MW01057143

# MESSIANIC ALEPH TAV INTERLINEAR SCRIPTURES

(MATIS)

VOLUME THREE

FIRST RED LETTER EDITION

# PROPHETS

*The Poetic Books and Prophetic Books of Major and Minor Prophets*

(*With Strong's Numbering*)



PALEO AND MODERN HEBREW-PHONETIC TRANSLATION-ENGLISH

STUDY BIBLE

**CCB Pulishing**
**British Columbia, Canada**

# The Messianic Aleph Tav Interlinear Scriptures
## (MATIS)

## FIRST EDITION VOLUME THREE

# THE PROPHETS



William H. Sanford

WHSanford@aol.com

## COPYRIGHT NOTICE



ISBN-13 978-1-77143-266-5
First Edition

Library and Archives Canada Cataloguing in Publication
Sanford, William H., 1952-
Messianic aleph tav interlinear scriptures volume three the prophets,
paleo and modern Hebrew-phonetic translation-English,
bold black edition study bible / Compiled by William H. Sanford – First edition.
Issued in print format.
ISBN 978-1-77143-266-5 (hbk.).--ISBN 978-1-77143-267-2 (pbk.).
Additional cataloguing data available from Library and Archives Canada



Publisher: CCB Publishing
British Columbia, Canada
www.ccbpublishing.com

א

םנןסצץפףעקרש

בגדהוזחטיכךלמ

ת

# The Messianic Aleph Tav Interlinear Scriptures

*First Edition Third Volume of the Prophets*



## TABLE OF CONTENTS

### *Poetic Books*



### *Prophetic Books of the Major Prophets*



### *Prophetic Books of the Minor Prophets*

# JOB
## (*Ayoub*)

The Book of Job begins the **Poetic Books** of the Tanakh between Job and the Song of Solomon. The Book of Job does not specifically name its author but tradition points to the most likely candidates as Job, Elihu, Moses or Solomon. The name Job in Hebrew means *persecuted* or *hated.* The date of the authorship of the book could only be determined by who the author of the Book of Job would be and if Moses was the author, the date would be around 1440 B.C.; if Solomon, the date would be around 950 B.C. But because we don't know the author, we cannot know the actual date of the writing. The book helps us to understand that Satan cannot bring either financial or physical destruction upon us unless it is by Elohim's divine permission. Suffering may sometimes be allowed in our lives to make restitution for sin and to purify, test and to teach and ultimately strengthen our faith. The book makes a profound statement on the justice of Yahuah our Elohim in light of human suffering.

**Job 1:1**

| איש 376 | היה 1961 | בארץ 776 | עוץ 5780 | איוב 347 | שמו 8034 | והיה 1961 | האיש 376 | ההוא 1931 | תם 8535 | וישר 3477 |
|---|---|---|---|---|---|---|---|---|---|---|
| 'aysh | hayah | ba'aretz | 'autz | 'ayoub | shamou; | uahayah | ha'aysh | hahua', | tam | uayashar |
| **a man** | **There was** | **in the land of** | **Uz** | ***was* Job** | **whose name** | **and was** | **man** | **that** | **perfect** | **and upright** |

| ויירא 3373 | אלהים 430 | וסר 5493 | מרע 7451: | **1:2** ויולדו 3205 | לו 3807a | שבעה 7651 | בנים 1121 | ושלוש 7969 |
|---|---|---|---|---|---|---|---|---|
| uiyrea' | 'alohiym | uasar | mera'. | uayiualadu | lou' | shib'ah | baniym | uashaloush |
| **and one that feared** | **Elohim** | **and eschewed** | **evil** | **And there were born** | **unto him** | **seven** | **sons** | **and three** |

| בנות 1323: | **1:3** ויהי 1961 | מקנהו 4735 | שבעת 7651 | אלפי 505 | צאן 6629 | ושלשת 7969 | אלפי 505 | גמלים 1581 | וחמש 2568 | מאות 3967 | צמד 6776 |
|---|---|---|---|---|---|---|---|---|---|---|---|
| banout. | uayahiy | miqnehu | shib'at | 'alpey | tza'n | uashloshet | 'alpey | gamaliym, | uachamesh | me'aut | tzemed |
| **daughters** | **also was** | **His substance** | **seven** | **thousand** | **sheep** | **and three** | **thousand** | **camels** | **and five** | **hundred** | **yoke of** |

| בקר 1241 | וחמש 2568 | מאות 3967 | אתונות 860 | ועבדה 5657 | רבה 7227 | מאד 3966 | ויהי 1961 | האיש 376 | ההוא 1931 | גדול 1419 | מכל 3605 |
|---|---|---|---|---|---|---|---|---|---|---|---|
| baqar | uachamesh | me'aut | atonout, | ua'abudah | rabah | ma'ad; | uayahiy | ha'aysh | hahua', | gadoul | mikal |
| **oxen** | **and five** | **hundred *of* his** | **she asses** | **and a household** | **great** | **very** | **so that was** | **man** | **this** | **the greatest** | **of all** |

| בני 1121 | קדם 6924: | **1:4** והלכו 1980 | בניו 1121 | ועשו 6213 | משתה 4960 | בית 1004 | איש 376 | יומו 3117 | ושלחו 7971 | וקראו 7121 |
|---|---|---|---|---|---|---|---|---|---|---|
| baney | qedem. | uahalaku | banayu | ua'asu | mishteh, | beyt | 'aysh | youmou; | uashalachu, | uaqar'au |
| **the men of** | **the east** | **And went** | **his sons** | **and hold** | **a feast** | ***in their* houses** | **every one** | **his day** | **and sent** | **and called** |

| לשלשת 7969 | אחיתיהם 269 | לאכל 398 | ולשתות 8354 | עמהם 5973: | **1:5** ויהי 1961 | כי 3588 | הקיפו 5362 | ימי 3117 | המשתה 4960 |
|---|---|---|---|---|---|---|---|---|---|
| lishloshet | 'achyoteyhem | le'akol | ualishtout | 'amahem. | uayahiy | kiy | hiqiypu | yamey | hamishteh |
| **for three** | **their sisters** | **to eat** | **and to drink** | **with them** | **And it was so** | **when** | **were gone about** | **days of *their*** | **the feasting** |

| וישלח 7971 | איוב 347 | ויקדשם 6942 | והשכים 7925 | בבקר 1242 | והעלה 5927 | עלות 5930 |
|---|---|---|---|---|---|---|
| uayishlach | 'ayoub | uayaqadshem, | uahishkiym | baboqer | uahe'alah | 'alout |
| **that sent** | **Job** | **and sanctified them** | **and rose up early** | **in the morning** | **and offered** | **burnt offerings** |

| מספר 4557 | כלם 3605 | כי 3588 | אמר 559 | איוב 347 | אולי 194 | חטאו 2398 | בני 1121 | וברכו 1288 | אלהים 430 |
|---|---|---|---|---|---|---|---|---|---|
| mispar | kulam | kiy | 'amar | 'ayoub, | 'aulay | chata'au | banay, | uaberaku | 'alohiym |
| ***according to* the number of** | **them all** | **for** | **said** | **Job** | **It may be that** | **have sinned** | **my sons** | **and cursed** | **Elohim** |

| בלבבם 3824 | ככה 3602 | יעשה 6213 | איוב 347 | כל 3605 | הימים 3117: | **1:6** ויהי 1961 | היום 3117 | ויבאו 935 | בני 1121 | האלהים 430 |
|---|---|---|---|---|---|---|---|---|---|---|
| bilbabam; | kakah | ya'aseh | 'ayoub | kal | hayamiym. | uayahiy | hayoum, | uayabo'au | baney | ha'alohiym, |
| **in their hearts** | **Thus** | **did** | **Job** | **all** | **continually** | **Now there was** | **a day** | **when came** | **the sons of** | **Elohim** |

**Job** 1:1 There was a man in the land of Uz, whose name was Job; and that man was perfect and upright, and one that feared G-d, and eschewed evil.2 And there were born unto him seven sons and three daughters.3 His substance also was seven thousand sheep, and three thousand camels, and five hundred yoke of oxen, and five hundred she asses, and a very great household; so that this man was the greatest of all the men of the east.4 And his sons went and feasted in their houses, everyone his day; and sent and called for their three sisters to eat and to drink with them.5 And it was so, when the days of their feasting were gone about, that Job sent and sanctified them, and rose up early in the morning, and offered burnt offerings according to the number of them all: for Job said, It may be that my sons have sinned, and cursed G-d in their hearts. Thus did Job continually.6 Now there was a day when the sons of G-d came to present themselves before YHUH, and Satan came also among them.

להתיצב 3320 על 5921 יהוה 3068 ויבוא 935 גם 1571 השטן 7854 בתוכם 8432: 1:7 ויאמר 559 יהוה 3068 אל 413 השטן 7854 מאין 370
lahityatzeb 'al Yahuah; uayabou'a gam hasatan batoukam. uaya'mer Yahuah 'al hasatan me'ayin
**to present themselves before Yahuah and came also the Satan among them And said Yahuah unto the Satan Where**

תבא 935 ויען 6030 השטן 7854 את 853 יהוה 3069 ויאמר 559 משוט 7751 בארץ 776
taba'; uaya'an hasatan 'at Yahuah uaya'mar, mishut ba'aretz,
**come you? Then answered the Satan Yahuah and said From going to and fro in the earth**

ומהתהלך 1980 בה 871a: 1:8 ויאמר 559 יהוה 3068 אל 413 השטן 7854 השמת 7760 לבך 3820 על 5921 עבדי 5650 איוב 347
uamehithalek bah. uaya'mer Yahuah 'al hasatan, hasamta libaka 'al 'abdiy 'ayoub;
**and from walking up and down in it And said Yahuah unto the Satan Have you considered of my servant Job**

כי 3588 אין 369 כמהו 3644 בארץ 776 איש 376 תם 8535 וישר 3477 ירא 3373 אלהים 430 וסר 5493 מרע 7451: 1:9
kiy 'aeyn kamohu ba'aretz, 'aysh tam uayashar yarea' 'alohiym uasar mera'.
**that *there is* none like him in the earth a man perfect and an upright one that fear Elohim and escheweth evil?**

ויען 6030 השטן 7854 את 853 יהוה 3068 ויאמר 559 החנם 2600 ירא 3372 איוב 347 אלהים 430: 1:10 הלא 3808 את 859
uaya'an hasatan 'at Yahuah uaya'mar; hachinam, yarea' 'ayoub 'alohiym. hala' 'at
**Then answered the Satan Yahuah and said for nought? Does fear Job Elohim not *You***

שכת 7753 בעדו 1157 ובעד 1157 ביתו 1004 ובעד 1157 כל 3605 אשר 834 לו 3807a מסביב 5439 מעשה 4639 ידיו 3027
sakta ba'adou uab'ad beytou uab'ad kal 'asher lou' misabiyb; ma'aseh yadayu
**Have made an hedge about him and about his house and about all that he has on every side? the work of his hands**

ברכת 1288 ומקנהו 4735 פרץ 6555 בארץ 776: 1:11 ואולם 199 שלח 7971 נא 4994 ידך 3027 וגע 5060 בכל 3605
berakta, uamiqnehu paratz ba'aretz. ua'aulam shalach naa' yadaka, uaga' bakal
**you haved blessed and his substance is increased in the land But put forth now your hand and touch all**

אשר 834 לו 3807a אם 518 לא 3808 על 5921 פניך 6440 יברכך 1288: 1:12 ויאמר 559 יהוה 3068 אל 413 השטן 7854 הנה 2009 כל 3605 אשר 834
'asher lou'; 'am la' 'al paneyka yabarakeka. uaya'mer Yahuah 'al hasatan, hineh kal 'asher
**that he has if not to your face he will curse you And said Yahuah unto the Satan Behold all that**

לו 3807a בידך 3027 רק 7535 אליו 413 אל 408 תשלח 7971 ידך 3027 ויצא 3318 השטן 7854 מעם 5973 פני 6440
lou' bayadeka, raq 'aelayu, 'al tishlach yadeka; uayetzea' hasatan, me'am paney
**he has *is* in your power only upon himself not put forth your hand So went forth the Satan from the presence of**

יהוה 3068: 1:13 ויהי 1961 היום 3117 ובניו 1121 ובנתיו 1323 אכלים 398 ושתים 8354 יין 3196 בבית 1004
Yahuah. uayahiy hayoum; uabanayu uabnotayu 'akliym uashotiym yayin, babeyt
**Yahuah And there was a day when his sons and his daughters *were* eating and drinking wine in house**

אחיהם 251 הבכור 1060: 1:14 ומלאך 4397 בא 935 אל 413 איוב 347 ויאמר 559 הבקר 1241 היו 1961 חרשות 2790 והאתנות 860
'achiyhem habakour. uamal'ak ba' 'al 'ayoub uaya'mar; habaqar hayu chorashout, uaha'atonout
**their brother's eldest And a messenger there came unto Job and said The oxen were plowing and his asses**

רעות 7462 על 5921 ידיהם 3027: 1:15 ותפל 5307 שבא 7614 ותקחם 3947 ואת 853 הנערים 5288 הכו 5221
ro'aut 'al yadeyhem. uatipol shaba' uatiqachem, ua'at hana'ariym hiku
**feeding beside them And fell *upon them* the Sabeans and took them away *yea* the servants they have slain**

Job 1:7 And YHUH said unto Satan, Where come you? Then Satan answered YHUH, and said, From going to and fro in the earth, and from walking up and down in it.8 And YHUH said unto Satan, Hast you considered my servant Job, that there is none like him in the earth, a perfect and an upright man, one that fear G-d, and escheweth evil?9 Then Satan answered YHUH, and said, Does Job fear G-d for nought?10 Hast not you made an hedge about him, and about his house, and about all that he has on every side? you have blessed the work of his hands, and his substance is increased in the land.11 But put forth your hand now, and touch all that he has, and he will curse you to your face.12 And YHUH said unto Satan, Behold, all that he has is in your power; only upon himself put not forth your hand. So Satan went forth from the presence of YHUH.13 And there was a day when his sons and his daughters were eating and drinking wine in their eldest brother's house:14 And there came a messenger unto Job, and said, The oxen were plowing, and the asses feeding beside them:15 And the Sabeans fell upon them, and took them away; yea, they have slain the servants with the edge of the sword; and I...

לפי 6310 חרב 2719 ואמלטה 4422 רק 7535 אני 589 לבדי 905 להגיד 5046 לך 3807a: **1:16** עוד 5750 זה 2088 מדבר 1696
lapiy chareb; ua'amalatah raq 'aniy labadiy lahagiyd lak. 'aud zeh madaber,
**with the edge of the sword and am escaped only I alone to tell to you While yet he *was* speaking**

וזה 2088 בא 935 ויאמר 559 אש 784 אלהים 430 נפלה 5307 מן 4480 השמים 8064 ותבער 1197 בצאן 6629
uazeh ba' uaya'mar 'aesh 'alohiym, naplah min hashamayim, uatib'ar batza'an
**also another there came and said The fire of Elohim is fallen from heaven and has burned up the sheep**

ובנערים 5288 ותאכלם 398 ואמלטה 4422 רק 7535 אני 589 לבדי 905 להגיד 5046 לך 3807a: **1:17** עוד 5750 זה 2088 מדבר 1696
uaban'ariym uata'kalem; ua'amalatah raq 'aniy labadiy lahagiyd lak. 'aud zeh madaber,
**and the servants and consumed them and am escaped only I alone to tell to you While yet he *was* speaking**

וזה 2088 בא 935 ויאמר 559 כשדים 3778 שמו 7760 שלשה 7969 ראשים 7218 ויפשטו 6584 על 5921 הגמלים 1581
uazeh ba' uaya'mar kasdiym samu shaloshah rashiym, uayipshatu 'al hagamaliym
**also another there came and said The Chaldeans made out three bands and fell upon the camels**

ויקחום 3947 ואת 853 הנערים 5288 הכו 5221 לפי 6310 חרב 2719 ואמלטה 4422 רק 7535 אני 589 לבדי 905
uayiqachum, ua'at hana'ariym hiku lapiy chareb; ua'amalatah raq 'aniy labadiy
**and have carried them away, *yea* and the servants slain with the edge of the sword and am escaped only I alone**

להגיד 5046 לך 3807a: **1:18** עד 5704 זה 2088 מדבר 1696 וזה 2088 בא 935 ויאמר 559 בניך 1121 ובנותיך 1323
lahagiyd lak. 'ad zeh madaber, uazeh ba' uaya'mar; baneyka uabnouteyka
**to tell to you While yet he *was* speaking also another there came and said Your sons and your daughters**

אכלים 398 ושתים 8354 יין 3196 בבית 1004 אחיהם 251 הבכור 1060: **1:19** והנה 2009 רוח 7307 גדולה 1419 באה 935 מעבר 5676
'akliym uashotiym yayin, babeyt 'achiyhem habakour. uahineh ruach gadoulah ba'ah me'aeber
***were* eating and drinking wine in house their brother's eldest And behold a wind great there came from**

המדבר 4057 ויגע 5060 בארבע 702 פנות 6438 הבית 1004 ויפל 5307 על 5921 הנערים 5288 וימותו 4191 ואמלטה 4422
hamidbar, uayiga' ba'arba pinout habayit, uayipol 'al hana'ariym uayamutu; ua'amalatah
**the wilderness and smote *the* four corners of the house and it fell upon the young men and they are dead and am escaped**

רק 7535 אני 589 לבדי 905 להגיד 5046 לך 3807a: **1:20** ויקם 6965 איוב 347 ויקרע 7167 את 853 מעלו 4598 ויגז 1494 את 853 ראשו 7218
raq 'aniy labadiy lahagiyd lak. uayaqam 'ayoub uayiqra' 'at ma'alou, uayagaz 'at ra'shou;
**only I alone to tell to you Then arose Job and rent his mantle and shaved his head**

ויפל 5307 ארצה 776 וישתחו 7812: **1:21** ויאמר 559 ערם 6174 יצתי 3318 מבטן 990 אמי 517 וערם 6174
uayipol 'artzah uayishtachu. uaya'mer 'arom yatza'tiy mibeten 'amiy, ua'arom
**and fell down upon the ground and worshipped And said Naked came I out of womb my mother's and naked**

אשוב 7725 שמה 8033 יהוה 3068 נתן 5414 ויהוה 3068 לקח 3947 יהי 1961 שם 8034 יהוה 3068 מברך 1288: **1:22** בכל 3605 זאת 2063
'ashub shamah, Yahuah natan, uaYahuah laqach; yahiy shem Yahuah maborak. bakal za't
**shall I return there Yahuah gave and Yahuah has taken away be the name of Yahuah blessed In all this**

לא 3808 חטא 2398 איוב 347 ולא 3808 נתן 5414 תפלה 8604 לאלהים 430:
la' chata' 'ayoub; uala' natan tiplah le'alohiym.
**not sinned Job nor charged foolishly to Elohim**

Job 1:15 only am escaped alone to tell you.16 While he was yet speaking, there came also another, and said, The fire of G-d is fallen from heaven, and has burned up the sheep, and the servants, and consumed them; and I only am escaped alone to tell you.17 While he was yet speaking, there came also another, and said, The Chaldeans made out three bands, and fell upon the camels, and have carried them away, yea, and slain the servants with the edge of the sword; and I only am escaped alone to tell you.18 While he was yet speaking, there came also another, and said, Thy sons and your daughters were eating and drinking wine in their eldest brother's house:19 And, behold, there came a great wind from the wilderness, and smote the four corners of the house, and it fell upon the young men, and they are dead; and I only am escaped alone to tell you.20 Then Job arose, and rent his mantle, and shaved his head, and fell down upon the ground, and worshipped,21 And said, Naked came I out of my mother's womb, and naked shall I return thither: YHUH gave, and YHUH has taken away; blessed be the name of YHUH.22 In all this Job sinned not, nor charged G-d foolishly.

**Job 2:1**

ויהי 1961 היום 3117 ויבאו 935 בני 1121 האלהים 430 להתיצב 3320 על 5921 יהוה 3068 ויבוא 935 גם 1571
uayahiy hayoum, uayabo'au baney ha'alohiym, lahityatzeb 'al Yahuah; uayabou'a gam
**Again there was a day when came the sons of Elohim to present themselves before Yahuah and came also**

**2:2**

השטן 7854 בתכם 8432 להתיצב 3320 על 5921 יהוה 3068: ויאמר 559 יהוה 3068 אל 413 השטן 7854 אי 335 מזה 2088 תבא 935
hasatan batoukam, lahityatzeb 'al Yahuah. uaya'mer Yahuah 'al hasatan, 'ay mizeh taba';
**the Satan among them to present himself before Yahuah And said Yahuah unto the Satan where From come you?**

ויען 6030 השטן 7854 את 853 יהוה 3068 ויאמר 559 משט 7751 בארץ 776 ומהתהלך 1980
uaya'an hasatan 'at Yahuah uaya'mar, mishut ba'aretz, uamehithalek
**And answered the Satan Yahuah and said From going to and fro in the earth and from walking up and down**

**2:3**

בה 871a: ויאמר 559 יהוה 3068 אל 413 השטן 7854 השמת 7760 לבך 3820 אל 413 עבדי 5650 איוב 347 כי 3588 אין 369 כמהו 3644
bah. uaya'mer Yahuah 'al hasatan, hasamta libaka 'al 'abdiy 'ayoub kiy 'aeyn kamohu
**in it And said Yahuah unto the Satan Have you considered about my servant Job that *there is* none like him**

בארץ 776 איש 376 תם 8535 וישר 3477 ירא 3373 אלהים 430 וסר 5493 מרע 7451 ועדנו 5750 מחזיק 2388 בתמתו 8538
ba'aretz, 'aysh tam uayashar yarea' 'alohiym uasar mera'; ua'adenu machaziyq batumatou,
**in the earth a man perfect and an upright one that fear Elohim and escheweth evil? and still he holds fast his integrity**

**2:4**

ותסיתני 5496 בו 871a לבלעו 1104 חנם 2600: ויען 6030 השטן 7854 את 853 יהוה 3068 ויאמר 559
uatasiyteniy bou labal'au chinam. uaya'an hasatan 'at Yahuah uaya'mar;
**although you movedst me against him to destroy him without cause And answered the Satan Yahuah and said**

**2:5**

עור 5785 בעד 1157 עור 5785 וכל 3605 אשר 834 לאיש 376 יתן 5414 בעד 1157 נפשו 5315: אולם 199 שלח 7971 נא 4994 ידך 3027
'aur ba'ad 'aur, uakol 'asher la'aysh, yiten ba'ad napshou. 'aulam shalach naa' yadaka,
**Skin for skin yea all that a man *has* will he give for his life But put forth now your hand**

**2:6**

וגע 5060 אל 413 עצמו 6106 ואל 413 בשרו 1320 אם 518 לא 3808 אל 413 פניך 6440 יברכך 1288: ויאמר 559 יהוה 3069 אל 413 השטן 7854
uaga' 'al atzamou ua'al basarou; 'am la' 'al paneyka yabarakeka. uaya'mer Yahuah 'al hasatan
**and touch to his bone and to his flesh if not to your face he will curse you And said Yahuah unto the Satan**

**2:7**

הנו 2005 בידך 3027 אך 389 את 853 נפשו 5315 שמר 8104: ויצא 3318 השטן 7854 מאת 853 פני 6440 יהוה 3068
hinou bayadeka; 'ak 'at napshou shamor. uayetzea' hasatan, me'at paney Yahuah;
**Behold he *is* in your hand but his life save So went forth the Satan from the presence of Yahuah**

**2:8**

ויך 5221 את 853 איוב 347 בשחין 7822 רע 7451 מכף 3709 רגלו 7272 עד 5704 קדקדו 6936: ויקח 3947 לו 3807a חרש 2789
uayak 'at 'ayoub bishachiyn ra', mikap raglou 'ad qadaqadou. uayiqach lou' cheres,
**and smote Job with boils sore from the sole of his foot unto his crown And he took him a potsherd**

**2:9**

להתגרד 1623 בו 871a והוא 1931 ישב 3427 בתוך 8432 האפר 665: ותאמר 559 לו 3807a אשתו 802 עדך 5750 מחזיק 2388
lahitgared bou; uahu'a yosheb batouk ha'aeper. uata'mer lou' ashtou, 'adaka machaziyq
**to scrape himself withal and he sat down among the ashes Then said unto him his wife still Do you retain**

**2:10**

בתמתך 8538 ברך 1288 אלהים 430 ומת 4191: ויאמר 559 אליה 413 כדבר 1696 אחת 259 הנבלות 5036 תדברי 1696 גם 1571
batumateka; barek 'alohiym uamut. uaya'mer 'aeleyha, kadaber 'achat hanabalout tadaberiy, gam
**your integrity? curse Elohim and die But he said unto her You speak as one of the foolish women speak What?**

**Job** 2:1 Again there was a day when the sons of G-d came to present themselves before YHUH, and Satan came also among them to present himself before YHUH.2 And YHUH said unto Satan, From whence come you? And Satan answered YHUH, and said, From going to and fro in the earth, and from walking up and down in it.3 And YHUH said unto Satan, Hast you considered my servant Job, that there is none like him in the earth, a perfect and an upright man, one that fear G-d, and escheweth evil? and still he holdeth fast his integrity, although you movedst me against him, to destroy him without cause.4 And Satan answered YHUH, and said, Skin for skin, yea, all that a man has will he give for his life.5 But put forth your hand now, and touch his bone and his flesh, and he will curse you to your face.6 And YHUH said unto Satan, Behold, he is in your hand; but save his life.7 So went Satan forth from the presence of YHUH, and smote Job with sore boils from the sole of his foot unto his crown.8 And he took him a potsherd to scrape himself withal; and he sat down among the ashes.9 Then said his wife unto him, Dost you still retain your integrity? curse G-d, and die. 10 But he said unto her, Thou speak as one of the foolish women speaketh. What? shall we receive good at the hand of G-d, and shall we not receive evil? In all this did not Job sin with his lips.

| את 853 | הטוב 2896 | נקבל 6901 | מאת 853 | האלהים 430 | ואת 853 | הרע 7451 | לא 3808 | נקבל 6901 | בכל 3605 | זאת 2063 | לא 3808 | חטא 2398 |
|---|---|---|---|---|---|---|---|---|---|---|---|---|
| 'at | hatoub, | naqabel | me'at | ha'alohiym, | ua'at | hara' | la' | naqabel; | bakal | za't | la' | chata' |
| | good | shall we receive at the hand of Elohim | | | *and* | evil? | not | shall we receive | In all | this | not | did sin |

| איוב 347 | בשפתיו 8193: | 2:11 | וישמעו 8085 | שלשת 7969 | רעי 7453 | איוב 347 | את 853 | כל 3605 | הרעה 7451 | הזאת 2063 | הבאה 935 |
|---|---|---|---|---|---|---|---|---|---|---|---|
| 'ayoub | bispatayu. | | uayishma'au | shaloshet | re'aey | 'ayoub, | 'at | kal | hara'ah | haza't | haba'ah |
| Job | with his lips | | Now when heard of | three | friends | Job's | | all | evil | this | that was come |

| עליו 5921 | ויבאו 935 | איש 376 | ממקמו 4725 | אליפז 464 | התימני 8489 | ובלדד 1085 | השוחי 7747 | וצופר 6691 |
|---|---|---|---|---|---|---|---|---|
| 'aelayu | uayabo'au | 'aysh | mimaqomou, | 'aliypaz | hateymaniy | uabildad | hashuchiy, | uatzoupar |
| upon him | they came | every one | from his own place | Eliphaz | the Temanite | and Bildad | the Shuhite | and Zophar |

| הנעמתי 5284 | ויועדו 3259 | יחדו 3162 | לבוא 935 | לנוד 5110 | לו 3807a | ולנחמו 5162: | 2:12 |
|---|---|---|---|---|---|---|---|
| hana'amatiy; | uayiua'adu | yachdau, | labou'a | lanud | lou' | ualnachamou. | |
| the Naamathite | for they had made an appointment | together | to come | to mourn | with him | and to comfort him | |

| וישאו 5375 | את 853 | עיניהם 5869 | מרחוק 7350 | ולא 3808 | הכירהו 5234 | וישאו 5375 | קולם 6963 | ויבכו 1058 |
|---|---|---|---|---|---|---|---|---|
| uayis'au | 'at | 'aeyneyhem | merachouq | uala' | hikiyruhu, | uayis'au | qoulam | uayibku; |
| And when they lifted up | | their eyes | afar off | and not | knew him | and they lifted up | their voice | and wept |

| ויקרעו 7167 | איש 376 | מעלו 4598 | ויזרקו 2236 | עפר 6083 | על 5921 | ראשיהם 7218 | השמימה 8064: | 2:13 | וישבו 3427 | אתו 854 |
|---|---|---|---|---|---|---|---|---|---|---|
| uayiqra'au | 'aysh | ma'alou, | uayizraqu | 'apar | 'al | ra'sheyhem | hashamayamah. | | uayeshabu | 'atou |
| and they rent | every one | his mantle | and sprinkled | dust | upon | their heads | toward heaven | | So they sat down | with him |

| לארץ 776 | שבעת 7651 | ימים 3117 | ושבעת 7651 | לילות 3915 | ואין 369 | דבר 1696 | אליו 413 | דבר 1697 | כי 3588 | ראו 7200 | כי 3588 | גדל 1431 |
|---|---|---|---|---|---|---|---|---|---|---|---|---|
| la'aretz, | shib'at | yamiym | uashib'at | leylout; | ua'aeyn | dober | 'aelayu | dabar, | kiy | ra'au, | kiy | gadal |
| upon the ground | seven | days | and seven | nights | and none | spoke | unto him | a word | for | they saw | that | was great |

| הכאב 3511 | מאד 3966: |
|---|---|
| haka'aeb | ma'ad. |
| *his* grief | very |

**Job 3:1**

| אחרי 310 | כן 3651 | פתח 6605 | איוב 347 | את 853 | פיהו 6310 | ויקלל 7043 | את 853 | יומו 3117: | 3:2 | ויען 6030 | איוב 347 | ויאמר 559: | 3:3 |
|---|---|---|---|---|---|---|---|---|---|---|---|---|---|
| 'acharey | ken, | patach | 'ayoub | 'at | piyhu, | uayaqalel | 'at | youmou. | | uaya'an | 'ayoub, | uaya'mar. | |
| After | this | opened | Job | | his mouth | and cursed | | his day | | And spoke | Job | and said | |

| יאבד 6 | יום 3117 | אולד 3205 | בו 871a | והלילה 3915 | אמר 559 | הרה 2030 | גבר 1397: | 3:4 | היום 3117 | ההוא 1931 |
|---|---|---|---|---|---|---|---|---|---|---|
| ya'bad | youm | 'aualed | bou; | uahalayalah | 'amar, | horah | gaber. | | hayoum | hahua', |
| Let perish | the day | I was born | wherein | and the night *in which* | it was said | There is conceive | a man child | | day | that |

| יהי 1961 | חשך 2822 | אל 408 | ידרשהו 1875 | אלוה 433 | ממעל 4605 | ואל 408 | תופע 3313 | עליו 5921 | נהרה 5105: | 3:5 | יגאלהו 1350 | חשך 2822 |
|---|---|---|---|---|---|---|---|---|---|---|---|---|
| yahiy | choshek | 'al | yidrashehu | 'alouah | mima'al; | ua'al | toupa' | 'aelayu | naharah. | | yig'aluhu | choshek |
| Let | be darkness | not | let regard it | Elohim | from above | neither | let shine | upon it | the light | | Let stain it | darkness |

| וצלמות 6757 | תשכן 7931 | עליו 5921 | עננה 6053 | יבעתהו 1204 | כמרירי 3650 | יום 3117: | 3:6 | הלילה 3915 | ההוא 1931 |
|---|---|---|---|---|---|---|---|---|---|
| uatzalmauet | tishkan | 'alayu | 'ananah; | yaba'atuhu, | kimriyrey | youm. | | halayalah | hahua' |
| and the shadow of death | let dwell | upon it | a cloud | let terrify it | the blackness of | the day | | *As for* night | that |

Job 2:11 Now when Job's three friends heard of all this evil that was come upon him, they came everyone from his own place; Eliphaz the Temanite, and Bildad the Shuhite, and Zophar the Naamathite: for they had made an appointment together to come to mourn with him and to comfort him.12 And when they lifted up their eyes afar off, and knew him not, they lifted up their voice, and wept; and they rent everyone his mantle, and sprinkled dust upon their heads toward heaven.13 So they sat down with him upon the ground seven days and seven nights, and none spoke a word unto him: for they saw that his grief was very great. **Job** 3:1 After this opened Job his mouth, and cursed his day.2 And Job spoke, and said,3 Let the day perish wherein I was born, and the night in which it was said, There is a man child conceived.4 Let that day be darkness; let not G-d regard it from above, neither let the light shine upon it.5 Let darkness and the shadow of death stain it; let a cloud dwell upon it; let the blackness of the day terrify it.6 As for that night, let darkness seize upon it; let it not be joined unto the days of the year, let it not come into the number of the months.

| יקחהו 3947 | אפל 652 | אל 408 | יחד 2302 | בימי 3117 | שנה 8141 | במספר 4557 | ירחים 3391 | אל 408 | יבא 935: | 3:7 |
|---|---|---|---|---|---|---|---|---|---|---|
| yiqachehu | 'apel | 'al | yichad | biymey | shanah; | bamispar | yarachiym, | 'al | yaba'. | |
| **let seize upon it** | **darkness** | **not** | **let it be joined** | **unto the days of** | **the year** | **into the number of** | **the months** | **not** | **let it come** | |

| הנה 2009 | הלילה 3915 | ההוא 1931 | יהי 1961 | גלמוד 1565 | אל 408 | תבא 935 | רננה 7445 | בו 871a: | 3:8 | יקבהו 5344 | אררי 779 | יום 3117 |
|---|---|---|---|---|---|---|---|---|---|---|---|---|
| hineh | halayalah | hahu' | yahiy | galmud; | 'al | taba' | rananah | bou. | | yiqbuhu | 'ararey | youm; |
| **Lo'** | **night** | **that** | **let be** | **solitary** | **no** | **let come** | **joyful voice** | **therein** | | **Let them curse it** | **that curse** | **the day** |

| העתידים 6264 | עורר 5782 | לויתן 3882: | 3:9 | יחשכו 2821 | כוכבי 3556 | נשפו 5399 | יקו 6960 | לאור 216 | ואין 369 |
|---|---|---|---|---|---|---|---|---|---|
| ha'atiydiym, | 'auer | liuyatan. | | yechshaku | koukabey | nishpou | yaqau | la'aur | ua'ayin; |
| **who are ready** | **to raise up** | **their mourning** | | **Let be dark** | **the stars of** | **the twilight thereof** | **let it look** | **for light** | **but *have* none** |

| ואל 408 | יראה 7200 | בעפעפי 6079 | שחר: | 3:10 | כי 3588 | לא 3808 | סגר 5462 | דלתי 1817 | בטני 990 | ויסתר 5641 | עמל 5999 |
|---|---|---|---|---|---|---|---|---|---|---|---|
| ua'al | yir'ah, | ba'ap'apey | shachar. | | kiy | la' | sagar | daltey | bitniy; | uayaster | 'amal, |
| **neither** | **let it see** | **the dawning of** | **the day** | | **Because** | **not** | **it shut up** | **the doors of** | **my *mother's* womb** | **nor hid** | **sorrow** |

| מעיני 5869: | 3:11 | למה 4100 | לא 3808 | מרחם 7358 | אמות 4191 | מבטן 990 | יצאתי 3318 |
|---|---|---|---|---|---|---|---|
| me'aeynay. | | lamah | la' | merechem | 'amut; | mibeten | yatza'tiy |
| **from mine eyes** | | **Why** | **not** | **from the womb?** | **died I** | **of the belly?** | **I came out** |

| ואגוע 1478: | 3:12 | מדוע 4069 | קדמוני 6923 | ברכים 1290 | ומה 4100 | שדים 7699 | כי 3588 |
|---|---|---|---|---|---|---|---|
| ua'agua'. | | madua' | qidmuniy | birkayim; | uamah | shadayim, | kiy |
| **and *why* did I not give up the ghost when** | | **Why** | **did prevent me?** | **the knees** | **or why** | **the breasts** | **that** |

| אינק 3243: | 3:13 | כי 3588 | עתה 6258 | שכבתי 7901 | ואשקוט 8252 | ישנתי 3462 | אז 227 | ינוח 5117 |
|---|---|---|---|---|---|---|---|---|
| 'aynaq. | | kiy | 'atah | shakabtiy | ua'ashqout; | yashantiy, | 'az | yanuach |
| **I should suck?** | | **For** | **now** | **should I have lain still** | **and been quiet** | **I should have slept** | **then** | **had been at rest** |

| לי 3807a: | 3:14 | עם 5973 | מלכים 4428 | ויעצי 3289 | ארץ 776 | הבנים 1129 | חרבות 2723 | למו 3807a: | 3:15 | או 176 | עם 5973 |
|---|---|---|---|---|---|---|---|---|---|---|---|
| liy. | | 'am | malakiym | uayo'atzey | 'aretz; | haboniym | charabout | lamou. | | 'au | 'am |
| **I** | | **With** | **kings** | **and counsellors of** | **the earth** | **which built** | **desolate places** | **for themselves** | | **Or** | **with** |

| שרים 8269 | זהב 2091 | להם 1992 | הממלאים 4390 | בתיהם 1004 | כסף 3701: | 3:16 | או 176 | כנפל 5309 | טמון 2934 | לא 3808 | אהיה 1961 |
|---|---|---|---|---|---|---|---|---|---|---|---|
| sariym | zahab | lahem; | hamamal'aym | bateyhem | kasep. | | 'au | kanepel | tamun | la' | 'ahayeh; |
| **princes *had*** | **gold** | **that** | **who filled** | **their houses with** | **silver** | | **Or** | **as an untimely birth** | **hidden** | **not** | **I had been** |

| כעללים 5768 | לא 3808 | ראו 7200 | אור 216: | 3:17 | שם 8033 | רשעים 7563 | חדלו 2308 | רגז 7267 | ושם 8033 | ינוחו 5117 | יגיעי 3019 |
|---|---|---|---|---|---|---|---|---|---|---|---|
| ka'alaliym, | la' | ra'au | 'aur. | | sham | rasha'aym | chadalu | rogez; | uasham | yanuchu, | yagiy'aey |
| **as infants *which*** | **never** | **saw** | **light** | | **There** | **the wicked** | **cease *from*** | **troubling** | **and there** | **be at rest** | **the weary of** |

| כח 3581: | 3:18 | יחד 3162 | אסירים 615 | שאננו 7599 | לא 3808 | שמעו 8085 | קול 6963 | נגש 5065: | 3:19 | קטן 6996 | וגדול 1419 |
|---|---|---|---|---|---|---|---|---|---|---|---|
| koach. | | yachad | 'asiyriym | sha'ananu; | la' | shama'au, | qoul | noges. | | qaton | uagadoul |
| **vigor** | | ***There* together** | **the prisoners** | **rest** | **not** | **they hear** | **the voice of** | **the oppressor** | | **The small** | **and great** |

| שם 8033 | הוא 1931 | ועבד 5650 | חפשי 2670 | מאדניו 113: | 3:20 | למה 4100 | יתן 5414 | לעמל 6001 | אור 216 |
|---|---|---|---|---|---|---|---|---|---|
| sham | hua'; | ua'abed, | chapashiy | me'adonayu. | | lamah | yiten | la'amel | 'aur; |
| ***are* there** | **they** | **and the servant *is*** | **free** | **from his master** | | **Wherefore** | **is given** | **to him that is in misery** | **light** |

Job 3:7 Lo, let that night be solitary, let no joyful voice come therein.8 Let them curse it that curse the day, who are ready to raise up their mourning.9 Let the stars of the twilight thereof be dark; let it look for light, but have none; neither let it see the dawning of the day:10 Because it shut not up the doors of my mother's womb, nor hid sorrow from mine eyes.11 Why died I not from the womb? why did I not give up the ghost when I came out of the belly?12 Why did the knees prevent me? or why the breasts that I should suck?13 For now should I have lain still and been quiet, I should have slept: then had I been at rest,14 With kings and counsellers of the earth, which built desolate places for themselves;15 Or with princes that had gold, who filled their houses with silver:16 Or as an hidden untimely birth I had not been; as infants which never saw light.17 There the wicked cease from troubling; and there the weary be at rest.18 There the prisoners rest together; they hear not the voice of the oppressor.19 The small and great are there; and the servant is free from his master.20 Wherefore is light given to him that is in misery, and life unto the bitter in soul;

| וחיים 2416 | למרי 4751 | נפש 5315: | 3:21 | המחכים 2442 | למות 4191 | ואיננו 369 | ויחפרהו 2658 |
|---|---|---|---|---|---|---|---|
| uachayiym, | lamarey | napesh. | | hamchakiym | lamauet | ua'aeynenu; | uayachparuhu, |
| **and life** | **unto the bitter** | ***in* soul** | | **Which long** | **for death** | **but it *comes* not** | **and dig for it** |

| ממטמונים 4301: | 3:22 | השמחים 8055 | אלי 413 | גיל 1524 | ישישו 7797 | כי 3588 | ימצאו 4672 | קבר 6913: | 3:23 |
|---|---|---|---|---|---|---|---|---|---|
| mimatmouniym. | | hasamechiym | 'aley | giyl; | yasiysu, | kiy | yimtz'au | qaber. | |
| **more than for hid treasures** | | **Which rejoice** | **about** | **exceedingly** | ***and* are glad** | **when** | **they can find** | **the grave?** | |

| לגבר 1397 | אשר 834 | דרכו 1870 | נסתרה 5641 | ויסך 5526 | אלוה 433 | בעדו 1157: | 3:24 | כי 3588 | לפני 6440 | לחמי 3899 |
|---|---|---|---|---|---|---|---|---|---|---|
| lageer | 'asher | darkou | nistarah; | uayasek | 'alouah | ba'adou. | | kiy | lipney | lachmiy |
| ***Why is light given* to a man** | **whose** | **way** | **is hid** | **and has hedged** | **Elohim** | **whom in?** | | **For** | **before** | **I eat** |

| אנחתי 585 | תבא 935 | ויתכו 5413 | כמים 4325 | שאגתי 7581: | 3:25 | כי 3588 | פחד 6343 | פחדתי 6342 | ויאתיני 857 |
|---|---|---|---|---|---|---|---|---|---|
| 'anchatiy | taba'; | uayitku | kamayim, | sha'agotay. | | kiy | pachad | pachadtiy | uaye'atayeniy; |
| **my sighing** | **comes** | **and are poured out** | **like the waters** | **my roarings** | | **For** | **the thing** | **I greatly feared** | **is come upon me** |

| ואשר 834 | יגרתי 3025 | יבא 935 | לי 3807a: | 3:26 | לא 3808 | שלותי 7951 | ולא 3808 | שקטתי 8252 | ולא 3808 | נחתי 5117 | ויבא 935 |
|---|---|---|---|---|---|---|---|---|---|---|---|
| ua'asher | yagoratiy, | yaba' | liy. | | la' | shalauatiy | uala' | shaqatatiy | uala' | nachatiy, | uayaba' |
| **that which** | **I was afraid of** | **is come** | **upon me** | | **not** | **I was in safety** | **neither** | **had I rest** | **neither** | **was I quiet** | **yet came** |

| רגז 7267: |
|---|
| rogez. |
| **trouble** |

| **Job 4:1** | ויען 6030 | אליפז 464 | התימני 8489 | ויאמר 559: | 4:2 | הנסה 5254 | דבר 1697 | אליך 413 | תלאה 3811 |
|---|---|---|---|---|---|---|---|---|---|
| | uaya'an | 'aliypaz | hateymaniy, | uaya'mar. | | hanisah | dabar | 'aeleyka | til'ah; |
| | **Then answered** | **Eliphaz** | **the Temanite** | **and said** | | ***If* we assay** | **to commune** | **with you** | **will you be grieved?** |

| ועצר 6113 | במלין 4405 | מי 4310 | יוכל 3201: | 4:3 | הנה 2009 | יסרת 3256 | רבים 7227 | וידים 3027 | רפות 7504 |
|---|---|---|---|---|---|---|---|---|---|
| ua'atzor | bamiliyn, | miy' | yukal. | | hineh | yisarta | rabiym; | uayadayim | rapout |
| **but withhold himself** | **from speaking?** | **who** | **can** | | **Behold** | **you have instructed** | **many** | **and hands** | ***the* weak** |

| תחזק 2388: | 4:4 | כושל 3782 | יקימון 6965 | מליך 4405 | וברכים 1290 | כרעות 3766 | תאמץ 553: | 4:5 |
|---|---|---|---|---|---|---|---|---|
| tachazeq. | | koushel | yaqiymun | mileyka; | uabirkayim | kora'aut | ta'ametz. | |
| **you have strengthened** | | **him that was falling** | **have upholden** | **Your words** | **and knees** | ***the* feeble** | **you have strengthened** | |

| כי 3588 | עתה 6258 | תבוא 935 | אליך 413 | ותלא 3811 | תגע 5060 | עדיך 5704 | ותבהל 926: | 4:6 | הלא 3808 | יראתך 3373 |
|---|---|---|---|---|---|---|---|---|---|---|
| kiy | 'atah | tabou'a | 'aeleyka | uatela'; | tiga' | 'adeyka, | uatibahel. | | hala' | yir'ataka |
| **But** | **now** | **it is come** | **upon you** | **and you faint** | **it touch** | **unto you** | **and you are troubled** | | ***Is* not** | ***this* your fear** |

| כסלתך 3690 | תקותך 8615 | ותם 8537 | דרכיך 1870: | 4:7 | זכר 2142 | נא 4994 | מי 4310 | הוא 1931 | נקי 5355 |
|---|---|---|---|---|---|---|---|---|---|
| kislateka; | tiquataka, | uatom | darakeyka. | | zakar | na', | miy' | hua' | naqiy |
| **your confidence** | **your hope** | **and the uprightness of** | **your ways?** | | **Remember** | **I pray you** | **who** | **he** | ***being* innocent?** |

| אבד 6 | ואיפה 375 | ישרים 3477 | נכחדו 3582: | 4:8 | כאשר 834 | ראיתי 7200 | חרשי 2790 | און 205 | וזרעי 2232 | עמל 5999 |
|---|---|---|---|---|---|---|---|---|---|---|
| 'abad; | ua'aeypoh, | yashariym | nikchadu. | | ka'asher | ra'aytiy | chorashey | 'auen; | uazora'aey | 'amal |
| ***ever* perished** | **or where** | ***were* the righteous** | **cut off?** | | **Even as** | **I have seen** | **they that plow** | **iniquity** | **and sow** | **wickedness** |

Job 3:21 Which long for death, but it cometh not; and dig for it more than for hid treasures;22 Which rejoice exceedingly, and are glad, when they can find the grave?23 Why is light given to a man whose way is hid, and whom G-d has hedged in?24 For my sighing cometh before I eat, and my roarings are poured out like the waters.25 For the thing which I greatly feared is come upon me, and that which I was afraid of is come unto me.26 I was not in safety, neither had I rest, neither was I quiet; yet trouble came. **Job** 4:1 Then Eliphaz the Temanite answered and said,2 If we assay to commune with you, will you be grieved? but who can withhold himself from speaking?3 Behold, you have instructed many, and you have strengthened the weak hands.4 Thy words have upholden him that was falling, and you have strengthened the feeble knees.5 But now it is come upon you, and you faintest; it touch you, and you are troubled.6 Is not this your fear, your confidence, your hope, and the uprightness of your ways?7 Remember, I pray you, who ever perished, being innocent? or where were the righteous cut off?8 Even as I have seen, they that plow iniquity, and sow wickedness, reap the same.

| יקצרהו 7114: | 4:9 | מנשמת 5397 | אלוה 433 | יאבדו 6 | ומרוח 7307 | אפו 639 | יכלו 3615: | 4:10 |
|---|---|---|---|---|---|---|---|---|
| yiqtzaruhu. | | minishmat | 'alouah | ya'bedu; | uameruach | 'apou | yiklu. | |
| **reap the same** | | **By the blast of** | **Elohim** | **they perish** | **and by the breath of** | **his nostrils** | **are they consumed** | |

| שאגת 7581 | אריה 738 | וקול 6963 | שחל 7826 | ושני 8127 | כפירים 3715 | נתעו 5421: | 4:11 | ליש 3918 | אבד 6 |
|---|---|---|---|---|---|---|---|---|---|
| sha'agat | 'aryeh | uaqoul | shachal; | uashiney | kapiyriym | nita'au. | | layish | 'abed |
| **The roaring of** | **the lion** | **and the voice of** | **the fierce lion** | **and the teeth of** | **the young lions** | **are broken** | | **The old lion** | **perish** |

| מבלי 1097 | טרף 2964 | ובני 1121 | לביא 3833 | יתפרדו 6504: | 4:12 | ואלי 413 | דבר 1697 | יגנב 1589 |
|---|---|---|---|---|---|---|---|---|
| mibaliy | tarep; | uabney | labiy'a, | yitparadu. | | ua'aelay | dabar | yagunab; |
| **for lack of** | **prey** | **and whelps** | **the stout lion's** | **are scattered abroad** | | **Now to me** | **a thing** | **was secretly brought** |

| ותקח 3947 | אזני 241 | שמץ 8102 | מנהו 4480: | 4:13 | בשעפים 5587 | מחזינות 2384 | לילה 3915 | בנפל 5307 | תרדמה 8639 | על 5921 |
|---|---|---|---|---|---|---|---|---|---|---|
| uatiqach | 'azaniy, | shemetz | menhu. | | bis'apiym | mechezyonout | layalah; | binpol | tardemah, | 'al |
| **and received** | **mine ear** | **a little** | **thereof** | | **In thoughts** | **from the visions of** | **the night** | **when fall** | **deep sleep** | **on** |

| אנשים 582: | 4:14 | פחד 6343 | קראני 7122 | ורעדה 7461 | ורב 7230 | עצמותי 6106 | הפחיד 6342: | 4:15 | ורוח 7307 | על 5921 |
|---|---|---|---|---|---|---|---|---|---|---|
| 'anashiym. | | pachad | qara'aniy | uar'adah; | uarob | atzmoutay | hipchiyd. | | uaruach | 'al |
| **men** | | **Fear** | **came upon me** | **and trembling** | **all** | **my bones** | **which made to shake** | | **Then a spirit** | **before** |

| פני 6440 | יחלף 2498 | תסמר 5568 | שערת 8185 | בשרי 1320: | 4:16 | יעמד 5975 | ולא 3808 | אכיר 5234 | מראהו 4758 | תמונה 8544 |
|---|---|---|---|---|---|---|---|---|---|---|
| panay | yachalop; | tasamer, | sa'arat | basariy. | | ya'amod | uala' | 'akiyr | mar'aehu, | tamunah |
| **my face** | **passed** | **stood up** | **the hair of** | **my flesh** | | **It stood still** | **but not** | **I could discern** | **the form thereof** | **an image** |

| לנגד 5048 | עיני 5869 | דממה 1827 | וקול 6963 | אשמע 8085: | 4:17 | האנוש 582 | מאלוה 433 | יצדק 6663 | אם 518 |
|---|---|---|---|---|---|---|---|---|---|
| laneged | 'aeynay; | damamah | uaqoul | 'ashma. | | ha'anoush | me'alouah | yitzdaq; | 'am |
| ***was* before** | **mine eyes** | ***there was* silence** | **and a voice** | **I heard *saying*** | | **mortal man** | **than Elohim?** | **Shall be more just** | **or** |

| מעשהו 6213 | יטהר 2891 | גבר 1397: | 4:18 | הן 2005 | בעבדיו 5650 | לא 3808 | יאמין 539 | ובמלאכיו 4397 | ישים 7760 |
|---|---|---|---|---|---|---|---|---|---|
| me'asehu, | yitahar | gaber. | | hen | ba'abadayu | la' | ya'amiyn; | uabmal'akayu, | yasiym |
| **than his maker?** | **shall be more pure** | **a man** | | **Behold** | **in his servants** | **no** | **he put trust** | **and his angels** | **he charged with** |

| תהלה 8417: | 4:19 | אף 637 | שכני 7931 | בתי 1004 | חמר 2563 | אשר 834 | בעפר 6083 | יסודם 3247 | ידכאום 1792 |
|---|---|---|---|---|---|---|---|---|---|
| tahalah. | | 'ap | shokaney | batey | chamor, | 'asher | be'apar | yasoudam; | yadak'aum, |
| **folly** | | **How much less *in* them that dwell in** | | **houses of** | **clay** | **whose** | ***is* in the dust** | **foundation** | ***which* are crushed** |

| לפני 6440 | עש 6211: | 4:20 | מבקר 1242 | לערב 6153 | יכתו 3807 | מבלי 1097 | משים 7760 | לנצח 5331 | יאבדו 6: | 4:21 |
|---|---|---|---|---|---|---|---|---|---|---|
| lipney | 'ash. | | miboqer | la'areb | yukatu; | mibaliy | mesiym, | lanetzach | ya'bedu. | |
| **before** | **the moth?** | | **from morning** | **to evening** | **They are destroyed** | **without any** | **regarding *it*** | **for ever** | **they perish** | |

| הלא 3808 | נסע 5265 | יתרם 3499 | בם 871a | ימותו 4191 | ולא 3808 | בחכמה 2451: |
|---|---|---|---|---|---|---|
| hala' | nisa' | yitram | bam; | yamutu, | uala' | bachakamah. |
| **not** | **Does go away?** | **their excellency *which is*** | **in them** | **they die** | **even without** | **wisdom** |

| Job 5:1 | קרא 7121 | נא 4994 | היש 3426 | עונך 6030 | ואל 413 | מי 4310 | מקדשים 6918 | תפנה 6437: | 5:2 | כי 3588 |
|---|---|---|---|---|---|---|---|---|---|---|
| | qara' | naa' | hayesh | 'aneka; | ua'al | miy' | miqdoshiym | tipneh. | | kiy |
| | **Call** | **now** | ***if* there be any** | **that will answer you** | **and to which** | **of** | **the saints** | **will you turn?** | | **For** |

Job 4:9 By the blast of G-d they perish, and by the breath of his nostrils are they consumed.10 The roaring of the lion, and the voice of the fierce lion, and the teeth of the young lions, are broken.11 The old lion perisheth for lack of prey, and the stout lion's whelps are scattered abroad.12 Now a thing was secretly brought to me, and mine ear received a little thereof.13 In thoughts from the visions of the night, when deep sleep fall on men,14 Fear came upon me, and trembling, which made all my bones to shake.15 Then a spirit passed before my face; the hair of my flesh stood up:16 It stood still, but I could not discern the form thereof: an image was before mine eyes, there was silence, and I heard a voice, saying,17 Shall mortal man be more just than G-d? shall a man be more pure than his maker?18 Behold, he put no trust in his servants; and his angels he charged with folly:19 How much less in them that dwell in houses of clay, whose foundation is in the dust, which are crushed before the moth?20 They are destroyed from morning to evening: they perish forever without any regarding it.21 Does not their excellency which is in them go away? they die, even without wisdom. **Job** 5:1 Call now,

לאויל 191 יהרג 2026 כעש 3708 ופתה 6601 תמית 4191 קנאה 7068: 5:3 אני 589 ראיתי 7200 אויל 191 משריש 8327 ואקוב 5344
le'auiyl yaharag ka'as; uapoteh, tamiyt qin'ah. 'aniy ra'aytiy 'auiyl mashriysh; ua'aqoub
**the foolish man kills wrath and the silly one slay envy I have seen the foolish taking root but I cursed**

נוהו 5116 פתאם 6597: 5:4 ירחקו 7368 בניו 1121 מישע 3468 וידכאו 1792 בשער 8179 ואין 369
nauehu pit'am. yirchaqu banayu miyesha'; uayidake'au basha'ar, ua'aeyn
**his habitation suddenly are far His children from safety and they are crushed in the gate and neither**

מציל 5337: 5:5 אשר 834 קצירו 7105 רעב 7456 יאכל 398 ואל 413 מצנים 6791 יקחהו 3947
matziyl. 'asher qatziyrou ra'aeb ya'kel, ua'al mitziniym yiqachehu;
***is there* any to deliver *them* Whose harvest the hungry eat up and for *even* out of the thorns takes it**

ושאף 7602 צמים 6782 חילם 2428: 5:6 כי 3588 לא 3808 יצא 3318 מעפר 6083 און 205 ומאדמה 127 לא 3808
uasha'ap tzamiym cheylam. kiy la' yetzea' me'apar 'auen; uame'adamah, la'
**and swallow up the robber their substance Although not comes forth of the dust affliction out of the ground neither**

יצמח 6779 עמל 5999: 5:7 כי 3588 אדם 120 לעמל 5999 יולד 3205 ובני 1121 רשף 7565 יגביהו 1361 עוף 5774: 5:8 אולם 199 אני 589 אדרש 1875
yitzmach 'amal. kiy 'adam la'amal yulad; uabaney reshep, yagbiyhu 'aup. 'aulam, 'aniy 'adrosh
**does spring trouble Yet man unto trouble is born as one sparks upward fly however I would seek**

אל 413 אל 410 ואל 413 אלהים 430 אשים 7760 דברתי 1700: 5:9 עשה 6213 גדלות 1419 ואין 369 חקר 2714
'al al; ua'al 'alohiym, 'asiym dibratiy. 'aseh gadolout ua'aeyn cheqer;
**unto El and unto Elohim would I commit my cause Which does great things as else unsearchable**

נפלאות 6381 עד 5704 אין 369 מספר 4557: 5:10 הנתן 5414 מטר 4306 על 5921 פני 6440 ארץ 776 ושלח 7971 מים 4325 על 5921 פני 6440
nipla'aut, 'ad 'aeyn mispar. hanoten mator 'al paney 'aretz; uasholeach mayim 'al paney
**marvellous things as without number Who gives rain up upon the earth and send waters up upon**

חוצות 2351: 5:11 לשום 7760 שפלים 8217 למרום 4791 וקדרים 6937 שגבו 7682 ישע 3468: 5:12 מפר 6565
chutzout. lasum shapaliym lamaroum; uaqodariym, sagabu yesha'. meper
**the fields To set up those that be low on high that those which mourn may be exalted to safety He disappoints**

מחשבות 4284 ערומים 6175 ולא 3808 תעשינה 6213 ידיהם 3027 תושיה 8454: 5:13 לכד 3920 חכמים 2450
machashabout 'arumiym; uala' ta'aseynah yadeyhem, tushiyah. loked chakamiym
**the devices of the crafty so that cannot perform hands *their* enterprise He takes the wise**

בערמם 6193 ועצת 6098 נפתלים 6617 נמהרה 4116: 5:14 יומם 3119 יפגשו 6298 חשך 2822
ba'aramam; ua'atzat niptaliym nimharah. youmam yapagshu choshek;
**in their own craftiness and the counsel of the froward is carried headlong in the daytime They meet with darkness**

וכלילה 3915 ימששו 4959 בצהרים 6672: 5:15 וישע 3467 מחרב 2719 מפיהם 6310 ומיד 3027
uakalayalah, yamashashu batzaharayim. uayosha' mechereb mipiyhem; uamiyad
**and as in the night grope in the noonday But he save from the sword from their mouth and from the hand of**

חזק 2389 אביון 34: 5:16 ותהי 1961 לדל 1800 תקוה 8615 ועלתה 5766 קפצה 7092 פיה 6310: 5:17 הנה 2009 אשרי 835 אנוש 582
chazaq abyoun. uatahiy ladal tiquah; ua'alatah, qapatzah piyha. hineh 'ashrey 'anoush
**the mighty the poor So has the poor hope and iniquity stop her mouth Behold happy *is* the man**

Job 5:if there be any that will answer you; and to which of the saints will you turn?2 For wrath kill the foolish man, and envy slayeth the silly one.3 I have seen the foolish taking root: but suddenly I cursed his habitation.4 His children are far from safety, and they are crushed in the gate, neither is there any to deliver them.5 Whose harvest the hungry eateth up, and take it even out of the thorns, and the robber swalloweth up their substance.6 Although affliction cometh not forth of the dust, neither doth trouble spring out of the ground;7 Yet man is born unto trouble, as the sparks fly upward.8 I would seek unto G-d, and unto G-d would I commit my cause:9 Which doeth great things and unsearchable; marvellous things without number:10 Who give rain upon the earth, and send waters upon the fields:11 To set up on high those that be low; that those which mourn may be exalted to safety.12 He disappointeth the devices of the crafty, so that their hands cannot perform their enterprise.13 He take the wise in their own craftiness: and the counsel of the froward is carried headlong.14 They meet with darkness in the daytime, and grope in the noonday as in the night.15 But he save the poor from the sword, from their mouth, and from the hand of the mighty.16 So the poor has hope, and iniquity stoppeth her mouth. 17 Behold, happy is the man whom G-d correcteth:

| יוכחנו 3198 | אלוה 433 | ומוסר 4148 | שדי 7706 | אל 408 | תמאס 3988: | 5:18 כי 3588 | הוא 1931 | יכאיב 3510 | ויחבש 2280 |
|---|---|---|---|---|---|---|---|---|---|
| youkichenu | 'alouah; | uamusar | shaday, | 'al | tim'as. | kiy | hua' | yak'ayb | uayechbash; |
| **whom correct** | **Elohim** | **therefore the chastening of** | **the Almighty** | **not** | **despise you** | **For** | **he** | **make sore** | **and bind up** |

| ימחץ 4272 | וידו 3027 | תרפינה 7495: | 5:19 בשש 8337 | צרות 6869 | יצילך 5337 | ובשבע 7651 | לא 3808 | יגע 5060 |
|---|---|---|---|---|---|---|---|---|
| yimchatz, | uayadou | tirpeynah. | bashesh | tzarout | yatziyleka; | uabsheba' | la' | yiga' |
| **he wound** | **and his hands** | **make whole** | **in six** | **troubles** | **He shall deliver you** | **yea in seven** | **no** | **there shall touch** |

| בך 871a | רע 7451: | 5:20 ברעב 7458 | פדך 6299 | ממות 4194 | ובמלחמה 4421 | מידי 3027 | חרב 2719: | 5:21 |
|---|---|---|---|---|---|---|---|---|
| baka | ra'. | bara'ab | padaka | mimauet; | uabmilchamah, | miydey | chareb. | |
| **against you** | **evil** | **In famine** | **he shall redeem you** | **from death** | **and in war** | **from the power of** | **the sword** | |

| בשוט 7752 | לשון 3956 | תחבא 2244 | ולא 3808 | תירא 3372 | משד 7701 | כי 3588 | יבוא 935: | 5:22 |
|---|---|---|---|---|---|---|---|---|
| bashout | lashoun | techabea'; | uala' | tiyraa' | mishod, | kiy | yabou'a. | |
| **from the scourge of** | **the tongue** | **You shall be hid** | **and neither** | **shall you be afraid** | **of destruction** | **when** | **it comes** | |

| לשד 7701 | ולכפן 3720 | תשחק 7832 | ומחית 2416 | הארץ 776 | אל 408 | תירא 3372: | 5:23 כי 3588 | עם 5973 |
|---|---|---|---|---|---|---|---|---|
| lashod | ualkapan | tischaq; | uamechayat | ha'aretz, | 'al | tiyraa'. | kiy | 'am |
| **At destruction** | **and famine** | **you shall laugh** | **of the beasts of** | **the earth** | **neither** | **shall you be afraid** | **For** | **with** |

| אבני 68 | השדה 7704 | בריתך 1285 | וחית 2416 | השדה 7704 | השלמה 7999 | לך 3807a: | 5:24 וידעת 3045 |
|---|---|---|---|---|---|---|---|
| 'abney | hasadeh | bariyteka; | uachayat | hasadeh, | hashelemah | lak. | uayada'ata |
| **the stones of** | **the field** | **you shall be in league** | **and the beasts of** | **the field** | **shall be at peace** | **with you** | **And you shall know** |

| כי 3588 | שלום 7965 | אהלך 168 | ופקדת 6485 | נוך 5116 | ולא 3808 | תחטא 2398: | 5:25 וידעת 3045 | כי 3588 |
|---|---|---|---|---|---|---|---|---|
| kiy | shaloum | 'ahaleka; | uapaqadta | nauaka | uala' | techeta'. | uayada'ata | kiy |
| **that** | ***shall be in* peace** | **your tabernacle** | **and you shall visit** | **your habitation** | **and not** | **shall sin** | **You shall know also** | **that** |

| רב 7227 | זרעך 2233 | וצאצאיך 6631 | כעשב 6212 | הארץ 776: | 5:26 תבוא 935 | בכלח 3624 | אלי 413 | קבר 6913 |
|---|---|---|---|---|---|---|---|---|
| rab | zar'aka; | uatze'atza'ayka, | ka'aeseb | ha'aretz. | tabou'a | bakelach | 'aley | qaber; |
| ***shall be* great** | **your seed** | **and your offspring** | **as the grass of** | **the earth** | **You shall come** | **in a full age** | **to** | ***your* grave** |

| כעלות 5927 | גדיש 1430 | בעתו 6256: | 5:27 הנה 2009 | זאת 2063 | חקרנוה 2713 | כן 3651 | היא 1931 | שמענה 8085 | ואתה 859 |
|---|---|---|---|---|---|---|---|---|---|
| ka'alout | gadiysh | ba'atou. | hineh | za't | chaqarnuha | ken | hiy'a; | shama'anah, | ua'atah |
| **like as comes in** | **a shock of corn** | **in his season** | **Lo'** | **this** | **we have searched it** | **so** | **it** | ***is* hear it** | **and you** |

| דע 3045 | לך 3807a: |
|---|---|
| da' | lak. |
| **know *it*** | **for your good** |

| Job 6:1 | ויען 6030 | איוב 347 | ויאמר 559: | 6:2 לו 3863 | שקול 8254 | ישקל 8254 | כעשי 3708 | והיתי 1962 | במאזנים 3976 |
|---|---|---|---|---|---|---|---|---|---|
| | uaya'an | 'ayoub, | uaya'mar. | lou', | shaqoul | yishaqel | ka'asiy; | uahayatiy | bama'zanayim |
| | **But answered** | **Job** | **and said** | **Oh that** | **were throughly** | **weighed** | **my grief** | **and my calamity** | **in the balances** |

| ישאו 5375 | יחד 3162: | 6:3 כי 3588 | עתה 6258 | מחול 2344 | ימים 3220 | יכבד 3513 | על 5921 | כן 3651 | דברי 1697 |
|---|---|---|---|---|---|---|---|---|---|
| yis'au | yachad. | kiy | 'atah, | mechoul | yamiym | yikbad; | 'al | ken, | dabaray |
| **laid** | **together** | **For** | **now** | **than the sand of** | **the sea** | **it would be heavier** | **after** | **therefore** | **my words** |

Job 5:17 therefore despise not you the chastening of the Almighty:18 For he make sore, and bindeth up: he woundeth, and his hands make whole.19 He shall deliver you in six troubles: yea, in seven there shall no evil touch you.20 In famine he shall redeem you from death: and in war from the power of the sword.21 Thou shall be hid from the scourge of the tongue: neither shall you be afraid of destruction when it cometh.22 At destruction and famine you shall laugh: neither shall you be afraid of the beasts of the earth.23 For you shall be in league with the stones of the field: and the beasts of the field shall be at peace with you.24 And you shall know that your tabernacle shall be in peace; and you shall visit your habitation, and shall not sin.25 Thou shall know also that your seed shall be great, and your offspring as the grass of the earth.26 Thou shall come to your grave in a full age, like as a shock of corn cometh in in his season.27 Lo this, we have searched it, so it is; hear it, and know you it for your good. **Job** 6:1 But Job answered and said,2 Oh that my grief were throughly weighed, and my calamity laid in the balances together!3 For now it would be heavier than the sand of the sea:

לעו 3886: 6:4 כי 3588 חצי 2671 שדי 7706 עמדי 5978 אשר 834 חמתם 2534 שתה 8354 רוחי 7307 בעותי 1161
la'au. kiy chitzey shaday 'amadiy, 'asher chamatam shotah ruchiy; bi'autey
**are swallowed up For *the* arrows of the Almighty *are* within me whereof the poison drink up my spirit the terrors of**

אלוה 433 יערכוני 6186: 6:5 הינהק 5101 פרא 6501 עלי 5921 דשא 1877 אם 518 יגעה 1600 שור 7794 על 5921
'alouah ya'arkuniy. hayinhaq pera' 'aley desha'; 'am yig'ah, shour 'al
**Elohim do set themselves in array against me Does bray the wild ass when *he has* grass? Or low the ox over**

בלילו 1098: 6:6 היאכל 398 תפל 8602 מבלי 1097 מלח 4417 אם 518 יש 3426 טעם 2940 בריר 7388 חלמות 2495: 6:7
baliylou. haye'akel tapel mibaliy melach; 'am yesh ta'am, bariyr chalamut.
**his fodder? Can be eaten that which is unsavoury without salt? or is there *any* taste in the white of an egg?**

מאנה 3985 לנגוע 5060 נפשי 5315 המה 1992 כדוי 1741 לחמי 3899: 6:8 מי 4310 יתן 5414 תבוא 935 שאלתי 7596
me'anah lingoua' napshiy; hemah, kiduey lachmiy. miy' yiten tabou'a she'alatiy;
***The things that* refused to touch my soul *are* like as sorrowful my meat Oh that would grant I might have my request**

ותקותי 8615 יתן 5414 אלוה 433: 6:9 ויאל 2974 אלוה 433 וידכאני 1792
uatiquatiy, yiten 'alouah. uayo'ael 'alouah uiydak'aeniy;
**and the thing that I long for would grant *me* *that* Elohim Even that it would please Elohim to destroy me**

יתר 5425 ידו 3027 ויבצעני 1214: 6:10 ותהי 1961 עוד 5750 נחמתי 5165 ואסלדה 5539
yater yadou, uiybatza'aeniy. 'uatahiy 'aud nechamatiy, ua'asaldah
**that he would let loose his hand and cut me off Then should I have yet comfort yea I would harden myself**

בחילה 2427 לא 3808 יחמול 2550 כי 3588 לא 3808 כחדתי 3582 אמרי 561 קדוש 6918: 6:11 מה 4100 כחי 3581 כי 3588
bachiylah la' yachmoul; kiy la' kichadtiy, 'amrey qadoush. mah kochiy kiy
**in sorrow not let him spare for not I have concealed the words of the Holy One What *is* my strength that**

איחל 3176 ומה 4100 קצי 7093 כי 3588 אאריך 748 נפשי 5315: 6:12 אם 518 כח 3581 אבנים 68 כחי 3581 אם 518
'ayachel; uamah qitziy, kiy 'a'ariyk napshiy. 'am koach 'abaniym kochiy; 'am
**I should hope? and what *is* mine end that I should prolong my life? *Is* or my strength stones? the strength of if**

בשרי 1320 נחוש 5153: 6:13 האם 518 אין 369 עזרתי 5833 בי 871a ותשיה 8454 נדחה 5080 ממני 4480: 6:14 למס 4523
basariy nachush. ha'am 'aeyn 'azratiy biy; uatushiyah, nidchah mimeniy. lamas
***is* my flesh of brass? *Is* if not my help in me? and wisdom is driven quite from me? To him that is afflicted**

מרעהו 4453 חסד 2617 ויראת 3374 שדי 7706 יעזוב 5800: 6:15 אחי 251 בגדו 898
mere'aehu chased; uayir'at shaday ya'azoub. 'achay bagadu
***should be showed* from his friend pity but the fear of the Almighty he forsake My brethren have dealt deceitfully**

כמו 3644 נחל 5158 כאפיק 650 נחלים 5158 יעברו 5674: 6:16 הקדרים 6937 מני 4480 קרח 7140 עלימו 5921
kamou nachal; ka'apiyq nachaliym ya'aboru. haqodariym miniy qarach; 'aleymou,
**as a brook *and* as the stream of brooks they pass away Which are blackish by reason of the ice *and* wherein**

יתעלם 5956 שלג 7950: 6:17 בעת 6256 יזרבו 2215 נצמתו 6789 בחמו 2527 נדעכו 1846 ממקומם 4725:
yit'alem shaleg. ba'aet yazorabu nitzmatu; bachumou, nid'aku mimqoumam.
**is hid the snow What time they wax warm they vanish when it is hot they are consumed out of their place**

Job 6:3 therefore my words are swallowed up.4 For the arrows of the Almighty are within me, the poison whereof drinketh up my spirit: the terrors of G-d do set themselves in array against me.5 Does the wild ass bray when he has grass? or loweth the ox over his fodder?6 Can that which is unsavoury be eaten without salt? or is there any taste in the white of an egg?7 The things that my soul refused to touch are as my sorrowful meat.8 Oh that I might have my request; and that G-d would grant me the thing that I long for!9 Even that it would please G-d to destroy me; that he would let loose his hand, and cut me off!10 Then should I yet have comfort; yea, I would harden myself in sorrow: let him not spare; for I have not concealed the words of the Holy One.11 What is my strength, that I should hope? and what is mine end, that I should prolong my life?12 Is my strength the strength of stones? or is my flesh of brass?13 Is not my help in me? and is wisdom driven quite from me?14 To him that is afflicted pity should be showed from his friend; but he forsaketh the fear of the Almighty.15 My brethren have dealt deceitfully as a brook, and as the stream of brooks they pass away;16 Which are blackish by reason of the ice, and wherein the snow is hid:17 What time they wax warm, they vanish: when it is hot, they are consumed out of their place.

| 6:18 | | | | | | 6:19 | | |
|---|---|---|---|---|---|---|---|---|
| ילפתו 3943 | ארחות 734 | דרכם 1870 | יעלו 5927 | בתהו 8414 | ויאבדו 6: | הביטו 5027 | ארחות 734 | תמא 8485 |
| yilapatu | 'arachout | darkam; | ya'alu | batohu | uaya'bedu. | hibiytu | 'arachout | tema'; |
| **are turned aside** | **The paths of** | **their way** | **they go** | **to nothing** | **and perish** | **looked** | **The troops of** | **Tema** |

| | | | | 6:20 | | | | |
|---|---|---|---|---|---|---|---|---|
| הליכת 1979 | שבא 7614 | קוו 6960 | למו 3807a: | בשו 954 | כי 3588 | בטח 982 | באו 935 | עדיה 5704 |
| haliykot | shaba', | qiuu | lamou. | boshu | kiy | batach; | ba'au | 'adeyha, |
| **the companies of** | **Sheba** | **waited** | **for them** | **They were confounded** | **because** | **they had hoped** | **they came** | **there** |

| | 6:21 | | | | | | | 6:22 | | |
|---|---|---|---|---|---|---|---|---|---|---|
| ויחפרו: | כי 3588 | עתה 6258 | הייתם 1961 | לא 3808 | תראו 7200 | חתת 2866 | ותיראו 3372: | הכי 3588 | אמרתי 559 | הבו 3051 |
| uayechparu. | kiy | 'atah | heyiytem | la' | tir'au | chatat, | uatiyra'au. | hakiy | 'amartiy | habu |
| **and were ashamed** | **For** | **now** | **you are** | **nothing** | **you see** | ***my* casting down** | **and are afraid** | **Did** | **I say** | **Bring** |

| | | | | 6:23 | | |
|---|---|---|---|---|---|---|
| לי 3807a | ומכחכם 3581 | שחדו 7809 | בעדי 1157: | ומלטוני 4422 | מיד 3027 | צר 6862 |
| liy; | uamikochakem, | shichadu | ba'adiy. | uamaltuniy | miyad | tzar; |
| **unto me?** | **or of your substance?** | **Give a reward** | **for me** | **Or, Deliver me** | **from the hand of** | ***the* enemy's** |

| | | | 6:24 | | | | |
|---|---|---|---|---|---|---|---|
| ומיד 3027 | עריצים 6184 | תפדוני 6299: | הורוני 3384 | ואני 589 | אחריש 2790 | ומה 4100 | שגיתי 7686 |
| uamiyad | 'ariytziym | tipduniy. | houruniy | ua'aniy | 'achariysh; | uamah | shagiytiy, |
| **and from the hand of** | **the mighty?** | **Redeem me** | **Teach me** | **and I** | **will hold my tongue** | **and wherein** | **I have erred** |

| | | 6:25 | | | | | | | 6:26 |
|---|---|---|---|---|---|---|---|---|---|
| הבינו 995 | לי 3807a: | מה 4100 | נמרצו 4834 | אמרי 561 | ישר 3476 | ומה 4100 | יוכיח 3198 | הוכח 3198 | מכם 4480: |
| habiynu | liy. | mah | nimratzu | 'amrey | yosher; | uamah | youkiyach | houkeach | mikem. |
| **cause to understand** | **me** | **How** | **forcible are** | **words** | **right** | **but what** | **does arguing** | **reprove?** | **your** |

| | | | | | | 6:27 | |
|---|---|---|---|---|---|---|---|
| הלהוכח 3198 | מלים 4405 | תחשבו 2803 | ולרוח 7307 | אמרי 561 | נאש 2976: | אף 637 | על 5921 |
| halahoukach | miliym | tachshobu; | ualruach, | 'amrey | no'ash. | 'ap | 'al |
| **to reprove** | **words** | **Do you imagine** | ***which are* and as wind?** | **the speeches of** | **one that is desperate** | **Yea** | **for** |

| | | | | | 6:28 | | | |
|---|---|---|---|---|---|---|---|---|
| יתום 3490 | תפילו 5307 | ותכרו 3738 | על 5921 | ריעכם 7453: | ועתה 6258 | הואילו 2974 | פנו 6437 | בי 871a |
| yatoum | tapiylu; | uatikru, | 'al | rey'akem. | ua'atah | hou'aylu | panu | biy; |
| **the fatherless** | **you overwhelm** | **and you dig *a pit*** | **for** | **your friend** | **Now therefore** | **be content** | **look** | **upon me** |

| | | | | 6:29 | | | | | | |
|---|---|---|---|---|---|---|---|---|---|---|
| ועל 5921 | פניכם 6440 | אם 518 | אכזב 3576: | שבו 7725 | נא 4994 | אל 408 | תהי 1961 | עולה 5766 | ושבי 7725 | עוד 5750 |
| ua'al | paneykem, | 'am | 'akazeb. | shubu | naa' | 'al | tahiy | 'aulah; | uashubiy | 'aud |
| **for *it is* evident** | **unto you** | **if** | **I lie** | **Return** | **I pray you** | **not** | **let it be** | **iniquity** | **yea, return** | **again** |

| | | 6:30 | | | | | | | |
|---|---|---|---|---|---|---|---|---|---|
| צדקי 6664 | בה 871a: | היש 3426 | בלשוני 3956 | עולה 5766 | אם 518 | חכי 2441 | לא 3808 | יבין 995 | הוות 1942: |
| tzidqiy | bah. | hayesh | bilshouniy | 'aulah; | 'am | chikiy, | la' | yabiyn | hauout. |
| **my righteousness *is*** | **in it** | **Is there** | **my tongue?** | **iniquity** | **in that** | **my taste** | **cannot** | **discern** | **perverse things?** |

| Job 7:1 | | | | | | | | 7:2 |
|---|---|---|---|---|---|---|---|---|
| הלא 3808 | צבא 6635 | לאנוש 582 | על 5921 | ארץ 776 | וכימי 3117 | שכיר 7916 | ימיו 3117: | |
| hala' | tzaba' | le'anoush | 'al | 'aretz; | uakiymey | sakiyr | yamayu. | |
| ***Is there* not** | **an appointed time** | **to man** | **upon** | **earth?** | ***are not* his days** | **an hireling?** | **also like the days of** | |

| | | | | | | 7:3 | |
|---|---|---|---|---|---|---|---|
| כעבד 5650 | ישאף 7602 | צל 6738 | וכשכיר 7916 | יקוה 6960 | פעלו 6467: | כן 3651 | הנחלתי 5157 |
| ka'abed | yish'ap | tzel; | uaksakiyr, | yaqaueh | pa'alou. | ken | hanachaltiy |
| **As a servant** | **earnestly desire** | **the shadow** | **and as an hireling** | **looks for** | ***the reward of* his work** | **So** | **am made to possess** |

Job 6:18 The paths of their way are turned aside; they go to nothing, and perish.19 The troops of Tema looked, the companies of Sheba waited for them.20 They were confounded because they had hoped; they came thither, and were ashamed.21 For now you are nothing; you see my casting down, and are afraid.22 Did I say, Bring unto me? or, Give a reward for me of your substance?23 Or, Deliver me from the enemy's hand? or, Redeem me from the hand of the mighty?24 Teach me, and I will hold my tongue: and cause me to understand wherein I have erred.25 How forcible are right words! but what doth your arguing reprove?26 Do you imagine to reprove words, and the speeches of one that is desperate, which are as wind?27 Yea, you overwhelm the fatherless, and you dig a pit for your friend.28 Now therefore be content, look upon me; for it is evident unto you if I lie.29 Return, I pray you, let it not be iniquity; yea, return again, my righteousness is in it.30 Is there iniquity in my tongue? cannot my taste discern perverse things? **Job** 7:1 Is there not an appointed time to man upon earth? are not his days also like the days of an hireling?2 As a servant earnestly desire the shadow, and as an hireling look for the reward of his work:3 So am I made to possess months of vanity, and wearisome nights are appointed to me.

7:4

לי 3807a ירחי 3391 שוא 7723 ולילות 3915 עמל 5999 מנו 4487 לי 3807a: אם 518 שכבתי 7901 ואמרתי 559 מתי 4970 אקום 6965

liy yarchey shau'a; ualeylout 'amal, minu liy. 'am shakabtiy, ua'amartiy, matay 'aqum

**I months of vanity and nights wearisome are appointed to me When I lie down and I say When shall I arise**

7:5

ומדד 4059 ערב 6153 ושבעתי 7646 נדדים 7076 עדי 5704 נשף 5399: לבש 3847 בשרי 1320 רמה 7415

uamidad 'areb; uasaba'atiy nadudiym 'adey nashep. labash basariy rimah

**and be gone the night and I am full of tossings to and fro unto *the* dawning of the day is clothed My flesh *with* worms**

7:6

וגיש 1487 עפר 6083 עורי 5785 רגע 7280 וימאס 3988: ימי 3117 קלו 7043 מני 4480 ארג 708 ויכלו 3615

uagiysh 'apar; 'aouriy raga', uayima'aes. yamay qalu miniy 'areg; uayiklu,

**the clods of dust my skin is broken and become loathsome My days are swifter than a weaver's shuttle and are spent**

7:7 7:8

באפס 657 תקוה 8615: זכר 2142 כי 3588 רוח 7307 חיי 2416 לא 3808 תשוב 7725 עיני 5869 לראות 7200 טוב 2896: לא 3808 תשורני 7789

ba'apes tiquah. zakor kiy ruach chayay; la' tashub 'aeyniy, lir'aut toub. la' tashureniy

**without hope O remember that *is* wind my life no more mine eye shall see good no *more* shall see me**

7:9

עין 5869 ראי 7210 עיניך 5869 בי 871a ואינני 369: כלה 3615 ענן 6051 וילך 1980 כן 3651

'aeyn ro'ay; 'aeyneyka biy ua'aeyneniy. kalah 'anan uayelak; ken

**The eye of him that has seen me your eyes *are* upon me and I am not *As* is consumed the cloud and vanishes away so**

7:10

יורד 3381 שאול 7585 לא 3808 יעלה 5927: לא 3808 ישוב 7725 עוד 5750 לביתו 1004 ולא 3808

youred sha'aul, la' ya'aleh. la' yashub 'aud labeytou; uala'

**he that goes down to the grave no *more* shall come up no He shall return more to his house neither**

7:11

יכירנו 5234 עוד 5750 מקמו 4725: גם 1571 אני 589 לא 3808 אחשך 2820 פי 6310 אדברה 1696 בצר 6862

yakiyrenu 'aud maqomou. gam 'aniy la' 'achesak piy 'adabrah batzar

**shall know him anymore his place Therefore I not will refrain my mouth I will speak in the anguish of**

7:12

רוחי 7307 אשיחה 7878 במר 4751 נפשי 5315: הים 3220 אני 589 אם 518 תנין 8577 כי 3588 תשים 7760 עלי 5921

ruchiy; 'asiychah, bamar napshiy. hayam 'aniy 'am taniyn; kiy tasiym 'alay

**my spirit I will complain in the bitterness of my soul Am a sea I or a whale that you set over me?**

7:13 7:14

משמר 4929: כי 3588 אמרתי 559 תנחמני 5162 ערשי 6210 ישא 5375 בשיחי 7878 משכבי 4904: וחתתני 2865

mishmar. kiy 'amartiy tanachameniy 'arsiy; yisa' basiychiy, mishkabiy. uachitataniy

**a watch When I say shall comfort me My bed shall ease my complaint my couch Then you scarest me**

7:15 7:16

בחלמות 2472 ומחזינות 2384 תבעתני 1204: ותבחר 977 מחנק 4267 נפשי 5315 מות 4194 מעצמותי 6106:

bachalomout; uamechezyonout taba'ataniy. uatibchar machanaq napshiy; mauet, me'atzmoutay.

**with dreams and through visions terrifiest me So that choose strangling my soul *and* death rather than my life**

7:17

מאסתי 3988 לא 3808 לעלם 5769 אחיה 2421 חדל 2308 ממני 4480 כי 3588 הבל 1892 ימי 3117: מה 4100 אנוש 582 כי 3588

ma'astiy la' la'alam 'achayeh; chadal mimeniy, kiy hebel yamay. mah 'anoush kiy

**I loathe *it* not alway I would live let alone me for *are* vanity my days What *is* man that**

7:18

תגדלנו 1431 וכי 3588 תשית 7896 אליו 413 לבך 3820: ותפקדנו 6485 לבקרים 1242

tagadlenu; uakiy tashiyt 'aelayu libeka. uatipqadenu libqariym;

**you should magnify him? and that you should set upon him? your heart And *that* you should visit him every morning**

Job 7:4 When I lie down, I say, When shall I arise, and the night be gone? and I am full of tossings to and fro unto the dawning of the day.5 My flesh is clothed with worms and clods of dust; my skin is broken, and become loathsome.6 My days are swifter than a weaver's shuttle, and are spent without hope.7 O remember that my life is wind: mine eye shall no more see good.8 The eye of him that has seen me shall see me no more: your eyes are upon me, and I am not.9 As the cloud is consumed and vanisheth away: so he that go down to the grave shall come up no more.10 He shall return no more to his house, neither shall his place know him anymore.11 Therefore I will not refrain my mouth; I will speak in the anguish of my spirit; I will complain in the bitterness of my soul.12 Am I a sea, or a whale, that you settest a watch over me?13 When I say, My bed shall comfort me, my couch shall ease my complaint;14 Then you scarest me with dreams, and terrifiest me through visions:15 So that my soul chooseth strangling, and death rather than my life.16 I loathe it; I would not live alway: let me alone; for my days are vanity.17 What is man, that you should magnify him? and that you should set your heart upon him?18 And that you should visit him every morning, and try him every moment?

7:19
לרגעים 7281 תבחננו 974: כמה 4100 לא 3808 תשעה 8159 ממני 4480 לא 3808 תרפני 7503 עד 5704 בלעי 1104
lirga'aym, tibchanenu. kamah la' tish'ah mimeniy; la' tarpeniy, 'ad bil'ay
**every moment? *and* try him How long not will you depart from me nor let me alone till I swallow down**

7:20
רקי 7536: חטאתי 2398 מה 4100 אפעל 6466 לך 3807a נצר 5341 האדם 120 למה 4100 שמתני 7760 למפגע 4645
ruqiy. chata'tiy mah 'ap'al lak notzer ha'adam lamah samtaniy lamipga'
**my spittle? I have sinned what shall I do unto you O you preserver of men? why have you set me as a mark**

7:21
לך 3807a ואהיה 1961 עלי 5921 למשא 4853: ומה 4100 לא 3808 תשא 5375 פשעי 6588 ותעביר 5674 את 853
lak; ua'ahayeh 'alay lamasa'. uameh la' tisa' pish'ay uata'abiyr 'at
**against you so that I am to myself? a burden And why not do you pardon my transgression and take away**

עוני 5771 כי 3588 עתה 6258 לעפר 6083 אשכב 7901 ושחרתני 7836 ואינני 369:
'auoniy kiy 'atah le'apar 'ashkab; uashichartaniy ua'aeyneniy.
**my iniquity? for now in the dust shall I sleep and you shall seek me in the morning but I shall not *be***

**Job 8:1** 8:2
ויען 6030 בלדד 1085 השוחי 7747 ויאמר 559: עד 5704 אן 575 תמלל 4448 אלה 428 ורוח 7307 כביר 3524
uaya'an bildad hashuchiy, uaya'mar 'ad 'an tamalel 'aeleh; uaruach kabiyr
**Then answered Bildad the Shuhite and said How long will you speak these *things*? and a wind? strong**

8:3
אמרי 561 פיך 6310: האל 410 יעות 5791 משפט 4941 ואם 518 שדי 7706 יעות 5791
'amrey piyka. ha'ael ya'auet mishapat; ua'am shaday, ya'auet
***how long shall* the words of your mouth *be like* El Does pervert judgment? or the Almighty does pervert**

8:4 8:5
צדק 6664: אם 518 בניך 1121 חטאו 2398 לו 3807a וישלחם 7971 ביד 3027 פשעם 6588: אם 518
tzedeq. 'am baneyka chata'au lou'; uayashalchem, bayad pish'am. 'am
**justice? If your children have sinned against him and he have cast them away for their transgression If**

8:6
אתה 859 תשחר 7836 אל 413 אל 410 ואל 413 שדי 7706 תתחנן 2603: אם 518 זך 2134 וישר 3477 אתה 859
'atah tashacher 'al 'ael; ua'al shaday, titchanan. 'am zak uayashar, 'atah
**you would seek betimes unto El and to the Almighty make your supplication If *wert* pure and upright you**

8:7
כי 3588 עתה 6258 יעיר 5782 עליך 5921 ושלם 7999 נות 5116 צדקך 6664: והיה 1961
kiy 'atah ya'ayr 'aleyka; uashilam, nauat tzidqeka. uahayah
**surely now he would awake for you and make prosperous the habitation of your righteousness Though was**

8:8
ראשיתך 7225 מצער 4705 ואחריתך 319 ישגה 7685 מאד 3966: כי 3588 שאל 7592 נא 4994 לדר 1755 רישון 7223
rea'shiytaka mitz'ar; ua'achariytaka, yisgeh ma'ad. kiy sha'al naa' lador riyshoun;
**your beginning small yet your latter end should increase greatly For inquire I pray you of age *the* former**

8:9
וכונן 3559 לחקר 2714 אבותם 1: כי 3588 תמול 8543 אנחנו 587 ולא 3808 נדע 3045 כי 3588
uakounen, lacheqer aboutam. kiy tamoul 'anachnu uala' neda'; kiy
**and prepare yourself to the search of their fathers For *are but of* yesterday we and nothing know because *are***

8:10
צל 6738 ימינו 3117 עלי 5921 ארץ 776: הלא 3808 הם 1992 יורוך 3384 יאמרו 559 לך 3807a ומלבם 3820 יוצאו 3318
tzel yameynu 'aley 'aretz. hala' hem youruka ya'maru lak; uamilibam, youtzi'au
**a shadow our days upon earth not they Shall teach you *and* tell to you and out of their heart? utter**

Job 8:19 How long will you not depart from me, nor let me alone till I swallow down my spittle?20 I have sinned; what shall I do unto you, O you preserver of men? why have you set me as a mark against you, so that I am a burden to myself?21 And why dost you not pardon my transgression, and take away mine iniquity? for now shall I sleep in the dust; and you shall seek me in the morning, but I shall not be. **Job** 8:1 Then answered Bildad the Shuhite, and said,2 How long will you speak these things? and how long shall the words of your mouth be like a strong wind?3 Does G-d pervert judgment? or doth the Almighty pervert justice?4 If your children have sinned against him, and he have cast them away for their transgression;5 If you would seek unto G-d betimes, and make your supplication to the Almighty;6 If you wert pure and upright; surely now he would awake for you, and make the habitation of your righteousness prosperous.7 Though your beginning was small, yet your latter end should greatly increase.8 For inquire, I pray you, of the former age, and prepare thyself to the search of their fathers:9(For we are but of yesterday, and know nothing, because our days upon earth are a shadow:) 10 Shall not they teach you, and tell you, and utter words out of their heart?

| | 8:11 | | | | | | | | 8:12 |
|---|---|---|---|---|---|---|---|---|---|
| מלים 4405: | היגאה 1342 | גמא 1573 | בלא 3808 | בצה 1207 | ישגה 7685 | אחו 260 | בלי 1097 | מים 4325: | עדנו 5750 |
| miliym. | hayig'ah | goma' | bala' | bitzah; | yisgeh | 'achu | baliy | mayim. | 'adenu |
| **words** | **Can grow up** | **the bulrush** | **without** | **mire?** | **can grow** | **the flag** | **without** | **water?** | **While it *is* yet** |

| | | | | | | | 8:13 | | | | |
|---|---|---|---|---|---|---|---|---|---|---|---|
| באבו 3 | לא 3808 | יקטף 6998 | ולפני 6440 | כל 3605 | חציר 2682 | ייבש 3001: | כן 3651 | ארחות 734 | כל 3605 | שכחי 7911 | אל 410 |
| ba'abou | la' | yiqatep; | ualipaney | kal | chatziyr | yiybash. | ken, | 'arachout | kal | shokachey | 'ael; |
| **in his greenness *and*** | **not** | **cut down** | **before** | **any *other*** | **herb** | **it wither** | **So *are*** | **the paths of** | **all** | **that forget** | **El** |

| | | | 8:14 | | | | | | 8:15 |
|---|---|---|---|---|---|---|---|---|---|
| ותקות 8615 | חנף 2611 | תאבד 6: | אשר 834 | יקוט 6962 | כסלו 3689 | ובית 1004 | עכביש 5908 | מבטחו 4009: | |
| uatiquat | chanep | ta'bed. | 'asher | yaqout | kislou; | uabeyt | 'akabiysh, | mibtachou. | |
| **hope** | **the hypocrite's** | **shall perish** | **Whose** | **shall be cut off** | **hope** | **and a web** | **a spider's** | **whose trust *shall be*** | |

| | | | | | | | | | 8:16 | |
|---|---|---|---|---|---|---|---|---|---|---|
| ישען 8172 | על 5921 | ביתו 1004 | ולא 3808 | יעמד 5975 | יחזיק 2388 | בו 871a | ולא 3808 | יקום 6965: | רטב 7373 | הוא 1931 |
| yisha'aen | 'al | beytou | uala' | ya'amod; | yachaziyq | bou, | uala' | yaqum. | ratob | hua' |
| **He shall lean** | **upon** | **his house** | **but not** | **it shall stand** | **he shall hold fast** | **it** | **but not** | **it shall endure** | ***is* green** | **He** |

| | | | | | | 8:17 | | | | |
|---|---|---|---|---|---|---|---|---|---|---|
| לפני 6440 | שמש 8121 | ועל 5921 | גנתו 1593 | ינקתו 3127 | תצא 3318: | על 5921 | גל 1530 | שרשיו 8328 | יסבכו 5440 | בית 1004 |
| lipaney | shamesh; | ua'al | ganatou, | yonaqtou | tetzea'. | 'al | gal | sharashayu | yasubaku; | beyt |
| **before** | **the sun** | **and in** | **his garden** | **his branch** | **shoot forth** | **about** | **the heap** | **His roots** | **are wrapped** | **the place of** |

| | | 8:18 | | | | | | | 8:19 |
|---|---|---|---|---|---|---|---|---|---|
| אבנים 68 | יחזה 2372: | אם 518 | יבלענו 1104 | ממקומו 4725 | וכחש 3584 | בו 871a | לא 3808 | ראיתיך 7200: | |
| 'abaniym | yechazeh. | 'am | yabala'anu | mimaqoumou; | uakichesh | bou, | la' | ra'aytiyka. | |
| **stones** | ***and* see** | **If** | **he destroy him** | **from his place** | **then *it* shall deny** | **him** | **not** | ***saying* I have seen you** | |

| | | | | | | | 8:20 | | | |
|---|---|---|---|---|---|---|---|---|---|---|
| הן 2005 | הוא 1931 | משוש 4885 | דרכו 1870 | ומעפר 6083 | אחר 312 | יצמחו 6779: | הן 2005 | אל 410 | לא 3808 | ימאס 3988 |
| hen | hua' | masous | darkou; | uame'apar, | 'acher | yitzmachu. | hen | 'ael | la' | yim'as |
| **Behold** | **this** | ***is* the joy of** | **his way** | **and out of the earth** | **others** | **shall grow** | **Behold** | **El** | **not** | **will cast away** |

| | | | | | 8:21 | | | | |
|---|---|---|---|---|---|---|---|---|---|
| תם 8535 | ולא 3808 | יחזיק 2388 | ביד 3027 | מרעים 7489: | עד 5704 | ימלה 4390 | שחוק 7814 | פיך 6310 | ושפתיך 8193 |
| tam; | uala' | yachaziyq, | bayad | mere'aym. | 'ad | yamaleh | sachouq | piyka; | uaspateyka |
| **a perfect *man*** | **neither** | **will he help** | **in hand** | **the evil doers** | **Till** | **he fill with** | **laughing** | **your mouth** | **and your lips** |

| | 8:22 | | | | | |
|---|---|---|---|---|---|---|
| תרועה 8643: | שנאיך 8130 | ילבשו 3847 | בשת 1322 | ואהל 168 | רשעים 7563 | איננו 369: |
| taru'ah. | son'ayka | yilbashu | boshet; | ua'ahel | rasha'aym | 'aeynenu. |
| ***with* rejoicing** | **They that hate you** | **shall be clothed** | **in shame** | **and the dwelling place of** | **the wicked** | ***shall come to* nought** |

| Job 9:1 | | | 9:2 | | | | | | | |
|---|---|---|---|---|---|---|---|---|---|---|
| ויען 6030 | איוב 347 | ויאמר 559: | אמנם 551 | ידעתי 3045 | כי 3588 | כן 3651 | ומה 4100 | יצדק 6663 | אנוש 582 | עם 5973 |
| uaya'an | 'ayoub, | uaya'mar. | 'amanam | yada'tiy | kiy | ken; | uamah | yitzdaq | 'anoush | 'am |
| **Then answered** | **Job** | **and said** | **of a truth** | **I know *it is*** | **for** | **so** | **but how** | **should be just** | **man** | **with** |

| | 9:3 | | | | | | | | | 9:4 | |
|---|---|---|---|---|---|---|---|---|---|---|---|
| אל 410: | אם 518 | יחפץ 2654 | לריב 7378 | עמו 5973 | לא 3808 | יעננו 6030 | אחת 259 | מני 4480 | אלף 505: | חכם 2450 | לבב 3824 |
| 'ael. | 'am | yachpotz | lariyb | 'amou; | la' | ya'anenu, | 'achat | miniy | 'alep. | chakam | lebab |
| **El?** | **If** | **he will** | **contend** | **with him** | **cannot** | **he answer him** | **one** | **of** | **a thousand** | ***He is* wise in** | **heart** |

| | | | | | | 9:5 | |
|---|---|---|---|---|---|---|---|
| ואמיץ 533 | כח 3581 | מי 4310 | הקשה 7185 | אליו 413 | וישלם 7999: | המעתיק 6275 | הרים 2022 |
| ua'amiytz | koach; | miy' | hiqashah | 'aelayu, | uayishlam. | hama'atiyq | hariym |
| **and mighty in** | **strength** | **who** | **has hardened *himself*** | **against him** | **and has prospered?** | **Which remove** | **the mountains** |

Job 8:11 Can the rush grow up without mire? can the flag grow without water?12 Whilst it is yet in his greenness, and not cut down, it withereth before any other herb.13 So are the paths of all that forget G-d; and the hypocrite's hope shall perish:14 Whose hope shall be cut off, and whose trust shall be a spider's web.15 He shall lean upon his house, but it shall not stand: he shall hold it fast, but it shall not endure.16 He is green before the sun, and his branch shooteth forth in his garden.17 His roots are wrapped about the heap, and see the place of stones.18 If he destroy him from his place, then it shall deny him, saying, I have not seen you.19 Behold, this is the joy of his way, and out of the earth shall others grow.20 Behold, G-d will not cast away a perfect man, neither will he help the evil doers:21 Till he fill your mouth with laughing, and your lips with rejoicing.22 They that hate you shall be clothed with shame; and the dwelling place of the wicked shall come to nought. **Job** 9:1 Then Job answered and said,2 I know it is so of a truth: but how should man be just with G-d?3 If he will contend with him, he cannot answer him one of a thousand. 4 He is wise in heart, and mighty in strength: who has hardened himself against him, and has prospered?5 Which removeth the mountains, and they know not: which overturneth them in his anger.

| | | | | | | | | | |
|---|---|---|---|---|---|---|---|---|---|
| ולא 3808 | ידעו 3045 | אשר 834 | הפכם 2015 | באפו 639: | 9:6 | המרגיז 7264 | ארץ 776 | ממקומה 4725 | ועמודיה 5982 |
| uala' | yada'au; | 'asher | hapakam | ba'apou. | | hamargiyz | 'aretz | mimaqoumah; | ua'amudeyha, |
| **and not** | **they know** | **which** | **overturn them** | **in his anger** | | **Which shake** | **the earth** | **out of her place** | **and the pillars thereof** |

| | | | | | | | | | | | |
|---|---|---|---|---|---|---|---|---|---|---|---|
| יתפלצון 6426: | 9:7 | האמר 559 | לחרס 2775 | ולא 3808 | יזרח 2224 | ובעד 1157 | כוכבים 3556 | יחתם 2856: | 9:8 | נטה 5186 | שמים 8064 |
| yitpalatzun | | ha'amer | lacheres | uala' | yizrach; | uab'ad | koukabiym | yachtom. | | noteh | shamayim |
| **tremble** | | **Which command** | **the sun** | **and not** | **it rise** | **and upon** | **the stars** | **seal up** | | **spread out** | **the heavens** |

| | | | | | | | | | |
|---|---|---|---|---|---|---|---|---|---|
| לבדו 905 | ודורך 1869 | על 5921 | במתי 1116 | ים 3220: | 9:9 | עשה 6213 | עש 5906 | כסיל 3685 | וכימה 3598 |
| labadou; | uadourek, | 'al | bamatey | yam. | | 'aseh | 'ash | kasiyl | uakiymah, |
| **Which alone** | **and tread** | **and** | **upon the waves of** | **the sea** | | **Which make** | **Arcturus** | **Orion** | **and Pleiades** |

| | | | | | | | | | | |
|---|---|---|---|---|---|---|---|---|---|---|
| וחדרי 2315 | תמן 8486: | 9:10 | עשה 6213 | גדלות 1419 | עד 5704 | אין 369 | חקר 2714 | ונפלאות 6381 | עד 5704 | אין 369 |
| uachadrey | teman. | | 'aseh | gadolout | 'ad | 'aeyn | cheqer; | uanipla'aut, | 'ad | 'aeyn |
| **and the chambers of** | **the south** | | ***Which* does** | **great things** | **even** | **past** | **finding out** | ***yea* and wonders** | **even** | **without** |

| | | | | | | | | | | | |
|---|---|---|---|---|---|---|---|---|---|---|---|
| מספר 4557: | 9:11 | הן 2005 | יעבר 5674 | עלי 5921 | ולא 3808 | אראה 7200 | ויחלף 2498 | ולא 3808 | אבין 995 | לו 3807a: | 9:12 הן 2005 |
| mispar. | | hen | ya'abor | 'alay | uala' | 'ar'ah; | uayachalop, | uala' | 'abiyn | lou'. | hen |
| **number** | | **Lo'** | **he goes** | **by me** | **andnot** | **I see** | ***him* he passed on also** | **but not** | **I perceive** | **him** | **Behold** |

| | | | | | | | | | | | |
|---|---|---|---|---|---|---|---|---|---|---|---|
| יחתף 2862 | מי 4310 | ישיבנו 7725 | מי 4310 | יאמר 559 | אליו 413 | מה 4100 | תעשה 6213: | 9:13 אלוה 433 | לא 3808 | ישיב 7725 | אפו 639 |
| yachtop | miy' | yashiybenu; | miy' | ya'mar | 'aelayu, | mah | ta'aseh. | 'alouah | la' | yashiyb | 'apou; |
| **he takes away** | **who** | **can hinder him?** | **who** | **will say** | **unto him** | **What** | **do you?** | ***If* Elohim** | **not** | **will withdraw** | **his anger** |

| | | | | | | | | | | | |
|---|---|---|---|---|---|---|---|---|---|---|---|
| תחתו 8478 | שחחו 7817 | עזרי 5826 | רהב 7293: | 9:14 | אף 637 | כי 3588 | אנכי 595 | אעננו 6030 | אבחרה 977 | דברי 1697 | |
| tachatau | shachachu, | 'azarey | rahab. | | 'ap | kiy | 'anokiy | 'a'anenu; | 'abcharah | dabaray | |
| **under him** | **do stoop** | **helpers** | **the proud** | | **How** | **much less** | **I** | **shall answer him** | ***and* choose out** | **my words** | ***to reason*** |

| | | | | | | | | | | |
|---|---|---|---|---|---|---|---|---|---|---|
| עמו 5973: | 9:15 | אשר 834 | אם 518 | צדקתי 6663 | לא 3808 | אענה 6030 | למשפטי 8199 | אתחנן 2603: | | 9:16 |
| 'amou. | | 'asher | 'am | tzadaqtiy | la' | 'a'aneh; | limshopatiy, | 'atchanan. | | |
| **with him?** | | **Whom** | **though** | **I were righteous** | **not** | ***yet* would I answer** | **to my judge** | ***but* I would make supplication** | | |

| | | | | | | | | | |
|---|---|---|---|---|---|---|---|---|---|
| אם 518 | קראתי 7121 | ויענני 6030 | לא 3808 | אאמין 539 | כי 3588 | יאזין 238 | קולי 6963: | 9:17 | אשר 834 |
| 'am | qaraa'tiy | uaya'aneniy; | la' | 'a'amiyn, | kiy | ya'aziyn | qouliy. | | 'asher |
| **If** | **I had called** | **and he had answered me** | **not** | ***yet* would I believe** | **that** | **he had hearkened unto** | **my voice** | | **For** |

| | | | | | | | | | | |
|---|---|---|---|---|---|---|---|---|---|---|
| בשערה 8183 | ישופני 7779 | והרבה 7235 | פצעי 6482 | חנם 2600: | 9:18 | לא 3808 | יתנני 5414 | השב 7725 | רוחי 7307 | כי 3588 |
| bis'arah | yashupeniy; | uahirbah | patza'ay | chinam. | | la' | yitaneniy | hasheb | ruchiy; | kiy |
| **with a tempest** | **he break me** | **and multiply** | **my wounds** | **without cause** | | **not** | **He will suffer** | **to take** | **my breath** | **but** |

| | | | | | | | | | | |
|---|---|---|---|---|---|---|---|---|---|---|
| ישבעני 7646 | ממררים 4472: | 9:19 | אם 518 | לכח 3581 | אמיץ 533 | הנה 2009 | ואם 518 | למשפט 4941 | מי 4310 |
| yasbi'aniy, | mamroriym. | | 'am | lakoach | 'amitz | hineh; | ua'am | lamishpat, | miy' |
| **fill me with** | **bitterness** | | **If** | ***I speak* of strength *he is*** | **strong** | **lo'** | **and if** | **of judgment** | **who** |

| | | | | | | | |
|---|---|---|---|---|---|---|---|
| יועידני 3259: | 9:20 | אם 518 | אצדק 6663 | פי 6310 | ירשיעני 7561 | תם 8535 | אני 589 |
| you'aydeniy. | | 'am | 'atzdaq | piy | yarshiy'aeniy; | tam | 'aniy, |
| **shall set me a time *to plead*?** | | **If** | **I justify myself** | **mine own mouth** | **shall condemn me: *am*** | **perfect, *if I say,*** | **I** |

Job 9:6 Which shaketh the earth out of her place, and the pillars thereof tremble.7 Which commandeth the sun, and it rise not; and sealeth up the stars.8 Which alone spreadeth out the heavens, and treadeth upon the waves of the sea.9 Which make Arcturus, Orion, and Pleiades, and the chambers of the south.10 Which doeth great things past finding out; yea, and wonders without number.11 Lo, he go by me, and I see him not: he pass on also, but I perceive him not.12 Behold, he take away, who can hinder him? who will say unto him, What does you?13 If G-d will not withdraw his anger, the proud helpers do stoop under him.14 How much less shall I answer him, and choose out my words to reason with him?15 Whom, though I were righteous, yet would I not answer, but I would make supplication to my judge.16 If I had called, and he had answered me; yet would I not believe that he had hearkened unto my voice.17 For he breaketh me with a tempest, and multiplieth my wounds without cause.18 He will not suffer me to take my breath, but filleth me with bitterness.19 If I speak of strength, lo, he is strong: and if of judgment, who shall set me a time to plead? 20 If I justify myself, mine own mouth shall

9:21 9:22

ויעקשני 6140: תם 8535 אני 589 לא 3808 אדע 3045 נפשי 5315 אמאס 3988 חיי 2416:

uaya'qasheniy. tam 'aniy la' 'aeda napshiy, 'am'as chayay.

**it shall also prove me perverse *Though were* perfect I not *yet* would I know my soul I would despise my life**

9:23

אחת 259 היא 1931 על 5921 כן 3651 אמרתי 559 תם 8535 ורשע 7563 הוא 1931 מכלה 3615: אם 518 שוט 7752 ימית 4191

'achat, hiy'a 'al ken 'amartiy; tam uarashaa', hua' makaleh. 'am shout yamiyt

***is* one *thing* This therefore after I said *it* the perfect and the wicked He destroy If the scourge slay**

9:24

פתאם 6597 למסת 4531 נקים 5355 ילעג 3932: ארץ 776 נתנה 5414 ביד 3027 רשע 7563 פני 6440

pit'am; lamasat naqiyim yil'ag. 'aretz nitanah bayad rasha', paney

**suddenly at the trial of the innocent he will laugh The earth is given into the hand of the wicked the faces of**

9:25

שפטיה 8199 יכסה 3680 אם 518 לא 3808 אפוא 645 מי 4310 הוא 1931: וימי 3117 קלו 7043 מני 4480 רץ 7323 ברחו 1272

shopateyha yakaseh; 'am la' aepou'a miy' hua'. uayamay qalu miniy ratz; barachu,

**the judges thereof he cover if not where *and* who *is* he? Now my days are swifter than a post they flee away**

9:26 9:27

לא 3808 ראו 7200 טובה 2896: חלפו 2498 עם 5973 אניות 591 אבה 16 כנשר 5404 יטוש 2907 עלי 5921 אכל 400:

la' ra'au toubah. chalapu 'am aniyout 'aebeh; kanesher, yatus 'aley 'akel.

**no they see good They are passed away as ships *the* swift as the eagle *that* hasten to the prey**

9:28

אם 518 אמרי 559 אשכחה 7911 שיחי 7879 אעזבה 5800 פני 6440 ואבליגה 1082: יגרתי 3025 כל 3605

'am 'amariy 'ashkachah siychiy; 'a'azbah panay ua'abliygah. yagoratiy kal

**If I say I will forget my complaint I will leave off my heaviness and comfort myself I am afraid of all**

9:29 9:30

עצבתי 6094 ידעתי 3045 כי 3588 לא 3808 תנקני 5352: אנכי 595 ארשע 7561 למה 4100 זה 2088 הבל 1892 איגע 3021: אם 518

'atzbotay; yada'tiy, kiy la' tanaqeniy. 'anokiy 'arsha'; lamah zeh, hebel 'ayga'. 'am

**my sorrows I know that not you will hold me innocent *If* I be wicked why then in vain? labour I If**

9:31

התרחצתי 7364 במו 1119 שלג 7950 והזכותי 2141 בבר 1253 כפי 3709: אז 227 בשחת 7845 תטבלני 2881

hitrachatztiy bamou shaleg; uahazikoutiy, babor kapay. 'az bashachat titbaleniy;

**I wash myself with *water* snow and make clean never so my hands Yet in the ditch shall you plunge me**

9:32

ותעבוני 8581 שלמותי 8008: כי 3588 לא 3808 איש 376 כמני 3644 אעננו 6030

uati'abuniy, salmoutay. kiy la' 'aysh kamoniy 'a'anenu;

**and shall abhor me mine own clothes For *he is* not a man as I *am that* I should answer him**

9:33

נבוא 935 יחדו 3162 במשפט 4941: לא 3808 יש 3426 בינינו 996 מוכיח 3198 ישת 7896 ידו 3027 על 5921

nabua' yachdau, bamishpat. la' yesh beyneynu moukiyach; yashet yadou 'al

***and* we should come together in judgment Neither is there any between us daysman *that* might lay his hand upon**

9:34 9:35

שנינו 8147: יסר 5493 מעלי 5921 שבטו 7626 ואמתו 367 אל 408 תבעתני 1204: אדברה 1696 ולא 3808

shaneynu. yasor me'alay shibtou; ua'aematou, 'al taba'ataniy. 'adabrah uala'

**us both Let him take away from me his rod and his fear not let terrify me *Then* would I speak and not**

איראנו 3372 כי 3588 לא 3808 כן 3651 אנכי 595 עמדי 5978:

'ayra'anu; kiy la' ken 'anokiy, 'amadiy.

**fear him but *it is* not so I with me**

Job 9:20 condemn me: if I say, I am perfect, it shall also prove me perverse.21 Though I were perfect, yet would I not know my soul: I would despise my life.22 This is one thing, therefore I said it, He destroyeth the perfect and the wicked.23 If the scourge slay suddenly, he will laugh at the trial of the innocent.24 The earth is given into the hand of the wicked: he covereth the faces of the judges thereof; if not, where, and who is he?25 Now my days are swifter than a post: they flee away, they see no good.26 They are passed away as the swift ships: as the eagle that hasteth to the prey.27 If I say, I will forget my complaint, I will leave off my heaviness, and comfort myself:28 I am afraid of all my sorrows, I know that you will not hold me innocent.29 If I be wicked, why then labour I in vain?30 If I wash myself with snow water, and make my hands never so clean;31 Yet shall you plunge me in the ditch, and mine own clothes shall abhor me.32 For he is not a man, as I am, that I should answer him, and we should come together in judgment.33 Neither is there any daysman betwixt us, that might lay his hand upon us both.34 Let him take his rod away from me, and let not his fear terrify me: 35 Then would I speak, and not fear him; but it is not so with me.

**Job 10:1** **10:2**

נקטה 5354 נפשי 5315 בחיי 2416 אעזבה 5800 עלי 5921 שיחי 7879 אדברה 1696 במר 4751 נפשי 5315:
naqatah napshiy, bachayay 'a'azbah 'alay siychiy; 'adabrah, bamar napshiy.
**is weary My soul of my life I will leave upon myself my complaint I will speak in the bitterness of my soul**

**10:3**

אמר 559 אל 413 אלוה 433 אל 408 תרשיעני 7561 הודיעני 3045 על 5921 מה 4100 תריבני 7378: הטוב 2895
'amar 'al 'alouah 'al tarshiy'aeniy; houdiy'aeniy, 'al mah tariybeniy. hatoub
**I will say unto Elohim not Do condemn me show me wherefore how long you contendest with me** ***Is it* good**

לך 3807a כי 3588 תעשק 6231 כי 3588 תמאס 3988 יגיע 3018 כפיך 3709 ועל 5921 עצת 6098 רשעים 7563
laka kiy ta'ashoq, kiy tim'as yagiya' kapeyka; ua'al 'atzat rasha'aym
**unto you that you should oppress that you should despise the work of your hands and upon the counsel of the wicked?**

**10:4** **10:5**

הופעת 3313: העיני 5869 בשר 1320 לך 3807a אם 518 כראות 7200 אנוש 582 תראה 7200: הכימי 3117 אנוש 582 ימיך 3117
houpa'ata. ha'aeyney basar lak; 'am kir'aut 'anoush tir'ah. hakiymey 'anoush yameyka;
**shine** ***Have* eyes of flesh? to you or see you as man see?** ***Are* your days man? as the days of *are***

**10:6** **10:7**

אם 518 שנותיך 8141 כימי 3117 גבר 1397: כי 3588 תבקש 1245 לעוני 5771 ולחטאתי 2403 תדרוש 1875: על 5921
'am shanouteyka, kiymey gaber. kiy tabaqesh la'auoniy; ualchata'tiy tidroush. 'al
**or your years as days man's That you inquire after mine iniquity and after my sin? search according**

**10:8**

דעתך 1847 כי 3588 לא 3808 ארשע 7561 ואין 369 מידך 3027 מציל 5337: ידיך 3027 עצבוני 6087
da'taka kiy la' 'arsha'; ua'aeyn miyadaka matziyl. yadeyka 'atzbuniy
**You know that not I am wicked and *there is* none out of your hand that can deliver Thine hands have made me**

**10:9**

ויעשוני 6213 יחד 3162 סביב 5439 ותבלעני 1104: זכר 2142 נא 4994 כי 3588 כחמר 2563
uaya'asuniy; yachad sabiyb, uatbal'aeniy. zakar naa' kiy kachomer
**and fashioned me together round about yet you do destroy me Remember I beseech you that as the clay**

**10:10**

עשיתני 6213 ואל 413 עפר 6083 תשיבני 7725: הלא 3808 כחלב 2461 תתיכני 5413
'asiytaniy; ua'al 'apar tashiybeniy. hala' kechalab tatiykeniy;
**you have made me and into dust will you bring me again? not as milk Have you poured me out**

**10:11**

וכגבנה 1385 תקפיאני 7087: עור 5785 ובשר 1320 תלבישני 3847 ובעצמות 6106 וגידים 1517
uakagbinah, taqpiy'aeniy. 'aur uabasar talbiysheniy; uaba'atzamout uagiydiym,
**and like cheese? curdled me *with* skin and flesh You have clothed me and with bones and sinews**

**10:12** **10:13**

תסככני 5526: חיים 2416 וחסד 2617 עשית 6213 עמדי 5978 ופקדתך 6486 שמרה 8104 רוחי 7307:
tasokakeniy. chayiym uachesed 'ashiyta 'amadiy; uapqudataka, shamarah ruchiy.
**have fensed me life and favor You have granted me and your visitation has preserved my spirit**

**10:14**

ואלה 428 צפנת 6845 בלבבך 3824 ידעתי 3045 כי 3588 זאת 2063 עמך 5973: אם 518 חטאתי 2398 ושמרתני 8104
ua'aeleh tzapanta bilbabeka; yada'tiy, kiy za't 'amak. 'am chata'tiy uashmartaniy;
**And these *things* have you hid in your heart I know that this *is* with you If I sin then you mark me**

**10:15**

ומעוני 5771 לא 3808 תנקני 5352: אם 518 רשעתי 7561 אללי 480 לי 3807a וצדקתי 6663 לא 3808
uame'auoniy, la' tanaqeniy. 'am rasha'atiy 'allay liy, uatzadaqtiy la'
**and from mine iniquity not you will acquit me If I be wicked woe unto me and *if* I be righteous not**

**Job** 10:1 My soul is weary of my life; I will leave my complaint upon myself; I will speak in the bitterness of my soul.2 I will say unto G-d, Do not condemn me; show me wherefore you contendest with me.3 Is it good unto you that you should oppress, that you should despise the work of your hands, and shine upon the counsel of the wicked?4 Hast you eyes of flesh? or seest you as man see?5 Are your days as the days of man? are your years as man's days,6 That you inquirest after mine iniquity, and searchest after my sin?7 Thou know that I am not wicked; and there is none that can deliver out of your hand.8 Thine hands have made me and fashioned me together round about; yet you dost destroy me.9 Remember, I beseech you, that you have made me as the clay; and will you bring me into dust again?10 Hast you not poured me out as milk, and curdled me like cheese?11 Thou have clothed me with skin and flesh, and have fenced me with bones and sinews.12 Thou have granted me life and favor, and your visitation has preserved my spirit.13 And these things have you hid in your heart: I know that this is with you.14 If I sin, then you markest me, and you will not acquit me from mine iniquity. 15 If I be wicked, woe unto me; and if I be righteous, yet will I not lift up my head. I am full of confusion; therefore see you mine affliction;

10:16
אשא 5375 | ראשי 7218 | שבע 7646 | קלון 7036 | וראה 7200 | עניי 6040: | ויגאה 1342 | כשחל 7826
'asa' | ra'shiy; | saba' | qaloun, | uar'aeh | 'anyiy. | uayig'ah | kashachal
**yet will I lift up | my head | I am full of | confusion | therefore see you | mine affliction | For it increase | as a fierce lion**

10:17
תצודני 6679 | ותשב 7725 | תתפלא 6381 | בי 871a: | תחדש 2318 | עדיך 5707 | נגדי 5048 | ותרב 7235
tatzudeniy; | uatashob, | titpala' | biy. | tachadesh | 'aedeyka | negdiy, | uatereb
**You hunt me | and again | you show yourself marvellous | upon me | You renew | your witnesses | against me | and increasest**

10:18
כעשך 3708 | עמדי 5978 | חליפות 2487 | וצבא 6635 | עמי 5973: | ולמה 4100 | מרחם 7358
ka'aska | 'amadiy; | chaliypout | uatzaba' | 'amiy. | ualamah | merechem
**your indignation | upon me | changes | and war | are against me | Wherefore then | out of the womb?**

10:19
הצאתני 3318 | אגוע 1478 | ועין 5869 | לא 3808 | תראני 7200: | כאשר 834 | לא 3808
hotzea'taniy; | 'agua', | ua'ayin | la' | tir'aeniy. | ka'asher | la'
**have you brought me forth | Oh that I had given up the ghost | and eye | no | had seen me | as though | not**

10:20
הייתי 1961 | אהיה 1961 | מבטן 990 | לקבר 6913 | אובל 2986: | הלא 3808 | מעט 4592 | ימי 3117 | יחדל 2308
hayiytiy | 'ahayeh; | mibeten, | laqeber | 'uabal. | hala' | ma'at | yamay | yechdal
**I should have been | I had been | from the womb | to the grave | I should have been carried | Are not few? | my days cease**

10:21
ישית 7896 | ממני 4480 | ואבליגה 1082 | מעט 4592: | בטרם 2962 | אלך 1980 | ולא 3808 | אשוב 7725 | אל 413
yashiyt | mimeniy, | ua'abliygah | ma'at. | baterem | 'aelek | uala' | 'ashub; | 'al
**then and let | me alone | that I may take comfort | a little | Before | I go | not | where I shall return | to**

10:22
ארץ 776 | חשך 2822 | וצלמות 6757: | ארץ 776 | עיפתה 5890 | כמו 3644 | אפל 652
'aretz | choshek | uatzalmauet. | 'aretz | 'aeypatah | kamou | 'apel,
***even* to the land of | darkness | and the shadow of death | A land of | darkness | as | darkness**

צלמות 6757 | ולא 3808 | סדרים 5468 | ותפע 3313 | כמו 3644 | אפל 652:
tzalmauet | uala' | sadariym, | uatopa' | kamou | 'apel.
***itself* of the shadow of death | and without *any* order | and *where* the light *is* | as | darkness**

**Job 11:1**
ויען 6030 | צפר 6691 | הנעמתי 5284 | ויאמר 559: | 11:2 הרב 7230 | דברים 1697 | לא 3808 | יענה 6030
uaya'an | tzopor | hana'amatiy, | uaya'mar. | harob | dabariym | la' | ye'aneh;
**Then answered | Zophar | the Naamathite | and said | the multitude of | words | not | Should be answered?**

11:3
ואם 518 | איש 376 | שפתים 8193 | יצדק 6663: | בדיך 907 | מתים 4962 | יחרישו 2790 | ותלעג 3932
ua'am | 'aysh | sapatayim | yitzdaq. | badeyka | matiym | yachariyshu; | uatil'ag,
**and | a man | *full of* talk | should be justified? | Should your lies | men | make hold their peace? | and when you mock**

11:4
ואין 369 | מכלם 3637: | ותאמר 559 | זך 2134 | לקחי 3948 | ובר 1249 | הייתי 1961 | בעיניך 5869:
ua'aeyn | maklim. | uata'mer | zak | liqchiy; | uabar, | hayiytiy | ba'aeyneyka.
**and no man | shall make you ashamed? | For you have said | *is* pure | My doctrine | and clean | I am | in your eyes**

11:5
ואולם 199 | מי 4310 | יתן 5414 | אלוה 433 | דבר 1696 | ויפתח 6605 | שפתיו 8193 | עמך 5973: | 11:6 ויגד 5046 | לך 3807a | תעלמות 8587
ua'aulam, | miy' | yiten | 'alouah | daber; | uayiptach | sapatayu | 'amak. | uayaged | laka | ta'alumout
**But | oh that | would | Elohim | speak | and open | his lips | against you | And that he would show | to you | the secrets of**

Job 10:16 For it increaseth. Thou hunt me as a fierce lion: and again you shewest thyself marvellous upon me.17 Thou renewest your witnesses against me, and increasest your indignation upon me; changes and war are against me.18 Wherefore then have you brought me forth out of the womb? Oh that I had given up the ghost, and no eye had seen me!19 I should have been as though I had not been; I should have been carried from the womb to the grave.20 Are not my days few? cease then, and let me alone, that I may take comfort a little,21 Before I go whence I shall not return, even to the land of darkness and the shadow of death;22 A land of darkness, as darkness itself; and of the shadow of death, without any order, and where the light is as darkness. **Job** 11:1 Then answered Zophar the Naamathite, and said,2 Should not the multitude of words be answered? and should a man full of talk be justified?3 Should your lies make men hold their peace? and when you mockest, shall no man make you ashamed?4 For you have said, My doctrine is pure, and I am clean in your eyes.5 But oh that G-d would speak, and open his lips against you;6 And that he would show you the secrets of wisdom,

| חכמה 2451 | כי 3588 | כפלים 3718 | לתושיה 8454 | ודע 3045 | כי 3588 | ישה 5382 | לך 3807a | אלוה 433 |
|---|---|---|---|---|---|---|---|---|
| chakamah | kiy | kiplayim | latushiyah | uada' | kiy | yasheh | laka | 'alouah, |
| **wisdom** | **that** | ***they are* double** | **to that which is!** | **Know therefore** | **that** | **exact** | **of you** | **Elohim** |

| מעונך 5771: | 11:7 | החקר 2714 | אלוה 433 | תמצא 4672 | אם 518 | עד 5704 | תכלית 8503 | שדי 7706 |
|---|---|---|---|---|---|---|---|---|
| me'auoneka. | | hacheqer | 'alouah | timtzaa'; | 'am | 'ad | takliyt | shaday |
| ***less* than your iniquity deserve** | | ***by* searching** | **Elohim?** | **Can you find out** | **or** | **unto** | **perfection?** | **the Almighty** |

| תמצא 4672: | 11:8 | גבהי 1363 | שמים 8064 | מה 4100 | תפעל 6466 | עמקה 6013 | משאול 7585 | מה 4100 | תדע 3045: | 11:9 | ארכה 752 |
|---|---|---|---|---|---|---|---|---|---|---|---|
| timtzaa'. | | gabahey | shamayim | mah | tip'al; | 'amuqah | misha'aul, | mah | teda'. | | 'arukah |
| **can you find out** | | ***It is as* high** | ***as* heaven** | **what** | **can you do?** | **deeper** | **than hell** | **what** | **can you know?** | | ***is* longer** |

| מארץ 776 | מדה 4055 | ורחבה 7342 | מני 4480 | ים 3220: | 11:10 | אם 518 | יחלף 2498 | ויסגיר 5462 | ויקהיל 6950 |
|---|---|---|---|---|---|---|---|---|---|
| me'aretz | midah; | uarchabah, | miniy | yam. | | 'am | yachalop | uayasgiyr; | uayaqhiyl, |
| **than the earth** | **The measure thereof** | **and broader** | **than** | **the sea** | | **If** | **he cut off** | **and shut up** | **or gather together** |

| ומי 4310 | ישיבנו 7725: | 11:11 | כי 3588 | הוא 1931 | ידע 3045 | מתי 4962 | שוא 7723 | וירא 7200 | און 205 | ולא 3808 |
|---|---|---|---|---|---|---|---|---|---|---|
| uamiy | yashiybenu. | | kiy | hua' | yada' | matey | shau'a; | uayar'a | 'auen, | uala' |
| **then who** | **can hinder him?** | | **For** | **he** | **knows** | **men** | **vain** | **he see also** | **wickedness** | **not then** |

| יתבונן 995: | 11:12 | ואיש 376 | נבוב 5014 | ילבב 3823 | ועיר 5895 | פרא 6501 | אדם 120 | יולד 3205: | 11:13 | אם 518 | אתה 859 |
|---|---|---|---|---|---|---|---|---|---|---|---|
| yitbounan. | | ua'aysh | nabub | yilabeb; | ua'ayir | pera', | 'adam | yiualed. | | 'am | 'atah, |
| **will he consider *it*?** | | **For man** | **vain** | **would be wise** | **though colt** | ***like* a wild ass's** | **man** | **be born** | | **If** | **you** |

| הכינות 3559 | לבך 3820 | ופרשת 6566 | אליו 413 | כפך 3709: | 11:14 | אם 518 | און 205 | בידך 3027 | הרחיקהו 7368 | ואל 408 |
|---|---|---|---|---|---|---|---|---|---|---|
| hakiynouta | libeka; | uaparasta | 'aelayu | kapeka. | | 'am | 'auen | bayadaka | harchiyqehu; | ua'al |
| **prepare** | **your heart** | **and stretch out** | **toward him** | **your hands** | | **If** | **iniquity** | ***be* in your hand** | **put it far away** | **and not** |

| תשכן 7931 | באהליך 168 | עולה 5766: | 11:15 | כי 3588 | אז 227 | תשא 5375 | פניך 6440 | ממום 3971 | והיית 1961 | מצק 3332 |
|---|---|---|---|---|---|---|---|---|---|---|
| tashken | ba'ahaleyka | 'aulah. | | kiy | 'az | tisa' | paneyka | mimum; | uahayiyta | mutzaq, |
| **let dwell** | **in your tabernacles** | **wickedness** | | **For** | **then** | **shall you lift up** | **your face** | **without spot** | **yea you shall be** | **stedfast** |

| ולא 3808 | תירא 3372: | 11:16 | כי 3588 | אתה 859 | עמל 5999 | תשכח 7911 | כמים 4325 | עברו 5674 | תזכר 2142: | 11:17 |
|---|---|---|---|---|---|---|---|---|---|---|
| uala' | tiyraa'. | | kiy | 'atah | 'amal | tishkach; | kamayim | 'abaru | tizkor. | |
| **and not** | **shall fear** | | **Because** | **you** | ***your* misery** | **shall forget** | ***it* as waters** | ***that* pass away** | ***and* remember** | |

| ומצהרים 6672 | יקום 6965 | חלד 2465 | תעפה 5774 | כבקר 1242 | תהיה 1961: | 11:18 |
|---|---|---|---|---|---|---|
| uamitzaharayim | yaqum | chaled; | ta'upah, | kaboqer | tihayeh. | |
| **And than the noonday** | **shall be clearer** | ***your* age** | **you shall shine forth** | **as the morning** | **you shall be** | |

| ובטחת 982 | כי 3588 | יש 3426 | תקוה 8615 | וחפרת 2658 | לבטח 983 | תשכב 7901: | 11:19 |
|---|---|---|---|---|---|---|---|
| uabatachta | kiy | yesh | tiquah; | uachaparta, | labetach | tishkab. | |
| **And you shall be secure** | **because** | **there is** | **hope** | **yea you shall dig *about you and*** | **in safety** | **you shall take your rest** | |

| ורבצת 7257 | ואין 369 | מחריד 2729 | וחלו 2470 | פניך 6440 | רבים 7227: | 11:20 | ועיני 5869 |
|---|---|---|---|---|---|---|---|
| uarabatzata | ua'aeyn | machariyd; | uachilu | paneyka | rabiym. | | ua'aeyney |
| **Also you shall lie down** | **and none** | **shall make *you* afraid** | **yea shall make suit** | **unto you** | **many** | | **But the eyes of** |

Job 11:6 that they are double to that which is! Know therefore that G-d exacteth of you less than your iniquity deserveth.7 Canst you by searching find out G-d? canst you find out the Almighty unto perfection?8 It is as high as heaven; what canst you do? deeper than hell; what canst you know?9 The measure thereof is longer than the earth, and broader than the sea.10 If he cut off, and shut up, or gather together, then who can hinder him?11 For he know vain men: he see wickedness also; will he not then consider it?12 For vain man would be wise, though man be born like a wild ass's colt.13 If you prepare your heart, and stretch out your hands toward him;14 If iniquity be in your hand, put it far away, and let not wickedness dwell in your tabernacles.15 For then shall you lift up your face without spot; yea, you shall be stedfast, and shall not fear:16 Because you shall forget your misery, and remember it as waters that pass away:17 And your age shall be clearer than the noonday; you shall shine forth, you shall be as the morning.18 And you shall be secure, because there is hope; yea, you shall dig about you, and you shall take your rest in safety. 19 Also you shall lie down, and none shall make you afraid; yea, many shall make suit unto you.

רשעים 7563 תכלינה 3615 ומנוס 4498 אבד 6 מנהם 4480 ותקותם 8615 מפח 4646 נפש 5315:
rasha'aym, tikleynah uamanous 'abad minhem; uatiquatam, mapach napesh.
**the wicked shall fail and escape shall not they and their hope *shall be as* the giving up of the ghost**

**Job 12:1** 12:2 12:3
ויען 6030 איוב 347 ויאמר 559: אמנם 551 כי 3588 אתם 859 עם 5971 ועמכם 5973 תמות 4191 חכמה 2451:
uaya'an 'ayoub, uaya'mar. 'amanam kiy 'atem 'am; ua'amakem, tamut chakamah
**And answered Job and said No doubt but you *are* the people and with you shall die wisdom**

גם 1571 לי 3807a לבב 3824 כמוכם 3644 לא 3808 נפל 5307 אנכי 595 מכם 4480 ואת 854 מי 4310 אין 369 כמו 3644
gam liy lebab kamoukem, la' nopel 'anokiy mikem; ua'at miy' 'aeyn kamou
**But I have understanding as well as you not inferior I *am* to you *yea* who *knows* not such things as**

12:4
אלה 428: שחק 7814 לרעהו 7453 אהיה 1961 קרא 7121 לאלוה 433 ויענהו 6030 שחוק 7814 צדיק 6662
'aeleh. sachoq lare'aehu 'ahayeh, qorea' le'alouah uaya'anehu; sachouq, tzadiyq
**these? *as one* mocked of his neighbour I am who call upon El and he answer him *man is* laughed to scorn the just**

12:5 12:6
תמים 8549: לפיד 3940 בוז 937 לעשתות 6248 שאנן 7600 נכון 3559 למועדי 4571 רגל 7272: ישליו 7951
tamiym. lapiyd buz la'ashtut sha'anan; nakoun, lamou'adey ragel. yishlayu
**upright *is as* a lamp despised in the thought of him that is at ease He that is ready to slip with *his* feet prosper**

12:7
אהלים 168 לשדדים 7703 ובטחות 987 למרגיזי 7264 אל 410 לאשר 834 הביא 935 אלוה 433 בידו 3027:
'ahaliym lashodadiym, uabatuchout lamargiyzey al; la'asher hebiy'a 'alouah bayadou.
**The tabernacles of robbers and are secure they that provoke El into whose bring *abundantly* Elohim hand**

12:8
ואולם 199 שאל 7592 נא 4994 בהמות 929 ותרך 3384 ועוף 5775 השמים 8064 ויגד 5046 לך 3807a:
ua'aulam, sha'al naa' bahemout uatoreka; ua'aup hashamayim, uayaged lak.
**But ask now the beasts and they shall teach you and the fowls of the air and they shall tell to you**

12:9
או 176 שיח 7878 לארץ 776 ותרך 3384 ויספרו 5608 לך 3807a דגי 1709 הים 3220: מי 4310 לא 3808 ידע 3045
'au siyach la'aretz uatoreka; uiysapru laka, dagey hayam. miy' la' yada'
**Or speak to the earth and it shall teach you and shall declare unto you the fishes of the sea Who not knows**

12:10
בכל 3605 אלה 428 כי 3588 יד 3027 יהוה 3069 עשתה 6213 זאת 2063: אשר 834 בידו 3027 נפש 5315 כל 3605 חי 2416
bakal 'aeleh; kiy yad Yahuah 'astah za't. 'asher bayadou nepesh kal chay;
**in all these that the hand of Yahuah has wrought this? whose In hand *is* the soul of every living thing**

12:11 12:12
ורוח 7307 כל 3605 בשר 1320 איש 376: הלא 3808 אזן 241 מלין 4405 תבחן 974 וחך 2441 אכל 400 יטעם 2938 לו 3807a:
uaruach, kal basar 'aysh. hala' 'azen miliyn tibchan; uachek, 'akel yit'am lou'.
**and the breath of all kind man not the ear words? Does try as the mouth meat? taste his**

12:13
בישישים 3453 חכמה 2451 וארך 753 ימים 3117 תבונה 8394: עמו 5973 חכמה 2451 וגבורה 1369 לו 3807a
biyshiyshiym chakamah ua'arek yamiym tabunah. amou chakamah uagaburah; lou',
**With the ancient *is* wisdom and in length of days understanding With him *is* wisdom and strength he**

12:14
עצה 6098 ותבונה 8394: הן 2005 יהרוס 2040 ולא 3808 יבנה 1129 יסגר 5462 על 5921 איש 376 ולא 3808
'aetzah uatbunah. hen yaharous uala' yibaneh; yisgor 'al 'aysh, uala'
***has* counsel and understanding Behold he break down and cannot it be built *again* he shut up a man and no**

Job 12:20 But the eyes of the wicked shall fail, and they shall not escape, and their hope shall be as the giving up of the ghost. **Job** 12:1 And Job answered and said,2 No doubt but you are the people, and wisdom shall die with you.3 But I have understanding as well as you; I am not inferior to you: yea, who know not such things as these?4 I am as one mocked of his neighbor, who call upon G-d, and he answer him: the just upright man is laughed to scorn.5 He that is ready to slip with his feet is as a lamp despised in the thought of him that is at ease.6 The tabernacles of robbers prosper, and they that provoke G-d are secure; into whose hand G-d bring abundantly.7 But ask now the beasts, and they shall teach you; and the fowls of the air, and they shall tell you:8 Or speak to the earth, and it shall teach you: and the fishes of the sea shall declare unto you.9 Who know not in all these that the hand of YHUH has wrought this?10 In whose hand is the soul of every living thing, and the breath of all mankind.11 Does not the ear try words? and the mouth taste his meat?12 With the ancient is wisdom; and in length of days understanding.13 With him is wisdom and strength, he has counsel and understanding.14 Behold, he breaketh down, and it cannot be built again: he shutteth up a man, and there can be no opening.

12:15

יפתח 6605: | הן 2005 | יעצר 6113 | במים 4325 | ויבשו 3001 | וישלחם 7971 | ויהפכו 2015
yipateach. | hen | ya'tzor | bamayim | uayibashu; | uiyshalchem, | uayahapku
**there can be opening | Behold | he withholdeth | the waters | and they dry up | also he send them out | and they overturn**

12:16 ... 12:17

ארץ 776: | עמו 5973 | עז 5797 | ותושיה 8454 | לו 3807a | שגג 7683 | ומשגה 7686: | מוליך 1980 | יועצים 3289
'aretz. | amou | 'az | uatushiyah; | lou', | shogeg | uamashgeh. | mouliyk | you'atziym
**the earth | With him *is* | strength | and wisdom *are* | his | the deceived | and the deceiver | He lead away | counsellors**

12:18 ... 12:19

שולל 7758 | ושפטים 8199 | יהולל 1984: | מוסר 4148 | מלכים 4428 | פתח 6605 | ויאסר 631 | אזור 232 | במתניהם 4975:
shoulal; | uashopatiym | yahoulel. | musar | malakiym | piteach; | uaye'asor | 'aezour, | bamataneyhem.
**spoiled | and the judges | make fools | the bond of | kings | He loose | and gird | *with* a girdle | their loins**

12:20

מוליך 1980 | כהנים 3548 | שולל 7758 | ואתנים 386 | יסלף 5557: | מסיר 5493 | שפה 8193 | לנאמנים 539
mouliyk | kohaniym | shoulal; | ua'aetaniym | yasalep. | mesiyr | sapah | lane'amaniym;
**He lead away | princes | spoiled | and the mighty | overthrow | He remove away | the speech | of the trusty**

12:21

וטעם 2940 | זקנים 2205 | יקח 3947: | שופך 8210 | בוז 937 | על 5921 | נדיבים 5081 | ומזיח 4206 | אפיקים 650
uata'am | zaqeniym | yiqach. | shoupek | buz | 'al | nadiybiym; | uamziyach | 'apiyqiym
**and the understanding of | the aged | takes away | He pour | contempt | upon | princes | the strength of | the mighty**

12:22 ... 12:23

רפה 7503: | מגלה 1540 | עמקות 6013 | מני 4480 | חשך 2822 | ויצא 3318 | לאור 216 | צלמות 6757: | משגיא 7679
ripah. | magaleh | 'amuqout | miniy | choshek; | uayotzea' | la'aur | tzalmauet. | masgiy'a
**and weaken | He discover | deep things | out of | darkness | and bring out | to light | the shadow of death | He increase**

12:24

לגוים 1471 | ויאבדם 6 | שטח 7849 | לגוים 1471 | וינחם 5148: | מסיר 5493 | לב 3820 | ראשי 7218
lagouyim | uaya'abdem; | shoteach | lagouyim, | uayanchem. | mesiyr, | leb | ra'shey
**the nations | and destroy them | he enlarge | the nations | and straiten them *again* | He takes away | the heart of | the chief of**

12:25

עם 5971 | הארץ 776 | ויתעם 8582 | בתהו 8414 | לא 3808 | דרך 1870: | ימששו 4959 | חשך 2822
'am | ha'aretz; | uayat'aem, | batohu | la' | darek. | yamashashu | choshek
**the people of | the earth | and cause them to wander | in a wilderness | *where there is* no | way | They grope in | the dark**

ולא 3808 | אור 216 | ויתעם 8582 | כשכור 7910:
uala' | 'aur; | uayat'aem, | kashikour.
**without | light | and he make them to stagger | like *a* drunken *man***

**Job 13:1** ... 13:2

הן 2005 | כל 3605 | ראתה 7200 | עיני 5869 | שמעה 8085 | אזני 241 | ותבן 995 | לה 3807a: | כדעתכם 1847
hen | kal | ra'atah | 'aeyniy; | sham'ah | 'azaniy, | uataben | lah. | kada'takem
**Lo | all | *this* has seen | mine eye | has heard | mine ear | and understood | it | What you know**

13:3

ידעתי 3045 | גם 1571 | אני 589 | לא 3808 | נפל 5307 | אנכי 595 | מכם 4480: | אולם 199 | אני 589 | אל 413 | שדי 7706 | אדבר 1696
yada'tiy | gam | 'aniy; | la' | nopel | 'anokiy | mikem. | 'aulam, | 'aniy | 'al | shaday | 'adaber;
***the same* do know | also | I | not | inferior | I | *am* unto you | Surely | I | to | the Almighty | would speak**

13:4

והוכח 3198 | אל 413 | אל 410 | אחפץ 2654: | ואולם 199 | אתם 859 | טפלי 2950 | שקר 8267 | רפאי 7495 | אלל 457 | כלכם 3605:
uahoukeach | 'al | 'ael | 'achpatz. | ua'aulam, | 'atem | topaley | shaqer; | ropa'aey | 'alil | kulkem.
**and to reason with | El | I desire | But | you | *are* forgers of | lies | physicians of | no value | you are all**

Job 12:15 Behold, he withholdeth the waters, and they dry up: also he send them out, and they overturn the earth.16 With him is strength and wisdom: the deceived and the deceiver are his.17 He leadeth counsellers away spoiled, and make the judges fools.18 He looseth the bond of kings, and gird their loins with a girdle.19 He leadeth princes away spoiled, and overthroweth the mighty.20 He removeth away the speech of the trusty, and take away the understanding of the aged.21 He poureth contempt upon princes, and weakeneth the strength of the mighty.22 He discovereth deep things out of darkness, and bring out to light the shadow of death.23 He increaseth the nations, and destroyeth them: he enlargeth the nations, and straiteneth them again.24 He take away the heart of the chief of the people of the earth, and causeth them to wander in a wilderness where there is no way.25 They grope in the dark without light, and he make them to stagger like a drunken man. **Job** 13:1 Lo, mine eye has seen all this, mine ear has heard and understood it.2 What you know, the same do I know also: I am not inferior unto you.3 Surely I would speak to the Almighty, and I desire to reason with G-d.4 But you are forgers of lies, you are all physicians of no value.

13:5 מי 4310 יתן 5414 החרש 2790 תחרישון 2790 ותהי 1961 לכם 3807a לחכמה 2451: 13:6 שמעו 8085 נא 4994 תוכחתי 8433
miy' yiten hacharesh tachariyshun; uathiy lakem lachakamah. shim'au naa' toukachatiy;
**O that you would altogether hold your peace and it should be to your wisdom Hear now my reasoning**

ורבות 7379 שפתי 8193 הקשיבו 7181: 13:7 הלאל 410 תדברו 1696 עולה 5766 ולו 3807a תדברו 1696 רמיה 7423: 13:8
uaribout sapatay haqashiybu. hal'ael tadabru 'aulah; ualou, tadabru ramiyah.
**and the pleadings of my lips listen *to* for El? Will you speak wickedly and for him? talk deceitfully**

הפניו 6440 תשאון 5375 אם 518 לאל 410 תריבון 7378: 13:9 הטוב 2895 כי 3588 יחקר 2713 אתכם 853 אם 518 כהתל 2048
hapanayu tisa'un; 'am la'ael tariybun. hatoub kiy yachqor 'atkem; 'am kahatel
**his person? Will you accept or for El? will you contend Is it good that he should search out? you or as one**

באנוש 582 תהתלו 2048 בו 871a: 13:10 הוכח 3198 יוכיח 3198 אתכם 853 אם 518 בסתר 5643 פנים 6440
be'anoush, tahatelu bou. houkeach youkiyach 'atkem; 'am baseter, paniym
**man mock another, do you *so* mock him? He will surely reprove you if secretly persons**

תשאון 5375: 13:11 הלא 3808 שאתו 7613 תבעת 1204 אתכם 853 ופחדו 6343 יפל 5307 עליכם 5921: 13:12
tisa'un. hala' sa'aetou taba'aet 'atkem; uapachdou, yipol 'aleykem.
**you do accept not his excellency Shall make afraid? you and his dread fall upon you?**

זכרניכם 2146 משלי 4911 אפר 665 לגבי 1354 חמר 2563 גביכם 1354: 13:13 החרישו 2790 ממני 4480
zikroneykem mishley 'aeper; lagabey chomor, gabeykem. hachariyshu mimeniy
**Your remembrances *are* like unto ashes your bodies to clay bodies of Hold your peace *let* me**

ואדברה 1696 אני 589 ויעבר 5674 עלי 5921 מה 4100: 13:14 על 5921 מה 4100 אשא 5375 בשרי 1320 בשני 8127
ua'adabrah 'aniy; uaya'abor 'alay mah. 'al mah 'asa' basariy bashinay;
***alone* that may speak I and let come on me what *will* Wherefore why do I take my flesh in my teeth**

ונפשי 5315 אשים 7760 בכפי 3709: 13:15 הן 2005 יקטלני 6991 לא 3808 איחל 3176 אך 389 דרכי 1870 אל 413 פניו 6440
uanapshiy, 'asiym bakapiy. hen yiqtaleniy la' 'ayachel; 'ak darakay, 'al panayu
**and my life put in my hand? Though he slay me in him: *yet* will I trust but mine own ways before him**

אוכיח 3198: 13:16 גם 1571 הוא 1931 לי 3807a לישועה 3444 כי 3588 לא 3808 לפניו 6440 חנף 2611 יבוא 935: 13:17 שמעו 8085
'aukiyach. gam hua' liy liyshu'ah; kiy la' lapanayu, chanep yabou'a. shim'au
**I will maintain also He *shall be* my salvation for not before him an hypocrite shall come Hear**

שמוע 8085 מלתי 4405 ואחותי 262 באזניכם 241: 13:18 הנה 2009 נא 4994 ערכתי 6186 משפט 4941 ידעתי 3045 כי 3588 אני 589
shamoua' milatiy; ua'achauatiy, ba'azaneykem. hineh naa' 'arakatiy mishapat; yada'tiy, kiy 'aniy
**diligently my speech and my declaration with your ears Behold now I have ordered *my* cause I know that I**

אצדק 6663: 13:19 מי 4310 הוא 1931 יריב 7378 עמדי 5978 כי 3588 עתה 6258 אחריש 2790
'atzdaq. miy' hua' yariyb 'amadiy; kiy 'atah 'achariysh
**shall be justified Who *is* he *that* will plead with me? for now *if* I hold my tongue**

ואגוע 1478: 13:20 אך 389 שתים 8147 אל 408 תעש 6213 עמדי 5978 אז 227 מפניך 6440 לא 3808 אסתר 5641:
ua'agua'. 'ak shatayim 'ael ta'as 'amadiy; 'az mipaneyka, la' 'asater.
**I shall give up the ghost Only two not do *things* unto me then *myself* from you not will I hide**

Job 13:5 O that you would altogether hold your peace! and it should be your wisdom.6 Hear now my reasoning, and hear to the pleadings of my lips.7 Will you speak wickedly for G-d? and talk deceitfully for him?8 Will you accept his person? will you contend for G-d?9 Is it good that he should search you out? or as one man mocketh another, do you so mock him?10 He will surely reprove you, if you do secretly accept persons.11 Shall not his excellency make you afraid? and his dread fall upon you?12 Your remembrances are like unto ashes, your bodies to bodies of clay.13 Hold your peace, let me alone, that I may speak, and let come on me what will.14 Wherefore do I take my flesh in my teeth, and put my life in mine hand?15 Though he slay me, yet will I trust in him: but I will maintain mine own ways before him.16 He also shall be my salvation: for an hypocrite shall not come before him.17 Hear diligently my speech, and my declaration with your ears.18 Behold now, I have ordered my cause; I know that I shall be justified.19 Who is he that will plead with me? for now, if I hold my tongue, I shall give up the ghost.20 Only do not two things unto me: then will I not hide myself from you.

**13:21**
כפך 3709 | מעלי 5921 | הרחק 7368 | ואמתך 367 | אל 408 | תבעתני 1204: | **13:22** וקרא 7121 | ואנכי 595 | אענה 6030
kapka | me'alay | harchaq; | ua'amataka, | 'al | taba'ataniy. | uqra' | ua'anokiy | 'a'aneh;
**your hand from me withdraw far and your dread not let make me afraid Then call you and I will answer**

או 176 | אדבר 1696 | והשיבני 7725: | **13:23** כמה 4100 | לי 3807a | עונות 5771 | וחטאות 2403 | פשעי 6588 | וחטאתי 2403
'au | 'adaber, | uahashibeniy. | kamah | liy | 'auonout | uachata'aut; | pish'ay | uachata'tiy,
**or let me speak and answer you me How many *are* my iniquities and sins? my transgression and my sin**

הדיעני 3045: | **13:24** למה 4100 | פניך 6440 | תסתיר 5641 | ותחשבני 2803 | לאויב 341 | לך 3807a: | **13:25** העלה 5929 | נדף 5086
houdiy'aeniy | lamah | paneyka | tastiyr; | uatachshabeniy | la'auyeb | lak. | he'aleh | nidap
**make me to know Wherefore your face hide you and hold me for enemy? to your a leaf driven to and fro?**

תערוץ 6206 | ואת 853 | קש 7179 | יבש 3002 | תרדף 7291: | **13:26** כי 3588 | תכתב 3789 | עלי 5921 | מררות 4846
ta'aroutz; | ua'at | qash | yabesh | tirdop. | kiy | tiktob | 'alay | marorout;
**Will you break *and* stubble? *the* dry will you pursue For you write against me bitter things**

ותורישני 3423 | עונות 5771 | נעורי 5271: | **13:27** ותשם 7760 | בסד 5465 | רגלי 7272 | ותשמור 8104 | כל 3605
uatouriysheniy, | 'auonout | na'auray. | uatasem | basad | raglay, | uatishmour | kal
**and make me to possess the iniquities of my youth You put also in the stocks my feet and look narrowly unto all**

ארחותי 734 | על 5921 | שרשי 8328 | רגלי 7272 | תתחקה 2707: | **13:28** והוא 1931 | כרקב 7538 | יבלה 1086 | כבגד 899 | אכלו 398
arachoutay; | 'al | sharashey | raglay, | titchaqeh. | uahu'a | karaqab | yibleh; | kabeged, | 'akalou
**my paths upon the heels of my feet you set a print And he as a rotten thing consume as a garment *that* is eaten**

עש 6211:
'ash.
**moth**

**Job 14:1**
אדם 120 | ילוד 3205 | אשה 802 | קצר 7116 | ימים 3117 | ושבע 7646 | רגז 7267: | **14:2** כציץ 6731 | יצא 3318
'adam | yalud | 'ashah; | qatzar | yamiym, | uasba' | rogez. | katziytz | yatza'
**Man *that is* born of a woman *is of* few days and full of trouble like a flower He comes forth**

וימל 5243 | ויברח 1272 | כצל 6738 | ולא 3808 | יעמוד 5975: | **14:3** אף 637 | על 5921 | זה 2088 | פקחת 6491 | עינך 5869 | ואתי 853
uayimal; | uayibrach | katzel, | uala' | ya'amoud. | 'ap | 'al | zeh | paqachta | 'aeyneka; | ua'atiy
**and is cut down he flee also as a shadow and not continue And yet upon such *an one* do you open your eyes and me**

תביא 935 | במשפט 4941 | עמך 5973: | **14:4** מי 4310 | יתן 5414 | טהור 2889 | מטמא 2931 | לא 3808 | אחד 259: | **14:5** אם 518
tabiy'a | bamishpat | 'amak. | miy' | yiten | tahour | mitamea', | la' | 'achad. | 'am
**bring into judgment with you? Who can bring a clean *thing* out of an unclean? not one Seeing**

חרוצים 2782 | ימיו 3117 | מספר 4557 | חדשיו 2320 | אתך 854 | חקו 2706 | עשית 6213 | ולא 3808 | יעבור 5674: | **14:6**
charutziym | yamayu, | mispar | chadashayu | 'atak; | chuqou | 'ashiyta, | uala' | ya'abour.
***are* determined his days the number of his months *are* with you his bounds you have appointed that cannot he pass**

שעה 8159 | מעליו 5921 | ויחדל 2308 | עד 5704 | ירצה 7521 | כשכיר 7916 | יומו 3117: | **14:7** כי 3588 | יש 3426 | לעץ 6086 | תקוה 8615
sha'aeh | me'alayu | uayechdal; | 'ad | yirtzeh, | kasakiyr | youmou. | kiy | yesh | la'aetz, | tiquah
**Turn from him that he may rest till he shall accomplish as an hireling his day For there is of a tree hope**

Job 14:21 Withdraw your hand far from me: and let not your dread make me afraid.22 Then call you, and I will answer: or let me speak, and answer you me.23 How many are mine iniquities and sins? make me to know my transgression and my sin.24 Wherefore hidest you your face, and holdest me for your enemy?25 Wilt you break a leaf driven to and fro? and will you pursue the dry stubble?26 For you writest bitter things against me, and make me to possess the iniquities of my youth.27 Thou puttest my feet also in the stocks, and lookest narrowly unto all my paths; you settest a print upon the heels of my feet.28 And he, as a rotten thing, consumeth, as a garment that is moth eaten. **Job** 14:1 Man that is born of a woman is of few days, and full of trouble.2 He cometh forth like a flower, and is cut down: he fleeth also as a shadow, and continueth not.3 And dost you open your eyes upon such an one, and bringest me into judgment with you?4 Who can bring a clean thing out of an unclean? not one.5 Seeing his days are determined, the number of his months are with you, you have appointed his bounds that he cannot pass;6 Turn from him, that he may rest, till he shall accomplish, as an hireling, his day.

| אם 518 | יכרת 3772 | ועוד 5750 | יחליף 2498 | וינקתו 3127 | לא 3808 | תחדל 2308: | 14:8 אם 518 | יזקין 2204 |
|---|---|---|---|---|---|---|---|---|
| 'am | yikaret | ua'aud | yachaliyp; | uayonaqtou, | la' | techadal. | 'am | yazqiyn |
| **if** | **it be cut down** | **that again** | **it will sprout** | **and that the tender branch thereof** | **not** | **will cease** | **Though** | **wax old** |

| בארץ 776 | שרשו 8328 | ובעפר 6083 | ימות 4191 | גזעו 1503: | 14:9 מריח 7381 | מים 4325 | יפרח 6524 |
|---|---|---|---|---|---|---|---|
| ba'aretz | sharashou; | uabe'apar, | yamut | giz'au. | mereyach | mayim | yapriach; |
| **in the earth** | **the root thereof** | **and in the ground** | **die** | **the stock thereof** | ***Yet* through the scent of** | **water** | **it will bud** |

| ועשה 6213 | קציר 7105 | כמו 3644 | נטע 5194: | 14:10 וגבר 1397 | ימות 4191 | ויחלש 2522 | ויגוע 1478 | אדם 120 |
|---|---|---|---|---|---|---|---|---|
| ua'asah | qatziyr | kamou | nata'. | uageber | yamut | uayechelash; | uayigua' | 'adam |
| **and bring forth** | **boughs** | **like** | **a plant** | **But man** | **die** | **and waste away** | **yea gives up the ghost** | **man** |

| ואיו 346: | 14:11 אזלו 235 | מים 4325 | מני 4480 | ים 3220 | ונהר 5104 | יחרב 2717 | ויבש 3001: | 14:12 ואיש 376 | שכב 7901 | ולא 3808 |
|---|---|---|---|---|---|---|---|---|---|---|
| ua'ayou. | 'azelu | mayim | miniy | yam; | uanahar, | yecherab | uayabesh. | ua'aysh | shakab, | uala' |
| **and where is he?** | ***As* fail** | **the waters** | **from** | **the sea** | **and the flood** | **decay** | **and dries up** | **So man** | **lies down** | **and not** |

| יקום 6965 | עד 5704 | בלתי 1115 | שמים 8064 | לא 3808 | יקיצו 6974 | ולא 3808 | יערו 5782 | משנתם 8142: | 14:13 מי 4325 | יתן 5414 |
|---|---|---|---|---|---|---|---|---|---|---|
| yaqum | 'ad | biltiy | shamayim | la' | yaqiytzu; | uala' | ye'aru, | mishnatam. | miy' | yiten |
| **rise** | **till** | ***be* no more** | **the heavens** | **not** | **they shall awake** | **nor** | **be raised** | **out of their sleep** | **O that** | **bring** |

| בשאול 7585 | תצפנני 6845 | תסתירני 5641 | עד 5704 | שוב 7725 | אפך 639 | תשית 7896 | לי 3807a |
|---|---|---|---|---|---|---|---|
| bish'aul | tatzapineniy, | tastiyreniy | 'ad | shub | 'apeka; | tashiyt | liy |
| **in the grave** | **you would hide me** | **that you would keep me secret** | **until** | **be past** | **your wrath** | **that you would appoint** | **me** |

| חק 2706 | ותזכרני 2142: | 14:14 אם 518 | ימות 4191 | גבר 1397 | היחיה 2421 | כל 3605 | ימי 3117 | צבאי 6635 | איחל 3176 |
|---|---|---|---|---|---|---|---|---|---|
| choq | uatizkareniy. | 'am | yamut | geber, | hayichayeh | kal | yamey | tzaba'ay | 'ayachel; |
| **a set time** | **and remember** | **If** | **die** | **a man** | **shall he live *again*?** | **all** | **the days of** | **my appointed time** | **will I wait** |

| עד 5704 | בוא 935 | חליפתי 2487: | 14:15 תקרא 7121 | ואנכי 595 | אענך 6030 | למעשה 4639 | ידיך 3027 |
|---|---|---|---|---|---|---|---|
| 'ad | bou'a, | chaliypatiy. | tiqraa' | ua'anokiy | 'a'aneka; | lama'aseh | yadeyka |
| **till** | **come** | **my change** | **You shall call** | **and I** | **will answer you** | **to the work of** | **your hands** |

| תכסף 3700: | 14:16 כי 3588 | עתה 6258 | צעדי 6806 | תספור 5608 | לא 3808 | תשמור 8104 | על 5921 | חטאתי 2403: | 14:17 חתם 2856 |
|---|---|---|---|---|---|---|---|---|---|
| tiksop. | kiy | 'atah | tza'aday | tispour; | la' | tishmour, | 'al | chata'tiy. | chatum |
| **you will have a desire** | **For** | **now** | **my steps** | **you number** | **not** | **do you watch** | **over** | **my sin?** | ***is* sealed up** |

| בצרור 6872 | פשעי 6588 | ותטפל 2950 | על 5921 | עוני 5771: | 14:18 ואולם 199 | הר 2022 | נופל 5307 | יבול 5034 |
|---|---|---|---|---|---|---|---|---|
| bitzarour | pish'ay; | uatitpol, | 'al | 'auniy. | ua'ulam | har | noupel | yiboul; |
| **in a bag** | **My transgression** | **and you sew** | **up** | **my iniquity** | **And surely** | **the mountain** | **falling** | **comes to nought** |

| וצור 6697 | יעתק 6275 | ממקמו 4725: | 14:19 אבנים 68 | שחקו 7833 | מים 4325 | תשטף 7857 | ספיחיה 5599 |
|---|---|---|---|---|---|---|---|
| uatzur, | ye'ataq | mimaqomou. | 'abaniym | shachaqu | mayim, | tishtop | sapiycheyha |
| **and the rock** | **is removed** | **out of his place** | **the stones** | **wear** | **The waters** | **you wash away** | **the things which grow *out* of** |

| עפר 6083 | ארץ 776 | ותקות 8615 | אנוש 582 | האבדת 6: | 14:20 תתקפהו 8630 | לנצח 5331 | ויהלך 1980 | משנה 8138 |
|---|---|---|---|---|---|---|---|---|
| 'apar | 'aretz; | uatiquat | 'anoush | he'abadta. | titqapehu | lanetzach | uayahalok; | mashaneh |
| **the dust of** | **the earth** | **and the hope of** | **man** | **you destroy** | **You prevail against him** | **for ever** | **and he passes** | **you change** |

Job 14:7 For there is hope of a tree, if it be cut down, that it will sprout again, and that the tender branch thereof will not cease.8 Though the root thereof wax old in the earth, and the stock thereof die in the ground;9 Yet through the scent of water it will bud, and bring forth boughs like a plant.10 But man die, and wasteth away: yea, man give up the ghost, and where is he?11 As the waters fail from the sea, and the flood decayeth and drieth up:12 So man lie down, and rise not: till the heavens be no more, they shall not awake, nor be raised out of their sleep.13 O that you would hide me in the grave, that you would keep me secret, until your wrath be past, that you would appoint me a set time, and remember me!14 If a man die, shall he live again? all the days of my appointed time will I wait, till my change come.15 Thou shall call, and I will answer you: you will have a desire to the work of your hands.16 For now you numberest my steps: dost you not watch over my sin?17 My transgression is sealed up in a bag, and you sewest up mine iniquity.18 And surely the mountain falling cometh to nought, and the rock is removed out of his place.19 The waters wear the stones: you washest away the things which grow out of the dust of the earth; and you destroyest the hope of man.20 Thou prevailest forever against him, and he pass: you changest his countenance, and send him away.

פניו 6440 ותשלחהו 7971: **14:21** יכבדו 3513 בניו 1121 ולא 3808 ידע 3045 ויצערו 6819 ולא 3808
panayu, uatashalchehu. yikbadu banayu uala' yeda'; uayitza'aru, uala'
**his countenance and send him away come to honor His sons and not he knows *it* and they are brought low but not**

יבין 995 למו 3807a: **14:22** אך 389 בשרו 1320 עליו 5921 יכאב 3510 ונפשו 5315 עליו 5921 תאבל 56:
yabiyn lamou. 'ak basarou 'alayu yik'ab; uanapshou, 'alayu te'abal.
**he perceive *it* of them But his flesh upon him shall have pain and his soul within him shall mourn**

**Job 15:1** ויען 6030 אליפז 464 התימני 8489 ויאמר 559: **15:2** החכם 2450 יענה 6030 דעת 1847 רוח 7307
uaya'an 'aliypaz hateymaniy, uaya'mar. hechakam, ya'aneh da'at ruach;
**Then answered Eliphaz the Temanite and said a wise man Should utter knowledge vain wind?**

וימלא 4390 קדים 6921 בטנו 990: **15:3** הוכח 3198 בדבר 1697 לא 3808 יסכון 5532 ומלים 4405 לא 3808 יועיל 3276
uiymalea' qadiym bitnou. houkeach badabar la' yiskoun; uamiliym, la' you'ayl
**and fill *with the* east his belly Should he reason with talk? not profitable or with speeches no he can do good?**

בם 871a: **15:4** אף 637 אתה 859 תפר 6565 יראה 3374 ותגרע 1639 שיחה 7881 לפני 6440 אל 410: **15:5** כי 3588 יאלף 502 עונך 5771
bam. 'ap 'atah taper yir'ah; uatigra' siychah, lipney 'ael. kiy ya'alep 'auonaka
**wherewith Yea you cast off fear and restrain prayer before El For utter your iniquity**

פיך 6310 ותבחר 977 לשון 3956 ערומים 6175: **15:6** ירשיעך 7561 פיך 6310 ולא 3808 אני 589 ושפתיך 8193
piyka; uatibchar, lashoun 'arumiym. yarshiy'aka piyka uala' 'aniy; uaspateyka,
**your mouth and you choose the tongue of the crafty condemn you Thine own mouth and not I yea your own lips**

יענו 6030 בך 871a: **15:7** הראישון 7223 אדם 120 תולד 3205 ולפני 6440 גבעות 1389 חוללת 2342: **15:8** הבסוד 5475 אלוה 433
ya'anu bak. hara'yshoun 'adam tiualed; ualipaney gaba'aut choulalata. habsoud 'alouah
**testify against you *Are* the first man *that* was born? or before the hill? were you made the secret of Elohim?**

תשמע 8085 ותגרע 1639 אליך 413 חכמה 2451: **15:9** מה 4100 ידעת 3045 ולא 3808 נדע 3045 תבין 995
tishma'; uatigra' 'aeleyka chakamah mah yada'ta uala' neda'; tabiyn,
**Have you heard and do you restrain to yourself? wisdom What know you that not? we know *what* understand you**

ולא 3808 עמנו 5973 הוא 1931: **15:10** גם 1571 שב 7867 גם 1571 ישיש 3453 בנו 871a כביר 3524 מאביך 1
uala' 'amanu hua'. gam shab gam yashiysh ba'nu; kabiyr me'abiyka
**not in us? which *is* *are* both the grayheaded both very aged men With us much than your father**

ימים 3117: **15:11** המעט 4592 ממך 4480 תנחמות 8575 אל 410 ודבר 1697 לאט 328 עמך 5973: **15:12** מה 4100
yamiym. hama'at mimaka tanchumout 'ael; uadabar, la'at 'amak. mah
**elder *Are* small with you? the consolations of El thing *is there any* secret with you? Why**

יקחך 3947 לבך 3820 ומה 4100 ירזמון 7335 עיניך 5869: **15:13** כי 3588 תשיב 7725 אל 413 אל 410 רוחך 7307
yiqachaka libeka; uamah yirzamun 'aeyneyka. kiy tashiyb 'al 'ael rucheka;
**does carry you away? your heart and what do wink at your eyes That you turn against El your spirit**

והצאת 3318 מפיך 6310 מלין 4405: **15:14** מה 4100 אנוש 582 כי 3588 יזכה 2135 וכי 3588 יצדק 6663
uahotzea'ta mipiyka miliyn. mah 'anoush kiy yizkeh; uakiy yitzdaq,
**and let go out of your mouth? *such* words What *is* man that he should be clean? and that he should be righteous?**

Job 14:21 His sons come to honor, and he know it not; and they are brought low, but he perceiveth it not of them.22 But his flesh upon him shall have pain, and his soul within him shall mourn. **Job** 15:1 Then answered Eliphaz the Temanite, and said,2 Should a wise man utter vain knowledge, and fill his belly with the east wind?3 Should he reason with unprofitable talk? or with speeches wherewith he can do no good?4 Yea, you castest off fear, and restrainest prayer before G-d.5 For your mouth uttereth your iniquity, and you choosest the tongue of the crafty.6 Thine own mouth condemneth you, and not I: yea, your own lips testify against you.7 Art you the first man that was born? or were you made before the hills?8 Hast you heard the secret of G-d? and dost you restrain wisdom to thyself?9 What know you, that we know not? what understandest you, which is not in us?10 With us are both the grayheaded and very aged men, much elder than your father.11 Are the consolations of G-d small with you? is there any secret thing with you?12 Why doth your heart carry you away? and what do your eyes wink at,13 That you turn your spirit against G-d, and lettest such words go out of your mouth?14 What is man, that he should be clean? and he which is born of a woman, that he should be righteous?

| ילוד 3205 | אשה 802: | 15:15 | הן 2005 | בקדשו 6918 | לא 3808 | יאמין 539 | ושמים 8064 | לא 3808 | זכו 2141 |
|---|---|---|---|---|---|---|---|---|---|
| yalud | 'ashah. | | hen | biqdoshou | la' | ya'amiyn; | uashamayim, | la' | zaku |
| ***he which is* born of** | **a woman** | | **Behold** | **in his saints;** | **no** | **he put no trust** | **yea the heavens** | **not** | **are clean** |

| בעיניו 5869: | 15:16 | אף 637 | כי 3588 | נתעב 8581 | ונאלח 444 | איש 376 | שתה 8354 | כמים 4325 | עולה 5766: | 15:17 |
|---|---|---|---|---|---|---|---|---|---|---|
| ba'aeynayu. | | 'ap | kiy | nit'ab | uane'alach; | 'aysh | shoteh | kamayim | 'aulah. | |
| **in his sight** | | **How much more** | **even** | **abominable** | **and filthy** | ***is* man** | **which drink** | **like water?** | **iniquity** | |

| אחוך 2331 | שמע 8085 | לי 3807a | וזה 2088 | חזיתי 2372 | ואספרה 5608: | 15:18 | אשר 834 | חכמים 2450 | יגידו 5046 | ולא 3808 |
|---|---|---|---|---|---|---|---|---|---|---|
| 'achauaka | shama' | liy; | uazeh | chaziytiy, | ua'asaperah. | | 'asher | chakamiym | yagiydu; | uala' |
| **I will show you** | **hear** | **me** | **and that** | ***which* I have seen** | **I will declare** | | **Which** | **wise men** | **have told** | **and not** |

| כחדו 3582 | מאבותם 1: | 15:19 | להם 3807a | לבדם 905 | נתנה 5414 | הארץ 776 | ולא 3808 | עבר 5674 | זר 2114 | בתוכם 8432: | 15:20 |
|---|---|---|---|---|---|---|---|---|---|---|---|
| kichadu, | me'aboutam. | | lahem | labadam | nitanah | ha'aretz; | uala' | 'abar | zar | batoukam. | |
| **have hid *it*** | **from their fathers** | | **Unto whom** | **alone** | **was given** | **the earth** | **and no** | **passed** | **stranger** | **among them** | |

| כל 3605 | ימי 3117 | רשע 7563 | הוא 1931 | מתחולל 2342 | ומספר 4557 | שנים 8141 | נצפנו 6845 | לעריץ 6184: | 15:21 |
|---|---|---|---|---|---|---|---|---|---|
| kal | yamey | rasha' | hua' | mitchoulel; | uamispar | shaniym, | nitzpanu | le'ariytz. | |
| **all *his*** | **days** | **The wicked man** | **he** | **travail with pain** | **and the number of** | **years** | **is hidden** | **to the oppressor** | |

| קול 6963 | פחדים 6343 | באזניו 241 | בשלום 7965 | שודד 7703 | יבואנו 935: | 15:22 | לא 3808 | יאמין 539 | שוב 7725 |
|---|---|---|---|---|---|---|---|---|---|
| qoul | pachadiym | ba'azanayu; | bashaloum, | shouded | yabou'anu. | | la' | ya'amiyn | shub |
| **A sound** | **dreadful *is*** | **in his ears** | **in prosperity** | **the destroyer** | **shall come upon him** | | **not** | **He believe** | **that he shall return** |

| מני 4480 | חשך 2822 | וצפו 6822 | הוא 1931 | אלי 413 | חרב 2719: | 15:23 | נדד 5074 | הוא 1931 | ללחם 3899 | איה 344 |
|---|---|---|---|---|---|---|---|---|---|---|
| miniy | choshek; | uatzapu | hua' | 'aley | chareb. | | noded | hua' | lalechem | 'ayeh; |
| **out of** | **darkness** | **and waited for** | **he *is*** | **of** | **the sword** | | **wander abroad** | **He** | **for bread *saying*** | **Where *is it*?** |

| ידע 3045 | כי 3588 | נכון 3559 | בידו 3027 | יום 3117 | חשך 2822: | 15:24 | יבעתהו 1204 | צר 6862 | ומצוקה 4691 |
|---|---|---|---|---|---|---|---|---|---|
| yada' | kiy | nakoun | bayadou | youm | choshek. | | yaba'atuhu | tzar | uamtzuqah; |
| **he knows** | **that** | **is ready** | **at his hand** | **the day** | **darkness** | | **shall make him afraid** | **Trouble** | **and anguish** |

| תתקפהו 8630 | כמלך 4428 | עתיד 6264 | לכידור 3593: | 15:25 | כי 3588 | נטה 5186 | אל 413 | אל 410 | ידו 3027 | ואל 413 |
|---|---|---|---|---|---|---|---|---|---|---|
| titqapehu, | kamelek | 'atiyd | lakiydour. | | kiy | natah | 'al | 'ael | yadou; | ua'al |
| **they shall prevail against him** | **as a king** | **ready** | **to the battle** | | **For** | **he stretch out** | **against** | **El** | **his hand** | **and against** |

| שדי 7706 | יתגבר 1396: | 15:26 | ירוץ 7323 | אליו 413 | בצואר 6677 | בעבי 5672 | גבי 1354 | מגניו 4043: | 15:27 |
|---|---|---|---|---|---|---|---|---|---|
| shaday, | yitgabar. | | yarutz | 'aelayu | batzaua'r; | ba'abiy, | gabey | maginayu. | |
| **the Almighty** | **strengthen himself** | | **He run** | **upon him *even*** | **on *his* neck** | **upon the thick** | **bosses of** | **his bucklers** | |

| כי 3588 | כסה 3680 | פניו 6440 | בחלבו 2459 | ויעש 6213 | פימה 6371 | עלי 5921 | כסל 6389: | 15:28 | וישכון 7931 | ערים 5892 |
|---|---|---|---|---|---|---|---|---|---|---|
| kiy | kisah | panayu | bachelbou; | uaya'as | piymah | 'aley | kasel. | | uayishkoun | 'ariym |
| **Because** | **he cover** | **his face** | **with his fatness** | **and make** | **collops of fat** | **on** | ***his* flanks** | | **And he dwell in** | **cities** |

| נכחדות 3582 | בתים 1004 | לא 3808 | ישבו 3427 | למו 3807a | אשר 834 | התעתדו 6257 | לגלים 1530: | 15:29 | לא 3808 | יעשר 6238 |
|---|---|---|---|---|---|---|---|---|---|---|
| nikchadout, | batiym | la' | yeshabu | lamou; | 'asher | hit'atdu | lagaliym. | | la' | ye'ashar |
| **desolate** | ***and* in houses** | **no** | **which inhabiteth man** | | **which** | **are ready** | ***to become* heaps** | | **nor** | **He shall be rich** |

Job 15:15 Behold, he put no trust in his saints; yea, the heavens are not clean in his sight.16 How much more abominable and filthy is man, which drinketh iniquity like water?17 I will show you, hear me; and that which I have seen I will declare;18 Which wise men have told from their fathers, and have not hid it:19 Unto whom alone the earth was given, and no stranger passed among them.20 The wicked man travaileth with pain all his days, and the number of years is hidden to the oppressor.21 A dreadful sound is in his ears: in prosperity the destroyer shall come upon him.22 He believeth not that he shall return out of darkness, and he is waited for of the sword.23 He wandereth abroad for bread, saying, Where is it? he know that the day of darkness is ready at his hand.24 Trouble and anguish shall make him afraid; they shall prevail against him, as a king ready to the battle.25 For he stretcheth out his hand against G-d, and strengtheneth himself against the Almighty.26 He runneth upon him, even on his neck, upon the thick bosses of his bucklers:27 Because he covereth his face with his fatness, and make collops of fat on his flanks. 28 And he dwell in desolate cities, and in houses which no man inhabiteth, which are ready to become heaps.

15:30
ולא 3808 יקום 6965 חילו 2428 ולא 3808 יטה 5186 לארץ 776 מנלם 4512: לא 3808
uala' yaqum cheylou; uala' yiteh la'aretz minlam. la'
**neither continue shall his substance neither shall he prolong upon the earth the perfection thereof not**

15:31
יסור 5493 מני 4480 חשך 2822 ינקתו 3127 תיבש 3001 שלהבת 7957 ויסור 5493 ברוח 7307 פיו 6310:
yasur miniy choshek, yonaqtou tayabesh shalhabet; uayasur, baruach piyu.
**He shall depart out of darkness his branches shall dry up the flame and shall he go away by the breath of his mouth**

15:32
אל 408 יאמן 539 בשו 7723 נתעה 8582 כי 3588 שוא 7723 תהיה 1961 תמורתו 8545: בלא 3808 יומו 3117
'al ya'amen bashou nit'ah; kiy, shau'a tihayeh tamuratou. bala' yomou
**not Let trust in vanity: him that is deceived for vanity shall be his recompence before his time**

15:33
תמלא 4390 וכפתו 3712 לא 3808 רעננה 7488: יחמס 2554 כגפן 1612 בסרו 1154
timalea'; uakipatou, la' ra'ananah. yachmos kagepen bisrou;
**It shall be accomplished and his branch not shall be green He shall shake off as the vine his unripe grape**

15:34
וישלך 7993 כזית 2132 נצתו 5328: כי 3588 עדת 5712 חנף 2611 גלמוד 1565 ואש 784 אכלה 398
uayashlek kazayit, nitzatou. kiy 'adat chanep galmud; ua'aesh, 'akalah
**and shall cast off as the olive his flower For the congregation of hypocrites *shall be* desolate and fire shall consume**

15:35
אהלי 168 שחד 7810: הרה 2029 עמל 5999 וילד 3205 און 205 ובטנם 990 תכין 3559 מרמה 4820:
'ahaley shochad. haroh 'amal uayalod 'auen; uabitnam, takiyn mirmah.
**the tabernacles of bribery They conceive mischief and bring forth vanity and their belly prepare deceit**

**Job 16:1** ... **16:2** ... **16:3**
ויען 6030 איוב 347 ויאמר 559: שמעתי 8085 כאלה 428 רבות 7227 מנחמי 5162 עמל 5999 כלכם 3605:
uaya'an 'ayoub, uaya'mar. shama'atiy ka'aeleh rabout; manachamey 'amal kulkem.
**Then answered Job and said I have heard such things many comforters miserable *are* you all**

16:4
הקץ 7093 לדברי 1697 רוח 7307 או 176 מה 4100 ימריצך 4834 כי 3588 תענה 6030: גם 1571 אנכי 595 ככם 3509a אדברה 1696
haqetz ladibrey ruach; 'au mah yamriytzaka, kiy ta'aneh. gam 'anokiy kakem 'adaberah
***Shall have* an end? words vain or what embolden you that you answer? also I as you *do* could speak**

16:5
לו 3863 יש 3426 נפשכם 5315 תחת 8478 נפשי 5315 אחבירה 2266 עליכם 5921 במלים 4405 ואניעה 5128 עליכם 5921 במו 1119 ראשי 7218:
lou' yesh napshakem tachat napshiy, 'achbiyrah 'aleykem bamiliym; ua'aniy'ah 'aleykem, bamou ra'shiy.
**if were your soul in stead my soul's I could heap up against you words and shake at you in mine head**

16:6
אאמצכם 553 במו 1119 פי 6310 וניד 5205 שפתי 8193 יחשך 2820: אם 518 אדברה 1696
'a'amitzkem bamou piy; uaniyd sapatay yachsok. 'am 'adabrah
***But* I would strengthen you with my mouth and the moving of my lips should asswage *your grief* Though I speak**

16:7
לא 3808 יחשך 2820 כאבי 3511 ואחדלה 2308 מה 4100 מני 4480 יהלך 1980: אך 389 עתה 6258 הלאני 3811
la' yechasek ka'aebiy; ua'achdalah, mah miniy yahalok. 'ak 'atah hel'aniy;
**not is asswaged my grief and *though* I forbear what I am eased? But now he has made me weary**

16:8
השמות 8074 כל 3605 עדתי 5712: ותקמטני 7059 לעד 5707 היה 1961
hashimouta, kal 'adatiy. uatiqmateniy la'aed hayah;
**you have made desolate all my company And you have filled me with wrinkles a witness *against me* which is**

Job 15:29 He shall not be rich, neither shall his substance continue, neither shall he prolong the perfection thereof upon the earth.30 He shall not depart out of darkness; the flame shall dry up his branches, and by the breath of his mouth shall he go away.31 Let not him that is deceived trust in vanity: for vanity shall be his recompence.32 It shall be accomplished before his time, and his branch shall not be green.33 He shall shake off his unripe grape as the vine, and shall cast off his flower as the olive.34 For the congregation of hypocrites shall be desolate, and fire shall consume the tabernacles of bribery.35 They conceive mischief, and bring forth vanity, and their belly prepareth deceit. **Job** 16:1 Then Job answered and said,2 I have heard many such things: miserable comforters are you all.3 Shall vain words have an end? or what emboldeneth you that you answerest?4 I also could speak as you do: if your soul were in my soul's stead, I could heap up words against you, and shake mine head at you.5 But I would strengthen you with my mouth, and the moving of my lips should asswage your grief.6 Though I speak, my grief is not asswaged: and though I forbear, what am I eased? 7 But now he has made me weary: you have made desolate all my company.8 And you have filled me with wrinkles, which is a witness against me: and my leanness rising up in me...

| ויקם 6965 | בי 871a | כחשי 3585 | בפני 6440 | יענה 6030: | 16:9 | אפו 639 | טרף 2963 | וישטמני 7852 | חרק 2786 | עלי 5921 |
|---|---|---|---|---|---|---|---|---|---|---|
| uayaqam | biy | kachashiy, | bapanay | ya'aneh. | | 'apou | tarap | uayistameniy, | charaq | 'alay |
| **and rising up** | **in me** | **my leanness** | **to my face** | **bear witness** | | ***me in* his wrath** | **He tear** | **who hate me** | **he gnash** | **upon me** |

| בשניו 8127 | צרי 6862 | ילטוש 3913 | עיניו 5869 | לי 3807a: | 16:10 | פערו 6473 | עלי 5921 | בפיהם 6310 | בחרפה 2781 |
|---|---|---|---|---|---|---|---|---|---|
| bashinayu; | tzariy | yiltoush | 'aeynayu | liy. | | pa'aru | 'alay | bapiyhem, | bacherpah |
| **with his teeth** | **mine enemy** | **sharpen** | **his eyes** | **upon me** | | **They have gaped** | **upon me** | **with their mouth** | **reproachfully** |

| הכו 5221 | לחיי 3895 | יחד 3162 | עלי 5921 | יתמלאון 4390: | 16:11 | יסגירני 5462 | אל 410 | אל 413 |
|---|---|---|---|---|---|---|---|---|
| hiku | lachayay; | yachad, | 'alay | yitmala'aun. | | yasgireniy | 'ael | 'al |
| **they have smitten me** | **upon the cheek** | **together** | **against me** | **they have gathered themselves** | | **has delivered me** | **El** | **to** |

| עויל 5760 | ועל 5921 | ידי 3027 | רשעים 7563 | ירטני 3399: | 16:12 | שלו 7961 | הייתי 1961 | ויפרפרני 6565 |
|---|---|---|---|---|---|---|---|---|
| 'auiyl; | ua'al | yadey | rasha'aym | yirteniy. | | shaleu | hayiytiy | uayaparpareniy, |
| **the ungodly** | **and into** | **the hands of** | **the wicked** | **turned me over** | | **at ease** | **I was** | **but he has broken me asunder** |

| ואחז 270 | בערפי 6203 | ויפצפצני 6327 | ויקימני 6965 | לו 3807a | למטרה 4307: | 16:13 | יסבו 5437 |
|---|---|---|---|---|---|---|---|
| ua'achaz | ba'arapiy | uaypatzpatzeniy; | uayaqiymeniy | lou', | lamatarah. | | yasobu |
| **he has also taken** | ***me* by my neck** | **and shaken me to pieces** | **and set up** | **me** | **for his mark** | | **compass round about** |

| עלי 5921 | רביו 7228 | יפלח 6398 | כליותי 3629 | ולא 3808 | יחמול 2550 | ישפך 8210 | לארץ 776 | מררתי 4845: | 16:14 |
|---|---|---|---|---|---|---|---|---|---|
| 'alay | rabayu, | yapalach | kilyoutay | uala' | yachmoul; | yishpok | la'aretz, | mareratiy. | |
| **me** | **His archers** | **he cleave asunder** | **my reins** | **and not** | **does spare** | **he pour out** | **upon the ground** | **my gall** | |

| יפרצני 6555 | פרץ 6556 | על 5921 | פני 6440 | פרץ 6556 | ירץ 7323 | עלי 5921 | כגבור 1368: | 16:15 | שק 8242 | תפרתי 8609 | עלי 5921 | גלדי 1539 |
|---|---|---|---|---|---|---|---|---|---|---|---|---|
| yipratzeniy | peretz | 'al | paney | paretz; | yarutz | 'alay | kagibour. | | saq | tapartiy | 'aley | gildiy; |
| **He break me with** | **breach** | **on** | **before** | **breach** | **he run** | **upon me** | **like a giant** | | **sackcloth** | **I have sewed** | **upon** | **my skin** |

| ועללתי 5953 | בעפר 6083 | קרני 7161: | 16:16 | פני 6440 | חמרמרה 2560 | מני 4480 | בכי 1065 | ועל 5921 | עפעפי 6079 | צלמות 6757: | 16:17 |
|---|---|---|---|---|---|---|---|---|---|---|---|
| ua'alaltiy | be'apar | qarniy. | | panay | chamarmarah | miniy | bekiy; | ua'al | 'ap'apay | tzalmauet. | |
| **and defiled** | **in the dust** | **my horn** | | **My face** | **is foul** | **with** | **weeping** | **and my** | **eyelids *is*** | ***the* shadow of death** | |

| על 5921 | לא 3808 | חמס 2555 | בכפי 3709 | ותפלתי 8605 | זכה 2134: | 16:18 | ארץ 776 | אל 408 | תכסי 3680 | דמי 1818 | ואל 408 | יהי 1961 |
|---|---|---|---|---|---|---|---|---|---|---|---|---|
| 'al | la' | chamas | bakapay; | utapilatiy | zakah. | | 'aretz | 'al | takasiy | damiy; | ua'al | yahiy |
| **for** | **Not** | ***any* injustice** | **in mine hands** | **also my prayer *is*** | **pure** | | **O earth** | **not** | **cover you** | **my blood** | **and no** | **let have** |

| מקום 4725 | לזעקתי 2201: | 16:19 | גם 1571 | עתה 6258 | הנה 2009 | בשמים 8064 | עדי 5707 | ושהדי 7717 | במרומים 4791: | 16:20 | מליצי 3887 |
|---|---|---|---|---|---|---|---|---|---|---|---|
| maqoum, | laza'aqatiy. | | gam | 'atah | hineh | bashamayim | 'aediy; | uasahadiy, | bamroumiym. | | maliytziy |
| **place** | **my cry** | | **Also** | **now** | **behold** | ***is* in heaven** | **my witness** | **and my record** | ***is* on high** | | **scorn me** |

| רעי 7453 | אל 413 | אלוה 433 | דלפה 1811 | עיני 5869: | 16:21 | ויוכח 3198 | לגבר 1397 | עם 5973 | אלוה 433 | ובן 1121 |
|---|---|---|---|---|---|---|---|---|---|---|
| re'ay; | 'al | 'alouah, | dalapah | 'aeyniy. | | uayoukach | lageber | 'am | 'alouah; | uaben |
| **My friends *tears*** | **unto** | **Elohim** | **pour out** | ***but* mine eye** | | **O that one might plead** | **for a man** | **with** | **Elohim** | **as a son of** |

| אדם 120 | לרעהו 7453: | 16:22 | כי 3588 | שנות 8141 | מספר 4557 | יאתיו 857 | וארח 734 | לא 3808 | אשוב 7725 | אהלך 1980: |
|---|---|---|---|---|---|---|---|---|---|---|
| 'adam | lare'aehu. | | kiy | shanout | mispar | ye'atayu; | ua'arach | la' | 'ashub | 'ahelok. |
| **a man *plead*** | **for his neighbor** | | **When** | **a years** | **few** | **they are come** | **then the way** | **not** | ***where* I shall return** | **I shall go** |

Job 16:9 beareth witness to my face.9 He teareth me in his wrath, who hateth me: he gnasheth upon me with his teeth; mine enemy sharpeneth his eyes upon me.10 They have gaped upon me with their mouth; they have smitten me upon the cheek reproachfully; they have gathered themselves together against me.11 G-d has delivered me to the ungodly, and turned me over into the hands of the wicked.12 I was at ease, but he has broken me asunder: he has also taken me by my neck, and shaken me to pieces, and set me up for his mark.13 His archers compass me round about, he cleaveth my reins asunder, and doth not spare; he poureth out my gall upon the ground.14 He breaketh me with breach upon breach, he runneth upon me like a giant.15 I have sewed sackcloth upon my skin, and defiled my horn in the dust.16 My face is foul with weeping, and my eyelids is the shadow of death;17 Not for any injustice in mine hands: also my prayer is pure.18 O earth, cover not you my blood, and let my cry have no place.19 Also now, behold, my witness is in heaven, and my record is on high.20 My friends scorn me: but mine eye poureth out tears unto G-d.21 O that one might plead for a man with G-d, as a man pleadeth for his neighbor!22 When a few years are come, then I shall go the way whence I shall not return.

**Job 17:1** רוחי 7307 חבלה 2254 ימי 3117 נזעכו 2193 קברים 6913 לי 3807a: **17:2** אם 518 לא 3808 התלים 2049
ruchiy chubalah yamay niz'aku, qabariym liy. 'am la' hatuliym
**My breath is corrupt my days are extinct the graves *are ready* for me *Are there* surely not mockers**

עמדי 5978 ובהמרותם 4784 תלן 3885 עיני 5869: **17:3** שימה 7760 נא 4994 ערבני 6148 עמך 5973 מי 4310
'amadiy; uabhamroutam, talan 'aeyniy. siymah naa' 'arabeniy 'amak; miy'
**with me? and in their provocation? do continue *not* mine eye Lay down now put me in a surety with you who *is***

הוא 1931 לידי 3027 יתקע 8628: **17:4** כי 3588 לבם 3820 צפנת 6845 משכל 7922 על 5921 כן 3651 לא 3808
hua' layadiy yitaqea'. kiy libam tzapanta misakel; 'al ken, la'
**he hands *that* will strike *with me*? For their heart you have hid from understanding therefore after not**

תרמם 7311: **17:5** לחלק 2506 יגיד 5046 רעים 7453 ועיני 5869 בניו 1121 תכלנה 3615: **17:6**
taromem. lacheleq yagiyd re'aym; ua'aeyney banayu tiklenah.
**shall you exalt *them* flattery He that speak *to his* friends even the eyes of his children shall fail**

והצגני 3322 למשל 4914 עמים 5971 ותפת 8611 לפנים 6440 אהיה 1961: **17:7** ותכה 3543 מכעש 3708 עיני 5869
uahitziganiy limshol 'amiym; uatopet lapaniym 'ahayeh. uatekah mika'as 'aeyniy;
**He has made me also a byword of the people and a tabret aforetime I was *as* also is dim by reason of sorrow Mine eye**

ויצרי 3338 כצל 6738 כלם 3605: **17:8** ישמו 8074 ישרים 3477 על 5921 זאת 2063 ונקי 5355 על 5921
uiytzuray katzel kulam. yashomu yashariym 'al za't; uanaqiy, 'al
**and my members *are* as a shadow all *men* shall be astonied Upright at this and the innocent against**

חנף 2611 יתערר 5782: **17:9** ויאחז 270 צדיק 6662 דרכו 1870 וטהר 2891 ידים 3027
chanep yit'arar. uaya'chez tzadiyq darkou; uatahar yadayim,
**the hypocrite shall stir up himself also shall hold on The righteous his way and he that has clean hands**

יסיף 3254 אמץ 555: **17:10** ואולם 199 כלם 3605 תשבו 7525 ובאו 935 נא 4994 ולא 3808 אמצא 4672 בכם 871a
yosiyp 'ametz. ua'aulam, kulam tashubu uabo'au na; uala' 'amtzaa' bakem
**shall be stronger *and* stronger But as for you all do you return and come now for cannot I find among you**

חכם 2450: **17:11** ימי 3117 עברו 5674 זמתי 2154 נתקו 5423 מורשי 4180 לבבי 3824: **17:12** לילה 3915 ליום 3117
chakam. yamay 'abaru zimotay nitqu; mourashey lababiy. layalah layoum
***one* wise man My days are past my purposes are broken off *even* the thoughts of my heart the night into day**

ישימו 7760 אור 216 קרוב 7138 מפני 6440 חשך 2822: **17:13** אם 518 אקוה 6960 שאול 7585 ביתי 1004 בחשך 2822 רפדתי 7502
yasiymu; 'aur, qaroub mipaney choshek. 'am 'aqaueh sha'aul beytiy; bachoshek, ripadtiy
**They change the light *is* short because of darkness If I wait the grave *is* mine house in the darkness I have made**

יצועי 3326: **17:14** לשחת 7843 קראתי 7121 אבי 1 אתה 859 אמי 517 ואחתי 269 לרמה 7415: **17:15**
yatzu'ay. lashachat qara'tiy 'abiy 'atah; 'amiy ua'achotiy, larimah.
**my bed to corruption I have said *are* my father You *You are* my mother and my sister to the worm**

ואיה 346 אפו 645 תקותי 8615 ותקותי 8615 מי 4325 ישורנה 7789: **17:16** בדי 905 שאל 7585 תרדנה 3381 אם 518
ua'ayeh aepou tiquatiy; uatiquatiy, miy' yashurenah. badey sha'al teradnah; 'am
**And where *is* now my hope? as for my hope who shall see it? the bars of the pit They shall go down to when**

**Job** 17:1 My breath is corrupt, my days are extinct, the graves are ready for me.2 Are there not mockers with me? and doth not mine eye continue in their provocation?3 Lay down now, put me in a surety with you; who is he that will strike hands with me?4 For you have hid their heart from understanding: therefore shall you not exalt them.5 He that speaketh flattery to his friends, even the eyes of his children shall fail.6 He has made me also a byword of the people; and aforetime I was as a tabret.7 Mine eye also is dim by reason of sorrow, and all my members are as a shadow.8 Upright men shall be astonied at this, and the innocent shall stir up himself against the hypocrite.9 The righteous also shall hold on his way, and he that has clean hands shall be stronger and stronger.10 But as for you all, do you return, and come now: for I cannot find one wise man among you.11 My days are past, my purposes are broken off, even the thoughts of my heart.12 They change the night intoday: the light is short because of darkness.13 If I wait, the grave is mine house: I have made my bed in the darkness.14 I have said to corruption, Thou are my father: to the worm, Thou are my mother, and my sister. 15 And where is now my hope? as for my hope, who shall see it?16 They shall go down to the bars of the pit, when our rest together is in the dust.

יחד 3162 על 5921 עפר 6083 נחת 5183:
yachad 'al 'apar nachat.
**together *is* in the dust *our* rest**

**Job 18:1** ויען 6030 בלדד 1085 השחי 7747 ויאמר 559: **18:2** עד 5704 אנה 575 תשימון 7760 קנצי 7093 למלין 4405
uaya'an bildad hashchiy, uaya'mar. 'ad 'anah tasiymun qintzey lamiliyn;
**Then answered Bildad the Shuhite and said How long when *will it be ere* you make an end of words?**

תבינו 995 ואחר 310 נדבר 1696: **18:3** מדוע 4069 נחשבנו 2803 כבהמה 929 נטמינו 2933 בעיניכם 5869: **18:4** טרף 2963
tabiynu, ua'achar nadaber. madua' nechshabnu chabahemah; nitmiynu, ba'aeyneykem. torep
**mark and afterwards we will speak Wherefore are we counted as beasts *and* reputed vile in your sight? He tear**

נפשו 5315 באפו 639 הלמענך 4616 תעזב 5800 ארץ 776 ויעתק 6275 צור 6697 ממקמו 4725: **18:5** גם 1571
napshou, ba'apou halama'anka te'azab 'aretz; uaye'ataq tzur, mimaqomou. gam
**himself in his anger for you? shall be forsaken the earth and shall be removed the rock out of his place? Yea**

אור 216 רשעים 7563 ידעך 1846 ולא 3808 יגה 5050 שביב 7632 אשו 784: **18:6** אור 216 חשך 2821
'aur rasha'aym yid'ak; uala' yigah, shabiyb 'ashou. 'aur chashak
**the light of the wicked shall be put out and not shall shine the spark of his fire The light shall be dark**

באהלו 168 ונרו 5216 עליו 5921 ידעך 1846: **18:7** יצרו 3334 צעדי 6806 אונו 202
ba'ahalou; uanerou, 'alayu yid'ak. yetzaru tza'adey 'aunou;
**in his tabernacle and his candle with him shall be put out shall be straitened The steps of his strength**

ותשליכהו 7993 עצתו 6098: **18:8** כי 3588 שלח 7971 ברשת 7568 ברגליו 7272 ועל 5921 שבכה 7639 יתהלך 1980: **18:9**
uatashliykehu atzatou. kiy shulach bareshet baraglayu; ua'al sabakah, yithalak.
**and shall cast him down his own counsel For he is cast into a net by his own feet and upon a snare he walk**

יאחז 270 בעקב 6119 פח 6341 יחזק 2388 עליו 5921 צמים 6782: **18:10** טמון 2934 בארץ 776 חבלו 2256
ya'chez ba'aqeb pach; yachazeq 'alayu tzamiym. tamun ba'aretz chablou;
**shall take *him* by the heel The gin shall prevail against him *and* the robber *is* laid in the ground The snare for him**

ומלכדתו 4434 עלי 5921 נתיב 5410: **18:11** סביב 5439 בעתהו 1204 בלהות 1091 והפיצהו 6327 לרגליו 7272: **18:12**
uamalkudtou, 'aley natiyb. sabiyb bi'atuhu balahout; uahepiytzuhu laraglayu.
**and a trap for him in the way on every side shall make him afraid Terrors and shall drive him to his feet**

יהי 1961 רעב 7457 אנו 202 ואיד 343 נכון 3559 לצלעו 6763: **18:13** יאכל 398 בדי 905 עורו 5785
yahiy ra'aeb 'anou; ua'aeyd, nakoun latzal'au. ya'kal badey arou;
**shall be hungerbitten His strength and destruction *shall be* ready at his side It shall devour the strength of his skin**

יאכל 398 בדיו 905 בכור 1060 מות 4194: **18:14** ינתק 5423 מאהלו 168 מבטחו 4009
ya'kal badayu, bakour mauet. yinateq me'ahalou mibtachou;
**shall devour his strength *even* the firstborn of death shall be rooted out of his tabernacle His confidence**

ותצעדהו 6805 למלך 4428 בלהות 1091: **18:15** תשכון 7931 באהלו 168 מבלי 1097 לו 3807a
uatatz'adehu, lamelek balahout. tishkoun ba'ahalou mibaliy lou';
**and it shall bring him to the king of terrors It shall dwell in his tabernacle because *it is* none of**

**Job** 18:1 Then answered Bildad the Shuhite, and said,2 How long will it be ere you make an end of words? mark, and afterwards we will speak.3 Wherefore are we counted as beasts, and reputed vile in your sight?4 He teareth himself in his anger: shall the earth be forsaken for you? and shall the rock be removed out of his place?5 Yea, the light of the wicked shall be put out, and the spark of his fire shall not shine.6 The light shall be dark in his tabernacle, and his candle shall be put out with him.7 The steps of his strength shall be straitened, and his own counsel shall cast him down.8 For he is cast into a net by his own feet, and he walk upon a snare.9 The gin shall take him by the heel, and the robber shall prevail against him.10 The snare is laid for him in the ground, and a trap for him in the way.11 Terrors shall make him afraid on every side, and shall drive him to his feet.12 His strength shall be hungerbitten, and destruction shall be ready at his side.13 It shall devour the strength of his skin: even the firstborn of death shall devour his strength.14 His confidence shall be rooted out of his tabernacle, and it shall bring him to the king of terrors. 15 It shall dwell in his tabernacle, because it is none of his:

18:16
יזרה 2219 על 5921 נוהו 5116 גפרית 1614: מתחת 8478 שרשיו 8328 יבשו 3001 וממעל 4605 ימל 5243
yazoreh 'al nauehu gapriyt. mitachat sharashayu yibashu; uamima'al, yimal
**shall be scattered upon his habitation his brimstone beneath His roots shall be dried up and above shall be cut off**

18:17 18:18
קצירו 7105: זכרו 2143 אבד 6 מני 4480 ארץ 776 ולא 3808 שם 8034 לו 3807a על 5921 פני 6440 חוץ 2351:
qatziyrou. zikrou 'abad miniy 'aretz; uala' shem lou', 'al paney chutz.
**his branch His remembrance shall perish from the earth and no name he *shall have* on in the street**

18:19
יהדפהו 1920 מאור 216 אל 413 חשך 2822 ומתבל 8398 ינדהו 5074: לא 3808 נין 5209 לו 3807a ולא 3808 נכד 5220
yehdapuhu me'aur 'al choshek; uamitebel yaniduhu. la' niyn lou' uala' neked
**He shall be driven from light into darkness and out of the world chased neither *have* son He *shall* nor nephew**

18:20
בעמו 5971 ואין 369 שריד 8300 במגוריו 4033: על 5921 יומו 3117 נשמו 8074 אחרנים 314
ba'amou; ua'aeyn sariyd, bimgurayu. 'al youmou nashamu 'acharoniym;
**among his people nor any remaining in his dwellings *They that come* at his day *him* shall be astonied after**

18:21
וקדמנים 6931 אחזו 270 שער 8178: אך 389 אלה 428 משכנות 4908 עול 5767 וזה 2088 מקום 4725 לא 3808
uaqadmoniym, 'achazu sa'ar. 'ak 'aeleh mishkanout 'aual; uazeh, maqoum la'
**as they that went before were affrighted Surely such *are* the dwellings of the wicked and this *is* the place not**

ידע 3045 אל 410:
yada' 'ael.
***of him that* knows El**

**Job 19:1** 19:2
ויען 6030 איוב 347 ויאמר 559: עד 5704 אנה 575 תוגיון 3013 נפשי 5315 ותדכאונני 1792
uaya'an 'ayoub, uaya'mar. 'ad 'anah tougayun napshiy; uatdak'aunaniy
**Then answered Job and said How long when will you vex my soul and break me in pieces**

19:3
במלים 4405: זה 2088 עשר 6235 פעמים 6471 תכלימוני 3637 לא 3808 תבשו 954
bamiliym. zeh 'aser pa'amiym takliymuniy; la' teboshu,
**with words? These ten times have you reproached me not you are ashamed**

19:4 19:5
תהכרו 1970 לי 3807a: ואף 637 אמנם 551 שגיתי 7686 אתי 854 תלין 3885 משוגתי 4879:
tahkaru liy. ua'ap 'amanam shagiytiy; 'atiy, taliyn mashugatiy.
***that* you make yourselves strange to me And yet *be it* indeed *that* I have erred with myself remains mine error**

19:6
אם 518 אמנם 551 עלי 5921 תגדילו 1431 ותוכיחו 3198 עלי 5921 חרפתי 2781: דעו 3045 אפו 645 כי 3588 אלוה 433
'am 'amanam 'alay tagdiylu; uatoukiychu 'alay, cherpatiy da'au 'aepou kiy 'alouah
**If indeed against me you will magnify *yourselves* and plead against me my reproach Know now that Elohim**

19:7
עותני 5791 ומצודו 4686 עלי 5921 הקיף 5362: הן 2005 אצעק 6817 חמס 2555 ולא 3808 אענה 6030
'auataniy; uamtzudou, 'alay hiqiyp. hen 'atz'aq chamas uala' 'ae'aneh;
**has overthrown me and with his net me *with* has compassed Behold I cry *out of* wrong but not I am heard**

19:8
אשוע 7768 ואין 369 משפט 4941: ארחי 734 גדר 1443 ולא 3808 אעבור 5674 ועל 5921 נתיבותי 5410 חשך 2822
'ashaua', ua'aeyn mishapat. 'arachiy gadar uala' 'a'abour; ua'al natiyboutay, choshek
**I cry aloud but *there is* no judgment my way He has fenced up that cannot I pass and in my paths darkness**

Job 18:15brimstone shall be scattered upon his habitation.16 His roots shall be dried up beneath, and above shall his branch be cut off.17 His remembrance shall perish from the earth, and he shall have no name in the street.18 He shall be driven from light into darkness, and chased out of the world.19 He shall neither have son nor nephew among his people, nor any remaining in his dwellings.20 They that come after him shall be astonied at his day, as they that went before were affrighted.21 Surely such are the dwellings of the wicked, and this is the place of him that know not G-d. **Job** 19:1 Then Job answered and said,2 How long will you vex my soul, and break me in pieces with words?3 These ten times have you reproached me: you are not ashamed that you make yourselves strange to me.4 And be it indeed that I have erred, mine error remain with myself.5 If indeed you will magnify yourselves against me, and plead against me my reproach:6 Know now that G-d has overthrown me, and has compassed me with his net.7 Behold, I cry out of wrong, but I am not heard: I cry aloud, but there is no judgment.8 He has fenced up my way that I cannot pass, and he has set darkness in my paths.

19:9 … 19:10

ישים 7760: כבודי 3519 מעלי 5921 הפשיט 6584 ויסר 5493 עטרת 5850 ראשי 7218: יתצני 5422

yasiym. kaboudiy me'alay hipshiyt; uayasar, 'ateret ra'shiy. yittzeniy

**he has set *of* my glory me He has stripped and taken the crown *from* my head He has destroyed me**

19:11

סביב 5439 ואלך 1980 ויסע 5265 כעץ 6086 תקותי 8615: ויחר 2734 עלי 5921 אפו 639

sabiyb ua'aelak; uayasa' ka'aetz, tiquatiy. uayachar 'alay 'apou;

**on every side and I am gone and has he removed like a tree mine hope He has also kindled against me his wrath**

19:12

ויחשבני 2803 לו 3807a כצריו 6862: יחד 3162 יבאו 935 גדודיו 1416 ויסלו 5549 עלי 5921 דרכם 1870

uayachshabeniy lou' katzarayu. yachad yabo'au gadudayu, uayasolu 'alay darkam;

**and he count me unto him as *one of* his enemies together come His troops and raise up against me their way**

19:13

ויחנו 2583 סביב 5439 לאהלי 168: אחי 251 מעלי 5921 הרחיק 7368 וידעי 3045 אך 389

uayachanu sabiyb la'ahaliy. 'achay me'alay hirchiyq; uayoda'ay, 'ak

**and encamp round about my tabernacle my brethren from me He has put far and mine acquaintance verily**

19:14 … 19:15

זרו 2114 ממני 4480: חדלו 2308 קרובי 7138 ומידעי 3045 שכחוני 7911: גרי 1481

zaru mimeniy. chadalu qaroubay; uamyuda'ay shakechuniy. garey

**are estranged from me have failed My kinsfolk and my familiar friends have forgotten me They that dwell in**

19:16

ביתי 1004 ואמהתי 519 לזר 2114 תחשבני 2803 נכרי 5237 הייתי 1961 בעיניהם 5869: לעבדי 5650 קראתי 7121 ולא 3808

beytiy ua'amhotay lazar tachshabuniy; nakariy, hayiytiy ba'aeyneyhem. la'abdiy qara'tiy uala'

**mine house and my maids for a stranger count me an alien I am in their sight my servant I called and no**

19:17

יענה 6030 במו 1119 פי 6310 אתחנן 2603 לו 3807a: רוחי 7307 זרה 2114 לאשתי 802 וחנתי 2603

ya'aneh; bamou piy, 'atchanen lou'. ruchiy zarah la'ashtiy; uachanotiy,

**he gave answer *me* with my mouth I intreated him My breath is strange to my wife though I intreated**

19:18

לבני 1121 בטני 990: גם 1571 עוילים 5759 מאסו 3988 בי 871a אקומה 6965 וידברו 1696

libney bitniy. gam 'auiyliym ma'asu biy; 'aqumah, uaydabru

**for the children *sake* of mine own body Yea young children despised me I arose and they spoke**

19:19 … 19:20

בי 871a: תעבוני 8581 כל 3605 מתי 4962 סודי 5475 וזה 2088 אהבתי 157 נהפכו 2015 בי 871a: בעורי 5785

biy. ti'abuniy kal matey soudiy; uazeh 'ahabtiy, nehpaku biy. ba'auriy

**against me abhorred me All friends my inward and those whom I loved are turned against me to my skin**

19:21

ובבשרי 1320 דבקה 1692 עצמי 6106 ואתמלטה 4422 בעור 5785 שני 8127: חנני 2603 חנני 2603

uabibsariy dabqah 'atzmiy; ua'atmaltah, ba'aur shinay. chanuniy chanuniy

**and to my flesh cleave My bone and I am escaped with the skin of my teeth Have pity upon me have pity upon me**

19:22

אתם 859 רעי 7453 כי 3588 יד 3027 אלוה 433 נגעה 5060 בי 871a: למה 4100 תרדפני 7291 כמו 3644 אל 410

'atem re'ay; kiy yad 'alouah, naga'ah biy. lamah tirdapuniy kamou 'ael;

**O you my friends for the hand of Elohim has touched me Why do you persecute me as El**

19:23

ומבשרי 1320 לא 3808 תשבעו 7646: מי 4310 יתן 5414 אפו 645 ויכתבון 3789 מלי 4405 מי 4310 יתן 5414 בספר 5612

uamibsariy, la' tisba'au. miy' yiten 'aepou uayikatabun milay; miy' yiten baseper

**and with my flesh? not are satisfied Oh that were now written my words oh that they were in a book**

Job 19:9 He has stripped me of my glory, and taken the crown from my head.10 He has destroyed me on every side, and I am gone: and mine hope has he removed like a tree.11 He has also kindled his wrath against me, and he counteth me unto him as one of his enemies.12 His troops come together, and raise up their way against me, and encamp round about my tabernacle.13 He has put my brethren far from me, and mine acquaintance are verily estranged from me.14 My kinsfolk have failed, and my familiar friends have forgotten me.15 They that dwell in mine house, and my maids, count me for a stranger: I am an alien in their sight.16 I called my servant, and he gave me no answer; I entreated him with my mouth.17 My breath is strange to my wife, though I entreated for the children's sake of mine own body.18 Yea, young children despised me; I arose, and they spoke against me.19 All my inward friends abhorred me: and they whom I loved are turned against me.20 My bone cleaveth to my skin and to my flesh, and I am escaped with the skin of my teeth.21 Have pity upon me, have pity upon me, O you my friends; for the hand of G-d has touched me.22 Why do you persecute me as G-d, and are not satisfied with my flesh?23 Oh that my words were now written! oh that they were printed in a book!

19:24 … 19:25

ויחקו 2710: | בעט 5842 | ברזל 1270 | ועפרת 5777 | לעד 5703 | בצור 6697 | יחצבון 2672: | ואני 589 | ידעתי 3045

uayuchaqu. | ba'aet | barzel | ua'aparet; | la'ad, | batzur | yechatzabun. | ua'aniy | yada'tiy

**printed** | ***That* with an pen** | **iron** | **and lead** | **for ever** | **in the rock** | **they were graven** | **For I** | **know**

19:26

גאלי 1350 | חי 2416 | ואחרון 314 | על 5921 | עפר 6083 | יקום 6965: | ואחר 310 | עורי 5785

go'aliy | chay; | ua'acharoun, | 'al | 'apar | yaqum. | ua'achar | 'auriy

***that* my redeemer** | **live, *day*** | **and the latter** | **upon** | **the earth** | ***that* he shall stand *at*** | **And *though* after** | **my skin**

19:27

נקפו 5362 | זאת 2063 | ומבשרי 1320 | אחזה 2372 | אלוה 433: | אשר 834 | אני 589 | אחזה 2372 | לי 3807a | ועיני 5869

niqpu | za't; | uamibsariy, | 'achezeh | 'alouah. | 'asher | 'aniy | 'achezeh | liy, | ua'aeynay

***worms* destroy** | **this** | ***body* yet in my flesh** | **shall I see** | **Elohim** | **Whom** | **I** | **shall see** | **for myself** | **and mine eyes**

19:28

ראו 7200 | ולא 3808 | זר 2114 | כלו 3615 | כליתי 3629 | בחקי 2436: | כי 3588 | תאמרו 559 | מה 4100 | נרדף 7291 | לו 3807a

ra'au | uala' | zar; | kalu | kilyotay | bacheqiy. | kiy | ta'maru | mah | nirdap | lou';

**shall behold and not another be consumed *though* my reins within me** | **But** | **you should say Why** | **persecute we** | **him**

19:29

ושרש 8328 | דבר 1697 | נמצא 4672 | בי 871a: | גורו 1481 | לכם 3807a | מפני 6440 | חרב 2719 | כי 3588 | חמה 2534

uashoresh | dabar, | nimtza | biy. | guru | lakem | mipaney | chereb, | kiy | chemah

**seeing the root of** | **the matter** | **is found** | **in me?** | **Be afraid** | **to you** | **of** | **the sword** | **for** | **wrath**

עונות 5771 | חרב 2719 | למען 4616 | תדעון 3045 | שדין 1779:

'auonout | chareb; | lama'an | teda'un | shadiyn

***bring* the punishments of the sword that** | **you may know *there is* a judgment.**

**Job 20:1** … 20:2

ויען 6030 | צפר 6691 | הנעמתי 5284 | ויאמר 559: | לכן 3651 | שעפי 5587 | ישיבוני 7725 | ובעבור 5668

uaya'an | tzipor | hana'amatiy, | uaya'mar. | laken | sa'apay | yashiybuniy; | uaba'abur,

**Then answered Zophar the Naamathite and said** | **Therefore my thoughts do cause me to answer and for *this***

20:3

חושי 2363 | בי 871a: | מוסר 4148 | כלמתי 3639 | אשמע 8085 | ורוח 7307 | מבינתי 998

chushiy | biy. | musar | kalimatiy | 'ashma; | uaruach, | mibiynatiy

**I make haste** | **I** | **the check of** | **my reproach** | **I have heard** | **and the spirit of** | **my understanding**

20:4 … 20:5

יענני 6030: | הזאת 2063 | ידעת 3045 | מני 4480 | עד 5703 | מני 4480 | שים 7760 | אדם 120 | עלי 5921 | ארץ 776: | כי 3588

ya'aneniy. | haza't | yada'ta | miniy | 'ad; | miniy | siym | 'adam | 'aley | 'aretz. | kiy

**cause me to answer** | ***not* this** | **Know you** | **of** | **old** | **since** | **was placed** | **man** | **upon** | **earth** | **That**

20:6

רננת 7445 | רשעים 7563 | מקרוב 7138 | ושמחת 8057 | חנף 2611 | עדי 5704 | רגע 7281: | אם 518 | יעלה 5927

rinat | rasha'aym | miqaroub; | uasimchat | chanep | 'adey | raga'. | 'am | ya'aleh

**the triumphing of** | **the wicked *is*** | **short** | **and the joy of** | **the hypocrite *but*** | **for** | **a moment?** | **Though** | **mount up**

20:7

לשמים 8064 | שיאו 7863 | וראשו 7218 | לעב 5645 | יגיע 5060: | כגללו 1561 | לנצח 5331 | יאבד 6

lashamayim | siy'au; | uarashou, | la'ab | yagiya'. | kagelalou | lanetzach | ya'bed;

**to the heavens** | **his excellency** | **and his head** | **unto the clouds** | **reach** | ***Yet* like his own dung** | **for ever** | **he shall perish**

20:8

ראיו 7200 | יאמרו 559 | איו 335: | כחלום 2472 | יעוף 5774 | ולא 3808 | ימצאוהו 4672

ro'ayu, | ya'maru | 'ayou. | kachaloum | ya'aup | uala' | yimtza'auhu;

**they which have seen him** | **shall say Where is he?** | **as a dream He shall fly away and not** | **shall be found**

Job 19:24 That they were graven with an iron pen and lead in the rock forever!25 For I know that my redeemer live, and that he shall stand at the latter day upon the earth:26 And though after my skin worms destroy this body, yet in my flesh shall I see G-d:27 Whom I shall see for myself, and mine eyes shall behold, and not another; though my reins be consumed within me.28 But you should say, Why persecute we him, seeing the root of the matter is found in me?29 Be you afraid of the sword: for wrath bring the punishments of the sword, that you may know there is a judgment. **Job** 20:1 Then answered Zophar the Naamathite, and said,2 Therefore do my thoughts cause me to answer, and for this I make haste.3 I have heard the check of my reproach, and the spirit of my understanding causeth me to answer.4 Know you not this of old, since man was placed upon earth,5 That the triumphing of the wicked is short, and the joy of the hypocrite but for a moment?6 Though his excellency mount up to the heavens, and his head reach unto the clouds;7 Yet he shall perish forever like his own dung: they which have seen him shall say, Where is he?8 He shall fly away as a dream, and shall not be found:

| וידד 5074 | כחזיון 2384 | לילה 3915: | 20:9 עין 5869 | שזפתו 7805 | ולא 3808 | תוסיף 3254 | ולא 3808 |
|---|---|---|---|---|---|---|---|
| uayudad, | kachezyoun | layalah. | 'ayin | shazapatu | uala' | tousiyp; | uala' |
| **yea he shall be chased away** | **as a vision of** | **the night** | **The eye** | ***which* saw him *shall see him*** | **also no** | **more** | **neither** |

| עוד 5750 | תשורנו 7789 | מקומו 4725: | 20:10 בניו 1121 | ירצו 7521 | דלים 1800 | וידיו 3027 | תשבנה 7725 |
|---|---|---|---|---|---|---|---|
| 'aud, | tashurenu | maqoumou. | banayu | yaratzu | daliym; | uayadayu, | tashebanah |
| **any more** | **shall behold him** | **his place** | **His children** | **shall seek to please** | **the poor** | **and his hands** | **shall restore** |

| אונו 202: | 20:11 עצמותיו 6106 | מלאו 4390 | עלומו 5934 | ועמו 5973 | על 5921 | עפר 6083 | תשכב 7901: | 20:12 אם 518 |
|---|---|---|---|---|---|---|---|---|
| 'aunou. | 'atzamoutayu | mala'au | 'alumou | ua'amou, | 'al | 'apar | tishkab. | 'am |
| **their goods** | **His bones** | **are full of** | ***the sin of* his youth,** | **with him** | **in** | **the dust** | ***which* shall lie down** | **Though** |

| תמתיק 4985 | בפיו 6310 | רעה 7451 | יכחידנה 3582 | תחת 8478 | לשונו 3956: | 20:13 יחמל 2550 | עליה 5921 | ולא 3808 | יעזבנה 5800 |
|---|---|---|---|---|---|---|---|---|---|
| tamtiyq | bapiyu | ra'ah; | yakchiydenah, | tachat | lashounou. | yachmol | 'aleyha | uala' | ya'azbenah; |
| **be sweet** | **in his mouth** | **wickedness** | ***though* he hide it** | **under** | **his tongue** | ***Though* he spare** | **it** | **and not** | **forsake it** |

| וימנענה 4513 | בתוך 8432 | חכו 2441: | 20:14 לחמו 3899 | במעיו 4578 | נהפך 2015 | מרורת 4846 | פתנים 6620 | בקרבו 7130: | 20:15 חיל 2428 |
|---|---|---|---|---|---|---|---|---|---|
| uayimna'anah, | batouk | chikou. | lachmou | bame'ayu | nehapak; | marourat | pataniym | baqirbou. | chayil |
| **but keep it still within** | | **his mouth** | ***Yet* his meat** | **in his bowels** | **is turned** | ***it is* the gall of** | **asps** | **within him** | **riches** |

| בלע 1104 | ויקאנו 6958 | מבטנו 990 | יורשנו 3423 | אל 410: | 20:16 ראש 7219 |
|---|---|---|---|---|---|
| bala' | uayaqi'anu; | mibitnou, | yourishenu | 'ael. | ra'sh |
| **He has swallowed down** | **and he shall vomit them up again** | **out of his belly** | **shall cast them** | **El** | **the poison of** |

| פתנים 6620 | יינק 3243 | תהרגהו 2026 | לשון 3956 | אפעה 660: | 20:17 אל 408 | ירא 7200 | בפלגות 6390 | נהרי 5104 | נחלי 5158 | דבש 1706 |
|---|---|---|---|---|---|---|---|---|---|---|
| pataniym | yiynaq; | tahargehu, | lashoun | 'ap'ah. | 'al | yera' | biplagout; | naharey | nachaley, | dabash |
| **asps** | **He shall suck** | **shall slay him** | **tongue** | ***the* viper's** | **not** | **He shall see** | **the rivers** | **the floods** | **the brooks of** | **honey** |

| וחמאה 2529: | 20:18 משיב 7725 | יגע 3022 | ולא 3808 | יבלע 1104 | כחיל 2428 |
|---|---|---|---|---|---|
| uachem'ah. | meshiyb | yaga' | uala' | yibla'; | kacheyl |
| **and butter** | **shall he restore** | **That which he laboured for** | **and not** | **shall swallow *it* down** | **according to *his* substance** |

| תמורתו 8545 | ולא 3808 | יעלס 5965: | 20:19 כי 3588 | רצץ 7533 | עזב 5800 | דלים 1800 | בית 1004 |
|---|---|---|---|---|---|---|---|
| tamuratou, | uala' | ya'alos. | kiy | ritzatz | 'azab | daliym; | bayit |
| ***shall* the restitution *be*** | **and not** | **he shall rejoice *therein*** | **Because** | **he has oppressed** | ***and* has forsaken** | **the poor** | **an house** |

| גזל 1497 | ולא 3808 | יבנהו 1129: | 20:20 כי 3588 | לא 3808 | ידע 3045 | שלו 7961 | בבטנו 990 |
|---|---|---|---|---|---|---|---|
| gazal, | uala' | yibenehu. | kiy | la' | yada' | shaleu | babitnou; |
| ***because* he has violently taken away** | **which not** | **he builded** | **Surely** | **not** | **he shall feel** | **quietness** | **in his belly** |

| בחמודו 2530 | לא 3808 | ימלט 4422: | 20:21 אין 369 | שריד 8300 | לאכלו 400 | על 5921 | כן 3651 | לא 3808 |
|---|---|---|---|---|---|---|---|---|
| bachamudou, | la' | yamalet. | 'aeyn | sariyd | la'akalou; | 'al | ken, | la' |
| **of that which he desired** | **not** | **he shall save** | **There shall none** | **be left** | **of his meat** | **therefore** | **after** | **no *man*** |

| יחיל 2342 | טובו 2898: | 20:22 במלאות 4390 | שפקו 5607 | יצר 3334 | לו 3807a | כל 3605 | יד 3027 | עמל 6001 |
|---|---|---|---|---|---|---|---|---|
| yachiyl | tubou. | bimla'ut | sipqou | yetzer | lou'; | kal | yad | 'amel |
| **shall look for** | **his goods** | **In the fullness of** | **his sufficiency** | **shall be in straits** | **he** | **every** | **hand of** | **the wicked** |

Job 20:8 yea, he shall be chased away as a vision of the night.9 The eye also which saw him shall see him no more; neither shall his place anymore behold him.10 His children shall seek to please the poor, and his hands shall restore their goods.11 His bones are full of the sin of his youth, which shall lie down with him in the dust.12 Though wickedness be sweet in his mouth, though he hide it under his tongue;13 Though he spare it, and forsake it not; but keep it still within his mouth:14 Yet his meat in his bowels is turned, it is the gall of asps within him.15 He has swallowed down riches, and he shall vomit them up again: G-d shall cast them out of his belly.16 He shall suck the poison of asps: the viper's tongue shall slay him.17 He shall not see the rivers, the floods, the brooks of honey and butter.18 That which he laboured for shall he restore, and shall not swallow it down: according to his substance shall the restitution be, and he shall not rejoice therein.19 Because he has oppressed and has forsaken the poor; because he has violently taken away an house which he built not;20 Surely he shall not feel quietness in his belly, he shall not save of that which he desired.21 There shall none of his meat be left; therefore shall no man look for his goods.22 In the fulness of his sufficiency he shall be in straits: every hand of the wicked shall come upon him.

| | | | | | | | | |
|---|---|---|---|---|---|---|---|---|
| תבואנו 935: | **20:23** | יהי 1961 | למלא 4390 | בטנו 990 | ישלח 7971 | בו 871a | חרון 2740 | אפו 639 |
| tabou'anu. | | yahiy | lamalea' | bitnou, | yashalach | bou | charoun | 'apou; |
| **shall come upon him** | | ***When* he is** | **about to fill** | **his belly** | ***Elohim* shall cast** | **upon him** | **the fury of** | **his wrath** |

| | | | | | | | |
|---|---|---|---|---|---|---|---|
| וימטר 4305 | עלימו 5921 | בלחומו 3894: | **20:24** | יברח 1272 | מנשק 5402 | ברזל 1270 | תחלפהו 2498 |
| uayamter | 'aleymou, | bilchumou. | | yibrach | mineshеq | barzel; | tachlapehu, |
| **and shall rain *it*** | **upon him** | **while he is eating** | | **He shall flee** | **from weapon** | ***the* iron** | **shall strike him through** |

| | | | | | | | | |
|---|---|---|---|---|---|---|---|---|
| קשת 7198 | נחושה 5154: | **20:25** | שלף 8025 | ויצא 3318 | מגוה 1465 | וברק 1300 | ממררתו 4846 | יהלך 1980 |
| qeshet | nachushah. | | shalap | uayetzea' | migeuah | uabaraq | mimroratou | yahalok, |
| ***and* the bow of** | **steel** | | **It is drawn** | **and comes out** | **of the body** | **yea the glittering sword** | **outof his gall** | **comes** |

| | | | | | | | | | | |
|---|---|---|---|---|---|---|---|---|---|---|
| עליו 5921 | אמים 368: | **20:26** | כל 3605 | חשך 2822 | טמון 2934 | לצפוניו 6845 | תאכלהו 398 | אש 784 | לא 3808 | נפח 5301 |
| 'alayu | 'aemiym. | | kal | choshek | tamun | litzpunayu | ta'akalehu | 'aesh | la' | nupach; |
| **upon him** | **terrors *are*** | | **All** | **darkness** | ***shall be* hid** | **in his secret places** | **shall consume him** | **a fire** | **not** | **blown** |

| | | | | | | | |
|---|---|---|---|---|---|---|---|
| ירע 3415 | שריד 8300 | באהלו 168: | **20:27** | יגלו 1540 | שמים 8064 | עונו 5771 | וארץ 776 | מתקוממה 6965 |
| yera' | sariyd | ba'ahalou. | | yagalu | shamayim | auonou; | ua'aretz, | mitqoumamah |
| **it shall go ill** | **with him that is left** | **in his tabernacle** | | **shall reveal** | **The heaven** | **his iniquity** | **and the earth** | **shall rise up** |

| | | | | | | | | | |
|---|---|---|---|---|---|---|---|---|---|
| לו 3807a: | **20:28** | יגל 1540 | יבול 2981 | ביתו 1004 | נגרות 5064 | ביום 3117 | אפו 639: | **20:29** | זה 2088 |
| lou'. | | yigel | yabul | beytou; | nigarout, | bayoum | 'apou. | | zeh |
| **against him** | | **shall depart** | **The increase of** | **his house** | ***and his goods* shall flow away** | **in the day of** | **his wrath** | | **This** |

| | | | | | | |
|---|---|---|---|---|---|---|
| חלק 2506 | אדם 120 | רשע 7563 | מאלהים 430 | ונחלת 5159 | אמרו 561 | מאל 410: |
| cheleq | 'adam | rasha' | me'alohiym; | uanachalat | 'amrou | me'ael. |
| ***is* the portion of** | **a man** | **wicked** | **from Elohim** | **and the heritage** | **appointed unto him** | **by El** |

| | | | | | | | | | | |
|---|---|---|---|---|---|---|---|---|---|---|
| **Job 21:1** | ויען 6030 | איוב 347 | ויאמר 559: | **21:2** | שמעו 8085 | שמוע 8085 | מלתי 4405 | ותהי 1961 | זאת 2063 | תנחומתיכם 8575: | **21:3** |
| | uaya'an | 'ayoub, | uaya'mar. | | shim'au | shamoua' | milatiy; | uatahiy | za't, | tanchumoteykem. | |
| | **But answered** | **Job** | **and said** | | **Hear** | **diligently** | **my speech** | **and let be** | **this** | **your consolations** | |

| | | | | | | | | | | |
|---|---|---|---|---|---|---|---|---|---|---|
| שאוני 5375 | ואנכי 595 | אדבר 1696 | ואחר 310 | דברי 1697 | תלעיג 3932: | **21:4** | האנכי 595 | לאדם 120 | שיחי 7879 | ואם 518 |
| 'sa'auniy | ua'anokiy | 'adaber; | ua'achar | dabriy | tal'ayg. | | he'anokiy | la'adam | siychiy; | ua'am |
| **Suffer me** | **that I** | **may speak** | **and after that** | **I have spoken** | **mock on** | | ***As for* me** | **to man?** | ***is* my complaint** | **and if** |

| | | | | | | | | | | |
|---|---|---|---|---|---|---|---|---|---|---|
| מדוע 4069 | לא 3808 | תקצר 7114 | רוחי 7307: | **21:5** | פנו 6437 | אלי 413 | והשמו 8074 | ושימו 7760 | יד 3027 | על 5921 |
| madua', | la' | tiqtzar | ruchiy. | | panu | 'aelay | uahashamu; | uasiymu | yad | 'al |
| ***it were not so* why** | **not** | **should be troubled?** | **my spirit** | | **Mark** | **me** | **and be astonished** | **and lay** | ***your* hand** | **upon** |

| | | | | | | | | | |
|---|---|---|---|---|---|---|---|---|---|
| פה 6310: | **21:6** | ואם 518 | זכרתי 2142 | ונבהלתי 926 | ואחז 270 | בשרי 1320 | פלצות 6427: | **21:7** | מדוע 4069 | רשעים 7563 |
| peh. | | ua'am | zakartiy | uanibhalatiy; | ua'achaz | basariy, | palatzut. | | madua' | rasha'aym |
| ***your* mouth** | | **Even when** | **I remember** | **I am afraid** | **and takes hold** | **on my flesh** | **trembling** | | **Wherefore** | **the wicked** |

| | | | | | | | | | | |
|---|---|---|---|---|---|---|---|---|---|---|
| יחיו 2421 | עתקו 6275 | גם 1571 | גברו 1396 | חיל 2428: | **21:8** | זרעם 2233 | נכון 3559 | לפניהם 6440 | עמם 5973 | וצאצאיהם 6631 |
| yichayu; | 'ataqu, | gam | gabaru | chayil. | | zar'am | nakoun | lipneyhem | 'amam; | uatze'atza'aeyhem, |
| **do live** | **become old** | **yea** | **are mighty** | ***in* power?** | | **Their seed** | **is established** | **in their sight** | **with them** | **and their offspring** |

Job 23:23 When he is about to fill his belly, G-d shall cast the fury of his wrath upon him, and shall rain it upon him while he is eating.24 He shall flee from the iron weapon, and the bow of steel shall strike him through.25 It is drawn, and cometh out of the body; yea, the glittering sword cometh out of his gall: terrors are upon him.26 All darkness shall be hid in his secret places: a fire not blown shall consume him; it shall go ill with him that is left in his tabernacle.27 The heaven shall reveal his iniquity; and the earth shall rise up against him.28 The increase of his house shall depart, and his goods shall flow away in the day of his wrath.29 This is the portion of a wicked man from G-d, and the heritage appointed unto him by G-d. **Job** 21:1 But Job answered and said,2 Hear diligently my speech, and let this be your consolations.3 Suffer me that I may speak; and after that I have spoken, mock on.4 As for me, is my complaint to man? and if it were so, why should not my spirit be troubled?5 Mark me, and be astonished, and lay your hand upon your mouth.6 Even when I remember I am afraid, and trembling take hold on my flesh.7 Wherefore do the wicked live, become old, yea, are mighty in power?8 Their seed is established in their sight with them, and their offspring before their eyes.

לעיניהם 5869: 21:9 בתיהם 1004 שלום 7965 מפחד 6343 ולא 3808 שבט 7626 אלוה 433 עליהם 5921: 21:10 שורו 7794 עבר 5674
la'aeyneyhem. bateyhem shaloum mipachad; uala' shebet 'alouah 'aleyhem. shourou 'abar
**before their eyes Their houses *are* safe from fear neither *is* the rod of Elohim upon them Their bull breeds**

ולא 3808 יגעל 1602 תפלט 6403 פרתו 6510 ולא 3808 תשכל 7921: 21:11 ישלחו 7971 כצאן 6629 עויליהם 5759 וילדיהם 3206
uala' yag'al; tapalet paratou, uala' tashakel. yashalchu katza'n 'auyleyhem; uayaldeyhem,
**and not fail calve their cow and not cast her calf They send forth like a flock their little ones and their children**

ירקדון 7540: 21:12 ישאו 5375 כתף 8596 וכנור 3658 וישמחו 8055 לקול 6963 עוגב 5748: 21:13 יבלו 1086 בטוב 2896
yaraqedun. yis'au katop uakinour; uayismachu, laqoul 'augab. yabalu batoub
**dance They take the timbrel and harp and rejoice at the sound of the organ They spend in wealth**

ימיהם 3117 וברגע 7281 שאול 7585 יחתו 5181: 21:14 ויאמרו 559 לאל 410 סור 5493 ממנו 4480 ודעת 1847
yameyhem; uabrega', sha'aul yechatu. uaya'maru la'ael sur mimenu; uada'at
**their days and in a moment *to* the grave go down Therefore they say unto El Depart from us for the knowledge of**

דרכיך 1870 לא 3808 חפצנו 2654: 21:15 מה 4100 שדי 7706 כי 3588 נעבדנו 5647 ומה 4100 נועיל 3276 כי 3588
darakeyka, la' chapatzanu. mah shaday kiy na'abdenu; uamah nou'ayl, kiy
**your ways not we desire What *is* the Almighty that we should serve him? and what profit should we have if**

נפגע 6293 בו 871a: 21:16 הן 2005 לא 3808 בידם 3027 טובם 2898 עצת 6098 רשעים 7563 רחקה 7368 מני 4480: 21:17
nipga' bou. hen la' bayadam tubam; 'atzat rasha'aym, rachaqah meniy.
**we pray unto him? Lo not *is* in their hand their good *is* the counsel of the wicked is far from me**

כמה 4100 נר 5216 רשעים 7563 ידעך 1846 ויבא 935 עלימו 5921 אידם 343 חבלים 2256 יחלק 2505
kamah ner rasha'aym yid'ak, uayaba' 'aleymou 'aeydam; chabaliym, yachaleq
**How oft the candle of the wicked is put out and *how oft* comes upon them their destruction sorrows *Elohim* distributeth**

באפו 639: 21:18 יהיו 1961 כתבן 8401 לפני 6440 רוח 7307 וכמץ 4671 גנבתו 1589 סופה 5492: 21:19 אלוה 433 יצפן 6845
ba'apou. yihayu, kateben lipney ruach; uakmotz, ganabatu supah. 'alouah, yitzpon
**in his anger They are as stubble before the wind and as chaff that carry away the storm Elohim lay up**

לבניו 1121 אונו 205 ישלם 7999 אליו 413 וידע 3045: 21:20 יראו 7200 עינו 5869 כידו 3589
labanayu 'aunou; yashalem 'aelayu uayeda'. yir'au 'aeynou kiydou;
**for his children his iniquity he reward him and he shall know *it* shall see His eyes his destruction**

ומחמת 2534 שדי 7706 ישתה 8354: 21:21 כי 3588 מה 4100 חפצו 2656 בביתו 1004 אחריו 310
uamechamat shaday yishteh. kiy mah cheptzou babeytou 'acharayu;
**and of the wrath of the Almighty he shall drink For what pleasure *has he* in his house after him**

ומספר 4557 חדשיו 2320 חצצו 2686: 21:22 הלאל 410 ילמד 3925 דעת 1847 והוא 1931
uamispar chadashayu chutzatzu. hal'ael yalamed da'at; uahu'a,
**when the number of his months is cut off in the midst? to El Shall *any* teach knowledge? seeing he**

רמים 7311 ישפוט 8199: 21:23 זה 2088 ימות 4191 בעצם 6106 תמו 8537 כלו 3605 שלאנן 7946 ושליו 7961: 21:24 עטיניו 5845
ramiym yishpout. zeh, yamut ba'atzem tumou; kulou, shal'anan uashaleyu. 'atiynayu
**those that are high judge One die in strength his full wholly being at ease and quiet His breasts**

Job 21:9 Their houses are safe from fear, neither is the rod of G-d upon them.10 Their bull gendereth, and faileth not; their cow calveth, and casteth not her calf.11 They send forth their little ones like a flock, and their children dance.12 They take the timbrel and harp, and rejoice at the sound of the organ.13 They spend their days in wealth, and in a moment go down to the grave.14 Therefore they say unto G-d, Depart from us; for we desire not the knowledge of your ways.15 What is the Almighty, that we should serve him? and what profit should we have, if we pray unto him?16 Lo, their good is not in their hand: the counsel of the wicked is far from me.17 How oft is the candle of the wicked put out! and how oft cometh their destruction upon them! G-d distributeth sorrows in his anger.18 They are as stubble before the wind, and as chaff that the storm carrieth away.19 G-d layeth up his iniquity for his children: he rewardeth him, and he shall know it.20 His eyes shall see his destruction, and he shall drink of the wrath of the Almighty.21 For what pleasure has he in his house after him, when the number of his months is cut off in the midst?22 Shall any teach G-d knowledge? seeing he judgeth those that are high.23 One die in his full strength, being wholly at ease and quiet.

| מלאו 4390 | חלב 2461 | ומח 4221 | עצמותיו 6106 | ישקה 8248: | 21:25 וזה 2088 | ימות 4191 | בנפש 5315 | מרה 4751 |
|---|---|---|---|---|---|---|---|---|
| mala'au | chalab; | uamoach | atzamoutayu | yashuqeh. | uazeh, | yamut | banepesh | marah; |
| **are full of** | **milk** | **and marrow** | **his bones** | **are moistened *with*** | **And another** | **die** | **in soul** | **the bitterness *of his*** |

| ולא 3808 | אכל 398 | בטובה 2896: | 21:26 יחד 3162 | על 5921 | עפר 6083 | ישכבו 7901 | ורמה 7415 | תכסה 3680 | עליהם 5921: 21:27 |
|---|---|---|---|---|---|---|---|---|---|
| uala' | 'akal, | batoubah. | yachad | 'al | 'apar | yishkabu; | uarimah, | takaseh | 'aleyhem. |
| **and never** | **eat** | **with pleasure** | **alike** | **in** | **the dust** | **They shall lie down** | **and the worms** | **shall cover** | **them** |

| הן 2005 | ידעתי 3045 | מחשבותיכם 4284 | ומזמות 4209 | עלי 5921 | תחמסו 2554: | 21:28 כי 3588 | תאמרו 559 | איה 346 |
|---|---|---|---|---|---|---|---|---|
| hen | yada'tiy | machshabouteykem; | uamzimout, | 'alay | tachmosu. | kiy | ta'maru, | 'ayeh |
| **Behold** | **I know** | **your thoughts** | **and the devices** | **against me *which*** | **you wrongfully imagine** | **For** | **you say** | **Where *is*** |

| בית 1004 | נדיב 5081 | ואיה 346 | אהל 168 | משכנות 4908 | רשעים 7563: | 21:29 הלא 3808 | שאלתם 7592 | עוברי 5674 |
|---|---|---|---|---|---|---|---|---|
| beyt | nadiyb; | ua'ayeh, | 'ahel | mishkanout | rasha'aym. | hala' | sh'altem | 'aubarey |
| **the house of** | **the prince?** | **and where** | **places of** | ***are the* dwelling** | **the wicked?** | **not** | **Have you asked** | **them that go by** |

| דרך 1870 | ואתתם 226 | לא 3808 | תנכרו 5234: | 21:30 כי 3588 | ליום 3117 | איד 343 | יחשך 2820 | רע 7451 | ליום 3117 |
|---|---|---|---|---|---|---|---|---|---|
| darek; | ua'atotam, | la' | tanakeru. | kiy | layoum | 'aeyd | yechasek | ra'; | layoum |
| **the way?** | **and their tokens** | **not** | **do you know** | **That** | **to the day of** | **destruction?** | **is reserved** | **the wicked** | **to the day of** |

| עברות 5678 | יובלו 2986: | 21:31 מי 4310 | יגיד 5046 | על 5921 | פניו 6440 | דרכו 1870 | והוא 1931 | עשה 6213 | מי 4310 | ישלם 7999 |
|---|---|---|---|---|---|---|---|---|---|---|
| abarout | yubalu. | miy' | yagiyd | 'al | panayu | darkou; | uahu'a | 'asah, | miy' | yashalem |
| **wrath** | **they shall be brought forth** | **Who** | **shall declare** | **to** | **his face?** | **his way** | **and he** | **has done?** | **who** | **shall repay** |

| לו 3807a: | 21:32 והוא 1931 | לקברות 6913 | יובל 2986 | ועל 5921 | גדיש 1430 | ישקוד 8245: | 21:33 מתקו 4985 | לו 3807a |
|---|---|---|---|---|---|---|---|---|
| lou'. | uahu'a | liqbarout | yubal; | ua'al | gadiysh | yishqoud. | mataqu | lou', |
| **him *what*** | **Yet he** | **to the grave** | **shall be brought** | **and in** | **the tomb** | **shall remain** | **shall be sweet** | **unto him** |

| רגבי 7263 | נחל 5158 | ואחריו 310 | כל 3605 | אדם 120 | ימשוך 4900 | ולפניו 6440 | אין 369 | מספר 4557: | 21:34 ואיך 349 |
|---|---|---|---|---|---|---|---|---|---|
| rigbey | nachal | ua'acharayu | kal | 'adam | yimshouk; | ualpanayu, | 'aeyn | mispar. | ua'aeyk |
| **The clods of** | **the valley** | **and after him** | **every** | **man** | **shall draw** | **as before him** | **there are** | **innumerable** | **How then** |

| תנחמוני 5162 | הבל 1892 | ותשובתיכם 8666 | נשאר 7604 | מעל 4604: |
|---|---|---|---|---|
| tanachamuniy | habel; | uatshuboteykem, | nish'ar | ma'al. |
| **comfort you me** | **in vain** | **seeing in your answers** | **there remains** | **falsehood?** |

**Job 22:1**

| ויען 6030 | אליפז 464 | התמני 8489 | ויאמר 559: | 22:2 הלאל 410 | יסכן 5532 | גבר 1397 | כי 3588 | יסכן 5532 |
|---|---|---|---|---|---|---|---|---|
| uaya'an | 'aliypaz | hatemaniy, | uaya'mar. | hal'ael | yiskan | gaber; | kiy | yiskon |
| **Then answered** | **Eliphaz** | **the Temanite** | **and said** | **unto El** | **Can be profitable** | **a man** | **as** | **may be profitable** |

| עלימו 5921 | משכיל 7919: | 22:3 החפץ 2656 | לשדי 7706 | כי 3588 | תצדק 6663 | ואם 518 | בצע 1215 | כי 3588 |
|---|---|---|---|---|---|---|---|---|
| 'aleymou | maskiyl. | hachepetz | lashaday | kiy | titzdaq; | ua'am | betza', | kiy |
| **unto himself?** | **he that is wise** | ***Is it* any pleasure** | **to the Almighty** | **that** | **you are righteous?** | **or** | ***is it* gain** | ***to him* that** |

| תתם 8552 | דרכיך 1870: | 22:4 המיראתך 3374 | יכיחך 3198 | יבוא 935 | עמך 5973 | במשפט 4941: | 22:5 הלא 3808 |
|---|---|---|---|---|---|---|---|
| tatem | darakeyka. | hamiyir'ataka | yokiycheka; | yabou'a | 'amaka, | bamishpat. | hala' |
| **you make perfect?** | **your ways** | ***for* fear of you?** | **Will he reprove you** | **will he enter** | **with you** | **into judgment?** | ***Is* not** |

Job 21:24 His breasts are full of milk, and his bones are moistened with marrow.25 And another die in the bitterness of his soul, and never eateth with pleasure.26 They shall lie down alike in the dust, and the worms shall cover them.27 Behold, I know your thoughts, and the devices which you wrongfully imagine against me.28 For you say, Where is the house of the prince? and where are the dwelling places of the wicked?29 Have you not asked them that go by the way? and do you not know their tokens,30 That the wicked is reserved to the day of destruction? they shall be brought forth to the day of wrath.31 Who shall declare his way to his face? and who shall repay him what he has done?32 Yet shall he be brought to the grave, and shall remain in the tomb.33 The clods of the valley shall be sweet unto him, and every man shall draw after him, as there are innumerable before him.34 How then comfort you me in vain, seeing in your answers there remain falsehood? **Job** 22:1 Then Eliphaz the Temanite answered and said,2 Can a man be profitable unto G-d, as he that is wise may be profitable unto himself?3 Is it any pleasure to the Almighty, that you are righteous? or is it gain to him that you make your ways perfect? 4 Will he reprove you for fear of you? will he enter with you into judgment?

| רעתך 7451 | רבה 7227 | ואין 369 | קץ 7093 | לעונתיך 5771: | 22:6 | כי 3588 | תחבל 2254 | אחיך 251 | חנם 2600 |
|---|---|---|---|---|---|---|---|---|---|
| ra'ataka | rabah; | ua'aeyn | qetz, | la'auonoteyka. | | kiy | tachbol | 'acheyka | chinam; |
| **your wickedness** | **great?** | **and no** | **end** | **to your iniquities** | | **For** | **you have taken a pledge** | **your brother** | **for nought** |

| ובגדי 899 | ערומים 6174 | תפשיט 6584: | 22:7 | לא 3808 | מים 4325 | עיף 5889 | תשקה 8248 | ומרעב 7456 |
|---|---|---|---|---|---|---|---|---|
| uabigdey | 'arumiym | tapshiyt. | | la' | mayim | 'ayep | tashqeh; | uamera'aeb, |
| **and their clothing** | **the naked *of*** | **stripped** | | **not** | **water to** | **the weary** | **You have given to drink** | **and from the hungry** |

| תמנע 4513 | לחם 3899: | 22:8 | ואיש 376 | זרוע 2220 | לו 3807a | הארץ 776 | ונשוא 5375 | פנים 6440 | ישב 3427 |
|---|---|---|---|---|---|---|---|---|---|
| timna' | lachem. | | ua'aysh | zaroua' | lou' | ha'aretz; | uansa' | paniym, | yesheb |
| **you have withholden** | **bread** | | **But man** | ***as for the* mighty** | **he** | ***had* the earth** | **and the honorable** | **of *man*** | **dwelt** |

| בה 871a: | 22:9 | אלמנות 490 | שלחת 7971 | ריקם 7387 | וזרעות 2220 | יתמים 3490 | ידכא 1792: | 22:10 | על 5921 | כן 3651 |
|---|---|---|---|---|---|---|---|---|---|---|
| bah. | | 'almanout | shilachta | reyqam; | uazro'aut | yatomiym | yaduka'. | | 'al | ken |
| **in it** | | **widows** | **You have sent away** | **empty** | **and the arms of** | **the fatherless** | **have been broken** | | **Therefore** | **after** |

| סביבותיך 5439 | פחים 6341 | ויבהלך 926 | פחד 6343 | פתאם 6597: | 22:11 | או 176 | חשך 2822 | לא 3808 | תראה 7200 |
|---|---|---|---|---|---|---|---|---|---|
| sabiybouteyka | pachiym; | uiybahelka | pachad | pit'am. | | 'au | choshek | la' | tir'ah; |
| ***are* round about you** | **snares** | **and trouble you** | **fear** | **sudden** | | **Or** | **darkness** | **not** | ***that* you can see** |

| ושפעת 8229 | מים 4325 | תכסך 3680: | 22:12 | הלא 3808 | אלוה 433 | גבה 1363 | שמים 8064 | וראה 7200 | ראש 7218 | כוכבים 3556 |
|---|---|---|---|---|---|---|---|---|---|---|
| uaship'at | mayim | takaseka. | | hala' | 'alouah | gobah | shamayim; | uar'aeh | ra'sh | koukabiym |
| **and abundance of** | **waters** | **cover you** | | ***Is* not** | **Elohim** | ***in* the height of** | **heaven?** | **and behold** | **the height of** | **the stars** |

| כי 3588 | רמו 7411: | 22:13 | ואמרת 559 | מה 4100 | ידע 3045 | אל 410 | הבעד 1157 | ערפל 6205 | ישפוט 8199: | 22:14 | עבים 5645 |
|---|---|---|---|---|---|---|---|---|---|---|---|
| kiy | ramu. | | ua'amarta | mah | yada' | 'ael; | hab'ad | 'arapel | yishpout. | | 'abiym |
| **how** | **high *they are*** | | **And you say** | **How** | **does know** | **El** | **through** | **the dark cloud?** | **can he judge** | | **Thick clouds** |

| סתר 5643 | לו 3807a | ולא 3808 | יראה 7200 | וחוג 2329 | שמים 8064 | יתהלך 1980: | 22:15 | הארח 734 | עולם 5769 | תשמר 8104 |
|---|---|---|---|---|---|---|---|---|---|---|
| seter | lou' | uala' | yir'ah; | uachug | shamayim, | yithalak. | | ha'arach | 'aulam | tishmor; |
| ***are* a covering** | **to him** | **that not** | **he see** | **and in the circuit of** | **heaven** | **he walk *in*** | | **the way** | **old** | **Have you marked** |

| אשר 834 | דרכו 1869 | מתי 4962 | און 205: | 22:16 | אשר 834 | קמטו 7059 | ולא 3808 | עת 6256 | נהר 5104 | יוצק 3332 |
|---|---|---|---|---|---|---|---|---|---|---|
| 'asher | daraku | matey | 'auen. | | 'asher | qumtu | uala' | 'aet; | nahar, | yutzaq |
| **which** | **have trodden** | **men** | **wicked** | | **Which** | **were cut down** | **out of** | **time** | ***with* a flood** | **was overflown** |

| יסודם 3247: | 22:17 | האמרים 559 | לאל 410 | סור 5493 | ממנו 4480 | ומה 4100 | יפעל 6466 | שדי 7706 | למו 3807a: | 22:18 | והוא 1931 |
|---|---|---|---|---|---|---|---|---|---|---|---|
| yasoudam. | | ha'amariym | la'ael | sur | mimenu; | uamah | yip'al | shaday | lamou. | | uahu'a |
| **whose foundation** | | **Which said** | **unto El** | **Depart** | **from us** | **and what** | **can do** | **the Almighty** | **for them?** | | **Yet he** |

| מלא 4390 | בתיהם 1004 | טוב 2896 | ועצת 6098 | רשעים 7563 | רחקה 7368 | מני 4480: | 22:19 | יראו 7200 | צדיקים 6662 |
|---|---|---|---|---|---|---|---|---|---|
| milea' | bateyhem | toub; | ua'atzat | rasha'aym, | rachaqah | meniy. | | yir'au | tzadiyqiym |
| **filled** | **their houses** | ***with* good** | ***things* but the counsel of** | **the wicked** | **is far** | **from me** | | **see *it*** | **The righteous** |

| וישמחו 8055 | ונקי 5355 | ילעג 3932 | למו 3807a: | 22:20 | אם 518 | לא 3808 | נכחד 3582 | קימנו 7009 |
|---|---|---|---|---|---|---|---|---|
| uayismachu; | uanaqiy, | yil'ag | lamou. | | 'am | la' | nikchad | qiymanu; |
| **and are glad** | **and the innocent** | **laugh to scorn** | **them** | | **Whereas** | **not** | **is cut down** | **our substance** |

Job 22:5 Is not your wickedness great? and your iniquities infinite?6 For you have taken a pledge from your brother for nought, and stripped the naked of their clothing.7 Thou have not given water to the weary to drink, and you have withholden bread from the hungry.8 But as for the mighty man, he had the earth; and the honourable man dwelt in it.9 Thou has sent widows away empty, and the arms of the fatherless have been broken.10 Therefore snares are round about you, and sudden fear trouble you;11 Or darkness, that you canst not see; and abundance of waters cover you.12 Is not G-d in the height of heaven? and behold the height of the stars, how high they are!13 And you say, How doth G-d know? can he judge through the dark cloud?14 Thick clouds are a covering to him, that he see not; and he walk in the circuit of heaven.15 Hast you marked the old way which wicked men have trodden?16 Which were cut down out of time, whose foundation was overflown with a flood:17 Which said unto G-d, Depart from us: and what can the Almighty do for them?18 Yet he filled their houses with good things: but the counsel of the wicked is far from me.19 The righteous see it, and are glad:

| ויתרם 3499 | אכלה 398 | אש 784: | 22:21 | הסכן 5532 | נא 4994 | עמו 5973 | ושלם 7999 | בהם 871a |
|---|---|---|---|---|---|---|---|---|
| uayitram, | 'akalah | 'aesh. | | hasken | naa' | 'amou; | uashlam | bahem, |
| **but the remnant of them** | **consume** | **the fire** | | **Acquaint** | **now *yourself*** | **with him** | **and be at peace** | **thereby** |

| תבואתך 935 | טובה 2896: | 22:22 | קח 3947 | נא 4994 | מפיו 6310 | תורה 8451 | ושים 7760 | אמריו 561 | בלבבך 3824: | 22:23 |
|---|---|---|---|---|---|---|---|---|---|---|
| tabou'ataka | toubah. | | qach | naa' | mipiyu | tourah; | uasiym | 'amarayu, | bilbabeka. | |
| **shall come unto you** | **good** | | **Receive** | **I pray you** | **from his mouth** | **the law** | **and lay up** | **his words** | **in your heart** | |

| אם 518 | תשוב 7725 | עד 5704 | שדי 7706 | תבנה 1129 | תרחיק 7368 | עולה 5766 | מאהלך 168: | 22:24 |
|---|---|---|---|---|---|---|---|---|
| 'am | tashub | 'ad | shaday | tibaneh; | tarchiyq | 'aulah, | me'ahaleka. | |
| **If** | **you return** | **to** | **the Almighty** | **you shall be built up** | **you shall put away far** | **iniquity** | **from your tabernacles** | |

| ושית 7896 | על 5921 | עפר 6083 | בצר 1220 | ובצור 6697 | נחלים 5158 | אופיר 211: | 22:25 | והיה 1961 |
|---|---|---|---|---|---|---|---|---|
| uashiyt | 'al | 'apar | batzer; | uabtzur | nachaliym | 'aupiyr. | | uahayah |
| **Then shall you lay up** | **as** | **dust** | **gold** | **and as the stones of** | **the brooks** | ***the gold of* Ophir** | | **Yea shall be** |

| שדי 7706 | בצריך 1220 | וכסף 3701 | תועפות 8443 | לך 3807a: | 22:26 | כי 3588 | אז 227 | על 5921 | שדי 7706 |
|---|---|---|---|---|---|---|---|---|---|
| shaday | batzareyka; | uakesep | tou'apout | lak. | | kiy | 'az | 'al | shaday |
| **the Almighty** | **your defence** | **and silver** | ***shall have* plenty of** | **to you** | | **For** | **then** | **in** | **the Almighty** |

| תתענג 6026 | ותשא 5375 | אל 413 | אלוה 433 | פניך 6440: | 22:27 | תעתיר 6279 | אליו 413 |
|---|---|---|---|---|---|---|---|
| tit'anag; | uatisa' | 'al | 'alouah | paneyka. | | ta'atiyr | 'aelayu |
| **shall you have your delight** | **and shall lift up** | **unto** | **Elohim** | **your face** | | **You shall make your prayer** | **unto him** |

| וישמעך 8085 | ונדריך 5088 | תשלם 7999: | 22:28 | ותגזר 1504 | אומר 562 | ויקם 6965 | לך 3807a |
|---|---|---|---|---|---|---|---|
| uayishma'aka; | uandareyka | tashalem. | | uatigzar | 'aumer | uayaqam | lak; |
| **and he shall hear** | **and your vows** | **you shall pay** | | **You shall also decree** | **a thing** | **and it shall be established** | **unto you** |

| ועל 5921 | דרכיך 1870 | נגה 5050 | אור 216: | 22:29 | כי 3588 | השפילו 8213 | ותאמר 559 | גוה 1466 | ושח 7807 |
|---|---|---|---|---|---|---|---|---|---|
| ua'al | darakeyka, | nagah | 'aur. | | kiy | hishpiylu | uata'mer | geuah; | uashach |
| **and upon** | **your ways** | **shall shine** | **the light** | | **When** | ***men* are cast down** | **then you shall say** | ***There is* lifting up** | **and humble** |

| עינים 5869 | יושע 3467: | 22:30 | ימלט 4422 | אי 336 | נקי 5355 | ונמלט 4422 | בבר 1252 |
|---|---|---|---|---|---|---|---|
| 'aeynayim | youshia'. | | yamalet | 'ay | naqiy; | uanimlat, | babor |
| **person** | **he shall save *the*** | | **He shall deliver** | **the island of** | **the innocent** | **and it is delivered** | **by the pureness of** |

| כפיך 3709: |
|---|
| kapeyka. |
| **your hands** |

| **Job 23:1** | ויען 6030 | איוב 347 | ויאמר 559: | 23:2 | גם 1571 | היום 3117 | מרי 4805 | שחי 7879 | ידי 3027 | כבדה 3513 | על 5921 |
|---|---|---|---|---|---|---|---|---|---|---|---|
| | uaya'an | 'ayoub, | uaya'mar. | | gam | hayoum | mariy | sichiy; | yadiy, | kabdah | 'al |
| | **Then answered** | **Job** | **and said** | | **Even** | **to day** | **bitter** | ***is* my complaint** | **my stroke** | **is heavier** | **than** |

| אנחתי 585: | 23:3 | מי 4310 | יתן 5414 | ידעתי 3045 | ואמצאהו 4672 | אבוא 935 | עד 5704 | תכונתו 8499: | 23:4 | אערכה 6186 |
|---|---|---|---|---|---|---|---|---|---|---|
| 'anchatiy. | | miy' | yiten | yada'tiy | ua'amtza'aehu; | abou'a, | 'ad | takunatou. | | 'a'arkah |
| **my groaning** | | **Oh** | **that** | **I knew** | **where I might find him** | ***that* I might come *even*** | **to** | **his seat** | | **I would order** |

Job 22:20 and the innocent laugh them to scorn.20 Whereas our substance is not cut down, but the remnant of them the fire consumeth.21 Acquaint now thyself with him, and be at peace: thereby good shall come unto you.22 Receive, I pray you, the law from his mouth, and lay up his words in your heart.23 If you return to the Almighty, you shall be built up, you shall put away iniquity far from your tabernacles.24 Then shall you lay up gold as dust, and the gold of Ophir as the stones of the brooks.25 Yea, the Almighty shall be your defence, and you shall have plenty of silver.26 For then shall you have your delight in the Almighty, and shall lift up your face unto G-d.27 Thou shall make your prayer unto him, and he shall hear you, and you shall pay your vows.28 Thou shall also decree a thing, and it shall be established unto you: and the light shall shine upon your ways.29 When men are cast down, then you shall say, There is lifting up; and he shall save the humble person.30 He shall deliver the island of the innocent: and it is delivered by the pureness of your hands. **Job** 23:1 Then Job answered and said,2 Even today is my complaint bitter: my stroke is heavier than my groaning.3 Oh that I knew where I might find him! that I might come even to his seat!4 I would order my cause before him,

| לפניו 6440 | משפט 4941 | ופי 6310 | אמלא 4390 | תוכחות 8433: | 23:5 | אדעה 3045 | מלים 4405 | יעננו 6030 |
|---|---|---|---|---|---|---|---|---|
| lapanayu | mishapat; | uapiy, | 'amalea' | toukachout. | | 'aeda'ah | miliym | ya'aneniy; |
| **before him** | ***my* cause** | **and my mouth** | **fill *with*** | **arguments** | | **I would know** | **the words** | ***which* he would answer me** |

| ואבינה 995 | מה 4100 | יאמר 559 | לי 3807a: | 23:6 | הברב 7227 | כח 3581 | יריב 7378 | עמדי 5978 | לא 3808 | אך 389 | הוא 1931 |
|---|---|---|---|---|---|---|---|---|---|---|---|
| ua'abiynah, | mah | ya'mar | liy. | | habrab | koach | yariyb | 'amadiy; | la' | 'ak | hua', |
| **and understand** | **what** | **he would say** | **unto me** | | **with his great** | **power?** | **Will he plead** | **against me** | **No** | **but** | **he** |

| ישם 7760 | בי 871a: | 23:7 | שם 8033 | ישר 3477 | נוכח 3198 | עמו 5973 | ואפלטה 6403 | לנצח 5331 |
|---|---|---|---|---|---|---|---|---|
| yasim | biy. | | sham, | yashar | noukach | 'amou; | ua'apaltah | lanetzach, |
| **would put *strength*** | **in me** | | **There** | **the righteous** | **might dispute** | **with him** | **so should I be delivered** | **for ever** |

| משפטי 8199: | 23:8 | הן 2005 | קדם 6924 | אהלך 1980 | ואיננו 369 | ואחור 268 | ולא 3808 | אבין 995 | לו 3807a: | 23:9 |
|---|---|---|---|---|---|---|---|---|---|---|
| mishshopatiy. | | hen | qedem | 'ahelok | ua'aeynenu; | ua'achour, | uala' | 'abiyn | lou'. | |
| **from my judge** | | **Behold** | **forward** | **I go** | **but he *is* not *there*** | **and backward** | **but cannot** | **I perceive** | **him** | |

| שמאול 8040 | בעשתו 6213 | ולא 3808 | אחז 2372 | יעטף 5848 | ימין 3225 | ולא 3808 |
|---|---|---|---|---|---|---|
| sama'ul | ba'asotou | uala' | 'achaz; | ya'atop | yamiyn, | uala' |
| ***On* the left hand** | **where he does work** | **but cannot *him*** | **I behold** | **he hides** | ***himself on* the right hand** | **that cannot** |

| אראה 7200: | 23:10 | כי 3588 | ידע 3045 | דרך 1870 | עמדי 5978 | בחנני 974 | כזהב 2091 | אצא 3318: | 23:11 | באשרו 838 |
|---|---|---|---|---|---|---|---|---|---|---|
| 'ar'ah. | | kiy | yada' | derek | 'amadiy; | bachananiy, | kazahab | 'aetzea'. | | ba'ashurou |
| **I see *him*** | | **But** | **he knows** | **the way** | **that I take** | ***when* he has tried me** | **as gold** | **I shall come forth** | | **his steps** |

| אחזה 270 | רגלי 7272 | דרכו 1870 | שמרתי 8104 | ולא 3808 | אט 5186: | 23:12 | מצות 4687 | שפתיו 8193 | ולא 3808 | אמיש 4185 |
|---|---|---|---|---|---|---|---|---|---|---|
| 'achazah | ragliy; | darkou | shamartiy | uala' | 'at. | | mitzuat | sapatayu | uala' | 'amiysh; |
| **has held** | **My foot** | **his way** | **have I kept** | **and not** | **declined** | | ***from* the commandment of** | **his lips** | **Neither** | **have I gone back** |

| מחקי 2706 | צפנתי 6845 | אמרי 561 | פיו 6310: | 23:13 | והוא 1931 | באחד 259 | ומי 4310 | ישיבנו 7725 |
|---|---|---|---|---|---|---|---|---|
| mechuqiy, | tzapantiy | 'amrey | piyu. | | uahu'a | ba'achad | uamiy | yashiybenu; |
| **more than my necessary *food*** | **I have esteemed** | **the words of** | **his mouth** | | **But he *is*** | **in one *mind*** | **and who** | **can turn him?** |

| ונפשו 5315 | אותה 853 | ויעש 6213: | 23:14 | כי 3588 | ישלים 7999 | חקי 2706 | וכהנה 2007 |
|---|---|---|---|---|---|---|---|
| uanapshou | 'auatah | uaya'as. | | kiy | yashliym | chuqiy; | uakahenah |
| **and *what* his soul** | **desire** | **even *that* he does** | | **For** | **he performed** | ***the thing that is* appointed for me** | **and such** |

| רבות 7227 | עמו 5973: | 23:15 | על 5921 | כן 3651 | מפניו 6440 | אבהל 926 | אתבונן 995 | ואפחד 6342 | ממנו 4480: | 23:16 |
|---|---|---|---|---|---|---|---|---|---|---|
| rabout | 'amou. | | 'al | ken | mipanayu | 'abahel; | 'atbounen, | ua'apchad | mimenu. | |
| **many *things are*** | **with him** | | **Therefore** | **so** | **at his presence** | **am I troubled** | **I consider** | **when I am afraid** | **of him** | |

| ואל 410 | הרך 7401 | לבי 3820 | ושדי 7706 | הבהילני 926: | 23:17 | כי 3588 | לא 3808 | נצמתי 6789 | מפני 6440 | חשך 2822 |
|---|---|---|---|---|---|---|---|---|---|---|
| ua'ael | herak | libiy; | uashaday, | hibhiylaniy. | | kiy | la' | nitzmatiy | mipaney | choshek; |
| **For El** | **make soft** | **my heart** | **and the Almighty** | **trouble me** | | **Because** | **not** | **I was cut off** | **before** | **the darkness *neither*** |

| ומפני 6440 | כסה 3680 | אפל 652: |
|---|---|---|
| uamipanay, | kisah | 'apel. |

**from my face has he covered the darkness**

Job 23:4 and fill my mouth with arguments.5 I would know the words which he would answer me, and understand what he would say unto me.6 Will he plead against me with his great power? No; but he would put strength in me.7 There the righteous might dispute with him; so should I be delivered forever from my judge.8 Behold, I go forward, but he is not there; and backward, but I cannot perceive him:9 On the left hand, where he doth work, but I cannot behold him: he hide himself on the right hand, that I cannot see him:10 But he know the way that I take: when he has tried me, I shall come forth as gold.11 My foot has held his steps, his way have I kept, and not declined.12 Neither have I gone back from the commandment of his lips; I have esteemed the words of his mouth more than my necessary food.13 But he is in one mind, and who can turn him? and what his soul desire, even that he doeth.14 For he performeth the thing that is appointed for me: and many such things are with him.15 Therefore am I troubled at his presence: when I consider, I am afraid of him.16 For G-d make my heart soft, and the Almighty trouble me:17 Because I was not cut off before the darkness, neither has he covered the darkness from my face.

**Job 24:1** … **24:2**

מדוע 4069 משדי 7706 לא 3808 נצפנו 6845 עתים 6256 וידעו 3045 לא 3808 חזו 2372 ימיו 3117:

madua', mishaday la' nitzpanu 'atiym; uayoda'au la' chazu yamayu.

**Why from the Almighty not are hidden *seeing* times do they that know him not see his days?**

גבלות 1367 ישיגו 5381 עדר 5739 גזלו 1497 וירעו 7462: **24:3** חמור 2543 יתומים 3490 ינהגו 5090

gabulout yasiygu; 'aeder gazlu, uayari'au. chamour yatoumiym yinhagu;

***Some* the landmarks remove flocks they violently take away and feed *thereof* the ass of the fatherless They drive away**

יחבלו 2254 שור 7794 אלמנה 490: **24:4** יטו 5186 אביונים 34 מדרך 1870 יחד 3162 חבאו 2244 עניי 6035

yachbalu, shour 'almanah. yatu 'abyouniym midarek; yachad chub'au, 'aniyey

**they take for a pledge ox the widow's They turn the needy out of the way together hide themselves the poor of**

ארץ 776: **24:5** הן 2005 פראים 6501 במדבר 4057 יצאו 3318 בפעלם 6467 משחרי 7836 לטרף 2964 ערבה 6160

'aretz. hen para'aym bamidbar, yatza'ua bapa'alam mashacharey latarep; 'arabah

**the earth Behold *as* wild asses in the desert go they forth to their work rising betimes for a prey the wilderness**

לו 3807a לחם 3899 לנערים 5288: **24:6** בשדה 7704 בלילו 1098 יקצירו 7114 וכרם 3754 רשע 7563

lou' lechem, lana'ariym. basadeh baliylou yaqtziyru uakerem rasha'

**for them *yield* food *and* for *their* children in the field *every one* his corn They reap and the vintage of the wicked**

ילקשו 3953: **24:7** ערום 6174 ילינו 3885 מבלי 1097 לבוש 3830 ואין 369 כסות 3682 בקרה 7135: **24:8**

yalaqeshu. 'aroum yaliynu mibaliy labush; ua'aeyn kasut, baqarah.

**they gather the naked They cause to lodge without clothing and that *they have* no covering in the cold**

מזרם 2230 הרים 2022 ירטבו 7372 ומבלי 1097 מחסה 4268 חבקו 2263 צור 6697: **24:9** יגזלו 1497

mizerem hariym yirtabu; uamibaliy machseh, chibqu tzur. yigzalu

**with the showers of the mountains They are wet and for want of a shelter embrace the rock They pluck**

משד 7699 יתום 3490 ועל 5921 עני 6041 יחבלו 2254: **24:10** ערום 6174 הלכו 1980 בלי 1097

mishod yatoum; ua'al 'aniy yachbolu. 'aroum halaku baliy

**from the breast the fatherless and sucking child of the poor take a pledge naked They cause *him* to go without**

לבוש 3830 ורעבים 7456 נשאו 5375 עמר 6016: **24:11** בין 996 שורתם 7791 יצהירו 6671 יקבים 3342 דרכו 1869

labush; uara'aebiym, nasa'au 'amer. beyn shurotam yatzhiyru; yaqabiym daraku,

**clothing and the hungry they take away the sheaf *from* *Which* within their walls make oil *their* winepresses *and* tread**

ויצמאו 6770: **24:12** מעיר 5892 מתים 4962 ינאקו 5008 ונפש 5315 חללים 2491 תשוע 7768 ואלוה 433 לא 3808

uayitzma'u. me'ayr metiym yin'aqu, uanepesh chalaliym tashauea'; ua'alouah, la'

**and suffer thirst *from* out of the city Men groan and the soul of the wounded cry out yet Elohim not**

ישים 7760 תפלה 8604: **24:13** המה 1992 היו 1961 במרדי 4775 אור 216 לא 3808 הכירו 5234 דרכיו 1870 ולא 3808 ישבו 3427

yasiym tiplah. hemah hayu bamoradey 'aur la' hikiyru darakayu; uala' yashabu,

**lay folly *to them* They are of those that rebel the light not they know the ways thereof nor abide**

בנתיבתיו 5410: **24:14** לאור 216 יקום 6965 רוצח 7523 יקטל 6991 עני 6041 ואביון 34 ובלילה 3915 יהי 1961

bintiybotayu. la'aur yaqum routzeach, yiqtal 'aniy ua'abyoun; uabalayalah, yahiy

**in the paths thereof with the light rising The murderer kills the poor and needy and in the night is**

**Job** 24:1 Why, seeing times are not hidden from the Almighty, do they that know him not see his days?2 Some remove the landmarks; they violently take away flocks, and feed thereof.3 They drive away the ass of the fatherless, they take the widow's ox for a pledge.4 They turn the needy out of the way: the poor of the earth hide themselves together.5 Behold, as wild asses in the desert, go they forth to their work; rising betimes for a prey: the wilderness yieldeth food for them and for their children.6 They reap everyone his corn in the field: and they gather the vintage of the wicked.7 They cause the naked to lodge without clothing, that they have no covering in the cold.8 They are wet with the showers of the mountains, and embrace the rock for want of a shelter.9 They pluck the fatherless from the breast, and take a pledge of the poor.10 They cause him to go naked without clothing, and they take away the sheaf from the hungry;11 Which make oil within their walls, and tread their winepresses, and suffer thirst.12 Men groan from out of the city, and the soul of the wounded crieth out: yet G-d layeth not folly to them.13 They are of those that rebel against the light; they know not the ways thereof, nor abide in the paths thereof.14 The murderer rising with the light kill the poor and needy, and in the night is as a thief.

24:15

כגנב 1590: ועין 5870 נאף 5003 שמרה 8104 נשף 5399 לאמר 559 לא 3808 תשורני 7789 עין 5869 וסתר 5643 פנים 6440

kaganab. ua'aeyn no'aep shamarah neshep lea'mor la' tashureniy 'ayin; uaseter paniym

**as a thief The eye also of the adulterer wait for the twilight saying No shall see me eye and disguises *his* face**

24:16

ישים 7760: חתר 2864 בחשך 2822 בתים 1004 יומם 3119 חתמו 2856 למו 3807a לא 3808 ידעו 3045

yasiym. chatar bachoshek, batiym youmam chitmu lamou, la' yada'au

**he does they dig through In the dark houses in the daytime *which* they had marked for themselves not they know**

24:17

אור 216: כי 3588 יחדו 3162 בקר 1242 למו 3807a צלמות 6757 כי 3588 יכיר 5234 בלהות 1091

'aur. kiy yachdau boqer lamou tzalmauet; kiy yakiyr, balahout

**the light For even as the morning *is* to them the shadow of death if *one* know *them they are in* the terrors of**

24:18

צלמות 6757: קל 7031 הוא 1931 על 5921 פני 6440 מים 4325 תקלל 7043 חלקתם 2513 בארץ 776 לא 3808 יפנה 6437

tzalmauet. qal hua' 'al paney mayim, taqulal chelqatam ba'aretz; la' yipneh

**the shadow of death *is* swift He on as the waters is cursed their portion in the earth not he behold**

24:19

דרך 1870 כרמים 3754: ציה 6723 גם 1571 חם 2527 יגזלו 1497 מימי 4325 שלג 7950 שאול 7585

derek karamiym. tziyah gam chom, yigzalu miymey sheleg, sha'aul

**the way of the vineyards Drought then heat consume waters *the* snow *so does* the grave**

24:20

חטאו 2398: ישכחהו 7911 רחם 7358 מתקו 4988 רמה 7415 עוד 5750 לא 3808

chata'au. yishkachehu rechem mataqou rimah, 'aud la'

***those which* have sinned shall forget him The womb shall feed sweetly on him the worm more no**

24:21

יזכר 2142 ותשבר 7665 כעץ 6086 עולה 5766: רעה 7462 עקרה 6135 לא 3808 תלד 3205

yizaker; uatishaber ka'aetz 'aulah. ro'ah 'aqarah la' teled;

**he shall be remembered and shall be broken as a tree wickedness *He* evil entreateth the barren not *that* bear**

24:22

ואלמנה 490 לא 3808 ייטיב 3190: ומשך 4900 אבירים 47 בכחו 3581 יקום 6965 ולא 3808 יאמין 539

ua'almanah, la' yayetiyb. uamashach 'abiyriym bakochou; yaqum, uala' ya'amiyn

**and the widow *to* not does good He draw also the mighty with his power he rise up and no *man* is sure**

24:23 ... 24:24

בחיין 2416: יתן 5414 לו 3807a לבטח 983 וישען 8172 ועיניהו 5869 על 5921 דרכיהם 1870:

bachayiyn. yiten lou' labetach uayisha'aen; ua'aeyneyhu, 'al darkeyhem.

**of life *Though* it be given him *to be* in safety whereon he rest yet his eyes *are* upon their ways**

רומו 7426 מעט 4592 ואיננו 369 והמכו 4355 ככל 3605 יקפצון 7092 וכראש 7218

roumu ma'at ua'aeynenu, uahumku, kakol yiqapatzun; uakra'sh

**They are exalted for a little while but are gone and brought low as all *other* they are taken out of the way and as the tops of**

24:25

שבלת 7641 ימלו 5243: ואם 518 לא 3808 אפו 645 מי 4310 יכזיבני 3576 וישם 7760 לאל 408 מלתי 4405:

shibolet yimalu. ua'am la' 'aepou miy' yakziybeniy; uayasem la'al, milatiy.

**the ears of corn cut off And if *it be* not *so* now who will make me a liar and make nothing *worth*? my speech**

**Job 25:1** ... 25:2

ויען 6030 בלדד 1085 השחי 7747 ויאמר 559: המשל 4910 ופחד 6343 עמו 5973 עשה 6213 שלום 7965

uaya'an bildad hashchiy, uaya'mar. hamshel uapachad 'amou; 'aseh shaloum,

**Then answered Bildad the Shuhite and said Dominion and fear *are* with him he make peace**

Job 24:15 The eye also of the adulterer waiteth for the twilight, saying, No eye shall see me: and disguiseth his face.16 In the dark they dig through houses, which they had marked for themselves in the daytime: they know not the light.17 For the morning is to them even as the shadow of death: if one know them, they are in the terrors of the shadow of death.18 He is swift as the waters; their portion is cursed in the earth: he beholdeth not the way of the vineyards.19 Drought and heat consume the snow waters: so doth the grave those which have sinned.20 The womb shall forget him; the worm shall feed sweetly on him; he shall be no more remembered; and wickedness shall be broken as a tree.21 He evil entreateth the barren that beareth not: and doeth not good to the widow.22 He draweth also the mighty with his power: he rise up, and no man is sure of life.23 Though it be given him to be in safety, whereon he resteth; yet his eyes are upon their ways.24 They are exalted for a little while, but are gone and brought low; they are taken out of the way as all other, and cut off as the tops of the ears of corn.25 And if it be not so now, who will make me a liar, and make my speech nothing worth? **Job** 25:1 Then answered Bildad the Shuhite, and said,2 Dominion and fear are with him, he make peace in his high places.

25:3 25:4

במרומיו 4791: היש 3426 מספר 4557 לגדודיו 1416 ועל 5921 מי 4310 לא 3808 יקום 6965 אורהו 216: ומה 4100
bimroumayu. hayesh mispar ligdudayu; ua'al miy, la' yaqum 'aurehu. uamah
**in his high places Is there any number of his armies? and upon whom not does arise? his light How then**

25:5

יצדק 6663 אנוש 582 עם 5973 אל 410 ומה 4100 יזכה 2135 ילוד 3205 אשה 802: הן 2005 עד 5704 ירח 3394 ולא 3808
yitzdaq 'anoush 'am 'ael; uamah yizkeh, yalud 'ashah. hen 'ad yareach uala'
**can be justified man with El? or how can he be clean *that is* born of a woman? Behold even to the moon and not**

25:6

יאהיל 166 וכוכבים 3556 לא 3808 זכו 2141 בעיניו 5869: אף 637 כי 3588 אנוש 582 רמה 7415 ובן 1121
ya'ahiyl; uakoukabiym, la' zaku ba'aeynayu. 'ap kiy 'anoush rimah; uaben
**it shine yea the stars not are pure in his sight How much less for man *that is* a worm? and the son of**

אדם 120 תולעה 8438:
'adam, toule'ah.
**man *which is* a worm?**

**Job 26:1** 26:2

ויען 6030 איוב 347 ויאמר 559: מה 4100 עזרת 5826 ללא 3808 כח 3581 הושעת 3467 זרוע 2220
uaya'an 'ayoub, uaya'mar. meh 'azarta lala' koach; housha'ta, zaroua'
**But answered Job and said How have you helped *him that has* without power? *how* saved you the arm**

26:3

לא 3808 עז 5797: מה 4100 יעצת 3289 ללא 3808 חכמה 2451 ותושיה 8454 לרב 7230
la' 'az. mah ya'atzata lala' chakamah uatushiyah, larob
***that has* no strength? How have you counselled *him that has* no wisdom? and the thing as it is? plentifully *how***

26:4 26:5

הודעת 3045: את 854 מי 4310 הגדת 5046 מלין 4405 ונשמת 5397 מי 4310 יצאה 3318 ממך 4480: הרפאים 7496
houda'ata. 'at miy' higadta miliyn; uanishmat miy' yatz'ah mimeka. harapa'aym
**have you declared *To* whom have you uttered words? and spirit whose came from you? Dead *things***

26:6

יחוללו 2342 מתחת 8478 מים 4325 ושכניהם 7931: ערום 6174 שאול 7585 נגדו 5048 ואין 369 כסות 3682
yachoulalu; mitachat mayim, uashokaneyhem. 'aroum sha'aul negdou; ua'aeyn kasut,
**are formed from under the waters and the inhabitants thereof *is* naked Hell (*grave*) before him and has no covering**

26:7 26:8

לאבדון 11: נטה 5186 צפון 6828 על 5921 תהו 8414 תלה 8518 ארץ 776 על 5921 בלי 1099 מה 4100:
la'abadoun. noteh tzapoun 'al tohu; toleh 'aretz, 'al baliy mah.
**destruction He stretch out the north over the empty place *and* hangeth the earth upon nothing what**

26:9

צרר 6887 מים 4325 בעביו 5645 ולא 3808 נבקע 1234 ענן 6051 תחתם 8478: מאחז 270 פני 6440 כסה 3678
tzorer mayim ba'abayu; uala' nibqa' 'anan tachtam. ma'achez paney kaseh;
**He bind up the waters in his thick clouds and not is rent the cloud under them He holds back the face of his throne**

26:10

פרשז 6576 עליו 5921 עננו 6051: חק 2706 חג 2328 על 5921 פני 6440 מים 4325 עד 5704 תכלית 8503
parshez 'alayu 'ananou. choq chag 'al paney mayim; 'ad takliyt
***and* spread over it his cloud *with* bounds He has compassed on the surface of the waters until *come to* an end**

26:11 26:12

אור 216 עם 5973 חשך 2822: עמודי 5982 שמים 8064 ירופפו 7322 ויתמהו 8539 מגערתו 1606: בכחו 3581
'aur 'am choshek. 'amudey shamayim yaroupapu; uayitmahu, miga'aratou. bakochou
**the day with night The pillars of heaven tremble and are astonished at his reproof with his power**

Job 25:3 Is there any number of his armies? and upon whom doth not his light arise?4 How then can man be justified with G-d? or how can he be clean that is born of a woman?5 Behold even to the moon, and it shineth not; yea, the stars are not pure in his sight.6 How much less man, that is a worm? and the son of man, which is a worm? **Job** 26:1 But Job answered and said,2 How have you helped him that is without power? how save you the arm that has no strength?3 How have you counseled him that has no wisdom? and how have you plentifully declared the thing as it is?4 To whom have you uttered words? and whose spirit came from you?5 Dead things are formed from under the waters, and the inhabitants thereof.6 Hell is naked before him, and destruction has no covering.7 He stretcheth out the north over the empty place, and hangeth the earth upon nothing.8 He bindeth up the waters in his thick clouds; and the cloud is not rent under them.9 He holdeth back the face of his throne, and spreadeth his cloud upon it.10 He has compassed the waters with bounds, until the day and night come to an end.11 The pillars of heaven tremble and are astonished at his reproof.

| רגע 7280 | הים 3220 | ובתובנתו 8394 | מחץ 4272 | רהב 7293: | 26:13 ברוחו 7307 | שמים 8064 | שפרה 8235 |
|---|---|---|---|---|---|---|---|
| raga' | hayam; | uabitubenatou | machatz | rahab. | baruchou | shamayim | shiprah; |
| **He divides** | **the sea** | **and by his understanding** | **he smite through** | **the proud** | **By his spirit** | **the heavens** | **he has garnished** |

| חללה 2342 | ידו 3027 | נחש 5175 | בריח 1280: | 26:14 הן 2005 | אלה 428 | קצות 7098 | דרכו 1870 | ומה 4100 | שמץ 8102 | דבר 1697 | נשמע 8085 |
|---|---|---|---|---|---|---|---|---|---|---|---|
| cholalah | yadou, | nachash | bariyach. | hen | 'aeleh | qatzout | darkou | uamah | shemetz | dabar | nishma' |
| **has pierced** | **his hand** | **serpent** | **the crooked** | **Lo** | **these** | ***are* parts of** | **his ways** | **but how** | **little** | **a portion** | **is heard** |

| בו 871a | ורעם 7482 | גבורתו 1369 | מי 4310 | יתבונן 995: |
|---|---|---|---|---|
| bou; | uara'am | gaburatou | miy' | yitbounan. |
| **of him?** | **but the thunder** | **of his power** | **who** | **can understand?** |

| Job 27:1 ויסף 3254 | איוב 347 | שאת 5375 | משלו 4912 | ויאמר 559: | 27:2 חי 2416 | אל 410 | הסיר 5493 |
|---|---|---|---|---|---|---|---|
| uayosep | 'ayoub | sa'aet | mashalou, | uaya'mar. | chay | 'ael | hesiyr |
| **Moreover continued** | **Job** | **you bring forth** | **his parable** | **and said** | ***As* live** | **El** | ***who* has taken away** |

| משפטי 4941 | ושדי 7706 | המר 4843 | נפשי 5315: | 27:3 כי 3588 | כל 3605 | עוד 5750 | נשמתי 5397 | בי 871a | ורוח 7307 |
|---|---|---|---|---|---|---|---|---|---|
| mishpatiy; | uashaday, | hemar | napshiy. | kiy | kal | 'aud | nishmatiy | biy; | uaruach |
| **my judgment** | **and the Almighty** | ***who* has vexed** | **my soul** | **for** | **All** | **the while** | **my breath** | ***is* in me** | **and the spirit of** |

| אלוה 433 | באפי 639: | 27:4 אם 518 | תדברנה 1696 | שפתי 8193 | עולה 5766 | ולשוני 3956 | אם 518 | יהגה 1897 | רמיה 7423: | 27:5 חלילה 2486 |
|---|---|---|---|---|---|---|---|---|---|---|
| 'alouah | ba'apiy. | 'am | tadaberanah | sapatay | 'aulah; | ualshouniy, | 'am | yehageh | ramiyah. | chaliylah |
| **Elohim** | ***is* in my nostrils** | **not** | **shall speak** | **My lips** | **wickedness** | **my tongue** | **nor** | **utter** | **deceit** | ***Elohim* forbid** |

| לי 3807a | אם 518 | אצדיק 6663 | אתכם 853 | עד 5704 | אגוע 1478 | לא 3808 | אסיר 5493 | תמתי 8538 | ממני 4480: | 27:6 בצדקתי 6666 |
|---|---|---|---|---|---|---|---|---|---|---|
| liy | 'am | 'atzdiyq | 'atkem | 'ad | 'agua'; | la' | 'asiyr | tumatiy | mimeniy. | batzidqatiy |
| **me** | **that** | **I should justify** | **you** | **till** | **I die** | **not** | **I will remove** | **mine integrity** | **from me** | **My righteousness** |

| החזקתי 2388 | ולא 3808 | ארפה 7503 | לא 3808 | יחרף 2778 | לבבי 3824 | מימי 3117: | 27:7 יהי 1961 | כרשע 7563 | איבי 341 |
|---|---|---|---|---|---|---|---|---|---|
| hechezaqtiy | uala' | 'arpeha; | la' | yecherap | lababiy, | miyamay. | yahiy | karasha' | 'ayabiy; |
| **I hold fast** | **and not** | **will let it go** | **not** | **shall reproach *me*** | **my heart** | **so long as I live** | **Let be** | **as the wicked** | **mine enemy** |

| ומתקוממי 6965 | כעול 5767: | 27:8 כי 3588 | מה 4100 | תקות 8615 | חנף 2611 | כי 3588 | יבצע 1214 | כי 3588 |
|---|---|---|---|---|---|---|---|---|
| uamitqoumamiy | ka'aual. | kiy | mah | tiquat | chanep | kiy | yibtza'; | kiy |
| **and he that rise up against me** | **as the unrighteous** | **For** | **what** | ***is* the hope of** | **the hypocrite** | **though** | **he has gained** | **when** |

| ישל 7953 | אלוה 433 | נפשו 5315: | 27:9 הצעקתו 6818 | ישמע 8085 | אל 410 | כי 3588 | תבוא 935 | עליו 5921 | צרה 6869: | 27:10 אם 518 | על 5921 |
|---|---|---|---|---|---|---|---|---|---|---|---|
| yeshel | 'alouah | napshou. | hatza'aqatou | yishma' | 'ael; | kiy | tabou'a | 'alayu | tzarah. | 'am | 'al |
| **takes away** | **Elohim** | **his soul?** | **his cry** | **Will hear** | **El** | **when** | **comes** | **upon him?** | **trouble** | **moreover** | **in** |

| שדי 7706 | יתענג 6026 | יקרא 7121 | אלוה 433 | בכל 3605 | עת 6256: | 27:11 אורה 3384 | אתכם 853 | ביד 3027 |
|---|---|---|---|---|---|---|---|---|
| shaday | yit'anag; | yiqra' | 'alouah | bakal | 'aet. | 'areh | 'atkem | bayad |
| **the Almighty?** | **Will he delight himself** | **will he call upon** | **Elohim?** | **in all** | **ways** | **I will teach** | **you** | **by the hand of** |

| אל 410 | אשר 834 | עם 5973 | שדי 7706 | לא 3808 | אכחד 3582: | 27:12 הן 2005 | אתם 859 | כלכם 3605 | חזיתם 2372 | ולמה 4100 | זה 2088 |
|---|---|---|---|---|---|---|---|---|---|---|---|
| 'ael; | 'asher | 'am | shaday, | la' | 'akached. | hen | 'atem | kulkem | chaziytem; | ualamah | zeh, |
| **El** | ***that* which** | ***is* with** | **the Almighty** | **not** | **will I conceal** | **Behold** | **yourselves** | **all you** | **have seen *it,*** | **why then** | **thus** |

Job 26:12 He divideth the sea with his power, and by his understanding he smite through the proud.13 By his spirit he has garnished the heavens; his hand has formed the crooked serpent.14 Lo, these are parts of his ways: but how little a portion is heard of him? but the thunder of his power who can understand? **Job** 27:1 Moreover Job continued his parable, and said,2 As G-d live, who has taken away my judgment; and the Almighty, who has vexed my soul;3 All the while my breath is in me, and the spirit of G-d is in my nostrils;4 My lips shall not speak wickedness, nor my tongue utter deceit.5 G-d forbid that I should justify you: till I die I will not remove mine integrity from me.6 My righteousness I hold fast, and will not let it go: my heart shall not reproach me so long as I live.7 Let mine enemy be as the wicked, and he that rise up against me as the unrighteous.8 For what is the hope of the hypocrite, though he has gained, when G-d take away his soul?9 Will G-d hear his cry when trouble cometh upon him?10 Will he delight himself in the Almighty? will he always call upon G-d?11 I will teach you by the hand of G-d: that which is with the Almighty will I not conceal.12 Behold, all you yourselves have seen it; why then are you thus altogether vain?

| הבל 1892 | תהבלו 1891: | 27:13 זה 2088 | חלק 2506 | אדם 120 | רשע 7563 | עם 5973 | אל 410 | ונחלת 5159 | עריצים 6184 |
|---|---|---|---|---|---|---|---|---|---|
| hebel | tehbalu. | zeh | cheleq | 'adam | rasha' | 'am | 'ael; | uanachalat | 'ariytziym, |
| **altogether** | **are you vain?** | **This** | ***is* the portion of** | **a man** | **wicked** | **with** | **El** | **and the heritage of** | **oppressors** |

| משדי 7706 | יקחו 3947: | 27:14 אם 518 | ירבו 7235 | בניו 1121 | למו 3926 | חרב 2719 | וצאצאיו 6631 | לא 3808 |
|---|---|---|---|---|---|---|---|---|
| mishaday | yiqachu. | 'am | yirbu | banayu | lamou | chareb; | uatze'atza'ayu, | la' |
| **of the Almighty** | ***which* they shall receive** | **If** | **be multiplied** | **his children** | ***it is* for** | **the sword** | **and his offspring** | **not** |

| ישבעו 7646 | לחם 3899: | 27:15 שרידו 8300 | במות 4194 | יקברו 6912 | ואלמנתיו 490 | לא 3808 |
|---|---|---|---|---|---|---|
| yisba'u | lachem. | seriydou | bamauet | yiqaberu; | ua'almanotayu, | la' |
| **shall be satisfied with** | **bread** | **Those that remain of him** | **in death** | **shall be buried** | **and his widows** | **not** |

| תבכינה 1058: | 27:16 אם 518 | יצבר 6651 | כעפר 6083 | כסף 3701 | וכחמר 2563 | יכין 3559 | מלבוש 4403: | 27:17 יכין 3559 |
|---|---|---|---|---|---|---|---|---|
| tibkeynah. | 'am | yitzbor | ke'apar | kasep; | uakachomer, | yakiyn | malbush. | yakiyn |
| **shall weep** | **Though** | **he heap up** | **as the dust** | **silver** | **and as the clay** | **prepare** | **raiment** | **He may prepare** |

| וצדיק 6662 | ילבש 3847 | וכסף 3701 | נקי 5355 | יחלק 2505: | 27:18 בנה 1129 | כעש 6211 | ביתו 1004 | וכסכה 5521 |
|---|---|---|---|---|---|---|---|---|
| uatzadiyq | yilbash; | uakesep, | naqiy | yachaloq. | banah | ka'ash | beytou; | uaksukah, |
| ***it* but the just** | **shall put *it* on** | **and the silver** | **the innocent** | **shall divide** | **He builds** | **as a moth** | **his house** | **and as a booth** |

| עשה 6213 | נצר 5341: | 27:19 עשיר 6223 | ישכב 7901 | ולא 3808 | יאסף 622 | עיניו 5869 | פקח 6491 | ואיננו 369: | 27:20 |
|---|---|---|---|---|---|---|---|---|---|
| 'asah | notzer. | 'ashiyr | yishkab | uala' | ye'asep; | 'aeynayu | paqach | ua'aeynenu. | |
| **make** | ***that* the keeper** | **The rich man** | **shall lie down** | **but not** | **he shall be gathered** | **his eyes** | **he open** | **and he is not** | |

| תשיגהו 5381 | כמים 4325 | בלהות 1091 | לילה 3915 | גנבתו 1589 | סופה 5492: | 27:21 ישאהו 5375 | קדים 6921 |
|---|---|---|---|---|---|---|---|
| tasiygehu | kamayim | balahout; | layalah, | ganabatu | supah. | yisa'aehu | qadiym |
| **take hold on him** | **as waters** | **Terrors** | **in the night** | **steal him away** | **a tempest** | **carry him away** | **The east wind** |

| וילך 1980 | וישערהו 8175 | ממקמו 4725: | 27:22 וישלך 7993 | עליו 5921 | ולא 3808 | יחמל 2550 |
|---|---|---|---|---|---|---|
| uayelak; | uiysa'arehu, | mimaqomou. | uayashlek | 'alayu | uala' | yachmol; |
| **and he depart** | **and as a storm hurleth him** | **out of his place** | **For *Elohim* shall cast** | **upon him** | **and not** | **spare** |

| מידו 3027 | ברוח 1272 | יברח 1272: | 27:23 ישפק 5606 | עלימו 5921 | כפימו 3709 | וישרק 8319 | עליו 5921 | ממקמו 4725: |
|---|---|---|---|---|---|---|---|---|
| miyadou, | barouach | yibrach. | yispoq | 'aleymou | kapeymou; | uayishroq | 'alayu, | mimaqomou. |
| **out of his hand** | **he would fain** | **flee** | ***Men* shall clap** | **at him** | **their hands** | **and shall hiss** | **him** | **out of his place** |

| Job 28:1 כי 3588 | יש 3426 | לכסף 3701 | מוצא 4161 | ומקום 4725 | לזהב 2091 | יזקו 2212: | 28:2 ברזל 1270 | מעפר 6083 | יקח 3947 |
|---|---|---|---|---|---|---|---|---|---|
| kiy | yesh | lakesep | moutza'; | uamaqoum, | lazahab | yazoqu. | barzel | me'apar | yuqach; |
| **Surely** | **there is** | **for the silver** | **a vein** | **and a place** | **for gold** | ***where* they fine *it*** | **Iron** | **out of the earth** | **is taken** |

| ואבן 68 | יצוק 6694 | נחושה 5154: | 28:3 קץ 7093 | שם 7760 | לחשך 2822 | ולכל 3605 | תכלית 8503 | הוא 1931 | חוקר 2713 | אבן 68 |
|---|---|---|---|---|---|---|---|---|---|---|
| ua'aben, | yatzuq | nachushah. | qetz | sam | lachoshek, | ualkal | takliyt | hua' | chouqer; | 'aben |
| **and the stone** | ***is* molten** | ***out of* brass** | **an end** | **He set** | **to darkness** | **and all** | **perfection** | **he** | **searches out** | **the stones of** |

| אפל 652 | וצלמות 6757: | 28:4 פרץ 6555 | נחל 5158 | מעם 5973 | גר 1481 | הנשכחים 7911 | מני 4480 | רגל 7272 |
|---|---|---|---|---|---|---|---|---|
| 'apel | uatzalmauet. | paratz | nachal | me'am | gar, | hanishkachiym | miniy | ragel; |
| **darkness** | **and the shadow of death** | **break out** | **The flood** | **from** | **the inhabitant** | ***even the waters* forgotten of** | | **the foot** |

Job 27:13 This is the portion of a wicked man with G-d, and the heritage of oppressors, which they shall receive of the Almighty.14 If his children be multiplied, it is for the sword: and his offspring shall not be satisfied with bread.15 Those that remain of him shall be buried in death: and his widows shall not weep.16 Though he heap up silver as the dust, and prepare raiment as the clay;17 He may prepare it, but the just shall put it on, and the innocent shall divide the silver.18 He buildeth his house as a moth, and as a booth that the keeper make.19 The rich man shall lie down, but he shall not be gathered: he openeth his eyes, and he is not.20 Terrors take hold on him as waters, a tempest stealeth him away in the night.21 The east wind carrieth him away, and he departeth: and as a storm hurleth him out of his place.22 For G-d shall cast upon him, and not spare: he would fain flee out of his hand.23 Men shall clap their hands at him, and shall hiss him out of his place. **Job** 28:1 Surely there is a vein for the silver, and a place for gold where they fine it.2 Iron is taken out of the earth, and brass is molten out of the stone.3 He set an end to darkness, and searcheth out all perfection: the stones of darkness, and the shadow of death.4 The flood breaketh out from the inhabitant; even the waters forgotten of the foot: they are dried up, they are gone away from men.

דלו 1809 מאנוש 582 נעו 5128: 28:5 ארץ 776 ממנה 4480 יצא 3318 לחם 3899 ותחתיה 8478 נהפך 2015
dalu me'anoush na'au. 'aretz, mimenah yetzea' lachem; uatachteyha, nehapak
**they are dried up from men they are gone away *As for* the earth out of it comes bread and under it is turned up**

כמו 3644 אש 784: 28:6 מקום 4725 ספיר 5601 אבניה 68 ועפרת 6083 זהב 2091 לו 3807a: 28:7 נתיב 5410 לא 3808
kamou 'aesh. maqoum sapiyr 'abaneyha; ua'aprot zahab lou'. natiyb la'
**as it were fire *are* the place of sapphires The stones of it and dust of gold it *has* *There is* a path which no**

ידעו 3045 עיט 5861 ולא 3808 שזפתו 7805 עין 5869 איה 344: 28:8 לא 3808 הדריכהו 1869 בני 1121 שחץ 7830 לא 3808 עדה 5710
yada'au 'ayit; uala' shazapatu, 'aeyn 'ayah. la' hidriykuhu baney shachatz; la' 'adah
**knows fowl not has seen eye *and which the* vulture's *The* not have trodden it whelps lion's nor passed**

עליו 5921 שחל 7826: 28:9 בחלמיש 2496 שלח 7971 ידו 3027 הפך 2015 משרש 8328 הרים 2022: 28:10
'alayu shachal. bachalamiysh shalach yadou; hapak mishoresh hariym.
**by it the fierce lion upon the rock He put forth his hand he overturn by the roots the mountains**

בצורות 6697 יארים 2975 בקע 1234 וכל 3605 יקר 3366 ראתה 7200 עינו 5869: 28:11 מבכי 1065 נהרות 5104 חבש 2280
batzurout ya'ariym biqea'; uakal yaqar, ra'atah 'aeynou. mibkiy naharout chibesh;
**among the rocks rivers He cuts out and every precious thing see his eye from overflowing the floods He bind**

ותעלמה 8587 יצא 3318 אור 216: 28:12 והחכמה 2451 מאין 370 תמצא 4672 ואי 335 זה 2088
uata'alumah, yotza' 'aur. uahachakamah me'ayin timatzea'; ua'aey zeh
**and *the thing that is* hid bring he forth to light But wisdom where shall be found? and where *is* he**

מקום 4725 בינה 998: 28:13 לא 3808 ידע 3045 אנוש 582 ערכה 6187 ולא 3808 תמצא 4672 בארץ 776 החיים 2416: 28:14
maqoum biynah. la' yada' 'anoush 'arkah; uala' timatzea', ba'aretz hachayiym.
**the place of understanding? not knows Man the price thereof neither is it found in the land of the living**

תהום 8415 אמר 559 לא 3808 בי 871a היא 1931 וים 3220 אמר 559 אין 369 עמדי 5978: 28:15 לא 3808 יתן 5414 סגור 5458 תחתיה 8478
tahoum 'amar la' biy hiy'a; uayam 'amar, 'aeyn 'amadiy. la' yutan sagour tachteyha;
**The depth saith not in me It *is* and the sea saith *It is* not with me cannot It be gotten for gold beneath**

ולא 3808 ישקל 8254 כסף 3701 מחירה 4242: 28:16 לא 3808 תסלה 5541 בכתם 3800 אופיר 211 בשהם 7718
uala' yishaqel, kesep machiyrah. la' tasuleh baketem 'aupiyr; bashoham
**neither shall be weighed silver *for* the price thereof cannot It be valued with the gold of Ophir with onyx**

יקר 3368 וספיר 5601: 28:17 לא 3808 יערכנה 6186 זהב 2091 וזכוכית 2137 ותמורתה 8545
yaqar uasapiyr. la' ya'arkenah zahab uazkoukiyt; uatmuratah
**the precious or the sapphire cannot equal it The gold and the crystal and the exchange of it *shall not be for***

כלי 3627 פז 6337: 28:18 ראמות 7215 וגביש 1378 לא 3808 יזכר 2142 ומשך 4901 חכמה 2451 מפנינים 6443: 28:19
kaliy paz. ra'mout uagabiysh la' yizaker; uameshek chakamah mipniyniym.
**jewels of fine gold *of* coral or of pearls No mention shall be made for the price of wisdom *is* above rubies**

לא 3808 יערכנה 6186 פטדת 6357 כוש 3568 בכתם 3800 טהור 2889 לא 3808 תסלה 5541: 28:20 והחכמה 2451 מאין 370 תבוא 935
la' ya'arkenah pitdat kush; baketem tahour, la' tasuleh. uahachakamah me'ayin tabou'a;
**not shall equal it The topaz of Ethiopia with gold pure neither shall it be valued then wisdom? Where comes**

Job 28:5 As for the earth, out of it cometh bread: and under it is turned up as it were fire.6 The stones of it are the place of sapphires: and it has dust of gold.7 There is a path which no fowl know, and which the vulture's eye has not seen:8 The lion's whelps have not trodden it, nor the fierce lion passed by it.9 He put forth his hand upon the rock; he overturneth the mountains by the roots.10 He cutteth out rivers among the rocks; and his eye see every precious thing.11 He bindeth the floods from overflowing; and the thing that is hid bring he forth to light.12 But where shall wisdom be found? and where is the place of understanding?13 Man know not the price thereof; neither is it found in the land of the living.14 The depth saith, It is not in me: and the sea saith, It is not with me.15 It cannot be gotten for gold, neither shall silver be weighed for the price thereof.16 It cannot be valued with the gold of Ophir, with the precious onyx, or the sapphire.17 The gold and the crystal cannot equal it: and the exchange of it shall not be for jewels of fine gold.18 No mention shall be made of coral, or of pearls: for the price of wisdom is above rubies.19 The topaz of Ethiopia shall not equal it, neither shall it be valued with pure gold.20 Where then cometh wisdom? and where is the place of understanding?

ואי 335 זה 2088 מקום 4725 בינה 998: 28:21 ונעלמה 5956 מעיני 5869 כל 3605 חי 2416 ומעוף 5775
ua'aey zeh, maqoum biynah. uane'almah me'aeyney kal chay; uame'aup
**and where *is* he the place of understanding? Seeing it is hid from the eyes of all living and from the fowls of**

השמים 8064 נסתרה 5641: 28:22 אבדון 11 ומות 4194 אמרו 559 באזנינו 241 שמענו 8085 שמעה 8088: 28:23 אלהים 430
hashamayim nistarah. abadoun uamauet 'amaru; ba'azaneynu, shama'anu shim'ah. 'alohiym
**the air kept close Destruction and death say with our ears We have heard the fame thereof Elohim**

הבין 995 דרכה 1870 והוא 1931 ידע 3045 את 853 מקומה 4725: 28:24 כי 3588 הוא 1931 לקצות 7098 הארץ 776 יביט 5027
hebiyn darkah; uahu'a, yada' 'at maqoumah. kiy hua' liqtzout ha'aretz yabiyt;
**understands the way thereof and he knows the place thereof For he to the ends of the earth looks**

תחת 8478 כל 3605 השמים 8064 יראה 7200: 28:25 לעשות 6213 לרוח 7307 משקל 4948 ומים 4325 תכן 8505 במדה 4060: 28:26
tachat kal hashamayim yir'ah. la'asout laruach mishqal; uamayim, tiken bamidah.
**under the whole heaven *and* see To make for the winds the weight and the waters he weigh by measure**

בעשתו 6213 למטר 4306 חק 2706 ודרך 1870 לחזיז 2385 קלות 6963: 28:27 אז 227 ראה 7200 ויספרה 5608
ba'astou lamatar choq; uaderek, lachaziyz qolout. 'az ra'ah uayasaprah;
**When he made for the rain a decree and a way for the lightning of the thunder Then did he see it and declare it**

הכינה 3559 וגם 1571 חקרה 2713: 28:28 ויאמר 559 לאדם 120 הן 2005 יראת 3374 אדני 136 היא 1931 חכמה 2451
hekiynah, uagam chaqarah. uaya'mer la'adam, hen yir'at 'adonay hiy'a chakamah
**he prepared it and yea searched it out And he said unto man Behold the fear of Adonai that *is* wisdom**

וסור 5493 מרע 7451 בינה 998:
uasur mera' biynah.
**and to depart from evil *is* understanding**

**Job 29:1** ויסף 3254 איוב 347 שאת 5375 משלו 4912 ויאמר 559: 29:2 מי 4310 יתנני 5414 כירחי 3391 קדם 6924
uayosep 'ayoub sa'aet mashalou, uaya'mar. miy' yitaneniy kayarchey qedem;
**Moreover continued Job you bring forth his parable and said Oh that I were as *in* months past**

כימי 3117 אלוה 433 ישמרני 8104: 29:3 בהלו 1984 נרו 5216 עלי 5921 ראשי 7218 לאורו 216 אלך 1980
kiymey, 'alouah yishmareniy. bahilou nerou 'aley ra'shiy; la'aurou 'aelek
**as *in* the days *when* Elohim preserved me When shined his candle upon my head *and when* by his light I walked**

חשך 2822: 29:4 כאשר 834 הייתי 1961 בימי 3117 חרפי 2779 בסוד 5475 אלוה 433 עלי 5921 אהלי 168: 29:5
choshek. ka'asher hayiytiy biymey charapiy; basoud 'alouah, 'aley 'ahaliy.
***through* darkness As I was in the days of my youth when the secret of Elohim *was* upon my tabernacle**

בעוד 5750 שדי 7706 עמדי 5978 סביבותי 5439 נערי 5288: 29:6 ברחץ 7364 הליכי 1978 בחמה 2529
ba'aud shaday 'amadiy; sabiyboutay na'aray. birchotz haliykay bachemah;
**When yet the Almighty *was* with me *were* about me *when* my children When I washed my steps with butter**

וצור 6697 יצוק 6694 עמדי 5978 פלגי 6388 שמן 8081: 29:7 בצאתי 3318 שער 8179 עלי 5921 קרת 7176 ברחוב 7339
uatzur yatzuq 'amadiy, palgey shamen. batzea'tiy sha'ar 'aley qaret; barchoub,
**and the rock poured out me rivers of oil When I went out to the gate through the city in the street**

Job 28:21 Seeing it is hid from the eyes of all living, and kept close from the fowls of the air.22 Destruction and death say, We have heard the fame thereof with our ears.23 G-d understandeth the way thereof, and he know the place thereof.24 For he look to the ends of the earth, and see under the whole heaven;25 To make the weight for the winds; and he weigheth the waters by measure.26 When he made a decree for the rain, and a way for the lightning of the thunder:27 Then did he see it, and declare it; he prepared it, yea, and searched it out.28 And unto man he said, Behold, the fear of the Adonai, that is wisdom; and to depart from evil is understanding. **Job** 29:1 Moreover Job continued his parable, and said,2 Oh that I were as in months past, as in the days when G-d preserved me;3 When his candle shined upon my head, and when by his light I walked through darkness;4 As I was in the days of my youth, when the secret of G-d was upon my tabernacle;5 When the Almighty was yet with me, when my children were about me;6 When I washed my steps with butter, and the rock poured me out rivers of oil;7 When I went out to the gate through the city, when I prepared my seat in the street!

29:8 | 29:9

אכין 3559 מושבי 4186: ראוני 7200 נערים 5288 ונחבאו 2244 וישישים 3453 קמו 6965 עמדו 5975:
'akiyn moushabiy. ra'auniy na'ariym uanechba'au; uiyshiyshiym qamu 'amadu.
***when*** **I prepared** **my seat** **saw me** **The young men** **and hid themselves** **and the aged** **arose** ***and*** **stood up**

29:10

שרים 8269 עצרו 6113 במלים 4405 וכף 3709 ישימו 7760 לפיהם 6310: קול 6963 נגידים 5057 נחבאו 2244
sariym 'atzaru bamiliym; uakap, yasiymu lapiyhem. qoul nagiydiym nechba'au;
**The princes** **refrained** **talking** **and hand** **laid** ***their*** **on their mouth** **held their peace** **The nobles** **they held**

29:11

ולשונם 3956 לחכם 2441 דבקה 1692: כי 3588 אזן 241 שמעה 8085 ותאשרני 833 ועין 5869
ualshounam, lachikam dabeqah. kiy 'azen sham'ah uat'ashreniy; ua'ayin
**and their tongue** **to the roof of their mouth** **cleaved** **When** **the ear** **heard** ***me*** **then it blessed me** **and when the eye**

29:12

ראתה 7200 ותעידני 5749: כי 3588 אמלט 4422 עני 6041 משוע 7768 ויתום 3490 ולא 3808
ra'atah, uat'aydeniy. kiy 'amalet 'aniy mashauea'; uayatoum, uala'
**saw** ***me*** **it gave witness to me** **Because** **I delivered** **the poor** **that cried** **and the fatherless** **and** ***him that had*** **none**

29:13

עזר 5826 לו 3807a: ברכת 1293 אבד 6 עלי 5921 תבא 935 ולב 3820 אלמנה 490
'azer lou'. birkat 'abed 'alay taba'; ualeb 'almanah
**to help** **him** **The blessing of** **him that was ready to perish** **upon me** **came** **and heart** ***the*** **widow's**

29:14 | 29:15

ארנן 7442: צדק 6664 לבשתי 3847 וילבשני 3847 כמעיל 4598 וצניף 6797 משפטי 4941:
'arnin. tzedeq labashtiy uayilbasheniy; kim'ayl uatzaniyp, mishpatiy.
**I caused to sing for joy** **righteousness** **I put on** **and it clothed me** ***was*** **as a robe** **and a diadem** **my judgment**

29:16

עינים 5869 הייתי 1961 לעור 5787 ורגלים 7272 לפסח 6455 אני 589: אב 1 אנכי 595 לאביונים 34 ורב 7379 לא 3808
'aeynayim hayiytiy la'auer; uaraglayim lapiseach 'aniy. 'ab 'anokiy la'abyouniym; uarib la'
**eyes** **I was** **to the blind** **and feet** **to the lame** ***was*** **I** ***was*** **a father** **I** **to the poor** **and the cause** **not**

29:17 | 29:18

ידעתי 3045 אחקרהו 2713: ואשברה 7665 מתלעות 4973 עול 5767 ומשניו 8127 אשליך 7993 טרף 2964:
yada'tiy 'achqarehu. ua'ashabrah matal'aut 'aual; uamishinayu, 'ashliyk tarep.
***which*** **I knew** **I searched out** **And I brake** **the jaws of** **the wicked** **and out of his teeth** **plucked** **the spoil**

29:19

ואמר 559 עם 5973 קני 7064 אגוע 1478 וכחול 2344 ארבה 7235 ימים 3117: שרשי 8328 פתוח 6605 אלי 413
ua'amar 'am qiniy 'agua'; uakachoul, 'arbeh yamiym. sharashiy patuach 'aley
**Then I said** **in** **my nest** **I shall die** **and as the sand** **I shall multiply** ***my*** **days** **My root** ***was*** **spread out** **by**

29:20

מים 4325 וטל 2919 ילין 3885 בקצירי 7105: כבודי 3519 חדש 2319 עמדי 5978 וקשתי 7198 בידי 3027
mayim; uatal, yaliyn biqtziyriy. kaboudiy chadash 'amadiy; uaqashtiy, bayadiy
**the waters** **and the dew** **lay all night** **upon my branch** **My glory** ***was*** **fresh** **in me** **and my bow** **in my hand**

29:21 | 29:22

תחליף 2498: לי 3807a שמעו 8085 ויחלו 3176 וידמו 1826 למו 3926 עצתי 6098: אחרי 310 דברי 1697 לא 3808
tachaliyp. liy shama'au uayichelu; uayidmu, lamou 'atzatiy. 'acharey dabariy la'
**was renewed** **Unto me** ***men*** **gave ear** **and waited** **and kept silence** **at** **my counsel** **After** **my words** **not**

29:23

ישנו 8138 ועלימו 5921 תטף 5197 מלתי 4405: ויחלו 3176 כמטר 4306 לי 3807a ופיהם 6310
yishnu; ua'aleymou, titop milatiy. uayichalu kamatar liy; uapiyhem,
**they spoke again** **and upon them** **dropped** **my speech** **And they waited** **as for the rain** **for me** **and their mouth**

Job 29:8 The young men saw me, and hid themselves: and the aged arose, and stood up.9 The princes refrained talking, and laid their hand on their mouth.10 The nobles held their peace, and their tongue cleaved to the roof of their mouth.11 When the ear heard me, then it blessed me; and when the eye saw me, it gave witness to me:12 Because I delivered the poor that cried, and the fatherless, and him that had none to help him.13 The blessing of him that was ready to perish came upon me: and I caused the widow's heart to sing for joy.14 I put on righteousness, and it clothed me: my judgment was as a robe and a diadem.15 I was eyes to the blind, and feet was I to the lame.16 I was a father to the poor: and the cause which I knew not I searched out.17 And I break the jaws of the wicked, and plucked the spoil out of his teeth.18 Then I said, I shall die in my nest, and I shall multiply my days as the sand.19 My root was spread out by the waters, and the dew lay all night upon my branch.20 My glory was fresh in me, and my bow was renewed in my hand.21 Unto me men gave ear, and waited, and kept silence at my counsel.22 After my words they spoke not again; and my speech dropped upon them.23 And they waited for me as for the rain; and they opened their mouth wide as for the latter rain.

פערו 6473 | למלקוש 4456: | 29:24 אשחק 7832 | אלהם 413 | לא 3808 | יאמינו 539 | ואור 216 | פני 6440
pa'aru | lamalqoush. | 'aschaq | 'alehem | la' | ya'amiynu; | ua'aur | panay,
**they opened wide** | ***as* for the latter rain** | ***If* I laughed** | **on them** | **not** | **they believed *it*** | **and the light of** | **my countenance**

לא 3808 | יפילון 5307: | 29:25 אבחר 977 | דרכם 1870 | ואשב 3427 | ראש 7218 | ואשכון 7931 | כמלך 4428 | בגדוד 1416 | כאשר 834 | אבלים 57
la' | yapiylun. | 'abachar | darkam | ua'aesheb | ra'sh | ua'ashkoun | kamelek | bagadud; | ka'asher | 'abeliym
**not** | **they cast down** | **I chose out** | **their way** | **and sat** | **chief** | **and dwelt** | **as a king** | **in the army** | **as** | **the mourners**

ינחם 5162:
yanachem.
**one *that* comforts**

**Job 30:1** ועתה 6258 | שחקו 7832 | עלי 5921 | צעירים 6810 | ממני 4480 | לימים 3117 | אשר 834 | מאסתי 3988 | אבותם 1
ua'atah | sachaqu | 'alay | tza'ayriym | mimeniy, | layamiym | 'asher | ma'astiy | aboutam;
**But now** | **have in derision** | **me** | ***they that are* younger than I** | **younger** | **whose** | **I would have disdained** | **fathers**

לשית 7896 | עם 5973 | כלבי 3611 | צאני 6629: | 30:2 גם 1571 | כח 3581 | ידיהם 3027 | למה 4100 | לי 3807a | עלימו 5921
lashiyt, | 'am | kalbey | tza'niy. | gam | koach | yadeyhem | lamah | liy; | 'aleymou,
**to have set** | **with** | **the dogs of** | **my flock** | **Yea** | ***might* the strength of** | **their hands** | **whereto *profit*** | **me** | **in whom**

אבד 6 | כלח 3624: | 30:3 בחסר 2639 | ובכפן 3720 | גלמוד 1565 | הערקים 6207 | ציה 6723 | אמש 570 | שואה 7722
'abad | kalach. | bacheser | uabkapan, | galmud | ha'araqiym | tziyah; | 'amesh, | shou'ah
**was perished?** | **old age** | **For want** | **and famine** | ***they were* solitary** | **fleeing into** | **the wilderness** | **in former time** | **desolate**

ומשאה 4875: | 30:4 הקטפים 6998 | מלוח 4408 | עלי 5921 | שיח 7880 | ושרש 8328 | רתמים 7574 | לחמם 3899: | 30:5 מן 4480 | גו 1460
uamsho'ah. | haqotapiym | maluach | 'aley | siyach; | uashoresh | ratamiym | lachmam. | min | geu
**and waste** | **Who cut up** | **mallows** | **by** | **the bushes** | **and roots** | **juniper *for*** | **their meat** | **from** | **among *men***

יגרשו 1644 | יריעו 7321 | עלימו 5921 | כגנב 1590: | 30:6 בערוץ 6178 | נחלים 5158 | לשכן 7931 | חרי 2356 | עפר 6083
yagorashu; | yariy'au | 'aleymou, | kaganab. | ba'arutz | nachaliym | lishkon; | chorey | 'apar
**They were driven forth** | **they cried** | **after them** | **as after a thief** | **in the clifts of** | **the valleys** | **To dwell** | ***in* caves of** | **the earth**

וכפים 3710: | 30:7 בין 996 | שיחים 7880 | ינהקו 5101 | תחת 8478 | חרול 2738 | יספחו 5596: | 30:8
uakepiym. | beyn | siychiym | yinhaqu; | tachat | charul | yasupachu.
**and *in* the rocks** | **Among** | **the bushes** | **they brayed** | **under** | **the nettles** | **they were gathered together**

בני 1121 | נבל 5036 | גם 1571 | בני 1121 | בלי 1097 | שם 8034 | נכאו 5217 | מן 4480 | הארץ 776: | 30:9 ועתה 6258 | נגינתם 5058
baney | nabal | gam | baney | baliy | shem; | nik'au, | min | ha'aretz. | ua'atah | nagiynatam
***They were* children of** | **fools** | **yea** | **children of** | **without base *men*** | **they were viler than** | **the earth** | **And now** | **their song**

הייתי 1961 | ואהי 1961 | להם 3807a | למלה 4405: | 30:10 תעבוני 8581 | רחקו 7368 | מני 4480 | ומפני 6440 | לא 3808 | חשכו 2820
hayiytiy; | ua'ahiy | lahem | lamilah. | ti'abuniy | rachaqu | meniy; | uamipanay, | la' | chasaku
**am I** | **yea I am** | **their** | **byword** | **They abhor me** | **they flee far** | **from me** | **and in my face** | **not** | **spare**

רק 7536: | 30:11 כי 3588 | יתרו 3499 | פתח 6605 | ויענני 6031 | ורסן 7448 | מפני 6440 | שלחו 7971: | 30:12 על 5921
roq. | kiy | yitrou | pitach | uay'aneniy; | uaresen, | mipanay | shilechu. | 'al
**to spit** | **Because my cord he has loosed and afflicted me** | **also the bridle before me they have let loose** | **Upon**

Job 29:24 If I laughed on them, they believed it not; and the light of my countenance they cast not down.25 I chose out their way, and sat chief, and dwelt as a king in the army, as one that comforteth the mourners. **Job** 30:1 But now they that are younger than I have me in derision, whose fathers I would have disdained to have set with the dogs of my flock.2 Yea, whereto might the strength of their hands profit me, in whom old age was perished?3 For want and famine they were solitary; fleeing into the wilderness in former time desolate and waste.4 Who cut up mallows by the bushes, and juniper roots for their meat.5 They were driven forth from among men, (they cried after them as after a thief;)6 To dwell in the clifts of the valleys, in caves of the earth, and in the rocks.7 Among the bushes they brayed; under the nettles they were gathered together.8 They were children of fools, yea, children of base men: they were viler than the earth.9 And now am I their song, yea, I am their byword.10 They abhor me, they flee far from me, and spare not to spit in my face.11 Because he has loosed my cord, and afflicted me, they have also let loose the bridle before me.

30:13
ימין 3225 פרחח 6526 יקומו 6965 רגלי 7272 שלחו 7971 ויסלו 5549 עלי 5921 ארחות 734 אידם 343:
yamiyn pirchach yaqumu raglay shilechu; uayasolu 'alay, 'arachout 'aeydam.
**my right the youth hand rise my feet they push away and they raise up against me the ways of their destruction**

30:14
נתסו 5420 נתיבתי 5410 להותי 1942 יעילו 3276 לא 3808 עזר 5826 למו 3807a: כפרץ 6556 רחב 7342
natasu, natiybatiy lahauatiy yo'aylu; la' 'azer lamou. kaperetz rachab
**They mar my path my calamity they set forward no helper they *have* as a breaking in *of waters* wide**

30:15
יאתיו 857 תחת 8478 שאה 7722 התגלגלו 1556: ההפך 2015 עלי 5921 בלהות 1091 תרדף 7291
ye'atayu; tachat sho'ah, hitgalgalu. hahapak 'alay, balahout tirdop
**They came *upon me* in the desolation they rolled themselves *upon me* are turned upon me Terrors they pursue**

30:16
כרוח 7307 נדבתי 5082 וכעב 5645 עברה 5674 ישעתי 3444: ועתה 6258 עלי 5921 תשתפך 8210 נפשי 5315
karuach nadibatiy; uak'ab, 'abarah yashu'atiy. ua'atah, 'alay tishtapek napshiy;
**as the wind my soul and as a cloud passed away my welfare And now upon me is poured out my soul**

30:17
יאחזוני 270 ימי 3117 עני 6040: לילה 3915 עצמי 6106 נקר 5365 מעלי 5921 וערקי 6207 לא 3808
ya'chazuniy yamey 'aniy. layalah, 'atzamay niqar me'alay; ua'araqay, la'
**have taken hold upon me the days of affliction in the night season My bones are pierced in me and my sinews no**

30:18 30:19
ישכבון 7901: ברב 7227 כח 3581 יתחפש 2664 לבושי 3830 כפי 6310 כתנתי 3801 יאזרני 247:
yishkabun. barab koach yitchapes labushiy; kapiy kutanatiy ya'azreniy.
**take rest By the great force *of my disease* is changed my garment as the collar of my coat it bind me about**

30:20
הרני 3384 לחמר 2563 ואתמשל 4911 כעפר 6083 ואפר 665: אשוע 7768 אליך 413 ולא 3808 תענני 6030
horaniy lachomer; ua'atmashel, ke'apar ua'aeper. 'ashaua' 'aeleyka uala' ta'aneniy;
**He has cast me into the mire and I am become like dust and ashes I cry unto you and not you do hear me**

30:21
עמדתי 5975 ותתבנן 995 בי 871a: תהפך 2015 לאכזר 393 לי 3807a בעצם 6108 ידך 3027
'amadtiy, uatitbonen biy. tehapek la'akzar liy; ba'atzem yadaka
**I stand up and you regard me *not* You are become cruel to me with strong your hand**

30:22
תשטמני 7852: תשאני 5375 אל 413 רוח 7307 תרכיבני 7392 ותמגגני 4127
tistameniy. tisa'aeniy 'al ruach tarkiybeniy; uatmogageniy,
**you opposest yourself against me You lift me up to the wind you cause me to ride *upon it* and dissolve**

30:23 30:24
תשוה 7738 כי 3588 ידעתי 3045 מות 4194 תשיבני 7725 ובית 1004 מועד 4150 לכל 3605 חי 2416: אך 389
teshueh kiy yada'tiy mauet tashiybeniy; uabeyt mou'aed lakal chay. 'ak
**my substance For I know *to* death *that* you will bring me and *to* the house appointed for all living Howbeit**

30:25
לא 3808 בעי 1164 ישלח 7971 יד 3027 אם 518 בפידו 6365 להן 3807a שוע 7769: אם 518 לא 3808 בכיתי 1058
la' ba'ay yishlach yad; 'am bapiydou, lahen shua'. 'am la' bakiytiy
**not *to* the grave he will stretch out *his* hand though in his destruction they cry surely not Did I weep**

30:26
לקשה 7186 יום 3117 עגמה 5701 נפשי 5315 לאביון 34: כי 3588 טוב 2896 קויתי 6960
liqsheh youm; 'agamah napshiy, la'abyoun. kiy toub qiuiytiy
**for him that was in trouble? daily was grieved *not* my soul for the poor? When good I looked for**

Job 30:12 Upon my right hand rise the youth; they push away my feet, and they raise up against me the ways of their destruction.13 They mar my path, they set forward my calamity, they have no helper.14 They came upon me as a wide breaking in of waters: in the desolation they rolled themselves upon me.15 Terrors are turned upon me: they pursue my soul as the wind: and my welfare pass away as a cloud.16 And now my soul is poured out upon me; the days of affliction have taken hold upon me.17 My bones are pierced in me in the night season: and my sinews take no rest.18 By the great force of my disease is my garment changed: it bindeth me about as the collar of my coat.19 He has cast me into the mire, and I am become like dust and ashes.20 I cry unto you, and you dost not hear me: I stand up, and you regardest me not.21 Thou are become cruel to me: with your strong hand you opposest thyself against me.22 Thou liftest me up to the wind; you causest me to ride upon it, and dissolvest my substance.23 For I know that you will bring me to death, and to the house appointed for all living.24 Howbeit he will not stretch out his hand to the grave, though they cry in his destruction.25 Did not I weep for him that was in trouble? was not my soul grieved for the poor?26 When I looked for good, then evil came unto me: and when I waited for light, there came darkness.

ויבא 935 | רע 7451 | ואיחלה 3176 | לאור 216 | ויבא 935 | אפל 652: | 30:27 מעי 4578 | רתחו 7570 | ולא 3808 | דמו 1826
uayaba' | ra'; | ua'ayachalah | la'aur, | uayaba' | 'apel. | me'ay | rutchu | uala' | damu,
**and then came *unto me*** | **evil** | **and when I waited** | **for light** | **there came** | **darkness** | **My bowels** | **boiled** | **and not** | **rested**

קדמני 6923 | ימי 3117 | עני 6040: | 30:28 קדר 6937 | הלכתי 1980 | בלא 3808 | חמה 2535 | קמתי 6965 | בקהל 6951
qidmuniy | yamey | 'aniy. | qoder | hilaktiy | bala' | chamah; | qamtiy | baqahal
**prevented me** | **the days of** | **affliction** | **mourning** | **I went** | **without** | **the sun** | **I stood up** | **in the congregation**

אשוע 7768: | 30:29 אח 251 | הייתי 1961 | לתנים 8577 | ורע 7453 | לבנות 1323 | יענה 3284: | 30:30 עורי 5785 | שחר 7835 | מעלי 5921
'ashauea'. | 'ach | hayiytiy | lataniym; | uarea', | libnout | ya'anah. | 'auriy | shachar | me'alay;
***and* I cried** | **a brother** | **I am** | **to dragons** | **and a companion** | **first** | **to owls** | **My skin** | **is black** | **upon me**

ועצמי 6106 | חרה 2787 | מני 4480 | חרב 2721: | 30:31 ויהי 1961 | לאבל 60 | כנרי 3658 | ועגבי 5748 | לקול 6963
ua'atzmiy | charah, | miniy | choreb. | uayahiy | la'aebel | kinoriy; | ua'ugabiy, | laqoul
**and my bones** | **are burned** | **with** | **heat** | **also is** | ***turned* to mourning** | **My harp** | **and my organ** | **into the voice of**

בכים 1058:
bokiym.
**them that weep**

**Job 31:1** ברית 1285 | כרתי 3772 | לעיני 5869 | ומה 4100 | אתבונן 995 | על 5921 | בתולה 1330: | 31:2 ומה 4100 | חלק 2506
bariyt | karatiy | la'aeynay; | uamah | 'atbounen, | 'al | batulah. | uameh | cheleq
**a covenant** | **I made** | **with mine eyes** | **why then** | **should I think** | **upon** | **a maid? (*virgin*)** | **For what** | **portion of**

אלוה 433 | ממעל 4605 | ונחלת 5159 | שדי 7706 | ממרמים 4791: | 31:3 הלא 3808 | איד 343 | לעול 5767
'alouah | mima'al; | uanachalat | shaday, | mimromiym. | hala' | 'aeyd | la'aual;
**Elohim** | ***is there* from above?** | **and what heritage of** | **the Almighty** | **from on high?** | ***Is* not** | **destruction** | **to the wicked?**

ונכר 5235 | לפעלי 6466 | און 205: | 31:4 הלא 3808 | הוא 1931 | יראה 7200 | דרכי 1870 | וכל 3605 | צעדי 6806 | 31:5 יספור 5608:
uaneker, | lapo'aley | 'auen. | hala' | hua' | yir'ah | darakay; | uakal | tza'aday | yispour.
**and a strange *punishment*** | **to the workers of** | **iniquity?** | **not** | **he** | **Does see** | **my ways** | **and all** | **my steps?** | **count**

אם 518 | הלכתי 1980 | עם 5973 | שוא 7723 | ותחש 2363 | על 5921 | מרמה 4820 | רגלי 7272: | 31:6 ישקלני 8254 | במאזני 3976 | צדק 6664
'am | halaktiy | 'am | shau'a; | uatachash | 'al | mirmah | ragliy. | yishqaleniy | bama'zaney | tzedeq;
**If** | **I have walked** | **with** | **vanity** | **or has hasted** | **to** | **deceit** | ***if* my foot** | **Let me be weighed** | **in an balance** | **even**

וידע 3045 | אלוה 433 | תמתי 8538: | 31:7 אם 518 | תטה 5186 | אשרי 838 | מני 4480 | הדרך 1870 | ואחר 310 | עיני 5869 | הלך 1980 | לבי 3820
uayeda' | 'alouah, | tumatiy. | 'am | titeh | 'ashuriy | miniy | hadarek | ua'achar | 'aeynay | halak | libiy;
**that may know** | **Elohim** | **mine integrity** | **If** | **has turned** | **my step** | **out of** | **the way** | **and after** | **mine eyes** | **walked** | **mine heart**

ובכפי 3709 | דבק 1692 | מאום 3971: | 31:8 אזרעה 2232 | ואחר 312 | יאכל 398 | וצאצאי 6631 | ישרשו 8327: | 31:9
uabkapay, | dabaq | ma'um | 'azra'ah | ua'acher | ya'kel; | uatza'atza'ay | yashorashu.
**and to mine hands** | **has cleaved** | ***if any* blot** | ***Then* let me sow** | **and another** | **let eat** | **yea my offspring** | **let be rooted out**

אם 518 | נפתה 6601 | לבי 3820 | על 5921 | אשה 802 | ועל 5921 | פתח 6607 | רעי 7453 | ארבתי 693: | 31:10 תטחן 2912
'am | niptah | libiy | 'al | 'ashah; | ua'al | petach | rea'ay | 'arabatiy. | titchan
**If** | **have been deceived** | **mine heart** | **by** | **a woman** | **or at** | **door** | **my neighbour's** | ***if* I have laid wait** | ***Then* let grind**

Job 30:27 My bowels boiled, and rested not: the days of affliction prevented me.28 I went mourning without the sun: I stood up, and I cried in the congregation.29 I am a brother to dragons, and a companion to owls.30 My skin is black upon me, and my bones are burned with heat.31 My harp also is turned to mourning, and my organ into the voice of them that weep. **Job** 31:1 I made a covenant with mine eyes; why then should I think upon a maid?2 For what portion of G-d is there from above? and what inheritance of the Almighty from on high?3 Is not destruction to the wicked? and a strange punishment to the workers of iniquity?4 Does not he see my ways, and count all my steps?5 If I have walked with vanity, or if my foot has hasted to deceit;6 Let me be weighed in an even balance, that G-d may know mine integrity.7 If my step has turned out of the way, and mine heart walked after mine eyes, and if any blot has cleaved to mine hands;8 Then let me sow, and let another eat; yea, let my offspring be rooted out.9 If mine heart have been deceived by a woman, or if I have laid wait at my neighbor's door;10 Then let my wife grind unto another, and let others bow down upon her.

31:11

לאחר 312 אשתי 802 ועליה 5921 יכרעון 3766 אחרין 312: כי 3588 הוא 1931 זמה 2154 והיא 1931 עון 5771
la'acher 'ashtiy; ua'aleyha, yikra'aun 'acheriyn. kiy hua' zimah; uahiy'a 'auon
**unto another my wife and upon her let bow down others For this *is* an heinous crime yea, it *is* an iniquity**

31:12

פלילים 6414: כי 3588 אש 784 היא 1931 עד 5704 אבדון 11 תאכל 398 ובכל 3605 תבואתי 8393
paliyliym. kiy 'aesh hiy'a 'ad abadoun ta'kel; uabkal tabu'atiy
***to be punished by* the judges For it *is* a fire it to destruction *that* consume and all mine increase**

31:13

תשרש 8327: אם 518 אמאס 3988 משפט 4941 עבדי 5650 ואמתי 519 ברבם 7378
tasharesh. 'am 'am'as, mishpat 'abdiy ua'amatiy; baribam,
**would root out If I did despise the cause of my manservant or of my maidservant when they contended**

31:14 31:15

עמדי 5978: ומה 4100 אעשה 6213 כי 3588 יקום 6965 אל 410 וכי 3588 יפקד 6485 מה 4100 אשיבנו 7725: הלא 3808
'amadiy. uamah 'a'aseh kiy yaqum 'ael; uakiy yipqod, mah 'ashiybenu. hala'
**with me What then shall I do when rise up? El and when he visit what shall I answer him? not**

31:16

בבטן 990 עשני 6213 עשהו 6213 ויכננו 3559 ברחם 7358 אחד 259: אם 518 אמנע 4513
babeten 'aseniy 'asahu; uayakunenu, barechem 'achad. 'am 'amna'
**me in the womb Did he that made me make him? and did fashion us in the womb? *not* one If I have withheld**

31:17

מחפץ 2656 דלים 1800 ועיני 5869 אלמנה 490 אכלה 3615: ואכל 398 פתי 6595 לבדי 905
mechepetz daliym; ua'aeyney 'almanah 'akaleh. ua'akal pitiy labadiy;
**from *their* desire the poor or the eyes of the widow have caused to fail Or have eaten my morsel *myself* alone**

31:18

ולא 3808 אכל 398 יתום 3490 ממנה 4480: כי 3588 מנעורי 5271 גדלני 1431 כאב 1
uala' 'akal yatoum mimenah. kiy min'auray gadelaniy ka'ab;
**and not has eaten the fatherless thereof For from my youth he was brought up with me as *with* a father**

31:19

ומבטן 990 אמי 517 אנחנה 5148: אם 518 אראה 7200 אובד 6 מבלי 1097 לבוש 3830 ואין 369 כסות 3682
uamibeten 'amiy 'anchenah. 'am 'ar'ah 'aubed mibaliy labush; ua'aeyn kasut,
**and from womb my mother's I have guided her If I have seen *any* perish for want of clothing or without covering**

31:20 31:21

לאביון 34: אם 518 לא 3808 ברכוני 1288 חלצו 2504 ומגז 1488 כבשי 3532 יתחמם 2552: אם 518
la'abyoun. 'am la' berakuniy chalatzou uamigez kabasay yitchamam. 'am
***any* poor If not have blessed me his loins and with the fleece of my sheep *if* he were *not* warmed If**

31:22

הניפותי 5130 על 5921 יתום 3490 ידי 3027 כי 3588 אראה 7200 בשער 8179 עזרתי 5833: כתפי 3802
haniypoutiy 'al yatoum yadiy; kiy 'ar'ah basha'ar, 'azratiy. katepiy
**I have lifted up against the fatherless my hand when I saw in the gate my help *Then* mine arm**

31:23

משכמה 7929 תפול 5307 ואזרעי 248 מקנה 7070 תשבר 7665: כי 3588 פחד 6343 אלי 413 איד 343 אל 410
mishikmah tipoul; ua'azro'ay, miqanah tishaber. kiy pachad 'aelay 'aeyd 'ael;
**from my shoulder blade let fall and mine arm from the bone be broken For *was* a terror to me destruction *from* El**

31:24

ומשאתו 7613 לא 3808 אוכל 3201: אם 518 שמתי 7760 זהב 2091 כסלי 3689 ולכתם 3800 אמרתי 559
uamis'aetou, la' 'aukal. 'am samtiy zahab kisliy; ualaketem, 'amartiy
**and by reason of his highness not I could endure If I have made gold my hope or to the fine gold have said**

Job 31:11 For this is an heinous crime; yea, it is an iniquity to be punished by the judges.12 For it is a fire that consumeth to destruction, and would root out all mine increase.13 If I did despise the cause of my manservant or of my maidservant, when they contended with me;14 What then shall I do when G-d rise up? and when he visiteth, what shall I answer him?15 Did not he that made me in the womb make him? and did not one fashion us in the womb?16 If I have withheld the poor from their desire, or have caused the eyes of the widow to fail;17 Or have eaten my morsel myself alone, and the fatherless has not eaten thereof;18(For from my youth he was brought up with me, as with a father, and I have guided her from my mother's womb;)19 If I have seen any perish for want of clothing, or any poor without covering;20 If his loins have not blessed me, and if he were not warmed with the fleece of my sheep;21 If I have lifted up my hand against the fatherless, when I saw my help in the gate:22 Then let mine arm fall from my shoulder blade, and mine arm be broken from the bone.23 For destruction from G-d was a terror to me, and by reason of his highness I could not endure. 24 If I have made gold my hope, or have said to the fine gold, Thou are my confidence;

31:25 31:26

מבטחי 4009: אם 518 אשמח 8055 כי 3588 רב 7227 חילי 2428 וכי 3588 כביר 3524 מצאה 4672 ידי 3027:

mibtachiy. 'am 'asmach kiy rab cheyliy; uakiy kabiyr, matz'ah yadiy.

***You are* my confidence If I rejoiced because *was* great my wealth and because much had gotten mine hand**

31:27

אם 518 אראה 7200 אור 216 כי 3588 יהל 1984 וירח 3394 יקר 3368 הלך 1980: ויפת 6601 בסתר 5643 לבי 3820

'am 'ar'ah 'aur kiy yahel; uayareach, yaqar holek. uayipt baseter libiy;

**If I beheld the sun when it shined or the moon *in* brightness walking And has been enticed secretly my heart**

31:28

ותשק 5401 ידי 3027 לפי 6310: גם 1571 הוא 1931 עון 5771 פלילי 6416 כי 3588 כחשתי 3584

uatishaq yadiy lapiy. gam hua' 'auon paliyliy; kiy kichashtiy

**or has kissed my hand my mouth also This *were* an iniquity *to be punished by* the judge for I should have denied**

31:29

לאל 410 ממעל 4605: אם 518 אשמח 8055 בפיד 6365 משנאי 8130 והתעררתי 5782 כי 3588 מצאו 4672

la'ael mima'al. 'am 'asmach bapiyd masan'ay; uahit'arartiy, kiy matza'au

**the El *that is* above If I rejoiced at the destruction of him that hated me or lifted up myself when found him**

31:30 31:31

רע 7451: ולא 3808 נתתי 5414 לחטא 2398 חכי 2441 לשאל 7592 באלה 423 נפשו 5315: אם 518 לא 3808 אמרו 559

ra'. uala' natatiy lachata' chikiy; lisha'al ba'alah napshou. 'am la' 'amaru

**evil Neither have I suffered to sin my mouth by wishing a curse *to* his soul If not said**

31:32

מתי 4962 אהלי 168 מי 4310 יתן 5414 מבשרו 1320 לא 3808 נשבע 7646: בחוץ 2351 לא 3808 ילין 3885

matey 'ahaliy; miy' yiten mibasarou, la' nisba'. bachutz la' yaliyn

**the men of my tabernacle Oh that we had of his flesh cannot we be satisfied in the street not did lodge**

31:33

גר 1616 דלתי 1817 לארח 734 אפתח 6605: אם 518 כסיתי 3680 כאדם 121 פשעי 6588 לטמון 2934

ger; dalatay, la'areach 'aptach. 'am kasiytiy ka'adam pasha'ay; litmoun

**The stranger my doors to the traveller *but* I opened If I covered as Adam my transgressions by hiding**

31:34

בחבי 2243 עוני 5771: כי 3588 אערוץ 6206 המון 1995 רבה 7227 ובוז 937 משפחות 4940 יחתני 2865

bachubiy 'auoniy. kiy 'a'aroutz hamoun rabah, uabuz mishpachout yachiteniy;

**in my bosom mine iniquity that Did I fear a multitude great or the contempt of families did terrify me**

31:35

ואדם 1826 לא 3808 אצא 3318 פתח 6607: מי 4310 יתן 5414 לי 3807a שמע 8085 לי 3807a הן 2005 תוי 8420

ua'adom, la' 'aetzea' patach. miy' yiten liy shomea' liy, hen tauiy

**that I kept silence not *and* went out of door? Oh that one would me hear for behold my desire**

31:36

שדי 7706 יענני 6030 וספר 5612 כתב 3789 איש 376 ריבי 7379: אם 518 לא 3808 על 5921

shaday ya'aneniy; uaseper katab, 'aysh riybiy. 'am la' 'al

***is that* the Almighty would answer me and a book had written that which my adversary Surely not upon**

31:37

שכמי 7926 אשאנו 5375 אענדנו 6029 עטרות 5850 לי 3807a: מספר 4557 צעדי 6806 אגידנו 5046 כמו 3644

shikmiy 'asa'anu; 'a'andenu atarout liy. mispar tza'aday 'agiydenu; kamou

**my shoulder I would take it *and* bind it *as* a crown to me the number of my steps I would declare unto him as**

31:38

נגיד 5057 אקרבנו 7126: אם 518 עלי 5921 אדמתי 127 תזעק 2199 ויחד 3162 תלמיה 8525

nagiyd, 'aqarabenu. 'am 'alay 'admatiy tiz'aq; uayachad, talameyha

**a prince would I go near unto him If against me my land cry or likewise the furrows thereof**

Job 31:25 If I rejoiced because my wealth was great, and because mine hand had gotten much;26 If I beheld the sun when it shined, or the moon walking in brightness;27 And my heart has been secretly enticed, or my mouth has kissed my hand:28 This also were an iniquity to be punished by the judge: for I should have denied the G-d that is above.29 If I rejoiced at the destruction of him that hated me, or lifted up myself when evil found him:30 Neither have I suffered my mouth to sin by wishing a curse to his soul.31 If the men of my tabernacle said not, Oh that we had of his flesh! we cannot be satisfied.32 The stranger did not lodge in the street: but I opened my doors to the traveler.33 If I covered my transgressions as Adam, by hiding mine iniquity in my bosom:34 Did I fear a great multitude, or did the contempt of families terrify me, that I kept silence, and went not out of the door?35 Oh that one would hear me! behold, my desire is, that the Almighty would answer me, and that mine adversary had written a book.36 Surely I would take it upon my shoulder, and bind it as a crown to me.37 I would declare unto him the number of my steps; as a prince would I go near unto him.38 If my land cry against me, or that the furrows likewise thereof complain;

| | 31:39 | | | | | | | |
|---|---|---|---|---|---|---|---|---|
| יבכיון 1058: | אם 518 | כחה 3581 | אכלתי 398 | בלי 1097 | כסף 3701 | ונפש 5315 | בעליה 1167 |
| yibkayun. | 'am | kochah | 'akaltiy | baliy | kasep; | uanepesh | ba'aleyha |
| **that complain** | **If** | **the fruits thereof** | **I have eaten** | **without** | **money** | **or their life** | **the owners thereof** |

| | 31:40 | | | | | | | | |
|---|---|---|---|---|---|---|---|---|---|
| הפחתי 5301: | תחת 8478 | חטה 2406 | יצא 3318 | חוח 2336 | ותחת 8478 | שערה 8184 | באשה 890 | תמו 8552 | דברי 1697 |
| hipachatiy. | tachat | chitah | yetzea' | chouach, | uatachat | sa'arah | ba'ashah; | tamu, | dibrey |
| **have caused to lose** | **instead of** | **wheat** | **Let grow** | **thistles** | **and instead of** | **barley** | **cockle** | **are ended** | **The words of** |

איוב 347:
'ayoub.
**Job**

| Job 32:1 | | | | | | | | | | |
|---|---|---|---|---|---|---|---|---|---|---|
| וישבתו 7673 | שלשת 7969 | האנשים 582 | האלה 428 | מענות 6030 | את 853 | איוב 347 | כי 3588 | הוא 1931 | צדיק 6662 | בעיניו 5869: |
| uayishbatu | shaloshet | ha'anashiym | ha'aeleh | me'anout | 'at | 'ayoub; | kiy | hua' | tzadiyq | ba'aeynayu. |
| **So ceased** | **three** | **men** | **these** | **to answer** | | **Job** | **because** | **he** | ***was* righteous** | **in his own eyes** |

| 32:2 | | | | | | | | |
|---|---|---|---|---|---|---|---|---|
| ויחר 2734 | אף 639 | אליהוא 453 | בן 1121 | ברכאל 1292 | הבוזי 940 | ממשפחת 4940 | רם 7410 | באיוב 347 |
| uayichar | 'ap | 'aliyhu'a | ben | barak'ael | habuziy | mimishpachat | ram | ba'ayoub |
| **Then was kindled** | **the wrath of** | **Elihu** | **the son of** | **Barachel** | **the Buzite** | **of the kindred of** | **Ram** | **against Job** |

| | | | | | | 32:3 | | |
|---|---|---|---|---|---|---|---|---|
| חרה 2734 | אפו 639 | על 5921 | צדקו 6663 | נפשו 5315 | מאלהים 430: | ובשלשת 7969 | רעיו 7453 | חרה 2734 |
| charah | 'apou; | 'al | tzadqou | napshou, | me'alohiym. | uabishloshet | re'ayu | charah |
| **was kindled** | **his wrath** | **because** | **he justified** | **himself** | **rather than Elohim** | **Also against three** | **his friends** | **was kindled** |

| | | | | | | | | | 32:4 |
|---|---|---|---|---|---|---|---|---|---|
| אפו 639 | על 5921 | אשר 834 | לא 3808 | מצאו 4672 | מענה 4617 | וירשיעו 7561 | את 853 | איוב 347: | ואליהו 453 |
| 'apou | 'al | 'asher | la' | matza'au | ma'aneh; | uayarshiy'au, | 'at | 'ayoub. | ua'aliyhu', |
| **his wrath** | **because** | **after** | **no** | **they had found** | **answer** | **and *yet* had condemned** | | **Job** | **Now Elihu** |

| | | | | | | | | | 32:5 | |
|---|---|---|---|---|---|---|---|---|---|---|
| חכה 2442 | את 853 | איוב 347 | בדברים 1697 | כי 3588 | זקנים 2205 | המה 1992 | ממנו 4480 | לימים 3117: | וירא 7200 | אליהוא 453 |
| chikah | 'at | 'ayoub | bidbariym; | kiy | zaqeniym | hemah | mimenu | layamiym. | uayar'a | 'aliyhu'a, |
| **had waited *till*** | | **Job** | **had spoken** | **because *were*** | **elder** | **they** | **than he** | **to age** | **When saw** | **Elihu** |

| | | | | | | | | 32:6 |
|---|---|---|---|---|---|---|---|---|
| כי 3588 | אין 369 | מענה 4617 | בפי 6310 | שלשת 7969 | האנשים 582 | ויחר 2734 | אפו 639: | ויען 6030 |
| kiy | 'aeyn | ma'aneh, | bapiy | shaloshet | ha'anashiym, | uayichar | 'apou. | uaya'an |
| **that *there was*** | **no** | **answer** | **in the mouth of** | ***these* three** | **men** | **then was kindled** | **his wrath** | **And answered** |

| | | | | | | | | | | | |
|---|---|---|---|---|---|---|---|---|---|---|---|
| אליהוא 453 | בן 1121 | ברכאל 1292 | הבוזי 940 | ויאמר 559 | צעיר 6810 | אני 589 | לימים 3117 | ואתם 859 | ישישים 3453 | על 5921 | כן 3651 |
| 'aliyhu'a | ben | barak'ael | habuziy, | uaya'mar | tza'ayr | 'aniy | layamiym | ua'atem | yashiyshiym; | 'al | ken |
| **Elihu** | **the son of** | **Barachel** | **the Buzite** | **and said** | ***am* young** | **I** | **to age** | **and you *are*** | **very old** | **wherefore** | **after that** |

| | | | | | 32:7 | | | | |
|---|---|---|---|---|---|---|---|---|---|
| זחלתי 2119 | ואירא 3372 | מחות 2331 | דעי 1843 | אתכם 853: | אמרתי 559 | ימים 3117 | ידברו 1696 | ורב 7230 | שנים 8141 |
| zachaltiy | ua'ayra' | mechauot | de'ay | 'atkem. | 'amartiy | yamiym | yadaberu; | uarob | shaniym, |
| **I was afraid** | **and dread not** | **show** | **mine opinion** | **you** | **I said** | **Days** | **should speak** | **and multitude of** | **years** |

| | | 32:8 | | | | | |
|---|---|---|---|---|---|---|---|
| ידיעו 3045 | חכמה 2451: | אכן 403 | רוח 7307 | היא 1931 | באנוש 582 | ונשמת 5397 | שדי 7706 |
| yodiy'au | chakamah | 'aken | ruach | hiy'a | ba'anoush; | uanishmat | shaday |
| **should teach** | **wisdom** | **But** | ***there is* a spirit** | **he** | **in man** | **and the inspiration of** | **the Almighty** |

Job 32:39 If I have eaten the fruits thereof without money, or have caused the owners thereof to lose their life:40 Let thistles grow instead of wheat, and cockle instead of barley. The words of Job are ended. **Job** 32:1 So these three men ceased to answer Job, because he was righteous in his own eyes.2 Then was kindled the wrath of Elihu the son of Barachel the Buzite, of the kindred of Ram: against Job was his wrath kindled, because he justified himself rather than G-d.3 Also against his three friends was his wrath kindled, because they had found no answer, and yet had condemned Job.4 Now Elihu had waited till Job had spoken, because they were elder than he.5 When Elihu saw that there was no answer in the mouth of these three men, then his wrath was kindled.6 And Elihu the son of Barachel the Buzite answered and said, I am young, and you are very old; wherefore I was afraid, and durst not show you mine opinion.7 I said, Days should speak, and multitude of years should teach wisdom.8 But there is a spirit in man: and the inspiration of the Almighty give them understanding.

32:9 ... 32:10
תבינם 995: | לא 3808 | רבים 7227 | יחכמו 2449 | וזקנים 2205 | יבינו 995 | משפט 4941: | לכן 3651
tabiynem. la' rabiym yechkamu; uazqeniym, yabiynu mishapat. laken
**gives them understanding not *always* Great men are wise neither the aged do understand judgment Therefore**

32:11
אמרתי 559 | שמעה 8085 | לי 3807a | אחוה 2331 | דעי 1843 | אף 637 | אני 589: | הן 2005 | הוחלתי 3176 | לדבריכם 1697 | אזין 238 | עד 5704
'amartiy shim'ah liy; 'achaueh de'ay 'ap 'aniy. hen houchaltiy ladibreykem, 'aziyn 'ad
**I said Hearken to me will show mine opinion also I Behold I waited for your words I gave ear to**

32:12
תבונתיכם 8394 | עד 5704 | תחקרון 2713 | מלין 4405: | ועדיכם 5704 | אתבונן 995 | והנה 2009 | אין 369 | לאיוב 347
tabunouteykem; 'ad tachqarun miliyn. ua'adeykem, 'atbounan uahineh 'aeyn la'ayoub
**your reasons while you searched out what to say Yea unto you I attended and behold *there was* none Job**

32:13
מוכיח 3198 | עונה 6030 | אמריו 561 | מכם 4480: | פן 6435 | תאמרו 559 | מצאנו 4672 | חכמה 2451 | אל 410
moukiyach; 'auneh 'amarayu mikem. pen ta'maru matza'nu chakamah 'ael
**that convinced *or* that answered his words of you Lest you should say We have found out wisdom El**

32:14
ידפנו 5086 | לא 3808 | איש 376: | ולא 3808 | ערך 6186 | אלי 413 | מלין 4405 | ובאמריכם 561 | לא 3808
yidpenu la' 'aysh. uala' 'arak 'aelay miliyn; uab'amreykem, la'
**thrust him down not man Now not he has directed against me *his* words with your speeches neither**

32:15 ... 32:16
אשיבנו 7725: | חתו 2865 | לא 3808 | ענו 6030 | עוד 5750 | העתיקו 6275 | מהם 1992 | מלים 4405:
'ashiybenu. chatu la' 'anu 'aud; he'atiyqu mehem miliym.
**will I answer him They were amazed no they answered more left off they speaking**

32:17
והוחלתי 3176 | כי 3588 | לא 3808 | ידברו 1696 | כי 3588 | עמדו 5975 | לא 3808 | ענו 6030 | עוד 5750: | אענה 6030 | אף 637 | אני 589
uahouchaltiy kiy la' yadaberu; kiy 'amadu, la' 'anu 'aud. 'a'neh 'ap 'aniy
**When I had waited for not they spoke but stood still no *and* answered more *I said* will answer also I**

32:18 ... 32:19
חלקי 2506 | אחוה 2331 | דעי 1843 | אף 637 | אני 589: | כי 3588 | מלתי 4390 | מלים 4405 | הציקתני 6693 | רוח 7307 | בטני 990: | הנה 2009
chelqiy; 'achaueh da'ay 'ap 'aniy. kiy maletiy miliym; hetziyqatniy, ruach bitniy. hineh
**my part will show mine opinion also I For I am full of matter constrained the spirit within me Behold**

32:20
בטני 990 | כיין 3196 | לא 3808 | יפתח 6605 | כאבות 178 | חדשים 2319 | יבקע 1234: | אדברה 1696
bitniy, kayayin la' yipateach; ka'about chadashiym, yibaqea'. 'adabrah
**my belly *is* as wine no *which* has vent like bottles new it is ready to burst I will speak**

32:21
וירוח 7304 | לי 3807a | אפתח 6605 | שפתי 8193 | ואענה 6030: | אל 408 | נא 4994 | אשא 5375 | פני 6440 | איש 376
uayiruach liy; 'aptach sapatay ua'a'aneh. 'al naa' 'asa' paney 'aysh;
**that I may be refreshed to me I will open my lips and answer not I pray you Let me accept person *any* man's**

32:22
ואל 413 | אדם 120 | לא 3808 | אכנה 3655: | כי 3588 | לא 3808 | ידעתי 3045 | אכנה 3655 | כמעט 4592
ua'al 'adam, la' 'akaneh. kiy la' yada'tiy 'akaneh; kima'at,
**unto man neither let me give flattering titles For not I know to give flattering titles soon**

ישאני 5375 | עשני 6213:
yisa'aeniy 'aseniy.
**would take me away *in so doing* my maker**

Job 32:9 Great men are not always wise: neither do the aged understand judgment.10 Therefore I said, Hearken to me; I also will show mine opinion.11 Behold, I waited for your words; I gave ear to your reasons, whilst you searched out what to say.12 Yea, I attended unto you, and, behold, there was none of you that convinced Job, or that answered his words:13 Lest you should say, We have found out wisdom: G-d thrusteth him down, not man.14 Now he has not directed his words against me: neither will I answer him with your speeches.15 They were amazed, they answered no more: they left off speaking.16 When I had waited, (for they spoke not, but stood still, and answered no more;)17 I said, I will answer also my part, I also will show mine opinion.18 For I am full of matter, the spirit within me constraineth me.19 Behold, my belly is as wine which has no vent; it is ready to burst like new bottles.20 I will speak, that I may be refreshed: I will open my lips and answer.21 Let me not, I pray you, accept any man's person, neither let me give flattering titles unto man.22 For I know not to give flattering titles; in so doing my maker would soon take me away.

**Job 33:1** … **33:2**

199 ואולם | 8085 שמע | 4994 נא | 347 איוב | 4405 מלי | 3605 וכל | 1697 דברי | 238: האזינה | 2009 הנה | 4994 נא | 6605 פתחתי

ua'aulam, shama' naa' 'ayoub milay; uakal dabaray ha'aziynah. hineh naa' patachtiy

**Wherefore hear I pray you Job my speeches and all my words listen to Behold now I have opened**

**33:3**

6310 פי | 1696 דברה | 3956 לשוני | 2441: בחכי | 3476 ישר | 3820 לבי | 561 אמרי | 1847 ודעת

piy; dibrah lashouniy bachikiy. yosher libiy 'amaray; uada'at

**my mouth has spoken my tongue in my mouth *shall be of* the uprightness of my heart My words and knowledge**

**33:4** … **33:5**

8193 שפתי | 1305 ברור | 4448: מללו | 7307 רוח | 410 אל | 6213 עשתני | 5397 ונשמת | 7706 שדי | 2421: תחיני

sapatay, barur milelu. ruach 'ael 'asataniy; uanishmat shaday tachayeniy.

**my lips clearly shall utter The Spirit of El has made me and the breath of the Almighty has given me life**

**33:6**

518 אם | 3201 תוכל | 7725 השיבני | 6186 ערכה | 6440 לפני | 3320: התיצבה | 2005 הן | 589 אני | 6310 כפיך

'am tukal hashiybeniy; 'arkah lapanay, hityatzabah. hen 'aniy kapiyka

**If you can answer me set *your words* in order before me stand up Behold I *am* according to your wish**

**33:7**

410 לאל | 2563 מחמר | 7169 קרצתי | 1571 גם | 589: אני | 2009 הנה | 367 אמתי | 3808 לא | 1204 תבעתך | 405 ואכפי | 5921 עליך

la'ael; mechomer, qoratzatiy gam 'aniy. hineh 'aematiy la' taba'ateka; ua'akpiy, 'aleyka

**in El's *stead* out of the clay am formed also I Behold my terror not shall make you afraid my hand upon you**

**33:8** … **33:9**

3808 לא | 3513: יכבד | 389 אך | 559 אמרת | 241 באזני | 6963 וקול | 4405 מלין | 8085: אשמע

la' yikbad. 'ak 'amarta ba'azanay; uaqoul miliyn 'ashma.

**neither shall be heavy Surely you have spoken in mine hearing and the voice of *your* words *saying* I have heard**

**33:10**

2134 זך | 589 אני | 1097 בלי | 6588 פשע | 2643 חף | 595 אנכי | 3808 ולא | 5771 עון | 3807a: לי | 2005 הן | 8569 תנואות

zak 'aniy, baliy pasha' chap 'anokiy; uala' 'auon liy. hen tanu'aut

***am* clean I without transgression *am* innocent I and neither *is there* iniquity in me Behold occasions**

**33:11** … **33:12**

5921 עלי | 4672 ימצא | 2803 יחשבני | 341 לאויב | 3807a: לו | 7760 ישם | 5465 בסד | 7272 רגלי | 8104 ישמר | 3605 כל | 734: ארחתי

'alay yimtza'; yachshabeniy la'auyeb lou'. yasem basad raglay; yishmor, kal 'arachotay.

**against me he finds he count me for enemy his He put in the stocks my feet he mark all my paths**

**33:13**

2005 הן | 2063 זאת | 3808 לא | 6663 צדקת | 6030 אענך | 3588 כי | 7235 ירבה | 433 אלוה | 582: מאנוש | 4069 מדוע | 413 אליו

hen za't la' tzadaqta 'a'aneka; kiy yirbeh 'alouah, me'anoush. madua' 'aelayu

**Behold *in* this not you are just I will answer you that is greater Elohim than man Why against him?**

**33:14**

7378 ריבות | 3588 כי | 3605 כל | 1697 דבריו | 3808 לא | 6030: יענה | 3588 כי | 259 באחת | 1696 ידבר | 410 אל | 8147 ובשתים | 3808 לא

riybouta; kiy kal dabarayu, la' ya'aneh. kiy ba'achat yadaber 'ael; uabishtayim, la'

**do you strive for any of his matters not he gives account of For once speak El yea twice not**

**33:15**

7789: ישורנה | 2472 בחלום | 2384 חזיון | 3915 לילה | 5307 בנפל | 8639 תרדמה | 5921 על | 582 אנשים | 8572 בתנומות | 5921 עלי

yashurenah. bachaloum chezyoun layalah, binpol tardemah 'al 'anashiym; bitnumout, 'aley

***yet man* perceive it In a dream in a vision of the night when fall deep sleep upon men in slumberings upon**

**33:16** … **33:17**

4904: משכב | 227 אז | 1540 יגלה | 241 אזן | 582 אנשים | 4561 ובמסרם | 2856: יחתם | 5493 להסיר | 120 אדם

mishkab. 'az yigleh 'azen 'anashiym; uabmosaram yachtem. lahasiyr 'adam

**the bed Then he open the ears of men and their instruction seal That he may withdraw man**

**Job** 33:1 Wherefore, Job, I pray you, hear my speeches, and hear to all my words.2 Behold, now I have opened my mouth, my tongue has spoken in my mouth.3 My words shall be of the uprightness of my heart: and my lips shall utter knowledge clearly.4 The Spirit of G-d has made me, and the breath of the Almighty has given me life.5 If you canst answer me, set your words in order before me, stand up.6 Behold, I am according to your wish in G-d's stead: I also am formed out of the clay.7 Behold, my terror shall not make you afraid, neither shall my hand be heavy upon you.8 Surely you have spoken in mine hearing, and I have heard the voice of your words, saying,9 I am clean without transgression, I am innocent; neither is there iniquity in me.10 Behold, he findeth occasions against me, he counteth me for his enemy,11 He put my feet in the stocks, he marketh all my paths.12 Behold, in this you are not just: I will answer you, that G-d is greater than man.13 Why dost you strive against him? for he give not account of any of his matters.14 For G-d speaketh once, yea twice, yet man perceiveth it not.15 In a dream, in a vision of the night, when deep sleep fall upon men, in slumberings upon the bed; 16 Then he openeth the ears of men, and sealeth their instruction,17 That he may withdraw man from his purpose, and hide pride from man.

33:18

מעשה 4639 | וגוה 1466 | מגבר 1397 | יכסה 3680: | יחשך 2820 | נפשו 5315 | מני 4480 | שחת 7845 | וחיתו 2416 | מעבר 5674

ma'aseh; uageuah migeber yakaseh. yachsok napshou miniy shachat; uachayatou, me'abor

*from his* purpose and pride from man hide He keep back his soul from the pit and his life from perishing

33:19 ... 33:20

בשלח 7973: | והוכח 3198 | במכאוב 4341 | על 5921 | משכבו 4904 | וריב 7379 | עצמיו 6106 | אתן 386:

bashalach. uahukach bamak'aub 'al mishkabou; uariyb 'atzamayu 'aetan.

by the sword He is chastened also with pain upon his bed and the multitude of his bones with strong *pain*

33:21

וזהמתו 2092 | חיתו 2416 | לחם 3899 | ונפשו 5315 | מאכל 3978 | תאוה 8378: | יכל 3615 | בשרו 1320 | מראי 7210

uazihamatu chayatou lachem; uanapshou, ma'akal ta'auah. yikel basarou mero'ay;

So that abhore his life bread and his soul meat dainty is consumed away His flesh that it cannot be seen

33:22

ושפי 8205 | עצמותיו 6106 | לא 3808 | ראו 7200: | ותקרב 7126 | לשחת 7845 | נפשו 5315 | וחיתו 2416

uashepiy atzamoutayu, la' ru'au. uatiqrab lashachat napshou; uachayatou,

and stick out. his bones not *that* were seen Yea draw near unto the grave his soul and his life

33:23

לממתים 4191: | אם 518 | יש 3426 | עליו 5921 | מלאך 4397 | מליץ | אחד 259 | מני 4480 | אלף 505 | להגיד 5046 | לאדם 120

lamitiym. 'am yesh 'alayu mal'ak, meliytz, 'achad miniy 'alep; lahagiyd la'adam

to the destroyers If there be with him a messenger an interpreter one among a thousand to show unto man

33:24

ישרו 3476: | ויחננו 2603 | ויאמר 559 | פדעהו 6308 | מרדת 3381 | שחת 7845 | מצאתי 4672

yasharou. uayachunenu, uaya'mer, pada'aehu meredet shachat, matza'tiy

his uprightness Then he is gracious unto him and saith Deliver him from going down to the pit I have found

33:25 ... 33:26

כפר 3724: | רטפש 7375 | בשרו 1320 | מנער 5290 | ישוב 7725 | לימי 3117 | עלומיו 5934: | יעתר 6279 | אל 413

koper. rutapash basarou mino'ar; yashub, liymey 'alumayu. ye'atar 'al

a ransom shall be fresher His flesh than a child's he shall return to the days of his youth He shall pray unto

אלוה 433 | וירצהו 7521 | וירא 7200 | פניו 6440 | בתרועה 8643 | וישב 7725 | לאנוש 582

'alouah uayirtzehu, uayar'a panayu bitaru'ah; uayasheb le'anoush,

Elohim and he will be favourable unto him and he shall see his face with joy for he will render unto man

33:27

צדקתו 6666: | ישר 7789 | על 5921 | אנשים 582 | ויאמר 559 | חטאתי 2398 | וישר 3477 | העויתי 5753 | ולא 3808

tzidqatou. yashor 'al 'anashiym, uaya'mer, chata'tiy uayashar he'aueytiy, uala'

his righteousness He looks upon men and *if any* say I have sinned and right perverted *that which was* and not

33:28 ... 33:29

שוה 7737 | לי 3807a: | פדה 6299 | נפשי 5315 | מעבר 5674 | בשחת 7845 | וחיתי 2416 | באור 216 | תראה 7200: | הן 2005 | כל 3605

shabah liy. padah napshiy me'abor bashachat; uachayatiy ba'aur tir'ah. hen kal

it profited me He will deliver his soul from going into the pit and his life the light shall see Lo' all

33:30

אלה 428 | יפעל 6466 | אל 410 | פעמים 6471 | שלוש 7969 | עם 5973 | גבר 1397: | להשיב 7725 | נפשו 5315 | מני 4480 | שחת 7845 | לאור 215

'aeleh yip'al 'ael; pa'amayim shaloush 'am gaber. lahashiyb napshou miniy shachat; lea'aur,

these *things* work El often times with man To bring back his soul from the pit to be enlightened

33:31 ... 33:32

באור 216 | החיים 2416: | הקשב 7181 | איוב 347 | שמע 8085 | לי 3807a | החרש 2790 | ואנכי 595 | אדבר 1696: | אם 518

ba'aur hachayiyim. haqsheb 'ayoub shama' liy; hacharesh, ua'anokiy 'adaber. 'am

with the light of the living Mark well O Job listen unto me hold your peace and I will speak If

Job 33:18 He keep back his soul from the pit, and his life from perishing by the sword.19 He is chastened also with pain upon his bed, and the multitude of his bones with strong pain:20 So that his life abhorreth bread, and his soul dainty meat.21 His flesh is consumed away, that it cannot be seen; and his bones that were not seen stick out.22 Yea, his soul draweth near unto the grave, and his life to the destroyers.23 If there be a messenger with him, an interpreter, one among a thousand, to show unto man his uprightness:24 Then he is gracious unto him, and saith, Deliver him from going down to the pit: I have found a ransom.25 His flesh shall be fresher than a child's: he shall return to the days of his youth:26 He shall pray unto G-d, and he will be favorable unto him: and he shall see his face with joy: for he will render unto man his righteousness.27 He look upon men, and if any say, I have sinned, and perverted that which was right, and it profited me not;28 He will deliver his soul from going into the pit, and his life shall see the light.29 Lo, all these things worketh G-d oftentimes with man,30 To bring back his soul from the pit, to be enlightened with the light of the living. 31 Mark well, O Job, hear unto me: hold your peace, and I will speak.

33:33

יש 3426 מלין 4405 השיבני 7725 דבר 1696 כי 3588 חפצתי 2654 צדקך 6663: אם 518 אין 369 אתה 859 שמע 8085 לי 3807a

yesh miliyn hashiybeniy; daber, kiy chapatztiy tzadqeka. 'am 'ayin 'atah shama' liy;

**you have any thing to say answer me speak for I desire to justify you If not you listen unto me**

החרש 2790 ואאלפך 502 חכמה 2451:

hacharesh, ua'a'alepka chakamah

**hold your peace and I shall teach you wisdom**

**Job 34:1** 34:2

ויען 6030 אליהוא 453 ויאמר 559: שמעו 8085 חכמים 2450 מלי 4405 וידעים 3045

uaya'an 'aliyhu'a, uaya'mar. shim'au chakamiym milay; uayoda'aym,

**Furthermore answered Elihu and said Hear O you wise *men* my words and you that have knowledge**

34:3 34:4

האזינו 238 לי 3807a: כי 3588 אזן 241 מלין 4405 תבחן 974 וחך 2441 יטעם 2938 לאכל 398: משפט 4941 נבחרה 977 לנו 3807a

ha'aziynu liy. kiy 'azen miliyn tibchan; uachek, yit'am le'akol. mishapat nibcharah lanu;

**give ear unto me For the ear words tries as the mouth taste meat judgment Let us choose to us**

34:5

נדעה 3045 בינינו 996 מה 4100 טוב 2896: כי 3588 אמר 559 איוב 347 צדקתי 6663 ואל 410 הסיר 5493

neda'ah beyneynu mah toub. kiy 'amar 'ayoub tzadaqtiy; ua'ael, hesiyr

**let us know among ourselves what *is* good For has said Job I am righteous and El has taken away**

34:6 34:7

משפטי 4941: על 5921 משפטי 4941 אכזב 3576 אנוש 605 חצי 2671 בלי 1097 פשע 6588: מי 4310 גבר 1397 כאיוב 347

mishpatiy. 'al mishpatiy 'akazeb; 'anush chitziy baliy pasha'. miy' geber ka'ayoub;

**my judgment against my right? Should I lie *is* incurable my wound without transgression What man *is* like Job**

34:8

ישתה 8354 לעג 3933 כמים 4325: וארח 732 לחברה 2274 עם 5973 פעלי 6466 און 205 וללכת 1980 עם 5973 אנשי 582

yishteh la'ag kamayim. ua'arach lachebrah 'am po'aley 'auen; ualaleket, 'am 'anshey

***who* drink up scorning like water? Which goes in company with the workers of iniquity and walks with men**

34:9 34:10

רשע 7562: כי 3588 אמר 559 לא 3808 יסכן 5532 גבר 1397 ברצתו 7521 עם 5973 אלהים 430: לכן 3651

resha'. kiy 'amar la' yiskan gaber; birtzotou, 'am 'alohiym. laken

**wicked For he has said nothing It profiteth a man that he should delight himself with Elohim Therefore**

אנשי 582 לבב 3824 שמעו 8085 לי 3807a חלילה 2486 לאל 410 מרשע 7562 ושדי 7706

'anshey lebab, shim'au liy chalilah la'ael meresha', uashaday

**you men of understanding listen unto me far be it from El *that he should do* wickedness and *from* the Almighty**

34:11

מעול 7566: כי 3588 פעל 6467 אדם 120 ישלם 7999 לו 3807a וכארח 734

me'auel. kiy po'al 'adam yashalem lou'; uak'arach

***that he should commit* iniquity For the work of a man shall he render unto him and according to *his* ways**

34:12 34:13

איש 376 ימצאנו 4672: אף 637 אמנם 551 אל 410 לא 3808 ירשיע 7561 ושדי 7706 לא 3808 יעות 5791 משפט 4941:

'aysh, yamtzi'anu. 'ap 'amnam, 'ael la' yarshiya'; uashaday, la' ya'auet mishapat.

**every man cause to find Yea surely El not will do wickedly the Almighty neither will pervert judgment**

34:14

מי 4310 פקד 6485 עליו 5921 ארצה 776 ומי 4310 שם 7760 תבל 8398 כלה 3605: אם 518 ישים 7760 אליו 413

miy' paqad 'alayu 'aratzah; uamiy sam tebel kulah. 'am yasiym 'aelayu

**Who has given him a charge him over the earth? or who has disposed world? the whole If he set upon man**

Job 33:32 If you have anything to say, answer me: speak, for I desire to justify you.33 If not, hear unto me: hold your peace, and I shall teach you wisdom. **Job** 34:1 Furthermore Elihu answered and said,2 Hear my words, O you wise men; and give ear unto me, you that have knowledge.3 For the ear trieth words, as the mouth tasteth meat.4 Let us choose to us judgment: let us know among ourselves what is good.5 For Job has said, I am righteous: and G-d has taken away my judgment.6 Should I lie against my right? my wound is incurable without transgression.7 What man is like Job, who drinketh up scorning like water?8 Which go in company with the workers of iniquity, and walk with wicked men.9 For he has said, It profiteth a man nothing that he should delight himself with G-d.10 Therefore hear unto me, you men of understanding: far be it from G-d, that he should do wickedness; and from the Almighty, that he should commit iniquity.11 For the work of a man shall he render unto him, and cause every man to find according to his ways.12 Yea, surely G-d will not do wickedly, neither will the Almighty pervert judgment.13 Who has given him a charge over the earth? or who has disposed the whole world?14 If he set his heart upon man, if he gather unto himself his spirit and his breath;

34:15
לבו 3820 רוחו 7307 ונשמתו 5397 אליו 413 יאסף 622: יגוע 1478 כל 3605 בשר 1320 יחד 3162 ואדם 120 על 5921 עפר 6083
libou; ruachou uanishmatou, 'aelayu ye'asop. yigua' kal basar yachad; ua'adam, 'al 'apar
**his heart his spirit and his breath unto himself *if* he gather shall perish All flesh together and man unto dust**

34:16 34:17
ישוב 7725: ואם 518 בינה 998 שמעה 8085 זאת 2063 האזינה 238 לקול 6963 מלי 4405: האף 637
yashub. ua'am biynah shim'ah za't; ha'aziynah, laqoul milay. ha'ap
**shall turn again If now *you have* understanding hear this listen to the voice of my words even**

34:18
שונא 8130 משפט 4941 יחבוש 2280 ואם 518 צדיק 6662 כביר 3524 תרשיע 7561: האמר 559 למלך 4428
sounea' mishapat yachaboush; ua'am tzadiyq kabiyr tarshiya'. ha'amour lamelek
**he that hate right Shall govern? and if just? *him that is* most will you condemn *Is it fit* to say to a king**

34:19
בליעל 1100 רשע 7563 אל 413 נדיבים 5081: אשר 834 לא 3808 נשא 5375 פני 6440
baliya'al; rasha', 'al nadiybiym. 'asher la' nasa' paney
***You are* wicked? *You are* ungodly? *and* to princes *How much less to him* that not accept the persons of**

34:20
שרים 8269 ולא 3808 נכר 5234 שוע 7771 לפני 6440 דל 1800 כי 3588 מעשה 4639 ידיו 3027 כלם 3605: רגע 7281
sariym, uala' nikar shoua' lipney dal; kiy ma'aseh yadayu kulam. rega'
**princes nor regard the rich more than the poor? for *are* the work of his hands they all In a moment**

ימתו 4191 וחצות 2676 לילה 3915 יגעשו 1607 עם 5971 ויעברו 5674 ויסירו 5493 אביר 47 לא 3808
yamutu uachatzout layalah yago'ashu 'am uaya'abiru; uayasiyru 'abiyr, la'
**shall they die and at mid night shall be troubled the people and pass away and shall be taken away the mighty without**

34:21 34:22
ביד 3027: כי 3588 עיניו 5869 על 5921 דרכי 1870 איש 376 וכל 3605 צעדיו 6806 יראה 7200: אין 369 חשך 2822 ואין 369
bayad. kiy 'aeynayu 'al darkey 'aysh; uakal tza'adayu yir'ah. 'aeyn choshek ua'aeyn
**hand For his eyes *are* upon the ways of man and all his goings he see *There is* no darkness nor**

34:23
צלמות 6757 להסתר 5641 שם 8033 פעלי 6466 און 205: כי 3588 לא 3808 על 5921 איש 376 ישים 7760
tzalmauet; lahisater sham po'aley 'auen. kiy la' 'al 'aysh yasiym
**shadow of death may hide *themselves* where the workers of iniquity For not upon man he will lay**

34:24
עוד 5750 להלך 1980 אל 413 אל 410 במשפט 4941: ירע 7489 כבירים 3524 לא 3808 חקר 2714
'aud; lahalok 'al 'ael, bamishpat. yaroa' kabiyriym la' cheqer;
**more *than right* that he should enter with El into judgment He shall break in pieces mighty men without number**

34:25
ויעמד 5975 אחרים 312 תחתם 8478: לכן 3651 יכיר 5234 מעבדיהם 4566 והפך 2015 לילה 3915
uaya'amed 'acheriym tachtam. laken, yakiyr ma'abadeyhem; uahapak layalah,
**and set others in their stead Therefore he knows their works and he overturn *them* in the night**

34:26 34:27
וידכאו 1792: תחת 8478 רשעים 7563 ספקם 5606 במקום 4725 ראים 7200: אשר 834 על 5921 כן 3651
uayidaka'au. tachat rasha'aym sapaqam, bimaqoum ro'aym. 'asher 'al ken
**so that they are destroyed as wicked men He strike them in the open sight of others Because after that**

34:28
סרו 5493 מאחריו 310 וכל 3605 דרכיו 1870 לא 3808 השכילו 7919: להביא 935 עליו 5921
saru me'acharayu; uakal darakayu, la' hiskiylu. lahabiy'a 'alayu
**they turned back from him and any of his ways not would consider So that they cause to come unto him**

Job 34:15 All flesh shall perish together, and man shall turn again unto dust.16 If now you have understanding, hear this: hear to the voice of my words.17 Shall even he that hateth right govern? and will you condemn him that is most just?18 Is it fit to say to a king, Thou are wicked? and to princes, You are ungodly?19 How much less to him that accepteth not the persons of princes, nor regardeth the rich more than the poor? for they all are the work of his hands.20 In a moment shall they die, and the people shall be troubled at midnight, and pass away: and the mighty shall be taken away without hand.21 For his eyes are upon the ways of man, and he see all his goings.22 There is no darkness, nor shadow of death, where the workers of iniquity may hide themselves.23 For he will not lay upon man more than right; that he should enter into judgment with G-d.24 He shall break in pieces mighty men without number, and set others in their stead.25 Therefore he know their works, and he overturneth them in the night, so that they are destroyed.26 He striketh them as wicked men in the open sight of others;27 Because they turned back from him, and would not consider any of his ways:28 So that they cause the cry of the poor to come unto him, and he hear the cry of the afflicted.

34:29
צעקת 6818 דל 1800 וצעקת 6818 עניים 6041 ישמע 8085: והוא 1931 ישקט 8252 ומי 4310 ירשיע 7561
tza'aqat dal; uatza'aqat 'aniyiym yishma'. uahu'a yashqit uamiy yarshiya',
**the cry of the poor the cry of the afflicted he hear When he gives quietness who then can make trouble?**

34:30
ויסתר 5641 פנים 6440 ומי 4310 ישורנו 7789 ועל 5921 גוי 1471 ועל 5921 אדם 120 יחד 3162:
uayaster paniym uamiy yashurenu; ua'al gouy ua'al 'adam yachad.
**and when he hides *his* face who then can behold him? whether *it be done* against a nation or against a man only**

34:31
ממלך 4427 אדם 120 חנף 2611 ממקשי 4170 עם 5971: כי 3588 אל 413 אל 410 האמר 559
mimalok 'adam chanep, mimoqashey 'am. kiy 'al 'ael he'amar
**That reign *the* men hypocrite *not* lest be ensnared the people Surely unto El *it is meet* to be said**

34:32
נשאתי 5375 לא 3808 אחבל 2254: בלעדי 1107 אחזה 2372 אתה 859 הרני 3384 אם 518 עול 5766
nasa'tiy, la' 'achbol. bil'adey 'achezeh 'atah horeniy; 'am 'auel
**I have borne *chastisement* not I will offend *anymore* *That which* not I see you teach me if iniquity**

34:33
פעלתי 6466 לא 3808 אסיף 3254: המעמך 5973 ישלמנה 7999 כי 3588 מאסת 3988
pa'altiy, la' 'asiyp. hame'amaka yashalmenah kiy ma'asta,
**I have done no I will do more *Should it be* according to your mind? he will recompense it whether you refuse *or***

34:34
כי 3588 אתה 859 תבחר 977 ולא 3808 אני 589 ומה 4100 ידעת 3045 דבר 1696: אנשי 582 לבב 3824 יאמרו 559 לי 3807a
kiy 'atah tibchar uala' 'aniy; uamah yada'ta daber. 'anshey lebab ya'maru liy;
**whether you choose and not I therefore what you know speak men of understanding Let tell me**

34:35
וגבר 1397 חכם 2450 שמע 8085 לי 3807a: איוב 347 לא 3808 בדעת 1847 ידבר 1696 ודבריו 1697 לא 3808
uageber chakam, shomea' liy. 'ayoub la' bada'at yadaber; uadbarayu, la'
**and a man wise let listen unto me Job without knowledge has spoken and his words *were* without**

34:36
בהשכיל 7919: אבי 15 יבחן 974 איוב 347 עד 5704 נצח 5331 על 5921 תשבת 8666 באנשי 582 און 205:
bahaskeyl. 'abiy, yibachen 'ayoub 'ad netzach; 'al tashubot, ba'anshey 'auen.
**wisdom My desire may be tried *is that* Job unto the end because of *his* answers for men wicked**

34:37
כי 3588 יסיף 3254 על 5921 חטאתו 2403 פשע 6588 בינינו 996 יספוק 5606 וירב 7235 אמריו 561 לאל 410:
kiy yosiyp 'al chata'tou pesha' beyneynu yispouq; uayereb 'amarayu la'ael.
**For he add unto his sin rebellion *his hands* among us he clappeth and multiply his words against El**

**Job 35:1**
ויען 6030 אליהו 452 ויאמר 559:
uaya'an 'aliyhu', uaya'mar.
**spoke moreover Elihu and said**

35:2
הזאת 2063 חשבת 2803 למשפט 4941 אמרת 559 צדקי 6664
haza't chashabta lamishpat; 'amarta, tzidqiy
**this Think you to be right *that* you said My righteousness**

מאל 410:
me'ael.
**more than El's?**

35:3
כי 3588 תאמר 559 מה 4100 יסכן 5532 לך 3807a מה 4100 אעיל 3276
kiy ta'mar mah yiskan lak; mah 'a'ayl,
**For you said What advantage will it be unto you? *and,* What profit shall I have**

מחטאתי 2403:
mechata'tiy.
***if I be cleansed* from my sin?**

35:4
אני 589 אשיבך 7725 מלין 4405 ואת 853 רעיך 7453 עמך 5973:
'aniy 'ashibaka miliyn; ua'at re'ayka 'amak.
**I again will answer you *and* your companions with you**

35:5
הבט 5027
habet
**Look unto**

Job 34:29 When he give quietness, who then can make trouble? and when he hide his face, who then can behold him? whether it be done against a nation, or against a man only:30 That the hypocrite reign not, lest the people be ensnared.31 Surely it is meet to be said unto G-d, I have borne chastisement, I will not offend anymore:32 That which I see not teach you me: if I have done iniquity, I will do no more.33 Should it be according to your mind? he will recompense it, whether you refuse, or whether you choose; and not I: therefore speak what you know.34 Let men of understanding tell me, and let a wise man hear unto me.35 Job has spoken without knowledge, and his words were without wisdom.36 My desire is that Job may be tried unto the end because of his answers for wicked men.37 For he addeth rebellion unto his sin, he clappeth his hands among us, and multiplieth his words against G-d. **Job** 35:1 Elihu spoke moreover, and said,2 Thinkest you this to be right, that you saidst, My righteousness is more than G-d's?3 For you saidst, What advantage will it be unto you? and, What profit shall I have, if I be cleansed from my sin?4 I will answer you, and your companions with you.

35:6

שמים 8064 וראה 7200 ושור 7789 שחקים 7834 גבהו 1361 ממך 4480: אם 518 חטאת 2398 מה 4100 תפעל 6466 בו 871a

shamayim uar'aeh; uashur shachaqiym, gabahu mimeka. 'am chata'ta mah tip'al bou;

**the heavens and see and behold the clouds *which* are higher than you If you sin what do you against him?**

35:7

ורבו 7231 פשעיך 6588 מה 4100 תעשה 6213 לו 3807a: אם 518 צדקת 6663 מה 4100 תתן 5414 לו 3807a או 176

uarabu pasha'ayka, mah ta'aseh lou'. 'am tzadaqta mah titen lou'; 'au

**or be multiplied *if* your transgressions what do you unto him? If you be righteous what give you him? or**

35:8

מה 4100 מידך 3027 יקח 3947: לאיש 376 כמוך 3644 רשעך 7562 ולבן 1121 אדם 120

mah miyadaka yiqach. la'aysh kamouka rish'aka; ualben 'adam,

**what of your hand? receive he *may hurt* a man as you *are* Your wickedness and the son of man**

35:9

צדקתך 6666: מרב 7230 עשוקים 6217 יזעיקו 2199 ישועו 7768

tzidqateka. merob 'ashuqiym yaz'ayqu; yashaua'au

**your righteousness *may profit* By reason of the multitude of oppressions they make *the oppressed* to cry they cry out**

35:10

מזרוע 2220 רבים 7227: ולא 3808 אמר 559 איה 335 אלוה 433 עשי 6213 נתן 5414 זמרות 2158

mizroua' rabiym. uala' 'amar, 'ayeh 'alouah 'asay; noten zamirout

**by reason of the arm of the mighty But none saith Where *is* Elohim my maker who gives songs**

35:11 35:12

בלילה 3915: מלפנו 502 מבהמות 929 ארץ 776 ומעוף 5775 השמים 8064 יחכמנו 2449:

balayalah. malpenu mibahamout 'aretz; uame'aup hashamayim yachakmenu.

**in the night Who teaches us more than the beasts of the earth and than the fowls of heaven? make us wiser**

35:13

שם 8033 יצעקו 6817 ולא 3808 יענה 6030 מפני 6440 גאון 1347 רעים 7451: אך 389 שוא 7723 לא 3808 ישמע 8085 אל 410

sham yitz'aqu uala' ya'aneh; mipaney, ga'aun ra'aym. 'ak shau'a la' yishma' 'ael;

**There they cry but none gives answer because of the pride of evil men Surely vanity not will hear El**

35:14

ושדי 7706 לא 3808 ישורנה 7789: אף 637 כי 3588 תאמר 559 לא 3808 תשורנו 7789 דין 1779 לפניו 6440

uashaday, la' yashurenah. 'ap kiy ta'mar la' tashurenu; diyn lapanayu,

**the Almighty neither will regard it Although when you say not you shall see him *yet* judgment *is* before him**

35:15

ותחולל 2342 לו 3807a: ועתה 6258 כי 3588 אין 369 פקד 6485 אפו 639 ולא 3808 ידע 3045 בפש 6580

uatchoulel lou'. ua'atah, kiy 'ayin paqad 'apou; uala' yada' bapash

**therefore trust you in him But now because *it is* not *so* bhe has visited in his anger yet not he know *it* in extremity**

35:16

מאד 3966: ואיוב 347 הבל 1892 יפצה 6475 פיהו 6310 בבלי 1097 דעת 1847 מלין 4405 יכבר 3527:

ma'ad. ua'ayoub hebel yiptzeh piyhu; bibliy da'at, miliyn yakbir.

**great Therefore Job in vain does open his mouth without knowledge words he multiply**

**Job 36:1** 36:2

ויסף 3254 אליהוא 453 ויאמר 559: כתר 3803 לי 3807a זעיר 2191 ואחוך 2331 כי 3588 עוד 5750

uayosep 'aliyhu'a, uaya'mar. katar liy za'aeyr ua'achaueka; kiy 'aud

**also proceeded Elihu and said Suffer me a little and I will show you that *I have* yet**

36:3 36:4

לאלוה 433 מלים 4405: אשא 5375 דעי 1843 למרחוק 7350 ולפעלי 6466 אתן 5414 צדק 6664: כי 3588

le'alouah miliym. 'asa' de'ay lamerachouq; ualapo'aliy, 'aten tzedeq. kiy

**on El's behalf to speak I will fetch my knowledge from afar and to my Maker will ascribe righteousness For**

Job 35:5 Look unto the heavens, and see; and behold the clouds which are higher than you.6 If you sinnest, what does you against him? or if your transgressions be multiplied, what does you unto him?7 If you be righteous, what givest you him? or what receive he of your hand?8 Thy wickedness may hurt a man as you are; and your righteousness may profit the son of man.9 By reason of the multitude of oppressions they make the oppressed to cry: they cry out by reason of the arm of the mighty.10 But none saith, Where is G-d my maker, who give songs in the night;11 Who teach us more than the beasts of the earth, and make us wiser than the fowls of heaven?12 There they cry, but none give answer, because of the pride of evil men.13 Surely G-d will not hear vanity, neither will the Almighty regard it.14 Although you say you shall not see him, yet judgment is before him; therefore trust you in him.15 But now, because it is not so, he has visited in his anger; yet he know it not in great extremity:16 Therefore doth Job open his mouth in vain; he multiplieth words without knowledge. **Job** 36:1 Elihu also proceeded, and said,2 Suffer me a little, and I will show you that I have yet to speak on G-d's behalf.3 I will fetch my knowledge from afar, and will ascribe righteousness to my Maker.

36:5

אמנם 551 לא 3808 שקר 8267 מלי 4405 תמים 8549 דעות 1844 עמך 5973: הן 2005 אל 410 כביר 3524 ולא 3808
'amanam la' sheqer milay; tamiym de'aut 'amak. hen 'ael kabiyr uala'
**truly not *be* false my words *shall* he that is perfect in knowledge *is* with you Behold El *is* mighty and not**

36:6

ימאס 3988 כביר 3524 כח 3581 לב 3820: לא 3808 יחיה 2421 רשע 7563 ומשפט 4941 עניים 6041
yim'as; kabiyr, koach leb. la' yachayeh rasha'; uamishpat 'aniyiym
**despise *any, he is* mighty in strength *and* wisdom not He preserve the life of the wicked but right to the poor**

36:7

יתן 5414: לא 3808 יגרע 1639 מצדיק 6662 עיניו 5869 ואת 854 מלכים 4428 לכסא 3678 וישיבם 3427
yiten. la' yigra' mitzadiyq, 'aeynayu ua'at melakiym lakisea'; uayoshiybem
**gives not He withdraw from the righteous his eyes *but with* kings *are they* on the throne yea he does establish them**

36:8 36:9

לנצח 5331 ויגבהו 1361: ואם 518 אסורים 631 בזקים 2131 ילכדון 3920 בחבלי 2256 עני 6040: ויגד 5046
lanetzach, uayigbahu. ua'am 'asuriym baziqiym; yilakdun, bachabley 'aniy. uayaged
**for ever and they are exalted And if *they be* bound in fetters *and* be holden in cords of affliction Then he shows**

36:10

להם 1992 פעלם 6467 ופשעיהם 6588 כי 3588 יתגברו 1396: ויגל 1540 אזנם 241 למוסר 4148
lahem pa'alam; uapish'aeyhem, kiy yitgabaru. uayigel 'azanam lamusar;
**them their work and their transgressions that they have exceeded He open also their ear to discipline**

36:11

ויאמר 559 כי 3588 ישבון 7725 מאון 205: אם 518 ישמעו 8085 ויעבדו 5647 יכלו 3615 ימיהם 3117 בטוב 2896
uaya'mer, kiy yashubun me'auen. 'am yishma'au, uaya'abodu yakalu yameyhem batoub;
**and command that they return from iniquity If they obey and serve *him* they shall spend their days in prosperity**

36:12

ושניהם 8141 בנעימים 5273: ואם 518 לא 3808 ישמעו 8085 בשלח 7973 יעברו 5674 ויגועו 1478 כבלי 1097
uashneyhem, bana'aymiym. ua'am la' yishma'au bashelach ya'aboru; uayigua'au, bibliy
**and their years in pleasures But if not they obey by the sword they shall perish and they shall die without**

36:13 36:14

דעת 1847: וחנפי 2611 לב 3820 ישימו 7760 אף 639 לא 3808 ישועו 7768 כי 3588 אסרם 631: תמת 4191 בנער 5290
da'at uachanpey leb yasiymu 'aap; la' yashaua'au, kiy 'asaram. tamot bano'ar
**knowledge But the hypocrites heart heap up wrath not they cry when he bind them die in youth**

36:15

נפשם 5315 וחיתם 2416 בקדשים 6945: יחלץ 2502 עני 6041 בעניו 6040 ויגל 1540 בלחץ 3906
napsham; uachayatam, baqdeshiym. yachaletz 'aniy ba'anyou; uayigel balachatz
**They and their life *is* among the unclean He deliver the poor in his affliction and open in oppression**

36:16

אזנם 241: ואף 637 הסיתך 5496 מפי 6310 צר 6862 רחב 7338 לא 3808 מוצק 4164 תחתיה 8478
'azanam. ua'ap hasiytaka mipiy tzar, rachab la' mutzaq tachteyha;
**their ears Even so would he have removed you out of the strait *into* a broad place *there is* no straitness where**

36:17

ונחת 5183 שלחנך 7979 מלא 4390 דשן 1880: ודין 1779 רשע 7563
uanachat shulchanaka, malea' dashen. uadiyn rasha'
**and that which should be set on your table *should be* full of fatness But the judgment of the wicked**

36:18

מלאת 4390 דין 1779 ומשפט 4941 יתמכו 8551: כי 3588 חמה 2534 פן 6435 יסיתך 5496
malea'ta; diyn uamishpat yitmoku. kiy chemah pen yasiytaka
**you have fulfilled judgment and justice take hold *on you* Because *there is* wrath *beware* lest he take you away**

Job 36:4 For truly my words shall not be false: he that is perfect in knowledge is with you.5 Behold, G-d is mighty, and despiseth not any: he is mighty in strength and wisdom.6 He preserveth not the life of the wicked: but give right to the poor.7 He withdraweth not his eyes from the righteous: but with kings are they on the throne; yea, he doth establish them forever, and they are exalted.8 And if they be bound in fetters, and be holden in cords of affliction;9 Then he show them their work, and their transgressions that they have exceeded.10 He openeth also their ear to discipline, and commandeth that they return from iniquity.11 If they obey and serve him, they shall spend their days in prosperity, and their years in pleasures.12 But if they obey not, they shall perish by the sword, and they shall die without knowledge.13 But the hypocrites in heart heap up wrath: they cry not when he bindeth them.14 They die in youth, and their life is among the unclean.15 He delivereth the poor in his affliction, and openeth their ears in oppression.16 Even so would he have removed you out of the strait into a broad place, where there is no straitness; and that which should be set on your table should be full of fatness.17 But you have fulfilled the judgment of the wicked: judgment and justice take hold on you.18 Because there is wrath, beware lest he take you away with his stroke:

| | | | | | | | | | | |
|---|---|---|---|---|---|---|---|---|---|---|
| בספק 5607 | ורב 7227 | כפר 3724 | אל 408 | יטך 5186: | 36:19 | היערך 6186 | שועך 7769 | לא 3808 | בצר 1222 | וכל 3605 |
| basapeq; | uarab | koper, | 'al | yateka. | | haya'arok | shu'aka | la' | batzar; | uakol, |
| **with *his* stroke** | **and then a great** | **ransom** | **cannot** | **deliver you** | | **Will he esteem** | **your riches?** | ***no* not** | **gold** | **nor all** |

| | | | | | | | | | | | | |
|---|---|---|---|---|---|---|---|---|---|---|---|---|
| מאמצי 3981 | כח 3581: | 36:20 | אל 408 | תשאף 7602 | הלילה 3915 | לעלות 5927 | עמים 5971 | תחתם 8478: | 36:21 | השמר 8104 | אל 408 | תפן 6437 |
| ma'amatzey | koach. | | 'al | tish'ap | halayalah; | la'alout | 'amiym | tachtam. | | hishamer | 'al | tepen |
| **the forces of** | **strength** | | **not** | **Desire** | **the night** | **when are cut off** | **people** | **in their place** | | **Take heed** | **not** | **regard** |

| | | | | | | | | | | | | |
|---|---|---|---|---|---|---|---|---|---|---|---|---|
| אל 413 | און 205 | כי 3588 | על 5921 | זה 2088 | בחרת 977 | מעני 6040: | 36:22 | הן 2005 | אל 410 | ישגיב 7682 | בכחו 3581 | מי 4310 |
| 'al | 'auen; | kiy | 'al | zeh, | bacharta | me'aniy. | | hen | 'ael | yasgiyb | bakochou; | miy' |
| **to** | **iniquity** | **for** | **on** | **this** | **have you chosen** | **rather than affliction** | | **Behold** | **El** | **exalt** | **by his power** | **who** |

| | | | | | | | | | | | |
|---|---|---|---|---|---|---|---|---|---|---|---|
| כמהו 3644 | מורה 3384: | 36:23 | מי 4310 | פקד 6485 | עליו 5921 | דרכו 1870 | ומי 4310 | אמר 559 | פעלת 6466 | עולה 5766: | 36:24 | זכר 2142 |
| kamohu | moureh. | | miy' | paqad | 'alayu | darkou; | uamiy | 'amar, | pa'alta | 'aulah. | | zakor |
| **like him?** | **teach** | | **Who** | **has enjoined** | **him** | **his way?** | **or who can** | **said** | **You have wrought** | **iniquity?** | | **Remember** |

| | | | | | | | | | | | | |
|---|---|---|---|---|---|---|---|---|---|---|---|---|
| כי 3588 | תשגיא 7696 | פעלו 6467 | אשר 834 | שררו 7891 | אנשים 582: | 36:25 | כל 3605 | אדם 120 | חזו 2372 | בו 871a | אנוש 582 | יביט 5027 |
| kiy | tasgiy'a | pa'alou; | 'asher | shoraru | 'anashiym. | | kal | 'adam | chazu | bou; | 'anoush, | yabiyt |
| **that** | **you magnify** | **his work** | **which** | **behold** | **men** | | **Every** | **man** | **may see** | **it** | **man** | **may behold** |

| | | | | | | | | | | |
|---|---|---|---|---|---|---|---|---|---|---|
| מרחוק 7350: | 36:26 | הן 2005 | אל 410 | שגיא 7689 | ולא 3808 | נדע 3045 | מספר 4557 | שניו 8141 | ולא 3808 | חקר 2714: | 36:27 |
| merachouq. | | hen | 'ael | sagiy'a | uala' | neda'; | mispar | shanayu | uala' | cheqer. | |
| ***it* afar off** | | **Behold** | **El** | ***is* great** | **and not** | **we know *him*** | **the number of** | **his years** | **and neither** | **can be searched out** | |

| | | | | | | | | | |
|---|---|---|---|---|---|---|---|---|---|
| כי 3588 | יגרע 1639 | נטפי 5198 | מים 4325 | יזקו 2212 | מטר 4306 | לאדו 108: | 36:28 | אשר 834 | יזלו 5140 |
| kiy | yagara' | nitpey | mayim; | yazoqu | matar | la'aedou. | | 'asher | yizlu |
| **For** | **he make small** | **the drops of** | **water** | **they pour down** | **rain** | **according to the vapour thereof** | | **Which** | **do drop** |

| | | | | | | | | | | |
|---|---|---|---|---|---|---|---|---|---|---|
| שחקים 7834 | ירעפו 7491 | עלי 5921 | אדם 120 | רב 7227: | 36:29 | אף 637 | אם 518 | יבין 995 | מפרשי 4666 | עב 5645 |
| shachaqiym; | yir'apu, | 'aley | 'adam | rab. | | 'ap | 'am | yabiyn | miprasey | 'ab; |
| **the clouds** | ***and* distil** | **upon** | **man** | **abundantly** | | **yet** | **Also** | **can *any* understand** | **the spreadings of** | **the clouds** |

| | | | | | | | | | | |
|---|---|---|---|---|---|---|---|---|---|---|
| תשאות 8663 | סכתו 5521: | 36:30 | הן 2005 | פרש 6566 | עליו 5921 | אורו 216 | ושרשי 8328 | הים 3220 | כסה 3680: | 36:31 | כי 3588 |
| tashu'aut, | sukatou. | | hen | paras | 'alayu | 'auru; | uasharashey | hayam | kisah. | | kiy |
| ***or* the noise of** | **his tabernacle?** | | **Behold** | **he spread** | **upon it** | **his light** | **and the bottom of** | **the sea** | **cover** | | **For** |

| | | | | | | | | | | |
|---|---|---|---|---|---|---|---|---|---|---|
| בם 871a | ידין 1777 | עמים 5971 | יתן 5414 | אכל 400 | למכביר 4342: | 36:32 | על 5921 | כפים 3709 | כסה 3680 | אור 216 |
| bam | yadiyn | 'amiym; | yiten | 'akel | lamakbiyr. | | 'al | kapayim | kisah | 'aur; |
| **by them** | **judge he** | **the people** | **he gives** | **meat** | **in abundance** | | **With** | **clouds** | **he cover** | **the light** |

| | | | | | | | | |
|---|---|---|---|---|---|---|---|---|
| ויצו 6680 | עליה 5921 | במפגיע 6293: | 36:33 | יגיד 5046 | עליו 5921 | רעו 7452 | מקנה 4735 |
| uayatzau | 'aleyha | bamapgiya'. | | yagiyd | 'alayu | re'au; | miqneh, |
| **and command it *not to shine*** | **by** | ***the cloud* that comes betwixt** | | **shows** | **concerning it** | **The noise thereof** | **the cattle** |

| | | |
|---|---|---|
| אף 637 | על 5921 | עולה 5927: |
| 'ap | 'al | auleh. |
| **also** | **concerning** | **the vapour** |

Job 36:18 then a great ransom cannot deliver you.19 Will he esteem your riches? no, not gold, nor all the forces of strength.20 Desire not the night, when people are cut off in their place.21 Take heed, regard not iniquity: for this have you chosen rather than affliction.22 Behold, G-d exalteth by his power: who teach like him?23 Who has enjoined him his way? or who can say, Thou have wrought iniquity?24 Remember that you magnify his work, which men behold.25 Every man may see it; man may behold it afar off.26 Behold, G-d is great, and we know him not, neither can the number of his years be searched out.27 For he make small the drops of water: they pour down rain according to the vapour thereof:28 Which the clouds do drop and distil upon man abundantly.29 Also can any understand the spreadings of the clouds, or the noise of his tabernacle?30 Behold, he spreadeth his light upon it, and covereth the bottom of the sea.31 For by them judgeth he the people; he give meat in abundance.32 With clouds he covereth the light; and commandeth it not to shine by the cloud that cometh betwixt.33 The noise thereof show concerning it, the cattle also concerning the vapour.

| Job 37:1 | | | | | | 37:2 | | | |
|---|---|---|---|---|---|---|---|---|---|
| אף 637 | לזאת 2063 | יחרד 2729 | לבי 3820 | ויתר 5425 | ממקומו 4725: | שמעו 8085 | שמוע 8085 | ברגז 7267 | קלו 6963 |
| 'ap | laza't | yecherad | libiy; | uayitar, | mimaqoumou. | shim'au | shamoua' | barogez | qolou; |
| **also** | **At this** | **tremble** | **my heart** | **and is moved** | **outof his place** | **Hear** | **attentively** | **the noise of** | **his voice** |

| | | | 37:3 | | | | | | |
|---|---|---|---|---|---|---|---|---|---|
| והגה 1899 | מפיו 6310 | יצא 3318: | תחת 8478 | כל 3605 | השמים 8064 | ישרהו 3474 | ואורו 216 | על 5921 | כנפות 3671 |
| uahegeh, | mipiyu | yetzea'. | tachat | kal | hashamayim | yishrehu; | ua'arou, | 'al | kanpout |
| **and the sound** | **his mouth** | ***that* goes out** | **under** | **the whole** | **heaven** | **He direct it** | **and his lightning** | **unto** | **the ends of** |

| | 37:4 | | | | | | | | |
|---|---|---|---|---|---|---|---|---|---|
| הארץ 776: | אחריו 310 | ישאג 7580 | קול 6963 | ירעם 7481 | בקול 6963 | גאונו 1347 | ולא 3808 | יעקבם 6117 | כי 3588 |
| ha'aretz. | 'acharayu | yish'ag | qoul, | yar'aem | baqoul | ga'anou; | uala' | ya'aqbem, | kiy |
| **the earth** | **After it** | **roars** | **a voice** | **he thunders** | **with the voice of** | **his excellency** | **and not** | **he will stay them** | **when** |

| | | 37:5 | | | | | | | 37:6 |
|---|---|---|---|---|---|---|---|---|---|
| ישמע 8085 | קולו 6963: | ירעם 7481 | אל 410 | בקולו 6963 | נפלאות 6381 | עשה 6213 | גדלות 1419 | ולא 3808 | נדע 3045: |
| yishama' | qoulou. | yar'aem | 'ael | baqoulou | nipla'aut; | 'aseh | gadolout, | uala' | neda'. |
| **is heard** | **his voice** | **thunders** | **El** | **with his voice** | **marvellously** | **does he** | **great things** | **cannot** | ***which* we comprehend** |

| | | | | | | | | | 37:7 |
|---|---|---|---|---|---|---|---|---|---|
| כי 3588 | לשלג 7950 | יאמר 559 | הוא 1933 | ארץ 776 | וגשם 1653 | מטר 4306 | וגשם 1653 | מטרות 4306 | עזו 5797: |
| kiy | lashelag | ya'mar, | heuea' | 'aretz | uageshem | matar; | uageshem, | mitrout | 'azu. |
| **For** | **to the snow** | **he saith** | **Be you *on*** | **the earth** | **and rain** | **to the small** | **and rain** | **likewise to the great** | ***of* his strength** |

| | | | | | | | | 37:8 | | | |
|---|---|---|---|---|---|---|---|---|---|---|---|
| ביד 3027 | כל 3605 | אדם 120 | יחתום 2856 | לדעת 3045 | כל 3605 | אנשי 582 | מעשהו 4639: | ותבא 935 | חיה 2416 | במו 1119 | ארב 695 |
| bayad | kal | 'adam | yachtoum; | lada'at, | kal | 'anshey | ma'asehu. | uataba' | chayah | bamou | 'areb; |
| **the hand of** | **every** | **man** | **He seal up** | **that may know** | **all** | **men** | **his work** | **Then go** | **the beasts** | **into** | **dens** |

| | | 37:9 | | | | | 37:10 |
|---|---|---|---|---|---|---|---|
| ובמעונתיה 4585 | תשכן 7931: | מן 4480 | החדר 2315 | תבוא 935 | סופה 5492 | וממזרים 4215 | קרה 7135: |
| uabim'aunoteyha | tishkon. | min | hacheder | tabou'a | supah; | uamimzariym | qarah. |
| **and in their places** | **remain** | **Out of** | **the south** | **comes** | **the whirlwind** | **and out of the north** | **cold** |

| | | | | | | | 37:11 | | |
|---|---|---|---|---|---|---|---|---|---|
| מנשמת 5397 | אל 410 | יתן 5414 | קרח 7140 | ורחב 7341 | מים 4325 | במוצק 4164: | אף 637 | ברי 7377 | יטריח 2959 |
| minishmat | 'ael | yiten | qarach; | uarochab | mayim | bamutzaq. | 'ap | bariy | yatriyach |
| **By the breath of** | **El** | **is given** | **frost** | **and the breadth of** | **the waters** | **is straitened** | **Also** | **by watering** | **he weary** |

| | | | | 37:12 | | | | |
|---|---|---|---|---|---|---|---|---|
| עב 5645 | יפיץ 6327 | ענן 6051 | אורו 216: | והוא 1931 | מסבות 4524 | מתהפך 2015 | בתחבולתו 8458 | לפעלם 6467 |
| 'ab; | yapiytz, | 'anan | 'auru. | uahu'a | masibout | mithapek | batachbulatou | lapa'alam; |
| **the thick cloud** | **he scatters** | **cloud** | **his bright** | **And it** | **round about** | **is turned** | **by his counsels** | **that they may do** |

| | | | | | | | 37:13 | | |
|---|---|---|---|---|---|---|---|---|---|
| כל 3605 | אשר 834 | יצום 6680 | על 5921 | פני 6440 | תבל 8398 | ארצה 776: | אם 518 | לשבט 7626 | אם 518 |
| kal | 'asher | yatzauem | 'al | paney | tebel | 'aratzah. | 'am | lashebet | 'am |
| **whatsoever** | **which** | **he command them** | **upon** | **the face of** | **the world in** | **the earth** | **whether** | **for correction** | **or** |

| | | | | 37:14 | | | | |
|---|---|---|---|---|---|---|---|---|
| לארצו 776 | אם 518 | לחסד 2617 | ימצאהו 4672: | האזינה 238 | זאת 2063 | איוב 347 | עמד 5975 | והתבונן 995 |
| la'artzou; | 'am | lachesed, | yamtzi'aehu. | ha'aziynah | za't | 'ayoub; | 'amod, | uahitbounen |
| **for his land** | **or** | **for mercy** | **He cause it to come** | **Hearken unto** | **this** | **O Job** | **stand still** | **and consider** |

| | | 37:15 | | | | | |
|---|---|---|---|---|---|---|---|
| נפלאות 6381 | אל 410: | התדע 3045 | בשום 7760 | אלוה 433 | עליהם 5921 | והופיע 3313 | אור 216 |
| nipla'aut | 'ael. | hateda' | basum | 'alouah | 'aleyhem; | uahoupiya', | 'aur |
| ***the* wondrous works of** | **El** | **Do you know when** | **disposed** | **Elohim** | **them** | **and caused to shine** | **the light of** |

**Job** 37:1 At this also my heart trembleth, and is moved out of his place.2 Hear attentively the noise of his voice, and the sound that go out of his mouth.3 He directeth it under the whole heaven, and his lightning unto the ends of the earth.4 After it a voice roareth: he thundereth with the voice of his excellency; and he will not stay them when his voice is heard.5 G-d thundereth marvellously with his voice; great things doeth he, which we cannot comprehend.6 For he saith to the snow, Be you on the earth; likewise to the small rain, and to the great rain of his strength.7 He sealeth up the hand of every man; that all men may know his work.8 Then the beasts go into dens, and remain in their places.9 Out of the south cometh the whirlwind: and cold out of the north.10 By the breath of G-d frost is given: and the breadth of the waters is straitened.11 Also by watering he wearieth the thick cloud: he scattereth his bright cloud:12 And it is turned round about by his counsels: that they may do whatsoever he commandeth them upon the face of the world in the earth.13 He causeth it to come, whether for correction, or for his land, or for mercy. 14 Hearken unto this, O Job: stand still, and consider the wondrous works of G-d.15 Dost you know when G-d disposed them, and caused the light of his cloud to shine?

עננו 6051: | **37:16** התדע 3045 | על 5921 | מפלשי 4657 | עב 5645 | מפלאות 4652 | תמים 8549
'ananou. hateda' 'al miplasey 'ab; mipla'aut, tamiym
**his cloud Do you know about the balancings of the clouds the wondrous works of him which is perfect in**

דעים 1843: | **37:17** אשר 834 | בגדיך 899 | חמים 2525 | בהשקט 8252 | ארץ 776 | מדרום 1864: | **37:18**
de'aym. 'asher bagadeyka chamiym; bahashqit 'aretz, midaroum.
**knowledge? How your garments *are* warm when he quieteth the earth by the south *wind*?**

תרקיע 7554 | עמו 5973 | לשחקים 7834 | חזקים 2389 | כראי 7209 | מוצק 3332: | **37:19** הודיענו 3045 | מה 4100
tarqiya' amou lishchaqiym; chazaqiym, kir'ay mutzaq. houdiy'aenu mah
**Have you spread out with him the sky *which is* strong *and* as looking glass? a molten Teach us what**

נאמר 559 | לו 3807a | לא 3808 | נערך 6186 | מפני 6440 | חשך 2822: | **37:20** היספר 5608 | לו 3807a | כי 3588 | אדבר 1696
na'mar lou'; la' na'arok, mipaney choshek. hayasupar lou' kiy 'adaber;
**we shall say unto him cannot *for* we order *our speech* by reason of darkness Shall it be told him that I speak?**

אם 518 | אמר 559 | איש 376 | כי 3588 | יבלע 1104: | **37:21** ועתה 6258 | לא 3808 | ראו 7200 | אור 216 | בהיר 925 | הוא 1931 | בשחקים 7834
'am 'amar 'aysh, kiy yabula'. ua'atah la' ra'au 'aur, bahiyr hua' bashchaqiym;
**if speak a man surely he shall be swallowed up And now not *men* see light *the* bright which *is* in the clouds**

ורוח 7307 | עברה 5674 | ותטהרם 2891: | **37:22** מצפון 6828 | זהב 2091 | יאתה 857 | על 5921 | אלוה 433 | נורא 3372
uaruach 'abarah, uattaharem. mitzapoun zahab ye'ateh; 'al 'alouah, noura'
**but the wind passed and cleanses them out of the north Fair weather he comes with Elohim *is* terrible**

הוד 1935: | **37:23** שדי 7706 | לא 3808 | מצאנהו 4672 | שגיא 7689 | כח 3581 | ומשפט 4941 | ורב 7230
houd. shaday la' matza'nuhu sagiy'a koach; uamishpat uarob
**majesty *Touching* the Almighty cannot we find him out *he is* excellent in power and in judgment and in plenty of**

צדקה 6666 | לא 3808 | יענה 6031: | **37:24** לכן 3651 | יראוהו 3372 | אנשים 582 | לא 3808 | יראה 3372 | כל 3605 | חכמי 2450 | לב 3820:
tzadaqah, la' ya'aneh. laken yarea'uhu 'anashiym; la' yir'ah, kal chakmey leb.
**justice not he will afflict therefore do fear him Men not he respect any *that are* wise of heart**

**Job 38:1** ויען 6030 | יהוה 3068 | את 853 | איוב 347 | מן 4480 | הסערה 5591 | ויאמר 559 | **38:2** מי 4310 | זה 2088 | מחשיך 2821 | עצה 6098
uaya'an Yahuah 'at 'ayoub min has'arah, uaya'mar miy' zeh machshiyk 'aetzah
**Then answered Yahuah Job out of the whirlwind, and said, Who *is* this that darken counsel**

במלין 4405 | בלי 1097 | דעת 1847: | **38:3** אזר 247 | נא 4994 | כגבר 1397 | חלציך 2504 | ואשאלך 7592 | והודיעני 3045: | **38:4**
bamiliyn, baliy da'at. 'azar naa' kageber chalatzeyka; ua'ash'alaka, uahoudiy'aeniy.
**by words without knowledge? Gird up now like a man your loins for I will demand of you and answer you me**

איפה 375 | היית 1961 | ביסדי 3245 | ארץ 776 | הגד 5046 | אם 518 | ידעת 3045 | בינה 998: | **38:5** מי 4310 | שם 7760
'aeypoh hayiyta bayasadiy 'aretz; haged, 'am yada'ta biynah. miy' sam
**Where were you when I laid the foundations of the earth? declare if you have understanding Who has laid**

ממדיה 4461 | כי 3588 | תדע 3045 | או 176 | מי 4310 | נטה 5186 | עליה 5921 | קו 6957: | **38:6** על 5921 | מה 4100
mamadeyha kiy teda'; 'au miy' natah 'aeleyha qau. 'al mah
**the measures thereof if you know? or who has stretched upon it? the line Whereupon how**

Job 37:16 Dost you know the balancings of the clouds, the wondrous works of him which is perfect in knowledge?17 How your garments are warm, when he quieteth the earth by the south wind?18 Hast you with him spread out the sky, which is strong, and as a molten looking glass?19 Teach us what we shall say unto him; for we cannot order our speech by reason of darkness.20 Shall it be told him that I speak? if a man speak, surely he shall be swallowed up.21 And now men see not the bright light which is in the clouds: but the wind pass, and cleanseth them.22 Fair weather cometh out of the north: with G-d is terrible majesty.23 Touching the Almighty, we cannot find him out: he is excellent in power, and in judgment, and in plenty of justice: he will not afflict.24 Men do therefore fear him: he respecteth not any that are wise of heart. **Job** 38:1 Then YHUH answered Job out of the whirlwind, and said,2 Who is this that darkeneth counsel by words without knowledge?3 Gird up now your loins like a man; for I will demand of you, and answer you me.4 Where were you when I laid the foundations of the earth? declare, if you have understanding.5 Who has laid the measures thereof, if you know?

| אדניה 134 | הטבעו 2883 | או 176 | מי 4310 | ירה 3384 | אבן 68 | פנתה 6438: | 38:7 ברן 7442 | יחד 3162 | כוכבי 3556 |
|---|---|---|---|---|---|---|---|---|---|
| 'adaneyha | hataba'au; | 'au | miy' | yarah, | 'aben | pinatah. | baran | yachad | koukabey |
| **the foundations thereof** | **are fastened?** | **or** | **who** | **laid** | **stone** | **the corner thereof** | **When sang** | **together** | **stars** |

| בקר 1242 | ויריעו 7321 | כל 3605 | בני 1121 | אלהים 430: | 38:8 ויסך 5526 | בדלתים 1817 | ים 3220 | בגיחו 1518 |
|---|---|---|---|---|---|---|---|---|
| boqer; | uayariy'au, | kal | baney | 'alohiym. | uayasek | bidlatayim | yam; | bagiychou, |
| ***the* morning** | **and shouted for joy?** | **all** | **all the sons of** | **Elohim** | **Or *who* shut up** | **with doors** | **the sea** | **when it brake forth** |

| מרחם 7358 | יצא 3318: | 38:9 בשומי 7760 | ענן 6051 | לבשו 3830 | וערפל 6205 |
|---|---|---|---|---|---|
| merechem | yetzea'. | basumiy | 'anan | labushou; | ua'arapel, |
| **out of the womb?** | ***as if* it had issued** | **When I made** | **the cloud** | **the garment thereof** | **and thick darkness** |

| חתלתו 2854: | 38:10 ואשבר 7665 | עליו 5921 | חקי 2706 | ואשים 7760 | בריח 1280 | ודלתים 1817: | 38:11 ואמר 559 | עד 5704 |
|---|---|---|---|---|---|---|---|---|
| chatulatou. | ua'ashbor | 'alayu | chuqiy; | ua'asiym, | bariyach | uadlatayim. | ua'amar, | 'ad |
| **a swaddlingband for it** | **And brake up** | **for it** | **my decreed *place*** | **and set** | **bars** | **and doors** | **And said** | **Hitherto** |

| פה 6311 | תבוא 935 | ולא 3808 | תסיף 3254 | ופא 6311 | ישית 7896 | בגאון 1347 | גליך 1530: | 38:12 המימיך 3117 |
|---|---|---|---|---|---|---|---|---|
| poh | tabou'a | uala' | tosiyp; | uapa' | yashiyt, | big'aun | galeyka. | hamiyameyka |
| **here** | **shall you come** | **but no** | **further** | **and here** | **shall be stayed?** | **proud** | **your waves** | **since your days** |

| צוית 6680 | בקר 1242 | ידעתה 3045 | שחר 7837 | מקמו 4725 | 38:13 לאחז 270 |
|---|---|---|---|---|---|
| tziuiyta | boqer; | yida'atah | shachar | maqomou | la'achoz |
| **Have you commanded** | **the morning** | ***and* caused to know** | ***the* dayspring** | **his place** | **That it might take hold** |

| בכנפות 3671 | הארץ 776 | וינערו 5287 | רשעים 7563 | ממנה 4480: | 38:14 תתהפך 2015 | כחמר 2563 | חותם 2368 | ויתיצבו 3320 |
|---|---|---|---|---|---|---|---|---|
| bakanpout | ha'aretz; | uayina'aru | rasha'aym | mimenah. | tithapek | kachomer | choutam; | uayityatzabu, |
| **of the ends of** | **the earth** | **that might be shaken** | **the wicked** | **out of it?** | **It is turned** | **as clay** | ***to* the seal** | **and they stand** |

| כמו 3644 | לבוש 3830: | 38:15 וימנע 4513 | מרשעים 7563 | אורם 216 | וזרוע 2220 | רמה 7311 | תשבר 7665: | 38:16 |
|---|---|---|---|---|---|---|---|---|
| kamou | labush. | uayimana' | merasha'aym | 'auram; | uazaoua' | ramah, | tishaber. | |
| **as** | **a garment** | **And is withholden** | **from the wicked** | **their light** | **and arm** | ***the* high** | **shall be broken** | |

| הבאת 935 | עד 5704 | נבכי 5033 | ים 3220 | ובחקר 2714 | תהום 8415 | התהלכת 1980: | 38:17 הנגלו 1540 |
|---|---|---|---|---|---|---|---|
| haba'ta | 'ad | nibkey | yam; | uabcheqer | tahoum, | hithalakata. | haniglu |
| **Have you entered** | **into** | **the springs of** | **the sea?** | **or in the search of** | **the depth?** | **have you walked** | **Have been opened** |

| לך 3807a | שערי 8179 | מות 4194 | ושערי 8179 | צלמות 6757 | תראה 7200: | 38:18 התבננת 995 | עד 5704 |
|---|---|---|---|---|---|---|---|
| laka | sha'arey | mauet; | uasha'arey | tzalmauet | tir'ah. | hitbonanta | 'ad |
| **unto you?** | **the gates of** | **death** | **or the doors of** | **the shadow of death?** | **have you seen** | **Have you perceived** | **unto** |

| רחבי 7338 | ארץ 776 | הגד 5046 | אם 518 | ידעת 3045 | כלה 3605: | 38:19 אי 335 | זה 2088 | הדרך 1870 | ישכן 7931 | אור 216 |
|---|---|---|---|---|---|---|---|---|---|---|
| rachabey | 'aretz; | haged, | 'am | yada'ta | kulah. | 'aey | zeh | haderek | yishkan | 'aur; |
| **the breadth of** | **the earth?** | **declare** | **if** | **you know** | **it all** | **Where *is*** | **this** | **the way** | **dwell?** | ***where* light** |

| וחשך 2822 | אי 335 | זה 2088 | מקמו 4725: | 38:20 כי 3588 | תקחנו 3947 | אל 413 | גבולו 1366 | וכי 3588 |
|---|---|---|---|---|---|---|---|---|
| uachoshek, | 'aey | zeh | maqomou. | kiy | tiqachenu | 'al | gabulou; | uakiy |
| **and *as for* darkness** | **where *is*** | **its** | **the place thereof** | **That** | **you should take it** | **to** | **the bound thereof** | **and that** |

Job 38:5 or who has stretched the line upon it?6 Whereupon are the foundations thereof fastened? or who laid the corner stone thereof;7 When the morning stars sang together, and all the sons of G-d shouted for joy?8 Or who shut up the sea with doors, when it break forth, as if it had issued out of the womb?9 When I made the cloud the garment thereof, and thick darkness a swaddlingband for it,10 And break up for it my decreed place, and set bars and doors,11 And said, Hitherto shall you come, but no further: and here shall your proud waves be stayed?12 Hast you commanded the morning since your days; and caused the dayspring to know his place;13 That it might take hold of the ends of the earth, that the wicked might be shaken out of it?14 It is turned as clay to the seal; and they stand as a garment.15 And from the wicked their light is withholden, and the high arm shall be broken.16 Hast you entered into the springs of the sea? or have you walked in the search of the depth?17 Have the gates of death been opened unto you? or have you seen the doors of the shadow of death?18 Hast you perceived the breadth of the earth? declare if you know it all.19 Where is the way where light dwell? and as for darkness, where is the place thereof,20 That you should take it to the bound thereof, and that you should know the paths to the house thereof?

| תבין 995 | נתיבות 5410 | ביתו 1004: | 38:21 | ידעת 3045 | כי 3588 | אז 227 | תולד 3205 |
|---|---|---|---|---|---|---|---|
| tabiyn, | natiybout | beytou. | | yada'ta | kiy | 'az | tiualed; |
| **you should know** | **the paths** | ***to* the house thereof?** | | **Know you *it*** | **because** | **then** | **you were born?** |

| ומספר 4557 | ימיך 3117 | רבים 7227: | 38:22 | הבאת 935 | אל 413 | אצרות 214 | שלג 7950 | ואצרות 214 |
|---|---|---|---|---|---|---|---|---|
| uamispar | yameyka | rabiym. | | haba'ta | 'al | 'atzarout | shaleg; | ua'atzarout |
| **or *because* the number of** | **your days** | ***is* great?** | | **Have you entered** | **into** | **the treasures of** | **the snow?** | **the treasures of** |

| ברד 1259 | תראה 7200: | 38:23 | אשר 834 | חשכתי 2820 | לעת 6256 | צר 6862 | ליום 3117 | קרב 7128 |
|---|---|---|---|---|---|---|---|---|
| barad | tir'ah. | | 'asher | chasaktiy | la'et | tzar; | layoum | qarab, |
| **the hail** | **or have you seen** | | **Which** | **I have reserved** | **against the time of** | **trouble** | **against the day of** | **battle** |

| ומלחמה 4421: | 38:24 | אי 335 | זה 2088 | הדרך 1870 | יחלק 2505 | אור 216 | יפץ 6327 | קדים 6921 | עלי 5921 | ארץ 776: | 38:25 | מי 4310 |
|---|---|---|---|---|---|---|---|---|---|---|---|---|
| uamilchamah. | | 'aey | zeh | haderek | yechaleq | 'aur; | yapetz | qadiym | 'aley | 'aretz. | | miy' |
| **and war?** | | ***By* what** | **this** | **the way** | **is parted** | **the light** | ***which* scatters** | **the east wind** | **upon** | **the earth?** | | **Who** |

| פלג 6385 | לשטף 7858 | תעלה 8585 | ודרך 1870 | לחזיז 2385 | קלות 6963: | 38:26 | להמטיר 4305 |
|---|---|---|---|---|---|---|---|
| pilag | lashetep | ta'alah; | uaderek, | lachaziyz | qolout. | | lahamtiyr |
| **has divided** | **for the overflowing of waters** | **a watercourse** | **or a way** | **for the lightning of** | **thunder** | | **To cause it to rain** |

| על 5921 | ארץ 776 | לא 3808 | איש 376 | מדבר 4057 | לא 3808 | אדם 120 | בו 871a: | 38:27 | להשביע 7646 | שאה 7722 |
|---|---|---|---|---|---|---|---|---|---|---|
| 'al | 'aretz | la' | 'aysh; | midbar, | la' | 'adam | bou. | | lahasbiya' | sho'ah |
| **on** | **the earth *where*** | **no** | **man** | ***is on* the wilderness** | ***there is* no** | **man** | **wherein** | | **To satisfy** | **the desolate** |

| ומשאה 4875 | ולהצמיח 6779 | מצא 4161 | דשא 1877: | 38:28 | היש 3426 | למטר 4306 | אב 1 | או 176 | מי 4310 |
|---|---|---|---|---|---|---|---|---|---|
| uamsho'ah; | ualhatzmiyach, | motza' | desha'. | | hayesh | lamatar | 'ab; | 'au | miy' |
| **and waste *ground*** | **and to cause to spring forth** | **the bud** | **the tender herb** | | **Has** | **the rain** | **a father?** | **or** | **who** |

| הוליד 3205 | אגלי 96 | טל 2919: | 38:29 | מבטן 990 | מי 4310 | יצא 3318 | הקרח 7140 | וכפר 3713 | שמים 8064 | מי 4310 |
|---|---|---|---|---|---|---|---|---|---|---|
| houliyd, | 'agley | tal. | | mibeten | miy' | yatza' | haqarach; | uakpor | shamayim | miy' |
| **has begotten** | **the drops of** | **dew?** | | **Out of womb** | **whose** | **came** | **the ice?** | **and the hoary frost of** | **heaven** | **who** |

| ילדו 3205: | 38:30 | כאבן 68 | מים 4325 | יתחבאו 2244 | ופני 6440 | תהום 8415 | יתלכדו 3920: | 38:31 | התקשר 7194 |
|---|---|---|---|---|---|---|---|---|---|
| yaladou. | | ka'aben | mayim | yitchaba'au; | uapaney | tahoum, | yitlakadu. | | hataqasher |
| **has gendered it?** | | **as *with* a stone** | **The waters** | **are hid** | **and the face** | **the deep** | **is frozen** | | **Can you bind** |

| מעדנות 4575 | כימה 3598 | או 176 | משכות 4189 | כסיל 3685 | תפתח 6605: | 38:32 | התציא 3318 | מזרות 4216 |
|---|---|---|---|---|---|---|---|---|
| ma'adanout | kiymah; | 'au | moshakout | kasiyl | tapateach. | | hatotziy'a | mazarout |
| ***the* sweet influences of** | **Pleiades (*seven stars*)** | **or** | **the bands of** | **Orion?** | **loose** | | **Can you bring forth** | **Mazzaroth** |

| בעתו 6256 | ועיש 5906 | על 5921 | בניה 1121 | תנחם 5148: | 38:33 | הידעת 3045 | חקות 2708 | שמים 8064 | אם 518 | תשים 7760 |
|---|---|---|---|---|---|---|---|---|---|---|
| ba'atou; | ua'ayish, | 'al | baneyha | tanchem. | | hayada'ata | chuqout | shamayim; | 'am | tasiym |
| **in his season?** | **or Arcturus wit** | | **his sons?** | **can you guide** | | **Know you** | **the ordinances of** | **the heavens?** | **or** | **can your set** |

| משטרו 4896 | בארץ 776: | 38:34 | התרים 7311 | לעב 5645 | קולך 6963 | ושפעת 8229 | מים 4325 |
|---|---|---|---|---|---|---|---|
| mishtarou | ba'aretz. | | hatariym | la'ab | qouleka; | uaship'at | mayim |
| **the dominion thereof in the earth?** | | | **Can you lift up to the clouds your voice that abundance of** | | | | **waters** |

Job 38:21 Know you it, because you were then born? or because the number of your days is great?22 Hast you entered into the treasures of the snow? or have you seen the treasures of the hail,23 Which I have reserved against the time of trouble, against the day of battle and war?24 By what way is the light parted, which scattereth the east wind upon the earth?25 Who has divided a watercourse for the overflowing of waters, or a way for the lightning of thunder;26 To cause it to rain on the earth, where no man is; on the wilderness, wherein there is no man;27 To satisfy the desolate and waste ground; and to cause the bud of the tender herb to spring forth?28 Hath the rain a father? or who has begotten the drops of dew?29 Out of whose womb came the ice? and the hoary frost of heaven, who has gendered it?30 The waters are hid as with a stone, and the face of the deep is frozen.31 Canst you bind the sweet influences of Pleiades, or loose the bands of Orion?32 Canst you bring forth Mazzaroth in his season? or canst you guide Arcturus with his sons?33 Know you the ordinances of heaven? canst you set the dominion thereof in the earth?34 Canst you lift up your voice to the clouds,

| | 38:35 | | | | | | 38:36 | |
|---|---|---|---|---|---|---|---|---|
| תכסך 3680: | התשלח 7971 | ברקים 1300 | וילכו 1980 | ויאמרו 559 | לך 3807a | הננו 2005: | מי 4310 | שת 7896 |
| takaseka. | hatshalach | baraqiym | uayeleku; | uaya'maru | laka | hinenu. | miy | shat |
| **may cover you?** | **Can you send** | **lightnings** | **that they may go** | **and say** | **unto you** | **Here we *are*?** | **Who** | **has put** |

| | | | | | | | 38:37 | | |
|---|---|---|---|---|---|---|---|---|---|
| בטחות 2910 | חכמה 2451 | או 176 | מי 4310 | נתן 5414 | לשכוי 7907 | בינה 998: | מי 4310 | יספר 5608 | שחקים 7834 |
| batuchout | chakamah | 'au | miy' | natan | lasekuiy | biynah. | miy' | yasaper | shachaqiym |
| **the innermost parts?** | **wisdom** | **or** | **who** | **has given** | **to the heart?** | **understanding** | **Who** | **can number** | **the clouds** |

| | | | | | 38:38 | | | |
|---|---|---|---|---|---|---|---|---|
| בחכמה 2451 | ונבלי 5035 | שמים 8064 | מי 4310 | ישכיב 7901: | בצקת 3332 | עפר 6083 | למוצק 4165 | ורגבים 7263 |
| bachakamah; | uanibley | shamayim, | miy' | yashkiyb. | batzeqet | 'apar | lamutzaq; | uargabiym |
| **in wisdom?** | **or the bottles of** | **heaven** | **who** | **can stay** | **When grow** | **the dust** | **into hardness** | **and the clods** |

| | 38:39 | | | | | | 38:40 |
|---|---|---|---|---|---|---|---|
| ידבקו 1692: | התצוד 6679 | ללביא 3833 | טרף 2964 | וחית 2416 | כפירים 3715 | תמלא 4390: | כי 3588 |
| yadubaqu. | hatatzud | lalabiy'a | tarep; | uachayat | kapiyriym | tamalea'. | kiy |
| **cleave fast together?** | **Will you hunt** | **for the lion?** | **the prey** | **or the appetite of** | **the young lions** | **fill** | **When** |

| | | | | | | 38:41 | | | | |
|---|---|---|---|---|---|---|---|---|---|---|
| ישחו 7817 | במעונות 4585 | ישבו 3427 | בסכה 5521 | למו 3926 | ארב 695: | מי 4310 | יכין 3559 | לערב 6158 | צידו 6718 | כי 3588 |
| yashochu | bam'aunout; | yeshabu | basukah | lamou | 'areb. | miy' | yakiyn | la'aureb, | tzeydou | kiy |
| **they couch** | **in *their* dens** | ***and* abide** | **in the covert** | **in** | **to lie wait?** | **Who** | **provide** | **for the raven** | **his food?** | **when** |

| | | | | | | |
|---|---|---|---|---|---|---|
| ילדו 3206 | אל 413 | אל 410 | ישועו 7768 | יתעו 8582 | לבלי 1097 | אכל 400: |
| yaladou | 'al | 'ael | yashaue'au; | yit'au, | libaliy | 'akel. |
| **his young ones** | **unto** | **El** | **cry** | **they wander** | **for lack of** | **meat** |

| Job 39:1 | | | | | | | 39:2 |
|---|---|---|---|---|---|---|---|
| הידעת 3045 | עת 6256 | לדת 3205 | יעלי 3277 | סלע 5553 | חלל 2342 | אילות 355 | תשמר 8104: |
| hayada'ata, | 'at | ledet | ya'aley | sala'; | cholel | ayalout | tishmor. |
| **Know you** | **the time** | **bring forth?** | ***when* the wild goats of** | **the rock** | **do calve?** | ***when* the hinds?** | ***or* can you mark** |

| | | | | | | 39:3 |
|---|---|---|---|---|---|---|
| תספר 5608 | ירחים 3391 | תמלאנה 4390 | וידעת 3045 | עת 6256 | לדתנה 3205: | תכרענה 3766 |
| tispor | yarachiym | tamale'anah; | uayada'ta, | 'at | lidtanah. | tikra'anah |
| **Can you number** | **the months** | ***that* they fulfill?** | **or know you** | **the time** | **when they bring forth?** | **They bow themselves** |

| | | | | 39:4 | | |
|---|---|---|---|---|---|---|
| ילדיהן 3206 | תפלחנה 6398 | חבליהם 2256 | תשלחנה 7971: | יחלמו 2492 | בניהם 1121 | ירבו 7235 |
| yaldeyhen | tapalachnah; | chebleyhem | tashalachnah. | yachlamu | baneyhem | yirbu |
| **their young ones** | **they bring forth** | **their sorrows** | **they cast out** | **are in good liking** | **Their young ones** | **they grow up** |

| | | | | | 39:5 | | | | |
|---|---|---|---|---|---|---|---|---|---|
| בבר 1250 | יצאו 3318 | ולא 3808 | שבו 7725 | למו 3807a: | מי 4310 | שלח 7971 | פרא 6501 | חפשי 2670 | ומסרות 4147 |
| babar; | yatza'ua, | uala' | shabu | lamou. | miy' | shilach | pera' | chapashiy; | uamosarout |
| **with corn** | **they go forth** | **and not** | **return** | **unto them** | **Who** | **has sent out** | **the wild ass** | **free?** | **or the bands of** |

| | | | 39:6 | | | | | 39:7 |
|---|---|---|---|---|---|---|---|---|
| ערוד 6171 | מי 4310 | פתח 6605: | אשר 834 | שמתי 7760 | ערבה 6160 | ביתו 1004 | ומשכנותיו 4908 | מלחה 4420: |
| aroud, | miy' | piteach. | 'asher | samtiy | 'arabah | beytou; | uamishkanoutayu | malechah. |
| **the wild ass?** | **who** | **has loosed** | **Whose** | **I have made** | **the wilderness** | **house** | **and his dwellings** | **the barren land** |

| | | | | | | | 39:8 | |
|---|---|---|---|---|---|---|---|---|
| ישחק 7832 | להמון 1995 | קריה 7151 | תשאות 8663 | נוגש 5065 | לא 3808 | ישמע 8085: | יתור 3491 | הרים 2022 |
| yischaq | lahamoun | qiryah; | tashu'aut | nouges, | la' | yishma'. | yatur | hariym |
| **He scorn** | **the multitude of** | **the city** | **the crying of** | **the driver** | **neither** | **regard he** | **The range of** | **the mountains** |

Job 38:34 that abundance of waters may cover you?35 Canst you send lightnings, that they may go, and say unto you, Here we are?36 Who has put wisdom in the inward parts? or who has given understanding to the heart?37 Who can number the clouds in wisdom? or who can stay the bottles of heaven,38 When the dust groweth into hardness, and the clods cleave fast together?39 Wilt you hunt the prey for the lion? or fill the appetite of the young lions,40 When they couch in their dens, and abide in the covert to lie in wait?41 Who provideth for the raven his food? when his young ones cry unto G-d, they wander for lack of meat. **Job** 39:1 Know you the time when the wild goats of the rock bring forth? or canst you mark when the hinds do calve?2 Canst you number the months that they fulfil? or know you the time when they bring forth? 3 They bow themselves, they bring forth their young ones, they cast out their sorrows.4 Their young ones are in good liking, they grow up with corn; they go forth, and return not unto them.5 Who has sent out the wild ass free? or who has loosed the bands of the wild ass?6 Whose house I have made the wilderness, and the barren land his dwellings. 7 He scorneth the multitude of the city, neither regardeth he the crying of the driver.8 The range of the mountains is his pasture, and he searcheth after every green thing.

| מרעהו 4829 | ואחר 310 | כל 3605 | ירוק 3387 | ידרוש 1875: | 39:9 | היאבה 14 | רים 7214 | עבדך 5647 | אם 518 | ילין 3885 | על 5921 |
|---|---|---|---|---|---|---|---|---|---|---|---|
| mir'aehu; | ua'achar | kal | yarouq | yidroush. | | haya'beh | reym | 'abadeka; | 'am | yaliyn, | 'al |
| ***is* his pasture** | **and after** | **every** | **green thing** | **he searches** | | **Will be willing** | **the unicorn** | **to serve you** | **or** | **abide** | **by** |

| אבוסך 18: | 39:10 | התקשר 7194 | רים 7214 | בתלם 8525 | עבתו 5688 | אם 518 | ישדד 7702 | עמקים 6010 | אחריך 310: | 39:11 |
|---|---|---|---|---|---|---|---|---|---|---|
| 'abuseka. | | hatiqshar | reym | batelem | abotou; | 'am | yasaded | 'amaqiym | 'achareyka. | |
| **your crib?** | | **Can you bind** | **the unicorn** | **in the furrow?** | ***with* his band** | **or** | **will he harrow** | **the valleys** | **after you?** | |

| התבטח 982 | בו 871a | כי 3588 | רב 7227 | כחו 3581 | ותעזב 5800 | אליו 413 | יגיעך 3018: | 39:12 | התאמין 539 | בו 871a | כי 3588 |
|---|---|---|---|---|---|---|---|---|---|---|---|
| hatibtach | bou | kiy | rab | kochou; | uata'azob | 'aelayu | yagiy'aka. | | hata'amiyn | bou | kiy |
| **Will you trust** | **him** | **because** | ***is* great?** | **his strength** | **or will you leave** | **to him?** | **your labour** | | **Will you believe** | **him** | **that** |

| ישוב 7725 | זרעך 2233 | וגרנך 1637 | יאסף 622: | 39:13 | כנף 3671 | רננים 7443 | נעלסה 5965 | אם 518 |
|---|---|---|---|---|---|---|---|---|
| yashub | zar'aka; | uagarnaka | ye'asop. | | kanap | rananiym | ne'alasah; | 'am |
| **he will bring home** | **your seed** | **and your barn?** | **gather *it into*** | | **wings** | ***Gavest you the* goodly** | **unto the peacocks?** | **or** |

| אברה 84 | חסידה 2624 | ונצה 5133: | 39:14 | כי 3588 | תעזב 5800 | לארץ 776 | ביציה 1000 | ועל 5921 | עפר 6083 | תחמם 2552: | 39:15 |
|---|---|---|---|---|---|---|---|---|---|---|---|
| 'abrah, | chasiydah | uanotzah. | | kiy | ta'azob | la'aretz | betzeyha; | ua'al | 'apar | tachamem. | |
| **wings** | **feathers *unto*** | **and the ostrich?** | | **Which** | **leave** | **in the earth** | **her eggs** | **and in** | **dust** | **warm them** | |

| ותשכח 7911 | כי 3588 | רגל 7272 | תזורה 2115 | וחית 2416 | השדה 7704 | תדושה 1758: | 39:16 | הקשיח 7188 |
|---|---|---|---|---|---|---|---|---|
| uatishkach | kiy | regel | tazureha; | uachayat | hasadeh | tadusheha. | | hiqshiyach |
| **And forget** | **that** | **the foot** | **may crush them** | **or beast** | ***that* the wild** | **may break them** | | **She is hardened against** |

| בניה 1121 | ללא 3808 | לה 3807a | לריק 7385 | יגיעה 3018 | בלי 1097 | פחד 6343: | 39:17 | כי 3588 | השה 5382 |
|---|---|---|---|---|---|---|---|---|---|
| baneyha | lala' | lah; | lariyq | yagiy'ah | baliy | pachad. | | kiy | hishah |
| **her young ones** | **as though *they were* not** | **hers** | ***is* in vain** | **her labour** | **without** | **fear** | | **Because** | **has deprived her of** |

| אלוה 433 | חכמה 2451 | ולא 3808 | חלק 2505 | לה 3807a | בבינה 998: | 39:18 | כעת 6256 | במרום 4791 | תמריא 4754 |
|---|---|---|---|---|---|---|---|---|---|
| 'alouah | chakamah | uala' | chalaq | lah, | babiynah. | | ka'aet | bamaroum | tamriy'a; |
| **Elohim** | **wisdom** | **and neither** | **has he imparted** | **to her** | **understanding** | | **What time** | **on high** | **she lift up herself** |

| תשחק 7832 | לסוס 5483 | ולרכבו 7392: | 39:19 | התתן 5414 | לסוס 5483 | גבורה 1369 | התלביש 3847 | צוארו 6677 | רעמה 7483: | 39:20 |
|---|---|---|---|---|---|---|---|---|---|---|
| tischaq | lasus, | ualrokabou. | | hatiten | lasus | gaburah; | hatalbiysh | tzaua'rou | ra'mah. | |
| **she scorn** | **the horse** | **and his rider** | | **Have you given** | **the horse** | **strength?** | **have you clothed** | **his neck** | ***with* thunder?** | |

| התרעישנו 7493 | כארבה 697 | הוד 1935 | נחרו 5170 | אימה 367: | 39:21 | יחפרו 2658 | בעמק 6010 | וישיש 7797 |
|---|---|---|---|---|---|---|---|---|
| hatar'ayshenu | ka'arbeh; | houd | nacharou | 'aeymah. | | yachparu | ba'aemeq | uayasiys |
| **Can you make him afraid** | **as a grasshopper?** | **the glory of** | **his nostrils** | ***is* terrible** | | **He paw** | **in the valley** | **and rejoice** |

| בכח 3581 | יצא 3318 | לקראת 7125 | נשק 5402: | 39:22 | ישחק 7832 | לפחד 6343 | ולא 3808 | יחת 2865 | ולא 3808 |
|---|---|---|---|---|---|---|---|---|---|
| bakoach; | yetzea', | liqra't | nasheq. | | yischaq | lapachad | uala' | yechat; | uala' |
| **in *his* strength** | **he goes on** | **to meet** | **the armed men** | | **He mock** | **at fear** | **and not** | **is affrighted** | **and neither** |

| ישוב 7725 | מפני 6440 | חרב 2719: | 39:23 | עליו 5921 | תרנה 7439 | אשפה 827 | להב 3851 | חנית 2595 | וכידון 3591: |
|---|---|---|---|---|---|---|---|---|---|
| yashub, | mipaney | chareb. | | 'alayu | tirneh | 'ashpah; | lahab | chaniyt | uakiydoun. |
| **turned he back** | **from** | **the sword** | | **against him** | **rattleth** | **The quiver** | ***the* glittering** | **spear** | **and the shield** |

Job 39:9 Will the unicorn be willing to serve you, or abide by your crib?10 Canst you bind the unicorn with his band in the furrow? or will he harrow the valleys after you?11 Wilt you trust him, because his strength is great? or will you leave your labour to him?12 Wilt you believe him, that he will bring home your seed, and gather it into your barn?13 Gavest you the goodly wings unto the peacocks? or wings and feathers unto the ostrich?14 Which leaveth her eggs in the earth, and warmeth them in dust,15 And forgetteth that the foot may crush them, or that the wild beast may break them.16 She is hardened against her young ones, as though they were not hers: her labour is in vain without fear;17 Because G-d has deprived her of wisdom, neither has he imparted to her understanding.18 What time she lift up herself on high, she scorneth the horse and his rider.19 Hast you given the horse strength? have you clothed his neck with thunder?20 Canst you make him afraid as a grasshopper? the glory of his nostrils is terrible.21 He paweth in the valley, and rejoice in his strength: he go on to meet the armed men.22 He mocketh at fear, and is not affrighted; neither turneth he back from the sword. 23 The quiver rattleth against him, the glittering spear and the shield.

**39:24** **39:25**
ברעש 7494 ורגז 7267 יגמא 1572 ארץ 776 ולא 3808 יאמין 539 כי 3588 קול 6963 שופר 7782:
bara'ash uarogez yagama' 'aretz; uala' ya'amiyn, kiy qoul shoupar.
**with fierceness and rage He swallow the ground and neither believe he that *it is* the sound of the trumpet**

**39:26**
בדי 1767 שפר 7782 יאמר 559 האח 1889 ומרחוק 7350 יריח 7306 מלחמה 4421 רעם 7482 שרים 8269 ותרועה 8643:
badey shopar ya'mar he'ach, uamerachouq yariyach milchamah; ra'am sariym uatru'ah.
**among the trumpets He saith Ha ha and afar off he smell the battle the thunder of the captains and the shouting**

**39:27**
המבינתך 998 יאבר 82 נץ 5322 יפרש 6566 כנפו 3671 לתימן 8486: אם 518 על 5921 פיך 6310
hamibiynataka ya'aber netz; yipros kanapou lateyman. 'am 'al piyka
**by your wisdom Does fly the hawk *and* stretch her wings toward the south? or at your command**

**39:28**
יגביה 1361 נשר 5404 וכי 3588 ירים 7311 קנו 7064: סלע 5553 ישכן 7931 ויתלנן 3885 על 5921 שן 8127 סלע 5553
yagbiyah nasher; uakiy, yariym qinou. sela' yishkon uayitlonan; 'al shen sela',
**Does mount up the eagle and for make on high? her nest *on* the rock She dwell and abide upon the crag of the rock**

**39:29** **39:30**
ומצודה 4686: משם 8033 חפר 2658 אכל 400 למרחוק 7350 עיניו 5869 יביטו 5027: ואפרחו 667
uamtzudah. misham chapar 'akel; lamerachouq, 'aeynayu yabiytu. ua'aprochou
**and the strong place From there she seek the prey afar off *and* her eyes behold Her young ones also**

יעלעו 5966 דם 1818 ובאשר 834 חללים 2491 שם 8033 הוא 1931:
ya'al'au dam; uaba'asher chalaliym, sham hua'.
**suck up blood and where the slain *are* there there *is* she**

**Job 40:1** **40:2**
ויען 6030 יהוה 3068 את 853 איוב 347 ויאמר 559: הרב 7378 עם 5973 שדי 7706 יסור 3250
uaya'an Yahuah 'at 'ayoub, uaya'mar. harob 'am shaday yisour;
**Moreover answered Yahuah Job and said Shall he that contend with the Almighty instruct**

**40:3** **40:4**
מוכיח 3198 אלוה 433 יעננה 6030: ויען 6030 איוב 347 את 853 יהוה 3068 ויאמר 559: הן 2005 קלתי 7043
moukiyach 'alouah ya'anenah. uaya'an 'ayoub 'at Yahuah uaya'mar. hen qalotiy
***him?* he that reprove Elohim let him answer it Then answered Job Yahuah and said Behold I am vile**

**40:5**
מה 4100 אשיבך 7725 ידי 3027 שמתי 7760 למו 3926 פי 6310: אחת 259 דברתי 1696 ולא 3808 אענה 6030 ושתים 8147
mah 'ashiybeka; yadiy, samtiy lamou piy. 'achat dibartiy uala' 'a'aneh; uashtayim,
**what shall I answer you? mine hand I will lay upon my mouth Once have I spoken but not I will answer yea twice**

**40:6** **40:7**
ולא 3808 אוסיף 3254: ויען 6030 יהוה 3068 את 853 איוב 347 מן 4480 סערה 5591 ויאמר 559 אזר 247
uala' 'ausiyp. uaya'an Yahuah 'at 'ayoub min has'arah, uaya'mar 'azar
**but no I will proceed further Then answered Yahuah *unto* Job out of the whirlwind, and said, Gird up**

**40:8**
נא 4994 כגבר 1397 חלציך 2504 אשאלך 7592 והודיעני 3045: האף 637 תפר 6565 משפטי 4941
naa' kageber chalatzeyka; 'ash'alaka, uahoudiy'aeniy. ha'ap taper mishpatiy;
**now like a man your loins I will demand of you and declare you unto me also Will you disannul my judgment?**

**40:9**
תרשיעני 7561 למען 4616 תצדק 6663: ואם 518 זרוע 2220 כאל 410 לך 3807a ובקול 6963 כמהו 3644
tarshiy'aeniy, lama'an titzdaq. ua'am zaroua' ka'ael lak; uabqoul, kamohu
**will you condemn me that you may be righteous? *Has* and if an arm Elohim? to you or with a voice like**

Job 39:24 He swalloweth the ground with fierceness and rage: neither believeth he that it is the sound of the trumpet.25 He saith among the trumpets, Ha, ha; and he smelleth the battle afar off, the thunder of the captains, and the shouting.26 Does the hawk fly by your wisdom, and stretch her wings toward the south?27 Does the eagle mount up at your command, and make her nest on high?28 She dwell and abideth on the rock, upon the crag of the rock, and the strong place.29 From thence she seek the prey, and her eyes behold afar off.30 Her young ones also suck up blood: and where the slain are, there is she. **Job** 40:1 Moreover YHUH answered Job, and said,2 Shall he that contendeth with the Almighty instruct him? he that reproveth G-d, let him answer it.3 Then Job answered YHUH, and said,4 Behold, I am vile; what shall I answer you? I will lay mine hand upon my mouth.5 Once have I spoken; but I will not answer: yea, twice; but I will proceed no further.6 Then answered YHUH unto Job out of the whirlwind, and said,7 Gird up your loins now like a man: I will demand of you, and declare you unto me.8 Wilt you also disannul my judgment? will you condemn me, that you may be righteous?9 Hast you an arm like G-d? or canst you thunder with a voice like him?

| | 40:10 | | | | | | | | 40:11 |
|---|---|---|---|---|---|---|---|---|---|
| תרעם 7481: | | עדה 5710 | נא 4994 | גאון 1347 | וגבה 1363 | והוד 1935 | והדר 1926 | תלבש 3847: | |
| tar'aem. | | 'adeh | naa' | ga'aun | uagobah; | uahoud | uahadar | tilbash. | |
| **can you thunder** | | **Deck yourself** | **now** | ***with* majesty** | **and excellency** | **and glory** | **and beauty** | **array yourself *with*** | |

| | | | | | | | 40:12 | | | |
|---|---|---|---|---|---|---|---|---|---|---|
| הפץ 6327 | עברות 5678 | אפך 639 | וראה 7200 | כל 3605 | גאה 1343 | והשפילהו 8213: | | ראה 7200 | כל 3605 | גאה 1343 |
| hapetz | 'abrout | 'apeka; | uar'aeh | kal | ge'ah, | uahashpiylehu. | | ra'aeh | kal | ge'ah |
| **Cast abroad** | **the rage of** | **your wrath** | **and behold** | **everyone** | ***that is* proud** | **and abasehim** | | **Look on** | **everyone** | ***that is* proud** |

| | | | | 40:13 | | | | | |
|---|---|---|---|---|---|---|---|---|---|
| הכניעהו 3665 | והדך 1915 | רשעים 7563 | תחתם 8478: | | טמנם 2934 | בעפר 6083 | יחד 3162 | פניהם 6440 | חבש 2280 |
| hakaniy'aehu; | uahadok | rasha'aym | tachtam. | | tamanem | be'apar | yachad; | paneyhem, | chabosh |
| ***and* bring him low** | **and tread down** | **the wicked** | **in their place** | | **Hide them** | **in the dust** | **together** | **their faces** | ***and* bind** |

| | 40:14 | | | | | | | | 40:15 | | |
|---|---|---|---|---|---|---|---|---|---|---|---|
| בטמון 2934: | | וגם 1571 | אני 589 | אודך 3034 | כי 3588 | תושע 3467 | לך 3807a | ימינך 3225: | | הנה 2009 | נא 4994 |
| batamun. | | uagam | 'aniy | 'adeka; | kiy | toushiya' | laka | yamiyneka. | | hineh | naa' |
| **in secret** | | **Then also** | **I** | **will confess unto you** | **that** | **can save** | **to you** | **your own right hand** | | **Behold** | **now** |

| | | | | | | | 40:16 | | | | | |
|---|---|---|---|---|---|---|---|---|---|---|---|---|
| בהמות 930 | אשר 834 | עשיתי 6213 | עמך 5973 | חציר 2682 | כבקר 1241 | יאכל 398: | | הנה 2009 | נא 4994 | כחו 3581 | במתניו 4975 | ואנו 202 |
| bahemout | 'asher | 'asiytiy | 'amak; | chatziyr, | kabaqar | ya'kel. | | hineh | naa' | kokou | bamatanayu; | ua'anou, |
| **behemoth** | **which** | **I made** | **with you** | **grass** | **as an ox** | **he eat** | | **Lo** | **now** | **his strength** | ***is* in his loins** | **and his force** |

| | | 40:17 | | | | | | | | 40:18 |
|---|---|---|---|---|---|---|---|---|---|---|
| בשרירי 8306 | בטנו 990: | | יחפץ 2654 | זנבו 2180 | כמו 3644 | ארז 730 | גידי 1517 | פחדו 6344 | ישרגו 8276: | |
| bishriyrey | bitnou. | | yachpotz | zanabou | kamou | 'arez; | giydey | pachadou | yasoragu. | |
| ***is* in the navel of** | **his belly** | | **He moves** | **his tail** | **like** | **a cedar** | **the sinews of** | **his stones** | **are wrapped together** | |

| | | | | | | 40:19 | | | |
|---|---|---|---|---|---|---|---|---|---|
| עצמיו 6106 | אפיקי 650 | נחושה 5154 | גרמיו 1634 | כמטיל 4300 | ברזל 1270: | | הוא 1931 | ראשית 7225 | דרכי 1870 |
| 'atzamayu | 'apiyqey | nachushah; | garamayu, | kimtiyl | barzel. | | hua' | ra'shiyt | darkey |
| **His bones** | ***are as* strong pieces of** | **brass** | **his bones** | ***are* like bars of** | **iron** | | **He** | ***is* the chief of** | **the ways of** |

| | | | | 40:20 | | | | | |
|---|---|---|---|---|---|---|---|---|---|
| אל 410 | העשו 6213 | יגש 5066 | חרבו 2719: | | כי 3588 | בול 944 | הרים 2022 | ישאו 5375 | לו 3807a |
| 'ael; | ha'asou | yagesh | charbou. | | kiy | bul | hariym | yis'au | lou'; |
| **El** | **he that made him** | **can make to approach *unto him*** | **his sword** | | **Surely** | **food** | **the mountains** | **bring forth** | **him** |

| | | | | | 40:21 | | | | | |
|---|---|---|---|---|---|---|---|---|---|---|
| וכל 3605 | חית 2416 | השדה 7704 | ישחקו 7832 | שם 8033: | | תחת 8478 | צאלים 6628 | ישכב 7901 | בסתר 5643 | קנה 7070 |
| uakal | chayat | hasadeh, | yasachaqu | sham. | | tachat | tze'aliym | yishkab; | baseter | qaneh |
| **and all** | **the beasts of** | **the field** | **play** | **where** | | **under** | **the shady trees** | **He lies** | **in the covert of** | **the reed** |

| | 40:22 | | | | | | | 40:23 | |
|---|---|---|---|---|---|---|---|---|---|
| ובצה 1207: | | יסכהו 5526 | צאלים 6628 | צללו 6752 | יסבוהו 5437 | ערבי 6155 | נחל 5158: | | הן 2005 |
| uabitzah. | | yasukuhu | tze'aliym | tzilalou; | yasubuhu, | 'arbey | nachal. | | hen |
| **and fens** | | **cover him** | **The shady trees** | ***with* their shadow** | **compass him about** | **the willows of** | **the brook** | | **Behold** |

| | | | | | | | | | | 40:24 | | |
|---|---|---|---|---|---|---|---|---|---|---|---|---|
| יעשק 6231 | נהר 5104 | לא 3808 | יחפוז 2648 | יבטח 982 | כי 3588 | יגיח 1518 | ירדן 3383 | אל 413 | פיהו 6310: | | בעיניו 5869 | יקחנו 3947 |
| ya'ashoq | nahar | la' | yachpouz; | yibtach | kiy | yagiyach | yarden | 'al | piyhu. | | ba'aeynayu | yiqachenu; |
| **he drink up** | **a river** | **not** | ***and* hasten** | **he trust** | **that** | **he can draw up** | **Jordan** | **into** | **his mouth** | | **with his eyes** | **He takes it** |

| | | |
|---|---|---|
| במוקשים 4170 | ינקב 5344 | אף 639: |
| bamouqshiym, | yinqab | 'aap. |
| **through snares** | **pierce** | ***his* nose** |

Job 40:10 Deck thyself now with majesty and excellency; and array thyself with glory and beauty.11 Cast abroad the rage of your wrath: and behold everyone that is proud, and abase him.12 Look on everyone that is proud, and bring him low; and tread down the wicked in their place.13 Hide them in the dust together; and bind their faces in secret.14 Then will I also confess unto you that your own right hand can save you.15 Behold now behemoth, which I made with you; he eateth grass as an ox.16 Lo now, his strength is in his loins, and his force is in the navel of his belly.17 He moveth his tail like a cedar: the sinews of his stones are wrapped together.18 His bones are as strong pieces of brass; his bones are like bars of iron.19 He is the chief of the ways of G-d: he that made him can make his sword to approach unto him.20 Surely the mountains bring him forth food, where all the beasts of the field play.21 He lie under the shady trees, in the covert of the reed, and fens.22 The shady trees cover him with their shadow; the willows of the brook compass him about.23 Behold, he drinketh up a river, and hasteth not: he trusteth that he can draw up Jordan into his mouth.24 He take it with his eyes: his nose pierceth through snares.

**Job 41:1** תמשך 4900 timshok | לויתן 3882 liuyatan | בחכה 2443 bachakah; | ובחבל 2256 uabchebel, | תשקיע 8257 tashqiya' | לשנו 3956: lashonou. | **41:2** התשים 7760 hatasiym | אגמון 100 agmoun

**Can you draw out leviathan with a hook? or with a cord *which* you let down? his tongue Can you put an hook**

באפו 639 ba'apou; | ובחוח 2336 uabchouach, | תקוב 5344 tiqoub | לחיו 3895: lecheyou. | **41:3** הירבה 7235 hayarbeh | אליך 413 'aeleyka | תחנונים 8469 tachanuniym; | אם 518 'am

**into his nose? or with a thron? borethrough his jaw many unto you? Will he make supplications or**

ידבר 1696 yadaber | אליך 413 'aeleyka | רכות 7390: rakout. | **41:4** היכרת 3772 hayikrot | ברית 1285 bariyt | עמך 5973 'amak; | תקחנו 3947 tiqachenu, | לעבד 5650 la'abed

**will he speak *words* unto you? soft Will he make a covenant will you? will you take him for a servant**

עולם 5769: 'aulam. | **41:5** התשחק 7832 hatsacheq | בו 871a bou | כצפור 6833 katzipour; | ותקשרנו 7194 uatiqsharenu, | לנערותיך 5291: lana'arouteyka. | **41:6** יכרו 3738 yikru

**for ever? Will you play with him as with a bird? or will you bind him for your maidens? Shall make a banquet**

עליו 5921 'alayu | חברים 2271 chabariym; | יחצוהו 2673 yechetzuhu, | בין 996 beyn | כנענים 3669: kana'aniym. | **41:7** התמלא 4390 hatamalea' | בשכות 7905 uasukout | עורו 5785 'aurou;

**of him? the companions shall they part him among the merchants? Can you fill with barbed iron? his skin**

ובצלצל 6767 uabtziltzal | דגים 1709 dagiym | ראשו 7218: ra'shou. | **41:8** שים 7760 siym | עליו 5921 'alayu | כפך 3709 kapeka; | זכר 2142 zakor | מלחמה 4421 milchamah, | אל 408 'al | תוסף 3254: tousap. | **41:9** הן 2005 hen

**or with spears? fish his head Lay upon him your hand remember the battle no do more Behold**

תחלתו 8431 tochaltou | נכזבה 3576 nikzabah; | הגם 1571 hagam | אל 413 'al | מראיו 4758 mar'ayu | יטל 2904: yutal. | **41:10** לא 3808 la' | אכזר 393 'akzar | כי 3588 kiy

**the hope of him is in vain even not *one* at the sight of him? shall be cast down None *is so* fierce that *dare***

יעורנו 5782 ya'urenu; | ומי 4310 uamiy | הוא 1931 hua', | לפני 6440 lapanay | יתיצב 3320: yityatzab. | **41:11** מי 4310 miy' | הקדימני 6923 hiqdiymaniy

**stir him up who then he before me? *is* able to stand Who has prevented me**

ואשלם 7999 ua'ashalem; | תחת 8478 tachat | כל 3605 kal | השמים 8064 hashamayim | לי 3807a liy | הוא 1931: hua'. | **41:12** לא 3808 la' | אחריש 2790 'achariysh | בדיו 907 badayu;

**that I should repay *him? whatsoever is* under the whole heaven *is* mine he not I will conceal his parts**

ודבר 1697 uadbar | גבורות 1369 gaburout, | וחין 2433 uachiyn | ערכו 6187: 'arkou. | **41:13** מי 4310 miy' | גלה 1540 gilah | פני 6440 paney | לבושו 3830 labushou; | בכפל 3718 bakepel

**nor his power nor comely his proportion Who can discover the face of his garment? *to him* with double**

רסנו 7448 risnou, | מי 4310 miy' | יבוא 935: yabou'a. | **41:14** דלתי 1817 daltey | פניו 6440 panayu | מי 4310 miy' | פתח 6605 piteach; | סביבות 5439 sabiybout | שניו 8127 shinayu | אימה 367: 'aeymah. | **41:15** גאוה 1346 geauoh

**his bridle? or who can come the doors of his face? Who can open round about his teeth *are* terrible *are his* pride**

אפיקי 650 'apiyqey | מגנים 4043 maginiym; | סגור 5462 sagur, | חותם 2368 choutam | צר 6862: tzar. | **41:16** אחד 259 'achad | באחד 259 ba'achad | יגשו 5066 yigashu; | ורוח 7307 uaruach, | לא 3808 la' | יבוא 935 yabou'a

***His* mighty scales shut up together *as with* a seal close One to another is so near that air no can come**

**Job** 41:1 Canst you draw out leviathan with an hook? or his tongue with a cord which you lettest down?2 Canst you put an hook into his nose? or bore his jaw through with a thorn?3 Will he make many supplications unto you? will he speak soft words unto you?4 Will he make a covenant with you? will you take him for a servant forever?5 Wilt you play with him as with a bird? or will you bind him for your maidens?6 Shall the companions make a banquet of him? shall they part him among the merchants?7 Canst you fill his skin with barbed iron? or his head with fish spears?8 Lay your hand upon him, remember the battle, do no more.9 Behold, the hope of him is in vain: shall not one be cast down even at the sight of him?10 None is so fierce that dare stir him up: who then is able to stand before me?11 Who has prevented me, that I should repay him? whatsoever is under the whole heaven is mine.12 I will not conceal his parts, nor his power, nor his comely proportion.13 Who can discover the face of his garment? or who can come to him with his double bridle?14 Who can open the doors of his face? his teeth are terrible round about.15 His scales are his pride, shut up together as with a close seal. 16 One is so near to another, that no air can come between them.

| | 41:17 | | | | | | 41:18 |
|---|---|---|---|---|---|---|---|
| ביניהם 996: | איש 376 | באחיהו 251 | ידבקו 1692 | יתלכדו 3920 | ולא 3808 | יתפרדו 6504: | עטישתיו 5846 |
| beyneyhem. | 'aysh | ba'achiyhu | yadubaqu; | yitlakdu, | uala' | yitparadu. | 'atiyshotayu |
| **between them** | **one** | **to another** | **They are joined** | **they stick together** | **and cannot** | **they be sundered** | **By his neesings** |

| | | | | | 41:19 | | | |
|---|---|---|---|---|---|---|---|---|
| תהל 1984 | אור 216 | ועיניו 5869 | כעפעפי 6079 | שחר 7837: | מפיו 6310 | לפידים 3940 | יהלכו 1980 | כידודי 3590 |
| tahel | 'aur; | ua'aeynayu, | ka'ap'apey | shachar. | mipiyu | lapidiym | yahaloku; | kiydoudey |
| **does shine** | **a light** | **and his eyes *are*** | **like the eyelids of** | **the morning** | **Out of his mouth** | **burning lamps** | **go *and*** | **sparks of** |

| | | 41:20 | | | | | | 41:21 | |
|---|---|---|---|---|---|---|---|---|---|
| אש 784 | יתמלטו 4422: | מנחיריו 5156 | יצא 3318 | עשן 6227 | כדוד 1731 | נפוח 5301 | ואגמן 100: | נפשו 5315 | גחלים 1513 |
| 'aesh, | yitmalatu. | minchiyrayu | yetzea' | 'ashan; | kadud | napuach | ua'agmon. | napshou | gechaliym |
| **fire** | **leap out** | **Out of his nostrils** | **goes** | **smoke** | **as *out* of a pot** | **seething** | **or caldron** | **His breath** | **coals** |

| | | | | 41:22 | | | | |
|---|---|---|---|---|---|---|---|---|
| תלהט 3857 | ולהב 3851 | מפיו 6310 | יצא 3318: | בצוארו 6677 | ילין 3885 | עז 5797 | ולפניו 6440 | תדוץ 1750 |
| talahet; | ualahab, | mipiyu | yetzea'. | batzaua'arou | yaliyn | 'az; | ualpanayu, | tadutz |
| **kindle** | **and a flame** | **of his mouth** | **goes out** | **In his neck** | **remains** | **strength** | **and before him** | **is turned *into joy*** |

| | 41:23 | | | | | | | 41:24 |
|---|---|---|---|---|---|---|---|---|
| דאבה 1670: | מפלי 4651 | בשרו 1320 | דבקו 1692 | יצוק 3332 | עליו 5921 | בל 1077 | ימוט 4131: | |
| da'abah. | mapley | basarou | dabequ; | yatzuq | 'alayu, | bal | yimout. | |
| **sorrow** | **The flakes of** | **his flesh** | **are joined together** | **they are firm** | **in themselves** | **cannot** | **they be moved** | |

| | | | | | | | 41:25 | |
|---|---|---|---|---|---|---|---|---|
| לבו 3820 | יצוק 3332 | כמו 3644 | אבן 68 | ויצוק 3332 | כפלח 6400 | תחתית 8482: | משתו 7613 | יגורו 1481 |
| libou | yatzuq | kamou | 'aben; | uayatzuq, | kapelach | tachtiyt. | misetou | yaguru |
| **His heart** | **is as firm** | **as** | **a stone** | **yea as hard** | **as a piece of** | **the nether *millstone*** | **When he raises up himself** | **are afraid** |

| | | | 41:26 | | | | |
|---|---|---|---|---|---|---|---|
| אלים 352 | משברים 7667 | יתחטאו 2398: | משיגהו 5381 | חרב 2719 | בלי 1097 | תקום 6965 | חנית 2595 |
| 'aeliym; | mishbariym, | yitchata'au. | masiygehu | chereb | baliy | taqum; | chaniyt |
| **the mighty** | **by reason of breakings** | **they purify themselves** | **of him that lay at him** | **The sword** | **cannot** | **hold** | **the spear** |

| | | 41:27 | | | | | | 41:28 | |
|---|---|---|---|---|---|---|---|---|---|
| מסע 4551 | ושריה 8302: | יחשב 2803 | לתבן 8401 | ברזל 1270 | לעץ 6086 | רקבון 7539 | נחושה 5154: | לא 3808 | יבריחנו 1272 |
| masa' | uashiryah. | yachshob | lateben | barzel; | la'aetz | riqaboun | nachushah. | la' | yabriychenu |
| **the dart** | **nor the habergeon** | **He esteem** | **as straw** | **iron** | **as wood** | **rotten** | ***and* brass** | **cannot** | **make him flee** |

| | | | | | | | 41:29 | | | |
|---|---|---|---|---|---|---|---|---|---|---|
| בן 1121 | קשת 7198 | לקש 7179 | נהפכו 2015 | לו 3807a | אבני 68 | קלע 7050: | כקש 7179 | נחשבו 2803 | תותח 8455 | וישחק 7832 |
| ben | qashet; | laqash, | nehpaku | lou' | 'abney | qala'. | kaqash | nechshabu | toutach; | uayischaq, |
| **arrow** | ***The* archers** | **into stubble** | **are turned with him** | **to** | **stones** | **sling** | **as stubble** | **are counted** | **Darts** | **he laugheth** |

| | | 41:30 | | | | | | | 41:31 |
|---|---|---|---|---|---|---|---|---|---|
| לרעש 7494 | כידון 3591: | תחתיו 8478 | חדודי 2303 | חרש 2789 | ירפד 7502 | חרוץ 2742 | עלי 5921 | טיט 2916: | |
| lara'ash | kiydoun. | tachtayu | chadudey | chares; | yirpad | charutz | 'aley | tiyt. | |
| **at the shaking of** | **a spear** | ***are* under him** | **Sharp** | **stones** | **he spread** | **sharp pointed things** | **upon** | **the mire** | |

| | | | | | | 41:32 | | |
|---|---|---|---|---|---|---|---|---|
| ירתיח 7570 | כסיר 5518 | מצולה 4688 | ים 3220 | ישים 7760 | כמרקחה 4841: | אחריו 310 | יאיר 215 | נתיב 5410 |
| yartiyach | kasiyr | matzulah; | yam, | yasiym | kamerqachah. | 'acharayu | ya'ayr | natiyb; |
| **He make to boil** | **like a pot** | **the deep** | **the sea** | **he make** | **like a pot of ointment** | **after him** | **He make to shine** | **a path** |

| | | | 41:33 | | | | | | | 41:34 |
|---|---|---|---|---|---|---|---|---|---|---|
| יחשב 2803 | תהום 8415 | לשיבה 7872: | אין 369 | על 5921 | עפר 6083 | משלו 4915 | העשו 6213 | לבלי 1097 | חת 2844: | את 853 |
| yachshob | tahoum | laseybah. | 'aeyn | 'al | 'apar | mashalou; | he'asu, | libliy | chat. | 'at |
| ***one* would think** | **the deep** | ***to be* hoary** | **there is not** | **Upon** | **earth** | **his like** | **who is made** | **without** | **fear** | |

Job 41:17 They are joined one to another, they stick together, that they cannot be sundered.18 By his neesings a light doth shine, and his eyes are like the eyelids of the morning.19 Out of his mouth go burning lamps, and sparks of fire leap out.20 Out of his nostrils go smoke, as out of a seething pot or caldron.21 His breath kindleth coals, and a flame go out of his mouth.22 In his neck remain strength, and sorrow is turned into joy before him.23 The flakes of his flesh are joined together: they are firm in themselves; they cannot be moved.24 His heart is as firm as a stone; yea, as hard as a piece of the nether millstone.25 When he raise up himself, the mighty are afraid: by reason of breakings they purify themselves.26 The sword of him that layeth at him cannot hold: the spear, the dart, nor the habergeon.27 He esteemeth iron as straw, and brass as rotten wood.28 The arrow cannot make him flee: slingstones are turned with him into stubble.29 Darts are counted as stubble: he laugheth at the shaking of a spear.30 Sharp stones are under him: he spreadeth sharp pointed things upon the mire.31 He make the deep to boil like a pot: he make the sea like a pot of ointment.32 He make a path to shine after him; one would think the deep to be hoary.33 Upon earth there is not his like, who is made without fear.

כל 3605 גבה 1364 יראה 7200 הוא 1931 מלך 4428 על 5921 כל 3605 בני 1121 שחץ 7830:
kal gaboah yir'ah; hua', melek 'al kal baney shachatz.
**all high *things* He behold he *is* a king over all the children of pride**

**Job 42:1** ויען 6030 איוב 347 את 853 יהוה 3068 ויאמר 559: **42:2** ידעת 3045 כי 3588 כל 3605 תוכל 3201 ולא 3808
uaya'an 'ayoub 'at Yahuah uaya'mar. yada'ta kiy kal tukal; uala'
**Then answered Job Yahuah and said I know that every *thing* you can do and *that* no**

יבצר 1219 ממך 4480 מזמה 4209: **42:3** מי 4310 זה 2088 מעלים 5956 עצה 6098 בלי 1097 דעת 1847 לכן 3651 הגדתי 5046
yibatzer mimaka mazimah. miy' zeh ma'aliym 'aetzah, baliy da'at laken higadtiy
**can be withholden from you thought Who *is* he that hides counsel without knowledge? therefore have I uttered**

ולא 3808 אבין 995 נפלאות 6381 ממני 4480 ולא 3808 אדע 3045: **42:4** שמע 8085 נא 4994 ואנכי 595 אדבר 1696
uala' 'abiyn; nipla'aut mimeniy, uala' 'aeda. shama' naa' ua'anokiy 'adaber;
**that not I understood *things* too wonderful for me which not I knew Hear I beseech you and I will speak**

אשאלך 7592 והודיעני 3045: **42:5** לשמע 8085 אזן 241 שמעתיך 8085 ועתה 6258 עיני 5869
'ash'alaka, uahoudiy'aeniy. lashema' 'azen shama'atiyka; ua'atah, 'aeyniy
**I will demand of you and declare you unto me I have heard of you the ear by the hearing of but now mine eye**

ראתך 7200: **42:6** על 5921 כן 3651 אמאס 3988 ונחמתי 5162 על 5921 עפר 6083 ואפר 665: **42:7** ויהי 1961 אחר 310
ra'ataka. 'al ken 'am'as uanichamtiy; 'al 'apar ua'aeper. uayahiy, 'achar
**see you Wherefore after I abhor *myself* and repent in dust and ashes And it was *so that* after**

דבר 1696 יהוה 3068 את 853 הדברים 1697 האלה 428 אל 413 איוב 347 ויאמר 559 יהוה 3068 אל 413 אליפז 464 התימני 8489 חרה 2734
diber Yahuah 'at hadabariym ha'aeleh 'al 'ayoub; uaya'mer Yahuah 'al 'aliypaz hateymaniy, charah
**had spoken Yahuah words these unto Job and said Yahuah to Eliphaz the Temanite is kindled**

אפי 639 בך 871a ובשני 8147 רעיך 7453 כי 3588 לא 3808 דברתם 1696 אלי 413 נכונה 3559 כעבדי 5650
'apiy baka uabishney re'ayka, kiy la' dibartem 'aelay nakounah ka'abdiy
**My wrath against you and against two your friends for not you have spoken of me *the thing that is* right as my servant**

איוב 347: **42:8** ועתה 6258 קחו 3947 לכם 3807a שבעה 7651 פרים 6499 ושבעה 7651 אילים 352 ולכו 1980 אל 413 עבדי 5650 איוב 347
'ayoub. ua'atah qachu lakem shib'ah pariym uashib'ah 'aeyliym ualku 'al 'abdiy 'ayoub,
**Job *has* Therefore now take unto you seven bullocks and seven rams and go to my servant Job**

והעליתם 5927 עולה 5930 בעדכם 1157 ואיוב 347 עבדי 5650 יתפלל 6419 עליכם 5921 כי 3588 אם 518 פניו 6440 אשא 5375
uaha'aliytem aulah ba'adkem, ua'ayoub 'abdiy, yitpalel 'aleykem; kiy 'am panayu 'asa',
**and offer up a burnt offering for yourselves and Job my servant shall pray for you for if him will I accept**

לבלתי 1115 עשות 6213 עמכם 5973 נבלה 5039 כי 3588 לא 3808 דברתם 1696 אלי 413 נכונה 3559 כעבדי 5650
labiltiy asout 'amakem nabalah, kiy la' dibartem 'aelay nakounah ka'abdiy
**lest I deal with you *after your* folly in that not you have spoken of me *the thing which is* right like my servant**

איוב 347: **42:9** וילכו 1980 אליפז 464 התימני 8489 ובלדד 1085 השוחי 7747 צפר 6691 הנעמתי 5284 ויעשו 6213 כאשר 834
'ayoub. uayelaku 'aliypaz hateymaniy uabildad hashuchiy, tzipor hana'amatiy, uaya'asu, ka'asher
**Job So went Eliphaz the Temanite and Bildad the Shuhite *and* Zophar the Naamathite and did according as**

Job 41:34 He beholdeth all high things: he is a king over all the children of pride. **Job** 42:1 Then Job answered YHUH, and said,2 I know that you canst do every thing, and that no thought can be withholden from you.3 Who is he that hide counsel without knowledge? therefore have I uttered that I understood not; things too wonderful for me, which I knew not.4 Hear, I beseech you, and I will speak: I will demand of you, and declare you unto me.5 I have heard of you by the hearing of the ear: but now mine eye see you.6 Wherefore I abhor myself, and repent in dust and ashes.7 And it was so, that after YHUH had spoken these words unto Job, YHUH said to Eliphaz the Temanite, My wrath is kindled against you, and against your two friends: for you have not spoken of me the thing that is right, as my servant Job has.8 Therefore take unto you now seven bullocks and seven rams, and go to my servant Job, and offer up for yourselves a burnt offering; and my servant Job shall pray for you: for him will I accept: lest I deal with you after your folly, in that you have not spoken of me the thing which is right, like my servant Job.9 So Eliphaz the Temanite and Bildad the Shuhite and Zophar the Naamathite went, and did according as YHUH commanded them: YHUH also accepted Job.

42:10

דבר 1696 אליהם 413 יהוה 3068 וישא 5375 יהוה 3068 את 853 פני 6440 איוב 347: ויהוה 3068 שב 7725 את 853 שבית 7622

diber 'aleyhem Yahuah; uayisaa' Yahuah 'at paney 'ayoub. uaYahuah shab 'at shabiyt

**commanded them Yahuah also accepted Yahuah them Job And Yahuah turned the captivity of**

42:11

איוב 347 בהתפללו 6419 בעד 1157 רעהו 7453 ויסף 3254 יהוה 3068 את 853 כל 3605 אשר 834 לאיוב 347 למשנה 4932:

'ayoub, bahitpallou ba'ad re'aehu; uayosep Yahuah 'at kal 'asher la'ayoub lamishneh.

**Job when he prayed for his friends also gave Yahuah all as *had before* Job twice as much**

ויבאו 935 אליו 413 כל 3605 אחיו 251 וכל 3605 אחיתיו 269 וכל 3605 ידעיו 3045 לפנים 6440

uayabo'au 'aelayu kal 'achiyu uakal 'achyotayu uakal yoda'ayu lapaniym,

**Then came *there* unto him all his brethren and all his sisters and all they that had been of his acquaintance before**

ויאכלו 398 עמו 5973 לחם 3899 בביתו 1004 וינדו 5110 לו 3807a וינחמו 5162 אתו 853 על 5921 כל 3605 הרעה 7451 אשר 834

uayo'akalu 'amou lechem babeytou uayanudu lou' uayanachamu 'atou, 'al kal hara'ah, 'asher

**and did eat with him bread in his house and they bemoaned him and comforted him over all the evil that**

הביא 935 יהוה 3068 עליו 5921 ויתנו 5414 לו 3807a איש 376 קשיטה 7192 אחת 259 ואיש 376 נזם 5141 זהב 2091

habiy'a Yahuah 'alayu; uayitanu lou', 'aysh qasiytah 'achat, ua'aysh nezem zahab

**had brought Yahuah upon him also gave him every man piece of money a and every one earring of gold**

42:12

אחד 259: ויהוה 3068 ברך 1288 את 853 אחרית 319 איוב 347 מראשתו 7225 ויהי 1961 לו 3807a ארבעה 702 עשר 6240

'achad. uaYahuah berak 'at 'achariyt 'ayoub mere'ashitou; uayahiy lou' 'arba'ah 'asar

**an So Yahuah blessed the latter end of Job more than his beginning for had he four ten**

42:13

אלף 505 צאן 6629 וששת 8337 אלפים 505 גמלים 1581 ואלף 505 צמד 6776 בקר 1241 ואלף 505 אתונות 860: ויהי 1961

'alep tza'n, uasheshet 'alapiym gamaliym, ua'alep tzemed baqar ua'alep 'atounout. uayahiy

**thousand sheep and six thousand camels and a thousand yoke of oxen and a thousand his she asses had also**

42:14

לו 3807a שבענה 7658 בנים 1121 ושלוש 7969 בנות 1323: ויקרא 7121 שם 8034 האחת 259 ימימה 3224 ושם 8034

lou' shib'anah baniym uashaloush banout. uayiqra' shem ha'achat yamiymah, uashem

**He seven sons and three daughters And he called the name of the first Jemima and the name of**

42:15

השנית 8145 קציעה 7103 ושם 8034 השלישית 7992 קרן 7163 הפוך 6320: ולא 3808 נמצא 4672 נשים 802 יפות 3303

hasheniyt qatziy'ah; uashem hashaliyshiyt qeren hapuk. uala' nimtza' nashiym yapout

**the second Kezia and the name of the third Keren happuch And no were found women *so* fair**

42:16

כבנות 1323 איוב 347 בכל 3605 הארץ 776 ויתן 5414 להם 1992 אביהם 1 נחלה 5159 בתוך 8432 אחיהם 251: ויחי 2421

kibanout 'ayoub bakal ha'aretz; uayiten lahem 'abiyhem nachalah batouk 'acheyhem. uaychiy

**as the daughters of Job in all the land and gave them their father inheritance among their brethren lived**

איוב 347 אחרי 310 זאת 2063 מאה 3967 וארבעים 705 שנה 8141 וירא 7200 את 853 בניו 1121 ואת 853 בני 1121 בניו 1121 ארבעה 702

'ayoub 'acharey za't, me'ah ua'arba'aym shanah; uayar'a 'at banayu ua'at baney banayu, 'arba'ah

**Job After this an hundred and forty years and saw his sons *and* his sons' sons *even* four**

42:17

דרות 1755: וימת 4191 איוב 347 זקן 2205 ושבע 7649 ימים 3117:

dorout. uayamat 'ayoub, zaqen uasba' yamiym.

**generations So died Job *being* old and full of days**

Job 42:10 And YHUH turned the captivity of Job, when he prayed for his friends: also YHUH gave Job twice as much as he had before.11 Then came there unto him all his brethren, and all his sisters, and all they that had been of his acquaintance before, and did eat bread with him in his house: and they bemoaned him, and comforted him over all the evil that YHUH had brought upon him: every man also gave him a piece of money, and everyone an earring of gold.12 So YHUH blessed the latter end of Job more than his beginning: for he had fourteen thousand sheep, and six thousand camels, and a thousand yoke of oxen, and a thousand she asses.13 He had also seven sons and three daughters.14 And he called the name of the first, Jemima; and the name of the second, Kezia; and the name of the third, Keren-happuch.15 And in all the land were no women found so fair as the daughters of Job: and their father gave them inheritance among their brethren.16 After this lived Job an hundred and forty years, and saw his sons, and his sons' sons, even four generations.17 So Job died, being old and full of days.

# PSALMS
## (*Tehillim*)

David is listed as the author of Psalms in 73 instances but he is definitely not the author of the entire collection. Psalms gives up a look into David's personality and identity. There are 150 Psalms and it is the longest book in the Tanakh and is also one of the most diverse. Both Psalms 72 and 127 are attributed to Solomon, David's son and successor to his throne. Psalm 90 is a prayer written about Moses and some scholars believe Moses may have been the author, which would make it the oldest Psalm. Some 12 Psalms are attributed to the family of Asaph while the sons of Korah wrote 11 Psalms. Psalm 88 is attributed to Heman and Psalm 89 is attributed to Ethan the Ezrahite. There are fifty Psalms that do not designate a specific author but with the exception of Solomon and Moses, all the authors were either priests or Levites who were responsible for providing the music for worship in the sanctuary during King David's reign. The writings actually span a period of many centuries with the youngest Psalm 137, which is a song of lament, which was clearly written during the days when the Israelites were being held captive in Babylon, from about 586 to 538 B.C. It is clear that all 150 Psalms were written by many different people across a period of a thousand years or more of Israel's history and were compiled in their present form by an unknown editor shortly after the end of the Babylonian captivity in 537 B.C.

| **Psalms 1:1** | | | | | | | | | | |
|---|---|---|---|---|---|---|---|---|---|---|
| אשרי 835 | האיש 376 | אשר 834 | לא 3808 | הלך 1980 | בעצת 6098 | רשעים 7563 | ובדרך 1870 | חטאים 2400 | לא 3808 | עמד 5975 |
| 'ashrey | ha'aysh, | 'asher | la' | halak | ua'atzat | rasha'aym | uabderek | chata'aym | la' | 'amad; |
| **Blessed *is* the man** | | **that** | **not** | **walk** | **in the counsel of** | **the ungodly** | **in the way of** | **sinners** | **nor** | **stands** |

| | | | | **1:2** | | | | | | | |
|---|---|---|---|---|---|---|---|---|---|---|---|
| ובמושב 4186 | לצים 3887 | לא 3808 | ישב 3427: | | כי 3588 | אם 518 | בתורת 8451 | יהוה 3069 | חפצו 2656 | ובתורתו 8451 | יהגה 1897 |
| uabmoushab | letziym, | la' | yashab. | | kiy | 'am | batourat | Yahuah | cheptzou | uabtouratou | yehageh, |
| **in the seat of** | **the scornful** | **nor** | **sit** | | **But** | **rather** | ***is* in the law** | **Yahuah** | **his delight** | **and in his law** | **does he meditate** |

| | | **1:3** | | | | | | | | | |
|---|---|---|---|---|---|---|---|---|---|---|---|
| יומם 3119 | ולילה 3915: | | והיה 1961 | כעץ 6086 | שתול 8362 | על 5921 | פלגי 6388 | מים 4325 | אשר 834 | פריו 6529 | יתן 5414 |
| youmam | ualayalah. | | uahayah, | ka'aetz | shatul | 'al | palgey | mayim | 'asher | piryou | yiten |
| **day** | **and night** | | **And he shall be** | **like a tree** | **planted** | **by** | **the rivers of** | **water** | **that** | **his fruit** | **bring forth** |

| | | | | | | | | **1:4** | | | |
|---|---|---|---|---|---|---|---|---|---|---|---|
| בעתו 6256 | ועלהו 5929 | לא 3808 | יבול 5034 | וכל 3605 | אשר 834 | יעשה 6213 | יצליח 6743: | | לא 3808 | כן 3651 | הרשעים 7563 |
| ba'atou, | ua'alehu | la' | yiboul; | uakol | 'asher | ya'aseh | yatzliyach. | | la' | ken | harasha'aym; |
| **in his season** | **his leaf also** | **not** | **shall wither** | **whatsoever** | **that** | **he does** | **shall prosper** | | **not** | **so** | **The ungodly *are*** |

| | | | | | | **1:5** | | | | | |
|---|---|---|---|---|---|---|---|---|---|---|---|
| כי 3588 | אם 518 | כמץ 4671 | אשר 834 | תדפנו 5086 | רוח 7307: | | על 5921 | כן 3651 | לא 3808 | יקמו 6965 | רשעים 7563 |
| kiy | 'am | kamotz, | 'asher | tidpenu | ruach. | | 'al | ken | la' | yaqumu | rasha'aym |
| **but** | **rather *are*** | **like the chaff** | **which** | **drive away** | **the wind** | | **Therefore** | **this** | **not** | **shall stand** | **the ungodly** |

| | | | | **1:6** | | | | | |
|---|---|---|---|---|---|---|---|---|---|
| במשפט 4941 | וחטאים 2400 | בעדת 5712 | צדיקים 6662: | | כי 3588 | יודע 3045 | יהוה 3068 | דרך 1870 | צדיקים 6662 |
| bamishpat; | uachata'aym, | ba'adat | tzadiyqiym. | | kiy | youdea' | Yahuah | derek | tzadiyqiym; |
| **in the judgment** | **nor sinners** | **in the congregation of** | **the righteous** | | **For** | **knows** | **Yahuah** | **the way of** | **the righteous** |

| | | |
|---|---|---|
| ודרך 1870 | רשעים 7563 | תאבד 6: |
| uaderek | rasha'aym | ta'bed. |
| **but the way of** | **the ungodly shall perish** | |

| **Ps 2:1** | | | | | | **2:2** | | | |
|---|---|---|---|---|---|---|---|---|---|
| למה 4100 | רגשו 7283 | גוים 1471 | ולאמים 3816 | יהגו 1897 | ריק 7385: | | יתיצבו 3320 | מלכי 4428 | ארץ 776 |
| lamah | ragashu | gouyim; | uala'amiym, | yehagu | riyq. | | yityatzbu | malkey | 'aretz, |
| **Why** | **do rage** | **the heathen** | **and the people** | **imagine** | **a vain thing?** | | **set themselves** | **The kings of** | **the earth** |

**Psalms** 1:1 Blessed is the man that walk not in the counsel of the ungodly, nor stand in the way of sinners, nor sitteth in the seat of the scornful.2 But his delight is in the law of YHUH; and in his law doth he meditate day and night.3 And he shall be like a tree planted by the rivers of water, that bring forth his fruit in his season; his leaf also shall not where; and whatsoever he doeth shall prosper.4 The ungodly are not so: but are like the chaff which the wind drive away.5 Therefore the ungodly shall not stand in the judgment, nor sinners in the congregation of the righteous.6 For YHUH know the way of the righteous: but the way of the ungodly shall perish. **Psalms** 2:1 Why do the heathen rage, and the people imagine a vain thing? 2 The kings of the earth set themselves, and the rulers take counsel together, against YHUH, and against his anointed, saying,

ורוזנים 7336 | נוסדו 3245 | יחד 3162 | על 5921 | יהוה 3068 | ועל 5921 | משיחו 4899: | **2:3** ננתקה 5423 | את 853
uarouzaniym nousadu yachad; 'al Yahuah ua'al mashiychou. nanatqah 'at
**and the rulers take counsel together against Yahuah and against his anointed *saying* Let us break asunder**

מוסרותימו 4147 | ונשליכה 7993 | ממנו 4480 | עבתימו 5688: | **2:4** יושב 3427 | בשמים 8064 | ישחק 7832 | אדני 136 | ילעג 3932
mousarouteymou; uanashliykah mimenu 'aboteymou. yousheb bashamayim yischaq; 'adonay, yil'ag
**their bands and cast away from us their cords He that sit in the heavens shall laugh Adonai shall have in derision**

למו 3807a: | **2:5** אז 227 | ידבר 1696 | אלימו 413 | באפו 639 | ובחרונו 2740 | יבהלמו 926: | **2:6** ואני 589 | נסכתי 5258
lamou. 'az yadaber 'aeleymou ba'apou; uabacharounou yabahalemou. ua'aniy nasaktiy
**them Then shall he speak unto them in his wrath and in his sore displeasure vex them Yet I have set**

מלכי 4428 | על 5921 | ציון 6726 | הר 2022 | קדשי 6944: | **2:7** אספרה 5608 | אל 413 | חק 2706 | יהוה 3069 | אמר 559 | אלי 413 | בני 1121 | אתה 859 | אני 589
malkiy; 'al tziyoun, har qadashiy 'asaprah, 'al choq Yahuah 'amar 'aelay baniy 'atah; 'aniy,
**my king upon Zion hill of my holy I will declare unto the decree Yahuah has said *are* to me my Son You I**

היום 3117 | ילדתיך 3205: | **2:8** שאל 7592 | ממני 4480 | ואתנה 5414 | גוים 1471 | נחלתך 5159 | ואחזתך 272
hayoum yalidtiyka. sha'al mimeniy, ua'atanah gouyim nachalateka; ua'achuzataka,
**this day have begotten you Ask of me and I shall give *you* the heathen *for* your inheritance and your possession**

אפסי 657 | ארץ 776: | **2:9** תרעם 7489 | בשבט 7626 | ברזל 1270 | ככלי 3627 | יוצר 3335
'apsey 'aretz. taro'aem bashebet barzel; kikliy youtzer
**the uttermost parts of the earth *for* You shall break them with a rod of iron like a vessel potter's**

תנפצם 5310: | **2:10** ועתה 6258 | מלכים 4428 | השכילו 7919 | הוסרו 3256 | שפטי 8199 | ארץ 776: | **2:11** עבדו 5647
tanaptzem. ua'atah malakiym hasakiylu; hiuasaru, shopatey 'aretz. 'abdu
**you shall dash them in pieces now therefore O you kings Be wise be instructed you judges of the earth Serve**

את 853 | יהוה 3068 | ביראה 3374 | וגילו 1523 | ברעדה 7461: | **2:12** נשקו 5401 | בר 1248 | פן 6435 | יאנף 599 | ותאבדו 6 | דרך 1870
'at Yahuah bayir'ah; uagiylu, bir'adah. nashqu bar pen ye'anap uata'badu derek,
**Yahuah with fear and rejoice with trembling Kiss the Son lest he be angry and you perish *from* the way**

כי 3588 | יבער 1197 | כמעט 4592 | אפו 639 | אשרי 835 | כל 3605 | חוסי 2620 | בו 871a:
kiy yib'ar kima'at 'apou; 'ashrey, kal chousey bou.
**when is kindled but a little his wrath Blessed *are* all they that put their trust in him**

**Ps 3:1** מזמור 4210 | לדוד 1732 | בברחו 1272 | מפני 6440 | אבשלום 53 | בנו 1121: | יהוה 3068 | מה 4100 | רבו 7231 | צרי 6862
mizmour ladauid; babarchou, mipaney 'abshaloum banou. Yahuah mah rabu tzaray;
**A Psalm of David when he fled from Absalom his son Yahuah how are they increased that trouble me**

רבים 7227 | קמים 6965 | עלי 5921: | **3:2** רבים 7227 | אמרים 559 | לנפשי 5315 | אין 369 | ישועתה 3444 | לו 3807a | באלהים 430
rabiym, qamiym 'alay. rabiym 'amariym lanapshiy 'aeyn yashu'atah lou' be'alohiym
**many *are* they that rise up against me Many *there be* which say of my soul *There is* no help for him in Elohim**

סלה 5542: | **3:3** ואתה 859 | יהוה 3068 | מגן 4043 | בעדי 1157 | כבודי 3519 | ומרים 7311 | ראשי 7218: | **3:4** קולי 6963 | אל 413 | יהוה 3069
selah. ua'atah Yahuah magen ba'adiy; kaboudiy, uameriym ra'shiy. qouliy 'al Yahuah
**Selah But you O Yahuah *are* a shield for me my glory and the lifter up of mine head *with* my voice unto Yahuah**

3 Let us break their bands asunder, and cast away their cords from us.4 He that sitteth in the heavens shall laugh: YHUH shall have them in derision.5 Then shall he speak unto them in his wrath, and vex them in his sore displeasure.6 Yet have I set my king upon my holy hill of Zion.7 I will declare the decree: YHUH has said unto me, Thou are my Son; this day have I begotten you.8 Ask of me, and I shall give you the heathen for your inheritance, and the uttermost parts of the earth for your possession.9 Thou shall break them with a rod of iron; you shall dash them in pieces like a potter's vessel.10 Be wise now therefore, O you kings: be instructed, you judges of the earth.11 Serve YHUH with fear, and rejoice with trembling.12 Kiss the Son, lest he be angry, and you perish from the way, when his wrath is kindled but a little. Blessed are all they that put their trust in him. **Psalms** 3:1 A Psalm of David, when he fled from Ab'sa-lom his son. YHUH, how are they increased that trouble me! many are they that rise up against me.2 Many there be which say of my soul, There is no help for him in G-d. Selah.3 But you, O YHUH, are a shield for me; my glory, and the lifter up of mine head.

3:5
אקרא 7121 ויענני 6030 מהר 2022 קדשו 6944 סלה 5542: אני 589 שכבתי 7901 ואישנה 3462 הקיצותי 6974 כי 3588 יהוה 3068
'aqraa'; uaya'aneniy mehar qadashou selah. 'aniy shakabtiy, ua'ayshanah heqiytzoutiy; kiy Yahuah
**I cried and he heard me out of hill his holy Selah I laid me down and slept I awaked for Yahuah**

3:6 3:7
יסמכני 5564: לא 3808 אירא 3372 מרבבות 7233 עם 5971 אשר 834 סביב 5439 שתו 7896 עלי 5921:
yismakeniy. la' 'ayra' meribbout 'am; 'asher sabiyb, shatu 'alay.
**sustained me not I will be afraid of ten thousands of people that round about have set *themselves* against me**

קומה 6965 יהוה 3068 הושיעני 3467 אלהי 430 כי 3588 הכית 5221 את 853 כל 3605 איבי 341 לחי 3895
qumah Yahuah houshiy'aeniy 'alohay, kiy hikiyta 'at kal 'ayabay lechiy;
**Arise O Yahuah save me O my Elohim for you have smitten all mine enemies *upon* the cheek bone**

3:8
שני 8127 רשעים 7563 שברת 7665: ליהוה 3068 הישועה 3444 על 5921 עמך 5971 ברכתך 1293 סלה 5542:
shiney rasha'aym shibarta. laYahuah hayashu'ah; 'al 'ameka birkateka selah.
**the teethof the ungodly you have broken *belongs* unto Yahuah Salvation upon your people your blessing *is* Selah**

Ps 4:1
למנצח 5329 בנגינות 5058 מזמור 4210 לדוד 1732: בקראי 7121 ענני 6030 אלהי 430 צדקי 6664
lamanatzeach binagiynout, mizmour ladauid. baqara'ay 'aneniy 'alohey tzidqiy,
**To the chief Musician on Neginoth A Psalm of David when I call Hear me O Elohim of my righteousness**

4:2
בצר 6862 הרחבת 7337 לי 3807a חנני 2603 ושמע 8085 תפלתי 8605: בני 1121 איש 376 עד 5704
batzar hirchabta liy; chaneniy uashma' tapilatiy. baney 'aysh 'ad
***when I was* in distress you have enlarged me have mercy upon me and hear my prayer O you sons of men long**

4:3
מה 4100 כבודי 3519 לכלמה 3639 תאהבון 157 ריק 7385 תבקשו 1245 כזב 3577 סלה 5542: ודעו 3045 כי 3588
meh kaboudiy likalimah te'ahabun riyq; tabaqshu kazab selah. uad'au, kiy
**how *will you turn* my glory into shame? *how long* will you love vanity *and* seek after leasing? Selah But know that**

4:4
הפלה 6395 יהוה 3068 חסיד 2623 לו 3807a יהוה 3068 ישמע 8085 בקראי 7121 אליו 413: רגזו 7264 ואל 408
hiplah Yahuah chasiyd lou'; Yahuah yishma', baqara'ay 'aelayu. rigzu, ua'al
**has set apart Yahuah him that is godly for himself Yahuah will hear when I call unto him Stand in awe and not**

4:5
תחטאו 2398 אמרו 559 בלבבכם 3824 על 5921 משכבכם 4904 ודמו 1826 סלה 5542: זבחו 2076 זבחי 2077 צדק 6664
techata'au 'amru bilbabkem 'al mishkabakem, uadomu selah. zibchu zibchey tzedeq;
**sin commune with your own heart upon your bed and be still Selah Offer the sacrifices of righteousness**

4:6
ובטחו 982 אל 413 יהוה 3068: רבים 7227 אמרים 559 מי 4310 יראנו 7200 טוב 2896 נסה 5375 עלינו 5921 אור 216
uabitchu, 'al Yahuah. rabiym 'amariym miy' yar'aenu toub nasah 'aleynu 'aur
**and put your trust in Yahuah *There be* many that say Who will show us *any* good? lift you up upon us the light of**

4:7
פניך 6440 יהוה 3068: נתתה 5414 שמחה 8057 בלבי 3820 מעת 6256 דגנם 1715 ותירושם 8492
paneyka Yahuah. natatah simchah balibiy; me'aut daganam uatiyrousham
**your countenance Yahuah You have put gladness in my heart more than in the time *that* their corn and their wine**

4:8
רבו 7231: בשלום 7965 יחדו 3162 אשכבה 7901 ואישן 3462 כי 3588 אתה 859 יהוה 3068 לבדד 910 לבטח 983 תושיבני 3427:
rabu. bashaloum yachdau 'ashkabah ua'ayshan kiy 'atah Yahuah labadad; labetach, toushiybeniy.
**increased in peace both I will lay me down and sleep for you Yahuah only in safety make me dwell**

Ps 3:4 I cried unto YHUH with my voice, and he heard me out of his holy hill. Selah.5 I laid me down and slept; I awaked; for YHUH sustained me.6 I will not be afraid of ten thousands of people, that have set themselves against me round about.7 Arise, O YHUH; save me, O my G-d: for you have smitten all mine enemies upon the cheek bone; you have broken the teeth of the ungodly.8 Salvation belong unto YHUH: your blessing is upon your people. Selah. **Psalms** 4:1 To the chief Musician on Neg'-i-noth, A Psalm of David. Hear me when I call, O G-d of my righteousness: you have enlarged me when I was in distress; have mercy upon me, and hear my prayer.2 O you sons of men, how long will you turn my glory into shame? how long will you love vanity, and seek after leasing? Selah.3 But know that YHUH has set apart him that is godly for himself: YHUH will hear when I call unto him.4 Stand in awe, and sin not: commune with your own heart upon your bed, and be still. Selah.5 Offer the sacrifices of righteousness, and put your trust in YHUH.6 There be many that say, Who will show us any good? YHUH, lift you up the light of your countenance upon us.7 Thou have put gladness in my heart, more than in the time that their corn and their wine increased.8 I will both lay me down in peace, and sleep: for you, YHUH, only make me dwell in safety.

**Ps 5:1**
למנצח 5329 אל 413 הנחילות 5155 מזמור 4210 לדוד 1732: אמרי 561 האזינה 238 יהוה 3068 בינה 995
lamanatzeach 'al hanachiylout, mizmour ladauid. 'amaray ha'aziynah Yahuah biynah
**To the chief Musician upon Nehiloth A Psalm of David my words Give ear to O Yahuah consider**

**5:2**
הגיגי 1901: הקשיבה 7181 לקול 6963 שועי 7773 מלכי 4428 ואלהי 430 כי 3588 אליך 413 אתפלל 6419: **5:3** יהוה 3068
hagiygiy. haqashiybah laqoul shau'ay, malkiy ua'alohay; kiy 'aeleyka, 'atpalal. Yahuah
**my meditation Hearken unto the voice of my cry my King and my Elohim for unto you will I pray O Yahuah**

**5:4**
בקר 1242 תשמע 8085 קולי 6963 בקר 1242 אערך 6186 לך 3807a ואצפה 6822: כי 3588 לא 3808
boqer tishma' qouliy; boqer 'a'arok laka, ua'atzapeh. kiy la'
***in* the morning shall you hear My voice *in* the morning will I direct *my prayer* unto you and will look up For not**

**5:5**
אל 410 חפץ 2655 רשע 7562 אתה 859 לא 3808 יגרך 1481 רע 7451: לא 3808 יתיצבו 3320 הוללים 1984 לנגד 5048
'ael chapetz resha' 'atah; la' yagurka ra'. la' yityatzbu houlaliym laneged
***a* El that has pleasure in wickedness you *are* neither dwell with you shall evil not shall stand The foolish in**

**5:6**
עיניך 5869 שנאת 8130 כל 3605 פעלי 6466 און 205: תאבד 6 דברי 1696 כזב 3577 איש 376 דמים 1818 ומרמה 4820
'aeyneyka; sanea'ta, kal po'aley 'auen. ta'abed dobarey kazab 'aysh damiym uamirmah,
**your sight you hate all workers of iniquity You shall destroy them that speak leasing man the bloody and deceitful**

**5:7**
יתעב 8581 יהוה 3068: ואני 589 ברב 7230 חסדך 2617 אבוא 935 ביתך 1004 אשתחוה 7812 אל 413
yata'aeb Yahuah. ua'aniy, barob chasdaka abou'a beytaka; 'ashtachaueh 'al
**will abhor Yahuah But as for me in the multitude of your mercy I will come *into* your house will I worship toward**

**5:8**
היכל 1964 קדשך 6944 ביראתך 3374: יהוה 3068 נחני 5148 בצדקתך 6666 למען 4616 שוררי 8324 הושר 3474
heykal qadashaka bayir'ateka. Yahuah nacheniy batzidqateka, lama'an shourray; houshar
**temple your holy *and* in your fear O Yahuah Lead me in your righteousness because of mine enemies make straight**

**5:9**
לפני 6440 דרכך 1870: כי 3588 אין 369 בפיהו 6310 נכונה 3559 קרבם 7130 הוות 1942
lapanay darkeka. kiy 'aeyn bapiyhu nakounah qirbam hauout
**before my face your way For *there* is no in their mouth faithfulness their inward part *is* very wickedness**

**5:10**
קבר 6913 פתוח 6605 גרונם 1627 לשונם 3956 יחליקון 2505: האשימם 816 אלהים 430 יפלו 5307
qeber patuach garounam; lashounam, yachaliyqun. ha'ashiymem 'alohiym, yiplu
***is* an sepulchre open their throat with their tongue they flatter Destroy you them O Elohim let them fall**

**5:11**
ממעצותיהם 4156 ברב 7230 פשעיהם 6588 הדיחמו 5080 כי 3588 מרו 4784 בך 871a:
mimo'atzouteyhem barob pish'aeyhem hadiychemou; kiy maru bak.
**by their own counsels in the multitude of their transgressions cast them out for they have rebelled against you**

וישמחו 8055 כל 3605 חוסי 2620 בך 871a לעולם 5769 ירננו 7442 ותסך 5526 עלימו 5921
uayismachu kal chousey bak la'aulam yaranenu uatasek 'aleymou;
**But let rejoice all those that put their trust in you ever let them shout for joy because you defend them**

**5:12**
ויעלצו 5970 בך 871a אהבי 157 שמך 8034: כי 3588 אתה 859 תברך 1288 צדיק 6662 יהוה 3068 כצנה 6793
uaya'altzu baka, 'ahabey shameka. kiy 'atah tabarek tzadiyq Yahuah; katzinah,
**and let them also be joyful in you that love your name For you will bless the righteous Yahuah as with a shield**

**Psalms** 5:1 To the chief Musician upon Ne'-hi-loth, A Psalm of David. Give ear to my words, O YHUH, consider my meditation.2 Hearken unto the voice of my cry, my King, and my G-d: for unto you will I pray.3 My voice shall you hear in the morning, O YHUH; in the morning will I direct my prayer unto you, and will look up.4 For you are not a G-d that has pleasure in wickedness: neither shall evil dwell with you.5 The foolish shall not stand in your sight: you hate all workers of iniquity.6 Thou shall destroy them that speak leasing: YHUH will abhor the bloody and deceitful man.7 But as for me, I will come into your house in the multitude of your mercy: and in your fear will I worship toward your holy temple.8 Lead me, O YHUH, in your righteousness because of mine enemies; make your way straight before my face.9 For there is no faithfulness in their mouth; their inward part is very wickedness; their throat is an open sepulcher; they flatter with their tongue.10 Destroy you them, O G-d; let them fall by their own counsels; cast them out in the multitude of their transgressions; for they have rebelled against you.11 But let all those that put their trust in you rejoice: let them ever shout for joy, because you defendest them: let them also that love your name be joyful in you.12 For you, YHUH, will bless the righteous; with favor will you compass him as with a shield.

רצון 7522 תעטרנו 5849:
ratzoun ta'atrenu.
***with* favor will you compass him**

**Ps 6:1** למנצח 5329 בנגינות 5058 על 5921 השמינית 8067 מזמור 4210 לדוד 1732: יהוה 3068 אל 408 באפך 639 תוכיחני 3198
lamanatzeach binagiynout 'al hashamiynit, mizmour ladauid. Yahuah 'al ba'apaka toukiycheniy;
**To the chief Musician on Neginoth upon Sheminith A Psalm of David O Yahuah not in your anger rebuke me**

ואל 408 בחמתך 2534 תיסרני 3256: **6:2** חנני 2603 יהוה 3069 כי 3588 אמלל 536 אני 589 רפאני 7495 יהוה 3069 כי 3588
ua'al bachamataka tayasreniy. chaneniy Yahuah kiy 'amlal 'aniy rapa'aeniy Yahuah; kiy
**neither in your hot displeasure chasten me Have mercy upon me Yahuah for *am* weak I heal me Yahuah for**

נבהלו 926 עצמי 6106: **6:3** ונפשי 5315 נבהלה 926 מאד 3966 ואת 859 יהוה 3068 עד 5704 מתי 4970: **6:4** שובה 7725 יהוה 3068 חלצה 2502
nibhalu 'atzamay. uanapshiy nibhalah ma'ad; ua'at Yahuah 'ad matay. shubah Yahuah chaltzah
**are vexed my bones My soul also is vexed sore *but* You O Yahuah how long? Return O Yahuah deliver**

נפשי 5315 הושיעני 3467 למען 4616 חסדך 2617: **6:5** כי 3588 אין 369 במות 4194 זכרך 2143 בשאול 7585 מי 4310
napshiy; houshiy'aeniy, lama'an chasadeka. kiy 'aeyn bamauet zikreka; bish'aul, miy'
**my soul oh save me for sake your mercies' For *there* is no in death remembrance of you in the grave who**

יודה 3034 לך 3807a: **6:6** יגעתי 3021 באנחתי 585 אשחה 7811 בכל 3605 לילה 3915 מטתי 4296 בדמעתי 1832
youdeh lak. yaga'atiy ba'anchatiy, 'ascheh bakal layalah mitatiy; badim'atiy,
**shall give thanks? to you I am weary with my groaning make I to swim all the night my bed with my tears**

ערשי 6210 אמסה 4529: **6:7** עששה 6244 מכעס 3708 עיני 5869 עתקה 6275 בכל 3605 צוררי 6887: **6:8** סורו 5493
'arsiy 'amseh. 'ashashah mika'as 'aeyniy; 'ataqah, bakal tzouraray. suru
**my couch I water is consumed because of grief Mine eye it waxeth old because of all mine enemies Depart**

ממני 4480 כל 3605 פעלי 6466 און 205 כי 3588 שמע 8085 יהוה 3068 קול 6963 בכיי 1065: **6:9** שמע 8085 יהוה 3068
mimeniy kal po'aley 'auen; kiy shama' Yahuah qoul bikyiy. shama' Yahuah
**from me all you workers of iniquity for has heard Yahuah the voice of my weeping has heard Yahuah**

תחנתי 8467 יהוה 3068 תפלתי 8605 יקח 3947: **6:10** יבשו 954 ויבהלו 926 מאד 3966 כל 3605 איבי 341 ישבו 3425
tachinatiy; Yahuah tapilatiy yiqach. yeboshu yeyibahalu ma'ad kal 'ayabay; yashubu,
**my supplication Yahuah my prayer will receive Let be ashamed and vexed sore all mine enemies let them return**

יבשו 954 רגע 7281:
yeboshu raga'.
***and* be ashamed suddenly**

**Ps 7:1** שגיון 7692 לדוד 1732 אשר 834 שר 7891 ליהוה 3068 על 5921 דברי 1697 כוש 3568 בן 1145 ימיני 3225: יהוה 3068
shigayoun, ladauid 'asher shar laYahuah; 'al dibrey kush, ben yamiyniy. Yahuah
**Shiggaion of David which he sang unto Yahuah concerning the words of Cush the Ben jamite O Yahuah**

אלהי 430 בך 871a חסיתי 2620 הושיעני 3467 מכל 3605 רדפי 7291 והצילני 5337: **7:2** פן 6435 יטרף 2963
'alohay baka chasiytiy; houshiy'aeniy mikal rodapay, uahatziyleniy. pen yitrop
**my Elohim in you do I put my trust save me from all them that persecute me and deliver me Lest he tear**

**Psalms** 6:1 To the chief Musician on Neg'-i-noth upon Shem'-i-nith, A Psalm of David. O YHUH, rebuke me not in your anger, neither chasten me in your hot displeasure.2 Have mercy upon me, O YHUH; for I am weak: O YHUH, heal me; for my bones are vexed.3 My soul is also sore vexed: but you, O YHUH, how long?4 Return, O YHUH, deliver my soul: oh save me for your mercies' sake.5 For in death there is no remembrance of you: in the grave who shall give you thanks?6 I am weary with my groaning; all the night make I my bed to swim; I water my couch with my tears.7 Mine eye is consumed because of grief; it waxeth old because of all mine enemies.8 Depart from me, all you workers of iniquity; for YHUH has heard the voice of my weeping.9 YHUH has heard my supplication; YHUH will receive my prayer.10 Let all mine enemies be ashamed and sore vexed: let them return and be ashamed suddenly. **Psalms** 7:1 Shig-ga'-ion of David, which he sang unto the Adonai, concerning the words of Cush the Benjamite. O Adonai my G-d, in you do I put my trust: save me from all them that persecute me, and deliver me:

כאריה 738 נפשי 5315 פרק 6561 ואין 369 מציל 5337: 7:3 יהוה 3068 אלהי 430 אם 518 עשיתי 6213 זאת 2063
ka'aryeh napshiy; poreq, ua'aeyn matziyl. Yahuah 'alohay 'am 'asiytiy za't;
**like a lion my soul rending *it* in pieces and while *there is* none to deliver O Yahuah my Elohim if I have done this**

אם 518 יש 3426 עול 5766 בכפי 3709: 7:4 אם 518 גמלתי 1580 שולמי 7999 רע 7451
'am yesh 'auel bakapay. 'am gamaltiy shoulamiy ra';
**if there be iniquity in my hands If I have rewarded unto him that was at peace with me evil**

ואחלצה 2502 צוררי 6887 ריקם 7387: 7:5 ירדף 7291 אויב 341 נפשי 5315 וישג 5381
ua'achaltzah tzourariy reyqam. yiradop auyeb napshiy uayaseg,
**yea I have delivered him *is* mine enemy *that* without cause Let persecute the enemy my soul and take**

וירמס 7429 לארץ 776 חיי 2416 וכבודי 3519 לעפר 6083 ישכן 7931 סלה 5542: 7:6 קומה 6965 יהוה 3068
uayirmos la'aretz chayay; uakboudiy le'apar yashken selah. qumah Yahuah
***it* yea, let him tread down upon the earth my life and mine honor in the dust lay Selah Arise O Yahuah**

באפך 639 הנשא 5375 בעברות 5678 צוררי 6887 ועורה 5782 אלי 413 משפט 4941
ba'apeka, hinasea' ba'abrout tzouraray; ua'aurah 'aelay, mishapat
**in your anger lift up *yourself* because of the rage of mine enemies and awake for me *to* the judgment**

צוית 6680: 7:7 ועדת 5712 לאמים 3816 תסובבך 5437 ועליה 5921
tziuiyta. ua'adat la'amiym tasoubaka; ua'aleyha,
***that* you have commanded So shall the congregation of the people shall compass you about and for their sakes therefore**

למרום 4791 שובה 7725: 7:8 יהוה 3068 ידין 1777 עמים 5971 שפטני 8199 יהוה 3068 כצדקי 6664
lamaroum shubah. Yahuah yadiyn 'amiym shapateniy Yahuah; katzidqiy
**on high return you Yahuah shall judge the people judge me O Yahuah according to my righteousness**

וכתמי 8537 עלי 5921: 7:9 יגמר 1584 נא 4994 רע 7451 רשעים 7563 ותכונן 3559 צדיק 6662
uaktumiy 'alay. yigmor naa' ra' rasha'aym uatkounen tzadiyq
**and according to mine integrity *that is* in me let come to an end Oh the wickedness of the wicked but establish the just**

ובחן 974 לבות 3826 וכליות 3629 אלהים 430 צדיק 6662: 7:10 מגני 4043 על 5921 אלהים 430 מושיע 3467 ישרי 3477 לב 3820: 7:11
uabochen libout, uaklayout, 'alohiym tzadiyq. maginiy 'al 'alohiym; moushiya', yishrey leb.
**for tries the hearts and reins Elohim the righteous My defence *is* of Elohim which save the upright in heart**

אלהים 430 שופט 8199 צדיק 6662 ואל 410 זעם 2194 בכל 3605 יום 3117: 7:12 אם 518 לא 3808 ישוב 7725 חרבו 2719 ילטוש 3913
'alohiym shoupet tzadiyq; ua'ael, zo'aem bakal youm. 'am la' yashub charbou yiltoush;
**Elohim judge the righteous and El is angry *with the wicked* every day If not he turn his sword he will whet**

קשתו 7198 דרך 1869 ויכוננה 3559: 7:13 ולו 3807a הכין 3559 כלי 3627 מות 4194 חציו 2671
qashtou darak, uayakounaneha. ualou hekiyn kaley mauet; chitzayu,
**his bow he has bent and made it ready for him He has also prepared the instruments of death his arrows**

לדלקים 1814 יפעל 6466: 7:14 הנה 2009 יחבל 2254 און 205 והרה 2029 עמל 5999 וילד 3205
ladolaqiym yip'al. hineh yachabel 'auen; uaharah 'amal, uayalad
**against the persecutors he ordaineth Behold he travail with iniquity and has conceived mischief and brought forth**

Ps 7:2 Lest he tear my soul like a lion, rending it in pieces, while there is none to deliver.3 O YHUH my G-d, if I have done this; if there be iniquity in my hands;4 If I have rewarded evil unto him that was at peace with me; (yea, I have delivered him that without cause is mine enemy:)5 Let the enemy persecute my soul, and take it; yea, let him tread down my life upon the earth, and lay mine honor in the dust. Selah.6 Arise, O YHUH, in your anger, lift up thyself because of the rage of mine enemies: and awake for me to the judgment that you have commanded.7 So shall the congregation of the people compass you about: for their sakes therefore return you on high.8 YHUH shall judge the people: judge me, O YHUH, according to my righteousness, and according to mine integrity that is in me.9 Oh let the wickedness of the wicked come to an end; but establish the just: for the righteous G-d trieth the hearts and reins.10 My defence is of G-d, which save the upright in heart.11 G-d judgeth the righteous, and G-d is angry with the wicked every day.12 If he turn not, he will whet his sword; he has bent his bow, and made it ready.13 He has also prepared for him the instruments of death; he ordaineth his arrows against the persecutors.14 Behold, he travaileth with iniquity, and has conceived mischief, and brought forth falsehood.

| | | | | | | | | |
|---|---|---|---|---|---|---|---|---|
| | 7:15 | | | | | | 7:16 | |
| שקר 8267: | בור 953 | כרה 3738 | ויחפרהו 2658 | ויפל 5307 | בשחת 7845 | יפעל 6466: | ישוב 7725 | עמלו 5999 |
| shaqer. | bour | karah | uayachparehu; | uayipol, | bashachat | yip'al. | yashub | 'amalou |
| **falsehood** | **a pit** | **He made** | **and digged it** | **and is fallen** | **into the ditch** | ***which* he made** | **shall return** | **His mischief** |

| | | | | | | |
|---|---|---|---|---|---|---|
| | | | | | 7:17 | |
| בראשו 7218 | ועל 5921 | קדקדו 6936 | חמסו 2555 | ירד 3381: | אודה 3034 | יהוה 3068 |
| bara'shou; | ua'al | qadaqadou, | chamasou | yered. | 'audeh | Yahuah |
| **upon his own head** | **and upon** | **his own pate** | **his violent dealing** | **shall come down** | **I will praise** | **Yahuah** |

| | | | | |
|---|---|---|---|---|
| כצדקו 6664 | ואזמרה 2167 | שם 8034 | יהוה 3068 | עליון 5945: |
| katzidqou; | ua'azamarah, | shem | Yahuah | 'alyoun. |
| **according to his righteousness** | **and will sing praise to** | **the name of** | **Yahuah** | **most high** |

| | | | | | | | | | | |
|---|---|---|---|---|---|---|---|---|---|---|
| **Ps 8:1** | | | | | | | | | | |
| למנצח 5329 | על 5921 | הגתית 1665 | מזמור 4210 | לדוד 1732: | יהוה 3068 | אדנינו 113 | מה 4100 | אדיר 117 | שמך 8034 | בכל 3605 |
| lamanatzeach | 'al | hagitiyt, | mizmour | ladauid. | Yahuah | 'adoneynu, | mah | 'adiyr | shimeka | bakal |
| **To the chief Musician** | **upon** | **Gittith** | **A Psalm** | **of David** | **O Yahuah** | **our Adonai** | **how** | **excellent *is*** | **your name** | **in all** |

| | | | | | | | | | |
|---|---|---|---|---|---|---|---|---|---|
| | | | | | | 8:2 | | | |
| הארץ 776 | אשר 834 | תנה 5414 | הודך 1935 | על 5921 | השמים 8064: | מפי 6310 | עוללים 5768 | וינקים 3243 | יסדת 3245 |
| ha'aretz; | 'asher | tanah | houdaka, | 'al | hashamayim. | mipiy | 'aulaliym | uayonaqiym | yisadta |
| **the earth** | **who** | **have set** | **your glory** | **above** | **the heavens** | **Out of the mouth of** | **babes** | **and sucklings** | **have you ordained** |

| | | | | | | | | |
|---|---|---|---|---|---|---|---|---|
| | | | | | | 8:3 | | |
| עז 5797 | למען 4616 | צורריך 6887 | להשבית 7673 | אויב 341 | ומתנקם 5358: | כי 3588 | אראה 7200 | שמיך 8064 |
| 'az | lama'an | tzourareyka; | lahashbiyt | auyeb, | uamitanaqem. | kiy | 'ar'ah | shameyka |
| **strength** | **because of** | **your enemies** | **that you might still** | **the enemy** | **and the avenger** | **When** | **I consider** | **your heavens** |

| | | | | | | | | | |
|---|---|---|---|---|---|---|---|---|---|
| | | | | | | 8:4 | | | |
| מעשי 4639 | אצבעתיך 676 | ירח 3394 | וכוכבים 3556 | אשר 834 | כוננתה 3559: | מה 4100 | אנוש 582 | כי 3588 | תזכרנו 2142 |
| ma'asey | 'atzb'ateyka; | yareach | uakoukabiym, | 'asher | kounanatah. | mah | 'anoush | kiy | tizkarenu; |
| **the work of** | **your fingers** | **the moon** | **and the stars** | **which** | **you have ordained** | **What *is*** | **man** | **that** | **you are mindful of him?** |

| | | | | | | | |
|---|---|---|---|---|---|---|---|
| | | | | 8:5 | | | |
| ובן 1121 | אדם 120 | כי 3588 | תפקדנו 6485: | ותחסרהו 2637 | מעט 4592 | מאלהים 430 | וכבוד 3519 |
| uaben | 'adam, | kiy | tipqadenu. | uatachasrehu | ma'at | me'alohiym; | uakaboud |
| **and the son of** | **man** | **that** | **you visit him?** | **For you have made him lower** | **a little** | **than the angels (*El*)** | **and glory** |

| | | | | | |
|---|---|---|---|---|---|
| | | 8:6 | | | |
| והדר 1926 | תעטרהו 5849: | תמשילהו 4910 | במעשי 4639 | ידיך 3027 | כל 3605 |
| uahadar | ta'atrehu. | tamashiylehu | bam'asey | yadeyka; | kol |
| **and honor** | **have crowned him *with*** | **You made him to have dominion** | **over the works of** | **your hands** | **all** |

| | | | | | | | | | | |
|---|---|---|---|---|---|---|---|---|---|---|
| | | | 8:7 | | | | | | 8:8 | |
| שתה 7896 | תחת 8478 | רגליו 7272: | צנה 6792 | ואלפים 504 | כלם 3605 | וגם 1571 | בהמות 929 | שדי 7704: | צפור 6833 | שמים 8064 |
| shatah | tachat | raglayu. | tzoneh | ua'alapiym | kulam; | ua'gam, | bahamout | saday. | tzipour | shamayim |
| **you have put *things*** | **under** | **his feet** | **sheep** | **and oxen** | **All** | **yea and** | **the beasts of the field** | | **The fowl of** | **the air** |

| | | | | | | | | |
|---|---|---|---|---|---|---|---|---|
| | | | | | 8:9 | | | |
| ודגי 1709 | הים 3220 | עבר 5674 | ארחות 734 | ימים 3220: | יהוה 3068 | אדנינו 113 | מה 4100 | אדיר 117 |
| uadgey | hayam; | 'aber, | 'arachout | yamiym. | Yahuah | 'adoneynu; | mah | 'adiyr |
| **and the fish of** | **the sea** | ***and whatsoever* passed through** | **the paths of** | **the seas** | **O Yahuah** | **our Adonai** | **how** | **excellent** |

| | | |
|---|---|---|
| שמך 8034 | בכל 3605 | הארץ 776: |
| shimka, | bakal | ha'aretz. |
| ***is* your name** | **in all** | **the earth** |

Ps 7:15 He made a pit, and digged it, and is fallen into the ditch which he made.16 His mischief shall return upon his own head, and his violent dealing shall come down upon his own pate.17 I will praise YHUH according to his righteousness: and will sing praise to the name of YHUH most high. **Psalms** 8:1 To the chief Musician upon Git'-tith, A Psalm of David. O YHUH our Adonai, how excellent is your name in all the earth! who have set your glory above the heavens.2 Out of the mouth of babes and sucklings have you ordained strength because of your enemies, that you might still the enemy and the avenger.3 When I consider your heavens, the work of your fingers, the moon and the stars, which you have ordained;4 What is man, that you are mindful of him? and the son of man, that you visitest him?5 For you have made him a little lower than the angels, and have crowned him with glory and honor.6 Thou madest him to have dominion over the works of your hands; you have put all things under his feet:7 All sheep and oxen, yea, and the beasts of the field;8 The fowl of the air, and the fish of the sea, and whatsoever pass through the paths of the seas.9 O YHUH our Adonai, how excellent is your name in all the earth!

**Ps 9:1**

| למנצח 5329 | עלמות 4192 | לבן 4192 | מזמור 4210 | לדוד 1732: | אודה 3034 | יהוה 3068 | בכל 3605 | לבי 3820 |
|---|---|---|---|---|---|---|---|---|
| lamanatzeach | 'alamout | laben, | mizmour | ladauid. | 'audeh | Yahuah | bakal | libiy; |
| **To the chief Musician** | **upon Muth** | **labben** | **A Psalm** | **of David** | **I will praise** | ***you* O Yahuah** | **with whole** | **my heart** |

| אספרה 5608 | כל 3605 | נפלאותיך 6381: | 9:2 | אשמחה 8055 | ואעלצה 5970 | בך 871a | אזמרה 2167 | שמך 8034 |
|---|---|---|---|---|---|---|---|---|
| 'asaprah, | kal | nipla'auteyka. | | 'asmachah | ua'a'altzah | bak; | 'azamrah | shimka |
| **I will show forth** | **all** | **your marvellous works** | | **I will be glad** | **and rejoice** | **in you** | **I will sing praise** | **your name** |

| עליון 5945: | 9:3 | בשוב 7725 | אויבי 341 | אחור 268 | יכשלו 3782 | ויאבדו 6 | מפניך 6440: | 9:4 | כי 3588 |
|---|---|---|---|---|---|---|---|---|---|
| 'alyoun. | | bashub | 'auyabay | 'achour; | yikashalu | uaya'badu, | mipaneyka. | | kiy |
| **O you most High** | | **When are turned** | **mine enemies** | **back** | **they shall fall** | **and perish** | **at your presence** | | **For** |

| עשית 6213 | משפטי 4941 | ודיני 1779 | ישבת 3427 | לכסא 3678 | שופט 8199 | צדק 6664: | 9:5 | גערת 1605 | גוים 1471 |
|---|---|---|---|---|---|---|---|---|---|
| 'asiyta | mishpatiy | uadiyniy; | yashabta | lakisea', | shoupet | tzedeq. | | ga'arta | gouyim |
| **you have maintained** | **my right** | **and my cause** | **you sat** | **in the throne** | **judging** | **right** | | **You have rebuked** | **the heathen** |

| אבדת 6 | רשע 7563 | שמם 8034 | מחית 4229 | לעולם 5769 | ועד 5703: | 9:6 | האויב 341 | תמו 8552 | חרבות 2723 |
|---|---|---|---|---|---|---|---|---|---|
| 'abadata | rasha'; | shamam | machiyta, | la'aulam | ua'ad. | | ha'auyeb | tamu | charabout, |
| **you have destroyed** | **the wicked** | **their name** | **you have put out** | **for ever** | **and ever** | | **O you enemy** | **are come end** | **destructions** |

| לנצח 5331 | וערים 5892 | נתשת 5428 | אבד 6 | זכרם 2143 | המה 1992: | 9:7 | ויהוה 3068 | לעולם 5769 | ישב 3427 |
|---|---|---|---|---|---|---|---|---|---|
| lanetzach | ua'ariym | natashta; | 'abad | zikram | hemah. | | uaYahuah | la'aulam | yesheb; |
| **to a perpetual** | **and cities** | **you have destroyed** | **is perished** | **their memorial** | ***with* them** | | **But Yahuah** | **for ever** | **shall endure** |

| כונן 3559 | למשפט 4941 | כסאו 3678: | 9:8 | והוא 1931 | ישפט 8199 | תבל 8398 | בצדק 6664 | ידין 1777 |
|---|---|---|---|---|---|---|---|---|
| kounen | lamishpat | kis'au. | | uahu'a, | yishpot | tebel | batzedeq; | yadiyn |
| **he has prepared** | **for judgment** | **his throne** | | **And he** | **shall judge** | **the world** | **in righteousness** | **he shall minister judgment** |

| לאמים 3816 | במישרים 4339: | 9:9 | ויהי 1961 | יהוה 3068 | משגב 4869 | לדך 1790 | משגב 4869 | לעתות 6256 | בצרה 6869: | 9:10 |
|---|---|---|---|---|---|---|---|---|---|---|
| la'amiym, | bameyshariym. | | uiyhiy | Yahuah | misgab | ladak; | misgab, | la'atout | batzarah. | |
| **to the people** | **in uprightness** | | **also will be** | **Yahuah** | **a refuge** | **for the oppressed** | **a refuge** | **in times** | **of trouble** | |

| ויבטחו 982 | בך 871a | יודעי 3045 | שמך 8034 | כי 3588 | לא 3808 | עזבת 5800 | דרשיך 1875 | יהוה 3068: | 9:11 |
|---|---|---|---|---|---|---|---|---|---|
| uayibtachu | baka | youda'aey | shameka; | kiy | la' | 'azabta | dorasheyka | Yahuah. | |
| **And they will put their trust** | **in you** | **that know** | **your name** | **for** | **not** | **you have forsaken** | **them that seek you** | **Yahuah** | |

| זמרו 2167 | ליהוה 3068 | ישב 3427 | ציון 6726 | הגידו 5046 | בעמים 5971 | עלילותיו 5949: | 9:12 | כי 3588 | דרש 1875 |
|---|---|---|---|---|---|---|---|---|---|
| zamru, | laYahuah | yosheb | tziyoun; | hagiydu | ba'amiym, | aliyloutayu. | | kiy | doresh |
| **Sing praises** | **to Yahuah** | **which dwell in** | **Zion** | **declare** | **among the people** | **his doings** | | **When** | **he make inquisition for** |

| דמים 1818 | אותם 853 | זכר 2142 | לא 3808 | שכח 7911 | צעקת 6818 | עניים 6041 | 9:13 | חנני 2603 | יהוה 3068 | ראה 7200 |
|---|---|---|---|---|---|---|---|---|---|---|
| damiym | 'autam | zakar; | la' | shakach, | tzea'aqat | 'aniyiym | | chananeniy | Yahuah | ra'aeh |
| **blood** | **them** | **he remembers** | **not** | **he forget** | **the cry of** | **the humble** | | **Have mercy upon me** | **O Yahuah** | **consider** |

| עניי 6040 | משנאי 8130 | מרוממי 7311 | משערי 8179 | מות 4194: | 9:14 | למען 4616 | אספרה 5608 |
|---|---|---|---|---|---|---|---|
| 'anyiy | misona'ay; | maroumamiy, | misha'arey | mauet. | | lama'an | 'asaprah, |
| **my trouble *which I suffer* of them that hate me** | | **you that lift me up** | **from the gates of** | **death** | | **That** | **I may show forth** |

**Psalms** 9:1 To the chief Musician upon Muth-lab'-ben, A Psalm of David. I will praise you, O YHUH, with my whole heart; I will show forth all your marvellous works.2 I will be glad and rejoice in you: I will sing praise to your name, O you most High.3 When mine enemies are turned back, they shall fall and perish at your presence.4 For you have maintained my right and my cause; you satest in the throne judging right.5 Thou have rebuked the heathen, you have destroyed the wicked, you have put out their name forever and ever.6 O you enemy, destructions are come to a perpetual end: and you have destroyed cities; their memorial is perished with them.7 But YHUH shall endure forever: he has prepared his throne for judgment.8 And he shall judge the world in righteousness, he shall minister judgment to the people in uprightness.9 YHUH also will be a refuge for the oppressed, a refuge in times of trouble.10 And they that know your name will put their trust in you: for you, YHUH, have not forsaken them that seek you.11 Sing praises to YHUH, which dwell in Zion: declare among the people his doings.12 When he make inquisition for blood, he remembereth them: he forgetteth not the cry of the humble.13 Have mercy upon me, O YHUH; consider my trouble which I suffer of them that hate me, you that liftest me up from the gates of death:

9:15

כל 3605 תהלתיך 8416 בשערי 8179 בת 1323 ציון 6726 אגילה 1523 בישועתך 3444: טבעו 2883 גוים 1471

kal tahilateyka basha'arey bat tziyoun; 'agiylah, biyshu'ateka. taba'au gouyim

**all your praise in the gates of the daughter of Zion I will rejoice in your salvation are sunk down The heathen**

9:16

בשחת 7845 עשו 6213 ברשת 7568 זו 2098 טמנו 2934 נלכדה 3920 רגלם 7272: נודע 3045 יהוה 3068 משפט 4941

bashachat 'asu; bareshet zu tamanu, nilkadah raglam. nouda' Yahuah mishapat

**in the pit *that* they made in the net which they hid is taken their own foot is known Yahuah *by* the judgment**

9:17

עשה 6213 בפעל 6467 כפיו 3709 נוקש 5367 רשע 7563 הגיון 1902 סלה 5542: ישובו 7725 רשעים 7563

'asah bapo'al kapayu nouqesh rasha'; higayoun selah. yashubu rasha'aym

***which* he execute in the work of his own hands is snared the wicked Higgaion Selah shall be turned The wicked**

9:18

לשאולה 7585 כל 3605 גוים 1471 שכחי 7913 אלהים 430: כי 3588 לא 3808 לנצח 5331 ישכח 7911 אביון 34 תקות 8615

lisha'aulah; kal gouyim, shakechey 'alohiym. kiy la' lanetzach yishakach abyoun; tiquat

**into hell all the nations that forget Elohim For not always shall be forgotten the needy the expectation of**

9:19

ענוים 6035 תאבד 6 לעד 5703: קומה 6965 יהוה 3069 אל 408 יעז 5810 אנוש 582 ישפטו 8199 גוים 1471 על 5921

'anauiym ta'bad la'ad. qumah Yahuah 'al ya'az 'anoush; yishapatu gouyim, 'al

**the poor shall *not* perish for ever Arise Yahuah not let prevail man let be judged the heathen in**

9:20

פניך 6440: שיתה 7896 יהוה 3068 מורה 4172 להם 1992 ידעו 3045 גוים 1471 אנוש 582 המה 1992 סלה 5542:

paneyka. shiytah Yahuah mourah, lahem yeda'au gouyim; 'anoush hemah selah.

**your sight Put Yahuah *in* fear them may know *that* the nations *to be but* men themselves Selah**

**Ps 10:1** 10:2

למה 4100 יהוה 3068 תעמד 5975 ברחוק 7350 תעלים 5956 לעתות 6256 בצרה 6869: בגאות 1346 רשע 7563

lamah Yahuah ta'amod barachouq; ta'aliym, la'atout batzarah. baga'auat rasha'

**Why Yahuah standest you afar off, *why* hide you *yourself* in times of trouble? in *his* pride The wicked**

10:3

ידלק 1814 עני 6041 יתפשו 8610 במזמות 4209 זו 2098 חשבו 2803: כי 3588 הלל 1984 רשע 7563 על 5921

yidlaq 'aniy; yitapasu bimazimout zu chashabu. kiy hilel rasha' 'al

**does persecute the poor let them be taken in the devices that they have imagined For boast the wicked of**

10:4

תאות 8378 נפשו 5315 ובצע 1214 ברך 1288 נאץ 5006 יהוה 3068: רשע 7563 כגבה 1363 אפו 639

ta'auat napshou; uabotzea' berek, ni'aetz Yahuah. rasha', kagobah 'apou

**desire his heart's the covetous and bless abhore *whom* Yahuah The wicked through the pride of his countenance**

10:5

בל 1077 ידרש 1875 אין 369 אלהים 430 כל 3605 מזמותיו 4209: יחילו 2342 דרכו 1870 בכל 3605 עת 6256 מרום 4791

bal yidrosh; 'aeyn 'alohiym, kal mazimoutayu. yachiylu daraku bakal 'aet, maroum

**not will seek *after Elohim is* not Elohim *in* all his thoughts are grievous His ways all ways *are* far above**

10:6

משפטיך 4941 מנגדו 5048 כל 3605 צורריו 6887 יפיח 6315 בהם 871a: אמר 559 בלבו 3820 בל 1077 אמוט 4131

mishpateyka minegdou; kal tzourayu, yapiyach bahem. 'amar balibou bal 'amout;

**your judgments out of his sight *as for* all his enemies he puff at them He has said in his heart not I shall be moved**

10:7

לדר 1755 ודר 1755 אשר 834 לא 3808 ברע 7451: אלה 423 פיהו 6310 מלא 4390 ומרמות 4820 ותך 8496 תחת 8478

lador uador, 'asher la' bara'. 'alah piyhu malea' uamirmout uatok; tachat

**ever and ever *for I shall* which nvere *be* in adversity cursing His mouth is full of and deceit and fraud under**

Ps 9:14 That I may show forth all your praise in the gates of the daughter of Zion: I will rejoice in your salvation.15 The heathen are sunk down in the pit that they made: in the net which they hid is their own foot taken.16 YHUH is known by the judgment which he executeth: the wicked is snared in the work of his own hands. Higgaion. Selah.17 The wicked shall be turned into hell, and all the nations that forget G-d.18 For the needy shall not alway be forgotten: the expectation of the poor shall not perish forever.19 Arise, O YHUH; let not man prevail: let the heathen be judged in your sight.20 Put them in fear, O YHUH: that the nations may know themselves to be but men. Selah. **Psalms** 10 :1 Why standest you afar off, O YHUH? why hidest you thyself in times of trouble?2 The wicked in his pride doth persecute the poor: let them be taken in the devices that they have imagined.3 For the wicked boasteth of his heart's desire, and blesseth the covetous, whom YHUH abhorreth.4 The wicked, through the pride of his countenance, will not seek after G-d: G-d is not in all his thoughts.5 His ways are always grievous; your judgments are far above out of his sight: as for all his enemies, he puffeth at them.6 He has said in his heart, I shall not be moved: for I shall never be in adversity.7 His mouth is full of cursing and deceit and fraud: under his tongue is mischief and vanity.

| לשונו 3956 | עמל 5999 | ואון 205: | 10:8 | ישב 3427 | במארב 3993 | חצרים 2691 | במסתרים 4565 | יהרג 2026 |
|---|---|---|---|---|---|---|---|---|
| lashounou, | 'amal | ua'auen. | | yesheb | bama'arab | chatzeriym, | bamistariym | yaharog |
| **his tongue** | ***is* mischief** | **and vanity** | | **He sit** | **in the lurking places of** | **the villages** | **in the secret places** | **does he murder** |

| נקי 5355 | עיניו 5869 | לחלכה 2489 | יצפנו 6845: | 10:9 | יארב 693 | במסתר 4565 | כאריה 738 | בסכה 5520 | יארב 693 |
|---|---|---|---|---|---|---|---|---|---|
| naqiy; | 'aeynayu, | lachelakah | yitzponu. | | ye'arob | bamistar | ka'aryeh | basukoh, | ye'arob |
| **the innocent** | **his eyes** | **against the poor** | **are privily set** | | **He lies in wait** | **secretly** | **as a lion** | **in his den** | **he lies in wait** |

| לחטוף 2414 | עני 6041 | יחטף 2414 | עני 6041 | במשכו 4900 | ברשתו 7568: | 10:10 | ודכה 1794 | ישח 7817 |
|---|---|---|---|---|---|---|---|---|
| lachatoup | 'aniy; | yachtop | 'aniy, | bamashakou | barishtou. | | uadkeh | yashoach; |
| **to catch** | **the poor** | **he does catch** | **the poor** | **when he draw him** | **into his net** | | **He croucheth,** | ***and* humble himself** |

| ונפל 5307 | בעצומיו 6099 | חלכאים 2489 | 10:11 | אמר 559 | בלבו 3820 | שכח 7911 | אל 410 | הסתיר 5641 | פניו 6440 | בל 1077 |
|---|---|---|---|---|---|---|---|---|---|---|
| uanapal | ba'atzumayu, | chelka'aym | | 'amar | balibou | shakach | 'ael; | histiyr | panayu, | bal |
| **that may fall** | **by his strong ones** | **the poor** | | **He has said** | **in his heart** | **has forgotten** | **El** | **he hides** | **his face** | **never** |

| ראה 7200 | לנצח 5331: | 10:12 | קומה 6965 | יהוה 3068 | אל 410 | נשא 5375 | ידך 3027 | אל 408 | תשכח 7911 | עניים 6041 | 10:13 | על 5921 |
|---|---|---|---|---|---|---|---|---|---|---|---|---|
| ra'ah | lanetzach. | | qumah | Yahuah | 'ael | nasa' | yadeka; | 'al | tishkach | 'aniyiym | | 'al |
| **he will see *it*** | **never** | | **Arise** | **O Yahuah** | **O El** | **lift up** | **your hand** | **not** | **forget** | **the humble** | | **Wherefore** |

| מה 4100 | נאץ 5006 | רשע 7563 | אלהים 430 | אמר 559 | בלבו 3820 | לא 3808 | תדרש 1875: | 10:14 | ראתה 7200 | כי 3588 |
|---|---|---|---|---|---|---|---|---|---|---|
| meh | ni'aetz | rasha' | 'alohiym; | 'amar | balibou, | la' | tidrosh. | | ra'aytah | kiy |
| **how *long*** | **does contemn** | **the wicked** | **Elohim?** | **he has said** | **in his heart** | **not** | **You will require *it*** | | **You have seen *it*** | **for** |

| אתה 859 | עמל 5999 | וכעס 3708 | תביט 5027 | לתת 5414 | בידך 3027 | עליך 5921 | יעזב 5800 | חלכה 2489 | יתום 3490 | אתה 859 |
|---|---|---|---|---|---|---|---|---|---|---|
| 'atah | 'amal | uaka'as | tabiyt | latet | bayadeka | 'aeleyk | ya'azob | chelekah; | yatoum, | 'atah |
| **you** | **mischief** | **and spite** | **behold** | **to requite *it*** | **with your hand** | **unto you** | **commit *himself*** | **the poor** | **the fatherless** | **you** |

| היית 1961 | עוזר 5826: | 10:15 | שבר 7665 | זרוע 2220 | רשע 7563 | ורע 7451 | תדרוש 1875 | רשעו 7562 | בל 1077 |
|---|---|---|---|---|---|---|---|---|---|
| hayiyta | 'auzer. | | shabor | zaroua' | rasha'; | bara', | tidroush | rish'au | bal |
| **are** | **the helper of** | | **Break you** | **the arm of** | **the wicked** | **and the evil** | ***man* seek out** | **his wickedness** | **none** |

| תמצא 4672: | 10:16 | יהוה 3068 | מלך 4428 | עולם 5769 | ועד 5703 | אבדו 6 | גוים 1471 | מארצו 776: | 10:17 | תאות 8378 | ענוים 6035 |
|---|---|---|---|---|---|---|---|---|---|---|---|
| timtzaa'. | | Yahuah | melek | 'aulam | ua'ad; | 'abadu | gouyim, | me'artzou. | | ta'auat | 'anauiym |
| ***till* you find** | | **Yahuah** | ***is* King** | **for ever** | **and ever** | **are perished** | **the heathen** | **out of his land** | | **the desire of** | **the humble** |

| שמעת 8085 | יהוה 3068 | תכין 3559 | לבם 3820 | תקשיב 7181 | אזנך 241: | 10:18 | לשפט 8199 | יתום 3490 |
|---|---|---|---|---|---|---|---|---|
| shama'ata | Yahuah; | takiyn | libam, | taqshiyb | 'azaneka. | | lishpot | yatoum, |
| **you have heard** | **Yahuah** | **you will prepare** | **their heart** | **you will cause to hear** | **your ear** | | **To judge** | **the fatherless** |

| ודך 1790 | בל 1077 | יוסיף 3254 | עוד 5750 | לערץ 6206 | אנוש 582 | מן 4480 | הארץ 776: |
|---|---|---|---|---|---|---|---|
| uadak | bal | yousiyp | 'aud; | la'arotz | 'anoush, | min | ha'aretz. |
| **and the oppressed** | **no** | **more** | **again** | **may oppress** | ***that* the man** | **of** | **the earth** |

| Ps 11:1 | למנצח 5329 | לדוד 1732 | ביהוה 3068 | חסיתי 2620 | איך 349 | תאמרו 559 | לנפשי 5315 | נודו 5110 |
|---|---|---|---|---|---|---|---|---|
| | lamanatzeach, | ladauid | baYahuah | chasiytiy, | 'aeyk | ta'maru | lanapshiy; | nudu |
| | **To the chief Musician** | ***A Psalm* of David** | **In Yahuah** | **put I my trust** | **How** | **say you** | **to my soul** | **Flee** |

Ps 10:8 He sitteth in the lurking places of the villages: in the secret places doth he murder the innocent: his eyes are privily set against the poor.9 He lie in wait secretly as a lion in his den: he lie in wait to catch the poor: he doth catch the poor, when he draweth him into his net.10 He croucheth, and humbleth himself, that the poor may fall by his strong ones.11 He has said in his heart, G-d has forgotten: he hide his face; he will never see it.12 Arise, O YHUH; O G-d, lift up your hand: forget not the humble.13 Wherefore doth the wicked contemn G-d? he has said in his heart, Thou will not require it.14 Thou have seen it; for you beholdest mischief and spite, to requite it with your hand: the poor committeth himself unto you; you are the helper of the fatherless.15 Break you the arm of the wicked and the evil man: seek out his wickedness till you find none.16 YHUH is King forever and ever: the heathen are perished out of his land.17 YHUH, you have heard the desire of the humble: you will prepare their heart, you will cause your ear to hear:18 To judge the fatherless and the oppressed, that the man of the earth may no more oppress. **Psalms** 11:1 To the chief Musician, A Psalm of David.

11:2

הרכם 2022 צפור 6833: כי 3588 הנה 2009 הרשעים 7563 ידרכון 1869 קשת 7198 כוננו 3559 חצם 2671 על 5921 יתר 3499
harakem tzipour. kiy hineh harasha'aym yidrakun qeshet, kounanu chitzam 'al yeter;
**_to_ your mountain? _as_ a bird For lo the wicked bend _their_ bow they make ready their arrow upon the string**

11:3

לירות 3384 במו 1119 אפל 652 לישרי 3477 לב 3820: כי 3588 השתות 8356 יהרסון 2040 צדיק 6662 מה 4100
liyrout bamou 'apel, layishrey leb. kiy hashatout yeharesun; tzadiyq, mah
**that they may shoot by privily at the uprightin heart If the foundations be destroyed the righteous what**

11:4

פעל 6466: יהוה 3068 בהיכל 1964 קדשו 6944 יהוה 3068 בשמים 8064 כסאו 3678 עיניו 5869 יחזו 2372 עפעפיו 6079 יבחנו 974
pa'al. Yahuah baheykal qadashou, Yahuah bashamayim kis'au 'aeynayu yechazu; 'ap'apayu yibchanu,
**can do? Yahuah _is_ in temple his holy Yahuah's _is_ in heaven throne his eyes behold his eyelids try**

11:5 11:6

בני 1121 אדם 120: יהוה 3068 צדיק 6662 יבחן 974 ורשע 7563 ואהב 157 חמס 2555 שנאה 8130 נפשו 5315:
baney 'adam. Yahuah tzadiyq yibchan uarashaa' ua'aheb chamas; sana'ah napshou.
**the children of men Yahuah the righteous tries but the wicked and him that love violence hate his soul**

ימטר 4305 על 5921 רשעים 7563 פחים 6341 אש 784 וגפרית 1614 ורוח 7307 זלעפות 2152 מנת 4521
yamter 'al rasha'aym, pachiym 'aesh uagapariyt uaruach zil'apout, manat
**he shall rain Upon the wicked snares fire and brimstone and an tempest horrible _this shall be_]the portion of**

11:7

כוסם 3563: כי 3588 צדיק 6662 יהוה 3068 צדקות 6666 אהב 157 ישר 3477 יחזו 2372 פנימו 6440:
kousam. kiy tzadiyq Yahuah tzadaqout 'aheb; yashar, yechezu paneymou.
**their cup For the righteous Yahuah righteousness love the upright does behold his countenance**

**Ps 12:1**

למנצח 5329 על 5921 השמינית 8067 מזמור 4210 לדוד 1732: הושיעה 3467 יהוה 3068 כי 3588 גמר 1584 חסיד 2623 כי 3588
lamanatzeach 'al hashamiynit, mizmour ladauid. houshiy'ah Yahuah kiy gamar chasiyd; kiy
**To the chief Musician upon Sheminith A Psalm of David Help Yahuah for cease the godly man for**

12:2

פסו 6461 אמונים 539 מבני 1121 אדם 120: שוא 7723 ידברו 1696 איש 376 את 854 רעהו 7453 שפת 8193
pasu 'amuniym, mibney 'adam. shau'a yadabru 'aysh 'at re'aehu sapat
**fail the faithful from among the children of men vanity They speak every one _with_ his neighbour lips**

12:3

חלקות 2513 בלב 3820 ולב 3820 ידברו 1696: יכרת 3772 יהוה 3068 כל 3605 שפתי 8193 חלקות 2513 לשון 3956
chalaqout; baleb ualeb yadaberu. yakret Yahuah kal siptey chalaqout; lashoun,
**_with_ flattering _and_ with a double heart do they speak shall cut off Yahuah all lips flattering _and_ the tongue**

12:4

מדברת 1696 גדלות 1419: אשר 834 אמרו 559 ללשננו 3956 נגביר 1396 שפתינו 8193 אתנו 853 מי 4310 אדון 113
madaberet gadolout. 'asher 'amaru lilshonenu nagbiyr sapateynu 'atanu; miy' 'adoun
**that speak proud things Who have said With our tongue will we prevail our lips _are_ our own who _is_ adonai**

12:5

לנו 3807a: משד 7701 עניים 6041 מאנקת 603 אביונים 34 עתה 6258 אקום 6965 יאמר 559 יהוה 3068 אשית 7896
lanu. mishod 'aniyiym me'anqat 'abyouniym 'atah 'aqum ya'mar Yahuah; 'ashiyt
**over us? For the oppression of the poor for the sighing of the needy now will I arise saith Yahuah I will set**

12:6

בישע 3468 יפיח 6315 לו 3807a: אמרות 565 יהוה 3068 אמרות 565 טהרות 2889 כסף 3701 צרוף 6884 בעליל 5948
bayesha', yapiyach lou'. 'amarout Yahuah 'amarout tahorout kesep tzarup ba'aliyl
**_him_ in safety _from him that_ puff at him The words of Yahuah words _are_ pure _as_ silver tried in a furnace**

Ps 11:1 In YHUH put I my trust: How say you to my soul, Flee as a bird to your mountain?2 For, lo, the wicked bend their bow, they make ready their arrow upon the string, that they may privily shoot at the upright in heart.3 If the foundations be destroyed, what can the righteous do?4 YHUH is in his holy temple, YHUH's throne is in heaven: his eyes behold, his eyelids try, the children of men.5 YHUH trieth the righteous: but the wicked and him that love violence his soul hateth.6 Upon the wicked he shall rain snares, fire and brimstone, and an horrible tempest: this shall be the portion of their cup.7 For the righteous YHUH love righteousness; his countenance doth behold the upright. **Psalms** 12:1 To the chief Musician upon Shem'-i-nith, A Psalm of David. Help, YHUH; for the godly man ceaseth; for the faithful fail from among the children of men.2 They speak vanity everyone with his neighbor: with flattering lips and with a double heart do they speak.3 YHUH shall cut off all flattering lips, and the tongue that speaketh proud things:4 Who have said, With our tongue will we prevail; our lips are our own: who is lord over us?5 For the oppression of the poor, for the sighing of the needy, now will I arise, saith YHUH; I will set him in safety from him that puffeth at him.6 The words of YHUH are pure words: as silver tried in a furnace of earth, purified seven times.

12:7

לארץ 776 מזקק 2212 שבעתים 7659: אתה 859 יהוה 3068 תשמרם 8104 תצרנו 5341 מן 4480 הדור 1755 זו 2098
la'aretz; mazuqaq, shib'atayim. 'atah Yahuah tishmarem; titzrenu min hadour zu
**of earth purified seven times You O Yahuah shall keep them you shall preserve them from generation this**

12:8

לעולם 5769: סביב 5439 רשעים 7563 יתהלכון 1980 כרם 7311 זלות 2149 לבני 1121 אדם 120:
la'aulam. sabiyb, rasha'aym yithalakun; karum zulut, libney 'adam.
**for ever on every side The wicked walk when are exalted *the* vilest the sons of men**

Ps 13:1

למנצח 5329 מזמור 4210 לדוד 1732: עד 5704 אנה 575 יהוה 3068 תשכחני 7911 נצח 5331 עד 5704 אנה 575
lamanatzeach, mizmour ladauid. 'ad 'anah Yahuah tishkacheniy netzach; 'ad 'anah
**To the chief Musician A Psalm of David How long when? Yahuah will you forget me for ever? how long when**

13:2

תסתיר 5641 את 853 פניך 6440 ממני 4480: עד 5704 אנה 575 אשית 7896 עצות 6098 בנפשי 5315 יגון 3015 בלבבי 3824
tastiyr 'at paneyka mimeniy. 'ad 'anah 'ashiyt aetzout banapashiy, yagoun bilbabiy
**will you hide your face from me? How long shall I take counsel in my soul *having* sorrow in my heart**

13:3

יומם 3119 עד 5704 אנה 575 ירום 7311 איבי 341 עלי 5921: הביטה 5027 ענני 6030 יהוה 3068 אלהי 430 האירה 215
youmam; 'ad 'anah yarum 'ayabiy 'alay. habiytah 'aneniy Yahuah 'alohay; ha'ayrah
**daily? how long shall be exalted mine enemy over me? Consider *and* hear me O Yahuah my Elohim lighten**

13:4

עיני 5869 פן 6435 אישן 3462 המות 4194: פן 6435 יאמר 559 איבי 341 יכלתיו 3201
'aeynay, pen 'ayshan hamauet. pen ya'mar 'ayabiy yakaltiyu;
**mine eyes lest I sleep the *sleep of* death Lest say mine enemy I have prevailed against him**

13:5

צרי 6862 יגילו 1523 כי 3588 אמוט 4131: ואני 589 בחסדך 2617 בטחתי 982 יגל 1523 לבי 3820
tzaray yagiylu, kiy 'amout. ua'aniy bachasdaka batachtiy yagel libiy,
***and* those that trouble me rejoice when I am moved But I in your mercy have trusted shall rejoice my heart**

13:6

בישועתך 3444 אשירה 7891 ליהוה 3068 כי 3588 גמל 1580 עלי 5921:
biyshu'ateka 'ashiyrah laYahuah; kiy gamal 'alay.
**in your salvation I will sing unto Yahuah because he has dealt bountifully with me**

Ps 14:1

למנצח 5329 לדוד 1732 אמר 559 נבל 5036 בלבו 3820 אין 369 אלהים 430 השחיתו 7843
lamanatzeach, ladauid 'amar nabal balibou 'aeyn 'alohiym; hishchiytu,
**To the chief Musician *A Psalm* of David has said The fool in his heart *There is* no Elohim They are corrupt**

14:2

התעיבו 8581 עלילה 5949 אין 369 עשה 6213 טוב 2896: יהוה 3068 משמים 8064 השקיף 8259 על 5921
hit'aybu 'aliylah, 'aeyn 'aseh toub. Yahuah mishamayim hishqiyp 'al
**they have done abominable works *there is* none that does good Yahuah from heaven looked down upon**

14:3

בני 1121 אדם 120 לראות 7200 היש 3426 משכיל 7919 דרש 1875 את 853 אלהים 430: הכל 3605
baney 'adam lir'aut hayesh maskiyl; doresh 'at 'alohiym. hakol
**the children of men to see *if* there were any that did understand *and* seek Elohim all**

14:4

סר 5493 יחדו 3162 נאלחו 444 אין 369 עשה 6213 טוב 2896 אין 369 גם 1571 אחד 259: הלא 3808
sar yachdau ne'alachu 'aeyn 'aseh toub; 'aeyn, gam 'achad. hala'
**They are gone aside *all* together they are become filthy *there is* none that does good no not one no**

Ps 12:7 Thou shall keep them, O YHUH, you shall preserve them from this generation forever.8 The wicked walk on every side, when the vilest men are exalted. **Psalms** 13:1 To the chief Musician, A Psalm of David. How long will you forget me, O YHUH? forever? how long will you hide your face from me?2 How long shall I take counsel in my soul, having sorrow in my heart daily? how long shall mine enemy be exalted over me?3 Consider and hear me, O YHUH my G-d: lighten mine eyes, lest I sleep the sleep of death;4 Lest mine enemy say, I have prevailed against him; and those that trouble me rejoice when I am moved.5 But I have trusted in your mercy; my heart shall rejoice in your salvation.6 I will sing unto YHUH, because he has dealt bountifully with me. **Psalms** 14:1 To the chief Musician, A Psalm of David. The fool has said in his heart, There is no G-d. They are corrupt, they have done abominable works, there is none that doeth good.2 YHUH looked down from heaven upon the children of men, to see if there were any that did understand, and seek G-d.3 They are all gone aside, they are all together become filthy: there is none that doeth good, no, not one.

ידעו 3045 כל 3605 פעלי 6466 און 205 אכלי 398 עמי 5971 אכלו 398 לחם 3899 יהוה 3068 לא 3808 קראו 7121: **14:5**
yada'au kal po'aley 'auen 'akley 'amiy 'akalu lechem; Yahuah la' qara'au.
**Have knowledge? all the workers of iniquity who eat up my people *as* they eat bread Yahuah not *and* call upon**

שם 8033 פחדו 6342 פחד 6343 כי 3588 אלהים 430 בדור 1755 צדיק 6662: **14:6** עצת 6098 עני 6041
sham pachadu pachad; kiy 'alohiym, badour tzadiyq. 'atzat 'aniy
**There *were* they fear *in* great for Elohim *is* in the generation of the righteous the counsel of the poor**

תבישו 954 כי 3588 יהוה 3068 מחסהו 4268: **14:7** מי 4310 יתן 5414 מציון 6726 ישועת 3444 ישראל 3478 בשוב 7725
tabiyshu; kiy Yahuah machsehu. miy' yiten mitziyoun yashu'at yisra'ael bashub
**You have shamed because Yahuah *is* his refuge Oh that were come out of Zion the salvation of Israel bring back**

יהוה 3068 שבות 7622 עמו 5971 יגל 1523 יעקב 3290 ישמח 8055 ישראל 3478:
Yahuah shabut 'amou; yagel ya'aqob, yismach yisra'ael
**Yahuah the captivity of his people shall rejoice Jacob shall be glad *and* Israel**

**Ps 15:1** **15:2**
מזמור 4210 לדוד 1732 יהוה 3068 מי 4310 יגור 1481 באהלך 168 מי 4310 ישכן 7931 בהר 2022 קדשך 6944:
mizmour, ladauid Yahuah miy' yagur ba'ahaleka; miy' yishkan, bahar qadasheka
**A Psalm of David Yahuah who shall abide in your tabernacle? who may dwell in hill? your holy**

הולך 1980 תמים 8549 ופעל 6466 צדק 6664 ודבר 1696 אמת 571 בלבבו 3824: **15:3** לא 3808 רגל 7270 על 5921
houlek tamiym uapo'ael tzedeq; uadober 'amet, bilbabou. la' ragal 'al
**He that walk uprightly and work righteousness and speak the truth in his heart *He that* not backbiteth with**

לשנו 3956 לא 3808 עשה 6213 לרעהו 7453 רעה 7451 וחרפה 2781 לא 3808 נשא 5375 על 5921 קרבו 7138: **15:4** נבזה 959
lashonou, la' 'asah lare'aehu ra'ah; uacherpah, la' nasa' 'al qarobou. nibzeh
**his tongue nor does to his neighbour evil a reproach nor takes up against his neighbour is contemned**

בעיניו 5869 נמאס 3988 ואת 853 יראי 3373 יהוה 3068 יכבד 3513 נשבע 7650 להרע 7489 ולא 3808 ימר 4171: **15:5**
ba'aeynayu nim'as, ua'at yira'aey Yahuah yakabed; nishba' lahara', uala' yamiyr.
**In whose eyes a vile person *but* them that fear Yahuah he honors *He that* swears to *his own* hurt and not changes**

כספו 3701 לא 3808 נתן 5414 בנשך 5392 ושחד 7810 על 5921 נקי 5355 לא 3808 לקח 3947 עשה 6213 אלה 428 לא 3808
kaspou la' natan baneshek uashochad 'al naqiy, la' laqach 'aseh 'aeleh; la'
***He that* his money not put out to usury reward against the innocent nor takes He that does these never *things***

ימוט 4131 לעולם 5769:
yimout la'aulam.
**shall be moved never**

**Ps 16:1** **16:2**
מכתם 4387 לדוד 1732 שמרני 8104 אל 410 כי 3588 חסיתי 2620 בך 871a: אמרת 559 ליהוה 3068
miktam ladauid; shamareniy 'ael, kiy chasiytiy bak. 'amart laYahuah
**Michtam of David Preserve me O El for do I put my trust in you *O my soul* you have said unto Yahuah**

אדני 136 אתה 859 טובתי 2896 בל 1077 עליך 5921: **16:3** לקדושים 6918 אשר 834 בארץ 776 המה 1992
'adonay 'atah; toubatiy, bal 'aleyka. liqdoushiym 'asher ba'aretz hemah;
**You *are* my Adonai you my goodness *extends* not to you *But* to the saints that *are* in the earth they**

Ps 14:4 Have all the workers of iniquity no knowledge? who eat up my people as they eat bread, and call not upon YHUH.5 There were they in great fear: for G-d is in the generation of the righteous.6 You have shamed the counsel of the poor, because YHUH is his refuge.7 Oh that the salvation of Israel were come out of Zion! when YHUH bring back the captivity of his people, Jacob shall rejoice, and Israel shall be glad. **Psalms** 15:1 A Psalm of David YHUH, who shall abide in your tabernacle? who shall dwell in your holy hill?2 He that walk uprightly, and worketh righteousness, and speaketh the truth in his heart.3 He that backbiteth not with his tongue, nor doeth evil to his neighbor, nor take up a reproach against his neighbor.4 In whose eyes a vile person is contemned; but he honoureth them that fear YHUH. He that sweareth to his own hurt, and changeth not.5 He that put not out his money to usury, nor take reward against the innocent. He that doeth these things shall never be moved. **Psalms** 16:1 Mich'-tam of David. Preserve me, O G-d: for in you do I put my trust.2 O my soul, you have said unto YHUH, Thou are my Adonai: my goodness extendeth not to you;3 But to the saints that are in the earth, and to the excellent, in whom is all my delight.

16:4
ואדירי 117 כל 3605 חפצי 2656 בם 871a: ירבו 7235 עצבותם 6094 אחר 312 מהרו 4116 בל 1077
ua'adiyrey, kal cheptziy bam. yirbu 'atzboutam 'acher maharu bal
**and *to* the excellent *is* all my delight in whom shall be multiplied *that* Their sorrows another *god* hasten *after* not**

16:5
אסיך 5258 נסכיהם 5262 מדם 1818 ובל 1077 אשא 5375 את 853 שמותם 8034 על 5921 שפתי 8193: יהוה 3068 מנת 4490
'asiyk niskeyhem midam; uabal 'asa' 'at shamoutam, 'al sapatay. Yahuah manot
**will I offer their drink offerings of blood nor take up their names into my lips Yahuah *is* the portion of**

16:6
חלקי 2506 וכוסי 3563 אתה 859 תומיך 8551 גורלי 1486: חבלים 2256 נפלו 5307 לי 3807a בנעמים 5273 אף 637
chelqiy uakousiy; 'atah, toumiyk gouraliy. chabaliym naplu liy bana'amiym; 'ap
**mine inheritance and of my cup you maintainest my lot *The* lines are fallen unto me in pleasant *places* yea *have***

16:7
נחלת 5159 שפרה 8231 עלי 5921: אברך 1288 את 853 יהוה 3068 אשר 834 יעצני 3289 אף 637 לילות 3915 יסרוני 3256
nachalat, shaparah 'alay. 'abarek, 'at Yahuah 'asher ya'atzaniy; 'ap leylout, yisruniy
**a heritage goodly I I will bless Yahuah who has given me counsel also *in* the night seasons instruct me**

16:8
כליותי 3629: שויתי 7737 יהוה 3068 לנגדי 5048 תמיד 8548 כי 3588 מימיני 3225 בל 1077 אמוט 4131:
kilyoutay. shiuiytiy Yahuah lanegdiy tamiyd; kiy miymiyniy, bal 'amout.
**my reins I have set Yahuah before me always because *he is* at my right hand not I shall be moved**

16:9
לכן 3651
laken
**Therefore**

16:10
שמח 8055 לבי 3820 ויגל 1523 כבודי 3519 אף 637 בשרי 1320 ישכן 7931 לבטח 983: כי 3588 לא 3808 תעזב 5800 נפשי 5315 לשאול 7585
samak libiy uayagel kaboudiy; 'ap basariy, yishkon labetach. kiy la' ta'azob napshiy lisha'ul;
**is glad my heart and rejoice my glory also my flesh shall rest in hope For not you will leave my soul in hell**

16:11
לא 3808 תתן 5414 חסידך 2623 לראות 7200 שחת 7845: תודיעני 3045 ארח 734 חיים 2416 שבע 7648
la' titen chasiydaka, lir'aut shachat toudiy'aeniy 'arach chayiym soba'
**neither will you suffer your Holy One to see corruption You will show me the path of life *is* fulness of**

שמחות 8057 את 853 פניך 6440 נעמות 5273 בימינך 3225 נצח 5331:
samachout 'at paneyka; na'amout biymiynaka netzach.
**joy in your presence *there are* pleasures at your right hand for evermore**

Ps 17:1
תפלה 8605 לדוד 1732 שמעה 8085 יהוה 3068 צדק 6664 הקשיבה 7181 רנתי 7440 האזינה 238 תפלתי 8605 בלא 3808 שפתי 8193
tapilah, ladauid shim'ah Yahuah tzedeq, haqashiybah rinatiy, ha'aziynah tapilatiy; bala', siptey
**A Prayer of David Hear O Yahuah the right attend unto my cry give ear unto my prayer *that goes* not lips**

17:2
17:3
מרמה 4820: מלפניך 6440 משפטי 4941 יצא 3318 עיניך 5869 תחזינה 2372 מישרים 4339:
mirmah. milpaneyka mishpatiy yetzea'; 'aeyneyka, techazeynah meyshariym.
***out of* feigned from your presence my sentence Let come forth your eyes let behold *the things* that are equal**

בחנת 974 לבי 3820 פקדת 6485 לילה 3915 צרפתני 6884 בל 1077 תמצא 4672 זמתי 2161 בל 1077
bachanta libiy paqadta layalah, tzaraptaniy bal timtzaa'; zamotiy, bal
**You have proved mine heart you have visited *me* in the night you have tried me nothing *and* shall find I am purposed not**

17:4
יעבר 5674 פי 6310: לפעלות 6468 אדם 120 בדבר 1697 שפתיך 8193 אני 589 שמרתי 8104
ya'abar piy. lipa'alout 'adam bidbar sapateyka; 'aniy shamartiy,
**shall transgress *that* my mouth Concerning the works of men by the word of your lips I have kept**

Ps 16:5 YHUH is the portion of mine inheritance and of my cup: you maintainest my lot.6 The lines are fallen unto me in pleasant places; yea, I have a goodly heritage.7 I will bless YHUH, who has given me counsel: my reins also instruct me in the night seasons.8 I have set YHUH always before me: because he is at my right hand, I shall not be moved.9 Therefore my heart is glad, and my glory rejoice: my flesh also shall rest in hope.10 For you will not leave my soul in hell; neither will you suffer your Holy One to see corruption.11 Thou will show me the path of life: in your presence is fulness of joy; at your right hand there are pleasures forevermore. **Psalms** 17:1 A Prayer of David. Hear the right, O YHUH, attend unto my cry, give ear unto my prayer, that go not out of feigned lips.2 Let my sentence come forth from your presence; let your eyes behold the things that are equal.3 Thou has proved mine heart; you have visited me in the night; you has tried me, and shall find nothing; I am purposed that my mouth shall not transgress.4 Concerning the works of men, by the word of your lips I have kept me from the paths of the destroyer.

| ארחות 734 | פריץ 6530: | 17:5 | תמך 8551 | אשרי 838 | במעגלותיך 4570 | בל 1077 | נמוטו 4131 | פעמי 6471: | 17:6 | אני 589 |
|---|---|---|---|---|---|---|---|---|---|---|
| 'arachout | pariytz. | | tamok | 'ashuray | bama'aglouteyka; | bal | namoutu | pa'amay. | | 'aniy |
| ***me from* the paths of** | **the destroyer** | | **Hold up** | **my goings** | **in your paths** | **not** | **slip** | ***that* my footsteps** | | **I** |

| קראתיך 7121 | כי 3588 | תענני 6030 | אל 410 | הט 5186 | אזנך 241 | לי 3807a | שמע 8085 | אמרתי 565: | 17:7 |
|---|---|---|---|---|---|---|---|---|---|
| qaraa'tiyka | kiy | ta'aneniy | 'ael; | hat | 'aznaka | liy, | shama' | 'amratiy. | |
| **have called upon you** | **for** | **you will hear me** | **O El** | **incline** | **your ear** | **unto me** | ***and* hear** | **my speech** | |

| הפלה 6395 | חסדיך 2617 | מושיע 3467 | חוסים 2620 | ממתקוממים 6965 |
|---|---|---|---|---|
| hapaleh | chasadeyka | moushiya' | chousiym; | mimitqoumamiym, |
| **Shew your marvellous** | **lovingkindness** | ***O you* that save** | **them which put their trust** | ***in you* from those that rise up** |

| בימינך 3225: | 17:8 | שמרני 8104 | כאישון 380 | בת 1323 | עין 5869 | בצל 6738 | כנפיך 3671 | תסתירני 5641: | 17:9 |
|---|---|---|---|---|---|---|---|---|---|
| biymiyneka. | | shamareniy | ka'ayshoun | bat | 'ayin; | batzel | kanapeyka, | tastiyreniy. | |
| **by your right hand** | | **Keep me** | **as the apple of** | **first (*daughter*)** | **the eye** | **under the shadow of** | **your wings** | **hide me** | |

| מפני 6440 | רשעים 7563 | זו 2098 | שדוני 7703 | איבי 341 | בנפש 5315 | יקיפו 5362 | עלי 5921: | 17:10 | חלבמו 2459 |
|---|---|---|---|---|---|---|---|---|---|
| mipaney | rasha'aym | zu | shaduniy; | 'ayabay | banepesh, | yaqiypu | 'alay. | | chelbamou |
| **From** | **the wicked** | **that** | **oppress me** | ***from* my enemies** | **deadly** | ***who* compass about** | **me** | | **in their own fat** |

| סגרו 5462 | פימו 6310 | דברו 1696 | בגאות 1348: | 17:11 | אשרינו 838 | עתה 6258 | סבבוני 5437 | עיניהם 5869 |
|---|---|---|---|---|---|---|---|---|
| sagaru; | piymou, | dibru | bage'aut. | | 'ashureynu | 'atah | sababuniy | 'aeyneyhem |
| **They are inclosed** | ***with* their mouth** | **they speak** | **proudly** | | ***in* our steps** | **now** | **They have compassed us** | **their eyes** |

| ישיתו 7896 | לנטות 5186 | בארץ 776: | 17:12 | דמינו 1825 | כאריה 738 | יכסוף 3700 | לטרוף 2963 | וככפיר 3715 |
|---|---|---|---|---|---|---|---|---|
| yashiytu, | linatout | ba'aretz. | | dimyonou, | ka'aryeh | yiksoup | litaroup; | uakikapiyr, |
| **they have set** | **bowing down** | **to the earth** | | **Like** | **as a lion** | ***that* is greedy** | **of his prey** | **and as it were a young lion** |

| ישב 3427 | במסתרים 4565: | 17:13 | קומה 6965 | יהוה 3068 | קדמה 6923 | פניו 6440 | הכריעהו 3766 | פלטה 6403 | נפשי 5315 | מרשע 7563 |
|---|---|---|---|---|---|---|---|---|---|---|
| yosheb | bamistariym. | | qumah | Yahuah | qadmah | panayu | hakariy'aehu; | paltah | napshiy, | merasha' |
| **lurking** | **in secret places** | | **Arise** | **O Yahuah** | **disappoint** | **him** | **cast him down** | **deliver** | **my soul** | **from the wicked** |

| חרבך 2719: | 17:14 | ממתים 4962 | ידך 3027 | יהוה 3068 | ממתים 4962 | מחלד 2465 | חלקם 2506 |
|---|---|---|---|---|---|---|---|
| charbeka. | | mimatiym | yadaka | Yahuah | mimatiym | mecheled, | chelaqam |
| ***which is* your sword** | | **From men** | ***which are* your hand** | **O Yahuah** | **from men** | **of the world** | ***which have* their portion** |

| בחיים 2416 | וצפינך 6840 | תמלא 4390 | בטנם 990 | ישבעו 7646 | בנים 1121 | והניחו 3240 | יתרם 3499 |
|---|---|---|---|---|---|---|---|
| bachayiym | uatzpiynaka | tamalea' | bitnam | yisba'au | baniym; | uahiniychu | yitram, |
| **in *this* life** | **your hid *treasure*:** | **you fillest with** | ***and* whose belly** | **they are full of** | **children** | **and leave** | **the rest of** |

| לעולליהם 5768: | 17:15 | אני 589 | בצדק 6664 | אחזה 2372 | פניך 6440 | אשבעה 7646 | בהקיץ 6974 |
|---|---|---|---|---|---|---|---|
| la'aulaleyhem. | | 'aniy, | batzedeq | 'achezeh | paneyka; | 'asba'ah | bahaqiytz, |
| ***their substance* to their babes** | | **As for me** | **in righteousness** | **I will behold** | **your face** | **I shall be satisfied** | **when I awake** |

| תמונתך 8544: |
|---|
| tamunateka. |
| ***with* your likeness** |

Ps 17:5 Hold up my goings in your paths, that my footsteps slip not.6 I have called upon you, for you will hear me, O G-d: incline your ear unto me, and hear my speech.7 Shew your marvellous lovingkindness, O you that save by your right hand them which put their trust in you from those that rise up against them.8 Keep me as the apple of the eye, hide me under the shadow of your wings,9 From the wicked that oppress me, from my deadly enemies, who compass me about.10 They are enclosed in their own fat: with their mouth they speak proudly.11 They have now compassed us in our steps: they have set their eyes bowing down to the earth;12 Like as a lion that is greedy of his prey, and as it were a young lion lurking in secret places.13 Arise, O YHUH, disappoint him, cast him down: deliver my soul from the wicked, which is your sword:14 From men which are your hand, O YHUH, from men of the world, which have their portion in this life, and whose belly you fillest with your hid treasure: they are full of children, and leave the rest of their substance to their babes.15 As for me, I will behold your face in righteousness: I shall be satisfied, when I awake, with your likeness.

| **Ps 18:1** | למנצח 5329 | לעבד 5650 | יהוה 3068 | לדוד 1732 | אשר 834 | דבר 1696 | ליהוה 3068 | את 853 | דברי 1697 |
|---|---|---|---|---|---|---|---|---|---|
| | lamanatzeach | la'abed | Yahuah | ladauid | 'asher | diber | laYahuah | 'at | dibrey |
| | **To the chief Musician** | **the servant** | **of Yahuah** | ***A Psalm* of David** | **who** | **spoke** | **unto Yahuah** | | **the words of** |

| השירה 7892 | הזאת 2063 | ביום 3117 | הציל 5337 | יהוה 3068 | אותו 853 | מכף 3709 | כל 3605 | איביו 341 | ומיד 3027 | שאול 7586: |
|---|---|---|---|---|---|---|---|---|---|---|
| hashiyrah | haza't; | bayoum | hitziyl | Yahuah | 'autou | mikap | kal | 'ayabayu, | uamiyad | sha'aul. |
| **song** | **this** | **in the day *that*** | **delivered** | **Yahuah** | **him** | **from the hand of** | **all** | **his enemies** | **and from the hand of** | **Saul** |

| ויאמר 559 | ארחמך 7355 | יהוה 3068 | חזקי 2391: | **18:2** | יהוה 3068 | סלעי 5553 | ומצודתי 4686 | ומפלטי 6403 | אלי 410 |
|---|---|---|---|---|---|---|---|---|---|
| uaya'mar | 'archamaka | Yahuah | chizqiy. | | Yahuah | sala'ay | uamtzudatiy, | uampaltiy | 'aeliy |
| **And he said** | **I will love you** | **O Yahuah** | **my strength** | | **Yahuah** | ***is* my rock** | **and my fortress** | **and my deliverer** | ***my* El** |

| צורי 6697 | אחסה 2620 | בו 871a | מגני 4043 | וקרן 7161 | ישעי 3468 | משגבי 4869: | **18:3** |
|---|---|---|---|---|---|---|---|
| tzuriy | 'acheseh | bou; | maginiy | uaqeren | yish'ay, | misgabiy. | |
| **my strength** | **I will trust** | **in whom** | **my buckler** | **and the horn of** | **my salvation** | ***and* my high tower** | |

| מהלל 1984 | אקרא 7121 | יהוה 3068 | ומן 4480 | איבי 341 | אושע 3467: | **18:4** | אפפוני 661 |
|---|---|---|---|---|---|---|---|
| mahulal | 'aqraa' | Yahuah; | uamin | 'ayabay, | 'auashea'. | | 'apapuniy |
| ***who is worthy* to be praised** | **I will call upon** | **Yahuah** | **so shall** | **mine enemies** | **shall I be saved** | | **compassed me** |

| חבלי 2256 | מות 4194 | ונחלי 5158 | בליעל 1100 | יבעתוני 1204: | **18:5** | חבלי 2256 | שאול 7585 |
|---|---|---|---|---|---|---|---|
| chebley | mauet; | uanachaley | baliya'al | yaba'atuniy. | | chebley | sha'aul |
| **The sorrows of** | **death** | **and the floods of** | **ungodly men** | **made me afraid** | | **The sorrows of** | **hell (*grave*)** |

| סבבוני 5437 | קדמוני 6923 | מוקשי 4170 | מות 4194: | **18:6** | בצר 6862 | לי 3807a | אקרא 7121 | יהוה 3068 | ואל 413 |
|---|---|---|---|---|---|---|---|---|---|
| sababuniy; | qidmuniy, | mouqashey | mauet. | | batzar | liy | 'aqraa' | Yahuah | ua'al |
| **compassed me about** | **prevented me** | **the snares of** | **death** | | **In distress** | **my** | **I called upon** | **Yahuah** | **and unto** |

| אלהי 430 | אשוע 7768 | ישמע 8085 | מהיכלו 1964 | קולי 6963 | ושועתי 7775 | לפניו 6440 | תבוא 935 | באזניו 241: | **18:7** | ותגעש 1607 |
|---|---|---|---|---|---|---|---|---|---|---|
| 'alohay | 'ashauea' | yishma' | meheykalou | qouliy; | uashaua'atiy, | lapanayu | tabou'a | ba'azanayu. | | uatig'ash |
| **my Elohim** | **cried** | **he heard** | **out of his temple** | **my voice** | **and my cry** | **before him** | **came *even*** | **into his ears** | | **Then shook** |

| ותרעש 7493 | הארץ 776 | ומוסדי 4146 | הרים 2022 | ירגזו 7264 | ויתגעשו 1607 | כי 3588 | חרה 2734 | לו 3807a: | **18:8** |
|---|---|---|---|---|---|---|---|---|---|
| uatir'ash | ha'aretz, | uamousadey | hariym | yiragazu; | uayitga'ashu, | kiy | charah | lou'. | |
| **and trembled** | **the earth** | **the foundations also of** | **the hills** | **moved** | **and were shaken** | **because** | **was wroth** | **he** | |

| עלה 5927 | עשן 6227 | באפו 639 | ואש 784 | מפיו 6310 | תאכל 398 | גחלים 1513 | בערו 1197 | ממנו 4480: | **18:9** |
|---|---|---|---|---|---|---|---|---|---|
| 'alah | 'ashan | ba'apou, | ua'aesh | mipiyu | ta'kel; | gechaliym, | ba'aru | mimenu. | |
| **There went up** | **a smoke** | **out of his nostrils** | **and fire** | **out of his mouth** | **devoured** | **coals** | **were kindled** | **by it** | |

| ויט 5186 | שמים 8064 | וירד 3381 | וערפל 6205 | תחת 8478 | רגליו 7272: | **18:10** | וירכב 7392 | על 5921 | כרוב 3742 |
|---|---|---|---|---|---|---|---|---|---|
| uayet | shamayim | uayerad; | ua'arapel, | tachat | raglayu. | | uayirkab | 'al | karub |
| **He bowed also** | **the heavens** | **and came down** | **and darkness *was*** | **under** | **his feet** | | **And he rode** | **upon** | **a cherub** |

| ויעף 5774 | וידא 1675 | על 5921 | כנפי 3671 | רוח 7307: | **18:11** | ישת 7896 | חשך 2822 | סתרו 5643 | סביבותיו 5439 |
|---|---|---|---|---|---|---|---|---|---|
| uaya'ap; | uaya'ap, | 'al | kanpey | ruach. | | yashet | choshek | sitrou, | sabiyboutayu |
| **and did fly** | **yea he did fly** | **upon** | **the wings of** | **the wind** | | **He made** | **darkness** | **his secret place** | **round about him** |

**Psalms** 18:1 To the chief Musician, A Psalm of David, the servant of the Adonai, who spoke unto YHUH the words of this song in the day that YHUH delivered him from the hand of all his enemies, and from the hand of Saul: And he said, I will love you, O YHUH, my strength.2 YHUH is my rock, and my fortress, and my deliverer; my G-d, my strength, in whom I will trust; my buckler, and the horn of my salvation, and my high tower.3 I will call upon YHUH, who is worthy to be praised: so shall I be saved from mine enemies.4 The sorrows of death compassed me, and the floods of ungodly men made me afraid.5 The sorrows of hell compassed me about: the snares of death prevented me.6 In my distress I called upon YHUH, and cried unto my G-d: he heard my voice out of his temple, and my cry came before him, even into his ears.7 Then the earth shook and trembled; the foundations also of the hills moved and were shaken, because he was wroth.8 There went up a smoke out of his nostrils, and fire out of his mouth devoured: coals were kindled by it.9 He bowed the heavens also, and came down: and darkness was under his feet.10 And he rode upon a cherub, and did fly: yea, he did fly upon the wings of the wind. 11 He made darkness his secret place; his pavilion round about him were dark waters and thick clouds of the skies.

18:12

סכתו 5521 חשכת 2824 מים 4325 עבי 5645 שחקים 7834: מנגה 5051 נגדו 5048 עביו 5645

sukatou; cheshchat mayim, 'abey shachaqiym. minogah, negdou 'abayu

**his pavilion *were* dark waters *and* thick clouds of the skies At the brightness *that was* before him his thick clouds**

18:13

עברו 5674 ברד 1259 וגחלי 1513 אש 784: וירעם 7481 בשמים 8064 יהוה 3068 ועליון 5945 יתן 5414 קלו 6963

'abaru; barad, uagachaley 'aesh. uayar'aem bashamayim Yahuah ua'alyoun yiten qolou;

**passed hail *stones* and coals of fire also thundered in the heavens Yahuah and the Highest gave his voice**

18:14

ברד 1259 וגחלי 1513 אש 784: וישלח 7971 חציו 2671 ויפיצם 6327 וברקים 1300 רב 7232

barad, uagachaley 'aesh. uayishlach chitzayu uayapiytzem; uabraqiym rab

**hail *stones* and coals of fire Yea he sent out his arrows and scattered and lightnings he shot out**

18:15

ויהמם 2000: ויראו 7200 אפיקי 650 מים 4325 ויגלו 1540 מוסדות 4146 תבל 8398

uayhumem. uayera'au 'apiqey mayim, uayigalu mousadout tebel

**and discomfited them Then were seen the channels of waters and were discovered the foundations of the world**

18:16

מגערתך 1606 יהוה 3068 מנשמת 5397 רוח 7307 אפך 639: ישלח 7971 ממרום 4791 יקחני 3847 ימשני 4871

miga'arataka Yahuah; minishmat, ruach 'apeka. yishlach mimaroum yiqacheniy; yamsheniy,

**at your rebuke O Yahuah at the blast of the breath of your nostrils He sent from above he took me he drew me**

18:17

ממים 4325 רבים 7227: יצילני 5337 מאיבי 341 עז 5794 ומשנאי 8130 כי 3588

mimayim rabiym. yatziyleniy, me'ayabiy 'az; uamisona'ay, kiy

**out of waters many He delivered me from my enemy strong and from them which hated me for**

18:18 18:19

אמצו 553 ממני 4480: יקדמוני 6923 ביום 3117 אידי 343 ויהי 1961 יהוה 3068 למשען 4937 לי 3807a:

'amatzu mimeniy. yaqadmuniy bayoum 'aeydiy; uayahiy Yahuah lamish'an liy.

**they were too strong for too They prevented me in the day of my calamity but was Yahuah stay my**

18:20

ויוציאני 3318 למרחב 4800 יחלצני 2502 כי 3588 חפץ 2654 בי 871a: יגמלני 1580 יהוה 3068

uayoutziy'aeniy lamerchab; yachaltzeniy, kiy chapetz biy. yigmaleniy Yahuah

**He brought me forth also into a large place he delivered me because he delighted in me rewarded me Yahuah**

18:21

כצדקי 6664 כבר 1252 ידי 3027 ישיב 7725 לי 3807a: כי 3588 שמרתי 8104

katzidqiy; kabor yaday, yashiyb liy. kiy shamartiy

**according to my righteousness according to the cleanness of my hands has he recompensed me For I have kept**

18:22

דרכי 1870 יהוה 3068 ולא 3808 רשעתי 7561 מאלהי 430: כי 3588 כל 3605 משפטיו 4941 לנגדי 5048

darkey Yahuah; uala' rasha'atiy, me'alohay. kiy kal mishpatayu lanegdiy;

**the ways of Yahuah and not have wickedly departed from my Elohim For all his judgments *were* before me**

18:23

וחקתיו 2708 לא 3808 אסיר 5493 מני 4480: ואהי 1961 תמים 8549 עמו 5973 ואשתמר 8104

uachuqotayu, la' 'asiyr meniy. ua'ahiy tamiym 'amou; ua'ashtamer,

**and his statutes not I did put away from me I was also upright before him and I kept myself**

18:24

מעוני 5771: וישב 7725 יהוה 3068 לי 3807a כצדקי 6664

me'auoniy. uayasheb Yahuah liy katzidqiy;

**from mine iniquity Therefore has recompensed Yahuah me according to my righteousness**

Ps 18:12 At the brightness that was before him his thick clouds passed, hail stones and coals of fire.13 YHUH also thundered in the heavens, and the Highest gave his voice; hail stones and coals of fire.14 Yea, he sent out his arrows, and scattered them; and he shot out lightnings, and discomfited them.15 Then the channels of waters were seen, and the foundations of the world were discovered at your rebuke, O YHUH, at the blast of the breath of your nostrils.16 He sent from above, he took me, he drew me out of many waters.17 He delivered me from my strong enemy, and from them which hated me: for they were too strong for me.18 They prevented me in the day of my calamity: but YHUH was my stay.19 He brought me forth also into a large place; he delivered me, because he delighted in me.20 YHUH rewarded me according to my righteousness; according to the cleanness of my hands has he recompensed me.21 For I have kept the ways of YHUH, and have not wickedly departed from my G-d.22 For all his judgments were before me, and I did not put away his statutes from me.23 I was also upright before him, and I kept myself from mine iniquity.24 Therefore has YHUH recompensed me according to my righteousness, according to the cleanness of my hands in his eyesight.

כבר 1252 ידי 3027 לנגד 5048 עיניו 5869: 18:25 עם 5973 חסיד 2623 תתחסד 2616 עם 5973
kabor yaday, laneged 'aeynayu. 'am chasiyd titchasad; 'am
**according to the cleanness of my hands in his eyesight With the merciful you will show yourself merciful with**

גבר 1399 תמים 8549 תתמם 8552: 18:26 עם 5973 נבר 1305 תתברר 1305 ועם 5973 עקש 6141
gabar tamiym, titamam. 'am nabar titbarar; ua'am 'aqesh,
**an man upright you will show yourself upright With the pure you will show yourself pure and with the froward**

תתפתל 6617: 18:27 כי 3588 אתה 859 עם 5971 עני 6041 תושיע 3467 ועינים 5869 רמות 7311 תשפיל 8213: 18:28
titpatal. kiy 'atah 'am 'aniy toushiya'; ua'aynayim ra'mout tashpiyl.
**you will show yourself froward For you people *the* afflicted will save but looks high will bring down**

כי 3588 אתה 859 תאיר 215 נרי 5216 יהוה 3068 אלהי 430 יגיה 5050 חשכי 2822: 18:29 כי 3588 בך 871a ארץ 7323
kiy 'atah ta'ayr neriy; Yahuah 'alohay, yagiyha chashakiy. kiy baka 'arutz
**For you will light my candle Yahuah my Elohim will enlighten my darkness For by you I have run through**

גדוד 1416 ובאלהי 430 אדלג 1801 שור 7791: 18:30 האל 410 תמים 8549 דרכו 1870 אמרת 565 יהוה 3068 צרופה 6884
gadud; uabe'alohay, 'adaleg shour. ha'ael tamiym darkou 'amrat Yahuah tzarupah;
**a troop and by my Elohim have I leaped over a wall *As for* El *is* perfect his way the word of Yahuah is tried**

מגן 4043 הוא 1931 לכל 3605 החסים 2620 בו 871a: 18:31 כי 3588 מי 4310 אלוה 433 מבלעדי 1107 יהוה 3068 ומי 4310 צור 6697 זולתי 2108
magen hua', lakol hachosiym bou. kiy miy' 'alouah mibala'adey Yahuah; uamiy tzur, zulatiy
***is* a buckler he to all those that trust in him For who *is* Elohim save Yahuah? or who a rock save**

אלהינו 430: 18:32 האל 410 המאזרני 247 חיל 2428 ויתן 5414 תמים 8549 דרכי 1870: 18:33 משוה 7737 רגלי 7272 כאילות 355
'aloheynu. ha'ael hama'azreniy chayil; uayiten tamiym darkiy. mashaueh raglay ka'ayalout;
**our Elohim? *It is* El that gird me with strength and make perfect my way He make my feet like hinds' *feet***

ועל 5921 במתי 1116 יעמידני 5975: 18:34 מלמד 3925 ידי 3027 למלחמה 4421 ונחתה 5181 קשת 7198 נחושה 5154
ua'al bamoutay, ya'amideniy. malamed yaday lamilchamah; uanichatah qeshet nachushah,
**and upon my high places set me He teach my hands to war so that is broken a bow of steel**

זרועתי 2220: 18:35 ותתן 5414 לי 3807a מגן 4043 ישעך 3468 וימינך 3225 תסעדני 5582
zarou'atay. uatiten liy magen yish'aka uiymiynaka tis'adeniy;
**mine arms You have also given me the shield of your salvation and your right hand has holden me up**

וענותך 6037 תרבני 7235: 18:36 תרחיב 7337 צעדי 6806 תחתי 8478 ולא 3808 מעדו 4571 קרסלי 7166: 18:37
ua'anuataka tarbeniy. tarchiyb tza'adiy tachtay; uala' ma'adu, qarsulay.
**and your gentleness has made me great You have enlarged my steps under me that not did slip my feet**

ארדוף 7291 אויבי 341 ואשיגם 5381 ולא 3808 אשוב 7725 עד 5704 כלותם 3615: 18:38
'ardoup 'auyabay ua'asiygem; uala' 'ashub 'ad kaloutam.
**I have pursued mine enemies and overtaken them and neither did I turn again till they were consumed**

אמחצם 4272 ולא 3808 יכלו 3201 קום 6965 יפלו 5307 תחת 8478 רגלי 7272: 18:39 ותאזרני 247
'amchatzem uala' yuklu qum; yiplu, tachat raglay. uata'azereniy
**I have wounded them that not they were able to rise they are fallen under my feet For you have girded me with**

Ps 18:25 With the merciful you will show thyself merciful; with an upright man you will show thyself upright;26 With the pure you will show thyself pure; and with the froward you will show thyself froward.27 For you will save the afflicted people; but will bring down high looks.28 For you will light my candle: YHUH my G-d will enlighten my darkness.29 For by you I have run through a troop; and by my G-d have I leaped over a wall.30 As for G-d, his way is perfect: the word of YHUH is tried: he is a buckler to all those that trust in him.31 For who is G-d save YHUH? or who is a rock save our G-d?32 It is G-d that gird me with strength, and make my way perfect.33 He make my feet like hinds' feet, and set me upon my high places.34 He teach my hands to war, so that a bow of steel is broken by mine arms.35 Thou have also given me the shield of your salvation: and your right hand has holden me up, and your gentleness has made me great.36 Thou have enlarged my steps under me, that my feet did not slip.37 I have pursued mine enemies, and overtaken them: neither did I turn again till they were consumed.38 I have wounded them that they were not able to rise: they are fallen under my feet.

| חיל 2428 | למלחמה 4421 | תכריע 3766 | קמי 6965 | תחתי 8478: | 18:40 | ואיבי 341 | נתתה 5414 | לי 3807a |
|---|---|---|---|---|---|---|---|---|
| chayil | lamilchamah; | takriya' | qamay | tachtay. | | ua'ayabay, | natatah | liy |
| **strength** | **unto the battle** | **you have subdued** | **those that rose up** | **under me** | | **also mine enemies** | **You have given** | **me** |

| ערף 6203 | ומשנאי 8130 | אצמיתם 6789: | 18:41 | ישועו 7768 | ואין 369 | מושיע 3467 | על 5921 |
|---|---|---|---|---|---|---|---|
| 'arep; | uamsana'ay, | 'atzmiytem. | | yashaua'au | ua'aeyn | moushiya'; | 'al |
| **the necks of** | **them that hate** | **that I might destroy** | | **They cried** | **there** | **but *there was* none to save *them even*** | **unto** |

| יהוה 3068 | ולא 3808 | ענם 6030: | 18:42 | ואשחקם 7833 | כעפר 6083 | על 5921 | פני 6440 | רוח 7307 | כטיט 2916 |
|---|---|---|---|---|---|---|---|---|---|
| Yahuah | uala' | 'anam. | | ua'ashchaqem, | ka'apar | 'al | paney | ruach; | katiyt |
| **Yahuah** | **but not** | **he answered them** | | **Then did I beat them small** | **as the dust** | **on** | **before** | **the wind** | **as the dirt in** |

| חוצות 2351 | אריקם 7324: | 18:43 | תפלטני 6403 | מריבי 7379 | עם 5971 | תשימני 7760 |
|---|---|---|---|---|---|---|
| chutzout | 'ariyqem. | | tapalteniy | meriybey | 'am | tasiymeniy |
| **the streets** | **I did cast them out** | | **You have delivered me** | **from the strivings of** | **the people** | ***and* you have made me** |

| לראש 7218 | גוים 1471 | עם 5971 | לא 3808 | ידעתי 3045 | יעבדוני 5647: | 18:44 | לשמע 8088 | אזן 241 |
|---|---|---|---|---|---|---|---|---|
| lara'sh | gouyim; | 'am | la' | yada'tiy | ya'abduniy. | | lashema' | 'azen |
| **the head of** | **the heathen** | **a people** | **not** | ***whom* I have known** | **shall serve me** | | **As soon as hear** | **they** |

| ישמעו 8085 | לי 3807a | בני 1121 | נכר 5236 | יכחשו 3584 | לי 3807a: | 18:45 | בני 1121 | נכר 5236 |
|---|---|---|---|---|---|---|---|---|
| yishama'au | liy; | baney | nekar, | yakachashu | liy. | | baney | nekar |
| ***of me* they shall obey** | **me** | **sons of** | **the strangers** | **shall submit themselves** | **unto me** | | **sons of** | **the strangers** |

| יבלו 5034 | ויחרגו 2727 | ממסגרותיהם 4526: | 18:46 | חי 2416 | יהוה 3068 | וברוך 1288 | צורי 6697 | וירום 7311 |
|---|---|---|---|---|---|---|---|---|
| yibolu; | uayachragu, | mimisgarouteyhem. | | chay | Yahuah | uabaruk | tzuriy; | uayarum, |
| **shall fade away** | **and be afraid** | **out of their close places** | | **live** | **Yahuah** | **and blessed** | ***be* my rock** | **and let be exalted** |

| אלוהי 430 | ישעי 3468: | 18:47 | האל 410 | הנותן 5414 | נקמות 5360 | לי 3807a | וידבר 1696 | עמים 5971 | תחתי 8478: | 18:48 | מפלטי 6403 |
|---|---|---|---|---|---|---|---|---|---|---|---|
| 'alouhey | yish'ay. | | ha'ael, | hanouten | naqamout | liy; | uayadaber | 'amiym | tachtay. | | mapaltiy, |
| **Elohim of** | **my salvation** | | ***It is* El** | **that executes** | **vengeance** | **me** | **and subdue** | **the people** | **under me** | | **He deliver me** |

| מאיבי 341 | אף 637 | מן 4480 | קמי 6965 | תרוממני 7311 | מאיש 376 | חמס 2555 |
|---|---|---|---|---|---|---|
| me'ayabay | 'ap | min | qamay | taroumameniy; | me'aysh | chamas, |
| **from mine enemies** | **yea** | **above** | **those that rise up against me** | **you lift me up** | **from man** | ***the* violent** |

| תצילני 5337: | 18:49 | על 5921 | כן 3651 | אודך 3034 | בגוים 1471 | יהוה 3068 |
|---|---|---|---|---|---|---|
| tatziyleniy. | | 'al | ken | 'audaka | bagouyim | Yahuah; |
| **you have delivered me** | | **Therefore** | **after that** | **will I give thanks unto you** | **among the heathen** | **O Yahuah** |

| ולשמך 8034 | אזמרה 2167: | 18:50 | מגדל 1431 | ישועות 3444 | מלכו 4428 | ועשה 6213 | חסד 2617 | למשיחו 4899 | לדוד 1732 |
|---|---|---|---|---|---|---|---|---|---|
| ualshimaka | 'azamerah. | | migdol | yashu'aut | malkou | ua'aseh | chesed | limashiychou, | ladauid |
| **and unto your name** | **sing praises** | | **Great** | **deliverance** | ***gives he to* his king** | **and shows** | **mercy** | **to his anointed** | **to David** |

| ולזרעו 2233 | עד 5704 | עולם 5769: |
|---|---|---|
| ualzar'au, | 'ad | 'aulam. |
| **and to his seed for** | | **evermore** |

Ps 18:39 For you have girded me with strength unto the battle: you have subdued under me those that rose up against me.40 Thou have also given me the necks of mine enemies; that I might destroy them that hate me.41 They cried, but there was none to save them: even unto YHUH, but he answered them not.42 Then did I beat them small as the dust before the wind: I did cast them out as the dirt in the streets.43 Thou have delivered me from the strivings of the people; and you have made me the head of the heathen: a people whom I have not known shall serve me.44 As soon as they hear of me, they shall obey me: the strangers shall submit themselves unto me.45 The strangers shall fade away, and be afraid out of their close places.46 YHUH live; and blessed be my rock; and let the G-d of my salvation be exalted.47 It is G-d that avengeth me, and subdueth the people under me.48 He delivereth me from mine enemies: yea, you liftest me up above those that rise up against me: you have delivered me from the violent man.49 Therefore will I give thanks unto you, O YHUH, among the heathen, and sing praises unto your name.50 Great deliverance give he to his king; and show mercy to his anointed, to David, and to his seed forevermore.

**Ps 19:1**
למנצח 5329 מזמור 4210 לדוד 1732: השמים 8064 מספרים 5608 כבוד 3519 אל 410 ומעשה 4639 ידיו 3027
lamanatzeach, mizmour ladauid. hashamayim, masapriym kaboud 'ael; uama'aseh yadayu,
**To the chief Musician A Psalm of David The heavens declare the glory of El and the work of his hands**

**19:2**
מגיד 5046 הרקיע 7549: יום 3117 ליום 3117 יביע 5042 אמר 562 ולילה 3915 ללילה 3915 יחוה 2331 דעת 1847: **19:3** אין 369
magiyd haraqiya'. youm layoum yabiya' 'amer; ualayalah lalaylah, yachaueh da'at. 'aeyn
**shows the firmament Day unto day utter speech and night unto night shows knowledge *There is* no**

**19:4**
אמר 562 ואין 369 דברים 1697 בלי 1097 נשמע 8085 קולם 6963: בכל 3605 הארץ 776 יצא 3318 קום 6957 ובקצה 7097
'amer ua'aeyn dabariym; baliy, nishma' qoulam. bakal ha'aretz yatza' qauam, uabiqtzeh
**speech nor language not is heard *where* their voice through all the earth is gone out Their line and to the end of**

**19:5**
תבל 8398 מליהם 4405 לשמש 8121 שם 7760 אהל 168 בהם 871a: והוא 1931 כחתן 2860 יצא 3318 מחפתו 2646
tebel mileyhem; lashemesh, sam 'ahel bahem. uahu'a, kachatan yotzea' mechupatou;
**the world their words for the sun has he set a tabernacle In them Which *is* as a bridegroom coming out of his chamber**

**19:6**
ישיש 7797 כגבור 1368 לרוץ 7323 ארח 734: מקצה 7097 השמים 8064 מוצאו 4161 ותקופתו 8622 על 5921
yasiys kagibour, larutz 'arach. miqtzeh hashamayim moutza'au, uatqupatou 'al
***and* rejoice as a strong man to run a race *is* from the end of the heaven His going forth and his circuit unto**

**19:7**
קצותם 7098 ואין 369 נסתר 5641 מחמתו 2535: תורת 8451 יהוה 3068 תמימה 8549 משיבת 7725 נפש 5315
qatzoutam; ua'aeyn nistar, mechamatou tourat Yahuah tamiymah mashiybat napesh;
**the ends of it and there is nothing hid from the heat thereof The law of Yahuah *is* perfect converting the soul**

**19:8**
עדות 5715 יהוה 3068 נאמנה 539 מחכימת 2449 פתי 6612: פקודי 6490 יהוה 3068 ישרים 3477 משמחי 8055 לב 3820
'aedut Yahuah ne'amanah, machkiymat petiy. piqudey Yahuah yashariym masamchey leb;
**the testimony of Yahuah *is* sure making wise the simple *The* statutes of Yahuah *are* right rejoicing *the* heart**

**19:9**
מצות 4687 יהוה 3068 ברה 1249 מאירת 215 עינים 5869: יראת 3374 יהוה 3068 טהורה 2889 עומדת 5975 לעד 5703
mitzuat Yahuah barah, ma'ayrat 'aeynayim. yir'at Yahuah tahourah 'amedet la'ad
***the* commandment of Yahuah *is* pure enlightening the eyes The fear of Yahuah *is* clean enduring for ever**

**19:10**
משפטי 4941 יהוה 3068 אמת 571 צדקו 6663 יחדו 3162: הנחמדים 2530 מזהב 2091 ומפז 6337
mishpatey Yahuah 'amet; tzadaqu yachdau. hanechamadiym, mizahab uamipaz
**the judgments of Yahuah *are* true *and* righteous altogether More to be desired *are they* than gold yea than fine gold**

**19:11**
רב 7227 ומתוקים 4966 מדבש 1706 ונפת 5317 צופים 6688: גם 1571 עבדך 5650 נזהר 2094 בהם 871a
rab; uamtuqiym midbash, uanopet tzupiym. gam 'abdaka nizhar bahem;
**much sweeter also than honey and the drippings of the honeycomb Moreover your servant is warned by them**

**19:12**
בשמרם 8104 עקב 6118 רב 7227: שגיאות 7691 מי 4310 יבין 995 מנסתרות 5641
bashamaram, 'aeqeb rab. shagiy'aut miy' yabiyn; ministarout
***and* in keeping of them reward *there is* great *his* errors? Who can understand from secret *faults***

**19:13**
נקני 5352: גם 1571 מזדים 2086 חשך 2820 עבדך 5650 אל 408 ימשלו 4910 בי 871a
naqeniy. gam mizediym chasok 'abdeka, 'al yimshalu biy
**cleanse you me also from presumptuous *sins* Keep back your servant not let them not have dominion over me**

**Psalms** 19:1 To the chief Musician, A Psalm of David. The heavens declare the glory of G-d; and the firmament show his handywork.2 Day untoday uttereth speech, and night untonight show knowledge.3 There is no speech nor language, where their voice is not heard.4 Their line is gone out through all the earth, and their words to the end of the world. In them has he set a tabernacle for the sun,5 Which is as a bridegroom coming out of his chamber, and rejoice as a strong man to run a race.6 His going forth is from the end of the heaven, and his circuit unto the ends of it: and there is nothing hid from the heat thereof.7 The law of YHUH is perfect, converting the soul: the testimony of YHUH is sure, making wise the simple.8 The statutes of YHUH are right, rejoicing the heart: the commandment of YHUH is pure, enlightening the eyes.9 The fear of YHUH is clean, enduring forever: the judgments of YHUH are true and righteous altogether.10 More to be desired are they than gold, yea, than much fine gold: sweeter also than honey and the honeycomb.11 Moreover by them is your servant warned: and in keeping of them there is great reward.12 Who can understand his errors? cleanse you me from secret faults.13 Keep back your servant also from presumptuous sins; let them not have dominion over me: then shall I be upright, and I shall be innocent from the great transgression.

19:14

אז 227 איתם 8552 ונקיתי 5352 מפשע 6588 רב 7227: יהיו 1961 לרצון 7522 אמרי 561 פי 6310
'az 'aeytam; uaniqeytiy, mipesha' rab. yihayu laratzoun 'amrey piy
**then shall I be upright and I shall be innocent from transgression *the* great Let be acceptable the words of my mouth**

והגיון 1902 לבי 3820 לפניך 6440 יהוה 3068 צורי 6697 וגאלי 1350:
uahegyoun libiy lapaneyka; Yahuah tzuriy uago'aliy.
**and the meditation of my heart in your sight O Yahuah my strength and my redeemer**

**Ps 20:1**

למנצח 5329 מזמור 4210 לדוד 1732: יענך 6030 יהוה 3068 ביום 3117 צרה 6869 ישגבך 7682 שם 8034
lamanatzeach, mizmour ladauid. ya'anka Yahuah bayoum tzarah; yasagebaka, shem
**To the chief Musician A Psalm of David hear you Yahuah in the day of trouble defend you the name of**

20:2 20:3

אלהי 430 יעקב 3290: ישלח 7971 עזרך 5828 מקדש 6944 ומציון 6726 יסעדך 5582: יזכר 2142 כל 3605
'alohey ya'aqob. yishlach 'azraka miqodesh; uamitziyoun, yis'adeka. yizkor kal
**the Elohim of Jacob Send you help from the sanctuary and out of Zion strengthen you Remember all**

20:4

מנחתך 4503 ועולתך 5930 ידשנה 1878 סלה 5542: יתן 5414 לך 3807a כלבבך 3824 וכל 3605
minchotaka; ua'aulataka yadashneh selah. yiten laka kilbabeka; uakal
**your offerings and your burnt sacrifice accept Selah Grant unto you according to your own heart and all**

20:5

עצתך 6098 ימלא 4390: נרננה 7442 בישועתך 3444 ובשם 8034 אלהינו 430 נדגל 1713
'atzataka yamalea'. narannah biyshu'ateka, uabshem 'aloheynu nidgol;
**your counsel fulfill We will rejoice in your salvation and in the name of our Elohim we will set up *our* banners**

20:6

ימלא 4390 יהוה 3068 כל 3605 משאלותיך 4862: עתה 6258 ידעתי 3045 כי 3588 הושיע 3467 יהוה 3068 משיחו 4899 יענהו 6030
yamalea' Yahuah kal mish'alouteyka. 'atah yada'tiy, kiy houshiya' Yahuah mashiychou ya'anehu
**fulfill Yahuah all your petitions Now know I that save Yahuah his anointed he will hear him**

20:7

משמי 8064 קדשו 6944 בגברות 1369 ישע 3468 ימינו 3225: אלה 428 ברכב 7393 ואלה 428 בסוסים 5483 ואנחנו 587
mishmey qadashou; bigabarout, yesha' yamiynou. 'aeleh barekeb ua'aleh uasusiym; ua'anachnu
**from heaven his holy with strength of *the* saving his right hand Some *trust* in chariots and some in horses but we**

20:8

בשם 8034 יהוה 3068 אלהינו 430 נזכיר 2142: המה 1992 כרעו 3766 ונפלו 5307 ואנחנו 587 קמנו 6965
bashem Yahuah 'aloheynu nazkiyr. hemah kara'u uanapalu; ua'anachnu qamnu,
**the name of Yahuah our Elohim will remember They are brought down and fallen but we are risen**

20:9

ונתעודד 5749: יהוה 3068 הושיעה 3467 המלך 4428 יעננו 6030 ביום 3117 קראנו 7121:
uanita'audad. Yahuah houshiy'ah; hamelek, ya'anenu bayoum qara'aenu.
**and stand upright Yahuah Save the king let hear us when we call**

**Ps 21:1**

למנצח 5329 מזמור 4210 לדוד 1732: יהוה 3068 בעזך 5797 ישמח 8055 מלך 4428 ובישועתך 3444 מה 4100
lamanatzeach, mizmour ladauid. Yahuah ba'azaka yismach melek; uabiyshu'ataka, mah
**To the chief Musician A Psalm of David O Yahuah in your strength shall joy The king and in your salvation how**

21:2

יגיל 1523 מאד 3966: תאות 8378 לבו 3820 נתתה 5414 לו 3807a וארשת 782 שפתיו 8193 בל 1077 מנעת 4513
yageyl ma'ad. ta'auat libou natatah lou'; ua'areshet sapatayu, bal mana'ta
**shall he rejoice greatly desire his heart's You have given him and the request of his lips not have withholden**

Ps 19:14 Let the words of my mouth, and the meditation of my heart, be acceptable in your sight, O YHUH, my strength, and my redeemer. **Psalms** 20:1 To the chief Musician, A Psalm of David. YHUH hear you in the day of trouble; the name of the G-d of Jacob defend you;2 Send you help from the sanctuary, and strengthen you out of Zion;3 Remember all your offerings, and accept your burnt sacrifice; Selah.4 Grant you according to your own heart, and fulfil all your counsel.5 We will rejoice in your salvation, and in the name of our G-d we will set up our banners: YHUH fulfil all your petitions.6 Now know I that YHUH save his anointed; he will hear him from his holy heaven with the saving strength of his right hand.7 Some trust in chariots, and some in horses: but we will remember the name of YHUH our G-d.8 They are brought down and fallen: but we are risen, and stand upright.9 Save, YHUH: let the king hear us when we call. **Psalms** 21:1 To the chief Musician, A Psalm of David. The king shall joy in your strength, O YHUH; and in your salvation how greatly shall he rejoice!2 Thou have given him his heart's desire, and have not withholden the request of his lips. Selah.

21:3 21:4
סלה 5542: כי 3588 תקדמנו 6923 ברכות 1293 טוב 2896 תשית 7896 לראשו 7218 עטרת 5850 פז 6337: חיים 2416
selah. kiy taqadmenu birkout toub; tashiyt lara'shou, 'ateret paz. chayiym
**Selah For you prevent him with the blessings of goodness you set on his head a crown of pure gold life**

21:5
שאל 7592 ממך 4480 נתתה 5414 לו 3807a ארך 753 ימים 3117 עולם 5769 ועד 5703: גדול 1419 כבודו 3519 בישועתך 3444
sha'al mimaka natatah lou'; 'arek yamiym, 'aulam ua'ad. gadoul kaboudou biyshu'ateka;
**He asked of you *and* you gave *it* him *even* length of days for ever and ever *is* great His glory in your salvation**

21:6
הוד 1935 והדר 1926 תשוה 7737 עליו 5921: כי 3588 תשיתהו 7896 ברכות 1293 לעד 5703 תחדהו 2302
houd uahadar tashaueh 'alayu. kiy tashiytehu barakout la'ad; tachadehu
**honor and majesty have you laid upon him For you have made him *most* blessed for ever you have made him glad**

21:7
בשמחה 8057 את 854 פניך 6440: כי 3588 המלך 4428 בטח 982 ביהוה 3068 ובחסד 2617 עליון 5945 בל 1077
basimchah, 'at paneyka. kiy hamelek boteach baYahuah; uabchesed 'alyoun, bal
**exceeding *with* your countenance For the king trust in Yahuah and through the mercy of the most High not**

21:8 21:9
ימוט 4131: תמצא 4672 ידך 3027 לכל 3605 איביך 341 ימינך 3225 תמצא 4672 שנאיך 8130:
yimout. timtzaa' yadaka lakal 'ayabeyka; yamiynaka timtzaa' son'ayka.
**he shall be moved shall find out Thine hand all your enemies your right hand shall find out those that hate you**

תשיתמו 7896 כתנור 8574 אש 784 לעת 6256 פניך 6440 יהוה 3068 באפו 639 יבלעם 1104
tashiytemou katanur 'aesh la'at paneyka Yahuah ba'apou yabala'aem;
**You shall make them as a oven fiery in the time of your anger Yahuah in his wrath shall swallow them up**

21:10
ותאכלם 398 אש 784: פרימו 6529 מארץ 776 תאבד 6 וזרעם 2233 מבני 1121
uata'kalem 'aesh. piryamo me'aretz ta'abed; uazar'am, mibney
**and shall devour them the fire Their fruit from the earth shall you destroy and their seed from among the children of**

21:11
אדם 120: כי 3588 נטו 5186 עליך 5921 רעה 7451 חשבו 2803 מזמה 4209 בל 1077
'adam. kiy natu 'aleyka ra'ah; chashabu mazimah, bal
**men For they intended against you evil they imagined a mischievous device not**

21:12
יוכלו 3201: כי 3588 תשיתמו 7896 שכם 7926 במיתריך 4340
yukalu. kiy tashiytemou shekem; bameytareyka,
***which* they are able *to perform* Therefore shall you make them turn their back *your arrows* upon your strings**

21:13
תכונן 3559 על 5921 פניהם 6440: רומה 7311 יהוה 3068 בעזך 5797 נשירה 7891
takounen 'al paneyhem. rumah Yahuah ba'uzeka; nashiyrah
***when* you shall make ready against the face of them Be you exalted Yahuah in your own strength *so* will we sing**

ונזמרה 2167 גבורתך 1369:
uanzamrah gaburateka.
**and praise your power**

Ps 22:1
למנצח 5329 על 5921 אילת 365 השחר 7837 מזמור 4210 לדוד 1732: אלי 410 אלי 410 למה 4100 עזבתני 5800
lamanatzeach 'al 'ayelet hashachar, mizmour ladauid. 'aeliy 'aeliy lamah 'azabtaniy;
**To the chief Musician upon Aijeleth Shahar A Psalm of David My El my El why have you forsaken me?**

Ps 21:3 For you preventest him with the blessings of goodness: you settest a crown of pure gold on his head.4 He asked life of you, and you gave it him, even length of days forever and ever.5 His glory is great in your salvation: honor and majesty have you laid upon him.6 For you have made him most blessed forever: you have made him exceeding glad with your countenance. 7 For the king trusteth in YHUH, and through the mercy of the most High he shall not be moved.8 Thine hand shall find out all your enemies: your right hand shall find out those that hate you.9 Thou shall make them as a fiery oven in the time of your anger: YHUH shall swallow them up in his wrath, and the fire shall devour them.10 Their fruit shall you destroy from the earth, and their seed from among the children of men.11 For they intended evil against you: they imagined a mischievous device, which they are not able to perform.12 Therefore shall you make them turn their back, when you shall make ready your arrows upon your strings against the face of them.13 Be you exalted, YHUH, in your own strength: so will we sing and praise your power. **Ps** 22:1 To the chief Musician upon Ai'-je-leth Sha'-har, A Psalm of David. My G-d, my G-d, why have you forsaken me? why are you so far from helping me, and from the words of my roaring?

| רחוק 7350 | מישועתי 3444 | דברי 1697 | שאגתי 7581: | 22:2 | אלהי 430 | אקרא 7121 | יומם 3119 | ולא 3808 |
|---|---|---|---|---|---|---|---|---|
| rachouq | mishu'atiy, | dibrey | sha'agatiy. | | 'alohay, | 'aqraa' | youmam | uala' |
| ***why are you so* far** | **from helping me** | ***and from* the words of** | **my roaring?** | | **O my Elohim** | **I cry in** | **the daytime** | **but not** |

| תענה 6030 | ולילה 3915 | ולא 3808 | דומיה 1747 | לי 3807a: | 22:3 | ואתה 859 | קדוש 6918 | יושב 3427 | תהלות 8416 |
|---|---|---|---|---|---|---|---|---|---|
| ta'aneh; | ualayalah, | uala' | dumiyah | liy. | | ua'atah | qadoush; | yousheb, | tahilout |
| **you hear** | **and in the night season** | **and not** | **am silent** | **for me** | | **But you** | ***are* holy** | ***O you* that inhabitest** | **the praises of** |

| ישראל 3478: | 22:4 | בך 871a | בטחו 982 | אבתינו 1 | בטחו 982 | ותפלטמו 6403: | 22:5 | אליך 413 | זעקו 2199 |
|---|---|---|---|---|---|---|---|---|---|
| yisra'ael. | | baka | batachu | 'aboteynu; | batachu, | uatapaltemou. | | 'aeleyka | za'aqu |
| **Israel** | | **in you** | **trusted** | **Our fathers** | **they trusted** | **and you did deliver them** | | **unto you** | **They cried** |

| ונמלטו 4422 | בך 871a | בטחו 982 | ולא 3808 | בושו 954: | 22:6 | ואנכי 595 | תולעת 8438 | ולא 3808 | איש 376 | חרפת 2781 |
|---|---|---|---|---|---|---|---|---|---|---|
| uanimlatu; | baka | batachu | uala' | boushu. | | ua'anokiy | toula'at | uala' | 'aysh; | cherpat |
| **and were delivered** | **in you** | **they trusted** | **and not** | **were confounded** | | **But I** | ***am* a worm** | **and no** | **man** | **a reproach of** |

| אדם 120 | ובזוי 959 | עם 5971: | 22:7 | כל 3605 | ראי 7200 | ילעגו 3932 | לי 3807a | יפטירו 6362 | בשפה 8193 | יניעו 5128 |
|---|---|---|---|---|---|---|---|---|---|---|
| 'adam, | uabzuy | 'am. | | kal | ro'ay | yala'agu | liy; | yaptiyru | basapah, | yaniy'au |
| **men** | **and despised of** | **the people** | | **All** | **they that see me** | **laugh to scorn** | **me** | **they shoot** | **out the lip** | **they shake** |

| ראש 7218: | 22:8 | גל 1556 | אל 413 | יהוה 3068 | יפלטהו 6403 | יצילהו 5337 | כי 3588 | חפץ 2654 | בו 871a: | 22:9 |
|---|---|---|---|---|---|---|---|---|---|---|
| ra'sh. | | gol | 'al | Yahuah | yapaltehu; | yatziylehu, | kiy | chapetz | bou. | |
| **the head *saying*** | | **He trusted on** | | **Yahuah** | ***that* he would deliver him** | **let him deliver him** | **seeing** | **he delighted in him** | | |

| כי 3588 | אתה 859 | גחי 1518 | מבטן 990 | מבטיחי 982 | על 5921 | שדי 7699 | אמי 517: | 22:10 |
|---|---|---|---|---|---|---|---|---|
| kiy | 'atah | gochiy | mibaten; | mabtiychiy, | 'al | shadey | 'amiy. | |
| **But** | **you** | ***are* he that took me** | **out of the womb** | **you did make me hope *when I was*** | **upon** | **breasts** | **my mother's** | |

| עליך 5921 | השלכתי 7993 | מרחם 7358 | מבטן 990 | אמי 517 | אלי 410 | אתה 859: | 22:11 | אל 408 | תרחק 7368 | ממני 4480 | כי 3588 | צרה 6869 |
|---|---|---|---|---|---|---|---|---|---|---|---|---|
| 'aleyika | hashalaktiy | merachem; | mibeten | 'amiy, | 'aeliy | 'atah. | | 'al | tirchaq | mimeniy | kiy | tzarah |
| **upon you** | **I was cast** | **from the womb** | **from belly** | **my mother's** | ***are* my El** | **you** | | **not** | **Be far** | **from me** | **for** | **trouble** |

| קרובה 7138 | כי 3588 | אין 369 | עוזר 5826: | 22:12 | סבבוני 5437 | פרים 6499 | רבים 7227 | אבירי 47 | בשן 1316 |
|---|---|---|---|---|---|---|---|---|---|
| qaroubah; | kiy | 'aeyn | 'auzer. | | sababuniy | pariym | rabiym; | 'abiyrey | bashan |
| ***is* near** | **for** | ***there is* none** | **to help** | | **have compassed me** | **bulls** | **Many** | **strong *bulls* of** | **Bashan** |

| כתרוני 3803: | 22:13 | פצו 6475 | עלי 5921 | פיהם 6310 | אריה 738 | טרף 2963 | ושאג 7580: | 22:14 | כמים 4325 |
|---|---|---|---|---|---|---|---|---|---|
| kitaruniy. | | patzu | 'alay | piyhem; | 'aryeh, | torep | uasha'aeg. | | kamayim |
| **have beset me round** | | **They gaped** | **upon me *with*** | **their mouths** | **lion** | ***as* a ravening** | **and a roaring** | | **like water** |

| נשפכתי 8210 | והתפרדו 6504 | כל 3605 | עצמותי 6106 | היה 1961 | לבי 3820 | כדונג 1749 | נמס 4549 | בתוך 8432 | מעי 4578: | 22:15 |
|---|---|---|---|---|---|---|---|---|---|---|
| nishpaktiy | uahitparadu, | kal | atzmoutay | hayah | libiy | kadounag; | names, | batouk | me'ay. | |
| **I am poured out** | **are out of joint** | **all** | **my bones** | **is** | **my heart** | **like wax** | **it is melted** | **in the midst of** | **my bowels** | |

| יבש 3001 | כחרש 2789 | כחי 3581 | ולשוני 3956 | מדבק 1692 | מלקוחי 4455 | ולעפר 6083 | מות 4194 |
|---|---|---|---|---|---|---|---|
| yabesh | kacheres | kochiy, | ualshouniy | mudbaq | malqouchay; | uala'apar | mauet |
| **is dried up** | **like a potsherd** | **My strength** | **and my tongue** | **cleave to** | **my jaws** | **and into the dust of** | **death** |

Ps 22:2 O my G-d, I cry in the daytime, but you hear not; and in the night season, and am not silent.3 But you are holy, O you that inhabitest the praises of Israel.4 Our fathers trusted in you: they trusted, and you did deliver them.5 They cried unto you, and were delivered: they trusted in you, and were not confounded.6 But I am a worm, and no man; a reproach of men, and despised of the people.7 All they that see me laugh me to scorn: they shoot out the lip, they shake the head saying,8 He trusted on YHUH that he would deliver him: let him deliver him, seeing he delighted in him.9 But you are he that took me out of the womb: you did make me hope when I was upon my mother's breasts.10 I was cast upon you from the womb: you are my G-d from my mother's belly.11 Be not far from me; for trouble is near; for there is none to help.12 Many bulls have compassed me: strong bulls of Bashan have beset me round.13 They gaped upon me with their mouths, as a ravening and a roaring lion.14 I am poured out like water, and all my bones are out of joint: my heart is like wax; it is melted in the midst of my bowels.15 My strength is dried up like a potsherd; and my tongue cleaveth to my jaws; and you have brought me into the dust of death.

| תשפתני 8239: | 22:16 כי 3588 | סבבוני 5437 | כלבים 3611 | עדת 5712 | מרעים 7489 | הקיפוני 5362 | כארי 3738/738 |
|---|---|---|---|---|---|---|---|
| tishpateniy. | kiy | sababuniy, | kalabiym | 'adat | mare'aym | hiqiypuniy; | ka'ariy, |
| **you have brought me** | **For** | **have compassed me** | **dogs** | **the assembly of** | **the wicked** | **have inclosed me** | **they pierced** |

| ידי 3027 | ורגלי 7272: | 22:17 אספר 5608 | כל 3605 | עצמותי 6106 | המה 1992 | יביטו 5027 | יראו 7200 | בי 871a: | 22:18 יחלקו 2505 | בגדי 899 |
|---|---|---|---|---|---|---|---|---|---|---|
| yaday | uaraglay. | 'asaper | kal | atzmoutay; | hemah | yabiytu, | yir'au | biy. | yachalaqu | bagaday |
| **my hands** | **and my feet** | **I may tell** | **all** | **my bones** | **they** | **look** | ***and* stare** | **upon me** | **They part** | **my garments** |

| להם 1992 | ועל 5921 | לבושי 3830 | יפילו 5307 | גורל 1486: | 22:19 ואתה 859 | יהוה 3068 | אל 408 | תרחק 7368 | אילותי 360 |
|---|---|---|---|---|---|---|---|---|---|
| lahem; | ua'al | labushiy, | yapiylu | goural. | ua'atah | Yahuah | 'al | tirchaq; | 'ayalutiy, |
| **among them** | **and upon** | **my vesture** | **cast** | **lots** | **But you** | **O Yahuah** | **not** | **be far from me** | **O my strength** |

| לעזרתי 5833 | חושה 2363: | 22:20 הצילה 5337 | מחרב 2719 | נפשי 5315 | מיד 3027 | כלב 3611 | יחידתי 3173: | 22:21 הושיעני 3467 |
|---|---|---|---|---|---|---|---|---|
| la'azratiy | chushah. | hatziylah | mechereb | napshiy; | miyad | keleb, | yachiydatiy. | houshiy'aeniy |
| **to help me** | **haste you** | **Deliver** | **from the sword** | **my soul** | **from the power of** | **the dog** | **my darling** | **Save me** |

| מפי 6310 | אריה 738 | ומקרני 7161 | רמים 7214 | עניתני 6030: | 22:22 אספרה 5608 | שמך 8034 |
|---|---|---|---|---|---|---|
| mipiy | 'aryeh; | uamiqarney | remiym | 'aniytaniy. | 'asaprah | shimka |
| **from mouth** | ***the* lion's** | **for from the horns of** | **the unicorns** | **you have heard me** | **I will declare** | **your name** |

| לאחי 251 | בתוך 8432 | קהל 6951 | אהללך 1984: | 22:23 יראי 3373 | יהוה 3068 | הללוהו 1984 | כל 3605 |
|---|---|---|---|---|---|---|---|
| la'achay; | batouk | qahal | 'ahalaleka. | yira'aey | Yahuah | halauhu, | kal |
| **unto my brethren** | **in the midst of** | **the congregation** | **will I praise** | **You that fear** | **Yahuah** | **praise you him** | **all** |

| זרע 2233 | יעקב 3290 | כבדוהו 3513 | וגורו 1481 | ממנו 4480 | כל 3605 | זרע 2233 | ישראל 3478: | 22:24 כי 3588 | לא 3808 | בזה 959 |
|---|---|---|---|---|---|---|---|---|---|---|
| zera' | ya'aqob | kabduhu; | uaguru | mimenu, | kal | zera' | yisra'ael. | kiy | la' | bazah |
| ***you* the seed of** | **Jacob** | **glorify him** | **and fear** | **him** | **all** | ***you* the seed of** | **Israel** | **For** | **not** | **he has despised** |

| ולא 3808 | שקץ 8262 | ענות 6039 | עני 6041 | ולא 3808 | הסתיר 5641 | פניו 6440 | ממנו 4480 | ובשועו 7768 | אליו 413 |
|---|---|---|---|---|---|---|---|---|---|
| uala' | shiqatz | 'anut | 'aniy, | uala' | histiyr | panayu | mimenu; | uabshaua'au | 'aelayu |
| **nor** | **abhorred** | **the affliction of** | **the afflicted** | **neither** | **has he hid** | **his face** | **from him** | **but when he cried** | **unto him** |

| שמע 8085: | 22:25 מאתך 853 | תהלתי 8416 | בקהל 6951 | רב 7227 | נדרי 5088 | אשלם 7999 | נגד 5048 | יראיו 3373: | 22:26 |
|---|---|---|---|---|---|---|---|---|---|
| shamea'. | me'ataka, | tahilatiy | baqahal | rab; | nadaray | 'ashalem, | neged | yare'ayu. | |
| **he heard** | **of you** | **My praise *shall be*** | **in congregation** | ***the* great** | **my vows** | **I will pay** | **before** | **them that fear him** | |

| יאכלו 398 | ענוים 6035 | וישבעו 7646 | יהללו 1984 | יהוה 3068 | דרשיו 1875 | יחי 2421 | לבבכם 3824 | לעד 5703: | 22:27 |
|---|---|---|---|---|---|---|---|---|---|
| ya'kalu | 'anauiym | uayisaba'au, | yahalalu | Yahuah | dorashayu; | yachiy | lababkem | la'ad. | |
| **shall eat** | **The meek** | **and be satisfied** | **they shall praise** | **Yahuah** | **that seek him** | **shall live** | **your heart** | **for ever** | |

| יזכרו 2142 | וישבו 7725 | אל 413 | יהוה 3068 | כל 3605 | אפסי 657 | ארץ 776 | וישתחוו 7812 | לפניך 6440 | כל 3605 | משפחות 4940 |
|---|---|---|---|---|---|---|---|---|---|---|
| yizkaru | uayashubu | 'al | Yahuah | kal | 'apsey | 'aretz; | uayishtachauu | lapaneyka, | kal | mishpachout |
| **shall remember** | **and turn** | **unto** | **Yahuah** | **All** | **the ends of** | **the world** | **shall worship** | **before you** | **all** | **the kindreds of** |

| גוים 1471: | 22:28 כי 3588 | ליהוה 3068 | המלוכה 4410 | ומשל 4910 | בגוים 1471: | 22:29 אכלו 398 | וישתחוו 7812 |
|---|---|---|---|---|---|---|---|
| gouyim. | kiy | laYahuah | hamalukah; | uamoshel, | bagouyim. | 'akalu | uayishtachauu |
| **the nations** | **For** | ***is* Yahuah's** | **the kingdom** | **and he *is* the governor** | **among the nations** | **shall eat** | **and worship** |

Ps 22:16 For dogs have compassed me: the assembly of the wicked have enclosed me: they pierced my hands and my feet.17 I may tell all my bones: they look and stare upon me.18 They part my garments among them, and cast lots upon my vesture.19 But be not you far from me, O YHUH: O my strength, haste you to help me.20 Deliver my soul from the sword; my darling from the power of the dog.21 Save me from the lion's mouth: for you have heard me from the horns of the unicorns.22 I will declare your name unto my brethren: in the midst of the congregation will I praise you.23 You that fear YHUH, praise him; all you the seed of Jacob, glorify him; and fear him, all you the seed of Israel.24 For he has not despised nor abhorred the affliction of the afflicted; neither has he hid his face from him; but when he cried unto him, he heard.25 My praise shall be of you in the great congregation: I will pay my vows before them that fear him.26 The meek shall eat and be satisfied: they shall praise YHUH that seek him: your heart shall live forever.27 All the ends of the world shall remember and turn unto YHUH: and all the kindreds of the nations shall worship before you.28 For the kingdom is YHUH's: and he is the governor among the nations.

כל 3605 דשני 1879 ארץ 776 לפניו 6440 יכרעו 3766 כל 3605 יורדי 3381 עפר 6083 ונפשו 5315 לא 3808
kal dishney 'aretz, lapanayu yikra'au kal youradey 'apar; uanapshou, la'
**All *they that be* fat upon earth before him shall bow all they that go down to the dust and his own soul none**

חיה 2421: 22:30 זרע 2233 יעבדנו 5647 יספר 5608 לאדני 136 לדור 1755: 22:31 יבאו 935
chiyah. zera' ya'abdenu; yasupar la'adonay ladour. yabo'au
**can keep alive A seed shall serve him it shall be accounted to Adonai for a generation They shall come**

ויגידו 5046 צדקתו 6666 לעם 5971 נולד 3205 כי 3588 עשה 6213:
uayagiydu tzidqatou; la'am noulad, kiy 'asah.
**and shall declare his righteousness unto a people that shall be born that he has done *this***

**Ps 23:1** מזמור 4210 לדוד 1732 יהוה 3068 רעי 7462 לא 3808 אחסר 2637: 23:2 בנאות 4999 דשא 1877 ירביצני 7257
mizmour ladauid; Yahuah ro'ay, la' 'achsar. bin'aut desha' yarbiytzeniy;
**A Psalm of David Yahuah *is* my shepherd not I shall want in pastures green He make me to lie down**

על 5921 מי 4325 מנחות 4496 ינהלני 5095: 23:3 נפשי 5315 ישובב 7725 ינחני 5148 במעגלי 4570 צדק 6664 למען 4616
'al mey manuchout yanahaleniy. napshiy yashoubeb; yancheniy bama'agley tzedeq, lama'an
**beside waters *the* still he lead me my soul He restoreth he lead me in the paths of righteousness for sake**

שמו 8034: 23:4 גם 1571 כי 3588 אלך 1980 בגיא 1516 צלמות 6757 לא 3808 אירא 3372 רע 7451 כי 3588 אתה 859
shamou. gam kiy 'aelek bagey'a tzalmauet la' 'ayra' ra', kiy 'atah
**his name's Yea though I walk through the valley of the shadow of death no I will fear evil for you *are***

עמדי 5978 שבטך 7626 ומשענתך 4938 המה 1992 ינחמני 5162: 23:5 תערך 6186 לפני 6440 שלחן 7979 נגד 5048
'amadiy; shibtaka uamish'anteka, hemah yanachamuniy. ta'arok lapanay shulchan, neged
**with me your rod and your staff they comfort You preparest before me a table in the presence of**

צררי 6887 דשנת 1878 בשמן 8081 ראשי 7218 כוסי 3563 רויה 7310: 23:6 אך 389 טוב 2896 וחסד 2617 ירדפוני 7291 כל 3605
tzoraray; dishanta bashemen ra'shiy, kousiy rauayah. 'ak toub uachesed yirdapuniy kal
**mine enemies you anointest with oil my head my cup run over Surely goodness and mercy shall follow me all**

ימי 3117 חיי 2416 ושבתי 3427 בבית 1004 יהוה 3068 לארך 753 ימים 3117:
yamey chayay; uashabtiy babeyt Yahuah la'arek yamiym.
**the days of my life and I will dwell in the house Yahuah for ever**

**Ps 24:1** לדוד 1732 מזמור 4210 ליהוה 3068 הארץ 776 ומלואה 4393 תבל 8398 וישבי 3427 בה 871a: 24:2 כי 3588
ladauid, mizmour laYahuah ha'aretz uamlou'ah; tebel, uayoshabey bah. kiy
**of David A Psalm *is* Yahuah's The earth and the fulness thereof the world and they that dwell therein For**

הוא 1931 על 5921 ימים 3220 יסדה 3245 ועל 5921 נהרות 5104 יכוננה 3559: 24:3 מי 4310 יעלה 5927 בהר 2022 יהוה 3068
hua' 'al yamiym yasadah; ua'al naharout, yakounaneha. miy' ya'aleh bahar Yahuah;
**he upon the seas has founded it and upon the floods *and* established it Who shall ascend into the hill of Yahuah?**

ומי 4310 יקום 6965 במקום 4725 קדשו 6944: 24:4 נקי 5355 כפים 3709 ובר 1249 לבב 3824 אשר 834 לא 3808 נשא 5375
uamiy yaqum bimaqoum qadashou. naqiy kapayim, uabar labab 'asher la' nasa'
**or who shall stand in place? his holy He that has clean hands and a pure heart who not has lifted up**

Ps 22:29 All they that be fat upon earth shall eat and worship: all they that go down to the dust shall bow before him: and none can keep alive his own soul.30 A seed shall serve him; it shall be accounted to YHUH for a generation.31 They shall come, and shall declare his righteousness unto a people that shall be born, that he has done this. **Ps** 23:1 A Psalm of David. YHUH is my shepherd; I shall not want.2 He make me to lie down in green pastures: he leadeth me beside the still waters.3 He restoreth my soul: he leadeth me in the paths of righteousness for his name's sake.4 Yea, though I walk through the valley of the shadow of death, I will fear no evil: for you are with me; your rod and your staff they comfort me.5 Thou preparest a table before me in the presence of mine enemies: you anointest my head with oil; my cup runneth over.6 Surely goodness and mercy shall follow me all the days of my life: and I will dwell in the house of YHUH forever. **Ps** 24:1 A Psalm of David. The earth is YHUH's, and the fulness thereof; the world, and they that dwell therein.2 For he has founded it upon the seas, and established it upon the floods.3 Who shall ascend into the hill of YHUH? or who shall stand in his holy place?4 He that has clean hands, and a pure heart; who has not lifted up his soul unto vanity, nor sworn deceitfully.

לשוא 7723 נפשי 5315 ולא 3808 נשבע 7650 למרמה 4820: 24:5 ישא 5375 ברכה 1293 מאת 853 יהוה 3068 וצדקה 6666
lashau'a napshiy; uala' nishba' lamirmah. yisa' barakah me'at Yahuah; uatzdaqah,
**unto vanity his soul and nor sworn deceitfully He shall receive the blessing from Yahuah and righteousness**

מאלהי 430 ישעו 3468: 24:6 זה 2088 דור 1755 דרשו 1875 מבקשי 1245 פניך 6440 יעקב 3290
me'alohey yish'au. zeh dour dorashau mabaqshey paneyka ya'aqob
**from the Elohim of his salvation This *is* the generation of them that seek him, that seek your face O Jacob**

סלה 5542: 24:7 שאו 5375 שערים 8179 ראשיכם 7218 והנשאו 5375 פתחי 6607 עולם 5769 ויבוא 935 מלך 4428
selah. sa'au sha'ariym ra'sheykem, uahinasa'au pitchey 'aulam; uayabou'a, melek
**Selah Lift up O you gates your heads and be you lift up doors *you* everlasting and shall come in the King of**

הכבוד 3519: 24:8 מי 4310 זה 2088 מלך 4428 הכבוד 3519 יהוה 3068 עזוז 5808 וגבור 1368 יהוה 3068 גבור 1368 מלחמה 4421: 24:9 שאו 5375
hakaboud. miy' zeh melek hakaboud Yahuah 'azuz uagibour; Yahuah gibour milchamah. sa'au
**glory Who *is* this King of glory? Yahuah strong and mighty Yahuah mighty in battle Lift up**

שערים 8179 ראשיכם 7218 ושאו 5375 פתחי 6607 עולם 5769 ויבא 935 מלך 4428 הכבוד 3519: 24:10 מי 4310
sha'ariym ra'sheykem, uasa'au pitchey 'aulam; uayaba' melek hakaboud. miy'
**O you gates your heads even lift *them* up you doors everlasting and shall come in *the* King of glory Who *is***

הוא 1931 זה 2088 מלך 4428 הכבוד 3519 יהוה 3068 צבאות 6635 הוא 1931 מלך 4428 הכבוד 3519 סלה 5542:
hua' zeh melek hakaboud Yahuah tzaba'aut; hua' melek hakaboud selah.
**he this King of glory? Yahuah of hosts he *is the* King of glory Selah**

**Ps 25:1** לדוד 1732 אליך 413 יהוה 3068 נפשי 5315 אשא 5375: 25:2 אלהי 430 בך 871a בטחתי 982 אל 408
ladauid 'aeleyka Yahuah napshiy 'asa'. 'alohay, baka batachtiy 'al
***A Psalm* of David Unto you O Yahuah my soul do I lift up O my Elohim in you I trust not**

אבושה 954 אל 408 יעלצו 5970 איבי 341 לי 3807a: 25:3 גם 1571 כל 3605 קויך 6960 לא 3808 יבשו 954
'aeboushah; 'al ya'altzu 'ayabay liy. gam kal qoueyka la' yeboshu;
**let me be ashamed not let triumph mine enemies over me Yea none let that wait on you none be ashamed**

יבשו 954 הבוגדים 898 ריקם 7387: 25:4 דרכיך 1870 יהוה 3068 הודיעני 3045 ארחותיך 734 למדני 3925: 25:5
yeboshu, habougadiym reyqam. darakeyka Yahuah houdiy'aeniy; 'arachouteyka lamadeniy.
**let them be ashamed which transgress without cause your ways O Yahuah Shew me your paths teach me**

הדריכני 1869 באמתך 571 ולמדני 3925 כי 3588 אתה 859 אלהי 430 ישעי 3468 אותך 854 קויתי 6960 כל 3605 היום 3117: 25:6
hadariykeniy ba'amiteka ualamadeniy, kiy 'atah 'alohey yish'ay; 'autaka qiuiytiy, kal hayoum.
**Lead me in your truth and teach me for you *are* the Elohim of my salvation on you do I wait all the day**

זכר 2142 רחמיך 7356 יהוה 3068 וחסדיך 2617 כי 3588 מעולם 5769 המה 1992: 25:7
zakar rachameyka Yahuah uachasadeyka; kiy me'aulam hemah.
**Remember your tender mercies O Yahuah and your lovingkindnesses for they *have been* ever of old they**

חטאות 2403 נעורי 5271 ופשעי 6588 אל 408 תזכר 2142 כחסדך 2617 זכר 2142 לי 3807a אתה 859 למען 4616
chata'ut na'auray uapsha'ay, 'al tizkor kachasdaka zakar liy 'atah; lama'an
**the sins of my youth nor my transgressions not Remember according to your mercy remember me you for sake**

Ps 24:5 He shall receive the blessing from YHUH, and righteousness from the G-d of his salvation.6 This is the generation of them that seek him, that seek your face, O Jacob. Selah.7 Lift up your head, O you gates; and be you lift up, you everlasting doors; and the King of glory shall come in.8 Who is this King of glory? YHUH strong and mighty, YHUH mighty in battle.9 Lift up your heads, O you gates; even lift them up, you everlasting doors; and the King of glory shall come in.10 Who is this King of glory? YHUH of hosts, he is the King of glory. Selah. **Ps** 25:1 A Psalm of David. Unto you, O YHUH, do I lift up my soul.2 O my G-d, I trust in you: let me not be ashamed, let not mine enemies triumph over me.3 Yea, let none that wait on you be ashamed: let them be ashamed which transgress without cause.4 Shew me your ways, O YHUH; teach me your paths.5 Lead me in your truth, and teach me: for you are the G-d of my salvation; on you do I wait all the day.6 Remember, O YHUH, your tender mercies and your lovingkindnesses; for they have been ever of old.7 Remember not the sins of my youth, nor my transgressions: according to your mercy remember you me for your goodness' sake, O YHUH.

25:8 25:9

טובך 2898 יהוה 3068: טוב 2896 וישר 3477 יהוה 3068 על 5921 כן 3651 יורה 3384 חטאים 2400 בדרך 1870:
tubaka Yahuah. toub uayashar Yahuah; 'al ken youreh chata'aym badarek.
**your goodness' O Yahuah Good and upright *is* Yahuah therefore after that will he teach sinners in the way**

25:10

ידרך 1869 ענוים 6035 במשפט 4941 וילמד 3925 ענוים 6035 דרכו 1870: כל 3605 ארחות 734 יהוה 3068 חסד 2617
yadrek 'anauiym bamishpat; uiylamed 'anauiym darkou. kal 'arachout Yahuah chesed
**will he guide The meek in judgment and will he teach the meek his way All the paths of Yahuah *are* mercy**

25:11

ואמת 571 לנצרי 5341 בריתו 1285 ועדתיו 5713: למען 4616 שמך 8034 יהוה 3068 וסלחת 5545 לעוני 5771
ua'amet; lanotzarey bariytou, ua'aedotayu. lama'an shimka Yahuah; uasalachta la'auoniy,
**and truth unto such as keep his covenant and his testimonies For sake your name's O Yahuah pardon mine iniquity**

25:12

כי 3588 רב 7227 הוא 1931: מי 4310 זה 2088 האיש 376 ירא 3373 יהוה 3068 יורנו 3384 בדרך 1870
kiy rab hua'. miy' zeh ha'aysh yarea' Yahuah; yourenu, baderek
**for *is* great it What he man *is* he that fear Yahuah him shall he teach in the way**

25:13 25:14

יבחר 977: נפשו 5315 בטוב 2896 תלין 3885 וזרעו 2233 יירש 3423 ארץ 776: סוד 5475 יהוה 3068
yibchar. napshou batoub taliyn; uazar'au, yiyrash 'aretz. coud Yahuah
***that* he shall choose His soul at ease shall dwell and his seed shall inherit the earth The secret of Yahuah**

25:15

ליראיו 3373 ובריתו 1285 להודיעם 3045: עיני 5869 תמיד 8548 אל 413 יהוה 3068 כי 3588 הוא 1931
liyre'ayu; uabriytou, lahoudiy'am. 'aeynay tamiyd 'al Yahuah; kiy hua'
***is* with them that fear him and his covenant he will show them Mine eyes *are* ever toward Yahuah for he**

25:16

יוציא 3318 מרשת 7568 רגלי 7272: פנה 6437 אלי 413 וחנני 2603 כי 3588 יחיד 3173 ועני 6041
youtziy'a mereshet raglay. paneh 'aelay uachaneniy kiy yachiyd ua'aniy
**shall pluck out of the net my feet Turn you unto me and have mercy upon me for I *am* desolate and afflicted**

25:17 25:18

אני 589: צרות 6869 לבבי 3824 הרחיבו 7337 ממצוקותי 4691 הוציאני 3318: ראה 7200 עניי 6040
'aniy. tzarout lababiy hirachiybu; mimatzuqoutay, houtziy'aeniy. ra'aeh 'anyiy
**I The troubles of my heart are enlarged out of my distresses *O* bring you me Look upon mine affliction**

25:19

ועמלי 5999 ושא 5375 לכל 3605 חטאותי 2403: ראה 7200 אויבי 341 כי 3588 רבו 7231 ושנאת 8130 חמס 2555
ua'amaliy; uasa', lakal chata'utay. ra'aeh 'auyabay kiy rabu; uasin'at chamas
**and my pain and forgive all my sins Consider mine enemies for they are many and they hate me *with* cruel**

25:20 25:21

שנאוני 8135: שמרה 8104 נפשי 5315 והצילני 5337 אל 408 אבוש 954 כי 3588 חסיתי 2620 בך 871a: תם 8537
sane'auniy. shamarah napshiy uahatziyleniy; 'al 'aeboush, kiy chasiytiy bak. tom
**hatred *O* keep my soul and deliver me not let me be ashamed for I put my trust in you integrity**

25:22

וישר 3476 יצרוני 5341 כי 3588 קויתיך 6960: פדה 6299 אלהים 430 את 853 ישראל 3478 מכל 3605 צרותיו 6869:
uayosher yitzruniy; kiy, qiuiytiyka. padeh 'alohiym 'at yisra'ael; mikol, tzaroutayu
**and uprightness Let preserve me for I wait on you Redeem O Elohim Israel out of all his troubles**

Ps 26:1

לדוד 1732 שפטני 8199 יהוה 3068 כי 3588 אני 589 בתמי 8537 הלכתי 1980 וביהוה 3068 בטחתי 982
ladauid shapateniy Yahuah kiy 'aniy batumiy halaktiy; uabaYahuah batachtiy,
***A Psalm* of David Judge me O Yahuah for I in mine integrity have walked also in Yahuah I have trusted**

Ps 25:8 Good and upright is YHUH: therefore will he teach sinners in the way.9 The meek will he guide in judgment: and the meek will he teach his way.10 All the paths of YHUH are mercy and truth unto such as keep his covenant and his testimonies.11 For your name's sake, O YHUH, pardon mine iniquity; for it is great.12 What man is he that fear YHUH? him shall he teach in the way that he shall choose.13 His soul shall dwell at ease; and his seed shall inherit the earth.14 The secret of YHUH is with them that fear him; and he will show them his covenant.15 Mine eyes are ever toward YHUH; for he shall pluck my feet out of the net.16 Turn you unto me, and have mercy upon me; for I am desolate and afflicted.17 The troubles of my heart are enlarged: O bring you me out of my distresses.18 Look upon mine affliction and my pain; and forgive all my sins.19 Consider mine enemies; for they are many; and they hate me with cruel hatred.20 O keep my soul, and deliver me: let me not be ashamed; for I put my trust in you.21 Let integrity and uprightness preserve me; for I wait on you.22 Redeem Israel, O G-d, out of all his troubles. **Ps** 26:1 A Psalm of David. Judge me, O YHUH; for I have walked in mine integrity: I have trusted also in YHUH; therefore I shall not slide.

26:2 26:3

לא 3808 אמעד 4571: בחנני 974 יהוה 3068 ונסני 5254 צרופה 6884 כליותי 3629 ולבי 3820: כי 3588
la' 'am'ad. bachaneniy Yahuah uanaseniy; tzaroupah kilyoutay ualibiy. kiy
**not *therefore* I shall slide Examine me O Yahuah and prove me try my reins and my heart For**

26:4

חסדך 2617 לנגד 5048 עיני 5869 והתהלכתי 1980 באמתך 571: לא 3808 ישבתי 3427 עם 5973 מתי 4962 שוא 7723 ועם 5973
chasdaka laneged 'aeynay; uahithalaktiy, ba'amiteka. la' yashabtiy 'am matey shau'a; ua'am
**your lovingkindness *is* before mine eyes and I have walked in your truth not I have sat with persons vain with**

26:5 26:6

נעלמים 5956 לא 3808 אבוא 935: שנאתי 8130 קהל 6951 מרעים 7489 ועם 5973 רשעים 7563 לא 3808 אשב 3427:
na'alamiym, la' abou'a. sanea'tiy qahal mere'aym; ua'am rasha'aym, la' 'aesheb.
**dissemblers neither will I go in I have hated the congregation of evil doers and with the wicked not will sit**

26:7

ארחץ 7364 בנקיון 5356 כפי 3709 ואסבבה 5437 את 853 מזבחך 4196 יהוה 3068: לשמע 8085 בקול 6963
'archatz baniqayoun kapay; ua'asobah 'at mizbachaka Yahuah. lashmia' baqoul
**I will wash in innocency mine hands so will I compass your altar O Yahuah That I may publish with the voice of**

26:8

תודה 8426 ולספר 5608 כל 3605 נפלאותיך 6381: יהוה 3068 אהבתי 157 מעון 4583 ביתך 1004 ומקום 4725
toudah; ualsaper, kal nipla'auteyka. Yahuah 'ahabtiy ma'aun beytaka; uamqoum,
**thanksgiving and tell of all your wondrous works Yahuah I have loved the habitation of your house and the place**

26:9 26:10

משכן 4908 כבודך 3519: אל 408 תאסף 622 עם 5973 חטאים 2400 נפשי 5315 ועם 5973 אנשי 582 דמים 1818 חיי 2416: אשר 834
mishkan kaboudeka. 'al ta'asop 'am chata'aym napshiy; ua'am 'anshey damiym chayay. 'asher
**where dwell your honor not You gather with sinners my soul with men bloody my life *In* whose**

26:11

בידיהם 3027 זמה 2154 וימינם 3225 מלאה 4390 שחד 7810: ואני 589 בתמי 8537 אלך 1980 פדני 6299
biydeyhem zimah; uiymiynam, mal'ah shochad. ua'aniy batumiy 'aelek, padeniy
**hands *is* mischief and their right hand is full of bribes But as for me in mine integrity I will walk redeem**

26:12

וחנני 2603: רגלי 7272 עמדה 5975 במישור 4334 במקהלים 4721 אברך 1288 יהוה 3068:
uachaneniy ragliy 'amdah bamiyshour; bamaqheliym, 'abarek Yahuah.
**me and be merciful unto me My foot stands in an even place in the congregations will I bless Yahuah**

**Ps 27:1**

לדוד 1732 יהוה 3068 אורי 216 וישעי 3468 ממי 4310 אירא 3372 יהוה 3068 מעוז 4581 חיי 2416
ladauid Yahuah 'aouriy uayish'ay mimiy 'ayra'; Yahuah ma'auz chayay,
***A Psalm* of David Yahuah *is* my light and my salvation whom shall I fear? Yahuah *is* the strength of my life**

27:2

ממי 4310 אפחד 6342: בקרב 7126 עלי 5921 מרעים 7489 לאכל 398 את 853 בשרי 1320 צרי 6862 ואיבי 341
mimiy 'apchad. biqrob 'alay mere'aym le'akol 'at basariy tzaray ua'ayabay
**of whom shall I be afraid? When came upon me the wicked to eat up my flesh *even* mine enemies and foes**

27:3

לי 3807a המה 1992 כשלו 3782 ונפלו 5307: אם 518 תחנה 2583 עלי 5921 מחנה 4264 לא 3808 יירא 3372 לבי 3820 אם 518
liy; hemah kashalu uanapalu. 'am tachaneh 'alay machaneh la' yiyra' libiy 'am
**my they stumbled and fell Though should encamp against me an host not shall fear my heart though**

27:4

תקום 6965 עלי 5921 מלחמה 4421 בזאת 2063 אני 589 בוטח 982: אחת 259 שאלתי 7592 מאת 853 יהוה 3068 אותה 853
taqum 'alay milchamah; baza't, 'aniy bouteach. 'achat sha'altiy me'at Yahuah 'autah
**should rise against me war in this *will* I *be* confident One *thing* have I desired of Yahuah that**

Ps 26:2 Examine me, O YHUH, and prove me; try my reins and my heart.3 For your lovingkindness is before mine eyes: and I have walked in your truth.4 I have not sat with vain persons, neither will I go in with dissemblers.5 I have hated the congregation of evil doers; and will not sit with the wicked.6 I will wash mine hands in innocency: so will I compass your altar, O YHUH:7 That I may publish with the voice of thanksgiving, and tell of all your wondrous works.8 YHUH, I have loved the habitation of your house, and the place where your honor dwell.9 Gather not my soul with sinners, nor my life with bloody men:10 In whose hands is mischief, and their right hand is full of bribes.11 But as for me, I will walk in mine integrity: redeem me, and be merciful unto me.12 My foot stand in an even place: in the congregations will I bless YHUH. **Ps** 27:1 A Psalm of David. YHUH is my light and my salvation; whom shall I fear? YHUH is the strength of my life; of whom shall I be afraid?2 When the wicked, even mine enemies and my foes, came upon me to eat up my flesh, they stumbled and fell.3 Though an host should encamp against me, my heart shall not fear: though war should rise against me, in this will I be confident.4 One thing have I desired of YHUH, that will I seek after; that I may dwell in the house of YHUH all the days of my life, to behold the beauty of YHUH,

אבקש 1245 שבתי 3427 בבית 1004 יהוה 3068 כל 3605 ימי 3117 חיי 2416 לחזות 2372 בנעם 5278 יהוה 3068
'abaqesh shibtiy babeyt Yahuah kal yamey chayay; lachazout bano'am Yahuah
**will I seek after that I may dwell in the house of Yahuah all the days of my life to behold the beauty of Yahuah**

ולבקר 1239 בהיכלו 1964: 27:5 כי 3588 יצפנני 6845 בסכה 5520 ביום 3117 רעה 7451 יסתרני 5641
ualbaqer baheykalou. kiy yitzpaneniy basukoh bayoum ra'ah yastireniy
**and to inquire in his temple For he shall hide me in his pavilion in the time of trouble shall he hide me**

בסתר 5643 אהלו 168 בצור 6697 ירוממני 7311: 27:6 ועתה 6258 ירום 7311 ראשי 7218 על 5921
baseter 'ahalou; batzur, yaroumameniy. ua'atah yarum ra'shiy 'al
**in the secret of his tabernacle upon a rock he shall set me up And now shall be lifted up mine head above**

איבי 341 סביבותי 5439 ואזבחה 2076 באהלו 168 זבחי 2077 תרועה 8643 אשירה 7891 ואזמרה 2167
'ayabay sabiyoutay, ua'azbachah ba'ahalou zibchey taru'ah; 'ashiyrah ua'azamarah,
**mine enemies round about me therefore will I offer in his tabernacle sacrifices of joy I will sing yea I will sing praises**

ליהוה 3068: 27:7 שמע 8085 יהוה 3068 קולי 6963 אקרא 7121 וחנני 2603 ועונני 6030: 27:8
laYahuah. shama' Yahuah qouliy 'aqraa', uachaneniy ua'aneniy.
**unto Yahuah Hear O Yahuah *with* my voice when I cry have mercy also upon me and answer me**

לך 3807a אמר 559 לבי 3820 בקשו 1245 פני 6440 את 853 פניך 6440 יהוה 3068 אבקש 1245: 27:9 אל 408 תסתר 5641
laka 'amar libiy baqashu panay; 'at paneyka Yahuah 'abaqesh. 'al taster
***When you said* unto you said my heart Seek you my face Your face Yahuah will I seek nor Hide**

פניך 6440 ממני 4480 אל 408 תט 5186 באף 639 עבדך 5650 עזרתי 5833 היית 1961 אל 408 תטשני 5203 ואל 408 תעזבני 5800
paneyka mimeniy 'al tat ba'ap, 'abdeka 'azratiy hayiyta; 'al titsheniy ua'al ta'azbeniy,
**your face *far* from me not put away in anger your servant my help you have been not leave me neither forsake me**

אלהי 430 ישעי 3468: 27:10 כי 3588 אבי 1 ואמי 517 עזבוני 5800 ויהוה 3068 יאספני 622: 27:11 הורני 3384
'alohey yish'ay. kiy 'abiy ua'amiy 'azabuniy; uaYahuah ya'aspeniy. houreniy
**O Elohim of my salvation When my father and my mother forsake me then Yahuah will take me up Teach me**

יהוה 3068 דרכך 1870 ונחני 5148 בארח 734 מישור 4334 למען 4616 שוררי 8324: 27:12 אל 408 תתנני 5414 בנפש 5315
Yahuah darkeka uancheniy ba'arach miyshour; lama'an, shourray. 'al titaneniy banepesh
**O Yahuah your way and lead me in a path plain because of mine enemies not Deliver me over unto the will of**

צרי 6862 כי 3588 קמו 6965 בי 871a עדי 5707 שקר 8267 ויפח 3307 חמס 2555: 27:13 לולא 3884
tzaray; kiy qamu biy 'aedey, sheqer uiypeach chamas. lulea',
**mine enemies for are risen up against me witnesses false and such as breathe out cruelty *I had fainted* unless**

האמנתי 539 לראות 7200 בטוב 2898 יהוה 3068 בארץ 776 חיים 2416: 27:14 קוה 6960 אל 413 יהוה 3068 חזק 2388
he'amantiy lir'aut batub Yahuah ba'aretz chayiym. qaueh, 'al Yahuah chazaq
**I had believed to see *the* goodness of Yahuah in the land of the living Wait on Yahuah be of good courage**

ויאמץ 553 לבך 3820 וקוה 6960 אל 413 יהוה 3068:
uaya'ametz libeka; uaqaueh, 'al Yahuah.
**and he shall strengthen your heart wait I say on Yahuah**

Ps 27:4 and to inquire in his temple.5 For in the time of trouble he shall hide me in his pavilion: in the secret of his tabernacle shall he hide me; he shall set me up upon a rock.6 And now shall mine head be lifted up above mine enemies round about me: therefore will I offer in his tabernacle sacrifices of joy; I will sing, yea, I will sing praises unto YHUH.7 Hear, O YHUH, when I cry with my voice: have mercy also upon me, and answer me.8 When you saidst, Seek you my face; my heart said unto you, Thy face, YHUH, will I seek.9 Hide not your face far from me; put not your servant away in anger: you have been my help; leave me not, neither forsake me, O G-d of my salvation.10 When my father and my mother forsake me, then YHUH will take me up.11 Teach me your way, O YHUH, and lead me in a plain path, because of mine enemies.12 Deliver me not over unto the will of mine enemies: for false witnesses are risen up against me, and such as breathe out cruelty.13 I had fainted, unless I had believed to see the goodness of YHUH in the land of the living.14 Wait on YHUH: be of good courage, and he shall strengthen your heart: wait, I say, on YHUH.

**Ps 28:1**
לדוד 1732 | אליך 413 | יהוה 3068 | אקרא 7121 | צורי 6697 | אל 408 | תחרש 2790 | ממני 4480 | פן 6435 | תחשה 2790 | ממני 4480
ladauid 'aeleyka Yahuah 'aqraa', tzuriy 'al techarash mimeniy pen techeSheh mimeniy;
***A Psalm* of David** **Unto you** **O Yahuah** **will I cry** **my rock** **not** **be silent** **to me** **lest *if*** **you be silent** **to me**

ונמשלתי 4911 | עם 5973 | יורדי 3381 | בור 953: | **28:2** שמע 8085 | קול 6963 | תחנוני 8469 | בשועי 7768 | אליך 413
uanimshaltiy, 'am youradey bour. shama' qoul tachanunay bashaua'ay 'aeleyka;
**I become** **like** **them that go down into** **the pit** **Hear** **the voice of** **my supplications** **when I cry** **unto you**

בנשאי 5375 | ידי 3027 | אל 413 | דביר 1687 | קדשך 6944: | **28:3** אל 408 | תמשכני 4900 | עם 5973 | רשעים 7563 | ועם 5973 | פעלי 6466
banasa'ay yaday, 'al dabiyr qadasheka 'al timshakeniy 'am rasha'aym ua'am po'aley
**when I lift up** **my hands** **toward** **oracle** **your holy** **not** **Draw me away** **with** **the wicked** **and with** **the workers of**

און 205 | דברי 1696 | שלום 7965 | עם 5973 | רעיהם 7453 | ורעה 7451 | בלבבם 3824: | **28:4** תן 5414 | להם 1992
'auen dobarey shaloum 'am re'aeyhem; uara'ah, bilbabam. ten lahem
**iniquity** **which speak** **peace** **to** **their neighbours** **but mischief** ***is* in their hearts** **Give** **them**

כפעלם 6467 | וכרע 7455 | מעלליהם 4611 | כמעשה 4639 | ידיהם 3027 | תן 5414 | להם 1992
kapa'alam uakroa' ma'aleyhem kama'aseh yadeyhem ten lahem;
**according to their deeds** **and according to the wickedness of** **their endeavours** **after the work of** **their hands** **give** **them**

השב 7725 | גמולם 1576 | להם 1992: | **28:5** כי 3588 | לא 3808 | יבינו 995 | אל 413 | פעלת 6468 | יהוה 3068 | ואל 413 | מעשה 4639 | ידיו 3027
hasheb gamulam lahem. kiy la' yabiynu 'al pa'alot Yahuah ua'al ma'aseh yadayu;
**render** **their desert** **to them** **Because** **not** **they regard** **nor** **the works of** **Yahuah** **and to** **the operation of** **his hands**

יהרסם 2040 | ולא 3808 | יבנם 1129: | **28:6** ברוך 1288 | יהוה 3068 | כי 3588 | שמע 8085 | קול 6963
yehersem, uala' yibnem. baruk Yahuah; kiy shama' qoul
**he shall destroy** **Nor** **them and not build them up** **Blessed** ***be* Yahuah** **because** **he has heard** **the voice of**

תחנוני 8469: | **28:7** יהוה 3068 | עזי 5797 | ומגני 4043 | בו 871a | בטח 982 | לבי 3820 | ונעזרתי 5826
tachanunay. Yahuah 'aziy uamaginiy bou batach libiy, uane'azaratiy
**my supplications** **Yahuah** ***is* my strength** **and my shield** **in him** **trusted** **my heart** **and I am helped**

ויעלז 5937 | לבי 3820 | ומשירי 7892 | אהודנו 3034: | **28:8** יהוה 3068 | עז 5797 | למו 3807a | ומעוז 4581
uaya'aloz libiy; uamishiyriy ahoudenu. Yahuah 'az lamou; uama'auz
**therefore greatly rejoice** **my heart** **and with my song** **will I praise him** **Yahuah** **strength *is*** **their** **and strength of**

ישועות 3444 | משיחו 4899 | הוא 1931: | **28:9** הושיעה 3467 | את 853 | עמך 5971 | וברך 1288 | את 853 | נחלתך 5159 | ורעם 7462
yashu'aut mashiychou hua'. houshiy'ah 'at 'ameka, uabarek 'at nachalateka; uara'aem
***is* the saving** **his anointed** **he** **Save** **your people** **and bless** **your inheritance** **feed them also**

ונשאם 5375 | עד 5704 | העולם 5769:
uanasa'aem, 'ad ha'aulam.
**and lift them up for** **ever**

**Ps 29:1**
מזמור 4210 | לדוד 1732 | הבו 3051 | ליהוה 3068 | בני 1121 | אלים 410 | הבו 3051 | ליהוה 3068 | כבוד 3519 | ועז 5797: | **29:2** הבו 3051
mizmour, ladauid habu laYahuah baney 'aeliym; habu laYahuah kaboud ua'az. habu
**A Psalm** **of David** **Give** **unto Yahuah** **sons of** **O you mighty** **give** **unto Yahuah** **glory** **and strength** **Give**

**Ps** 28:1 A Psalm of David. Unto you will I cry, O YHUH my rock; be not silent to me: lest, if you be silent to me, I become like them that go down into the pit.2 Hear the voice of my supplications, when I cry unto you, when I lift up my hands toward your holy oracle.3 Draw me not away with the wicked, and with the workers of iniquity, which speak peace to their neighbors, but mischief is in their hearts.4 Give them according to their deeds, and according to the wickedness of their endeavours: give them after the work of their hands; render to them their desert.5 Because they regard not the works of YHUH, nor the operation of his hands, he shall destroy them, and not build them up.6 Blessed be YHUH, because he has heard the voice of my supplications.7 YHUH is my strength and my shield; my heart trusted in him, and I am helped: therefore my heart greatly rejoice; and with my song will I praise him.8 YHUH is their strength, and he is the saving strength of his anointed.9 Save your people, and bless your inheritance: feed them also, and lift them up forever. **Ps** 29:1 A Psalm of David. Give unto YHUH, O you mighty, give unto YHUH glory and strength.

29:3

ליהוה 3068 כבוד 3519 שמו 8034 השתחוו 7812 ליהוה 3068 בהדרת 1927 קדש 6944: קול 6963 יהוה 3068 על 5921

laYahuah kaboud shamou; hishtachauu laYahuah bahadrat qodesh. qoul Yahuah 'al

**unto Yahuah the glory *due unto* his name worship Yahuah in the beauty of holiness The voice of Yahuah *is* upon**

29:4

המים 4325 אל 410 הכבוד 3519 הרעים 7481 יהוה 3068 על 5921 מים 4325 רבים 7227: קול 6963 יהוה 3068 בכח 3581 קול 6963

hamayim 'ael hakaboud hir'aym; Yahuah 'al mayim rabiym. qoul Yahuah bakoach; qoul

**the waters El *of* glory thunders Yahuah *is* upon waters many The voice of Yahuah *is* powerful the voice of**

29:5

יהוה 3068 בהדר 1926: קול 6963 יהוה 3068 שבר 7665 ארזים 730 וישבר 7665 יהוה 3068 את 853 ארזי 730

Yahuah behadar. qoul Yahuah shober 'araziym; uayashaber Yahuah 'at 'arzey

**Yahuah *is* full of majesty The voice of Yahuah break yea the cedars and break Yahuah cedars of**

29:6 29:7

הלבנון 3844: וירקידם 7540 כמו 3644 עגל 5695 לבנון 3844 ושרין 8303 כמו 3644 בן 1121 ראמים 7214: קול 6963

halabanoun. uayarqiydem kamou 'aegel; labanoun uasiryon, kamou ben ra'aemiym. qoul

**the Lebanon He make them also to skip like a calf Lebanon and Sirion like a young unicorn The voice of**

29:8

יהוה 3068 חצב 2672 להבות 3852 אש 784: קול 6963 יהוה 3068 יחיל 2342 מדבר 4057 יחיל 2342 יהוה 3068 מדבר 4057

Yahuah chotzeb, lahabout 'aesh. qoul Yahuah yachiyl midbar; yachiyl Yahuah midbar

**Yahuah divides the flames of fire The voice of Yahuah shake the wilderness shake Yahuah the wilderness of**

29:9

קדש 6946: קול 6963 יהוה 3068 יחולל 2342 אילות 355 ויחשף 2834 יערות 3295 ובהיכלו 1964 כלו 3605

qadesh. qoul Yahuah yachoulel 'ayalout uayechasop ya'arout uabheykalou; kulou,

**Kadesh The voice of Yahuah make to calve the hinds and discover the forests and in his temple every one**

29:10 29:11

אמר 559 כבוד 3519: יהוה 3068 למבול 3999 ישב 3427 וישב 3427 יהוה 3068 מלך 4428 לעולם 5769: יהוה 3068 עז 5797

'amer kaboud. Yahuah lamabul yashab; uayesheb Yahuah melek la'aulam. Yahuah 'az

**does speak of *his* glory Yahuah upon the flood sit yea sit Yahuah King for ever Yahuah strength**

לעמו 5971 יתן 5414 יהוה 3068 יברך 1288 את 853 עמו 5971 בשלום 7965:

la'amou yiten; Yahuah yabarek 'at 'amou bashaloum.

**unto his people will give Yahuah will bless his people with peace**

**Ps 30:1**

מזמור 4210 שיר 7892 חנכת 2598 הבית 1004 לדוד 1732: ארוממך 7311 יהוה 3068 כי 3588 דליתני 1802

mizmour shiyr chanukat habayit ladauid. aroumimaka Yahuah kiy diliytaniy;

**A Psalm *and* Song *at* the dedication of the house of David I will extol you O Yahuah for you have lifted me up**

30:2 30:3

ולא 3808 שמחת 8055 איבי 341 לי 3807a: יהוה 3068 אלהי 430 שועתי 7768 אליך 413 ותרפאני 7495:

uala' simachta 'ayabay liy. Yahuah 'alohay; shiua'atiy 'aeleyka, uatirpa'aeniy.

**and not have made to rejoice my foes over me O Yahuah my Elohim I cried unto you and you have healed me**

30:4

יהוה 3068 העלית 5927 מן 4480 שאול 7585 נפשי 5315 חייתני 2421 מיורדי 3381 בור 953:

Yahuah he'aliyta min sha'aul napshiy; chiyiytaniy, miyouradiy bour.

**O Yahuah you have brought up from the grave my soul you have kept me alive that I should not go down to the pit**

30:5

זמרו 2167 ליהוה 3068 חסידיו 2623 והודו 3034 לזכר 2143 קדשו 6944: כי 3588

zamru laYahuah chasiydayu; uahoudu, lezeker qadashou. kiy

**Sing praise unto Yahuah O you saints of his and give thanks at the remembrance of his holiness For**

Ps 29:2 Give unto YHUH the glory due unto his name; worship YHUH in the beauty of holiness.3 The voice of YHUH is upon the waters: the G-d of glory thundereth: YHUH is upon many waters.4 The voice of YHUH is powerful; the voice of YHUH is full of majesty.5 The voice of YHUH breaketh the cedars; yea, YHUH breaketh the cedars of Lebanon.6 He make them also to skip like a calf; Lebanon and Sirion like a young unicorn.7 The voice of YHUH divideth the flames of fire.8 The voice of YHUH shaketh the wilderness; YHUH shaketh the wilderness of Kadesh.9 The voice of YHUH make the hinds to calve, and discovereth the forests: and in his temple doth everyone speak of his glory.10 YHUH sitteth upon the flood; yea, YHUH sitteth King forever.11 YHUH will give strength unto his people; YHUH will bless his people with peace. **Ps** 30:1 A Psalm and Song at the dedication of the house of David. I will extol you, O YHUH; for you have lifted me up, and have not made my foes to rejoice over me.2 O YHUH my G-d, I cried unto you, and you have healed me.3 O YHUH, you have brought up my soul from the grave: you have kept me alive, that I should not go down to the pit.4 Sing unto YHUH, O you saints of his, and give thanks at the remembrance of his holiness.

| רגע 7281 | באפו 639 | חיים 2416 | ברצונו 7522 | בערב 6153 | ילין 3885 | בכי 1065 | ולבקר 1242 | רנה 7440: | 30:6 |
|---|---|---|---|---|---|---|---|---|---|
| rega' | ba'apou | chayiym | birtzounou | ba'areb | yaliyn | bekiy, | ualaboqer | rinah. | |
| ***endures but*** **a moment** | **his anger** | ***is*** **life** | **in his favor** | **for a night** | **may endure** | **weeping** | **but in the morning** | **joy *comes*** | |

| ואני 589 | אמרתי 559 | בשלוי 7959 | בל 1077 | אמוט 4131 | לעולם 5769: | 30:7 | יהוה 3068 | ברצונך 7522 | העמדתה 5975 |
|---|---|---|---|---|---|---|---|---|---|
| ua'aniy | 'amartiy | bashaluiy; | bal | 'amout | la'aulam. | | Yahuah | birtzounaka | he'amadtah |
| **And I** | **said** | **in my prosperity** | **never** | **I shall be moved** | **never** | | **Yahuah** | **by your favor** | **you have made to stand** |

| להררי 2042 | עז 5797 | הסתרת 5641 | פניך 6440 | הייתי 1961 | נבהל 926: | 30:8 | אליך 413 | יהוה 3068 | אקרא 7121 | ואל 413 | אדני 136 |
|---|---|---|---|---|---|---|---|---|---|---|---|
| laharriy | 'az | histarta | paneyka, | hayiytiy | nibhal. | | 'aeleyka | Yahuah | 'aqraa'; | ua'al | 'adonay, |
| **my mountain** | **strong** | **you did hide** | **your face** | ***and*** **I was** | **troubled** | | **to you** | **O Yahuah** | **I cried** | **and unto** | **Adonai** |

| אתחנן 2603: | 30:9 | מה 4100 | בצע 1215 | בדמי 1818 | ברדתי 3381 | אל 413 | שחת 7845 | היודך 3034 | עפר 6083 |
|---|---|---|---|---|---|---|---|---|---|
| 'atchanan. | | mah | betza' | badamiy | baridtiy | al | shachat | hayoudaka | 'apar; |
| **I made supplication** | | **What** | **profit** | ***is there*** **in my blood** | **when I go down** | **to** | **the pit?** | **shall praise you?** | **the dust** |

| היגיד 5046 | אמתך 571: | 30:10 | שמע 8085 | יהוה 3068 | וחנני 2603 | יהוה 3068 | היה 1961 | עזר 5826 | לי 3807a: | 30:11 |
|---|---|---|---|---|---|---|---|---|---|---|
| hayagiyd | 'amiteka. | | shama' | Yahuah | uachaneniy | Yahuah | heyeh | 'azer | liy. | |
| **shall it declare** | **your truth?** | | **Hear** | **O Yahuah** | **and have mercy upon me** | **Yahuah** | **be you** | **helper** | **my** | |

| הפכת 2015 | מספדי 4553 | למחול 4234 | לי 3807a | פתחת 6605 | שקי 8242 | ותאזרני 247 | שמחה 8057: | 30:12 |
|---|---|---|---|---|---|---|---|---|
| hapakta | mispadiy | lamachoul | liy | pitachta | saqiy; | uata'azereniy | simchah. | |
| **You have turned** | **my mourning** | **into dancing** | **for me** | **you have put off** | **my sackcloth** | **and you girded me with** | **gladness** | |

| למען 4616 | יזמרך 2167 | כבוד 3519 | ולא 3808 | ידם 1826 | יהוה 3068 | אלהי 430 | לעולם 5769 |
|---|---|---|---|---|---|---|---|
| lama'an | yazameraka | kaboud | uala' | yidom; | Yahuah | 'alohay, | la'aulam |
| **To the end of** | **may sing praise to you** | **that *my* glory** | **and not** | **be silent** | **O Yahuah** | **my Elohim** | **for ever** |

| אודך 3034: |
|---|
| 'audeka. |
| **I will give thanks unto you** |

| Ps 31:1 | למנצח 5329 | מזמור 4210 | לדוד 1732: | בך 871a | יהוה 3068 | חסיתי 2620 | אל 408 | אבושה 954 | לעולם 5769 |
|---|---|---|---|---|---|---|---|---|---|
| | lamanatzeach, | mizmour | ladauid. | baka | Yahuah | chasiytiy | 'al | 'aeboushah | la'aulam; |
| | **To the chief Musician** | **A Psalm** | **of David** | **In you** | **O Yahuah** | **do I put my trust** | **never** | **let me be ashamed** | **for** |

| בצדקתך 6666 | פלטני 6403: | 31:2 | הטה 5186 | אלי 413 | אזנך 241 | מהרה 4120 | הצילני 5337 | היה 1961 | לי 3807a | לצור 6697 | מעוז 4581 |
|---|---|---|---|---|---|---|---|---|---|---|---|
| batzidqataka | palteniy. | | hateh | 'aelay | 'aznaka | maherah | hatziyleniy | hayeh | liy | latzur | ma'auz |
| **in your righteousness** | **deliver me** | | **Bow down** | **to me** | **your ear** | **speedily** | **deliver me** | **be you** | **my** | **rock** | **strong** |

| לבית 1004 | מצודות 4686 | להושיעני 3467: | 31:3 | כי 3588 | סלעי 5553 | ומצודתי 4686 | אתה 859 | ולמען 4616 | שמך 8034 |
|---|---|---|---|---|---|---|---|---|---|
| labeyt | matzudout, | lahoushiy'aeniy. | | kiy | sala'ay | uamtzudatiy | 'atah; | ualma'an | shimka, |
| **for an house of** | **defence** | **to save me** | | **For** | ***are*** **my rock** | **and my fortress** | **you** | **therefore for sake** | **your name's** |

| תנחני 5148 | ותנהלני 5095: | 31:4 | תוציאני 3318 | מרשת 7568 | זו 2098 | טמנו 2934 | לי 3807a | כי 3588 | אתה 859 | מעוזי 4581: |
|---|---|---|---|---|---|---|---|---|---|---|
| tanacheniy | uatnahaleniy. | | toutziy'aeniy, | mereshet | zu | tamanu | liy; | kiy | 'atah | ma'auziy. |
| **lead me** | **and guide me** | | **Pull me out** | **of the net** | **that** | **they have laid privily** | **for me** | **for** | **you** | ***are*** **my strength** |

Ps 30:5 For his anger endureth but a moment; in his favor is life: weeping may endure for a night, but joy cometh in the morning.6 And in my prosperity I said, I shall never be moved.7 YHUH, by your favor you have made my mountain to stand strong: you did hide your face, and I was troubled.8 I cried to you, O YHUH; and unto YHUH I made supplication.9 What profit is there in my blood, when I go down to the pit? Shall the dust praise you? shall it declare your truth?10 Hear, O YHUH, and have mercy upon me: YHUH, be you my helper.11 Thou have turned for me my mourning into dancing: you have put off my sackcloth, and girded me with gladness;12 To the end that my glory may sing praise to you, and not be silent. O YHUH my G-d, I will give thanks unto you forever. **Ps** 31:1 To the chief Musician, A Psalm of David. In you, O YHUH, do I put my trust; let me never be ashamed: deliver me in your righteousness.2 Bow down your ear to me; deliver me speedily: be you my strong rock, for an house of defence to save me.3 For you are my rock and my fortress; therefore for your name's sake lead me, and guide me.4 Pull me out of the net that they have laid privily for me: for you are my strength.

| 31:5 בידך 3027 | אפקיד 6485 | רוחי 7307 | פדיתה 6299 | אותי 853 | יהוה 3068 | אל 410 | אמת 571: | 31:6 שנאתי 8130 |
|---|---|---|---|---|---|---|---|---|
| bayadaka | 'apqiyd | ruchiy | padiytah | 'autiy | Yahuah | 'ael | 'amet. | sanea'tiy, |
| **Into your hand** | **I commit** | **my spirit** | **you have redeemed** | **me** | **O Yahuah** | **El *of*** | **truth** | **I have hated them** |

| השמרים 8104 | הבלי 1892 | שוא 7723 | ואני 589 | אל 413 | יהוה 3068 | בטחתי 982: | 31:7 אגילה 1523 | ואשמחה 8055 | בחסדך 2617 | אשר 834 |
|---|---|---|---|---|---|---|---|---|---|---|
| hashomariym | habley | shau'a; | ua'aniy, | 'al | Yahuah | batachatiy. | 'agiylah | ua'asmachah, | bachasdeka | 'asher |
| **that regard** | **vanities** | **lying** | **but I** | **in** | **Yahuah** | **trust** | **I will be glad** | **and rejoice** | **in your mercy** | **for** |

| ראית 7200 | את 853 | עניי 6040 | ידעת 3045 | בצרות 6869 | נפשי 5315: | 31:8 ולא 3808 | הסגרתני 5462 |
|---|---|---|---|---|---|---|---|
| ra'ayta | 'at | 'anyiy; | yada'ta, | batzarout | napshiy. | uala' | hisagartaniy |
| **you have considered** | | **my trouble** | **you have known** | **in adversities** | **my soul** | **And not** | **have shut me up** |

| ביד 3027 | אויב 341 | העמדת 5975 | במרחב 4800 | רגלי 7272: | 31:9 חנני 2603 | יהוה 3068 | כי 3588 | צר 6887 |
|---|---|---|---|---|---|---|---|---|
| bayad | auyeb; | he'amadta | bamerchab | raglay. | chaneniy | Yahuah | kiy | tzar |
| **into the hand of** | **the enemy** | **you have set** | **in a large room** | **my feet** | **Have mercy upon me** | **O Yahuah** | **for *am*** | **in trouble** |

| לי 3807a | עששה 6244 | בכעס 3708 | עיני 5869 | נפשי 5315 | ובטני 990: | 31:10 כי 3588 | כלו 3615 | ביגון 3015 | חיי 2416 | ושנותי 8141 |
|---|---|---|---|---|---|---|---|---|---|---|
| liy | 'ashashah | baka'as | 'aeyniy, | napshiy | uabitniy. | kiy | kalu | bayagoun | chayay | uashnoutay |
| **I** | **is consumed** | **with grief** | **mine eye** | ***yea* my soul** | **and my belly** | **For** | **is spent** | **with grief** | **my life** | **and my years** |

| באנחה 585 | כשל 3782 | בעוני 5771 | כחי 3581 | ועצמי 6106 | עששו 6244: | 31:11 מכל 3605 | צררי 6887 |
|---|---|---|---|---|---|---|---|
| ba'anachah | kashal | ba'auoniy | kochiy; | ua'atzamay | 'asheshu. | mikal | tzoraray |
| **with sighing** | **fail** | **because of mine iniquity** | **my strength** | **and my bones** | **are consumed** | **among all** | **mine enemies** |

| הייתי 1961 | חרפה 2781 | ולשכני 7934 | מאד 3966 | ופחד 6343 | למידעי 3045 | ראי 7200 | בחוץ 2351 |
|---|---|---|---|---|---|---|---|
| hayiytiy | cherpah | ualishakenay | ma'ad | uapachad | limayuda'ay | ro'ay | bachutz; |
| **I was** | **a reproach** | **but among my neighbours** | **especially** | **and a fear** | **to mine acquaintance** | **they that did see me** | **without** |

| נדדו 5074 | ממני 4480: | 31:12 נשכחתי 7911 | כמת 4191 | מלב 3820 | הייתי 1961 | ככלי 3627 | אבד 6: | 31:13 כי 3588 | שמעתי 8085 |
|---|---|---|---|---|---|---|---|---|---|
| nadadu | mimeniy. | nishkachtiy | kamet | mileb; | hayiytiy, | kikliy | 'abed. | kiy | shama'atiy |
| **fled** | **from me** | **I am forgotten** | **as a dead man** | **out of mind** | **I am** | **like a vessel** | **broken** | **For** | **I have heard** |

| דבת 1681 | רבים 7227 | מגור 4032 | מסביב 5439 | בהוסדם 3245 | יחד 3162 | עלי 5921 | לקחת 3947 | נפשי 5315 |
|---|---|---|---|---|---|---|---|---|
| dibat | rabiym | magour | misabiyb | bahiuasadam | yachad | 'alay; | laqachat | napshiy |
| **the slander of** | **many** | **fear** | ***was* on every side** | **while they took counsel** | **together** | **against me** | **to take away** | **my life** |

| זממו 2161: | 31:14 ואני 589 | עליך 5921 | בטחתי 982 | יהוה 3068 | אמרתי 559 | אלהי 430 | אתה 859: | 31:15 בידך 3027 | עתתי 6256 |
|---|---|---|---|---|---|---|---|---|---|
| zamamu. | ua'aniy | 'aleyka | batachtiy | Yahuah; | 'amartiy, | 'alohay | 'atah. | bayadaka | 'atotay; |
| **they devised** | **But I** | **in you** | **trusted** | **O Yahuah** | **I said** | **You *are* my Elohim** | **you** | ***are* in your hand** | **My times** |

| הצילני 5337 | מיד 3027 | אויבי 341 | ומרדפי 7291: | 31:16 האירה 215 | פניך 6440 | על 5921 |
|---|---|---|---|---|---|---|
| hatziyleniy | miyad | 'auyabay, | uamerodapay. | ha'ayrah | paneyka | 'al |
| **deliver me** | **from the hand of** | **mine enemies** | **and from them that persecute me** | **Make to shine** | **your face** | **upon** |

| עבדך 5650 | הושיעני 3467 | בחסדך 2617: | 31:17 יהוה 3068 | אל 408 | אבושה 954 | כי 3588 | קראתיך 7121 |
|---|---|---|---|---|---|---|---|
| 'abdeka; | houshiy'aeniy | bachasdeka. | Yahuah | 'al | 'aeboushah | kiy | qaraa'tiyka; |
| **your servant** | **save me** | **for your mercies' sake** | **O Yahuah** | **not** | **Let me be ashamed** | **for** | **I have called upon you** |

Ps 31:5 Into your hand I commit my spirit: you have redeemed me, O YHUH G-d of truth.6 I have hated them that regard lying vanities: but I trust in YHUH.7 I will be glad and rejoice in your mercy: for you have considered my trouble; you have known my soul in adversities;8 And have not shut me up into the hand of the enemy: you have set my feet in a large room.9 Have mercy upon me, O YHUH, for I am in trouble: mine eye is consumed with grief, yea, my soul and my belly.10 For my life is spent with grief, and my years with sighing: my strength faileth because of mine iniquity, and my bones are consumed.11 I was a reproach among all mine enemies, but especially among my neighbors, and a fear to mine acquaintance: they that did see me without fled from me.12 I am forgotten as a dead man out of mind: I am like a broken vessel.13 For I have heard the slander of many: fear was on every side: while they took counsel together against me, they devised to take away my life.14 But I trusted in you, O YHUH: I said, Thou are my G-d.15 My times are in your hand: deliver me from the hand of mine enemies, and from them that persecute me.16 Make your face to shine upon your servant: save me for your mercies' sake.17 Let me not be ashamed, O YHUH; for I have called upon you: let the wicked be ashamed, and let them be silent in the grave.

31:18
יבשו 954 רשעים 7563 ידמו 1826 לשאול 7585: תאלמנה 481 שפתי 8193 שקר 8267 הדברות 1696
yeboshu rasha'aym, yidamu lisha'aul. te'alamnah, siptey shaqer hadobarout
**let be ashamed the wicked *and* let them be silent in the grave Let they be put to silence lips *the* lying which speak**

31:19
על 5921 צדיק 6662 עתק 6277 בגאוה 1346 ובוז 937: מה 4100 רב 7227 טובך 2898 אשר 834
'al tzadiyq 'ataq, baga'auah uabuz. mah rab tubaka 'asher
**against the righteous grievous things proudly and contemptuously *Oh* how great *is* your goodness which**

31:20
צפנת 6845 ליראיך 3373 פעלת 6466 לחסים 2620 בך 871a נגד 5048 בני 1121 אדם 120:
tzapanta liyre'ayka pa'alta lachosiym bak; neged, baney 'adam
**you have laid up for them that fear you *which* you have wrought for them that trust in you before the sons of men**

תסתירם 5641 בסתר 5643 פניך 6440 מרכסי 7407 איש 376 תצפנם 6845 בסכה 5521
tastiyrem baseter paneyka meruksey 'aysh titzpanem basukah,
**You shall hide them in the secret of your presence from the pride of man you shall keep them secretly in a pavilion**

31:21
מריב 7379 לשנות 3956: ברוך 1288 יהוה 3069 כי 3588 הפליא 6381 חסדו 2617 לי 3807a בעיר 5892
mariyb lashonout. baruk Yahuah; kiy hipliy'a chasdou liy, ba'ayr
**from the strife of tongues Blessed Yahuah for he has showed marvellous his kindness me in a city**

31:22
מצור 4692: ואני 589 אמרתי 559 בחפזי 2648 נגרזתי 1629 מנגד 5048 עיניך 5869 אכן 403 שמעת 8085 קול 6963
matzour. ua'aniy 'amartiy bachapaziy, nigraztiy mineged 'aeyneyka 'aken, shama'ata qoul
**strong For I said in my haste I am cut off from before your eyes nevertheless you heard the voice of**

31:23
תחנוני 8469 בשועי 7768 אליך 413: אהבו 157 את 853 יהוה 3068 כל 3605 חסידיו 2623 אמונים 539 נצר 5341 יהוה 3068
tachanunay, bashaua'ay 'aeleyka. 'ahabu 'at Yahuah kal chasiydayu 'amuniym notzer Yahuah;
**my supplications when I cried unto you O love Yahuah all *you* his saints the faithful preserve *for* Yahuah**

31:24
ומשלם 7999 על 5921 יתר 3499 עשה 6213 גאוה 1346: חזקו 2388 ויאמץ 553 לבבכם 3824 כל 3605
uamshalem 'al yeter, 'aseh ga'auah. chizqu uaya'ametz lababkem; kal
**and reward on plentifully doer the proud Be of good courage and he shall strengthen your heart all**

המיחלים 3176 ליהוה 3068:
hamayachaliym, laYahuah.
**you that hope in Yahuah**

Ps 32:1
32:2
לדוד 1732 משכיל 4905 אשרי 835 נשוי 5375 פשע 6588 כסוי 3680 חטאה 2401: אשרי 835
ladauid, maskiyl 'ashrey nasuy pesha', kasuy chata'ah. 'ashrey
***A Psalm* of David Maschil Blessed *is* forgiven *is he whose* transgression *is* covered *whose* sin Blessed**

32:3
אדם 120 לא 3808 יחשב 2803 יהוה 3068 לו 3807a עון 5771 ואין 369 ברוחו 7307 רמיה 7423: כי 3588 החרשתי 2790
'adam, la' yachshob Yahuah lou' 'auon; ua'aeyn baruchou ramiyah kiy hecherashtiy
***is* the man not imputeth Yahuah unto whom iniquity and *there is* no in whose spirit guile When I kept silence**

32:4
בלו 1086 עצמי 6106 בשאגתי 7581 כל 3605 היום 3117: כי 3588 יומם 3119 ולילה 3915 תכבד 3513 עלי 5921 ידך 3027
balu 'atzamay; basha'agatiy, kal hayoum. kiy youmam ualayalah tikbad 'alay, yadeka
**waxed old my bones through my roaring all the day *long* For day and night was heavy upon me your hand**

Ps 31:18 Let the lying lips be put to silence; which speak grievous things proudly and contemptuously against the righteous.19 Oh how great is your goodness, which you have laid up for them that fear you; which you have wrought for them that trust in you before the sons of men!20 Thou shall hide them in the secret of your presence from the pride of man: you shall keep them secretly in a pavilion from the strife of tongues.21 Blessed be YHUH: for he has showed me his marvellous kindness in a strong city.22 For I said in my haste, I am cut off from before your eyes: nevertheless you heardest the voice of my supplications when I cried unto you.23 O love YHUH, all you his saints: for YHUH preserveth the faithful, and plentifully rewardeth the proud doer.24 Be of good courage, and he shall strengthen your heart, all you that hope in YHUH. **Ps** 32:1 A Psalm of David, Mas'-chil. Blessed is he whose transgression is forgiven, whose sin is covered.2 Blessed is the man unto whom YHUH imputeth not iniquity, and in whose spirit there is no guile.3 When I kept silence, my bones waxed old through my roaring all the day long.4 For day and night your hand was heavy upon me: my moisture is turned into the drought of summer. Selah.

נהפך 2015 לשדי 3955 בחרבני 2725 קיץ 7019 סלה 5542: **32:5** חטאתי 2403 אודיעך 3045 ועוני 5771 לא 3808
nehapak lashadiy; bacharboney qayitz selah. chata'tiy 'audiy'aka ua'auoniy la'
**is turned my moisture into the drought of summer Selah my sin unto you I acknowledged and mine iniquity not**

כסיתי 3680 אמרתי 559 אודה 3034 עלי 5921 פשעי 6588 ליהוה 3068 ואתה 859 נשאת 5375 עון 5771 חטאתי 2403
kisiytiy, 'amartiy, 'audeh 'aley pasha'ay laYahuah; ua'atah nasa'ta 'auon chata'tiy
**have I hid I said I will confess of my transgressions unto Yahuah and you forgave the iniquity of my sin**

סלה 5542: **32:6** על 5921 זאת 2063 יתפלל 6419 כל 3605 חסיד 2623 אליך 413 לעת 6256 מצא 4672 רק 7535
selah. 'al za't yitpalel kal chasiyd 'aeleyka la'at matza' raq,
**Selah For this shall pray every one that is godly unto you in a time when you may be found surely**

לשטף 7858 מים 4325 רבים 7227 אליו 413 לא 3808 יגיעו 5060: **32:7** אתה 859 סתר 5643 לי 3807a מצר 6862
lashetep mayim rabiym; 'aelayu, la' yagiy'au. 'atah seter liy mitzar
**in the floods of waters great unto him not they shall come near You hiding place *are* my from trouble**

תצרני 5341 רני 7438 פלט 6405 תסובבני 5437 סלה 5542: **32:8** אשכילך 7919 ואורך 3384
titzreniy raney palet; tasoubabeniy selah. 'askiylaka ua'auraka,
**you shall preserve me *with* songs of deliverance you shall compass me about Selah I will instruct you and teach**

בדרך 1870 זו 2098 תלך 1980 איעצה 3289 עליך 5921 עיני 5869: **32:9** אל 408 תהיו 1961 כסוס 5483 כפרד 6505
baderek zu telek; 'ay'atzah 'aleyka 'aeyniy. 'al tihayu kasus kapered
**in the way which you shall go I will guide you *with* mine eye not Be you as the horse *or* as the mule**

אין 369 הבין 995 במתג 4964 ורסן 7448 עדיו 5716 לבלום 1102 בל 1077 קרב 7126 אליך 413: **32:10**
'aeyn habiyn bameteg uaresen 'adyou libaloum; bal, qarob 'aeleyka.
***which* have no understanding with bit and bridle whose mouth must be held in lest they come near unto you**

רבים 7227 מכאובים 4341 לרשע 7563 והבוטח 982 ביהוה 3068 חסד 2617 יסובבנו 5437: **32:11** שמחו 8055
rabiym maka'aubiym, larasha' uahabouteach baYahuah; chesed, yasoubabenu. simchu
**Many sorrows *shall be* to the wicked but he that trust in Yahuah mercy shall compasshim about Be glad**

ביהוה 3068 וגילו 1523 צדיקים 6662 והרנינו 7442 כל 3605 ישרי 3477 לב 3820:
baYahuah uagiylu tzadiyqiym; uaharniynu, kal yishrey leb.
**in Yahuah and rejoice you righteous and shout for joy all *you that are* upright in heart**

**Ps 33:1** רננו 7442 צדיקים 6662 ביהוה 3068 לישרים 3477 נאוה 5000 תהלה 8416: **33:2** הודו 3034 ליהוה 3068 בכנור 3658
rannu tzadiyqiym baYahuah; layshariym, na'uah tahilah. houdu laYahuah bakinour;
**Rejoice O you righteous in Yahuah for the upright is comely *for* praise Praise unto Yahuah with harp**

בנבל 5035 עשור 6218 זמרו 2167 לו 3807a: **33:3** שירו 7891 לו 3807a שיר 7892 חדש 2319 היטיבו 3190
banebel 'asour, zamru lou'. shiyru lou' shiyr chadash; heytiybu
**with the psaltery *and* an instrument of ten strings sing praise unto him Sing unto him a song new skilfully**

נגן 5059 בתרועה 8643: **33:4** כי 3588 ישר 3477 דבר 1697 יהוה 3068 וכל 3605 מעשהו 4639 באמונה 530: **33:5** אהב 157
nagen, bitaru'ah. kiy yashar dabar Yahuah; uakal ma'asehu, be'amunah. 'aheb
**play with a loud noise For *is* right the word of Yahuah and all his works *are done* in truth He love**

Ps 32:5 I acknowledged my sin unto you, and mine iniquity have I not hid. I said, I will confess my transgressions unto YHUH; and you forgavest the iniquity of my sin. Selah.6 For this shall everyone that is godly pray unto you in a time when you may be found: surely in the floods of great waters they shall not come nigh unto him.7 Thou are my hiding place; you shall preserve me from trouble; you shall compass me about with songs of deliverance. Selah.8 I will instruct you and teach you in the way which you shall go: I will guide you with mine eye.9 Be you not as the horse, or as the mule, which have no understanding: whose mouth must be held in with bit and bridle, lest they come near unto you.10 Many sorrows shall be to the wicked: but he that trusteth in YHUH, mercy shall compass him about.11 Be glad in YHUH, and rejoice, you righteous: and shout for joy, all you that are upright in heart. **Ps**33:1 Rejoice in YHUH, O you righteous: for praise is comely for the upright.2 Praise YHUH with harp: sing unto him with the psaltery and an instrument of ten strings.3 Sing unto him a new song; play skilfully with a loud noise.4 For the word of YHUH is right; and all his works are done in truth.

| | | | | | | 33:6 | | |
|---|---|---|---|---|---|---|---|---|
| צדקה 6666 | ומשפט 4941 | חסד 2617 | יהוה 3068 | מלאה 4390 | הארץ 776: | בדבר 1697 | יהוה 3068 | שמים 8064 |
| tzadaqah | uamishpat; | chesed | Yahuah | mal'ah | ha'aretz. | bidbar | Yahuah | shamayim |
| **righteousness** | **and judgment** | **the goodness of** | **Yahuah** | **is full of** | **the earth** | **By the word of** | **Yahuah** | **the heavens** |

| | | | | | 33:7 | | |
|---|---|---|---|---|---|---|---|
| נעשו 6213 | וברוח 7307 | פיו 6310 | כל 3605 | צבאם 6635: | כנס 3664 | כנד 5067 | מי 4325 |
| naa'asu; | uabruach | piyu, | kal | tzaba'am. | kones | kaned | mey |
| **were made** | **and by the breath of** | **his mouth** | **all** | **the host of them** | **He gathered together** | **as an heap** | **the waters of** |

| | | | | 33:8 | | | | | | |
|---|---|---|---|---|---|---|---|---|---|---|
| הים 3220 | נתן 5414 | באצרות 214 | תהומות 8415: | ייראו 3372 | מיהוה 3068 | כל 3605 | הארץ 776 | ממנו 4480 | יגורו 1481 | כל 3605 |
| hayam; | noten | ba'atzarout | tahoumout. | yiyra'au | meYahuah | kal | ha'aretz; | mimenu | yaguru, | kal |
| **the sea** | **he lay up** | **in storehouses** | **the depth** | **Let fear** | **of Yahuah** | **all** | **the earth** | **of him** | **let stand in awe** | **all** |

| | | 33:9 | | | | | | | 33:10 |
|---|---|---|---|---|---|---|---|---|---|
| ישבי 3427 | תבל 8398: | כי 3588 | הוא 1931 | אמר 559 | ויהי 1961 | הוא 1931 | צוה 6680 | ויעמד 5975: | יהוה 3068 |
| yoshabey | tebel. | kiy | hua' | 'amar | uayehiy; | hua' | tziuah, | uaya'amod. | Yahuah |
| **the inhabitants of** | **the world** | **For** | **he** | **spoke** | **and was *done*** | **it** | **he commanded** | **and it stood fast** | **Yahuah** |

| | | | | | | 33:11 | |
|---|---|---|---|---|---|---|---|
| הפיר 6331 | עצת 6098 | גוים 1471 | הניא 5106 | מחשבות 4284 | עמים 5971: | עצת 6098 | יהוה 3068 |
| hepiyr | 'atzat | gouyim; | heniy'a, | machashabout | 'amiym. | 'atzat | Yahuah |
| **bring to nought** | **the counsel of** | **the heathen** | **he make of none effect** | **the devices of** | **the people** | **The counsel of** | **Yahuah** |

| | | | | | | 33:12 | | | | |
|---|---|---|---|---|---|---|---|---|---|---|
| לעולם 5769 | תעמד 5975 | מחשבות 4284 | לבו 3820 | לדר 1755 | ודר 1755: | אשרי 835 | הגוי 1471 | אשר 834 | יהוה 3068 | אלהיו 430 |
| la'aulam | ta'amod; | machashabout | libou, | lador | uador. | 'ashrey | hagouy | 'asher | Yahuah | 'alohayu; |
| **for ever** | **stands** | **the thoughts of** | **his heart** | **to all** | **generations** | **Blessed *is*** | **the nation** | **whose *is*** | **Yahuah** | **their Elohim** |

| | | | | 33:13 | | | | | |
|---|---|---|---|---|---|---|---|---|---|
| העם 5971 | בחר 977 | לנחלה 5159 | לו 3807a: | משמים 8064 | הביט 5027 | יהוה 3068 | ראה 7200 | את 853 | כל 3605 |
| ha'am | bachar | lanachalah | lou'. | mishamayim | hibiyt | Yahuah; | ra'ah, | 'at | kal |
| ***and* the people** | ***whom* he has chosen** | **own inheritance** | **for his** | **from heaven** | **looks** | **Yahuah** | **he behold** | | **all** |

| | | 33:14 | | | | | | | 33:15 |
|---|---|---|---|---|---|---|---|---|---|
| בני 1121 | האדם 120: | ממכון 4349 | שבתו 3427 | השגיח 7688 | אל 413 | כל 3605 | ישבי 3427 | הארץ 776: | |
| baney | ha'adam. | mimakoun | shibatou | hishgiyach; | 'al | kal | yoshabey | ha'aretz. | |
| **the sons of** | **men** | **From the place of** | **his habitation** | **he looks** | **upon** | **all** | **the inhabitants of** | **the earth** | |

| | | | | | | | 33:16 | | |
|---|---|---|---|---|---|---|---|---|---|
| היצר 3335 | יחד 3162 | לבם 3820 | המבין 995 | אל 413 | כל 3605 | מעשיהם 4639: | אין 369 | המלך 4428 | נושע 3467 |
| hayotzer | yachad | libam; | hamebiyn, | 'al | kal | ma'aseyhem. | 'aeyn | hamelek | nousha' |
| **He fashioned** | **alike** | **their hearts** | **he consider** | **to** | **all** | **their works** | **There is no** | **king** | **saved** |

| | | | | | | | 33:17 | | |
|---|---|---|---|---|---|---|---|---|---|
| ברב 7230 | חיל 2428 | גבור 1368 | לא 3808 | ינצל 5337 | ברב 7230 | כח 3581: | שקר 8267 | הסוס 5483 | לתשועה 8668 |
| barab | chayil; | gibour, | la' | yinatzel | barab | koach. | sheqer | hasus | litshu'ah; |
| **by the multitude of** | **an host** | **a mighty man** | **not** | **is delivered** | **by much** | **strength** | ***is* a vain thing** | **An horse** | **for safety** |

| | | | | 33:18 | | | | |
|---|---|---|---|---|---|---|---|---|
| וברב 7230 | חילו 2428 | לא 3808 | ימלט 4422: | הנה 2009 | עין 5869 | יהוה 3068 | אל 413 | יראיו 3373 |
| uabrob | cheylou, | la' | yamalet. | hineh | 'aeyn | Yahuah | 'al | yare'ayu; |
| ***any* by great** | **his strength** | **neither** | **shall he deliver** | **Behold** | **the eye of** | **Yahuah** | ***is* upon** | **them that fear him** |

| | | 33:19 | | | | | 33:20 |
|---|---|---|---|---|---|---|---|
| למיחלים 3176 | לחסדו 2617: | להציל 5337 | ממות 4194 | נפשם 5315 | ולחיותם 2421 | ברעב 7458: | נפשנו 5315 |
| lamayachaliym | lachasdou. | lahatziyl | mimauet | napsham; | ualchayoutam, | bara'ab. | napshenu |
| **upon them that hope** | **in his mercy** | **To deliver** | **from death** | **their soul** | **and to keep them alive** | **in famine** | **Our soul** |

Ps 33:5 He love righteousness and judgment: the earth is full of the goodness of YHUH.6 By the word of YHUH were the heavens made; and all the host of them by the breath of his mouth.7 He gathereth the waters of the sea together as an heap: he layeth up the depth in storehouses.8 Let all the earth fear YHUH: let all the inhabitants of the world stand in awe of him.9 For he spoke, and it was done; he commanded, and it stood fast.10 YHUH bring the counsel of the heathen to nought: he make the devices of the people of none effect.11 The counsel of YHUH stand forever, the thoughts of his heart to all generations.12 Blessed is the nation whose G-d is YHUH: and the people whom he has chosen for his own inheritance.13 YHUH look from heaven; he beholdeth all the sons of men.14 From the place of his habitation he look upon all the inhabitants of the earth.15 He fashioneth their hearts alike; he considereth all their works.16 There is no king saved by the multitude of an host: a mighty man is not delivered by much strength.17 An horse is a vain thing for safety: neither shall he deliver any by his great strength.18 Behold, the eye of YHUH is upon them that fear him, upon them that hope in his mercy;19 To deliver their soul from death, and to keep them alive in famine.

חכתה 2442 ליהוה 3068 עזרנו 5828 ומגננו 4043 הוא 1931: **33:21** כי 3588 בו 871a ישמח 8055 לבנו 3820 כי 3588 בשם 8034 קדשו 6944
chiktah laYahuah; 'azrenu uamaginenu hua'. kiy bou yismach libenu; kiy bashem qadashou
**wait for Yahuah *is* our help and our shield he For in him shall rejoice our heart because in name his holy**

בטחנו 982: **33:22** יהי 1961 חסדך 2617 יהוה 3068 עלינו 5921 כאשר 834 יחלנו 3176 לך 3807a:
batachanu. yahiy chasdaka Yahuah 'aleynu; ka'asher, yichalnu lak.
**we have trusted Let be your mercy O Yahuah upon us according as we hope in you**

**Ps 34:1** לדוד 1732 בשנותו 8138 את 853 טעמו 2940 לפני 6440 אבימלך 40 ויגרשהו 1644 וילך 1980:
ladauid, bashanoutou 'at ta'amou lipney 'abiymelek; uayagarashehu, uayelak.
***A Psalm* of David when he changed his behaviour before Abimelek *who* drove him away and he departed**

אברכה 1288 את 853 יהוה 3068 בכל 3605 עת 6256 תמיד 8548 תהלתו 8416 בפי 6310: **34:2** ביהוה 3068 תתהלל 1984
'abarakah 'at Yahuah bakal 'aet; tamiyd, tahilatou bapiy. baYahuah tithalel
**I will bless Yahuah at all times *shall* continually his praise *be* in my mouth in Yahuah shall make her boast**

נפשי 5315 ישמעו 8085 ענוים 6035 וישמחו 8055: **34:3** גדלו 1431 ליהוה 3068 אתי 854 ונרוממה 7311 שמו 8034
napshiy; yishma'au 'anauiym uayismachu. gadalu laYahuah 'atiy; uanroumamah shamou
**My soul shall hear *thereof* the humble and be glad *O* magnify unto Yahuah with me and let us exalt his name**

יחדו 3162: **34:4** דרשתי 1875 את 853 יהוה 3068 וענני 6030 ומכל 3605 מגורותי 4035 הצילני 5337: **34:5** הביטו 5027 אליו 413
yachdau. darashtiy 'at Yahuah ua'ananiy; uamikal magouroutay, hitziylaniy. hibiytu 'aelayu
**together I sought Yahuah and he heard me and from all my fears delivered me They looked unto him**

ונהרו 5102 ופניהם 6440 אל 408 יחפרו 2659: **34:6** זה 2088 עני 6041 קרא 7121 ויהוה 3068 שמע 8085 ומכל 3605
uanaharu; uapneyhem, 'al yechaparu. zeh 'aniy qara' uaYahuah shamea'; uamikal
**and were lightened and their faces not were ashamed This poor *man* cried and Yahuah heard *him* and out of all**

צרותיו 6869 הושיעו 3467: **34:7** חנה 2583 מלאך 4397 יהוה 3068 סביב 5439 ליראיו 3373 ויחלצם 2502: **34:8** טעמו 2938
tzaroutayu, houshiy'au. choneh mal'ak Yahuah sabiyb liyre'ayu, uayachaltzem. ta'amu
**his troubles saved him encamp The angel of Yahuah round about them that fear him and deliver them O taste**

וראו 7200 כי 3588 טוב 2896 יהוה 3068 אשרי 835 הגבר 1397 יחסה 2620 בו 871a: **34:9** יראו 3372 את 853 יהוה 3068 קדשיו 6918 כי 3588 אין 369
uar'au kiy toub Yahuah; 'ashrey hageber, yecheseh bou. yar'au 'at Yahuah qadoshayu; kiy 'aeyn
**and see that *is* good Yahuah blessed *is* the man *that* trust in him O fear Yahuah you his saints for *there is* no**

מחסור 4270 ליראיו 3373: **34:10** כפירים 3715 רשו 7326 ורעבו 7456 ודרשי 1875 יהוה 3068 לא 3808
machsour, liyre'ayu. kapiyriym rashu uara'aebu; uadorashey Yahuah la'
**want to them that fear him The young lions do lack and suffer hunger but they that seek Yahuah not**

יחסרו 2637 כל 3605 טוב 2896: **34:11** לכו 1980 בנים 1121 שמעו 8085 לי 3807a יראת 3374 יהוה 3068 אלמדכם 3925: **34:12** מי 4310
yachsaru kal toub. laku baniym shim'au liy; yir'at Yahuah 'alamedakem. miy'
**shall want any good *thing* Come you children listen unto me the fear of Yahuah I will teach you What**

האיש 376 החפץ 2655 חיים 2416 אהב 157 ימים 3117 לראות 7200 טוב 2896: **34:13** נצר 5341 לשונך 3956 מרע 7451
ha'aysh hechapetz chayiym; 'aheb yamiym, lir'aut toub. natzor lashounaka mera';
**man *is he that* desire life *and* love *many* days that he may see good? Keep your tongue from evil**

Ps 33:20 Our soul waiteth for YHUH: he is our help and our shield.21 For our heart shall rejoice in him, because we have trusted in his holy name.22 Let your mercy, O YHUH, be upon us, according as we hope in you. **Ps** 34:1 A Psalm of David, when he changed his behavior before A-bim'-e-lech; who drove him away, and he departed. I will bless YHUH at all times: his praise shall continually be in my mouth.2 My soul shall make her boast in YHUH: the humble shall hear thereof, and be glad.3 O magnify YHUH with me, and let us exalt his name together.4 I sought YHUH, and he heard me, and delivered me from all my fears.5 They looked unto him, and were lightened: and their faces were not ashamed.6 This poor man cried, and YHUH heard him, and saved him out of all his troubles.7 The angel of YHUH encampeth round about them that fear him, and delivereth them.8 O taste and see that YHUH is good: blessed is the man that trusteth in him.9 O fear YHUH, you his saints: for there is no want to them that fear him.10 The young lions do lack, and suffer hunger: but they that seek YHUH shall not want any good thing.11 Come, you children, hear unto me: I will teach you the fear of YHUH.12 What man is he that desire life, and love many days, that he may see good?

34:14 ... 34:15

ושפתיך 8193 | מדבר 1696 | מרמה 4820: | סור 5493 | מרע 7451 | ועשה 6213 | טוב 2896 | בקש 1245 | שלום 7965 | ורדפהו 7291:
uaspateyka, midaber mirmah. sur mera' ua'aseh toub; baqesh shaloum uaradapehu.
**and your lips from speaking guile Depart from evil and do good; seek peace and pursue it**

34:16

עיני 5869 | יהוה 3068 | אל 413 | צדיקים 6662 | ואזניו 241 | אל 413 | שועתם 7775: | פני 6440 | יהוה 3068
'aeyney Yahuah 'al tzadiyqiym; ua'azanayu, 'al shau'atam. paney Yahuah
**The eyes of Yahuah *are* upon the righteous and his ears *are open* unto their cry The face of Yahuah**

34:17

בעשי 6213 | רע 7451 | להכרית 3772 | מארץ 776 | זכרם 2143: | צעקו 6817 | ויהוה 3068
ba'asey ra'; lahakriyt me'aretz zikram. tza'aqu uaYahuah
***is* against them that do evil to cut off from the earth the remembrance of them *The righteous* cry and Yahuah**

34:18

שמע 8085 | ומכל 3605 | צרותם 6869 | הצילם 5337: | קרוב 7138 | יהוה 3068 | לנשברי 7665 | לב 3820 | ואת 853
shamea'; uamikal tzaroutam, hitziylam. qaroub Yahuah lanishbarey leb; ua'at
**hear and out of all their troubles deliver them *is* near Yahuah unto them that are of a broken heart *and***

34:19

דכאי 1793 | רוח 7307 | יושיע 3467: | רבות 7227 | רעות 7451 | צדיק 6662 | ומכלם 3605 | יצילנו 5337
daka'aey ruach youshiya'. rabout ra'aut tzadiyq; uamikulam, yatziylenu
**such as be of a contrite spirit save Many *are* the afflictions of the righteous but out of them all deliver him**

34:20 ... 34:21

יהוה 3068: | שמר 8104 | כל 3605 | עצמותיו 6106 | אחת 259 | מהנה 2007 | לא 3808 | נשברה 7665: | תמותת 4191 | רשע 7563 | רעה 7451
Yahuah. shomer kal atzamoutayu; 'achat mehenah, la' nishbarah. tamoutet rasha' ra'ah;
**Yahuah He keep all his bones one of them not is broken shall slay the wicked Evil**

34:22

ושנאי 8130 | צדיק 6662 | יאשמו 816: | פודה 6299 | יהוה 3068 | נפש 5315 | עבדיו 5650 | ולא 3808
uasona'aey tzadiyq ye'ashamu. poudeh Yahuah nepesh 'abadayu; uala'
**and they that hate the righteous shall be desolate redeem Yahuah the soul of his servants and none of**

יאשמו 816 | כל 3605 | החסים 2620 | בו 871a:
ya'shamu, kal hachosiym bou.
**shall be desolate any of them that trust in him**

**Ps 35:1**

לדוד 1732 | ריבה 7378 | יהוה 3068 | את 853 | יריבי 3401 | לחם 3898 | את 853
ladauid riybah Yahuah 'at yariybay; lachem, 'at
***A Psalm* of David Plead *my cause* O Yahuah with them that strive with me fight**

35:2 ... 35:3

לחמי 3898: | החזק 2388 | מגן 4043 | וצנה 6793 | וקומה 6965 | בעזרתי 5833: | והרק 7324
lochamay. hachazeq magen uatzinah; uaqumah, ba'azratiy. uahareq
**against them that fight against me Take hold of shield and buckler and stand up for mine help Draw out also**

35:4

חנית 2595 | וסגר 5462 | לקראת 7125 | רדפי 7291 | אמר 559 | לנפשי 5315 | ישעתך 3444 | אני 589:
chaniyt uasgor liqra't rodapay; 'amor lanapshiy, yashu'atek 'aniy.
**the spear and stop *the way* against them that persecute me say unto my soul *am* your salvation I**

יבשו 954 | ויכלמו 3637 | מבקשי 1245 | נפשי 5315 | יסגו 5472 | אחור 268 | ויחפרו 2659
yeboshu uayikalamu mabaqshey napshiy yisogu 'achour uayachparu;
**Let them be confounded and put to shame that seek after my soul let them be turned back and brought to confusion**

Ps 34:13 Keep your tongue from evil, and your lips from speaking guile.14 Depart from evil, and do good; seek peace, and pursue it.15 The eyes of YHUH are upon the righteous, and his ears are open unto their cry.16 The face of YHUH is against them that do evil, to cut off the remembrance of them from the earth.17 The righteous cry, and YHUH hear, and delivereth them out of all their troubles.18 YHUH is nigh unto them that are of a broken heart; and save such as be of a contrite spirit.19 Many are the afflictions of the righteous: but YHUH delivereth him out of them all.20 He keep all his bones: not one of them is broken.21 Evil shall slay the wicked: and they that hate the righteous shall be desolate.22 YHUH redeemeth the soul of his servants: and none of them that trust in him shall be desolate. **Ps** 35:1 A Psalm of David. Plead my cause, O YHUH, with them that strive with me: fight against them that fight against me.2 Take hold of shield and buckler, and stand up for mine help.3 Draw out also the spear, and stop the way against them that persecute me: say unto my soul, I am your salvation.4 Let them be confounded and put to shame that seek after my soul: let them be turned back and brought to confusion that devise my hurt.

חשבי 2803 | רעתי 7451: | 35:5 יהיו 1961 | כמץ 4671 | לפני 6440 | רוח 7307 | ומלאך 4397 | יהוה 3068 | דוחה 1760: | 35:6 יהי 1961
choshbey, ra'atiy. yihayu, kamotz lipney ruach; uamal'ak Yahuah doucheh. yahiy
**that devise my hurt Let them be as chaff before the wind and the angel of Yahuah let chase them Let be**

דרכם 1870 | חשך 2822 | וחלקלקות 2519 | ומלאך 4397 | יהוה 3068 | רדפם 7291: | 35:7 כי 3588 | חנם 2600 | טמנו 2934
darkam, choshek uachalaqlaqout; uamal'ak Yahuah rodapam. kiy chinam tamanu
**their way dark and slippery and the angel of Yahuah let persecute them For without cause have they hid**

לי 3807a | שחת 7845 | רשתם 7568 | חנם 2600 | חפרו 2658 | לנפשי 5315: | 35:8 תבואהו 935 | שואה 7722 | לא 3808
liy shachat rishtam; chinam, chaparu lanapshiy. tabou'aehu shou'ah la'
**for me *in* a pit their net *which* without cause they have digged for my soul Let come upon him destruction as**

ידע 3045 | ורשתו 7568 | אשר 834 | טמן 2934 | תלכדו 3920 | בשואה 7722 | יפל 5307 | בה 871a: | 35:9 ונפשי 5315
yeda' uarishtou 'asher taman tilkadou; bashou'ah, yipal bah. uanapshiy
**unawares and his net that he has hid let catch himself into that very destruction let fall him And my soul**

תגיל 1523 | ביהוה 3068 | תשיש 7797 | בישועתו 3444: | 35:10 כל 3605 | עצמותי 6106 | תאמרנה 559 | יהוה 3068 | מי 4310 | כמוך 3644
tagiyl baYahuah; tasiys biyshu'atou. kal atzmoutay ta'marnah Yahuah miy' kamouka
**shall be joyful in Yahuah it shall rejoice in his salvation All my bones shall say Yahuah who *is* like unto you**

מציל 5337 | עני 6041 | מחזק 2389 | ממנו 4480 | ועני 6041 | ואביון 34 | מגזלו 1497: | 35:11
matziyl 'aniy mechazaq mimenu; ua'aniy ua'abyoun, migozalou.
**which deliverest the poor from him that is too strong for him yea the poor and the needy from him that spoil him?**

יקומון 6965 | עדי 5707 | חמס 2555 | אשר 834 | לא 3808 | ידעתי 3045 | ישאלוני 7592: | 35:12 ישלמוני 7999 | רעה 7451 | תחת 8478
yaqumun 'aedey chamas; 'asher la' yada'tiy, yish'aluniy. yashalmuniy ra'ah tachat
**did rise up witnesses False *things* that not I knew they laid to my charge They rewarded me evil for**

טובה 2896 | שכול 7908 | לנפשי 5315: | 35:13 ואני 589 | בחלותם 2470 | לבושי 3830 | שק 8242 | עניתי 6031
toubah, shakoul lanapshiy. ua'aniy bachaloutam labushiy saq, 'aneytiy
**good *to* the spoiling of my soul But as for me when they were sick my clothing *was* sackcloth I humbled**

בצום 6685 | נפשי 5315 | ותפלתי 8605 | על 5921 | חיקי 2436 | תשוב 7725: | 35:14 כרע 7453 | כאח 251
batzoum napshiy; utapilatiy, 'al cheyqiy tashub. karea' ka'ach
**with fasting my soul and my prayer into mine own bosom returned as though my friend *or* brother *he had been***

לי 3807a | התהלכתי 1980 | כאבל 57 | אם 517 | קדר 6937 | שחותי 7817: | 35:15 ובצלעי 6761 | שמחו 8055
liy hithalakatiy; ka'abel 'aem, qoder shachoutiy. uabtzal'ay samachu
**my I behaved myself as one that mourns *for his* mother heavily I bowed down But in mine adversity they rejoiced**

ונאספו 622 | נאספו 622 | עלי 5921 | נכים 5222 | ולא 3808 | ידעתי 3045
uane'asapu ne'aspu 'alay nekiym uala' yada'tiy;
**and gathered themselves together gathered themselves together against me *yea* the abjects and not I knew**

קרעו 7167 | ולא 3808 | דמו 1826: | 35:16 בחנפי 2611 | לעגי 3934 | מעוג 4580 | חרק 2786 | עלי 5921
qara'au uala' damu. bachanpey la'agey ma'aug; charoq 'alay
***it* they did tear *me* and not ceased With hypocritical mockers in feasts they gnashed upon me**

Ps 35:5 Let them be as chaff before the wind: and let the angel of YHUH chase them.6 Let their way be dark and slippery: and let the angel of YHUH persecute them.7 For without cause have they hid for me their net in a pit, which without cause they have digged for my soul.8 Let destruction come upon him at unawares; and let his net that he has hid catch himself: into that very destruction let him fall.9 And my soul shall be joyful in YHUH: it shall rejoice in his salvation.10 All my bones shall say, YHUH, who is like unto you, which deliverest the poor from him that is too strong for him, yea, the poor and the needy from him that spoileth him?11 False witnesses did rise up; they laid to my charge things that I knew not.12 They rewarded me evil for good to the spoiling of my soul.13 But as for me, when they were sick, my clothing was sackcloth: I humbled my soul with fasting; and my prayer returned into mine own bosom.14 I behaved myself as though he had been my friend or brother: I bowed down heavily, as one that mourn for his mother.15 But in mine adversity they rejoiced, and gathered themselves together: yea, the abjects gathered themselves together against me, and I knew it not; they did tear me, and ceased not:16 With hypocritical mockers in feasts, they gnashed upon me with their teeth.

| שנימו 8127: | 35:17 | אדני 136 | כמה 4100 | תראה 7200 | השיבה 7725 | נפשי 5315 | משאיהם 7722 | מכפירים 3715 |
|---|---|---|---|---|---|---|---|---|
| shineymou. | | 'adonay | kamah | tir'ah | hashiybah | napshiy | misho'aeyhem; | mikapiyriym, |
| **_with_ their teeth** | | **Adonai** | **how long** | **will you look on?** | **rescue** | **my soul** | **from their destructions** | **from the lions** |

| יחידתי 3173: | 35:18 | אודך 3034 | בקהל 6951 | רב 7227 | בעם 5971 | עצום 6099 | אהללך 1984: | 35:19 | אל 408 |
|---|---|---|---|---|---|---|---|---|---|
| yachiydatiy. | | 'audaka | baqahal | rab; | ba'am | 'atzum | 'ahalaleka. | | 'al |
| **my darling** | | **I will give you thanks** | **in congregation** | **_the_ great** | **among people** | **much** | **I will praise you** | | **not** |

| ישמחו 8055 | לי 3807a | איבי 341 | שקר 8267 | שנאי 8130 | חנם 2600 | יקרצו 7169 |
|---|---|---|---|---|---|---|
| yismachu | liy | 'ayabay | sheqer; | son'ay | chinam, | yiqratzu |
| **Let rejoice** | **over me** | **them that are mine enemies** | **wrongfully** | **that hate me** | **without a cause** | **_neither_ let them wink with** |

| עין 5869: | 35:20 | כי 3588 | לא 3808 | שלום 7965 | ידברו 1696 | ועל 5921 | רגעי 7282 | ארץ 776 | דברי 1697 | מרמות 4820 |
|---|---|---|---|---|---|---|---|---|---|---|
| 'ayin. | | kiy | la' | shaloum, | yadaberu | ua'al | rig'aey | 'aretz; | dibrey | mirmout |
| **the eye** | | **For** | **not** | **peace** | **they speak** | **but against** | **_them that are_ quiet in** | **the land** | **matters** | **deceitful** |

| יחשבון 2803: | 35:21 | וירחיבו 7337 | עלי 5921 | פיהם 6310 | אמרו 559 | האח 1889 | האח 1889 | ראתה 7200 | עינינו 5869: | 35:22 |
|---|---|---|---|---|---|---|---|---|---|---|
| yachashobun. | | uayarchiybu | 'alay, | piyhem | 'amaru | he'ach | he'ach; | ra'atah | 'aeyneynu. | |
| **they devise** | | **Yea they opened wide** | **against me** | **their mouth** | **_and_ said** | **Aha** | **aha** | **has seen _it_** | **our eye** | |

| ראיתה 7200 | יהוה 3068 | אל 408 | תחרש 2790 | אדני 136 | אל 408 | תרחק 7368 | ממני 4480: | 35:23 | העירה 5782 | והקיצה 6974 |
|---|---|---|---|---|---|---|---|---|---|---|
| ra'aytah | Yahuah | 'al | techarash; | 'adonay, | 'al | tirchaq | mimeniy. | | ha'ayrah | uahaqiytzah |
| **_This_ you have seen** | **O Yahuah** | **not** | **keep silence** | **O Adonai** | **not** | **be far** | **from me** | | **Stir up yourself** | **and awake** |

| למשפטי 4941 | אלהי 430 | ואדני 136 | לריבי 7379: | 35:24 | שפטני 8199 | כצדקך 6664 | יהוה 3068 |
|---|---|---|---|---|---|---|---|
| lamishpatiy; | 'alohay | ua'adonay | lariybiy. | | shapateniy | katzidqaka | Yahuah |
| **to my judgment** | **my Elohim** | **and my Adonai** | **_even_ unto my cause** | | **Judge me** | **according to your righteousness** | **O Yahuah** |

| אלהי 430 | ואל 408 | ישמחו 8055 | לי 3807a: | 35:25 | אל 408 | יאמרו 559 | בלבם 3820 | האח 1889 | נפשנו 5315 | אל 408 |
|---|---|---|---|---|---|---|---|---|---|---|
| 'alohay, | ua'al | yismachu | liy. | | 'al | ya'maru | balibam | he'ach | napshenu; | 'al |
| **my Elohim** | **and not** | **let them rejoice** | **over me** | | **not** | **Let them say** | **in their hearts** | **Ah** | **_so_ would we have it** | **not** |

| יאמרו 559 | בלענוהו 1104: | 35:26 | יבשו 954 | ויחפרו 2659 | יחדו 3162 | שמחי 8056 |
|---|---|---|---|---|---|---|
| ya'maru, | bila'anuhu. | | yeboshu | uayachparu | yachdau | samechey |
| **let them say** | **We have swallowed him up** | | **Let them be ashamed** | **and brought to confusion** | **together** | **that rejoice at** |

| רעתי 7451 | ילבשו 3847 | בשת 1322 | וכלמה 3639 | המגדילים 1431 | עלי 5921: | 35:27 | ירנו 7442 |
|---|---|---|---|---|---|---|---|
| ra'atiy | yilbashu | boshet | uaklimah; | hamagadiyliym | 'alay. | | yaronu |
| **mine hurt** | **let them be clothed with** | **shame** | **and dishonour** | **that magnify _themselves_** | **against me** | | **Let them shout for joy** |

| וישמחו 8055 | חפצי 2655 | צדקי 6664 | ויאמרו 559 | תמיד 8548 | יגדל 1431 | יהוה 3068 | החפץ 2655 |
|---|---|---|---|---|---|---|---|
| uayismachu | chapetzey | tzidqiy | uaya'maru | tamiyd | yigdal | Yahuah; | hechapetz, |
| **and be glad** | **that favor** | **my righteous cause** | **yea let them say** | **continually** | **Let be magnified** | **Yahuah** | **which has pleasure in** |

| שלום 7965 | עבדו 5650: | 35:28 | ולשוני 3956 | תהגה 1897 | צדקך 6664 | כל 3605 | היום 3117 | תהלתך 8416: |
|---|---|---|---|---|---|---|---|---|
| shaloum | abdou. | | ualshouniy | tehageh | tzidqeka; | kal | hayoum | tahilateka. |
| **the prosperity of** | **his servant** | | **And my tongue shall speak of** | **your righteousness** | **all** | **the day _long and of_** | **your praise** |

Ps 35:17 Adonai, how long will you look on? rescue my soul from their destructions, my darling from the lions.18 I will give you thanks in the great congregation: I will praise you among much people.19 Let not them that are mine enemies wrongfully rejoice over me: neither let them wink with the eye that hate me without a cause.20 For they speak not peace: but they devise deceitful matters against them that are quiet in the land.21 Yea, they opened their mouth wide against me, and said, Aha, aha, our eye has seen it.22 This you have seen, O YHUH: keep not silence: O Adonai, be not far from me.23 Stir up thyself, and awake to my judgment, even unto my cause, my G-d and my Adonai.24 Judge me, O YHUH my G-d, according to your righteousness; and let them not rejoice over me.25 Let them not say in their hearts, Ah, so would we have it: let them not say, We have swallowed him up.26 Let them be ashamed and brought to confusion together that rejoice at mine hurt: let them be clothed with shame and dishonour that magnify themselves against me.27 Let them shout for joy, and be glad, that favor my righteous cause: yea, let them say continually, Let YHUH be magnified, which has pleasure in the prosperity of his servant.28 And my tongue shall speak of your righteousness and of your praise all the day long.

| Ps 36:1 | למנצח 5329 | לעבד 5650 | יהוה 3068 | לדוד 1732: | נאם 5002 | פשע 6588 | לרשע 7563 | בקרב 7130 |
|---|---|---|---|---|---|---|---|---|
| | lamanatzeach | la'abed | Yahuah | ladauid. | na'am | pesha' | larasha' | baqereb |
| | **To the chief Musician** | **the servant of** | **Yahuah** | ***A Psalm* of David** | **saith** | **The transgression** | **of the wicked** | **within** |

| לבי 3820 | אין 369 | פחד 6343 | אלהים 430 | לנגד 5048 | עיניו 5869: | 36:2 | כי 3588 | החליק 2505 | אליו 413 | בעיניו 5869 | למצא 4672 |
|---|---|---|---|---|---|---|---|---|---|---|---|
| libiy; | 'aeyn | pachad | 'alohiym, | laneged | 'aeynayu. | | kiy | hecheliyq | 'aelayu | ba'aeynayu; | limtza' |
| **my heart** | ***that there is* no** | **fear of** | **Elohim** | **before** | **his eyes** | | **For** | **he flatter** | **himself** | **in his own eyes** | **be found** |

| עונו 5771 | לשנא 8130: | 36:3 | דברי 1697 | פיו 6310 | און 205 | ומרמה 4820 | חדל 2308 | להשכיל 7919 |
|---|---|---|---|---|---|---|---|---|
| auonou | lisna'. | | dibrey | piyu | 'auen | uamirmah; | chadal | lahshkiyl |
| ***until* his iniquity** | **to be hateful** | | **The words of** | **his mouth** | ***are* iniquity** | **and deceit** | **he has left off** | **to be wise** |

| להיטיב 3190: | 36:4 | און 205 | יחשב 2803 | על 5921 | משכבו 4904 | יתיצב 3320 | על 5921 | דרך 1870 | לא 3808 | טוב 2896 | רע 7451 | לא 3808 |
|---|---|---|---|---|---|---|---|---|---|---|---|---|
| laheytiyb. | | 'auen | yachshob, | 'al | mishkabou | yityatzeb | 'al | derek | la' | toub; | ra', | la' |
| ***and* to do good** | | **mischief** | **He devise** | **upon** | **his bed** | **he set himself** | **in** | **a way *that is*** | **not** | **good** | **evil** | **not** |

| ימאס 3988: | 36:5 | יהוה 3068 | בהשמים 8064 | חסדך 2617 | אמונתך 530 | עד 5704 | שחקים 7834: | 36:6 |
|---|---|---|---|---|---|---|---|---|
| yim'as. | | Yahuah | behashshaMayim | chasadeka; | 'emunatecha, | 'ad | shachaqiym. | |
| **he abhore** | | **O Yahuah** | ***is* in the heavens** | **Your mercy** | ***and* your faithfulness *reaches*** | **unto** | **the clouds** | |

| צדקתך 6666 | כהררי 2042 | אל 410 | משפטך 4941 | תהום 8415 | רבה 7227 | אדם 120 | ובהמה 929 | תושיע 3467 |
|---|---|---|---|---|---|---|---|---|
| tzidqataka | kaharey | 'ael, | mishpateka | tahoum | rabah; | 'adam | uabahemah | toushiya' |
| **Your righteousness *is*** | **like mountains** | ***the* great** | **your judgments *are*** | **a deep** | **great** | **man** | **and beast** | **you preserve** |

| יהוה 3068: | 36:7 | מה 4100 | יקר 3368 | חסדך 2617 | אלהים 430 | ובני 1121 | אדם 120 | בצל 6738 |
|---|---|---|---|---|---|---|---|---|
| Yahuah. | | mah | yaqar | chasdaka, | 'alohiym | uabney | 'adam; | batzel |
| **O Yahuah** | | **How** | **excellent** | ***is* your lovingkindness** | **O Elohim** | **therefore the children of** | **men** | **under the shadow of** |

| כנפיך 3671 | יחסיון 2620: | 36:8 | ירוין 7301 | מדשן 1880 | ביתך 1004 | ונחל 5158 |
|---|---|---|---|---|---|---|
| kanapeyka, | yechesayun. | | yiruayun | mideshen | beytaka; | uanachal |
| **your wings** | **put their trust** | | **They shall be abundantly satisfied** | **with the fatness of** | **your house** | **of the river of** |

| עדניך 5730 | תשקם 8248: | 36:9 | כי 3588 | עמך 5973 | מקור 4726 | חיים 2416 | באורך 216 | נראה 7200 |
|---|---|---|---|---|---|---|---|---|
| 'adaneyka | tashqem. | | kiy | 'amaka | maqour | chayiym; | ba'auraka, | nir'ah |
| **your pleasures** | **and you shall make them drink *of*** | | **For** | **with you *is*** | **the fountain of** | **life** | **in your light** | **shall we see** |

| אור 216: | 36:10 | משך 4900 | חסדך 2617 | לידעיך 3045 | וצדקתך 6666 | לישרי 3477 |
|---|---|---|---|---|---|---|
| 'aur. | | mashok | chasdaka | layoda'ayka; | uatzidqataka, | layishrey |
| **light** | | **O continue** | **your lovingkindness** | **unto them that know you** | **and your righteousness** | **to the upright in** |

| לב 3820: | 36:11 | אל 408 | תבואני 935 | רגל 7272 | גאוה 1346 | ויד 3027 | רשעים 7563 | אל 408 | תנדני 5110: | 36:12 | שם 8033 |
|---|---|---|---|---|---|---|---|---|---|---|---|
| leb. | | 'al | tabou'aeniy | regel | ga'auah; | uayad | rasha'aym, | 'al | tanideniy. | | sham |
| **heart** | | **not** | **Let come against me** | **the foot of** | **pride** | **and the hand of** | **the wicked** | **not** | **let remove me** | | **There** |

| נפלו 5307 | פעלי 6466 | און 205 | דחו 1760 | ולא 3808 | יכלו 3201 | קום 6965: |
|---|---|---|---|---|---|---|
| naplu | po'aley | 'auen; | dochu, | uala' | yakalu | qum. |
| **are fallen** | **the workers of** | **iniquity** | **they are cast down** | **and not** | **shall be able** | **to rise** |

**Ps** 36:1 To the chief Musician, A Psalm of David, the servant of the Adonai. The transgression of the wicked saith within my heart, that there is no fear of G-d before his eyes.2 For he flattereth himself in his own eyes, until his iniquity be found to be hateful.3 The words of his mouth are iniquity and deceit: he has left off to be wise, and to do good.4 He deviseth mischief upon his bed; he set himself in a way that is not good; he abhorreth not evil.5 Thy mercy, O YHUH, is in the heavens; and your faithfulness reacheth unto the clouds.6 Thy righteousness is like the great mountains; your judgments are a great deep: O YHUH, you preservest man and beast.7 How excellent is your lovingkindness, O G-d! therefore the children of men put their trust under the shadow of your wings.8 They shall be abundantly satisfied with the fatness of your house; and you shall make them drink of the river of your pleasures.9 For with you is the fountain of life: in your light shall we see light.10 O continue your lovingkindness unto them that know you; and your righteousness to the upright in heart.11 Let not the foot of pride come against me, and let not the hand of the wicked remove me.

**Ps 37:1**
לדוד 1732 | אל 408 | תתחר 2734 | במרעים 7489 | אל 408 | תקנא 7065 | בעשי 6213
ladauid | 'al | titchar | bamare'aym; | 'al | taqanea', | ba'asey
***A Psalm* of David** | **not** | **Fret yourself** | **because of evildoers** | **neither** | **be you envious** | **against the workers of**

עולה 5766: | **37:2** כי 3588 | כחציר 2682 | מהרה 4120 | ימלו 5243 | וכירק 3418 | דשא 1877 | יבולון 5034: | **37:3** בטח 982 | ביהוה 3068
'aulah. | kiy | kechatziyr | maherah | yimalu; | uakyereq | desha', | yiboulun. | batach | baYahuah
**iniquity** | **For** | **like the grass** | **soon** | **they shall be cut down** | **and as the green** | **herb** | **wither** | **Trust** | **in Yahuah**

ועשה 6213 | טוב 2896 | שכן 7931 | ארץ 776 | ורעה 7462 | אמונה 530: | **37:4** והתענג 6026 | על 5921 | יהוה 3068
ua'aseh | toub; | shakan | 'aretz, | uar'aeh | 'amunah. | uahit'anag | 'al | Yahuah;
**and do** | **good** | ***so* shall you dwell in** | **the land** | **and you shall be fed** | **verily** | **Delight yourself also** | **in** | **Yahuah**

ויתן 5414 | לך 3807a | משאלת 4862 | לבך 3820: | **37:5** גול 1556 | על 5921 | יהוה 3068 | דרכך 1870 | ובטח 982 | עליו 5921 | והוא 1931
uayiten | laka, | mish'alot | libeka. | goul | 'al | Yahuah | darkeka; | uabtach | 'alayu, | uahu'a
**and he shall give** | **to you** | **the desires of** | **your heart** | **Commit** | **unto** | **Yahuah** | **your way** | **trust also** | **in him** | **and he**

יעשה 6213: | **37:6** והוציא 3318 | כאור 216 | צדקך 6664 | ומשפטך 4941 | כצהרים 6672: | **37:7**
ya'aseh. | uahoutziy'a | ka'aur | tzidqeka; | uamishpateka, | katzaharayim.
**shall bring *it* to pass** | **And he shall bring forth** | **as the light** | **your righteousness** | **and your judgment** | **as the noonday**

דום 1826 | ליהוה 3068 | והתחולל 2342 | לו 3807a | אל 408 | תתחר 2734 | במצליח 6743 | דרכו 1870
doum | laYahuah | uahitchoulel | lou' | 'al | titchar | bamatzliyach | darkou;
**Rest** | **in Yahuah** | **and wait patiently** | **for him** | **not** | **fret yourself** | **because of him who prospers in** | **his way**

באיש 376 | עשה 6213 | מזמות 4209: | **37:8** הרף 7503 | מאף 639 | ועזב 5800 | חמה 2534 | אל 408 | תתחר 2734
ba'aysh, | 'aseh | mazimout. | herep | me'ap | ua'azob | chemah; | 'al | titchar,
**because of the man** | **who bring to pass** | **wicked devices** | **Cease** | **from anger** | **and forsake** | **wrath** | **not** | **fret yourself**

אך 389 | להרע 7489: | **37:9** כי 3588 | מרעים 7489 | יכרתון 3772 | וקוי 6960 | יהוה 3068 | המה 1992 | יירשו 3423
'ak | laharea'. | kiy | mare'aym | yikaretun; | uaqouey | Yahuah | hemah | yiyrashu
**in any wise** | **to do evil** | **For** | **evildoers** | **shall be cut off** | **but those that wait upon** | **Yahuah** | **they** | **shall inherit**

ארץ 776: | **37:10** ועוד 5750 | מעט 4592 | ואין 369 | רשע 7563 | והתבוננת 995 | על 5921 | מקומו 4725
'aretz. | ua'aud | ma'at | ua'aeyn | rasha'; | uahitbounanta | 'al | maqoumou
**the earth** | **For yet** | **a little while** | **and no** | ***be* the wicked** | ***shall* yea you shall diligently consider** | **for** | **his place**

ואיננו 369: | **37:11** וענוים 6035 | יירשו 3423 | ארץ 776 | והתענגו 6026 | על 5921 | רב 7230
ua'aeynenu. | ua'anauiym | yiyrashu | 'aretz; | uahit'anagu, | 'al | rob
**and it shall not be** | **But the meek** | **shall inherit** | **the earth** | **and shall delight themselves** | **in** | **the abundance of**

שלום 7965: | **37:12** זמם 2161 | רשע 7563 | לצדיק 6662 | וחרק 2786 | עליו 5921 | שניו 8127: | **37:13** אדני 136 | ישחק 7832 | לו 3807a
shaloum. | zomem | rasha' | latzadiyq; | uachoreq | 'alayu | shinayu. | 'adonay | yischak | lou';
**peace** | **plot** | **The wicked** | **against the just** | **and gnash** | **upon him** | ***with* his teeth** | **Adonai** | **shall laugh** | **at him**

כי 3588 | ראה 7200 | כי 3588 | יבא 935 | יומו 3117: | **37:14** חרב 2719 | פתחו 6605 | רשעים 7563 | ודרכו 1869 | קשתם 7198 | להפיל 5307
kiy | ra'ah, | kiy | yaba' | youmou. | chereb | patachu | rasha'aym | uadaraku | qashtam | lahapiyl
**for** | **he see** | **that** | **is coming his day** | **the sword** | **have drawn out** | **The wicked** | **and have bent** | **their bow** | **to cast down**

Ps 36:12 There are the workers of iniquity fallen: they are cast down, and shall not be able to rise. **Ps** 37:1 A Psalm of David. Fret not thyself because of evildoers, neither be you envious against the workers of iniquity.2 For they shall soon be cut down like the grass, and where as the green herb.3 Trust in YHUH, and do good; so shall you dwell in the land, and verily you shall be fed.4 Delight thyself also in YHUH; and he shall give you the desires of your heart.5 Commit your way unto YHUH; trust also in him; and he shall bring it to pass.6 And he shall bring forth your righteousness as the light, and your judgment as the noonday.7 Rest in YHUH, and wait patiently for him: fret not thyself because of him who prospereth in his way, because of the man who bring wicked devices to pass.8 Cease from anger, and forsake wrath: fret not thyself in any wise to do evil.9 For evildoers shall be cut off: but those that wait upon YHUH, they shall inherit the earth.10 For yet a little while, and the wicked shall not be: yea, you shall diligently consider his place, and it shall not be.11 But the meek shall inherit the earth; and shall delight themselves in the abundance of peace.12 The wicked plotteth against the just, and gnasheth upon him with his teeth.13 The Adonai shall laugh at him: for he see that his day is coming.

37:15

עני 6041 ואביון 34 לטבוח 2873 ישרי 3477 דרך 1870: חרבם 2719 תבוא 935 בלבם 3820
'aniy ua'abyoun; litabouach, yishrey darek. charbam tabou'a balibam;
**the poor and needy *and* to slay such as be of upright conversation Their sword shall enter into their own heart**

37:16 37:17

וקשתותם 7198 תשברנה 7665: טוב 2896 מעט 4592 לצדיק 6662 מהמון 1995 רשעים 7563 רבים 7227: כי 3588
uaqashtoutam, tishabarnah. toub ma'at latzadiyq; mehamoun, rasha'aym rabiym. kiy
**and their bows shall be broken *is* better A little *that* a righteous man than the riches of wicked many For**

37:18

זרועות 2220 רשעים 7563 תשברנה 7665 וסומך 5564 צדיקים 6662 יהוה 3068: יודע 3045 יהוה 3068 ימי 3117 תמימם 8549
zarou'aut rasha'aym tishabarnah; uasomek tzadiyqiym Yahuah. youdea' Yahuah yamey tamiymim;
**the arms of the wicked shall be broken but uphold the righteous Yahuah knows Yahuah the days of the upright**

37:19

ונחלתם 5159 לעולם 5769 תהיה 1961: לא 3808 יבשו 954 בעת 6256 רעה 7451 ובימי 3117 רעבון 7459
uanachalatam, la'aulam tihayeh. la' yeboshu ba'aet ra'ah; uabiymey ra'aboun
**and their inheritance for ever shall be not They shall be ashamed in time *the* evil and in the days of famine**

37:20

ישבעו 7646: כי 3588 רשעים 7563 יאבדו 6 ואיבי 341 יהוה 3068 כיקר 3368 כרים 3733
yisba'au. kiy rasha'aym ya'bedu, ua'ayabey Yahuah kiyqar kariym;
**they shall be satisfied But the wicked shall perish and the enemies of Yahuah *shall be* as the fat of lambs**

37:21

כלו 3615 בעשן 6227 כלו 3615: לוה 3867 רשע 7563 ולא 3808 ישלם 7999 וצדיק 6662
kalu ba'ashan kalu. loueh rasha' uala' yashalem; uatzadiyq,
**they shall consume into smoke shall they consume away borrow The wicked and not pay again but the righteous**

37:22

חונן 2603 ונותן 5414: כי 3588 מברכיו 1288 יירשו 3423 ארץ 776 ומקלליו 7043
chounen uanouten. kiy maborakayu yiyrashu 'aretz; uamqulalayu,
**shows mercy and gives For *such as be* blessed of him shall inherit the earth and *they that be* cursed of him**

37:23 37:24

יכרתו 3772: מיהוה 3068 מצעדי 4703 גבר 1397 כוננו 3559 ודרכו 1870 יחפץ 2654: כי 3588 יפל 5307 לא 3808
yikaretu. meYahuah mitz'adey geber kounanu, uadarkou yechpatz. kiy yipol la'
**shall be cut off by Yahuah The steps of a *good* man are ordered and his way he delight in Though he fall not**

37:25

יוטל 2904 כי 3588 יהוה 3068 סומך 5564 ידו 3027: נער 5288 הייתי 1961 גם 1571 זקנתי 2204
yutal; kiy Yahuah soumek yadou. na'ar hayiytiy, gam zaqantiy
**he shall be utterly cast down for Yahuah uphold *him with* his hand young I have been moreover *now* am old**

37:26

ולא 3808 ראיתי 7200 צדיק 6662 נעזב 5800 וזרעו 2233 מבקש 1245 לחם 3899: כל 3605 היום 3117 חונן 2603 ומלוה 3867
uala' ra'aytiy tzadiyq ne'azab; uazar'au, mabaqesh lachem. kal hayoum chounen uamalueh;
**yet not have I seen the righteous forsaken nor his seed begging bread *He is* all ever merciful and lend**

37:27 37:28

וזרעו 2233 לברכה 1293: סור 5493 מרע 7451 ועשה 6213 טוב 2896 ושכן 7931 לעולם 5769: כי 3588 יהוה 3068 אהב 157 משפט 4941
uazar'au, librakah. sur mera' ua'aseh toub, uashkon la'aulam. kiy Yahuah 'aheb mishapat,
**and his seed *is* blessed Depart from evil and do good and dwell for evermore For Yahuah love judgment**

37:29

ולא 3808 יעזב 5800 את 853 חסידיו 2623 לעולם 5769 נשמרו 8104 וזרע 2233 רשעים 7563 נכרת 3772: צדיקים 6662
uala' ya'azob 'at chasiydayu la'aulam nishmaru; uazera' rasha'aym nikrat. tzadiyqiym
**and not forsake his saints for ever they are preserved but the seed of the wicked shall be cut off The righteous**

Ps 37:14 The wicked have drawn out the sword, and have bent their bow, to cast down the poor and needy, and to slay such as be of upright conversation.15 Their sword shall enter into their own heart, and their bows shall be broken.16 A little that a righteous man has is better than the riches of many wicked.17 For the arms of the wicked shall be broken: but YHUH upholdeth the righteous.18 YHUH know the days of the upright: and their inheritance shall be forever.19 They shall not be ashamed in the evil time: and in the days of famine they shall be satisfied.20 But the wicked shall perish, and the enemies of YHUH shall be as the fat of lambs: they shall consume; into smoke shall they consume away.21 The wicked borroweth, and payeth not again: but the righteous show mercy, and give.22 For such as be blessed of him shall inherit the earth; and they that be cursed of him shall be cut off.23 The steps of a good man are ordered by YHUH: and he delighteth in his way.24 Though he fall, he shall not be utterly cast down: for YHUH upholdeth him with his hand.25 I have been young, and now am old; yet have I not seen the righteous forsaken, nor his seed begging bread.26 He is ever merciful, and lendeth; and his seed is blessed.27 Depart from evil, and do good; and dwell forevermore.28 For YHUH love judgment, and forsaketh not his saints; they are preserved forever:

37:30

ירשו 3423 ארץ 776 וישכנו 7931 לעד 5703 עליה 5921: פי 6310 צדיק 6662 יהגה 1897 חכמה 2451 ולשונו 3956
yiyrashu 'aretz; uayishkanu la'ad 'aleyha. piy tzadiyq yehageh chakamah ualshounou,
**shall inherit the land and dwell for ever therein The mouth of the righteous speak wisdom and his tongue**

37:31 37:32

תדבר 1696 משפט 4941: תורת 8451 אלהיו 430 בלבו 3820 לא 3808 תמעד 4571 אשריו 838: צופה 6822 רשע 7563
tadaber mishapat. tourat 'alohayu balibou; la' tim'ad 'ashurayu. tzoupeh rasha'
**talk of judgment The law of his Elohim *is* in his heart none of shall slide his steps watch The wicked**

37:33

לצדיק 6662 ומבקש 1245 להמיתו 4191: יהוה 3068 לא 3808 יעזבנו 5800 בידו 3027 ולא 3808 ירשיענו 7561
latzadiyq; uambaqesh, lahamiytou Yahuah la' ya'azbenu bayadou; uala' yarshiy'anu,
**the righteous and seek to slay him Yahuah not will leave him in his hand nor condemn him**

37:34

בהשפטו 8199: קוה 6960 אל 413 יהוה 3068 ושמר 8104 דרכו 1870 וירוממך 7311 לרשת 3423 ארץ 776 בהכרת 3772
bahishapatou. qaueh 'al Yahuah uashmor darkou, uiyroumimaka lareshet 'aretz; bahikaret
**when he is judged Wait on Yahuah and keep his way and he shall exalt you to inherit the land when are cut off**

37:35 37:36

רשעים 7563 תראה 7200: ראיתי 7200 רשע 7563 עריץ 6184 ומתערה 6168 כאזרח 249 רענן 7488:
rasha'aym tir'ah. ra'aytiy rasha' 'ariytz; uamit'areh, ka'azrach ra'anan.
**the wicked you shall see *it* I have seen the wicked in great power and spreading himself like a bay tree green**

37:37

ויעבר 5674 והנה 2009 איננו 369 ואבקשהו 1245 ולא 3808 נמצא 4672: שמר 8104 תם 8535
uaya'abor uahineh 'aeynenu; ua'abaqshehu, uala' nimtza'. shamar tam
**Yet he passed away and lo he *was* not yea I sought him but not he could be found Mark *the* perfect**

37:38

וראה 7200 ישר 3477 כי 3588 אחרית 319 לאיש 376 שלום 7965: ופשעים 6586 נשמדו 8045 יחדו 3162
uar'aeh yashar; kiy 'achariyt la'aysh shaloum. uaposha'aym nishmadu yachdau;
***man* and behold the upright for the end of *that* man *is* peace But the transgressors shall be destroyed together**

37:39

אחרית 319 רשעים 7563 נכרתה 3772: ותשועת 8668 צדיקים 6662 מיהוה 3068 מעוזם 4581 בעת 6256
'achariyt rasha'aym nikratah. uatshu'at tzadiyqiym meYahuah; ma'uzam, ba'aet
**the end of the wicked shall be cut off But the salvation of the righteous *is* of Yahuah *he is* their strength in the time of**

37:40

צרה 6869: ויעזרם 5826 יהוה 3068 ויפלטם 6403 יפלטם 6403 מרשעים 7563 ויושיעם 3467
tzarah. uaya'azrem Yahuah uayapaltem yapaltem merasha'aym uayoushiy'aem;
**trouble And shall help them Yahuah and deliver them he shall deliver them from the wicked and save them**

כי 3588 חסו 2620 בו 871a:
kiy chasu bou.
**because they trust in him**

**Ps 38:1**

מזמור 4210 לדוד 1732 להזכיר 2142: יהוה 3068 אל 408 בקצפך 7110 תוכיחני 3198
mizmour ladauid lahazkiyr. Yahuah 'al baqetzpaka toukiycheniy;
**A Psalm of David to bring to remembrance O Yahuah not in your wrath rebuke me**

38:2

ובחמתך 2534 תיסרני 3256: כי 3588 חציך 2671 נחתו 5181 בי 871a ותנחת 5181 עלי 5921
uabachamataka tayasreniy. kiy chitzeyka nichatu biy; uatinchat 'alay
**neither in your hot displeasure chasten me For your arrows stick fast and in me and press sore me**

Ps 37:28 but the seed of the wicked shall be cut off.29 The righteous shall inherit the land, and dwell therein forever.30 The mouth of the righteous speaketh wisdom, and his tongue talketh of judgment.31 The law of his G-d is in his heart; none of his steps shall slide.32 The wicked watcheth the righteous, and seek to slay him.33 YHUH will not leave him in his hand, nor condemn him when he is judged.34 Wait on YHUH, and keep his way, and he shall exalt you to inherit the land: when the wicked are cut off, you shall see it.35 I have seen the wicked in great power, and spreading himself like a green bay tree.36 Yet he passed away, and, lo, he was not: yea, I sought him, but he could not be found.37 Mark the perfect man, and behold the upright: for the end of that man is peace.38 But the transgressors shall be destroyed together: the end of the wicked shall be cut off.39 But the salvation of the righteous is of YHUH: he is their strength in the time of trouble.40 And YHUH shall help them and deliver them: he shall deliver them from the wicked, and save them, because they trust in him. **Ps** 38:1 A Psalm of David, to bring to remembrance. O YHUH, rebuke me not in your wrath: neither chasten me in your hot displeasure.2 For your arrows stick fast in me, and your hand presseth me sore.

| | | | | | | | | | |
|---|---|---|---|---|---|---|---|---|---|
| ידך 3027: | 38:3 | אין 369 | מתם 4974 | בבשרי 1320 | מפני 6440 | זעמך 2195 | אין 369 | שלום 7965 | בעצמי 6106 |
| yadeka. | | 'aeyn | matom | bibasariy | mipaney | za'ameka; | 'aeyn | shaloum | ba'atzamay, |
| **your hand** | | ***There is* no** | **soundness** | **in my flesh** | **because of** | **your anger** | **neither *is there any*** | **rest** | **in my bones** |

| | | | | | | | | | |
|---|---|---|---|---|---|---|---|---|---|
| מפני 6440 | חטאתי 2403: | 38:4 | כי 3588 | עונתי 5771 | עברו 5674 | ראשי 7218 | כמשא 4853 | כבד 3515 | יכבדו 3513 |
| mipaney | chata'tiy. | | kiy | 'auonotay | 'abaru | ra'shiy; | kamasa' | kabed, | yikbadu |
| **because of** | **my sin** | | **For** | **mine iniquities** | **are gone over** | **mine head** | **as an burden** | **heavy** | **they are too heavy** |

| | | | | | | | | | | |
|---|---|---|---|---|---|---|---|---|---|---|
| ממני 4480: | 38:5 | הבאישו 887 | נמקו 4743 | חבורתי 2250 | מפני 6440 | אולתי 200: | 38:6 | נעויתי 5753 | שחתי 7817 | עד 5704 |
| mimeniy. | | hiba'ayshu | namaqu | chaburotay; | mipaney, | 'aualtiy. | | na'aueytiy | shachotiy | 'ad |
| **for me** | | **stink *and*** | **are corrupt** | **My wounds** | **because of** | **my foolishness** | | **I am troubled** | **I am bowed down** | **to** |

| | | | | | | | | | | | |
|---|---|---|---|---|---|---|---|---|---|---|---|
| מאד 3966 | כל 3605 | היום 3117 | קדר 6937 | הלכתי 1980: | 38:7 | כי 3588 | כסלי 3689 | מלאו 4390 | נקלה 7033 | ואין 369 | מתם 4974 |
| ma'ad; | kal | hayoum, | qoder | hilakatiy. | | kiy | kasalay | mala'au | niqleh; | ua'aeyn | matom, |
| **greatly** | **all** | **the day** | **mourning** | **I go** | | **For** | **my loins** | **are filled with** | **a loathsome *disease*** | **and *there is* no** | **soundness** |

| | | | | | | | | | |
|---|---|---|---|---|---|---|---|---|---|
| בבשרי 1320: | 38:8 | נפוגותי 6313 | ונדכיתי 1794 | עד 5704 | מאד 3966 | שאגתי 7580 | מנהמת 5100 | לבי 3820: | 38:9 |
| bibsariy. | | napugoutiy | uanidkeytiy | 'ad | ma'ad; | 'sha'agtiy, | minahamat | libiy. | |
| **in my flesh** | | **I am feeble** | **and broken** | **against** | **sore** | **I have roared** | **by reason of the disquietness of** | **my heart** | |

| | | | | | | | | | | | |
|---|---|---|---|---|---|---|---|---|---|---|---|
| אדני 136 | נגדך 5048 | כל 3605 | תאותי 8378 | ואנחתי 585 | ממך 4480 | לא 3808 | נסתרה 5641: | 38:10 | לבי 3820 | סחרחר 5503 | עזבני 5800 |
| 'adonay | negdaka | kal | ta'auatiy; | ua'anchatiy, | mimaka | la' | nistarah. | | libiy | sacharchar | 'azabaniy |
| **Adonai *is*** | **before you** | **all** | **my desire** | **and my groaning** | **from you** | **not** | **is hid** | | **My heart** | **pant** | **fail me** |

| | | | | | | | | | | | |
|---|---|---|---|---|---|---|---|---|---|---|---|
| כחי 3581 | ואור 216 | עיני 5869 | גם 1571 | הם 1992 | אין 369 | אתי 854: | 38:11 | אהבי 157 | ורעי 7453 | מנגד 5048 | נגעי 5061 |
| kochiy; | ua'aur | 'aeynay | gam | hem, | 'aeyn | 'atiy. | | 'ahabay | uare'ay, | mineged | nig'ay |
| **my strength** | **as for the light of** | **mine eyes** | **also** | **it** | **is gone** | **from me** | | **My lovers** | **and my friends** | **aloof from** | **my sore** |

| | | | | | | | | | |
|---|---|---|---|---|---|---|---|---|---|
| יעמדו 5975 | וקרובי 7138 | מרחק 7350 | עמדו 5975: | 38:12 | וינקשו 5367 | מבקשי 1245 | נפשי 5315 | ודרשי 1875 | |
| ya'amodu; | uaqroubay, | merachoq | 'amadu. | | uaynaqshu | mabaqshey | napshiy, | uadorashey | |
| **stand** | **and my kinsmen** | **afar off** | **stand** | | **They also lay snares *for me*** | **that seek after** | **my life** | **and they that seek** | |

| | | | | | | | | | | | |
|---|---|---|---|---|---|---|---|---|---|---|---|
| רעתי 7451 | דברו 1696 | הוות 1942 | ומרמות 4820 | כל 3605 | היום 3117 | יהגו 1897: | 38:13 | ואני 589 | כחרש 2795 | לא 3808 | אשמע 8085 |
| ra'atiy | dibru | hauout; | uamirmout, | kal | hayoum | yehagu. | | ua'aniy | kacheresh | la' | 'ashma; |
| **my hurt** | **speak** | **mischievous things** | **and deceits** | **all** | **the day *long*** | **imagine** | | **But I** | **as a deaf *man*** | **not** | **heard** |

| | | | | | | | | | | |
|---|---|---|---|---|---|---|---|---|---|---|
| וכאלם 483 | לא 3808 | יפתח 6605 | פיו 6310: | 38:14 | ואהי 1961 | כאיש 376 | אשר 834 | לא 3808 | שמע 8085 | ואין 369 |
| uak'alem, | la' | yiptach | piyu. | | ua'ahiy, | ka'aysh | 'asher | la' | shomea'; | ua'aeyn |
| **and *I was* as a dumb man** | **not** | ***that* open** | **his mouth** | | **Thus I was** | **as a man** | **that** | **not** | **hear** | **and *are* no** |

| | | | | | | | | | | | |
|---|---|---|---|---|---|---|---|---|---|---|---|
| בפיו 6310 | תוכחות 8433: | 38:15 | כי 3588 | לך 3807a | יהוה 3069 | הוחלתי 3176 | אתה 859 | תענה 6030 | אדני 136 | אלהי 430: | 38:16 כי 3588 |
| bapiyu, | toukachout. | | kiy | laka | Yahuah | houchaltiy; | 'atah | ta'aneh, | 'adonay | 'alohay. | kiy |
| **in whose mouth** | **no reproofs** | | **For** | **in you** | **O Yahuah** | **do I hope** | **you** | **will hear** | **O Adonai** | **my Elohim** | **For** |

| | | | | | | | |
|---|---|---|---|---|---|---|---|
| אמרתי 559 | פן 6435 | ישמחו 8055 | לי 3807a | במוט 4131 | רגלי 7272 | עלי 5921 | הגדילו 1431: |
| 'amartiy | pen | yismachu | liy; | bamout | ragliy, | 'alay | higdiylu. |
| **I said *Hear me* lest** | ***otherwise*** | **they should rejoice** | **over me** | **when slip** | **my foot** | **against me** | **they magnify *themselves*** |

Ps 37:3 There is no soundness in my flesh because of your anger; neither is there any rest in my bones because of my sin.4 For mine iniquities are gone over mine head: as an heavy burden they are too heavy for me.5 My wounds stink and are corrupt because of my foolishness.6 I am troubled; I am bowed down greatly; I go mourning all the day long.7 For my loins are filled with a loathsome disease: and there is no soundness in my flesh.8 I am feeble and sore broken: I have roared by reason of the disquietness of my heart.9 Adonai, all my desire is before you; and my groaning is not hid from you.10 My heart panteth, my strength faileth me: as for the light of mine eyes, it also is gone from me.11 My lovers and my friends stand aloof from my sore; and my kinsmen stand afar off.12 They also that seek after my life lay snares for me: and they that seek my hurt speak mischievous things, and imagine deceits all the day long.13 But I, as a deaf man, heard not; and I was as a dumb man that openeth not his mouth.14 Thus I was as a man that hear not, and in whose mouth are no reproofs.15 For in you, O YHUH, do I hope: you will hear, O Adonai my G-d.16 For I said, Hear me, lest otherwise they should rejoice over me: when my foot slippeth, they magnify themselves against me.

**38:17** כי 3588 אני 589 לצלע 6761 נכון 3559 ומכאובי 4341 נגדי 5048 תמיד 8548: **38:18** כי 3588 עוני 5771 אגיד 5046
kiy 'aniy latzela' nakoun; uamak'aubiy negdiy tamiyd. kiy 'auniy 'agiyd;
**For I to halt *am* ready and my sorrow before me *is* continually For mine iniquity I will declare**

אדאג 1672 מחטאתי 2403: **38:19** ואיבי 341 חיים 2416 עצמו 6105 ורבו 7231 שנאי 8130
'ad'ag, mechata'tiy. ua'ayabay chayiym 'atzemu; uarabu son'ay
**I will be sorry for my sin But mine enemies *are* lively *and* they are strong and are multiplied they that hate me**

שקר 8267: **38:20** ומשלמי 7999 רעה 7451 תחת 8478 טובה 2896 ישטנוני 7853 תחת 8478 רדופי 7291 טוב 2896:
shaqer. uamshalmey ra'ah tachat toubah; yistanuniy, tachat radoupiy toub.
**wrongfully They also that render evil for good *are* mine adversaries because I follow *the thing that* good *is***

**38:21** אל 408 תעזבני 5800 יהוה 3068 אלהי 430 אל 408 תרחק 7368 ממני 4480: **38:22** חושה 2363 לעזרתי 5833 אדני 136
'al ta'azbeniy Yahuah; 'alohay, 'al tirchaq mimeniy. chushah la'azratiy; 'adonay,
**not Forsake me O Yahuah O my Elohim not be far from me Make haste to help me O Adonai**

תשועתי 8668:
tashu'atiy.
**my salvation**

**Ps 39:1** למנצח 5329 לידיתון 3038 מזמור 4210 לדוד 1732: אמרתי 559 אשמרה 8104 דרכי 1870 מחטוא 2398
lamanatzeach liydiytun mizmour ladauid. 'amartiy, 'ashmarah darakay mechata'
**To the chief Musician *even* to Jeduthun A Psalm of David I said I will take heed to my ways that I sin not**

בלשוני 3956 אשמרה 8104 לפי 6310 מחסום 4269 בעד 1157 רשע 7563 לנגדי 5048: **39:2** נאלמתי 481 דומיה 1747
bilshouniy 'ashmarah lapiy machsoum; ba'aud rasha' lanegdiy. ne'alamtiy dumiyah
**with my tongue I will keep my mouth *with* a bridle while *the* wicked *is* before me I was dumb with silence**

החשיתי 2814 מטוב 2896 וכאבי 3511 נעכר 5916: **39:3** חם 2552 לבי 3820 בקרבי 7130 בהגיגי 1901 תבער 1197
hecheshеytiy mitoub; uak'aebiy ne'akar. cham libiy baqirbiy, bahagiygiy tib'ar
**I held my peace *even* from good and my sorrow was stirred was hot My heart within me while I was musing burned**

אש 784 דברתי 1696 בלשוני 3956: **39:4** הודיעני 3045 יהוה 3068 קצי 7093 ומדת 4060 ימי 3117 מה 4100 היא 1931
'aesh; dibartiy, bilshouniy. houdiy'aeniy Yahuah qitziy, uamidat yamay mah hiy'a;
**the fire *then* spoke I with my tongue make me to know Yahuah mine end and the measure of my days what it**

אדעה 3045 מה 4100 חדל 2310 אני 589: **39:5** הנה 2009 טפחות 2947 נתתה 5414 ימי 3117 וחלדי 2465 כאין 369
'aeda'ah, meh chadel 'aniy. hineh tapachout natatah yamay, uacheldiy ka'ayin
***is that* I may know how frail I *am* Behold *as* an handbreadth you have made my days and mine age *is* as nothing**

נגדך 5048 אך 389 כל 3605 הבל 1892 כל 3605 אדם 120 נצב 5324 סלה 5542: **39:6** אך 389 בצלם 6754 יתהלך 1980 איש 376 אך 389
negdeka; 'ak kal hebel kal 'adam, nitzab selah. 'ak batzelem yithalek 'aysh, 'ak
**before you verily every vanity *is* altogether man at his best state Selah Surely in a show walk every man Surely**

הבל 1892 יהמיון 1993 יצבר 6651 ולא 3808 ידע 3045 מי 4325 אספם 622: **39:7** ועתה 6258 מה 4100 קויתי 6960
hebel yehamayun; yitzbor, uala' yeda' miy' 'asapam. ua'atah mah qiuiytiy
**vain they are disquieted he heapeth up *riches* and not knows who shall gather them And now what wait I for?**

Ps 38:17 For I am ready to halt, and my sorrow is continually before me.18 For I will declare mine iniquity; I will be sorry for my sin.19 But mine enemies are lively, and they are strong: and they that hate me wrongfully are multiplied.20 They also that render evil for good are mine adversaries; because I follow the thing that good is.21 Forsake me not, O YHUH: O my G-d, be not far from me.22 Make haste to help me, O Adonai my salvation. **Ps** 39:1 To the chief Musician, even to Je-du'-thun, A Psalm of David. I said, I will take heed to my ways, that I sin not with my tongue: I will keep my mouth with a bridle, while the wicked is before me.2 I was dumb with silence, I held my peace, even from good; and my sorrow was stirred.3 My heart was hot within me, while I was musing the fire burned: then spoke I with my tongue,4 YHUH, make me to know mine end, and the measure of my days, what it is; that I may know how frail I am.5 Behold, you have made my days as an handbreadth; and mine age is as nothing before you: verily every man at his best state is altogether vanity. Selah.6 Surely every man walk in a vain show: surely they are disquieted in vain: he heapeth up riches, and know not who shall gather them.7 And now, Adonai, what wait I for? my hope is in you.

| אדני 136 | תוחלתי 8431 | לך 3807a | היא 1931: | 39:8 | מכל 3605 | פשעי 6588 | הצילני 5337 | חרפת 2781 | נבל 5036 | אל 408 |
|---|---|---|---|---|---|---|---|---|---|---|
| 'adonay; | touchaltiy, | laka | hiy'a. | | mikal | pasha'ay | hatziyleniy; | cherpat | nabal, | 'al |
| **Adonai** | **my hope *is*** | **in you** | **he** | | **from all** | **my transgressions** | **Deliver me** | **the reproach of** | **the foolish** | **not** |

| תשימני 7760: | 39:9 | נאלמתי 481 | לא 3808 | אפתח 6605 | פי 6310 | כי 3588 | אתה 859 | עשית 6213: | 39:10 | הסר 5493 | מעלי 5921 | נגעך 5061 |
|---|---|---|---|---|---|---|---|---|---|---|---|---|
| tasiymeniy. | | ne'alamtiy | la' | 'aptach | piy; | kiy | 'atah | 'ashiyta. | | haser | me'alay | nig'aka; |
| **make** | | **I was dumb** | **not** | **I opened** | **my mouth** | **because** | **you** | **did *it*** | | **Remove away** | **from me** | **your stroke** |

| מתגרת 8409 | ידך 3027 | אני 589 | כליתי 3615: | 39:11 | בתוכחות 8433 | על 5921 | עון 5771 | יסרת 3256 | איש 376 |
|---|---|---|---|---|---|---|---|---|---|
| mitigrat | yadaka, | 'aniy | kaliytiy. | | batoukachout | 'al | 'auon | yisarta | 'aysh, |
| **by the blow of** | **your hand** | **I** | **I consumed** | | **When you with rebukes** | **for** | **iniquity** | **do correct** | **man** |

| ותמס 4529 | כעש 6211 | חמודו 2530 | אך 389 | הבל 1892 | כל 3605 | אדם 120 | סלה 5542: | 39:12 | שמעה 8085 | תפלתי 8605 |
|---|---|---|---|---|---|---|---|---|---|---|
| uatemes | ka'ash | chamudou; | 'ak | hebel | kal | 'adam | selah. | | shim'ah | tapilatiy |
| **you make to consume away** | **like a moth** | **his beauty** | **surely** | ***is* vanity** | **every** | **man** | **Selah** | | **Hear** | **my prayer** |

| יהוה 3068 | ושועתי 7775 | האזינה 238 | אל 413 | דמעתי 1832 | אל 408 | תחרש 2790 | כי 3588 | גר 1616 | אנכי 595 | עמך 5973 |
|---|---|---|---|---|---|---|---|---|---|---|
| Yahuah | uashaua'atiy | ha'aziynah | 'al | dim'atiy, | 'al | techarash | kiy | ger | 'anokiy | 'amak; |
| **O Yahuah** | **and my cry** | **give ear *unto*** | **at** | **my tears** | **not** | **hold your peace** | **for** | ***am* a stranger** | **I** | **with you** |

| תושב 8453 | ככל 3605 | אבותי 1: | 39:13 | השע 8159 | ממני 4480 | ואבליגה 1082 | בטרם 2962 | אלך 1980 |
|---|---|---|---|---|---|---|---|---|
| toushab, | kakal | aboutay. | | hasha' | mimeniy | ua'abliygah; | baterem | 'aelek |
| ***and* a sojourner** | **as all** | **my fathers *were*** | | **O spare** | **me** | **that I may recover strength** | **before** | **I go hence** |

| ואינני 369: |
|---|
| ua'aeyneniy. |
| **and be no more** |

| Ps 40:1 | למנצח 5329 | לדוד 1732 | מזמור 4210: | קוה 6960 | קויתי 6960 | יהוה 3068 | ויט 5186 | אלי 413 | וישמע 8085 |
|---|---|---|---|---|---|---|---|---|---|
| | lamanatzeach, | ladauid | mizmour. | qauoh | qiuiytiy | Yahuah; | uayet | 'aelay, | uayishma' |
| | **To the chief Musician** | **of David** | **A Psalm** | **I waited** | **patiently for the** | **Yahuah** | **and he inclined** | **unto me** | **and heard** |

| שועתי 7775: | 40:2 | ויעלני 5927 | מבור 953 | שאון 7588 | מטיט 2916 | היון 3121 | ויקם 6965 | על 5921 | סלע 5553 | רגלי 7272 |
|---|---|---|---|---|---|---|---|---|---|---|
| shaua'atiy. | | uaya'aleniy | mibour | sha'aun | mitiyt | hayauen | uayaqem | 'al | sela' | raglay, |
| **my cry** | | **He brought me up also** | **out of an pit** | **horrible** | **out of clay** | **the miry** | **and set** | **upon** | **a rock** | **my feet** |

| כונן 3559 | אשרי 838: | 40:3 | ויתן 5414 | בפי 6310 | שיר 7892 | חדש 2319 | תהלה 8416 | לאלהינו 430 | יראו 7200 | רבים 7227 |
|---|---|---|---|---|---|---|---|---|---|---|
| kounen | 'ashuray. | | uayiten | bapiy | shiyr | chadash | tahilah | le'aloheynu | yir'au | rabiym |
| ***and* established** | **my goings** | | **And he has put** | **in my mouth** | **a song** | **new *even*** | **praise** | **unto our Elohim** | **shall see** | **many** |

| וייראו 3372 | ויבטחו 982 | ביהוה 3068: | 40:4 | אשרי 835 | הגבר 1397 | אשר 834 | שם 7760 | יהוה 3068 | מבטחו 4009 | ולא 3808 | פנה 6437 | אל 413 |
|---|---|---|---|---|---|---|---|---|---|---|---|---|
| uayiyra'au; | uayibtachu, | baYahuah. | | 'ashrey | hageber, | 'asher | sam | Yahuah | mibtachou; | uala' | panah | 'al |
| **[it] and fear** | **and shall trust** | **in Yahuah** | | **Blessed** | ***is* that man** | **that** | **make** | **Yahuah** | **his trust** | **and not** | **respect** | **to** |

| רהבים 7295 | ושטי 7750 | כזב 3577: | 40:5 | רבות 7227 | עשית 6213 | אתה 859 | יהוה 3068 | אלהי 430 |
|---|---|---|---|---|---|---|---|---|
| rahabiym, | uasatey | kazab. | | rabout | 'ashiyta | 'atah | Yahuah | 'alohay |
| **the proud** | **nor such as turn aside to** | **lies** | | **Many** | **have done *which*** | **you** | **O Yahuah** | **my Elohim** |

Ps 39:8 Deliver me from all my transgressions: make me not the reproach of the foolish.9 I was dumb, I opened not my mouth; because you did it.10 Remove your stroke away from me: I am consumed by the blow of your hand.11 When you with rebukes dost correct man for iniquity, you make his beauty to consume away like a moth: surely every man is vanity. Selah.12 Hear my prayer, O YHUH, and give ear unto my cry; hold not your peace at my tears: for I am a stranger with you, and a sojourner, as all my fathers were.13 O spare me, that I may recover strength, before I go hence, and be no more. **Ps** 40:1 To the chief Musician, A Psalm of David. I waited patiently for YHUH; and he inclined unto me, and heard my cry.2 He brought me up also out of an horrible pit, out of the miry clay, and set my feet upon a rock, and established my goings.3 And he has put a new song in my mouth, even praise unto our G-d: many shall see it, and fear, and shall trust in YHUH.4 Blessed is that man that make YHUH his trust, and respecteth not the proud, nor such as turn aside to lies.5 Many, O YHUH my G-d, are your wonderful works which you have done, and your thoughts which are to us-ward: they cannot be reckoned up in order unto you: if I would declare and speak of them, they are more than can be numbered.

נפלאתיך 6381 ומחשבתיך 4284 אלינו 413 אין 369 ערך 6186 אליך 413
nipl'ateyka uamachshaboteyka, 'aleynu 'aeyn 'arok 'aeleyka,
***are*** **your wonderful works and your thoughts *which are* to us-ward cannot they be reckoned up in order unto you**

אגידה 5046 ואדברה 1696 עצמו 6105 מספר 5608: 40:6 זבח 2077 ומנחה 4503 לא 3808 חפצת 2654
'agiydah ua'adaberah; 'atzamu, misaper. zebach uaminchah la' chapatzta,
***if*** **I would declare and speak *of them* they are more than can be numbered Sacrifice and offering not you did desire**

אזנים 241 כרית 3738 לי 3807a עולה 5930 וחטאה 2401 לא 3808 שאלת 7592: 40:7 אז 227 אמרתי 559 הנה 2009 באתי 935
'azanayim kariyta liy; aulah uachata'ah, la' sha'alta. 'az 'amartiy hineh ba'tiy;
**ears have you opened mine burnt offering and sin offering not have you required Then said I Lo I come**

במגלת 4039 ספר 5612 כתוב 3789 עלי 5921: 40:8 לעשות 6213 רצונך 7522 אלהי 430 חפצתי 2654 ותורתך 8451 בתוך 8432
bimagilat seper, katub 'alay. la'asout ratzounaka 'alohay chapatzatiy; uatourataka, batouk
**in the volume of the book *it is* written of me to do your will O my Elohim I delight yea your law *is* within**

מעי 4578: 40:9 בשרתי 1319 צדק 6664 בקהל 6951 רב 7227 הנה 2009 שפתי 8193 לא 3808 אכלא 3607 יהוה 3068
me'ay. bisartiy tzedeq baqahal rab, hineh sapatay la' 'akala'; Yahuah
**my heart I have preached righteousness in congregation *the* great Lo my lips not I have refrained O Yahuah**

אתה 859 ידעת 3045: 40:10 צדקתך 6666 לא 3808 כסיתי 3680 בתוך 8432 לבי 3820 אמונתך 530 ותשועתך 8668
'atah yada'ta. tzidqataka la' kisiytiy batouk libiy, 'amunataka uatshu'ataka
**you know your righteousness not I have hid within my heart your faithfulness and your salvation**

אמרתי 559 לא 3808 כחדתי 3582 חסדך 2617 ואמתך 571 לקהל 6951 רב 7227: 40:11 אתה 859
'amaratiy; la' kichadtiy chasdaka ua'amataka, laqahal rab. 'atah
**I have declared not I have concealed your lovingkindness and your truth from congregation *the* great you**

יהוה 3068 לא 3808 תכלא 3607 רחמיך 7356 ממני 4480 חסדך 2617 ואמתך 571 תמיד 8548
Yahuah la' tikla' rachameyka mimeniy; chasdaka ua'amataka, tamiyd
**O Yahuah not Withhold your tender mercies from me your lovingkindness and your truth continually**

יצרוני 5341: 40:12 כי 3588 אפפו 661 עלי 5921 רעות 7451 עד 5704 אין 369 מספר 4557 השיגוני 5381
yitzruniy. kiy 'apapu 'alay ra'aut 'ad 'aeyn mispar, hisiyguniy
**let preserve me For have compassed about me evils against else innumerable have taken hold upon me**

עונתי 5771 ולא 3808 יכלתי 3201 לראות 7200 עצמו 6105 משערות 8185 ראשי 7218 ולבי 3820
'auonotay uala' yakoltiy lir'aut; 'atzamu misa'arout ra'shiy, ualibiy
**mine iniquities so that not I am able to look up they are more than the hairs of mine head therefore my heart**

עזבני 5800: 40:13 רצה 7521 יהוה 3068 להצילני 5337 יהוה 3068 לעזרתי 5833 חושה 2363: 40:14 יבשו 954
'azabaniy. ratzeh Yahuah lahatziyleniy; Yahuah la'azratiy chushah. yeboshu
**fail me Be pleased O Yahuah to deliver me O Yahuah to help me make haste Let them be ashamed**

ויחפרו 2659 יחד 3162 מבקשי 1245 נפשי 5315 לספותה 5595 יסגו 5472 אחור 268 ויכלמו 3637 חפצי 2655
uayachparu yachad mabaqshey napshiy, lispoutah yisogu 'achour uayikalamu; chapetzey,
**and confounded together that seek after my soul to destroy it let them be driven backward and put to shame that wish me**

Ps 40:6 Sacrifice and offering you did not desire; mine ears have you opened: burnt offering and sin offering have you not required.7 Then said I, Lo, I come: in the volume of the book it is written of me,8 I delight to do your will, O my G-d: yea, your law is within my heart.9 I have preached righteousness in the great congregation: lo, I have not refrained my lips, O YHUH, you know.10 I have not hid your righteousness within my heart; I have declared your faithfulness and your salvation: I have not concealed your lovingkindness and your truth from the great congregation.11 Withhold not you your tender mercies from me, O YHUH: let your lovingkindness and your truth continually preserve me.12 For innumerable evils have compassed me about: mine iniquities have taken hold upon me, so that I am not able to look up; they are more than the hairs of mine head: therefore my heart faileth me.13 Be pleased, O YHUH, to deliver me: O YHUH, make haste to help me.14 Let them be ashamed and confounded together that seek after my soul to destroy it; let them be driven backward and put to shame that wish me evil.

40:15 40:16

רעתי 7451: ישמו 8074 על 5921 עקב 6118 בשתם 1322 האמרים 559 לי 3807a האח 1889 האח 1889: ישישו 7797

ra'atiy. yashomu 'al 'aeqeb bashatam; ha'amariym liy, he'ach he'ach. yasiysu

**evil Let them be desolate for a reward of their shame that say unto me Aha aha Let rejoice**

40:17

וישמחו 8055 בך 871a כל 3605 מבקשיך 1245 יאמרו 559 תמיד 8548 יגדל 1431 יהוה 3068 אהבי 157 תשועתך 8668:

uayismachu baka, kal mabaqsheyka ya'maru tamiyd yigdal Yahuah; 'ahabey, tashu'ateka.

**and be glad in you all those that seek you let say continually be magnified Yahuah such as love your salvation**

ואני 589 עני 6041 ואביון 34 אדני 136 יחשב 2803 לי 3807a עזרתי 5833 ומפלטי 6403 אתה 859 אלהי 430 אל 408

ua'aniy 'aniy ua'abyoun 'adonay yachashab liy 'azratiy uampaltiy 'atah; 'alohay, 'al

**But I *am* poor and needy *yet* Adonai think upon me *are* my help and my deliverer you O my Elohim no**

תאחר 309:

ta'achar.

**make tarrying**

**Ps 41:1**

למנצח 5329 מזמור 4210 לדוד 1732: אשרי 835 משכיל 7919 אל 413 דל 1800 ביום 3117 רעה 7451

lamanatzeach, mizmour ladauid. 'ashrey maskiyl 'al dal; bayoum ra'ah,

**To the chief Musician A Psalm of David Blessed *is* he that consider to the poor in time of trouble**

41:2

ימלטהו 4422 יהוה 3068: יהוה 3068 ישמרהו 8104 ויחיהו 2421 יאשר 833 בארץ 776 ואל 408

yamaltehu Yahuah. Yahuah yishmarehu uiychayehu ya'ashar ba'aretz; ua'al

**will deliver him Yahuah Yahuah will preserve him and keep him alive *and* he shall be blessed upon the earth and not**

41:3

תתנהו 5414 בנפש 5315 איביו 341: יהוה 3068 יסעדנו 5582 על 5921 ערש 6210 דוי 1741 כל 3605

titanehu, banepesh 'ayabayu. Yahuah yis'adenu 'al 'ares dauay; kal

**you will deliver him unto the will of his enemies Yahuah will strengthen him upon the bed of languishing all**

41:4

משכבו 4904 הפכת 2015 בחליו 2483: אני 589 אמרתי 559 יהוה 3068 חנני 2603 רפאה 7495 נפשי 5315 כי 3588

mishkabou, hapakta bachalayou. 'aniy 'amartiy Yahuah chaneniy rapa'ah napshiy, kiy

**his bed you will make in his sickness I said Yahuah be merciful unto me heal my soul for**

41:5 41:6

חטאתי 2398 לך 3807a: אויבי 341 יאמרו 559 רע 7451 לי 3807a מתי 4970 ימות 4191 ואבד 6 שמו 8034: ואם 518

chata'tiy lak. 'auyabay, ya'maru ra' liy; matay yamut, ua'abad shamou. ua'am

**I have sinned against you Mine enemies speak evil of me When shall he die and perish? his name And if**

41:7

בא 935 לראות 7200 שוא 7723 ידבר 1696 לבו 3820 יקבץ 6908 און 205 לו 3807a יצא 3318 לחוץ 2351 ידבר 1696: יחד 3162

ba' lir'aut shau'a yadaber, libou, yiqbatz 'auen lou'; yetzea' lachutz yadaber. yachad,

**he come to see *me* vanity he speak his heart gathered iniquity to itself he goes *when* abroad he tell it together**

41:8

עלי 5921 יתלחשו 3907 כל 3605 שנאי 8130 עלי 5921 יחשבו 2803 רעה 7451 לי 3807a: דבר 1699 בליעל 1100 יצוק 3332

'alay yitlachashu kal son'ay; 'alay yachshabu ra'ah liy. dabar baliya'al yatzuq

**against me whisper All that hate me against me do they devise hurt my An disease evil *say they* cleave fast**

41:9

בו 871a ואשר 834 שכב 7901 לא 3808 יוסיף 3254 לקום 6965: גם 1571 איש 376 שלומי 7965 אשר 834

bou; ua'asher shakab, la' yousiyp laqum. gam 'aysh shaloumiy 'asher

**unto him and *now* that he lies no more he shall rise up Yea man mine own familiar friend in whom**

Ps 41:15 Let them be desolate for a reward of their shame that say unto me, Aha, aha.16 Let all those that seek you rejoice and be glad in you: let such as love your salvation say continually, YHUH be magnified.17 But I am poor and needy; yet YHUH thinketh upon me: you are my help and my deliverer; make no tarrying, O my G-d. **Ps** 41:1 To the chief Musician, A Psalm of David. Blessed is he that considereth the poor: YHUH will deliver him in time of trouble.2 YHUH will preserve him, and keep him alive; and he shall be blessed upon the earth: and you will not deliver him unto the will of his enemies.3 YHUH will strengthen him upon the bed of languishing: you will make all his bed in his sickness.4 I said, YHUH, be merciful unto me: heal my soul; for I have sinned against you.5 Mine enemies speak evil of me, When shall he die, and his name perish?6 And if he come to see me, he speaketh vanity: his heart gathereth iniquity to itself; when he go abroad, he tell it.7 All that hate me whisper together against me: against me do they devise my hurt.8 An evil disease, say they, cleaveth fast unto him: and now that he lie he shall rise up no more.9 Yea, mine own familiar friend, in whom I trusted, which did eat of my bread, has lifted up his heel against me.

בטחתי 982 בו 871a אוכל 398 לחמי 3899 הגדיל 1431 עלי 5921 עקב 6119: 41:10 ואתה 859 יהוה 3069 חנני 2603
batachtiy bou 'aukel lachmiy; higdiyl 'alay 'aqeb. ua'atah Yahuah chaneniy
**I trusted in him which did eat of my bread has lifted up against me *his* heel But you Yahuah be merciful unto me**

והקימני 6965 ואשלמה 7999 להם 3807a: 41:11 בזאת 2063 ידעתי 3045 כי 3588 חפצת 2654 בי 871a כי 3588 לא 3808 יריע 7321
uahaqiymeniy; ua'ashalmah lahem. baza't yada'tiy kiy chapatzta biy; kiy la' yariya'
**and raise me up that I may requite them By this I know that you favor me because not does triumph**

איבי 341 עלי 5921: 41:12 ואני 589 בתמי 8537 תמכת 8551 בי 871a ותציבני 5324 לפניך 6440 לעולם 5769: 41:13
'ayabiy 'alay. ua'aniy, batumiy tamakta biy; uatatziybeniy lapaneyka la'aulam.
**mine enemy over me And as for me in mine integrity you uphold me and set me before your face for ever**

ברוך 1288 יהוה 3068 אלהי 430 ישראל 3478 מהעולם 5769 ועד 5704 העולם 5769 אמן 543 ואמן 543:
baruk Yahuah 'alohey yisra'ael, meha'aulam ua'ad ha'aulam, 'amen ua'amen.
**Blessed *be* Yahuah Elohim of Israel from everlasting and to everlasting Amen and Amen**

Ps 42:1 למנצח 5329 משכיל 4905 לבני 1121 קרח 7141: כאיל 354 תערג 6165 על 5921 אפיקי 650 מים 4325 כן 3651 נפשי 5315
lamanatzeach, maskiyl libney qorach. ka'ayal, ta'arog 'al 'apiyqey mayim; ken napshiy
**To the chief Musician Maschil for the sons of Korah As the hart pant after brooks *the* water so my soul**

תערג 6165 אליך 413 אלהים 430: 42:2 צמאה 6770 נפשי 5315 לאלהים 430 לאל 410 חי 2416 מתי 4970 אבוא 935 ואראה 7200 פני 6440
ta'arog 'aeleyka 'alohiym. tzama'ah napshiy le'alohiym la'ael chay matay abou'a; ua'aera'ah, paney
**pant after you O Elohim thirst My soul for Elohim for El *the* living when shall I come and appear before**

אלהים 430: 42:3 היתה 1961 לי 3807a דמעתי 1832 לחם 3899 יומם 3119 ולילה 3915 באמר 559 אלי 413 כל היום 3117 איה 346
'alohiym. hayatah liy dim'atiy lechem youmam ualayalah; be'amor 'aelay kal hayoum, 'ayeh
**Elohim? have been my My tears meat day and night while they say unto me all continually Where**

אלהיך 430: 42:4 אלה 428 אזכרה 2142 ואשפכה 8210 עלי 5921 נפשי 5315 כי 3588 אעבר 5674 בסך 5519
'aloheyka. 'aeleh 'azkarah ua'ashpakah 'alay napshiy, kiy 'aabor basak
***is* your Elohim these *things* I remember When I pour out in me my soul for I had gone with the multitude**

אדדם 1718 עד 5704 בית 1004 אלהים 430 בקול 6963 רנה 7440 ותודה 8426 המון 1995 חוגג 2287: 42:5
'adadem, 'ad beyt 'alohiym baqoul rinah uatoudah, hamoun chougeg.
**I went with them to the house of Elohim with the voice of joy and praise *with* a multitude that kept holyday**

מה 4100 תשתוחחי 7817 נפשי 5315 ותהמי 1993 עלי 5921 הוחילי 3176 לאלהים 430 כי 3588 עוד 5750
mah tishtouchachiy napshiy uatehemiy 'alay houchiyliy le'alohiym kiy 'aud
**Why are you cast down O my soul? and why are you disquieted in me? hope you in Elohim for yet**

אודנו 3034 ישועות 3444 פניו 6440: 42:6 אלהי 430 עלי 5921 נפשי 5315 תשתוחח 7817 על 5921 כן 3651
audenu, yashu'aut panayu. 'alohay, 'alay napshiy tishtouchach 'al ken,
**I shall praise him *for* the help of his countenance O my Elohim within me my soul is cast down therefore after that**

אזכרך 2142 מארץ 776 ירדן 3383 וחרמונים 2769 מהר 2022 מצער 4706: 42:7 תהום 8415 אל 413 תהום 8415
'azkaraka me'aretz yarden; uachermouniym, mehar mitz'ar. tahoum 'al tahoum
**will I remember you from the land of Jordan and of the Hermonites from the hill Mizar Deep unto deep**

Ps 41:10 But you, O YHUH, be merciful unto me, and raise me up, that I may requite them.11 By this I know that you favourest me, because mine enemy doth not triumph over me.12 And as for me, you upholdest me in mine integrity, and settest me before your face forever.13 Blessed be YHUH G-d of Israel from everlasting, and to everlasting. Amen, and Amen. **Ps** 42:1 To the chief Musician, Mas'-chil, for the sons of Ko'rah. As the hart panteth after the water brooks, so panteth my soul after you, O G-d.2 My soul thirsteth for G-d, for the living G-d: when shall I come and appear before G-d?3 My tears have been my meat day and night, while they continually say unto me, Where is your G-d?4 When I remember these things, I pour out my soul in me: for I had gone with the multitude, I went with them to the house of G-d, with the voice of joy and praise, with a multitude that kept holyday.5 Why are you cast down, O my soul? and why are you disquieted in me? hope you in G-d: for I shall yet praise him for the help of his countenance.6 O my G-d, my soul is cast down within me: therefore will I remember you from the land of Jordan, and of the Hermonites, from the hill Mizar.

42:8
קורא 7121 לקול 6963 צנוריך 6794 כל 3605 משבריך 4867 וגליך 1530 עלי 5921 עברו 5674: יומם 3119
qourea' laqoul tzinoureyka; kal mishbareyka uagaleyka, 'alay 'abaru. youmam
**call at the noise of your waterspouts all your waves and your billows over me are gone *Yet in* the daytime**

יצוה 6680 יהוה 3068 חסדו 2617 ובלילה 3915 שירה עמי 5973 תפלה 8605 לאל 410
yatzaueh Yahuah chasdou, uabalayalah shiyrah 'amiy; tapilah, la'ael
**will command Yahuah his lovingkindness and in the night his song *shall be* with me *and* my prayer unto *the* El *of***

42:9
חיי 2416: אומרה 559 לאל 410 סלעי 5553 למה 4100 שכחתני 7911 למה 4100 קדר 6937 אלך 1980
chayay. 'amarah la'ael sala'ay lamah shakachtaniy lamah qoder 'aelek,
**my life I will say unto El my rock Why have you forgotten me? why mourning go I**

42:10
בלחץ 3906 אויב 341: ברצח 7524 בעצמותי 6106 חרפוני 2778 צוררי 6887 באמרם 559
balachatz auyeb. baretzach ba'atzmoutay, cherapuniy tzouraray; ba'amaram
**because of the oppression of the enemy? *As* with a sword in my bones reproach me mine enemies while they say**

42:11
אלי 413 כל 3605 היום 3117 איה 346 אלהיך 430: מה 4100 תשתוחחי 7817 נפשי 5315 ומה 4100 תהמי 1993
'aelay kal hayoum, 'ayeh 'aloheyka. mah tishtouchachiy napshiy uamah tehamiy
**unto me all daily Where *is* your Elohim? Why are you cast down O my soul? and why are you disquieted**

עלי 5921 הוחילי 3176 לאלהים 430 כי 3588 עוד 5750 אודנו 3034 ישועת 3444 פני 6440 ואלהי 430:
'alay houchiyliy le'alohiym kiy 'aud audenu; yashu'at panay, ua'alohay.
**within me? hope you in Elohim for yet I shall yet praise him *who is* the health of my countenance and my Elohim**

**Ps 43:1**
שפטני 8199 אלהים 430 וריבה 7378 ריבי 7379 מגוי 1471 לא 3808 חסיד 2623 מאיש 376 מרמה 4820 ועולה 5766
shapateniy 'alohiym uariybah riybiy, migouy la' chasiyd; me'aysh mirmah ua'aulah
**Judge me O Elohim and plead my cause against an nation not godly from man the deceitful and unjust**

43:2
תפלטני 6403: כי 3588 אתה 859 אלהי 430 מעוזי 4581 למה 4100 זנחתני 2186 למה 4100 קדר 6937 אתהלך 1980
tapalteniy. kiy 'atah 'alohey ma'auziy lamah zanachtaniy lamah qoder 'athalek,
**O deliver me For you *are* the Elohim of my strength why do you cast me off? why mourning go I**

43:3
בלחץ 3906 אויב 341: שלח 7971 אורך 216 ואמתך 571 המה 1992 ינחוני 5148 יביאוני 935
balachatz auyeb. shalach 'auraka ua'amataka hemah yanchuniy; yabiy'aniy
**because of the oppression of the enemy? O send out your light and your truth them let lead me let them bring me**

43:4
אל 413 הר 2022 קדשך 6944 ואל 413 משכנותיך 4908: ואבואה 935 אל 413 מזבח 4196 אלהים 430 אל 413 אל 410 שמחת 8057 גילי 1524
'al har qadashaka ua'al mishkanouteyka. ua'abou'ah 'al mizbach 'alohiym, 'al 'ael simchat giyliy
**unto hill your holy and to your tabernacles Then will I go unto the altar of Elohim unto El exceeding my joy**

43:5
ואודך 3034 בכנור 3658 אלהים 430 אלהי 430: מה 4100 תשתוחחי 7817 נפשי 5315 ומה 4100
ua'audaka bakinour, 'alohiym 'alohay. mah tishtouchachiy napshiy uamah
**yea will I praise you upon the harp O Elohim my Elohim Why are you cast down O my soul? and why**

תהמי 1993 עלי 5921 הוחילי 3176 לאלהים 430 כי 3588 עוד 5750 אודנו 3034 ישועת 3444 פני 6440
tehamiy 'alay houchiyliy le'alohiym kiy 'aud audenu; yashu'at panay,
**are you disquieted within me? hope in Elohim for yet I shall praise him *who is* the health of my countenance**

Ps 42:7 Deep call unto deep at the noise of your waterspouts: all your waves and your billows are gone over me.8 Yet YHUH will command his lovingkindness in the daytime, and in the night his song shall be with me, and my prayer unto the G-d of my life.9 I will say unto G-d my rock, Why have you forgotten me? why go I mourning because of the oppression of the enemy?10 As with a sword in my bones, mine enemies reproach me; while they say daily unto me, Where is your G-d?11 Why are you cast down, O my soul? and why are you disquieted within me? hope you in G-d: for I shall yet praise him, who is the health of my countenance, and my G-d. **Ps** 43:1 Judge me, O G-d, and plead my cause against an ungodly nation: O deliver me from the deceitful and unjust man.2 For you are the G-d of my strength: why dost you cast me off? why go I mourning because of the oppression of the enemy?3 O send out your light and your truth: let them lead me; let them bring me unto your holy hill, and to your tabernacles.4 Then will I go unto the altar of G-d, unto G-d my exceeding joy: yea, upon the harp will I praise you, O G-d my G-d.5 Why are you cast down, O my soul? and why are you disquieted within me? hope in G-d: for I shall yet praise him, who is the health of my countenance, and my G-d.

ואלהי 430:
ua'alohay.
**and my Elohim**

Ps 44:1 למנצח 5329 לבני 1121 קרח 7141 משכיל 4905: אלהים 430 באזנינו 241 שמענו 8085 אבותינו 1 ספרו 5608
lamanatzeach libney qorach maskiyl. 'alohiym ba'azaneynu shama'anu, abouteynu sipru
**To the chief Musician for the sons of Korah Maschil O Elohim with our ears We have heard our fathers have told**

לנו 3807a פעל 6467 פעלת 6466 בימיהם 3117 בימי 3117 קדם 6924: 44:2 אתה 859 ידך 3027 גוים 1471 הורשת 3423
lanu; po'al pa'alta biymeyhem, biymey qedem. 'atah yadaka gouyim hourashta
**us *what* work you did in their days in the times of old *How* you *with* your hand the heathen did drive out**

ותטעם 5193 תרע 7489 לאמים 3816 ותשלחם 7971: 44:3 כי 3588 לא 3808 בחרבם 2719 ירשו 3423
uatita'aem; tara' la'amiym, uatashalchem. kiy la' bacharbam yarashu
**and plant them *how* you did afflict the people and cast them out For not by their own sword they got in possession**

ארץ 776 וזרועם 2220 לא 3808 הושיעה 3467 למו 3807a כי 3588 ימינך 3225 וזרועך 2220 ואור 216 פניך 6440
'aretz, uazrou'am la' houshiy'ah lamou kiy yamiynaka uazrou'aka ua'aur paneyka,
**the land their own arm neither did save them but your right hand and your arm and the light of your countenance**

כי 3588 רציתם 7521: 44:4 אתה 859 הוא 1931 מלכי 4428 אלהים 430 צוה 6680 ישועות 3444 יעקב 3290: 44:5
kiy ratziytam. 'atah hua' malkiy 'alohiym; tzaueh, yashu'aut ya'aqob.
**because you had a favor unto them You *are* he my King O Elohim command deliverances for Jacob**

בך 871a צרינו 6862 ננגח 5055 בשמך 8034 נבוס 947 קמינו 6965: 44:6 כי 3588
baka tzareynu nanageach; bashimka, nabus qameynu. kiy
**Through you our enemies will we push down through your name will we tread them under that rise up against us For**

לא 3808 בקשתי 7198 אבטח 982 וחרבי 2719 לא 3808 תושיעני 3467: 44:7 כי 3588 הושעתנו 3467 מצרינו 6862
la' baqashtiy 'abtach; uacharbiy, la' toushiy'aeniy. kiy housha'atanu mitzareynu;
**not in my bow I will trust my sword neither shall save me But you have saved us from our enemies**

ומשנאינו 8130 הבישות 954: 44:8 באלהים 430 הללנו 1984 כל 3605 היום 3117 ושמך 8034 לעולם 5769 נודה 3034
uamsan'aeynu hebiyshouta. be'alohiym hilalnu kal hayoum; uashimaka la'aulam noudeh
**and that hated us have put them to shame In Elohim we boast all the day *long* and your name for ever praise**

סלה 5542: 44:9 אף 637 זנחת 2186 ותכלימנו 3637 ולא 3808 תצא 3318 בצבאותינו 6635: 44:10 תשיבנו 7725 אחור 268
selah. 'ap zanachta uatakliymenu; uala' tetzea', batzib'auteynu. tashiybenu 'achour
**Selah But you have cast off and put us to shame and not go forth with our armies You make us to turn back**

מני 4480 צר 6862 ומשנאינו 8130 שסו 8154 למו 3807a: 44:11 תתננו 5414 כצאן 6629 מאכל 3978
miniy tzar; uamsan'aeynu, shasu lamou. titanenu katza'n ma'akal;
**from the enemy and they which hate us spoil for themselves You have given us like sheep *appointed* for meat**

ובגוים 1471 זריתנו 2219: 44:12 תמכר 4376 עמך 5971 בלא 3808 הון 1952 ולא 3808 רבית 7235
uabagouyim, zeriytanu. timkor 'amaka bala' houn; uala' ribiyta,
**and among the heathen have scattered us You sell your people for nought and not do increase**

**Ps** 44:1 To the chief Musician for the sons of Ko'-rah, Mas'-chil. We have heard with our ears, O G-d, our fathers have told us, what work you did in their days, in the times of old.2 How you did drive out the heathen with your hand, and plantedst them; how you did afflict the people, and cast them out.3 For they got not the land in possession by their own sword, neither did their own arm save them: but your right hand, and your arm, and the light of your countenance, because you had a favor unto them.4 Thou are my King, O G-d: command deliverances for Jacob.5 Through you will we push down our enemies: through your name will we tread them under that rise up against us.6 For I will not trust in my bow, neither shall my sword save me.7 But you have saved us from our enemies, and have put them to shame that hated us.8 In G-d we boast all the day long, and praise your name forever. Selah.9 But you have cast off, and put us to shame; and go not forth with our armies.10 Thou make us to turn back from the enemy: and they which hate us spoil for themselves.11 Thou have given us like sheep appointed for meat; and have scattered us among the heathen.12 Thou sellest your people for nought, and dost not increase your wealth by their price.

44:13

במחיריהם 4242: | תשימנו 7760 | חרפה 2781 | לשכנינו 7934 | לעג 3933 | וקלס 7047
bimachiyreyhem. | tasiymenu | cherpah | lishkeneynu; | la'ag | uaqeles,
***your wealth* by their price** | **You make us** | **a reproach** | **to our neighbours** | **a scorn** | **and a derision**

44:14

לסביבותינו 5439: | תשימנו 7760 | משל 4912 | בגוים 1471 | מנוד 4493 | ראש 7218 | בל 3816
lisbiybouteynu. | tasiymenu | mashal | bagouyim; | manoud | ra'sh, | bal
**to them that are round about us** | **You make us** | **a byword** | **among the heathen** | **a shaking of** | **the head** | **among**

44:15 ... 44:16

אמים 3816: | כל 3605 | היום 3117 | כלמתי 3639 | נגדי 5048 | ובשת 1322 | פני 6440 | כסתני 3680:
'aumiym. | kal | hayoum | kalimatiy | negdiy; | uaboshet | panay | kisataniy.
**the peoples** | **All** | ***is* continually** | **My confusion** | ***is* before me** | **and the shame of** | **my face** | **has covered me**

44:17

מקול 6963 | מחרף 2778 | ומגדף 1442 | מפני 6440 | אויב 341 | ומתנקם 5358: | כל 3605 | זאת 2063 | באתנו 935
miqoul | macharep | uamgadep; | mipaney | auyeb, | uamitanaqem. | kal | za't | ba'atnu
**For the voice of** | **him that reproach** | **and blasphem** | **by reason of** | **the enemy** | **and avenger** | **All** | **this** | **is come upon us**

44:18

ולא 3808 | שכחנוך 7911 | ולא 3808 | שקרנו 8266 | בבריתך 1285: | לא 3808 | נסוג 5472 | אחור 268 | לבנו 3820
uala' | shakachanuka; | uala' | shiqarnu, | bibriyteka. | la' | nasoug | 'achour | libenu;
**yet not** | **have we forgotten** | **neither** | **have we dealt falsely** | **in your covenant** | **not** | **is turned** | **back** | **Our heart**

44:19

ותט 5186 | אשרינו 838 | מני 4480 | ארחך 734: | כי 3588 | דכיתנו 1794 | במקום 4725 | תנים 8577
uatet | 'ashureynu, | miniy | 'aracheka. | kiy | dikiytanu | bimaqoum | taniym;
**neither have declined** | **our steps** | **from** | **your way** | **Though** | **you have sore broken us** | **in the place of** | **dragons**

44:20

ותכס 3680 | עלינו 5921 | בצלמות 6757: | אם 518 | שכחנו 7911 | שם 8034 | אלהינו 430 | ונפרש 6566
uatakas | 'aleynu | uatzalmauet. | 'am | shakachnu | shem | 'aloheynu; | uanipros
**and covered** | **us** | **with the shadow of death** | **If** | **we have forgotten** | **the name of** | **our Elohim** | **or stretched out**

44:21

כפינו 3709 | לאל 410 | זר 2114: | הלא 3808 | אלהים 430 | יחקר 2713 | זאת 2063 | כי 3588 | הוא 1931 | ידע 3045 | תעלמות 8587
kapeynu, | la'ael | zar. | hala' | 'alohiym | yachaqar | za't; | kiy | hua' | yodea', | ta'alumout
**our hands** | **to *a* god** | **strange** | **not** | **Elohim** | **Shall search out?** | **this** | **for** | **he** | **knows** | **the secrets of**

44:22 ... 44:23

לב 3820: | כי 3588 | עליך 5921 | הרגנו 2026 | כל 3605 | היום 3117 | נחשבנו 2803 | כצאן 6629 | טבחה 2878:
leb. | kiy | 'aleyka | horagnu | kal | hayoum; | nechshabnu, | katza'n | tibchah.
**the heart** | **Yea** | **for your sake** | **are we killed** | **all** | **the day** | ***long* we are counted** | **as sheep for** | **the slaughter**

44:24

עורה 5782 | למה 4100 | תישן 3462 | אדני 136 | הקיצה 6974 | אל 408 | תזנח 2186 | לנצח 5331: | למה 4100 | פניך 6440 | תסתיר 5641 | תשכח 7911
'uarah | lamah | tiyshan | 'adonay; | haqiytzah, | 'al | tiznach | lanetzach. | lamah | paneyka | tastiyr; | tishkach
**Awake** | **why** | **sleep you** | **Adonai** | **arise, *us*** | **not** | **cast off** | **for ever** | **Wherefore** | **your face** | **hide you** | ***and* forget**

44:25 ... 44:26

ענינו 6040 | ולחצנו 3906: | כי 3588 | שחה 7743 | לעפר 6083 | נפשנו 5315 | דבקה 1692 | לארץ 776 | בטננו 990:
'anayenu | ualachatzenu. | kiy | shachah | le'apar | napshenu; | dabqah | la'aretz | bitnenu.
**our affliction** | **and our oppression?** | **For** | **is bowed down** | **to the dust** | **our soul** | **cleave** | **unto the earth** | **our belly**

קומה 6965 | עזרתה 5833 | לנו 3807a | ופדנו 6299 | למען 4616 | חסדך 2617:
qumah | 'azratah | lanu; | uapdenu, | lama'an | chasadeka.
**Arise** | **help** | ***for* our** | **and redeem us** | **for sake** | **your mercies'**

Ps 44:13 Thou make us a reproach to our neighbors, a scorn and a derision to them that are round about us.14 Thou make us a byword among the heathen, a shaking of the head among the people.15 My confusion is continually before me, and the shame of my face has covered me,16 For the voice of him that reproacheth and blasphemeth; by reason of the enemy and avenger.17 All this is come upon us; yet have we not forgotten you, neither have we dealt falsely in your covenant.18 Our heart is not turned back, neither have our steps declined from your way;19 Though you have sore broken us in the place of dragons, and covered us with the shadow of death.20 If we have forgotten the name of our G-d, or stretched out our hands to a strange god;21 Shall not G-d search this out? for he know the secrets of the heart.22 Yea, for your sake are we killed all the day long; we are counted as sheep for the slaughter.23 Awake, why sleepest you, O Adonai? arise, cast us not off forever.24 Wherefore hidest you your face, and forgettest our affliction and our oppression?25 For our soul is bowed down to the dust: our belly cleaveth unto the earth.26 Arise for our help, and redeem us for your mercies' sake.

**Ps 45:1**
למנצח 5329 על 5921 ששנים 7799 לבני 1121 קרח 7141 משכיל 4905 שיר 7892 ידידת 3039: רחש 7370 לבי 3820
lamanatzeach 'al shoshaniym libney qorach; maskiyl, shiyr yadiydot. rachash libiy
**To the chief Musician upon Shoshannim for the sons of Korah Maschil A Song of loves is inditing My heart**

דבר 1697 טוב 2896 אמר 559 אני 589 מעשי 4639 למלך 4428 לשוני 3956 עט 5842 סופר 5608
dabar toub, 'amer 'aniy ma'asay lamelek; lashouniy, 'aet souper
**a matter good speak of I the things which I have made touching the king my tongue *is* the pen of a writer**

**45:2**
מהיר 4106: יפיפית 3302 מבני 1121 אדם 120 הוצק 3332 חן 2580 בשפתותיך 8193 על 5921 כן 3651 ברכך 1288
mahiyr. yapayapiyta mibney 'adam, hutzaq chen baseptouteyka; 'al ken berakaka
**ready You are fairer than the children of men is poured grace into your lips therefore after that has blessed you**

**45:3** **45:4**
אלהים 430 לעולם 5769: חגור 2296 חרבך 2719 על 5921 ירך 3409 גבור 1368 הודך 1935 והדרך 1926:
'alohiym la'aulam. chagour charbaka 'al yarek gibour; houdaka, uahadareka.
**Elohim for ever Gird your sword upon *your* thigh O *most* mighty *with* your glory and your majesty**

והדרך 1926 צלח 6743 רכב 7392 על 5921 דבר 1697 אמת 571 וענוה 6037 צדק 6664 ותורך 3384
uahadaraka tzalach rakab, 'al dabar 'amet ua'anuah tzedeq; uatouraka
**And in your majesty prosperously ride for because of truth and meekness *and* righteousness shall teach you**

**45:5**
נוראות 3372 ימינך 3225: חציך 2671 שנונים 8150 עמים 5971 תחתיך 8478 יפלו 5307 בלב 3820 אויבי 341
noura'aut yamiyneka. chitzeyka, shanuniym 'amiym tachteyka yiplu; baleb, 'auyabey
**terrible things your right hand Thine arrows *are* sharp *whereby* the people under you fall in the heart of enemies**

**45:6** **45:7**
המלך 4428: כסאך 3678 אלהים 430 עולם 5769 ועד 5703 שבט 7626 מישר 4334 שבט 7626 מלכותך 4438: אהבת 157
hamelek. kis'aka 'alohiym 'aulam ua'ad; shebet miyshor, shebet malakuteka. 'ahabta
**the king's Your throne O Elohim *is* for ever and ever the sceptre *is* a right sceptre your kingdom You love**

צדק 6664 ותשנא 8130 רשע 7562 על 5921 כן 3651 משחך 4886 אלהים 430 אלהיך 430 שמן 8081 ששון 8342
tzedeq uatisna' resha' 'al ken mashachaka 'alohiym 'aloheyka shemen sasoun,
**righteousness and hate wickedness therefore after that has anointed you Elohim your Elohim *with* the oil of gladness**

**45:8**
מחבריך 2270: מר 4753 ואהלות 174 קציעות 7102 כל 3605 בגדתיך 899 מן 4480 היכלי 1964 שן 8127 מני 4482
mechabereyka. mor ua'ahalout qatziy'aut kal bigadoteyka; min heykaley shen miniy
**above your fellows *smell* of myrrh and aloes *an* cassia All your garments out of palaces *the* ivory whereby**

**45:9**
שמחוך 8055: בנות 1323 מלכים 4428 ביקרותיך 3368 נצבה 5324 שגל 7694
simchuka. banout malakiym bayiqrouteyka; nitzbah shegal
**they have made you glad daughters Kings' *were* among your honorable women did stand the queen**

**45:10**
לימינך 3225 בכתם 3800 אופיר 211: שמעי 8085 בת 1323 וראי 7200 והטי 5186 אזנך 241 ושכחי 7911
liymiynaka, baketem 'aupiyr. shim'ay bat uar'ay uahatiy 'azanek; uashikchiy
**upon your right hand in gold of Ophir Hearken O daughter and consider and incline your ear forget also**

**45:11**
עמך 5971 ובית 1004 אביך 1: ויתאו 183 המלך 4428 יפיך 3308 כי 3588 הוא 1931 אדניך 113
'amek, uabeyt 'abiyk. uayit'au hamelek yapayek; kiy hua' 'adonayik,
**your own people and house your father's So shall greatly desire the king your beauty for he *is* your Adonai**

**Ps** 45:1 To the chief Musician upon Sho-shan'-nim, for the sons of Ko'rah, Mas'chil, A Song of loves. My heart is inditing a good matter: I speak of the things which I have made touching the king: my tongue is the pen of a ready writer.2 Thou are fairer than the children of men: grace is poured into your lips: therefore G-d has blessed you forever.3 Gird your sword upon your thigh, O most mighty, with your glory and your majesty.4 And in your majesty ride prosperously because of truth and meekness and righteousness; and your right hand shall teach you terrible things.5 Thine arrows are sharp in the heart of the king's enemies; whereby the people fall under you.6 Thy throne, O G-d, is forever and ever: the sceptre of your kingdom is a right sceptre.7 Thou love righteousness, and hate wickedness: therefore G-d, your G-d, has anointed you with the oil of gladness above your fellows.8 All your garments smell of myrrh, and aloes, and cassia, out of the ivory palaces, whereby they have made you glad.9 Kings' daughters were among your honourable women: upon your right hand did stand the queen in gold of Ophir.10 Hearken, O daughter, and consider, and incline your ear; forget also your own people, and your father's house;11 So shall the king greatly desire your beauty: for he is your Adonai; and worship you him.

| והשתחוי 7812 | לו 3807a: | 45:12 | ובת 1323 | צר 6865 | במנחה 4503 | פניך 6440 | יחלו 2470 |
|---|---|---|---|---|---|---|---|
| uahishtachauiy | lou'. | | uabat | tzor | baminchah | panayik | yachalu, |
| **and worship you** | **him** | | **And the daughter of** | **Tyre** | ***shall be there* with a gift** | **your favor** | **shall intreat** |

| עשירי 6223 | עם 5971: | 45:13 | כל 3605 | כבודה 3520 | בת 1323 | מלך 4428 | פנימה 6441 | ממשבצות 4865 | זהב 2091 |
|---|---|---|---|---|---|---|---|---|---|
| 'ashiyrey | 'am. | | kal | kabudah | bat | melek | paniymah; | mimishbatzout | zahab |
| ***even* the rich among** | **the people** | | ***The is* all** | **glorious** | **daughter** | **king's** | **within** | ***is* of wrought** | **gold** |

| לבושה 3830: | 45:14 | לרקמות 7553 | תובל 2986 | למלך 4428 | בתולות 1330 | אחריה 310 | רעותיה 7464 |
|---|---|---|---|---|---|---|---|
| labushah. | | liraqamout | tubal | lamelek | batulout | 'achareyha | re'ateyha; |
| **her clothing** | | **in raiment of needlework** | **She shall be brought** | **unto the king** | **the virgins** | **that follow her** | **companions** |

| מובאות 935 | לך 3807a: | 45:15 | תובלנה 2986 | בשמחת 8057 | וגיל 1524 | תבאינה 935 | בהיכל 1964 |
|---|---|---|---|---|---|---|---|
| muba'aut | lak. | | tubalnah | bismachot | uagiyl; | tabo'aynah, | baheykal |
| **shall be brought** | **unto you** | | **shall they be brought** | **With gladness** | **and rejoicing** | **they shall enter** | **into palace** |

| מלך 4428: | 45:16 | תחת 8478 | אבתיך 1 | יהיו 1961 | בניך 1121 | תשיתמו 7896 | לשרים 8269 | בכל 3605 | הארץ 776: | 45:17 |
|---|---|---|---|---|---|---|---|---|---|---|
| melek. | | tachat | 'aboteykha | yihayu | baneyka; | tashiytemou | lasariym, | bakal | ha'aretz. | |
| ***the* king's** | | **Instead of** | **your fathers** | **shall be** | **your children** | **whom you may make** | **princes** | **in all** | **the earth** | |

| אזכירה 2142 | שמך 8034 | בכל 3605 | דר 1755 | ודר 1755 | על 5921 | כן 3651 | עמים 5971 | יהודך 3034 |
|---|---|---|---|---|---|---|---|---|
| 'azkiyrah | shimka | bakal | dor | uador; | 'al | ken | 'amiym | yahouduka, |
| **I will make to be remembered** | **your name** | **in all** | **generation** | **and generation** | **therefore** | **after that** | **the people** | **shall praise you** |

| לעלם 5769 | ועד 5703: |
|---|---|
| la'alam | ua'ad. |
| **for ever** | **and ever** |

| Ps 46:1 | למנצח 5329 | לבני 1121 | קרח 7141 | על 5921 | עלמות 5961 | שיר 7892: | אלהים 430 | לנו 3807a | מחסה 4268 | ועז 5797 | עזרה 5833 |
|---|---|---|---|---|---|---|---|---|---|---|---|
| | lamanatzeach | libney | qorach; | 'al | 'alamout | shiyr. | 'alohiym | lanu | machaseh | ua'az; | 'azrah |
| | **To the chief Musician** | **for the sons of** | **Korah** | **upon** | **Alamoth** | **A Song** | **Elohim** | ***is* our** | **refuge** | **and strength** | **help** |

| בצרות 6869 | נמצא 4672 | מאד 3966: | 46:2 | על 5921 | כן 3651 | לא 3808 | נירא 3372 | בהמיר 4171 | ארץ 776 |
|---|---|---|---|---|---|---|---|---|---|
| uatzarout, | nimtza' | ma'ad. | | 'al | ken | la' | niyra' | bahamiyr | 'aretz; |
| **in trouble** | **a present** | **very** | | **Therefore** | **after that** | **not** | **will we fear** | **though be removed** | **the earth** |

| ובמוט 4131 | הרים 2022 | בלב 3820 | ימים 3220: | 46:3 | יהמו 1993 | יחמרו 2560 | מימיו 4325 |
|---|---|---|---|---|---|---|---|
| uabmout | hariym, | baleb | yamiym. | | yehamu | yechmaru | meymayu; |
| **and though be carried** | **the mountains** | **into the midst of** | **the sea** | | ***Though* roar** | ***and* be troubled** | **the waters thereof** |

| ירעשו 7493 | הרים 2022 | בגאותו 1346 | סלה 5542: | 46:4 | נהר 5104 | פלגיו 6388 | ישמחו 8055 |
|---|---|---|---|---|---|---|---|
| yir'ashu | hariym | baga'auatou | selah. | | nahar, | palagayu, | yasamchu |
| **shake** | ***though* the mountains** | **with the swelling thereof** | **Selah** | | ***There is* a river** | **the streams whereof** | **shall make glad** |

| עיר 5892 | אלהים 430 | קדש 6918 | משכני 4908 | עליון 5945: | 46:5 | אלהים 430 | בקרבה 7130 | בל 1077 |
|---|---|---|---|---|---|---|---|---|
| 'ayr | 'alohiym; | qadosh, | mishkaney | 'alyoun. | | 'alohiym | baqirbah | bal |
| **the city of** | **Elohim** | **the holy *place* of** | **the tabernacles of** | **the most High** | | **Elohim *is*** | **in the midst of her** | **not** |

Ps 45:12 And the daughter of Tyre shall be there with a gift; even the rich among the people shall entreat your favor.13 The king's daughter is all glorious within: her clothing is of wrought gold.14 She shall be brought unto the king in raiment of needlework: the virgins her companions that follow her shall be brought unto you.15 With gladness and rejoicing shall they be brought: they shall enter into the king's palace.16 Instead of your fathers shall be your children, whom you may make princes in all the earth.17 I will make your name to be remembered in all generations: therefore shall the people praise you forever and ever. **Ps** 46:1 To the chief Musician for the sons of Ko'-rah, A Song upon Al'-a-moth. G-d is our refuge and strength, a very present help in trouble.2 Therefore will not we fear, though the earth be removed, and though the mountains be carried into the midst of the sea;3 Though the waters thereof roar and be troubled, though the mountains shake with the swelling thereof. Selah.4 There is a river, the streams whereof shall make glad the city of G-d, the holy place of the tabernacles of the most High.5 G-d is in the midst of her; she shall not be moved: G-d shall help her, and that right early.

תמוט 4131 | יעזרה 5826 | אלהים 430 | לפנות 6437 | בקר 1242: | **46:6** | המו 1993 | גוים 1471 | מטו 4131 | ממלכות 4467
timout; ya'azreha 'alohiym, lipnout boqer. hamu gouyim matu mamlakout;
**she shall be moved shall help her Elohim *and that* right early raged The heathen were moved the kingdoms**

נתן 5414 | בקולו 6963 | תמוג 4127 | ארץ 776: | **46:7** | יהוה 3068 | צבאות 6635 | עמנו 5973 | משגב 4869 | לנו 3807a | אלהי 430 | יעקב 3290 | סלה 5542: | **46:8**
natan baqolou, tamug 'aretz. Yahuah tzaba'aut 'amanu; misgab lanu 'alohey ya'aqob selah.
**he uttered his voice melted the earth Yahuah of hosts *is* with us refuge *is* our the Elohim of Jacob Selah**

לכו 1980 | חזו 2372 | מפעלות 4659 | יהוה 3068 | אשר 834 | שם 7760 | שמות 8047 | בארץ 776: | **46:9** | משבית 7673 | מלחמות 4421 | עד 5704
laku chazu mipa'alout Yahuah; 'asher sam shamout ba'aretz. mashbiyt milchamout 'ad
**Come behold the works of Yahuah what he has made desolations in the earth He make to cease wars unto**

קצה 7097 | הארץ 776 | קשת 7198 | ישבר 7665 | וקצץ 7112 | חנית 2595 | עגלות 5699 | ישרף 8313 | באש 784: | **46:10** | הרפו 7503 | ודעו 3045
qatzeh ha'aretz qeshet yashaber uaqitzetz chaniyt; agalout, yisrop ba'aesh. harapu uad'au
**the end of the earth the bow he break and cut in sunder the spear the chariot he burn in the fire Be still and know**

כי 3588 | אנכי 595 | אלהים 430 | ארום 7311 | בגוים 1471 | ארום 7311 | בארץ 776: | **46:11** | יהוה 3068 | צבאות 6635 | עמנו 5973
kiy 'anokiy 'alohiym; 'arum bagouyim, 'arum ba'aretz. Yahuah tzaba'aut 'amanu;
**that I *am* Elohim I will be exalted among the heathen I will be exalted in the earth Yahuah of hosts *is* with us**

משגב 4869 | לנו 3807a | אלהי 430 | יעקב 3290 | סלה 5542:
misgab lanu 'alohey ya'aqob selah.
**refuge *is* our the Elohim of Jacob Selah**

**Ps 47:1** | למנצח 5329 | לבני 1121 | קרח 7141 | מזמור 4210: | כל 3605 | העמים 5971 | תקעו 8628 | כף 3709 | הריעו 7321 | לאלהים 430
lamanatzeach libney qorach mizmour. kal ha'amiym tiq'au kap; hariy'au le'alohiym,
**To the chief Musician for the sons of Korah A Psalm all you people O clap your hands shout unto Elohim**

בקול 6963 | רנה 7440: | **47:2** | כי 3588 | יהוה 3068 | עליון 5945 | נורא 3372 | מלך 4428 | גדול 1419 | על 5921 | כל 3605 | הארץ 776: | **47:3**
baqoul rinah. kiy Yahuah 'alyoun noura'; melek gadoul 'al kal ha'aretz.
**with the voice of triumph For Yahuah most high *is* terrible *he is* a King great over all the earth**

ידבר 1696 | עמים 5971 | תחתינו 8478 | ולאמים 3816 | תחת 8478 | רגלינו 7272: | **47:4** | יבחר 977 | לנו 3807a | את 853 | נחלתנו 5159
yadber 'amiym tachteynu; uala'amiym, tachat ragleynu. yibchar lanu 'at nachalatenu;
**He shall subdue the people under us and the nations under our feet He shall choose for us our inheritance**

את 853 | גאון 1347 | יעקב 3290 | אשר 834 | אהב 157 | סלה 5542: | **47:5** | עלה 5927 | אלהים 430 | בתרועה 8643 | יהוה 3068 | בקול 6963
'at ga'aun ya'aqob 'asher 'aheb selah. 'alah 'alohiym bitaru'ah; Yahuah baqoul
**the excellency of Jacob whom he loved Selah is gone up Elohim with a shout Yahuah with the sound of**

שופר 7782: | **47:6** | זמרו 2167 | אלהים 430 | זמרו 2167 | זמרו 2167 | למלכנו 4428 | זמרו 2167: | **47:7** | כי 3588 | מלך 4428 | כל 3605
shoupar. zamru 'alohiym zameru; zamru lamalkenu zameru. kiy melek kal
**a trumpet Sing praises to Elohim sing praises sing praises unto our King sing praises For *is* the King of all**

הארץ 776 | אלהים 430 | זמרו 2167 | משכיל 7919: | **47:8** | מלך 4427 | אלהים 430 | על 5921 | גוים 1471 | אלהים 430 | ישב 3427 | על 5921
ha'aretz 'alohiym, zamru maskiyl. malak 'alohiym 'al gouyim; 'alohiym, yashab 'al
**the earth Elohim sing you praises with understanding reigns Elohim over the heathen Elohim sit upon**

Ps 47:6 The heathen raged, the kingdoms were moved: he uttered his voice, the earth melted.7 YHUH of hosts is with us; the G-d of Jacob is our refuge. Selah.8 Come, behold the works of YHUH, what desolations he has made in the earth.9 He make wars to cease unto the end of the earth; he breaketh the bow, and cutteth the spear in sunder; he burneth the chariot in the fire.10 Be still, and know that I am G-d: I will be exalted among the heathen, I will be exalted in the earth.11 YHUH of hosts is with us; the G-d of Jacob is our refuge. Selah. **Ps** 47:1 To the chief Musician, A Psalm for the sons of Ko'-rah. O clap your hands, all you people; shout unto G-d with the voice of triumph.2 For YHUH most high is terrible; he is a great King over all the earth.3 He shall subdue the people under us, and the nations under our feet.4 He shall choose our inheritance for us, the excellency of Jacob whom he loved. Selah.5 G-d is gone up with a shout, YHUH with the sound of a trumpet.6 Sing praises to G-d, sing praises: sing praises unto our King, sing praises.7 For G-d is the King of all the earth: sing you praises with understanding.8 G-d reigned over the heathen: G-d sitteth upon the throne of his holiness.

כסא 3678 קדשו 6944: **47:9** נדיבי 5081 עמים 5971 נאספו 622 עם 5971 אלהי 430 אברהם 85
kisea' qadashou. nadiybey 'amiym ne'asapu, 'am 'alohey 'abraham
**the throne of his holiness The princes of the people are gathered together *even* the people of the Elohim of Abraham**

כי 3588 לאלהים 430 מגני 4043 ארץ 776 מאד 3966 נעלה 5927:
kiy le'alohiym maginey 'aretz, ma'ad na'alah.
**for *belong* unto Elohim the shields of the earth greatly he is exalted**

**Ps 48:1** שיר 7892 מזמור 4210 לבני 1121 קרח 7141: גדול 1419 יהוה 3068 ומהלל 1984 מאד 3966 בעיר 5892 אלהינו 430
shiyr mizmour libney qorach. gadoul Yahuah uamahulal ma'ad; ba'ayr 'aloheynu,
**A Song *and* Psalm for the sons of Korah Great *is* Yahuah and to be praised greatly in the city of our Elohim**

הר 2022 קדשו 6944: **48:2** יפה 3303 נוף 5131 משוש 4885 כל 3605 הארץ 776 הר 2022 ציון 6726 ירכתי 3411
har qadashou. yapeh noup masous kal ha'aretz har tziyoun yarkatey
***in* the mountain of his holiness Beautiful for situation the joy of whole the earth *is* mount Zion *on* the sides of**

צפון 6828 קרית 7151 מלך 4428 רב 7227: **48:3** אלהים 430 בארמנותיה 759 נודע 3045 למשגב 4869: **48:4** כי 3588 הנה 2009 המלכים 4428
tzapoun; qiryat, melek rab. 'alohiym ba'armanouteyha, nouda' lamisgab. kiy hineh hamalakiym
**the north the city of King *the* great Elohim in her palaces is known for a refuge For lo the kings**

נועדו 3259 עברו 5674 יחדו 3162: **48:5** המה 1992 ראו 7200 כן 3651 תמהו 8539 נבהלו 926
nou'adu; 'abaru yachdau. hemah ra'au ken tamahu; nibhalu
**were assembled they passed by together They saw *it and* so they marvelled they were troubled**

נחפזו 2648: **48:6** רעדה 7461 אחזתם 270 שם 8033 חיל 2427 כיולדה 3205: **48:7** ברוח 7307 קדים 6921
nechapazu. ra'adah 'achazatam sham; chiyl, kayouledah. baruach qadiym;
***and* hasted away Fear took hold upon them there *and* pain as of a woman in travail with an wind east**

תשבר 7665 אניות 591 תרשיש 8659: **48:8** כאשר 834 שמענו 8085 כן 3651 ראינו 7200 בעיר 5892 יהוה 3068 צבאות 6635
tashaber, aniyout tarshiysh. ka'asher shama'anu ken ra'aynu, ba'ayr Yahuah tzaba'aut
**You breakest the ships of Tarshish As we have heard so have we seen in the city of Yahuah of hosts**

בעיר 5892 אלהינו 430 אלהים 430 יכוננה 3559 עד 5704 עולם 5769 סלה 5542: **48:9** דמינו 1819 אלהים 430
ba'ayr 'aloheynu; 'alohiym yakounaneha 'ad 'aulam selah. dimiynu 'alohiym
**in the city of our Elohim Elohim will establish it for ever Selah We have thought O Elohim**

חסדך 2617 בקרב 7130 היכלך 1964: **48:10** כשמך 8034 אלהים 430 כן 3651 תהלתך 8416 על 5921
chasadeka; baqereb, heykaleka. kashimaka 'alohiym, ken tahilataka 'al
***of* your lovingkindness in the midst of your temple According to your name O Elohim so *is* your praise unto**

קצוי 7099 ארץ 776 צדק 6664 מלאה 4390 ימינך 3225: **48:11** ישמח 8055 הר 2022 ציון 6726 תגלנה 1523 בנות 1323
qatzuey 'aretz; tzedeq, mal'ah yamiyneka. yismach har tziyoun, tagelanah banout
**the ends of the earth righteousness is full of your right hand Let rejoice mount Zion let be glad the daughters of**

יהודה 3063 למען 4616 משפטיך 4941: **48:12** סבו 5437 ציון 6726 והקיפוה 5362 ספרו 5608 מגדליה 4026:
yahudah; lama'an, mishpateyka. sobu tziyoun uahaqiypuha; sipru, migdaleyha.
**Judah because of your judgments Walk about Zion and go round about her tell the towers thereof**

Ps 47:9 The princes of the people are gathered together, even the people of the G-d of Abraham: for the shields of the earth belong unto G-d: he is greatly exalted. **Ps** 48:1 A Song and Psalm for the sons of Ko'-rah. Great is YHUH, and greatly to be praised in the city of our G-d, in the mountain of his holiness.2 Beautiful for situation, the joy of the whole earth, is mount Zion, on the sides of the north, the city of the great King.3 G-d is known in her palaces for a refuge.4 For, lo, the kings were assembled, they passed by together.5 They saw it, and so they marvelled; they were troubled, and hasted away.6 Fear took hold upon them there, and pain, as of a woman in travail.7 Thou breakest the ships of Tarshish with an east wind.8 As we have heard, so have we seen in the city of YHUH of hosts, in the city of our G-d: G-d will establish it forever. Selah.9 We have thought of your lovingkindness, O G-d, in the midst of your temple.10 According to your name, O G-d, so is your praise unto the ends of the earth: your right hand is full of righteousness.11 Let mount Zion rejoice, let the daughters of Judah be glad, because of your judgments.12 Walk about Zion, and go round about her: tell the towers thereof.

**48:13** **48:14**
שיתו 7896 לבכם 3820 לחילה 2430 פסגו 6448 ארמנותיה 759 למען 4616 תספרו 5608 לדור 1755 אחרון 314:
shiytu libakem lacheylah, pasgu armanouteyha; lama'an tasapru, ladour 'acharoun.
**Mark you well her bulwarks consider her palaces that you may tell *it* to the generation following**

כי 3588 זה 2088 אלהים 430 אלהינו 430 עולם 5769 ועד 5703 הוא 1931 ינהגנו 5090 על 5921 מות 4192:
kiy zeh 'alohiym 'aloheynu 'aulam ua'ad; hua' yanahagenu 'al mut.
**For this Elohim *is* our Elohim for ever and ever he will be our guide *even* unto death**

**Ps 49:1**
למנצח 5329 לבני 1121 קרח 7141 מזמור 4210: שמעו 8085 זאת 2063 כל 3605 העמים 5971 האזינו 238 כל 3605
lamanatzeach libney qorach mizmour. shim'au za't kal ha'amiym; ha'aziynu, kal
**To the chief Musician for the sons of Korah A Psalm Hear this all *you* people give ear all**

**49:2** **49:3**
ישבי 3427 חלד 2465: גם 1571 בני 1121 אדם 120 גם 1571 בני 1121 איש 376 יחד 3162 עשיר 6223 ואביון 34: פי 6310
yoshabey chaled. gam baney 'adam gam baney 'aysh; yachad, 'ashiyr ua'abyoun. piy
***you* inhabitants of the world Both sons of man both sons of high together rich and poor My mouth**

**49:4**
ידבר 1696 חכמות 2454 והגות 1900 לבי 3820 תבונות 8394: אטה 5186 למשל 4912 אזני 241
yadaber chakmout; uahagut libiy tabunout. 'ateh lamashal 'azaniy;
**shall speak of wisdom and the meditation of my heart *shall be* of understanding I will incline to a parable mine ear**

**49:5**
אפתח 6605 בכנור 3658 חידתי 2420: למה 4100 אירא 3372 בימי 3117 רע 7451 עון 5771 עקבי 6120
'aptach bakinour, chiydatiy. lamah 'ayra' biymey ra'; 'auon 'aqebay
**I will open upon the harp my dark saying Wherefore should I fear in the days of evil *when* the iniquity of my heels**

**49:6** **49:7**
יסובני 5437: הבטחים 982 על 5921 חילם 2428 וברב 7230 עשרם 6239 יתהללו 1984:
yasubeniy. habotachiym 'al cheylam; uabrob 'asharam, yitahalalu.
**shall compass me about? They that trust in their wealth and in the multitude of their riches boast themselves**

**49:8**
אח 251 לא 3808 פדה 6299 יפדה 6299 איש 376 לא 3808 יתן 5414 לאלהים 430 כפרו 3724: ויקר 3365
'ach, la' padoh yipdeh 'aysh; la' yiten le'alohiym kaparou. uayeqar
**his brother None *of them* can by any means redeem man nor give to Elohim a ransom for him For precious**

**49:9**
פדיון 6306 נפשם 5315 וחדל 2308 לעולם 5769: ויחי 2421 עוד 5750 לנצח 5331 לא 3808 יראה 7200
pidyon napsham, uachadal la'aulam. uiychiy 'aud lanetzach; la' yir'ah
**the redemption of their soul *is* and it cease for ever That he should live still for ever *and* not see**

**49:10**
השחת 7845: כי 3588 יראה 7200 חכמים 2450 ימותו 4191 יחד 3162 כסיל 3684 ובער 1198 יאבדו 6 ועזבו 5800
hashachat. kiy yir'ah chakamiym yamutu, yachad kasiyl uaba'ar ya'bedu; ua'azabu
**corruption For he see *that* wise men die likewise the fool and the brutish person perish and leave**

**49:11**
לאחרים 312 חילם 2428: קרבם 7130 בתימו 1004 לעולם 5769 משכנתם 4908
la'acheriym cheylam. qirbam bateymou la'aulam, mishkanotam
**to others their wealth Their inward thought *is that* their houses *shall continue* for ever *and* their dwelling places**

**49:12**
לדר 1755 ודר 1755 קראו 7121 בשמותם 8034 עלי 5921 אדמות 127: ואדם 120 ביקר 3366 בל 1077
lador uador; qara'au bishmoutam, 'aley adamout. ua'adam biyqar bal
**to all generations they call after their own names. *their* on lands Nevertheless man *being* in honor not**

Ps 49:13 Mark you well her bulwarks, consider her palaces; that you may tell it to the generation following.14 For this G-d is our G-d forever and ever: he will be our guide even unto death. **Ps** 49:1 To the chief Musician, A Psalm for the sons of Ko'-rah. Hear this, all you people; give ear, all you inhabitants of the world:2 Both low and high, rich and poor, together.3 My mouth shall speak of wisdom; and the meditation of my heart shall be of understanding.4 I will incline mine ear to a parable: I will open my dark saying upon the harp.5 Wherefore should I fear in the days of evil, when the iniquity of my heels shall compass me about?6 They that trust in their wealth, and boast themselves in the multitude of their riches;7 None of them can by any means redeem his brother, nor give to G-d a ransom for him:8(For the redemption of their soul is precious, and it ceaseth forever:)9 That he should still live forever, and not see corruption.10 For he see that wise men die, likewise the fool and the brutish person perish, and leave their wealth to others.11 Their inward thought is, that their houses shall continue forever, and their dwelling places to all generations; they call their lands after their own names. 12 Nevertheless man being in honor abideth not: he is like the beasts that perish.

49:13
ילין 3885 נמשל 4911 כבהמות 929 נדמו 1820: זה 2088 דרכם 1870 כסל 6389 למו 3807a ואחריהם 310 בפיהם 6310 ירצו 7521
yaliyn; nimshal kabahemout nidmu. zeh darkam kesel lamou; ua'achareyhem bapiyhem yirtzu
**abide he is like the beasts *that* perish This their way folly *is* their yet their posterity their sayings approve**

49:14
סלה 5542: כצאן 6629 לשאול 7585 שתו 8371 מות 4194 ירעם 7462 וירדו 7287 בם 871a
selah. katza'n lisha'aul shatu mauet yir'aem uayirdu bam
**Selah Like sheep in the grave they are laid death shall feed on them and shall have dominion over them**

49:15
ישרים 3477 לבקר 1242 וצירם 6736 לבלות 1086 שאול 7585 מזבל 2073 לו 3807a: אך 389 אלהים 430
yashariym laboqer, uatziyram labalout sha'aul, mizabul lou'. 'ak 'alohiym,
**the upright in the morning and their beauty *shall* consume in the grave from dwelling their But Elohim**

49:16
יפדה 6299 נפשי 5315 מיד 3027 שאול 7585 כי 3588 יקחני 3847 סלה 5542: אל 408 תירא 3372 כי 3588
yipdeh napshiy miyad sha'aul; kiy yiqacheniy selah. 'al tiyraa' kiy
**will redeem my soul from the power of the grave for he shall receive me Selah not Be you afraid when**

49:17
יעשר 6238 איש 376 כי 3588 ירבה 7235 כבוד 3519 ביתו 1004: כי 3588 לא 3808 במותו 4194 יקח 3947 הכל 3605
ya'ashir 'aysh; kiy yirbeh kaboud beytou. kiy la' bamoutou yiqach hakol;
**is made rich one when is increased the glory of his house For nothing when he die he shall carry away nothing**

49:18
לא 3808 ירד 3381 אחריו 310 כבודו 3519: כי 3588 נפשו 5315 בחייו 2416 יברך 1288 ויודך 3034 כי 3588
la' yered 'acharayu kaboudou. kiy napshou bachayayu yabarek; uayoudua, kiy
**not shall descend after him his glory Though his soul while he lived he blessed and *men* will praise you when**

49:19
תיטיב 3190 לך 3807a: תבוא 935 עד 5704 דור 1755 אבותיו 1 עד 5704 נצח 5331 לא 3808 יראו 7200
teytiyb lak. tabou'a 'ad dour aboutayu; 'ad netzach, la' yir'au
**you do well to yourself He shall go to the generation of his fathers to ever not they shall see**

49:20
אור 216: אדם 120 ביקר 3366 ולא 3808 יבין 995 נמשל 4911 כבהמות 929 נדמו 1820:
'aur. 'adam biyqar uala' yabiyn; nimshal kabahemout nidmu.
**light man *that is* in honor and not understands is like the beasts *that* perish**

**Ps 50:1**
מזמור 4210 לאסף 623 אל 410 אלהים 430 יהוה 3068 דבר 1696 ויקרא 7121 ארץ 776 ממזרח 4217 שמש 8121
mizmour, la'asap 'ael 'alohiym Yahuah diber uayiqra' 'aretz; mimizrach, shemesh
**A Psalm of Asaph El The mighty *even* Yahuah has spoken and called the earth from the rising of the sun**

50:2 50:3
עד 5704 מבאו 3996: מציון 6726 מכלל 4359 יפי 3308 אלהים 430 הופיע 3313: יבא 935 אלהינו 430
'ad mabo'au. mitziyoun miklal yopiy, 'alohiym houpiya'. yaba' 'aloheynu,
**unto the going down thereof Out of Zion the perfection of beauty Elohim has shined shall come Our Elohim**

50:4
ואל 408 יחרש 2790 אש 784 לפניו 6440 תאכל 398 וסביביו 5439 נשערה 8175 מאד 3966:
ua'al yecharash 'aesh lapanayu ta'kel; uasbiybayu, nis'arah ma'ad.
**and not shall keep silence a fire before him shall devour and round about him it shall be tempestuous very**

50:5
יקרא 7121 אל 413 השמים 8064 מעל 5920 ואל 413 הארץ 776 לדין 1777 עמו 5971: אספו 622 לי 3807a
yiqra' 'al hashamayim me'al; ua'al ha'aretz, ladiyn 'amou. 'aspu liy
**He shall call to the heavens from above and to the earth that he may judge his people Gather together unto me**

Ps 49:13 This their way is their folly: yet their posterity approve their sayings. Selah.14 Like sheep they are laid in the grave; death shall feed on them; and the upright shall have dominion over them in the morning; and their beauty shall consume in the grave from their dwelling.15 But G-d will redeem my soul from the power of the grave: for he shall receive me. Selah.16 Be not you afraid when one is made rich, when the glory of his house is increased;17 For when he die he shall carry nothing away: his glory shall not descend after him.18 Though while he lived he blessed his soul: and men will praise you, when you does well to thyself.19 He shall go to the generation of his fathers; they shall never see light.20 Man that is in honor, and understandeth not, is like the beasts that perish. **Ps** 50:1 A Psalm of A'-saph. The mighty G-d, even YHUH, has spoken, and called the earth from the rising of the sun unto the going down thereof.2 Out of Zion, the perfection of beauty, G-d has shined.3 Our G-d shall come, and shall not keep silence: a fire shall devour before him, and it shall be very tempestuous round about him.4 He shall call to the heavens from above, and to the earth, that he may judge his people.5 Gather my saints together unto me; those that have made a covenant with me by sacrifice.

חסידי 2623 כרתי 3772 בריתי 1285 עלי 5921 זבח 2077: 50:6 ויגידו 5046 שמים 8064 צדקו 6664
chasiyday; koratey bariytiy 'aley zabach. uayagiydu shamayim tzidqou;
**my saints those that have made a covenant with me by sacrifice And shall declare the heavens his righteousness**

כי 3588 אלהים 430 שפט 8199 הוא 1931 סלה 5542: 50:7 שמעה 8085 עמי 5971 ואדברה 1696 ישראל 3478 ואעידה 5749 בך 871a
kiy 'alohiym shopet hua' selah. shim'ah 'amiy ua'adaberah, yisra'ael ua'a'aydah bak;
**for Elohim *is* judge himself Selah Hear O my people and I will speak O Israel and I will testify against you**

אלהים 430 אלהיך 430 אנכי 595: 50:8 לא 3808 על 5921 זבחיך 2077 אוכיחך 3198 ועולתיך 5930 לנגדי 5048
'alohiym 'aloheyka 'anokiy. la' 'al zabacheyka 'awkiycheka; ua'auloteyka lanegdiy
***am* Elohim *even* your Elohim I not for your sacrifices I will reprove you or your burnt offerings before me**

תמיד 8548: 50:9 לא 3808 אקח 3947 מביתך 1004 פר 6499 ממכלאתיך 4356 עתודים 6260: 50:10 כי 3588 לי 3807a
tamiyd. la' 'aqach mibeytaka par; mimikla'ateyka, 'atudiym. kiy liy
***to have been* continually no I will take out of your house bullock out of your folds *nor* he goats For *is* mine**

כל 3605 חיתו 2416 יער 3293 בהמות 929 בהררי 2042 אלף 505: 50:11 ידעתי 3045 כל 3605 עוף 5775 הרים 2022
kal chaytou ya'ar; bahemout, baharrey 'alep. yada'tiy kal 'aup hariym;
**every beast of the forest *and* the cattle upon a hills thousand I know all the fowls of the mountains**

וזיז 2123 שדי 7704 עמדי 5978: 50:12 אם 518 ארעב 7456 לא 3808 אמר 559 לך 3807a כי 3588 לי 3807a תבל 8398
uaziyz shaday, 'amadiy. 'am 'ar'ab la' 'amar lak; kiy liy tebel,
**and the wild beasts of the field *are* mine If I were hungry not I would tell to you for *is* mine the world**

ומלאה 4393: 50:13 האוכל 398 בשר 1320 אבירים 47 ודם 1818 עתודים 6260 אשתה 8354: 50:14 זבח 2076 לאלהים 430
uamlo'ah. ha'aukal basar 'abiyriym; uadam 'atudiym 'ashteh. zabach le'alohiym
**and the fulness thereof Will I eat the flesh of bulls or the blood of goats? drink Offer unto Elohim**

תודה 8426 ושלם 7999 לעליון 5954 נדריך 5088: 50:15 וקראני 7121 ביום 3117 צרה 6869 אחלצך 2502
toudah; uashalem la'alyoun nadareyka. uaqra'aeniy bayoum tzarah; 'achaletzaka,
**thanksgiving and pay unto the most High your vows And call upon me in the day of trouble I will deliver you**

ותכבדני 3513: 50:16 ולרשע 7563 אמר 559 אלהים 430 מה 4100 לך 3807a לספר 5608 חקי 2706
uatkabdeniy. ualarasha' 'amar 'alohiym, mah laka lasaper chuqay;
**and you shall glorify me But unto the wicked saith Elohim What *have* to you *to do* to declare my statutes**

ותשא 5375 בריתי 1285 עלי 5921 פיך 6310: 50:17 ואתה 859 שנאת 8130 מוסר 4148 ותשלך 7993 דברי 1697
uatisa' bariytiy 'aley piyka. ua'atah sanea'ta musar; uatashlek dabaray
**or *that* you should take my covenant in your mouth? Seeing you hate instruction and cast my words**

אחריך 310: 50:18 אם 518 ראית 7200 גנב 1590 ותרץ 7521 עמו 5973 ועם 5973 מנאפים 5003 חלקך 2506: 50:19
'achareyka. 'am ra'ayta ganab uatiretz 'amou; ua'am mana'apiym chelqeka.
**behind you When you saw a thief then you consentedst with him and with adulterers *have been* partaker**

פיך 6310 שלחת 7971 ברעה 7451 ולשונך 3956 תצמיד 6775 מרמה 4820: 50:20 תשב 3427 באחיך 251 תדבר 1696 בבן 1121
piyka shalachta bara'ah; ualshounaka, tatzmiyd mirmah. tesheb ba'achiyka tadaber; baben
**your mouth You give to evil and your tongue frameth deceit You sit against your brother *and* speak son**

Ps 50:6 And the heavens shall declare his righteousness: for G-d is judge himself. Selah.7 Hear, O my people, and I will speak; O Israel, and I will testify against you: I am G-d, even your G-d.8 I will not reprove you for your sacrifices or your burnt offerings, to have been continually before me.9 I will take no bullock out of your house, nor he goats out of your folds.10 For every beast of the forest is mine, and the cattle upon a thousand hills.11 I know all the fowls of the mountains: and the wild beasts of the field are mine.12 If I were hungry, I would not tell you: for the world is mine, and the fulness thereof.13 Will I eat the flesh of bulls, or drink the blood of goats?14 Offer unto G-d thanksgiving; and pay your vows unto the most High:15 And call upon me in the day of trouble: I will deliver you, and you shall glorify me.16 But unto the wicked G-d saith, What have you to do to declare my statutes, or that you should take my covenant in your mouth?17 Seeing you hate instruction, and castest my words behind you.18 When you saw a thief, then you consentedst with him, and have been partaker with adulterers.19 Thou givest your mouth to evil, and your tongue frameth deceit.20 Thou sittest and speak against your brother; you slanderest your own mother's son.

50:21

אמך 517 תתן 5414 דפי 1848: אלה 428 עשית 6213 והחרשתי 2790 דמית 1819 היות 1961 אהיה 1961
'amaka, titen dopiy. 'aeleh 'ashiyta uahecharashtiy, dimiyta, heyout 'ahayeh
**your own mother's you slander These *things* have you done and I kept silence you thought that I was altogether**

50:22

כמוך 3644 אוכיחך 3198 ואערכה 6186 לעיניך 5869: בינו 995 נא 4994 זאת 2063
kamouka; 'aukiychaka ua'a'arkah la'aeyneyka. biynu naa' za't
***such an one* as yourself *but* I will reprove you and set *them* in order before your eyes consider Now this**

50:23

שכחי 7911 אלוה 433 פן 6435 אטרף 2963 ואין 369 מציל 5337: זבח 2076 תודה 8426 יכבדנני 3513
shokachey 'alouah; pen 'atrop, ua'aeyn matziyl. zobeach toudah, yakabdananiy
**you that forget Elohim lest I tear *you* in pieces and *there be* none to deliver Whoso offer praise glorify me**

ושם 7760 דרך 1870 אראנו 7200 בישע 3468 אלהים 430:
uasam derek; 'ar'anu, bayesha' 'alohiym.
**and to him that order *his* conversation *aright* will I show the salvation of Elohim**

Ps 51:1

למנצח 5329 מזמור 4210 לדוד 1732: בבוא 935 אליו 413 נתן 5416 הנביא 5030 כאשר 834 בא 935 אל 413
lamanatzeach, mizmour ladauid. babou'a 'aelayu natan hanabiy'a; ka'asher ba', 'al
**To the chief Musician A Psalm of David when came unto him Nathan the prophet after he had gone in to**

בת 1339 שבע 7651: חנני 2603 אלהים 430 כחסדך 2617 כרב 7230
bat shaba'. chaneniy 'alohiym kachasdeka; karob
**Bath sheba Have mercy upon me O Elohim according to your lovingkindness according unto the multitude of**

51:2

רחמיך 7356 מחה 4229 פשעי 6588: הרבה 7235 כבסני 3526 מעוני 5771 ומחטאתי 2403
rachameyka, macheh pasha'ay. harbeh kabaseniy me'auoniy; uamechata'tiy
**your tender mercies blot out my transgressions throughly Wash me from mine iniquity and from my sin**

51:3 51:4

טהרני 2891: כי 3588 פשעי 6588 אני 589 אדע 3045 וחטאתי 2403 נגדי 5048 תמיד 8548: לך 3807a לבדך 905
tahareniy. kiy pasha'ay 'aniy 'aeda; uachata'tiy negdiy tamiyd. laka labadaka
**cleanse me For my transgressions I acknowledge and my sin before me *is* ever Against you you only**

חטאתי 2398 והרע 7451 בעיניך 5869 עשיתי 6213 למען 4616 תצדק 6663 בדברך 1696 תזכה 2135
chata'tiy uahara' ba'aeyneyka, 'asiytiy lama'an titzdaq badabareka, tizkeh
**have I sinned and evil in your sight done *this* that you might be justified when you speak *and* be clear**

51:5 51:6

בשפטך 8199: הן 2005 בעוון 5771 חוללתי 2342 ובחטא 2399 יחמתני 3179 אמי 517: הן 2005 אמת 571 חפצת 2654
bashapateka. hen ba'auoun choulalatiy; uabchet'a, yechamatniy 'amiy. hen 'amet chapatzta
**when you judge Behold in iniquity I was shapen and in sin did conceive me my mother Behold truth you desirest**

51:7

בטחות 2910 ובסתם 5640 חכמה 2451 תודיעני 3045: תחטאני 2398 באזוב 231
batuchout; uabsatum, chakamah toudiy'aeniy. tachat'aeniy ba'aezoub
**in the inward parts and in the hidden wisdom *part* you shall make me to know Purge me with hyssop**

51:8

ואטהר 2891 תכבסני 3526 ומשלג 7950 אלבין 3835: תשמיעני 8085 ששון 8342 ושמחה 8057 תגלנה 1523
ua'athar; takabseniy, uamisheleg 'albiyn. tashmiy'aeniy sasoun uasimchah; tagelanah,
**and I shall be clean wash me and than snow I shall be whiter Make me to hear joy and gladness may rejoice**

Ps 50:21 These things have you done, and I kept silence; you thoughtest that I was altogether such an one as thyself: but I will reprove you, and set them in order before your eyes.22 Now consider this, you that forget G-d, lest I tear you in pieces, and there be none to deliver.23 Whoso offereth praise glorifieth me: and to him that ordereth his conversation aright will I show the salvation of G-d. **Ps** 51:1 To the chief Musician, A Psalm of David, when Nathan the prophet came unto him, after he had gone in to Bath-she'-ba Have mercy upon me, O G-d, according to your lovingkindness: according unto the multitude of your tender mercies blot out my transgressions.2 Wash me throughly from mine iniquity, and cleanse me from my sin.3 For I acknowledge my transgressions: and my sin is ever before me.4 Against you, you only, have I sinned, and done this evil in your sight: that you might be justified when you speak, and be clear when you judgest.5 Behold, I was shapen in iniquity; and in sin did my mother conceive me.6 Behold, you desirest truth in the inward parts: and in the hidden part you shall make me to know wisdom.7 Purge me with hyssop, and I shall be clean: wash me, and I shall be whiter than snow.8 Make me to hear joy and gladness; that the bones which you have broken may rejoice.

51:9 ... 51:10

עצמות 6106 דכית 1794: הסתר 5641 פניך 6440 מחטאי 2399 וכל 3605 עונתי 5771 מחה 4229: לב 3820
'atzmout dikiyta. hasater paneyka mechata'ay; uakal 'auonotay macheh. leb
***that*** **the bones** ***which*** **you have broken Hide your face from my sins and all mine iniquities blot out a heart**

51:11

טהור 2889 ברא 1254 לי 3807a אלהים 430 ורוח 7307 נכון 3559 חדש 2318 בקרבי 7130: אל 408 תשליכני 7993 מלפניך 6440
tahour bara' liy 'alohiym; uaruach nakoun, chadesh baqirbiy. 'al tashliykeniy milpaneyka;
**clean Create in me O Elohim and a spirit right renew within me not Cast me away from your presence**

51:12

ורוח 7307 קדשך 6944 אל 408 תקח 3947 ממני 4480: השיבה 7725 לי 3807a ששון 8342 ישעך 3468 ורוח 7307 נדיבה 5081
uaruach qadashaka 'al tiqach mimeniy. hashiybah liy sasoun yish'aka; uaruach nadiybah
**and spirit your holy not take from me Restore unto me the joy of your salvation and spirit** ***with your*** **free**

51:13 ... 51:14

תסמכני 5564: אלמדה 3925 פשעים 6586 דרכיך 1870 וחטאים 2400 אליך 413 ישובו 7725: הצילני 5337
tismakeniy. 'alamdah posha'aym darakeyka; uachata'aym, 'aeleyka yashubu. hatziyleniy
**uphold me** ***Then*** **will I teach transgressors your ways and sinners unto you shall be converted Deliver me**

51:15

מדמים 1818 אלהים 430 אלהי 430 תשועתי 8668 תרנן 7442 לשוני 3956 צדקתך 6666:
midamiym 'alohiym, 'alohey tashu'atiy; taranen lashouniy, tzidqateka.
**from bloodguiltiness O Elohim you Elohim of my salvation shall sing aloud** ***and*** **my tongue** ***of*** **your righteousness**

51:16

אדני 136 שפתי 8193 תפתח 6605 ופי 6310 יגיד 5046 תהלתך 8416: כי 3588 לא 3808 תחפץ 2654 זבח 2077
'adonay sapatay tiptach; uapiy, yagiyd tahilateka. kiy la' tachapotz zebach
**O Adonai my lips open you and my mouth shall show forth your praise For not you desirest sacrifice**

51:17

ואתנה 5414 עולה 5930 לא 3808 תרצה 7521: זבחי 2077 אלהים 430 רוח 7307 נשברה 7665 לב 3820 נשבר 7665
ua'atenah; aulah, la' tirtzeh. zibchey 'alohiym ruach nishbarah leb nishbar
**else would I give** ***it in*** **burnt offering not you delight The sacrifices of Elohim spirit** ***are*** **a broken a heart broken**

51:18

ונדכה 1794 אלהים 430 לא 3808 תבזה 959: היטיבה 3190 ברצונך 7522 את 853 ציון 6726 תבנה 1129
uanidkeh; 'alohiym, la' tibzeh. heytiybah birtzounaka 'at tziyoun; tibneh,
**and a contrite O Elohim not you will despise Do good in your good pleasure** ***unto*** **Zion build you**

51:19

חומות 2346 ירושלם 3389: אז 227 תחפץ 2654 זבחי 2077 צדק 6664 עולה 5930
choumout yarushalaim. 'az tachapotz zibchey tzedeq aulah
**the walls of Jerusalem Then shall you be pleased with the sacrifices of righteousness** ***with*** **burnt offering**

וכליל 3632 אז 227 יעלו 5927 על 5921 מזבחך 4196 פרים 6499:
uachaliyl; 'az ya'alu 'al mizbachaka pariym.
**and whole burnt offering then shall they offer upon your altar bullocks**

Ps 52:1

למנצח 5329 משכיל 4905 לדוד 1732: בבוא 935 דואג 1673 האדמי 130 ויגד 5046 לשאול 7586 ויאמר 559
lamanatzeach, maskiyl ladauid. babou'a do'aeg ha'adomiy uayaged lasha'aul uaya'mer
**To the chief Musician Maschil** ***A Psalm*** **of David when came Doeg the Edomite and told Saul and said**

לו 3807a בא 935 דוד 1732 אל 413 בית 1004 אחימלך 288: מה 4100 תתהלל 1984 ברעה 7451 הגבור 1368
lou'; ba' dauid, 'al beyt 'achiymelek. mah tithalel bara'ah hagibour;
**unto him is come David to the house of Ahimelek Why boast you yourself in mischief O mighty man?**

Ps 51:9 Hide your face from my sins, and blot out all mine iniquities.10 Create in me a clean heart, O G-d; and renew a right spirit within me.11 Cast me not away from your presence; and take not your holy spirit from me.12 Restore unto me the joy of your salvation; and uphold me with your free spirit.13 Then will I teach transgressors your ways; and sinners shall be converted unto you.14 Deliver me from bloodguiltiness, O G-d, you G-d of my salvation: and my tongue shall sing aloud of your righteousness.15 O Adonai, open you my lips; and my mouth shall show forth your praise.16 For you desirest not sacrifice; else would I give it: you delightest not in burnt offering.17 The sacrifices of G-d are a broken spirit: a broken and a contrite heart, O G-d, you will not despise.18 Do good in your good pleasure unto Zion: build you the walls of Jerusalem.19 Then shall you be pleased with the sacrifices of righteousness, with burnt offering and whole burnt offering: then shall they offer bullocks upon your altar. **Ps** 52:1 To the chief Musician, Mas'-chil, A Psalm of David, when Do'-eg the E'dom-ite came and told Saul, and said unto him, David is come to the house of A'him'-e-lech. Why boastest you thyself in mischief, O mighty man? the goodness of G-d endureth continually.

**52:2**
חסד 2617 · אל 410 · כל 3605 · היום 3117: · הוות 1942 · תחשב 2803 · לשונך 3956 · כתער 8593 · מלטש 3913 · עשה 6213
chesed · 'ael, · kal · hayoum. · hauout · tachashob · lashouneka; · kata'ar · malutash, · 'aseh
**the goodness of · El · *endures* all of · continually · mischiefs · devise · Your tongue · like a razor · sharp · working**

**52:3**
רמיה 7423: · אהבת 157 · רע 7451 · מטוב 2896 · שקר 8267 · מדבר 1696 · צדק 6664 · סלה 5542: · **52:4** · אהבת 157 · כל 3605
ramiyah. · 'ahabta · ra' · mitoub; · sheqer · midaber · tzedeq · selah. · 'ahabta · kal
**deceitfully · You love · evil · more than good · *and* lying · rather than to speak · righteousness · Selah · You love · all**

**52:5**
דברי 1697 · בלע 1105 · לשון 3956 · מרמה 4820: · גם 1571 · אל 410 · יתצך 5422 · לנצח 5331 · יחתך 2846
dibrey · bala', · lashoun · mirmah. · gam · 'al · yitatzaka · lanetzach · yachtaka
**words · devouring · tongue · O *you* deceitful · likewise · El · shall destroy you · for ever · he shall take you away**

**52:6**
ויסחך 5255 · מאהל 168 · ושרשך 8327 · מארץ 776 · חיים 2416 · סלה 5542: · ויראו 7200 · צדיקים 6662
uayisachaka · me'ahel; · uashereshaka · me'aretz · chayiym · selah. · uayir'au · tzadiyqiym
**and pluck you · out of *your* dwelling place · and root you · out of the land of · the living · Selah · also shall see · The righteous**

**52:7**
וייראו 3372 · ועליו 5921 · ישחקו 7832: · הנה 2009 · הגבר 1397 · לא 3808 · ישים 7760 · אלהים 430 · מעוזו 4581 · ויבטח 982
uayiyra'au, · ua'alayu · yisachaqu. · hineh · hageber, · la' · yasiym · 'alohiym, · ma'auzou · uayibtach
**and fear · and at him · shall laugh · Lo · *this is* the man · not · *that* made · Elohim · his strength · but trusted**

**52:8**
ברב 7230 · עשרו 6239 · יעז 5810 · בהותו 1942: · ואני 589 · כזית 2132 · רענן 7488
barob · 'asharou; · ya'az, · bahauatou. · ua'aniy · kazayit · ra'anan
**in the abundance of · his riches · *and* strengthened himself · in his wickedness · But I *am* · like a olive tree · green**

**52:9**
בבית 1004 · אלהים 430 · בטחתי 982 · בחסד 2617 · אלהים 430 · עולם 5769 · ועד 5703: · אודך 3034 · לעולם 5769 · כי 3588
babeyt · 'alohiym; · batachtiy · bachesed · 'alohiym, · 'aulam · ua'ad. · 'audaka · la'aulam · kiy
**in the house of · Elohim · I trust · in the mercy of · Elohim · for ever · and ever · I will praise you · for ever · because**

עשית 6213 · ואקוה 6960 · שמך 8034 · כי 3588 · טוב 2896 · נגד 5048 · חסידיך 2623:
'ashiyta; · ua'aqaueh · shimka · kiy · toub, · neged · chasiydeyka.
**you have done *it* · and I will wait on · your name · for · *it is* good · before · your saints**

**Ps 53:1**
למנצח 5329 · על 5921 · מחלת 4257 · משכיל 4905 · לדוד 1732: · אמר 559 · נבל 5036 · בלבו 3820 · אין 369
lamanatzeach · 'al · machalat, · maskiyl · ladauid. · 'amar · nabal · balibou · 'aeyn
**To the chief Musician · upon · Mahalath · Maschil · *A Psalm* of David · has said · The fool · in his heart · *There is* no**

**53:2**
אלהים 430 · השחיתו 7843 · והתעיבו 8581 · עול 5766 · אין 369 · עשה 6213 · טוב 2896: · אלהים 430 · משמים 8064
'alohiym; · hishchiytu, · uahit'aybu · 'auel, · 'aeyn · 'aseh · toub. · 'alohiym, · mishamayim
**Elohim · Corrupt are they · and have done abominable · iniquity · *there is* none · that does · good · Elohim · from heaven**

**53:3**
השקיף 8259 · על 5921 · בני 1121 · אדם 120 · לראות 7200 · היש 3426 · משכיל 7919 · דרש 1875 · את 853 · אלהים 430:
hishqiyp · 'al · baney · 'adam · lir'aut · hayesh · maskiyl; · doresh, · 'at · 'alohiym.
**looked down · upon · the children of · men · to see · if there were *any* that did understand · that did seek · Elohim**

כלו 3605 · סג 5472 · יחדו 3162 · נאלחו 444 · אין 369 · עשה 6213 · טוב 2896 · אין 369 · גם 1571 · אחד 259:
kulou · sag · yachdau · ne'alachu · 'aeyn · 'aseh · toub; · 'aeyn, · gam · 'achad.
**Every one of them · is gone back · altogether · they are become filthy · *there is* none · that does good · no · not · one**

Ps 52:2 Thy tongue deviseth mischiefs; like a sharp razor, working deceitfully.3 Thou love evil more than good; and lying rather than to speak righteousness. Selah.4 Thou love all devouring words, O you deceitful tongue.5 G-d shall likewise destroy you forever, he shall take you away, and pluck you out of your dwelling place, and root you out of the land of the living. Selah.6 The righteous also shall see, and fear, and shall laugh at him:7 Lo, this is the man that made not G-d his strength; but trusted in the abundance of his riches, and strengthened himself in his wickedness.8 But I am like a green olive tree in the house of G-d: I trust in the mercy of G-d forever and ever.9 I will praise you forever, because you have done it: and I will wait on your name; for it is good before your saints. **Ps** 53:1 To the chief Musician upon Ma'-ha-lath, Mas'-chil, A Psalm of David. The fool has said in his heart, There is no G-d. Corrupt are they, and have done abominable iniquity: there is none that doeth good.2 G-d looked down from heaven upon the children of men, to see if there were any that did understand, that did seek G-d.

**53:4**
הלא 3808 | ידעו 3045 | פעלי 6466 | און 205 | אכלי 398 | עמי 5971 | אכלו 398 | לחם 3899 | אלהים 430 | לא 3808
hala' | yada'au | po'aley | 'auen | 'akley | 'amiy | 'akalu | lechem; | 'alohiym, | la'
**no | Have knowledge? | the workers of | iniquity | who eat up | my people | *as* they eat | bread | Elohim | not**

קראו 7121: | **53:5** שם 8033 | פחדו 6342 | פחד 6343 | לא 3808 | היה 1961 | פחד 6343 | כי 3588 | אלהים 430 | פזר 6340 | עצמות 6106
qara'au. | sham | pachadu | pachad | la' | hayah | pachad | kiy | 'alohiym, | pizar | atzmout
**they have called | There | were they in fear | great *where* | no | was | fear | for | Elohim | has scattered | the bones of**

חנך 2583 | הבשתה 954 | כי 3588 | אלהים 430 | מאסם 3988: | **53:6** מי 4310 | יתן 5414
chonak; | habishotah, | kiy | 'alohiym | ma'asam. | miy' | yiten
**him that encamp *against you:* | you have put *them* to shame | because | Elohim | has despised | Oh that | were come**

מציון 6726 | ישעות 3444 | ישראל 3478 | בשוב 7725 | אלהים 430 | שבות 7622 | עמו 5971 | יגל 1523 | יעקב 3290
mitziyoun | yashu'aut | yisra'ael | bashub | 'alohiym | shabut | 'amou; | yagel | ya'aqob,
**out of Zion | the salvation of | Israel | When bring back | Elohim | the captivity of | his people | shall rejoice | Jacob**

ישמח 8055 | ישראל 3478:
yismach | yisra'ael.
**shall be glad *and* Israel**

**Ps 54:1**
למנצח 5329 | בנגינת 5058 | משכיל 4905 | לדוד 1732: | בבוא 935 | הזיפים 2130 | ויאמרו 559 | לשאול 7586
lamanatzeach | binagiynout, | maskiyl | ladauid. | babou'a | haziypiym | uaya'maru | lasha'aul;
**To the chief Musician | on Neginoth | Maschil | *A Psalm* of David | when came | the Ziphims | and said | to Saul**

הלא 3808 | דוד 1732 | מסתתר 5641 | עמנו 5973: | אלהים 430 | בשמך 8034 | הושיעני 3467 | ובגבורתך 1369 | תדינני 1777: | **54:2** אלהים 430
hala' | dauid, | mistater | 'amanu. | 'alohiym | bashimka | houshiy'aeniy; | uabigburataka | tadiyneniy. | 'alohiym
**Does not | David | hide himself with us? | O Elohim | by your name | Save me | by your strength | and judge me | O Elohim**

שמע 8085 | תפלתי 8605 | האזינה 238 | לאמרי 561 | פי 6310: | **54:3** כי 3588 | זרים 2114 | קמו 6965 | עלי 5921 | ועריצים 6184
shama' | tapilatiy; | ha'aziynah, | la'amrey | piy. | kiy | zariym | qamu | 'alay, | ua'ariytziym
**Hear | my prayer | give ear | to the words of | my mouth | For | strangers | are risen up | against me | and oppressors**

בקשו 1245 | נפשי 5315 | לא 3808 | שמו 7760 | אלהים 430 | לנגדם 5048 | סלה 5542: | **54:4** הנה 2009 | אלהים 430 | עזר 5826 | לי 3807a | אדני 136
biqshu | napshiy; | la' | samu | 'alohiym | lanegdam | selah. | hineh | 'alohiym | 'azer | liy; | 'adonay,
**seek after | my soul | not | they have set | Elohim | before them | Selah | Behold | Elohim | helper | *is* mine | Adonai**

בסמכי 5564 | נפשי 5315: | **54:5** ישוב 7725 | הרע 7451 | לשררי 8324 | באמתך 571 | הצמיתם 6789: | **54:6** בנדבה 5071
basomakey | napshiy. | yashoub | hara' | lashoraray; | ba'amitaka, | hatzamiytem. | binadabah
***is* with them that uphold | my soul | He shall reward evil | unto mine enemies | in your truth | cut them off | freely**

אזבחה 2076 | לך 3807a | אודה 3034 | שמך 8034 | יהוה 3068 | כי 3588 | טוב 2896: | **54:7** כי 3588 | מכל 3605 | צרה 6869 | הצילני 5337
'azbachah | lak; | 'audeh | shimka | Yahuah | kiy | toub. | kiy | mikal | tzarah | hitziylaniy;
**I will sacrifice unto you | I will praise your name | O Yahuah | for | *it is* good | For | out of all | trouble | he has delivered me**

ובאיבי 341 | ראתה 7200 | עיני 5869:
uab'ayabay, | ra'atah | 'aeyniy.
**and upon mine enemies | has seen *his desire* | mine eye**

Ps 53:3 Every one of them is gone back: they are altogether become filthy; there is none that doeth good, no, not one.4 Have the workers of iniquity no knowledge? who eat up my people as they eat bread: they have not called upon G-d.5 There were they in great fear, where no fear was: for G-d has scattered the bones of him that encampeth against you: you have put them to shame, because G-d has despised them.6 Oh that the salvation of Israel were come out of Zion! When G-d bring back the captivity of his people, Jacob shall rejoice, and Israel shall be glad. **Ps** 54:1 To the chief Musician of Neg'-i-noth, Mas'-chil, A Psalm of David, when the Ziph'ims came and said to Saul, Does not David hide himself with us? Save me, O G-d, by your name, and judge me by your strength.2 Hear my prayer, O G-d; give ear to the words of my mouth.3 For strangers are risen up against me, and oppressors seek after my soul: they have not set G-d before them. Selah.4 Behold, G-d is mine helper: YHUH is with them that uphold my soul.5 He shall reward evil unto mine enemies: cut them off in your truth.6 I will freely sacrifice unto you: I will praise your name, O YHUH; for it is good.7 For he has delivered me out of all trouble: and mine eye has seen his desire upon mine enemies.

**Ps 55:1** למנצח 5329 | בנגינת 5058 | משכיל 4905 | לדוד 1732: | האזינה 238 | אלהים 430 | תפלתי 8605 | ואל 408
lamanatzeach | binagiynout, | maskiyl | ladauid. | ha'aziynah | 'alohiym | tapilatiy; | ua'al
**To the chief Musician | on Neginoth | Maschil | *A Psalm* of David | Give ear to | O Elohim | my prayer | and not**

תתעלם 5956 | מתחנתי 8467: | **55:2** הקשיבה 7181 | לי 3807a | ועניני 6030 | אריד 7300 | בשיחי 7879 | ואהימה 1949: | **55:3**
tit'alam, | mitchinatiy. | haqashiybah | liy | ua'aneniy; | 'ariyd | basiychiy | ua'ahiymah.
**hide yourself | from my supplication | Attend | unto me | and hear me | I mourn | in my complaint | and make a noise**

מקול 6963 | אויב 341 | מפני 6440 | עקת 6125 | רשע 7563 | כי 3588 | ימיטו 4131 | עלי 5921 | און 205 | ובאף 639
miqoul | auyeb, | mipaney | 'aqat | rasha'; | kiy | yamiytu | 'alay | 'auen, | uab'ap
**Because of the voice of | the enemy | because of | the oppression of | the wicked | for | they cast | upon me | iniquity | and in wrath**

ישטמוני 7852: | **55:4** לבי 3820 | יחיל 2342 | בקרבי 7130 | ואימות 367 | מות 4194 | נפלו 5307 | עלי 5921: | **55:5** יראה 3374
yistamuniy. | libiy | yachiyl | baqirbiy; | ua'aeymout | mauet, | naplu | 'alay. | yir'ah
**they hate me | My heart | is sore pained | within me | and the terrors of | death | are fallen | upon me | Fearfulness**

ורעד 7461 | יבא 935 | בי 871a | ותכסני 3680 | פלצות 6427: | **55:6** ואמר 559 | מי 4310 | יתן 5414 | לי 3807a | אבר 83
uara'ad | yaba' | biy; | uatakaseniy, | palatzut. | ua'amar, | miy' | yiten | liy | 'aeber
**and trembling | are come | upon me | and has overwhelmed me | horror | And I said | Oh that | had | I | wings**

כיונה 3123 | אעופה 5774 | ואשכנה 7931: | **55:7** הנה 2009 | ארחיק 7368 | נדד 5074 | אלין 3885 | במדבר 4057
kayounah, | 'a'aupah | ua'ashkonah. | hineh | 'archiyq | nadod; | 'aliyn | bamidbar
**like a dove *for then* would I fly away | and be at rest | Lo | far off | *then* would I wander | *and* remain | in the wilderness**

סלה 5542: | **55:8** אחישה 2363 | מפלט 4655 | לי 3807a | מרוח 7307 | סעה 5584 | מסער 5591: | **55:9** בלע 1104 | אדני 136 | פלג 6385
selah. | 'achiyshah | miplat | liy; | meruach | so'ah | misa'ar. | bala' | 'adonay | palag
**Selah | I would hasten | escape | my | from the windy | storm | *and* tempest | Destroy | O Adonai | *and* divide**

לשונם 3956 | כי 3588 | ראיתי 7200 | חמס 2555 | וריב 7379 | בעיר 5892: | **55:10** יומם 3119 | ולילה 3915 | יסובבה 5437 | על 5921
lashounam; | kiy | ra'aytiy | chamas | uariyb | ba'ayr. | youmam | ualayalah, | yasoubabuha | 'al
**their tongues | for | I have seen | violence | and strife | in the city | Day | and night | they go about it | upon**

חומתיה 2346 | ואון 205 | ועמל 5999 | בקרבה 7130: | **55:11** הוות 1942 | בקרבה 7130 | ולא 3808 | ימיש 4185
choumoteyha; | ua'auen | ua'amal | baqirbah. | hauout | baqirbah; | uala' | yamiysh
**the walls thereof | mischief also | and sorrow | *are* in the midst of it | Wickedness | *is* in the midst thereof | not | depart**

מרחבה 7339 | תך 8496 | ומרמה 4820: | **55:12** כי 3588 | לא 3808 | אויב 341 | יחרפני 2778 | ואשא 5375 | לא 3808
merachobah, | tok | uamirmah. | kiy | la' | auyeb | yacharapeniy, | ua'asa' | la'
**from her streets | deceit | and guile | For *it was* | not | an enemy | *that* reproached me | then I could have borne *it* | neither**

משנאי 8130 | עלי 5921 | הגדיל 1431 | ואסתר 5641 | ממנו 4480: | **55:13** ואתה 859
masan'ay | 'alay | higdiyl; | ua'asater | mimenu. | ua'atah
***was it* he that hated me | against me | *that* did magnify *himself* | then I would have hid myself | from him | But *it was* you**

אנוש 582 | כערכי 6187 | אלופי 441 | ומידעי 3045: | **55:14** אשר 834 | יחדו 3162 | נמתיק 4985 | סוד 5475 | בבית 1004
'anoush | ka'arkiy; | 'alupiy, | uamyuda'ay. | 'asher | yachdau | namtiyq | coud; | babeyt
**a man | mine equal | my guide | and mine acquaintance | who | together | We took sweet | counsel | unto the house of**

**Ps** 55:1 To the chief Musician on Neg'-i-noth, Mas'-chil, A Psalm of David. Give ear to my prayer, O G-d; and hide not thyself from my supplication.2 Attend unto me, and hear me: I mourn in my complaint, and make a noise;3 Because of the voice of the enemy, because of the oppression of the wicked: for they cast iniquity upon me, and in wrath they hate me.4 My heart is sore pained within me: and the terrors of death are fallen upon me.5 Fearfulness and trembling are come upon me, and horror has overwhelmed me.6 And I said, Oh that I had wings like a dove! for then would I fly away, and be at rest.7 Lo, then would I wander far off, and remain in the wilderness. Selah.8 I would hasten my escape from the windy storm and tempest.9 Destroy, O Adonai, and divide their tongues: for I have seen violence and strife in the city.10 Day and night they go about it upon the walls thereof: mischief also and sorrow are in the midst of it.11 Wickedness is in the midst thereof: deceit and guile depart not from her streets.12 For it was not an enemy that reproached me; then I could have borne it: neither was it he that hated me that did magnify himself against me; then I would have hid myself from him:13 But it was you, a man mine equal, my guide, and mine acquaintance.14 We took sweet counsel together, and walked unto the house of G-d in company.

55:15
אלהים 430 נהלך 1980 ברגש 7285: ישימות 3451 עלימו 5921 ירדו 3381 שאול 7585 חיים 2416 כי 3588
'alohiym, nahalek baragesh. yashiymauat 'aleymou yeradu sha'aul chayiym; kiy
**Elohim *and* walked in company Let seize death upon them *and* let them go down into hell (*grave*) quick for**

55:16 55:17
רעות 7451 במגורם 4033 בקרבם 7130: אני 589 אל 413 אלהים 430 אקרא 7121 ויהוה 3068 יושיעני 3467:
ra'aut bimaguram baqirbam. 'aniy 'al 'alohiym 'aqraa'; uaYahuah youshiy'aeniy.
**wickedness *is* in their dwellings *and* among them As for me upon Elohim I will call and Yahuah shall save me**

55:18
ערב 6153 ובקר 1242 וצהרים 6672 אשיחה 7878 ואהמה 1993 וישמע 8085 קולי 6963: פדה 6299 בשלום 7965
'areb uaboqer uatzaharayim 'asiychah ua'ahameh; uayishma' qouliy. padah uashaloum
**Evening and morning and at noon will I pray and cry aloud and he shall hear my voice He has delivered in peace**

55:19
נפשי 5315 מקרב 7128 לי 3807a כי 3588 ברבים 7227 היו 1961 עמדי 5978: ישמע 8085 אל 410 ויענם 6031
napshiy miqarab liy; kiy barabiym, hayu 'amadiy. yishma' 'ael uaya'anem
**my soul from the battle *that was* against me for many there were with me shall hear El and afflict them**

55:20
וישב 3427 קדם 6924 סלה 5542 אשר 834 אין 369 חליפות 2487 למו 3807a ולא 3808 יראו 3372 אלהים 430:
uayosheb qedem, selah 'asher 'aeyn chaliypout lamou; uala' yara'au 'alohiym.
**even he that abide of old Selah Because have no changes they therefore not they fear Elohim**

55:21
שלח 7971 ידיו 3027 בשלמיו 7965 חלל 2490 בריתו 1285:
shalach yadayu bishlomayu, chilel bariytou.
**He has put forth his hands against such as be at peace with him he has broken his covenant**

חלקו 2505 מחמאת 4260 פיו 6310 וקרב 7128 לבו 3820 רכו 7401 דבריו 1697 משמן 8081 והמה 1992
chalaqu machma'at piyu uaqarab libou raku dabarayu mishemen, uahemah
***The words of* were smoother *than* butter his mouth but war *was* in his heart were softer his words than oil yet *were* they**

55:22
פתחות 6609: השלך 7993 על 5921 יהוה 3068 יהבך 3053 והוא 1931 יכלכלך 3557 לא 3808 יתן 5414 לעולם 5769
patichout. hashalek 'al Yahuah yahabaka uahu'a yakalkaleka la' yiten la'aulam
**drawn swords Cast upon Yahuah your burden and he shall sustain you not he shall suffer ever**

55:23
מוט 4131 לצדיק 6662: ואתה 859 אלהים 430 תורדם 3381 לבאר 875 שחת 7845 אנשי 582 דמים 1818
mout, latzadiyq. ua'atah 'alohiym touridem lib'aer shachat, 'anshey damiym
**to be moved the righteous But you O Elohim shall bring them down into the pit of destruction men bloody**

ומרמה 4820 לא 3808 יחצו 2673 ימיהם 3117 ואני 589 אבטח 982 בך 871a:
uamirmah la' yechetzu yameyhem; ua'aniy, 'abtach bak.
**and deceitful not shall live out half their days but I will trust in you**

Ps 56:1
למנצח 5329 על 5921 יונת 3128 אלם 3128 רחקים 3128 לדוד 1732 מכתם 4387 באחז 270 אתו 853 פלשתים 6430
lamanatzeach 'al younat 'aelem rachoqiym ladauid miktam; be'achoz 'atou palishtiym
**To the chief Musician upon dove congregation far abroad of David Michtam took him the Philistines**

בגת 1661: חנני 2603 אלהים 430 כי 3588 שאפני 7602 אנוש 582 כל 3605 היום 3117 לחם 3898 ילחצני 3905:
bagat. chaneniy 'alohiym kiy sha'apaniy 'anoush; kal hayoum, lachem yilchatzeniy.
**in Gath Be merciful unto me O Elohim for would swallow me up man all daily he fighting oppress me**

Ps 55:15 Let death seize upon them, and let them go down quick into hell: for wickedness is in their dwellings, and among them.16 As for me, I will call upon G-d; and YHUH shall save me.17 Evening, and morning, and at noon, will I pray, and cry aloud: and he shall hear my voice.18 He has delivered my soul in peace from the battle that was against me: for there were many with me.19 G-d shall hear, and afflict them, even he that abideth of old. Selah. Because they have no changes, therefore they fear not G-d.20 He has put forth his hands against such as be at peace with him: he has broken his covenant.21 The words of his mouth were smoother than butter, but war was in his heart: his words were softer than oil, yet were they drawn swords.22 Cast your burden upon YHUH, and he shall sustain you: he shall never suffer the righteous to be moved.23 But you, O G-d, shall bring them down into the pit of destruction: bloody and deceitful men shall not live out half their days; but I will trust in you. **Ps** 56:1 To the chief Musician upon Jo'-nath-e'-lem-re-cho'-kim, Mich'-tam of David, when the Phi-lis'-times took him in Gath. Be merciful unto me, O G-d: for man would swallow me up;

**56:2** שאפו 7602 sha'apu **would swallow *me* up** | שוררי 8324 shourray **Mine enemies** | כל 3605 kal **all** | היום 3117 hayoum; **daily** | כי 3588 kiy **for** | רבים 7227 rabiym ***they be* many** | לחמים 3898 lochamiym **that fight** | לי 3807a liy **against me** | מרום 4791: maroum. **O you most High** **56:3**

יום 3117 youm **What time** | אירא 3372 'ayra'; **I am afraid** | אני 589 'aniy, **I** | אליך 413 'aeleyka **in you** | אבטח 982: 'abtach. **will trust** | **56:4** באלהים 430 be'alohiym **In Elohim** | אהלל 1984 'ahalel **I will praise** | דברו 1697 dabarou **his word** | באלהים 430 be'alohiym **in Elohim** | בטחתי 982 batachtiy **I have put my trust** | לא 3808 la' **not**

אירא 3372 'ayra'; **I will fear** | מה 4100 mah **what** | יעשה 6213 ya'aseh **can do** | בשר 1320 basar **flesh** | לי 3807a: liy. **unto me** | **56:5** כל 3605 kal **Every** | היום 3117 hayoum **day** | דברי 1697 dabaray **my words** | יעצבו 6087 ya'atzebu; **they wrest** | עלי 5921 'alay **against me** | כל 3605 kal **all** | מחשבתם 4284 machshabotam **their thoughts**

לרע 7451: lara'. ***are* for evil** | **56:6** יגורו 1481 yaguru **They gather themselves together** | יצפינו 6845 yatzpiynu **they hide them selves,** | המה 1992 hemah **they** | עקבי 6119 'aqebay **my steps** | ישמרו 8104 yishmoru; **mark** | כאשר 834 ka'asher, **when** | קוו 6960 qiuu **they wait for**

נפשי 5315: napshiy. **my soul** | **56:7** על 5921 'al **by** | און 205 'auen **iniquity?** | פלט 6405 palet **Shall escape** | למו 3807a lamou; **they** | באף 639 ba'ap, **in your anger** | עמים 5971 'amiym **the people** | הורד 3381 houred **cast down** | אלהים 430: 'alohiym. **O Elohim** | **56:8** נדי 5112 nodiy **my wanderings**

ספרתה 5608 sapartah **tell** | אתה 859 'atah **You** | שימה 7760 siymah **put you** | דמעתי 1832 dim'atiy **my tears** | בנאדך 4997 bana'deka; **into your bottle** | הלא 3808 hala', **are they not** | בספרתך 5612: basiprateka. **in your book?** | **56:9** אז 227 'az **then** | ישובו 7725 yashubu **shall turn** | אויבי 341 'auyabay **mine enemies** | אחור 268 'achour **back**

ביום 3117 bayoum **When** | אקרא 7121 'aqraa'; **I cry *unto you*** | זה 2088 zeh **this** | ידעתי 3045 yada'tiy, **I know** | כי 3588 kiy **for** | אלהים 430 'alohiym **Elohim** | לי 3807a: liy. **for me** | **56:10** באלהים 430 be'alohiym **In Elohim** | אהלל 1984 'ahalel **will I praise** | דבר 1697 dabar; ***his* word** | ביהוה 3068 baYahuah **in Yahuah** | אהלל 1984 'ahalel **will I praise**

דבר 1697: dabar. ***his* word** | **56:11** באלהים 430 be'alohiym **In Elohim** | בטחתי 982 batachtiy **have I put my trust** | לא 3808 la' **not** | אירא 3372 'ayra'; **I will be afraid** | מה 4100 mah **what** | יעשה 6213 ya'aseh **can do** | אדם 120 'adam **man** | לי 3807a: liy. **unto me** | **56:12** עלי 5921 'alay **upon me**

אלהים 430 'alohiym **O Elohim** | נדריך 5088 nadareyka; **Your vows *are*** | אשלם 7999 'ashalem **I will render** | תודת 8426 toudot **praises** | לך 3807a: lak. **unto me** | **56:13** כי 3588 kiy **For** | הצלת 5337 hitzalta **you have delivered** | נפשי 5315 napshiy **my soul** | ממות 4194 mimauet **from death** | הלא 3808 hala' ***will* not**

רגלי 7272 raglay, ***you deliver* my feet** | מדחי 1762 midechiy **from falling** | להתהלך 1980 lahithalek **that I may walk** | לפני 6440 lipney **before** | אלהים 430 'alohiym; **Elohim** | באור 216 ba'aur, **in the light of** | החיים 2416: hachayiym. **the living?**

**Ps 57:1** למנצח 5329 lamanatzeach **To the chief Musician** | אל 516 'al **Al** | תשחת 7843 tashchet **taschith** | לדוד 1732 ladauid **of David** | מכתם 4387 miktam; **Michtam** | בברחו 1272 babarchou **when he fled** | מפני 6440 mipaney **from** | שאול 7586 sha'aul, **Saul** | במערה 4631: bam'arah. **in the cave**

חנני 2603 chaneniy **Be merciful unto me** | אלהים 430 'alohiym **O Elohim** | חנני 2603 chaneniy **be merciful unto me** | כי 3588 kiy **for** | בך 871a baka **in you** | חסיה 2620 chasayah **trust** | נפשי 5315 napshiy **my soul** | ובצל 6738 uabtzel **yea in the shadow of** | כנפיך 3671 kanapeyka **your wings**

Ps 56:1 he fighting daily oppresseth me.2 Mine enemies would daily swallow me up: for they be many that fight against me, O you most High.3 What time I am afraid, I will trust in you.4 In G-d I will praise his word, in G-d I have put my trust; I will not fear what flesh can do unto me.5 Every day they wrest my words: all their thoughts are against me for evil.6 They gather themselves together, they hide themselves, they mark my steps, when they wait for my soul.7 Shall they escape by iniquity? in your anger cast down the people, O G-d.8 Thou tellest my wanderings: put you my tears into your bottle: are they not in your book?9 When I cry unto you, then shall mine enemies turn back: this I know; for G-d is for me.10 In G-d will I praise his word: in YHUH will I praise his word.11 In G-d have I put my trust: I will not be afraid what man can do unto me.12 Thy vows are upon me, O G-d: I will render praises unto you.13 For you have delivered my soul from death: will not you deliver my feet from falling, that I may walk before G-d in the light of the living? **Ps** 57:1 To the chief Musician, Al-tas'-chith, Mich'-tam of David, when he fled from Saul in the cave. Be merciful unto me, O G-d, be merciful unto me: for my soul trusteth in you: yea, in the shadow of your wings will I make my refuge, until these calamities be overpast.

57:2
אחסה 2620 עד 5704 יעבר 5674 הוות 1942: אקרא 7121 לאלהים 430 עליון 5945 לאל 410
'achseh; 'ad, ya'abor hauout. 'aqraa' le'alohiym 'alyoun; la'ael,
**will I make my refuge until be overpast *these* calamities I will cry unto Elohim most high unto El**

57:3
גמר 1584 עלי 5921: ישלח 7971 משמים 8064 ויושיעני 3467 חרף 2778
gomer 'alay. yishlach mishamayim uayoushiy'aeniy, cherep
**that perform *all things* for me He shall send from heaven and save me *from* the reproach of him**

57:4
שאפי 7602 סלה 5542 ישלח 7971 אלהים 430 חסדו 2617 ואמתו 571: נפשי 5315 בתוך 8432 לבאם 3833
sho'apiy selah; yishlach 'alohiym, chasdou ua'amitou. napshiy batouk laba'am
**that would swallow me up Selah shall send forth Elohim his mercy and his truth My soul *is* among lions**

אשכבה 7901 להטים 3857 בני 1121 אדם 120 שניהם 8127 חנית 2595 וחצים 2671 ולשונם 3956
'ashkabah lohatiym baney 'adam, shineyhem chaniyt uachitziym; ualshounam,
***and* I lie *even among* them that are set on fire *even* the sons of men whose teeth *are* spears and arrows and their tongue**

57:5 57:6
חרב 2719 חדה 2299: רומה 7311 על 5921 השמים 8064 אלהים 430 על 5921 כל 3605 הארץ 776 כבודך 3519: רשת 7568
chereb chadah. rumah 'al hashamayim 'alohiym; 'al kal ha'aretz kaboudeka. reshet
**a sword sharp Be you exalted above the heavens O Elohim above all the earth *let* your glory *be* a net**

הכינו 3559 לפעמי 6471 כפף 3721 נפשי 5315 כרו 3738 לפני 6440 שיחה 7882 נפלו 5307
hekiynu lipa'amay kapap napshiy karu lapanay shiychah; naplu
**They have prepared for my steps is bowed down my soul they have digged before me a pit they are fallen *themselves***

57:7 57:8
בתוכה 8432 סלה 5542: נכון 3559 לבי 3820 אלהים 430 נכון 3559 לבי 3820 אשירה 7891 ואזמרה 2167: עורה 5782
batoukah selah. nakoun libiy 'alohiym nakoun libiy; 'ashiyrah, ua'azamerah. 'uarah
**into the midst whereof Selah is fixed My heart O Elohim is fixed my heart I will sing and give praise Awake up**

57:9
כבודי 3519 עורה 5782 הנבל 5035 וכנור 3658 אעירה 5782 שחר 7837: אודך 3034 בעמים 5971 אדני 136
kaboudiy, 'uarah hanebel uakinour, 'a'ayrah shachar. 'audaka ba'amiym 'adonay;
**my glory awake psaltery and harp I *myself* will awake early I will praise you among the people O Adonai**

57:10
אזמרך 2167 בל 3816 אמים 3816: כי 3588 גדל 1419 עד 5704 שמים 8064 חסדך 2617 ועד 5704 שחקים 7834
'azameraka, bal 'aumiym. kiy gadoul 'ad shamayim chasadeka; ua'ad shachaqiym
**I will sing unto you among the nations For *is* great unto the heavens your mercy and unto the clouds**

57:11
אמתך 571: רומה 7311 על 5921 שמים 8064 אלהים 430 על 5921 כל 3605 הארץ 776 כבודך 3519:
'amiteka. rumah 'al shamayim 'alohiym; 'al kal ha'aretz kaboudeka.
**your truth Be you exalted above the heavens O Elohim above all the earth *let* your glory *be***

**Ps 58:1**
למנצח 5329 אל 516 תשחת 7843 לדוד 1732 מכתם 4387: האמנם 552 אלם 482 צדק 6664 תדברון 1696
lamanatzeach 'al tashchet, ladauid miktam. ha'amnam, 'aelem tzedeq tadabrun;
**To the chief Musician Al taschith of David Michtam indeed O congregation? righteousness Do you speak**

58:2
מישרים 4339 תשפטו 8199 בני 1121 אדם 120: אף 637 בלב 3820 עולת 5766 תפעלון 6466 בארץ 776 חמס 2555
meyshariym tishpatu, baney 'adam. 'ap baleb 'aulot tip'alun ba'aretz chamas
**uprightly do you judge O you sons of men? Yea in heart wickedness you work in the earth the violence of**

Ps 57:2 I will cry unto G-d most high; unto G-d that performeth all things for me.3 He shall send from heaven, and save from the reproach of him that would swallow me up. Selah. G-d shall send forth his mercy and his truth.4 My soul is among lions: and I lie even among them that are set on fire, even the sons of men, whose teeth are spears and arrows, and their tongue a sharp sword.5 Be you exalted, O G-d, above the heavens; let your glory be above all the earth.6 They have prepared a net for my steps; my soul is bowed down: they have digged a pit before me, into the midst whereof they are fallen themselves. Selah.7 My heart is fixed, O G-d, my heart is fixed: I will sing and give praise.8 Awake up, my glory; awake, psaltery and harp: I myself will awake early.9 I will praise you, O Adonai, among the people: I will sing unto you among the nations.10 For your mercy is great unto the heavens, and your truth unto the clouds.11 Be you exalted, O G-d, above the heavens: let your glory be above all the earth. **Ps** 58:1 To the chief Musician, Al-tas'-chith, Mich'-tam of David. Do you indeed speak righteousness, O congregation? do you judge uprightly, O you sons of men? 2 Yea, in heart you work wickedness; you weigh the violence of your hands in the earth.

58:3

ידיכם 3027 תפלסון 6424: זרו 2114 רשעים 7563 מרחם 7358 תעו 8582 מבטן 990 דברי 1697
yadeykem, tapalesun. zoru rasha'aym merachem; ta'au mibeten, dobarey
**your hands you weigh are estranged The wicked from the womb they go astray as soon as they be born speaking**

58:4 58:5

כזב 3577: חמת 2534 למו 3807a כדמות 1823 חמת 2534 נחש 5175 כמו 3644 פתן 6620 חרש 2795 יאטם 331 אזנו 241: אשר 834
kazab. chamat lamou, kidmut chamat nachash; kamou peten cheresh, ya'atem 'azanou. 'asher
**lies poison Their *is* like the poison of a serpent *they are* like adder the deaf *that* stop her ear Which**

58:6

לא 3808 ישמע 8085 לקול 6963 מלחשים 3907 חובר 2266 חברים 2267 מחכם 2449: אלהים 430 הרס 2040 שנימו 8127
la' yishma' laqoul melachashiym; chouber chabariym machukam. 'alohiym, haros shineymou
**not will listen to the voice of charmers ones charming charmings never so wisely O Elohim Break their teeth**

58:7

בפימו 6310 מלתעות 4459 כפירים 3715 נתץ 5422 יהוה 3068: ימאסו 3988 כמו 3644 מים 4325 יתהלכו 1980
bapiymou; malta'aut kapiyriym, natotz Yahuah. yima'asu kamou mayim yithalku
**in their mouth *the* great teeth of the young lions break out O Yahuah Let them melt away as waters *which* run**

58:8

למו 3807a ידרך 1869 חצו 2671 כמו 3644 יתמללו 4135: כמו 3644 שבלול 7642 תמס 8557
lamou; yidrok chitzou kamou yitmolalu. kamou shablul temes
**continually *when* he bends *his bow to shoot* his arrows as let them be cut in pieces As a snail *which* melts**

58:9

יהלך 1980 נפל 5309 אשת 802 בל 1077 חזו 2372 שמש 8121: בטרם 2962 יבינו 995
yahalok; nepel 'aeshet, bal chazu shamesh. baterem yabiynu
**let *every one of them* pass away *like* the untimely birth of a woman not *that* they may see the sun Before can feel**

58:10

סירתיכם 5518 אטד 329 כמו 3644 חי 2416 כמו 3644 חרון 2740 ישערנו 8175: ישמח 8055
siyroteykem 'atad; kamou chay kamou charoun, yis'arenu. yismach
**your pots the thorns *and* in *both* living *his* like wrath he shall take them away as with a whirlwind shall rejoice**

58:11

צדיק 6662 כי 3588 חזה 2372 נקם 5359 פעמיו 6471 ירחץ 7364 בדם 1818 הרשע 7563: ויאמר 559 אדם 120
tzadiyq kiy chazah naqam; pa'amayu yirchatz, badam harasha'. uaya'mar 'adam
**The righteous when he see the vengeance his feet he shall wash in the blood of the wicked So that shall say a man**

אך 389 פרי 6529 לצדיק 6662 אך 389 יש 3426 אלהים 430 שפטים 8199 בארץ 776:
'ak pariy latzadiyq; 'ak yesh 'alohiym, shopatiym ba'aretz.
**Verily *there is* a reward for the righteous verily he is a Elohim that judge in the earth**

**Ps 59:1**

למנצח 5329 אל 516 תשחת 7843 לדוד 1732 מכתם 4387 בשלח 7971 שאול 7586 וישמרו 8104 את 853 הבית 1004
lamanatzeach 'al tashchet ladauid miktam bishloach sha'aul; uayishmaru 'at habayit,
**To the chief Musician Al taschith of David Michtam when sent Saul *and* they watched the house**

59:2

להמיתו 4191: הצילני 5337 מאיבי 341 אלהי 430 ממתקוממי 6965 תשגבני 7682: הצילני 5337
lahamiytou. hatziyleniy me'ayabay 'alohay; mimitqoumay tasagbeniy. hatziyleniy
**to kill him Deliver me from mine enemies O my Elohim from them that rise up against me defend me Deliver me**

59:3

מפעלי 6466 און 205 ומאנשי 582 דמים 1818 הושיעני 3467: כי 3588 הנה 2009 ארבו 693 לנפשי 5315
mipo'aley 'auen; uame'anshey damiym, houshiy'aeniy. kiy hineh 'arabu lanapshiy,
**from the workers of iniquity and from men bloody save me For lo they lie in wait for my soul**

Ps 58:3 The wicked are estranged from the womb: they go astray as soon as they be born, speaking lies.4 Their poison is like the poison of a serpent: they are like the deaf adder that stoppeth her ear;5 Which will not hear to the voice of charmers, charming never so wisely.6 Break their teeth, O G-d, in their mouth: break out the great teeth of the young lions, O YHUH.7 Let them melt away as waters which run continually: when he bendeth his bow to shoot his arrows, let them be as cut in pieces.8 As a snail which melteth, let everyone of them pass away: like the untimely birth of a woman, that they may not see the sun.9 Before your pots can feel the thorns, he shall take them away as with a whirlwind, both living, and in his wrath.10 The righteous shall rejoice when he see the vengeance: he shall wash his feet in the blood of the wicked.11 So that a man shall say, Verily there is a reward for the righteous: verily he is a G-d that judgeth in the earth. **Ps** 59:1 To the chief Musician, Al-tas'-chith, Mich'-tam of David; when Saul sent, and they watched the house to kill him. Deliver me from mine enemies, O my G-d: defend me from them that rise up against me.2 Deliver me from the workers of iniquity, and save me from bloody men.3 For, lo, they lie in wait for my soul: the mighty are gathered against me; not for my transgression, nor for my sin, O YHUH.

| יגורו 1481 | עלי 5921 | עזים 5794 | לא 3808 | פשעי 6588 | ולא 3808 | חטאתי 2403 | יהוה 3068: | 59:4 | בלי 1097 | עון 5771 |
|---|---|---|---|---|---|---|---|---|---|---|
| yaguru | 'alay | 'aziym; | la' | pish'ay | uala' | chata'tiy | Yahuah. | | baliy | 'auon |
| **are gathered** | **against me** | **the mighty** | **not** | ***for* my transgression** | **nor** | ***for* my sin** | **O Yahuah** | | **without** | ***my* fault** |

| ירוצון 7323 | ויכוננו 3559 | עורה 5782 | לקראתי 7125 | וראה 7200: | 59:5 | ואתה 859 | יהוה 3068 | אלהים 430 | צבאות 6635 |
|---|---|---|---|---|---|---|---|---|---|
| yarutzun | uayikounanu; | 'uarah | liqra'tiy | ur'aeh. | | ua'atah | Yahuah | 'alohiym | tzaba'aut |
| **They run** | **and prepare themselves** | **awake** | **to help me** | **and behold** | | **You therefore** | **O Yahuah** | **Elohim of** | **hosts** |

| אלהי 430 | ישראל 3478 | הקיצה 6974 | לפקד 6485 | כל 3605 | הגוים 1471 | אל 408 | תחן 2603 | כל 3605 | בגדי 898 | און 205 | סלה 5542: | 59:6 |
|---|---|---|---|---|---|---|---|---|---|---|---|---|
| 'alohey | yisra'ael, | haqiytzah, | lipqod | kal | hagouyim; | 'al | tachon | kal | bogadey | 'auen | selah. | |
| **the Elohim of** | **Israel** | **awake** | **to visit** | **all** | **the heathen** | **not** | **be merciful to** | **any** | **transgressors** | **wicked** | **Selah** | |

| ישובו 7725 | לערב 6153 | יהמו 1993 | ככלב 3611 | ויסובבו 5437 | עיר 5892: | 59:7 | הנה 2009 | יביעון 5042 |
|---|---|---|---|---|---|---|---|---|
| yashubu | la'areb | yehamu | kakaleb, | uiysoubabu | 'ayr. | | hineh | yabiy'un |
| **They return** | **at evening** | **they make a noise** | **like a dog** | **and go round about** | **the city** | | **Behold** | **they belch out** |

| בפיהם 6310 | חרבות 2719 | בשפתותיהם 8193 | כי 3588 | מי 4310 | שמע 8085: | 59:8 | ואתה 859 | יהוה 3068 | תשחק 7832 | למו 3807a |
|---|---|---|---|---|---|---|---|---|---|---|
| bapiyhem, | charabout | basiptouteyhem; | kiy | miy' | shomea'. | | ua'atah | Yahuah | tischaq | lamou; |
| **with their mouth** | **swords** | ***are* in their lips** | **for** | **who** | ***say they* does hear?** | | **But you** | **O Yahuah** | **shall laugh** | **at them** |

| תלעג 3932 | לכל 3605 | גוים 1471: | 59:9 | עזו 5797 | אליך 413 | אשמרה 8104 | כי 3588 | אלהים 430 |
|---|---|---|---|---|---|---|---|---|
| til'ag, | lakal | gouyim. | | 'azou | 'aeleyka | 'ashmorah; | kiy | 'alohiym, |
| **you shall have in derision** | **all** | **the heathen** | | ***Because of* his strength** | **upon you** | **will I wait** | **for** | **Elohim** |

| משגבי 4869: | 59:10 | אלהי 430 | חסדו 2617 | יקדמני 6923 | אלהים 430 | יראני 7200 | בשררי 8324: | 59:11 |
|---|---|---|---|---|---|---|---|---|
| misgabiy. | | 'alohey | chasdou | yaqadmeniy; | 'alohiym, | yar'aeniy | bashoraray. | |
| ***is* my defence** | | **The Elohim of** | **my mercy** | **shall prevent me** | **Elohim** | **shall let me see *my desire*** | **upon mine enemies** | |

| אל 408 | תהרגם 2026 | פן 6435 | ישכחו 7911 | עמי 5971 | הניעמו 5128 | בחילך 2428 | והורידמו 3381 | מגננו 4043 | אדני 136: | 59:12 |
|---|---|---|---|---|---|---|---|---|---|---|
| 'al | tahargem | pen | yishkachu | 'amiy, | haniy'aemou | bacheylaka | uahouriydemou; | maginenu | 'adonay. | |
| **not** | **Slay them** | **lest** | **forget** | **my people** | **scatter them** | **by your power** | **and bring them down** | **our shield** | **O Adonai** | |

| חטאת 2403 | פימו 6310 | דבר 1697 | שפתימו 8193 | וילכדו 3920 | בגאונם 1347 | ומאלה 423 | ומכחש 3585 |
|---|---|---|---|---|---|---|---|
| chata't | piymou, | dabar | sapateymou | uayilakadu | big'aunam; | uame'alah | uamikachash |
| ***For* the sin of** | **their mouth** | ***and* the words of** | **their lips** | **let them even be taken** | **in their pride** | **and for cursing** | **and lying** |

| יספרו 5608: | 59:13 | כלה 3615 | בחמה 2534 | כלה 3615 | ואינמו 369 | וידעו 3045 | כי 3588 | אלהים 430 |
|---|---|---|---|---|---|---|---|---|
| yasaperu. | | kaleh | bachemah | kaleh | ua'aeynemou | uayeda'au, | kiy | 'alohiym |
| ***which* they speak** | | **Consume** | ***them* in wrath** | **consume *them*** | **that they *may* not** | ***be* and let them know** | **that** | **Elohim** |

| משל 4910 | ביעקב 3290 | לאפסי 657 | הארץ 776 | סלה 5542: | 59:14 | וישובו 7725 | לערב 6153 | יהמו 1993 |
|---|---|---|---|---|---|---|---|---|
| moshel | baya'aqob; | la'apsey | ha'aretz | selah. | | uayashubu | la'areb | yehamu |
| **rule** | **in Jacob** | **unto the ends** | **the earth** | **Selah** | | **And let them return** | **at evening** | ***and* let them make a noise** |

| ככלב 3611 | ויסובבו 5437 | עיר 5892: | 59:15 | המה 1992 | ינועון 5128 | לאכל 398 | אם 518 | לא 3808 | ישבעו 7646 |
|---|---|---|---|---|---|---|---|---|---|
| kakaleb, | uiysoubabu | 'ayr. | | hemah | yanu'aun | le'akol; | 'am | la' | yisba'au, |
| **like a dog** | **and go round about** | **the city** | | **them** | **Let wonder up and down** | **for meat** | **if** | **not** | **if they be satisfied** |

Ps 59:4 They run and prepare themselves without my fault: awake to help me, and behold.5 Thou therefore, O YHUH G-d of hosts, the G-d of Israel, awake to visit all the heathen: be not merciful to any wicked transgressors. Selah.6 They return at evening: they make a noise like a dog, and go round about the city.7 Behold, they belch out with their mouth: swords are in their lips: for who, say they, doth hear?8 But you, O YHUH, shall laugh at them; you shall have all the heathen in derision.9 Because of his strength will I wait upon you: for G-d is my defence.10 The G-d of my mercy shall prevent me: G-d shall let me see my desire upon mine enemies.11 Slay them not, lest my people forget: scatter them by your power; and bring them down, O Adonai our shield.12 For the sin of their mouth and the words of their lips let them even be taken in their pride: and for cursing and lying which they speak.13 Consume them in wrath, consume them, that they may not be: and let them know that G-d rule in Jacob unto the ends of the earth. Selah.14 And at evening let them return; and let them make a noise like a dog, and go round about the city.15 Let them wander up and down for meat, and grudge if they be not satisfied.

**59:16**

וילינו 3885: | ואני 589 | אשיר 7891 | עזך 5797 | וארנן 7442 | לבקר 1242 | חסדך 2617 | כי 3588

uayaliynu. ua'aniy 'ashiyr 'azeka ua'aranen laboqer, chasadeka kiy

**and grudge | But I | will sing of | your power | yea I will sing aloud | in the morning | *of* your mercy | for**

**59:17**

היית 1961 | משגב 4869 | לי 3807a | ומנוס 4498 | ביום 3117 | צר 6862 | לי 3807a: | עזי 5797 | אליך 413 | אזמרה 2167 | כי 3588

hayiyta misgab liy; uamanous, bayoum tzar liy. 'aziy 'aeleyka 'azamerah; kiy

**for you have been | defence | my | and refuge | in the day of | trouble | my | O my strength | Unto you | will I sing | for**

אלהים 430 | משגבי 4869 | אלהי 430 | חסדי 2617:

'alohiym misgabiy, 'alohey chasdiy.

**Elohim *is* my defence *and* the Elohim of my mercy**

**Ps 60:1**

למנצח 5329 | על 5921 | שושן 7802 | עדות 5715 | מכתם 4387 | לדוד 1732 | ללמד 3925: | בהצותו 5327 | את 854 | ארם 763 | נהרים 5104

lamanatzeach 'al shushan 'aedut; miktam ladauid lalamed. bahatzoutou 'at 'aram naharayim

**To the chief Musician | upon | Shushan | eduth | Michtam | of David | to teach | when he strove | *with* | Aham | naharaim**

ואת 854 | ארם 760 | צובה 6678 | וישב 7725 | יואב 3097 | ויך 5221 | את 853 | אדום 123 | בגיא 1516 | מלח 4417 | שנים 8147 | עשר 6240 | אלף 505:

ua'at 'aram tzoubah uayashab you'ab, uayak 'at 'adoum bagey'a melach; shaneym 'asar 'alep.

***and with* | Aram zobah | when returned | Joab | and smote | *of* Edom | in the valley of | salt | two | ten | thousand**

**60:2**

אלהים 430 | זנחתנו 2186 | פרצתנו 6555 | אנפת 599 | תשובב 7725 | לנו 3807a:

'alohiym zanachtanu paratztanu; 'anapta, tashoubeb lanu.

**O Elohim | you have cast us off | you have scattered us | you have been displeased | O turn yourself again | to us**

**60:3**

הרעשתה 7493 | ארץ 776 | פצמתה 6480 | רפה 7495 | שבריה 7667 | כי 3588 | מטה 4131: | הראיתה 7200

hir'ashtah 'aretz patzamtah; rapah shabareyha kiy matah. hir'aytah

**You have made to tremble | the earth | you have broken it | heal | the breaches thereof | for | it shake | You have showed**

**60:4**

עמך 5971 | קשה 7186 | השקיתנו 8248 | יין 3196 | תרעלה 8653: | נתתה 5414 | ליראיך 3373

'ameka qashah; hishqiytanu, yayin tar'aelah. natatah liyre'aeyka

**your people | hard things | you have made us to drink | the wine of | astonishment | You have given | to them that fear you**

**60:5**

נס 5251 | להתנוסס 5127 | מפני 6440 | קשט 7189 | סלה 5542: | למען 4616 | יחלצון 2502 | ידידיך 3039 | הושיעה 3467

nes lahitnouses; mipaney, qoshet selah. lama'an yechalatzun yadiydeyka; houshiy'ah

**a banner | that it may be displayed | because of | the truth | Selah | That | may be delivered | your beloved | save**

**60:6**

ימינך 3225 | ועננו 6030: | אלהים 430 | דבר 1696 | בקדשו 6944 | אעלזה 5937 | אחלקה 2505 | שכם 7927

yamiynaka ua'anenu 'alohiym diber baqadashou, 'a'alozah 'achalaqah shakem;

***with* your right hand | and hear me. | Elohim | has spoken | in his holiness | I will rejoice | I will divide | Shechem**

**60:7**

ועמק 6010 | סכות 5523 | אמדד 4058: | לי 3807a | גלעד 1568 | ולי 3807a | מנשה 4519 | ואפרים 669 | מעוז 4581 | ראשי 7218

ua'ameq sukout 'amaded. liy gil'ad ualiy manasheh, ua'aprayim ma'auz ra'shiy;

**and the valley of | Succoth | mete out | *is* mine | Gilead | and mine | Manasseh *is* | Ephraim also | *is* the strength of | mine head**

**60:8**

יהודה 3063 | מחקקי 2710: | מואב 4124 | סיר 5518 | רחצי 7366 | על 5921 | אדום 123 | אשליך 7993 | נעלי 5275 | עלי 5921 | פלשת 6429

yahudah, machoqaqiy. mou'ab siyr rachatziy, 'al 'adoum 'ashliyk na'aliy; 'alay, paleshet

**Judah | *is* my lawgiver | Moab *is* | my | washbowl | over | Edom | will I cast out | my shoe | because of me | Philistia**

Ps 59:16 But I will sing of your power; yea, I will sing aloud of your mercy in the morning: for you have been my defence and refuge in the day of my trouble.17 Unto you, O my strength, will I sing: for G-d is my defence, and the G-d of my mercy. **Ps** 60:1 To the chief Musician upon Shu'-shan-e'-duth, Mich'-tam of David, to teach; when he strove with A'-ram-na-ha-ra'-im and with A'-ram-zo'-bah, when Jo'-ab returned, and smote of E'-dom in the valley of salt twelve thousand. O G-d, you have cast us off, you have scattered us, you have been displeased; O turn thyself to us again.2 Thou have made the earth to tremble; you have broken it: heal the breaches thereof; for it shaketh.3 Thou have showed your people hard things: you have made us to drink the wine of astonishment.4 Thou have given a banner to them that fear you, that it may be displayed because of the truth. Selah.5 That your beloved may be delivered; save with your right hand, and hear me.6 G-d has spoken in his holiness; I will rejoice, I will divide Shechem, and mete out the valley of Succoth.7 Gilead is mine, and Manasseh is mine; Ephraim also is the strength of mine head; Judah is my lawgiver;8 Moab is my washpot; over Edom will I cast out my shoe: Philistia, triumph you because of me.

60:9 … 60:10

התרעעי 7321: מי 4310 יבלני 2986 עיר 5892 מצור 4692 מי 4310 נחני 5148 עד 5704 אדום 123: הלא 3808 אתה 859

hitro'a'ay. miy' yobileniy 'ayr matzour; miy' nachaniy 'ad 'adoum. hala' 'atah

**triumph you Who will bring me city? *into the* strong who will lead me into Edom? *Will* not you**

60:11

אלהים 430 זנחתנו 2186 ולא 3808 תצא 3318 אלהים 430 בצבאותינו 6635: הבה 3051 לנו 3807a עזרת 5833

'alohiym zanachtanu; uala' tetzea' 'alohiym, batzib'auteynu. habah lanu 'azrat

**O Elohim *which* had cast us off? and not *you* *which* did go out O Elohim with our armies? Give us help**

60:12

מצר 6862 ושוא 7723 תשועת 8668 אדם 120: באלהים 430 נעשה 6213 חיל 2428 והוא 1931 יבוס 947

mitzar; uashau, tashu'at 'adam be'alohiym na'aseh chayil; uahu'a, yabus

**from trouble for vain *is* the help of man Through Elohim we shall do valiantly for he *it is that* shall tread down**

צרינו 6862:

tzareynu.

**our enemies**

Ps 61:1 … 61:2

למנצח 5329 על 5921 נגינת 5058 לדוד 1732: שמעה 8085 אלהים 430 רנתי 7440 הקשיבה 7181 תפלתי 8605:

lamanatzeach 'al nagiynat ladauid. shim'ah 'alohiym rinatiy; haqashiybah, tapilatiy.

**To the chief Musician upon Neginah *A Psalm* of David Hear O Elohim my cry attend unto my prayer**

מקצה 7097 הארץ 776 אליך 413 אקרא 7121 בעטף 5848 לבי 3820 בצור 6697 ירום 7311 ממני 4480

miqtzeh ha'aretz 'aeleyka 'aqraa' ba'atop libiy; batzur yarum mimeniy

**From the end of the earth unto you will I cry when is overwhelmed my heart to the rock *that* is higher than I**

61:3 … 61:4

תנחני 5148: כי 3588 היית 1961 מחסה 4268 לי 3807a מגדל 4026 עז 5797 מפני 6440 אויב 341: אגורה 1481

tanacheniy. kiy hayiyta machseh liy; migdal 'az, mipaney auyeb. 'agurah

**lead me For you have been a shelter for me *and* a tower strong from the enemy I will abide**

61:5

באהלך 168 עולמים 5769 אחסה 2620 בסתר 5643 כנפיך 3671 סלה 5542: כי 3588 אתה 859 אלהים 430 שמעת 8085

ua'ahalaka 'aulamiym; 'achaseh uaseter kanapeyka selah. kiy 'atah 'alohiym shama'ata

**in your tabernacle for ever I will trust in the covert of your wings Selah For you O Elohim have heard**

61:6

לנדרי 5088 נתת 5414 ירשת 3425 יראי 3373 שמך 8034: ימים 3117 על 5921 ימי 3117 מלך 4428 תוסיף 3254

lindaray; natata yarushat, yira'aey shameka. yamiym 'al yamey melek tousiyp;

**my vows you have given *me* the heritage of those that fear your name life on life of *the* king's You will prolong**

61:7

שנותיו 8141 כמו 3644 דר 1755 ודר 1755: ישב 3427 עולם 5769 לפני 6440 אלהים 430 חסד 2617 ואמת 571 מן 4487

shanoutayu, kamou dor uador. yesheb 'aulam lipney 'alohiym; chesed ua'amet, man

***and* his years will be as many generations He shall abide for ever before Elohim mercy and truth O prepare**

61:8

ינצרהו 5341: כן 3651 אזמרה 2167 שמך 8034 לעד 5703 לשלמי 7999 נדרי 5088 יום 3117 יום 3117:

yintzaruhu. ken 'azamrah shimka la'ad; lashalmiy nadaray, youm youm.

***which* may preserve him So will I sing praise unto your name for ever that I may perform my vows day to day**

Ps 62:1

למנצח 5329 על 5921 ידותון 3038 מזמור 4210 לדוד 1732: אך 389 אל 413 אלהים 430 דומיה 1747 נפשי 5315 ממנו 4480

lamanatzeach 'al yadutun, mizmour ladauid. 'ak 'al 'alohiym dumiyah napshiy; mimenu,

**To the chief Musician to Jeduthun A Psalm of David Truly upon Elohim wait my soul from him *come***

Ps 60:9 Who will bring me into the strong city? who will lead me into Edom?10 Wilt not you, O G-d, which had cast us off? and you, O G-d, which did not go out with our armies?11 Give us help from trouble: for vain is the help of man.12 Through G-d we shall do valiantly: for he it is that shall tread down our enemies. **Ps** 61:1 To the chief Musician upon Neg'-i-nah, A Psalm of David. Hear my cry, O G-d; attend unto my prayer.2 From the end of the earth will I cry unto you, when my heart is overwhelmed: lead me to the rock that is higher than I.3 For you have been a shelter for me, and a strong tower from the enemy.4 I will abide in your tabernacle forever: I will trust in the covert of your wings. Selah.5 For you, O G-d, have heard my vows: you have given me the heritage of those that fear your name.6 Thou will prolong the king's life: and his years as many generations.7 He shall abide before G-d forever: O prepare mercy and truth, which may preserve him.8 So will I sing praise unto your name forever, that I may daily perform my vows. **Ps** 62:1 To the chief Musician, to Je-du'-thun, A Psalm of David. Truly my soul waiteth upon G-d: from him cometh my salvation.

62:2 … 62:3

ישועתי 3444: אך 389 הוא 1931 צורי 6697 וישועתי 3444 משגבי 4869 לא 3808 אמוט 4131 רבה 7227: עד 5704

yashu'atiy. 'ak hua' tzuriy uiyshu'atiy; misgabiy, la' 'amout rabah. 'ad

**my salvation only He *is* my rock and my salvation *he is* my defence not I shall be moved greatly How long**

אנה 575 תהותתו 2050 על 5921 איש 376 תרצחו 7523 כלכם 3605 כקיר 7023 נטוי 5186 גדר 1447

'anah tahoutau 'al 'aysh taratzachu kulkem kaqiyr natuy; gader,

**now will you imagine mischief against a man? you shall be slain all of you as a wall *shall you be and as* bowing a fence**

62:4

הדחויה 1760: אך 389 משאתו 7613 יעצו 3289 להדיח 5080 ירצו 7521 כזב 3577 בפיו 6310 יברכו 1288

hadachuyah. 'ak misa'aetou ya'atzu lahadiyach yirtzu kazab bapiyu yabareku;

**tottering only from his excellency They consult to cast *him* down they delight in lies with their mouth they bless**

62:5 … 62:6

ובקרבם 7130 יקללו 7043 סלה 5542: אך 389 לאלהים 430 דומי 1826 נפשי 5315 כי 3588 ממנו 4480 תקותי 8615: אך 389

uabqirbam, yaqalalu selah. 'ak le'alohiym domiy napshiy; kiy mimenu, tiquatiy. 'ak

**but inwardly they curse Selah only upon Elohim wait you My soul for *is* from him my expectation only**

62:7

הוא 1931 צורי 6697 וישועתי 3444 משגבי 4869 לא 3808 אמוט 4131: על 5921 אלהים 430 ישעי 3468

hua' tzuriy uiyshu'atiy; misgabiy, la' 'amout. 'al 'alohiym yish'ay

**He *is* my rock and my salvation *he is* my defence not I shall be moved In Elohim *is* my salvation**

62:8

וכבודי 3519 צור 6697 עזי 5797 מחסי 4268 באלהים 430: בטחו 982 בו 871a בכל 3605 עת 6256 עם 5971 שפכו 8210

uakboudiy; tzur 'aziy machasiy, be'alohiym. bitchu bou bakal 'at 'am, shipku

**and my glory the rock of my strength *and* my refuge *is* in Elohim Trust in him at all times *you* people pour out**

62:9

לפניו 6440 לבבכם 3824 אלהים 430 מחסה 4268 לנו 3807a סלה 5542: אך 389 הבל 1892 בני 1121 אדם 120 כזב 3577 בני 1121

lapanayu lababkem; 'alohiym machaseh lanu selah. 'ak hebel baney 'adam kazab baney

**before him your heart Elohim *is* a refuge for us Selah Surely *are* vanity man of low degree *are* a lie *and* men of**

62:10

איש 376 במאזנים 3976 לעלות 5927 המה 1992 מהבל 1892 יחד 3162: אל 408 תבטחו 982 בעשק 6233

'aysh bama'zanayim la'alout; hemah, mehebel yachad. 'al tibtachu ba'asheq

**high degree in the balance to be laid they *lighter* than vanity *are* altogether not Trust in oppression**

62:11

ובגזל 1498 אל 408 תהבלו 1891 חיל 2428 כי 3588 ינוב 5107 אל 408 תשיתו 7896 לב 3820: אחת 259 דבר 1696 אלהים 430

uabgazel 'al tehbalu chayil kiy yanub; 'al tashiytu leb. 'achat diber 'alohiym,

**and in robbery not become vain riches if increase not set your heart once has spoken Elohim**

62:12

שתים 8147 זו 2098 שמעתי 8085 כי 3588 עז 5797 לאלהים 430: ולך 3807a אדני 136 חסד 2617 כי 3588 אתה 859

shatayim zu shama'atiy; kiy 'az, le'alohiym. uleka 'adonay chased; kiy 'atah

**twice this have I heard that power *belongs* unto Elohim Also unto you O Adonai *belongs* mercy for you**

תשלם 7999 לאיש 376 כמעשהו 4639:

tashalem la'aysh kama'asehu.

**renderest to every man according to his work**

**Ps 63:1**

מזמור 4210 לדוד 1732 בהיותו 1961 במדבר 4057 יהודה 3063: אלהים 430 אלי 410 אתה 859 אשחרך 7836

mizmour ladauid; bihayotou, bamidbar yahudah. 'alohiym 'aeliy 'atah, 'ashachareka

**A Psalm of David when he was in the wilderness of Judah O Elohim *are* my El you early will I seek you**

Ps 62:2 He only is my rock and my salvation; he is my defence; I shall not be greatly moved.3 How long will you imagine mischief against a man? you shall be slain all of you: as a bowing wall shall you be, and as a tottering fence.4 They only consult to cast him down from his excellency: they delight in lies: they bless with their mouth, but they curse inwardly. Selah.5 My soul, wait you only upon G-d; for my expectation is from him.6 He only is my rock and my salvation: he is my defence; I shall not be moved.7 In G-d is my salvation and my glory: the rock of my strength, and my refuge, is in G-d.8 Trust in him at all times; you people, pour out your heart before him: G-d is a refuge for us. Selah.9 Surely men of low degree are vanity, and men of high degree are a lie: to be laid in the balance, they are altogether lighter than vanity.10 Trust not in oppression, and become not vain in robbery: if riches increase, set not your heart upon them.11 G-d has spoken once; twice have I heard this; that power belong unto G-d.12 Also unto you, O Adonai, belong mercy: for you renderest to every man according to his work. **Ps** 63:1 A Psalm of David, when he was in the wilderness of Judah. O G-d, you are my G-d; early will I seek you: my soul thirsteth for you, my flesh longeth for you in a dry and thirsty land, where no water is;

63:2
צמאה 6770 לך 3807a נפשי 5315 כמה 3642 לך 3807a בשרי 1320 בארץ 776 ציה 6723 ועיף 5889 בלי 1097 מים 4325: כן 3651
tzama'ah laka napshiy, kamah laka basariy; ba'aretz tziyah ua'ayep baliy mayim. ken
**thirst for you my soul long for you my flesh in land a dry and thirsty where no is water so**

63:3
בקדש 6944 חזיתיך 2372 לראות 7200 עזך 5797 וכבודך 3519: כי 3588 טוב 2896 חסדך 2617
baqodesh chaziytiyka; lir'aut 'uzaka, uakboudeka. kiy toub chasdaka
**in the sanctuary *as* I have seen you To see your power and your glory Because *is* better your lovingkindness**

63:4 63:5
מחיים 2416 שפתי 8193 ישבחונך 7623: כן 3651 אברכך 1288 בחיי 2416 בשמך 8034 אשא 5375 כפי 3709: כמו 3644
mechayiym, sapatay yashabchunaka. ken 'abarekka bachayay; bashimka 'asa' kapay. kamou
**than life my lips shall praise you Thus will I bless you while I live in your name I will lift up my hands as**

63:6
חלב 2459 ודשן 1880 תשבע 7646 נפשי 5315 ושפתי 8193 רננות 7445 יהלל 1984 פי 6310: אם 518
cheleb uadeshen tisba' napshiy; uasiptey rananout, yahalel piy. 'am
***with* marrow and fatness shall be satisfied My soul and lips *you with* joyful shall praise my mouth When**

63:7
זכרתיך 2142 על 5921 יצועי 3326 באשמרות 821 אהגה 1897 בך 871a: כי 3588 היית 1961 עזרתה 5833 לי 3807a
zakartiyka 'al yatzu'ay; ba'ashmurout, 'ahageh bak. kiy hayiyta 'azratah liy;
**I remember you upon my bed in the *night* watches *and* meditate on you Because you have been help my**

63:8
ובצל 6738 כנפיך 3671 ארנן 7442: דבקה 1692 נפשי 5315 אחריך 310 בי 871a תמכה 8551
uabtzel kanapeyka 'arnen. dabqah napshiy 'achareyka; biy, tamakah
**therefore in the shadow of your wings will I rejoice follows hard My soul after you me uphold**

63:9 63:10
ימינך 3225: והמה 1992 לשואה 7722 יבקשו 1245 נפשי 5315 יבאו 935 בתחתיות 8482 הארץ 776: יגירהו 5064
yamiyneka. uahemah, lashou'ah yabaqshu napshiy; yabo'au, batachtiyout ha'aretz. yagiyruhu
**your right hand But those to destroy *it that* seek my soul shall go into the lower parts of the earth They shall fall**

63:11
על 5921 ידי 3027 חרב 2719 מנת 4521 שעלים 7776 יהיו 1961: והמלך 4428 ישמח 8055 באלהים 430 יתהלל 1984
'al yadey chareb; manat shu'aliym yihayu. uahamelek yismach be'alohiym yithalel
**on by the sword a portion for foxes they shall be But the king shall rejoice in Elohim shall glory**

כל 3605 הנשבע 7650 בו 871a כי 3588 יסכר 5534 פי 6310 דוברי 1696 שקר 8267:
kal hanishba' bou; kiy yisaker, piy doubarey shaqer.
**every one that swears by him but shall be stopped the mouth of them that speak lies**

**Ps 64:1**
למנצח 5329 מזמור 4210 לדוד 1732: שמע 8085 אלהים 430 קולי 6963 בשיחי 7879 מפחד 6343 אויב 341 תצר 5341
lamanatzeach, mizmour ladauid. shama' 'alohiym qouliy basiychiy; mipachad auyeb, titzor
**To the chief Musician A Psalm of David Hear O Elohim my voice in my prayer from fear of the enemy preserve**

64:2 64:3
חיי 2416: תסתירני 5641 מסוד 5475 מרעים 7489 מרגשת 7285 פעלי 6466 און 205: אשר 834
chayay. tastiyreniy misoud mere'aym; merigshat, po'aley 'auen. 'asher
**my life Hide me from the secret counsel of the wicked from the insurrection of the workers of iniquity Who**

64:4
שננו 8150 כחרב 2719 לשונם 3956 דרכו 1869 חצם 2671 דבר 1697 מר 4751: לירות 3384
shananu kachereb lashounam; daraku chitzam, dabar mar. liyrout
**whet like a sword their tongue *and* bend *their bows to shoot* their arrows words *even* bitter That they may shoot**

Ps 63:2 To see your power and your glory, so as I have seen you in the sanctuary.3 Because your lovingkindness is better than life, my lips shall praise you.4 Thus will I bless you while I live: I will lift up my hands in your name.5 My soul shall be satisfied as with marrow and fatness; and my mouth shall praise you with joyful lips:6 When I remember you upon my bed, and meditate on you in the night watches.7 Because you have been my help, therefore in the shadow of your wings will I rejoice.8 My soul followed hard after you: your right hand upholdeth me.9 But those that seek my soul, to destroy it, shall go into the lower parts of the earth.10 They shall fall by the sword: they shall be a portion for foxes.11 But the king shall rejoice in G-d; everyone that sweareth by him shall glory: but the mouth of them that speak lies shall be stopped. **Ps** 64:1 To the chief Musician, A Psalm of David. Hear my voice, O G-d, in my prayer: preserve my life from fear of the enemy.2 Hide me from the secret counsel of the wicked; from the insurrection of the workers of iniquity:3 Who whet their tongue like a sword, and bend their bows to shoot their arrows, even bitter words:

| במסתרים 4565 | תם 8535 | פתאם 6597 | ירהו 3384 | ולא 3808 | ייראו 3372: | 64:5 יחזקו 2388 | למו 3807a | דבר 1697 |
|---|---|---|---|---|---|---|---|---|
| bamistariym | tam; | pit'am | yoruhu, | uala' | yiyra'au. | yachazqu | lamou | dabar |
| **in secret at** | **the perfect** | **suddenly** | **do they shoot at him** | **and not** | **fear** | **They encourage** | **themselves *in*** | **an matter** |

| רע 7451 | יספרו 5608 | לטמון 2934 | מוקשים 4170 | אמרו 559 | מי 4310 | יראה 7200 | למו 3807a: | 64:6 יחפשו 2664 | עולת 5766 |
|---|---|---|---|---|---|---|---|---|---|
| ra', | yasaparu | litamoun | mouqashiym; | 'amaru, | miy' | yir'ah | lamou. | yachpasu | 'aulot, |
| **evil** | **they commune** | **of laying privily** | **snares** | **they say** | **Who** | **shall see** | **them?** | **They search out** | **iniquities** |

| תמנו 8552 | חפש 2664 | מחפש 2665 | וקרב 7130 | איש 376 | ולב 3820 | 64:7 עמק 6013: |
|---|---|---|---|---|---|---|
| tamnu | chepes | machupas; | uaqereb | 'aysh, | ualeb | 'amoq. |
| **they accomplish** | **a diligent** | **search** | **both the inward** | ***thought of* every one** | ***of them* and the heart** | ***is* deep** |

| וירם 3384 | אלהים 430 | חץ 2671 | פתאום 6597 | היו 1961 | מכותם 4347: | 64:8 ויכשילוהו 3782 |
|---|---|---|---|---|---|---|
| uayorem, | 'alohiym | chetz | pit'aum; | hayu, | makoutam. | uayakshiyluhu |
| **But shall shoot at them** | **Elohim** | ***with* an arrow** | **suddenly** | **shall they be** | **wounded** | **So they shall make to fall** |

| עלימו 5921 | לשונם 3956 | יתנדדו 5074 | כל 3605 | ראה 7200 | בם 871a: | 64:9 וייראו 3372 | כל 3605 | אדם 120 | ויגידו 5046 |
|---|---|---|---|---|---|---|---|---|---|
| 'aleymou | lashounam; | yitnodadu, | kal | ro'aeh | bam. | uayiyra'au, | kal | 'adam | uayagiydu |
| **upon themselves** | **their own tongue** | **shall flee away** | **all** | **that see** | **them** | **And shall fear** | **all** | **men** | **and shall declare** |

| פעל 6467 | אלהים 430 | ומעשהו 4639 | השכילו 7919: | 64:10 ישמח 8055 | צדיק 6662 | ביהוה 3069 | וחסה 2620 |
|---|---|---|---|---|---|---|---|
| po'al | 'alohiym, | uama'asehu | hiskiylu. | yismach | tzadiyq | baYahuah | uachasah |
| **the work of** | **Elohim** | **for his doing** | **they shall wisely consider *of*** | **shall be glad** | **The righteous** | **in Yahuah** | **and shall trust** |

| בו 871a | ויתהללו 1984 | כל 3605 | ישרי 3477 | לב 3820: |
|---|---|---|---|---|
| bou; | uayithallu, | kal | yishrey | leb. |
| **in him** | **and shall glory** | **all** | **the upright in** | **heart** |

| Ps 65:1 למנצח 5329 | מזמור 4210 | לדוד 1732 | שיר 7892: | לך 3807a | דמיה 1747 | תהלה 8416 | אלהים 430 | בציון 6726 | ולך 3807a |
|---|---|---|---|---|---|---|---|---|---|
| lamanatzeach | mizmour, | ladauid | shiyr. | laka | dumiyah | tahilah | 'alohiym | batziyoun; | ualka, |
| **To the chief Musician** | **A Psalm** | **of David** | ***and* Song** | **for you** | **wait** | **Praise** | **O Elohim** | **in Sion** | **and unto you** |

| ישלם 7999 | נדר 5088: | 65:2 שמע 8085 | תפלה 8605 | עדיך 5704 | כל 3605 | בשר 1320 | יבאו 935: | 65:3 דברי 1697 | עונת 5771 | גברו 1396 |
|---|---|---|---|---|---|---|---|---|---|---|
| yashulam | neder. | shomea' | tapilah; | 'adeyka, | kal | basar | yabo'au. | dibrey | 'auonot | gabaru |
| **shall be performed** | **the vow** | **O you that hear** | **prayer** | **unto you** | **all** | **flesh** | **shall come** | **act** | **Iniquities** | **prevail** |

| מני 4480 | פשעינו 6588 | אתה 859 | תכפרם 3722: | 65:4 אשרי 835 | תבחר 977 |
|---|---|---|---|---|---|
| meniy; | pasha'aeynu, | 'atah | takaprem. | 'ashrey | tibchar |
| **against me** | ***as for* our transgressions** | **you** | **shall purge them away** | **Blessed** | ***is the man whom* you choose** |

| ותקרב 7126 | ישכן 7931 | חצריך 2691 | נשבעה 7646 | בטוב 2896 | ביתך 1004 |
|---|---|---|---|---|---|
| uatqareb | yishkan | chatzereyka | nisba'ah | batub | beytaka; |
| **and cause to approach** | ***unto you that* he may dwell in** | **your courts** | **we shall be satisfied** | **with the goodness of** | **your house** |

| קדש 6918 | היכלך 1964: | 65:5 נוראות 3372 | בצדק 6664 | תעננו 6030 | אלהי 430 | ישענו 3468 |
|---|---|---|---|---|---|---|
| qadosh, | heykaleka. | noura'aut | batzedeq | ta'anenu | 'alohey | yish'aenu; |
| ***even of* holy** | **your temple** | ***By* terrible things** | **in righteousness** | **will you answer us** | **O Elohim of** | **our salvation** |

Ps 64:4 That they may shoot in secret at the perfect: suddenly do they shoot at him, and fear not.5 They encourage themselves in an evil matter: they commune of laying snares privily; they say, Who shall see them?6 They search out iniquities; they accomplish a diligent search: both the inward thought of everyone of them, and the heart, is deep.7 But G-d shall shoot at them with an arrow; suddenly shall they be wounded.8 So they shall make their own tongue to fall upon themselves: all that see them shall flee away.9 And all men shall fear, and shall declare the work of G-d; for they shall wisely consider of his doing.10 The righteous shall be glad in YHUH, and shall trust in him; and all the upright in heart shall glory. **Ps** 65:1 To the chief Musician, A Psalm and Song of David. Praise waiteth for you, O G-d, in Sion: and unto you shall the vow be performed.2 O you that hear prayer, unto you shall all flesh come.3 Iniquities prevail against me: as for our transgressions, you shall purge them away.4 Blessed is the man whom you choosest, and causest to approach unto you, that he may dwell in your courts: we shall be satisfied with the goodness of your house, even of your holy temple.5 By terrible things in righteousness will you answer us, O G-d of our salvation; who are the confidence of all the ends of the earth, and of them that are afar off upon the sea:

מבטח 4009 כל 3605 קצוי 7099 ארץ 776 וים 3220 רחקים 7350: 65:6 מכין 3559
mibtach kal qatzuey 'aretz, uayam rachouqiym. mekiyn
***who are*** **the confidence of all the ends of the earth and the sea** ***of*** **them that are afar off** ***upon*** ***Which*** **set fast**

הרים 2022 בכחו 3581 נאזר 247 בגבורה 1369: 65:7 משביח 7623 שאון 7588 ימים 3220 שאון 7588 גליהם 1530
hariym bakochou; ne'azar, bigburah. mashbiyach sha'aun yamiym sha'aun galeyhem,
**the mountains by his strength** ***being*** **girded with power Which still the noise of the seas the noise of their waves**

והמון 1995 לאמים 3816: 65:8 וייראו 3372 ישבי 3427 קצות 7099 מאותתיך 226 מוצאי 4161
uahamoun la'amiym. uayiyra'au yoshabey qatzauot me'autoteyka; moutza'aey
**and the tumult of the people They also that are afraid dwell in the utter most parts at your tokens the outgoings of**

בקר 1242 וערב 6153 תרנין 7442: 65:9 פקדת 6485 הארץ 776 ותשקקה 7783 רבת 7227 תעשרנה 6238
boqer ua'areb tarniyn. paqadta ha'aretz uatashoqaqeha rabat ta'ashrenah,
**the morning and evening you make to rejoice You visit the earth and water it greatly you enrichest it**

פלג 6388 אלהים 430 מלא 4390 מים 4325 תכין 3559 דגנם 1715 כי 3588 כן 3651
peleg 'alohiym malea' mayim; takiyn daganam, kiy ken
***with*** **the river of Elohim** ***which*** **is full of water you preparest them corn when so**

תכינה 3559: 65:10 תלמיה 8525 רוה 7301 נחת 5181 גדודיה 1417 ברביבים 7241
takiyneha. talameyha raueh nachet gadudeyha; birabiybiym
**thusyou have provided for it the ridges thereof You water abundantly you settle the furrows thereof with showers**

תמגגנה 4127 צמחה 6780 תברך 1288: 65:11 עטרת 5849 שנת 8141 טובתך 2896 ומעגליך 4570 ירעפון 7491
tamogagenah, tzimchah tabarek. 'ateret shanat toubateka; uama'agaleyka, yir'apun
**you make it soft the springing thereof you blessest You crown the year** ***with*** **your goodness and your paths drop**

דשן 1880: 65:12 ירעפו 7491 נאות 4999 מדבר 4057 וגיל 1524 גבעות 1389 תחגרנה 2296: 65:13 לבשו 3847
dashen. yir'apu na'aut midbar; uagiyl, gaba'aut tachgoranah. labashu
**fatness They drop** ***upon*** **the pastures of the wilderness and rejoice** ***the*** **little hills on every side are clothed with**

כרים 3733 הצאן 6629 ועמקים 6010 יעטפו 5848 בר 1250 יתרועעו 7321 אף 637 ישירו 7891:
kariym hatza'an, ua'amaqiym ya'atapu bar; yitrou'a'au, 'ap yashiyru.
**The pastures flocks the valleys also are covered over with corn they shout for joy also they sing**

**Ps 66:1** למנצח 5329 שיר 7892 מזמור 4210 הריעו 7321 לאלהים 430 כל 3605 הארץ 776: 66:2 זמרו 2167
lamanatzeach shiyr mizmour; hariy'au le'alohiym kal ha'aretz. zamru
**To the chief Musician A Song** ***or*** **Psalm Make a joyful noise unto Elohim all you lands Sing forth**

כבוד 3519 שמו 8034 שימו 7760 כבוד 3519 תהלתו 8416: 66:3 אמרו 559 לאלהים 430 מה 4100 נורא 3372 מעשיך 4639
kaboud shamou; siymu kaboud, tahilatou. 'amru le'alohiym mah noura' ma'aseyka;
**the honor of his name make glorious his praise Say unto Elohim How terrible** ***are you in*** **your works**

ברב 7230 עזך 5797 יכחשו 3584 לך 3807a איביך 341: 66:4 כל 3605 הארץ 776 ישתחוו 7812
barob 'uzaka, yakachashu laka 'ayabeyka. kal ha'aretz yishtachauu
**through the greatness of your power shall submit themselves unto you your enemies All the earth shall worship**

Ps 65:6 Which by his strength set fast the mountains; being girded with power:7 Which stilleth the noise of the seas, the noise of their waves, and the tumult of the people.8 They also that dwell in the uttermost parts are afraid at your tokens: you make the outgoings of the morning and evening to rejoice.9 Thou visitest the earth, and waterest it: you greatly enrichest it with the river of G-d, which is full of water: you preparest them corn, when you have so provided for it.10 Thou waterest the ridges thereof abundantly: you settlest the furrows thereof: you make it soft with showers: you blessest the springing thereof.11 Thou crownest the year with your goodness; and your paths drop fatness.12 They drop upon the pastures of the wilderness: and the little hills rejoice on every side.13 The pastures are clothed with flocks; the valleys also are covered over with corn; they shout for joy, they also sing. **Ps** 66:1 To the chief Musician, A Song or Psalm. Make a joyful noise unto G-d, all you lands:2 Sing forth the honor of his name: make his praise glorious.3 Say unto G-d, How terrible are you in your works! through the greatness of your power shall your enemies submit themselves unto you.

| | | | | | 66:5 | | | | |
|---|---|---|---|---|---|---|---|---|---|
| לך 3807a | ויזמרו 2167 | לך 3807a | יזמרו 2167 | שמך 8034 | סלה 5542: | לכו 1980 | וראו 7200 | מפעלות 4659 | אלהים 430 |
| laka | uiyzamru | lak; | yazamru | shimka | selah. | laku | uar'au | mipa'alout | 'alohiym; |
| **unto you** | **and shall sing** | **unto you** | **they shall sing** | ***to* your name** | **Selah** | **Come** | **and see** | **the works of** | **Elohim** |

| | | | | | 66:6 | | | | |
|---|---|---|---|---|---|---|---|---|---|
| נורא 3372 | עלילה 5949 | על 5921 | בני 1121 | אדם 120: | הפך 2015 | ים 3220 | ליבשה 3004 | בנהר 5104 | יעברו 5674 |
| noura' | 'aliylah, | 'al | baney | 'adam. | hapak | yam | layabashah, | banahar | ya'abru |
| ***he is* terrible** | ***in his* doing** | **toward** | **the children of** | **men** | **He turned** | **the sea** | **into dry *land*** | **through the flood** | **they went** |

| | | | | 66:7 | | | | | |
|---|---|---|---|---|---|---|---|---|---|
| ברגל 7272 | שם 8033 | נשמחה 8055 | בו 871a: | משל 4910 | בגבורתו 1369 | עולם 5769 | עיניו 5869 | בגוים 1471 | תצפינה 6822 | הסוררים 5637 |
| baragel; | sham | nismachah | bou. | moshel | bigaburatou | 'aulam, | 'aeynayu | bagouyim | titzpeynah; | hasourariym |
| **on foot** | **there** | **did we rejoice** | **in him** | **He rule** | **by his power** | **for ever** | **his eyes** | **the nations** | **behold** | **let the rebellious** |

| | | | | 66:8 | | | | | | 66:9 |
|---|---|---|---|---|---|---|---|---|---|---|
| אל 408 | ירימו 7311 | למו 3807a | סלה 5542: | ברכו 1288 | עמים 5971 | אלהינו 430 | והשמיעו 8085 | קול 6963 | תהלתו 8416: | |
| 'al | yariymu | lamou | selah. | baraku | 'amiym | 'aloheynu; | uahashamiy'au, | qoul | tahilatou. | |
| **not** | **exalt** | **themselves** | **Selah** | **O bless** | **you people** | **our Elohim** | **and make to be heard** | **the voice of** | **his praise** | |

| | | | | | | | 66:10 | | |
|---|---|---|---|---|---|---|---|---|---|
| השם 7760 | נפשנו 5315 | בחיים 2416 | ולא 3808 | נתן 5414 | למוט 4132 | רגלנו 7272: | כי 3588 | בחנתנו 974 | אלהים 430 |
| hasam | napshenu | bachayiym; | uala' | natan | lamout | raglenu. | kiy | bachantanu | 'alohiym; |
| **Which holds** | **our soul** | **in life** | **and not** | **suffer** | **to be moved** | **our feet** | **For** | **you have proved us** | **O Elohim** |

| | | | 66:11 | | | | | 66:12 |
|---|---|---|---|---|---|---|---|---|
| צרפתנו 6884 | כצרף 6884 | כסף 3701: | הבאתנו 935 | במצודה 4686 | שמת 7760 | מועקה 4157 | במתנינו 4975: | |
| tzaraptanu, | kitzrap | kasep. | habea'tanu | bamtzudah; | samta | mu'aqah | bamataneynu. | |
| **you have tried us** | **as is tried** | **silver** | **You brought us** | **into the net** | **you laid** | **affliction** | **upon our loins** | |

| הרכבת 7392 | אנוש 582 | לראשנו 7218 | באנו 935 | באש 784 | ובמים 4325 | ותוציאנו 3318 |
|---|---|---|---|---|---|---|
| hirkabta | 'anoush, | lara'shenu | banu | ba'ash | uabamayim; | uatoutziy'aenu, |
| **You have caused to ride** | **men** | **over our heads** | **we went** | **through fire** | **and through water** | **but you brought us out** |

| | 66:13 | | | | | | 66:14 |
|---|---|---|---|---|---|---|---|
| לרויה 7310: | אבוא 935 | ביתך 1004 | בעולות 5930 | אשלם 7999 | לך 3807a | נדרי 5088: | אשר 834 |
| larauayah. | abou'a | beytaka | ua'alout; | 'ashalem | laka | nadaray. | 'asher |
| **into a wealthy *place*** | **I will go into** | **your house** | **with burnt offerings** | **I will pay** | **unto you** | **my vows** | **Which** |

| | | | | | | 66:15 | | |
|---|---|---|---|---|---|---|---|---|
| פצו 6475 | שפתי 8193 | ודבר 1696 | פי 6310 | בצר 6862 | לי 3807a: | עלות 5930 | מחים 4220 | אעלה 5927 |
| patzu | sapatay; | uadiber | piy, | batzar | liy. | 'alout | mechiym | 'a'aleh |
| **have uttered** | **my lips** | **and has spoken** | **my mouth** | **when was in trouble** | **I** | **burnt sacrifices of** | **fatlings** | **I will offer** |

| | | | | | | | | | 66:16 | |
|---|---|---|---|---|---|---|---|---|---|---|
| לך 3807a | עם 5973 | קטרת 7004 | אילים 352 | אעשה 6213 | בקר 1241 | עם 5973 | עתודים 6260 | סלה 5542: | לכו 1980 | שמעו 8085 |
| lak | 'am | qatoret | 'aeyliym; | 'a'aseh | baqar | 'am | 'atudiym | selah. | laku | shim'au |
| **unto you** | **with** | **the incense of** | **rams** | **I will offer** | **bullocks** | **with** | **goats** | **Selah** | **Come** | ***and* hear** |

| | | | | | | | 66:17 | | |
|---|---|---|---|---|---|---|---|---|---|
| ואספרה 5608 | כל 3605 | יראי 3373 | אלהים 430 | אשר 834 | עשה 6213 | לנפשי 5315: | אליו 413 | פי 6310 | קראתי 7121 |
| ua'asaprah | kal | yira'aey | 'alohiym; | 'asher | 'asah | lanapshiy. | 'aelayu | piy | qaraa'tiy; |
| **and I will declare** | **all** | **you that fear** | **Elohim** | **what** | **he has done** | **for my soul** | **unto him** | ***with* my mouth** | **I cried** |

| | | | 66:18 | | | | | | |
|---|---|---|---|---|---|---|---|---|---|
| ורומם 7318 | תחת 8478 | לשוני 3956: | און 205 | אם 518 | ראיתי 7200 | בלבי 3820 | לא 3808 | ישמע 8085 | אדני 136: |
| uaroumam, | tachat | lashouniy. | 'auen | 'am | ra'aytiy | balibiy; | la' | yishma' | 'adonay. |
| **and he was extolled with** | | **my tongue** | **iniquity** | **If** | **I regard** | **in my heart** | **not** | **will hear *me*** | **Adonai** |

Ps 66:4 All the earth shall worship you, and shall sing unto you; they shall sing to your name. Selah.5 Come and see the works of G-d: he is terrible in his doing toward the children of men.6 He turned the sea into dry land: they went through the flood on foot: there did we rejoice in him.7 He rule by his power forever; his eyes behold the nations: let not the rebellious exalt themselves. Selah.8 O bless our G-d, you people, and make the voice of his praise to be heard:9 Which holdeth our soul in life, and suffereth not our feet to be moved.10 For you, O G-d, have proved us: you have tried us, as silver is tried.11 Thou brought us into the net; you laidst affliction upon our loins.12 Thou have caused men to ride over our heads; we went through fire and through water: but you brought us out into a wealthy place.13 I will go into your house with burnt offerings: I will pay you my vows,14 Which my lips have uttered, and my mouth has spoken, when I was in trouble.15 I will offer unto you burnt sacrifices of fatlings, with the incense of rams; I will offer bullocks with goats. Selah.16 Come and hear, all you that fear G-d, and I will declare what he has done for my soul.17 I cried unto him with my mouth, and he was extolled with my tongue.18 If I regard iniquity in my heart, YHUH will not hear me:

**66:19** | **66:20**

אכן 403 שמע 8085 אלהים 430 הקשיב 7181 בקול 6963 תפלתי 8605: ברוך 1288 אלהים 430 אשר 834 לא 3808

'aken shama' 'alohiym; hiqshiyb, baqoul tapilatiy. baruk 'alohiym; 'asher la'

***But* verily has heard *me* Elohim he has attended to the voice of my prayer Blessed *be* Elohim which not**

הסיר 5493 תפלתי 8605 וחסדו 2617 מאתי 854:

hesiyr tapilatiy uachasdou, me'atiy.

**has turned away my prayer nor his mercy from me.**

**Ps 67:1**

למנצח 5329 בנגינת 5058 מזמור 4210 שיר 7892: אלהים 430 יחננו 2603 ויברכנו 1288 יאר 215

lamnatzech binagiynout, mizmour shiyr. 'alohiym, yachanenu uivbarakenu; ya'aer

**To the chief Musician on Neginoth A Psalm *or* Song Elohim be merciful unto us and bless us to shine**

**67:2**

פניו 6440 אתנו 854 סלה 5542: לדעת 3045 בארץ 776 דרכך 1870 בכל 3605 גוים 1471

panayu 'atanu selah. lada'at ba'aretz darkeka; bakal gouyim,

***and* cause his face upon us Selah That may be known upon earth your way among all nations**

**67:3** | **67:4**

ישועתך 3444: יודוך 3034 עמים 5971 אלהים 430 יודוך 3034 עמים 5971 כלם 3605: ישמחו 8055

yashu'ateka. youduka 'amiym 'alohiym; youduka, 'amiym kulam. yismachu

**your saving health Let praise you the people O Elohim let praise you the people all O let be glad**

**67:5**

וירננו 7442 לאמים 3816 כי 3588 תשפט 8199 עמים 5971 מישור 4334 ולאמים 3816 בארץ 776 תנחם 5148 סלה 5542:

uiyrannu, la'amiym kiy tishpat 'amiym miyshour; uala'amiym ba'aretz tanachem selah.

**and sing for joy the nations for you shall judge the people righteously and the nations upon earth govern Selah**

**67:6**

יודוך 3034 עמים 5971 אלהים 430 יודוך 3034 עמים 5971 כלם 3605: ארץ 776 נתנה 5414 יבולה 2981

youduka 'amiym 'alohiym; youduka, 'amiym kulam. 'aretz natanah yabulah;

**Let praise you the people O Elohim let praise you the people all *Then* the earth shall yield her increase**

**67:7**

יברכנו 1288 אלהים 430 אלהינו 430: יברכנו 1288 אלהים 430 וייראו 3372 אתו 853 כל 3605 אפסי 657 ארץ 776:

yabarakenu, 'alohiym 'aloheynu. yabarakenu 'alohiym; uayiyra'au 'atou, kal 'apsey 'aretz.

**shall bless us *and* Elohim *even* our own Elohim shall bless Elohim and shall fear him all the ends of the earth**

**Ps 68:1**

למנצח 5329 לדוד 1732 מזמור 4210 שיר 7892: יקום 6965 אלהים 430 יפוצו 6327 אויביו 341 וינוסו 5127

lamanatzeach ladauid, mizmour shiyr. yaqum 'alohiym yaputzu 'auyabayu; uayanusu

**To the chief Musician of David A Psalm *or* Song Let arise Elohim let be scattered his enemies let them also flee**

**68:2**

משנאיו 8130 מפניו 6440: כהנדף 5086 עשן 6227 תנדף 5086 כהמס 4549 דונג 1749 מפני 6440 אש 784 יאבדו 6

masan'ayu, mipanayu. kahindop 'ashan, tindop kahimes dounag mipaney 'aesh; ya'badu

**that hate him before him As is driven away smoke *so* drive *them* away as melt wax before the fire *so* let perish**

**68:3**

רשעים 7563 מפני 6440 אלהים 430: וצדיקים 6662 ישמחו 8055 יעלצו 5970 לפני 6440 אלהים 430

rasha'aym, mipaney 'alohiym. uatzadiyqiym, yismachu ya'altzu lipney 'alohiym,

**the wicked at the presence of Elohim But let the righteous let be glad let them rejoice before Elohim**

**68:4**

וישישו 7797 בשמחה 8057: שירו 7891 לאלהים 430 זמרו 2167 שמו 8034 סלו 5549 לרכב 7392 בערבות 6160

uayasiysu basimchah. shiyru le'alohiym zamru shamou solu larokeb ba'arabout

**yea let them rejoice exceedingly Sing unto Elohim sing praises to his name extol him that ride upon the heavens**

Ps 67:19 But verily G-d has heard me; he has attended to the voice of my prayer.20 Blessed be G-d, which has not turned away my prayer, nor his mercy from me. **Ps** 67:1 To the chief Musician on Neg'-i-noth, A Psalm or Song. G-d be merciful unto us, and bless us; and cause his face to shine upon us; Selah.2 That your way may be known upon earth, your saving health among all nations.3 Let the people praise you, O G-d; let all the people praise you.4 O let the nations be glad and sing for joy: for you shall judge the people righteously, and govern the nations upon earth. Selah.5 Let the people praise you, O G-d; let all the people praise you.6 Then shall the earth yield her increase; and G-d, even our own G-d, shall bless us.7 G-d shall bless us; and all the ends of the earth shall fear him. **Ps** 68:1 To the chief Musician, A Psalm or Song of David. Let G-d arise, let his enemies be scattered: let them also that hate him flee before him.2 As smoke is driven away, so drive them away: as wax melteth before the fire, so let the wicked perish at the presence of G-d.3 But let the righteous be glad; let them rejoice before G-d: yea, let them exceedingly rejoice.4 Sing unto G-d, sing praises to his name: extol him that rideth upon the heavens by his name YAH, and rejoice before him.

ביה 3050 שמו 8034 ועלזו 5937 לפניו 6440: **68:5** אבי 1 יתומים 3490 ודין 1781 אלמנות 490 אלהים 430 במעון 4583
bayah shamou, ua'alzu lapanayu. 'abiy yatoumiym uadayan almanout; 'alohiym, bima'aun
**by YAH his name and rejoice before him A father of the fatherless and a judge of the widows *is* Elohim in habitation**

קדשו 6944: **68:6** אלהים 430 מושיב 3427 יחידים 3173 ביתה 1004 מוציא 3318 אסירים 615 בכושרות 3574 אך 389
qadashou. 'alohiym moushiyb yachiydiym bayatah, moutziy'a 'asiyriym bakousharout; 'ak
**his holy Elohim set the solitary in families he brings out those which are bound with chains but**

סוררים 5637 שכנו 7931 צחיחה 6707: **68:7** אלהים 430 בצאתך 3318 לפני 6440 עמך 5971 בצעדך 6805
sourariym, shakanu tzachiychah. 'alohiym, batzea'taka lipney 'ameka; batza'adaka
**the rebellious dwell in a dry land O Elohim when you went forth before your people when you did march**

בישימון 3452 סלה 5542: **68:8** ארץ 776 רעשה 7493 אף 637 שמים 8064 נטפו 5197 מפני 6440 אלהים 430 זה 2088
biyshiymoun selah. 'aretz ra'ashah 'ap shamayim natapu mipaney 'alohiym zeh
**through the wilderness Selah The earth shook also the heavens dropped at the presence of Elohim itself**

סיני 5514 מפני 6440 אלהים 430 אלהי 430 ישראל 3478: **68:9** גשם 1653 נדבות 5071 תניף 5130 אלהים 430
siynay; mipaney 'alohiym, 'alohey yisra'ael. geshem nadabout taniyp 'alohiym;
***even* Sinai *was moved* at the presence of Elohim the Elohim of Israel a rain plentiful You did send O Elohim**

נחלתך 5159 ונלאה 3811 אתה 859 כוננתה 3559: **68:10** חיתך 2416 ישבו 3427 בה 871a
nachalataka uanil'ah, 'atah kounantah. chayataka yashabu bah;
**your inheritance *when* it was weary you whereby did confirm Your congregation has dwelt therein**

תכין 3559 בטובתך 2896 לעני 6041 אלהים 430: **68:11** אדני 136 יתן 5414 אמר 562 המבשרות 1319
takiyn batoubataka le'aniy 'alohiym. 'adonay yiten 'amer; hamabasrout,
**you have prepared of your goodness for the poor O Elohim Adonai gave the word of those that published *it***

צבא 6635 רב 7227: **68:12** מלכי 4428 צבאות 6635 ידדון 5074 ידדון 5074 ונות 5116 בית 1004 תחלק 2505 שלל 7998: **68:13**
tzaba' rab. malkey tzaba'aut yidodun yidodun; uanuat bayit, tachaleq shalal.
***was* the company of great Kings of armies did flee apace and she that tarried at home divided the spoil**

אם 518 תשכבון 7901 בין 996 שפתים 8240 כנפי 3671 יונה 3123 נחפה 2645 בכסף 3701 ואברותיה 84
'am tishkabun beyn shapatayim kanpey younah nechapah bakesep; ua'abrouteyha,
**Though you have lien among the pots *yet shall you be as* the wings of a dove covered with silver and yellow**

בירקרק 3422 חרוץ 2742: **68:14** בפרש 6566 שדי 7706 מלכים 4428 בה 871a תשלג 7949 בצלמון 6756: **68:15** הר 2022
biyraqraq charutz. bapares shaday malakiym bah, tashleg batzalmoun. har
**her feathers *with* gold When scattered the Almighty kings in it, *it was white* as snow in Salmon The hill of**

אלהים 430 הר 2022 בשן 1316 הר 2022 גבננים 1386 הר 2022 בשן 1316: **68:16** למה 4100 תרצדון 7520 הרים 2022 גבננים 1386
'alohiym har bashan; har gabnuniym, har bashan. lamah taratzadun hariym gabnuniym
**Elohim *is as* the hill of Bashan an high hill *as* the hill of Bashan Why leap you hills? *you* high *this is***

ההר 2022 חמד 2530 אלהים 430 לשבתו 3427 אף 637 יהוה 3068 ישכן 7931 לנצח 5331: **68:17** רכב 7393 אלהים 430
hahar, chamad 'alohiym lashibtou; 'ap Yahuah yishkon lanetzach. rekeb 'alohiym,
**the hill desire *which* Elohim to dwell in yea Yahuah will dwell *in it* for ever The chariots of Elohim**

Ps 68:5 A father of the fatherless, and a judge of the widows, is G-d in his holy habitation.6 G-d set the solitary in families: he bring out those which are bound with chains: but the rebellious dwell in a dry land.7 O G-d, when you went forth before your people, when you did march through the wilderness; Selah:8 The earth shook, the heavens also dropped at the presence of G-d: even Sinai itself was moved at the presence of G-d, the G-d of Israel.9 Thou, O G-d, did send a plentiful rain, whereby you did confirm your inheritance, when it was weary.10 Thy congregation has dwelt therein: you, O G-d, have prepared of your goodness for the poor.11 The Adonai gave the word: great was the company of those that published it.12 Kings of armies did flee apace: and she that tarried at home divided the spoil.13 Though you have lien among the pots, yet shall you be as the wings of a dove covered with silver, and her feathers with yellow gold.14 When the Almighty scattered kings in it, it was white as snow in Salmon.15 The hill of G-d is as the hill of Bashan; an high hill as the hill of Bashan.16 Why leap you, you high hills? this is the hill which G-d desire to dwell in; yea, YHUH will dwell in it forever.

68:18
רבתים 7239 | אלפי 505 | שנאן 8136 | אדני 136 | בם 871a | סיני 5514 | בקדש 6944:
ribotayim | 'alpey | shin'an; | 'adonay | bam, | siynay | baqodesh.
***are*** **twenty thousand** | ***even*** **thousands of** | **angels** | **Adonai** | ***is*** **among them** | ***as in*** **Sinai** | **in the holy place**

עלית 5927 | למרום 4791 | שבית 7617 | שבי 7628 | לקחת 3947 | מתנות 4979 | באדם 120 | ואף 637 | סוררים 5637
'aliyta | lamaroum | shabiyta | shebiy, | laqachta | matanout | ba'adam; | ua'ap | sourariym,
**You have ascended** | **on high** | **you have led captive** | **captivity** | **you have received** | **gifts** | **for men** | **yea also** | ***for*** **the rebellious**

לשכן 7931 | יה 3050 | אלהים 430: | 68:19 | ברוך 1288 | אדני 136 | יום 3117 | יום 3117 | יעמס 6006 | לנו 3807a
lishkon | Yah | 'alohiym. | baruk | 'adonay | youm | youm | ya'amos | lanu,
***among them*** **that might dwell** | **Yah** | **Elohim** | **Blessed** | ***be*** **Adonai** | ***who*** **day** | ***to*** **day** | **loads** | **us**

האל 410 | ישועתנו 3444 | סלה 5542: | 68:20 | האל 410 | לנו 3807a | אל 410 | למושעות 4190 | וליהוה 3069
ha'ael | yashu'atenu | selah. | ha'ael | lanu | 'ael | lamousha'aut | ualeYahuah
***with benefits even*** **the El** ***of*** | **our salvation** | **Selah** | ***He that is*** **the El** | **our** | ***is the*** **El** | **of salvation** | **and unto Yahuah**

אדני 136 | למות 4194 | תוצאות 8444: | 68:21 | אך 389 | אלהים 430 | ימחץ 4272 | ראש 7218 | איביו 341 | קדקד 6936 | שער 8181
'adonay; | lamauet, | totza'aut. | 'ak | 'alohiym, | yimchatz | ra'sh | 'ayabayu | qadaqod | se'ar;
**Adonai** | **from death** | ***belong*** **the issues** | **But** | **Elohim** | **shall wound** | **the head of** | **his enemies** | **scalp of** | ***and the*** **hairy**

מתהלך 1980 | באשמיו 817: | 68:22 | אמר 559 | אדני 136 | מבשן 1316 | אשיב 7725 | אשיב 7725
mithalek, | ba'ashamayu. | 'amar | 'adonay | mibashan | 'ashiyb; | 'ashiyb,
**such an one as goes on still** | **in his trespasses** | **said** | **Adonai** | **from Bashan** | **I will bring again** | **I will bring** ***my people*** **again**

ממצלות 4688 | ים 3220: | 68:23 | למען 4616 | תמחץ 4272 | רגלך 7272 | בדם 1818 | לשון 3956 | כלביך 3611 | מאיבים 341
mimatzulout | yam. | lama'an | timchatz | raglaka, | badam | lashoun | kalabeyka; | me'ayabiym
**from the depths of** | **the sea** | **That** | **may be dipped** | **your foot** | **in the blood of** | ***and*** **the tongue of** | **your dogs** | ***your*** **enemies**

מנהו 4480: | 68:24 | ראו 7200 | הליכותיך 1979 | אלהים 430 | הליכות 1979 | אלי 410 | מלכי 4428 | בקדש 6944: | 68:25
minehu. | ra'au | haliykouteyka | 'alohiym; | haliykout | 'aeliy | malkiy | baqodesh.
**in the same** | **They have seen** | **your goings** | **O Elohim** | ***even*** **the goings of** | **my El** | **my King** | **in the sanctuary**

קדמו 6923 | שרים 7891 | אחר 310 | נגנים 5059 | בתוך 8432 | עלמות 5959
qidmu | shariym | 'achar | noganiym; | batouk | 'alamout,
**went before** | **The singers** | ***followed*** **after** | **the players on instruments** | **among** | ***them were*** **the damsels**

תופפות 8608: | 68:26 | במקהלות 4721 | ברכו 1288 | אלהים 430 | יהוה 3068 | ממקור 4726 | ישראל 3478: | 68:27 | שם 8033
toupepout. | Bemakhelot | baraku | 'alohiym; | Yahuah | mimaqour | yisra'ael. | sham
**playing with timbrels** | **in the congregations** | **Bless you** | **Elohim** | **Yahuah** | **from the fountain of** | **Israel** | **There**

בנימן 1144 | צעיר 6810 | רדם 7287 | שרי 8269 | יהודה 3063 | רגמתם 7277 | שרי 8269 | זבלון 2074 | שרי 8269
binyamin | tza'ayr | rodem, | sarey | yahudah | rigmatam; | sarey | zabulun, | sarey
**Benjamin** | ***is*** **little** | ***with*** **their ruler** | **the princes of** | **Judah** | ***and*** **their council** | **the princes of** | **Zebulun** | ***and*** **the princes of**

נפתלי 5321: | 68:28 | צוה 6680 | אלהיך 430 | עזך 5797 | עוזה 5810 | אלהים 430 | זו 2098 | פעלת 6466
naptaliy. | tziuah | 'aloheyka, | 'azeka | 'azah | 'alohiym; | zu, | pa'alta
**Naphtali** | **has commanded** | **Your Elohim** | **your strength** | **strengthen** | **O Elohim** | **that which** | **you have wrought**

Ps 68:17 The chariots of G-d are twenty thousand, even thousands of angels: YHUH is among them, as in Sinai, in the holy place.18 Thou have ascended on high, you have led captivity captive: you have received gifts for men; yea, for the rebellious also, that YHUH G-d might dwell among them.19 Blessed be the Adonai, who daily loadeth us with benefits, even the G-d of our salvation. Selah.20 He that is our G-d is the G-d of salvation; and unto G-d YHUH belong the issues from death.21 But G-d shall wound the head of his enemies, and the hairy scalp of such an one as go on still in his trespasses.22 The Adonai said, I will bring again from Bashan, I will bring my people again from the depths of the sea:23 That your foot may be dipped in the blood of your enemies, and the tongue of your dogs in the same.24 They have seen your goings, O G-d; even the goings of my G-d, my King, in the sanctuary.25 The singers went before, the players on instruments followed after; among them were the damsels playing with timbrels.26 Bless you G-d in the congregations, even the Adonai, from the fountain of Israel.27 There is little Benjamin with their ruler, the princes of Judah and their council, the princes of Zebulun, and the princes of Naphtali.28 Thy G-d has commanded your strength: strengthen, O G-d, that which you have wrought for us.

| לנו 3807a: | 68:29 מהיכלך 1964 | על 5921 | ירושלם 3389 | לך 3807a | יובילו 2986 | מלכים 4428 | שי 7862: | 68:30 גער 1605 |
|---|---|---|---|---|---|---|---|---|
| lanu. | meheykaleka | 'al | yarushalaim; | laka | youbiylu | malakiym | shay. | ga'ar |
| **for us** | **Because of your temple** | **at** | **Jerusalem** | **unto you** | **shall bring** | **kings** | **presents** | **Rebuke** |

| חית 2416 | קנה 7070 | עדת 5712 | אבירים 47 | בעגלי 5695 | עמים 5971 | מתרפס 7511 |
|---|---|---|---|---|---|---|
| chayat | qaneh | 'adat | 'abiyriym | ba'agley | 'amiym, | mitrapes |
| **the company of** | **spearmen** | **the multitude of** | **the bulls** | **with the calves of** | **the people** | ***till every one* submit himself** |

| ברצי 7518 | כסף 3701 | בזר 967 | עמים 5971 | קרבות 7128 | יחפצו 2654: | 68:31 יאתיו 857 | חשמנים 2831 | מני 4480 | מצרים 4714 |
|---|---|---|---|---|---|---|---|---|---|
| baratzey | kasep; | bizar | 'amiym, | qarabout | yechpatzu. | ye'atayu | chashmaniym | miniy | mitzrayim; |
| **with pieces of** | **silver** | **scatter you** | **the people** | **in war** | ***that* delight** | **they shall come** | **Princes** | **out of** | **Egypt** |

| כוש 3568 | תריץ 7323 | ידיו 3027 | לאלהים 430: | 68:32 ממלכות 4467 | הארץ 776 | שירו 7891 | לאלהים 430 |
|---|---|---|---|---|---|---|---|
| kush | tariytz | yadayu, | le'alohiym. | mamlakout | ha'aretz | shiyru | le'alohiym; |
| **Ethiopia** | **shall soon stretch out** | **her hands** | **unto Elohim** | **you kingdoms of** | **the earth** | **Sing** | **unto Elohim** |

| זמרו 2167 | אדני 136 | סלה 5542: | 68:33 לרכב 7392 | בשמי 8064 | שמי 8064 | קדם 6924 | הן 2005 |
|---|---|---|---|---|---|---|---|
| zamru | 'adonay | selah. | larokeb | bishmey | shamey | qedem; | hen |
| **O sing praises unto** | **Adonai** | **Selah** | **To him that ride** | **upon the heavens of** | **heavens** | ***which were* of old** | **lo** |

| יתן 5414 | בקולו 6963 | קול 6963 | עז 5797: | 68:34 תנו 5414 | עז 5797 | לאלהים 430 | על 5921 | ישראל 3478 | גאותו 1346 |
|---|---|---|---|---|---|---|---|---|---|
| yiten | baqoulou | qoul | 'az. | tanu | 'az, | le'alohiym | 'al | yisra'ael | ga'auatou; |
| **he does send out** | **his voice** | ***and that* voice** | **a mighty** | **Ascribe you** | **strength** | **unto Elohim** | **over** | **Israel** | **his excellency *is*** |

| ועזו 5797 | בשחקים 7834: | 68:35 נורא 3372 | אלהים 430 | ממקדשיך 4720 | אל 410 | ישראל 3478 | הוא 1931 | נתן 5414 |
|---|---|---|---|---|---|---|---|---|
| ua'azou, | bashchaqiym. | noura' | 'alohiym, | mimiqdasheyka | 'ael | yisra'ael, | hua' | noten |
| **and his strength *is*** | **in the clouds** | ***you are* terrible** | **O Elohim** | **out of your holy places** | ***the* El *of*** | **Israel** | ***is* he** | **that gives** |

| עז 5797 | ותעצמות 8592 | לעם 5971 | ברוך 1288 | אלהים 430: |
|---|---|---|---|---|
| 'az | uata'atzumout | la'am, | baruk | 'alohiym. |
| **strength** | **and power** | **unto *his* people** | **Blessed *be*** | **Elohim** |

| Ps 69:1 למנצח 5329 | על 5921 | שושנים 7799 | לדוד 1732: | הושיעני 3467 | אלהים 430 | כי 3588 | באו 935 | מים 4325 |
|---|---|---|---|---|---|---|---|---|
| lamanatzeach | 'al | shoushaniym | ladauid. | houshiy'aeniy | 'alohiym; | kiy | ba'au | mayim |
| **To the chief Musician** | **upon** | **Shoshannim** | ***A Psalm* of David** | **Save me** | **O Elohim** | **for** | **are come in** | **the waters** |

| עד 5704 | נפש 5315: | 69:2 טבעתי 2883 | ביון 3121 | מצולה 4688 | ואין 369 | מעמד 4613 | באתי 935 | במעמקי 4615 | מים 4325 |
|---|---|---|---|---|---|---|---|---|---|
| 'ad | napesh. | taba'atiy | biyuen | matzulah | ua'aeyn | ma'amad; | ba'tiy | bama'amaqey | mayim, |
| **unto** | ***my* soul** | **I sink** | **in mire** | **deep** | **and where *there is* no** | **standing** | **I am come** | **into deep** | **waters** |

| ושבלת 7641 | שטפתני 7857: | 69:3 יגעתי 3021 | בקראי 7121 | נחר 2787 | גרוני 1627 | כלו 3615 | עיני 5869 | מיחל 3176 |
|---|---|---|---|---|---|---|---|---|
| washibolet | shatapataniy. | yaga'atiy | baqara'ay | nichar | garouniy | kalu | 'aeynay; | mayachel, |
| **where the floods** | **overflow me** | **I am weary** | **of my crying** | **is dried** | **my throat** | **fail** | **mine eyes** | **while I wait** |

| לאלהי 430: | 69:4 רבו 7231 | משערות 8185 | ראשי 7218 | שנאי 8130 | חנם 2600 | עצמו 6105 |
|---|---|---|---|---|---|---|
| le'alohay. | rabu | misa'arout | ra'shiy | son'ay | chinam | 'atzamu |
| **for my Elohim** | **are more than** | **the hairs of** | **mine head** | **They that hate me** | **without a cause** | **are mighty** |

Ps 68:29 Because of your temple at Jerusalem shall kings bring presents unto you.30 Rebuke the company of spearmen, the multitude of the bulls, with the calves of the people, till everyone submit himself with pieces of silver: scatter you the people that delight in war.31 Princes shall come out of Egypt; Ethiopia shall soon stretch out her hands unto G-d.32 Sing unto G-d, you kingdoms of the earth; O sing praises unto the Adonai; Selah:33 To him that rideth upon the heavens of heavens, which were of old; lo, he doth send out his voice, and that a mighty voice.34 Ascribe you strength unto G-d: his excellency is over Israel, and his strength is in the clouds.35 O G-d, you are terrible out of your holy places: the G-d of Israel is he that give strength and power unto his people. Blessed be G-d. **Ps** 69:1 To the chief Musician upon Sho-shan'-nim, A Psalm of David. Save me, O G-d; for the waters are come in unto my soul.2 I sink in deep mire, where there is no standing: I am come into deep waters, where the floods overflow me.3 I am weary of my crying: my throat is dried: mine eyes fail while I wait for my G-d.4 They that hate me without a cause are more than the hairs of mine head: they that would destroy me, being mine enemies wrongfully, are mighty: then I restored that which I took not away.

| מצמיתי 6789 | איבי 341 | שקר 8267 | אשר 834 | לא 3808 | גזלתי 1497 | אז 227 | אשיב 7725: | 69:5 אלהים 430 |
|---|---|---|---|---|---|---|---|---|
| matzmiytay | 'ayabay | sheqer; | 'asher | la' | gazaltiy, | 'az | 'ashiyb. | 'alohiym, |
| **they that would destroy me** | ***being* mine enemies** | **wrongfully** | ***that* which** | **not** | **I took away** | **then** | **I restored** | **O Elohim** |

| אתה 859 | ידעת 3045 | לאולתי 200 | ואשמותי 819 | ממך 4480 | לא 3808 | נכחדו 3582: | 69:6 אל 408 | יבשו 954 | בי 871a |
|---|---|---|---|---|---|---|---|---|---|
| 'atah | yada'ta | la'aualtiy; | ua'ashmoutay, | mimaka | la' | nikchadu. | 'al | yeboshu | biy |
| **you** | **know** | **my foolishness** | **and my sins** | **from you** | **not** | **are hid** | **not** | **be ashamed *for my sake*** | **on you** |

| קויך 6960 | אדני 136 | יהוה 3069 | צבאות 6635 | אל 408 | יכלמו 3637 | בי 871a | מבקשיך 1245 | אלהי 430 |
|---|---|---|---|---|---|---|---|---|
| qoueyka | 'adonay | Yahuah | tzaba'aut | 'al | yikalamu | biy | mabaqsheyka; | 'alohey, |
| **Let them that wait** | **O Adonai** | **Yahuah** | **of hosts** | **not** | **let be confounded** | **for my sake** | **those that seek you** | **O Elohim of** |

| ישראל 3478: | 69:7 כי 3588 | עליך 5921 | נשאתי 5375 | חרפה 2781 | כסתה 3680 | כלמה 3639 | פני 6440: | 69:8 מוזר 2114 | הייתי 1961 |
|---|---|---|---|---|---|---|---|---|---|
| yisra'ael. | kiy | 'aleyka | nasa'tiy | cherpah; | kistah | kalimah | panay. | muzar | hayiytiy |
| **Israel** | **Because** | **for your sake** | **I have borne** | **reproach** | **has covered** | **shame** | **my face** | **a stranger** | **I am become** |

| לאחי 251 | ונכרי 5237 | לבני 1121 | אמי 517: | 69:9 כי 3588 | קנאת 7068 | ביתך 1004 | אכלתני 398 |
|---|---|---|---|---|---|---|---|
| la'achay; | uanakariy, | libney | 'amiy. | kiy | qin'at | beytaka | 'akalataniy; |
| **unto my brethren** | **and an alien** | **unto children** | **my mother's** | **For** | **the zeal of** | **your house** | **has eaten me up** |

| וחרפות 2781 | חורפיך 2778 | נפלו 5307 | עלי 5921: | 69:10 ואבכה 1058 | בצום 6685 | נפשי 5315 |
|---|---|---|---|---|---|---|
| uacherapout | chourapeyka, | naplu | 'alay. | ua'abkeh | batzoum | napshiy; |
| **and the reproaches of** | **them that reproached you** | **are fallen** | **upon me** | **When I wept** | **with fasting *and chastened*** | **my soul** |

| ותהי 1961 | לחרפות 2781 | לי 3807a: | 69:11 ואתנה 5414 | לבושי 3830 | שק 8242 | ואהי 1961 | להם 1992 | למשל 4912: | 69:12 |
|---|---|---|---|---|---|---|---|---|---|
| uatahiy | lacharapout | liy. | ua'atnah | labushiy | saq; | ua'ahiy | lahem | lamashal. | |
| **that was** | **to reproach** | **my** | **I made also** | **my garment** | **sackcloth** | **and I became** | **to them** | **a proverb** | |

| ישיחו 7878 | בי 871a | ישבי 3427 | שער 8179 | ונגינות 5058 | שותי 8354 | שכר 7941: | 69:13 ואני 589 |
|---|---|---|---|---|---|---|---|
| yasiychu | biy | yoshabey | sha'ar; | ungiynout, | shoutey | shekar. | ua'aniy |
| **They that speak** | **against me** | **sit in** | **the gate** | **and I *was* the song of** | **assuredly** | **the drunkards** | **But as for me** |

| תפלתי 8605 | לך 3807a | יהוה 3068 | עת 6256 | רצון 7522 | אלהים 430 | ברב 7230 | חסדך 2617 | ענני 6030 | באמת 571 |
|---|---|---|---|---|---|---|---|---|---|
| tapilatiy | laka | Yahuah | 'at | ratzoun, | 'alohiym | barab | chasadeka; | 'aneniy, | be'amet |
| **my prayer** | ***is* unto you** | **O Yahuah** | ***in* an time** | **acceptable** | **O Elohim** | **in the multitude of** | **your mercy** | **hear me** | **in the truth of** |

| ישעך 3468: | 69:14 הצילני 5337 | מטיט 2916 | ואל 408 | אטבעה 2883 | אנצלה 5337 | משנאי 8130 |
|---|---|---|---|---|---|---|
| yish'aka. | hatziyleniy | mitiyt | ua'al | 'atba'ah; | 'anatzalah | misona'ay, |
| **your salvation** | **Deliver me** | **out of the mire** | **and not** | **let me sink** | **let me be delivered** | **from them that hate me** |

| וממעמקי 4615 | מים 4325: | 69:15 אל 408 | תשטפני 7857 | שבלת 7641 | מים 4325 | ואל 408 | תבלעני 1104 | מצולה 4688 |
|---|---|---|---|---|---|---|---|---|
| uamima'amaqey | mayim. | 'al | tishtapeniy | shibolet | mayim | ua'al | tibla'aeniy | matzulah; |
| **and out of the deep** | **waters** | **not** | **Let overflow me** | **branch** | **the waterflood** | **neither** | **let swallow me up** | **the deep** |

| ואל 408 | תאטר 332 | עלי 5921 | באר 875 | פיה 6310: | 69:16 ענני 6030 | יהוה 3068 | כי 3588 | טוב 2896 | חסדך 2617 |
|---|---|---|---|---|---|---|---|---|---|
| ua'al | te'atar | 'alay | ba'aer | piyha. | 'aneniy | Yahuah | kiy | toub | chasadeka; |
| **and not** | **let shut** | **upon me** | **the pit** | **her mouth** | **Hear me** | **O Yahuah** | **for** | ***is* good** | **your lovingkindness** |

Ps 69:5 O G-d, you know my foolishness; and my sins are not hid from you.6 Let not them that wait on you, O Adonai G-D of hosts, be ashamed for my sake: let not those that seek you be confounded for my sake, O G-d of Israel.7 Because for your sake I have borne reproach; shame has covered my face.8 I am become a stranger unto my brethren, and an alien unto my mother's children.9 For the zeal of your house has eaten me up; and the reproaches of them that reproached you are fallen upon me.10 When I wept, and chastened my soul with fasting, that was to my reproach.11 I made sackcloth also my garment; and I became a proverb to them.12 They that sit in the gate speak against me; and I was the song of the drunkards.13 But as for me, my prayer is unto you, O YHUH, in an acceptable time: O G-d, in the multitude of your mercy hear me, in the truth of your salvation.14 Deliver me out of the mire, and let me not sink: let me be delivered from them that hate me, and out of the deep waters.15 Let not the waterflood overflow me, neither let the deep swallow me up, and let not the pit shut her mouth upon me.16 Hear me, O YHUH; for your lovingkindness is good: turn unto me according to the multitude of your tender mercies.

כרב 7230 רחמיך 7356 פנה 6437 אלי 413: **69:17** ואל 408 תסתר 5641 פניך 6440 מעבדך 5650
karob rachameyka, paneh 'aelay. ua'al taster paneyka me'abdeka;
**according to the multitude of your tender mercies turn unto me And not hide your face from your servant**

כי 3588 צר 6887 לי 3807a מהר 4118 ענני 6030: **69:18** קרבה 7126 אל 413 נפשי 5315 גאלה 1350 למען 4616 איבי 341
kiy tzar liy, maher 'aneniy. qarabah 'al napshiy ga'alah; lama'an 'ayabay
**for *am* in trouble I speedily hear me Draw near unto my soul *and* redeem it because of mine enemies**

פדני 6299: **69:19** אתה 859 ידעת 3045 חרפתי 2781 ובשתי 1322 וכלמתי 3639 נגדך 5048 כל 3605
padeniy. 'atah yada'ta, cherpatiy uabashatiy uaklimatiy; negdaka, kal
**deliver me You have known my reproach and my shame and my dishonour *are* before you all**

צוררי 6887: **69:20** חרפה 2781 שברה 7665 לבי 3820 ואנושה 5136 ואקוה 6960 לנוד 5110
tzouraray. cherpah shabarah libiy, ua'anushah ua'aqaueh lanud
**mine adversaries Reproach has broken my heart and I am full of heaviness and I looked *for some* to take pity**

ואין 369 ולמנחמים 5162 ולא 3808 מצאתי 4672: **69:21** ויתנו 5414 בברותי 1267 ראש 7219 ולצמאי 6772
ua'ayin; ualamanachamiym, uala' matza'tiy. uayitanu babarutiy ra'sh; ualitzma'ay,
**but *there was* none and for comforters but none I found They gave me also for my meat gall and in my thirst**

ישקוני 8248 חמץ 2558: **69:22** יהי 1961 שלחנם 7979 לפניהם 6440 לפח 6341
yashquni chometz. yahiy shulchanam lipneyhem lapach;
**they gave me to drink vinegar Let become their table before them a snare**

ולשלומים 7965 למוקש 4170: **69:23** תחשכנה 2821 עיניהם 5869 מראות 7200
ualishloumiym lamouqesh. techshaknah 'aeyneyhem mera'aut;
**and *that which should have been* for *their* welfare *let it become* a trap Let be darkened their eyes that they see not**

ומתניהם 4975 תמיד 8548 המעד 4571: **69:24** שפך 8210 עליהם 5921 זעמך 2195 וחרון 2740 אפך 639
uamataneyhem, tamiyd hama'ad. shapak 'aleyhem za'ameka; uacharoun 'apaka,
**and their loins continually make to shake Pour out upon them your indignation and your wrathful anger**

ישיגם 5381: **69:25** תהי 1961 טירתם 2918 נשמה 8074 באהליהם 168 אל 408 יהי 1961 ישב 3427: **69:26** כי 3588 אתה 859
yasiygem. tahiy tiyratam nashamah; ba'ahaleyhem, 'al yahiy yosheb. kiy 'atah
**let take hold of them Let be their habitation desolate in their tents none *and* let dwell For you**

אשר 834 הכית 5221 רדפו 7291 ואל 413 מכאוב 4341 חלליך 2491 יספרו 5608: **69:27** תנה 5414 עון 5771
'asher hikiyta radapu; ua'al mak'aub chalaleyka yasaperu. tanah 'auon
***him* whom have smitten they persecute and to the grief of those whom you have wounded they talk Add iniquity**

על 5921 עונם 5771 ואל 408 יבאו 935 בצדקתך 6666: **69:28** ימחו 4229 מספר 5612 חיים 2416
'al 'auonam; ua'al yabo'au, batzidqateka. yimachu miseper chayiym;
**unto their iniquity and not let them come into your righteousness Let them be blotted out of the book of the living**

ועם 5973 צדיקים 6662 אל 408 יכתבו 3789: **69:29** ואני 589 עני 6041 וכואב 3510 ישועתך 3444 אלהים 430
ua'am tzadiyqiym, 'al yikatebu. ua'aniy 'aniy uakou'aeb; yashu'ataka 'alohiym
**and with the righteous not be written But I *am* poor and sorrowful your salvation O Elohim**

Ps 69:17 And hide not your face from your servant; for I am in trouble: hear me speedily.18 Draw nigh unto my soul, and redeem it: deliver me because of mine enemies.19 Thou have known my reproach, and my shame, and my dishonour: mine adversaries are all before you.20 Reproach has broken my heart; and I am full of heaviness: and I looked for some to take pity, but there was none; and for comforters, but I found none.21 They gave me also gall for my meat; and in my thirst they gave me vinegar to drink.22 Let their table become a snare before them: and that which should have been for their welfare, let it become a trap.23 Let their eyes be darkened, that they see not; and make their loins continually to shake.24 Pour out your indignation upon them, and let your wrathful anger take hold of them.25 Let their habitation be desolate; and let none dwell in their tents.26 For they persecute him whom you have smitten; and they talk to the grief of those whom you have wounded.27 Add iniquity unto their iniquity: and let them not come into your righteousness.28 Let them be blotted out of the book of the living, and not be written with the righteous.29 But I am poor and sorrowful: let your salvation, O G-d, set me up on high.

69:30 ... 69:31

תשגבני 7682: אהללה 1984 שם 8034 אלהים 430 בשיר 7892 ואגדלנו 1431 בתודה 8426:
tasagbeniy. 'ahalalah shem 'alohiym bashiyr; ua'agadlenu batoudah.
**let set me up on high I will praise the name of Elohim with a song and will magnify him with thanksgiving**

69:32

ותיטב 3190 ליהוה 3068 משור 7794 פר 6499 מקרן 7160 מפריס 6536: ראו 7200 ענוים 6035
uatiytab laYahuah mishour par, maqrin mapriys. ra'au 'anauiym
**This also shall please better Yahuah than an ox *or* bullock that has horns *and* hoofs shall see *this, and* The humble**

69:33

ישמחו 8055 דרשי 1875 אלהים 430 ויחי 2421 לבבכם 3824: כי 3588 שמע 8085 אל 413 אביונים 34 יהוה 3068 ואת 853 אסיריו 615
yismachu; dorashey 'alohiym, uaychiy lababkem. kiy shomea' 'al 'abyouniym Yahuah; ua'at 'asiyrayu,
**be glad that seek Elohim and shall live your heart For hear about the poor Yahuah *and* his prisoners**

69:34 69:35

לא 3808 בזה 959: יהללוהו 1984 שמים 8064 וארץ 776 ימים 3220 וכל 3605 רמש 7430 בם 871a: כי 3588 אלהים 430
la' bazah. yahalaluhu shamayim ua'aretz; yamiym, uakal romes bam. kiy 'alohiym
**not despise Let praise him the heaven and earth the seas and every thing that moves therein For Elohim**

69:36

יושיע 3467 ציון 6726 ויבנה 1129 ערי 5892 יהודה 3063 וישבו 3427 שם 8033 וירשוה 3423:
youshiya' tziyoun, uayibneh 'arey yahudah; uayashabu sham uiyreshuha.
**will save Zion and will build the cities of Judah that they may dwell there and have it in possession**

וזרע 2233 עבדיו 5650 ינחלוה 5157 ואהבי 157 שמו 8034 ישכנו 7931 בה 871a:
uazera' 'abadayu yinchaluha; ua'ahabey shamou, yishkanu bah.
**The seed also of his servants shall inherit it and they that love his name shall dwell therein**

**Ps 70:1**

למנצח 5329 לדוד 1732 להזכיר 2142: אלהים 430 להצילני 5337 יהוה 3068
lamanatzeach, ladauid lahazkiyr. 'alohiym lahatziyleniy; Yahuah
**To the chief Musician *A Psalm* of David to bring to remembrance O Elohim *Make haste* to deliver me O Yahuah**

70:2

לעזרתי 5833 חושה 2363: יבשו 954 ויחפרו 2659 מבקשי 1245 נפשי 5315 יסגו 5472 אחור 268
la'azratiy chushah. yeboshu uayachparu mabaqshey napshiy yisogu 'achour
**to help me make haste Let them be ashamed and confounded that seek after my soul let them be turned backward**

70:3

ויכלמו 3637 חפצי 2655 רעתי 7451: ישובו 7725 על 5921 עקב 6118 בשתם 1322 האמרים 559 האח 1889
uayikalamu; chapetzey, ra'atiy. yashubu 'al 'aeqeb bashatam; ha'amariym, he'ach
**and put to confusion that desire my hurt Let them be turned back for a reward of their shame that say Aha**

70:4

האח 1889: ישישו 7797 וישמחו 8055 בך 871a כל 3605 מבקשיך 1245 ויאמרו 559 תמיד 8548 יגדל 1431 אלהים 430
he'ach. yasiysu uayismachu baka, kal mabaqsheyka uaya'maru tamiyd yigdal 'alohiym;
**aha Let rejoice and be glad in you all those that seek you and let say continually Let be magnified Elohim**

70:5

אהבי 157 ישועתך 3444: ואני 589 עני 6041 ואביון 34 אלהים 430 חושה 2363 לי 3807a עזרי 5828 ומפלטי 6403
'ahabey, yashu'ateka. ua'aniy 'aniy ua'abyoun 'alohiym chushah liy 'azriy uampaltiy
**such as love your salvation But I *am* poor and needy O Elohim make haste unto me *are* my help and my deliverer**

אתה 859 יהוה 3068 אל 408 תאחר 309:
'atah; Yahuah 'al ta'achar.
**you O Yahuah no make tarrying**

Ps 69:30 I will praise the name of G-d with a song and will magnify him with thanksgiving.31 This also shall please YHUH better than an ox or bullock that has horns and hoofs.32 The humble shall see this, and be glad: and your heart shall live that seek G-d.33 For YHUH hear the poor and despiseth not his prisoners.34 Let the heaven and earth praise him, the seas, and everything that moveth therein.35 For G-d will save Zion and will build the cities of Judah: that they may dwell there, and have it in possession.36 The seed also of his servants shall inherit it: and they that love his name shall dwell therein. **Ps**70:1 To the chief Musician, A Psalm of David, to bring to remembrance. Make haste, O G-d, to deliver me; make haste to help me, O YHUH.2 Let them be ashamed and confounded that seek after my soul: let them be turned backward, and put to confusion, that desire my hurt.3 Let them be turned back for a reward of their shame that say, Aha, aha.4 Let all those that seek you rejoice and be glad in you: and let such as love your salvation say continually, Let G-d be magnified.5 But I am poor and needy: make haste unto me O G-d: you are my help and my deliverer; O YHUH make no tarrying.

**Ps 71:1** … **71:2**

בך 871a | יהוה 3068 | חסיתי 2620 | אל 408 | אבושה 954 | לעולם 5769: | בצדקתך 6666

baka | Yahuah | chasiytiy; | 'al | 'aeboushah | la'aulam. | batzidqataka,

**In you | O Yahuah | do I put my trust | never | let me be put to confusion | never | in your righteousness**

… **71:3** …

תצילני 5337 | ותפלטני 6403 | הטה 5186 | אלי 413 | אזנך 241 | והושיעני 3467: | היה 1961 | לי 3807a | לצור 6697 | מעון 4583

tatziyleniy | uatpalteniy; | hateh | 'aelay | 'aznaka, | uahoushiy'aeniy. | hayeh | liy | latzur | ma'aun

**Deliver me | and cause me to escape | incline | unto me | your ear | and save me | Be you | my | strong | habitation**

לבוא 935 | תמיד 8548 | צוית 6680 | להושיעני 3467 | כי 3588 | סלעי 5553 | ומצודתי 4686

labou'a, | tamiyd, | tziuiyta | lahoushiy'aeniy; | kiy | sala'ay | uamtzudatiy

**whereunto resort | I may continually | you have given commandment | to save me | for | *are* my rock | and my fortress**

… **71:4** … **71:5**

אתה 859: | אלהי 430 | פלטני 6403 | מיד 3027 | רשע 7563 | מכף 3709 | מעול 5765 | וחומץ 2556:

'atah. | 'alohay, | palteniy | miyad | rasha'; | mikap | ma'auel | uachoumetz

**you | O my Elohim | Deliver me | out of the hand of | the wicked | out of the hand | of the unrighteous | and cruel man**

… **71:6** …

כי 3588 | אתה 859 | תקותי 8615 | אדני 136 | יהוה 3068 | מבטחי 4009 | מנעורי 5271: | עליך 5921 | נסמכתי 5564

kiy | 'atah | tiquatiy; | 'adonay | Yahuah | mibtachiy | mina'auray. | 'aleyka | nismaktiy

**For | you | *are* my hope | O Adonai | Yahuah | *you are* my trust | from my youth | By you | have I been holden up**

… **71:7**

מבטן 990 | ממעי 4578 | אמי 517 | אתה 859 | גוזי 1491 | בך 871a | תהלתי 8416 | תמיד 8548:

mibeten, | mim'aey | 'amiy | 'atah | gouziy; | baka | tahilatiy | tamiyd.

**from the womb | out of bowels | my mother's | you | *are* he that took me | of you | my praise | *shall be* continually**

… **71:8** …

כמופת 4159 | הייתי 1961 | לרבים 7227 | ואתה 859 | מחסי 4268 | עז 5797: | ימלא 4390 | פי 6310 | תהלתך 8416 | כל 3605 | היום 3117

kamoupet | hayiytiy | larabiym; | ua'atah, | machasiy | 'az. | yimalea' | piy | tahilateka; | kal | hayoum,

**as a wonder | I am | unto many | but you | *are* my refuge | strong | Let be filled | my mouth | *with* your praise | all | the day**

… **71:9** … **71:10** …

תפארתך 8597: | אל 408 | תשליכני 7993 | לעת 6256 | זקנה 2209 | ככלות 3615 | כחי 3581 | אל 408 | תעזבני 5800: | כי 3588

tip'arteka. | 'al | tashliykeniy | la'aet | ziqnah; | kiklout | kochiy, | 'al | ta'azbeniy. | kiy

***and with* your honor | not | Cast me off | in the time of | old age | when fail | my strength | not | forsake me | For**

… **71:11** …

אמרו 559 | אויבי 341 | לי 3807a | ושמרי 8104 | נפשי 5315 | נועצו 3289 | יחדו 3162: | לאמר 559 | אלהים 430

'amaru | 'auyabay | liy; | uashomarey | napshiy, | nou'atzu | yachdau. | lea'mor | 'alohiym

**speak | mine enemies | against me | and they that lay wait for | my soul | take counsel | together | Saying | Elohim**

… **71:12** …

עזבו 5800 | רדפו 7291 | ותפשוהו 8610 | כי 3588 | אין 369 | מציל 5337: | אלהים 430 | אל 408 | תרחק 7368 | ממני 4480

azabou; | ridpu | uatipsuhu, | kiy | 'aeyn | matziyl. | 'alohiym | 'al | tirchaq | mimeniy;

**has forsaken him | persecute | and take him | for | *there is* none | to deliver *him* | O Elohim | not | be far | from me**

… **71:13** …

אלהי 430 | לעזרתי 5833 | חישה 2363: | יבשו 954 | יכלו 3615 | שטני 7853 | נפשי 5315

'alohay, | la'azratiy | chiyshah | yeboshu | yiklu | sotaney | napshiy

**O my Elohim | for my help | make haste | Let them be confounded | *and* consumed | that are adversaries to | my soul**

… **71:14** …

יעטו 5844 | חרפה 2781 | וכלמה 3639 | מבקשי 1245 | רעתי 7451: | ואני 589 | תמיד 8548 | איחל 3176

ya'atou | cherpah | uaklimah; | mabaqshey, | ra'atiy. | ua'aniy | tamiyd | 'ayachel;

**let them be covered | *with* reproach | and dishonour | that seek | my hurt | But I | continually | will hope**

**Ps** 71:1 In you, O YHUH, do I put my trust: let me never be put to confusion.2 Deliver me in your righteousness, and cause me to escape: incline your ear unto me, and save me.3 Be you my strong habitation, whereunto I may continually resort: you have given commandment to save me; for you are my rock and my fortress.4 Deliver me, O my G-d, out of the hand of the wicked, out of the hand of the unrighteous and cruel man.5 For you are my hope, O Adonai G-D: you are my trust from my youth.6 By you have I been holden up from the womb: you are he that took me out of my mother's bowels: my praise shall be continually of you.7 I am as a wonder unto many; but you are my strong refuge.8 Let my mouth be filled with your praise and with your honor all the day.9 Cast me not off in the time of old age; forsake me not when my strength faileth.10 For mine enemies speak against me; and they that lay wait for my soul take counsel together,11 Saying, G-d has forsaken him: persecute and take him; for there is none to deliver him.12 O G-d, be not far from me: O my G-d, make haste for my help.13 Let them be confounded and consumed that are adversaries to my soul; let them be covered with reproach and dishonour that seek my hurt.14 But I will hope continually, and will yet praise you more and more.

והוספתי 3254 | על 5921 | כל 3605 | תהלתך 8416: | **71:15** | פי 6310 | יספר 5608 | צדקתך 6666 | כל 3605 | היום 3117
uahosaptiy, | 'al | kal | tahilateka. | | piy | yasaper | tzidqateka, | kal | hayoum
**and yet more and more | on | all of | will praise | | My mouth | shall show forth | your righteousness | all | the day**

תשועתך 8668 | כי 3588 | לא 3808 | ידעתי 3045 | ספרות 5615: | **71:16** | אבוא 935 | בגברות 1369 | אדני 136 | יהוה 3069
tashu'ateka; | kiy | la' | yada'tiy | saporout. | | abou'a, | bigaurout | 'adonay | Yahuah;
***and* your salvation | for | not | I know | the numbers *thereof* | | I will go | in the strength of | Adonai | Yahuah**

אזכיר 2142 | צדקתך 6666 | לבדך 905: | **71:17** | אלהים 430 | למדתני 3925 | מנעורי 5271 | ועד 5704
'azkiyr | tzidqataka | labadeka. | | 'alohiym, | limadtaniy | mina'auray; | ua'ad
**I will make mention of | your righteousness *even* | of you only | | O Elohim | you have taught me | from my youth | and unto**

הנה 2008 | אגיד 5046 | נפלאותיך 6381: | **71:18** | וגם 1571 | עד 5704 | זקנה 2209 | ושיבה 7872 | אלהים 430 | אל 408 | תעזבני 5800
henah, | 'agiyd | nipla'auteyka. | | ua'gam | 'ad | ziqnah | uaseybah | 'alohiym | 'al | ta'azbeniy
**here to | have I declared | your wondrous works | | Now also | when | *I am* old | and grayheaded | O Elohim | not | forsake me**

עד 5704 | אגיד 5046 | זרועך 2220 | לדור 1755 | לכל 3605 | יבוא 935 | גבורתך 1369: | **71:19**
'ad | 'agiyd | zarou'aka | ladour; | lakal | yabou'a, | gaburateka.
**until | I have showed | your strength | unto *this* generation | to every one | *that* is to come | *and* your power**

וצדקתך 6666 | אלהים 430 | עד 5704 | מרום 4791 | אשר 834 | עשית 6213 | גדלות 1419 | אלהים 430 | מי 4310 | כמוך 3644: | **71:20**
uatzidqataka | 'alohiym, | 'ad | maroum | 'asher | 'ashiyta | gadolout; | 'alohiym, | miy' | kamouka.
**Your righteousness also | O Elohim *is* | very | high | who | have done | great things | O Elohim | who | *is* like unto you**

אשר 834 | הראיתנו 7200 | צרות 6869 | רבות 7227 | ורעות 7451 | תשוב 7725 | תחיינו 2421 | ומתהמות 8415 | הארץ 776 | תשוב 7725
'asher | hir'aytanu | tzarout | rabout, | uara'aut | tashub | tachayeynu | uamitahomout | ha'aretz, | tashub
**You which | has shown me | troubles | great | and sore | again | shall quicken me | and from the depths of | the earth | again**

תעלני 5927: | **71:21** | תרב 7235 | גדלתי 1420 | ותסב 5437 | תנחמני 5162: | **71:22** | גם 1571 | אני 589 | אודך 3034
ta'aleniy. | | tereb | gadulatiy, | uatisob | tanachameniy. | | gam | 'aniy | 'audaka
**shall bring me up | | You shall increase | my greatness | and on every side | comfort me | | also | I | will praise you**

בכלי 3627 | נבל 5035 | אמתך 571 | אלהי 430 | אזמרה 2167 | לך 3807a | בכנור 3658 | קדוש 6918
bikley | nebel | 'amitaka | 'alohay | 'azamrah | laka | bakinour; | qadoush,
**in instrument | with the psaltery *even* | your truth | O my Elohim | will I sing | unto you | with the harp | O *you* Holy One of**

ישראל 3478: | **71:23** | תרננה 7442 | שפתי 8193 | כי 3588 | אזמרה 2167 | לך 3807a | ונפשי 5315 | אשר 834 | פדית 6299: | **71:24** | גם 1571
yisra'ael. | | taranenah | sapatay | kiy | 'azamrah | lak; | uanapshiy, | 'asher | padiyta. | | gam
**Israel | | shall greatly rejoice | My lips | when | I sing | unto you | and my soul | which | you have redeemed | | also**

לשוני 3956 | כל 3605 | היום 3117 | תהגה 1897 | צדקתך 6666 | כי 3588 | בשו 954 | כי 3588
lashouniy, | kal | hayoum | tehageh | tzidqateka; | kiy | boshu | kiy
**My tongue | all | the day *long* | shall talk of | your righteousness | for | they are confounded | for**

חפרו 2659 | מבקשי 1245 | רעתי 7451:
chaparu, | mabaqshey | ra'atiy.
**they are brought unto shame | that seek | my hurt**

Ps 71:15 My mouth shall show forth your righteousness and your salvation all the day; for I know not the numbers thereof.16 I will go in the strength of YHUH G-D: I will make mention of your righteousness, even of your only.17 O G-d, you have taught me from my youth: and hitherto have I declared your wondrous works.18 Now also when I am old and grayheaded, O G-d, forsake me not; until I have showed your strength unto this generation, and your power to everyone that is to come.19 Thy righteousness also, O G-d, is very high, who have done great things: O G-d, who is like unto you!20 Thou, which have showed me great and sore troubles, shall quicken me again, and shall bring me up again from the depths of the earth.21 Thou shall increase my greatness, and comfort me on every side.22 I will also praise you with the psaltery, even your truth, O my G-d: unto you will I sing with the harp, O you Holy One of Israel.23 My lips shall greatly rejoice when I sing unto you; and my soul, which you have redeemed.24 My tongue also shall talk of your righteousness all the day long: for they are confounded, for they are brought unto shame, that seek my hurt.

| Ps 72:1 | לשלמה 8010 | אלהים 430 | משפטיך 4941 | למלך 4428 | תן 5414 | וצדקתך 6666 | לבן 1121 | מלך 4428: | 72:2 |
|---|---|---|---|---|---|---|---|---|---|
| | lishalomoh | 'alohiym, | mishpateyka | lamelek | ten; | uatzidqataka | laben | melek. | |
| | ***A Psalm* for Solomon** | **O Elohim** | **your judgments** | **the king** | **Give** | **and your righteousness** | **unto son** | ***the* king's** | |

| ידין 1777 | עמך 5971 | בצדק 6664 | ועניך 6041 | במשפט 4941: | 72:3 | ישאו 5375 | הרים 2022 | שלום 7965 |
|---|---|---|---|---|---|---|---|---|
| yadiyn | 'amaka | batzedeq; | ua'aniyeyka | bamishpat. | | yis'au | hariym | shaloum |
| **He shall judge** | **your people** | **with righteousness** | **and your poor** | **with judgment** | | **shall bring** | **The mountains** | **peace** |

| לעם 5971 | וגבעות 1389 | בצדקה 6666: | 72:4 | ישפט 8199 | עניי 6041 | עם 5971 | יושיע 3467 | לבני 1121 |
|---|---|---|---|---|---|---|---|---|
| la'am; | uagba'aut, | bitzadaqah. | | yishpot | 'aniyey | 'am, | youshiya' | libney |
| **to the people** | **and the little hills** | **by righteousness** | | **He shall judge** | **the poor of** | ***the* people** | **he shall save** | **the children of** |

| אביון 34 | וידכא 1792 | עושק 6231: | 72:5 | ייראוך 3372 | עם 5973 | שמש 8121 | ולפני 6440 | ירח 3394 |
|---|---|---|---|---|---|---|---|---|
| abyoun; | uiydakea' | 'ausheq. | | yiyra'auka | 'am | shamesh; | ualipaney | yareach, |
| **the needy** | **and shall break in pieces** | **the oppressor** | | **They shall fear you** | **as long as** | **the sun** | **and endure** | **moon** |

| דור 1755 | דורים 1755: | 72:6 | ירד 3381 | כמטר 4306 | על 5921 | גז 1488 | כרביבים 7241 | זרזיף 2222 | ארץ 776: | 72:7 |
|---|---|---|---|---|---|---|---|---|---|---|
| dour | douriym. | | yered | kamatar | 'al | gez; | kirbiybiym, | zarziyp | 'aretz. | |
| ***throughout* all** | **generations** | | **He shall come down** | **like rain** | **upon** | **the mown grass** | **as showers** | ***that* water** | **the earth** | |

| יפרח 6524 | בימיו 3117 | צדיק 6662 | ורב 7230 | שלום 7965 | עד 5704 | בלי 1097 | ירח 3394: | 72:8 |
|---|---|---|---|---|---|---|---|---|
| yiprach | bayamayu | tzadiyq; | uarob | shaloum, | 'ad | baliy | yareach. | |
| **shall flourish** | **In his days** | **the righteous** | **and abundance of** | **peace** | **so long as** | **endures** | **the moon** | |

| וירד 7287 | מים 3220 | עד 5704 | ים 3220 | ומנהר 5104 | עד 5704 | אפסי 657 | ארץ 776: | 72:9 | לפניו 6440 |
|---|---|---|---|---|---|---|---|---|---|
| uayered | miyam | 'ad | yam; | uaminahar, | 'ad | 'apsey | 'aretz. | | lapanayu |
| **He shall have dominion also** | **from sea** | **to** | **sea** | **and from the river** | **unto** | **the ends of** | **the earth** | | **before him** |

| יכרעו 3766 | ציים 6728 | ואיביו 341 | עפר 6083 | ילחכו 3897: | 72:10 | מלכי 4428 | תרשיש 8659 | ואיים 339 |
|---|---|---|---|---|---|---|---|---|
| yikra'au | tziyiym; | ua'ayabayu, | 'apar | yalacheku. | | malkey | tarshiysh | ua'ayiym |
| **shall bow** | **They that dwell in the wilderness** | **and his enemies** | **the dust** | **shall lick** | | **The kings of** | **Tarshish** | **and of the isles** |

| מנחה 4503 | ישיבו 7725 | מלכי 4428 | שבא 7614 | וסבא 5434 | אשכר 814 | יקריבו 7126: | 72:11 | וישתחוו 7812 | לו 3807a | כל 3605 | מלכים 4428 |
|---|---|---|---|---|---|---|---|---|---|---|---|
| minchah | yashiybu; | malkey | shaba' | uasaba', | 'ashkar | yaqriybu. | | uayishatachauu | lou' | kal | malakiym; |
| **presents** | **shall bring** | **the kings of** | **Sheba** | **and Seba** | **gifts** | **shall offer** | | **Yea shall fall down** | **before him** | **all** | **kings** |

| כל 3605 | גוים 1471 | יעבדוהו 5647: | 72:12 | כי 3588 | יציל 5337 | אביון 34 | משוע 7768 | ועני 6041 | ואין 369 | עזר 5826 |
|---|---|---|---|---|---|---|---|---|---|---|
| kal | gouyim | ya'abduhu. | | kiy | yatziyl | abyoun | mashauea'; | ua'aniy, | ua'aeyn | 'azer |
| **all** | **nations** | **shall serve him** | | **For** | **he shall deliver** | **the needy** | ***when* he cry** | **the poor also** | **and has no** | **helper** |

| לו 3807a: | 72:13 | יחס 2347 | על 5921 | דל 1800 | ואביון 34 | ונפשות 5315 | אביונים 34 | יושיע 3467: | 72:14 | מתוך 8496 |
|---|---|---|---|---|---|---|---|---|---|---|
| lou'. | | yachos | 'al | dal | ua'abyoun; | uanapshout | 'abyouniym | youshiya'. | | mitouk |
| **him *that*** | | **He shall spare** | **on** | **the poor** | **and needy** | **and the souls of** | **the needy** | **shall save** | | **from deceit** |

| ומחמס 2555 | יגאל 1350 | נפשם 5315 | וייקר 3365 | דמם 1818 | בעיניו 5869: | 72:15 | ויחי 2421 |
|---|---|---|---|---|---|---|---|
| uamechamas | yig'al | napsham; | uayeyqar | damam | ba'aeynayu. | | uiychiy, |
| **and violence** | **He shall redeem** | **their soul** | **and precious shall be** | **their blood** | **in his sight** | | **And he shall live** |

**Ps** 72:1 A Psalm for Solomon. Give the king your judgments, O G-d, and your righteousness unto the king's son.2 He shall judge your people with righteousness, and your poor with judgment.3 The mountains shall bring peace to the people, and the little hills, by righteousness.4 He shall judge the poor of the people, he shall save the children of the needy, and shall break in pieces the oppressor.5 They shall fear you as long as the sun and moon endure, throughout all generations.6 He shall come down like rain upon the mown grass: as showers that water the earth.7 In his days shall the righteous flourish; and abundance of peace so long as the moon endureth.8 He shall have dominion also from sea to sea, and from the river unto the ends of the earth.9 They that dwell in the wilderness shall bow before him; and his enemies shall lick the dust.10 The kings of Tarshish and of the isles shall bring presents: the kings of Sheba and Seba shall offer gifts.11 Yea, all kings shall fall down before him: all nations shall serve him.12 For he shall deliver the needy when he crieth; the poor also, and him that has no helper.13 He shall spare the poor and needy, and shall save the souls of the needy.

ויתן 5414 לו 3807a מזהב 2091 שבא 7614 ויתפלל 6419 בעדו 1157 תמיד 8548 כל 3605 היום 3117
uayiten lou' mizhab shaba' uayitpalel ba'adou tamiyd; kal hayoum,
**and shall be given to him of the gold of Sheba prayer also shall be made for him continually *and* all daily**

72:16
יברכנהו 1288: יהי 1961 פסת 6451 בר 1250 בארץ 776 בראש 7218 הרים 2022 ירעש 7493
yabarakenhu. yahiy pisat bar ba'aretz bara'sh hariym yir'ash
**shall he be praised There shall be an handful of corn in the earth upon the top of the mountains shall shake**

72:17
כלבנון 3844 פריו 6529 ויציצו 6692 מעיר 5892 כעשב 6212 הארץ 776: יהי 1961 שמו 8034
kalabanoun piryou; uayatziytzu me'ayr, ka'aeseb ha'aretz. yahiy shamou
**like Lebanon the fruit thereof and shall flourish *they* of the city like grass of the earth shall endure His name**

לעולם 5769 לפני 6440 שמש 8121 ינין 5125 שמו 8034 ויתברכו 1288 בו 871a כל 3605 גוים 1471
la'aulam, lipaney shemesh yaniyn shamou uayitbaraku bou; kal gouyim
**for ever as long as the sun shall be continued his name and *men* shall be blessed in him all nations**

72:18 72:19
יאשרוהו 833: ברוך 1288 יהוה 3068 אלהים 430 אלהי 430 ישראל 3478 עשה 6213 נפלאות 6381 לבדו 905:
ya'ashruhu. baruk Yahuah 'alohiym 'alohey yisra'ael; 'aseh nipla'aut labadou.
**shall call him blessed Blessed *be* Yahuah Elohim the Elohim of Israel who does wondrous things only**

72:20
וברוך 1288 שם 8034 כבודו 3519 לעולם 5769 וימלא 4390 כבודו 3519 את 853 כל 3605 הארץ 776 אמן 543 ואמן 543:
uabaruk shem kaboudou, la'aulam uayimalea' kaboudou 'at kal ha'aretz, 'amen ua'amen.
**And blessed name *be* his glorious for ever and let be filled *with* his glory whole the earth Amen and Amen**

כלו 3615 תפלות 8605 דוד 1732 בן 1121 ישי 3448:
kalu tapilout; dauid, ben yishay.
**are ended The prayers of David the son of Jesse**

**Ps 73:1** 73:2
מזמור 4210 לאסף 623 אך 389 טוב 2896 לישראל 3478 אלהים 430 לברי 1249 לבב 3824: ואני 589
mizmour, la'asap 'ak toub layisra'ael 'alohiym, labarey labab. ua'aniy,
**A Psalm of Asaph Truly *is* good to Israel Elohim *even* to such as are of a clean heart But as for me**

73:3
כמעט 4592 נטוי 5186 רגלי 7272 כאין 369 שפכה 8210 אשרי 838: כי 3588 קנאתי 7065 בהוללים 1984 שלום 7965
kima'at natuiy raglay; ka'ayin, shupakah 'ashuray. kiy qinea'tiy bahoulaliym; shaloum
**almost were gone my feet well near had slipped my steps For I was envious at the foolish the prosperity of**

73:4 73:5
רשעים 7563 אראה 7200: כי 3588 אין 369 חרצבות 2784 למותם 4194 ובריא 1277 אולם 193: בעמל 5999
rasha'aym 'ar'ah. kiy 'aeyn chartzubout lamoutam, uabariy'a 'aulam. ba'amal
**the wicked *when* I saw For *there are* no bands in their death but firm their strength *is* in trouble**

73:6
אנוש 582 אינמו 369 ועם 5973 אדם 120 לא 3808 ינגעו 5060: לכן 3651 ענקתמו 6059
'anoush 'aeynemou; ua'am 'adam, la' yanuga'au. laken 'anaqatmou
***as other* men They *are* not like *other* men neither are they plagued Therefore compass them about as a chain**

73:7
גאוה 1346 יעטף 5848 שית 7897 חמס 2555 למו 3807a: יצא 3318 מחלב 2459 עינמו 5869 עברו 5674 משכיות 4906
ga'auah; ya'atap, shiyt chamas lamou. yatza' mecheleb 'aeynemou; 'abaru, maskiyout
**pride cover *as* a garment violence them stand out with fatness Their eyes they have more than could wish**

Ps 72:14 He shall redeem their soul from deceit and violence: and precious shall their blood be in his sight.15 And he shall live, and to him shall be given of the gold of Sheba: prayer also shall be made for him continually; and daily shall he be praised.16 There shall be an handful of corn in the earth upon the top of the mountains; the fruit thereof shall shake like Lebanon: and they of the city shall flourish like grass of the earth.17 His name shall endure forever: his name shall be continued as long as the sun: and men shall be blessed in him: all nations shall call him blessed.18 Blessed be YHUH G-d, the G-d of Israel, who only doeth wondrous things.19 And blessed be his glorious name forever: and let the whole earth be filled with his glory; Amen, and Amen.20 The prayers of David the son of Jesse are ended. **Ps** 73:1 A Psalm of A'-saph. Truly G-d is good to Israel, even to such as are of a clean heart.2 But as for me, my feet were almost gone; my steps had well nigh slipped.3 For I was envious at the foolish, when I saw the prosperity of the wicked.4 For there are no bands in their death: but their strength is firm.5 They are not in trouble as other men; neither are they plagued like other men.6 Therefore pride compass them about as a chain; violence covereth them as a garment.7 Their eyes stand out with fatness: they have more than heart could wish.

73:8 | 73:9

לבב 3824: ימיקו 4167 וידברו 1696 ברע 7451 עשק 6233 ממרום 4791 ידברו 1696: שתו 8371

labab. yamiyqu uiydabaru bara' 'asheq; mimaroum yadaberu. shatu

**heart They are corrupt and speak wickedly *concerning* oppression loftily they speak They set**

73:10

בשמים 8064 פיהם 6310 ולשונם 3956 תהלך 1980 בארץ 776: לכן 3651 ישיב 7725 עמו 5971 הלם 1988

bashamayim piyhem; ualshounam, tihalak ba'aretz. laken yashiyb 'amou halom;

**against the heavens their mouth and their tongue walk through the earth Therefore return his people here**

73:11

ומי 4325 מלא 4392 ימצו 4680 למו 3807a: ואמרו 559 איכה 349 ידע 3045 אל 410 ויש 3426 דעה 1844

uamey malea', yimatzu lamou. ua'amaru, 'aeykah yada' 'ael; uayesh de'ah

**and waters of a full *cup* are wrung out to them And they say How does know El and is there knowledge**

73:12 | 73:13

בעליון 5945: הנה 2009 אלה 428 רשעים 7563 ושלוי 7961 עולם 5769 השגו 7685 חיל 2428: אך 389 ריק 7385

ba'alyoun. hineh 'aeleh rasha'aym; uashaluey 'aulam, hisgu chayil. 'ak riyq

**in the most high? Behold these *are* the ungodly who prosper in the world they increase *in* riches Verily *in* vain**

73:14

זכיתי 2135 לבבי 3824 וארחץ 7364 בנקיון 5356 כפי 3709: ואהי 1961 נגוע 5060 כל 3605 היום 3117

zikiytiy lababiy; ua'archatz baniqayoun kapay. ua'ahiy nagua' kal hayoum;

**I have cleansed my heart and washed in innocency my hands For have I been plagued all the day *long***

73:15

ותוכחתי 8433 לבקרים 1242: אם 518 אמרתי 559 אספרה 5608 כמו 3644 הנה 2009 דור 1755 בניך 1121

uatoukachtiy, labaqariym. 'am 'amartiy 'asaprah kamou; hineh dour baneyka

**and chastened *every* morning If I say I will speak thus behold *against* the generation of your children**

73:16 | 73:17

בגדתי 898: ואחשבה 2803 לדעת 3045 זאת 2063 עמל 5999 היא 1931 בעיני 5869: עד 5704 אבוא 935 אל 413

bagadatiy. ua'achashbah lada'at za't; 'amal hiy'a ba'aeynay. 'ad 'abou'a 'al

**I should offend When I thought to know this *was too* painful it for me Until I went into**

73:18

מקדשי 4720 אל 410 אבינה 995 לאחריתם 319: אך 389 בחלקות 2513 תשית 7896 למו 3807a

miqdashey 'ael; 'abiynah, la'achariytam. 'ak bachalaqout tashiyt lamou;

**the sanctuary of El *then* understood I their end Surely in slippery places you did set them**

73:19

הפלתם 5307 למשואות 4876: איך 349 היו 1961 לשמה 8047 כרגע 7281 ספו 5486 תמו 8552

hipaltam, lamashu'aut. 'aeyk hayu lashamah karaga'; sapu tamu,

**you cast them down into destruction How are they *brought* into desolation as in a moment they utterly are consumed**

73:20 | 73:21

מן 4480 בלהות 1091: כחלום 2472 מהקיץ 6974 אדני 136 בעיר 5782 צלמם 6754 תבזה 959: כי 3588

min balahout. kachaloum mehaqiytz; 'adonay ba'ayr tzalmam tibzeh. kiy

**with terrors As a dream when *one* awaken *so* O Adonai when you awake their image you shall despise Thus**

73:22

יתחמץ 2556 לבבי 3824 וכליותי 3629 אשתונן 8150: ואני 589 בער 1198 ולא 3808 אדע 3045 בהמות 929 הייתי 1961

yitchametz lababiy; uakilyoutay, 'ashtounan. ua'aniy ba'ar uala' 'aeda; bahemout, hayiytiy

**was grieved my heart and in my reins I was pricked So I foolish *was* I and ignorant *as* a beast I was**

73:23 | 73:24

עמך 5973: ואני 589 תמיד 8548 עמך 5973 אחזת 270 ביד 3027 ימיני 3225: בעצתך 6098

'amak. ua'aniy tamiyd 'amak; 'achazta, bayad yamiyniy. ba'atzataka

**before you Nevertheless I *am* continually with you: you have holden *me* by hand my right with your counsel**

Ps 73:8 They are corrupt, and speak wickedly concerning oppression: they speak loftily.9 They set their mouth against the heavens, and their tongue walk through the earth.10 Therefore his people return hither: and waters of a full cup are wrung out to them.11 And they say, How doth G-d know? and is there knowledge in the most High?12 Behold, these are the ungodly, who prosper in the world; they increase in riches.13 Verily I have cleansed my heart in vain, and washed my hands in innocency.14 For all the day long have I been plagued, and chastened every morning.15 If I say, I will speak thus; behold, I should offend against the generation of your children.16 When I thought to know this, it was too painful for me;17 Until I went into the sanctuary of G-d; then understood I their end.18 Surely you did set them in slippery places: you castedst them down into destruction.19 How are they brought into desolation, as in a moment! they are utterly consumed with terrors.20 As a dream when one awaketh; so, O Adonai, when you awakest, you shall despise their image.21 Thus my heart was grieved, and I was pricked in my reins.22 So foolish was I, and ignorant: I was as a beast before you.23 Nevertheless I am continually with you: you have holden me by my right hand.

73:25

תנחני 5148 ואחר 310 כבוד 3519 תקחני 3947: מי 4310 לי 3807a בשמים 8064 ועמך 5973
tanacheniy; ua'achar, kaboud tiqacheniy. miy' liy bashamayim; ua'amaka,
**You shall guide me and afterward *to* glory receive me Whom *have* I in heaven *but you?* and besides you *there is***

73:26

לא 3808 חפצתי 2654 בארץ 776: כלה 3615 שארי 7607 ולבבי 3824 צור 6697 לבבי 3824 וחלקי 2506 אלהים 430
la' chapatztiy ba'aretz. kalah sha'aeriy, ualbabiy tzur lababiy uachelqiy, 'alohiym
**none *that* I desire upon earth fail My flesh and my heart *is* the strength of my heart and my portion *but* Elohim**

73:27

לעולם 5769: כי 3588 הנה 2009 רחקיך 7369 יאבדו 6 הצמתה 6789 כל 3605 זונה 2181
la'aulam. kiy hineh racheqeyka ya'bedu; hitzmatah, kal zouneh
**for ever For lo they that are far from you shall perish you have destroyed all them that go a whoring**

73:28

ממך 4480: ואני 589 קרבת 7132 אלהים 430 לי 3807a טוב 2896 שתי 7896 באדני 136 יהוה 3069 מחסי 4268 לספר 5608
mimeka. ua'aniy qirabat 'alohiym, liy toub shatiy ba'adonay Yahuah machasiy; lasaper,
**from you But to draw near to Elohim for me *it is* good I have put in Adonai Yahuah my trust that I may declare**

כל 3605 מלאכותיך 4399:
kal mal'akouteyka.
**all your works**

**Ps 74:1**

משכיל 4905 לאסף 623 למה 4100 אלהים 430 זנחת 2186 לנצח 5331 יעשן 6225 אפך 639 בצאן 6629
maskiyl, la'asap lamah 'alohiym zanachta lanetzach; ye'ashan 'apaka, batza'an
**Maschil of Asaph why O Elohim have you cast *us* off for ever? *why* do smoke your anger against the sheep of**

74:2

מרעיתך 4830: זכר 2142 עדתך 5712 קנית 7069 קדם 6924 גאלת 1350 שבט 7626
mar'ayteka. zakor 'adataka qaniyta qedem, ga'alta shebet
**your pasture? Remember your congregation *which* you have purchased of old *which* you have redeemed the rod of**

74:3

נחלתך 5159 הר 2022 ציון 6726 זה 2088 שכנת 7931 בו 871a: הרימה 7311 פעמיך 6471 למשאות 4876 נצח 5331
nachalateka; har tziyoun, zeh shakanta bou. hariymah pa'ameyka lamashu'aut netzach;
**your inheritance mount Zion this you have dwelt wherein Lift up your feet unto desolations *the* perpetual**

74:4

כל 3605 הרע 7489 אויב 341 בקדש 6944: שאגו 7580 צרריך 6887 בקרב 7130 מועדך 4150
kal hera' auyeb baqodesh. sha'agu tzorareyka baqereb mou'adeka;
***even* all has done wickedly *that* the enemy in the sanctuary roar Thine enemies in the midst of your congregations**

74:5

שמו 7760 אותתם 226 אתות 226: יודע 3045 כמביא 935 למעלה 4605 בסבך 5442 עץ 6086
samu 'autotam 'autot. yiuada' kamebiy'a lama'alah; bisabak 'aetz,
**they set up their ensigns *for* signs *A man* was famous according as he had lifted up upon the thick trees**

74:6 74:7

קרדמות 7134: ועת 6256 פתוחיה 6603 יחד 3162 בכשיל 3781 וכילפת 3597 יהלמון 1986: שלחו 7971
qardumout. ua'ata pitucheyha yachad; bakashshiyl uakeylapot, yahalomun. shilchu
**axes But now the carved work thereof at once with axes and hammers they break down They have cast**

74:8

באש 784 מקדשך 4720 לארץ 776 חללו 2490 משכן 4908 שמך 8034: אמרו 559
ba'esh miqadasheka; la'aretz, chillu mishkan shameka. 'amaru
**fire into your sanctuary to the ground they have defiled *by casting down* the dwelling place of your name They said**

Ps 73:24 Thou shall guide me with your counsel, and afterward receive me to glory.25 Whom have I in heaven but you? and there is none upon earth that I desire beside you.26 My flesh and my heart faileth: but G-d is the strength of my heart, and my portion forever.27 For, lo, they that are far from you shall perish: you have destroyed all them that go a whoring from you.28 But it is good for me to draw near to G-d: I have put my trust in YHUH G-D, that I may declare all your works. **Ps** 74:1 Mas'-chil of A'-saph. O G-d, why have you cast us off forever? why doth your anger smoke against the sheep of your pasture?2 Remember your congregation, which you have purchased of old; the rod of your inheritance, which you have redeemed; this mount Zion, wherein you have dwelt.3 Lift up your feet unto the perpetual desolations; even all that the enemy has done wickedly in the sanctuary.4 Thine enemies roar in the midst of your congregations; they set up their ensigns for signs.5 A man was famous according as he had lifted up axes upon the thick trees.6 But now they break down the carved work thereof at once with axes and hammers.7 They have cast fire into your sanctuary, they have defiled by casting down the dwelling place of your name to the ground.

| בלבם 3820 | נינם 3238 | יחד 3162 | שרפו 8313 | כל 3605 | מועדי 4150 | אל 410 | בארץ 776: | 74:9 אותתינו 226 |
|---|---|---|---|---|---|---|---|---|
| balibam | niynam | yachad; | sarapu | kal | mou'adey | 'ael | ba'aretz. | 'autoteynu, |
| in their hearts | Let us destroy them | together | they have burned up | all | the synagogues of | El | in the land | our signs |

| לא 3808 | ראינו 7200 | אין 369 | עוד 5750 | נביא 5030 | ולא 3808 | אתנו 854 | ידע 3045 | עד 5704 | 74:10 מה 4100: |
|---|---|---|---|---|---|---|---|---|---|
| la' | ra'aynu | 'aeyn | 'aud | nabiy'a; | uala' | 'atanu, | yodea' | 'ad | mah. |
| not | We see | *there is* no | more | *any* prophet | and neither *is there* | among us | any that knows | how long | what |

| עד 5704 | מתי 4970 | אלהים 430 | יחרף 2778 | צר 6862 | ינאץ 5006 | אויב 341 | שמך 8034 | לנצח 5331: | 74:11 למה 4100 |
|---|---|---|---|---|---|---|---|---|---|
| 'ad | matay | 'alohiym | yacharep | tzar; | yana'aetz | auyeb | shimka | lanetzach. | lamah |
| how long | when | O Elohim | shall reproach? | the adversary | shall blaspheme | the enemy | your name | for ever? | Why |

| תשיב 7725 | ידך 3027 | וימינך 3225 | מקרב 7130 | חוקך 2436 | כלה 3615: | 74:12 ואלהים 430 | מלכי 4428 | מקדם 6924 |
|---|---|---|---|---|---|---|---|---|
| tashiyb | yadaka | uiymiyneka; | miqereb | chouqaka | kaleh. | ua'alohiym | malkiy | miqedem; |
| withdraw you | your hand | even your right hand? | *it* out of | your bosom | pluck | For Elohim | *is* my King | of old |

| פעל 6466 | ישועות 3444 | בקרב 7130 | הארץ 776: | 74:13 אתה 859 | פוררת 6565 | בעזך 5797 | ים 3220 | שברת 7665 | ראשי 7218 |
|---|---|---|---|---|---|---|---|---|---|
| po'ael | yashu'aut, | baqereb | ha'aretz. | 'atah | pourarta | ba'azaka | yam; | shibarta | ra'shey |
| working | salvation | in the midst of | the earth | You | did divide | by your strength | the sea | you brake | the heads of |

| תנינים 8577 | על 5921 | המים 4325: | 74:14 אתה 859 | רצצת 7533 | ראשי 7218 | לויתן 3882 | תתננו 5414 | מאכל 3978 | לעם 5971 |
|---|---|---|---|---|---|---|---|---|---|
| taniyniym, | 'al | hamayim. | 'atah | ritzatzta | ra'shey | liuyatan; | titanenu | ma'akal, | la'am |
| the dragons | in | the waters | You | brake in pieces | the heads of | leviathan | *and* gave him | *to be* meat | to the people |

| לציים 6728: | 74:15 אתה 859 | בקעת 1234 | מעין 4599 | ונחל 5158 | אתה 859 | הובשת 3001 | נהרות 5104 | 74:16 איתן 386: |
|---|---|---|---|---|---|---|---|---|
| latziyiym. | 'atah | baqa'ata | ma'ayan | uanachal; | 'atah | houbashta, | naharout | 'aeytan. |
| inhabiting the wilderness | You | did cleave | the fountain | and the flood | you | dry up | rivers | mighty |

| לך 3807a | יום 3117 | אף 637 | לך 3807a | לילה 3915 | אתה 859 | הכינות 3559 | מאור 3974 | ושמש 8121: | 74:17 אתה 859 | הצבת 5324 | כל 3605 |
|---|---|---|---|---|---|---|---|---|---|---|---|
| laka | youm | 'ap | laka | layalah; | 'atah | hakiynouta, | ma'our | uashamesh. | 'atah | hitzabta | kal |
| *is* to your | The day | also | *is* to your | the night | you | have prepared | the light | and the sun | You | have set | all |

| גבולות 1367 | ארץ 776 | קיץ 7019 | וחרף 2779 | אתה 859 | יצרתם 3335: | 74:18 זכר 2142 | זאת 2063 | אויב 341 | חרף 2778 |
|---|---|---|---|---|---|---|---|---|---|
| gabulout | 'aretz; | qayitz | uachorep, | 'atah | yatzartam | zakar | za't, | 'auyeb | cherep |
| the borders of | the earth | summer | and winter | you | have made | Remember | this | *that* the enemy | has reproached |

| יהוה 3068 | ועם 5971 | נבל 5036 | נאצו 5006 | שמך 8034: | 74:19 אל 408 | תתן 5414 | לחית 2416 |
|---|---|---|---|---|---|---|---|
| Yahuah; | ua'am | nabal, | ni'atzu | shameka. | 'al | titen | lachayat |
| O Yahuah | and people | *that the* foolish | have blasphemed | your name | not | O deliver | unto the multitude *of the wicked* |

| נפש 5315 | תורך 8449 | חית 2416 | ענייך 6041 | אל 408 | תשכח 7911 | לנצח 5331: | 74:20 הבט 5027 | לברית 1285 |
|---|---|---|---|---|---|---|---|---|
| nepesh | toureka; | chayat | 'aniyeyka, | 'al | tishkach | lanetzach. | habet | labriyt; |
| the soul of | your turtledove | the congregation of | your poor | not | forget | for ever | Have respect | unto the covenant |

| כי 3588 | מלאו 4390 | מחשכי 4285 | ארץ 776 | נאות 4999 | חמס 2555: | 74:21 אל 408 | ישב 7725 | דך 1790 | נכלם 3637 |
|---|---|---|---|---|---|---|---|---|---|
| kiy | mala'au | machashakey | 'aretz, | na'aut | chamas. | 'al | yashob | dak | niklam; |
| for | are full of | *the* dark places of | the earth | the habitations of | cruelty | not | O let return | the oppressed | ashamed |

Ps 74:8 They said in their hearts, Let us destroy them together: they have burned up all the synagogues of G-d in the land.9 We see not our signs: there is no more any prophet: neither is there among us any that know how long.10 O G-d, how long shall the adversary reproach? shall the enemy blaspheme your name forever?11 Why withdrawest you your hand, even your right hand? pluck it out of your bosom.12 For G-d is my King of old, working salvation in the midst of the earth.13 Thou did divide the sea by your strength: you brakest the heads of the dragons in the waters.14 Thou brakest the heads of leviathan in pieces, and gave him to be meat to the people inhabiting the wilderness.15 Thou did cleave the fountain and the flood: you driedst up mighty rivers.16 The day is your, the night also is your: you have prepared the light and the sun.17 Thou have set all the borders of the earth: you have made summer and winter.18 Remember this, that the enemy has reproached, O YHUH, and that the foolish people have blasphemed your name.19 O deliver not the soul of your turtledove unto the multitude of the wicked: forget not the congregation of your poor forever.20 Have respect unto the covenant: for the dark places of the earth are full of the habitations of cruelty.21 O let not the oppressed return ashamed: let the poor and needy praise your name.

74:22

עני 6041 ואביון 34 יהללו 1984 שמך 8034: קומה 6965 אלהים 430 ריבה 7378 ריבך 7379 זכר 2142 חרפתך 2781 מני 4480
'aniy ua'abyoun, yahalalu shameka. qumah 'alohiym riybah riybeka; zakor cherpataka miniy
**the poor and needy let praise your name Arise O Elohim plead your own cause remember reproach you how**

74:23

נבל 5036 כל 3605 היום 3117: אל 408 תשכח 7911 קול 6963 צרריך 6887 שאון 7588 קמיך 6965
nabal, kal hayoum. 'al tishkach qoul tzorareyka; sha'aun qameyka,
**the foolish man all daily not Forget the voice of your enemies the tumult of those that rise up against you**

עלה 5927 תמיד 8548:
'aleh tamiyd.
**increase continually**

**Ps 75:1**

למנצח 5329 אל 516 תשחת 7843 מזמור 4210 לאסף 623 שיר 7892: הודינו 3034 לך 3807a אלהים 430
lamanatzeach 'al tashchet; mizmour la'asap shiyr. houdiynu laka 'alohiym,
**To the chief Musician Al taschith A Psalm of Asaph *or* Song do we give thanks Unto you O Elohim**

75:2

הודינו 3034 וקרוב 7138 שמך 8034 ספרו 5608 נפלאותיך 6381: כי 3588 אקח 3947
houdiynu uaqaroub shameka; sipru, nipla'auteyka. kiy 'aqach
***unto you* do we give thanks for is near *that* your name declare your wondrous works When I shall receive**

75:3

מועד 4150 אני 589 מישרים 4339 אשפט 8199: נמגים 4127 ארץ 776 וכל 3605 ישביה 3427 אנכי 595 תכנתי 8505
mou'aed; 'aniy, meyshariym 'ashpot. namogiym, 'aretz uakal yoshabeyha; 'anokiy tikantiy
**the congregation I uprightly will judge are dissolved The earth and all the inhabitants thereof I bear up**

75:4 75:5

עמודיה 5982 סלה 5542: אמרתי 559 להוללים 1984 אל 408 תהלו 1984 ולרשעים 7563 אל 408 תרימו 7311 קרן 7161: אל 408
'amudeyha selah. 'amartiy lahoulaliym 'al taholu; ualarasha'aym, 'al tariymu qaren. 'al
**the pillars of it Selah I said unto the fools not Deal foolishly and to the wicked not Lift up the horn not**

75:6

תרימו 7311 למרום 4791 קרנכם 7161 תדברו 1696 בצואר 6677 עתק 6277: כי 3588 לא 3808 ממוצא 4161 וממערב 4628 ולא 3808
tariymu lamaroum qarnakem; tadabru batzaua'ar 'ataq. kiy la' mimoutzaa' uamima'arab; uala',
**Lift up on high your horn speak neck *not with* a stiff For neither from the east nor from the west and nor**

75:7 75:8

ממדבר 4057 הרים 7311: כי 3588 אלהים 430 שפט 8199 זה 2088 ישפיל 8213 וזה 2088 ירים 7311: כי 3588
mimidbar hariym. kiy 'alohiym shopet; zeh yashpiyl, uazeh yariym. kiy
**from the south promotion *comes* But Elohim *is* the judge one he put down and another set up For**

כוס 3563 ביד 3027 יהוה 3068 ויין 3196 חמר 2560 מלא 4392 מסך 4538 ויגר 5064 מזה 2088 אך 389
kous bayad Yahuah uayayin chamar malea' mesek uayager mizeh 'ak
***there is* a cup in the hand of Yahuah and the wine is red it is full of mixture and he pour out of the same but**

75:9

שמריה 8105 ימצו 4680 ישתו 8354 כל 3605 רשעי 7563 ארץ 776: ואני 589 אגיד 5046 לעלם 5769
shamareyha yimtzu yishtu; kol, rish'aey 'aretz. ua'aniy 'agiyd la'alam;
**the dregs thereof shall wring them out *and* drink *them* all the wicked of the earth But I will declare for ever**

75:10

אזמרה 2167 לאלהי 430 יעקב 3290: וכל 3605 קרני 7161 רשעים 7563 אגדע 1438 תרוממנה 7311
'azamrah, le'alohey ya'aqob. uakal qarney rasha'aym 'agadea'; taroumamnah,
**I will sing praises to the Elohim of Jacob All also the horns of the wicked will I cut off shall be exalted**

Ps 74:22 Arise, O G-d, plead your own cause: remember how the foolish man reproacheth you daily.23 Forget not the voice of your enemies: the tumult of those that rise up against you increaseth continually. **Ps** 75:1 To the chief Musician, Al-tas'-chith, A Psalm or Song of A'-saph. Unto you, O G-d, do we give thanks, unto you do we give thanks: for that your name is near your wondrous works declare.2 When I shall receive the congregation I will judge uprightly.3 The earth and all the inhabitants thereof are dissolved: I bear up the pillars of it. Selah.4 I said unto the fools, Deal not foolishly: and to the wicked, Lift not up the horn:5 Lift not up your horn on high: speak not with a stiff neck.6 For promotion cometh neither from the east, nor from the west, nor from the south.7 But G-d is the judge: he put down one, and set up another.8 For in the hand of YHUH there is a cup, and the wine is red; it is full of mixture; and he poureth out of the same: but the dregs thereof, all the wicked of the earth shall wring them out, and drink them.9 But I will declare forever; I will sing praises to the G-d of Jacob.10 All the horns of the wicked also will I cut off; but the horns of the righteous shall be exalted.

קרנות 7161 | צדיק 6662:
qarnout | tzadiyq.
***but* the horns of | the righteous**

**Ps 76:1** למנצח 5329 | בנגינת 5058 | מזמור 4210 | לאסף 623 | שיר 7892: | נודע 3045 | ביהודה 3063 | אלהים 430 | בישראל 3478 | גדול 1419
lamanatzeach | binagiynout; | mizmour | la'asap | shiyr. | nouda' | biyahudah | 'alohiym; | bayisra'ael, | gadoul
**To the chief Musician | on Neginoth | A Psalm | of Asaph | *or* Song | known | In Judah | *is* Elohim | in Israel | *is* great**

שמו 8034: | **76:2** ויהי 1961 | בשלם 8004 | סכו 5520 | ומעונתו 4585 | בציון 6726: | **76:3** שמה 8033 | שבר 7665 | רשפי 7565
shamou. | uayahiy | bashalem | sukou; | uam'aunatou | batziyoun. | shamah | shibar | rishpey
**his name | also is | In Salem | his tabernacle | and his dwelling place | in Zion | There | brake he | the arrows of**

קשת 7198 | מגן 4043 | וחרב 2719 | ומלחמה 4421 | סלה 5542: | **76:4** נאור 215 | אתה 859 | אדיר 117 | מהררי 2042
qashet; | magen | uachereb | uamilchamah | selah. | na'aur | 'atah | 'adiyr, | meharey
**the bow | the shield | and the sword | and the battle | Selah | *are more* glorious | You | *and* excellent | than the mountains of**

טרף 2964: | **76:5** אשתוללו 7997 | אבירי 47 | לב 3820 | נמו 5123 | שנתם 8142 | ולא 3808 | מצאו 4672 | כל 3605 | אנשי 582
tarep. | 'ashtoulalu | 'abiyrey | leb | namu | shanatam; | uala' | matza'au | kal | 'anshey
**prey | they are spoiled | The stout | hearted | they have slept | their sleep | and none of | have found | none of | the men of**

חיל 2428 | ידיהם 3027: | **76:6** מגערתך 1606 | אלהי 430 | יעקב 3290 | נרדם 7290 | ורכב 7393 | וסוס 5483: | **76:7**
chayil | yadeyhem. | miga'arataka | 'alohey | ya'aqob; | nirdam, | uarekeb | uasus.
**might | their hands | At your rebuke | O Elohim of | Jacob | are cast into a dead sleep | both the chariot | and horse**

אתה 859 | נורא 3372 | אתה 859 | ומי 4310 | יעמד 5975 | לפניך 6440 | מאז 227 | אפך 639: | **76:8** משמים 8064
'atah | noura' | 'atah, | uamiy | ya'amod | lapaneyka, | me'az | 'apeka. | mishamayim
**You | *are* to be feared *even* | you | and who | may stand | in your sight | when once | you are angry? | from heaven**

השמעת 8085 | דין 1779 | ארץ 776 | יראה 3372 | ושקטה 8252: | **76:9** בקום 6965 | למשפט 4941 | אלהים 430 | להושיע 3467 | כל 3605
hishma'ata | diyn; | 'aretz | yara'ah | uashaqatah. | baqum | lamishpat | 'alohiym; | lahoushiya' | kal
**You did cause to be heard | judgment | the earth | feared | and was still | When arose | to judgment | Elohim | to save | all**

ענוי 6035 | ארץ 776 | סלה 5542: | **76:10** כי 3588 | חמת 2534 | אדם 120 | תודך 3034 | שארית 7611 | חמת 2534
'anuey | 'aretz | selah. | kiy | chamat | 'adam | toudeka; | sha'aeriyt | chemot
**the meek of | the earth | Selah | Surely | the wrath of | man | shall praise you | the remainder of | wrath**

תחגר 2296: | **76:11** נדרו 5087 | ושלמו 7999 | ליהוה 3068 | אלהיכם 430 | כל 3605 | סביביו 5439 | יובילו 2986 | שי 7862
tachagor. | nidaru | uashalmu | laYahuah | 'aloheykem | kal | sabiybayu; | youbiylu | shay
**shall you restrain | Vow | and pay | unto Yahuah | your Elohim | all | that be round about him | let bring | presents**

למורא 4172: | **76:12** יבצר 1219 | רוח 7307 | נגידים 5057 | נורא 3372 | למלכי 4428 | ארץ 776:
lamoura'. | yibtzor | ruach | nagiydiym; | noura', | lamalkey | 'aretz.
**unto him that ought to be feared | He shall cut off | the spirit of | princes | *he is* terrible | to the kings of | the earth**

**Ps 77:1** למנצח 5329 | על 5921 | ידיתון 3038 | לאסף 623 | מזמור 4210: | קולי 6963 | אל 413 | אלהים 430 | ואצעקה 6817 | קולי 6963
lamanatzeach | 'al | yadiytun | la'asap | mizmour. | qouliy | 'al | 'alohiym | ua'atz'aqah; | qouliy
**To the chief Musician | to | Jeduthun | of Asaph | A Psalm | *with* my voice | unto | Elohim | I cried | *with* my voice**

**Ps** 76:1 To the chief Musician on Neg'-i-noth, A Psalm or Song of A'-saph. In Judah is G-d known: his name is great in Israel.2 In Salem also is his tabernacle, and his dwelling place in Zion.3 There break he the arrows of the bow, the shield, and the sword, and the battle. Selah.4 Thou are more glorious and excellent than the mountains of prey.5 The stouthearted are spoiled, they have slept their sleep: and none of the men of might have found their hands.6 At your rebuke, O G-d of Jacob, both the chariot and horse are cast into a dead sleep.7 Thou, even you, are to be feared: and who may stand in your sight when once you are angry?8 Thou did cause judgment to be heard from heaven; the earth feared, and was still,9 When G-d arose to judgment, to save all the meek of the earth. Selah.10 Surely the wrath of man shall praise you: the remainder of wrath shall you restrain.11 Vow, and pay unto YHUH your G-d: let all that be round about him bring presents unto him that ought to be feared.12 He shall cut off the spirit of princes: he is terrible to the kings of the earth. **Ps** 77:1 To the chief Musician, to Je-du'-thun, A Psalm of A'-saph. I cried unto G-d with my voice, even unto G-d with my voice; and he gave ear unto me.

77:2
אל 413 | אלהים 430 | והאזין 238 | אלי 413: | ביום 3117 | צרתי 6869 | אדני 136 | דרשתי 1875 | ידי 3027 | לילה 3915 | נגרה 5064
'al 'alohiym, uaha'aziyn 'aelay. bayoum tzaratiy 'adonay darashatiy yadiy layalah nigrah
***even* unto Elohim and he gave ear unto me In the day of my trouble Adonai I sought my sore in the night ran**

77:3
ולא 3808 | תפוג 6313 | מאנה 3985 | הנחם 5162 | נפשי 5315: | אזכרה 2142 | אלהים 430 | ואהמיה 1993 | אשיחה 7878
uala' tapug; me'anah hinachem napshiy. 'azkarah 'alohiym ua'ahemayah; 'asiychah
**and not ceased refused to be comforted my soul I remembered Elohim and was troubled I complained**

77:4 77:5
ותתעטף 5848 | רוחי 7307 | סלה 5542: | אחזת 270 | שמרות 8109 | עיני 5869 | נפעמתי 6470 | ולא 3808 | אדבר 1696:
uatit'atep ruchiy selah. 'achazta shamurout 'aeynay; nip'amtiy, uala' 'adaber.
**and was overwhelmed my spirit Selah You hold waking mine eyes I am so troubled that cannot I speak**

77:6
חשבתי 2803 | ימים 3117 | מקדם 6924 | שנות 8141 | עולמים 5769: | אזכרה 2142 | נגינתי 5058 | בלילה 3915 | עם 5973
chishabtiy yamiym miqedem; shanout, 'aulamiym. 'azkarah nagiynatiy, balayalah 'am
**I have considered the days of old the years of ancient times I call to remembrance my song in the night with**

77:7
לבבי 3824 | אשיחה 7878 | ויחפש 2664 | רוחי 7307: | הלעולמים 5769 | יזנח 2186 | אדני 136 | ולא 3808
lababiy 'asiychah; uaychapes ruchiy. hala'aulamiym yiznach 'adonay; uala'
**mine own heart I commune and made diligent search my spirit for ever? Will cast off Adonai and no**

77:8 77:9
יסיף 3254 | לרצות 7521 | עוד 5750: | האפס 656 | לנצח 5331 | חסדו 2617 | גמר 1584 | אמר 562 | לדר 1755 | ודר 1755:
yosiyp liratzout 'aud. he'apes lanetzach chasdou; gamar 'amer, lador uador.
**will he be more? favourable more? Is clean gone for ever? his mercy does fail *his* promise for all and evermore?**

77:10
השכח 7911 | חנות 2589 | אל 410 | אם 518 | קפץ 7092 | באף 639 | רחמיו 7356 | סלה 5542: | ואמר 559
hashakach chanout 'ael; 'am qapatz ba'ap, rachamayu selah. ua'amar
**Has forgotten to be gracious? El or has he shut up in anger his tender mercies? Selah And I said**

77:11
חלותי 2470 | היא 1931 | שנות 8141 | ימין 3225 | עליון 5945: | אזכיר 2142 | מעללי 4611
chaloutiy hiy'a; shanout, yamiyn 'alyoun. 'azkiyr ma'alley
***is* my infirmity This *but I will remember* the years of the right hand the most High I will remember the works of**

77:12
יה 3050 | כי 3588 | אזכרה 2142 | מקדם 6924 | פלאך 6382: | והגיתי 1897 | בכל 3605 | פעלך 6467 | ובעלילותיך 5949
Yah; kiy 'azkarah miqedem pila'aka. uahagiytiy bakal pa'aleka; uaba'aliylouteyka
**Yah surely I will remember old your wonders of I will meditate also of all your work and of your doings**

77:13 77:14
אשיחה 7878: | אלהים 430 | בקדש 6944 | דרכך 1870 | מי 4310 | אל 410 | גדול 1419 | כאלהים 430: | אתה 859 | האל 410
'asiychah. 'alohiym baqodesh darkeka; miy' 'ael gadoul, ke'alohiym. 'atah ha'ael
**talk O Elohim *is* in the sanctuary Your way who a El *is so* great as our Elohim? You *are* the El**

77:15
עשה 6213 | פלא 6382 | הודעת 3045 | בעמים 5971 | עזך 5797: | גאלת 1350 | בזרוע 2220 | עמך 5971
'asheh pela'; houda'ata ba'amiym 'azeka. ga'alta bizroua' 'ameka;
**that do wonders you have declared among the people your strength You have redeemed with *your* arm your people**

77:16
בני 1121 | יעקב 3290 | ויוסף 3130 | סלה 5542: | ראוך 7200 | מים 4325 | אלהים 430 | ראוך 7200 | מים 4325 | יחילו 2342 | אף 637
baney ya'aqob uayousep selah. ra'auka mayim 'alohiym, ra'auka mayim yachiylu; 'ap,
**the sons of Jacob and Joseph Selah saw you The waters O Elohim saw you the waters they were afraid also**

Ps 77:2 In the day of my trouble I sought the Adonai: my sore ran in the night, and ceased not: my soul refused to be comforted.3 I remembered G-d, and was troubled: I complained, and my spirit was overwhelmed. Selah.4 Thou holdest mine eyes waking: I am so troubled that I cannot speak.5 I have considered the days of old, the years of ancient times.6 I call to remembrance my song in the night: I commune with mine own heart: and my spirit made diligent search.7 Will YHUH cast off forever? and will he be favorable no more?8 Is his mercy clean gone forever? doth his promise fail forevermore?9 Hath G-d forgotten to be gracious? has he in anger shut up his tender mercies? Selah.10 And I said, This is my infirmity: but I will remember the years of the right hand of the most High.11 I will remember the works of YHUH: surely I will remember your wonders of old.12 I will meditate also of all your work, and talk of your doings.13 Thy way, O G-d, is in the sanctuary: who is so great a G-d as our G-d?14 Thou are the G-d that does wonders: you have declared your strength among the people.15 Thou have with your arm redeemed your people, the sons of Jacob and Joseph. Selah.16 The waters saw you, O G-d, the waters saw you; they were afraid: the depths also were troubled.

77:17
ירגזו 7264 תהמות 8415: זרמו 2229 מים 4325 עבות 5645 קול 6963 נתנו 5414 שחקים 7834 אף 637 חצציך 2687
yirgazu tahomout. zoramu mayim about, qoul natanu shachaqiym; 'ap chatzatzeyka,
**were troubled the depths poured out water The clouds a sound sent out the skies also your arrows**

77:18
יתהלכו 1980: קול 6963 רעמך 7482 בגלגל 1534 האירו 215 ברקים 1300 תבל 8398 רגזה 7264 ותרעש 7493
yithalaku. qoul ra'amka bagalgal, he'ayru baraqiym tebel; ragazah uatir'ash
**went abroad The voice of your thunder *was* in the heaven lightened the lightnings the world trembled and shook**

77:19 77:20
הארץ 776: בים 3220 דרכך 1870 ושביליך 7635 במים 4325 רבים 7227 ועקבותיך 6119 לא 3808 נדעו 3045: נחית 5148
ha'aretz. bayam darkeka, uashbiyleyka bamayim rabiym; ua'aqbouteyka, la' noda'au. nachiyta
**the earth *is* in the sea Your way and your path in waters *the* great and your footsteps not are known You led**

כצאן 6629 עמך 5971 ביד 3027 משה 4872 ואהרן 175:
katzo'an 'ameka; bayad mosheh ua'aharon.
**like a flock your people by the hand of Moses and Aaron**

**Ps 78:1** 78:2
משכיל 4905 לאסף 623 האזינה 238 עמי 5971 תורתי 8451 הטו 5186 אזנכם 241 לאמרי 561 פי 6310: אפתחה 6605
maskiyl, la'asap ha'aziynah 'amiy touratiy; hatu 'aznakem, la'amrey piy. 'aptachah
**Maschil of Asaph Give ear O my people *to* my law incline your ears to the words of my mouth I will open**

78:3
במשל 4912 פי 6310 אביעה 5042 חידות 2420 מני 4480 קדם 6924: אשר 834 שמענו 8085 ונדעם 3045 ואבותינו 1
bamashal piy; 'abiy'ah chiydout, miniy qedem. 'asher shama'anu uaneda'aem; ua'abouteynu,
**in a parable my mouth I will utter dark sayings of old Which we have heard and known and our fathers**

78:4
ספרו 5608 לנו 3807a: לא 3808 נכחד 3582 מבניהם 1121 לדור 1755 אחרון 314 מספרים 5608 תהלות 8416
sipru lanu. la' nakached mibneyhem, ladour 'acharoun, masapriym tahilout
**have told us not We will hide *them* from their children to the generation to come shewing the praises of**

78:5
יהוה 3068 ועזוזו 5807 ונפלאותיו 6381 אשר 834 עשה 6213: ויקם 6965 עדות 5715 ביעקב 3290
Yahuah; ua'azuzou uanipla'autayu, 'asher 'asah. uayaqem 'aedut baya'aqob,
**Yahuah and his strength and his wonderful works that he has done For he established a testimony in Jacob**

ותורה 8451 שם 7760 בישראל 3478 אשר 834 צוה 6680 את 853 אבותינו 1 להודיעם 3045
uatourah sam bayisra'ael 'asher tziuah 'at abouteynu; lahoudiy'am,
**and a law appointed in Israel which he commanded our fathers that they should make them known**

78:6
לבניהם 1121: למען 4616 ידעו 3045 דור 1755 אחרון 314 בנים 1121 יולדו 3205
libneyhem. lama'an yeda'au dour 'acharoun baniym yiualedu;
**to their children That might know the generation to come *them even* the children of *which* should be born**

78:7
יקמו 6965 ויספרו 5608 לבניהם 1121: וישימו 7760 באלהים 430 כסלם 3689 ולא 3808 ישכחו 7911
yaqumu, uiysapru libneyhem. uayasiymu be'alohiym, kislam uala' yishkachu
***who* should arise and declare *them* to their children That they might set in Elohim their hope and not forget**

78:8
מעללי 4611 אל 410 ומצותיו 4687 ינצרו 5341: ולא 3808 יהיו 1961 כאבותם 1 דור 1755 סורר 5637
ma'alley 'ael; uamitzuotayu yintzoru. uala' yihayu ka'aboutam, dour sourer
**the works of El but his commandments keep And not might be as their fathers generation a stubborn**

Ps 77:17 The clouds poured out water: the skies sent out a sound: your arrows also went abroad.18 The voice of your thunder was in the heaven: the lightnings lightened the world: the earth trembled and shook.19 Thy way is in the sea, and your path in the great waters, and your footsteps are not known.20 Thou led your people like a flock by the hand of Moses and Aaron. **Ps** 78:1 Mas'-chil of A'-saph. Give ear, O my people, to my law: incline your ears to the words of my mouth.2 I will open my mouth in a parable: I will utter dark sayings of old:3 Which we have heard and known, and our fathers have told us.4 We will not hide them from their children, shewing to the generation to come the praises of YHUH, and his strength, and his wonderful works that he has done.5 For he established a testimony in Jacob, and appointed a law in Israel, which he commanded our fathers, that they should make them known to their children:6 That the generation to come might know them, even the children which should be born; who should arise and declare them to their children:7 That they might set their hope in G-d, and not forget the works of G-d, but keep his commandments:8 And might not be as their fathers, a stubborn and rebellious generation; a generation that set not their heart aright, and whose spirit was not stedfast with G-d.

78:9
ומרה 4784 דור 1755 לא 3808 הכין 3559 לבו 3820 ולא 3808 נאמנה 539 את 854 אל 410 רוחו 7307:
uamoreh dour la' hekiyn libou; uala' ne'amnah 'at 'al ruachou.
**and rebellious a generation and not *that* set aright their heart and not was stedfast *with* El whose spirit**

78:10
בני 1121 אפרים 669 נושקי 5401 רומי 7411 קשת 7198 הפכו 2015 ביום 3117 קרב 7128: לא 3808 שמרו 8104
baney 'aprayim, noushaqey roumey qashet; hapaku, bayoum qarab. la' shamaru
**The children of Ephraim *being* armed *and* carrying bows turned back in the day of battle not They kept**

78:11
ברית 1285 אלהים 430 ובתורתו 8451 מאנו 3985 ללכת 1980: וישכחו 7911 עלילותיו 5949 ונפלאותיו 6381 אשר 834
bariyt 'alohiym; uabtouratou, me'anu laleket. uayishkachu aliyloutayu; uanipla'autayu, 'asher
**the covenant of Elohim and in his law refused to walk And forgot his works and his wonders that**

78:12
הראם 7200: נגד 5048 אבותם 1 עשה 6213 פלא 6382 בארץ 776 מצרים 4714 שדה 7704
her'am. neged 'aboutam 'asah pela'; ba'aretz mitzrayim sadeh
**he had showed them in the sight of their fathers did he Marvellous things in the land of Egypt *in* the field of**

78:13 78:14
צען 6814: בקע 1234 ים 3220 ויעבירם 5674 ויצב 5324 מים 4325 כמו 3644 נד 5067:
tzo'an. baqa' yam uaya'abiyrem; uayatzeb mayim kamou ned.
**Zoan He divided the sea and caused them to pass through and he made to stand the waters as an heap**

78:15
וינחם 5148 בענן 6051 יומם 3119 וכל 3605 הלילה 3915 באור 216 אש 784: יבקע 1234 צרים 6697
uayanchem be'anan youmam; uakal halayalah, ba'aur 'aesh. yabaqa' tzuriym
**also he led them with a cloud In the daytime and all the night with a light of fire He clave the rocks**

78:16
במדבר 4057 וישק 8248 כתהמות 8415 רבה 7227: ויוצא 3318 נוזלים 5140 מסלע 5553
bamidbar; uayashq, kitahomout rabah. uayoutza' nouzaliym misala';
**in the wilderness and gave *them* drink as depths *out of the* great He brought also streams out of the rock**

78:17
ויורד 3381 כנהרות 5104 מים 4325: ויוסיפו 3254 עוד 5750 לחטא 2398 לו 3807a למרות 4784 עליון 5945
uayoured kanaharout mayim. uayousiypu 'aud lachato'a lou'; lamarout 'alyoun,
**and caused to run down like rivers waters And more yet they sinned against him by provoking the most High**

78:18 78:19
בציה 6723: וינסו 5254 אל 410 בלבבם 3824 לשאל 7592 אכל 400 לנפשם 5315: וידברו 1696
batziyah. uayanasu 'ael bilbabam; lish'al 'akel lanapsham. uayadabru,
**in the wilderness And they tempted El in their heart by asking meat for their lust Yea they spoke**

78:20
באלהים 430 אמרו 559 היוכל 3201 אל 410 לערך 6186 שלחן 7979 במדבר 4057: הן 2005 הכה 5221 צור 6697 ויזובו 2100
be'alohiym 'amaru hayukal 'ael; la'arok shulchan, bamidbar. hen hikah tzur uayazubu
**against Elohim thcy said Can El furnish a table in the wilderness? Behold he smote the rock that gushed out**

78:21
מים 4325 ונחלים 5158 ישטפו 7857 הגם 1571 לחם 3899 יוכל 3201 תת 5414 אם 518 יכין 3559 שאר 7607 לעמו 5971:
mayim uanchaliym yishtopu hagam lechem yukal tet; 'am yakiyn sha'aer la'amou.
**the waters and the streams overflowed also? bread can he give *can* or he provide flesh for his people?**

לכן 3651 שמע 8085 יהוה 3068 ויתעבר 5674 ואש 784 נשקה 5400 ביעקב 3290 וגם 1571 אף 639 עלה 5927 בישראל 3478:
laken shama' Yahuah uayit'abar ua'aesh nisqah uaya'aqob; uagam 'ap, 'alah bayisra'ael.
**Therefore heard *this* Yahuah and was wroth so a fire was kindled against Jacob and also anger came up against Israel**

Ps 78:9 The children of Ephraim, being armed, and carrying bows, turned back in the day of battle.10 They kept not the covenant of G-d, and refused to walk in his law;11 And forgot his works, and his wonders that he had showed them.12 Marvellous things did he in the sight of their fathers, in the land of Egypt, in the field of Zoan.13 He divided the sea, and caused them to pass through; and he made the waters to stand as an heap.14 In the daytime also he led them with a cloud, and all the night with a light of fire.15 He clave the rocks in the wilderness, and gave them drink as out of the great depths.16 He brought streams also out of the rock, and caused waters to run down like rivers.17 And they sinned yet more against him by provoking the most High in the wilderness.18 And they tempted G-d in their heart by asking meat for their lust.19 Yea, they spoke against G-d; they said, Can G-d furnish a table in the wilderness?20 Behold, he smote the rock, that the waters gushed out, and the streams overflowed; can he give bread also? can he provide flesh for his people?21 Therefore YHUH heard this, and was wroth: so a fire was kindled against Jacob, and anger also came up against Israel;

78:22
כי 3588 לא 3808 האמינו 539 באלהים 430 ולא 3808 בטחו 982 בישועתו 3444: 78:23 ויצו 6680
kiy la' he'amiynu be'alohiym; uala' batachu, biyshu'atou. uayatzau
**Because not they believed in Elohim and not trusted in his salvation Though he had commanded**

שחקים 7834 ממעל 4605 ודלתי 1817 שמים 8064 פתח 6605: 78:24 וימטר 4305 עליהם 5921 מן 4478 לאכל 398
shachaqiym mima'al; uadaltey shamayim patach. uayamter 'aleyhem man le'akol;
**the clouds from above and the doors of heaven opened And had rained down upon them manna to eat**

ודגן 1715 שמים 8064 נתן 5414 למו 3807a: 78:25 לחם 3899 אבירים 47 אכל 398 איש 376 צידה 6720 שלח 7971 להם 1992
uadgan shamayim, natan lamou. lechem 'abyiyriym 'akal 'aysh; tzeydah shalach lahem
**and the corn of heaven had given them *of* food angels' did eat Man meat he sent them**

לשבע 7648: 78:26 יסע 5265 קדים 6921 בשמים 8064 וינהג 5090 בעזו 5797 תימן 8486: 78:27
lasoba'. yasa' qadiym bashamayim; uayanaheg ba'azou teyman.
**to the full He caused to blow an east *wind* in the heaven and he brought in by his power the south *wind***

וימטר 4305 עליהם 5921 כעפר 6083 שאר 7607 וכחול 2344 ימים 3220 עוף 5775 כנף 3671: 78:28 ויפל 5307
uayamter 'aleyhem ke'apar sha'aer; uakchoul yamiym, 'aup kanap. uayapel
**He rained also upon them as dust flesh and like as the sand of the sea fowls feathered And he let *it* fall**

בקרב 7130 מחנהו 4264 סביב 5439 למשכנתיו 4908: 78:29 ויאכלו 398 וישבעו 7646 מאד 3966 ותאותם 8378
baqereb machanehu; sabiyb, lamishkanotayu. uayo'akalu uayisba'au ma'ad; uata'auatam,
**in the midst of their camp round about their habitations So they did eat and were filled well for their own desire**

יבא 935 להם 1992: 78:30 לא 3808 זרו 2114 מתאותם 8378 עוד 5750 אכלם 400 בפיהם 6310: 78:31
yaba' lahem. la' zaru mita'auatam; 'aud, 'aklam bapiyhem.
**he gave them not They were estranged from their lust *was* yet *But while* their meat in their mouths**

ואף 639 אלהים 430 עלה 5927 בהם 871a ויהרג 2026 במשמניהם 4924 ובחורי 970 ישראל 3478 הכריע 3766: 78:32
ua'ap 'alohiym 'alah bahem, uayaharog bamishmaneyhem; uabachurey yisra'ael hikriya'.
**The wrath of Elohim came upon them and slew the fattest of them and the chosen *men* of Israel smote down**

בכל 3605 זאת 2063 חטאו 2398 עוד 5750 ולא 3808 האמינו 539 בנפלאותיו 6381: 78:33 ויכל 3615 בהבל 1892
bakal za't chata'au 'aud; uala' he'amiynu, banipla'autayu. uayakal bahebel
**For all this they sinned still and not believed for his wondrous works Therefore did he consume in vanity**

ימיהם 3117 ושנותם 8141 בבהלה 928: 78:34 אם 518 הרגם 2026 ודרשוהו 1875 ושבו 7725
yameyhem; uashnoutam, babehalah. 'am haragam uadrashuhu; uashabu,
**their days and their years in trouble When he slew them then they sought him and they returned**

ושחרו 7836 אל 410: 78:35 ויזכרו 2142 כי 3588 אלהים 430 צורם 6697 ואל 410 עליון 5945
uashicharu 'ael. uayizkaru kiy 'alohiym tzuram; ua'ael 'alyoun
**and inquired early after El And they remembered that Elohim *was* their rock and El *the* high**

גאלם 1350: 78:36 ויפתוהו 6601 בפיהם 6310 ובלשונם 3956 יכזבו 3576 לו 3807a:
go'alam. uayapatuhu bapiyhem; uabilshounam, yakazbu lou'.
**their redeemer Nevertheless they did flatter him with their mouth *with* their tongues and they lied unto him**

Ps 78:22 Because they believed not in G-d, and trusted not in his salvation:23 Though he had commanded the clouds from above, and opened the doors of heaven,24 And had rained down manna upon them to eat, and had given them of the corn of heaven.25 Man did eat angels' food: he sent them meat to the full.26 He caused an east wind to blow in the heaven: and by his power he brought in the south wind.27 He rained flesh also upon them as dust, and feathered fowls like as the sand of the sea:28 And he let it fall in the midst of their camp, round about their habitations.29 So they did eat, and were well filled: for he gave them their own desire;30 They were not estranged from their lust. But while their meat was yet in their mouths,31 The wrath of G-d came upon them, and slew the fattest of them, and smote down the chosen men of Israel.32 For all this they sinned still, and believed not for his wondrous works.33 Therefore their days did he consume in vanity, and their years in trouble.34 When he slew them, then they sought him: and they returned and inquired early after G-d.35 And they remembered that G-d was their rock, and the high G-d their redeemer.36 Nevertheless they did flatter him with their mouth, and they lied unto him with their tongues.

| 78:37 | ולבם 3820 | לא 3808 | נכון 3559 | עמו 5973 | ולא 3808 | נאמנו 539 | בבריתו 1285: | 78:38 | והוא 1931 |
|---|---|---|---|---|---|---|---|---|---|
| | ualibam | la' | nakoun | 'amou; | uala' | ne'amanu, | bibriytou. | | uahu'a |
| | **For their heart** | **not** | **was right** | **with him** | **and neither** | **were they stedfast** | **in his covenant** | | **But he** |

| רחום 7349 | יכפר 3722 | עון 5771 | ולא 3808 | ישחית 7843 | והרבה 7235 | להשיב 7725 | אפו 639 | ולא 3808 |
|---|---|---|---|---|---|---|---|---|
| rachum | yakaper | 'auon | uala' | yashchiyt | uahirbah | lahashiyb | 'apou; | uala' |
| ***being* full of compassion** | **forgave** | ***their* iniquity** | **and not** | **destroyed** | ***them* yea many a time** | **turned he away** | **his anger** | **and not** |

| יעיר 5782 | כל 3605 | חמתו 2534: | 78:39 | ויזכר 2142 | כי 3588 | בשר 1320 | המה 1992 | רוח 7307 | הולך 1980 | ולא 3808 |
|---|---|---|---|---|---|---|---|---|---|---|
| ya'ayr | kal | chamatou. | | uayizkor | kiy | basar | hemah; | ruach | houlek, | uala' |
| **did stir up** | **all** | **his wrath** | | **For he remembered** | **that** | **they *were but* flesh** | **they** | **a wind** | **that passed away** | **and not** |

| ישוב 7725: | 78:40 | כמה 4100 | ימרוהו 4784 | במדבר 4057 | יעציבוהו 6087 | בישימון 3452: | 78:41 |
|---|---|---|---|---|---|---|---|
| yashub. | | kamah | yamaruhu | bamidbar; | ya'atzybuhu, | biyshiymoun. | |
| **comes again** | | **How oft** | **did they provoke him** | **in the wilderness** | ***and* grieve him** | **in the desert** | |

| וישובו 7725 | וינסו 5254 | אל 410 | וקדוש 6918 | ישראל 3478 | התוו 8428: | 78:42 | לא 3808 | זכרו 2142 | את 853 |
|---|---|---|---|---|---|---|---|---|---|
| uayashubu | uayanasu | 'ael; | uaqadoush | yisra'ael | hitauu. | | la' | zakaru | 'at |
| **Yea they turned back** | **and tempted** | **El** | **and the Holy One of** | **Israel** | **limited** | | **not** | **They remembered** | |

| ידו 3027 | יום 3117 | אשר 834 | פדם 6299 | מני 4480 | צר 6862: | 78:43 | אשר 834 | שם 7760 | במצרים 4714 | אתותיו 226 |
|---|---|---|---|---|---|---|---|---|---|---|
| yadou; | youm, | 'asher | padam | miniy | tzar. | | 'asher | sam | bamitzrayim | 'atoutayu; |
| **his hand** | ***nor* the day** | **when** | **he delivered** | ***them* from** | **the enemy** | | **How** | **he had wrought** | **in Egypt** | **his signs** |

| ומופתיו 4159 | בשדה 7704 | צען 6814: | 78:44 | ויהפך 2015 | לדם 1818 | יאריהם 2975 | ונזליהם 5140 | בל 1077 |
|---|---|---|---|---|---|---|---|---|
| uamoupatayu, | bisdeh | tzo'an. | | uayahapok | ladam | ya'areyhem; | uanozaleyhem, | bal |
| **and his wonders** | **in the field of** | **Zoan** | | **And had turned** | **into blood** | **their rivers** | **and their floods** | **not** |

| ישתיון 8354: | 78:45 | ישלח 7971 | בהם 871a | ערב 6157 | ויאכלם 398 | וצפרדע 6854 |
|---|---|---|---|---|---|---|
| yishtayun. | | yashalach | bahem | 'arob | uaya'kalem; | uatzpardea', |
| **that they could drink** | | **He sent** | **among them** | **divers sorts of flies** | **which devoured them** | **and frogs** |

| ותשחיתם 7843: | 78:46 | ויתן 5414 | לחסיל 2625 | יבולם 2981 | ויגיעם 3018 | לארבה 697: | 78:47 |
|---|---|---|---|---|---|---|---|
| uatashchiytem. | | uayiten | lechasiyl | yabulam; | uiygiy'am, | la'arbeh. | |
| **which destroyed them** | | **He gave also** | **unto the caterpiller** | **their increase** | **and their labour** | **unto the locust** | |

| יהרג 2026 | בברד 1259 | גפנם 1612 | ושקמותם 8256 | בחנמל 2602: | 78:48 | ויסגר 5462 | לברד 1259 | בעירם 1165 |
|---|---|---|---|---|---|---|---|---|
| yaharog | babarad | gapnam; | uashiqmoutam, | bachanamal. | | uayasger | labarad | ba'ayram; |
| **He destroyed** | **with hail** | **their vines** | **and their sycomore trees** | **with frost** | | **He gave up also** | **to the hail** | **their cattle** |

| ומקניהם 4735 | לרשפים 7565: | 78:49 | ישלח 7971 | בם 871a | חרון 2740 | אפו 639 | עברה 5678 | וזעם 2195 |
|---|---|---|---|---|---|---|---|---|
| uamiqneyhem, | larashapiym. | | yashalach | bam | charoun | 'apou, | 'abrah | uaza'am |
| **and their flocks** | **to hot thunderbolts** | | **He cast** | **upon them** | **the fierceness of** | **his anger** | **wrath** | **and indignation** |

| וצרה 6869 | משלחת 4917 | מלאכי 4397 | רעים 7451: | 78:50 | יפלס 6424 | נתיב 5410 | לאפו 639 | לא 3808 | חשך 2820 | ממות 4194 |
|---|---|---|---|---|---|---|---|---|---|---|
| uatzarah; | mishlachat, | mal'akey | ra'aym. | | yapales | natiyb, | la'apou | la' | chasak | mimauet |
| **and trouble *by*** | **sending** | **angels *among them*** | **evil** | | **He made a way** | | **to his anger** | **not** | **he spared** | **from death** |

Ps 78:37 For their heart was not right with him, neither were they stedfast in his covenant.38 But he, being full of compassion, forgave their iniquity, and destroyed them not: yea, many a time turned he his anger away, and did not stir up all his wrath.39 For he remembered that they were but flesh; a wind that pass away, and cometh not again.40 How oft did they provoke him in the wilderness, and grieve him in the desert!41 Yea, they turned back and tempted G-d, and limited the Holy One of Israel.42 They remembered not his hand, nor the day when he delivered them from the enemy.43 How he had wrought his signs in Egypt, and his wonders in the field of Zoan:44 And had turned their rivers into blood; and their floods, that they could not drink.45 He sent divers sorts of flies among them, which devoured them; and frogs, which destroyed them.46 He gave also their increase unto the caterpiller, and their labour unto the locust.47 He destroyed their vines with hail, and their sycomore trees with frost.48 He gave up their cattle also to the hail, and their flocks to hot thunderbolts.49 He cast upon them the fierceness of his anger, wrath, and indignation, and trouble, by sending evil angels among them.50 He made a way to his anger; he spared not their soul from death, but gave their life over to the pestilence;

| נפשם 5315 | וחיתם 2416 | לדבר 1698 | הסגיר 5462: | 78:51 | ויך 5221 | כל 3605 | בכור 1060 | במצרים 4714 | ראשית 7225 |
|---|---|---|---|---|---|---|---|---|---|
| napsham; | uachayatam, | ladeber | hisgiyr. | | uayak | kal | bakour | bamitzrayim; | ra'shiyt |
| **their soul** | **but their life** | **to the pestilence** | **gave over** | | **And smote** | **all** | **the firstborn** | **in Egypt** | **the chief of** |

| אונים 202 | באהלי 168 | חם 2526: | 78:52 | ויסע 5265 | כצאן 6629 | עמו 5971 | וינהגם 5090 |
|---|---|---|---|---|---|---|---|
| 'auniym, | ba'ahaley | cham. | | uayasa' | katza'n | 'amou; | uayanahagem |
| ***their* strength** | **in the tabernacles of** | **Ham** | | **But made to go forth** | **like sheep** | **his own people** | **and guided them** |

| כעדר 5739 | במדבר 4057: | 78:53 | וינחם 5148 | לבטח 983 | ולא 3808 | פחדו 6342 | ואת 853 | אויביהם 341 | כסה 3680 |
|---|---|---|---|---|---|---|---|---|---|
| ka'aeder, | bamidbar. | | uayanchem | labetach | uala' | pachadu; | ua'at | 'auyabeyhem, | kisah |
| **like a flock** | **in the wilderness** | | **And he led them on** | **safely** | **so that not** | **they feared** | ***but*** | **their enemies** | **overwhelmed** |

| הים 3220: | 78:54 | ויביאם 935 | אל 413 | גבול 1366 | קדשו 6944 | הר 2022 | זה 2088 | קנתה 7069 |
|---|---|---|---|---|---|---|---|---|
| hayam. | | uayabiy'aem | 'al | gabul | qadashou; | har | zeh, | qanatah |
| **the sea** | | **And he brought them** | **to** | **the border of** | **his sanctuary** | **this mountain *even to*** | **this** | **had purchased** |

| ימינו 3225: | 78:55 | ויגרש 1644 | מפניהם 6440 | גוים 1471 | ויפילם 5307 | בחבל 2256 | נחלה 5159 |
|---|---|---|---|---|---|---|---|
| yamiynou. | | uayagaresh | mipaneyhem | gouyim, | uayapiylem | bachebel | nachalah; |
| ***which* his right hand** | | **He cast out also** | **before them** | **the heathen** | **and divided them** | **by line** | **an inheritance** |

| וישכן 7931 | באהליהם 168 | שבטי 7626 | ישראל 3478: | 78:56 | וינסו 5254 | וימרו 4784 | את 853 | אלהים 430 | עליון 5945 |
|---|---|---|---|---|---|---|---|---|---|
| uayashken | ba'ahaleyhem, | shibtey | yisra'ael. | | uayanasu | uayamru | 'at | 'alohiym | 'alyoun; |
| **and made to dwell** | **in their tents** | **the tribes of** | **Israel** | | **Yet they tempted** | **and provoked** | | **Elohim** | **the most high** |

| ועדותיו 5713 | לא 3808 | שמרו 8104: | 78:57 | ויסגו 5472 | ויבגדו 898 | כאבותם 1 | נהפכו 2015 |
|---|---|---|---|---|---|---|---|
| ua'aedoutayu, | la' | shamaru. | | uayisogu | uayibgadu | ka'aboutam; | nehpaku, |
| **and his testimonies** | **not** | **kept** | | **But turned back** | **and dealt unfaithfully** | **like their fathers** | **they were turned aside** |

| כקשת 7198 | רמיה 7423: | 78:58 | ויכעיסוהו 3707 | בבמותם 1116 | ובפסיליהם 6456 |
|---|---|---|---|---|---|
| kaqeshet | ramiyah. | | uayaka'aysuhu | babamoutam; | uabipsiyleyhem, |
| **like a bow** | **deceitful** | | **For they provoked him to anger** | **with their high places** | **and with their graven images** |

| יקניאוהו 7065: | 78:59 | שמע 8085 | אלהים 430 | ויתעבר 5674 | וימאס 3988 | מאד 3966 | בישראל 3478: | 78:60 |
|---|---|---|---|---|---|---|---|---|
| yaqniy'auhu. | | shama' | 'alohiym | uayit'abar; | uayim'as | ma'ad, | bayisra'ael. | |
| **moved him to jealousy** | | **heard *this*** | **Elohim** | **When he was wroth** | **and abhorred** | **greatly** | **Israel** | |

| ויטש 5203 | משכן 4908 | שלו 7887 | אהל 168 | שכן 7931 | באדם 120: | 78:61 | ויתן 5414 | לשבי 7628 |
|---|---|---|---|---|---|---|---|---|
| uayitosh | mishkan | shilou; | 'ahel, | shiken | ba'adam. | | uayiten | lashbiy |
| **So that he forsook** | **the tabernacle of** | **Shiloh** | **the tent** | ***which* he placed** | **among men** | | **And delivered** | **into captivity** |

| עזו 5797 | ותפארתו 8597 | ביד 3027 | צר 6862: | 78:62 | ויסגר 5462 | לחרב 2719 | עמו 5971 | ובנחלתו 5159 |
|---|---|---|---|---|---|---|---|---|
| 'azou; | uatip'artou | bayad | tzar. | | uayasger | lachereb | 'amou; | uabnachalatou, |
| **his strength** | **and his glory** | **into hand** | ***the* enemy's** | | **He gave over also** | **unto the sword** | **his people** | **and with his inheritance** |

| התעבר 5674: | 78:63 | בחוריו 970 | אכלה 398 | אש 784 | ובתולתיו 1330 | לא 3808 | הוללו 1984: | 78:64 | כהניו 3548 |
|---|---|---|---|---|---|---|---|---|---|
| hit'abar. | | bachurayu | 'akalah | 'aesh; | uabtulotayu, | la' | hulalu. | | kohanayu |
| **was wroth** | | **their young men** | **consumed** | **The fire** | **and their maidens** | **not** | **were given to marriage** | | **Their priests** |

Ps 78:51 And smote all the firstborn in Egypt; the chief of their strength in the tabernacles of Ham:52 But made his own people to go forth like sheep, and guided them in the wilderness like a flock.53 And he led them on safely, so that they feared not: but the sea overwhelmed their enemies.54 And he brought them to the border of his sanctuary, even to this mountain, which his right hand had purchased.55 He cast out the heathen also before them, and divided them an inheritance by line, and made the tribes of Israel to dwell in their tents.56 Yet they tempted and provoked the most high G-d, and kept not his testimonies:57 But turned back, and dealt unfaithfully like their fathers: they were turned aside like a deceitful bow.58 For they provoked him to anger with their high places, and moved him to jealousy with their graven images.59 When G-d heard this, he was wroth, and greatly abhorred Israel:60 So that he forsook the tabernacle of Shiloh, the tent which he placed among men;61 And delivered his strength into captivity, and his glory into the enemy's hand.62 He gave his people over also unto the sword; and was wroth with his inheritance.63 The fire consumed their young men; and their maidens were not given to marriage.

בחרב 2719 | נפלו 5307 | ואלמנתיו 490 | לא 3808 | תבכינה 1058: | **78:65** | ויקץ 3364 | כישן 3463 | אדני 136
bachereb napalu; ua'almanotayu, la' tibkeynah. uayiyqatz kayashen 'adonay;
**by the sword fell and their widows no made lamentation Then awaked as one out of sleep Adonai**

כגבור 1368 | מתרונן 7442 | מיין 3196: | **78:66** | ויך 5221 | צריו 6862 | אחור 268 | חרפת 2781
kagibour, mitrounen miyayin. uayak tzarayu 'achour; cherpat
***and* like a mighty man that shout by reason of wine And he smote his enemies *in* the hinder parts *to* a reproach**

עולם 5769 | נתן 5414 | למו 3807a: | **78:67** | וימאס 3988 | באהל 168 | יוסף 3130 | ובשבט 7626 | אפרים 669 | לא 3808
'aulam, natan lamou. uayim'as ba'ahel yousep; uabshebet 'aprayim, la'
**perpetual he put them Moreover he refused the tabernacle of Joseph and the tribe of Ephraim not**

בחר 977: | **78:68** | ויבחר 977 | את 853 | שבט 7626 | יהודה 3063 | את 853 | הר 2022 | ציון 6726 | אשר 834 | אהב 157: | **78:69** | ויבן 1129 | כמו 3644
bachar. uayibchar 'at shebet yahudah; 'at har tziyoun, 'asher 'aheb. uayiben kamou
**chose But chose the tribe of Judah the mount Zion which he loved And he built like**

רמים 7311 | מקדשו 4720 | כארץ 776 | יסדה 3245 | לעולם 5769: | **78:70** | ויבחר 977 | בדוד 1732 | עבדו 5650
ramiym miqadashou; ka'aretz, yasadah la'aulam. uayibchar badauid abdou;
**high *palaces* his sanctuary like the earth which he has established for ever He chose also David his servant**

ויקחהו 3947 | ממכלאת 4356 | צאן 6629: | **78:71** | מאחר 310 | עלות 5763 | הביאו 935 | לרעות 7462 | ביעקב 3290
uayiqachehu, mimikla'at tza'n. me'achar 'alout, hebiy'au lir'aut baya'aqob
**and took him from the fold sheep From following the ewes great with young he brought him to feed Jacob**

עמו 5971 | ובישראל 3478 | נחלתו 5159: | **78:72** | וירעם 7462 | כתם 8537 | לבבו 3824 | ובתבונות 8394
'amou; uabyisra'ael, nachalatou. uayira'aem katom lababou; uabitbunout
**his people and Israel his inheritance So he fed them according to the integrity of his heart and by the skilfulness of**

כפיו 3709 | ינחם 5148:
kapayu yanchem.
**his hands guided them**

**Ps 79:1** | מזמור 4210 | לאסף 623 | אלהים 430 | באו 935 | גוים 1471 | בנחלתך 5159 | טמאו 2930 | את 853 | היכל 1964 | קדשך 6944
mizmour, la'asap 'alohiym ba'au gouyim banachalateka, tima'au 'at heykal qadasheka
**A Psalm of Asaph O Elohim are come the heathen into your inheritance have they defiled temple your holy**

שמו 7760 | את 853 | ירושלם 3389 | לעיים 5856: | **79:2** | נתנו 5414 | את 853 | נבלת 5038 | עבדיך 5650 | מאכל 3978
samu 'at yarushalaim la'ayiym. natanu 'at niblat 'abadeyka, ma'akal
**they have laid Jerusalem on heaps have they given The dead bodies of your servants *to be* meat**

לעוף 5775 | השמים 8064 | בשר 1320 | חסידיך 2623 | לחיתו 2416 | ארץ 776: | **79:3** | שפכו 8210 | דמם 1818
la'oup hashamayim; basar chasiydeyka, lachaytou 'aretz. shapaku damam
**unto the fowls of the heaven the flesh of your saints unto the beasts of the earth have they shed Their blood**

כמים 4325 | סביבות 5439 | ירושלם 3389 | ואין 369 | קובר 6912: | **79:4** | היינו 1961 | חרפה 2781 | לשכנינו 7934
kamayim, sabiybout yarushalaim, ua'aeyn qouber. hayiynu cherpah lishkeneynu;
**like water round about Jerusalem and *there was* none to bury *them* We are become a reproach to our neighbours**

Ps 78:64 Their priests fell by the sword; and their widows made no lamentation.65 Then YHUH awaked as one out of sleep, and like a mighty man that shouteth by reason of wine.66 And he smote his enemies in the hinder parts: he put them to a perpetual reproach.67 Moreover he refused the tabernacle of Joseph, and chose not the tribe of Ephraim:68 But chose the tribe of Judah, the mount Zion which he loved.69 And he built his sanctuary like high palaces, like the earth which he has established forever.70 He chose David also his servant, and took him from the sheepfolds:71 From following the ewes great with young he brought him to feed Jacob his people, and Israel his inheritance.72 So he fed them according to the integrity of his heart; and guided them by the skilfulness of his hands. **Ps** 79:1 A Psalm of A'-saph. O G-d, the heathen are come into your inheritance; your holy temple have they defiled; they have laid Jerusalem on heaps.2 The dead bodies of your servants have they given to be meat unto the fowls of the heaven, the flesh of your saints unto the beasts of the earth.3 Their blood have they shed like water round about Jerusalem; and there was none to bury them.

79:5

לעג 3933 וקלס 7047 לסביבותינו 5439: עד 5704 מה 4100 יהוה 3068 תאנף 599 לנצח 5331 תבער 1197
la'ag uaqeles, lisbiybouteynu. 'ad mah Yahuah te'anap lanetzach; tib'ar
**a scorn and derision to them that are round about us Howlong what Yahuah will you be angry for ever? shall burn**

79:6

כמו 3644 אש 784 קנאתך 7068: שפך 8210 חמתך 2534 אל 413 הגוים 1471 אשר 834 לא 3808 ידעוך 3045 ועל 5921
kamou 'aesh, qin'ateka. shapok chamataka 'al hagouyim 'asher la' yada'auka ua'al
**like fire? your jealousy Pour out your wrath upon the heathen that not have known you and upon**

79:7

ממלכות 4467 אשר 834 בשמך 8034 לא 3808 קראו 7121: כי 3588 אכל 398 את 853 יעקב 3290 ואת 853
mamlakout; 'asher bashimka, la' qara'au. kiy 'akal 'at ya'aqob; ua'at
**the kingdoms that upon your name not have called For they have devoured Jacob *and***

79:8

נוהו 5116 השמו 8074: אל 408 תזכר 2142 לנו 3807a עונת 5771 ראשנים 7223 מהר 4118 יקדמונו 6923
nauehu heshamu. 'al tizkar lanu 'auonot ra'shoniym maher yaqadmunu
**his dwelling place laid waste not O remember against us iniquities former speedily let prevent us**

79:9

רחמיך 7356 כי 3588 דלונו 1809 מאד 3966: עזרנו 5826 אלהי 430 ישענו 3468 על 5921 דבר 1697 כבוד 3519
rachameyka; kiy dalounu ma'ad. 'azarenu 'alohey yish'aenu, 'al dabar kaboud
**your tender mercies for we are brought low very Help us O Elohim of our salvation for matter of the glory of**

79:10

שמך 8034 והצילנו 5337 וכפר 3722 על 5921 חטאתינו 2403 למען 4616 שמך 8034: למה 4100 יאמרו 559 הגוים 1471
shameka; uahatziylenu uakaper 'al chata'teynu, lama'an shameka. lamah ya'maru hagouyim
**your name and deliver us and purge away over our sins for sake your name's Wherefore should say the heathen**

איה 346 אלהיהם 430 יודע 3045 בגיים 1471 לעינינו 5869 נקמת 5360 דם 1818 עבדיך 5650
'ayeh 'aloheyhem yiuada' bagiyiym la'aeyneynu; naqmat, dam 'abadeyka
**Where *is* their Elohim? let him be known among the heathen in our sight *by* the revenging of the blood of your servants**

79:11

השפוך 8210: תבוא 935 לפניך 6440 אנקת 603 אסיר 616 כגדל 1433 זרועך 2220 הותר 3498
hashapuk. tabou'a lapaneyka 'anqat 'asiyr kagodel zarou'aka; houter,
***which is* shed Let come before you the sighing of the prisoner according to the greatness of your power preserve you**

79:12

בני 1121 תמותה 8546: והשב 7725 לשכנינו 7934 שבעתים 7659 אל 413 חיקם 2436 חרפתם 2781
baney tamutah. uahasheb lishkeneynu shib'atayim 'al cheyqam; cherpatam
**those that are appointed to die And render unto our neighbours sevenfold into their bosom their reproach**

79:13

אשר 834 חרפוך 2778 אדני 136: ואנחנו 587 עמך 5971 וצאן 6629 מרעיתך 4830 נודה 3034
'asher cherapuka 'adonay. ua'anachnu 'amaka uatza'n mar'ayteka noudeh
**wherewith they have reproached you O Adonai So we your people and sheep of your pasture will give thanks**

לך 3807a לעולם 5769 לדר 1755 ודר 1755 נספר 5608 תהלתך 8416:
laka, la'aulam lador uador; nasaper, tahilateka.
**to you for ever to all generations we will show forth your praise**

**Ps 80:1**

למנצח 5329 אל 413 ששנים 7802 עדות 5715 לאסף 623 מזמור 4210: רעה 7462 ישראל 3478 האזינה 238
lamanatzeach 'al shoshaniym; 'aedut la'asap mizmour. ro'aeh yisra'ael ha'aziynah,
**To the chief Musician upon Shoshannim eduth of Asaph A Psalm O Shepherd of Israel Give ear**

Ps 79:4 We are become a reproach to our neighbors, a scorn and derision to them that are round about us.5 How long, YHUH? will you be angry forever? shall your jealousy burn like fire?6 Pour out your wrath upon the heathen that have not known you, and upon the kingdoms that have not called upon your name.7 For they have devoured Jacob, and laid waste his dwelling place.8 O remember not against us former iniquities: let your tender mercies speedily prevent us: for we are brought very low.9 Help us, O G-d of our salvation, for the glory of your name: and deliver us, and purge away our sins, for your name's sake.10 Wherefore should the heathen say, Where is their G-d? let him be known among the heathen in our sight by the revenging of the blood of your servants which is shed.11 Let the sighing of the prisoner come before you; according to the greatness of your power preserve you those that are appointed to die;12 And render unto our neighbors sevenfold into their bosom their reproach, wherewith they have reproached you, O Adonai.13 So we your people and sheep of your pasture will give you thanks forever: we will show forth your praise to all generations. **Ps**80:1 To the chief Musician upon Sho-shan'-nim-E'-duth, A Psalm of A'-saph. Give ear,

80:2

נהג 5090 כצאן 6629 יוסף 3130 ישב 3427 הכרובים 3742 הופיעה 3313: לפני 6440 אפרים 669 ובנימן 1144
noheg katza'n yousep; yosheb hakarubiym houpiy'ah. lipney 'aprayim uabinyamin
**you that lead like a flock Joseph you that dwell *between* the cherubims shine forth Before Ephraim and Benjamin**

80:3

ומנשה 4519 עוררה 5782 את 853 גבורתך 1369 ולכה 1980 לישעתה 3444 לנו 3807a: אלהים 430 השיבנו 7725 והאר 215
uamanasheh, 'aurarah 'at gaburateka; ualkah liyshu'atah lanu. 'alohiym hashiybenu; uaha'aer
**and Manasseh stir up your strength and come *and* save us O Elohim Turn us again and cause to shine**

80:4

פניך 6440 ונושעה 3467: יהוה 3068 אלהים 430 צבאות 6635 עד 5704 מתי 4970 עשנת 6225 בתפלת 8605
paneyka, uaniuashe'ah. Yahuah 'alohiym tzaba'aut; 'ad matay 'ashanta, bitapilat
**your face and we shall be saved O Yahuah Elohim of hosts how long when will you be angry against the prayer of**

80:5 80:6

עמך 5971: האכלתם 398 לחם 3899 דמעה 1832 ותשקמו 8248 בדמעות 1832 שליש 7991:
'ameka. he'akaltam lechem dim'ah; uatashqemou, bidma'aut shaliysh.
**your people? You feed them with the bread of tears and give them to drink tears *in* great measure**

80:7

תשימנו 7760 מדון 4066 לשכנינו 7934 ואיבינו 341 ילעגו 3932 למו 3807a: אלהים 430 צבאות 6635
tasiymenu madoun lishkeneynu; ua'ayabeynu, yil'agu lamou. 'alohiym tzaba'aut
**You make us a strife unto our neighbours and our enemies laugh among themselves O Elohim of hosts**

80:8

השיבנו 7725 והאר 215 פניך 6440 ונושעה 3467: גפן 1612 ממצרים 4714 תסיע 5265
hashiybenu; uaha'aer paneyka, uaniuashe'ah. gepen mimitzrayim tasiya';
**Turn us again and cause to shine your face and we shall be saved a vine out of Egypt You have brought**

80:9

תגרש 1644 גוים 1471 ותטעה 5193: פנית 6437 לפניה 6440 ותשרש 8327 שרשיה 8328
tagaresh gouyim, uatita'aha. piniyta lapaneyha; uatashresh sharasheyha,
**you have cast out the heathen and planted it You preparedst *room* before it and did cause it to take root deep**

80:10

ותמלא 4390 ארץ 776: כסו 3680 הרים 2022 צלה 6738 וענפיה 6057 ארזי 730
uatamalea' 'aretz. kasu hariym tzilah; ua'anapeyha, 'arzey
**and it filled the land were covered The hills *with* the shadow of it and the boughs thereof cedars**

80:11 80:12

אל 410: תשלח 7971 קציריה 7105 עד 5704 ים 3220 ואל 413 נהר 5104 יונקותיה 3127: למה 4100
'ael. tashalach qatziyreha 'ad yam; ua'al nahar, younaqouteyha. lamah
***were like the* goodly She sent out her boughs unto the sea and unto the river her branches Why**

80:13

פרצת 6555 גדריה 1447 וארוה 717 כל 3605 עברי 5674 דרך 1870: יכרסמנה 3765
paratzta gadereyha; ua'aruha, kal 'abarey darek. yakarsamenah
**have you *then* broken down her hedges so that do pluck her? all they which pass by the way does waste it**

80:14

חזיר 2386 מיער 3293 וזיז 2123 שדי 7704 ירענה 7462: אלהים 430 צבאות 6635 שוב 7725 נא 4994
chaziyr miya'ar; uaziyz saday yir'anah. 'alohiym tzaba'aut shub naa'
**The boar out of the wood and the wild beast of the field does devour it O Elohim of hosts Return we beseech you**

80:15

הבט 5027 משמים 8064 וראה 7200 ופקד 6485 גפן 1612 זאת 2063: וכנה 3657 אשר 834 נטעה 5193 ימינך 3225
habet mishamayim uar'aeh; uapqod, gepen za't. uakanah 'asher nata'ah yamiyneka;
**look down from heaven and behold and visit vine this and the vineyard which has planted your right hand**

Ps 80:1 O Shepherd of Israel, you that leadest Joseph like a flock; you that dwellest between the cherubims, shine forth.2 Before Ephraim and Benjamin and Manasseh stir up your strength, and come and save us.3 Turn us again, O G-d, and cause your face to shine; and we shall be saved.4 O YHUH G-d of hosts, how long will you be angry against the prayer of your people?5 Thou feedest them with the bread of tears; and givest them tears to drink in great measure.6 Thou make us a strife unto our neighbors: and our enemies laugh among themselves.7 Turn us again, O G-d of hosts, and cause your face to shine; and we shall be saved.8 Thou have brought a vine out of Egypt: you have cast out the heathen, and planted it.9 Thou preparedst room before it, and did cause it to take deep root, and it filled the land.10 The hills were covered with the shadow of it, and the boughs thereof were like the goodly cedars.11 She sent out her boughs unto the sea, and her branches unto the river.12 Why have you then broken down her hedges, so that all they which pass by the way do pluck her?13 The boar out of the wood doth waste it, and the wild beast of the field doth devour it.14 Return, we beseech you, O G-d of hosts: look down from heaven, and behold, and visit this vine;15 And the vineyard which your right hand has planted, and the branch that you madest strong for thyself.

| ועל 5921 | בן 1121 | אמצתה 553 | לך 3807a: | 80:16 | שרפה 8313 | באש 784 | כסוחה 3683 | מגערת 1606 |
|---|---|---|---|---|---|---|---|---|
| ua'al | ben, | 'amatzatah | lak. | | sarupah | ba'aesh | kasuchah; | miga'arat |
| **and on** | **the Branch (*son*)** | ***that* you made strong** | **for yourself** | | ***It is* burned** | **with fire** | ***it is* cut down** | **at the rebuke of** |

| פניך 6440 | יאבדו 6: | 80:17 | תהי 1961 | ידך 3027 | על 5921 | איש 376 | ימינך 3225 | על 5921 | בן 1121 | אדם 120 |
|---|---|---|---|---|---|---|---|---|---|---|
| paneyka | ya'bedu. | | tahiy | yadaka | 'al | 'aysh | yamiyneka; | 'al | ben | 'adam, |
| **your countenance** | **they perish** | | **Let be** | **your hand** | **upon** | **the man of** | **your right hand** | **upon** | **the son of** | **man** |

| אמצת 553 | לך 3807a: | 80:18 | ולא 3808 | נסוג 5472 | ממך 4480 | תחינו 2421 | ובשמך 8034 |
|---|---|---|---|---|---|---|---|
| 'amatzata | lak. | | uala' | nasoug | mimeka; | tachayenu, | uabshimka |
| ***whom* you made strong** | **for yourself** | | **So not** | **will we go back** | **from you** | **quicken us** | **and upon your name** |

| נקרא 7121: | 80:19 | יהוה 3068 | אלהים 430 | צבאות 6635 | השיבנו 7725 | האר 215 | פניך 6440 | ונושעה 3467: |
|---|---|---|---|---|---|---|---|---|
| niqra'. | | Yahuah | 'alohiym | tzaba'aut | hashiybenu; | ha'aer | paneyka, | uaniuashe'ah. |
| **we will call** | | **O Yahuah** | **Elohim of** | **hosts** | **Turn us again** | **cause to shine** | **your face** | **and we shall be saved** |

| Ps 81:1 | למנצח 5329 | על 5921 | הגתית 1665 | לאסף 623: | הרנינו 7442 | לאלהים 430 | עוזנו 5797 | הריעו 7321 |
|---|---|---|---|---|---|---|---|---|
| | lamanatzeach | 'al | hagitiyt | la'asap. | haraniynu | le'alohiym | 'uazenu; | hariy'au, |
| | **To the chief Musician** | **upon** | **Gittith** | ***A Psalm* of Asaph** | **Sing aloud** | **unto Elohim** | **our strength** | **make a joyful noise** |

| לאלהי 430 | יעקב 3290: | 81:2 | שאו 5375 | זמרה 2172 | ותנו 5414 | תף 8596 | כנור 3658 | נעים 5273 | עם 5973 | נבל 5035: | 81:3 |
|---|---|---|---|---|---|---|---|---|---|---|---|
| le'alohey | ya'aqob. | | sa'au | zimrah | uatnu | top; | kinour | na'aym | 'am | nabel. | |
| **unto the Elohim of** | **Jacob** | | **Take** | **a psalm** | **and bring *here*** | **the timbrel** | **harp** | ***the* pleasant** | **with** | **the psaltery** | |

| תקעו 8628 | בחדש 2320 | שופר 7782 | בכסה 3677 | ליום 3117 | חגנו 2282: | 81:4 | כי 3588 | חק 2706 | לישראל 3478 |
|---|---|---|---|---|---|---|---|---|---|
| tiq'au | bachodesh | shoupar; | bakeseh, | layoum | chagenu. | | kiy | choq | layisra'ael |
| **Blow up** | **in the new moon** | **the trumpet** | **in the time appointed** | **on day** | **our solemn feast** | | **For** | ***was* a statute** | **for Israel** |

| הוא 1931 | משפט 4941 | לאלהי 430 | יעקב 3290: | 81:5 | עדות 5715 | ביהוסף 3084 | שמו 7760 | בצאתו 3318 | על 5921 |
|---|---|---|---|---|---|---|---|---|---|
| hua'; | mishapat, | le'alohey | ya'aqob. | | 'aedut | biyahousep | samou, | batzea'tou | 'al |
| **this** | ***and* a law** | **of the Elohim of** | **Jacob** | | ***This for* a testimony** | **in Joseph** | **he ordained** | **when he went out** | **through** |

| ארץ 776 | מצרים 4714 | שפת 8193 | לא 3808 | ידעתי 3045 | אשמע 8085: | 81:6 | הסירותי 5493 | מסבל 5447 | שכמו 7926 |
|---|---|---|---|---|---|---|---|---|---|
| 'aretz | mitzrayim; | sapat | la' | yada'tiy | 'ashma. | | hasiyroutiy | misebel | shikmou; |
| **the land of** | **Egypt** | **a language** | **not** | ***that* I understood** | ***where* I heard** | | **I removed** | **from the burden** | **his shoulder** |

| כפיו 3709 | מדוד 1731 | תעברנה 5674: | 81:7 | בצרה 6869 | קראת 7121 | ואחלצך 2502 | אענך 6030 | בסתר 5643 |
|---|---|---|---|---|---|---|---|---|
| kapayu, | midud | ta'aboranah. | | batzarah | qara'ta, | ua'achaltzeka | 'a'anaka | baseter |
| **his hands** | **from the pots** | **were delivered** | | **in trouble** | **You called** | **and I delivered you** | **I answered you** | **in the secret place of** |

| רעם 7482 | אבחנך 974 | על 5921 | מי 4325 | מריבה 4809 | סלה 5542: | 81:8 | שמע 8085 | עמי 5971 | ואעידה 5749 | בך 871a | ישראל 3478 |
|---|---|---|---|---|---|---|---|---|---|---|---|
| ra'am; | 'abchanaka | 'al | mey | mariybah | selah. | | shama' | 'amiy | ua'a'aydah | bak; | yisra'ael, |
| **thunder** | **I proved you** | **at** | **the waters of** | **Meribah** | **Selah** | | **Hear** | **O my people** | **and I will testify** | **unto you** | **O Israel** |

| אם 518 | תשמע 8085 | לי 3807a: | 81:9 | לא 3808 | יהיה 1961 | בך 871a | אל 410 | זר 2114 | ולא 3808 | תשתחוה 7812 | לאל 410 |
|---|---|---|---|---|---|---|---|---|---|---|---|
| 'am | tishma' | liy. | | la' | yihayeh | baka | 'ael | zar; | uala' | tishtachaueh, | la'ael |
| **if** | **you will listen** | **unto me** | | **no** | **There shall be** | **in you** | **god** | **strange** | **neither** | **shall you worship** | **to god** |

Ps 80:16 It is burned with fire, it is cut down: they perish at the rebuke of your countenance.17 Let your hand be upon the man of your right hand, upon the son of man whom you madest strong for thyself.18 So will not we go back from you: quicken us, and we will call upon your name.19 Turn us again, O YHUH G-d of hosts, cause your face to shine; and we shall be saved. **Ps** 81:1 To the chief Musician upon Git'-tith, A Psalm of A'-saph. Sing aloud unto G-d our strength: make a joyful noise unto the G-d of Jacob.2 Take a psalm, and bring hither the timbrel, the pleasant harp with the psaltery.3 Blow up the trumpet in the new moon, in the time appointed, on our solemn feast day.4 For this was a statute for Israel, and a law of the G-d of Jacob.5 This he ordained in Joseph for a testimony, when he went out through the land of Egypt: where I heard a language that I understood not.6 I removed his shoulder from the burden: his hands were delivered from the pots.7 Thou called in trouble, and I delivered you; I answered you in the secret place of thunder: I proved you at the waters of Meribah. Selah.8 Hear, O my people, and I will testify unto you: O Israel, if you will hear unto me;9 There shall no strange god be in you; neither shall you worship any strange god.

| נכר 5236: | 81:10 אנכי 595 | יהוה 3068 | אלהיך 430 | המעלך 5927 | מארץ 776 | מצרים 4714 | הרחב 7337 | פיך 6310 |
|---|---|---|---|---|---|---|---|---|
| nekar. | 'anokiy | Yahuah | 'aloheyka, | mama'alaka | me'aretz | mitzrayim; | harcheb | piyka, |
| ***any* strange** | **I *am*** | **Yahuah** | **your Elohim** | **which brought you** | **out of the land of** | **Egypt** | **open wide** | **your mouth** |

| ואמלאהו 4390: | 81:11 ולא 3808 | שמע 8085 | עמי 5971 | לקולי 6963 | וישראל 3478 | לא 3808 | אבה 14 | לי 3807a: | 81:12 ואשלחהו 7971 |
|---|---|---|---|---|---|---|---|---|---|
| ua'amal'aehu. | uala' | shama' | 'amiy | laqouliy; | uayisra'ael, | la' | 'abah | liy. | ua'ashalchehu |
| **and I will fill** | **But not** | **would listen** | **my people** | **to my voice** | **and Israel** | **none** | **would** | **of me** | **So I gave them up** |

| בשרירות 8307 | לבם 3820 | ילכו 1980 | במועצותיהם 4156: | 81:13 לו 3807a | עמי 5971 | שמע 8085 | לי 3807a |
|---|---|---|---|---|---|---|---|
| bishriyrut | libam; | yelaku, | bamou'atzouteyhem. | lou', | 'amiy | shomea' | liy; |
| **unto lust** | **their own hearts'** | ***and* they walked** | **in their own counsels** | **Oh that** | **my people** | **had hearkened** | **unto me** |

| ישראל 3478 | בדרכי 1870 | יהלכו 1980: | 81:14 כמעט 4592 | אויביהם 341 | אכניע 3665 | ועל 5921 | צריהם 6862 | אשיב 7725 |
|---|---|---|---|---|---|---|---|---|
| yisra'ael, | bidrakay | yahaleku. | kima'at | 'auyabeyhem | 'akniya'; | ua'al | tzareyhem, | 'ashiyb |
| ***and* Israel** | **in my ways** | **had walked** | **soon** | **their enemies** | **I should have subdued** | **and against** | **their adversaries** | **turned** |

| ידי 3027: | 81:15 משנאי 8130 | יהוה 3068 | יכחשו 3584 | לו 3807a | ויהי 1961 | עתם 6256 |
|---|---|---|---|---|---|---|
| yadiy. | masan'aey | Yahuah | yakachashu | lou'; | uiyhiy | 'atam |
| **my hand** | **The haters of** | **Yahuah** | **should have submitted themselves** | **unto him** | **but should have endured** | **their time** |

| לעולם 5769: | 81:16 ויאכילהו 398 | מחלב 2459 | חטה 2406 | ומצור 6697 | דבש 1706 |
|---|---|---|---|---|---|
| la'aulam. | uaya'akiylehu | mecheleb | chitah; | uamitzur, | dabash |
| **for ever** | **He should have fed them also** | **with the finest of** | **the wheat** | **and out of the rock** | ***with* honey** |

| אשביעך 7646: |
|---|
| 'asbiy'aka. |
| **should I have satisfied you** |

| Ps 82:1 מזמור 4210 | לאסף 623 | אלהים 430 | נצב 5324 | בעדת 5712 | אל 410 | בקרב 7130 | אלהים 430 | ישפט 8199: |
|---|---|---|---|---|---|---|---|---|
| mizmour, | la'asap | 'alohiym, | nitzab | ba'adat | 'ael; | baqereb | 'alohiym | yishpot. |
| **A Psalm *Song or*** | **of Asaph** | **Elohim** | **stands** | **in the congregation** | **of the mighty** | **among** | **the gods** | **he judge** |

| 82:2 עד 5704 | מתי 4970 | תשפטו 8199 | עול 5766 | ופני 6440 | רשעים 7563 | תשאו 5375 | סלה 5542: | 82:3 שפטו 8199 | דל 1800 |
|---|---|---|---|---|---|---|---|---|---|
| 'ad | matay | tishpatu | 'auel; | uapaney | rasha'aym, | tis'au | selah. | shiptu | dal |
| **How long** | **when** | **will you judge** | **unjustly** | **and the persons of** | **the wicked?** | **accept** | **Selah** | **Defend** | **the poor** |

| ויתום 3490 | עני 6041 | ורש 7326 | הצדיקו 6663: | 82:4 פלטו 6403 | דל 1800 | ואביון 34 | מיד 3027 | רשעים 7563 |
|---|---|---|---|---|---|---|---|---|
| uayatoum; | 'aniy | uarash | hatzdiyqu. | paltu | dal | ua'abyoun; | miyad | rasha'aym |
| **and fatherless** | **the afflicted** | **and needy** | **do justice to** | **Deliver** | **the poor** | **and needy** | **out of the hand of** | **the wicked** |

| הצילו 5337: | 82:5 לא 3808 | ידעו 3045 | ולא 3808 | יבינו 995 | בחשכה 2825 | יתהלכו 1980 | ימוטו 4131 | כל 3605 |
|---|---|---|---|---|---|---|---|---|
| hatziylu. | la' | yada'au | uala' | yabiynu, | bachashekah | yithalaku; | yimoutu, | kal |
| **rid *them*** | **not** | **They know** | **and neither** | **will they understand** | **in darkness** | **they walk on** | **are out of course** | **all** |

| מוסדי 4144 | ארץ 776: | 82:6 אני 589 | אמרתי 559 | אלהים 430 | אתם 859 | ובני 1121 | עליון 5945 | כלכם 3605: |
|---|---|---|---|---|---|---|---|---|
| mousadey | 'aretz. | 'aniy | 'amartiy | 'alohiym | 'atem; | uabney | 'alyoun | kulkem. |
| **the foundations of** | **the earth** | **I** | **have said *are*** | **gods** | **You** | **and children of** | **the most High** | **all of you *are*** |

Ps 81:10 I am YHUH your G-d, which brought you out of the land of Egypt: open your mouth wide, and I will fill it.11 But my people would not hear to my voice; and Israel would none of me.12 So I gave them up unto their own hearts' lust: and they walked in their own counsels.13 Oh that my people had hearkened unto me, and Israel had walked in my ways!14 I should soon have subdued their enemies, and turned my hand against their adversaries.15 The haters of YHUH should have submitted themselves unto him: but their time should have endured forever.16 He should have fed them also with the finest of the wheat: and with honey out of the rock should I have satisfied you. **Ps** 82:1 A Song or Psalm of A'-saph. G-d stand in the congregation of the mighty; he judgeth among the gods.2 How long will you judge unjustly, and accept the persons of the wicked? Selah.3 Defend the poor and fatherless: do justice to the afflicted and needy.4 Deliver the poor and needy: rid them out of the hand of the wicked.5 They know not, neither will they understand; they walk on in darkness: all the foundations of the earth are out of course.6 I have said, You are gods; and all of you are children of the most High.

82:7 82:8
אכן 403 כאדם 120 תמותון 4191 וכאחד 259 השרים 8269 תפלו 5307: קומה 6965 אלהים 430 שפטה 8199 הארץ 776 כי 3588
'aken ka'adam tamutun; uak'achad hasariym tipolu. qumah 'alohiym shapatah ha'aretz; kiy
**But like men you shall die and like one of the princes fall Arise O Elohim judge the earth for**

אתה 859 תנחל 5157 בכל 3605 הגוים 1471:
'atah tinchal, bakal hagouyim.
**you shall inherit all nations**

Ps 83:1 83:2
שיר 7892 מזמור 4210 לאסף 623: אלהים 430 אל 408 דמי 1824 לך 3807a אל 408 תחרש 2790 ואל 408 תשקט 8252 אל 410:
shiyr mizmour la'asap. 'alohiym 'al damiy lak; 'al techarash ua'al tishqot 'ael.
**A Song *or* Psalm of Asaph O Elohim not Keep silence to you not hold your peace and not be still O El**

83:3
כי 3588 הנה 2009 אויביך 341 יהמיון 1993 ומשנאיך 8130 נשאו 5375 ראש 7218: על 5921 עמך 5971
kiy hineh 'auyabeyka yehamayun; uamsan'ayka, nasa'au ra'sh. 'al 'amaka
**For lo your enemies make a tumult and they that hate you have lifted up the head against your people**

83:4
יערימו 6191 סוד 5475 ויתיעצו 3289 על 5921 צפוניך 6845: אמרו 559 לכו 1980 ונכחידם 3582
ya'ariymu coud; ayitya'atzu, 'al tzapuneyka. 'amaru, laku uanakchiydem
**They have taken crafty counsel and consulted against your hidden ones They have said Come and let us cut them off**

83:5
מגוי 1471 ולא 3808 יזכר 2142 שם 8033 ישראל 3478 עוד 5750: כי 3588 נועצו 3289
migouy; uala' yizaker shem yisra'ael 'aud. kiy nou'atzu
**from *being* a nation that no may be in remembrance the name of Israel more For they have consulted**

83:6
לב 3820 יחדו 3162 עליך 5921 ברית 1285 יכרתו 3772: אהלי 168 אדום 123 וישמעאלים 3459
leb yachdau; 'aleyka, bariyt yikrotu. 'ahaley 'adoum uayishma'aeliym,
***with* one consent together *they are* against you confederate they are The tabernacles of Edom and the Ishmaelites**

83:7 83:8
מואב 4124 והגרים 1905: גבל 1381 ועמון 5983 ועמלק 6002 פלשת 6429 עם 5973 ישבי 3427 צור 6865:
mou'ab uahagriym. gabal ua'amoun ua'amaleq; paleshet, 'am yoshabey tzour.
***of* Moab and the Hagarenes Gebal and Ammon and Amalek the Philistines with the inhabitants of Tyre**

83:9
גם 1571 אשור 804 נלוה 3867 עמם 5973 היו 1961 זרוע 2220 לבני 1121 לוט 3876 סלה 5542: עשה 6213 להם 1992
gam 'ashur niluah 'amam; hayu zaroua' libney lout selah. 'aseh lahem
**also Assur is joined with them they have holpen the children of Lot Selah Do unto them**

83:10
כמדין 4080 כסיסרא 5516 כיבין 2985 בנחל 5158 קישון 7028: נשמדו 8045 בעין 5874 דאר 1756 היו 1961
kamidayan; kasiysara' kayabiyn, banachal qiyshoun. nishmadu ba'aeyn do'ar; hayu
**as *unto* the Midianites as *to* Sisera as *to* Jabin at the brook of Kison *Which* perished at En dor they became**

83:11
דמן 1828 לאדמה 127: שיתמו 7896 נדיבמו 5081 כערב 6159 וכזאב 2062 וכזבח 2078 וכצלמנע 6759 כל 3605
domen, la'adamah. shiytemou nadiybenou ka'aureb uakiz'aeb; uakzebach uaktzalmuna', kal
***as* dung for the earth Make their nobles like Oreb and like Zeeb yea, as Zebah and as Zalmunna all**

83:12 83:13
נסיכמו 5257: אשר 834 אמרו 559 נירשה 3423 לנו 3807a את 853 נאות 4999 אלהים 430: אלהי 430
nasiykemou. 'asher 'amaru niyrashah lanu; 'aet, na'aut 'alohiym. 'alohay,
**their princes Who said Let us take in possession to ourselves the houses of Elohim O my Elohim**

Ps 82:7 But you shall die like men, and fall like one of the princes.8 Arise, O G-d, judge the earth: for you shall inherit all nations. **Ps** 83:1 A Song or Psalm of A'-saph Keep not you silence, O G-d: hold not your peace, and be not still, O G-d.2 For, lo, your enemies make a tumult: and they that hate you have lifted up the head.3 They have taken crafty counsel against your people, and consulted against your hidden ones.4 They have said, Come, and let us cut them off from being a nation; that the name of Israel may be no more in remembrance.5 For they have consulted together with one consent: they are confederate against you:6 The tabernacles of Edom, and the Ishmaelites; of Moab, and the Hagarenes;7 Gebal, and Ammon, and Amalek; the Philistines with the inhabitants of Tyre;8 Assur also is joined with them: they have holpen the children of Lot. Selah.9 Do unto them as unto the Midianites; as to Sisera, as to Jabin, at the brook of Kison:10 Which perished at Endor: they became as dung for the earth.11 Make their nobles like Oreb, and like Zeeb: yea, all their princes as Zebah, and as Zalmunna:12 Who said, Let us take to ourselves the houses of G-d in possession.

| | | | | | | | | | |
|---|---|---|---|---|---|---|---|---|---|
| שיתמו 7896 | כגלגל 1534 | קש 7179 | לפני 6440 | רוח 7307: | 83:14 כאש 784 | תבער 1197 | יער 3293 | וכלהבה 3852 | תלהט 3857 |
| shiytemou | kagalgal; | kaqash, | lipney | ruach. | ka'aesh | tib'ar | ya'ar; | uaklehabah, | talahet |
| **make them** | **like a wheel** | **as the stubble** | **before** | **the wind** | **As the fire** | **burn** | **a wood** | **and as the flame** | **set on fire** |

| | | | | | | |
|---|---|---|---|---|---|---|
| הרים 2022: | 83:15 כן 3651 | תרדפם 7291 | בסערך 5591 | ובסופתך 5492 | תבהלם 926: | 83:16 מלא 4390 |
| hariym. | ken | tirdapem | basa'areka; | uabsupataka | tabahalem. | malea' |
| **the mountains** | **So** | **persecute them** | **with your tempest** | **and with your storm** | **make them afraid** | **Fill with** |

| | | | | | | | | |
|---|---|---|---|---|---|---|---|---|
| פניהם 6440 | קלון 7036 | ויבקשו 1245 | שמך 8034 | יהוה 3068: | 83:17 יבשו 954 | ויבהלו 926 | עדי 5703 | עד 5704 |
| paneyhem | qaloun; | uiybaqshu | shimka | Yahuah. | yeboshu | uayibahalu | 'adey | 'ad, |
| **their faces** | **shame** | **that they may seek** | **your name** | **O Yahuah** | **Let them be confounded** | **and troubled** | **ever** | **for** |

| | | | | | | | |
|---|---|---|---|---|---|---|---|
| ויחפרו 2659 | ויאבדו 6: | 83:18 וידעו 3045 | כי 3588 | אתה 859 | שמך 8034 | יהוה 3068 | לבדך 905 |
| uayachparu | uaya'bedu. | uayeda'au, | kiy | 'atah | shimka | Yahuah | labadeka; |
| **yea let them be put to shame** | **and perish** | **That *men* may know** | **that** | **you** | **whose name *is*** | **YAHUAH** | **alone** |

| | | | |
|---|---|---|---|
| עליון 5945 | על 5921 | כל 3605 | הארץ 776: |
| 'alyoun, | 'al | kal | ha'aretz. |
| ***are* the most high over** | | **all** | **the earth** |

| | | | | | | | | |
|---|---|---|---|---|---|---|---|---|
| Ps 84:1 למנצח 5329 | על 5921 | הגתית 1665 | לבני 1121 | קרח 7141 | מזמור 4210: | מה 4100 | ידידות 3039 | משכנותיך 4908 |
| lamanatzeach | 'al | hagitiyt; | libney | qorach | mizmour. | mah | yadiydout | mishkanouteyka, |
| **To the chief Musician** | **upon** | **Gittith** | **for the sons of** | **Korah** | **A Psalm** | **How** | **amiable** | ***are* your tabernacles** |

| | | | | | | | | | | |
|---|---|---|---|---|---|---|---|---|---|---|
| יהוה 3068 | צבאות 6635: | 84:2 נכספה 3700 | וגם 1571 | כלתה 3615 | נפשי 5315 | לחצרות 2691 | יהוה 3068 | לבי 3820 | ובשרי 1320 | ירננו 7442 |
| Yahuah | tzaba'aut. | niksapah | uagam | kaltah | napshiy | lachatzrout | Yahuah | libiy | uabsariy; | yarannu, |
| **O Yahuah** | **of hosts** | **long** | **yea even** | **faint** | **My soul** | **for the courts of** | **Yahuah** | **my heart** | **and my flesh** | **cry out** |

| | | | | | | | | | | | |
|---|---|---|---|---|---|---|---|---|---|---|---|
| אל 413 | אל 410 | חי 2416: | 84:3 גם 1571 | צפור 6833 | מצאה 4672 | בית 1004 | ודרור 1866 | קן 7064 | לה 3807a | אשר 834 | שתה 7896 |
| 'al | 'ael | chay. | gam | tzipour | matz'ah | bayit | uadrour | qen | lah | 'asher | shatah |
| **for** | **El** | ***the* living** | **Yea** | **the sparrow** | **has found** | **an house** | **and the swallow** | **a nest** | **for herself** | **where** | **she may lay** |

| | | | | | | | | |
|---|---|---|---|---|---|---|---|---|
| אפרחיה 667 | את 853 | מזבחותיך 4196 | יהוה 3068 | צבאות 6635 | מלכי 4428 | ואלהי 430: | 84:4 אשרי 835 | יושבי 3427 |
| 'aprocheyha | 'at | mizbachouteyka | Yahuah | tzaba'aut; | malkiy, | ua'alohay. | 'ashrey | youshabey |
| **her young** | | ***even* your altars** | **O Yahuah** | **of hosts** | **my King** | **and my Elohim** | **Blessed** | ***are* they that dwell in** |

| | | | | | | | | | |
|---|---|---|---|---|---|---|---|---|---|
| ביתך 1004 | עוד 5750 | יהללוך 1984 | סלה 5542: | 84:5 אשרי 835 | אדם 120 | עוז 5797 | לו 3807a | בך 871a | מסלות 4546 |
| beytaka; | 'aud, | yahalaluka | selah. | 'ashrey | 'adam | 'auz | lou' | bak; | masilout, |
| **your house** | **still** | **they will be praising you** | **Selah** | **Blessed *is*** | **the man** | **strength** | **whose *is*** | **in you** | ***are* the ways *of them*** |

| | | | | | | | | | |
|---|---|---|---|---|---|---|---|---|---|
| בלבבם 3824: | 84:6 עברי 5674 | בעמק 6010 | הבכא 1056 | מעין 4599 | ישיתוהו 7896 | גם 1571 | ברכות 1293 | יעטה 5844 | מורה 4175: |
| bilbabam. | 'abarey | ba'aemeq | habaka' | ma'ayan | yashiytuhu; | gam | barakout, | ya'ateh | moureh. |
| **in whose heart** | ***Who* passing** | **through the valley of** | **Baca** | **a well** | **make it** | **also** | **the pools** | **fill** | **the rain** |

| | | | | | | | | | | |
|---|---|---|---|---|---|---|---|---|---|---|
| 84:7 ילכו 1980 | מחיל 2428 | אל 413 | חיל 2428 | יראה 7200 | אל 413 | אלהים 430 | בציון 6726: | 84:8 יהוה 3068 | אלהים 430 | צבאות 6635 |
| yelaku | mechayil | 'al | chayil; | yera'ah | 'al | 'alohiym | batziyoun. | Yahuah | 'alohiym | tzaba'aut |
| **They go from strength to** | | | **strength** | **appear** | **before** | **Elohim** | ***every one of them* in Zion** | **O Yahuah** | **Elohim of** | **hosts** |

Ps 83:13 O my G-d, make them like a wheel; as the stubble before the wind.14 As the fire burneth a wood, and as the flame set the mountains on fire;15 So persecute them with your tempest, and make them afraid with your storm.16 Fill their faces with shame; that they may seek your name, O YHUH.17 Let them be confounded and troubled forever; yea, let them be put to shame, and perish:18 That men may know that you, whose name alone is JEHOVAH, are the most high over all the earth. **Ps** 84:1 To the chief Musician upon Git'-tith, A Psalm for the sons of Ko'rah. How amiable are your tabernacles, O YHUH of hosts!2 My soul longeth, yea, even fainteth for the courts of YHUH: my heart and my flesh crieth out for the living G-d.3 Yea, the sparrow has found an house, and the swallow a nest for herself, where she may lay her young, even your altars, O YHUH of hosts, my King, and my G-d.4 Blessed are they that dwell in your house: they will be still praising you. Selah.5 Blessed is the man whose strength is in you; in whose heart are the ways of them.6 Who passing through the valley of Baca make it a well; the rain also filleth the pools.7 They go from strength to strength, everyone of them in Zion appeareth before G-d.8 O YHUH G-d of hosts, hear my prayer: give ear, O G-d of Jacob. Selah.

שמעה 8085 תפלתי 8605 האזינה 238 אלהי 430 יעקב 3290 סלה 5542: **84:9** מגננו 4043 ראה 7200 אלהים 430 והבט 5027 פני 6440
shim'ah tapilatiy; ha'aziynah 'alohey ya'aqob selah. maginenu ra'aeh 'alohiym; uahabet, paney
**hear my prayer give ear O Elohim of Jacob Selah our shield Behold O Elohim and look upon the face of**

משיחך 4899: **84:10** כי 3588 טוב 2896 יום 3117 בחצריך 2691 מאלף 505 בחרתי 977 הסתופף 5605 בבית 1004
mashiycheka. kiy toub youm bachatzereyka, me'alep bachartiy, histoupep babeyt
**your anointed For *is* better a day in your courts than a thousand I had rather be a doorkeeper in the house of**

אלהי 430 מדור 1752 באהלי 168 רשע 7562: **84:11** כי 3588 שמש 8121 ומגן 4043 יהוה 3068 אלהים 430 חן 2580 וכבוד 3519
'alohay; midur, ba'ahaley resha'. kiy shemesh uamagen Yahuah 'alohiym chen uakaboud
**my Elohim than to dwell in the tents of wickedness For *is* a sun and shield Yahuah Elohim grace and glory**

יתן 5414 יהוה 3068 לא 3808 ימנע 4513 טוב 2896 להלכים 1980 בתמים 8549: **84:12** יהוה 3068 צבאות 6635 אשרי 835
yiten Yahuah; la' yimna' toub, laholakiym batamiym. Yahuah tzaba'aut; 'ashrey
**will give Yahuah no *thing* will he withhold good from them that walk uprightly O Yahuah of hosts blessed**

אדם 120 בטח 982 בך 871a:
'adam, boteach bak.
***is* the man that trust in you**

**Ps 85:1** למנצח 5329 לבני 1121 קרח 7141 מזמור 4210: רצית 7521 יהוה 3068 ארצך 776
lamanatzeach libney qorach mizmour. ratziyta Yahuah 'artzeka;
**To the chief Musician for the sons of Korah A Psalm you have been favourable unto Yahuah your land**

שבת 7725 שבות 7622 יעקב 3290: **85:2** נשאת 5375 עון 5771 עמך 5971 כסית 3680 כל 3605
shabata shebut ya'aqob. Nasa'ta 'auon 'ameka; kisiyta kal
**you have brought back the captivity of Jacob You have forgiven the iniquity of your people you have covered all**

חטאתם 2403 סלה 5542: **85:3** אספת 622 כל 3605 עברתך 5678 השיבות 7725 מחרון 2740
chata'tam selah. 'asapta kal 'abrateka; heshiybouta, mecharoun
**their sin Selah You have taken away all your wrath you have turned *yourself* from the fierceness of**

אפך 639: **85:4** שובנו 7725 אלהי 430 ישענו 3468 והפר 6565 כעסך 3708 עמנו 5973: **85:5** הלעולם 5769
'apeka. shubenu 'alohey yish'aenu; uahaper ka'asaka 'amanu. hal'aulam
**your anger Turn us O Elohim of our salvation and cause to cease your anger toward us for ever?**

תאנף 599 בנו 871a תמשך 4900 אפך 639 לדר 1755 ודר 1755: **85:6** הלא 3808 אתה 859 תשוב 7725
te'anap ba'nu; timshok 'apaka, lador uador. hala' 'atah tashub
**Will you be angry with us will you draw out your anger to all generations? not Your again**

תחינו 2421 ועמך 5971 ישמחו 8055 בך 871a: **85:7** הראנו 7200 יהוה 3068 חסדך 2617 וישעך 3468 תתן 5414
tachayenu; ua'amaka, yismachu bak. har'aenu Yahuah chasadeka; uayesh'aka, titen
**Will you revive us that your people may rejoice in you? Shew us O Yahuah your mercy and your salvation grant**

לנו 3807a: **85:8** אשמעה 8085 מה 4100 ידבר 1696 האל 410 יהוה 3068 כי 3588 ידבר 1696 שלום 7965 אל 413 עמו 5971 ואל 413 חסידיו 2623
lanu. 'ashma'ah, mah yadaber ha'ael Yahuah kiy yadaber shaloum, 'al 'amou ua'al chasiydayu;
**us I will hear what will speak El Yahuah for he will speak peace unto his people and to his saints**

Ps 84:9 Behold, O G-d our shield, and look upon the face of your anointed.10 For a day in your courts is better than a thousand. I had rather be a doorkeeper in the house of my G-d, than to dwell in the tents of wickedness.11 For YHUH G-d is a sun and shield: YHUH will give grace and glory: no good thing will he withhold from them that walk uprightly.12 O YHUH of hosts, blessed is the man that trusteth in you. **Ps** 85:1 To the chief Musician, A Psalm for the sons of Ko'rah. YHUH, you have been favorable unto your land: you have brought back the captivity of Jacob.2 Thou have forgiven the iniquity of your people, you have covered all their sin. Selah.3 Thou have taken away all your wrath: you have turned thyself from the fierceness of your anger.4 Turn us, O G-d of our salvation, and cause your anger toward us to cease.5 Wilt you be angry with us forever? will you draw out your anger to all generations?6 Wilt you not revive us again: that your people may rejoice in you?7 Shew us your mercy, O YHUH, and grant us your salvation.8 I will hear what G-d YHUH will speak: for he will speak peace unto his people, and to his saints: but let them not turn again to folly.

| ואל 408 | ישובו 7725 | לכסלה 3690: | 85:9 | אך 389 | קרוב 7138 | ליראיו 3373 | ישעו 3468 | לשכן 7931 | כבוד 3519 |
|---|---|---|---|---|---|---|---|---|---|
| ua'al | yashubu | lakislah. | | 'ak | qaroub | liyre'ayu | yish'au; | lishkon | kaboud |
| **but not** | **let them turn again** | **to folly** | | **Surely** | ***is* near** | **them that fear him** | **his salvation** | **that may dwell** | **glory** |

| בארצנו 776: | 85:10 | חסד 2617 | ואמת 571 | נפגשו 6298 | צדק 6664 | ושלום 7965 | נשקו 5401: | 85:11 | אמת 571 |
|---|---|---|---|---|---|---|---|---|---|
| ba'artzenu. | | chesed | ua'amet | nipgashu; | tzedeq | uashaloum | nashaqu. | | 'amet |
| **in our land** | | **Mercy** | **and truth** | **are met together** | **righteousness** | **and peace** | **have kissed *each other*** | | **Truth** |

| מארץ 776 | תצמח 6779 | וצדק 6664 | משמים 8064 | נשקף 8259: | 85:12 | גם 1571 | יהוה 3068 | יתן 5414 |
|---|---|---|---|---|---|---|---|---|
| me'aretz | tatzmiach; | batzedeq, | mishamayim | nishqap. | | gam | Yahuah | yiten |
| **outof the earth** | **shall spring** | **and righteousness** | **from heaven** | **shall look down** | | **Yea** | **Yahuah** | **shall give** |

| הטוב 2896 | וארצנו 776 | תתן 5414 | יבולה 2981: | 85:13 | צדק 6664 | לפניו 6440 | יהלך 1980 | וישם 7760 |
|---|---|---|---|---|---|---|---|---|
| hatoub; | ua'artzenu, | titen | yabulah. | | tzedeq | lapanayu | yehalek; | uayasem |
| ***that which is* good** | **and our land** | **shall yield** | **her increase** | | **Righteousness** | **before him** | **shall go** | **and shall set** |

| לדרך 1870 | פעמיו 6471: |
|---|---|
| laderek | pa'amayu. |
| ***us* in the way of** | **his steps** |

| Ps 86:1 | תפלה 8605 | לדוד 1732 | הטה 5186 | יהוה 3068 | אזנך 241 | ענני 6030 | כי 3588 | עני 6041 | ואביון 34 | אני 589: | 86:2 | שמרה 8104 | נפשי 5315 |
|---|---|---|---|---|---|---|---|---|---|---|---|---|---|
| | tapilah, | ladauid | hateh | Yahuah | 'aznaka | 'aneniy; | kiy | 'aniy | ua'abyoun | 'aniy. | | shamarah | napshiy |
| | **A Prayer** | **of David** | **Bow down** | **O Yahuah** | **your ear** | **hear me** | **for** | ***am* poor** | **and needy** | **I** | | **Preserve** | **my soul** |

| כי 3588 | חסיד 2623 | אני 589 | הושע 3467 | עבדך 5650 | אתה 859 | אלהי 430 | הבוטח 982 | אליך 413: | 86:3 | חנני 2603 | אדני 136 |
|---|---|---|---|---|---|---|---|---|---|---|---|
| kiy | chasiyd | 'aniy | housha' | 'abdeka | 'atah | 'alohay; | habouteach | 'aeleyka. | | chaneniy | 'adonay; |
| **for *am*** | **holy** | **I** | **save** | **your servant** | **O you** | **my Elohim** | **that trust** | **in you** | | **Be merciful unto me** | **O Adonai** |

| כי 3588 | אליך 413 | אקרא 7121 | כל 3605 | היום 3117: | 86:4 | שמח 8056 | נפש 5315 | עבדך 5650 | כי 3588 | אליך 413 | אדני 136 | נפשי 5315 |
|---|---|---|---|---|---|---|---|---|---|---|---|---|
| kiy | 'aeleyka | 'aqraa', | kal | hayoum. | | sameach | nepesh | 'abdeka; | kiy | 'aeleyka | 'adonay, | napshiy |
| **for** | **unto you** | **I cry** | **all** | **daily** | | **Rejoice** | **the soul of** | **your servant** | **for** | **unto you** | **O Adonai** | **my soul** |

| אשא 5375: | 86:5 | כי 3588 | אתה 859 | אדני 136 | טוב 2896 | וסלח 5546 | ורב 7227 | חסד 2617 | לכל 3605 |
|---|---|---|---|---|---|---|---|---|---|
| 'asa'. | | kiy | 'atah | 'adonay | toub | uasalach; | uarab | chesed, | lakal |
| **do I lift up** | | **For** | **you** | **Adonai** | ***are* good** | **and ready to forgive** | **and plenteous in** | **mercy** | **unto all** |

| קראיך 7121: | 86:6 | האזינה 238 | יהוה 3068 | תפלתי 8605 | והקשיבה 7181 | בקול 6963 | תחנונותי 8469: | 86:7 |
|---|---|---|---|---|---|---|---|---|
| qora'ayka. | | ha'aziynah | Yahuah | tapilatiy; | uahaqshiybah, | baqoul | tachanunoutay. | |
| **them that call unto you** | | **Give ear** | **O Yahuah** | ***unto* my prayer** | **and attend** | **to the voice of** | **my supplications** | |

| ביום 3117 | צרתי 6869 | אקראך 7121 | כי 3588 | תענני 6030: | 86:8 | אין 369 | כמוך 3644 | באלהים 430 |
|---|---|---|---|---|---|---|---|---|
| bayoum | tzaratiy | 'aqra'aka, | kiy | ta'aneniy. | | 'aeyn | kamouka | ba'alohiym |
| **In the day of** | **my trouble** | **I will call upon you** | **for** | **you will answer me** | | ***there is* none** | **like unto you** | **Among the gods** |

| אדני 136 | ואין 369 | כמעשיך 4639: | 86:9 | כל 3605 | גוים 1471 | אשר 834 | עשית 6213 | יבואו 935 |
|---|---|---|---|---|---|---|---|---|
| 'adonay, | ua'aeyn | kama'aseyka. | | kal | gouyim | 'asher | 'ashiyta, | yabou'au |
| **O Adonai** | **and neither *are there any works*** | **like unto your works** | | **All** | **nations** | **whom** | **you have made** | **shall come** |

Ps 85:9 9 Surely his salvation is nigh them that fear him; that glory may dwell in our land.10 Mercy and truth are met together; righteousness and peace have kissed each other.11 Truth shall spring out of the earth; and righteousness shall look down from heaven.12 Yea, YHUH shall give that which is good; and our land shall yield her increase.13 Righteousness shall go before him; and shall set us in the way of his steps. **Ps** 86:1 A Prayer of David. Bow down your ear, O YHUH, hear me: for I am poor and needy.2 Preserve my soul; for I am holy: O you my G-d, save your servant that trusteth in you.3 Be merciful unto me, O Adonai: for I cry unto you daily.4 Rejoice the soul of your servant: for unto you, O Adonai, do I lift up my soul.5 For you, Adonai, are good, and ready to forgive; and plenteous in mercy unto all them that call upon you.6 Give ear, O YHUH, unto my prayer; and attend to the voice of my supplications.7 In the day of my trouble I will call upon you: for you will answer me.8 Among the gods there is none like unto you, O Adonai; neither are there any works like unto your works.9 All nations whom you have made shall come and worship before you,

86:10

7812 וישתחוו 6440 לפניך 136 אדני 3513 ויכבדו 8034 לשמך: 3588 כי 1419 גדול 859 אתה 6213 ועשה 6381 נפלאות

uayishtachauu lapaneyka 'adonay; uiykabdu lishmeka. kiy gadoul 'atah ua'auseh nipla'aut;

**and worship before you O Adonai and shall glorify your name For *are* great you and do wondrous things**

86:11

859 אתה 430 אלהים 905 לבדך: 3384 הורני 3068 יהוה 1870 דרכך 1980 אהלך 571 באמתך 3161 יחד 3824 לבבי 3372 ליראה

'atah 'alohiym labadeka. houreniy Yahuah darkeka, 'ahalek ba'amiteka; yached lababiy, layir'ah

**you *are* Elohim alone Teach me O Yahuah your way I will walk in your truth unite my heart to fear**

86:12 86:13

8034 שמך: 3034 אודך 136 אדני 430 אלהי 3605 בכל 3824 לבבי 3513 ואכבדה 8034 שמך 5769 לעולם:

shameka. 'audaka 'adonay 'alohay bakal lababiy; ua'akabdah shimka la'aulam.

**your name I will praise you O Adonai my Elohim with all my heart and I will glorify your name for evermore**

86:14

3588 כי 2617 חסדך 1419 גדול 5921 עלי 5337 והצלת 5315 נפשי 7585 משאול 8482 תחתיה: 430 אלהים 2086 זדים

kiy chasdaka gadoul 'alay; uahitzalta napshiy, misha'aul tachtiyah. 'alohiym zediym

**For *is* your mercy great toward me and you have delivered my soul from hell *the* lowest O Elohim the proud**

6965 קמו 5921 עלי 5712 ועדת 6184 עריצים 1245 בקשו 5315 נפשי 3808 ולא 7760 שמוך

qamu 'alay, ua'adat 'ariytziym biqshu napshiy; uala' samuka

**are risen against me and the assemblies of violent *men* have sought after my soul and not have set you**

86:15

5048 לנגדם: 859 ואתה 136 אדני 410 אל 7349 רחום 2587 וחנון 750 ארך 639 אפים 7227 ורב 2617 חסד

lanegdam. ua'atah 'adonay 'ael rachum uachanun; 'arek 'apayim, uarab chesed

**before them But you O Adonai *are* a El full of compassion and gracious long suffering and plenteous in mercy**

86:16

571 ואמת: 6437 פנה 413 אלי 2603 וחנני 5414 תנה 5797 עזך 5650 לעבדך 3467 והושיעה 1121 לבן

ua'amet. paneh 'aelay, uachaneniy tanah 'azeka la'abdeka; uahoushiy'ah, laben

**and truth O turn unto me and have mercy upon me give your strength unto your servant and save the son of**

86:17

519 אמתך: 6213 עשה 5973 עמי 226 אות 2896 לטובה 7200 ויראו 8130 שנאי 954 ויבשו 3588 כי 859 אתה

'amateka. 'aseh 'amiy 'aut, latoubah uayir'au son'ay uayeboshu; kiy 'atah

**your handmaid Shew me a token for good that may see *it* they which hate me and be ashamed because you**

3068 יהוה 5826 עזרתני 5162 ונחמתני:

Yahuah 'azartaniy uanichamtaniy.

**Yahuah have holpen me and comforted me**

Ps 87:1 87:2

1121 לבני 7141 קרח 4210 מזמור 7892 שיר 3248 יסודתו 2042 בהררי 6944 קדש: 157 אהב 3068 יהוה 8179 שערי

libney qorach mizmour shiyr; yasudatou, baharrey qodesh. 'aheb Yahuah sha'arey

**for the sons of Korah A Psalm *or* Song His foundation *is in the* mountains holy love Yahuah the gates of**

87:3 87:4

6726 ציון 3605 מכל 4908 משכנות 3290 יעקב: 3513 נכבדות 1696 מדבר 871a בך 5892 עיר 430 האלהים 5542 סלה:

tziyoun; mikol, mishkanout ya'aqob. nikbadout madubar bak; 'ayr ha'alohiym selah.

**Zion *more* than all the dwellings of Jacob Glorious things are spoken of you O city of Elohim Selah**

2142 אזכיר 7294 רהב 894 ובבל 3045 לידעי 2009 הנה 6429 פלשת 6865 וצור 5973 עם 3568 כוש 2088 זה

'azkiyr rahab uababel, layoda'ay hineh paleshet uatzour 'am kush; zeh,

**I will make mention of Rahab and Babylon to them that know me behold Philistia and Tyre with Ethiopia this**

Ps 86:9 O Adonai; and shall glorify your name.10 For you are great, and does wondrous things: you are G-d alone.11 Teach me your way, O YHUH; I will walk in your truth: unite my heart to fear your name.12 I will praise you, O Adonai my G-d, with all my heart: and I will glorify your name forevermore.13 For great is your mercy toward me: and you have delivered my soul from the lowest hell.14 O G-d, the proud are risen against me, and the assemblies of violent men have sought after my soul; and have not set you before them.15 But you, O Adonai, are a G-d full of compassion, and gracious, longsuffering, and plenteous in mercy and truth.16 O turn unto me, and have mercy upon me; give your strength unto your servant, and save the son of your handmaid.17 Shew me a token for good; that they which hate me may see it, and be ashamed: because you, YHUH, have holpen me, and comforted me. **Ps** 87:1 A Psalm or Song for the sons of Ko'-rah. His foundation is in the holy mountains.2 YHUH love the gates of Zion more than all the dwellings of Jacob.3 Glorious things are spoken of you, O city of G-d. Selah.4 I will make mention of Rahab and Babylon to them that know me: behold Philistia, and Tyre, with Ethiopia; this man was born there.

87:5

ילד 3205 | שם 8033: | ולציון 6726 | יאמר 559 | איש 376 | ואיש 376 | ילד 3205 | בה 871a | והוא 1931 | יכוננה 3559

yulad sham. ualatziyoun ye'amar, 'aysh ua'aysh yulad bah; uahu'a yakounaneha

***man*** **was born there And of Zion it shall be said This and that man was born in her and himself shall establish her**

87:6 ... 87:7

עליון 5945: | יהוה 3068 | יספר 5608 | בכתוב 3789 | עמים 5971 | זה 2088 | ילד 3205 | שם 8033 | סלה 5542:

'alyoun. Yahuah yispor biktoub 'amiym; zeh yulad sham selah.

**the highest Yahuah shall count when he writeth up the people *that* this *man* was born there Selah**

ושרים 7891 | כחללים 2490 | כל 3605 | מעיני 4599 | בך 871a:

uashariym kacholaliym; kal ma'ayanay bak.

**As well the singers as the players on instruments *shall be there* all my springs *are* in you**

Ps 88:1

שיר 7892 | מזמור 4210 | לבני 1121 | קרח 7141 | למנצח 5329 | על 5921 | מחלת 4257 | לענות 6031 | משכיל 4905 | להימן 1968

shiyr mizmour, libney qorach lamanatzeach 'al machalat le'anout; maskiyl, laheyman

**A Song *or* Psalm for the sons of Korah to the chief Musician upon Mahalath Leannoth Maschil of Heman**

88:2

האזרחי 250: | יהוה 3068 | אלהי 430 | ישועתי 3444 | יום 3117 | צעקתי 6817 | בלילה 3915 | נגדך 5048: | תבוא 935 | לפניך 6440

ha'ezrachiy. Yahuah 'alohey yashu'atiy; youm tza'aqtiy balayalah negdeka. tabou'a lapaneyka

**the Ezrahite O Yahuah Elohim of my salvation day I have cried *and* night before you Let come before you**

88:3 ... 88:4

תפלתי 8605 | הטה 5186 | אזנך 241 | לרנתי 7440: | כי 3588 | שבעה 7646 | ברעות 7451 | נפשי 5315 | וחיי 2416 | לשאול 7585 | הגיעו 5060:

tapilatiy; hateh 'aznaka, larinatiy. kiy saba'ah bara'aut napshiy; uachayay, lisha'aul higiy'au.

**my prayer incline your ear unto my cry For is full of troubles my soul and my life unto the grave draw near**

88:5

נחשבתי 2803 | עם 5973 | יורדי 3381 | בור 953 | הייתי 1961 | כגבר 1397 | אין 369 | איל 353: | במתים 4191 | חפשי 2670

nechshabtiy 'am youradey bour; hayiytiy, kageber 'aeyn 'ayal. bametiym, chapashiy

**I am counted with them that go down into the pit I am as a man *that has* no strength among the dead Free**

88:6

כמו 3644 | חללים 2491 | שכבי 7901 | קבר 6913 | אשר 834 | לא 3808 | זכרתם 2142 | עוד 5750 | והמה 1992 | מידך 3027 | נגזרו 1504:

kamou chalaliym shokabey qeber, 'asher la' zakartam 'aud; uahemah, miyadaka nigzaru.

**like the slain that lie in the grave whom no you remember more and they from your hand are cut off**

88:7

שתני 7896 | בבור 953 | תחתיות 8482 | במחשכים 4285 | במצלות 4688: | עלי 5921 | סמכה 5564 | חמתך 2534 | וכל 3605 | משבריך 4867

shataniy babour tachtiyout; bamachashakiym, bimtzolout. 'alay samakah chamateka; uakal mishbareyka,

**You have laid me in pit *the* lowest in darkness in the deeps upon me lies hard Your wrath and all your waves**

88:8

ענית 6031 | סלה 5542: | הרחקת 7368 | מידעי 3045 | ממני 4480 | שתני 7896

'aniyta selah. hirchaqta mayuda'ay, mimeniy shataniy

**you have afflicted *me with* Selah You have put away far mine acquaintance from me you have made me**

88:9

תועבות 8441 | למו 3807a | כלא 3607 | ולא 3808 | אצא 3318: | עיני 5869 | דאבה 1669 | מני 4480 | עני 6040

tou'aebout lamou; kalu, uala' 'aetzea'. 'aeyniy da'abah, miniy 'aniy

**an abomination unto them *I am* shut up and cannot I come forth Mine eye mourns by reason of affliction**

88:10

קראתיך 7121 | יהוה 3068 | בכל 3605 | יום 3117 | שטחתי 7849 | אליך 413 | כפי 3709: | הלמתים 4191 | תעשה 6213

qaraa'tiyka Yahuah bakal youm; shitachtiy 'aeleyka kapay. halametiym ta'aseh

**I have called upon you Yahuah every daily I have stretched out unto you my hands to the dead? Will you show**

Ps 87:5 And of Zion it shall be said, This and that man was born in her: and the highest himself shall establish her.6 YHUH shall count, when he writeth up the people, that this man was born there. Selah.7 As well the singers as the players on instruments shall be there: all my springs are in you. **Ps** 88:1 A Song or Psalm for the sons of Ko'-rah, to the chief Musician upon Ma'-ha-lath Le-an'-noth, Mas'-chil of He'-man the Ez'-ra-hite. O YHUH G-d of my salvation, I have cried day and night before you:2 Let my prayer come before you: incline your ear unto my cry;3 For my soul is full of troubles: and my life draweth nigh unto the grave.4 I am counted with them that go down into the pit: I am as a man that has no strength:5 Free among the dead, like the slain that lie in the grave, whom you rememberest no more: and they are cut off from your hand.6 Thou have laid me in the lowest pit, in darkness, in the deeps.7 Thy wrath lie hard upon me, and you have afflicted me with all your waves. Selah.8 Thou have put away mine acquaintance far from me; you have made me an abomination unto them: I am shut up, and I cannot come forth.9 Mine eye mourn by reason of affliction: YHUH, I have called daily upon you, I have stretched out my hands unto you.10 Wilt you show wonders to the dead?

88:11
פלא 6382 אם 518 רפאים 7496 יקומו 6965 יודוך 3034 סלה 5542: היספר 5608 בקבר 6913 חסדך 2617
pela'; 'am rapa'aym, yaqumu youduka selah. hayasupar baqeber chasadeka;
**wonders lo the dead shall arise *and* praise you? Selah Shall be declared in the grave? your lovingkindness *or***

88:12
אמונתך 530 באבדון 11: היודע 3045 בחשך 2822 פלאך 6382 וצדקתך 6666 בארץ 776
'amunataka, ba'abadoun. hayiuada' bachoshek pila'aka; uatzidqataka, ba'aretz
**your faithfulness in destruction? be known in the dark? Shall your wonders and your righteousness in the land of**

88:13 88:14
נשיה 5388: ואני 589 אליך 413 יהוה 3068 שועתי 7768 ובבקר 1242 תפלתי 8605 תקדמך 6923: למה 4100
nashiyah. ua'aniy 'aeleyka Yahuah shiua'atiy; uababoqer, tapilatiy taqadmeka. lamah
**forgetfulness? But I unto you O Yahuah have cried and in the morning my prayer shall prevent you why**

88:15
יהוה 3068 תזנח 2186 נפשי 5315 תסתיר 5641 פניך 6440 ממני 4480: עני 6041 אני 589 וגוע 1478 מנער 5290
Yahuah tiznach napshiy; tastiyr paneyka mimeniy. 'aniy 'aniy uagouea' mino'ar;
**Yahuah cast you off my soul? *why* hide you your face from me? *am* afflicted I and ready to die from *my* youth**

88:16 88:17
נשאתי 5375 אמיך 367 אפונה 6323: עלי 5921 עברו 5674 חרוניך 2740 בעותיך 1161 צמתותני 6789:
nasa'tiy 'aemeyka 'apunah. 'alay 'abaru charouneyka; bi'auteyka, tzimtutuniy.
***up while* I suffer your terrors I am distracted over me goes Your fierce wrath your terrors have cut me off**

88:18
סבוני 5437 כמים 4325 כל 3605 היום 3117 הקיפו 5362 עלי 5921 יחד 3162: הרחקת 7368
sabuniy kamayim kal hayoum; hiqiypu 'alay yachad. hirchaqta
**They came round about me like water all daily they compassed about me together have you put far**

ממני 4480 אהב 157 ורע 7453 מידעי 3045 מחשך 4285:
mimeniy 'aheb uarea'; mayuda'ay machshak.
**from me Lover and friend *and* mine acquaintance into darkness**

**Ps 89:1**
משכיל 4905 לאיתן 387 האזרחי 250: חסדי 2617 יהוה 3068 עולם 5769 אשירה 7891 לדר 1755 ודר 1755
maskiyl, la'aeytan ha'azrachiy. chasdey Yahuah 'aulam 'ashiyrah; lador uador
**Maschil of Ethan the Ezrahite of the mercies of Yahuah for ever I will sing of to all generations**

89:2
אודיע 3045 אמונתך 530 בפי 6310: כי 3588 אמרתי 559 עולם 5769 חסד 2617 יבנה 1129 שמים 8064
'audiya' 'amunataka bapiy. kiy 'amartiy, 'aulam chesed yibaneh; shamayim
**will I make known your faithfulness with my mouth For I have said for ever Mercy shall be built up *very* heavens**

89:3
תכן 8559 אמונתך 530 בהם 871a: כרתי 3772 ברית 1285 לבחירי 972 נשבעתי 7650 לדוד 1732
takiyn 'amunataka bahem. karatiy bariyt libchiyriy; nishba'atiy, ladauid
**shall you establish your faithfulness in the I have made a covenant with my chosen I have sworn unto David**

89:4 89:5
עבדי 5650: עד 5704 עולם 5769 אכין 3559 זרעך 2233 ובניתי 1129 לדר 1755 ודור 1755 כסאך 3678 סלה 5542:
'abdiy. 'ad 'aulam 'akiyn zar'aka; uabaniytiy lador uadour kis'aka selah.
**my servant for ever will I establish Your seed and build up all to generations your throne Selah**

89:6
ויודו 3034 שמים 8064 פלאך 6382 יהוה 3068 אף 637 אמונתך 530 בקהל 6951 קדשים 6918: כי 3588
uayoudu shamayim pila'aka Yahuah; 'ap 'amunataka, biqahal qadoshiym. kiy
**And shall praise the heavens your wonders O Yahuah also your faithfulness in the congregation of the saints For**

Ps 88:10 shall the dead arise and praise you? Selah.11 Shall your lovingkindness be declared in the grave? or your faithfulness in destruction?12 Shall your wonders be known
in the dark? and your righteousness in the land of forgetfulness?13 But unto you have I cried, O YHUH; and in the morning shall my prayer prevent you.14 YHUH, why
castest you off my soul? why hidest you your face from me?15 I am afflicted and ready to die from my youth up: while I suffer your terrors I am distracted.16 Thy fierce wrath
go over me; your terrors have cut me off.17 They came round about me daily like water; they compassed me about together.18 Lover and friend have you put far from me, and
mine acquaintance into darkness. **Ps** 89:1 Mas'-chil of E'-than the Ez'-ra-hite. I will sing of the mercies of YHUH forever: with my mouth will I make known your faithfulness
to all generations.2 For I have said, Mercy shall be built up forever: your faithfulness shall you establish in the very heavens.3 I have made a covenant with my chosen, I have
sworn unto David my servant,4 Thy seed will I establish forever, and build up your throne to all generations. Selah.5 And the heavens shall praise your wonders,

| מי 4310 | בשחק 7834 | יערך 6186 | ליהוה 3068 | ידמה 1819 | ליהוה 3068 | בבני 1121 | אלים 410: | 89:7 |
|---|---|---|---|---|---|---|---|---|
| miy' | bashachaq | ya'arok | laYahuah; | yidameh | laYahuah | bibney | 'aeliym | |
| **who** | **in the heaven** | **can be compared** | **unto Yahuah?** | **can be likened** | **unto Yahuah?** | ***who*** **among the sons of** | **the mighty** | |

| אל 410 | נערץ 6206 | בסוד 5475 | קדשים 6918 | רבה 7227 | ונורא 3372 | על 5921 | כל 3605 |
|---|---|---|---|---|---|---|---|
| 'ael | na'aratz | basoud | qadoshiym | rabah; | uanoura', | 'al | kal |
| **El** | **is to be feared** | **in the assembly of** | **the saints** | **greatly** | **and to be had in reverence** | **of** | **all** |

| סביביו 5439: | 89:8 | יהוה 3068 | אלהי 430 | צבאות 6635 | מי 4310 | כמוך 3644 | חסין 2626 | יה 3050 | ואמונתך 530 |
|---|---|---|---|---|---|---|---|---|---|
| sabiybayu. | | Yahuah | 'alohey | tzaba'aut, | miy' | kamouka | chasiyn | Yah; | ua'amunataka, |
| ***them that are*** **about him** | | **O Yahuah** | **Elohim of** | **hosts** | **who** | ***is*** **like unto you?** | ***is*** **a strong** | **Yah** | **or to your faithfulness** |

| סביבותיך 5439: | 89:9 | אתה 859 | מושל 4910 | בגאות 1348 | הים 3220 | בשוא 5375 | גליו 1530 | אתה 859 | תשבחם 7623: | 89:10 | אתה 859 |
|---|---|---|---|---|---|---|---|---|---|---|---|
| sabiybouteyka. | | 'atah | moushel | bage'aut | hayam; | basou'a | galayu, | 'atah | tashabchem. | | 'atah |
| **round about you?** | | **You** | **rulest** | **the raging of** | **the sea** | **when arise** | **the waves thereof** | **You** | **still them** | | **You** |

| דכאת 1792 | כחלל 2491 | רהב 7294 | בזרוע 2220 | עזך 5797 | פזרת 6340 | אויביך 341: | 89:11 |
|---|---|---|---|---|---|---|---|
| diki'ata | kechalal | rahab; | bizroua' | 'uzaka, | pizarta | 'auyabeyka. | |
| **you have broken in pieces** | **as one that is slain** | **Rahab** | **with arm** | **your strong** | **you have scattered** | **your enemies** | |

| לך 3807a | שמים 8064 | אף 637 | לך 3807a | ארץ 776 | תבל 8398 | ומלאה 4393 | אתה 859 | יסדתם 3245: | 89:12 |
|---|---|---|---|---|---|---|---|---|---|
| laka | shamayim | 'ap | laka | 'aretz; | tebel | uamlo'ah, | 'atah | yasadtam. | |
| ***are*** **to your** | **The heavens** | **also** ***is*** | **to your** | **the earth** | ***as for*** **the world** | **and the fulness** ***thereof*** | **you** | **have founded them** | |

| צפון 6828 | וימין 3225 | אתה 859 | בראתם 1254 | תבור 8396 | וחרמון 2768 | בשמך 8034 | ירננו 7442: | 89:13 | לך 3807a |
|---|---|---|---|---|---|---|---|---|---|
| tzapoun | uayamiyn | 'atah | bara'tam; | tabour | uachermoun, | bashimka | yaranenu. | | laka |
| **The north** | **and the south** | **you** | **you have created them** | **Tabor** | **and Hermon** | **in your name** | **shall rejoice** | | **You** ***have*** |

| זרוע 2220 | עם 5973 | גבורה 1369 | תעז 5810 | ידך 3027 | תרום 7311 | ימינך 3225: | 89:14 | צדק 6664 | ומשפט 4941 | מכון 4349 |
|---|---|---|---|---|---|---|---|---|---|---|
| zaroua' | 'am | gaburah; | ta'az | yadaka, | tarum | yamiyneka. | | tzedeq | uamishpat | makoun |
| **a arm** | **with** | **mighty** | **strong is** | **your hand** | ***and*** **high is** | **your right hand** | | **Justice** | **and judgment** | ***are*** **the habitation of** |

| כסאך 3678 | חסד 2617 | ואמת 571 | יקדמו 6923 | פניך 6440: | 89:15 | אשרי 835 | העם 5971 | יודעי 3045 | תרועה 8643 | יהוה 3068 |
|---|---|---|---|---|---|---|---|---|---|---|
| kis'aka; | chesed | ua'amet, | yaqadmu | paneyka. | | 'ashrey | ha'am | youda'aey | taru'ah; | Yahuah |
| **your throne** | **mercy** | **and truth** | **shall go before** | **your face** | | **Blessed** | ***is*** **the people** | **that know** | **the joyful sound** | **O Yahuah** |

| באור 216 | פניך 6440 | יהלכון 1980: | 89:16 | בשמך 8034 | יגילון 1523 | כל 3605 | היום 3117 |
|---|---|---|---|---|---|---|---|
| ba'aur | paneyka | yahalekun. | | bashimka | yagiylun | kal | hayoum; |
| **in the light of** | **your countenance** | **they shall walk** | | **In your name** | **shall they rejoice** | **all** | **the day** |

| ובצדקתך 6666 | ירומו 7311: | 89:17 | כי 3588 | תפארת 8597 | עזמו 5797 | אתה 859 | וברצנך 7522 |
|---|---|---|---|---|---|---|---|
| uabtzidqataka | yarumu. | | kiy | tip'aret | 'uazamou | 'atah; | uabirtzonaka, |
| **and in your righteousness** | **shall they be exalted** | | **For** ***are*** | **the glory of** | **their strength** | **you** | **and in your favor** |

| תרים 7311 | קרננו 7161: | 89:18 | כי 3588 | ליהוה 3068 | מגננו 4043 | ולקדוש 6918 | ישראל 3478 | מלכנו 4428: | 89:19 | אז 227 |
|---|---|---|---|---|---|---|---|---|---|---|
| tariym | qarnenu. | | kiy | laYahuah | maginenu; | ualiqadoush | yisra'ael | malkenu. | | 'az |
| **shall be exalted** | **our horn** | | **For** | **to Yahuah** ***is*** | **our defence** | **and the Holy One of** | **Israel** | ***is*** **our king** | | **Then** |

Ps 89:5 O YHUH: your faithfulness also in the congregation of the saints.6 For who in the heaven can be compared unto YHUH? who among the sons of the mighty can be likened unto YHUH?7 G-d is greatly to be feared in the assembly of the saints, and to be had in reverence of all them that are about him.8 O YHUH G-d of hosts, who is a strong YHUH like unto you? or to your faithfulness round about you?9 Thou rulest the raging of the sea: when the waves thereof arise, you stillest them.10 Thou have broken Rahab in pieces, as one that is slain; you have scattered your enemies with your strong arm.11 The heavens are your, the earth also is your: as for the world and the fulness thereof, you have founded them.12 The north and the south you have created them: Tabor and Hermon shall rejoice in your name.13 Thou have a mighty arm: strong is your hand, and high is your right hand.14 Justice and judgment are the habitation of your throne: mercy and truth shall go before your face.15 Blessed is the people that know the joyful sound: they shall walk, O YHUH, in the light of your countenance.16 In your name shall they rejoice all the day: and in your righteousness shall they be exalted.17 For you are the glory of their strength: and in your favor our horn shall be exalted.18 For YHUH is our defence; and the Holy One of Israel is our king.

1696 דברת 2377 בחזון 2623 לחסידיך 559 ותאמר 7737 שויתי 5828 עזר 5921 על 1368 גבור 7311 הרימותי 970 בחור
dibarta bachazoun lachasiydeyka, uata'mer, shiuiytiy 'azer 'al gibour; hariymoutiy bachur
**you spoke in vision to your holy one and said I have laid help unto *one that is* mighty I have exalted *one* chosen**

89:20 — 89:21

5971: מעם 4672 מצאתי 1732 דוד 5650 עבדי 8081 בשמן 6944 קדשי 4886: משחתיו 834 אשר 3027 ידי
me'am. matza'tiy dauid 'abdiy; bashemen qadashiy mashachtiyu. 'asher yadiy
**out of the people I have found David my servant with oil my holy have I anointed him whom my hand**

89:22

3559 תכון 5973 עמו 637 אף 2220 זרועי 553: תאמצנו 3808 לא 5378 ישא 341 אויב 871a בו 1121 ובן
tikoun 'amou; 'ap zarou'ay ta'amtzenu. la' yasha' auyeb bou; uaben
**shall be established With also mine arm shall strengthen him not shall exact The enemy upon him nor the son of**

89:23 — 89:24

5766 עולה 3808 לא 6031: יעננו 3807 וכתותי 6440 מפניו 6862 צריו 8130 ומשנאיו 5062: אגוף
'aulah, la' ya'anenu. uakatoutiy mipanayu tzarayu; uamsan'ayu 'agoup.
**wickedness nor afflict him And I will beat down before his face his foes and them that hate him plague**

89:25

530 ואמונתי 2617 וחסדי 5973 עמו 8034 ובשמי 7311 תרום 7161: קרנו 7760 ושמתי 3220 בים
ua'amunatiy uachasdiy 'amou; uabishmiy, tarum qarnou. uasamtiy bayam
**But my faithfulness and my mercy *shall be* with him and in my name shall be exalted his horn I will set also in the sea**

89:26

3027 ידו 5104 ובנהרות 3225: ימינו 1931 הוא 7121 יקראני 1 אבי 859 אתה 410 אלי 6697 וצור
yadou; uabanharout yamiynou. hua' yiqra'aeniy 'abiy 'atah; 'aeliy, uatzur
**his hand and in the rivers his right hand He shall cry unto me *are* my father you my El and the rock of**

89:27 — 89:28

3444: ישועתי 637 אף 589 אני 1060 בכור 5414 אתנהו 5945 עליון 4428 למלכי 776: ארץ 5769 לעולם
yashu'atiy. 'ap 'aniy bakour 'atanehu; 'alyoun, lamalkey 'aretz. la'aulam,
**my salvation Also I *my* firstborn I will make him higher than the kings of the earth for evermore**

89:29

8104 אשמור 3807a לו 2617 חסדי 1285 ובריתי 539 נאמנת 3807a: לו 7760 ושמתי 5703 לעד 2233 זרעו
'ashmour lou' chasdiy; uabriytiy, ne'amenet lou'. uasamtiy la'ad zar'au;
**will I keep for him My mercy and my covenant shall stand fast with him also will I make *to endure* for ever His seed**

89:30

3678 וכסאו 3117 כימי 8064: שמים 518 אם 5800 יעזבו 1121 בניו 8451 תורתי 4941 ובמשפטי 3808 לא
uakis'au, kiymey shamayim. 'am ya'azbu banayu touratiy; uabmishpatay, la'
**and his throne as the days of heaven If forsake his children my law not in my judgments not**

89:31 — 89:32

1980: ילכון 518 אם 2708 חקתי 2490 יחללו 4687 ומצותי 3808 לא 8104: ישמרו 6485 ופקדתי 7626 בשבט
yelekun. 'am chuqotay yachalelu; uamitzuotay, la' yishmoru. uapaqadtiy bashebet
**walk If my statutes they break and my commandments not keep Then will I visit with the rod**

89:33

6588 פשעם 5061 ובנגעים 5771: עונם 2617 וחסדי 3808 לא 6331 אפיר 5973 מעמו
pish'am; uabinga'aym 'auonam. uachasdiy la' 'apiyr me'amou;
**their transgression and with stripes their iniquity Nevertheless my lovingkindness not will I utterly take from him**

89:34

3808 ולא 8266 אשקר 530: באמונתי 3808 לא 2490 אחלל 1285 בריתי 4161 ומוצא 8193 שפתי 3808 לא
uala' 'ashaqer, be'amunatiy. la' 'achalel bariytiy; uamoutza' sapatay, la'
**nor suffer to fail my faithfulness not will I break My covenant the thing that is gone out of my lips nor**

Ps 89:19 Then you spoke in vision to your holy one, and saidst, I have laid help upon one that is mighty; I have exalted one chosen out of the people.20 I have found David my servant; with my holy oil have I anointed him:21 With whom my hand shall be established: mine arm also shall strengthen him.22 The enemy shall not exact upon him; nor the son of wickedness afflict him.23 And I will beat down his foes before his face, and plague them that hate him.24 But my faithfulness and my mercy shall be with him: and in my name shall his horn be exalted.25 I will set his hand also in the sea, and his right hand in the rivers.26 He shall cry unto me, Thou are my father, my G-d, and the rock of my salvation.27 Also I will make him my firstborn, higher than the kings of the earth.28 My mercy will I keep for him forevermore, and my covenant shall stand fast with him.29 His seed also will I make to endure forever, and his throne as the days of heaven.30 If his children forsake my law, and walk not in my judgments;31 If they break my statutes, and keep not my commandments;32 Then will I visit their transgression with the rod, and their iniquity with stripes.33 Nevertheless my lovingkindness will I not utterly take from him, nor suffer my faithfulness to fail.34 My covenant will I not break, nor alter the thing that is gone out of my lips.

| אשנה 8138: | 89:35 | אחת 259 | נשבעתי 7650 | בקדשי 6944 | אם 518 | לדוד 1732 | אכזב 3576: | 89:36 | זרעו 2233 | לעולם 5769 | יהיה 1961 |
|---|---|---|---|---|---|---|---|---|---|---|---|
| 'ashaneh. | | 'achat | nishba'atiy | baqadashiy; | 'am | ladauid | 'akazeb. | | zar'au | la'aulam | yihayeh; |
| **alter** | | **Once** | **have I sworn** | **by my holiness** | **not** | **unto David** | **that I will lie** | | **His seed** | **for ever** | **shall endure** |

| וכסאו 3678 | כשמש 8121 | נגדי 5048: | 89:37 | כירח 3394 | יכון 3559 | עולם 5769 | ועד 5707 | בשחק 7834 | נאמן 539 |
|---|---|---|---|---|---|---|---|---|---|
| uakis'au | kashemesh | negdiy. | | kayareach | yikoun | 'aulam; | ua'aed | bashachaq, | ne'aman |
| **and his throne** | **as the sun** | **before me** | | **as the moon** | **It shall be established** | **for ever** | **and *as* a witness** | **in heaven** | **faithful** |

| סלה 5542: | 89:38 | ואתה 859 | זנחת 2186 | ותמאס 3988 | התעברת 5674 | עם 5973 | משיחך 4899: | 89:39 | נארתה 5010 |
|---|---|---|---|---|---|---|---|---|---|
| selah. | | ua'atah | zanachta | uatim'as; | hit'abarta, | 'am | mashiycheka. | | ne'artah |
| **Selah** | | **But you** | **have cast off** | **and abhorred** | **you have been wroth** | **with** | **your anointed** | | **You have made void** |

| ברית 1285 | עבדך 5650 | חללת 2490 | לארץ 776 | נזרו 5145: | 89:40 | פרצת 6555 | כל 3605 |
|---|---|---|---|---|---|---|---|
| bariyt | 'abdeka; | chilalta | la'aretz | nizrou. | | paratzta | kal |
| **the covenant of** | **your servant** | **you have profaned** | ***by casting it* to the ground** | **his crown** | | **You have broken down** | **all** |

| גדרתיו 1448 | שמת 7760 | מבצריו 4013 | מחתה 4288: | 89:41 | שסהו 8155 | כל 3605 | עברי 5674 | דרך 1870 | היה 1961 | חרפה 2781 |
|---|---|---|---|---|---|---|---|---|---|---|
| gaderotayu; | samta | mibtzarayu | machitah | | shasuhu | kal | 'abarey | darek; | hayah | cherpah, |
| **his hedges** | **you have brought** | **his strong holds** | **to ruin** | | **spoil him** | **All** | **that pass by** | **the way** | **he is** | **a reproach** |

| לשכניו 7934: | 89:42 | הרימות 7311 | ימין 3225 | צריו 6862 | השמחת 8055 | כל 3605 | אויביו 341: | 89:43 |
|---|---|---|---|---|---|---|---|---|
| lishkenayu. | | hariymouta | yamiyn | tzarayu; | hismachta, | kal | 'auyabayu. | |
| **to his neighbours** | | **You have set up** | **the right hand of** | **his adversaries** | **you have made to rejoice** | **all** | **his enemies** | |

| אף 637 | תשיב 7725 | צור 6697 | חרבו 2719 | ולא 3808 | הקימתו 6965 | במלחמה 4421: | 89:44 | השבת 7673 |
|---|---|---|---|---|---|---|---|---|
| 'ap | tashiyb | tzur | charbou; | uala' | haqeymotou, | bamilchamah. | | hishbata |
| **also** | **You have turned** | **the edge of** | **his sword** | **and not** | **have made him to stand** | **in the battle** | | **You have made to cease** |

| מטהרו 2892 | וכסאו 3678 | לארץ 776 | מגרתה 4048: | 89:45 | הקצרת 7114 | ימי 3117 | עלומיו 5934 | העטית 5844 | עליו 5921 |
|---|---|---|---|---|---|---|---|---|---|
| mitaharou; | uakis'au, | la'aretz | migartah. | | hiqtzarta | yamey | 'alumayu; | he'atiyta | 'alayu |
| **his glory** | **and his throne** | **to the ground** | **cast down** | | **have you shortened** | **The days of** | **his youth** | **you have covered** | **him** |

| בושה 955 | סלה 5542: | 89:46 | עד 5704 | מה 4100 | יהוה 3068 | תסתר 5641 | לנצח 5331 | תבער 1197 | כמו 3644 | אש 784 |
|---|---|---|---|---|---|---|---|---|---|---|
| bushah | selah. | | 'ad | mah | Yahuah | tisater | lanetzach; | tib'ar | kamou | 'aesh |
| ***with* shame** | **Selah** | | **How long** | **what** | **Yahuah** | **will you hide yourself** | **for ever?** | **shall burn** | **like** | **fire?** |

| חמתך 2534: | 89:47 | זכר 2142 | אני 589 | מה 4100 | חלד 2465 | על 5921 | מה 4100 | שוא 7723 | בראת 1254 | כל 3605 | בני 1121 |
|---|---|---|---|---|---|---|---|---|---|---|---|
| chamateka. | | zakar | 'aniy | meh | chaled; | 'al | mah, | shau'a | bara'ta | kal | baney |
| **your wrath** | | **Remember** | **my** | **how** | **short time *is*** | **wherefore** | **what** | **in vain?** | **have you made** | **all** | **the sons of** |

| אדם 120: | 89:48 | מי 4310 | גבר 1397 | יחיה 2421 | ולא 3808 | יראה 7200 | מות 4194 | ימלט 4422 | נפשו 5315 | מיד 3027 | שאול 7585 |
|---|---|---|---|---|---|---|---|---|---|---|---|
| 'adam. | | miy' | geber | yichayeh | uala' | yir'ah | mauet; | yamalet | napshou | miyad | sha'aul |
| **men** | | **What** | **man *is he that*** | **live** | **and not** | **shall see** | **death?** | **shall he deliver** | **his soul** | **from the hand of** | **the grave?** |

| סלה 5542: | 89:49 | איה 346 | חסדיך 2617 | הראשנים 7223 | אדני 136 | נשבעת 7650 | לדוד 1732 | באמונתך 530: |
|---|---|---|---|---|---|---|---|---|
| selah. | | 'ayeh | chasadeyka | hara'shoniym | 'adonay; | nishba'ta | ladauid, | be'amunateka. |
| **Selah** | | **where *are*** | **your lovingkindnesses** | **former** | **Adonai** | ***which* you sware** | **unto David** | **in your truth?** |

Ps 89:35 Once have I sworn by my holiness that I will not lie unto David.36 His seed shall endure forever, and his throne as the sun before me.37 It shall be established forever as the moon, and as a faithful witness in heaven. Selah.38 But you have cast off and abhorred, you have been wroth with your anointed.39 Thou have made void the covenant of your servant: you have profaned his crown by casting it to the ground.40 Thou have broken down all his hedges; you have brought his strong holds to ruin.41 All that pass by the way spoil him: he is a reproach to his neighbors.42 Thou have set up the right hand of his adversaries; you have made all his enemies to rejoice.43 Thou have also turned the edge of his sword, and have not made him to stand in the battle.44 Thou have made his glory to cease, and cast his throne down to the ground.45 The days of his youth have you shortened: you have covered him with shame. Selah.46 How long, YHUH? will you hide thyself forever? shall your wrath burn like fire?47 Remember how short my time is: wherefore have you made all men in vain?48 What man is he that live, and shall not see death? shall he deliver his soul from the hand of the grave? Selah.49 Adonai, where are your former lovingkindnesses, which you swarest unto David in your truth?

89:50 זכר 2142 אדני 136 חרפת 2781 עבדיך 5650 שאתי 5375 בחיקי 2436 כל 3605 רבים 7227
zakor 'adonay cherpat 'abadeyka; sa'aetiy bacheyqiy, kal rabiym
**Remember Adonai the reproach of your servants *how* I do bear in my bosom *the reproach of* all *the* mighty**

עמים 5971: 89:51 אשר 834 חרפו 2778 אויביך 341 יהוה 3068 אשר 834 חרפו 2778 עקבות 6119
'amiym. 'asher cherapu 'auyabeyka Yahuah; 'asher cherapu, 'aqabout
**people Wherewith have reproached your enemies O Yahuah wherewith they have reproached the footsteps of**

משיחך 4899: 89:52 ברוך 1288 יהוה 3068 לעולם 5769 אמן 543 ואמן 543:
mashiycheka. baruk Yahuah la'aulam, 'amen ua'amen.
**your anointed Blessed *be* Yahuah for evermore Amen and Amen**

Ps 90:1 תפלה 8605 למשה 4872 איש 376 האלהים 430 אדני 136 מעון 4583 אתה 859 היית 1961 לנו 3807a בדר 1755 ודר 1755: 90:2
tapilah lamosheh 'aysh ha'alohiym 'adonay, ma'aun 'atah hayiyta lanu, bador uador.
**A Prayer of Moses the man of Elohim Adonai dwelling place you have been our in all generations**

בטרם 2962 הרים 2022 ילדו 3205 ותחולל 2342 ארץ 776 ותבל 8398 ומעולם 5769 עד 5704
baterem hariym yuladu, uatachoulel 'aretz uatebel; uame'aulam 'ad
**Before the mountains were brought forth or ever you had formed the earth and the world even from everlasting to**

עולם 5769 אתה 859 אל 410: 90:3 תשב 7725 אנוש 582 עד 5704 דכא 1793 ותאמר 559 שובו 7725 בני 1121 אדם 120: 90:4 כי 3588
'aulam, 'atah 'ael. tasheb 'anoush 'ad daka'; uata'mer, shubu baney 'adam. kiy
**everlasting you *are* El You turn man to destruction and say Return you children of men For**

אלף 505 שנים 8141 בעיניך 5869 כיום 3117 אתמול 865 כי 3588 יעבר 5674 ואשמורה 821 בלילה 3915: 90:5
'alep shaniym ba'aeyneyka, kayoum 'atmoul kiy ya'abor; ua'ashmurah balayalah.
**a thousand years in your sight *are but* as yesterday when it is past and *as* a watch in the night**

זרמתם 2229 שנה 8142 יהיו 1961 בבקר 1242 כחציר 2682 יחלף 2498: 90:6
zaramtam shenah yihayu; baboqer, kechatziyr yachalop.
**You carry them away as with a flood *as* a sleep they are in the morning *they are* like grass *which* grow up**

בבקר 1242 יציץ 6692 וחלף 2498 לערב 6153 ימולל 4135 ויבש 3001: 90:7 כי 3588 כלינו 3615 באפך 639
baboqer yatziytz uachalap; la'areb, yamoulel uayabesh. kiy kaliynu ba'apeka;
**In the morning it flourish and grow up in the evening it is cut down and wither For we are consumed by your anger**

ובחמתך 2534 נבהלנו 926: 90:8 שת 7896 עונתינו 5771 לנגדך 5048 עלמנו 5956 למאור 3974
uabachamataka nibhalanu. shata 'auonoteynu lanegdeka; 'alumenu, lima'aur
**and by your wrath are we troubled You have set our iniquities before you our secret *sins* in the light of**

פניך 6440: 90:9 כי 3588 כל 3605 ימינו 3117 פנו 6437 בעברתך 5678 כלינו 3615 שנינו 8141 כמו 3644
paneyka. kiy kal yameynu panu ba'abrateka; kiliynu shaneynu kamou
**your countenance For all our days are passed away in your wrath we spend our years as**

הגה 1899: 90:10 ימי 3117 שנותינו 8141 בהם 871a שבעים 7657 שנה 8141 ואם 518 בגבורת 1369
hegeh. yamey shanouteynu bahem shib'aym shanah ua'am bigabarout
**a tale *that is told* The days of our years in them threescore and ten (*seventy*) years and if by reason of strength**

Ps 89:50 Remember, Adonai, the reproach of your servants; how I do bear in my bosom the reproach of all the mighty people;51 Wherewith your enemies have reproached, O YHUH; wherewith they have reproached the footsteps of your anointed.52 Blessed be YHUH forevermore. Amen, and Amen. **Ps** 90:1 A Prayer of Moses the man of G-d. YHUH, you have been our dwelling place in all generations.2 Before the mountains were brought forth, or ever you had formed the earth and the world, even from everlasting to everlasting, you are G-d.3 Thou turn man to destruction; and say, Return, you children of men.4 For a thousand years in your sight are but as yesterday when it is past, and as a watch in the night.5 Thou carriest them away as with a flood; they are as a sleep: in the morning they are like grass which groweth up.6 In the morning it flourisheth, and groweth up; in the evening it is cut down, and withereth.7 For we are consumed by your anger, and by your wrath are we troubled.8 Thou have set our iniquities before you, our secret sins in the light of your countenance.9 For all our days are passed away in your wrath: we spend our years as a tale that is told.10 The days of our years are threescore years and ten; and if by reason of strength they be fourscore years, yet is their strength labour and sorrow; for it is soon cut off, and we fly away.

שמונים 8084 | שנה 8141 | ורהבם 7296 | עמל 5999 | ואון 205 | כי 3588 | גז 1468 | חיש 2440 | ונעפה 5774: | **90:11** מי 4310 | יודע 3045
shamouniym shanah, uarahabam 'amal ua'auen; kiy gaz chiysh, uana'apah. miy' youdea'
**_they be_ fourscore years yet _is_ their strength labour and sorrow for cut off _it is_ soon and we fly away Who knows**

עז 5797 | אפך 639 | וכיראתך 3374 | עברתך 5678: | **90:12** למנות 4487 | ימינו 3117 | כן 3651 | הודע 3045
'az 'apeka; uakyir'ataka, 'abrateka. limnout yameynu ken houda';
**the power of your anger? even according to your fear _so is_ your wrath _us_ to number our days So teach**

ונבא 935 | לבב 3824 | חכמה 2451: | **90:13** שובה 7725 | יהוה 3068 | עד 5704 | מתי 4970 | והנחם 5162 | על 5921
uanabi'a, labab chakamah shubah Yahuah 'ad matay; uahinachem, 'al
**that we may apply _our_ hearts unto wisdom Return O Yahuah how long when? and let it repent you concerning**

עבדיך 5650: | **90:14** שבענו 7646 | בבקר 1242 | חסדך 2617 | ונרננה 7442 | ונשמחה 8055 | בכל 3605 | ימינו 3117: | **90:15**
'abadeyka. sab'aenu baboqer chasadeka; uanrannah uanismachah, bakal yameynu.
**your servants O satisfy us early _with_ your mercy that we may rejoice and be glad all our days**

שמחנו 8055 | כימות 3117 | עניתנו 6031 | שנות 8141 | ראינו 7200 | רעה 7451: | **90:16**
samchenu kiymout 'aniytanu; shanout, ra'aynu ra'ah.
**Make us glad according to the days _wherein_ you have afflicted us _and_ the years _wherein_ we have seen evil**

יראה 7200 | אל 413 | עבדיך 5650 | פעלך 6467 | והדרך 1926 | על 5921 | בניהם 1121: | **90:17** ויהי 1961 | נעם 5278 | אדני 136
yera'ah 'al 'abadeyka pa'aleka; uahadaraka, 'al baneyhem. uiyhiy no'am 'adonay
**Let appear unto your servants your work and your glory unto their children And let be the beauty of Adonai**

אלהינו 430 | עלינו 5921 | ומעשה 4639 | ידינו 3027 | כוננה 3559 | עלינו 5921 | ומעשה 4639 | ידינו 3027 | כוננהו 3559:
'aloheynu, 'aleynu uama'aseh yadeynu kounanah 'aleynu; uama'aseh yadeynu, kounanehu.
**our Elohim upon us and the work of our hands establish you upon us yea the work of our hands establish you it**

**Ps 91:1** ישב 3427 | בסתר 5643 | עליון 5945 | בצל 6738 | שדי 7706 | יתלונן 3885: | **91:2** אמר 559
yosheb baseter 'alyoun; batzel shaday, yitlounan. 'amar,
**He that dwell in the secret place of the most High under the shadow of the Almighty shall abide I will say**

ליהוה 3068 | מחסי 4268 | ומצודתי 4686 | אלהי 430 | אבטח 982 | בו 871a: | **91:3** כי 3588 | הוא 1931 | יצילך 5337
laYahuah machasiy uamtzudatiy; 'alohay, 'abtach bou. kiy hua' yatziylaka
**of Yahuah _He is_ my refuge and my fortress my Elohim will I trust in him Surely he shall deliver you**

מפח 6341 | יקוש 3353 | מדבר 1698 | הוות 1942: | **91:4** באברתו 84 | יסך 5526 | לך 3807a | ותחת 8478
mipach yaqush, mideber hauout. ba'abratou yasek lak uatachat
**from the snare of the fowler _and_ from pestilence _the_ noisome with his feathers He shall cover to you and under**

כנפיו 3671 | תחסה 2620 | צנה 6793 | וסחרה 5507 | אמתו 571: | **91:5** לא 3808 | תירא 3372 | מפחד 6343 | לילה 3915
kanapayu techaseh; tzinah uasocherah 'amitou. la' tiyraa' mipachad layalah;
**his wings shall you trust _shall be your_ shield and buckler his truth not You shall be afraid for the terror by night**

מחץ 4271 | יעוף 5774 | יומם 3119: | **91:6** מדבר 1698 | באפל 652 | יהלך 1980 | מקטב 6986 | ישוד 7736
mechetz, ya'aup youmam. Mideber ba'apel yahalok; miqeteb, yashud
**_nor_ for the arrow _that_ flies by day _Nor_ for the pestilence in darkness _that_ walk _nor_ for the destruction _that_ waste at**

Ps 90:11 Who know the power of your anger? even according to your fear, so is your wrath.12 So teach us to number our days, that we may apply our hearts unto wisdom.13 Return, O YHUH, how long? and let it repent you concerning your servants.14 O satisfy us early with your mercy; that we may rejoice and be glad all our days.15 Make us glad according to the days wherein you have afflicted us, and the years wherein we have seen evil.16 Let your work appear unto your servants, and your glory unto their children.17 And let the beauty of YHUH our G-d be upon us: and establish you the work of our hands upon us; yea, the work of our hands establish you it. **Ps** 91:1 He that dwell in the secret place of the most High shall abide under the shadow of the Almighty.2 I will say of YHUH, He is my refuge and my fortress: my G-d; in him will I trust.3 Surely he shall deliver you from the snare of the fowler, and from the noisome pestilence.4 He shall cover you with his feathers, and under his wings shall you trust: his truth shall be your shield and buckler.5 Thou shall not be afraid for the terror by night; nor for the arrow that flieth by day;6 Nor for the pestilence that walk in darkness; nor for the destruction that wasteth at noonday.

| 91:7 | | | | | | | |
|---|---|---|---|---|---|---|---|
| צהרים 6672: | יפל 5307 | מצדך 6654 | אלף 505 | ורבבה 7233 | מימינך 3225 | אליך 413 | לא 3808 |
| tzaharayim. | yipol | mitzidaka | 'alep, | uarbabah | miymiyneka; | 'aeleyka, | la' |
| **noonday** | **shall fall** | **at your side** | **A thousand** | **and ten thousand** | **at your right hand** | **you** | **not** |

| 91:8 | | | | | | 91:9 | |
|---|---|---|---|---|---|---|---|
| יגש 5066: | רק 7535 | בעיניך 5869 | תביט 5027 | ושלמת 8011 | רשעים 7563 | תראה 7200: | כי 3588 |
| yigash. | raq | ba'aeyneyka | tabiyt; | uashilumat | rasha'aym | tir'ah. | kiy |
| ***but*** **it shall come near** | **Only** | **with your eyes** | **shall you behold** | **and the reward of** | **the wicked** | **see** | **Because** |

| | | | | | 91:10 | | | |
|---|---|---|---|---|---|---|---|---|
| אתה 859 | יהוה 3068 | מחסי 4268 | עליון 5945 | שמת 7760 | מעונך 4583: | לא 3808 | תאנה 579 | אליך 413 |
| 'atah | Yahuah | machasiy; | 'alyoun, | samta | ma'auneka. | la' | ta'aneh | 'aeleyka |
| **you** | **Yahuah** | ***which is*** **my refuge** | ***even*** **the most High** | **have made** | **your habitation** | **no** | **There shall befall** | **you** |

| | | | | | 91:11 | | | |
|---|---|---|---|---|---|---|---|---|
| רעה 7451 | ונגע 5061 | לא 3808 | יקרב 7126 | באהלך 168: | כי 3588 | מלאכיו 4397 | יצוה 6680 | לך 3807a | לשמרך 8104 |
| ra'ah; | uanega', | la' | yiqrab | ba'ahaleka. | kiy | mala'akayu | yatzaueh | lak; | lishmaraka, |
| **evil** | ***any*** **plague** | **neither** | **shall come near** | **your dwelling** | **For** | **his angels** | **he shall give charge** | **over you** | **to keep you** |

| | | 91:12 | | | | | | 91:13 |
|---|---|---|---|---|---|---|---|---|
| בכל 3605 | דרכיך 1870: | על 5921 | כפים 3709 | ישאונך 5375 | פן 6435 | תגף 5062 | באבן 68 | רגלך 7272: | על 5921 |
| bakal | darakeyka. | 'al | kapayim | yisa'aunaka; | pen | tigop | ba'aben | ragleka. | 'al |
| **in all** | **your ways** | **in** | ***their*** **hands** | **They shall bear you up** | **lest** | **you dash** | **against a stone** | **your foot** | **upon** |

| | | | | | | 91:14 | |
|---|---|---|---|---|---|---|---|
| שחל 7826 | ופתן 6620 | תדרך 1869 | תרמס 7429 | כפיר 3715 | ותנין 8577: | כי 3588 | בי 871a |
| shachal | uapeten | tidrok; | tirmos | kapiyr | uataniyn. | kiy | biy |
| **the lion** | **and adder** | **You shall tread** | **shall you trample under feet** | **the young lion** | **and the dragon** | **Because** | **upon me** |

| | | | | | 91:15 |
|---|---|---|---|---|---|
| חשק 2836 | ואפלטהו 6403 | אשגבהו 7682 | כי 3588 | ידע 3045 | שמי 8034: |
| chashaq | ua'apaltehu; | 'asagbehu, | kiy | yada' | shamiy. |
| **he has set his love** | **therefore will I deliver him** | **I will set him on high** | **because** | **he has known** | **my name** |

| | | | | | | | 91:16 |
|---|---|---|---|---|---|---|---|
| יקראני 7121 | ואענהו 6030 | עמו 5973 | אנכי 595 | בצרה 6869 | אחלצהו 2502 | ואכבדהו 3513: | |
| yiqra'aeniy | ua'a'anehu, | 'amou | 'anokiy | batzarah; | 'achalatzehu, | ua'akabdehu. | |
| **He shall call upon me** | **and I will answer him** | ***will be*** **with him** | **I** | **in trouble** | **I will deliver him** | **and honor him** | |

| | | | | |
|---|---|---|---|---|
| ארך 753 | ימים 3117 | אשביעהו 7646 | ואראהו 7200 | בישועתי 3444: |
| 'arek | yamiym | 'asbiy'aehu; | ua'ar'ah, | biyshu'atiy. |
| ***With*** **long life** | | **will I satisfy him** | **and show him** | **my salvation** |

| Ps 92:1 | | | | | | | |
|---|---|---|---|---|---|---|---|
| מזמור 4210 | שיר 7892 | ליום 3117 | השבת 7676: | טוב 2896 | להדות 3034 | ליהוה 3068 | ולזמר 2167 |
| mizmour | shiyr, | layoum | hashabat. | toub, | lahodout | laYahuah; | ualzamer |
| **A Psalm** | ***or*** **Song** | **for day** | **the sabbath** | ***It is a*** **good** | ***thing*** **to give thanks** | **unto Yahuah** | **and to sing praises** |

| | | 92:2 | | | | |
|---|---|---|---|---|---|---|
| לשמך 8034 | עליון 5945: | להגיד 5046 | בבקר 1242 | חסדך 2617 | ואמונתך 530 | בלילות 3915: |
| lashimka | 'alyoun. | lahagiyd | baboqer | chasadeka; | ua'amunataka, | baleyhout. |
| **unto your name** | **O most High** | **To show forth** | **in the morning** | **your lovingkindness** | **and your faithfulness** | **every night** |

| 92:3 | | | | | | | 92:4 |
|---|---|---|---|---|---|---|---|
| עלי 5921 | עשור 6218 | ועלי 5921 | נבל 5035 | עלי 5921 | הגיון 1902 | בכנור 3658: | כי 3588 |
| 'aley | 'asour | ua'aley | nabel; | 'aley | higayoun | bakinour. | kiy |
| **Upon** | **an instrument of ten strings** | **and upon** | **the psaltery** | **with** | **a solemn sound** | **upon the harp** | **For** |

Ps 91:7 A thousand shall fall at your side, and ten thousand at your right hand; but it shall not come nigh you.8 Only with your eyes shall you behold and see the reward of the wicked.9 Because you have made YHUH, which is my refuge, even the most High, your habitation;10 There shall no evil befall you, neither shall any plague come nigh your dwelling.11 For he shall give his angels charge over you, to keep you in all your ways.12 They shall bear you up in their hands, lest you dash your foot against a stone.13 Thou shall tread upon the lion and adder: the young lion and the dragon shall you trample under feet.14 Because he has set his love upon me, therefore will I deliver him: I will set him on high, because he has known my name.15 He shall call upon me, and I will answer him: I will be with him in trouble; I will deliver him, and honor him.16 With long life will I satisfy him, and show him my salvation. **Ps** 92:1 A Psalm or Song for the Sabbath day. It is a good thing to give thanks unto YHUH, and to sing praises unto your name, O most High:2 To show forth your lovingkindness in the morning, and your faithfulness every night,3 Upon an instrument of ten strings, and upon the psaltery; upon the harp with a solemn sound.

| | | | | | | 92:5 | | |
|---|---|---|---|---|---|---|---|---|
| שמחתני 8055 | יהוה 3068 | בפעלך 6467 | במעשי 4639 | ידיך 3027 | ארנן 7442: | מה 4100 | גדלו 1431 | מעשיך 4639 |
| simachtaniy | Yahuah | bapa'aleka; | bam'asey | yadeyka | 'arnen. | mah | gadalu | ma'aseyka |
| **have made me glad** | **Yahuah** | **through your work** | **in the works of** | **your hands** | **I will triumph** | **how** | **great are** | **your works!** |

| | | | | 92:6 | | | | | | | |
|---|---|---|---|---|---|---|---|---|---|---|---|
| יהוה 3068 | מאד 3966 | עמקו 6009 | מחשבתיך 4284: | איש 376 | בער 1198 | לא 3808 | ידע 3045 | וכסיל 3684 | לא 3808 | יבין 995 | את 853 |
| Yahuah; | ma'ad, | 'amaqu | machshaboteyka. | 'aysh | ba'ar | la' | yeda'; | uakasiyl, | la' | yabiyn | 'at |
| **O Yahuah** | **very** | **are deep** | ***and* your thoughts** | **A man** | **brutish** | **not** | **knows** | **a fool** | **neither** | **does understand** | |

| | 92:7 | | | | | | | |
|---|---|---|---|---|---|---|---|---|
| זאת 2063: | בפרח 6524 | רשעים 7563 | כמו 3644 | עשב 6212 | ויציצו 6692 | כל 3605 | פעלי 6466 | און 205 |
| za't. | biparoach | rasha'aym | kamou | 'aeseb, | uayatziytzu | kal | po'aley | 'auen; |
| **this** | **When spring** | ***the* wicked** | **as** | **the grass** | **and when do flourish** | **all** | **the workers of** | **iniquity** |

| | | | 92:8 | | | 92:9 | | |
|---|---|---|---|---|---|---|---|---|
| להשמדם 8045 | עדי 5703 | עד 5704: | ואתה 859 | מרום 4791 | לעלם 5769 | יהוה 3068: | כי 3588 | הנה 2009 |
| lahishamadam | 'adey | 'ad. | ua'atah | maroum, | la'alam | Yahuah. | kiy | hineh |
| ***it is* that they shall be destroyed** | **for** | **ever** | **But you** | ***are* most high** | **for evermore** | **Yahuah** | **For** | **lo** |

| | | | | | | | | | 92:10 |
|---|---|---|---|---|---|---|---|---|---|
| איביך 341 | יהוה 3068 | כי 3588 | הנה 2009 | איביך 341 | יאבדו 6 | יתפרדו 6504 | כל 3605 | פעלי 6466 | און 205: |
| 'ayabeyka | Yahuah | kiy | hineh | 'ayabeyka | ya'bedu; | yitparadu, | kal | po'aley | 'auen. |
| **your enemies** | **O Yahuah** | **for** | **lo** | **your enemies** | **shall perish** | **shall be scattered** | **all** | **the workers of** | **iniquity** |

| | | | | | | 92:11 | |
|---|---|---|---|---|---|---|---|
| ותרם 7311 | כראים 7214 | קרני 7161 | בלתי 1101 | בשמן 8081 | רענן 7488: | ותבט 5027 | עיני 5869 |
| uatarem | kir'aeym | qarniy; | balotiy, | bashemen | ra'anan. | uatabet | 'aeyniy, |
| **But shall you exalt** | **like *the horn of* an unicorn** | **my horn** | **I shall be anointed** | **with oil** | **fresh** | **also shall see** | **Mine eye** |

| | | | | | | 92:12 |
|---|---|---|---|---|---|---|
| בשורי 7790 | בקמים 6965 | עלי 5921 | מרעים 7489 | תשמענה 8085 | אזני 241: | צדיק 6662 |
| bashuray | baqamiym | 'alay | mare'aym, | tishma'anah | 'azanay. | tzadiyq |
| ***my desire* on mine enemies** | **that rise up** | **against me** | ***my desire* of the wicked** | **shall hear** | ***and* mine ears** | **The righteous** |

| | | | | | 92:13 | | |
|---|---|---|---|---|---|---|---|
| כתמר 8558 | יפרח 6524 | כארז 730 | בלבנון 3844 | ישגה 7685: | שתולים 8362 | בבית 1004 | יהוה 3068 |
| katamar | yiprach; | ka'arez | balabanoun | yisgeh. | shatuliym | babeyt | Yahuah; |
| **like the palm tree** | **shall flourish** | **like a cedar** | **in Lebanon** | **he shall grow** | **Those that be planted** | **in the house of** | **Yahuah** |

| | | | 92:14 | | | | |
|---|---|---|---|---|---|---|---|
| בחצרות 2691 | אלהינו 430 | יפריחו 6524: | עוד 5750 | ינובון 5107 | בשיבה 7872 | דשנים 1879 | ורעננים 7488 |
| bachatzarout | 'aloheynu | yapriychu. | 'aud | yanubun | baseybah; | dasheniym | uara'ananiym |
| **in the courts of** | **our Elohim** | **shall flourish** | **still** | **They shall bring forth fruit** | **in old age** | **fat** | **and flourishing** |

| | 92:15 | | | | | | | |
|---|---|---|---|---|---|---|---|---|
| יהיו 1961: | להגיד 5046 | כי 3588 | ישר 3477 | יהוה 3068 | צורי 6697 | ולא 3808 | עלתה 5766 | בו 871a: |
| yihayu. | lahagiyd | kiy | yashar | Yahuah; | tzuriy, | uala' | 'alatah | bou. |
| **they shall be** | **To show** | **that** | ***is* upright** | **Yahuah** | ***he is* my rock** | **and there is no** | **unrighteousness** | **in him** |

| Ps 93:1 | | | | | | | | |
|---|---|---|---|---|---|---|---|---|
| יהוה 3068 | מלך 4427 | גאות 1348 | לבש 3847 | לבש 3847 | יהוה 3068 | עז 5797 | התאזר 247 | אף 637 |
| Yahuah | malak | ge'aut | labesh | labesh | Yahuah | 'az | hit'azar; | 'ap |
| **Yahuah** | **reigns** | **majesty** | **he is clothed with** | **is clothed with** | **Yahuah** | **strength** | ***wherewith* he has girded *himself*** | **also** |

| | | | | 93:2 | | | | |
|---|---|---|---|---|---|---|---|---|
| תכון 3559 | תבל 8398 | בל 1077 | תמוט 4131: | נכון 3559 | כסאך 3678 | מאז 227 | מעולם 5769 | אתה 859: |
| tikoun | tebel, | bal | timout. | nakoun | kis'aka | me'az; | me'aulam | 'atah. |
| **is stablished** | **the world** | **cannot** | **that it be moved** | ***is* established** | **Your throne** | **of old** | ***are* from everlasting** | **you** |

Ps 92:4 For you, YHUH, have made me glad through your work: I will triumph in the works of your hands.5 O YHUH, how great are your works! and your thoughts are very deep.6 A brutish man know not; neither doth a fool understand this.7 When the wicked spring as the grass, and when all the workers of iniquity do flourish; it is that they shall be destroyed forever:8 But you, YHUH, are most high forevermore.9 For, lo, your enemies, O YHUH, for, lo, your enemies shall perish; all the workers of iniquity shall be scattered.10 But my horn shall you exalt like the horn of an unicorn: I shall be anointed with fresh oil.11 Mine eye also shall see my desire on mine enemies, and mine ears shall hear my desire of the wicked that rise up against me.12 The righteous shall flourish like the palm tree: he shall grow like a cedar in Lebanon.13 Those that be planted in the house of YHUH shall flourish in the courts of our G-d.14 They shall still bring forth fruit in old age; they shall be fat and flourishing;15 To show that YHUH is upright: he is my rock, and there is no unrighteousness in him. **Ps** 93:1 YHUH reigned, he is clothed with majesty; YHUH is clothed with strength, wherewith he has girded himself: the world also is stablished, that it cannot be moved.2 Thy throne is established of old: you are from everlasting.

93:3 ... 93:4
נשאו 5375 נהרות 5104 יהוה 3068 נשאו 5375 נהרות 5104 קולם 6963 ישאו 5375 נהרות 5104 דכים 1796:
nasa'au naharout Yahuah nasa'au naharout qoulam; yis'au naharout dakayam.
**have lifted up The floods O Yahuah have lifted up the floods their voice lift up the floods their waves**

מקלות 6963 מים 4325 רבים 7227 אדירים 117 משברי 4867 ים 3220 אדיר 117 במרום 4791 יהוה 3068: 93:5 עדתיך 5713
miqolout mayim rabiym, 'adiyriym mishbareiy yam; 'adiyr bamaroum Yahuah. 'aedoteyka
**than the noise of waters many *is* mightier waves of the sea *yea than the* mighty on high Yahuah Your testimonies**

נאמנו 539 מאד 3966 לביתך 1004 נאוה 4998 קדש 6944 יהוה 3068 לארך 753 ימים 3117:
ne'amanu ma'ad, labeytaka na'abah qodesh; Yahuah la'arek yamiym.
**are sure very your house become holiness O Yahuah for ever**

Ps 94:1
אל 410 נקמות 5360 יהוה 3068 אל 410 נקמות 5360 הופיע 3313: 94:2 הנשא 5375
'ael naqamout Yahuah; 'ael naqamout houpiya'. hinasea'
**El *to whom* vengeance O Yahuah *belongs* O El *to whom* vengeance *belongs* show yourself Lift up**

שפט 8199 הארץ 776 השב 7725 גמול 1576 על 5921 גאים 1343: 94:3 עד 5704 מתי 4970 רשעים 7563 יהוה 3068 עד 5704
shopet ha'aretz; hasheb gamul, 'al ge'aym. 'ad matay rasha'aym Yahuah; 'ad
***yourself* you judge of the earth render a reward to the proud how long when *shall* the wicked Yahuah how long**

מתי 4970 רשעים 7563 יעלזו 5937: 94:4 יביעו 5042 ידברו 1696 עתק 6277 יתאמרו 559 כל 3605
matay, rasha'aym ya'alozu. yabiy'au yadabru 'ataq; yit'amaru, kal
**when the wicked shall triumph? *How long* shall they utter *and* speak hard things? boast themselves? *and* all**

פעלי 6466 און 205: 94:5 עמך 5971 יהוה 3068 ידכאו 1792 ונחלתך 5159 יענו 6031: 94:6 אלמנה 490
po'aley 'auen. 'amaka Yahuah yadak'au; uanachalataka ya'anu. 'almanah
**the workers of iniquity your people O Yahuah They break in pieces and your heritage afflict the widow**

וגר 1616 יהרגו 2026 ויתומים 3490 ירצחו 7523: 94:7 ויאמרו 559 לא 3808 יראה 7200 יה 3050 ולא 3808
uager yaharogu; uiytoumiym yaratzechu. uaya'maru la' yir'ah Yah; uala'
**and the stranger They slay and the fatherless murder Yet they say not shall see Yahuah and neither**

יבין 995 אלהי 430 יעקב 3290: 94:8 בינו 995 בערים 1197 בעם 5971 וכסילים 3684 מתי 4970
yabiyn, 'alohey ya'aqob. biynu bo'ariym ba'am; uaksiyliym, matay
**shall regard *it* the Elohim of Jacob Understand *you* brutish among the people and *you* fools when**

תשכילו 7919: 94:9 הנטע 5193 אזן 241 הלא 3808 ישמע 8085 אם 518 יצר 3335 עין 5869 הלא 3808 יביט 5027: 94:10
taskiylu. hanota' 'azen hala' yishma'; 'am yotzer 'ayin, hala' yabiyt.
**will you be wise? He that planted the ear not shall he hear? or he that formed the eye not shall he see**

היסר 3256 גוים 1471 הלא 3808 יוכיח 3198 המלמד 3925 אדם 120 דעת 1847: 94:11 יהוה 3068
hayoser gouyim hala' youkiyacha; hamalamed 'adam da'at. Yahuah
**He that chastise the heathen not shall he correct? he that teach man knowledge *shall not he know*? Yahuah**

ידע 3045 מחשבות 4284 אדם 120 כי 3588 המה 1992 הבל 1892: 94:12 אשרי 835 הגבר 1397 אשר 834 תיסרנו 3256 יה 3050 ומתורתך 8451
yodea' machashabout 'adam; kiy hemah habel. 'ashrey hageber 'asher tayasrenu Yah; uamitourataka
**knows the thoughts of man that they *are* vanity Blessed *is* the man whom you chasten O Yah out of your law**

Ps 93:3 The floods have lifted up, O YHUH, the floods have lifted up their voice; the floods lift up their waves.4 YHUH on high is mightier than the noise of many waters, yea, than the mighty waves of the sea.5 Thy testimonies are very sure: holiness becometh your house, O YHUH, forever. **Ps** 94:1 O YHUH G-d, to whom vengeance belong; O G-d, to whom vengeance belong, show thyself.2 Lift up thyself, you judge of the earth: render a reward to the proud.3 YHUH, how long shall the wicked, how long shall the wicked triumph?4 How long shall they utter and speak hard things? and all the workers of iniquity boast themselves?5 They break in pieces your people, O YHUH, and afflict your heritage.6 They slay the widow and the stranger, and murder the fatherless.7 Yet they say, YHUH shall not see, neither shall the G-d of Jacob regard it.8 Understand, you brutish among the people: and you fools, when will you be wise?9 He that planted the ear, shall he not hear? he that formed the eye, shall he not see?10 He that chastiseth the heathen, shall not he correct? he that teach man knowledge, shall not he know?11 YHUH know the thoughts of man, that they are vanity.12 Blessed is the man whom you chastenest, O YHUH, and teachest him out of your law;

| תלמדנו 3925: | 94:13 להשקיט 8252 | לו 3807a | מימי 3117 | רע 7451 | עד 5704 | יכרה 3738 | לרשע 7563 |
|---|---|---|---|---|---|---|---|
| talamdenu. | lahashqiyt | lou' | miymey | ra'; | 'ad | yikareh | larasha' |
| **and teach him** | **That you may give rest** | **him** | **from the days of** | **adversity** | **until** | **be digged** | **for the wicked** |

| שחת 7845: | 94:14 כי 3588 | לא 3808 | יטש 5203 | יהוה 3068 | עמו 5971 | ונחלתו 5159 | לא 3808 | יעזב 5800: | 94:15 כי 3588 | עד 5704 |
|---|---|---|---|---|---|---|---|---|---|---|
| shachat. | kiy | la' | yitosh | Yahuah | 'amou; | uanachalatou, | la' | ya'azob. | kiy | 'ad |
| **the pit** | **For** | **not** | **will cast off** | **Yahuah** | **his people** | **his inheritance** | **neither** | **will he forsake** | **But** | **unto** |

| צדק 6664 | ישוב 7725 | משפט 4941 | ואחריו 310 | כל 3605 | ישרי 3477 | לב 3820: | 94:16 מי 4325 | יקום 6965 | לי 3807a | עם 5973 |
|---|---|---|---|---|---|---|---|---|---|---|
| tzedeq | yashub | mishapat; | ua'acharayu, | kal | yishrey | leb. | miy' | yaqum | liy | 'am |
| **righteousness** | **shall return** | **judgment** | **and shall follow it** | **all** | **the upright in** | **heart** | **Who** | **will rise up** | **for me** | **against** |

| מרעים 7489 | מי 4310 | יתיצב 3320 | לי 3807a | עם 5973 | פעלי 6466 | און 205: | 94:17 לולי 3884 | יהוה 3068 | עזרתה 5833 | לי 3807a |
|---|---|---|---|---|---|---|---|---|---|---|
| mare'aym; | miy' | yityatzeb | liy | 'am | po'aley | 'auen. | luley | Yahuah | 'azratah | liy; |
| **the evildoers?** | ***or* who** | **will stand up** | **for me** | **against** | **the workers of** | **iniquity?** | **Unless** | **Yahuah** | **help *had been*** | **my** |

| כמעט 4592 | שכנה 7931 | דומה 1745 | נפשי 5315: | 94:18 אם 518 | אמרתי 559 | מטה 4131 | רגלי 7272 | חסדך 2617 | יהוה 3068 | יסעדני 5582: 94:19 |
|---|---|---|---|---|---|---|---|---|---|---|
| kima'at | shakanah | dumah | napshiy. | 'am | 'amartiy | matah | ragliy; | chasdaka | Yahuah | yis'adeniy. |
| **almost** | **had dwelt in** | **silence** | **my soul** | **When** | **I said** | **slip** | **My foot** | **your mercy** | **O Yahuah** | **held me up** |

| ברב 7230 | שרעפי 8312 | בקרבי 7130 | תנחומיך 8575 | ישעשעו 8173 | נפשי 5315: | 94:20 היחברך 2266 |
|---|---|---|---|---|---|---|
| barob | sar'apay | baqirbiy; | tanchumeyka, | yasha'ash'au | napshiy. | hayachabraka |
| **In the multitude of** | **my thoughts** | **within me** | **your comforts** | **delight** | **my soul** | **Shall have fellowship with you** |

| כסא 3678 | הוות 1942 | יצר 3335 | עמל 5999 | עלי 5921 | חק 2706: | 94:21 יגודו 1413 | על 5921 | נפש 5315 |
|---|---|---|---|---|---|---|---|---|
| kisea' | hauout; | yotzer | 'amal | 'aley | choq. | yagoudu | 'al | nepesh |
| **the throne of** | **iniquity** | **which frameth** | **mischief** | **by** | **a law?** | **They gather themselves together** | **against** | **the soul of** |

| צדיק 6662 | ודם 1818 | נקי 5355 | ירשיעו 7561: | 94:22 ויהי 1961 | יהוה 3068 | לי 3807a | למשגב 4869 | ואלהי 430 | לצור 6697 |
|---|---|---|---|---|---|---|---|---|---|
| tzadiyq; | uadam | naqiy | yarshiy'au. | uayahiy | Yahuah | liy | lamisgab; | ua'alohay, | latzur |
| **the righteous** | **and blood** | ***the* innocent** | **condemn** | **But is** | **Yahuah** | **my** | **defence** | **and my Elohim** | ***is* the rock of** |

| מחסי 4268: | 94:23 וישב 7725 | עליהם 5921 | את 853 | אונם 205 | וברעתם 7451 | יצמיתם 6789 |
|---|---|---|---|---|---|---|
| machasiy. | uayasheb | 'aleyhem | 'at | 'aunam, | uabra'atam | yatzmiytem; |
| **my refuge** | **And he shall bring** | **upon them** | | **their own iniquity** | **and in their own wickedness** | **shall cut them off** |

| יצמיתם 6789 | יהוה 3068 | אלהינו 430: |
|---|---|---|
| yatzmiytem, | Yahuah | 'aloheynu. |
| **shall cut them off *yea*** | **Yahuah** | **our Elohim** |

| **Ps 95:1** לכו 1980 | נרננה 7442 | ליהוה 3068 | נריעה 7321 | לצור 6697 | ישענו 3468: | 95:2 נקדמה 6923 |
|---|---|---|---|---|---|---|
| laku | narannah | laYahuah; | nariy'ah, | latzur | yish'aenu. | naqadmah |
| **O come** | **let us sing** | **unto Yahuah** | **let us make a joyful noise** | **to the rock of** | **our salvation** | **Let us come before** |

| פניו 6440 | בתודה 8426 | בזמרות 2158 | נריע 7321 | לו 3807a: | 95:3 כי 3588 | אל 410 | גדול 1419 | יהוה 3068 | ומלך 4428 |
|---|---|---|---|---|---|---|---|---|---|
| panayu | batoudah; | bizmirout, | nariya' | lou'. | kiy | 'ael | gadoul | Yahuah; | uamelek |
| **his presence** | **with thanksgiving** | **with psalms *and*** | **make a joyful noise** | **unto him** | **For *is*** | ***a* El** | **great** | **Yahuah** | **and a King** |

Ps 94:13 That you may give him rest from the days of adversity, until the pit be digged for the wicked.14 For YHUH will not cast off his people, neither will he forsake his inheritance.15 But judgment shall return unto righteousness: and all the upright in heart shall follow it.16 Who will rise up for me against the evildoers? or who will stand up for me against the workers of iniquity?17 Unless YHUH had been my help, my soul had almost dwelt in silence.18 When I said, My foot slippeth; your mercy, O YHUH, held me up.19 In the multitude of my thoughts within me your comforts delight my soul.20 Shall the throne of iniquity have fellowship with you, which frameth mischief by a law?21 They gather themselves together against the soul of the righteous, and condemn the innocent blood.22 But YHUH is my defence; and my G-d is the rock of my refuge.23 And he shall bring upon them their own iniquity, and shall cut them off in their own wickedness; yea, YHUH our G-d shall cut them off. **Ps** 95:1 O come, let us sing unto YHUH: let us make a joyful noise to the rock of our salvation.2 Let us come before his presence with thanksgiving, and make a joyful noise unto him with psalms.3 For YHUH is a great G-d, and a great King above all gods.

גדול 1419 על 5921 כל 3605 אלהים 430: **95:4** אשר 834 בידו 3027 מחקרי 4278 ארץ 776 ותועפות 8443 הרים 2022
gadoul, 'al kal 'alohiym. 'asher bayadou mechqarey 'aretz; uatou'apout hariym
**great above all gods who In his hand *are* the deep places of the earth the strength of also the hills *is***

לו 3807a: **95:5** אשר 834 לו 3807a הים 3220 והוא 1931 עשהו 6213 ויבשת 3006 ידיו 3027 יצרו 3335: **95:6** באו 935 נשתחוה 7812
lou'. 'asher lou' hayam uahu'a 'asahu; uayabeshet, yadayu yatzaru. bo'au nishtachaueh
**his *is* who his The sea and he made it *land* and dry his hands formed *the* O come let us worship**

ונכרעה 3766 נברכה 1288 לפני 6440 יהוה 3068 עשנו 6213: **95:7** כי 3588 הוא 1931 אלהינו 430 ואנחנו 587 עם 5971
uanikra'ah; nibrakah, lipney Yahuah 'asenu. kiy hua' 'aloheynu, ua'anachnu 'am
**and bow down let us kneel before Yahuah our maker For he *is* our Elohim and we *are* the people of**

מרעיתו 4830 וצאן 6629 ידו 3027 היום 3117 אם 518 בקלו 6963 תשמעו 8085: **95:8** אל 408 תקשו 7185 לבבכם 3824
mar'aytou uatza'n yadou; hayoum, 'am baqolou tishma'au. 'al taqshu lababkem
**his pasture and the sheep of his hand To day if his voice you will hear not Harden your heart**

כמריבה 4808 כיום 3117 מסה 4531 במדבר 4057: **95:9** אשר 834 נסוני 5254 אבותיכם 1 בחנוני 974
kimariybah; kayoum masah, bamidbar. 'asher nisuniy abouteykem; bachanuniy,
**as in the provocation *and* as in the day of temptation in the wilderness When tempted me your fathers proved me**

גם 1571 ראו 7200 פעלי 6467: **95:10** ארבעים 705 שנה 8141 אקוט 6962 בדור 1755 ואמר 559 עם 5971 תעי 8582
gam ra'au pa'aliy. 'arba'aym shanah 'aqut badour, ua'amar, 'am to'aey
**though and saw my work Forty years *long* was I grieved with *this* generation and said *is* a people that do err**

לבב 3824 הם 1992 והם 1992 לא 3808 ידעו 3045 דרכי 1870: **95:11** אשר 834 נשבעתי 7650 באפי 639 אם 518
labab hem; uahem, la' yada'au darakay. 'asher nishba'atiy ba'apiy; 'am
**in their heart It and they not have known my ways *Unto* whom I sware in my wrath that not**

יבאון 935 אל 413 מנוחתי 4496:
yabo'aun, 'al manuchatiy.
**they should enter into my rest**

**Ps 96:1** שירו 7891 ליהוה 3068 שיר 7892 חדש 2319 שירו 7891 ליהוה 3068 כל 3605 הארץ 776: **96:2** שירו 7891 ליהוה 3068 ברכו 1288
shiyru laYahuah shiyr chadash; shiyru laYahuah kal ha'aretz. shiyru laYahuah baraku
**O sing unto Yahuah a song new sing unto Yahuah all the earth Sing unto Yahuah bless**

שמו 8034 בשרו 1319 מיום 3117 ליום 3117 ישועתו 3444: **96:3** ספרו 5608 בגוים 1471 כבודו 3519 בכל 3605 העמים 5971
shamou; basru miyoum layoum, yashu'atou. sapru bagouyim kaboudou; bakal ha'amiym,
**his name show forth from day to day his salvation Declare among the heathen his glory among all people**

נפלאותיו 6381: **96:4** כי 3588 גדול 1419 יהוה 3068 ומהלל 1984 מאד 3966 נורא 3372 הוא 1931 על 5921 כל 3605 אלהים 430: **96:5** כי 3588
nipla'autayu. kiy gadoul Yahuah uamahulal ma'ad; noura' hua', 'al kal 'alohiym. kiy
**his wonders For *is* great Yahuah and to be praised greatly *is* to be feared he above all gods For**

כל 3605 אלהי 430 העמים 5971 אלילים 457 ויהוה 3068 שמים 8064 עשה 6213: **96:6** הוד 1935 והדר 1926 לפניו 6440 עז 5797
kal 'alohey ha'amiym 'aliyliym; laYahuah shamayim 'asah. houd uahadar lapanayu; 'az
**all the gods of the nations *are* idols but Yahuah the heavens made Honour and majesty *are* before him strength**

Ps 95:4 In his hand are the deep places of the earth: the strength of the hills is his also.5 The sea is his, and he made it: and his hands formed the dry land.6 O come, let us worship and bow down: let us kneel before YHUH our maker.7 For he is our G-d; and we are the people of his pasture, and the sheep of his hand. To day if you will hear his voice,8 Harden not your heart, as in the provocation, and as in the day of temptation in the wilderness:9 When your fathers tempted me, proved me, and saw my work.10 Forty years long was I grieved with this generation, and said, It is a people that do err in their heart, and they have not known my ways:11 Unto whom I sware in my wrath that they should not enter into my rest. **Ps** 96:1 O sing unto YHUH a new song: sing unto YHUH, all the earth.2 Sing unto YHUH, bless his name; show forth his salvation from day today.3 Declare his glory among the heathen, his wonders among all people.4 For YHUH is great, and greatly to be praised: he is to be feared above all gods.5 For all the gods of the nations are idols: but YHUH made the heavens.6 Honour and majesty are before him: strength and beauty are in his sanctuary.

96:7
ותפארת 8597 במקדשו 4720: הבו 3051 ליהוה 3068 משפחות 4940 עמים 5971 הבו 3051 ליהוה 3068 כבוד 3519
uatip'aret, bamiqdashou. habu laYahuah mishpachout 'amiym; habu laYahuah kaboud
**and beauty *are* in his sanctuary Give unto Yahuah O you kindreds of the people give unto Yahuah glory**

96:8 96:9
ועז 5797: הבו 3051 ליהוה 3068 כבוד 3519 שמו 8034 שאו 5375 מנחה 4503 ובאו 935 לחצרותיו 2691:
ua'az. habu laYahuah kaboud shamou; sa'au minchah, uabo'au lachatzroutayu.
**and strength Give unto Yahuah the glory *due unto* his name bring an offering and come into his courts**

96:10
השתחוו 7812 ליהוה 3068 בהדרת 1927 קדש 6944 חילו 2342 מפניו 6440 כל 3605 הארץ 776: אמרו 559 בגוים 1471
hishtachauu laYahuah bahadrat qodesh; chiylu mipanayu, kal ha'aretz. 'amru bagouyim
**O worship unto Yahuah in the beauty of holiness fear before him all the earth Say among the heathen**

יהוה 3068 מלך 4427 אף 637 תכון 3559 תבל 8398 בל 1077 תמוט 4131 ידין 1777 עמים 5971
Yahuah malak, 'ap tikoun tebel bal timout; yadiyn 'amiym,
***that* Yahuah reigns also shall be established the world not *that* it shall be moved he shall judge the people**

96:11 96:12
במישרים 4339: ישמחו 8055 השמים 8064 ותגל 1523 הארץ 776 ירעם 7481 הים 3220 ומלאו 4393:
bameyshariym. yismachu hashamayim uatagel ha'aretz; yir'am hayam, uamlo'au.
**righteously Let rejoice the heavens and let be glad the earth let roar the sea and the fulness thereof**

96:13
יעלז 5937 שדי 7704 וכל 3605 אשר 834 בו 871a אז 227 ירננו 7442 כל 3605 עצי 6086 יער 3293: לפני 6440 יהוה 3068 כי 3588
ya'aloz shaday uakal 'asher bou; 'az yarannu, kal 'atzey ya'ar. lipney Yahuah kiy
**Let be joyful the field and all that *is* therein then shall rejoice all the trees of the wood Before Yahuah for**

בא 935 כי 3588 בא 935 לשפט 8199 הארץ 776 ישפט 8199 תבל 8398 בצדק 6664 ועמים 5971 באמונתו 530:
ba', kiy ba' lishpot ha'aretz yishpot tebel batzedeq; ua'amiym, be'amunatou.
**he comes for he comes to judge the earth he shall judge the world with righteousness and the people with his truth**

**Ps 97:1** 97:2
יהוה 3068 מלך 4427 תגל 1523 הארץ 776 ישמחו 8055 איים 339 רבים 7227: ענן 6051 וערפל 6205
Yahuah malak tagel ha'aretz; yismachu, 'ayiym rabiym. 'anan ua'arapel
**Yahuah reigns let rejoice the earth let be glad *thereof* isles the multitude of Clouds and darkness**

97:3
סביביו 5439 צדק 6664 ומשפט 4941 מכון 4349 כסאו 3678: אש 784 לפניו 6440 תלך 1980
sabiybayu; tzedeq uamishpat, makoun kis'au. 'aesh lapanayu telek;
***are* round about him righteousness and judgment *are* the habitation of his throne A fire before him goes**

97:4 97:5
ותלהט 3857 סביב 5439 צריו 6862: האירו 215 ברקיו 1300 תבל 8398 ראתה 7200 ותחל 2342 הארץ 776:
uatlahet sabiyb tzarayu. he'ayru baraqayu tebel; ra'atah uatachel ha'aretz.
**and burn up round about his enemies enlightened His lightnings the world saw and trembled the earth**

97:6
הרים 2022 כדונג 1749 נמסו 4549 מלפני 6440 יהוה 3068 מלפני 6440 אדון 136 כל 3605 הארץ 776: הגידו 5046
hariym, kadounag, namasu milipney Yahuah; milipney, 'adoun kal ha'aretz. higiydu
**The hills like wax melted at the presence of Yahuah at the presence of Adonai *of* whole the earth declare**

97:7
השמים 8064 צדקו 6664 וראו 7200 כל 3605 העמים 5971 כבודו 3519: יבשו 954 כל 3605 עבדי 5647 פסל 6459
hashamayim tzidqou; uar'au kal ha'amiym kaboudou. yeboshu kal 'abadey pesel,
**The heavens his righteousness and see all the people his glory Confounded be all they that serve graven images**

Ps 97:7 Give unto YHUH, O you kindreds of the people, give unto YHUH glory and strength.8 Give unto YHUH the glory due unto his name: bring an offering, and come into his courts.9 O worship YHUH in the beauty of holiness: fear before him, all the earth.10 Say among the heathen that YHUH reigned: the world also shall be established that it shall not be moved: he shall judge the people righteously.11 Let the heavens rejoice, and let the earth be glad; let the sea roar, and the fulness thereof.12 Let the field be joyful, and all that is therein: then shall all the trees of the wood rejoice 13 Before YHUH: for he cometh, for he cometh to judge the earth: he shall judge the world with righteousness, and the people with his truth. **Ps** 97:1 YHUH reigned; let the earth rejoice; let the multitude of isles be glad thereof.2 Clouds and darkness are round about him: righteousness and judgment are the habitation of his throne.3 A fire go before him, and burneth up his enemies round about.4 His lightnings enlightened the world: the earth saw, and trembled.5 The hills melted like wax at the presence of YHUH, at the presence of YHUH of the whole earth.6 The heavens declare his righteousness, and all the people see his glory.7 Confounded be all they that serve graven images, that boast themselves of idols: worship him, all you gods.

97:8
המתהללים 1984 באלילים 457 השתחוו 7812 לו 3807a כל 3605 אלהים 430: שמעה 8085 ותשמח 8055 ציון 6726 ותגלנה 1523
hamithalaliym ba'aliyliym; hishtachauu lou' kal 'alohiym. sham'ah uatismach tziyoun, uatagelanah
**that boast themselves of idols worship him all *you* gods heard and was glad Zion and rejoiced**

97:9
בנות 1323 יהודה 3063 למען 4616 משפטיך 4941 יהוה 3068: כי 3588 אתה 859 יהוה 3068 עליון 5945 על 5921 כל 3605 הארץ 776
banout yahudah; lama'an mishpateyka Yahuah. kiy 'atah Yahuah 'alyoun 'al kal ha'aretz;
**the daughters of Judah because of your judgments O Yahuah For you Yahuah *are* high above all the earth**

97:10
מאד 3966 נעלית 5927 על 5921 כל 3605 אלהים 430: אהבי 157 יהוה 3068 שנאו 8130 רע 7451 שמר 8104 נפשות 5315 חסידיו 2623
ma'ad na'aleyta, 'al kal 'alohiym. 'ahabey Yahuah sin'au ra' shomer napshout chasiydayu;
**far you are exalted above all gods You that love Yahuah hate evil he preserve the souls of his saints**

97:11
מיד 3027 רשעים 7563 יצילם 5337: אור 216 זרע 2232 לצדיק 6662 ולישרי 3477 לב 3820
miyad rasha'aym, yatziylem. 'aur zarua' latzadiyq; ualyishrey leb
**out of the hand of the wicked he deliver them Light is sown for the righteous and for the upright in heart**

97:12
שמחה 8057: שמחו 8055 צדיקים 6662 ביהוה 3068 והודו 3034 לזכר 2143 קדשו 6944:
simchah. simchu tzadiyqiym baYahuah; uahoudu, lazeker qadashou.
**gladness Rejoice you righteous in Yahuah and give thanks at the remembrance of his holiness**

Ps 98:1
מזמור 4210 שירו 7891 ליהוה 3068 שיר 7892 חדש 2319 כי 3588 נפלאות 6381 עשה 6213 הושיעה 3467 לו 3807a
mizmour shiyru laYahuah shiyr chadash kiy nipla'aut 'asah; houshiy'ah lou'
**A Psalm O sing unto Yahuah a song new for marvellous things he has done has gotten the victory him**

98:2
ימינו 3225 וזרוע 2220 קדשו 6944: הודיע 3045 יהוה 3068 ישועתו 3444 לעיני 5869 הגוים 1471
yamiynou, uazaoua' qadashou. houdiya' Yahuah yashu'atou; la'aeyney hagouyim,
**his right hand and arm his holy has made known Yahuah his salvation in the sight of the heathen**

98:3
גלה 1540 צדקתו 6666: זכר 2142 חסדו 2617 ואמונתו 530 לבית 1004 ישראל 3478
gilah tzidqatou. zakar chasdou ua'amunatou labeyt yisra'ael
**has he openly showed his righteousness He has remembered his mercy and his truth toward the house of Israel**

98:4
ראו 7200 כל 3605 אפסי 657 ארץ 776 את 853 ישועת 3444 אלהינו 430: הריעו 7321 ליהוה 3068 כל 3605
ra'au kal 'apsey 'aretz; 'aet, yashu'at 'aloheynu. hariy'au laYahuah kal
**have seen all the ends of the earth the salvation of our Elohim Make a joyful noise unto Yahuah all**

98:5
הארץ 776 פצחו 6476 ורננו 7442 וזמרו 2167: זמרו 2167 ליהוה 3068 בכנור 3658 בכנור 3658
ha'aretz; pitzchu uarannu uazameru. zamru laYahuah bakinour; bakinour,
**the earth make a loud noise and rejoice and sing praise Sing praises unto Yahuah with the harp with the harp**

98:6 98:7
וקול 6963 זמרה 2172: בחצצרות 2689 וקול 6963 שופר 7782 הריעו 7321 לפני 6440 המלך 4428 יהוה 3068:
uaqoul zimrah. bachatzotzarout uaqoul shoupar; hariy'au, lipney hamelek Yahuah.
**and the voice of a psalm With trumpets and sound of cornet make a joyful noise before the King Yahuah**

98:8
ירעם 7481 הים 3220 ומלאו 4393 תבל 8398 וישבי 3427 בה 871a: נהרות 5104 ימחאו 4222 כף 3709
yir'am hayam uamlo'au; tebel, uayoshabey bah. naharout yimcha'au kap;
**Let roar the sea and the fulness thereof the world and they that dwell therein the floods Let clap *their* hands**

Ps 97:8 Zion heard, and was glad; and the daughters of Judah rejoiced because of your judgments, O YHUH.9 For you, YHUH, are high above all the earth: you are exalted far above all gods.10 You that love YHUH, hate evil: he preserveth the souls of his saints; he delivereth them out of the hand of the wicked.11 Light is sown for the righteous, and gladness for the upright in heart.12 Rejoice in YHUH, you righteous; and give thanks at the remembrance of his holiness. **Ps** 98:1 A Psalm. O sing unto YHUH a new song; for he has done marvellous things: his right hand, and his holy arm, has gotten him the victory.2 YHUH has made known his salvation: his righteousness has he openly showed in the sight of the heathen.3 He has remembered his mercy and his truth toward the house of Israel: all the ends of the earth have seen the salvation of our G-d.4 Make a joyful noise unto YHUH, all the earth: make a loud noise, and rejoice, and sing praise.5 Sing unto YHUH with the harp; with the harp, and the voice of a psalm.6 With trumpets and sound of cornet make a joyful noise before YHUH, the King.7 Let the sea roar, and the fulness thereof; the world, and they that dwell therein.8 Let the floods clap their hands:

98:9

3162 יחד 2022 הרים 7442: ירננו 6440 לפני 3068 יהוה 3588 כי 935 בא 8199 לשפט 776 הארץ 8199 ישפט 8398 תבל
yachad, hariym yaranenu. lipney Yahuah kiy ba' lishpot ha'aretz yishpot tebel
**together the hills let be joyful Before Yahuah for he comes to judge the earth shall he judge the world**

6664 בצדק 5971 ועמים 4339: במישרים
batzedeq; ua'amiym, bameyshariym.
**with righteousness and the people with equity**

**Ps 99:1** 99:2

3068 יהוה 4427 מלך 7264 ירגזו 5971 עמים 3427 ישב 3742 כרובים 5120 תנוט 776: הארץ 3068 יהוה 6726 בציון
Yahuah malak yirgazu 'amiym; yosheb karubiym, tanut ha'aretz. Yahuah batziyoun
**Yahuah reigns let tremble the people he sit *between* the cherubims let be moved the earth Yahuah in Zion**

99:3 99:4

1419 גדול 7311 ורם 1931 הוא 5921 על 3605 כל 5971: העמים 3034 יודו 8034 שמך 1419 גדול 3372 ונורא 6918 קדוש 1931: הוא
gadoul; uaram hua', 'al kal ha'amiym. youdu shimka gadoul uanoura', qadoush hua'.
***is* great and high he *is* above all the people Let them praise your name great and terrible *is* holy *for* it**

5797 ועז 4428 מלך 4941 משפט 157 אהב 859 אתה 3559 כוננת 4339 מישרים 4941 משפט 6666 וצדקה 3290 ביעקב 859 אתה
ua'az melek mishapat 'aheb 'atah kounanta meyshariym; mishapat uatzdaqah, baya'aqob 'atah
***The* strength also king's judgment love you do establish equity judgment and righteousness in Jacob you**

99:5 99:6

6213: עשית 7311 רוממו 3068 יהוה 430 אלהינו 7812 והשתחוו 1916 להדם 7272 רגליו 6918 קדוש 1931: הוא 4872 משה 175 ואהרן
'ashiyta. roumamu Yahuah 'aloheynu, uahishtachauu lahadom raglayu, qadoush hua'. mosheh ua'aharon
**executest Exalt you Yahuah our Elohim and worship at stool his foot *is* holy *for* he Moses and Aaron**

99:7

3548 בכהניו 8050 ושמואל 7121 בקראי 8034 שמו 7121 קראים 413 אל 3068 יהוה 1931 והוא 6030: יענם
bakohanayu, uashamu'ael baqora'aey shamou; qora'ym 'al Yahuah uahu'a ya'anem.
**among his priests and Samuel among them that call upon his name they called upon Yahuah and he answered them**

99:8

5982 בעמוד 6051 ענן 1696 ידבר 413 אליהם 8104 שמרו 5713 עדתיו 2706 וחק 5414 נתן 3807a: למו 3069 יהוה
ba'amud 'anan yadaber 'aleyhem; shamaru 'aedotayu, uachoq natan lamou. Yahuah
**in pillar *the* cloudy He spoke unto them they kept his testimonies and the ordinance *that* he gave them Yahuah**

430 אלהינו 859 אתה 6030 עניתם 410 אל 5375 נשא 1961 היית 1992 להם 5359 ונקם 5921 על
'aloheynu 'atah 'aniytam 'al nosea' hayiyta lahem; uanoqem, 'al
**our Elohim You answered them *a* El that forgave you were them though you took vengeance of**

99:9

5949: עלילותם 7311 רוממו 3068 יהוה 430 אלהינו 7812 והשתחוו 2022 להר 6944 קדשו 3588 כי 6918 קדוש 3068 יהוה 430: אלהינו
aliyloutam. roumamu Yahuah 'aloheynu, uahishtachauu lahar qadashou; kiy qadoush, Yahuah 'aloheynu.
**their inventions Exalt Yahuah our Elohim and worship at hill his holy for *is* holy Yahuah our Elohim**

**Ps 100:1** 100:2

4210 מזמור 8426 לתודה 7321 הריעו 3068 ליהוה 3605 כל 776: הארץ 5647 עבדו 853 את 3068 יהוה 8057 בשמחה
mizmour latoudah; hariy'au laYahuah kal ha'aretz. 'abdu 'at Yahuah basimchah;
**A Psalm of praise Make a joyful noise unto Yahuah all you lands Serve Yahuah with gladness**

100:3

935 באו 6440 לפניו 6440: ברננה 3045 דעו 3588 כי 3068 יהוה 1931 הוא 430 אלהים 1931 הוא 6213 עשנו 3808 ולא
bo'au lapanayu, birnanah. da'au, kiy Yahuah hua' 'alohiym hua' 'asanu uala'
**come before his presence with singing Know you that Yahuah he *is* Elohim *it is* he *that* has made us and not**

Ps 99:8 let the hills be joyful together 9 Before YHUH; for he cometh to judge the earth: with righteousness shall he judge the world, and the people with equity. **Ps** 99:1 YHUH reigned; let the people tremble: he sitteth between the cherubims; let the earth be moved.2 YHUH is great in Zion; and he is high above all the people.3 Let them praise your great and terrible name; for it is holy.4 The king's strength also love judgment; you dost establish equity, you executest judgment and righteousness in Jacob.5 Exalt you YHUH our G-d, and worship at his footstool; for he is holy.6 Moses and Aaron among his priests, and Samuel among them that call upon his name; they called upon YHUH, and he answered them.7 He spoke unto them in the cloudy pillar: they kept his testimonies, and the ordinance that he gave them.8 Thou answeredst them, O YHUH our G-d: you were a G-d that forgavest them, though you tookest vengeance of their inventions.9 Exalt YHUH our G-d, and worship at his holy hill; for YHUH our G-d is holy. **Ps** 100:1 A Psalm of praise. Make a joyful noise unto YHUH, all you lands.2 Serve YHUH with gladness: come before his presence with singing.3 Know you that YHUH he is G-d: it is he that has made us, and not we ourselves; we are his people, and the sheep of his pasture.

100:4
אנחנו 587 | עמו 5971 | וצאן 6629 | מרעיתו 4830: | באו 935 | שעריו 8179 | בתודה 8426 | חצרתיו 2691
'anachnu; 'amou, uatza'n mar'aytou. bo'au sha'arayu batoudah, chatzerotayu
**we ourselves *we are* his people and the sheep of his pasture Enter into his gates with thanksgiving *and into* his courts**

100:5
בתהלה 8416 | הודו 3034 | לו 3807a | ברכו 1288 | שמו 8034: | כי 3588 | טוב 2896 | יהוה 3068 | לעולם 5769 | חסדו 2617 | ועד 5704 | דר 1755
bitahilah; hodu lou', baraku shamou. kiy toub Yahuah la'aulam chasdou; ua'ad dor
**with praise be thankful unto him *and* bless his name For *is* good Yahuah *is* everlasting his mercy and to all**

ודר 1755 | אמונתו 530:
uador, 'amunatou.
**generations his truth *endures***

Ps 101:1
לדוד 1732 | מזמור 4210 | חסד 2617 | ומשפט 4941 | אשירה 7891 | לך 3807a | יהוה 3068 | אזמרה 2167:
ladauid, mizmour chesed uamishpat 'ashiyrah; laka Yahuah 'azamerah.
**of David A Psalm mercy and judgment I will sing of unto you O Yahuah will I sing**

101:2
אשכילה 7919 | בדרך 1870 | תמים 8549 | מתי 4970 | תבוא 935 | אלי 413 | אתהלך 1980 | בתם 8537 | לבבי 3824 | בקרב 7130
'askiylah baderek tamiym, matay tabou'a 'aelay; 'athalek batam lababiy, baqereb
**I will behave myself wisely in a way perfect O when will you come unto me? I will walk with a perfect heart within**

ביתי 1004: | לא 3808 | אשית 7896 | לנגד 5048 | עיני 5869 | דבר 1697 | בליעל 1100 | עשה 6213 | סטים 7750 | שנאתי 8130 | לא 3808
beytiy. la' 'ashiyt laneged 'aeynay, dabar baliya'al 'asoh setiym sanea'tiy; la'
**my house no I will set before mine eyes thing wicked the work of them that turn aside I hate not**

101:3

ידבק 1692 | בי 871a: | לבב 3824 | עקש 6141 | יסור 5493 | ממני 4480 | רע 7451 | לא 3808 | אדע 3045: | מלושני 3960
yidbaq biy. leabab 'aqesh yasur mimeniy; ra', la' 'aeda. melousheniy
***it* shall cleave to me A heart froward shall depart from me a wicked *person* not I will know Whoso slander**

101:4

101:5

בסתר 5643 | רעהו 7453 | אותו 853 | אצמית 6789 | גבה 1362 | עינים 5869 | ורחב 7342 | לבב 3824 | אתו 853 | לא 3808 | אוכל 3201:
baseter re'aehu 'autou 'atzmiyt gabah 'aeynayim uarchab labab; 'atou, la' 'aukal.
**privily his neighbour him will I cut off *that has* an high look and a proud heart him not will I suffer**

101:6
עיני 5869 | בנאמני 539 | ארץ 776 | לשבת 3427 | עמדי 5978 | הלך 1980 | בדרך 1870 | תמים 8549 | הוא 1931
'aeynay bane'amney 'aretz lashabet 'amadiy halok baderek tamiym; hua',
**Mine eyes *shall be* upon the faithful of the land that they may dwell with me he that walk in a way perfect he**

ישרתני 8334: | לא 3808 | ישב 3427 | בקרב 7130 | ביתי 1004 | עשה 6213 | רמיה 7423 | דבר 1696 | שקרים 8267 | לא 3808 | יכון 3559
yasharateniy. la' yesheb baqereb beytiy 'aseh ramiyah dober shaqariym; la' yikoun,
**shall serve me not shall dwell within my house He that work deceit he that tell lies not shall tarry**

101:7

לנגד 5048 | עיני 5869: | לבקרים 1242 | אצמית 6789 | כל 3605 | רשעי 7563 | ארץ 776 | להכרית 3772 | מעיר 5892 | יהוה 3068
laneged 'aeynay. labaqariym, 'atzmiyt kal rish'aey 'aretz; lahakriyt me'ayr Yahuah
**in my sight early I will destroy all the wicked of the land that I may cut off from the city of Yahuah**

101:8

כל 3605 | פעלי 6466 | און 205:
kal po'aley 'auen.
**all doers wicked**

Ps 100:4 Enter into his gates with thanksgiving, and into his courts with praise: be thankful unto him, and bless his name.5 For YHUH is good; his mercy is everlasting; and his truth endureth to all generations. **Ps** 101:1 A Psalm of David. I will sing of mercy and judgment: unto you, O YHUH, will I sing.2 I will behave myself wisely in a perfect way. O when will you come unto me? I will walk within my house with a perfect heart.3 I will set no wicked thing before mine eyes: I hate the work of them that turn aside; it shall not cleave to me.4 A froward heart shall depart from me: I will not know a wicked person.5 Whoso privily slandereth his neighbor, him will I cut off: him that has an high look and a proud heart will not I suffer.6 Mine eyes shall be upon the faithful of the land, that they may dwell with me: he that walk in a perfect way, he shall serve me.7 He that worketh deceit shall not dwell within my house: he that tell lies shall not tarry in my sight.8 I will early destroy all the wicked of the land; that I may cut off all wicked doers from the city of YHUH.

**Ps 102:1**
תפלה 8605 לעני 6041 כי 3588 יעטף 5848 ולפני 6440 יהוה 3068 ישפך 8210 שיחו 7879: יהוה 3068 שמעה 8085
tapilah la'aniy kiy ya'atop; ualipaney Yahuah yishpok siychou. Yahuah shim'ah
**A Prayer of the afflicted when he is overwhelmed and before Yahuah pour out his complaint O Yahuah Hear**

תפלתי 8605 ושועתי 7775 אליך 413 תבוא 935: **102:2** אל 408 תסתר 5641 פניך 6440 ממני 4480 ביום 3117 צר 6862 לי 3807a
tapilatiy; uashaua'atiy, 'aeleyka tabou'a. 'al taster paneyka mimeniy bayoum tzar liy
**my prayer and let my cry unto you let come not Hide your face from me in the day *am in* trouble *when* I**

הטה 5186 אלי 413 אזנך 241 ביום 3117 אקרא 7121 מהר 4118 ענני 6030: **102:3** כי 3588 כלו 3615 בעשן 6227 ימי 3117
hateh 'aelay 'azeneka; bayoum 'aqraa', maher 'aneniy. kiy kalu ba'ashan yamay;
**incline unto me your ear in the day *when* I call speedily answer me For are consumed in smoke my days**

ועצמותי 6106 כמו 3644 קד 4168 נחרו 2787: **102:4** הוכה 5221 כעשב 6212 ויבש 3001 לבי 3820 כי 3588 שכחתי 7911 מאכל 398
ua'atzmoutay, kamou qed nicharu. hukah ka'aeseb uayibash libiy; kiy shakachtiy, me'akol
**and my bones like are burned as an hearth is smitten like grass and withered My heart so that I forget to eat**

לחמי 3899: **102:5** מקול 6963 אנחתי 585 דבקה 1692 עצמי 6106 לבשרי 1320: **102:6** דמיתי 1819 לקאת 6893
lachmiy. miqoul 'anchatiy; dabqah 'atzmiy, libsariy. damiytiy liq'at
**my bread By reason of the voice of my groaning cleave my bones to my skin I am like a pelican of**

מדבר 4057 הייתי 1961 ככוס 3563 חרבות 2723: **102:7** שקדתי 8245 ואהיה 1961 כצפור 6833 בודד 909 על 5921 גג 1406: **102:8**
midbar; hayiytiy, kakous charabout. shaqadtiy ua'ahayeh; katzipour, bouded 'al gag.
**the wilderness I am like an owl of the desert I watch and am as a sparrow alone upon the house top**

כל 3605 היום 3117 חרפוני 2778 אויבי 341 מהוללי 1984 בי 871a נשבעו 7650: **102:9** כי 3588 אפר 665
kal hayoum cherapuniy 'auyabay; mahoulalay, biy nishba'au. kiy 'aeper
**all the day reproach me Mine enemies *and* they that are mad against me are sworn against me For ashes**

כלחם 3899 אכלתי 398 ושקוי 8249 בבכי 1065 מסכתי 4537: **102:10** מפני 6440 זעמך 2195 וקצפך 7110 כי 3588
kalechem 'akalatiy; uashiquay, bibkiy masakatiy. mipaney za'amaka uaqitzpeka; kiy
**like bread I have eaten and my drink with weeping mingled Because of your indignation and your wrath for**

נשאתני 5375 ותשליכני 7993: **102:11** ימי 3117 כצל 6738 נטוי 5186 ואני 589 כעשב 6212
nasa'taniy, uatashliykeniy. yamay katzel natuy; ua'aniy, ka'aeseb
**you have lifted me up and cast me down My days *are* like a shadow that declineth and I like grass**

איבש 3001: **102:12** ואתה 859 יהוה 3068 לעולם 5769 תשב 3427 וזכרך 2143 לדר 1755 ודר 1755: **102:13** אתה 859
'aybash. ua'atah Yahuah la'aulam tesheb; uazikraka, lador uador. 'atah
***am* withered But you O Yahuah for ever shall endure and your remembrance unto all generations You**

תקום 6965 תרחם 7355 ציון 6726 כי 3588 עת 6256 לחננה 2603 כי 3588 בא 935 מועד 4150: **102:14** כי 3588
taqum tarachem tziyoun; kiy 'at lachennah, kiy ba' mou'aed. kiy
**shall arise *and* have mercy upon Zion for the time to favor her yea is come the set time For**

רצו 7521 עבדיך 5650 את 853 אבניה 68 ואת 853 עפרה 6083 יחננו 2603: **102:15** וייראו 3372 גוים 1471 את 853
ratzu 'abadeyka 'at 'abaneyha; ua'at 'aparah yachonenu. uayiyra'au gouyim 'at
**take pleasure in your servants her stones *and* the dust thereof favor So shall fear the heathen**

**Ps** 102:1 A Prayer of the afflicted, when he is overwhelmed, and poureth out his complaint before the Adonai. Hear my prayer, O YHUH, and let my cry come unto you.2 Hide not your face from me in the day when I am in trouble; incline your ear unto me: in the day when I call answer me speedily.3 For my days are consumed like smoke, and my bones are burned as an hearth.4 My heart is smitten, and withered like grass; so that I forget to eat my bread.5 By reason of the voice of my groaning my bones cleave to my skin.6 I am like a pelican of the wilderness: I am like an owl of the desert.7 I watch, and am as a sparrow alone upon the house top.8 Mine enemies reproach me all the day; and they that are mad against me are sworn against me.9 For I have eaten ashes like bread, and mingled my drink with weeping,10 Because of your indignation and your wrath: for you have lifted me up, and cast me down.11 My days are like a shadow that declineth; and I am withered like grass.12 But you, O YHUH, shall endure forever; and your remembrance unto all generations.13 Thou shall arise, and have mercy upon Zion: for the time to favor her, yea, the set time, is come.14 For your servants take pleasure in her stones, and favor the dust thereof.15 So the heathen shall fear the name of YHUH, and all the kings of the earth your glory.

שם 8034 | יהוה 3068 | וכל 3605 | מלכי 4428 | הארץ 776 | את 853 | כבודך 3519: | **102:16** | כי 3588 | בנה 1129 | יהוה 3068 | ציון 6726
shem | Yahuah; | uakal | malkey | ha'aretz, | 'at | kaboudeka. | | kiy | banah | Yahuah | tziyoun;
**the name of** | **Yahuah** | **and all** | **the kings of** | **the earth** | | **your glory** | | **When** | **shall build up** | **Yahuah** | **Zion**

נראה 7200 | בכבודו 3519: | **102:17** | פנה 6437 | אל 413 | תפלת 8605 | הערער 6199 | ולא 3808 | בזה 959 | את 853
nir'ah, | bikboudou. | | panah | 'al | tapilat | ha'ar'ar; | uala' | bazah, | 'at
**he shall appear** | **in his glory** | | **He will regard** | **to** | **the prayer of** | **the destitute** | **and not** | **despise** |

תפלתם 8605: | **102:18** | תכתב 3789 | זאת 2063 | לדור 1755 | אחרון 314 | ועם 5971 | נברא 1254 | יהלל 1984
tapilatam. | | tikateb | za't | ladour | 'acharoun; | ua'am | nibraa', | yahalel
**their prayer** | | **shall be written** | **This** | **for the generation** | **to come** | **and the people** | **which shall be created** | **shall praise**

יה 3050: | **102:19** | כי 3588 | השקיף 8259 | ממרום 4791 | קדשו 6944 | יהוה 3068 | משמים 8064 | אל 413 | ארץ 776
Yah. | | kiy | hishqiyp | mimaroum | qadashou; | Yahuah | mishamayim | 'al | 'aretz
**Yah** | | **For** | **he has looked down** | **from the height of** | **his sanctuary** | **Yahuah** | **from heaven** | **upon** | **the earth**

הביט 5027: | **102:20** | לשמע 8085 | אנקת 603 | אסיר 615 | לפתח 6605 | בני 1121 | תמותה 8546: | **102:21** | לספר 5608
hibiyt. | | lishmoa' | 'anqat | 'asiyr; | lapateach, | baney | tamutah. | | lasaper
**did behold** | | **To hear** | **the groaning of** | **the prisoner** | **to loose** | **those that are appointed to** | **death** | | **To declare**

בציון 6726 | שם 8034 | יהוה 3068 | ותהלתו 8416 | בירושלם 3389: | **102:22** | בהקבץ 6908 | עמים 5971 | יחדו 3162
batziyoun | shem | Yahuah; | uatahilatou, | biyarushalaim. | | bahiqabetz | 'amiym | yachdau;
**in Zion** | **the name of** | **Yahuah** | **and his praise** | **in Jerusalem** | | **When are gathered** | **the people** | **together**

וממלכות 4467 | לעבד 5647 | את 853 | יהוה 3068: | **102:23** | ענה 6031 | בדרך 1870 | כחו 3581 | קצר 7114 | ימי 3117: | **102:24** | אמר 559
uamamlakout, | la'abod | 'at | Yahuah. | | 'anah | baderek | kochou | qitzar | yamay. | | 'amar,
**and the kingdoms** | **to serve** | | **Yahuah** | | **He weakened** | **in the way** | **my strength** | **he shortened** | **my days** | | **I said**

אלי 410 | אל 408 | תעלני 5927 | בחצי 2677 | ימי 3117 | בדור 1755 | דורים 1755 | שנותיך 8141: | **102:25** | לפנים 6440 | הארץ 776
'aeliy, | 'al | ta'aleniy | bachatziy | yamay; | badour | douriym | shanouteyka. | | lapaniym | ha'aretz
**O my El** | **not** | **take me away** | **in the midst of** | **my days** | ***are* throughout all** | **generations** | **your years** | | **Of old** | **the earth**

יסדת 3245 | ומעשה 4639 | ידיך 3027 | שמים 8064: | **102:26** | המה 1992 | יאבדו 6 | ואתה 859
yasadta; | uama'aseh | yadeyka | shamayim. | | hemah | ya'bedu | ua'atah
**have you laid the foundation of** | **and the work of** | **your hands** | **and the heavens *are*** | | **They** | **shall perish** | **but you**

תעמד 5975 | וכלם 3605 | כבגד 899 | יבלו 1086 | כלבוש 3830 | תחליפם 2498
ta'amod | uakulam | kabeged | yiblu; | kalabush | tachaliypem
**shall endure** | **yea all of them** | **like a garment** | **shall wax old** | **as a vesture** | **shall you change them**

ויחלפו 2498: | **102:27** | ואתה 859 | הוא 1931 | ושנותיך 8141 | לא 3808 | יתמו 8552: | **102:28** | בני 1121
uayachalopu. | | ua'atah | hua'; | ushnouteyka, | la' | yitamu. | | baney
**and they shall be changed** | | **But you *are*** | **the same** | **and your years** | **no** | **shall have end** | | **The children of**

עבדיך 5650 | ישכונו 7931 | וזרעם 2233 | לפניך 6440 | יכון 3559:
'abadeyka | yishkounu; | uazar'am, | lapaneyka | yikoun.
**your servants** | **shall continue** | **and their seed** | **before you** | **shall be established**

Ps 102:16 When YHUH shall build up Zion, he shall appear in his glory.17 He will regard the prayer of the destitute, and not despise their prayer.18 This shall be written for the generation to come: and the people which shall be created shall praise YHUH.19 For he has looked down from the height of his sanctuary; from heaven did YHUH behold the earth;20 To hear the groaning of the prisoner; to loose those that are appointed to death;21 To declare the name of YHUH in Zion, and his praise in Jerusalem;22 When the people are gathered together, and the kingdoms, to serve YHUH.23 He weakened my strength in the way; he shortened my days.24 I said, O my G-d, take me not away in the midst of my days: your years are throughout all generations.25 Of old have you laid the foundation of the earth: and the heavens are the work of your hands.26 They shall perish, but you shall endure: yea, all of them shall wax old like a garment; as a vesture shall you change them, and they shall be changed:27 But you are the same, and your years shall have no end.28 The children of your servants shall continue, and their seed shall be established before you.

**Ps 103:1** ... **103:2**
לדוד 1732 ברכי 1288 נפשי 5315 את 853 יהוה 3068 וכל 3605 קרבי 7130 את 853 שם 8034 קדשו 6944:
ladauid barakiy napshiy 'at Yahuah; uakal qarabay, 'at shem qadashou.
***A Psalm* of David Bless O my soul Yahuah and all that is within me name *bless* his holy**

**103:3**
ברכי 1288 נפשי 5315 את 853 יהוה 3068 ואל 408 תשכחי 7911 כל 3605 גמוליו 1576: הסלח 5545 לכל 3605 עונכי 5771 הרפא 7495
barakiy napshiy 'at Yahuah; ua'al tishkachiy, kal gamulayu. hasoleach lakal 'auonekiy; haropea',
**Bless O my soul Yahuah and not forget all his benefits Who forgives all your iniquities who heals**

**103:4**
לכל 3605 תחלאיכי 8463: הגואל 1350 משחת 7845 חייכי 2416 המעטרכי 5849 חסד 2617
lakal tachalu'ayakiy. hagou'ael mishachat chayayakiy; hama'atrekiy, chesed
**all your diseases Who redeem from destruction your life who crowns you with lovingkindness**

**103:5** **103:6**
ורחמים 7356: המשביע 7646 בטוב 2896 עדיך 5716 תתחדש 2318 כנשר 5404 נעוריכי 5271:
uarachamiym. hamasabiya' batoub 'adyek; titchadesh kanesher na'urayakiy.
**and tender mercies Who satisfies with good *things so that* your mouth is renewed like the eagle's your youth**

**103:7**
עשה 6213 צדקות 6666 יהוה 3068 ומשפטים 4941 לכל 3605 עשוקים 6231: יודיע 3045 דרכיו 1870 למשה 4872
'aseh tzadaqout Yahuah; uamishpatiym, lakal 'ashuqiym. youdiya' darakayu lamosheh;
**execute righteousness Yahuah and judgment for all that are oppressed He made known his ways unto Moses**

**103:8**
לבני 1121 ישראל 3478 עלילותיו 5949: רחום 7349 וחנון 2587 יהוה 3068 ארך 750 אפים 639 ורב 7227
libney yisra'ael, aliyloutayu. rachum uachanun Yahuah; 'arek 'apayim uarab
**unto the children of Israel his acts *is* merciful and gracious Yahuah slow to anger and plenteous in**

**103:9** **103:10**
חסד 2617: לא 3808 לנצח 5331 יריב 7378 ולא 3808 לעולם 5769 יטור 5201: לא 3808 כחטאינו 2399 עשה 6213
chased. la' lanetzach yariyb; uala' la'aulam yitour. la' kachata'aeynu 'asah
**mercy not always He will chide neither *his anger* for ever will he keep not after our sins He has dealt**

**103:11**
לנו 3807a ולא 3808 כעונתינו 5771 גמל 1580 עלינו 5921: כי 3588 כגבה 1361 שמים 8064 על 5921 הארץ 776 גבר 1396
lanu; uala' ka'auonoteynu, gamal 'aleynu. kiy kigboah shamayim 'al ha'aretz; gabar
**with us nor according to our iniquities rewarded us For as is high the heaven above the earth *so* great is**

**103:12**
חסדו 2617 על 5921 יראיו 3373: כרחק 7368 מזרח 4217 ממערב 4628 הרחיק 7368 ממנו 4480 את 853
chasdou, 'al yare'ayu. kirchoq mizrach mima'arab; hirchiyq mimenu, 'at
**his mercy toward them that fear him As far as the east *is* from the west *so* far has he removed from us**

**103:13** **103:14**
פשעינו 6588: כרחם 7355 אב 1 על 5921 בנים 1121 רחם 7355 יהוה 3068 על 5921 יראיו 3373:
pasha'aeynu. karachem 'ab 'al baniym; richam Yahuah 'al yare'ayu.
**our transgressions Like as pities a father *his* on children pities *so* Yahuah that them that fear him**

**103:15**
כי 3588 הוא 1931 ידע 3045 יצרנו 3336 זכור 2142 כי 3588 עפר 6083 אנחנו 587: אנוש 582 כחציר 2682 ימיו 3117 כציץ 6731
kiy hua' yada' yitzrenu; zakur, kiy 'apar 'anachanu. 'anoush kechatziyr yamayu; katziytz
**For he knows our frame he remembers that *are* dust we *as for* man *are* grass his days as a flower of**

**103:16**
השדה 7704 כן 3651 יציץ 6692: כי 3588 רוח 7307 עברה 5674 בו 871a ואיננו 369 ולא 3808 יכירנו 5234 עוד 5750
hasadeh, ken yatziytz. kiy ruach 'abarah bou ua'aeynenu; uala' yakiyrenu 'aud
**the field so he flourish For the wind passes over it and it is gone and no shall know it more**

**Ps** 103:1 A Psalm of David. Bless YHUH, O my soul: and all that is within me, bless his holy name.2 Bless YHUH, O my soul, and forget not all his benefits:3 Who forgiveth all your iniquities; who healeth all your diseases;4 Who redeemeth your life from destruction; who crowneth you with lovingkindness and tender mercies;5 Who satisfieth your mouth with good things; so that your youth is renewed like the eagle's.6 YHUH executeth righteousness and judgment for all that are oppressed.7 He made known his ways unto Moses, his acts unto the children of Israel.8 YHUH is merciful and gracious, slow to anger, and plenteous in mercy.9 He will not always chide: neither will he keep his anger forever.10 He has not dealt with us after our sins; nor rewarded us according to our iniquities.11 For as the heaven is high above the earth, so great is his mercy toward them that fear him.12 As far as the east is from the west, so far has he removed our transgressions from us.13 Like as a father pitieth his children, so YHUH pitieth them that fear him.14 For he know our frame; he remembereth that we are dust.15 As for man, his days are as grass: as a flower of the field, so he flourisheth.16 For the wind pass over it, and it is gone; and the place thereof shall know it no more.

103:17

מקומו 4725: וחסד 2617 יהוה 3068 מעולם 5769 ועד 5704 עולם 5769 על 5921 יראיו 3373
maqoumou. uachesed Yahuah me'aulam ua'ad 'aulam 'al yare'ayu;
**the place thereof But the mercy of Yahuah *is* from everlasting to everlasting upon them that fear him**

103:18

וצדקתו 6666 לבני 1121 בנים 1121: לשמרי 8104 בריתו 1285 ולזכרי 2142
uatzidqatou, libney baniym. lashomarey bariytou; ualzokarey
**and his righteousness unto children's children To such as keep his covenant and to those that remember**

103:19

פקדיו 6490 לעשותם 6213: יהוה 3068 בשמים 8064 הכין 3559 כסאו 3678 ומלכותו 4438 בכל 3605
piqudayu, la'asoutam. Yahuah bashamayim hekiyn kis'au; uamalkutou, bakol
**his commandments to do them Yahuah in the heavens has prepared his throne and his kingdom over all**

103:20

משלה 4910: ברכו 1288 יהוה 3068 מלאכיו 4397 גברי 1368 כח 3581 עשי 6213 דברו 1697 לשמע 8085
mashalah. baraku Yahuah mal'akayu giborey koach 'asey dabarou; lishmoa',
**rule Bless Yahuah you his angels that excel in strength that do his commandments hearkening**

103:21

103:22

בקול 6963 דברו 1697: ברכו 1288 יהוה 3068 כל 3605 צבאיו 6635 משרתיו 8334 עשי 6213 רצונו 7522:
baqoul dabarou. baraku Yahuah kal tzaba'ayu; masharatayu, 'asey ratzounou.
**unto the voice of his word Bless you Yahuah all *you* his hosts *you* ministers of his that do his pleasure**

ברכו 1288 יהוה 3068 כל 3605 מעשיו 4639 בכל 3605 מקמות 4725 ממשלתו 4475 ברכי 1288 נפשי 5315 את 853 יהוה 3068:
baraku Yahuah kal ma'asayu, bakal maqomout memshaltou; barakiy napshiy, 'at Yahuah.
**Bless Yahuah all his works in all places of his dominion bless O my soul Yahuah**

Ps 104:1

ברכי 1288 נפשי 5315 את 853 יהוה 3068 יהוה 3068 אלהי 430 גדלת 1431 מאד 3966 הוד 1935 והדר 1926
barakiy napshiy, 'at Yahuah Yahuah 'alohay gadalta ma'ad; houd uahadar
**Bless O my soul Yahuah O Yahuah my Elohim you are great very honor and majesty**

104:2

לבשת 3847: עטה 5844 אור 216 כשלמה 8008 נוטה 5186 שמים 8064
labashata. 'ateh 'aur kasalmah; nouteh shamayim,
**you are clothed with Who cover *yourself* with light as *with* a garment who stretches out the heavens**

104:3

כיריעה 3407: המקרה 7136 במים 4325 עליותיו 5944 השם 7760 עבים 5645 רכובו 7398 המהלך 1980 על 5921
kayariy'ah. hamqareh bamayim, aliyoutayua hasam 'abiym rakubou; hamahalek, 'al
**like a curtain Who lay the beams of in the waters his chambers who make the clouds his chariot who walk upon**

104:4

104:5

כנפי 3671 רוח 7307: עשה 6213 מלאכיו 4397 רוחות 7307 משרתיו 8334 אש 784 להט 3857: יסד 3245 ארץ 776 על 5921
kanpey ruach. 'aseh mal'akayu ruchout; masharatayu, 'aesh lohet. yasad 'aretz 'al
**the wings of the wind Who make his angels spirits his ministers a fire flaming *Who* laid the earth upon**

104:6

מכוניה 4349 בל 1077 תמוט 4131 עולם 5769 ועד 5703: תהום 8415 כלבוש 3830 כסיתו 3680
makouneyha; bal timout, 'aulam ua'ad. tahoum kalabush kisiytou;
**the foundations of not *that* it should be removed for ever and ever the deep as *with* a garment You covered it with**

104:7

על 5921 הרים 2022 יעמדו 5975 מים 4325: מן 4480 גערתך 1606 ינוסון 5127 מן 4480 קול 6963 רעמך 7482
'al hariym, ya'amdu mayim. min ga'arataka yanusun; min qoul ra'amka,
**above the mountains stood the waters At your rebuke they fled at the voice of your thunder**

Ps 103:17 But the mercy of YHUH is from everlasting to everlasting upon them that fear him, and his righteousness unto children's children;18 To such as keep his covenant, and to those that remember his commandments to do them.19 YHUH has prepared his throne in the heavens; and his kingdom rule over all.20 Bless YHUH, you his angels, that excel in strength, that do his commandments, hearkening unto the voice of his word.21 Bless you YHUH, all you his hosts; you ministers of his, that do his pleasure.22 Bless YHUH, all his works in all places of his dominion: bless YHUH, O my soul. **Ps** 104:1 Bless YHUH, O my soul. O YHUH my G-d, you are very great; you are clothed with honor and majesty.2 Who coverest thyself with light as with a garment: who stretchest out the heavens like a curtain:3 Who layeth the beams of his chambers in the waters: who make the clouds his chariot: who walk upon the wings of the wind:4 Who make his angels spirits; his ministers a flaming fire:5 Who laid the foundations of the earth, that it should not be removed forever.6 Thou coverest it with the deep as with a garment: the waters stood above the mountains.7 At your rebuke they fled; at the voice of your thunder they hasted away.

104:8

יחפזון 2648: יעלו 5927 הרים 2022 ירדו 3381 בקעות 1237 אל 413 מקום 4725 זה 2088 יסדת 3245

yechapezun. ya'alu hariym yeradu baqa'aut; 'al maqoum, zeh yasadta

**they hasted away They go up by the mountains they go down by the valleys unto the place which you have founded**

104:9 104:10

להם 1992: גבול 1366 שמת 7760 בל 1077 יעברון 5674 בל 1077 ישובון 7725 לכסות 3680 הארץ 776:

lahem. gabul samta bal ya'aborun; bal yashubun, lakasout ha'aretz.

**for them a bound You have set not *that* they may pass over not *that* they turn again to cover the earth**

104:11

המשלח 7971 מעינים 4599 בנחלים 5158 בין 996 הרים 2022 יהלכון 1980: ישקו 8248 כל 3605 חיתו 2416 שדי 7704

hamashaleach ma'ayaniym banachaliym; beyn hariym, yahalekun. yashqu kal chaytou saday;

**He send the springs into the valleys among the hills *which* run They give drink to every beast of the field**

104:12

ישברו 7665 פראים 6501 צמאם 6772: עליהם 5921 עוף 5775 השמים 8064 ישכון 7931 מבין 996

yishbaru para'aym tzama'am. 'aleyhem 'aup hashamayim yishkoun; mibeyn

**quench the wild asses their thirst By them the fowls of the heaven shall have their habitation among**

104:13

עפאים 6073 יתנו 5414 קול 6963: משקה 8248 הרים 2022 מעליותיו 5944 מפרי 6529 מעשיך 4639 תשבע 7646

'apaa'yim, yitanu qoul. mashqeh hariym me'aliyoutayu; mipriy ma'aseyka, tisba'

**the branches *which* lift up sing He watereth the hills from his chambers with the fruit of your works is satisfied**

104:14

הארץ 776: מצמיח 6779 חציר 2682 לבהמה 929 ועשב 6212 לעבדת 5656 האדם 120 להוציא 3318

ha'aretz. matzmiyach chatziyr labahemah, ua'aeseb la'abodat ha'adam; lahoutziy'a

**the earth He cause to grow the grass for the cattle and herb for the service of man that he may bring forth**

104:15

לחם 3899 מן 4480 הארץ 776: ויין 3196 ישמח 8055 לבב 3824 אנוש 582 להצהיל 6670 פנים 6440 משמן 8081

lechem, min ha'aretz. uayayin yasamach labab 'anoush, lahatzhiyl paniym mishamen;

**food out of the earth And wine *that* make glad the heart of man to make to shine *his* face *and* oil**

104:16

ולחם 3899 לבב 3824 אנוש 582 יסעד 5582: ישבעו 7646 עצי 6086 יהוה 3068 ארזי 730 לבנון 3844 אשר 834

ua'alechem, labab 'anoush yis'ad. yisba'au 'atzey Yahuah; 'arzey labanoun, 'asher

**and bread heart man's *which* strengthen are full The trees of Yahuah *of sap* the cedars of Lebanon which**

104:17 104:18

נטע 5193: אשר 834 שם 8033 צפרים 6833 יקננו 7077 חסידה 2624 ברושים 1265 ביתה 1004: הרים 2022

nata'. 'asher sam tzipariym yaqanenu; chasiydah, baroushiym beytah. hariym

**he has planted Where in it the birds make their nests *as for* the stork the fir trees *are* her house hills**

104:19

הגבהים 1364 ליעלים 3277 סלעים 5553 מחסה 4268 לשפנים 8227: עשה 6213 ירח 3394 למועדים 4150 שמש 8121

hagabohiym laya'aeliym; sala'aym, machseh lashpaniym. 'asah yareach lamou'adiym; shemesh

**The high for the wild goats *and* the rocks *are* a refuge for the conies He appointed the moon for seasons the sun**

104:20 104:21

ידע 3045 מבואו 3996: תשת 7896 חשך 2822 ויהי 1961 לילה 3915 בו 871a תרמש 7430 כל 3605 חיתו 2416 יער 3293:

yada' mabou'au. tashet choshek uiyhiy layalah; bou tirmos, kal chaytou ya'ar.

**knows his going down You make darkness and it is night wherein do creep all the beasts of the forest**

104:22

הכפירים 3715 שאגים 7580 לטרף 2964 ולבקש 1245 מאל 410 אכלם 400: תזרח 2224 השמש 8121

hakapiyriym sho'agiym latarep; ualbaqesh me'ael 'akelam. tizrach hashemesh

**The young lions roar after their prey and seek from El their meat arise The sun**

Ps 104:8 They go up by the mountains; they go down by the valleys unto the place which you have founded for them.9 Thou have set a bound that they may not pass over; that they turn not again to cover the earth.10 He send the springs into the valleys, which run among the hills.11 They give drink to every beast of the field: the wild asses quench their thirst.12 By them shall the fowls of the heaven have their habitation, which sing among the branches.13 He watereth the hills from his chambers: the earth is satisfied with the fruit of your works.14 He causeth the grass to grow for the cattle, and herb for the service of man: that he may bring forth food out of the earth;15 And wine that make glad the heart of man, and oil to make his face to shine, and bread which strengtheneth man's heart.16 The trees of YHUH are full of sap; the cedars of Lebanon, which he has planted;17 Where the birds make their nests: as for the stork, the fir trees are her house.18 The high hills are a refuge for the wild goats; and the rocks for the conies.19 He appointed the moon for seasons: the sun know his going down.20 Thou make darkness, and it is night: wherein all the beasts of the forest do creep forth.21 The young lions roar after their prey, and seek their meat from G-d.

יאספון 622 ואל 413 מעונתם 4585 ירבצון 7257: 104:23 יצא 3318 אדם 120 לפעלו 6467 ולעבדתו 5656
ye'asepun; ua'al ma'aunotam, yirbatzun. yetzea' 'adam lapa'alou; uala'abodatou
**they gather themselves together and in their dens lay them down goes forth man unto his work and to his labour**

עדי 5704 ערב 6153: 104:24 מה 4100 רבו 7231 מעשיך 4639 יהוה 3068 כלם 3605 בחכמה 2451 עשית 6213 מלאה 4390
'adey 'areb. mah rabu ma'aseyka Yahuah kulam bachakamah 'ashiyta; mal'ah
**until the evening how how manifold are your works O Yahuah them all in wisdom have you made is full of**

הארץ 776 קנינך 7075: 104:25 זה 2088 הים 3220 גדול 1419 ורחב 7342 ידים 3027 שם 8033 רמש 7431 ואין 369
ha'aretz, qinyaneka. zeh hayam gadoul uarchab yadayim sham remes ua'aeyn
**the earth your riches *So is* this sea great and wide border wherein *are* things creeping and without**

מספר 4557 חיות 2416 קטנות 6996 עם 5973 גדלות 1419: 104:26 שם 8033 אניות 591 יהלכון 1980 לויתן 3882 זה 2088
mispar; chayout qatanout, 'am gadolout. sham aniyout yahalekun; liuyatan, zeh
**numerable beasts *both* small with great There the ships go *there is* that leviathan whom**

יצרת 3335 לשחק 7832 בו 871a: 104:27 כלם 3605 אליך 413 ישברון 7663 לתת 5414 אכלם 400
yatzarta lasacheq bou. kulam 'aeleyka yasaberun; latet 'aklam
**you have made to play therein all upon you These wait that you may give *them* their meat**

בעתו 6256: 104:28 תתן 5414 להם 1992 ילקטון 3950 תפתח 6605 ידך 3027 ישבעון 7646 טוב 2896: 104:29 תסתיר 5641
ba'atou. titen lahem yilqotun; tiptach yadaka, yisba'aun toub. tastiyr
**in due season *That* you give them they gather you open your hand they are filled with good You hide**

פניך 6440 יבהלון 926 תסף 622 רוחם 7307 יגועון 1478 ואל 413 עפרם 6083 ישובון 7725: 104:30 תשלח 7971
paneyka yibahelun tosep rucham yigua'aun; ua'al 'aparam yashubun. tashalach
**your face they are troubled you take away their breath they die and to their dust return You send forth**

רוחך 7307 יבראון 1254 ותחדש 2318 פני 6440 אדמה 127: 104:31 יהי 1961 כבוד 3519 יהוה 3068 לעולם 5769
ruchaka yibare'aun; uatchadesh, paney 'adamah. yahiy kaboud Yahuah la'aulam;
**your spirit they are created and you renew the face of the earth shall endure The glory of Yahuah for ever**

ישמח 8055 יהוה 3068 במעשיו 4639: 104:32 המביט 5027 לארץ 776 ותרעד 7460 יגע 5060 בהרים 2022 ויעשנו 6225: 104:33
yismach Yahuah bama'asayu. hamabiyt la'aretz uatir'ad; yiga' behariym uaye'ashanu.
**shall rejoice Yahuah in his works He looks on the earth and it tremble he touch the hills and they smoke**

אשירה 7891 ליהוה 3068 בחיי 2416 אזמרה 2167 לאלהי 430 בעודי 5750: 104:34 יערב 6149 עליו 5921
'ashiyrah laYahuah bachayay; 'azamrah le'alohay ba'audiy. ye'arab 'alayu
**I will sing unto Yahuah as long as I live I will sing praise to my Elohim while I have my being shall be sweet of him**

שיחי 7879 אנכי 595 אשמח 8055 ביהוה 3068: 104:35 יתמו 8552 חטאים 2400 מן 4480 הארץ 776 ורשעים 7563 עוד 5750
siychiy; 'anokiy, 'asmach baYahuah. yitamu chata'aym min ha'aretz uarsha'aym 'aud
**My meditation I will be glad in Yahuah Let be consumed the sinners out of the earth and the wicked more**

אינם 369 ברכי 1288 נפשי 5315 את 853 יהוה 3068 הללו 1984 יה 3050:
'aeynam, barakiy napshiy 'at Yahuah halalu Yah.
**let be no Bless you O my soul Yahuah Praise you Yah**

Ps 104:22 The sun arise, they gather themselves together, and lay them down in their dens.23 Man go forth unto his work and to his labour until the evening.24 O YHUH, how manifold are your works! in wisdom have you made them all: the earth is full of your riches.25 So is this great and wide sea, wherein are things creeping innumerable, both small and great beasts.26 There go the ships: there is that leviathan, whom you have made to play therein.27 These wait all upon you; that you may give them their meat in due season.28 That you givest them they gather: you openest your hand, they are filled with good.29 Thou hidest your face, they are troubled: you takest away their breath, they die, and return to their dust.30 Thou send forth your spirit, they are created: and you renewest the face of the earth.31 The glory of YHUH shall endure forever: YHUH shall rejoice in his works.32 He look on the earth, and it trembleth: he touch the hills, and they smoke.33 I will sing unto YHUH as long as I live: I will sing praise to my G-d while I have my being.34 My meditation of him shall be sweet: I will be glad in YHUH.35 Let the sinners be consumed out of the earth, and let the wicked be no more. Bless you YHUH, O my soul. Praise you YHUH.

**Ps 105:1** ... **105:2**

הודו 3034 ליהוה 3068 קראו 7121 בשמו 8034 הודיעו 3034 בעמים 5971 עלילותיו 5949: שירו 7891
houdu laYahuah qir'au bishmou; houdiy'au ba'amiym, aliyloutayu. shiyru
**O give thanks unto Yahuah call upon his name make known among the people his deeds Sing**

**105:3**

לו 3807a זמרו 2167 לו 3807a שיחו 7878 בכל 3605 נפלאותיו 6381: התהללו 1984 בשם 8034 קדשו 6944 ישמח 8055
lou' zamru lou'; siychu bakal nipla'autayu. hitahallu bashem qadashou; yismach,
**unto him sing psalms unto him talk you of all his wondrous works Glory you in name his holy let rejoice**

**105:4** **105:5**

לב 3820 מבקשי 1245 יהוה 3068: דרשו 1875 יהוה 3068 ועזו 5797 בקשו 1245 פניו 6440 תמיד 8548: זכרו 2142
leb mabaqshey Yahuah. dirshu Yahuah ua'azou; baqashu panayu tamiyd. zikru,
**the heart of them that seek Yahuah Seek Yahuah and his strength seek his face evermore Remember**

**105:6**

נפלאותיו 6381 אשר 834 עשה 6213 מפתיו 4159 ומשפטי 4941 פיו 6310: זרע 2233 אברהם 85
nipla'autayu 'asher 'asah; mopatayu, uamishpatey piyu. zera' 'abraham
**his marvellous works that he has done his wonders and the judgments of his mouth O you seed of Abraham**

**105:7** **105:8**

עבדו 5650 בני 1121 יעקב 3290 בחיריו 972: הוא 1931 יהוה 3068 אלהינו 430 בכל 3605 הארץ 776 משפטיו 4941:
abdou; baney ya'aqob bachiyrayu. hua' Yahuah 'aloheynu; bakal ha'aretz, mishpatayu.
**his servant you children of Jacob his chosen He *is* Yahuah our Elohim *are* in all the earth his judgments**

**105:9**

זכר 2142 לעולם 5769 בריתו 1285 דבר 1697 צוה 6680 לאלף 505 דור 1755: אשר 834
zakar la'aulam bariytou; dabar tziuah, la'alep dour. 'asher
**He has remembered for ever his covenant the word *which* he commanded to a thousand generations Which**

**105:10**

כרת 3772 את 854 אברהם 85 ושבועתו 7621 לישחק 3446: ויעמידה 5975 ליעקב 3290 לחק 2706 לישראל 3478
karat 'at 'abraham; uashbu'atou layischaq. uaya'amiydeha laya'aqob lachoq; layisra'ael,
***covenant* he made *with* Abraham and his oath unto Isaac And confirmed *the same* unto Jacob for a law *and* to Israel**

**105:11** **105:12**

ברית 1285 עולם 5769: לאמר 559 לך 3807a אתן 5414 את 853 ארץ 776 כנען 3667 חבל 2256 נחלתכם 5159:
bariyt 'aulam. lea'mor, laka, 'aten 'at 'aretz kana'an; chebel, nachalatkem.
***for* an covenant everlasting Saying Unto you will I give the land of Canaan the lot of your inheritance**

**105:13**

בהיותם 1961 מתי 4962 מספר 4557 כמעט 4592 וגרים 1481 בה 871a: ויתהלכו 1980 מגוי 1471 אל 413
bihayoutam matey mispar; kima'at, uagariym bah. uayithalaku migouy 'al
**When they were *but* a few men in number *yea* very few and strangers in it When they went from one nation to**

**105:14**

גוי 1471 ממלכה 4467 אל 413 עם 5971 אחר 312: לא 3808 הניח 3240 אדם 120 לעשקם 6231 ויוכח 3198
gouy; mimamalakah, 'al 'am 'acher. la' hiniyach 'adam la'ashaqam; uayoukach
**another from *one* kingdom to people another no He suffered man to do them wrong yea he reproved**

**105:15** **105:16**

עליהם 5921 מלכים 4428: אל 408 תגעו 5060 במשיחי 4899 ולנביאי 5030 אל 408 תרעו 7489:
'aleyhem malakiym. 'al tig'au bimshiychay; ualinabiy'ay 'al tare'au.
**for their sakes kings *Saying* not Touch mine anointed and my prophets no do harm**

**105:17**

ויקרא 7121 רעב 7458 על 5921 הארץ 776 כל 3605 מטה 4294 לחם 3899 שבר 7665: שלח 7971 לפניהם 6440 איש 376
uayiqra' ra'au 'al ha'aretz; kal mateh lechem shabar. shalach lipneyhem 'aysh;
**Moreover he called for a famine upon the land the whole staff of bread he brake He sent before them a man**

**Ps** 105:1 O give thanks unto YHUH; call upon his name: make known his deeds among the people.2 Sing unto him, sing psalms unto him: talk you of all his wondrous works.3 Glory you in his holy name: let the heart of them rejoice that seek YHUH.4 Seek YHUH, and his strength: seek his face evermore.5 Remember his marvellous works that he has done; his wonders, and the judgments of his mouth;6 O you seed of Abraham his servant, you children of Jacob his chosen.7 He is YHUH our G-d: his judgments are in all the earth.8 He has remembered his covenant forever, the word which he commanded to a thousand generations.9 Which covenant he made with Abraham, and his oath unto Isaac;10 And confirmed the same unto Jacob for a law, and to Israel for an everlasting covenant:11 Saying, Unto you will I give the land of Canaan, the lot of your inheritance:12 When they were but a few men in number; yea, very few, and strangers in it.13 When they went from one nation to another, from one kingdom to another people;14 He suffered no man to do them wrong: yea, he reproved kings for their sakes;15 Saying, Touch not mine anointed, and do my prophets no harm.16 Moreover he called for a famine upon the land: he break the whole staff of bread.17 He sent a man before them, even Joseph, who was sold for a servant:

105:18 105:19

לעבד 5650 נמכר 4376 יוסף 3130: ענו 6031 בכבל 3525 רגליו 7272 ברזל 1270 באה 935 נפשו 5315: עד 5704

la'abed, nimkar yousep. 'anu bakebel raglayu barzel, ba'ah napshou. 'ad

**for a servant *who* was sold *even* Joseph they hurt with fetters Whose feet iron was laid in he Until**

105:20

עת 6256 בא 935 דברו 1697 אמרת 565 יהוה 3068 צרפתהו 6884: שלח 7971 מלך 4428 ויתירהו 5425 משל 4910

'at ba' dabarou; 'amrat Yahuah tzarapatahu. shalach melek uayatiyrehu; moshel

**the time that came his word the word of Yahuah tried him sent The king and loosed him *even* the ruler of**

105:21 105:22

עמים 5971 ויפתחהו 6605: שמו 7760 אדון 113 לביתו 1004 ומשל 4910 בכל 3605 קנינו 7075: לאסר 631

'amiym, uayapatchehu. samou 'adoun labeytou; uamoshel, bakal qinyanou. le'asor

**the people and let him go free He made him adonai of his house and ruler of all his substance To bind**

105:23

שריו 8269 בנפשו 5315 וזקניו 2205 יחכם 2449: ויבא 935 ישראל 3478 מצרים 4714 ויעקב 3290 גר 1481

sarayu banapshou; uazqenayu yachakem. uayaba' yisra'ael mitzrayim; uaya'aqob, gar

**his princes at his pleasure and his senators teach wisdom also came into Israel Egypt and Jacob sojourned**

105:24 105:25

בארץ 776 חם 2526: ויפר 6509 את 853 עמו 5971 מאד 3966 ויעצמהו 6105 מצריו 6862:

ba'aretz cham. uayeper 'at 'amou ma'ad; uaya'atzimehu mitzarayu.

**in the land of Ham And he increased his people greatly and made them stronger than their enemies**

105:26

הפך 2015 לבם 3820 לשנא 8130 עמו 5971 להתנכל 5230 בעבדיו 5650: שלח 7971 משה 4872 עבדו 5650 אהרן 175

hapak libam lisna' 'amou; lahitnakel, ba'abadayu. shalach mosheh abdou; 'aharon,

**He turned their heart to hate his people to deal subtilly with his servants He sent Moses his servant *and* Aaron**

105:27

אשר 834 בחר 977 בו 871a: שמו 7760 בם 871a דברי 1697 אתותיו 226 ומפתים 4159 בארץ 776

'asher bachar bou. samu bam dibrey 'atoutayu; uamopatiym, ba'aretz

**whom he had chosen in him They showed among them his signs wondrous and wonders in the land of**

105:28 105:29

חם 2526: שלח 7971 חשך 2822 ויחשך 2821 ולא 3808 מרו 4784 את 854 דברוו 1697: הפך 2015 את 853

cham. shalach choshek uayachshik; uala' maru, 'at dabarauu hapak 'at

**Ham He sent darkness and made it dark did not they rebelled *against* his word He turned**

105:30

מימיהם 4325 לדם 1818 וימת 4191 את 853 דגתם 1710: שרץ 8317 ארצם 776 צפרדעים 6854

meymeyhem ladam; uayamet, 'at dagatam. sharatz 'artzam tzaparda'aym;

**their waters into blood and slew their fish brought forth in abundance Their land frogs**

105:31 105:32

בחדרי 2315 מלכיהם 4428: אמר 559 ויבא 935 ערב 6157 כנים 3654 בכל 3605 גבולם 1366:

bachadrey, malkeyhem. 'amar uayaba' arob; kiniym, bakal gabulam.

**in the chambers of their kings He spoke and there came divers sorts of flies *and* lice in all their coasts**

105:33

נתן 5414 גשמיהם 1653 ברד 1259 אש 784 להבות 3852 בארצם 776: ויך 5221 גפנם 1612 ותאנתם 8384

natan gishmeyhem barad; 'aesh lehabout ba'artzam. uayak gapnam uat'anatam;

**He gave *for* rain *them* hail fire *and* flaming in their land He smote also their vines and their fig trees**

105:34

וישבר 7665 עץ 6086 גבולם 1366: אמר 559 ויבא 935 ארבה 697 וילק 3218 ואין 369

uayashaber, 'aetz gabulam. 'amar uayaba' 'arbeh; uayeleq, ua'aeyn

**and brake the trees of their coasts He spoke and came the locusts and caterpillers and that without**

Ps 105:18 Whose feet they hurt with fetters: he was laid in iron:19 Until the time that his word came: the word of YHUH tried him.20 The king sent and loosed him; even the ruler of the people, and let him go free.21 He made him lord of his house, and ruler of all his substance:22 To bind his princes at his pleasure; and teach his senators wisdom.23 Israel also came into Egypt; and Jacob sojourned in the land of Ham.24 And he increased his people greatly; and made them stronger than their enemies.25 He turned their heart to hate his people, to deal subtilly with his servants.26 He sent Moses his servant; and Aaron whom he had chosen.27 They showed his signs among them, and wonders in the land of Ham.28 He sent darkness, and made it dark; and they rebelled not against his word.29 He turned their waters into blood, and slew their fish.30 Their land brought forth frogs in abundance, in the chambers of their kings.31 He spoke, and there came divers sorts of flies, and lice in all their coasts.32 He gave them hail for rain, and flaming fire in their land.33 He smote their vines also and their fig trees; and break the trees of their coasts.34 He spoke, and the locusts came, and caterpillers, and that without number,

105:35 105:36

מספר 4557: | ויאכל 398 | כל 3605 | עשב 6212 | בארצם 776 | ויאכל 398 | פרי 6529 | אדמתם 127: | ויך 5221
mispar. uaya'kal kal 'aeseb ba'artzam; uaya'kal, pariy 'admatam. uayak
**number And did eat up all the herbs in their land and devoured the fruit of their ground He smote also**

105:37

כל 3605 | בכור 1060 | בארצם 776 | ראשית 7225 | לכל 3605 | אונם 202: | ויוציאם 3318 | בכסף 3701 | וזהב 2091
kal bakour ba'artzam; ra'shiyt, lakal 'aunam. uayoutziy'aem bakesep uazahab;
**all the firstborn in their land the chief of all their strength He brought them forth also with silver and gold**

105:38

ואין 369 | בשבטיו 7626 | כושל 3782: | שמח 8056 | מצרים 4714 | בצאתם 3318 | כי 3588 | נפל 5307
ua'aeyn bishbatayu koushel. samak mitzrayim batzea'tam; kiy napal
**and *there was* not one *person* among their tribes feeble was glad Egypt when they departed for fell**

105:39 105:40

פחדם 6343 | עליהם 5921: | פרש 6566 | ענן 6051 | למסך 4539 | ואש 784 | להאיר 215 | לילה 3915:
pachdam 'aleyhem. paras 'anan lamasak; ua'aesh, laha'ayr layalah.
**the fear of them upon them He spread a cloud for a covering and fire to give light in the night**

105:41

שאל 7592 | ויבא 935 | שלו 7958 | ולחם 3899 | שמים 8064 | ישביעם 7646: | פתח 6605 | צור 6697
sha'al uayabea' salau; ua'alechem shamayim, yasbiy'aem. patach tzur
***The people* asked and he brought quails and with the bread of heaven satisfied them He opened the rock**

105:42

ויזובו 2100 | מים 4325 | הלכו 1980 | בציות 6723 | נהר 5104: | כי 3588 | זכר 2142 | את 853 | דבר 1697 | קדשו 6944 | את 853
uayazubu mayim; halaku, batziyout nahar. kiy zakar 'at dabar qadashou; 'at
**and gushed out the waters they ran in the dry places *like* a river For he remembered promise his holy**

105:43 105:44

אברהם 85 | עבדו 5650: | ויוצא 3318 | עמו 5971 | בששון 8342 | ברנה 7440 | את 853 | בחיריו 972:
'abraham abdou. uayoutza' 'amou basasoun; barinah, 'at bachiyrayu.
***and* Abraham his servant And he brought forth his people with joy with gladness *and* his chosen**

105:45

ויתן 5414 | להם 1992 | ארצות 776 | גוים 1471 | ועמל 5999 | לאמים 3816 | יירשו 3423: | בעבור 5668 | ישמרו 8104
uayiten lahem 'artzout gouyim; ua'amal la'amiym yiyrashu. ba'abur yishmaru
**And gave them the lands of the heathen and the labour of the people they inherited That they might observe**

חקיו 2706 | ותורתיו 8451 | ינצרו 5341 | הללו 1984 | יה 3050:
chuqayu uatourotayu yintzoru, halalu Yah.
**his statutes and his laws keep Praise you Yah**

**Ps 106:1** 106:2

הללויה 1984 | הודו 3034 | ליהוה 3068 | כי 3588 | טוב 2896 | כי 3588 | לעולם 5769 | חסדו 2617: | מי 4310 | ימלל 4448
halaluyah houdu laYahuah kiy toub; kiy la'aulam chasdou. miy, yamalel
**Praise you O give thanks unto Yahuah for *he is* good for *endures* for ever his mercy Who can utter**

106:3

גבורות 1369 | יהוה 3068 | ישמיע 8085 | כל 3605 | תהלתו 8416: | אשרי 835 | שמרי 8104 | משפט 4941 | עשה 6213
gaburout Yahuah; yashmiya', kal tahilatou. 'ashrey shomrey mishapat; 'aseh
**the mighty acts of Yahuah who can show forth all his praise? Blessed *are* they that keep judgment *and* he that does**

106:4

צדקה 6666 | בכל 3605 | עת 6256: | זכרני 2142 | יהוה 3068 | ברצון 7522 | עמך 5971 | פקדני 6485
tzadaqah bakal 'aet. zakareniy Yahuah birtzoun 'ameka; paqadeniy,
**righteousness at all times Remember me O Yahuah with the favor *that you bear unto* your people O visit me**

Ps 105:35 And did eat up all the herbs in their land, and devoured the fruit of their ground.36 He smote also all the firstborn in their land, the chief of all their strength.37 He brought them forth also with silver and gold: and there was not one feeble person among their tribes.38 Egypt was glad when they departed: for the fear of them fell upon them.39 He spread a cloud for a covering; and fire to give light in the night.40 The people asked, and he brought quails, and satisfied them with the bread of heaven.41 He opened the rock, and the waters gushed out; they ran in the dry places like a river.42 For he remembered his holy promise, and Abraham his servant.43 And he brought forth his people with joy, and his chosen with gladness:44 And gave them the lands of the heathen: and they inherited the labour of the people;45 That they might observe his statutes, and keep his laws. Praise you YHUH. **Ps** 106:1 Praise you YHUH. O give thanks unto YHUH; for he is good: for his mercy endureth forever.2 Who can utter the mighty acts of YHUH? who can show forth all his praise?3 Blessed are they that keep judgment, and he that doeth righteousness at all times.4 Remember me, O YHUH, with the favor that you bear unto your people: O visit me with your salvation;

106:5
ביְשׁוּעָתֶךָ 3444: | לִרְאוֹת 7200 | בְּטוֹבַת 2896 | בְּחִירֶיךָ 972 | לִשְׂמֹחַ 8055 | בְּשִׂמְחַת 8057 | גּוֹיֶךָ 1471
biyshu'ateka. | lir'aut | batoubat | bachiyreyka, | lismoach | basimchat | gouyeka;
**with your salvation | That I may see | the good of | your chosen | that I may rejoice | in the gladness of | your nation**

106:6
להתהלל 1984 | עם 5973 | נחלתך 5159: | חטאנו 2398 | עם 5973 | אבותינו 1 | העוינו 5753
lahithalel, | 'am | nachalateka. | chata'nu | 'am | abouteynu, | he'auiynu
**that I may glory | with | your inheritance | We have sinned | with | our fathers | we have committed iniquity**

106:7
הרשענו 7561: | אבותינו 1 | במצרים 4714 | לא 3808 | השכילו 7919 | נפלאותיך 6381 | לא 3808 | זכרו 2142 | את 853
hirsha'anu. | 'abouteynu | bamitzrayim | la' | hiskiylu | nipla'auteyka, | la' | zakaru | 'at
**we have done wickedly | Our fathers | in Egypt | not | understood | your wonders | not | they remembered**

106:8
רב 7230 | חסדיך 2617 | וימרו 4784 | על 5921 | ים 3220 | בים 3220 | סוף 5488: | ויושיעם 3467
rob | chasadeyka; | uayamru | 'al | yam | bayam | sup. | uayoushiy'aem
**the multitude of | your mercies | but provoked *him* | at | the sea *even at* | sea | the Red | Nevertheless he saved them**

106:9
למען 4616 | שמו 8034 | להודיע 3045 | את 853 | גבורתו 1369: | ויגער 1605 | בים 3220 | סוף 5488
lama'an | shamou; | lahoudiya', | 'at | gaburatou. | uayig'ar | bayam | sup
**for sake | his name's | that he might make to be known | his mighty power | He rebuked also | sea | the Red**

106:10
ויחרב 2717 | ויוליכם 1980 | בתהמות 8415 | כמדבר 4057: | ויושיעם 3467
uayecherab; | uayouliykem | batahomout, | kamidbar. | uayoushiy'aem
**and it was dried up | so he led them | through the depths | as through the wilderness | And he saved them**

106:11
מיד 3027 | שונא 8130 | ויגאלם 1350 | מיד 3027 | אויב 341: | ויכסו 3680 | מים 4325
miyad | sounea'; | uayig'alem, | miyad | auyeb. | uayakasu | mayim
**from the hand of | him that hated | *them* and redeemed them | from the hand of | the enemy | And covered | the waters**

106:12
צריהם 6862 | אחד 259 | מהם 1992 | לא 3808 | נותר 3498: | ויאמינו 539 | בדבריו 1697 | ישירו 7891 | תהלתו 8416: | מהרו 4116
tzareyhem; | 'achad | mehem, | la' | noutar. | uaya'amiynu | bidbarayu; | yashiyru, | tahilatou. | miharu
**their enemies | one | of them | not | there was left | Then believed they | his words | they sang | his praise | soon**

106:13
106:14
שכחו 7911 | מעשיו 4639 | לא 3808 | חכו 2442 | לעצתו 6098: | ויתאוו 183 | תאוה 8378 | במדבר 4057 | וינסו 5254 | אל 410
shakachu | ma'asayu; | la' | chiku, | la'atzatou. | uayit'auu | ta'abah | bamidbar; | uayanasu | 'ael,
**They forgot | his works | not | they waited | for his counsel | But lusted | exceedingly | in the wilderness | and tempted | El**

106:15
בישימון 3452: | ויתן 5414 | להם 1992 | שאלתם 7596 | וישלח 7971 | רזון 7332 | בנפשם 5315: | ויקנאו 7065
biyshiymoun. | uayiten | lahem | she'alatam; | uayashalach | razoun | banapsham. | uayaqan'au
**in the desert | And he gave | them | their request | but sent | leanness | into their soul | They envied also**

106:16
106:17
למשה 4872 | במחנה 4264 | לאהרן 175 | קדוש 6918 | יהוה 3068: | תפתח 6605 | ארץ 776 | ותבלע 1104 | דתן 1885 | ותכס 3680
lamosheh | bamachaneh; | la'aharon, | qadoush | Yahuah. | tiptach | 'aretz | uatibla' | datan; | uatakas,
**Moses | in the camp | *and* Aaron | the saint of | Yahuah | opened | The earth | and swallowed up | Dathan | and covered**

106:18
על 5921 | עדת 5712 | אבירם 48: | ותבער 1197 | אש 784 | בעדתם 5712 | להבה 3852 | תלהט 3857 | רשעים 7563:
'al | 'adat | 'abiyram. | uatib'ar | 'aesh | ba'adatam; | lehabah, | talahet | rasha'aym.
**over | the company of | Abiram | And was kindled | a fire | in their company | the flame | burned up | the wicked**

Ps 106:5 That I may see the good of your chosen, that I may rejoice in the gladness of your nation, that I may glory with your inheritance.6 We have sinned with our fathers, we have committed iniquity, we have done wickedly.7 Our fathers understood not your wonders in Egypt; they remembered not the multitude of your mercies; but provoked him at the sea, even at the Red sea.8 Nevertheless he saved them for his name's sake, that he might make his mighty power to be known.9 He rebuked the Red sea also, and it was dried up: so he led them through the depths, as through the wilderness.10 And he saved them from the hand of him that hated them, and redeemed them from the hand of the enemy.11 And the waters covered their enemies: there was not one of them left.12 Then believed they his words; they sang his praise.13 They soon forgot his works; they waited not for his counsel:14 But lusted exceedingly in the wilderness, and tempted G-d in the desert.15 And he gave them their request; but sent leanness into their soul.16 They envied Moses also in the camp, and Aaron the saint of YHUH.17 The earth opened and swallowed up Dathan, and covered the company of Abiram.18 And a fire was kindled in their company; the flame burned up the wicked.

**106:19** יעשו 6213 | עגל 5695 | בחרב 2722 | וישתחוו 7812 | למסכה 4541: | **106:20** וימירו 4171 | את 853 | כבודם 3519
ya'asu 'aegel bachoreb; uayishtachauu, lamasekah. uayamiyru 'at kaboudam;
**They made a calf in Horeb and worshipped the molten image Thus they changed their glory**

בתבנית 8403 | שור 7794 | אכל 398 | עשב 6212: | **106:21** שכחו 7911 | אל 410 | מושיעם 3467 | עשה 6213 | גדלות 1419
batabniyt shour 'akel 'aeseb. shakachu 'ael moushiy'am; 'aseh gadolout
**into the similitude of an ox that eat grass They forgot El their saviour which had done great things**

במצרים 4714: | **106:22** נפלאות 6381 | בארץ 776 | חם 2526 | נוראות 3372 | על 5921 | ים 3220 | סוף 5488: | **106:23** ויאמר 559
bamitzrayim. nipla'aut ba'aretz cham; noura'aut, 'al yam sup. uaya'mer,
**in Egypt Wondrous works in the land of Ham *and* terrible things by sea the Red Therefore he said**

להשמידם 8045 | לולי 3884 | משה 4872 | בחירו 972 | עמד 5975 | בפרץ 6556 | לפניו 6440 | להשיב 7725 | חמתו 2534
lahashmiydam luley mosheh bachiyrou, 'amad baperetz lapanayu; lahashiyb chamatou,
**that he would destroy them had not Moses his chosen stood in the breach before him to turn away his wrath**

מהשחית 7843: | **106:24** וימאסו 3988 | בארץ 776 | חמדה 2532 | לא 3808 | האמינו 539 | לדברו 1697: | **106:25**
mehashachiyt. uayim'asu ba'aretz chemdah; la' he'amiynu, lidbarou.
**lest he should destroy *them* Yea they despised land *the* pleasant not they believed his word**

וירגנו 7279 | באהליהם 168 | לא 3808 | שמעו 8085 | בקול 6963 | יהוה 3068: | **106:26** וישא 5375 | ידו 3027
uayeraganu ua'ahaleyhem; la' shama'au, baqoul Yahuah. uayisaa' yadou
**But murmured in their tents not *and* hearkened unto the voice of Yahuah Therefore he lifted up his hand**

להם 1992 | להפיל 5307 | אותם 853 | במדבר 4057: | **106:27** ולהפיל 5307 | זרעם 2233 | בגוים 1471
lahem; lahapiyl 'autam, bamidbar. ualhapiyl zar'am bagouyim;
**against them to overthrow them in the wilderness To overthrow also their seed among the nations**

ולזרותם 2219 | בארצות 776: | **106:28** ויצמדו 6775 | לבעל 1187 | פעור 6465 | ויאכלו 398 | זבחי 2077
ualzaroutam, ba'aratzout. uayitzamadu laba'al pa'aur; uayo'akalu, zibchey
**and to scatter them in the lands They joined themselves also unto Baal peor and ate the sacrifices of**

מתים 4191: | **106:29** ויכעיסו 3707 | במעלליהם 4611 | ותפרץ 6555 | בם 871a | מגפה 4046: | **106:30**
metiym. uayaka'aysu bama'alleyhem; uatipratz bam, magepah.
**the dead Thus they provoked *him* to anger with their inventions and brake in upon them the plague**

ויעמד 5975 | פינחס 6372 | ויפלל 6419 | ותעצר 6113 | המגפה 4046: | **106:31** ותחשב 2803 | לו 3807a
uaya'amod piynachas uayapalel; uate'atzar, hamagepah. uatechasheb lou'
**Then stood up Phinehas and executed judgment and was stayed *so* the plague And that was counted unto him**

לצדקה 6666 | לדר 1755 | ודר 1755 | עד 5704 | עולם 5769: | **106:32** ויקציפו 7107 | על 5921 | מי 4325 | מריבה 4808
litzdaqah; lador uador, 'ad 'aulam. uayaqtziypu 'al mey mariybah;
**for righteousness unto all generations for evermore They angered *him* also at the waters of strife**

וירע 3415 | למשה 4872 | בעבורם 5668: | **106:33** כי 3588 | המרו 4784 | את 853 | רוחו 7307 | ויבטא 981
uayera' lamosheh, ba'aburam. kiy himaru 'at ruachou; uayabatea',
**so that it went ill with Moses for their sakes Because they provoked his spirit so that he spoke unadvisedly**

Ps 106:19 They made a calf in Horeb, and worshipped the molten image.20 Thus they changed their glory into the similitude of an ox that eateth grass.21 They forgot G-d their savior, which had done great things in Egypt;22 Wondrous works in the land of Ham, and terrible things by the Red sea.23 Therefore he said that he would destroy them, had not Moses his chosen stood before him in the breach, to turn away his wrath, lest he should destroy them.24 Yea, they despised the pleasant land, they believed not his word:25 But murmured in their tents, and hearkened not unto the voice of YHUH.26 Therefore he lifted up his hand against them, to overthrow them in the wilderness:27 To overthrow their seed also among the nations, and to scatter them in the lands.28 They joined themselves also unto Baal-peor, and ate the sacrifices of the dead.29 Thus they provoked him to anger with their inventions: and the plague break in upon them.30 Then stood up Phinehas, and executed judgment: and so the plague was stayed.31 And that was counted unto him for righteousness unto all generations forevermore.32 They angered him also at the waters of strife, so that it went ill with Moses for their sakes:33 Because they provoked his spirit, so that he spoke unadvisedly with his lips.

106:34 106:35

בשפתיו 8193: לא 3808 השמידו 8045 את 853 העמים 5971 אשר 834 אמר 559 יהוה 3068 להם 1992:
bispatayu. la' hishmiydu 'at ha'amiym; 'asher 'amar Yahuah lahem.
**with his lips not They did destroy the nations *concerning* whom commanded Yahuah them**

106:36

ויתערבו 6148 בגוים 1471 וילמדו 3925 מעשיהם 4639: ויעבדו 5647 את 853 עצביהם 6091 ויהיו 1961
uayita'arabu bagouyim; uayilmadu, ma'aseyhem. uaya'abdu 'at 'atzabeyhem; uayihayu
**But were mingled among the heathen and learned their works And they served their idols which were**

106:37 106:38

להם 1992 למוקש 4170: ויזבחו 2076 את 853 בניהם 1121 ואת 853 בנותיהם 1323 לשדים 7700: וישפכו 8210 דם 1818
lahem lamouqesh. uayizbachu 'at baneyhem ua'at banouteyhem, lashediym. uayishpaku dam
**unto them a snare Yea they sacrificed their sons *and* their daughters unto devils And shed blood**

נקי 5355 דם 1818 בניהם 1121 ובנותיהם 1323 אשר 834 זבחו 2076 לעצבי 6091 כנען 3667
naqiy dam baneyhem uabnouteyhem, 'asher zibchu la'atzabey kana'an;
**innocent *even* the blood of their sons and of their daughters whom they sacrificed unto the idols of Canaan**

106:39

ותחנף 2610 הארץ 776 בדמים 1818: ויטמאו 2930 במעשיהם 4639 ויזנו 2181
uatechanap ha'aretz, badamiym. uayitma'au bama'aseyhem; uayiznu,
**and was polluted the land with blood Thus were they defiled with their own works and went a whoring**

106:40

במעלליהם 4611: ויחר 2734 אף 639 יהוה 3068 בעמו 5971 ויתעב 8581
bama'alleyhem. uayichar 'ap Yahuah ba'amou; uayata'aeb,
**with their own inventions Therefore was kindled the wrath of Yahuah against his people insomuch that he abhorred**

106:41

את 853 נחלתו 5159: ויתנם 5414 ביד 3027 גוים 1471 וימשלו 4910 בהם 871a
'at nachalatou. uayitanem bayad gouyim; uayimshalu bahem,
**his own inheritance And he gave them into the hand of the heathen and ruled over them**

106:42

שנאיהם 8130: וילחצום 3905 אויביהם 341 ויכנעו 3665 תחת 8478
son'aeyhem. uayilchatzum 'auyabeyhem; uayikana'au, tachat
**they that hated them also oppressed them Their enemies and they were brought into subjection under**

106:43

ידם 3027: פעמים 6471 רבות 7227 יצילם 5337 והמה 1992 ימרו 4784 בעצתם 6098 וימכו 4355
yadam. pa'amiym rabout, yatziylem uahemah yamaru ba'atzatam; uayamoku,
**their hand times Many did he deliver them but they provoked *him* with their counsel and were brought low**

106:44 106:45

בעונם 5771: וירא 7200 בצר 6862 להם 1992 בשמעו 8085 את 853 רנתם 7440:
ba'auonam. uayar'a batzar lahem; bashama'au, 'at rinatam.
**for their iniquity Nevertheless he regarded affliction their when he heard their cry**

106:46

ויזכר 2142 להם 1992 בריתו 1285 וינחם 5162 כרב 7230 חסדו 2617 ויתן 5414
uayizkor lahem bariytou; uayinachem, karob chasdou uayiten
**And he remembered for them his covenant and repented according to the multitude of his mercies. He made also**

106:47

אותם 853 לרחמים 7356 לפני 6440 כל 3605 שוביהם 7617: הושיענו 3467 יהוה 3068 אלהינו 430
'autam larachamiym; lipney kal shoubeyhem. houshiy'aenu Yahuah 'aloheynu,
**them to be pitied of all those that carried them captives Save us O Yahuah our Elohim**

Ps 106:34 They did not destroy the nations, concerning whom YHUH commanded them:35 But were mingled among the heathen, and learned their works.36 And they served their idols: which were a snare unto them.37 Yea, they sacrificed their sons and their daughters unto devils,38 And shed innocent blood, even the blood of their sons and of their daughters, whom they sacrificed unto the idols of Canaan: and the land was polluted with blood.39 Thus were they defiled with their own works, and went a whoring with their own inventions.40 Therefore was the wrath of YHUH kindled against his people, insomuch that he abhorred his own inheritance.41 And he gave them into the hand of the heathen; and they that hated them ruled over them.42 Their enemies also oppressed them, and they were brought into subjection under their hand.43 Many times did he deliver them; but they provoked him with their counsel, and were brought low for their iniquity.44 Nevertheless he regarded their affliction, when he heard their cry:45 And he remembered for them his covenant, and repented according to the multitude of his mercies.46 He made them also to be pitied of all those that carried them captives.47 Save us, O YHUH our G-d, and gather us from among the heathen, to give thanks unto your holy name, and to triumph in your praise.

**106:48**

וקבצנו 6908 מן 4480 הגוים 1471 להדות 3034 לשם 8034 קדשך 6944 להשתבח 7623 בתהלתך 8416: ברוך 1288
uaqabtzenu min hagouyim lahodout lashem qadasheka lahishtabeach, bithilateka. baruk
**and gather us from *among* the heathen to give thanks unto name your holy *and* to triumph in your praise Blessed**

יהוה 3068 אלהי 430 ישראל 3478 מן 4480 העולם 5769 ועד 5704 העולם 5769 ואמר 559 כל 3605 העם 5971 אמן 543 הללו 1984 יה 3050:
Yahuah 'alohey yisra'ael min ha'aulam ua'ad ha'aulam, ua'amar kal ha'am 'amen, halalu Yah.
***be* Yahuah Elohim of Israel from everlasting and to everlasting and let say all the people Amen Praise you Yah**

**Ps 107:1** הדו 3034 ליהוה 3068 כי 3588 טוב 2896 כי 3588 לעולם 5769 חסדו 2617: **107:2** יאמרו 559 גאולי 1350
hodu laYahuah kiy toub; kiy la'aulam chasdou. ya'maru ga'auley
**O give thanks unto Yahuah for *he is* good for *endures* for ever his mercy Let say *so* the redeemed of**

יהוה 3068 אשר 834 גאלם 1350 מיד 3027 צר 6862: **107:3** ומארצות 776 קבצם 6908 ממזרח 4217
Yahuah; 'asher ga'alam, miyad tzar. uame'aratzout, qibtzam mimizrach
**Yahuah whom he has redeemed from the hand of the enemy And out of the lands gathered them from the east**

וממערב 4628 מצפון 6828 ומים 3220: **107:4** תעו 8582 במדבר 4057 בישימון 3452 דרך 1870 עיר 5892
uamima'arab; mitzapoun uamiyam. ta'au bamidbar biyshiymoun darek; 'ayr
**and from the west from the north and from the south They wandered in the wilderness in a solitary way city**

מושב 4186 לא 3808 מצאו 4672: **107:5** רעבים 7457 גם 1571 צמאים 6771 נפשם 5315 בהם 871a תתעטף 5848: **107:6** ויצעקו 6817 אל 413
moushab, la' matza'au. ra'aebiym gam tzame'aym; napsham, bahem tit'atap. uayitz'aqu 'al
**to dwell in no they found Hungry moreover thirsty their soul in them fainted Then they cried unto**

יהוה 3069 בצר 6862 להם 1992 ממצוקותיהם 4691 יצילם 5337: **107:7** וידריכם 1869 בדרך 1870 ישרה 3477
Yahuah batzar lahem; mimatzuqouteyhem, yatziylem. uayadriykem baderek yasharah;
**Yahuah in trouble their out of their distresses *and* he delivered them And he led them forth by way *the* right**

ללכת 1980 אל 413 עיר 5892 מושב 4186: **107:8** יודו 3034 ליהוה 3068 חסדו 2617
laleket, 'al 'ayr moushab. youdu laYahuah chasdou;
**that they might go to a city of habitation Oh that *men* would praise Yahuah *for* his goodness**

ונפלאותיו 6381 לבני 1121 אדם 120: **107:9** כי 3588 השביע 7646 נפש 5315 שקקה 8264 ונפש 5315 רעבה 7457
uanipla'autayu, libney 'adam. kiy hisbiya' nepesh shoqeqah; uanepesh ra'aebah
**and *for* his wonderful works to the children of men For he satisfies soul *the* longing and soul *the* hungry**

מלא 4390 טוב 2896: **107:10** ישבי 3427 חשך 2822 וצלמות 6757 אסירי 615 עני 6040 וברזל 1270: **107:11**
milea' toub. yoshabey choshek uatzalmauet; 'asiyrey 'aniy uabarzel.
**fill with goodness Such as sit in darkness and in the shadow of death *being* bound in affliction and iron**

כי 3588 המרו 4784 אמרי 561 אל 410 ועצת 6098 עליון 5945 נאצו 5006: **107:12**
kiy himaru 'amrey 'ael; ua'atzat 'alyoun na'atzu.
**Because they rebelled against the words of El and the counsel of the most High contemned**

ויכנע 3665 בעמל 5999 לבם 3820 כשלו 3782 ואין 369 עזר 5826: **107:13** ויזעקו 2199 אל 413
uayakana' be'amal libam; kashalu, ua'aeyn 'azer. uayiz'aqu 'al
**Therefore he brought down with labour their heart they fell down and *there was* none to help Then they cried unto**

Ps 106:48 Blessed be YHUH G-d of Israel from everlasting to everlasting: and let all the people say, Amen. Praise you YHUH. **Ps** 107:1 O give thanks unto YHUH, for he is good: for his mercy endureth forever.2 Let the redeemed of YHUH say so, whom he has redeemed from the hand of the enemy;3 And gathered them out of the lands, from the east, and from the west, from the north, and from the south.4 They wandered in the wilderness in a solitary way; they found no city to dwell in.5 Hungry and thirsty, their soul fainted in them.6 Then they cried unto YHUH in their trouble, and he delivered them out of their distresses.7 And he led them forth by the right way, that they might go to a city of habitation.8 Oh that men would praise YHUH for his goodness, and for his wonderful works to the children of men!9 For he satisfieth the longing soul, and filleth the hungry soul with goodness.10 Such as sit in darkness and in the shadow of death, being bound in affliction and iron;11 Because they rebelled against the words of G-d, and contemned the counsel of the most High:12 Therefore he brought down their heart with labour; they fell down, and there was none to help.

107:14
יהוה 3069 בצר 6862 להם 1992 ממצקותיהם 4691 יושיעם 3467: יוציאם 3318 מחשך 2822
Yahuah batzar lahem; mimatzuqouteyhem, youshiy'aem. youtziy'aem mechoshek
**Yahuah in trouble their out of their distresses *and* he saved them He brought them out of darkness**

107:15
וצלמות 6757 ומוסרותיהם 4147 ינתק 5423: יודו 3034 ליהוה 3068 חסדו 2617
uatzalmauet; uamousarouteyhem yanateq. youdu laYahuah chasdou;
**and the shadow of death and their bands brake in sunder *Oh that men* would praise unto Yahuah *for* his goodness**

107:16
ונפלאותיו 6381 לבני 1121 אדם 120: כי 3588 שבר 7665 דלתות 1817 נחשת 5178 ובריחי 1280
uanipla'autayu, libney 'adam. kiy bar daltout nachoshet; uabriychey
**and *for* his wonderful works to the children of men For he has broken the gates of brass and the bars of**

107:17 107:18
ברזל 1270 גדע 1438: אולים 191 מדרך 1870 פשעם 6588 ומעונתיהם 5771 יתענו 6031:
barzel gidea'. 'auiliym miderek pish'am; uame'auonoteyhem, yit'anu.
**iron cut in sunder Fools because of their transgression and because of their iniquities are afflicted**

107:19
כל 3605 אכל 400 תתעב 8581 נפשם 5315 ויגיעו 5060 עד 5704 שערי 8179 מות 4194: ויזעקו 2199 אל 413 יהוה 3069
kal 'akel tata'aeb napsham; uayagiy'au, 'ad sha'arey mauet. uayiz'aqu 'al Yahuah
**all manner of meat abhore Their soul and they draw near unto the gates of death Then they cry unto Yahuah**

107:20
בצר 6862 להם 1992 ממצקותיהם 4691 יושיעם 3467: ישלח 7971 דברו 1697 וירפאם 7495 וימלט 4422
batzar lahem; mimatzuqouteyhem, youshiy'aem. yishlach dabarou uayirpa'aem; uiymalet,
**in trouble their out of their distresses *and* he save them He sent his word and healed them and delivered**

107:21
משחיתותם 7825: יודו 3034 ליהוה 3068 חסדו 2617 ונפלאותיו 6381
mishchiytoutam. youdu laYahuah chasdou; uanipla'autayu,
***them* from their destructions Oh that *men* would praise to Yahuah *for* his goodness and *for* his wonderful works**

107:22
לבני 1121 אדם 120: ויזבחו 2076 זבחי 2077 תודה 8426 ויספרו 5608 מעשיו 4639 ברנה 7440:
libney 'adam. uayizbachu zibchey toudah; uiysapru ma'asayu barinah.
**to the children of men And let them sacrifice the sacrifices of thanksgiving and declare his works with rejoicing**

107:23 107:24
יורדי 3381 הים 3220 באניות 591 עשי 6213 מלאכה 4399 במים 4325 רבים 7227: המה 1992 ראו 7200 מעשי 4639
youradey hayam ba'aniyout; 'asey mala'kah, bamayim rabiym. hemah ra'au ma'asey
**They that go down to the sea in ships that do business in waters great These see the works of**

107:25
יהוה 3068 ונפלאותיו 6381 במצולה 4688: ויאמר 559 ויעמד 5975 רוח 7307 סערה 5591 ותרומם 7311 גליו 1530:
Yahuah; uanipla'autayu, bimatzulah. uaya'mer, uaya'amed ruach sa'arah; uataroumem galayu.
**Yahuah and his wonders in the deep For he command and raises wind *the* stormy which lift up the waves thereof**

107:26 107:27
יעלו 5927 שמים 8064 ירדו 3381 תהומות 8415 נפשם 5315 ברעה 7451 תתמוגג 4127:
ya'alu shamayim yeradu tahoumout; napsham, bara'ah titmougag.
**They mount up to the heaven they go down again to the depths their soul because of trouble is melted**

107:28
יחוגו 2287 וינועו 5128 כשכור 7910 וכל 3605 חכמתם 2451 תתבלע 1104: ויצעקו 6817 אל 413 יהוה 3069
yachougu uayanu'au kashikour; uakal chakamatam, titbala'. uayitz'aqu 'al Yahuah
**They reel to and fro and stagger like a drunken man and are at their wits' end Then they cry unto Yahuah**

Ps 107:13 Then they cried unto YHUH in their trouble, and he saved them out of their distresses.14 He brought them out of darkness and the shadow of death, and break their bands in sunder.15 Oh that men would praise YHUH for his goodness, and for his wonderful works to the children of men!16 For he has broken the gates of brass, and cut the bars of iron in sunder.17 Fools because of their transgression, and because of their iniquities, are afflicted.18 Their soul abhorreth all manner of meat; and they draw near unto the gates of death.19 Then they cry unto YHUH in their trouble, and he save them out of their distresses.20 He sent his word, and healed them, and delivered them from their destructions.21 Oh that men would praise YHUH for his goodness, and for his wonderful works to the children of men!22 And let them sacrifice the sacrifices of thanksgiving, and declare his works with rejoicing.23 They that go down to the sea in ships, that do business in great waters;24 These see the works of YHUH, and his wonders in the deep.25 For he commandeth, and raise the stormy wind, which lift up the waves thereof.26 They mount up to the heaven, they go down again to the depths: their soul is melted because of trouble.27 They reel to and fro, and stagger like a drunken man, and are at their wits' end.

| בצר 6862 | להם 1992 | וממצוקתיהם 4691 | יוציאם 3318: | 107:29 | יקם 6965 | סערה 5591 | לדממה 1827 | ויחשו 2814 |
|---|---|---|---|---|---|---|---|---|
| batzar | lahem; | uamimtzuqoteyhem, | youtziy'aem. | | yaqem | sa'arah | lidamamah; | uayecheshu, |
| **in trouble** | **their** | **and outof their distresses** | **he bring them** | | **He make** | **the storm** | **a calm** | **so that are still** |

| גליהם 1530: | 107:30 | וישמחו 8055 | כי 3588 | ישתקו 8367 | וינחם 5148 | אל 413 | מחוז 4231 | חפצם 2656: | 107:31 |
|---|---|---|---|---|---|---|---|---|---|
| galeyhem. | | uayismachu | kiy | yishtoqu; | uayanchem, | 'al | machouz | cheptzam. | |
| **the waves thereof** | | **Then are they glad** | **because** | **they be quiet** | **so he bring them** | **unto** | **haven** | **their desired** | |

| יודו 3034 | ליהוה 3068 | חסדו 2617 | ונפלאותיו 6381 | לבני 1121 | אדם 120: | 107:32 |
|---|---|---|---|---|---|---|
| youdu | laYahuah | chasdou; | uanipla'autayu, | libney | 'adam. | |
| **Oh that *men* would praise** | **to Yahuah** | ***for* his goodness** | **and *for* his wonderful works** | **to the children of** | **men** | |

| וירממוהו 7311 | בקהל 6951 | עם 5971 | ובמושב 4186 | זקנים 2205 | יהללוהו 1984: | 107:33 |
|---|---|---|---|---|---|---|
| uiyromamuhu | biqahal | 'am; | uabmoushab | zaqeniym | yahalaluhu. | |
| **Let them exalt him also** | **in the congregation of** | **the people** | **him in the assembly of** | **the elders** | **and praise him** | |

| ישם 7760 | נהרות 5104 | למדבר 4057 | ומצאי 4161 | מים 4325 | לצמאון 6774: | 107:34 | ארץ 776 | פרי 6529 | למלחה 4420 |
|---|---|---|---|---|---|---|---|---|---|
| yasem | naharout | lamidbar; | uamotza'aey | mayim, | latzima'aun. | | 'aretz | pariy | limalechah; |
| **He turned** | **rivers** | **into a wilderness** | **and springs** | **of water** | **into dry ground** | | **A land** | **fruitful** | **into barrenness** |

| מרעת 7451 | ישבי 3427 | בה 871a: | 107:35 | ישם 7760 | מדבר 4057 | לאגם 98 | מים 4325 | וארץ 776 | ציה 6723 |
|---|---|---|---|---|---|---|---|---|---|
| mera'at, | yoshabey | bah. | | yasem | midbar | la'agam | mayim; | ua'aretz | tziyah, |
| **for the wickedness of** | **them that dwell** | **therein** | | **He turned** | **the wilderness** | **into a standing** | **water** | **and ground** | **dry** |

| למצאי 4161 | מים 4325: | 107:36 | ויושב 3427 | שם 8033 | רעבים 7457 | ויכוננו 3559 | עיר 5892 | מושב 4186: | 107:37 |
|---|---|---|---|---|---|---|---|---|---|
| lamotza'aey | mayim. | | uayousheb | sham | ra'aebiym; | uayakounanu, | 'ayr | moushab. | |
| **into springs** | **of water** | | **And he make to dwell** | **there** | **the hungry** | **that they may prepare** | **a city for** | **habitation** | |

| ויזרעו 2232 | שדות 7704 | ויטעו 5193 | כרמים 3754 | ויעשו 6213 | פרי 6529 | תבואה 8393: | 107:38 | ויברכם 1288 |
|---|---|---|---|---|---|---|---|---|
| uayizra'au | sadout | uayita'au | karamiym; | uaya'asu, | pariy | tabu'ah. | | uayabarakem |
| **And sow** | **the fields** | **and plant** | **vineyards** | **which may yield** | **fruits of** | **increase** | | **He bless them also** |

| וירבו 7235 | מאד 3966 | ובהמתם 929 | לא 3808 | ימעיט 4591: | 107:39 | וימעטו 4591 | וישחו 7817 |
|---|---|---|---|---|---|---|---|
| uayirbu | ma'ad; | uabhemtam, | la' | yama'ayt. | | uayim'atu | uayashochu; |
| **so that they are multiplied** | **greatly** | **their cattle** | **not** | **suffer to decrease** | | **Again they are minished** | **and brought low** |

| מעצר 6115 | רעה 7451 | ויגון 3015: | 107:40 | שפך 8210 | בוז 937 | על 5921 | נדיבים 5081 | ויתעם 8582 |
|---|---|---|---|---|---|---|---|---|
| me'atzer | ra'ah | uayagoun. | | shopek | buz | 'al | nadiybiym; | uayat'aem, |
| **through oppression** | **affliction** | **and sorrow** | | **He pour** | **contempt** | **upon** | **princes** | **and cause them to wander** |

| בתהו 8414 | לא 3808 | דרך 1870: | 107:41 | וישגב 7682 | אביון 34 | מעוני 6040 | וישם 7760 | כצאן 6629 |
|---|---|---|---|---|---|---|---|---|
| batohu | la' | darek. | | uayasageb | abyoun | me'auniy; | uayasem | katza'n, |
| **in the wilderness *where there is*** | **no** | **way** | | **Yet set he on high** | **the poor** | **from affliction** | **and make** | **like a flock** |

| משפחות 4940: | 107:42 | יראו 7200 | ישרים 3477 | וישמחו 8055 | וכל 3605 | עולה 5766 | קפצה 7092 | פיה 6310: | 107:43 | מי 4310 | חכם 2450 |
|---|---|---|---|---|---|---|---|---|---|---|---|
| mishpachout. | | yir'au | yashariym | uayismachu; | uakal | 'aulah, | qapatzah | piyha. | | miy' | chakam |
| ***him* families** | | **shall see** | **The righteous *it*** | **and rejoice** | **and all** | **iniquity** | **shall stop** | **her mouth** | | **Whoso** | ***is* wise** |

Ps 107:28 Then they cry unto YHUH in their trouble, and he bring them out of their distresses.29 He make the storm a calm, so that the waves thereof are still.30 Then are they glad because they be quiet; so he bring them unto their desired haven.31 Oh that men would praise YHUH for his goodness, and for his wonderful works to the children of men!32 Let them exalt him also in the congregation of the people, and praise him in the assembly of the elders.33 He turneth rivers into a wilderness, and the watersprings into dry ground;34 A fruitful land into barrenness, for the wickedness of them that dwell therein.35 He turneth the wilderness into a standing water, and dry ground into watersprings.36 And there he make the hungry to dwell, that they may prepare a city for habitation;37 And sow the fields, and plant vineyards, which may yield fruits of increase.38 He blesseth them also, so that they are multiplied greatly; and suffereth not their cattle to decrease.39 Again, they are minished and brought low through oppression, affliction, and sorrow.40 He poureth contempt upon princes, and causeth them to wander in the wilderness, where there is no way.41 Yet set he the poor on high from affliction, and make him families like a flock.42 The righteous shall see it, and rejoice: and all iniquity shall stop her mouth.

וישמר 8104 אלה 428 ויתבוננו 995 חסדי 2617 יהוה 3068:
uayishmar 'aeleh; uayitbounanu, chasdey Yahuah.
**and will observe these *things* even they shall understand the lovingkindness of Yahuah**

**Ps 108:1** **108:2**
שיר 7892 מזמור 4210 לדוד 1732: נכון 3559 לבי 3820 אלהים 430 אשירה 7891 ואזמרה 2167 אף 637 כבודי 3519: עורה 5782
shiyr mizmour ladauid. nakoun libiy 'alohiym; 'ashiyrah ua'azamarah, 'ap kaboudiy. 'uarah
**A Song *or* Psalm of David is fixed my heart O Elohim I will sing and give praise even *with* my glory Awake**

**108:3**
הנבל 5035 וכנור 3658 אעירה 5782 שחר 7837: אודך 3034 בעמים 5971 יהוה 3068
hanebel uakinour, 'a'ayrah shachar. 'audaka ba'amiym Yahuah;
**psaltery and harp I *myself* will awake early I will praise you among the people O Yahuah**

**108:4**
ואזמרך 2167 בל 3816 אמים 3816: כי 3588 גדול 1419 מעל 5921 שמים 8064 חסדך 2617 ועד 5704
ua'azameraka, bal 'aumiym. kiy gadoul me'al shamayim chasadeka; ua'ad
**and I will sing praises unto you among the nations For *is* great above the heavens your mercy and unto**

**108:5**
שחקים 7834 אמתך 571: רומה 7311 על 5921 שמים 8064 אלהים 430 ועל 5921 כל 3605 הארץ 776
shachaqiym 'amiteka. rumah 'al shamayim 'alohiym; ua'al kal ha'aretz
**the clouds your truth *reaches* Be you exalted above the heavens O Elohim and above all the earth**

**108:6** **108:7**
כבודך 3519: למען 4616 יחלצון 2502 ידידיך 3039 הושיעה 3467 ימינך 3225 ועניני 6030: אלהים 430
kaboudeka. lama'an yechalatzun yadiydeyka; houshiy'ah yamiynaka ua'aneniy. 'alohiym
**your glory That may be delivered your beloved save *with* your right hand and answer me Elohim**

**108:8**
דבר 1696 בקדשו 6944 אעלזה 5937 אחלקה 2505 שכם 7927 ועמק 6010 סכות 5523 אמדד 4058: לי 3807a גלעד 1568
diber baqadashou, 'a'alozah 'achalaqah shakem; ua'ameq sukout 'amaded. liy gil'ad
**has spoken in his holiness I will rejoice I will divide Shechem and the valley of Succoth mete out *is* mine Gilead**

**108:9**
לי 3807a מנשה 4519 ואפרים 669 מעוז 4581 ראשי 7218 יהודה 3063 מחקקי 2710: מואב 4124 סיר 5518 רחצי 7366
liy manasheh, ua'aprayim ma'auz ra'shiy; yahudah, machoqaqiy. mou'ab siyr rachatziy,
***is* mine Manasseh and Ephraim also *is* the strength of mine head Judah *is* my lawgiver Moab *is* bowl my wash**

**108:10**
על 5921 אדום 123 אשליך 7993 נעלי 5275 עלי 5921 פלשת 6429 אתרועע 7321: מי 4310 יבלני 2986 עיר 5892 מבצר 4013 מי 4310
'al 'adoum 'ashliyk na'aliy; 'aley paleshet, 'atrou'aa'. miy' yobileniy 'ayr mibtzar; miy'
**over Edom will I cast out my shoe over Philistia will I triumph Who will bring me into city? *the* strong who**

**108:11**
נחני 5148 עד 5704 אדום 123: הלא 3808 אלהים 430 זנחתנו 2186 ולא 3808 תצא 3318 אלהים 430
nachaniy 'ad 'adoum. hala' 'alohiym zanachtanu; uala' tetzea' 'alohiym,
**will lead me into Edom? *Will* not *you* O Elohim *who* have cast us off? and not will you go forth O Elohim**

**108:12** **108:13**
בצבאתינו 6635: הבה 3051 לנו 3807a עזרת 5833 מצר 6862 ושוא 7723 תשועת 8668 אדם 120: באלהים 430
batzib'ateynu. habah lanu 'azrat mitzar; uashau', tashu'at 'adam. be'alohiym
**with our armies Give us help from trouble for vain *is* the help of man Through Elohim**

נעשה 6213 חיל 2428 והוא 1931 יבוס 947 צרינו 6862:
na'aseh chayil; uahu'a, yabus tzareynu.
**we shall do valiantly for he *it is that* shall tread down our enemies**

Ps 107:43 Whoso is wise, and will observe these things, even they shall understand the lovingkindness of YHUH. **Ps** 108:1 A Song or Psalm of David. O G-d, my heart is fixed; I will sing and give praise, even with my glory.2 Awake, psaltery and harp: I myself will awake early.3 I will praise you, O YHUH, among the people: and I will sing praises unto you among the nations.4 For your mercy is great above the heavens: and your truth reacheth unto the clouds.5 Be you exalted, O G-d, above the heavens: and your glory above all the earth;6 That your beloved may be delivered: save with your right hand, and answer me.7 G-d has spoken in his holiness; I will rejoice, I will divide Shechem, and mete out the valley of Succoth.8 Gilead is mine; Manasseh is mine; Ephraim also is the strength of mine head; Judah is my lawgiver;9 Moab is my washpot; over Edom will I cast out my shoe; over Philistia will I triumph.10 Who will bring me into the strong city? who will lead me into Edom?11 Wilt not you, O G-d, who have cast us off? and will not you, O G-d, go forth with our hosts?12 Give us help from trouble: for vain is the help of man.13 Through G-d we shall do valiantly: for he it is that shall tread down our enemies.

**Ps 109:1** … **109:2**

למנצח 5329 לדוד 1732 מזמור 4210 אלהי 430 תהלתי 8416 אל 408 תחרש 2790: כי 3588 פי 6310

lamanatzeach ladauid mizmour; 'alohey tahilatiy, 'al techarash. kiy piy

**To the chief Musician of David A Psalm O Elohim of my praise not Hold your peace For the mouth of**

רשע 7563 ופי 6310 מרמה 4820 עלי 5921 פתחו 6605 דברו 1696 אתי 854 לשון 3956

rasha' uapiy mirmah 'alay patachu; dibru 'atiy, lashoun

**the wicked and the mouth of the deceitful against me are opened they have spoken against me with a tongue**

**109:3** … **109:4**

שקר 8267: ודברי 1697 שנאה 8135 סבבוני 5437 וילחמוני 3898 חנם 2600: תחת 8478

shaqer. uadibrey sin'ah sababuniy; uayilachamuniy chinam. tachat

**lying also with words of hatred They compassed me about and fought against me without a cause For**

**109:5**

אהבתי 160 ישטנוני 7853 ואני 589 תפלה 8605: וישימו 7760 עלי 5921 רעה 7451 תחת 8478

'ahabatiy yistanuniy, ua'aniy tapilah. uayasiymu 'alay ra'ah tachat

**my love they are my adversaries but I *give myself unto* prayer And they have rewarded me evil for**

**109:6** … **109:7**

טובה 2896 ושנאה 8135 תחת 8478 אהבתי 160: הפקד 6485 עליו 5921 רשע 7563 ושטן 7854 יעמד 5975 על 5921 ימינו 3225:

toubah; uasin'ah, tachat 'ahabatiy. hapqed 'alayu rasha'; uasatan, ya'amod 'al yamiynou.

**good and hatred for my love Set you over him a wicked man and Satan let stand at his right hand**

**109:8**

בהשפטו 8199 יצא 3318 רשע 7563 ותפלתו 8605 תהיה 1961 לחטאה 2401: יהיו 1961 ימיו 3117 מעטים 4592

bahishapatou yetzea' rasha'; uatpilatou, tihayeh lachata'ah. yihayu yamayu ma'atiym;

**When he shall be judged let him be condemned and his prayer let become sin Let be his days few**

**109:9** … **109:10**

פקדתו 6486 יקח 3947 אחר 312: יהיו 1961 בניו 1121 יתומים 3490 ואשתו 802 אלמנה 490: ונוע 5128

paqudatou, yiqach 'acher. yihayu banayu yatoumiym; ua'ashtou 'almanah. uanoua'

**his office *and* let take another Let be his children fatherless and his wife a widow Let be continually**

**109:11**

ינועו 5128 בניו 1121 ושאלו 7592 ודרשו 1875 מחרבותיהם 2723: ינקש 5367 נושה 5383

yanu'au banayu uashi'aelu; uadarashu, mecharabouteyhem. yanaqesh nousheh

**vagabonds his children and beg let them seek *their bread* also out of their desolate places Let catch *the* extortioner**

**109:12**

לכל 3605 אשר 834 לו 3807a ויבזו 962 זרים 2114 יגיעו 3018: אל 408 יהי 1961 לו 3807a משך 4900 חסד 2617 ואל 408

lakal 'asher lou'; uayabozu zariym yagiy'au. 'al yahiy lou' moshek chased; ua'al

**all that he *has* and let spoil the strangers his labour none Let there be unto him to extend mercy neither**

**109:13**

יהי 1961 חונן 2603 ליתומיו 3490: יהי 1961 אחריתו 319 להכרית 3772 בדור 1755 אחר 312

yahiy chounen, liytoumayu. yahiy 'achariytou lahakriyt; badour 'acher,

**let there be *any* to favor his fatherless children Let be his posterity cut off *and* in the generation following**

**109:14**

ימח 4229 שמם 8034: יזכר 2142 עון 5771 אבתיו 1 אל 413 יהוה 3068 וחטאת 2403 אמו 517

yimach shamam. yizaker 'auon 'abotayu 'al Yahuah; uachata't 'amou,

**let be blotted out their name Let be remembered the iniquity of his fathers with Yahuah and the sin of his mother**

**109:15**

אל 408 תמח 4229: יהיו 1961 נגד 5048 יהוה 3068 תמיד 8548 ויכרת 3772 מארץ 776

'al timach. yihayu neged Yahuah tamiyd; uayakret me'aretz

**not let be blotted out Let them be before Yahuah continually that he may cut off from the earth**

**Ps** 109:1 To the chief Musician, A Psalm of David. Hold not your peace, O G-d of my praise;2 For the mouth of the wicked and the mouth of the deceitful are opened against me: they have spoken against me with a lying tongue.3 They compassed me about also with words of hatred; and fought against me without a cause.4 For my love they are my adversaries: but I give myself unto prayer.5 And they have rewarded me evil for good, and hatred for my love.6 Set you a wicked man over him: and let Satan stand at his right hand.7 When he shall be judged, let him be condemned: and let his prayer become sin.8 Let his days be few; and let another take his office.9 Let his children be fatherless, and his wife a widow.10 Let his children be continually vagabonds, and beg: let them seek their bread also out of their desolate places.11 Let the extortioner catch all that he has; and let the strangers spoil his labour.12 Let there be none to extend mercy unto him: neither let there be any to favor his fatherless children.13 Let his posterity be cut off; and in the generation following let their name be blotted out.14 Let the iniquity of his fathers be remembered with YHUH; and let not the sin of his mother be blotted out.15 Let them be before YHUH continually, that he may cut off the memory of them from the earth.

109:16
זכרם 2143: יען 3282 אשר 834 לא 3808 זכר 2142 עשות 6213 חסד 2617 וירדף 7291 איש 376 עני 6041
zikram. ya'an, 'asher la' zakar asout chased uayirdop 'aysh 'aniy
**the memory of them Because that not he remembered to show mercy but persecuted man the poor**

109:17
ואביון 34 ונכאה 5218 לבב 3824 למותת 4191: ויאהב 157 קללה 7045 ותבואהו 935 ולא 3808
ua'abyoun uanik'aeh lebab lamoutet. uaye'ahab qalalah uatabou'aehu; uala'
**and needy the broken in heart that he might even slay As he loved cursing so let it come unto him as not**

109:18
חפץ 2654 בברכה 1293 ותרחק 7368 ממנו 4480: וילבש 3847 קללה 7045 כמדו 4055
chapetz bibarakah, uatirchaq mimenu. uayilbash qalalah, kamadou
**he delighted in blessing so let it be far from him As he clothed himself with cursing like as with his garment**

109:19
ותבא 935 כמים 4325 בקרבו 7130 וכשמן 8081 בעצמותיו 6106: תהי 1961 לו 3807a כבגד 899
uataba' kamayim baqirbou; uakashemen, ba'atzamoutayu. tahiy lou' kabeged
**so let it come like water into his bowels and like oil into his bones Let it be unto him as the garment**

109:20
יעטה 5844 ולמזח 4206 תמיד 8548 יחגרה 2296: זאת 2063 פעלת 6468 שטני 7853
ya'ateh; ualmezach, tamiyd yachgareha. za't pa'alat sotanay
***which* cover him and for a girdle continually *wherewith* he is girded *Let* this *be* the reward of mine adversaries**

109:21
מאת 853 יהוה 3068 והדברים 1696 רע 7451 על 5921 נפשי 5315: ואתה 859 יהוה 3069 אדני 136 עשה 6213 אתי 854 למען 4616
me'at Yahuah; uahadobariym ra', 'al napshiy. ua'atah Yahuah 'adonay, 'aseh 'atiy lama'an
**from Yahuah and of them that speak evil against my soul But you O Yahuah Adonai do for me for sake**

109:22
שמך 8034 כי 3588 טוב 2896 חסדך 2617 הצילני 5337: כי 3588 עני 6041 ואביון 34 אנכי 595 ולבי 3820 חלל 2490
shameka; kiy toub chasdaka, hatziyleniy. kiy 'aniy ua'abyoun 'anokiy; ualibiy, chalal
**your name's because *is* good your mercy deliver you me For *am* poor and needy I and my heart is wounded**

109:23 109:24
בקרבי 7130: כצל 6738 כנטותו 5186 נהלכתי 1980 ננערתי 5287 כארבה 697: ברכי 1290
baqirbiy. katzel kintoutou nehelakatiy; nin'artiy, ka'arbeh. birkay
**within me like the shadow when it declineth I am gone I am tossed up and down as the locust My knees**

109:25
כשלו 3782 מצום 6685 ובשרי 1320 כחש 3584 משמן 8081: ואני 589 הייתי 1961 חרפה 2781 להם 1992
kashalu mitzoum; uabsariy, kachash mishamen. ua'aniy hayiytiy cherpah lahem;
**are weak through fasting and my flesh fail of fatness I also become a reproach unto them**

109:26
יראוני 7200 יניעון 5128 ראשם 7218: עזרני 5826 יהוה 3068 אלהי 430 הושיעני 3467
yir'auniy, yaniy'aun ra'sham. 'azareniy Yahuah 'alohay; houshiy'aeniy
***when* they looked upon me they shaked their heads Help me O Yahuah my Elohim O save me**

109:27 109:28
כחסדך 2617: וידעו 3045 כי 3588 ידך 3027 זאת 2063 אתה 859 יהוה 3068 עשיתה 6213:
kachasadeka. uayeda'au kiy yadaka za't; 'atah Yahuah 'asiytah.
**according to your mercy That they may know that *is* your hand this *that* you Yahuah have done it**

109:29
יקללו 7043 המה 1992 ואתה 859 תברך 1288 קמו 6965 ויבשו 954 ועבדך 5650 ישמח 8055: ילבשו 3847
yaqalalu hemah ua'atah tabarek qamu uayeboshu, ua'abdaka yismach. yilbshu
**Let curse them but you bless *when* they arise let them be ashamed but your servant let rejoice Let be clothed**

Ps 109:16 Because that he remembered not to show mercy, but persecuted the poor and needy man, that he might even slay the broken in heart.17 As he loved cursing, so let it come unto him: as he delighted not in blessing, so let it be far from him.18 As he clothed himself with cursing like as with his garment, so let it come into his bowels like water, and like oil into his bones.19 Let it be unto him as the garment which covereth him, and for a girdle wherewith he is girded continually.20 Let this be the reward of mine adversaries from YHUH, and of them that speak evil against my soul.21 But do you for me, O G-D the Adonai, for your name's sake: because your mercy is good, deliver you me.22 For I am poor and needy, and my heart is wounded within me.23 I am gone like the shadow when it declineth: I am tossed up and down as the locust.24 My knees are weak through fasting; and my flesh faileth of fatness.25 I became also a reproach unto them: when they looked upon me they shaked their heads.26 Help me, O YHUH my G-d: O save me according to your mercy:27 That they may know that this is your hand; that you, YHUH, have done it.28 Let them curse, but bless you: when they arise, let them be ashamed; but let your servant rejoice.

שוטני 7853 כלמה 3639 ויעטו 5844 כמעיל 4598 בשתם 1322: **109:30** אודה 3034
soutanay kalimah; uaya'atou kama'ayl bashatam. 'audeh
**mine adversaries with shame and let them cover themselves as with a mantle with their own confusion I will praise**

יהוה 3068 מאד 3966 בפי 6310 ובתוך 8432 רבים 7227 אהללנו 1984: **109:31** כי 3588 יעמד 5975 לימין 3225
Yahuah ma'ad bapiy; uabtouk rabiym 'ahalalenu. kiy ya'amod liyamiyn
**Yahuah greatly with my mouth yea among the multitude I will praise him For he shall stand at the right hand of**

אביון 34 להושיע 3467 משפטי 8199 נפשו 5315:
abyoun; lahoushiya', mishopatey napshou.
**the poor to save *him* from those that condemn his soul**

**Ps 110:1** לדוד 1732 מזמור 4210 נאם 5002 יהוה 3068 לאדני 113 שב 3427 לימיני 3225 עד 5704 אשית 7896 איביך 341 הדם 1916
ladauid, mizmour na'am Yahuah la'adoniy, shaeb liymiyniy; 'ad 'ashiyt 'ayabeyka, hadom
**of David A Psalm said Yahuah unto my Adonai Sit you at my right hand until I make your enemies stool**

לרגליך 7272: **110:2** מטה 4294 עזך 5797 ישלח 7971 יהוה 3068 מציון 6726 רדה 7287 בקרב 7130 איביך 341: **110:3**
laragleyka. mateh 'azaka, yishlach Yahuah mitziyoun; radeh, baqereb 'ayabeyka.
**your foot the rod of your strength shall send Yahuah out of Zion rule you in the midst of your enemies**

עמך 5971 נדבת 5071 ביום 3117 חילך 2428 בהדרי 1926 קדש 6944 מרחם 7358 משחר 4891 לך 3807a
'amaka nadabot bayoum cheyleka bahadrey qodesh merechem mishchar; laka,
**Your people *shall be* willing in the day of your power in the beauties of holiness from the womb of the morning to you**

טל 2919 ילדתיך 3208: **110:4** נשבע 7650 יהוה 3068 ולא 3808 ינחם 5162 אתה 859 כהן 3548 לעולם 5769 על 5921 דברתי 1700
tal yalduteyka. nishba' Yahuah uala' yinachem, 'atah kohen la'aulam; 'al dibratiy,
***have* the dew of your youth has sworn Yahuah and not will repent You *are* a priest for ever after the order of**

מלכי 4442 צדק 6664: **110:5** אדני 136 על 5921 ימינך 3225 מחץ 4272 ביום 3117 אפו 639 מלכים 4428: **110:6**
malkiy tzedeq. 'adonay 'al yamiynaka; machatz bayoum 'apou malakiym.
**Melchi zedek Adonai at your right hand shall strike through in the day of his wrath kings**

ידין 1777 בגוים 1471 מלא 4390 גויות 1472 מחץ 4272 ראש 7218 על 5921 ארץ 776
yadiyn bagouyim malea' gauiyat; machatz ra'sh, 'al 'aretz
**He shall judge among the heathen he shall fill *the places* with the dead bodies he shall wound the heads over countries**

רבה 7227: **110:7** מנחל 5158 בדרך 1870 ישתה 8354 על 5921 כן 3651 ירים 7311 ראש 7218:
rabah. minachal baderek yishteh; 'al ken, yariym ra'sh.
**many of the brook in the way He shall drink therefore after that shall he lift up the head**

**Ps 111:1** הללו 1984 יה 3050 אודה 3034 יהוה 3068 בכל 3605 לבב 3824 בסוד 5475 ישרים 3477
halalu Yah 'audeh Yahuah bakal labab; basoud yashariym
**Praise you Yah I will praise Yahuah with *my* whole heart in the assembly of the upright**

ועדה 5712: **111:2** גדלים 1419 מעשי 4639 יהוה 3068 דרושים 1875 לכל 3605 חפציהם 2656:
ua'aedah. gadoliym ma'asey Yahuah; darushiym, lakal chepatzeyhem.
**and *in* the congregation *are* great The works of Yahuah sought out of all them that have pleasure**

Ps 109:29 Let mine adversaries be clothed with shame, and let them cover themselves with their own confusion, as with a mantle.30 I will greatly praise YHUH with my mouth; yea, I will praise him among the multitude.31 For he shall stand at the right hand of the poor, to save him from those that condemn his soul. **Ps** 110:1 A Psalm of David YHUH said unto my Adonai, Sit you at my right hand, until I make your enemies your footstool.2 YHUH shall send the rod of your strength out of Zion: rule you in the midst of your enemies.3 Thy people shall be willing in the day of your power, in the beauties of holiness from the womb of the morning: you have the dew of your youth.4 YHUH has sworn, and will not repent, Thou are a priest forever after the order of Melchizedek.5 The Adonai at your right hand shall strike through kings in the day of his wrath.6 He shall judge among the heathen, he shall fill the places with the dead bodies; he shall wound the heads over many countries.7 He shall drink of the brook in the way: therefore shall he lift up the head. **Ps** 111:1 Praise you YHUH. I will praise YHUH with my whole heart, in the assembly of the upright, and in the congregation.2 The works of YHUH are great, sought out of all them that have pleasure therein.

111:3 · 111:4
הוד 1935 | והדר 1926 | פעלו 6467 | וצדקתו 6666 | עמדת 5975 | לעד 5703: | זכר 2143 | עשה 6213
houd | uahadar | pa'alou; | uatzidqatou, | 'amedet | la'ad. | zeker | 'asah
*is* honorable | and glorious | His work | and his righteousness | endures | for ever | to be remembered | He has made

111:5
לנפלאתיו 6381 | חנון 2587 | ורחום 7349 | יהוה 3068: | טרף 2964 | נתן 5414 | ליראיו 3373
lanipla'atayu; | chanun | uarachum | Yahuah. | terep | natan | liyre'ayu;
his wonderful works | *is* gracious | and full of compassion | Yahuah | meat | He has given | unto them that fear him

111:6
יזכר 2142 | לעולם 5769 | בריתו 1285: | כח 3581 | מעשיו 4639 | הגיד 5046 | לעמו 5971 | לתת 5414
yizkor | la'aulam | bariytou. | koach | ma'asayu | higiyd | la'amou; | latet
he will be mindful of | ever | his covenant | the power of | his works | He has showed | his people | that he may give

111:7
להם 3807a | נחלת 5159 | גוים 1471: | מעשי 4639 | ידיו 3027 | אמת 571 | ומשפט 4941 | נאמנים 539 | כל 3605
lahem, | nachalat | gouyim. | ma'asey | yadayu | 'amet | uamishpat; | ne'amaniym, | kal
them | the heritage of | the heathen | The works of | his hands | *are* verity | and judgment | *are* sure | all

111:8 · 111:9
פקודיו 6490: | סמוכים 5564 | לעד 5703 | לעולם 5769 | עשוים 6213 | באמת 571 | וישר 3477: | פדות 6304 | שלח 7971
piqudayu. | samukiym | la'ad | la'aulam; | 'asuyim, | be'amet | uayashar. | padut | shalach
his commandments | They stand fast for ever and ever *and are* done in truth and uprightness | redemption | He sent

111:10
לעמו 5971 | צוה 6680 | לעולם 5769 | בריתו 1285 | קדוש 6918 | ונורא 3372 | שמו 8034: | ראשית 7225
la'amou, | tziuah | la'aulam | bariytou; | qadoush | uanoura' | shamou. | ra'shiyt
unto his people | he has commanded | for ever | his covenant | holy | and reverend | *is* his name | *is* the beginning of

חכמה 2451 | יראת 3374 | יהוה 3068 | שכל 7922 | טוב 2896 | לכל 3605 | עשיהם 6213 | תהלתו 8416 | עמדת 5975 | לעד 5703:
chakamah | yir'at | Yahuah | sekel | toub | lakal | 'aseyhem; | tahilatou, | 'amedet | la'ad.
wisdom | The fear of | Yahuah | a understanding | good | *have* all they that do *his commandments* | his praise | endures | for ever

Ps 112:1 · 112:2
הללו 1984 | יה 3050 | אשרי 835 | איש 376 | ירא 3372 | את 853 | יהוה 3068 | במצותיו 4687 | חפץ 2654 | מאד 3966:
halalu | Yah | 'ashrey | 'aysh | yarea' | 'at | Yahuah; | bamitzuotayu, | chapetz | ma'ad.
Praise you | Yah | Blessed | *is* the man | *that* fear | | Yahuah | in his commandments | *that* delight | greatly

112:3
גבור 1368 | בארץ 776 | יהיה 1961 | זרעו 2233 | דור 1755 | ישרים 3477 | יברך 1288: | הון 1952 | ועשר 6239
gibour | ba'aretz | yihayeh | zar'au; | dour | yashariym | yaborak. | houn | ua'asher
mighty | upon earth | shall be | His seed | the generation of | the upright | shall be blessed | Wealth | and riches

112:4
בביתו 1004 | וצדקתו 6666 | עמדת 5975 | לעד 5703: | זרח 2224 | בחשך 2822 | אור 216 | לישרים 3477
babeytou; | uatzidqatou, | 'amedet | la'ad. | zarach | bachoshek | 'aur | layshariym;
*shall be* in his house | and his righteousness | endures | for ever | there arise | in the darkness | light | Unto the upright

112:5
חנון 2587 | ורחום 7349 | וצדיק 6662: | טוב 2896 | איש 376 | חונן 2603 | ומלוה 3867 | יכלכל 3557 | דבריו 1697
chanun | uarachum | uatzadiyq. | toub | 'aysh | chounen | uamalueh; | yakalkel | dabarayu
*he is* gracious | and full of compassion | and righteous | good | A man | shows favor | and lend | he will guide | his affairs

112:6
במשפט 4941: | כי 3588 | לעולם 5769 | לא 3808 | ימוט 4131 | לזכר 2143 | עולם 5769 | יהיה 1961 | צדיק 6662:
bamishpat. | kiy | la'aulam | la' | yimout; | lazeker | 'aulam, | yihayeh | tzadiyq.
with discretion | Surely | for ever | not | he shall be moved | in remembrance | everlasting | shall be | the righteous

Ps 111:3 His work is honourable and glorious: and his righteousness endureth forever.4 He has made his wonderful works to be remembered: YHUH is gracious and full of compassion.5 He has given meat unto them that fear him: he will ever be mindful of his covenant.6 He has showed his people the power of his works, that he may give them the heritage of the heathen.7 The works of his hands are verity and judgment; all his commandments are sure.8 They stand fast forever and ever, and are done in truth and uprightness.9 He sent redemption unto his people: he has commanded his covenant forever: holy and reverend is his name.10 The fear of YHUH is the beginning of wisdom: a good understanding have all they that do his commandments: his praise endureth forever. **Ps** 112:1 Praise you YHUH. Blessed is the man that fear YHUH, that delighteth greatly in his commandments.2 His seed shall be mighty upon earth: the generation of the upright shall be blessed.3 Wealth and riches shall be in his house: and his righteousness endureth forever.4 Unto the upright there arise light in the darkness: he is gracious, and full of compassion, and righteous.5 A good man show favor, and lendeth: he will guide his affairs with discretion.6 Surely he shall not be moved forever: the righteous shall be in everlasting remembrance.

| | | | | | | | | | | | |
|---|---|---|---|---|---|---|---|---|---|---|---|
| **112:7** | משמועה 8052 | רעה 7451 | לא 3808 | יירא 3372 | נכון 3559 | לבו 3820 | בטח 982 | ביהוה 3068: | **112:8** | סמוך 5564 | לבו 3820 |
| | mishmu'ah | ra'ah | la' | yiyra'; | nakoun | libou, | batuach | baYahuah. | | samuk | libou |
| | **tidings** | **evil** | **not** | **He shall be afraid of** | **is fixed** | **his heart** | **trusting** | **in Yahuah** | | ***is* established** | **His heart** |

| | | | | | | | | | |
|---|---|---|---|---|---|---|---|---|---|
| לא 3808 | יירא 3372 | עד 5704 | אשר 834 | יראה 7200 | בצריו 6862: | **112:9** | פזר 6340 | נתן 5414 | לאביונים 34 |
| la' | yiyra'; | 'ad | 'asher | yir'ah | batzarayu. | | pizar | natan | la'abyouniym, |
| **not** | **he shall be afraid** | **until** | **which** | **he see** | ***his desire* upon his enemies** | | **He has dispersed** | **he has given** | **to the poor** |

| | | | | | | | | | |
|---|---|---|---|---|---|---|---|---|---|
| צדקתו 6666 | עמדת 5975 | לעד 5703 | קרנו 7161 | תרום 7311 | בכבוד 3519: | **112:10** | רשע 7563 | יראה 7200 | וכעס 3707 |
| tzidqatou | 'amedet | la'ad; | qarnou, | tarum | bakaboud. | | rasha' | yir'ah | uaka'as, |
| **his righteousness** | **endures** | **for ever** | **his horn** | **shall be exalted** | **with honor** | | **The wicked** | **shall see** | ***it* and be grieved** |

| | | | | | |
|---|---|---|---|---|---|
| שניו 8127 | יחרק 2786 | ונמס 4549 | תאות 8378 | רשעים 7563 | תאבד 6: |
| shinayu | yacharoq | uanamas; | ta'auat | rasha'aym | ta'bed. |
| ***with* his teeth** | **he shall gnash** | **and melt away** | **the desire of** | **the wicked** | **shall perish** |

| | | | | | | | | | | | |
|---|---|---|---|---|---|---|---|---|---|---|---|
| **Ps 113:1** | הללו 1984 | יה 3050 | הללו 1984 | עבדי 5650 | יהוה 3068 | הללו 1984 | את 853 | שם 8034 | יהוה 3068: | **113:2** יהי 1961 | שם 8034 |
| | halalu | Yah | halalu | 'abdey | Yahuah; | halalu | 'at | shem | Yahuah. | yahiy | shem |
| | **Praise you** | **Yah** | **Praise** | **O you servants of** | **Yahuah** | **praise** | | **the name of** | **Yahuah** | **be** | **the name of** |

| | | | | | | | | | |
|---|---|---|---|---|---|---|---|---|---|
| יהוה 3068 | מברך 1288 | מעתה 6258 | ועד 5704 | עולם 5769: | **113:3** | ממזרח 4217 | שמש 8121 | עד 5704 | מבואו 3996 |
| Yahuah | maborak; | me'atah, | ua'ad | 'aulam. | | mimizrach | shemesh | 'ad | mabou'au; |
| **Yahuah** | **Blessed** | **from this time forth** | **and for** | **evermore** | | **From the rising of** | **the sun** | **unto** | **the going down of** |

| | | | | | | | | | | | |
|---|---|---|---|---|---|---|---|---|---|---|---|
| מהלל 1984 | שם 8034 | יהוה 3068: | **113:4** רם 7311 | על 5921 | כל 3605 | גוים 1471 | יהוה 3068 | על 5921 | השמים 8064 | כבודו 3519: | **113:5** |
| mahulal, | shem | Yahuah. | ram | 'al | kal | gouyim | Yahuah; | 'al | hashamayim | kaboudou. | |
| ***is* to be praised** | **name** | ***the same* Yahuah's** | ***is* high** | **above** | **all** | **nations** | **Yahuah** | **above** | **the heavens** | ***and* his glory** | |

| | | | | | | | |
|---|---|---|---|---|---|---|---|
| מי 4310 | כיהוה 3068 | אלהינו 430 | המגביהי 1361 | לשבת 3427: | **113:6** | המשפילי 8213 | לראות 7200 |
| miy' | baYahuah | 'aloheynu; | hamagabiyhiy | lashabet. | | hamashapiyliy | lir'aut; |
| **Who *is* like** | **unto Yahuah** | **our Elohim** | **high** | **who dwell on** | | **Who humble** | ***himself* to behold** |

| | | | | | | | |
|---|---|---|---|---|---|---|---|
| בשמים 8064 | ובארץ 776: | **113:7** | מקימי 6965 | מעפר 6083 | דל 1800 | מאשפת 830 | ירים 7311 |
| bashamayim | uaba'aretz. | | maqiymiy | me'apar | dal; | me'ashpot, | yariym |
| ***the things that are* in heaven** | **and in the earth** | | **He raises up** | **out of the dust** | **the poor** | **out of the dunghill** | ***and* lift** |

| | | | | | | | | | |
|---|---|---|---|---|---|---|---|---|---|
| אביון 34: | **113:8** | להושיבי 3427 | עם 5973 | נדיבים 5081 | עם 5973 | נדיבי 5081 | עמו 5971: | **113:9** | מושיבי 3427 |
| abyoun. | | lahoushiybiy | 'am | nadiybiym; | 'am, | nadiybey | 'amou. | | moushiybiy |
| **the needy** | | **That he may set *him*** | **with** | **princes *even*** | **with** | **the princes of** | **his people** | | **He make to keep** |

| | | | | | | |
|---|---|---|---|---|---|---|
| עקרת 6135 | הבית 1004 | אם 517 | הבנים 1121 | שמחה 8056 | הללו 1984 | יה 3050: |
| 'aqeret | habayit, | 'am | habaniym | samechah, | halalu | Yah. |
| **the barren woman** | **house** | ***and to be* a mother of** | **children** | **joyful** | **Praise you** | **Yah** |

| | | | | | | | | | |
|---|---|---|---|---|---|---|---|---|---|
| **Ps 114:1** | בצאת 3318 | ישראל 3478 | ממצרים 4714 | בית 1004 | יעקב 3290 | מעם 5971 | לעז 3937: | **114:2** | היתה 1961 |
| | batzea't | yisra'ael | mimitzrayim; | beyt | ya'aqob, | me'am | la'aez. | | hayatah |
| | **When went out** | **Israel** | **of Egypt** | **the house of** | **Jacob** | **from a people of** | **strange language** | | **was** |

Ps 112:7 He shall not be afraid of evil tidings: his heart is fixed, trusting in YHUH.8 His heart is established, he shall not be afraid, until he see his desire upon his enemies.9 He has dispersed, he has given to the poor; his righteousness endureth forever; his horn shall be exalted with honor.10 The wicked shall see it, and be grieved; he shall gnash with his teeth, and melt away: the desire of the wicked shall perish. **Ps** 113:1 Praise you YHUH. Praise, O you servants of YHUH, praise the name of YHUH.2 Blessed be the name of YHUH from this time forth and forevermore.3 From the rising of the sun unto the going down of the same YHUH's name is to be praised.4 YHUH is high above all nations, and his glory above the heavens.5 Who is like unto YHUH our G-d, who dwell on high,6 Who humbleth himself to behold the things that are in heaven, and in the earth!7 He raise up the poor out of the dust, and lift the needy out of the dunghill;8 That he may set him with princes, even with the princes of his people.9 He make the barren woman to keep house, and to be a joyful mother of children. Praise you YHUH. **Ps** 114:1 When Israel went out of Egypt, the house of Jacob from a people of strange language;

יהודה 3063 לקדשו 6944 ישראל 3478 ממשלותיו 4475: **114:3** הים 3220 ראה 7200 וינס 5127 הירדן 3383 יסב 5437 לאחור 268: **114:4**
yahudah laqadashou; yisra'ael, mamshaloutayu. hayam ra'ah uayanos; hayarden, yisob la'achour.
**Judah his sanctuary *and* Israel his dominion The sea saw *it* and fled the Jordan was driven back**

ההרים 2022 רקדו 7540 כאילים 352 גבעות 1389 כבני 1121 צאן 6629: **114:5** מה 4100 לך 3807a הים 3220 כי 3588 תנוס 5127
hehariym raqadu ka'aeyliym; gaba'aut, kibney tza'n. mah laka hayam kiy tanus;
**The mountains skipped like rams *and* the little hills like lambs flock What *ailed* to you O sea that you fled**

הירדן 3383 תסב 5437 לאחור 268: **114:6** ההרים 2022 תרקדו 7540 כאילים 352 גבעות 1389 כבני 1121
hayarden, tisob la'achour. hehariym tirqadu ka'aeyliym; gaba'aut, kibney
**the Jordan *that* you were driven back? You mountains *that* you skipped like rams *and* you little hills like lambs**

צאן 6629: **114:7** מלפני 6440 אדון 136 חולי 2342 ארץ 776 מלפני 6440 אלוה 433 יעקב 3290: **114:8** ההפכי 2015
tza'n. milipney 'adoun chuliy 'aretz; milipney, 'alouah ya'aqob. hahopakiy
**flock at the presence of Adonai Tremble you earth at the presence of *the* Elohim *of* Jacob Which turned**

הצור 6697 אגם 98 מים 4325 חלמיש 2496 למעינו 4599 מים 4325:
hatzur 'agam mayim; chalamiysh, lama'aynou mayim.
**the rock *into* a standing water the flint into a fountain of waters**

**Ps 115:1** לא 3808 לנו 3807a יהוה 3068 לא 3808 לנו 3807a כי 3588 לשמך 8034 תן 5414 כבוד 3519 על 5921 חסדך 2617 על 5921
la' lanu Yahuah la' lanu kiy lashimka ten kaboud; 'al chasdaka, 'al
**Not unto us O Yahuah not unto us but unto your name give glory for your mercy *and* for**

אמתך 571: **115:2** למה 4100 יאמרו 559 הגוים 1471 איה 346 נא 4994 אלהיהם 430: **115:3** ואלהינו 430
'amiteka. lamah ya'maru hagouyim; 'ayeh na, 'aloheyhem. ua'aloheynu
**your truth's sake Wherefore should say the heathen Where *is* now their Elohim? But our Elohim**

בשמים 8064 כל 3605 אשר 834 חפץ 2654 עשה 6213: **115:4** עצביהם 6091 כסף 3701 וזהב 2091 מעשה 4639 ידי 3027
bashamayim; kal 'asher chapetz 'asah. 'atzabeyhem kesep uazahab; ma'aseh, yadey
***is* in the heavens whatsoever which he has pleased he has done Their idols *are* silver and gold the work of hands**

אדם 120: **115:5** פה 6310 להם 1992 ולא 3808 ידברו 1696 עינים 5869 להם 1992 ולא 3808 יראו 7200: **115:6** אזנים 241 להם 3807a ולא 3808
'adam. peh lahem uala' yadaberu; 'aeynayim lahem, uala' yir'au. 'azanayim lahem uala'
**men's *have* mouths They but not they speak eyes *have* they but not they see *have* ears They but not**

ישמעו 8085 אף 639 להם 3807a ולא 3808 יריחון 7306: **115:7** ידיהם 3027 ולא 3808 ימישון 4184 רגליהם 7272 ולא 3808 יהלכו 1980
yishma'au; 'ap lahem, uala' yariychun. yadeyhem uala' yamiyshun, ragleyhem uala' yahaleku;
**they hear noses *have* they but not they smell They have hands but not they handle feet have they but not they walk**

לא 3808 יהגו 1897 בגרונם 1627: **115:8** כמוהם 3644 יהיו 1961 עשיהם 6213 כל 3605 אשר 834 בטח 982
la' yehagu, bigrounam. kamouhem yihayu 'aseyhem; kal 'asher boteach
**neither speak they through their throat like unto them are They that make them *so is* every one that trust**

בהם 871a: **115:9** ישראל 3478 בטח 982 ביהוה 3068 עזרם 5828 ומגנם 4043 הוא 1931: **115:10** בית 1004 אהרן 175 בטחו 982
bahem. yisra'ael batach baYahuah; 'azram uamaginam hua'. beyt 'aharon bitchu
**in them O Israel trust you in Yahuah *is* their help and their shield he O house of Aaron trust**

Ps 114:2 Judah was his sanctuary, and Israel his dominion.3 The sea saw it, and fled: Jordan was driven back.4 The mountains skipped like rams, and the little hills like lambs.5 What ailed you, O you sea, that you fleddest? you Jordan, that you were driven back?6 You mountains, that you skipped like rams; and you little hills, like lambs?7 Tremble, you earth, at the presence of the Adonai, at the presence of the G-d of Jacob;8 Which turned the rock into a standing water, the flint into a fountain of waters. **Ps** 115:1 Not unto us, O YHUH, not unto us, but unto your name give glory, for your mercy, and for your truth's sake.2 Wherefore should the heathen say, Where is now their G-d?3 But our G-d is in the heavens: he has done whatsoever he has pleased.4 Their idols are silver and gold, the work of men's hands.5 They have mouths, but they speak not: eyes have they, but they see not:6 They have ears, but they hear not: noses have they, but they smell not:7 They have hands, but they handle not: feet have they, but they walk not: neither speak they through their throat.8 They that make them are like unto them; so is everyone that trusteth in them.9 O Israel, trust you in YHUH: he is their help and their shield.

115:11

ביהוה 3068 עזרם 5828 ומגנם 4043 הוא 1931: יראי 3373 יהוה 3068 בטחו 982 ביהוה 3068 עזרם 5828 ומגנם 4043
baYahuah; 'azram uamaginam hua'. yira'aey Yahuah bitchu baYahuah; 'azram uamaginam
**in Yahuah *is* their help and their shield he You that fear Yahuah trust in Yahuah *is* their help and their shield**

115:12

הוא 1931: יהוה 3068 זכרנו 2142 יברך 1288 יברך 1288 את 853 בית 1004 ישראל 3478 יברך 1288 את 853
hua'. Yahuah zakaranu yabarek yabarek 'at beyt yisra'ael; yabarek, 'at
**he Yahuah has been mindful of us he will bless *us* he will bless the house of Israel he will bless**

115:13 115:14

בית 1004 אהרן 175: יברך 1288 יראי 3373 יהוה 3068 הקטנים 6996 עם 5973 הגדלים 1419:
beyt 'aharon. yabarek yira'aey Yahuah; haqataniym, 'am hagadoliym.
**the house of Aaron He will bless them that fear Yahuah *both* small with great**

115:15

יסף 3254 יהוה 3068 עליכם 5921 עליכם 5921 ועל 5921 בניכם 1121: ברוכים 1288 אתם 859 ליהוה 3068
yasap Yahuah 'aleykem; 'aleykem, ua'al baneykem. barukiym 'atem laYahuah;
**shall increase more and more Yahuah you you and on your children *are* blessed You of Yahuah**

115:16

עשה 6213 שמים 8064 וארץ 776: השמים 8064 שמים 8064 ליהוה 3068 והארץ 776 נתן 5414
'aseh, shamayim ua'aretz. hashamayim shamayim laYahuah; uaha'aretz, natan
**which made heaven and earth The heaven *even* the heavens *are* to Yahuah's but the earth has he given**

115:17 115:18

לבני 1121 אדם 120: לא 3808 המתים 4191 יהללו 1984 יה 3050 ולא 3808 כל 3605 ירדי 3381 דומה 1745:
libney 'adam. la' hametiym yahalalu Yah; uala', kal yoradey dumah.
**to the children of men not The dead let praise Yah neither any that go down into silence**

ואנחנו 587 נברך 1288 יה 3050 מעתה 6258 ועד 5704 עולם 5769 הללו 1984 יה 3050:
ua'anachnu nabarek Yah, me'atah ua'ad 'aulam, halalu Yah.
**But we will bless Yah from this time forth and for evermore Praise Yah**

**Ps 116:1** 116:2

אהבתי 157 כי 3588 ישמע 8085 יהוה 3068 את 853 קולי 6963 תחנוני 8469: כי 3588 הטה 5186 אזנו 241
'ahabtiy kiy yishma' Yahuah; 'at qouliy, tachanunay. kiy hitah 'azanou
**I love because he has heard Yahuah my voice *and* my supplications Because he has inclined his ear**

116:3

לי 3807a ובימי 3117 אקרא 7121: אפפוני 661 חבלי 2256 מות 4194 ומצרי 4712 שאול 7585
liy; uabyamay 'aqraa'. 'apapuniy chebley mauet, uamtzarey sha'aul
**upon me therefore as long as I live will I call *him* compassed me The sorrows of death and the pains of hell (*grave*)**

116:4

מצאוני 4672 צרה 6869 ויגון 3015 אמצא 4672: ובשם 8034 יהוה 3068 אקרא 7121 אנה 577 יהוה 3068
matza'uniy; tzarah uayagoun 'amtzaa'. uabshem Yahuah 'aqraa'; 'anah Yahuah
**got hold upon me trouble and sorrow I found Then upon the name of Yahuah called I I beseech you O Yahuah**

116:5 116:6

מלטה 4422 נפשי 5315: חנון 2587 יהוה 3068 וצדיק 6662 ואלהינו 430 מרחם 7355: שמר 8104 פתאים 6612 יהוה 3068
maltah napshiy. chanun Yahuah uatzadiyq; ua'aloheynu marachem. shomer pata'yim Yahuah;
**deliver my soul Gracious *is* Yahuah and righteous yea our Elohim *is* merciful preserve the simple Yahuah**

116:7

דלותי 1809 ולי 3807a יהושיע 3467: שובי 7725 נפשי 5315 למנוחיכי 4496 כי 3588 יהוה 3068 גמל 1580
daloutiy, ualiy yahoushiya'. shubiy napshiy limanuchayakiy; kiy Yahuah gamal
**I was brought low and me he helped Return O my soul unto your rest For Yahuah has dealt bountifully**

Ps 116:10 O house of Aaron, trust in YHUH: he is their help and their shield.11 You that fear YHUH, trust in YHUH: he is their help and their shield.12 YHUH has been mindful of us: he will bless us; he will bless the house of Israel; he will bless the house of Aaron.13 He will bless them that fear YHUH, both small and great.14 YHUH shall increase you more and more, you and your children.15 You are blessed of YHUH which made heaven and earth.16 The heaven, even the heavens, are YHUH's: but the earth has he given to the children of men.17 The dead praise not YHUH, neither any that go down into silence.18 But we will bless YHUH from this time forth and forevermore. Praise YHUH. **Ps** 116:1 I love YHUH, because he has heard my voice and my supplications.2 Because he has inclined his ear unto me, therefore will I call upon him as long as I live.3 The sorrows of death compassed me, and the pains of hell got hold upon me: I found trouble and sorrow.4 Then called I upon the name of YHUH; O YHUH, I beseech you, deliver my soul.5 Gracious is YHUH, and righteous; yea, our G-d is merciful.6 YHUH preserveth the simple: I was brought low, and he helped me.7 Return unto your rest, O my soul; for YHUH has dealt bountifully with you.

116:8

עליכי 5921: כי 3588 חלצת 2502 נפשי 5315 ממות 4194 את 853 עיני 5869 מן 4480 דמעה 1832 את 853 רגלי 7272
'alayakiy. kiy chilatzta napshiy, mimauet 'at 'aeyniy min dim'ah; 'at ragliy
**with you For you have delivered my soul from death mine eyes from tears *and* my feet**

116:9 116:10

מדחי 1762: אתהלך 1980 לפני 6440 יהוה 3068 בארצות 776 החיים 2416: האמנתי 539 כי 3588 אדבר 1696 אני 589
midechiy. 'athalek lipney Yahuah; ba'artzout, hachayiym. he'amantiy kiy 'adaber; 'aniy,
**from falling I will walk before Yahuah in the land of the living I believed therefore have I spoken I**

116:11 116:12

עניתי 6031 מאד 3966: אני 589 אמרתי 559 בחפזי 2648 כל 3605 האדם 120 כזב 3576: מה 4100 אשיב 7725 ליהוה 3068
'aniytiy ma'ad. 'aniy 'amartiy bachapaziy; kal ha'adam kozeb. mah 'ashiyb laYahuah;
**was afflicted greatly I I said in my haste All men *are* liars What shall I render unto Yahuah**

116:13 116:14

כל 3605 תגמולוהי 8408 עלי 5921: כוס 3563 ישועות 3444 אשא 5375 ובשם 8034 יהוה 3068 אקרא 7121:
kal tagmulouhiy 'alay. kos yashu'aut 'asa'; uabshem Yahuah 'aqraa'.
***for* all his benefits toward me? the cup of salvation I will take and upon the name of Yahuah call**

116:15

נדרי 5088 ליהוה 3068 אשלם 7999 נגדה 5048 נא 4994 לכל 3605 עמו 5971: יקר 3368 בעיני 5869 יהוה 3068
nadaray laYahuah 'ashalem; negdah na, lakal 'amou. yaqar ba'aeyney Yahuah;
**my vows unto Yahuah I will pay in the presence of now all his people Precious in the sight of Yahuah**

116:16

המותה 4194 לחסידיו 2623: אנה 575 יהוה 3068 כי 3588 אני 589 עבדך 5650 אני 589 עבדך 5650 בן 1121
hamauatah, lachasiydayu. 'anah Yahuah kiy 'aniy 'abdeka 'aniy 'abdaka ben
***is* the death of his saints truly O Yahuah surely I *am* your servant I *am* your servant *and* the son of**

116:17

אמתך 519 פתחת 6605 למוסרי 4147: לך 3807a אזבח 2076 זבח 2077 תודה 8426 ובשם 8034
'amateka; pitachta, lamouseray. laka 'azbach zebach toudah; uabshem
**your handmaid you have loosed my bonds to you I will offer the sacrifice of thanksgiving and upon the name of**

116:18 116:19

יהוה 3068 אקרא 7121: נדרי 5088 ליהוה 3068 אשלם 7999 נגדה 5048 נא 4994 לכל 3605 עמו 5971: בחצרות 2691
Yahuah 'aqraa'. nadaray laYahuah 'ashalem; negdah na, lakal 'amou. bachatzarout
**Yahuah will call my vows unto Yahuah I will pay in the presence of now all his people In the courts of**

בית 1004 יהוה 3068 בתוככי 8432 ירושלם 3389 הללו 1984 יה 3050:
beyt Yahuah batoukekiy yarushalaim, halalu Yah.
**house Yahuah's in the midst of you O Jerusalem Praise you Yah**

**Ps 117:1** 117:2

הללו 1984 את 853 יהוה 3068 כל 3605 גוים 1471 שבחוהו 7623 כל 3605 האמים 523: כי 3588 גבר 1396 עלינו 5921
halalu 'at Yahuah kal gouyim; shabchuhu, kal ha'amiym. kiy gabar 'aleynu
**O praise Yahuah all you nations praise him all you people For is great toward us**

חסדו 2617 ואמת 571 יהוה 3068 לעולם 5769 הללו 1984 יה 3050:
chasdou, ua'amet Yahuah la'aulam, halalu Yah.
**his merciful kindness and the truth of Yahuah *endures* for ever Praise you Yah**

**Ps 118:1** 118:2

הודו 3034 ליהוה 3068 כי 3588 טוב 2896 כי 3588 לעולם 5769 חסדו 2617: יאמר 559 נא 4994 ישראל 3478 כי 3588
houdu laYahuah kiy toub; kiy la'aulam chasdou. ya'mar naa' yisra'ael; kiy
**O give thanks unto Yahuah for *he is* good for *endures* for ever his mercy Let say now Israel that**

Ps 116:8 For you have delivered my soul from death, mine eyes from tears, and my feet from falling.9 I will walk before YHUH in the land of the living.10 I believed, therefore have I spoken: I was greatly afflicted:11 I said in my haste, All men are liars.12 What shall I render unto YHUH for all his benefits toward me?13 I will take the cup of salvation, and call upon the name of YHUH.14 I will pay my vows unto YHUH now in the presence of all his people.15 Precious in the sight of YHUH is the death of his saints.16 O YHUH, truly I am your servant; I am your servant, and the son of your handmaid: you have loosed my bonds.17 I will offer to you the sacrifice of thanksgiving, and will call upon the name of YHUH.18 I will pay my vows unto YHUH now in the presence of all his people,19 In the courts of YHUH's house, in the midst of you, O Jerusalem. Praise you YHUH. **Ps** 117:1 O praise YHUH, all you nations: praise him, all you people.2 For his merciful kindness is great toward us: and the truth of YHUH endureth forever. Praise you YHUH. **Ps** 118:1 O give thanks unto YHUH; for he is good: because his mercy endureth forever.2 Let Israel now say, that his mercy endureth forever.

118:3 118:4

לעולם 5769 חסדו 2617: יאמרו 559 נא 4994 בית 1004 אהרן 175 כי 3588 לעולם 5769 חסדו 2617: יאמרו 559 נא 4994
la'aulam chasdou. yomeru naa' beyt 'aharon; kiy la'aulam chasdou. ya'maru naa'
***endures* for ever his mercy Let say now the house of Aaron that *endures* for ever his mercy Let say now**

118:5

יראי 3373 יהוה 3068 כי 3588 לעולם 5769 חסדו 2617: מן 4480 המצר 4712 קראתי 7121 יה 3050 ענני 6030
yira'aey Yahuah; kiy la'aulam chasdou. min hametzar qaraa'tiy Yah; 'ananiy
**them that fear Yahuah that *endures* for ever his mercy in distress I called upon Yah answered me**

118:6 118:7

במרחב 4800 יה 3050: יהוה 3068 לי 3807a לא 3808 אירא 3372 מה 4100 יעשה 6213 לי 3807a אדם 120:
bamerchab Yah. Yahuah liy la' 'ayra'; mah ya'aseh liy 'adam.
***and set me* in a large place Yah Yahuah *is* on my side not I will fear what can do unto me? man**

118:8

יהוה 3068 לי 3807a בעזרי 5826 ואני 589 אראה 7200 בשנאי 8130: טוב 2896
Yahuah liy ba'azaray; ua'aniy, 'ar'ah basona'ay. toub,
**Yahuah me *takes my part* with them that help therefore I shall see *my desire* upon them that hate me *It is* better**

118:9

לחסות 2620 ביהוה 3068 מבטח 982 באדם 120: טוב 2896 לחסות 2620 ביהוה 3068 מבטח 982
lachasout baYahuah; mibtoach, ba'adam. toub, lachasout baYahuah; mibtoach,
**to trust in Yahuah than to put confidence in man *It is* better to trust in Yahuah than to put confidence**

118:10 118:11

בנדיבים 5081: כל 3605 גוים 1471 סבבוני 5437 בשם 8034 יהוה 3068 כי 3588 אמילם 4135:
binadiybiym. kal gouyim sababuniy; bashem Yahuah kiy 'amiylam.
**in princes All nations compassed me about in the name of Yahuah but will I destroy them**

118:12

סבוני 5437 גם 1571 סבבוני 5437 בשם 8034 יהוה 3068 כי 3588 אמילם 4135:
sabuniy gam sababuniy; bashem Yahuah kiy 'amiylam.
**They compassed me about yea they compassed me about in the name of Yahuah but I will destroy them**

סבוני 5437 כדבורים 1682 דעכו 1846 כאש 784 קוצים 6975 בשם 8034 יהוה 3068 כי 3588
sabuniy kidbouriym, do'aku ka'aesh qoutziym; bashem Yahuah kiy
**They compassed me about like bees they are quenched as the fire of thorns for in the name of Yahuah for**

118:13 118:14

אמילם 4135: דחה 1760 דחיתני 1760 לנפל 5307 ויהוה 3068 עזרני 5826: עזי 5797
'amiylam. dachoh dachiytaniy linpol; uaYahuah 'azaraniy. 'aziy
**I will destroy them You have thrust sore at me that I might fall but Yahuah helped me *is* my strength**

118:15

וזמרת 2176 יה 3050 ויהי 1961 לי 3807a לישועה 3444: קול 6963 רנה 7440 וישועה 3444 באהלי 168
uazimrat Yah; uayahiy liy, liyshu'ah. qoul rinah uiyshu'ah, ba'ahaley
**and song Yah and is become to me for salvation The voice of rejoicing and salvation *is* in the tabernacles of**

118:16

צדיקים 6662 ימין 3225 יהוה 3068 עשה 6213 חיל 2428: ימין 3225 יהוה 3068 רוממה 7426 ימין 3225
tzadiyqiym; yamiyn Yahuah 'asah chayil. yamiyn Yahuah roumemah; yamiyn
**the righteous the right hand of Yahuah does valiantly The right hand of Yahuah is exalted the right hand of**

118:17 118:18

יהוה 3068 עשה 6213 חיל 2428: לא 3808 אמות 4191 כי 3588 אחיה 2421 ואספר 5608 מעשי 4639 יה 3050: יסר 3256
Yahuah 'asah chayil. la' 'amut kiy 'achayeh; ua'asaper, ma'asey Yah. yasor
**Yahuah does valiantly not I shall die but live and declare the works of Yah has chastened me**

Ps 118:3 Let the house of Aaron now say, that his mercy endureth forever.4 Let them now that fear YHUH say, that his mercy endureth forever.5 I called upon YHUH in distress: YHUH answered me, and set me in a large place.6 YHUH is on my side; I will not fear: what can man do unto me?7 YHUH take my part with them that help me: therefore shall I see my desire upon them that hate me.8 It is better to trust in YHUH than to put confidence in man.9 It is better to trust in YHUH than to put confidence in princes.10 All nations compassed me about: but in the name of YHUH will I destroy them.11 They compassed me about; yea, they compassed me about: but in the name of YHUH I will destroy them.12 They compassed me about like bees; they are quenched as the fire of thorns: for in the name of YHUH I will destroy them.13 Thou have thrust sore at me that I might fall: but YHUH helped me.14 YHUH is my strength and song, and is become my salvation.15 The voice of rejoicing and salvation is in the tabernacles of the righteous: the right hand of YHUH doeth valiantly.16 The right hand of YHUH is exalted: the right hand of YHUH doeth valiantly.17 I shall not die, but live, and declare the works of YHUH.

118:19
יסרני 3256 יה 3050 ולמות 4194 לא 3808 נתנני 5414: פתחו 6605 לי 3807a שערי 8179 צדק 6664 אבא 935
yisraniy Yah; ualamauet, la' natananiy. pitchu liy sha'arey tzedeq; 'aaba'
**sore Yah but unto death not he has given me over Open to me the gates of righteousness I will go**

118:20 118:21
בם 871a אודה 3034 יה 3050: זה 2088 השער 8179 ליהוה 3068 צדיקים 6662 יבאו 935 בו 871a:
bam 'audeh Yah. zeh hasha'ar laYahuah; tzadiyqiym, yabo'au bou.
**into them *and* I will praise Yah This gate of Yahuah the righteous shall enter into which**

118:22
אודך 3034 כי 3588 עניתני 6030 ותהי 1961 לי 3807a לישועה 3444: אבן 68 מאסו 3988 הבונים 1129
'audaka kiy 'aniytaniy; uatahiy liy, liyshu'ah. 'aben ma'asu haboniym;
**I will praise you for you have heard me and are become my salvation The stone refused *which* the builders**

118:23 118:24
היתה 1961 לראש 7218 פנה 6438: מאת 853 יהוה 3068 היתה 1961 זאת 2063 היא 1931 נפלאת 6381 בעינינו 5869:
hayatah, lara'sh pinah. me'at Yahuah hayatah za't; hiy'a nipla't ba'aeyneynu.
**is become the head *stone* of the corner from Yahuah's is doing This it *is* marvellous in our eyes**

118:25
זה 2088 היום 3117 עשה 6213 יהוה 3068 נגילה 1523 ונשמחה 8055 בו 871a: אנא 577 יהוה 3068 הושיעה 3467 נא 4994
zeh hayoum 'asah Yahuah; nagiylah uanismachah bou. 'ana' Yahuah houshiy'ah na;
**This *is* the day has made *which* Yahuah we will rejoice and be glad in it I beseech you O Yahuah Save now**

118:26
אנא 577 יהוה 3068 הצליחה 6743 נא 4994: ברוך 1288 הבא 935 בשם 8034 יהוה 3068
'ana' Yahuah hatzaliychah na'. baruk habaa' bashem Yahuah;
**I beseech you O Yahuah send prosperity now Blessed *be* he that comes in the name of Yahuah**

118:27
ברכנוכם 1288 מבית 1004 יהוה 3068: אל 410 יהוה 3068 ויאר 216 לנו 3807a אסרו 631 חג 2282
beraknukem, mibeyt Yahuah. 'ael Yahuah uaya'ar lanu 'asru chag
**we have blessed you out of the house of Yahuah El *is* Yahuah light *which has showed* us bind the sacrifice**

118:28
בעבתים 5688 עד 5704 קרנות 7161 המזבח 4196: אלי 410 אתה 859 ואודך 3034 אלהי 430
ba'abotiym; 'ad qarnout, hamizbeach. 'aeliy 'atah ua'adeka; 'alohay,
**with cords *even* unto the horns of the altar *are* my El You and I will praise you: *you are* my Elohim**

118:29
ארוממך 7311: הודו 3034 ליהוה 3068 כי 3588 טוב 2896 כי 3588 לעולם 5769 חסדו 2617:
'aroumaka. houdu laYahuah kiy toub; kiy la'aulam chasdou.
**I will exalt you O give thanks unto Yahuah for *he is* good for *endures* for ever his mercy**

**Ps 119:1** 119:2
אשרי 835 תמימי 8549 דרך 1870 ההלכים 1980 בתורת 8451 יהוה 3069: אשרי 835 נצרי 5341
'ashrey tamiymey darek; haholakiym, batourat Yahuah. 'ashrey notzarey
**ALEPH: Blessed *are* the undefiled in the way who walk in the law of Yahuah Blessed *are* they that keep**

119:3 119:4
עדתיו 5713 בכל 3605 לב 3820 ידרשוהו 1875: אף 637 לא 3808 פעלו 6466 עולה 5766 בדרכיו 1870 הלכו 1980:
'aedotayu, bakal leb yidrashuhu. 'ap la' pa'alu 'aulah; bidrakayu halaku.
**his testimonies with the whole heart *and that* seek him also no They do iniquity in his ways they walk**

119:5
אתה 859 צויתה 6680 פקדיך 6490 לשמר 8104 מאד 3966: אחלי 305 יכנו 3559 דרכי 1870 לשמר 8104
'atah tziuiytah piqudeyka, lishmor ma'ad. 'achalay yikonu darakay, lishmor
**You have commanded your precepts *us* to keep diligently O that were directed my ways to keep**

Ps 118:18 YHUH has chastened me sore: but he has not given me over unto death.19 Open to me the gates of righteousness: I will go into them, and I will praise YHUH:20 This gate of YHUH, into which the righteous shall enter.21 I will praise you: for you have heard me, and are become my salvation.22 The stone which the builders refused is become the head stone of the corner.23 This is YHUH's doing; it is marvellous in our eyes.24 This is the day which YHUH has made; we will rejoice and be glad in it.25 Save now, I beseech you, O YHUH: O YHUH, I beseech you, send now prosperity.26 Blessed be he that cometh in the name of YHUH: we have blessed you out of the house of YHUH.27 G-d is YHUH, which has showed us light: bind the sacrifice with cords, even unto the horns of the altar.28 Thou are my G-d, and I will praise you: you are my G-d, I will exalt you.29 O give thanks unto YHUH; for he is good: for his mercy endureth forever. **Ps** 119:1 Blessed are the undefiled in the way, who walk in the law of YHUH.2 Blessed are they that keep his testimonies, and that seek him with the whole heart.3 They also do no iniquity: they walk in his ways.4 Thou have commanded us to keep your precepts diligently.5 O that my ways were directed to keep your statutes!

119:6 119:7
חקיך 2706: אז 227 לא 3808 אבוש 954 בהביטי 5027 אל 413 כל 3605 מצותיך 4687:
chuqeyka. 'az la' 'aeboush; bahabiytiy, 'al kal mitzuoteyka.
**your statutes Then not shall I be ashamed when I have respect unto all your commandments**

119:8
אודך 3034 בישר 3476 לבב 3824 בלמדי 3925 משפטי 4941 צדקך 6664: את 853 חקיך 2706
'audaka bayosher lebab; balamadiy, mishpatey tzidqeka. 'at chuqeyka
**I will praise you with uprightness of heart when I shall have learned judgments your righteous your statutes**

119:9
אשמר 8104 אל 408 תעזבני 5800 עד 5704 מאד 3966: במה 1400 יזכה 2135 נער 5288 את 853 ארחו 734
'ashmor; 'al ta'azbeniy 'ad ma'ad. bameh yazakeh na'ar 'at 'arachou;
**I will keep not O forsake me unto utterly BETH: Wherewithal shall cleanse a young man his way?**

119:10
לשמר 8104 כדברך 1697: בכל 3605 לבי 3820 דרשתיך 1875 אל 408 תשגני 7686
lishmor, kidbareka. bakal libiy darashtiyka; 'al tashgeniy,
**by taking heed *thereto* according to your word With whole my heart have I sought you not O let me wander**

119:11 119:12
ממצותיך 4687: בלבי 3820 צפנתי 6845 אמרתך 565 למען 4616 לא 3808 אחטא 2398 לך 3807a:
mimitzuoteyka. balibiy tzapantiy 'amrateka; lama'an, la' 'achetaa' lak.
**from your commandments in mine heart have I hid Your word that not I might sin against you**

119:13
ברוך 1288 אתה 859 יהוה 3068 למדני 3925 חקיך 2706: בשפתי 8193 ספרתי 5608 כל 3605 משפטי 4941
baruk 'atah Yahuah lamadeniy chuqeyka. bisapatay sipartiy; kol, mishpatey
**Blessed *are* you Yahuah teach me your statutes With my lips have I declared all the judgments of**

119:14 119:15
פיך 6310: בדרך 1870 עדותיך 5715 ששתי 7797 כעל 5921 כל 3605 הון 1952: בפקדיך 6490
piyka. baderek 'aedauoteyka sastiy, ka'al kal houn. bapiqudeyka
**your mouth in the way of your testimonies I have rejoiced as *much as* in all riches in your precepts**

119:16
אשיחה 7878 ואביטה 5027 ארחתיך 734: בחקתיך 2708 אשתעשע 8173 לא 3808 אשכח 7911
'asiychah; ua'abiytah, 'arachoteyka. bachuqoteyka 'ashata'asha'; la' 'ashkach
**I will meditate and have respect unto your ways in your statutes I will delight myself not I will forget**

119:17 119:18
דברך 1697: גמל 1580 על 5921 עבדך 5650 אחיה 2421 ואשמרה 8104 דברך 1697: גל 1540
dabareka. gamol 'al 'abdaka 'achayeh, ua'ashmarah dabareka. gal
**your word GIMEL: Deal bountifully with your servant *that* I may live and keep your word Open you**

119:19
עיני 5869 ואביטה 5027 נפלאות 6381 מתורתך 8451: גר 1616 אנכי 595 בארץ 776 אל 408 תסתר 5641
'aeynay ua'abiytah; nipla'aut, mitourateka. ger 'anokiy ba'aretz; 'al taster
**mine eyes that I may behold wondrous things out of your law *am* a stranger I in the earth not hide**

119:20
ממני 4480 מצותיך 4687: גרסה 1638 נפשי 5315 לתאבה 8375 אל 413 משפטיך 4941 בכל 3605
mimeniy, mitzuoteyka. garasah napshiy lata'abah; 'al mishpateyka bakal
**from me your commandments break My soul for the longing *that it has* unto your judgments at all**

119:21 119:22
עת 6256: גערת 1605 זדים 2086 ארורים 779 השגים 7686 ממצותיך 4687: גל 1556
'aet. ga'arta zediym 'aruriym; hashogiym mimitzuoteyka. gal
**times You have rebuked the proud *that are* cursed which do err from your commandments Remove**

Ps 119:6 Then shall I not be ashamed, when I have respect unto all your commandments.7 I will praise you with uprightness of heart, when I shall have learned your righteous judgments.8 I will keep your statutes: O forsake me not utterly.9 Wherewithal shall a young man cleanse his way? by taking heed thereto according to your word.10 With my whole heart have I sought you: O let me not wander from your commandments.11 Thy word have I hid in mine heart, that I might not sin against you.12 Blessed are you, O YHUH: teach me your statutes.13 With my lips have I declared all the judgments of your mouth.14 I have rejoiced in the way of your testimonies, as much as in all riches.15 I will meditate in your precepts, and have respect unto your ways.16 I will delight myself in your statutes: I will not forget your word.17 Deal bountifully with your servant, that I may live, and keep your word.18 Open you mine eyes, that I may behold wondrous things out of your law.19 I am a stranger in the earth: hide not your commandments from me.20 My soul breaketh for the longing that it has unto your judgments at all times.21 Thou have rebuked the proud that are cursed, which do err from your commandments.

119:23

מעלי 5921 חרפה 2781 ובוז 937 נצרתי 5341 כי 3588 עדתיך 5713 נצרתי 5341: גם 1571 ישבו 3427 שרים 8269 בי 871a נדברו 1696
me'alay cherpah uabuz; kiy 'aedoteyka natzaratiy. gam yashabu sariym biy nidbaru;
**from me reproach and contempt for your testimonies I have kept also did sit Princes against me *and* speak**

119:24 119:25

עבדך 5650 ישיח 7878 בחקיך 2706: גם 1571 עדתיך 5713 שעשעי 8191 אנשי 582 עצתי 6098:
'abdaka, yasiyach bachuqeyka. gam 'aedoteyka sha'ashu'ay, 'anshey 'atzatiy.
***but* your servant did meditate in your statutes also Your testimonies *are* my delight *and* my counsellors**

119:26

דבקה 1692 לעפר 6083 נפשי 5315 חיני 2421 כדברך 1697: דרכי 1870 ספרתי 5608
dabqah le'apar napshiy; chayeniy, kidbareka. darakay sipartiy
**DALETH: cleave unto the dust My soul quicken you me according to your word my ways I have declared**

119:27

ותענני 6030 למדני 3925 חקיך 2706: דרך 1870 פקודיך 6490 הבינני 995 ואשיחה 7878
uata'aneniy, lamadeniy chuqeyka. derek piqudeyka habiyneniy; ua'asiychah,
**and you heard me teach me your statutes the way of your precepts Make me to understand so shall I talk**

119:28 119:29

בנפלאותיך 6381: דלפה 1811 נפשי 5315 מתוגה 8424 קימני 6965 כדברך 1697:
banipla'auteyka. dalapah napshiy mitugah; qayameniy, kidbareka.
**of your wondrous works melt My soul for heaviness strengthen you me according unto your word**

119:30

דרך 1870 שקר 8267 הסר 5493 ממני 4480 ותורתך 8451 חנני 2603: דרך 1870 אמונה 530 בחרתי 977
dereka sheqer haser mimeniy; uatorataka chaneniy derek 'amunah bacharatiy;
**the way of lying Remove from me and your law grant me graciously the way of truth I have chosen**

119:31 119:32

משפטיך 4941 שויתי 7737: דבקתי 1692 בעדותיך 5715 יהוה 3069 אל 408 תבישני 954:
mishpateyka shiuiytiy. dabaqtiy ba'aedauoteyka; Yahuah 'al tabiysheniy.
**your judgments have I laid *before me* I have stuck unto your testimonies Yahuah not put me to shame**

119:33

דרך 1870 מצותיך 4687 ארוץ 7323 כי 3588 תרחיב 7337 לבי 3820: הורני 3384 יהוה 3069 דרך 1870
derek mitzuoteyka 'arutz; kiy tarchiyb libiy. houreniy Yahuah derek
**the way of your commandments I will run when you shall enlarge my heart HE: Teach me Yahuah the way of**

119:34

חקיך 2706 ואצרנה 5341 עקב 6118: הבינני 995 ואצרה 5341 תורתך 8451 ואשמרנה 8104
chuqeyka, ua'atzrenah 'aeqeb. habiyneniy ua'atzrah tourateka, ua'ashmarenah
**your statutes and I shall keep it *unto* the end Give me understanding and I shall keep your law yea I shall observe it**

119:35 119:36

בכל 3605 לב 3820: הדריכני 1869 בנתיב 5410 מצותיך 4687 כי 3588 בו 871a חפצתי 2654: הט 5186
bakal leb. hadariykeniy binatiyb mitzuoteyka; kiy bou chapatzatiy. hat
**with *my* whole heart Make me to go in the path of your commandments for therein do I delight Incline**

119:37

לבי 3820 אל 413 עדותיך 5715 ואל 408 אל 413 בצע 1215: העבר 5674 עיני 5869 מראות 7200 שוא 7723
libiy 'al 'aedauoteyka, ua'al 'al batza'. ha'aber 'aeynay mera'aut shau'a;
**my heart unto your testimonies and not to covetousness Turn away mine eyes from beholding vanity**

119:38

בדרכך 1870 חיני 2421: הקם 6965 לעבדך 5650 אמרתך 565 אשר 834 ליראתך 3374:
bidrakeka chayeniy. haqem la'abdaka 'amrateka; 'asher, layir'ateka.
**in your way *and* quicken you me Establish unto your servant your word who *is devoted* to your fear**

Ps 119:22 Remove from me reproach and contempt; for I have kept your testimonies.23 Princes also did sit and speak against me: but your servant did meditate in your statutes.24 Thy testimonies also are my delight and my counsellors.25 My soul cleaveth unto the dust: quicken you me according to your word.26 I have declared my ways, and you heardest me: teach me your statutes.27 Make me to understand the way of your precepts: so shall I talk of your wondrous works.28 My soul melteth for heaviness: strengthen you me according unto your word.29 Remove from me the way of lying: and grant me your law graciously.30 I have chosen the way of truth: your judgments have I laid before me.31 I have stuck unto your testimonies: O YHUH, put me not to shame.32 I will run the way of your commandments, when you shall enlarge my heart.33 Teach me, O YHUH, the way of your statutes; and I shall keep it unto the end.34 Give me understanding, and I shall keep your law; yea, I shall observe it with my whole heart.35 Make me to go in the path of your commandments; for therein do I delight.36 Incline my heart unto your testimonies, and not to covetousness.37 Turn away mine eyes from beholding vanity; and quicken you me in your way.38 Stablish your word unto your servant, who is devoted to your fear.

**119:39** העבר 5674 חרפתי 2781 אשר 834 יגרתי 3025 כי 3588 משפטיך 4941 טובים 2896: **119:40** הנה 2009 תאבתי 8373
ha'aber cherpatiy 'asher yagoratiy; kiy mishpateyka toubiym. hineh ta'abtiy
**Turn away my reproach which I fear For your judgments *are* good Behold I have longed after**

לפקדיך 6490 בצדקתך 6666 חיני 2421: **119:41** ויבאני 935 חסדך 2617 יהוה 3069
lapiqudeyka; batzidqataka chayeniy. uiybo'aniy chasadeka Yahuah;
**your precepts in your righteousness quicken me VAU: Let come also unto me your mercies Yahuah**

תשועתך 8668 כאמרתך 565: **119:42** ואענה 6030 חרפי 2778 דבר 1697 כי 3588
tashu'ataka, ka'amrateka. ua'a'aneh chorapiy dabar; kiy
***even* your salvation according to your word So shall I have to answer him that reproach me wherewith for**

בטחתי 982 בדברך 1697: **119:43** ואל 408 תצל 5337 מפי 6310 דבר 1697 אמת 571 עד 5704 מאד 3966 כי 3588 למשפטך 4941
batachtiy biddareka. ua'al tatzel mipiy dabar 'amet 'ad ma'ad; kiy lamishpateka
**I trust in your word And not take out of my mouth the word of truth unto utterly for in your judgments**

יחלתי 3176: **119:44** ואשמרה 8104 תורתך 8451 תמיד 8548 לעולם 5769 ועד 5703: **119:45** ואתהלכה 1980 ברחבה 7342 כי 3588
yichalatiy. ua'ashmarah tourataka tamiyd, la'aulam ua'ad. ua'athalkah barachabah; kiy
**I have hoped So shall I keep your law continually for ever and ever And I will walk at liberty for**

פקדיך 6490 דרשתי 1875: **119:46** ואדברה 1696 בעדתיך 5713 נגד 5048 מלכים 4428 ולא 3808 אבוש 954: **119:47**
piqudeyka darashatiy. ua'adabarah ba'aedoteyka neged malakiym, uala' 'aeboush.
**your precepts I seek I will speak also of your testimonies before kings and not will be ashamed**

ואשתעשע 8173 במצותיך 4687 אשר 834 אהבתי 157: **119:48** ואשא 5375 כפי 3709 אל 413
ua'ashta'asha' bamitzuoteyka, 'asher 'ahabatiy. ua'asaa' kapay, 'al
**And I will delight myself in your commandments which I have loved also will I lift up My hands unto**

מצותיך 4687 אשר 834 אהבתי 157 ואשיחה 7878 בחקיך 2706: **119:49** זכר 2142 דבר 1697
mitzuoteyka 'asher 'ahabatiy, ua'asiychah uachuqeyka. zakor dabar
**your commandments which I have loved and I will meditate in your statutes ZAYIN: Remember the word**

לעבדך 5650 על 5921 אשר 834 יחלתני 3176: **119:50** זאת 2063 נחמתי 5165 בעניי 6040 כי 3588 אמרתך 565
la'abdeka; 'aal, 'asher yichaltaniy. za't nechamatiy ba'anyiy; kiy 'amrataka
**unto your servant on which you have caused me to hope This *is* my comfort in my affliction for your word**

חיתני 2421: **119:51** זדים 2086 הליצני 3887 עד 5704 מאד 3966 מתורתך 8451 לא 3808 נטיתי 5186: **119:52**
chiyataniy. zediym heliytzuniy 'ad ma'ad; mitourataka, la' natiytiy.
**has quickened me The proud have had me in derision unto greatly from your law not *yet* have I declined**

זכרתי 2142 משפטיך 4941 מעולם 5769 יהוה 3069 ואתנחם 5162: **119:53** זלעפה 2152
zakartiy mishpateyka me'aulam Yahuah ua'atnecham. zal'apah
**I remembered your judgments of old Yahuah and have comforted myself Horror**

אחזתני 270 מרשעים 7563 עזבי 5800 תורתך 8451: **119:54** זמרות 2158 היו 1961 לי 3807a חקיך 2706
'achazatniy merasha'aym; 'azabey, tourateka. zamirout hayu liy chuqeyka,
**(*she*) has taken hold upon me because of the wicked that forsake your law songs have been my Your statutes**

Ps 119:39 Turn away my reproach which I fear: for your judgments are good.40 Behold, I have longed after your precepts: quicken me in your righteousness.41 Let your mercies come also unto me, O YHUH, even your salvation, according to your word.42 So shall I have wherewith to answer him that reproacheth me: for I trust in your word.43 And take not the word of truth utterly out of my mouth; for I have hoped in your judgments.44 So shall I keep your law continually forever and ever.45 And I will walk at liberty: for I seek your precepts.46 I will speak of your testimonies also before kings, and will not be ashamed.47 And I will delight myself in your commandments, which I have loved.48 My hands also will I lift up unto your commandments, which I have loved; and I will meditate in your statutes.49 Remember the word unto your servant, upon which you have caused me to hope.50 This is my comfort in my affliction: for your word has quickened me.51 The proud have had me greatly in derision: yet have I not declined from your law.52 I remembered your judgments of old, O YHUH; and have comforted myself.53 Horror has taken hold upon me because of the wicked that forsake your law.54 Thy statutes have been my songs in the house of my pilgrimage.

| | | 119:55 | | | | | | 119:56 |
|---|---|---|---|---|---|---|---|---|
| בבית 1004 | מגורי 4033: | זכרתי 2142 | בלילה 3915 | שמך 8034 | יהוה 3069 | ואשמרה 8104 | תורתך 8451: | |
| babeyt | maguray. | zakartiy | balayalah | shimka | Yahuah; | ua'ashmarah, | tourateka. | |
| **in the house of** | **my pilgrimage** | **I have remembered** | **in the night** | **your name** | **Yahuah** | **and have kept** | **your law** | |

| | | | | | | 119:57 | | |
|---|---|---|---|---|---|---|---|---|
| זאת 2063 | היתה 1961 | לי 3807a | כי 3588 | פקדיך 6490 | נצרתי 5341: | חלקי 2506 | יהוה 3069 | אמרתי 559 |
| za't | hayatah | liy; | kiy | piqudeyka | natzaratiy. | chelqiy | Yahuah | 'amartiy, |
| **This** | **had** | **I** | **because** | **your precepts** | **I kept** | **CHETH: *You are* my portion** | **Yahuah** | **I have said** |

| | | 119:58 | | | | |
|---|---|---|---|---|---|---|
| לשמר 8104 | דבריך 1697: | חליתי 2470 | פניך 6440 | בכל 3605 | לב 3820 | חנני 2603 |
| lishmor | dabareyka. | chiliytiy | paneyka | bakal | leb; | chaneniy |
| **that I would keep** | **your words** | **I intreated** | **your favor** | **with *my* whole** | **heart** | **be merciful unto me** |

| | 119:59 | | | | | | 119:60 |
|---|---|---|---|---|---|---|---|
| כאמרתך 565: | חשבתי 2803 | דרכי 1870 | ואשיבה 7725 | רגלי 7272 | אל 413 | עדתיך 5713: | חשתי 2363 |
| ka'amrateka. | chishabtiy | darakay; | ua'ashiybah | raglay, | 'al | 'aedoteyka. | chashtiy |
| **according to your word** | **I thought on** | **my ways** | **and turned** | **my feet** | **unto** | **your testimonies** | **I made haste** |

| | | | | 119:61 | | | | |
|---|---|---|---|---|---|---|---|---|
| ולא 3808 | התמהמהתי 4102 | לשמר 8104 | מצותיך 4687: | חבלי 2256 | רשעים 7563 | עודני 5749 | תורתך 8451 | לא 3808 |
| uala' | hitmahamahatiy; | lishmor, | mitzuoteyka. | chebley | rasha'aym | 'auaduniy; | tourataka, | la' |
| **and not** | **delayed** | **to keep** | **your commandments** | **The bands of** | **the wicked** | **have robbed me** | **your law** | **not** |

| | 119:62 | | | | | | | | 119:63 |
|---|---|---|---|---|---|---|---|---|---|
| שכחתי 7911: | חצות 2676 | לילה 3915 | אקום 6965 | להודות 3034 | לך 3807a | על 5921 | משפטי 4941 | צדקך 6664: | |
| shakachatiy. | chatzout | layalah, | 'aqum | lahadout | lak; | 'aal, | mishpatey | tzidqeka. | |
| ***but* I have forgotten** | ***At* mid** | **night** | **I will rise** | **to give thanks** | **unto you** | **because of** | **judgments** | **your righteous** | |

| | | | | | | | 119:64 | |
|---|---|---|---|---|---|---|---|---|
| חבר 2270 | אני 589 | לכל 3605 | אשר 834 | יראוך 3372 | ולשמרי 8104 | פקודיך 6490: | חסדך 2617 | יהוה 3069 |
| chaber | 'aniy | lakal | 'asher | yare'auka; | ualshomarey, | piqudeyka. | chasdaka | Yahuah |
| ***am* a companion of** | **I** | **all** | ***them* that** | **fear you** | **and of them that keep** | **your precepts** | **your mercy** | **Yahuah** |

| | | | | 119:65 | | | | |
|---|---|---|---|---|---|---|---|---|
| מלאה 4390 | הארץ 776 | חקיך 2706 | למדני 3925: | טוב 2896 | עשית 6213 | עם 5973 | עבדך 5650 | יהוה 3069 |
| mal'ah | ha'aretz, | chuqeyka | lamadeniy. | toub | 'ashiyta | 'am | 'abdaka; | Yahuah |
| **is full of** | **The earth** | **your statutes** | **teach me** | **TETH: well** | **You have dealt** | **with** | **your servant** | **Yahuah** |

| | 119:66 | | | | | |
|---|---|---|---|---|---|---|
| כדברך 1697: | טוב 2898 | טעם 2940 | ודעת 1847 | למדני 3925 | כי 3588 | במצותיך 4687 |
| kidbareka. | toub | ta'am | uada'at | lamadeniy; | kiy | bamitzuoteyka |
| **according unto your word** | **good** | **judgment** | **and knowledge** | **Teach me** | **for** | **your commandments** |

| | 119:67 | | | | | | | 119:68 | |
|---|---|---|---|---|---|---|---|---|---|
| האמנתי 539: | טרם 2962 | אענה 6031 | אני 589 | שגג 7683 | ועתה 6258 | אמרתך 565 | שמרתי 8104: | טוב 2896 | אתה 859 |
| he'amanatiy. | terem | 'a'aneh | 'aniy | shogeg; | ua'atah, | 'amrataka | shamaratiy. | toub | 'atah |
| **I have believed** | **Before** | **I was afflicted** | **I** | **went astray** | **but now** | **your word** | **have I kept** | ***are* good** | **You** |

| | | | 119:69 | | | | | | |
|---|---|---|---|---|---|---|---|---|---|
| ומטיב 2895 | למדני 3925 | חקיך 2706: | טפלו 2950 | עלי 5921 | שקר 8267 | זדים 2086 | אני 589 | בכל 3605 | לב 3820 |
| uametiyb, | lamadeniy | chuqeyka. | tapalu | 'alay | sheqer | zediym; | 'aniy, | bakal | leb |
| **and do good** | **teach me** | **your statutes** | **have forged** | **against me** | **a lie** | **The proud *but*** | **I** | **with *my* whole** | **heart** |

| | | 119:70 | | | | | | 119:71 | | |
|---|---|---|---|---|---|---|---|---|---|---|
| אצר 5341 | פקודיך 6490: | טפש 2954 | כחלב 2459 | לבם 3820 | אני 589 | תורתך 8451 | שעשעתי 8173: | טוב 2896 | לי 3807a | כי 3588 |
| 'atzor | piqudeyka. | tapash | kacheleb | libam; | 'aniy, | tourataka | shi'asha'atiy. | toub | liy | kiy |
| **will keep** | **your precepts** | **is as fat** | **as grease** | **Their heart *but*** | **I** | **your law** | **delight in** | ***It is* good** | **for me** | **that** |

Ps 119:55 I have remembered your name, O YHUH, in the night, and have kept your law.56 This I had, because I kept your precepts.57 Thou are my portion, O YHUH: I have said that I would keep your words.58 I entreated your favor with my whole heart: be merciful unto me according to your word.59 I thought on my ways, and turned my feet unto your testimonies.60 I made haste, and delayed not to keep your commandments.61 The bands of the wicked have robbed me: but I have not forgotten your law.62 At midnight I will rise to give thanks unto you because of your righteous judgments.63 I am a companion of all them that fear you, and of them that keep your precepts.64 The earth, O YHUH, is full of your mercy: teach me your statutes.65 Thou have dealt well with your servant, O YHUH, according unto your word.66 Teach me good judgment and knowledge: for I have believed your commandments.67 Before I was afflicted I went astray: but now have I kept your word.68 Thou are good, and does good; teach me your statutes.69 The proud have forged a lie against me: but I will keep your precepts with my whole heart.70 Their heart is as fat as grease; but I delight in your law.

| | | | | 119:72 | | | | |
|---|---|---|---|---|---|---|---|---|
| עניתי 6031 | למען 4616 | אלמד 3925 | חקיך 2706: | | טוב 2896 | לי 3807a | תורת 8451 | פיך 6310 |
| 'aneytiy; | lama'an, | 'almad | chuqeyka. | | toub | liy | tourat | piyka; |
| **I have been afflicted** | **that** | **I might learn** | **your statutes** | | ***is* better** | **unto me** | **The law of** | **your mouth** |

| | | | 119:73 | | | | |
|---|---|---|---|---|---|---|---|
| מאלפי 505 | זהב 2091 | וכסף 3701: | | ידיך 3027 | עשוני 6213 | ויכוננוני 3559 | הבינני 995 |
| me'alpey, | zahab | uakasep. | | yadeyka | 'asuniy | uayakounanuniy; | habiyneniy, |
| **than thousands of** | **gold** | **and silver** | | **YOD: Your hands** | **have made me** | **and fashioned me** | **give me understanding** |

| | | 119:74 | | | | | |
|---|---|---|---|---|---|---|---|
| ואלמדה 3925 | מצותיך 4687: | | יראיך 3373 | יראוני 7200 | וישמחו 8055 | כי 3588 | לדברך 1697 |
| ua'almadah | mitzuoteyka. | | yare'ayka | yir'auniy | uayismachu; | kiy | lidbaraka |
| **that I may learn** | **your commandments** | | **They that fear you** | ***when* they see me** | **will be glad** | **because** | **in your word** |

| | 119:75 | | | | | | | | 119:76 |
|---|---|---|---|---|---|---|---|---|---|
| יחלתי 3176: | | ידעתי 3045 | יהוה 3069 | כי 3588 | צדק 6664 | משפטיך 4941 | ואמונה 530 | עניתני 6031: | |
| yichalatiy. | | yada'tiy | Yahuah | kiy | tzedeq | mishpateyka; | ua'amunah, | 'aniytaniy. | |
| **I have hoped** | | **I know** | **Yahuah** | **that** | ***are* right** | **your judgments** | **and faithfulness *that*** | **you have afflicted me *in*** | |

| | | | | | | 119:77 |
|---|---|---|---|---|---|---|
| יהי 1961 | נא 4994 | חסדך 2617 | לנחמני 5162 | כאמרתך 565 | לעבדך 5650: | |
| yahiy | naa' | chasdaka | lanachameniy; | ka'amrataka | la'abdeka. | |
| **Let be** | **I pray you** | **your merciful kindness** | **for my comfort** | **according to your word** | **unto your servant** | |

| | | | | | | 119:78 | | | |
|---|---|---|---|---|---|---|---|---|---|
| יבאוני 935 | רחמיך 7356 | ואחיה 2421 | כי 3588 | תורתך 8451 | שעשעי 8191: | | יבשו 954 | זדים 2086 | כי 3588 |
| yabo'auniy | rachameyka | ua'achayeh; | kiy | tourataka, | sha'ashu'ay. | | yeboshu | zediym | kiy |
| **Let come unto me** | **your tender mercies** | **that I may live** | **for** | **your law *is*** | **my delight** | | **Let be ashamed** | **the proud** | **for** |

| | | | | | 119:79 | | |
|---|---|---|---|---|---|---|---|
| שקר 8267 | עותוני 5791 | אני 589 | אשיח 7878 | בפקודיך 6490: | | ישובו 7725 | לי 3807a |
| sheqer | 'auatuniy; | 'aniy, | 'asiyach | bapiqudeyka. | | yashubu | liy |
| **without a cause** | **they dealt perversely with me** | ***but* I** | **will meditate** | **in your precepts** | | **Let turn** | **unto me** |

| | | | 119:80 | | | | | |
|---|---|---|---|---|---|---|---|---|
| יראיך 3373 | וידעו 3045 | עדתיך 5713: | | יהי 1961 | לבי 3820 | תמים 8549 | בחקיך 2706 | למען 4616 |
| yare'ayka; | uayada'au | 'aedoteyka. | | yahiy | libiy | tamiym | bachuqeyka; | lama'an, |
| **those that fear you** | **and those that have known** | **your testimonies** | | **Let be** | **my heart** | **sound** | **in your statutes** | **that** |

| | | 119:81 | | | | | | 119:82 | | |
|---|---|---|---|---|---|---|---|---|---|---|
| לא 3808 | אבוש 954: | | כלתה 3615 | לתשועתך 8668 | נפשי 5315 | לדברך 1697 | יחלתי 3176: | | כלו 3615 | עיני 5869 |
| la' | 'aeboush. | | kaltah | litshu'ataka | napshiy; | lidbaraka | yichalatiy. | | kalu | 'aeynay |
| **not** | **I be ashamed** | | **KAPH: faint** | **for your salvation** | **My soul** | **in your word** | ***but* I hope** | | **fail** | **Mine eyes** |

| | | | | 119:83 | | | | | | |
|---|---|---|---|---|---|---|---|---|---|---|
| לאמרתך 565 | לאמר 559 | מתי 4970 | תנחמני 5162: | | כי 3588 | הייתי 1961 | כנאד 4997 | בקיטור 7008 | חקיך 2706 | לא 3808 |
| la'amrateka; | lea'mor, | matay | tanachameniy. | | kiy | hayiytiy | kana'd | baqiytour; | chuqeyka, | la' |
| **for your word** | **saying** | **When** | **will you comfort me?** | | **For** | **I am become** | **like a bottle** | **in the smoke** | **your statutes** | **not** |

| | 119:84 | | | | | | |
|---|---|---|---|---|---|---|---|
| שכחתי 7911: | | כמה 4100 | ימי 3117 | עבדך 5650 | מתי 4970 | תעשה 6213 | ברדפי 7291 |
| shakachatiy. | | kamah | yamey | 'abdeka; | matay | ta'aseh | barodapay |
| ***yet* do I forget** | | **How many** | ***are* the days of** | **your servant?** | **when** | **will you execute** | **on them that persecute me?** |

| | 119:85 | | | | | | | | 119:86 | |
|---|---|---|---|---|---|---|---|---|---|---|
| משפט 4941: | | כרו 3738 | לי 3807a | זדים 2086 | שיחות 7882 | אשר 834 | לא 3808 | כתורתך 8451: | | כל 3605 |
| mishapat. | | karu | liy | zediym | shiychout; | 'asher, | la' | katourateka. | | kal |
| **judgment** | | **have digged** | **for me** | **The proud** | **pits** | **which** | **not** | ***are* after your law** | | **All** |

Ps 119:71 It is good for me that I have been afflicted; that I might learn your statutes.72 The law of your mouth is better unto me than thousands of gold and silver.73 Thy hands have made me and fashioned me: give me understanding, that I may learn your commandments.74 They that fear you will be glad when they see me; because I have hoped in your word.75 I know, O YHUH, that your judgments are right, and that you in faithfulness have afflicted me.76 Let, I pray you, your merciful kindness be for my comfort, according to your word unto your servant.77 Let your tender mercies come unto me, that I may live: for your law is my delight.78 Let the proud be ashamed; for they dealt perversely with me without a cause: but I will meditate in your precepts.79 Let those that fear you turn unto me, and those that have known your testimonies.80 Let my heart be sound in your statutes; that I be not ashamed.81 My soul fainteth for your salvation: but I hope in your word.82 Mine eyes fail for your word, saying, When will you comfort me?83 For I am become like a bottle in the smoke; yet do I not forget your statutes.84 How many are the days of your servant? when will you execute judgment on them that persecute me?85 The proud have digged pits for me, which are not after your law.

| מצותיך 4687 | אמונה 530 | שקר 8267 | רדפוני 7291 | עזרני 5826: | 119:87 | כמעט 4592 | כלוני 3615 |
|---|---|---|---|---|---|---|---|
| mitzuoteyka | 'amunah; | sheqer | radapuniy | 'azareniy. | | kima'at | kiluniy |
| **your commandments** | ***are* faithful** | **wrongfully** | **they persecute me** | **help you me** | | **almost** | **They had consumed me** |

| בארץ 776 | ואני 589 | לא 3808 | עזבתי 5800 | פקודיך 6490: | 119:88 | כחסדך 2617 | חיני 2421 | ואשמרה 8104 |
|---|---|---|---|---|---|---|---|---|
| ba'aretz; | ua'aniy, | la' | 'azabtiy | piqudeyka | | kachasdaka | chayeniy; | ua'ashmarah, |
| **upon earth** | **but I** | **not** | **forsook** | **your precepts** | | **after your lovingkindness** | **Quicken me** | **so shall I keep** |

| עדות 5715 | פיך 6310: | 119:89 | לעולם 5769 | יהוה 3069 | דברך 1697 | נצב 5324 | בשמים 8064: | 119:90 | לדר 1755 |
|---|---|---|---|---|---|---|---|---|---|
| 'aedut | piyka. | | la'aulam | Yahuah; | dabaraka, | nitzab | bashamayim. | | lador |
| **the testimony of** | **your mouth** | | **LAMED: For ever** | **Yahuah** | **your word** | **is settled** | **in heaven** | | ***is* unto all** |

| ודר 1755 | אמונתך 530 | כוננת 3559 | ארץ 776 | ותעמד 5975: | 119:91 | למשפטיך 4941 |
|---|---|---|---|---|---|---|
| uador | 'amunateka; | kounanta | 'aretz, | uata'amod. | | lamishpateyka |
| **generations** | **Your faithfulness** | **you have established** | **the earth** | **and it abide** | | **according to your ordinances** |

| עמדו 5975 | היום 3117 | כי 3588 | הכל 3605 | עבדיך 5650: | 119:92 | לולי 3884 | תורתך 8451 | שעשעי 8191 | אז 227 |
|---|---|---|---|---|---|---|---|---|---|
| 'amadu | hayoum; | kiy | hakol | 'abadeyka. | | luley | tourataka | sha'ashu'ay; | 'az, |
| **They continue** | **this day** | **for** | **all** | ***are* your servants** | | **Unless** | **your law** | ***had been* my delights** | **then** |

| אבדתי 6 | בעניי 6040: | 119:93 | לעולם 5769 | לא 3808 | אשכח 7911 | פקודיך 6490 | כי 3588 | בם 871a |
|---|---|---|---|---|---|---|---|---|
| 'abadtiy | ba'anyiy. | | la'aulam | la' | 'ashkach | piqudeyka; | kiy | bam, |
| **I should have perished** | **in mine affliction** | | **never** | **not** | **I will forget** | **your precepts** | **for** | **with them** |

| חייתני 2421: | 119:94 | לך 3807a | אני 589 | הושיעני 3467 | כי 3588 | פקודיך 6490 | דרשתי 1875: | 119:95 | לי 3807a |
|---|---|---|---|---|---|---|---|---|---|
| chiyiytaniy. | | leka | 'aniy | houshiy'aeniy; | kiy | piqudeyka | darashatiy. | | liy |
| **you have quickened me** | | ***am* to your** | **I** | **I save me** | **for** | **your precepts** | **I have sought** | | **for me** |

| קוו 6960 | רשעים 7563 | לאבדני 6 | עדתיך 5713 | אתבונן 995: | 119:96 | לכל 3605 | תכלה 8502 | ראיתי 7200 | קץ 7093 |
|---|---|---|---|---|---|---|---|---|---|
| qiuu | rasha'aym | la'abdeniy; | 'aedoteyka, | 'atbounan. | | lakal | tiklah | ra'aytiy | qetz; |
| **have waited** | **The wicked** | **to destroy me** | **your testimonies** | ***but* I will consider** | | **of all** | **perfection** | **I have seen** | **an end** |

| רחבה 7342 | מצותך 4687 | מאד 3966: | 119:97 | מה 4100 | אהבתי 157 | תורתך 8451 | כל 3605 | היום 3117 | היא 1931 |
|---|---|---|---|---|---|---|---|---|---|
| rachabah | mitzuataka | ma'ad. | | mah | 'ahabtiy | tourateka; | kal | hayoum, | hiy'a |
| **broad** | ***but* your commandment** | ***is* exceeding** | | **MEM: O how** | **love I** | **your law** | **all** | **the day** | **it** |

| שיחתי 7881: | 119:98 | מאיבי 341 | תחכמני 2449 | מצותך 4687 | כי 3588 | לעולם 5769 | היא 1931 |
|---|---|---|---|---|---|---|---|
| siychatiy. | | me'ayabay | tachakmeniy | mitzauoteka; | kiy | la'aulam | hiy'a |
| ***is* my meditation** | | **than mine enemies** | **You have made me wiser** | ***through* your commandments** | **for *are*** | **ever** | **they** |

| לי 3807a: | 119:99 | מכל 3605 | מלמדי 3925 | השכלתי 7919 | כי 3588 | עדותיך 5715 | שיחה 7881 | לי 3807a: | 119:100 |
|---|---|---|---|---|---|---|---|---|---|
| liy. | | mikal | malamday | hiskaltiy; | kiy | 'aedauoteyka, | siychah | liy. | |
| **with me** | | **than all** | **my teachers** | **I have more understanding** | **for** | **your testimonies** | **meditation** | ***are* my** | |

| מזקנים 2205 | אתבונן 995 | כי 3588 | פקודיך 6490 | נצרתי 5341: | 119:101 | מכל 3605 | ארח 734 | רע 7451 | כלאתי 3607 |
|---|---|---|---|---|---|---|---|---|---|
| mizqeniym | 'atbounan; | kiy | piqudeyka | natzaratiy. | | mikal | 'arach | ra' | kala'tiy |
| **more than the ancients** | **I understand** | **because** | **your precepts** | **I keep** | | **from every** | **way** | **evil** | **I have refrained** |

Ps 119:86 All your commandments are faithful: they persecute me wrongfully; help you me.87 They had almost consumed me upon earth; but I forsook not your precepts.88 Quicken me after your lovingkindness; so shall I keep the testimony of your mouth.89 For ever, O YHUH, your word is settled in heaven.90 Thy faithfulness is unto all generations: you have established the earth, and it abideth.91 They continue this day according to your ordinances: for all are your servants.92 Unless your law had been my delights, I should then have perished in mine affliction.93 I will never forget your precepts: for with them you have quickened me.94 I am your, save me; for I have sought your precepts.95 The wicked have waited for me to destroy me: but I will consider your testimonies.96 I have seen an end of all perfection: but your commandment is exceeding broad.97 O how love I your law! it is my meditation all the day.98 Thou through your commandments have made me wiser than mine enemies: for they are ever with me.99 I have more understanding than all my teachers: for your testimonies are my meditation.100 I understand more than the ancients, because I keep your precepts.101 I have refrained my feet from every evil way, that I might keep your word.

רגלי 7272 למען 4616 אשמר 8104 דברך 1697: 119:102 ממשפטיך 4941 לא 3808 סרתי 5493 כי 3588 אתה 859
raglay; lama'an, 'ashmor dabareka. mimishpateyka la' saratiy; kiy 'atah,
**my feet that I might keep your word from your judgments not I have departed for you**

הורתני 3384: 119:103 מה 4100 נמלצו 4452 לחכי 2441 אמרתך 565 מדבש 1706 לפי 6310: 119:104
houretaniy. mah nimlatzu lachikiy 'amrateka, midbash lapiy.
**have taught me How sweet are unto my taste your words *yea sweeter* than honey to my mouth**

מפקודיך 6490 אתבונן 995 על 5921 כן 3651 שנאתי 8130 כל 3605 ארח 734 שקר 8267: 119:105 נר 5216
mipiqudeyka 'atbounan; 'al ken, sanea'tiy kal 'arach shaqer. ner
**Through your precepts I get understanding therefore so I hate every way false NUN: *is* a lamp**

לרגלי 7272 דברך 1697 ואור 216 לנתיבתי 5410: 119:106 נשבעתי 7650 ואקימה 6965 לשמר 8104 משפטי 4941
laragliy dabareka; ua'aur, linatiybatiy. nishba'atiy ua'aqayemah; lishmor, mishpatey
**unto my feet Your word and a light unto my path I have sworn and I will perform *it* that I will keep judgments**

צדקך 6664: 119:107 נעניתי 6031 עד 5704 מאד 3966 יהוה 3069 חיני 2421 כדברך 1697: 119:108
tzidqeka. na'aneytiy 'ad ma'ad; Yahuah chayeniy kidbareka.
**your righteous I am afflicted very much Yahuah quicken me according unto your word**

נדבות 5071 פי 6310 רצה 7521 נא 4994 יהוה 3069 ומשפטיך 4941 למדני 3925: 119:109 נפשי 5315
nidbout piy retzeh naa' Yahuah; uamishpateyka lamadeniy. napshiy
**the freewill offerings of my mouth Accept I beseech you Yahuah and your judgments teach me My soul**

בכפי 3709 תמיד 8548 ותורתך 8451 לא 3808 שכחתי 7911: 119:110 נתנו 5414 רשעים 7563 פח 6341 לי 3807a
bakapiy tamiyd; uatourataka, la' shakachatiy. natanu rasha'aym pach liy;
**in my hand *is* continually yet your law not do I forget have laid The wicked a snare for me**

ומפקודיך 6490 לא 3808 תעיתי 8582: 119:111 נחלתי 5157 עדותיך 5715 לעולם 5769 כי 3588
uamipiqudeyka, la' ta'aytiy. nachaltiy 'aedauoteyka la'aulam; kiy
**yet from your precepts not I erred have I taken as an heritage Your testimonies for ever for**

ששון 8342 לבי 3820 המה 1992: 119:112 נטיתי 5186 לבי 3820 לעשות 6213 חקיך 2706 לעולם 5769
sasoun libiy hemah. natiytiy libiy la'asout chuqeyka, la'aulam
***are* the rejoicing of my heart they I have inclined mine heart to perform your statutes alway**

עקב 6118: 119:113 סעפים 5588 שנאתי 8130 ותורתך 8451 אהבתי 157: 119:114 סתרי 5643
'aeqeb. se'apiym sanea'tiy; uatourataka 'ahabatiy. sitriy
***even unto* the end SAMEKH: *vain* thoughts I hate but your law do I love *are* my hiding place**

ומגני 4043 אתה 859 לדברך 1697 יחלתי 3176: 119:115 סורו 5493 ממני 4480 מרעים 7489 ואצרה 5341 מצות 4687
uamaginiy 'atah; lidbaraka yichalatiy. suru mimeniy mere'aym; ua'atzrah, mitzuot
**and my shield You in your word I hope Depart from me you evildoers for I will keep the commandments of**

אלהי 430: 119:116 סמכני 5564 כאמרתך 565 ואחיה 2421 ואל 408 תבישני 954 משברי 7664:
'alohay. samakeniy ka'amrataka ua'achayeh; ua'al tabiysheniy, misibriy.
**my Elohim Uphold me according unto your word that I may live and not let me be ashamed of my hope**

Ps 119:102 I have not departed from your judgments: for you have taught me.103 How sweet are your words unto my taste! yea, sweeter than honey to my mouth!104 Through your precepts I get understanding: therefore I hate every false way.105 Thy word is a lamp unto my feet, and a light unto my path.106 I have sworn, and I will perform it, that I will keep your righteous judgments.107 I am afflicted very much: quicken me, O YHUH, according unto your word.108 Accept, I beseech you, the freewill offerings of my mouth, O YHUH, and teach me your judgments.109 My soul is continually in my hand: yet do I not forget your law.110 The wicked have laid a snare for me: yet I erred not from your precepts.111 Thy testimonies have I taken as an heritage forever: for they are the rejoicing of my heart.112 I have inclined mine heart to perform your statutes alway, even unto the end.113 I hate vain thoughts: but your law do I love.114 Thou are my hiding place and my shield: I hope in your word.115 Depart from me, you evildoers: for I will keep the commandments of my G-d.116 Uphold me according unto your word, that I may live: and let me not be ashamed of my hope.

119:117 סעדני 5582 ואושעה 3467 ואשעה 8159 בחקיך 2706 תמיד 8548: 119:118
sa'adeniy ua'auashe'ah; ua'ash'Ah uachuqeyka tamiyd.
**Hold you me up and I shall be safe and I will have respect unto your statutes continually**

סלית 5541 כל 3605 שוגים 7686 מחקיך 2706 כי 3588 שקר 8267 תרמיתם 8649: 119:119 סגים 5509
saliyta kal shougiym mechuqeyka; kiy, sheqer tarmiytam. sigiym,
**You have trodden down all them that err from your statutes for *is* falsehood their deceit *like* dross**

השבת 7673 כל 3605 רשעי 7563 ארץ 776 לכן 3651 אהבתי 157 עדתיך 5713: 119:120 סמר 5568 מפחדך 6343 בשרי 1320
hishbata kal rish'aey 'aretz; laken, 'ahabtiy 'aedoteyka. samar mipachdaka basariy;
**You put away all the wicked of the earth therefore I love your testimonies tremble for fear of you My flesh**

וממשפטיך 4941 יראתי 3372: 119:121 עשיתי 6213 משפט 4941 וצדק 6664 בל 1077 תניחני 3240
uamimishpateyka yara'tiy. 'asiytiy mishapat uatzedeq; bal taniycheniy,
**and of your judgments I am afraid AYIN: I have done judgment and justice not leave me**

לעשקי 6231: 119:122 ערב 6148 עבדך 5650 לטוב 2896 אל 408 יעשקני 6231 זדים 2086: 119:123 עיני 5869 כלו 3615
la'ashaqay. arob 'abdaka latoub; 'al ya'ashquniy zediym. 'aeynay kalu
**to mine oppressors Be surety for your servant for good not let oppress me the proud Mine eyes fail**

לישועתך 3444 ולאמרת 565 צדקך 6664: 119:124 עשה 6213 עם 5973 עבדך 5650 כחסדך 2617
liyshu'ateka; ual'amrat tzidqeka. 'aseh 'am 'abdaka kachasadeka,
**for your salvation and for the word of your righteousness Deal with your servant according unto your mercy**

וחקיך 2706 למדני 3925: 119:125 עבדך 5650 אני 589 הבינני 995 ואדעה 3045
uachuqeyka lamadeniy. 'abdaka 'aniy habiyneniy; ua'aeda'ah,
**and your statutes teach me *am* your servant I give me understanding that I may know**

עדתיך 5713: 119:126 עת 6256 לעשות 6213 ליהוה 3069 הפרו 6565 תורתך 8451: 119:127 על 5921 כן 3651
'aedoteyka. 'at la'asout laYahuah; heperu, tourateka. 'al ken
**your testimonies *It is* time to work: *for you,* Yahuah *for* they have made void your law Therefore after that**

אהבתי 157 מצותיך 4687 מזהב 2091 ומפז 6337: 119:128 על 5921 כן 3651 כל 3605
'ahabtiy mitzuoteyka; mizahab uamipaz. 'al ken kal
**I love your commandments above gold yea above fine gold Therefore after that *I esteem* all *your***

פקודי 6490 כל 3605 ישרתי 3474 כל 3605 ארח 734 שקר 8267 שנאתי 8130: 119:129 פלאות 6382
piqudey kal yisharatiy; kal 'arach sheqer sanea'tiy. pala'aut
**all precepts *concerning* all *things to be* right every way false *and* I hate PEY: *are* wonderful**

עדותיך 5715 על 5921 כן 3651 נצרתם 5341 נפשי 5315: 119:130 פתח 6608 דבריך 1697 יאיר 215
'aedauoteyka; 'al ken, natzaratam napshiy. petach dabareyka ya'ayr,
**Your testimonies therefore after that does keep them my soul The entrance of your words gives light**

מבין 995 פתיים 6612: 119:131 פי 6310 פערתי 6473 ואשאפה 7602 כי 3588 למצותיך 4687
mebiyn pata'yiym. piy pa'artiy ua'ash'apah; kiy lamitzuoteyka
**it gives understanding unto the simple my mouth I opened and panted for your commandments**

Ps 119:117 Hold you me up, and I shall be safe: and I will have respect unto your statutes continually.118 Thou have trodden down all them that err from your statutes: for their deceit is falsehood.119 Thou puttest away all the wicked of the earth like dross: therefore I love your testimonies.120 My flesh trembleth for fear of you; and I am afraid of your judgments.121 I have done judgment and justice: leave me not to mine oppressors.122 Be surety for your servant for good: let not the proud oppress me.123 Mine eyes fail for your salvation, and for the word of your righteousness.124 Deal with your servant according unto your mercy, and teach me your statutes.125 I am your servant; give me understanding, that I may know your testimonies.126 It is time for you, YHUH, to work: for they have made void your law.127 Therefore I love your commandments above gold; yea, above fine gold.128 Therefore I esteem all your precepts concerning all things to be right; and I hate every false way.129 Thy testimonies are wonderful: therefore doth my soul keep them.130 The entrance of your words give light; it give understanding unto the simple.131 I opened my mouth, and panted: for I longed for your commandments.

119:132

יאבתי 2968: | פנה 6437 | אלי 413 | וחנני 2603 | כמשפט 4941 | לאהבי 157
ya'abatiy. | paneh | 'aelay | uachaneniy | kamishpat, | la'ahabey
**I longed for | Look you | upon me | and be merciful upon me | as you usest to do | unto those that love**

119:133 ... 119:134

שמך 8034: | פעמי 6471 | הכן 3559 | באמרתך 565 | ואל 408 | תשלט 7980 | בי 871a | כל 3605 | און 205: | פדני 6299
shameka. | pa'amay | hakan | ba'amrateka; | ua'al | tashlet | biy | kal | 'auen. | padeniy
**your name | my steps | Order | in your word | and not | let have dominion | over me | any | iniquity | Deliver me**

119:135

מעשק 6233 | אדם 120 | ואשמרה 8104 | פקודיך 6490: | פניך 6440 | האר 215 | בעבדך 5650
me'asheq | 'adam; | ua'ashmarah, | piqudeyka. | paneyka | ha'aer | ba'abdeka;
**from the oppression of | man | so will I keep | your precepts | your face | Make to shine | upon your servant**

119:136

ולמדני 3925 | את 853 | חקיך 2706: | פלגי 6388 | מים 4325 | ירדו 3381 | עיני 5869 | על 5921 | לא 3808 | שמרו 8104
ualamadeniy, | 'at | chuqeyka. | palgey | mayim | yaradu | 'aeynay; | 'aal, | la' | shamaru
**and teach me | your statutes | Rivers of | waters | run down | mine eyes | because | not | they keep**

119:137 ... 119:138

תורתך 8451: | צדיק 6662 | אתה 859 | יהוה 3069 | וישר 3477 | משפטיך 4941:
tourateka. | tzadiyq | 'atah | Yahuah; | uayashar, | mishpateyka.
**your law | TZADHE: Righteous *are* | you | O Yahuah | and upright | *are* your judgments**

119:139

צוית 6680 | צדק 6664 | עדתיך 5713 | ואמונה 530 | מאד 3966: | צמתתני 6789 | קנאתי 7068 | כי 3588
tziuiyta | tzedeq | 'aedoteyka; | ua'amunah | ma'ad. | tzimtatniy | qin'atiy; | kiy
***that* you have commanded | *are* righteous | Your testimonies | and faithful | very | has consumed me | My zeal | because**

119:140 ... 119:141

שכחו 7911 | דבריך 1697 | צרי 6862: | צרופה 6884 | אמרתך 565 | מאד 3966 | ועבדך 5650 | אהבה 157:
shakachu | dabareyka | tzaray. | tzarupah | 'amrataka | ma'ad, | ua'abdaka | 'ahebah.
**have forgotten | your words | mine enemies | pure | Your word | *is* very | therefore your servant | love it**

119:142

צעיר 6810 | אנכי 595 | ונבזה 959 | פקדיך 6490 | לא 3808 | שכחתי 7911: | צדקתך 6666 | צדק 6664 | לעולם 5769
tza'ayr | 'anokiy | uanibzeh; | piqudeyka, | la' | shakachatiy. | tzidqataka | tzedeq | la'aulam;
***am* small | I | and despised | your precepts | not | *yet* do I forget | Your righteousness *is* | an righteousness | everlasting**

119:143

ותורתך 8451 | אמת 571: | צר 6862 | ומצוק 4689 | מצאוני 4672 | מצותיך 4687
uatourataka | 'amet. | tzar | uamatzouq | matza'uniy; | mitzuoteyka,
**and your law | *is* the truth | Trouble | and anguish | have taken hold on me | *yet* your commandments**

119:144 ... 119:145

שעשעי 8191: | צדק 6664 | עדותיך 5715 | לעולם 5769 | הבינני 995 | ואחיה 2421:
sha'ashu'ay. | tzedeq | 'aedauoteyka | la'aulam, | habiyneniy | ua'achayeh.
***are* my delights | The righteousness of | your testimonies *is* | everlasting | give me understanding | and I shall live**

119:146

קראתי 7121 | בכל 3605 | לב 3820 | ענני 6030 | יהוה 3069 | חקיך 2706 | אצרה 5341: | קראתיך 7121 | הושיעני 3467
qaraa'tiy | bakal | leb | 'aneniy | Yahuah | chuqeyka | 'atzorah. | qaraa'tiyka | houshiy'aeniy;
**QOPH: I cried | with *my* whole | heart | hear me | O Yahuah | your statutes | I will keep | I cried unto you | save me**

119:147

ואשמרה 8104 | עדתיך 5713: | קדמתי 6923 | בנשף 5399 | ואשועה 7768 | לדבריך 1697
ua'ashmarah, | 'aedoteyka. | qidamtiy | baneshep | ua'ashaue'ah; | lidbarayka
**and I shall keep | your testimonies | I prevented | the dawning of the morning | and cried | in your word**

Ps 119:132 Look you upon me, and be merciful unto me, as you usest to do unto those that love your name.133 Order my steps in your word: and let not any iniquity have dominion over me.134 Deliver me from the oppression of man: so will I keep your precepts.135 Make your face to shine upon your servant; and teach me your statutes.136 Rivers of waters run down mine eyes, because they keep not your law.137 Righteous are you, O YHUH, and upright are your judgments.138 Thy testimonies that you have commanded are righteous and very faithful.139 My zeal has consumed me, because mine enemies have forgotten your words.140 Thy word is very pure: therefore your servant love it.141 I am small and despised: yet do not I forget your precepts.142 Thy righteousness is an everlasting righteousness, and your law is the truth.143 Trouble and anguish have taken hold on me: yet your commandments are my delights.144 The righteousness of your testimonies is everlasting: give me understanding, and I shall live.145 I cried with my whole heart; hear me, O YHUH: I will keep your statutes.146 I cried unto you; save me, and I shall keep your testimonies.147 I prevented the dawning of the morning, and cried: I hoped in your word.

| יחלתי 3176: | 119:148 | קדמו 6923 | עיני 5869 | אשמרות 821 | לשיח 7878 | באמרתך 565: | 119:149 | קולי 6963 | שמעה 8085 |
|---|---|---|---|---|---|---|---|---|---|
| yichalatiy. | | qidmu | 'aeynay | 'ashmurout; | lasiyach, | ba'amrateka. | | qouliy | shim'ah |
| **I hoped** | | **prevent** | **Mine eyes** | ***the night* watches** | **that I might meditate** | **in your word** | | **my voice** | **Hear** |

| כחסדך 2617 | יהוה 3069 | כמשפטך 4941 | חיני 2421: | 119:150 | קרבו 7126 |
|---|---|---|---|---|---|
| kachasadeka; | Yahuah | kamishpateka | chayeniy. | | qarabu |
| **according unto your lovingkindness** | **Yahuah** | **according to your judgment** | **quicken me** | | **They draw near** |

| רדפי 7291 | זמה 2154 | מתורתך 8451 | רחקו 7368: | 119:151 | קרוב 7138 | אתה 859 | יהוה 3069 | וכל 3605 | מצותיך 4687 |
|---|---|---|---|---|---|---|---|---|---|
| rodapey | zimah; | mitourataka | rachaqu. | | qaroub | 'atah | Yahuah; | uakal | mitzuoteyka |
| **that follow after** | **mischief** | **from your law** | **they are far** | | ***are* near** | **You** | **Yahuah** | **and all** | **your commandments** |

| אמת 571: | 119:152 | קדם 6924 | ידעתי 3045 | מעדתיך 5713 | כי 3588 | לעולם 5769 | יסדתם 3245: | 119:153 |
|---|---|---|---|---|---|---|---|---|
| 'amet. | | qedem | yada'tiy | me'aedoteyka; | kiy | la'aulam | yasadtam. | |
| ***are* truth** | | **old** | **I have known of** | **Concerning your testimonies** | **that** | **for ever** | **you have founded them** | |

| ראה 7200 | עניי 6040 | וחלצני 2502 | כי 3588 | תורתך 8451 | לא 3808 | שכחתי 7911: | 119:154 | ריבה 7378 | ריבי 7379 |
|---|---|---|---|---|---|---|---|---|---|
| ra'aeh | 'anyiy | uachaltzeniy; | kiy | tourataka, | la' | shakachatiy. | | riybah | riybiy |
| **RESH: Consider** | **mine affliction** | **and deliver me** | **for** | **your law** | **not** | **I do forget** | | **Plead** | **my cause** |

| וגאלני 1350 | לאמרתך 565 | חיני 2421: | 119:155 | רחוק 7350 | מרשעים 7563 | ישועה 3444 | כי 3588 | חקיך 2706 | לא 3808 |
|---|---|---|---|---|---|---|---|---|---|
| uag'aleniy; | la'amrataka | chayeniy. | | rachouq | merasha'aym | yashu'ah; | kiy | chuqeyka | la' |
| **and deliver me** | **according to your word** | **quicken me** | | ***is* far** | **from the wicked** | **Salvation** | **for** | **your statutes** | **not** |

| דרשו 1875: | 119:156 | רחמיך 7356 | רבים 7227 | יהוה 3068 | כמשפטיך 4941 | חיני 2421: | 119:157 | רבים 7227 |
|---|---|---|---|---|---|---|---|---|
| darashu. | | rachameyka | rabiym | Yahuah; | kamishpateyka | chayeniy. | | rabiym |
| **they seek** | | ***are* your tender mercies** | **Great** | **Yahuah** | **according to your judgments** | **quicken me** | | **Many** |

| רדפי 7291 | וצרי 6862 | מעדותיך 5715 | לא 3808 | נטיתי 5186: | 119:158 | ראיתי 7200 | בגדים 898 |
|---|---|---|---|---|---|---|---|
| rodapay | uatzaray; | me'adauoteyka, | la' | natiytiy. | | ra'aytiy | bogadiym |
| ***are* my persecutors** | **and mine enemies** | **from your testimonies** | **not** | ***yet* do I decline** | | **I beheld** | **the transgressors** |

| ואתקוטטה 6962 | אשר 834 | אמרתך 565 | לא 3808 | שמרו 8104: | 119:159 | ראה 7200 | כי 3588 | פקודיך 6490 | אהבתי 157 | יהוה 3069 |
|---|---|---|---|---|---|---|---|---|---|---|
| ua'atqoutatah; | 'asher | 'amrataka, | la' | shamaru. | | ra'aeh | kiy | piqudeyka | 'ahabatiy; | Yahuah |
| **and was grieved** | **because** | **your word** | **not** | **they kept** | | **Consider** | **how** | **your precepts** | **I love** | **Yahuah** |

| כחסדך 2617 | חיני 2421: | 119:160 | ראש 7218 | דברך 1697 | אמת 571 | ולעולם 5769 | כל 3605 |
|---|---|---|---|---|---|---|---|
| kachasdaka | chayeniy. | | ra'sh | dabaraka | 'amet; | ual'aulam, | kal |
| **according to your lovingkindness** | **quicken me** | | ***from* the beginning** | **Your word** | ***is* true** | **and for ever** | **every one of** |

| משפט 4941 | צדקך 6664: | 119:161 | שרים 8269 | רדפוני 7291 | חנם 2600 | ומדבריך 1697 |
|---|---|---|---|---|---|---|
| mishapat | tzidqeka. | | sariym | radapuniy | chinam; | uamidebareyaka |
| **judgments *endure*** | **your righteous** | | **SHIN: Princes** | **have persecuted me** | **without a cause** | **but of your word** |

| פחד 6342 | לבי 3820: | 119:162 | שש 7797 | אנכי 595 | על 5921 | אמרתך 565 | כמוצא 4672 | שלל 7998 | רב 7227: | 119:163 | שקר 8267 | שנאתי 8130 |
|---|---|---|---|---|---|---|---|---|---|---|---|---|
| pachad | libiy. | | sas | 'anokiy | 'al | 'amrateka; | kamoutzea', | shalal | rab. | | sheqer | sanea'tiy |
| **stands in awe** | **my heart** | | **rejoice** | **I** | **at** | **your word** | **as one that finds** | **spoil** | **great** | | **lying** | **I hate** |

Ps 119:148 Mine eyes prevent the night watches, that I might meditate in your word.149 Hear my voice according unto your lovingkindness: O YHUH, quicken me according to your judgment.150 They draw nigh that follow after mischief: they are far from your law.151 Thou are near, O YHUH; and all your commandments are truth.152 Concerning your testimonies, I have known of old that you have founded them forever.153 Consider mine affliction, and deliver me: for I do not forget your law.154 Plead my cause, and deliver me: quicken me according to your word.155 Salvation is far from the wicked: for they seek not your statutes.156 Great are your tender mercies, O YHUH: quicken me according to your judgments.157 Many are my persecutors and mine enemies; yet do I not decline from your testimonies.158 I beheld the transgressors, and was grieved; because they kept not your word.159 Consider how I love your precepts: quicken me, O YHUH, according to your lovingkindness.160 Thy word is true from the beginning: and everyone of your righteous judgments endureth forever.161 Princes have persecuted me without a cause: but my heart stand in awe of your word.162 I rejoice at your word, as one that findeth great spoil.

| 8581 ואתעבה | 8451 תורתך | 157 אהבתי: | 119:164 | 7651 שבע | 3117 ביום | 1984 הללתיך | 5921 על | 4941 משפטי |
|---|---|---|---|---|---|---|---|---|
| ua'ata'aebah; | tourataka | 'ahabatiy. | | sheba' | bayoum | hilaltiyka; | 'aal, | mishpatey |
| **and abhor** | ***but* your law** | **I do love** | | **Seven *times*** | **a day** | **do I praise you** | **because of** | **judgments** |

| 6664 צדקך: | 119:165 | 7965 שלום | 7227 רב | 157 לאהבי | 8451 תורתך | 369 ואין | 3807a למו | 4383 מכשול: | 119:166 |
|---|---|---|---|---|---|---|---|---|---|
| tzidqeka. | | shaloum | rab | la'ahabey | tourateka; | ua'aeyn | lamou | mikshoul. | |
| **your righteous** | | **peace** | **Great** | ***have* they which love** | **your law** | **and nothing** | **them** | **shall offend** | |

| 7663 שברתי | 3444 לישועתך | 3069 יהוה | 4687 ומצותיך | 6213 עשיתי: | 119:167 | 8104 שמרה | 5315 נפשי | 5713 עדתיך |
|---|---|---|---|---|---|---|---|---|
| sibartiy | liyshu'ataka | Yahuah; | uamitzuoteyka | 'asiytiy. | | shamarah | napshiy | 'aedoteyka; |
| **I have hoped** | **for your salvation** | **Yahuah** | **and your commandments** | **done** | | **has kept** | **My soul** | **your testimonies** |

| 157 ואהבם | 3966 מאד: | 119:168 | 8104 שמרתי | 6490 פקודיך | 5713 ועדתיך | 3588 כי | 3605 כל | 1870 דרכי |
|---|---|---|---|---|---|---|---|---|
| ua'ahabem | ma'ad. | | shamartiy | piqudeyka | ua'aedoteyka; | kiy | kal | darakay |
| **and I love them** | **exceedingly** | | **I have kept** | **your precepts** | **and your testimonies** | **for** | **all** | **my ways** |

| 5048 נגדך: | 119:169 | 7126 תקרב | 7440 רנתי | 6440 לפניך | 3069 יהוה | 1697 כדברך |
|---|---|---|---|---|---|---|
| negdeka. | | tiqrab | rinatiy | lapaneyka | Yahuah; | kidbaraka |
| ***are* before you** | | **TAU: Let come near** | **my cry** | **before you** | **O Yahuah** | **according to your word** |

| 995 הבינני: | 119:170 | 935 תבוא | 8467 תחנתי | 6440 לפניך | 565 כאמרתך | 5337 הצילני: | 119:171 |
|---|---|---|---|---|---|---|---|
| habiyneniy. | | tabou'a | tachinatiy | lapaneyka; | ka'amrataka, | hatziyleniy. | |
| **give me understanding** | | **Let come** | **my supplication** | **before you** | **according to your word** | **deliver me** | |

| 5042 תבענה | 8193 שפתי | 8416 תהלה | 3588 כי | 3925 תלמדני | 2706 חקיך: | 119:172 | 6030 תען | 3956 לשוני | 565 אמרתך | 3588 כי |
|---|---|---|---|---|---|---|---|---|---|---|
| taba'anah | sapatay | tahilah; | kiy | talamdeniy | chuqeyka. | | ta'an | lashouniy | 'amrateka; | kiy |
| **shall utter** | **My lips** | **praise** | **when** | **you have taught me** | **your statutes** | | **shall speak of** | **My tongue** | **your word** | **for** |

| 3605 כל | 4687 מצותיך | 6664 צדק: | 119:173 | 1961 תהי | 3027 ידך | 5826 לעזרני | 3588 כי | 6490 פקודיך |
|---|---|---|---|---|---|---|---|---|
| kal | mitzuoteyka | tzedeq. | | tahiy | yadaka | la'azareniy; | kiy | piqudeyka |
| **all** | **your commandments** | ***are* righteousness** | | **Let** | **your hand** | **help me** | **for** | **your precepts** |

| 977 בחרתי: | 119:174 | 8373 תאבתי | 3444 לישועתך | 3069 יהוה | 8451 ותורתך | 8191 שעשעי: | 119:175 | 2421 תחי | 5315 נפשי |
|---|---|---|---|---|---|---|---|---|---|
| bacharatiy. | | ta'abtiy | liyshu'ataka | Yahuah; | uatourataka, | sha'ashu'ay. | | tachiy | napshiy |
| **I have chosen** | | **I have longed for** | **your salvation** | **O Yahuah** | **and your law** | ***is* my delight** | | **Let live** | **my soul** |

| 1984 ותהללך | 4941 ומשפטך | 5826 יעזרני: | 119:176 | 8582 תעיתי | 7716 כשה | 6 אבד | 1245 בקש | 5650 עבדך |
|---|---|---|---|---|---|---|---|---|
| uatahaleka; | uamishpateka | ya'azruniy. | | ta'aytiy, | kaseh | 'abed | baqesh | 'abdeka; |
| **and it shall praise you** | **and your judgments** | **let help me** | | **I have gone astray** | **like a sheep** | **lost** | **seek** | **your servant** |

| 3588 כי | 4687 מצותיך | 3808 לא | 7911 שכחתי: |
|---|---|---|---|
| kiy | mitzuoteyka, | la' | shakachatiy. |
| **for** | **your commandments** | **not** | **I do forget** |

| **Ps 120:1** | 7892 שיר | 4609 המעלות | 413 אל | 3068 יהוה | 6869 בצרתה | 3807a לי | 7121 קראתי | 6030 ויענני: | **120:2** | 3068 יהוה | 5337 הצילה | 5315 נפשי |
|---|---|---|---|---|---|---|---|---|---|---|---|---|
| | shiyr, | hama'alout | 'al | Yahuah | batzaratah | liy; | qaraa'tiy, | uaya'aneniy. | | Yahuah | hatziylah | napshiy |
| | **A Song** | **of degrees** | **unto** | **Yahuah** | **In distress** | **my** | **I cried** | **and he heard me** | | **O Yahuah** | **Deliver** | **my soul** |

Ps 119:163 I hate and abhor lying: but your law do I love.164 Seven times a day do I praise you because of your righteous judgments.165 Great peace have they which love your law: and nothing shall offend them.166 YHUH, I have hoped for your salvation, and done your commandments.167 My soul has kept your testimonies; and I love them exceedingly.168 I have kept your precepts and your testimonies: for all my ways are before you.169 Let my cry come near before you, O YHUH: give me understanding according to your word.170 Let my supplication come before you: deliver me according to your word.171 My lips shall utter praise, when you have taught me your statutes.172 My tongue shall speak of your word: for all your commandments are righteousness.173 Let your hand help me; for I have chosen your precepts.174 I have longed for your salvation, O YHUH; and your law is my delight.175 Let my soul live, and it shall praise you; and let your judgments help me.176 I have gone astray like a lost sheep; seek your servant; for I do not forget your commandments. **Ps** 120:1 A Song of degrees. In my distress I cried unto YHUH, and he heard me.

משפת 8193 שקר 8267 מלשון 3956 רמיה 7423: **120:3** מה 4100 יתן 5414 לך 3807a ומה 4100 יסיף 3254 לך 3807a
mispat sheqer; milashoun ramiyah. mah yiten laka uamah yosiyp lak,
**from lips lying *and* from a tongue deceitful What shall be given unto you? and what shall be done unto you**

לשון 3956 רמיה 7423: **120:4** חצי 2671 גבור 1368 שנונים 8150 עם 5973 גחלי 1513 רתמים 7574: **120:5** אויה 190 לי 3807a כי 3588 גרתי 1481
lashoun ramiyah. chitzey gibour shanuniym; 'am, gachaley ratamiym. 'auyah liy kiy gartiy
**tongue? *you* false arrows of the mighty Sharp with coals of juniper Woe *is* me that I sojourn in**

משך 4902 שכנתי 7931 עם 5973 אהלי 168 קדר 6938: **120:6** רבת 7227 שכנה 7931 לה 3807a נפשי 5315 עם 5973 שונא 8130 שלום 7965: **120:7**
meshek; shakantiy, 'am 'ahaley qedar. rabat shakanah lah napshiy; 'am, sounea' shaloum.
**Mesech *that* I dwell in the tents of Kedar long has dwelt to My soul with him that hate peace**

אני 589 שלום 7965 וכי 3588 אדבר 1696 המה 1992 למלחמה 4421:
'aniy shaloum uakiy 'adaber; hemah, lamilchamah.
**I *am* *for* peace but when I speak they *are* war**

**Ps 121:1** שיר 7892 למעלות 4609 אשא 5375 עיני 5869 אל 413 ההרים 2022 מאין 370 יבא 935 עזרי 5828: **121:2** עזרי 5828 מעם 5973
shiyr, lama'alout 'asa' 'aeynay 'al hehariym; me'ayin, yaba' 'azriy. 'azriy me'am
**A Song of degrees I will lift up mine eyes unto the hills from where comes my help My help *comes* from**

יהוה 3068 עשה 6213 שמים 8064 וארץ 776: **121:3** אל 408 יתן 5414 למוט 4132 רגלך 7272 אל 408 ינום 5123
Yahuah; 'aseh, shamayim ua'aretz. 'al yiten lamout ragleka; 'al yanum,
**Yahuah which made heaven and earth not He will suffer to be moved your foot not will slumber**

שמרך 8104: **121:4** הנה 2009 לא 3808 ינום 5123 ולא 3808 יישן 3462 שומר 8104 ישראל 3478: **121:5** יהוה 3068 שמרך 8104
shomareka. hineh la' yanum uala' yiyshan; shoumer, yisra'ael. Yahuah shomareka;
**he that keep you Behold neither shall slumber nor sleep he that keep Israel Yahuah *is* your keeper**

יהוה 3068 צלך 6738 על 5921 יד 3027 ימינך 3225: **121:6** יומם 3119 השמש 8121 לא 3808 יככה 5221 וירח 3394
Yahuah tzilaka, 'al yad yamiyneka. youmam, hashemesh la' yakekah, uayareach
**Yahuah *is* your shade upon hand your right by day The sun not shall smite you nor the moon**

בלילה 3915: **121:7** יהוה 3068 ישמרך 8104 מכל 3605 רע 7451 ישמר 8104 את 853 נפשך 5315: **121:8** יהוה 3068 ישמר 8104
balayalah. Yahuah yishmaraka mikal ra'; yishmor, 'at napsheka. Yahuah yishmar
**by night Yahuah shall preserve you from all evil he shall preserve your soul Yahuah shall preserve**

צאתך 3318 ובואך 935 מעתה 6258 ועד 5704 עולם 5769:
tzea'taka uabou'aka; me'atah, ua'ad 'aulam.
**your going out and your coming in from this time forth and even for evermore**

**Ps 122:1** שיר 7892 המעלות 4609 לדוד 1732 שמחתי 8055 באמרים 559 לי 3807a בית 1004 יהוה 3068 נלך 1980: **122:2**
shiyr hama'alout, ladauid samachtiy ba'amariym liy; beyt Yahuah nelek.
**A Song of degrees of David I was glad when they said unto me the house of Yahuah Let us go into**

עמדות 5975 היו 1961 רגלינו 7272 בשעריך 8179 ירושלם 3389: **122:3** ירושלם 3389 הבנויה 1129 כעיר 5892 שחברה 2266 לה 3807a
'amadout hayu ragleynu; bish'arayik, yarushalaim. yarushalaim habanuyah; ka'ayr, shechubarah lah
**stand shall Our feet within your gates O Jerusalem Jerusalem is builded as a city that is compact to**

Ps 120:2 Deliver my soul, O YHUH, from lying lips, and from a deceitful tongue.3 What shall be given unto you? or what shall be done unto you, you false tongue?4 Sharp arrows of the mighty, with coals of juniper.5 Woe is me, that I sojourn in Mesech, that I dwell in the tents of Kedar!6 My soul has long dwelt with him that hateth peace.7 I am for peace: but when I speak, they are for war. **Ps** 121:1 A Song of degrees. I will lift up mine eyes unto the hills, from whence cometh my help.2 My help cometh from YHUH, which made heaven and earth.3 He will not suffer your foot to be moved: he that keep you will not slumber.4 Behold, he that keep Israel shall neither slumber nor sleep.5 YHUH is your keeper: YHUH is your shade upon your right hand.6 The sun shall not smite you by day, nor the moon by night.7 YHUH shall preserve you from all evil: he shall preserve your soul.8 YHUH shall preserve your going out and your coming in from this time forth, and even forevermore. **Ps** 122:1 A Song of degrees of David. I was glad when they said unto me, Let us go into the house of YHUH.2 Our feet shall stand within your gates, O Jerusalem.3 Jerusalem is built as a city that is compact together:

122:4
יחדו 3162: ששם 8033 עלו 5927 שבטים 7626 שבטי 7626 יה 3050 עדות 5715 לישראל 3478 להדות 3034
yachdau. shesham 'alu shabatiym shibtey Yah 'aedut layisra'ael; lahodout,
**together Whither go up the tribes the tribes of Yah unto the testimony of Israel to give thanks**

122:5 122:6
לשם 8034 יהוה 3068: כי 3588 שמה 8033 ישבו 3427 כסאות 3678 למשפט 4941 כסאות 3678 לבית 1004 דויד 1732:
lashem Yahuah. kiy shamah yashabu kis'aut lamishpat; kis'aut, labeyt dauiyd.
**unto the name of Yahuah For there are set thrones of judgment the thrones of the house of David**

122:7
שאלו 7592 שלום 7965 ירושלם 3389 ישליו 7951 אהביך 157: יהי 1961 שלום 7965 בחילך 2426 שלוה 7962
sha'alu shaloum yarushalaim; yishlayu, 'ahabayik. yahiy shaloum bacheylek; shaluah,
**Pray for the peace of Jerusalem they shall prosper that love you be Peace within your walls *and* prosperity**

122:8 122:9
בארמנותיך 759: למען 4616 אחי 251 ורעי 7453 אדברה 1696 נא 4994 שלום 7965 בך 871a: למען 4616
ba'armanoutayik. lama'an 'achay uare'ay; 'adabrah naa' shaloum bak. lama'an
**within your palaces For sake my brethren and companions' I will say now Peace *be* within you Because of**

בית 1004 יהוה 3068 אלהינו 430 אבקשה 1245 טוב 2896 לך 3807a:
beyt Yahuah 'aloheynu; 'abaqshah toub lak.
**the house of Yahuah our Elohim I will seek good to your**

**Ps 123:1** 123:2
שיר 7892 המעלות 4609 אליך 413 נשאתי 5375 את 853 עיני 5869 הישבי 3427 בשמים 8064: הנה 2009 כעיני 5869
shiyr, hama'alout 'aeleyka nasa'tiy 'at 'aeynay; hayoshabiy, bashamayim. hineh ka'aeyney
**A Song of degrees Unto you lift I up mine eyes O you that dwell in the heavens Behold as the eyes of**

עבדים 5650 אל 413 יד 3027 אדוניהם 113 כעיני 5869 שפחה 8198 אל 413 יד 3027 גברתה 1404 כן 3651
'abadiym 'al yad adouneyhema, ka'aeyney shipchah 'al yad gabirtah ken
**servants *look* unto the hand of their masters *and* as the eyes of a maiden unto the hand of her mistress so**

123:3
עינינו 5869 אל 413 יהוה 3068 אלהינו 430 עד 5704 שיחננו 2603: חננו 2603 יהוה 3068
'aeyneynu 'al Yahuah 'aloheynu; 'ad, sheyachanenu. chanenu Yahuah
**our eyes *wait* upon Yahuah our Elohim until that he have mercy upon us Have mercy upon us O Yahuah**

123:4
חננו 2603 כי 3588 רב 7227 שבענו 7646 בוז 937: רבת 7227 שבעה 7646 לה 3807a נפשנו 5315
chanenu; kiy rab, saba'anu buz. rabat saba'ah lah napshenu
**have mercy upon us for exceedingly we are filled with contempt exceedingly is filled with Our soul**

הלעג 3933 השאננים 7600 הבוז 937 לגאיונים 1349:
hala'ag hasha'ananiym; habuz, lig'aeyouniym
**the scorning of those that are at ease *and with* the contempt of the proud**

**Ps 124:1**
שיר 7892 המעלות 4609 לדוד 1732 לולי 3884 יהוה 3068 שהיה 1961 לנו 3807a יאמר 559 נא 4994 ישראל 3478:
shiyr hama'alout, ladauid luley Yahuah shehayah lanu; ya'mar naa' yisra'ael.
**A Song of degrees of David If *it had not been* Yahuah who was on our side may say now Israel**

124:2 124:3
לולי 3884 יהוה 3068 שהיה 1961 לנו 3807a בקום 6965 עלינו 5921 אדם 120: אזי 233 חיים 2416
luley Yahuah shehayah lanu; baqum 'aleynu 'adam. 'azay chayiym
**If *it had not been* Yahuah who was on our side when rose up against us men Then quick**

Ps 122:4 Whither the tribes go up, the tribes of YHUH, unto the testimony of Israel, to give thanks unto the name of YHUH.5 For there are set thrones of judgment, the thrones of the house of David.6 Pray for the peace of Jerusalem: they shall prosper that love you.7 Peace be within your walls, and prosperity within your palaces.8 For my brethren and companions' sakes, I will now say, Peace be within you.9 Because of the house of YHUH our G-d I will seek your good. **Ps** 123:1 A Song of degrees. Unto you lift I up mine eyes, O you that dwellest in the heavens.2 Behold, as the eyes of servants look unto the hand of their masters, and as the eyes of a maiden unto the hand of her mistress; so our eyes wait upon YHUH our G-d, until that he have mercy upon us.3 Have mercy upon us, O YHUH, have mercy upon us: for we are exceedingly filled with contempt.4 Our soul is exceedingly filled with the scorning of those that are at ease, and with the contempt of the proud. **Ps** 124:1 A Song of degrees of David. If it had not been YHUH who was on our side, now may Israel say;2 If it had not been YHUH who was on our side, when men rose up against us:

124:4

בלעונו 1104 בחרות 2734 אפם 639 בנו 871a: אזי 233 המים 4325 שטפונו 7857 נחלה 5158

bala'aunu; bacharout 'apam banu. 'azay hamayim shatapunu; nachalah,

**they had swallowed us up when was kindled their wrath against us Then the waters had overwhelmed us the stream**

124:5 124:6

עבר 5674 על 5921 נפשנו 5315: אזי 233 עבר 5674 על 5921 נפשנו 5315 המים 4325 הזידונים 2121: ברוך 1288 יהוה 3068 שלא 3808

'abar 'al napshenu. 'azay 'abar 'al napshenu; hamayim, hazeydouniym. baruk Yahuah; shela'

**had gone over our soul Then had gone over our soul waters the proud Blessed *be* Yahuah not**

124:7

נתננו 5414 טרף 2964 לשניהם 8127: נפשנו 5315 כצפור 6833 נמלטה 4422 מפח 6341 יוקשים 3369 הפח 6341

natananu terep, lashineyhem. napshenu, katzipour nimalatah mipach youqashiym hapach

**who has given us *as* a prey to their teeth Our soul as a bird is escaped out of the snare of the fowlers the snare**

124:8

נשבר 7665 ואנחנו 587 נמלטנו 4422: עזרנו 5828 בשם 8034 יהוה 3068 עשה 6213 שמים 8064 וארץ 776:

nishbar, ua'anachnu nimlatanu. 'azrenu bashem Yahuah; 'aseh, shamayim ua'aretz.

**is broken and we are escaped Our help *is* in the name of Yahuah who made heaven and earth**

Ps 125:1

שיר 7892 המעלות 4609 הבטחים 982 ביהוה 3068 כהר 2022 ציון 6726 לא 3808 ימוט 4131 לעולם 5769

shiyr, hama'alout habotachiym baYahuah; kahar tziyoun la' yimout, la'aulam

**A Song of degrees They that trust in Yahuah *shall be* as mount Zion *which* cannot be removed for ever**

125:2

ישב 3427: ירושלם 3389 הרים 2022 סביב 5439 לה 3807a ויהוה 3068 סביב 5439 לעמו 5971 מעתה 6258

yesheb. yarushalaim, hariym sabiyb lah laYahuah sabiyb la'amou; me'atah,

***but* abide *As* Jerusalem the mountains *are* round about to so Yahuah *is* round about his people from henceforth**

125:3

ועד 5704 עולם 5769: כי 3588 לא 3808 ינוח 5117 שבט 7626 הרשע 7562 על 5921 גורל 1486 הצדיקים 6662 למען 4616 לא 3808 ישלחו 7971

ua'ad 'aulam. kiy la' yanuach shebet haresha', 'al goural hatzadiyqiym lama'an la' yishlachu

**and even for ever For not shall rest the rod of the wicked upon the lot of the righteous lest not put forth**

125:4

הצדיקים 6662 בעולתה 5766 ידיהם 3027: היטיבה 2895 יהוה 3068 לטובים 2896 ולישרים 3477

hatzadiyqim ba'aualatah yadeyhem. heytiybah Yahuah latoubiym; ualiyshariym,

**the righteous unto iniquity their hands Do good O Yahuah unto *those that be* good and *to them that are* upright**

125:5

בלבותם 3826: והמטים 5186 עקלקלותם 6128 יוליכם 1980 יהוה 3068 את 854 פעלי 6466

baliboutam. uahamatiym aqalqaloutam, youliykem Yahuah 'at po'aley

**in their hearts As for such as turn aside *unto* their crooked ways shall lead them forth Yahuah *with* the workers of**

האון 205 שלום 7965 על 5921 ישראל 3478:

ha'auen; shaloum, 'al yisra'ael.

**iniquity *but* peace *shall be* upon Israel**

Ps 126:1 126:2

שיר 7892 המעלות 4609 בשוב 7725 יהוה 3068 את 853 שיבת 7870 ציון 6726 היינו 1961 כחלמים 2492:

shiyr, hama'alout bashub Yahuah 'at shiybat tziyoun; hayiynu, kacholamiym.

**A Song of degrees When turned again Yahuah the captivity of Zion we were like them that dream**

אז 227 ימלא 4390 שחוק 7814 פינו 6310 ולשוננו 3956 רנה 7440 אז 227 יאמרו 559 בגוים 1471 הגדיל 1431

'az yimalea' sachouq piynu ualshounenu rinah 'az ya'maru bagouyim; higdiyl

**Then was filled with laughter our mouth and our tongue *with* singing then said they among the heathen great things**

Ps 124:3 Then they had swallowed us up quick, when their wrath was kindled against us:4 Then the waters had overwhelmed us, the stream had gone over our soul:5 Then the proud waters had gone over our soul.6 Blessed be YHUH, who has not given us as a prey to their teeth.7 Our soul is escaped as a bird out of the snare of the fowlers: the snare is broken, and we are escaped.8 Our help is in the name of YHUH, who made heaven and earth. **Ps** 125:1 A Song of degrees. They that trust in YHUH shall be as mount Zion, which cannot be removed, but abideth forever.2 As the mountains are round about Jerusalem, so YHUH is round about his people from henceforth even forever.3 For the rod of the wicked shall not rest upon the lot of the righteous; lest the righteous put forth their hands unto iniquity.4 Do good, O YHUH, unto those that be good, and to them that are upright in their hearts.5 As for such as turn aside unto their crooked ways, YHUH shall lead them forth with the workers of iniquity: but peace shall be upon Israel. **Ps** 126:1 A Song of Degrees. When YHUH turned again the captivity of Zion, we were like them that dream.2 Then was our mouth filled with laughter, and our tongue with singing: then said they among the heathen, YHUH has done great things for them.

126:3 ... 126:4

יהוה 3068 לעשות 6213 עם 5973 אלה 428: הגדיל 1431 יהוה 3068 לעשות 6213 עמנו 5973 היינו 1961 שמחים 8056: שובה 7725

Yahuah la'asout 'am 'aeleh. higdiyl Yahuah la'asout 'amanu, hayiynu samechiym. shubah

**Yahuah has done for them great Yahuah has done *things* for us *whereof* we are glad Turn again**

126:5 ... 126:6

יהוה 3068 את 853 שבותנו 7622 כאפיקים 650 בנגב 5045: הזרעים 2232 בדמעה 1832 ברנה 7440 יקצרו 7114: הלוך 1980

Yahuah 'at shebutenu ka'apiyqiym banegeb. hazora'aym badim'ah, barinah yiqtzoru. halouk

**O Yahuah our captivity, as the streams in the south They that sow in tears in joy shall reap He that**

ילך 1980 ובכה 1058 נשא 5375 משך 4901 הזרע 2233 בא 935 יבוא 935 ברנה 7440 נשא 5375 אלמתיו 485:

yelek uabakoh nosea' meshek hazara' ba' yabou'a barinah; nosea', 'alumotayu.

**goes forth and weeps bearing precious seed shall doubtless come again with rejoicing bringing his sheaves *with him***

Ps 127:1

שיר 7892 המעלות 4609 לשלמה 8010 אם 518 יהוה 3068 לא 3808 יבנה 1129 בית 1004 שוא 7723 עמלו 5998 בוניו 1129 בו 871a

shiyr hama'alout, lishalomoh 'am Yahuah la' yibneh bayit, shau'a 'amalu bounayu bou;

**A Song of degrees for Solomon Except Yahuah not build the house in vain they labour that build it**

127:2

אם 518 יהוה 3068 לא 3808 ישמר 8104 עיר 5892 שוא 7723 שקד 8245 שומר 8104: שוא 7723 לכם 3807a משכימי 7925 קום 6965

'am Yahuah la' yishmor 'ayr, shau'a shaqad shoumer. shau'a lakem mashkiymey qum

**except Yahuah not keep the city *but* in vain wake the watchman *It is* vain for you early to rise up**

127:3

מאחרי 309 שבת 3427 אכלי 398 לחם 3899 העצבים 6089 כן 3651 יתן 5414 לידידו 3039 שנא 8142: הנה 2009 נחלת 5159

ma'acharey shebet, 'akley lechem ha'atzabiym; ken yiten liydiydou shenaa'. hineh nachalat

**late to sit up to eat bread of the sorrows *for* so he gives his beloved sleep Lo *are* an heritage of**

127:4

יהוה 3068 בנים 1121 שכר 7939 פרי 6529 הבטן 990: כחצים 2671 ביד 3027 גבור 1368 כן 3651

Yahuah baniym; sakar, pariy habaten. kachitziym bayad gibour; ken,

**Yahuah children *is his* reward *and* the fruit of the womb As arrows *are* in the hand of a mighty man so**

127:5

בני 1121 הנעורים 5271: אשרי 835 הגבר 1397 אשר 834 מלא 4390 את 853 אשפתו 827 מהם 1992 לא 3808 יבשו 954

baney hana'auriym. 'ashrey hageber, 'asher milea' 'at 'ashpatou, mehem la' yeboshu;

***are* children of the youth Happy *is* the man that has full his quiver of them not they shall be ashamed**

כי 3588 ידברו 1696 את 854 אויבים 341 בשער 8179:

kiy yadabru 'at 'auyabiym basha'ar.

**but they shall speak *with* the enemies in the gate**

Ps 128:1 ... 128:2

שיר 7892 המעלות 4609 אשרי 835 כל 3605 ירא 3373 יהוה 3069 ההלך 1980 בדרכיו 1870: יגיע 3018 כפיך 3709

shiyr, hama'alout 'ashrey kal yarea' Yahuah; haholek, bidrakayu. yagiya' kapeyka

**A Song of degrees Blessed *is* every one that fear Yahuah that walk in his ways the labour of your hands**

128:3

כי 3588 תאכל 398 אשריך 835 וטוב 2896 לך 3807a: אשתך 802 כגפן 1612 פריה 6509 בירכתי 3411

kiy ta'kel; 'ashreyka, uatoub lak. 'ashtaka kagepen poriyah bayarkatey

**For you shall eat happy *shall* you *be* and *it shall be* well with you Your wife *shall be* as a vine fruitful by the sides of**

128:4

ביתך 1004 בניך 1121 כשתלי 8363 זיתים 2132 סביב 5439 לשלחנך 7979: הנה 2009 כי 3588 כן 3651 יברך 1288 גבר 1397

beyteka baneyka kishtiley zeytiym; sabiyb, lashulachaneka. hineh kiy ken yaborak gaber,

**your house your children like plants olive round about your table Behold that thus shall be blessed the man**

Ps 126:3 YHUH has done great things for us; whereof we are glad.4 Turn again our captivity, O YHUH, as the streams in the south.5 They that sow in tears shall reap in joy.6 He that go forth and weep, bearing precious seed, shall doubtless come again with rejoicing, bringing his sheaves with him. **Ps** 127:1 A Song of degrees for Solomon. Except YHUH build the house, they labour in vain that build it: except YHUH keep the city, the watchman waketh but in vain.2 It is vain for you to rise up early, to sit up late, to eat the bread of sorrows: for so he give his beloved sleep.3 Lo, children are an heritage of YHUH. and the fruit of the womb is his reward.4 As arrows are in the hand of a mighty man; so are children of the youth.5 Happy is the man that has his quiver full of them: they shall not be ashamed, but they shall speak with the enemies in the gate. **Ps** 128:1 A Song of degrees. Blessed is everyone that fear YHUH; that walk in his ways.2 For you shall eat the labour of your hands: happy shall you be, and it shall be well with you.3 Thy wife shall be as a fruitful vine by the sides of your house: your children like olive plants round about your table.4 Behold, that thus shall the man be blessed that fear YHUH.

128:5
ירא 3373 | יהוה 3068: | יברכך 1288 | יהוה 3068 | מציון 6726 | וראה 7200 | בטוב 2898 | ירושלם 3389 | כל 3605 | ימי 3117
yarea' | Yahuah. | yabarekka | Yahuah | mitziyoun | uar'aeh | batub | yarushalaim; | kol, | yamey
**that fear | Yahuah | shall bless you | Yahuah | out of Zion | and you shall see | the good of | Jerusalem | all | the days of**

128:6
חייך 2416: | וראה 7200 | בנים 1121 | לבניך 1121 | שלום 7965 | על 5921 | ישראל 3478:
chayeyka. | ur'aeh | baniym | labaneyka; | shaloum, | 'al | yisra'ael.
**your life | Yea you shall see | your children's | children | *and* peace | upon | Israel**

Ps 129:1 | 129:2
שיר 7892 | המעלות 4609 | רבת 7227 | צררוני 6887 | מנעורי 5271 | יאמר 559 | נא 4994 | ישראל 3478:
shiyr, | hama'alout | rabat | tzararuniy | min'auray; | ya'mar | naa' | yisra'ael.
**A Song | of degrees | Many a time | have they afflicted me | from my youth | may say | now | Israel**

129:3
רבת 7227 | צררוני 6887 | מנעורי 5271 | גם 1571 | לא 3808 | יכלו 3201 | לי 3807a: | על 5921 | גבי 1354
rabat | tzararuniy | mina'auray; | gam | la' | yukalu | liy. | 'al | gabiy
**Many a time | have they afflicted me | from my youth | yet | not | they have prevailed | against me | upon | my back**

129:4
חרשו 2790 | חרשים 2790 | האריכו 748 | למענותם 4618 | יהוה 3068 | צדיק 6662 | קצץ 7112 | עבות 5688
charashu | chorashiym; | he'ariyku, | lema'anoutam | Yahuah | tzadiyq; | qitzetz, | about
**The plowers | plowed | they made long | their furrows | Yahuah | *is* righteous | he has cut asunder | the cords of**

129:5 | 129:6
רשעים 7563: | יבשו 954 | ויסגו 5472 | אחור 268 | כל 3605 | שנאי 8130 | ציון 6726: | יהיו 1961 | כחציר 2682
rasha'aym. | yeboshu | uayisogu | 'achour; | kol, | sona'aey | tziyoun. | yihayu | kachatziyr
**the wicked | Let them all be confounded | and turned | back | all | that hate | Zion | Let them be | as the grass**

129:7
גגות 1406 | שקדמת 6927 | שלף 8025 | יבש 3001: | שלא 3808 | מלא 4390 | כפו 3709 | קוצר 7114 | וחצנו 2683
gagout; | sheqadmat | shalap | yabesh. | shela' | milea' | kapou | qoutzer, | uachitznou
***upon* the housetops | which afore | it grow up | wither | *Wherewith* not | fill | his hand | the mower | nor his bosom**

129:8
מעמר 6014: | ולא 3808 | אמרו 559 | העברים 5674 | ברכת 1293 | יהוה 3068 | אליכם 413 | ברכנו 1288 | אתכם 853
ma'amer. | uala' | 'amaru | ha'abariym, | birkat | Yahuah | 'aleykem; | beraknu | 'atkem,
**he that bind sheaves | Neither | do say | they which go by | The blessing of | Yahuah | *be* upon you | we bless | you**

בשם 8034 | יהוה 3068:
bashem | Yahuah.
**in the name of | Yahuah**

Ps 130:1 | 130:2
שיר 7892 | המעלות 4609 | ממעמקים 4615 | קראתיך 7121 | יהוה 3068: | אדני 136 | שמעה 8085 | בקולי 6963 | תהיינה 1961
shiyr | hama'alout; | mima'amaqiym | qaraa'tiyka | Yahuah. | 'adonay | shim'ah | baqouliy | tihayeynah
**A Song of degrees | Out of the depths | have I cried unto you | O Yahuah | Adonai | hear | my voice | let be**

130:3
אזניך 241 | קשבות 7183 | לקול 6963 | תחנוני 8469: | אם 518 | עונות 5771 | תשמר 8104 | יה 3050 | אדני 136 | מי 4310
'azaneyka | qashubout; | laqoul, | tachanunay. | 'am | 'auonout | tishmor | Yah; | 'adonay, | miy'
**your ears | attentive | to the voice of | my supplications | If *you* | iniquities | should mark | Yah | O Adonai | who**

130:4 | 130:5
יעמד 5975: | כי 3588 | עמך 5973 | הסליחה 5547 | למען 4616 | תורא 3372: | קויתי 6960 | יהוה 3068 | קותה 6960 | נפשי 5315
ya'amod. | kiy | 'amaka | hasaliychah; | lama'an, | tiuarea'. | qiuiytiy | Yahuah | qiuatah | napshiy;
**shall stand? | But | with you *there is* forgiveness | that | you may be feared | I wait for | Yahuah | does wait | my soul**

Ps 128:5 YHUH shall bless you out of Zion: and you shall see the good of Jerusalem all the days of your life.6 Yea, you shall see your children's children, and peace upon Israel. **Ps** 129:1 A Song of Degrees. Many a time have they afflicted me from my youth, may Israel now say:2 Many a time have they afflicted me from my youth: yet they have not prevailed against me.3 The plowers plowed upon my back: they made long their furrows.4 YHUH is righteous: he has cut asunder the cords of the wicked.5 Let them all be confounded and turned back that hate Zion.6 Let them be as the grass upon the housetops, which withereth afore it groweth up:7 Wherewith the mower filleth not his hand; nor he that bindeth sheaves his bosom.8 Neither do they which go by say, The blessing of YHUH be upon you: we bless you in the name of YHUH. **Ps** 130:1 A Song of degrees. Out of the depths have I cried unto you, O YHUH.2 Adonai, hear my voice: let your ears be attentive to the voice of my supplications.3 If you, YHUH, should mark iniquities, O Adonai, who shall stand?4 But there is forgiveness with you, that you may be feared.5 I wait for YHUH, my soul doth wait, and in his word do I hope.

| ולדברו 1697 | הוחלתי 3176: | 130:6 | נפשי 5315 | לאדני 136 | משמרים 8104 | לבקר 1242 |
|---|---|---|---|---|---|---|
| ualidbarou | houchaltiy. | | napshiy | la'adonay; | mishomariym | laboqer, |
| **and in his word** | **do I hope** | | **My soul** | ***wait* for Adonai** | **more than they that watch** | **for the morning** |

| שמרים 8104 | לבקר 1242: | 130:7 | יחל 3176 | ישראל 3478 | אל 413 | יהוה 3068 | כי 3588 | עם 5973 | יהוה 3068 | החסד 2617 |
|---|---|---|---|---|---|---|---|---|---|---|
| shomriym | laboqer. | | yachel | yisra'ael, | 'al | Yahuah | kiy | 'am | Yahuah | hachesed; |
| ***I say more than* they that watch** | **for the morning** | | **Let hope** | **Israel** | **in** | **Yahuah** | **for** | **with** | **Yahuah *there is*** | **mercy** |

| והרבה 7235 | עמו 5973 | פדות 6304: | 130:8 | והוא 1931 | יפדה 6299 | את 853 | ישראל 3478 | מכל 3605 | עונתיו 5771: |
|---|---|---|---|---|---|---|---|---|---|
| uaharbeh | 'amou | padut. | | uahu'a | yipdeh | 'at | yisra'ael; | mikol, | 'auonotayu. |
| **and plenteous** | **with him *is*** | **redemption** | | **And he** | **shall redeem** | | **Israel** | **from all** | **his iniquities** |

| Ps 131:1 | שיר 7892 | המעלות 4609 | לדוד 1732 | יהוה 3068 | לא 3808 | גבה 1361 | לבי 3820 | ולא 3808 | רמו 7411 | עיני 5869 | ולא 3808 |
|---|---|---|---|---|---|---|---|---|---|---|---|
| | shiyr | hama'alout, | ladauid | Yahuah | la' | gabah | libiy | uala' | ramu | 'aeynay; | uala' |
| | **A Song** | **of degrees** | **of David** | **Yahuah** | **not** | **is haughty** | **my heart** | **nor** | **lofty** | **mine eyes** | **neither** |

| הלכתי 1980 | בגדלות 1419 | ובנפלאות 6381 | ממני 4480: | 131:2 | אם 518 | לא 3808 | שויתי 7737 | ודוממתי 1826 |
|---|---|---|---|---|---|---|---|---|
| hilaktiy | bigadolout | uabnipla'aut | mimeniy. | | 'am | la' | shiuiytiy | uadoumamtiy, |
| **do I exercise myself** | **in great matters** | **or in things too high** | **for me** | | **Surely** | **not** | **I have behaved** | **and quieted** |

| נפשי 5315 | כגמל 1580 | עלי 5921 | אמו 517 | כגמל 1580 | עלי 5921 | נפשי 5315: | 131:3 | יחל 3176 | ישראל 3478 | אל 413 |
|---|---|---|---|---|---|---|---|---|---|---|
| napshiy | kagamul | 'aley | 'amou; | kagamul | 'alay | napshiy. | | yachel | yisra'ael | 'al |
| **myself** | **as a child that is weaned** | **of** | **his mother *is even*** | **as a weaned child** | **with** | **my soul** | | **Let hope** | **Israel** | **in** |

| יהוה 3068 | מעתה 6258 | ועד 5704 | עולם 5769: |
|---|---|---|---|
| Yahuah; | me'atah, | ua'ad | 'aulam. |
| **Yahuah** | **from henceforth** | **and for** | **ever** |

| Ps 132:1 | שיר 7892 | המעלות 4609 | זכור 2142 | יהוה 3068 | לדוד 1732 | את 854 | כל 3605 | ענותו 6031: | 132:2 | אשר 834 | נשבע 7650 | ליהוה 3068 |
|---|---|---|---|---|---|---|---|---|---|---|---|---|
| | shiyr, | hama'alout | zakour | Yahuah | ladauid; | 'at | kal | 'anoutou. | | 'asher | nishba' | laYahuah; |
| | **A Song** | **of degrees** | **remember** | **Yahuah** | **David** | ***and*** | **all** | **his afflictions** | | **How** | **he sware** | **unto Yahuah** |

| נדר 5087 | לאביר 46 | יעקב 3290: | 132:3 | אם 518 | אבא 935 | באהל 168 | ביתי 1004 | אם 518 | אעלה 5927 |
|---|---|---|---|---|---|---|---|---|---|
| nadar, | la'abiyr | ya'aqob. | | 'am | 'aba' | ba'ahel | beytiy; | 'am | 'a'aleh, |
| ***and* vowed** | **unto the mighty** | ***Elohim of* Jacob** | | **Surely not** | **I will come** | **into the tabernacle of** | **my house** | **nor** | **go up** |

| על 5921 | ערש 6210 | יצועי 3326: | 132:4 | אם 518 | אתן 5414 | שנת 8153 | לעיני 5869 | לעפעפי 6079 | תנומה 8572: | 132:5 | עד 5704 | אמצא 4672 | מקום 4725 |
|---|---|---|---|---|---|---|---|---|---|---|---|---|---|
| 'al | 'ares | yatzu'ay. | | 'am | 'aten | shanat | la'aeynay; | la'ap'apay | tanumah. | | 'ad | 'amtzaa' | maqoum |
| **into** | **couch** | **my bed** | | **not** | **I will give** | **sleep** | **to mine eyes** | **to mine eyelids** | ***or* slumber** | | **Until** | **I find out** | **a place** |

| ליהוה 3068 | משכנות 4908 | לאביר 46 | יעקב 3290: | 132:6 | הנה 2009 | שמענוה 8085 | באפרתה 672 | מצאנוה 4672 |
|---|---|---|---|---|---|---|---|---|
| laYahuah; | mishkanout, | la'abiyr | ya'aqob. | | hineh | shama'anuha | ba'apratah; | matzaa'nuha, |
| **for Yahuah** | **an habitation** | **for the mighty** | ***Elohim of* Jacob** | | **Lo** | **we heard of it** | **at Ephratah** | **we found it** |

| בשדי 7704 | יער 3293: | 132:7 | נבואה 935 | למשכנותיו 4908 | נשתחוה 7812 | להדם 1916 | רגליו 7272: | 132:8 | קומה 6965 | יהוה 3068 |
|---|---|---|---|---|---|---|---|---|---|---|
| bisdey | ya'ar. | | nabou'ah | lamishkanoutayu; | nishtachaueh, | lahadom | raglayu. | | qumah | Yahuah |
| **in the fields of** | **the wood** | | **We will go** | **into his tabernacles** | **we will worship** | **at stool** | **his foot** | | **Arise** | **O Yahuah** |

Ps 130:6 My soul waiteth for YHUH more than they that watch for the morning: I say, more than they that watch for the morning.7 Let Israel hope in YHUH: for with YHUH there is mercy, and with him is plenteous redemption.8 And he shall redeem Israel from all his iniquities. **Ps** 131:1 A Song of degrees of David. YHUH, my heart is not haughty, nor mine eyes lofty: neither do I exercise myself in great matters, or in things too high for me.2 Surely I have behaved and quieted myself, as a child that is weaned of his mother: my soul is even as a weaned child.3 Let Israel hope in YHUH from henceforth and forever. **Ps** 132:1 A Song of degrees. YHUH, remember David, and all his afflictions:2 How he sware unto YHUH, and vowed unto the mighty G-d of Jacob;3 Surely I will not come into the tabernacle of my house, nor go up into my bed;4 I will not give sleep to mine eyes, or slumber to mine eyelids,5 Until I find out a place for YHUH, an habitation for the mighty G-d of Jacob.6 Lo, we heard of it at Ephratah: we found it in the fields of the wood.7 We will go into his tabernacles: we will worship at his footstool.8 Arise, O YHUH, into your rest; you, and the ark of your strength.

132:9

למנוחתך 4496 אתה 859 וארון 727 עזך 5797: כהניך 3548 ילבשו 3847 צדק 6664 וחסידיך 2623
limanuchateka; 'atah, ua'aroun 'azeka. kohaneyka yilbeshu tzedeq; uachasiydeyka
**into your rest you and the ark of your strength your priests Let be clothed with righteousness and your saints**

132:10 132:11

ירננו 7442: בעבור 5668 דוד 1732 עבדך 5650 אל 408 תשב 7725 פני 6440 משיחך 4899: נשבע 7650 יהוה 3068
yaranenu. ba'abur dauid 'abdeka; 'al tasheb, paney mashiycheka. nishba' Yahuah
**let shout for joy For sake David's your servant not turn away the face of your anointed has sworn Yahuah**

132:12

לדוד 1732 אמת 571 לא 3808 ישוב 7725 ממנה 4480 מפרי 6529 בטנך 990 אשית 7896 לכסא 3678 לך 3807a: אם 518
ladauid 'amet la' yashub mimenah mipriy bitnaka; 'ashiyt, lakisea' lak. 'am
**unto David *in* truth not he will turn from it Of the fruit of your body will I set upon throne to your If**

ישמרו 8104 בניך 1121 בריתי 1285 ועדתי 5713 זו 2090 אלמדם 3925 גם 1571 בניהם 1121 עדי 5703 עד 5703
yishmaru baneyka bariytiy ua'aedotiy zou, 'alamdem gam baneyhem 'adey 'ad;
**will keep your children my covenant and my testimony that I shall teach them also their children for evermore**

132:13 132:14

ישבו 3427 לכסא 3678 לך 3807a: כי 3588 בחר 977 יהוה 3068 בציון 6726 אוה 183 למושב 4186 לו 3807a:
yeshabu, lakisea' lak. kiy bachar Yahuah batziyoun; 'auah, lamoushab lou'.
**shall sit upon throne to your For has chosen Yahuah Zion he has desired *it* for habitation his**

132:15

זאת 2063 מנוחתי 4496 עדי 5703 עד 5703 פה 6311 אשב 3427 כי 3588 אותיה 183: צידה 6718 ברך 1288 אברך 1288
za't manuchatiy 'adey 'ad; poh 'aesheb, kiy 'auitiyha. tzeydah barek 'abarek;
**This *is* my rest for ever here will I dwell for I have desired it her provision I will abundantly bless**

132:16

אביוניה 34 אשביע 7646 לחם 3899: וכהניה 3548 אלביש 3847 ישע 3468 וחסידיה 2623 רנן 7442
'abyouneyha, 'asbiya' lachem. uakohaneyha 'albiysh yesha'; uachasiydeyha, ranen
**her poor I will satisfy *with* bread also her priests I will clothe with salvation and her saints shall shout**

132:17 132:18

ירננו 7442: שם 8033 אצמיח 6779 קרן 7161 לדוד 1732 ערכתי 6186 נר 5216 למשיחי 4899:
yaranenu. sham 'atzmiyach qeren ladauid; 'arakatiy ner, limashiychiy.
**aloud for joy There will I make to bud the horn of David I have ordained a lamp for mine anointed**

אויביו 341 אלביש 3847 בשת 1322 ועליו 5921 יציץ 6692 נזרו 5145:
'auyabayu 'albiysh boshet; ua'alayu, yatziytz nizrou.
**His enemies will I clothe with shame but upon himself shall flourish his crown**

**Ps 133:1**

שיר 7892 המעלות 4609 לדוד 1732 הנה 2009 מה 4100 טוב 2896 ומה 4100 נעים 5273 שבת 3427 אחים 251 גם 1571
shiyr hama'alout, ladauid hineh mah toub uamah na'aym; shebet 'achiym gam
**A Song of degrees of David Behold how good and how pleasant to dwell brethren *it is* for in unity**

133:2

יחד 3162: כשמן 8081 הטוב 2896 על 5921 הראש 7218 ירד 3381 על 5921 הזקן 2206 זקן 2206 אהרן 175
yachad. kashemen hatoub 'al hara'sh, yored, 'al hazaqan zaqan 'aharon;
**together *It is* like ointment the precious upon the head that ran down upon the beard beard *even* Aaron's**

133:3

שירד 3381 על 5921 פי 6310 מדותיו 4060: כטל 2919 חרמון 2768 שירד 3381 על 5921
sheyored, 'al piy midoutayu. katal chermoun, sheyored 'al
**that went down to the skirts of his garments As the dew of Hermon *and as the dew* that descended upon**

Ps 132:9 Let your priests be clothed with righteousness; and let your saints shout for joy.10 For your servant David's sake turn not away the face of your anointed.11 YHUH has sworn in truth unto David; he will not turn from it; Of the fruit of your body will I set upon your throne.12 If your children will keep my covenant and my testimony that I shall teach them, their children shall also sit upon your throne forevermore.13 For YHUH has chosen Zion; he has desired it for his habitation.14 This is my rest forever: here will I dwell; for I have desired it.15 I will abundantly bless her provision: I will satisfy her poor with bread.16 I will also clothe her priests with salvation: and her saints shall shout aloud for joy.17 There will I make the horn of David to bud: I have ordained a lamp for mine anointed.18 His enemies will I clothe with shame: but upon himself shall his crown flourish. **Ps** 133:1 A Song of degrees of David. Behold, how good and how pleasant it is for brethren to dwell together in unity!2 It is like the precious ointment upon the head, that ran down upon the beard, even Aaron's beard: that went down to the skirts of his garments;3 As the dew of Hermon, and as the dew that descended upon the mountains of Zion: for there YHUH commanded the blessing, even life forevermore.

הררי 2042 ציון 6726 כי 3588 שם 8033 צוה 6680 יהוה 3068 את 853 הברכה 1293 חיים 2416 עד 5704 העולם 5769:
harrey tziyoun kiy sham tziuah Yahuah 'at habarakah; chayiym, 'ad ha'aulam.
**the mountains of Zion for there commanded Yahuah the blessing *even* life for evermore**

**Ps 134:1**
שיר 7892 המעלות 4609 הנה 2009 ברכו 1288 את 853 יהוה 3068 כל 3605 עבדי 5650 יהוה 3068 העמדים 5975 בבית 1004
shiyr, hama'alout hineh baraku 'at Yahuah kal 'abdey Yahuah; ha'amadiym babeyt
**A Song of degrees Behold bless you Yahuah all *you* servants of Yahuah which stand in the house of**

**134:2** **134:3**
יהוה 3068 בלילות 3915: שאו 5375 ידכם 3027 קדש 6944 וברכו 1288 את 853 יהוה 3068: יברכך 1288 יהוה 3068 מציון 6726
Yahuah baleyhout. sa'au yadekem qodesh; uabaraku 'at Yahuah. yabarekka Yahuah mitziyoun;
**Yahuah by night Lift up your hands *in* the sanctuary and bless Yahuah bless you Yahuah out of Zion**

עשה 6213 שמים 8064 וארץ 776:
'aseh, shamayim ua'aretz.
**that made heaven and earth**

**Ps 135:1** **135:2**
הללו 1984 יה 3050 הללו 1984 את 853 שם 8034 יהוה 3068 הללו 1984 עבדי 5650 יהוה 3068:
halalu Yah halalu 'at shem Yahuah; halalu 'abadey Yahuah.
**Praise you Yah Praise you the name of Yahuah praise *him* O you servants of Yahuah**

**135:3**
שעמדים 5975 בבית 1004 יהוה 3068 בחצרות 2691 בית 1004 אלהינו 430: הללו 1984 יה 3050 כי 3588 טוב 2896 יהוה 3068
she'amadiym babeyt Yahuah; bachatzarout, beyt 'aloheynu. halalu Yah kiy toub Yahuah;
**You that stand in the house of Yahuah in the courts of the house of our Elohim Praise Yah for *is* good Yahuah**

**135:4**
זמרו 2167 לשמו 8034 כי 3588 נעים 5273: כי 3588 יעקב 3290 בחר 977 לו 3807a יה 3050 ישראל 3478
zamru lishmou, kiy na'aym. kiy ya'aqob, bachar lou' Yah; yisra'ael,
**sing praises unto his name for *it is* pleasant For Jacob has chosen unto himself Yah *and* Israel**

**135:5** **135:6**
לסגלתו 5459: כי 3588 אני 589 ידעתי 3045 כי 3588 גדול 1419 יהוה 3068 ואדנינו 113 מכל 3605 אלהים 430:
lisgulatou. kiy 'aniy yada'tiy kiy gadoul Yahuah; ua'adoneynu, mikal 'alohiym.
**for his peculiar treasure For I know that *is* great Yahuah and that our Adonai *is* above all gods**

**135:7**
כל 3605 אשר 834 חפץ 2654 יהוה 3068 עשה 6213 בשמים 8064 ובארץ 776 בימים 3220 וכל 3605 תהומות 8415:
kal 'asher chapetz Yahuah 'asah bashamayim uaba'aretz; bayamiym, uakal tahoumout.
**Whatsoever after pleased Yahuah *that* did he in heaven and in earth in the seas and all deep places**

מעלה 4627 נשאים 5387 מקצה 7097 הארץ 776 ברקים 1300 למטר 4306 עשה 6213 מוצא 3318 רוח 7307
ma'aleh nashi'aym miqtzeh ha'aretz baraqiym lamatar 'asah; moutzea' ruach
**He cause to ascend the vapours from the ends of the earth lightnings for the rain he make he bring the wind**

**135:8** **135:9**
מאוצרותיו 214: שהכה 5221 בכורי 1060 מצרים 4714 מאדם 120 עד 5704 בהמה 929: שלח 7971 אתות 226
me'autzaroutayu. shehikah bakourey mitzrayim; me'adam, 'ad bahemah. shalach 'autot
**out of his treasuries Who smote the firstborn of Egypt *both* of man unto beast *Who* sent tokens**

**135:10**
ומפתים 4159 בתוככי 8432 מצרים 4714 בפרעה 6547 ובכל 3605 עבדיו 5650: שהכה 5221 גוים 1471 רבים 7227
uamoptiym batoukekiy mitzrayim; bapar'ah, uabkal 'abadayu. shehikah gouyim rabiym;
**and wonders into the midst of you O Egypt upon Pharaoh and upon all his servants Who smote nations great**

**Ps** 134:1 A Song of degrees. Behold, bless you YHUH, all you servants of YHUH, which by night stand in the house of YHUH.2 Lift up your hands in the sanctuary, and bless YHUH.3 YHUH that made heaven and earth bless you out of Zion. **Ps** 135:1 Praise you YHUH. Praise you the name of YHUH; praise him, O you servants of YHUH.2 You that stand in the house of YHUH, in the courts of the house of our G-d,3 Praise YHUH; for YHUH is good: sing praises unto his name; for it is pleasant.4 For YHUH has chosen Jacob unto himself, and Israel for his peculiar treasure.5 For I know that YHUH is great, and that our Adonai is above all gods.6 Whatsoever YHUH pleased, that did he in heaven, and in earth, in the seas, and all deep places.7 He causeth the vapours to ascend from the ends of the earth; he make lightnings for the rain; he bring the wind out of his treasuries.8 Who smote the firstborn of Egypt, both of man and beast.9 Who sent tokens and wonders into the midst of you, O Egypt, upon Pharaoh, and upon all his servants.10 Who smote great nations, and slew mighty kings;

135:11

והרג 2026 מלכים 4428 עצומים 6099: לסיחון 5511 מלך 4428 האמרי 567 ולעוג 5747 מלך 4428 הבשן 1316 ולכל 3605 ממלכות 4467

uaharag, malakiym 'atzumiym. lasiychoun melek ha'amoriy, ual'aug melek habashan; ualkal, mamlakout

**and slew kings mighty Sihon king of the Amorites and Og king of Bashan and all the kingdoms of**

135:12 135:13

כנען 3667: ונתן 5414 ארצם 776 נחלה 5159 נחלה 5159 לישראל 3478 עמו 5971: יהוה 3068 שמך 8034

kana'an. uanatan 'artzam nachalah; nachalah, layisra'ael 'amou. Yahuah shimka

**Canaan And gave their land *for* an heritage an heritage unto Israel his people O Yahuah Your name**

135:14

לעולם 5769 יהוה 3068 זכרך 2143 לדר 1755 ודר 1755: כי 3588 ידין 1777 יהוה 3068 עמו 5971

la'aulam; Yahuah zikraka lador uador. kiy yadiyn Yahuah 'amou;

***endures* for ever O Yahuah *and* your memorial throughout all generations For will judge Yahuah his people**

135:15

ועל 5921 עבדיו 5650 יתנחם 5162: עצבי 6091 הגוים 1471 כסף 3701 וזהב 2091 מעשה 4639 ידי 3027

ua'al 'abadayu, yitnecham. 'atzabey hagouyim kesep uazahab; ma'aseh, yadey

**and concerning his servants he will repent himself The idols of the heathen *are* silver and gold the work of hands**

135:16 135:17

אדם 120: פה 6310 להם 1992 ולא 3808 ידברו 1696 עינים 5869 להם 1992 ולא 3808 יראו 7200: אזנים 241 להם 1992 ולא 3808

'adam. peh lahem uala' yadaberu; 'aeynayim lahem, uala' yir'au. 'azanayim lahem uala'

**men's *have* mouths They but not they speak eyes *have* they but not they see *have* ears They but not**

135:18

יאזינו 238 אף 637 אין 369 יש 3426 רוח 7307 בפיהם 6310: כמוהם 3644 יהיו 1961 עשיהם 6213 כל 3605

ya'aziynu; 'ap, 'aeyn yesh ruach bapiyhem. kamouhem yihayu 'aseyhem; kal

**they hear also neither is there *any* breath in their mouths like unto them They are that make them *so is* every one**

135:19

אשר 834 בטח 982 בהם 871a: בית 1004 ישראל 3478 ברכו 1288 את 853 יהוה 3068 בית 1004 אהרן 175 ברכו 1288 את 853

'asher boteach bahem. beyt yisra'ael baraku 'at Yahuah; beyt 'aharon, baraku 'at

**that trust in them O house of Israel Bless Yahuah O house of Aaron bless**

135:20 135:21

יהוה 3068: בית 1004 הלוי 3878 ברכו 1288 את 853 יהוה 3068 יראי 3373 יהוה 3068 ברכו 1288 את 853 יהוה 3068: ברוך 1288

Yahuah. beyt haleuiy baraku 'at Yahuah; yira'aey Yahuah baraku 'at Yahuah. baruk

**Yahuah O house of Levi Bless Yahuah you that fear Yahuah bless Yahuah Blessed be**

יהוה 3068 מציון 6726 שכן 7931 ירושלם 3389 הללו 1984 יה 3050:

Yahuah mitziyoun, shoken yarushalaim, halalu Yah.

**Yahuah out of Zion which dwell at Jerusalem Praise you Yah**

**Ps 136:1** 136:2

הודו 3034 ליהוה 3068 כי 3588 טוב 2896 כי 3588 לעולם 5769 חסדו 2617: הודו 3034

houdu laYahuah kiy toub; kiy la'aulam chasdou. houdu

**O give thanks unto Yahuah for *he is* good for *endures* for ever his mercy O give thanks**

136:3

לאלהי 430 האלהים 430 כי 3588 לעולם 5769 חסדו 2617: הודו 3034 לאדני 113 האדנים 113 כי 3588

le'alohey ha'alohiym; kiy la'aulam chasdou. houdu la'adoney ha'adoniym; kiy

**unto the Elohim of gods for *endures* for ever his mercy O give thanks to Adonai of lords for**

136:4

לעלם 5769 חסדו 2617: לעשה 6213 נפלאות 6381 גדלות 1419 לבדו 905 כי 3588 לעולם 5769 חסדו 2617:

la'alam chasdou. la'aseh nipla'aut gadolout labadou; kiy la'aulam chasdou.

***endures* for ever his mercy To him who does wonders great alone for *endures* for ever his mercy**

Ps 135:11 Sihon king of the Amorites, and Og king of Bashan, and all the kingdoms of Canaan:12 And gave their land for an heritage, an heritage unto Israel his people.13 Thy name, O YHUH, endureth forever; and your memorial, O YHUH, throughout all generations.14 For YHUH will judge his people, and he will repent himself concerning his servants.15 The idols of the heathen are silver and gold, the work of men's hands.16 They have mouths, but they speak not; eyes have they, but they see not;17 They have ears, but they hear not; neither is there any breath in their mouths.18 They that make them are like unto them: so is everyone that trusteth in them.19 Bless YHUH, O house of Israel: bless YHUH, O house of Aaron:20 Bless YHUH, O house of Levi: you that fear YHUH, bless YHUH.21 Blessed be YHUH out of Zion, which dwell at Jerusalem. Praise you YHUH. **Ps** 136:1 O give thanks unto YHUH; for he is good: for his mercy endureth forever.2 O give thanks unto the G-d of gods: for his mercy endureth forever.3 O give thanks to YHUH of lords: for his mercy endureth forever.4 To him who alone doeth great wonders: for his mercy endureth forever.

**136:5** לעשה 6213 השמים 8064 בתבונה 8394 כי 3588 לעולם 5769 חסדו 2617: **136:6** לרקע 7554 הארץ 776
la'aseh hashamayim bitabunah; kiy la'aulam chasdou. laroqa' ha'aretz
**To him that made the heavens by wisdom for *endures* for ever his mercy To him that stretched out the earth**

על 5921 המים 4325 כי 3588 לעולם 5769 חסדו 2617: **136:7** לעשה 6213 אורים 216 גדלים 1419 כי 3588 לעולם 5769
'al hamayim; kiy la'aulam chasdou. la'aseh 'auriym gadoliym; kiy la'aulam
**above the waters for *endures* for ever his mercy To him that made lights great for *endures* for ever**

חסדו 2617: **136:8** את 853 השמש 8121 לממשלת 4475 ביום 3117 כי 3588 לעולם 5769 חסדו 2617: **136:9** את 853 הירח 3394 וכוכבים 3556
chasdou. 'at hashemesh lamemshelet bayoum; kiy la'aulam chasdou. 'at hayareach uakoukabiym
**his mercy The sun to rule by day for endures for ever his mercy The moon and stars**

לממשלות 4475 בלילה 3915 כי 3588 לעולם 5769 חסדו 2617: **136:10** למכה 5221 מצרים 4714 בבכוריהם 1060 כי 3588
lamemshalout balayalah; kiy la'aulam chasdou. lamakeh mitzrayim bibakoureyhem; kiy
**to rule by night for *endures* for ever his mercy To him that smote Egypt in their firstborn for**

לעולם 5769 חסדו 2617: **136:11** ויוצא 3318 ישראל 3478 מתוכם 8432 כי 3588 לעולם 5769 חסדו 2617: **136:12**
la'aulam chasdou. uayoutzea' yisra'ael mitoukam; kiy la'aulam chasdou.
***endures* for ever his mercy And brought out Israel from among them for *endures* for ever his mercy**

ביד 3027 חזקה 2389 ובזרוע 2220 נטויה 5186 כי 3588 לעולם 5769 חסדו 2617: **136:13** לגזר 1504 ים 3220
bayad chazaqah uabizroua' natuyah; kiy la'aulam chasdou. lagozer yam
**With a hand strong and with arm a stretched out for *endures* for ever his mercy To him which divided sea**

סוף 5488 לגזרים 1506 כי 3588 לעולם 5769 חסדו 2617: **136:14** והעביר 5674 ישראל 3478 בתוכו 8432 כי 3588
sup ligazariym; kiy la'aulam chasdou. uahe'abiyr yisra'ael batoukou; kiy
**the Red into parts for *endures* for ever his mercy And made to pass Israel through the midst of it for**

לעולם 5769 חסדו 2617: **136:15** ונער 5287 פרעה 6547 וחילו 2428 בים 3220 סוף 5488 כי 3588 לעולם 5769
la'aulam chasdou. uaniy'aer par'ah uacheylou bayam sup; kiy la'aulam
***endures* for ever his mercy But overthrew Pharaoh and his host sea in the Red for *endures* for ever**

חסדו 2617: **136:16** למוליך 1980 עמו 5971 במדבר 4057 כי 3588 לעולם 5769 חסדו 2617: **136:17**
chasdou. lamouliyk 'amou bamidbar; kiy la'aulam chasdou.
**his mercy To him which led his people through the wilderness for *endures* for ever his mercy**

למכה 5221 מלכים 4428 גדלים 1419 כי 3588 לעולם 5769 חסדו 2617: **136:18** ויהרג 2026 מלכים 4428 אדירים 117 כי 3588
lamakeh malakiym gadoliym; kiy la'aulam chasdou. uayaharog malakiym 'adiyriym; kiy
**To him which smote kings great for *endures* for ever his mercy And slew kings famous for**

לעולם 5769 חסדו 2617: **136:19** לסיחון 5511 מלך 4428 האמרי 567 כי 3588 לעולם 5769 חסדו 2617: **136:20** ולעוג 5747
la'aulam chasdou. lasiychoun melek ha'amoriy; kiy la'aulam chasdou. ual'aug
***endures* for ever his mercy Sihon king of the Amorites for *endures* for ever his mercy And Og**

מלך 4428 הבשן 1316 כי 3588 לעולם 5769 חסדו 2617: **136:21** ונתן 5414 ארצם 776 לנחלה 5159 כי 3588 לעולם 5769
melek habashan; kiy la'aulam chasdou. uanatan 'artzam lanachalah; kiy la'aulam
**the king of Bashan for *endures* for ever his mercy And gave their land for an heritage for *endures* for ever**

Ps 136:5 To him that by wisdom made the heavens: for his mercy endureth forever.6 To him that stretched out the earth above the waters: for his mercy endureth forever.7 To him that made great lights: for his mercy endureth forever:8 The sun to rule by day: for his mercy endureth forever:9 The moon and stars to rule by night: for his mercy endureth forever.10 To him that smote Egypt in their firstborn: for his mercy endureth forever:11 And brought out Israel from among them: for his mercy endureth forever:12 With a strong hand, and with a stretched out arm: for his mercy endureth forever.13 To him which divided the Red sea into parts: for his mercy endureth forever:14 And made Israel to pass through the midst of it: for his mercy endureth forever:15 But overthrew Pharaoh and his host in the Red sea: for his mercy endureth forever.16 To him which led his people through the wilderness: for his mercy endureth forever.17 To him which smote great kings: for his mercy endureth forever:18 And slew famous kings: for his mercy endureth forever:19 Sihon king of the Amorites: for his mercy endureth forever:20 And Og the king of Bashan: for his mercy endureth forever:21 And gave their land for an heritage: for his mercy endureth forever:

**136:22**
חסדו 2617: | נחלה 5159 | לישראל 3478 | עבדו 5650 | כי 3588 | לעולם 5769 | חסדו 2617: | **136:23** שבשפלנו 8216
chasdou. | nachalah | layisra'ael | abdou; | kiy | la'aulam | chasdou. | shebashiplenu
**his mercy** | ***Even* an heritage** | **unto Israel** | **his servant** | **for** | ***endures* for ever** | **his mercy** | ***in* our low estate**

זכר 2142 | לנו 3807a | כי 3588 | לעולם 5769 | חסדו 2617: | **136:24** ויפרקנו 6561 | מצרינו 6862 | כי 3588
zakar | lanu; | kiy | la'aulam | chasdou. | uayipraqenu | mitzareynu; | kiy
**Who remembered** | **us** | **for** | ***endures* for ever** | **his mercy** | **And has redeemed us** | **from our enemies** | **for**

לעולם 5769 | חסדו 2617: | **136:25** נתן 5414 | לחם 3899 | לכל 3605 | בשר 1320 | כי 3588 | לעולם 5769 | חסדו 2617: | **136:26** הודו 3034
la'aulam | chasdou. | noten | lechem | lakal | basar; | kiy | la'aulam | chasdou. | houdu
***endures* for ever** | **his mercy** | **Who gives** | **food** | **to all** | **flesh** | **for** | ***endures* for ever** | **his mercy** | **O give thanks**

לאל 410 | השמים 8064 | כי 3588 | לעולם 5769 | חסדו 2617:
la'ael | hashamayim; | kiy | la'aulam | chasdou.
**unto *the* El *of*** | **heaven** | **for** | ***endures* for ever** | **his mercy**

**Ps 137:1**
על 5921 | נהרות 5104 | בבל 894 | שם 8033 | ישבנו 3427 | גם 1571 | בכינו 1058 | בזכרנו 2142 | את 853 | ציון 6726: | **137:2** על 5921
'al | naharout | babel, | sham | yashabnu | gam | bakiynu; | bazakarenu, | 'at | tziyoun. | 'al
**By** | **the rivers of** | **Babylon** | **there** | **we sat down** | **yea** | **we wept** | **when we remembered** | | **Zion** | **upon**

ערבים 6155 | בתוכה 8432 | תלינו 8518 | כנרותינו 3658: | **137:3** כי 3588 | שם 8033 | שאלונו 7592
'arabiym | batoukah; | taliynu, | kinorouteynu. | kiy | sham | sha'aelunu
**the willows** | **in the midst thereof** | **We hanged** | **our harps** | **For** | **there** | **required of us**

שובינו 7617 | דברי 1697 | שיר 7892 | ותוללינו 8437 | שמחה 8057 | שירו 7891 | לנו 3807a
shoubeynu | dibrey | shiyr | uatoulaleynu | simchah; | shiyru | lanu,
**they that carried us away captive** | **words of** | **a song** | **and they that wasted us** | ***required of us* mirth** | ***saying* Sing** | **us *one***

משיר 7892 | ציון 6726: | **137:4** איך 349 | נשיר 7891 | את 853 | שיר 7892 | יהוה 3068 | על 5921 | אדמת 127 | נכר 5236: | **137:5** אם 518 | אשכחך 7911
mishiyr | tziyoun. | 'aeyk, | nashiyr | 'at | shiyr | Yahuah; | 'al, | 'admat | nekar. | 'am | 'ashkachek
**of the songs of** | **Zion** | **How** | **shall we sing** | | **song** | **Yahuah's** | **in** | **a land?** | **strange** | **If** | **I forget you, *let***

ירושלם 3389 | תשכח 7911 | ימיני 3225: | **137:6** תדבק 1692 | לשוני 3956 | לחכי 2441 | אם 518 | לא 3808
yarushalaim, | tishkach | yamiyniy. | tidbaq | lashouniy | lachikiy | 'am | la'
**O Jerusalem** | **forget *her cunning*** | **my right hand** | **let cleave** | **my tongue** | **to the roof of my mouth** | **If** | **not**

אזכרכי 2142 | אם 518 | לא 3808 | אעלה 5927 | את 853 | ירושלם 3389 | על 5921 | ראש 7218 | שמחתי 8057: | **137:7** זכר 2142 | יהוה 3068
'azkarekiy | 'am | la' | 'a'aleh | 'at | yarushalaim; | 'al, | ra'sh | simchatiy. | zakor | Yahuah
**If I do remember you** | **if** | **not** | **I prefer** | | **Jerusalem** | **above** | **chief** | **my joy** | **Remember** | **O Yahuah**

לבני 1121 | אדום 123 | את 853 | יום 3117 | ירושלם 3389 | האמרים 559 | ערו 6168 | ערו 6168 | עד 5704 | היסוד 3247 | בה 871a: | **137:8**
libney | 'adoum, | 'at | youm | yarushalaim | ha'amariym | 'aru | 'aru; | 'ad, | hayasoud | bah.
**the children of** | **Edom *in*** | | **the day of** | **Jerusalem** | **who said** | **Rase *it*** | **rase *it even*** | **to** | **the foundation** | **thereof**

בת 1323 | בבל 894 | השדודה 7703 | אשרי 835 | שישלם 7999 | לך 3807a | את 853 | גמולך 1576
bat | babel, | hashadudah | 'ashrey | sheyashalem | lak; | 'at | gamulek,
**O daughter of** | **Babylon** | **who are to be destroyed** | **happy** | ***shall he be* that reward to you** | | | ***as* the recompense**

Ps 136:22 Even an heritage unto Israel his servant: for his mercy endureth forever.23 Who remembered us in our low estate: for his mercy endureth forever:24 And has redeemed us from our enemies: for his mercy endureth forever.25 Who give food to all flesh: for his mercy endureth forever.26 O give thanks unto the G-d of heaven: for his mercy endureth forever. **Ps** 137:1 By the rivers of Babylon, there we sat down, yea, we wept, when we remembered Zion.2 We hanged our harps upon the willows in the midst thereof.3 For there they that carried us away captive required of us a song; and they that wasted us required of us mirth, saying, Sing us one of the songs of Zion.4 How shall we sing YHUH's song in a strange land?5 If I forget you, O Jerusalem, let my right hand forget her cunning.6 If I do not remember you, let my tongue cleave to the roof of my mouth; if I prefer not Jerusalem above my chief joy.7 Remember, O YHUH, the children of Edom in the day of Jerusalem; who said, Rase it, rase it, even to the foundation thereof.8 O daughter of Babylon, who are to be destroyed; happy shall he be, that rewardeth you as you have served us.

137:9

שגמלת 1580 | לנו 3807a: | אשרי 835 | שיאחז 270 | ונפץ 5310 | את 853 | עלליך 5768 | אל 413 | הסלע 5553:

shegamalt | lanu. | 'ashrey | sheya'chez | uanipetz | 'at | 'alalayik, | 'al | hasala'.

**you have served us | Happy *shall he be* that takes and dash | your little ones against | the stones**

**Ps 138:1** | **138:2**

לדוד 1732 | אודך 3034 | בכל 3605 | לבי 3820 | נגד 5048 | אלהים 430 | אזמרך 2167:

ladauid | 'audaka | bakal | libiy; | neged | 'alohiym | 'azamreka.

***A Psalm* of David | I will praise you | with whole | my heart | before | the gods | will I sing praise unto you**

אשתחוה 7812 | אל 413 | היכל 1964 | קדשך 6944 | ואודה 3034 | את 853 | שמך 8034 | על 5921 | חסדך 2617 | ועל 5921 | אמתך 571 | כי 3588

'ashtachaueh | 'al | heykal | qadashaka | ua'audeh | 'at | shameka, | 'al | chasdaka | ua'al | 'amiteka; | kiy

**I will worship | toward | temple | your holy | and praise | your name | for | your lovingkindness | and for | your truth | for**

138:3

הגדלת 1431 | על 5921 | כל 3605 | שמך 8034 | אמרתך 565: | ביום 3117 | קראתי 7121 | ותענני 6030

higdalta | 'al | kal | shimka, | 'amrateka. | bayoum | qara'tiy | uata'aneniy;

**you have magnified | above | all | your name | your word | In the day | I cried | when you answered me**

138:4

תרהבני 7292 | בנפשי 5315 | עז 5797: | יודוך 3034 | יהוה 3068 | כל 3605 | מלכי 4428 | ארץ 776 | כי 3588

tarhibeniy | uanapshiy | 'az. | youduka | Yahuah | kal | malkey | 'aretz; | kiy

***and* strengthened me | in my soul | *with* strength | shall praise you | O Yahuah | All | the kings of | the earth | when**

138:5

שמעו 8085 | אמרי 561 | פיך 6310: | וישירו 7891 | בדרכי 1870 | יהוה 3068 | כי 3588 | גדול 1419 | כבוד 3519

shama'au, | 'amrey | piyka. | uayashiyru | badarkey | Yahuah; | kiy | gadoul, | kaboud

**they hear | the words of | your mouth | Yea they shall sing | in the ways of | Yahuah | for | great | *is* the glory of**

138:6 | 138:7

יהוה 3068: | כי 3588 | רם 7311 | יהוה 3068 | ושפל 8217 | יראה 7200 | וגבה 1364 | ממרחק 4801 | יידע 3045: | אם 518

Yahuah. | kiy | ram | Yahuah | uashapal | yir'ah; | uagaboah, | mimerchaq | yayeda'. | 'am

**Yahuah | Though *be* high | Yahuah | yet the lowly | has he respect unto | but the proud | afar off | he knows | Though**

אלך 1980 | בקרב 7130 | צרה 6869 | תחיני 2421 | על 5921 | אף 639 | איבי 341 | תשלח 7971 | ידך 3027

'aelek | baqereb | tzarah, | tachayeniy | 'al | 'ap | 'ayabay | tishlach | yadeka;

**I walk | in the midst of | trouble | you will revive me | against | the wrath of | mine enemies | you shall stretch forth | your hand**

138:8

ותושיעני 3467 | ימינך 3225: | יהוה 3068 | יגמר 1584 | בעדי 1157 | יהוה 3068 | חסדך 2617 | לעולם 5769

uatoushiy'aeniy | yamiyneka. | Yahuah | yigmor | ba'adiy | Yahuah | chasdaka | la'aulam;

**and shall save me | your right hand | Yahuah will perfect *that which* concern me | O Yahuah | your mercy *endures* for ever**

מעשי 4639 | ידיך 3027 | אל 408 | תרף 7503:

ma'asey | yadeyka | 'al | terep.

**the works of | your own hands | not | forsake**

**Ps 139:1** | **139:2**

למנצח 5329 | לדוד 1732 | מזמור 4210 | יהוה 3068 | חקרתני 2713 | ותדע 3045: | אתה 859 | ידעת 3045

lamanatzeach | ladauid | mizmour; | Yahuah | chaqartaniy, | uateda'. | 'atah | yada'ta

**To the chief Musician | of David | A Psalm | O Yahuah | you have searched me | and known *me* | You | know**

139:3

שבתי 3427 | וקומי 6965 | בנתה 995 | לרעי 7454 | מרחוק 7350: | ארחי 734 | ורבעי 7252 | זרית 2219

shibtiy | uaqumiy; | banatah | lare'ay, | merachouq. | 'arachiy | uarib'ay | zeriyta;

**my downsitting | and mine uprising | you understand | my thought | afar off | my path | and my lying down | You compass**

Ps 137:9 Happy shall he be, that take and dasheth your little ones against the stones. **Ps** 138:1 A Psalm of David. I will praise you with my whole heart: before the gods will I sing praise unto you.2 I will worship toward your holy temple, and praise your name for your lovingkindness and for your truth: for you have magnified your word above all your name.3 In the day when I cried you answeredst me, and strengthenedst me with strength in my soul.4 All the kings of the earth shall praise you, O YHUH, when they hear the words of your mouth.5 Yea, they shall sing in the ways of YHUH: for great is the glory of YHUH.6 Though YHUH be high, yet has he respect unto the lowly: but the proud he know afar off.7 Though I walk in the midst of trouble, you will revive me: you shall stretch forth your hand against the wrath of mine enemies, and your right hand shall save me.8 YHUH will perfect that which concerneth me: your mercy, O YHUH, endureth forever: forsake not the works of your own hands. **Ps** 139:1 To the chief Musician, A Psalm of David. O YHUH, you have searched me, and known me.2 Thou know my downsitting and mine uprising, you understandest my thought afar off.3 Thou compassest my path and my lying down, and are acquainted with all my ways.

139:4

וכל 3605 דרכי 1870 הסכנתה 5532: כי 3588 אין 369 מלה 4405 בלשוני 3956 הן 2005 יהוה 3068 ידעת 3045

uakal darakay hiskantah. kiy 'aeyn milah bilshouniy; hen Yahuah yada'ta

**and all my ways are acquainted *with* For *there is* not a word in my tongue *but* lo O Yahuah you know it**

139:5 139:6

כלה 3605: אחור 268 וקדם 6924 צרתני 6696 ותשת 7896 עלי 5921 כפכה 3709: פלאיה 6383 דעת 1847

kulah. 'achour uaqedem tzartaniy; uatashet 'alay kapekah. pal'ayah da'at

**altogether behind and before You have beset me and laid upon me your hand *is too* wonderful *Such* knowledge**

139:7

ממני 4480 נשגבה 7682 לא 3808 אוכל 3201 לה 3807a: אנה 575 אלך 1980 מרוחך 7307 ואנה 575 מפניך 6440

mimeniy; nisgabah, la' 'aukal lah. 'anah 'aelek merucheka; ua'anah, mipaneyka

**for me it is high not I can unto it Where shall I go from your spirit? or where from your presence?**

139:8

אברח 1272: אם 518 אסק 5266 שמים 8064 שם 8033 אתה 859 ואציעה 3331 שאול 7585

'abrach. 'am 'asaq shamayim sham 'atah; ua'atziy'ah sha'aul

**shall I flee If I ascend up into heaven *are* there you if I make my bed in hell (*grave*)**

139:9 139:10

הנך 2005: אשא 5375 כנפי 3671 שחר 7837 אשכנה 7931 באחרית 319 ים 3220: גם 1571

hineka. 'asa' kanpey shachar; 'ashkanah, ba'achariyt yam. gam

**behold, you *are there* *If* I take the wings of the morning *and* dwell in the uttermost parts of the sea Even**

139:11

שם 8033 ידך 3027 תנחני 5148 ותאחזני 270 ימינך 3225: ואמר 559 אך 389 חשך 2822 ישופני 7779

sham yadaka tanacheniy; uata'chazeniy yamiyneka. ua'amar 'ak choshek yashupeniy;

**there your hand shall lead me and shall hold me your right hand If I say Surely the darkness shall cover me**

139:12

ולילה 3915 אור 216 בעדני 1157: גם 1571 חשך 2822 לא 3808 יחשיך 2821 ממך 4480 ולילה 3915 כיום 3117 יאיר 215

ualayalah, 'aur ba'adeniy. gam choshek la' yachshiyk mimeka ualaylah kayoum ya'ayr;

**even the night shall be light about me Yea the darkness not hides from you but the night as the day shine**

139:13

כחשיכה 2825 כאורה 219: כי 3588 אתה 859 קנית 7069 כליתי 3629 תסכני 5526 בבטן 990

kachasheykah, ka'aurah. kiy 'atah qaniyta kilyotay; tasukeniy, babeten

**the darkness and the light *are both alike to you* For you have possessed my reins you have covered me in womb**

139:14

אמי 517: אודך 3034 על 5921 כי 3588 נוראות 3372 נפליתי 6395 נפלאים 6381 מעשיך 4639

'amiy. 'audaka, 'al kiy noura'aut, nipleytiy nipla'aym ma'aseyka;

**my mother's I will praise you on for I am fearfully *and* wonderfully made marvellous *are* your works**

139:15

ונפשי 5315 ידעת 3045 מאד 3966: לא 3808 נכחד 3582 עצמי 6108 ממך 4480 אשר 834 עשיתי 6213 בסתר 5643

uanapshiy, yoda'at ma'ad. la' nikchad 'atzamiy, mimeka 'asher 'aseytiy baseter;

**and *that* my soul knows right well not was hid My substance from you when I was made in secret**

139:16

רקמתי 7551 בתחתיות 8482 ארץ 776: גלמי 1564 ראו 7200 עיניך 5869 ועל 5921

ruqamtiy, batachtiyout 'aretz. galamiy ra'au 'ayneyka, ua'al

***and* curiously wrought in the lowest parts of the earth my substance yet being unperfect did see Thine eyes and in**

ספרך 5612 כלם 3605 יכתבו 3789 ימים 3117 יצרו 3335 ולא 3808 אחד 259

sipraka kulam yikatebu yamiym yutzaru; uala' 'achad

**your book all *my members* were written *in* continuance *which* were fashioned when *as yet there was* not one**

Ps 139:4 For there is not a word in my tongue, but, lo, O YHUH, you know it altogether.5 Thou have beset me behind and before, and laid your hand upon me.6 Such knowledge is too wonderful for me; it is high, I cannot attain unto it.7 Whither shall I go from your spirit? or whither shall I flee from your presence?8 If I ascend up into heaven, you are there: if I make my bed in hell, behold, you are there.9 If I take the wings of the morning, and dwell in the uttermost parts of the sea;10 Even there shall your hand lead me, and your right hand shall hold me.11 If I say, Surely the darkness shall cover me; even the night shall be light about me.12 Yea, the darkness hide not from you; but the night shineth as the day: the darkness and the light are both alike to you.13 For you have possessed my reins: you have covered me in my mother's womb.14 I will praise you; for I am fearfully and wonderfully made: marvellous are your works; and that my soul know right well.15 My substance was not hid from you, when I was made in secret, and curiously wrought in the lowest parts of the earth.16 Thine eyes did see my substance, yet being unperfect; and in your book all my members were written, which in continuance were fashioned, when as yet there was none of them.

בהם 871a: **139:17** ולי 3807a מה 4100 יקרו 3365 רעיך 7454 אל 410 מה 4100 עצמו 6105 ראשיהם 7218: **139:18**
bahem. ualiy, mah yaqaru re'ayka 'ael; meh 'atzamu ra'sheyhem.
**of them also unto me How precious are your thoughts O El how great is the sum of them**

אספרם 5608 מחול 2344 ירבון 7235 הקיצתי 6974 ועודי 5750 עמך 5973: **139:19** אם 518
'asparem mechoul yirbun; heqiytzotiy, ua'audiy 'amak. 'am
***If* I should count them than the sand they are more in number I awake when I am still with you Surely**

תקטל 6991 אלוה 433 רשע 7563 ואנשי 582 דמים 1818 סורו 5493 מני 4480: **139:20** אשר 834 יאמרך 559
tiqtol 'alouah rasha'; ua'anshey damiym, suru meniy. 'asher ya'maruka
**you will slay O Elohim the wicked men *ye* bloody depart you from me therefore For they speak against you**

למזמה 4209 נשא 5375 לשוא 7723 עריך 5892 [6145]: **139:21** הלוא 3808 משנאיך 8130 יהוה 3068 אשנא 8130
limazimah; nasa' lashau'a 'areyka. halou'a masan'ayka Yahuah 'asna';
**wickedly take *your name* in vain *and* your enemies not Do I hate them O Yahuah that hate you?**

ובתקוממיך 8618 אתקוטט 6962: **139:22** תכלית 8503 שנאה 8135 שנאתים 8130 לאויבים 341 היו 1961
uabitqoumameyka, 'atqoutat. takliyt sin'ah sana'tiym; la'auyabiym, hayu
**and with those that rise up against you? am not I grieved *with* perfect hatred I hate them mine enemies I count**

לי 3807a: **139:23** חקרני 2713 אל 410 ודע 3045 לבבי 3824 בחנני 974 ודע 3045 שרעפי 8312: **139:24** וראה 7200 אם 518 דרך 1870
liy. chaqareniy 'ael uada' lababiy; bachaneniy, uada' sar'apay. uar'aeh, 'am derek
**them Search me O El and know my heart try me and know my thoughts And see if way**

עצב 6090 בי 871a ונחני 5148 בדרך 1870 עולם 5769:
'atzeb biy; uancheniy, baderek 'aulam.
***there be any* wicked in me and lead me in the way everlasting**

**Ps 140:1** למנצח 5329 מזמור 4210 לדוד 1732: חלצני 2502 יהוה 3068 מאדם 120 רע 7451 מאיש 376 חמסים 2555
lamanatzeach, mizmour ladauid. chaltzeniy Yahuah me'adam ra'; me'aysh chamasiym
**To the chief Musician A Psalm of David Deliver me O Yahuah from man *the* evil from man *the* violent**

תנצרני 5341: **140:2** אשר 834 חשבו 2803 רעות 7451 בלב 3820 כל 3605 יום 3117 יגורו 1481
tintzareniy. 'asher chashabu ra'aut baleb; kal youm, yaguru
**preserve me Which imagine mischiefs in *their* heart all manner continually are they gathered together**

מלחמות 4421: **140:3** שננו 8150 לשונם 3956 כמו 3644 נחש 5175 חמת 2534 עכשוב 5919 תחת 8478 שפתימו 8193 סלה 5542: **140:4**
milchamout. shananu lashounam kamou nachash chamat 'akshub; tachat sapateymou selah.
***for* war They have sharpened their tongues like a serpent poison adders' *is* under their lips Selah**

שמרני 8104 יהוה 3068 מידי 3027 רשע 7563 מאיש 376 חמסים 2555 תנצרני 5341 אשר 834 חשבו 2803 לדחות 1760
shamareniy Yahuah miydey rasha', me'aysh chamasiym tintzareniy; 'asher chashabu, lidachout
**Keep me O Yahuah from the hands of the wicked from man *the* violent preserve me who have purposed to overthrow**

פעמי 6471: **140:5** טמנו 2934 גאים 1343 פח 6341 לי 3807a וחבלים 2256 פרשו 6566 רשת 7568 ליד 3027 מעגל 4570 מקשים 4170
pa'amay. tamanu ge'aym pach liy, uachabaliym, parasu reshet layad ma'gal; moqashiym
**my goings have hid The proud a snare for me and cords they have spread a net by side *the* way gins**

Ps 139:17 How precious also are your thoughts unto me, O G-d! how great is the sum of them! 18 If I should count them, they are more in number than the sand: when I awake,
I am still with you. 19 Surely you will slay the wicked, O G-d: depart from me therefore, you bloody men. 20 For they speak against you wickedly, and your enemies take your
name in vain. 21 Do not I hate them, O YHUH, that hate you? and am not I grieved with those that rise up against you? 22 I hate them with perfect hatred: I count them mine
enemies. 23 Search me, O G-d, and know my heart: try me, and know my thoughts: 24 And see if there be any wicked way in me, and lead me in the way everlasting. **Ps** 140:1
To the chief Musician, A Psalm of David. Deliver me, O YHUH, from the evil man: preserve me from the violent man; 2 Which imagine mischiefs in their heart; continually
are they gathered together for war. 3 They have sharpened their tongues like a serpent; adders' poison is under their lips. Selah. 4 Keep me, O YHUH, from the hands of the
wicked; preserve me from the violent man; who have purposed to overthrow my goings. 5 The proud have hid a snare for me, and cords; they have spread a net by the wayside;
they have set gins for me. Selah.

| שתו 7896 | לי 3807a | סלה 5542: | 140:6 | אמרתי 559 | ליהוה 3068 | אלי 410 | אתה 859 | האזינה 238 | יהוה 3068 | קול 6963 |
|---|---|---|---|---|---|---|---|---|---|---|
| shatu | liy | selah. | | 'amartiy | laYahuah | 'aeliy | 'atah; | ha'aziynah | Yahuah | qoul |
| **they have set** | **for me** | **Selah** | | **I said** | **unto Yahuah** | ***are* my El** | **You** | **hear** | **O Yahuah** | **the voice of** |

| תחנוני 8469: | 140:7 | יהוה 3068 | אדני 136 | עז 5797 | ישועתי 3444 | סכתה 5526 | לראשי 7218 | ביום 3117 |
|---|---|---|---|---|---|---|---|---|
| tachanunay. | | Yahuah | 'adonay | 'az | yashu'atiy; | sakotah | lara'shiy, | bayoum |
| **my supplications** | | **O Yahuah** | **Adonai** | **the strength of** | **my salvation** | **you have covered** | **my head** | **in the day of** |

| נשק 5402: | 140:8 | אל 408 | תתן 5414 | יהוה 3068 | מאויי 3970 | רשע 7563 | זממו 2162 | אל 408 | תפק 6329 | ירומו 7311 |
|---|---|---|---|---|---|---|---|---|---|---|
| nasheq. | | 'al | titen | Yahuah | ma'auayey | rasha'; | zamamou | 'al | tapeq, | yarumu |
| **battle** | | **not** | **Grant** | **O Yahuah** | **the desires of** | **the wicked** | **his wicked device** | **not** | **further** | ***lest* they exalt themselves** |

| סלה 5542: | 140:9 | ראש 7218 | מסבי 4524 | עמל 5999 | שפתימו 8193 | יכסומו 3680: | 40:10 | ימיטו 4131 |
|---|---|---|---|---|---|---|---|---|
| selah. | | ra'sh | masibay; | 'amal | sapateymou | yakasumou | | yamiytu |
| **Selah** | | ***As for* the head of** | **those that compass me about** | **the mischief of** | **their own lips** | **let cover them.** | | **Let fall** |

| עליהם 5921 | גחלים 1513 | באש 784 | יפלם 5307 | במהמרות 4113 | בל 1077 | יקומו 6965: | 140:11 | איש 376 |
|---|---|---|---|---|---|---|---|---|
| 'aleyhem, | gechaliym | ba'aesh | yapilem; | bamahamorout, | bal | yaqumu. | | 'aysh |
| **upon them** | **burning coals** | **into the fire** | **let them be cast** | **into deep pits** | **not** | **that they rise up again** | | **man** |

| לשון 3956 | בל 1077 | יכון 3559 | בארץ 776 | איש 376 | חמס 2555 | רע 7451 | יצודנו 6679 | למדחפת 4073: | 140:12 | ידעת 3045 |
|---|---|---|---|---|---|---|---|---|---|---|
| lashoun | bal | yikoun | ba'aretz | 'aysh | chamas | ra'; | yatzudenu, | lamadchepot. | | yada'ta |
| **an evil speaker** | **not** | **Let be established** | **in the earth** | **man** | ***the* violent** | **evil** | **shall hunt** | **to overthrow *him*** | | **I know** |

| כי 3588 | יעשה 6213 | יהוה 3068 | דין 1779 | עני 6041 | משפט 4941 | אבינים 34: | 140:13 | אך 389 | צדיקים 6662 |
|---|---|---|---|---|---|---|---|---|---|
| kiy | ya'aseh | Yahuah | diyn | 'aniy; | mishapat, | 'abyoniym. | | 'ak | tzadiyqiym |
| **that** | **will maintain** | **Yahuah** | **the cause of** | **the afflicted** | ***and* the right of** | **the poor** | | **Surely** | **the righteous** |

| יודו 3034 | לשמך 8034 | ישבו 3427 | ישרים 3477 | את 853 | פניך 6440: |
|---|---|---|---|---|---|
| youdu | lishmeka; | yeshabu | yashariym, | 'at | paneyka. |
| **shall give thanks** | **unto your name** | **shall dwell in** | **the upright** | | **your presence** |

| Ps 141:1 | מזמור 4210 | לדוד 1732 | יהוה 3068 | קראתיך 7121 | חושה 2363 | לי 3807a | האזינה 238 | קולי 6963 | בקראי 7121 | לך 3807a: | 141:2 |
|---|---|---|---|---|---|---|---|---|---|---|---|
| | mizmour, | ladauid | Yahuah | qara'tiyka | chushah | liy; | ha'aziynah | qouliy, | baqara'ay | lak. | |
| | **A Psalm** | **of David** | **Yahuah** | **I cry unto you** | **make haste** | **unto me** | **give ear unto** | **my voice** | **when I cry** | **unto you** | |

| תכון 3559 | תפלתי 8605 | קטרת 7004 | לפניך 6440 | משאת 4864 | כפי 3709 | מנחת 4503 | ערב 6153: | 141:3 | שיתה 7896 |
|---|---|---|---|---|---|---|---|---|---|
| tikoun | tapilatiy | qatoret | lapaneyka; | mas'at | kapay, | minchat | 'areb. | | shiytah |
| **Let be set forth** | **my prayer** | ***as* incense** | **before you** | ***and* the lifting up of** | **my hands** | **sacrifice** | ***as the* evening** | | **Set** |

| יהוה 3068 | שמרה 8108 | לפי 6310 | נצרה 5341 | על 5921 | דל 1817 | שפתי 8193: | 141:4 | אל 408 | תט 5186 | לבי 3820 | לדבר 1697 | רע 7451 |
|---|---|---|---|---|---|---|---|---|---|---|---|---|
| Yahuah | shamarah | lapiy; | nitzrah, | 'al | dal | sapatay. | | 'al | tat | libiy | ladabar | ra' |
| **O Yahuah** | **a watch** | **before my mouth** | **keep** | **over** | **the door of** | **my lips** | | **not** | **Incline** | **my heart** | **to thing** | ***any* evil** |

| להתעולל 5953 | עללות 5949 | ברשע 7562 | את 854 | אישים 376 | פעלי 6466 | און 205 | ובל 1077 | אלחם 3898 | במנעמיהם 4516: | 141:5 | יהלמני 1986 |
|---|---|---|---|---|---|---|---|---|---|---|---|
| lahit'aulel | alilout | baresha', | 'at | 'ayshiym | po'aley | 'auen; | uabal | 'alcham, | baman'ameyhem. | | yehelmeniy |
| **to practise** | **works** | **wicked** | ***with*** | **men** | **that work** | **iniquity** | **and not** | **let me eat** | **of their dainties** | | **Let smite me** |

Ps 140:6 I said unto YHUH, Thou are my G-d: hear the voice of my supplications, O YHUH.7 O G-D the Adonai, the strength of my salvation, you have covered my head in the day of battle.8 Grant not, O YHUH, the desires of the wicked: further not his wicked device; lest they exalt themselves. Selah.9 As for the head of those that compass me about, let the mischief of their own lips cover them.10 Let burning coals fall upon them: let them be cast into the fire; into deep pits, that they rise not up again.11 Let not an evil speaker be established in the earth: evil shall hunt the violent man to overthrow him.12 I know that YHUH will maintain the cause of the afflicted, and the right of the poor.13 Surely the righteous shall give thanks unto your name: the upright shall dwell in your presence. **Ps** 141:1 A Psalm of David. YHUH, I cry unto you: make haste unto me; give ear unto my voice, when I cry unto you.2 Let my prayer be set forth before you as incense; and the lifting up of my hands as the evening sacrifice.3 Set a watch, O YHUH, before my mouth; keep the door of my lips.4 Incline not my heart to any evil thing, to practise wicked works with men that work iniquity: and let me not eat of their dainties.

צדיק 6662 חסד 2617 ויוכיחני 3198 שמן 8081 ראש 7218 אל 408 יני 5106 ראשי 7218
tzadiyq chesed uayoukiycheniy, shemen ra'sh 'al yaniy' ra'shiy;
**the righteous *it shall be* a kindness and let him reprove me *it shall be* an oil excellent not *which* shall break my head**

כי 3588 עוד 5750 ותפלתי 8605 ברעותיהם 7451: **141:6** נשמטו 8058 בידי 3027 סלע 5553 שפטיהם 8199
kiy 'aud utapilatiy, bara'auteyhem. nishmatu biydey sela' shopateyhem;
**for yet my prayer also *shall be* in their calamities are overthrown in places stony their judges**

ושמעו 8085 אמרי 561 כי 3588 נעמו 5276: **141:7** כמו 3644 פלח 6398 ובקע 1234 בארץ 776 נפזרו 6340
uashama'au 'amaray, kiy na'aemu. kamou poleach uaboqea' ba'aretz; nipzaru
**When they shall hear my words for they are sweet as when one cuts and cleave *wood* upon the earth are scattered**

עצמינו 6106 לפי 6310 שאול 7585: **141:8** כי 3588 אליך 413 יהוה 3068 אדני 136 עיני 5869 בכה 871a חסיתי 2620 אל 408
'atzameynu, lapiy sha'aul. kiy 'aeleyka Yahuah 'adonay 'aeynay; bakah chasiytiy, 'al
**Our bones at mouth *the* grave's But *are* unto you O Yahuah Adonai mine eyes in you is my trust not**

תער 6168 נפשי 5315: **141:9** שמרני 8104 מידי 3027 פח 6341 יקשו 3369 לי 3807a ומקשות 4170 פעלי 6466
ta'ar napshiy. shamareniy, miydey pach yaqashu liy; uamoqashout, po'aley
**leave destitute my soul Keep me from the snares *which* they have laid for me and the gins of the workers of**

און 205: **141:10** יפלו 5307 במכמריו 4364 רשעים 7563 יחד 3162 אנכי 595 עד 5704 אעבור 5674:
'auen. yiplu bamakmorayu rasha'aym; yachad 'anokiy, 'ad 'a'abour.
**iniquity Let fall into their own nets the wicked withal *that* I while escape**

**Ps 142:1** משכיל 4905 לדוד 1732 בהיותו 1961 במערה 4631 תפלה 8605: קולי 6963 אל 413 יהוה 3068 אזעק 2199 קולי 6963 אל 413
maskiyl ladauid; bihayotou bama'arah tapilah. qouliy 'al Yahuah 'az'aq; qouliy, 'al
**Maschil of David when he was in the cave A Prayer *with* my voice unto Yahuah I cried *with* my voice unto**

יהוה 3068 אתחנן 2603: **142:2** אשפך 8210 לפניו 6440 שיחי 7879 צרתי 6869 לפניו 6440 אגיד 5046: **142:3**
Yahuah 'atchanan. 'ashpok lapanayu siychiy; tzaratiy, lapanayu 'agiyd.
**Yahuah did I make my supplication I poured out before him my complaint my trouble before him I showed**

בהתעטף 5848 עלי 5921 רוחי 7307 ואתה 859 ידעת 3045 נתיבתי 5410 בארח 734 זו 2098 אהלך 1980 טמנו 2934
bahit'atep 'alay ruchiy, ua'atah yada'ta natiybatiy ba'orach zu 'ahalek; tamanu
**When was overwhelmed within me my spirit then you knew my path In the way wherein I walked have they privily laid**

פח 6341 לי 3807a: **142:4** הביט 5027 ימין 3225 וראה 7200 ואין 369 לי 3807a מכיר 5234 אבד 6 מנוס 4498
pach liy. habeyt yamiyn uar'aeh ua'aeyn liy makiyr 'abad manous
**a snare for me I looked on *my* right hand and beheld but *there was* no me *man* that would know failed refuge**

ממני 4480 אין 369 דורש 1875 לנפשי 5315: **142:5** זעקתי 2199 אליך 413 יהוה 3068 אמרתי 559 אתה 859 מחסי 4268 חלקי 2506
mimeniy; 'aeyn douresh lanapshiy. za'aqtiy 'aeleyka, Yahuah 'amartiy 'atah machasiy; chelqiy,
**me no *man* cared for my soul I cried unto you O Yahuah I said You *are* my refuge *and* my portion**

בארץ 776 החיים 2416: **142:6** הקשיבה 7181 אל 413 רנתי 7440 כי 3588 דלותי 1809 מאד 3966 הצילני 5337 מרדפי 7291
ba'aretz hachayiyim. haqashiybah 'al rinatiy kiy daloutiy ma'ad hatziyleniy merodapay;
**in the land of the living Attend unto my cry for I am brought low very deliver me from my persecutors**

Ps 141:5 Let the righteous smite me; it shall be a kindness: and let him reprove me; it shall be an excellent oil, which shall not break my head: for yet my prayer also shall be in their calamities.6 When their judges are overthrown in stony places, they shall hear my words; for they are sweet.7 Our bones are scattered at the grave's mouth, as when one cutteth and cleaveth wood upon the earth.8 But mine eyes are unto you, O G-D the Adonai: in you is my trust; leave not my soul destitute.9 Keep me from the snares which they have laid for me, and the gins of the workers of iniquity.10 Let the wicked fall into their own nets, whilst that I withal escape. **Ps** 142:1 Mas'-chil of David; A Prayer when he was in the cave. I cried unto YHUH with my voice; with my voice unto YHUH did I make my supplication.2 I poured out my complaint before him; I showed before him my trouble.3 When my spirit was overwhelmed within me, then you knew my path. In the way wherein I walked have they privily laid a snare for me.4 I looked on my right hand, and beheld, but there was no man that would know me: refuge failed me; no man cared for my soul.5 I cried unto you, O YHUH: I said, Thou are my refuge and my portion in the land of the living.

| | | 142:7 | | | | | | | |
|---|---|---|---|---|---|---|---|---|---|
| כי 3588 | אמצו 553 | ממני 4480: | הוציאה 3318 | ממסגר 4525 | נפשי 5315 | להודות 3034 | את 853 | שמך 8034 | בי 871a |
| kiy | 'amatzu | mimeniy. | houtziy'ah | mimasger | napshiy | lahoudout | 'at | shameka | biy |
| **for** | **they are stronger** | **than I** | **Bring** | **out of prison** | **my soul** | **that I may praise** | | **your name** | **me** |

| | | | | |
|---|---|---|---|---|
| יכתרו 3803 | צדיקים 6662 | כי 3588 | תגמל 1580 | עלי 5921: |
| yaktiru | tzadiyqiym; | kiy | tigmol | 'alay. |
| **shall compass about** | **the righteous** | **for** | **you shall deal bountifully** | **with me** |

| Ps 143:1 | | | | | | | | | |
|---|---|---|---|---|---|---|---|---|---|
| מזמור 4210 | לדוד 1732 | יהוה 3068 | שמע 8085 | תפלתי 8605 | האזינה 238 | אל 413 | תחנוני 8469 | באמנתך 530 | ענני 6030 |
| mizmour, | ladauid | Yahuah | shama' | tapilatiy, | ha'aziynah | 'al | tachanunay; | be'amunataka | 'aneniy, |
| **A Psalm** | **of David** | **O Yahuah** | **Hear** | **my prayer** | **give ear** | **to** | **my supplications** | **in your faithfulness** | **answer me** |

| | 143:2 | | | | | | | |
|---|---|---|---|---|---|---|---|---|
| בצדקתך 6666: | ואל 408 | תבוא 935 | במשפט 4941 | את 854 | עבדך 5650 | כי 3588 | לא 3808 | יצדק 6663 |
| batzidqateka. | ua'al | tabou'a | bamishpat | 'at | 'abdeka; | kiy | la' | yitzdaq |
| ***and* faithfulness answer me** | **And not** | **enter** | **into judgment** | ***with*** | **your servant** | **for** | **no** | **shall be justified** |

| | | | 143:3 | | | | | | |
|---|---|---|---|---|---|---|---|---|---|
| לפניך 6440 | כל 3605 | חי 2416: | כי 3588 | רדף 7291 | אויב 341 | נפשי 5315 | דכא 1792 | לארץ 776 | חיתי 2416 |
| lapaneyka | kal | chay. | kiy | radap | auyeb | napshiy, | dikaa' | la'aretz | chayatiy; |
| **in your sight** | **no** | ***man* living** | **For** | **has persecuted** | **the enemy** | **my soul** | **he has struck down** | **to the ground** | **my life** |

| | | | 143:4 | |
|---|---|---|---|---|
| הושיבני 3427 | במחשכים 4285 | כמתי 4191 | עולם 5769: ותתעטף 5848 | עלי 5921 |
| hoshiybaniy | bamachashakiym, | kametey | 'aulam. uatit'atep | 'alay |
| **he has made me to dwell** | **in darkness** | **as those that have been dead** | **long** **Therefore is overwhelmed** | **within me** |

| | | | | 143:5 | | | | | |
|---|---|---|---|---|---|---|---|---|---|
| רוחי 7307 | בתוכי 8432 | ישתומם 8074 | לבי 3820: | זכרתי 2142 | ימים 3117 | מקדם 6924 | הגיתי 1897 | בכל 3605 | פעלך 6467 |
| ruchiy; | batoukiy, | yishtoumem | libiy. | zakartiy | yamiym | miqedem, | hagiytiy | bakal | pa'aleka; |
| **my spirit** | **within me** | **is desolate** | **my heart** | **I remember** | **the days** | **of old** | **I meditate** | **on all** | **your works** |

| | | | 143:6 | | | | | | |
|---|---|---|---|---|---|---|---|---|---|
| במעשה 4639 | ידיך 3027 | אשוחח 7878: | פרשתי 6566 | ידי 3027 | אליך 413 | נפשי 5315 | כארץ 776 | עיפה 5889 | לך 3807a |
| bama'aseh | yadeyka | 'asoucheach. | perastiy | yaday | 'aeleyka; | napshiy | ka'aretz | 'ayepah | laka |
| **on the work of** | **your hands** | **I muse** | **I stretch forth** | **my hands** | **unto you** | **my soul** | **as a land** | **thirsty** | ***thirst* after you** |

| | 143:7 | | | | | | | | | | |
|---|---|---|---|---|---|---|---|---|---|---|---|
| סלה 5542: | מהר 4118 | ענני 6030 | יהוה 3068 | כלתה 3615 | רוחי 7307 | אל 408 | תסתר 5641 | פניך 6440 | ממני 4480 | ונמשלתי 4911 | עם 5973 |
| selah. | maher | 'aneniy | Yahuah | kalatah | ruchiy | 'al | taster | paneyka | mimeniy; | uanimshaltiy, | 'am |
| **Selah** | **speedily** | **Hear me** | **O Yahuah** | **fail** | **my spirit** | **not** | **hide** | **your face** | **from me** | **lest I be like** | **unto** |

| | | 143:8 | | | | | |
|---|---|---|---|---|---|---|---|
| ירדי 3381 | בור 953: | השמיעני 8085 | בבקר 1242 | חסדך 2617 | כי 3588 | בך 871a | בטחתי 982 |
| yoradey | bour. | hashamiy'aeniy | baboqer | chasdeka | kiy | baka | batachatiy |
| **them that go down into** | **the pit** | **Cause me to hear** | **in the morning** | **your lovingkindness** | **for** | **in you** | **do I trust** |

| | | | | | | | | 143:9 | |
|---|---|---|---|---|---|---|---|---|---|
| הודיעני 3045 | דרך 1870 | זו 2098 | אלך 1980 | כי 3588 | אליך 413 | נשאתי 5375 | נפשי 5315: | הצילני 5337 | מאיבי 341 |
| houdiy'aeniy, | derek | zu | 'aelek; | kiy | 'aeleyka | nasa'tiy | napshiy. | hatziyleniy | me'ayabay |
| **cause me to know** | **the way** | **wherein** | **I should walk** | **for** | **unto you** | **I lift up** | **my soul** | **Deliver me** | **from mine enemies** |

| | | | 143:10 | | | | | | | |
|---|---|---|---|---|---|---|---|---|---|---|
| יהוה 3068 | אליך 413 | כסתי 3680: | למדני 3925 | לעשות 6213 | רצונך 7522 | כי 3588 | אתה 859 | אלוהי 430 | רוחך 7307 | טובה 2896 |
| Yahuah | 'aeleyka | kisitiy. | lamadeniy | la'asout | ratzouneka | kiy | 'atah | 'alouhay | ruchaka | toubah; |
| **O Yahuah** | **unto you** | **I flee to hide me** | **Teach me** | **to do** | **your will** | **for** | **you *are*** | **my Elohim** | **your spirit *is*** | **good** |

Ps 142:6 Attend unto my cry; for I am brought very low: deliver me from my persecutors; for they are stronger than I.7 Bring my soul out of prison, that I may praise your name: the righteous shall compass me about; for you shall deal bountifully with me. **Ps** 143:1 A Psalm of David. Hear my prayer, O YHUH, give ear to my supplications: in your faithfulness answer me, and in your righteousness.2 And enter not into judgment with your servant: for in your sight shall no man living be justified.3 For the enemy has persecuted my soul; he has smitten my life down to the ground; he has made me to dwell in darkness, as those that have been long dead.4 Therefore is my spirit overwhelmed within me; my heart within me is desolate.5 I remember the days of old; I meditate on all your works; I muse on the work of your hands.6 I stretch forth my hands unto you: my soul thirsteth after you, as a thirsty land. Selah.7 Hear me speedily, O YHUH: my spirit faileth: hide not your face from me, lest I be like unto them that go down into the pit.8 Cause me to hear your lovingkindness in the morning; for in you do I trust: cause me to know the way wherein I should walk; for I lift up my soul unto you.9 Deliver me, O YHUH, from mine enemies: I flee unto you to hide me.10 Teach me to do your will; for you are my G-d: your spirit is good; lead me into the land of uprightness.

143:11

תנחני 5148 בארץ 776 מישור 4334: למען 4616 שמך 8034 יהוה 3068 תחיני 2421 בצדקתך 6666
tanacheniy, ba'aretz miyshour. lama'an shimka Yahuah tachayeniy; batzidqataka
**lead me into the land of uprightness for sake your name's O Yahuah Quicken me for your righteousness' sake**

143:12

תוציא 3318 מצרה 6869 נפשי 5315: ובחסדך 2617 תצמית 6789 איבי 341 והאבדת 6 כל 3605 צררי 6887
toutziy'a mitzarah napshiy. uabchasdaka tatzmiyt 'ayabay uaha'abadta kal tzorarey
**you bring out of trouble my soul And of your mercy cut off mine enemies and you destroy all them that afflict**

נפשי 5315 כי 3588 אני 589 עבדך 5650:
napshiy; kiy, 'aniy 'abdeka.
**my soul for I *am* your servant**

**Ps 144:1**

לדוד 1732 ברוך 1288 יהוה 3068 צורי 6697 המלמד 3925 ידי 3027 לקרב 7128 אצבעותי 676
ladauid baruk Yahuah tzuriy, hamalamed yaday laqarab; 'atzba'autay,
***A Psalm* of David Blessed *be* Yahuah my strength which teach my hands to war *and* my fingers**

144:2

למלחמה 4421: חסדי 2617 ומצודתי 4686 משגבי 4869 ומפלטי 6403 לי 3807a מגני 4043 ובו 871a חסיתי 2620
lamilchamah. chasdiy uamtzudatiy misgabiy uampaltiy liy maginiy uabou chasiytiy;
**to fight My goodness and my fortress my high tower and deliverer my my shield and *he* in whom I trust**

144:3

הרודד 7286 עמי 5971 תחתי 8478: יהוה 3069 מה 4100 אדם 120 ותדעהו 3045 בן 1121 אנוש 582
harouded 'amiy tachtay. Yahuah mah 'adam uateda'aehu; ben 'anoush,
**who subdue my people under me Yahuah what *is* man that you take knowledge of him *or* the son of man**

144:4

ותחשבהו 2803: אדם 120 להבל 1892 דמה 1819 ימיו 3117 כצל 6738 עובר 5674:
uatachashbehu. 'adam lahebel damah; yamayu, katzel 'auber.
**that you make account of him man *to* vanity is like his days *are* as a shadow that passed away**

144:5

יהוה 3068
Yahuah
**O Yahuah**

הט 5186 שמיך 8064 ותרד 3381 גע 5060 בהרים 2022 ויעשנו 6225:
hat shameyka uatered; ga' behariym uaye'ashanu.
**Bow your heavens and come down touch the mountains and they shall smoke**

144:6

ברוק 1299 ברק 1300 ותפיצם 6327
barouq baraq uatpiytzem;
**Cast forth lightning and scatter them**

שלח 7971 חציך 2671 ותהמם 2000:
shalach chitzeyka, uathumem.
**shoot out your arrows and destroy them**

144:7

שלח 7971 ידיך 3027 ממרום 4791 פצני 6475 והצילני 5337 ממים 4325 רבים 7227
shalach yadeyka, mimaroum patzeniy uahatziyleniy mimayim rabiym;
**Send your hand from above rid me and deliver me out of waters great**

מיד 3027 בני 1121 נכר 5236:
miyad, baney nekar.
**from the hand of children strange**

144:8

אשר 834 פיהם 6310 דבר 1696 שוא 7723 וימינם 3225 ימין 3225
'asher piyhem diber shau'a; uiymiynam, yamiyn
**Whose mouth speak vanity and their right hand *is* a right hand of**

שקר 8267:
shaqer.
**falsehood**

144:9

אלהים 430 שיר 7892 חדש 2319 אשירה 7891 לך 3807a בנבל 5035 עשור 6218
'alohiym, shiyr chadash 'ashiyrah lak; banebel 'asour,
**O Elohim I will sing a new song unto you upon a psaltery *and* an instrument of ten strings**

אזמרה 2167 לך 3807a:
'azamrah lak.
**will I sing praises unto you**

144:10

הנותן 5414 תשועה 8668 למלכים 4428 הפוצה 6475 את 853 דוד 1732 עבדו 5650 מחרב 2719
hanouten tashu'ah, lamalakiym hapoutzeh 'at dauid abdou, mechereb
***It is he* that gives salvation unto kings who deliver David his servant from sword**

Ps 143:11 Quicken me, O YHUH, for your name's sake: for your righteousness' sake bring my soul out of trouble.12 And of your mercy cut off mine enemies, and destroy all them that afflict my soul: for I am your servant. **Ps** 144:1 A Psalm of David. Blessed be YHUH my strength, which teach my hands to war, and my fingers to fight:2 My goodness, and my fortress; my high tower, and my deliverer; my shield, and he in whom I trust; who subdueth my people under me.3 YHUH, what is man, that you takest knowledge of him! or the son of man, that you make account of him!4 Man is like to vanity: his days are as a shadow that pass away.5 Bow your heavens, O YHUH, and come down: touch the mountains, and they shall smoke.6 Cast forth lightning, and scatter them: shoot out your arrows, and destroy them.7 Send your hand from above; rid me, and deliver me out of great waters, from the hand of strange children;8 Whose mouth speaketh vanity, and their right hand is a right hand of falsehood.9 I will sing a new song unto you, O G-d: upon a psaltery and an instrument of ten strings will I sing praises unto you.10 It is he that give salvation unto kings: who delivereth David his servant from the hurtful sword.

| רעה 7451: | 144:11 | פצני 6475 | והצילני 5337 | מיד 3027 | בני 1121 | נכר 5236 | אשר 834 | פיהם 6310 | דבר 1696 | שוא 7723 |
|---|---|---|---|---|---|---|---|---|---|---|
| ra'ah. | | patzeniy | uahatziyleniy | miyad | baney | nekar | 'asher | piyhem | diber | shau'a; |
| ***the* hurtful** | | **Rid me** | **and deliver me** | **from the hand of** | **children** | **strange** | **whose** | **mouth** | **speak** | **vanity** |

| וימינם 3225 | ימין 3225 | שקר 8267: | 144:12 | אשר 834 | בנינו 1121 | כנטעים 5195 | מגדלים 1431 | בנעוריהם 5271 |
|---|---|---|---|---|---|---|---|---|
| uiymiynam, | yamiyn | shaqer. | | 'asher | baneynu | kinti'aym | magudaliym | bin'aureyhem |
| **and their right hand** | ***is* a right hand of** | **falsehood** | | **That** | **our sons** | ***may be* as plants** | **grown up** | **in their youth** |

| בנותינו 1323 | כזוית 2106 | מחטבות 2404 | תבנית 8403 | היכל 1964: | 144:13 | מזוינו 4200 | מלאים 4392 |
|---|---|---|---|---|---|---|---|
| banouteynu | kazauiyot; | machutabout, | tabaniyt | heykal. | | mazaueynu | male'aym |
| ***that* our daughters *may be*** | **as corner stones** | **polished** | ***after* the similitude of** | **a palace** | | ***That* our garners *may be*** | **full** |

| מפיקים 6329 | מזן 2177 | אל 413 | זן 2177 | צאוננו 6629 | מאליפות 503 | מרבבות 7231 | בחוצותינו 2351: | 144:14 |
|---|---|---|---|---|---|---|---|---|
| mapiyqiym | mizan, | al | zan | tza'unenu | ma'aliypout | marubabout, | bachutzouteynu. | |
| **affording** | **all manner** | **of** | **store** | ***that* our sheep** | **may bring forth thousands** | ***and* ten thousands** | **in our streets** | |

| אלופינו 441 | מסבלים 5445 | אין 369 | פרץ 6556 | ואין 369 | יוצאת 3318 | ואין 369 | צוחה 6682 |
|---|---|---|---|---|---|---|---|
| 'alupeynu, | masubaliym | 'aeyn | peretz | ua'aeyn | yatzea't; | ua'aeyn | tzauachah, |
| ***That* our oxen** | ***may be* strong to labour** | ***that there be* no** | **breaking in** | **nor** | **going out** | **that *there be* no** | **complaining** |

| ברחבתינו 7339: | 144:15 | אשרי 835 | העם 5971 | שככה 3602 | לו 3807a | אשרי 835 | העם 5971 | שיהוה 3068 |
|---|---|---|---|---|---|---|---|---|
| birchoboteynu. | | 'ashrey | ha'am | shekakah | lou'; | 'ashrey | ha'am, | sheYahuah |
| **in our streets** | | **Happy** | ***is* that people** | **that is in such a case** | ***yea* to him** | **happy** | ***is* that people** | ***is* who Yahuah** |

| אלהיו 430: |
|---|
| 'alohayu. |
| **whose Elohim** |

| Ps 145:1 | תהלה 8416 | לדוד 1732 | ארוממך 7311 | אלוהי 430 | המלך 4428 | ואברכה 1288 | שמך 8034 | לעולם 5769 | ועד 5703: | 145:2 |
|---|---|---|---|---|---|---|---|---|---|---|
| | tahilah, | ladauid | aroumimaka | 'alouhay | hamelek; | ua'abarakah | shimka, | la'aulam | ua'ad. | |
| | ***Psalm* of praise** | **David's** | **I will extol you** | **my Elohim** | **O king** | **and I will bless** | **your name** | **for ever** | **and ever** | |

| בכל 3605 | יום 3117 | אברכך 1288 | ואהללה 1984 | שמך 8034 | לעולם 5769 | ועד 5703: | 145:3 | גדול 1419 | יהוה 3068 | ומהלל 1984 |
|---|---|---|---|---|---|---|---|---|---|---|
| bakal | youm | 'abarakeka; | ua'ahalalah | shimka, | la'aulam | ua'ad. | | gadoul | Yahuah | uamahulal |
| **Every** | **day** | **will I bless you** | **and I will praise** | **your name** | **for ever** | **and ever** | | **Great** | ***is* Yahuah** | **and to be praised** |

| מאד 3966 | ולגדלתו 1420 | אין 369 | חקר 2714: | 145:4 | דור 1755 | לדור 1755 | ישבח 7623 | מעשיך 4639 | וגבורתיך 1369 |
|---|---|---|---|---|---|---|---|---|---|
| ma'ad; | ualigadulatou, | 'aeyn | cheqer. | | dour | ladour | yashabach | ma'aseyka; | uagaburoteyka |
| **greatly** | **and his greatness** | ***is* not** | **searchable** | | **One generation** | **to another** | **shall praise** | **your works** | **and your mighty acts** |

| יגידו 5046: | 145:5 | הדר 1926 | כבוד 3519 | הודך 1935 | ודברי 1697 | נפלאותיך 6381 | אשיחה 7878: | 145:6 | ועזוז 5807 |
|---|---|---|---|---|---|---|---|---|---|
| yagiydu. | | hadar | kaboud | houdeka; | uadibrey | nipla'auteyka | 'asiychah. | | ue'azuz |
| **shall declare** | | **honor of** | ***the* glorious** | **your majesty** | **and works** | ***of* your wondrous** | **I will speak of** | | **And the might of** |

| נוראתיך 3372 | יאמרו 559 | וגדולתיך 1420 | אספרנה 5608: | 145:7 | זכר 2143 | רב 7227 | טובך 2898 |
|---|---|---|---|---|---|---|---|
| noura'ateyka | ya'meru; | uagadulateyka | 'asaprenah. | | zeker | rab | tubaka |
| **your terrible acts** | ***men* shall speak *of*** | **and your greatness** | **I will declare** | | **the memory of** | **great** | **your goodness** |

Ps 144:11 Rid me, and deliver me from the hand of strange children, whose mouth speaketh vanity, and their right hand is a right hand of falsehood:12 That our sons may be as plants grown up in their youth; that our daughters may be as corner stones, polished after the similitude of a palace:13 That our garners may be full, affording all manner of store: that our sheep may bring forth thousands and ten thousands in our streets:14 That our oxen may be strong to labour; that there be no breaking in, nor going out; that there be no complaining in our streets.15 Happy is that people, that is in such a case: yea, happy is that people, whose G-d is YHUH. **Ps** 145:1 David's Psalm of praise. I will extol you, my G-d, O king; and I will bless your name forever and ever.2 Every day will I bless you; and I will praise your name forever and ever.3 Great is YHUH, and greatly to be praised; and his greatness is unsearchable.4 One generation shall praise your works to another, and shall declare your mighty acts.5 I will speak of the glorious honor of your majesty, and of your wondrous works.6 And men shall speak of the might of your terrible acts: and I will declare your greatness.7 They shall abundantly utter the memory of your great goodness, and shall sing of your righteousness.

יביעו 5042 וצדקתך 6666 ירננו 7442: 145:8 חנון 2587 ורחום 7349 יהוה 3068 ארך 750
yabiy'au; uatzidqataka yaranenu. chanun uarachum Yahuah; 'arek
**They shall abundantly utter and your righteousness shall sing *of* *is* gracious and full of compassion Yahuah slow**

אפים 639 וגדל 1419 חסד 2617: 145:9 טוב 2896 יהוה 3068 לכל 3605 ורחמיו 7356 על 5921 כל 3605 מעשיו 4639: 145:10
'apayim, uagdal chased. toub Yahuah lakol; uarachamayu, 'al kal ma'asayu.
**to anger and of great mercy *is* good Yahuah to all and his tender mercies *are* over all his works**

יודוך 3034 יהוה 3068 כל 3605 מעשיך 4639 וחסידיך 2623 יברכוכה 1288: 145:11 כבוד 3519 מלכותך 4438
youduka Yahuah kal ma'aseyka; uachasiydeyka, yabarakukah. kaboud malkutaka
**shall praise you O Yahuah All your works and your saints shall bless you the glory of your kingdom**

יאמרו 559 וגבורתך 1369 ידברו 1696: 145:12 להודיע 3045 לבני 1121 האדם 120 גבורתיו 1369 וכבוד 3519
ya'meru; uagburataka yadaberu. lahoudiya' libney ha'adam gaburotayu; uakboud,
**They shall speak of and your power talk of To make known to the sons of men his mighty acts and the glorious**

הדר 1926 מלכותו 4438: 145:13 מלכותך 4438 מלכות 4438 כל 3605 עלמים 5769 וממשלתך 4475 בכל 3605
hadar malkutou. malkutaka, malkut kal 'aulamiym; uamemsheltaka, bakal
**majesty of his kingdom Your kingdom *is* an kingdom throughout everlasting and your dominion *endures* in every**

דור 1755 ודור 1755: 145:14 סומך 5564 יהוה 3068 לכל 3605 הנפלים 5307 וזוקף 2210 לכל 3605 הכפופים 3721: 145:15
dour uadour. soumek Yahuah lakal hanopliym; uazouqep, lakal hakapupiym.
**generation and generation uphold Yahuah all that fall and raises up all *those that be* bowed down**

עיני 5869 כל 3605 אליך 413 ישברו 7663 ואתה 859 נותן 5414 להם 1992 את 853 אכלם 400 בעתו 6256: 145:16 פותח 6605 את 853
'aeyney kal 'aeleyka yasaberu; ua'atah nouten lahem 'at 'aklam ba'atou. pouteach 'at
**The eyes of all upon you wait and you give them their meat in due season You open**

ידך 3027 ומשביע 7646 לכל 3605 חי 2416 רצון 7522: 145:17 צדיק 6662 יהוה 3068 בכל 3605 דרכיו 1870 וחסיד 2623 בכל 3605
yadeka; uamasbiya' lakal chay ratzoun. tzadiyq Yahuah bakal darakayu; uachasiyd, bakal
**your hand and satisfiest every living thing the desire of *is* righteous Yahuah in all his ways and holy in all**

מעשיו 4639: 145:18 קרוב 7138 יהוה 3068 לכל 3605 קראיו 7121 לכל 3605 אשר 834 יקראהו 7121 באמת 571: 145:19
ma'asayu. qaroub Yahuah lakal qora'ayu; lakol 'asher yiqra'ahu be'amet.
**his works *is* near Yahuah unto all them that call upon him to all that call upon him in truth**

רצון 7522 יראיו 3373 יעשה 6213 ואת 853 שועתם 7775 ישמע 8085 ויושיעם 3467: 145:20 שומר 8104 יהוה 3068
ratzoun yare'ayu ya'aseh; ua'at shau'atam yishma', uayoushiy'aem. shoumer Yahuah
**the desire of them that fear him He will fulfill *also* their cry he will hear and will save them preserve Yahuah**

את 853 כל 3605 אהביו 157 ואת 853 כל 3605 הרשעים 7563 ישמיד 8045: 145:21 תהלת 8416 יהוה 3068 ידבר 1696 פי 6310
'at kal 'ahabayu; ua'at kal harasha'aym yashmiyd. tahilat Yahuah yadaber piy
**all them that love him *but* all the wicked will he destroy the praise of Yahuah shall speak My mouth**

ויברך 1288 כל 3605 בשר 1320 שם 8034 קדשו 6944 לעולם 5769 ועד 5703:
uiybarek kal basar shem qadashou, la'aulam ua'ad.
**and let bless all flesh name his holy for ever and ever**

Ps 145:8 YHUH is gracious, and full of compassion; slow to anger, and of great mercy.9 YHUH is good to all: and his tender mercies are over all his works.10 All your works shall praise you, O YHUH; and your saints shall bless you.11 They shall speak of the glory of your kingdom, and talk of your power;12 To make known to the sons of men his mighty acts, and the glorious majesty of his kingdom.13 Thy kingdom is an everlasting kingdom, and your dominion endureth throughout all generations.14 YHUH upholdeth all that fall, and raise up all those that be bowed down.15 The eyes of all wait upon you; and you givest them their meat in due season.16 Thou openest your hand, and satisfiest the desire of every living thing.17 YHUH is righteous in all his ways, and holy in all his works.18 YHUH is nigh unto all them that call upon him, to all that call upon him in truth.19 He will fulfil the desire of them that fear him: he also will hear their cry, and will save them.20 YHUH preserveth all them that love him: but all the wicked will he destroy.21 My mouth shall speak the praise of YHUH: and let all flesh bless his holy name forever and ever.

**Ps 146:1** הללו 1984 יה 3050 הללי 1984 נפשי 5315 את 853 יהוה 3068: **146:2** אהללה 1984 יהוה 3068 בחיי 2416 אזמרה 2167
halalu Yah halaliy napshiy, 'at Yahuah. 'ahalalah Yahuah bachayay; 'azamrah
**Praise you Yah Praise O my soul Yahuah will I praise Yahuah While I live I will sing praises**

לאלהי 430 בעודי 5750: **146:3** אל 408 תבטחו 982 בנדיבים 5081 בבן 1121 אדם 120 שאין 369 לו 3807a
le'alohay ba'audiy. 'al tibtachu binadiybiym; baben 'adam she'aeyn lou'
**unto my Elohim while I have any being not Put your trust in princes *nor* in the son of man *there is* no in whom**

תשועה 8668: **146:4** תצא 3318 רוחו 7307 ישב 7725 לאדמתו 127 ביום 3117 ההוא 1931 אבדו 6 עשתנתיו 6250: **146:5** אשרי 835
tashu'ah. tetzea' ruachou yashub la'admatou; bayoum hahua', 'abadu 'ashtonotayu. 'ashrey,
**help goes forth His breath he return to his earth in day that *very* perish his thoughts Happy *is he***

שאל 410 יעקב 3290 בעזרו 5828 שברו 7664 על 5921 יהוה 3068 אלהיו 430: **146:6** עשה 6213 שמים 8064 וארץ 776 את 853
she'ael ya'aqob ba'azrou; sibrou, 'al Yahuah 'alohayu. 'aseh shamayim ua'aretz, 'at
**that *has* the El of Jacob for his help whose hope *is* in Yahuah his Elohim Which made heaven and earth**

הים 3220 ואת 853 כל 3605 אשר 834 בם 871a השמר 8104 אמת 571 לעולם 5769: **146:7** עשה 6213 משפט 4941 לעשוקים 6231
hayam ua'at kal 'asher bam; hashomer 'amet la'aulam. 'aseh mishapat la'ashuqiym,
**the sea *and* all that therein *is* which keep truth for ever Which execute judgment for the oppressed**

נתן 5414 לחם 3899 לרעבים 7457 יהוה 3068 מתיר 5425 אסורים 631: **146:8** יהוה 3068 פקח 6491 עורים 5787 יהוה 3068 זקף 2210
noten lechem lara'aebiym; Yahuah matiyr 'asuriym. Yahuah poqeach 'auriym, Yahuah zoqep
**which gives food to the hungry Yahuah loose the prisoners Yahuah open *the eyes of* the blind Yahuah raises**

כפופים 3721 יהוה 3068 אהב 157 צדיקים 6662: **146:9** יהוה 3068 שמר 8104 את 853 גרים 1616 יתום 3490 ואלמנה 490
kapupiym; Yahuah 'aheb tzadiyqiym. Yahuah shomer 'at geriym, yatoum ua'almanah
**them that are bowed down Yahuah love the righteous Yahuah preserve the strangers the fatherless and widow**

יעודד 5749 ודרך 1870 רשעים 7563 יעות 5791: **146:10** ימלך 4427 יהוה 3068 לעולם 5769 אלהיך 430 ציון 6726
ya'auded; uaderek rasha'aym ya'auet. yimlok Yahuah la'aulam, 'alohayik tziyoun
**he relieveth but the way of the wicked he turned upside down shall reign Yahuah for ever *even* your Elohim O Zion**

לדר 1755 ודר 1755 הללו 1984 יה 3050:
lador uador, halalu Yah.
**unto all generations Praise you Yah**

**Ps 147:1** הללו 1984 יה 3050 כי 3588 טוב 2896 זמרה 2167 אלהינו 430 כי 3588 נעים 5273 נאוה 5000 תהלה 8416: **147:2**
halalu Yah kiy toub zamrah 'aloheynu; kiy na'aym na'uah tahilah.
**Praise you Yah for *it is* good to sing praises unto our Elohim for *it is* pleasant is comely *and* praise**

בונה 1129 ירושלם 3389 יהוה 3068 נדחי 1760 ישראל 3478 יכנס 3664: **147:3** הרפא 7495 לשבורי 7665 לב 3820
bouneh yarushalaim Yahuah; nidchey yisra'ael yakanes. haropea' lishburey leb;
**does build up Jerusalem Yahuah the outcasts of Israel he gathered together He heals the broken in heart**

ומחבש 2280 לעצבותם 6094: **147:4** מונה 4487 מספר 4557 לכוכבים 3556 לכלם 3605 שמות 8034 יקרא 7121: **147:5** גדול 1419
uamchabesh, la'atzboutam. mouneh mispar lakoukabiym; lakulam, shemout yiqra'. gadoul
**and bind up their wounds He tell the number of the stars them all *by their* names he call Great**

**Ps** 146:1 Praise you YHUH. Praise YHUH, O my soul.2 While I live will I praise YHUH: I will sing praises unto my G-d while I have any being.3 Put not your trust in princes, nor in the son of man, in whom there is no help.4 His breath go forth, he returneth to his earth; in that very day his thoughts perish.5 Happy is he that has the G-d of Jacob for his help, whose hope is in YHUH his G-d:6 Which made heaven, and earth, the sea, and all that therein is: which keep truth forever:7 Which executeth judgment for the oppressed: which give food to the hungry. YHUH looseth the prisoners:8 YHUH openeth the eyes of the blind: YHUH raise them that are bowed down: YHUH love the righteous:9 YHUH preserveth the strangers; he relieveth the fatherless and widow: but the way of the wicked he turneth upside down.10 YHUH shall reign forever, even your G-d, O Zion, unto all generations. Praise you YHUH. **Ps** 147:1 Praise you YHUH: for it is good to sing praises unto our G-d; for it is pleasant; and praise is comely.2 YHUH doth build up Jerusalem: he gathereth together the outcasts of Israel.3 He healeth the broken in heart, and bindeth up their wounds.4 He tell the number of the stars; he call them all by their names.

147:6

113 אדונינו | 7227 ורב | 3581 כח | 8394 לתבונתו | 369 אין | 4557: מספר | 5749 מעודד | 6035 ענוים | 3068 יהוה | 8213 משפיל
'adouneynu | uarab | koach; | litabunatou, | 'aeyn | mispar. | ma'auded | 'anauiym | Yahuah; | mashpiyl
**_is_ our Adonai | and of great | power | his understanding | _is_ no | numbering | lift up | the meek | Yahuah | he cast down**

147:7 | 147:8

7563 רשעים | 5704 עדי | 776: ארץ | 6030 ענו | 3068 ליהוה | 8426 בתודה | 2167 זמרו | 430 לאלהינו | 3658: בכנור
rasha'aym | 'adey | 'aretz. | 'anu | laYahuah | batoudah; | zamru | le'aloheynu | bakinour.
**the wicked | to | the ground | Sing | unto Yahuah | with thanksgiving | sing praise | unto our Elohim | upon the harp**

147:9

3680 המכסה | 8064 שמים | 5645 בעבים | 3559 המכין | 776 לארץ | 4306 מטר | 6779 המצמיח | 2022 הרים | 2682: חציר
hamkaseh | shamayim | ba'abiym, | hamekiyn | la'aretz | matar; | hamatzamiyach | hariym | chatziyr.
**Who cover | the heaven | with clouds | who prepare | for the earth | rain | who make to grow upon | the mountains | grass**

147:10

5414 נותן | 929 לבהמה | 3899 לחמה | 1121 לבני | 6158 ערב | 834 אשר | 7121: יקראו | 3808 לא | 1369 בגבורת | 5483 הסוס
nouten | libahemah | lachamah; | libney | 'areb, | 'asher | yiqra'au. | la' | bigaburat | hasus
**He gives | to the beast | his food | _and_ to the young | ravens | which | cry | not | in the strength of | the horse**

147:11

2654 יחפץ | 3808 לא | 7785 בשוקי | 376 האיש | 7521: ירצה | 7521 רוצה | 3068 יהוה | 853 את | 3373 יראיו | 853 את
yechpatz; | la' | bashouqey | ha'aysh | yirtzeh. | routzeh | Yahuah | 'at | yare'ayu; | 'at
**He delight | not | in the legs of | a man | he takes pleasure | takes pleasure in | Yahuah | them that fear him**

147:12 | 147:13

3176 המיחלים | 2617: לחסדו | 7623 שבחי | 3389 ירושלם | 853 את | 3068 יהוה | 1984 הללי | 430 אלהיך | 6726: ציון | 3588 כי
hamayachaliym | lachasdou. | shabchiy | yarushalaim | 'at | Yahuah; | halaliy | 'alohayik | tziyoun. | kiy
**_in_ those that hope | in his mercy | Praise | O Jerusalem | Yahuah | praise | your Elohim | O Zion | For**

147:14

2388 חזק | 1280 בריחי | 8179 שעריך | 1288 ברך | 1121 בניך | 7130: בקרבך | 7760 השם | 1366 גבולך
chizaq | bariychey | sha'arayik; | berak | banayik | baqirbek. | hasam | gabulek
**he has strengthened | the bars of | your gates | he has blessed | your children | within you | He make | _in_ your borders**

147:15

7965 שלום | 2459 חלב | 2406 חטים | 7646: ישביעך | 7971 השלח | 565 אמרתו | 776 ארץ | 5704 עד | 4120 מהרה
shaloum; | cheleb | chitiym, | yasbiy'aek. | hasholeach | 'amratou | 'aretz; | 'ad | maherah,
**peace | the finest of | the wheat | _and_ fill you with | He send forth | his commandment | _upon_ earth | very | swiftly**

147:16 | 147:17

7323 ירוץ | 1697: דברו | 5414 הנתן | 7950 שלג | 6785 כצמר | 3713 כפור | 665 כאפר | 6340: יפזר | 7993 משליך | 7140 קרחו
yarutz | dabarou. | hanoten | sheleg | katzamer; | kapour, | ka'aeper | yapazer. | mashliyk | qarchou
**run | his word | He gives | snow | like wool | the hoarfrost | like ashes | he scatters | He cast forth | his ice**

147:18

6595 כפתים | 6440 לפני | 7135 קרתו | 4310 מי | 5975: יעמד | 7971 ישלח | 1697 דברו | 4529 וימסם | 5380 ישב | 7307 רוחו | 5140 יזלו
kapitiym; | lipney | qaratou, | miy' | ya'amod. | yishlach | dabarou | uayamsem; | yasheb | ruachou, | yizlu
**like morsels | before | his cold? | Who | can stand | He send out | his word | and melt them | he cause to blow | his wind | flow**

147:19 | 147:20

4325: מים | 5046 מגיד | 1697 דברו | 3290 ליעקב | 2706 חקיו | 4941 ומשפטיו | 3478: לישראל | 3808 לא | 6213 עשה
mayim. | magiyd | dabarou | laya'aqob; | chuqayu | uamishpatayu, | layisra'ael. | la' | 'asah
**_and_ the waters | He shows | his word | unto Jacob | his statutes | and his judgments | unto Israel | not | He has dealt**

3651 כן | 3605 לכל | 1471 גוי | 4941 ומשפטים | 1077 בל | 3045 ידעום | 1984 הללו | 3050: יה
ken | lakal | gouy, | uamishpatiym | bal | yada'aum, | halalu | Yah.
**so | with any | nation | and _as for his_ judgments | not | they have known them | Praise you | Yah**

Ps 147:5 Great is our Adonai, and of great power: his understanding is infinite.6 YHUH lift up the meek: he casteth the wicked down to the ground.7 Sing unto YHUH with thanksgiving; sing praise upon the harp unto our G-d:8 Who covereth the heaven with clouds, who prepareth rain for the earth, who make grass to grow upon the mountains.9 He give to the beast his food, and to the young ravens which cry.10 He delighteth not in the strength of the horse: he take not pleasure in the legs of a man.11 YHUH take pleasure in them that fear him, in those that hope in his mercy.12 Praise YHUH, O Jerusalem; praise your G-d, O Zion.13 For he has strengthened the bars of your gates; he has blessed your children within you.14 He make peace in your borders, and filleth you with the finest of the wheat.15 He send forth his commandment upon earth: his word runneth very swiftly.16 He give snow like wool: he scattereth the hoarfrost like ashes.17 He casteth forth his ice like morsels: who can stand before his cold?18 He send out his word, and melteth them: he causeth his wind to blow, and the waters flow.19 He show his word unto Jacob, his statutes and his judgments unto Israel.20 He has not dealt so with any nation: and as for his judgments, they have not known them. Praise you YHUH.

**Ps 148:1**
הללו 1984 | יה 3050 | הללו 1984 | את 853 | יהוה 3068 | מן 4480 | השמים 8064 | הללוהו 1984 | במרומים 4791:
halalu Yah halalu 'at Yahuah min hashamayim; halauhu, bamroumiym.
**Praise you Yah Praise you Yahuah from the heavens praise you him in the heights**

**148:2**
הללוהו 1984 | כל 3605 | מלאכיו 4397 | הללוהו 1984 | כל 3605 | צבאו 6635
halauhu kal mal'akayu; halaluhu, kal tzaba'au
**Praise you him all his angels praise you him all his host**

**148:3**
הללוהו 1984 | שמש 8121 | וירח 3394 | הללוהו 1984 | כל 3605 | כוכבי 3556 | אור 216:
halaluhu shemesh uayareach; halauhu, kal koukabey 'aur.
**Praise you him sun and moon praise you him all you stars of light**

**148:4**
הללוהו 1984 | שמי 8064 | השמים 8064 | והמים 4325 | אשר 834 | מעל 5921 | השמים 8064:
halaluhu shamey hashamayim; uahamayim, 'asher me'al hashamayim.
**Praise you him you heavens of heavens and you waters that *be* above the heavens**

**148:5**
יהללו 1984 | את 853 | שם 8034 | יהוה 3068 | כי 3588 | הוא 1931 | צוה 6680 | ונבראו 1254:
yahalalu 'at shem Yahuah; kiy hua' tziuah uanibra'au.
**Let them praise the name of Yahuah for he commanded and they were created**

**148:6**
ויעמידם 5975 | לעד 5703 | לעולם 5769 | חק 2706 | נתן 5414 | ולא 3808 | יעבור 5674:
uaya'amiydem la'ad la'aulam; chaq natan, uala' ya'abour.
**He has also stablished them for ever and ever a decree he has made which not shall pass**

**148:7**
הללו 1984 | את 853 | יהוה 3068 | מן 4480 | הארץ 776 | תנינים 8577 | וכל 3605 | תהמות 8415:
halalu 'at Yahuah min ha'aretz; taniyniym, uakal tahomout.
**Praise Yahuah from the earth you dragons and all deeps**

**148:8**
אש 784 | וברד 1259 | שלג 7950 | וקיטור 7008 | רוח 7307 | סערה 5591 | עשה 6213 | דברו 1697:
'aesh uabarad sheleg uaqiytour; ruach sa'arah, 'asah dabarou.
**Fire and hail snow and vapour wind stormy fulfilling his word**

**148:9**
ההרים 2022 | וכל 3605 | גבעות 1389 | עץ 6086 | פרי 6529 | וכל 3605 | ארזים 730:
hehariym uakal gaba'aut; 'aetz pariy, uakal 'araziym.
**Mountains and all hills trees fruitful and all cedars**

**148:10**
החיה 2416 | וכל 3605 | בהמה 929 | רמש 7431 | וצפור 6833 | כנף 3671:
hachayah uakal bahemah; remes, uatzipour kanap.
**Beasts and all cattle creeping things and fowl flying**

**148:11**
מלכי 4428 | ארץ 776 | וכל 3605 | לאמים 3816 | שרים 8269 | וכל 3605 | שפטי 8199 | ארץ 776:
malkey 'aretz uakal la'amiym; sariym, uakal shopatey 'aretz.
**Kings of the earth and all the people princes and all judges of the earth**

**148:12**
בחורים 970 | וגם 1571 | בתולות 1330 | זקנים 2205 | עם 5973 | נערים 5288:
bachuriym uagam batulout; zaqeniym, 'am na'ariym.
**young men Both and maidens old men and with children**

**148:13**
יהללו 1984 | את 853 | שם 8034 | יהוה 3068 | כי 3588 | נשגב 7682 | שמו 8034 | לבדו 905 | הודו 3035 | על 5921 | ארץ 776 | ושמים 8064:
yahalalu 'at shem Yahuah kiy nisgab shamou labadou; houdou, 'al 'aretz uashamayim.
**Let them praise the name of Yahuah for is excellent his name alone his glory *is* above the earth and heaven**

**148:14**
וירם 7311 | קרן 7161 | לעמו 5971 | תהלה 8416 | לכל 3605 | חסידיו 2623 | לבני 1121 | ישראל 3478 | עם 5971 | קרבו 7138 | הללו 1984 | יה 3050:
uayarem qeren la'amou tahilah lakal chasiydayu, libney yisra'ael 'am qarobou, halalu Yah.
**He also exalt the horn of his people the praise for all his saints *even* of the children of Israel a people near unto him Praise you Yah**

**Ps 149:1**
הללו 1984 | יה 3050 | שירו 7891 | ליהוה 3068 | שיר 7892 | חדש 2319 | תהלתו 8416 | בקהל 6951 | חסידים 2623:
halalu Yah shiyru laYahuah shiyr chadash; tahilatou, biqahal chasiydiym.
**Praise you Yah Sing unto Yahuah a song new *and* his praise in the congregation of saints**

**Ps** 148:1 Praise you YHUH. Praise you YHUH from the heavens: praise him in the heights.2 Praise you him, all his angels: praise you him, all his hosts.3 Praise you him, sun and moon: praise him, all you stars of light.4 Praise him, you heavens of heavens, and you waters that be above the heavens.5 Let them praise the name of YHUH: for he commanded, and they were created.6 He has also stablished them forever and ever: he has made a decree which shall not pass.7 Praise YHUH from the earth, you dragons, and all deeps:8 Fire, and hail; snow, and vapour; stormy wind fulfilling his word:9 Mountains, and all hills; fruitful trees, and all cedars:10 Beasts, and all cattle; creeping things, and flying fowl:11 Kings of the earth, and all people; princes, and all judges of the earth:12 Both young men, and maidens; old men, and children:13 Let them praise the name of YHUH: for his name alone is excellent; his glory is above the earth and heaven.14 He also exalteth the horn of his people, the praise of all his saints; even of the children of Israel, a people near unto him. Praise you YHUH. **Ps** 149:1 Praise you YHUH. Sing unto YHUH a new song, and his praise in the congregation of saints.

| **149:2** | | | | | | | **149:3** |
|---|---|---|---|---|---|---|---|
| ישמח 8055 | ישראל 3478 | בעשיו 6213 | בני 1121 | ציון 6726 | יגילו 1523 | במלכם 4428: | יהללו 1984 |
| yismach | yisra'ael | ba'asayu; | baney | tziyoun, | yagiylu | bamalkam. | yahalalu |
| **Let rejoice** | **Israel** | **in him that made him** | **the children of** | **Zion** | **let be joyful** | **in their King** | **Let them praise** |

| | | | | | | **149:4** | | |
|---|---|---|---|---|---|---|---|---|
| שמו 8034 | במחול 4234 | בתף 8596 | וכנור 3658 | יזמרו 2167 | לו 3807a: | כי 3588 | רוצה 7521 | יהוה 3068 |
| shamou | bamachoul; | batop | uakinour, | yazamru | lou'. | kiy | routzeh | Yahuah |
| **his name** | **in the dance** | **with the timbrel** | **and harp** | **let them sing praises** | **unto him** | **For** | **takes pleasure** | **Yahuah** |

| | | | | **149:5** | | | | |
|---|---|---|---|---|---|---|---|---|
| בעמו 5971 | יפאר 6286 | ענוים 6035 | בישועה 3444: | יעלזו 5937 | חסידים 2623 | בכבוד 3519 | ירננו 7442 | על 5921 |
| ba'amou; | yapa'aer | 'anauiym, | biyshu'ah. | ya'alzu | chasiydiym | bakaboud; | yarannu, | 'al |
| **in his people** | **he will beautify** | **the meek** | **with salvation** | **Let be joyful** | **the saints** | **in glory** | **let them sing aloud** | **upon** |

| | **149:6** | | | | | | **149:7** |
|---|---|---|---|---|---|---|---|
| משכבותם 4904: | רוממות 7319 | אל 410 | בגרונם 1627 | וחרב 2719 | פיפיות 6374 | בידם 3027: | לעשות 6213 |
| mishkaboutam. | roumamout | 'ael | bigrounam; | uachereb | piypiyout | bayadam. | la'asout |
| **their beds** | ***Let the* high *praises* of** | **El** | ***be* in their mouth** | **and a sword** | **twoedged** | **in their hand** | **To execute** |

| | | | | | **149:8** | | | |
|---|---|---|---|---|---|---|---|---|
| נקמה 5360 | בגוים 1471 | תוכחת 8433 | בל 3816 | אמים 3816: | לאסר 631 | מלכיהם 4428 | בזקים 2131 | ונכבדיהם 3513 |
| naqamah | bagouyim; | toukechot, | bal | 'aumiym. | le'asor | malkeyhem | baziqiym; | uanikbadeyhem, |
| **vengeance** | **upon the heathen** | ***and* punishments** | **upon** | **the people** | **To bind** | **their kings** | **with chains** | **and their nobles** |

| | | **149:9** | | | | | | | | | |
|---|---|---|---|---|---|---|---|---|---|---|---|
| בכבלי 3525 | ברזל 1270: | לעשות 6213 | בהם 871a | משפט 4941 | כתוב 3789 | הדר 1926 | הוא 1931 | לכל 3605 | חסידיו 2623 | הללו 1984 |
| bakabley | barzel. | la'asout | bahem | mishapat | katub, | hadar | hua' | lakal | chasiydayu, | halalu |
| **with fetters of** | **iron** | **To execute** | **upon them** | **the judgment** | **written** | **honor** | **this** | ***have* all** | **his saints** | **Praise you** |

יה 3050:
Yah.
**Yah**

| **Ps 150:1** | | | | | | | **150:2** |
|---|---|---|---|---|---|---|---|
| הללו 1984 | יה 3050 | הללו 1984 | אל 410 | בקדשו 6944 | הללוהו 1984 | ברקיע 7549 | עזו 5797: |
| halalu | Yah | halalu | 'ael | baqadashou; | halauhu, | birqiya' | 'azou. |
| **Praise you** | **Yah** | **Praise** | **El** | **in his sanctuary** | **praise you him** | **in the firmament of** | **his power** |

| | | | | | **150:3** |
|---|---|---|---|---|---|
| הללוהו 1984 | בגבורתיו 1369 | הללוהו 1984 | כרב 7230 | גדלו 1433: | הללוהו 1984 |
| halauhu | bigaburotayu; | halauhu, | karob | gudlou. | halaluhu |
| **Praise you him** | **for his mighty acts** | **praise you him** | **according to excellent** | **his greatness** | **Praise you him** |

| | | | | | **150:4** | | |
|---|---|---|---|---|---|---|---|
| בתקע 8629 | שופר 7782 | הללוהו 1984 | בנבל 5035 | וכנור 3658: | הללוהו 1984 | בתף 8596 | ומחול 4234 |
| bateqa' | shoupar; | halauhu, | banebel | uakinour. | halaluhu | batop | uamachoul; |
| **with the sound of** | **the trumpet** | **praise you him** | **with the psaltery** | **and harp** | **Praise you him** | **with the timbrel** | **and dance** |

| | | | **150:5** | | | |
|---|---|---|---|---|---|---|
| הללוהו 1984 | במנים 4482 | ועוגב 5748: | הללוהו 1984 | בצלצלי 6767 | שמע 8088 | הללוהו 1984 |
| halauhu, | baminiym | ua'augab. | halauhu | batziltzaley | shama'; | halauhu, |
| **praise you him** | **with stringed instruments** | **and organs** | **Praise you him** | **upon cymbals** | ***the* loud** | **praise you him** |

| | | **150:6** | | | | | |
|---|---|---|---|---|---|---|---|
| בצלצלי 6767 | תרועה 8643: | כל 3605 | הנשמה 5397 | תהלל 1984 | יה 3050 | הללו 1984 | יה 3050: |
| batziltzaley | taru'ah. | kal | hanashamah | tahalel | Yah, | halalu | Yah. |
| **upon cymbals** | ***the* high sounding** | **every thing** | **that has breath** | **Let praise** | **Yah** | **Praise you** | **Yah** |

Ps 149:2 Let Israel rejoice in him that made him: let the children of Zion be joyful in their King.3 Let them praise his name in the dance: let them sing praises unto him with the timbrel and harp.4 For YHUH take pleasure in his people: he will beautify the meek with salvation.5 Let the saints be joyful in glory: let them sing aloud upon their beds.6 Let the high praises of G-d be in their mouth, and a twoedged sword in their hand;7 To execute vengeance upon the heathen, and punishments upon the people;8 To bind their kings with chains, and their nobles with fetters of iron;9 To execute upon them the judgment written: this honor have all his saints. Praise you YHUH. **Ps** 150:1 Praise you YHUH. Praise G-d in his sanctuary: praise him in the firmament of his power.2 Praise him for his mighty acts: praise him according to his excellent greatness.3 Praise him with the sound of the trumpet: praise him with the psaltery and harp.4 Praise him with the timbrel and dance: praise him with stringed instruments and organs.5 Praise him upon the loud cymbals: praise him upon the high sounding cymbals.6 Let everything that has breath praise YHUH. Praise you YHUH.

# PROVERBS
## (*Mishlei*)

King Solomon was the principal writer of Proverbs according to the first sentence and the word Proverbs in Hebrew means *examples of* or *rules of.* The book will forever be a look into the beautiful wisdom and character of Solomon, which was composed around 900 B.C. During Solomon's reign the nation of Israel reached its height in spiritually, as well as politically as the world's most superior nation, which gave glory both to Solomon and Elohim's kingdom. As Israel's reputation soared throughout the world, rulers and peoples from foreign nations traveled great distances to hear the wise king speak (1 Kgs 4:34) and to see the Kingdom.

**Proverbs 1:1**
משלי 4912 | שלמה 8010 | בן 1121 | דוד 1732 | מלך 4428 | ישראל 3478: | **1:2** לדעת 3045 | חכמה 2451 | ומוסר 4148
mishley | shalomoh | ben | dauid; | melek, | yisra'ael. | lada'at | chakamah | uamusar;
**The proverbs of | Solomon | the son of | David | king of | Israel | To know | wisdom | and instruction**

להבין 995 | אמרי 561 | בינה 998: | **1:3** לקחת 3947 | מוסר 4148 | השכל 7919 | צדק 6664 | ומשפט 4941 | ומישרים 4339: | **1:4**
lahabiyn, | 'amrey | biynah. | laqachat | musar | hasKel; | tzedeq | uamishpat, | uameyshariym.
**to perceive | the words of | understanding | To receive | the instruction of | wisdom | justice | and judgment | and equity**

לתת 5414 | לפתאים 6612 | ערמה 6195 | לנער 5288 | דעת 1847 | ומזמה 4209: | **1:5** ישמע 8085 | חכם 2450 | ויוסף 3254
latet | liptaa'yim | 'armah; | lana'ar, | da'at | uamazimah. | yishma' | chakam | uayousep
**To give | to the simple | subtilty | to the young man | knowledge | and discretion | *man* will hear | A wise | and will increase**

לקח 3948 | ונבון 995 | תחבלות 8458 | יקנה 7069: | **1:6** להבין 995 | משל 4912 | ומליצה 4426
laqach; | uanaboun, | tachabulout | yiqneh. | lahabiyn | mashal | uamliytzah;
**learning | and a man of understanding | *unto* wise counsels | shall attain | To understand | a proverb | and the interpretation**

דברי 1697 | חכמים 2450 | וחידתם 2420: | **1:7** יראת 3374 | יהוה 3068 | ראשית 7225 | דעת 1847 | חכמה 2451
dibrey | chakamiym, | uachiydotam. | yir'at | Yahuah | rea'shiyt | da'at; | chakamah
**the words of | the wise | and their dark sayings | The fear of | Yahuah | *is* the beginning of | knowledge | wisdom**

ומוסר 4148 | אוילים 191 | בזו 936: | **1:8** שמע 8085 | בני 1121 | מוסר 4148 | אביך 1 | ואל 408 | תטש 5203 | תורת 8451
uamusar, | 'auiyliym | bazu. | shama' | baniy | musar | 'abiyka; | ua'al | titosh, | tourat
**and instruction | *but* fools | despise | hear | My son | the instruction of | your father | and not | forsake | the law of**

אמך 517: | **1:9** כי 3588 | לוית 3880 | חן 2580 | הם 1992 | לראשך 7218 | וענקים 6060 | לגרגרתיך 1621: | **1:10** בני 1121 | אם 518
'ameka. | kiy | liuayat | chen | hem | lara'sheka; | ua'anaqiym, | lagargaroteyka. | baniy | 'am
**your mother | For shall *be* | an ornament of | grace | they | unto your head | and chains | about your neck | My son | if**

יפתוך 6601 | חטאים 2400 | אל 408 | תבא 14: | **1:11** אם 518 | יאמרו 559 | לכה 1980 | אתנו 854 | נארבה 693 | לדם 1818 | נצפנה 6845
yapatuka | chata'aym, | 'al | tobea'. | 'am | ya'maru | lakah | 'atanu | ne'arabah | ladam; | nitzpanah
**entice you | sinners | not | consent you | If | they say | Come | with us | let us lay wait | for blood | let us lurk privily**

לנקי 5355 | חנם 2600: | **1:12** נבלעם 1104 | כשאול 7585 | חיים 2416 | ותמימים 8549 | כיורדי 3381
lanaqiy | chinam. | nibla'aem | kiysha'aul | chayiym; | uatamiymiym, | kayouradey
**for the innocent | without cause | Let us swallow them up | as the grave | alive | and whole | as those that go down**

בור 953: | **1:13** כל 3605 | הון 1952 | יקר 3368 | נמצא 4672 | נמלא 4390 | בתינו 1004 | שלל 7998: | **1:14** גורלך 1486 | תפיל 5307 | בתוכנו 8432
bour. | kal | houn | yaqar | nimtza'; | namalea' | bateynu | shalal. | gouralaka | tapiyl | batoukenu;
***into* the pit | all | substance | precious | We shall find | we shall fill | our houses | *with* spoil | in your lot | Cast | among us**

**Proverbs** 1:1 The proverbs of Solomon the son of David, king of Israel;2 To know wisdom and instruction; to perceive the words of understanding;3 To receive the instruction of wisdom, justice, and judgment, and equity;4 To give subtilty to the simple, to the young man knowledge and discretion.5 A wise man will hear, and will increase learning; and a man of understanding shall attain unto wise counsels:6 To understand a proverb, and the interpretation; the words of the wise, and their dark sayings.7 The fear of YHUH is the beginning of knowledge: but fools despise wisdom and instruction.8 My son, hear the instruction of your father, and forsake not the law of your mother:9 For they shall be an ornament of grace unto your head, and chains about your neck.10 My son, if sinners entice you, consent you not.11 If they say, Come with us, let us lay wait for blood, let us lurk privily for the innocent without cause:12 Let us swallow them up alive as the grave; and whole, as those that go down into the pit: 13 We shall find all precious substance, we shall fill our houses with spoil:

1:15 1:16

כיס 3599 אחד 259 יהיה 1961 לכלנו 3605: בני 1121 אל 408 תלך 1980 בדרך 1870 אתם 854 מנע 4513 רגלך 7272 מנתיבתם 5410:

kiys 'achad, yihayeh lakulanu. baniy, 'al telek baderek 'atam; mana' raglaka, mintiybatam.

**purse one let have us all My son not walk you in the way with them refrain your foot from their path**

1:17

כי 3588 רגליהם 7272 לרע 7451 ירוצו 7323 וימהרו 4116 לשפך 8210 דם 1818: כי 3588 חנם 2600 מזרה 2219 הרשת 7568 בעיני 5869 כל 3605

kiy ragleyhem lara' yarutzu; uiymaharu, lishpak dam. kiy chinam mazorah harashet; ba'aeyney, kal

**For their feet to evil run and make haste to shed blood Surely in vain is spread the net in the sight of any**

1:18 1:19

בעל 1167 כנף 3671: והם 1992 לדמם 1818 יארבו 693 יצפנו 6845 לנפשתם 5315: כן 3651 ארחות 734

ba'al kanap. uahem ladamam ye'arobu; yitzpanu, lanapshotam. ken, 'arachout

**owner bird And they for their *own* blood lay wait they lurk privily for their *own* lives So *are* the ways of**

1:20

כל 3605 בצע 1214 בצע 1215 את 853 נפש 5315 בעליו 1167 יקח 3947: חכמות 2454 בחוץ 2351 תרנה 7442

kal botzea' batza'; 'at nepesh ba'alayu yiqach. chakmout bachutz taronah;

**every one that is greedy of gain the life of the owners thereof *which* takes away Wisdom without cry**

1:21

ברחבות 7339 תתן 5414 קולה 6963: בראש 7218 המיות 1993 תקרא 7121 בפתחי 6607 שערים 8179 בעיר 5892

barachobout, titen qoulah. bara'sh homiyout, tiqraa' bapitchey sha'ariym ba'ayr,

**in the streets she utter her voice *in the* chief place of concourse She cry in the openings of the gates in the city**

1:22

אמריה 561 תאמר 559: עד 5704 מתי 4970 פתים 6612 תאהבו 157 פתי 6612 ולצים 3887 לצון 3944

'amareyha ta'mer. 'ad matay patayim ta'aehabu petiy ualetziym, latzoun

**her words *saying* she utter How long when you simple ones will you love simplicity? and the scorners in scorning**

1:23

חמדו 2530 להם 1992 וכסילים 3684 ישנאו 8130 דעת 1847: תשובו 7725 לתוכחתי 8433 הנה 2009 אביעה 5042 לכם 3807a רוחי 7307

chamadu lahem; uaksiyliym, yisna'au da'at. tashubu, latoukachtiy hineh 'abiy'ah lakem ruchiy;

**delight their and fools hate knowledge? Turn you at my reproof behold I will pour out unto you my spirit**

1:24

אודיעה 3045 דברי 1697 אתכם 853: יען 3282 קראתי 7121 ותמאנו 3985 נטיתי 5186 ידי 3027

'audiy'ah dabaray 'atkem. ya'an qara'tiy uatama'aenu; natiytiy yadiy,

**I will make known my words unto you Because I have called and you refused I have stretched out my hand**

1:25 1:26

ואין 369 מקשיב 7181: ותפרעו 6544 כל 3605 עצתי 6098 ותוכחתי 8433 לא 3808 אביתם 14: גם 1571

ua'aeyn maqshiyb. uatipra'au kal 'atzatiy; uatoukachtiy, la' 'abiytem. gam

**and no man regarded But you have set at nought all my counsel and my reproof none *of* you would also**

1:27

אני 589 באידכם 343 אשחק 7832 אלעג 3932 בבא 935 פחדכם 6343: בבא 935 כשאוה 7584 פחדכם 6343

'aniy ba'aeydakem 'aschaq; 'al'ag, baba' pachdakem. baba' kasha'auah pachdakem,

**I at your calamity will laugh I will mock when comes your fear When comes as desolation your fear**

1:28

ואידכם 343 כסופה 5492 יאתה 857 בבא 935 עליכם 5921 צרה 6869 וצוקה 6695: אז 227 יקראנני 7121

ua'aeydakem kasupah ye'ateh; baba' 'aleykem, tzarah uatzuqah. 'az yiqra'ananiy

**and your destruction as a whirlwind he comes when comes upon you distress and anguish Then shall they call upon me**

1:29

ולא 3808 אענה 6030 ישחרנני 7836 ולא 3808 ימצאנני 4672: תחת 8478 כי 3588 שנאו 8130 דעת 1847

uala' 'a'aneh; yashacharuniy, uala' yimtza'ananiy. tachat kiy sana'au da'at;

**but not I will answer they shall seek me early but not they shall find me For that they hated knowledge**

Pro 1:14 Cast in your lot among us; let us all have one purse:15 My son, walk not you in the way with them; refrain your foot from their path:16 For their feet run to evil, and make haste to shed blood.17 Surely in vain the net is spread in the sight of any bird.18 And they lay wait for their own blood; they lurk privily for their own lives.19 So are the ways of everyone that is greedy of gain; which take away the life of the owners thereof.20 Wisdom crieth without; she uttereth her voice in the streets:21 She crieth in the chief place of concourse, in the openings of the gates: in the city she uttereth her words, saying,22 How long, you simple ones, will you love simplicity? and the scorners delight in their scorning, and fools hate knowledge?23 Turn you at my reproof: behold, I will pour out my spirit unto you, I will make known my words unto you.24 Because I have called, and you refused; I have stretched out my hand, and no man regarded;25 But you have set at nought all my counsel, and would none of my reproof:26 I also will laugh at your calamity; I will mock when your fear cometh;27 When your fear cometh as desolation, and your destruction cometh as a whirlwind; when distress and anguish cometh upon you. 28 Then shall they call upon me, but I will not answer; they shall seek me early, but they shall not find me:29 For that they hated knowledge,

| ויראת 3374 | יהוה 3068 | לא 3808 | בחרו 977: | 1:30 | לא 3808 | אבו 14 | לעצתי 6098 | נאצו 5006 | כל 3605 | תוכחתי 8433: | 1:31 |
|---|---|---|---|---|---|---|---|---|---|---|---|
| uayir'at | Yahuah | la' | bacharu. | | la' | 'abu | la'atzatiy; | na'atzu, | kal | toukachatiy. | |
| **and the fear of** | **Yahuah** | **not** | **did choose** | | **none** | **They would** | **of my counsel** | **they despised** | **all** | **my reproof** | |

| ויאכלו 398 | מפרי 6529 | דרכם 1870 | וממעצתיהם 4156 | ישבעו 7646: | 1:32 | כי 3588 | משובת 4878 |
|---|---|---|---|---|---|---|---|
| uaya'kalu | mipriy | darkam; | uamima'atzoteyhem | yisba'au. | | kiy | meshuba'at |
| **Therefore shall they eat** | **of the fruit of** | **their own way** | **and with their own devices** | **be filled** | | **For** | **the turning away** |

| פתים 6612 | תהרגם 2026 | ושלות 7962 | כסילים 3684 | תאבדם 6: | 1:33 | ושמע 8085 | לי 3807a |
|---|---|---|---|---|---|---|---|
| pata'yim | tahargem; | uashaluat | kasiyliym | ta'abdem. | | uashomea' | liy |
| ***of* the simple** | **shall slay them** | **and the prosperity of** | **fools** | **shall destroy them** | | **But whoso hearken** | **unto me** |

| ישכן 7931 | בטח 982 | ושאנן 7599 | מפחד 6343 | רעה 7451: |
|---|---|---|---|---|
| yishkan | betach; | uasha'anan, | mipachad | ra'ah. |
| **shall dwell safely** | | **and shall be quiet** | **from fear of** | **evil** |

| **Prov 2:1** | בני 1121 | אם 518 | תקח 3947 | אמרי 561 | ומצותי 4687 | תצפן 6845 | אתך 854: | 2:2 | להקשיב 7181 |
|---|---|---|---|---|---|---|---|---|---|
| | baniy | 'am | tiqach | 'amaray; | uamitzuotay, | titzpon | 'atak. | | lahaqshiyb |
| | **My son** | **if** | **you will receive** | **my words** | **and my commandments** | **hide** | **within you** | | **So that you incline** |

| לחכמה 2451 | אזנך 241 | תטה 5186 | לבך 3820 | לתבונה 8394: | 2:3 | כי 3588 | אם 518 | לבינה 998 | תקרא 7121 | לתבונה 8394 |
|---|---|---|---|---|---|---|---|---|---|---|
| lachakamah | 'azeneka; | tateh | libaka, | latabunah. | | kiy | 'am | labiynah | tiqraa'; | latabunah, |
| **unto wisdom** | **your ear** | ***and* apply** | **your heart** | **to understanding** | | **Yea** | **if** | **after knowledge** | **you cry** | **for understanding** |

| תתן 5414 | קולך 6963: | 2:4 | אם 518 | תבקשנה 1245 | ככסף 3701 | וכמטמונים 4301 | תחפשנה 2664: | 2:5 | אז 227 | תבין 995 |
|---|---|---|---|---|---|---|---|---|---|---|
| titen | qouleka. | | 'am | tabaqshenah | kakasep; | uakamatmouniym | tachpasenah. | | 'az, | tabiyn |
| ***and* lift up** | **your voice** | | **If** | **you seek her** | **as silver** | **and hid treasures** | **search for her *as for*** | | **Then** | **shall you understand** |

| יראת 3374 | יהוה 3068 | ודעת 1847 | אלהים 430 | תמצא 4672: | 2:6 | כי 3588 | יהוה 3068 | יתן 5414 | חכמה 2451 | מפיו 6310 |
|---|---|---|---|---|---|---|---|---|---|---|
| yir'at | Yahuah; | uada'at | 'alohiym | timtzaa'. | | kiy | Yahuah | yiten | chakamah | mipiyu, |
| **the fear of** | **Yahuah** | **the knowledge of** | **Elohim** | **find** | | **For** | **Yahuah** | **gives** | **wisdom** | **out of his mouth** |

| דעת 1847 | ותבונה 8394: | 2:7 | וצפן 6845 | לישרים 3477 | תושיה 8454 | מגן 4043 | להלכי 1980 |
|---|---|---|---|---|---|---|---|
| da'at | uatbunah. | | yitzapan | layashariym | tushiyah; | magen, | laholakey |
| ***comes* knowledge** | **and understanding** | | **He lay up** | **for the righteous** | **sound wisdom** | ***he is* a buckler** | **to them that walk** |

| תם 8537: | 2:8 | לנצר 5341 | ארחות 734 | משפט 4941 | ודרך 1870 | חסידו 2623 | ישמר 8104: | 2:9 | אז 227 | תבין 995 |
|---|---|---|---|---|---|---|---|---|---|---|
| tom. | | lintzor | 'arachout | mishapat; | uaderek | chasiydau | yishmor. | | 'az, | tabiyn |
| **uprightly** | | **He keep** | **the paths of** | **judgment** | **and the way of** | **his saints.** | **preserve** | | **Then** | **shall you understand** |

| צדק 6664 | ומשפט 4941 | ומישרים 4339 | כל 3605 | מעגל 4570 | טוב 2896: | 2:10 | כי 3588 | תבוא 935 | חכמה 2451 | בלבך 3820 |
|---|---|---|---|---|---|---|---|---|---|---|
| tzedeq | uamishpat; | uameyshariym, | kal | ma'gal | toub. | | kiy | tabou'a | chakamah | balibeka; |
| **righteousness** | **and judgment** | **and equity** | ***yea* every** | **path** | **good** | | **When** | **enter** | **wisdom** | **into your heart** |

| ודעת 1847 | לנפשך 5315 | ינעם 5276: | 2:11 | מזמה 4209 | תשמר 8104 | עליך 5921 | תבונה 8394 | תנצרכה 5341: |
|---|---|---|---|---|---|---|---|---|
| uada'at, | lanapshaka | yina'am. | | mazimah | tishmor | 'aleyka, | tabunah | tintzarekah. |
| **and knowledge** | **unto your soul** | **is pleasant** | | **Discretion** | **shall preserve** | **over you** | **understanding** | **shall keep you** |

Pro 1:29 and did not choose the fear of YHUH:30 They would none of my counsel: they despised all my reproof.31 Therefore shall they eat of the fruit of their own way, and be filled with their own devices.32 For the turning away of the simple shall slay them, and the prosperity of fools shall destroy them.33 But whoso hearkeneth unto me shall dwell safely, and shall be quiet from fear of evil. **Pro** 2:1 My son, if you will receive my words, and hide my commandments with you;2 So that you incline your ear unto wisdom, and apply your heart to understanding;3 Yea, if you criest after knowledge, and liftest up your voice for understanding;4 If you seek her as silver, and searchest for her as for hid treasures;5 Then shall you understand the fear of YHUH, and find the knowledge of G-d.6 For YHUH give wisdom: out of his mouth cometh knowledge and understanding.7 He layeth up sound wisdom for the righteous: he is a buckler to them that walk uprightly.8 He keep the paths of judgment, and preserveth the way of his saints.9 Then shall you understand righteousness, and judgment, and equity; yea, every good path. 10 When wisdom entereth into your heart, and knowledge is pleasant unto your soul;11 Discretion shall preserve you, understanding shall keep you:

**2:12** … **2:13**

להצילך 5337 מדרך 1870 רע 7451 מאיש 376 מדבר 1696 תהפכות 8419: העזבים 5800 ארחות 734
lahatziylaka miderek ra'; me'aysh, madaber tahpukout. ha'azabiym 'arachout
**To deliver you from the way of the evil *man* from the man that speak froward things Who leave the paths of**

ישר 3476 ללכת 1980 בדרכי 1870 חשך 2822: **2:14** השמחים 8056 לעשות 6213 רע 7451 יגילו 1523 בתהפכות 8419
yosher; laleket, badarkey choshek. hasamechiym la'asout ra'; yagiylu, batahpukout
**uprightness to walk in the ways of darkness Who rejoice to do evil *and* delight in the frowardness of**

רע 7451: **2:15** אשר 834 ארחתיהם 734 עקשים 6141 ונלוזים 3868 במעגלותם 4570: **2:16** להצילך 5337 מאשה 802
ra'. 'asher 'arachoteyhem 'aqshiym; uanalouziym, bam'agloutam. lahatziylaka me'ashah
**the wicked Whose ways of them *are* crooked and *they* froward in their paths To deliver you from woman**

זרה 2114 מנכריה 5237 אמריה 561 החליקה 2505: **2:17** העזבת 5800 אלוף 441 נעוריה 5271 ואת 853
zarah; minakariyah, 'amareyha hecheliyqah. ha'azebet 'alup na'aureyha; ua'at
***the* strange *even* from the stranger *with* her words *which* flatter Which forsake the guide of her youth *and***

ברית 1285 אלהיה 430 שכחה 7911: **2:18** כי 3588 שחה 7743 אל 413 מות 4194 ביתה 1004 ואל 413 רפאים 7496 מעגלתיה 4570: **2:19**
bariyt 'aloheyha shakechah. kiy shachah 'al mauet beytah; ua'al rapa'aym, ma'agloteyha.
**the covenant of her Elohim forget For inclineth unto death her house and unto *the* dead her paths**

כל 3605 באיה 935 לא 3808 ישובון 7725 ולא 3808 ישיגו 5381 ארחות 734 חיים 2416: **2:20** למען 4616 תלך 1980
kal ba'ayha la' yashubun; uala' yasiygu, 'arachout chayiym. lama'an, telek
**None that go unto her Nor return again and neither take they hold of the paths of life That you may walk**

בדרך 1870 טובים 2896 וארחות 734 צדיקים 6662 תשמר 8104: **2:21** כי 3588 ישרים 3477 ישכנו 7931 ארץ 776
baderek toubiym; ua'arachout tzadiyqiym tishmor. kiy yashariym yishkanu 'aretz;
**in the way of good *men* and the paths of the righteous keep For the upright shall dwell in the land**

ותמימים 8549 יותרו 3498 בה 871a: **2:22** ורשעים 7563 מארץ 776 יכרתו 3772 ובוגדים 898 יסחו 5255
uatamiymiym, yiuataru bah. uarsha'aym me'aretz yikaretu; uabougadiym, yisachu
**and the perfect shall remain in it But the wicked from the earth shall be cut off and the transgressors shall be rooted**

ממנה 4480:
mimenah.
**out of it**

**Prov 3:1** … **3:2**

בני 1121 תורתי 8451 אל 408 תשכח 7911 ומצותי 4687 יצר 5341 לבך 3820: כי 3588 ארך 753 ימים 3117 ושנות 8141
baniy touratiy 'al tishkach; uamitzuotay, yitzor libeka. kiy 'arek yamiym uashanout
**My son my law not forget but my commandments let keep your heart For length of days and long**

חיים 2416 ושלום 7965 יוסיפו 3254 לך 3807a: **3:3** חסד 2617 ואמת 571 אל 408 יעזבך 5800 קשרם 7194 על 5921 גרגרותיך 1621
chayiym; uashaloum, yousiypu lak. chesed ua'amet, 'al ya'azbuka qasharem 'al gargarouteyka;
**life and peace shall they add to you mercy and truth not Let forsake you bind them about your neck**

כתבם 3789 על 5921 לוח 3871 לבך 3820: **3:4** ומצא 4672 חן 2580 ושכל 7922 טוב 2896 בעיני 5869 אלהים 430
katabem, 'al luach libeka. umatzaa' chen uasekel toub; ba'aeyney 'alohiym
**write them upon the table of your heart So shall you find favor and understanding good in the sight of Elohim**

Pro 2:12 To deliver you from the way of the evil man, from the man that speaketh froward things;13 Who leave the paths of uprightness, to walk in the ways of darkness;14 Who rejoice to do evil, and delight in the frowardness of the wicked;15 Whose ways are crooked, and they froward in their paths:16 To deliver you from the strange woman, even from the stranger which flattereth with her words;17 Which forsaketh the guide of her youth, and forgetteth the covenant of her G-d.18 For her house inclineth unto death, and her paths unto the dead.19 None that go unto her return again, neither take they hold of the paths of life.20 That you may walk in the way of good men, and keep the paths of the righteous.21 For the upright shall dwell in the land, and the perfect shall remain in it.22 But the wicked shall be cut off from the earth, and the transgressors shall be rooted out of it. **Pro** 3:1 My son, forget not my law; but let your heart keep my commandments:2 For length of days, and long life, and peace, shall they add to you.3 Let not mercy and truth forsake you: bind them about your neck; write them upon the table of your heart: 4 So shall you find favor and good understanding in the sight of G-d and man.

3:5 3:6
ואדם 120: בטח 982 אל 413 יהוה 3068 בכל 3605 לבך 3820 ואל 413 בינתך 998 אל 408 תשען 8172: בכל 3605
ua'adam. batach 'al Yahuah bakal libeka; ua'al biynataka, 'al tisha'aen. bakal
**and man Trust in Yahuah with all your heart and unto your own understanding not lean In all**

3:7
דרכיך 1870 דעהו 3045 והוא 1931 יישר 3474 ארחתיך 734: אל 408 תהי 1961 חכם 2450 בעיניך 5869 ירא 3372 את 853
darakeyka da'aehu; uahu'a, yayasher 'arachoteyka. 'al tahiy chakam ba'aeyneyka; yara' 'at
**your ways acknowledge him and he shall direct your paths not Be wise in your own eyes fear**

3:8 3:9
יהוה 3069 וסור 5493 מרע 7451: רפאות 7500 תהי 1961 לשרך 8270 ושקוי 8250 לעצמותיך 6106: כבד 3513 את 853 יהוה 3068
Yahuah uasur mera'. rip'aut tahiy lashareka; uashiquy, la'atzmouteyka. kabed 'at Yahuah
**Yahuah and depart from evil health It shall be to your navel and marrow to your bones Honour Yahuah**

3:10
מהונך 1952 ומראשית 7225 כל 3605 תבואתך 8393: וימלאו 4390 אסמיך 618 שבע 7647
mehouneka; uamerea'shiyt, kal tabu'ateka. uayimala'au 'asameyka saba';
**with your substance and with the firstfruits of all your increase So shall be filled your barns *with* plenty**

3:11
ותירוש 8492 יקביך 3342 יפרצו 6555: מוסר 4148 יהוה 3068 בני 1121 אל 408 תמאס 3988 ואל 408 תקץ 6973
uatiyroush, yaqabeyka yiprotzu. musar Yahuah baniy 'al tim'as; ua'al taqotz,
**with new wine your presses shall burst out *with* the chastening of Yahuah My son not despise and neither be weary**

3:12 3:13
בתוכחתו 8433: כי 3588 את 853 אשר 834 יאהב 157 יהוה 3068 יוכיח 3198 וכאב 1 את 853 בן 1121 ירצה 7521:
batoukachatou. kiy 'at 'asher ye'ahab Yahuah youkiyach; uak'ab, 'at ben yirtzeh.
**of his correction For whom love Yahuah he correct even as a father the son *in whom* he delight**

3:14
אשרי 835 אדם 120 מצא 4672 חכמה 2451 ואדם 120 יפיק 6329 תבונה 8394: כי 3588 טוב 2896 סחרה 5504
'ashrey 'adam matza' chakamah ua'adam, yapiyq tabunah. kiy toub sacharah
**Happy *is* the man *that* finds wisdom and the man *that* get understanding For *is* better the merchandise of it**

3:15
מסחר 5505 כסף 3701 ומחרוץ 2742 תבואתה 8393: יקרה 3368 היא 1931 מפניים 6443 וכל 3605
mischar kasep; uamecharutz, tabu'atah. yaqarah hiy'a mipniyniym uakal
**than the merchandise of silver and than fine gold the gain thereof *is more* precious She than rubies and all**

3:16
חפציך 2656 לא 3808 ישוו 7737 בה 871a: ארך 753 ימים 3117 בימינה 3225 בשמאולה 8040
chapatzeyka, la' yishauu bah. 'arek yamiym biymiynah; bisma'ulah,
**the things you can desire not are to be compared unto her Length of days *is* in her right hand *and* in her left hand**

3:17 3:18
עשר 6239 וכבוד 3519: דרכיה 1870 דרכי 1870 נעם 5278 וכל 3605 נתיבותיה 5410 שלום 7965: עץ 6086 חיים 2416 היא 1931
'asher uakaboud. darakeyha darkey no'am; uakal natiybouteyha shaloum. 'aetz chayiym hiy'a
**riches and honor Her ways *are* ways of pleasantness and all her paths *are* peace *is* a tree of life She**

3:19
למחזיקים 2388 בה 871a ותמכיה 8551 מאשר 833: יהוה 3068 בחכמה 2451 יסד 3245
lamachaziyqiym bah; uatomakeyha ma'ashar. Yahuah bachakamah yasad
**to them that lay hold upon her and *is every one* that retain happy *is every one* Yahuah by wisdom has founded**

3:20
ארץ 776 כונן 3559 שמים 8064 בתבונה 8394: בדעתו 1847 תהומות 8415 נבקעו 1234 ושחקים 7834
'aretz; kounen shamayim, bitabunah. bada'ato tahoumout nibqa'au; uashchaqiym,
**the earth has he established the heavens by understanding By his knowledge the depths are broken up and the clouds**

Pro 3:5 Trust in YHUH with all your heart; and lean not unto your own understanding.6 In all your ways acknowledge him, and he shall direct your paths.7 Be not wise in your own eyes: fear YHUH, and depart from evil.8 It shall be health to your navel, and marrow to your bones.9 Honour YHUH with your substance, and with the firstfruits of all your increase:10 So shall your barns be filled with plenty, and your presses shall burst out with new wine.11 My son, despise not the chastening of YHUH; neither be weary of his correction:12 For whom YHUH love he correcteth; even as a father the son in whom he delighteth.13 Happy is the man that findeth wisdom, and the man that get understanding.14 For the merchandise of it is better than the merchandise of silver, and the gain thereof than fine gold.15 She is more precious than rubies: and all the things you canst desire are not to be compared unto her.16 Length of days is in her right hand; and in her left hand riches and honor.17 Her ways are ways of pleasantness, and all her paths are peace.18 She is a tree of life to them that lay hold upon her: and happy is everyone that retaineth her.19 YHUH by wisdom has founded the earth; by understanding has he established the heavens. 20 By his knowledge the depths are broken up, and the clouds drop down the dew.

3:21 ... 3:22

ירעפו 7491 טל 2919: בני 1121 אל 408 ילזו 3868 מעיניך 5869 נצר 5341 תשיה 8454 ומזמה 4209:
yira'apu tal. baniy 'al yaluzu me'aeyneyka; natzor tshiyah, uamazimah.
**drop down the dew My son not let them depart from your eyes keep sound wisdom and discretion**

3:23

ויהיו 1961 חיים 2416 לנפשך 5315 וחן 2580 לגרגרתיך 1621: אז 227 תלך 1980 לבטח 983 דרכך 1870
uayihayu chayiym lanapsheka; uachen, lagargaroteyka. 'az telek labetach darkeka;
**So shall they be life unto your soul and grace to your neck Then shall you walk safely in your way**

3:24

ורגלך 7272 לא 3808 תגוף 5062: אם 518 תשכב 7901 לא 3808 תפחד 6342 ושכבת 7901
uaraglaka, la' tigoup. 'am tishkab la' tipchad; uashakabta,
**and your foot not shall stumble When you liest down not you shall be afraid yea you shall lie down**

3:25

וערבה 6149 שנתך 8142: אל 408 תירא 3372 מפחד 6343 פתאם 6597 ומשאת 7722 רשעים 7563 כי 3588
ua'arabah shanateka. 'al tiyraa' mipachad pit'am; uamisho'at rasha'aym, kiy
**and shall be sweet your sleep not Be afraid of fear sudden neither of the desolation of the wicked when**

3:26 ... 3:27

תבא 935: כי 3588 יהוה 3068 יהיה 1961 בכסלך 3689 ושמר 8104 רגלך 7272 מלכד 3921: אל 408 תמנע 4513 טוב 2896
tabo'a. kiy Yahuah yihayeh bakisleka; uashamar raglaka milaked. 'al timna' toub
**it comes For Yahuah shall be your confidence and shall keep your foot from being taken no Withold good**

3:28

מבעליו 1167 בהיות 1961 לאל 410 ידיך 3027 לעשות 6213: אל 408 תאמר 559 לרעיך 7453 לך 1980
miba'alayu; bihayout la'ael yadeyka la'asout. 'al ta'mar lare'ayka lek
**from them to whom it is due when it is in the power (*El*) your hand to do *it* not Say unto your neighbor Go you**

3:29

ושוב 7725 ומחר 4279 אתן 5414 ויש 3426 אתך 854: אל 408 תחרש 2790 על 5921 רעך 7453 רעה 7451
uashub uamachar 'aten, uayesh 'atak. 'al tacharosh 'al re'aka ra'ah;
**and come again and to morrow I will give when you have it by you not evil against your neighbour Devise**

3:30

והוא 1931 יושב 3427 לבטח 983 אתך 854: אל 408 תרוב 7378 עם 5973 אדם 120 חנם 2600 אם 518 לא 3808 גמלך 1580
uahu'a yousheb labetach 'atak. 'al taroub 'am 'adam chinam; 'am la' gamalaka
**seeing he dwell securely by you not Strive with a man without cause if no he have done you**

3:31 ... 3:32

רעה 7451: אל 408 תקנא 7065 באיש 376 חמס 2555 ואל 408 תבחר 977 בכל 3605 דרכיו 1870: כי 3588 תועבת 8441 יהוה 3068
ra'ah. 'al taqanea' ba'aysh chamas; ua'al tibchar, bakal darakayu. kiy tou'abat Yahuah
**harm not Envy you man the oppressor and none choose of his ways For *is* abomination Yahuah**

3:33

נלוז 3868 ואת 853 ישרים 3477 סודו 5475: מארת 3994 יהוה 3068 בבית 1004 רשע 7563
nalouz; ua'at yashariym soudou. ma'aerat Yahuah babeyt rasha';
**the froward *but is with* the righteous his secret The curse of Yahuah *is* in the house of the wicked**

3:34 ... 3:35

ונוה 5116 צדיקים 6662 יברך 1288: אם 518 ללצים 3887 הוא 1931 יליץ 3887 ולעניים 6041 יתן 5414 חן 2580:
uanaueh tzadiyqiym yabarek. 'am laletziym hua' yaliytz; uala'aniyiym yiten chen.
**but the habitation of the just he bless Surely scorn he the scorners unto the lowly *but* he gives grace**

כבוד 3519 חכמים 2450 ינחלו 5157 וכסילים 3684 מרים 7311 קלון 7036:
kaboud chakamiym yinchalu; uaksiyliym, meriym qaloun.
**glory The wise shall inherit but fools *shall be* the promotion of shame**

Pro 3: 21 My son, let not them depart from your eyes: keep sound wisdom and discretion:22 So shall they be life unto your soul, and grace to your neck.23 Then shall you walk in your way safely, and your foot shall not stumble.24 When you liest down, you shall not be afraid: yea, you shall lie down, and your sleep shall be sweet.25 Be not afraid of sudden fear, neither of the desolation of the wicked, when it cometh.26 For YHUH shall be your confidence, and shall keep your foot from being taken.27 Withhold not good from them to whom it is due, when it is in the power of your hand to do it.28 Say not unto your neighbor, Go, and come again, and tomorrow I will give; when you have it by you.29 Devise not evil against your neighbor, seeing he dwell securely by you.30 Strive not with a man without cause, if he have done you no harm.31 Envy you not the oppressor, and choose none of his ways.32 For the froward is abomination to YHUH: but his secret is with the righteous.33 The curse of YHUH is in the house of the wicked: but he blesseth the habitation of the just.34 Surely he scorneth the scorners: but he give grace unto the lowly. 35 The wise shall inherit glory: but shame shall be the promotion of fools.

**Prov 4:1** … **4:2**

שמעו 8085 בנים 1121 מוסר 4148 אב 1 והקשיבו 7181 לדעת 3045 בינה 998: כי 3588 לקח 3948 טוב 2896

shim'au baniym musar 'ab; uahaqshiybu, lada'at biynah. kiy laqach toub

**Hear you children the instruction of a father and attend to know understanding For doctrine good**

**4:3**

נתתי 5414 לכם 3807a תורתי 8451 אל 408 תעזבו 5800: כי 3588 בן 1121 הייתי 1961 לאבי 1 רך 7390 ויחיד 3173 לפני 6440

natatiy lakem; touratiy, 'al ta'azobu. kiy ben hayiytiy la'abiy; rak uayachiyd, lipney

**I give to you my law not forsake you For son I was my father's tender and only *beloved* in the sight of**

**4:4**

אמי 517: וירני 3384 ויאמר 559 לי 3807a יתמך 8551 דברי 1697 לבך 3820 שמר 8104 מצותי 4687

'amiy. uayoreniy, uaya'mer liy, yitamak dabaray libeka; shamor mitzuotay

**my mother He taught me also and said unto me Let retain my words your heart keep my commandments**

**4:5** **4:6**

וחיה 2421: קנה 7069 חכמה 2451 קנה 7069 בינה 998 אל 408 תשכח 7911 ואל 408 תט 5186 מאמרי 561 פי 6310:

uachayeh. qaneh chakamah qaneh biynah; 'al tishkach ua'al tet, me'amrey piy.

**and live Get wisdom get understanding *it* not forget and neither decline from the words of my mouth**

**4:7**

אל 408 תעזבה 5800 ותשמרך 8104 אהבה 157 ותצרך 5341: ראשית 7225 חכמה 2451

'al ta'azbeha uatishmareka; 'ahabeha uatitzreka. ra'shiyt chakamah

**not Forsake her and she shall preserve you love her and she shall keep you *is* the principal thing Wisdom**

**4:8**

קנה 7069 חכמה 2451 ובכל 3605 קנינך 7075 קנה 7069 בינה 998: סלסלה 5549 ותרוממך 7311

qaneh chakamah uabkal qinyanaka, qaneh biynah. salsaleha uataroumameka;

***therefore* get wisdom and with all your getting get understanding Exalt her and she shall promote you**

**4:9**

תכבדך 3513 כי 3588 תחבקנה 2263: תתן 5414 לראשך 7218 לוית 3880 חן 2580 עטרת 5850

takabedaka, kiy tachabqenah. titen lara'shaka liuayat chen; 'ateret

**she shall bring you to honor when you do embrace her She shall give to your head an ornament of grace a crown of**

**4:10**

תפארת 8597 תמגנך 4042: שמע 8085 בני 1121 וקח 3947 אמרי 561 וירבו 7235 לך 3807a שנות 8141

tip'aret tamagneka. shama' baniy uaqach 'amaray; uayirbu laka, shanout

**glory shall she deliver to you Hear O my son and receive my sayings and shall be many to your the years of**

**4:11** **4:12**

חיים 2416: בדרך 1870 חכמה 2451 הרתיך 3384 הדרכתיך 1869 במעגלי 4570 ישר 3476: בלכתך 1980 לא 3808

chayiym. baderek chakamah horetiyka; hidraktiyka, bama'agley yosher. balektaka la'

**life in the way of wisdom I have taught you I have led you in paths right When you go not**

**4:13**

יצר 3334 צעדך 6806 ואם 518 תרוץ 7323 לא 3808 תכשל 3782: החזק 2388 במוסר 4148 אל 408 תרף 7503

yetzar tza'adeka; ua'am tarutz, la' tikashel. hachazeq bamusar 'al terep;

**shall be straitened your steps and when you run not you shall stumble Take fast hold of instruction *her* not let go**

**4:14**

נצרה 5341 כי 3588 היא 1931 חייך 2416: בארח 734 רשעים 7563 אל 408 תבא 935 ואל 408 תאשר 833 בדרך 1870 רעים 7451:

nitzreha, kiy hiy'a chayeyka. ba'arach rasha'aym 'al tabo'a; ua'al ta'asher, baderek ra'aym.

**keep her for she *is* your life into the path of the wicked not Enter and not go in the way of evil *men***

**4:15** **4:16**

פרעהו 6544 אל 408 תעבר 5674 בו 871a שטה 7847 מעליו 5921 ועבור 5674: כי 3588 לא 3808 ישנו 3462 אם 518 לא 3808

para'aehu 'al ta'abar bou; sateh me'alayu ua'abour. kiy la' yishanu 'am la'

**Avoid it no pass by it turn from it and pass away For not they sleep except for**

**Pro** 4:1 Hear, you children, the instruction of a father, and attend to know understanding.2 For I give you good doctrine, forsake you not my law.3 For I was my father's son, tender and only beloved in the sight of my mother.4 He taught me also, and said unto me, Let your heart retain my words: keep my commandments, and live.5 Get wisdom, get understanding: forget it not; neither decline from the words of my mouth.6 Forsake her not, and she shall preserve you: love her, and she shall keep you.7 Wisdom is the principal thing; therefore get wisdom: and with all your getting get understanding.8 Exalt her, and she shall promote you: she shall bring you to honor, when you dost embrace her.9 She shall give to your head an ornament of grace: a crown of glory shall she deliver to you.10 Hear, O my son, and receive my sayings; and the years of your life shall be many.11 I have taught you in the way of wisdom; I have led you in right paths.12 When you go, your steps shall not be straitened; and when you runnest, you shall not stumble.13 Take fast hold of instruction; let her not go: keep her; for she is your life. 14 Enter not into the path of the wicked, and go not in the way of evil men.15 Avoid it, pass not by it, turn from it, and pass away.16 For they sleep not, except they have done mischief; and their sleep is taken away, unless they cause some to fall.

4:17
ירעו 7489 ונגזלה 1497 שנתם 8142 אם 518 לא 3808 יכשולו 3782: כי 3588 לחמו 3898 לחם 3899
yare'au; uanigzalah shanatam, 'am la' yakshoulu kiy lachamu lachem
**they have done mischief and is taken away their sleep unless not they cause some to fall. For they eat the bread of**

4:18
רשע 7562 ויין 3196 חמסים 2555 ישתו 8354: וארח 734 צדיקים 6662 כאור 216 נגה 5051 הולך 1980
resha'; uayeyn chamasiym yishtu. ua'arach tzadiyqiym ka'aur nogah; houlek
**wickedness and the wine of violence drink But the path of the just *is* as light *the* shining more and more**

4:19 4:20
ואור 215 עד 5704 נכון 3559 היום 3117: דרך 1870 רשעים 7563 כאפלה 653 לא 3808 ידעו 3045 במה 1400 יכשלו 3782:
ua'aur, 'ad nakoun hayoum. derek rasha'aym ka'apelah; la' yada'au, bameh yikashelu.
**that shine until perfect the day The way of the wicked *is* as darkness not they know at what they stumble**

4:21
בני 1121 לדברי 1697 הקשיבה 7181 לאמרי 561 הט 5186 אזנך 241: אל 408 יליזו 3868 מעיניך 5869 שמרם 8104
baniy lidbaray haqashiybah; la'amaray, hat 'azaneka. 'al yaliyzu me'aeyneyka; shamarem,
**My son to my words attend unto my sayings incline your ear not Let them depart from your eyes keep them**

4:22 4:23
בתוך 8432 לבבך 3824: כי 3588 חיים 2416 הם 1992 למצאיהם 4672 ולכל 3605 בשרו 1320 מרפא 4832: מכל 3605
batouk lababeka. kiy chayiym hem lamotza'aeyhem; ualkal basarou marpea'. mikal
**in the midst of your heart For *are* life they unto those that find them and to all their flesh health with all**

4:24
משמר 4929 נצר 5341 לבך 3820 כי 3588 ממנו 4480 תוצאות 8444 חיים 2416: הסר 5493 ממך 4480 עקשות 6143 פה 6310
mishmar natzor libeka; kiy mimenu, totz'aut chayiym. haser mimaka 'aqashut peh;
**diligence Keep your heart for out of it *are* the issues of life Put away from you a froward mouth**

4:25
ולזות 3891 שפתים 8193 הרחק 7368 ממך 4480: עיניך 5869 לנכח 5227 יביטו 5027 ועפעפיך 6079 יישרו 3474
ualzut sapatayim, harcheq mimeka. 'aeyneyka lanokach yabiytu; ua'ap'apeyka, yayashiru
**and perverse lips put far from you your eyes right on Let look and let your eyelids let look straight**

4:26 4:27
נגדך 5048: פלס 6424 מעגל 4570 רגלך 7272 וכל 3605 דרכיך 1870 יכנו 3559: אל 408 תט 5186 ימין 3225
negdeka. pales ma'gal ragleka; uakal darakeyka yikonu. 'al tet yamiyn
**before you Ponder the path of your feet and all your ways let be established not Turn *to the* right hand**

ושמאול 8040 הסר 5493 רגלך 7272 מרע 7451:
uasma'ul; haser raglaka mera'.
**nor to the left remove your foot from evil**

**Prov 5:1** 5:2
בני 1121 לחכמתי 2451 הקשיבה 7181 לתבונתי 8394 הט 5186 אזנך 241: לשמר 8104 מזמות 4209
baniy lachakamatiy haqashiybah; litabunatiy, hat 'azaneka. lishmor mazimout;
**My son unto my wisdom attend to my understanding *and* bow your ear That you may regard discretion**

5:3
ודעת 1847 שפתיך 8193 ינצרו 5341: כי 3588 נפת 5317 תטפנה 5197 שפתי 8193 זרה 2114 וחלק 2509
uada'at, sapateyka yintzoru. kiy nopet titopanah siptey zarah; uachalaq
**and knowledge *that* your lips may keep For *as* an honeycomb drop the lips of a strange woman and smoother**

5:4 5:5
משמן 8081 חכה 2441: ואחריתה 319 מרה 4751 כלענה 3939 חדה 2299 כחרב 2719 פיות 6310: רגליה 7272 ירדות 3381 מות 4194
mishemen chikah. ua'achariytah marah kala'anah; chadah, kachereb piyout. ragleyha yoradout mauet;
**than oil her mouth *is* But her end *is* bitter as wormwood sharp as a sword twoedged Her feet go down *to* death**

Pro 4:17 For they eat the bread of wickedness, and drink the wine of violence.18 But the path of the just is as the shining light, that shineth more and more unto the perfect day.19 The way of the wicked is as darkness: they know not at what they stumble.20 My son, attend to my words; incline your ear unto my sayings.21 Let them not depart from your eyes; keep them in the midst of your heart.22 For they are life unto those that find them, and health to all their flesh.23 Keep your heart with all diligence; for out of it are the issues of life.24 Put away from you a froward mouth, and perverse lips put far from you.25 Let your eyes look right on, and let your eyelids look straight before you.26 Ponder the path of your feet, and let all your ways be established.27 Turn not to the right hand nor to the left: remove your foot from evil. **Pro** 5 1 My son, attend unto my wisdom, and bow your ear to my understanding:2 That you may regard discretion, and that your lips may keep knowledge.3 For the lips of a strange woman drop as an honeycomb, and her mouth is smoother than oil: 4 But her end is bitter as wormwood, sharp as a twoedged sword.5 Her feet go down to death; her steps take hold on hell.

5:6

שאול 7585 צעדיה 6806 יתמכו 8551: ארח 734 חיים 2416 פן 6435 תפלס 6424 נעו 5128 מעגלתיה 4570 לא 3808
sha'aul, tza'adeyha yitmoku. 'arach chayiym pen tapales; na'au ma'agloteyha, la'
**hell (*grave*) her steps take hold on the path of life Lest you should ponder are moveable her ways not**

5:7

תדע 3045: ועתה 6258 בנים 1121 שמעו 8085 לי 3807a ואל 408 תסורו 5493 מאמרי 561
teda'. ua'atah baniym shim'au liy; ua'al tasuru, me'amrey
***that* you can know *them* now therefore O you children Hear me and not depart from the words of**

5:8 5:9

פי 6310: הרחק 7368 מעליה 5921 דרכך 1870 ואל 408 תקרב 7126 אל 413 פתח 6607 ביתה 1004: פן 6435 תתן 5414 לאחרים 312
piy. harcheq me'aleyha darkeka; ua'al tiqrab, 'al petach beytah. pen titen la'acheriym
**my mouth Remove far from her your way and not come near to the door of her house Lest you give unto others**

5:10

הודך 1935 ושנתיך 8141 לאכזרי 394: פן 6435 ישבעו 7646 זרים 2114 כחך 3581 ועצביך 6089
houdeka; uashanoteyka, la'akzariy. pen yisba'au zariym kocheka; ua'atzabeyka,
**your honor and your years unto the cruel Lest be filled strangers *with* your wealth and your labours**

5:11 5:12

בבית 1004 נכרי 5237: ונהמת 5098 באחריתך 319 בכלות 3615 בשרך 1320 ושארך 7607:
babeyt nakariy. uanahamta ba'achariyteka; biklout basarka, uasha'aereka.
***be* in the house of a stranger And you mourn at the last when are consumed your flesh and your body**

5:13

ואמרת 559 איך 349 שנאתי 8130 מוסר 4148 ותוכחת 8433 נאץ 5006 לבי 3820: ולא 3808 שמעתי 8085 בקול 6963
ua'amarta, 'aeyk sanea'tiy musar; uatoukachat, na'atz libiy. uala' shama'atiy baqoul
**And you say How have I hated instruction and reproof despised my heart And not have obeyed the voice of**

5:14

מורי 3384 ולמלמדי 3925 לא 3808 הטיתי 5186 אזני 241: כמעט 4592 הייתי 1961 בכל 3605 רע 7451 בתוך 8432
mouray; ualimlamday, la' hitiytiy 'azaniy. kima'at hayiytiy bakal ra'; batouk
**my teachers to them that instructed me nor inclined mine ear almost I was in all evil in the midst of**

5:15 5:16

קהל 6951 ועדה 5712: שתה 8354 מים 4325 מבורך 953 ונזלים 5140 מתוך 8432 בארך 875:
qahal ua'aedah. shateh mayim miboureka; uanozaliym, mitouk ba'aereka.
**the congregation and assembly Drink waters out of your own cistern and running waters out of your own well**

5:17

יפוצו 6327 מעינתיך 4599 חוצה 2351 ברחבות 7339 פלגי 6388 מים 4325: יהיו 1961 לך 3807a לבדך 905 ואין 369
yaputzu ma'ayanoteyka chutzah; barachobout, palgey mayim. yihayu laka labadeka; ua'aeyn
**Let be dispersed your fountains abroad in the streets *and* rivers of waters Let them be your own only and not**

5:18 5:19

לזרים 2114 אתך 854: יהי 1961 מקורך 4726 ברוך 1288 ושמח 8055 מאשת 802 נעורך 5271: אילת 365
lazariym 'atak. yahiy maqouraka baruk; uasamach, me'aeshet na'aureka. 'ayelet
**strangers' with you Let be your fountain blessed and rejoice with the wife of your youth *Let her be as* hind**

5:20

אהבים 158 ויעלת 3280 חן 2580 דדיה 1717 ירוך 7301 בכל 3605 עת 6256 באהבתה 160 תשגה 7686 תמיד 8548:
'ahabiym, uaya'alat chen dadeyha yarauuka bakal 'aet; ba'ahabatah, tishgeh tamiyd.
**loving and roe pleasant her breasts let satisfy you at all times *and* with her love be you ravished always**

5:21

ולמה 4100 תשגה 7686 בני 1121 בזרה 2114 ותחבק 2263 חק 2436 נכריה 5237: כי 3588 נכח 5227
ualamah tishgeh baniy bazarah; uatachabeq, chek nakariyah. kiy nokach
**And why will you be ravished my son with a strange woman and embrace the bosom of a stranger? For *are* before**

Pro 5:6 Lest you should ponder the path of life, her ways are moveable, that you canst not know them.7 Hear me now therefore, O you children, and depart not from the words of my mouth.8 Remove your way far from her, and come not nigh the door of her house:9 Lest you give your honor unto others, and your years unto the cruel:10 Lest strangers be filled with your wealth; and your labours be in the house of a stranger;11 And you mourn at the last, when your flesh and your body are consumed,12 And say, How have I hated instruction, and my heart despised reproof;13 And have not obeyed the voice of my teachers, nor inclined mine ear to them that instructed me!14 I was almost in all evil in the midst of the congregation and assembly.15 Drink waters out of your own cistern, and running waters out of your own well.16 Let your fountains be dispersed abroad, and rivers of waters in the streets.17 Let them be only your own, and not strangers' with you.18 Let your fountain be blessed: and rejoice with the wife of your youth.19 Let her be as the loving hind and pleasant roe; let her breasts satisfy you at all times; and be you ravished always with her love. 20 And why will you, my son, be ravished with a strange woman, and embrace the bosom of a stranger?21 For the ways of man are before the eyes of YHUH, and he pondereth all his goings.

עיני 5869 | יהוה 3069 | דרכי 1870 | איש 376 | וכל 3605 | מעגלתיו 4570 | מפלס 6424: | **5:22** | עוונותיו 5771 | ילכדנו 3920 | את 853
'aeyney | Yahuah | darkey | 'aysh; | uakal | ma'aglotayu | mapales. | | auounoutayu, | yilkadunou | 'at
**the eyes of** | **Yahuah** | **the ways of** | **man** | **and all** | **his goings** | **he ponder** | | **His own iniquities** | **shall take**

הרשע 7563 | ובחבלי 2256 | חטאתו 2403 | יתמך 8551: | **5:23** | הוא 1931 | ימות 4191 | באין 369 | מוסר 4148
harasha'; | uabchabley | chata'tou, | yitamek. | | hua', | yamut | ba'aeyn | musar;
**the wicked himself** | **and he shall be holden** | **his sins** | ***with* the cords of** | | **He** | **shall die** | **without** | **instruction**

וברב 7230 | אולתו 200 | ישגה 7686:
uabrob | 'aualtou | yishgeh.
**and in the greatness of** | **his folly** | **he shall go astray**

**Prov 6:1** | בני 1121 | אם 518 | ערבת 6148 | לרעך 7453 | תקעת 8628 | לזר 2114 | כפיך 3709: | **6:2** | נוקשת 3369
| baniy | 'am | 'arabta | lare'aka; | taqa'ata | lazar | kapeyka. | | nouqashta
| **My son** | **if** | **you be surety** | **for your friend** | ***if* you have stricken** | **with a stranger** | **your hand** | | **You are snared**

באמרי 561 | פיך 6310 | נלכדת 3920 | באמרי 561 | פיך 6310: | **6:3** | עשה 6213 | זאת 2063 | אפוא 645 | בני 1121
ba'amrey | piyka; | nilkadta, | ba'amrey | piyka. | | 'aseh | za't | aepou'a | baniy
**with the words of** | **your mouth** | **you are taken** | **with the words of** | **your mouth** | | **Do** | **this** | **now** | **my son**

והנצל 5337 | כי 3588 | באת 935 | בכף 3709 | רעך 7453 | לך 1980 | התרפס 7511 | ורהב 7292
uahinatzel, | kiy | ba'ta | bakap | re'aka; | lek | hitrapes, | uarahab
**and deliver yourself** | **when** | **you are come** | **into the hand of** | **your friend** | **Go you** | **humble yourself** | **and make sure**

רעיך 7453: | **6:4** | אל 408 | תתן 5414 | שנה 8142 | לעיניך 5869 | ותנומה 8572 | לעפעפיך 6079: | **6:5** | הנצל 5337 | כצבי 6643 | מיד 3027
re'ayka. | | 'al | titen | shenah | la'aeyneyka; | uatanumah, | la'ap'apeyka. | | hinatzel | kitzbiy | miyad;
**your friend** | | **not** | **Give** | **sleep** | **to your eyes** | **nor slumber** | **to your eyelids** | | **Deliver yourself** | **as a roe** | **from the hand**

וכצפור 6833 | מיד 3027 | יקוש 3353: | **6:6** | לך 1980 | אל 413 | נמלה 5244 | עצל 6102 | ראה 7200 | דרכיה 1870
uaktzipour, | miyad | yaqush. | | lek | 'al | namalah | 'atzel; | ra'aeh | darakeyha
***of the hunter* and as a bird** | **from the hand of** | **the fowler** | | **Go you** | **to** | **the ant** | **you sluggard** | **consider** | **her ways**

וחכם 2449: | **6:7** | אשר 834 | אין 369 | לה 3807a | קצין 7101 | שטר 7860 | ומשל 4910: | **6:8** | תכין 3559 | בקיץ 7019 | לחמה 3899 | אגרה 103
uachakam. | | 'asher | 'aeyn | lah | qatziyn, | shoter | uamoshel. | | takiyn | baqayitz | lachamah; | 'agarah
**and be wise** | | **Which** | **no** | **having** | **guide** | **overseer** | **or ruler** | | **Provide** | **in the summer** | **her meat** | ***and* gathered**

בקציר 7105 | מאכלה 3978: | **6:9** | עד 5704 | מתי 4970 | עצל 6102 | תשכב 7901 | מתי 4970 | תקום 6965 | משנתך 8142: | **6:10**
baqatziyr, | ma'akalah. | | 'ad | matay | 'atzel | tishkab; | matay, | taqum | mishnateka.
**in the harvest** | **her food** | | **How long** | **when** | **O sluggard?** | **will you sleep** | **when** | **will you arise** | **out of your sleep?**

מעט 4592 | שנות 8142 | מעט 4592 | תנומות 8572 | מעט 4592 | חבק 2264 | ידים 3027 | לשכב 7901: | **6:11** | ובא 935 | כמהלך 1980
ma'at | shenout | ma'at | tanumout; | ma'at | chibuq | yadayim | lishkab. | | uaba' | kimhalek
***Yet* a little** | **sleep** | **a little** | **slumber** | **a little** | **folding of** | **the hands** | **to sleep** | | **So shall come** | **as one that travel**

ראשך 7389 | ומחסרך 4270 | כאיש 376 | מגן 4043: | **6:12** | אדם 120 | בליעל 1100 | איש 376 | און 205 | הולך 1980 | עקשות 6143 | פה 6310:
rea'sheka; | uamachasoraka, | ka'aysh | magen. | | 'adam | baliya'al | 'aysh | 'auen; | houlek, | 'aqashut | peh.
**your poverty** | **and your want** | **as an man** | **armed** | | **A person** | **naughty** | **a man** | **wicked** | **walk** | ***with* a froward** | **mouth**

Pro 5:22 His own iniquities shall take the wicked himself, and he shall be holden with the cords of his sins.23 He shall die without instruction; and in the greatness of his folly he shall go astray. **Pro** 6:1 My son, if you be surety for your friend, if you have stricken your hand with a stranger,2 Thou are snared with the words of your mouth, you are taken with the words of your mouth.3 Do this now, my son, deliver thyself, when you are come into the hand of your friend; go, humble thyself, and make sure your friend.4 Give not sleep to your eyes, nor slumber to your eyelids.5 Deliver thyself as a roe from the hand of the hunter, and as a bird from the hand of the fowler.6 Go to the ant, you sluggard; consider her ways, and be wise:7 Which having no guide, overseer, or ruler,8 Provideth her meat in the summer, and gathereth her food in the harvest.9 How long will you sleep, O sluggard? when will you arise out of your sleep?10 Yet a little sleep, a little slumber, a little folding of the hands to sleep: 11 So shall your poverty come as one that travelleth, and your want as an armed man.12 A naughty person, a wicked man, walk with a froward mouth.

6:13 קרץ 7169 | בעיניו 5869 | מלל 4448 | ברגלו 7272 | מרה 3384 | באצבעתיו 676: | 6:14 תהפכות 8419 | בלבו 3820 | חרש 2790
qoretz | ba'aeynayu | molel | baraglayu; | moreh, | ba'atzba'atayu. | tahpukout | balibou, | choresh
**He wink | with his eyes | he speak | with his feet | he teach | with his fingers | Frowardness | *is* in his heart | he devise**

רע 7451 | בכל 3605 | עת 6256 | מדנים 4090 | ישלח 7971: | 6:15 על 5921 | כן 3651 | פתאם 6597 | יבוא 935 | אידו 343 | פתע 6621
ra' | bakal | 'aet; | medaniym | yashaleach. | 'al | ken, | pit'am | yabou'a | 'aeydou; | peta'
**mischief | in all | continually | discord. | he sow | Therefore | after that | suddenly | shall come | his calamity | suddenly**

ישבר 7665 | ואין 369 | מרפא 4832: | 6:16 שש 8337 | הנה 2007 | שנא 8130 | יהוה 3068 | ושבע 7651 | תועבות 8441
yishaber, | ua'aeyn | marpea'. | shesh | henah | sanea' | Yahuah; | uasheba', | tou'about
**shall he be broken | and without | remedy | six | These | *things* does hate | Yahuah | yea seven | *are* an abomination unto**

נפשו 5315: | 6:17 עינים 5869 | רמות 7311 | לשון 3956 | שקר 8267 | וידים 3027 | שפכות 8210 | דם 1818 | נקי 5355: | 6:18 לב 3820 | חרש 2790
napshou. | 'aeynayim | ramout | lashoun | shaqer; | uayadayim, | shopakout | dam | naqiy. | leb, | choresh
**him | A look | proud | a tongue | lying | and hands | that shed | blood | innocent | An heart | that devise**

מחשבות 4284 | און 205 | רגלים 7272 | ממהרות 4116 | לרוץ 7323 | לרעה 7451: | 6:19 יפיח 6315 | כזבים 3577 | עד 5704 | שקר 8267
machashabout | 'auen; | raglayim | mamaharout, | larutz | lara'ah. | yapiyach | kazabiym | 'aed | shaqer;
**imaginations | wicked | feet | that be swift | in running | to mischief | *that* speak | lies | A witness | false**

ומשלח 7971 | מדנים 4090 | בין 996 | אחים 251: | 6:20 נצר 5341 | בני 1121 | מצות 4687 | אביך 1 | ואל 408 | תטש 5203 | תורת 8451
uamashaleach | madaniym, | beyn | 'achiym. | natzor | baniy | mitzuat | 'abiyka; | ua'al | titosh, | tourat
**and he that sow | discord | among | brethren | keep | My son | commandment | your father's | and not | forsake | the law of**

אמך 517: | 6:21 קשרם 7194 | על 5921 | לבך 3820 | תמיד 8548 | ענדם 6029 | על 5921 | גרגרתך 1621: | 6:22 בהתהלכך 1980
'ameka. | qasharem | 'al | libaka | tamiyd; | 'anadem, | 'al | gargaroteka. | bahithalekka
**your mother | Bind them | upon | your heart | continually | *and* tie them | around about | your neck | When you go**

תנחה 5148 | אתך 853 | בשכבך 7901 | תשמר 8104 | עליך 5921 | והקיצות 6974 | היא 1931 | תשיחך 7878: | 6:23 כי 3588 | נר 5216
tancheh | 'atak, | bashakbaka | tishmor | 'aleyka; | uahaqiytzouta, | hiy'a | tasiycheka. | kiy | ner
**it shall lead | you | when you sleep | it shall keep | you over | and *when* you awake | it | shall talk with you | For *is* | a lamp**

מצוה 4687 | ותורה 8451 | אור 216 | ודרך 1870 | חיים 2416 | תוכחות 8433 | מוסר 4148: | 6:24 לשמרך 8104 | מאשת 802
mitzuah | uatourah | 'aur; | uaderek | chayiym, | toukachout | musar. | lishmaraka | me'aeshet
**the commandment | and the law *is* | light | and the way of | life | reproofs of | instruction *are* | To keep you | from woman**

רע 7451 | מחלקת 2513 | לשון 3956 | נכריה 5237: | 6:25 אל 408 | תחמד 2530 | יפיה 3308 | בלבבך 3824 | ואל 408
ra'; | mechelqat, | lashoun | nakariyah. | 'al | tachmod | yapayah | bilbabeka; | ua'al
***the* evil | from the flattery of | the tongue of | a strange woman | not | Lust after | her beauty | in your heart | and neither**

תקחך 3947 | בעפעפיה 6079: | 6:26 כי 3588 | בעד 1157 | אשה 802 | זונה 2181 | עד 5704 | ככר 3603 | לחם 3899
tiqachaka, | ba'ap'apeyha. | kiy | ba'ad | 'ashah | zounah, | 'ad | kikar | lachem
**let her take you | with her eyelids | For | by means of | a woman *a man is brought* | whorish | to | a piece of | bread**

ואשת 802 | איש 376 | נפש 5315 | יקרה 3368 | תצוד 6679: | 6:27 היחתה 2846 | איש 376 | אש 784 | בחיקו 2436 | ובגדיו 899 | לא 3808
ua'ashet | 'aysh; | nepesh | yaqarah | tatzud. | hayachateh | 'aysh | 'aesh | bacheyqou; | uabgadayu, | la'
**and the adulteress | he | life | *the* precious | will hunt for | Can take | a man | fire | in his bosom | and his clothes | not**

Pro 6:13 He winketh with his eyes, he speaketh with his feet, he teach with his fingers;14 Frowardness is in his heart, he deviseth mischief continually; he soweth discord.15 Therefore shall his calamity come suddenly; suddenly shall he be broken without remedy.16 These six things doth YHUH hate: yea, seven are an abomination unto him:17 A proud look, a lying tongue, and hands that shed innocent blood,18 An heart that deviseth wicked imaginations, feet that be swift in running to mischief,19 A false witness that speaketh lies, and he that soweth discord among brethren.20 My son, keep your father's commandment, and forsake not the law of your mother:21 Bind them continually upon your heart, and tie them about your neck.22 When you go, it shall lead you; when you sleepest, it shall keep you; and when you awakest, it shall talk with you.23 For the commandment is a lamp; and the law is light; and reproofs of instruction are the way of life:24 To keep you from the evil woman, from the flattery of the tongue of a strange woman.25 Lust not after her beauty in your heart; neither let her take you with her eyelids. 26 For by means of a whorish woman a man is brought to a piece of bread: and the adulteress will hunt for the precious life.27 Can a man take fire in his bosom, and his clothes not be burned?

6:28 6:29

תשרפנה 8313: אם 518 יהלך 1980 איש 376 על 5921 הגחלים 1513 ורגליו 7272 לא 3808 תכוינה 3554: כן 3651 הבא 935 אל 413

tisarapnah. 'am yahalek 'aysh 'al hagechaliym; uaraglayu, la' tikaueynah. ken, habaa' 'al

**be burned if Can go one upon hot coals and his feet not be burned? So he that goes in to**

6:30

אשת 802 רעהו 7453 לא 3808 ינקה 5352 כל 3605 הנגע 5060 בה 871a: לא 3808 יבוזו 936 לגנב 1590 כי 3588 יגנוב 1589

'aeshet re'aehu; la' yinaqeh, kal hanogea' bah. la' yabuzu laganab kiy yignoub;

**wife his neighbour's will not shall be innocent whosoever touch her *Men* not do despise a thief if he steal**

6:31

למלא 4390 נפשו 5315 כי 3588 ירעב 7456: ונמצא 4672 ישלם 7999 שבעתים 7659 את 853 כל 3605 הון 1952

lamalea' napshou, kiy yir'ab. uanimtzaa' yashalem shib'atayim; 'at kal houn

**to satisfy his soul when he is hungry But *if* he be found he shall restore sevenfold all the substance of**

6:32

ביתו 1004 יתן 5414: נאף 5003 אשה 802 חסר 2638 לב 3820 משחית 7843 נפשו 5315 הוא 1931

beytou yiten. no'aep 'ashah chasar leb; mashchiyt napshou, hua'

**his house he shall give *But* whoso commit adultery *with* a woman lack understanding destroy his own soul he**

6:33 6:34

יעשנה 6213: נגע 5061 וקלון 7036 ימצא 4672 וחרפתו 2781 לא 3808 תמחה 4229: כי 3588 קנאה 7068

ya'asenah. nega' uaqaloun yimtza'; uacherpatou, la' timacheh. kiy qin'ah

***that* does it A wound and dishonour shall he get and his reproach not shall be wiped away For jealousy**

6:35

חמת 2534 גבר 1397 ולא 3808 יחמול 2550 ביום 3117 נקם 5359: לא 3808 ישא 5375 פני 6440 כל 3605 כפר 3724

chamat gaber; uala' yachmoul, bayoum naqam. la' yisaa' paney kal koper;

***is* the rage of a man and therefore not he will spare in the day of vengeance not He will regard accept any ransom**

ולא 3808 יאבה 14 כי 3588 תרבה 7235 שחד 7810:

uala' ya'beh, kiy tarbeh shochad.

**and neither will he rest content though you give many gifts**

**Prov 7:1** 7:2

בני 1121 שמר 8104 אמרי 561 ומצותי 4687 תצפן 6845 אתך 854: שמר 8104 מצותי 4687 וחיה 2421

baniy shamor 'amaray; uamitzuotay, titzpon 'atak. shamor mitzuotay uachayeh;

**My son keep my words and my commandments lay up with you Keep my commandments and live**

7:3 7:4

ותורתי 8451 כאישון 380 עיניך 5869: קשרם 7194 על 5921 אצבעתיך 676 כתבם 3789 על 5921 לוח 3871 לבך 3820:

uatouratiy, ka'ayshoun 'aeyneyka. qasharem 'al 'atzba'ateyka; katabem, 'al luach libeka.

**and my law as the apple of your eye Bind them upon your fingers write them upon the table of your heart**

7:5

אמר 559 לחכמה 2451 אחתי 269 את 859 ומדע 4129 לבינה 998 תקרא 7121: לשמרך 8104 מאשה 802

'amor lachakamah 'achotiy 'at; uamodaa', labiynah tiqraa'. lishmaraka me'ashah

**Say unto wisdom *are* my sister *You* and kinswoman understanding *your* call That they may keep you from woman**

7:6

זרה 2114 מנכריה 5237 אמריה 561 החליקה 2505: כי 3588 בחלון 2474 ביתי 1004 בעד 1157 אשנבי 822

zarah; minakariyah, 'amareyha hecheliyqah. kiy bachaloun beytiy; ba'ad 'ashnabiy

***the* strange from the stranger *with* her words *which* flatter For at the window of my house through my casement**

7:7

נשקפתי 8259: וארא 7200 בפתאים 6612 אבינה 995 בבנים 1121 נער 5288 חסר 2638 לב 3820:

nishqapatiy. ua'aera' bapataa'yim, 'abiynah babaniym, na'ar chasar leb.

**I looked And beheld among the simple ones I discerned among the youths a young man void of understanding**

Pro 6:28 Can one go upon hot coals, and his feet not be burned?29 So he that go in to his neighbor's wife; whosoever touch her shall not be innocent.30 Men do not despise a thief, if he steal to satisfy his soul when he is hungry;31 But if he be found, he shall restore sevenfold; he shall give all the substance of his house.32 But whoso committeth adultery with a woman lacketh understanding: he that doeth it destroyeth his own soul.33 A wound and dishonour shall he get; and his reproach shall not be wiped away.34 For jealousy is the rage of a man: therefore he will not spare in the day of vengeance.35 He will not regard any ransom; neither will he rest content, though you givest many gifts. **Pro** 7:1 My son, keep my words, and lay up my commandments with you.2 Keep my commandments, and live; and my law as the apple of your eye.3 Bind them upon your fingers, write them upon the table of your heart.4 Say unto wisdom, Thou are my sister; and call understanding your kinswoman:5 That they may keep you from the strange woman, from the stranger which flattereth with her words.6 For at the window of my house I looked through my casement, 7 And beheld among the simple ones, I discerned among the youths, a young man void of understanding,

7:8 עבר 5674 בשוק 7784 אצל 681 פנה 6438 ודרך 1870 ביתה 1004 יצעד 6805: 7:9 בנשף 5399 בערב 6153 יום 3117
'aber bashuq 'aetzel pinah; uaderek beytah yitza'ad. baneshep ba'areb youm;
**Passing through the street near her corner and the way to her house he went In the twilight in the evening time**

באישון 380 לילה 3915 ואפלה 653: 7:10 והנה 2009 אשה 802 לקראתו 7125 שית 7897 זונה 2181 ונצרת 5341
ba'ayshoun layalah, ua'apelah. uahineh 'ashah liqra'tou; shiyt zounah, uanatzurat
**in the black night and dark And behold a woman *there* met him *with* the attire of an harlot and subtil of**

לב 3820: 7:11 המיה 1993 היא 1931 וסררת 5637 בביתה 1004 לא 3808 ישכנו 7931 רגליה 7272: 7:12 פעם 6471 בחוץ 2351 פעם 6471
leb. homiyah hiy'a uasoraret; babeytah, la' yishkanu ragleyha. pa'am bachutz, pa'am
**heart *is* loud She and stubborn in her house not abide her feet Now *is she* without now**

ברחבות 7339 ואצל 681 כל 3605 פנה 6438 תארב 693: 7:13 והחזיקה 2388 בו 871a ונשקה 5401 לו 3807a העזה 5810 פניה 6440
barachobout; ua'aetzel kal pinah te'arob. uahecheziyqah bou uanashaqah lou'; he'aezah paneyha,
**in the streets and at every corner lies in wait So she caught him and kissed him *and with* an impudent face**

ותאמר 559 לו 3807a: 7:14 זבחי 2077 שלמים 8002 עלי 5921 היום 3117 שלמתי 7999 נדרי 5088: 7:15 על 5921 כן 3651
uata'mar lou'. zibchey shalamiym 'alay; hayoum, shilamtiy nadaray. 'al ken
**and said unto him *I have* offerings peace with me this day have I payed my vows Therefore after that**

יצאתי 3318 לקראתך 7125 לשחר 7836 פניך 6440 ואמצאך 4672: 7:16 מרבדים 4765 רבדתי 7234
yatza'tiy liqra'teka; lashacher paneyka, ua'amtzaa'aka. marbadiym rabadtiy
**came I forth to meet you diligently to seek your face and I have found you *with* coverings of tapestry I have decked**

ערשי 6210 חטבות 2405 אטון 330 מצרים 4714: 7:17 נפתי 5130 משכבי 4904 מר 4753 אהלים 174
'arsiy; chatubout, 'aetun mitzrayim. naptiy mishkabiy; mor 'ahaliym,
**my bed *with* carved *works with* fine linen of Egypt I have perfumed my bed *with* myrrh aloes**

וקנמון 7076: 7:18 לכה 1980 נרוה 7301 דדים 1730 עד 5704 הבקר 1242 נתעלסה 5965 באהבים 159: 7:19 כי 3588
uaqinamoun. lakah nirueh dodiym 'ad haboqer; nit'alsah, ba'ahabiym. kiy
**and cinnamon Come let us take our fill of love until the morning let us solace ourselves with loves For**

אין 369 האיש 376 בביתו 1004 הלך 1980 בדרך 1870 מרחוק 7350: 7:20 צרור 6872 הכסף 3701 לקח 3947 בידו 3027 ליום 3117
'aeyn ha'aysh babeytou; halak, baderek merachouq. tzarour hakesep laqach bayadou; layoum
***is* not the goodman at home he is gone a journey long a bag of money He has taken with him at the day**

הכסא 3677 יבא 935 ביתו 1004: 7:21 הטתו 5186 ברב 7230 לקחה 3948 בחלק 2506 שפתיה 8193
hakesa', yaba' beytou. hitatu barob liqchah; bacheleq sapateyha,
**appointed *and* will come home she caused him to yield With much her fair speech with the flattering of her lips**

תדיחנו 5080: 7:22 הולך 1980 אחריה 310 פתאם 6597 כשור 7794 אל 413 טבח 2874 יבוא 935 וכעכס 5914 אל 413
tadiychenu. houlek 'achareyha, pit'am kashour 'al tabach yabou'a; uak'akes, 'al
**she forced him He goes after her straightway as an ox to *the* slaughter goes or as the stocks to**

מוסר 4148 אויל 191: 7:23 עד 5704 יפלח 6398 חץ 2671 כבדו 3516 כמהר 4116 צפור 6833 אל 413 פח 6341 ולא 3808 ידע 3045 כי 3588
musar 'auiyl. 'ad yapalach chetz kabedou, kamaher tzipour 'al pach; uala' yada', kiy
**the correction of a fool Till strike through a dart his liver as hasten a bird to the snare and not knows that**

Pro 7:8 Passing through the street near her corner; and he went the way to her house,9 In the twilight, in the evening, in the black and dark night:10 And, behold, there met him a woman with the attire of an harlot, and subtle of heart.11(She is loud and stubborn; her feet abide not in her house:12 Now is she without, now in the streets, and lie in wait at every corner.)13 So she caught him, and kissed him, and with an impudent face said unto him,14 I have peace offerings with me; this day have I payed my vows.15 Therefore came I forth to meet you, diligently to seek your face, and I have found you.16 I have decked my bed with coverings of tapestry, with carved works, with fine linen of Egypt.17 I have perfumed my bed with myrrh, aloes, and cinnamon.18 Come, let us take our fill of love until the morning: let us solace ourselves with loves.19 For the goodman is not at home, he is gone a long journey:20 He has taken a bag of money with him, and will come home at the day appointed.21 With her much fair speech she caused him to yield, with the flattering of her lips she forced him.22 He go after her straightway, as an ox go to the slaughter, or as a fool to the correction of the stocks; 23 Till a dart strike through his liver; as a bird hasteth to the snare, and know not that it is for his life.

7:24
בנפשו 5315 הוא 1931: ועתה 6258 בנים 1121 שמעו 8085 לי 3807a והקשיבו 7181 לאמרי 561 פי 6310: 7:25
banapshou hua'. ua'atah baniym shim'au liy; uahaqshiybu, la'amrey piy.
***is* for his life it now therefore O you children Hearken unto me and attend to the words of my mouth**

אל 408 ישט 7847 אל 413 דרכיה 1870 לבך 3820 אל 408 תתע 8582 בנתיבותיה 5410: 7:26 כי 3588 רבים 7227 חללים 2491 הפילה 5307
'al yest 'al darakeyha libeka; 'al teta' bintiybouteyha. kiy rabiym chalaliym hipiylah;
**not Let decline to her ways your heart not go astray in her paths For many wounded she has cast down**

ועצמים 6099 כל 3605 הרגיה 2026: 7:27 דרכי 1870 שאול 7585 ביתה 1004 ירדות 3381 אל 413 חדרי 2315
ua'atzumiym, kal harugeyha. darkey sha'aul beytah; yoradout, 'al chadrey
**yea strong many *men* have been slain by her *is* the way to hell (*grave*) Her house going down to the chambers of**

מות 4194:
mauet.
**death**

**Prov 8:1** הלא 3808 חכמה 2451 תקרא 7121 ותבונה 8394 תתן 5414 קולה 6963: 8:2 בראש 7218 מרומים 4791 עלי 5921 דרך 1870
hala' chakamah tiqraa'; uatbunah, titen qoulah. bara'sh maroumiym 'aley darek;
**not wisdom Does cry? and understanding put forth her voice? in the top of high places by the way**

בית 1004 נתיבות 5410 נצבה 5324: 8:3 ליד 3027 שערים 8179 לפי 6310 קרת 7176 מבוא 3996 פתחים 6607 תרנה 7442: 8:4
beyt natiybout nitzabah. layad sha'ariym lapiy qaret; mabou'a patachiym taronah.
***in* the places of the paths She stands at *the* gates at the entry of *the* city *at* the coming in *at* the doors She cry**

אליכם 413 אישים 376 אקרא 7121 וקולי 6963 אל 413 בני 1121 אדם 120: 8:5 הבינו 995 פתאים 6612 ערמה 6195 וכסילים 3684
'aleykem 'ayshiym 'aqraa'; uaqouliy, 'al baney 'adam. habiynu pataa'yim 'armah; uaksiyliym,
**Unto you O men I call and my voice *is* to the sons of man understand O you simple wisdom and you fools**

הבינו 995 לב 3820: 8:6 שמעו 8085 כי 3588 נגידים 5057 אדבר 1696 ומפתח 4669 שפתי 8193
habiynu leb. shim'au kiy nagiydiym 'adaber; uamiptach sapatay,
**be you of an understanding heart Hear for excellent things I will speak of and the opening of my lips**

מישרים 4339: 8:7 כי 3588 אמת 571 יהגה 1897 חכי 2441 ותועבת 8441 שפתי 8193 רשע 7562: 8:8
meyshariym. kiy 'amet yehageh chikiy; uatou'abat sapatay resha'.
***shall be* right things For truth shall speak my mouth and an abomination to my lips wickedness *is***

בצדק 6664 כל 3605 אמרי 561 פי 6310 אין 369 בהם 871a נפתל 6617 ועקש 6141: 8:9 כלם 3605 נכחים 5228
batzedeq kal 'amrey piy; 'aeyn bahem, niptal ua'aqesh. kulam nakochiym
***are* in righteousness All the words of my mouth *there is* nothing in them froward or perverse They *are* all plain**

למבין 995 וישרים 3477 למצאי 4672 דעת 1847: 8:10 קחו 3947 מוסרי 4147 ואל 408 כסף 3701
lamebiyn; uiyshariym, lamotza'aey da'at. qachu musariy ua'al kasep;
**to him that understands and right to them that find knowledge Receive my instruction and not rather silver**

ודעת 1847 מחרוץ 2742 נבחר 977: 8:11 כי 3588 טובה 2896 חכמה 2451 מפנינים 6443 וכל 3605 חפצים 2656 לא 3808
uada'at, mecharutz nibchar. kiy toubah chakamah mipniyniym; uakal chapatziym, la'
**and knowledge than gold choice For *is* better wisdom than rubies and all *the things* that may be desired not**

Pro 7:24 Hearken unto me now therefore, O you children, and attend to the words of my mouth.25 Let not your heart decline to her ways, go not astray in her paths.26 For she has cast down many wounded: yea, many strong men have been slain by her.27 Her house is the way to hell, going down to the chambers of death. **Pro** 8:1 Does not wisdom cry? and understanding put forth her voice?2 She stand in the top of high places, by the way in the places of the paths.3 She crieth at the gates, at the entry of the city, at the coming in at the doors.4 Unto you, O men, I call; and my voice is to the sons of man.5 O you simple, understand wisdom: and, you fools, be you of an understanding heart.6 Hear; for I will speak of excellent things; and the opening of my lips shall be right things.7 For my mouth shall speak truth; and wickedness is an abomination to my lips.8 All the words of my mouth are in righteousness; there is nothing froward or perverse in them.9 They are all plain to him that understandeth, and right to them that find knowledge.10 Receive my instruction, and not silver; and knowledge rather than choice gold.11 For wisdom is better than rubies; and all the things that may be desired are not to be compared to it.

**8:12** **8:13**

ישוו 7737 בה 871a: אני 589 חכמה 2451 שכנתי 7931 ערמה 6195 ודעת 1847 מזמות 4209 אמצא 4672:

yishauu bah. 'aniy chakamah shakantiy 'armah; uada'at mazimout 'amtzaa'.

**are to be compared to it I wisdom dwell *with* prudence and knowledge of witty inventions find out**

**8:14**

יראת 3374 יהוה 3068 שנאת 8130 רע 7451 גאה 1344 וגאון 1347 ודרך 1870 רע 7451 ופי 6310 תהפכות 8419 שנאתי 8130: לי 3807a

yir'at Yahuah sana't ra' ge'ah uaga'aun uaderek ra' uapiy tahpukout sanea'tiy. liy

**The fear of Yahuah *is* to hate evil pride and arrogancy and way *the* evil and mouth *the* froward do I hate *is* mine**

**8:15**

עצה 6098 ותושיה 8454 אני 589 בינה 998 לי 3807a גבורה 1369: בי 871a מלכים 4428 ימלכו 4427 ורוזנים 7336

'aetzah uatushiyah; 'aniy biynah, liy gaburah. biy malakiym yimloku; uarouzaniym,

**Counsel and sound wisdom I *am* understanding I have strength By me kings reign and princes**

**8:16** **8:17**

יחקקו 2710 צדק 6664: בי 871a שרים 8269 ישרו 8323 ונדיבים 5081 כל 3605 שפטי 8199 צדק 6664: אני 589 אהביה 157

yachoqaqu tzedeq. biy sariym yasouru; uanadiybiym, kal shopatey tzedeq. 'aniy 'ahabayha

**decree justice By me princes rule and nobles *even* all the judges of the earth I love**

**8:18**

אהב 157 ומשחרי 7836 ימצאנני 4672: עשר 6239 וכבוד 3519 אתי 854 הון 1952 עתק 6276

'aehab; uamashacharay, yimtza'ananiy. 'asher uakaboud 'atiy; houn 'ateq,

**them that love me and those that seek me early shall find me Riches and honor *are* with me riches *yea* durable**

**8:19** **8:20**

וצדקה 6666: טוב 2896 פריי 6529 מחרוץ 2742 ומפז 6337 ותבואתי 8393 מכסף 3701 נבחר 977: בארח 734

uatzdaqah. toub piryiy mecharutz uamipaz; uatabu'atiy, mikesep nibchar. ba'arach

**and righteousness *is* better My fruit than gold yea than fine gold and my revenue than silver choice in the way of**

**8:21**

צדקה 6666 אהלך 1980 בתוך 8432 נתיבות 5410 משפט 4941: להנחיל 5157 אהבי 157 יש 3426

tzadaqah 'ahalek; batouk, natiybout mishapat. lahanachiyl 'ahabay yesh;

**righteousness I lead in the midst of the paths of judgment That I may cause to inherit those that love me substance**

**8:22** **8:23**

ואצרתיהם 214 אמלא 4390: יהוה 3068 קנני 7069 ראשית 7225 דרכו 1870 קדם 6924 מפעליו 4659 מאז 227:

ua'atzaroteyhem 'amalea'. Yahuah qananiy rea'shiyt darkou; qedem mipa'alayu me'az.

**and their treasures I will fill Yahuah possessed me *in* the beginning of his way before his works of old**

**8:24**

מעולם 5769 נסכתי 5258 מראש 2718 מקדמי 6924 ארץ 776: באין 369 תהמות 8415

me'aulam nisaktiy mera'sh, miqadmey 'aretz. ba'aeyn tahomout

**from everlasting I was set up from the beginning *or* ever the earth *was* When *there were* no depths**

**8:25**

חוללתי 2342 באין 369 מעינות 4599 נכבדי 3513 מים 4325: בטרם 2962 הרים 2022 הטבעו 2883

choulalatiy; ba'aeyn ma'yanout, nikbadey mayim. baterem hariym hataba'au;

**I was brought forth when *there were* no fountains abounding with water Before the mountains were settled**

**8:26**

לפני 6440 גבעות 1389 חוללתי 2342: עד 5704 לא 3808 עשה 6213 ארץ 776 וחוצות 2351 וראש 7218

lipney gaba'aut choulalatiy. 'ad la' 'asah 'aretz uachutzout; uara'sh,

**before the hills was I brought forth *While* as yet not he had made the earth nor the fields nor the highest part of**

**8:27**

עפרות 6083 תבל 8398: בהכינו 3559 שמים 8064 שם 8033 אני 589 בחוקו 2710 חוג 2329 על 5921 פני 6440

aparout tebel. bahakiynou shamayim sham 'aniy; bachuqou chug, 'al paney

**the dust of the world When he prepared the heavens *was* there I when he set a compass upon the face of**

Pro 8:12 I wisdom dwell with prudence, and find out knowledge of witty inventions.13 The fear of YHUH is to hate evil: pride, and arrogance, and the evil way, and the froward mouth, do I hate.14 Counsel is mine, and sound wisdom: I am understanding; I have strength.15 By me kings reign, and princes decree justice.16 By me princes rule, and nobles, even all the judges of the earth.17 I love them that love me; and those that seek me early shall find me.18 Riches and honor are with me; yea, durable riches and righteousness.19 My fruit is better than gold, yea, than fine gold; and my revenue than choice silver.20 I lead in the way of righteousness, in the midst of the paths of judgment:21 That I may cause those that love me to inherit substance; and I will fill their treasures.22 YHUH possessed me in the beginning of his way, before his works of old.23 I was set up from everlasting, from the beginning, or ever the earth was.24 When there were no depths, I was brought forth; when there were no fountains abounding with water.25 Before the mountains were settled, before the hills was I brought forth:26 While as yet he had not made the earth, nor the fields, nor the highest part of the dust of the world. 27 When he prepared the heavens, I was there: when he set a compass upon the face of the depth:

8:28 8:29

תהום 8415: באמצו 553 שחקים 7834 ממעל 4605 בעזוז 5810 עינות 5869 תהום 8415: בשומו 7760

tahoum. ba'amtzou shachaqiym mima'al; ba'azouz, 'aynout tahoum basumou

**the depth When he established the clouds above when he strengthened the fountains of the deep When he gave**

לים 3220 חקו 2706 ומים 4325 לא 3808 יעברו 5674 פיו 6310 בחוקו 2710 מוסדי 4144

layam chuqou, uamayim la' ya'abru piyu; bachuqou, mousadey

**to the sea his decree that the waters not should pass his commandment when he appointed the foundations of**

8:30

ארץ 776: ואהיה 1961 אצלו 681 אמון 525 ואהיה 1961 שעשעים 8191 יום 3117 יום 3117 משחקת 7832 לפניו 6440

'aretz. ua'ahayeh 'atzlou, 'amoun ua'ahayeh sha'ashu'aym youm youm; masacheqet lapanayu

**the earth Then I was by him *as* one brought up *with him* and I was *his* delight day daily rejoicing before him**

8:31 8:32

בכל 3605 עת 6256: משחקת 7832 בתבל 8396 ארצו 776 ושעשעי 8191 את 854 בני 1121 אדם 120:

bakal 'aet. masacheqet batebel artzou; uasha'ashu'ay, 'at baney 'adam.

**in all ways Rejoicing in the habitable part of his earth and my delights *were* with the sons of men**

8:33

ועתה 6258 בנים 1121 שמעו 8085 לי 3807a ואשרי 835 דרכי 1870 ישמרו 8104: שמעו 8085 מוסר 4148 וחכמו 2449

ua'atah baniym shim'au liy; ua'ashrey, darakay yishmoru. shim'au musar uachakamu,

**Now therefore O you children listen unto me for blessed my ways *are they that* keep Hear instruction and be wise**

8:34

ואל 408 תפרעו 6544: אשרי 835 אדם 120 שמע 8085 לי 3807a לשקד 8245 על 5921 דלתתי 1817 יום 3117 יום 3117 לשמר 8104 מזוזת 4201

ua'al tipra'au. 'ashrey 'adam shomea' liy lishqod 'al daltotay youm youm; lishmor, mazuzot

**and not refuse Blessed *is* the man that hear me watching at my gates day to day waiting at the posts of**

8:35 8:36

פתחי 6607: כי 3588 מצאי 4672 מצאי 4672 חיים 2416 ויפק 6329 רצון 7522 מיהוה 3068: וחטאי 2398

patachay. kiy motz'ay motz'ay chayiym; uayapeq ratzoun, meYahuah. uachota'ay

**my doors For whoso finds me finds life and shall obtain favor of Yahuah But he that sin against me**

חמס 2554 נפשו 5315 כל 3605 משנאי 8130 אהבו 157 מות 4194:

chomes napshou; kal masan'ay, 'ahabu mauet.

**wrongeth his own soul all they that hate me love death**

**Prov 9:1** 9:2

חכמות 2454 בנתה 1129 ביתה 1004 חצבה 2672 עמודיה 5982 שבעה 7651: טבחה 2873 טבחה 2874

chakmout banatah beytah; chatzabah 'amudeyha shib'ah. tabachah tibchah

**Wisdom has builded her house she has hewn out her pillars seven She has killed her beasts**

9:3

מסכה 4537 יינה 3196 אף 637 ערכה 6186 שלחנה 7979: שלחה 7971 נערתיה 5291 תקרא 7121 על 5921 גפי 1610

masakah yeynah; 'aap, 'arakah shulchanah. shalchah na'aroteyha tiqraa'; 'al gapey,

**she has mingled her wine also she has furnished her table She has sent forth her maidens she cry upon *the* highest**

9:4 9:5

מרמי 4791 קרת 7176: מי 4310 פתי 6612 יסר 5493 הנה 2008 חסר 2638 לב 3820 אמרה 559 לו 3807a:

maromey qaret. miy' petiy yasur henah; chasar leb, 'amarah lou'.

**places of the city Whoever *is* simple let him turn in here *as for* him that want understanding she saith to him**

9:6

לכו 1980 לחמו 3898 בלחמי 3899 ושתו 8354 ביין 3196 מסכתי 4537: עזבו 5800 פתאים 6612 וחיו 2421 ואשרו 833

laku lachamu balachamiy; uashtu, bayayin masakatiy. 'azbu pataa'yim uachayu; ua'ashru,

**Come eat of my bread and drink of the wine *which* I have mingled Forsake the foolish and live and go**

Pro 8:28 When he established the clouds above: when he strengthened the fountains of the deep:29 When he gave to the sea his decree, that the waters should not pass his commandment: when he appointed the foundations of the earth:30 Then I was by him, as one brought up with him: and I was daily his delight, rejoicing always before him;31 Rejoicing in the habitable part of his earth; and my delights were with the sons of men.32 Now therefore hear unto me, O you children: for blessed are they that keep my ways.33 Hear instruction, and be wise, and refuse it not.34 Blessed is the man that hear me, watching daily at my gates, waiting at the posts of my doors.35 For whoso findeth me findeth life, and shall obtain favor of YHUH.36 But he that sin against me wrongeth his own soul: all they that hate me love death. **Pro** 9:1 Wisdom has built her house, she has hewn out her seven pillars:2 She has killed her beasts; she has mingled her wine; she has also furnished her table.3 She has sent forth her maidens: she crieth upon the highest places of the city,4 Whoso is simple, let him turn in hither: as for him that wanteth understanding, she saith to him, 5 Come, eat of my bread, and drink of the wine which I have mingled.6 Forsake the foolish, and live; and go in the way of understanding.

בדרך 1870 בינה 998: **9:7** יסר 3256 לץ 3887 לקח 3947 לו 3807a קלון 7036 ומוכיח 3198 לרשע 7563
baderek biynah. yoser letz, loqeach lou' qaloun; uamoukiyach larasha'
**in the way of understanding He that reprove a scorner get to himself shame and he that rebuke a wicked**

מומו 3971: **9:8** אל 408 תוכח 3198 לץ 3887 פן 6435 ישנאך 8130 הוכח 3198 לחכם 2450 ויאהבך 157: **9:9** תן 5414
mumou. 'al toukach letz pen yisna'aka; houkach lachakam, uaye'ahabeka. ten
***man get* himself a blot not Reprove a scorner lest he hate you rebuke a wise man and he will love you Give**

לחכם 2450 ויחכם 2449 עוד 5750 הודע 3045 לצדיק 6662 ויוסף 3254 לקח 3948: **9:10**
lachakam uayechakam 'aud; houda' latzadiyq, uayousep leqach.
***instruction* to a wise *man* and he will be wiser yet teach a just *man* and he will increase in learning**

תחלת 8462 חכמה 2451 יראת 3374 יהוה 3069 ודעת 1847 קדשים 6918 בינה 998: **9:11** כי 3588 בי 871a
tachilat chakamah yir'at Yahuah; uada'at qadoshiym biynah. kiy biy
***is* the beginning of wisdom The fear of Yahuah and the knowledge of the holy *is* understanding For by me**

ירבו 7235 ימיך 3117 ויוסיפו 3254 לך 3807a שנות 8141 חיים 2416: **9:12** אם 518 חכמת 2449 חכמת 2449
yirbu yameyka; uayousipu leka, shanout chayiym. 'am chakamat chakamat
**shall be multiplied your days and shall be increased to your the years of life If you be wise you shall be wise**

לך 3807a ולצת 3887 לבדך 905 תשא 5375: **9:13** אשת 802 כסילות 3687 המיה 1993 פתיות 6615 ובל 1077
lak; ualatzta, labadaka tisa'. 'aeshet kasiylut homiyah; patayut, uabal
**for yourself but *if* you scornest you alone shall bear *it* A woman foolish *is* clamorous *she is* simple and nothing**

ידעה 3045 מה 4100: **9:14** וישבה 3427 לפתח 6607 ביתה 1004 על 5921 כסא 3678 מרמי 4791 קרת 7176: **9:15** לקרא 7121
yada'ah mah. uayashabah lapetach beytah; 'al kisea', maromey qaret. liqra'
**knows what For she sit at the door of her house on a seat *in the* high places of the city To call**

לעברי 5674 דרך 1870 המישרים 3474 ארחותם 734: **9:16** מי 4310 פתי 6612 יסר 5493 הנה 2008 וחסר 2638
la'abarey darek; hamayashariym, 'arachoutam. miy' petiy yasur henah; uachasar
**passengers along who go right on their ways Whoever *is* simple let him turn in here and *as for* him that want**

לב 3820 ואמרה 559 לו 3807a: **9:17** מים 4325 גנובים 1589 ימתקו 4985 ולחם 3899 סתרים 5643 ינעם 5276: **9:18** ולא 3808
leb, ua'amarah lou'. mayim ganubiym yimataqu; ua'alechem satariym yina'am. uala'
**understanding she saith to him waters Stolen are sweet and bread *eaten* in secret is pleasant But not**

ידע 3045 כי 3588 רפאים 7496 שם 8033 בעמקי 6012 שאול 7585 קראיה 7121:
yada' kiy rapa'aym sham; ba'amqey sha'aul qaru'ayha.
**he knows that *the* dead *are* there *are* in the depths of hell (*grave*) *and that* her guests**

**Prov 10:1** משלי 4912 שלמה 8010 בן 1121 חכם 2450 ישמח 8055 אב 1 ובן 1121 כסיל 3684 תוגת 8424 אמו 517:
mishley, shalomoh ben chakam yasamach 'ab; uaben kasiyl, tugat 'amou.
**The proverbs of Solomon A son wise make glad a father but a son foolish *is* the heaviness of his mother**

**10:2** לא 3808 יועילו 3276 אוצרות 214 רשע 7562 וצדקה 6666 תציל 5337 ממות 4194: **10:3** לא 3808 ירעיב 7456
la' you'aylu 'autzarout resha'; uatzdaqah, tatziyl mimauet. la' yara'ayb
**nothing profit Treasures of wickedness but righteousness deliver from death not will suffer to famish**

Pro 9:7 He that reproveth a scorner get to himself shame: and he that rebuketh a wicked man get himself a blot.8 Reprove not a scorner, lest he hate you: rebuke a wise man, and he will love you.9 Give instruction to a wise man, and he will be yet wiser: teach a just man, and he will increase in learning.10 The fear of YHUH is the beginning of wisdom: and the knowledge of the holy is understanding.11 For by me your days shall be multiplied, and the years of your life shall be increased.12 If you be wise, you shall be wise for thyself: but if you scornest, you alone shall bear it.13 A foolish woman is clamourous: she is simple, and know nothing.14 For she sitteth at the door of her house, on a seat in the high places of the city,15 To call passengers who go right on their ways:16 Whoso is simple, let him turn in hither: and as for him that wanteth understanding, she saith to him,17 Stolen waters are sweet, and bread eaten in secret is pleasant.18 But he know not that the dead are there; and that her guests are in the depths of hell. **Pro** 10:1 The proverbs of Solomon. A wise son make a glad father: but a foolish son is the heaviness of his mother. 2 Treasures of wickedness profit nothing: but righteousness delivereth from death.3 YHUH will not suffer the soul of the righteous to famish: but he casteth away the substance of the wicked.

| | | | | | | 10:4 | | |
|---|---|---|---|---|---|---|---|---|
| יהוה 3068 | נפש 5315 | צדיק 6662 | והות 1942 | רשעים 7563 | יהדף 1920: | ראש 7326 | עשה 6213 | כף 3709 |
| Yahuah | nepesh | tzadiyq; | uahauat | rasha'aym | yehadop. | ra'sh, | 'aseh | kap |
| **Yahuah** | **the soul of** | **the righteous** | **but the substance of** | **the wicked** | **he cast away** | ***become* poor** | **He that deal** | ***with* a hand** |

| | | | 10:5 | | | | | |
|---|---|---|---|---|---|---|---|---|
| רמיה 7423 | ויד 3027 | חרוצים 2742 | תעשיר 6238: | אגר 103 | בקיץ 7019 | בן 1121 | משכיל 7919 | נרדם 7290 |
| ramiyah; | uayad | charutziym | ta'ashiyr. | 'ager | baqayitz | ben | maskiyl; | nirdam |
| **slack** | **but the hand of** | **the diligent** | **make rich** | **He that gathered** | **in summer** | ***is* a son** | **wise** | ***but* he that sleep** |

| | | | 10:6 | | | | | |
|---|---|---|---|---|---|---|---|---|
| בקציר 7105 | בן 1121 | מביש 954: | ברכות 1293 | לראש 7218 | צדיק 6662 | ופי 6310 | רשעים 7563 | יכסה 3680 |
| baqatziyr, | ben | mebiysh. | barakout | lara'sh | tzadiyq; | uapiy | rasha'aym, | yakaseh |
| **in harvest** | ***is* a son** | **that cause shame** | **Blessings** | ***are* upon the head of** | **the just** | **but the mouth of** | **the wicked** | **cover** |

| | 10:7 | | | | | | 10:8 | | |
|---|---|---|---|---|---|---|---|---|---|
| חמס 2555: | זכר 2143 | צדיק 6662 | לברכה 1293 | ושם 8034 | רשעים 7563 | ירקב 7537: | חכם 2450 | לב 3820 | יקח 3947 |
| chamas. | zeker | tzadiyq | librakah; | uashem | rasha'aym | yirqab. | chakam | leb | yiqach |
| **violence** | **The memory of** | **the just** | ***is* blessed** | **but the name of** | **the wicked** | **shall rot** | **The wise in** | **heart** | **will receive** |

| | | | | 10:9 | | | | | |
|---|---|---|---|---|---|---|---|---|---|
| מצות 4687 | ואויל 191 | שפתים 8193 | ילבט 3832: | הולך 1980 | בתם 8537 | ילך 1980 | בטח 983 | ומעקש 6140 | דרכיו 1870 |
| mitzuot; | ua'auiyl | sapatayim, | yilabet. | houlek | batom | yelek | betach; | uama'aqesh | darakayu, |
| **commandments** | **but a fool** | **prating** | **shall fall** | **He that walk** | **uprightly** | **walks** | **surely** | **but he that pervert** | **his ways** |

| | 10:10 | | | | | | | 10:11 |
|---|---|---|---|---|---|---|---|---|
| יודע 3045: | קרץ 7169 | עין 5869 | יתן 5414 | עצבת 6094 | ואויל 191 | שפתים 8193 | ילבט 3832: | מקור 4726 |
| yiuadea'. | qoretz | 'ayin | yiten | 'atzabet; | ua'auiyl | sapatayim, | yilabet. | maqour |
| **shall be known** | **He that wink with** | **the eye** | **cause** | **sorrow** | **but a fool** | **prating** | **shall fall** | ***man is* a well of** |

| | | | | | | | 10:12 | | | |
|---|---|---|---|---|---|---|---|---|---|---|
| חיים 2416 | פי 6310 | צדיק 6662 | ופי 6310 | רשעים 7563 | יכסה 3680 | חמס 2555: | שנאה 8135 | תעורר 5782 | מדנים 4090 | ועל 5921 |
| chayiym | piy | tzadiyq; | uapiy | rasha'aym, | yakaseh | chamas. | sin'ah | ta'aurer | madaniym; | ua'al |
| **life** | **The mouth of** | **a righteous** | **but the mouth of** | **the wicked** | **cover** | **violence** | **Hatred** | **stir up** | **strifes** | **but** |

| | | | | 10:13 | | | | |
|---|---|---|---|---|---|---|---|---|
| כל 3605 | פשעים 6588 | תכסה 3680 | אהבה 160: | בשפתי 8193 | נבון 995 | תמצא 4672 | חכמה 2451 | ושבט 7626 |
| kal | pasha'aym, | takaseh | 'ahabah. | basiptey | naboun | timatzea' | chakamah | uashebet, |
| **all** | **sins** | **cover** | **love** | **In the lips of** | **him that has understanding** | **is found** | **wisdom** | **but a rod** |

| | | | 10:14 | | | | |
|---|---|---|---|---|---|---|---|
| לגו 1460 | חסר 2638 | לב 3820: | חכמים 2450 | יצפנו 6845 | דעת 1847 | ופי 6310 | אויל 191 |
| lageu | chasar | leb. | chakamiym | yitzpanu | da'at; | uapiy | 'auiyl |
| ***is* for the back of** | **him that is void of** | **understanding** | **Wise *men*** | **lay up** | **knowledge** | **but the mouth** | **the foolish** |

| | | 10:15 | | | | | | 10:16 |
|---|---|---|---|---|---|---|---|---|
| מחתה 4288 | קרבה 7138: | הון 1952 | עשיר 6223 | קרית 7151 | עזו 5797 | מחתת 4288 | דלים 1800 | רישם 7389: |
| machitah | qarobah. | houn | 'ashiyr | qiryat | 'azou; | machitat | daliym | reysham. |
| **destruction** | ***is* near** | ***The* wealth** | **rich man's** | **city *is*** | **his strong** | **the destruction of** | **the poor** | ***is* their poverty** |

| | | | | | | 10:17 | | |
|---|---|---|---|---|---|---|---|---|
| פעלת 6468 | צדיק 6662 | לחיים 2416 | תבואת 8393 | רשע 7563 | לחטאת 2403: | ארח 734 | לחיים 2416 | שומר 8104 |
| pa'alat | tzadiyq | lachayiym; | tabu'at | rasha' | lachata't. | 'arach | lachayiym | shoumer |
| **The labour of** | **the righteous** | ***tend* to life** | **the fruit of** | **the wicked** | **to sin** | **He *is in* the way** | **of life** | **that keep** |

| | | | | 10:18 | | | | | |
|---|---|---|---|---|---|---|---|---|---|
| מוסר 4148 | ועוזב 5800 | תוכחת 8433 | מתעה 8582: | מכסה 3680 | שנאה 8135 | שפתי 8193 | שקר 8267 | ומוצא 3318 | דבה 1681 |
| musar; | ua'azeb | toukachat | mata'ah. | makaseh | sin'ah | siptey | shaqer; | uamoutza' | dibah, |
| **instruction** | **but he that refuse** | **reproof** | **err** | **He that hides** | **hatred** | **lips** | ***with* lying** | **and that utter** | **a slander** |

Pro 10: 4 He becometh poor that deal with a slack hand: but the hand of the diligent make rich.5 He that gathereth in summer is a wise son: but he that sleep in harvest is a son that causeth shame.6 Blessings are upon the head of the just: but violence covereth the mouth of the wicked.7 The memory of the just is blessed: but the name of the wicked shall rot.8 The wise in heart will receive commandments: but a prating fool shall fall.9 He that walk uprightly walk surely: but he that perverteth his ways shall be known.10 He that winketh with the eye causeth sorrow: but a prating fool shall fall.11 The mouth of a righteous man is a well of life: but violence covereth the mouth of the wicked.12 Hatred stirreth up strifes: but love covereth all sins.13 In the lips of him that has understanding wisdom is found: but a rod is for the back of him that is void of understanding.14 Wise men lay up knowledge: but the mouth of the foolish is near destruction.15 The rich man's wealth is his strong city: the destruction of the poor is their poverty.16 The labour of the righteous tendeth to life: the fruit of the wicked to sin.17 He is in the way of life that keep instruction: but he that refuseth reproof erreth. 18 He that hide hatred with lying lips, and he that uttereth a slander, is a fool.

10:19 10:20
הוא 1931 כסיל 3684: ברב 7230 דברים 1697 לא 3808 יחדל 2308 פשע 6588 וחשך 2820 שפתיו 8193 משכיל 7919:
hua' kasiyl. barob dabariym la' yechdal pasha'; uachosek sapatayu maskiyl.
**he *is* a fool In the multitude of words not there want sin but he that refrain his lips *is* wise**

10:21
כסף 3701 נבחר 977 לשון 3956 צדיק 6662 לב 3820 רשעים 7563 כמעט 4592: שפתי 8193 צדיק 6662 ירעו 7462
kesep nibchar lashoun tzadiyq; leb rasha'aym kima'at. siptey tzadiyq yir'au
**silver *is as* choice The tongue of the just the heart of the wicked *is* little *worth* The lips of the righteous feed**

10:22
רבים 7227 ואוילים 191 בחסר 2638 לב 3820 ימותו 4191: ברכת 1293 יהוה 3068 היא 1931 תעשיר 6238 ולא 3808 יוסף 3254 עצב 6089
rabiym; ua'auiyliym, bachasar leb yamutu. birkat Yahuah hiy'a ta'ashiyr; uala' yosiyp 'atzeb
**many but fools for want of wisdom die The blessing of Yahuah it make rich and no he add sorrow**

10:23 10:24
עמה 5973: כשחוק 7814 לכסיל 3684 עשות 6213 זמה 2154 וחכמה 2451 לאיש 376 תבונה 8394: מגורת 4034
'amah. kischouq liksiyl asout zimah; uachakamah, la'aysh tabunah. magourat
**with it *It is* as sport to a fool to do mischief but wisdom a man of understanding *has* The fear of**

10:25
רשע 7563 היא 1931 תבואנו 935 ותאות 8378 צדיקים 6662 יתן 5414: כעבור 5674 סופה 5492
rasha' hiy'a tabou'anu; uata'auat tzadiyqiym yiten. ka'abour supah
**the wicked it shall come upon him but the desire of the righteous shall be granted As passed the whirlwind**

10:26
ואין 369 רשע 7563 וצדיק 6662 יסוד 3247 עולם 5769: כחמץ 2558 לשנים 8127 וכעשן 6227
ua'aeyn rasha'; uatzadiyq, yasoud 'aulam. kachometz lashinayim, uake'ashan
**so *is* no *more* the wicked but the righteous *is* an foundation everlasting As vinegar to the teeth and as smoke**

10:27
לעינים 5869 כן 3651 העצל 6102 לשלחיו 7971: יראת 3374 יהוה 3068 תוסיף 3254 ימים 3117 ושנות 8141
la'aeynayim; ken he'atzel, lasholachayu. yir'at Yahuah tousiyp yamiym; uashanout
**to the eyes so *is* the sluggard to them that send him The fear of Yahuah prolong days but the years of**

10:28
רשעים 7563 תקצרנה 7114: תוחלת 8431 צדיקים 6662 שמחה 8057 ותקות 8615 רשעים 7563
rasha'aym tiqtzoranah. touchelet tzadiyqiym simchah; uatiquat rasha'aym
**the wicked shall be shortened The hope of the righteous *shall be* gladness but the expectation of the wicked**

10:29 10:30
תאבד 6: מעוז 4581 לתם 8537 דרך 1870 יהוה 3068 ומחתה 4288 לפעלי 6466 און 205:
ta'bed. ma'auz latom derek Yahuah; uamachitah, lapo'aley 'auen.
**shall perish *is* strength to the upright The way of Yahuah but destruction *shall be* to the workers of iniquity**

10:31
צדיק 6662 לעולם 5769 בל 1077 ימוט 4131 ורשעים 7563 לא 3808 ישכנו 7931 ארץ 776: פי 6310 צדיק 6662
tzadiyq la'aulam bal yimout; uarsha'aym, la' yishkanu 'aretz. piy tzadiyq
**The righteous never lest shall be removed but the wicked not shall inhabit the earth The mouth of the just**

10:32
ינוב 5107 חכמה 2451 ולשון 3956 תהפכות 8419 תכרת 3772: שפתי 8193 צדיק 6662 ידעון 3045 רצון 7522
yanub chakamah ualshoun tahpukout, tikaret. siptey tzadiyq yeda'un ratzoun;
**bring forth wisdom but tongue *the* froward shall be cut out The lips of the righteous know what is acceptable**

ופי 6310 רשעים 7563 תהפכות 8419:
uapiy rasha'aym, tahpukout.
**but the mouth of the wicked *speak* frowardness**

Pro 10:19 In the multitude of words there wanteth not sin: but he that refraineth his lips is wise.20 The tongue of the just is as choice silver: the heart of the wicked is little worth.21 The lips of the righteous feed many: but fools die for want of wisdom.22 The blessing of YHUH, it make rich, and he addeth no sorrow with it.23 It is as sport to a fool to do mischief: but a man of understanding has wisdom.24 The fear of the wicked, it shall come upon him: but the desire of the righteous shall be granted.25 As the whirlwind pass, so is the wicked no more: but the righteous is an everlasting foundation.26 As vinegar to the teeth, and as smoke to the eyes, so is the sluggard to them that send him.27 The fear of YHUH prolongeth days: but the years of the wicked shall be shortened.28 The hope of the righteous shall be gladness: but the expectation of the wicked shall perish.29 The way of YHUH is strength to the upright: but destruction shall be to the workers of iniquity.30 The righteous shall never be removed: but the wicked shall not inhabit the earth.31 The mouth of the just bring forth wisdom: but the froward tongue shall be cut out.32 The lips of the righteous know what is acceptable: but the mouth of the wicked speaketh frowardness.

**Prov 11:1** … **11:2**
מאזני 3976 מרמה 4820 תועבת 8441 יהוה 3068 ואבן 68 שלמה 8003 רצונו 7522: בא 935 זדון 2087
ma'zaney mirmah tou'abat Yahuah; ua'aben shalemah ratzounou. ba' zadoun
**A balance false *is* abomination to Yahuah but a weight just *is* his delight *When* comes pride**

**11:3**
ויבא 935 קלון 7036 ואת 854 צנועים 6800 חכמה 2451: תמת 8538 ישרים 3477 תנחם 5148 וסלף 5558
uayaba' qaloun; ua'at tzanu'aym chakamah tumat yashariym tanchem; uaselep
**then comes shame *but with* the lowly *is* wisdom The integrity of the upright shall guide them but the perverseness of**

**1:4** … **11:5**
בוגדים 898 ושדם 7703 לא 3808 יועיל 3276 הון 1952 ביום 3117 עברה 5678 וצדקה 6666 תציל 5337 ממות 4194:
bougadiym uashadem la' you'ayl houn bayoum 'abrah; uatzdaqah, tatziyl mimauet.
**transgressors shall destroy them. not profit Riches in the day of wrath but righteousness deliver from death**

**11:6**
צדקת 6666 תמים 8549 תישר 3474 דרכו 1870 וברשעתו 7564 יפל 5307 רשע 7563:
tzadaqta tamiym tayasher darkou; uabrish'atou, yipol rasha'.
**The righteousness of the perfect shall direct his way but by his own wickedness shall fall the wicked**

**11:7**
צדקת 6666 ישרים 3477 תצילם 5337 ובהות 1942 בגדים 898 ילכדו 3920: במות 4194
tzadqta yashariym tatziylem; uabhauat, bogadiym yilakedu. bamout
**The righteousness of the upright shall deliver them but in *their own* naughtiness transgressors shall be taken When die**

**11:8**
אדם 120 רשע 7563 תאבד 6 תקוה 8615 ותוחלת 8431 אונים 205 אבדה 6: צדיק 6662 מצרה 6869 נחלץ 2502
'adam rasha' ta'bad tiquah; uatouchelet 'auniym 'abadah. tzadiyq mitzarah nechelatz;
**a man wicked shall perish *his* expectation and the hope of unjust *men* perish The righteous out of trouble is delivered**

**11:9**
ויבא 935 רשע 7563 תחתיו 8478: בפה 6310 חנף 2611 ישחת 7843 רעהו 7453 ובדעת 1847
uayaba' rasha' tachtayu. bapeh, chanep yashchit re'aehu; uabda'at,
**and comes the wicked in his place with *his* mouth An hypocrite destroy his neighbour but through knowledge**

**11:10**
צדיקים 6662 יחלצו 2502: בטוב 2896 צדיקים 6662 תעלץ 5970 קריה 7151 ובאבד 6 רשעים 7563
tzadiyqiym yechaletzu. batub tzadiyqiym ta'alotz qiryah; uaba'abod rasha'aym
**the just shall be delivered When it goes well with the righteous rejoice the city and when perish the wicked**

**11:11**
רנה 7440: בברכת 1293 ישרים 3477 תרום 7311 קרת 7176 ובפי 6310 רשעים 7563
rinah. babirkat yashariym tarum qaret; uabpiy rasha'aym,
***there is* shouting By the blessing of the upright is exalted the city but by the mouth of the wicked**

**11:12** … **11:13**
תהרס 2040: בז 936 לרעהו 7453 חסר 2638 לב 3820 ואיש 376 תבונות 8394 יחריש 2790:
tehares. baz lare'aehu chasar leb; ua'aysh tabunout yachariysh.
**it is overthrown despise his neighbour He that is void of wisdom but a man of understanding holds his peace**

**11:14**
הולך 1980 רכיל 7400 מגלה 1540 סוד 5475 ונאמן 539 רוח 7307 מכסה 3680 דבר 1697: באין 369 תחבלות 8458
houlek rakiyl magaleh coud; uane'aman ruach, makaseh dabar. ba'aeyn tachabulout
**goes A talebearer reveal secrets but he that is of faithful a spirit conceals the matter Where no *is* counsel**

**11:15**
יפל 5307 עם 5971 ותשועה 8668 ברב 7230 יועץ 3289: רע 7451 ירוע 7489 כי 3588
yipal 'am; uatashu'ah, barob you'aetz. ra' yeroua' kiy
**fall the people but safety in the multitude of counsellors *there is* shall surely smart *for it* for**

**Pro** 11:1 A false balance is abomination to YHUH: but a just weight is his delight.2 When pride cometh, then cometh shame: but with the lowly is wisdom.3 The integrity of the upright shall guide them: but the perverseness of transgressors shall destroy them.4 Riches profit not in the day of wrath: but righteousness delivereth from death.5 The righteousness of the perfect shall direct his way: but the wicked shall fall by his own wickedness.6 The righteousness of the upright shall deliver them: but transgressors shall be taken in their own naughtiness.7 When a wicked man die, his expectation shall perish: and the hope of unjust men perisheth.8 The righteous is delivered out of trouble, and the wicked cometh in his stead.9 An hypocrite with his mouth destroyeth his neighbor: but through knowledge shall the just be delivered.10 When it go well with the righteous, the city rejoice: and when the wicked perish, there is shouting.11 By the blessing of the upright the city is exalted: but it is overthrown by the mouth of the wicked.12 He that is void of wisdom despiseth his neighbor: but a man of understanding holdeth his peace.13 A talebearer revealeth secrets: but he that is of a faithful spirit concealeth the matter. 14 Where no counsel is, the people fall: but in the multitude of counsellers there is safety.15 He that is surety for a stranger shall smart for it:

11:16

ערב 6148 זר 2114 ושנא 8130 תקעים 8628 בוטח 982: אשת 802 חן 2580 תתמך 8551 כבוד 3519 ועריצים 6184

'arab zar; uasonea' toqa'aym bouteach. 'aeshet chen titmok kaboud; ua'ariytziym,

**He that is surety for a stranger and he that hate suretiship *is* sure A woman gracious retain honor and strong**

11:17 11:18

יתמכו 8551 עשר 6239: גמל 1580 נפשו 5315 איש 376 חסד 2617 ועכר 5916 שארו 7607 אכזרי 394:

yitmaku 'asher. gomel napshou 'aysh chased; ua'aker sha'aerou, 'akzariy.

***men* retain riches *The* does good *to* his own soul man merciful but trouble his own flesh *he that is* cruel**

11:19

רשע 7563 עשה 6213 פעלת 6468 שקר 8267 וזרע 2232 צדקה 6666 שכר 7938 אמת 571: כן 3651 צדקה 6666

rasha', 'aseh pa'alat shaqer; uazorea' tzadaqah, seker 'amet. ken tzadaqah

**The wicked work a work deceitful but to him that sow righteousness *shall be* a reward sure As righteousness**

11:20

לחיים 2416 ומרדף 7291 רעה 7451 למותו 4194: תועבת 8441 יהוה 3068 עקשי 6141

lachayiym; uamaradep ra'ah lamoutou. tou'abat Yahuah 'aqshey

***tend* to life so he that pursue evil *pursue it* to his own death *are* abomination to Yahuah They that are of a froward**

11:21

לב 3820 ורצונו 7522 תמימי 8549 דרך 1870: יד 3027 ליד 3027 לא 3808 ינקה 5352

leb; uaratzounou, tamiymey darek. yad layad la' yinaqeh

**heart but his delight *such as are* upright in *their* way *are* *Though* hand *join* in hand not shall be unpunished**

11:22

רע 7451 וזרע 2233 צדיקים 6662 נמלט 4422: נזם 5141 זהב 2091 באף 639 חזיר 2386 אשה 802

ra'; uazera' tzadiyqiym nimlat. nezem zahab ba'ap chaziyr; 'ashah

**the wicked but the seed of the righteous shall be delivered *As* a jewel of gold in a snout swine's *so is* a woman**

11:23

יפה 3303 וסרת 5493 טעם 2940: תאות 8378 צדיקים 6662 אך 389 טוב 2896 תקות 8615 רשעים 7563

yapah, uasarat ta'am. ta'auat tzadiyqiym 'ak toub; tiquat rasha'aym

**fair which is without discretion The desire of the righteous *is* only good *but* the expectation of the wicked**

11:24

עברה 5678: יש 3426 מפזר 6340 ונוסף 3254 עוד 5750 וחושך 2820 מישר 3476 אך 389

'abrah. yesh mapazer uanousap 'aud; uachousek miyosher, 'ak

***is* wrath There is that scatters and increase yet and *there is* that withholdeth *more than is* meet but**

11:25 11:26

למחסור 4270: נפש 5315 ברכה 1293 תדשן 1878 ומרוה 7301 גם 1571 הוא 1931 יורא 3384:

lamachsour. nepesh barakah tadushan; uamarueh, gam hua' youra'.

***it tend* to poverty *The* soul liberal shall be made fat and he that watereth also himself shall be watered**

11:27

מנע 4513 בר 1250 יקבהו 5344 לאום 3816 וברכה 1293 לראש 7218 משביר 7666:

monea' bar yiqbuhu la'aum; uabarakah, lara'sh mashbiyr.

**He that withholdeth corn shall curse him the people but blessing *shall be* upon the head of him that sell *it***

11:28

שחר 7836 טוב 2896 יבקש 1245 רצון 7522 ודרש 1875 רעה 7451 תבואנו 935: בוטח 982

shocher toub yabaqesh ratzoun; uadoresh ra'ah tabou'anu. bouteach

**He that diligently seek good procure favor but he that seek mischief it shall come unto him He that trust**

11:29

בעשרו 6239 הוא 1931 יפל 5307 וכעלה 5929 צדיקים 6662 יפרחו 6524: עוכר 5916 ביתו 1004 ינחל 5157

ba'asharou hua' yipol; uake'aleh, tzadiyqiym yiprachu. 'auker beytou yinchal

**in his riches he shall fall but as a branch the righteous shall flourish He that trouble his own house shall inherit**

Pro 11:15 and he that hateth suretiship is sure.16 A gracious woman retaineth honor: and strong men retain riches. 17 The merciful man doeth good to his own soul: but he that is cruel trouble his own flesh.18 The wicked worketh a deceitful work: but to him that soweth righteousness shall be a sure reward.19 As righteousness tendeth to life: so he that pursueth evil pursueth it to his own death.20 They that are of a froward heart are abomination to YHUH: but such as are upright in their way are his delight.21 Though hand join in hand, the wicked shall not be unpunished: but the seed of the righteous shall be delivered.22 As a jewel of gold in a swine's snout, so is a fair woman which is without discretion.23 The desire of the righteous is only good: but the expectation of the wicked is wrath.24 There is that scattereth, and yet increaseth; and there is that withholdeth more than is meet, but it tendeth to poverty.25 The liberal soul shall be made fat: and he that watereth shall be watered also himself.26 He that withholdeth corn, the people shall curse him: but blessing shall be upon the head of him that sell it.27 He that diligently seek good procureth favor: but he that seek mischief, it shall come unto him.28 He that trusteth in his riches shall fall: but the righteous shall flourish as a branch.29 He that trouble his own house shall inherit the wind:

רוח 7307 | ועבד 5650 | אויל 191 | לחכם 2450 | לב 3820: | **11:30** פרי 6529 | צדיק 6662 | עץ 6086 | חיים 2416
ruach; | ua'abed | 'auiyl, | lachacham | leb. | pariy | tzadiyq | 'aetz | chayiym;
**the wind | and servant | the fool *shall be* | to the wise of | heart | The fruit of | the righteous | *is* a tree of | life**

ולקח 3947 | נפשות 5315 | חכם 2450: | **11:31** הן 2005 | צדיק 6662 | בארץ 776 | ישלם 7999 | אף 637 | כי 3588
ualoqeach | napasout | chakam. | hen | tzadiyq | ba'aretz | yashulam; | 'aap, | kiy
**and he that win | souls | *is* wise | Behold | the righteous | in the earth | shall be recompensed | much more | that**

רשע 7563 | וחוטא 2398:
rasha' | uachoutea'.
**the wicked and the sinner**

**Prov 12:1** אהב 157 | מוסר 4148 | אהב 157 | דעת 1847 | ושנא 8130 | תוכחת 8433 | בער 1197: | **12:2** טוב 2896 | יפיק 6329 | רצון 7522
'aheb | musar | 'aheb | da'at; | uasonea' | toukachat | ba'ar. | toub, | yapiyq | ratzoun
**Whoso love | instruction | love | knowledge | but he that hate | reproof | is brutish | A good *man* | obtains | favor**

מיהוה 3069 | ואיש 376 | מזמות 4209 | ירשיע 7561: | **12:3** לא 3808 | יכון 3559 | אדם 120 | ברשע 7562
meYahuah; | ua'aysh | mazimout | yarshiya'. | la' | yikoun | 'adam | baresha';
**of Yahuah | but a man of | wicked devices | will he condemn | not | shall be established | A man | by wickedness**

ושרש 8328 | צדיקים 6662 | בל 1077 | ימוט 4131: | **12:4** אשת 802 | חיל 2428 | עטרת 5850 | בעלה 1167 | וכרקב 7538
uashoresh | tzadiyqiym, | bal | yimout. | 'aeshet | chayil | 'ateret | ba'lah; | uakraqab
**but the root of | the righteous | not | shall be moved | *A* woman | virtuous | *is* a crown | to her husband | but as rottenness**

בעצמותיו 6106 | מבישה 954: | **12:5** מחשבות 4284 | צדיקים 6662 | משפט 4941 | תחבלות 8458 | רשעים 7563
ba'atzamoutayu | mabiyshah. | machashabout | tzadiyqiym | mishapat; | tachabulout | rasha'aym
**in his bones | she that make ashamed *is* | The thoughts of | the righteous | *are* right | *but* the counsels of | the wicked**

מרמה 4820: | **12:6** דברי 1697 | רשעים 7563 | ארב 693 | דם 1818 | ופי 6310 | ישרים 3477 | יצילם 5337: | **12:7**
mirmah. | dibrey | rasha'aym | 'arab | dam; | uapiy | yashariym, | yatziylem.
***are* deceit | The words of | the wicked | *are* to lie in wait | *for* blood | but the mouth of | the upright | shall deliver them**

הפוך 2015 | רשעים 7563 | ואינם 369 | ובית 1004 | צדיקים 6662 | יעמד 5975: | **12:8** לפי 6310 | שכלו 7922
hapouk | rasha'aym | ua'aeynam; | uabeyt | tzadiyqiym | ya'amod. | lapiy | siklou
**are overthrown | The wicked | and *are* not | but the house of | the righteous | shall stand | according to | his wisdom**

יהלל 1984 | איש 376 | ונעוה 5753 | לב 3820 | יהיה 1961 | לבוז 937: | **12:9** טוב 2896 | נקלה 7034
yahulal | 'aysh; | uana'aueh | leb, | yihayeh | labuz. | toub | niqleh
**shall be commended | A man | but he that is of perverse | a heart | shall be | despised | *He that is* better | despised**

ועבד 5650 | לו 3807a | ממתכבד 3513 | וחסר 2638 | לחם 3899: | **12:10** יודע 3045 | צדיק 6662 | נפש 5315 | בהמתו 929
ua'abed | lou'; | mimtakabed, | uachasar | lachem. | youdea' | tzadiyq | nepesh | bahemtou;
**and has a servant | himself | than he that honors | and lack | bread | *man* regard | A righteous | the life of | his beast**

ורחמי 7356 | רשעים 7563 | אכזרי 394: | **12:11** עבד 5647 | אדמתו 127 | ישבע 7646 | לחם 3899 | ומרדף 7291
uarachamey | rasha'aym, | 'akzariy. | 'abed | admatou | yisba' | lachem; | uamaradep
**but the tender mercies of | the wicked *are* cruel | He that tills | his land | shall be satisfied *with* | bread | but he that follows**

Pro 11:29 and the fool shall be servant to the wise of heart.30 The fruit of the righteous is a tree of life; and he that winneth souls is wise.31 Behold, the righteous shall be recompensed in the earth: much more the wicked and the sinner. **Pro** 12:1 Whoso love instruction love knowledge: but he that hateth reproof is brutish.2 A good man obtaineth favor of YHUH: but a man of wicked devices will he condemn.3 A man shall not be established by wickedness: but the root of the righteous shall not be moved.4 A virtuous woman is a crown to her husband: but she that make ashamed is as rottenness in his bones.5 The thoughts of the righteous are right: but the counsels of the wicked are deceit.6 The words of the wicked are to lie in wait for blood: but the mouth of the upright shall deliver them.7 The wicked are overthrown, and are not: but the house of the righteous shall stand.8 A man shall be commended according to his wisdom: but he that is of a perverse heart shall be despised.9 He that is despised, and has a servant, is better than he that honoureth himself, and lacketh bread.10 A righteous man regardeth the life of his beast: but the tender mercies of the wicked are cruel.11 He that tilleth his land shall be satisfied with bread: but he that followed vain persons is void of understanding.

12:12

ריקים 7386 חסר 2638 לב 3820: חמד 2530 רשע 7563 מצוד 4685 רעים 7451 ושרש 8328 צדיקים 6662
reyqiym chasar leb. chamad rasha' matzoud ra'aym; uashoresh tzadiyqiym
**vain *persons is* void of understanding desire The wicked the net of evil *men* but the root of the righteous**

12:13 12:14

יתן 5414: בפשע 6588 שפתים 8193 מוקש 4170 רע 7451 ויצא 3318 מצרה 6869 צדיק 6662:
yiten. bapesha' sapatayim mouqesh ra'; uayetzea' mitzarah tzadiyq.
**yield *fruit* by the transgression of *his* lips is snared The wicked but shall come out of trouble the just**

מפרי 6529 פי 6310 איש 376 ישבע 7646 טוב 2896 וגמול 1576 ידי 3027 אדם 120 ישוב 7725
mipriy piy 'aysh yisba' toub; uagmul yadey 'adam, yashub
**by the fruit of *his* mouth A man shall be satisfied *with* good and the recompence of a hands man's shall be rendered**

12:15 12:16

לו 3807a: דרך 1870 אויל 191 ישר 3477 בעיניו 5869 ושמע 8085 לעצה 6098 חכם 2450: אויל 191 ביום 3117
lou'. derek 'auiyl yashar ba'aeynayu; uashomea' la'atzah chakam. 'auiyl, bayoum
**unto him The way of a fool *is* right in his own eyes but he that hearken unto counsel *is* wise A fool's presently**

12:17

יודע 3045 כעסו 3708 וכסה 3680 קלון 7036 ערום 6175: יפיח 6315 אמונה 530 יגיד 5046 צדק 6664 ועד 5707
yiuada' ka'asou; uakoseh qaloun 'arum. yapiyach 'amunah yagiyd tzedeq; ua'aed
**is known wrath cover shame a prudent *man He that* speak truth shows forth righteousness but a witness**

12:18 12:19

שקרים 8267 מרמה 4820: יש 3426 בוטה 981 כמדקרות 4094 חרב 2719 ולשון 3956 חכמים 2450 מרפא 4832:
shaqariym mirmah. yesh bouteh kamadqarout chareb; ualshoun chakamiym marpea'.
**false deceit There is that speak like the piercings of a sword but the tongue of the wise *is* health**

12:20

שפת 8193 אמת 571 תכון 3559 לעד 5703 ועד 5704 ארגיעה 7281 לשון 3956 שקר 8267: מרמה 4820 בלב 3820
sapat 'amet tikoun la'ad; ua'ad 'argiy'ah, lashoun shaqer. mirmah baleb
**The lip of truth shall be established for ever but for a moment a tongue *is but* lying Deceit *is* in the heart of**

12:21

חרשי 2790 רע 7451 וליעצי 3289 שלום 7965 שמחה 8057: לא 3808 יאנה 579 לצדיק 6662 כל 3605 און 205
chorashey ra'; ualyo'atzey shaloum simchah. la' ya'aneh latzadiyq kal 'auen;
**them that imagine evil but to the counsellors of peace *is* joy no There shall happen to the just all evil**

12:22

ורשעים 7563 מלאו 4390 רע 7451: תועבת 8441 יהוה 3068 שפתי 8193 שקר 8267 ועשי 6213 אמונה 530
uarsha'aym, mala'au ra'. tou'abat Yahuah siptey shaqer; ua'ausey 'amunah
**but the wicked shall be filled *with* mischief *are* abomination to Yahuah lips Lying but they that deal truly**

12:23 12:24

רצונו 7522: אדם 120 ערום 6175 כסה 3680 דעת 1847 ולב 3820 כסילים 3684 יקרא 7121 אולת 200:
ratzounou. 'adam 'arum koseh da'at; ualeb kasiyliym, yiqra' 'auelet.
***are* his delight A man prudent conceals knowledge but the heart of fools proclaims foolishness**

12:25

יד 3027 חרוצים 2742 תמשול 4910 ורמיה 7423 תהיה 1961 למס 4522: דאגה 1674 בלב 3820 איש 376
yad charutziym timshoul; uaramiyah, tihayeh lamas. da'agah baleb 'aysh
**The hand of the diligent shall bear rule but the slothful shall be under tribute Heaviness in the heart of man**

12:26

ישחנה 7812 ודבר 1697 טוב 2896 ישמחנה 8055: יתר 8446 מרעהו 7453 צדיק 6662 ודרך 1870
yashchenah; uadabar toub yasamchenah. yater mere'aehu tzadiyq; uaderek
**make it stoop but a word good make it glad *is more* excellent than his neighbour The righteous but the way of**

Pro 12:12 The wicked desire the net of evil men: but the root of the righteous yieldeth fruit.13 The wicked is snared by the transgression of his lips: but the just shall come out of trouble.14 A man shall be satisfied with good by the fruit of his mouth: and the recompence of a man's hands shall be rendered unto him.15 The way of a fool is right in his own eyes: but he that hearkeneth unto counsel is wise.16 A fool's wrath is presently known: but a prudent man covereth shame.17 He that speaketh truth show forth righteousness: but a false witness deceit.18 There is that speaketh like the piercings of a sword: but the tongue of the wise is health.19 The lip of truth shall be established forever: but a lying tongue is but for a moment.20 Deceit is in the heart of them that imagine evil: but to the counsellers of peace is joy.21 There shall no evil happen to the just: but the wicked shall be filled with mischief.22 Lying lips are abomination to YHUH: but they that deal truly are his delight.23 A prudent man concealeth knowledge: but the heart of fools proclaimeth foolishness. 24 The hand of the diligent shall bear rule: but the slothful shall be under tribute. 25 Heaviness in the heart of man make it stoop: but a good word make it glad.26 The righteous is more excellent than his neighbor: but the way of the wicked seduceth them.

12:27
רשעים 7563 תתעם 8582: לא 3808 יחרך 2760 רמיה 7423 צידו 6718 והון 1952 אדם 120
rasha'aym tata'aem. la' yacharok ramiyah tzeydou; uahoun 'adam
**the wicked seduceth them *The* not *man* roast slothful that which he took in hunting but the substance of a man**

12:28
יקר 3368 חרוץ 2742: בארח 734 צדקה 6666 חיים 2416 ודרך 1870 נתיבה 5410 אל 408 מות 4194:
yaqar charutz. ba'arach tzadaqah chayiym; uaderek natiybah 'al mauet.
***is* precious diligent In the way of righteousness *is* life and in the way path *thereof there is* no death**

**Prov 13:1** 13:2
בן 1121 חכם 2450 מוסר 4148 אב 1 ולץ 3887 לא 3808 שמע 8085 גערה 1606: מפרי 6529 פי 6310
ben chakam musar 'ab; ualetz, la' shama' ga'arah. mapriy piy
**A son wise instruction *hear* his father's but a scorner not hear rebuke by the fruit of *his* mouth**

13:3
איש 376 יאכל 398 טוב 2896 ונפש 5315 בגדים 898 חמס 2555: נצר 5341 פיו 6310 שמר 8104 נפשו 5315
'aysh ya'kal toub; uanepesh bogadiym chamas. notzer piyu shomer napshou;
**A man shall eat good but the soul of the transgressors *shall eat* violence He that keep his mouth keep his life**

13:4
פשק 6589 שפתיו 8193 מחתה 4288 לו 3807a: מתאוה 183 ואין 369 נפשו 5315 עצל 6102
poseq sapatayu, machitah lou'. mita'auah ua'ayin napshou 'atzel;
***but* he that open wide his lips destruction shall have desire and *has* nothing The soul of the sluggard**

13:5
ונפש 5315 חרצים 2742 תדשן 1878: דבר 1697 שקר 8267 ישנא 8130 צדיק 6662 ורשע 7563 יבאיש 887
uanepesh charutziym tadushan. dabar sheqer yisnaa' tzadiyq; uarashaa', yaba'aysh
**but the soul of the diligent shall be made fat words lying *man* hate A righteous but a wicked *man* is loathsome**

13:6 13:7
ויחפיר 2659: צדקה 6666 תצר 5341 תם 8537 דרך 1870 ורשעה 7564 תסלף 5557 חטאת 2403:
uayachpiyr. tzadaqah titzor tam darek; uarish'ah, tasalep chata't.
**and comes to shame Righteousness keep *him that is* upright in the way but wickedness overthrow the sinner**

13:8
יש 3426 מתעשר 6238 ואין 369 כל 3605 מתרושש 7326 והון 1952 רב 7227: כפר 3724
yesh mita'asher ua'aeyn kol; mitroushesh, uahoun rab. koper
**There is that make himself rich nothing *there is* yet *has* that make himself poor yet riches *has* great The ransom of**

13:9
נפש 5315 איש 376 עשרו 6239 ורש 7326 לא 3808 שמע 8085 גערה 1606: אור 216 צדיקים 6662 ישמח 8055 ונר 5216
nepesh 'aysh 'asharou; uarash, la' shama' ga'arah. 'aur tzadiyqiym yismach; uaner
**a life man's *are* his riches but the poor not hear rebuke The light of the righteous rejoice but the lamp of**

13:10 13:11
רשעים 7563 ידעך 1846: רק 7535 בזדון 2087 יתן 5414 מצה 4683 ואת 854 נועצים 3289 חכמה 2451: הון 1952
rasha'aym yid'ak. raq bazadoun yiten matzah; ua'at nou'atziym chakamah houn
**the wicked shall be put out Only by pride comes contention *but with* the well advised *is* wisdom Wealth**

13:12
מהבל 1892 ימעט 4591 וקבץ 6908 על 5921 יד 3027 ירבה 7235: תוחלת 8431 ממשכה 4900 מחלה 2470
mehebel yim'at; uaqobetz 'al yad yarbeh. touchelet mamushakah machalah
***gotten* by vanity shall be diminished but he that gathered by labour shall increase Hope deferred make sick**

13:13
לב 3820 ועץ 6086 חיים 2416 תאוה 8378 באה 935: בז 936 לדבר 1697 יחבל 2254 לו 3807a
leb; ua'aetz chayiym, ta'auah ba'ah. baz ladabar yechabel lou';
**the heart *it is* but a tree of life *when* the desire comes despise the word shall be destroyed Whoso**

Pro 12:27 The slothful man roasteth not that which he took in hunting: but the substance of a diligent man is precious.28 In the way of righteousness is life; and in the pathway thereof there is no death. **Pro** 13:1 A wise son hear his father's instruction: but a scorner hear not rebuke.2 A man shall eat good by the fruit of his mouth: but the soul of the transgressors shall eat violence.3 He that keep his mouth keep his life: but he that openeth wide his lips shall have destruction.4 The soul of the sluggard desire, and has nothing: but the soul of the diligent shall be made fat.5 A righteous man hateth lying: but a wicked man is loathsome, and cometh to shame.6 Righteousness keep him that is upright in the way: but wickedness overthroweth the sinner.7 There is that make himself rich, yet has nothing: there is that make himself poor, yet has great riches.8 The ransom of a man's life are his riches: but the poor hear not rebuke.9 The light of the righteous rejoice: but the lamp of the wicked shall be put out.10 Only by pride cometh contention: but with the well advised is wisdom.11 Wealth gotten by vanity shall be diminished: but he that gathereth by labour shall increase. 12 Hope deferred make the heart sick: but when the desire cometh, it is a tree of life. 13 Whoso despiseth the word shall be destroyed: but he that fear the commandment shall be rewarded.

13:14

וירא 3373 מצוה 4687 הוא 1931 ישלם 7999: תורת 8451 חכם 2450 מקור 4726 חיים 2416 לסור 5493
uiyrea' mitzuah, hua' yashulam. tourat chakam maqour chayiym; lasur,
**but he that fear the commandment he shall be rewarded The law of the wise *is* a fountain of life to depart**

13:15 13:16

ממקשי 4170 מות 4194: שכל 7922 טוב 2896 יתן 5414 חן 2580 ודרך 1870 בגדים 898 איתן 386: כל 3605
mimoqashey mauet. sekel toub yiten chen; uaderek bogadiym 'aeytan. kal
**from the snares of death understanding Good gives favor but the way of transgressors *is* hard Every**

13:17

ערום 6175 יעשה 6213 בדעת 1847 וכסיל 3684 יפרש 6566 אולת 200: מלאך 4397 רשע 7563 יפל 5307 ברע 7451
'arum ya'aseh bada'at; uakasiyl, yipros 'auelet. mal'ak rasha' yipol bara';
**prudent *man* deal with knowledge but a fool lay open *his* folly A messenger wicked fall into mischief**

13:18

וציר 6735 אמונים 529 מרפא 4832: ריש 7389 וקלון 7036 פורע 6544 מוסר 4148 ושומר 8104
uatziyr 'amuniym marpea'. reysh uaqaloun pourea' musar; uashoumer
**but a ambassador faithful *is* health Poverty and shame *shall be to* him that refuse instruction but he that regard**

13:19

תוכחת 8433 יכבד 3513: תאוה 8378 נהיה 1961 תערב 6149 לנפש 5315 ותועבת 8441 כסילים 3684 סור 5493
toukachat yakubad. ta'auah nihayah te'arab lanapesh; uatou'abat kasiyliym, sur
**reproof shall be honoured The desire accomplished is sweet to the soul but *it is* abomination to fools to depart**

13:20 13:21

מרע 7451: הלוך 1980 את 854 חכמים 2450 וחכם 2449 ורעה 7462 כסילים 3684 ירוע 7321:
mera'. halouk 'at chakamiym uachakam uaro'ah kasiyliym yeroua'.
**from evil He that walks *with* wise *men* shall be wise: but a companion of fools shall be destroyed**

13:22

חטאים 2400 תרדף 7291 רעה 7451 ואת 853 צדיקים 6662 ישלם 7999 טוב 2896: טוב 2896 ינחיל 5157
chata'aym taradep ra'ah; ua'at tzadiyqiym, yashalem toub. toub, yanchiyl
**sinners pursue Evil *but to* the righteous shall be repayed good A good *man* leave an inheritance to**

13:23

בני 1121 בנים 1121 וצפון 6845 לצדיק 6662 חיל 2428 חוטא 2398: רב 7230 אכל 400 ניר 5215 ראשים 7326
baney baniym; uatzapun latzadiyq, cheyl choutea'. rab 'akel niyr rashiym;
***his* children's children and laid up for the just the wealth of the sinner *is* Much food *is in* the tillage of the poor**

13:24

ויש 3426 נספה 5595 בלא 3808 משפט 4941: חושך 2820 שבטו 7626 שונא 8130 בנו 1121 ואהבו 157
uayesh nispeh, bala' mishapat. chousek shibtou sounea' banou; ua'ahabou,
**but there is *that is* destroyed for want of judgment He that spares his rod hate his son but he that love him**

13:25

שחרו 7836 מוסר 4148: צדיק 6662 אכל 398 לשבע 7648 נפשו 5315 ובטן 990 רשעים 7563 תחסר 2637:
shicharou musar. tzadiyq, 'akel lasoba' napshou; uabeten rasha'aym techsar.
**him betimes chasteneth The righteous eat to the satisfying of his soul but the belly of the wicked shall want**

**Prov 14:1** 14:2

חכמות 2454 נשים 802 בנתה 1129 ביתה 1004 ואולת 200 בידיה 3027 תהרסנו 2040: הולך 1980
chakmout nashiym banatah beytah; ua'auelet, bayadeyha tehersenu. houlek
***Every* wise woman builds her house but the foolish with her hands plucks it down He that walk**

14:3

בישרו 3476 ירא 3373 יהוה 3068 ונלוז 3868 דרכיו 1870 בוזהו 959: בפי 6310 אויל 191 חטר 2415
bayasharou yarea' Yahuah; uanalouz darakayu bouzehu. bapiy 'auiyl choter
**in his uprightness fear Yahuah but *he that is* perverse in his ways despise him In the mouth of the foolish *is* a rod of**

Pro 13:14 The law of the wise is a fountain of life, to depart from the snares of death.15 Good understanding give favor: but the way of transgressors is hard.16 Every prudent man deal with knowledge: but a fool layeth open his folly. 17 A wicked messenger fall into mischief: but a faithful ambassador is health.18 Poverty and shame shall be to him that refuseth instruction: but he that regardeth reproof shall be honoured.19 The desire accomplished is sweet to the soul: but it is abomination to fools to depart from evil.20 He that walk with wise men shall be wise: but a companion of fools shall be destroyed.21 Evil pursueth sinners: but to the righteous good shall be repayed.22 A good man leaveth an inheritance to his children's children: and the wealth of the sinner is laid up for the just.23 Much food is in the tillage of the poor: but there is that is destroyed for want of judgment.24 He that spareth his rod hateth his son: but he that love him chasteneth him betimes.25 The righteous eateth to the satisfying of his soul: but the belly of the wicked shall want. **Pro** 14:1 Every wise woman buildeth her house: but the foolish plucketh it down with her hands. 2 He that walk in his uprightness fear YHUH: but he that is perverse in his ways despiseth him.3 In the mouth of the foolish is a rod of pride: but the lips of the wise shall preserve them.

14:4

1346 גאוה | 8193 ושפתי | 2450 חכמים | 8104: תשמורם | 369 באין | 505 אלפים | 18 אבוס | 1249 בר | 7230 ורב | 8393 תבואות

ga'auah; uasiptey chakamiym, tishmurem. ba'aeyn 'alapiym 'aebus bar; uarab tabu'aut,

**pride but the lips of the wise shall preserve them Where no *are* oxen the crib *is* clean but much increase**

14:5 14:6

3581 בכח | 7794: שור | 5707 עד | 529 אמונים | 3808 לא | 3576 יכזב | 6315 ויפיח | 3577 כזבים | 5707 עד | 8267: שקר | 1245 בקש

bakoach shour. 'aed 'amuniym la' yakazeb; uayapiyach kazabiym, 'aed shaqer. biqesh

***is* by the strength of the ox A witness faithful not will lies but will utter lies a witness false seek**

14:7

3887 לץ | 2451 חכמה | 369 ואין | 1847 ודעת | 995 לנבון | 7043: נקל | 1980 לך | 5048 מנגד

letz chakamah ua'ayin; uada'at lanaboun naqal. lek mineged

**A scorner wisdom and *finds it* not but knowledge unto him that understands *is* easy Go you from the presence of**

14:8

376 לאיש | 3684 כסיל | 1077 ובל | 3045 ידעת | 8193 שפתי | 1847: דעת | 2451 חכמת | 6175 ערום | 995 הבין

la'aysh kasiyl; uabal yada'ta, siptey da'at. chakamat 'arum habiyn

**a man foolish when not you perceive *in him* the lips of knowledge The wisdom of the prudent *is* to understand**

14:9

1870 דרכו | 200 ואולת | 3684 כסילים | 4820: מרמה | 191 אולים | 3887 יליץ | 817 אשם | 996 ובין | 3477 ישרים

darkou; ua'auelet kasiyliym mirmah. 'auiliym yaliytz 'asham; uabeyn yashariym

**his way but the folly of fools *is* deceit Fools make a mock at sin but among the righteous**

14:10 14:11

7522: רצון | 3820 לב | 3045 יודע | 4751 מרת | 5315 נפשו | 8057 ובשמחתו | 3808 לא | 6148 יתערב | 2114: זר

ratzoun. leb, youdea' marat napshou; uabsimchatou, la' yit'arab zar.

***there is* favor The heart knows bitterness his own and with his joy not does intermeddle a stranger**

14:12

1004 בית | 7563 רשעים | 8045 ישמד | 168 ואהל | 3477 ישרים | 6524: יפריח | 3426 יש | 1870 דרך

beyt rasha'aym yishamed; ua'ahel yashariym yapariyach. yesh derek

**The house of the wicked shall be overthrown but the tabernacle of the upright shall flourish There is a way**

14:13

3477 ישר | 6440 לפני | 376 איש | 319 ואחריתה | 1870 דרכי | 4194: מות | 1571 גם | 7814 בשחוק | 3510 יכאב | 3820 לב

yashar lipney 'aysh; ua'achariytah, darkey mauet. gam bisachouq yika'ab leb;

***which seems* right unto a man but the end thereof *are* the ways of death Even in laughter is sorrowful the heart**

14:14

319 ואחריתה | 8057 שמחה | 8424: תוגה | 1870 מדרכיו | 7646 ישבע | 5472 סוג | 3820 לב | 5921 ומעליו

ua'achariytah simchah tugah. midrakayu yisba' sug leb; uame'alayu,

**and the end of *that* mirth *is* heaviness with his own ways shall be filled The backslider in heart and from himself**

14:15 14:16

376 איש | 2896: טוב | 6612 פתי | 539 יאמין | 3605 לכל | 1697 דבר | 6175 וערום | 995 יבין | 838: לאשרו

'aysh toub. petiy ya'amiyn lakal dabar; ua'arum, yabiyn la'ashurou.

**a man *shall be satisfied* good The simple believe every word but the prudent *man* looks well to his going**

14:17

2450 חכם | 3373 ירא | 5493 וסר | 7451 מרע | 3684 וכסיל | 5674 מתעבר | 982: ובוטח | 7116 קצר | 639 אפים | 6213 יעשה | 200 אולת

chakam yarea' uasar mera'; uakasiyl, mita'aber uabouteach. qatzar 'apayim ya'aseh 'auelet;

**A wise *man* fear and depart from evil but the fool rageth and is confident *He that is* soon angry deal foolishly**

14:18

376 ואיש | 4209 מזמות | 8130: ישנא | 5157 נחלו | 6612 פתאים | 200 אולת | 6175 וערומים | 3803 יכתרו | 1847: דעת

ua'aysh mazimout, yisanea'. nachalu pataa'yim 'auelet; ua'arumiym, yaktiru da'at.

**and a man of wicked devices is hated inherit The simple folly but the prudent are crowned *with* knowledge**

Pro 14:4 Where no oxen are, the crib is clean: but much increase is by the strength of the ox.5 A faithful witness will not lie: but a false witness will utter lies.6 A scorner seek wisdom, and findeth it not: but knowledge is easy unto him that understandeth.7 Go from the presence of a foolish man, when you perceivest not in him the lips of knowledge.8 The wisdom of the prudent is to understand his way: but the folly of fools is deceit.9 Fools make a mock at sin: but among the righteous there is favor.10 The heart know his own bitterness; and a stranger doth not intermeddle with his joy.11 The house of the wicked shall be overthrown: but the tabernacle of the upright shall flourish.12 There is a way which seem right unto a man, but the end thereof are the ways of death.13 Even in laughter the heart is sorrowful; and the end of that mirth is heaviness.14 The backslider in heart shall be filled with his own ways: and a good man shall be satisfied from himself.15 The simple believeth every word: but the prudent man look well to his going.16 A wise man fear, and departeth from evil: but the fool rageth, and is confident.17 He that is soon angry deal foolishly: 17 and a man of wicked devices is hated.18 The simple inherit folly: but the prudent are crowned with knowledge.

14:19 שחו 7817 רעים 7451 לפני 6440 טובים 2896 ורשעים 7563 על 5921 שערי 8179 צדיק 6662: 14:20 גם 1571 לרעהו 7453
shachu ra'aym lipney toubiym; uarsha'aym, 'al sha'arey tzadiyq. gam lare'aehu
**bow The evil before the good and the wicked at the gates of the righteous even of his own neighbour**

ישנא 8130 רש 7326 ואהבי 157 עשיר 6223 רבים 7227: 14:21 בז 936 לרעהו 7453 חוטא 2398 ומחונן 2603
yisanea' ra'sh; ua'ahabey 'ashiyr rabiym. baz lare'aehu choutea'; uamachounen
**is hated The poor but friends the rich *has* many He that despise his neighbour sin but he that has mercy on**

עניים 6041 אשריו 835: 14:22 הלוא 3808 יתעו 8582 חרשי 2790 רע 7451 וחסד 2617 ואמת 571 חרשי 2790
'anayim 'ashrayu. halou'a yita'au chorashey ra'; uachesed ua'amet, chorashey
**the poor happy is he not Do they err that devise evil? but mercy and truth *shall be* to them that devise**

טוב 2896: 14:23 בכל 3605 עצב 6089 יהיה 1961 מותר 4195 ודבר 1697 שפתים 8193 אך 389 למחסור 4270: 14:24 עטרת 5850
toub. bakal 'atzeb yihayeh moutar; uadbar sapatayim, 'ak lamachsour. 'ateret
**good In all labour there is profit but the talk of the lips *tend* only to penury The crown of**

חכמים 2450 עשרם 6239 אולת 200 כסילים 3684 אולת 200: 14:25 מציל 5337 נפשות 5315 עד 5704 אמת 571 ויפח 6315 כזבים 3577
chakamiym 'asharam; 'auelet kasiyliym 'auelet. matziyl napashout 'aed 'amet; uayapiach kazabiym
**the wise *is* their riches *but* the foolishness of fools *is* folly deliver souls A witness true but speak lies**

מרמה 4820: 14:26 ביראת 3374 יהוה 3069 מבטח 4009 עז 5797 ולבניו 1121 יהיה 1961 מחסה 4268: 14:27
mirmah. bayir'at Yahuah mibtach 'az; ualbanayu, yihayeh machseh.
**a deceitful *witness* In the fear of Yahuah confidence *is* strong and his children shall have a place of refuge**

יראת 3374 יהוה 3068 מקור 4726 חיים 2416 לסור 5493 ממקשי 4170 מות 4194: 14:28 ברב 7230 עם 5971 הדרת 1927
yir'at Yahuah maqour chayiym; lasur, mimoqashey mauet. barab 'am hadrat
**The fear of Yahuah *is* a fountain of life to depart from the snares of death In the multitude of people honor**

מלך 4428 ובאפס 657 לאם 3816 מחתת 4288 רזון 7333: 14:29 ארך 750 אפים 639 רב 7227
melek; uab'apes la'am, machitat razoun. 'arek 'apayim rab
***is the* king's but in the want of people *is* the destruction of the prince *He that is* slow to wrath *is* of great**

תבונה 8394 וקצר 7116 רוח 7307 מרים 7311 אולת 200: 14:30 חיי 2416 בשרים 1320 לב 3820 מרפא 4832
tabunah; uaqatzar ruach, meriym 'auelet. chayey basariym leb marpea';
**understanding but *he that is* hasty of spirit exalt folly *is* the life of the flesh A heart sound**

ורקב 7538 עצמות 6106 קנאה 7068: 14:31 עשק 6231 דל 1800 חרף 2778 עשהו 6213 ומכבדו 3513
uaraqab 'atzmout qin'ah. 'asheq dal cherep 'asehu; uamkabadou,
**but the rottenness of the bones envy He that oppress the poor reproach his Maker but he that honors him**

חנן 2603 אביון 34: 14:32 ברעתו 7451 ידחה 1760 רשע 7563 וחסה 2620 במותו 4194 צדיק 6662:
chonen abyoun. bara'atou yidacheh rasha'; uachoseh bamoutou tzadiyq.
**has mercy on the poor in his wickedness is driven away The wicked but has hope in his death the righteous**

14:33 בלב 3820 נבון 995 תנוח 5117 חכמה 2451 ובקרב 7130 כסילים 3684
baleb naboun tanuach chakamah uabqereb kasiyliym,
**in the heart of him that has understanding rest Wisdom but *that which is* in the midst of fools**

Pro 14:19 The evil bow before the good; and the wicked at the gates of the righteous.20 The poor is hated even of his own neighbor: but the rich has many friends.21 He that despiseth his neighbor sin: but he that has mercy on the poor, happy is he.22 Do they not err that devise evil? but mercy and truth shall be to them that devise good.23 In all labour there is profit: but the talk of the lips tendeth only to penury.24 The crown of the wise is their riches: but the foolishness of fools is folly.25 A true witness delivereth souls: but a deceitful witness speaketh lies.26 In the fear of YHUH is strong confidence: and his children shall have a place of refuge.27 The fear of YHUH is a fountain of life, to depart from the snares of death.28 In the multitude of people is the king's honor: but in the want of people is the destruction of the prince.29 He that is slow to wrath is of great understanding: but he that is hasty of spirit exalteth folly. 30 A sound heart is the life of the flesh: but envy the rottenness of the bones.31 He that oppresseth the poor reproacheth his Maker: but he that honoureth him has mercy on the poor.32 The wicked is driven away in his wickedness: but the righteous has hope in his death. 33 Wisdom resteth in the heart of him that has understanding: but that which is in the midst of fools is made known.

| | 14:34 | | | | | | 14:35 | |
|---|---|---|---|---|---|---|---|---|
| תודע 3045: | צדקה 6666 | תרומם 7311 | גוי 1471 | וחסד 2617 | לאמים 3816 | חטאת 2403: | רצון 7522 | מלך 4428 |
| tiuadea'. | tzadaqah | taroumem | gouy; | uachesed | la'amiym | chata't. | ratzoun | melek |
| **is made known** | **Righteousness** | **exalt** | **a nation** | ***is* but a reproach** | **to any people** | **sin *is*** | ***The* favor** | **king's** |

| | | | | |
|---|---|---|---|---|
| לעבד 5650 | משכיל 7919 | ועברתו 5678 | תהיה 1961 | מביש 954: |
| la'abed | maskiyl; | ua'abratou, | tihayeh | mebiysh. |
| ***is* toward a servant** | **wise** | **but his wrath** | **is** | ***against* him that cause shame** |

| Prov 15:1 | | | | | | | | 15:2 | |
|---|---|---|---|---|---|---|---|---|---|
| מענה 4617 | רך 7390 | ישיב 7725 | חמה 2534 | ודבר 1697 | עצב 6089 | יעלה 5927 | אף 639: | לשון 3956 | חכמים 2450 |
| ma'aneh | rak | yashiyb | chemah; | uadbar | 'atzeb, | ya'aleh | 'aap. | lashoun | chakamiym |
| **A answer** | **soft** | **turned away** | **wrath** | **but words** | **grievous** | **stir up** | **anger** | **The tongue of** | **the wise** |

| | | | | | | 15:3 | | | |
|---|---|---|---|---|---|---|---|---|---|
| תיטיב 3190 | דעת 1847 | ופי 6310 | כסילים 3684 | יביע 5042 | אולת 200: | בכל 3605 | מקום 4725 | עיני 5869 | יהוה 3068 |
| teytiyb | da'at; | uapiy | kasiyliym, | yabiya' | 'auelet. | bakal | maqoum | 'aeyney | Yahuah; |
| **use aright** | **knowledge** | **but the mouth of** | **fools** | **pour out** | **foolishness** | ***are* in every** | **place** | **The eyes of** | **Yahuah** |

| | | | 15:4 | | | | | | |
|---|---|---|---|---|---|---|---|---|---|
| צפות 6822 | רעים 7451 | וטובים 2896: | מרפא 4832 | לשון 3956 | עץ 6086 | חיים 2416 | וסלף 5558 | בה 871a | שבר 7667 |
| tzopout, | ra'aym | uatoubiym | marpea' | lashoun | 'aetz | chayiym; | uaselep | bah, | sheber |
| **beholding** | **the evil** | **and the good** | **A wholesome** | **tongue** | ***is* a tree of** | **life** | **but perverseness** | **therein** | ***is* a breach** |

| | 15:5 | | | | | | | 15:6 |
|---|---|---|---|---|---|---|---|---|
| ברוח 7307: | אויל 191 | ינאץ 5006 | מוסר 4148 | אביו 1 | ושמר 8104 | תוכחת 8433 | יערם 6191: | בית 1004 |
| baruach. | 'auiyl, | yina'atz | musar | 'abiyu; | uashomer | toukachat | ya'arim. | beyt |
| **in the spirit** | **A fool** | **despise** | **instruction** | **his father's** | **but he that regard** | **reproof** | **is prudent** | **In the house of** |

| | | | | | | 15:7 | | | |
|---|---|---|---|---|---|---|---|---|---|
| צדיק 6662 | חסן 2633 | רב 7227 | ובתבואת 8393 | רשע 7563 | נעכרת 5916: | שפתי 8193 | חכמים 2450 | יזרו 2219 | דעת 1847 |
| tzadiyq | chosen | rab; | uabitbu'at | rasha' | ne'akaret. | siptey | chakamiym | yazaru | da'at; |
| **the righteous** | **treasure** | ***is* much** | **but in the revenues of** | **the wicked** | **is trouble** | **The lips of** | **the wise** | **disperse** | **knowledge** |

| | | | | 15:8 | | | | |
|---|---|---|---|---|---|---|---|---|
| ולב 3820 | כסילים 3684 | לא 3808 | כן 3651: | זבח 2077 | רשעים 7563 | תועבת 8441 | יהוה 3068 | ותפלת 8605 |
| ualeb | kasiyliym | la' | ken. | zebach | rasha'aym | tou'abat | Yahuah; | uatpilat |
| **but the heart of** | **the foolish** | ***do* not** | **so** | **The sacrifice of** | **the wicked** | ***is* an abomination to** | **Yahuah** | **but the prayer of** |

| | | 15:9 | | | | |
|---|---|---|---|---|---|---|
| ישרים 3477 | רצונו 7522: | תועבת 8441 | יהוה 3068 | דרך 1870 | רשע 7563 | ומרדף 7291 |
| yashariym | ratzounou. | tou'abat | Yahuah | derek | rasha'; | uamaradep |
| **the upright** | ***is* his delight** | ***is* an abomination unto** | **Yahuah** | **The way of** | **the wicked** | **but him that follows after** |

| | | 15:10 | | | | | | | 15:11 |
|---|---|---|---|---|---|---|---|---|---|
| צדקה 6666 | יאהב 157: | מוסר 4148 | רע 7451 | לעזב 5800 | ארח 734 | שונא 8130 | תוכחת 8433 | ימות 4191: | |
| tzadaqah | ye'ahab. | musar | ra' | la'azeb | 'arach; | sounea' | toukachat | yamut. | |
| **righteousness** | **he love** | **Correction** | ***is* grievous** | **unto him that forsake** | **the way** | ***and* he that hate** | **reproof** | **shall die** | |

| | | | | | | | | | 15:12 |
|---|---|---|---|---|---|---|---|---|---|
| שאול 7585 | ואבדון 11 | נגד 5048 | יהוה 3069 | אף 637 | כי 3588 | לבות 3826 | בני 1121 | אדם 120: | לא 3808 |
| sha'aul | ua'abadoun | neged | Yahuah; | 'aap, | kiy | libout | baney | 'adam. | la' |
| **Hell (*grave*)** | **and destruction *are*** | **before** | **Yahuah** | **how much more** | **then** | **the hearts of** | **the children of** | **man** | **not** |

| | | | | | | | 15:13 | | |
|---|---|---|---|---|---|---|---|---|---|
| יאהב 157 | לץ 3887 | הוכח 3198 | לו 3807a | אל 413 | חכמים 2450 | לא 3808 | ילך 1980: | לב 3820 | שמח 8056 | ייטב 3190 |
| ye'ahab | letz | houkeach | lou'; | 'al | chakamiym, | la' | yelek. | leb | sameach | yeytiyb |
| **love** | **A scorner** | **one that reprove him** | | **unto** | **the wise** | **neither will he go** | | **A heart** | **merry** | **make cheerful** |

Pro 14:34 Righteousness exalteth a nation: but sin is a reproach to any people.35 The king's favor is toward a wise servant: but his wrath is against him that causeth shame. **Pro** 15:1 A soft answer turneth away wrath: but grievous words stir up anger.2 The tongue of the wise useth knowledge aright: but the mouth of fools poureth out foolishness.3 The eyes of YHUH are in every place, beholding the evil and the good.4 A wholesome tongue is a tree of life: but perverseness therein is a breach in the spirit.5 A fool despiseth his father's instruction: but he that regardeth reproof is prudent.6 In the house of the righteous is much treasure: but in the revenues of the wicked is trouble.7 The lips of the wise disperse knowledge: but the heart of the foolish doeth not so.8 The sacrifice of the wicked is an abomination to YHUH: but the prayer of the upright is his delight.9 The way of the wicked is an abomination unto YHUH: but he love him that followed after righteousness.10 Correction is grievous unto him that forsaketh the way: and he that hateth reproof shall die.11 Hell and destruction are before YHUH: how much more then the hearts of the children of men? 12 A scorner love not one that reproveth him: neither will he go unto the wise.13 A merry heart make a cheerful countenance: but by sorrow of the heart the spirit is broken.

15:14
פנים 6440 ובעצבת 6094 לב 3820 רוח 7307 נכאה 5218: לב 3820 נבון 995 יבקש 1245
paniym; uab'atzbat leb ruach nake'ah. leb naboun yabaqesh
**a countenance but by sorrow of the heart the spirit is broken The heart of him that has understanding seek**

15:15
דעת 1847 ופני 6440 כסילים 3684 ירעה 7462 אולת 200: כל 3605 ימי 3117 עני 6041 רעים 7451
da'at; uapeniy kasiyliym, yir'ah 'auelet. kal yamey 'aniy ra'aym;
**knowledge but the mouth of fools feed on foolishness All the days of the afflicted *are* evil**

15:16
וטוב 2896 לב 3820 משתה 4960 תמיד 8548: טוב 2896 מעט 4592 ביראת 3374 יהוה 3068 מאוצר 214 רב 7227
uatoub leb, mishteh tamiyd. toub ma'at bayir'at Yahuah; me'autzar rab,
**but merry *he that is of* a heart *has* a feast continual Better *is* little with the fear of Yahuah than treasure great**

15:17
ומהומה 4103 בו 871a: טוב 2896 ארחת 737 ירק 3419 ואהבה 160 שם 8033 משור 7794 אבוס 75 ושנאה 8135
uamahumah bou. toub 'aruchat yaraq ua'ahabah sham; mishour 'abus, uasin'ah
**and trouble therewith Better *is* a dinner (*ration*) of herbs love *is* where than a ox stalled and hatred therewith**

15:18 15:19
בו 871a: איש 376 חמה 2534 יגרה 1624 מדון 4066 וארך 750 אפים 639 ישקיט 8252 ריב 7379: דרך 1870 עצל 6102
bou. 'aysh chemah yagareh madoun; ua'arek 'apayim, yashqiyt riyb. derek 'atzel
**in him A man wrathful stir up strife but *he that is* slow *to* anger appeaseth strife The way of the slothful**

15:20
כמשכת 4881 חדק 2312 וארח 734 ישרים 3477 סללה 5549: בן 1121 חכם 2450 ישמח 8055 אב 1
kimsukat chadeq; ua'arach yashariym salulah. ben chakam yasamach 'ab;
***man is* as an hedge of thorns but the way of the righteous *is* made plain A son wise make glad a father**

15:21
וכסיל 3684 אדם 120 בוזה 959 אמו 517: אולת 200 שמחה 8057 לחסר 2638 לב 3820 ואיש 376 תבונה 8394
uakasiyl 'adam, bouzeh 'amou. 'auelet simchah lachasar leb; ua'aysh tabunah,
**but a foolish man despise his mother Folly *is* joy to *him that is* destitute of wisdom but a man of understanding**

15:22
יישר 3474 לכת 1980: הפר 6565 מחשבות 4284 באין 369 סוד 5475 וברב 7230 יועצים 3289
yayasher laket. haper machashabout ba'aeyn coud; uabrob you'atziym
**uprightly walks are disappointed purposes Without counsel but in the multitude of counsellors**

15:23
תקום 6965: שמחה 8057 לאיש 376 במענה 4617 פיו 6310 ודבר 1697 בעתו 6256 מה 4100
taqum. simchah la'aysh bama'aneh piyu; uadabar ba'atou mah
**they are established *has* joy A man by the answer of his mouth and a word *spoken* in due season how**

15:24 15:25
טוב 2896: ארח 734 חיים 2416 למעלה 4605 למשכיל 7919 למען 4616 סור 5493 משאול 7585 מטה 4295: בית 1004
toub. 'arach chayiym lama'alah lamaskiyl; lama'an sur, misha'aul matah. beyt
**good is it The way of life *is* above to the wise that he may depart from hell beneath the house of**

15:26
גאים 1343 יסח 5255 יהוה 3068 ויצב 5324 גבול 1366 אלמנה 490: תועבת 8441 יהוה 3068
ge'aym yisach Yahuah; uayatzeb, gabul 'almanah. tou'abat Yahuah
**the proud will destroy Yahuah but he will establish the border of the widow *are* an abomination to Yahuah**

15:27
מחשבות 4284 רע 7451 וטהרים 2889 אמרי 561 נעם 5278: עכר 5916 ביתו 1004 בוצע 1214
machashabout ra'; uatahoriym, 'amrey no'am. 'aker beytou boutzea'
**The thoughts of the wicked but *the words* of the pure words *are* pleasant trouble his own house He that is greedy of**

Pro 15:14 The heart of him that has understanding seek knowledge: but the mouth of fools feedeth on foolishness.15 All the days of the afflicted are evil: but he that is of a merry heart has a continual feast.16 Better is little with the fear of YHUH than great treasure and trouble therewith.17 Better is a dinner of herbs where love is, than a stalled ox and hatred therewith.18 A wrathful man stirreth up strife: but he that is slow to anger appeaseth strife.19 The way of the slothful man is as an hedge of thorns: but the way of the righteous is made plain.20 A wise son make a glad father: but a foolish man despiseth his mother.21 Folly is joy to him that is destitute of wisdom: but a man of understanding walk uprightly.22 Without counsel purposes are disappointed: but in the multitude of counsellers they are established.23 A man has joy by the answer of his mouth: and a word spoken in due season, how good is it!24 The way of life is above to the wise, that he may depart from hell beneath.25 YHUH will destroy the house of the proud: but he will establish the border of the widow.26 The thoughts of the wicked are an abomination to YHUH: but the words of the pure are pleasant words.27 He that is greedy of gain trouble his own house; but he that hateth gifts shall live.

15:28

בצע 1215 ושונא 8130 מתנת 4979 יחיה 2421: לב 3820 צדיק 6662 יהגה 1897 לענות 6030 ופי 6310 רשעים 7563

batza'; uasounea' matanot yichayeh. leb tzadiyq yehageh la'anout; uapiy rasha'aym,

**gain but he that hate gifts shall live The heart of the righteous study to answer but the mouth of the wicked**

15:29 15:30

יביע 5042 רעות 7451: רחוק 7350 יהוה 3068 מרשעים 7563 ותפלת 8605 צדיקים 6662 ישמע 8085: מאור 3974

yabiya' ra'aut. rachouq Yahuah merasha'aym; uatpilat tzadiyqiym yishma'. ma'aur

**pour out evil things *is* far Yahuah from the wicked but the prayer of the righteous he hear The light of**

15:31

עינים 5869 ישמח 8055 לב 3820 שמועה 8052 טובה 2896 תדשן 1878 עצם 6106: אזן 241 שמעת 8085 תוכחת 8433 חיים 2416

'aeynayim yasamach leb; shamu'ah toubah, tadashen 'atzem. 'azen, shoma'at toukachat chayiym;

**the eyes rejoice the heart *and* a report good make fat the bones The ear that hear the reproof of life**

15:32

בקרב 7130 חכמים 2450 תלין 3885: פורע 6544 מוסר 4148 מואס 3988 נפשו 5315 ושומע 8085 תוכחת 8433 קונה 7069

baqereb chakamiym taliyn. pourea' musar mou'aes napshou; uashomea' toukachat, qouneh

**among the wise abide He that refuse instruction despise his own soul but he that hear reproof get**

15:33

לב 3820: יראת 3374 יהוה 3068 מוסר 4148 חכמה 2451 ולפני 6440 כבוד 3519 ענוה 6038:

leb. yir'at Yahuah musar chakamah ualipaney kaboud 'anauah.

**understanding The fear of Yahuah *is* the instruction of wisdom and before honor *is* humility**

**Prov 16:1** 16:2

לאדם 120 מערכי 4633 לב 3820 ומיהוה 3068 מענה 4617 לשון 3956: כל 3605 דרכי 1870

la'adam ma'arkey leb; uameYahuah ma'aneh lashoun. kal darkey

**in man The preparations of the heart *is* and from Yahuah the answer of the tongue All the ways of**

16:3

איש 376 זך 2134 בעיניו 5869 ותכן 8505 רוחות 7307 יהוה 3069: גל 1556 אל 413 יהוה 3068 מעשיך 4639

'aysh zak ba'aeynayu; uatoken ruchout Yahuah. gol 'al Yahuah ma'aseyka;

**a man *are* clean in his own eyes but weigh the spirits Yahuah Commit unto Yahuah your works**

16:4

ויכנו 3559 מחשבתיך 4284: כל 3605 פעל 6466 יהוה 3068 למענהו 4617 וגם 1571 רשע 7563 ליום 3117

uayikonu, machshaboteyka. kol pa'al Yahuah lama'anehu; uagam rasha', layoum

**and shall be established your thoughts all has made Yahuah *things* for himself yea even the wicked for the day of**

16:5

רעה 7451: תועבת 8441 יהוה 3068 כל 3605 גבה 1362 לב 3820 יד 3027 ליד 3027 לא 3808

ra'ah. tou'abat Yahuah kal gabah leb; yad layad, la'

**evil *is* an abomination to Yahuah Everyone *that is* proud in heart *though* hand *join* in hand not**

16:6 16:7

ינקה 5352: בחסד 2617 ואמת 571 יכפר 3722 עון 5771 וביראת 3374 יהוה 3068 סור 5493 מרע 7451:

yinaqeh. bachesed ua'amet yakupar 'auon; uabyir'at Yahuah sur mera'.

**he shall be unpunished By mercy and truth is purged iniquity and by the fear of Yahuah *men* depart from evil**

16:8

ברצות 7521 יהוה 3068 דרכי 1870 איש 376 גם 1571 אויביו 341 ישלם 7999 אתו 854: טוב 2896 מעט 4592

birtzout Yahuah darkey 'aysh; gam 'auyabayu, yashlim 'atou. toub ma'at

**When please Yahuah a ways man's even his enemies he make to be at peace with him Better *is* a little**

16:9

בצדקה 6666 מרב 7230 תבואות 8393 בלא 3808 משפט 4941: לב 3820 אדם 120 יחשב 2803 דרכו 1870 ויהוה 3068 יכין 3559

bitzadaqah; merob tabu'aut, bala' mishapat. leb 'adam yachasheb darkou; uaYahuah yakiyn

**with righteousness than great revenues without right A heart man's devise his way but Yahuah direct**

Pro 15:28 The heart of the righteous studieth to answer: but the mouth of the wicked poureth out evil things.29 YHUH is far from the wicked: but he hear the prayer of the righteous.30 The light of the eyes rejoice the heart: and a good report make the bones fat.31 The ear that hear the reproof of life abideth among the wise.32 He that refuseth instruction despiseth his own soul: but he that hear reproof get understanding.33 The fear of YHUH is the instruction of wisdom; and before honor is humility. **Pro** 16 :1 The preparations of the heart in man, and the answer of the tongue, is from YHUH.2 All the ways of a man are clean in his own eyes; but YHUH weigheth the spirits.3 Commit your works unto YHUH, and your thoughts shall be established.4 YHUH has made all things for himself: yea, even the wicked for the day of evil.5 Every one that is proud in heart is an abomination to YHUH: though hand join in hand, he shall not be unpunished.6 By mercy and truth iniquity is purged: and by the fear of YHUH men depart from evil. 7 When a man's ways please YHUH, he make even his enemies to be at peace with him. 8 Better is a little with righteousness than great revenues without right.9 A man's heart deviseth his way: but YHUH directeth his steps.

17:7 17:8
אבותם 1: | לא 3808 | נאוה 5000 | לנבל 5036 | שפת 8193 | יתר 3499 | אף 637 | כי 3588 | לנדיב 5081 | שפת 8193 | שקר 8267: | אבן 68
aboutam. la' na'uah lanabal sapat yeter; 'aap, kiy lanadiyb sapat shaqer. 'aben
***are* their fathers** **not** **become** **a fool** **speech** **Excellent** **much less** **for** **a prince** **lips** ***do* lying** **stone**

17:9
חן 2580 | השחד 7810 | בעיני 5869 | בעליו 1167 | אל 413 | כל 3605 | אשר 834 | יפנה 6437 | ישכיל 7919: | מכסה 3680
chen hashochad ba'aeyney ba'alayu; 'al kal 'asher yipneh yaskiyl. makaseh
***is as* a precious** **A gift** **in the eyes of** **him that has it** **to** **whithersoever** **after** **it turned** **it prospers** **He that cover**

17:10
פשע 6588 | מבקש 1245 | אהבה 160 | ושנה 8138 | בדבר 1697 | מפריד 6504 | אלוף 441: | תחת 5181 | גערה 1606
pesha' mabaqesh 'ahabah; uashanah badabar, mapriyd 'alup. techat ga'arah
**a transgression** **seek** **love** **but he that repeats** **a matter** **separates** ***very* friends** **enter** **A reproof**

17:11
במבין 995 | מהכות 5221 | כסיל 3684 | מאה 3967: | אך 389 | מרי 4805 | יבקש 1245 | רע 7451 | ומלאך 4397
bamebiyn; mehakout kasiyl me'ah. 'ak mariy yabaqesh ra'; uamal'ak
***more* into a wise man** **than an stripes** ***into* a fool** **hundred** **only** **rebellion** ***man* seek** **An evil** **therefore a messenger**

17:12 17:13
אכזרי 394 | ישלח 7971 | בו 871a: | פגוש 6298 | דב 1677 | שכול 7909 | באיש 376 | ואל 408 | כסיל 3684 | באולתו 200:
'akzariy, yashulach bou. pagoush dob shakul ba'aysh; ua'al kasiyl, ba'aualtou.
**cruel** **shall be sent against him** **Let meet a bear robbed of her whelps** **a man** **rather than a fool** **in his folly**

17:14
משיב 7725 | רעה 7451 | תחת 8478 | טובה 2896 | לא 3808 | תמיש 4185 | רעה 7451 | מביתו 1004: | פוטר 6362 | מים 4325
meshiyb ra'ah tachat toubah; la' tamiysh ra'ah, mibeytou. pouter mayim
**Whoso reward** **evil** **for** **good** **not** **shall depart** **evil** **from his house** ***is as* when one let out** **water**

17:15
ראשית 7225 | מדון 4066 | ולפני 6440 | התגלע 1566 | הריב 7379 | נטוש 5203: | מצדיק 6663 | רשע 7563
ra'shiyt madoun; ualipaney hitgala', hariyb natoush. matzdiyq rasha'
**The beginning of** **strife** **therefore before** **it be meddled with** **contention** **leave off** **He that justifies** **the wicked**

17:16
ומרשיע 7561 | צדיק 6662 | תועבת 8441 | יהוה 3068 | גם 1571 | שניהם 8147: | למה 4100 | זה 2088 | מחיר 4242
uamarshiya' tzadiyq; tou'abat Yahuah gam shaneyhem. lamah zeh machiyr
**and he that condemn** **the just** ***are* abomination to** **Yahuah** **even** **they both** **Wherefore** **this** ***is there* a price**

17:17
ביד 3027 | כסיל 3684 | לקנות 7069 | חכמה 2451 | ולב 3820 | אין 369: | בכל 3605 | עת 6256 | אהב 157 | הרע 7453 | ואח 251
bayad kasiyl; liqnout chakamah ualeb 'ayin. bakal 'at 'aheb harea'; ua'ach
**in the hand of** **a fool** **to get** **wisdom *to it*? seeing *he has* heart** **no** **at all** **times** **love** **A friend** **and a brother**

17:18
לצרה 6869 | יולד 3205: | אדם 120 | חסר 2638 | לב 3820 | תוקע 8628 | כף 3709 | ערב 6148 | ערבה 6161 | לפני 6440
latzarah, yiualed. 'adam chasar leb touqea' kap; 'areb 'arubah, lipney
**for adversity** **is born** **A man** **void of** **understanding** **strike** **hands** ***and* become** **surety** **in the presence of**

17:19 17:20
רעהו 7453: | אהב 157 | פשע 6588 | אהב 157 | מצה 4683 | מגביה 1361 | פתחו 6607 | מבקש 1245 | שבר 7667:
re'aehu. 'aheb pesha' 'aheb matzah; magabiyah pitchou, mabaqesh shaber.
**his friend** **He love** **transgression** **that love** **strife** ***and* he that exalt** **his gate** **seek** **destruction**

עקש 6141 | לב 3820 | לא 3808 | ימצא 4672 | טוב 2896 | ונהפך 2015 | בלשונו 3956 | יפול 5307 | ברעה 7451:
'aqesh leb la' yimtza toub; uanehpak bilshounou, yipoul bara'ah.
**He that has a froward heart** **no** **finds** **good** **and he that has a perverse tongue** **fall** **into mischief**

Pro 17:7 Excellent speech becometh not a fool: much less do lying lips a prince.8 A gift is as a precious stone in the eyes of him that has it: whithersoever it turneth, it prospereth.9 He that covereth a transgression seek love; but he that repeateth a matter separateth very friends. 10 A reproof entereth more into a wise man than an hundred stripes into a fool.11 An evil man seek only rebellion: therefore a cruel messenger shall be sent against him.12 Let a bear robbed of her whelps meet a man, rather than a fool in his folly.13 Whoso rewardeth evil for good, evil shall not depart from his house.14 The beginning of strife is as when one lets out water: therefore leave off contention, before it be meddled with.15 He that justifieth the wicked, and he that condemneth the just, even they both are abomination to YHUH.16 Wherefore is there a price in the hand of a fool to get wisdom, seeing he has no heart to it?17 A friend love at all times, and a brother is born for adversity.18 A man void of understanding striketh hands, and becometh surety in the presence of his friend. 19 He love transgression that love strife: and he that exalteth his gate seek destruction. 20 He that has a froward heart findeth no good: and he that has a perverse tongue fall into mischief.

**17:21** ילד 3205 כסיל 3684 לתוגה 8424 לו 3807a ולא 3808 ישמח 8055 אבי 1 נבל 5036: **17:22** לב 3820 שמח 8056
yoled kasiyl latugah lou'; uala' yismach, 'abiy nabal. leb sameach
**He that beget a fool *does it* to his sorrow: do it and no has joy the father of a fool A heart merry**

ייטב 3190 גהה 1456 ורוח 7307 נכאה 5218 תיבש 3001 גרם 1634: **17:23** שחד 7810 מחיק 2436 רשע 7563 יקח 3947
yeytiyb gehah; uaruach nake'ah, tayabesh garem. shochad mecheyq rasha' yiqach;
**does good *like* a medicine but a spirit broken dries the bones a gift out of the bosom A wicked *man* takes**

להטות 5186 ארחות 734 משפט 4941: **17:24** את 854 פני 6440 מבין 995 חכמה 2451 ועיני 5869 כסיל 3684
lahatout, 'arachout mishapat. 'at paney mebiyn chakamah ua'aeyney kasiyl,
**to pervert the ways of judgment before him that has understanding Wisdom *is* but the eyes of a fool**

בקצה 7097 ארץ 776: **17:25** כעס 3708 לאביו 1 בן 1121 כסיל 3684 וממר 4470 ליולדתו 3205: **17:26** גם 1571
biqtzeh 'aretz. ka'as la'abiyu ben kasiyl; uamemer, layouladtou. gam
***are* in the ends of the earth *is* a grief to his father A son foolish and bitterness to her that bare him Also**

ענוש 6064 לצדיק 6662 לא 3808 טוב 2896 להכות 5221 נדיבים 5081 על 5921 ישר 3476: **17:27** חושך 2820 אמריו 561 יודע 3045 דעת 1847
anoush latzadiyq la' toub; lahakout nadiybiym 'al yosher. chousek 'amarayu youdea' da'at;
**to punish the just *is* not good *nor* to strike princes for equity spares his words He that has knowledge**

וקר 7119 רוח 7307 איש 376 תבונה 8394: **17:28** גם 1571 אויל 191 מחריש 2790 חכם 2450 יחשב 2803
uaqar ruach, 'aysh tabunah. gam 'auiyl machariysh chakam yechasheb;
***is of* an excellent spirit *and* a man of understanding Even a fool when he holds his peace wise is counted**

אטם 331 שפתיו 8193 נבון 995:
'atem sapatayu naboun.
***and* he that shut his lips *is esteemed* a man of understanding**

**Prov 18:1** לתאוה 8378 יבקש 1245 נפרד 6504 בכל 3605 תושיה 8454 יתגלע 1566: **18:2** לא 3808
lata'auah yabaqesh niprad; bakal tushiyah, yitgala'. la'
**Through desire seek a man having separated himself with all wisdom *and* intermeddle no**

יחפץ 2654 כסיל 3684 בתבונה 8394 כי 3588 אם 518 בהתגלות 1540 לבו 3820: **18:3** בבוא 935 רשע 7563 בא 935 גם 1571
yachpotz kasiyl bitabunah; kiy, 'am bahitgalout libou. babou'a rasha' ba' gam
**has delight A fool in understanding that but may discover his heart When comes the wicked *then* comes also**

בוז 937 ועם 5973 קלון 7036 חרפה 2781: **18:4** מים 4325 עמקים 6013 דברי 1697 פי 6310 איש 376 נחל 5158 נבע 5042
buz; ua'am qaloun cherpah. mayim 'amuqiym dibrey piy 'aysh; nachal nobea',
**contempt and with ignominy reproach waters *are as* deep The words of a mouth man's *as* a brook flowing**

מקור 4726 חכמה 2451: **18:5** שאת 5375 פני 6440 רשע 7563 לא 3808 טוב 2896 להטות 5186 צדיק 6662
maqour chakamah sa'aet paney rasha' la' toub; lahatout tzadiyq,
***and* the wellspring of wisdom you to accept the person of the wicked not *It is* good to overthrow the righteous**

במשפט 4941: **18:6** שפתי 8193 כסיל 3684 יבאו 935 בריב 7379 ופיו 6310 למהלמות 4112 יקרא 7121: **18:7** פי 6310 כסיל 3684
bamishpat. siptey kasiyl yabo'au bariyb; uapiyu, lamahalumout yiqra'. piy kasiyl
**in judgment A lips fool's enter into contention and his mouth for strokes call A mouth fool's**

Pro 17:21 He that begetteth a fool doeth it to his sorrow: and the father of a fool has no joy.22 A merry heart doeth good like a medicine: but a broken spirit drieth the bones.23 A wicked man take a gift out of the bosom to pervert the ways of judgment.24 Wisdom is before him that has understanding; but the eyes of a fool are in the ends of the earth. 25 A foolish son is a grief to his father, and bitterness to her that bare him.26 Also to punish the just is not good, nor to strike princes for equity.27 He that has knowledge spareth his words: and a man of understanding is of an excellent spirit.28 Even a fool, when he holdeth his peace, is counted wise: and he that shutteth his lips is esteemed a man of understanding. **Pro** 18:1 Through desire a man, having separated himself, seek and intermeddleth with all wisdom.2 A fool has no delight in understanding, but that his heart may discover itself.3 When the wicked cometh, then cometh also contempt, and with ignominy reproach.4 The words of a man's mouth are as deep waters, and the wellspring of wisdom as a flowing brook.5 It is not good to accept the person of the wicked, to overthrow the righteous in judgment. 6 A fool's lips enter into contention, and his mouth call for strokes.

18:8

מחתה 4288 | לו 3807a | ושפתיו 8193 | מוקש 4170 | נפשו 5315: | דברי 1697 | נרגן 5372 | כמתלהמים 3859 | והם 1992

machitah lou'; uasapatayu, mouqesh napshou. dibrey nirgan kamitlahamiym; uahem,

***is*** **his destruction his and his lips *are* the snare of his soul The words of a talebearer *are* as wounds and they**

18:9

ירדו 3381 | חדרי 2315 | בטן 990: | גם 1571 | מתרפה 7503 | במלאכתו 4399 | אח 251 | הוא 1931 | לבעל 1167

yaradu chadrey baten. gam mitrapeh bimla'ktou; 'ach hua', laba'al

**go down *into* the innermost parts of the belly also that is slothful in his work *is* brother He to him that is a great**

18:10 18:11

משחית 7843: | מגדל 4026 | עז 5797 | שם 8034 | יהוה 3069 | בו 871a | ירוץ 7323 | צדיק 6662 | ונשגב 7682: | הון 1952 | עשיר 6223

mashchiyt. migdal 'az shem Yahuah; bou yarutz tzadiyq uanisgab. houn 'ashiyr

**waster *is* a tower strong The name of Yahuah into it run the righteous and is safe The wealth rich man's**

18:12

קרית 7151 | עזו 5797 | וכחומה 2346 | נשגבה 7682 | במשכיתו 4906: | לפני 6440 | שבר 7667 | יגבה 1361 | לב 3820 | איש 376

qiryat 'azou; uakchoumah nisgabah, bamaskiytou. lipney sheber yigabah leb 'aysh;

**city *is* his strong and as an wall high in his own conceit Before destruction is haughty the heart of man**

18:13 18:14

ולפני 6440 | כבוד 3519 | ענוה 6038: | משיב 7725 | דבר 1697 | בטרם 2962 | ישמע 8085 | אולת 200 | היא 1931 | לו 3807a | וכלמה 3639:

ualipney kaboud 'anauah. meshiyb dabar baterem yishma'; 'auelet hiy'a lou', uaklimah.

**and before honor *is* humility He that answer a matter before he hear *it, is* folly it unto him and shame**

18:15

רוח 7307 | איש 376 | יכלכל 3557 | מחלהו 4245 | ורוח 7307 | נכאה 5218 | מי 4310 | ישאנה 5375: | לב 3820 | נבון 995 | יקנה 7069

ruach 'aysh yakalkel machalehu; uaruach nake'ah, miy' yisa'anah. leb naboun yiqneh

**The spirit of a man will sustain his infirmity but a spirit wounded who can bear? The heart of the prudent get**

18:16

דעת 1847 | ואזן 241 | חכמים 2450 | תבקש 1245 | דעת 1847: | מתן 4976 | אדם 120 | ירחיב 7337 | לו 3807a | ולפני 6440 | גדלים 1419

da'at; ua'azen chakamiym, tabaqesh da'at. matan 'adam yarchiyb lou'; ualipaney gadoliym

**knowledge and the ear of the wise seek knowledge A gift man's make room for him and before great *men***

18:17 18:18

ינחנו 5148: | צדיק 6662 | הראשון 7223 | בריבו 7379 | יבא 935 | רעהו 7453 | וחקרו 2713: | מדינים 4079

yanchenu. tzadiyq hara'shoun bariybou; yaba' re'aehu, uachaqarou. midyaniym

**bring him *seems* just *He that is* first in his own cause but comes his neighbor and searches him contentions**

18:19

ישבית 7673 | הגורל 1486 | ובין 996 | עצומים 6099 | יפריד 6504: | אח 251 | נפשע 6586 | מקרית 7151 | עז 5797

yashbiyt hagoural; uabeyn 'atzumiym yapriyd. 'ach, nipsha' miqiryat 'az;

**cause to cease The lot and between the mighty part A brother offended *is harder to be won* than a city strong**

18:20

ומדונים 4066 | כבריח 1280 | ארמון 759: | מפרי 6529 | פי 6310 | איש 376 | תשבע 7646 | בטנו 990

uamedouniym kibriyach 'armoun. mipriy piy 'aysh tisba' bitnou;

**and their contentions *are* like the bars of a castle with the fruit of his mouth A man's shall be satisfied belly**

18:21

תבואת 8393 | שפתיו 8193 | ישבע 7646: | מות 4194 | וחיים 2416 | ביד 3027 | לשון 3956

tabu'at sapatayu yisba'. mauet uachayiym bayad lashoun;

***and*** **with the increase of his lips shall he be filled Death and life *are* in the power of the tongue**

18:22

ואהביה 157 | יאכל 398 | פריה 6529: | מצא 4672 | אשה 802 | מצא 4672 | טוב 2896 | ויפק 6329 | רצון 7522

ua'ahabeyha, ya'kal piryah. matza' 'ashah matza' toub; uayapeq ratzoun,

**and they that love it shall eat the fruit thereof *Whoso* finds a wife finds a good *thing* and obtains favor**

Pro 18:7 A fool's mouth is his destruction, and his lips are the snare of his soul.8 The words of a talebearer are as wounds, and they go down into the innermost parts of the belly.9 He also that is slothful in his work is brother to him that is a great waster.10 The name of YHUH is a strong tower: the righteous runneth into it, and is safe.11 The rich man's wealth is his strong city, and as an high wall in his own conceit.12 Before destruction the heart of man is haughty, and before honor is humility.13 He that answer a matter before he hear it, it is folly and shame unto him.14 The spirit of a man will sustain his infirmity; but a wounded spirit who can bear?15 The heart of the prudent get knowledge; and the ear of the wise seek knowledge.16 A man's gift make room for him, and bring him before great men.17 He that is first in his own cause seem just; but his neighbor cometh and searcheth him.18 The lot causeth contentions to cease, and parteth between the mighty.19 A brother offended is harder to be won than a strong city: and their contentions are like the bars of a castle.20 A man's belly shall be satisfied with the fruit of his mouth; and with the increase of his lips shall he be filled.21 Death and life are in the power of the tongue: 21 and they that love it shall eat the fruit thereof.22 Whoso findeth a wife findeth a good thing, and obtaineth favor of YHUH.

**18:23** **18:24**

מיהוה 3068: תחנונים 8469 ידבר 1696 רש 7326 ועשיר 6223 יענה 6030 עזות 5794: איש 376 רעים 7453
meYahuah. tachanuniym yadaber ra'sh; ua'ashiyr, ya'aneh azout. 'aysh re'aym
**of Yahuah intreaties use The poor but the rich answer roughly A man *that has* friends**

להתרעע 7489 ויש 3426 אהב 157 דבק 1695 מאח 251:
lahitro'aea'; uayesh 'aheb, dabeq me'ach.
**must show himself friendly and there is a friend *that* sticks closer than a brother**

**Prov 19:1** **19:2**

טוב 2896 רש 7326 הולך 1980 בתמו 8537 מעקש 6141 שפתיו 8193 והוא 1931 כסיל 3684: גם 1571
toub rash houlek batumou; me'aqesh sapatayu, uahu'a kasiyl. gam
**Better *is* the poor that walk in his integrity than *he that is* perverse in his lips and he *is* a fool Also**

**19:3**

בלא 3808 דעת 1847 נפש 5315 לא 3808 טוב 2896 ואץ 213 ברגלים 7272 חוטא 2398: אולת 200 אדם 120
bala' da'at nepesh la' toub; ua'atz baraglayim choutea'. 'auelet 'adam
***be* without knowledge *that* the soul *it is* not good and he that hasten with *his* feet sin The foolishness of man**

**19:4**

תסלף 5557 דרכו 1870 ועל 5921 יהוה 3068 יזעף 2196 לבו 3820: הון 1952 יסיף 3254 רעים 7453 רבים 7227 ודל 1800 מרעהו 7453
tasalep darkou; ua'al Yahuah yiz'ap libou. houn, yosiyp re'aym rabiym; uadal, mera'hua'
**pervert his way and against Yahuah fret his heart Wealth make friends many but the poor from his neighbour**

**19:5** **19:6**

יפרד 6504: עד 5707 שקרים 8267 לא 3808 ינקה 5352 ויפיח 6315 כזבים 3577 לא 3808 ימלט 4422:
yipared. 'aed shaqariym la' yinaqeh; uayapiyach kazabiym, la' yimalet.
**is separated A witness false not shall be unpunished and *he that* speak lies not shall escape**

**19:7**

רבים 7227 יחלו 2470 פני 6440 נדיב 5081 וכל 3605 הרע 7453 לאיש 376 מתן 4976: כל 3605 אחי 251
rabiym yachalu paney nadiyb; uakal harea', la'aysh matan. kal 'achey
**Many will intreat the favor of the prince and every man *is* a friend to him that gives gifts All the brethren of**

רש 7326 שנאהו 8130 אף 637 כי 3588 מרעהו 4828 רחקו 7368 ממנו 4480 מרדף 7291 אמרים 561 לא 3808
rash sane'ahu, 'ap kiy mare'aehu rachaqu mimenu; maradep 'amariym la'
**the poor do hate him how much more that his friends do go far from him? he pursue *them with* words *are* wanting *to him.***

**19:8** **19:9**

המה 1992: קנה 7069 לב 3820 אהב 157 נפשו 5315 שמר 8104 תבונה 8394 למצא 4672 טוב 2896: עד 5704 שקרים 8267
hemah. qoneh leb 'aheb napshou; shomer tabunah, limtza' toub. 'aed shaqariym
***yet* they He that get wisdom love his own soul he that keep understanding shall find good A witness false**

**19:10**

לא 3808 ינקה 5352 ויפיח 6315 כזבים 3577 יאבד 6: לא 3808 נאוה 5000 לכסיל 3684 תענוג 8588 אף 637
la' yinaqeh; uayapiyach kazabiym ya'bed. la' naa'ueh liksiyl ta'anug; 'aap,
**not shall be unpunished and *he that* speak lies shall perish not is seemly for a fool Delight much less**

**19:11**

כי 3588 לעבד 5650 משל 4910 בשרים 8269: שכל 7922 אדם 120 האריך 748 אפו 639 ותפארתו 8597 עבר 5674 על 5921
kiy la'abed mashol basariym. sekel 'adam he'ariyk 'apou; uatip'artou, 'abor 'al
**for a servant to have rule over princes The discretion of a man defer his anger and *it is* his glory to pass over**

**19:12**

פשע 6588: נהם 5099 ככפיר 3715 זעף 2197 מלך 4428 וכטל 2919 על 5921 עשב 6212 רצונו 7522:
pasha'. naham kakapiyr za'ap melek; uakatal 'al 'aeseb ratzounou.
**a transgression *is* as the roaring of a lion wrath *The* king's but as dew upon the grass his favor *is***

Pro 18:23 The poor useth intreaties; but the rich answer roughly.24 A man that has friends must show himself friendly: and there is a friend that sticketh closer than a brother. **Pro** 19:1 Better is the poor that walk in his integrity, than he that is perverse in his lips, and is a fool.2 Also, that the soul be without knowledge, it is not good; and he that hasteth with his feet sin. 3 The foolishness of man perverteth his way: and his heart fretteth against YHUH.4 Wealth make many friends; but the poor is separated from his neighbor. 5 A false witness shall not be unpunished, and he that speaketh lies shall not escape.6 Many will entreat the favor of the prince: and every man is a friend to him that give gifts. 7 All the brethren of the poor do hate him: how much more do his friends go far from him? he pursueth them with words, yet they are wanting to him.8 He that get wisdom love his own soul: he that keep understanding shall find good.9 A false witness shall not be unpunished, and he that speaketh lies shall perish.10 Delight is not seemly for a fool; much less for a servant to have rule over princes. 11 The discretion of a man deferreth his anger; and it is his glory to pass over a transgression. 12 The king's wrath is as the roaring of a lion; but his favor is as dew upon the grass.13 A foolish son is the calamity of his father: and the contentions of a wife are a continual dropping.

**19:13** … **19:14**
הות 1942 לאביו 1 בן 1121 כסיל 3684 ודלף 1812 טרד 2956 מדיני 4079 אשה 802: בית 1004
hauot la'abiyu ben kasiyl; uadelep tored, midyaney 'ashah. bayit
**is the calamity of his father A son foolish and a dropping continual the contentions of a wife are House**

**19:15**
והון 1952 נחלת 5159 אבות 1 ומיהוה 3068 אשה 802 משכלת 7919: עצלה 6103 תפיל 5307 תרדמה 8639
uahoun nachalat about; uameYahuah 'ashah maskalet. 'atzlah tapiyl tardemah;
**and riches *are* the inheritance of fathers and from Yahuah *is* a wife prudent Slothfulness cast *into* a deep sleep**

**19:16**
ונפש 5315 רמיה 7423 תרעב 7456: שמר 8104 מצוה 4687 שמר 8104 נפשו 5315 בוזה 959
uanepesh ramiyah tir'ab. shomer mitzuah shomer napshou; bouzeh
**and an soul idle shall suffer hunger He that keep the commandment keep his own soul *but* he that despise**

**9:17**
דרכיו 1870 יומת 4191 מלוה 3867 יהוה 3068 חונן 2603 דל 1800 וגמלו 1576 ישלם 7999
darakayu yumat malueh Yahuah chounen dal; uagmulou, yashalem
**his ways shall die. lend unto Yahuah He that has pity upon the poor and that which he has given will he pay again**

**19:18** … **19:19**
לו 3807a: יסר 3256 בנך 1121 כי 3588 יש 3426 תקוה 8615 ואל 413 המיתו 4191 אל 408 תשא 5375 נפשך 5315: גרל 1632
lou'. yaser binka kiy yesh tiquah; ua'al hamiytou, 'al tisa' napsheka. goral
**him Chasten your son while there is hope and for his crying not let spare your soul A man of great**

**19:20**
חמה 2534 נשא 5375 ענש 6066 כי 3588 אם 518 תציל 5337 ועוד 5750 תוסף 3254: שמע 8085 עצה 6098 וקבל 6901
chemah nosea' 'anesh; kiy 'am tatziyl, ua'aud tousip. shama' 'aetzah uaqabel
**wrath shall suffer punishment for if you deliver *him* yet you must do it again Hear counsel and receive**

**19:21**
מוסר 4148 למען 4616 תחכם 2449 באחריתך 319: רבות 7227 מחשבות 4284 בלב 3820 איש 376
musar; lama'an, techakam ba'achariyteka. rabout machashabout baleb 'aysh;
**instruction that you may be wise in your latter end *There are* many devices in a heart man's**

**19:22**
ועצת 6098 יהוה 3068 היא 1931 תקום 6965: תאות 8378 אדם 120 חסדו 2617 וטוב 2896 רש 7326
ua'atzat Yahuah hiy'a taqum. ta'auat 'adam chasdou; uatoub rash
**nevertheless the counsel of Yahuah that he shall stand The desire of a man *is* his kindness and better a poor man**

**19:23**
מאיש 376 כזב 3577: יראת 3374 יהוה 3068 לחיים 2416 ושבע 7649 ילין 3885 בל 1077 יפקד 6485
me'aysh kazab. yir'at Yahuah lachayiym; uasabea' yaliyn, bal yipaqed
***is* than man a liar The fear of Yahuah *tend* to life and satisfied *he that has it* shall abide not he shall be visited**

**19:24** … **19:25**
רע 7451: טמן 2934 עצל 6102 ידו 3027 בצלחת 6747 גם 1571 אל 413 פיהו 6310 לא 3808 ישיבנה 7725:
ra'. taman 'atzel yadou batzalachat; gam 'al piyhu, la' yashiybenah.
***with* evil *man* hides A slothful his hand in *his* bosom and so much as to his mouth not will bring it again**

לץ 3887 תכה 5221 ופתי 6612 יערם 6191 והוכיח 3198 לנבון 995 יבין 995
letz takeh uapetiy ya'arim; uahoukiyach lanaboun, yabiyn
**a scorner Smite and the simple will beware and reprove one that has understanding *and* he will understand**

**19:26** … **19:27**
דעת 1847: משדד 7703 מוסר 4148 לשגות 7686 מאמרי 561 דעת 1847: חדל 2308 בני 1121 לשמע 8085
da'at. mashaded musar; lishgout, me'amrey da'at. chadal baniy lishmoa'
**knowledge He that waste the instruction *that cause* to err from the words of knowledge Cease my son to hear**

Pro 19:14 House and riches are the inheritance of fathers and a prudent wife is from YHUH.15 Slothfulness casteth into a deep sleep; and an idle soul shall suffer hunger.16 He that keep the commandment keep his own soul; but he that despiseth his ways shall die.17 He that has pity upon the poor lendeth unto YHUH; and that which he has given will he pay him again.18 Chasten your son while there is hope, and let not your soul spare for his crying.19 A man of great wrath shall suffer punishment: for if you deliver him, yet you must do it again.20 Hear counsel, and receive instruction, that you may be wise in your latter end.21 There are many devices in a man's heart; nevertheless the counsel of YHUH, that shall stand.22 The desire of a man is his kindness: and a poor man is better than a liar.23 The fear of YHUH tendeth to life: and he that has it shall abide satisfied; he shall not be visited with evil.24 A slothful man hide his hand in his bosom, and will not so much as bring it to his mouth again.25 Smite a scorner, and the simple will beware: and reprove one that has understanding, and he will understand knowledge. 26 He that wasteth his father, and chaseth away his mother, is a son that causeth shame, and bring reproach. 27 Cease, my son, to hear the instruction that causeth to err from the words of knowledge.

19:28

מוסר 4148 לשגות 7686 מאמרי 561 דעת 1847: עד 5704 בליעל 1100 יליץ 3887 משפט 4941 ופי 6310

musar; lishgout, me'amrey da'at. 'aed baliya'al yaliytz mishapat; uapiy

**the instruction *that cause* to err from the words of knowledge An witness ungodly scorn judgment and the mouth of**

19:29

רשעים 7563 יבלע 1104 און 205: נכונו 3559 ללצים 3887 שפטים 8201 ומהלמות 4112 לגו 1460 כסילים 3684:

rasha'aym, yabala' 'auen. nakounu laletziym shapatiym; uamahalumout, lageu kasiyliym.

**the wicked devour iniquity are prepared for scorners Judgments and stripes for the back of fools**

**Prov 20:1** 20:2

לץ 3887 היין 3196 המה 1993 שכר 7941 וכל 3605 שגה 7686 בו 871a לא 3808 יחכם 2449:

letz hayayin homeh shekar; uakal shogeh bou, la' yechakam.

***is* a mocker Wine *is* raging strong drink and whosoever is deceived thereby not is wise**

20:3

נהם 5099 ככפיר 3715 אימת 367 מלך 4428 מתעברו 5674 חוטא 2398 נפשו 5315: כבוד 3519

naham kakapiyr 'aeymat melek; mita'abarou, choutea' napshou. kaboud

**the roaring of *is* as a lion The fear of a king *whoso* provoke him to anger sin *against* his own soul *It is* an honor**

20:4

לאיש 376 שבת 7674 מריב 7379 וכל 3605 אויל 191 יתגלע 1566: מחרף 2779 עצל 6102 לא 3808 יחרש 2790

la'aysh shebet mariyb; uakal 'auiyl, yitgala'. mechorep 'atzel la' yacharosh;

**for a man to cease from strife but every fool will be meddling by reason of the cold The sluggard not will plow**

20:5

ישאל 7592 בקציר 7105 ואין 369: מים 4325 עמקים 6013 עצה 6098 בלב 3820 איש 376 ואיש 376

yish'al baqatziyr ua'ayin. mayim 'amuqiym 'aetzah baleb 'aysh; ua'aysh

**therefore shall he beg in harvest and have nothing water *is like* deep Counsel in the heart of man but a man of**

20:6

תבונה 8394 ידלנה 1802: רב 7230 אדם 120 יקרא 7121 איש 376 חסדו 2617 ואיש 376 אמונים 529 מי 4310

tabunah yidlenah. rab 'adam, yiqraa' 'aysh chasdou; ua'aysh 'amuniym, miy'

**understanding will draw it out Most men will proclaim every one his own goodness but *a* man faithful who**

20:7 20:8

ימצא 4672: מתהלך 1980 בתמו 8537 צדיק 6662 אשרי 835 בניו 1121 אחריו 310: מלך 4428 יושב 3427 על 5921 כסא 3678

yimtza'. mithalek batumou tzadiyq; 'ashrey banayu 'acharayu. melek, yousheb 'al kisea'

**can find? *man* walk in his integrity *The* just *are* blessed his children after him A king that sit in the throne of**

20:9

דין 1779 מזרה 2219 בעיניו 5869 כל 3605 רע 7451: מי 4310 יאמר 559 זכיתי 2135 לבי 3820 טהרתי 2891

diyn; mazareh ba'aeynayu kal ra'. miy' ya'mar zikiytiy libiy; tahartiy,

**judgment scatters away with his eyes all evil Who can say I have made clean my heart I am pure**

20:10 20:11

מחטאתי 2403: אבן 68 ואבן 68 איפה 374 ואיפה 374 תועבת 8441 יהוה 3068 גם 1571 שניהם 8147: גם 1571

mechata'tiy. 'aben ua'aben 'aeypah ua'aeypah; tou'abat Yahuah gam shaneyhem. gam

**from my sin? Differing weights and differing measures abomination to Yahuah *are* alike both of them Even**

20:12

במעלליו 4611 יתנכר 5234 נער 5288 אם 518 זך 2134 ואם 518 ישר 3477 פעלו 6467: אזן 241 שמעת 8085 ועין 5869 ראה 7200

bama'alalayu yitnaker na'ar; 'am zak ua'am yashar pa'alou. 'azen shoma'at ua'ayin ro'ah;

**by his doings is known a child whether *be* pure and whether *it be* right his work *The* ear hearing and eye *the* seeing**

20:13

יהוה 3068 עשה 6213 גם 1571 שניהם 8147: אל 408 תאהב 157 שנה 8142 פן 6435 תורש 3423 פקח 6491 עיניך 5869

Yahuah 'asah gam shaneyhem. 'al te'ahab shenah pen tiuaresh; paqach 'aeyneyka

**Yahuah has made even both of them not Love sleep lest you come to poverty open your eyes**

Pro 19:28 An ungodly witness scorneth judgment: and the mouth of the wicked devour iniquity.29 Judgments are prepared for scorners, and stripes for the back of fools. **Pro** 20:1 Wine is a mocker, strong drink is raging: and whosoever is deceived thereby is not wise.2 The fear of a king is as the roaring of a lion: whoso provoketh him to anger sin against his own soul.3 It is an honor for a man to cease from strife: but every fool will be meddling.4 The sluggard will not plow by reason of the cold; therefore shall he beg in harvest, and have nothing.5 Counsel in the heart of man is like deep water; but a man of understanding will draw it out.6 Most men will proclaim everyone his own goodness: but a faithful man who can find?7 The just man walk in his integrity: his children are blessed after him.8 A king that sitteth in the throne of judgment scattereth away all evil with his eyes.9 Who can say, I have made my heart clean, I am pure from my sin?10 Divers weights and divers measures both of them are alike abomination to YHUH.11 Even a child is known by his doings whether his work be pure and whether it be right. 12 The hearing ear, and the seeing eye, YHUH has made even both of them.13 Love not sleep,

| שבע 7646 | לחם 3899: | 20:14 | רע 7451 | רע 7451 | יאמר 559 | הקונה 7069 | ואזל 235 | לו 3807a | אז 227 |
|---|---|---|---|---|---|---|---|---|---|
| saba' | lachem. | | ra' | ra' | ya'mar | haqouneh; | ua'azel | lou', | 'az |
| ***and*** **you shall be satisfied** | ***with*** **bread** | | ***It is*** **naught** | ***it is*** **naught** | **saith** | **the buyer** | **but when he is gone** | **his way** | **then** |

| יתהלל 1984: | 20:15 | יש 3426 | זהב 2091 | ורב 7230 | פנינים 6443 | וכלי 3627 | יקר 3366 | שפתי 8193 | דעת 1847: | 20:16 | לקח 3947 |
|---|---|---|---|---|---|---|---|---|---|---|---|
| yitahalal. | | yesh | zahab | uarab | paniyniym; | uakliy | yaqar, | siptey | da'at. | | laqach |
| **he boast** | | **There is** | **gold** | **and a multitude of** | **rubies** | **but a jewel** | **precious** | **the lips of** | **knowledge** ***are*** | | **Take** |

| בגדו 899 | כי 3588 | ערב 6148 | זר 2114 | ובעד 1157 | נכרים 5237 | חבלהו 2254: | 20:17 | ערב 6149 | לאיש 376 | לחם 3899 |
|---|---|---|---|---|---|---|---|---|---|---|
| bigdou | kiy | 'arab | zar; | uab'ad | nakeriym | chablehu. | | 'areb | la'aysh | lechem |
| **his garment** | **that** | **is surety** ***for*** | **a stranger** | **and for** | **a strange woman.** | **take a pledge of him** | | **is sweet** | **to a man** | **Bread of** |

| שקר 8267 | ואחר 310 | ימלא 4390 | פיהו 6310 | חצץ 2687: | 20:18 | מחשבות 4284 | בעצה 6098 | תכון 3559 |
|---|---|---|---|---|---|---|---|---|
| shaqer; | ua'achar, | yimalea' | piyhu | chatzatz. | | machashabout | ba'aetzah | tikoun; |
| **deceit** | **but afterwards** | **shall be filled** | **his mouth** | ***with*** **gravel** | | ***Every*** **purpose** | **by counsel** | **is established** |

| ובתחבלות 8458 | עשה 6213 | מלחמה 4421: | 20:19 | גולה 1540 | סוד 5475 | הולך 1980 | רכיל 7400 |
|---|---|---|---|---|---|---|---|
| uabtachabulout, | 'aseh | milchamah. | | gouleh | coud | houlek | rakiyl; |
| **and with good advice** | **make** | **war** | | **reveal** | **secrets** | **He that goes about** | ***as*** **a talebearer** |

| ולפתה 6601 | שפתיו 8193 | לא 3808 | תתערב 6148: | 20:20 | מקלל 7043 | אביו 1 | ואמו 517 | ידעך 1846 |
|---|---|---|---|---|---|---|---|---|
| ualpoteh | sapatayu, | la' | tit'arab. | | maqalel | 'abiyu | ua'amou; | yida'ak |
| **therefore with him that flatter** | ***with*** **his lips** | **not** | **meddle** | | **Whoso curses** | **his father** | **or his mother** | **shall be put out** |

| נרו 5216 | באישון 380 | חשך 2822: | 20:21 | נחלה 5159 | מבחלת 973 | בראשנה 7223 | ואחריתה 319 | לא 3808 |
|---|---|---|---|---|---|---|---|---|
| nerou, | be'ayshun | choshek. | | nachalah | mabochelet | bara'shonah; | ua'achariytah, | la' |
| **his lamp** | **in obscure** | **darkness** | | **An inheritance** ***may be*** | **gotten hastily** | **at the beginning** | **but the end thereof** | **not** |

| תברך 1288: | 20:22 | אל 408 | תאמר 559 | אשלמה 7999 | רע 7451 | קוה 6960 | ליהוה 3068 | וישע 3467 | לך 3807a: | 20:23 |
|---|---|---|---|---|---|---|---|---|---|---|
| taborak. | | 'al | ta'mar | 'ashalmah | ra'; | qaueh | laYahuah | uayosha' | lak. | |
| **shall be blessed** | | **not** | **Say you** | **I will recompense** | **evil** | ***but*** **wait** | **onYahuah** | **and he shall save** | **to you** | |

| תועבת 8441 | יהוה 3068 | אבן 68 | ואבן 68 | ומאזני 3976 | מרמה 4820 | לא 3808 | טוב 2896: | 20:24 | מיהוה 3068 | מצעדי 4703 |
|---|---|---|---|---|---|---|---|---|---|---|
| tou'abat | Yahuah | 'aben | ua'aben; | uama'zaney | mirmah | la' | toub. | | meYahuah | mitz'adey |
| ***are*** **an abomination unto** | **Yahuah** | **Differing** | **weights** | ***is*** **and a balance** | **false** | **not** | **good** | | ***are*** **of Yahuah** | **goings** |

| גבר 1397 | ואדם 120 | מה 4100 | יבין 995 | דרכו 1870: | 20:25 | מוקש 4170 | אדם 120 | ילע 3216 | קדש 6944 |
|---|---|---|---|---|---|---|---|---|---|
| gaber; | ua'adam, | mah | yabiyn | darkou. | | mouqesh | 'adam | yala' | qodesh; |
| **man's** | **a man then** | **how** | **can understand** | **his own way?** | | ***It is*** **a snare** | ***to*** **the man** | ***who*** **devours** | ***that which is*** **holy** |

| ואחר 310 | נדרים 5088 | לבקר 1239: | 20:26 | מזרה 2219 | רשעים 7563 | מלך 4428 | חכם 2450 | וישב 7725 | עליהם 5921 | אופן 212: | 20:27 |
|---|---|---|---|---|---|---|---|---|---|---|---|
| ua'achar | nadariym | labaqer. | | mazareh | rasha'aym | melek | chakam; | uayasheb | 'aleyhem | 'aupan. | |
| **and after** | **vows** | **to make enquiry** | | **scatters** | **the wicked** | **A king** | **wise** | **and bring** | **over them** | **the wheel** | |

| נר 5216 | יהוה 3068 | נשמת 5397 | אדם 120 | חפש 2664 | כל 3605 | חדרי 2315 | בטן 990: | 20:28 | חסד 2617 | ואמת 571 | יצרו 5341 |
|---|---|---|---|---|---|---|---|---|---|---|---|
| ner | Yahuah | nishmat | 'adam; | chopes, | kal | chadrey | baten. | | chesed | ua'amet | yitzru |
| ***is*** **the candle of** | **Yahuah** | **The spirit of** | **man** | **searching** | **all** | **the inward parts of** | **the belly** | | **Mercy** | **and truth** | **preserve** |

Pro 20:13 lest you come to poverty; open your eyes, and you shall be satisfied with bread.14 It is naught, it is naught, saith the buyer: but when he is gone his way, then he boasteth.15 There is gold, and a multitude of rubies: but the lips of knowledge are a precious jewel.16 Take his garment that is surety for a stranger: and take a pledge of him for a strange woman.17 Bread of deceit is sweet to a man; but afterwards his mouth shall be filled with gravel.18 Every purpose is established by counsel: and with good advice make war.19 He that go about as a talebearer revealeth secrets: therefore meddle not with him that flattereth with his lips.20 Whoso curseth his father or his mother, his lamp shall be put out in obscure darkness.21 An inheritance may be gotten hastily at the beginning; but the end thereof shall not be blessed.22 Say not you, I will recompense evil; but wait on YHUH, and he shall save you.23 Divers weights are an abomination unto YHUH; and a false balance is not good.24 Man's goings are of YHUH; how can a man then understand his own way?25 It is a snare to the man who devour that which is holy, and after vows to make inquiry. 26 A wise king scattereth the wicked, and bring the wheel over them.27 The spirit of man is the candle of YHUH, searching all the inward parts of the belly.28 Mercy and truth preserve the king:

| מלך 4428 | וסעד 5582 | בחסד 2617 | כסאו 3678: | 20:29 | תפארת 8597 | בחורים 970 | כחם 3581 | והדר 1926 | זקנים 2205 |
|---|---|---|---|---|---|---|---|---|---|
| melek; | uasa'ad | bachesed | kis'au. | | tip'aret | bachuriym | kocham; | uahadar | zaqeniym |
| **the king** | **and is upholden** | **by mercy** | **his throne** | | **The glory of** | **young men** | ***is* their strength** | **and the beauty of** | **old men** |

| שיבה 7872: | 20:30 | חברות 2250 | פצע 6482 | תמריק 8562 | ברע 7451 | ומכות 4347 | חדרי 2315 | בטן 990: |
|---|---|---|---|---|---|---|---|---|
| seybah. | | chaburout | petza' | tamriyq | bara'; | uamakout, | chadrey | baten. |
| ***is* the gray head** | | **The blueness of** | **a wound** | **cleanses away** | **evil** | **so *do* stripes** | **the inward parts of** | **the belly** |

| Prov 21:1 | פלגי 6388 | מים 4325 | לב 3820 | מלך 4428 | ביד 3027 | יהוה 3068 | על 5921 | כל 3605 | אשר 834 | יחפץ 2654 |
|---|---|---|---|---|---|---|---|---|---|---|
| | palgey | mayim | leb | melek | bayad | Yahuah; | 'al | kal | 'asher | yachpotz |
| | ***as* the rivers of** | **water** | **heart** | ***The* king's** | ***is* in the hand of** | **Yahuah** | **whithersoever** | **all manner** | **which** | **he will** |

| יטנו 5186: | 21:2 | כל 3605 | דרך 1870 | איש 376 | ישר 3477 | בעיניו 5869 | ותכן 8505 | לבות 3826 | יהוה 3068: | 21:3 | עשה 6213 | צדקה 6666 |
|---|---|---|---|---|---|---|---|---|---|---|---|---|
| yatenu. | | kal | derek | 'aysh | yashar | ba'aeynayu; | uatoken | libout | Yahuah. | | 'asoh | tzadaqah |
| **he turned it** | | **Every** | **way of** | **a man** | ***is* right** | **in his own eyes** | **but ponder** | **the hearts** | **Yahuah** | | **To do** | **justice** |

| ומשפט 4941 | נבחר 977 | ליהוה 3068 | מזבח 2077: | 21:4 | רום 7311 | עינים 5869 | ורחב 7342 | לב 3820 | נר 5215 |
|---|---|---|---|---|---|---|---|---|---|
| uamishpat; | nibchar | laYahuah | mizabach. | | rum | 'aeynayim | uarachab | leb; | nir |
| **and judgment** | ***is* more acceptable** | **to Yahuah** | **than sacrifice** | | **An high** | **look** | **and a proud** | **heart** | ***and* the plowing of** |

| רשעים 7563 | חטאת 2403: | 21:5 | מחשבות 4284 | חרוץ 2742 | אך 389 | למותר 4195 | וכל 3605 | אץ 213 | אך 389 |
|---|---|---|---|---|---|---|---|---|---|
| rasha'aym | chata't. | | machashabout | charutz | 'ak | lamoutar; | uakal | 'atz, | 'ak |
| **the wicked** | ***is* sin** | | **The thoughts of** | **the diligent** | ***tend* only** | **to plenteousness** | **but of every one** | ***that is* hasty** | **only** |

| למחסור 4270: | 21:6 | פעל 6467 | אוצרות 214 | בלשון 3956 | שקר 8267 | הבל 1892 | נדף 5086 | מבקשי 1245 | מות 4194: | 21:7 |
|---|---|---|---|---|---|---|---|---|---|---|
| lamachsour. | | po'al | 'autzarout | bilshoun | shaqer; | hebel | nidap, | mabaqshey | mauet. | |
| **to want** | | **The getting of** | **treasures** | **by a tongue** | **lying** | ***is* a vanity** | **tossed to and fro of** | **them that seek** | **death** | |

| שד 7701 | רשעים 7563 | יגורם 1641 | כי 3588 | מאנו 3985 | לעשות 6213 | משפט 4941: | 21:8 | הפכפך 2019 | דרך 1870 | איש 376 |
|---|---|---|---|---|---|---|---|---|---|---|
| shod | rasha'aym | yagourem; | kiy | me'anu, | la'asout | mishapat. | | hapakpak | derek | 'aysh |
| **The robbery of** | **the wicked** | **shall destroy them** | **because** | **they refuse** | **to do** | **judgment** | | ***is* froward** | **The way of** | **man** |

| וזר 2054 | וזך 2134 | ישר 3477 | פעלו 6467: | 21:9 | טוב 2896 | לשבת 3427 | על 5921 | פנת 6438 | גג 1406 | מאשת 802 |
|---|---|---|---|---|---|---|---|---|---|---|
| uazar; | uazak, | yashar | pa'alou. | | toub, | lashabet | 'al | pinat | gag; | me'aeshet |
| **and strange** | **but *as for* the pure** | ***is* right** | **his work** | | ***It is* better** | **to dwell** | **in** | **a corner of** | **the housetop** | **than with a woman** |

| מדינים 4079 | ובית 1004 | חבר 2267: | 21:10 | נפש 5315 | רשע 7563 | אותה 183 | רע 7451 | לא 3808 | יחן 2603 | בעיניו 5869 | רעהו 7453: | 21:11 |
|---|---|---|---|---|---|---|---|---|---|---|---|---|
| midyaniym, | uabeyt | chaber. | | nepesh | rasha' | 'autah | ra'; | la' | yuchan | ba'aeynayu | re'aehu. | |
| **brawling** | **in a house** | **wide** | | **The soul of** | **the wicked** | **desire** | **evil** | **no** | **finds favor** | **in his eyes** | **his neighbour** | |

| בענש 6064 | לץ 3887 | יחכם 2449 | פתי 6612 | ובהשכיל 7919 | לחכם 2450 | יקח 3947 | דעת 1847: | 21:12 |
|---|---|---|---|---|---|---|---|---|
| ba'nash | letz | yechakam | petiy; | uabhaskiyl | lachakam, | yiqach | da'at. | |
| **When is punished** | **the scorner** | **is made wise** | **the simple** | **and when is instructed** | **the wise** | **he receive** | **knowledge** | |

| משכיל 7919 | צדיק 6662 | לבית 1004 | רשע 7563 | מסלף 5557 | רשעים 7563 | לרע 7451: |
|---|---|---|---|---|---|---|
| maskiyl | tzadiyq | labeyt | rasha'; | masalep | rasha'aym | lara'. |
| ***man* wisely consider** | ***The* righteous** | **the house of** | **the wicked** | ***but Elohim* overthrow** | **the wicked** | **for *their* wickedness** |

Pro 20:28 and his throne is upholden by mercy.29 The glory of young men is their strength: and the beauty of old men is the gray head.30 The blueness of a wound cleanseth away evil: so do stripes the inward parts of the belly. **Pro** 21:1 The king's heart is in the hand of YHUH, as the rivers of water: he turneth it whithersoever he will.2 Every way of a man is right in his own eyes: but YHUH pondereth the hearts.3 To do justice and judgment is more acceptable to YHUH than sacrifice. 4 An high look, and a proud heart, and the plowing of the wicked, is sin.5 The thoughts of the diligent tend only to plenteousness; but of everyone that is hasty only to want.6 The getting of treasures by a lying tongue is a vanity tossed to and fro of them that seek death.7 The robbery of the wicked shall destroy them; because they refuse to do judgment.8 The way of man is froward and strange: but as for the pure, his work is right.9 It is better to dwell in a corner of the housetop, than with a brawling woman in a wide house.10 The soul of the wicked desire evil: his neighbor findeth no favor in his eyes. 11 When the scorner is punished, the simple is made wise: and when the wise is instructed, he receive knowledge.12 The righteous man wisely considereth the house of the wicked: but G-d overthroweth the wicked for their wickedness.

21:13 21:14
אטם 331 אזנו 241 מזעקת 2201 דל 1800 גם 1571 הוא 1931 יקרא 7121 ולא 3808 יענה 6030: מתן 4976 בסתר 5643
'atem azanou miza'aqat dal; gam hua' yiqra', uala' ye'aneh. matan baseter
**Whoso stop his ears at the cry of the poor also himself he shall cry but not shall be heard A gift in secret**

21:15
יכפה 3711 אף 639 ושחד 7810 בחק 2436 חמה 2534 עזה 5794: שמחה 8057 לצדיק 6662 עשות 6213 משפט 4941 ומחתה 4288
yichapeh 'aap; uashochad bacheq, chemah 'azah. simchah latzadiyq asout mishapat; uamachitah,
**pacify anger and a reward in the bosom wrath strong *It is* joy to the just to do judgment but destruction**

21:16
לפעלי 6466 און 205: אדם 120 תועה 8582 מדרך 1870 השכל 7919 בקהל 6951
lapo'aley 'auen. 'adam, tou'ah miderek haskel; biqahal
***shall be* to the workers of iniquity The man that wander out of the way of understanding in the congregation of**

21:17
רפאים 7496 ינוח 5117: איש 376 מחסור 4270 אהב 157 שמחה 8057 אהב 157 יין 3196 ושמן 8081 לא 3808
rapa'aym yanuach. 'aysh machsour 'aheb simchah; 'aheb yayin uashemen, la'
**the dead shall remain *shall be* a man poor He that love pleasure he that love wine and oil not**

21:18 21:19
יעשיר 6238: כפר 3724 לצדיק 6662 רשע 7563 ותחת 8478 ישרים 3477 בוגד 898: טוב 2896
ya'ashiyr. koper latzadiyq rasha'; uatachat yashariym bouged. toub,
**shall be rich *shall be* a ransom for the righteous The wicked and for the upright the transgressor *It is* better**

21:20
שבת 3427 בארץ 776 מדבר 4057 מאשת 802 מדונים 4066 וכעס 3708: אוצר 214 נחמד 2530 ושמן 8081
shebet ba'aretz midbar; me'aeshet medouniym uaka'as. 'autzar nechmad uashemen
**to dwell in land the wilderness than with woman a contentious and an angry *There is* treasure to be desired and oil**

21:21
בנוה 5116 חכם 2450 וכסיל 3684 אדם 120 יבלענו 1104: רדף 7291 צדקה 6666 וחסד 2617 ימצא 4672
binueh chakam; uakasiyl 'adam yabala'anu. rodep tzadaqah uachased; yimtza'
**in the dwelling of the wise but a foolish man spend it up He that follows after righteousness and mercy finds**

21:22
חיים 2416 צדקה 6666 וכבוד 3519: עיר 5892 גברים 1368 עלה 5927 חכם 2450 וירד 3381 עז 5797
chayiym, tzadaqah uakaboud. 'ayr giboriym 'alah chakam; uayored, 'az
**life righteousness and honor the city of the mighty *man* scaleth A wise and cast down the strength of**

21:23 21:24
מבטחה 4009: שמר 8104 פיו 6310 ולשונו 3956 שמר 8104 מצרות 6869 נפשו 5315: זד 2086 יהיר 3093
mibtechah. shomer piyu ualshounou; shomer mitzarout napshou. zed yahiyr
**the confidence thereof Whoso keep his mouth and his tongue keep from troubles his soul Proud *and* haughty**

21:25
לץ 3887 שמו 8034 עושה 6213 בעברת 5678 זדון 2087: תאות 8378 עצל 6102 תמיתנו 4191 כי 3588 מאנו 3985 ידיו 3027
letz shamou; 'auseh, ba'abrat zadoun. ta'auat 'atzel tamiytenu; kiy me'anu yadayu
**scorner *is* his name who deal in wrath proud The desire of the slothful kills him for refuse his hands**

21:26 21:27
לעשות 6213: כל 3605 היום 3117 התאוה 183 תאוה 8378 וצדיק 6662 יתן 5414 ולא 3808 יחשך 2820: זבח 2077
la'asout. kal hayoum hit'auah ta'auah; uatzadiyq yiten, uala' yachsok. zebach
**to labour all the day long He covet greedily but the righteous gives and not spares The sacrifice of**

21:28
רשעים 7563 תועבה 8441 אף 637 כי 3588 בזמה 2154 יביאנו 935: עד 5707 כזבים 3577 יאבד 6
rasha'aym tou'aebah; 'aap, kiy bazimah yabiy'anu. 'aed kazabiym ya'bed;
**the wicked *is* abomination how much more when with a wicked mind? he bring it A witness false shall perish**

Pro 21:13 Whoso stoppeth his ears at the cry of the poor, he also shall cry himself, but shall not be heard.14 A gift in secret pacifieth anger: and a reward in the bosom strong wrath.15 It is joy to the just to do judgment: but destruction shall be to the workers of iniquity.16 The man that wandereth out of the way of understanding shall remain in the congregation of the dead.17 He that love pleasure shall be a poor man: he that love wine and oil shall not be rich.18 The wicked shall be a ransom for the righteous, and the transgressor for the upright.19 It is better to dwell in the wilderness, than with a contentious and an angry woman.20 There is treasure to be desired and oil in the dwelling of the wise; but a foolish man spendeth it up.21 He that followed after righteousness and mercy findeth life, righteousness, and honor.22 A wise man scaleth the city of the mighty, and casteth down the strength of the confidence thereof.23 Whoso keep his mouth and his tongue keep his soul from troubles.24 Proud and haughty scorner is his name, who deal in proud wrath.25 The desire of the slothful kill him; for his hands refuse to labour. 26 He coveteth greedily all the day long: but the righteous give and spareth not.27 The sacrifice of the wicked is abomination: how much more, when he bring it with a wicked mind?28 A false witness shall perish:

21:29
ואיש 376 שומע 8085 לנצח 5331 ידבר 1696: העז 5810 איש 376 רשע 7563 בפניו 6440 וישר 3477 הוא 1931 יכין 3559
ua'aysh shoumea', lanetzach yadaber. he'aez 'aysh rasha' bapanayu; uayashar, hua' yakiyn
**but the man that hear constantly speak hardens A man wicked his face but *as for* the upright he directs**

21:30 21:31
דרכיו 1870 אין 369 חכמה 2451 ואין 369 תבונה 8394 ואין 369 עצה 6098 לנגד 5048 יהוה 3069: סוס 5483 מוכן 3559
darkayu 'aeyn chakamah ua'aeyn tabunah; ua'aeyn 'aetzah, laneged Yahuah. sus, mukan
**his way. *There is* no wisdom nor understanding and nor counsel against Yahuah The horse *is* prepared**

ליום 3117 מלחמה 4421 וליהוה 3068 התשועה 8668:
layoum milchamah; ualeYahuah hatashu'ah.
**against the day of battle but of Yahuah but safety *is***

**Prov 22:1** 22:2
נבחר 977 שם 8034 מעשר 6239 רב 7227 מכסף 3701 ומזהב 2091 חן 2580 טוב 2896:
nibchar sam me'asher rab; mikesep uamizahab, chen toub.
***is* rather to be chosen A *good* name riches *than* great *rather* than silver and gold favor *and* loving**

22:3
עשיר 6223 ורש 7326 נפגשו 6298 עשה 6213 כלם 3605 יהוה 3068: ערום 6175 ראה 7200 רעה 7451 ויסתר 5641
'ashiyr uarash nipgashu; 'aseh kulam Yahuah. 'arum ra'ah ra'ah uayistar
**The rich and poor meet together *is* the maker of them all Yahuah A prudent *man* foresees the evil and hides himself**

22:4 22:5
ופתיים 6612 עברו 5674 ונענשו 6064: עקב 6118 ענוה 6038 יראת 3374 יהוה 3068 עשר 6239 וכבוד 3519 וחיים 2416:
uapatayiym, 'abaru uane'anashu. 'aeqeb 'anauah yir'at Yahuah; 'asher uakaboud uachayiym.
**but the simple pass on and are punished By humility *and* the fear of Yahuah *are* riches and honor and life**

22:6
צנים 6791 פחים 6341 בדרך 1870 עקש 6141 שומר 8104 נפשו 5315 ירחק 7368 מהם 1992: חנך 2596 לנער 5288
tziniym pachiym baderek 'aqesh; shoumer napshou, yirchaq mehem. chanok lana'ar
**Thorns *and* snares *are* in the way of the froward he that does keep his soul shall be far from them Train up a child**

22:7
על 5921 פי 6310 דרכו 1870 גם 1571 כי 3588 יזקין 2204 לא 3808 יסור 5493 ממנה 4480: עשיר 6223 ברשים 7326 ימשול 4910
'al piy darkou; gam kiy yazaqiyn, la' yasur mimenah. 'ashiyr barashiym yimshoul;
**in he should go the way and even when he is old not he will depart from it The rich over the poor rule**

22:8
ועבד 5650 לוה 3867 לאיש 376 מלוה 3867: זורע 2232 עולה 5766 יקצור 7114 און 205 ושבט 7626 עברתו 5678
ua'abed loueh, la'aysh malueh. zourea' 'aulah yiqatzou 'auen; uashebet 'abratou
**and servant the borrower *is* to man the lender He that sow iniquity shall reap vanity: and the rod of his anger**

22:9 22:10
יכלה 3615: טוב 2896 עין 5869 הוא 1931 יברך 1288 כי 3588 נתן 5414 מלחמו 3899 לדל 1800: גרש 1644
yikleh. toub 'ayin hua' yaborak; kiy natan milachmou ladal. garesh
**shall fail *that has a* bountiful eye He shall be blessed for he gives of his bread to the poor Cast out**

22:11
לץ 3887 ויצא 3318 מדון 4066 וישבת 7673 דין 1779 וקלון 7036: אהב 157 טהור 2889 לב 3820
letz uayetzea' madoun; uayishbot, diyn uaqaloun. 'aheb tehour leb;
**the scorner and shall go out contention yea shall cease strife and reproach He that love pureness of heart**

22:12
חן 2580 שפתיו 8193 רעהו 7453 מלך 4428: עיני 5869 יהוה 3068 נצרו 5341 דעת 1847 ויסלף 5557
chen sapatayu, re'aehu melek. 'aeyney Yahuah natzaru da'at; uayasalep,
***for* the grace of his lips *shall be* his friend the king The eyes of Yahuah preserve knowledge and he overthrow**

Pro 21:28 but the man that hear speaketh constantly. 29 A wicked man hardeneth his face: but as for the upright, he directeth his way.30 There is no wisdom nor understanding nor counsel against YHUH.31 The horse is prepared against the day of battle: but safety is of YHUH. **Pro** 22:1 A good name is rather to be chosen than great riches, and loving favor rather than silver and gold.2 The rich and poor meet together: YHUH is the maker of them all.3 A prudent man foreseeth the evil, and hide himself: but the simple pass on, and are punished.4 By humility and the fear of YHUH are riches, and honor, and life. 5 Thorns and snares are in the way of the froward: he that doth keep his soul shall be far from them.6 Train up a child in the way he should go: and when he is old, he will not depart from it. 7 The rich rule over the poor, and the borrower is servant to the lender.8 He that soweth iniquity shall reap vanity: and the rod of his anger shall fail.9 He that has a bountiful eye shall be blessed; for he give of his bread to the poor. 10 Cast out the scorner, and contention shall go out; yea, strife and reproach shall cease.11 He that love pureness of heart, for the grace of his lips the king shall be his friend. 12 The eyes of YHUH preserve knowledge, and he overthroweth the words of the transgressor.

22:13 | 22:14

דברי 1697 בגד 898: אמר 559 עצל 6102 ארי 738 בחוץ 2351 בתוך 8432 רחבות 7339 ארצח 7523:
dibrey boged. 'amar 'atzel 'ariy bachutz; batouk rachobout, 'aeratzeach.
**the words of the transgressor *man* saith *The* slothful *There is* a lion without in the streets I shall be slain**

22:15

שוחה 7745 עמקה 6013 פי 6310 זרות 2114 זעום 2194 יהוה 3068 יפול 5307 שם 8033: אולת 200
shuchah 'amuqah piy zarout; za'um Yahuah yipoul sham. 'auelet
***is* a pit deep The mouth of strange women he that is abhorred of Yahuah shall fall therein. Foolishness**

22:16

קשורה 7194 בלב 3820 נער 5288 שבט 7626 מוסר 4148 ירחיקנה 7368 ממנו 4480: עשק 6231 דל 1800
qashurah baleb na'ar; shebet musar, yarchiyqenah mimenu. 'asheq dal
***is* bound in the heart of a child *but* the rod of correction shall drive it far from him He that oppress the poor**

22:17

להרבות 7235 לו 3807a נתן 5414 לעשיר 6223 אך 389 למחסור 4270: הט 5186 אזנך 241 ושמע 8085
laharbout lou'; noten la'ashiyr, 'ak lamachsour. hat 'aznaka, uashma'
**to increase his *riches and* he that gives to the rich *shall* surely *come* to want Bow down your ear and hear**

22:18

דברי 1697 חכמים 2450 ולבך 3820 תשית 7896 לדעתי 1847: כי 3588 נעים 5273 כי 3588 תשמרם 8104
dibrey chakamiym; ualibaka, tashiyt lada'atiy. kiy na'aym kiy tishmarem
**the words of the wise and your heart apply unto my knowledge For *it is* a pleasant thing if you keep them**

22:19

בבטנך 990 יכנו 3559 יחדו 3162 על 5921 שפתיך 8193: להיות 1961 ביהוה 3068 מבטחך 4009
babitneka; yikonu yachdau, 'al sapateyka. lihayout baYahuah mibtacheka;
**within you they shall be fitted withal in your lips That may be in Yahuah your trust**

22:20

הודעתיך 3045 היום 3117 אף 637 אתה 859: הלא 3808 כתבתי 3789 לך 3807a שלשום 8032 במועצת 4156
houda'tiyka hayoum 'ap 'atah. hala' katabtiy laka shilshoum bamou'aetzot
**I have made known to you this day even to you not Have I written to you excellent *things* in counsels**

22:21

ודעת 1847: להודיעך 3045 קשט 7189 אמרי 561 אמת 571 להשיב 7725 אמרים 561
uada'at. lahoudiy'aka, qosht 'amrey 'amet; lahashiyb 'amariym
**and knowledge That I might make you know *the* certainty of *the* words of truth that you might answer the words of**

22:22

אמת 571 לשלחיך 7971: אל 408 תגזל 1497 דל 1800 כי 3588 דל 1800 הוא 1931 ואל 408 תדכא 1792 עני 6041
'amet, lasholacheyka. 'al tigzal dal kiy dal hua'; ua'al tadakea' 'aniy
**truth to them that send unto you? no Rob the poor because *is* poor he neither oppress the afflicted**

22:23 | 22:24

בשער 8179: כי 3588 יהוה 3069 יריב 7378 ריבם 7379 וקבע 6906 את 853 קבעיהם 6906 נפש 5315: אל 408
basha'ar. kiy Yahuah yariyb riybam; uaqaba' 'at qoba'aeyhem napesh. 'al
**in the gate For Yahuah will plead their cause and spoil those that spoiled them the soul of no**

22:25

תתרע 7462 את 854 בעל 1167 אף 639 ואת 854 איש 376 חמות 2534 לא 3808 תבוא 935: פן 6435 תאלף 502 ארחתו 734
titra' 'at ba'al 'aap; ua'at 'aysh chemout la' tabou'a. pen te'alap 'arachatou
**Make friendship *with* an man angry *and with* a man furious not you shall go Lest you learn his ways,**

22:26

ולקחת 3947 מוקש 4170 לנפשך 5315: אל 408 תהי 1961 בתקעי 8628 כף 3709 בערבים 6148
ualaqachta mouqesh lanapsheka. 'al tahiy batoqa'aey kap; ba'arabiym,
**and get a snare to your soul not Be you *one* of them that strike hands *or* of them that are sureties for**

Pro 22:13 The slothful man saith, There is a lion without, I shall be slain in the streets.14 The mouth of strange women is a deep pit: he that is abhorred of YHUH shall fall therein. 15 Foolishness is bound in the heart of a child; but the rod of correction shall drive it far from him.16 He that oppresseth the poor to increase his riches, and he that give to the rich, shall surely come to want.17 Bow down your ear, and hear the words of the wise, and apply your heart unto my knowledge.18 For it is a pleasant thing if you keep them within you; they shall withal be fitted in your lips. 19 That your trust may be in YHUH, I have made known to you this day, even to you.20 Have not I written to you excellent things in counsels and knowledge,21 That I might make you know the certainty of the words of truth; that you might answer the words of truth to them that send unto you?22 Rob not the poor, because he is poor: neither oppress the afflicted in the gate:23 For YHUH will plead their cause, and spoil the soul of those that spoiled them. 24 Make no friendship with an angry man; and with a furious man you shall not go:25 Lest you learn his ways, and get a snare to your soul.26 Be not you one of them that strike hands, or of them that are sureties for debts.

22:27 ... 22:28

משאות 4859: אם 518 אין 369 לך 3807a לשלם 7999 למה 4100 יקח 3947 משכבך 4904 מתחתיך 8478:

mashsha'aut. 'am 'aeyn laka lashalem; lamah yiqach mishkabaka, mitachateyka.

**debts If have nothing to you to pay why should he take away your bed from under you?**

22:29

אל 408 תסג 5253 גבול 1366 עולם 5769 אשר 834 עשו 6213 אבותיך 1: חזית 2372 איש 376 מהיר 4106 במלאכתו 4399 לפני 6440

'al taseg gabul 'aulam; 'asher 'asu abouteyka. chaziyta 'aysh mahiyr bimla'ktou, lipney

**not Remove landmark *the* ancient which have set your fathers See you a man diligent in his business? before**

מלכים 4428 יתיצב 3320 בל 1077 יתיצב 3320 לפני 6440 חשכים 2823:

malakiym yityatzab; bal yityatzeb lipney chashukiym.

**kings he shall stand not he shall stand before mean *men***

**Prov 23:1** ... 23:2

כי 3588 תשב 3427 ללחום 3898 את 854 מושל 4910 בין 995 תבין 995 את 853 אשר 834 לפניך 6440: ושמת 7760 שכין 7915

kiy tesheb lilchoum 'at moushel; biyn tabiyn, 'at 'asher lapaneyka. uasamta sakiyn

**When you sit to eat *with with* a ruler consider diligently what *is* before you And put a knife**

23:3

בלעך 3930 אם 518 בעל 1167 נפש 5315 אתה 859: אל 408 תתאו 183 למטעמותיו 4303 והוא 1931 לחם 3899

bala'aka; 'am ba'al nepesh 'atah. 'al tit'au lamat'amoutayu; uahu'a, lechem

**to your throat if *be* a man *given to* appetite you not Be you desirous of his dainties for they meat**

23:4 ... 23:5

כזבים 3577: אל 408 תיגע 3021 להעשיר 6238 מבינתך 998 חדל 2308: התעוף 5774 עיניך 5869 בו 871a

kazabiym. 'al tiyga' laha'ashiyr; mibiynataka chadal. hata'ayp 'ayneyka bou,

***are* deceitful not Labour to be rich from your own wisdom cease Will you set your eyes upon that**

23:6

ואיננו 369 כי 3588 עשה 6213 יעשה 6213 לו 3807a כנפים 3671 כנשר 5404 ועיף 5774 השמים 8064: אל 408

ua'aeynenu kiy 'asoh ya'aseh lou' kanapayim; kanesher, ua'ayep hashamayim. 'al

**which is not? for *riches* certainly make themselves wings as an eagle they fly away *toward* heaven not**

23:7

תלחם 3898 את 853 לחם 3899 רע 7451 עין 5869 ואל 408 תתאו 183 למטעמתיו 4303: כי 3588 כמו 3644 שער 8176

tilcham, 'at lechem ra' 'ayin; ua'al tit'ay lamat'amotayu. kiy kamou sha'ar

**Eat you the bread of *him that has* an evil eye neither desire you his dainty meats For as he think**

23:8

בנפשו 5315 כן 3651 הוא 1931 אכל 398 ושתה 8354 יאמר 559 לך 3807a ולבו 3820 בל 1077 עמך 5973: פתך 6595

banapshou, ken hua' 'akol uashteh ya'mar lak; ualibou, bal 'amak. pitaka

**in his heart so *is* he Eat and drink saith he to you but his heart *is* not with you The morsel**

23:9

אכלת 398 תקיאנה 6958 ושחת 7843 דבריך 1697 הנעימים 5273: באזני 241 כסיל 3684 אל 408 תדבר 1696

'akalta taqiy'anah; uashichata, dabareyka hana'aymiym. ba'azaney kasiyl 'al tadaber;

***which* you have eaten shall you vomit up and lose your words sweet in the ears of a fool not Speak**

23:10

כי 3588 יבוז 936 לשכל 7922 מליך 4405: אל 408 תסג 5253 גבול 1366 עולם 5769 ובשדי 7704 יתומים 3490

kiy yabuz, lasekel mileyka. 'al taseg gabul 'aulam; uabisdey yatoumiym,

**for he will despise the wisdom of your words not Remove landmark *the* old and into the fields of the fatherless**

23:11 ... 23:12

אל 408 תבא 935: כי 3588 גאלם 1350 חזק 2388 הוא 1931 יריב 7378 את 853 ריבם 7379 אתך 854: הביאה 935

'al tobea'. kiy go'alam chazaq; hua' yariyb 'at riybam 'atak. habiy'a'ah

**not enter For their redeemer *is* mighty he shall plead their cause with you Apply**

Pro 22:27 If you have nothing to pay, why should he take away your bed from under you?28 Remove not the ancient landmark, which your fathers have set.29 See you a man diligent in his business? he shall stand before kings; he shall not stand before mean men. **Pro** 23:1 When you sittest to eat with a ruler, consider diligently what is before you:2 And put a knife to your throat, if you be a man given to appetite.3 Be not desirous of his dainties: for they are deceitful meat.4 Labour not to be rich: cease from your own wisdom.5 Wilt you set your eyes upon that which is not? for riches certainly make themselves wings; they fly away as an eagle toward heaven.6 Eat you not the bread of him that has an evil eye, neither desire you his dainty meats:7 For as he thinketh in his heart, so is he: Eat and drink, saith he to you; but his heart is not with you.8 The morsel which you have eaten shall you vomit up, and lose your sweet words.9 Speak not in the ears of a fool: 9 for he will despise the wisdom of your words.10 Remove not the old landmark; and enter not into the fields of the fatherless:11 For their redeemer is mighty; he shall plead their cause with you.

23:13

למוסר 4148 לבך 3820 ואזנך 241 לאמרי 561 דעת 1847: אל 408 תמנע 4513 מנער 5288 מוסר 4148 כי 3588

lamusar libeka; ua'azaneka, la'amrey da'at. 'al timna' mina'ar musar; kiy

**unto instruction your heart and your ears to the words of knowledge not Withhold from the child correction for**

23:14

תכנו 5221 בשבט 7626 לא 3808 ימות 4191: אתה 859 בשבט 7626 תכנו 5221 ונפשו 5315 משאול 7585

takenu bashebet, la' yamut. 'atah bashebet takenu; uanapshou, misha'aul

***if* you beat him with the rod not he shall die You with the rod shall beat him and his soul from hell**

23:15 23:16

תציל 5337: בני 1121 אם 518 חכם 2449 לבך 3820 ישמח 8055 לבי 3820 גם 1571 אני 589: ותעלזנה 5937 כליותי 3629

tatziyl. baniy 'am chakam libeka; yismach libiy gam 'aniy. uata'alozanah kilyoutay;

**shall deliver My son if be wise your heart shall rejoice my heart even mine Yea shall rejoice my reins**

23:17

בדבר 1696 שפתיך 8193 מישרים 4339: אל 408 יקנא 7065 לבך 3820 בחטאים 2400 כי 3588 אם 518 ביראת 3374 יהוה 3068

badaber sapateyka, meyshariym. 'al yaqanea' libaka bachata'aym; kiy 'am bayir'at Yahuah

**when speak your lips right things not Let envy your heart sinners for but *be you* in the fear of Yahuah**

23:18 23:19

כל 3605 היום 3117: כי 3588 אם 518 יש 3426 אחרית 319 ותקותך 8615 לא 3808 תכרת 3772: שמע 8085 אתה 859

kal hayoum. kiy 'am yesh 'achariyt; uatiquataka, la' tikaret. shama' 'atah

**all the day long For surely there is an end and your expectation not shall be cut off Hear you**

23:20

בני 1121 וחכם 2449 ואשר 833 בדרך 1870 לבך 3820: אל 408 תהי 1961 בסבאי 5433 יין 3196 בזללי 2151

baniy uachakam; ua'asher baderek libeka. 'al tahiy basoba'aey yayin; bazolaley

**my son and be wise and guide in the way your heart not Be among bibbers of wine among riotous eaters of**

23:21

בשר 1320 למו 3807a: כי 3588 סבא 5433 וזולל 2151 יורש 3423 וקרעים 7168 תלביש 3847

basar lamou. kiy sobea' uazoulel yiuaresh; uaqara'aym, talbiysh

**flesh for them For the drunkard and the glutton shall come to poverty and rags shall clothe**

23:22 23:23

נומה 5124: שמע 8085 לאביך 1 זה 2088 ילדך 3205 ואל 408 תבוז 936 כי 3588 זקנה 2204 אמך 517:

numah. shama' la'abiyka zeh yaladeka; ua'al tabuz, kiy zaqanah 'ameka.

***a man with* drowsiness Hearken unto your father that begat you and not despise when she is old your mother**

23:24

אמת 571 קנה 7069 ואל 408 תמכר 4376 חכמה 2451 ומוסר 4148 ובינה 998: גול 1523 יגול 1523 אבי 1

'amet qaneh ua'al timakor; chakamah uamusar uabiynah. goul yagoul 'abiy

**the truth Buy and not sell *it* *also* wisdom and instruction and understanding greatly shall rejoice: The father of**

23:25

צדיק 6662 יולד 3205 חכם 2450 וישמח 8055 בו 871a: ישמח 8055 אביך 1 ואמך 517

tzadiyq; youled chakam, uayismach bou. yismach 'abiyka ua'ameka;

**the righteous and he that beget a wise *child* shall have joy of him. shall be glad Your father and your mother**

23:26 23:27

ותגל 1523 יולדתך 3205: תנה 5414 בני 1121 לבך 3820 לי 3807a ועיניך 5869 דרכי 1870 תרצנה 7521 כי 3588

uatagel, youladteka. tanah baniy libaka liy; ua'aeyneyka, darakay tirtzenah kiy

**you shall rejoice and she that bare give My son your heart me and your eyes my ways let observe For *is***

23:28

שוחה 7745 עמקה 6013 זונה 2181 ובאר 875 צרה 6862 נכריה 5237: אף 637 היא 1931 כחתף 2863 תארב 693

shuchah 'amuqah zounah; uab'aer tzarah, nakariyah. 'ap hiy'a kachetep te'arob;

**a ditch deep a whore and a pit narrow a strange woman *is* also She as *for* a prey lies in wait**

Pro 23:12 Apply your heart unto instruction, and your ears to the words of knowledge.13 Withhold not correction from the child: for if you beatest him with the rod, he shall not die.14 Thou shall beat him with the rod, and shall deliver his soul from hell.15 My son, if your heart be wise, my heart shall rejoice, even mine.16 Yea, my reins shall rejoice, when your lips speak right things. 17 Let not your heart envy sinners: but be you in the fear of YHUH all the day long.18 For surely there is an end; and your expectation shall not be cut off.19 Hear you, my son, and be wise, and guide your heart in the way.20 Be not among winebibbers; among riotous eaters of flesh:21 For the drunkard and the glutton shall come to poverty: and drowsiness shall clothe a man with rags.22 Hearken unto your father that begat you, and despise not your mother when she is old.23 Buy the truth, and sell it not; also wisdom, and instruction, and understanding.24 The father of the righteous shall greatly rejoice: and he that begetteth a wise child shall have joy of him.25 Thy father and your mother shall be glad, and she that bare you shall rejoice. 26 My son, give me your heart, and let your eyes observe my ways.27 For a whore is a deep ditch; and a strange woman is a narrow pit.28 She also lie in wait as for a prey, and increaseth the transgressors among men.

ובוגדים 898 באדם 120 תוסף 3254: **23:29** למי 4310 אוי 188 למי 4310 אבוי 17 למי 4310 מדונים 4066 למי 4310
uabougadiym, ba'adam tousip. lamiy 'auy lamiy 'abouy lamiy midouniym lamiy
**and the transgressors among men increase Who *has* woe? Who *has* sorrow? Who *has* contentions? Who**

שיח 7879 למי 4310 פצעים 6482 חנם 2600 למי 4310 חכללות 2448 עינים 5869: **23:30** למאחרים 309 על 5921 היין 3196
siyach, lamiy patza'aym chinam; lamiy, chaklilut 'aeynayim. lama'achariym 'al hayayin;
***has* babbling? Who *has* wounds without cause? Who *has* redness of eyes? They that tarry long at the wine**

לבאים 935 לחקר 2713 ממסך 4469: **23:31** אל 408 תרא 7200 יין 3196 כי 3588 יתאדם 119 כי 3588 יתן 5414 בכיס 3599 עינו 5869
laba'aym, lachqor misak. 'al tera' yayin kiy yit'adam kiy yiten bakiys 'aeynou;
**they that go to seek mixed wine not Look you upon the wine when it is red when it gives in the cup his colour**

יתהלך 1980 במישרים 4339: **23:32** אחריתו 319 כנחש 5175 ישך 5391 וכצפעני 6848 יפרש 6567: **23:33** עיניך 5869
yithalek, bameyshariym. 'achariytou kanachash yishak; uaktzip'aniy yaprish. 'aeyneyka
***when* it moves *itself* aright *At* the last like a serpent it bite and like an adder sting Thine eyes**

יראו 7200 זרות 2114 ולבך 3820 ידבר 1696 תהפכות 8419: **23:34** והיית 1961 כשכב 7901
yir'au zarout; ualibaka, yadaber tahpukout. uahayiyta kashokeb
**shall behold strange women and your heart shall utter perverse things Yea you shall be as he that lies down**

בלב 3820 ים 3220 וכשכב 7901 בראש 7218 חבל 2260: **23:35** הכוני 5221 בל 1077
baleb yam; uakshokeb, bara'sh chibel. hikuniy bal
**in the midst of the sea or as he that lies upon the top of a mast They have stricken me not**

חליתי 2470 הלמוני 1986 בל 1077 ידעתי 3045 מתי 4970 אקיץ 6974 אוסיף 3254 אבקשנו 1245 עוד 5750:
chaliytiy halamuniy, bal yadaa'tiy matay 'aqiytz; 'ausiyp, 'abaqshenu 'aud.
***shall you say and* I was sick they have beaten me *it* not *and* I felt when shall I awake? yet I will seek it again**

**Prov 24:1** אל 408 תקנא 7065 באנשי 582 רעה 7451 ואל 408 תתאו 183 להיות 1961 אתם 854: **24:2** כי 3588 שד 7701 יהגה 1897
'al taqanea' ba'anshey ra'ah; ua'al tit'ayu lihayout 'atam. kiy shod yehageh
**not Be you envious against men evil neither desire you to be with them. For destruction study**

לבם 3820 ועמל 5999 שפתיהם 8193 תדברנה 1696: **24:3** בחכמה 2451 יבנה 1129 בית 1004 ובתבונה 8394
libam; ua'amal, sipteyhem tadaberanah. bachakamah yibaneh bayit; uabitbunah,
**their heart and mischief their lips talk *of* Through wisdom is builded an house and by understanding**

יתכונן 3559: **24:4** ובדעת 1847 חדרים 2315 ימלאו 4390 כל 3605 הון 1952 יקר 3368 ונעים 5273: **24:5** גבר 1397 חכם 2450
yitkounan. uabda'at chadariym yimala'au; kal houn yaqar uana'aym. geber chakam
**it is established And by knowledge the chambers shall be filled all riches precious and pleasant A man wise**

בעוז 5797 ואיש 376 דעת 1847 מאמץ 553 כח 3581: **24:6** כי 3588 בתחבלות 8458 תעשה 6213 לך 3807a מלחמה 4421
ba'auz; ua'aysh da'at, ma'ametz koach. kiy batachbulout ta'aseh laka milchamah;
***is* strong yea a man of knowledge increase strength For by wise counsel you shall make to your war**

ותשועה 8668 ברב 7230 יועץ 3289: **24:7** ראמות 7311 לאויל 191 חכמות 2454 בשער 8179 לא 3808 יפתח 6605 פיהו 6310:
uatashu'ah, barob you'aetz. ra'mout le'auiyl chakmout; basha'ar, la' yiptach piyhu.
**and safety in multitude of counsellors *there is* *is* too high for a fool Wisdom in the gate not he open his mouth**

Pro 23:29 Who has woe? who has sorrow? who has contentions? who has babbling? who has wounds without cause? who has redness of eyes?30 They that tarry long at the wine; they that go to seek mixed wine.31 Look not you upon the wine when it is red, when it give his colour in the cup, when it moveth itself aright.32 At the last it biteth like a serpent, and stingeth like an adder.33 Thine eyes shall behold strange women, and your heart shall utter perverse things.34 Yea, you shall be as he that lie down in the midst of the sea, or as he that lie upon the top of a mast.35 They have stricken me, shall you say, and I was not sick; they have beaten me, and I felt it not: when shall I awake? I will seek it yet again. **Pro** 24:1 Be not you envious against evil men, neither desire to be with them.2 For their heart studieth destruction, and their lips talk of mischief.3 Through wisdom is an house built; and by understanding it is established: 4 And by knowledge shall the chambers be filled with all precious and pleasant riches. 5 A wise man is strong; yea, a man of knowledge increaseth strength.6 For by wise counsel you shall make your war: and in multitude of counsellers there is safety.7 Wisdom is too high for a fool: he openeth not his mouth in the gate.

24:8 מחשב 2803 להרע 7489 לו 3807a בעל 1167 מזמות 4209 יקראו 7121: 24:9 זמת 2154 אולת 200 חטאת 2403
machasheb laharea'; lou', ba'al mazimout yiqra'au. zimat 'auelet chata't;
**He that devise to do evil to him a person mischievous shall be called The thought of foolishness *is* sin**

ותועבת 8441 לאדם 120 לץ 3887: 24:10 התרפית 7503 ביום 3117 צרה 6869 צר 6862 כחכה 3581: 24:11 הצל 5337
uatou'abat la'adam letz. hitrapiyta bayoum tzarah, tzar kochekah. hatzel
**and an abomination to men the scorner *is* *If* you faint in the day of adversity *is* small your strength to deliver**

לקחים 3947 למות 4194 ומטים 4131 להרג 2027 אם 518 תחשוך 2820: 24:12 כי 3588 תאמר 559 הן 2005 לא 3808
laquchiym lamauet; uamatiym lahereg, 'am tachsouk. kiy ta'mar, hen la'
***them that are* drawn unto death and *those that are* ready to be slain If you forbear If you say Behold not**

ידענו 3045 זה 2088 הלא 3808 תכן 8505 לבות 3826 הוא 1931 יבין 995 ונצר 5341 נפשך 5315 הוא 1931 ידע 3045
yada'nu zeh hala' token libout hua' yabiyn, uanotzer napshaka hua' yeda';
**we knew it not he that ponder the heart it? do consider and he that keep your soul it? does *not* he know**

והשיב 7725 לאדם 120 כפעלו 6467: 24:13 אכל 398 בני 1121 דבש 1706 כי 3588 טוב 2896
uaheshiyb la'adam kapa'alou. 'akal baniy dabash kiy toub;
**and shall *not* he render to *every* man according to his works? eat you My son honey because *it is* good**

ונפת 5317 מתוק 4966 על 5921 חכך 2441: 24:14 כן 3651 דעה 3045 חכמה 2451 לנפשך 5315 אם 518
uanopet matouq, 'al chikeka. ken da'ah chakamah lanapsheka 'am
**and the honeycomb *which is* sweet to your taste So *shall* the knowledge of wisdom *be* unto your soul when**

מצאת 4672 ויש 3426 אחרית 319 ותקותך 8615 לא 3808 תכרת 3772: 24:15 אל 408 תארב 693 רשע 7563
matza'ta uayesh 'achariyt; uatiquataka, la' tikaret. 'al te'arob rasha'
**you have found *it* then there shall be a reward and your expectation not shall be cut off not Lay wait O wicked**

לנוה 5116 צדיק 6662 אל 408 תשדד 7703 רבצו 7258: 24:16 כי 3588 שבע 7651 יפול 5307 צדיק 6662
linueh tzadiyq; 'al tashaded ribtzou. kiy sheba' yipoul tzadiyq
***man* against the dwelling of the righteous not spoil his resting place For seven *times* *man* fall a just**

וקם 6965 ורשעים 7563 יכשלו 3782 ברעה 7451: 24:17 בנפל 5307 אויביך 341 אל 408 תשמח 8055 ובכשלו 3782
uaqam; uarsha'aym, yikashalu bara'ah. binpol 'auyabeyka 'al tismach; uabikashalou,
**and rise up again but the wicked shall fall into mischief when fall your enemy not Rejoice and when he stumbleth**

אל 408 יגל 1523 לבך 3820: 24:18 פן 6435 יראה 7200 יהוה 3069 ורע 7489 בעיניו 5869 והשיב 7725 מעליו 5921
'al yagel libeka. pen yir'ah Yahuah uara' ba'aeynayu; uaheshiyb me'alayu
**not let be glad your heart Lest see *it* Yahuah and displease it him and he turn away from him**

אפו 639: 24:19 אל 408 תתחר 2734 במרעים 7489 אל 408 תקנא 7065 ברשעים 7563: 24:20 כי 3588 לא 3808
'apou. 'al titchar bamare'aym; 'al taqanea', barasha'aym. kiy la'
**his wrath not Fret yourself because of evil *men* neither be you envious at the wicked For no**

תהיה 1961 אחרית 319 לרע 7451 נר 5216 רשעים 7563 ידעך 1846: 24:21 ירא 3372 את 853 יהוה 3068 בני 1121
tihayeh 'achariyt lara'; ner rasha'aym yid'ak. yara' 'at Yahuah baniy
**there shall be reward to the evil *man* the candle of the wicked shall be put out fear you Yahuah My son**

Pro 24:8 He that deviseth to do evil shall be called a mischievous person.9 The thought of foolishness is sin: and the scorner is an abomination to men.10 If you faint in the day of adversity, your strength is small.11 If you forbear to deliver them that are drawn unto death, and those that are ready to be slain;12 If you say, Behold, we knew it not; doth not he that pondereth the heart consider it? and he that keep your soul, doth not he know it? and shall not he render to every man according to his works?13 My son, eat you honey, because it is good; and the honeycomb, which is sweet to your taste:14 So shall the knowledge of wisdom be unto your soul: when you have found it, then there shall be a reward, and your expectation shall not be cut off.15 Lay not wait, O wicked man, against the dwelling of the righteous; spoil not his resting place:16 For a just man fall seven times, and rise up again: but the wicked shall fall into mischief.17 Rejoice not when your enemy fall, and let not your heart be glad when he stumbleth:18 Lest YHUH see it, and it displease him, and he turn away his wrath from him. 19 Fret not thyself because of evil men, neither be you envious at the wicked;20 For there shall be no reward to the evil man; the candle of the wicked shall be put out.21 My son, fear you YHUH and the king: and meddle not with them that are given to change:

24:22

ומלך 4428 | עם 5973 | שונים 8138 | אל 408 | תתערב 6148: | כי 3588 | פתאם 6597 | יקום 6965 | אידם 343

uamelek; 'am shouniym, 'al tit'arab. kiy pit'am yaqum 'aeydam;

**and the king with them that are given to change not *and* meddle For suddenly shall rise their calamity**

24:23

ופיד 6365 | שניהם 8147 | מי 4310 | יודע 3045: | גם 1571 | אלה 428 | לחכמים 2450 | הכר 5234 | פנים 6440 | במשפט 4941

uapiyd shaneyhem, miy' youdea'. gam 'aeleh lachakamiym; haker paniym bamishpat

**and the ruin of them both? who knows *things* also These *belong* to the wise to have respect of persons in judgment**

24:24

בל 1077 | טוב 2896: | אמר 559 | לרשע 7563 | צדיק 6662 | אתה 859 | יקבהו 5344 | עמים 5971 | יזעמוהו 2194

bal toub. 'amer larasha' tzadiyq 'atah yiqbuhu 'amiym; yiz'amuhu

***It is* not good He that saith unto the wicked *are* righteous You him shall curse the people shall abhor him**

24:25

לאמים 3816: | ולמוכיחים 3198 | ינעם 5276 | ועליהם 5921 | תבוא 935 | ברכת 1293 | טוב 2896: | שפתים 8193

la'amiym. ualamoukiychiym yina'am; ua'aleyhem, tabou'a birkat toub. sapatayim

**nations But to them that rebuke *him* shall be delight and upon them shall come a blessing good *his* lips**

24:26

ישק 5401 | משיב 7725 | דברים 1697 | נכחים 5228: | הכן 3559 | בחוץ 2351 | מלאכתך 4399 | ועתדה 6257 | בשדה 7704

yishaq; meshiyb, dabariym nakochiym. hakan bachutz mala'kteka, ua'atdah basadeh

***Every man* shall kiss that gives answer a right Prepare without your work and make it fit in the field**

24:27

לך 3807a | אחר 310 | ובנית 1129 | ביתך 1004: | אל 408 | תהי 1961 | עד 5704 | חנם 2600 | ברעך 7453

lak; 'achar, uabaniyta beyteka. 'al tahiy 'aed chinam bare'aka;

**for yourself afterwards and build your house not Be a witness without cause against your neighbour**

24:28

והפתית 6601 | בשפתיך 8193: | אל 408 | תאמר 559 | כאשר 834 | עשה 6213 | לי 3807a | כן 3651 | אעשה 6213 | לו 3807a | אשיב 7725 | לאיש 376

uahapitiyta, bispateyka. 'al ta'mar, ka'asher 'asah liy ken 'aaseh lou'; 'ashiyb la'aysh

**and deceive *not* with your lips not Say as I will do to him so he has done to me I will render to the man**

24:29

כפעלו 6467: | על 5921 | שדה 7704 | איש 376 | עצל 6102 | עברתי 5674 | ועל 5921 | כרם 3754 | אדם 120 | חסר 2638

kapa'alou. 'al sadeh 'aysh 'atzel 'abartiy; ua'al kerem, 'adam chasar

**according to his work by the field of man the sluggard I went and by the vineyard of the man void of**

24:30

לב 3820: | והנה 2009 | עלה 5927 | כלו 3605 | קמשנים 7063 | כסו 3680 | פניו 6440 | חרלים 2738 | וגדר 1444

leb. uahineh 'alah kulou qimsoniym, kasu panayu charuliym; uageder

**understanding And lo it was grown over all *and* nettles had covered the face thereof *with* thorns and wall**

24:31

אבניו 68 | נהרסה 2040: | ואחזה 2372 | אנכי 595 | אשית 7896 | לבי 3820 | ראיתי 7200 | לקחתי 3947

'abanayu neherasah. ua'achazeh 'anokiy 'ashiyt libiy; ra'aytiy, laqachtiy

***the* stone thereof was broken down Then saw I *and* considered care for I looked *upon it, and* received**

24:32

מוסר 4148: | מעט 4592 | שנות 8142 | מעט 4592 | תנומות 8572 | מעט 4592 | חבק 2264 | ידים 3027 | לשכב 7901: | ובא 935

musar. ma'at shenout ma'at tanumout; ma'at chibuq yadayim lishkab. uaba'

**instruction *Yet* a little sleep a little slumber a little folding of the hands to sleep So shall come**

24:33

24:34

מתהלך 1980 | רישך 7389 | ומחסריך 4270 | כאיש 376 | מגן 4043:

mithalek reysheka; uamachasoreyka, ka'aysh magen.

***as* one that travel your poverty and your want as an man armed**

Pro 24:22 For their calamity shall rise suddenly; and who know the ruin of them both?23 These things also belong to the wise. It is not good to have respect of persons in judgment.24 He that saith unto the wicked, Thou are righteous; him shall the people curse, nations shall abhor him:25 But to them that rebuke him shall be delight, and a good blessing shall come upon them.26 Every man shall kiss his lips that give a right answer.27 Prepare your work without, and make it fit for thyself in the field; and afterwards build your house.28 Be not a witness against your neighbor without cause; and deceive not with your lips.29 Say not, I will do so to him as he has done to me: I will render to the man according to his work.30 I went by the field of the slothful, and by the vineyard of the man void of understanding;31 And, lo, it was all grown over with thorns, and nettles had covered the face thereof, and the stone wall thereof was broken down.32 Then I saw, and considered it well: I looked upon it, and received instruction. 33 Yet a little sleep, a little slumber, a little folding of the hands to sleep:34 So shall your poverty come as one that travelleth; and your want as an armed man.

**Prov 25:1** ... **25:2**
גם 1571 אלה 428 משלי 4912 שלמה 8010 אשר 834 העתיקו 6275 אנשי 582 חזקיה 2396 מלך 4428 יהודה 3063:
gam 'aeleh mishley shalomoh; 'asher he'atiyqu, 'anshey chizqiyah melek yahudah.
***are* also These proverbs of Solomon which copied out the men of Hezekiah king of Judah**

**25:3**
כבד 3519 אלהים 430 הסתר 5641 דבר 1697 וכבד 3519 מלכים 4428 חקר 2713 דבר 1697: שמים 8064 לרום 7312
kabod 'alohiym hasater dabar; uakabod malakiym, chaqor dabar. shamayim larum
***It is* the glory of Elohim to conceal a thing but the honor of kings *is* to search out a matter The heaven for height**

**25:4**
וארץ 776 לעמק 6011 ולב 3820 מלכים 4428 אין 369 חקר 2714: הגו 1898 סיגים 5509 מכסף 3701
ua'aretz la'ameq; ualeb malakiym, 'aeyn cheqer. hagou siygiym mikasep;
**and the earth for depth and the heart of kings *is* not searchable Take away the dross from the silver**

**25:5**
ויצא 3318 לצרף 6884 כלי 3627: הגו 1898 רשע 7563 לפני 6440 מלך 4428 ויכון 3559
uayetzea' latzorep keliy. hagou rasha' lipney melek; uayikoun
**and there shall come forth for the finer a vessel Take away the wicked *from* before the king and shall be established**

**25:6**
בצדק 6664 כסאו 3678: אל 408 תתהדר 1921 לפני 6440 מלך 4428 ובמקום 4725 גדלים 1419 אל 408
batzedeq kis'au. 'al tithadar lipney melek; uabimqoum gadoliym, 'al
**in righteousness his throne not Put forth yourself in the presence of the king and in the place of great *men* not**

**25:7**
תעמד 5975: כי 3588 טוב 2896 אמר 559 לך 3807a עלה 5927 הנה 2008 מהשפילך 8213
ta'amod. kiy toub 'amar laka, 'aleh henah mehashapiylaka
**stand For better *it is* that it be said unto you Come up here than that you should be put lower**

**25:8**
לפני 6440 נדיב 5081 אשר 834 ראו 7200 עיניך 5869: אל 408 תצא 3318 לרב 7378 מהר 4118 פן 6435 מה 4100
lipney nadiyb; 'asher ra'au 'aeyneyka. 'al tetzea' larib, maher pen mah
**in the presence of the prince whom have seen your eyes not Go forth to strive hastily lest *you know not* what**

**25:9**
תעשה 6213 באחריתה 319 בהכלים 3637 אתך 853 רעך 7453: ריבך 737 ריב 7379 את 854
ta'aseh ba'achariytah; bahakliym 'atka re'aka. riybaka riyb 'at
**to do in the end thereof when has put to shame you your neighbour Debate your cause *with***

**25:10**
רעך 7453 וסוד 5475 אחר 312 אל 408 תגל 1540: פן 6435 יחסדך 2616 שמע 8085 ודבתך 1681
re'aka; uasoud 'acher 'al tagal. pen yachasedka shomea'; uadibataka,
**your neighbour *himself* and a secret to another not discover Lest *it* put you to shame he that hear and your infamy**

**25:11** ... **25:12**
לא 3808 תשוב 7725: תפוחי 8598 זהב 2091 במשכיות 4906 כסף 3701 דבר 1697 דבר 1696 על 5921 אפניו 655: נזם 5141
la' tashub. tapuchey zahab bamaskiyout kasep; dabar, dabur 'al 'apanayu. nezem
**not turn away *is like* apples of gold in pictures of silver A word spoken on fitly *As* an earring of**

**25:13**
זהב 2091 וחלי 2481 כתם 3800 מוכיח 3198 חכם 2450 על 5921 אזן 241 שמעת 8085: כצנת 6793 שלג 7950
zahab uachaliy katem; moukiyach chakam, 'al 'azen shoma'at. katzinat sheleg
**gold and an ornament of fine gold *so is* a reprover wise upon an ear obedient As the cold of snow**

ביום 3117 קציר 7105 ציר 6735 נאמן 539 לשלחיו 7971 ונפש 5315 אדניו 113 ישיב 7725:
bayoum qatziyr, tziyr ne'aman lasholachayu; uanepesh 'adonayu yashiyb.
**in the time of harvest *so is* a messenger faithful to them that send him for the soul of his masters he refresheth**

**Pro** 25:1 These are also proverbs of Solomon, which the men of Hezekiah king of Judah copied out.2 It is the glory of G-d to conceal a thing: but the honor of kings is to search out a matter.3 The heaven for height, and the earth for depth, and the heart of kings is unsearchable.4 Take away the dross from the silver, and there shall come forth a vessel for the finer.5 Take away the wicked from before the king, and his throne shall be established in righteousness.6 Put not forth thyself in the presence of the king, and stand not in the place of great men:7 For better it is that it be said unto you, Come up hither; than that you should be put lower in the presence of the prince whom your eyes have seen.8 Go not forth hastily to strive, lest you know not what to do in the end thereof, when your neighbor has put you to shame.9 Debate your cause with your neighbor himself; and discover not a secret to another:10 Lest he that hear it put you to shame, and your infamy turn not away.11 A word fitly spoken is like apples of gold in pictures of silver. 12 As an earring of gold, and an ornament of fine gold, so is a wise reprover upon an obedient ear.13 As the cold of snow in the time of harvest, so is a faithful messenger to them that send him: for he refresheth the soul of his masters.

| 25:14 | | | | | | | | 25:15 | |
|---|---|---|---|---|---|---|---|---|---|
| נשיאים 5387 | ורוח 7307 | וגשם 1653 | אין 369 | איש 376 | מתהלל 1984 | במתת 4991 | שקר 8267: | בארך 753 | אפים 639 |
| nasiy'aym | uaruach | uageshem | 'ayin; | 'aysh | mithalel, | bamatat | shaqer. | ba'arek | 'apayim |
| ***is like* clouds** | **and wind** | **rain** | **without** | **Whoso** | **boast himself** | **of a gift** | **false** | **By long** | **forbearing** |

| | | | | | | 25:16 | | |
|---|---|---|---|---|---|---|---|---|
| יפתה 6601 | קצין 7101 | ולשון 3956 | רכה 7390 | תשבר 7665 | גרם 1634: | דבש 1706 | מצאת 4672 | אכל 398 |
| yaputeh | qatziyn; | ualashoun | rakah, | tishbar | garem. | dabash | matza'ta | 'akol |
| **is persuaded** | **a prince** | **and a tongue** | **soft** | **break** | **the bone** | **honey?** | **Have you found** | **eat** |

| | | | | 25:17 | | |
|---|---|---|---|---|---|---|
| דיך 1767 | פן 6435 | תשבענו 7646 | והקאתו 6958: | הקר 3365 | רגלך 7272 | מבית 1004 |
| dayeka; | pen | tisba'anu, | uahaqea'tou. | hoqar | raglaka | mibeyt |
| **so much as is sufficient for you** | **lest** | **you be filled therewith** | **and you vomit it** | **Withdraw** | **your foot** | **from house** |

| | | | | 25:18 | | | | |
|---|---|---|---|---|---|---|---|---|
| רעך 7453 | פן 6435 | ישבעך 7646 | ושנאך 8130: | מפיץ 4650 | וחרב 2719 | וחץ 2671 | שנון 8150 | איש 376 |
| re'aka; | pen | yisba'aka, | uasane'aka. | mepiytz | uachereb | uachetz | shanun; | 'aysh |
| **your neighbour's** | **lest** | **he be weary of you** | **and *so* hate you** | ***is* a maul** | **and a sword** | **and a arrow** | **sharp** | **A man** |

| | | | | 25:19 | | | | |
|---|---|---|---|---|---|---|---|---|
| ענה 6030 | ברעהו 7453 | עד 5707 | שקר 8267: | שן 8127 | רעה 7465 | ורגל 7272 | מועדת 4154 | מבטח 4009 |
| 'aneh | bare'aehu, | 'aed | shaqer. | shen | ro'ah | uaregel | mu'adet; | mibtach |
| **that bear** | **against his neighbour** | **witness** | **false.** | ***is like* a tooth** | **broken** | **and a foot** | **out of joint** | **Confidence in** |

| | | | 25:20 | | | | | | |
|---|---|---|---|---|---|---|---|---|---|
| בוגד 898 | ביום 3117 | צרה 6869: | מעדה 5710 | בגד 899 | ביום 3117 | קרה 7135 | חמץ 2558 | על 5921 | נתר 5427 |
| bouged, | bayoum | tzarah. | ma'adeh | beged | bayoum | qarah | chometz | 'al | nater; |
| **an unfaithful man** | **in time of** | **trouble** | ***As* he that takes away** | **a garment** | **in weather** | **cold** | ***and as* vinegar** | **upon** | **nitre** |

| | | | | | 25:21 | | | | | |
|---|---|---|---|---|---|---|---|---|---|---|
| ושר 7891 | בשרים 7892 | על 5921 | לב 3820 | רע 7451: | אם 518 | רעב 7456 | שנאך 8130 | האכלהו 398 | לחם 3899 | ואם 518 |
| uashar | bashiriym, | 'al | leb | ra'. | 'am | ra'aeb | sona'aka | ha'akilehu | lachem; | ua'am |
| **so *is* he that sing** | **songs** | **to** | **an heart** | **heavy** | **If** | **be hungry** | **your enemy** | **give him to eat** | **bread** | **and if** |

| | | | 25:22 | | | | | | | |
|---|---|---|---|---|---|---|---|---|---|---|
| צמא 6771 | השקהו 8248 | מים 4325: | כי 3588 | גחלים 1513 | אתה 859 | חתה 2846 | על 5921 | ראשו 7218 | ויהוה 3068 | ישלם 7999 |
| tzamea', | hashaqehu | mayim. | kiy | gechaliym, | 'atah | choteh | 'al | ra'shou; | uaYahuah | yashalem |
| **he be thirsty** | **give him to drink** | **water** | **For** | **coals *of fire*** | **you** | **shall heap** | **upon** | **his head** | **and Yahuah** | **shall reward** |

| | 25:23 | | | | | | | | 25:24 |
|---|---|---|---|---|---|---|---|---|---|
| לך 3807a: | רוח 7307 | צפון 6828 | תחולל 2342 | גשם 1653 | ופנים 6440 | נזעמים 2194 | לשון 3956 | סתר 5643: | טוב 2896 |
| lak. | ruach | tzapoun | tachoulel | gashem; | uapaniym | niz'amiym, | lashoun | sater. | toub, |
| **to you** | **wind** | ***The* north** | **drive away** | **rain** | **countenance** | **so *does* an angry** | **a tongue** | **backbiting** | ***It is* better** |

| | | | | | | | | 25:25 | | |
|---|---|---|---|---|---|---|---|---|---|---|
| שבת 3427 | על 5921 | פנת 6438 | גג 1406 | מאשת 802 | מדונים 4066 | ובית 1004 | חבר 2267: | מים 4325 | קרים 7119 | על 5921 |
| shebet | 'al | pinat | gag; | me'aeshet | midouniym | uabeyt | chaber. | mayim | qariym | 'al |
| **to dwell in** | | **the corner of** | **the housetop *than*** | **with a woman** | **brawling** | **and in a house** | **wide** | **waters** | ***As* cold** | **to** |

| | | | | | | 25:26 | | | |
|---|---|---|---|---|---|---|---|---|---|
| נפש 5315 | עיפה 5889 | ושמועה 8052 | טובה 2896 | מארץ 776 | מרחק 7801: | מעין 4599 | נרפש 7515 | ומקור 4726 | משחת 7843 |
| nepesh | 'ayepah; | uashmu'ah | toubah, | me'aretz | merchaq. | ma'ayan | nirpas | uamaqour | mashachat; |
| **a soul** | **thirsty** | **so news** | ***is* good** | **from a country** | **far** | ***is as* a fountain** | **troubled** | **and a spring** | **corrupt** |

| | | | | 25:27 | | | | | |
|---|---|---|---|---|---|---|---|---|---|
| צדיק 6662 | מט 4131 | לפני 6440 | רשע 7563: | אכל 398 | דבש 1706 | הרבות 7235 | לא 3808 | טוב 2896 | וחקר 2714 |
| tzadiyq, | mat | lipney | rasha'. | 'akol | dabash | harabout | la' | toub; | uacheqer |
| **A righteous man** | **falling down** | **before** | **the wicked** | ***It is* to eat** | **honey** | **much** | **not** | **good** | **so *for men* to search** |

Pro 25:14 Whoso boasteth himself of a false gift is like clouds and wind without rain.15 By long forbearing is a prince persuaded, and a soft tongue breaketh the bone.16 Hast you found honey? eat so much as is sufficient for you, lest you be filled therewith, and vomit it.17 Withdraw your foot from your neighbor's house; lest he be weary of you, and so hate you.18 A man that beareth false witness against his neighbor is a maul, and a sword, and a sharp arrow.19 Confidence in an unfaithful man in time of trouble is like a broken tooth, and a foot out of joint.20 As he that take away a garment in cold weather, and as vinegar upon nitre, so is he that singeth songs to an heavy heart.21 If your enemy be hungry, give him bread to eat; and if he be thirsty, give him water to drink:22 For you shall heap coals of fire upon his head, and YHUH shall reward you.23 The north wind drive away rain: so doth an angry countenance a backbiting tongue.24 It is better to dwell in the corner of the housetop, than with a brawling woman and in a wide house.25 As cold waters to a thirsty soul, so is good news from a far country. 26 A righteous man falling down before the wicked is as a troubled fountain, and a corrupt spring.27 It is not good to eat much honey: so for men to search their own glory is not glory.

25:28

כבדם 3519 כבוד 3519: עיר 5892 פרוצה 6555 אין 369 חומה 2346 איש 376 אשר 834 אין 369 מעצר 4623
kabodam kaboud. 'ayr parutzah 'aeyn choumah; 'aysh, 'asher 'aeyn ma'atzar
**their own glory *is not* glory *is like* a city *that is* broken down *has* no walls He that *and* without rule**

לרוחו 7307:
laruchou.
**over his own spirit**

**Prov 26:1** 26:2

כשלג 7950 בקיץ 7019 וכמטר 4306 בקציר 7105 כן 3651 לא 3808 נאוה 5000 לכסיל 3684 כבוד 3519: כצפור 6833 לנוד 5110
kasheleg baqayitz, uakamatar baqatziyr; ken la' naa'ueh liksiyl kaboud. katzipour lanud
**As snow in summer and as rain in harvest so not seemly for a fool honor *is* As the bird by wandering**

26:3

כדרור 1866 לעוף 5774 כן 3651 קללת 7045 חנם 2600 לא 3808 תבא 935: שוט 7752 לסוס 5483 מתג 4964 לחמור 2543 ושבט 7626
kadarour la'up; ken qilalat chinam, la' taboa'. shout lasus meteg lachamour; uashebet,
**as the swallow by flying so *the* curse causeless not shall come A whip for the horse a bridle for the ass and a rod**

26:4 26:5

לגו 1460 כסילים 3684: אל 408 תען 6030 כסיל 3684 כאולתו 200 פן 6435 תשוה 7737 לו 3807a גם 1571 אתה 859: ענה 6030
lageu kasiyliym. 'al ta'an kasiyl ka'aualtou; pen tishueh lou' gam 'atah. 'aneh
**for back *the* fool's not Answer a fool according to his folly lest be like unto him also you Answer**

26:6

כסיל 3684 כאולתו 200 פן 6435 יהיה 1961 חכם 2450 בעיניו 5869: מקצה 7097 רגלים 7272 חמס 2555 שתה 8354
kasiyl ka'aualtou; pen yihayeh chakam ba'aeynayu. maqatzeh raglayim chamas shoteh;
**a fool according to his folly lest he be wise in his own conceit cuts off the feet damage *and* drink**

26:7

שלח 7971 דברים 1697 ביד 3027 כסיל 3684: דליו 1809 שקים 7785 מפסח 6455 ומשל 4912 בפי 6310
sholeach dabariym bayad kasiyl. dalyu shoqayim mipiseach; uamashal, bapiy
**He that send a message by the hand of a fool are not equal The legs of the lame so *is* a parable in the mouth of**

26:8 26:9

כסילים 3684: כצרור 6887 אבן 68 במרגמה 4773 כן 3651 נותן 5414 לכסיל 3684 כבוד 3519: חוח 2336 עלה 5927
kasiyliym. kitzrour 'aben bamargemah; ken nouten liksiyl kaboud. chouach 'alah
**fools As he that binds a stone in a sling so *is* he that gives to a fool honor *As* a thorn goes up**

26:10

ביד 3027 שכור 7910 ומשל 4912 בפי 6310 כסילים 3684: רב 7227 מחולל 2342 כל 3605
bayad shikour; uamashal, bapiy kasiyliym. rab machoulel kol;
**into the hand of a drunkard so *is* a parable in the mouth of fools *The* great *Elohim* that formed all *things***

26:11 26:12

ושכר 7936 כסיל 3684 ושכר 7936 עברים 5674: ככלב 3611 שב 7725 על 5921 קאו 6892 כסיל 3684 שונה 8138 באולתו 200:
uasoker kasiyl, uasoker 'abariym. kakeleb shab 'al qe'au; kasiyl, shouneh ba'aualtou.
**both reward the fool and reward transgressors As a dog return to his vomit *so* a fool return to his folly**

26:13

ראית 7200 איש 376 חכם 2450 בעיניו 5869 תקוה 8615 לכסיל 3684 ממנו 4480: אמר 559 עצל 6102
ra'ayta, 'aysh chakam ba'aeynayu; tiquah liksiyl mimenu. 'amar 'atzel
**See you a man wise in his own conceit? *there is more* hope of a fool than of him *man* saith *The* slothful**

26:14

שחל 7826 בדרך 1870 ארי 738 בין 996 הרחבות 7339: הדלת 1817 תסוב 5437 על 5921 צירה 6735 ועצל 6102 על 5921
shachal badarek; 'ariy, beyn harachobout. hadelet tisoub 'al tziyrah; ua'atzel, 'al
***There is* a lion in the way a lion *is* in the streets *As* the door turned upon his hinges so *does* the slothful upon**

Pro 25:28 He that has no rule over his own spirit is like a city that is broken down, and without walls. **Pro** 26:1 As snow in summer, and as rain in harvest, so honor is not seemly for a fool.2 As the bird by wandering, as the swallow by flying, so the curse causeless shall not come.3 A whip for the horse, a bridle for the ass, and a rod for the fool's back.4 Answer not a fool according to his folly, lest you also be like unto him.5 Answer a fool according to his folly, lest he be wise in his own conceit.6 He that send a message by the hand of a fool cutteth off the feet, and drinketh damage.7 The legs of the lame are not equal: so is a parable in the mouth of fools.8 As he that bindeth a stone in a sling, so is he that give honor to a fool.9 As a thorn go up into the hand of a drunkard, so is a parable in the mouth of fools.10 The great G-d that formed all things both rewardeth the fool, and rewardeth transgressors.11 As a dog returneth to his vomit, so a fool returneth to his folly.12 See you a man wise in his own conceit? there is more hope of a fool than of him. 13 The slothful man saith, There is a lion in the way; a lion is in the streets.14 As the door turneth upon his hinges, so doth the slothful upon his bed.

26:15 … 26:16

מטתו 4296: טמן 2934 עצל 6102 ידו 3027 בצלחת 6747 נלאה 3811 להשיבה 7725 אל 413 פיו 6310: חכם 2450

mitatou. taman 'atzel yadou batzalachat; nila'ah, lahashiybah 'al piyu. chakam

**his bed hides *The* slothful his hand in *his* bosom it grieves him to bring it again to his mouth *is* wiser**

26:17

עצל 6102 בעיניו 5869 משבעה 7651 משיבי 7725 טעם 2940: מחזיק 2388 באזני 241 כלב 3611

'atzel ba'aeynayu; mishib'ah, mashiybey ta'am. machaziyq ba'azaney kaleb;

**The sluggard in his own conceit than seven *men* that can render a reason *is like* one that takes by the ears a dog**

26:18

עבר 5674 מתעבר 5674 על 5921 ריב 7379 לא 3808 לו 3807a: כמתלהלה 3856 הירה 3384 זקים 2131 חצים 2671

'aber mita'aber, 'al riyb la' lou'. kamitlahaleah hayoreh ziqiym, chitziym

**He that passed by *and* meddle with strife *belonging* not to him As a mad *man* who cast firebrands arrows**

26:19 … 26:20

ומות 4194: כן 3651 איש 376 רמה 7411 את 853 רעהו 7453 ואמר 559 הלא 3808 משחק 7832 אני 589: באפס 657

uamauet. ken 'aysh rimah 'at re'aehu; ua'amar, hala' masacheq 'aniy. ba'apes

**and death So *is* the man *that* deceive his neighbour and saith not Am in sport? I Where no is**

26:21

עצים 6086 תכבה 3518 אש 784 ובאין 369 נרגן 5372 ישתק 8367 מדון 4066: פחם 6352 לגחלים 1513

'aetziym tikbeh 'aesh; uab'aeyn nirgan, yishtoq madoun. pecham lagechaliym

**wood goes out *there* the fire *so where* there is no talebearer cease the strife *As* coals *are* to burning coals**

26:22

ועצים 6086 לאש 784 ואיש 376 מדונים 4066 לחרחר 2787 ריב 7379: דברי 1697 נרגן 5372 כמתלהמים 3859 והם 1992

ua'aetziym la'aesh; ua'aysh midouniym lacharchar riyb. dibrey nirgan kamitlahamiym; uahem,

**and wood to fire so man *is* a contentious to kindle strife The words of a talebearer *are* as wounds and they**

26:23

ירדו 3381 חדרי 2315 בטן 990: כסף 3701 סיגים 5509 מצפה 6823 על 5921 חרש 2789 שפתים 8193 דלקים 1814

yaradu chadrey baten. kesep siygiym matzupeh 'al chares; sapatayim dolaqiym

**go down into *the* innermost parts of the belly silver dross covered with *are like* a potsherd lips Burning**

26:24 … 26:25

ולב 3820 רע 7451: בשפתו 8193 ינכר 5234 שונא 8130 ובקרבו 7130 ישית 7896 מרמה 4820: כי 3588 יחנן 2603

ualeb ra'. bispatou yinaker sounea'; uabqirbou, yashiyt mirmah. kiy yachanen

**and a heart wicked with his lips dissemble He that hate and within him lay up deceit When fair**

26:26

קולו 6963 אל 408 תאמן 539 בו 871a כי 3588 שבע 7651 תועבות 8441 בלבו 3820: תכסה 3680 שנאה 8135

qoulou 'al ta'amen bou; kiy sheba' tou'aebout balibou. tikaseh sin'ah

**he speak not you believe him for *there are* seven abominations in his heart *Whose* is covered hatred**

26:27

במשאון 4860 תגלה 1540 רעתו 7451 בקהל 6951: כרה 3738 שחת 7845 בה 871a יפל 5307

bamasha'aun; tigaleh ra'atou baqahal. koreh shachat bah yipol;

**by deceit shall be showed his wickedness before the *whole* congregation Whoso digs a pit therein shall fall**

26:28

וגלל 1556 אבן 68 אליו 413 תשוב 7725: לשון 3956 שקר 8267 ישנא 8130 דכיו 1790 ופה 6310

uagolel 'aben 'aelayu tashub. lashoun sheqer yisnaa' dakayu; uapeh

**and he that rolls a stone upon him it will return A tongue lying hate *those that are* afflicted *by it;* and a mouth**

חלק 2509 יעשה 6213 מדחה 4072:

chalaq, ya'aseh midcheh.

**flattering work ruin**

Pro2 6:15 The slothful hide his hand in his bosom; it grieve him to bring it again to his mouth.16 The sluggard is wiser in his own conceit than seven men that can render a reason.17 He that pass by, and meddleth with strife belonging not to him, is like one that take a dog by the ears.18 As a mad man who casteth firebrands, arrows, and death,19 So is the man that deceiveth his neighbor, and saith, Am not I in sport?20 Where no wood is, there the fire go out: so where there is no talebearer, the strife ceaseth.21 As coals are to burning coals, and wood to fire; so is a contentious man to kindle strife.22 The words of a talebearer are as wounds, and they go down into the innermost parts of the belly.23 Burning lips and a wicked heart are like a potsherd covered with silver dross.24 He that hateth dissembleth with his lips, and layeth up deceit within him;25 When he speaketh fair, believe him not: for there are seven abominations in his heart.26 Whose hatred is covered by deceit, his wickedness shall be showed before the whole congregation.27 Whoso diggeth a pit shall fall therein: and he that rolleth a stone, it will return upon him.28 A lying tongue hateth those that are afflicted by it; and a flattering mouth worketh ruin.

**Prov 27:1** אל 408 תתהלל 1984 ביום 3117 מחר 4279 כי 3588 לא 3808 תדע 3045 מה 4100 ילד 3205 יום 3117: **27:2**
'al tithalel bayoum machar; kiy la' teda', mah yeled youm.
**not Boast *yourself* of what to morrow for not you know what may bring forth a day**

יהללך 1984 זר 2114 ולא 3808 פיך 6310 נכרי 5237 ואל 408 שפתיך 8193: **27:3** כבד 3514 אבן 68 ונטל 5192
yahalelaka zar uala' piyka; nakariy, ua'al sapateyka. koed 'aben uanetel
**Let praise you another man and not your own mouth a stranger and not your own lips *is* heavy A stone and weighty**

החול 2344 וכעס 3708 אויל 191 כבד 3515 משניהם 8147: **27:4** אכזריות 395 חמה 2534 ושטף 7858 אף 639 ומי 4310
hachoul; uaka'as 'auiyl, kabed mishneyhem. 'akzariyut chemah uashetep 'aap; uamiy
**the sand but wrath a fool's *is* heavier than them both *is* cruel Wrath and outrageous anger *is* but who**

יעמד 5975 לפני 6440 קנאה 7068: **27:5** טובה 2896 תוכחת 8433 מגלה 1540 מאהבה 160 מסתרת 5641: **27:6** נאמנים 539 פצעי 6482
ya'amod lipney qin'ah. toubah toukachat magulah; me'ahabah masutaret. ne'amaniym pitza'aey
***is* able to stand before envy? *is* better rebuke Open than love secret Faithful *are* the wounds of**

אוהב 157 ונעתרות 6280 נשיקות 5390 שונא 8130: **27:7** נפש 5315 שבעה 7649 תבוס 947 נפת 5317 ונפש 5315 רעבה 7457 כל 3605
'auheb; uana'tarout, nashiyqout sounea'. nepesh sabe'ah tabus nopet; uanepesh ra'aebah, kal
**a friend but deceitful the kisses of an enemy *are* soul *The* full loathe an honeycomb but soul *to* the hungry every**

מר 4751 מתוק 4966: **27:8** כצפור 6833 נודדת 5074 מן 4480 קנה 7064 כן 3651 איש 376 נודד 5074 ממקומו 4725: **27:9** שמן 8081
mar matouq. katzipour noudedet min qinah; ken 'aysh, nouded mimaqoumou. shemen
**bitter thing *is* sweet As a bird that wander from her nest so *is* a man that wander from his place Ointment**

וקטרת 7004 ישמח 8055 לב 3820 ומתק 4986 רעהו 7453 מעצת 6098 נפש 5315: **27:10** רעך 7453
uaqtoret yasamach leb; uameteq re'aehu, me'atzat napesh. re'aka
**and perfume rejoice the heart so *does* the sweetness of a man's friend by counsel hearty Thine own friend**

ורעה 7453 אביך 1 אל 408 תעזב 5800 ובית 1004 אחיך 251 אל 408 תבוא 935 ביום 3117 אידך 343 טוב 2896
uare'ah 'abiyka 'al ta'azob, uabeyt 'achiyka, 'al tabou'a bayoum 'aeydeka; toub
**and friend your father's not forsake house your brother's neither go into in the day of your calamity *for* better**

שכן 7934 קרוב 7138 מאח 251 רחוק 7350: **27:11** חכם 2449 בני 1121 ושמח 8056 לבי 3820 ואשיבה 7725
shaken qaroub, me'ach rachouq. chakam baniy uasamach libiy; ua'ashiybah
***is* a neighbour *that is* near than a brother far off be wise My son and make glad my heart that I may answer him**

חרפי 2778 דבר 1697: **27:12** ערום 6175 ראה 7200 רעה 7451 נסתר 5641 פתאים 6612 עברו 5674
chorapiy dabar. 'arum ra'ah ra'ah nistar; pata'yim, 'abaru
**that reproach me *with* words A prudent *man* foresees the evil *and* hides himself *but* the simple pass on**

נענשו 6064: **27:13** קח 3947 בגדו 899 כי 3588 ערב 6148 זר 2114 ובעד 1157 נכריה 5237
ne'anashu. qach bigdou kiy 'arab zar; uab'ad nakariyah
***and* are punished Take his garment that is surety for a stranger and for a strange woman**

חבלהו 2254: **27:14** מברך 1288 רעהו 7453 בקול 6963 גדול 1419 בבקר 1242 השכים 7925 קללה 7045
chablehu. mabarek re'aehu baqoul gadoul baboqer hashkeym; qalalah,
**take a pledge of him He that bless his friend with a voice loud in the morning rising early a curse**

**Pro** 27:1 Boast not thyself of tomorrow; for you know not what a day may bring forth.2 Let another man praise you, and not your own mouth; a stranger, and not your own lips.3 A stone is heavy, and the sand weighty; but a fool's wrath is heavier than them both.4 Wrath is cruel, and anger is outrageous; but who is able to stand before envy? 5 Open rebuke is better than secret love.6 Faithful are the wounds of a friend; but the kisses of an enemy are deceitful.7 The full soul loatheth an honeycomb; but to the hungry soul every bitter thing is sweet. 8 As a bird that wandereth from her nest, so is a man that wandereth from his place.9 Ointment and perfume rejoice the heart: so doth the sweetness of a man's friend by hearty counsel.10 Thine own friend, and your father's friend, forsake not; neither go into your brother's house in the day of your calamity: for better is a neighbor that is near than a brother far off.11 My son, be wise, and make my heart glad, that I may answer him that reproacheth me.12 A prudent man foreseeth the evil, and hide himself; but the simple pass on, and are punished.13 Take his garment that is surety for a stranger, and take a pledge of him for a strange woman. 14 He that blesseth his friend with a loud voice, rising early in the morning, it shall be counted a curse to him.

27:15 ... 27:16
תחשב 2803 | לו 3807a: | דלף 1812 | טורד 2956 | ביום 3117 | סגריר 5464 | ואשת 802 | מדונים 4066 | נשתוה 7737:
techasheb | lou'. | delep | toured | bayoum | sagriyr; | ua'aeshet | midouniym | nishtauah.
**it shall be counted | to him | A dropping | continual | in a day | very rainy | and a woman | contenious | are alike**

27:17
צפניה 6845 | צפן 6845 | רוח 7307 | ושמן 8081 | ימינו 3225 | יקרא 7121: | ברזל 1270 | בברזל 1270
tzopaneyha | tzapan | ruach; | uashemen | yamiynou | yiqra'. | barzel | babarzel
**Whosoever hides her | hides | the wind | and the ointment of | his right hand | *which* bewray *itself* | Iron | iron**

27:18
יחד 2300 | ואיש 376 | יחד 2300 | פני 6440 | רעהו 7453: | נצר 5341 | תאנה 8384 | יאכל 398 | פריה 6529
yachad; | ua'aysh, | yachad | paney | re'aehu. | notzer | ta'aenah | ya'kal | piryah;
**sharpen | so a man | sharpen | the countenance of | his friend | Whoso keep | the fig tree | shall eat | the fruit thereof**

27:19
ושמר 8104 | אדניו 113 | יכבד 3513: | כמים 4325 | הפנים 6440 | לפנים 6440 | כן 3651 | לב 3820 | האדם 120
uashomer | 'adonayu | yakubad. | kamayim | hapaniym | lapaniym; | ken | leb | ha'adam,
**so he that wait on | his master | shall be honoured | As in water | face | *answer* to face | so | the heart of | man**

27:20 ... 27:21
לאדם 120: | שאול 7585 | ואבדה 10 | לא 3808 | תשבענה 7646 | ועיני 5869 | האדם 120 | לא 3808 | תשבענה 7646:
la'adam. | sha'aul | ua'abadoh | la' | tisba'anah; | ua'aeyney | ha'adam, | la' | tisba'anah.
**to man | Hell (*grave*) | and destruction | never | are full | so the eyes of | man | never | are satisfied**

27:22
מצרף 4715 | לכסף 3701 | וכור 3564 | לזהב 2091 | ואיש 376 | לפי 6310 | מהללו 4110: | אם 518 | תכתוש 3806 | את 853
matzrep | lakesep | uakur | lazahab; | ua'aysh, | lapiy | mahalalou. | 'am | tiktoush | 'at
***As* the fining pot | for silver | and the furnace | for gold | so *is* a man | to | his praise | Though | you should bray**

27:23
האויל 191 | במכתש 4388 | בתוך 8432 | הריפות 7383 | בעלי 5940 | לא 3808 | תסור 5493 | מעליו 5921 | אולתו 200: | ידע 3045
ha'auiyl | bamakatesh | batouk | hariypout | ba'aliy; | la' | tasur | me'alayu, | 'aualtou. | yadoa'
**a fool | in a mortar | among | wheat | with a pestle | not | *yet* will depart | from him | his foolishness | Be you diligent**

27:24
תדע 3045 | פני 6440 | צאנך 6629 | שית 7896 | לבך 3820 | לעדרים 5739: | כי 3588 | לא 3808 | לעולם 5769 | חסן 2633 | ואם 518 | נזר 5145
teda' | paney | tza'neka; | shiyt | libaka, | la'adariym. | kiy | la' | la'aulam | chosen; | ua'am | nezer,
**to know | the state of | your flocks *and* look well | to your herds | For | not | for ever | riches *are* and | *does* the crown**

7:25
לדור 1755 | דור 1755 | גלה 1540 | חציר 2682 | ונראה 7200 | דשא 1877 | ונאספו 622 | עשבות 6212
ladour | dour | galah | chatziyr | uanir'ah | desha'; | uane'aspu, | 'asbout
***endure* to every | generation? | appear | The hay | and shows itself | *the* tender grass | and are gathered | herbs of**

27:26 ... 27:27
הרים 2022: | כבשים 3532 | ללבושך 3830 | ומחיר 4242 | שדה 7704 | עתודים 6260: | ודי 1767 | חלב 2461
hariym. | kabasiym | lilbusheka; | uamachiyr | sadeh, | 'atudiym. | uadey | chaleb
**the mountains | The lambs | *are* for your clothing | and the price of | the field | the goats *are* | And enough | milk**

עזים 5795 | ללחמך 3899 | ללחם 3899 | ביתך 1004 | וחיים 2416 | לנערותיך 5291:
aziym, | lalachmaka | lalechem | beyteka; | uachayiym, | lana'arouteyka.
***you shall have* goats' | for your food | for the food of | your household | and *for* the maintenance | for your maidens**

**Prov 28:1** ... 28:2
נסו 5127 | ואין 369 | רדף 7291 | רשע 7563 | וצדיקים 6662 | ככפיר 3715 | יבטח 982: | בפשע 6588 | ארץ 776
nasu | ua'aeyn | rodep | rasha'; | uatzadiyqiym, | kikapiyr | yibtach. | bapesha' | 'aretz
**flee | when no man pursue | The wicked | but the righteous | as a lion | are bold | For the transgression of | a land**

Pro 27:15 A continual dropping in a very rainy day and a contentious woman are alike.16 Whosoever hide her hide the wind, and the ointment of his right hand, which bewrayeth itself.17 Iron sharpeneth iron; so a man sharpeneth the countenance of his friend.18 Whoso keep the fig tree shall eat the fruit thereof: so he that waiteth on his master shall be honoured.19 As in water face answer to face, so the heart of man to man.20 Hell and destruction are never full; so the eyes of man are never satisfied.21 As the fining pot for silver, and the furnace for gold; so is a man to his praise.22 Though you should bray a fool in a mortar among wheat with a pestle, yet will not his foolishness depart from him.23 Be you diligent to know the state of your flocks, and look well to your herds.24 For riches are not forever: and doth the crown endure to every generation?25 The hay appeareth, and the tender grass show itself, and herbs of the mountains are gathered.26 The lambs are for your clothing, and the goats are the price of the field.27 And you shall have goats' milk enough for your food, for the food of your household, and for the maintenance for your maidens. **Pro** 28:1 The wicked flee when no man pursueth: but the righteous are bold as a lion.2 For the transgression of a land many are the princes thereof:

רבים 7227 שריה 8269 ובאדם 120 מבין 995 ידע 3045 כן 3651 יאריך 748: **28:3**
rabiym sareyha; uab'adam mebiyn yodea', ken ya'ariyk.
**many *are* the princes thereof but by a man of understanding *and* knowledge the state *thereof* shall be prolonged**

גבר 1397 רש 7326 ועשק 6231 דלים 1800 מטר 4306 סחף 5502 ואין 369 לחם 3899: **28:4** עזבי 5800 תורה 8451
geber rash ua'asheq daliym; matar sochep, ua'aeyn lachem. 'azabey tourah
**A man poor that oppress the poor *is like* a rain sweeping which leave no food They that forsake the law**

יהללו 1984 רשע 7563 ושמרי 8104 תורה 8451 יתגרו 1624 בם 871a: **28:5** אנשי 582 רע 7451 לא 3808 יבינו 995 משפט 4941
yahalalu rasha'; uashomarey tourah, yitgaru bam. 'anshey ra' la' yabiynu mishapat;
**let praise the wicked but such as keep the law contend with them men Evil not understand judgment**

ומבקשי 1245 יהוה 3069 יבינו 995 כל 3605: **28:6** טוב 2896 רש 7326 הולך 1980 בתמו 8537 מעקש 6141
uamabaqshey Yahuah yabiynu kol. toub rash houlek batumou; me'aqesh
**but they that seek Yahuah understand all *things* Better *is* the poor that walk in his uprightness than *he that is* perverse**

דרכים 1870 והוא 1931 עשיר 6223: **28:7** נוצר 5341 תורה 8451 בן 1121 מבין 995 ורעה 7462 זוללים 2151
darakayim, uahu'a 'ashiyr. noutzer tourah ben mebiyn; uaro'ah zoulaliym,
***in his* ways though he *be* rich Whoso keep the law *is* a son wise but he that is a companion of riotous**

יכלים 3637 אביו 1: **28:8** מרבה 7235 הונו 1952 בנשך 5392 ובתרבית 8636 לחונן 2603 דלים 1800
yakliym 'abiyu. marbeh hounou baneshek uabetarbiyt lachounen daliym
***men* shame his father He that increase his substance by usury and unjust gain for him that will pity the poor**

יקבצנו 6908: **28:9** מסיר 5493 אזנו 241 משמע 8085 תורה 8451 גם 1571 תפלתו 8605 תועבה 8441: **28:10**
yiqbatzenu. mesiyr azanou mishmoa' tourah; gam tapilatou, tou'aebah.
**he shall gather it He that turned away his ear from hearing the law even his prayer *shall be* abomination**

משגה 7686 ישרים 3477 בדרך 1870 רע 7451 בשחותו 7816 הוא 1931 יפול 5307 ותמימים 8549
mashgeh yashariym baderek ra', bishchutou hua' yipoul; uatamiymiym,
**Whoso cause to go astray the righteous in an way evil into his own pit himself he shall fall but the upright**

ינחלו 5157 טוב 2896: **28:11** חכם 2450 בעיניו 5869 איש 376 עשיר 6223 ודל 1800 מבין 995
yinchalu toub. chakam ba'aeynayu 'aysh 'ashiyr; uadal mebiyn
**shall have in possession good *things* *is* wise in his own conceit man *The* rich but the poor that has understanding**

יחקרנו 2713: **28:12** בעלץ 5970 צדיקים 6662 רבה 7227 תפארת 8597 ובקום 6965 רשעים 7563 יחפש 2664
yachqarenu. ba'alotz tzadiyqiym rabah tip'aret; uabqum rasha'aym, yachupas
**searches him out When do rejoice righteous *men* *there is* great glory but when rise the wicked is hidden**

אדם 120: **28:13** מכסה 3680 פשעיו 6588 לא 3808 יצליח 6743 ומודה 3034 ועזב 5800 ירחם 7355: **28:14**
'adam. makaseh pasha'ayu la' yatzliyach; uamoudeh ua'azeb yarucham.
**a man He that cover his sins not shall prosper but whoso confesseth and forsake *them* shall have mercy**

אשרי 835 אדם 120 מפחד 6342 תמיד 8548 ומקשה 7185 לבו 3820 יפול 5307 ברעה 7451: **28:15** ארי 738 נהם 5098 ודב 1677
'ashrey 'adam mapached tamiyd; uamaqasheh libou, yipoul bara'ah. 'ariy nohem uadob
**Happy *is* the man that fear alway but he that hardens his heart shall fall into mischief *As* a lion roaring and a bear**

Pro 28:2 but by a man of understanding and knowledge the state thereof shall be prolonged.3 A poor man that oppresseth the poor is like a sweeping rain which leaveth no food.4 They that forsake the law praise the wicked: but such as keep the law contend with them.5 Evil men understand not judgment: but they that seek YHUH understand all things.6 Better is the poor that walk in his uprightness, than he that is perverse in his ways, though he be rich.7 Whoso keep the law is a wise son: but he that is a companion of riotous men shameth his father.8 He that by usury and unjust gain increaseth his substance, he shall gather it for him that will pity the poor.9 He that turneth away his ear from hearing the law, even his prayer shall be abomination.10 Whoso causeth the righteous to go astray in an evil way, he shall fall himself into his own pit: but the upright shall have good things in possession.11 The rich man is wise in his own conceit; but the poor that has understanding searcheth him out.12 When righteous men do rejoice, there is great glory: but when the wicked rise, a man is hidden.13 He that covereth his sins shall not prosper: but whoso confesseth and forsaketh them shall have mercy. 14 Happy is the man that fear alway: but he that hardeneth his heart shall fall into mischief.15 As a roaring lion, and a ranging bear; so is a wicked ruler over the poor people.

| | | | | | | 28:16 | | | | |
|---|---|---|---|---|---|---|---|---|---|---|
| שוקק 8264 | משל 4910 | רשע 7563 | על 5921 | עם 5971 | דל 1800: | נגיד 5057 | חסר 2638 | תבונות 8394 | ורב 7227 | מעשקות 4642 |
| shouqeq; | moshel | rasha', | 'al | 'am | dal. | nagiyd, | chasar | tabunout | uarab | ma'ashaqout; |
| **ranging *so is*** | **a ruler** | **wicked** | **over** | **people** | ***the* poor** | **The prince** | **that want** | **understanding** | ***is* also a great** | **oppressor** |

| | | | | 28:17 | | | | |
|---|---|---|---|---|---|---|---|---|
| שנאי 8130 | בצע 1215 | יאריך 748 | ימים 3117: | אדם 120 | עשק 6231 | בדם 1818 | נפש 5315 | עד 5704 |
| sone'ay | betza', | ya'ariyk | yamiym. | 'adam | 'ashuq | badam | napesh; | 'ad |
| ***but* he that hates** | **covetousness** | **shall prolong** | ***his* days** | **A man** | **that does violence** | **to the blood of** | ***any* person** | **to** |

| | | | | | 28:18 | | | | |
|---|---|---|---|---|---|---|---|---|---|
| בור 953 | ינוס 5127 | אל 408 | יתמכו 8551 | בו 871a: | הולך 1980 | תמים 8549 | יושע 3467 | ונעקש 6140 | דרכים 1870 |
| bour | yanus, | 'al | yitmaku | bou. | houlek | tamiym | yiuashea'; | uane'aqash | darakayim, |
| **the pit** | **shall flee** | **no *man*** | **let stay** | **him** | **Whoso walk** | **uprightly** | **shall be saved** | **but *he that is* perverse** | ***in his* ways** |

| | | 28:19 | | | | | |
|---|---|---|---|---|---|---|---|
| יפול 5307 | באחת 259: | עבד 5647 | אדמתו 127 | ישבע 7646 | לחם 3899 | ומרדף 7291 | רקים 7386 |
| yipoul | ba'achat. | 'abed | admatou | yisba' | lachem; | uamaradep | reqiym, |
| **shall fall** | **at once** | **He that tills** | **his land** | **shall have plenty of** | **bread** | **but he that follows after** | **vain *persons*** |

| | | 28:20 | | | | | | |
|---|---|---|---|---|---|---|---|---|
| ישבע 7646 | ריש 7389: | איש 376 | אמונות 530 | רב 7227 | ברכות 1293 | ואץ 213 | להעשיר 6238 | לא 3808 |
| yisba' | riysh. | 'aysh | 'amunout | rab | barakout; | ua'atz | laha'ashiyr, | la' |
| **shall have enough** | **poverty** | **A man** | **faithful** | **shall abound with** | **blessings** | **but he that make haste** | **to be rich** | **not** |

| | 28:21 | | | | | | | | | 28:22 |
|---|---|---|---|---|---|---|---|---|---|---|
| ינקה 5352: | הכר 5234 | פנים 6440 | לא 3808 | טוב 2896 | ועל 5921 | פת 6595 | לחם 3899 | יפשע 6586 | גבר 1397: | |
| yinaqeh. | haker | paniym | la' | toub; | ua'al | pat | lechem, | yipasha' | gaber. | |
| **shall be innocent** | **To have respect of** | **persons *is*** | **not** | **good** | **for for** | **a piece of** | **bread** | **will transgress** | ***that* man** | |

| | | | | | | | | | | 28:23 |
|---|---|---|---|---|---|---|---|---|---|---|
| נבהל 926 | להון 1952 | איש 376 | רע 7451 | עין 5869 | ולא 3808 | ידע 3045 | כי 3588 | חסר 2639 | יבאנו 935: | מוכיח 3198 |
| nibahal | lahoun, | 'aysh | ra' | 'ayin; | uala' | yeda' | kiy | cheser | yabo'anu. | moukiyach |
| **that hasten** | **to be rich** | **He** | **evil** | ***has* an eye** | **and not** | **consider** | **that** | **poverty** | **shall come upon him** | **He that rebuke** |

| | | | | | | 28:24 | | |
|---|---|---|---|---|---|---|---|---|
| אדם 120 | אחרי 310 | חן 2580 | ימצא 4672 | ממחליק 2505 | לשון 3956: | גוזל 1497 | אביו 1 | ואמו 517 |
| 'adam | 'acharay | chen | yimtza'; | mimachaliyq | lashoun. | gouzel | 'abiyu | ua'amou, |
| **a man** | **afterwards** | ***more* favor** | **shall find** | **than he that flatter** | **with the tongue** | **Whoso robs** | **his father** | **or his mother** |

| | | | | | | | 28:25 | | |
|---|---|---|---|---|---|---|---|---|---|
| ואמר 559 | אין 369 | פשע 6588 | חבר 2270 | הוא 1931 | לאיש 376 | משחית 7843: | רחב 7342 | נפש 5315 | יגרה 1624 |
| ua'amer | 'aeyn | pasha'; | chaber | hua', | la'aysh | mashchiyt. | rachab | nepesh | yagareh |
| **and saith *It is*** | **no** | **transgression** | ***is* the companion of** | **the same** | **man** | **a destroys** | ***He that is of* a proud** | **heart** | **stir up** |

| | | | | | 28:26 | | | |
|---|---|---|---|---|---|---|---|---|
| מדון 4066 | ובוטח 982 | על 5921 | יהוה 3068 | ידשן 1878: | בוטח 982 | בלבו 3820 | הוא 1931 | כסיל 3684 |
| madoun; | uabouteach | 'al | Yahuah | yadushan. | bouteach | balibou | hua' | kasiyl; |
| **strife** | **but he that put his trust** | **in** | **Yahuah** | **shall be made fat** | **He that trust** | **in his own heart** | **he** | ***is* a fool** |

| | | | | 28:27 | | | | |
|---|---|---|---|---|---|---|---|---|
| והולך 1980 | בחכמה 2451 | הוא 1931 | ימלט 4422: | נותן 5414 | לרש 7326 | אין 369 | מחסור 4270 | ומעלים 5956 |
| uahoulek | bachakamah, | hua' | yimalet. | nouten | larash | 'aeyn | machsour; | uama'aliym |
| **but whoso walk** | **wisely** | **he** | **shall be delivered** | **He that gives** | **unto the poor** | **not** | **shall lack** | **but he that hides** |

| | | | 28:28 | | | | | |
|---|---|---|---|---|---|---|---|---|
| עיניו 5869 | רב 7227 | מארות 3994: | בקום 6965 | רשעים 7563 | יסתר 5641 | אדם 120 | ובאבדם 6 | ירבו 7235 |
| 'aeynayu, | rab | ma'aerout. | baqum | rasha'aym | yisater | 'adam; | uab'abadam, | yirbu |
| **his eyes** | ***shall have* many** | **a curse** | **When rise** | **the wicked** | **hide themselves** | **men** | **but when they perish** | **increase** |

Pro 28:16 The prince that wanteth understanding is also a great oppressor: but he that hateth covetousness shall prolong his days.17 A man that doeth violence to the blood of any person shall flee to the pit; let no man stay him.18 Whoso walk uprightly shall be saved: but he that is perverse in his ways shall fall at once.19 He that tilleth his land shall have plenty of bread: but he that followed after vain persons shall have poverty enough.20 A faithful man shall abound with blessings: but he that make haste to be rich shall not be innocent.21 To have respect of persons is not good: for for a piece of bread that man will transgress.22 He that hasteth to be rich has an evil eye, and considereth not that poverty shall come upon him.23 He that rebuketh a man afterwards shall find more favor than he that flattereth with the tongue.24 Whoso robbeth his father or his mother, and saith, It is no transgression; the same is the companion of a destroyer.25 He that is of a proud heart stirreth up strife: but he that put his trust in YHUH shall be made fat.26 He that trusteth in his own heart is a fool: but whoso walk wisely, he shall be delivered.27 He that give unto the poor shall not lack: 27 but he that hide his eyes shall have many a curse.28 When the wicked rise, men hide themselves: but when they perish, the righteous increase.

צדיקים 6662:
tzadiyqiym.
**the righteous**

**Prov 29:1** איש 376 תוכחות 8433 מקשה 7185 ערף 6203 פתע 6621 ישבר 7665 ואין 369 מרפא 4832: **29:2**
'aysh toukachout maqsheh 'arep; peta' yishaber, ua'aeyn marpea'.
**He that being often reproved hardens *his* neck suddenly shall be destroyed and that without remedy**

ברבות 7235 צדיקים 6662 ישמח 8055 העם 5971 ובמשל 4910 רשע 7563 יאנח 584 עם 5971: **29:3** איש 376
birbout tzadiyqiym yismach ha'am; uabimshol rasha', ye'anach 'am. 'aysh
**When are in authority the righteous rejoice the people but when bear rule the wicked mourn the people Whoso**

אהב 157 חכמה 2451 ישמח 8055 אביו 1 ורעה 7462 זונות 2181 יאבד 6 הון 1952: **29:4** מלך 4428
'aheb chakamah yasamach 'abiyu; uaro'ah zounout, ya'abed houn. melek,
**love wisdom rejoice his father but he that keep company with harlots spend *his* substance The king**

במשפט 4941 יעמיד 5975 ארץ 776 ואיש 376 תרומות 8641 יהרסנה 2040: **29:5** גבר 1397 מחליק 2505 על 5921 רעהו 7453 רשת 7568
bamishpat ya'amiyd 'aretz; ua'aysh tarumout yeherasenah. geber machaliyq 'al re'aehu; reshet,
**by judgment establish the land but he *that receive* gifts overthrow it A man that flatter on his neighbour a net**

פורש 6566 על 5921 פעמיו 6471: **29:6** בפשע 6588 איש 376 רע 7451 מוקש 4170 וצדיק 6662 ירון 7442
poures 'al pa'amayu. bapesha' 'aysh ra' mouqesh; uatzadiyq, yarun
**spread for his feet In the transgression of an man evil *there is* a snare but the righteous does sing**

ושמח 8055: **29:7** ידע 3045 צדיק 6662 דין 1779 דלים 1800 רשע 7563 לא 3808 יבין 995 דעת 1847: **29:8** אנשי 582 לצון 3944
uasameach. yodea' tzadiyq diyn daliym; rasha', la' yabiyn da'at. 'anshey latzoun
**and rejoices consider The righteous the cause of the poor *but* the wicked not regard to know *it* men Scornful**

יפיחו 6315 קריה 7151 וחכמים 2450 ישיבו 7725 אף 639: **29:9** איש 376 חכם 2450 נשפט 8199 את 854 איש 376 אויל 191
yapiychu qiryah; uachakamiym, yashiybu 'aap. 'aysh chakam, nishpat 'at 'aysh 'auiyl;
**bring into a snare a city but wise *men* turn away wrath *If* a man wise will contend *with* a man foolish**

ורגז 7264 ושחק 7832 ואין 369 נחת 5183: **29:10** אנשי 582 דמים 1818 ישנאו 8130 תם 8535 וישרים 3477 יבקשו 1245
uaragaz uasachaq, ua'aeyn nachat. 'anshey damiym yisna'au tam; uiyshariym, yabaqshu
**whether he rage or laugh and *there is* no rest The thirsty of blood hate the upright but the just seek**

נפשו 5315: **29:11** כל 3605 רוחו 7307 יוציא 3318 כסיל 3684 וחכם 2450 באחור 268 ישבחנה 7623: **29:12** משל 4910 מקשיב 7181 על 5921
napshou. kal ruachou youtziy'a kasiyl; uachakam, ba'achour yashabchenah. moshel maqshiyb 'al
**his soul all his mind utter A fool but a wise *in till* afterwards *man* keep it *If* a ruler listen to**

דבר 1697 שקר 8267 כל 3605 משרתיו 8334 רשעים 7563: **29:13** רש 7326 ואיש 376 תככים 8501 נפגשו 6298 מאיר 215 עיני 5869
dabar shaqer; kal masharatayu rasha'aym. rash ua'aysh takakiym nipgashu; me'ayr 'aeyney
**lies false all his servants *are* wicked The poor and man *the* deceitful meet together lighten their eyes**

שניהם 8147 יהוה 3068: **29:14** מלך 4428 שופט 8199 באמת 571 דלים 1800 כסאו 3678 לעד 5703 יכון 3559: **29:15** שבט 7626
shaneyhem Yahuah. melek shoupet be'amet daliym; kis'au, la'ad yikoun. shebet
**both Yahuah The king that judge faithfully the poor his throne for ever shall be established The rod**

**Pro** 29:1 He, that being often reproved hardeneth his neck, shall suddenly be destroyed, and that without remedy.2 When the righteous are in authority, the people rejoice: but when the wicked beareth rule, the people mourn.3 Whoso love wisdom rejoice his father: but he that keep company with harlots spendeth his substance.4 The king by judgment establisheth the land: but he that receive gifts overthroweth it.5 A man that flattereth his neighbor spreadeth a net for his feet.6 In the transgression of an evil man there is a snare: but the righteous doth sing and rejoice.7 The righteous considereth the cause of the poor: but the wicked regardeth not to know it.8 Scornful men bring a city into a snare: but wise men turn away wrath.9 If a wise man contendeth with a foolish man, whether he rage or laugh, there is no rest.10 The bloodthirsty hate the upright: but the just seek his soul.11 A fool uttereth all his mind: but a wise man keep it in till afterwards.12 If a ruler hear to lies, all his servants are wicked.13 The poor and the deceitful man meet together: 13 YHUH lighteneth both their eyes.14 The king that faithfully judgeth the poor, his throne shall be established forever.15 The rod and reproof give wisdom: but a child left to himself bring his mother to shame.

| | | | | | | | 29:16 | |
|---|---|---|---|---|---|---|---|---|
| ותוכחת 8433 | יתן 5414 | חכמה 2451 | ונער 5288 | משלח 7971 | מביש 954 | אמו 517: | | ברבות 7235 |
| uatoukachat | yiten | chakamah | uana'ar | mashulach, | mebiysh | 'amou. | | birbout |
| **and reproof** | **give** | **wisdom** | **but a child** | **left** | ***to himself* bring to shame** | **his mother** | | **When are multiplied** |

| | | | | | | 29:17 | | | |
|---|---|---|---|---|---|---|---|---|---|
| רשעים 7563 | ירבה 7235 | פשע 6588 | וצדיקים 6662 | במפלתם 4658 | יראו 7200: | | יסר 3256 | בנך 1121 | ויניחך 5117 |
| rasha'aym | yirbeh | pasha'; | uatzadiyqiym, | bamapaltam | yir'au. | | yaser | binka | uiyniycheka; |
| **the wicked** | **increase** | **transgression** | **but the righteous** | **their fall** | **shall see** | | **Correct** | **your son** | **and he shall give you rest** |

| | | | 29:18 | | | | | | |
|---|---|---|---|---|---|---|---|---|---|
| ויתן 5414 | מעדנים 4574 | לנפשך 5315: | | באין 369 | חזון 2377 | יפרע 6544 | עם 5971 | ושמר 8104 | תורה 8451 |
| uayiten | ma'adaniym | lanapsheka. | | ba'aeyn | chazoun | yipara' | 'am; | uashomer | tourah |
| **yea he shall give** | **delight** | **unto your soul** | | **Where *there is* no** | **vision** | **perish** | **the people** | **but he that keep** | **the law** |

| | 29:19 | | | | | | | | | 29:20 |
|---|---|---|---|---|---|---|---|---|---|---|
| אשרהו 835: | | בדברים 1697 | לא 3808 | יוסר 3256 | עבד 5650 | כי 3588 | יבין 995 | ואין 369 | מענה 4617: | |
| 'ashrehu. | | bidbariym | la' | yiuaser | 'abed; | kiy | yabiyn, | ua'aeyn | ma'aneh. | |
| **happy is he** | | **by words** | **not** | **will be corrected** | **A servant** | **for though** | **he understand** | **not** | **he will answer** | |

| | | | | | | | 29:21 | |
|---|---|---|---|---|---|---|---|---|
| חזית 2372 | איש 376 | אץ 213 | בדבריו 1697 | תקוה 8615 | לכסיל 3684 | ממנו 4480: | | מפנק 6445 |
| chaziyta, | 'aysh | 'aetz | bidbarayu; | tiquah | liksiyl | mimenu. | | mapaneq |
| **See you** | **a man** | ***that is* hasty** | **in his words?** | ***there is more* hope** | **of a fool** | **than of him** | | **He that delicately bring up** |

| | | | | | 29:22 | | | | | |
|---|---|---|---|---|---|---|---|---|---|---|
| מנער 5290 | עבדו 5650 | ואחריתו 319 | יהיה 1961 | מנון 4497: | | איש 376 | אף 639 | יגרה 1624 | מדון 4066 | ובעל 1167 |
| mino'ar | abdou; | ua'achariytou, | yihayeh | manoun. | | 'aysh | 'ap | yagareh | madoun; | uaba'al |
| **from a child** | **his servant** | **at the length** | **shall have him to become** | ***his* son** | | **An man** | **angry** | **stir up** | **strife** | **and a man** |

| | | | 29:23 | | | | | | |
|---|---|---|---|---|---|---|---|---|---|
| חמה 2534 | רב 7227 | פשע 6588: | | גאות 1346 | אדם 120 | תשפילנו 8213 | ושפל 8217 | רוח 7307 | יתמך 8551 |
| chemah | rab | pasha'. | | ga'auat | 'adam | tashpiylenu; | ushpal | ruach, | yitmok |
| **furious** | **abound in** | **transgression** | | **A pride** | **man's** | **shall bring him low** | **but the humble in** | **spirit** | **shall uphold** |

| | 29:24 | | | | | | | | | | 29:25 | |
|---|---|---|---|---|---|---|---|---|---|---|---|---|
| כבוד 3519: | | חולק 2505 | עם 5973 | גנב 1590 | שונא 8130 | נפשו 5315 | אלה 423 | ישמע 8085 | ולא 3808 | יגיד 5046: | | חרדת 2731 |
| kaboud. | | chouleq | 'am | ganab | sounea' | napshou; | 'alah | yishma', | uala' | yagiyd. | | cherdat |
| **honor** | | **Whoso is partner** | **with** | **a thief** | **hate** | **his own soul** | **cursing** | **he hear** | **and not** | **bewray *it*** | | **The fear of** |

| | | | | | | 29:26 | | | | |
|---|---|---|---|---|---|---|---|---|---|---|
| אדם 120 | יתן 5414 | מוקש 4170 | ובוטח 982 | ביהוה 3068 | ישגב 7682: | | רבים 7227 | מבקשים 1245 | פני 6440 | מושל 4910 |
| 'adam | yiten | mouqesh; | uabouteach | baYahuah | yasugab. | | rabiym | mabaqshiym | paney | moushel; |
| **man** | **bring** | **a snare** | **but whoso put his trust** | **in Yahuah** | **shall be safe** | | **Many** | **seek** | **favor** | ***the* ruler's** |

| | | | 29:27 | | | | | |
|---|---|---|---|---|---|---|---|---|
| ומיהוה 3068 | משפט 4941 | איש 376: | | תועבת 8441 | צדיקים 6662 | איש 376 | עול 5766 | ותועבת 8441 |
| uameYahuah | mishapat | 'aysh. | | tou'abat | tzadiyqiym | 'aysh | 'auel; | uatou'abat |
| **but from Yahuah** | **judgment *comes*** | ***every* man's** | | ***is* an abomination to** | **the just** | **An man** | **unjust** | ***is* an abomination to** |

| | | |
|---|---|---|
| רשע 7563 | ישר 3477 | דרך 1870: |
| rasha' | yashar | darek. |
| **the wicked** | ***he that is* upright in** | **the way** |

| Prov 30:1 | | | | | | | | | |
|---|---|---|---|---|---|---|---|---|---|
| | דברי 1697 | אגור 94 | בן 1121 | יקה 3348 | המשא 4853 | נאם 5002 | הגבר 1397 | לאיתיאל 384 | לאיתיאל 384 |
| | dibrey | 'agur | bin | yaqeh, | hamasaa' | na'am | hageber | la'aytiy'ael; | la'aytiy'ael |
| | **The words of** | **Agur** | **the son of** | **Jakeh** | ***even* the prophecy** | **spoke** | **the man** | **unto Ithiel** | **even unto Ithiel** |

Pro 29:16 When the wicked are multiplied, transgression increaseth: but the righteous shall see their fall. 17 Correct your son, and he shall give you rest; yea, he shall give delight unto your soul.18 Where there is no vision, the people perish: but he that keep the law, happy is he.19 A servant will not be corrected by words: for though he understand he will not answer.20 See you a man that is hasty in his words? there is more hope of a fool than of him.21 He that delicately bring up his servant from a child shall have him become his son at the length.22 An angry man stirreth up strife, and a furious man aboundeth in transgression.23 A man's pride shall bring him low: but honor shall uphold the humble in spirit.24 Whoso is partner with a thief hateth his own soul: he hear cursing, and bewrayeth it not.25 The fear of man bring a snare: but whoso put his trust in YHUH shall be safe.26 Many seek the ruler's favor; but every man's judgment cometh from YHUH.27 An unjust man is an abomination to the just: and he that is upright in the way is abomination to the wicked. **Pro** 30:1 The words of Agur the son of Jakeh, even the prophecy: the man spoke unto Ithiel, even unto Ithiel and Ucal,

30:2 30:3
ואכל 401: כי 3588 בער 1198 אנכי 595 מאיש 376 ולא 3808 בינת 998 אדם 120 לי 3807a: ולא 3808
ua'akal. kiy ba'ar 'anokiy me'aysh; uala' biynat 'adam liy. uala'
**and Ucal Surely *am* more brutish I than *any* man and not the understanding of a man have neither**

30:4
למדתי 3925 חכמה 2451 ודעת 1847 קדשים 6918 אדע 3045: מי 4310 עלה 5927 שמים 8064 וירד 3381
lamadtiy chakamah uada'at qadoshiym 'aeda. miy' 'alah shamayim uayerad
**I learned wisdom nor the knowledge of the holy have Who has ascended up into heaven or descended?**

מי 4310 אסף 622 רוח 7307 בחפניו 2651 מי 4310 צרר 6887 מים 4325 בשמלה 8071 מי 4310 הקים 6965 כל 3605 אפסי 657
miy' 'asap ruach bachapanayu miy' tzarar mayim basimlah, miy' heqiym kal 'apsey
**who has gathered the wind in his fists? who has bound the waters in a garment? who has established all the ends of**

30:5
ארץ 776 מה 4100 שמו 8034 ומה 4100 שם 8034 בנו 1121 כי 3588 תדע 3045: כל 3605 אמרת 565 אלוה 433 צרופה 6884 מגן 4043
'aretz; mah shamou uamah shem banou, kiy teda'. kal 'amrat 'alouah tzarupah; magen
**the earth? what *is* his name and what name *is* his son's if you can tell? Every word of Elohim *is* pure *is* a shield**

30:6
הוא 1931 לחסים 2620 בו 871a: אל 408 תוסף 3254 על 5921 דבריו 1697 פן 6435 יוכיח 3198 בך 871a
hua', lachosiym bou. 'al tousp 'al dabarayu; pen youkiyacha baka
**he unto them that put their trust in him not Add you unto his words lest he reprove in you**

30:7 30:8
ונכזבת 3576: שתים 8147 שאלתי 7592 מאתך 853 אל 408 תמנע 4513 ממני 4480 בטרם 2962 אמות 4191: שוא 7723
uanikzabata. shatayim sha'altiy me'atak; 'al timna' mimeniy, baterem 'amut. shau'a
**and you be found a liar Two *things* have I required of you *them* not deny me before I die vanity**

30:9
ודבר 1697 כזב 3577 הרחק 7368 ממני 4480 ראש 7289 ועשר 6239 אל 408 תתן 5414 לי 3807a הטריפני 2963 לחם 3899 חקי 2706:
uadbar kazab harcheq mimeniy, rea'sh ua'asher 'al titen liy; hatariypeniy, lechem chuqiy.
**and word lies Remove far from me poverty nor riches neither give me feed me with food convenient for me**

פן 6435 אשבע 7646 וכחשתי 3584 ואמרתי 559 מי 4310 יהוה 3069 ופן 6435 אורש 3423 וגנבתי 1589 ותפשתי 8610 שם 8034
pen 'ashbea uakichashtiy ua'amartiy, miy' Yahuah uapen 'auaresh uaganabtiy; uatapastiy, shem
**Lest I be full and deny *you* and say Who *is* Yahuah or lest I be poor and steal and take the name of**

30:10 30:11
אלהי 430: אל 408 תלשן 3960 עבד 5650 אל 413 אדנו 113 פן 6435 יקללך 7043 ואשמת 816:
'alohay. 'al talshen 'abed 'al 'adonou pen yaqalelaka ua'ashamata.
**my Elohim *in vain* not Accuse a servant unto his master, lest he curse you and you be found guilty**

30:12
דור 1755 אביו 1 יקלל 7043 ואת 853 אמו 517 לא 3808 יברך 1288: דור 1755 טהור 2889
dour 'abiyu yaqalel; ua'at 'amou, la' yabarek. dour tahour
***There is* a generation their father *that* curses *and* their mother not does bless *There is* a generation *that are* pure**

30:13
בעיניו 5869 ומצאתו 6675 לא 3808 רחץ 7364: דור 1755 מה 4100 רמו 7411 עיניו 5869
ba'aeynayu; uamitzo'atou, la' ruchatz. dour mah ramu 'aeynayu;
**in their own eyes from their filthiness not and *yet* is washed *There is* a generation O how lofty *are* their eyes**

30:14
ועפעפיו 6079 ינשאו 5375: דור 1755 חרבות 2719 שניו 8127 ומאכלות 3979 מתלעתיו 4973
ua'ap'apayu, yinase'au. dour charabout shinayu uama'akalout matala'atayu
**and their eyelids are lifted up *There is* a generation *are as* swords whose teeth and knives their jaw teeth *as***

Pro 30:2 Surely I am more brutish than any man, and have not the understanding of a man.3 I neither learned wisdom, nor have the knowledge of the holy.4 Who has ascended up into heaven, or descended? who has gathered the wind in his fists? who has bound the waters in a garment? who has established all the ends of the earth? what is his name, and what is his son's name, if you canst tell?5 Every word of G-d is pure: he is a shield unto them that put their trust in him.6 Add you not unto his words, lest he reprove you, and you be found a liar.7 Two things have I required of you; deny me them not before I die:8 Remove far from me vanity and lies: give me neither poverty nor riches; feed me with food convenient for me:9 Lest I be full, and deny you, and say, Who is YHUH? or lest I be poor, and steal, and take the name of my G-d in vain.10 Accuse not a servant unto his master, lest he curse you, and you be found guilty.11 There is a generation that curseth their father, and doth not bless their mother.12 There is a generation that are pure in their own eyes, and yet is not washed from their filthiness.13 There is a generation, O how lofty are their eyes! and their eyelids are lifted up.14 There is a generation, whose teeth are as swords, and their jaw teeth as knives, to devour the poor from off the earth, and the needy from among men.

30:15
לאכל 398 עניים 6041 מארץ 776 ואביונים 34 מאדם 120: לעלוקה 5936 שתי 8147 בנות 1323 הב 3051
le'akol 'aniyiym me'aretz; ua'abyouniym, me'adam. la'aluqah shatey banout hab
**to devour the poor from off the earth and the needy from *among* men The horseleach *has* two daughters *crying* Give**

30:16
הב 3051 שלוש 7969 הנה 2007 לא 3808 תשבענה 7646 ארבע 702 לא 3808 אמרו 559 הון 1952: שאול 7585 ועצר 6115
hab shaloush henah la' tisba'anah; 'arba, la' 'amaru houn. sha'al ua'atzer
**give *are* three There never *things that* are satisfied *yea* four not *things* say *It is* enough The grave and the barren**

30:17
רחם 7356 ארץ 776 לא 3808 שבעה 7646 מים 4325 ואש 784 לא 3808 אמרה 559 הון 1952: עין 5869 תלעג 3932
racham 'aretz la' saba'ah mayim; ua'aesh, la' 'amarah houn. 'ayin til'ag
**womb the earth *that is* not filled with water and the fire not *that* saith *It is* enough The eye *that* mock**

לאב 1 ותבוז 936 ליקהת 3349 אם 517 יקרוה 5365 ערבי 6158 נחל 5158 ויאכלוה 398 בני 1121 נשר 5404:
la'ab uatabuz liyqahat 'aem yiqaruha 'arabey nachal; uaya'kaluha baney nasher.
**at *his* father and despise to obey *his* mother shall pick it out the ravens of the valley and shall eat it *the* young eagles**

30:18 30:19
שלשה 7969 המה 1992 נפלאו 6381 ממני 4480 וארבע 702 לא 3808 ידעתים 3045: דרך 1870 הנשר 5404
shaloshah hemah nipla'au mimeniy; ua'arba la' yada'atiym. derek hanesher
***be* three There *things which are* too wonderful for me yea, four not which I know The way of an eagle**

בשמים 8064 דרך 1870 נחש 5175 עלי 5921 צור 6697 דרך 1870 אניה 591 בלב 3820 ים 3220 ודרך 1870 גבר 1397
bashamayim derek nachash, 'aley tzur derek 'aniyah baleb yam; uaderek geber
**in the air the way of a serpent upon a rock the way of a ship in the midst of the sea and the way of a man**

30:20
בעלמה 5959: כן 3651 דרך 1870 אשה 802 מנאפת 5003 אכלה 398 ומחתה 4229 פיה 6310 ואמרה 559 לא 3808 פעלתי 6466
ba'almah. ken derek 'ashah, mana'apet 'akalah uamachatah piyha; ua'amarah, la' pa'altiy
**with a maid Such *is* the way of an woman adulterous she eat and wipe her mouth and saith no I have done**

30:21 30:22
און 205: תחת 8478 שלוש 7969 רגזה 7264 ארץ 776 ותחת 8478 ארבע 702 לא 3808 תוכל 3201 שאת 5375: תחת 8478
'auen. tachat shaloush ragazah 'aretz; uatachat 'arba, la' tukal sa'aet. tachat
**wickedness For three is disquieted *things* the earth and for four *which* it cannot you bear For**

30:23
עבד 5650 כי 3588 ימלוך 4427 ונבל 5036 כי 3588 ישבע 7646 לחם 3899: תחת 8478 שנואה 8130 כי 3588 תבעל 1166
'abed kiy yimlok; uanabal, kiy yisba' lachem. tachat sanu'ah kiy tiba'ael;
**a servant when he reigns and a fool when he is filled with meat For an odious *woman* when she is married**

30:24
ושפחה 8198 כי 3588 תירש 3423 גברתה 1404: ארבעה 702 הם 1992 קטני 6996 ארץ 776 והמה 1992
uashipchah, kiy tiyrash gabirtah. 'arba'ah hem qataney 'aretz; uahemah,
**and an handmaid that is heir to her mistress *be* four There *things which are* little upon the earth but they**

30:25 30:26
חכמים 2450 מחכמים 2449: הנמלים 5244 עם 5971 לא 3808 עז 5794 ויכינו 3559 בקיץ 7019 לחמם 3899:
chakamiym machukamiym. hanamaliym 'am la' 'az; uayakiynu baqayitz lachmam.
**wise *are* exceeding The ants *are* a people not strong yet they prepare in the summer their meat**

30:27
שפנים 8227 עם 5971 לא 3808 עצום 6099 וישימו 7760 בסלע 5553 ביתם 1004: מלך 4428 אין 369 לארבה 697
shapaniym 'am la' 'atzum; uayasiymu basela' beytam. melek 'aeyn la'arbeh;
**The conies *are but* a folk not feeble yet make they in the rocks their houses king have no The locusts**

Pro 30:15 The horseleach has two daughters, crying, Give, give. There are three things that are never satisfied, yea, four things say not, It is enough:16 The grave; and the barren womb; the earth that is not filled with water; and the fire that saith not, It is enough.17 The eye that mocketh at his father, and despiseth to obey his mother, the ravens of the valley shall pick it out, and the young eagles shall eat it.18 There be three things which are too wonderful for me, yea, four which I know not:19 The way of an eagle in the air; the way of a serpent upon a rock; the way of a ship in the midst of the sea; and the way of a man with a maid.20 Such is the way of an adulterous woman; she eateth, and wipeth her mouth, and saith, I have done no wickedness.21 For three things the earth is disquieted, and for four which it cannot bear:22 For a servant when he reigned; and a fool when he is filled with meat;23 For an odious woman when she is married; and an handmaid that is heir to her mistress.24 There be four things which are little upon the earth, but they are exceeding wise:25 The ants are a people not strong, yet they prepare their meat in the summer; 26 The conies are but a feeble folk, yet make they their houses in the rocks;27 The locusts have no king, yet go they forth all of them by bands;

30:28 ... 30:29

ויצא 3318 חצץ 2686 כלו 3605: שממית 8079 בידים 3027 תתפש 8610 והיא 1931 בהיכלי 1964 מלך 4428:

uayetzea' chotzetz kulou. samamiyt bayadayim tatapes; uahiy'a, baheykaley melek.

**yet go they forth *by* bands all of them The spider with her hands takes hold and he *is* in palaces kings'**

30:30

שלשה 7969 המה 1992 מיטיבי 3190 צעד 6806 וארבעה 702 מיטבי 3190 לכת 1980: ליש 3918 גבור 1368 בבהמה 929 ולא 3808

shaloshah hemah meytiybey tza'ad; ua'arbah, meytibey laket. layish gibour babahemah; uala'

***be* three There well *things* which go yea four are comely in going A lion *which is* strongest among beasts and not**

30:31

ישוב 7725 מפני 6440 כל 3605: זרזיר 2223 מתנים 4975 או 176 תיש 8495 ומלך 4428 אלקום 510

yashub, mipaney kol. zarziyr matanayim 'au tayish; uamelek, 'alqum

**turned away for any A grey hound (*loins*) also an he goat and a king *there is* no rising up**

30:32

עמו 5973: אם 518 נבלת 5034 בהתנשא 5375 ואם 518 זמות 2161 יד 3027

'amou. 'am nabalta bahitnasea'; ua'am zamouta, yad

**against whom If you have done foolishly in lifting up yourself or if you have thought evil *lay* your hand**

30:33

לפה 6310: כי 3588 מיץ 4330 חלב 2461 יוציא 3318 חמאה 2529 ומיץ 4330 אף 639 יוציא 3318 דם 1818

lapeh. kiy mitz chalab youtziy'a chem'ah, uamiytz 'ap youtziy'a dam;

**upon your mouth Surely the churning of milk bring forth butter and the wringing of the nose bring forth blood**

ומיץ 4330 אפים 639 יוציא 3318 ריב 7379:

uamiytz 'apayim, youtziy'a riyb.

**so the forcing of wrath bring forth strife**

**Prov 31:1** ... 31:2

דברי 1697 למואל 3927 מלך 4428 משא 4853 אשר 834 יסרתו 3256 אמו 517: מה 4100 ברי 1248 ומה 4100

dibrey lamu'ael melek; masa', 'asher yisaratu 'amou. mah bariy uamah

**The words of Lemuel king the prophecy that taught him his mother What my son? and what**

31:3

בר 1248 בטני 990 ומה 4100 בר 1248 נדרי 5088: אל 408 תתן 5414 לנשים 802 חילך 2428 ודרכיך 1870

bar bitniy; uameh bar nadaray. 'al titen lanashiym cheyleka; uadrakeyka,

**the son of my womb? and what the son of my vows? not Give unto women your strength nor your ways**

31:4

למחות 4229 מלכין 4428: אל 408 למלכים 4428 למואל 3927 אל 408 למלכים 4428 שתו 8354 יין 3196 ולרוזנים 7336 או 176

lamchout malakiyn. 'al lamalakiym lamou'ael, 'al lamalakiym shatou yayin; ualrouzaniym, 'au

**to that which destroy kings *It is* not for kings O Lemuel *it is* not for kings to drink wine nor for princes or**

31:5 ... 31:6

שכר 7941: פן 6435 ישתה 8354 וישכח 7911 מחקק 2710 וישנה 8138 דין 1779 כל 3605 בני 1121 עני 6040:

shekar. pen yishteh uayishkach machuqaq; uiyshaneh diyn kal baney 'aniy.

**strong drink Lest they drink and forget the law (*statute*) and pervert the judgment of any of sons of the afflicted**

31:7

תנו 5414 שכר 7941 לאובד 6 ויין 3196 למרי 4751 נפש 5315: ישתה 8354

tanu shekar la'aubed; uayayin lamarey napesh. yishteh

**Give strong drink unto him that is ready to perish and wine unto those that be of heavy hearts Let him drink**

31:8

וישכח 7911 רישו 7389 ועמלו 5999 לא 3808 יזכר 2142 עוד 5750: פתח 6605 פיך 6310 לאלם 483 אל 413 דין 1779

uayishkach riyshou; ua'amalou, la' yizkar 'aud. patach piyka la'alem; 'al diyn,

**and forget his poverty and his misery no remember more Open your mouth for the dumb in the cause of**

Pro 30:28 The spider take hold with her hands, and is in kings' palaces.29 There be three things which go well, yea, four are comely in going:30 A lion which is strongest among beasts, and turneth not away for any;31 A greyhound; an he goat also; and a king, against whom there is no rising up.32 If you have done foolishly in lifting up thyself, or if you have thought evil, lay your hand upon your mouth.33 Surely the churning of milk bring forth butter, and the wringing of the nose bring forth blood: so the forcing of wrath bring forth strife. **Pro** 31:1 The words of king Lemuel, the prophecy that his mother taught him.2 What, my son? and what, the son of my womb? and what, the son of my vows?3 Give not your strength unto women, nor your ways to that which destroyeth kings.4 It is not for kings, O Lemuel, it is not for kings to drink wine; nor for princes strong drink:5 Lest they drink, and forget the law, and pervert the judgment of any of the afflicted.6 Give strong drink unto him that is ready to perish, and wine unto those that be of heavy hearts. 7 Let him drink, and forget his poverty, and remember his misery no more.8 Open your mouth for the dumb in the cause of all such as are appointed to destruction.

31:9
כל 3605 בני 1121 חלוף 2475: פתח 6605 פיך 6310 שפט 8199 צדק 6664 ודין 1777 עני 6041
kal baney chaloup. patach piyka shapat tzedeq; uadiyn, 'aniy
**all *such as are* appointed to destruction Open your mouth judge righteously and plead *the cause of* the poor**

31:10 31:11
ואביון 34: אשת 802 חיל 2428 מי 4310 ימצא 4672 ורחק 7350 מפנינים 6443 מכרה 4377: בטח 982 בה 871a
ua'abyoun. 'aeshet chayil miy' yimtza'; uarachoq mipniyniym mikrah. batach bah
**and needy a woman? virtuous Who can find *is* far above rubies her price *is* does safely trust in her**

31:12
לב 3820 בעלה 1167 ושלל 7998 לא 3808 יחסר 2637: גמלתהו 1580 טוב 2896 ולא 3808 רע 7451 כל 3605
leb ba'alah; uashalal, la' yechsar. gamalatahu toub uala' ra'; kol,
**The heart her husband so that spoil no he shall have need *of* She will do him good and not evil all**

31:13 31:14
ימי 3117 חייה 2416: דרשה 1875 צמר 6785 ופשתים 6593 ותעש 6213 בחפץ 2656 כפיה 3709: היתה 1961 כאניות 591
yamey chayeyha darashah tzemer uapishtiym; uata'as, bachepetz kapeyha. hayatah ka'aniyout
**the days of her life She seek wool and flax and work willingly *with* her hands She is like the ships**

31:15
סוחר 5503 ממרחק 4801 תביא 935 לחמה 3899: ותקם 6965 בעוד 5750 לילה 3915 ותתן 5414 טרף 2964 לביתה 1004
soucher; mimerchaq, tabiy'a lachamah. uataqam ba'aud layalah, uatiten terep labeytah;
**merchants' from afar she bring her food She rise also while it is yet night and gives meat to her household**

31:16
וחק 2706 לנערתיה 5291: זממה 2161 שדה 7704 ותקחהו 3947 מפרי 6529 כפיה 3709 נטע 5193
uachoq, lana'aroteyha. zamamah deh uatiqachehu; mipriy kapeyha, neta'a
**and a portion to her maidens She consider a field and buy it with the fruit of her hands she planted**

31:17 31:18
כרם 3754: חגרה 2296 בעוז 5797 מתניה 4975 ותאמץ 553 זרועתיה 2220: טעמה 2938 כי 3588 טוב 2896
karem. chagarah ba'auz mataneyha; uata'ametz, zaro'ateyha. ta'amah kiy toub
**a vineyard She gird with strength her loins and strengthen her arms She perceive that *is* good**

31:19
סחרה 5504 לא 3808 יכבה 3518 בליל 3915 נרה 5216: ידיה 3027 שלחה 7971 בכישור 3601 וכפיה 3709 תמכו 8551
sacharah; la' yikbeh balayal nerah. yadeyah shilchah bakiyshour; uakapeyha, tamaku
**her merchandise not goes out by night her candle her hands She lay to the spindle and her hands hold**

31:20 31:21
פלך 6418: כפה 3709 פרשה 6566 לעני 6041 וידיה 3027 שלחה 7971 לאביון 34: לא 3808 תירא 3372
palek. kapah parasah la'aniy; uayadeyha, shilchah la'abyoun. la' tiyraa'
**the distaff her hand She stretch out to the poor yea her hands she reached forth to the needy not She is afraid**

31:22
לביתה 1004 משלג 7950 כי 3588 כל 3605 ביתה 1004 לבש 3847 שנים 8144: מרבדים 4765 עשתה 6213
labeytah mishaleg; kiy kal beytah, labush shaniym. marbadiym 'astah
**for her household of the snow for all her household *are* clothed *with* scarlet coverings of tapestry She make**

31:23
לה 3807a שש 8336 וארגמן 713 לבושה 3830: נודע 3045 בשערים 8179 בעלה 1167 בשבתו 3427 עם 5973 זקני 2205
lah; shesh ua'argaman labushah. nouda' bash'ariym ba'alah; bashibtou, 'am ziqaney
**herself *is* silk and purple her clothing is known in the gates Her husband when he sit among the elders of**

31:24 31:25
ארץ 776: סדין 5466 עשתה 6213 ותמכר 4376 וחגור 2289 נתנה 5414 לכנעני 3669: עז 5797 והדר 1926
'aretz. sadiyn 'astah uatimkor; uachagour, natanah lakana'aniy. 'az uahadar
**the land fine linen She make and sell *it* and girdles deliver unto the merchant Strength and honor**

Pro 31:9 Open your mouth, judge righteously, and plead the cause of the poor and needy.10 Who can find a virtuous woman? for her price is far above rubies.11 The heart of her husband doth safely trust in her, so that he shall have no need of spoil.12 She will do him good and not evil all the days of her life.13 She seek wool, and flax, and worketh willingly with her hands.14 She is like the merchants' ships; she bring her food from afar.15 She rise also while it is yet night, and give meat to her household, and a portion to her maidens.16 She considereth a field, and buyeth it: with the fruit of her hands she planteth a vineyard.17 She gird her loins with strength, and strengtheneth her arms.18 She perceiveth that her merchandise is good: her candle go not out by night.19 She layeth her hands to the spindle, and her hands hold the distaff.20 She stretcheth out her hand to the poor; yea, she reacheth forth her hands to the needy.21 She is not afraid of the snow for her household: for all her household are clothed with scarlet.22 She make herself coverings of tapestry; her clothing is silk and purple. 23 Her husband is known in the gates, when he sitteth among the elders of the land. 24 She make fine linen, and sell it; and delivereth girdles unto the merchant.25 Strength and honor are her clothing; and she shall rejoice in time to come.

| | | | | | | | | | |
|---|---|---|---|---|---|---|---|---|---|
| לבושה 3830 | ותשחק 7832 | ליום 3117 | אחרון 314: | **31:26** | פיה 6310 | פתחה 6605 | בחכמה 2451 | ותורת 8451 | חסד 2617 |
| labushah; | uatischaq, | layoum | 'acharoun. | | piyha | patachah | bachakamah; | uatourat | chesed, |
| ***are*** **her clothing** | **and she shall rejoice** | **in time** | **to come** | | **her mouth** | **She open** | **with wisdom** | **and the law of** | **kindness** |

| | | | | | | | | | |
|---|---|---|---|---|---|---|---|---|---|
| על 5921 | לשונה 3956: | **31:27** | צופיה 6822 | הליכות 1979 | ביתה 1004 | ולחם 3899 | עצלות 6104 | לא 3808 | תאכל 398: **31:28** |
| 'al | lashounah. | | tzoupiyah | haliykout | beytah; | ua'alechem | 'atzlut, | la' | ta'kel. |
| **in** | **her tongue** ***is*** | | **She looks well to** | **the ways of** | **her household** | **and the bread of** | **idleness** | **not** | **and eat** |

| | | | | | | | | | |
|---|---|---|---|---|---|---|---|---|---|
| קמו 6965 | בניה 1121 | ויאשרוה 833 | בעלה 1167 | ויהללה 1984: | **31:29** | רבות 7227 | בנות 1323 | עשו 6213 | חיל 2428 |
| qamu | baneyha | uaya'ashruha; | ba'alah, | uayahalalah. | | rabout | banout | 'asu | chayil; |
| **arise up** | **Her children** | **and call her blessed** | **her husband** ***also*** | **and he praise her** | | **Many** | **daughters** | **have done** | **virtuously** |

| | | | | | | | | | | | | |
|---|---|---|---|---|---|---|---|---|---|---|---|---|
| ואת 859 | עלית 5927 | על 5921 | כלנה 3605: | **31:30** | שקר 8267 | החן 2580 | והבל 1892 | היפי 3308 | אשה 802 | יראת 3373 | יהוה 3069 | היא 1931 |
| ua'at, | 'aliyt | 'al | kulanah. | | sheqer | hachen | uahebel | hayopiy; | 'ashah | yir'at | Yahuah | hiy'a |
| ***but you*** | **excellest** | **over** | **them all** | | ***is*** **deceitful** | **Favour** | **and vain** | **beauty** ***is*** | ***but*** **a woman** | ***that*** **fear** | **Yahuah** | **she** |

| | | | | | | | | | |
|---|---|---|---|---|---|---|---|---|---|
| תתהלל 1984: | **31:31** | תנו 5414 | לה 3807a | מפרי 6529 | ידיה 3027 | ויהללוה 1984 | בשערים 8179 | מעשיה 4639: |
| tithalal. | | tanu | lah | mipriy | yadeyha; | uiyhalaluha | basha'ariym | ma'aseyha. |
| **shall be praised** | | **Give** | **her** | **of the fruit of** | **her hands** | **and let praise her** | **in the gates** | **her own works** |

Pro 31:26 She openeth her mouth with wisdom; and in her tongue is the law of kindness.27 She look well to the ways of her household, and eateth not the bread of idleness.28 Her children arise up, and call her blessed; her husband also, and he praiseth her.29 Many daughters have done virtuously, but you excellest them all.30 Favour is deceitful, and beauty is vain: but a woman that fear YHUH, she shall be praised.31 Give her of the fruit of her hands; and let her own works praise her in the gates.

# ECCLESIASTES
## (*Kohelet*)

The Book of Ecclesiastes does not directly identify its author but there are many verses that imply it was Solomon. The name Ecclesiastes in Hebrew means *member of an assembly* but is often thought to mean *Preacher*. There are some verses that may suggest a different person wrote the book after Solomon's death, which could have been several hundred years later, but the conventional belief is that Solomon is indeed the author. Solomon's reign as king of Israel lasted from around 970 B.C. to approximately 930 B.C. and the book is believed to have been written towards the end of his reign. Ecclesiastes is a book which puts into perspective a narrative of "the Preacher", or "the Teacher", and reveals the depression that inevitably results from seeking happiness through worldly possessions. The book is a perspective of the world through the eyes of wisdom and explores the meaning of humanity in regard to most every form of worldly pleasure. In the end he decides to except the fact that life is brief and ultimately worthless without personal commitment and obedience to Yahuah our Elohim instead of temporary pleasure.

**Ecclesiates 1:1** דברי 1697 | קהלת 6953 | בן 1121 | דוד 1732 | מלך 4428 | בירושלם 3389: | **1:2** הבל 1892 | הבלים 1892 | אמר 559
dibrey qohelet ben dauid, melek biyarushalaim. habel habaliym 'amar
**The words of the Preacher the son of David king in Jerusalem Vanity of vanities saith**

קהלת 6953 | הבל 1892 | הבלים 1892 | הכל 3605 | הבל 1892: | **1:3** מה 4100 | יתרון 3504 | לאדם 120 | בכל 3605 | עמלו 5999 | שיעמל 5998 | תחת 8478
qohelet, habel habaliym hakol habel. mah yitroun la'adam; bakal 'amalou, sheya'amol tachat
**the Preacher vanity of vanities all *is* vanity What profit *has* a man of all his labour which he takes under**

השמש 8121: | **1:4** דור 1755 | הלך 1980 | ודור 1755 | בא 935 | והארץ 776 | לעולם 5769 | עמדת 5975: | **1:5** וזרח 2224
hashamesh. dour halok uadour ba', uaha'aretz la'aulam 'amadet. uazarach
**the sun? *One* generation passed away and *another* generation comes but the earth for ever abide also arise**

השמש 8121 | ובא 935 | השמש 8121 | ואל 413 | מקומו 4725 | שואף 7602 | זורח 2224 | הוא 1931 | שם 8033: | **1:6** הולך 1980 | אל 413 | דרום 1864
hashemesh uaba' hashamesh; ua'ael maqoumou, shou'aep zoureach hua' sham. houlek 'al daroum,
**The sun and goes down the sun and to his place hasten arose he where goes toward the south**

וסובב 5437 | אל 413 | צפון 6828 | סובב 5437 | סבב 5437 | הולך 1980 | הרוח 7307 | ועל 5921 | סביבתיו 5439 | שב 7725
uasoubeb 'al tzapoun; soubeb soubeb houlek haruach, ua'al sabiybotayu shab
**and turned about unto the north it whirling about continually The wind and according to his circuits return again**

הרוח 7307: | **1:7** כל 3605 | הנחלים 5158 | הלכים 1980 | אל 413 | הים 3220 | והים 3220 | איננו 369 | מלא 4392 | אל 413 | מקום 4725 | שהנחלים 5158
haruach. kal hanachaliym holakiym 'al hayam, uahayam 'aeynenu malea'; 'al maqoum, shehanachaliym
**the wind All the rivers run into the sea yet the sea *is* not full unto the place from where the rivers**

הלכים 1980 | שם 8033 | הם 1992 | שבים 7725 | ללכת 1980: | **1:8** כל 3605 | הדברים 1697 | יגעים 3023 | לא 3808 | יוכל 3201 | איש 376 | לדבר 1696 | לא 3808
holakiym, sham hem shabiym lalaket. kal hadabariym yage'aym, la' yukal 'aysh ladaber; la'
**come there they return again All things *are* full of labour not can man utter *it* not**

תשבע 7646 | עין 5869 | לראות 7200 | ולא 3808 | תמלא 4390 | אזן 241 | משמע 8085: | **1:9** מה 4100 | שהיה 1961 | הוא 1931 | שיהיה 1961
tisba' 'ayin lir'aut, uala' timalea' 'azen mishmoa'. mah shehayah hua' sheyihayeh,
**is satisfied the eye with seeing nor filled the ear with hearing *The* thing that has been it *is that* which shall be**

ומה 4100 | שנעשה 6213 | הוא 1931 | שיעשה 6213 | ואין 369 | כל 3605 | חדש 2319 | תחת 8478 | השמש 8121: | **1:10** יש 3426
uamah shena'asah, hua' sheye'aseh; ua'aeyn kal chadash tachat hashamesh. yesh
**and that which is done *is* that which shall be done and *there is* no any new *thing* under the sun Is there**

**Ecclesiastes** 1:1 The words of the Preacher, the son of David, king in Jerusalem.2 Vanity of vanities, saith the Preacher, vanity of vanities; all is vanity.3 What profit has a man of all his labour which he take under the sun?4 One generation pass away, and another generation cometh: but the earth abideth forever.5 The sun also arise, and the sun go down, and hasteth to his place where he arose.6 The wind go toward the south, and turneth about unto the north; it whirleth about continually, and the wind returneth again according to his circuits.7 All the rivers run into the sea; yet the sea is not full; unto the place from whence the rivers come, thither they return again.8 All things are full of labour; man cannot utter it: the eye is not satisfied with seeing, nor the ear filled with hearing.9 The thing that has been, it is that which shall be; and that which is done is that which shall be done: and there is no new thing under the sun.

1:11
דבר 1697 שיאמר 559 ראה 7200 זה 2088 חדש 2319 הוא 1931 כבר 3528 היה 1961 לעלמים 5769 אשר 834 היה 1961 מלפננו 6440:
dabar sheya'mar ra'aeh zeh chadash hua'; kabar hayah la'aulamiym, 'asher hayah milpanenu.
***any* thing whereof it may be said See this *is* new? it already has been of old time which has before us**

אין 369 זכרון 2146 לראשנים 7223 וגם 1571 לאחרנים 314 שיהיו 1961 לא 3808 יהיה 1961 להם 1992
'aeyn zikroun lara'shoniym; ua'gam la'acharoniym sheyihayu, la' yihayeh lahem
***There is* no remembrance of former *things* and neither to come shall there be neither *things* that are *any* to them**

זכרון 2146 עם 5973 שיהיו 1961 לאחרנה 314: 1:12 אני 589 קהלת 6953 הייתי 1961 מלך 4428 על 5921 ישראל 3478
zikaroun, 'am sheyihayu la'acharonah. 'aniy qohelet, hayiytiy melek 'al yisra'ael
**remembrance of with *those* that shall come after I the Preacher I was king over Israel**

בירושלם 3389: 1:13 ונתתי 5414 את 853 לבי 3820 לדרוש 1875 ולתור 8446 בחכמה 2451 על 5921 כל 3605 אשר 834 נעשה 6213
biyarushalaim. uanatatiy 'at libiy, lidroush ualatur bachakamah, 'al kal 'asher na'asah
**in Jerusalem And I gave my heart to seek and search out by wisdom concerning all *things* that are done**

תחת 8478 השמים 8064 הוא 1931 ענין 6045 רע 7451 נתן 5414 אלהים 430 לבני 1121 האדם 120 לענות 6031 בו 871a: 1:14
tachat hashamayim; hua' 'anyan ra', natan 'alohiym libney ha'adam la'anout bou.
**under heaven this travail sore has given Elohim to the sons of man to be exercised therewith**

ראיתי 7200 את 853 כל 3605 המעשים 4639 שנעשו 6213 תחת 8478 השמש 8121 והנה 2009 הכל 3605 הבל 1892 ורעות 7469
ra'aytiy 'at kal hama'asiym, shena'asu tachat hashamesh; uahineh hakol hebel uar'aut
**I have seen all the works that are done under the sun and behold all *is* vanity and vexation of**

רוח 7307: 1:15 מעות 5791 לא 3808 יוכל 3201 לתקן 8626 וחסרון 2642 לא 3808 יוכל 3201
ruach. ma'auat la' yukal litqon; uachesroun la' yukal
**spirit *That which is* crooked not can be made straight and that which is wanting not can**

להמנות 4487: 1:16 דברתי 1696 אני 589 עם 5973 לבי 3820 לאמר 559 אני 589 הנה 2009 הגדלתי 1431
lahimanout. dibartiy 'aniy 'am libiy lea'mor, 'aniy, hineh higdaltiy
**be numbered communed I with mine own heart saying I Lo am come to great estate**

והוספתי 3254 חכמה 2451 על 5921 כל 3605 אשר 834 היה 1961 לפני 6440 על 5921 ירושלם 3389 ולבי 3820
uahousaptiy chakamah 'al kal 'asher hayah lapanay 'al yarushalaim; ualibiy
**and have gotten more wisdom than all *they* that have been before me in Jerusalem yea my heart**

ראה 7200 הרבה 7235 חכמה 2451 ודעת 1847: 1:17 ואתנה 5414 לבי 3820 לדעת 3045 חכמה 2451 ודעת 3045 הוללות 1947
ra'ah harbeh chakamah uada'at. ua'atnah libiy lada'at chakamah uada'at houlelout
**had experience of great wisdom and knowledge And I gave my heart to know wisdom and to know madness**

ושכלות 5531 ידעתי 3045 שגם 1571 זה 2088 הוא 1931 רעיון 7475 רוח 7307: 1:18 כי 3588 ברב 7230 חכמה 2451 רב 7227 כעס 3708
uasiklut; yada'tiy shegam zeh hua' ra'youn ruach. kiy barob chakamah rab ka'as;
**and folly I perceived also this that *is* vexation of spirit For in much wisdom *is* much grief**

ויוסיף 3254 דעת 1847 יוסיף 3254 מכאוב 4341:
uayousiyp da'at yousiyp mak'aub.
**and he that increase knowledge increase sorrow**

Ecc 1:10 Is there anything whereof it may be said, See, this is new? it has been already of old time, which was before us.11 There is no remembrance of former things; neither shall there be any remembrance of things that are to come with those that shall come after.12 I the Preacher was king over Israel in Jerusalem.13 And I gave my heart to seek and search out by wisdom concerning all things that are done under heaven: this sore travail has G-d given to the sons of man to be exercised therewith.14 I have seen all the works that are done under the sun; and, behold, all is vanity and vexation of spirit.15 That which is crooked cannot be made straight: and that which is wanting cannot be numbered.16 I communed with mine own heart, saying, Lo, I am come to great estate, and have gotten more wisdom than all they that have been before me in Jerusalem: yea, my heart had great experience of wisdom and knowledge.17 And I gave my heart to know wisdom, and to know madness and folly: I perceived that this also is vexation of spirit.18 For in much wisdom is much grief: and he that increaseth knowledge increaseth sorrow.

**Eccl 2:1** 559 אמרתי 589 אני 3820 בלבי 1980 לכה 4994 נא 5254 אנסכה 8057 בשמחה 7200 וראה 2896 בטוב 2009 והנה 1571 גם
'amartiy 'aniy balibiy, lakah naa' 'anaskah basimchah uar'aeh batoub; uahineh gam
**I said I in mine heart Go to now I will prove you with mirth therefore enjoy pleasure and behold also**

1931 הוא 1892 הבל: **2:2** 7814 לשחוק 559 אמרתי 1984 מהולל 8057 ולשמחה 4100 מה 2090 זה 6213 עשה: **2:3** 8446 תרתי 3820 בלבי 4900 למשוך
hua' habel. lischouq 'amartiy mahoulal; ualsimchah mah zoh 'asah. tartiy balibiy, limshouk
**this *is* vanity of laughter I said *It is* mad and of mirth What it? does I sought in mine heart to give**

3196 ביין 853 את 1320 בשרי 3820 ולבי 5090 נהג 2451 בחכמה 270 ולאחז 5531 בסכלות 5704 עד 834 אשר 7200 אראה
bayayin 'at basariy; ualibiy noheg bachakamah uale'achoz basiklut, 'ad 'asher 'ar'ah,
**unto wine myself yet mine heart acquainting with wisdom and to lay hold on folly till which I might see**

335 אי 2088 זה 2896 טוב 1121 לבני 120 האדם 834 אשר 6213 יעשו 8478 תחת 8064 השמים 4557 מספר 3117 ימי
'ay zeh toub libney ha'adam 'asher ya'asu tachat hashamayim, mispar yamey
**what *was* that good for the sons of men which they should do under the heaven all the days of**

2416 חייהם: **2:4** 1431 הגדלתי 4639 מעשי 1129 בניתי 3807a לי 1004 בתים 5193 נטעתי 3807a לי 3754 כרמים: **2:5** 6213 עשיתי 3807a לי 1593 גנות
chayeyhem. higdaltiy ma'asay; baniytiy liy batiym, nata'atiy liy karamiym. 'asiytiy liy, ganout
**their life I made great me works I builded me houses I planted me vineyards I made me gardens**

6508 ופרדסים 5193 ונטעתי 871a בהם 6086 עץ 3605 כל 6529 פרי: **2:6** 6213 עשיתי 3807a לי 1295 ברכות 4325 מים 8248 להשקות
uapardesiym; uanata'atiy bahem 'aetz kal periy. 'asiytiy liy barekout mayim; lahashqout
**and orchards and I planted in them trees of all *kind of* fruits I made me pools of water to water (*irrigate*)**

1992 מהם 3293 יער 6779 צומח 6086 עצים: **2:7** 7069 קניתי 5650 עבדים 8198 ושפחות 1121 ובני 1004 בית 1961 היה 3807a לי
mehem, ya'ar tzoumeach 'aetziym. qaniytiy 'abadiym uashpachout, uabney bayit hayah liy;
**therewith the wood that bring forth trees I got *me* servants and maidens and servants born house had *in* my**

1571 גם 4735 מקנה 1241 בקר 6629 וצאן 7235 הרבה 1961 היה 3807a לי 3605 מכל 1961 שהיו 6440 לפני 3389 בירושלם: **2:8**
gam miqneh baqar uatza'n harbeh hayah liy, mikol shehayu lapanay biyarushalaim.
**also possessions of great and small cattle great had I above all that were before me in Jerusalem**

3664 כנסתי 3807a לי 1571 גם 3701 כסף 2091 וזהב 5459 וסגלת 4428 מלכים 4082 והמדינות 6213 עשיתי 3807a לי
kanastiy liy gam kesep uazahab, uasgulat malakiym uahamadiynout; 'asiytiy liy
**I gathered me also silver and gold and the peculiar treasure of kings and of the provinces I got me**

7891 שרים 7891 ושרות 8588 ותענוגת 1121 בני 120 האדם 7705 שדה 7705 ושדות: **2:9**
shariym uasharout, uata'anugot baney ha'adam shidah uashidout.
**men singers and women singers and the delights of the sons of men *as* musical instruments and that of all sorts**

1431 וגדלתי 3254 והוספתי 3605 מכל 1961 שהיה 6440 לפני 3389 בירושלם 637 אף 2451 חכמתי 5975 עמדה 3807a לי: **2:10**
agadaltiy uahousaptiy, mikol shehayah lapanay biyarushalaim; 'ap chakamatiy 'amdah liy.
**So I was great and increased more than all that were before me in Jerusalem also my wisdom remained with me**

3605 וכל 834 אשר 7592 שאלו 5869 עיני 3808 לא 680 אצלתי 1992 מהם 3808 לא 4513 מנעתי 853 את 3820 לבי 3605 מכל 8057 שמחה
uakol 'asher sha'alu 'aeynay, la' 'atzaltiy mehem; la' mana'atiy 'at libiy mikal simchah,
**And whatsoever after desired mine eyes not I kept from them not I withheld my heart from any joy**

**Ecc** 2:1 I said in mine heart, Go to now, I will prove you with mirth, therefore enjoy pleasure: and, behold, this also is vanity.2 I said of laughter, It is mad: and of mirth, What doeth it?3 I sought in mine heart to give myself unto wine, yet acquainting mine heart with wisdom; and to lay hold on folly, till I might see what was that good for the sons of men, which they should do under the heaven all the days of their life.4 I made me great works; I built me houses; I planted me vineyards:5 I made me gardens and orchards, and I planted trees in them of all kind of fruits:6 I made me pools of water, to water therewith the wood that bring forth trees:7 I got me servants and maidens, and had servants born in my house; also I had great possessions of great and small cattle above all that were in Jerusalem before me:8 I gathered me also silver and gold, and the peculiar treasure of kings and of the provinces: I got me men singers and women singers, and the delights of the sons of men, as musical instruments, and that of all sorts.9 So I was great, and increased more than all that were before me in Jerusalem: also my wisdom remained with me.10 And whatsoever mine eyes desired I kept not from them, I withheld not my heart from any joy; for my heart rejoiced in all my labour: and this was my portion of all my labour.

2:11

כי 3588 לבי 3820 שמח 8055 מכל 3605 עמלי 5999 וזה 2088 היה 1961 חלקי 2506 מכל 3605 עמלי 5999: ופניתי 6437 אני 589 בכל 3605
kiy libiy sameach mikal 'amaliy, uazeh hayah chelqiy mikal 'amaliy. uapaniytiy 'aniy, bakal
**for my heart rejoiced in all my labour and this was my portion of all my labour Then looked I on all**

מעשי 4639 שעשו 6213 ידי 3027 ובעמל 5999 שעמלתי 5998 לעשות 6213 והנה 2009 הכל 3605 הבל 1892
ma'asay she'asu yaday, uabe'amal she'amaltiy la'asout; uahineh hakol habel
**the works that had wrought my hands and on the labour that I had laboured to do and behold all *was* vanity**

2:12

ורעות 7469 רוח 7307 ואין 369 יתרון 3504 תחת 8478 השמש 8121: ופניתי 6437 אני 589 לראות 7200 חכמה 2451
uar'aut ruach, ua'aeyn yitroun tachat hashamesh. uapaniytiy 'aniy lir'aut chakamah
**and vexation of spirit and *there was* no profit under the sun And turned myself I to behold wisdom**

והוללות 1947 וסכלות 5531 כי 3588 מה 4100 האדם 120 שיבוא 935 אחרי 310 המלך 4428 את 853 אשר 834 כבר 3528
uahoulelout uasiklut; kiy meh ha'adam, sheyabou'a 'acharey hamelek, 'at 'asher kabar
**and madness and folly for what *can* the man *do* that comes after the king? *even* that which already**

2:13

עשוהו 6213: וראיתי 7200 אני 589 שיש 3426 יתרון 3504 לחכמה 2451 מן 4480 הסכלות 5531 כיתרון 3504 האור 216 מן 4480
'asuhu. uara'aytiy 'aniy, sheyesh yitroun lachakamah min hasiklut; kayitroun ha'aur min
**has been done Then saw I that excell as far as wisdom from folly excell light from**

2:14

החשך 2822: החכם 2450 עיניו 5869 בראשו 7218 והכסיל 3684 בחשך 2822 הולך 1980 וידעתי 3045 גם 1571 אני 589 שמקרה 4745
hachoshek. hechakam 'aeynayu bara'shou, uahakasiyl bachoshek houlek; uayada'atiy gam 'aniy, shemiqreh
**darkness The wise man's eyes *are* in his head but the fool in darkness walk and perceived also I myself that event**

2:15

אחד 259 יקרה 7136 את 853 כלם 3605: ואמרתי 559 אני 589 בלבי 3820 כמקרה 4745 הכסיל 3684 גם 1571 אני 589 יקרני 7136
'achad yiqreh 'at kulam. ua'amartiy 'aniy balibiy, kamiqreh hakasiyl gam 'aniy yiqreniy,
**one happen to them all Then said I in my heart As it happen to the fool even I *so* it happen to me**

2:16

ולמה 4100 חכמתי 2449 אני 589 אז 227 יותר 3148 ודברתי 1696 בלבי 3820 שגם 1571 זה 2088 הבל 1892: כי 3588 אין 369
ualamah chakamtiy 'aniy 'az youter; uadibartiy balibiy, shegam zeh habel. kiy 'aeyn
**and why was wise? I then more Then I said in my heart that also this *is* vanity For *there is* no**

זכרון 2146 לחכם 2450 עם 5973 הכסיל 3684 לעולם 5769 בשכבר 3528 הימים 3117 הבאים 935 הכל 3605
zikaroun lachakam 'am hakasiyl la'aulam; bashekbar hayamiym haba'aym hakol
**remembrance of the wise more than of the fool for ever seeing that which now *is* in the days to come all**

2:17

נשכח 7911 ואיך 349 ימות 4191 החכם 2450 עם 5973 הכסיל 3684: ושנאתי 8130 את 853 החיים 2416 כי 3588
nishkach, ua'aeyk yamut hechakam 'am hakasiyl. uasanea'tiy 'at hachayiym, kiy
**shall be forgotten And how die the wise *man*? as the fool Therefore I hated life because**

2:18

רע 7451 עלי 5921 המעשה 4639 שנעשה 6213 תחת 8478 השמש 8121 כי 3588 הכל 3605 הבל 1892 ורעות 7469 רוח 7307:
ra' 'alay hama'aseh, shena'asah tachat hashamesh; kiy hakol hebel uar'aut ruach.
***is* grievous unto me the work that is wrought under the sun for all *is* vanity and vexation of spirit**

ושנאתי 8130 אני 589 את 853 כל 3605 עמלי 5999 שאני 589 עמל 6001 תחת 8478 השמש 8121 שאניחנו 3240 לאדם 120
uasanea'tiy 'aniy 'at kal 'amaliy, she'aniy 'amel tachat hashamesh; she'aniychenu, la'adam
**Yea hated I all my labour which I had taken under the sun because I should leave it unto the man**

Ecc 2:11 Then I looked on all the works that my hands had wrought, and on the labour that I had laboured to do: and, behold, all was vanity and vexation of spirit, and there was no profit under the sun.12 And I turned myself to behold wisdom, and madness, and folly: for what can the man do that cometh after the king? even that which has been already done.13 Then I saw that wisdom excelleth folly, as far as light excelleth darkness.14 The wise man's eyes are in his head; but the fool walk in darkness: and I myself perceived also that one event happeneth to them all.15 Then said I in my heart, As it happeneth to the fool, so it happeneth even to me; and why was I then more wise? Then I said in my heart, that this also is vanity.16 For there is no remembrance of the wise more than of the fool forever; seeing that which now is in the days to come shall all be forgotten. And how die the wise man? as the fool.17 Therefore I hated life; because the work that is wrought under the sun is grievous unto me: for all is vanity and vexation of spirit.18 Yea, I hated all my labour which I had taken under the sun: because I should leave it unto the man that shall be after me.

2:19

שיהיה 1961 | אחרי 310: | ומי 4310 | יודע 3045 | החכם 2450 | יהיה 1961 | או 176 | סכל 5530 | וישלט 7980 | בכל 3605
sheyihayeh 'acharay. uamiy youdea', hechakam yihayeh 'au sakal, uayishlat bakal
**that shall be after me And who knows a wise man *whether* he shall be or a fool? yet shall he have rule over all**

2:20

עמלי 5999 | שעמלתי 5998 | ושחכמתי 2449 | תחת 8478 | השמש 8121 | גם 1571 | זה 2088 | הבל 1892:
'amaliy, she'amaltiy uashechakamtiy tachat hashamesh; gam zeh habel.
**my labour wherein I have laboured and wherein I have showed myself wise under the sun *is* also This vanity**

2:21

וסבותי 5437 | אני 589 | ליאש 2976 | את 853 | לבי 3820 | על 5921 | כל 3605 | העמל 5999 | שעמלתי 5998 | תחת 8478 | השמש 8121:
uasaboutiy 'aniy laya'aesh 'at libiy; 'al kal he'amal, she'amaltiy tachat hashamesh.
**Therefore went about I to cause to despair my heart of all the labour which I took under the sun**

כי 3588 | יש 3426 | אדם 120 | שעמלו 5999 | בחכמה 2451 | ובדעת 1847 | ובכשרון 3788 | ולאדם 120 | שלא 3808 | עמל 5998
kiy yesh 'adam, she'amalou bachakamah uabda'at uabkishroun; ual'adam shela' 'amal
**For there is a man whose labour *is* in wisdom and in knowledge and in equity yet to a man not that has laboured**

2:22

בו 871a | יתננו 5414 | חלקו 2506 | גם 1571 | זה 2088 | הבל 1892 | ורעה 7451 | רבה 7227: | כי 3588 | מה 4100 | הוה 1933 | לאדם 120 | בכל 3605
bou yitanenu chelqou, gam zeh hebel uara'ah rabah. kiy meh houeh la'adam bakal
**therein shall he leave it *for* his portion also This *is* vanity and a evil great For what has man of all**

2:23

עמלו 5999 | וברעיון 7475 | לבו 3820 | שהוא 1931 | עמל 6001 | תחת 8478 | השמש 8121: | כי 3588 | כל 3605 | ימיו 3117
'amalou, uabra'youn libou; shehua' 'amel tachat hashamesh. kiy kal yamayu
**his labour and of the vexation of his heart wherein he has laboured under the sun? For all his days**

2:24

מכאבים 4341 | וכעס 3708 | ענינו 6045 | גם 1571 | בלילה 3915 | לא 3808 | שכב 7901 | לבו 3820 | גם 1571 | זה 2088 | הבל 1892 | הוא 1931:
mak'abiym, uaka'as anyanou, gam balayalah la' shakab libou; gam zeh hebel hua'.
***are* sorrows and grief his travail yea in the night not takes rest his heart *is* also This vanity he**

אין 369 | טוב 2896 | באדם 120 | שיאכל 398 | ושתה 8354 | והראה 7200 | את 853 | נפשו 5315 | טוב 2896
'aeyn toub ba'adam sheya'kal uashatah, uahera'ah 'at napshou toub
***There is* nothing better for a man *than* that he should eat and drink and *that* he should make his soul *enjoy* good**

2:25

בעמלו 5999 | גם 1571 | זה 2090 | ראיתי 7200 | אני 589 | כי 3588 | מיד 3027 | האלהים 430 | היא 1931: | כי 3588 | מי 43210 | יאכל 398
ba'amalou; gam zoh ra'aytiy 'aniy, kiy miyad ha'alohiym hiy'a. kiy miy' ya'kal
**in his labour also This saw I that *was* from the hand of the Elohim it For who can eat**

2:26

ומי 4310 | יחוש 2363 | חוץ 2351 | ממני 4480: | כי 3588 | לאדם 120 | שטוב 2896 | לפניו 6440 | נתן 5414 | חכמה 2451
uamiy yachush chutz mimeniy. kiy la'adam shetoub lapanayu, natan chakamah
**or who *else* can hasten *hereunto* more than I? For to a man that *is* good in his sight *Elohim* gives wisdom**

ודעת 1847 | ושמחה 8057 | ולחוטא 2398 | נתן 5414 | ענין 6045 | לאסוף 622 | ולכנוס 3664 | לתת 5414 | לטוב 2896
uada'at uasimchah; ualachouta' natan 'anyan le'asoup ualiknous, latet latoub
**and knowledge and joy but to the sinner he gives travail to gather and to heap up that he may give to *him that is* good**

לפני 6440 | האלהים 430 | גם 1571 | זה 2088 | הבל 1892 | ורעות 7469 | רוח 7307:
lipney ha'alohiym, gam zeh hebel uar'aut ruach.
**before Elohim also This *is* vanity and vexation of spirit**

Ecc 2:19 And who know whether he shall be a wise man or a fool? yet shall he have rule over all my labour wherein I have laboured, and wherein I have showed myself wise under the sun. This is also vanity.20 Therefore I went about to cause my heart to despair of all the labour which I took under the sun.21 For there is a man whose labour is in wisdom, and in knowledge, and in equity; yet to a man that has not laboured therein shall he leave it for his portion. This also is vanity and a great evil.22 For what has man of all his labour, and of the vexation of his heart, wherein he has laboured under the sun?23 For all his days are sorrows, and his travail grief; yea, his heart take not rest in the night. This is also vanity.24 There is nothing better for a man, than that he should eat and drink, and that he should make his soul enjoy good in his labour. This also I saw, that it was from the hand of G-d.25 For who can eat, or who else can hasten hereunto, more than I?26 For G-d give to a man that is good in his sight wisdom, and knowledge, and joy: but to the sinner he give travail, to gather and to heap up, that he may give to him that is good before G-d. This also is vanity and vexation of spirit.

**Eccl 3:1** ... **3:2**

לכל 3605 זמן 2165 ועת 6256 לכל 3605 חפץ 2656 תחת 8478 השמים 8064: עת 6256 ללדת 3205 ועת 6256
lakol zaman; ua'at lakal chepetz tachat hashamayim. 'at laledet ua'at
**To every *thing there is* a season and a time to every purpose under the heaven A time to be born and a time**

**3:3**

למות 4191 עת 6256 לטעת 5193 ועת 6256 לעקור 6131 נטוע 5193: עת 6256 להרוג 2026 ועת 6256 לרפוא 7495 עת 6256
lamut; 'at lata'at, ua'at la'aqour natua'. 'at laharoug ua'at lirpou'a, 'at
**to die a time to plant and a time to pluck up *that which is* planted A time to kill and a time to heal a time**

**3:4** **3:5**

לפרוץ 6555 ועת 6256 לבנות 1129: עת 6256 לבכות 1058 ועת 6256 לשחוק 7832 עת 6256 ספוד 5594 ועת 6256 רקוד 7540:
liproutz ua'at libnout. 'at libkout ua'at lischouq, 'at sapoud ua'at raqoud.
**to break down and a time to build up A time to weep and a time to laugh a time to mourn and a time to dance**

**3:6**

עת 6256 להשליך 7993 אבנים 68 ועת 6256 כנוס 3664 אבנים 68 עת 6256 לחבוק 2263 ועת 6256 לרחק 7368 מחבק 2263:
'at lahashliyk 'abaniym, ua'at kanous 'abaniym; 'at lachabouq, ua'at lirchoq mechabeq.
**A time to cast away stones and a time to gether stones a time to embrace and a time to refrain from embracing**

**3:7**

עת 6256 לבקש 1245 ועת 6256 לאבד 6 עת 6256 לשמור 8104 ועת 6256 להשליך 7993: עת 6256 לקרוע 7167 ועת 6256 לתפור 8609 עת 6256
'at labaqesh ua'at la'abed, 'at lishmour ua'at lahashliyk. 'at liqroua' ua'at litpour, 'at
**A time to get and a time to lose a time to keep and a time to cast away A time to rend and a time to sew a time**

**3:8** **3:9**

לחשות 2814 ועת 6256 לדבר 1696: עת 6256 לאהב 157 ועת 6256 לשנא 8130 עת 6256 מלחמה 4421 ועת 6256 שלום 7965:
lachashout ua'at ladaber. 'at le'ahob ua'at lisna', 'at milchamah ua'at shaloum.
**to keep silence and a time to speak A time to love and a time to hate a time of war and a time of peace**

**3:10**

מה 4100 יתרון 3504 העושה 6213 באשר 834 הוא 1931 עמל 6001: ראיתי 7200 את 853 הענין 6045 אשר 834 נתן 5414 אלהים 430
mah yitroun ha'aseh, ba'asher hua' 'amel. ra'aytiy 'at ha'anyan, 'asher natan 'alohiym
**What profit *has* he that work in that wherein he labors? I have seen the travail which has given Elohim**

**3:11**

לבני 1121 האדם 120 לענות 6031 בו 871a: את 853 הכל 3605 עשה 6213 יפה 3303 בעתו 6256 גם 1571 את 853 העלם 5769
libney ha'adam la'anout bou. 'at hakol 'asah yapeh ba'atou; gam 'at ha'aulam
**to the sons of men to be exercised in it every *thing* He has made beautiful in his time also the world**

נתן 5414 בלבם 3820 מבלי 1097 אשר 834 לא 3808 ימצא 4672 האדם 120 את 853 המעשה 4639 אשר 834 עשה 6213 האלהים 430
natan balibam, mibliy 'asher la' yimtza' ha'adam, 'at hama'aseh 'asher 'asah ha'alohiym
**he has set in their heart so that which will not can find out no man the work that make Elohim**

**3:12**

מראש 2718 ועד 5704 סוף 5490: ידעתי 3045 כי 3588 אין 369 טוב 2896 בם 871a כי 3588 אם 518 לשמוח 8055 ולעשות 6213
mera'sh ua'ad soup. yada'tiy kiy 'aeyn toub bam; kiy 'am lismouach, uala'asout
**from the beginning and to the end I know that *there is* no good in them for but *a man* to rejoice and to do**

**3:13**

טוב 2896 בחייו 2416: וגם 1571 כל 3605 האדם 120 שיאכל 398 ושתה 8354 וראה 7200 טוב 2896 בכל 3605 עמלו 5999 מתת 4991
toub bachayayu. ua'gam kal ha'adam sheya'kal uashatah, uara'ah toub bakal 'amalou; matat
**good in his life And also *that* every man should eat and drink and enjoy the good of all his labour *is* the gift of**

**3:14**

אלהים 430 היא 1931: ידעתי 3045 כי 3588 כל 3605 אשר 834 יעשה 6213 האלהים 430 הוא 1931 יהיה 1961 לעולם 5769 עליו 5921 אין 369
'alohiym hiy'a. yada'tiy, kiy kal 'asher ya'aseh ha'alohiym hua' yihayeh la'aulam, 'alayu 'aeyn
**Elohim it I know that whatsoever after does Elohim it shall be for ever to it nothing**

**Ecc** 3:1 To everything there is a season, and a time to every purpose under the heaven:2 A time to be born, and a time to die; a time to plant, and a time to pluck up that which is planted;3 A time to kill, and a time to heal; a time to break down, and a time to build up;4 A time to weep, and a time to laugh; a time to mourn, and a time to dance;5 A time to cast away stones, and a time to gather stones together; a time to embrace, and a time to refrain from embracing;6 A time to get, and a time to lose; a time to keep, and a time to cast away;7 A time to rend, and a time to sew; a time to keep silence, and a time to speak;8 A time to love, and a time to hate; a time of war, and a time of peace.9 What profit has he that worketh in that wherein he laboureth?10 I have seen the travail, which G-d has given to the sons of men to be exercised in it.11 He has made everything beautiful in his time: also he has set the world in their heart, so that no man can find out the work that G-d make from the beginning to the end.12 I know that there is no good in them, but for a man to rejoice, and to do good in his life.13 And also that every man should eat and drink, and enjoy the good of all his labour, it is the gift of G-d.14 I know that, whatsoever G-d doeth, it shall be forever: nothing can be put to it, nor anything taken from it: and G-d doeth it, that men should fear before him.

3:15
להוסיף 3254 וממנו 4480 אין 369 לגרע 1639 והאלהים 430 עשה 6213 שיראו 3372 מלפניו 6440: מה 4100
lahousiyp, uamimenu 'aeyn ligroa'; uaha'alohiym 'asah, sheyir'au milpanayu. mah
**can be put from it nor *any thing* taken and Elohim does *it* that *men* should fear before him That**

3:16
שהיה 1961 כבר 3528 הוא 1931 ואשר 834 להיות 1961 כבר 3528 היה 1961 והאלהים 430 יבקש 1245 את 853 נרדף 7291:
shehayah kabar hua', ua'asher lihayout kabar hayah; uaha'alohiym yabaqesh 'at nirdap.
**which has been *is* now he and that which is to be already been and Elohim require that which is past**

ועוד 5750 ראיתי 7200 תחת 8478 השמש 8121 מקום 4725 המשפט 4941 שמה 8033 הרשע 7562 ומקום 4725
ua'aud ra'aytiy tachat hashamesh; maqoum hamishpat shamah haresha', uamqoum
**And moreover I saw under the sun place of the judgment *was* there *that* wickedness and place of**

3:17
הצדק 6664 שמה 8033 הרשע 7562: אמרתי 559 אני 589 בלבי 3820 את 853 הצדיק 6662 ואת 853 הרשע 7563 ישפט 8199
hatzedeq shamah harasha'. 'amartiy 'aniy balibiy, 'at hatzadiyq ua'at harasha', yishpot
**the righteousness there *that* iniquity said I in mine heart the righteous *and* the wicked shall judge**

3:18
האלהים 430 כי 3588 עת 6256 לכל 3605 חפץ 2656 ועל 5921 כל 3605 המעשה 4639 שם 8033: אמרתי 559 אני 589 בלבי 3820
ha'alohiym; kiy 'at lakal chepetz, ua'al kal hama'aseh sham. 'amartiy 'aniy balibiy,
**Elohim for *there is* a time for every purpose and for every work there said I in mine heart**

על 5921 דברת 1700 בני 1121 האדם 120 לברם 1305 האלהים 430 ולראות 7200 שהם 1992 בהמה 929
'al dibrat baney ha'adam, labaram ha'alohiym; ualira'aut shahem bahemah
**concerning the estate of the sons of men that might manifest them Elohim and that might see which they *are* beasts**

3:19
המה 1992 להם 1992: כי 3588 מקרה 4745 בני 1121 האדם 120 ומקרה 4745 הבהמה 929 ומקרה 4745 אחד 259 להם 3807a
hemah lahem. kiy miqreh baney ha'adam uamiqreh habahemah, uamiqreh 'achad lahem,
**they themselves For that which befall the sons of men befall even beasts befall one thing them**

כמות 4194 זה 2088 כן 3651 מות 4194 זה 2088 ורוח 7307 אחד 259 לכל 3605 ומותר 4195 האדם 120 מן 4480 הבהמה 929
kamout zeh ken mout zeh, uaruach 'achad lakol; uamoutar ha'adam min habahemah
**as die the one so die the other yea, breath one they have all has no preeminence a man above a beast**

3:20
אין 369 כי 3588 הכל 3605 הבל 1892: הכל 3605 הולך 1980 אל 413 מקום 4725 אחד 259 הכל 3605 היה 1961 מן 4480 העפר 6083 והכל 3605 שב 7725
'ayin, kiy hakol habel. hakol houlek 'al maqoum 'achad; hakol hayah min he'apar, uahakol shab
**has no for all *is* vanity All go unto place one all are of the dust and all turn again**

3:21
אל 413 העפר 6083: מי 4310 יודע 3045 רוח 7307 בני 1121 האדם 120 העלה 5927 היא 1931 למעלה 4605 ורוח 7307 הבהמה 929
'al he'apar. miy' youdea', ruach baney ha'adam, ha'aelah hiy'a lama'alah; uaruach habehemah,
**to the dust Who knows the spirit of sons of man goes that upward and the spirit of the beast**

3:22
הירדת 3381 היא 1931 למטה 4295 לארץ 776: וראיתי 7200 כי 3588 אין 369 טוב 2896 מאשר 834 ישמח 8055
hayoredet hiy'a lamatah la'aretz. uara'aytiy, kiy 'aeyn toub me'asher yismach
**goes that downward to the earth? Wherefore I perceive that *there is* nothing better than that should rejoice**

האדם 120 במעשיו 4639 כי 3588 הוא 1931 חלקו 2506 כי 3588 מי 4310 יביאנו 935 לראות 7200 במה 1400 שיהיה 1961 אחריו 310:
ha'adam bama'asayu, kiy hua' chelqou; kiy miy' yabiy'anu lir'aut, bameh sheyihayeh 'acharayu.
**a man in his own works for that *is* his portion for who shall bring him to see what shall be after him?**

Ecc 3:15 That which has been is now; and that which is to be has already been; and G-d requireth that which is past.16 And moreover I saw under the sun the place of judgment, that wickedness was there; and the place of righteousness, that iniquity was there.17 I said in mine heart, G-d shall judge the righteous and the wicked: for there is a time there forevery purpose and forevery work.18 I said in mine heart concerning the estate of the sons of men, that G-d might manifest them, and that they might see that they themselves are beasts.19 For that which befalleth the sons of men befalleth beasts; even one thing befalleth them: as the one die, so die the other; yea, they have all one breath; so that a man has no preeminence above a beast: for all is vanity.20 All go unto one place; all are of the dust, and all turn to dust again.21 Who know the spirit of man that go upward, and the spirit of the beast that go downward to the earth?22 Wherefore I perceive that there is nothing better, than that a man should rejoice in his own works; for that is his portion: for who shall bring him to see what shall be after him?

**Eccl 4:1**

ושבתי 7725 אני 589 ואראה 7200 את 853 כל 3605 העשקים 6217 אשר 834 נעשים 6213 תחת 8478 השמש 8121 והנה 2009
uashabtiy 'aniy, ua'ar'ah 'at kal ha'ashuqiym, 'asher na'asiym tachat hashamesh; uahineh
**So returned I and considered all the oppressions that are done under the sun and behold**

דמעת 1832 העשקים 6217 ואין 369 להם 3807a מנחם 5162 ומיד 3027 עשקיהם 6231 כח 3581
dim'at ha'ashuqiym, ua'aeyn lahem manachem, uamiyad 'ashaqeyhem koach,
**the tears of *such as were* oppression and had no they comforter and on the side of there oppressed *there was* power**

ואין 369 להם 3807a מנחם 5162: **4:2** ושבח 7623 אני 589 את 853 המתים 4191 שכבר 3528 מתו 4191 מן 4480
ua'aeyn lahem manachem. uashabeach 'aniy 'at hametiym shekabar metu; min
**but had no they comforter Wherefore praised I the dead are which already dead more than**

החיים 2416 אשר 834 המה 1992 חיים 2416 עדנה 5728: **4:3** וטוב 2896 משניהם 8147 את 853 אשר 834 עדן 5728 לא 3808 היה 1961
hachayiym, 'asher hemah chayiym 'adenah. uatoub mishneyhem, 'at 'asher 'aeden la' hayah;
**the living which they they alive *are* yet Yea better *is he* than both they which yet not has been**

אשר 834 לא 3808 ראה 7200 את 853 המעשה 4639 הרע 7451 אשר 834 נעשה 6213 תחת 8478 השמש 8121: **4:4** וראיתי 7200 אני 589 את 853 כל 3605
'asher la' ra'ah 'at hama'aseh hara', 'asher na'asah tachat hashamesh. uara'aytiy 'aniy 'at kal
**who not has seen work the evil that is done under the sun Again considered I all**

עמל 5999 ואת 853 כל 3605 כשרון 3788 המעשה 4639 כי 3588 היא 1931 קנאת 7068 איש 376 מרעהו 7453 גם 1571 זה 2088 הבל 1892
'amal, ua'at kal kishroun hama'aseh, kiy hiy'a qin'at 'aysh mere'aehu; gam zeh hebel
**travail *and* every right work that *for* this is envied a man of his neighbour *is* also This vanity**

ורעות 7469 רוח 7307: **4:5** הכסיל 3684 חבק 2263 את 853 ידיו 3027 ואכל 398 את 853 בשרו 1320: **4:6** טוב 2896 מלא 4393
uar'aut ruach. hakasiyl chobeq 'at yadayu, ua'akel 'at basarou. toub mala
**and vexation of spirit The fool fold together his hands and eat his own flesh Better *is* full**

כף 3709 נחת 5183 ממלא 4393 חפנים 2651 עמל 5999 ורעות 7469 רוח 7307: **4:7** ושבתי 7725 אני 589 ואראה 7200
kap nachat; mimala' chapanayim 'amal uar'aut ruach. uashabtiy 'aniy ua'ar'ah
**an handful *with* quietness than full both the hands *with* travail and vexation of spirit Then returned I and I saw**

הבל 1892 תחת 8478 השמש 8121: **4:8** יש 3426 אחד 259 ואין 369 שני 8147 גם 1571 בן 1121 ואח 251 אין 369 לו 3807a
hebel tachat hashamesh. yesh 'achad ua'aeyn sheniy gam ben ua'ach 'aeyn lou',
**vanity under the sun There is one *alone* and *there is* not a second yea, neither child nor brother neither he**

ואין 369 קץ 7093 לכל 3605 עמלו 5999 גם 1571 עיניו 5869 לא 3808 תשבע 7646 עשר 6239 ולמי 4310 אני 589
ua'aeyn qetz lakal 'amalou, gam 'aeynayu la' tisba' 'asher; ualmiy 'aniy
**has yet *is there* no end of all his labour neither *saith he* his eye neither is satisfied with riches For whom I**

עמל 6001 ומחסר 2637 את 853 נפשי 5315 מטובה 2896 גם 1571 זה 2088 הבל 1892 וענין 6045 רע 7451 הוא 1931: **4:9** טובים 2896 השנים 8147
'amel, uamchaser 'at napshiy mitoubah, gam zeh hebel ua'anyan ra' hua'. toubiym hashanayim
**do labour and bereave my soul of good? *is* also This vanity yea, a travail sore it *is* better Two *are***

מן 4480 האחד 259 אשר 834 יש 3426 להם 1992 שכר 7939 טוב 2896 בעמלם 5999: **4:10** כי 3588 אם 518 יפלו 5307 האחד 259 יקים 6965 את 853
min ha'achad; 'asher yesh lahem sakar toub ba'amalam. kiy 'am yipolu, ha'achad yaqiym 'at
**than one because have they a reward good for their labour For if they fall the one will lift up**

**Ecc** 4:1 So I returned, and considered all the oppressions that are done under the sun: and behold the tears of such as were oppressed, and they had no comforter; and on the side of their oppressors there was power; but they had no comforter.2 Wherefore I praised the dead which are already dead more than the living which are yet alive.3 Yea, better is he than both they, which has not yet been, who has not seen the evil work that is done under the sun.4 Again, I considered all travail, and every right work, that for this a man is envied of his neighbor. This is also vanity and vexation of spirit.5 The fool foldeth his hands together, and eateth his own flesh.6 Better is an handful with quietness, than both the hands full with travail and vexation of spirit.7 Then I returned, and I saw vanity under the sun.8 There is one alone, and there is not a second; yea, he has neither child nor brother: yet is there no end of all his labour; neither is his eye satisfied with riches; neither saith he, For whom do I labour, and bereave my soul of good? This is also vanity, yea, it is a sore travail.9 Two are better than one; because they have a good reward for their labour.10 For if they fall, the one will lift up his fellow: but woe to him that is alone when he fall; for he has not another to help him up.

| חברו 2270 | ואילו 337 | האחד 259 | שיפול 5307 | ואין 369 | שני 8147 | להקימו 6965: | **4:11** | גם 1571 | אם 518 | ישכבו 7901 |
|---|---|---|---|---|---|---|---|---|---|---|
| chaberou; | ua'aylou, | ha'achad | sheyipoul, | ua'aeyn | sheniy | lahaqiymou. | | gam | 'am | yishkabu |
| **his fellow** | **but woe to him** | ***that is* alone** | **when he fall** | **for *he has* not** | **another** | **to help him up** | | **Again** | **if** | **lie together** |

| שנים 8147 | וחם 2552 | להם 3807a | ולאחד 259 | איך 349 | יחם 3179: | **4:12** | ואם 518 | יתקפו 8630 | האחד 259 | השנים 8147 |
|---|---|---|---|---|---|---|---|---|---|---|
| shanayim | uacham | lahem; | ual'achad | 'aeyk | yecham. | | ua'am | yitqapou | ha'achad, | hashanayim |
| **two** | **then have heat** | **they** | **but one** | **how** | **can be warm *alone*?** | | **And if** | **prevail against him** | **one** | **two** |

| יעמדו 5975 | נגדו 5048 | והחוט 2339 | המשלש 8027 | לא 3808 | במהרה 4120 | ינתק 5423: | **4:13** | טוב 2896 | ילד 3206 | מסכן 4542 | וחכם 2450 |
|---|---|---|---|---|---|---|---|---|---|---|---|
| ya'amdu | negdou; | uahachut | hamshulash, | la' | bimherah | yinateq. | | toub | yeled | misken | uachakam; |
| **shall withstand** | **before him** | **and a cord** | **threefold** | **not** | **quickly** | **is broken** | | **Better *is*** | **a child** | **poor** | **and a wise** |

| ממלך 4428 | זקן 2205 | וכסיל 3684 | אשר 834 | לא 3808 | ידע 3045 | להזהר 2094 | עוד 5750: | **4:14** | כי 3588 | מבית 1004 | הסורים 612 |
|---|---|---|---|---|---|---|---|---|---|---|---|
| mimelek | zaqen | uakasiyl, | 'asher | la' | yada' | lahizaher | 'aud. | | kiy | mibeyt | hasuriym |
| **than an king** | **old** | **and foolish** | **who** | **no** | **will** | **be admonished** | **more** | | **For** | **out of prison** | **the ones bound** |

| יצא 3318 | למלך 4427 | כי 3588 | גם 1571 | במלכותו 4438 | נולד 3205 | רש 7326: | **4:15** | ראיתי 7200 | את 853 | כל 3605 | החיים 2416 |
|---|---|---|---|---|---|---|---|---|---|---|---|
| yatza' | limlok; | kiy | gam | bamalkutou | noulad | ra'sh. | | ra'aytiy | 'at | kal | hachayiym, |
| **he comes** | **to reign** | **whereas** | **also** | **in his kingdom** | ***he that is* born** | **become poor** | | **I considered** | | **all** | **the living** |

| המהלכים 1980 | תחת 8478 | השמש 8121 | עם 5973 | הילד 3206 | השני 8145 | אשר 834 | יעמד 5975 | תחתיו 8478: | **4:16** | אין 369 | קץ 7093 | לכל 3605 |
|---|---|---|---|---|---|---|---|---|---|---|---|---|
| hamhalkiym | tachat | hashamesh; | 'am | hayeled | hasheniy, | 'asher | ya'amod | tachtayu. | | 'aeyn | qetz | lakal |
| **which walk** | **under** | **the sun** | **with** | **child** | **the second** | **that** | **shall stand up** | **in his stead** | | ***There is* no** | **end** | **of all** |

| העם 5971 | לכל 3605 | אשר 834 | היה 1961 | לפניהם 6440 | גם 1571 | האחרונים 314 | לא 3808 | ישמחו 8055 | בו 871a | כי 3588 | גם 1571 |
|---|---|---|---|---|---|---|---|---|---|---|---|
| ha'am, | lakol | 'asher | hayah | lipneyhem, | gam | ha'acharouniym | la' | yismachu | bou; | kiy | gam |
| **the people** | ***even* of all** | **that** | **have been** | **before them** | **also** | **they that come after** | **not** | **shall rejoice** | **in him** | **Surely** | **also** |

| זה 2088 | הבל 1892 | ורעיון | רוח 7307: |
|---|---|---|---|
| zeh | hebel | uara'youn | ruach. |
| **this** | ***is* vanity** | **and vexation of** | **spirit** |

| **Eccl 5:1** | שמר 8104 | רגליך 7272 | כאשר 834 | תלך 1980 | אל 413 | בית 1004 | האלהים 430 | וקרוב 7138 | לשמע 8085 | מתת 5414 | הכסילים 3684 |
|---|---|---|---|---|---|---|---|---|---|---|---|
| | shamor | ragleyka | ka'asher | telek | 'al | beyt | ha'alohiym, | uaqaroub | lishmoa', | mitet | hakasiyliym |
| | **Keep** | **your foot** | **when** | **you go** | **to** | **house of** | **the Elohim** | **and be more ready** | **to hear** | **than to give** | **the fools** |

| זבח 2077 | כי 3588 | אינם 369 | יודעים 3045 | לעשות 6213 | רע 7451: | **5:2** | אל 408 | תבהל 926 | על 5921 | פיך 6310 | ולבך 3820 | אל 408 |
|---|---|---|---|---|---|---|---|---|---|---|---|---|
| zabach; | kiy | 'aeynam | youda'aym | la'asout | ra'. | | 'al | tabahel | 'al | piyka | ualibaka | 'al |
| **sacrifice *of*** | **for** | **not** | **they consider** | **that they do** | **evil** | | **not** | **Be rash** | **with** | **your mouth** | **and your heart** | **not** |

| ימהר 4116 | להוציא 3318 | דבר 1697 | לפני 6440 | האלהים 430 | כי 3588 | האלהים 430 | בשמים 8064 | ואתה 859 | על 5921 | הארץ 776 | על 5921 | כן 3651 |
|---|---|---|---|---|---|---|---|---|---|---|---|---|
| yamaher | lahoutziy'a | dabar | lipney | ha'alohiym; | kiy | ha'alohiym | bashamayim | ua'atah | 'al | ha'aretz, | 'al | ken |
| **let be hasty** | **to utter** | ***any* thing** | **before** | **Elohim** | **for** | **Elohim *is*** | **in heaven** | **and you** | **upon** | **the earth** | **therefore** | **so** |

| יהיו 1961 | דבריך 1697 | מעטים 4592: | **5:3** | כי 3588 | בא 935 | החלום 2472 | ברב 7230 | ענין 6045 | וקול 6963 | כסיל 3684 |
|---|---|---|---|---|---|---|---|---|---|---|
| yihayu | dabareyka | ma'atiym. | | kiy | ba' | hachaloum | barob | 'anyan; | uaqoul | kasiyl |
| **let be** | **your words** | **few** | | **For** | **comes** | **a dream** | **through the multitude of** | **business** | **and a voice** | **fool's** |

Ecc 4:11 Again, if two lie together, then they have heat: but how can one be warm alone?12 And if one prevail against him, two shall withstand him; and a threefold cord is not quickly broken.13 Better is a poor and a wise child than an old and foolish king, who will no more be admonished.14 For out of prison he cometh to reign; whereas also he that is born in his kingdom becometh poor.15 I considered all the living which walk under the sun, with the second child that shall stand up in his stead.16 There is no end of all the people, even of all that have been before them: they also that come after shall not rejoice in him. Surely this also is vanity and vexation of spirit. **Ecc** 5:1 Keep your foot when you go to the house of G-d, and be more ready to hear, than to give the sacrifice of fools: for they consider not that they do evil.2 Be not rash with your mouth, and let not your heart be hasty to utter anything before G-d: for G-d is in heaven, and you upon earth: therefore let your words be few.3 For a dream cometh through the multitude of business; and a fool's voice is known by multitude of words.

ברב 7230 דברים 1697: 5:4 כאשר 834 תדר 5087 נדר 5088 לאלהים 430 אל 408 תאחר 309 לשלמו 7999 כי 3588 אין 369
barob dabariym. ka'asher tidor neder le'alohiym, 'al ta'acher lashalmou, kiy 'aeyn
**_is known_ by multitude of words When you vowest a vow unto Elohim not defer to pay it for _he has_ no**

חפץ 2656 בכסילים 3684 את 853 אשר 834 תדר 5087 שלם 7999: 5:5 טוב 2896 אשר 834 לא 3808 תדר 5087
chepetz baksiyliym; 'at 'asher tidor shalem. toub 'asher la' tidor;
**pleasure in fools that which you have vowed pay Better _is it_ that not you should vow**

משתדור 5087 ולא 3808 תשלם 7999: 5:6 אל 408 תתן 5414 את 853 פיך 6310 לחטיא 2398 את 853 בשרך 1320 ואל 408
mishetidour uala' tashalem. 'al titen 'at piyka lachatiy'a 'at basareka, ua'al
**than that you should vow and not pay not Suffer your mouth to cause to sin your flesh neither**

תאמר 559 לפני 6440 המלאך 4397 כי 3588 שגגה 7684 היא 1931 למה 4100 יקצף 7107 האלהים 430 על 5921 קולך 6963 וחבל 2254
ta'mar lipney hamal'ak, kiy shagagah hiy'a; lamah yiqtzop ha'alohiym 'al qouleka, uachibel
**say you before the angel that _was_ an error it wherefore should be angry Elohim at your voice and destroy**

את 853 מעשה 4639 ידיך 3027: 5:7 כי 3588 ברב 7230 חלמות 2472 והבלים 1892 ודברים 1697 הרבה 7235 כי 3588
'at ma'aseh yadeyka. kiy barob chalomout uahabaliym, uadbariym harbeh; kiy
**the work of your hands? For in the multitude of dreams _there are_ also _divers_ vanities and words many but**

את 853 האלהים 430 ירא 3372: 5:8 אם 518 עשק 6233 רש 7326 וגזל 1499 משפט 4941 וצדק 6664 תראה 7200
'at ha'alohiym yara'. 'am 'asheq rash uagezel mishapat uatzedeq tir'ah
**Elohim fear you If the oppression of the poor and violent perverting of judgment and justice you see**

במדינה 4082 אל 408 תתמה 8539 על 5921 החפץ 2656 כי 3588 גבה 1364 מעל 5921 גבה 1364 שמר 8104 וגבהים 1364
bamdiinah, 'al titamah 'al hachepetz; kiy gaboah me'al gaboah shomer, uagbohiym
**in a province not marvel at the matter for _he that is_ higher than the highest regard and _there be_ higher**

עליהם 5921: 5:9 ויתרון 3504 ארץ 776 בכל 3605 היא 1931 מלך 4428 לשדה 7704 נעבד 5647: 5:10 אהב 157 כסף 3701
'aleyhem. uayitroun 'aretz bakol hiy'a melek lasadeh ne'abad. 'aheb kesep
**than they Moreover the profit of the earth _is_ for all himself the king by the field is served He that love silver**

לא 3808 ישבע 7646 כסף 3701 ומי 4310 אהב 157 בהמון 1995 לא 3808 תבואה 8393 גם 1571 זה 2088 הבל 1892: 5:11
la' yisba' kesep, uamiy 'aheb behamoun la' tabu'ah; gam zeh habel.
**not shall be satisfied with silver he that love abundance nor _with_ increase _is_ also this vanity**

ברבות 7235 הטובה 2896 רבו 7235 אוכליה 398 ומה 4100 כשרון 3788 לבעליה 1167 כי 3588 אם 518
birbout hatoubah, rabu 'aukaleyha; uamah kishroun lib'aleyha, kiy 'am
**When increase goods they are increase that eat them and what good _is there_ to the owners thereof saving**

ראית 7212 עיניו 5869: 5:12 מתוקה 4966 שנת 8142 העבד 5647 אם 518 מעט 4592 ואם 518 הרבה 7235 יאכל 398
re'ayat 'aeynayu. matuqah shanat ha'abed, 'am ma'at ua'am harbeh ya'kel;
**the beholding of them with their eyes? _is_ sweet The sleep of a labouring man whether little or much he eat**

והשבע 7647 לעשיר 6223 איננו 369 מניח 3240 לו 3807a לישון 3462: 5:13 יש 3426 רעה 7451 חולה 2470 ראיתי 7200 תחת 8478
uahasaba' le'ashiyr, 'aeynenu maniyach lou' liyshoun. yesh ra'ah choulah, ra'aytiy tachat
**but the abundance of the rich not will suffer him to sleep There is a evil sore _which_ I have seen under**

Ecc 5:4 When you vowest a vow unto G-d, defer not to pay it; for he has no pleasure in fools: pay that which you have vowed.5 Better is it that you should not vow, than that you should vow and not pay.6 Suffer not your mouth to cause your flesh to sin; neither say you before the angel, that it was an error: wherefore should G-d be angry at your voice, and destroy the work of your hands?7 For in the multitude of dreams and many words there are also divers vanities: but fear you G-d.8 If you seest the oppression of the poor, and violent perverting of judgment and justice in a province, marvel not at the matter: for he that is higher than the highest regardeth; and there be higher than they.9 Moreover the profit of the earth is for all: the king himself is served by the field.10 He that love silver shall not be satisfied with silver; nor he that love abundance with increase: this is also vanity.11 When goods increase, they are increased that eat them: and what good is there to the owners thereof, saving the beholding of them with their eyes?12 The sleep of a labouring man is sweet, whether he eat little or much: but the abundance of the rich will not suffer him to sleep.13 There is a sore evil which I have seen under the sun, namely, riches kept for the owners thereof to their hurt.

5:14

השמש 8121 עשר 6239 שמור 8104 לבעליו 1167 לרעתו 7451: ואבד 6 העשר 6239 ההוא 1931 בענין 6045 רע 7451
hashamesh; 'asher shamur liba'alayu lara'atou. ua'abad ha'asher hahua' ba'anyan ra';
**the sun *namely* riches kept for the owners thereof to their hurt But perish riches those by travail evil**

5:15

והוליד 3205 בן 1121 ואין 369 בידו 3027 מאומה 3972: כאשר 834 יצא 3318 מבטן 990 אמו 517 ערום 6174
uahouliyd ben, ua'aeyn bayadou ma'aumah. ka'asher yatza' mibeten 'amou, 'aroum
**and he beget a son and *there is* not in his hand nothing As he came forth of womb his mother's naked**

5:16

ישוב 7725 ללכת 1980 כשבא 935 ומאומה 3972 לא 3808 ישא 5375 בעמלו 5999 שילך 1980 בידו 3027:
yashub laleket kasheba'; uam'uamah la' yisa' ba'amalou, sheyolek bayadou.
**shall he return to go as he came and thing no shall take of his labour which he may carry away in his hand**

וגם 1571 זה 2090 רעה 7451 חולה 2470 כל 3605 עמת 5980 שבא 935 כן 3651 ילך 1980 ומה 4100 יתרון 3504 לו 3807a שיעמל 5998
uagam zoh ra'ah choulah, kal 'amat sheba' ken yelek; uamah yitroun lou', sheya'amol
**And also this *is* a evil sore *that* in all points *as* he came so shall he go and what profit has he that has laboured**

5:17 5:18

לרוח 7307: גם 1571 כל 3605 ימיו 3117 בחשך 2822 יאכל 398 וכעס 3708 הרבה 7235 וחליו 2483 וקצף 7110:
laruach. gam kal yamayu bachoshek ya'kel; uaka'as harbeh uachalayou uaqatzep.
**for the wind? also All his days in darkness he eat and sorrow *he has* much with his sickness and wrath**

הנה 2009 אשר 834 ראיתי 7200 אני 589 טוב 2896 אשר 834 יפה 3303 לאכול 398 ולשתות 8354 ולראות 7200 טובה 2896 בכל 3605
hineh 'asher ra'aytiy 'aniy, toub 'asher yapeh le'akoul ualishtout ualira'aut toubah bakal
**Behold *that* which have seen I *it is* good which comely *for one* to eat and to drink and to enjoy the good of all**

עמלו 5999 שיעמל 5998 תחת 8478 השמש 8121 מספר 4557 ימי 3117 חיו 2416 אשר 834 נתן 5414 לו 3807a האלהים 430 כי 3588 הוא 1931
'amalou sheya'amol tachat hashemesh, mispar yamey chayau 'asher natan lou' ha'alohiym kiy hua'
**his labour that he takes under the sun all the days of his life, which gives him Elohim for it**

5:19

חלקו 2506: גם 1571 כל 3605 האדם 120 אשר 834 נתן 5414 לו 3807a האלהים 430 עשר 6239 ונכסים 5233 והשליטו 7980
chelqou. gam kal ha'adam 'asher natan lou' ha'alohiym 'asher uankasiym uahishliytou
***is* his portion also Every man whom has given to Elohim riches and wealth and has given him power**

5:20

לאכל 398 ממנו 4480 ולשאת את 853 חלקו 2506 ולשמח 8055 בעמלו 5999 זה 2090 מתת 4991 אלהים 430 היא 1931: כי 3588
le'akol mimenu ualasa't 'at chelqou, ualismoach ba'amalou; zoh matat 'alohiym hiy'a. kiy
**to eat thereof and to take his portion and to rejoice in his labour this *is* the gift of Elohim he For**

לא 3808 הרבה 7235 יזכר 2142 את 853 ימי 3117 חייו 2416 כי 3588 האלהים 430 מענה 6031 בשמחת 8057 לבו 3820:
la' harbeh, yizkor 'at yamey chayayu; kiy ha'alohiym ma'aneh basimchat libou.
**not much he shall remember the days of his life because Elohim answer *him* in the joy of his heart**

Eccl 6:1 6:2

יש 3426 רעה 7451 אשר 834 ראיתי 7200 תחת 8478 השמש 8121 ורבה 7227 היא 1931 על 5921 האדם 120: איש 376 אשר 834
yesh ra'ah, 'asher ra'aytiy tachat hashamesh; uarabah hiy'a 'al ha'adam. 'aysh 'asher
**There is an evil which I have seen under the sun and common it *is* among men A man whom**

יתן 5414 לו 3807a האלהים 430 עשר 6239 ונכסים 5233 וכבוד 3519 ואיננו 369 חסר 2638 לנפשו 5315 מכל 3605 אשר 834 יתאוה 183
yiten lou' ha'alohiym 'asher uankasiym uakaboud ua'aeynenu chaser lanapshou mikol 'asher yit'aueh,
**has given to the Elohim riches wealth and honor so that nothing he want for his soul of all that he desire**

Ecc 5:14 But those riches perish by evil travail: and he begetteth a son, and there is nothing in his hand.15 As he came forth of his mother's womb, naked shall he return to go as he came, and shall take nothing of his labour, which he may carry away in his hand.16 And this also is a sore evil, that in all points as he came, so shall he go: and what profit has he that has laboured for the wind?17 All his days also he eateth in darkness, and he has much sorrow and wrath with his sickness.18 Behold that which I have seen: it is good and comely for one to eat and to drink, and to enjoy the good of all his labour that he take under the sun all the days of his life, which G-d give him: for it is his portion.19 Every man also to whom G-d has given riches and wealth, and has given him power to eat thereof, and to take his portion, and to rejoice in his labour; this is the gift of G-d.20 For he shall not much remember the days of his life; because G-d answer him in the joy of his heart. **Ecc** 6:1 There is an evil which I have seen under the sun, and it is common among men:2 A man to whom G-d has given riches, wealth, and honor, so that he wanteth nothing for his soul of all that he desire, yet G-d give him not power to eat thereof, but a stranger eateth it: this is vanity, and it is an evil disease.

ולא 3808 ישליטנו 7980 האלהים 430 לאכל 398 ממנו 4480 כי 3588 איש 376 נכרי 5237 יאכלנו 398 זה 2088 הבל 1892 וחלי 2483 רע 7451
uala' yashliytenu ha'alohiym le'akol mimenu, kiy 'aysh nakariy ya'kalenu; zeh hebel uachaliy ra'
**yet not gives him power Elohim to eat thereof but man a stranger eat it this *is* vanity an disease evil**

הוא 1931: 6:3 אם 518 יוליד 3205 איש 376 מאה 3967 ושנים 8141 רבות 7227 יחיה 2421 ורב 7227 שיהיו 1961 ימי 3117
hua'. 'am youliyd 'aysh me'ah uashaniym rabout yichayeh uarab sheyihayu yamey
**it If beget a man an hundred *children* and years many so that live many be the days of**

שניו 8141 ונפשו 5315 לא 3808 תשבע 7646 מן 4480 הטובה 2896 וגם 1571 קבורה 6900 לא 3808 היתה 1961 לו 3807a אמרתי 559 טוב 2896 ממנו 4480
shanayu, uanapshou la' tisba' min hatoubah, uagam qaburah la' hayatah lou'; 'amartiy toub mimenu
**his years and his soul not be filled with good and also burial no have *that* he I say *is* better than he**

הנפל 5309: 6:4 כי 3588 בהבל 1892 בא 935 ובחשך 2822 ילך 1980 ובחשך 2822 שמו 8034
hanapel. kiy bahebel ba' uabachoshek yelek; uabachoshek shamou
***that* an untimely birth For with vanity he comes in and in darkness depart and with darkness his name**

יכסה 3680: 6:5 גם 1571 שמש 8121 לא 3808 ראה 7200 ולא 3808 ידע 3045 נחת 5183 לזה 2088 מזה 2088: 6:6
yakuseh. gam shemesh la' ra'ah uala' yada'; nachat lazeh mizeh.
**shall be covered Moreover the sun not he has seen nor known *any thing* *has* more rest this than the other**

ואלו 432 חיה 2421 אלף 505 שנים 8141 פעמים 6471 וטובה 2896 לא 3808 ראה 7200 הלא 3808 אל 413 מקום 4725 אחד 259 הכל 3605
ua'alu chayah, 'alep shaniym pa'amayim, uatoubah la' ra'ah; hala' 'al maqoum 'achad hakol
**Yea though he live a thousand years twice *told* yet good no has he seen not to place? one all**

הולך 1980: 6:7 כל 3605 עמל 5999 האדם 120 לפיהו 6310 וגם 1571 הנפש 5315 לא 3808 תמלא 4390: 6:8 כי 3588 מה 4100 יותר 3148
houlek. kal 'amal ha'adam lapiyhu; uagam hanepesh la' timalea'. kiy mah youter
**do go All labour of the man *is* for his mouth and yet the appetite not is filled For what more**

לחכם 2450 מן 4480 הכסיל 3684 מה 4100 לעני 6041 יודע 3045 להלך 1980 נגד 5048 החיים 2416: 6:9 טוב 2896 מראה 4758 עינים 5869
lechakam min hakasiyl; mah le'aniy youdea', lahalok neged hachayiym. toub mar'aeh 'aeynayim
**has the wise than the fool? what has the poor that knows to walk before the living? Better *is* the sight of the eyes**

מהלך 1980 נפש 5315 גם 1571 זה 2088 הבל 1892 ורעות 7469 רוח 7307: 6:10 מה 4100 שהיה 1961 כבר 3528
mehalak napesh; gam zeh hebel uar'aut ruach. mah shehayah, kabar
**than the wandering of the desire *is* also this vanity and vexation of spirit That which has been already**

נקרא 7121 שמו 8034 ונודע 3045 אשר 834 הוא 1931 אדם 120 ולא 3808 יוכל 3201 לדין 1777 עם 5973 שהתקיף 8630 ממנו 4480: 6:11
niqra' shamou, uanouda' 'asher hua' 'adam; uala' yukal ladiyn, 'am shehataqiyp mimenu.
**is called name and it is known that it *is* man neither may he contend with him that is mightier than he**

כי 3588 יש 3426 דברים 1697 הרבה 7235 מרבים 7235 הבל 1892 מה 4100 יתר 3148 לאדם 120: 6:12 כי 3588 מי 4310 יודע 3045 מה 4100 טוב 2896
kiy yesh dabariym harbeh marbiym habel; mah yoter la'adam. kiy miy' youdea' mah toub
**Seeing there be things many that increase vanity what the better? *is* man For who knows what *is* good**

לאדם 120 בחיים 2416 מספר 4557 ימי 3117 חיי 2416 הבלו 1892 ויעשם 6213 כצל 6738 אשר 834 מי 4310 יגיד 5046 לאדם 120 מה 4100
la'adam bachayiym, mispar yamey chayey heblou uaya'asem katzel; 'asher miy' yagiyd la'adam, mah
**for man in *this* life all the days of life his vain which he spend as a shadow? for who can tell a man what**

Ecc 6:3 If a man beget an hundred children, and live many years, so that the days of his years be many, and his soul be not filled with good, and also that he have no burial; I say, that an untimely birth is better than he.4 For he cometh in with vanity, and departeth in darkness, and his name shall be covered with darkness.5 Moreover he has not seen the sun, nor known anything: this has more rest than the other.6 Yea, though he live a thousand years twice told, yet has he seen no good: do not all go to one place?7 All the labour of man is for his mouth, and yet the appetite is not filled.8 For what has the wise more than the fool? what has the poor, that know to walk before the living?9 Better is the sight of the eyes than the wandering of the desire: this is also vanity and vexation of spirit.10 That which has been is named already, and it is known that it is man: neither may he contend with him that is mightier than he.11 Seeing there be manythings that increase vanity, what is man the better?12 For who know what is good for man in this life, all the days of his vain life which he spendeth as a shadow? for who can tell a man what shall be after him under the sun?

יהיה 1961 אחריו 310 תחת 8478 השמש 8121:
yihayeh 'acharayu tachat hashamesh.
**shall be after him under the sun?**

**Eccl 7:1** טוב 2896 שם 8034 משמן 8081 טוב 2896 ויום 3117 המות 4194 מיום 3117 הולדו 3205: **7:2** טוב 2896
toub shem mishemen toub; uayoum hamauet, miyoum hiualdou. toub
***is* better A good name than ointment precious and day of the death than day of the one's birth *It is* better**

ללכת 1980 אל 413 בית 1004 אבל 60 מלכת 1980 אל 413 בית 1004 משתה 4960 באשר 834 הוא 1931 סוף 5490 כל 3605 האדם 120
laleket 'al beyt 'aebel, mileket 'al beyt mishteh, ba'asher hua' soup kal ha'adam;
**to go to the house of mourning than to go to the house of feasting for that *is* the end of all men**

והחי 2416 יתן 5414 אל 413 לבו 3820: **7:3** טוב 2896 כעס 3708 משחק 7814 כי 3588 ברע 7455 פנים 6440
uahachay yiten 'al libou. toub ka'as mischoq; kiy baroa' paniym
**and the living will lay *it* to his heart *is* better Sorrow than laughter for by the sadness of the countenance**

ייטב 3190 לב 3820: **7:4** לב 3820 חכמים 2450 בבית 1004 אבל 60 ולב 3820 כסילים 3684 בבית 1004
yiytab leb. leb chakamiym babeyt 'abel, ualeb kasiyliym babeyt
**is made better the heart The heart of the wise *is* in the house of mourning but the heart of fools *is* in the house of**

שמחה 8057: **7:5** טוב 2896 לשמע 8085 גערת 1606 חכם 2450 מאיש 376 שמע 8085 שיר 7892 כסילים 3684: **7:6** כי 3588
simchah. toub lishmoa' ga'arat chakam; me'aysh shomea' shiyr kasiyliym. kiy
**mirth *It is* better to hear the rebuke of the wise than for a man to hear the song of fools For**

כקול 6963 הסירים 5518 תחת 8478 הסיר 5518 כן 3651 שחק 7814 הכסיל 3684 וגם 1571 זה 2088 הבל 1892: **7:7** כי 3588 העשק 6233
kaqoul hasiyriym tachat hasiyr, ken sachoq hakasiyl; uagam zeh habel. kiy ha'asheq
**as crackling of the thorns under a pot so *is* the laughter of the fool also this *is* vanity Surely oppression**

יהולל 1984 חכם 2450 ויאבד 6 את 853 לב 3820 מתנה 4979: **7:8** טוב 2896 אחרית 319 דבר 1697 מראשיתו 7225
yahoulel chakam; uiy'abed 'at leb matanah. toub 'achariyt dabar merea'shiytou;
**make mad a wise man and destroy the heart a gift Better *is* the end of a thing than the beginning thereof**

טוב 2896 ארך 750 רוח 7307 מגבה 1362 רוח 7307: **7:9** אל 408 תבהל 926 ברוחך 7307 לכעוס 3707 כי 3588 כעס 3708
toub 'arek ruach migbah ruach. 'al tabahel baruchaka lik'aus; kiy ka'as,
***is* better *and* the patient in spirit than the proud in spirit not Be hasty in your spirit to be angry for anger**

בחיק 2436 כסילים 3684 ינוח 5117: **7:10** אל 408 תאמר 559 מה 4100 היה 1961 שהימים 3117 הראשנים 7223 היו 1961 טובים 2896
bacheyq kasiyliym yanuach. 'al ta'mar meh hayah, shehaiyamiym hara'shoniym, hayu toubiym
**in the bosom of fools rest not Say you What is *the cause* that days the former were better**

מאלה 428 כי 3588 לא 3808 מחכמה 2451 שאלת 7592 על 5921 זה 2088: **7:11** טובה 2896 חכמה 2451 עם 5973 נחלה 5159
me'aeleh; kiy la' mechakamah sha'alta 'al zeh. toubah chakamah 'am nachalah;
**than these? for not wisely you do inquire concerning this *is* good Wisdom with an inheritance**

ויתר 3148 לראי 7200 השמש 8121: **7:12** כי 3588 בצל 6738 החכמה 2451 בצל 6738 הכסף 3701
uayoter laro'aey hashamesh. kiy batzel hachakamah batzel hakasep;
**and *by it there is* profit to them that see the sun For *is* a defence wisdom *is* a defence *and* money**

**Ecc** 7:1 A good name is better than precious ointment; and the day of death than the day of one's birth.2 It is better to go to the house of mourning, than to go to the house of feasting: for that is the end of all men; and the living will lay it to his heart.3 Sorrow is better than laughter: for by the sadness of the countenance the heart is made better.4 The heart of the wise is in the house of mourning; but the heart of fools is in the house of mirth.5 It is better to hear the rebuke of the wise, than for a man to hear the song of fools.6 For as the crackling of thorns under a pot, so is the laughter of the fool: this also is vanity.7 Surely oppression make a wise man mad; and a gift destroyeth the heart.8 Better is the end of a thing than the beginning thereof: and the patient in spirit is better than the proud in spirit.9 Be not hasty in your spirit to be angry: for anger resteth in the bosom of fools.10 Say not you, What is the cause that the former days were better than these? for you dost not inquire wisely concerning this.11 Wisdom is good with an inheritance: and by it there is profit to them that see the sun.12 For wisdom is a defence, and money is a defence: but the excellency of knowledge is, that wisdom give life to them that have it.

ויתרון 3504 דעת 1847 החכמה 2451 תחיה 2421 בעליה 1167: 7:13 ראה 7200 את 853 מעשה 4639 האלהים 430 כי 3588
uayitroun da'at, hachakamah tachayeh ba'aleyha. ra'aeh 'at ma'aseh ha'alohiym; kiy
**but the excellency of knowledge *is that* wisdom gives life to them that have it Consider work of the Elohim for**

מי 4310 יוכל 3201 לתקן 8626 את 853 אשר 834 עותו 5791: 7:14 ביום 3117 טובה 2896 היה 1961 בטוב 2896
miy' yukal lataqen, 'at 'asher 'auatou. bayoum toubah hayeh batoub,
**who can make *that* straight which he has made crooked? In the day of prosperity be joyful**

וביום 3117 רעה 7451 ראה 7200 גם 1571 את 853 זה 2088 לעמת 5980 זה 2088 עשה 6213 האלהים 430 על 5921 דברת 1700
uabyoum ra'ah ra'aeh; gam 'at zeh la'amat zeh 'asah ha'alohiym, 'al dibrat,
**but in the day of adversity consider also the one over against the other has set Elohim to the end**

שלא 3808 ימצא 4672 האדם 120 אחריו 310 מאומה 3972: 7:15 את 853 הכל 3605 ראיתי 7200 בימי 3117 הבלי 1892 יש 3426
shela' yimtza' ha'adam 'acharayu ma'aumah. 'at hakol ra'aytiy biymey hebliy; yesh
**that nothing should find man after him nothing All *things* have I seen in the days of my vanity there is**

צדיק 6662 אבד 6 בצדקו 6664 ויש 3426 רשע 7563 מאריך 748 ברעתו 7451: 7:16 אל 408
tzadiyq 'abed batzidqou, uayesh rasha', ma'ariyk bara'atou. 'al
**a just *man* that perish in his righteousness and there is a wicked *man* that prolong *his life* in his wickedness not**

תהי 1961 צדיק 6662 הרבה 7235 ואל 408 תתחכם 2449 יותר 3148 למה 4100 תשומם 8074: 7:17 אל 408 תרשע 7561
tahiy tzadiyq harbeh, ua'al titchakam youter; lamah tishoumem. 'al tirsha'
**Be righteous over much neither make yourself wise over why should you destroy yourself? not Be wicked**

הרבה 7235 ואל 408 תהי 1961 סכל 5530 למה 4100 תמות 4191 בלא 3808 עתך 6256: 7:18 טוב 2896 אשר 834 תאחז 270
harbeh ua'al tahiy sakal; lamah tamut bala' 'ateka. toub 'asher te'achoz
**over much neither be you foolish why should you die before your time? *It is* good that you should take hold**

בזה 2088 וגם 1571 מזה 2088 אל 408 תנח 3240 את 853 ידך 3027 כי 3588 ירא 3373 אלהים 430 יצא 3318 את 854
bazeh, uagam mizeh 'al tanach 'at yadeka; kiy yarea' 'alohiym yetzea' 'at
**of this and yea also from this not withdraw your hand for he that fear Elohim shall come forth *of***

כלם 3605: 7:19 החכמה 2451 תעז 5810 לחכם 2450 מעשרה 6235 שליטים 7989 אשר 834 היו 1961 בעיר 5892: 7:20 כי 3588 אדם 120
kulam. hachakamah ta'az lechakam; me'asarah shaliytiym, 'asher hayu ba'ayr. kiy 'adam,
**them all Wisdom strengthen the wise more than ten mighty *men* which are in the city For a man**

אין 369 צדיק 6662 בארץ 776 אשר 834 יעשה 6213 טוב 2896 ולא 3808 יחטא 2398: 7:21 גם 1571 לכל 3605 הדברים 1697 אשר 834 ידברו 1696
'aeyn tzadiyq ba'aretz; 'asher ya'aseh toub uala' yecheta'. gam lakal hadabariym 'asher yadaberu,
***there is* not just upon earth that does good and not sin Also unto all words that are spoken**

אל 408 תתן 5414 לבך 3820 אשר 834 לא 3808 תשמע 8085 את 853 עבדך 5650 מקללך 7043: 7:22 כי 3588 גם 1571 פעמים 6471 רבות 7227 ידע 3045
'al titen libeka; 'asher la' tishma' 'at 'abdaka maqalleka. kiy gam pa'amiym rabout yada'
**no take heed lest so you hear your servant curse you For also times often knows**

לבך 3820 אשר 834 גם 1571 את 859 קללת 7043 אחרים 312: 7:23 כל 3605 זה 2090 נסיתי 5254 בחכמה 2451 אמרתי 559
libeka; 'asher gam 'at qilalta 'acheriym. kal zoh nisiytiy bachakamah; 'amartiy
**your own heart that likewise *yourself you* have cursed others All this have I proved by wisdom I said**

Ecc 7:13 Consider the work of G-d: for who can make that straight, which he has made crooked?14 In the day of prosperity be joyful, but in the day of adversity consider: G-d also has set the one over against the other, to the end that man should find nothing after him.15 All things have I seen in the days of my vanity: there is a just man that perisheth in his righteousness, and there is a wicked man that prolongeth his life in his wickedness.16 Be not righteous over much; neither make thyself over wise: why should you destroy thyself?17 Be not over much wicked, neither be you foolish: why should you die before your time?18 It is good that you should take hold of this; yea, also from this withdraw not your hand: for he that fear G-d shall come forth of them all.19 Wisdom strengtheneth the wise more than ten mighty men which are in the city.20 For there is not a just man upon earth, that doeth good, and sin not.21 Also take no heed unto all words that are spoken; lest you hear your servant curse you:22 For oftentimes also your own heart know that you thyself likewise have cursed others.23 All this have I proved by wisdom: I said, I will be wise; but it was far from me.

7:24 7:25
אחכמה 2449 והיא 1931 רחוקה 7350 ממני 4480: רחוק 7350 מה 4100 שהיה 1961 ועמק 6013 עמק 6013 מי 4310 ימצאנו 4672:
'achkamah, uahiy'a rachouqah mimeniy. rachouq mah shehayah; ua'amoq 'amoq miy' yimtza'anu.
**I will be wise but it *was* far from me far off That which is and exceeding deep who can find it out?**

סבותי 5437 אני 589 ולבי 3820 לדעת 3045 ולתור 8446 ובקש 1245 חכמה 2451 וחשבון 2808 ולדעת 1847
saboutiy 'aniy ualibiy lada'at ualatur, uabaqesh chakamah uacheshboun; ualada'at
**applied I mine heart to know and to search and to seek out wisdom and the reason *of things* and to know**

7:26
רשע 7562 כסל 6389 והסכלות 5531 הוללות 1947: ומוצא 4672 אני 589 מר 4751 ממות 4194 את 853 האשה 802
resha' kesel, uahasiklut houlelout. uamoutza' 'aniy mar mimauet, 'at ha'ashah
**the wickedness of folly even of foolishness *and* madness And find I more bitter than death the woman**

אשר 834 היא 1931 מצודים 4685 וחרמים 2764 לבה 3820 אסורים 612 ידיה 3027 טוב 2896 לפני 6440 האלהים 430 ימלט 4422 ממנה 4480
'asher hiy'a matzoudiym uacharamiym libah 'asuriym yadeyha; toub lipney ha'alohiym yimalet mimenah,
**whose she *is* snares and nets heart *as* bands *and* her hands please accept Elohim shall escape from her**

7:27
וחוטא 2398 ילכד 3920 בה 871a: ראה 7200 זה 2088 מצאתי 4672 אמרה 559 קהלת 6953 אחת 259 לאחת 259 למצא 4672
uachoutea' yilaked bah. ra'aeh zeh matza'tiy, 'amarah qohelet; 'achat la'achat limtza'
**but the sinner shall be taken by her Behold this have I found saith the preacher *counting* one by one to find out**

7:28
חשבון 2808: אשר 834 עוד 5750 בקשה 1245 נפשי 5315 ולא 3808 מצאתי 4672 אדם 120 אחד 259 מאלף 505 מצאתי 4672
cheshboun. 'asher 'aud biqshah napshiy uala' matza'tiy; 'adam 'achad me'alep matza'tiy,
**the account Which yet seek my soul but not I find man one among a thousand have I found**

7:29
ואשה 802 בכל 3605 אלה 428 לא 3808 מצאתי 4672: לבד 905 ראה 7200 זה 2088 מצאתי 4672 אשר 834 עשה 6213 האלהים 430 את 853
ua'ashah bakal 'aeleh la' matza'tiy. labad ra'aeh zeh matza'tiy, 'asher 'asah ha'alohiym 'at
**but a woman among all those not have I found only Lo this have I found that has made the Elohim**

האדם 120 ישר 3477 והמה 1992 בקשו 1245 חשבנות 2810 רבים 7227:
ha'adam yashar; uahemah biqshu chishabonout rabiym.
**man upright but they have sought out inventions many**

**Eccl 8:1**
מי 4310 כהחכם 2450 ומי 4310 יודע 3045 פשר 6592 דבר 1697 חכמת 2451 אדם 120 תאיר 215 פניו 6440
miy' kahechakam, uamiy youdea' pesher dabar; chakamat 'adam ta'ayr panayu,
**Who *is* as the wise *man*? and who knows the interpretation of a thing? a wisdom man's make to shine his face**

8:2
ועז 5797 פניו 6440 ישנא 8132: אני 589 פי 6310 מלך 4428 שמור 8104 ועל 5921
ua'az panayu yashuna'. 'aniy piy melek shamor, ua'al
**and the boldness of his face shall be changed I commandment *the* king's *counsel you* to keep and on**

8:3
דברת 1700 שבועת 7621 אלהים 430: אל 408 תבהל 926 מפניו 6440 תלך 1980 אל 408 תעמד 5975 בדבר 1697 רע 7451 כי 3588
dibrat shabu'at 'alohiym. 'al tibahel mipanayu telek, 'al ta'amod badabar ra'; kiy
***that* in regard of the oath of Elohim not Be hasty of his sight to go out not stand in an thing evil for**

8:4
כל 3605 אשר 834 יחפץ 2654 יעשה 6213: באשר 834 דבר 1697 מלך 4428 שלטון 7983 ומי 4310 יאמר 559 לו 3807a מה 4100
kal 'asher yachpotz ya'aseh. ba'asher dabar melek shiltoun; uamiy ya'mar lou' mah
**whatsoever he please him he does Where the word of a king *is there is* power and who may say unto him What**

Ecc 7:24 That which is far off, and exceeding deep, who can find it out?25 I applied mine heart to know, and to search, and to seek out wisdom, and the reason of things, and to know the wickedness of folly, even of foolishness and madness:26 And I find more bitter than death the woman, whose heart is snares and nets, and her hands as bands: whoso pleaseth G-d shall escape from her; but the sinner shall be taken by her.27 Behold, this have I found, saith the preacher, counting one by one, to find out the account:28 Which yet my soul seek, but I find not: one man among a thousand have I found; but a woman among all those have I not found.29 Lo, this only have I found, that G-d has made man upright; but they have sought out many inventions. **Ecc** 8:1 Who is as the wise man? and who know the interpretation of a thing? a man's wisdom make his face to shine, and the boldness of his face shall be changed.2 I counsel you to keep the king's commandment, and that in regard of the oath of G-d.3 Be not hasty to go out of his sight: stand not in an evil thing; for he doeth whatsoever pleaseth him.4 Where the word of a king is, there is power: and who may say unto him, What does you?

8:5

תעשה 6213: שומר 8104 מצוה 4687 לא 3808 ידע 3045 דבר 1697 רע 7451 ועת 6256 ומשפט 4941 ידע 3045 לב 3820

ta'aseh. shoumer mitzuah, la' yeda' dabar ra'; ua'at uamishpat, yeda' leb

**do you? Whoso keep the commandment no shall feel thing evil and both time and judgment discerneth heart**

8:6

חכם 2450: כי 3588 לכל 3605 חפץ 2656 יש 3426 עת 6256 ומשפט 4941 כי 3588 רעת 7451 האדם 120 רבה 7227

chakam. kiy lakal chepetz, yesh 'at uamishpat; kiy ra'at ha'adam rabah

**a wise man's Because to every purpose there is time and judgment therefore the misery of the man *is* great**

8:7 8:8

עליו 5921: כי 3588 איננו 369 ידע 3045 מה 4100 שיהיה 1961 כי 3588 כאשר 834 יהיה 1961 מי 4310 יגיד 5046 לו 3807a: אין 369

'alayu. kiy 'aeynenu yodea' mah sheyihayeh; kiy ka'asher yihayeh, miy' yagiyd lou'. 'aeyn

**upon him For not he knows that which shall be for when it shall be? who can tell him *There is* no**

אדם 120 שליט 7989 ברוח 7307 לכלוא 3607 את 853 הרוח 7307 ואין 369 שלטון 7983 ביום 3117 המות 4194 ואין 369

'adam shaliyt baruach liklou'a 'at haruach, ua'aeyn shiltoun bayoum hamauet, ua'aeyn

**man that has power over the spirit to retain the spirit neither *has he* power in day of the death and *there is* no**

8:9

משלחת 4917 במלחמה 4421 ולא 3808 ימלט 4422 רשע 7562 את 853 בעליו 1167: את 853 כל 3605 זה 2088 ראיתי 7200

mishlachat bamilchamah; uala' yamalet resha' 'at ba'alayu. 'at kal zeh ra'aytiy

**discharge in *that* war neither shall deliver wickedness those that are given to it All this have I seen**

ונתון 5414 את 853 לבי 3820 לכל 3605 מעשה 4639 אשר 834 נעשה 6213 תחת 8478 השמש 8121 עת 6256 אשר 834 שלט 7980 האדם 120

uanatoun 'at libiy, lakal ma'aseh, 'asher na'asah tachat hashamesh; 'aet, 'asher shalat ha'adam

**and applied my heart unto every work that is done under the sun *there is* a time wherein rule one man**

8:10

באדם 120 לרע 7451 לו 3807a: ובכן 3651 ראיתי 7200 רשעים 7563 קברים 6912 ובאו 935 וממקום 4725 קדוש 6918 יהלכו 1980

ba'adam lara' lou'. uabken ra'aytiy rasha'aym qaburiym uaba'au, umimaqum qadoush yahaleku,

**over another to hurt his own And so I saw the wicked buried who had come from the place of *the* holy gone**

8:11

וישתכחו 7911 בעיר 5892 אשר 834 כן 3651 עשו 6213 גם 1571 זה 2088 הבל 1892: אשר 834 אין 369 נעשה 6213

uayishtakchu ba'ayr 'asher ken 'asu; gam zeh habel. 'asher 'aeyn na'asah

**and they were forgotten in the city where so they had done *is* also this vanity Because not is executed**

פתגם 6599 מעשה 4639 הרעה 7451 מהרה 4120 על 5921 כן 3651 מלא 4390 לב 3820 בני 1121 האדם 120 בהם 871a לעשות 6213

pitgam, ma'aseh hara'ah maherah; 'al ken malea' leb baney ha'adam bahem la'asout

**sentence against an work evil speedily therefore so is fully set the heart of the sons of men in them to do**

8:12

רע 7451: אשר 834 חטא 2398 עשה 6213 רע 7451 מאת 3967 ומאריך 748 לו 3807a כי 3588 גם 1571 יודע 3045 אני 589 אשר 834

ra'. 'asher chotea', 'aseh ra' me'at uama'ariyk lou'; kiy gam youdea' 'aniy, 'asher

**evil Though a sinner do evil an hundred *times* and be prolonged his *days* yet surely I know I that**

8:13

יהיה 1961 טוב 2896 ליראי 3372 האלהים 430 אשר 834 ייראו 3372 מלפניו 6440: וטוב 2896 לא 3808 יהיה 1961 לרשע 7563

yihayeh toub layir'aey ha'alohiym, 'asher yiyra'au milpanayu. uatoub la' yihayeh larasha',

**it shall be well with them that fear Elohim which fear before him But well not it shall be with the wicked**

8:14

ולא 3808 יאריך 748 ימים 3117 כצל 6738 אשר 834 איננו 369 ירא 3373 מלפני 6440 אלהים 430: יש 3426 הבל 1892

uala' ya'ariyk yamiym katzel; 'asher 'aeynenu yarea' milipney 'alohiym. yesh hebel

**neither shall he prolong *his* days *which are* as a shadow because not he fear before Elohim There is a vanity**

Ecc 8:5 Whoso keep the commandment shall feel no evil thing: and a wise man's heart discerneth both time and judgment.6 Because to every purpose there is time and judgment, therefore the misery of man is great upon him.7 For he know not that which shall be: for who can tell him when it shall be?8 There is no man that has power over the spirit to retain the spirit; neither has he power in the day of death: and there is no discharge in that war; neither shall wickedness deliver those that are given to it.9 All this have I seen, and applied my heart unto every work that is done under the sun: there is a time wherein one man rule over another to his own hurt.10 And so I saw the wicked buried, who had come and gone from the place of the holy, and they were forgotten in the city where they had so done: this is also vanity.11 Because sentence against an evil work is not executed speedily, therefore the heart of the sons of men is fully set in them to do evil.12 Though a sinner do evil an hundred times, and his days be prolonged, yet surely I know that it shall be well with them that fear G-d, which fear before him:13 But it shall not be well with the wicked, neither shall he prolong his days, which are as a shadow; because he fear not before G-d.

אשר 834 נעשה 6213 על 5921 הארץ 776 אשר 834 יש 3426 צדיקים 6662 אשר 834 מגיע 5060 אלהם 413 כמעשה 4639
'asher na'asah 'al ha'aretz 'asher yesh tzadiyqiym, 'asher magiya' 'alehem kama'aseh
**which is done upon the earth that there be just *men* whom it happen unto whom according to the work of**

הרשעים 7563 ויש 3426 רשעים 7563 שמגיע 5060 אלהם 413 כמעשה 4639 הצדיקים 6662 אמרתי 559 שגם 1571
harasha'aym, uayesh rasha'aym, shemagiya' 'alehem kama'aseh hatzadiyqim; 'amartiy shegam
**the wicked again there be wicked *men* it happen to whom according to the work of the righteous I said that also**

זה 2088 הבל 1892: **8:15** ושבחתי 7623 אני 589 את 853 השמחה 8057 אשר 834 אין 369 טוב 2896 לאדם 120 תחת 8478 השמש 8121 כי 3588
zeh habel. uashibachtyi 'aniy 'at hasimchah, 'asher 'aeyn toub la'adam tachat hashemesh, kiy
**this *is* vanity Then commended I mirth because has no better a man *thing* under the sun than**

אם 518 לאכול 398 ולשתות 8354 ולשמוח 8055 והוא 1931 ילונו 3867 בעמלו 5999 ימי 3117 חייו 2416 אשר 834 נתן 5414
'am le'akoul ualishtout ualismoach; uahu'a yiluenu ba'amalou, yamey chayayu 'asher natan
**only to eat and to drink and to be merry for that shall abide with him of his labour the days of his life which gives**

לו 3807a האלהים 430 תחת 8478 השמש 8121: **8:16** כאשר 834 נתתי 5414 את 853 לבי 3820 לדעת 3045 חכמה 2451 ולראות 7200 את 853 הענין 6045
lou' ha'alohiym tachat hashamesh. ka'asher natatiy 'at libiy lada'at chakamah ualira'aut 'at ha'anyan,
**him Elohim under the sun When I applied mine heart to know wisdom and to see the business**

אשר 834 נעשה 6213 על 5921 הארץ 776 כי 3588 גם 1571 ביום 3117 ובלילה 3915 שנה 8142 בעיניו 5869 איננו 369 ראה 7200: **8:17**
'asher na'asah 'al ha'aretz; kiy gam bayoum uabalayalah, shenah ba'aeynayu 'aeynenu ro'ah.
**that is done upon the earth for also day nor night sleep with his eyes *there is that* neither see**

וראיתי 7200 את 853 כל 3605 מעשה 4639 האלהים 430 כי 3588 לא 3808 יוכל 3201 האדם 120 למצוא 4672 את 853 המעשה 4639 אשר 834 נעשה 6213
uara'aytiy 'at kal ma'aseh ha'alohiym kiy la' yukal ha'adam, limtzua' 'at hama'aseh 'asher na'asah
**Then I beheld all work of the Elohim that not can a man find out the work that is done**

תחת 8478 השמש 8121 בשל 7945 אשר 834 יעמל 5998 האדם 120 לבקש 1245 ולא 3808 ימצא 4672 וגם 1571 אם 518 יאמר 559
tachat hashemesh, bashel 'asher ya'amol ha'adam labaqesh uala' yimtza'; ua'gam 'am ya'mar
**under the sun because though labour a man to seek *it* out yet not he shall find *it* yea further though *man* think**

החכם 2450 לדעת 3045 לא 3808 יוכל 3201 למצא 4672:
hechakam lada'at, la' yukal limtza'.
**a wise to know *it, yet* not shall he be able to find *it***

**Eccl 9:1** כי 3588 את 853 כל 3605 זה 2088 נתתי 5414 אל 413 לבי 3820 ולבור 952 את 853 כל 3605 זה 2088 אשר 834 הצדיקים 6662
kiy 'at kal zeh natatiy 'al libiy ualabur 'at kal zeh, 'asher hatzadiyqim
**For all this I considered in my heart even to declare all this that the righteous**

והחכמים 2450 ועבדיהם 5652 ביד 3027 האלהים 430 גם 1571 אהבה 160 גם 1571 שנאה 8135 אין 369 יודע 3045 האדם 120 הכל 3605
uahachakamiym ua'abadeyhem bayad ha'alohiym; gam 'ahabah gam sin'ah, 'aeyn youdea' ha'adam, hakol
**and the wise and their works *are* in hand of the Elohim either love or hatred no knows man *by* all**

לפניהם 6440: **9:2** הכל 3605 כאשר 834 לכל 3605 מקרה 4745 אחד 259 לצדיק 6662 ולרשע 7563 לטוב 2896
lipneyhem. hakol ka'asher lakol, miqreh 'achad latzadiyq ualarasha' latoub
***that is* before them All *things come* alike to all event *there is* one to the righteous and to the wicked to the good**

Ecc 8:14 There is a vanity which is done upon the earth; that there be just men, unto whom it happeneth according to the work of the wicked; again, there be wicked men, to whom it happeneth according to the work of the righteous: I said that this also is vanity.15 Then I commended mirth, because a man has no better thing under the sun, than to eat, and to drink, and to be merry: for that shall abide with him of his labour the days of his life, which G-d give him under the sun.16 When I applied mine heart to know wisdom, and to see the business that is done upon the earth: (for also there is that neither day nor night see sleep with his eyes:)17 Then I beheld all the work of G-d, that a man cannot find out the work that is done under the sun: because though a man labour to seek it out, yet he shall not find it; yea further; though a wise man think to know it, yet shall he not be able to find it. **Ecc** 9:1 For all this I considered in my heart even to declare all this, that the righteous, and the wise, and their works, are in the hand of G-d: no man know either love or hatred by all that is before them.2 All things come alike to all: there is one event to the righteous, and to the wicked; to the good and to the clean, and to the unclean; to him that sacrificeth, and to him that sacrificeth not: as is the good, so is the sinner; and he that sweareth, as he that fear an oath.

| 2889 ולטהור | 2931 ולטמא | 2076 ולזבח | 834 ולאשר | 369 איננו | 2076 זבח | 2896 כטוב | 2398 כחטא |
|---|---|---|---|---|---|---|---|
| ualatahour | ualatamea', | ualazobeach, | uala'asher | 'aeynenu | zobeach; | katoub | kachotea', |
| **and to the clean** | **and to the unclean** | **to him that sacrifice** | **and to him** | **not** | **that sacrifice** | **as *is* the good** | **so *is* the sinner** |

| 7650 הנשבע | 834 כאשר | 7621 שבועה | 3372: ירא | 9:3 2088 זה | 7451 רע | 3605 בכל | 834 אשר | 6213 נעשה | 8478 תחת | 8121 השמש |
|---|---|---|---|---|---|---|---|---|---|---|
| hanishba' | ka'asher | shabu'ah | yarea'. | zeh | ra', | bakal | 'asher | na'asah | tachat | hashemesh, |
| ***and* he that swears** | **as he that** | **an oath** | **afraid** | **This** | ***is* an evil** | **among all *things*** | **that** | **are done** | **under** | **the sun** |

| 3588 כי | 4745 מקרה | 259 אחד | 3605 לכל | 1571 וגם | 3820 לב | 1121 בני | 120 האדם | 4390 מלא | 7451 רע | 1947 והוללות | 3824 בלבבם |
|---|---|---|---|---|---|---|---|---|---|---|---|
| kiy | miqreh | 'achad | lakol; | ua'gam | leb | baney | ha'adam | malea' | ra' | uahoulelout | bilbabam |
| **that** | **event** | ***there is* one** | **unto all** | **yea, also** | **the heart of** | **sons of** | **the men** | **is full of** | **evil** | **and madness** | ***is* in their heart** |

| 2416 בחייהם | 310 ואחריו | 413 אל | 4191: המתים | 9:4 3588 כי | 4310 מי | 834 אשר | 977 יבחר | 413 אל | 3605 כל | 2416 החיים | 3426 יש |
|---|---|---|---|---|---|---|---|---|---|---|---|
| bachayeyhem, | ua'acharayu | 'al | hametiym. | kiy | miy' | 'asher | yibacher | 'al | kal | hachayiym | yesh |
| **while they live** | **and after that *they go*** | **to** | **the dead** | **For** | **to him** | **that** | **is joined** | **to** | **all** | **the living** | **there is** |

| 986 בטחון | 3588 כי | 3611 לכלב | 2416 חי | 1931 הוא | 2896 טוב | 4480 מן | 738 האריה | 4191: המת | 9:5 3588 כי | 2416 החיים | 3045 יודעים | 4191 שימתו |
|---|---|---|---|---|---|---|---|---|---|---|---|---|
| bitachoun; | kiy | lakeleb | chay | hua' | toub, | min | ha'aryeh | hamet. | kiy | hachayiym | youda'aym | sheyamutu; |
| **hope** | **for** | **a dog** | **living** | ***is* he** | **better** | **than** | **a lion** | **dead** | **For** | **the living** | **know** | **that they shall die** |

| 4191 והמתים | 369 אינם | 3045 יודעים | 3972 מאומה | 369 ואין | 5750 עוד | 3807a להם | 7939 שכר | 3588 כי | 7911 נשכח |
|---|---|---|---|---|---|---|---|---|---|
| uahametiym | 'aeynam | youda'aym | ma'aumah, | ua'aeyn | 'aud | lahem | sakar, | kiy | nishkach |
| **but the dead** | **not** | **know** | **any thing** | **neither have** | **any more** | **they** | **a reward** | **for** | **is forgotten** |

| 2143: זכרם | 9:6 1571 גם | 160 אהבתם | 1571 גם | 8135 שנאתם | 1571 גם | 7068 קנאתם | 3528 כבר | 6 אבדה | 2506 וחלק |
|---|---|---|---|---|---|---|---|---|---|
| zikram. | gam | 'ahabatam | gam | sin'atam | gam | qin'atam | kabar | 'abadah; | uacheleq |
| **for the memory of them** | **Also** | **their love** | **moreover** | **their hatred** | **also** | **their envy** | **now** | **is perished** | **a portion** |

| 369 אין | 1992 להם | 5750 עוד | 5769 לעולם | 3605 בכל | 834 אשר | 6213 נעשה | 8478 תחת | 8121: השמש | 9:7 1980 לך | 398 אכל | 8057 בשמחה |
|---|---|---|---|---|---|---|---|---|---|---|---|
| 'aeyn | lahem | 'aud | la'aulam, | bakol | 'asher | na'asah | tachat | hashemesh. | lek | 'akol | basimchah |
| **neither have** | **they** | **any more** | **for ever** | **in any *thing*** | **that** | **is done** | **under** | **the sun** | **Go your way** | **eat** | **with joy** |

| 3899 לחמך | 8354 ושתה | 3820 בלב | 2896 טוב | 3196 יינך | 3588 כי | 3528 כבר | 7521 רצה | 430 האלהים | 854 את | 4639: מעשיך | 9:8 3605 בכל | 6256 עת |
|---|---|---|---|---|---|---|---|---|---|---|---|---|
| lachmeka, | uashateh | baleb | toub | yeyneka; | kiy | kabor, | ratzah | ha'alohiym | 'at | ma'aseyka. | bakal | 'at |
| **your bread** | **and drink** | **with a heart** | **merry** | **your wine** | **for** | **now** | **accept** | **Elohim** | | **your works** | **all** | **ways** |

| 1961 יהיו | 899 בגדיך | 3836 לבנים | 8081 ושמן | 5921 על | 7218 ראשך | 408 אל | 2637: יחסר | 9:9 7200 ראה | 2416 חיים | 5973 עם | 802 אשה | 834 אשר |
|---|---|---|---|---|---|---|---|---|---|---|---|---|
| yihayu | bagadeyka | labaniym; | uashemen | 'al | ra'shaka | 'al | yechsar. | ra'aeh | chayiym | 'am | 'ashah | 'asher |
| **Let be** | **your garments** | **white** | **and ointment** | **on** | **your head** | **no** | **let lack** | **joyfully** | **Live** | **with** | **the wife** | **whom** |

| 157 אהבת | 3605 כל | 3117 ימי | 2416 חיי | 1892 הבלך | 834 אשר | 5414 נתן | 3807a לך | 8478 תחת | 8121 השמש | 3605 כל | 3117 ימי |
|---|---|---|---|---|---|---|---|---|---|---|---|
| 'ahabta, | kal | yamey | chayey | hebleka, | 'asher | natan | laka | tachat | hashemesh, | kol | yamey |
| **you love** | **all** | **the days of** | **the life of** | **your vanity** | **which** | **he has given** | **to you** | **under** | **the sun** | **all** | **the days of** |

| 1892 הבלך | 3588 כי | 1931 הוא | 2506 חלקך | 2416 בחיים | 5999 ובעמלך | 834 אשר | 859 אתה | 6001 עמל | 8478 תחת | 8121: השמש |
|---|---|---|---|---|---|---|---|---|---|---|
| hebleka; | kiy | hua' | chelqaka | bachayiym, | uaba'amalaka, | 'asher | 'atah | 'amel | tachat | hashemesh. |
| **your vanity** | **for** | **that** | ***is* your portion** | **in *this* life** | **and in your labour** | **which** | **you** | **take** | **under** | **the sun** |

Ecc 9:3 This is an evil among all things that are done under the sun, that there is one event unto all: yea, also the heart of the sons of men is full of evil, and madness is in their heart while they live, and after that they go to the dead.4 For to him that is joined to all the living there is hope: for a living dog is better than a dead lion.5 For the living know that they shall die: but the dead know not anything, neither have they anymore a reward; for the memory of them is forgotten.6 Also their love, and their hatred, and their envy, is now perished; neither have they anymore a portion forever in anything that is done under the sun.7 Go your way, eat your bread with joy, and drink your wine with a merry heart; for G-d now accepteth your works.8 Let your garments be always white; and let your head lack no ointment.9 Live joyfully with the wife whom you love all the days of the life of your vanity, which he has given you under the sun, all the days of your vanity: for that is your portion in this life, and in your labour which you takest under the sun.

**9:10**
כל 3605 | אשר 834 | תמצא 4672 | ידך 3027 | לעשות 6213 | בכחך 3581 | עשה 6213 | כי 3588 | אין 369 | מעשה 4639 | וחשבון 2808
kal 'asher timtzaa' yadaka la'asout bakochaka 'aseh; kiy 'aeyn ma'aseh uacheshboun
**Whatsoever after finds your hand to do *it* with your might do for *there is* no work nor device**

ודעת 1847 | וחכמה 2451 | בשאול 7585 | אשר 834 | אתה 859 | הלך 1980 | שמה 8033: | **9:11** שבתי 7725 | וראה 7200 | תחת 8478 | השמש 8121 | כי 3588
uada'at uachakamah, bisha'aul 'asher 'atah holek shamah. shabtiy uara'ah tachat hashemesh, kiy
**nor knowledge nor wisdom in the grave where you go there I returned and saw under the sun that**

לא 3808 | לקלים 7031 | המרוץ 4793 | ולא 3808 | לגבורים 1368 | המלחמה 4421 | וגם 1571 | לא 3808 | לחכמים 2450 | לחם 3899 | וגם 1571 | לא 3808
la' laqaliym hameroutz uala' lagibouriym hamilchamah, uagam la' lachakamiym lechem ua'gam la'
**not to the swift the race *is* nor to the strong the battle yet neither to the wise bread yet nor**

לנבנים 995 | עשר 6239 | וגם 1571 | לא 3808 | לידעים 3045 | חן 2580 | כי 3588 | עת 6256 | ופגע 6294 | יקרה 7136 | את 853 | כלם 3605: | **9:12**
lanboniym 'asher, ua'gam la' layoda'aym chen; kiy 'at uapega' yiqreh 'at kulam.
**to men of understanding riches yet nor to men of skill favor but time and chance happen *to* them all**

כי 3588 | גם 1571 | לא 3808 | ידע 3045 | האדם 120 | את 853 | עתו 6256 | כדגים 1709 | שנאחזים 270 | במצודה 4685 | רעה 7451 | וכצפרים 6833
kiy gam la' yeda' ha'adam 'at 'atou, kadagiym shene'achaziym bimtzoudah ra'ah, uakatzipariym,
**For also not knows man his time as the fishes that are taken in an net evil and as the birds**

האחזות 270 | בפח 6341 | כהם 1992 | יוקשים 3369 | בני 1121 | האדם 120 | לעת 6256 | רעה 7451 | כשתפול 5307 | עליהם 5921
ha'achuzout bapach; kahem, yuqashiym baney ha'adam, la'at ra'ah, kashetipoul 'aleyhem
**ones that are caught in the snare so snared sons of *are* the men in an time evil when it fall upon them**

פתאם 6597: | **9:13** גם 1571 | זה 2090 | ראיתי 7200 | חכמה 2451 | תחת 8478 | השמש 8121 | וגדולה 1419 | היא 1931 | אלי 413: | **9:14** עיר 5892
pit'am. gam zoh ra'aytiy chakamah tachat hashamesh; uagdoulah hiy'a 'aelay. 'ayr
**suddenly also This have I seen wisdom under the sun and great it *seemed* unto me *There was* a city**

קטנה 6996 | ואנשים 582 | בה 871a | מעט 4592 | ובא 935 | אליה 413 | מלך 4428 | גדול 1419 | וסבב 5437 | אתה 853 | ובנה 1129 | עליה 5921
qatanah, ua'anashiym bah ma'at; uaba' 'aeleyha melek gadoul uasabab 'atah, uabanah 'aeleyha
**little and men within it few and there came against it a king great and besieged it and built against it**

מצודים 4685 | גדלים 1419: | **9:15** ומצא 4672 | בה 871a | איש 376 | מסכן 4542 | חכם 2450 | ומלט 4422 | הוא 1931 | את 853 | העיר 5892
matzoudiym gadoliym. uamatza' bah, 'aysh misken chakam, uamilat hua' 'at ha'ayr
**bulwarks great Now there was found in it a man poor wise and delivered he the city**

בחכמתו 2451 | ואדם 120 | לא 3808 | זכר 2142 | את 853 | האיש 376 | המסכן 4542 | ההוא 1931: | **9:16** ואמרתי 559 | אני 589 | טובה 2896 | חכמה 2451
bachakamatou; ua'adam la' zakar, 'at ha'aysh hamisken hahua'. ua'amartiy 'aniy, toubah chakamah
**by his wisdom yet man no remembered man poor that same Then said I *is* better Wisdom**

מגבורה 1369 | וחכמת 2451 | המסכן 4542 | בזויה 959 | ודבריו 1697 | אינם 369 | נשמעים 8085: | **9:17** דברי 1697
migburah; uachakamat hamisken bazuyah, uadbarayu 'aeynam nishma'aym. dibrey
**than strength nevertheless wisdom the poor man's *is* despised and his words not are heard The words of**

חכמים 2450 | בנחת 5183 | נשמעים 8085 | מזעקת 2201 | מושל 4910 | בכסילים 3684: | **9:18** טובה 2896 | חכמה 2451
chakamiym, banachat nishma'aym; miza'aqat moushel baksiyliym. toubah chakamah
**wise in quiet *men are* heard more than the cry of him that rule among fools *is* better Wisdom**

Ecc 9:10 Whatsoever your hand findeth to do, do it with your might; for there is no work, nor device, nor knowledge, nor wisdom, in the grave, whither you go.11 I returned, and saw under the sun, that the race is not to the swift, nor the battle to the strong, neither yet bread to the wise, nor yet riches to men of understanding, nor yet favor to men of skill; but time and chance happeneth to them all.12 For man also know not his time: as the fishes that are taken in an evil net, and as the birds that are caught in the snare; so are the sons of men snared in an evil time, when it fall suddenly upon them.13 This wisdom have I seen also under the sun, and it seemed great unto me:14 There was a little city, and few men within it; and there came a great king against it, and besieged it, and built great bulwarks against it:15 Now there was found in it a poor wise man, and he by his wisdom delivered the city; yet no man remembered that same poor man.16 Then said I, Wisdom is better than strength: nevertheless the poor man's wisdom is despised, and his words are not heard.17 The words of wise men are heard in quiet more than the cry of him that rule among fools.

מכלי 3627 קרב 7128 וחוטא 2398 אחד 259 יאבד 6 טובה 2896 הרבה 7235:
mikley qarab; uachoutea' 'achad, ya'abed toubah harbeh.
**than weapons of war but sinner one destroy good much**

**Eccl 10:1**
זבובי 2070 מות 4194 יבאיש 887 יביע 5042 שמן 8081 רוקח 7543 יקר 3368
zabubey mauet, yab'aysh yabiya' shemen rouqeach; yaqar
**flies Dead cause a stinking savour to send forth the ointment of the apothecary *him that is in* reputation**

מחכמה 2451 מכבוד 3519 סכלות 5531 מעט 4592: **10:2** לב 3820 חכם 2450 לימינו 3225 ולב 3820 כסיל 3684
mechakamah mikaboud siklut ma'at. leb chakam liymiynou, ualeb kasiyl
**for wisdom *and* honor *so does* a folly little A heart wise man's *is* at his right hand but a heart fool's**

לשמאלו 8040: **10:3** וגם 1571 בדרך 1870 כשהסכל 5530 הלך 1980 לבו 3820 חסר 2638 ואמר 559 לכל 3605 סכל 5530
lisma'lou. uagam baderek keshehasakal holek libou chaser; ua'amar lakol sakal
**at his left Yea also by the way when he that is a fool walk his wisdom fail *him* and he saith to every one *is* a fool**

הוא 1931: **10:4** אם 518 רוח 7307 המושל 4910 תעלה 5927 עליך 5921 מקומך 4725 אל 408 תנח 3240 כי 3588 מרפא 4832 יניח 3240 חטאים 2399
hua'. 'am ruach hamoushel ta'aleh 'aleyka, maqoumaka 'al tanach; kiy marpea', yaniyach chata'aym
***that* he If the spirit of the ruler rise up against you your place not leave for yielding pacify offences**

גדולים 1419: **10:5** יש 3426 רעה 7451 ראיתי 7200 תחת 8478 השמש 8121 כשגגה 7684 שיצא 3318 מלפני 6440 השליט 7989: **10:6**
gadouliym. yesh ra'ah, ra'aytiy tachat hashamesh; kishgagah sheyotza' milipney hashaliyt.
**great There is an evil *which* I have seen under the sun as an error *which* proceed from the ruler**

נתן 5414 הסכל 5529 במרומים 4791 רבים 7227 ועשירים 6223 בשפל 8216 ישבו 3427: **10:7** ראיתי 7200 עבדים 5650 על 5921 סוסים 5483 ושרים 8269
nitan hasekel, bamroumiym rabiym; ua'ashiyriym bashepel yeshebu. ra'aytiy 'abadiym 'al susiym; uasariym
**is set Folly in dignity great and the rich in low place sit I have seen servants upon horses and princes**

הלכים 1980 כעבדים 5650 על 5921 הארץ 776: **10:8** חפר 2658 גומץ 1475 בו 871a יפול 5307 ופרץ 6555 גדר 1447 ישכנו 5391
holakiym ka'abadiym 'al ha'aretz. choper gumatz bou yipoul; uaporetz gader yishkenu
**walking as servants upon the earth He that dig a pit into it shall fall and whoso break an hedge shall bite him**

נחש 5175: **10:9** מסיע 5265 אבנים 68 יעצב 6087 בהם 871a בוקע 1234 עצים 6086 יסכן 5533
nachash. masiya' 'abaniym, ye'atzeb bahem; bouqea' 'aetziym yisaken
**a serpent Whoso remove stones shall be hurt therewith *and* he that cleave wood shall be endangered**

בם 871a: **10:10** אם 518 קהה 6949 הברזל 1270 והוא 1931 לא 3808 פנים 6440 קלקל 7043 וחילים 2428 יגבר 1396 ויתרון 3504
bam. 'am qehah habarzel, uahu'a la' paniym qilqal, uachayaliym yagaber; uayitroun
**thereby If be blunt the iron and he not the edge do whet then more strength must he put to but profitable**

הכשיר 3787 חכמה 2451: **10:11** אם 518 ישך 5391 הנחש 5175 בלוא 3808 לחש 3908 ואין 369 יתרון 3504 לבעל 1167
haksheyr chakamah 'am yishok hanachash balou'a lachash; ua'aeyn yitroun, laba'al
**to direct wisdom *is* Surely will bite the serpent without enchantment and is no better to those given to it**

הלשון 3956: **10:12** דברי 1697 פי 6310 חכם 2450 חן 2580 ושפתות 8193 כסיל 3684 תבלענו 1104:
halashoun. dibrey piy chakam chen; uasiptout kasiyl tabal'anu.
**a babbler The words of mouth a wise man's *are* gracious but the lips of a fool will swallow up himself**

Ecc 9:18 Wisdom is better than weapons of war: but one sinner destroyeth much good. **Ecc** 10:1 Dead flies cause the ointment of the apothecary to send forth a stinking savour: so doth a little folly him that is in reputation for wisdom and honor.2 A wise man's heart is at his right hand; but a fool's heart at his left.3 Yea also, when he that is a fool walk by the way, his wisdom faileth him, and he saith to everyone that he is a fool.4 If the spirit of the ruler rise up against you, leave not your place; for yielding pacifieth great offences.5 There is an evil which I have seen under the sun, as an error which proceed from the ruler:6 Folly is set in great dignity, and the rich sit in low place.7 I have seen servants upon horses, and princes walking as servants upon the earth.8 He that diggeth a pit shall fall into it; and whoso breaketh an hedge, a serpent shall bite him.9 Whoso removeth stones shall be hurt therewith; and he that cleaveth wood shall be endangered thereby.10 If the iron be blunt, and he do not whet the edge, then must he put to more strength: but wisdom is profitable to direct.11 Surely the serpent will bite without enchantment; and a babbler is no better.12 The words of a wise man's mouth are gracious; but the lips of a fool will swallow up himself.

**10:13** **10:14**

תחלת 8462 דברי 1697 פיהו 6310 סכלות 5531 ואחרית 319 פיהו 6310 הוללות 1948 רעה 7451:

tachilat dibrey piyhu siklut; ua'achariyt piyhu, houlelut ra'ah.

**The beginning of the words of his mouth *is* foolishness and the end of his talk madness *is* mischievous**

והסכל 5530 ירבה 7235 דברים 1697 לא 3808 ידע 3045 האדם 120 מה 4100 שיהיה 1961 ואשר 834 יהיה 1961 מאחריו 310 מי 4310 יגיד 5046

uahasakal yarbeh dabariym; la' yeda' ha'adam mah sheyihayeh, ua'asher yihayeh me'acharayu, miy' yagiyd

**A fool also is full of words cannot tell a man what shall be and what shall be after him who can tell**

**10:15** **10:16**

לו 3807a: עמל 5999 הכסילים 3684 תיגענו 3021 אשר 834 לא 3808 ידע 3045 ללכת 1980 אל 413 עיר 5892:

lou'. 'amal hakasiyliym tayag'anu; 'asher la' yada' laleket 'al 'ayr.

**him? The labour of the foolish weary every one of them because not he knows to go to the city**

**10:17**

אי 337 לך 3807a ארץ 776 שמלכך 4428 נער 5288 ושריך 8269 בבקר 1242 יאכלו 398: אשריך 835 ארץ 776

'ay lak 'aretz, shemalkek na'ar; uasarayik baboqer ya'kelu. 'ashreyk 'aretz,

**Woe to you O land when your king *is* a child and your princes in the morning eat Blessed *are* you O land**

**10:18**

שמלכך 4428 בן 1121 חורים 2715 ושריך 8269 בעת 6256 יאכלו 398 בגבורה 1369 ולא 3808 בשתי 8358:

shemalkek ben chouriym; uasarayik ba'aet ya'kelu, bigburah uala' bashtiy.

**when your king *is* the son of nobles and your princes in due season eat for strength and not for drunkenness**

**10:19**

בעצלתים 6103 ימך 4355 המקרה 4746 ובשפלות 8220 ידים 3027 ידלף 1811 הבית 1004: לשחוק 7814

ba'atzaltayim yimach hamqareh; uabshiplut yadayim yidlop habayit. lischouq

**By much slothfulness decay the building and through idleness of the hands droppeth through the house for laughter**

**10:20**

עשים 6213 לחם 3899 ויין 3196 ישמח 8055 חיים 2416 והכסף 3701 יענה 6030 את 853 הכל 3605: גם 1571 במדעך 4093 מלך 4428

'asiym lechem, uayayin yasamach chayiym; uahakesep ya'aneh 'at hakol. gam bamada'aka, melek

**is made A feast and wine makes merry lives but money answer all *things* no not in your thought the king**

אל 408 תקלל 7043 ובחדרי 2315 משכבך 4904 אל 408 תקלל 7043 עשיר 6223 כי 3588 עוף 5775 השמים 8064 יוליך 1980 את 853 הקול 6963

'al taqalel, uabchadrey mishkabaka, 'al taqalel 'ashiyr; kiy 'aup hashamayim youliyk 'at haqoul,

**not Curse and in chamber your bed not curse the rich for a bird of the air shall carry the voice**

ובעל 1167 הכנפים 3671 יגיד 5046 דבר 1697:

uaba'al hakenapayim yageyd dabar.

**and that which has wings shall tell the matter**

**Eccl 11:1** **11:2**

שלח 7971 לחמך 3899 על 5921 פני 6440 המים 4325 כי 3588 ברב 7230 הימים 3117 תמצאנו 4672: תן 5414 חלק 2506

shalach lachmaka 'al paney hamayim; kiy barob hayamiym timtza'anu. ten cheleq

**Cast your bread upon suffface of the waters for it after many days you shall find it Give a portion**

**11:3**

לשבעה 7651 וגם 1571 לשמונה 8083 כי 3588 לא 3808 תדע 3045 מה 4100 יהיה 1961 רעה 7451 על 5921 הארץ 776: אם 518 ימלאו 4390

lashib'ah ua'gam lishmounah; kiy la' teda', mah yihayeh ra'ah 'al ha'aretz. 'am yimala'au

**to seven and also to eight for not you know what shall be evil upon the earth If be full of**

העבים 5645 גשם 1653 על 5921 הארץ 776 יריקו 7324 ואם 518 יפול 5307 עץ 6086 בדרום 1864 ואם 518 בצפון 6828

he'abiym geshem 'al ha'aretz yariyqu, ua'am yipoul 'aetz badaroum ua'am batzapoun;

**the clouds rain upon the earth they empty *themselves* and if fall the tree toward the south or toward the north**

Ecc 10:13 The beginning of the words of his mouth is foolishness: and the end of his talk is mischievous madness.14 A fool also is full of words: a man cannot tell what shall be; and what shall be after him, who can tell him? 15 The labour of the foolish wearieth everyone of them, because he know not how to go to the city.16 Woe to you, O land, when your king is a child, and your princes eat in the morning!17 Blessed are you, O land, when your king is the son of nobles, and your princes eat in due season, for strength, and not for drunkenness!18 By much slothfulness the building decayeth; and through idleness of the hands the house droppeth through.19 A feast is made for laughter, and wine make merry: but money answer all things.20 Curse not the king, no not in your thought; and curse not the rich in your bedchamber: for a bird of the air shall carry the voice, and that which has wings shall tell the matter. **Ecc** 11:1 Cast your bread upon the waters: for you shall find it after many days.2 Give a portion to seven, and also to eight; for you know not what evil shall be upon the earth.3 If the clouds be full of rain, they empty themselves upon the earth: and if the tree fall toward the south, or toward the north, in the place where the tree fall, there it shall be.

מקום 4725 שיפול 5307 העץ 6086 שם 8033 יהוא 1933: 11:4 שמר 8104 רוח 7307 לא 3808 יזרע 2232 וראה 7200 בעבים 5645
maqoum sheyipoul ha'aetz sham yahu'a. shomer ruach la' yizra'; uaro'ah be'abiym
**in the place where fall the tree there it shall be He that observe the wind not shall sow and he that regard the clouds**

לא 3808 יקצור 7114: 11:5 כאשר 834 אינך 369 יודע 3045 מה 4100 דרך 1870 הרוח 7307 כעצמים 6106 בבטן 990
la' yiqtzour. ka'asher 'aeynaka youdea' mah derek haruach, ka'atzamiym babeten
**not shall reap As not you know what *is* the way of the spirit *nor* how the bones *do grow* in the womb of**

המלאה 4392 ככה 3602 לא 3808 תדע 3045 את 853 מעשה 4639 האלהים 430 אשר 834 יעשה 6213 את 853 הכל 3605: 11:6 בבקר 1242
hamale'ah; kakah, la' teda' 'at ma'aseh ha'alohiym, 'asher ya'aseh 'at hakol. baboqer
**her that is with child even so not you know works of the Elohim who make all In the morning**

זרע 2232 את 853 זרעך 2233 ולערב 6153 אל 408 תנח 3240 ידך 3027 כי 3588 אינך 369 יודע 3045 אי 335 זה 2088
zara' 'at zar'aka, uala'areb 'al tanach yadeka; kiy 'aeynaka youdea' 'aey zeh
**sow your seed and in the evening not withhold your hand for not you know whether this**

יכשר 3787 הזה 2088 או 176 זה 2088 ואם 518 שניהם 8147 כאחד 259 טובים 2896: 11:7 ומתוק 4966 האור 216
yikshar hazeh 'au zeh, ua'am shaneyhem ka'aechad toubiym. uamatouq ha'aur;
**shall prosper *either* this or that or whether they both *shall be* alike good Truly sweet the light *is***

וטוב 2896 לעינים 5869 לראות 7200 את 853 השמש 8121: 11:8 כי 3588 אם 518 שנים 8141 הרבה 7235 יחיה 2421 האדם 120
uatoub la'aeynayim lir'aut 'at hashamesh. kiy 'am shaniym harbeh yichayeh ha'adam
**and a pleasant *thing it is* for the eyes to behold the sun But if years many live a man**

בכלם 3605 ישמח 8055 ויזכר 2142 את 853 ימי 3117 החשך 2822 כי 3588 הרבה 7235 יהיו 1961 כל 3605 שבא 935
bakulam yismach; uayizkor 'at yamey hachoshek, kiy harbeh yihayu kal sheba'
**in them all *and* rejoice yet let him remember days of the darkness for many they shall be All that comes**

הבל 1892: 11:9 שמח 8055 בחור 970 בילדותיך 3208 ויטיבך 3190 לבך 3820 בימי 3117 בחורותך 979 והלך 1980
habel. samach bachur bayalduteyka, uiytiybaka libaka biymey bachurouteka, uahalek
***is* vanity Rejoice O young man in your youth and let cheer you your heart you in the days of your youth and walk**

בדרכי 1870 לבך 3820 ובמראי 4758 עיניך 5869 ודע 3045 כי 3588 על 5921 כל 3605 אלה 428 יביאך 935
badarkey libaka, uabmar'aey 'aeyneyka; uada' kiy 'al kal 'aeleh yabiy'aka
**in the ways of your heart and in the sight of your eyes but know you that for all these will bring you *things***

האלהים 430 במשפט 4941: 11:10 והסר 5493 כעס 3708 מלבך 3820 והעבר 5674 רעה 7451 מבשרך 1320 כי 3588
ha'alohiym bamishpat. uahaser ka'as milibeka, uaha'aber ra'ah mibasareka; kiy
**Elohim into judgment Therefore remove sorrow from your heart and put away evil from your flesh for**

הילדות 3208 והשחרות 7839 הבל 1892:
hayaldut uahashacharut habel.
**childhood and youth *are* vanity**

**Eccl 12:1**
וזכר 2142 את 853 בוראיך 1254 בימי 3117 בחורתיך 979 עד 5704 אשר 834 לא 3808 יבאו 935 ימי 3117 הרעה 7451
uazkor 'at boura'ayka, biymey bachuroteyka; 'ad 'asher la' yabo'au yamey hara'ah,
**Remember now your Creator in the days of your youth while which not come days the evil**

Ecc 11:4 He that observeth the wind shall not sow; and he that regardeth the clouds shall not reap.5 As you know not what is the way of the spirit, nor how the bones do grow in the womb of her that is with child: even so you know not the works of G-d who make all.6 In the morning sow your seed, and in the evening withhold not your hand: for you know not whether shall prosper, either this or that, or whether they both shall be alike good.7 Truly the light is sweet, and a pleasant thing it is for the eyes to behold the sun:8 But if a man live many years, and rejoice in them all; yet let him remember the days of darkness; for they shall be many. All that cometh is vanity.9 Rejoice, O young man, in your youth; and let your heart cheer you in the days of your youth, and walk in the ways of your heart, and in the sight of your eyes: but know you, that for all these things G-d will bring you into judgment.10 Therefore remove sorrow from your heart, and put away evil from your flesh: for childhood and youth are vanity. **Ecc** 12:1 Remember now your Creator in the days of your youth, while the evil days come not, nor the years draw nigh, when you shall say, I have no pleasure in them;

| 𐤅𐤄𐤂𐤉𐤏𐤅 | 𐤔𐤍𐤉𐤌 | 𐤀𐤔𐤓 | 𐤕𐤀𐤌𐤓 | 𐤀𐤉𐤍 | 𐤋𐤉 | 𐤁𐤄𐤌 | 𐤇𐤐𐤑 | 12:2 𐤏𐤃 | 𐤀𐤔𐤓 | 𐤋𐤀 | 𐤕𐤇𐤔𐤊 |
|---|---|---|---|---|---|---|---|---|---|---|---|
| והגיעו 5060 | שנים 8141 | אשר 834 | תאמר 559 | אין 369 | לי 3807a | בהם 871a | חפץ 2656: | עד 5704 | אשר 834 | לא 3808 | תחשך 2821 |
| uahigiy'au | shaniym, | 'asher | ta'mar, | 'aeyn | liy | bahem | chepetz. | 'ad | 'asher | la' | techshak |
| **nor draw near** | **the years** | **when** | **you shall say** | **have no** | **I** | **in them** | **pleasure** | **While** | **which** | **not** | **be darkened** |

| 𐤄𐤔𐤌𐤔 | 𐤅𐤄𐤀𐤅𐤓 | 𐤅𐤄𐤉𐤓𐤇 | 𐤅𐤄𐤊𐤅𐤊𐤁𐤉𐤌 | 𐤅𐤔𐤁𐤅 | 𐤄𐤏𐤁𐤉𐤌 | 𐤀𐤇𐤓 | 𐤄𐤂𐤔𐤌 | 12:3 𐤁𐤉𐤅𐤌 |
|---|---|---|---|---|---|---|---|---|
| השמש 8121 | והאור 216 | והירח 3394 | והכוכבים 3556 | ושבו 7725 | העבים 5645 | אחר 310 | הגשם 1653: | ביום 3117 |
| hashemesh | uaha'aur, | uahayareach | uahakoukabiym; | uashabu | he'abiym | 'achar | hagashem. | bayoum, |
| **the sun** | **or the light** | **or the moon** | **or the stars** | **nor return** | **the clouds** | **after** | **the rain** | **In the day** |

| 𐤔𐤉𐤆𐤏𐤅 | 𐤔𐤌𐤓𐤉 | 𐤄𐤁𐤉𐤕 | 𐤅𐤄𐤕𐤏𐤅𐤕𐤅 | 𐤀𐤍𐤔𐤉 | 𐤄𐤇𐤉𐤋 | 𐤅𐤁𐤈𐤋𐤅 | 𐤄𐤈𐤇𐤍𐤅𐤕 | 𐤊𐤉 |
|---|---|---|---|---|---|---|---|---|
| שיזעו 2111 | שמרי 8104 | הבית 1004 | והתעותו 5791 | אנשי 582 | החיל 2428 | ובטלו 988 | הטחנות 2912 | כי 3588 |
| sheyazu'au | shomrey | habayit, | uahit'auatu | 'anshey | hechayil; | uabatalu | hatochanout | kiy |
| **when shall tremble** | **the keepers of** | **the house** | **and shall bow themselves** | **men** | **the strong** | **and cease** | **the grinders** | **because** |

| 𐤌𐤏𐤈𐤅 | 𐤅𐤇𐤔𐤊𐤅 | 𐤄𐤓𐤀𐤅𐤕 | 𐤁𐤀𐤓𐤁𐤅𐤕 | 12:4 𐤅𐤎𐤂𐤓𐤅 | 𐤃𐤋𐤕𐤉𐤌 | 𐤁𐤔𐤅𐤒 | 𐤁𐤔𐤐𐤋 |
|---|---|---|---|---|---|---|---|
| מעטו 4592 | וחשכו 2821 | הראות 7200 | בארבות 699: | וסגרו 5462 | דלתים 1817 | בשוק 7784 | בשפל 8217 |
| mi'aetu, | uachashaku | haro'aut | ba'arubout. | uasugru | dalatayim | bashuq, | bishpal |
| **they are few** | **and be darkened** | **those that look** | **out of the windows** | **And shall be shut** | **the doors** | **in the streets** | **when is low** |

| 𐤒𐤅𐤋 | 𐤄𐤈𐤇𐤍𐤄 | 𐤅𐤉𐤒𐤅𐤌 | 𐤋𐤒𐤅𐤋 | 𐤄𐤑𐤐𐤅𐤓 | 𐤅𐤉𐤔𐤇𐤅 | 𐤊𐤋 | 𐤁𐤍𐤅𐤕 |
|---|---|---|---|---|---|---|---|
| קול 6963 | הטחנה 2913 | ויקום 6965 | לקול 6963 | הצפור 6833 | וישחו 7817 | כל 3605 | בנות 1323 |
| qoul | hatachanah; | uayaqum | laqoul | hatzipour, | uayishachu | kal | banout |
| **the sound of** | **the grinding** | **and he shall rise up** | **at the voice of** | **the bird** | **and shall be brought low** | **all** | **daughters of** |

| 𐤄𐤔𐤉𐤓 | 12:5 𐤂𐤌 | 𐤌𐤂𐤁𐤄 | 𐤉𐤓𐤀𐤅 | 𐤅𐤇𐤕𐤇𐤕𐤉𐤌 | 𐤁𐤃𐤓𐤊 | 𐤅𐤉𐤍𐤀𐤑 |
|---|---|---|---|---|---|---|
| השיר 7892: | גם 1571 | מגבה 1364 | יראו 3372 | וחתחתים 2849 | בדרך 1870 | וינאץ 5006 |
| hashiyr. | gam | migaboah | yiyra'au | uachatchatiym | baderek, | uayanea'tz |
| **the music** | **Also** | **of *that which is* high** | ***when* they shall be afraid** | **and fears** | ***shall be* in the way** | **and shall flourish** |

| 𐤄𐤔𐤒𐤃 | 𐤅𐤉𐤎𐤕𐤁𐤋 | 𐤄𐤇𐤂𐤁 | 𐤅𐤕𐤐𐤓 | 𐤄𐤀𐤁𐤉𐤅𐤍𐤄 | 𐤊𐤉 | 𐤄𐤋𐤊 | 𐤄𐤀𐤃𐤌 | 𐤀𐤋 | 𐤁𐤉𐤕 |
|---|---|---|---|---|---|---|---|---|---|
| השקד 8247 | ויסתבל 5445 | החגב 2284 | ותפר 6565 | האביונה 35 | כי 3588 | הלך 1980 | האדם 120 | אל 413 | בית 1004 |
| hashaqed | uayistabel | hechagab, | uataper | ha'abiyounah; | kiy | hokek | ha'adam | 'al | beyt |
| **the almond tree** | **and shall be a burden** | **the grasshopper** | **and shall fail** | **the desire** | **because** | **goes** | **man** | **to** | **home** |

| 𐤏𐤅𐤋𐤌𐤅 | 𐤅𐤎𐤁𐤁𐤅 | 𐤁𐤔𐤅𐤒 | 𐤄𐤎𐤐𐤃𐤉𐤌 | 12:6 𐤏𐤃 | 𐤀𐤔𐤓 | 𐤋𐤀 | 𐤉𐤓𐤇𐤒 | 𐤇𐤁𐤋 | 𐤄𐤊𐤎𐤐 | 𐤅𐤕𐤓𐤑 | 𐤂𐤋𐤕 |
|---|---|---|---|---|---|---|---|---|---|---|---|
| עולמו 5769 | וסבבו 5437 | בשוק 7784 | הספדים 5594: | עד 5704 | אשר 834 | לא 3808 | ירחק 7368 | חבל 2256 | הכסף 3701 | ותרץ 7533 | גלת 1543 |
| 'aulamou, | uasababu | bashuq | hasopadiym. | 'ad | 'asher | la' | yirchaq | chebel | hakesep, | uatarutz | gulat |
| **his long** | **and go about** | **the streets** | **the mourners** | **Or** | **ever** | **not** | **be loosed** | **cord** | **the silver** | **or be broken** | **bowl** |

| 𐤄𐤆𐤄𐤁 | 𐤅𐤕𐤔𐤁𐤓 | 𐤊𐤃 | 𐤏𐤋 | 𐤄𐤌𐤁𐤅𐤏 | 𐤅𐤍𐤓𐤑 | 𐤄𐤂𐤋𐤂𐤋 | 𐤀𐤋 | 𐤄𐤁𐤅𐤓 | 12:7 𐤅𐤉𐤔𐤁 | 𐤄𐤏𐤐𐤓 |
|---|---|---|---|---|---|---|---|---|---|---|
| הזהב 2091 | ותשבר 7665 | כד 3537 | על 5921 | המבוע 4002 | ונרץ 7533 | הגלגל 1534 | אל 413 | הבור 953: | וישב 7725 | העפר 6083 |
| hazahab; | uatishaber | kad | 'al | hamabua', | uanarotz | hagalgal | 'al | habour. | uayashob | he'apar |
| **the golden** | **or be broken** | **the pitcher** | **at** | **the fountain** | **or broken** | **the wheel** | **at** | **the cistern** | **Then shall return** | **the dust** |

| 𐤏𐤋 | 𐤄𐤀𐤓𐤑 | 𐤊𐤔𐤄𐤉𐤄 | 𐤅𐤄𐤓𐤅𐤇 | 𐤕𐤔𐤅𐤁 | 𐤀𐤋 | 𐤄𐤀𐤋𐤄𐤉𐤌 | 𐤀𐤔𐤓 | 𐤍𐤕𐤍𐤄 | 12:8 𐤄𐤁𐤋 | 𐤄𐤁𐤋𐤉𐤌 | 𐤀𐤌𐤓 |
|---|---|---|---|---|---|---|---|---|---|---|---|
| על 5921 | הארץ 776 | כשהיה 1961 | והרוח 7307 | תשוב 7725 | אל 413 | האלהים 430 | אשר 834 | נתנה 5414: | הבל 1892 | הבלים 1892 | אמר 559 |
| 'al | ha'aretz | kashehayah; | uaharuach | tashub, | 'al | ha'alohiym | 'asher | natanah. | habel | habaliym | 'amar |
| **to** | **the earth** | **as it was** | **and the spirit** | **shall return** | **unto** | **Elohim** | **who** | **gave it** | **Vanity of** | **vanities** | **saith** |

| 𐤄𐤒𐤅𐤄𐤋𐤕 | 𐤄𐤊𐤋 | 𐤄𐤁𐤋 | 12:9 𐤅𐤉𐤕𐤓 | 𐤔𐤄𐤉𐤄 | 𐤒𐤄𐤋𐤕 | 𐤇𐤊𐤌 | 𐤏𐤅𐤃 | 𐤋𐤌𐤃 | 𐤃𐤏𐤕 | 𐤀𐤕 |
|---|---|---|---|---|---|---|---|---|---|---|
| הקוהלת 6953 | הכל 3605 | הבל 1892: | ויתר 3148 | שהיה 1961 | קהלת 6953 | חכם 2450 | עוד 5750 | למד 3925 | דעת 1847 | את 853 |
| haqouhelet | hakol | habel. | uayoter | shehayah | qohelet | chakam; | 'aud, | limad | da'at | 'at |
| **the preacher** | **all** | ***is* vanity** | **And moreover** | **because was** | **the preacher** | **wise** | **still** | **he taught** | **knowledge** | |

| 𐤄𐤏𐤌 | 𐤅𐤀𐤆𐤍 | 𐤅𐤇𐤒𐤓 | 𐤕𐤒𐤍 | 𐤌𐤔𐤋𐤉𐤌 | 𐤄𐤓𐤁𐤄 | 12:10 𐤁𐤒𐤔 | 𐤒𐤄𐤋𐤕 |
|---|---|---|---|---|---|---|---|
| העם 5971 | ואזן 238 | וחקר 2713 | תקן 8626 | משלים 4912 | הרבה 7235: | בקש 1245 | קהלת 6953 |
| ha'am, | ua'azen | uachiqer, | tiqen | mashaliym | harbeh. | biqesh | qohelet, |
| **the people** | **yea, he gave good heed** | **and sought out** | ***and* set in order** | **proverbs** | **many** | **sought** | **The preacher** |

Ecc 12:2 While the sun, or the light, or the moon, or the stars, be not darkened, nor the clouds return after the rain:3 In the day when the keepers of the house shall tremble, and the strong men shall bow themselves, and the grinders cease because they are few, and those that look out of the windows be darkened,4 And the doors shall be shut in the streets, when the sound of the grinding is low, and he shall rise up at the voice of the bird, and all the daughters of musick shall be brought low;5 Also when they shall be afraid of that which is high, and fears shall be in the way, and the almond tree shall flourish, and the grasshopper shall be a burden, and desire shall fail: because man go to his long home, and the mourners go about the streets:6 Or ever the silver cord be loosed, or the golden bowl be broken, or the pitcher be broken at the fountain, or the wheel broken at the cistern.7 Then shall the dust return to the earth as it was: and the spirit shall return unto G-d who gave it.8 Vanity of vanities, saith the preacher; all is vanity.9 And moreover, because the preacher was wise, he still taught the people knowledge; yea, he gave good heed, and sought out, and set in order many proverbs.

| למצא 4672 | דברי 1697 | חפץ 2656 | וכתוב 3789 | ישר 3476 | דברי 1697 | אמת 571: | 12:11 דברי 1697 | חכמים 2450 |
|---|---|---|---|---|---|---|---|---|
| limtza' | dibrey | chepetz; | uakatub | yosher | dibrey | 'amet. | dibrey | chakamiym |
| **to find out** | **words** | **acceptable** | **and *that which was* written** | ***was* upright** | ***even* words of** | **truth** | **The words of** | **the wise** |

| כדרבנות 1861 | וכמשמרות 4930 | נטועים 5193 | בעלי 1167 | אספות 627 | נתנו 5414 | מרעה 7462 | אחד 259: | 12:12 |
|---|---|---|---|---|---|---|---|---|
| kadarabonout, | uakmasmarout | natu'aym | ba'aley | asupout; | nitanu | mero'ah | 'achad. | |
| ***are* as goads** | **and as nails** | **fastened** | ***by* the masters of** | **assemblies** | ***which* are given** | **from shepherd** | **one** | |

| ויתר 3148 | מהמה 1992 | בני 1121 | הזהר 2094 | עשות 6213 | ספרים 5612 | הרבה 7235 | אין 369 | קץ 7093 | ולהג 3854 | הרבה 7235 |
|---|---|---|---|---|---|---|---|---|---|---|
| uayoter | mehemah | baniy | hizaher; | asout | sapariym | harbeh | 'aeyn | qetz, | ualahag | harbeh |
| **And further** | **by these** | **my son** | **be admonished** | ***of* making** | **books** | **many** | **no** | ***there is* no end** | **and study** | **much** |

| יגעת 3024 | בשר 1320: | 12:13 סוף 5490 | דבר 1697 | הכל 3605 | נשמע 8085 | את 853 | האלהים 430 | ירא 3372 | ואת 853 |
|---|---|---|---|---|---|---|---|---|---|
| yagi'at | basar. | soup | dabar | hakol | nishma'; | 'at | ha'alohiym | yara' | ua'at |
| ***is* a weariness of** | **the flesh** | **the conclusion of** | **matter** | **the whole** | **Let us hear** | | **Elohim** | **Fear** | ***and*** |

| מצותיו 4687 | שמור 8104 | כי 3588 | זה 2088 | כל 3605 | האדם 120: | 12:14 כי 3588 | את 853 | כל 3605 | מעשה 4639 | האלהים 430 | יבא 935 |
|---|---|---|---|---|---|---|---|---|---|---|---|
| mitzuotayu | shamor, | kiy | zeh | kal | ha'adam. | kiy | 'at | kal | ma'aseh, | ha'alohiym | yaba' |
| **his commandments** | **keep** | **for** | **this *is*** | **the whole *duty* of** | **man** | **For** | | **every** | **work** | **Elohim** | **shall bring** |

| במשפט 4941 | על 5921 | כל 3605 | נעלם 5956 | אם 518 | טוב 2896 | ואם 518 | רע 7451: |
|---|---|---|---|---|---|---|---|
| bamishpat | 'al | kal | ne'alam; | 'am | toub | ua'am | ra'. |
| **into judgment** | **with** | **every** | **secret thing** | **whether *it be*** | **good** | **or whether** | ***it be* evil** |

Ecc 12:10 The preacher sought to find out acceptable words: and that which was written was upright, even words of truth.11 The words of the wise are as goads, and as nails fastened by the masters of assemblies, which are given from one shepherd.12 And further, by these, my son, be admonished: of making many books there is no end; and much study is a weariness of the flesh.13 Let us hear the conclusion of the whole matter: Fear G-d, and keep his commandments: for this is the whole duty of man.14 For G-d shall bring every work into judgment, with every secret thing, whether it be good, or whether it be evil.

# SONG OF SOLOMON
## (*Shir Ha-Shirim*)

Without question Solomon wrote Song of Solomon, according to the first verse. This Song is one of 1,005 that Solomon wrote according to 1 Kings 4:32. The title "Song of Songs" is a superlative, meaning this is his best one and it was most likely written during the early part of his reign around 965 B.C. before his heart turned away from Elohim. The placement of the Aleph/ Tavs in the Song actually enhances the lyric poem to extol the virtues of love between a husband, symbolic of Messiah and his wife, symbolic of the bride. The poem clearly presents marriage between a husband and wife as Elohim's design for the human race. A man and woman are to live together only within the context and commitment by covenant marriage, loving each other both physically and emotionally in their obedience to Elohim's commandments. The marriage profile and description in the Song is a model for believers of how true commitment brings both physical and spiritual fulfillment. I have segregated the speaking parts so the reader will know who is speaking and when, so there will be no confusion in the dialog. If you wish the audio version email me.

| **Song of Songs 1:1** | | | | **1:2** | | | |
|---|---|---|---|---|---|---|---|
| שיר 7892 | השירים 7892 | אשר 834 | לשלמה 8010: | ישקני 5401 | מנשיקות 5390 | פיהו 6310 | כי 3588 |
| shiyr | hashiyriym | 'asher | lishalomoh. | yishaqeniy | minshiyqout | piyhu, | kiy |
| **The song of** | **songs** | **which** | ***is* Solomon's** | **Let him kiss me** | **with the kisses of** | **his mouth** | **for** |

| | | | **1:3** | | | | | |
|---|---|---|---|---|---|---|---|---|
| טובים 2896 | דדיך 1730 | מיין 3196: | לריח 7381 | שמניך 8081 | טובים 2896 | שמן 8081 | תורק 7324 | שמך 8034 |
| toubiym | dodeyka | miyayin. | lareyach | shamaneyka | toubiym, | shemen | turaq | shameka; |
| ***is* better** | **your love** | **than wine** | **Because of the savour of** | **your ointments** | **good** | ***is as* ointment** | **poured forth** | **your name** |

| | | | | **1:4** | | | | | |
|---|---|---|---|---|---|---|---|---|---|
| על 5921 | כן 3651 | עלמות 5959 | אהבוך 157: | משכני 4900 | אחריך 310 | נרוצה 7323 | הביאני 935 | המלך 4428 | חדריו 2315 |
| 'al | ken | 'alamout | 'ahebuka. | mashakeniy | 'achareyka | narutzah; | hebiy'aniy | hamelek | chadarayu, |
| **therefore** | **after** | **the virgins** | **do love you** | **Draw me** | **after you** | **we will run** | **has brought me** | **the king** | ***into* his chambers** |

| | | | | | | | | **1:5** | |
|---|---|---|---|---|---|---|---|---|---|
| נגילה 1523 | ונשמחה 8055 | בך 871a | נזכירה 2142 | דדיך 1730 | מיין 3196 | מישרים 4339 | אהבוך 157: | שחורה 7838 | אני 589 |
| nagiylah | uanismachah | bak, | nazkiyrah | dodeyka | miyayin, | meyshariym | 'ahebuka. | shachourah | 'aniy |
| **we will be glad** | **and rejoice** | **in you** | **we will remember** | **your love** | **more than wine** | **the upright** | **love you** | ***am* black** | **I** |

| | | | | | | | **1:6** | |
|---|---|---|---|---|---|---|---|---|
| ונאוה 5000 | בנות 1323 | ירושלם 3389 | כאהלי 168 | קדר 6938 | כיריעות 3407 | שלמה 8010: | אל 408 | תראוני 7200 |
| uana'auh, | banout | yarushalaim; | ka'ahaley | qedar, | kiyriy'aut | shalomoh. | 'al | tir'auniy |
| **but comely** | **O you daughters of** | **Jerusalem** | **as the tents of** | **Kedar** | **as the curtains of** | **Solomon** | **not** | **Look upon me** |

| | | | | | | | | |
|---|---|---|---|---|---|---|---|---|
| שאני 589 | שחרחרת 7840 | ששזפתני 7805 | השמש 8121 | בני 1121 | אמי 517 | נחרו 2787 | בי 871a | שמני 7760 |
| she'aniy | shacharchoret, | sheshezapatniy | hashamesh; | baney | 'amiy | nicharu | biy, | samuniy |
| **because I** | ***am* black** | **because has looked upon me** | **the sun** | **children** | **my mother's** | **were angry** | **with me** | **they made me** |

| | | | | | | | **1:7** | | |
|---|---|---|---|---|---|---|---|---|---|
| נטרה 5201 | את 853 | הכרמים 3754 | כרמי 3754 | שלי 3807a | לא 3808 | נטרתי 5201: | הגידה 5046 | לי 3807a | שאהבה 157 |
| noterah | 'at | hakaramiym, | karmiy | sheliy | la' | nataratiy. | hagiydah | liy, | she'ahabah |
| **the keeper of** | | **the vineyards** | ***but* mine own vineyard** | **have I** | **not** | **kept** | **Tell** | **me *O you*** | **whom love** |

| | | | | | | | | |
|---|---|---|---|---|---|---|---|---|
| נפשי 5315 | איכה 349 | תרעה 7462 | איכה 349 | תרביץ 7257 | בצהרים 6672 | שלמה 4100 | אהיה 1961 | כעטיה 5844 |
| napshiy, | 'aeykah | tir'ah, | 'aeykah | tarbiytz | batzaharayim; | shalamah | 'ahayeh | ka'atayah, |
| **my soul** | **where** | **you feed** | **where** | **you make *your flock* to rest** | **at noon** | ***for* why** | **should I be** | **as one that turned aside** |

| | | | **1:8** | | | | | | | |
|---|---|---|---|---|---|---|---|---|---|---|
| על 5921 | עדרי 5739 | חבריך 2270: | אם 518 | לא 3808 | תדעי 3045 | לך 3807a | היפה 3303 | בנשים 802 | צאי 3318 | לך 3807a |
| 'al | 'adrey | chabereyka. | 'am | la' | teda'ay | lak, | hayapah | banashiym; | tza'ay | lak |
| **by** | **the flocks of** | **your companion?** | **If** | **not** | **you know** | **O you** | **fairest** | **among women** | **go forth** | **your way** |

**Song of Songs** 1:1 The song of songs, which is Solomon's.2 Let him kiss me with the kisses of his mouth: for your love is better than wine.3 Because of the savour of your good ointments your name is as ointment poured forth, therefore do the virgins love you.4 Draw me, we will run after you: the king has brought me into his chambers: we will be glad and rejoice in you, we will remember your love more than wine: the upright love you.5 I am black, but comely, O you daughters of Jerusalem, as the tents of Kedar, as the curtains of Solomon.6 Look not upon me, because I am black, because the sun has looked upon me: my mother's children were angry with me; they made me the keeper of the vineyards; but mine own vineyard have I not kept.7 Tell me, O you whom my soul love, where you feedest, where you make your flock to rest at noon: for why should I be as one that turneth aside by the flocks of your companions?8 If you know not, O you fairest among women, go your way forth by the footsteps of the flock, and feed your kids beside the shepherds' tents.

| בעקבי 6119 | הצאן 6629 | ורעי 7462 | את 853 | גדיתיך 1429 | על 5921 | משכנות 4908 | הרעים 7462: | 1:9 לססתי 5484 |
|---|---|---|---|---|---|---|---|---|
| ba'aqbey | hatza'an, | uara'ay | 'at | gadiyotayik, | 'al | mishkanout | haro'aym. | lasusatiy |
| **by the footsteps of** | **the flock** | **and feed** | | **your kids** | **beside** | **tents** | **the shepherds'** | **to a company of horses** |

| ברכבי 7393 | פרעה 6547 | דמיתיך 1819 | רעיתי 7474: | 1:10 נאוו 4998 | לחייך 3895 | בתרים 8447 | צוארך 6677 |
|---|---|---|---|---|---|---|---|
| barikbey | par'ah, | dimiytiyk | ra'yatiy. | na'auu | lachayayik | batoriym, | tzaua'rek |
| **in chariots** | **Pharaoh's** | **I have compared you** | **O my love** | ***are* comely** | **Your cheeks** | **with rows** | ***of jewels* your neck** |

| בחרוזים 2737: | 1:11 תורי 8447 | זהב 2091 | נעשה 6213 | לך 3807a | עם 5973 | נקדות 5351 | הכסף 3701: | 1:12 עד 5704 | שהמלך 4428 |
|---|---|---|---|---|---|---|---|---|---|
| bacharuziym. | tourey | zahab | na'aseh | lak, | 'am | naqudout | hakasep. | 'ad | shehamelek |
| **with chains of gold** | **borders of** | **gold** | **We will make** | **to you** | **with** | **studs of** | **silver** | **While** | **the king** |

| במסבו 4524 | נרדי 5373 | נתן 5414 | ריחו 7381: | 1:13 צרור 6872 | המר 4753 | דודי 1730 | לי 3807a | בין 996 |
|---|---|---|---|---|---|---|---|---|
| bimsibou, | nirdiy | natan | reychou. | tzarour | hamor | doudiy | liy, | beyn |
| ***sit* at his table** | **my spikenard** | **send forth** | **the smell thereof** | **A bundle of** | **myrrh** | ***is* my wellbeloved** | **unto me** | **betwixt** |

| שדי 7699 | ילין 3885: | 1:14 אשכל 811 | הכפר 3724 | דודי 1730 | לי 3807a | בכרמי 3754 | עין 5872 | גדי 1423: 1:15 |
|---|---|---|---|---|---|---|---|---|
| shaay | yaliyn. | 'ashkol | hakoper | doudiy | liy, | bakarmey | 'aeyn | gediy. |
| **my breasts** | **he shall lie all night** | ***as* a cluster of** | **camphire** | **My beloved *is*** | **unto me** | **in the vineyards of** | **En** | **gedi** |

| הנך 2005 | יפה 3303 | רעיתי 7474 | הנך 2005 | יפה 3303 | עיניך 5869 | יונים 3123: | 1:16 הנך 2005 | יפה 3303 | דודי 1730 | אף 637 |
|---|---|---|---|---|---|---|---|---|---|---|
| hinak | yapah | ra'yatiy, | hinak | yapah | 'aeynayik | youniym. | hinaka | yapeh | doudiy | 'ap |
| **Behold you** | ***are* fair** | **my love** | **behold you** | ***are* fair** | **you *have* eyes** | **doves'** | **Behold you** | ***are* fair** | **my beloved** | **yea** |

| נעים 5273 | אף 637 | ערשנו 6210 | רעננה 7488: | 1:17 קרות 6982 | בתינו 1004 | ארזים 730 | רחיטנו 7351 | ברותים 1266: |
|---|---|---|---|---|---|---|---|---|
| na'aym, | 'ap | 'arsenu | ra'ananah. | qarout | bateynu | 'araziym, | rachiytenu | baroutiym. |
| **pleasant** | **also** | **our bed** | ***is* green** | **The beams of** | **our house** | ***are* cedar** | ***and* our rafters of fir** | |

| Song 2:1 אני 589 | חבצלת 2261 | השרון 8289 | שושנת 7799 | העמקים 6010: | 2:2 כשושנה 7799 | בין 996 | החוחים 2336 | כן 3651 | רעיתי 7474 |
|---|---|---|---|---|---|---|---|---|---|
| 'aniy | chabatzelet | hasharoun, | shoushanat | ha'amaqiym. | kashoushanah | beyn | hachouchiym, | ken | ra'yatiy |
| **I** | **rose of *am*** | **the Sharon** | ***and* the lily of** | **the valleys** | **As the lily** | **among** | **thorns** | **so** | ***is* my love** |

| בין 996 | הבנות 1323: | 2:3 כתפוח 8598 | בעצי 6086 | היער 3293 | כן 3651 | דודי 1730 | בין 996 | הבנים 1121 |
|---|---|---|---|---|---|---|---|---|
| beyn | habanout. | katapuach | ba'atzey | haya'ar, | ken | doudiy | beyn | habaniym; |
| **among** | **the daughters** | **As the apple tree** | **among the trees of** | **the wood** | **so** | ***is* my beloved** | **among** | **the sons** |

| בצלו 6738 | חמדתי 2530 | וישבתי 3427 | ופריו 6529 | מתוק 4966 | לחכי 2441: | 2:4 הביאני 935 | אל 413 | בית 1004 |
|---|---|---|---|---|---|---|---|---|
| batzilou | chimadtiy | uayashabtiy, | uapiryou | matouq | lachikiy. | hebiy'aniy | 'al | beyt |
| **under his shadow with** | **great delight** | **I sat down** | **and his fruit** | ***was* sweet** | **to my taste** | **He brought me** | **to** | **house** |

| היין 3196 | ודגלו 1714 | עלי 5921 | אהבה 160: | 2:5 סמכוני 5564 | באשישות 809 | רפדוני 7502 | בתפוחים 8598 | כי 3588 | חולת 2470 |
|---|---|---|---|---|---|---|---|---|---|
| hayayin, | uadiglou | 'alay | 'ahabah. | samkuniy | ba'ashiyshout, | rapduniy | batapuchiym; | kiy | choulat |
| **the banqueting** | **and his banner** | **over me** | ***was* love** | **Stay me** | **with raisin cakes** | **comfort me** | **with apples** | **for** | ***am* sick of** |

| אהבה 160 | אני 589: | 2:6 שמאלו 8040 | תחת 8478 | לראשי 7218 | וימינו 3225 | תחבקני 2263: | 2:7 השבעתי 7650 | אתכם 853 |
|---|---|---|---|---|---|---|---|---|
| 'ahabah | 'aniy. | sama'lou | tachat | lara'shiy, | uiymiynou | tachabqeniy. | hishba'atiy | 'atkem |
| **love** | **I** | **His left hand *is* under** | | **my head** | **and his right hand does embrace me** | | **I charge** | **you** |

Song 1:9 I have compared you, O my love, to a company of horses in Pharaoh's chariots.10 Thy cheeks are comely with rows of jewels, your neck with chains of gold.11 We will make you borders of gold with studs of silver.12 While the king sitteth at his table, my spikenard send forth the smell thereof.13 A bundle of myrrh is my wellbeloved unto me; he shall lie all night betwixt my breasts.14 My beloved is unto me as a cluster of camphire in the vineyards of En-gedi.15 Behold, you are fair, my love; behold, you are fair; you have doves' eyes.16 Behold, you are fair, my beloved, yea, pleasant: also our bed is green.17 The beams of our house are cedar, and our rafters of fir. **Song** 2:1 I am the rose of Sharon, and the lily of the valleys.2 As the lily among thorns, so is my love among the daughters.3 As the apple tree among the trees of the wood, so is my beloved among the sons. I sat down under his shadow with great delight, and his fruit was sweet to my taste.4 He brought me to the banqueting house, and his banner over me was love.5 Stay me with flagons, comfort me with apples: for I am sick of love.6 His left hand is under my head, and his right hand doth embrace me.

1323 בנות 3389 ירושלם 6643 בצבאות 176 או 355 באילות 7704 השדה 518 אם 5782 תעירו 518 ואם 5782 תעוררו 853 את
banout yarushalaim bitzaba'aut, 'au ba'aylout hasadeh; 'am ta'ayru ua'am ta'auraru 'at
**O you daughters of Jerusalem by the roes or by the hinds of the field that not you stir up nor awake**

160 האהבה 5704 עד 2654: שתחפץ **2:8** 6963 קול 1730 דודי 2009 הנה 2088 זה 935 בא 1801 מדלג 5921 על 2022 ההרים 7092 מקפץ
ha'ahabah 'ad shetechpatz. qoul doudiy, hineh zeh ba'; madaleg 'al hehariym, maqapetz
***my* love till he please The voice of my beloved behold this one he comes leaping upon the mountains skipping**

5921 על 1389: הגבעות **2:9** 1819 דומה 1730 דודי 6643 לצבי 176 או 6082 לעפר 354 האילים 2009 הנה 2088 זה 5975 עומד 310 אחר 3796 כתלנו
'al hagaba'aut. doumeh doudiy litzbiy, 'au la'aper ha'aeyliym; hineh zeh aumed 'achar katalenu,
**upon the hills is like My beloved a roe or young a hart behold this one he stands behind our wall**

7688 משגיח 4480 מן 2474 החלנות 6692 מציץ 4480 מן 2762: החרכים **2:10** 6030 ענה 1730 דודי 559 ואמר 3807a לי 6965 קומי
mashgiyach min hachalonout, metziytz min hacharakiym. 'anah doudiy ua'amar liy; quamiy
**he looks forth at the windows shewing himself through the lattice spoke My beloved and said unto me Rise up**

3807a לך 7474 רעיתי 3303 יפתי 1980 ולכי 3807a: לך **2:11** 3588 כי 2009 הנה 5638 הסתו 5674 עבר 1653 הגשם 2498 חלף 1980 הלך 3807a: לו **2:12**
lak ra'yatiy yapatiy ualkiy lak. kiy hineh hasatau 'abar; hageshem chalap halak lou'.
**to you my love my fair one and come away For lo the winter is past the rain is over *and* gone to him**

5339 הנצנים 7200 נראו 776 בארץ 6256 עת 2158 הזמיר 5060 הגיע 6963 וקול 8449 התור 8085 נשמע 776: בארצנו **2:13**
hanitzaniym nir'au ba'aretz, 'at hazamiyr higiya'; uaqoul hatour nishma' ba'artzenu.
**The flowers appear on the earth the time of the singing *of birds* is come and the voice of the turtle is heard in our land**

8384 התאנה 2590 חנטה 6291 פגיה 1612 והגפנים 5563 סמדר 5414 נתנו 7381 ריח 6965 קומי 1980 לכי
hata'aenah chantah pageyha, uahagapaniym samadar natanu reyach; quamiy lakiy
**The fig tree put forth her green figs and the vines *with the* tender grape give a *good* smell Arise and come away**

7474 רעיתי 3303 יפתי 1980 ולכי 3807a: לך **2:14** 3123 יונתי 2288 בחגוי 5553 הסלע 5643 בסתר
ra'yatiy yapatiy ualkiy lak. younatiy bachaguey hasela', baseter
**my love my fair one and come away to you O my dove *that are* in the clefts of the rock in the secret *places* of**

4095 המדרגה 7200 הראיני 853 את 4758 מראיך 8085 השמיעיני 853 את 6963 קולך 3588 כי 6963 קולך 6156 ערב
hamadaregah, hara'ayniy 'at mar'ayik, hashamiy'ayniy 'at qoulek; kiy qoulek 'areb
**the stairs let me see your countenance let me hear your voice for *is* your voice sweet**

4758 ומראיך 5000: נאוה **2:15** 270 אחזו 3807a לנו 7776 שועלים 7776 שועלים 6996 קטנים 2254 מחבלים 3754 כרמים 3754 וכרמינו
uamar'aeyk naa'ueh. 'achezu lanu shu'aliym, shu'aliym qataniym machabliym karamiym; uakrameynu
**and your countenance *is* comely Take us the foxes foxes *the* little that spoil the vines for our vines**

5563: סמדר **2:16** 1730 דודי 3807a לי 589 ואני 3807a לו 7462 הרעה 7799: בשושנים **2:17** 5704 עד 6315 שיפוח 3117 היום
samadar. doudiy liy ua'aniy lou', hara'ah bashoushaniym. 'ad sheyapuach hayoum,
***have* tender grapes My beloved *is* mine and I *am* his he feed among the lilies Until break the day**

5127 ונסו 6752 הצללים 5437 סב 1819 דמה 3807a לך 1730 דודי 6643 לצבי 176 או 6082 לעפר 354 האילים 5921 על 2022 הרי
uanasu hatzalaliym; so dameh laka doudiy litzbiy, 'au la'aper ha'ayliym 'al harey
**and flee away the shadows turn *and* be like to you my beloved a roe or a young hart upon the mountains of**

Song 2:7 I charge you, O you daughters of Jerusalem, by the roes, and by the hinds of the field, that you stir not up, nor awake my love, till he please.8 The voice of my beloved! behold, he cometh leaping upon the mountains, skipping upon the hills.9 My beloved is like a roe or a young hart: behold, he stand behind our wall, he look forth at the windows, shewing himself through the lattice.10 My beloved spoke, and said unto me, Rise up, my love, my fair one, and come away.11 For, lo, the winter is past, the rain is over and gone;12 The flowers appear on the earth; the time of the singing of birds is come, and the voice of the turtle is heard in our land;13 The fig tree put forth her green figs, and the vines with the tender grape give a good smell. Arise, my love, my fair one, and come away.14 O my dove, that are in the clefts of the rock, in the secret places of the stairs, let me see your countenance, let me hear your voice; for sweet is your voice, and your countenance is comely.15 Take us the foxes, the little foxes, that spoil the vines: for our vines have tender grapes.16 My beloved is mine, and I am his: he feedeth among the lilies.17 Until the day break, and the shadows flee away, turn, my beloved, and be you like a roe or a young hart upon the mountains of Bether.

בתר 1335:
bater.
**Bether**

**Song 3:1** על 5921 משכבי 4904 בלילות 3915 בקשתי 1245 את 853 שאהבה 157 נפשי 5315 בקשתיו 1245 ולא 3808 מצאתיו 4672: **3:2**
'al mishkabiy baleyhout, biqashtiy 'at she'ahabah napshiy; biqashtiyu uala' matza'tiyu.
**on my bed By night I sought him whom love my soul I sought him but not I found him**

אקומה 6965 נא 4994 ואסובבה 5437 בעיר 5892 בשוקים 7784 וברחבות 7339 אבקשה 1245 את 853 שאהבה 157 נפשי 5315
'aqumah naa' ua'asoubah ba'ayr, bashauaqiym uabarachobout, 'abaqshah 'at she'ahabah napshiy;
**I will rise now and go about the city in the streets and in the broad ways I will seek him whom love my soul**

בקשתיו 1245 ולא 3808 מצאתיו 4672: **3:3** מצאוני 4672 השמרים 8104 הסבבים 5437 בעיר 5892 את 853 שאהבה 157 נפשי 5315
biqashtiyu uala' matza'tiyu. matza'uniy hashomariym, hasobabiym ba'ayr; 'at she'ahabah napshiy
**I sought him but not I found him found me The watchmen that go about the city *him* whom love? my soul**

ראיתם 7200: **3:4** כמעט 4592 שעברתי 5674 מהם 1992 עד 5704 שמצאתי 4672 את 853 שאהבה 157 נפשי 5315
ra'aytem. kima'at she'abartiy mehem, 'ad shematza'tiy, 'at she'ahabah napshiy;
***to whom I said* Saw you *It was* but a little that I passed from them but I found him whom love my soul**

אחזתיו 270 ולא 3808 ארפנו 7503 עד 5704 שהביאתיו 935 אל 413 בית 1004 אמי 517 ואל 413 חדר 2315
'achaztiyu uala' 'arpenu, 'ad shehabey'tiyu 'al beyt 'amiy, ua'al cheder
**I held him and not would let him go until I had brought him into house my mother's and into the chamber of**

הורתי 2029: **3:5** השבעתי 7650 אתכם 853 בנות 1323 ירושלם 3389 בצבאות 6643 או 176 באילות 355 השדה 7704
houratiy. hishba'atiy 'atkem banout yarushalaim bitzaba'aut, 'au ba'aylout hasadeh;
**her that conceived me I charge you O you daughters of Jerusalem by the roes or by the hinds of the field**

אם 518 תעירו 5782 ואם 518 תעוררו 5782 את 853 האהבה 160 עד 5704 שתחפץ 2654: **3:6** מי 4310 זאת 2063 עלה 5927 מן 4480 המדבר 4057
'am ta'ayru ua'am ta'auraru 'at ha'ahabah 'ad shetechpatz. miy' za't, 'alah min hamidbar,
**that not you stir up nor awake *my* love till he please Who *is* this that comes out of the wilderness**

כתימרות 8490 עשן 6227 מקטרת 6999 מור 4753 ולבונה 3828 מכל 3605 אבקת 81 רוכל 7402: **3:7** הנה 2009 מטתו 4296
katiymarout 'ashan; maquteret mour ualabounah, mikol 'abqat roukel. hineh, mitatou
**like pillars of smoke perfumed with myrrh and frankincense with all powders of the merchant? Behold his bed**

שלשלמה 8010 ששים 8346 גברים 1368 סביב 5439 לה 3807a מגברי 1368 ישראל 3478: **3:8** כלם 3605 אחזי 270 חרב 2719
shelishalomoh, shishiym giboriym sabiyb lah; migiborey yisra'ael. kulam 'achuzey chereb,
**which *is* Solomon's threescore valiant men *are* about it of the valiant of Israel They all hold swords**

מלמדי 3925 מלחמה 4421 איש 376 חרבו 2719 על 5921 ירכו 3409 מפחד 6343 בלילות 3915: **3:9** אפריון 668 עשה 6213
malumdey milchamah; 'aysh charbou 'al yarekou, mipachad baleyhout. 'apiryoun, 'asah
***being* expert in war every man *has* his sword upon his thigh because of fear in the night a chariot made**

לו 3807a המלך 4428 שלמה 8010 מעצי 6086 הלבנון 3844: **3:10** עמודיו 5982 עשה 6213 כסף 3701 רפידתו 7507 זהב 2091
lou' hamelek shalomoh, me'atzey halabanoun. 'amudayu 'asah kesep, rapiydatou zahab,
**himself King Solomon of wood of the Lebanon the pillars thereof He made *of* silver the bottom thereof *of* gold**

**Song** 3:1 By night on my bed I sought him whom my soul love: I sought him, but I found him not.2 I will rise now, and go about the city in the streets, and in the broad ways I will seek him whom my soul love: I sought him, but I found him not.3 The watchmen that go about the city found me: to whom I said, Saw you him whom my soul love?4 It was but a little that I passed from them, but I found him whom my soul love: I held him, and would not let him go, until I had brought him into my mother's house, and into the chamber of her that conceived me.5 I charge you, O you daughters of Jerusalem, by the roes, and by the hinds of the field, that you stir not up, nor awake my love, till he please.6 Who is this that cometh out of the wilderness like pillars of smoke, perfumed with myrrh and frankincense, with all powders of the merchant?7 Behold his bed, which is Solomon's; threescore valiant men are about it, of the valiant of Israel.8 They all hold swords, being expert in war: every man has his sword upon his thigh because of fear in the night.9 King Solomon made himself a chariot of the wood of Lebanon.10 He made the pillars thereof of silver, the bottom thereof of gold, the covering of it of purple, the midst thereof being paved with love, for the daughters of Jerusalem.

מרכבו 4817 | ארגמן 713 | תוכו 8432 | רצוף 7532 | אהבה 160 | מבנות 1323 | ירושלם 3389: | **3:11** צאינה 3318
merkabou | 'argaman; | toukou | ratzup | 'ahabah, | mibanout | yarushalaim. | tza'aynah
**the covering of it | *of* purple | the midst thereof | being paved | *with* love | for the daughters of | Jerusalem | Go forth**

וראינה 7200 | בנות 1323 | ציון 6726 | במלך 4428 | שלמה 8010 | בעטרה 5850 | שעטרה 5849 | לו 3807a | אמו 517
uar'aynah | banout | tziyoun | bamelek | shalomoh; | ba'atarah, | she'atrah | lou' | 'amou
**and behold | O you daughters of | Zion | king | Solomon | with the crown | crowned | him | *wherewith* his mother**

ביום 3117 | חתנתו 2861 | וביום 3117 | שמחת 8057 | לבו 3820:
bayoum | chatunatou, | uabyoum | simchat | libou.
**in the day of | his espousals | and in the day of | the gladness of | his heart**

**Song 4:1**
הנך 2005 | יפה 3303 | רעיתי 7474 | הנך 2005 | יפה 3303 | עיניך 5869 | יונים 3123 | מבעד 1157 | לצמתך 6777 | שערך 8181
hinak | yapah | ra'yatiy | hinak | yapah, | 'aeynayik | youniym, | miba'ad | latzamatek; | sa'arek
**Behold you | *are* fair | my love | behold you | *are* fair | you *have* eyes | doves' | within | your locks | your hair**

כעדר 5739 | העזים 5795 | שגלשו 1570 | מהר 2022 | גלעד 1568: | **4:2** שניך 8127 | כעדר 5739 | הקצובות 7094
ka'aeder | ha'aziym, | shegalashu | mehar | gil'ad. | shinayik | ka'aeder | haqatzubout,
***is* as a flock of | goats | that appear | from mount | Gilead | Your teeth | *are* like a flock | *of sheep that are even* shorn**

שעלו 5927 | מן 4480 | הרחצה 7367 | שכלם 3605 | מתאימות 8382 | ושכלה 7909 | אין 369 | בהם 871a: | **4:3** כחוט 2339
she'alu | min | harachatzah; | shekulam | mat'aymout, | uashakulah | 'aeyn | bahem. | kachut
**which came up | from | the washing | whereof every | one bear twins | and *is* barren | none | among them | *are* like a thread of**

השני 8144 | שפתתיך 8193 | ומדבריך 4057 | נאוה 5000 | כפלח 6400 | הרמון 7416 | רקתך 7541 | מבעד 1157 | לצמתך 6777: | **4:4**
hashaniy | siptotayik, | uamidbareyk | naa'ueh; | kapelach | harimoun | raqatek, | miba'ad | latzamatek.
**scarlet | Your lips | and your speech | *is* comely | *are* like a piece of | a pomegranate | your temples | within | your locks**

כמגדל 4026 | דויד 1732 | צוארך 6677 | בנוי 1129 | לתלפיות 8530 | אלף 505 | המגן 4043 | תלוי 8518 | עליו 5921 | כל 3605 | שלטי 7982
kamigdal | dauiyd | tzaua'rek, | banuy | latalpiyout; | 'alep | hamagen | taluy | 'alayu, | kal | shiltey
***is* like the tower of | David | Your neck | builded | for an armoury | a thousand | bucklers | there hang | whereon | all | shields of**

הגבורים 1368: | **4:5** שני 8147 | שדיך 7699 | כשני 8147 | עפרים 6082 | תאומי 8380 | צביה 6646 | הרועים 7462 | בשושנים 7799: | **4:6** עד 5704
hagibouriym. | shaney | shadayik | kishney | 'apariym | ta'amey | tzabiyah; | harou'aym | bashoushaniym. | 'ad
**mighty men | two | Your breasts | *are* like two | young | *that are* twins | roes | which feed | among the lilies | Until**

שיפוח 6315 | היום 3117 | ונסו 5127 | הצללים 6752 | אלך 1980 | לי 3807a | אל 413 | הר 2022 | המור 4753 | ואל 413 | גבעת 1389
sheyapuach | hayoum, | uanasu | hatzalaliym; | 'aelek | liy | 'al | har | hamour, | ua'al | gib'at
**break | the day | and flee away | the shadows | I will get | me | to | the mountain of | myrrh | and to | hill of**

הלבונה 3828: | **4:7** כלך 3605 | יפה 3303 | רעיתי 7474 | ומום 3971 | אין 369 | בך 871a: | **4:8** אתי 854 | מלבנון 3844 | כלה 3618 | אתי 854
halabounah. | kulak | yapah | ra'yatiy, | uamum | 'aeyn | bak. | 'atiy | milabanoun | kalah, | 'atiy
**the frankincense | You *are* all | fair | my love | and spot | *there is* no | in you | with me | from Lebanon | *my* spouse | with me**

מלבנון 3844 | תבואי 935 | תשורי 7789 | מראש 2718 | אמנה 549 | מראש 2718 | שניר 8149 | וחרמון 2768 | ממענות 4585 | אריות 738
milabanoun | tabou'ay; | tashuriy | mera'sh | 'amanah, | mera'sh | saniyr | uachermoun, | mima'anout | arayout,
**from Lebanon | Come | look | from the top of | Amana | from the top of | Shenir | and Hermon | from dens | *the* lions'**

Song 3:11 Go forth, O you daughters of Zion, and behold king Solomon with the crown wherewith his mother crowned him in the day of his espousals, and in the day of the gladness of his heart. **Song** 4:1 Behold, you are fair, my love; behold, you are fair; you have doves' eyes within your locks: your hair is as a flock of goats, that appear from mount Gilead.2 Thy teeth are like a flock of sheep that are even shorn, which came up from the washing; whereof everyone bear twins, and none is barren among them.3 Thy lips are like a thread of scarlet, and your speech is comely: your temples are like a piece of a pomegranate within your locks.4 Thy neck is like the tower of David built for an armoury, whereon there hang a thousand bucklers, all shields of mighty men.5 Thy two breasts are like two young roes that are twins, which feed among the lilies.6 Until the day break, and the shadows flee away, I will get me to the mountain of myrrh, and to the hill of frankincense.7 Thou are all fair, my love; there is no spot in you. 8 Come with me from Lebanon, my spouse, with me from Lebanon: look from the top of Amana, from the top of Shenir and Hermon, from the lions' dens, from the mountains of the leopards.

4:9
מהררי 2042 | נמרים 5246: | לבבתני 3823 | אחתי 269 | כלה 3618 | לבבתיני 3823
meharrey | nameriym. | libabtiniy | 'achotiy | kalah; | libabtiyniy
**from the mountains of | the leopards | You have ravished my heart | my sister | *my* spouse | you have ravished my heart**

4:10
באחד 259 | מעיניך 5869 | באחד 259 | ענק 6060 | מצורניך 6677: | מה 4100 | יפו 3302 | דדיך 1730 | אחתי 269 | כלה 3618 | מה 4100 | טבו 2895
ba'achad | me'aeynayik, | ba'achad | 'anaq | mitzauaronayik. | mah | yapu | dodayik | 'achotiy | kalah; | mah | tobu
**with one of your eyes | with one chain | of your neck | How | fair is | your love | my sister | *my* spouse | how | much better is**

4:11
דדיך 1730 | מיין 3196 | וריח 7381 | שמניך 8081 | מכל 3605 | בשמים 1314: | נפת 5317 | תטפנה 5197 | שפתותיך 8193
dodayik | miyayin, | uareyach | shamanayik | mikal | basamiym. | nopet | titopanah | siptoutayik
**your love | than wine | and the smell of | your ointments | than all | spices | *as* the honeycomb | drop | Your lips**

4:12
כלה 3618 | דבש 1706 | וחלב 2461 | תחת 8478 | לשונך 3956 | וריח 7381 | שלמתיך 8008 | כריח 7381 | לבנון 3844:
kalah; | dabash | uachalab | tachat | lashounek, | uareyach | salmotayik | kareyach | labanoun.
**O *my* spouse | honey | and milk | *are* under | your tongue | and the smell of | your garments | *is* like the smell of | Lebanon**

4:13
גן 1588 | נעול 5274 | אחתי 269 | כלה 3618 | גל 1530 | נעול 5274 | מעין 4599 | חתום 2856: | שלחיך 7973 | פרדס 6508
gan | na'aul | 'achotiy | kalah; | gal | na'aul | ma'ayan | chatum. | shalachayik | pardes
**A garden | inclosed | *is* my sister | *my* spouse | a spring | shut up | a fountain | sealed | Your plants | *are* an orchard of**

4:14
רמונים 7416 | עם 5973 | פרי 6529 | מגדים 4022 | כפרים 3724 | עם 5973 | נרדים 5373: | נרד 5373 | וכרכם 3750 | קנה 7070 | וקנמון 7076
rimouniym, | 'am | pariy | magadiym; | kapariym | 'am | naradiym. | nerd | uakarkom, | qaneh | uaqinamoun,
**pomegranates | with | fruits | pleasant | camphire | with | spikenard | Spikenard | and saffron | calamus | and cinnamon**

4:15
עם 5973 | כל 3605 | עצי 6086 | לבונה 3828 | מר 4753 | ואהלות 174 | עם 5973 | כל 3605 | ראשי 7218 | בשמים 1314: | מעין 4599 | גנים 1588 | באר 875
'am | kal | 'atzey | labounah; | mor | ua'ahalout, | 'am | kal | ra'shey | basamiym. | ma'ayan | ganiym, | ba'aer
**with | all | trees of | frankincense | myrrh | and aloes | with | all | the chief spices | A fountain of | gardens | a well of**

4:16
מים 4325 | חיים 2416 | ונזלים 5140 | מן 4480 | לבנון 3844: | עורי 5782 | צפון 6828 | ובואי 935 | תימן 8486 | הפיחי 6315 | גני 1588
mayim | chayiym; | uanozaliym | min | labanoun. | 'auriy | tzapoun | uaboa'ay | teyman, | hapiychiy | ganiy
**waters | living | and streams | from | Lebanon | Awake | O north wind | and come you | south | blow upon | my garden**

יזלו 5140 | בשמיו 1314 | יבא 935 | דודי 1730 | לגנו 1588 | ויאכל 398 | פרי 6529 | מגדיו 4022:
yizlu | basamayu; | yaba' | doudiy | laganou, | uaya'kal | pariy | magadayu.
**may flow out *that* | the spices thereof | Let come | my beloved | into his garden | and eat | fruits | his pleasant**

Song 5:1
באתי 935 | לגני 1588 | אחתי 269 | כלה 3618 | אריתי 717 | מורי 4753 | עם 5973 | בשמי 1314 | אכלתי 398
ba'tiy | laganiy | 'achotiy | kalah | 'ariytiy | mouriy | 'am | basamiy, | 'akaltiy
**I am come | into my garden | my sister | *my* spouse | I have gathered | my myrrh | with | my spice | I have eaten**

יערי 3296 | עם 5973 | דבשי 1706 | שתיתי 8354 | ייני 3196 | עם 5973 | חלבי 2461 | אכלו 398 | רעים 7453 | שתו 8354 | ושכרו 7937
ya'ariy | 'am | dibshiy, | shatiytiy | yeyniy | 'am | chalabiy; | 'aklu | re'aym, | shatu | uashikaru
**my honeycomb | with | my honey | I have drunk | my wine | with | my milk | eat | O friends | drink | yea drink abundantly**

5:2
דודים 1730: | אני 589 | ישנה 3462 | ולבי 3820 | ער 5782 | קול 6963 | דודי 1730 | דופק 1849 | פתחי 6605 | לי 3807a | אחתי 269
doudiym. | 'aniy | yashenah | ualibiy | 'aer; | qoul | doudiy | doupeq, | pitchiy | liy | 'achotiy
**O beloved | I | sleep | but my heart wake | *it is* the voice of | my beloved | that knocketh *saying* | Open | to me | my sister**

Song 4:9 Thou have ravished my heart, my sister, my spouse; you have ravished my heart with one of your eyes, with one chain of your neck.10 How fair is your love, my sister, my spouse! how much better is your love than wine! and the smell of your ointments than all spices!11 Thy lips, O my spouse, drop as the honeycomb: honey and milk are under your tongue; and the smell of your garments is like the smell of Lebanon.12 A garden enclosed is my sister, my spouse; a spring shut up, a fountain sealed.13 Thy plants are an orchard of pomegranates, with pleasant fruits; camphire, with spikenard,14 Spikenard and saffron; calamus and cinnamon, with all trees of frankincense; myrrh and aloes, with all the chief spices:15 A fountain of gardens, a well of living waters, and streams from Lebanon.16 Awake, O north wind; and come, you south; blow upon my garden, that the spices thereof may flow out. Let my beloved come into his garden, and eat his pleasant fruits. **Song** 5:1 I am come into my garden, my sister, my spouse: I have gathered my myrrh with my spice; I have eaten my honeycomb with my honey; I have drunk my wine with my milk: eat, O friends; drink, yea, drink abundantly, O beloved.2 I sleep, but my heart waketh: it is the voice of my beloved that knocketh, saying, Open to me, my sister, my love, my dove, my undefiled:

רעיתי 7474 יונתי 3123 תמתי 8535 שראשי 7218 נמלא 4390 טל 2919 קוצותי 6977 רסיסי 7447 לילה 3915: 5:3 פשטתי 6584
ra'yatiy younatiy tamatiy, shera'shiy nimlaa' tal, qautzoutay rasiysey layalah. pashattiy
**my love my dove my undefiled for my head is filled with dew *and* my locks with the drops of the night I have put off**

את 853 כתנתי 3801 איככה 349 אלבשנה 3847 רחצתי 7364 את 853 רגלי 7272 איככה 349 אטנפם 2936: 5:4 דודי 1730 שלח 7971
'at kutanatiy, 'aeykakah 'albashenah; rachatztiy 'at raglay 'aeykakah 'atanpem. doudiy, shalach
**my coat how shall I put it on? I have washed my feet how shall I defile them? My beloved put in**

ידו 3027 מן 4480 החר 2356 ומעי 4578 המו 1993 עליו 5921: 5:5 קמתי 6965 אני 589 לפתח 6605 לדודי 1730
yadou min hachor, uame'ay hamu 'alayu. qamtiy 'aniy liptoach ladoudiy;
**his hand by the hole *of the door* and my bowels were moved for him rose up I to open to my beloved**

וידי 3027 נטפו 5197 מור 4753 ואצבעתי 676 מור 4753 עבר 5674 על 5921 כפות 3709 המנעול 4514: 5:6 פתחתי 6605
uayaday natapu mour, ua'atzba'autay mour 'aber, 'al kapout hamana'aul. patachtiy
**and my hands dropped *with* myrrh and my fingers myrrh *with* sweet smelling upon the handles of the lock opened**

אני 589 לדודי 1730 ודודי 1730 חמק 2559 עבר 5674 נפשי 5315 יצאה 3318 בדברו 1696 בקשתיהו 1245
'aniy ladoudiy, uadoudiy chamaq 'abar; napshiy yatz'ah badabrou, biqashtiyhu
**I to my beloved but my beloved had withdrawn himself *and* was gone my soul failed when he spoke I sought him**

ולא 3808 מצאתיהו 4672 קראתיו 7121 ולא 3808 ענני 6030: 5:7 מצאני 4672 השמרים 8104 הסבבים 5437 בעיר 5892
uala' matza'tiyhu, qara'tiyu uala' 'ananiy. matza'uniy hashomariym hasobabiym ba'ayr
**but not I could find him I called him but no he gave me answer found me The watchmen that went about the city**

הכוני 5221 פצעוני 6481 נשאו 5375 את 853 רדידי 7289 מעלי 5921 שמרי 8104 החמות 2346: 5:8 השבעתי 7650 אתכם 853
hikuniy patza'auniy; nasa'au 'at radiydiy me'alay, shomrey hachomout. hishba'atiy 'atkem
**they smote me they wounded me took away my veil from me the keepers of the walls I charge you**

בנות 1323 ירושלם 3389 אם 518 תמצאו 4672 את 853 דודי 1730 מה 4100 תגידו 5046 לו 3807a שחולת 2470 אהבה 160 אני 589: 5:9 מה 4100
banout yarushalaim; 'am timtza'au 'at doudiy, mah tagiydu lou', shechoulat 'ahabah 'aniy. mah
**O daughters of Jerusalem if you find my beloved that you tell him that sick of love I *am* What**

דודך 1730 מדוד 1730 היפה 3303 בנשים 802 מה 4100 דודך 1730 מדוד 1730
doudek midoud, hayapah banashiym; mah doudek midoud,
***is* your beloved more than *another* beloved O you fairest among women? what *is* your beloved more than *another* beloved**

שככה 3602 השבעתנו 7650: 5:10 דודי 1730 צח 6703 ואדום 122 דגול 1713 מרבבה 7233: 5:11 ראשו 7218 כתם 3800
shekakah hishba'atanu. doudiy tzach ua'adoum, dagul merababah. ra'shou ketem
**that so youdo charge us? My beloved *is* white and ruddy the chief among ten thousand His head *is as the* most**

פז 6337 קוצותיו 6977 תלתלים 8534 שחרות 7838 כעורב 6158: 5:12 עיניו 5869 כיונים 3123 על 5921 אפיקי 650 מים 4325
paz; qautzoutayu taltaliym, shachorout ka'aureb. 'aeynayu kayouniym 'al 'apiyqey mayim;
**fine gold his locks *are* bushy *and* black as a raven His eyes *are* as *the eyes* of doves by the rivers of waters**

רחצות 7364 בחלב 2461 ישבות 3327 על 5921 מלאת 4402: 5:13 לחיו 3895 כערוגת 6170 הבשם 1314 מגדלות 4026 מרקחים 4840 שפתותיו 8193
rochatzout bechalab, yoshabout 'al milea't. lachayau ka'arugat habosem, migdalout merqachiym; siptoutayu
**washed with milk *and* set beside filty His cheeks *are* as a bed of spices flowers *as* sweet his lips**

Song 5:2 for my head is filled with dew, and my locks with the drops of the night.3 I have put off my coat; how shall I put it on? I have washed my feet; how shall I defile them?4 My beloved put in his hand by the hole of the door, and my bowels were moved for him.5 I rose up to open to my beloved; and my hands dropped with myrrh, and my fingers with sweet smelling myrrh, upon the handles of the lock.6 I opened to my beloved; but my beloved had withdrawn himself, and was gone: my soul failed when he spoke: I sought him, but I could not find him; I called him, but he gave me no answer.7 The watchmen that went about the city found me, they smote me, they wounded me; the keepers of the walls took away my veil from me.8 I charge you, O daughters of Jerusalem, if you find my beloved, that you tell him, that I am sick of love.9 What is your beloved more than another beloved, O you fairest among women? what is your beloved more than another beloved, that you dost so charge us?10 My beloved is white and ruddy, the chief among ten thousand.11 His head is as the most fine gold, his locks are bushy, and black as a raven.12 His eyes are as the eyes of doves by the rivers of waters, washed with milk, and fitly set.13 His cheeks are as a bed of spices, as sweet flowers: his lips like lilies, dropping sweet smelling myrrh.

7799 שושנים | 5197 נטפות | 4753 מור | 5674: עבר | **5:14** | 3027 ידיו | 1550 גלילי | 2091 זהב | 4390 ממלאים | 8658 בתרשיש | 4578 מעיו
shoushaniym, notapout mour 'aber. yadayu galiyley zahab, mamula'aym batarshiysh; me'ayu
***like* lilies dropping myrrh sweet smelling His hands rings *are as* gold set with the beryl his belly**

6247 עשת | 8127 שן | 5968 מעלפת | 5601: ספירים | **5:15** | 7785 שוקיו | 5982 עמודי | 8336 שש | 3245 מיסדים | 5921 על | 134 אדני | 6337 פז
'ashet shen, ma'alepet sapiyriym. shouqayu 'amudey shesh, mayusadiym 'al 'adney paz;
***is as* bright ivory overlaid *with* sapphires His legs *are as* pillars of marble set upon sockets of fine gold**

4758 מראהו | 3844 כלבנון | 977 בחור | 730: כארזים | **5:16** | 2441 חכו | 4477 ממתקים | 3605 וכלו | 4261 מחמדים | 2088 זה
mar'aehu kalabanoun, bachur ka'araziym. chikou mamtaqiym, uakulou machamadiym; zeh
**his countenance *is* as Lebanon excellent as the cedars His mouth *is* most sweet yea he *is* altogether lovely This**

1730 דודי | 2088 וזה | 7453 רעי | 1323 בנות | 3389: ירושלם
doudiy uazeh ra'ay, banout yarushalaim.
***is* my beloved and this my friend O daughters of Jerusalem**

**Song 6:1** | 575 אנה | 1980 הלך | 1730 דודך | 3303 היפה | 802 בנשים | 575 אנה | 6437 פנה | 1730 דודך
'anah halak doudek, hayapah banashiym; 'anah panah doudek,
**Where is gone your beloved O you fairest among women? where is turned aside? your beloved**

1245 ונבקשנו | 5973: עמך | **6:2** | 1730 דודי | 3381 ירד | 1588 לגנו | 6170 לערוגות | 1314 הבשם | 7462 לרעות | 1588 בגנים
uanbaqshenu 'amak. doudiy yarad laganou, la'arugout habosem; lir'aut baganiym,
**that we may seek him with you My beloved is gone down into his garden to the beds of spices to feed in the gardens**

3950 וללקט | 7799: שושנים | **6:3** | 589 אני | 1730 לדודי | 1730 ודודי | 3807a לי | 7462 הרעה | 7799: בשושנים | **6:4** | 3303 יפה | 859 את
ualilqot shoushaniym. 'aniy ladoudiy uadoudiy liy, hara'ah bashoushaniym. yapah 'at
**and to gather lilies I *am* my beloved's and my beloved *is* mine he feed among the lilies *are* beautiful *You***

7474 רעיתי | 8656 כתרצה | 5000 נאוה | 3389 כירושלם | 366 אימה | 1713: כנדגלות | **6:5** | 5437 הסבי | 5869 עיניך | 5048 מנגדי | 1992 שהם
ra'yatiy katirtzah, na'uah kiyarushalaim; 'ayumah kanidgalout. hasebiy 'aeynayik minegdiy, shehem
**O my love as Tirzah comely as Jerusalem terrible as *an army* with banners Turn away your eyes from me for they**

7292 הרהיבני | 8181 שערך | 5739 כעדר | 5795 העזים | 1570 שגלשו | 4480 מן | 5168: הגלעד | **6:6** | 8127 שניך | 5739 כעדר
hirhiybuniy; sa'arek ka'aeder ha'aziym, shegalashu min hagil'ad. shinayik ka'aeder
**have overcome me your hair *is* as a flock of goats that appear from Gilead Your teeth *are* as a flock of**

7353 הרחלים | 5927 שעלו | 4480 מן | 7367 הרחצה | 3605 שכלם | 8382 מתאימות | 7909 ושכלה | 369 אין | 871a: בהם | **6:7**
haracheliym, she'alu min harachatzah; shekulam mat'aymout, uashakulah 'aeyn bahem.
**sheep which go up from the washing whereof every one bear twins and one barren *there is* not among them**

6400 כפלח | 7416 הרמון | 7541 רקתך | 1157 מבעד | 6777: לצמתך | **6:8** | 8346 ששים | 1992 המה | 4436 מלכות | 8084 ושמנים
kapelach harimoun raqatek, miba'ad latzamatek. shishiym hemah malakout, uashmuniym
**As a piece of a pomegranate *are* your temples within your locks threescore There are queens and fourscore**

6370 פילגשים | 5959 ועלמות | 369 אין | 4557: מספר | **6:9** | 259 אחת | 1931 היא | 3123 יונתי | 8535 תמתי | 259 אחת | 1931 היא | 517 לאמה
pilagshiym; ua'alamout 'aeyn mispar. 'achat hiy'a younatiy tamatiy, 'achat hiy'a la'amah,
**concubines and virgins without number *is but* one she My dove my undefiled *is the only* one she of her mother**

Song 5:14 His hands are as gold rings set with the beryl: his belly is as bright ivory overlaid with sapphires.15 His legs are as pillars of marble, set upon sockets of fine gold: his countenance is as Lebanon, excellent as the cedars.16 His mouth is most sweet: yea, he is altogether lovely. This is my beloved, and this is my friend, O daughters of Jerusalem. **Song** 6:1 Whither is your beloved gone, O you fairest among women? whither is your beloved turned aside? that we may seek him with you.2 My beloved is gone down into his garden, to the beds of spices, to feed in the gardens, and to gather lilies.3 I am my beloved's, and my beloved is mine: he feedeth among the lilies.4 Thou are beautiful, O my love, as Tirzah, comely as Jerusalem, terrible as an army with banners.5 Turn away your eyes from me, for they have overcome me: your hair is as a flock of goats that appear from Gilead.6 Thy teeth are as a flock of sheep which go up from the washing, whereof everyone beareth twins, and there is not one barren among them.7 As a piece of a pomegranate are your temples within your locks.8 There are threescore queens, and fourscore concubines, and virgins without number.9 My dove, my undefiled is but one; she is the only one of her mother, she is the choice one of her that bare her.

| ברה 1249 | היא 1931 | ליולדתה 3205 | ראוה 7200 | בנות 1323 | ויאשרוה 833 | מלכות 4436 | ופילגשים 6370 |
|---|---|---|---|---|---|---|---|
| barah | hiy'a | layouladatah; | ra'auha | banout | uaya'ashruha, | malakout | uapiylagshiym |
| ***is*** **the choice** | **she** | ***one*** **of her that bare her** | **saw her** | **The daughters** | **and blessed her** | ***yea*** **the queens** | **and the concubines** |

| ויהללוה 1984: | 6:10 | מי 4310 | זאת 2063 | הנשקפה 8259 | כמו 3644 | שחר 7837 | יפה 3303 | כלבנה 3842 | ברה 1249 | כחמה 2535 |
|---|---|---|---|---|---|---|---|---|---|---|
| uayahalaluha. | | miy' | za't | hanishqapah | kamou | shachar; | yapah | kalabanah, | barah | kachamah, |
| **and they praised her** | | **Who** ***is*** | **this** | ***that*** **looks forth** | **as** | **the morning** | **fair** | **as the moon** | **clear** | **as the sun** |

| אימה 366 | כנדגלות 1713: | 6:11 | אל 413 | גנת 1594 | אגוז 93 | ירדתי 3381 | לראות 7200 | באבי 3 | הנחל 5158 |
|---|---|---|---|---|---|---|---|---|---|
| 'ayumah | kanidgalout. | | 'al | ginat | 'agouz | yaradtiy, | lir'aut | ba'abey | hanachal; |
| ***and*** **terrible** | **as** ***an army*** **with banners?** | | **into** | **the garden of** | **nuts** | **I went down** | **to see** | **the fruits of** | **the valley** |

| לראות 7200 | הפרחה 6524 | הגפן 1612 | הנצו 5132 | הרמנים 7416: | 6:12 | לא 3808 | ידעתי 3045 | נפשי 5315 | שמתני 7760 |
|---|---|---|---|---|---|---|---|---|---|
| lir'aut | haparachah | hagapen, | henetzu | harimoniym. | | la' | yada'tiy, | napshiy | samatniy, |
| ***and*** **to see** | **flourished** | ***whether*** **the vine** | **budded** | ***and*** **the pomegranates** | | ***Or*** **ever** | **I was aware** | **my soul** | **made me** |

| מרכבות 4818 | עמי 5971 | נדיב 5081: | 6:13 | שובי 7725 | שובי 7725 | השולמית 7759 | שובי 7725 | שובי 7725 | ונחזה 2372 | בך 871a | מה 4100 |
|---|---|---|---|---|---|---|---|---|---|---|---|
| markabout | 'amiy | nadiyb. | | shubiy | shubiy | hashulamiyt, | shubiy | shubiy | uanechezeh | bak; | mah |
| ***like*** **the chariots of** | **Ammi** | **nadib** | | **Return** | **return** | **O Shulamite** | **return** | **return** | **that we may look** | **upon you** | **What** |

| תחזו 2372 | בשולמית 7759 | כמחלת 4246 | המחנים 4264: |
|---|---|---|---|
| techazu | bashulamiyt, | kimcholat | hamachanayim. |

**will you see the Shulammite? as it were the company of two armies**

| Song 7:1 | מה 4100 | יפו 3303 | פעמיך 6471 | בנעלים 5275 | בת 1323 | נדיב 5081 | חמוקי 2542 | ירכיך 3409 | כמו 3644 | חלאים 2481 |
|---|---|---|---|---|---|---|---|---|---|---|
| | mah | yapu | pa'amayik | bana'aliym | bat | nadiyb; | chamuqey | yarekayik, | kamou | chala'aym, |
| | **How** | **beautiful** | ***are*** **your feet** | **with shoes** | **daughter** | **O prince's** | **the joints of** | **your thighs** | ***are*** **like** | **jewels** |

| מעשה 4639 | ידי 3027 | אמן 542: | 7:2 | שררך 8326 | אגן 101 | הסהר 5469 | אל 408 | יחסר 2637 | המזג 4197 | בטנך 990 |
|---|---|---|---|---|---|---|---|---|---|---|
| ma'aseh | yadey | 'aman. | | shararek | 'agan | hasahar, | 'al | yechsar | hamazeg; | bitnek |
| **the work of** | **the hands of** | **a cunning workman** | | **Your navel** ***is like*** | **a goblet** | **round** | **not** | ***which*** **want** | **liquor** | **your belly** |

| ערמת 6194 | חטים 2406 | סוגה 5473 | בשושנים 7799: | 7:3 | שני 8147 | שדיך 7699 | כשני 8147 | עפרים 6082 | תאמי 8380 | צביה 6646: | 7:4 |
|---|---|---|---|---|---|---|---|---|---|---|---|
| 'aremat | chitiym, | sugah | bashoushaniym. | | shaney | shadayik | kishney | 'apariym | ta'amey | tzabiyah. | |
| ***is like*** **an heap of** | **wheat** | **set about** | **with lilies** | | **two** | **Your breasts** | ***are*** **like two** | **young** | ***that are*** **twins** | **roes** | |

| צוארך 6677 | כמגדל 4026 | השן 8127 | עיניך 5869 | ברכות 1295 | בחשבון 2809 | על 5921 | שער 8179 | בת 1323 | רבים 7227 | אפך 639 |
|---|---|---|---|---|---|---|---|---|---|---|
| tzaua'rek | kamigdal | hashen; | 'aeynayik | barekout | bacheshboun, | 'al | sha'ar | bat | rabiym, | 'apek |
| **Your neck** | ***is*** **as a tower of** | **ivory** | **your eyes** ***like*** | **the fishpools** | **in Heshbon** | **by** | **the gate of** | **Bath** | **rabbim** | **your nose** |

| כמגדל 4026 | הלבנון 3844 | צופה 6822 | פני 6440 | דמשק 1834: | 7:5 | ראשך 7218 | עליך 5921 | ככרמל 3760 | ודלת 1803 |
|---|---|---|---|---|---|---|---|---|---|
| kamigdal | halabanoun, | tzoupeh | paney | damaseq. | | ra'shek | 'aleyka | kakarmel, | uadalat |
| ***is*** **as tower of** | **the Lebanon** | **which looks** | **toward** | **Damascus** | | **Thine head** | **upon you** | ***is*** **like Carmel** | **and the hair of** |

| ראשך 7218 | כארגמן 713 | מלך 4428 | אסור 631 | ברהטים 7298: | 7:6 | מה 4100 | יפית 3302 | ומה 4100 | נעמת 5276 | אהבה 160 | בתענוגים 8588: |
|---|---|---|---|---|---|---|---|---|---|---|---|
| ra'shek | ka'argaman; | melek | 'asur | barahatiym. | | mah | yapiyt | uamah | na'amt, | 'ahabah | bata'anugiym. |
| **your head** | **like purple** | **the king** | ***is*** **held** | **in the galleries** | | **How** | **fair** | **and how** | **pleasant are you** | **O love** | **for delights** |

Song 6:9 yea, the queens and the concubines, and they praised her.10 Who is she that look forth as the morning, fair as the moon, clear as the sun, and terrible as an army with banners?11 I went down into the garden of nuts to see the fruits of the valley, and to see whether the vine flourished, and the pomegranates budded.12 Or ever I was aware, my soul made me like the chariots of Amminadib.13 Return, return, O Shulamite; return, return, that we may look upon you. What will you see in the Shulamite? As it were the company of two armies. **Song** 7:1 How beautiful are your feet with shoes, O prince's daughter! the joints of your thighs are like jewels, the work of the hands of a cunning workman.2 Thy navel is like a round goblet, which wanteth not liquor: your belly is like an heap of wheat set about with lilies.3 Thy two breasts are like two young roes that are twins.4 Thy neck is as a tower of ivory; your eyes like the fishpools in Heshbon, by the gate of Bath-rabbim: your nose is as the tower of Lebanon which look toward Damascus.5 Thine head upon you is like Carmel, and the hair of your head like purple; the king is held in the galleries.6 How fair and how pleasant are you, O love, for delights!

| 7:7 | | | | | | 7:8 | |
|---|---|---|---|---|---|---|---|
| זאת 2063 | קומתך 6967 | דמתה 1819 | לתמר 8558 | ושדיך 7699 | לאשכלות 811: | אמרתי 559 | אעלה 5927 |
| za't | qoumatek | damatah | latamar, | uashadayik | la'ashkolout. | 'amartiy | 'a'aleh |
| **This** | **your stature** | **is like** | **to a palm tree** | **and your breasts** | **to clusters *of grapes*** | **I said** | **I will go up** |

| | | | | | | | |
|---|---|---|---|---|---|---|---|
| בתמר 8558 | אחזה 270 | בסנסניו 5577 8598 | ויהיו 1961 | נא 4994 | שדיך 7699 | כאשכלות 811 | הגפן 1612 |
| batamar, | 'achazah | basansinayu; | uayihayu | naa' | shadayik | ka'ashkalout | hagapen, |
| **to the palm tree** | **I will take hold** | **of the boughs thereof** | **also shall be** | **now** | **your breasts** | **as clusters of** | **the vine** |

| | | | 7:9 | | | | |
|---|---|---|---|---|---|---|---|
| וריח 7381 | אפך 639 | כתפוחים 8598: | וחכך 2441 | כיין 3196 | הטוב 2896 | הולך 1980 | לדודי 1730 |
| uareyach | 'apek | katapuchiym. | uachikek | kayeyn | hatoub | houlek | ladoudiy |
| **and the smell of** | **your nose** | **like apples** | **And the roof of your mouth** | **like wine** | **the best** | **that goes** | **for my beloved** |

| | | | | 7:10 | | | 7:11 |
|---|---|---|---|---|---|---|---|
| למישרים 4339 | דובב 1680 | שפתי 8193 | ישנים 3462: | אני 589 | לדודי 1730 | ועלי 5921 | תשוקתו 8669: |
| lameysharìym; | doubeb | siptey | yasheniym. | 'aniy | ladoudiy, | ua'alay | tashuqatou. |
| ***down* sweetly** | **causing to speak** | **the lips of** | **those that are asleep** | **I *am*** | **my beloved's** | **and toward me** | **his desire *is*** |

| | | | | | | 7:12 | | |
|---|---|---|---|---|---|---|---|---|
| לכה 1980 | דודי 1730 | נצא 3318 | השדה 7704 | נלינה 3885 | בכפרים 3723: | נשכימה 7925 | לכרמים 3754 | נראה 7200 |
| lakah | doudiy | netzea' | hasadeh, | naliynah | bakpariym. | nashkiymah | lakaramiym, | nir'ah |
| **Come** | **my beloved** | **let us go forth into** | **the field** | **let us lodge in the villages** | | **Let us get up early** | **to the vineyards** | **let us see** |

| | | | | | | | | | | |
|---|---|---|---|---|---|---|---|---|---|---|
| אם 518 | פרחה 6524 | הגפן 1612 | פתח 6605 | הסמדר 5563 | הנצו 5132 | הרמונים 7416 | שם 8033 | אתן 5414 | את 853 | דדי 1730 |
| 'am | parachah | hagapen | pitach | hasamadar, | henetzu | harimouniym; | sham | 'aten | 'at | doday |
| **if** | **flourish** | **the vine** | **appear** | ***whether* the tender grape** | **bud forth** | ***and* the pomegranates** | **there** | **will I give** | | **my loves** |

| | 7:13 | | | | | | | | |
|---|---|---|---|---|---|---|---|---|---|
| לך 3807a: | הדודאים 1736 | נתנו 5414 | ריח 7381 | ועל 5921 | פתחינו 6607 | כל 3605 | מגדים 4022 | חדשים 2319 | גם 1571 |
| lak. | haduda'aym | natanu | reyach, | ua'al | patacheynu | kal | magadiym, | chadashiym | gam |
| **to you** | **The mandrakes** | **give** | **a smell** | **and at** | **our gates** | ***are* all manner of** | **pleasant** | ***fruits* new** | **and again** |

| | | | |
|---|---|---|---|
| ישנים 3465 | דודי 1730 | צפנתי 6845 | לך 3807a: |
| yashaniym; | doudiy | tzapantiy | lak. |
| **old** | **O my beloved *which* I have laid up for you** | | |

| Song 8:1 | | | | | | | | |
|---|---|---|---|---|---|---|---|---|
| מי 4310 | יתנך 5414 | כאח 251 | לי 3807a | יונק 3243 | שדי 7699 | אמי 517 | אמצאך 4672 | בחוץ 2351 |
| miy' | yitenaka | ka'ach | liy, | youneq | shadey | 'amiy; | 'amtza'aka | bachutz |
| **O that** | **you *wert*** | **as brother** | **my** | **that sucked** | **the breasts of** | **my mother** | ***when* I should find you** | **without** |

| | | | | | 8:2 | | | | |
|---|---|---|---|---|---|---|---|---|---|
| אשקך 5401 | גם 1571 | לא 3808 | יבוזו 936 | לי 3807a: | אנהגך 5090 | אביאך 935 | אל 413 | בית 1004 | אמי 517 |
| 'ashaqaka, | gam | la' | yabuzu | liy. | 'anhagaka, | 'abiy'aka | 'al | beyt | 'amiy |
| **I would kiss you** | **yea** | **not** | **should be despised** | **I** | **I would lead you** | ***and* bring you** | **into** | **house** | **my mother's** |

| | | | | | | 8:3 |
|---|---|---|---|---|---|---|
| תלמדני 3925 | אשקך 8248 | מיין 3196 | הרקח 7544 | מעסיס 6071 | רמני 7416: | |
| talamdeniy; | 'ashqaka | miyayin | hareqach, | me'asiys | rimoniy. | |
| ***who* would instruct me** | **I would cause you to drink of** | **wine** | **spiced** | **of the juice of** | **my pomegranate** | |

| | | | | | 8:4 | | |
|---|---|---|---|---|---|---|---|
| שמאלו 8040 | תחת 8478 | ראשי 7218 | וימינו 3225 | תחבקני 2263: | השבעתי 7650 | אתכם 853 | בנות 1323 |
| sama'lou | tachat | ra'shiy, | uiymiynou | tachabqeniy. | hishba'atiy | 'atkem | banout |
| **His left hand *should be*** | **under** | **my head and his right hand should embrace me** | | | **I charge** | **you** | **O daughters of** |

Song 7:7 This your stature is like to a palm tree, and your breasts to clusters of grapes.8 I said, I will go up to the palm tree, I will take hold of the boughs thereof: now also your breasts shall be as clusters of the vine, and the smell of your nose like apples;9 And the roof of your mouth like the best wine for my beloved, that go down sweetly, causing the lips of those that are asleep to speak.10 I am my beloved's, and his desire is toward me.11 Come, my beloved, let us go forth into the field; let us lodge in the villages.12 Let us get up early to the vineyards; let us see if the vine flourish, whether the tender grape appear, and the pomegranates bud forth: there will I give you my loves.13 The mandrakes give a smell, and at our gates are all manner of pleasant fruits, new and old, which I have laid up for you, O my beloved. **Song** 8:1 O that you wert as my brother, that sucked the breasts of my mother! when I should find you without, I would kiss you; yea, I should not be despised.2 I would lead you, and bring you into my mother's house, who would instruct me: I would cause you to drink of spiced wine of the juice of my pomegranate.3 His left hand should be under my head, and his right hand should embrace me.4 I charge you, O daughters of Jerusalem, that you stir not up, nor awake my love, until he please.

8:5

ירושלם 3389 מה 4100 תעירו 5782 ומה 4100 תעררו 5782 את 853 האהבה 160 עד 5704 שתחפץ 2654: מי 4310 זאת 2063 עלה 5927 מן 4480
yarushalaim; mah ta'ayru uamah ta'槽araru 'at ha'ahabah 'ad shetechpatz. miy' za't, 'alah min
**Jerusalem that not you stir up nor awake *my* love until he please Who *is* this that comes up from**

המדבר 4057 מתרפקת 7514 על 5921 דודה 1730 תחת 8478 התפוח 8598 עוררתיך 5782 שמה 8033 חבלתך 2254 אמך 517
hamidbar, mitrapeqet 'al doudah; tachat hatapuach 'aurartiyka, mah chiblataka 'ameka,
**the wilderness leaning upon her beloved? under the apple tree I raise you up there brought you forth your mother**

8:6

שמה 8033 חבלה 2254 ילדתך 3205: שימני 7760 כחותם 2368 על 5921 לבך 3820 כחותם 2368 על 5921 זרועך 2220 כי 3588
shamah chiblah yaladataka. siymeniy kachoutam 'al libeka, kachoutam 'al zarou'aka, kiy
**there she brought you forth *that* bare you Set me as a seal upon your heart as a seal upon your arm for**

עזה 5794 כמות 4194 אהבה 160 קשה 7186 כשאול 7585 קנאה 7068 רשפיה 7565 רשפי 7565 אש 784
'azah kamauet 'ahabah, qashah kisha'aul qin'ah; rashapeyha rishpey 'aesh
***is* strong as death love *is* cruel as the grave jealousy the coals thereof *are* coals of fire**

8:7

שלהבתיה 7957: מים 4325 רבים 7227 לא 3808 יוכלו 3201 לכבות 3518 את 853 האהבה 160 ונהרות 5104 לא 3808
shalhebetyah. mayim rabiym, la' yukalu lakabout 'at ha'ahabah, uanharout la'
***which has a* most vehement flame waters Many not can quench love the floods neither**

ישטפוה 7857 אם 518 יתן 5414 איש 376 את 853 כל 3605 הון 1952 ביתו 1004 באהבה 160 בוז 936 יבוזו 936
yishtapuha; 'am yiten 'aysh 'at kal houn beytou ba'ahabah, bouz yabuzu
**can drown it if would give *a* man all the substance of his house for love it would utterly be contemned**

8:8

לו 3807a: אחות 269 לנו 3807a קטנה 6996 ושדים 7699 אין 369 לה 3807a מה 4100 נעשה 6213 לאחתנו 269 ביום 3117
lou'. achout lanu qatanah, uashadayim 'aeyn lah; mah na'aseh la'achoutenu, bayoum
**to him *have* a sister We little and breasts has no she what shall we do for our sister in the day**

8:9

שידבר 1696 בה 871a: אם 518 חומה 2346 היא 1931 נבנה 1129 עליה 5921 טירת 2918 כסף 3701 ואם 518 דלת 1817
sheyadubar bah. 'am choumah hiy'a, nibneh 'aleyha tiyrat kasep; ua'am delet
**when shall be spoken for she If *be* a wall she we will build upon her a palace of silver and if *be* a door**

8:10

היא 1931 נצור 6696 עליה 5921 לוח 3871 ארז 730: אני 589 חומה 2346 ושדי 7699 כמגדלות 4026 אז 227 הייתי 1961 בעיניו 5869
hiy'a, natzur 'aleyha luach 'arez. 'aniy choumah, uashaday kamigdalout; 'az hayiytiy ba'aeynayu
**she we will inclose her *with* boards of cedar I *am* a wall and my breasts like towers then was I in his eyes**

8:11

כמוצאת 4672 שלום 7965: כרם 3754 היה 1961 לשלמה 8010 בבעל 1174 המון 1995 נתן 5414 את 853 הכרם 3754 לנטרים 5201
kamoutza'aet shaloum. kerem hayah lishalomoh baba'al hamoun, natan 'at hakerem lanotariym;
**as one that found favor a vineyard had Solomon at Baal hamon he let out the vineyard unto keepers**

8:12

איש 376 יבא 935 בפריו 6529 אלף 505 כסף 3701: כרמי 3754 שלי 3807a לפני 6440
'aysh yaba' bapiryou 'alep kasep. karmiy sheliy lapanay;
**every one was to bring for the fruit thereof a thousand *pieces* of silver My vineyard which *is* mine *is* before me**

8:13

האלף 505 לך 3807a שלמה 8010 ומאתים 3967 לנטרים 5201 את 853 פריו 6529: היושבת 3427
ha'alep laka shalomoh, uama'tayim lanotariym 'at piryou. hayoushebet
***must have* a thousand to you O Solomon and two hundred those that keep the fruit thereof You that dwell**

Song 8:5 Who is this that cometh up from the wilderness, leaning upon her beloved? I raised you up under the apple tree: there your mother brought you forth: there she brought you forth that bare you.6 Set me as a seal upon your heart, as a seal upon your arm: for love is strong as death; jealousy is cruel as the grave: the coals thereof are coals of fire, which has a most vehement flame.7 Many waters cannot quench love, neither can the floods drown it: if a man would give all the substance of his house for love, it would utterly be contemned.8 We have a little sister, and she has no breasts: what shall we do for our sister in the day when she shall be spoken for?9 If she be a wall, we will build upon her a palace of silver: and if she be a door, we will inclose her with boards of cedar.10 I am a wall, and my breasts like towers: then was I in his eyes as one that found favor.11 Solomon had a vineyard at Baal-hamon; he let out the vineyard unto keepers; everyone for the fruit thereof was to bring a thousand pieces of silver.12 My vineyard, which is mine, is before me: you, O Solomon, must have a thousand, and those that keep the fruit thereof two hundred.

| | | | | | | | | |
|---|---|---|---|---|---|---|---|---|
| בגנים 1588 | חברים 2270 | מקשיבים 7181 | לקולך 6963 | השמיעני 8085: | **8:14** | ברח 1272 | דודי 1730 | ודמה 1819 |
| baganiym, | chaberiym | maqshiybiym | laqoulek | hashamiy'ayniy. | | barak | doudiy, | uadmeh |
| **in the gardens** | **the companions** | **listen** | **to your voice** | **cause me to hear *it*** | | **Make haste** | **my beloved** | **and be like** |

| | | | | | | | |
|---|---|---|---|---|---|---|---|
| לך 3807a | לצבי 6643 | או 176 | לעפר 6083 | האילים 354 | על 5921 | הרי 2022 | בשמים 1314: |
| laka | litzbiy | 'au | la'aper | ha'ayliym, | 'al | harey | basamiym. |
| **to you** | **to a roe** | **or** | **to young** | **a hart** | **upon** | **the mountains of** | **spices** |

Song 8:13 Thou that dwellest in the gardens, the companions hear to your voice: cause me to hear it.14 Make haste, my beloved, and be you like to a roe or to a young hart upon the mountains of spices.

# ISAIAH
## (*Yashayahu*)

The Book of Isaiah begins the **Major Prophets** from Isaiah through Daniel. The author is identified as the Prophet Isaiah, written between 701 and 681 B.C. Isaiah was called to prophesy to the southern Kingdom, the House of Judah, which was going through times of rebellion against Yahuah's Torah. Isaiah's name in Hebrew means *Yah is salvation.* Isaiah prophesied that Judah was going to be destroyed by Assyria and Egypt. Isaiah proclaimed a message of repentance from sin with a hopeful expectation of Elohim's deliverance as he presented, in undeniable detail, how the messiah would come and suffer for our sin and iniquity described in chapter 53, and yet, come also as the conquering and ruling King and Prince of Peace described in Isaiah 9:6.

**Isaiah 1:1**

| חזון 2377 | ישעיהו 3470 | בן 1121 | אמוץ 531 | אשר 834 | חזה 2372 | על 5921 | יהודה 3063 | וירושלם 3389 | בימי 3117 |
|---|---|---|---|---|---|---|---|---|---|
| chazoun | yasha'yahu | ben | amoutz, | 'asher | chazah, | 'al | yahudah | uiyarushalaim; | biymey |
| **The vision of** | **Isaiah** | **the son of** | **Amoz** | **which** | **he saw** | **concerning** | **Judah** | **and Jerusalem** | **in the days of** |

| עזיהו 5818 | יותם 3147 | אחז 271 | יחזקיהו 2396 | מלכי 4428 | יהודה 3063: | **1:2** שמעו 8085 | שמים 8064 | והאזיני 238 | ארץ 776 | כי 3588 | יהוה 3068 |
|---|---|---|---|---|---|---|---|---|---|---|---|
| 'aziyahu | youtam | 'achaz | yachizqiyahu | malkey | yahudah. | shim'au | shamayim | uaha'aziynim | 'aretz, | kiy | Yahuah |
| **Uzziah** | **Jotham** | **Ahaz** | ***and*** **Hezekiah** | **kings of** | **Judah** | **Hear** | **O heavens** | **and give ear** | **O earth** | **for** | **Yahuah** |

| דבר 1696 | בנים 1121 | גדלתי 1431 | ורוממתי 7311 | והם 1992 | פשעו 6586 | בי 871a: | **1:3** ידע 3045 | שור 7794 | קנהו 7069 |
|---|---|---|---|---|---|---|---|---|---|
| diber; | baniym | gidaltiy | uaroumamtiy, | uahem | pasha'au | biy. | yada' | shour | qonehu, |
| **has spoken** | **children** | **I have nourished** | **and brought up** | **and they** | **have rebelled** | **against me** | **knows** | **The ox** | **his owner** |

| וחמור 2543 | אבוס 18 | בעליו 1167 | ישראל 3478 | לא 3808 | ידע 3045 | עמי 5971 | לא 3808 | התבונן 995: | **1:4** הוי 1945 | גוי 1471 | חטא 2398 | עם 5971 |
|---|---|---|---|---|---|---|---|---|---|---|---|---|
| uachamour | 'aebus | ba'alayu; | yisra'el | la' | yada', | 'amiy | la' | hitbounan. | houy | gouy | chotea', | 'am |
| **and the ass** | **crib** | **his master's** | ***but*** **Israel** | **not** | **does know** | **my people** | **not** | **does consider** | **Ah** | **nation** | **sinful** | **a people** |

| כבד 3515 | עון 5771 | זרע 2233 | מרעים 7489 | בנים 1121 | משחיתים 7843 | עזבו 5800 | את 853 | יהוה 3068 |
|---|---|---|---|---|---|---|---|---|
| kebed | 'auon, | zera' | mere'aym, | baniym | mashchitiym; | 'azabu | 'at | Yahuah |
| **laden with** | **iniquity** | **a seed** | **of evildoers** | **children** | **that are corrupters** | **they have forsaken** | | **Yahuah** |

| נאצו 5006 | את 853 | קדוש 6918 | ישראל 3478 | נזרו 2114 | אחור 268: | **1:5** על 5921 | מה 4100 |
|---|---|---|---|---|---|---|---|
| ni'atzu | 'at | qadoush | yisra'el | nazoru | 'achour. | 'al | meh |
| **they have provoked unto anger** | | ***the*** **Holy One** ***of*** | **Israel** | **they are gone away** | **backward** | **for** | **Why** |

| תכו 5221 | עוד 5750 | תוסיפו 3254 | סרה 5627 | כל 3605 | ראש 7218 | לחלי 2483 | וכל 3605 | לבב 3824 |
|---|---|---|---|---|---|---|---|---|
| tuku | 'aud | tousiypu | sarah; | kal | ra'sh | lachaliy, | uakal | lebab |
| **should you be stricken** | **any more?** | **you will more and more** | **revolt** | **the whole** | **head** | **is sick** | **and the whole** | **heart** |

| דוי 1742: | **1:6** מכף 3709 | רגל 7272 | ועד 5704 | ראש 7218 | אין 369 | בו 871a | מתם 4974 | פצע 6482 | וחבורה 2250 | ומכה 4347 |
|---|---|---|---|---|---|---|---|---|---|---|
| dauay. | mikap | regel | ua'ad | ra'sh | 'aeyn | bou | matom, | petza' | uachaburah | uamakah |
| **faint** | **From the sole of** | **the foot** | **even unto** | **the head** | ***there is*** **no** | **in it** | **soundness** | ***but*** **wounds** | **and bruises** | **and sores** |

| טריה 2961 | לא 3808 | זרו 2115 | ולא 3808 | חבשו 2280 | ולא 3808 | רככה 7401 | בשמן 8081: | **1:7** ארצכם 776 | שממה 8077 |
|---|---|---|---|---|---|---|---|---|---|
| tariyah; | la' | zoru | uala' | chubashu, | uala' | rukakah | bashamen. | 'artzakem | shamamah, |
| **putrifying** | **not** | **they have been closed** | **neither** | **bound up** | **neither** | **mollified** | **with ointment** | **Your country** | ***is*** **desolate** |

| עריכם 5892 | שרפות 8313 | אש 784 | אדמתכם 127 | לנגדכם 5048 | זרים 2114 | אכלים 398 | אתה 853 | ושממה 8077 | כמהפכת 4114 |
|---|---|---|---|---|---|---|---|---|---|
| 'areykem | sarupout | 'aesh; | 'admatkem, | lanegdakem | zariym | 'akliym | 'atah, | uashmamah | kamahpekat |
| **your cities** ***are*** | **burned with** | **fire** | **your land** | **in your presence** | **strangers** | **devour** | **it** | **and** ***it is*** **desolate** | **as overthrown by** |

**Isaiah** 1:1 The vision of Isaiah the son of Amoz, which he saw concerning Judah and Jerusalem in the days of Uzziah, Jotham, Ahaz, and Hezekiah, kings of Judah.2 Hear, O heavens, and give ear, O earth: for YHUH has spoken, I have nourished and brought up children, and they have rebelled against me.3 The ox know his owner, and the ass his master's crib: but Israel doth not know, my people doth not consider.4 Ah sinful nation, a people laden with iniquity, a seed of evildoers, children that are corrupters: they have forsaken YHUH, they have provoked the Holy One of Israel unto anger, they are gone away backward.5 Why should you be stricken anymore? you will revolt more and more: the whole head is sick, and the whole heart faint.6 From the sole of the foot even unto the head there is no soundness in it; but wounds, and bruises, and putrifying sores: they have not been closed, neither bound up, neither mollified with ointment.7 Your country is desolate, your cities are burned with fire: your land, strangers devour it in your presence, and it is desolate, as overthrown by strangers.

| | 1:8 | | | | | | | | |
|---|---|---|---|---|---|---|---|---|---|
| זרים 2114: | | ונותרה 3498 | בת 1323 | ציון 6726 | כסכה 5521 | בכרם 3754 | כמלונה 4412 | במקשה 4750 | כעיר 5892 |
| zariym. | | uanoutarah | bat | tziyoun | kasukah | bakarem; | kimlunah | bamiqshah | ka'ayr |
| **strangers** | | **And is left** | **the daughter of** | **Zion** | **as a cottage** | **in a vineyard** | **as a lodge** | **in a garden of cucumbers** | **as a city** |

| | 1:9 | | | | | | | | | |
|---|---|---|---|---|---|---|---|---|---|---|
| נצורה 5341: | | לולי 3884 | יהוה 3068 | צבאות 6635 | הותיר 3498 | לנו 3807a | שריד 8300 | כמעט 4592 | כסדם 5467 | היינו 1961 |
| natzurah. | | luley | Yahuah | tzaba'aut, | houtiyr | lanu | sariyd | kima'at; | kisadom | hayiynu, |
| **besieged** | | **Except** | **Yahuah** | **of hosts** | **had left** | **unto us** | **a remnant** | **very small** | **as Sodom** | **we should have been *like*** |

| | | 1:10 | | | | | | | |
|---|---|---|---|---|---|---|---|---|---|
| לעמרה 6017 | דמינו 1819: | | שמעו 8085 | דבר 1697 | יהוה 3069 | קציני 7101 | סדם 5467 | האזינו 238 | תורת 8451 |
| la'amorah | damiynu. | | shim'au | dabar | Yahuah | qatziyney | sadom; | ha'aziynu | tourat |
| **unto Gomorrah** | ***and* we should have been** | | **Hear** | **the word of** | **Yahuah** | **you rulers of** | **Sodom** | **give ear unto** | **the law of** |

| | | | 1:11 | | | | | | |
|---|---|---|---|---|---|---|---|---|---|
| אלהינו 430 | עם 5971 | עמרה 6017: | | למה 4100 | לי 3807a | רב 7230 | זבחיכם 2077 | יאמר 559 | יהוה 3068 |
| 'aloheynu | 'am | 'amorah. | | lamah | liy | rab | zibcheykem | ya'mar | Yahuah, |
| **our Elohim** | **you people of** | **Gomorrah** | | **To what** | **unto me?** | ***purpose is* the multitude of** | **your sacrifices** | **saith** | **Yahuah** |

| | | | | | | | | |
|---|---|---|---|---|---|---|---|---|
| שבעתי 7646 | עלות 5930 | אילים 352 | וחלב 2459 | מריאים 4806 | ודם 1818 | פרים 6499 | וכבשים 3532 | ועתודים 6260 |
| saba'atiy | 'alout | 'aeyliym | uacheleb | mariy'aym; | uadam | pariym | uakbasiym | ua'atudiym |
| **I am full of** | **the burnt offerings of** | **rams** | **and the fat of** | **fed beasts** | **and the blood of** | **bullocks** | **or of lambs** | **or of he goats** |

| | | 1:12 | | | | | | | | | |
|---|---|---|---|---|---|---|---|---|---|---|---|
| לא 3808 | חפצתי 2654: | | כי 3588 | תבאו 935 | לראות 7200 | פני 6440 | מי 4310 | בקש 1245 | זאת 2063 | מידכם 3027 | רמס 7429 |
| la' | chapatzatiy. | | kiy | tabo'au, | lera'aut | panay; | miy' | biqesh | za't | miyedkem | ramos |
| **not** | **I delight in** | | **When** | **you come** | **to appear** | **before me** | **who** | **has required** | **this** | **at your hand** | **to tread** |

| | 1:13 | | | | | | | | | | |
|---|---|---|---|---|---|---|---|---|---|---|---|
| חצרי 2691: | | לא 3808 | תוסיפו 3254 | הביא 935 | מנחת 4503 | שוא 7723 | קטרת 7004 | תועבה 8441 | היא 1931 | לי 3807a | חדש 2320 |
| chatzeray. | | la' | tousiypu, | habiy'a | minchat | shau'a, | qatoret | tou'aebah | hiy'a | liy; | chodesh |
| **my courts?** | | **no** | **more** | **Bring** | **oblations** | **vain** | **incense** | ***is* an abomination** | **he** | **unto me** | **the new moons** |

| | | | | | | | 1:14 | |
|---|---|---|---|---|---|---|---|---|
| ושבת 7676 | קרא 7121 | מקרא 4744 | לא 3808 | אוכל 3201 | און 205 | ועצרה 6116: | | חדשיכם 2320 |
| uashabat | qara' | miqraa', | la' | 'aukal | 'auen | ua'atzarah. | | chadasheykem |
| **and sabbaths** | **the calling of** | **assemblies** | **cannot** | **I away with** | ***it is* iniquity** | **even the solemn meeting** | | **Your new moons** |

| | | | | | | | | 1:15 |
|---|---|---|---|---|---|---|---|---|
| ומועדיכם 4150 | שנאה 8130 | נפשי 5315 | היו 1961 | עלי 5921 | לטרח 2960 | נלאיתי 3811 | נשא 5375: | |
| uamou'adeykem | sana'ah | napshiy, | hayu | 'alay | latorach; | nil'aeytiy | nasa'. | |
| **and your appointed feasts** | **hate** | **my soul** | **they are** | **unto me** | **a trouble** | **I am weary** | **to bear *them*** | |

| | | | | | | | | | |
|---|---|---|---|---|---|---|---|---|---|
| ובפרשכם 6566 | כפיכם 3709 | אעלים 5956 | עיני 5869 | מכם 4480 | גם 1571 | כי 3588 | תרבו 7235 | תפלה 8605 | אינני 369 |
| uabpariskem | kapeykem, | 'a'liym | 'aeynay | mikem, | gam | kiy | tarbu | tapilah | 'aeyneniy |
| **And when you spread forth** | **your hands** | **I will hide** | **mine eyes** | **from you** | **yea** | **when** | **you make many** | **prayers** | **I not** |

| | | | | 1:16 | | | | | | |
|---|---|---|---|---|---|---|---|---|---|---|
| שמע 8085 | ידיכם 3027 | דמים 1818 | מלאו 4390: | | רחצו 7364 | הזכו 2135 | הסירו 5493 | רע 7455 | מעלליכם 4611 | מנגד 5048 |
| shomea'; | yadeykem | damiym | male'au. | | rachatzu | hizaku, | hasiyru | roa' | ma'alleykem | mineged |
| **will hear** | **your hands** | **blood** | **are full of** | | **Wash you** | **make you clean** | **put away** | **the evil of** | **your doings** | **from before** |

| | | | 1:17 | | | | | | | | |
|---|---|---|---|---|---|---|---|---|---|---|---|
| עיני 5869 | חדלו 2308 | הרע 7489: | | למדו 3925 | היטב 3190 | דרשו 1875 | משפט 4941 | אשרו 833 | חמוץ 2541 | שפטו 8199 | יתום 3490 |
| 'aeynay; | chidlu | harea'. | | limdu | heyteb | dirshu | mishapat | 'ashru | chamoutz; | shiptu | yatoum, |
| **mine eyes** | **cease** | **to do evil** | | **Learn** | **to do well** | **seek** | **judgment** | **relieve** | **the oppressed** | **judge** | **the fatherless** |

Isa 1:8 And the daughter of Zion is left as a cottage in a vineyard, as a lodge in a garden of cucumbers, as a besieged city.9 Except YHUH of hosts had left unto us a very small remnant, we should have been as Sodom, and we should have been like unto Gomorrah.10 Hear the word of YHUH, you rulers of Sodom; give ear unto the law of our G-d, you people of Gomorrah.11 To what purpose is the multitude of your sacrifices unto me? saith YHUH: I am full of the burnt offerings of rams, and the fat of fed beasts; and I delight not in the blood of bullocks, or of lambs, or of he goats.12 When you come to appear before me, who has required this at your hand, to tread my courts?13 Bring no more vain oblations; incense is an abomination unto me; the new moons and sabbaths, the calling of assemblies, I cannot away with; it is iniquity, even the solemn meeting.14 Your new moons and your appointed feasts my soul hateth: they are a trouble unto me; I am weary to bear them.15 And when you spread forth your hands, I will hide mine eyes from you: yea, when you make many prayers, I will not hear: your hands are full of blood.16 Wash you, make you clean; put away the evil of your doings from before mine eyes; cease to do evil;17 Learn to do well; seek judgment, relieve the oppressed, judge the fatherless, plead for the widow.

1:18

| ריבו 7378 | אלמנה 490: | לכו 1980 | נא 4994 | ונוכחה 3198 | יאמר 559 | יהוה 3068 | אם 518 | יהיו 1961 | חטאיכם 2399 | כשנים 8144 |
|---|---|---|---|---|---|---|---|---|---|---|
| riybu | 'almanah. | laku | naa' | uaniuakachah | ya'mar | Yahuah; | 'am | yihayu | chata'aeykem | kashaniym |
| **plead for** | **the widow** | **Come** | **now** | **and let us reason together** | **saith** | **Yahuah** | **though** | **be** | **your sins** | **as scarlet** |

1:19

| כשלג 7950 | ילבינו 3835 | אם 518 | יאדימו 119 | כתולע 8438 | כצמר 6785 | יהיו 1961: | אם 518 | תאבו 14 |
|---|---|---|---|---|---|---|---|---|
| kasheleg | yalbiynu, | 'am | ya'adiymu | katoula' | katzemer | yihayu. | 'am | ta'bu |
| **as snow** | **they shall be as white** | **though** | **they be red** | **like crimson** | **as wool** | **they shall be** | **If** | **you be willing** |

1:20

| ושמעתם 8085 | טוב 2896 | הארץ 776 | תאכלו 398: | ואם 518 | תמאנו 3985 | ומריתם 4784 | חרב 2719 | תאכלו 398 |
|---|---|---|---|---|---|---|---|---|
| uashma'tem; | toub | ha'aretz | ta'kelu. | ua'am | tama'anu | uamriytem; | chereb | ta'aklu, |
| **and obedient** | **the good of** | **the land** | **you shall eat** | **But if** | **you refuse** | **and rebel** | ***with* the sword** | **you shall be devoured** |

1:21

| כי 3588 | פי 6310 | יהוה 3068 | דבר 1696: | איכה 349 | היתה 1961 | לזונה 2181 | קריה 7151 | נאמנה 539 | מלאתי 4395 | משפט 4941 |
|---|---|---|---|---|---|---|---|---|---|---|
| kiy | piy | Yahuah | diber. | 'aeykah | hayatah | lazounah, | qiryah | ne'amanah; | male'atiy | mishapat, |
| **for** | **the mouth of** | **Yahuah** | **has spoken *it*** | **How** | **is become** | **an harlot** | **city** | ***the* faithful *it was*** | **full of** | **judgment** |

1:22 1:23

| צדק 6664 | ילין 3885 | בה 871a | ועתה 6258 | מרצחים 7523: | כספך 3701 | היה 1961 | לסיגים 5509 | סבאך 5435 | מהול 4107 | במים 4325: |
|---|---|---|---|---|---|---|---|---|---|---|
| tzedeq | yaliyn | bah | ua'atah | maratzchiym. | kaspek | hayah | lasiygiym; | saba'aek | mahul | bamayim. |
| **righteousness** | **lodged** | **in it** | **but now** | **murderers** | **Your silver** | **is become** | **dross** | **your wine** | **mixed** | **with water** |

| שריך 8269 | סוררים 5637 | וחברי 2270 | גנבים 1590 | כלו 3605 | אהב 157 | שחד 7810 | ורדף 7291 | שלמנים 8021 |
|---|---|---|---|---|---|---|---|---|
| sarayik | sourariym, | uachabrey | ganabiym, | kulou | 'aheb | shochad, | uarodep | shalmoniym; |
| **Your princes** | ***are* rebellious** | **and companions of** | **thieves** | **every one** | **love** | **gifts** | **and follows after** | **rewards** |

1:24

| יתום 3490 | לא 3808 | ישפטו 8199 | וריב 7379 | אלמנה 490 | לא 3808 | יבוא 935 | אליהם 413: | לכן 3651 | נאם 5002 | האדון 113 |
|---|---|---|---|---|---|---|---|---|---|---|
| yatoum | la' | yishpotu, | uariyb | 'almanah | la' | yabou'a | 'aleyhem. | laken, | na'am | ha'adoun |
| **the fatherless** | **not** | **they judge** | **the cause of** | **the widow** | **neither** | **does come** | **unto them** | **Therefore** | **saith** | **Adonai** |

| יהוה 3068 | צבאות 6635 | אביר 46 | ישראל 3478 | הוי 1945 | אנחם 5162 | מצרי 6862 | ואנקמה 5358 |
|---|---|---|---|---|---|---|---|
| Yahuah | tzaba'aut, | 'abiyr | yisra'ael; | houy | 'anachem | mitzaray, | ua'anaqamah |
| **Yahuah** | **of hosts** | **the mighty One of** | **Israel** | **Ah** | **I will ease me** | **of mine adversaries** | **and avenge me** |

1:25

| מאויבי 341: | ואשיבה 7725 | ידי 3027 | עליך 5921 | ואצרף 6884 | כבר 1252 | סיגיך 5509 | ואסירה 5493 | כל 3605 |
|---|---|---|---|---|---|---|---|---|
| me'auyabay. | ua'ashiybah | yadiy | 'alayik, | ua'atzrop | kabor | siygayik; | ua'asiyrah | kal |
| **of mine enemies** | **And I will turn** | **my hand** | **upon you** | **and purge away** | **purely** | **your dross** | **and take away** | **all** |

1:26

| בדיליך 913: | ואשיבה 7725 | שפטיך 8199 | כבראשנה 7223 | ויעציך 3289 | כבתחלה 8462 | אחרי 310 | כן 3651 |
|---|---|---|---|---|---|---|---|
| badiylayik. | ua'ashiybah | shopatayik | kabara'shonah, | uayo'atzayik | kabatchilah; | 'acharey | ken, |
| **your tin** | **And I will restore** | **your judges** | **as at the first** | **and your counsellors** | **as at the beginning** | **afterward** | **so** |

1:27

| יקרא 7121 | לך 3807a | עיר 5892 | הצדק 6664 | קריה 7151 | נאמנה 539: | ציון 6726 | במשפט 4941 | תפדה 6299 |
|---|---|---|---|---|---|---|---|---|
| yiqaraea' | lak | 'ayr | hatzedeq, | qiryah | ne'amanah. | tziyoun | bamishpat | tipadeh; |
| **shall be called** | **to you** | **city of** | **The righteousness** | **city** | ***the* faithful** | **Zion** | **with judgment** | **shall be redeemed** |

1:28

| ושביה 7725 | בצדקה 6666: | ושבר 7667 | פשעים 6586 | וחטאים 2400 | יחדו 3162 |
|---|---|---|---|---|---|
| uashabeyha | bitzadaqah. | uasheber | posha'aym | uachata'aym | yachdau; |
| **and her converts** | **with righteousness** | **And the destruction of** | **the transgressors** | **and of the sinners** | ***shall be* together** |

Isa 1:18 Come now, and let us reason together, saith YHUH: though your sins be as scarlet, they shall be as white as snow; though they be red like crimson, they shall be as wool.19 If you be willing and obedient, you shall eat the good of the land:20 But if you refuse and rebel, you shall be devoured with the sword: for the mouth of YHUH has spoken it.21 How is the faithful city become an harlot! it was full of judgment; righteousness lodged in it; but now murderers.22 Thy silver is become dross, your wine mixed with water:23 Thy princes are rebellious, and companions of thieves: everyone love gifts, and followed after rewards: they judge not the fatherless, neither doth the cause of the widow come unto them.24 Therefore saith the Adonai, YHUH of hosts, the mighty One of Israel, Ah, I will ease me of mine adversaries, and avenge me of mine enemies:25 And I will turn my hand upon you, and purely purge away your dross, and take away all your tin:26 And I will restore your judges as at the first, and your counsellers as at the beginning: afterward you shall be called, The city of righteousness, the faithful city.27 Zion shall be redeemed with judgment, and her converts with righteousness.28 And the destruction of the transgressors and of the sinners shall be together, and they that forsake YHUH shall be consumed.

| ועזבי 5800 | יהוה 3068 | יכלו 3615: | 1:29 כי 3588 | יבשו 954 | מאילים 352 | אשר 834 | חמדתם 2530 |
|---|---|---|---|---|---|---|---|
| ua'azabey | Yahuah | yiklu. | kiy | yeboshu, | me'aeyliym | 'asher | chamadtem; |
| **and they that forsake** | **Yahuah** | **shall be consumed** | **For** | **they shall be ashamed** | **of the oaks** | **which** | **you have desired** |

| ותחפרו 2659 | מהגנות 1593 | אשר 834 | בחרתם 977: | 1:30 כי 3588 | תהיו 1961 | כאלה 424 | נבלת 5034 | עלה 5929 |
|---|---|---|---|---|---|---|---|---|
| uatachparu, | mehaganout | 'asher | bacharatem. | kiy | tihayu, | ka'aelah | nobelet | 'aleha; |
| **and you shall be confounded** | **for the gardens** | **that** | **you have chosen** | **For** | **you shall be** | **as an oak** | **fade** | **whose leaf** |

| וכגנה 1593 | אשר 834 | מים 4325 | אין 369 | לה 3807a: | 1:31 והיה 1961 | החסן 2634 | לנערת 5296 | ופעלו 6467 | לניצוץ 5213 |
|---|---|---|---|---|---|---|---|---|---|
| uakganah, | 'asher | mayim | 'aeyn | lah. | uahayah | hechason | lin'aret, | uapo'alou | laniytzoutz; |
| **and as a garden** | **that** | **water** | **no** | **has** | **And shall be** | **the strong** | **as tow** | **and the maker of it** | **as a spark** |

| ובערו 1197 | שניהם 8147 | יחדו 3162 | ואין 369 | מכבה 3518: |
|---|---|---|---|---|
| uaba'aru | shaneyhem | yachdau | ua'aeyn | makabeh. |
| **and they shall burn** | **both** | **together** | **and none** | **shall quench *them*** |

| **Isa 2:1** | הדבר 1697 | אשר 834 | חזה 2372 | ישעיהו 3470 | בן 1121 | אמוץ 531 | על 5921 | יהודה 3063 | וירושלם 3389: | **2:2** |
|---|---|---|---|---|---|---|---|---|---|---|
| | hadabar | 'asher | chazah, | yasha'yahu | ben | amoutz; | 'al | yahudah | uiyarushalaim. | |
| | **The word** | **that** | **saw** | **Isaiah** | **the son of** | **Amoz** | **concerning** | **Judah** | **and Jerusalem** | |

| והיה 1961 | באחרית 319 | הימים 3117 | נכון 3559 | יהיה 1961 | הר 2022 | בית 1004 | יהוה 3068 | בראש 7218 |
|---|---|---|---|---|---|---|---|---|
| uahayah | ba'achariyt | hayamiym, | nakoun | yihayeh | har | beyt | Yahuah | bara'sh |
| **And it shall come to pass** | **in last** | **the days** | **established** | **shall be** | ***that* the mountain of** | **house** | **Yahuah's** | **in the top of** |

| ההרים 2022 | ונשא 5375 | מגבעות 1389 | ונהרו 5102 | אליו 413 | כל 3605 | הגוים 1471: | 2:3 והלכו 1980 | עמים 5971 | רבים 7227 |
|---|---|---|---|---|---|---|---|---|---|
| hehariym, | uanisa' | migba'aut; | uanaharu | 'aelayu | kal | hagouyim. | uahalaku | 'amiym | rabiym, |
| **the mountains** | **and shall be exalted** | **above the hills** | **and shall flow** | **unto it** | **all** | **nations** | **And shall go** | **people** | **many** |

| ואמרו 559 | לכו 1980 | ונעלה 5927 | אל 413 | הר 2022 | יהוה 3069 | אל 413 | בית 1004 | אלהי 430 | יעקב 3290 |
|---|---|---|---|---|---|---|---|---|---|
| ua'amaru | laku | uana'aleh | 'al | har | Yahuah | 'al | beyt | 'alohey | ya'aqob, |
| **and say** | **Come you** | **and let us go up** | **to** | **the mountain of** | **Yahuah** | **to** | **to the house of** | **the Elohim of** | **Jacob** |

| וירנו 3384 | מדרכיו 1870 | ונלכה 1980 | בארחתיו 734 | כי 3588 | מציון 6726 | תצא 3318 | תורה 8451 | ודבר 1697 |
|---|---|---|---|---|---|---|---|---|
| uayorenu | midrakayu, | uanelakah | ba'arachotayu; | kiy | mitziyoun | tetzea' | tourah, | uadbar |
| **and he will teach us** | **of his ways** | **and we will walk** | **in his paths** | **for** | **out of Zion** | **shall go forth** | **the law** | **and the word of** |

| יהוה 3069 | מירושלם 3389: | 2:4 ושפט 8199 | בין 996 | הגוים 1471 | והוכיח 3198 | לעמים 5971 | רבים 7227 | וכתתו 3807 |
|---|---|---|---|---|---|---|---|---|
| Yahuah | miyarushalaim. | uashapat | beyn | hagouyim, | uahoukiyach | la'amiym | rabiym; | uakitatu |
| **Yahuah** | **from Jerusalem** | **And he shall judge** | **among** | **the nations** | **and shall rebuke** | **people** | **many** | **and they shall beat** |

| חרבותם 2719 | לאתים 855 | וחניתותיהם 2595 | למזמרות 4211 | לא 3808 | ישא 5375 | גוי 1471 | אל 413 | גוי 1471 | חרב 2719 |
|---|---|---|---|---|---|---|---|---|---|
| charboutam | la'atiym, | uachaniytouteyhem | lamazmerout, | la' | yisa' | gouy | 'al | gouy | chereb, |
| **their swords** | **into plowshares** | **and their spears** | **into pruninghooks** | **not** | **shall lift up** | **nation** | **against** | **nation** | **sword** |

| ולא 3808 | ילמדו 3925 | עוד 5750 | מלחמה 4421: | 2:5 בית 1004 | יעקב 3290 | לכו 1980 | ונלכה 1980 | באור 216 |
|---|---|---|---|---|---|---|---|---|
| uala' | yilmadu | 'aud | milchamah. | beyt | ya'aqob; | laku | uanelakah | ba'aur |
| **and neither** | **shall they learn** | **any more** | **war** | **O house of** | **Jacob** | **come you** | **and let us walk** | **in the light of** |

Isa 1:29 For they shall be ashamed of the oaks which you have desired, and you shall be confounded for the gardens that you have chosen.30 For you shall be as an oak whose leaf fadeth, and as a garden that has no water.31 And the strong shall be as tow, and the maker of it as a spark, and they shall both burn together, and none shall quench them.
**Isa** 2:1 the word that Isaiah the son of Amoz saw concerning Judah and Jerusalem.2 And it shall come to pass in the last days, that the mountain of YHUH's house shall be established in the top of the mountains, and shall be exalted above the hills; and all nations shall flow unto it.3 And many people shall go and say, Come you, and let us go up to the mountain of YHUH, to the house of the G-d of Jacob; and he will teach us of his ways, and we will walk in his paths: for out of Zion shall go forth the law, and the word of YHUH from Jerusalem.4 And he shall judge among the nations, and shall rebuke many people: and they shall beat their swords into plowshares, and their spears into pruninghooks: nation shall not lift up sword against nation, neither shall they learn war anymore.5 O house of Jacob, come you, and let us walk in the light of YHUH.

2:6

יהוה 3068: | כי 3588 | נטשתה 5203 | עמך 5971 | בית 1004 | יעקב 3290 | כי 3588 | מלאו 4390 | מקדם 6924
Yahuah. | kiy | natashtah, | 'amaka | beyt | ya'aqob, | kiy | mala'au | miqedem,
**Yahuah** | **Therefore** | **you have forsaken** | **your people** | **the house of** | **Jacob** | **because** | **they be replenished** | **from the east**

ועננים 6049 | כפלשתים 6430 | ובילדי 3206 | נכרים 5237 | ישפיקו 5606: | 2:7 ותמלא 4390 | ארצו 776
ua'ananiym | kapalishtiym; | uabyaldey | nakariym | yaspiyqu. | uatimalea' | artzou
**and *are* soothsayers** | **like the Philistines** | **and in the children of** | **strangers** | **they please themselves** | **also is full** | **Their land**

כסף 3701 | וזהב 2091 | ואין 369 | קצה 7097 | לאצרתיו 214 | ותמלא 4390 | ארצו 776 | סוסים 5483 | ואין 369 | קצה 7097
kesep | uazahab, | ua'aeyn | qetzeh | la'atzarotayu; | uatimalea' | artzou | susiym, | ua'aeyn | qetzeh
***of* silver** | **and gold** | **and neither** | ***is there any* end** | **of their treasures** | **is also full** | **their land** | ***of* horses** | **neither** | ***is there any* end**

למרכבתיו 4818: | 2:8 ותמלא 4390 | ארצו 776 | אלילים 457 | למעשה 4639 | ידיו 3027 | ישתחוו 7812 | לאשר 834 | עשו 6213
lamarkabotayu. | uatimalea' | artzou | 'aliyliym; | lama'aseh | yadayu | yishtachauu, | la'asher | 'asu
**of their chariots** | **also is full** | **Their land** | ***of* idols** | **the work of** | **their own hands** | **they worship** | **that which** | **have made**

אצבעתיו 676: | 2:9 וישח 7817 | אדם 120 | וישפל 8213 | איש 376 | ואל 408 | תשא 5375 | להם 3807a: 2:10
'atzba'atayu. | uayishach | 'adam | uayishpal | 'aysh; | ua'al | tisa' | lahem.
**their own fingers** | **And bows down** | **the *mean* man** | **and humble himself** | **the great man** | **therefore not** | **forgive** | **them**

בוא 935 | בצור 6697 | והטמן 2934 | בעפר 6083 | מפני 6440 | פחד 6343 | יהוה 3068 | ומהדר 1926 | גאנו 1347: | 2:11 עיני 5869
bou'a | batzur, | uahitamen | be'apar; | mipaney | pachad | Yahuah, | uamehadar | ga'anou. | 'aeyney
**Enter** | **into the rock** | **and hide you** | **in the dust** | **for** | **fear of** | **Yahuah** | **and for the glory of** | **his majesty** | **looks of**

גבהות 1365 | אדם 120 | שפל 8213 | ושח 7817 | רום 7312 | אנשים 582 | ונשגב 7682 | יהוה 3068
gabhut | 'adam | shapel, | uashach | rum | 'anashiym; | uanisgab | Yahuah
**The lofty** | **man** | **shall be humbled** | **and shall be bowed down** | **the haughtiness of** | **men** | **and shall be exalted** | **Yahuah**

לבדו 905 | ביום 3117 | ההוא 1931: | 2:12 כי 3588 | יום 3117 | ליהוה 3068 | צבאות 6635 | על 5921 | כל 3605 | גאה 1343 | ורם 7311 | ועל 5921
labadou | bayoum | hahua'. | kiy | youm | laYahuah | tzaba'aut | 'al | kal | ge'ah | uaram; | ua'al
**alone** | **in day** | **that** | **For** | **the day** | **of Yahuah** | **of hosts *shall be*** | **upon** | **every one** | ***that is* proud** | **and lofty** | **and upon**

כל 3605 | נשא 5375 | ושפל 8213: | 2:13 ועל 5921 | כל 3605 | ארזי 730 | הלבנון 3844 | הרמים 7311
kal | nisa' | uashapel. | ua'al | kal | 'arzey | halabanoun, | haramiym
**every one** | ***that is* lifted up** | **and he shall be brought low** | **And upon** | **all** | **cedars of** | **the Lebanon** | ***that are* high**

והנשאים 5375 | ועל 5921 | כל 3605 | אלוני 437 | הבשן 1316: | 2:14 ועל 5921 | כל 3605 | ההרים 2022 | הרמים 7311 | ועל 5921 | כל 3605 | הגבעות 1389
uahanisa'aym; | ua'al | kal | 'alouney | habashan. | ua'al | kal | hehariym | haramiym; | ua'al | kal | hagaba'aut
**and lifted up** | **and upon** | **all** | **oaks of** | **the Bashan** | **And upon** | **all** | **mountains** | **the high** | **and upon** | **all** | **the hills**

הנשאות 5375: | 2:15 ועל 5921 | כל 3605 | מגדל 4026 | גבה 1364 | ועל 5921 | כל 3605 | חומה 2346 | בצורה 1219: | 2:16 ועל 5921 | כל 3605
hanisa'aut. | ua'al | kal | migdal | gaboha; | ua'al | kal | choumah | batzurah. | ua'al | kal
***that are* ones lifted up** | **And upon** | **every** | **tower** | **high** | **and upon** | **every** | **wall** | **fenced** | **And upon** | **all**

אניות 591 | תרשיש 8659 | ועל 5921 | כל 3605 | שכיות 7914 | החמדה 2532: | 2:17 ושח 7817 | גבהות 1365 | האדם 120
aniyout | tarshiysh; | ua'al | kal | sakiyout | hachemdah. | uashach | gabhut | ha'adam,
**the ships of** | **Tarshish** | **and upon** | **all** | **pictures** | **pleasant** | **And shall be bowed down** | **loftiness of** | **the man**

Isa 2:6 Therefore you have forsaken your people the house of Jacob, because they be replenished from the east, and are soothsayers like the Philistines, and they please themselves in the children of strangers.7 Their land also is full of silver and gold, neither is there any end of their treasures; their land is also full of horses, neither is there any end of their chariots:8 Their land also is full of idols; they worship the work of their own hands, that which their own fingers have made:9 And the mean man bow down, and the great man humbleth himself: therefore forgive them not.10 Enter into the rock, and hide you in the dust, for fear of YHUH, and for the glory of his majesty.11 The lofty looks of man shall be humbled, and the haughtiness of men shall be bowed down, and YHUH alone shall be exalted in that day.12 For the day of YHUH of hosts shall be upon everyone that is proud and lofty, and upon everyone that is lifted up; and he shall be brought low:13 And upon all the cedars of Lebanon, that are high and lifted up, and upon all the oaks of Bashan,14 And upon all the high mountains, and upon all the hills that are lifted up,15 And upon every high tower, and upon every fenced wall,16 And upon all the ships of Tarshish, and upon all pleasant pictures.17 And the loftiness of man shall be bowed down, and the haughtiness of men shall be made low:

ושפל 8213 רום 7312 אנשים 582 ונשגב 7682 יהוה 3068 לבדו 905 ביום 3117 ההוא 1931: **2:18**
uashapel rum 'anashiym; uanisgab Yahuah labadou bayoum hahua'.
**and shall be made low the haughtiness of men and shall be exalted Yahuah alone in day that**

והאלילים 457 כליל 3632 יחלף 2498: **2:19** ובאו 935 במערות 4631 צרים 6697 ובמחלות 4247 עפר 6083
uaha'aliyliym kaliyl yachalop. uaba'au bim'arout tzuriym, uabimchilout 'apar;
**And the idols utterly he shall abolish And they shall go into the holes of the rocks and into the caves of the earth**

מפני 6440 פחד 6343 יהוה 3068 ומהדר 1926 גאונו 1347 בקומו 6965 לערץ 6206 הארץ 776: **2:20** ביום 3117 ההוא 1931
mipaney pachad Yahuah uamehadar ga'aunou, baqumou la'arotz ha'aretz. bayoum hahua'
**for fear of Yahuah and for the glory of his majesty when he arise to shake terribly the earth In day that**

ישליך 7993 האדם 120 את 853 אלילי 457 כספו 3701 ואת 853 אלילי 457 זהבו 2091 אשר 834 עשו 6213 לו 3807a
yashliyk ha'adam, 'at 'aliyley kaspou, ua'at 'aliyley zahabou; 'asher 'asu lou'
**shall cast a man his idols of silver *and* his idols of gold which they made *each one* for himself**

להשתחות 7812 לחפר 2661 פרות 6512 ולעטלפים: 5847 **2:21** לבוא 935 בנקרות 5366 הצרים 6697 ובסעפי 5585
lahishtachauot, lachapor parout uala'atalepiym. labou'a baniqrout hatzuriym, uabis'apey
**to worship to the moles rats and to the bats To go into the clefts of the rocks and into the tops of**

הסלעים 5553 מפני 6440 פחד 6343 יהוה 3068 ומהדר 1926 גאונו 1347 בקומו 6965 לערץ 6206 הארץ 776: **2:22**
hasala'aym; mipaney pachad Yahuah uamehadar ga'aunou, baqumou la'arotz ha'aretz.
**the ragged rocks for fear of Yahuah and for the glory of his majesty when he arise to shake terribly the earth**

חדלו 2308 לכם 3807a מן 4480 האדם 120 אשר 834 נשמה 5397 באפו 639 כי 3588 במה 1400 נחשב 2803 הוא 1931:
chidlu lakem min ha'adam, 'asher nashamah ba'apou; kiy bameh nechshab hua'.
**Cease to you from man whose breath *is* in his nostrils for wherein is he to be accounted of? he**

**Isa 3:1** כי 3588 הנה 2009 האדון 113 יהוה 3068 צבאות 6635 מסיר 5493 מירושלם 3389 ומיהודה 3063 משען 4937 ומשענה 4938
kiy hineh ha'adoun Yahuah tzaba'aut, mesiyr miyarushalaim uamiyahudah, mash'aen uamash'aenah;
**For behold the Adonai Yahuah of hosts does take away from Jerusalem and from Judah the stay and the staff**

כל 3605 משען 4937 לחם 3899 וכל 3605 משען 4937 מים 4325: **3:2** גבור 1368 ואיש 376 מלחמה 4421 שופט 8199
kal mish'an lechem, uakol mish'an mayim. gibour ua'aysh milchamah; shoupet
**the whole stay of bread and the whole stay of water The mighty man and the man of war the judge**

ונביא 5030 וקסם 7080 וזקן 2205: **3:3** שר 8269 חמשים 2572 ונשוא 5375 פנים 6440 ויועץ 3289
uanabiy'a uaqosem uazaqen. sar chamishiym uansa' paniym; uayou'aetz
**and the prophet and the prudent and the ancient The captain of fifty and the man honorable and the counsellor**

וחכם 2450 חרשים 2798 ונבון 995 לחש 3908: **3:4** ונתתי 5414 נערים 5288 שריהם 8269 ותעלולים 8586 ימשלו 4910
uachakam charashiym uanboun lachash. uanatatiy na'ariym sareyhem; uata'aluliym yimshalu
**and the cunning artificer and eloquent the orator And I will give children *to be* their princes and babes shall rule**

בם 871a: **3:5** ונגש 5065 העם 5971 איש 376 באיש 376 ואיש 376 ברעהו 7453
bam. uanigas ha'am, 'aysh ba'aysh ua'aysh bare'aehu;
**over them And shall be oppressed the people every one by another and every one by his neighbour**

Ias 2:17 and YHUH alone shall be exalted in that day.18 And the idols he shall utterly abolish.19 And they shall go into the holes of the rocks, and into the caves of the earth, for fear of YHUH, and for the glory of his majesty, when he arise to shake terribly the earth.20 In that day a man shall cast his idols of silver, and his idols of gold, which they made each one for himself to worship, to the moles and to the bats;21 To go into the clefts of the rocks, and into the tops of the ragged rocks, for fear of YHUH, and for the glory of his majesty, when he arise to shake terribly the earth.22 Cease you from man, whose breath is in his nostrils: for wherein is he to be accounted of? **Isa** 3:1 For, behold, the Adonai, YHUH of hosts, doth take away from Jerusalem and from Judah the stay and the staff, the whole stay of bread, and the whole stay of water,2 The mighty man, and the man of war, the judge, and the prophet, and the prudent, and the ancient,3 The captain of fifty, and the honourable man, and the counselor, and the cunning artificer, and the eloquent orator.4 And I will give children to be their princes, and babes shall rule over them.5 And the people shall be oppressed, everyone by another, and everyone by his neighbor: the child shall behave himself proudly against the ancient, and the base against the honourable.

ירהבו 7292 הנער 5288 בזקן 2205 והנקלה 7034 בנכבד 3513: 3:6 כי 3588 יתפש 8610
yirhabu, hana'ar bazaqen, uahaniqleh banikbad. kiy yitpos
**shall behave himself proudly the child against the ancient and the base against the honorable When shall take hold**

איש 376 באחיו 251 בית 1004 אביו 1 שמלה 8071 לכה 1980 קצין 7101 תהיה 1961 לנו 3807a והמכשלה 4384 הזאת 2063
'aysh ba'achiyu beyt 'abiyu, simlah lakah, qatziyn tihayeh lanu; uahamakshelah haza't
**a man of his brother of the house of his father clothing *saying* You have ruler be you our and ruin *let* this**

תחת 8478 ידך 3027: 3:7 ישא 5375 ביום 3117 ההוא 1931 לאמר 559 לא 3808 אהיה 1961 חבש 2280 ובביתי 1004 אין 369 לחם 3899
tachat yadeka. yisa' bayoum hahua' lea'mor la' 'ahayeh chobesh, uabbeytiy 'aeyn lechem
***be* under your hand shall he swear In day that saying not I will be an healer for in my house *is* neither bread**

ואין 369 שמלה 8071 לא 3808 תשימני 7760 קצין 7101 עם 5971: 3:8 כי 3588 כשלה 3782 ירושלם 3389 ויהודה 3063 נפל 5307 כי 3588
ua'aeyn simlah; la' tasiymuniy qatziyn 'am. kiy kashalah yarushalaim, uayahudah napal; kiy
**nor clothing not make me a ruler of the people For is ruined Jerusalem and Judah is fallen because**

לשונם 3956 ומעלליהם 4611 אל 413 יהוה 3068 למרות 4784 עני 5869 כבודו 3519: 3:9 הכרת 1971 פניהם 6440
lashounam uama'alleyhem 'al Yahuah, lamarout 'aeney kaboudou. hakarat paneyhem
**their tongue and their doings *are* against Yahuah to provoke the eyes of his glory The show of their countenance**

ענתה 6030 בם 871a וחטאתם 2403 כסדם 5467 הגידו 5046 לא 3808 כחדו 3582 אוי 188 לנפשם 5315 כי 3588
'anatah bam, uachata'tam kisadom higiydu la' kichedu; 'auy lanapsham, kiy
**does witness against them and their sin as Sodom they declare not they hide *it* Woe unto their soul for**

גמלו 1580 להם 1992 רעה 7451: 3:10 אמרו 559 צדיק 6662 כי 3588 טוב 2896 כי 3588 פרי 6529
gamalu lahem ra'ah. 'amru tzadiyq kiy toub; kiy pariy
**they have rewarded unto themselves evil Say you *to* the righteous that *it shall be* well *with him:* for the fruit of**

מעלליהם 4611 יאכלו 398: 3:11 אוי 188 לרשע 7563 רע 7451 כי 3588 גמול 1576 ידיו 3027 יעשה 6213
ma'alleyhem ya'kelu. 'auy larasha' ra'; kiy gamul yadayu ye'aseh
**their doings they shall eat Woe unto the wicked *it shall be* ill *with him* for the reward of his hands shall be given**

לו 3807a: 3:12 עמי 5971 נגשיו 5065 מעולל 5768 ונשים 802 משלו 4910 בו 871a עמי 5971
lou'. 'amiy nogasayu ma'aulel, uanashiym mashalu bou; 'amiy
**him *As for* my people *are* their oppressors children and women rule over them O my people**

מאשריך 833 מתעים 8582 ודרך 1870 ארחתיך 734 בלעו 1104: 3:13 נצב 5324 לריב 7378 יהוה 3068 ועמד 5975
ma'ashreyka mat'aym, uaderek 'arachoteyka bile'au. nitzab lariyb Yahuah; ua'aumed
**they which lead you cause *you* to err and the way of your paths destroy stands up to plead Yahuah and stands**

לדין 1777 עמים 5971: 3:14 יהוה 3068 במשפט 4941 יבוא 935 עם 5973 זקני 2205 עמו 5971 ושריו 8269 ואתם 859
ladiyn 'amiym. Yahuah bamishpat yabou'a, 'am ziqney 'amou uasarayu; ua'atem
**to judge the people Yahuah into judgment will enter with the ancients of his people and the princes thereof for you**

בערתם 1197 הכרם 3754 גזלת 1500 העני 6041 בבתיכם 1004: 3:15 מלכם 4100 תדכאו 1792 עמי 5971
bi'artem hakerem, gazelat he'aniy babateykem. malakem tadak'au 'amiy,
**have eaten up the vineyard the spoil of the poor *is* in your houses What *mean* you *that* you beat to pieces my people**

Isa 3:6 When a man shall take hold of his brother of the house of his father, saying, Thou have clothing, be you our ruler, and let this ruin be under your hand:7 In that day shall he swear, saying, I will not be an healer; for in my house is neither bread nor clothing: make me not a ruler of the people.8 For Jerusalem is ruined, and Judah is fallen: because their tongue and their doings are against YHUH, to provoke the eyes of his glory.9 The show of their countenance doth witness against them; and they declare their sin as Sodom, they hide it not. Woe unto their soul! for they have rewarded evil unto themselves.10 Say you to the righteous, that it shall be well with him: for they shall eat the fruit of their doings.11 Woe unto the wicked! it shall be ill with him: for the reward of his hands shall be given him.12 As for my people, children are their oppressors, and women rule over them. O my people, they which lead you cause you to err, and destroy the way of your paths.13 YHUH stand up to plead, and stand to judge the people.14 YHUH will enter into judgment with the ancients of his people, and the princes thereof: for you have eaten up the vineyard; the spoil of the poor is in your houses.15 What mean you that you beat my people to pieces, and grind the faces of the poor? saith YHUH G-D of hosts.

| ופני 6440 | עניים 6041 | תטחנו 2912 | נאם 5002 | אדני 136 | יהוה 3069 | צבאות 6635: | 3:16 | ויאמר 559 | יהוה 3069 | יען 3282 | כי 3588 |
|---|---|---|---|---|---|---|---|---|---|---|---|
| uapaney | 'aniyiym | titchanu; | na'am | 'adonay | Yahuah | tzaba'aut. | | uaya'mer | Yahuah | ya'an | kiy |
| **and the faces of** | **the poor?** | ***and* grind** | **said** | **Adonai** | **Yahuah** | **of hosts** | | **Moreover saith** | **Yahuah** | **Because** | **that** |

| גבהו 1361 | בנות 1323 | ציון 6726 | ותלכנה 1980 | נטוות 5186 | גרון 1627 | ומשקרות 8265 | עינים 5869 | הלוך 1980 | וטפף 2952 |
|---|---|---|---|---|---|---|---|---|---|
| gabahu | banout | tziyoun, | uatelaknah | natuuot | garoun, | uamasaqrout | 'aeynayim; | halouk | uatapop |
| **are haughty** | **the daughters of** | **Zion** | **and walk with** | **stretched forth** | **necks** | **and wanton** | **eyes** | **walking** | **and mincing** |

| תלכנה 1980 | וברגליהם 7272 | תעכסנה 5913: | 3:17 | ושפח 5596 | אדני 136 | קדקד 6936 |
|---|---|---|---|---|---|---|
| telaknah, | uabragleyhem | ta'akasnah. | | uasipach | 'adonay, | qadaqod |
| ***as* they go** | **and with their feet** | **making a tinkling** | | **Therefore will smite with a scab** | **Adonai** | **the crown of the head of** |

| בנות 1323 | ציון 6726 | ויהוה 3068 | פתהן 6596 | יערה 6168: | 3:18 | ביום 3117 | ההוא 1931 | יסיר 5493 | אדני 136 | את 853 |
|---|---|---|---|---|---|---|---|---|---|---|
| banout | tziyoun; | uaYahuah | patahen | ya'areh. | | bayoum | hahua' | yasiyr | 'adonay, | 'at |
| **the daughters of** | **Zion** | **and Yahuah** | **their secret parts** | **will discover** | | **In day** | **that** | **will take away** | **Adonai** | |

| תפארת 8597 | העכסים 5914 | והשביסים 7636 | והשהרנים 7720: | 3:19 | הנטיפות 5188 |
|---|---|---|---|---|---|
| tip'aret | ha'akasiym | uahashabiysiym | uahasaharoniym. | | hanatiypout |
| **bravery of** | ***their* the tinkling ornaments** | ***about their feet* and *their* cauls** | **and *their* round tires like the moon** | | **The chains** |

| והשירות 8285 | והרעלות 7479: | 3:20 | הפארים 6287 | והצעדות 6807 | והקשרים 7196 | ובתי 1004 |
|---|---|---|---|---|---|---|
| uahasheyrout | uahara'alout. | | hapa'aeriym | uahatza'adout | uahaqishuriym, | uabatey |
| **and the bracelets** | **and the mufflers** | | **The bonnets** | **and the ornaments of the legs** | **and the headbands** | **and boxes of** |

| הנפש 5315 | והלחשים 3908: | 3:21 | הטבעות 2885 | ונזמי 5141 | האף 639: | 3:22 | המחלצות 4254 | והמעטפות 4595 |
|---|---|---|---|---|---|---|---|---|
| hanepesh | uahalchashiym. | | hataba'aut | uanizmey | ha'ap. | | hamachalatzout | uahama'atapout, |
| **the tablets** | **and the earrings** | | **The rings** | **and jewels** | **the nose** | | **The changeable suits of apparel** | **and the mantles** |

| והמטפחות 4304 | והחריטים 2754: | 3:23 | והגלינים 1549 | והסדינים 5466 | והצניפות 6797 | והרדידים 7289: | 3:24 |
|---|---|---|---|---|---|---|---|
| uahamitpachout | uahachariytiym. | | uahagilyoniym | uahasdiyniym, | uahatzaniypout | uaharadiydiym. | |
| **and the wimples** | **and the crisping pins** | | **The glasses** | **and the fine linen** | **and the hoods** | **and the vails** | |

| והיה 1961 | תחת 8478 | בשם 1314 | מק 4716 | יהיה 1961 | ותחת 8478 | חגורה 2290 | נקפה 5364 | ותחת 8478 |
|---|---|---|---|---|---|---|---|---|
| uahayah | tachat | boshem | maq | yihayeh, | uatachat | chagourah | niqpah | uatachat |
| **And it shall come to pass *that*** | **instead of** | **sweet smell stink** | | **there shall be** | **and instead of** | **a girdle** | **a rent** | **and instead of** |

| מעשה 4639 | מקשה 4748 | קרחה 7144 | ותחת 8478 | פתיגיל 6614 | מחגרת 4228 | שק 8242 | כי 3587 | תחת 8478 | יפי 3308: | 3:25 |
|---|---|---|---|---|---|---|---|---|---|---|
| ma'aseh | miqsheh | qarachah, | uatachat | patiygiyl | machagoret | saq; | kiy | tachat | yopiy. | |
| **well set** | **hair** | **baldness** | **and instead of** | **a stomacher** | **a girding of** | **sackcloth** | ***and* burning** | **instead of** | **beauty** | |

| מתיך 4962 | בחרב 2719 | יפלו 5307 | וגבורתך 1369 | במלחמה 4421: | 3:26 | ואנו 578 | ואבלו 56 | פתחיה 6607 | ונקתה 5352 |
|---|---|---|---|---|---|---|---|---|---|
| matayik | bachereb | yipolu; | uagaburatek | bamilchamah. | | ua'anu | ua'abalu | patacheyha; | uaniqatah |
| **Your men** | **by the sword** | **shall fall** | **and your mighty** | **in the war** | | **And shall lament** | **and mourn** | **her gates** | **and desolate** |

| לארץ 776 | תשב 3427: |
|---|---|
| la'aretz | tesheb. |
| **upon the ground she shall sit *being*** | |

Isa 3:16 Moreover YHUH saith, Because the daughters of Zion are haughty, and walk with stretched forth necks and wanton eyes, walking and mincing as they go, and making a tinkling with their feet:17 Therefore YHUH will smite with a scab the crown of the head of the daughters of Zion, and YHUH will discover their secret parts.18 In that day YHUH will take away the bravery of their tinkling ornaments about their feet, and their cauls, and their round tires like the moon,19 The chains, and the bracelets, and the mufflers,20 The bonnets, and the ornaments of the legs, and the headbands, and the tablets, and the earrings,21 The rings, and nose jewels,22 The changeable suits of apparel, and the mantles, and the wimples, and the crisping pins,23 The glasses, and the fine linen, and the hoods, and the vails.24 And it shall come to pass, that instead of sweet smell there shall be stink; and instead of a girdle a rent; and instead of well set hair baldness; and instead of a stomacher a girding of sackcloth; and burning instead of beauty.25 Thy men shall fall by the sword, and your mighty in the war.26 And her gates shall lament and mourn; and she being desolate shall sit upon the ground.

**Isa 4:1**
והחזיקו 2388 שבע 7651 נשים 802 באיש 376 אחד 259 ביום 3117 ההוא 1931 לאמר 559 לחמנו 3899 נאכל 398
uahecheziyqu sheba' nashiym ba'aysh 'achad, bayoum hahua' lea'mor, lachamenu na'kel,
**And shall take hold seven women of man one in day that saying our own bread We will eat**

ושמלתנו 8071 נלבש 3847 רק 7535 יקרא 7121 שמך 8034 עלינו 5921 אסף 622 חרפתנו 2781: **4:2** ביום 3117 ההוא 1931
uasimlatenu nilbash; raq, yiqarea' shimka 'aleynu, 'asop cherpatenu. bayoum hahua',
**and our own apparel wear only let be called by your name us to take away our reproach In day that**

יהיה 1961 צמח 6780 יהוה 3068 לצבי 6643 ולכבוד 3519 ופרי 6529 הארץ 776 לגאון 1347 ולתפארת 8597
yihayeh tzemach Yahuah, litzbiy ualkaboud; uapariy ha'aretz laga'aun ualtip'aret,
**shall be the Branch of Yahuah beautiful and glorious and the fruit of the earth** ***shall be*** **excellent and comely**

לפליטת 6413 ישראל 3478: **4:3** והיה 1961 הנשאר 7604 בציון 6726 והנותר 3498
lipleytat yisra'ael. uahayah hanish'ar batziyoun, uahanoutar
**for them that are escaped of Israel And it shall come to pass** ***that he that is*** **left in Zion and** ***he that*** **remains**

בירושלם 3389 קדוש 6918 יאמר 559 לו 3807a כל 3605 הכתוב 3789 לחיים 2416 בירושלם 3389: **4:4** אם 518
biyarushalaim, qadoush ye'amer lou'; kal hakatub lachayiym biyarushalaim. 'am
**in Jerusalem holy shall be called to him** ***even*** **every one that is written among the living in Jerusalem When**

רחץ 7364 אדני 136 את 853 צאת 6675 בנות 1323 ציון 6726 ואת 853 דמי 1818 ירושלם 3389 ידיח 1740
rachatz 'adonay, 'at tzo'at banout tziyoun, ua'at damey yarushalaim yadiyach
**shall have washed away Adonai the filth of the daughters of Zion** ***and*** **the blood of Jerusalem shall have purged**

מקרבה 7130 ברוח 7307 משפט 4941 וברוח 7307 בער 1197: **4:5** וברא 1254 יהוה 3068 על 5921 כל 3605
miqirbah; baruach mishapat uabruach ba'aer. uabara' Yahuah 'al kal
**from the midst thereof by the spirit of judgment and by the spirit of burning And will create Yahuah upon every**

מכון 4349 הר 2022 ציון 6726 ועל 5921 מקראה 4744 ענן 6051 יומם 3119 ועשן 6227 ונגה 5051 אש 784 להבה 3852
makoun har tziyoun ua'al miqra'aha, 'anan youmam ua'ashan, uanogah 'aesh lehabah
**dwelling place of mount Zion and upon her assemblies a cloud by day and smoke and the shining of a fire the flaming**

לילה 3915 כי 3588 על 5921 כל 3605 כבוד 3519 חפה 2646: **4:6** וסכה 5521 תהיה 1961 לצל 6738 יומם 3119
layalah; kiy 'al kal kaboud chupah. uasukah tihayeh latzel youmam
***by*** **night for upon all the glory** ***shall be*** **a defence And a tabernacle there shall be for a shadow in the daytime**

מחרב 2721 ולמחסה 4268 ולמסתור 4563 מזרם 2230 וממטר 4306:
mechoreb; ualmachseh ualmistour, mizerem uamimatar.
**from the heat and for a place of refuge and for a covert from storm and from rain**

**Isa 5:1**
אשירה 7891 נא 4994 לידידי 3039 שירת 7892 דודי 1730 לכרמו 3754 כרם 3754 היה 1961 לידידי 3039
'ashiyrah naa' liydiydiy, shiyrat doudiy lakarmou; kerem hayah liydiydiy
**will I sing Now my wellbeloved a song of to my beloved touching his vineyard a vineyard has My wellbeloved**

בקרן 7161 בן 1121 שמן 8081: **5:2** ויעזקהו 5823 ויסקלהו 5619 ויטעהו 5193 שרק 8321
baqeren ben shamen. uaya'azqehu uayasaqlehu, uayita'aehu soreq,
**in a hill very fruitful And he fenced it and gathered out the stones thereof and planted it with the choicest vine**

**Isa** 4:1 And in that day seven women shall take hold of one man, saying, We will eat our own bread, and wear our own apparel: only let us be called by your name, to take away our reproach.2 In that day shall the branch of YHUH be beautiful and glorious, and the fruit of the earth shall be excellent and comely for them that are escaped of Israel.3 And it shall come to pass, that he that is left in Zion, and he that remain in Jerusalem, shall be called holy, even everyone that is written among the living in Jerusalem:4 When YHUH shall have washed away the filth of the daughters of Zion, and shall have purged the blood of Jerusalem from the midst thereof by the spirit of judgment, and by the spirit of burning.5 And YHUH will create upon every dwelling place of mount Zion, and upon her assemblies, a cloud and smoke by day, and the shining of a flaming fire by night: for upon all the glory shall be a defence.6 And there shall be a tabernacle for a shadow in the daytime from the heat, and for a place of refuge, and for a covert from storm and from rain. **Isa** 5:1 Now will I sing to my wellbeloved a song of my beloved touching his vineyard. My wellbeloved has a vineyard in a very fruitful hill:2 And he fenced it, and gathered out the stones thereof, and planted it with the choicest vine, and built a tower in the midst of it, and also made a winepress therein:

ויבן 1129 מגדל 4026 בתוכו 8432 וגם 1571 יקב 3342 חצב 2672 בו 871a ויקו 6960 לעשות 6213 ענבים 6025
uayiben migdal batoukou, uagam yeqeb chatzeb bou; uayaqau la'asout 'anabiym
**and built a tower in the midst of it and also a winepress made therein and he looked that it should bring forth grapes**

ויעש 6213 באשים 891: 5:3 ועתה 6258 יושב 3427 ירושלם 3389 ואיש 376 יהודה 3063 שפטו 8199 נא 4994
uaya'as ba'ashiym. ua'atah yousheb yarushalaim ua'aysh yahudah; shiptu naa'
**and it brought forth wild grapes And now O inhabitants of Jerusalem and men of Judah judge I pray you**

ביני 996 ובין 996 כרמי 3754: 5:4 מה 4100 לעשות 6213 עוד 5750 לכרמי 3754 ולא 3808 עשיתי 6213 בו 871a
beyniy uabeyn karmiy. mah la'asout 'aud lakarmiy, uala' 'asiytiy bou;
**between me and between my vineyard What could have been done more to my vineyard that not I have done in it?**

מדוע 4069 קויתי 6960 לעשות 6213 ענבים 6025 ויעש 6213 באשים 891: 5:5 ועתה 6258 אודיעה 3045 נא 4994
madua' qiueytiy la'asout 'anabiym uaya'as ba'ashiym. ua'atah 'audiy'ah naa'
**wherefore when I looked that it should bring forth grapes brought it forth wild grapes? And now I will tell go to**

אתכם 853 את 853 אשר 834 אני 589 עשה 6213 לכרמי 3754 הסר 5493 משוכתו 4881 והיה 1961 לבער 1197
'atkem, 'at 'asher 'aniy 'aseh lakarmiy; haser masukatou uahayah laba'aer,
**you what I will do to my vineyard I will take away the hedge thereof and it shall be eaten up**

פרץ 6555 גדרו 1447 והיה 1961 למרמס 4823: 5:6 ואשיתהו 7896 בתה 1326 לא 3808 יזמר 2168 ולא 3808
parotz gaderou uahayah lamirmas. ua'ashiytehu batah, la' yizamer uala'
***and* break down the wall thereof and it shall be trodden down And I will lay it waste not it shall be pruned nor**

יעדר 5737 ועלה 5927 שמיר 8068 ושית 7898 ועל 5921 העבים 5645 אצוה 6680 מהמטיר 4305 עליו 5921
ye'ader, ua'alah shamiyr uashayit; ua'al he'abiym 'atzaueh, mehamtiyr 'alayu
**digged but there shall come up briers and thorns also the clouds I will command that they rain also upon it**

מטר 4306: 5:7 כי 3588 כרם 3754 יהוה 3068 צבאות 6635 בית 1004 ישראל 3478 ואיש 376 יהודה 3063 נטע 5194 שעשועיו 8191
matar. kiy kerem Yahuah tzaba'aut beyt yisra'el, ua'aysh yahudah, nata' sha'ashu'ayu;
**rain For the vineyard of Yahuah of hosts *is* the house of Israel and the men of Judah plant his pleasant**

ויקו 6960 למשפט 4941 והנה 2009 משפח 4939 לצדקה 6666 והנה 2009 צעקה 6818: 5:8 הוי 1945 מגיעי 5060
uayaqau lamishpat uahineh mispach, litzdaqah uahineh tza'aqah. houy, magiy'aey
**and he looked for judgment but behold oppression for righteousness but behold a cry Woe *unto* them that join**

בית 1004 בבית 1004 שדה 7704 בשדה 7704 יקריבו 7126 עד 5704 אפס 657 מקום 4725 והושבתם 3427 לבדכם 905 בקרב 7130
bayit babayit, sadeh uasadeh yaqriybu; 'ad 'apes maqoum, uahushabtem labadakem baqereb
**house to house field to field *that* lay till *there be* no place that they may be placed alone in the midst of**

הארץ 776: 5:9 באזני 241 יהוה 3068 צבאות 6635 אם 518 לא 3808 בתים 1004 רבים 7227 לשמה 8047 יהיו 1961 גדלים 1419 וטובים 2896
ha'aretz. ba'azanay Yahuah tzaba'aut; 'am la' batiym rabiym lashamah yihayu, gadoliym uatoubiym
**the earth In mine ears *said* Yahuah of hosts Of a truth not houses many desolate shall be *even* great and fair**

מאין 369 יושב 3427: 5:10 כי 3588 עשרת 6235 צמדי 6776 כרם 3754 יעשו 6213 בת 1324 אחת 259 וזרע 2233 חמר 2563 יעשה 6213
me'ayn yousheb. kiy, 'aseret tzimdey kerem, ya'asu bat 'achat; uazera' chamor ya'aseh
**without inhabitant Yea ten acres of vineyard shall yield bath one and the seed of an homer shall yield**

Isa 5:2 and he looked that it should bring forth grapes, and it brought forth wild grapes.3 And now, O inhabitants of Jerusalem, and men of Judah, judge, I pray you, betwixt me and my vineyard.4 What could have been done more to my vineyard, that I have not done in it? wherefore, when I looked that it should bring forth grapes, brought it forth wild grapes?5 And now go to; I will tell you what I will do to my vineyard: I will take away the hedge thereof, and it shall be eaten up; and break down the wall thereof, and it shall be trodden down:6 And I will lay it waste: it shall not be pruned, nor digged; but there shall come up briers and thorns: I will also command the clouds that they rain no rain upon it.7 For the vineyard of YHUH of hosts is the house of Israel, and the men of Judah his pleasant plant: and he looked for judgment, but behold oppression; for righteousness, but behold a cry.8 Woe unto them that join house to house, that lay field to field, till there be no place, that they may be placed alone in the midst of the earth!9 In mine ears said YHUH of hosts, Of a truth many houses shall be desolate, even great and fair, without inhabitant.10 Yea, ten acres of vineyard shall yield one bath, and the seed of an homer shall yield an ephah.

5:11

איפה 374: הוי 1945 משכימי 7925 בבקר 1242 שכר 7941 ירדפו 7291 מאחרי 309 בנשף 5399

'aeypah. houy mashkiymey baboqer shekar yirdopu; me'acharey baneshep,

**an ephah Woe *unto* them that rise up early in the morning strong drink *that* they may follow that continue until night**

5:12

יין 3196 ידליקם 1814: והיה 1961 כנור 3658 ונבל 5035 תף 8596 וחליל 2485 ויין 3196 משתיהם 4960 ואת 853 פעל 6467

yayin yadliyqem. uahayah kinour uanebel, top uachaliyl uayayin mishteyhem; ua'at po'al

***till* wine inflame them And are the harp and the viol the tabret and pipe and wine *in* their feasts *but* the work of**

5:13

יהוה 3068 לא 3808 יביטו 5027 ומעשה 4639 ידיו 3027 לא 3808 ראו 7200: לכן 3651 גלה 1540 עמי 5971

Yahuah la' yabiytu, uama'aseh yadayu la' ra'au. laken galah 'amiy

**Yahuah not they regard the operation of his hands neither consider Therefore are gone into captivity my people**

5:14

מבלי 1097 דעת 1847 וכבודו 3519 מתי 4962 רעב 7458 והמונו 1995 צחה 6704 צמא 6772:

mibaliy da'at; uakboudou metey ra'ab, uahamounou tzicheh tzama'.

**because *they have* no knowledge and their honorable men *are* famished and their multitude dried up with thirst**

לכן 3651 הרחיבה 7337 שאול 7585 נפשה 5315 ופערה 6473 פיה 6310 לבלי 1097 חק 2706 וירד 3381 הדרה 1926

laken, hirchiybah sha'al napshah, uapa'arah piyha libaliy choq; uayarad hadarah

**Therefore has enlarged hell (*grave*) herself and opened her mouth without measure and shall descend their glory**

5:15

והמונה 1995 ושאונה 7588 ועלז 5938 בה 871a: וישח 7817 אדם 120

uahamounah uash'aunah ua'alez bah. uayishach 'adam

**and their multitude and their pomp and he that rejoice into it And shall be brought down the *mean* man**

5:16

וישפל 8213 איש 376 ועיני 5869 גבהים 1364 תשפלנה 8213: ויגבה 1361 יהוה 3068 צבאות 6635

uayishpal 'aysh; ua'aeyney gabohiym tishpalnah. uayigbah Yahuah tzaba'aut

**and shall be humbled the mighty man and the eyes of the lofty shall be humbled But shall be exalted Yahuah of hosts**

5:17

במשפט 4941 והאל 410 הקדוש 6918 נקדש 6942 בצדקה 6666: ורעו 7462 כבשים 3532

bamishpat; uaha'ael haqadoush, niqdash bitzadaqah. uar'au kabasiym

**in judgment and the Elohim *that is* the holy shall be sanctified in righteousness Then shall feed the lambs**

5:18

כדברם 1699 וחרבות 2723 מחים 4220 גרים 1481 יאכלו 398: הוי 1945 משכי 4900 העון 5771

kadabaram; uacharabout mechiym gariym ya'kelu. houy moshakey he'auon

**after their manner and the waste places of the fat ones strangers shall eat Woe *unto* them that draw iniquity**

5:19

בחבלי 2256 השוא 7723 וכעבות 5688 העגלה 5699 חטאה 2403: האמרים 559 ימהר 4116 יחישה 2363 מעשהו 4639

bachabley hashab; uaka'about ha'agalah chata'ah. ha'amariym, yamaher yachiyshah ma'asehu

**with cords of vanity and as rope *it were with* a cart sin That say Let him make speed *and* hasten his work**

5:20

למען 4616 נראה 7200 ותקרב 7126 ותבואה 935 עצת 6098 קדוש 6918 ישראל 3478 ונדעה 3045:

lama'an nir'ah; uatiqrab uatabou'ah, 'atzat qadoush yisra'ael uaneda'ah.

**that we may see *it* and let draw near and come the counsel of *the* Holy One of Israel that we may know *it***

הוי 1945 האמרים 559 לרע 7451 טוב 2896 ולטוב 2896 רע 7451 שמים 7760 חשך 2822 לאור 216 ואור 216 לחשך 2822 שמים 7760 מר 4751

houy ha'amariym lara' toub ualatoub ra'; samiym choshek la'aur ua'aur lachoshek, samiym mar

**Woe *unto* them that call evil good and good evil that put darkness for light and light for darkness that put bitter**

Isa 5:11 Woe unto them that rise up early in the morning, that they may follow strong drink; that continue until night, till wine inflame them!12 And the harp, and the viol, the tabret, and pipe, and wine, are in their feasts: but they regard not the work of YHUH, neither consider the operation of his hands.13 Therefore my people are gone into captivity, because they have no knowledge: and their honourable men are famished, and their multitude dried up with thirst.14 Therefore hell has enlarged herself, and opened her mouth without measure: and their glory, and their multitude, and their pomp, and he that rejoice, shall descend into it.15 And the mean man shall be brought down, and the mighty man shall be humbled, and the eyes of the lofty shall be humbled:16 But YHUH of hosts shall be exalted in judgment, and G-d that is holy shall be sanctified in righteousness.17 Then shall the lambs feed after their manner, and the waste places of the fat ones shall strangers eat.18 Woe unto them that draw iniquity with cords of vanity, and sin as it were with a cart rope:19 That say, Let him make speed, and hasten his work, that we may see it: and let the counsel of the Holy One of Israel draw nigh and come, that we may know it!20 Woe unto them that call evil good, and good evil; that put darkness for light, and light for darkness; that put bitter for sweet, and sweet for bitter!

**5:21** … **5:22**

למתוק 4966 ומתוק 4966 למר 4751: הוי 1945 חכמים 2450 בעיניהם 5869 ונגד 5048 פניהם 6440 נבנים 995:
lamatouq uamatouq lamar. houy chakamiym ba'aeyneyhem; uaneged paneyhem naboniym.
**for sweet and sweet for bitter Woe *unto them that are* wise in their own eyes and in their own sight prudent**

**5:23**

הוי 1945 גבורים 1368 לשתות 8354 יין 3196 ואנשי 582 חיל 2428 למסך 4537 שכר 7941: מצדיקי 6663 רשע 7563
houy gibouriym lishtout yayin; ua'anshey chayil limsok shekar. matzdiyqey rasha'
**Woe *unto them that are* mighty to drink wine and men of strength to mingle strong drink Which justify the wicked**

**5:24**

עקב 6118 שחד 7810 וצדקת 6666 צדיקים 6662 יסירו 5493 ממנו 4480: לכן 3651 כאכל 398 קש 7179 לשון 3956
'aeqeb shochad; uatziydqat tzadiyqiym yasiyru mimenu. laken ke'akoul qash lashoun
**for reward and the righteousness of the righteous take away from him Therefore as devour the stubble a tongue**

אש 784 וחשש 2842 להבה 3852 ירפה 7503 שרשם 8328 כמק 4716 יהיה 1961 ופרחם 6525 כאבק 80 יעלה 5927 כי 3588
'aesh, uachashash lehabah yirpeh, sharasham kamaq yihayeh, uapircham ka'abaq ya'aleh; kiy
**the fire the chaff the flame consume *so* their root as rottenness shall be and their blossom as dust shall go up because**

**5:25**

מאסו 3988 את 853 תורת 8451 יהוה 3068 צבאות 6635 ואת 853 אמרת 565 קדוש 6918 ישראל 3478 נאצו 5006:
ma'asu, 'at tourat Yahuah tzaba'aut, ua'at 'amrat qadoush yisra'ael ni'aetzu.
**they have cast away the law of Yahuah of hosts *and* the word of *the* Holy One of Israel despised**

על 5921 כן 3651 חרה 2734 אף 639 יהוה 3068 בעמו 5971 ויט 5186 ידו 3027 עליו 5921
'al ken charah 'ap Yahuah ba'amou uayet yadou 'alayu
**Therefore this is kindled the anger of Yahuah against his people and he has stretched forth his hand against them**

ויכהו 5221 וירגזו 7264 ההרים 2022 ותהי 1961 נבלתם 5038 כסוחה 5478 בקרב 7130 חוצות 2351 בכל 3605 זאת 2063
uayakehu, uayirgazu heharyim, uatahiy niblatam kasuchah baqereb chutzout; bakal za't
**and has smitten them and did tremble the hills and lay their carcases *were* torn in the midst of the streets For all this**

**5:26**

לא 3808 שב 7725 אפו 639 ועוד 5750 ידו 3027 נטויה 5186: ונשא 5375 נס 5251 לגוים 1471 מרחוק 7350
la' shab 'apou, ua'aud yadou natuyah. uanasa' nes lagouyim merachouq,
**not is turned away his anger but still his hand *is* stretched out And he will lift up an ensign to the nations from far**

**5:27**

ושרק 8319 לו 3807a מקצה 7097 הארץ 776 והנה 2009 מהרה 4120 קל 7031 יבוא 935: אין 369 עיף 5889
uasharaq lou' miqtzeh ha'aretz; uahineh maherah qal yabou'a. 'aeyn 'ayep
**and will hiss unto them from the end of the earth and behold *with* speed swiftly they shall come None shall be weary**

ואין 369 כושל 3782 בו 871a לא 3808 ינום 5123 ולא 3808 יישן 3462 ולא 3808 נפתח 6605 אזור 232 חלציו 2504 ולא 3808
ua'aeyn koushel bou, la' yanum uala' yiyshan; uala' niptach 'aezour chalatzayu, uala'
**nor stumble among them none shall slumber nor sleep neither shall be loosed the girdle of their loins nor**

**5:28**

נתק 5423 שרוך 8288 נעליו 5275: אשר 834 חציו 2671 שנונים 8150 וכל 3605 קשתתיו 7198 דרכות 1869 פרסות 6541 סוסיו 5483
nitaq sarouk na'alayu. 'asher chitzayu shanuniym, uakal qashtotayu darukout; parsout susayu
**be broken the latchet of their shoes Whose arrows *are* sharp and all their bows bent hoofs their horses'**

**5:29**

כצר 6862 נחשבו 2803 וגלגליו 1534 כסופה 5492: שאגה 7581 לו 3807a כלביא 3833 ושאג 7580
katzar nechshabu, uagalgilayu kasupah. sha'agah lou' kalabiy'a; uasha'ag
**like flint shall be counted and their wheels like a whirlwind roaring Their *shall be* like a lion they shall roar**

Isa 5:21 Woe unto them that are wise in their own eyes, and prudent in their own sight!22 Woe unto them that are mighty to drink wine, and men of strength to mingle strong drink:23 Which justify the wicked for reward, and take away the righteousness of the righteous from him!24 Therefore as the fire devour the stubble, and the flame consumeth the chaff, so their root shall be as rottenness, and their blossom shall go up as dust: because they have cast away the law of YHUH of hosts, and despised the word of the Holy One of Israel.25 Therefore is the anger of YHUH kindled against his people, and he has stretched forth his hand against them, and has smitten them: and the hills did tremble, and their carcases were torn in the midst of the streets. For all this his anger is not turned away, but his hand is stretched out still.26 And he will lift up an ensign to the nations from far, and will hiss unto them from the end of the earth: and, behold, they shall come with speed swiftly:27 None shall be weary nor stumble among them; none shall slumber nor sleep; neither shall the girdle of their loins be loosed, nor the latchet of their shoes be broken:28 Whose arrows are sharp, and all their bows bent, their horses' hoofs shall be counted like flint, and their wheels like a whirlwind:29 Their roaring shall be like a lion, they shall roar like young lions:

כפירים 3715 | וינהם 5098 | ויאחז 270 | טרף 2964 | ויפליט 6403 | ואין 369 | מציל 5337: **5:30**
kakapiyriym | uayinhom | uaya'chez | terep, | uayapliyt | ua'aeyn | matziyl.
**like young lions | yea they shall roar | and lay hold of | the prey | and shall carry *it* away safe | and none | shall deliver *it***

וינהם 5098 | עליו 5921 | ביום 3117 | ההוא 1931 | כנהמת 5100 | ים 3220 | ונבט 5027 | לארץ 776 | והנה 2009 | חשך 2822
uayinhom | 'alayu | bayoum | hahua' | kanahamat | yam; | uanibat | la'aretz | uahineh | choshek,
**And they shall roar | against them | in day | that | like the roaring of | the sea | if *one* look | unto the land | and behold | darkness**

צר 6862 | ואור 216 | חשך 2821 | בעריפיה 6183:
tzar | ua'aur, | chashak | ba'ariypeyha.
***and* sorrow | and the light | is darkened | in the heavens thereof**

**Isa 6:1** בשנת 8141 | מות 4194 | המלך 4428 | עזיהו 5818 | ואראה 7200 | את 853 | אדני 136 | ישב 3427 | על 5921 | כסא 3678 | רם 7311 | ונשא 5375
bishnat | mout | hamelek | 'aziyahu, | ua'ar'ah | 'at | 'adonay | yosheb | 'al | kisea' | ram | uanisa';
**In the year | that died | king | Uzziah | I saw also | | Adonai | sitting | upon | a throne | high | and lifted up**

ושוליו 7757 | מלאים 4390 | את 853 | ההיכל 1964: | **6:2** שרפים 8314 | עמדים 5975 | ממעל 4605 | לו 3807a | שש 8337 | כנפים 3671 | שש 8337 | כנפים 3671
uashulayu | male'aym | 'at | haheykal. | sarapiym | 'amdiym | mima'al | lou', | shesh | kanapayim | shesh | kanapayim
**and his train | filled | | the temple | the seraphims | stood | Above | it | *had* six | wings | six | wings**

לאחד 259 | בשתים 8147 | יכסה 3680 | פניו 6440 | ובשתים 8147 | יכסה 3680 | רגליו 7272 | ובשתים 8147 | יעופף 5774: | **6:3** וקרא 7121 | זה 2088
la'achad; | bishtayim | yakaseh | panayu, | uabishtayim | yakaseh | raglayu | uabishtayim | ya'aupep. | uaqara' | zeh
**each one | with twain | he covered | his face | and with twain | he covered | his feet | and with twain | he did fly | And cried | one**

אל 413 | זה 2088 | ואמר 559 | קדוש 6918 | קדוש 6918 | קדוש 6918 | יהוה 3068 | צבאות 6635 | מלא 4393 | כל 3605 | הארץ 776 | כבודו 3519: | **6:4** וינעו 5128
'al | zeh | ua'amar, | qadoush | qadoush | qadoush | Yahuah | tzaba'aut; | mala | kal | ha'aretz | kaboudou. | uayanu'au
**unto | another | and said | Holy | holy | holy | *is* Yahuah | of hosts | *is* full | whole | the earth | *of* his glory | And moved**

אמות 520 | הספים 5592 | מקול 6963 | הקורא 7121 | והבית 1004 | ימלא 4390 | עשן 6227: | **6:5** ואמר 559 | אוי 188 | לי 3807a
'amout | hasipiym, | miqoul | haqourea'; | uahabayit | yimalea' | 'ashan. | ua'amar | 'auy | liy
**the posts of | the door | at the voice of | him that cried | and the house | was filled with | smoke | Then said I | Woe | *is* me**

כי 3588 | נדמיתי 1820 | כי 3588 | איש 376 | טמא 2931 | שפתים 8193 | אנכי 595 | ובתוך 8432 | עם 5971 | טמא 2931 | שפתים 8193 | אנכי 595
kiy | nidmeytiy, | kiy | 'aysh | tamea' | sapatayim | 'anokiy, | uabtouk | 'am | tamea' | sapatayim, | 'anokiy
**for | I am undone | because | a man of | unclean lips | | I *am* | and in the midst of | a people of | unclean lips | I**

יושב 3427 | כי 3588 | את 853 | המלך 4428 | יהוה 3068 | צבאות 6635 | ראו 7200 | עיני 5869: | **6:6** ויעף 5774 | אלי 413 | אחד 259 | מן 4480 | השרפים 8314
yousheb; | kiy, | 'at | hamelek | Yahuah | tzaba'aut | ra'au | 'aeynay. | uaya'ap | 'aelay, | 'achad | min | hasarapiym,
**dwell | for | | the King | Yahuah | of hosts | have seen | mine eyes | Then flew | unto me | one | of | the seraphims**

ובידו 3027 | רצפה 7531 | במלקחים 4457 | לקח 3947 | מעל 5921 | המזבח 4196: | **6:7** ויגע 5060 | על 5921 | פי 6310
uabyadou | ritzpah; | bamelqachayim, | laqach | me'al | hamizbeach. | uayaga' | 'al | piy,
**having in his hand | a live coal | with the tongs | *which* he had taken | from off | the altar | And he laid *it* | upon | my mouth**

ויאמר 559 | הנה 2009 | נגע 5060 | זה 2088 | על 5921 | שפתיך 8193 | וסר 5493 | עונך 5771 | וחטאתך 2403 | תכפר 3722: | **6:8** ואשמע 8085
uaya'mer | hineh | naga' | zeh | 'al | sapateyka; | uasar | 'auoneka, | uachata'taka | takupar. | ua'ashma'
**and said | Lo | has touched | this | on | your lips | and is taken away | your iniquity | and your sin | purged | Also I heard**

Isa 5:29 yea, they shall roar, and lay hold of the prey, and shall carry it away safe, and none shall deliver it.30 And in that day they shall roar against them like the roaring of the sea: and if one look unto the land, behold darkness and sorrow, and the light is darkened in the heavens thereof. **Isa** 6:1 In the year that king Uzziah died I saw also YHUH sitting upon a throne, high and lifted up, and his train filled the temple.2 Above it stood the seraphims: each one had six wings; with twain he covered his face, and with twain he covered his feet, and with twain he did fly.3 And one cried unto another, and said, Holy, holy, holy, is YHUH of hosts: the whole earth is full of his glory.4 And the posts of the door moved at the voice of him that cried, and the house was filled with smoke.5 Then said I, Woe is me! for I am undone; because I am a man of unclean lips, and I dwell in the midst of a people of unclean lips: for mine eyes have seen the King, YHUH of hosts.6 Then flew one of the seraphims unto me, having a live coal in his hand, which he had taken with the tongs from off the altar:7 And he laid it upon my mouth, and said, Lo, this has touched your lips; and your iniquity is taken away, and your sin purged.

את 853 קול 6963 אדני 136 אמר 559 את 853 מי 4310 אשלח 7971 ומי 4310 ילך 1980 לנו 3807a ואמר 559 הנני 2005 שלחני 7971: 6:9
'at qoul 'adonay 'amer, 'at miy' 'ashlach uamiy yelek lanu; ua'amar hinniy shalacheniy.
**the voice of Adonai saying Whom shall I send and who will go for us? Then said I Here *am* I send me**

ויאמר 559 לך 1980 ואמרת 559 לעם 5971 הזה 2088 שמעו 8085 שמוע 8085 ואל 408 תבינו 995 וראו 7200 ראו 7200 ואל 408
uaya'mer lek ua'amarta la'am hazeh; shim'au shamoua' ua'al tabiynu, uar'au ra'ou ua'al
**And he said Go you and tell people this Hear you indeed but not understand and see you indeed but not**

תדעו 3045: 6:10 השמן 8080 לב 3820 העם 5971 הזה 2088 ואזניו 241 הכבד 3513 ועיניו 5869 השע 8173 פן 6435 יראה 7200
teda'au. hashmen leb ha'am hazeh, ua'azanayu hakabed ua'aeynayu hasha'; pen yir'ah
**perceive Make fat the heart of the people this and make their ears heavy and their eyes shut lest they see**

בעיניו 5869 ובאזניו 241 ישמע 8085 ולבבו 3824 יבין 995 ושב 7725 ורפא 7495 לו 3807a: 6:11
ba'aeynayu uab'azanayu yishma', ualbabou yabiyn uashab uarapa' lou'.
**with their eyes and with their ears hear and with their heart understand and convert and be healed for himself**

ואמר 559 עד 5704 מתי 4970 אדני 136 ויאמר 559 עד 5704 אשר 834 אם 518 שאו 7582 ערים 5892 מאין 369 יושב 3427
ua'amar 'ad matay 'adonay; uaya'mer 'ad 'asher 'am sha'au 'ariym me'ayn yousheb,
**Then said I how long? when Adonai And he answered Until which if be wasted the cities without inhabitant**

ובתים 1004 מאין 369 אדם 120 והאדמה 127 תשאה 7582 שממה 8077: 6:12 ורחק 7368 יהוה 3069 את 853 האדם 120
uabatiym me'ayn 'adam, uaha'adamah tisha'ah shamamah. uarichaq Yahuah 'at ha'adam;
**and the houses without man and the land be utterly desolate And have removed far away Yahuah men**

ורבה 7227 העזובה 5805 בקרב 7130 הארץ 776: 6:13 ועוד 5750 בה 871a עשריה 6224 ושבה 7725 והיתה 1961
uarabah ha'azubah baqereb ha'aretz. ua'aud bah 'asiriyah, uashabah uahayatah
**and *there be* a great forsaking in the midst of the land But yet in it *shall be* a tenth and *it* shall return and shall be**

לבער 1197 כאלה 424 וכאלון 437 אשר 834 בשלכת 7995 מצבת 4678 בם 871a זרע 2233 קדש 6944
laba'aer; ka'aelah uaka'aloun, 'asher bashaleket matzebet bam, zera' qodesh
**eaten as a teil tree and as an oak whose when they cast *their leaves: so the* substance *is* in them seed holy**

מצבתה 4678:
matzabtah.
***shall be* the substance thereof**

Isa 7:1 ויהי 1961 בימי 3117 אחז 271 בן 1121 יותם 3147 בן 1121 עזיהו 5818 מלך 4428 יהודה 3063 עלה 5927 רצין 7526
uayahiy biymey 'achaz ben youtam ben 'aziyahu melek yahudah, 'alah ratziyn
**And it came to pass in the days of Ahaz the son of Jotham the son of Uzziah king of Judah went up *that* Rezin**

מלך 4428 ארם 758 ופקח 6492 בן 1121 רמליהו 7425 מלך 4428 ישראל 3478 ירושלם 3389 למלחמה 4421 עליה 5921 ולא 3808
melek 'aram uapeqach ben ramalyahu melek yisra'ael yarushalaim, lamilchamah 'aleyha; uala'
**the king of Syria and Pekah the son of Remaliah king of Israel *toward* Jerusalem to war against it but not**

יכל 3201 להלחם 3898 עליה 5921: 7:2 ויגד 5046 לבית 1004 דוד 1732 לאמר 559 נחה 5117 ארם 758 על 5921 אפרים 669
yakol lahilachem 'aleyha. uayugad, labeyt dauid lea'mor, nachah 'aram 'al 'aprayim;
**could prevail against it And it was told the house of David saying is confederate Syria with Ephraim**

Isa 6:8 Also I heard the voice of the Adonai, saying, Whom shall I send, and who will go for us? Then said I, Here am I; send me.9 And he said, Go, and tell this people, Hear you indeed, but understand not; and see you indeed, but perceive not.10 Make the heart of this people fat, and make their ears heavy, and shut their eyes; lest they see with their eyes, and hear with their ears, and understand with their heart, and convert, and be healed.11 Then said I, Adonai, how long? And he answered, Until the cities be wasted without inhabitant, and the houses without man, and the land be utterly desolate,12 And YHUH have removed men far away, and there be a great forsaking in the midst of the land.13 But yet in it shall be a tenth, and it shall return, and shall be eaten: as a teil tree, and as an oak, whose substance is in them, when they cast their leaves: so the holy seed shall be the substance thereof. **Isa** 7:1 And it came to pass in the days of Ahaz the son of Jotham, the son of Uzziah, king of Judah, that Rezin the king of Syria, and Pekah the son of Remaliah, king of Israel, went up toward Jerusalem to war against it, but could not prevail against it.2 And it was told the house of David, saying, Syria is confederate with Ephraim. And his heart was moved, and the heart of his people, as the trees of the wood are moved with the wind.

7:3

וינע 5128 לבבו 3824 ולבב 3824 עמו 5971 כנוע 5128 עצי 6086 יער 3293 מפני 6440 רוח 7307: ויאמר 559

uayana' lababou ualbab 'amou, kanoua' 'atzey ya'ar mipaney ruach. uaya'mer

**And was moved his heart and the heart of his people as are moved the trees of the wood with the wind Then said**

יהוה 3068 אל 413 ישעיהו 3470 צא 3318 נא 4994 לקראת 7125 אחז 271 אתה 859 ושאר 7610 ישוב 7725 בנך 1121 אל 413 קצה 7097 תעלת 8585

Yahuah 'al yasha'yahu tzea' naa' liqra't 'achaz, 'atah uash'ar yashub baneka; 'al qatzeh, ta'alat

**Yahuah unto Isaiah Go forth now to meet Ahaz you and Shear jashub your son at the end of the conduit of**

7:4

הברכה 1295 העליונה 5945 אל 413 מסלת 4546 שדה 7704 כובס 3526: ואמרת 559 אליו 413 השמר 8104 והשקט 8252 אל 408

habarekah ha'alyounah, 'al masilat sadeh koubes. ua'amarta 'aelayu hishamer uahashaqet 'al

**pool the upper in the highway of field *the* fuller's And say unto him Take heed and be quiet not**

תירא 3372 ולבבך 3824 אל 408 ירך 7401 משני 8147 זנבות 2180 האודים 181 העשנים 6226 האלה 428 בחרי 2750 אף 639

tiyraa', ualbabaka 'al yerak, mishney zanbout ha'udiym ha'asheniym ha'aeleh; bachariy 'ap

**fear be fainthearted neither faint for the two tails of the firebrands smoking these for the fierce anger of**

7:5

רצין 7526 וארם 758 ובן 1121 רמליהו 7425: יען 3282 כי 3588 יעץ 3289 עליך 5921 ארם 758 רעה 7451 אפרים 669

ratziyn ua'aram uaben ramalyahu. ya'an, kiy ya'atz 'alayik 'aram ra'ah; 'aprayim

**Rezin with Syria and of the son of Remaliah Because for have taken counsel against you Syria evil Ephraim**

7:6

ובן 1121 רמליהו 7425 לאמר 559: נעלה 5927 ביהודה 3063 ונקיצנה 6973 ונבקענה 1234 אלינו 413

uaben ramalyahu lea'mor. na'aleh bayahudah uanqiytzenah, uanabqi'anah 'aeleynu;

**and the son of Remaliah saying Let us go up against Judah and vex it and let us make a breach therein for us**

7:7

ונמליך 4427 מלך 4428 בתוכה 8432 את 853 בן 1121 טבאל 2870: כה 3541 אמר 559 אדני 136 יהוה 3069 לא 3808 תקום 6965

uanamliyk melek batoukah, 'at ben taba'al. koh 'amar 'adonay Yahuah; la' taqum

**and set a king in the midst of it *even* the son of Tabeal Thus saith Adonai Yahuah not It shall stand**

7:8

ולא 3808 תהיה 1961: כי 3588 ראש 7218 ארם 758 דמשק 1834 וראש 7218 דמשק 1834 רצין 7526 ובעוד 5750

uala' tihayeh. kiy ra'sh 'aram dameseq, uara'sh dameseq ratziyn; uab'aud,

**neither shall it come to pass For the head of Syria *is* Damascus and the head of Damascus *is* Rezin and within**

7:9

ששים 8346 וחמש 2568 שנה 8141 יחת 2844 אפרים 669 מעם 5971: וראש 7218 אפרים 669 שמרון 8111

shishiym uachamesh shanah, yechat 'aprayim me'am. uara'sh 'aprayim shomaroun,

**threescore and five years shall be broken Ephraim that it be not a people And the head of Ephraim *is* Samaria**

7:10

וראש 7218 שמרון 8111 בן 1121 רמליהו 7425 אם 518 לא 3808 תאמינו 539 כי 3588 לא 3808 תאמנו 539:

uara'sh shomaroun ben ramalyahu; 'am la' ta'amiynu, kiy la' te'amenu.

**and the head of Samaria son *is* Remaliah's If not you will believe surely not you shall be established**

7:11

ויוסף 3254 יהוה 3069 דבר 1696 אל 413 אחז 271 לאמר 559: שאל 7592 לך 3807a אות 226 מעם 5973 יהוה 3068 אלהיך 430

uayousep Yahuah, daber 'al 'achaz lea'mor. sha'al laka 'aut, me'am Yahuah 'aloheyka;

**Moreover again Yahuah spoke unto Ahaz saying Ask to you a sign of Yahuah your Elohim**

7:12

העמק 6009 שאלה 7592 או 176 הגבה 1361 למעלה 4605: ויאמר 559 אחז 271 לא 3808 אשאל 7592 ולא 3808 אנסה 5254 את 853

ha'ameq she'alah, 'au hagabeah lama'alah. uaya'mer 'achaz; la' 'aesh'al uala' 'anaseh 'at

***either in* the depth ask it or the height in above But said Ahaz not I will ask neither will I tempt**

Isa 7:3 Then said YHUH unto Isaiah, Go forth now to meet Ahaz, you, and Shear-jashub your son, at the end of the conduit of the upper pool in the highway of the fuller's field;4 And say unto him, Take heed, and be quiet; fear not, neither be fainthearted for the two tails of these smoking firebrands, for the fierce anger of Rezin with Syria, and of the son of Remaliah.5 Because Syria, Ephraim, and the son of Remaliah, have taken evil counsel against you, saying,6 Let us go up against Judah, and vex it, and let us make a breach therein for us, and set a king in the midst of it, even the son of Tabeal:7 Thus saith YHUH G-D, It shall not stand, neither shall it come to pass.8 For the head of Syria is Damascus, and the head of Damascus is Rezin; and within threescore and five years shall Ephraim be broken, that it be not a people.9 And the head of Ephraim is Samaria, and the head of Samaria is Remaliah's son. If you will not believe, surely you shall not be established.10 Moreover YHUH spoke again unto Ahaz, saying,11 Ask you a sign of YHUH your G-d; ask it either in the depth, or in the height above.12 But Ahaz said, I will not ask, neither will I tempt YHUH.

7:13

יהוה 3068: ויאמר 559 שמעו 8085 נא 4994 בית 1004 דוד 1732 המעט 4592 מכם 4480 הלאות 3811 אנשים 582 כי 3588

Yahuah. uaya'mer shim'au naa' beyt dauid; hama'at mikem hal'aut 'anashiym, kiy

**Yahuah And he said Hear you now O house of David *Is it* a small thing for you to weary men but**

7:14

תלאו 3811 גם 1571 את 853 אלהי 430: לכן 3651 יתן 5414 אדני 136 הוא 1931 לכם 3807a אות 226 הנה 2009 העלמה 5959

tal'au gam 'at 'alohay. laken yiten 'adonay hua' lakem 'aut; hineh ha'almah,

**will you weary also? my Elohim Therefore shall give Adonai himself to you a sign Behold a virgin**

7:15

הרה 2030 וילדת 3205 בן 1121 וקראת 7121 שמו 8034 עמנו 6005 אל 410: חמאה 2529 ודבש 1706 יאכל 398 לדעתו 3045

harah uayoledet ben, uaqara't shamou 'amanu 'ael. chem'ah uadbash ya'kel; lada'atou

**shall conceive and bear a son and shall call his name Immanu el Butter and honey shall he eat that he may know**

7:16

מאוס 3988 ברע 7451 ובחור 977 בטוב 2896: כי 3588 בטרם 2962 ידע 3045 הנער 5288 מאס 3988 ברע 7451 ובחר 977 בטוב 2896

ma'aus bara' uabachour batoub. kiy baterem yeda' hana'ar ma'as bara' uabachor batoub;

**to refuse the evil and choose the good For before shall know the child to refuse the evil and choose the good**

7:17

תעזב 5800 האדמה 127 אשר 834 אתה 859 קץ 6973 מפני 6440 שני 8147 מלכיה 4428: יביא 935 יהוה 3068 עליך 5921

te'azeb ha'adamah 'asher 'atah qatz, mipaney shaney malakeyha. yabiy'a Yahuah 'aleyka,

**shall be forsaken the land that you abhorrest of both her kings shall bring Yahuah upon you**

ועל 5921 עמך 5971 ועל 5921 בית 1004 אביך 1 ימים 3117 אשר 834 לא 3808 באו 935 למיום 3117 סור 5493 אפרים 669

ua'al 'amaka ua'al beyt 'abiyka yamiym 'asher la' ba'au, lamiyoum sur 'aprayim

**and upon your people and upon house your father's days that not have come from the day departed *that* Ephraim**

7:18

מעל 5921 יהודה 3063 את 853 מלך 4428 אשור 804: והיה 1961 ביום 3117 ההוא 1931 ישרק 8319 יהוה 3068

me'al yahudah; 'at melek 'ashur. uahayah bayoum hahua', yishroq Yahuah

**from Judah *even* the king of Assyria And it shall come to pass in day that shall hiss *that* Yahuah**

7:19

לזבוב 2070 אשר 834 בקצה 7097 יארי 2975 מצרים 4714 ולדבורה 1682 אשר 834 בארץ 776 אשור 804:

lazabub, 'asher biqtzeh ya'arey mitzrayim; ualadabourah, 'asher ba'aretz 'ashur.

**for the fly that *is* in the uttermost part of the rivers of Egypt and for the bee that *is* in the land of Assyria**

ובאו 935 ונחו 5117 כלם 3605 בנחלי 5158 הבתות 1327 ובנקיקי 5357 הסלעים 5553 ובכל 3605

uaba'au uanachu kulam banachaley habatout, uabinqiyqey hasala'aym; uabkol

**And they shall come and shall rest all of them in valleys the desolate and in the holes of the rocks and upon all**

7:20

הנעצוצים 5285 ובכל 3605 הנהללים 5097: ביום 3117 ההוא 1931 יגלח 1548 אדני 136 בתער 8593 השכירה 7917

hana'atzutziym, uabkol hanahaloliym. bayoum hahua' yagalach 'adonay bata'ar hasakiyrah

**bushes and upon all thorns In day the same shall shave Adonai with a rasor that is hired**

בעברי 5676 נהר 5104 במלך 4428 אשור 804 את 853 הראש 7218 ושער 8181 הרגלים 7272 וגם 1571 את 853 הזקן 2206

ba'abrey nahar bamelek 'ashur, 'at hara'sh uasa'ar haraglayim; ua'gam 'at hazaqan

***namely* by them beyond the river by the king of Assyria the head and the hair of the feet and also the beard**

7:21

תספה 5595: והיה 1961 ביום 3117 ההוא 1931 יחיה 2421 איש 376 עגלת 5697 בקר 1241 ושתי 8147

tispeh. uahayah bayoum hahua'; yachayeh 'aysh 'aglat baqar uashtey

**it shall consume And it shall come to pass in day that shall nourish *that* a man a cow young and two**

Isa 7:13 And he said, Hear you now, O house of David; Is it a small thing for you to weary men, but will you weary my G-d also? 14 Therefore YHUH himself shall give you a sign; Behold, a virgin shall conceive, and bear a son, and shall call his name Immanuel.15 Butter and honey shall he eat, that he may know to refuse the evil, and choose the good.16 For before the child shall know to refuse the evil, and choose the good, the land that you abhorrest shall be forsaken of both her kings.17 YHUH shall bring upon you, and upon your people, and upon your father's house, days that have not come, from the day that Ephraim departed from Judah; even the king of Assyria.18 And it shall come to pass in that day, that YHUH shall hiss for the fly that is in the uttermost part of the rivers of Egypt, and for the bee that is in the land of Assyria.19 And they shall come, and shall rest all of them in the desolate valleys, and in the holes of the rocks, and upon all thorns, and upon all bushes.20 In the same day shall YHUH shave with a razor that is hired, namely, by them beyond the river, by the king of Assyria, the head, and the hair of the feet: and it shall also consume the beard.21 And it shall come to pass in that day, that a man shall nourish a young cow, and two sheep;

**7:22**
צאן 6629: | והיה 1961 | מרב 7230 | עשות 6213 | חלב 2461 | יאכל 398 | חמאה 2529 | כי 3588 | חמאה 2529
tza'n. uahayah, merob asout chalab ya'kal chem'ah; kiy chem'ah
**sheep And it shall come to pass for the abundance of *that* they shall give milk he shall eat butter for butter**

**7:23**
ודבש 1706 | יאכל 398 | כל 3605 | הנותר 3498 | בקרב 7130 | הארץ 776: | והיה 1961 | ביום 3117 | ההוא 1931 | יהיה 1961
uadbash ya'kel, kal hanoutar baqereb ha'aretz. uahayah bayoum hahua', yihayeh
**and honey shall eat every one that is left in the land And it shall come to pass in day that shall be *that***

כל 3605 | מקום 4725 | אשר 834 | יהיה 1961 | שם 8033 | אלף 505 | גפן 1612 | באלף 505 | כסף 3701 | לשמיר 8068 | ולשית 7898
kal maqoum, 'asher yihayeh sham 'alep gepen ba'alep kasep; lashamiyr ualashayit
**every place where there were where a thousand vines at a thousand silverlings for briers and thorns**

**7:24**
יהיה 1961: | בחצים 2678 | ובקשת 7198 | יבוא 935 | שמה 8033 | כי 3588 | שמיר 8068 | ושית 7898 | תהיה 1961 | כל 3605
yihayeh. bachitziym uabaqeshet yabou'a shamah; kiy shamiyr uashayit tihayeh kal
**it shall *even* be With arrow and with bows shall *men* come there because briers and thorns shall become all**

**7:25** of
הארץ 776: | וכל 3605 | ההרים 2022 | אשר 834 | במעדר 4576 | יעדרון 5737 | לא 3808 | תבוא 935 | שמה 8033 | יראת 3374
ha'aretz. uakol hehariym, 'asher bama'ader ye'aderun, la' tabou'a shamah, yir'at
**the land And *on* all hills that with the mattock shall be digged not there shall come there the fear**

שמיר 8068 | ושית 7898 | והיה 1961 | למשלח 4916 | שור 7794 | ולמרמס 4823 | שה 7716:
shamiyr uashayit; uahayah lamishlach shour, ualmirmas seh.
**briers and thorns but it shall be for the sending forth of oxen and for the treading of lesser cattle**

**Isa 8:1**
ויאמר 559 | יהוה 3068 | אלי 413 | קח 3947 | לך 3807a | גליון 1549 | גדול 1419 | וכתב 3789 | עליו 5921 | בחרט 2747 | אנוש 582
uaya'mer Yahuah 'aelay, qach laka gilayoun gadoul; uaktob 'alayu bacheret 'anoush,
**Moreover said Yahuah unto me Take to you roll a great and write in it with a pen man's**

**8:2**
למהר 4122 | שלל 7998 | חש 2363 | בז 957: | ואעידה 5749 | לי 3807a | עדים 5707 | נאמנים 539 | את 853 | אוריה 223 | הכהן 3548
lamaher shalal chash baz. ua'a'aydah liy, 'aediym ne'amaniym; 'at 'uariyah hakohen,
**concerning Maher shalal hash baz And I took to record unto me witnesses faithful Uriah the priest**

**8:3**
ואת 853 | זכריהו 2148 | בן 1121 | יברכיהו 3000: | ואקרב 7126 | אל 413 | הנביאה 5031 | ותהר 2029 | ותלד 3205 | בן 1121 | ויאמר 559
ua'at zakaryahu ben yaberekyahu. ua'aqrab 'al hanabiy'ah, uatahar uateled ben; uaya'mer
***and* Zechariah the son of Jeberechiah And I went unto the prophetess and she conceived and bare a son Then said**

**8:4**
יהוה 3068 | אלי 413 | קרא 7121 | שמו 8034 | מהר 4122 | שלל 7998 | חש 2363 | בז 957: | כי 3588 | בטרם 2962 | ידע 3045 | הנער 5288 | קרא 7121
Yahuah 'aelay, qara' shamou, maher shalal chash baz. kiy, baterem yeda' hana'ar, qara'
**Yahuah to me Call his name Maher shalal hash baz For before shall have knowledge the child to cry**

אבי 1 | ואמי 517 | ישא 5375 | את 853 | חיל 2428 | דמשק 1834 | ואת 853 | שלל 7998 | שמרון 8111 | לפני 6440
'abiy ua'amiy; yisa' 'at cheyl dameseq, ua'at shalal shomaroun, lipney
**My father and my mother shall be taken away the riches of Damascus *and* the spoil of Samaria before**

**8:5** **8:6**
מלך 4428 | אשור 804: | ויסף 3254 | יהוה 3068 | דבר 1696 | אלי 413 | עוד 5750 | לאמר 559: | יען 3282 | כי 3588 | מאס 3988 | העם 5971 | הזה 2088
melek 'ashur. uayosep Yahuah, daber 'aelay 'aud lea'mor. ya'an, kiy ma'as ha'am hazeh,
**the king of Assyria also Yahuah spoke unto me again saying Forasmuch as refuse the people this**

Isa 7:22 And it shall come to pass, for the abundance of milk that they shall give he shall eat butter: for butter and honey shall everyone eat that is left in the land.23 And it shall come to pass in that day, that every place shall be, where there were a thousand vines at a thousand silverlings, it shall even be for briers and thorns.24 With arrows and with bows shall men come thither; because all the land shall become briers and thorns.25 And on all hills that shall be digged with the mattock, there shall not come thither the fear of briers and thorns: but it shall be for the sending forth of oxen, and for the treading of lesser cattle. **Isa** 8:1 Moreover YHUH said unto me, Take you a great roll, and write in it with a man's pen concerning Maher-shalal-hash-baz.2 And I took unto me faithful witnesses to record, Uriah the priest, and Zechariah the son of Jeberechiah.3 And I went unto the prophetess; and she conceived, and bare a son. Then said YHUH to me, Call his name Maher-shalal-hash-baz.4 For before the child shall have knowledge to cry, My father, and my mother, the riches of Damascus and the spoil of Samaria shall be taken away before the king of Assyria.5 YHUH spoke also unto me again, saying,6 Forasmuch as this people refuseth the waters of Shiloah that go softly, and rejoice in Rezin and Remaliah's son;

| את 853 | מי 4325 | השלח 7975 | ההלכים 1980 | לאט 328 | ומשוש 4885 | את 853 | רצין 7526 | ובן 1121 | רמליהו 7425: | 8:7 ולכן 3651 | הנה 2009 |
|---|---|---|---|---|---|---|---|---|---|---|---|
| 'at | mey | hashiloach, | haholakiym | la'at; | uamsous | 'at | ratziyn | uaben | ramalyahu. | ualaken | hineh |
| | **the waters of** | **Shiloah** | **that go** | **softly** | **and rejoice in** | | **Rezin** | **and son** | **Remaliah's** | **Now therefore** | **behold** |

| אדני 136 | מעלה 4627 | עליהם 5921 | את 853 | מי 4325 | הנהר 5104 | העצומים 6099 | והרבים 7227 | את 853 | מלך 4428 | אשור 804 | ואת 853 |
|---|---|---|---|---|---|---|---|---|---|---|---|
| 'adonay | ma'aleh | 'aleyhem | 'at | mey | hanahar, | ha'atzumiym | uaharabiym, | 'at | melek | 'ashur | ua'at |
| **Adonai** | **bring up** | **upon them** | | **the waters of** | **the river** | **strong** | **and many** | ***even*** | **the king of** | **Assyria** | ***and*** |

| כל 3605 | כבודו 3519 | ועלה 5927 | על 5921 | כל 3605 | אפיקיו 650 | והלך 1980 | על 5921 | כל 3605 | גדותיו 1415: | 8:8 וחלף 2498 |
|---|---|---|---|---|---|---|---|---|---|---|
| kal | kaboudou; | ua'alah | 'al | kal | 'apiyqayu, | uahalak | 'al | kal | gadoutayu. | uachalap |
| **all** | **his glory** | **and he shall come up** | **over** | **all** | **his channels** | **and go** | **over** | **all** | **his banks** | **And he shall pass** |

| ביהודה 3063 | שטף 7857 | ועבר 5674 | עד 5704 | צואר 6677 | יגיע 5060 | והיה 1961 | מטות 4298 | כנפיו 3671 |
|---|---|---|---|---|---|---|---|---|
| biyahudah | shatap | ua'abar, | 'ad | tzaua'ar | yagiya'; | uahayah | mutout | kanapayu, |
| **through Judah** | **he shall overflow** | **and go over** | **to** | **the neck** | **he shall reach *even*** | **and shall** | **the stretching out of** | **his wings** |

| מלא 4393 | רחב 7341 | ארצך 776 | עמנו 6005 | אל 410: | 8:9 רעו 7489 | עמים 5971 | וחתו 2865 |
|---|---|---|---|---|---|---|---|
| mala | rochab | 'artzaka | 'amanu | 'ael. | ro'au | 'amiym | uachotu, |
| **fill** | **the breadth of** | **your land** | **O Immanu** | **el** | **Associate yourselves** | **O you people** | **and you shall be broken in pieces** |

| והאזינו 238 | כל 3605 | מרחקי 4801 | ארץ 776 | התאזרו 247 | וחתו 2865 | התאזרו 247 |
|---|---|---|---|---|---|---|
| uaha'aziynu, | kal | merchaqey | 'aretz; | hit'azru | uachotu, | hit'azru |
| **and give ear** | **all** | ***you of* far** | **countries** | **gird yourselves** | **and you shall be broken in pieces** | **gird yourselves** |

| וחתו 2865: | 8:10 עצו 5779 | עצה 6098 | ותפר 6565 | דברו 1696 | דבר 1697 | ולא 3808 |
|---|---|---|---|---|---|---|
| uachotu. | 'atzu | 'aetzah | uatupar; | dabaru | dabar | uala' |
| **and you shall be broken in pieces** | **Take together** | **counsel** | **and it shall come to nought** | **speak** | **the word** | **and not** |

| יקום 6965 | כי 3588 | עמנו 5973 | אל 410: | 8:11 כי 3588 | כה 3541 | אמר 559 | יהוה 3068 | אלי 413 | כחזקת 2393 | היד 3027 | ויסרני 3256 |
|---|---|---|---|---|---|---|---|---|---|---|---|
| yaqum, | kiy | 'amanu | 'ael. | kiy | koh | 'amar | Yahuah | 'aelay | kachezqat | hayad; | uayisreniy |
| **it shall stand** | **for** | ***is* with us** | **El** | **For** | **thus** | **spoke** | **Yahuah** | **to me** | **with strong** | **a hand** | **and instructed me** |

| מלכת 1980 | בדרך 1870 | העם 5971 | הזה 2088 | לאמר 559: | 8:12 לא 3808 | תאמרון 559 | קשר 7195 | לכל 3605 | אשר 834 |
|---|---|---|---|---|---|---|---|---|---|
| mileket | baderek | ha'am | hazeh | lea'mor. | la' | ta'marun | qesher, | lakol | 'asher |
| **that I should not walk** | **in the way of** | **the people** | **this** | **saying** | **not** | **Say you** | **A confederacy** | **to all *them to*** | **whom** |

| יאמר 559 | העם 5971 | הזה 2088 | קשר 7195 | ואת 853 | מוראו 4172 | לא 3808 | תיראו 3372 | ולא 3808 | תעריצו 6206: | 8:13 את 853 | יהוה 3068 | צבאות 6635 |
|---|---|---|---|---|---|---|---|---|---|---|---|---|
| ya'mar | ha'am | hazeh | qasher; | ua'at | moura'au | la' | tiyra'au | uala' | ta'ariytzu. | 'at | Yahuah | tzaba'aut |
| **shall say** | **the people** | **this** | **A confederacy** | ***neither*** | **their fear** | **neither** | **fear you** | **nor** | **be afraid** | | **Yahuah** | **of hosts** |

| אתו 853 | תקדישו 6942 | והוא 1931 | מוראכם 4172 | והוא 1931 | מערצכם 6206: | 8:14 והיה 1961 | למקדש 4720 |
|---|---|---|---|---|---|---|---|
| 'atou | taqdiyshu; | uahu'a | moura'akem | uahu'a | ma'aritzakem. | uahayah | lamiqdash; |
| **himself** | **Sanctify** | **and *let* him** | ***be* your fear** | **and *let* him** | ***be* your dread** | **And he shall be** | **for a sanctuary** |

| ולאבן 68 | נגף 5063 | ולצור 6697 | מכשול 4383 | לשני 8147 | בתי 1004 | ישראל 3478 | לפח 6341 | ולמוקש 4170 |
|---|---|---|---|---|---|---|---|---|
| ual'aben | negep | ualtzur | mikshoul | lishney | batey | yisra'ael | lapach | ualmouqesh, |
| **but for a stone of** | **stumbling** | **and for a rock of** | **offence** | **to both** | **the houses of** | **Israel** | **for a gin** | **and for a snare** |

Isa 8:7 Now therefore, behold, YHUH bring up upon them the waters of the river, strong and many, even the king of Assyria, and all his glory: and he shall come up over all his channels, and go over all his banks:8 And he shall pass through Judah; he shall overflow and go over, he shall reach even to the neck; and the stretching out of his wings shall fill the breadth of your land, O Immanuel.9 Associate yourselves, O you people, and you shall be broken in pieces; and give ear, all you of far countries: gird yourselves, and you shall be broken in pieces; gird yourselves, and you shall be broken in pieces.10 Take counsel together, and it shall come to nought; speak the word, and it shall not stand: for G-d is with us.11 For YHUH spoke thus to me with a strong hand, and instructed me that I should not walk in the way of this people, saying,12 Say you not, A confederacy, to all them to whom this people shall say, A confederacy; neither fear you their fear, nor be afraid.13 Sanctify YHUH of hosts himself; and let him be your fear, and let him be your dread.14 And he shall be for a sanctuary; but for a stone of stumbling and for a rock of offence to both the houses of Israel, for a gin and for a snare to the inhabitants of Jerusalem.

8:15
ליושב 3427 | ירושלם 3389: | וכשלו 3782 | בם 871a | רבים 7227 | ונפלו 5307 | ונשברו 7665 | ונוקשו 3369
layousheb | yarushalaim. | uakashlu | bam | rabiym; | uanapalu | uanishbaru, | uanouqashu
**to the inhabitants of | Jerusalem | And shall stumble | among them | many | and fall | and be broken | and be snared**

8:16 ... 8:17
ונלכדו 3920: | צור 6887 | תעודה 8584 | חתום 2856 | תורה 8451 | בלמדי 3928: | וחכיתי 2442 | ליהוה 3068 | המסתיר 5641
uanilkadu. | tzour | ta'udah; | chatoum | tourah | balimuday. | uachikiytiy | laYahuah, | hamastiyr
**and be taken | Bind up | the testimony | seal | the law | among my disciples | And I will wait | upon Yahuah | that hides**

8:18
פניו 6440 | מבית 1004 | יעקב 3290 | וקויתי 6960 | לו 3807a: | הנה 2009 | אנכי 595 | והילדים 3206 | אשר 834 | נתן 5414 | לי 3807a
panayu | mibeyt | ya'aqob; | uaqiueytiy | lou'. | hineh | 'anokiy, | uahayaladiym | 'asher | natan | liy
**his face | from the house of | Jacob | and I will look | for them | Behold | I | and the children | whom | has given | me**

8:19
יהוה 3068 | לאתות 226 | ולמופתים 4159 | בישראל 3478 | מעם 5973 | יהוה 3068 | צבאות 6635 | השכן 7931 | בהר 2022 | ציון 6726: | וכי 3588
Yahuah, | la'atout | ualmoupatiym | bayisra'ael; | me'am | Yahuah | tzaba'aut, | hashoken | bahar | tziyoun. | uakiy
**Yahuah | *are* for signs | and for wonders | in Israel | from | Yahuah | of hosts | which dwell | in mount | Zion | And when**

יאמרו 559 | אליכם 413 | דרשו 1875 | אל 413 | האבות 178 | ואל 413 | הידענים 3049 | המצפצפים 6850
ya'maru | 'aleykem, | dirshu | 'al | ha'about | ua'al | haiyd'aniym, | hamtzaptzapiym
**they shall say | unto you | Seek should | unto | them that have familiar spirits | and | the wizards | that peep**

8:20
והמהגים 1897 | הלוא 3808 | עם 5971 | אל 413 | אלהיו 430 | ידרש 1875 | בעד 1157 | החיים 2416 | אל 413 | המתים 4191: | לתורה 8451
uahamahagiym; | halou'a | 'am | 'al | 'alohayu | yidrosh, | ba'ad | hachayiym | 'al | hametiym. | latourah
**and that mutter | not | a people | unto | their Elohim? | seek | for | the living | to | the dead? | To the law**

8:21
ולתעודה 8584 | אם 518 | לא 3808 | יאמרו 559 | כדבר 1697 | הזה 2088 | אשר 834 | אין 369 | לו 3807a | שחר 7837:
ualit'audah; | 'am | la' | ya'maru | kadabar | hazeh, | 'asher | 'aeyn | lou' | shachar.
**and to the testimony | if | not | they speak | according to word | this *it is* | because | *there is* no | in them | light**

ועבר 5674 | בה 871a | נקשה 7185 | ורעב 7457 | והיה 1961 | כי 3588 | ירעב 7456
ua'abar | bah | niqsheh | uara'aeb; | uahayah | kiy | yir'ab
**And they shall pass | through it | hardly bestead | and hungry | and it shall come to pass | when | they shall be hungry**

8:22
והתקצף 7107 | וקלל 7043 | במלכו 4428 | ובאלהיו 430 | ופנה 6437 | למעלה 4605: | ואל 413 | ארץ 776
uahitqatzap, | uaqilel | bamalkou | uabe'alohayu | uapanah | lama'alah. | ua'al | 'aretz
**that they shall fret themselves | and curse | their king | and their Elohim | and look | upward | And unto | the earth**

יביט 5027 | והנה 2009 | צרה 6869 | וחשכה 2825 | מעוף 4588 | צוקה 6695 | ואפלה 653 | מנדח 5080:
yabiyt; | uahineh | tzarah | uachashekah | ma'aup | tzuqah, | ua'apelah | manudach.
**they shall look | and behold | trouble | and darkness | dimness of | anguish | and darkness | *they shall be* driven *to***

Isa 9:1
כי 3588 | לא 3808 | מועף 4155 | לאשר 834 | מוצק 4165 | לה 3807a | כעת 6256 | הראשון 7223 | הקל 7043
kiy | la' | mu'ap | la'asher | mutzaq | lah | ka'aet | hara'shoun, | heqal
**Nevertheless | not *be* | the dimness *shall* | for her who *was* | in her vexation | to | when | at the first | he lightly afflicted**

ארצה 776 | זבלון 2074 | וארצה 776 | נפתלי 5321 | והאחרון 314 | הכביד 3513 | דרך 1870 | הים 3220 | עבר 5676
'artzah | zabulun | ua'artzah | naptaliy, | uaha'acharoun | hikbiyd; | derek | hayam | 'aeber
**the land of | Zebulun | and the land of | Naphtali | and afterward | did more grievously afflict *her by* | the way of | the sea | beyond**

Isa 8:15 And many among them shall stumble, and fall, and be broken, and be snared, and be taken.16 Bind up the testimony, seal the law among my disciples.17 And I will wait upon YHUH, that hide his face from the house of Jacob, and I will look for him.18 Behold, I and the children whom YHUH has given me are for signs and for wonders in Israel from YHUH of hosts, which dwell in mount Zion.19 And when they shall say unto you, Seek unto them that have familiar spirits, and unto wizards that peep, and that mutter: should not a people seek unto their G-d? for the living to the dead?20 To the law and to the testimony: if they speak not according to this word, it is because there is no light in them.21 And they shall pass through it, hardly bestead and hungry: and it shall come to pass, that when they shall be hungry, they shall fret themselves, and curse their king and their G-d, and look upward.22 And they shall look unto the earth; and behold trouble and darkness, dimness of anguish; and they shall be driven to darkness. **Isa** 9:1 Nevertheless the dimness shall not be such as was in her vexation, when at the first he lightly afflicted the land of Zebulun and the land of Naphtali, and afterward did more grievously afflict her by the way of the sea, beyond Jordan, in Galilee of the nations.

9:2

הירדן 3383 גליל 1551 הגוים 1471: העם 5971 ההלכים 1980 בחשך 2822 ראו 7200 אור 216 גדול 1419 ישבי 3427
hayarden, galiyl hagouyim. ha'am haholakiym bachoshek, ra'au 'aur gadoul; yoshabey
**the Jordan *in* Galilee of the nations The people that walked in darkness have seen a light great they that dwell**

9:3

בארץ 776 צלמות 6757 אור 216 נגה 5050 עליהם 5921: הרבית 7235 הגוי 1471 לא 3808 הגדלת 1431
ba'aretz tzalmauet, 'aur nagah 'aleyhem. hirbiyta hagouy, la' higdalta
**in the land of the shadow of death the light has shined upon them You have multiplied the nation *and* not increased**

9:4

השמחה 8057 שמחו 8055 לפניך 6440 כשמחת 8057 בקציר 7105 כאשר 834 יגילו 1523 בחלקם 2505 שלל 7998: כי 3588
hasimchah; samachu lapaneyka kasimchat baqatziyr, ka'asher yagiylu bachalqam shalal. kiy
**the joy they joy before you according to the joy in harvest *and* as *men* rejoice when they divide the spoil For**

את 853 על 5923 סבלו 5448 ואת 853 מטה 4294 שכמו 7926 שבט 7626 הנגש 5065 בו 871a החתת 2865 כיום 3117
'at 'al subalou, ua'at mateh shikmou, shebet hanoges bou; hachitota kayoum
**the yoke of his burden *and* the staff of his shoulder the rod of oppressor his you have broken as in the day of**

9:5

מדין 4080: כי 3588 כל 3605 סאון 5430 סאן 5431 ברעש 7494 ושמלה 8071 מגוללה 1556 בדמים 1818 והיתה 1961
midyan. kiy kal sa'aun so'aen bara'ash, uasimlah magoulalah badamiym; uahayatah
**Midian For every battle of the warrior *is* with confused noise and garments rolled in blood but *this* shall be**

9:6

לשרפה 8316 מאכלת 3980 אש 784: כי 3588 ילד 3206 ילד 3205 לנו 3807a בן 1121 נתן 5414 לנו 3807a ותהי 1961 המשרה 4951 על 5921
lisrepah ma'akolet 'aesh. kiy yeled yulad lanu, ben nitan lanu, uatahiy hamisrah 'al
**with burning *and* fuel of fire For a child is born unto us a son is given unto us and shall be the government upon**

שכמו 7926 ויקרא 7121 שמו 8034 פלא 6382 יועץ 3289 אל 410 גבור 1368 אביעד 5703 שר 8269
shikmou; uayiqra' shamou pela' you'aetz 'ael gibour, 'abiy'ad sar
**his shoulder and shall be called his name Wonderful Counsellor El *The* mighty *The* everlasting *The* Prince of**

9:7

שלום 7965: למרבה 4766 המשרה 4951 ולשלום 7965 אין 369 קץ 7093 על 5921 כסא 3678 דוד 1732 ועל 5921
shaloum. lamarbeh hamisrah ualshaloum 'aeyn qetz, 'al kisea' dauid ua'al
**Peace Of the increase of *his* government and peace *there shall be* no end upon the throne of David and upon**

ממלכתו 4467 להכין 3559 אתה 853 ולסעדה 5582 במשפט 4941 ובצדקה 6666 מעתה 6258 ועד 5704 עולם 5769
mamlaktou, lahakiyn 'atah ualsa'adah, bamishpat uabitzdaqah; me'atah ua'ad 'aulam,
**his kingdom to order it and to establish it with judgment and with justice from henceforth and even forever**

9:8 … 9:9

קנאת 7068 יהוה 3068 צבאות 6635 תעשה 6213 זאת 2063: דבר 1697 שלח 7971 אדני 136 ביעקב 3290 ונפל 5307 בישראל 3478:
qin'at Yahuah tzaba'aut ta'aseh za't. dabar shalach 'adonay baya'aqob; uanapal bayisra'ael.
**The zeal of Yahuah of hosts will perform this a word sent Adonai into Jacob and it has lighted upon Israel**

וידעו 3045 העם 5971 כלו 3605 אפרים 669 ויושב 3427 שמרון 8111 בגאוה 1346 ובגדל 1433 לבב 3824
uayada'aua ha'am kulou, 'aprayim uayousheb shomaroun; baga'auah uabgodel lebab
**And shall know the people all *even* Ephraim and the inhabitant of Samaria in the pride and stoutness of heart**

9:10

לאמר 559: לבנים 3843 נפלו 5307 וגזית 1496 נבנה 1129 שקמים 8256 גדעו 1438 וארזים 730
lea'mor. labeniym napalu uagaziyt nibneh; shiqmiym guda'au, ua'araziym
**that say The bricks are fallen down but hewn stones we will build *with* the sycomores are cut down but cedars**

Isa 9:2 The people that walked in darkness have seen a great light: they that dwell in the land of the shadow of death, upon them has the light shined.3 Thou have multiplied the nation, and not increased the joy: they joy before you according to the joy in harvest, and as men rejoice when they divide the spoil.4 For you have broken the yoke of his burden, and the staff of his shoulder, the rod of his oppressor, as in the day of Midian.5 For every battle of the warrior is with confused noise, and garments rolled in blood; but this shall be with burning and fuel of fire.6 For unto us a child is born, unto us a son is given: and the government shall be upon his shoulder: and his name shall be called Wonderful, Counseller, The mighty G-d, The everlasting Father, The Prince of Peace.7 Of the increase of his government and peace there shall be no end, upon the throne of David, and upon his kingdom, to order it, and to establish it with judgment and with justice from henceforth even forever. The zeal of YHUH of hosts will perform this.8 The Adonai sent a word into Jacob, and it has lighted upon Israel.9 And all the people shall know, even Ephraim and the inhabitant of Samaria, that say in the pride and stoutness of heart,10 The bricks are fallen down, but we will build with hewn stones: the sycomores are cut down, but we will change them into cedars.

9:11
נחליף 2498: וישגב 7682 יהוה 3068 את 853 צרי 6862 רצין 7526 עליו 5921 ואת 853 איביו 341
nachaliyp. uayasageb Yahuah 'at tzarey ratziyn 'alayu; ua'at 'ayabayu
**we will change *them into* Therefore shall set up Yahuah the adversaries of Rezin against him *and* his enemies**

9:12
יסכסך 5526: ארם 758 מקדם 6924 ופלשתים 6430 מאחור 268 ויאכלו 398 את 853 ישראל 3478 בכל 3605
yasaksek. 'aram miqedem, uapalishtiym me'achour, uayo'akalu 'at yisra'ael bakal
**join together The Syrians before and the Philistines behind and they shall devour Israel with open**

9:13
פה 6310 בכל 3605 זאת 2063 לא 3808 שב 7725 אפו 639 ועוד 5750 ידו 3027 נטויה 5186: והעם 5971 לא 3808 שב 7725
peh; bakal za't la' shab 'apou, ua'aud yadou natuyah. uaha'am la' shab
**mouth For all this not is turned away his anger but still his hand *is* stretched out For the people not turned**

9:14
עד 5704 המכהו 5221 ואת 853 יהוה 3068 צבאות 6635 לא 3808 דרשו 1875: ויכרת 3772 יהוה 3068 מישראל 3478
'ad hamakehu; ua'at Yahuah tzaba'aut la' darashu. uayakret Yahuah miyisra'ael,
**unto him that smite them *neither* Yahuah of hosts neither do they seek Therefore will cut off Yahuah from Israel**

9:15
ראש 7218 וזנב 2180 כפה 3712 ואגמון 100 יום 3117 אחד 259: זקן 2205 ונשוא 5375 פנים 6440 הוא 1931 הראש 7218
ra'sh uazanab kipah ua'agmoun youm 'achad. zaqen uansu'a paniym hua' hara'sh;
**head and tail branch and rush day *in* one The ancient and honorable before he *is* the head**

9:16
ונביא 5030 מורה 3384 שקר 8267 הוא 1931 הזנב 2180: ויהיו 1961 מאשרי 833 העם 5971 הזה 2088 מתעים 8582
uanabiy'a moureh sheqer hua' hazanab. uayihayu ma'ashrey ha'am hazeh mat'aym;
**and the prophet that teach lies he *is* the tail For the leaders of the people this cause *them* to err**

9:17
ומאשריו 833 מבלעים 1104: על 5921 כן 3651 על 5921 בחוריו 970 לא 3808 ישמח 8055 אדני 136
uam'usharayu mabula'aym. 'al ken 'al bachurayu la' yismach 'adonay,
**and *they that are* led of them *are* destroyed Therefore after in their young men no shall have joy Adonai**

ואת 853 יתמיו 3490 ואת 853 אלמנתיו 490 לא 3808 ירחם 7355 כי 3588 כלו 3605 חנף 2611 ומרע 7489
ua'at yatomayu ua'at 'almanotayu la' yarachem, kiy kulou chanep uamera',
***neither* their fatherless *and* widows neither shall have mercy on for every one *is* an hypocrite and an evildoer**

9:18
וכל 3605 פה 6310 דבר 1696 נבלה 5039 בכל 3605 זאת 2063 לא 3808 שב 7725 אפו 639 ועוד 5750 ידו 3027 נטויה 5186:
uakal peh dober nabalah; bakal za't la' shab 'apou, ua'aud yadou natuyah.
**and every mouth speak folly For all this not is turned away his anger but still his hand *is* stretched out**

כי 3588 בערה 1197 כאש 784 רשעה 7564 שמיר 8068 ושית 7898 תאכל 398 ותצת 3341 בסבכי 5442 היער 3293
kiy ba'arah ka'aesh rish'ah, shamiyr uashayit ta'kel; uatitzat basibkey haya'ar,
**For burn as the fire wickedness the briers and thorns it shall devour and shall kindle in the thickets of the forest**

9:19
ויתאבכו 55 גאות 1348 עשן 6227: בעברת 5678 יהוה 3069 צבאות 6635 נעתם 6272 ארץ 776
uayit'abku ge'aut 'ashan. ba'abrat Yahuah tzaba'aut ne'tam 'aretz;
**and they shall mount up *like* the lifting up of smoke Through the wrath of Yahuah hosts is darkened the land**

9:20
ויהי 1961 העם 5971 כמאכלת 3980 אש 784 איש 376 אל 413 אחיו 251 לא 3808 יחמלו 2550: ויגזר 1504 על 5921
uayahiy ha'am kama'akolet 'aesh, 'aysh 'al 'achiyu la' yachamolu. uayigzor 'al
**and shall be the people as the fuel of the fire man about his brother no shall spare And he shall snatch on**

Isa 9:11 Therefore YHUH shall set up the adversaries of Rezin against him, and join his enemies together;12 The Syrians before, and the Philistines behind; and they shall devour Israel with open mouth. For all this his anger is not turned away, but his hand is stretched out still.13 For the people turneth not unto him that smite them, neither do they seek YHUH of hosts.14 Therefore YHUH will cut off from Israel head and tail, branch and rush, in one day.15 The ancient and honourable, he is the head; and the prophet that teach lies, he is the tail.16 For the leaders of this people cause them to err; and they that are led of them are destroyed.17 Therefore YHUH shall have no joy in their young men, neither shall have mercy on their fatherless and widows: foreveryone is an hypocrite and an evildoer, and every mouth speaketh folly. For all this his anger is not turned away, but his hand is stretched out still.18 For wickedness burneth as the fire: it shall devour the briers and thorns, and shall kindle in the thickets of the forest, and they shall mount up like the lifting up of smoke.19 Through the wrath of YHUH of hosts is the land darkened, and the people shall be as the fuel of the fire: no man shall spare his brother. 20 And he shall snatch on the right hand, and be hungry;

ימין 3225 ורעב 7456 ויאכל 398 על 5921 שמאול 8040 ולא 3808 שבעו 7646 איש 376 בשר 1320
yamiyn uara'aeb, uaya'kal 'al sama'ul uala' sabe'au; 'aysh basar
**the right hand and are hungry and he shall eat on the left hand are not they shall be satisfied every man the flesh of**

9:21
זרעו 2220 יאכלו 398: מנשה 4519 את 853 אפרים 669 ואפרים 669 את 853 מנשה 4519 יחדו 3162 המה 1992 על 5921
zaro'au ya'kelu. manasheh 'at 'aprayim, ua'aprayim 'at manasheh, yachdau hemah 'al
**his own arm they shall eat Manasseh Ephraim and Ephraim Manasseh together *and* they *shall be* against**

יהודה 3063 בכל 3605 זאת 2063 לא 3808 שב 7725 אפו 639 ועוד 5750 ידו 3027 נטויה 5186:
yahudah; bakal za't la' shab 'apou, ua'aud yadou natuyah.
**Judah For all this not is turned away his anger but still his hand *is* stretched out**

**Isa 10:1** 10:2
הוי 1945 החקקים 2710 חקקי 2711 און 205 ומכתבים 3789 עמל 5999 כתבו 3789:
houy hachoqaqiym chiqqey 'auen; uamkatbiym 'amal kitebu.
**Woe unto them that decree decrees unrighteous and that write grievousness *which* they have prescribed**

להטות 5186 מדין 1779 דלים 1800 ולגזל 1497 משפט 4941 עניי 6041 עמי 5971 להיות 1961 אלמנות 490
lahatout midiyn daliym, ualigzol mishapat 'aniyey 'amiy; lihayout 'almanout
**To turn aside from judgment the needy and to take away the right from the poor of my people that may be widows**

10:3
שללם 7998 ואת 853 יתומים 3490 יבזו 962: ומה 4100 תעשו 6213 ליום 3117 פקדה 6486 ולשואה 7722
shalalam, ua'at yatoumiym yabozu. uamah ta'asu layoum paqudah, ualshou'ah
**their prey *and* the fatherless *that* they may rob And what will you do in the day of visitation and in the desolation**

10:4
ממרחק 4801 תבוא 935 על 5921 מי 4310 תנוסו 5127 לעזרה 5833 ואנה 575 תעזבו 5800 כבודכם 3519: בלתי 1115
mimerchaq tabou'a; 'al miy' tanusu la'azrah, ua'anah ta'azbu kaboudakem. biltiy
**from afar? *which* shall come to whom will you flee for help? and where will you leave your glory? Without me**

כרע 3766 תחת 8478 אסיר 616 ותחת 8478 הרוגים 2026 יפלו 5307 בכל 3605 זאת 2063 לא 3808 שב 7725 אפו 639
kara' tachat 'asiyr, uatachat harugiym yipolu; bakal za't la' shab 'apou,
**they shall bow down under the prisoners and under the slain they shall fall For all this not is turned away his anger**

10:5
ועוד 5750 ידו 3027 נטויה 5186: הוי 1945 אשור 804 שבט 7626 אפי 639 ומטה 4294 הוא 1931 בידם 3027
ua'aud yadou natuyah. houy 'ashur shebet 'apiy; uamateh hua' bayadam
**but still his hand *is* stretched out Woe Assyrian the rod of mine anger and the staff whose in their hand**

10:6
זעמי 2195: בגוי 1471 חנף 2611 אשלחנו 7971 ועל 5921 עם 5971 עברתי 5678
za'amiy. bagouy chanep 'ashalchenu, ua'al 'am 'abratiy
***is* mine indignation against an nation hypocritical I will send him and against the people of my wrath**

10:7
אצונו 6680 לשלל 7997 שלל 7998 ולבז 962 בז 957 ולשימו 7760 מרמס 4823 כחמר 2563 חוצות 2351:
'atzauenu; lishlol shalal ualaboz baz, ualsiymou mirmas kachomer chutzout.
**will I give him a charge to take the spoil and to take the prey and them to tread down like the mire of the streets**

והוא 1931 לא 3808 כן 3651 ידמה 1819 ולבבו 3824 לא 3808 כן 3651 יחשב 2803 כי 3588 להשמיד 8045 בלבבו 3824 ולהכרית 3772 גוים 1471
uahu'a la' ken yadameh, ualbabou la' ken yachshob; kiy lahashamiyd bilbabou, ualhakriyt gouyim
**Howbeit he not so mean his heart neither so does think but to destroy *it is* in his heart and cut off nations**

Isa 9:20 and he shall eat on the left hand, and they shall not be satisfied: they shall eat every man the flesh of his own arm:21 Manasseh, Ephraim; and Ephraim, Manasseh: and they together shall be against Judah. For all this his anger is not turned away, but his hand is stretched out still. **Isa** 10:1 Woe unto them that decree unrighteous decrees, and that write grievousness which they have prescribed;2 To turn aside the needy from judgment, and to take away the right from the poor of my people, that widows may be their prey, and that they may rob the fatherless!3 And what will you do in the day of visitation, and in the desolation which shall come from far? to whom will you flee for help? and where will you leave your glory?4 Without me they shall bow down under the prisoners, and they shall fall under the slain. For all this his anger is not turned away, but his hand is stretched out still.5 O Assyrian, the rod of mine anger, and the staff in their hand is mine indignation.6 I will send him against an hypocritical nation, and against the people of my wrath will I give him a charge, to take the spoil, and to take the prey, and to tread them down like the mire of the streets.7 Howbeit he mean not so, neither doth his heart think so; but it is in his heart to destroy and cut off nations not a few.

10:8 10:9

לא 3808 מעט 4592: כי 3588 יאמר 559 הלא 3808 שרי 8269 יחדו 3162 מלכים 4428: הלא 3808 ככרכמיש 3751 כלנו 3641 אם 518 לא 3808

la' ma'at. kiy ya'mar; hala' saray yachdau malakiym. hala' kakarkamiysh kalnou; 'am la'

**not a few For he saith *Are* not my princes altogether kings? *Is* not as Carchemish? Calno *is* also not**

10:10

כארפד 774 חמת 2574 אם 518 לא 3808 כדמשק 1834 שמרון 8111: כאשר 834 מצאה 4672 ידי 3027 לממלכת 4467 האליל 457

ka'arpad chamat, 'am la' kadameseq shomaroun. ka'asher matze'ah yadiy, lamamlakot ha'aliyl;

**as Arpad? Hamath *is* also not Damascus? Samaria As has found my hand the kingdoms of the idols**

10:11

ופסיליהם 6456 מירושלם 3389 ומשמרון 8111: הלא 3808 כאשר 834 עשיתי 6213 לשמרון 8111

uapsiyleyhem, miyarushalaim uamishomaroun. hala', ka'asher 'asiytiy lashomaroun

**and whose graven images *did excel them* of Jerusalem and of Samaria Shall I not as I have done unto Samaria**

10:12

ולאליליה 457 כן 3651 אעשה 6213 לירושלם 3389 ולעצביה 6091: והיה 1961 כי 3588 יבצע 1214

uale'aliyleyha; ken 'a'aseh liyarushalaim uala'atzabeyha. uahayah, kiy yabatza'

**and her idols so do to Jerusalem and her idols? Wherefore it shall come to pass *that* when has performed**

אדני 136 את 853 כל 3605 מעשהו 4639 בהר 2022 ציון 6726 ובירושלם 3389 אפקד 6485 על 5921 פרי 6529 גדל 1433 לבב 3824

'adonay 'at kal ma'asehu, bahar tziyoun uabiyarushalaim; 'apqod, 'al pariy godel labab

**Adonai whole his work upon mount Zion and on Jerusalem I will punish on the fruit of *the* stout heart of**

10:13

מלך 4428 אשור 804 ועל 5921 תפארת 8597 רום 7312 עיניו 5869: כי 3588 אמר 559 בכח 3581 ידי 3027 עשיתי 6213

melek 'ashur, ua'al tip'aret rum 'aeynayu. kiy 'amar, bakoach yadiy 'asiytiy,

**the king of Assyria and on the glory of high his looks For he saith By the strength of my hand I have done *it***

ובחכמתי 2451 כי 3588 נבנותי 995 ואסיר 5493 גבולת 1367 עמים 5971 ועתידתיהם 6264 שושתי 8154

uabchakamatiy kiy nabunoutiy; ua'asiyr gabulout 'amiym, ua'atiydoteyhem shousetiy,

**and by my wisdom for I am prudent and I have removed the bounds of the people and their treasures have robbed**

10:14

ואוריד 3381 כאביר 47 יושבים 3427: ותמצא 4672 כקן 7064 ידי 3027 לחיל 2428 העמים 5971

ua'ariyd kabiyr youshabiym. uatimtza' kaqen yadiy lacheyl ha'amiym,

**and I have put down like a valiant *man* the inhabitants And has found as a nest my hand the riches of the people**

וכאסף 622 ביצים 1000 עזבות 5800 כל 3605 הארץ 776 אני 589 אספתי 622 ולא 3808 היה 1961 נדד 5074 כנף 3671

uake'asop beytziym 'azubout, kal ha'aretz 'aniy 'asapatiy; uala' hayah noded kanap,

**and as one gathered have eggs *that are* left all the earth I gathered and none there was that moved the wing**

10:15

ופצה 6475 פה 6310 ומצפצף 6850: היתפאר 6286 הגרזן 1631 על 5921 החצב 2672 בו 871a אם 518

uapotzeh peh uamtzaptzep. hayitpa'aer hagarzen, 'al hachotzeb bou; 'am

**or opened the mouth or peeped Shall boast itself the axe against him that heweth therewith? or**

יתגדל 1431 המשור 4883 על 5921 מניפו 5130 כהניף 5130 שבט 7626 ואת 853 מרימיו 7311

yitgadel hamasour 'al maniypou, kahaniyp shebet ua'at mariymayu,

**shall magnify itself the saw against him that shake it? as should shake *if* the rod *and* *itself* against them that lift it up**

10:16

כהרים 7311 מטה 4294 לא 3808 עץ 6086: לכן 3651 ישלח 7971 האדון 113 יהוה 3068 צבאות 6635

kahariym mateh la' 'aetz. laken yashalach ha'adoun Yahuah tzaba'aut

***or* as should lift up *itself as if it were if* the staff no wood Therefore shall send the Adonai Yahuah of hosts**

Isa 10:8 For he saith, Are not my princes altogether kings?9 Is not Calno as Carchemish? is not Hamath as Arpad? is not Samaria as Damascus?10 As my hand has found the kingdoms of the idols, and whose graven images did excel them of Jerusalem and of Samaria;11 Shall I not, as I have done unto Samaria and her idols, so do to Jerusalem and her idols?12 Wherefore it shall come to pass, that when YHUH has performed his whole work upon mount Zion and on Jerusalem, I will punish the fruit of the stout heart of the king of Assyria, and the glory of his high looks.13 For he saith, By the strength of my hand I have done it, and by my wisdom; for I am prudent: and I have removed the bounds of the people, and have robbed their treasures, and I have put down the inhabitants like a valiant man:14 And my hand has found as a nest the riches of the people: and as one gathereth eggs that are left, have I gathered all the earth; and there was none that moved the wing, or opened the mouth, or peeped.15 Shall the axe boast itself against him that heweth therewith? or shall the saw magnify itself against him that shaketh it? as if the rod should shake itself against them that lift it up, or as if the staff should lift up itself, as if it were no wood.16 Therefore shall the Adonai, YHUH of hosts, send among his fat ones leanness;

10:17
במשמניו 4924 רזון 7332 ותחת 8478 כבדו 3519 יקד 3344 יקד 3350 כיקוד 3350 אש 784: והיה 1961
bamishmanayu razoun; uatachat kabodou yeqad yaqod kiyqoud 'aesh. uahayah
**among his fat ones leanness and under his glory he shall kindle a burning like the burning of a fire And shall be**

אור 216 ישראל 3478 לאש 784 וקדושו 6918 ללהבה 3852 ובערה 1197 ואכלה 398 שיתו 7898 ושמירו 8068 ביום 3117
'aur yisra'ael la'aesh, uaqdoushou lalehabah; uaba'arah, ua'akalah shiytou uashmiyrou bayoum
**the light of Israel for a fire and his Holy One for a flame and it shall burn and devour his thorns and his briers in day**

10:18
אחד 259: וכבוד 3519 יערו 3293 וכרמלו 3759 מנפש 5315 ועד 5704 בשר 1320 יכלה 3615
'achad. uakboud ya'arou uakarmilou, minepesh ua'ad basar yakaleh;
**one And the glory of his forest and of his fruitful field soul and both *and* body shall consume**

10:19
והיה 1961 כמסס 4549 נסס 5263: ושאר 7605 עץ 6086 יערו 3293 מספר 4557 יהיו 1961 ונער 5288
uahayah kimsos noses. uash'ar 'aetz ya'arou mispar yihayu; uana'ar
**and they shall be as when faint a standardbearer And the rest of the trees of his forest few shall be that a child**

10:20
יכתבם 3789: והיה 1961 ביום 3117 ההוא 1931 לא 3808 יוסיף 3254 עוד 5750 שאר 7605 ישראל 3478
yiktabem. uahayah bayoum hahua', la' yousiyp 'aud sha'ar yisra'ael
**may write them And it shall come to pass in day that no again more *that* the remnant of Israel**

ופליטת 6413 בית 1004 יעקב 3290 להשען 8172 על 5921 מכהו 5221 ונשען 8172 על 5921 יהוה 3068
uapleytat beyt ya'aqob, lahisha'aen 'al makehu; uanish'an, 'al Yahuah
**and such as are escaped of the house of Jacob shall upon him that smote them stay upon Yahuah**

10:21
קדוש 6918 ישראל 3478 באמת 571: שאר 7605 ישוב 7725 שאר 7605 יעקב 3290 אל 413 אל 410
qadoush yisra'ael be'amet. sha'ar yashub sha'ar ya'aqob; 'al 'ael
***the* Holy One of Israel in truth The remnant shall return *even* the remnant of Jacob unto El**

10:22
גבור 1368: כי 3588 אם 518 יהיה 1961 עמך 5971 ישראל 3478 כחול 2344 הים 3220 שאר 7605 ישוב 7725 בו 871a
gibour. kiy 'am yihayeh 'amaka yisra'ael kachoul hayam, sha'ar yashub bou;
***the* mighty For though be your people Israel as the sand of the sea *yet* a remnant shall return of them**

10:23
כליון 3631 חרוץ 2782 שוטף 7857 צדקה 6666: כי 3588 כלה 3617 ונחרצה 2782 אדני 136 יהוה 3069
kilayoun charutz shoutep tzadaqah. kiy kalah uanecheratzah; 'adonay Yahuah
**the consumption decreed shall overflow with righteousness For a consumption even determined Adonai Yahuah**

10:24
צבאות 6635 עשה 6213 בקרב 7130 כל 3605 הארץ 776: לכן 3651 כה 3541 אמר 559 אדני 136 יהוה 3068 צבאות 6635 אל 408 תירא 3372
tzaba'aut, 'aseh baqereb kal ha'aretz. laken, koh 'amar 'adonay Yahuah tzaba'aut, 'al tiyraa'
**of hosts shall make in the midst of all the land Therefore thus saith Adonai Yahuah of hosts not be afraid**

עמי 5971 ישב 3427 ציון 6726 מאשור 804 בשבט 7626 יככה 5221 ומטהו 4294 ישא 5375 עליך 5921
'amiy yosheb tziyoun me'ashur; bashebet yakekah, uamatehu yisaa' 'aleyka
**O my people that dwell in Zion of the Assyrian with a rod he shall smite you and his staff shall lift up against you**

10:25
בדרך 1870 מצרים 4714: כי 3588 עוד 5750 מעט 4592 מזער 4213 וכלה 3615 זעם 2195 ואפי 639
baderek mitzrayim. kiy 'aud ma'at miz'ar; uakalah za'am, ua'apiy
**after the manner of Egypt For yet a little while very and shall cease the indignation and mine anger**

Isa 10:16 and under his glory he shall kindle a burning like the burning of a fire.17 And the light of Israel shall be for a fire, and his Holy One for a flame: and it shall burn and devour his thorns and his briers in one day;18 And shall consume the glory of his forest, and of his fruitful field, both soul and body: and they shall be as when a standardbearer fainteth.19 And the rest of the trees of his forest shall be few, that a child may write them.20 And it shall come to pass in that day, that the remnant of Israel, and such as are escaped of the house of Jacob, shall no more again stay upon him that smote them; but shall stay upon YHUH, the Holy One of Israel, in truth.21 The remnant shall return, even the remnant of Jacob, unto the mighty G-d.22 For though your people Israel be as the sand of the sea, yet a remnant of them shall return: the consumption decreed shall overflow with righteousness.23 For YHUH G-D of hosts shall make a consumption, even determined, in the midst of all the land.24 Therefore thus saith YHUH G-D of hosts, O my people that dwellest in Zion, be not afraid of the Assyrian: he shall smite you with a rod, and shall lift up his staff against you, after the manner of Egypt.25 For yet a very little while, and the indignation shall cease, and mine anger in their destruction.

10:26

על 5921 תבליתם 8399: ועורר 5782 עליו 5921 יהוה 3068 צבאות 6635 שוט 7752 כמכת 4347 מדין 4080

'al tabliytam. ua'aurer 'alayu Yahuah tzaba'aut shout, kamakat midyan

**in their destruction And shall stir up for him Yahuah of hosts a scourge according to the slaughter of Midian**

10:27

בצור 6697 עורב 6159 ומטהו 4294 על 5921 הים 3220 ונשאו 5375 בדרך 1870 מצרים 4714:

batzur 'aureb; uamatehu 'al hayam, uansa'au baderek mitzrayim.

**at the rock of Oreb and *as* his rod *was* upon the sea so shall he lift it up after the manner of Egypt**

והיה 1961 ביום 3117 ההוא 1931 יסור 5493 סבלו 5448 מעל 5921 שכמך 7926 ועלו 5923

uahayah bayoum hahua', yasur subalou me'al shikmeka, ua'alou

**And it shall come to pass in day that shall be taken away *that* his burden from off your shoulder and his yoke**

10:28

מעל 5921 צוארך 6677 וחבל 2254 על 5923 מפני 6440 שמן 8081: בא 935 על 5921 עית 5857 עבר 5674

me'al tzaua'reka; uachubal 'al mipaney shamen. ba' 'al 'ayat 'abar

**from off your neck and shall be destroyed the yoke because of the anointing He is come to Aiath he is passed**

10:29

במגרון 4051 למכמש 4363 יפקיד 6485 כליו 3627: עברו 5674 מעברה 4569 גבע 1387

bamigroun; lamikmas yapqiyd kelayu. 'abaru ma'barah, geba'

**to Migron at Michmash he has laid up his carriages They are gone over the passage *at* Geba**

10:30

מלון 4411 לנו 3807a חרדה 2729 הרמה 7414 גבעת 1390 שאול 7586 נסה 5127: צהלי 6670 קולך 6963 בת 1323

maloun lanu; charadah haramah, gib'at sha'aul nasah. tzahaliy qoulek bat

**they have taken up lodging their is afraid Ramah Gibeah of Saul is fled Lift up your voice O daughter of**

10:31

גלים 1554 הקשיבי 7181 לישה 3919 עניה 6041 ענתות 6068: נדדה 5074 מדמנה 4088 ישבי 3427 הגבים 1374

galiym; haqashiybiy layashah 'aniyah 'anatout. nadadah madmenah; yoshabey hagebiym

**Gallim cause it to be heard unto Laish O poor Anathoth is removed Madmenah inhabitants of the Gebim**

10:32

העיזו 5756: עוד 5750 היום 3117 בנב 5011 לעמד 5975 ינפף 5130 ידו 3027 הר 2022

he'ayzu. 'aud hayoum banob la'amod; yanopep yadou har

**gather themselves to flee As yet that day at Nob shall he remain he shall shake his hand *against* the mount of**

10:33

בית 1004 ציון 6726 גבעת 1389 ירושלם 3389: הנה 2009 האדון 113 יהוה 3068 צבאות 6635 מסעף 5586 פארה 6288 במערצה 4637

beyt tziyoun, gib'at yarushalaim. hineh ha'adoun Yahuah tzaba'aut, masa'aep pa'rah bama'aratzah;

**the daughter of first the hill of Jerusalem Behold Adonai Yahuah of hosts shall lop the bough with terror**

10:34

ורמי 7311 הקומה 6967 גדועים 1438 והגבהים 1364 ישפלו 8213: ונקף 5362

uaramey haqoumah gadu'aym, uahagabohiym yishpalu. uanipaq

**and the high ones of stature *shall be* hewn down and the haughty shall be humbled And he shall cut down**

סבכי 5442 היער 3293 בברזל 1270 והלבנון 3844 באדיר 117 יפול 5307:

sibkey haya'ar babarzel; uahalabanoun ba'adiyr yipoul.

**the thickets of the forest with iron and the Lebanon by a mighty one shall fall**

**Isa 11:1**

ויצא 3318 חטר 2415 מגזע 1503 ישי 3448 ונצר 5342 משרשיו 8328 יפרה 6509:

uayatza' choter migeza' yishay; uanetzer misharashayu yipreh.

**And there shall come forth a rod out of the stem of Jesse and a Branch out of his roots shall grow**

Isa 10:26 And YHUH of hosts shall stir up a scourge for him according to the slaughter of Midian at the rock of Oreb: and as his rod was upon the sea, so shall he lift it up after the manner of Egypt.27 And it shall come to pass in that day, that his burden shall be taken away from off your shoulder, and his yoke from off your neck, and the yoke shall be destroyed because of the anointing.28 He is come to Aiath, he is passed to Migron; at Michmash he has laid up his carriages:29 They are gone over the passage: they have taken up their lodging at Geba; Ramah is afraid; Gibeah of Saul is fled.30 Lift up your voice, O daughter of Gallim: cause it to be heard unto Laish, O poor Anathoth.31 Madmenah is removed; the inhabitants of Gebim gather themselves to flee.32 As yet shall he remain at Nob that day: he shall shake his hand against the mount of the daughter of Zion, the hill of Jerusalem.33 Behold, the Adonai, YHUH of hosts, shall lop the bough with terror: and the high ones of stature shall be hewn down, and the haughty shall be humbled.34 And he shall cut down the thickets of the forest with iron, and Lebanon shall fall by a mighty one. **Isa** 11:1 And there shall come forth a rod out of the stem of Jesse, and a Branch shall grow out of his roots:

| 11:2 | ונחה 5117 | עליו 5921 | רוח 7307 | יהוה 3068 | רוח 7307 | חכמה 2451 | ובינה 998 | רוח 7307 | עצה 6098 |
|---|---|---|---|---|---|---|---|---|---|
| | uanachah | 'alayu | ruach | Yahuah; | ruach | chakamah | uabiynah, | ruach | 'aetzah |
| | **And shall rest** | **upon him** | **the spirit of** | **Yahuah** | **the spirit of** | **wisdom** | **and understanding** | **the spirit of** | **counsel** |

| וגבורה 1369 | רוח 7307 | דעת 1847 | ויראת 3374 | יהוה 3068: | 11:3 | והריחו 7306 |
|---|---|---|---|---|---|---|
| uagaburah, | ruach | da'at | uayir'at | Yahuah. | | uahariychou |
| **and might** | **the spirit of** | **knowledge** | **and of the fear of** | **Yahuah** | | **And shall make him of quick understanding** |

| ביראת 3374 | יהוה 3068 | ולא 3808 | למראה 4758 | עיניו 5869 | ישפוט 8199 | ולא 3808 | למשמע 4926 | אזניו 241 |
|---|---|---|---|---|---|---|---|---|
| bayir'at | Yahuah; | uala' | lamar'aeh | 'aeynayu | yishpout, | uala' | lamishma' | 'azanayu |
| **in the fear of** | **Yahuah** | **and not** | **after the sight of** | **his eyes** | **he shall judge** | **neither** | **after the hearing of** | **his ears** |

| יוכיח 3198: | 11:4 | ושפט 8199 | בצדק 6664 | דלים 1800 | והוכיח 3198 | במישור 4334 | לענוי 6035 | ארץ 776 |
|---|---|---|---|---|---|---|---|---|
| youkiyach. | | uashapat | batzedeq | daliym, | uahoukiyach | bamiyshour | la'anuey | 'aretz; |
| **reprove** | | **But shall he judge** | **with righteousness** | **the poor** | **and reprove** | **with equity** | **for the meek of** | **the earth** |

| והכה 5221 | ארץ 776 | בשבט 7626 | פיו 6310 | וברוח 7307 | שפתיו 8193 | ימית 4191 | רשע 7563: | 11:5 |
|---|---|---|---|---|---|---|---|---|
| uahikah | 'aretz | bashebet | piyu, | uabruach | sapatayu | yamiyt | rasha'. | |
| **and he shall smite** | **the earth** | **with the rod of** | **his mouth** | **and with the breath of** | **his lips** | **shall he slay** | **the wicked** | |

| והיה 1961 | צדק 6664 | אזור 232 | מתניו 4975 | והאמונה 530 | אזור 232 | חלציו 2504: | 11:6 | וגר 1481 | זאב 2061 |
|---|---|---|---|---|---|---|---|---|---|
| uahayah | tzedeq | 'aezour | matanayu; | uaha'amunah | 'aezour | chalatzayu. | | uagar | za'aeb |
| **And shall be** | **righteousness** | **the girdle of** | **his loins** | **and faithfulness** | **the girdle of** | **his reins** | | **also shall dwell** | **The wolf** |

| עם 5973 | כבש 3532 | ונמר 5246 | עם 5973 | גדי 1423 | ירבץ 7257 | ועגל 5695 | וכפיר 3715 | ומריא 4806 | יחדו 3162 |
|---|---|---|---|---|---|---|---|---|---|
| 'am | kebes, | uanamer | 'am | gadiy | yirbatz; | ua'aegel | uakpiyr | uamriy' | yachdau, |
| **with** | **the lamb** | **and the leopard** | **with** | **the kid** | **shall lie down** | **and the calf** | **and the young lion** | **and the fatling** | **together** |

| ונער 5288 | קטן 6996 | נהג 5090 | בם 871a: | 11:7 | ופרה 6510 | ודב 1677 | תרעינה 7462 | יחדו 3162 | ירבצו 7257 | ילדיהן 3206 |
|---|---|---|---|---|---|---|---|---|---|---|
| uana'ar | qaton | noheg | bam. | | uaparah | uadob | tir'aynah, | yachdau | yirbatzu | yaldeyhen; |
| **and a child** | **little** | **shall lead** | **them** | | **And the cow** | **and the bear** | **shall feed** | **together** | **shall lie down** | **their young ones** |

| ואריה 738 | כבקר 1241 | יאכל 398 | תבן 8401: | 11:8 | ושעשע 8173 | יונק 3243 | על 5921 | חר 2356 | פתן 6620 | ועל 5921 |
|---|---|---|---|---|---|---|---|---|---|---|
| ua'aryeh | kabaqar | ya'kal | teben. | | uashi'asha' | youneq | 'al | chur | paten; | ua'al |
| **and the lion** | **like the ox** | **shall eat** | **straw** | | **And shall play** | **the sucking child** | **on** | **the hole of** | **the asp** | **and on** |

| מאורת 3975 | צפעוני 6848 | גמול 1580 | ידו 3027 | הדה 1911: | 11:9 | לא 3808 | ירעו 7489 | ולא 3808 | ישחיתו 7843 | בכל 3605 |
|---|---|---|---|---|---|---|---|---|---|---|
| ma'aurat | tzip'auniy, | gamul | yadou | hadah. | | la' | yare'au | uala' | yashchiytu | bakal |
| **den (*light shaft*) *the*** | **cockatrice'** | **and the weaned child** | **his hand** | **shall put** | | **not** | **They shall hurt** | **nor** | **destroy** | **in all** |

| הר 2022 | קדשי 6944 | כי 3588 | מלאה 4390 | הארץ 776 | דעה 1844 | את 853 | יהוה 3069 | כמים 4325 | לים 3220 | מכסים 3680: | 11:10 |
|---|---|---|---|---|---|---|---|---|---|---|---|
| har | qadashiy | kiy | mal'ah | ha'aretz, | de'ah | 'at | Yahuah, | kamayim | layam | makasiym. | |
| **mountain** | **my holy** | **for** | **shall be full of** | **the earth** | **the knowledge of** | | **Yahuah** | **as the waters** | **the sea** | **cover** | |

| והיה 1961 | ביום 3117 | ההוא 1931 | שרש 8328 | ישי 3448 | אשר 834 | עמד 5975 | לנס 5251 | עמים 5971 | אליו 413 | גוים 1471 |
|---|---|---|---|---|---|---|---|---|---|---|
| uahayah | bayoum | hahua', | shoresh | yishay, | 'asher | 'amed | lanes | 'amiym, | 'aelayu | gouyim |
| **And there shall be** | **in day** | **that** | **a root of** | **Jesse** | **which** | **shall stand** | **for an ensign of** | **the people** | **to it** | **the Gentiles** |

Isa 11:2 And the spirit of YHUH shall rest upon him, the spirit of wisdom and understanding, the spirit of counsel and might, the spirit of knowledge and of the fear of YHUH;3 And shall make him of quick understanding in the fear of YHUH: and he shall not judge after the sight of his eyes, neither reprove after the hearing of his ears:4 But with righteousness shall he judge the poor, and reprove with equity for the meek of the earth: and he shall smite the earth with the rod of his mouth, and with the breath of his lips shall he slay the wicked.5 And righteousness shall be the girdle of his loins, and faithfulness the girdle of his reins.6 The wolf also shall dwell with the lamb, and the leopard shall lie down with the kid; and the calf and the young lion and the fatling together; and a little child shall lead them.7 And the cow and the bear shall feed; their young ones shall lie down together: and the lion shall eat straw like the ox.8 And the sucking child shall play on the hole of the asp, and the weaned child shall put his hand on the cockatrice' den.9 They shall not hurt nor destroy in all my holy mountain: for the earth shall be full of the knowledge of YHUH, as the waters cover the sea.10 And in that day there shall be a root of Jesse, which shall stand for an ensign of the people; to it shall the Gentiles seek: and his rest shall be glorious.

| ידרשו 1875 | והיתה 1961 | מנחתו 4496 | כבוד 3519: | 11:11 | והיה 1961 | ביום 3117 | ההוא 1931 | יוסיף 3254 | אדני 136 |
|---|---|---|---|---|---|---|---|---|---|
| yidroshu; | uahayatah | manuchatou | kaboud. | | uahayah | bayoum | hahua', | yousiyp | 'adonay |
| **shall seek** | **and shall be** | **his rest** | **glorious** | | **And it shall come to pass** | **in day** | **that** | **shall set again** | ***that* Adonai** |

| שנית 8145 | ידו 3027 | לקנות 7069 | את 853 | שאר 7605 | עמו 5971 | אשר 834 | ישאר 7604 | מאשור 804 | וממצרים 4714 |
|---|---|---|---|---|---|---|---|---|---|
| sheniyt | yadou, | liqnout | 'at | sha'ar | 'amou; | 'asher | yisha'aer | me'ashur | uamimitzrayim |
| **the second time** | **his hand** | **to recover** | | **the remnant of** | **his people** | **which** | **shall be left** | **from Assyria** | **and from Egypt** |

| ומפתרוס 6624 | ומכוש 3568 | ומעילם 5867 | ומשנער 8152 | ומחמת 2574 | ומאיי 339 | הים 3220: | 11:12 |
|---|---|---|---|---|---|---|---|
| uamipatrous | uamikush, | uame'aeylam | uamishin'ar | uamechamat, | uame'ayey | hayam. | |
| **and from Pathros** | **and from Cush** | **and from Elam** | **and from Shinar** | **and from Hamath** | **and from the islands of** | **the sea** | |

| ונשא 5375 | נס 5251 | לגוים 1471 | ואסף 622 | נדחי 1760 | ישראל 3478 | ונפצות 5310 | יהודה 3063 |
|---|---|---|---|---|---|---|---|
| uanasa' | nes | lagouyim, | ua'asap | nidchey | yisra'ael; | uanputzout | yahudah |
| **And he shall set up** | **an ensign** | **for the nations** | **and shall assemble** | **the outcasts of** | **Israel** | **the dispersed of** | **Judah** |

| יקבץ 6908 | מארבע 702 | כנפות 3671 | הארץ 776: | 11:13 | וסרה 5493 | קנאת 7068 | אפרים 669 | וצררי 6862 | יהודה 3063 |
|---|---|---|---|---|---|---|---|---|---|
| yaqabetz, | me'arba' | kanpout | ha'aretz. | | uasarah | qin'at | 'aprayim, | uatzorarey | yahudah |
| **and gather together** | **from the four** | **corners of** | **the earth** | | **also shall depart** | **The envy of** | **Ephraim** | **adversary of** | **Judah** |

| יכרתו 3772 | אפרים 669 | לא 3808 | יקנא 7065 | את 853 | יהודה 3063 | ויהודה 3063 | לא 3808 | יצר 6887 | את 853 | אפרים 669: | 11:14 | ועפו 5774 |
|---|---|---|---|---|---|---|---|---|---|---|---|---|
| yikaretu; | 'aprayim | la' | yaqanea' | 'at | yahudah, | uayahudah | la' | yatzor | 'at | 'aprayim. | | ua'apu |
| **shall be cut off** | **Ephraim** | **not** | **shall envy** | | **Judah** | **and Judah** | **not** | **shall vex** | | **Ephraim** | | **But they shall fly** |

| בכתף 3802 | פלשתים 6430 | ימה 3220 | יחדו 3162 | יבזו 962 | את 853 | בני 1121 | קדם 6924 | אדום 123 | ומואב 4124 |
|---|---|---|---|---|---|---|---|---|---|
| bakatep | palishtiym | yamah, | yachdau | yabozu | 'at | baney | qedem; | 'adoum | uamou'ab |
| **upon the shoulders of** | **the Philistines toward** | **the west** | **together** | **they shall spoil** | | **them of** | **the east *upon*** | **Edom** | **and Moab** |

| משלוח 4916 | ידם 3027 | ובני 1121 | עמון 5983 | משמעתם 8085: | 11:15 | והחרים 2763 | יהוה 3068 | את 853 |
|---|---|---|---|---|---|---|---|---|
| mishlouch | yadam, | uabney | 'amoun | mishma'tam. | | uahecheriym | Yahuah | 'at |
| **they shall lay** | **their hand** | **and the children of** | **Ammon** | **shall obey them** | | **And shall utterly destroy** | **Yahuah** | |

| לשון 3956 | ים 3220 | מצרים 4714 | והניף 5130 | ידו 3027 | על 5921 | הנהר 5104 | בעים 5868 | רוחו 7307 | והכהו 5221 |
|---|---|---|---|---|---|---|---|---|---|
| lashoun | yam | mitzrayim, | uaheniyp | yadou | 'al | hanahar | ba'yam | ruachou; | uahikahu |
| **the tongue of** | **sea** | **the Egyptian** | **and shall he shake** | **his hand** | **over** | **the river** | **with mighty** | **his wind** | **and shall smite it** |

| לשבעה 7651 | נחלים 5158 | והדריך 1869 | בנעלים 5275: | 11:16 | והיתה 1961 | מסלה 4546 | לשאר 7605 |
|---|---|---|---|---|---|---|---|
| lashib'ah | nachaliym, | uahidriyk | bana'aliym. | | uahayatah | masilah, | lish'ar |
| **in the seven** | **streams** | **and make *men* go over** | **dryshod** | | **And there shall be** | **an highway** | **for the remnant of** |

| עמו 5971 | אשר 834 | ישאר 7604 | מאשור 804 | כאשר 834 | היתה 1961 | לישראל 3478 | ביום 3117 | עלתו 5927 | מארץ 776 |
|---|---|---|---|---|---|---|---|---|---|
| 'amou, | 'asher | yisha'aer | me'ashur; | ka'asher | hayatah | layisra'ael, | bayoum | alotou | me'aretz |
| **his people** | **which** | **shall be left** | **from Assyria** | **like as** | **it was** | **to Israel** | **in the day** | **that he came up** | **out of the land of** |

| מצרים 4714: |
|---|
| mitzrayim. |
| **Egypt** |

Isa 11:11 And it shall come to pass in that day, that YHUH shall set his hand again the second time to recover the remnant of his people, which shall be left, from Assyria, and from Egypt, and from Pathros, and from Cush, and from Elam, and from Shinar, and from Hamath, and from the islands of the sea.12 And he shall set up an ensign for the nations, and shall assemble the outcasts of Israel, and gather together the dispersed of Judah from the four corners of the earth.13 The envy also of Ephraim shall depart, and the adversaries of Judah shall be cut off: Ephraim shall not envy Judah, and Judah shall not vex Ephraim.14 But they shall fly upon the shoulders of the Philistines toward the west; they shall spoil them of the east together: they shall lay their hand upon Edom and Moab; and the children of Ammon shall obey them.15 And YHUH shall utterly destroy the tongue of the Egyptian sea; and with his mighty wind shall he shake his hand over the river, and shall smite it in the seven streams, and make men go over dryshod.16 And there shall be an highway for the remnant of his people, which shall be left, from Assyria; like as it was to Israel in the day that he came up out of the land of Egypt.

**Isa 12:1**
ואמרת 559 ביום 3117 ההוא 1931 אודך 3034 יהוה 3068 כי 3588 אנפת 599 בי 871a ישב 7725
ua'amarta bayoum hahua', 'audaka Yahuah, kiy 'anapta biy; yashob
**And you shall say in day that I will praise you O Yahuah for though you were angry with me is turned away**

אפך 639 ותנחמני 5162: **12:2** הנה 2009 אל 410 ישועתי 3444 אבטח 982 ולא 3808 אפחד 6342 כי 3588 עזי 5797
'apaka uatnachameniy. hineh 'ael yashu'atiy 'abtach uala' 'apchad; kiy 'aziy
**your anger and you comforted me Behold El *is* my salvation I will trust and not be afraid for *is* my strength**

וזמרת 2176 יה 3050 יהוה 3068 ויהי 1961 לי 3807a לישועה 3444: **12:3** ושאבתם 7579 מים 4325 בששון 8342
uazimrat Yah Yahuah, uayahiy liy liyshu'ah. uash'abtem mayim basasoun;
**and *my* song for Yah YAHUAH he also is become my salvation Therefore shall you draw water with joy**

ממעיני 4599 הישועה 3444: **12:4** ואמרתם 559 ביום 3117 ההוא 1931 הודו 3034 ליהוה 3069 קראו 7121 בשמו 8034 הודיעו 3035
mima'ayaney hayashu'ah. ua'amartem bayoum hahua', houdu laYahuah qara'au bishmou, houdiy'au
**out of wells of the salvation And shall you say in day that Praise unto Yahuah call upon his name declare**

בעמים 5971 עלילתיו 5949 הזכירו 2142 כי 3588 נשגב 7682 שמו 8034: **12:5** זמרו 2167 יהוה 3068 כי 3588 גאות 1348
ba'amiym 'aliylotayu; hazakiryu kiy nisgab shamou. zamru Yahuah, kiy ge'aut
**among the people his doings make mention that is exalted his name Sing unto Yahuah for excellent things**

עשה 6213 מידעת 3045 זאת 2063 בכל 3605 הארץ 776: **12:6** צהלי 6670 ורני 7442 יושבת 3427 ציון 6726 כי 3588 גדול 1419
'asah; meyuda'at za't bakal ha'aretz. tzahaliy uaroniy youshebet tziyoun; kiy gadoul
**he has done is known this in all the earth Cry out and shout *you* inhabitant of Zion for great**

בקרבך 7130 קדוש 6918 ישראל 3478:
baqirbek qadoush yisra'ael.
**in the midst of you *is the* Holy One of Israel**

**Isa 13:1**
משא 4853 בבל 894 אשר 834 חזה 2372 ישעיהו 3470 בן 1121 אמוץ 531: **13:2** על 5921 הר 2022 נשפה 8192 שאו 5375
masa' babel; 'asher chazah, yasha'yahu ben amoutz. 'al har nishpeh sa'au
**The burden of Babylon which did see Isaiah the son of Amoz upon mountain *the* high Lift you up**

נס 5251 הרימו 7311 קול 6963 להם 3807a הניפו 5130 יד 3027 ויבאו 935 פתחי 6607 נדיבים 5081: **13:3** אני 589
nes, hariymu qoul lahem; haniypu yad, uayabo'au pitchey nadiybiym. 'aniy
**a banner exalt the voice unto them shake the hand that they may go into the gates of the nobles I**

צויתי 6680 למקדשי 6942 גם 1571 קראתי 7121 גבורי 1368 לאפי 639 עליזי 5947
tziueytiy limqudashay; gam qaraa'tiy gibouray la'apiy, 'aliyzey
**have commanded my sanctified ones also I have called my mighty ones for mine anger *even* them that rejoice in**

גאותי 1346: **13:4** קול 6963 המון 1995 בהרים 2022 דמות 1823 עם 5971 רב 7227 קול 6963 שאון 7588
ga'auatiy. qoul hamoun behariym damut 'am rab; qoul sha'aun
**my highness The noise of a multitude in the mountains like as *of* a people great a noise of tumultuous**

ממלכות 4467 גוים 1471 נאספים 622 יהוה 3068 צבאות 6635 מפקד 6485 צבא 6635 מלחמה 4421: **13:5** באים 935
mamlakout gouyim ne'asapiym, Yahuah tzaba'aut, mapaqed tzaba' milchamah. ba'aym
**the kingdoms of nations gathered together Yahuah of hosts mustereth the host of the battle They come**

**Isa** 12:1 And in that day you shall say, O YHUH, I will praise you: though you were angry with me, your anger is turned away, and you comfortedst me.2 Behold, G-d is my salvation; I will trust, and not be afraid: for YHUH JEHOVAH is my strength and my song; he also is become my salvation.3 Therefore with joy shall you draw water out of the wells of salvation.4 And in that day shall you say, Praise YHUH, call upon his name, declare his doings among the people, make mention that his name is exalted.5 Sing unto YHUH; for he has done excellent things: this is known in all the earth.6 Cry out and shout, you inhabitant of Zion: for great is the Holy One of Israel in the midst of you.
**Isa** 13:1 The burden of Babylon, which Isaiah the son of Amoz did see.2 Lift you up a banner upon the high mountain, exalt the voice unto them, shake the hand, that they may go into the gates of the nobles.3 I have commanded my sanctified ones, I have also called my mighty ones for mine anger, even them that rejoice in my highness.4 The noise of a multitude in the mountains, like as of a great people; a tumultuous noise of the kingdoms of nations gathered together: YHUH of hosts mustereth the host of the battle.

מארץ 776 מרחק 7801 מקצה 7097 השמים 8064 יהוה 3068 וכלי 3627 זעמו 2195 לחבל 2254 כל 3605
me'aretz merchaq miqtzeh hashamayim; Yahuah uakley za'amou, lachabel kal
**from a country far from the end of heaven *even* Yahuah and the weapons of his indignation to destroy whole**

13:6 13:7
הארץ 776: הילילו 3213 כי 3588 קרוב 7138 יום 3117 יהוה 3068 כשד 7701 משדי 7706 יבוא 935:
ha'aretz. heyliylu kiy qaroub youm Yahuah; kashod mishaday yabou'a.
**the land Howl you for *is* at hand for the day of Yahuah as a destruction from the Almighty it shall come**

13:8
על 5921 כן 3651 כל 3605 ידים 3027 תרפינה 7503 וכל 3605 לבב 3824 אנוש 582 ימס 4549: ונבהלו 926 צירים 6735
'al ken kal yadayim tirpeynah; uakal labab 'anoush yimas uanibhalu tziyriym
**Therefore after all hands shall be faint and every heart man's shall melt And they shall be afraid pangs**

וחבלים 2256 יאחזון 270 כיולדה 3205 יחילון 2342 איש 376 אל 413 רעהו 7453 יתמהו 8539
uachabaliym ya'chezun, kayouledah yachiylun; 'aysh 'al re'aehu yitmahu,
**and sorrows shall take hold of them as a woman that travail they shall be in pain one at another they shall be amazed**

13:9
פני 6440 להבים 3851 פניהם 6440: הנה 2009 יום 3117 יהוה 3068 בא 935 אכזרי 394 ועברה 5678 וחרון 2740 אף 639
paney lahabiym paneyhem. hineh youm Yahuah ba', 'akzariy ua'abrah uacharoun 'aap;
**faces of *shall be as* flames their faces Behold the day of Yahuah comes cruel both with wrath and fierce anger**

13:10
לשום 7760 הארץ 776 לשמה 8047 וחטאיה 2400 ישמיד 8045 ממנה 4480: כי 3588 כוכבי 3556 השמים 8064
lasum ha'aretz lashamah, uachata'ayha yashmiyd mimenah. kiy koukabey hashamayim
**to lay the land desolate and the sinners thereof he shall destroy out of it For stars of the heaven**

וכסיליהם 3685 לא 3808 יהלו 1984 אורם 216 חשך 2821 השמש 8121 בצאתו 3318 וירח 3394
uaksiyleyhem, la' yahelu 'auram; chashak hashemesh batzea'tou, uayareach
**and the constellations thereof not shall give their light shall be darkened the sun in his going forth and the moon**

13:11
לא 3808 יגיה 5050 אורו 216: ופקדתי 6485 על 5921 תבל 8398 רעה 7451 ועל 5921 רשעים 7563 עונם 5771
la' yagiyah 'auru. uapaqadtiy 'al tebel ra'ah, ua'al rasha'aym 'auonam;
**not shall cause to shine her light And I will punish for the world *their* evil and on the wicked for their iniquity**

13:12
והשבתי 7673 גאון 1347 זדים 2086 וגאות 1346 עריצים 6184 אשפיל 8213:
uahishbatiy ga'aun zediym, uaga'auat 'ariytziym 'ashpiyl.
**and I will cause to cease the arrogancy of the proud and the haughtiness of the terrible will lay low**

13:13
אוקיר 3365 אנוש 582 מפז 6337 ואדם 120 מכתם 3800 אופיר 211: על 5921 כן 3651
'auqiyr 'anoush mipaz; ua'adam miketem 'aupiyr. 'al ken
**I will make more precious a man than fine gold even a man than the golden wedge of Ophir Therefore after**

שמים 8064 ארגיז 7264 ותרעש 7493 הארץ 776 ממקומה 4725 בעברת 5678 יהוה 3068 צבאות 6635 וביום 3117
shamayim 'argiyz, uatir'ash ha'aretz mimaqoumah; ba'abrat Yahuah tzaba'aut, uabyoum
**the heavens I will shake and shall remove the earth out of her place in the wrath of Yahuah of hosts and in the day of**

13:14
חרון 2740 אפו 639: והיה 1961 כצבי 6643 מדח 5080 וכצאן 6629 ואין 369 מקבץ 6908 איש 376 אל 413
charoun 'apou. uahayah kitzbiy mudach, uaktza'n ua'aeyn maqabetz; 'aysh 'al
**fierce his anger And it shall be as roe *the* chased and as a sheep that no man takes up every man to**

Isa 13:5 They come from a far country, from the end of heaven, even YHUH, and the weapons of his indignation, to destroy the whole land.6 Howl you; for the day of YHUH is at hand; it shall come as a destruction from the Almighty.7 Therefore shall all hands be faint, and every man's heart shall melt:8 And they shall be afraid: pangs and sorrows shall take hold of them; they shall be in pain as a woman that travaileth: they shall be amazed one at another; their faces shall be as flames.9 Behold, the day of YHUH cometh, cruel both with wrath and fierce anger, to lay the land desolate: and he shall destroy the sinners thereof out of it.10 For the stars of heaven and the constellations thereof shall not give their light: the sun shall be darkened in his going forth, and the moon shall not cause her light to shine.11 And I will punish the world for their evil, and the wicked for their iniquity; and I will cause the arrogance of the proud to cease, and will lay low the haughtiness of the terrible.12 I will make a man more precious than fine gold; even a man than the golden wedge of Ophir.13 Therefore I will shake the heavens, and the earth shall remove out of her place, in the wrath of YHUH of hosts, and in the day of his fierce anger.14 And it shall be as the chased roe, and as a sheep that no man take up: they shall every man turn to his own people, and flee everyone into his own land.

| | | | | | | | | |
|---|---|---|---|---|---|---|---|---|
| עמו 5971 | יפנו 6437 | ואיש 376 | אל 413 | ארצו 776 | ינוסו 5127: | 13:15 | כל 3605 | הנמצא 4672 |
| 'amou | yipnu, | ua'aysh | 'al | artzou | yanusu. | | kal | hanimtza' |
| **his own people** | **they shall turn** | **and every one** | **into** | **his own land** | **flee** | | **Every one** | **that is found** |

| | | | | | | |
|---|---|---|---|---|---|---|
| ידקר 1856 | וכל 3605 | הנספה 5595 | יפול 5307 | בחרב 2719: | 13:16 | ועלליהם 5768 |
| yidaqer; | uakal | hanispeh | yipoul | bechareb. | | ua'alaleyhem |
| **shall be thrust through** | **and every one** | **that is joined** | ***unto them* shall fall** | **by the sword** | | **Their children also** |

| | | | | | | | |
|---|---|---|---|---|---|---|---|
| ירטשו 7376 | לעיניהם 5869 | ישסו 8155 | בתיהם 1004 | ונשיהם 802 | תשגלנה 7693: | 13:17 | הנני 2005 |
| yarutshu | la'aeyneyhem; | yishasu | bateyhem, | uansheyhem | tishagalnah | | hinniy |
| **shall be dashed to pieces** | **before their eyes** | **shall be spoiled** | **their houses** | **and their wives** | **ravished** | | **Behold, I** |

| | | | | | | | | | | |
|---|---|---|---|---|---|---|---|---|---|---|
| מעיר 5782 | עליהם 5921 | את 853 | מדי 4074 | אשר 834 | כסף 3701 | לא 3808 | יחשבו 2803 | וזהב 2091 | לא 3808 | יחפצו 2654 |
| me'ayr | 'aleyhem | 'at | maday; | 'asher | kesep | la' | yachshobu, | uazahab | la' | yachpatzu |
| **will stir up** | **against them** | | **the Medes** | **which** | **silver** | **not** | **shall regard** | **and *as for* gold** | **not** | **they shall delight** |

| | | | | | | | | | |
|---|---|---|---|---|---|---|---|---|---|
| בו 871a: | 13:18 | וקשתות 7198 | נערים 5288 | תרטשנה 7376 | ופרי 6529 | בטן 990 | לא 3808 | ירחמו 7355 | על 5921 |
| bou. | | uaqshatout | na'ariym | taratashnah; | uapriy | uaten | la' | yarachemu, | 'al |
| **in it** | | ***Their* archers also** | **the young men** | **shall dash to pieces** | **and fruit of** | **the womb** | **no** | **they shall have pity** | **on** |

| | | | | | | | | | | |
|---|---|---|---|---|---|---|---|---|---|---|
| בנים 1121 | לא 3808 | תחוס 2347 | עינם 5869: | 13:19 | והיתה 1961 | בבל 894 | צבי 6643 | ממלכות 4467 | תפארת 8597 | גאון 1347 | כשדים 3778 |
| baniym | la' | tachous | 'aeynam. | | uahayatah | babel | tzabiy | mamlakout, | tip'aret | ga'aun | kasdiym; |
| **children** | **not** | **shall spare** | **their eye** | | **And** | **Babylon** | **the glory of** | **kingdoms** | **the beauty of** | **excellency** | **the Chaldees'** |

| | | | | | | | | | | |
|---|---|---|---|---|---|---|---|---|---|---|
| כמהפכת 4114 | אלהים 430 | את 853 | סדם 5467 | ואת 853 | עמרה 6017: | 13:20 | לא 3808 | תשב 3427 | לנצח 5331 | ולא 3808 |
| kamahpekat | 'alohiym, | 'at | sadom | ua'at | 'amorah. | | la' | tesheb | lanetzach, | uala' |
| ***shall be* as when overthrew** | **Elohim** | | **Sodom** | ***and*** | **Gomorrah** | | **not** | **It shall be inhabited** | **never** | **and neither** |

| | | | | | | | | | |
|---|---|---|---|---|---|---|---|---|---|
| תשכן 7931 | עד 5704 | דור 1755 | ודור 1755 | ולא 3808 | יהל 167 | שם 8033 | ערבי 6163 | ורעים 7462 | לא 3808 |
| tishkon | 'ad | dour | uadour; | uala' | yahel | sham | 'arabiy, | uaro'aym | la' |
| **shall it be dwelt in** | **from** | **generation** | **to generation** | **and neither** | **shall pitch tent** | **there** | **the Arabian** | **the shepherds** | **neither** |

| | | | | | | | |
|---|---|---|---|---|---|---|---|
| ירבצו 7257 | שם 8033: | 13:21 | ורבצו 7257 | שם 8033 | ציים 6728 | ומלאו 4390 | בתיהם 1004 |
| yarbitzu | sham. | | uarabatzu | sham | tziyiym, | uamal'au | bateyhem |
| **shall make their fold** | **there** | | **But shall lie** | **there** | **wild beasts of the desert** | **and shall be full of** | **their houses** |

| | | | | | | | | | |
|---|---|---|---|---|---|---|---|---|---|
| אחים 255 | ושכנו 7931 | שם 8033 | בנות 1323 | יענה 3284 | ושעירים 8163 | ירקדו 7540 | שם 8033: | 13:22 | וענה 6030 |
| 'achiym; | uashakanu | sham | banout | ya'anah, | uas'ayriym | yaraqdu | sham. | | ua'anah |
| **doleful creatures** | **and shall dwell** | **there** | **company of** | **owls** | **and satyrs** | **shall dance** | **there** | | **And shall cry** |

| | | | | | | | |
|---|---|---|---|---|---|---|---|
| איים 338 | באלמנותיו 490 | ותנים 8577 | בהיכלי 1964 | ענג 6027 | וקרוב 7138 | לבוא 935 | עתה 6256 |
| 'ayiym | ba'almanoutayu, | uataniym | baheykaley | 'aneg; | uaqaroub | labou'a | 'atah, |
| **the wild beasts of the islands** | **in their desolate houses** | **and dragons** | **in palaces** | ***their* pleasant** | **and near** | **to come** | **her time *is*** |

| | | |
|---|---|---|
| וימיה 3117 | לא 3808 | ימשכו 4900: |
| uayameyha | la' | yimasheku. |
| **and her days** | **not** | **shall be prolonged** |

Isa 13:15 Every one that is found shall be thrust through; and everyone that is joined unto them shall fall by the sword.16 Their children also shall be dashed to pieces before their eyes; their houses shall be spoiled, and their wives ravished.17 Behold, I will stir up the Medes against them, which shall not regard silver; and as for gold, they shall not delight in it.18 Their bows also shall dash the young men to pieces; and they shall have no pity on the fruit of the womb; their eye shall not spare children.19 And Babylon, the glory of kingdoms, the beauty of the Chaldees' excellency, shall be as when G-d overthrew Sodom and Gomorrah.20 It shall never be inhabited, neither shall it be dwelt in from generation to generation: neither shall the Arabian pitch tent there; neither shall the shepherds make their fold there.21 But wild beasts of the desert shall lie there; and their houses shall be full of doleful creatures; and owls shall dwell there, and satyrs shall dance there.22 And the wild beasts of the islands shall cry in their desolate houses, and dragons in their pleasant palaces: and her time is near to come, and her days shall not be prolonged.

**Isa 14:1** כי 3588 ירחם 7355 יהוה 3068 את 853 יעקב 3290 ובחר 977 עוד 5750 בישראל 3478 והניחם 3240 על 5921
kiy yarachem Yahuah 'at ya'aqob, uabachar 'aud bayisra'ael, uahiniycham 'al
**For will have mercy on Yahuah Jacob and will choose yet Israel and set them in**

אדמתם 127 ונלוה 3867 הגר 1616 עליהם 5921 ונספחו 5596 על 5921 בית 1004 יעקב 3290: **14:2**
'admatam; uaniluah hager 'aleyhem, uanispachu 'al beyt ya'aqob.
**their own land and shall be joined the strangers with them and they shall cleave to the house of Jacob**

ולקחום 3947 עמים 5971 והביאום 935 אל 413 מקומם 4725 והתנחלום 5157 בית 1004 ישראל 3478 על 5921
ualqachum 'amiym uahebiy'am 'al maqoumam uahitnachalum beyt yisra'ael, 'al
**And shall take them the people and bring them to their place and shall possess them the house of Israel in**

אדמת 127 יהוה 3068 לעבדים 5650 ולשפחות 8198 והיו 1961 שבים 7617 לשביהם 7617
'admat Yahuah, la'abadiym ualishpachout; uahayu shobiym lashobeyhem,
**the land of Yahuah for servants and handmaids and they shall take them captives whose captives they were**

ורדו 7287 בנגשיהם 5065: **14:3** והיה 1961 ביום 3117 הניח 5117 יהוה 3068 לך 3807a
uaradu banogaseyhem. uahayah, bayoum haniyach Yahuah laka,
**and they shall rule over their oppressors And it shall come to pass in the day that shall give rest Yahuah to you**

מעצבך 6090 ומרגזך 7267 ומן 4480 העבדה 5656 הקשה 7186 אשר 834 עבד 5647 בך 871a: **14:4**
me'atzbaka uameragazeka; uamin ha'abodah haqashah 'asher 'abad bak.
**from your sorrow and from your fear and from bondage the hard where were made to serve in you**

ונשאת 5375 המשל 4912 הזה 2088 על 5921 מלך 4428 בבל 894 ואמרת 559 איך 349 שבת 7673 נגש 5065 שבתה 7673
uanasa'ta hamashal hazeh 'al melek babel ua'amarata; 'aeyk shabat noges, shabatah
**That you shall take up proverb this against the king of Babylon and say How has ceased the oppressor ceased**

מדהבה 4062: **14:5** שבר 7665 יהוה 3068 מטה 4294 רשעים 7563 שבט 7626 משלים 4910: **14:6** מכה 5221 עמים 5971
madhebah. shabar Yahuah mateh rasha'aym; shebet moshaliym. makeh 'amiym
**the golden city has broken Yahuah the staff of the wicked *and* the sceptre of the rulers He who smote the people**

בעברה 5678 מכת 4347 בלתי 1115 סרה 5627 רדה 7287 באף 639 גוים 1471 מרדף 7783 בלי 1097 חשך 2820: **14:7** נחה 5117
ba'abrah, makat biltiy sarah; rodeh ba'ap gouyim, murdap baliy chasak. nachah
**in wrath *with* a stroke because continual he that ruled in anger the nations is persecuted *and* none hinder is at rest**

שקטה 8252 כל 3605 הארץ 776 פצחו 6476 רנה 7440: **14:8** גם 1571 ברושים 1265 שמחו 8055 לך 3807a ארזי 730
shaqatah kal ha'aretz; patzachu rinah. gam baroushiym samachu laka 'arzey
***and* is quiet whole The earth they break forth into singing Yea the fir trees rejoice at you *and* the cedars of**

לבנון 3844 מאז 227 שכבת 7901 לא 3808 יעלה 5927 הכרת 3772 עלינו 5921: **14:9** שאול 7585 מתחת 8478 רגזה 7264
labanoun; me'az shakabta, la' ya'aleh hakoet 'aleynu. sha'aul, mitachat ragazah
**Lebanon *saying* Since you are laid down no is come up feller against us Hell (*grave*) from beneath is moved**

לך 3807a לקראת 7125 בואך 935 עורר 5782 לך 3807a רפאים 7496 כל 3605 עתודי 6260 ארץ 776 הקים 6965
laka liqra't bou'aka; 'aurer laka rapa'aym kal 'atudey 'aretz, heqiym
**for you to meet *you* at your coming it stir up for you *even* the dead all the chief ones of the earth it has raised up**

**Isa** 14:1 For YHUH will have mercy on Jacob, and will yet choose Israel, and set them in their own land: and the strangers shall be joined with them, and they shall cleave to the house of Jacob.2 And the people shall take them, and bring them to their place: and the house of Israel shall possess them in the land of YHUH for servants and handmaids: and they shall take them captives, whose captives they were; and they shall rule over their oppressors.3 And it shall come to pass in the day that YHUH shall give you rest from your sorrow, and from your fear, and from the hard bondage wherein you were made to serve,4 That you shall take up this proverb against the king of Babylon, and say, How has the oppressor ceased! the golden city ceased!5 YHUH has broken the staff of the wicked, and the sceptre of the rulers.6 He who smote the people in wrath with a continual stroke, he that ruled the nations in anger, is persecuted, and none hindereth.7 The whole earth is at rest, and is quiet: they break forth into singing.8 Yea, the fir trees rejoice at you, and the cedars of Lebanon, saying, Since you are laid down, no feller is come up against us.9 Hell from beneath is moved for you to meet you at your coming: it stirreth up the dead for you, even all the chief ones of the earth; it has raised up from their thrones all the kings of the nations.

| מכסאותם 3678 | כל 3605 | מלכי 4428 | גוים 1471: | 14:10 | כלם 3605 | יענו 6030 | ויאמרו 559 | אליך 413 | גם 1571 | אתה 859 |
|---|---|---|---|---|---|---|---|---|---|---|
| mikis'autam, | kal | malkey | gouyim. | | kulam | ya'anu, | uaya'maru | 'aeleyka; | gam | 'atah |
| **from their thrones** | **all** | **the kings of** | **the nations** | | **All** | **they shall speak** | **and say** | **unto you** | **also** | **you** |

| חלית 2470 | כמונו 3644 | אלינו 413 | נמשלת 4911: | 14:11 | הורד 3381 | שאול 7585 | גאונך 1347 | המית 1998 |
|---|---|---|---|---|---|---|---|---|
| chuleyta | kamounu | 'aeleynu | nimshalata. | | hurad | sha'aul | ga'auneka | hemyat |
| **Are become weak** | **as we?** | **unto us?** | **are you become like** | | **is brought down to** | **the grave** | **Your pomp** | ***and* the noise of** |

| נבליך 5035 | תחתיך 8478 | יצע 3331 | רמה 7415 | ומכסיך 4374 | תולעה 8438: | 14:12 | איך 349 | נפלת 5307 | משמים 8064 |
|---|---|---|---|---|---|---|---|---|---|
| nabaleyka; | tachteyka | yutza' | rimah, | uamkaseyka | toule'ah. | | 'aeyk | napalta | mishamayim |
| **your viols** | **under you** | **is spread** | **the worm** | **and cover you** | **the worms** | | **How** | **are you fallen** | **from heaven** |

| הילל 1966 | בן 1121 | שחר 7837 | נגדעת 1438 | לארץ 776 | חולש 2522 | על 5921 | גוים 1471: | 14:13 |
|---|---|---|---|---|---|---|---|---|
| heylel | ben | shachar; | nigda'ata | la'aretz, | choulesh | 'al | gouyim. | |
| **O Lucifer (*howl you*)** | **son of** | **the morning** | ***how* are you cut down** | **to the ground** | **which did weaken** | **over** | **the nations** | |

| ואתה 859 | אמרת 559 | בלבבך 3824 | השמים 8064 | אעלה 5927 | ממעל 4605 | לכוכבי 3556 | אל 410 | ארים 7311 | כסאי 3678 | ואשב 3427 |
|---|---|---|---|---|---|---|---|---|---|---|
| ua'atah | 'amarta | bilbabaka | hashamayim | 'a'aleh, | mima'al | lakoukabey | 'ael | 'ariym | kis'ay; | ua'aesheb |
| **For you** | **have said** | **in your heart** | ***into* heaven** | **I will ascend** | **above** | **the stars of** | **El** | **I will exalt** | **my throne** | **I will sit also** |

| בהר 2022 | מועד 4150 | בירכתי 3411 | צפון 6828: | 14:14 | אעלה 5927 | על 5921 | במתי 1116 | עב 5645 |
|---|---|---|---|---|---|---|---|---|
| bahar | mou'aed | bayarkatey | tzapoun. | | 'a'aleh | 'al | bamatey | 'ab; |
| **upon the mount of** | **the congregation** | **in the sides of** | **the north** | | **I will ascend** | **above** | **the heights of** | **the clouds** |

| אדמה 1819 | לעליון 5954: | 14:15 | אך 389 | אל 413 | שאול 7585 | תורד 3381 | אל 413 | ירכתי 3411 | בור 953: | 14:16 |
|---|---|---|---|---|---|---|---|---|---|---|
| 'adameh | la'alyoun. | | 'ak | 'al | sha'aul | turad | 'al | yarkatey | bour. | |
| **I will be like** | **the most High** | | **Yet** | **to** | **hell (*grave*)** | **you shall be brought down** | **to** | **the sides of** | **the pit** | |

| ראיך 7200 | אליך 413 | ישגיחו 7688 | אליך 413 | יתבוננו 995 | הזה 2088 | האיש 376 | מרגיז 7264 |
|---|---|---|---|---|---|---|---|
| ro'ayka | 'aeleyka | yashgiychu, | 'aeleyka | yitbounanu; | hazeh | ha'aysh | margiyz |
| **They that see** | **you** | **shall narrowly look upon you** | **you** | ***and* consider** | ***saying, Is* this** | **the man** | **that made to tremble** |

| הארץ 776 | מרעיש 7493 | ממלכות 4467: | 14:17 | שם 7760 | תבל 8398 | כמדבר 4057 | ועריו 5892 | הרס 2040 |
|---|---|---|---|---|---|---|---|---|
| ha'aretz, | mar'aysh | mamlakout. | | sam | tebel | kamidbar | ua'arayu | haras; |
| **the earth** | **that did shake** | **kingdoms** | | ***That* made** | **the world** | **as a wilderness** | **and the cities thereof** | **destroyed** |

| אסיריו 615 | לא 3808 | פתח 6605 | ביתה 1004: | 14:18 | כל 3605 | מלכי 4428 | גוים 1471 | כלם 3605 | שכבו 7901 | בכבוד 3519 |
|---|---|---|---|---|---|---|---|---|---|---|
| 'asiyrayu | la' | patach | bayatah. | | kal | malkey | gouyim | kulam; | shakabu | bakaboud |
| **his prisoners** | **not** | ***that* opened** | **the house of** | | **All** | **the kings of** | **the nations *even*** | **all of them** | **lie** | **in glory** |

| איש 376 | בביתו 1004: | 14:19 | ואתה 859 | השלכת 7993 | מקברך 6913 | כנצר 5342 | נתעב 8581 | לבוש 3830 |
|---|---|---|---|---|---|---|---|---|
| 'aysh | babeytou. | | ua'atah | hashalakta | miqibraka | kanetzer | nit'ab, | labush |
| **every one** | **in his own house** | | **But you** | **are cast** | **out of your grave** | **like an branch** | **abominable** | ***and as* the raiment of** |

| הרגים 2026 | מטעני 2944 | חרב 2719 | יורדי 3381 | אל 413 | אבני 68 | בור 953 | כפגר 6297 |
|---|---|---|---|---|---|---|---|
| harugiym | mato'aney | chareb; | youradey | 'al | 'abney | bour | kapeger |
| **those that are slain** | **thrust through with** | **a sword** | **that go down to** | | **the stones of** | **the pit** | **as a carcase** |

Isa 14:10 All they shall speak and say unto you, Art you also become weak as we? are you become like unto us?11 Thy pomp is brought down to the grave, and the noise of your viols: the worm is spread under you, and the worms cover you.12 How are you fallen from heaven, O Lucifer, son of the morning! how are you cut down to the ground, which did weaken the nations!13 For you have said in your heart, I will ascend into heaven, I will exalt my throne above the stars of G-d: I will sit also upon the mount of the congregation, in the sides of the north:14 I will ascend above the heights of the clouds; I will be like the most High.15 Yet you shall be brought down to hell, to the sides of the pit.16 They that see you shall narrowly look upon you, and consider you, saying, Is this the man that made the earth to tremble, that did shake kingdoms;17 That made the world as a wilderness, and destroyed the cities thereof; that opened not the house of his prisoners?18 All the kings of the nations, even all of them, lie in glory, everyone in his own house.19 But you are cast out of your grave like an abominable branch, and as the raiment of those that are slain, thrust through with a sword, that go down to the stones of the pit; as a carcase trodden under feet.

14:20

מובס 947: | לא 3808 | תחד 3161 | אתם 854 | בקבורה 6900 | כי 3588 | ארצך 776 | שחת 7843 | עמך 5971

mubas. | la' | techad | 'atam | biqaburah, | kiy | 'artzaka | shichata | 'ameka

**trodden under feet | not | You shall be joined with them | in burial | because | your land | you have destroyed | your people**

14:21

הרגת 2026 | לא 3808 | יקרא 7121 | לעולם 5769 | זרע 2233 | מרעים 7489: | הכינו 3559 | לבניו 1121 | מטבח 4293

haragata; | la' | yiqarea' | la'aulam | zera' | mere'aym. | hakiynu | labanayu | matbeach

***and* slain | not | shall be renowned | never | the seed of | evildoers | Prepare | for his children | slaughter**

14:22

בעון 5771 | אבותם 1 | בל 1077 | יקמו 6965 | וירשו 3423 | ארץ 776 | ומלאו 4390 | פני 6440 | תבל 8398 | ערים 5892:

ba'auon | aboutam; | bal | yaqumu | uayarashu | 'aretz, | uamal'au | paney | tebel | 'ariym.

**for the iniquity of | their fathers | not | that they do rise | nor possess | the land | nor fill | the face of | the world | *with* cities**

וקמתי 6965 | עליהם 5921 | נאם 5002 | יהוה 3069 | צבאות 6635 | והכרתי 3772 | לבבל 894 | שם 8034 | ושאר 7605 | ונין 5209

uaqamtiy | 'aleyhem, | na'am | Yahuah | tzaba'aut; | uahikratiy | lababel | shem | uash'ar | uaniyn

**For I will rise up | against them | saith | Yahuah | of hosts | and cut off | from Babylon | the name | and remnant | and son**

14:23

ונכד 5220 | נאם 5002 | יהוה 3069: | ושמתיה 7760 | למורש 4180 | קפד 7090 | ואגמי 98 | מים 4325 | וטאטאתיה 2894

uaneked | na'am | Yahuah. | uasamtiyha | lamourash | qipod | ua'agmey | mayim; | uatea'tea'tiyha

**and nephew | saith | Yahuah | I will also make it | a possession for | the bittern | and pools of | water | and I will sweep it**

14:24

במטאטא 4292 | השמד 8045 | נאם 5002 | יהוה 3068 | צבאות 6635: | נשבע 7650 | יהוה 3068 | צבאות 6635 | לאמר 559 | אם 518 | לא 3808 | כאשר 834

bamat'atea' | hashamed, | na'am | Yahuah | tzaba'aut. | nishba' | Yahuah | tzaba'aut | lea'mor; | 'am | la' | ka'asher

**with the besom of | destruction | saith | Yahuah | of hosts | has sworn | Yahuah | of hosts | saying | Surely | not | as**

14:25

דמיתי 1819 | כן 3651 | היתה 1961 | וכאשר 834 | יעצתי 3289 | היא 1931 | תקום 6965: | לשבר 7665

dimiytiy | ken | hayatah, | uaka'asher | ya'atzatiy | hiy'a | taqum. | lishbor

**I have thought | so | so shall it come to pass | and as | I have purposed | it | *so* shall stand | That I will break**

אשור 804 | בארצי 776 | ועל 5921 | הרי 2022 | אבוסנו 947 | וסר 5493 | מעליהם 5921 | עלו 5923

'ashur | ba'artziy, | ua'al | haray | 'abusenu; | uasar | me'aleyhem | 'alou,

**the Assyrian | in my land | and upon | my mountains | tread him under foot | then shall depart | from off them | his yoke**

14:26

וסבלו 5448 | מעל 5921 | שכמו 7926 | יסור 5493: | זאת 2063 | העצה 6098 | היעוצה 3289 | על 5921 | כל 3605 | הארץ 776 | וזאת 2063

uasubalou, | me'al | shikmou | yasur. | za't | ha'aetzah | haya'autzah | 'al | kal | ha'aretz; | uaza't

**and his burden | from off | their shoulders | depart | This | *is* the purpose | that is purpose | upon | whole | the earth | and this**

14:27

היד 3027 | הנטויה 5186 | על 5921 | כל 3605 | הגוים 1471: | כי 3588 | יהוה 3068 | צבאות 6635 | יעץ 3289 | ומי 4310

hayad | hanatuyah | 'al | kal | hagouyim. | kiy | Yahuah | tzaba'aut | ya'atz | uamiy

***is* the hand | that is stretched out | upon | all | the nations | For | Yahuah | of hosts | has purposed | and who**

14:28

יפר 6565 | וידו 3027 | הנטויה 5186 | ומי 4310 | ישיבנה 7725: | בשנת 8141 | מות 4194 | המלך 4428 | אחז 271

yaper; | uayadou | hanatuyah | uamiy | yashiybenah. | bishnat | mout | hamelek | 'achaz;

**shall disannul *it*? | and his hand | *is* stretched out | and who | shall turn it back? | In the year that | died | king | Ahaz**

14:29

היה 1961 | המשא 4853 | הזה 2088: | אל 408 | תשמחי 8055 | פלשת 6429 | כלך 3605 | כי 3588 | נשבר 7665 | שבט 7626 | מכך 5221 | כי 3588

hayah | hamasa' | hazeh. | 'al | tismachiy | paleshet | kulek, | kiy | nishbar | shebet | makek; | kiy

**was | burden | this | not | Rejoice you | Palestina | whole | because | *you* is broken | the rod of | him that smote | for**

Isa 14:20 Thou shall not be joined with them in burial, because you have destroyed your land, and slain your people: the seed of evildoers shall never be renowned.21 Prepare slaughter for his children for the iniquity of their fathers; that they do not rise, nor possess the land, nor fill the face of the world with cities.22 For I will rise up against them, saith YHUH of hosts, and cut off from Babylon the name, and remnant, and son, and nephew, saith YHUH.23 I will also make it a possession for the bittern, and pools of water: and I will sweep it with the besom of destruction, saith YHUH of hosts.24 YHUH of hosts has sworn, saying, Surely as I have thought, so shall it come to pass; and as I have purposed, so shall it stand:25 That I will break the Assyrian in my land, and upon my mountains tread him under foot: then shall his yoke depart from off them, and his burden depart from off their shoulders.26 This is the purpose that is purposed upon the whole earth: and this is the hand that is stretched out upon all the nations.27 For YHUH of hosts has purposed, and who shall disannul it? and his hand is stretched out, and who shall turn it back?28 In the year that king Ahaz died was this burden.29 Rejoice not you, whole Palestina, because the rod of him that smote you is broken: for out of the serpent's root shall come forth a cockatrice, and his fruit shall be a fiery flying serpent.

| משרש 8328 | נחש 5175 | יצא 3318 | צפע 6848 | ופריו 6529 | שרף 8314 | מעופף 5774: | 14:30 ורעו 7462 |
|---|---|---|---|---|---|---|---|
| mishoresh | nachash | yetzea' | tzepa', | uapiryou | sarap | ma'aupep. | uar'au |
| out of root | *the* serpent's | shall come forth | a cockatrice | and his fruit *shall be* | a fiery serpent | flying | And shall feed |

| בכורי 1060 | דלים 1800 | ואביונים 34 | לבטח 983 | ירבצו 7257 | והמתי 4191 | ברעב 7458 | שרשך 8328 | ושאריתך 7611 |
|---|---|---|---|---|---|---|---|---|
| bakourey | daliym, | ua'abyouniym | labetach | yirbatzu; | uahematiy | bara'ab | sharashek, | uash'aeriytek |
| the firstborn of | the poor | and the needy | in safety | shall lie down | and I will kill | with famine | your root | and your remnant |

| יהרג 2026: | 14:31 הילילי 3213 | שער 8179 | זעקי 2199 | עיר 5892 | נמוג 4127 | פלשת 6429 | כלך 3605 | כי 3588 | מצפון 6828 | עשן 6227 |
|---|---|---|---|---|---|---|---|---|---|---|
| yaharog. | heyliyliy | sha'ar | za'aqiy | 'ayr, | namoug | paleshet | kulek; | kiy | mitzapoun | 'ashan |
| he shall slay | Howl | O gate | cry | O city | *are* dissolved | Palestina *you* | whole | for | from the north | a smoke |

| בא 935 | ואין 369 | בודד 909 | במועדיו 4151: | 14:32 ומה 4100 | יענה 6030 | מלאכי 4397 |
|---|---|---|---|---|---|---|
| ba', | ua'aeyn | bouded | bamou'adayu. | uamah | ya'aneh | mal'akey |
| there shall come | and none *shall be* | alone | in his appointed times | What then | shall answer *one* | the messengers of |

| גוי 1471 | כי 3588 | יהוה 3068 | יסד 3245 | ציון 6726 | ובה 871a | יחסו 2620 | עניי 6041 | עמו 5971: |
|---|---|---|---|---|---|---|---|---|
| gouy; | kiy | Yahuah | yisad | tziyoun, | uabah | yechesu | 'aniyey | 'amou. |
| the nation? | That | Yahuah | has founded | Zion | and in it | shall trust | the poor of | his people |

| Isa 15:1 משא 4853 | מואב 4124 | כי 3588 | בליל 3915 | שדד 7703 | ער 6144 | מואב 4124 | נדמה 1820 | כי 3588 |
|---|---|---|---|---|---|---|---|---|
| masa' | mou'ab; | kiy | baleyl | shudad | 'ar | mou'ab | nidmah, | kiy, |
| The burden of | Moab | Because | in the night | is laid waste | Ar of | Moab | *and* brought to silence | because |

| בליל 3915 | שדד 7703 | קיר 7024 | מואב 4124 | נדמה 1820: | 15:2 עלה 5927 | הבית 1004 | ודיבן 1769 | הבמות 1116 |
|---|---|---|---|---|---|---|---|---|
| baleyl | shudad | qiyr | mou'ab | nidmah. | 'alah | habayit | uadiybon | habamout |
| in the night | is laid waste | Kir of | Moab | *and* brought to silence | He is gone up to | Bajith | and to Dibon | the high places |

| לבכי 1065 | על 5921 | נבו 5015 | ועל 5921 | מידבא 4311 | מואב 4124 | ייליל 3213 | בכל 3605 | ראשיו 7218 | קרחה 7144 | כל 3605 | זקן 2206 |
|---|---|---|---|---|---|---|---|---|---|---|---|
| labekiy; | 'al | nabou' | ua'al | meydaba' | mou'ab | yayeliyl, | bakal | ra'shayu | qarachah, | kal | zaqan |
| to weep | over | Nebo | and over | Medeba | Moab | shall howl | on all | their heads | *shall be* baldness | *and* every | beard |

| גרועה 1639: | 15:3 בחוצתיו 2351 | חגרו 2296 | שק 8242 | על 5921 | גגותיה 1406 | וברחבתיה 7339 |
|---|---|---|---|---|---|---|
| garu'ah. | bachutzotau | chagaru | saq; | 'al | gagouteyha | uabirchoboteyha |
| cut off | In their streets | they shall gird themselves with | sackcloth | on | the tops of their houses | and in their streets |

| כלה 3605 | ייליל 3213 | ירד 3381 | בבכי 1065: | 15:4 ותזעק 2199 | חשבון 2809 | ואלעלה 500 | עד 5704 | יהץ 3096 | נשמע 8085 |
|---|---|---|---|---|---|---|---|---|---|
| kuloh | yayeliyl | yored | babekiy. | uatiz'aq | cheshboun | ua'al'aleh, | 'ad | yahatz | nishma' |
| every one | shall howl | abundantly | weeping | And shall cry | Heshbon | and Elealeh | unto | Jahaz | shall be heard *even* |

| קולם 6963 | על 5921 | כן 3651 | חלצי 2502 | מואב 4124 | יריעו 7321 | נפשו 5315 | ירעה 3415 | לו 3807a: | 15:5 לבי 3820 |
|---|---|---|---|---|---|---|---|---|---|
| qoulam; | 'al | ken, | chalutzey | mou'ab | yariy'au, | napshou | yara'ah | lou'. | libiy |
| their voice | therefore | after | the armed soldiers of | Moab | shall cry out | his life | shall be grievous | unto him | My heart |

| למואב 4124 | יזעק 2199 | בריחה 1281 | עד 5704 | צער 6820 | עגלת 5697 | שלשיה 7992 | כי 3588 | מעלה 4608 |
|---|---|---|---|---|---|---|---|---|
| lamou'ab | yiz'aq, | bariycheha | 'ad | tzo'ar | 'aglat | shalishiyah; | kiy | ma'aleh |
| for Moab | shall cry out | his fugitives *shall flee* | unto | Zoar | an heifer of | three *years old* | for | *by* the mounting up of |

Isa 14:30 And the firstborn of the poor shall feed, and the needy shall lie down in safety: and I will kill your root with famine, and he shall slay your remnant.31 Howl, O gate; cry, O city; you, whole Palestina, are dissolved: for there shall come from the north a smoke, and none shall be alone in his appointed times.32 What shall one then answer the messengers of the nation? That YHUH has founded Zion, and the poor of his people shall trust in it. **Isa** 15:1 The burden of Moab. Because in the night Ar of Moab is laid waste, and brought to silence; because in the night Kir of Moab is laid waste, and brought to silence;2 He is gone up to Bajith, and to Dibon, the high places, to weep: Moab shall howl over Nebo, and over Medeba: on all their heads shall be baldness, and every beard cut off.3 In their streets they shall gird themselves with sackcloth: on the tops of their houses, and in their streets, everyone shall howl, weeping abundantly.4 And Heshbon shall cry, and Elealeh: their voice shall be heard even unto Jahaz: therefore the armed soldiers of Moab shall cry out; his life shall be grievous unto him.5 My heart shall cry out for Moab; his fugitives shall flee unto Zoar, an heifer of three years old: for by the mounting up of Luhith with weeping shall they go it up; for in the way of Horonaim they shall raise up a cry of destruction.

הלוחית 3872 בבכי 1065 יעלה 5927 בו 871a כי 3588 דרך 1870 חורנים 2773 זעקת 2201 שבר 7667 יעערו 5782: 15:6
haluchiyt, bibkiy ya'aleh bou, kiy derek chouronayim, za'aqat sheber ya'a'eru.
**Luhith with weeping shall they go up it for *in* the way of Horonaim a cry of destruction they shall raise up**

כי 3588 מי 4325 נמרים 5249 משמות 4923 יהיו 1961 כי 3588 יבש 3001 חציר 2682 כלה 3615 דשא 1877 ירק 3418 לא 3808
kiy mey nimriym mashamout yihayu; kiy yabesh chatziyr kalah deshe', yereq la'
**For the waters of Nimrim desolate shall be for is withered away the hay fail the grass green thing no**

היה 1961: 15:7 על 5921 כן 3651 יתרה 3502 עשה 6213 ופקדתם 6486 על 5921 נחל 5158
hayah. 'al ken yitrah 'asah; uapqudatam, 'al nachal
**there is Therefore after the abundance they have gotten and that which they have laid up to the brook of**

הערבים 6155 ישאום 5375: 15:8 כי 3588 הקיפה 5362 הזעקה 2201 את 853 גבול 1366 מואב 4124 עד 5704 אגלים 97
ha'arabiym yisa'um. kiy hiqiypah haza'aqah 'at gabul mou'ab; 'ad 'aglayim
**the willows shall they carry away For is gone round about the cry the borders of Moab unto Eglaim**

יללתה 3215 ובאר 879 אילים 352 יללתה 3215: 15:9 כי 3588 מי 4325 דימון 1775 מלאו 4390 דם 1818
yillatah, uab'aer 'aeyliym yillatah. kiy mey diymoun mala'au dam,
**the howling thereof and Beer elim the howling thereof *unto* For the waters of Dimon shall be full of blood**

כי 3588 אשית 7896 על 5921 דימון 1775 נוספות 3254 לפליטת 6413 מואב 4124 אריה 738 ולשארית 7611 אדמה 127:
kiy 'ashiyt 'al diymoun nousapout; lipleytat mou'ab 'aryeh, ualish'aeriyt 'adamah.
**for I will bring upon Dimon more upon him that escape of Moab lions and upon the remnant of the land**

**Isa 16:1** שלחו 7971 כר 3733 משל 4910 ארץ 776 מסלע 5554 מדברה 4057 אל 413 הר 2022 בת 1323
shilchu char moshel 'aretz misela' midbarah; 'al har bat
**Send you the lamb *to* the ruler of the land from Sela the wilderness unto the mount of the daughter of**

ציון 6726: 16:2 והיה 1961 כעוף 5775 נודד 5074 קן 7064 משלח 7971 תהיינה 1961 בנות 1323 מואב 4124 מעברת 4569
tziyoun. uahayah ka'oup nouded qen mashulach; tihayeynah banout mou'ab, ma'abarot
**Zion For it shall be *that* as a bird wandering the nest cast out of shall be *so* the daughters of Moab *at* the fords**

לארנון 769: 16:3 הביאו 935 עצה 6098 עשו 6213 פלילה 6415 שיתי 7896 כליל 3915 צלך 6738 בתוך 8432 צהרים 6672 סתרי 5641
la'arnoun. habiy'au 'aetzah 'asu paliylah, shiytiy kaliyl tzilek batouk tzaharayim; satriy
**of Arnon Take counsel execute judgment make as the night your shadow in the midst of the noonday hide**

נדחים 5080 נדד 5074 אל 408 תגלי 1540: 16:4 יגורו 1481 בך 871a נדחי 5080 מואב 4124 הוי 1933 סתר 5643 למו 3807a
nidachiym, noded 'al tagaliy. yaguru bak nidchey, mou'ab hauiy seter lamou
**the outcasts him that wander not bewray Let dwell with you mine outcasts Moab be you a covert to them**

מפני 6440 שודד 7703 כי 3588 אפס 656 המץ 4160 כלה 3615 שד 7701 תמו 8552 רמס 7429 מן 4480
mipaney shouded; kiy 'apes hametz kalah shod, tamu romes min
**from the face of the spoiler for is at an end the extortioner cease the spoiler are consumed the oppressors out of**

הארץ 776: 16:5 והוכן 3559 בחסד 2617 כסא 3678 וישב 3427 עליו 5921 באמת 571 באהל 168 דוד 1732
ha'aretz. uahukan bachesed kisea', uayashab 'aelayu be'amet ba'ahel dauid;
**the land And shall be established in mercy the throne and he shall sit upon it in truth in the tabernacle of David**

Isa 15:6 For the waters of Nimrim shall be desolate: for the hay is withered away, the grass faileth, there is no green thing.7 Therefore the abundance they have gotten, and that which they have laid up, shall they carry away to the brook of the willows.8 For the cry is gone round about the borders of Moab; the howling thereof unto Eglaim, and the howling thereof unto Beer-elim.9 For the waters of Dimon shall be full of blood: for I will bring more upon Dimon, lions upon him that escapeth of Moab, and upon the remnant of the land. **Isa** 16:1 Send you the lamb to the ruler of the land from Sela to the wilderness, unto the mount of the daughter of Zion.2 For it shall be, that, as a wandering bird cast out of the nest, so the daughters of Moab shall be at the fords of Arnon.3 Take counsel, execute judgment; make your shadow as the night in the midst of the noonday; hide the outcasts; bewray not him that wandereth.4 Let mine outcasts dwell with you, Moab; be you a covert to them from the face of the spoiler: for the extortioner is at an end, the spoiler ceaseth, the oppressors are consumed out of the land.5 And in mercy shall the throne be established: and he shall sit upon it in truth in the tabernacle of David, judging, and seeking judgment, and hasting righteousness.

16:6

שפט 8199 ודרש 1875 משפט 4941 ומהר 4106 צדק 6664: שמענו 8085 גאון 1347 מואב 4124 גא 1341 מאד 3966

shopet uadoresh mishapat uamhir tzedeq. shama'anu ga'aun mou'ab gea' ma'ad;

**judging and seeking judgment and hasting righteousness We have heard of the pride of Moab proud *he is* very**

16:7

גאותו 1346 וגאונו 1347 ועברתו 5678 לא 3808 כן 3651 בדיו 907: לכן 3651 יילל 3213 מואב 4124

ga'auatou uag'aunou ua'abratou la' ken badayu. laken, yayeliyl mou'ab

***even* of his haughtiness and his pride and his wrath not *be* so *but* his lies *shall* Therefore shall howl Moab**

16:8

למואב 4124 כלה 3605 יילל 3213 לאשישי 808 קיר 7025 חרשת 2889 תהגו 1897 אך 389 נכאים 5218: כי 3588

lamou'ab kuloh yayeliyl; la'ashiyshey qiyr chareset tehagu 'ak naka'aym. kiy

**for Moab every one shall howl for the foundations of Kir hareseth shall you mourn surely *they are* stricken For**

שדמות 7709 חשבון 2809 אמלל 536 גפן 1612 שבמה 7643 בעלי 1167 גוים 1471 הלמו 1986

shadmout cheshboun 'amlal gepen sibmah, ba'aley gouyim halamu

**the fields of Heshbon languish *and* the vine of Sibmah the lords of the heathen have broken down**

שרוקיה 8291 עד 5704 יעזר 3270 נגעו 5060 תעו 8582 מדבר 4057 שלחותיה 7976

saruqeyha, 'ad ya'azer naga'au ta'au midbar; shaluchouteyha,

**the principal plants thereof unto Jazer they are come *even* they wandered *through* the wilderness her branches**

16:9

נטשו 5203 עברו 5674 ים 3220: על 5921 כן 3651 אבכה 1058 בבכי 1065 יעזר 3270 גפן 1612

nitshu 'abaru yam. 'al ken 'abkeh bibkiy ya'azer gepen

**are stretched out they are gone over the sea Therefore after I will bewail with the weeping of Jazer the vine of**

שבמה 7643 אריוך 7301 דמעתי 1832 חשבון 2809 ואלעלה 500 כי 3588 על 5921 קיצך 7019 ועל 5921 קצירך 7105

sibmah, 'arayauek dim'atiy, cheshboun ua'al'aleh; kiy 'al qeytzek ua'al qatziyrek

**Sibmah I will water you with my tears O Heshbon and Elealeh for on your summer fruits and for your harvest**

16:10

הידד 1959 נפל 5307: ונאסף 622 שמחה 8057 וגיל 1524 מן 4480 הכרמל 3759 ובכרמים 3754 לא 3808

heydad napal. uane'asap simchah uagiyl min hakarmel, uabakramiym la'

**the shouting is fallen And is taken away gladness and joy out of the plentiful field and in the vineyards no**

ירנן 7442 לא 3808 ירעע 7321 יין 3196 ביקבים 3342 לא 3808 ידרך 1869 הדרך 1869

yarunan la' yaro'aa'; yayin, bayaqabiym la' yidrok hadorek

**there shall be singing neither shall there be shouting wine in *their* presses no the treaders shall tread out *their vintage***

16:11

הידד 1959 השבתי 7673: על 5921 כן 3651 מעי 4578 למואב 4124 ככנור 3658 יהמו 1993 וקרבי 7130

heydad hishbatiy. 'al ken me'ay lamou'ab, kakinour yehamu; uaqirbiy

**shouting I have made to cease Wherefore after my bowels for Moab like an harp shall sound and mine inward parts**

16:12

לקיר 7025 חרש 2789: והיה 1961 כי 3588 נראה 7200 כי 3588 נלאה 3811 מואב 4124 על 5921 הבמה 1116

laqiyr chares. uahayah kiy nir'ah kiy nila'ah mou'ab 'al habamah;

**for Kir haresh And it shall come to pass when it is seen that is weary Moab on the high place**

16:13

ובא 935 אל 413 מקדשו 4720 להתפלל 6419 ולא 3808 יוכל 3201: זה 2088 הדבר 1697 אשר 834 דבר 1696 יהוה 3069

uaba' 'al miqadashou lahitpalel uala' yukal. zeh hadabar, 'asher diber Yahuah

**that he shall come to his sanctuary to pray but not he shall prevail This *is* the word that has spoken Yahuah**

Isa 16:6 We have heard of the pride of Moab; he is very proud: even of his haughtiness, and his pride, and his wrath: but his lies shall not be so.7 Therefore shall Moab howl for Moab, everyone shall howl: for the foundations of Kir-hareseth shall you mourn; surely they are stricken.8 For the fields of Heshbon languish, and the vine of Sibmah: the lords of the heathen have broken down the principal plants thereof, they are come even unto Jazer, they wandered through the wilderness: her branches are stretched out, they are gone over the sea.9 Therefore I will bewail with the weeping of Jazer the vine of Sibmah: I will water you with my tears, O Heshbon, and Elealeh: for the shouting for your summer fruits and for your harvest is fallen.10 And gladness is taken away, and joy out of the plentiful field; and in the vineyards there shall be no singing, neither shall there be shouting: the treaders shall tread out no wine in their presses; I have made their vintage shouting to cease.11 Wherefore my bowels shall sound like an harp for Moab, and mine inward parts for Kir-haresh.12 And it shall come to pass, when it is seen that Moab is weary on the high place, that he shall come to his sanctuary to pray; but he shall not prevail. 13 This is the word that YHUH has spoken concerning Moab since that time.

| אל 413 | מואב 4124 | מאז 227: | 16:14 | ועתה 6258 | דבר 1696 | יהוה 3068 | לאמר 559 | בשלש 7969 | שנים 8141 | כשני 8141 |
|---|---|---|---|---|---|---|---|---|---|---|
| 'al | mou'ab | me'az. | | ua'atah, | diber | Yahuah | lea'mor | bashalosh | shaniym | kishney |
| **concerning** | **Moab** | **since that time** | | **But now** | **has spoken** | **Yahuah** | **saying** | **Within three** | **years** | **as the years of** |

| שכיר 7916 | ונקלה 7034 | כבוד 3519 | מואב 4124 | בכל 3605 | ההמון 1995 | הרב 7227 | ושאר 7605 | מעט 4592 |
|---|---|---|---|---|---|---|---|---|
| sakiyr, | uaniqlah | kaboud | mou'ab, | bakal | hehamoun | harab; | uash'ar | ma'at |
| **an hireling** | **and shall be contemned** | **the glory of** | **Moab** | **with all** | **that multitude** | **great** | **and the remnant** | ***shall be* very** |

| מזער 4213 | לוא 3808 | כביר 3524: |
|---|---|---|
| miz'ar | lua' | kabiyr. |
| **small** | ***and* not** | **feeble** |

| Isa 17:1 | משא 4853 | דמשק 1834 | הנה 2009 | דמשק 1834 | מוסר 5493 | מעיר 5892 | והיתה 1961 | מעי 4596 | מפלה 4654: | 17:2 |
|---|---|---|---|---|---|---|---|---|---|---|
| | masa' | damaseq; | hineh | dameseq | musar | me'ayr, | uahayatah | ma'ay | mapalah. | |
| | **The burden of** | **Damascus** | **Behold** | **Damascus** | **is taken away** | **from *being* a city** | **and it shall be** | **a heap** | **ruinous** | |

| עזבות 5800 | ערי 5892 | ערער 6177 | לעדרים 5739 | תהיינה 1961 | ורבצו 7257 | ואין 369 | מחריד 2729: | 17:3 |
|---|---|---|---|---|---|---|---|---|
| 'azubout | 'arey | 'aro'aer; | la'adariym | tihayeynah, | uarabatzu | ua'aeyn | machariyd. | |
| ***are* forsaken** | **The cities of** | **Aroer** | **for flocks** | **they shall be** | **which shall lie down** | **and none** | **shall make *them* afraid** | |

| ונשבת 7673 | מבצר 4013 | מאפרים 669 | וממלכה 4467 | מדמשק 1834 | ושאר 7605 | ארם 758 | ככבוד 3519 |
|---|---|---|---|---|---|---|---|
| uanishbat | mibtzar | me'aprayim, | uamamlakah | midameseq | uash'ar | 'aram; | kikaboud |
| **also shall cease** | **The fortress** | **from Ephraim** | **and the kingdom** | **from Damascus** | **and the remnant of** | **Syria** | **as the glory of** |

| בני 1121 | ישראל 3478 | יהיו 1961 | נאם 5002 | יהוה 3068 | צבאות 6635: | 17:4 | והיה 1961 | ביום 3117 | ההוא 1931 |
|---|---|---|---|---|---|---|---|---|---|
| baney | yisra'ael | yihayu, | na'am | Yahuah | tzaba'aut. | | uahayah | bayoum | hahua', |
| **the children of** | **Israel** | **they shall be** | **saith** | **Yahuah** | **of hosts** | | **And it shall come to pass** | **in day** | **that** |

| ידל 1809 | כבוד 3519 | יעקב 3290 | ומשמן 4924 | בשרו 1320 | ירזה 7329: | 17:5 | והיה 1961 |
|---|---|---|---|---|---|---|---|
| yidal | kaboud | ya'aqob; | uamishman | basarou | yerazeh. | | uahayah, |
| **shall be made thin** | ***that* the glory of** | **Jacob** | **and the fatness of** | **his flesh** | **shall wax lean** | | **And it shall be** |

| כאסף 622 | קציר 7105 | קמה 7054 | וזרעו 2220 | שבלים 7641 | יקצור 7114 | והיה 1961 | כמלקט 3950 | שבלים 7641 |
|---|---|---|---|---|---|---|---|---|
| ke'asop | qatziyr | qamah, | uazero'au | shibaliym | yiqtzour; | uahayah | kimlaqet | shibaliym |
| **as when gathered** | **the harvestman** | **the corn** | **and his arm** | **the ears *with*** | **reap** | **and it shall be** | **as he that gathered** | **ears** |

| בעמק 6010 | רפאים 7497: | 17:6 | ונשאר 7604 | בו 871a | עוללת 5955 | כנקף 5363 | זית 2132 | שנים 8147 | שלשה 7969 |
|---|---|---|---|---|---|---|---|---|---|
| ba'aemeq | rapa'aym. | | uanish'ar | bou | 'aulelot | kanoqep | zayit, | shanayim | shaloshah |
| **in the valley of** | **Rephaim** | | **Yet shall be left** | **in it** | **gleaning grapes** | **as the shaking of** | **an olive tree** | **two** | ***or* three** |

| גרגרים 1620 | בראש 7218 | אמיר 534 | ארבעה 702 | חמשה 2568 | בסעפיה 5585 | פריה 6509 | נאם 5002 | יהוה 3068 |
|---|---|---|---|---|---|---|---|---|
| gargariym | bara'sh | 'amiyr; | 'arba'ah | chamishah, | bis'apeyha | poriyah, | na'am | Yahuah |
| **berries** | **in the top of** | **the uppermost bough** | **four** | ***or* five** | **in the outmost branches thereof** | **fruitful** | **saith** | **Yahuah** |

| אלהי 430 | ישראל 3478: | 17:7 | ביום 3117 | ההוא 1931 | ישעה 8159 | האדם 120 | על 5921 | עשהו 6213 | ועיניו 5869 | אל 413 | קדוש 6918 | ישראל 3478 |
|---|---|---|---|---|---|---|---|---|---|---|---|---|
| 'alohey | yisra'ael. | | bayoum | hahua', | yish'ah | ha'adam | 'al | 'asehu; | ua'aeynayu | 'al | qadoush | yisra'ael |
| **Elohim of** | **Israel** | | **At day** | **that** | **shall look** | **a man** | **to** | **his Maker** | **and his eyes** | **to** | ***the* Holy One of** | **Israel** |

Isa 16:14 But now YHUH has spoken, saying, Within three years, as the years of an hireling, and the glory of Moab shall be contemned, with all that great multitude; and the remnant shall be very small and feeble. **Isa** 17:1 The burden of Damascus. Behold, Damascus is taken away from being a city, and it shall be a ruinous heap.2 The cities of Aroer are forsaken: they shall be for flocks, which shall lie down, and none shall make them afraid.3 The fortress also shall cease from Ephraim, and the kingdom from Damascus, and the remnant of Syria: they shall be as the glory of the children of Israel, saith YHUH of hosts.4 And in that day it shall come to pass, that the glory of Jacob shall be made thin, and the fatness of his flesh shall wax lean.5 And it shall be as when the harvestman gathereth the corn, and reapeth the ears with his arm; and it shall be as he that gathereth ears in the valley of Rephaim.6 Yet gleaning grapes shall be left in it, as the shaking of an olive tree, two or three berries in the top of the uppermost bough, four or five in the outmost fruitful branches thereof, saith YHUH G-d of Israel.7 At that day shall a man look to his Maker, and his eyes shall have respect to the Holy One of Israel.

17:8

תראינה 7200: ולא 3808 ישעה 8159 אל 413 המזבחות 4196 מעשה 4639 ידיו 3027 ואשר 834 עשו 6213 אצבעתיו 676

tir'aynah. uala' yish'ah, 'al hamizbachout ma'aseh yadayu; ua'asher 'asu 'atzba'atayu

**shall have respect And not he shall look to the altars the work of his hands *that* which have made his fingers**

17:9

לא 3808 יראה 7200 והאשרים 842 והחמנים 2553: ביום 3117 ההוא 1931 יהיו 1961 ערי 5892 מעזו 4581 כעזובת 5800 החרש 2793

la' yir'ah, uaha'asheriym uahachamaniym. bayoum hahua' yihayu 'arey ma'azu, ka'azubat hachoresh

**neither shall respect either the groves or the images In day that shall be cities his strong as forsaken a bough**

17:10

והאמיר 534 אשר 834 עזבו 5800 מפני 6440 בני 1121 ישראל 3478 והיתה 1961 שממה 8077:

uaha'amiyr, 'asher 'azabu, mipaney baney yisra'ael; uahayatah shamamah.

**and an uppermost branch which they left because of the children of Israel and there shall be desolation**

כי 3588 שכחת 7911 אלהי 430 ישעך 3468 וצור 6697 מעזך 4581 לא 3808 זכרת 2142

kiy shakachat 'alohey yish'aek, uatzur ma'uzek la' zakart;

**Because you have forgotten the Elohim of your salvation and the rock of your strength not have been mindful *of***

17:11

על 5921 כן 3651 תטעי 5193 נטעי 5194 נעמנים 5282 וזמרת 2156 זר 2114 תזרענו 2232: ביום 3117 נטעך 5194

'al ken, tit'ay nit'aey na'amaniym, uazmorat zar tizra'anu. bayoum nit'aek

**therefore after shall you plant plants pleasant and slips *with* strange shall set it In the day your plant**

תשגשגי 7735 ובבקר 1242 זרעך 2233 תפריחי 6524 נד 5067 קציר 7105 ביום 3117

tasagsegiy, uababoqer zar'aek tapriychiy; ned qatziyr bayoum

**shall you make to grow and in the morning your seed shall you make to flourish *shall be* a heap *but* the harvest in the day of**

17:12

נחלה 2470 וכאב 3511 אנוש 605: הוי 1945 המון 1995 עמים 5971 רבים 7227 כהמות 1993 ימים 3220

nachalah uak'aeb 'anush. houy, hamoun 'amiym rabiym, kahamout yamiym

**grief and sorrow *of* desperate Woe *to* the multitude of people many *which* make a noise the seas**

17:13

יהמיון 1993 ושאון 7588 לאמים 3816 כשאון 7588 מים 4325 כבירים 3524 ישאון 7582: לאמים 3816

yehamayun; uash'aun la'amiym, kish'aun mayim kabiyriym yisha'aun. la'amiym,

**like the noise of and to the rushing of nations *that* make a rushing waters! mighty like the rushing of The nations**

כשאון 7588 מים 4325 רבים 7227 ישאון 7582 וגער 1605 בו 871a ונס 5127 ממרחק 4801

kish'aun mayim rabiym yisha'aun, uaga'ar bou uanas mimerchaq;

**like the rushing of waters many shall rush but *Elohim* shall rebuke them and they shall flee far off**

17:14

ורדף 7291 כמץ 4671 הרים 2022 לפני 6440 רוח 7307 וכגלגל 1534 לפני 6440 סופה 5492:

uarudap, kamotz hariym lipaney ruach, uakgalgal lipaney supah.

**and shall be chased as the chaff of the mountains before the wind and like a rolling thing before the whirlwind**

לעת 6256 ערב 6153 והנה 2009 בלהה 1091 בטרם 2962 בקר 1242 איננו 369 זה 2088 חלק 2506 שוסינו 8154

la'aet 'areb uahineh balahah, baterem boqer 'aeynenu; zeh cheleq shouseynu,

**at evening tide And behold trouble *and* before the morning he *is* not This *is* the portion of them that spoil us**

וגורל 1486 לבזזינו 962:

uagoural labozazeynu.

**and the lot of them that rob us**

Isa 17:8 And he shall not look to the altars, the work of his hands, neither shall respect that which his fingers have made, either the groves, or the images.9 In that day shall his strong cities be as a forsaken bough, and an uppermost branch, which they left because of the children of Israel: and there shall be desolation.10 Because you have forgotten the G-d of your salvation, and have not been mindful of the rock of your strength, therefore shall you plant pleasant plants, and shall set it with strange slips:11 In the day shall you make your plant to grow, and in the morning shall you make your seed to flourish: but the harvest shall be a heap in the day of grief and of desperate sorrow.12 Woe to the multitude of many people, which make a noise like the noise of the seas; and to the rushing of nations, that make a rushing like the rushing of mighty waters!13 The nations shall rush like the rushing of many waters: but G-d shall rebuke them, and they shall flee far off, and shall be chased as the chaff of the mountains before the wind, and like a rolling thing before the whirlwind.14 And behold at eveningtide trouble and before the morning he is not. This is the portion of them that spoil us and the lot of them that rob us.

**Isa 18:1** הוי 1945 ארץ 776 צלצל 6767 כנפים 3671 אשר 834 מעבר 5676 לנהרי 5104 כוש 3568: **18:2** השלח 7971 בים 3220
houy 'aretz tziltzal kanapayim; 'asher me'aeber lanaharey kush. hasholeach bayam
**Woe *to* the land shadowing with wings which *is* beyond the rivers of Ethiopia That send by the sea**

צירים 6735 ובכלי 3627 גמא 1573 על 5921 פני 6440 מים 4325 לכו 1980 מלאכים 4397 קלים 7031 אל 413 גוי 1471
tziyriym, uabikaley goma' 'al paney mayim laku mal'akiym qaliym, 'al gouy
**ambassadors even in vessels of bulrushes upon surfaces the waters *saying* Go messengers *you* swift to a nation**

ממשך 4900 ומורט 4178 אל 413 עם 5971 נורא 3372 מן 4480 הוא 1931 והלאה 1973 גוי 1471 קו 6978 קו 6978 ומבוסה 4001
mamushak uamourat, 'al 'am noura' min hua' uahal'ah; gouy qau qau uambusah,
**scattered and peeled to a people terrible from their beginning hitherto a nation meted out and trodden down**

אשר 834 בזאו 958 נהרים 5104 ארצו 776: **18:3** כל 3605 ישבי 3427 תבל 8398 ושכני 7931 ארץ 776 כנשא 5375
'asher baza'au nahariym artzou. kal yoshabey tebel uashokaney 'aretz; kinsa'
**whose have spoiled the rivers land All *you* inhabitants of the world and dwellers on the earth when he lift up**

נס 5251 הרים 2022 תראו 7200 וכתקע 8628 שופר 7782 תשמעו 8085: **18:4** כי 3588 כה 3541 אמר 559 יהוה 3068 אלי 413
nes hariym tir'au, uakitqoa' shoupar tishma'au. kiy koh 'amar Yahuah 'aelay,
**an ensign on the mountains see you and when he blow a trumpet hear you For so said Yahuah unto me**

אשקוטה 8252 ואביטה 5027 במכוני 4349 כחם 2527 צח 6703 עלי 5921 אור 219 כעב 5645 טל 2919
'ashqutah ua'abiytah bimkouniy; kachom tzach 'aley 'aur, ka'ab tal
**I will take my rest and I will consider in my dwelling place like a heat clear upon herbs *and* like a cloud of dew**

בחם 2527 קציר 7105: **18:5** כי 3588 לפני 6440 קציר 7105 כתם 8552 פרח 6525 ובסר 1155 גמל 1580 יהיה 1961
bachom qatziyr. kiy lipaney qatziyr katam perach, uaboser gomel yihayeh
**in the heat of harvest For afore the harvest when is perfect the bud and the sour grape ripening is**

נצה 5328 וכרת 3772 הזלזלים 2150 במזמרות 4211 ואת 853 הנטישות 5189 הסיר 5493 התז 8456: **18:6**
nitzah; uakarat hazalzaliym bamazmerout, ua'at hanatiyshout hesiyr hetaz.
***in* the flower he shall both cut off the sprigs with pruning hooks *and* the branches take away *and* cut down**

יעזבו 5800 יחדו 3162 לעיט 5861 הרים 2022 ולבהמת 929 הארץ 776 וקץ 6972 עליו 5921
ye'azabu yachdau la'aeyt hariym, ualbehemat ha'aretz; uaqatz 'aelayu
**They shall be left together unto the fowls of the mountains and to the beasts of the earth and shall summer upon them**

העיט 5861 וכל 3605 בהמת 929 הארץ 776 עליו 5921 תחרף 2778: **18:7** בעת 6256 ההיא 1931 יובל 2986 שי 7862 ליהוה 3069
ha'ayit, uakal behemat ha'aretz 'alayu techerap. ba'aet hahiy'a yubal shay laYahuah
**the fowls and all the beasts of the earth upon them shall winter In time that shall be brought the present Yahuah**

צבאות 6635 עם 5971 ממשך 4900 ומורט 4178 ומעם 5971 נורא 3372 מן 4480 הוא 1931 והלאה 1973 גוי 1471 קו 6978 קו 6978
tzaba'aut, 'am mamushak uamourat, uame'am noura' min hua' uahal'ah; gouy qau qau
**of hosts of a people scattered and peeled and from a people terrible from their beginning hitherto a nation meted out**

ומבוסה 4001 אשר 834 בזאו 958 נהרים 5104 ארצו 776 אל 413 מקום 4725 שם 8034 יהוה 3069 צבאות 6635 הר 2022
uambusah, 'asher baza'au nahariym artzou, 'al maqoum shem Yahuah tzaba'aut har
**and trodden under foot whose have spoiled the rivers land to the place of the name of Yahuah of hosts the mount**

**Isa** 18:1 Woe to the land shadowing with wings, which is beyond the rivers of Ethiopia:2 That send ambassadors by the sea, even in vessels of bulrushes upon the waters, saying, Go, you swift messengers, to a nation scattered and peeled, to a people terrible from their beginning hitherto; a nation meted out and trodden down, whose land the rivers have spoiled!3 All you inhabitants of the world, and dwellers on the earth, see you, when he lift up an ensign on the mountains; and when he bloweth a trumpet, hear you.4 For so YHUH said unto me, I will take my rest, and I will consider in my dwelling place like a clear heat upon herbs, and like a cloud of dew in the heat of harvest.5 For afore the harvest, when the bud is perfect, and the sour grape is ripening in the flower, he shall both cut off the sprigs with pruning hooks, and take away and cut down the branches.6 They shall be left together unto the fowls of the mountains, and to the beasts of the earth: and the fowls shall summer upon them, and all the beasts of the earth shall winter upon them.7 In that time shall the present be brought unto YHUH of hosts of a people scattered and peeled, and from a people terrible from their beginning hitherto; a nation meted out and trodden under foot, whose land the rivers have spoiled, to the place of the name of YHUH of hosts, the mount Zion.

ציון 6726:
tziyoun.
**Zion**

**Isa 19:1**
משא 4853 | מצרים 4714 | הנה 2009 | יהוה 3068 | רכב 7392 | על 5921 | עב 5645 | קל 7031 | ובא 935 | מצרים 4714
masa' | mitzrayim; | hineh | Yahuah | rokeb | 'al | 'ab | qal | uaba' | mitzrayim,
**The burden of | Egypt | Behold | Yahuah | ride | upon | a cloud | swift | and shall come into | Egypt**

ונעו 5128 | אלילי 457 | מצרים 4714 | מפניו 6440 | ולבב 3824 | מצרים 4714 | ימס 4549 | בקרבו 7130: | **19:2**
uana'au | 'aliyley | mitzrayim | mipanayu, | ualbab | mitzrayim | yimas | baqirbou.
**and shall be moved | the idols of | Egypt | at his presence | and the heart of | Egypt | shall melt | in the midst of it**

וסכסכתי 5526 | מצרים 4714 | במצרים 4714 | ונלחמו 3898 | איש 376 | באחיו 251 | ואיש 376
uasiksaktiy | mitzrayim | bamitzrayim, | uanilchamu | 'aysh | ba'achiyu | ua'aysh
**And I will set | the Egyptians | against the Egyptians | and they shall fight | every one | against his brother | and every one**

ברעהו 7453 | עיר 5892 | בעיר 5892 | ממלכה 4467 | בממלכה 4467: | **19:3** ונבקה 1238 | רוח 7307 | מצרים 4714
bare'aehu; | 'ayr | ba'ayr, | mamlakah | bamamlakah. | uanabaqah | ruach | mitzrayim
**against his neighbour | city | against city | *and* kingdom | against kingdom | And shall fail | the spirit of | Egypt**

בקרבו 7130 | ועצתו 6098 | אבלע 1104 | ודרשו 1875 | אל 413 | האלילים 457 | ואל 413 | האטים 328 | ואל 413
baqirbou, | ua'atzatou | 'abalea'; | uadarashu | 'al | ha'aliyliym | ua'al | ha'atiym, | ua'al
**in the midst thereof | and the counsel thereof | I will destroy | and they shall seek to | the idols | and to | the charmers | and to**

האבות 178 | ואל 413 | הידענים 3049: | **19:4** וסכרתי 5534 | את 853 | מצרים 4714 | ביד 3027 | אדנים 113
ha'about | ua'al | haiyd'aniym. | uasikartiy | 'at | mitzrayim, | bayad | 'adoniym
**them that have familiar spirits | and to | the wizards | And will I give over | the Egyptians | into the hand of | a adonai**

קשה 7186 | ומלך 4428 | עז 5794 | ימשל 4910 | בם 871a | נאם 5002 | האדון 113 | יהוה 3068 | צבאות 6635: | **19:5** ונשתו 5405 | מים 4325 | מהים 3220
qasheh; | uamelek | 'az | yimshal | bam, | na'am | ha'adoun | Yahuah | tzaba'aut. | uanishtu | mayim | mehayam;
**cruel | and a king | fierce | shall rule over | them | saith | Adonai | Yahuah | of hosts | and dried up | the waters | from the sea**

ונהר 5104 | יחרב 2717 | ויבש 3001: | **19:6** והאזניחו 2186 | נהרות 5104 | דללו 1809 | וחרבו 2717
uanahar | yecherab | uayabesh. | uahe'azniychu | naharout, | dalalu | uacharabu
**and the river | shall be wasted | And shall fail | And they shall turn far away | the rivers | shall be emptied | and dried up**

יארי 2975 | מצור 4693 | קנה 7070 | וסוף 5488 | קמלו 7060: | **19:7** ערות 6169 | על 5921 | יאור 2975 | על 5921 | פי 6310
ya'arey | matzour; | qaneh | uasup | qamelu. | 'arout | 'al | ya'aur | 'al | piy
***and* the brooks of | defence | the reeds | and flags | shall wither | The paper reeds | by | the brooks | by | the mouth of**

יאור 2975 | וכל 3605 | מזרע 4218 | יאור 2975 | ייבש 3001 | נדף 5086 | ואיננו 369: | **19:8** ואנו 578
ya'aur; | uakol | mizra' | ya'aur, | yiybash | nidap | ua'aeynenu. | ua'anu
**the brooks | and every thing | sown by | the brooks | shall wither | be driven away | and be no *more* | also shall mourn**

הדיגים 1771 | ואבלו 56 | כל 3605 | משליכי 7993 | ביאור 2975 | חכה 2443 | ופרשי 6566 | מכמרת 4365 | על 5921 | פני 6440
hadayagiym, | ua'abalu, | kal | mashliykey | baya'aur | chakah; | uaporasey | mikmoret | 'al | paney
**The fishers | and shall lament | all | they that cast | into the brooks | angle | and they that spread | nets | up | upon**

**Isa** 19:1 The burden of Egypt. Behold, YHUH rideth upon a swift cloud, and shall come into Egypt: and the idols of Egypt shall be moved at his presence, and the heart of Egypt shall melt in the midst of it.2 And I will set the Egyptians against the Egyptians: and they shall fight everyone against his brother, and everyone against his neighbor; city against city, and kingdom against kingdom.3 And the spirit of Egypt shall fail in the midst thereof; and I will destroy the counsel thereof: and they shall seek to the idols, and to the charmers, and to them that have familiar spirits, and to the wizards.4 And the Egyptians will I give over into the hand of a cruel lord; and a fierce king shall rule over them, saith the Adonai, YHUH of hosts.5 And the waters shall fail from the sea, and the river shall be wasted and dried up.6 And they shall turn the rivers far away; and the brooks of defence shall be emptied and dried up: the reeds and flags shall where.7 The paper reeds by the brooks, by the mouth of the brooks, and everything sown by the brooks, shall where, be driven away, and be no more.8 The fishers also shall mourn, and all they that cast angle into the brooks shall lament, and they that spread nets upon the waters shall languish.

| מים 4325 | אמללו 535: | | ובשו 954 | עבדי 5647 | פשתים 6593 | שריקות 8305 | וארגים 707 |
|---|---|---|---|---|---|---|---|
| mayim | 'uamlalu. | 19:9 | uaboshu | 'abadey | pishtiym | sariyqout; | ua'aragiym |
| **the waters** | **shall languish** | | **Moreover shall be confounded** | **they that work in** | **flax** | **fine** | **and they that weave** |

| חורי 2355: | | והיו 1961 | שתתיה 8356 | מדכאים 1792 | כל 3605 | עשי 6213 | שכר 7938 | אגמי 99 |
|---|---|---|---|---|---|---|---|---|
| chouray. | 19:10 | uahayu | shatoteyha | meduka'aym; | kal | 'asey | seker | 'agmey |
| **networks** | | **And they shall be** | ***in* the purposes thereof** | **broken** | **all** | **that make** | **sluices** | ***and* ponds for** |

| נפש 5315: | | אך 389 | אולים 196 | שרי 8269 | צען 6814 | חכמי 2450 | יעצי 6098 | פרעה 6547 | עצה 6098 | נבערה 1197 |
|---|---|---|---|---|---|---|---|---|---|---|
| napesh. | 19:11 | 'ak | 'auiliym | sarey | tzo'an, | chakmey | yo'atzey | par'ah, | 'aetzah | nib'arah; |
| **fish** | | **Surely *are*** | **fools** | **the princes of** | **Zoan** | **the wise** | **the counsel of** | **Pharaoh** | **counsellers of** | **is become brutish** |

| איך 349 | תאמרו 559 | אל 413 | פרעה 6547 | בן 1121 | חכמים 2450 | אני 589 | בן 1121 | מלכי 4428 | קדם 6924: | | אים 335 | אפוא 645 |
|---|---|---|---|---|---|---|---|---|---|---|---|---|
| 'aeyk | ta'maru | 'al | par'ah, | ben | chakamiym | 'aniy | ben | malkey | qedem. | 19:12 | 'ayam | aepou'a |
| **how** | **say you** | **unto** | **Pharaoh** | ***am* the son of** | **the wise** | **I** | **the son of** | **kings?** | **ancient** | | **Where *are* they?** | **where** |

| חכמיך 2450 | ויגידו 5046 | נא 4994 | לך 3807a | וידעו 3045 | מה 4100 | יעץ 3289 | יהוה 3068 | צבאות 6635 | על 5921 |
|---|---|---|---|---|---|---|---|---|---|
| chakameyka, | uayagiydu | naa' | lak; | uayodi'au, | mah | ya'atz | Yahuah | tzaba'aut | 'al |
| ***are* your wise** | ***men*? and let them tell** | **now** | **to you** | **and let them know** | **what** | **has purposed** | **Yahuah** | **of hosts** | **upon** |

| מצרים 4714: | | נואלו 2973 | שרי 8269 | צען 6814 | נשאו 5377 | שרי 8269 | נף 5297 | התעו 8582 | את 853 |
|---|---|---|---|---|---|---|---|---|---|
| mitzrayim. | 19:13 | nou'alu | sarey | tzo'an, | nish'au | sarey | nop; | hit'au | 'at |
| **Egypt** | | **are become fools** | **The princes of** | **Zoan** | **are deceived** | **the princes of** | **Noph** | **they have also seduced** | |

| מצרים 4714 | פנת 6438 | שבטיה 7626: | | יהוה 3068 | מסך 4537 | בקרבה 7130 | רוח 7307 | עועים 5773 |
|---|---|---|---|---|---|---|---|---|
| mitzrayim | pinat | shabateyha. | 19:14 | Yahuah | masak | baqirbah | ruach | 'au'aym; |
| **Egypt** | ***even they that are* the stay of** | **the tribes thereof** | | **Yahuah** | **has mingled** | **in the midst thereof** | **a spirit** | **perverse** |

| והתעו 8582 | את 853 | מצרים 4714 | בכל 3605 | מעשהו 4639 | כהתעות 8582 | שכור 7910 | בקיאו 6892: | | ולא 3808 |
|---|---|---|---|---|---|---|---|---|---|
| uahit'au | 'at | mitzrayim | bakal | ma'asehu, | kahita'aut | shikour | baqiy'au. | 19:15 | uala' |
| **and they have caused to err** | | **Egypt** | **in every** | **work thereof** | **as staggereth** | **a drunken *man*** | **in his vomit** | | **Neither** |

| יהיה 1961 | למצרים 4714 | מעשה 4639 | אשר 834 | יעשה 6213 | ראש 7218 | וזנב 2180 | כפה 3712 | ואגמון 100: | | ביום 3117 | ההוא 1931 | יהיה 1961 |
|---|---|---|---|---|---|---|---|---|---|---|---|---|
| yihayeh | lamitzrayim | ma'aseh; | 'asher | ya'aseh | ra'sh | uazanab | kipah | ua'agmoun. | 19:16 | bayoum | hahua', | yihayeh |
| **shall there be** | **for Egypt** | ***any* work** | **which** | **may do** | **the head** | **or tail** | **branch** | **or rush** | | **In day** | **that** | **shall be** |

| מצרים 4714 | כנשים 802 | וחרד 2729 | ופחד 6342 | מפני 6440 | תנופת 8573 | יד 3027 | יהוה 3068 | צבאות 6635 | אשר 834 |
|---|---|---|---|---|---|---|---|---|---|
| mitzrayim | kanashiym; | uacharad | uapachad, | mipaney | tanupat | yad | Yahuah | tzaba'aut, | 'asher |
| **Egypt** | **like unto women** | **and it shall be afraid** | **and fear** | **because of** | **the shaking of** | **the hand of** | **Yahuah** | **of hosts** | **which** |

| הוא 1931 | מניף 5130 | עליו 5921: | | והיתה 1961 | אדמת 127 | יהודה 3063 | למצרים 4714 | לחגא 2283 | כל 3605 | אשר 834 | יזכיר 2142 |
|---|---|---|---|---|---|---|---|---|---|---|---|
| hua' | meniyp | 'alayu. | 19:17 | uahayatah | 'admat | yahudah | lamitzrayim | lachaga', | kal | 'asher | yazkiyr |
| **he** | **shake** | **over it** | | **And shall be** | **the land of** | **Judah** | **unto Egypt** | **a terror** | **every one** | **that** | **make mention** |

| אתה 853 | אליו 413 | יפחד 6342 | מפני 6440 | עצת 6098 | יהוה 3068 | צבאות 6635 | אשר 834 | הוא 1931 | יועץ 3289 |
|---|---|---|---|---|---|---|---|---|---|
| 'atah | 'aelayu | yipchad; | mipaney, | 'atzat | Yahuah | tzaba'aut, | 'asher | hua' | you'aetz |
| **thereof** | **in himself** | **shall be afraid** | **because of** | **the counsel of** | **Yahuah** | **of hosts** | **which** | **he** | **has determined** |

Isa 19:9 Moreover they that work in fine flax, and they that weave networks, shall be confounded.10 And they shall be broken in the purposes thereof, all that make sluices and ponds for fish.11 Surely the princes of Zoan are fools, the counsel of the wise counsellers of Pharaoh is become brutish: how say you unto Pharaoh, I am the son of the wise, the son of ancient kings?12 Where are they? where are your wise men? and let them tell you now, and let them know what YHUH of hosts has purposed upon Egypt.13 The princes of Zoan are become fools, the princes of Noph are deceived; they have also seduced Egypt, even they that are the stay of the tribes thereof.14 YHUH has mingled a perverse spirit in the midst thereof: and they have caused Egypt to err in every work thereof, as a drunken man staggereth in his vomit.15 Neither shall there be any work for Egypt, which the head or tail, branch or rush, may do.16 In that day shall Egypt be like unto women: and it shall be afraid and fear because of the shaking of the hand of YHUH of hosts, which he shaketh over it.17 And the land of Judah shall be a terror unto Egypt, everyone that make mention thereof shall be afraid in himself, because of the counsel of YHUH of hosts, which he has determined against it.

| עליו 5921: | 19:18 ביום 3117 | ההוא 1931 | יהיו 1961 | חמש 2568 | ערים 5892 | בארץ 776 | מצרים 4714 | מדברות 1696 | שפת 8193 | כנען 3667 |
|---|---|---|---|---|---|---|---|---|---|---|
| 'alayu. | bayoum | hahua' | yihayu | chamesh | 'ariym | ba'aretz | mitzrayim, | medabrout | sapat | kana'an, |
| **against it** | **In day** | **that** | **shall** | **five** | **cities** | **in the land of** | **Egypt** | **speak** | **the language of** | **Canaan** |

| ונשבעות 7650 | ליהוה 3068 | צבאות 6635 | עיר 5892 | ההרס 2041 | יאמר 559 | לאחת 259: | 19:19 ביום 3117 | ההוא 1931 | יהיה 1961 |
|---|---|---|---|---|---|---|---|---|---|
| uanishba'aut | laYahuah | tzaba'aut; | 'ayr | haheres, | ye'amer | la'achat. | bayoum | hahua', | yihayeh |
| **and swear** | **to Yahuah** | **of hosts** | **The city of** | **destruction** | **shall be called** | **one** | **In day** | **that** | **shall there be** |

| מזבח 4196 | ליהוה 3068 | בתוך 8432 | ארץ 776 | מצרים 4714 | ומצבה 4676 | אצל 681 | גבולה 1366 | ליהוה 3068: | 19:20 |
|---|---|---|---|---|---|---|---|---|---|
| mizbeach | laYahuah, | batouk | 'aretz | mitzrayim; | uamatzebah | 'aetzel | gabulah | laYahuah. | |
| **an altar** | **to Yahuah** | **in the midst of** | **the land of** | **Egypt** | **and a pillar** | **at** | **the border thereof** | **to Yahuah** | |

| והיה 1961 | לאות 226 | ולעד 5707 | ליהוה 3068 | צבאות 6635 | בארץ 776 | מצרים 4714 | כי 3588 | יצעקו 6817 | אל 413 |
|---|---|---|---|---|---|---|---|---|---|
| uahayah | la'aut | ual'aed | laYahuah | tzaba'aut | ba'aretz | mitzrayim; | kiy | yitz'aqu | 'al |
| **And it shall be** | **for a sign** | **and for a witness** | **unto Yahuah** | **of hosts** | **in the land of** | **Egypt** | **for** | **they shall cry** | **unto** |

| יהוה 3068 | מפני 6440 | לחצים 3905 | וישלח 7971 | להם 3807a | מושיע 3467 | ורב 7227 | והצילם 5337: | 19:21 |
|---|---|---|---|---|---|---|---|---|
| Yahuah | mipaney | lochatziym, | uayishlach | lahem | moushiya' | uarab | uahitzlam. | |
| **Yahuah** | **because of** | **the oppressors** | **and he shall send** | **them** | **a saviour** | **and a great one** | **and he shall deliver them** | |

| ונודע 3045 | יהוה 3068 | למצרים 4714 | וידעו 3045 | מצרים 4714 | את 853 | יהוה 3068 | ביום 3117 | ההוא 1931 | ועבדו 5647 | זבח 2077 |
|---|---|---|---|---|---|---|---|---|---|---|
| uanouda' | Yahuah | lamitzrayim, | uayada'aua | mitzrayim | 'at | Yahuah | bayoum | hahua'; | ua'abadu | zebach |
| **And shall be known** | **Yahuah** | **to Egypt** | **and shall know** | **the Egyptians** | | **Yahuah** | **in day** | **that** | **and shall do sacrifice** | |

| ומנחה 4503 | ונדרו 5087 | נדר 5088 | ליהוה 3068 | ושלמו 7999: | 19:22 ונגף 5062 | יהוה 3068 | את 853 | מצרים 4714 |
|---|---|---|---|---|---|---|---|---|
| uaminchah, | uanadaru | neder | laYahuah | uashilemu. | uanagap | Yahuah | 'at | mitzrayim |
| **and oblation** | **yea they shall vow** | **a vow** | **unto Yahuah** | **and perform *it*** | **And shall smite** | **Yahuah** | | **Egypt** |

| נגף 5062 | ורפוא 7495 | ושבו 7725 | עד 5704 | יהוה 3068 | ונעתר 6279 | להם 3807a |
|---|---|---|---|---|---|---|
| nagop | uarapou'a; | uashabu | 'ad | Yahuah, | uane'atar | lahem |
| **he shall smite** | **and heal** | ***it* and they shall return *even*** | **to** | **Yahuah** | **and he shall be intreated** | **of them** |

| ורפאם 7495: | 19:23 ביום 3117 | ההוא 1931 | תהיה 1961 | מסלה 4546 | ממצרים 4714 | אשורה 804 | ובא 935 | אשור 804 |
|---|---|---|---|---|---|---|---|---|
| uarpa'am. | bayoum | hahua', | tihayeh | masilah | mimitzrayim | 'ashurah, | uaba' | 'ashur |
| **and shall heal them** | **In day** | **that** | **shall there be** | **a highway** | **out of Egypt to** | **Assyria** | **and shall come** | **the Assyrian** |

| במצרים 4714 | ומצרים 4714 | באשור 804 | ועבדו 5647 | מצרים 4714 | את 853 | אשור 804: | 19:24 ביום 3117 | ההוא 1931 |
|---|---|---|---|---|---|---|---|---|
| bamitzrayim | uamitzrayim | ba'ashur; | ua'abadu | mitzrayim | 'at | 'ashur. | bayoum | hahua', |
| **into Egypt** | **and the Egyptian** | **into Assyria** | **and shall serve with** | **the Egyptians** | | **the Assyrians** | **In day** | **that** |

| יהיה 1961 | ישראל 3478 | שלישיה 7992 | למצרים 4714 | ולאשור 804 | ברכה 1293 | בקרב 7130 | הארץ 776: | 19:25 אשר 834 |
|---|---|---|---|---|---|---|---|---|
| yihayeh | yisra'ael | shaliyshiyah, | lamitzrayim | ual'ashur; | barakah | baqereb | ha'aretz. | 'asher |
| **shall be** | **Israel** | **the third** | **with Egypt** | **and with Assyria** | ***even* a blessing** | **in the midst of** | **the land** | **Whom** |

| ברכו 1288 | יהוה 3068 | צבאות 6635 | לאמר 559 | ברוך 1288 | עמי 5971 | מצרים 4714 | ומעשה 4639 | ידי 3027 | אשור 804 | ונחלתי 5159 |
|---|---|---|---|---|---|---|---|---|---|---|
| berakou | Yahuah | tzaba'aut | lea'mor; | baruk | 'amiy | mitzrayim, | uama'aseh | yaday | 'ashur, | uanachalatiy |
| **shall bless** | **Yahuah** | **of hosts** | **saying** | **Blessed** | **my people *be*** | **Egypt** | **and the work of** | **my hands** | **Assyria** | **and mine inheritance** |

Isa 19:18 In that day shall five cities in the land of Egypt speak the language of Canaan, and swear to YHUH of hosts; one shall be called, The city of destruction.19 In that day shall there be an altar to YHUH in the midst of the land of Egypt, and a pillar at the border thereof to YHUH.20 And it shall be for a sign and for a witness unto YHUH of hosts in the land of Egypt: for they shall cry unto YHUH because of the oppressors, and he shall send them a savior, and a great one, and he shall deliver them.21 And YHUH shall be known to Egypt, and the Egyptians shall know YHUH in that day, and shall do sacrifice and oblation; yea, they shall vow a vow unto YHUH, and perform it.22 And YHUH shall smite Egypt: he shall smite and heal it: and they shall return even to YHUH, and he shall be entreated of them, and shall heal them.23 In that day shall there be a highway out of Egypt to Assyria, and the Assyrian shall come into Egypt, and the Egyptian into Assyria, and the Egyptians shall serve with the Assyrians.24 In that day shall Israel be the third with Egypt and with Assyria, even a blessing in the midst of the land:25 Whom YHUH of hosts shall bless, saying, Blessed be Egypt my people, and Assyria the work of my hands, and Israel mine inheritance.

ישראל 3478:
yisra'ael.
**Israel**

**Isa 20:1** בשנת 8141 בא 935 תרתן 8661 אשדודה 795 בשלח 7971 אתו 853 סרגון 5623 מלך 4428 אשור 804 וילחם 3898
bishnat ba' tartan 'ashdoudah, bishlach 'atou, sargoun melek 'ashur; uayilachem
**In the year that came Tartan *unto* Ashdod when sent him Sargon the king of Assyria and fought**

באשדוד 795 וילכדה 3920: **20:2** בעת 6256 ההיא 1931 דבר 1696 יהוה 3069 ביד 3027 ישעיהו 3470 בן 1121 אמוץ 531 לאמר 559 לך 1980
ba'ashdoud uayilkadah. ba'aet hahiy'a, diber Yahuah bayad yasha'yahu ben 'amoutz lea'mor lek,
**against Ashdod and took it At time the same spoke Yahuah by Isaiah the son of Amoz saying Go you**

ופתחת 6605 השק 8242 מעל 5921 מתניך 4975 ונעלך 5275 תחלץ 2502 מעל 5921 רגליך 7272 ויעש 6213 כן 3651 הלך 1980 ערום 6174
uapitachta hasaq me'al mataneyka, uana'alka tachalotz me'al ragleyka; uaya'as ken, halok 'aroum
**and loose the sackcloth from off your loins and your shoe put off from your foot And he did so walking naked**

ויחף 3182: **20:3** ויאמר 559 יהוה 3068 כאשר 834 הלך 1980 עבדי 5650 ישעיהו 3470 ערום 6174 ויחף 3182 שלש 7969 שנים 8141
uayachep. uaya'mer Yahuah, ka'asher halak 'abdiy yasha'yahu 'aroum uayachep; shalosh shaniym
**and barefoot And said Yahuah Like as has walked my servant Isaiah naked and barefoot three years**

אות 226 ומופת 4159 על 5921 מצרים 4714 ועל 5921 כוש 3568: **20:4** כן 3651 ינהג 5090 מלך 4428 אשור 804 את 853 שבי 7628
'aut uamoupet, 'al mitzrayim ua'al kush. ken yinhag melek 'ashur 'at shabiy
***for* a sign and wonder upon Egypt and upon Ethiopia So shall lead away the king of Assyria prisoners**

מצרים 4714 ואת 853 גלות 1546 כוש 3568 נערים 5288 וזקנים 2205 ערום 6174 ויחף 3182 וחשופי 2834 שת 8357
mitzrayim ua'at galut kush na'ariym uazqeniym 'aroum uayachep; uachasupay shet
**the Egyptians *and* captives the Ethiopians young and old naked and barefoot even uncovered *with their* buttocks**

ערות 6172 מצרים 4714: **20:5** וחתו 2865 ובשו 954 מכוש 3568 מבטם 4007 ומן 4480 מצרים 4714
'aruat mitzrayim. uachatu uaboshu; mikush mabatam, uamin mitzrayim
***to* the shame of Egypt And they shall be afraid and ashamed of Ethiopia their expectation and of Egypt**

תפארתם 8597: **20:6** ואמר 559 ישב 3427 האי 339 הזה 2088 ביום 3117 ההוא 1931 הנה 2009 כה 3541 מבטנו 4007 אשר 834
tip'artam. ua'amar yosheb ha'ay hazeh bayoum hahua' hineh koh mabatenu, 'asher
**their glory And shall say the inhabitant of isle this in day that Behold such *is* our expectation where**

נסנו 5127 שם 8033 לעזרה 5833 להנצל 5337 מפני 6440 מלך 4428 אשור 804 ואיך 349 נמלט 4422 אנחנו 587:
nasnu sham la'azrah, lahinatzel, mipaney melek 'ashur; ua'aeyk nimalet 'anachanu.
**we flee there for help to be delivered from the king of Assyria and how shall escape we**

**Isa 21:1** משא 4853 מדבר 4057 ים 3220 כסופות 5492 בנגב 5045 לחלף 2498 ממדבר 4057 בא 935
masa' midbar yam; kasupout banegeb lachalop, mimidbar ba',
**The burden of the desert of the sea As whirlwinds in the south pass through from the desert *so* it comes**

מארץ 776 נוראה 3372: **21:2** חזות 2380 קשה 7186 הגד 5046 לי 3807a הבוגד 898 בוגד 898 והשודד 7703
me'aretz noura'ah. chazut qashah hugad liy; habouged bouged uahashouded
**from a land terrible A vision grievous is declared unto me the treacherous dealer deal treacherously and the spoiler**

**Isa** 20:1 In the year that Tartan came unto Ashdod, (when Sargon the king of Assyria sent him,) and fought against Ashdod, and took it;2 At the same time spoke YHUH by Isaiah the son of Amoz, saying, Go and loose the sackcloth from off your loins, and put off your shoe from your foot. And he did so, walking naked and barefoot.3 And YHUH said, Like as my servant Isaiah has walked naked and barefoot three years for a sign and wonder upon Egypt and upon Ethiopia;4 So shall the king of Assyria lead away the Egyptians prisoners, and the Ethiopians captives, young and old, naked and barefoot, even with their buttocks uncovered, to the shame of Egypt.5 And they shall be afraid and ashamed of Ethiopia their expectation, and of Egypt their glory.6 And the inhabitant of this isle shall say in that day, Behold, such is our expectation, whither we flee for help to be delivered from the king of Assyria: and how shall we escape? **Isa** 21:1 The burden of the desert of the sea. As whirlwinds in the south pass through; so it cometh from the desert, from a terrible land.2 A grievous vision is declared unto me; the treacherous dealer deal treacherously, and the spoiler spoileth. Go up, O Elam: besiege, O Media; all the sighing thereof have I made to cease.

21:3

שודד 7703 עלי 5927 עילם 5867 צורי 6696 מדי 4074 כל 3605 אנחתה 585 השבתי 7673: על 5921 כן 3651 מלאו 4390
shouded, 'aliy 'aeylam tzuriy maday, kal 'anchatah hishbatiy. 'al ken, mala'au
**spoil Go up O Elam besiege O Media all the sighing thereof have I made to cease Therefore this are filled**

מתני 4975 חלחלה 2479 צירים 6735 אחזוני 270 כצירי 6735 יולדה 3205 נעויתי 5753
matanay chalchalah, tziyriym 'achazuniy, katziyrey youledah; na'aueytiy
**my loins *with* pain pangs have taken hold upon me as the pangs of a woman that travail I was bowed down at**

21:4

משמע 8085 נבהלתי 926 מראות 7200: תעה 8582 לבבי 3824 פלצות 6427 בעתתני 1204 את 853 נשף 5399
mishmoa', nibhaltiy mera'aut. ta'ah lababiy, palatzut bi'atataniy; 'at neshep
**the hearing *of it* I was dismayed at the seeing *of it* panted My heart fearfulness affrighted me the night of**

21:5

חשקי 2837 שם 7760 לי 3807a לחרדה 2731: ערך 6186 השלחן 7979 צפה 6823 הצפית 6823 אכול 398 שתה 8354 קומו 6965
chishqiy, sam liy lacharadah. 'arok hashulchan tzapoh hatzapiyt 'akoul shatoh; qumu
**my pleasure has he turned unto me into fear Prepare the table watch *in* the watchtower eat drink arise**

21:6

השרים 8269 משחו 4886 מגן 4043: כי 3588 כה 3541 אמר 559 אלי 413 אדני 136 לך 1980 העמד 5975 המצפה 6822 אשר 834 יראה 7200
hasariym mishaku magen. kiy koh 'amar 'aelay 'adonay; lek ha'amed hamatzapeh, 'asher yir'ah
**you princes *and* anoint the shield For thus has said unto me Adonai Go you set a watchman what he see**

21:7

יגיד 5046: וראה 7200 רכב 7393 צמד 6776 פרשים 6571 רכב 7393 חמור 2543 רכב 7393 גמל 1581
yagiyd. uara'ah rekeb, tzemed parashiym, rekeb chamour rekeb gamal;
**let him declare And he saw a chariot *with* a couple of horsemen a chariot of asses *and* a chariot of camels**

21:8

והקשיב 7181 קשב 7182 רב 7227 קשב 7182: ויקרא 7121 אריה 738 על 5921 מצפה 4707 אדני 136 אנכי 595 עמד 5975
uahiqshiyb qesheb rab qasheb. uayiqra' 'aryeh; 'al mitzpeh 'adonay, 'anokiy 'amed
**and he hearkened diligently with much heed And he cried A lion upon the watchtower My adonai I stand**

21:9

תמיד 8548 יומם 3119 ועל 5921 משמרתי 4931 אנכי 595 נצב 5324 כל 3605 הלילות 3915: והנה 2009 זה 2088 בא 935 רכב 7393
tamiyd youmam, ua'al mishmartiy, 'anokiy nitzab kal haleylout. uahineh zeh ba' rekeb
**continually *in* the daytime in my ward I am set whole nights And behold here comes a chariot of**

איש 376 צמד 6776 פרשים 6571 ויען 6030 ויאמר 559 נפלה 5307 נפלה 5307 בבל 894 וכל 3605 פסילי 6456
'aysh, tzemed parashiym; uaya'an uaya'mer, naplah naplah babel, uakal pasiyley
**men *with* a couple of horsemen And he answered and said is fallen is fallen Babylon and all the graven images of**

21:10

אלהיה 430 שבר 7665 לארץ 776: מדשתי 4098 ובן 1121 גרני 1637 אשר 834 שמעתי 8085 מאת 853
'aloheyha shibar la'aretz. madushatiy uaben garaniy; 'asher shama'atiy, me'at
**her gods he has broken unto the ground O my threshing and the corn of my floor that which I have heard of**

21:11

יהוה 3068 צבאות 6635 אלהי 430 ישראל 3478 הגדתי 5046 לכם 3807a: משא 4853 דומה 1746 אלי 413 קרא 7121 משעיר 8165
Yahuah tzaba'aut 'alohey yisra'ael higadtiy lakem. masa' dumah; 'aelay qorea' mise'ayr,
**Yahuah of hosts the Elohim of Israel have I declared unto you The burden of Dumah to me He call out of Seir**

21:12

שמר 8104 מה 4100 מלילה 3915 שמר 8104 מה 4100 מליל 3915: אמר 559 שמר 8104 אתה 857 בקר 1242 וגם 1571
shomer mah milayalah, shomer mah mileyl. 'amar shomer, 'atah boqer uagam
**Watchman what of the night? Watchman what of the night? said The watchman comes The morning and also**

Isa 21:3 Therefore are my loins filled with pain: pangs have taken hold upon me, as the pangs of a woman that travaileth: I was bowed down at the hearing of it; I was dismayed at the seeing of it.4 My heart panted, fearfulness affrighted me: the night of my pleasure has he turned into fear unto me.5 Prepare the table, watch in the watchtower, eat, drink: arise, you princes, and anoint the shield.6 For thus has YHUH said unto me, Go, set a watchman, let him declare what he see.7 And he saw a chariot with a couple of horsemen, a chariot of asses, and a chariot of camels; and he hearkened diligently with much heed:8 And he cried, A lion: My lord, I stand continually upon the watchtower in the daytime, and I am set in my ward whole nights:9 And, behold, here cometh a chariot of men, with a couple of horsemen. And he answered and said, Babylon is fallen, is fallen; and all the graven images of her gods he has broken unto the ground.10 O my threshing, and the corn of my floor: that which I have heard of YHUH of hosts, the G-d of Israel, have I declared unto you.11 The burden of Dumah. He call to me out of Seir, Watchman, what of the night? Watchman, what of the night?12 The watchman said, The morning cometh, and also the night: if you will inquire, inquire you: return, come.

לילה 3915 אם 518 תבעיון 1158 בעיו 1158 שבו 7725 אתיו 857: **21:13** משא 4853 בערב 6152 ביער 3293 בערב 6152
layalah; 'am tib'ayun ba'ayu shubu 'atayu. masa' ba'rab; baya'ar ba'rab
**the night if you will inquire inquire you return come you The burden upon Arabia In the forest in Arabia**

תלינו 3885 ארחות 736 **21:14** דדנים 1720: לקראת 7125 צמא 6771 התיו 857 מים 4325
taliynu, 'arachout dadaniym. liqra't tzamea' hetayu mayim;
**shall you lodge O you travelling companies of Dedanim to meet him that was thirsty brought water**

ישבי 3427 ארץ 776 תימא 8485 בלחמו 3899 קדמו 6923 נדד 5074: **21:15** כי 3588 מפני 6440 חרבות 2719
yoshabey 'aretz teymaa', balachmou qidamu noded. kiy mipaney charabout
**The inhabitants of the land of Tema with their bread they prevented him that fled For from the swords**

נדדו 5074 מפני 6440 חרב 2719 נטושה 5203 ומפני 6440 קשת 7198 דרוכה 1869 ומפני 6440 כבד 3514 מלחמה 4421: **21:16** כי 3588
nadadu; mipaney chereb natushah, uamipaney qeshet darukah, uamipaney kobed milchamah. kiy
**they fled from sword *the* drawn and from bow the bent and from the grievousness of war For**

כה 3541 אמר 559 אדני 136 אלי 413 בעוד 5750 שנה 8141 כשני 8141 שכיר 7916 וכלה 3615 כל 3605 כבוד 3519
koh 'amar 'adonay 'aelay; be'aud shanah kishney sakiyr, uakalah kal kaboud
**thus has said Adonai unto me Within a year according to the years of an hireling and shall fail all the glory of**

קדר 6938: **21:17** ושאר 7605 מספר 4557 קשת 7198 גבורי 1368 בני 1121 קדר 6938 ימעטו 4591
qedar. uash'ar mispar qeshet gibourey baney qedar yim'atu;
**Kedar And the residue of the number of archers the mighty men of the children of Kedar shall be diminished**

כי 3588 יהוה 3068 אלהי 430 ישראל 3478 דבר 1696:
kiy Yahuah 'alohey yisra'ael diber.
**for Yahuah Elohim of Israel has spoken *it***

**Isa 22:1** משא 4853 גיא 1516 חזיון 2384 מה 4100 לך 3807a אפוא 645 כי 3588 עלית 5927 כלך 3605
masa' gey'a chizayoun; mah lak aepou'a, kiy 'aliyt kulak
**The burden of the valley of vision What *aileth* to you now that you are gone up wholly**

לגגות 1406: **22:2** תשאות 8663 מלאה 4395 עיר 5892 הומיה 1993 קריה 7151 עליזה 5947 חלליך 2491 לא 3808 חללי 2491
lagagout. tashu'aut male'ah, 'ayr houmiyah, qiryah 'aliyzah; chalalayik la' challey
**to the housetops? *You that are* stirs full of a city tumultuous a city joyous your slain *men are* not slain with**

חרב 2719 ולא 3808 מתי 4191 מלחמה 4421: **22:3** כל 3605 קציניך 7101 נדדו 5074 יחד 3162 מקשת 7198 אסרו 631 כל 3605
chereb, uala' matey milchamah. kal qatziynayik nadadu yachad miqeshet 'usaru; kal
**the sword nor dead in battle All your rulers are fled together by the archers they are bound all**

נמצאיך 4672 אסרו 631 יחדו 3162 מרחוק 7350 ברחו 1272: **22:4** על 5921 כן 3651 אמרתי 559 שעו 8159 מני 4480
nimtza'ayik 'usru yachdau, merachouq barachu. 'al ken 'amartiy sha'au miniy
**that are found in you are bound together from far *which* have fled Therefore after said I Look away from me**

אמרר 4843 בבכי 1065 אל 408 תאיצו 213 לנחמני 5162 על 5921 שד 7701 בת 1323 עמי 5971: **22:5** כי 3588
'amarer babekiy; 'al ta'aytzu lanachameniy, 'al shod bat 'amiy. kiy
**bitterly I will weep not labour to comfort me because of the spoiling of the daughter of my people For**

Isa 21:13 The burden upon Arabia. In the forest in Arabia shall you lodge, O you travelling companies of Dedanim.14 The inhabitants of the land of Tema brought water to him that was thirsty, they prevented with their bread him that fled.15 For they fled from the swords, from the drawn sword, and from the bent bow, and from the grievousness of war.16 For thus has YHUH said unto me, Within a year, according to the years of an hireling, and all the glory of Kedar shall fail:17 And the residue of the number of archers, the mighty men of the children of Kedar, shall be diminished: for YHUH G-d of Israel has spoken it. **Isa** 22:1 The burden of the valley of vision. What ail you now, that you are wholly gone up to the housetops?2 Thou that are full of stirs, a tumultuous city, a joyous city: your slain men are not slain with the sword, nor dead in battle.3 All your rulers are fled together, they are bound by the archers: all that are found in you are bound together, which have fled from far.4 Therefore said I, Look away from me; I will weep bitterly, labour not to comfort me, because of the spoiling of the daughter of my people.

| יום 3117 | מהומה 4103 | ומבוסה 4001 | ומבוכה 3998 | לאדני 136 | יהוה 3069 | צבאות 6635 | בגיא 1516 | חזיון 2384 |
|---|---|---|---|---|---|---|---|---|
| youm | mahumah | uambusah | uambukah, | la'adonay | Yahuah | tzaba'aut | bagey'a | chizayoun; |
| ***it is*** **a day of** | **trouble** | **and of treading down** | **and of perplexity** | **by Adonai** | **Yahuah** | **of hosts** | **in the valley of** | **vision** |

| מקרקר 6979 | קר 7023 | ושוע 7771 | אל 413 | ההר 2022: | 22:6 | ועילם 5867 | נשא 5375 | אשפה 827 | ברכב 7393 | אדם 120 |
|---|---|---|---|---|---|---|---|---|---|---|
| maqarqar | qir | uashoua' | 'al | hahar. | | ua'aeylam | nasa' | 'ashpah, | barekeb | 'adam |
| **breaking down** | **the walls** | **and of crying** | **to** | **the mountains** | | **And Elam** | **bare** | **the quiver** | **with chariots of** | **men** |

| פרשים 6571 | וקיר 7024 | ערה 6168 | מגן 4043: | 22:7 | ויהי 1961 | מבחר 4005 | עמקיך 6010 | מלאו 4390 | רכב 7393 |
|---|---|---|---|---|---|---|---|---|---|
| parashiym; | uaqiyr | 'aerah | magen. | | uayahiy | mibchar | 'amaqayik | mala'au | rakeb; |
| ***and*** **horsemen** | **and Kir** | **uncovered** | **the shield** | | **And it shall come to pass** | **choicest** | ***that*** **your valleys** | **shall be full of** | **chariots** |

| והפרשים 6571 | שת 7896 | שתו 7896 | השערה 8179: | 22:8 | ויגל 1540 | את 853 | מסך 4539 | יהודה 3063 |
|---|---|---|---|---|---|---|---|---|
| uahaparashiym, | shot | shatu | hasha'arah. | | uayagal | 'at | masak | yahudah; |
| **and the horsemen** | **shall set themselves in** | **array** | ***at*** **the gate** | | **And he discovered** | | **the covering of** | **Judah** |

| ותבט 5027 | ביום 3117 | ההוא 1931 | אל 413 | נשק 5402 | בית 1004 | היער 3293: | 22:9 | ואת 853 | בקיעי 1233 | עיר 5892 | דוד 1732 |
|---|---|---|---|---|---|---|---|---|---|---|---|
| uatabet | bayoum | hahua', | 'al | nesheq | beyt | haya'ar. | | ua'at | baqiy'aey | 'ayr | dauid |
| **and you did look** | **in day** | **that** | **to** | **the armour of** | **the house of** | **the forest** | | ***also*** | **the breaches of** | **the city of** | **David** |

| ראיתם 7200 | כי 3588 | רבו 7235 | ותקבצו 6908 | את 853 | מי 4325 | הברכה 1295 | התחתונה 8481: | 22:10 | ואת 853 |
|---|---|---|---|---|---|---|---|---|---|
| ra'aytem | kiy | rabu; | uataqabtzu, | 'at | mey | habarekah | hatachtonah. | | ua'at |
| **You have seen** | **that** | **they are many** | **and you gathered together** | | **the waters of** | **pool** | **the lower** | | ***And*** |

| בתי 1004 | ירושלם 3389 | ספרתם 5608 | ותתצו 5422 | הבתים 1004 | לבצר 1219 | החומה 2346: | 22:11 | ומקוה 4724 |
|---|---|---|---|---|---|---|---|---|
| batey | yarushalaim | sapartem; | uatitatzu | habatiym, | labatzer | hachoumah. | | uamiquah |
| **the houses of** | **Jerusalem** | **you have numbered** | **have you broken down** | **the houses** | **to fortify** | **the wall** | | **also a ditch** |

| עשיתם 6213 | בין 996 | החמתים 2346 | למי 4325 | הברכה 1295 | הישנה 3465 | ולא 3808 | הבטתם 5027 | אל 413 | עשיה 6213 |
|---|---|---|---|---|---|---|---|---|---|
| 'asiytem, | beyn | hachomotayim, | lamey | habarekah | hayashanah; | uala' | hibattem | 'al | 'aseyha, |
| **You made** | **between** | **the two walls** | **for the water of** | **pool** | **the old** | **but not** | **you have looked** | **unto** | **the maker thereof** |

| ויצרה 3335 | מרחוק 7350 | לא 3808 | ראיתם 7200: | 22:12 | ויקרא 7121 | אדני 136 | יהוה 3069 | צבאות 6635 | ביום 3117 | ההוא 1931 |
|---|---|---|---|---|---|---|---|---|---|---|
| uayotzarah | merachouq | la' | ra'aytem. | | uayiqra', | 'adonay | Yahuah | tzaba'aut | bayoum | hahua'; |
| ***unto*** **him that fashioned it** | **long ago** | **neither** | **had respect** | | **And did call** | **Adonai** | **Yahuah** | **of hosts** | **in day** | **that** |

| לבכי 1065 | ולמספד 4553 | ולקרחה 7144 | ולחגר 2296 | שק 8242: | 22:13 | והנה 2009 | ששון 8342 | ושמחה 8057 | הרג 2026 |
|---|---|---|---|---|---|---|---|---|---|
| libakiy | ualmisped, | ualqarachah | ualachagor | saq. | | uahineh | sasoun | uasimchah, | harog |
| **to weeping** | **and to mourning** | **and to baldness** | **and to girding with** | **sackcloth** | | **And behold** | **joy** | **and gladness** | **slaying** |

| בקר 1241 | ושחט 7819 | צאן 6629 | אכל 398 | בשר 1320 | ושתות 8354 | יין 3196 | אכול 398 | ושתו 8354 | כי 3588 | מחר 4279 | נמות 4191: | 22:14 |
|---|---|---|---|---|---|---|---|---|---|---|---|---|
| baqar | uashachot | tza'n, | 'akol | basar | uashatout | yayin; | 'akoul | uashatou, | kiy | machar | namut. | |
| **oxen** | **and killing** | **sheep** | **eating** | **flesh** | **and drinking** | **wine** | **let us eat** | **and drink** | **for** | **to morrow** | **we shall die** | |

| ונגלה 1540 | באזני 241 | יהוה 3069 | צבאות 6635 | אם 518 | יכפר 3722 | העון 5771 | הזה 2088 | לכם 3807a | עד 5704 | תמתון 2191 |
|---|---|---|---|---|---|---|---|---|---|---|
| uaniglah | ba'azanay | Yahuah | tzaba'aut; | 'am | yakupar | he'auon | hazeh | lakem | 'ad | tamutun, |
| **And it was revealed** | **in mine ears** | **Yahuah** | **of hosts** | **Surely not** | **shall be purged** | **iniquity** | **this** | **from you** | **till** | **you die** |

Isa 22:5 For it is a day of trouble, and of treading down, and of perplexity by YHUH G-D of hosts in the valley of vision, breaking down the walls, and of crying to the mountains.6 And Elam bare the quiver with chariots of men and horsemen, and Kir uncovered the shield.7 And it shall come to pass, that your choicest valleys shall be full of chariots, and the horsemen shall set themselves in array at the gate.8 And he discovered the covering of Judah, and you did look in that day to the armor of the house of the forest.9 You have seen also the breaches of the city of David, that they are many: and you gathered together the waters of the lower pool.10 And you have numbered the houses of Jerusalem, and the houses have you broken down to fortify the wall.11 You made also a ditch between the two walls for the water of the old pool: but you have not looked unto the maker thereof, neither had respect unto him that fashioned it long ago.12 And in that day did YHUH G-D of hosts call to weeping, and to mourning, and to baldness, and to girding with sackcloth:13 And behold joy and gladness, slaying oxen, and killing sheep, eating flesh, and drinking wine: let us eat and drink; for tomorrow we shall die.14 And it was revealed in mine ears by YHUH of hosts, Surely this iniquity shall not be purged from you till you die, saith YHUH G-D of hosts.

**22:15**

אמר 559 אדני 136 יהוה 3068 צבאות 6635: כה 3541 אמר 559 אדני 136 יהוה 3069 צבאות 6635 לך 1980 בא 935 אל 413 הסכן 5532 הזה 2088
'amar 'adonay Yahuah tzaba'aut. koh 'amar 'adonay Yahuah tzaba'aut; lek ba' 'al hasoken hazeh,
**saith Adonai Yahuah of hosts Thus saith Adonai Yahuah of hosts Go you get you unto treasurer this *even***

**22:16**

על 5921 שבנא 7644 אשר 834 על 5921 הבית 1004: מה 4100 לך 3807a פה 6311 ומי 4310 לך 3807a פה 6311 כי 3588
'al shebna' 'asher 'al habayit. mah laka poh uamiy laka poh, kiy
**unto Shebna which *is* over the house *and say* What *have* to you here? and whom *have* to you here that**

חצבת 2672 לך 3807a פה 6311 קבר 6913 חצבי 2672 מרום 4791 קברו 6913 חקקי 2710 בסלע 5553
chatzabta laka poh qaber; chotzabiy maroum qibrou, choqaqiy basela'
**you have hewed out to you here a sepulchre *as* he that hewed him out on high a sepulchre *and* that carves in a rock?**

**22:17** **22:18**

משכן 4908 לו 3807a: הנה 2009 יהוה 3068 מטלטלך 2904 טלטלה 2925 גבר 1397 ועטך 5844 עטה 5844:
mishkan lou'. hineh Yahuah mataltelka, taltelah gaber; ua'ataka 'atoh.
**an habitation for himself Behold Yahuah will carry you away *with* a captivity mighty and will surely cover you**

צנוף 6801 יצנפך 6801 צנפה 6802 כדור 1754 אל 413 ארץ 776 רחבת 7342 ידים 3027 שמה 8033 תמות 4191 ושמה 8033
tzanoup yitznapaka tzanepah, kadur 'al 'aretz rachabat yadayim; shamah tamut, uashamah
**He will surely violently turn *and* toss you *like* a ball into a country large borders there shall you die and there**

**22:19**

מרכבות 4818 כבודך 3519 קלון 7036 בית 1004 אדניך 113: והדפתיך 1920 ממצבך 4673
markabout kaboudeka, qaloun beyt 'adoneyka. uahadaptiyka mimatzabeka;
**the chariots of your glory *shall be* the shame of house your adonai's And I will drive you from your station**

**22:20**

וממעמדך 4612 יהרסך 2040: והיה 1961 ביום 3117 ההוא 1931 וקראתי 7121 לעבדי 5650
uamima'amadaka yeherseka. uahayah bayoum hahua'; uaqara'tiy la'abdiy,
**and from your state shall he pull you down And it shall come to pass in day that I will call my servant**

**22:21**

לאליקים 471 בן 1121 חלקיהו 2518: והלבשתיו 3847 כתנתך 3801 ואבנטך 73 אחזקנו 2388
la'alyaqiym ben chilqiyahu. uahilbashtiyu kutanateka, ua'abnetaka 'achazqenu,
**Eliakim the son of Hilkiah And I will clothe him *with* your robe and your girdle strengthen him**

וממשלתך 4475 אתן 5414 בידו 3027 והיה 1961 לאב 1 ליושב 3427 ירושלם 3389
uamemsheltaka 'aten bayadou; uahayah la'ab layousheb yarushalaim
***with* and your government I will commit into his hand and he shall be a father to the inhabitants of Jerusalem**

**22:22**

ולבית 1004 יהודה 3063: ונתתי 5414 מפתח 4668 בית 1004 דוד 1732 על 5921 שכמו 7926 ופתח 6605
ualbeyt yahudah. uanatatiy mapteach beyt dauid 'al shikmou; uapatach
**and to the house of Judah And will I lay the key of the house of David upon his shoulder so he shall open**

**22:23**

ואין 369 סגר 5462 וסגר 5462 ואין 369 פתח 6605: ותקעתיו 8628 יתד 3489 במקום 4725 נאמן 539
ua'aeyn soger, uasagar ua'aeyn poteach. uatqa'atiyu yated bamaqoum ne'aman;
**and none shall shut and he shall shut and none shall open And I will fasten him *as* a nail in a place sure**

**22:24**

והיה 1961 לכסא 3678 כבוד 3519 לבית 1004 אביו 1: ותלו 8518 עליו 5921 כל 3605 כבוד 3519 בית 1004
uahayah lakisea' kaboud labeyt 'abiyu. uatalu' 'aelayu kal kaboud beyt
**and he shall be for a throne glorious to house his father's And they shall hang upon him all the glory of house**

Isa 22:15 Thus saith YHUH G-D of hosts, Go, get you unto this treasurer, even unto Shebna, which is over the house, and say,16 What have you here? and whom have you here, that you have hewed you out a sepulcher here, as he that heweth him out a sepulcher on high, and that graveth an habitation for himself in a rock?17 Behold, YHUH will carry you away with a mighty captivity, and will surely cover you.18 He will surely violently turn and toss you like a ball into a large country: there shall you die, and there the chariots of your glory shall be the shame of your lord's house.19 And I will drive you from your station, and from your state shall he pull you down.20 And it shall come to pass in that day, that I will call my servant Eliakim the son of Hilkiah:21 And I will clothe him with your robe, and strengthen him with your girdle, and I will commit your government into his hand: and he shall be a father to the inhabitants of Jerusalem, and to the house of Judah.22 And the key of the house of David will I lay upon his shoulder; so he shall open, and none shall shut; and he shall shut, and none shall open.23 And I will fasten him as a nail in a sure place; and he shall be for a glorious throne to his father's house.24 And they shall hang upon him all the glory of his father's house, the offspring and the issue, all vessels of small quantity, from the vessels of cups,

אביו 1 | הצאצאים 6631 | והצפעות 6849 | כל 3605 | כלי 3627 | הקטן 6996 | מכלי 3627 | האגנות 101 | ועד 5704 | כל 3605 | כלי 3627
'abiyu, hatze'atza'aym uahatzapi'aut, kal kaley haqatan; mikley ha'aganout, ua'ad kal kaley
**his father's the offspring and the issue all vessels of small quantity from vessels of the cups even to all vessels of**

22:25 הנבלים 5035: | ביום 3117 | ההוא 1931 | נאם 5002 | יהוה 3068 | צבאות 6635 | תמוש 4185 | היתד 3489 | התקועה 8628 | במקום 4725 | נאמן 539
hanabaliym. bayoum hahua', na'am Yahuah tzaba'aut, tamush hayated, hataqu'ah bamaqoum ne'aman;
**the flagons In day that saith Yahuah of hosts shall be removed the nail that is fastened in place *the* sure**

ונגדעה 1438 | ונפלה 5307 | ונכרת 3772 | המשא 4853 | אשר 834 | עליה 5921 | כי 3588 | יהוה 3068 | דבר 1696:
uanigda'ah uanapalah, uanikrat hamasa' 'asher 'aleyha, kiy Yahuah diber.
**and be cut down and fall shall be cut off and the burden that *was* upon it for Yahuah has spoken *it***

**Isa 23:1** משא 4853 | צר 6865 | הילילו 3213 | אניות 591 | תרשיש 8659 | כי 3588 | שדד 7703 | מבית 1004 | מבוא 935
masa' tzor; heyliylu aniyout tarshiysh, kiy shudad mibayit mibou'a,
**The burden of Tyre Howl *you* ships of Tarshish for it is laid waste *so that there is* no house no entering in**

23:2 מארץ 776 | כתים 3794 | נגלה 1540 | למו 3807a: | דמו 1826 | ישבי 3427 | אי 339 | סחר 5503 | צידון 6721
me'aretz kitiym niglah lamou. domu yoshabey 'ay; socher tziydoun
**from the land of Chittim it is revealed to them Be still *you* inhabitants of the isle the merchants of Zidon**

23:3 עבר 5674 | ים 3220 | מלאוך 4390: | ובמים 4325 | רבים 7227 | זרע 2233 | שחר 7883 | קציר 7105 | יאור 2975
'aber yam mil'auk. uabmayim rabiym zera' shichor, qatziyr ya'aur
**that pass over the sea you whom have replenished And by waters great the seed of Sihor the harvest of the river**

23:4 תבואתה 8393 | ותהי 1961 | סחר 5505 | גוים 1471: | בושי 954 | צידון 6721 | כי 3588 | אמר 559 | ים 3220 | מעוז 4581
tabu'atah; uatahiy sakar gouyim. boushiy tziydoun, kiy 'amar yam, ma'auz
***is* her revenue and she is a mart of nations Be you ashamed O Zidon for has spoken the sea *even* the strength of**

23:5 הים 3220 | לאמר 559 | לא 3808 | חלתי 2342 | ולא 3808 | ילדתי 3205 | ולא 3808 | גדלתי 1431 | בחורים 970 | רוממתי 7311 | בתולות 1330:
hayam lea'mor; la' chaltiy uala' yaladtiy, uala' gidaltiy bachuriym roumamatiy batulout.
**the sea saying not I travail nor bring forth children neither do I nourish up young men *nor* bring up virgins**

23:6 כאשר 834 | שמע 8088 | למצרים 4714 | יחילו 2342 | כשמע 8085 | צר 6865: | עברו 5674
ka'asher shema' lamitzrayim; yachiylu kashema' tzor. 'abru
**As *at* the report concerning Egypt *so* shall they be sorely pained at the report of Tyre Pass you over to**

23:7 תרשישה 8659 | הילילו 3213 | ישבי 3427 | אי 339: | הזאת 2063 | לכם 3807a | עליזה 5947 | מימי 3117 | קדם 6924 | קדמתה 6927
tarshiyshah; heyliylu yoshabey 'ay. haza't lakem 'aliyzah; miymey qedem qadmatah
**Tarshish howl *you* inhabitants of the isle *Is* this to your joyous *city, is* of days? ancient whose antiquity**

23:8 יבלוה 2986 | רגליה 7272 | מרחוק 7350 | לגור 1481: | מי 4310 | יעץ 3289 | זאת 2063 | על 5921 | צר 6865 | המעטירה 5849
yobiluha ragleyha, merachouq lagur. miy' ya'atz za't, 'al tzor hama'atiyrah;
**shall carry her her own feet afar off to sojourn Who has taken this counsel this against Tyre the crowning *city***

23:9 אשר 834 | סחריה 5503 | שרים 8269 | כנעניה 3667 | נכבדי 3513 | ארץ 776: | יהוה 3069 | צבאות 6635 | יעצה 3289
'asher sochareyha sariym, kin'aneyha nikbadey 'aretz. Yahuah tzaba'aut ya'atzah;
**whose merchants *are* princes whose traffickers *are* the honorable of the earth? Yahuah of hosts has purposed it**

Isa 22:24 even to all the vessels of flagons.25 In that day, saith YHUH of hosts, shall the nail that is fastened in the sure place be removed, and be cut down, and fall; and the burden that was upon it shall be cut off: for YHUH has spoken it. **Isa** 23:1 The burden of Tyre. Howl, you ships of Tarshish; for it is laid waste, so that there is no house, no entering in: from the land of Chittim it is revealed to them.2 Be still, you inhabitants of the isle; you whom the merchants of Zidon, that pass over the sea, have replenished.3 And by great waters the seed of Sihor, the harvest of the river, is her revenue; and she is a mart of nations.4 Be you ashamed, O Zidon: for the sea has spoken, even the strength of the sea, saying, I travail not, nor bring forth children, neither do I nourish up young men, nor bring up virgins.5 As at the report concerning Egypt, so shall they be sorely pained at the report of Tyre.6 Pass you over to Tarshish; howl, you inhabitants of the isle.7 Is this your joyous city, whose antiquity is of ancient days? her own feet shall carry her afar off to sojourn.8 Who has taken this counsel against Tyre, the crowning city, whose merchants are princes, whose traffickers are the honourable of the earth?9 YHUH of hosts has purposed it, to stain the pride of all glory, and to bring into contempt all the honourable of the earth.

לחלל 2490 | גאון 1347 | כל 3605 | צבי 6643 | להקל 7043 | כל 3605 | נכבדי 3513 | ארץ 776: | **23:10** עברי 5674
lachalel | ga'aun | kal | tzabiy, | lahaqel | kal | nikbadey | 'aretz. | 'abriy
**to stain | the pride of | all | glory | *and* to bring into contempt | all | the honorable of | the earth | Pass through**

ארצך 776 | כיאר 2975 | בת 1323 | תרשיש 8659 | אין 369 | מזח 4206 | עוד 5750: | **23:11** ידו 3027 | נטה 5186 | על 5921 | הים 3220
'artzek | kaya'ar; | bat | tarshiysh | 'aeyn | mezach | 'aud. | yadou | natah | 'al | hayam,
**your land | as a river | O daughter of | Tarshish | *there is* no | strength | more | his hand | He stretched out | over | the sea**

הרגיז 7264 | ממלכות 4467 | יהוה 3068 | צוה 6680 | אל 413 | כנען 3667 | לשמד 8045
hirgiyz | mamlakout; | Yahuah | tziuah | 'al | kana'an, | lashmid
**he shook | the kingdoms | Yahuah | has given a commandment | against | the merchant | *city* to destroy**

מעזניה 4581: | **23:12** ויאמר 559 | לא 3808 | תוסיפי 3254 | עוד 5750 | לעלוז 5937 | המעשקה 6231 | בתולת 1330 | בת 1323
ma'azneyha. | uaya'mer | la' | tousiypiy | 'aud | la'alouz; | hama'ashaqah | batulat | bat
**the strong holds thereof | And he said | no | more | over | You shall rejoice | O you oppressed | virgin | daughter of**

צידון 6721 | כתיים 3794 | קומי 6965 | עברי 5674 | גם 1571 | שם 8033 | לא 3808 | ינוח 5117 | לך 3807a: | **23:13** הן 2005 | ארץ 776 | כשדים 3778
tziydoun, | kitiyiym | quamiy | 'aboriy, | gam | sham | la' | yanuach | lak. | hen | 'aretz | kasdiym,
**Zidon | Chittim | arise | pass over to | also | there | no | shall have rest | to you | Behold | the land of | the Chaldeans**

זה 2088 | העם 5971 | לא 3808 | היה 1961 | אשור 804 | יסדה 3245 | לציים 6728 | הקימו 6965 | בחיניו 971
zeh | ha'am | la' | hayah, | 'ashur | yasadah | latziyiym; | heqiymu | bachiynayu
**this | the people | not | was *till* | the Assyrian | founded it | for them that dwell in the wilderness | they set up | the towers thereof**

עררו 6209 | ארמנותיה 759 | שמה 7760 | למפלה 4654: | **23:14** הילילו 3213 | אניות 591 | תרשיש 8659 | כי 3588 | שדד 7703
'araru | armanouteyha, | samah | lamapelah. | heyliylu | aniyout | tarshiysh; | kiy | shudad
**they raised up | the palaces thereof *and* | he brought it | to ruin | Howl | *you* ships of | Tarshish | for | is laid waste**

מעזכן 4581: | **23:15** והיה 1961 | ביום 3117 | ההוא 1931 | ונשכחת 7911 | צר 6865 | שבעים 7657 | שנה 8141
ma'azken. | uahayah | bayoum | hahua', | uanishkachat | tzor | shib'aym | shanah,
**your strength | And it shall come to pass | in day | that | shall be forgotten | Tyre | seventy | years**

כימי 3117 | מלך 4428 | אחד 259 | מקץ 7093 | שבעים 7657 | שנה 8141 | יהיה 1961 | לצר 6865 | כשירת 7892 | הזונה 2181: | **23:16** קחי 3947
kiymey | melek | 'achad; | miqetz | shib'aym | shanah | yihayeh | latzor, | kashiyrat | hazounah. | qachiy
**according to the days of | king | one | after the end of | seventy | years | shall | Tyre | sing as | an harlot | Take**

כנור 3658 | סבי 5437 | עיר 5892 | זונה 2181 | נשכחה 7911 | היטיבי 3190 | נגן 5059 | הרבי 7235 | שיר 7892 | למען 4616
kinour | sobiy | 'ayr | zounah | nishkachah; | heytiybiy | nagen | harabiy | shiyr, | lama'an
**an harp | go about | the city | you harlot | that have been forgotten | make sweet | melody | many | sing songs | that**

תזכרי 2142: | **23:17** והיה 1961 | מקץ 7093 | שבעים 7657 | שנה 8141 | יפקד 6485 | יהוה 3068 | את 853
tizakeriy. | uahayah | miqetz | shib'aym | shanah, | yipqod | Yahuah | 'at
**you may be remembered | And it shall come to pass | after the end of | seventy | years | that will visit | Yahuah**

צר 6865 | ושבה 7725 | לאתננה 868 | וזנתה 2181 | את 854 | כל 3605 | ממלכות 4467 | הארץ 776 | על 5921 | פני 6440
tzor, | uashabah | la'atnanah; | uazanatah | 'at | kal | mamlakout | ha'aretz | 'al | paney
**Tyre | and she shall turn | to her hire | and shall commit fornication | *with* | all of | the kingdoms of | the world | upon | the face of**

Isa 23:10 Pass through your land as a river, O daughter of Tarshish: there is no more strength.11 He stretched out his hand over the sea, he shook the kingdoms: YHUH has given a commandment against the merchant city, to destroy the strong holds thereof.12 And he said, Thou shall no more rejoice, O you oppressed virgin, daughter of Zidon: arise, pass over to Chittim; there also shall you have no rest.13 Behold the land of the Chaldeans; this people was not, till the Assyrian founded it for them that dwell in the wilderness: they set up the towers thereof, they raised up the palaces thereof; and he brought it to ruin.14 Howl, you ships of Tarshish: for your strength is laid waste.15 And it shall come to pass in that day, that Tyre shall be forgotten seventy years, according to the days of one king: after the end of seventy years shall Tyre sing as an harlot.16 Take an harp, go about the city, you harlot that have been forgotten; make sweet melody, sing many songs, that you may be remembered.17 And it shall come to pass after the end of seventy years, that YHUH will visit Tyre, and she shall turn to her hire, and shall commit fornication with all the kingdoms of the world upon the face of the earth.

| האדמה 127: | 23:18 והיה 1961 | סחרה 5504 | ואתננה 868 | קדש 6944 | ליהוה 3068 | לא 3808 | יאצר 686 | ולא 3808 | יחסן 2630 |
|---|---|---|---|---|---|---|---|---|---|
| ha'adamah. | uahayah | sacharah | ua'atananah, | qodesh | laYahuah, | la' | ya'atzer | uala' | yechasen; |
| **the earth** | **And shall be** | **her merchandise** | **and her hire** | **holiness** | **to Yahuah** | **not** | **it shall be treasured** | **nor** | **laid up** |

| כי 3588 | לישבים 3427 | לפני 6440 | יהוה 3068 | יהיה 1961 | סחרה 5504 | לאכל 398 | לשבעה 7654 | ולמכסה 4374 | עתיק 6266: |
|---|---|---|---|---|---|---|---|---|---|
| kiy | layoshabiym | lipney | Yahuah | yihayeh | sacharah, | le'akol | lasaba'ah | ualimkaseh | 'atiyq. |
| **for** | **for them that dwell** | **before** | **Yahuah** | **shall be** | **her merchandise** | **to eat** | **sufficiently** | **and for clothing** | **durable** |

| Isa 24:1 | הנה 2009 | יהוה 3068 | בוקק 1238 | הארץ 776 | ובולקה 1110 | ועוה 5753 | פניה 6440 | והפיץ 6327 |
|---|---|---|---|---|---|---|---|---|
| | hineh | Yahuah | bouqeq | ha'aretz | uaboulaqah; | ua'auah | paneyha, | uahepiytz |
| | **Behold** | **Yahuah** | **make empty** | **the earth** | **and make it waste** | **and turned it** | **upside down** | **and scatters abroad** |

| ישביה 3427: | 24:2 והיה 1961 | כעם 5971 | ככהן 3548 | כעבד 5650 | כאדניו 113 |
|---|---|---|---|---|---|
| yoshabeyha. | uahayah | ka'am | kakohen, | ka'abed | ka'adonayu, |
| **the inhabitants thereof** | **And it shall be** | **as with the people** | **so with the priest** | **as with the servant** | **so with his master** |

| כשפחה 8198 | כגברתה 1404 | כקונה 7069 | כמוכר 4376 | כמלוה 3867 | כלוה 3867 |
|---|---|---|---|---|---|
| kashipchah | kagabirtah; | kaqouneh | kamouker, | kamalueh | kaloueh, |
| **as with the maid** | **so with her mistress** | **as with the buyer** | **so with the seller** | **as with the lender** | **so with the borrower** |

| כנשה 5383 | כאשר 834 נשא 5378 | בו 871a: | 24:3 הבוק 1238 | תבוק 1238 | הארץ 776 | והבוז 962 | תבוז 962 | כי 3588 |
|---|---|---|---|---|---|---|---|---|
| kanosheh | ka'asher nosha' | bou. | hibouq | tibouq | ha'aretz | uahibouz | tibouz; | kiy |
| **as with the taker of usury** | **so *with* the giver of usury** | **to him** | **shall be utterly emptied** | | **The land** | **and utterly spoiled** | | **for** |

| יהוה 3068 | דבר 1696 | את 853 | הדבר 1697 | הזה 2088: | 24:4 אבלה 56 | נבלה 5034 | הארץ 776 | אמללה 535 | נבלה 5034 | תבל 8398 |
|---|---|---|---|---|---|---|---|---|---|---|
| Yahuah, | diber | 'at | hadabar | hazeh. | 'abalah | nabalah | ha'aretz, | 'amlalah | nabalah | tebel; |
| **Yahuah** | **has spoken** | | **word** | **this** | **mourns** | ***and* fade away** | **The earth** | **languish** | ***and* fade away** | **the world** |

| אמללו 535 | מרום 4791 | עם 5971 | הארץ 776: | 24:5 והארץ 776 | חנפה 2610 | תחת 8478 | ישביה 3427 | כי 3588 |
|---|---|---|---|---|---|---|---|---|
| 'uamlalu | maroum | 'am | ha'aretz. | uaha'aretz | chanapah | tachat | yoshabeyha; | kiy |
| **do languish** | ***the* haughty** | **people of** | **the earth** | **The earth also** | **is defiled** | **under** | **the inhabitants thereof** | **because** |

| עברו 5674 | תורת 8451 | חלפו 2498 | חק 2706 | הפרו 6565 | ברית 1285 | עולם 5769: | 24:6 על 5921 | כן 3651 | אלה 423 |
|---|---|---|---|---|---|---|---|---|---|
| 'abaru | taurot | chalapu | choq, | heperu | bariyt | 'aulam. | 'al | ken, | 'alah |
| **they have transgressed** | **the laws** | **changed** | **the ordinance** | **broken** | **covenant** | ***the* everlasting** | **Therefore** | **after** | **the curse** |

| אכלה 398 | ארץ 776 | ויאשמו 816 | ישבי 3427 | בה 871a | על 5921 | כן 3651 | חרו 2787 | ישבי 3427 | ארץ 776 |
|---|---|---|---|---|---|---|---|---|---|
| 'akalah | 'aretz, | uaye'ashmu | yoshabey | bah; | 'al | ken, | charu | yoshabey | 'aretz, |
| **has devoured** | **the earth** | **and are desolate** | **they that dwell** | **therein** | **therefore** | **after** | **are burned** | **the inhabitants of** | **the earth** |

| ונשאר 7604 | אנוש 582 | מזער 4213: | 24:7 אבל 56 | תירוש 8492 | אמללה 535 | גפן 1612 | נאנחו 584 | כל 3605 | שמחי 8056 | לב 3820: | 24:8 שבת 7673 |
|---|---|---|---|---|---|---|---|---|---|---|---|
| uanish'ar | 'anoush | miz'ar. | 'abal | tiyroush | 'umlalah | gapen; | ne'anchu | kal | simchey | leb. | shabat |
| **and left** | **men** | **few** | **mourns** | **The new wine** | **languish** | **the vine** | **do sigh** | **all** | **the merry** | **hearted** | **cease** |

| משוש 4885 | תפים 8596 | חדל 2308 | שאון 7588 | עליזים 5947 | שבת 7673 | משוש 4885 | כנור 3658: | 24:9 בשיר 7892 | לא 3808 |
|---|---|---|---|---|---|---|---|---|---|
| masous | tupiym, | chadal | sha'aun | 'aliyziym; | shabat | masous | kinour. | bashiyr | la' |
| **The mirth of** | **tabrets** | **endeth** | **the noise of** | **them that rejoice** | **cease** | **the joy of** | **the harp** | **with a song** | **not** |

Isa 23:18 And her merchandise and her hire shall be holiness to YHUH: it shall not be treasured nor laid up; for her merchandise shall be for them that dwell before YHUH, to eat sufficiently, and for durable clothing. **Isa** 24:1 Behold, YHUH make the earth empty, and make it waste, and turneth it upside down, and scattereth abroad the inhabitants thereof.2 And it shall be, as with the people, so with the priest; as with the servant, so with his master; as with the maid, so with her mistress; as with the buyer, so with the seller; as with the lender, so with the borrower; as with the taker of usury, so with the giver of usury to him.3 The land shall be utterly emptied, and utterly spoiled: for YHUH has spoken this word.4 The earth mourn and fadeth away, the world languisheth and fadeth away, the haughty people of the earth do languish.5 The earth also is defiled under the inhabitants thereof; because they have transgressed the laws, changed the ordinance, broken the everlasting covenant.6 Therefore has the curse devoured the earth, and they that dwell therein are desolate: therefore the inhabitants of the earth are burned, and few men left.7 The new wine mourn, the vine languisheth, all the merryhearted do sigh.8 The mirth of tabrets ceaseth, the noise of them that rejoice endeth, the joy of the harp ceaseth.

24:10

ישתו 8354 | יין 3196 | ימר 4843 | שכר 7941 | לשתיו 8354: | נשברה 7665 | קרית 7151 | תהו 8414
yishtu | yayin; | yemar | shekar | lashotayu. | nishbarah | qiryat | tohu;
**They shall drink | wine | shall be bitter | strong drink | to them that drink it | is broken down | The city of | confusion**

24:11

סגר 5462 | כל 3605 | בית 1004 | מבוא 935: | צוחה 6682 | על 5921 | היין 3196 | בחוצות 2351 | ערבה 6150 | כל 3605
sugar | kal | bayit | mibou'a. | tzauachah | 'al | hayayin | bachutzout; | 'arabah | kal
**is shut up | every | house | that no man may come in | *There is* a crying | for | wine | in the streets | is darkened | all**

24:12 24:13

שמחה 8057 | גלה 1540 | משוש 4885 | הארץ 776: | נשאר 7604 | בעיר 5892 | שמה 8047 | ושאיה 7591 | יכת 3807 | שער 8179:
simchah, | galah | masous | ha'aretz. | nish'ar | ba'ayr | shamah; | uash'ayah | yukat | sha'ar.
**joy | is gone | the mirth of | the land | is left | In the city | desolation | and destruction | is smitten | *with* the gate**

כי 3588 | כה 3541 | יהיה 1961 | בקרב 7130 | הארץ 776 | בתוך 8432 | העמים 5971 | כנקף 5363 | זית 2132
kiy | koh | yihayeh | baqereb | ha'aretz | batouk | ha'amiym; | kanoqep | zayit,
**When | thus | it shall be | in the midst of | the land | among | the people | *there shall be* as the shaking of | an olive tree**

24:14

כעוללת 5955 | אם 518 | כלה 3615 | בציר 1210: | המה 1992 | ישאו 5375 | קולם 6963 | ירנו 7442 | בגאון 1347
ka'aulelot | 'am | kalah | batziyr. | hemah | yis'au | qoulam | yaronu; | big'aun
***and* as the gleaning grapes | when | is done | the vintage | They | shall lift up | their voice | they shall sing | for the majesty**

24:15

יהוה 3069 | צהלו 6670 | מים 3220: | על 5921 | כן 3651 | בארים 217 | כבדו 3513 | יהוה 3068 | באיי 339 | הים 3220
Yahuah, | tzahalu | miyam. | 'al | ken | ba'uriym | kabdu | Yahuah; | ba'ayey | hayam,
**Yahuah | they shall cry aloud | from the sea | Wherefore | as | in the fires | glorify you | Yahuah | in the isles of | the sea**

24:16

שם 8034 | יהוה 3068 | אלהי 430 | ישראל 3478: | מכנף 3671 | הארץ 776 | זמרת 2158 | שמענו 8085
shem | Yahuah | 'alohey | yisra'ael. | miknap | ha'aretz | zamirot | shama'anu
***even* the name of | Yahuah | Elohim of | Israel | From the uttermost part of | the earth | songs | have we heard**

צבי 6643 | לצדיק 6662 | ואמר 559 | רזי 7334 | לי 3807a | רזי 7334 | לי 3807a | אוי 188 | לי 3807a | בגדים 898
tzabiy | latzadiyq, | ua'amar | raziy | liy | raziy | liy | 'auy | liy; | bogadiym
***even* glory | to the righteous | But I said | leanness | My | leanness | my | woe | unto me | *the* treacherous dealers**

24:17

בגדו 898 | ובגד 899 | בוגדים 898 | בגדו 898: | פחד 6343 | ופחת 6354 | ופח 6341
bagadu, | uabeged | bougadiym | bagadu. | pachad | uapachat | uapach;
**have dealt treacherously | yea, very treacherous | have dealt | treacherously | Fear | and the pit | and the snare *are***

24:18

עליך 5921 | יושב 3427 | הארץ 776: | והיה 1961 | הנס 5127 | מקול 6963 | הפחד 6343 | יפל 5307
'aleyka | yousheb | ha'aretz. | uahayah | hanas | miqoul | hapachad | yipol
**upon you | O inhabitant of | the earth | And it shall come to pass | *that* he who flee | from the noise of | the fear | shall fall**

אל 413 | הפחת 6354 | והעולה 5927 | מתוך 8432 | הפחת 6354 | ילכד 3920 | בפח 6341 | כי 3588 | ארבות 699
'al | hapachat, | uaha'auleh | mitouk | hapachat, | yilaked | bapach; | kiy | arubout
**into | the pit | and he that comes up | out of the midst of | the pit | shall be taken | in the snare | for | the windows**

24:19

ממרום 4791 | נפתחו 6605 | וירעשו 7493 | מוסדי 4146 | ארץ 776: | רעה 7489 | התרעעה 7489 | הארץ 776 | פור 6565
mimaroum | niptachu, | uayir'ashu | mousadey | 'aretz. | ro'ah | hitro'a'ah | ha'aretz; | pour
**from on high | are open | and do shake | the foundations of | the earth | is utterly | broken down | The earth | is clean**

Isa 24:9 They shall not drink wine with a song; strong drink shall be bitter to them that drink it.10 The city of confusion is broken down: every house is shut up, that no man may come in.11 There is a crying for wine in the streets; all joy is darkened, the mirth of the land is gone.12 In the city is left desolation, and the gate is smitten with destruction.13 When thus it shall be in the midst of the land among the people, there shall be as the shaking of an olive tree, and as the gleaning grapes when the vintage is done.14 They shall lift up their voice, they shall sing for the majesty of YHUH, they shall cry aloud from the sea.15 Wherefore glorify you YHUH in the fires, even the name of YHUH G-d of Israel in the isles of the sea.16 From the uttermost part of the earth have we heard songs, even glory to the righteous. But I said, My leanness, my leanness, woe unto me! the treacherous dealers have dealt treacherously; yea, the treacherous dealers have dealt very treacherously.17 Fear, and the pit, and the snare, are upon you, O inhabitant of the earth.18 And it shall come to pass, that he who fleeth from the noise of the fear shall fall into the pit; and he that cometh up out of the midst of the pit shall be taken in the snare: for the windows from on high are open, and the foundations of the earth do shake.19 The earth is utterly broken down, the earth is clean dissolved,

| התפוררה 6565 | ארץ 776 | מוט 4131 | התמוטטה 4131 | ארץ 776: | 24:20 | נוע 5128 | תנוע 5128 | ארץ 776 | כשכור 7910 |
|---|---|---|---|---|---|---|---|---|---|
| hitpourarah | 'aretz, | mout | hitmoutatah | 'aretz. | | noua' | tanua' | 'aretz | kashikour, |
| **dissolved** | **the earth** | **is moved** | **exceedingly** | **the earth** | | **shall reel** | **to and fro** | **The earth** | **like a drunkard** |

| והתנודדה 5110 | כמלונה 4412 | וכבד 3513 | עליה 5921 | פשעה 6588 | ונפלה 5307 | ולא 3808 | תסיף 3254 |
|---|---|---|---|---|---|---|---|
| uahitnoudadah | kamlunah; | uakabad | 'aleyha | pish'ah, | uanapalah | uala' | tosiyp |
| **and shall be removed** | **like a cottage** | **shall be heavy** | **upon it** | **and the transgression thereof** | **and it shall fall** | **and not** | **again** |

| קום 6965: | 24:21 | והיה 1961 | ביום 3117 | ההוא 1931 | יפקד 6485 | יהוה 3068 | על 5921 | צבא 6635 | המרום 4791 |
|---|---|---|---|---|---|---|---|---|---|
| qum. | | uahayah | bayoum | hahua', | yipqod | Yahuah | 'al | tzaba' | hamaroum |
| **rise** | | **And it shall come to pass** | **in day** | **that** | **shall punish *that*** | **Yahuah** | **on** | **the host of** | **the high ones** |

| במרום 4791 | ועל 5921 | מלכי 4428 | האדמה 127 | על 5921 | האדמה 127: | 24:22 | ואספו 622 | אספה 626 |
|---|---|---|---|---|---|---|---|---|
| bamaroum; | ua'al | malkey | ha'adamah | 'al | ha'adamah. | | ua'aspu | 'asepah |
| ***that are* on high** | **and on** | **the kings of** | **the earth** | **upon** | **the earth** | | **And they shall be gathered together** | **are gathered** |

| אסיר 616 | על 5921 | בור 953 | וסגרו 5462 | על 5921 | מסגר 4525 | ומרב 7230 | ימים 3117 | יפקדו 6485: | 24:23 |
|---|---|---|---|---|---|---|---|---|---|
| 'asiyr | 'al | bour, | uasugru | 'al | masger; | uamerob | yamiym | yipaqedu. | |
| ***as* prisoners** | **in** | **the pit** | **and shall be shut up** | **in** | **the prison** | **and after many** | **days** | **shall they be visited** | |

| וחפרה 2659 | הלבנה 3842 | ובושה 954 | החמה 2535 | כי 3588 | מלך 4427 | יהוה 3068 | צבאות 6635 | בהר 2022 | ציון 6726 |
|---|---|---|---|---|---|---|---|---|---|
| uachaparah | halabanah, | uaboushah | hachamah; | kiy | malak | Yahuah | tzaba'aut, | bahar | tziyoun |
| **Then shall be confounded** | **the moon** | **and ashamed** | **the sun** | **when** | **shall reign** | **Yahuah** | **of hosts** | **in mount** | **Zion** |

| ובירושלם 3389 | ונגד 5048 | זקניו 2205 | כבוד 3519: |
|---|---|---|---|
| uabiyarushalaim, | uaneged | zaqenayu | kaboud. |

**and in Jerusalem and before his ancients gloriously**

| Isa 25:1 | יהוה 3068 | אלהי 430 | אתה 859 | ארוממך 7426 | אודה 3034 | שמך 8034 | כי 3588 | עשית 6213 | פלא 6382 |
|---|---|---|---|---|---|---|---|---|---|
| | Yahuah | 'alohay | 'atah, | aroumimaka | 'audeh | shimka, | kiy | 'ashiyta | pela'; |
| | **O Yahuah** | ***are* my Elohim** | **you** | **I will exalt you** | **I will praise** | **your name** | **for** | **you have done** | **wonderful** |

| עצות 6098 | מרחוק 7350 | אמונה 530 | אמן 544: | 25:2 | כי 3588 | שמת 7760 | מעיר 5892 | לגל 1530 | קריה 7151 | בצורה 1219 |
|---|---|---|---|---|---|---|---|---|---|---|
| aetzout | merachouq | 'amunah | 'amen. | | kiy | samta | me'ayr | lagal, | qiryah | batzurah |
| ***things your* counsels** | **of old** | ***are* faithfulness** | ***and* truth** | | **For** | **you have made** | **of a city** | **an heap *of*** | **a city** | **defenced** |

| למפלה 4654 | ארמון 759 | זרים 2114 | מעיר 5892 | לעולם 5769 | לא 3808 | יבנה 1129: | 25:3 | על 5921 | כן 3651 | יכבדוך 3513 | עם 5971 |
|---|---|---|---|---|---|---|---|---|---|---|---|
| lamapelah; | 'armoun | zariym | me'ayr, | la'aulam | la' | yibaneh. | | 'al | ken | yakabduka | 'am |
| **a ruin** | **a palace of** | **strangers** | **to be no city** | **never** | **not** | **it shall be built** | | **Therefore** | **after** | **shall glorify you** | **people** |

| עז 5794 | קרית 7151 | גוים 1471 | עריצים 6184 | ייראוך 3372: | 25:4 | כי 3588 | היית 1961 | מעוז 4581 | לדל 1800 | מעוז 4581 |
|---|---|---|---|---|---|---|---|---|---|---|
| 'az; | qiryat | gouyim | 'ariytziym | yiyra'auka. | | kiy | hayiyta | ma'auz | ladal | ma'auz |
| ***the* strong** | **the city of** | **nations** | ***the* terrible** | **shall fear you** | | **For** | **you have been** | **a strength** | **to the poor** | **a strength** |

| לאביון 34 | בצר 6862 | לו 3807a | מחסה 4268 | מזרם 2230 | צל 6738 | מחרב 2721 | כי 3588 | רוח 7307 | עריצים 6184 |
|---|---|---|---|---|---|---|---|---|---|
| la'abyoun | batzar | lou'; | machseh | mizerem | tzel | mechoreb, | kiy | ruach | 'ariytziym |
| **to the needy** | **in distress** | **his** | **a refuge** | **from the storm** | **a shadow** | **from the heat** | **when** | **the blast of** | **the terrible ones** |

Isa 24:19 the earth is moved exceedingly.20 The earth shall reel to and fro like a drunkard, and shall be removed like a cottage; and the transgression thereof shall be heavy upon it; and it shall fall, and not rise again.21 And it shall come to pass in that day, that YHUH shall punish the host of the high ones that are on high, and the kings of the earth upon the earth.22 And they shall be gathered together, as prisoners are gathered in the pit, and shall be shut up in the prison, and after many days shall they be visited.23 Then the moon shall be confounded, and the sun ashamed, when YHUH of hosts shall reign in mount Zion, and in Jerusalem, and before his ancients gloriously. **Isa** 25:1 O YHUH, you are my G-d; I will exalt you, I will praise your name; for you have done wonderful things; your counsels of old are faithfulness and truth.2 For you have made of a city an heap; of a defenced city a ruin: a palace of strangers to be no city; it shall never be built.3 Therefore shall the strong people glorify you, the city of the terrible nations shall fear you.4 For you have been a strength to the poor, a strength to the needy in his distress, a refuge from the storm, a shadow from the heat, when the blast of the terrible ones is as a storm against the wall.

| כזרם 2230 | קיר 7023: | 25:5 כחרב 2721 | בציון 6724 | שאון 7588 | זרים 2114 | תכניע 3665 | חרב 2721 |
|---|---|---|---|---|---|---|---|
| kazerem | qiyr. | kachoreb | batzayoun, | sha'aun | zariym | takniya'; | choreb |
| **is as a storm** | ***against* the wall** | **as the heat** | **in a dry place** | **the noise of** | **strangers** | **You shall bring down** | ***even* the heat** |

| בצל 6738 | עב 5645 | זמיר 2158 | עריצים 6184 | יענה 6030: | 25:6 ועשה 6213 | יהוה 3068 | צבאות 6635 |
|---|---|---|---|---|---|---|---|
| batzel | 'ab, | zamiyr | 'ariytziym | ya'aneh. | ua'asah | Yahuah | tzaba'aut |
| **with the shadow of** | **a cloud** | **the branch of** | **the terrible ones** | **shall be brought low** | **And shall make** | **Yahuah** | **of hosts** |

| לכל 3605 | העמים 5971 | בהר 2022 | הזה 2088 | משתה 4960 | שמנים 8081 | משתה 4960 | שמרים 8105 | שמנים 8081 | ממחים 4229 |
|---|---|---|---|---|---|---|---|---|---|
| lakal | ha'amiym | bahar | hazeh, | mishteh | shamaniym | mishteh | shamariym; | shamaniym | mamuchayim, |
| **unto all** | **people** | **in mountain** | **this** | **a feast of** | **fat things** | **a feast of** | **wines on the lees** | ***of* fat things** | **full of marrow** |

| שמרים 8105 | מזקקים 2212: | 25:7 ובלע 1104 | בהר 2022 | הזה 2088 | פני 6440 | הלוט 3875 | הלוט 3874 | על 5921 | כל 3605 |
|---|---|---|---|---|---|---|---|---|---|
| shamariym | mazuqaqiym. | uabila' | bahar | hazeh, | paney | halout | halout | 'al | kal |
| ***of* wines on the lees** | **well refined** | **And he will destroy** | **in mountain** | **this** | **the face of** | **the covering** | **cast** | **over** | **all** |

| העמים 5971 | והמסכה 4541 | הנסוכה 5259 | על 5921 | כל 3605 | הגוים 1471: | 25:8 בלע 1104 | המות 4194 | לנצח 5331 | ומחה 4229 |
|---|---|---|---|---|---|---|---|---|---|
| ha'amiym; | uahamasekah | hanasukah | 'al | kal | hagouyim. | bila' | hamauet | lanetzach, | uamachah |
| **people** | **and the vail** | **that is spread over** | | **all** | **nations** | **He will swallow up** | **death** | **in victory** | **and will wipe away** |

| אדני 136 | יהוה 3069 | דמעה 1832 | מעל 5921 | כל 3605 | פנים 6440 | וחרפת 2781 | עמו 5971 | יסיר 5493 | מעל 5921 | כל 3605 | הארץ 776 |
|---|---|---|---|---|---|---|---|---|---|---|---|
| 'adonay | Yahuah | dim'ah | me'al | kal | paniym; | uacherapat | 'amou, | yasiyr | me'al | kal | ha'aretz, |
| **Adonai** | **Yahuah** | **tears** | **from off** | **all** | **faces** | **and the rebuke of** | **his people** | **shall he take away** | **from off** | **all** | **the earth** |

| כי 3588 | יהוה 3068 | דבר 1696: | 25:9 ואמר 559 | ביום 3117 | ההוא 1931 | הנה 2009 | אלהינו 430 | זה 2088 | קוינו 6960 | לו 3807a |
|---|---|---|---|---|---|---|---|---|---|---|
| kiy | Yahuah | diber. | ua'amar | bayoum | hahua', | hineh | 'aloheynu | zeh | qiuiynu | lou' |
| **for** | **Yahuah** | **has spoken *it*** | **And it shall be said** | **in day** | **that** | **Lo, *is*** | **our Elohim** | **this** | **we have waited** | **for him** |

| ויושיענו 3467 | זה 2088 | יהוה 3069 | קוינו 6960 | לו 3807a | נגילה 1523 | ונשמחה 8055 | בישועתו 3444: | 25:10 כי 3588 | תנוח 5117 |
|---|---|---|---|---|---|---|---|---|---|
| uayoushiy'aenu; | zeh | Yahuah | qiuiynu | lou', | nagiylah | uanismachah | biyshu'atou. | kiy | tanuach |
| **and he will save us** | **this *is*** | **Yahuah** | **we have waited** | **for him** | **we will be glad** | **and rejoice** | **in his salvation** | **For** | **shall rest** |

| יד 3027 | יהוה 3068 | בהר 2022 | הזה 2088 | ונדוש 1758 | מואב 4124 | תחתיו 8478 | כהדוש 1758 | מתבן 4963 |
|---|---|---|---|---|---|---|---|---|
| yad | Yahuah | bahar | hazeh; | uanadoush | mou'ab | tachtayu, | kahidush | matben |
| **the hand of** | **Yahuah** | **in mountain** | **this** | **and shall be trodden down** | **Moab** | **under him** | **even as is trodden down** | **straw** |

| במי 4325 | מדמנה 4087: | 25:11 ופרש 6566 | ידיו 3027 | בקרבו 7130 | כאשר 834 | יפרש 6566 | השחה 7811 |
|---|---|---|---|---|---|---|---|
| bamey | madmenah. | uaperas | yadayu | baqirbou, | ka'asher | yapares | hasocheh |
| **for** | **the dunghill** | **And he shall spread forth** | **his hands** | **in the midst of them** | **as** | **spread forth** | **he that swimmeth** |

| לשחות 7811 | והשפיל 8213 | גאותו 1346 | עם 5973 | ארבות 698 | ידיו 3027: | 25:12 ומבצר 4013 |
|---|---|---|---|---|---|---|
| lischout; | uahishpiyl | ga'auatou, | 'am | 'arabout | yadayu. | uamibtzar |
| ***his hands* to swim** | **and he shall bring down together** | **their pride** | **with** | **the spoils of** | **their hands** | **And the fortress of** |

| משגב 4869 | חומתיך 2346 | השח 7817 | השפיל 8213 | הגיע 5060 | לארץ 776 | עד 5704 | עפר 6083: |
|---|---|---|---|---|---|---|---|
| misgab | chomoteyka, | heshach | hishpiyl | higiya' | la'aretz | 'ad | 'apar. |
| **the high fort of** | **your walls** | **shall he bring down** | **lay low** | ***and* bring** | **to the ground** | ***even* to** | **the dust** |

Isa25:5 Thou shall bring down the noise of strangers, as the heat in a dry place; even the heat with the shadow of a cloud: the branch of the terrible ones shall be brought low.6 And in this mountain shall YHUH of hosts make unto all people a feast of fat things, a feast of wines on the lees, of fat things full of marrow, of wines on the lees well refined.7 And he will destroy in this mountain the face of the covering cast over all people, and the vail that is spread over all nations.8 He will swallow up death in victory; and YHUH G-D will wipe away tears from off all faces; and the rebuke of his people shall he take away from off all the earth: for YHUH has spoken it.9 And it shall be said in that day, Lo, this is our G-d; we have waited for him, and he will save us: this is YHUH; we have waited for him, we will be glad and rejoice in his salvation.10 For in this mountain shall the hand of YHUH rest, and Moab shall be trodden down under him, even as straw is trodden down for the dunghill.11 And he shall spread forth his hands in the midst of them, as he that swimmeth spreadeth forth his hands to swim: and he shall bring down their pride together with the spoils of their hands.12 And the fortress of the high fort of your walls shall he bring down, lay low, and bring to the ground, even to the dust.

**Isa 26:1**
ביום 3117 ההוא 1931 יושר 7891 השיר 7892 הזה 2088 בארץ 776 יהודה 3063 עיר 5892 עז 5794 לנו 3807a ישועה 3444
bayoum hahua', yushar hashshiyr hazeh ba'aretz yahudah; 'ayr 'az lanu, yashu'ah
**In day that shall be sung song this in the land of Judah *have* a city strong We salvation**

ישית 7896 חומות 2346 וחל 2426: **26:2** פתחו 6605 שערים 8179 ויבא 935 גוי 1471 צדיק 6662 שמר 8104
yashiyt choumout uachel. pitchu sha'ariym; uayaba' gouy tzadiyq shomer
**will *Elohim* appoint *for* walls and bulwarks Open you the gates that may enter in nation *the* righteous which keep**

אמנים 529: **26:3** יצר 3336 סמוך 5564 תצר 5341 שלום 7965 שלום 7965 כי 3588 בך 871a בטוח 982: **26:4** בטחו 982
'amuniym. yetzer samuk, titzor shaloum shaloum; kiy baka batuach. bitchu
**the truth *whose* mind *is* stayed *on you:* You will keep *him* in perfect peace because in you he trust Trust you**

ביהוה 3068 עדי 5704 עד 5703 כי 3588 ביה 3050 יהוה 3068 צור 6697 עולמים 5769: **26:5** כי 3588 השח 7817 ישבי 3427 מרום 4791
baYahuah 'adey 'ad; kiy baYah Yahuah, tzur 'aulamiym. kiy heshach yoshabey maroum,
**in Yahuah for ever for in Yah Yahuah strength *is* everlasting For he bring down them that dwell on high**

קריה 7151 נשגבה 7682 ישפילנה 8213 ישפילה 8213 עד 5704 ארץ 776 יגיענה 5060 עד 5704 עפר 6083: **26:6** תרמסנה 7429 רגל 7272
qiryah nisgabah; yashpiylenah yashpiylah 'ad 'aretz, yagiy'anah 'ad 'apar. tirmasenah ragel;
**city *the* lofty he lay it low he lay it low *even* to the ground he bring it *even* to the dust shall tread it down The foot**

רגלי 7272 עני 6041 פעמי 6471 דלים 1800: **26:7** ארח 734 לצדיק 6662 מישרים 4339 ישר 3477 מעגל 4570
ragley 'aniy pa'amey daliym. 'arach latzadiyq meyshariym; yashar ma'gal
***even* the feet of the poor *and* the steps of the needy The way of the just *is* uprightness *you* most upright the path of**

צדיק 6662 תפלס 6424: **26:8** אף 637 ארח 734 משפטיך 4941 יהוה 3068 קוינוך 6960 לשמך 8034
tzadiyq tapales. 'ap 'arach mishpateyka Yahuah qiuiynuka; lashimka
**the just do weigh Yea *in* the way of your judgments O Yahuah have we waited for you *is* to your name**

ולזכרך 2143 תאות 8378 נפש 5315: **26:9** נפשי 5315 אויתיך 183 בלילה 3915 אף 637 רוחי 7307
ualzikraka ta'auat napesh. napshiy 'auiytiyka balayalah, 'ap ruchiy
**and to the remembrance of you the desire of *our* soul *With* my soul have I desired you in the night yea *with* my spirit**

בקרבי 7130 אשחרך 7836 כי 3588 כאשר 834 משפטיך 4941 לארץ 776 צדק 6664 למדו 3925 ישבי 3427
uaqirbiy 'ashachareka; kiy ka'asher mishpateyka la'aretz, tzedeq lamadu yoshabey
**within me will I seek you early for when your judgments *are* in the earth righteousness will learn the inhabitants of**

תבל 8398: **26:10** יחן 2603 רשע 7563 בל 1077 למד 3925 צדק 6664 בארץ 776 נכחות 5229
tebel. yuchan rasha' bal lamad tzedeq, ba'aretz nakochout
**the world Let favor be showed to the wicked *yet* not will he learn righteousness in the land of uprightness**

יעול 5765 ובל 1077 יראה 7200 גאות 1348 יהוה 3069: **26:11** יהוה 3068 רמה 7311 ידך 3027 בל 1077
ya'auel; uabal yir'ah ge'aut Yahuah. Yahuah ramah yadaka bal
**will he deal unjustly and not will behold the majesty of Yahuah Yahuah is lifted up *when* your hand not**

יחזיון 2372 יחזו 2372 ויבשו 954 קנאת 7068 עם 5971 אף 637 אש 784 צריך 6862
yechazayun; yechazu uayeboshu qin'at 'am, 'ap 'aesh tzareyka
**they will see *but* they shall see and be ashamed for *their* envy *at the* people yea the fire of your enemies**

**Isa** 26:1 In that day shall this song be sung in the land of Judah; We have a strong city; salvation will G-d appoint for walls and bulwarks.2 Open you the gates, that the righteous nation which keep the truth may enter in.3 Thou will keep him in perfect peace, whose mind is stayed on you: because he trusteth in you.4 Trust you in YHUH forever: for in YHUH JEHOVAH is everlasting strength:5 For he bring down them that dwell on high; the lofty city, he layeth it low; he layeth it low, even to the ground; he bring it even to the dust.6 The foot shall tread it down, even the feet of the poor, and the steps of the needy.7 The way of the just is uprightness: you, most upright, dost weigh the path of the just.8 Yea, in the way of your judgments, O YHUH, have we waited for you; the desire of our soul is to your name, and to the remembrance of you.9 With my soul have I desired you in the night; yea, with my spirit within me will I seek you early: for when your judgments are in the earth, the inhabitants of the world will learn righteousness.10 Let favor be showed to the wicked, yet will he not learn righteousness: in the land of uprightness will he deal unjustly, and will not behold the majesty of YHUH.11 YHUH, when your hand is lifted up they will not see but they shall see, and be ashamed for their envy at the people; yea, the fire of your enemies shall devour them.

תאכלם 398: ta'kalem. **shall devour them**

**26:12** יהוה 3068 Yahuah **Yahuah** | תשפת 8239 tishpot **you will ordain** | שלום 7965 shaloum **peace** | לנו 3807a lanu; **for us:** | כי 3588 kiy **for** | גם 1571 gam **also** | כל 3605 kal **all** | מעשינו 4639 ma'aseynu **our works** | פעלת 6466 pa'alta **you have wrought**

לנו 3807a: lanu. **in us**

**26:13** יהוה 3068 Yahuah **O Yahuah** | אלהינו 430 'aloheynu, **our Elohim** | בעלונו 1166 ba'alunu **you have had dominion** | אדנים 113 'adoniym ***other* adonai's** | זולתך 2108 zulateka; **beside you** | לבד 905 labad **only** | בך 871a baka ***but* by you**

נזכיר 2142 nazkiyr **will we make mention of** | שמך 8034: shameka. **your name**

**26:14** מתים 4191 metiym ***They are* dead** | בל 1077 bal **not** | יחיו 2421 yichayu, **they shall live** | רפאים 7496 rapa'aym ***they are* deceased** | בל 1077 bal **not** | יקמו 6965 yaqumu; **they shall rise**

לכן 3651 laken **therefore** | פקדת 6485 paqadta **have you visited** | ותשמידם 8045 uatashmiydem, **and destroyed them** | ותאבד 6 uata'abed **and made to perish** | כל 3605 kal **all** | זכר 2143 zeker **memory** | למו 3807a: lamou. **their**

**26:15** יספת 3254 yasapta **You have increased** | לגוי 1471 lagouy **the nation** | יהוה 3068 Yahuah, **O Yahuah** | יספת 3254 yasapta **you have increased** | לגוי 1471 lagouy **the nation** | נכבדת 3513 nikbadata; **you are glorified** | רחקת 7368 richaqta **you had removed *it* far** | כל 3605 kal ***unto* all** | קצוי 7099 qatzuey **the ends of**

ארץ 776: 'aretz. **the earth**

**26:16** יהוה 3068 Yahuah **Yahuah** | בצר 6862 batzar **in trouble** | פקדוך 6485 paqaduka; **have they visited you** | צקון 6694 tzaqun **they poured out** | לחש 3908 lachash, **a prayer** | מוסרך 4148 musaraka ***when* your chastening**

למו 3807a: lamou. ***was* upon them**

**26:17** כמו 3644 kamou **Like as** | הרה 2030 harah **a woman with child** | תקריב 7126 taqriyb ***that* draw near** | ללדת 3205 laledet, **the time of her delivery** | תחיל 2342 tachiyl **is in pain** | תזעק 2199 tiz'aq ***and* cry out**

בחבליה 2256 bachabaleyha; **in her pangs** | כן 3651 ken **so** | היינו 1961 hayiynu **have we been** | מפניך 6440 mipaneyka **in your sight** | יהוה 3068: Yahuah. **O Yahuah**

**26:18** הרינו 2030 hariynu **We have been with child** | חלנו 2342 chalnu, **we have been in pain** | כמו 3644 kamou **as it were**

ילדנו 3205 yaladnu **we have brought forth** | רוח 7307 ruach; **wind** | ישועת 3444 yashu'at **any deliverance** | בל 1077 bal **not** | נעשה 6213 na'aseh **we have wrought** | ארץ 776 'aretz, ***in* the earth** | ובל 1077 uabal **neither** | יפלו 5307 yiplu **have fallen** | ישבי 3427 yoshabey **the inhabitants of**

תבל 8398: tebel. **the world**

**26:19** יחיו 2421 yichayu **shall live** | מתיך 4191 meteyka, **Your dead *men*** | נבלתי 5038 niblotiy ***together with* my dead body** | יקומון 6965 yaqumun; **shall they arise** | הקיצו 6974 haqiytzu **Awake** | ורננו 7442 uarannu **and sing** | שכני 7931 shokaney **you that dwell in**

עפר 6083 'apar, **dust** | כי 3588 kiy **for** | טל 2919 tal **your dew *is as*** | אורת 219 aurot **herbs (*lights*)** | טלך 2919 taleka, **the dew of** | וארץ 776 ua'aretz **and the earth** | רפאים 7496 rapa'aym **the dead** | תפיל 5307: tapiyl. **shall cast out**

**26:20** לך 1980 lek **Come you** | עמי 5971 'amiy **my people**

בא 935 ba' **enter you** | בחדריך 2315 bachadareyka, **into your chambers** | וסגר 5462 uasgor **and shut** | דלתיך 1817 daltayka **your doors** | בעדך 1157 ba'adeka; **about you** | חבי 2247 chabiy **hide yourself** | כמעט 4592 chim'at **as it were for a little** | רגע 7281 rega' **moment** | עד 5704 'ad **Until** | יעבור 5674 ya'abour **be overpast**

Isa 26:12 YHUH, you will ordain peace for us: for you also have wrought all our works in us.13 O YHUH our G-d, other lords beside you have had dominion over us: but by you only will we make mention of your name.14 They are dead, they shall not live; they are deceased, they shall not rise: therefore have you visited and destroyed them, and made all their memory to perish.15 Thou have increased the nation, O YHUH, you have increased the nation: you are glorified: you had removed it far unto all the ends of the earth.16 YHUH, in trouble have they visited you, they poured out a prayer when your chastening was upon them.17 Like as a woman with child, that draweth near the time of her delivery, is in pain, and crieth out in her pangs; so have we been in your sight, O YHUH.18 We have been with child, we have been in pain, we have as it were brought forth wind; we have not wrought any deliverance in the earth; neither have the inhabitants of the world fallen.19 Thy dead men shall live, together with my dead body shall they arise. Awake and sing, you that dwell in dust: for your dew is as the dew of herbs, and the earth shall cast out the dead.20 Come, my people, enter you into your chambers, and shut your doors about you: hide thyself as it were for a little moment, until the indignation be overpast.

26:21
זעם 2195: | כי 3588 הנה 2009 יהוה 3068 יצא 3318 ממקומו 4725 לפקד 6485 עון 5771 ישב 3427 הארץ 776 עליו 5921
za'am. kiy hineh Yahuah yotzea' mimaqoumou, lipqod 'auon yosheb ha'aretz 'alayu;
**the indignation For behold Yahuah comes out of his place to punish iniquity the inhabitants of the earth for their**

וגלתה 1540 הארץ 776 את 853 דמיה 1818 ולא 3808 תכסה 3680 עוד 5750 על 5921 הרוגיה 2026:
uagiltah ha'aretz 'at dameyha, uala' takaseh 'aud 'al harugeyha.
**also shall disclose the earth her blood and no shall cover more over her slain**

**Isa 27:1**
ביום 3117 ההוא 1931 יפקד 6485 יהוה 3068 בחרבו 2719 הקשה 7186 והגדולה 1419 והחזקה 2389 על 5921 לויתן 3882 נחש 5175
bayoum hahua' yipqod Yahuah bacharbou haqashah uahagadoulah uahachazaqah, 'al liuyatan nachash
**In day that shall punish Yahuah with sword his sore and great and strong even leviathan serpent**

ברח 1281 ועל 5921 לויתן 3882 נחש 5175 עקלתון 6129 והרג 2026 את 853 התנין 8577 אשר 834 בים 3220: | 27:2 ביום 3117
bariach, ua'al liuyatan, nachash 'aqalatoun; uaharag 'at hataniyn 'asher bayam. bayoum
***the* piercing even leviathan serpent *that* crooked and he shall slay the dragon that *is* in the sea In day**

ההוא 1931 כרם 3754 חמד 2531 ענו 6030 לה 3807a: | 27:3 אני 589 יהוה 3068 נצרה 5341 לרגעים 7281 אשקנה 8248 פן 6435
hahua'; kerem chemed 'anu lah. 'aniy Yahuah notzarah, lirga'aym 'ashqenah; pen
**that A vineyard of red wine sing you unto her I Yahuah do keep it *every* moment I will water it lest**

יפקד 6485 עליה 5921 לילה 3915 ויום 3117 אצרנה 5341: | 27:4 חמה 2534 אין 369 לי 3807a מי 4310 יתנני 5414 שמיר 8068 שית 7898
yipqod 'aleyha, layalah uayoum 'atzarenah. chemah 'aeyn liy; miy' yitaneniy shamiyr shayit
***any* hurt it night and day I will keep it Fury *is* not in me who would set against me the briers *and* thorns**

במלחמה 4421 אפשעה 6585 בה 871a אציתנה 6702 יחד 3162: | 27:5 או 176 יחזק 2388 במעוזי 4581
bamilchamah, 'apsa'ah bah 'atziytenah yachad. 'au yachazeq bama'auziy,
**in battle? I would go through them I would burn them together Or let him take hold of my strength**

יעשה 6213 שלום 7965 לי 3807a שלום 7965 יעשה 6213 לי 3807a: | 27:6 הבאים 935 ישרש 8327
ya'aseh shaloum liy; shaloum ya'aseh liy. haba'aym yashresh
***that* he may make peace with me peace *and* he shall make with me them that come He shall cause to take root**

יעקב 3290 יציץ 6692 ופרח 6524 ישראל 3478 ומלאו 4390 פני 6440 תבל 8398 תנובה 8570: | 27:7 הכמכת 4347 מכהו 5221
ya'aqob, yatziytz uaparach yisra'ael; uamal'au paney tebel tanubah. hakamakat makehu
***of* Jacob shall blossom and bud Israel and fill the face of the world with fruit *as* he smote Has he smitten him**

הכהו 5221 אם 518 כהרג 2027 הרגיו 2026 הרג 2026: | 27:8 בסאסאה 5432
hikahu; 'am kahereg harugayu horag. basa'sa'ah
**those that smote him? or according to the slaughter of is he slain them that are slain him? In measure**

בשלחה 7971 תריבנה 7378 הגה 1898 ברוחו 7307 הקשה 7186 ביום 3117 קדים 6921: | 27:9 לכן 3651 בזאת 2063
bashalchah tariybenah; hagah baruchou haqashah bayoum qadiym. laken, baza't
**when it shoot forth you will debate with it he stayed wind his rough in the day of the east wind therefore By this**

יכפר 3722 עון 5771 יעקב 3290 וזה 2088 כל 3605 פרי 6529 הסר 5493 חטאתו 2403 בשומו 7760 כל 3605
yakupar 'auon ya'aqob, uazeh kal pariy hasir chata'tou; basumou kal
**shall be purged the iniquity of Jacob and this *is* all the fruit to take away his sin when he make all**

Isa 26:21 For, behold, YHUH cometh out of his place to punish the inhabitants of the earth for their iniquity: the earth also shall disclose her blood, and shall no more cover her slain. **Isa** 27:1 In that day YHUH with his sore and great and strong sword shall punish leviathan the piercing serpent, even leviathan that crooked serpent; and he shall slay the dragon that is in the sea.2 In that day sing you unto her, A vineyard of red wine.3 I YHUH do keep it; I will water it every moment: lest any hurt it, I will keep it night and day.4 Fury is not in me: who would set the briers and thorns against me in battle? I would go through them, I would burn them together.5 Or let him take hold of my strength, that he may make peace with me; and he shall make peace with me.6 He shall cause them that come of Jacob to take root: Israel shall blossom and bud, and fill the face of the world with fruit.7 Hath he smitten him, as he smote those that smote him? or is he slain according to the slaughter of them that are slain by him?8 In measure, when it shooteth forth, you will debate with it: he stayeth his rough wind in the day of the east wind.9 By this therefore shall the iniquity of Jacob be purged; and this is all the fruit to take away his sin; when he make all the stones of the altar as chalkstones that are beaten in sunder, the groves and images shall not stand up.

**27:10**

אבני 68 מזבח 4196 כאבני 68 גר 1615 מנפצות 5310 לא 3808 יקמו 6965 אשרים 842 וחמנים 2553:
'abney mizbeach, ka'abney gir manupatzout, la' yaqumu 'asheriym uachamaniym.
**the stones of the altar stones as chalk that are beaten in sunder not shall stand up the groves and images**

כי 3588 עיר 5892 בצורה 1219 בדד 910 נוה 5116 משלח 7971 ונעזב 5800 כמדבר 4057 שם 8033 ירעה 7462 עגל 5695
kiy 'ayr batzurah badad, naueh mashulach uane'azab kamidbar; sham yir'ah 'aegel
**Yet city *the* defenced *shall be* desolate *and* the habitation forsaken and left like a wilderness there shall feed the calf**

ושם 8033 ירבץ 7257 וכלה 3615 סעפיה 5585: **27:11** בּיבשׁ 3001 קצירה 7105
uasham yirbatz uakilah sa'apeyha. biybosh qatziyrah
**and there shall he lie down and consume the branches thereof When are withered the boughs thereof**

תשברנה 7665 נשים 802 באות 935 מאירות 215 אותה 853 כי 3588 לא 3808 עם 5971 בינות 998 הוא 1931
tishabarnah, nashiym ba'aut ma'ayrout 'autah; kiy la' 'am biynout hua',
**they shall be broken off the women one come *and* set on fire them for no *is* a people of understanding it**

על 5921 כן 3651 לא 3808 ירחמנו 7355 עשהו 6213 ויצרו 3335 לא 3808
'al ken la' yarachamenu 'asehu, uayotzarou la'
**therefore after not will have mercy on them he that made them and he that formed them no**

יחננו 2603: **27:12** והיה 1961 ביום 3117 ההוא 1931 יחבט 2251 יהוה 3069 משבלת 7641
yachunenu. uahayah bayoum hahua', yachbot Yahuah mishibolet
**will show them favor And it shall come to pass in day that shall beat off *that* Yahuah from the channel of**

הנהר 5104 עד 5704 נחל 5158 מצרים 4714 ואתם 859 תלקטו 3950 לאחד 259 אחד 259 בני 1121 ישראל 3478: **27:13**
hanahar 'ad nachal mitzrayim; ua'atem taluqtu la'achad 'achad baney yisra'ael.
**the river unto the stream of Egypt and you shall be gathered one by one O you children of Israel**

והיה 1961 ביום 3117 ההוא 1931 יתקע 8628 בשופר 7782 גדול 1419 ובאו 935
uahayah bayoum hahua', yitaqa' bashoupar gadoul uaba'au,
**And it shall come to pass in day that shall be blown trumpet *that* the great and they shall come**

האבדים 6 בארץ 776 אשור 804 והנדחים 5080 בארץ 776 מצרים 4714 והשתחוו 7812 ליהוה 3068
ha'abadiym ba'aretz 'ashur, uahanidachiym ba'aretz mitzrayim; uahishtachauu laYahuah
**which were ready to perish in the land of Assyria and the outcasts in the land of Egypt and shall worship Yahuah**

בהר 2022 הקדש 6944 בירושלם 3389:
bahar haqodesh biyarushalaim.
**in mount the holy at Jerusalem**

**Isa 28:1**

הוי 1945 עטרת 5850 גאות 1348 שכרי 7910 אפרים 669 וציץ 6731 נבל 5034 צבי 6643 תפארתו 8597 אשר 834
houy, ateret ge'aut shikorey 'aprayim, uatziytz nobel tzabiy tip'artou; 'asher
**Woe *to* the crown of pride *to* the drunkards of Ephraim *is* a flower fading glorious whose beauty which *are***

על 5921 ראש 7218 גיא 1516 שמנים 8081 הלומי 1986 יין 3196: **28:2** הנה 2009 חזק 2389 ואמץ 553
'al ra'sh gey'a shamaniym halumey yayin. hineh chazaq ua'amitz
**on the head of valleys of *the* fat them that are overcome with wine Behold *has* a mighty and strong one**

Isa 27:10 Yet the defenced city shall be desolate, and the habitation forsaken, and left like a wilderness: there shall the calf feed, and there shall he lie down, and consume the branches thereof.11 When the boughs thereof are withered, they shall be broken off: the women come, and set them on fire: for it is a people of no understanding: therefore he that made them will not have mercy on them, and he that formed them will show them no favor.12 And it shall come to pass in that day, that YHUH shall beat off from the channel of the river unto the stream of Egypt, and you shall be gathered one by one, O you children of Israel.13 And it shall come to pass in that day, that the great trumpet shall be blown, and they shall come which were ready to perish in the land of Assyria, and the outcasts in the land of Egypt, and shall worship YHUH in the holy mount at Jerusalem. **Isa 28:1** Woe to the crown of pride, to the drunkards of Ephraim, whose glorious beauty is a fading flower, which are on the head of the fat valleys of them that are overcome with wine!2 Behold, YHUH has a mighty and strong one, which as a tempest of hail and a destroying storm, as a flood of mighty waters overflowing, shall cast down to the earth with the hand.

לאדני 136 כזרם 2230 ברד 1259 שער 8178 קטב 6986 כזרם 2230 מים 4325 כבירים 3524 שטפים 7857 הניח 3240
la'adonay, kazerem barad sa'ar qateb; kazerem mayim kabiyriym shotapiym hiniyach
**Adonai *which* as a tempest of hail *and* a storm destroying as a flood of waters mighty overflowing shall cast down**

לארץ 776 ביד 3027: 28:3 ברגלים 7272 תרמסנה 7429 עטרת 5850 גאות 1348 שכורי 7910 אפרים 669: 28:4
la'aretz bayad. baraglayim teramasnah; ateret ge'aut shikourey 'aprayim.
**to the earth with the hand under feet shall be trodden The crown of pride the drunkards of Ephraim**

והיתה 1961 ציצת 6733 נבל 5034 צבי 6643 תפארתו 8597 אשר 834 על 5921 ראש 7218 גיא 1516 שמנים 8081 כבכורה 1061
uahayatah tziytzat nobel tzabiy tip'artou, 'asher 'al ra'sh gey'a shamaniym; kabikurah
**And shall be a flower fading *the* glorious beauty which *is* on the head of valley *the* fat *and* as the hasty fruit**

בטרם 2962 קיץ 7019 אשר 834 יראה 7200 הראה 7200 אותה 853 בעודה 5750 בכפו 3709 יבלענה 1104: 28:5 ביום 3117
baterem qayitz, 'asher yir'ah hara'ah 'autah, ba'audah bakapou yibla'anah. bayoum
**before the summer which *when* he that looks upon see it while it is yet in his hand he eat it up In day**

ההוא 1931 יהיה 1961 יהוה 3068 צבאות 6635 לעטרת 5850 צבי 6643 ולצפירת 6843 תפארה 8597 לשאר 7605 עמו 5971: 28:6
hahua', yihayeh Yahuah tzaba'aut, la'ateret tzabiy, ualitzpiyrat tip'arah; lish'ar 'amou.
**that shall be Yahuah of hosts for a crown of glory and for a diadem of beauty unto the residue of his people**

ולרוח 7307 משפט 4941 ליושב 3427 על 5921 המשפט 4941 ולגבורה 1369 משיבי 7725 מלחמה 4421 שערה 8179: 28:7
ualruach mishapat; layousheb 'al hamishpat, ualigaburah, mashiybey milchamah sha'arah.
**And for a spirit of judgment to him that sit in judgment and for strength to them that turn the battle to the gate**

וגם 1571 אלה 428 ביין 3196 שגו 7686 ובשכר 7941 תעו 8582 כהן 3548 ונביא 5030 שגו 7686
uagam 'aeleh bayayin shagu, uabashekar ta'au; kohen uanabiy'a shagu
**But also they through wine have erred and through strong drink are out of the way the priest and the prophet have erred**

בשכר 7941 נבלעו 1104 מן 4480 היין 3196 תעו 8582 מן 4480 השכר 7941 שגו 7686 בראה 7203
bashekar nibla'au min hayayin, ta'au min hashekar, shagu baro'ah,
**through strong drink they are swallowed up of wine they are out of the way through strong drink they err in vision**

פקו 6328 פליליה 6417: 28:8 כי 3588 כל 3605 שלחנות 7979 מלאו 4390 קיא 6892 צאה 6675 בלי 1097 מקום 4725: 28:9
paqu paliyliyah. kiy kal shulchanout, mala'au qiy'a tzo'ah; baliy maqoum.
**they stumble *in* judgment For all tables are full of vomit *and* filthiness *so that there is* no place *clean***

את 853 מי 4310 יורה 3384 דעה 1844 ואת 853 מי 4310 יבין 995 שמועה 8052 גמולי 1580
'at miy' youreh de'ah, ua'at miy' yabiyn shamu'ah; gamuley
**Whom shall he teach knowledge? *and* whom shall he make to understand doctrine? *them that are* weaned**

מחלב 2461 עתיקי 6267 משדים 7699: 28:10 כי 3588 צו 6673 לצו 6673 צו 6673 לצו 6673 קו 6957 לקו 6957
mechalab, 'atiyqey mishadayim. kiy tzau latzau tzau latzau, qau laqau
**from the milk *and* drawn from the breasts For precept *must be* upon precept precept upon precept line upon line**

קו 6957 לקו 6957 זעיר 2191 שם 8033 זעיר 2191 שם 8033: 28:11 כי 3588 בלעגי 3934 שפה 8193 ובלשון 3956 אחרת 312 ידבר 1696
qau laqau; za'aeyr sham za'aeyr sham. kiy bala'agey sapah, uablashoun 'acheret; yadaber
**line upon line a little here a little *and* there For with stammering lips and tongue another will he speak**

Isa 28:3 The crown of pride, the drunkards of Ephraim, shall be trodden under feet:4 And the glorious beauty, which is on the head of the fat valley, shall be a fading flower, and as the hasty fruit before the summer; which when he that look upon it see, while it is yet in his hand he eateth it up.5 In that day shall YHUH of hosts be for a crown of glory, and for a diadem of beauty, unto the residue of his people,6 And for a spirit of judgment to him that sitteth in judgment, and for strength to them that turn the battle to the gate.7 But they also have erred through wine, and through strong drink are out of the way; the priest and the prophet have erred through strong drink, they are swallowed up of wine, they are out of the way through strong drink; they err in vision, they stumble in judgment.8 For all tables are full of vomit and filthiness, so that there is no place clean.9 Whom shall he teach knowledge? and whom shall he make to understand doctrine? them that are weaned from the milk, and drawn from the breasts.10 For precept must be upon precept, precept upon precept; line upon line, line upon line; here a little, and there a little:11 For with stammering lips and another tongue will he speak to this people.

28:12

אל 413 העם 5971 הזה 2088: אשר 834 אמר 559 אליהם 413 זאת 2063 המנוחה 4496 הניחו 5117 לעיף 5889
'al ha'am hazeh. 'asher 'amar 'aleyhem, za't hamanuchah haniychu le'ayep,
**to the people this whom he said to them This *is* the rest *wherewith* you may cause to rest the weary**

28:13

וזאת 2063 המרגעה 4774 ולא 3808 אבוא 14 שמוע 8085: והיה 1961 להם 1992 דבר 1697 יהוה 3068 צו 6673 לצו 6673
uaza't hamarge'ah; uala' 'abua' shamoua'. uahayah lahem dabar Yahuah tzau latzau
**and this *is* the refreshing yet not they would hear But was unto them the word of Yahuah precept upon precept**

צו 6673 לצו 6673 קו 6957 לקו 6957 קו 6957 לקו 6957 זעיר 2191 שם 8033 זעיר 2191 שם 8033 למען 4616 ילכו 1980 וכשלו 3782
tzau latzau qau laqau qau laqau, za'aeyr sham za'aeyr sham; lama'an yelaku uakashlu
**precept upon precept line upon line line upon line a little here a little *and* there that they may go and fall**

28:14

אחור 268 ונשברו 7665 ונוקשו 3369 ונלכדו 3920: לכן 3651 שמעו 8085 דבר 1697 יהוה 3068 אנשי 582 לצון 3944
'achour uanishbaru, uanouqashu uanilkadu. laken shim'au dabar Yahuah 'anshey latzoun;
**backward and be broken and snared and taken Wherefore hear the word of Yahuah men *you* scornful**

28:15

משלי 4910 העם 5971 הזה 2088 אשר 834 בירושלם 3389: כי 3588 אמרתם 559 כרתנו 3772 ברית 1285 את 854 מות 4194
moshaley ha'am hazeh, 'asher biyarushalaim. kiy 'amartem, karatnu bariyt 'at mauet,
**that rule the people this which *is* in Jerusalem Because you have said We have made a covenant *with* death**

ועם 5973 שאול 7585 עשינו 6213 חזה 2374 שיט 7885 שוטף 7857 כי 3588 עבר 5674 לא 3808 יבואנו 935
ua'am sha'aul 'asiynu chozeh; shiyt shoutep kiy 'abar la' yabou'aenu,
**and with hell (*grave*) are we *at* agreement scourge *the* overflowing when shall pass through, not it shall come unto us**

28:16

כי 3588 שמנו 7760 כזב 3577 מחסנו 4268 ובשקר 8267 נסתרנו 5641: לכן 3651 כה 3541 אמר 559 אדני 136
kiy samnu kazab machasenu uabasheqer nistaranu. laken, koh 'amar 'adonay
**for we have made lies our refuge and under falsehood have we hid ourselves Therefore thus saith Adonai**

יהוה 3069 הנני 2005 יסד 3245 בציון 6726 אבן 68 אבן 68 בחן 976 פנת 6438 יקרת 3368 מוסד 4143 מוסד 3245
Yahuah, hinniy yosed batziyoun 'aben; 'aben bochan pinat yiqrat musad musad,
**Yahuah Behold I lay a foundation in Zion *for* a stone stone a tried corner *stone* a precious a foundation a sure**

28:17

המאמין 539 לא 3808 יחיש 2363: ושמתי 7760 משפט 4941 לקו 6957 וצדקה 6666 למשקלת 4949
hama'amiyn la' yachiysh. uasamtiy mishapat laqau, uatzdaqah lamishqalet;
**he that believe not shall make haste also will I lay Judgment to the line and righteousness to the plummet**

28:18

ויעה 3261 ברד 1259 מחסה 4268 כזב 3577 וסתר 5643 מים 4325 ישטפו 7857:
uaya'ah barad machseh kazab, uaseter mayim yishtopu.
**and shall sweep away the hail the refuge of lies and the hiding place the waters shall overflow**

וכפר 3722 בריתכם 1285 את 854 מות 4194 וחזותכם 2380 את 854 שאול 7585 לא 3808 תקום 6965 שוט 7752
uakupar bariytakem 'at mauet, uachazutakem 'at sha'aul la' taqum; shout
**And shall be disannulled your covenant *with* death and your agreement *with* hell (*grave*) not shall stand scourge**

28:19

שוטף 7857 כי 3588 יעבר 5674 והייתם 1961 לו 3807a למרמס 4823: מדי 1767 עברו 5674
shoutep kiy ya'abor, uihyiytem lou' lamirmas. midey 'abarou
***the* overflowing when shall pass through then you shall be by it trodden down From the time that it goes forth**

Isa 28:12 To whom he said, This is the rest wherewith you may cause the weary to rest; and this is the refreshing: yet they would not hear.13 But the word of YHUH was unto them precept upon precept, precept upon precept; line upon line, line upon line; here a little, and there a little; that they might go, and fall backward, and be broken, and snared, and taken.14 Wherefore hear the word of YHUH, you scornful men, that rule this people which is in Jerusalem.15 Because you have said, We have made a covenant with death, and with hell are we at agreement; when the overflowing scourge shall pass through, it shall not come unto us: for we have made lies our refuge, and under falsehood have we hid ourselves:16 Therefore thus saith YHUH G-D, Behold, I lay in Zion for a foundation a stone, a tried stone, a precious corner stone, a sure foundation: he that believeth shall not make haste.17 Judgment also will I lay to the line, and righteousness to the plummet: and the hail shall sweep away the refuge of lies, and the waters shall overflow the hiding place.18 And your covenant with death shall be disannulled, and your agreement with hell shall not stand; when the overflowing scourge shall pass through, then you shall be trodden down by it.19 From the time that it go forth it shall take you: for morning by morning shall it pass over, by day and by night:

יקח 3947 אתכם 853 כי 3588 בבקר 1242 בבקר 1242 יעבר 5674 ביום 3117 ובלילה 3915 והיה 1961 רק 7535 זועה 2113
yiqach 'atkem, kiy baboqer baboqer ya'abor bayoum uabalayalah; uahayah raq zaua'ah
**it shall take you for morning by morning shall it pass over by day and by night and it shall be only a vexation**

28:20
הבין 995 שמועה 8052: כי 3588 קצר 7114 המצע 4702 מהשתרע 8311 והמסכה 4541 צרה 6887
habiyn shamu'ah. kiy qatzar hamatza' mehistarea'; uahamasekah tzarah
***to* understand the report For is shorter the bed than that *a man* can stretch himself *on it* and the covering narrower**

28:21
כהתכנס 3664: כי 3588 כהר 2022 פרצים 6559 יקום 6965 יהוה 3068 כעמק 6010 בגבעון 1391
kahitkanes. kiy kahar paratziym yaqum Yahuah, ka'aemeq bagib'aun
**than that he can wrap himself *in it* For as *in* mount Perazim shall rise up Yahuah as *in* the valley of Gibeon**

28:22
ירגז 7264 לעשות 6213 מעשהו 4639 זר 2114 מעשהו 4639 ולעבד 5647 עבדתו 5656 נכריה 5237 עבדתו 5656:
yirgaz; la'asout ma'asehu zar ma'asehu, uala'abod abodatou, nakariyah abodatou.
**he shall be wroth that he may do his work strange his work and bring to pass his act strange his act**

ועתה 6258 אל 408 תתלוצצו 3887 פן 6435 יחזקו 2388 מוסריכם 4147 כי 3588 כלה 3617 ונחרצה 2782
ua'atah 'al titloutzatzu, pen yechzaqu mousareykem; kiy kalah uanecheratzah
**Now therefore not be you mockers lest be made strong your bands for a consumption even determined**

28:23
שמעתי 8085 מאת 853 אדני 136 יהוה 3068 צבאות 6635 על 5921 כל 3605 הארץ 776: האזינו 238 ושמעו 8085 קולי 6963 הקשיבו 7181
shama'atiy, me'at 'adonay Yahuah tzaba'aut 'al kal ha'aretz. ha'aziynu uashim'au qouliy; haqashiybu
**I have heard from Adonai Yahuah of hosts upon whole the earth Give you ear and hear my voice listen**

28:24
ושמעו 8085 אמרתי 565: הכל 3605 היום 3117 יחרש 2790 החרש 2790 לזרע 2232 יפתח 6605 וישדד 7702
uashim'au 'amratiy. hakol hayoum, yacharosh hachoresh lizroa'; yapatach uiysaded
**and hear my speech all day Does the plowman plow to sow? does he open and break the clods of**

28:25
אדמתו 127: הלוא 3808 אם 518 שוה 7737 פניה 6440 והפיץ 6327 קצח 7100 וכמן 3646 יזרק 2236
'admatou. halou'a 'am shiuah paneyha, uahepiytz qetzach uakamon yizroq;
**his ground? not When he has made plain the face thereof does he cast abroad the fitches the cummin and scatter**

28:26
ושם 7760 חטה 2406 שורה 7795 ושערה 8184 נסמן 5567 וכסמת 3698 גבלתו 1367: ויסרו 3256
uasam chitah sourah uas'arah nisman, uakusemet gabulatou. uayisrou
**and cast in wheat *the* principal and barley *the* appointed and rie in their place? For does instruct him**

28:27
למשפט 4941 אלהיו 430 יורנו 3384: כי 3588 לא 3808 בחרוץ 2742 יודש 1758 קצח 7100
lamishpat 'alohayu yourenu. kiy la' bacharutz yudash qetzach,
**to discretion his Elohim *and* does teach him For not with a threshing instrument are threshed the fitches**

ואופן 212 עגלה 5699 על 5921 כמן 3646 יוסב 5437 כי 3588 במטה 4294 יחבט 2251 קצח 7100 וכמן 3646
ua'aupan 'agalah, 'al kamon yusab; kiy bamateh yechabet qetzach uakamon
**neither a wheel cart upon the cummin is turned about but with a staff are beaten out the fitches and the cummin**

28:28
בשבט 7626: לחם 3899 יודק 1854 כי 3588 לא 3808 לנצח 5331 אדוש 156 ידושנו 1758 והמם 2000 גלגל 1536
bashabet. lechem yudaq, kiy la' lanetzach adoush yadushenu; uahamam gilgal
**with a rod Bread *corn* is bruised because not he will ever thresh be threshing it nor break *it with* the wheel of**

Isa 28:19 and it shall be a vexation only to understand the report.20 For the bed is shorter than that a man can stretch himself on it: and the covering narrower than that he can wrap himself in it.21 For YHUH shall rise up as in mount Perazim, he shall be wroth as in the valley of Gibeon, that he may do his work, his strange work; and bring to pass his act, his strange act.22 Now therefore be you not mockers, lest your bands be made strong: for I have heard from YHUH G-D of hosts a consumption, even determined upon the whole earth.23 Give you ear, and hear my voice; hear, and hear my speech.24 Does the plowman plow all day to sow? doth he open and break the clods of his ground?25 When he has made plain the face thereof, doth he not cast abroad the fitches, and scatter the cummin, and cast in the principal wheat and the appointed barley and rie in their place?26 For his G-d doth instruct him to discretion, and doth teach him.27 For the fitches are not threshed with a threshing instrument, neither is a cart wheel turned about upon the cummin; but the fitches are beaten out with a staff, and the cummin with a rod.28 Bread corn is bruised; because he will not ever be threshing it, nor break it with the wheel of his cart, nor bruise it with his horsemen.

28:29
עגלתו 5699 ופרשיו 6571 לא 3808 ידקנו 1854: גם 1571 זאת 2063 מעם 5973 יהוה 3068 צבאות 6635 יצאה 3318 הפליא 6381
'aglatou uaparashayu la' yaduqenu. gam za't me'am Yahuah tzaba'aut yatza'ah; hipliy'a
**his cart *with* his horsemen nor bruise it also This from Yahuah of hosts comes forth *which* is wonderful**

עצה 6098 הגדיל 1431 תושיה 8454:
'aetzah, higdiyl tushiyah.
**in counsel *and* excellent in working**

**Isa 29:1** **29:2**
הוי 1945 אריאל 740 אריאל 740 קרית 7151 חנה 2583 דוד 1732 ספו 5595 שנה 8141 על 5921 שנה 8141 חגים 2282 ינקפו 5362:
houy 'ariy'ael 'ariy'ael, qiryat chanah dauid; sapu shanah 'al shanah chagiym yinqopu.
**Woe *to* Ariel *to* Ariel the city dwelt *where* David add you year to year sacrifices let them kill**

**29:3**
והציקותי 6693 לאריאל 740 והיתה 1961 תאניה 8386 ואניה 592 והיתה 1961 לי 3807a כאריאל 740:
uahatziyqoutiy la'ariy'ael; uahayatah ta'aniyah ua'aniyah, uahayatah liy ka'ariy'ael.
**Yet I will distress Ariel and there shall be heaviness and sorrow and it shall be unto me as Ariel**

וחניתי 2583 כדור 1754 עליך 5921 וצרתי 6696 עליך 5921 מצב 4674 והקימתי 6965 עליך 5921
uachaniytiy kadur 'alayik; uatzartiy 'alayik mutzab, uahaqiymotiy 'alayik
**And I will camp round about against you and will lay siege against you *with* a mount and I will raise against you**

**29:4**
מצרת 4694: ושפלת 8213 מארץ 776 תדברי 1696 ומעפר 6083 תשח 7817 אמרתך 565
matzurot. uashapalt me'aretz tadaberiy, uame'apar tishach 'amratek;
**forts And you shall be brought down out of the ground *and* shall speak out of the dust shall be low your speech**

והיה 1961 כאוב 178 מארץ 776 קולך 6963 ומעפר 6083 אמרתך 565
uahayah ka'aub me'aretz qoulek, uame'apar 'amratek
**and shall be as of one that has a familiar spirit out of the ground your voice and out of the dust your speech**

**29:5**
תצפצף 6850: והיה 1961 כאבק 80 דק 1851 המון 1995 זריך 2114 וכמץ 4671 עבר 5674
tatzaptzep. uahayah ka'abaq daq hamoun zarayik; uakmotz 'aber
**shall whisper Moreover shall be like dust small the multitude of your strangers and as chaff that passed away**

**29:6**
המון 1995 עריצים 6184 והיה 1961 לפתע 6621 פתאם 6597: מעם 5973 יהוה 3068 צבאות 6635
hamoun 'ariytziym, uahayah lapeta' pit'am. me'am Yahuah tzaba'aut
**the multitude of the terrible ones *shall be* yea it shall be at an instant suddenly of Yahuah of hosts**

תפקד 6485 ברעם 7482 וברעש 7494 וקול 6963 גדול 1419 סופה 5492 וסערה 5591 ולהב 3851 אש 784
tipaqed, bara'am uabra'ash uaqoul gadoul; supah uas'arah, ualahab 'aesh
**You shall be visited with thunder and with earthquake and noise great *with* storm and tempest and the flame of fire**

**29:7**
אוכלה 398: והיה 1961 כחלום 2472 חזון 2377 לילה 3915 המון 1995 כל 3605 הגוים 1471 הצבאים 6633 על 5921 אריאל 740
'aukelah. uahayah, kachaloum chazoun layalah, hamoun kal hagouyim, hatzoba'aym 'al 'ariy'ael;
**devouring And shall be as a dream of vision a night the multitude of all the nations that fight against Ariel**

**29:8**
וכל 3605 צביה 6633 ומצדתה 4685 והמציקים 6693 לה 3807a: והיה 1961 כאשר 834 יחלם 2492
uakal tzobeyha uamtzodatah, uahamatziyqiym lah. uahayah ka'asher yachalom
**even all that fight against her and her munition and that distress her It shall even be as when dreams**

Isa 28:29 This also cometh forth from YHUH of hosts, which is wonderful in counsel, and excellent in working. **Isa** 29:1 Woe to Ariel, to Ariel, the city where David dwelt! add you year to year; let them kill sacrifices.2 Yet I will distress Ariel, and there shall be heaviness and sorrow: and it shall be unto me as Ariel.3 And I will camp against you round about, and will lay siege against you with a mount, and I will raise forts against you.4 And you shall be brought down, and shall speak out of the ground, and your speech shall be low out of the dust, and your voice shall be, as of one that has a familiar spirit, out of the ground, and your speech shall whisper out of the dust.5 Moreover the multitude of your strangers shall be like small dust, and the multitude of the terrible ones shall be as chaff that pass away: yea, it shall be at an instant suddenly.6 Thou shall be visited of YHUH of hosts with thunder, and with earthquake, and great noise, with storm and tempest, and the flame of devouring fire.7 And the multitude of all the nations that fight against Ariel, even all that fight against her and her munition, and that distress her, shall be as a dream of a night vision.8 It shall even be as when an hungry man dreameth, and, behold, he eateth; but he awaketh, and his soul is empty: or as when a thirsty man dreameth, and, behold, he drinketh;

| הרעב 7457 | והנה 2009 | אוכל 398 | והקיץ 6974 | וריקה 7386 | נפשו 5315 | וכאשר 834 | יחלם 2492 | הצמא 6771 | והנה 2009 |
|---|---|---|---|---|---|---|---|---|---|
| hara'aeb | uahineh | 'aukel, | uaheqiytz | uareyqah | napshou | uaka'asher | yachalom | hatzamea' | uahineh |
| **an hungry *man*** | **and behold** | **he eat** | **but he awaken** | **and is empty** | **his soul** | **or as when** | **dreams** | **a thirsty man** | **and behold** |

| שתה 8354 | והקיץ 6974 | והנה 2009 | עיף 5889 | ונפשו 5315 | שוקקה 8264 | כן 3651 | יהיה 1961 | המון 1995 | כל 3605 | הגוים 1471 |
|---|---|---|---|---|---|---|---|---|---|---|
| shoteh, | uaheqiytz | uahineh | 'ayep, | uanapshou | shouqeqah; | ken | yihayeh, | hamoun | kal | hagouyim, |
| **he drink** | **but he awaken** | **and behold** | ***he is* faint** | **and his soul** | **has appetite** | **so** | **shall be** | **the multitude of** | **all** | **the nations** |

| הצבאים 6633 | על 5921 | הר 2022 | ציון 6726: | 29:9 | התמהמהו 4102 | ותמהו 8539 | השתעשעו 8173 | ושעו 8173 | שכרו 7937 | ולא 3808 |
|---|---|---|---|---|---|---|---|---|---|---|
| hatzoba'aym | 'al | har | tziyoun. | | hitmahmahu | uatmahu, | hishta'ash'au | uasho'au; | shakaru | uala' |
| **that fight** | **against** | **mount** | **Zion** | | **Stay yourselves** | **and wonder** | **cry you out** | **and cry** | **they are drunken** | **but not** |

| יין 3196 | נעו 5128 | ולא 3808 | שכר 7941: | 29:10 | כי 3588 | נסך 5258 | עליכם 5921 | יהוה 3069 | רוח 7307 | תרדמה 8639 |
|---|---|---|---|---|---|---|---|---|---|---|
| yayin, | na'au | uala' | shekar. | | kiy | nasak | 'aleykem | Yahuah | ruach | tardemah, |
| ***with* wine** | **they stagger** | **but not** | ***with* strong drink** | | **For** | **has poured out** | **upon you** | **Yahuah** | **the spirit of** | **deep sleep** |

| ויעצם 6105 | את 853 | עיניכם 5869 | את 853 | הנביאים 5030 | ואת 853 | ראשיכם 7218 | החזים 2374 | כסה 3680: | 29:11 | ותהי 1961 |
|---|---|---|---|---|---|---|---|---|---|---|
| uaya'atzem | 'at | 'aeyneykem; | 'at | hanabiy'aym | ua'at | ra'sheykem | hachoziym | kisah. | | uatahiy |
| **and has closed** | | **your eyes** | | **the prophets** | ***and*** | **your rulers** | **the seers** | **has he covered** | | **And is become** |

| לכם 3807a | חזות 2380 | הכל 3605 | כדברי 1697 | הספר 5612 | החתום 2856 | אשר 834 | יתנו 5414 | אתו 853 | אל 413 | יודע 3045 |
|---|---|---|---|---|---|---|---|---|---|---|
| lakem | chazut | hakol, | kadibrey | haseper | hechatum | 'asher | yitanu | 'atou, | 'al | youdea' |
| **unto you** | **the vision of** | **all** | **as the words of** | **a book** | **that is sealed** | **which** | ***men* deliver** | **which** | **to** | **one that is learned** |

| הספר 5612 | לאמר 559 | קרא 7121 | נא 4994 | זה 2088 | ואמר 559 | לא 3808 | אוכל 3201 | כי 3588 | חתום 2856 | הוא 1931: | 29:12 | ונתן 5414 |
|---|---|---|---|---|---|---|---|---|---|---|---|---|
| haseper | lea'mor | qara' | naa' | zeh; | ua'amar | la' | 'aukal, | kiy | chatum | hua'. | | uanitan |
| **book** | **saying** | **Read** | **I pray you** | **this** | **and he saith** | **not** | **I can** | **for** | ***is* sealed** | **it** | | **And is delivered** |

| הספר 5612 | על 5921 | אשר 834 | לא 3808 | ידע 3045 | ספר 5612 | לאמר 559 | קרא 7121 | נא 4994 | זה 2088 | ואמר 559 | לא 3808 | ידעתי 3045 |
|---|---|---|---|---|---|---|---|---|---|---|---|---|
| haseper, | 'al | 'asher | la' | yada' | seper | lea'mor | qara' | naa' | zeh; | ua'amar | la' | yada'tiy |
| **the book** | **to** | **him that** | **not** | **is learned** | **book** | **saying** | **Read** | **I pray you** | **this** | **and he saith** | **not** | **I am learned** |

| ספר 5612: | 29:13 | ויאמר 559 | אדני 136 | יען 3282 | כי 3588 | נגש 5066 | העם 5971 | הזה 2088 | בפיו 6310 |
|---|---|---|---|---|---|---|---|---|---|
| seper. | | uaya'mer | 'adonay, | ya'an | kiy | nigash | ha'am | hazeh, | bapiyu |
| **book** | | **Wherefore said** | **Adonai** | **Forasmuch** | **as** | **draw near** | **the people** | **this** | ***me* with their mouth** |

| ובשפתיו 8193 | כבדוני 3513 | ולבו 3820 | רחק 7368 | ממני 4480 | ותהי 1961 | יראתם 3373 | אתי 853 | מצות 4687 |
|---|---|---|---|---|---|---|---|---|
| uabispatayu | kibaduniy, | ualibou | richaq | mimeniy; | uatahiy | yir'atam | 'atiy, | mitzuat |
| **and with their lips** | **do honor me** | **but their heart** | **have removed far** | **from me** | **and is** | **their fear** | **toward me** | ***by* the precept of** |

| אנשים 582 | מלמדה 3925: | 29:14 | לכן 3651 | הנני 2005 | יוסף 3254 | להפליא 6381 | את 853 | העם 5971 | הזה 2088 |
|---|---|---|---|---|---|---|---|---|---|
| 'anashiym | malumadah. | | laken, | hinniy | yosiyp | lahapliy'a | 'at | ha'am | hazeh |
| **men** | **taught** | | **Therefore** | **behold** | **I will proceed** | **to do a marvellous work** | | **among people** | **this** |

| הפלא 6381 | ופלא 6382 | ואבדה 6 | חכמת 2451 | חכמיו 2450 | ובינת 998 |
|---|---|---|---|---|---|
| haplea' | uapela'; | ua'abadah | chakamat | chakamayu, | uabiynat |

***even* a marvellous work and a wonder for shall perish the wisdom of their wise *men* and the understanding of**

Isa 29:8 but he awaketh, and, behold, he is faint, and his soul has appetite: so shall the multitude of all the nations be, that fight against mount Zion.9 Stay yourselves, and wonder; cry you out, and cry: they are drunken, but not with wine; they stagger, but not with strong drink.10 For YHUH has poured out upon you the spirit of deep sleep, and has closed your eyes: the prophets and your rulers, the seers has he covered.11 And the vision of all is become unto you as the words of a book that is sealed, which men deliver to one that is learned, saying, Read this, I pray you: and he saith, I cannot; for it is sealed:12 And the book is delivered to him that is not learned, saying, Read this, I pray you: and he saith, I am not learned.13 Wherefore YHUH said, Forasmuch as this people draw near me with their mouth, and with their lips do honor me, but have removed their heart far from me, and their fear toward me is taught by the precept of men:14 Therefore, behold, I will proceed to do a marvellous work among this people, even a marvellous work and a wonder: for the wisdom of their wise men shall perish, and the understanding of their prudent men shall be hid.

נבוניו 995 תסתתר 5641: 29:15 הוי 1945 המעמיקים 6009 מיהוה 3068 לסתר 5641 עצה 6098 והיה 1961
nabonayu tistatar. houy hama'amiyqiym meYahuah lastir 'aetzah; uahayah
**their prudent *men* shall be hid Woe *unto* them that seek deep from Yahuah to hide their counsel and are**

במחשך 4285 מעשיהם 4639 ויאמרו 559 מי 4310 ראנו 7200 ומי 4310 יודענו 3045: 29:16 הפככם 2017 אם 518
bamachashak ma'aseyhem, uaya'maru, miy' ro'aenu uamiy youda'aenu. hapkakem, 'am
**in the dark their works and they say Who see us? and who knows us? your turning of things upside down Surely**

כחמר 2563 היצר 3335 יחשב 2803 כי 3588 יאמר 559 מעשה 4639 לעשהו 6213 לא 3808 עשני 6213
kachomer hayotzer yechasheb; kiy ya'mar ma'aseh la'asehu la' 'asaniy,
**as clay the potter's shall be esteemed for shall say the work of him that made it not? He made me**

ויצר 3336 אמר 559 ליוצרו 3335 לא 3808 הבין 995: 29:17 הלוא 3808 עוד 5750 מעט 4592 מזער 4213
uayetzer 'amar layoutzarou la' hebiyn. halou'a 'aud ma'at miz'ar,
**or the thing framed shall say of him that framed it no He had understanding? *Is it* not yet a little while very**

ושב 7725 לבנון 3844 לכרמל 3759 והכרמל 3759 ליער 3293 יחשב 2803: 29:18 ושמעו 8085
uashab labanoun lakarmel; uahakarmel laya'ar yechasheb. uashama'au
**and shall be turned Lebanon into a fruitful field and the fruitful field as a forest? shall be esteemed And shall hear**

ביום 3117 ההוא 1931 החרשים 2795 דברי 1697 ספר 5612 ומאפל 652 ומחשך 2822 עיני 5869 עורים 5787
bayoum hahua' hacherashiym dibrey seper; uame'apel uamechoshek, 'aeyney 'auriym
**in day that the deaf the words of the book and out of obscurity and out of darkness the eyes of the blind**

תראינה 7200: 29:19 ויספו 3254 ענוים 6035 ביהוה 3068 שמחה 8057 ואביוני 34 אדם 120 בקדוש 6918 ישראל 3478
tir'aynah. uayasapu 'anauiym baYahuah simchah; ua'abyouney 'adam, biqdoush yisra'ael
**shall see also shall increase The meek in Yahuah *their* joy and the poor *among* men in the Holy One of Israel**

יגילו 1523: 29:20 כי 3588 אפס 656 עריץ 6184 וכלה 3615 לץ 3887 ונכרתו 3772 כל 3605
yagiylu. kiy 'apes 'ariytz uakalah letz; uanikratu kal
**shall rejoice For is brought to nought the terrible one and is consumed the scorner and are cut off all**

שקדי 8245 און 205: 29:21 מחטיאי 2398 אדם 120 בדבר 1697 ולמוכיח 3198 בשער 8179 יקשון 6983
shoqadey 'auen. machatiy'aey 'adam badabar, ualamoukiyach basha'ar yaqoshun;
**that watch for iniquity That make an offender a man for a word and for him that reprove in the gate lay a snare**

ויטו 5186 בתהו 8414 צדיק 6662: 29:22 לכן 3651 כה 3541 אמר 559 יהוה 3068 אל 413 בית 1004 יעקב 3290 אשר 834
uayatu batohu tzadiyq. laken, koh 'amar Yahuah 'al beyt ya'aqob, 'asher
**and turn aside for a thing of nought the just Therefore thus saith Yahuah concerning the house of Jacob who**

פדה 6299 את 853 אברהם 85 לא 3808 עתה 6258 יבוש 954 יעקב 3290 ולא 3808 עתה 6258 פניו 6440 יחורו 2357: 29:23 כי 3588
padah 'at 'abraham; la' 'atah yeboush ya'aqob, uala' 'atah panayu yecheuaru. kiy
**redeemed Abraham not now shall be ashamed Jacob neither now his face shall wax pale But**

בראתו 7200 ילדיו 3206 מעשה 4639 ידי 3027 בקרבו 7130 יקדישו 6942 שמי 8034 והקדישו 6942 את 853
bira'atou yaladayu ma'aseh yaday baqirbou yaqdiyshu shamiy; uahiqdiyshu 'at
**when he see his children the work of mine hands in the midst of him they shall sanctify my name and sanctify**

Isa 29:15 Woe unto them that seek deep to hide their counsel from YHUH, and their works are in the dark, and they say, Who see us? and who know us?16 Surely your turning of things upside down shall be esteemed as the potter's clay: for shall the work say of him that made it, He made me not? or shall the thing framed say of him that framed it, He had no understanding?17 Is it not yet a very little while, and Lebanon shall be turned into a fruitful field, and the fruitful field shall be esteemed as a forest?18 And in that day shall the deaf hear the words of the book, and the eyes of the blind shall see out of obscurity, and out of darkness.19 The meek also shall increase their joy in YHUH, and the poor among men shall rejoice in the Holy One of Israel.20 For the terrible one is brought to nought, and the scorner is consumed, and all that watch for iniquity are cut off:21 That make a man an offender for a word, and lay a snare for him that reproveth in the gate, and turn aside the just for a thing of nought.22 Therefore thus saith YHUH, who redeemed Abraham, concerning the house of Jacob, Jacob shall not now be ashamed, neither shall his face now wax pale.23 But when he see his children, the work of mine hands, in the midst of him, they shall sanctify my name, and sanctify the Holy One of Jacob, and shall fear the G-d of Israel.

מפני 6440 גערת 1606 אחד 259 מפני 6440 גערת 1606 חמשה 2568 תנסו 5127 עד 5704 אם 518 נותרתם 3498 כתרן 8650 על 5921
mipaney ga'arat 'achad, mipaney ga'arat chamishah tanusu; 'ad 'am noutartem, katoren 'al
***shall flee* at the rebuke of one at the rebuke of five shall you flee till when you be left as a beacon upon**

30:18
ראש 7218 ההר 2022 וכנס 5251 על 5921 הגבעה 1389: ולכן 3651 יחכה 2442 יהוה 3068
ra'sh hahar, uakanes 'al hagib'ah. ualaken yachakeh Yahuah
**the top of a mountain and as an ensign on an hill And therefore will wait Yahuah**

לחננכם 2603 ולכן 3651 ירום 7311 לרחמכם 7355 כי 3588 אלהי 430
lachanankem, ualaken yarum larachemkem; kiy 'alohey
**that he may be gracious unto you and therefore will he be exalted that he may have mercy upon you for *is* a Elohim of**

30:19
משפט 4941 יהוה 3068 אשרי 835 כל 3605 חוכי 2442 לו 3807a: כי 3588 עם 5971 בציון 6726 ישב 3427 בירושלם 3389
mishapat Yahuah, 'ashrey kal choukey lou'. kiy 'am batziyoun yesheb biyarushalaim;
**judgment Yahuah blessed *are* all they that wait for him For the people in Zion shall dwell at Jerusalem**

בכו 1058 לא 3808 תבכה 1058 חנון 2603 יחנך 2603 לקול 6963 זעקך 2201 כשמעתו 8085
bakou la' tibkeh, chanoun yachnaka laqoul za'aqeka, kashama'atou
**you shall weep no more he will be very gracious unto you at the voice of your cry when he shall hear it**

30:20
ענך 6030: ונתן 5414 לכם 3807a אדני 136 לחם 3899 צר 6862 ומים 4325 לחץ 3906 ולא 3808
'anak. uanatan lakem 'adonay lechem tzar uamayim lachatz; uala'
**he will answer you And give to you *though* Adonai the bread of adversity and the water of affliction yet not**

30:21
יכנף 3670 עוד 5750 מוריך 3384 והיו 1961 עיניך 5869 ראות 7200 את 853 מוריך 3384:
yikanep 'aud moureyka, uahayu 'aeyneyka ro'aut 'at moureyka.
**shall be removed into a corner any more your teachers but shall your eyes see your teachers**

ואזניך 241 תשמענה 8085 דבר 1697 מאחריך 310 לאמר 559 זה 2088 הדרך 1870 לכו 1980 בו 871a כי 3588 תאמינו 541
ua'azaneyka tishma'anah dabar, me'achareyka lea'mor; zeh haderek laku bou, kiy ta'amiynu
**And your ears shall hear a word behind you saying This *is* the way walk you in it when you turn to the right hand**

30:22
וכי 3588 תשמאילו 8041: וטמאתם 2930 את 853 צפוי 6826 פסילי 6456 כספך 3701 ואת 853
uakiy tasma'aylu. uatimea'tem, 'at tzipuy pasiyley kaspeka, ua'at
**and when you turn to the left You shall defile also the covering of your graven images of silver *and***

אפדת 642 מסכת 4541 זהבך 2091 תזרם 2219 כמו 3644 דוה 1739 צא 3318
'apudat masekat zahabeka; tizrem kamou dauah, tzea'
**the ornament of your molten images of gold you shall cast them away as a menstruous cloth Get you hence**

30:23
תאמר 559 לו 3807a: ונתן 5414 מטר 4306 זרעך 2233 אשר 834 תזרע 2232 את 853 האדמה 127
ta'mar lou'. uanatan matar zar'aka 'asher tizra' 'at ha'adamah,
**you shall say unto it Then shall he give the rain of your seed that you shall sow the ground withal**

ולחם 3899 תבואת 8393 האדמה 127 והיה 1961 דשן 1879 ושמן 8082 ירעה 7462 מקניך 4735 ביום 3117 ההוא 1931 כר 3733
ua'alechem tabu'at ha'adamah, uahayah dashen uashamen; yir'ah miqneyka bayoum hahua' kar
**and bread of the increase of the earth and it shall be fat and plenteous shall feed your cattle in day that pastures**

Isa 30:17 One thousand shall flee at the rebuke of one; at the rebuke of five shall you flee: till you be left as a beacon upon the top of a mountain, and as an ensign on an hill.18 And therefore will YHUH wait, that he may be gracious unto you, and therefore will he be exalted, that he may have mercy upon you: for YHUH is a G-d of judgment: blessed are all they that wait for him.19 For the people shall dwell in Zion at Jerusalem: you shall weep no more: he will be very gracious unto you at the voice of your cry; when he shall hear it, he will answer you.20 And though YHUH give you the bread of adversity, and the water of affliction, yet shall not your teachers be removed into a corner anymore, but your eyes shall see your teachers:21 And your ears shall hear a word behind you, saying, This is the way, walk you in it, when you turn to the right hand, and when you turn to the left.22 You shall defile also the covering of your graven images of silver, and the ornament of your molten images of gold: you shall cast them away as a menstruous cloth; you shall say unto it, Get you hence.23 Then shall he give the rain of your seed, that you shall sow the ground withal; and bread of the increase of the earth, and it shall be fat and plenteous: in that day shall your cattle feed in large pastures.

30:24

נרחב 7337: והאלפים 504 והעירים 5895 עבדי 5647 האדמה 127 בליל 1098 חמיץ 2548 יאכלו 398 אשר 834
nirchab. uaha'alapiym uaha'ayariym, 'abadey ha'adamah, baliyl chamiytz ya'kelu; 'asher
***in*** **large** **The oxen likewise** **and the young asses** **that ear** **the ground** **provender** **clean** **shall eat** **which**

30:25

זרה 2219 ברחת 7371 ובמזרה 4214: והיה 1961 על 5921 כל 3605 הר 2022 גבה 1364 ועל 5921
zoreh barachat uabamizreh. uahayah 'al kal har gaboha, ua'al
**has been winnowed** **with the shovel** **and with the fan** **And there shall be** **upon** **every** **mountain** **high** **and upon**

30:26

כל 3605 גבעה 1389 נשאה 5375 פלגים 6388 יבלי 2988 מים 4325 ביום 3117 הרג 2027 רב 7227 בנפל 5307 מגדלים 4026:
kal gib'ah nisa'ah, palagiym yibley mayim; bayoum hereg rab, binpol migdaliym.
**every** **hill** **high** **rivers** ***and*** **streams of** **waters** **in the day of** **slaughter** ***the*** **great** **when fall** **the towers**

והיה 1961 אור 216 הלבנה 3842 כאור 216 החמה 2535 ואור 216 החמה 2535 יהיה 1961 שבעתים 7659
uahayah 'aur halabanah ka'aur hachamah, ua'aur hachamah yihayeh shib'atayim,
**Moreover shall be** **the light of** **the moon** **as the light of** **the sun** **and the light of** **the sun** **shall be** **sevenfold**

כאור 216 שבעת 7651 הימים 3117 ביום 3117 חבש 2280 יהוה 3068 את 853 שבר 7667 עמו 5971 ומחץ 4273
ka'aur shib'at hayamiym; bayoum, chabosh Yahuah 'at sheber 'amou, uamachatz
**as the light of** **seven** **days** **in the day** **that bind up** **Yahuah** **the breach of** **his people** **and the stroke of**

30:27

מכתו 4347 ירפא 7495: הנה 2009 שם 8034 יהוה 3068 בא 935 ממרחק 4801 בער 1197 אפו 639 וכבד 3514
makatou yirpa'. hineh shem Yahuah ba' mimerchaq, bo'aer 'apou, uakobed
**their wound** **heals** **Behold** **the name of** **Yahuah** **comes** **from far** **burning** ***with*** **his anger** **and heavy**

30:28

משאה 4858 שפתיו 8193 מלאו 4390 זעם 2195 ולשונו 3956 כאש 784 אכלת 398: ורוחו 7307 כנחל 5158
masa'ah; sapatayu mala'au za'am, ualshounou ka'aesh 'akalet. uaruchou kanachal
**the burden *thereof is*** **his lips** **are full of** **indignation** **and his tongue** **as a fire** **devouring** **And his breath** **as an stream**

שוטף 7857 עד 5704 צואר 6677 יחצה 2673 להנפה 5130 גוים 1471 בנפת 5299 שוא 7723 ורסן 7448
shoutep 'ad tzaua'ar yechatzeh, lahanapah gouyim banapat shau'a; uaresen
**overflowing** **to** **of the neck** **shall reach the midst** **to sift** **the nations** **with the sieve of** **vanity** **and *there shall be*** **a bridle**

30:29

מתעה 8582 על 5921 לחיי 3895 עמים 5971: השיר 7892 יהיה 1961 לכם 3807a כליל 3915 התקדש 6942
mata'ah, 'al lachayey 'amiym. hashiyr yihayeh lakem, kaleyl hitkadesh
**causing *them* to err** **in** **the jaws of** **the people** **a song** **shall have** **To you** **as in the night** **holy is kept** ***when***

חג 2282 ושמחת 8057 לבב 3824 כהולך 1980 בחליל 2485 לבוא 935 בהר 2022 יהוה 3068 אל 413
chag; uasimchat lebab, kahoulek bechaliyl, labou'a bahar Yahuah 'al
**a solemnity** **and gladness of** **heart** **as when one goes** **with a pipe** **to come** **into the mountain of** **Yahuah** **to**

30:30

צור 6697 ישראל 3478: והשמיע 8085 יהוה 3068 את 853 הוד 1935 קולו 6963 ונחת 5183
tzur yisra'ael. uahishmiya' Yahuah 'at houd qoulou, uanachat
**the mighty One of** **Israel** **And shall cause to be heard** **Yahuah** **glorious** **his voice** **the lighting down of**

זרועו 2220 יראה 7200 בזעף 2197 אף 639 ולהב 3851 אש 784 אוכלה 398 נפץ 5311 וזרם 2230
zarou'au yara'ah, baza'ap 'aap, ualahab 'aesh 'aukelah; nepetz uazerem
**his arm** **shall show** **with the indignation of** ***his*** **anger** **and *with*** **the flame of** **a fire** **devouring** ***with*** **scattering** **and tempest**

Isa 30:24 The oxen likewise and the young asses that ear the ground shall eat clean provender, which has been winnowed with the shovel and with the fan.25 And there shall be upon every high mountain, and upon every high hill, rivers and streams of waters in the day of the great slaughter, when the towers fall.26 Moreover the light of the moon shall be as the light of the sun, and the light of the sun shall be sevenfold, as the light of seven days, in the day that YHUH bindeth up the breach of his people, and healeth the stroke of their wound.27 Behold, the name of YHUH cometh from far, burning with his anger, and the burden thereof is heavy: his lips are full of indignation, and his tongue as a devouring fire:28 And his breath, as an overflowing stream, shall reach to the midst of the neck, to sift the nations with the sieve of vanity: and there shall be a bridle in the jaws of the people, causing them to err.29 You shall have a song, as in the night when a holy solemnity is kept; and gladness of heart, as when one go with a pipe to come into the mountain of YHUH, to the mighty One of Israel.30 And YHUH shall cause his glorious voice to be heard, and shall show the lighting down of his arm, with the indignation of his anger, and with the flame of a devouring fire, with scattering, and tempest, and hailstones.

| | | 30:31 | | | | | | |
|---|---|---|---|---|---|---|---|---|
| ואבן 68 | ברד 1259: | | כי 3588 | מקול 6963 | יהוה 3068 | יחת 2865 | אשור 804 | בשבט 7626 |
| ua'aben | barad. | | kiy | miqoul | Yahuah | yechat | 'ashur; | bashebet |
| **and stones** | **hail** | | **For** | **through the voice of** | **Yahuah** | **shall be beaten down** | **the Assyrian** | **with a rod** |

| | 30:32 | | | | | | | | |
|---|---|---|---|---|---|---|---|---|---|
| יכה 5221: | והיה 1961 | כל 3605 | מעבר 4569 | מטה 4294 | מוסדה 4145 | אשר 834 | יניח 5117 | יהוה 3068 | עליו 5921 |
| yakeh. | uahayah, | kal | ma'abar | mateh | musadah, | 'asher | yaniyach | Yahuah | 'aelayu, |
| ***which* smote** | **And shall be** | ***in* every place** | **where shall pass** | **staff** | **the grounded** | **which** | **shall lay** | **Yahuah** | **upon him** |

| | | | | | | 30:33 | | | |
|---|---|---|---|---|---|---|---|---|---|
| בתפים 8596 | ובכנרות 3658 | ובמלחמות 4421 | תנופה 8573 | נלחם 3898 | בה 871a | כי 3588 | ערוך 6186 | מאתמול 865 | תפתה 8613 |
| batupiym | uabkinorout; | uabmilchamout | tanupah | nilcham | bah | kiy | 'aruk | me'atmul | tapateh, |
| ***it* shall be with tabrets** | **and harps** | **and in battles of** | **shaking** | **will he fight** | **with it.** | **For** | ***is* ordained** | **of old** | **Tophet** |

| | | | | | | | | | | |
|---|---|---|---|---|---|---|---|---|---|---|
| גם 1571 | הוא 1931 | למלך 4428 | הוכן 3559 | העמיק 6009 | הרחב 7337 | מדרתה 4071 | אש 784 | ועצים 6086 | הרבה 7235 | נשמת 5397 |
| gam | hua' | lamelek | hukan | he'miyq | hirchiyb; | maduratah, | 'aesh | ua'aetziym | harbeh, | nishmat |
| **yea** | **it** | **for the king** | **is prepared** | **he has made *it* deep** | ***and* large** | **the pile thereof** | ***is* fire** | **and wood** | **much** | **the breath of** |

| | | | | |
|---|---|---|---|---|
| יהוה 3068 | כנחל 5158 | גפרית 1614 | בערה 1197 | בה 871a: |
| Yahuah | kanachal | gapriyt, | bo'arahh | bah. |
| **Yahuah** | **like a stream of** | **brimstone** | **does kindle** | **it** |

| Isa 31:1 | | | | | | | | | | | |
|---|---|---|---|---|---|---|---|---|---|---|---|
| הוי 1945 | הירדים 3381 | מצרים 4714 | לעזרה 5833 | על 5921 | סוסים 5483 | ישענו 8172 | ויבטחו 982 | על 5921 | רכב 7393 | כי 3588 |
| houy | hayoradiym | mitzrayim | la'azrah, | 'al | susiym | yisha'aenu; | uayibtachu | 'al | rekeb | kiy |
| **Woe** | ***to* them that go down to** | **Egypt** | **for help** | **on** | **horses** | ***and* stay** | **and trust** | **in** | **chariots** | **because** |

| | | | | | | | | | | | |
|---|---|---|---|---|---|---|---|---|---|---|---|
| רב 7227 | ועל 5921 | פרשים 6571 | כי 3588 | עצמו 6105 | מאד 3966 | ולא 3808 | שעו 8159 | על 5921 | קדוש 6918 | ישראל 3478 | ואת 853 |
| rab, | ua'al | parashiym | kiy | 'atzamu | ma'ad, | uala' | sha'au | 'al | qadoush | yisra'ael, | ua'at |
| ***they are* many** | **and in** | **horsemen** | **because** | **they are strong** | **very** | **but not** | **they look** | **unto** | ***the* Holy One of** | **Israel** | ***neither*** |

| | | | 31:2 | | | | | | | | |
|---|---|---|---|---|---|---|---|---|---|---|---|
| יהוה 3068 | לא 3808 | דרשו 1875: | | וגם 1571 | הוא 1931 | חכם 2450 | ויבא 935 | רע 7451 | ואת 853 | דבריו 1697 | לא 3808 | הסיר 5493 |
| Yahuah | la' | darashu. | | uagam | hua' | chakam | uayabea' | ra', | ua'at | dabarayu | la' | hesiyr; |
| **Yahuah** | **neither** | **seek** | | **Yet also** | **he** | ***is* wise** | **and will bring** | **evil** | ***and*** | **his words** | **not** | **will call back** |

| | | | | | | | | 31:3 |
|---|---|---|---|---|---|---|---|---|
| וקם 6965 | על 5921 | בית 1004 | מרעים 7489 | ועל 5921 | עזרת 5833 | פעלי 6466 | און 205: | ומצרים 4714 |
| uaqam | 'al | beyt | mere'aym, | ua'al | 'azrat | po'aley | 'auen. | uamitzrayim |
| **but will arise** | **against** | **the house of** | **the evildoers** | **and against** | **the help of** | **them that work** | **iniquity** | **Now the Egyptians** |

| | | | | | | | | | | | |
|---|---|---|---|---|---|---|---|---|---|---|---|
| אדם 120 | ולא 3808 | אל 410 | וסוסיהם 5483 | בשר 1320 | ולא 3808 | רוח 7307 | ויהוה 3068 | יטה 5186 | ידו 3027 | וכשל 3782 |
| 'adam | uala' | al, | uasuseyhem | basar | uala' | ruach; | laYahuah | yateh | yadou, | uakashal |
| ***are* men** | **and not** | **El** | **and their horses** | **flesh** | **and not** | **spirit** | **When Yahuah** | **shall stretch out** | **his hand** | **both shall fall** |

| | | | | | | 31:4 | | | | |
|---|---|---|---|---|---|---|---|---|---|---|
| עוזר 5826 | ונפל 5307 | עזר 5826 | ויחדו 3162 | כלם 3605 | יכליון 3615: | כי 3588 | כה 3541 | אמר 559 | יהוה 3068 | אלי 413 |
| 'auzer | uanapal | 'azur, | uayachdau | kulam | yiklayun. | kiy | koh | 'amar | Yahuah | 'aelay |
| **he that helps** | **shall fall down** | **he that is holpen** | **and together** | **they all** | **shall fail** | **For** | **thus** | **has spoken** | **Yahuah** | **unto me** |

| | | | | | | | | | | |
|---|---|---|---|---|---|---|---|---|---|---|
| כאשר 834 | יהגה 1897 | האריה 738 | והכפיר 3715 | על 5921 | טרפו 2964 | אשר 834 | יקרא 7121 | עליו 5921 | מלא 4393 | רעים 7462 |
| ka'asher | yehageh | ha'aryeh | uahakapiyr | 'al | tarpou, | 'asher | yiqarea' | 'alayu | mala | ro'aym, |
| **Like as** | **roaring** | **the lion** | **and the young lion** | **on** | **his prey** | **when** | **is called forth** | **against him** | **a multitude of** | **shepherds** |

Isa 30:31 For through the voice of YHUH shall the Assyrian be beaten down, which smote with a rod.32 And in every place where the grounded staff shall pass, which YHUH shall lay upon him, it shall be with tabrets and harps: and in battles of shaking will he fight with it.33 For Tophet is ordained of old; yea, for the king it is prepared; he has made it deep and large: the pile thereof is fire and much wood; the breath of YHUH, like a stream of brimstone, doth kindle it. **Isa** 31:1 Woe to them that go down to Egypt for help; and stay on horses, and trust in chariots, because they are many; and in horsemen, because they are very strong; but they look not unto the Holy One of Israel, neither seek YHUH!2 Yet he also is wise, and will bring evil, and will not call back his words: but will arise against the house of the evildoers, and against the help of them that work iniquity.3 Now the Egyptians are men, and not G-d; and their horses flesh, and not spirit. When YHUH shall stretch out his hand, both he that helpeth shall fall, and he that is holpen shall fall down, and they all shall fail together.4 For thus has YHUH spoken unto me, Like as the lion and the young lion roaring on his prey, when a multitude of shepherds is called forth against him, he will not be afraid of their voice, nor abase himself for the noise of them:

6963 מקולם | 3808 לא | 2865 יחת | 1995 ומהמונם | 3808 לא | 6031 יענה | 3651 כן | 3381 ירד | 3068 יהוה | 6635 צבאות
miqoulam la' yechat, uamehamounam la' ya'aneh; ken, yered Yahuah tzaba'aut,
**of their voice not *he* will be afraid for the noise of them nor abase himself so shall come down Yahuah of hosts**

6633 לצבא | 5921 על | 2022 הר | 6726 ציון | 5921 ועל | 1389: גבעתה | **31:5** 6833 כצפרים | 5774 עפות | 3651 כן | 1598 יגן | 3068 יהוה | 6635 צבאות | 5921 על
litzba' 'al har tziyoun ua'al gib'atah. katzipariym 'apout, ken, yagen Yahuah tzaba'aut 'al
**to fight for mount Zion and for the hill thereof As birds flying so will defend Yahuah of hosts on**

3389 ירושלם | 1598 גנון | 5337 והציל | 6452 פסח | 4422: והמליט | **31:6** 7725 שובו | 834 לאשר
yarushalaim; ganoun uahitziyl pasoach uahimliyt. shubu, la'asher
**Jerusalem defending also he will deliver *it* passing over *it* and he will preserve Turn you unto *him from* whom**

6009 העמיקו | 5627 סרה | 1121 בני | 3478: ישראל | **31:7** 3588 כי | 3117 ביום | 1931 ההוא | 3988 ימאסון | 376 איש | 457 אלילי | 3701 כספו
he'miyqu sarah baney yisra'ael. kiy bayoum hahua', yim'asun, 'aysh 'aliyley kaspou,
**deeply have revolted the children of Israel For in day that shall cast away every man his idols of silver**

457 ואלילי | 2091 זהבו | 834 אשר | 6213 עשו | 3807a לכם | 3027 ידיכם | 2399: חטא | **31:8** 5307 ונפל | 804 אשור
ua'aliyley zahabou; 'asher 'asu lakem yadeykem chet'a. uanapal 'ashur
**and his idols of gold which have made unto you your own hands *for* a sin Then shall fall the Assyrian**

2719 בחרב | 3808 לא | 376 איש | 2719 וחרב | 3808 לא | 120 אדם | 398 תאכלנו | 5127 ונס | 3807a לו | 6440 מפני
bachereb la' 'aysh, uachereb la' 'adam ta'kalenu; uanas lou' mipaney
**with the sword not *of* a mighty man and the sword not *of* a *mean* man shall devour him but shall flee he from**

2719 חרב | 970 ובחוריו | 4522 למס | 1961: יהיו | **31:9** 5553 וסלעו | 4032 ממגור | 5674 יעבור | 2865 וחתו
chereb, uabachurayu lamas yihayu. uasal'au mimagour ya'abour, uachatu
**the sword and his young men discomfited shall be And to his strong hold for fear he shall pass over to shall be afraid**

5251 מנס | 8269 שריו | 5002 נאם | 3069 יהוה | 834 אשר | 217 אור | 3807a לו | 6726 בציון | 8574 ותנור | 3807a לו | 3389: בירושלם
mines sarayu; na'am Yahuah 'asher 'aur lou' batziyoun, uatanur lou' biyarushalaim.
**of the ensign his princes saith Yahuah whose fire to him *is* in Zion and furnace his in Jerusalem**

**Isa 32:1** 2005 הן | 6664 לצדק | 4427 ימלך | 4428 מלך | 8269 ולשרים | 4941 למשפט | 8323: ישרו | **32:2** 1961 והיה | 376 איש
hen latzedeq yimlak melek; ualsariym lamishpat yasouru. uahayah 'aysh
**Behold in righteousness shall reign a king and princes in judgment shall rule And shall be a man**

4224 כמחבא | 7307 רוח | 5643 וסתר | 2230 זרם | 6388 כפלגי | 4325 מים | 6724 בציון | 6738 כצל | 5553 סלע
kamachabea' ruach uaseter zarem; kapalgey mayim batzayoun, katzel sela'
**as an hiding place from the wind and a covert from the tempest as rivers of water in a dry place as the shadow of a rock**

3515 כבד | 776 בארץ | 5889: עיפה | **32:3** 3808 ולא | 8159 תשעינה | 5869 עיני | 7200 ראים | 241 ואזני | 8085 שמעים
kabed ba'aretz 'ayepah. uala' tish'aynah 'aeyney ro'aym; ua'azaney shoma'aym
**great in a land weary And not shall be dim the eyes of them that see and the ears of them that hear**

7181: תקשבנה | **32:4** 3824 ולבב | 4116 נמהרים | 995 יבין | 3045 לדעת | 3956 ולשון | 5926 עלגים
tiqshabnah. ualbab nimhariym yabiyn lada'at; ualshoun 'algiym,
**shall listen The heart also of the rash shall understand acknowledge and the tongue of the stammerers**

Isa 31:4 so shall YHUH of hosts come down to fight for mount Zion, and for the hill thereof.5 As birds flying, so will YHUH of hosts defend Jerusalem; defending also he will deliver it; and passing over he will preserve it.6 Turn you unto him from whom the children of Israel have deeply revolted.7 For in that day every man shall cast away his idols of silver, and his idols of gold, which your own hands have made unto you for a sin.8 Then shall the Assyrian fall with the sword, not of a mighty man; and the sword, not of a mean man, shall devour him: but he shall flee from the sword, and his young men shall be discomfited.9 And he shall pass over to his strong hold for fear, and his princes shall be afraid of the ensign, saith YHUH, whose fire is in Zion, and his furnace in Jerusalem. **Isa** 32:1 Behold, a king shall reign in righteousness, and princes shall rule in judgment.2 And a man shall be as an hiding place from the wind, and a covert from the tempest; as rivers of water in a dry place, as the shadow of a great rock in a weary land.3 And the eyes of them that see shall not be dim, and the ears of them that hear shall hear.4 The heart also of the rash shall understand knowledge, and the tongue of the stammerers shall be ready to speak plainly.

| תמהר 4116 | לדבר 1696 | צחות 6703: | 32:5 | לא 3808 | יקרא 7121 | עוד 5750 | לנבל 5036 | נדיב 5081 | ולכילי 3596 | לא 3808 | יאמר 559 |
|---|---|---|---|---|---|---|---|---|---|---|---|
| tamaher | ladaber | tzachout. | | la' | yiqarea' | 'aud | lanabal | nadiyb; | ualkiylay | la' | ye'amer |
| **shall be ready** | **to speak** | **plainly** | | **no** | **shall be called** | **more** | **The vile person** | **liberal** | **the churl** | **nor** | **said** |

| שוע 7771: | 32:6 | כי 3588 | נבל 5036 | נבלה 5039 | ידבר 1696 | ולבו 3820 | יעשה 6213 | און 205 | לעשות 6213 | חנף 2612 |
|---|---|---|---|---|---|---|---|---|---|---|
| shoua'. | | kiy | nabal | nabalah | yadaber, | ualibou | ya'aseh | 'auen; | la'asout | chonep, |
| ***to be* bountiful** | | **For** | **the vile person** | **villany** | **will speak** | **and his heart** | **will work** | **iniquity** | **to practise** | **hypocrisy** |

| ולדבר 1696 | אל 413 | יהוה 3069 | תועה 8442 | להריק 7324 | נפש 5315 | רעב 7457 | ומשקה 4945 | צמא 6771 |
|---|---|---|---|---|---|---|---|---|
| ualdaber | 'al | Yahuah | tou'ah, | lahariyq | nepesh | ra'aeb, | uamashqeh | tzamea' |
| **and to utter** | **against** | **Yahuah** | **error** | **to make empty** | **the soul of** | **the hungry** | **and the drink of** | **the thirsty** |

| יחסיר 2637: | 32:7 | וכלי 3596 | כליו 3627 | רעים 7451 | הוא 1931 | זמות 2154 | יעץ 3289 | לחבל 2254 | ענוים 6035 |
|---|---|---|---|---|---|---|---|---|---|
| yachsiyr. | | uakelay | kelayu | ra'aym; | hua' | zimout | ya'atz, | lachabel | 'anauiym |
| **he will cause to fail** | | **also of the churl** | **The instruments** | ***are* evil** | **he** | **wicked devices** | **devise** | **to destroy** | **the poor** |

| באמרי 561 | שקר 8267 | ובדבר 1696 | אביון 34 | משפט 4941: | 32:8 | ונדיב 5081 | נדיבות 5081 | יעץ 3289 | והוא 1931 | על 5921 |
|---|---|---|---|---|---|---|---|---|---|---|
| ba'amrey | sheqer, | uabdaber | abyoun | mishapat. | | uanadiyb | nadiybout | ya'atz; | uahu'a | 'al |
| **with words** | **lying** | **even when speak** | **the needy** | **right** | | **But the liberal** | **liberal things** | **devise** | **and he** | **by** |

| נדיבות 5081 | יקום 6965: | 32:9 | נשים 802 | שאננות 7600 | קמנה 6965 | שמענה 8085 | קולי 6963 | בנות 1323 | בטחות 982 |
|---|---|---|---|---|---|---|---|---|---|
| nadiybout | yaqum. | | nashiym | sha'ananout, | qomanah | shama'anah | qouliy; | banout | botachout, |
| **liberal things** | **shall he stand** | | **you women** | **ones that are at ease** | **Rise up** | **hear** | **my voice** | **daughters** | **you careless ones** |

| האזנה 238 | אמרתי 565: | 32:10 | ימים 3117 | על 5921 | שנה 8141 | תרגזנה 7264 | בטחות 982 | כי 3588 | כלה 3615 |
|---|---|---|---|---|---|---|---|---|---|
| ha'zenah | 'amratiy. | | yamiym | 'al | shanah, | tirgaznah | botachout; | kiy | kalah |
| **give ear unto** | **my speech** | | **Many days** | **of** | **years** | **shall you be troubled** | **you careless women** | **for** | **shall fail** |

| בציר 1210 | אסף 625 | בלי 1097 | יבוא 935: | 32:11 | חרדו 2729 | שאננות 7600 | רגזה 7264 | בטחות 982 |
|---|---|---|---|---|---|---|---|---|
| batziyr, | 'asep | baliy | yabou'a. | | chirdu | sha'ananout, | ragazah | botachout; |
| **the vintage** | **the gathering** | **not** | **shall come** | | **Tremble** | ***you* women that are at ease** | **be troubled** | **you careless ones** |

| פשטה 6584 | וערה 6209 | וחגורה 2296 | על 5921 | חלצים 2504: | 32:12 | על 5921 | שדים 7699 | ספדים 5594 | על 5921 | שדי 7704 |
|---|---|---|---|---|---|---|---|---|---|---|
| pashotah | ua'arah, | uachagourah | 'al | chalatzayim. | | 'al | shadayim | sopadiym; | 'al | sadey |
| **strip you** | **and make you bare** | **and gird *sackcloth*** | **upon** | ***your* loins** | | **for** | **the teats** | **They shall lament** | **for** | **fields** |

| חמד 2531 | על 5921 | גפן 1612 | פריה 6509: | 32:13 | על 5921 | אדמת 127 | עמי 5971 | קוץ 6975 | שמיר 8068 | תעלה 5927 | כי 3588 | על 5921 | כל 3605 |
|---|---|---|---|---|---|---|---|---|---|---|---|---|---|
| chemed | 'al | gepen | poriyah. | | 'al | 'admat | 'amiy, | qoutz | shamiyr | ta'aleh; | kiy | 'al | kal |
| ***the* pleasant** | **for** | **vine** | ***the* fruitful** | | **Upon** | **the land of** | **my people** | **thorns *and*** | **briers** | **shall come up** | **yea** | **upon** | **all** |

| בתי 1004 | משוש 4885 | קריה 7151 | עליזה 5947: | 32:14 | כי 3588 | ארמון 759 | נטש 5203 | המון 1995 | עיר 5892 |
|---|---|---|---|---|---|---|---|---|---|
| batey | masous, | qiryah | 'aliyzah. | | kiy | 'armoun | nutash, | hamoun | 'ayr |
| **the houses of** | **joy** | **city** | ***in* the joyous** | | **Because** | **the palaces** | **shall be forsaken** | **the multitude of** | **the city** |

| עזב 5800 | עפל 6076 | ובחן 975 | היה 1961 | בעד 5750 | מערות 4631 | עד 5704 | עולם 5769 | משוש 4885 | פראים 6501 | מרעה 4829 | עדרים 5739: |
|---|---|---|---|---|---|---|---|---|---|---|---|
| 'uzab; | 'apel | uabachan | hayah | ba'ad | ma'arout | 'ad | 'aulam, | masous | para'aym | mir'aeh | 'adariym. |
| **shall be left** | **the forts** | **and towers** | **shall be** | **for** | **dens** | **for** | **ever** | **a joy of** | **wild asses** | **a pasture of** | **flocks** |

Isa 32:5 The vile person shall be no more called liberal, nor the churl said to be bountiful.6 For the vile person will speak villany, and his heart will work iniquity, to practise hypocrisy, and to utter error against YHUH, to make empty the soul of the hungry, and he will cause the drink of the thirsty to fail.7 The instruments also of the churl are evil: he deviseth wicked devices to destroy the poor with lying words, even when the needy speaketh right.8 But the liberal deviseth liberal things; and by liberal things shall he stand.9 Rise up, you women that are at ease; hear my voice, you careless daughters; give ear unto my speech.10 Many days and years shall you be troubled, you careless women: for the vintage shall fail, the gathering shall not come.11 Tremble, you women that are at ease; be troubled, you careless ones: strip you, and make you bare, and gird sackcloth upon your loins.12 They shall lament for the teats, for the pleasant fields, for the fruitful vine.13 Upon the land of my people shall come up thorns and briers; yea, upon all the houses of joy in the joyous city:14 Because the palaces shall be forsaken; the multitude of the city shall be left; the forts and towers shall be for dens forever, a joy of wild asses, a pasture of flocks;

**32:15**
עד 5704 יערה 6168 עלינו 5921 רוח 7307 ממרום 4791 והיה 1961 מדבר 4057 לכרמל 3759 וכרמל 3759
'ad ya'areh 'aleynu ruach mimaroum; uahayah midbar lakarmel, uakarmel
**Until be poured upon us the spirit from on high and be the wilderness a fruitful field and the fruit fulfield**

ליער 3293 יחשב 2803: **32:16** ושכן 7931 במדבר 4057 משפט 4941 וצדקה 6666 בכרמל 3759
laya'ar yechasheb. uashakan bamidbar mishapat; uatzdaqah bakarmel
**for a forest be counted Then shall dwell in the wilderness judgment and righteousness in the fruitful field**

תשב 3427: **32:17** והיה 1961 מעשה 4639 הצדקה 6666 שלום 7965 ועבדת 5656 הצדקה 6666 השקט 8252 ובטח 983
tesheb. uahayah ma'aseh hatzadaqah shaloum; ua'abodat hatzadaqah, hashqet uabetach
**remain And shall be work of the righteousness peace and the effect of righteousness quietness and assurance**

עד 5704 עולם 5769: **32:18** וישב 3427 עמי 5971 בנוה 5116 שלום 7965 ובמשכנות 4908 מבטחים 4009 ובמנוחת 4496
'ad 'aulam. uayashab 'amiy binueh shaloum; uabmishkanout mibtachiym, uabimnuchot
**for ever And shall dwell my people in a habitation peaceable and in dwellings sure and in resting places**

שאננות 7600: **32:19** וברד 1258 ברדת 3381 היער 3293 ובשפלה 8218 תשפל 8213 העיר 5892: **32:20** אשריכם 835
sha'ananout. uabarad baredet haya'ar; uabashiplah tishpal ha'ayr. 'ashreykem
**quiet ones When it shall hail coming down on the forest and in a low place shall be low the city Blessed**

זרעי 2232 על 5921 כל 3605 מים 4325 משלחי 7971 רגל 7272 השור 7794 והחמור 2543:
zora'aey 'al kal mayim; mashalchey regel hashour uahachamour.
***are* you that sow beside all waters that send forth *there* the feet of the ox and the ass**

**Isa 33:1**
הוי 1945 שודד 7703 ואתה 859 לא 3808 שדוד 7703 ובוגד 898 ולא 3808 בגדו 898
houy shouded, ua'atah la' shadud, uabouged uala' bagadu
**Woe *to* you that spoil and you *were* not spoiled and dealest treacherously and not they dealt treacherously**

בו 871a כהתמך 8552 שודד 7703 תושד 7703 כנלתך 5239 לבגד 898
bou; kahatimka shouded tushad, kanlotaka libgod
**with you when you shall cease to spoil you shall be spoiled *and* when you shall make an end to deal treacherously**

יבגדו 898 בך 871a: **33:2** יהוה 3068 חננו 2603 לך 3807a קוינו 6960 היה 1961 זרעם 2220
yibgadu bak. Yahuah chanenu laka qiuiynu; hayeh zaro'am
**they shall deal treacherously with you O Yahuah be gracious unto us we have waited for you be you their arm**

לבקרים 1242 אף 637 ישועתנו 3444 בעת 6256 צרה 6869: **33:3** מקול 6963 המון 1995 נדדו 5074 עמים 5971
labaqariym, 'ap yashu'atenu ba'aet tzarah. miqoul hamoun, nadadu 'amiym;
**every morning also our salvation in the time of trouble At the noise of the tumult fled the people**

מרוממתך 7427 נפצו 5310 גוים 1471: **33:4** ואסף 622 שללכם 7998 אסף 625
meroumamuteka, napatzu gouyim. ua'usap shalalkem, 'asep
**at the lifting up of yourself were scattered the nations And shall be gathered your spoil *like* the gathering of**

החסיל 2625 כמשק 4944 גבים 1357 שוקק 8264 בו 871a: **33:5** נשגב 7682 יהוה 3068 כי 3588 שכן 7931 מרום 4791
hechasiyl; kamashaq gebiym shouqeq bou. nisgab Yahuah, kiy shoken maroum;
**the caterpiller as the running to and fro of locusts shall he run upon them is exalted Yahuah for he dwell on high**

Isa 32:15 Until the spirit be poured upon us from on high, and the wilderness be a fruitful field, and the fruitful field be counted for a forest.16 Then judgment shall dwell in the wilderness, and righteousness remain in the fruitful field.17 And the work of righteousness shall be peace; and the effect of righteousness quietness and assurance forever.18 And my people shall dwell in a peaceable habitation, and in sure dwellings, and in quiet resting places;19 When it shall hail, coming down on the forest; and the city shall be low in a low place.20 Blessed are you that sow beside all waters, that send forth thither the feet of the ox and the ass. **Isa** 33:1 Woe to you that spoilest, and you were not spoiled; and dealest treacherously, and they dealt not treacherously with you! when you shall cease to spoil, you shall be spoiled; and when you shall make an end to deal treacherously, they shall deal treacherously with you.2 O YHUH, be gracious unto us; we have waited for you: be you their arm every morning, our salvation also in the time of trouble.3 At the noise of the tumult the people fled; at the lifting up of thyself the nations were scattered.4 And your spoil shall be gathered like the gathering of the caterpiller: as the running to and fro of locusts shall he run upon them.5 YHUH is exalted; for he dwell on high: he has filled Zion with judgment and righteousness.

מלא 4390 ציון 6726 משפט 4941 וצדקה 6666: 33:6 והיה 1961 אמונת 530 עתיך 6256 חסן 2633
milea' tziyoun, mishapat uatzdaqah. uahayah 'amunat 'ateyka, chosen
**he has filled Zion with judgment and righteousness And shall be the stability of your times *and* strength of**

ישועת 3444 חכמת 2451 ודעת 1847 יראת 3374 יהוה 3068 היא 1931 אוצרו 214: 33:7 הן 2005 אראלם 691 צעקו 6817 חצה 2351
yashu'at chakamat uada'at; yir'at Yahuah hiy'a uatzarou. hen 'ar'alam, tza'aqu chutzah;
**salvation wisdom and knowledge the fear of Yahuah he *is* his treasure Behold their valiant ones shall cry without**

מלאכי 4397 שלום 7965 מר 4751 יבכיון 1058: 33:8 נשמו 8074 מסלות 4546 שבת 7673 עבר 5674 ארח 734 הפר 6565
mal'akey shaloum, mar yibkayun. nashamu masilout, shabat 'aber 'arach; heper
**the ambassadors of peace bitterly shall weep lie waste The highways cease faring man *the* way he has broken**

ברית 1285 מאס 3988 ערים 5892 לא 3808 חשב 2803 אנוש 582: 33:9 אבל 56 אמללה 535 ארץ 776 החפיר 2659 לבנון 3844
bariyt ma'as 'aeriym, la' chashab 'anoush. 'abal 'amlalah 'aretz, hechpiyr labanoun
**the covenant he has despised the cities no he regard man mourns *and* languish The earth is ashamed Lebanon**

קמל 7060 היה 1961 השרון 8289 כערבה 6160 ונער 5287 בשן 1316 וכרמל 3760: 33:10 עתה 6258 אקום 6965 יאמר 559
qamal; hayah hasharoun ka'arabah, uano'aer bashan uakarmel. 'atah 'aqum ya'mar
***and* hewn down is Sharon like a wilderness shake off *their fruits* Bashan and Carmel Now will I rise saith**

יהוה 3068 עתה 6258 ארומם 7311 עתה 6258 אנשא 5375: 33:11 תהרו 2029 חשש 2842 תלדו 3205 קש 7179
Yahuah; 'atah 'aeroumam, 'atah 'anasea'. taharu chashash teladu qash;
**Yahuah now will I be exalted now will I lift up myself You shall conceive chaff you shall bring forth stubble**

רוחכם 7307 אש 784 תאכלכם 398: 33:12 והיו 1961 עמים 5971 משרפות 4955 שיד 7875 קוצים 6975 כסוחים 3683 באש 784
ruchakem 'aesh ta'kalkem. uahayu 'amiym misrapout siyd; qoutziym kasuchiym ba'aesh
**your breath *as* fire shall devour you And shall be the people *as* the burnings of lime *as* thorns cut up in the fire**

יצתו 3341: 33:13 שמעו 8085 רחוקים 7350 אשר 834 עשיתי 6213 ודעו 3045 קרובים 7138 גברתי 1369: 33:14
yitzatu. shim'au rachouqiym 'asher 'asiytiy; uad'au qaroubiym gaburatiy.
**shall they be burned Hear you *that are* far off what I have done and acknowledge you *that are* near my might**

פחדו 6342 בציון 6726 חטאים 2400 אחזה 270 רעדה 7461 חנפים 2611 מי 4310 יגור 1481 לנו 3807a אש 784
pachadu batziyoun chata'aym, 'achazah ra'adah chanepiym; miy' yagur lanu, 'aesh
**are afraid in Zion The sinners has surprised fearfulness the hypocrites Who shall dwell among us fire?**

אוכלה 398 מי 4310 יגור 1481 לנו 3807a מוקדי 4168 עולם 5769: 33:15 הלך 1980 צדקות 6666 ודבר 1696
'aukelah, miy' yagur lanu mouqadey 'aulam. holek tzadaqout, uadober
***with the* devouring who shall dwell among us burnings? *with* everlasting He that walk righteously and speak**

מישרים 4339 מאס 3988 בבצע 1215 מעשקות 4642 נער 5287 כפיו 3709 מתמך 8551 בשחד 7810 אטם 331 אזנו 241
meyshariym; mo'aes babetza' ma'ashaqout, no'aer kapayu mitamok bashochad, 'atem 'azanou
**uprightly he that despise the gain of oppressions that shake his hands from holding of bribes that stop his ears**

משמע 8085 דמים 1818 ועצם 6105 עיניו 5869 מראות 7200 ברע 7451: 33:16 הוא 1931 מרומים 4791 ישכן 7931
mishmoa' damiym, ua'atzem 'aeynayu mera'aut bara'. hua' maroumiym yishkon,
**from hearing of blood and shut his eyes from seeing evil He on high shall dwell**

Isa 32:15 Until the spirit be poured upon us from on high, and the wilderness be a fruitful field, and the fruitful field be counted for a forest.16 Then judgment shall dwell in the wilderness, and righteousness remain in the fruitful field.17 And the work of righteousness shall be peace; and the effect of righteousness quietness and assurance forever.18 And my people shall dwell in a peaceable habitation, and in sure dwellings, and in quiet resting places;19 When it shall hail, coming down on the forest; and the city shall be low in a low place.20 Blessed are you that sow beside all waters, that send forth thither the feet of the ox and the ass. **Isa** 33:1 Woe to you that spoilest, and you were not spoiled; and dealest treacherously, and they dealt not treacherously with you! when you shall cease to spoil, you shall be spoiled; and when you shall make an end to deal treacherously, they shall deal treacherously with you.2 O YHUH, be gracious unto us; we have waited for you: be you their arm every morning, our salvation also in the time of trouble.3 At the noise of the tumult the people fled; at the lifting up of thyself the nations were scattered.4 And your spoil shall be gathered like the gathering of the caterpiller: as the running to and fro of locusts shall he run upon them.5 YHUH is exalted; for he dwell on high: he has filled Zion with judgment and righteousness.

| מצדות 4679 | סלעים 5553 | משגבו 4869 | לחמו 3899 | נתן 5414 | מימיו 4325 | נאמנים 539: | 33:17 | מלך 4428 |
|---|---|---|---|---|---|---|---|---|
| matzadout | sala'aym | misgabou; | lachmou | nitan, | meymayu | ne'amaniym. | | melek |
| ***shall be* the munitions of** | **rocks** | **his place of defence** | **bread** | **shall be given him** | **his waters** | ***shall be* sure** | | **the king** |

| ביפיו 3308 | תחזינה 2372 | עיניך 5869 | תראינה 7200 | ארץ 776 | מרחקים 4801: | 33:18 | לבך 3820 | יהגה 1897 | אימה 367 |
|---|---|---|---|---|---|---|---|---|---|
| bayapayou | techazeynah | 'aeyneyka; | tir'aynah | 'aretz | marchaqiym. | | libaka | yehageh | 'aeymah; |
| **in his beauty** | **shall see** | **Thine eyes** | **they shall behold** | **the land** | **that is very far off** | | **Thine heart** | **shall meditate** | **terror** |

| איה 346 | ספר 5608 | איה 346 | שקל 8254 | איה 346 | ספר 5608 | את 853 | המגדלים 4026: | 33:19 | את 853 | עם 5971 | נועז 3267 | לא 3808 |
|---|---|---|---|---|---|---|---|---|---|---|---|---|
| 'ayeh | soper | 'ayeh | shoqel, | 'ayeh | soper | 'at | hamigdaliym. | | 'at | 'am | nou'az | la' |
| **Where *is*** | **the scribe?** | **where** | ***is* the receiver?** | **where** | ***is* he that counted** | | **the towers?** | | | **a people** | **fierce** | **not** |

| תראה 7200 | עם 5971 | עמקי 6012 | שפה 8193 | משמוע 8085 | נלעג 3932 | לשון 3956 | אין 369 |
|---|---|---|---|---|---|---|---|
| tir'ah; | 'am | 'amqey | sapah | mishmoua', | nil'ag | lashoun | 'aeyn |
| **You shall see** | **a people of** | **a deeper** | **speech** | **than you can perceive** | ***of* a stammering** | **tongue *that you can*** | **not** |

| בינה 998: | 33:20 | חזה 2372 | ציון 6726 | קרית 7151 | מועדנו 4150 | עיניך 5869 | תראינה 7200 | ירושלם 3389 | נוה 5116 | שאנן 7600 |
|---|---|---|---|---|---|---|---|---|---|---|
| biynah. | | chazeh | tziyoun, | qiryat | mou'adenu; | 'aeyneyka | tir'aynah | yarushalaim | naueh | sha'anan, |
| **understand** | | **Look** | **upon Zion** | **the city of** | **our solemnities** | **your eyes** | **shall see** | **Jerusalem** | **a habitation** | **quiet** |

| אהל 168 | בל 1077 | יצען 6813 | בל 1077 | יסע 5265 | יתדתיו 3489 | לנצח 5331 | וכל 3605 |
|---|---|---|---|---|---|---|---|
| 'ahel | bal | yitz'an | bal | yisa' | yatedotayu | lanetzach, | uakal |
| **a tabernacle** | **not** | ***that* shall be taken down** | **not** | **shall be removed** | ***one of* the stakes thereof** | **ever** | **any of** |

| חבליו 2256 | בל 1077 | ינתקו 5423: | 33:21 | כי 3588 | אם 518 | שם 8033 | אדיר 117 | יהוה 3068 | לנו 3807a | מקום 4725 | נהרים 5104 |
|---|---|---|---|---|---|---|---|---|---|---|---|
| chabalayu | bal | yinatequ. | | kiy | 'am | sham | 'adiyr | Yahuah | lanu, | maqoum | nahariym |
| **the cords thereof** | **neither** | **shall be broken** | | **But** | **that** | **there** | **glorious** | **Yahuah** | ***will be* unto us** | **a place of** | **rivers** |

| יארים 2975 | רחבי 7342 | ידים 3027 | בל 1077 | תלך 1980 | בו 871a | אני 590 | שיט 7885 | וצי 6716 | אדיר 117 | לא 3808 | יעברנו 5674: | 33:22 |
|---|---|---|---|---|---|---|---|---|---|---|---|---|
| ya'ariym | rachabey | yadayim; | bal | telek | bou | 'aniy | shayit, | uatziy | 'adiyr | la' | ya'abrenu. | |
| ***and* streams** | **broad** | **sides** | **no** | **shall go** | **wherein** | **galley with** | **oars** | **ship** | **gallant** | **neither** | **shall pass therby** | |

| כי 3588 | יהוה 3068 | שפטנו 8199 | יהוה 3068 | מחקקנו 2710 | יהוה 3068 | מלכנו 4428 | הוא 1931 | יושיענו 3467: | 33:23 | נטשו 5203 | חבליך 2256 |
|---|---|---|---|---|---|---|---|---|---|---|---|
| kiy | Yahuah | shopatenu, | Yahuah | machoqaqenu; | Yahuah | malkenu | hua' | youshiy'aenu. | | nitshu | chabalayik; |
| **For** | **Yahuah** | ***is* our judge** | **Yahuah** | ***is* our lawgiver** | **Yahuah** | ***is* our king** | **he** | **will save us** | | **are loosed** | **Your tacklings** |

| בל 1077 | יחזקו 2388 | כן 3651 | תרנם 8650 | בל 1077 | פרשו 6566 | נס 5251 | אז 227 | חלק 2505 | עד 5706 | שלל 7998 | מרבה 4766 |
|---|---|---|---|---|---|---|---|---|---|---|---|
| bal | yachazqu | ken | taranam | bal | parasu | nes, | 'az | chulaq | 'ad | shalal | marbeh, |
| **not** | **they could strengthen** | **well** | **their mast** | **not** | **they could spread** | **the sail** | **then** | **is divided** | **the prey of** | **a spoil** | **great** |

| פסחים 6455 | בזזו 962 | בז 957: | 33:24 | ובל 1077 | יאמר 559 | שכן 7934 | חליתי 2470 | העם 5971 | הישב 3427 | בה 871a | נשא 5375 |
|---|---|---|---|---|---|---|---|---|---|---|---|
| pischiym | bazazu | baz. | | uabal | ya'mar | shaken | chaliytiy; | ha'am | hayosheb | bah | nasa' |
| **the lame** | **take** | **the prey** | | **And not** | **shall say** | **the inhabitant** | **I am sick** | **the people** | **that dwell** | **therein** | ***shall be* forgiven** |

| עון 5771: |
|---|
| 'auon. |
| ***their* iniquity** |

Isa 33:17 Thine eyes shall see the king in his beauty: they shall behold the land that is very far off.18 Thine heart shall meditate terror. Where is the scribe? where is the receiver? where is he that counted the towers?19 Thou shall not see a fierce people, a people of a deeper speech than you canst perceive; of a stammering tongue, that you canst not understand.20 Look upon Zion, the city of our solemnities: your eyes shall see Jerusalem a quiet habitation, a tabernacle that shall not be taken down; not one of the stakes thereof shall ever be removed, neither shall any of the cords thereof be broken.21 But there the glorious YHUH will be unto us a place of broad rivers and streams; wherein shall go no galley with oars, neither shall gallant ship pass thereby.22 For YHUH is our judge, YHUH is our lawgiver, YHUH is our king; he will save us.23 Thy tacklings are loosed; they could not well strengthen their mast, they could not spread the sail: then is the prey of a great spoil divided; the lame take the prey.24 And the inhabitant shall not say, I am sick: the people that dwell therein shall be forgiven their iniquity.

| Isa 34:1 | | | | | | | | |
|---|---|---|---|---|---|---|---|---|
| קרבו 7126 | גוים 1471 | לשמע 8085 | ולאמים 3816 | הקשיבו 7181 | תשמע 8085 | הארץ 776 | ומלאה 4393 | תבל 8398 |
| qirbu | gouyim | lishmoa', | uala'amiym | haqashiybu; | tishma' | ha'aretz | uamlo'ah, | tebel |
| **Come near you** | **nations** | **to hear** | **and people** | **listen you** | **let hear** | **the earth** | **and all that is therein** | **the world** |

| | | 34:2 | | | | | | | |
|---|---|---|---|---|---|---|---|---|---|
| וכל 3605 | צאצאיה 6631: | כי 3588 | קצף 7110 | ליהוה 3068 | על 5921 | כל 3605 | הגוים 1471 | וחמה 2534 | על 5921 |
| uakal | tze'atza'ayha. | kiy | qetzep | laYahuah | 'al | kal | hagouyim, | uachemah | 'al |
| **and all things** | **that come forth of it** | **For** | **the indignation of** | **Yahuah** | ***is* upon** | **all** | **nations** | **and *his* fury** | **upon** |

| | | | | | 34:3 |
|---|---|---|---|---|---|
| כל 3605 | צבאם 6635 | החרימם 2763 | נתנם 5414 | לטבח 2874: | וחלליהם 2491 |
| kal | tzaba'am; | hecheriymam | natanam | latabach. | uachaleyhem |
| **all** | **their armies** | **he has utterly destroyed them** | **he has delivered them** | **to the slaughter** | **Their slain also** |

| | | | | | | | 34:4 |
|---|---|---|---|---|---|---|---|
| ישלכו 7993 | ופגריהם 6297 | יעלה 5927 | באשם 889 | ונמסו 4549 | הרים 2022 | מדמם 1818: | |
| yushlaku, | uapigreyhem | ya'aleh | ba'asham; | uanamasu | hariym | midamam. | |
| **shall be cast out** | **and their carcases** | **shall come up *out of*** | **their stink** | **and shall be melted** | **the mountains** | **with their blood** | |

| | | | | | | | | |
|---|---|---|---|---|---|---|---|---|
| ונמקו 4743 | כל 3605 | צבא 6635 | השמים 8064 | ונגלו 1556 | כספר 5612 | השמים 8064 | וכל 3605 | צבאם 6635 |
| uanamaqu | kal | tzaba' | hashamayim, | uanagolu | kaseper | hashamayim; | uakal | tzaba'am |
| **And shall be dissolved** | **all** | **host of** | **the heaven** | **and shall be rolled together** | **as a scroll** | **the heavens** | **and all** | **their host** |

| | | | | | | 34:5 | | |
|---|---|---|---|---|---|---|---|---|
| יבול 5034 | כנבל 5034 | עלה 5929 | מגפן 1612 | וכנבלת 5034 | מתאנה 8384: | כי 3588 | רותה 7301 | בשמים 8064 |
| yiboul, | kinbol | 'aleh | migepen, | uaknobelet | mit'aenah. | kiy | riuatah | bashamayim |
| **shall fall down** | **as fall off** | **the leaf** | **from the vine** | **and as a falling *fig*** | **from the fig tree** | **For** | **shall be bathed** | **in heaven** |

| | | | | | | | | | 34:6 |
|---|---|---|---|---|---|---|---|---|---|
| חרבי 2719 | הנה 2009 | על 5921 | אדום 123 | תרד 3381 | ועל 5921 | עם 5971 | חרמי 2764 | למשפט 4941: | חרב 2719 |
| charbiy; | hineh | 'al | 'adoum | tered, | ua'al | 'am | chermiy | lamishpat. | chereb |
| **my sword** | **behold** | **upon** | **Idumea** | **it shall come down** | **and upon** | **the people of** | **my curse** | **to judgment** | **The sword** |

| | | | | | | | | |
|---|---|---|---|---|---|---|---|---|
| ליהוה 3068 | מלאה 4390 | דם 1818 | הדשנה 1878 | מחלב 2459 | מדם 1818 | כרים 3733 | ועתודים 6260 | מחלב 2459 |
| laYahuah | mal'ah | dam | hudashnah | mecheleb, | midam | kariym | ua'atudiym, | mecheleb |
| **of Yahuah** | **is filled with** | **blood** | **it is made fat** | **with fatness** | ***and* with the blood of** | **lambs** | **and goats** | **with the fat of** |

| | | | | | | | | | | 34:7 |
|---|---|---|---|---|---|---|---|---|---|---|
| כליות 3629 | אילים 352 | כי 3588 | זבח 2077 | ליהוה 3068 | בבצרה 1224 | וטבח 2874 | גדול 1419 | בארץ 776 | אדום 123: | |
| kilyout | 'aeyliym; | kiy | zebach | laYahuah | babatzarah, | uatebach | gadoul | ba'aretz | 'adoum. | |
| **the kidneys of** | **rams** | **for** | ***has* a sacrifice** | **unto Yahuah** | **in Bozrah** | **and a slaughter** | **great** | **in the land of** | **Idumea** | |

| | | | | | | | | |
|---|---|---|---|---|---|---|---|---|
| וירדו 3381 | ראמים 7214 | עמם 5973 | ופרים 6499 | עם 5973 | אבירים 47 | ורותה 7301 | ארצם 776 | מדם 1818 |
| uayaradu | ra'aemiym | 'amam, | uapariym | 'am | 'abiyriym; | uariuatah | 'artzam | midam, |
| **And shall come down** | **the unicorns** | **with them** | **and the bullocks** | **with** | **the bulls** | **and shall be soaked** | **their land** | **with blood** |

| | | | 34:8 | | | | | |
|---|---|---|---|---|---|---|---|---|
| ועפרם 6083 | מחלב 2459 | ידשן 1878: | כי 3588 | יום 3117 | נקם 5359 | ליהוה 3068 | שנת 8141 | שלומים 7966 |
| ua'aparam | mecheleb | yadushan. | kiy | youm | naqam | laYahuah; | shanat | shilumiym |
| **and their dust** | **with fatness** | **made fat** | **For** | ***it is* the day** | **vengeance** | **of Yahuah's** | ***and* the year of** | **recompences** |

| | | 34:9 | | | | |
|---|---|---|---|---|---|---|
| לריב 7379 | ציון 6726: | ונהפכו 2015 | נחליה 5158 | לזפת 2203 | ועפרה 6083 | לגפרית 1614 |
| lariyb | tziyoun. | uanehepku | nachaleyha | lazepet, | ua'aparah | lagapariyt; |
| **for the controversy of** | **Zion** | **And shall be turned** | **the streams thereof** | **into pitch** | **and the dust thereof** | **into brimstone** |

**Isa** 34:1 Come near, you nations, to hear; and hear, you people: let the earth hear, and all that is therein; the world, and all things that come forth of it.2 For the indignation of YHUH is upon all nations, and his fury upon all their armies: he has utterly destroyed them, he has delivered them to the slaughter.3 Their slain also shall be cast out, and their stink shall come up out of their carcases, and the mountains shall be melted with their blood.4 And all the host of heaven shall be dissolved, and the heavens shall be rolled together as a scroll: and all their host shall fall down, as the leaf fall off from the vine, and as a falling fig from the fig tree.5 For my sword shall be bathed in heaven: behold, it shall come down upon Idumea, and upon the people of my curse, to judgment.6 The sword of YHUH is filled with blood, it is made fat with fatness, and with the blood of lambs and goats, with the fat of the kidneys of rams: for YHUH has a sacrifice in Bozrah, and a great slaughter in the land of Idumea.7 And the unicorns shall come down with them, and the bullocks with the bulls; and their land shall be soaked with blood, and their dust made fat with fatness.8 For it is the day of YHUH's vengeance, and the year of recompences for the controversy of Zion.9 And the streams thereof shall be turned into pitch, and the dust thereof into brimstone,

והיתה 1961 | ארצה 776 | לזפת 2203 | בערה 1197: | **34:10** | לילה 3915 | ויומם 3119 | לא 3808 | תכבה 3518 | לעולם 5769
uahayatah | 'artzah, | lazepet | bo'aerah. | | layalah | uayoumam | la' | tikbeh, | la'aulam
**and shall become | the land thereof | pitch | burning | | night | nor day | not | It shall be quenched | for ever**

יעלה 5927 | עשנה 6227 | מדור 1755 | לדור 1755 | תחרב 2717 | לנצח 5331 | נצחים 5331 | אין 369 | עבר 5674
ya'aleh | 'ashanah; | midour | ladour | techarab, | lanetzach | natzachiym, | 'aeyn | 'aber
**shall go up | the smoke thereof | from generation | to generation | it shall lie waste | for ever | and ever | none | shall pass**

בה 871a: | **34:11** | וירשוה 3423 | קאת 6893 | וקפוד 7090 | וינשוף 3244 | וערב 6158 | ישכנו 7931 | בה 871a
bah. | | uiyreshuha | qa'at | uaqipoud, | uayanshoup | ua'areb | yishkanu | bah;
**through it | | But shall possess it | the cormorant | and the bittern | the owl also | and the raven | shall dwell | in it**

ונטה 5186 | עליה 5921 | קו 6957 | תהו 8414 | ואבני 68 | בהו 922: | **34:12** | חריה 2715 | ואין 369
uanatah | 'aleyha | qau | tohu | ua'abney | bohu. | | choreyha | ua'aeyn
**and he shall stretch out | upon it | the line of | confusion | and the stones of | emptiness | | the nobles thereof | but none** ***shall be***

שם 8033 | מלוכה 4410 | יקראו 7121 | וכל 3605 | שריה 8269 | יהיו 1961 | אפס 657: | **34:13** | ועלתה 5927 | ארמנתיה 759
sham | malukah | yiqra'au; | uakal | sareyha | yihayu | 'apes. | | ua'alatah | 'armanoteyha
**there |** ***to*** **the kingdom | They shall call | and all | her princes | shall be | nothing | | And shall come up in | her palaces**

סירים 5518 | קמוש 7057 | וחוח 2336 | במבצריה 4013 | והיתה 1961 | נוה 5116 | תנים 8577 | חציר 2681 | לבנות 1323
siyriym, | qimous | uachouach | bamibtzareyha; | uahayatah | naueh | taniym, | chatziyr | libnout
**thorns | nettles | and brambles | in the fortresses thereof | and it shall be | an habitation of | dragons |** ***and*** **a court | old**

יענה 3284: | **34:14** | ופגשו 6298 | ציים 6728 | את 854 | איים 338 | ושעיר 8163 | על 5921
ya'anah. | | uapagashu | tziyiym | 'at | 'ayiym, | uasa'ayr | 'al
**owls | | shall also meet | The wild beasts of the desert** ***with*** **|** ***with*** **the wild beasts of the island | and the satyr (*****goat*****) | to**

רעהו 7453 | יקרא 7121 | אך 389 | שם 8033 | הרגיעה 7280 | לילית 3917 | ומצאה 4672 | לה 3807a | מנוח 4494: | **34:15** | שמה 8033
re'aehu | yiqra'; | 'ak | sham | hirgiy'ah | liyliyt, | uamatza'ah | lah | manouach. | | shamah
**his fellow | shall cry | also | there | shall rest | the screech owl | and find | for herself | a place of rest | | There**

קננה 7077 | קפוז 7091 | ותמלט 4422 | ובקעה 1234 | ודגרה 1716 | בצלה 6738 | אך 389 | שם 8033 | נקבצו 6908
qinanah | qipouz | uatamalet, | uabaqa'ah | uadagarah | batzilah; | 'ak | sham | niqbatzu
**shall make her nest | the great owl | and lay | and hatch | and gather | under her shadow | also | there | shall be gathered**

דיות 1772 | אשה 802 | רעותה 7468: | **34:16** | דרשו 1875 | מעל 5921 | ספר 5612 | יהוה 3068 | וקראו 7121 | אחת 259 | מהנה 2007 | לא 3808 | נעדרה 5737
dayout | 'ashah | ra'utah. | | dirshu | me'al | seper | Yahuah | uaqra'au, | 'achat | mehenah | la' | ne'darah,
**the vultures | every one |** ***with*** **her mate | | Seek you | out of | the book of | Yahuah | and read | one | of these | no | shall fail**

אשה 802 | רעותה 7468 | לא 3808 | פקדו 6485 | כי 3588 | פי 6310 | הוא 1931 | צוה 6680 | ורוחו 7307 | הוא 1931 | קבצן 6908: | **34:17**
'ashah | ra'utah | la' | paqadu; | kiy | piy | hua' | tziuah, | uaruchou | hua' | qibtzan.
**none | her mate | none | shall want | for | my mouth | it | has commanded | and his spirit | it | has gathered them**

והוא 1931 | הפיל 5307 | להן 3807a | גורל 1486 | וידו 3027 | חלקתה 2505 | להם 1992 | בקו 6957 | עד 5704 | עולם 5769 | יירשוה 3423
uahu'a | hipiyl | lahen | goural, | uayadou | chilqatah | lahem | baqau; | 'ad | 'aulam | yiyrashuha,
**And he | has cast | for them | the lot | and his hand | has divided it | unto them | by line | for | ever | they shall possess it**

Isa 34:9 and the land thereof shall become burning pitch.10 It shall not be quenched night nor day; the smoke thereof shall go up forever: from generation to generation it shall lie waste; none shall pass through it forever and ever.11 But the cormorant and the bittern shall possess it; the owl also and the raven shall dwell in it: and he shall stretch out upon it the line of confusion, and the stones of emptiness.12 They shall call the nobles thereof to the kingdom, but none shall be there, and all her princes shall be nothing.13 And thorns shall come up in her palaces, nettles and brambles in the fortresses thereof: and it shall be an habitation of dragons, and a court for owls.14 The wild beasts of the desert shall also meet with the wild beasts of the island, and the satyr shall cry to his fellow; the screech owl also shall rest there, and find for herself a place of rest.15 There shall the great owl make her nest, and lay, and hatch, and gather under her shadow: there shall the vultures also be gathered, everyone with her mate.16 Seek you out of the book of YHUH, and read: no one of these shall fail, none shall want her mate: for my mouth it has commanded, and his spirit it has gathered them.17 And he has cast the lot for them, and his hand has divided it unto them by line: they shall possess it forever, from generation to generation shall they dwell therein.

לדור 1755 ודור 1755 ישכנו 7931 בה 871a:
ladour uadour yishkanu bah.
**from generation to generation shall they dwell therein**

**Isa 35:1** ישׂשום 7797 מדבר 4057 וציה 6723 ותגל 1523 ערבה 6160 ותפרח 6524
yasusum midbar uatziyah; uatagel 'arabah uatiprach
**shall be glad for them The wilderness and the solitary place and shall rejoice the desert and blossom**

כחבצלת 2261: **35:2** פרח 6524 תפרח 6524 ותגל 1523 אף 637 גילת 1525 ורנן 7442 כבוד 3519 הלבנון 3844 נתן 5414
kachabatzalet. parouach tiprach uatagel, 'ap giylat uaranen, kaboud halabanoun nitan
**as the rose It shall blossom abundantly and rejoice even *with* joy and singing glory of the Lebanon shall be given**

לה 3807a הדר 1926 הכרמל 3760 והשרון 8289 המה 1992 יראו 7200 כבוד 3519 יהוה 3068 הדר 1926 אלהינו 430: **35:3**
lah, hadar hakarmel uahasharoun; hemah yir'au kaboud Yahuah hadar 'aloheynu.
**unto it excellency of the Carmel and Sharon they shall see the glory of Yahuah *and* the excellency of our Elohim**

חזקו 2388 ידים 3027 רפות 7504 וברכים 1290 כשלות 3782 אמצו 553: **35:4** אמרו 559 לנמהרי 4116 לב 3820 חזקו 2388
chazqu yadayim rapout; uabirkayim koshalout 'ametzu. 'amru lanimharey leb, chizqu
**Strengthen you hands *the* weak and knees *the* feeble confirm Say to them *that are* of a fearful heart Be strong**

אל 408 תיראו 3372 הנה 2009 אלהיכם 430 נקם 5359 יבוא 935 גמול 1576 אלהים 430 הוא 1931 יבוא 935
'al tiyra'au; hineh 'aloheykem naqam yabou'a, gamul 'alohiym, hua' yabou'a
**not fear behold your Elohim *with* vengeance will come *with* a recompence *even* Elohim he will come**

וישעכם 3467: **35:5** אז 227 תפקחנה 6491 עיני 5869 עורים 5787 ואזני 241 חרשים 2795 תפתחנה 6605: **35:6** אז 227
uayosha'akem. 'az tipaqachnah 'aeyney 'auriym; ua'azaney cherashiym tipatachnah. 'az
**and save you Then shall be opened the eyes of the blind and the ears of the deaf shall be unstopped Then**

ידלג 1801 כאיל 354 פסח 6455 ותרן 7442 לשון 3956 אלם 483 כי 3588 נבקעו 1234 במדבר 4057 מים 4325
yadaleg ka'ayal piseach, uataron lashoun 'alem; kiy nibqa'au bamidbar mayim,
**shall leap as an hart the lame *man* and sing the tongue of the dumb for shall break out in the wilderness waters**

ונחלים 5158 בערבה 6160: **35:7** והיה 1961 השרב 8273 לאגם 98 וצמאון 6774 למבועי 4002 מים 4325
uanchaliym ba'arabah. uahayah hasharab la'agam, uatzima'oun lamabu'aey mayim;
**and streams in the desert And shall become the parched ground a pool and the thirsty land springs of water**

בנוה 5116 תנים 8577 רבצה 7258 חציר 2682 לקנה 7070 וגמא 1573: **35:8** והיה 1961 שם 8033 מסלול 4547
binueh taniym ribtzah, chatziyr laqaneh uagoma'. uahayah sham maslul
**in the habitation of dragons where each lay *shall be* grass with reeds and rushes And shall be there an highway**

ודרך 1870 ודרך 1870 הקדש 6944 יקרא 7121 לה 3807a לא 3808 יעברנו 5674 טמא 2931 והוא 1931 למו 3807a
uaderek, uaderek haqodesh yiqaraea' lah, la' ya'abrenu tamea' uahu'a lamou;
**and a way and way of The holiness shall be called it not shall pass over it the unclean but it *shall be* for those**

הלך 1980 דרך 1870 ואוילים 191 לא 3808 יתעו 8582: **35:9** לא 3808 יהיה 1961 שם 8033 אריה 738 ופריץ 6530 חיות 2416 בל 1077
halok derek ua'auiyliym la' yit'au. la' yihayeh sham 'aryeh, uapriytz chayout bal
**the faring *men* way though fools *therin* not shall err No shall be there lion *any* ravenous beast nor**

**Isa** 35:1 The wilderness and the solitary place shall be glad for them; and the desert shall rejoice, and blossom as the rose.2 It shall blossom abundantly, and rejoice even with joy and singing: the glory of Lebanon shall be given unto it, the excellency of Carmel and Sharon, they shall see the glory of YHUH, and the excellency of our G-d.3 Strengthen you the weak hands, and confirm the feeble knees.4 Say to them that are of a fearful heart, Be strong, fear not: behold, your G-d will come with vengeance, even G-d with a recompence; he will come and save you.5 Then the eyes of the blind shall be opened, and the ears of the deaf shall be unstopped.6 Then shall the lame man leap as an hart, and the tongue of the dumb sing: for in the wilderness shall waters break out, and streams in the desert.7 And the parched ground shall become a pool, and the thirsty land springs of water: in the habitation of dragons, where each lay, shall be grass with reeds and rushes.8 And an highway shall be there, and a way, and it shall be called The way of holiness; the unclean shall not pass over it; but it shall be for those: the wayfaring men, though fools, shall not err therein.9 No lion shall be there, nor any ravenous beast shall go up thereon, it shall not be found there; but the redeemed shall walk there:

| יעלנה 5927 | לא 3808 | תמצא 4672 | שם 8033 | והלכו 1980 | גאולים 1350: | 35:10 ופדויי 6299 | יהוה 3068 |
|---|---|---|---|---|---|---|---|
| ya'alenah, | la' | timatzea' | sham; | uahalaku | ga'uliym. | uapduyey | Yahuah |
| **shall go up thereon** | **not** | **it shall be found** | **there;** | **but shall walk *there*** | **the redeemed** | **And the ransomed of** | **Yahuah** |

| ישבון 7725 | ובאו 935 | ציון 6726 | ברנה 7440 | ושמחת 8057 | עולם 5769 | על 5921 | ראשם 7218 | ששון 8342 | ושמחה 8057 | ישיגו 5381 |
|---|---|---|---|---|---|---|---|---|---|---|
| yashubun, | uaba'au | tziyoun | barinah, | uasimchat | 'aulam | 'al | ra'sham; | sasoun | uasimchah | yasiygu, |
| **shall return** | **and come to** | **Zion** | **with songs** | **and joy** | **everlasting** | **upon** | **their heads** | **joy** | **and gladness** | **they shall obtain** |

| ונסו 5127 | יגון 3015 | ואנחה 585: |
|---|---|---|
| uanasu | yagoun | ua'anachah. |
| **shall flee away** | **sorrow** | **and sighing** |

| Isa 36:1 ויהי 1961 | בארבע 702 | עשרה 6240 | שנה 8141 | למלך 4428 | חזקיהו 2396 | עלה 5927 | סנחריב 5576 | מלך 4428 | אשור 804 |
|---|---|---|---|---|---|---|---|---|---|
| uayahiy | ba'arba | 'asreh | shanah | lamelek | chizqiyahu, | 'alah | sancheriyb | melek | 'ashur |
| **Now it came to pass** | **in the four** | **ten** | **year** | **of king** | **Hezekiah** | **came up** | ***that* Sennacherib** | **king of** | **Assyria** |

| על 5921 | כל 3605 | ערי 5892 | יהודה 3063 | הבצרות 1219 | ויתפשם 8610: | 36:2 וישלח 7971 | מלך 4428 | אשור 804 | את 853 | רב 7262 | שקה 8248 |
|---|---|---|---|---|---|---|---|---|---|---|---|
| 'al | kal | 'arey | yahudah | habatzurout | uayitpasem. | uayishlach | melek | 'ashur | 'at | rab | shaqeh |
| **against** | **all** | **cities of** | **Judah** | **the defenced** | **and took them** | **And sent** | **the king of** | **Assyria** | | **Rab** | **shakeh** |

| מלכיש 3923 | ירושלמה 3389 | אל 413 | המלך 4428 | חזקיהו 2396 | בחיל 2426 | כבד 3515 | ויעמד 5975 | בתעלת 8585 | הברכה 1295 |
|---|---|---|---|---|---|---|---|---|---|
| milakiysh | yarushalamah | 'al | hamelek | chizqiyahu | bacheyl | kabed; | uaya'amod, | bit'alat | habarekah |
| **from Lachish to** | **Jerusalem** | **unto** | **king** | **Hezekiah** | **with a army** | **great** | **And he stood** | **by the conduit of** | **pool** |

| העליונה 5945 | במסלת 4546 | שדה 7704 | כובס 3526: | 36:3 ויצא 3318 | אליו 413 | אליקים 471 | בן 1121 | חלקיהו 2518 | אשר 834 |
|---|---|---|---|---|---|---|---|---|---|
| ha'alyounah, | bimasilat | sadeh | koubes. | uayetzea' | 'aelayu | 'alyaqiym | ben | chilqiyahu | 'asher |
| **the upper** | **in the highway of** | **field** | ***the* fuller's** | **Then came forth** | **unto him** | **Eliakim** | **son** | **Hilkiah's** | **which** |

| על 5921 | הבית 1004 | ושבנא 7644 | הספר 5608 | ויואח 3098 | בן 1121 | אסף 623 | המזכיר 2142: | 36:4 ויאמר 559 | אליהם 413 | רב 7262 | שקה 8248 |
|---|---|---|---|---|---|---|---|---|---|---|---|
| 'al | habayit; | uashebna' | hasoper, | uayou'ach | ben | 'asap | hamazkiyr. | uaya'mer | 'aleyhem | rab | shaqeh, |
| ***was* over** | **the house** | **and Shebna** | **the scribe** | **and Joah** | **son** | **Asaph's** | **the recorder** | **And said** | **unto them** | **Rab** | **shakeh** |

| אמרו 559 | נא 4994 | אל 413 | חזקיהו 2396 | כה 3541 | אמר 559 | המלך 4428 | הגדול 1419 | מלך 4428 | אשור 804 | מה 4100 | הבטחון 986 | הזה 2088 | אשר 834 |
|---|---|---|---|---|---|---|---|---|---|---|---|---|---|
| 'amru | naa' | 'al | chizqiyahu; | koh | 'amar | hamelek | hagadoul | melek | 'ashur, | mah | habitachoun | hazeh | 'asher |
| **Say you** | **now** | **to** | **Hezekiah** | **Thus** | **saith** | **king** | **the great** | **the king of** | **Assyria** | **What** | **confidence** | ***is* this** | **wherein** |

| בטחת 982: | 36:5 אמרתי 559 | אך 389 | דבר 1697 | שפתים 8193 | עצה 6098 | וגבורה 1369 | למלחמה 4421 | עתה 6258 | על 5921 | מי 4310 |
|---|---|---|---|---|---|---|---|---|---|---|
| batachata. | 'amartiy | 'ak | dabar | sapatayim, | 'aetzah | uagaburah | lamilchamah; | 'atah | 'al | miy' |
| **you trust?** | **I say, *say you*** | **but** | **words** | ***they are but* vain** | ***I have* counsel** | **and strength** | **for war** | **now** | **on** | **whom** |

| בטחת 982 | כי 3588 | מרדת 4775 | בי 871a: | 36:6 הנה 2009 | בטחת 982 | על 5921 | משענת 4938 | הקנה 7070 | הרצוץ 7533 | הזה 2088 | על 5921 | מצרים 4714 |
|---|---|---|---|---|---|---|---|---|---|---|---|---|
| batachta, | kiy | maradta | biy. | hineh | batachta | 'al | mish'anet | haqaneh | haratzutz | hazeh | 'al | mitzrayim, |
| **do you trust that** | **you rebel against me?** | | | **Lo** | **you trust in** | | **the staff of** | **reed** | **broken** | **this** | **on** | **Egypt** |

| אשר 834 | יסמך 5564 | איש 376 | עליו 5921 | ובא 935 | בכפו 3709 | ונקבה 5344 | כן 3651 | פרעה 6547 | מלך 4428 | מצרים 4714 | לכל 3605 |
|---|---|---|---|---|---|---|---|---|---|---|---|
| 'asher | yisamek | 'aysh | 'alayu, | uaba' | bakapou | uanqabah; | ken | par'ah | melek | mitzrayim, | lakal |
| **whereon** | **lean** | ***if* a man** | **on him** | **it will go** | **into his hand** | **and pierce it** | **so** | ***is* Pharaoh** | **king of** | **Egypt** | **to all** |

Isa 35:10 And the ransomed of YHUH shall return, and come to Zion with songs and everlasting joy upon their heads: they shall obtain joy and gladness, and sorrow and sighing shall flee away. **Isa** 36:1 Now it came to pass in the fourteenth year of king Hezekiah, that Sennacherib king of Assyria came up against all the defenced cities of Judah, and took them.2 And the king of Assyria sent Rabshakeh from Lachish to Jerusalem unto king Hezekiah with a great army. And he stood by the conduit of the upper pool in the highway of the fuller's field.3 Then came forth unto him Eliakim, Hilkiah's son, which was over the house, and Shebna the scribe, and Joah, Asaph's son, the recorder.4 And Rabshakeh said unto them, Say you now to Hezekiah, Thus saith the great king, the king of Assyria, What confidence is this wherein you trustest?5 I say, say you, (but they are but vain words) I have counsel and strength for war: now on whom dost you trust, that you rebellest against me?6 Lo, you trustest in the staff of this broken reed, on Egypt; whereon if a man lean, it will go into his hand, and pierce it: so is Pharaoh king of Egypt to all that trust in him.

36:7
הבטחים 982 עליו 5921: וכי 3588 תאמר 559 אלי 413 אל 413 יהוה 3069 אלהינו 430 בטחנו 982 הלוא 3808 הוא 1931 אשר 834
habotachiym 'alayu. uakiy ta'mar 'aelay, 'al Yahuah 'aloheynu batachanu; halou'a hua', 'asher
**that trust in him But if you say to me in Yahuah our Elohim We trust *is it* not he whose**

הסיר 5493 חזקיהו 2396 את 853 במתיו 1116 ואת 853 מזבחתיו 4196 ויאמר 559 ליהודה 3063 ולירושלם 3389 לפני 6440
hesiyr chizqiyahu 'at bamotayu ua'at mizbachotayu, uaya'mer liyahudah ualiyarushalaim, lipney
**has taken away Hezekiah *whose* high places *and* whose altars and said to Judah and to Jerusalem before**

36:8
המזבח 4196 הזה 2088 תשתחוו 7812: ועתה 6258 התערב 6148 נא 4994 את 854 אדני 113 המלך 4428 אשור 804
hamizbeach hazeh tishtachauu. ua'atah hit'areb na, 'at 'adoniy hamelek 'ashur;
**altars? this You shall worship Now therefore give pledges I pray you *to* my master the king of Assyria**

36:9
ואתנה 5414 לך 3807a אלפים 505 סוסים 5483 אם 518 תוכל 3201 לתת 5414 לך 3807a רכבים 7392 עליהם 5921: ואיך 349
ua'atanah laka 'alpayim susiym, 'am tukal latet laka rokabiym 'aleyhem. ua'aeyk
**and I will give to you two thousand horses if you be able to set on your part riders upon them How then**

תשיב 7725 את 853 פני 6440 פחת 6346 אחד 259 עבדי 5650 אדני 113 הקטנים 6996 ותבטח 982 לך 3807a על 5921
tashiyb, 'at paney pachat 'achad 'abdey 'adoniy haqataniym; uatibtach laka 'al
**will you turn away the face of captain of one servants my master's the least of and put your trust to your on**

36:10
מצרים 4714 לרכב 7393 ולפרשים 6571: ועתה 6258 המבלעדי 1107 יהוה 3068 עליתי 5927 על 5921 הארץ 776 הזאת 2063
mitzrayim, larekeb ualparashiym. ua'atah hamibal'adey Yahuah, 'aliytiy 'al ha'aretz haza't
**Egypt for chariots and for horseman? And am I now without Yahuah come up against the land this**

36:11
להשחיתה 7843 יהוה 3068 אמר 559 אלי 413 עלה 5927 אל 413 הארץ 776 הזאת 2063 והשחיתה 7843: ויאמר 559 אליקים 471
lahashchiytah; Yahuah 'amar 'aelay, 'aleh 'al ha'aretz haza't uahashachiytah. uaya'mer 'alyaqiym
**to destroy it? Yahuah said unto me Go up against the land this and destroy it Then said Eliakim**

ושבנא 7644 ויואח 3098 אל 413 רב 7262 שקה 8248 דבר 1696 נא 4994 אל 413 עבדיך 5650 ארמית 762 כי 3588
uashebna' uayou'ach 'al rab shaqeh, daber naa' 'al 'abadeyka 'aramiyt, kiy
**and Shebna and Joah unto Rab shakeh Speak I pray you unto your servants in the Syrian language for**

שמעים 8085 אנחנו 587 ואל 408 תדבר 1696 אלינו 413 יהודית 3066 באזני 241 העם 5971 אשר 834 על 5921
shoma'aym 'anachanu; ua'al tadaber 'aeleynu yahudiyt, ba'azaney ha'am, 'asher 'al
**understand *it* we and not speak to us in the Jews' language in the ears of the people that *are* on**

36:12
החומה 2346: ויאמר 559 רב 7262 שקה 8248 האל 413 אדניך 113 ואליך 413 שלחני 7971 אדני 113 לדבר 1696 את 853 הדברים 1697
hachoumah. uaya'mer rab shaqeh, ha'ael 'adoneyka ua'aleyka shalachaniy 'adoniy, ladaber 'at hadabariym
**the wall But said Rab shakeh to my master and to you has sent me your master to speak words?**

האלה 428 הלא 3808 על 5921 האנשים 582 הישבים 3427 על 5921 החומה 2346 לאכל 398 את 853 חראיהם 2716 ולשתות 8354
ha'aeleh; hala' 'al ha'anashiym, hayoshbiym 'al hachoumah, le'akol 'at char'ayhem ualishtout
**these *has he* not *sent me* to the men that sit upon the wall that they may eat their own dung and drink**

36:13
את 853 שיניהם 7890 עמכם 5973 ויעמד 5975 רב 7262 שקה 8248 ויקרא 7121 בקול 6963 גדול 1419 יהודית 3066
'at sheyneyhem 'amakem. uaya'amod rab shaqeh, uayiqra' baqoul gadoul yahudiyt;
**their own piss with you? Then stood Rab shakeh and cried with a voice loud in the Jews' language**

Isa 36:7 But if you say to me, We trust in YHUH our G-d: is it not he, whose high places and whose altars Hezekiah has taken away, and said to Judah and to Jerusalem, You shall worship before this altar?8 Now therefore give pledges, I pray you, to my master the king of Assyria, and I will give you two thousand horses, if you be able on your part to set riders upon them.9 How then will you turn away the face of one captain of the least of my master's servants, and put your trust on Egypt for chariots and for horsemen?10 And am I now come up without YHUH against this land to destroy it? YHUH said unto me, Go up against this land, and destroy it.11 Then said Eliakim and Shebna and Joah unto Rabshakeh, Speak, I pray you, unto your servants in the Syrian language; for we understand it: and speak not to us in the Jews' language, in the ears of the people that are on the wall.12 But Rabshakeh said, Hath my master sent me to your master and to you to speak these words? has he not sent me to the men that sit upon the wall, that they may eat their own dung, and drink their own piss with you?13 Then Rabshakeh stood, and cried with a loud voice in the Jews' language, and said, Hear you the words of the great king, the king of Assyria.

36:14

ויאמר 559 שמעו 8085 את 853 דברי 1697 המלך 4428 הגדול 1419 מלך 4428 אשור 804: כה 3541 אמר 559 המלך 4428 אל 408 ישא 5377

uaya'mer shim'au, 'at dibrey hamelek hagadoul melek 'ashur. koh 'amar hamelek, 'al yasha'

**and said Hear you the words of king the great the king of Assyria Thus saith the king not Let deceive**

36:15

לכם 3807a חזקיהו 2396 כי 3588 לא 3808 יוכל 3201 להציל 5337 אתכם 853: ואל 408 יבטח 982 אתכם 853 חזקיהו 2396 אל 413

lakem chizqiyahu; kiy la' yukal lahatziyl 'atkem. ua'al yabtach 'atkem chizqiyahu 'al

**to you Hezekiah for not he shall be able to deliver you Neither let make trust you Hezekiah in**

יהוה 3068 לאמר 559 הצל 5337 יצילנו 5337 יהוה 3068 לא 3808 תנתן 5414 העיר 5892 הזאת 2063 ביד 3027 מלך 4428

Yahuah lea'mor, hatzel yatziylenu Yahuah; la' tinaten ha'ayr haza't, bayad melek

**Yahuah saying will surely deliver us Yahuah not shall be delivered city this into the hand of the king of**

36:16

אשור 804: אל 408 תשמעו 8085 אל 413 חזקיהו 2396 כי 3588 כה 3541 אמר 559 המלך 4428 אשור 804 עשו 6213 אתי 854

'ashur. 'al tishma'au 'al chizqiyahu; kiy koh 'amar hamelek 'ashur, 'asu 'atiy

**Assyria not Hearken to Hezekiah for thus saith the king of Assyria Make *an agreement* with me**

ברכה 1293 וצאו 3318 אלי 413 ואכלו 398 איש 376 גפנו 1612 ואיש 376 תאנתו 8384 ושתו 8354 איש 376

barakah uatz'au 'aelay, ua'aklu 'aysh gapnou ua'aysh ta'aenatou, uashtu 'aysh

***by* a present and come out to me and eat you every one *of* his vine and every one *of* his fig tree and drink you every one**

36:17

מי 4325 בורו 953: עד 5704 באי 935 ולקחתי 3947 אתכם 853 אל 413 ארץ 776 כארצכם 776 ארץ 776

mey bourou. 'ad bo'ay ualaqachtiy 'atkem 'al 'aretz ka'artzakem; 'aretz

**the waters of his own cistern Until I come and take you away you to a land like your own land a land of**

36:18

דגן 1715 ותירוש 8492 ארץ 776 לחם 3899 וכרמים 3754: פן 6435 יסית 5496 אתכם 853 חזקיהו 2396 לאמר 559 יהוה 3068

dagan uatiyroush, 'aretz lachem uakramiym. pen yasiyt 'atkem chizqiyahu lea'mor, Yahuah

**corn and wine a land of bread and vineyards *Beware* lest persuade you Hezekiah saying Yahuah**

36:19

יצילנו 5337 ההצילו 5337 אלהי 430 הגוים 1471 איש 376 את 853 ארצו 776 מיד 3027 מלך 4428 אשור 804:

yatziylenu; hahitziylu 'alohey hagouyim 'aysh 'at artzou, miyad melek 'ashur.

**will deliver us Has delivered the gods of the nations any of his land out of the hand of the king of Assyria?**

איה 346 אלהי 430 חמת 2574 וארפד 774 איה 346 אלהי 430 ספרוים 5617 וכי 3588 הצילו 5337 את 853

'ayeh 'alohey chamat ua'arpad, 'ayeh 'alohey saparuayim; uakiy hitziylu 'at

**Where *are* the gods of Hamath and Arpad? where *are* the gods of Sepharvaim? and that have they delivered**

36:20

שמרון 8111 מידי 3027: מי 4310 בכל 3605 אלהי 430 הארצות 776 האלה 428 אשר 834 הצילו 5337 את 853

shomaroun miyadiy. miy, bakal 'alohey ha'aratzout ha'aeleh, 'asher hitziylu 'at

**Samaria out of my hand? Who *are they* among all the gods of lands these that have delivered**

36:21

ארצם 776 מידי 3027 כי 3588 יציל 5337 יהוה 3068 את 853 ירושלם 3389 מידי 3027: ויחרישו 2790

'artzam miyadiy; kiy yatziyl Yahuah 'at yarushalaim miyadiy. uayachariyshu,

**their land out of my hand that should deliver Yahuah Jerusalem out of my hand? But they held their peace**

ולא 3808 ענו 6030 אתו 853 דבר 1697 כי 3588 מצות 4687 המלך 4428 היא 1931 לאמר 559 לא 3808 תענהו 6030:

uala' 'anu 'atou dabar; kiy mitzuat hamelek hiy'a lea'mor la' ta'anuhu.

**not and answered him a word for commandment *was* the king's he saying not Answer him**

Isa 36:14 Thus saith the king, Let not Hezekiah deceive you: for he shall not be able to deliver you.15 Neither let Hezekiah make you trust in YHUH, saying, YHUH will surely deliver us: this city shall not be delivered into the hand of the king of Assyria.16 Hearken not to Hezekiah: for thus saith the king of Assyria, Make an agreement with me by a present, and come out to me: and eat you everyone of his vine, and everyone of his fig tree, and drink you everyone the waters of his own cistern;17 Until I come and take you away to a land like your own land, a land of corn and wine, a land of bread and vineyards.18 Beware lest Hezekiah persuade you, saying, YHUH will deliver us. Hath any of the gods of the nations delivered his land out of the hand of the king of Assyria?19 Where are the gods of Hamath and Arphad? where are the gods of Sepharvaim? and have they delivered Samaria out of my hand?20 Who are they among all the gods of these lands, that have delivered their land out of my hand, that YHUH should deliver Jerusalem out of my hand?21 But they held their peace, and answered him not a word: for the king's commandment was, saying, Answer him not.

36:22 ויבא 935 אליקים 471 בן 1121 חלקיהו 2518 אשר 834 על 5921 הבית 1004 ושבנא 7644 הספר 5608 ויואח 3098 בן 1121
uayaba' 'alyaqiym ben chilqiyahu 'asher 'al habayit uashebna' hasouper uayou'ach ben
**Then came Eliakim the son of Hilkiah that *was* over the household and Shebna the scribe and Joah the son of**

אסף 623 המזכיר 2142 אל 413 חזקיהו 2396 קרועי 7167 בגדים 899 ויגידו 5046 לו 3807a את 853 דברי 1697 רב 7262 שקה 8248:
'asap hamazkiyr 'al chizqiyahu qaru'aey bagadiym; uayagiydu lou', 'at dibrey rab shaqeh.
**Asaph the recorder to Hezekiah rent with *their* clothes and told him the words of Rab shakeh**

Isa 37:1 ויהי 1961 כשמע 8085 המלך 4428 חזקיהו 2396 ויקרע 7167 את 853 בגדיו 899 ויתכס 3680
uayahiy, kishmoa' hamelek chizqiyahu, uayiqra' 'at bagadayu; uayitkas
**And it came to pass when heard *it* king Hezekiah that he rent his clothes and covered**

בשק 8242 ויבא 935 בית 1004 יהוה 3068: 37:2 וישלח 7971 את 853 אליקים 471 אשר 834 על 5921 הבית 1004
basaq, uayaba' beyt Yahuah. uayishlach 'at 'alyaqiym 'asher 'al habayit
***himself* with sackcloth and went into the house of Yahuah And he sent Eliakim who *was* over the household**

ואת 853 שבנא 7644 הספר 5608 ואת 853 זקני 2205 הכהנים 3548 מתכסים 3680 בשקים 8242 אל 413 ישעיהו 3470 בן 1121 אמוץ 531
ua'at shebna' hasouper, ua'at ziqney hakohaniym, mitkasiym basaqiym; 'al yasha'yahu ben amoutz
***and* Shebna the scribe *and* the elders of the priests covered with sackcloth unto Isaiah the son of Amoz**

הנביא 5030: 37:3 ויאמרו 559 אליו 413 כה 3541 אמר 559 חזקיהו 2396 יום 3117 צרה 6869 ותוכחה 8433 ונאצה 5007 היום 3117
hanabiy'a. uaya'maru 'aelayu, koh 'amar chizqiyahu, youm tzarah uatoukechah uan'atzah hayoum
**the prophet And they said unto him Thus saith Hezekiah day trouble and of rebuke and of blasphemy *is* a day of**

הזה 2088 כי 3588 באו 935 בנים 1121 עד 5704 משבר 4866 וכח 3581 אין 369 ללדה 3205: 37:4 אולי 194 ישמע 8085 יהוה 3069
hazeh; kiy ba'au baniym 'ad mashber, uakoach 'ayin laledah. 'aulay yishma' Yahuah
**This for are come the children to the birth and strength *there is* not to bring forth It may be will hear Yahuah**

אלהיך 430 את 853 דברי 1697 רב 7262 שקה 8248 אשר 834 שלחו 7971 מלך 4428 אשור 804 אדניו 113 לחרף 2778 אלהים 430
'aloheyka 'at dibrey rab shaqeh, 'asher shalachou melek 'ashur 'adonayu lacharep 'alohiym
**your Elohim the words of Rab shakeh whom has sent the king of Assyria his master to reproach Elohim**

חי 2416 והוכיח 3198 בדברים 1697 אשר 834 שמע 8085 יהוה 3069 אלהיך 430 ונשאת 5375 תפלה 8605 בעד 1157
chay, uahoukiyach badabariym, 'asher shama' Yahuah 'aloheyka; uanasa'ta tapilah, ba'ad
***the* living and will reprove the words which has heard Yahuah your Elohim wherefore lift up *your* prayer for**

השארית 7611 הנמצאה 4672: 37:5 ויבאו 935 עבדי 5650 המלך 4428 חזקיהו 2396 אל 413 ישעיהו 3470: 37:6 ויאמר 559 אליהם 413
hasha'aeriyt hanimtza'ah. uayabo'au, 'abdey hamelek chizqiyahu 'al yasha'yahu. uaya'mer 'aleyhem
**the remnant that is left So came servants of the king Hezekiah to Isaiah And said unto them**

ישעיהו 3470 כה 3541 תאמרון 559 אל 413 אדניכם 113 כה 3541 אמר 559 יהוה 3068 אל 408 תירא 3372 מפני 6440 הדברים 1697 אשר 834
yasha'yahu, koh ta'marun 'al 'adoneykem; koh 'amar Yahuah 'al tiyraa' mipaney hadabariym 'asher
**Isaiah Thus shall you say unto your master Thus saith Yahuah not Be afraid of the words that**

שמעת 8085 אשר 834 גדפו 1442 נערי 5288 מלך 4428 אשור 804 אותי 853: 37:7 הנני 2005 נותן 5414 בו 871a
shama'ata, 'asher gidpu na'arey melek 'ashur 'autiy. hinniy nouten bou
**you have heard wherewith have blasphemed the servants of the king of Assyria me Behold, I will send upon him**

Isa 36:22 Then came Eliakim, the son of Hilkiah, that was over the household, and Shebna the scribe, and Joah, the son of Asaph, the recorder, to Hezekiah with their clothes rent, and told him the words of Rabshakeh. **Isa** 37:1 And it came to pass, when king Hezekiah heard it, that he rent his clothes, and covered himself with sackcloth, and went into the house of YHUH.2 And he sent Eliakim, who was over the household, and Shebna the scribe, and the elders of the priests covered with sackcloth, unto Isaiah the prophet the son of Amoz.3 And they said unto him, Thus saith Hezekiah, This day is a day of trouble, and of rebuke, and of blasphemy: for the children are come to the birth, and there is not strength to bring forth.4 It may be YHUH your G-d will hear the words of Rabshakeh, whom the king of Assyria his master has sent to reproach the living G-d, and will reprove the words which YHUH your G-d has heard: wherefore lift up your prayer for the remnant that is left.5 So the servants of king Hezekiah came to Isaiah.6 And Isaiah said unto them, Thus shall you say unto your master, Thus saith YHUH, Be not afraid of the words that you have heard, wherewith the servants of the king of Assyria have blasphemed me.7 Behold, I will send a blast upon him, and he shall hear a rumour, and return to his own land;

| רוח 7307 | ושמע 8085 | שמועה 8052 | ושב 7725 | אל 413 | ארצו 776 | והפלתיו 5307 | בחרב 2719 |
|---|---|---|---|---|---|---|---|
| ruach, | uashama' | shamu'ah | uashab | 'al | artzou; | uahipaltiyu | bachereb |
| **a blast** | **and he shall hear** | **a rumour** | **and return** | **to** | **his own land** | **and I will cause him to fall** | **by the sword** |

| בארצו 776: | 37:8 | וישב 7725 | רב 7262 | שקה 8248 | וימצא 4672 | את 853 | מלך 4428 | אשור 804 | נלחם 3898 | על 5921 | לבנה 3841 | כי 3588 |
|---|---|---|---|---|---|---|---|---|---|---|---|---|
| ba'artzou. | | uayashab | rab | shaqeh, | uayimtza' | 'at | melek | 'ashur, | nilcham | 'al | libnah; | kiy |
| **in his own land** | | **So returned** | **Rab** | **shakeh** | **and found** | | **the king of** | **Assyria** | **warring** | **against** | **Libnah** | **for** |

| שמע 8085 | כי 3588 | נסע 5265 | מלכיש 3923: | 37:9 | וישמע 8085 | על 5921 | תרהקה 8640 | מלך 4428 | כוש 3568 | לאמר 559 |
|---|---|---|---|---|---|---|---|---|---|---|
| shama', | kiy | nasa' | milakiysh. | | uayishma', | 'al | tirhaqah | melek | kush | lea'mor, |
| **he had heard** | **that** | **he was departed** | **from Lachish** | | **And he heard** | **concerning** | **Tirhakah** | **king of** | **Ethiopia** | **say** |

| יצא 3318 | להלחם 3898 | אתך 854 | וישמע 8085 | וישלח 7971 | מלאכים 4397 | אל 413 | חזקיהו 2396 | לאמר 559: | 37:10 | כה 3541 |
|---|---|---|---|---|---|---|---|---|---|---|
| yatza' | lahilachem | 'atak; | uayishma' | uayishlach | mal'akiym, | 'al | chizqiyahu | lea'mor. | | koh |
| **He is come forth** | **to make war** | **with you** | **when he heard *it*** | **And he sent** | **messengers** | **to** | **Hezekiah** | **saying** | | **Thus** |

| תאמרון 559 | אל 413 | חזקיהו 2396 | מלך 4428 | יהודה 3063 | לאמר 559 | אל 408 | ישאך 5377 | אלהיך 430 | אשר 834 | אתה 859 | בוטח 982 |
|---|---|---|---|---|---|---|---|---|---|---|---|
| ta'marun, | 'al | chizqiyahu | melek | yahudah | lea'mor, | 'al | yashi'aka | 'aloheyka, | 'asher | 'atah | bouteach |
| **shall you speak** | **to** | **Hezekiah** | **king of** | **Judah** | **saying** | **not** | **Let deceive you** | **your Elohim** | **in whom** | **you** | **trust** |

| בו 871a | לאמר 559 | לא 3808 | תנתן 5414 | ירושלם 3389 | ביד 3027 | מלך 4428 | אשור 804: | 37:11 | הנה 2009 | אתה 859 | שמעת 8085 |
|---|---|---|---|---|---|---|---|---|---|---|---|
| bou | lea'mor; | la' | tinaten | yarushalaim, | bayad | melek | 'ashur. | | hineh | 'atah | shama'ata, |
| **in him** | **saying** | **not** | **shall be given** | **Jerusalem** | **into the hand of** | **the king of** | **Assyria** | | **Behold** | **you** | **have heard** |

| אשר 834 | עשו 6213 | מלכי 4428 | אשור 804 | לכל 3605 | הארצות 776 | להחרימם 2763 | ואתה 859 | תנצל 5337: | 37:12 |
|---|---|---|---|---|---|---|---|---|---|
| 'asher | 'asu | malkey | 'ashur | lakal | ha'aratzout | lahachariymam; | ua'atah | tinatzel. | |
| **what** | **have done** | **the kings of** | **Assyria** | **to all** | **lands** | **by destroying them utterly** | **and you** | **shall be delivered?** | |

| ההצילו 5337 | אותם 853 | אלהי 430 | הגוים 1471 | אשר 834 | השחיתו 7843 | אבותי 1 | את 853 | גוזן 1470 | ואת 853 | חרן 2771 | ורצף 7530 |
|---|---|---|---|---|---|---|---|---|---|---|---|
| hahitziylu | 'autam | 'alohey | hagouyim | 'asher | hishchiytu | aboutay, | 'at | gouzan | ua'at | charan; | uaretzep |
| **Have delivered** | **them** | **the gods of** | **the nations** | **which** | **have destroyed** | **my fathers** | *as* | **Gozan** | *and* | **Haran** | **and Rezeph** |

| ובני 1121 | עדן 5729 | אשר 834 | בתלשר 8515: | 37:13 | איה 346 | מלך 4428 | חמת 2574 | ומלך 4428 | ארפד 774 |
|---|---|---|---|---|---|---|---|---|---|
| uabney | 'aeden | 'asher | bitala'sar. | | 'ayeh | melek | chamat | uamelek | 'arpad, |
| **and the children of** | **Eden** | **which *were*** | **in Telassar?** | | **Where** | ***is* the king of** | **Hamath** | **and the king of** | **Arphad** |

| ומלך 4428 | לעיר 5892 | ספרוים 5617 | הנע 2012 | ועוה 5755: | 37:14 | ויקח 3947 | חזקיהו 2396 | את 853 | הספרים 5612 | מיד 3027 |
|---|---|---|---|---|---|---|---|---|---|---|
| uamelek | la'ayr | saparuayim; | hena' | ua'auah. | | uayiqach | chizqiyahu | 'at | hasapariym | miyad |
| **and the king of** | **the city of** | **Sepharvaim** | **Hena** | **and Ivah?** | | **And received** | **Hezekiah** | | **the letter** | **from the hand of** |

| המלאכים 4397 | ויקראהו 7121 | ויעל 5927 | בית 1004 | יהוה 3068 | ויפרשהו 6566 | חזקיהו 2396 | לפני 6440 | יהוה 3068: | 37:15 |
|---|---|---|---|---|---|---|---|---|---|
| hamal'akiym | uayiqra'aehu; | uaya'al | beyt | Yahuah, | uayiprasehu | chizqiyahu | lipney | Yahuah. | |
| **the messengers** | **and read it** | **and went up unto** | **the house of** | **Yahuah** | **and spread it** | **Hezekiah** | **before** | **Yahuah** | |

| ויתפלל 6419 | חזקיהו 2396 | אל 413 | יהוה 3068 | לאמר 559: | 37:16 | יהוה 3068 | צבאות 6635 | אלהי 430 | ישראל 3478 | ישב 3427 |
|---|---|---|---|---|---|---|---|---|---|---|
| uayitpalel | chizqiyahu, | 'al | Yahuah | lea'mor. | | Yahuah | tzaba'aut | 'alohey | yisra'ael | yosheb |
| **And prayed** | **Hezekiah** | **unto** | **Yahuah** | **saying** | | **O Yahuah** | **of hosts** | **Elohim of** | **Israel** | **that dwell** |

Isa 37:7 Behold, I will send a blast upon him, and he shall hear a rumour, and return to his own land; and I will cause him to fall by the sword in his own land.8 So Rabshakeh returned, and found the king of Assyria warring against Libnah: for he had heard that he was departed from Lachish.9 And he heard say concerning Tirhakah king of Ethiopia, He is come forth to make war with you. And when he heard it, he sent messengers to Hezekiah, saying,10 Thus shall you speak to Hezekiah king of Judah, saying, Let not your G-d, in whom you trustest, deceive you, saying, Jerusalem shall not be given into the hand of the king of Assyria.11 Behold, you have heard what the kings of Assyria have done to all lands by destroying them utterly; and shall you be delivered?12 Have the gods of the nations delivered them which my fathers have destroyed, as Gozan, and Haran, and Rezeph, and the children of Eden which were in Telassar?13 Where is the king of Hamath, and the king of Arphad, and the king of the city of Sepharvaim, Hena, and Ivah?14 And Hezekiah received the letter from the hand of the messengers, and read it: and Hezekiah went up unto the house of YHUH, and spread it before YHUH.15 And Hezekiah prayed unto YHUH, saying,16 O YHUH of hosts, G-d of Israel, that dwellest between the cherubims, you are the G-d, even you alone,

הכרבים 3742 אתה 859 הוא 1931 האלהים 430 לבדך 905 לכל 3605 ממלכות 4467 הארץ 776 אתה 859 עשית 6213
hakarubiym, 'atah hua' ha'alohiym labadaka, lakol mamlakout ha'aretz; 'atah 'ashiyta,
***between*** **the cherubims you you *are* the Elohim *even* you alone of all the kingdoms of the earth you have made**

37:17
את 853 השמים 8064 ואת 853 הארץ 776: הטה 5186 יהוה 3068 אזנך 241 ושמע 8085 פקח 6491 יהוה 3068 עינך 5869 וראה 7200 ושמע 8085
'at hashamayim ua'at ha'aretz. hateh Yahuah 'aznaka uashma', paqach Yahuah 'aeyneka uar'aeh; uashma',
**heaven *and* the earth Incline O Yahuah your ear and hear open O Yahuah your eyes and see and hear**

37:18
את 853 כל 3605 דברי 1697 סנחריב 5576 אשר 834 שלח 7971 לחרף 2778 אלהים 430 חי 2416: אמנם 551 יהוה 3068
'at kal dibrey sancheriyb, 'asher shalach, lacharep 'alohiym chay. 'amnam Yahuah;
**all the words of Sennacherib which has sent to reproach Elohim *the* living Of a truth Yahuah**

37:19
החריבו 2717 מלכי 4428 אשור 804 את 853 כל 3605 הארצות 776 ואת 853 ארצם 776: ונתן 5414 את 853 אלהיהם 430
hecheriybu malkey 'ashur 'at kal ha'aratzout ua'at 'artzam. uanaton 'at 'aloheyhem
**have laid waste the kings of Assyria all the nations *and* their countries And have cast their gods**

באש 784 כי 3588 לא 3808 אלהים 430 המה 1992 כי 3588 אם 518 מעשה 4639 ידי 3027 אדם 120 עץ 6086 ואבן 68
ba'aesh; kiy la' 'alohiym hemah, kiy 'am ma'aseh yadey 'adam 'aetz ua'aben
**into the fire for no gods they *were* but rather the work of hands men's wood and stone**

37:20
ויאבדום 6: ועתה 6258 יהוה 3068 אלהינו 430 הושיענו 3467 מידו 3027 וידעו 3045
uay'abdum. ua'atah Yahuah 'aloheynu, houshiy'aenu miyadou; uayeda'au
**therefore they have destroyed them Now therefore O Yahuah our Elohim save us from his hand that may know**

37:21
כל 3605 ממלכות 4467 הארץ 776 כי 3588 אתה 859 יהוה 3068 לבדך 905: וישלח 7971 ישעיהו 3470 בן 1121 אמוץ 531 אל 413
kal mamlakout ha'aretz, kiy 'atah Yahuah labadeka. uayishlach yasha'yahu ben amoutz, 'al
**all the kingdoms of the earth that you *are* Yahuah *even* you only Then sent Isaiah the son of Amoz unto**

חזקיהו 2396 לאמר 559 כה 3541 אמר 559 יהוה 3068 אלהי 430 ישראל 3478 אשר 834 התפללת 6419 אלי 413 אל 413 סנחריב 5576
chizqiyahu lea'mor; koh 'amar Yahuah 'alohey yisra'ael, 'asher hitpalalta 'aelay, 'al sancheriyb
**Hezekiah saying Thus saith Yahuah Elohim of Israel Whereas you have prayed to me against Sennacherib**

37:22
מלך 4428 אשור 804: זה 2088 הדבר 1697 אשר 834 דבר 1696 יהוה 3068 עליו 5921 בזה 959 לך 3807a
melek 'ashur. zeh hadabar, 'asher diber Yahuah 'alayu; bazah laka
**king of Assyria This *is* the word which has spoken Yahuah concerning him has despised to you**

לעגה 3932 לך 3807a בתולת 1330 בת 1323 ציון 6726 אחריך 310 ראש 7218 הניעה 5128 בת 1323
la'agah laka, batulat bat tziyoun, 'achareyka ra'sh heniy'a'ah, bat
***and* laughed to scorn to you The virgin the daughter of Zion at you her head has shaken the daughter of**

37:23
ירושלם 3389: את 853 מי 4310 חרפת 2778 וגדפת 1442 ועל 5921 מי 4310 הרימותה 7311 קול 6963
yarushalaim. 'at miy' cherapta uagidapta, ua'al miy' hariymoutah qoul;
**Jerusalem Whom have you reproached and blasphemed? and against whom have you exalted *your* voice**

37:24
ותשא 5375 מרום 4791 עיניך 5869 אל 413 קדוש 6918 ישראל 3478: ביד 3027 עבדיך 5650 חרפת 2778
uatisa' maroum 'aeyneyka 'al qadoush yisra'ael. bayad 'abadeyka cherapta
**and lifted up on high? your eyes *even* against *the* Holy of Israel By your servants have you reproached**

Isa 37:16 of all the kingdoms of the earth: you have made heaven and earth.17 Incline your ear, O YHUH, and hear; open your eyes, O YHUH, and see: and hear all the words of Sennacherib, which has sent to reproach the living G-d.18 Of a truth, YHUH, the kings of Assyria have laid waste all the nations, and their countries,19 And have cast their gods into the fire: for they were no gods, but the work of men's hands, wood and stone: therefore they have destroyed them.20 Now therefore, O YHUH our G-d, save us from his hand, that all the kingdoms of the earth may know that you are YHUH, even you only.21 Then Isaiah the son of Amoz sent unto Hezekiah, saying, Thus saith YHUH G-d of Israel, Whereas you have prayed to me against Sennacherib king of Assyria:22 This is the word which YHUH has spoken concerning him; The virgin, the daughter of Zion, has despised you, and laughed you to scorn; the daughter of Jerusalem has shaken her head at you.23 Whom have you reproached and blasphemed? and against whom have you exalted your voice, and lifted up your eyes on high? even against the Holy One of Israel.24 By your servants have you reproached the Adonai, and have said, By the multitude of my chariots am I come up to the height of the mountains, to the sides of Lebanon;

| 136 אדני | 559 ותאמר | 7230 ברב | 7393 רכבי | 589 אני | 5927 עליתי | 4791 מרום | 2022 הרים | 3411 ירכתי |
|---|---|---|---|---|---|---|---|---|
| 'adonay | uata'mer, | barob | rikbiy | 'aniy | 'aliytiy | maroum | hariym | yarkatey |
| **Adonai** | **and have said** | **By the multitude of** | **my chariots** | **I** | **am come up** | ***to* the height of** | **the mountains** | ***to* the sides of** |

| 3844 לבנון | 3772 ואכרת | 6967 קומת | 730 ארזיו | 4005 מבחר | 1265 ברשיו | 935 ואבוא | 4791 מרום |
|---|---|---|---|---|---|---|---|
| labanoun; | ua'akrot | qoumat | 'arazayu | mibchar | baroshayu, | ua'abou'a | maroum |
| **Lebanon** | **and I will cut down** | **the tall** | **cedars thereof** | ***and* the choice** | **fir trees thereof** | **and I will enter into** | **the height of** |

| 7093 קצו | 3293 יער | 3759: כרמלו | 37:25 | 589 אני | 6979 קרתי | 8354 ושתיתי | 4325 מים | 2717 ואחרב | 3709 בכף |
|---|---|---|---|---|---|---|---|---|---|
| qitzou, | ya'ar | karmilou. | | 'aniy | qartiy | uashatiytiy | mayim; | ua'achrib | bakap |
| **his border** | ***and* the forest of** | **his Carmel** | | **I** | **have digged** | **and drunk** | **water** | **and have I dried up** | **with the sole of** |

| 6471 פעמי | 3605 כל | 2975 יארי | 4692: מצור | 37:26 | 3808 הלוא | 8085 שמעת | 7350 למרחוק | 853 אותה | 6213 עשיתי |
|---|---|---|---|---|---|---|---|---|---|
| pa'amay, | kal | ya'arey | matzour. | | halou'a | shama'ata | lamerachouq | 'autah | 'asiytiy, |
| **my feet** | **all** | **the rivers of** | **the besieged places** | | **not** | **Have you heard** | **long ago** | **it** | ***how* I have done** |

| 3117 מימי | 6924 קדם | 3335 ויצרתיה | 6258 עתה | 935 הבאתיה | 1961 ותהי | 7582 להשאות | 1530 גלים |
|---|---|---|---|---|---|---|---|
| miymey | qedem | uiytzartiyha; | 'atah | habea'tiyha, | uatahiy, | lahash'aut | galiym |
| ***and* of times** | **ancient** | **that I have formed it?** | **now** | **have I brought it to pass** | **that you should be** | **to lay waste** | **heaps** |

| 5327 נצים | 5892 ערים | 1219: בצרות | 37:27 | 3427 וישביהן | 7116 קצרי | 3027 יד | 2865 חתו |
|---|---|---|---|---|---|---|---|
| nitziym | 'ariym | batzurout. | | uayoshabeyhen | qitzrey | yad, | chatu |
| ***into* ruinous** | **cities** | **defenced** | | **Therefore their inhabitants *were* of** | **small** | **power** | **they were dismayed** |

| 954 ובשו | 1961 היו | 6212 עשב | 7704 שדה | 3419 וירק | 1877 דשא | 2682 חציר | 1406 גגות |
|---|---|---|---|---|---|---|---|
| uaboshu; | hayu | 'aeseb | sadeh | uiyraq | desha', | chatziyr | gagout, |
| **and confounded** | **they were** | ***as* the grass of** | **the field** | **and *as* the green** | **herb** | ***as* the grass on** | **the housetops** |

| 7709 ושדמה | 6440 לפני | 7054: קמה | 37:28 | 3427 ושבתך | 3318 וצאתך | 935 ובואך | 3045 ידעתי | 853 ואת |
|---|---|---|---|---|---|---|---|---|
| uashdemah | lipney | qamah. | | uashibtaka | uatzea'taka | uabou'aka | yadaa'tiy; | ua'at |
| **and *as corn* blasted** | **before** | **it be grown up** | | **But your abode** | **and your going out** | **and your coming in** | **I know** | ***and*** |

| 7264 התרגזך | 413: אלי | 37:29 | 3282 יען | 7264 התרגזך | 413 אלי | 7600 ושאננך | 5927 עלה | 241 באזני | 7760 ושמתי |
|---|---|---|---|---|---|---|---|---|---|
| hitragezka | 'aelay. | | ya'an | hitragezka | 'aelay, | uasha'ananaka | 'alah | ba'azanay; | uasamtiy |
| **your rage** | **against me** | | **Because** | **your rage** | **against me** | **and your tumult** | **is come up** | **into mine ears** | **therefore will I put** |

| 2397 חחי | 639 באפך | 4964 ומתגי | 8193 בשפתיך | 7725 והשיבתיך | 1870 בדרך | 834 אשר | 935 באת | 871a: בה | 37:30 |
|---|---|---|---|---|---|---|---|---|---|
| chachiy | ba'apeka, | uamitgiy | bispateyka, | uahashibotiyka, | baderek | 'asher | ba'ta | bah. | |
| **my hook** | **in your nose** | **and my bridle** | **in your lips** | **and I will turn you back** | **by the way** | **which** | **you come** | **by** | |

| 2088 וזה | 3807a לך | 226 האות | 398 אכול | 8141 השנה | 5599 ספיח | 8141 ובשנה | 8145 השנית |
|---|---|---|---|---|---|---|---|
| uazeh | laka | ha'aut, | 'akoul | hashanah | sapiyach, | uabashanah | hasheniyt |
| **And this** | **unto you** | ***shall be* a sign** | **You shall eat** | ***this* year** | ***such as* grow of itself** | **and year** | **the second** |

| 7823 שחיס | 8141 ובשנה | 7992 השלישית | 2232 זרעו | 7114 וקצרו | 5193 ונטעו | 3754 כרמים | 398 ואכול | 6529: פרים |
|---|---|---|---|---|---|---|---|---|
| shachiys; | uabashanah | hashaliyshiyt, | zir'au | uaqitzru | uanit'au | karamiym | ua'akul | piryam. |
| **that which spring of the same** | **and in year** | **the third** | **sow you** | **and reap** | **and plant** | **vineyards** | **and eat** | **the fruit thereof** |

Isa 37:24 and I will cut down the tall cedars thereof, and the choice fir trees thereof: and I will enter into the height of his border, and the forest of his Carmel.25 I have digged, and drunk water; and with the sole of my feet have I dried up all the rivers of the besieged places.26 Hast you not heard long ago, how I have done it; and of ancient times, that I have formed it? now have I brought it to pass, that you should be to lay waste defenced cities into ruinous heaps.27 Therefore their inhabitants were of small power, they were dismayed and confounded: they were as the grass of the field, and as the green herb, as the grass on the housetops, and as corn blasted before it be grown up.28 But I know your abode, and your going out, and your coming in, and your rage against me.29 Because your rage against me, and your tumult, is come up into mine ears, therefore will I put my hook in your nose, and my bridle in your lips, and I will turn you back by the way by which you came.30 And this shall be a sign unto you, You shall eat this year such as growth of itself; and the second year that which spring of the same: and in the third year sow you, and reap, and plant vineyards, and eat the fruit thereof.

**37:31**

| 3254 ויספה | 6413 פליטת | 1004 בית | 3063 יהודה | 7604 הנשארה | 8328 שרש | 4295 למטה | 6213 ועשה | 6529 פרי |
|---|---|---|---|---|---|---|---|---|
| uayasapah | paleytat | beyt | yahudah | hanish'arah | shoresh | lamatah; | ua'asah | pariy |
| **And again** | **that is escaped of** | **the house of** | **Judah** | **the remnant** | **shall take root** | **downward** | **and bear** | **fruit** |

| 4605: למעלה | **37:32** | 3588 כי | 3389 מירושלם | 3318 תצא | 7611 שארית | 6413 ופליטה | 2022 מהר | 6726 ציון | 7068 קנאת |
|---|---|---|---|---|---|---|---|---|---|
| lama'alah. | | kiy | miyarushalaim | tetzea' | sha'aeriyt, | uapleytah | mehar | tziyoun; | qin'at |
| **upward** | | **For** | **out of Jerusalem** | **shall go forth** | **a remnant** | **and they that escape** | **out of mount** | **Zion** | **the zeal of** |

| 3068 יהוה | 6635 צבאות | 6213 תעשה | 2063: זאת | **37:33** | 3651 לכן | 3541 כה | 559 אמר | 3068 יהוה | 413 אל | 4428 מלך | 804 אשור | 3808 לא |
|---|---|---|---|---|---|---|---|---|---|---|---|---|
| Yahuah | tzaba'aut | ta'aseh | za't. | | laken, | koh | 'amar | Yahuah | 'al | melek | 'ashur, | la' |
| **Yahuah** | **of hosts** | **shall do** | **this** | | **Therefore** | **thus** | **saith** | **Yahuah** | **concerning** | **the king of** | **Assyria** | **not** |

| 935 יבוא | 413 אל | 5892 העיר | 2063 הזאת | 3808 ולא | 3384 יורה | 8033 שם | 2671 חץ | 3808 ולא | 6923 יקדמנה | 4043 מגן | 3808 ולא | 8210 ישפך |
|---|---|---|---|---|---|---|---|---|---|---|---|---|
| yabou'a | 'al | ha'ayr | haza't, | uala' | youreh | sham | chetz; | uala' | yaqadmenah | magen, | uala' | yishpok |
| **He shall come** | **into** | **city** | **this** | **nor** | **shoot** | **there** | **an arrow** | **nor** | **come before it** | ***with* shields** | **nor** | **cast** |

| 5921 עליה | 5550: סללה | **37:34** | 1870 בדרך | 834 אשר | 935 בא | 871a בה | 7725 ישוב | 413 ואל | 5892 העיר | 2063 הזאת | 3808 לא | 935 יבוא |
|---|---|---|---|---|---|---|---|---|---|---|---|---|
| 'aleyha | solalah. | | baderek | 'asher | ba' | bah | yashub; | ua'al | ha'ayr | haza't | la' | yabou'a |
| **against it** | **a bank** | | **By the way** | **that** | **he came** | **by the same** | **shall he return** | **and into** | **city** | **this** | **not** | **come** |

| 5002 נאם | 3068: יהוה | **37:35** | 1598 וגנותי | 5921 על | 5892 העיר | 2063 הזאת | 3467 להושיעה | 4616 למעני | 4616 ולמען | 1732 דוד |
|---|---|---|---|---|---|---|---|---|---|---|
| na'am | Yahuah. | | uaganoutiy | 'al | ha'ayr | haza't | lahoushiy'ah; | lama'aniy, | ualma'an | dauid |
| **saith** | **Yahuah** | | **For I will defend** | **on** | **city** | **this** | **to save it** | **for mine own sake** | **and for sake** | **David's** |

| 5650: עבדי | **37:36** | 3318 ויצא | 4397 מלאך | 3068 יהוה | 5221 ויכה | 4264 במחנה | 804 אשור | 3967 מאה | 8084 ושמנים |
|---|---|---|---|---|---|---|---|---|---|
| 'abdiy. | | uayetzea' | mal'ak | Yahuah | uayakeh | bamachaneh | 'ashur, | me'ah | uashmuniym |
| **my servant** | | **Then went forth** | **the angel of** | **Yahuah** | **and smote** | **in the camp of** | **the Assyrians** | **a hundred** | **and fourscore** |

| 2568 וחמשה | 505 אלף | 7925 וישכימו | 1242 בבקר | 2009 והנה | 3605 כלם | 6297 פגרים | 4191: מתים | **37:37** |
|---|---|---|---|---|---|---|---|---|
| uachamishah | 'alep; | uayashkiymu | baboqer, | uahineh | kulam | pagariym | metiym. | |
| **and five** | **thousand** | **and when they arose early** | **in the morning** | **and behold** | **they *were* all** | **corpses** | **dead** | |

| 5265 ויסע | 1980 וילך | 7725 וישב | 5576 סנחריב | 4428 מלך | 804 אשור | 3427 וישב | 5210: בנינוה | **37:38** 1961 ויהי | 1931 הוא |
|---|---|---|---|---|---|---|---|---|---|
| uayisa' | uayelek, | uayashab | sancheriyb | melek | 'ashur; | uayesheb | baniynaueh. | uayahiy | hua' |
| **So departed** | **and went** | **and returned** | **Sennacherib** | **king of** | **Assyria** | **and dwelt** | **at Nineveh** | **And it came to pass** | **he** |

| 7812 משתחוה | 1004 בית | 5268 נסרך | 430 אלהיו | 152 ואדרמלך | 8272 ושראצר | 1121 בניו | 5221 הכהו | 2719 בחרב |
|---|---|---|---|---|---|---|---|---|
| mishtachaueh | beyt | nisrok | 'alohayu, | ua'adramelek | uasar'atzer | banayu | hikuhu | bachereb, |
| **as was worshipping in** | **the house of** | **Nisroch** | **his god** | **that Adrammelek** | **and Sharezer** | **his sons** | **smote him** | **with the sword** |

| 1992 והמה | 4422 נמלטו | 776 ארץ | 780 אררט | 4427 וימלך | 634 אסר | n/a חדן | 1121 בנו | 8478: תחתיו |
|---|---|---|---|---|---|---|---|---|
| uahemah | nimlatu | 'aretz | 'ararat; | uayimlok | 'aesor | chadon | banou | tachtayu. |
| **and they** | **escaped into** | **the land of** | **Armenia** | **and reigned** | **Esar** | **haddon** | **his son** | **in his stead** |

**Isa 38:1**

| 3117 בימים | 1992 ההם | 2470 חלה | 2396 חזקיהו | 4191 למות | 935 ויבוא | 413 אליו | 3470 ישעיהו | 1121 בן | 531 אמוץ | 5030 הנביא |
|---|---|---|---|---|---|---|---|---|---|---|
| bayamiym | hahem, | chalah | chizqiyahu | lamut; | uayabou'a | 'aelayu | yasha'yahu | ben | amoutz | hanabiy'a, |
| **In days** | **those** | **was sick** | **Hezekiah** | **unto death** | **And came** | **unto him** | **Isaiah** | **the son of** | **Amoz** | **the prophet** |

Isa 37:31 And the remnant that is escaped of the house of Judah shall again take root downward, and bear fruit upward:32 For out of Jerusalem shall go forth a remnant, and they that escape out of mount Zion: the zeal of YHUH of hosts shall do this.33 Therefore thus saith YHUH concerning the king of Assyria, He shall not come into this city, nor shoot an arrow there nor come before it with shields, nor cast a bank against it.34 By the way that he came, by the same shall he return, and shall not come into this city, saith YHUH.35 For I will defend this city to save it for mine own sake, and for my servant David's sake.36 Then the angel of YHUH went forth, and smote in the camp of the Assyrians a hundred and fourscore and five thousand: and when they arose early in the morning, behold, they were all dead corpses.37 So Sennacherib king of Assyria departed, and went and returned, and dwelt at Nineveh.38 And it came to pass, as he was worshipping in the house of Nisroch his god, that Adrammelech and Sharezer his sons smote him with the sword; and they escaped into the land of Armenia: and Esar-haddon his son reigned in his stead. **Isa** 38:1 In those days was Hezekiah sick unto death. And Isaiah the prophet the son of Amoz came unto him, and said unto him, Thus saith YHUH, Set your house in order: for you shall die, and not live.

| 559 ויאמר | 413 אליו | 3541 כה | 559 אמר | 3068 יהוה | 6680 צו | 1004 לביתך | 3588 כי | 4191 מת | 859 אתה | 3808 ולא | 2421: תחיה | 38:2 5437 ויסב |
|---|---|---|---|---|---|---|---|---|---|---|---|---|
| uaya'mer | 'aelayu | koh | 'amar | Yahuah | tzau | labeyteka, | kiy | met | 'atah | uala' | tichayeh. | uayaseb |
| **and said** | **unto him** | **Thus** | **saith** | **Yahuah** | **Set in order** | **your house** | **for** | **shall die** | **you** | **and not** | **live** | **Then turned** |

| 2396 חזקיהו | 6440 פניו | 413 אל | 7023 הקיר | 6419 ויתפלל | 413 אל | 3068: יהוה | 38:3 559 ויאמר | 575 אנה | 3068 יהוה | 2142 זכר | 4994 נא |
|---|---|---|---|---|---|---|---|---|---|---|---|
| chizqiyahu | panayu | 'al | haqiyr; | uayitpalel | 'al | Yahuah. | uaya'mar, | 'anah | Yahuah | zakar | naa' |
| **Hezekiah** | **his face** | **toward** | **the wall** | **and prayed** | **unto** | **Yahuah** | **And said** | **I beseech you** | **now O Yahuah** | **Remember** | **now** |

| 853 את | 834 אשר | 1980 התהלכתי | 6440 לפניך | 571 באמת | 3820 ובלב | 8003 שלם | 2896 והטוב | 5869 בעיניך | 6213 עשיתי |
|---|---|---|---|---|---|---|---|---|---|
| 'at | 'asher | hithalaktiy | lapaneyka, | be'amet | uableb | shalem, | uahatoub | ba'aeyneyka | 'asiytiy; |
| | **how** | **I have walked** | **before you** | **in truth** | **and with a heart** | **perfect** | **and good** | **in your sight** | **have done** ***that which is*** |

| 1058 ויבך | 2396 חזקיהו | 1058 בכי | 1419: גדול | 38:4 1961 ויהי | 1697 דבר | 3068 יהוה | 413 אל | 3470 ישעיהו | 559: לאמר | 38:5 1980 הלוך | 559 ואמרת |
|---|---|---|---|---|---|---|---|---|---|---|---|
| uayebk | chizqiyahu | bakiy | gadoul. | uayahiy | dabar | Yahuah, | 'al | yasha'yahu | lea'mor. | halouk | ua'amarta |
| **And wept** | **Hezekiah** | **wept** | **sore** | **Then came** | **the word of** | **Yahuah** | **to** | **Isaiah** | **saying** | **Go** | **and say** |

| 413 אל | 2396 חזקיהו | 3541 כה | 559 אמר | 3069 יהוה | 430 אלהי | 1732 דוד | 1 אביך | 8085 שמעתי | 853 את | 8605 תפלתך | 7200 ראיתי | 853 את |
|---|---|---|---|---|---|---|---|---|---|---|---|---|
| 'al | chizqiyahu, | koh | 'amar | Yahuah | 'alohey | dauid | 'abiyka, | shama'atiy | 'at | tapilateka, | ra'aytiy | 'at |
| **to** | **Hezekiah** | **Thus** | **saith** | **Yahuah** | **the Elohim of** | **David** | **your father** | **I have heard** | | **your prayer** | **I have seen** | |

| 1832 דמעתך | 2005 הנני | 3254 יוסף | 5921 על | 3117 ימיך | 2568 חמש | 6240 עשרה | 8141: שנה | 38:6 3709 ומכף | 4428 מלך | 804 אשור |
|---|---|---|---|---|---|---|---|---|---|---|
| dim'ateka; | hinniy | yosiyp | 'al | yameyka, | chamesh | 'asreh | shanah. | uamikap | melek | 'ashur |
| **your tears** | **behold** | **I will add** | **unto** | **your days** | **five** | **ten** | **years** | **And out of the hand of** | **the king of** | **Assyria** |

| 5337 אצילך | 853 ואת | 5892 העיר | 2063 הזאת | 1598 וגנותי | 5921 על | 5892 העיר | 2063: הזאת | 38:7 2088 וזה | 3807a לך | 226 האות |
|---|---|---|---|---|---|---|---|---|---|---|
| 'atziylaka, | ua'at | ha'ayr | haza't; | uaganoutiy | 'al | ha'ayr | haza't. | uazeh | laka | ha'aut |
| **I will deliver you** | ***and*** | **city** | **this** | **and I will defend** | **on** | **city** | **this** | **And this** | **unto you** | ***shall be*** **a sign** |

| 853 מאת | 3068 יהוה | 834 אשר | 6213 יעשה | 3068 יהוה | 853 את | 1697 הדבר | 2088 הזה | 834 אשר | 1696: דבר | 38:8 2005 הנני | 7725 משיב | 853 את |
|---|---|---|---|---|---|---|---|---|---|---|---|---|
| me'at | Yahuah; | 'asher | ya'aseh | Yahuah, | 'at | hadabar | hazeh | 'asher | diber. | hinniy | meshiyb | 'at |
| **from** | **Yahuah** | **that** | **will do** | **Yahuah** | | **thing** | **this** | **that** | **he has spoken** | **Behold** | **I will bring again** | |

| 6738 צל | 4609 המעלות | 834 אשר | 3381 ירדה | 4609 במעלות | 271 אחז | 8121 בשמש | 322 אחרנית | 6235 עשר | 4609 מעלות | 7725 ותשב |
|---|---|---|---|---|---|---|---|---|---|---|
| tzel | hama'alout | 'asher | yaradah | bama'alot | 'achaz | bashemesh | 'achoraniyt | 'aser | ma'alout; | uatashab |
| **the shadow of** | **the degrees** | **which** | **is gone down** | **in dial of** | **Ahaz** | **in the sun** | **backward** | **ten** | **degrees** | **So returned** |

| 8121 השמש | 6235 עשר | 4609 מעלות | 4609 במעלות | 834 אשר | 3381: ירדה | 38:9 4385 מכתב | 2396 לחזקיהו | 4428 מלך | 3063 יהודה |
|---|---|---|---|---|---|---|---|---|---|
| hashemesh | 'aser | ma'alout, | bamma'alout | 'asher | yaradah. | miktab | lachizqiyahu | melek | yahudah; |
| **the sun** | **ten** | **degrees** | **by dial of** | **which** | **it was gone down** | **The writing** | **of Hezekiah** | **king of** | **Judah** |

| 2470 בחלתו | 2421 ויחי | 2483: מחליו | 38:10 589 אני | 559 אמרתי | 1824 בדמי | 3117 ימי | 1980 אלכה |
|---|---|---|---|---|---|---|---|
| bachalotou | uaychiy | mechalayou. | 'aniy | 'amartiy, | bidmiy | yamay | 'aelekah |
| **when he had been sick** | **and was recovered** | **of his sickness** | **I** | **said** | **in the cutting off of** | **my days** | **I shall go** |

| 8179 בשערי | 7585 שאול | 6485 פקדתי | 3499 יתר | 8141: שנותי | 38:11 559 אמרתי | 3808 לא | 7200 אראה | 3050 יה | 3050 יה |
|---|---|---|---|---|---|---|---|---|---|
| basha'arey | sha'aul; | puqadtiy | yeter | shanoutay. | 'amartiy | la' | 'ar'ah | Yah, | Yah |
| **to the gates of** | **the grave** | **I am deprived of** | **the residue of** | **my years** | **I said** | **not** | **I shall see** | **Yah** | ***even*** **Yah** |

Isa 38:2 Then Hezekiah turned his face toward the wall, and prayed unto YHUH,3 And said, Remember now, O YHUH, I beseech you, how I have walked before you in truth and with a perfect heart, and have done that which is good in your sight. And Hezekiah wept sore.4 Then came the word of YHUH to Isaiah, saying,5 Go, and say to Hezekiah, Thus saith YHUH, the G-d of David your father, I have heard your prayer, I have seen your tears: behold, I will add unto your days fifteen years.6 And I will deliver you and this city out of the hand of the king of Assyria: and I will defend this city.7 And this shall be a sign unto you from YHUH, that YHUH will do this thing that he has spoken;8 Behold, I will bring again the shadow of the degrees, which is gone down in the sun dial of Ahaz, ten degrees backward. So the sun returned ten degrees, by which degrees it was gone down.9 The writing of Hezekiah king of Judah, when he had been sick, and was recovered of his sickness:10 I said in the cutting off of my days, I shall go to the gates of the grave: I am deprived of the residue of my years.11 I said, I shall not see YHUH, even YHUH, in the land of the living: I shall behold man no more with the inhabitants of the world.

38:12

בארץ 776 החיים 2416 לא 3808 אביט 5027 אדם 120 עוד 5750 עם 5973 יושבי 3427 חדל 2309: דורי 1755 נסע 5265
ba'aretz hachayiym; la' 'abiyt 'adam 'aud 'am youshabey chadel. douriy, nisa'
**in the land of the living no I shall behold man more with the inhabitants of the world Mine age is departed**

ונגלה 1540 מני 4480 כאהל 168 רעי 7473 קפדתי 7088 כארג 707 חיי 2416 מדלה 1803 יבצעני 1214
uaniglah miniy ka'ahel ro'aey; qipadtiy ka'areg chayay midalah yabatza'aeniy,
**and is removed from me as a tent shepherd's I have cut off like a weaver my life with pining sickness he will cut me off**

38:13

מיום 3117 עד 5704 לילה 3915 תשלימני 7999: שויתי 7737 עד 5704 בקר 1242 כארי 738 כן 3651 ישבר 7665
miyoum 'ad layalah tashliymeniy. shiuiytiy 'ad boqer ka'ariy, ken yashaber
**from day *even* to night will you make an end of me I reckoned till morning *that* as a lion so will he break**

38:14

כל 3605 עצמותי 6106 מיום 3117 עד 5704 לילה 3915 תשלימני 7999: כסוס 5483 עגור 5693 כן 3651 אצפצף 6850
kal atzmoutay; miyoum 'ad layalah tashliymeniy. kasus 'agur ken 'atzaptzep,
**all my bones from day *even* to night will you make an end of me Like a crane *or* a swallow so did I chatter**

38:15

אהגה 1897 כיונה 3123 דלו 1809 עיני 5869 למרום 4791 אדני 136 עשקה 6234 לי 3807a ערבני 6148: מה 4100
'ahgeh kayounah; dalu 'aeynay lamaroum, 'adonay 'ashqah liy 'arabeniy. mah
**I did mourn as a dove fail mine eyes *with looking* upward Adonai I am oppressed I undertake for me What**

אדבר 1696 ואמר 559 לי 3807a והוא 1931 עשה 6213 אדדה 1718 כל 3605 שנותי 8141 על 5921 מר 4751
'adaber ua'amar liy uahu'a 'asah; 'adadeh kal shanoutay 'al mar
**shall I say? he has both spoken unto me and himself has done *it* I shall go softly all my years in the bitterness of**

38:16

נפשי 5315: אדני 136 עליהם 5921 יחיו 2421 ולכל 3605 בהן 871a חיי 2416 רוחי 7307 ותחלימני 2492
napshiy. 'adonay 'aleyhem yichayu; ualkal bahen chayey ruchiy, uatachaliymeniy
**my soul O Adonai by these *things men* live and in all these *things is* the life of my spirit so will you recover me**

38:17

והחיני 2421: הנה 2009 לשלום 7965 מר 4751 לי 3807a מר 4751 ואתה 859 חשקת 2836 נפשי 5315
uahachayeniy. hineh lashaloum mar liy mar; ua'atah chashaqta napshiy
**and make me to live Behold for peace *had* great I bitterness but you have in love to my soul**

38:18

משחת 7845 בלי 1097 כי 3588 השלכת 7993 אחרי 310 גוך 1460 כל 3605 חטאי 2399: כי 3588 לא 3808 שאול 7585
mishachat baliy, kiy hishlakta 'acharey gebaka kal chata'ay. kiy la' sha'aul
***delivered it* from the pit of corruption for you have cast behind your back all my sins For cannot the grave**

38:19

תודך 3034 מות 4194 יהללך 1984 לא 3808 ישברו 7663 יורדי 3381 בור 953 אל 413 אמתך 571: חי 2416
toudeka mauet yahalleka; la' yasabru youradey bour 'al 'amiteka. chay
**praise you death can *not* celebrate you cannot hope they that go down into the pit for your truth The living**

38:20

חי 2416 הוא 1931 יודך 3034 כמוני 3644 היום 3117 אב 1 לבנים 1121 יודיע 3045 אל 413 אמתך 571:
chay hua' youdeka kamouniy hayoum; 'ab labaniym, youdiya' 'al 'amiteka.
**the living he shall praise you as I *do* this day the father to the children shall make known to your truth**

יהוה 3068 להושיעני 3467 ונגנותי 5058 ננגן 5059 כל 3605 ימי 3117 חיינו 2416 על 5921
Yahuah lahoushiy'aeniy; uanginoutay nanagen kal yamey chayeynu 'al
**Yahuah *was ready* to save me therefore my songs we will sing to the stringed instruments all the days of our life in**

Isa 38:12 Mine age is departed, and is removed from me as a shepherd's tent: I have cut off like a weaver my life: he will cut me off with pining sickness: from day even tonight will you make an end of me.13 I reckoned till morning, that, as a lion, so will he break all my bones: from day even tonight will you make an end of me.14 Like a crane or a swallow, so did I chatter: I did mourn as a dove: mine eyes fail with looking upward: O YHUH, I am oppressed; undertake for me.15 What shall I say? he has both spoken unto me, and himself has done it: I shall go softly all my years in the bitterness of my soul.16 O Adonai, by these things men live, and in all these things is the life of my spirit: so will you recover me, and make me to live.17 Behold, for peace I had great bitterness: but you have in love to my soul delivered it from the pit of corruption: for you have cast all my sins behind your back.18 For the grave cannot praise you, death can not celebrate you: they that go down into the pit cannot hope for your truth.19 The living, the living, he shall praise you, as I do this day: the father to the children shall make known your truth.20 YHUH was ready to save me: therefore we will sing my songs to the stringed instruments all the days of our life in the house of YHUH.

| | 38:21 | | | | | | | |
|---|---|---|---|---|---|---|---|---|
| בית 1004 | יהוה 3068: | ויאמר 559 | ישעיהו 3470 | ישאו 5375 | דבלת 1690 | תאנים 8384 | וימרחו 4799 | על 5921 |
| beyt | Yahuah. | uaya'mer | yasha'yahu, | yis'au | dabelet | ta'aeniym; | uayimrachu | 'al |
| **the house of** | **Yahuah** | **For had said** | **Isaiah** | **Let them take** | **a lump of** | **figs** | **and lay *it* for a plaister** | **upon** |

| | | 38:22 | | | | | | | |
|---|---|---|---|---|---|---|---|---|---|
| השחין 7822 | ויחי 2421: | ויאמר 559 | חזקיהו 2396 | מה 4100 | אות 226 | כי 3588 | אעלה 5927 | בית 1004 | יהוה 3068: |
| hashachiyn | uayechiy. | uaya'mer | chizqiyahu | mah | 'aut; | kiy | 'a'aleh | beyt | Yahuah. |
| **the boil** | **and he shall recover** | **also had said** | **Hezekiah** | **What** | ***is* the sign** | **that** | **I shall go up to** | **the house of** | **Yahuah?** |

| Isa 39:1 | | | | | | | | | | | |
|---|---|---|---|---|---|---|---|---|---|---|---|
| בעת 6256 | ההוא 1931 | שלח 7971 | מרדך 4757 | בלאדן 1081 | בן 1121 | בלאדן 1081 | מלך 4428 | בבל 894 | ספרים 5612 | ומנחה 4503 | אל 413 |
| ba'aet | hahiua' | shalach | marodak | bal'adan | ben | bal'adan | melek | babel | sapariym | uaminchah | 'al |
| **At time** | **that** | **sent** | **Merodach** | **baladan** | **the son of** | **Baladan** | **king of** | **Babylon** | **letters** | **and a present** | **to** |

| | | | | | 39:2 | | |
|---|---|---|---|---|---|---|---|
| חזקיהו 2396 | וישמע 8085 | כי 3588 | חלה 2470 | ויחזק 2388: | וישמח 8055 | עליהם 5921 | חזקיהו 2396 |
| chizqiyahu; | uayishma' | kiy | chalah | uayechazaq. | uayismach | 'aleyhem | chizqiyahu |
| **Hezekiah** | **for he had heard** | **that** | **he had been sick** | **and was recovered** | **And was glad** | **of them** | **Hezekiah** |

| | | | | | | | | | | |
|---|---|---|---|---|---|---|---|---|---|---|
| ויראם 7200 | את 853 | בית 1004 | נכתה 5238 | את 853 | הכסף 3701 | ואת 853 | הזהב 2091 | ואת 853 | הבשמים 1314 | ואת 853 |
| uayar'aem | 'at | beyt | nakotah | 'at | hakesep | ua'at | hazahab | ua'at | habasamiym | ua'at |
| **and showed them** | | **the house of** | **his precious things,** | | **the silver** | ***and*** | **the gold** | ***and*** | **the spices** | ***and*** |

| | | | | | | | | | | | | |
|---|---|---|---|---|---|---|---|---|---|---|---|---|
| השמן 8081 | הטוב 2896 | ואת 853 | כל 3605 | בית 1004 | כליו 3627 | ואת 853 | כל 3605 | אשר 834 | נמצא 4672 | באצרתיו 214 | לא 3808 |
| hashemen | hatoub, | ua'at | kal | beyt | kelayu, | ua'at | kal | 'asher | nimtza' | ba'atzarotayu; | la' |
| **ointment** | **the precious** | ***and*** | **all** | **the house of** | **his armour** | ***and*** | **all** | **that** | **was found** | **in his treasures** | **nothing** |

| | | | | | | | | | | 39:3 | |
|---|---|---|---|---|---|---|---|---|---|---|---|
| היה 1961 | דבר 1697 | אשר 834 | לא 3808 | הראם 7200 | חזקיהו 2396 | בביתו 1004 | ובכל 3605 | ממשלתו 4474: | ויבא 935 | ישעיהו 3470 |
| hayah | dabar, | 'asher | la' | her'am | chizqiyahu | babeytou | uabkal | memshaltou. | uayaba' | yasha'yahu |
| **there was** | **nothing** | **that** | **not** | **showed them** | **Hezekiah** | **in his house** | **nor in all** | **his dominion** | **Then came** | **Isaiah** |

| | | | | | | | | | | | |
|---|---|---|---|---|---|---|---|---|---|---|---|
| הנביא 5030 | אל 413 | המלך 4428 | חזקיהו 2396 | ויאמר 559 | אליו 413 | מה 4100 | אמרו 559 | האנשים 582 | האלה 428 | ומאין 370 | יבאו 935 |
| hanabiy'a, | 'al | hamelek | chizqiyahu; | uaya'mer | 'aelayu | mah | 'amaru | ha'anashiym | ha'aeleh, | uame'ayin | yabo'au |
| **the prophet** | **unto** | **king** | **Hezekiah** | **and said** | **unto him** | **What** | **said** | **the men?** | **these** | **and from where** | **came they** |

| | | | | | | | | 39:4 |
|---|---|---|---|---|---|---|---|---|
| אליך 413 | ויאמר 559 | חזקיהו 2396 | מארץ 776 | רחוקה 7350 | באו 935 | אלי 413 | מבבל 894: | ויאמר 559 |
| 'aeleyka, | uaya'mer | chizqiyahu, | me'aretz | rachouqah | ba'au | 'aelay | mibabel. | uaya'mer |
| **unto you?** | **And said** | **Hezekiah** | **from a country** | **far** | **They are come** | **unto me** | ***even* from Babylon** | **Then said he** |

| | | | | | | | | | | | |
|---|---|---|---|---|---|---|---|---|---|---|---|
| מה 4100 | ראו 7200 | בביתך 1004 | ויאמר 559 | חזקיהו 2396 | את 853 | כל 3605 | אשר 834 | בביתי 1004 | ראו 7200 | לא 3808 |
| mah | ra'au | babeyteka; | uaya'mer | chizqiyahu, | 'at | kal | 'asher | babeytiy | ra'au, | la' |
| **What** | **have they seen** | **in mine house?** | **And answered** | **Hezekiah** | | **All** | **that *is*** | **in mine house** | **have they seen** | **nothing** |

| | | | | | | 39:5 | | | | |
|---|---|---|---|---|---|---|---|---|---|---|
| היה 1961 | דבר 1697 | אשר 834 | לא 3808 | הראיתים 7200 | באוצרתי 214: | ויאמר 559 | ישעיהו 3470 | אל 413 | חזקיהו 2396 | שמע 8085 |
| hayah | dabar | 'asher | la' | hir'aytim | ba'autzarotay. | uaya'mer | yasha'yahu | 'al | chizqiyahu; | shama' |
| **there is** | **nothing** | **that** | **not** | **I have showed them** | **among my treasures** | **Then said** | **Isaiah** | **to** | **Hezekiah** | **Hear** |

| | | | 39:6 | | | | | | |
|---|---|---|---|---|---|---|---|---|---|
| דבר 1697 | יהוה 3068 | צבאות 6635: | הנה 2009 | ימים 3117 | באים 935 | ונשא 5375 | כל 3605 | אשר 834 | בביתך 1004 |
| dabar | Yahuah | tzaba'aut. | hineh | yamiym | ba'aym | uanisa' | kal | 'asher | babeyteka, |
| **the word of** | **Yahuah** | **of hosts** | **Behold** | **the days** | **come** | **that shall be carried** | **all** | **that** | ***is* in your house** |

Isa 38:21 For Isaiah had said, Let them take a lump of figs, and lay it for a plaister upon the boil, and he shall recover.22 Hezekiah also had said, What is the sign that I shall go up to the house of YHUH? **Isa** 39:1 At that time Merodach-baladan, the son of Baladan, king of Babylon, sent letters and a present to Hezekiah: for he had heard that he had been sick, and was recovered.2 And Hezekiah was glad of them, and showed them the house of his precious things, the silver, and the gold, and the spices, and the precious ointment, and all the house of his armor, and all that was found in his treasures: there was nothing in his house, nor in all his dominion, that Hezekiah showed them not.3 Then came Isaiah the prophet unto king Hezekiah, and said unto him, What said these men? and from whence came they unto you? And Hezekiah said, They are come from a far country unto me, even from Babylon.4 Then said he, What have they seen in your house? And Hezekiah answered, All that is in mine house have they seen: there is nothing among my treasures that I have not showed them.5 Then said Isaiah to Hezekiah, Hear the word of YHUH of hosts:6 Behold, the days come, that all that is in your house, and that which your fathers have laid up in store until this day, shall be carried to Babylon: nothing shall be left, saith YHUH.

ואשר 834 אצרו 686 אבתיך 1 עד 5704 היום 3117 הזה 2088 בבל 894 לא 3808 יותר 3498 דבר 1697 אמר 559
ua'asher 'atzaru 'aboteyka 'ad hayoum hazeh babel; la' yiuater dabar 'amar
**and *that* which have laid up in store your fathers until day this *to* Babylon nothing shall be left nothing saith**

**39:7**
יהוה 3068: ומבניך 1121 אשר 834 יצאו 3318 ממך 4480 אשר 834 תוליד 3205 יקחו 3947 והיו 1961
Yahuah. uamibaneyka 'asher yetza'ua mimaka 'asher touliyd yiqachu; uahayu
**Yahuah And of your sons that shall issue from you which you shall beget shall they take away and they shall be**

**39:8**
סריסים 5631 בהיכל 1964 מלך 4428 בבל 894: ויאמר 559 חזקיהו 2396 אל 413 ישעיהו 3470 טוב 2896 דבר 1697 יהוה 3068
sariysiym, baheykal melek babel. uaya'mer chizqiyahu 'al yasha'yahu, toub dabar Yahuah
**eunuchs in the palace of the king of Babylon Then said Hezekiah to Isaiah Good *is* the word of Yahuah**

אשר 834 דברת 1696 ויאמר 559 כי 3588 יהיה 1961 שלום 7965 ואמת 571 בימי 3117:
'asher dibarta; uaya'mer kiy yihayeh shaloum ua'amet bayamay.
**which you have spoken He said moreover For there shall be peace and truth in my days**

**Isa 40:1** **40:2**
נחמו 5162 נחמו 5162 עמי 5971 יאמר 559 אלהיכם 430: דברו 1696 על 5921 לב 3820 ירושלם 3389
nachamu nachamu 'amiy; ya'mar 'aloheykem. dabaru 'al leb yarushalaim
**Comfort you comfort you my people saith your Elohim Speak you on comfortably *to* Jerusalem**

וקראו 7121 אליה 413 כי 3588 מלאה 4390 צבאה 6635 כי 3588 נרצה 7521 עונה 5771 כי 3588 לקחה 3947 מיד 3027 יהוה 3069
uaqir'au 'aleyha, kiy mal'ah tzaba'ah, kiy nirtzah 'auonah; kiy laqchah miyad Yahuah,
**and cry unto her that is accomplished her warfare that is pardoned her iniquity for she has received of hand Yahuah**

**40:3**
כפלים 3718 בכל 3605 חטאתיה 2403: קול 6963 קורא 7121 במדבר 4057 פנו 6437 דרך 1870 יהוה 3068 ישרו 3474
kiplayim bakal chata'teyha. qoul qourea', bamidbar panu derek Yahuah; yashru
**double for all her sins The voice of him that cry in the wilderness Prepare you the way of Yahuah make straight**

**40:4**
בערבה 6160 מסלה 4546 לאלהינו 430: כל 3605 גיא 1516 ינשא 5375 וכל 3605 הר 2022 וגבעה 1389 ישפלו 8213
ba'arabah, masilah le'aloheynu. kal gey'a yinasea', uakal har uagib'ah yishpalu;
**in the desert a highway for our Elohim Every valley shall be exalted and every mountain and hill shall be made low**

**40:5**
והיה 1961 העקב 6121 למישור 4334 והרכסים 7406 לבקעה 1237: ונגלה 1540 כבוד 3519 יהוה 3068
uahayah he'aqob lamiyshour, uaharakasiym labiq'ah. uaniglah kaboud Yahuah;
**and shall be the crooked made straight and the rough places plain And shall be revealed the glory of Yahuah**

**40:6**
וראו 7200 כל 3605 בשר 1320 יחדו 3162 כי 3588 פי 6310 יהוה 3068 דבר 1696: קול 6963 אמר 559 קרא 7121 ואמר 559
uar'au kal basar yachdau, kiy piy Yahuah diber. qoul 'amer qara', ua'amar
**and shall see all flesh *it* together for the mouth of Yahuah has spoken *it* The voice said Cry And he said**

**40:7**
מה 4100 אקרא 7121 כל 3605 הבשר 1320 חציר 2682 וכל 3605 חסדו 2617 כציץ 6731 השדה 7704: יבש 3001 חציר 2682
mah 'aqraa'; kal habasar chatziyr, uakal chasdou katziytz hasadeh. yabesh chatziyr
**What shall I cry? All flesh *is* grass and all the goodliness thereof *is* as the flower of the field wither The grass**

**40:8**
נבל 5034 ציץ 6731 כי 3588 רוח 7307 יהוה 3068 נשבה 5380 בו 871a אכן 403 חציר 2682 העם 5971: יבש 3001 חציר 2682 נבל 5034
nabel tziytz, kiy ruach Yahuah nashabah bou; 'aken chatziyr ha'am. yabesh chatziyr nabel
**fade the flower because the spirit Yahuah blows upon it surely *is* grass the people wither The grass fade**

Isa 39:7 And of your sons that shall issue from you, which you shall beget, shall they take away; and they shall be eunuchs in the palace of the king of Babylon.8 Then said Hezekiah to Isaiah, Good is the word of YHUH which you have spoken. He said moreover, For there shall be peace and truth in my days. **Isa** 40:1 Comfort you, comfort you my people, saith your G-d.2 Speak you comfortably to Jerusalem, and cry unto her, that her warfare is accomplished, that her iniquity is pardoned: for she has received of YHUH's hand double for all her sins.3 The voice of him that crieth in the wilderness, Prepare you the way of YHUH, make straight in the desert a highway for our G-d.4 Every valley shall be exalted, and every mountain and hill shall be made low: and the crooked shall be made straight, and the rough places plain:5 And the glory of YHUH shall be revealed, and all flesh shall see it together: for the mouth of YHUH has spoken it.6 The voice said, Cry. And he said, What shall I cry? All flesh is grass, and all the goodliness thereof is as the flower of the field:7 The grass withereth, the flower fadeth: because the spirit of YHUH bloweth upon it: surely the people is grass.8 The grass withereth, the flower fadeth: but the word of our G-d shall stand forever.

| ציץ 6731 | ודבר 1697 | אלהינו 430 | יקום 6965 | לעולם 5769: | **40:9** | על 5921 | הר 2022 | גבה 1364 | עלי 5927 | לך 3807a |
|---|---|---|---|---|---|---|---|---|---|---|
| tziytz; | uadbar | 'aloheynu | yaqum | la'aulam. | | 'al | har | gaboha | 'aliy | lak |
| **the flower** | **but the word of** | **our Elohim** | **shall stand** | **for ever** | | **into** | **mountain** | ***the* high** | **get up** | **to you** |

| מבשרת 1319 | ציון 6726 | הרימי 7311 | בכח 3581 | קולך 6963 | מבשרת 1319 | ירושלם 3389 | הרימי 7311 | אל 408 |
|---|---|---|---|---|---|---|---|---|
| mabaseret | tziyoun, | hariymiy | bakoach | qoulek, | mabaseret | yarushalaim; | hariymiy | 'al |
| **that bring good tidings** | **O Zion** | **lift up** | **with strength** | **your voice** | **that bring good tidings** | **O Jerusalem** | **lift *it* up** | **not** |

| תיראי 3372 | אמרי 559 | לערי 5892 | יהודה 3063 | הנה 2009 | אלהיכם 430: | **40:10** | הנה 2009 | אדני 136 | יהוה 3069 | בחזק 2389 | יבוא 935 |
|---|---|---|---|---|---|---|---|---|---|---|---|
| tiyra'ay, | 'amriy | la'arey | yahudah, | hineh | 'aloheykem. | | hineh | 'adonay | Yahuah | bachazaq | yabou'a, |
| **be afraid** | **say** | **unto the cities of** | **Judah** | **Behold** | **your Elohim** | | **Behold** | **Adonai** | **Yahuah** | **with strong *hand*** | **will come** |

| וזרעו 2220 | משלה 4910 | לו 3807a | הנה 2009 | שכרו 7939 | אתו 854 | ופעלתו 6468 | לפניו 6440: | **40:11** | כרעה 7462 | עדרו 5739 |
|---|---|---|---|---|---|---|---|---|---|---|
| uazro'au | moshalah | lou'; | hineh | sakarou | 'atou, | uap'alatou | lapanayu. | | kara'ah | 'adrou |
| **and his arm** | **shall rule** | **for him** | **behold** | **his reward *is*** | **with him** | **and his work** | **before him** | | **He shall feed** | **his flock** |

| ירעה 7462 | בזרעו 2220 | יקבץ 6908 | טלאים 2922 | ובחיקו 2436 | ישא 5375 | עלות 5763 |
|---|---|---|---|---|---|---|
| yir'ah, | bizro'au | yaqabetz | tala'aym, | uabcheyqou | yisa'; | 'alout |
| **like a shepherd** | **with his arm** | **he shall gather** | **the lambs** | **and in his bosom** | **carry *them*** | **those that are with young** |

| ינהל 5095: | **40:12** | מי 4310 | מדד 4058 | בשעלו 8168 | מים 4325 | ושמים 8064 | בזרת 2239 | תכן 8505 |
|---|---|---|---|---|---|---|---|---|
| yanahel. | | miy | madad | basha'alou | mayim, | uashamayim | bazeret | tiken, |
| ***and* shall gently lead** | | **Who** | **has measured** | **in the hollow of his hand** | **the waters** | **and heaven** | **with the span** | **meted out** |

| וכל 3605 | בשלש 7991 | עפר 6083 | הארץ 776 | ושקל 8254 | בפלס 6425 | הרים 2022 | וגבעות 1389 |
|---|---|---|---|---|---|---|---|
| uakal | bashalish | 'apar | ha'aretz; | uashaqal | bapeles | hariym, | uagba'aut |
| **and comprehended** | **in a measure** | **the dust of** | **the earth** | **and weighed** | **in scales** | **the mountains** | **and the hills** |

| במאזנים 3976: | **40:13** | מי 4310 | תכן 8505 | את 853 | רוח 7307 | יהוה 3068 | ואיש 376 | עצתו 6098 | יודיענו 3045: | **40:14** | את 854 |
|---|---|---|---|---|---|---|---|---|---|---|---|
| bama'zanayim. | | miy | tiken | 'at | ruach | Yahuah; | ua'aysh | atzatou | youdiy'anu. | | 'at |
| **in a balance?** | | **Who** | **has directed** | | **the Spirit of** | **Yahuah** | **or *being*** | **his counseller** | **has taught him?** | | ***With*** |

| מי 4310 | נועץ 3289 | ויבינהו 995 | וילמדהו 3925 | בארח 734 | משפט 4941 | וילמדהו 3925 | דעת 1847 |
|---|---|---|---|---|---|---|---|
| miy' | nou'atz | uayabiynehu, | uayalamdehu | ba'arach | mishapat; | uayalamdehu | da'at, |
| **whom** | **took he counsel** | **and *who* instructed him** | **and taught him** | **in the path of** | **judgment** | **and taught him** | **knowledge** |

| ודרך 1870 | תבונות 8394 | יודיענו 3045: | **40:15** | הן 2005 | גוים 1471 | כמר 4752 | מדלי 1805 | וכשחק 7834 |
|---|---|---|---|---|---|---|---|---|
| uaderek | tabunout | youdiy'anu. | | hen | gouyim | kamar | midliy, | uakshachaq |
| **and the way of understanding?** | | **showed to him** | | **Behold** | **the nations** | ***are* as a drop of** | **a bucket** | **and as the small dust of** |

| מאזנים 3976 | נחשבו 2803 | הן 2005 | איים 339 | כדק 1851 | יטול 5190: | **40:16** | ולבנון 3844 | אין 369 | די 1767 | בער 1197 |
|---|---|---|---|---|---|---|---|---|---|---|
| ma'zanayim | nechshabu; | hen | 'ayiym | kadaq | yitoul. | | ualabanoun | 'aeyn | diy | ba'aer; |
| **the balance** | **are counted** | **behold** | **the isles** | **as a very little thing** | **he takes up** | | **And Lebanon** | ***is* not** | **sufficient** | **to burn** |

| וחיתו 2416 | אין 369 | די 1767 | עולה 5930: | **40:17** | כל 3605 | הגוים 1471 | כאין 369 | נגדו 5048 | מאפס 657 |
|---|---|---|---|---|---|---|---|---|---|
| uachayatou, | 'aeyn | dey | 'aulah. | | kal | hagouyim | ka'ayin | negdou; | me'apes |
| **the beasts thereof** | **nor** | **sufficient for** | **a burnt offering** | | **All** | **nations** | **are as nothing** | **before him** | **less than nothing** |

Isa 40:9 O Zion, that bringest good tidings, get you up into the high mountain; O Jerusalem, that bringest good tidings, lift up your voice with strength; lift it up, be not afraid; say unto the cities of Judah, Behold your G-d!10 Behold, YHUH G-D will come with strong hand, and his arm shall rule for him: behold, his reward is with him, and his work before him.11 He shall feed his flock like a shepherd: he shall gather the lambs with his arm, and carry them in his bosom, and shall gently lead those that are with young.12 Who has measured the waters in the hollow of his hand, and meted out heaven with the span, and comprehended the dust of the earth in a measure, and weighed the mountains in scales, and the hills in a balance?13 Who has directed the Spirit of YHUH, or being his counselor has taught him?14 With whom took he counsel, and who instructed him, and taught him in the path of judgment, and taught him knowledge, and showed to him the way of understanding?15 Behold, the nations are as a drop of a bucket, and are counted as the small dust of the balance: behold, he take up the isles as a very little thing.16 And Lebanon is not sufficient to burn, nor the beasts thereof sufficient for a burnt offering.17 All nations before him are as nothing; and they are counted to him less than nothing, and vanity.

ותהו 8414 נחשבו 2803 לו 3807a: **40:18** ואל 413 מי 4310 תדמיון 1819 אל 410 ומה 4100 דמות 1823 תערכו 6123
uatohu nechshabu lou'. ua'al miy' tadamyun 'ael; uamah damut ta'arku
**and vanity *and* they are counted to him To then whom will you liken El? or what likeness will you compare**

לו 3807a: **40:19** הפסל 6459 נסך 5258 חרש 2796 וצרף 6884 בזהב 2091 ירקענו 7554 ורתקות 7577 כסף 3701
lou'. hapesel nasak charash, uatzorep bazahab yaraq'anu; uartuqout kesep
**unto him? a graven image melt The workman and the goldsmith with gold spread it over and chains silver**

צורף 6884: **40:20** המסכן 5533 תרומה 8641 עץ 6086 לא 3808 ירקב 7537 יבחר 977 חרש 2796 חכם 2450
tzourep. hamasukan tarumah, 'aetz la' yirqab yibchar; charash chakam
**cast He that is so impoverished *that he has no* oblation a tree not *that* will rot choose a workman cunning**

יבקש 1245 לו 3807a להכין 3559 פסל 6459 לא 3808 ימוט 4131: **40:21** הלוא 3808 תדעו 3045 הלוא 3808
yabaqesh lou', lahakiyn pesel la' yimout. halou'a teda'au halou'a
**he seek unto him to prepare a graven image not *that* shall be moved not Have you known? not**

תשמעו 8085 הלוא 3808 הגד 5046 מראש 2718 לכם 3807a הלוא 3808 הבינתם 995 מוסדות 4146
tishma'au, halou'a hugad mera'sh lakem; halou'a habiynotem, mousadout
**have you heard? not has it been told from the beginning? to you not have you understood *from* the foundations of**

הארץ 776: **40:22** הישב 3427 על 5921 חוג 2329 הארץ 776 וישביה 3427 כחגבים 2284
ha'aretz. hayosheb 'al chug ha'aretz, uayoshabeyha kachagabiym;
**the earth? *It is* he that sit upon the circle of the earth and the inhabitants thereof *are* as grasshoppers**

הנוטה 5186 כדק 1852 שמים 8064 וימתחם 4969 כאהל 168 לשבת 3427: **40:23** הנותן 5414 רוזנים 7336 לאין 369
hanouteh kadoq shamayim, uayimtachem ka'ahel lashabet. hanouten rouzniym la'ayin;
**that stretch out as a curtain the heavens and spread them out as a tent to dwell in That bring the princes to nothing**

שפטי 8199 ארץ 776 כתהו 8414 עשה 6213: **40:24** אף 637 בל 1077 נטעו 5193 אף 637 בל 1077 זרעו 2232 אף 637
shopatey 'aretz katohu 'asah. 'ap bal nita'au, 'ap bal zora'au, 'ap
**the judges of the earth as vanity he make Yea not they shall be planted yea not they shall be sown yet**

בל 1077 שרש 8327 בארץ 776 גזעם 1503 וגם 1571 נשף 5398 בהם 871a ויבשו 3001 וסערה 5591
bal shoresh ba'aretz giz'am; uagam nashap bahem uayibashu, uas'arah
**not shall take root in the earth their stock and also he shall blow upon them and they shall wither and the whirlwind**

כקש 7179 תשאם 5375: **40:25** ואל 413 מי 4310 תדמיוני 1819 ואשוה 7737 יאמר 559 קדוש 6918: **40:26**
kaqash tisa'aem. ua'al miy tadamyuniy ua'ashueh; ya'mar qadoush.
**as stubble shall take them away To then whom will you liken me or shall I be equal? saith *the* Holy One**

שאו 5375 מרום 4791 עיניכם 5869 וראו 7200 מי 4310 ברא 1254 אלה 428 המוציא 3318 במספר 4557 צבאם 6635 לכלם 3605
sa'au maroum 'aeyneykem uar'au miy' bara' 'aeleh, hamoutziy'a bamispar tzaba'am; lakulam
**Lift up on high your eyes and behold who has created these *things* that bring out by number their host them all**

בשם 8034 יקרא 7121 מרב 7230 אונים 202 ואמיץ 533 כח 3581 איש 376 לא 3808 נעדר 5737: **40:27** למה 4100 תאמר 559
bashem yiqra', merob 'auniym ua'amiytz koach, 'aysh la' ne'adar. lamah ta'mar
**by names he call by the greatness of his might for that *he is* strong in power one not fail Why say you**

Isa 40:18 To whom then will you liken G-d? or what likeness will you compare unto him?19 The workman melteth a graven image, and the goldsmith spreadeth it over with gold, and casteth silver chains.20 He that is so impoverished that he has no oblation chooseth a tree that will not rot; he seek unto him a cunning workman to prepare a graven image, that shall not be moved.21 Have you not known? have you not heard? has it not been told you from the beginning? have you not understood from the foundations of the earth?22 It is he that sitteth upon the circle of the earth, and the inhabitants thereof are as grasshoppers; that stretcheth out the heavens as a curtain, and spreadeth them out as a tent to dwell in:23 That bring the princes to nothing; he make the judges of the earth as vanity.24 Yea, they shall not be planted; yea, they shall not be sown: yea, their stock shall not take root in the earth: and he shall also blow upon them, and they shall where, and the whirlwind shall take them away as stubble.25 To whom then will you liken me, or shall I be equal? saith the Holy One.26 Lift up your eyes on high, and behold who has created these things, that bring out their host by number: he call them all by names by the greatness of his might, for that he is strong in power; not one faileth.

40:28
יעקב 3290 ותדבר 1696 ישראל 3478 נסתרה 5641 דרכי 1870 מיהוה 3068 ומאלהי 430 משפטי 4941 יעבור 5674:
ya'aqob, uatdaber yisra'ael; nistarah darkiy meYahuah, uame'alohay mishpatiy ya'abour.
**O Jacob and speak O Israel is hid My way from Yahuah and from my Elohim? my judgment is passed over**

הלוא 3808 ידעת 3045 אם 518 לא 3808 שמעת 8085 אלהי 430 עולם 5769 יהוה 3068 בורא 1254 קצות 7098
halou'a yada'ta 'am la' shama'ata, 'alohey 'aulam Yahuah bourea' qatzout
**not Have you known? or not have you heard Elohim *that* the everlasting Yahuah the Creator of the ends of**

הארץ 776 לא 3808 ייעף 3286 ולא 3808 ייגע 3021 אין 369 חקר 2714 לתבונתו 8394: 40:29 נתן 5414 ליעף 3287 כח 3581
ha'aretz, la' yiy'ap uala' yiyga'; 'aeyn cheqer litabunatou. noten laya'aep koach;
**the earth not faint neither is weary? *there is* no searching of his understanding He gives to the faint power**

ולאין 369 אונים 202 עצמה 6109 ירבה 7235: 40:30 ויעפו 3286 נערים 5288 ויגעו 3021 ובחורים 970
ual'aeyn 'auniym 'atzamah yarbeh. uayi'apu na'ariym uayiga'au; uabachuriym
**and to *them that have* no might strength he increase Even shall faint the youths and be weary and the young men**

כשול 3782 יכשלו 3782: 40:31 וקוי 6960 יהוה 3068 יחליפו 2498 כח 3581 יעלו 5927 אבר 83
kashoul yikashelu. uaqouye Yahuah yachaliypu koach, ya'alu 'aeber
**shall utterly fall But they that wait upon Yahuah shall renew *their* strength they shall mount up with wings**

כנשרים 5404 ירוצו 7323 ולא 3808 ייגעו 3021 ילכו 1980 ולא 3808 ייעפו:
kanashariym; yarutzu uala' yiyga'au, yelaku uala' yiy'apu.
**as eagles they shall run and not be weary *and* shall walk and not faint**

**Isa 41:1**
החרישו 2790 אלי 413 איים 339 ולאמים 3816 יחליפו 2498 כח 3581 יגשו 5066 אז 227 ידברו 1696
hachariyshu 'aelay 'ayiym, uala'amiym yachaliypu koach; yigshu 'az yadaberu,
**Keep silence before me O islands and the people let renew *their* strength let them come near then let them speak**

יחדו 3162 למשפט 4941 נקרבה 7126: 41:2 מי 4310 העיר 5782 ממזרח 4217 צדק 6664 יקראהו 7121 לרגלו 7272 יתן 5414
yachdau lamishpat niqrabah. miy' he'ayr mimizrach, tzedeq yiqra'aehu laraglou; yiten
**together to judgment let us come near Who raised up *man* from the east the righteous called him to his foot gave**

לפניו 6440 גוים 1471 ומלכים 4428 ירד 7287 יתן 5414 כעפר 6083 חרבו 2719 כקש 7179 נדף 5086
lapanayu gouyim uamalakiym yard, yiten ke'apar charbou, kaqash nidap
**before him the nations and kings? made *him* rule over he gave *them* as the dust *to* his sword *and* as stubble to driven**

קשתו 7198: 41:3 ירדפם 7291 יעבור 5674 שלום 7965 ארח 734 ברגליו 7272 לא 3808 יבוא 935: 41:4 מי 4310
qashtou. yirdapem ya'abour shaloum; 'arach baraglayu la' yabou'a. miy
**his bow He pursued them *and* passed safely *even* by the way with his feet not *that* he had gone Who**

פעל 6466 ועשה 6213 קרא 7121 הדרות 1755 מראש 2718 אני 589 יהוה 3068 ראשון 7223 ואת 853 אחרנים 314 אני 589
pa'al ua'asah, qorea' hadaurout mera'sh; 'aniy Yahuah ra'shoun, ua'at 'acharoniym 'aniy
**has wrought and done *it* calling the generations from the beginning? I Yahuah the first *and* *with* the last I *am***

הוא 1931: 41:5 ראו 7200 איים 339 וייראו 3372 קצות 7098 הארץ 776 יחרדו 2729 קרבו 7126 ויאתיון 857: 41:6 איש 376 את 853
hua'. ra'au 'ayiym uayiyra'au, qatzout ha'aretz yecharadu; qarabu uaye'atayun. 'aysh 'at
**he saw *it* The isles and feared the ends of the earth were afraid drew near and they came every one**

Isa 40:27 Why say you, O Jacob, and speak, O Israel, My way is hid from YHUH, and my judgment is passed over from my G-d?28 Hast you not known? have you not heard, that the everlasting G-d, YHUH, the Creator of the ends of the earth, fainteth not, neither is weary? there is no searching of his understanding.29 He give power to the faint; and to them that have no might he increaseth strength.30 Even the youths shall faint and be weary, and the young men shall utterly fall:31 But they that wait upon YHUH shall renew their strength; they shall mount up with wings as eagles; they shall run, and not be weary; and they shall walk, and not faint. **Isa** 41:1 Keep silence before me, O islands; and let the people renew their strength: let them come near; then let them speak: let us come near together to judgment.2 Who raised up the righteous man from the east, called him to his foot, gave the nations before him, and made him rule over kings? he gave them as the dust to his sword, and as driven stubble to his bow.3 He pursued them, and passed safely; even by the way that he had not gone with his feet.4 Who has wrought and done it, calling the generations from the beginning? I YHUH, the first, and with the last; I am he.

| | | | | 41:7 | | | |
|---|---|---|---|---|---|---|---|
| רעהו 7453 | יעזרו 5826 | ולאחיו 251 | יאמר 559 | חזק 2388: | ויחזק 2388 | חרש 2796 | את 853 |
| re'aehu | ya'zoru; | ual'achiyu | ya'mar | chazaq. | uaychazeq | charash | 'at |
| **his neighbour** | **They helped** | **and to his brother** | ***every one* said** | **Be of good courage** | **So encouraged** | **the carpenter** | |

| | | | | | | | | | |
|---|---|---|---|---|---|---|---|---|---|
| צרף 6884 | מחליק 2505 | פטיש 6360 | את 853 | הולם 1986 | פעם 6471 | אמר 559 | לדבק 1694 | טוב 2896 | הוא 1931 |
| tzorep, | machaliyq | patiysh | 'at | houlem | pa'am; | 'amer | ladebeq | toub | hua', |
| **the goldsmith** | ***and* he that smooth** | ***with* the hammer** | | **him that smote** | **the anvil** | **saying** | **for the sodering** | ***is* ready** | **It** |

| | | | | 41:8 | | | | |
|---|---|---|---|---|---|---|---|---|
| ויחזקהו 2388 | במסמרים 4548 | לא 3808 | ימוט 4131: | ואתה 859 | ישראל 3478 | עבדי 5650 | יעקב 3290 | אשר 834 |
| uayachazqehu | bamasmariym | la' | yimout. | ua'atah | yisra'el | 'abdiy, | ya'aqob | 'asher |
| **and he fastened it** | **with nails** | **not** | ***that* it should be moved** | **But you** | **Israel** | ***are* my servant** | **Jacob** | **whom** |

| | | | | 41:9 | | | |
|---|---|---|---|---|---|---|---|
| בחרתיך 977 | זרע 2233 | אברהם 85 | אהבי 157: | אשר 834 | החזקתיך 2388 | מקצות 7098 | הארץ 776 |
| bacharatiyka; | zera' | 'abraham | 'ahabiy. | 'asher | hechazaqtiyka | miqtzout | ha'aretz, |
| **I have chosen** | **the seed of** | **Abraham** | **my friend** | ***You* whom** | **I have taken** | **from the ends of** | **the earth** |

| | | | | | | | |
|---|---|---|---|---|---|---|---|
| ומאציליה 678 | קראתיך 7121 | ואמר 559 | לך 3807a | עבדי 5650 | אתה 859 | בחרתיך 977 | ולא 3808 |
| uame'atziyleyha | qaraa'tiyka; | ua'amar | laka | 'abdiy | 'atah, | bacharatiyka | uala' |
| **and from the chief men thereof** | **I called you** | **and said** | **unto you** | ***are* my servant** | **You** | **I have chosen you** | **and not** |

| | 41:10 | | | | | | | | | |
|---|---|---|---|---|---|---|---|---|---|---|
| מאסתיך 3988: | אל 408 | תירא 3372 | כי 3588 | עמך 5973 | אני 589 | אל 408 | תשתע 8159 | כי 3588 | אני 589 | אלהיך 430 |
| ma'astiyka. | 'al | tiyraa' | kiy | 'amaka | 'aniy, | 'al | tishta' | kiy | 'aniy | 'aloheyka; |
| **cast you away** | **not** | **Fear you** | **for *am*** | **with you** | **I** | **not** | **be dismayed** | **for** | **I** | ***am* your Elohim** |

| | | | | | | | 41:11 |
|---|---|---|---|---|---|---|---|
| אמצתיך 553 | אף 637 | עזרתיך 5826 | אף 637 | תמכתיך 8551 | בימין 3225 | צדקי 6664: | הן 2005 |
| 'amatztiyka | 'ap | 'azartiyka, | 'ap | tamaktiyka | biymiyn | tzidqiy. | hen |
| **I will strengthen you** | **yea** | **I will help you** | **yea** | **I will uphold you** | **with the right hand of** | **my righteousness** | **Behold** |

| | | | | | | | |
|---|---|---|---|---|---|---|---|
| יבשו 954 | ויכלמו 3637 | כל 3605 | הנחרים 2734 | בך 871a | יהיו 1961 | כאין 369 | ויאבדו 6 |
| yeboshu | uayikalamu, | kal | hanechariym | bak; | yihayu | ka'ayin | uaya'badu |
| **shall be ashamed** | **and confounded** | **all** | **they that were incensed** | **against you** | **they shall be** | **as nothing** | **and shall perish** |

| | | 41:12 | | | | | |
|---|---|---|---|---|---|---|---|
| אנשי 582 | ריבך 7379: | תבקשם 1245 | ולא 3808 | תמצאם 4672 | אנשי 582 | מצתך 4695 | יהיו 1961 |
| 'anshey | riybeka. | tabaqshem | uala' | timtza'em, | 'anshey | matzuteka; | yihayu |
| **they** | **that strive with you** | **You shall seek them** | **and not** | **shall find them** | ***even* them** | **that contended will you** | **shall be** |

| | | | | 41:13 | | | | |
|---|---|---|---|---|---|---|---|---|
| כאין 369 | וכאפס 657 | אנשי 582 | מלחמתך 4421: | כי 3588 | אני 589 | יהוה 3069 | אלהיך 430 | מחזיק 2388 |
| ka'ayin | uak'apes | 'anshey | milchamteka. | kiy, | 'aniy | Yahuah | 'aloheyka | machaziyq |
| **as nothing** | **and as a thing of nought** | **they** | **that war against you** | **For** | **I** | **Yahuah** | **your Elohim** | **will hold** |

| | | | | | | | 41:14 | | | | |
|---|---|---|---|---|---|---|---|---|---|---|---|
| ימינך 3225 | האמר 559 | לך 3807a | אל 408 | תירא 3372 | אני 589 | עזרתיך 5826: | אל 408 | תיראי 3372 | תולעת 8438 | יעקב 3290 | מתי 4962 |
| yamiyneka; | ha'amer | laka | 'al | tiyraa' | 'aniy | 'azartiyka. | 'al | tiyr'ay | toula'at | ya'aqob, | matey |
| **your right hand** | **saying** | **unto you** | **not** | **Fear** | **I** | **will help you** | **not** | **Fear** | ***you* worm** | **Jacob** | ***and* you men of** |

| | | | | | | | | 41:15 | |
|---|---|---|---|---|---|---|---|---|---|
| ישראל 3478 | אני 589 | עזרתיך 5826 | נאם 5002 | יהוה 3068 | וגאלך 1350 | קדוש 6918 | ישראל 3478: | הנה 2009 | שמתיך 7760 |
| yisra'el; | 'aniy | 'azartiyk | na'am | Yahuah, | uago'alek | qadoush | yisra'el. | hineh | samtiyk, |
| **Israel** | **I** | **will help you** | **saith** | **Yahuah** | **and your redeemer** | ***the* Holy One of** | **Israel** | **Behold** | **I will make you** |

Isa 41:5 The isles saw it, and feared; the ends of the earth were afraid, drew near, and came.6 They helped everyone his neighbor; and everyone said to his brother, Be of good courage.7 So the carpenter encouraged the goldsmith, and he that smootheth with the hammer him that smote the anvil, saying, It is ready for the sodering: and he fastened it with nails, that it should not be moved.8 But you, Israel, are my servant, Jacob whom I have chosen, the seed of Abraham my friend.9 Thou whom I have taken from the ends of the earth, and called you from the chief men thereof, and said unto you, Thou are my servant; I have chosen you, and not cast you away.10 Fear you not; for I am with you: be not dismayed; for I am your G-d: I will strengthen you; yea, I will help you; yea, I will uphold you with the right hand of my righteousness.11 Behold, all they that were incensed against you shall be ashamed and confounded: they shall be as nothing; and they that strive with you shall perish.12 Thou shall seek them, and shall not find them, even them that contended with you: they that war against you shall be as nothing, and as a thing of nought.13 For I YHUH your G-d will hold your right hand, saying unto you, Fear not; I will help you. 14 Fear not, you worm Jacob, and you men of Israel; I will help you, saith YHUH, and your redeemer, the Holy One of Israel.

למורג 4173 חרוץ 2742 חדש 2319 בעל 1167 פיפיות 6374 תדוש 1758 הרים 2022 ותדק 1854 וגבעות 1389
lamourag charutz chadash, ba'al piypiyout; tadush hariym uatadoq, uagba'aut
**a threshing instrument sharp new having teeth you shall thresh the mountains and beat *them* small and the hills**

כמץ 4671 תשים 7760: **41:16** תזרם 2219 ורוח 7307 תשאם 5375 וסערה 5591 תפיץ 6327 אותם 853
kamotz tasiym. tizrem uaruach tisa'aem, uas'arah tapiytz 'autam;
**as chaff shall make You shall fan them and the wind shall carry them away and the whirlwind shall scatter them**

ואתה 859 תגיל 1523 ביהוה 3068 בקדוש 6918 ישראל 3478 תתהלל 1984: **41:17** העניים 6041 והאביונים 34
ua'atah tagiyl baYahuah, biqdoush yisra'ael tithalal. ha'aniyiym uaha'abyouniym
**and you shall rejoice in Yahuah in the Holy One of Israel *and* shall glory *When* the poor and needy**

מבקשים 1245 מים 4325 ואין 369 לשונם 3956 בצמא 6772 נשתה 5405 אני 589 יהוה 3068 אענם 6030 אלהי 430
mabaqshiym mayim ua'ayin, lashounam batzama' nashatah; 'aniy Yahuah 'a'anem, 'alohey
**seek water and *there is* none *and* their tongue for thirst fail I Yahuah will hear them *I* the Elohim of**

ישראל 3478 לא 3808 אעזבם 5800: **41:18** אפתח 6605 על 5921 שפיים 8205 נהרות 5104 ובתוך 8432 בקעות 1237 מעינות 4599
yisra'ael la' 'a'azbem. 'aptach 'al shapayiym naharout, uabtouk baqa'aut ma'yanout;
**Israel not will forsake them I will open in high places rivers and in the midst of the valleys fountains**

אשים 7760 מדבר 4057 לאגם 98 מים 4325 וארץ 776 ציה 6723 למוצאי 4161 מים 4325: **41:19** אתן 5414 במדבר 4057
'asiym midbar la'agam mayim, ua'aretz tziyah lamoutza'aey mayim. 'aten bamidbar
**I will make the wilderness a pool of water and land *the* dry springs of water I will plant in the wilderness**

ארז 730 שטה 7848 והדס 1918 ועץ 6086 שמן 8081 אשים 7760 בערבה 6160 ברוש 1265 תדהר 8410 ותאשור 8391
'arez shitah, uahadas ua'aetz shamen; 'asiym ba'arabah, baroush tidhar uat'ashur
**the cedar the shittah tree and the myrtle and tree *the* oil I will set in the desert the fir tree *and* the pine and the box tree**

יחדו 3162: **41:20** למען 4616 יראו 7200 וידעו 3045 וישימו 7760 וישכילו 7919 יחדו 3162 כי 3588 יד 3027 יהוה 3068 עשתה 6213
yachdau. lama'an yir'au uayeda'au, uayasiymu uayaskiylu yachdau, kiy yad Yahuah 'astah
**together That they may see and know and consider and understand together that the hand of Yahuah has done**

זאת 2063 וקדוש 6918 ישראל 3478 בראה 1254: **41:21** קרבו 7126 ריבכם 7379 יאמר 559 יהוה 3068 הגישו 5066 עצמותיכם 6110
za't; uaqadoush yisra'ael bara'ah. qarabu riybakem ya'mar Yahuah; hagiyshu atzumouteykem,
**this and the Holy One of Israel has created it Produce your cause saith Yahuah bring forth your strong**

יאמר 559 מלך 4428 יעקב 3290: **41:22** יגישו 5066 ויגידו 5046 לנו 3807a את 853 אשר 834 תקרינה 7136
ya'mar melek ya'aqob. yagiyshu uayagiydu lanu, 'at 'asher tiqreynah;
***reasons* saith the King of Jacob Let them bring *them* forth and show us what shall happen**

הראשנות 7223 מה 4100 הנה 2007 הגידו 5046 ונשימה 7760 לבנו 3820 ונדעה 3045 אחריתן 319 או 176
hara'shonout mah henah, hagiydu uanasiymah libenu uaned'ah 'achariytan, 'au
**the former things what they *be* let them show that we may consider them and know the latter end of them or**

הבאות 935 השמיענו 8085: **41:23** הגידו 5046 האתיות 857 לאחור 268 ונדעה 3045 כי 3588 אלהים 430 אתם 859
haba'aut hashmiy'unu. hagiydu ha'atiyout la'achour, uaned'ah, kiy 'alohiym 'atem;
**things for to come declare us Shew the things that are to come hereafter that we may know that *are* gods you**

Isa 41:15 Behold, I will make you a new sharp threshing instrument having teeth: you shall thresh the mountains, and beat them small, and shall make the hills as chaff.16 Thou shall fan them, and the wind shall carry them away, and the whirlwind shall scatter them: and you shall rejoice in YHUH, and shall glory in the Holy One of Israel.17 When the poor and needy seek water, and there is none, and their tongue faileth for thirst, I YHUH will hear them, I the G-d of Israel will not forsake them.18 I will open rivers in high places, and fountains in the midst of the valleys: I will make the wilderness a pool of water, and the dry land springs of water.19 I will plant in the wilderness the cedar, the shittah tree, and the myrtle, and the oil tree; I will set in the desert the fir tree, and the pine, and the box tree together:20 That they may see, and know, and consider, and understand together, that the hand of YHUH has done this, and the Holy One of Israel has created it.21 Produce your cause, saith YHUH; bring forth your strong reasons, saith the King of Jacob.22 Let them bring them forth, and show us what shall happen: let them show the former things, what they be, that we may consider them, and know the latter end of them; or declare us things for to come. 23 Shew the things that are to come hereafter, that we may know that you are gods:

אף 637 תיטיבו 3190 ותרעו 7489 ונשתעה 8159 ונרא 7200 יחדו 3162: **41:24** הן 2005 אתם 859 מאין 369 ופעלכם 6467
'ap teytiybu uatare'au, uanishta'ah uanera' yachdau. hen 'atem me'ayin, uapa'alakem
**yea do good or do evil that we may be dismayed and behold *it* together Behold you *are* of nothing and your work**

מאפע 659 תועבה 8441 יבחר 977 בכם 871a: **41:25** העירותי 5782 מצפון 6828 ויאת 857
me'apa'; tou'aebah yibchar bakem. ha'ayroutiy mitzapoun uayat,
**of nought an abomination *is he that* choose you I have raised up *one* from the north and he shall come**

ממזרח 4217 שמש 8121 יקרא 7121 בשמי 8034 ויבא 935 סגנים 5461 כמו 3644 חמר 2563 וכמו 3644 יוצר 3335
mimizrach shemesh yiqra' bishmiy; uayaba' saganiym kamou chomer, uakmou youtzer
**from the rising of the sun shall he call upon my name and he shall come princes as *upon* morter and as the potter**

ירמס 7429 טיט 2916: **41:26** מי 4310 הגיד 5046 מראש 2718 ונדעה 3045 ומלפנים 6440 ונאמר 559
yirmos tiyt. miy' higiyd mera'sh uaneda'ah, uamilpaniym uana'mar
**tread clay Who has declared from the beginning that we may know? and beforetime that we may say**

צדיק 6662 אף 637 אין 369 מגיד 5046 אף 637 אין 369 משמיע 8085 אף 637 אין 369 שמע 8085
tzadiyq; 'ap 'aeyn magiyd, 'ap 'aeyn mashmiya', 'ap 'aeyn shomea'
***He is* righteous? yea *there is* none that show yea *there is* none that declareth yea *there is* none that hear**

אמריכם 561: **41:27** ראשון 7223 לציון 6726 הנה 2009 הנם 2005 ולירושלם 3389 מבשר 1319
'amreykem. ra'shoun latziyoun hineh hinam; ualiyarushalaim mabaser
**your words The first *shall say* to Zion Behold behold them and to Jerusalem one that bring good tidings**

אתן 5414: **41:28** וארא 7200 ואין 369 איש 376 ומאלה 428 ואין 369 יועץ 3289 ואשאלם 7592
'aten. ua'aera' ua'aeyn 'aysh, uame'aleh ua'aeyn you'aetz; ua'ash'alem
**I will give For I beheld and *there was* no man even among them and *there was* no counsellor when I asked of them**

וישיבו 7725 דבר 1697: **41:29** הן 2005 כלם 3605 און 205 אפס 657 מעשיהם 4639 רוח 7307 ותהו 8414
uayashiybu dabar. hen kulam, 'auen 'apes ma'aseyhem; ruach uatohu
**that could answer a word Behold they *are* all vanity *are* nothing their works *are* wind and confusion**

נסכיהם 5262:
niskeyhem.
**their molten images**

**Isa 42:1** הן 2005 עבדי 5650 אתמך 8551 בו 871a בחירי 972 רצתה 7521 נפשי 5315 נתתי 5414 רוחי 7307 עליו 5921 משפט 4941
hen 'abdiy 'atmak bou, bachiyriy ratzatah napshiy; natatiy ruchiy 'alayu, mishapat
**Behold my servant I uphold whom mine elect delight *in whom* my soul I have put my spirit upon him judgment**

לגוים 1471 יוציא 3318: **42:2** לא 3808 יצעק 6817 ולא 3808 ישא 5375 ולא 3808 ישמיע 8085 בחוץ 2351
lagouyim youtziy'a. la' yitz'aq uala' yisa'; uala' yashmiya' bachutz
**to the Gentiles he shall bring forth not He shall cry nor lift up nor cause to be heard in the street**

קולו 6963: **42:3** קנה 7070 רצוץ 7533 לא 3808 ישבור 7665 ופשתה 6594 כהה 3544 לא 3808 יכבנה 3518 לאמת 571
qoulou. qaneh ratzutz la' yishbour, uapishtah kehah la' yakabenah; le'amet
**his voice A reed bruised not shall he break and flax the smoking not shall he quench unto truth**

Isa 41:23yea, do good, or do evil, that we may be dismayed, and behold it together.24 Behold, you are of nothing, and your work of nought: an abomination is he that chooseth you.25 I have raised up one from the north, and he shall come: from the rising of the sun shall he call upon my name: and he shall come upon princes as upon morter, and as the potter treadeth clay.26 Who has declared from the beginning, that we may know? and beforetime, that we may say, He is righteous? yea, there is none that show, yea, there is none that declareth, yea, there is none that hear your words.27 The first shall say to Zion, Behold, behold them: and I will give to Jerusalem one that bring good tidings.28 For I beheld, and there was no man; even among them, and there was no counselor, that, when I asked of them, could answer a word.29 Behold, they are all vanity; their works are nothing: their molten images are wind and confusion. **Isa** 42:1 Behold my servant, whom I uphold; mine elect, in whom my soul delighteth; I have put my spirit upon him: he shall bring forth judgment to the Gentiles.2 He shall not cry, nor lift up, nor cause his voice to be heard in the street.3 A bruised reed shall he not break, and the smoking flax shall he not quench: he shall bring forth judgment unto truth.

| יוציא 3318 | משפט 4941: | 42:4 | לא 3808 | יכהה 3543 | ולא 3808 | ירוץ 7533 | עד 5704 | ישים 7760 | בארץ 776 | משפט 4941 |
|---|---|---|---|---|---|---|---|---|---|---|
| youtziy'a | mishapat. | | la' | yikheh | uala' | yarutz, | 'ad | yasiym | ba'aretz | mishapat; |
| **he shall bring forth** | **judgment** | | **not** | **He shall fail** | **nor** | **be discouraged** | **till** | **he have set** | **in the earth** | **judgment** |

| ולתורתו 8451 | איים 339 | ייחילו 3176: | 42:5 | כה 3541 | אמר 559 | האל 410 | יהוה 3068 | בורא 1254 | השמים 8064 | ונוטיהם 5186 |
|---|---|---|---|---|---|---|---|---|---|---|
| ualtouratou | 'ayiym | yayacheylu. | | koh | 'amar | ha'ael | Yahuah | bourea' | hashamayim | uanouteyhem, |
| **and for his law** | **the isles** | **shall wait** | | **Thus** | **saith** | **the El** | **Yahuah** | **he that created** | **the heavens** | **and stretched them out** |

| רקע 7554 | הארץ 776 | וצאצאיה 6631 | נתן 5414 | נשמה 5397 | לעם 5971 | עליה 5921 | ורוח 7307 |
|---|---|---|---|---|---|---|---|
| roqa' | ha'aretz | uatze'atza'ayha; | noten | nashamah | la'am | 'aleyha, | uaruach |
| **he that spread forth** | **the earth** | **and that which comes out of it** | **he that gives** | **breath** | **unto the people** | **upon it** | **and spirit** |

| להלכים 1980 | בה 871a: | 42:6 | אני 589 | יהוה 3068 | קראתיך 7121 | בצדק 6664 | ואחזק 2388 | בידך 3027 | ואצרך 5341 |
|---|---|---|---|---|---|---|---|---|---|
| laholakiym | bah. | | 'aniy | Yahuah | qaraa'tiyka | batzedeq | ua'achzeq | bayadeka; | ua'atzaraka, |
| **to them that walk** | **therein** | | **I** | **Yahuah** | **have called you** | **in righteousness** | **and will hold** | **your hand** | **and will keep you** |

| ואתנך 5414 | לברית 1285 | עם 5971 | לאור 216 | גוים 1471: | 42:7 | לפקח 6491 | עינים 5869 | עורות 5787 | להוציא 3318 |
|---|---|---|---|---|---|---|---|---|---|
| ua'atenka | libriyt | 'am | la'aur | gouyim. | | lipqoach | 'aeynayim | 'aurout; | lahoutziy'a |
| **and give you** | **for a covenant of** | **the people** | **for a light of** | **the Gentiles** | | **To open** | **eyes *the*** | **blind** | **to bring out** |

| ממסגר 4525 | אסיר 616 | מבית 1004 | כלא 3608 | ישבי 3427 | חשך 2822: | 42:8 | אני 589 | יהוה 3068 | הוא 1931 | שמי 8034 |
|---|---|---|---|---|---|---|---|---|---|---|
| mimasger | 'asiyr, | mibeyt | kele' | yoshabey | choshek. | | 'aniy | Yahuah | hua' | shamiy; |
| **from the prison** | **the prisoners** | **out of house** | ***the* prison** | ***and* them that sit in** | **darkness** | | **I *am*** | **Yahuah** | **that** | ***is* my name** |

| וכבודי 3519 | לאחר 312 | לא 3808 | אתן 5414 | ותהלתי 8416 | לפסילים 6456: | 42:9 | הראשנות 7223 | הנה 2009 |
|---|---|---|---|---|---|---|---|---|
| uakboudiy | la'acher | la' | 'aten, | uatahilatiy | lapasiyliym. | | hara'shonout | hineh |
| **and my glory** | **to another** | **not** | **will I give** | **neither my praise** | **to graven images** | | **the former things** | **Behold** |

| באו 935 | וחדשות 2319 | אני 589 | מגיד 5046 | בטרם 2962 | תצמחנה 6779 | אשמיע 8085 | אתכם 853: | 42:10 | שירו 7891 |
|---|---|---|---|---|---|---|---|---|---|
| ba'au; | uachadashout | 'aniy | magiyd, | baterem | titzmachnah | 'ashmiya' | 'atkem. | | shiyru |
| **are come to pass** | **and new things** | **I** | **do declare** | **before** | **they spring forth** | **I tell** | **you *of them*** | | **Sing** |

| ליהוה 3068 | שיר 7892 | חדש 2319 | תהלתו 8416 | מקצה 7097 | הארץ 776 | יורדי 3381 | הים 3220 | ומלאו 4393 |
|---|---|---|---|---|---|---|---|---|
| laYahuah | shiyr | chadash, | tahilatou | miqtzeh | ha'aretz; | youradey | hayam | uamlo'au, |
| **unto Yahuah** | **a song** | **new** | ***and* his praise** | **from the end of** | **the earth** | **you that go down to** | **the sea** | **and all that is therein** |

| איים 339 | וישביהם 3427: | 42:11 | ישאו 5375 | מדבר 4057 | ועריו 5892 | חצרים 2691 |
|---|---|---|---|---|---|---|
| 'ayiym | uayoshabeyhem. | | yis'au | midbar | ua'arayu, | chatzeriym |
| **the isles** | **and the inhabitants thereof** | | **Let lift up *their voice*** | **the wilderness** | **and the cities thereof** | **the villages** |

| תשב 3427 | קדר 6938 | ירנו 7442 | ישבי 3427 | סלע 5554 | מראש 2718 | הרים 2022 | יצוחו 6681: | 42:12 |
|---|---|---|---|---|---|---|---|---|
| tesheb | qedar; | yaronu | yoshabey | sela', | mera'sh | hariym | yitzuachu. | |
| **does inhabit** | ***that* Kedar** | **let sing** | **the inhabitants of** | **the rock** | **from the top of** | **the mountains** | **let them shout** | |

| ישימו 7760 | ליהוה 3068 | כבוד 3519 | ותהלתו 8416 | באיים 339 | יגידו 5046: | 42:13 | יהוה 3068 | כגבור 1368 | יצא 3318 |
|---|---|---|---|---|---|---|---|---|---|
| yasiymu | laYahuah | kaboud; | uatahilatou | ba'ayiym | yagiydu. | | Yahuah | kagibour | yetzea', |

**Let them give unto Yahuah glory** **and his praise in the islands declare** **Yahuah as a mighty man shall go forth**

Isa 42:4 He shall not fail nor be discouraged, till he have set judgment in the earth: and the isles shall wait for his law.5 Thus saith G-d YHUH, he that created the heavens, and stretched them out; he that spread forth the earth, and that which cometh out of it; he that give breath unto the people upon it, and spirit to them that walk therein:6 I YHUH have called you in righteousness, and will hold your hand, and will keep you, and give you for a covenant of the people, for a light of the Gentiles;7 To open the blind eyes, to bring out the prisoners from the prison, and them that sit in darkness out of the prison house.8 I am YHUH: that is my name: and my glory will I not give to another, neither my praise to graven images.9 Behold, the former things are come to pass, and new things do I declare: before they spring forth I tell you of them.10 Sing unto YHUH a new song, and his praise from the end of the earth, you that go down to the sea, and all that is therein; the isles, and the inhabitants thereof.11 Let the wilderness and the cities thereof lift up their voice, the villages that Kedar doth inhabit: let the inhabitants of the rock sing, let them shout from the top of the mountains.12 Let them give glory unto YHUH, and declare his praise in the islands.13 YHUH shall go forth as a mighty man, he shall stir up jealousy like a man of war: he shall cry, yea, roar; he shall prevail against his enemies.

42:14

כאיש 376 מלחמות 4421 יעיר 5782 קנאה 7068 יריע 7321 אף 637 יצריח 6873 על 5921 איביו 341 יתגבר 1396:

ka'aysh milchamout ya'ayr qin'ah; yariya' 'ap yatzriyach, 'al 'ayabayu yitgabar.

**like a man of war he shall stir up jealousy he shall cry yea roar against his enemies he shall prevail**

החשיתי 2814 מעולם 5769 אחריש 2790 אתאפק 662 כיולדה 3205 אפעה 6463 אשם 5395

hechesheytiy me'aulam, 'achariysh 'at'apaq; kayouledah 'ap'ah, 'ashom

**I have holden my peace long time I have been still *and* refrained myself like a travailing woman *now* will I cry I will destroy**

42:15

ואשאף 7602 יחד 3162: אחריב 2717 הרים 2022 וגבעות 1389 וכל 3605 עשבם 6212 אוביש 3001 ושמתי 7760 נהרות 5104

ua'ash'ap yachad. 'achariyb hariym uagba'aut, uakal 'asbam 'aubiysh; uasamtiy naharout

**and devour at once I will make waste mountains and hills and all their herbs dry up and I will make the rivers**

42:16

לאיים 339 ואגמים 98 אוביש 3001: והולכתי 1980 עורים 5787 בדרך 1870 לא 3808 ידעו 3045 בנתיבות 5410 לא 3808

la'ayiym, ua'agamiym 'aubiysh. uahoulaktiy 'auriym, baderek la' yada'au, bintiybout la'

**islands and the pools I will dry up And I will bring the blind by a way not *that* they knew in paths not**

ידעו 3045 אדריכם 1869 אשים 7760 מחשך 4285 לפניהם 6440 לאור 216 ומעקשים 4625 למישור 4334 אלה 428

yada'au 'adriykem; 'asiym machshak lipneyhem la'aur, uama'aqashiym lamiyshour, 'aeleh

***that* they have known I will lead them I will make darkness before them light and crooked things straight These**

42:17

הדברים 1697 עשיתם 6213 ולא 3808 עזבתים 5800: נסגו 5472 אחור 268 יבשו 954 בשת 1322

hadabariym, 'asiytim uala' 'azabtiym. nasougu 'achour yeboshu boshet,

**things will I do unto them and not forsake them They shall be turned back they shall be ashamed greatly**

42:18

הבטחים 982 בפסל 6459 האמרים 559 למסכה 4541 אתם 859 אלהינו 430: החרשים 2795 שמעו 8085

habotachiym bapasel; ha'amariym lamasekah 'atem 'aloheynu. hacherashiym shama'au;

**that trust in graven images that say to the molten images You *are* our gods you deaf Hear**

42:19

והעורים 5787 הביטו 5027 לראות 7200: מי 4310 עור 5787 כי 3588 אם 518 עבדי 5650 וחרש 2795 כמלאכי 4397 אשלח 7971

uaha'auariym habiytu lira'aut. miy' 'aur kiy 'am 'abdiy, uacheresh kamal'akiy 'ashlach;

**and you blind look that you may see Who *is* blind but only my servant? or deaf as my messenger *that* I sent?**

42:20

מי 4310 עור 5787 כמשלם 7999 ועור 5787 כעבד 5650 יהוה 3068: ראית 7200 רבות 7227 ולא 3808 תשמר 8104

miy' 'aur kimashulam, ua'auer ka'abed Yahuah. ra'ayta rabout uala' tishmor;

**who *is* blind as *he that is* perfect and blind as servant? Yahuah's Seeing many things but not you observest**

42:21

פקוח 6491 אזנים 241 ולא 3808 ישמע 8085: יהוה 3068 חפץ 2654 למען 4616 צדקו 6664 יגדיל 1431 תורה 8451

paqouach 'azanayim uala' yishma'. Yahuah chapetz lama'an tzidqou; yagdiyl tourah

**opening the ears but not he hear Yahuah is well pleased for sake his righteousness' he will magnify the law**

42:22

ויאדיר 142: והוא 1931 עם 5973 בזוז 962 ושסוי 8154 הפח 6351 בחורים 2352 כלם 3605 ובבתי 1004

uaya'diyr. uahu'a 'am bazuz uashasuy hapeach bachuriym kulam, uabbatey

**and make *it* honorable But this *is* a people robbed and spoiled snared in holes *they are* all of them and in houses**

42:23

כלאים 3608 החבאו 2244 היו 1961 לבז 957 ואין 369 מציל 5337 משסה 4933 ואין 369 אמר 559 השב 7725: מי 4310

kala'aym hachaba'au; hayu labaz ua'aeyn matziyl, mashisah ua'aeyn 'amer hashab. miy'

**prison they are hid they are for a prey and none deliver *for* a spoil and none saith Restore Who**

Isa 42:14 I have long time holden my peace; I have been still, and refrained myself: now will I cry like a travailing woman; I will destroy and devour at once.15 I will make waste mountains and hills, and dry up all their herbs; and I will make the rivers islands, and I will dry up the pools.16 And I will bring the blind by a way that they knew not; I will lead them in paths that they have not known: I will make darkness light before them, and crooked things straight. These things will I do unto them, and not forsake them.17 They shall be turned back, they shall be greatly ashamed, that trust in graven images, that say to the molten images, You are our gods.18 Hear, you deaf; and look, you blind, that you may see.19 Who is blind, but my servant? or deaf, as my messenger that I sent? who is blind as he that is perfect, and blind as YHUH's servant?20 Seeing manythings, but you observest not; opening the ears, but he hear not.21 YHUH is well pleased for his righteousness' sake; he will magnify the law, and make it honourable.22 But this is a people robbed and spoiled; they are all of them snared in holes, and they are hid in prison houses: they are for a prey, and none delivereth; for a spoil, and none saith, Restore.

בכם 871a יאזין 238 זאת 2063 יקשב 7181 וישמע 8085 לאחור 268: 42:24 מי 4310 נתן 5414 למשוסה 4882 יעקב 3290
bakem ya'aziyn za't; yaqshib uayishma' la'achour. miy' natan limshouseh ya'aqob
**among you will give ear to this? *who* will listen and hear for the time to come? Who gave for a spoil, Jacob**

וישראל 3478 לבוזים 962 הלוא 3808 יהוה 3069 זו 2098 חטאנו 2398 לו 3807a ולא 3808 אבו 14 בדרכיו 1870 הלוך 1980
uayisra'ael labozaziym halou'a Yahuah; zu chata'nu lou', uala' 'abu bidrakayu halouk,
**and Israel to the robbers? did not Yahuah whom we have sinned? he against for not they would in his ways walk**

ולא 3808 שמעו 8085 בתורתו 8451: 42:25 וישפך 8210 עליו 5921 חמה 2534 אפו 639 ועזוז 5807
uala' shama'au batouratou. uayishpok 'alayu chemah 'apou, ue'azuz
**neither were they obedient unto his law Therefore he has poured upon him the fury of his anger and the strength of**

מלחמה 4421 ותלהטהו 3857 מסביב 5439 ולא 3808 ידע 3045 ותבער 1197 בו 871a ולא 3808 ישים 7760 על 5921 לב 3820:
milchamah; uatalahatehu misabiyb uala' yada', uatib'ar bou uala' yasiym 'al leb.
**battle and it has set him on fire round about yet not he knew and it burned him yet not he laid *it* to heart**

Isa 43:1 ועתה 6258 כה 3541 אמר 559 יהוה 3068 בראך 1254 יעקב 3290 ויצרך 3335 ישראל 3478 אל 408 תירא 3372 כי 3588
ua'atah koh 'amar Yahuah bora'aka ya'aqob, uayotzerka yisra'ael; 'al tiyraa' kiy
**But now thus saith Yahuah that created you O Jacob and he that formed you O Israel not Fear for**

גאלתיך 1350 קראתי 7121 בשמך 8034 לי 3807a אתה 859: 43:2 כי 3588 תעבר 5674 במים 4325
ga'altiyka, qaraa'tiy bashimaka liy 'atah. kiy ta'abor bamayim
**I have redeemed you I have called *you* by your name *are* mine you When you passest throughthe waters**

אתך 854 אני 589 ובנהרות 5104 לא 3808 ישטפוך 7857 כי 3588 תלך 1980 במו 1119 אש 784 לא 3808
'ataka 'aniy, uabanharout la' yishtapuka; kiy telek bamou 'aesh la'
***will be* with you I and through the rivers not they shall overflow you when you walk through the fire not**

תכוה 3554 ולהבה 3852 לא 3808 תבער 1197 בך 871a: 43:3 כי 3588 אני 589 יהוה 3069 אלהיך 430 קדוש 6918
tikaueh, ualehabah la' tib'ar bak. kiy, 'aniy Yahuah 'aloheyka, qadoush
**you shall be burned the flame neither shall kindle upon you For I *am* Yahuah your Elohim *the* Holy One of**

ישראל 3478 מושיעך 3467 נתתי 5414 כפרך 3724 מצרים 4714 כוש 3568 וסבא 5434 תחתיך 8478: 43:4 מאשר 834 יקרת 3365
yisra'ael moushiy'aka; natatiy kapraka mitzrayim, kush uasaba' tachteyka. me'asher yaqarta
**Israel your Saviour I gave *for* your ransom Egypt Ethiopia and Seba for you Since you was precious**

בעיני 5869 נכבדת 3513 ואני 589 אהבתיך 157 ואתן 5414 אדם 120 תחתיך 8478 ולאמים 3816 תחת 8478
ba'aeynay nikbadta ua'aniy 'ahabtiyka; ua'aten 'adam tachteyka, uala'amiym tachat
**in my sight you have been honorable and I have loved you therefore will I give men for you and people for**

נפשך 5315: 43:5 אל 408 תירא 3372 כי 3588 אתך 854 אני 589 ממזרח 4217 אביא 935 זרעך 2233 וממערב 4628
napsheka. 'al tiyraa' kiy 'ataka 'aniy; mimizrach 'abiy'a zar'aka, uamima'arab
**your life not Fear for *am* with you I from the east I will bring your seed and from the west**

אקבצך 6908: 43:6 אמר 559 לצפון 6828 תני 5414 ולתימן 8486 אל 408 תכלאי 3607 הביאי 935 בני 1121 מרחוק 7350
'aqabtzeka. 'amar latzapoun teniy, ualteyman 'al tikla'ay; habiy'ay banay merachouq,
**gather you I will say to the north Give up and to the south not Keep back bring my sons from far**

Isa 42:23 Who among you will give ear to this? who will hear and hear for the time to come?24 Who gave Jacob for a spoil, and Israel to the robbers? did not YHUH, he against whom we have sinned? for they would not walk in his ways, neither were they obedient unto his law.25 Therefore he has poured upon him the fury of his anger, and the strength of battle: and it has set him on fire round about, yet he knew not; and it burned him, yet he laid it not to heart. **Isa** 43:1 But now thus saith YHUH that created you, O Jacob, and he that formed you, O Israel, Fear not: for I have redeemed you, I have called you by your name; you are mine.2 When you passest through the waters, I will be with you; and through the rivers, they shall not overflow you: when you walk through the fire, you shall not be burned; neither shall the flame kindle upon you.3 For I am YHUH your G-d, the Holy One of Israel, your Saviour: I gave Egypt for your ransom, Ethiopia and Seba for you.4 Since you were precious in my sight, you have been honourable, and I have loved you: therefore will I give men for you, and people for your life.5 Fear not: for I am with you: I will bring your seed from the east, and gather you from the west;6 I will say to the north, Give up; and to the south, Keep not back: bring my sons from far, and my daughters from the ends of the earth;

| ובנותי 1323 | מקצה 7097 | הארץ 776: | 43:7 כל 3605 | הנקרא 7121 | בשמי 8034 | ולכבודי 3519 |
|---|---|---|---|---|---|---|
| uabnoutay | miqtzeh | ha'aretz. | kal | haniqra' | bishmiy, | ualikboudiy |
| **and my daughters** | **from the ends of** | **the earth** | ***Even* every one** | **that is called** | **by my name** | **for my glory** |

| בראתיו 1254 | יצרתיו 3335 | אף 637 | עשיתיו 6213: | 43:8 הוציא 3318 | עם 5971 | עור 5787 | ועינים 5869 | יש 3426 |
|---|---|---|---|---|---|---|---|---|
| bara'tiyu; | yatzartiyu | 'ap | 'asiytiyu. | houtziy'a | 'am | 'aur | ua'aynayim | yesh; |
| **I have created him *for*** | **I have formed him** | **yea** | **I have made him** | **Bring forth** | **people** | ***the* blind** | **that eyes** | **have** |

| וחרשים 2795 | ואזנים 241 | למו 3807a: | 43:9 כל 3605 | הגוים 1471 | נקבצו 6908 | יחדו 3162 | ויאספו 622 | לאמים 3816 |
|---|---|---|---|---|---|---|---|---|
| uacherashiym | ua'azanayim | lamou. | kal | hagouyim | niqbatzu | yachdau, | uaye'asapu | la'amiym, |
| **and the deaf that** | **ears** | **have** | **all** | **the nations** | **Let be gathered** | **together** | **and let be assembled** | **the people** |

| מי 4310 | בהם 871a | יגיד 5046 | זאת 2063 | וראשנות 7223 | ישמיענו 8085 | יתנו 5414 | עדיהם 5707 |
|---|---|---|---|---|---|---|---|
| miy' | bahem | yagiyd | za't, | uara'shonout | yashmiy'anu; | yitanu | 'aedeyhem |
| **who** | **among them** | **can declare** | **this** | **and former things?** | **show us** | **let them bring forth** | **their witnesses** |

| ויצדקו 6663 | וישמעו 8085 | ויאמרו 559 | אמת 571: | 43:10 אתם 859 | עדי 5707 | נאם 5002 | יהוה 3068 |
|---|---|---|---|---|---|---|---|
| uayitzdaqu, | uayishma'au | uaya'maru | 'amet. | 'atem | 'aeday | na'am | Yahuah, |
| **that they may be justified** | **or let them hear** | **and say** | ***It is* truth** | **You** | ***are* my witnesses** | **saith** | **Yahuah** |

| ועבדי 5650 | אשר 834 | בחרתי 977 | למען 4616 | תדעו 3045 | ותאמינו 539 | לי 3807a | ותבינו 995 | כי 3588 | אני 589 | הוא 1931 |
|---|---|---|---|---|---|---|---|---|---|---|
| ua'abdiy | 'asher | bacharatiy; | lama'an | teda'au | uata'amiynu | liy | uatabiynu | kiy | 'aniy | hua', |
| **and my servant** | **whom** | **I have chosen** | **that** | **you may know** | **and believe** | **me** | **and understand** | **that** | **I *am*** | **he** |

| לפני 6440 | לא 3808 | נוצר 3335 | אל 410 | ואחרי 310 | לא 3808 | יהיה 1961: | 43:11 אנכי 595 | אנכי 595 | יהוה 3068 | ואין 369 |
|---|---|---|---|---|---|---|---|---|---|---|
| lapanay | la' | noutzar | 'ael, | ua'acharay | la' | yihayeh. | 'anokiy | 'anokiy | Yahuah; | ua'aeyn |
| **before me** | **no** | **there was formed** | **El** | **after me** | **neither** | **shall there be** | **I *even*** | **I *am*** | **Yahuah** | **and *there is* no** |

| מבלעדי 1107 | מושיע 3467: | 43:12 אנכי 595 | הגדתי 5046 | והושעתי 3467 | והשמעתי 8085 | ואין 369 | בכם 871a |
|---|---|---|---|---|---|---|---|
| mibal'aday | moushiya'. | 'anokiy | higadtiy | uahousha'tiy | uahishma'atiy, | ua'aeyn | bakem |
| **beside me** | **saviour** | **I** | **have declared** | **and have saved** | **and I have showed** | **and when *there was* no** | ***god* among you** |

| זר 2114 | ואתם 859 | עדי 5707 | נאם 5002 | יהוה 3068 | ואני 589 | אל 410: | 43:13 גם 1571 | מיום 3117 | אני 589 | הוא 1931 |
|---|---|---|---|---|---|---|---|---|---|---|
| zar; | ua'atem | 'aeday | na'am | Yahuah | ua'aniy | 'ael. | gam | miyoum | 'aniy | hua', |
| **strange** | **therefore you *are*** | **my witnesses** | **saith** | **Yahuah** | **that I *am*** | **El** | **Yea** | **before the day** | ***was* I** | ***am* he** |

| ואין 369 | מידי 3027 | מציל 5337 | אפעל 6466 | ומי 4310 | ישיבנה 7725: | 43:14 כה 3541 | אמר 559 | יהוה 3068 |
|---|---|---|---|---|---|---|---|---|
| ua'aeyn | miyadiy | matziyl; | 'ap'al | uamiy | yashiybenah. | koh | 'amar | Yahuah |
| **and *there is* none** | **out of my hand** | **that can deliver** | **I will work** | **and who** | **shall let it?** | **Thus** | **saith** | **Yahuah** |

| גאלכם 1350 | קדוש 6918 | ישראל 3478 | למענכם 4616 | שלחתי 7971 | בבלה 894 | והורדתי 3381 | בריחים 1281 | כלם 3605 |
|---|---|---|---|---|---|---|---|---|
| go'alkem | qadoush | yisra'ael; | lama'anakem | shilachtiy | babelah, | uahouradtiy | bariychiym | kulam, |
| **your redeemer *the*** | **Holy One of** | **Israel** | **For your sake** | **I have sent** | **to Babylon** | **and have brought down** | **their nobles** | **all** |

| וכשדים 3778 | באניות 591 | רנתם 7440: | 43:15 אני 589 | יהוה 3068 | קדושכם 6918 | בורא 1254 | ישראל 3478 | מלככם 4428: |
|---|---|---|---|---|---|---|---|---|
| uakasdiym | ba'aniyout | rinatam. | 'aniy | Yahuah | qadoushakem; | bourea' | yisra'ael | malkakem. |
| **and the Chaldeans *is*** | **in the ships** | **whose cry** | **I *am*** | **Yahuah** | **your Holy One** | **the creator of** | **Israel** | **your King** |

Isa 43:7 Even everyone that is called by my name: for I have created him for my glory, I have formed him; yea, I have made him.8 Bring forth the blind people that have eyes, and the deaf that have ears.9 Let all the nations be gathered together, and let the people be assembled: who among them can declare this, and show us former things? let them bring forth their witnesses, that they may be justified: or let them hear, and say, It is truth.10 You are my witnesses, saith YHUH, and my servant whom I have chosen: that you may know and believe me, and understand that I am he: before me there was no G-d formed, neither shall there be after me.11 I, even I, am YHUH; and beside me there is no savior.12 I have declared, and have saved, and I have showed, when there was no strange god among you: therefore you are my witnesses, saith YHUH, that I am G-d.13 Yea, before the day was I am he; and there is none that can deliver out of my hand: I will work, and who shall let it?14 Thus saith YHUH, your redeemer, the Holy One of Israel; For your sake I have sent to Babylon, and have brought down all their nobles, and the Chaldeans, whose cry is in the ships.15 I am YHUH, your Holy One, the creator of Israel, your King.

| 43:16 כה 3541 | אמר 559 | יהוה 3068 | הנותן 5414 | בים 3220 | דרך 1870 | ובמים 4325 | עזים 5794 | נתיבה 5410: | 43:17 המוציא 3318 |
|---|---|---|---|---|---|---|---|---|---|
| koh | 'amar | Yahuah, | hanouten | bayam | darek; | uabmayim | 'aziym | natiybah. | hamoutziy'a |
| **Thus** | **saith** | **Yahuah** | **which make** | **in the sea** | **a way** | **and in the waters** | **mighty** | **a path** | **Which bring forth** |

| רכב 7393 | וסוס 5483 | חיל 2428 | ועזוז 5808 | יחדו 3162 | ישכבו 7901 | בל 1077 | יקומו 6965 | דעכו 1846 | כפשתה 6594 |
|---|---|---|---|---|---|---|---|---|---|
| rekeb | uasus | chayil | ua'azuz; | yachdau | yishkabu | bal | yaqumu, | da'aku | kapishtah |
| **the chariot** | **and horse** | **the army** | **and the power** | **together** | **they shall lie down** | **not** | **they shall rise** | **they are extinct** | **as tow** |

| כבו 3518: | 43:18 אל 408 | תזכרו 2142 | ראשנות 7223 | וקדמניות 6931 | אל 408 | תתבננו 995: | 43:19 הנני 2005 | עשה 6213 |
|---|---|---|---|---|---|---|---|---|
| kabu. | 'al | tizkaru | ra'shonout; | uaqadmoniyout | 'al | titbonanu. | hinniy | 'aseh |
| **they are quenched** | **not** | **Remember you** | **the former things** | **the things of old** | **neither** | **consider** | **Behold I** | **will do** |

| חדשה 2319 | עתה 6258 | תצמח 6779 | הלוא 3808 | תדעוה 3045 | אף 637 | אשים 7760 | במדבר 4057 | דרך 1870 | בישמון 3452 |
|---|---|---|---|---|---|---|---|---|---|
| chadashah | 'atah | tatzmiach, | halou'a | teda'auha; | 'ap | 'asiym | bamidbar | derek, | biyshimoun |
| **a new thing** | **now** | **it shall spring forth** | **not** | **shall you know it?** | **even** | **I will make** | **in the wilderness** | **a way** | **in the desert** |

| נהרות 5104: | 43:20 תכבדני 3513 | חית 2416 | השדה 7704 | תנים 8577 | ובנות 1323 | יענה 3284 | כי 3588 | נתתי 5414 |
|---|---|---|---|---|---|---|---|---|
| naharout. | takabdeniy | chayat | hasadeh, | taniym | uabnout | ya'anah; | kiy | natatiy |
| ***and* rivers** | **shall honor me** | **The beast of** | **the field** | **the dragons** | **company** | **and the owls** | **because** | **I give** |

| במדבר 4057 | מים 4325 | נהרות 5104 | בישימן 3452 | להשקות 8248 | עמי 5971 | בחירי 972: | 43:21 עם 5971 | זו 2098 | יצרתי 3335 |
|---|---|---|---|---|---|---|---|---|---|
| bamidbar | mayim, | naharout | biyshiymoun, | lahashqout | 'amiy | bachiyriy. | 'am | zu | yatzartiy |
| **in the wilderness** | **waters** | ***and* rivers** | **in the desert** | **to give drink to** | **my people** | **my chosen** | **people** | **This** | **have I formed** |

| לי 3807a | תהלתי 8416 | יספרו 5608: | 43:22 ולא 3808 | אתי 853 | קראת 7121 | יעקב 3290 | כי 3588 | יגעת 3021 |
|---|---|---|---|---|---|---|---|---|
| liy, | tahilatiy | yasaperu. | uala' | 'atiy | qara'ta | ya'aqob; | kiy | yaga'ta |
| **for myself** | **my praise** | **they shall show forth** | **But not** | **me** | **you have called upon** | **O Jacob** | **but** | **you have been weary** |

| בי 871a | ישראל 3478: | 43:23 לא 3808 | הביאת 935 | לי 3807a | שה 7716 | עלתיך 5930 | וזבחיך 2077 | לא 3808 |
|---|---|---|---|---|---|---|---|---|
| biy | yisra'el. | la' | hebey'ata | liy | seh | 'aloteyka, | uazebacheyka | la' |
| **of me** | **O Israel** | **not** | **You have brought** | **me** | **the small cattle of** | **your burnt offerings** | **with your sacrifices** | **neither** |

| כבדתני 3513 | לא 3808 | העבדתיך 5647 | במנחה 4503 | ולא 3808 | הוגעתיך 3021 | בלבונה 3828: | 43:24 לא 3808 |
|---|---|---|---|---|---|---|---|
| kibadtaniy; | la' | he'abadtiyka | baminchah, | uala' | houga'atiyka | bilabounah. | la' |
| **have you honoured me** | **not** | **I have caused you to serve** | **with an offering** | **nor** | **wearied you** | **with incense** | **no** |

| קנית 7069 | לי 3807a | בכסף 3701 | קנה 7070 | וחלב 2459 | זבחיך 2077 | לא 3808 | הרויתני 7301 | אך 389 |
|---|---|---|---|---|---|---|---|---|
| qaniyta | liy | bakesep | qaneh, | uacheleb | zabacheyka | la' | hiruiytaniy; | 'ach, |
| **You have bought** | **me** | **with money** | **sweet cane** | **with the fat** | **of your sacrifices** | **neither** | **have you filled me** | **but** |

| העבדתני 5647 | בחטאותיך 2403 | הוגעתני 3021 | בעונתיך 5771: | 43:25 אנכי 595 | אנכי 595 | הוא 1931 |
|---|---|---|---|---|---|---|
| he'abadtaniy | bachata'uteyka, | houga'taniy | ba'auonoteyka. | 'anokiy | 'anokiy | hua' |
| **you have made me to serve** | **with your sins** | **you have wearied me** | **with your iniquities** | **I *even*** | **I *am*** | **he** |

| מחה 4229 | פשעיך 6588 | למעני 4616 | וחטאתיך 2403 | לא 3808 | אזכר 2142: | 43:26 הזכירני 2142 |
|---|---|---|---|---|---|---|
| mocheh | pasha'ayka | lama'aniy; | uachata'teyka | la' | 'azkor. | hazakiyreniy |
| **that blotted out** | **your transgressions** | **for mine own sake** | **and your sins** | **not** | **will remember** | **Put me in remembrance** |

Isa 43:16 Thus saith YHUH, which make a way in the sea, and a path in the mighty waters;17 Which bring forth the chariot and horse, the army and the power; they shall lie down together, they shall not rise: they are extinct, they are quenched as tow.18 Remember you not the former things, neither consider the things of old.19 Behold, I will do a new thing; now it shall spring forth; shall you not know it? I will even make a way in the wilderness, and rivers in the desert.20 The beast of the field shall honor me, the dragons and the owls: because I give waters in the wilderness, and rivers in the desert, to give drink to my people, my chosen.21 This people have I formed for myself; they shall show forth my praise.22 But you have not called upon me, O Jacob; but you have been weary of me, O Israel.23 Thou have not brought me the small cattle of your burnt offerings; neither have you honoured me with your sacrifices. I have not caused you to serve with an offering, nor wearied you with incense.24 Thou have bought me no sweet cane with money, neither have you filled me with the fat of your sacrifices: but you have made me to serve with your sins, you have wearied me with your iniquities.25 I, even I, am he that blotteth out your transgressions for mine own sake, and will not remember your sins.

נשפטה 8199 יחד 3162 ספר 5608 אתה 859 למען 4616 תצדק 6663: | 43:27 אביך 1 הראשון 7223 חטא 2398 ומליציך 3887
nishapatah yachad; saper 'atah lama'an titzdaq. 'abiyka hara'shoun chata'; uamliytzeyka
**let us plead together declare you that you may be justified father Your first has sinned and your teachers**

פשעו 6586 בי 871a: | 43:28 ואחלל 2490 שרי 8269 קדש 6944 ואתנה 5414 לחרם 2764
pasha'au biy. ua'achalel sarey qodesh; ua'atanah lacherem
**have transgressed against me Therefore I have profaned the princes of the sanctuary and have given to the curse**

יעקב 3290 וישראל 3478 לגדופים 1421:
ya'aqob, uayisra'ael lagidupiym.
**Jacob and Israel to reproaches**

**Isa 44:1** ועתה 6258 שמע 8085 יעקב 3290 עבדי 5650 וישראל 3478 בחרתי 977 בו 871a: | 44:2 כה 3541 אמר 559 יהוה 3068 עשך 6213
ua'atah shama' ya'aqob 'abdiy; uayisra'ael bachartiy bou. koh 'amar Yahuah 'aseka
**Yet now hear O Jacob my servant and Israel I have chosen whom Thus saith Yahuah that made you**

ויצרך 3335 מבטן 990 יעזרך 5826 אל 408 תירא 3372 עבדי 5650 יעקב 3290 וישרון 3484 בחרתי 977
uayotzerka mibeten ya'zareka; 'al tiyraa' 'abdiy ya'aqob, uiyashurun bachartiy
**and formed you from the womb *which* will help you not Fear my servant O Jacob and you Jesurun I have chosen**

בו 871a: | 44:3 כי 3588 אצק 3332 מים 4325 על 5921 צמא 6771 ונזלים 5140 על 5921 יבשה 3004 אצק 3332 רוחי 7307 על 5921
bou. kiy 'atzaq mayim 'al tzamea', uanozaliym 'al yabashah; 'atzoq ruchiy 'al
**whom For I will pour water upon him that is thirsty and floods upon the dry ground I will pour my spirit upon**

זרעך 2233 וברכתי 1293 על 5921 צאצאיך 6631: | 44:4 וצמחו 6779 בבין 996 חציר 2682 כערבים 6155 על 5921 יבלי 2988
zar'aka, uabirkatiy 'al tze'atza'ayka. uatzamachu babeyn chatziyr; ka'arabiym 'al yibley
**your seed and my blessing upon your offspring And they shall spring up *as* among the grass as willows by courses**

מים 4325: | 44:5 זה 2088 יאמר 559 ליהוה 3068 אני 589 וזה 2088 יקרא 7121 בשם 8034 יעקב 3290 וזה 2088
mayim. zeh ya'mar laYahuah 'aniy, uazeh yiqra' bashem ya'aqob; uazeh,
***the* water One shall say *am* Yahuah's I and another shall call *himself* by the name of Jacob and another**

יכתב 3789 ידו 3027 ליהוה 3068 ובשם 8034 ישראל 3478 יכנה 3655: | 44:6 כה 3541 אמר 559 יהוה 3068
yiktob yadou laYahuah, uabshem yisra'ael yakaneh. koh 'amar Yahuah
**shall subscribe *with* his hand unto Yahuah and by the name of Israel surname *himself* Thus saith Yahuah**

מלך 4428 ישראל 3478 וגאלו 1350 יהוה 3068 צבאות 6635 אני 589 ראשון 7223 ואני 589 אחרון 314 ומבלעדי 1107 אין 369
melek yisra'ael uago'alou Yahuah tzaba'aut; 'aniy ra'shoun ua'aniy 'acharoun, uamibal'aday 'aeyn
**the King of Israel and his redeemer Yahuah of hosts I *am* the first and I *am* the last and beside me *there is* no**

אלהים 430: | 44:7 ומי 4310 כמוני 3644 יקרא 7121 ויגידה 5046 ויערכה 6186 לי 3807a משומי 7760 עם 5971
'alohiym. uamiy kamouniy yiqra', uayagiydeha uaya'arkeha liy, misumiy 'am
**Elohim And who as I shall call and shall declare it and set it in order for me since I appointed people?**

עולם 5769 ואתיות 857 ואשר 834 תבאנה 935 יגידו 5046 למו 3807a: | 44:8 אל 408 תפחדו 6342 ואל 408
'aulam; ua'atiyout ua'asher taba'nah yagiydu lamou. 'al tipchadu ua'al
***the* ancient and the things that are coming and which shall come let them show unto them not Fear you neither**

Isa 43:26 Put me in remembrance: let us plead together: declare you, that you may be justified.27 Thy first father has sinned, and your teachers have transgressed against me.28 Therefore I have profaned the princes of the sanctuary, and have given Jacob to the curse, and Israel to reproaches. **Isa** 44:1 Yet now hear, O Jacob my servant; and Israel, whom I have chosen:2 Thus saith YHUH that made you, and formed you from the womb, which will help you; Fear not, O Jacob, my servant; and you, Jesurun, whom I have chosen.3 For I will pour water upon him that is thirsty, and floods upon the dry ground: I will pour my spirit upon your seed, and my blessing upon your offspring:4 And they shall spring up as among the grass, as willows by the water courses.5 One shall say, I am YHUH's; and another shall call himself by the name of Jacob; and another shall subscribe with his hand unto YHUH, and surname himself by the name of Israel.6 Thus saith YHUH the King of Israel, and his redeemer YHUH of hosts; I am the first, and I am the last; and beside me there is no G-d.7 And who, as I, shall call, and shall declare it, and set it in order for me, since I appointed the ancient people? and the things that are coming, and shall come, let them show unto them.

תרהו 7297 הלא 3808 מאז 227 השמעתיך 8085 והגדתי 5046 ואתם 859 עדי 5707 היש 3426 אלוה 433
tirhu, hala' me'az hishma'atiyka uahigadtiy ua'atem 'aeday; hayesh 'alouah
**be afraid not from that time have I told you and have declared *it*? and you *are* even my witnesses Is there *a* Elohim**

מבלעדי 1107 ואין 369 צור 6697 בל 1077 ידעתי 3045: 44:9 יצרי 3335 פסל 6459 כלם 3605 תהו 8414
mibal'aday, ua'aeyn tzur bal yadaa'tiy. yotzarey pesel kulam tohu,
**beside me? yea *there is* no rock (*Elohim*) not *any* I know They that make a graven image *are* all of them vanity**

וחמודיהם 2530 בל 1077 יועילו 3276 ועדיהם 5707 המה 1992 בל 1077 יראו 7200 ובל 1077 ידעו 3045 למען 4616
uachamudeyhem bal you'aylu; ua'adeyhem hemah, bal yir'au uabal yeda'au lama'an
**and their delectable things not shall profit and their own witnesses they *are* not they see nor know that**

יבשו 954: 44:10 מי 4310 יצר 3335 אל 410 ופסל 6459 נסך 5258 לבלתי 1115 הועיל 3276: 44:11 הן 2005
yeboshu. miy' yatzar 'ael uapesel nasak; labiltiy hou'ayl. hen
**they may be ashamed Who has formed a god or a graven image molten for nothing? *that* is profitable Behold**

כל 3605 חבריו 2270 יבשו 954 וחרשים 2796 המה 1992 מאדם 120 יתקבצו 6908 כלם 3605 יעמדו 5975
kal chaberayu yeboshu, uacharashiym hemah me'adam; yitqabtzu kulam ya'amodu,
**all his fellows shall be ashamed and the workmen they *are* of men let be gathered together them all let them stand up**

יפחדו 6342 יבשו 954 יחד 3162: 44:12 חרש 2796 ברזל 1270 מעצד 4621 ופעל 6466 בפחם 6352
yipchadu yeboshu yachad. charash barzel ma'atzad, uapa'al bapecham,
***yet* they shall fear *and* they shall be ashamed together *The* smith iron *with* the tongs both work in the coals**

ובמקבות 4717 יצרהו 3335 ויפעלהו 6466 בזרוע 2220 כחו 3581 גם 1571 רעב 7456 ואין 369 כח 3581 לא 3808
uabamaqabout yitzarehu; uayip'alehu bizroua' kochou, gam ra'aeb ua'aeyn koach, la'
**and with hammers fashioned it and work it with his arms the strength of yea he is hungry and fail his strength no**

שתה 8354 מים 4325 וייעף 3286: 44:13 חרש 2791 עצים 6086 נטה 5186 קו 6957 יתארהו 8388 בשרד 8279 יעשהו 6213
shatah mayim uayiy'ap. charash 'aetziym natah qau yata'arehu basered, ya'asehu
**he drink water and is faint The carpenter wood stretch out *his* rule he marked it out with a line he fitted it**

במקצעות 4741 ובמחוגה 4230 יתארהו 8388 ויעשהו 6213 כתבנית 8403 איש 376 כתפארת 8597 אדם 120
bamaqtzu'aut, uabamchugah yata'arehu; uay'asehu katabniyt 'aysh, katip'aret 'adam
**with planes and with the compass he mark it out and make it after the figure of a man according to the beauty of a man**

לשבת 3427 בית 1004: 44:14 לכרת 3772 לו 3807a ארזים 730 ויקח 3947 תרזה 8645 ואלון 437
lashabet bayit. likrat lou' 'araziym, uayiqach tirzah ua'aloun,
**that it may remain in the house He heweth down him cedars and takes the cypress and the oak**

ויאמץ 553 לו 3807a בעצי 6086 יער 3293 נטע 5193 ארן 766 וגשם 1653 יגדל 1431: 44:15
uaya'ametz lou' ba'atzey ya'ar; nata' 'aren uageshem yagadel.
**which he strengthen for himself among the trees of the forest he planteth an ash and the rain does nourish it**

והיה 1961 לאדם 120 לבער 1197 ויקח 3947 מהם 1992 ויחם 2552 אף 637 ישיק 5400 ואפה 644 לחם 3899 אף 637
uahayah la'adam laba'aer, uayiqach mehem uayacham, 'ap yasiyq ua'apah lachem; 'ap
**Then shall it be for a man to burn for he will take thereof and warm himself yea he kindle *it* and bake bread yea**

Isa 44:8 Fear you not, neither be afraid: have not I told you from that time, and have declared it? you are even my witnesses. Is there a G-d beside me? yea, there is no G-d; I know not any.9 They that make a graven image are all of them vanity; and their delectable things shall not profit; and they are their own witnesses; they see not, nor know; that they may be ashamed.10 Who has formed a god, or molten a graven image that is profitable for nothing?11 Behold, all his fellows shall be ashamed: and the workmen, they are of men: let them all be gathered together, let them stand up; yet they shall fear, and they shall be ashamed together.12 The smith with the tongs both worketh in the coals, and fashioneth it with hammers, and worketh it with the strength of his arms: yea, he is hungry, and his strength faileth: he drinketh no water, and is faint.13 The carpenter stretcheth out his rule; he marketh it out with a line; he fitteth it with planes, and he marketh it out with the compass, and make it after the figure of a man, according to the beauty of a man; that it may remain in the house.14 He heweth him down cedars, and take the cypress and the oak, which he strengtheneth for himself among the trees of the forest: he planteth an ash, and the rain doth nourish it.15 Then shall it be for a man to burn: for he will take thereof, and warm himself; yea, he kindleth it, and baketh bread;

44:16

יפעל 6466 אל 410 וישתחו 7812 עשהו 6213 פסל 6459 ויסגד 5456 למו 3807a: חציו 2677 שרף 8313 במו 1119 אש 784

yip'al 'ael uayishtachu, 'asahu pesel uayisgad lamou. chetzyou sarap bamou 'aesh,

**he make a god and worship *it* he make it a graven image and fall down thereto part thereof He burn in the fire**

על 5921 חציו 2677 בשר 1320 יאכל 398 יצלה 6740 צלי 6748 וישבע 7646 אף 637 יחם 2552 ויאמר 559 האח 1889 חמותי 2552

'al chetzyou basar ya'kel, yitzleh tzaliy uayisba'; 'ap yachom uaya'mar he'ach, chamoutiy

**with part thereof flesh he eat he roast roast and is satisfied yea he warm *himself* and saith Aha I am warm**

44:17

ראיתי 7200 אור 217: ושאריתו 7611 לאל 410 עשה 6213 לפסלו 6459 יסגוד 5456 לו 3807a וישתחו 7812

ra'aytiy 'aur. uash'aeriytou, la'ael 'asah lapislou; yisgoud lou' uayishtachu

**I have seen the fire And the residue thereof a god he make *even* his graven image he fall down unto it and worship *it***

44:18

ויתפלל 6419 אליו 413 ויאמר 559 הצילני 5337 כי 3588 אלי 410 אתה 859: לא 3808 ידעו 3045 ולא 3808 יבינו 995 כי 3588

uayitpalel 'aelayu, uaya'mar hatziyleniy, kiy 'aeliy 'atah. la' yada'au uala' yabiynu; kiy

**and prayed unto it and saith Deliver me for *are* my god you not They have known nor understood for**

44:19

טח 2902 מראות 7200 עיניהם 5869 מהשכיל 7919 לבתם 3826: ולא 3808 ישיב 7725 אל 413

tach mera'aut 'aeyneyhem, mehaskiyl libotam. uala' yashiyb 'al

**he has shut that they cannot see their eyes that they cannot understand *and* their hearts And none consider in**

לבו 3820 ולא 3808 דעת 1847 ולא 3808 תבונה 8394 לאמר 559 חציו 2677 שרפתי 8313 במו 1119 אש 784 ואף 637

libou, uala' da'at uala' tabunah lea'mor chetzyou saraptiy bamou 'aesh, ua'ap

**his heart neither *is there* knowledge nor understanding to say part of it I have burned in the fire yea also**

אפיתי 644 על 5921 גחליו 1513 לחם 3899 אצלה 6740 בשר 1320 ואכל 398 ויתרו 3499 לתועבה 8441

'apiytiy 'al gechalayu lechem, 'atzleh basar ua'akel; uayitrou latou'aebah

**I have baked upon the coals thereof bread I have roasted flesh and eaten *it* and the residue thereof an abomination**

44:20

אעשה 6213 לבול 944 עץ 6086 אסגוד 5456: רעה 7462 אפר 665 לב 3820 הותל 2048 הטהו 5186

'aaseh, labul 'aetz 'asgoud. ro'ah 'aeper, leb hutal hitahu;

**shall I make to the stock of a tree? shall I fall down He feed on ashes a heart deceived has turned him aside**

44:21

ולא 3808 יציל 5337 את 853 נפשו 5315 ולא 3808 יאמר 559 הלוא 3808 שקר 8267 בימיני 3225: זכר 2142 אלה 428 יעקב 3290

uala' yatziyl 'at napshou uala' ya'mar, halou'a sheqer biymiyniy. zakar 'aeleh ya'aqob,

**that cannot he deliver his soul nor say *Is there* not a lie in my right hand? Remember these O Jacob**

וישראל 3478 כי 3588 עבדי 5650 אתה 859 יצרתיך 3335 עבד 5650 לי 3807a אתה 859 ישראל 3478 לא 3808

uayisra'ael kiy 'abdiy 'atah; yatzartiyka 'abed liy 'atah, yisra'ael la'

**and Israel for *are* my servant you I have formed you servant *are* my you O Israel not**

44:22

תנשני 5382: מחיתי 4229 כעב 5645 פשעיך 6588 וכענן 6051 חטאותיך 2403

tinasheniy. machiytiy ka'ab pasha'ayka, uake'anan chata'uteyka;

**you shall be forgotten of me I have blotted out as a thick cloud your transgressions and as a cloud your sins**

44:23

שובה 7725 אלי 413 כי 3588 גאלתיך 1350: רנו 7442 שמים 8064 כי 3588 עשה 6213 יהוה 3069 הריעו 7321

shubah 'aelay kiy ga'altiyka. ranu shamayim kiy 'asah Yahuah hariy'au

**return unto me for I have redeemed you Sing O you heavens for has done *it* Yahuah shout**

Isa 44:15 yea, he make a god, and worshippeth it; he make it a graven image, and fall down thereto.16 He burneth part thereof in the fire; with part thereof he eateth flesh; he roasteth roast, and is satisfied: yea, he warmeth himself, and saith, Aha, I am warm, I have seen the fire:17 And the residue thereof he make a god, even his graven image: he fall down unto it, and worshippeth it, and pray unto it, and saith, Deliver me; for you are my god.18 They have not known nor understood: for he has shut their eyes, that they cannot see; and their hearts, that they cannot understand.19 And none considereth in his heart, neither is there knowledge nor understanding to say, I have burned part of it in the fire; yea, also I have baked bread upon the coals thereof; I have roasted flesh, and eaten it: and shall I make the residue thereof an abomination? shall I fall down to the stock of a tree?20 He feedeth on ashes: a deceived heart has turned him aside, that he cannot deliver his soul, nor say, Is there not a lie in my right hand?21 Remember these, O Jacob and Israel; for you are my servant: I have formed you; you are my servant: O Israel, you shall not be forgotten of me.22 I have blotted out, as a thick cloud, your transgressions, and, as a cloud, your sins: return unto me; for I have redeemed you. 23 Sing, O you heavens; for YHUH has done it:

תחתיות 8482 | ארץ 776 | פצחו 6476 | הרים 2022 | רנה 7440 | יער 3293 | וכל 3605 | עץ 6086 | בו 871a | כי 3588 | גאל 1350
tachtiyout 'aretz, pitzchu hariym rinah, ya'ar uakal 'aetz bou; kiy ga'al
**you lower parts of the earth break forth you mountains *into* singing O forest and every tree therein for has redeemed**

יהוה 3069 | יעקב 3290 | ובישראל 3478 | יתפאר 6286: | **44:24** כה 3541 | אמר 559 | יהוה 3068 | גאלך 1350 | ויצרך 3335
Yahuah ya'aqob, uabyisra'ael yitpa'ar. koh 'amar Yahuah go'aleka, uayotzerka
**Yahuah Jacob and in Israel glorified himself Thus saith Yahuah your redeemer and he that formed you**

מבטן 990 | אנכי 595 | יהוה 3068 | עשה 6213 | כל 3605 | נטה 5186 | שמים 8064 | לבדי 905 | רקע 7554 | הארץ 776
mibaten; 'anokiy Yahuah 'asheh kol, noteh shamayim labadiy, roqa' ha'aretz
**from the womb I *am* Yahuah that make all *things* that stretch forth the heavens alone that spread abroad the earth**

מי 4310 | אתי 854 | **44:25** מפר 6565 | אתות 226 | בדים 907 | וקסמים 7080 | יהולל 1984 | משיב 7725 | חכמים 2450 | אחור 268
miy' 'atiy meper 'autot badiym, uaqosamiym yahoulel; meshiyb chakamiym 'achour
**who by myself; That frustrateth the tokens of the liars and diviners make mad that turned wise *men* backward**

ודעתם 1847 | ישכל 5528: | **44:26** מקים 6965 | דבר 1697 | עבדו 5650 | ועצת 6098 | מלאכיו 4397 | ישלים 7999
uada'tam yasakel. meqiym dabar abdou, ua'atzat mal'akayu yashliym;
**and their knowledge make foolish That confirm the word of his servant and the counsel of his messengers performed**

האמר 559 | לירושלם 3389 | תושב 8427 | ולערי 5892 | יהודה 3063 | תבנינה 1129 | וחרבותיה 2723
ha'amer liyarushalaim tushab, ual'arey yahudah tibaneynah, uacharabouteyha
**that saith to Jerusalem You shall be inhabited and to the cities of Judah You shall be built and the decayed places thereof**

אקומם 6965: | **44:27** האמר 559 | לצולה 6683 | חרבי 2717 | ונהרתיך 5104 | אוביש 3001: | **44:28** האמר 559 | לכורש 3566
'aqoumem. ha'amer latzulah charabiy; uanaharotayik 'aubiysh. ha'amer lakouresh
**I will raise up That saith to the deep Be dry and your rivers I will dry up That saith of Cyrus**

רעי 7473 | וכל 3605 | חפצי 2656 | ישלם 7999 | ולאמר 559 | לירושלם 3389 | תבנה 1129 | והיכל 1964
ro'aey, uakal chepatziy yashlim; ualea'mor liyarushalaim tibaneh, uaheykal
**He is my shepherd and all my pleasure shall perform even saying to Jerusalem You shall be built and to the temple**

תוסד 3245:
tiuased.
**Your foundation shall be laid**

**Isa 45:1** כה 3541 | אמר 559 | יהוה 3068 | למשיחו 4899 | לכורש 3566 | אשר 834 | החזקתי 2388 | בימינו 3225 | לרד 7286 | לפניו 6440 | גוים 1471
koh 'amar Yahuah limashiychou lakouresh 'asher hechezaqtiy uiymiynou, larad lapanayu gouyim,
**Thus saith Yahuah to his anointed to Cyrus whose I have holden right hand to subdue before him nations**

ומתני 4975 | מלכים 4428 | אפתח 6605 | לפתח 6605 | לפניו 6440 | דלתים 1817 | ושערים 8179 | לא 3808 | יסגרו 5462: | **45:2** אני 589
uamataney melakiym 'apateach; liptoach lapanayu dalatayim, uash'ariym la' yisageru. 'aniy
**and the loins of kings I will loose to open before him the two leaved gates and the gates not shall be shut I**

לפניך 6440 | אלך 1980 | והדורים 1921 | אושר 3474 | דלתות 1817 | נחושה 5154 | אשבר 7665 | ובריחי 1280
lapaneyka 'aelek, uahaduriym 'ausher daltout nachushah 'ashaber, uabriychey
**before you will go and the crooked places make straight: the gates of brass I will break in pieces and the bars of**

Isa 44:23 shout, you lower parts of the earth: break forth into singing, you mountains, O forest, and every tree therein: for YHUH has redeemed Jacob, and glorified himself in Israel.24 Thus saith YHUH, your redeemer, and he that formed you from the womb, I am YHUH that make all things; that stretcheth forth the heavens alone; that spreadeth abroad the earth by myself;25 That frustrateth the tokens of the liars, and make diviners mad; that turneth wise men backward, and make their knowledge foolish;26 That confirmeth the word of his servant, and performeth the counsel of his messengers; that saith to Jerusalem, Thou shall be inhabited; and to the cities of Judah, You shall be built, and I will raise up the decayed places thereof:27 That saith to the deep, Be dry, and I will dry up your rivers:28 That saith of Cyrus, He is my shepherd, and shall perform all my pleasure: even saying to Jerusalem, Thou shall be built; and to the temple, Thy foundation shall be laid. **Isa** 45:1 Thus saith YHUH to his anointed, to Cyrus, whose right hand I have holden, to subdue nations before him; and I will loose the loins of kings, to open before him the two leaved gates; and the gates shall not be shut;2 I will go before you, and make the crooked places straight: I will break in pieces the gates of brass, and cut in sunder the bars of iron:

| ברזל 1270 | אגדע 1438: | 45:3 ונתתי 5414 | לך 3807a | אוצרות 214 | חשך 2822 | ומטמני 4301 | מסתרים 4565 | למען 4616 |
|---|---|---|---|---|---|---|---|---|
| barzel | 'agadea'. | uanatatiy | laka | 'autzarout | choshek, | uamatmuney | mistariym; | lama'an |
| **iron** | **cut in sunder** | **And I will give** | **to you** | **the treasures of** | **darkness** | **and hidden riches of** | **secret places** | **that** |

| תדע 3045 | כי 3588 | אני 589 | יהוה 3068 | הקורא 7121 | בשמך 8034 | אלהי 430 | ישראל 3478: | 45:4 למען 4616 | עבדי 5650 |
|---|---|---|---|---|---|---|---|---|---|
| teda', | kiy | 'aniy | Yahuah | haqourea' | bashimaka | 'alohey | yisra'ael. | lama'an | 'abdiy |
| **you may know** | **that it** | **I** | **Yahuah** | **which call *you*** | **by your name** | ***am* the Elohim of** | **Israel** | **For sake** | **my servant's** |

| יעקב 3290 | וישראל 3478 | בחירי 972 | ואקרא 7121 | לך 3807a | בשמך 8034 | אכנך 3655 | ולא 3808 |
|---|---|---|---|---|---|---|---|
| ya'aqob, | uayisra'ael | bachiyriy; | ua'aqra' | laka | bishameka, | 'akanka | uala' |
| **Jacob** | **and Israel** | **mine elect** | **I have even called** | **to you** | **by your name** | **I have surnamed you** | **though not** |

| ידעתני 3045: | 45:5 אני 589 | יהוה 3068 | ואין 369 | עוד 5750 | זולתי 2108 | אין 369 | אלהים 430 | אאזרך 247 | ולא 3808 |
|---|---|---|---|---|---|---|---|---|---|
| yada'ataniy. | 'aniy | Yahuah | ua'aeyn | 'aud, | zulatiy | 'aeyn | 'alohiym; | 'a'azerka | uala' |
| **you have known me** | **I *am*** | **Yahuah** | **and *there is* none** | **else** | **beside me** | ***there is* no** | **Elohim** | **I girded you** | **though not** |

| ידעתני 3045: | 45:6 למען 4616 | ידעו 3045 | ממזרח 4217 | שמש 8121 | וממערבה 4628 | כי 3588 | אפס 657 |
|---|---|---|---|---|---|---|---|
| yada'ataniy. | lama'an | yeda'au, | mimizrach | shemesh | uamima'arabah, | kiy | 'apes |
| **you have known me** | **That** | **they may know** | **from the rising of** | **the sun** | **and from the west** | **that** | ***there is* none** |

| בלעדי 1107 | אני 589 | יהוה 3068 | ואין 369 | עוד 5750: | 45:7 יוצר 3335 | אור 216 | ובורא 1254 | חשך 2822 | עשה 6213 | שלום 7965 | ובורא 1254 |
|---|---|---|---|---|---|---|---|---|---|---|---|
| bil'aday; | 'aniy | Yahuah | ua'aeyn | 'aud. | youtzer | 'aur | uabourea' | choshek, | 'aseh | shaloum | uabourea' |
| **beside me** | **I *am*** | **Yahuah** | **and *there is* none** | **else** | **I form** | **the light** | **and create** | **darkness** | **I make** | **peace** | **and create** |

| רע 7451 | אני 589 | יהוה 3068 | עשה 6213 | כל 3605 | אלה 428: | 45:8 הרעיפו 7491 | שמים 8064 | ממעל 4605 | ושחקים 7834 | יזלו 5140 |
|---|---|---|---|---|---|---|---|---|---|---|
| ra'; | 'aniy | Yahuah | 'aseh | kal | 'aeleh. | har'aypu | shamayim | mima'al, | uashchaqiym | yizlu |
| **evil** | **I** | **Yahuah** | **do** | **all** | **these *things*** | **Drop down** | **you heavens** | **from above** | **and the skies** | **let pour down** |

| צדק 6664 | תפתח 6605 | ארץ 776 | ויפרו 6509 | ישע 3468 | וצדקה 6666 | תצמיח 6779 | יחד 3162 | אני 589 | יהוה 3068 |
|---|---|---|---|---|---|---|---|---|---|
| tzedeq; | tiptach | 'aretz | uayipru | yesha', | uatzdaqah | tatzmiyach | yachad, | 'aniy | Yahuah |
| **righteousness** | **let open** | **the earth** | **and let them bring forth** | **salvation** | **and righteousness** | **let spring up** | **together** | **I** | **Yahuah** |

| בראתיו 1254: | 45:9 הוי 1945 | רב 7378 | את 853 | יצרו 3335 | חרש 2791 | את 853 | חרשי 2789 |
|---|---|---|---|---|---|---|---|
| bara'tiyu. | houy, | rab | 'at | yotzarou, | cheres | 'at | charsey |
| **have created *it*** | **Woe** | ***unto* him that strive with** | | **his Maker** | ***Let* the potsherd** | ***strive with*** | **the potsherds of** |

| אדמה 127 | היאמר 559 | חמר 2563 | ליצרו 3335 | מה 4100 | תעשה 6213 | ופעלך 6467 | אין 369 | ידים 3027 | לו 3807a: | 45:10 הוי 1945 |
|---|---|---|---|---|---|---|---|---|---|---|
| 'adamah; | haya'mar | chamor | layotzarou | mah | ta'aseh, | uapa'alaka | 'aeyn | yadayim | lou'. | houy |
| **the earth** | **Shall say** | **the clay** | **to him that fashioned it** | **What** | **make you?** | **or your work** | ***has* no** | **hands?** | **He** | **Woe** |

| אמר 559 | לאב 1 | מה 4100 | תוליד 3205 | ולאשה 802 | מה 4100 | תחילין 2342: | 45:11 כה 3541 | אמר 559 |
|---|---|---|---|---|---|---|---|---|
| 'amer | la'ab | mah | touliyd; | ual'ashah | mah | tachiyliyn. | koh | 'amar |
| ***unto* him that saith** | **unto *his* father** | **What** | **beget you?** | **or to the woman** | **What** | **have you brought forth?** | **Thus** | **saith** |

| יהוה 3068 | קדוש 6918 | ישראל 3478 | ויצרו 3335 | האתיות 857 | שאלוני 7592 | על 5921 | בני 1121 | ועל 5921 |
|---|---|---|---|---|---|---|---|---|
| Yahuah | qadoush | yisra'ael | uayotzarou; | ha'atiyout | sha'aluniy, | 'al | banay | ua'al |
| **Yahuah** | ***the* Holy One of** | **Israel** | **and his Maker** | ***of* things to come** | **Ask me** | **concerning** | **my sons** | **and concerning** |

Isa 45:3 And I will give you the treasures of darkness, and hidden riches of secret places, that you may know that I, YHUH, which call you by your name, am the G-d of Israel.4 For Jacob my servant's sake, and Israel mine elect, I have even called you by your name: I have surnamed you, though you have not known me.5 I am YHUH, and there is none else, there is no G-d beside me: I girded you, though you have not known me:6 That they may know from the rising of the sun, and from the west, that there is none beside me. I am YHUH, and there is none else.7 I form the light, and create darkness: I make peace, and create evil: I YHUH do all these things.8 Drop down, you heavens, from above, and let the skies pour down righteousness: let the earth open, and let them bring forth salvation, and let righteousness spring up together; I YHUH have created it.9 Woe unto him that striveth with his Maker! Let the potsherd strive with the potsherds of the earth. Shall the clay say to him that fashioneth it, What make you? or your work, He has no hands?10 Woe unto him that saith unto his father, What begettest you? or to the woman, What have you brought forth?11 Thus saith YHUH, the Holy One of Israel, and his Maker, Ask me of things to come concerning my sons, and concerning the work of my hands command you me.

פעל 6467 ידי 3027 תצוני 6680: **45:12** אנכי 595 עשיתי 6213 ארץ 776 ואדם 120 עליה 5921 בראתי 1254 אני 589
po'al yaday tatzauniy. 'anokiy 'asiytiy 'aretz, ua'adam 'aleyha bara'tiy; 'aniy,
**the work of my hands command you me I have made the earth and man upon it I created I**

ידי 3027 נטו 5186 שמים 8064 וכל 3605 צבאם 6635 צויתי 6680: **45:13** אנכי 595 העירתהו 5782
yaday natu shamayim, uakal tzaba'am tziueytiy. 'anokiy ha'ayrotihu
***even* my hands have stretched out the heavens and all their host have I commanded I have raised him up**

בצדק 6664 וכל 3605 דרכיו 1870 אישר 3474 הוא 1931 יבנה 1129 עירי 5892 וגלותי 1546 ישלח 7971 לא 3808 במחיר 4242
batzedeq, uakal darakayu 'ayasher; hua' yibneh 'ayriy uagalutiy yashaleach, la' bimachiyr
**in righteousness and all his ways I will direct he shall build my city and my captives he shall let go not for price**

ולא 3808 בשחד 7810 אמר 559 יהוה 3068 צבאות 6635: **45:14** כה 3541 אמר 559 יהוה 3069 יגיע 3018 מצרים 4714 וסחר 5505
uala' bashochad, 'amar Yahuah tzaba'aut. koh 'amar Yahuah yagiya' mitzrayim uaschar
**nor reward saith Yahuah of hosts Thus saith Yahuah The labour of Egypt and merchandise of**

כוש 3568 וסבאים 5436 אנשי 582 מדה 4060 עליך 5921 יעברו 5674 ולך 3807a יהיו 1961 אחריך 310
kush uasaba'aym 'anshey midah 'alayik ya'aboru ualak yihayu, 'acharayik
**Ethiopia and of the Sabeans men of stature unto you and shall come over to you they shall be your after you**

ילכו 1980 בזקים 2131 יעברו 5674 ואליך 413 ישתחוו 7812 אליך 413
yeleku, baziqiym ya'aboru; ua'aelayik yishtachauu 'aelayik
**they shall come in chains they shall come over and unto you they shall fall down unto you**

יתפללו 6419 אך 389 בך 871a אל 410 ואין 369 עוד 5750 אפס 657 אלהים 430: **45:15** אכן 403 אתה 859
yitpalalu, 'ak bach 'ael ua'aeyn 'aud 'apes 'alohiym. 'aken 'atah
**they shall make supplication *saying* Surely *is* in you El and *there is* none else *there is* no Elohim Verily you**

אל 410 מסתתר 5641 אלהי 430 ישראל 3478 מושיע 3467: **45:16** בושו 954 וגם 1571 נכלמו 3637
'ael mistater; 'alohey yisra'ael moushiya'. boushu uagam niklamu
***are a* El that hide yourself O Elohim of Israel the Saviour They shall be ashamed and also confounded**

כלם 3605 יחדו 3162 הלכו 1980 בכלמה 3639 חרשי 2796 צירים 6736: **45:17** ישראל 3478 נושע 3467 ביהוה 3068
kulam; yachdau halaku baklimah, charashey tziyriym. yisra'ael nousha' baYahuah,
**all of them together they shall go to confusion *that are* makers of idols *But* Israel shall be saved in Yahuah**

תשועת 8668 עולמים 5769 לא 3808 תבשו 954 ולא 3808 תכלמו 3637 עד 5704 עולמי 5769 עד 5703: **45:18** כי 3588 כה 3541
tashu'at 'aulamiym; la' teboshu uala' tikalamu 'ad 'aulamey 'ad. kiy koh
***with* an salvation everlasting not you shall be ashamed nor confounded unto world without end For thus**

אמר 559 יהוה 3068 בורא 1254 השמים 8064 הוא 1931 האלהים 430 יצר 3335 הארץ 776 ועשה 6213 הוא 1931 כוננה 3559
'amar Yahuah bourea' hashamayim hua' ha'alohiym, yotzer ha'aretz ua'asah hua' kounanah,
**saith Yahuah that created the heavens himself Elohim that formed the earth and made it he has established it**

לא 3808 תהו 8414 בראה 1254 לשבת 3427 יצרה 3335 אני 589 יהוה 3068 ואין 369 עוד 5750: **45:19** לא 3808 בסתר 5643
la' tohu bara'ah lashabet yatzarah; 'aniy Yahuah ua'aeyn 'aud. la' baseter
**not in vain he created it to be inhabited he formed it I *am* Yahuah and there is none else not in secret**

Isa 45:12 I have made the earth, and created man upon it: I, even my hands, have stretched out the heavens, and all their host have I commanded.13 I have raised him up in righteousness, and I will direct all his ways: he shall build my city, and he shall let go my captives, not for price nor reward, saith YHUH of hosts.14 Thus saith YHUH, The labour of Egypt, and merchandise of Ethiopia and of the Sabeans, men of stature, shall come over unto you, and they shall be your: they shall come after you; in chains they shall come over, and they shall fall down unto you, they shall make supplication unto you, saying, Surely G-d is in you; and there is none else, there is no G-d.15 Verily you are a G-d that hidest thyself, O G-d of Israel, the Saviour.16 They shall be ashamed, and also confounded, all of them: they shall go to confusion together that are makers of idols.17 But Israel shall be saved in YHUH with an everlasting salvation: you shall not be ashamed nor confounded world without end.18 For thus saith YHUH that created the heavens; G-d himself that formed the earth and made it; he has established it, he created it not in vain, he formed it to be inhabited: I am YHUH; and there is none else.

| דברתי 1696 | במקום 4725 | ארץ 776 | חשך 2822 | לא 3808 | אמרתי 559 | לזרע 2233 | יעקב 3290 | תהו 8414 | בקשוני 1245 | אני 589 | יהוה 3068 |
|---|---|---|---|---|---|---|---|---|---|---|---|
| dibartiy, | bimqoum | 'aretz | choshek, | la' | 'amartiy | lazera' | ya'aqob | tohu | baqashuniy; | 'aniy | Yahuah |
| **I have spoken** | **in a place of** | **the earth** | **dark** | **not** | **I said** | **unto the seed of** | **Jacob** | **in vain** | **Seek you me** | **I** | **Yahuah** |

| דבר 1696 | צדק 6664 | מגיד 5046 | מישרים 4339: | **45:20** | הקבצו 6908 | ובאו 935 | התנגשו 5066 | יחדו 3162 |
|---|---|---|---|---|---|---|---|---|
| dober | tzedeq, | magiyd | meyshariym. | | hiqabatzu | uaba'au | hitnagashu | yachdau |
| **speak** | **righteousness** | **I declare** | **things that are right** | | **Assemble yourselves** | **and come** | **draw near** | **together** |

| פליטי 6412 | הגוים 1471 | לא 3808 | ידעו 3045 | הנשאים 5375 | את 853 | עץ 6086 | פסלם 6459 |
|---|---|---|---|---|---|---|---|
| paliytey | hagouyim; | la' | yada'au, | hanos'aym | 'at | 'aetz | pislam, |
| **you *that are* escaped of** | **the nations** | **no** | **they have knowledge** | **that set up** | | **the wood of** | **their graven image** |

| ומתפללים 6419 | אל 413 | אל 410 | לא 3808 | יושיע 3467: | **45:21** | הגידו 5046 | והגישו 5066 | אף 637 | יועצו 3289 | יחדו 3162 |
|---|---|---|---|---|---|---|---|---|---|---|
| uamitpalliym, | 'al | 'ael | la' | youshiya'. | | hagiydu | uahagiyshu, | 'ap | yiua'atzu | yachdau; |
| **and pray** | **unto** | ***a* god** | ***that* cannot** | **save** | | **Tell you** | **and bring *them* near** | **yea** | **let them take counsel** | **together** |

| מי 4310 | השמיע 8085 | זאת 2063 | מקדם 6924 | מאז 227 | הגידה 5046 | הלוא 3808 | אני 589 | יהוה 3068 | ואין 369 | עוד 5750 |
|---|---|---|---|---|---|---|---|---|---|---|
| miy' | hishmia' | za't | miqedem | me'az | higiydah, | halou'a | 'aniy | Yahuah | ua'aeyn | 'aud |
| **who** | **has declared** | **this** | **from ancient time?** | **for then?** | ***who* has told it** | ***have* not** | **I** | **Yahuah?** | **and *there is* no** | **else** |

| אלהים 430 | מבלעדי 1107 | אל 410 | צדיק 6662 | ומושיע 3467 | אין 369 | זולתי 2108: | **45:22** פנו 6437 | אלי 413 | והושעו 3467 | כל 3605 |
|---|---|---|---|---|---|---|---|---|---|---|
| 'alohiym | mibal'aday, | 'ael | tzadiyq | uamoushiya', | 'ayin | zulatiy. | panu | 'aelay | uahiuasha'au | kal |
| **Elohim** | **beside me** | ***a* El** | **just** | **and a Saviour** | **there is none** | **beside me** | **Look** | **unto me** | **and be you saved** | **all** |

| אפסי 657 | ארץ 776 | כי 3588 | אני 589 | אל 410 | ואין 369 | עוד 5750: | **45:23** בי 871a | נשבעתי 7650 | יצא 3318 | מפי 6310 |
|---|---|---|---|---|---|---|---|---|---|---|
| 'apsey | 'aretz; | kiy | 'aniy | 'al | ua'aeyn | 'aud. | biy | nishba'atiy, | yatza' | mipiy |
| **the ends of** | **the earth** | **for** | **I** | ***am* El** | **and there is none** | **else** | **by myself** | **I have sworn** | **is gone out** | **of my mouth** |

| צדקה 6666 | דבר 1697 | ולא 3808 | ישוב 7725 | כי 3588 | לי 3807a | תכרע 3766 | כל 3605 | ברך 1290 | תשבע 7650 | כל 3605 | לשון 3956: | **45:24** |
|---|---|---|---|---|---|---|---|---|---|---|---|---|
| tzadaqah | dabar | uala' | yashub; | kiy | liy | tikra' | kal | berek, | tishaba' | kal | lashoun. | |
| ***in* righteousness** | **the word** | **and not** | **shall return** | **That** | **unto me** | **shall bow** | **every** | **knee** | **shall swear** | **every** | **tongue** | |

| אך 389 | ביהוה 3068 | לי 3807a | אמר 559 | צדקות 6666 | ועז 5797 | עדיו 5704 | יבוא 935 | ויבשו 954 |
|---|---|---|---|---|---|---|---|---|
| 'ak | baYahuah | liy | 'amar | tzadaqout | ua'az; | 'adayu | yabou'a | uayeboshu, |
| **Surely** | **in Yahuah** | **to me** | **shall *one* say have I** | **righteousness** | **and strength** | ***even* to him** | **shall *men* come** | **and shall be ashamed** |

| כל 3605 | הנחרים 2734 | בו 871a: | **45:25** ביהוה 3068 | יצדקו 6663 | ויתהללו 1984 | כל 3605 | זרע 2233 | ישראל 3478: |
|---|---|---|---|---|---|---|---|---|
| kal | hanechariym | bou. | Yahuah | yitzdaqu | uayithallu | kal | zera' | yisra'ael. |
| **all** | **that are incensed** | **against him** | **In Yahuah** | **shall be justified** | **and shall glory** | **all** | **the seed of** | **Israel** |

| **Isa 46:1** | כרע 3766 | בל 1078 | קרס 7164 | נבו 5015 | היו 1961 | עצביהם 6091 | לחיה 2416 | ולבהמה 929 | נשאתיכם 5385 |
|---|---|---|---|---|---|---|---|---|---|
| | karea' | bel | qores | nabou', | hayu | 'atzabeyhem, | lachayah | ualabahemah; | nasu'ateykem |
| | **bows down** | **Bel** | **stooped** | **Nebo** | **were** | **their idols** | **upon the beasts** | **and upon the cattle** | **your carriages** |

| עמוסות 6006 | משא 4853 | לעיפה 5889: | **46:2** קרסו 7164 | כרעו 3766 | יחדו 3162 | לא 3808 | יכלו 3201 | מלט 4422 |
|---|---|---|---|---|---|---|---|---|
| amusout, | masa' | la'ayepah. | qarasu | kara'u | yachdau, | la' | yukalu | malet |
| ***were* heavy loaden** | ***they are* a burden** | **to the weary *beast*** | **They stoop** | **they bow down** | **together** | **not** | **they could** | **deliver** |

Isa 45:19 I have not spoken in secret, in a dark place of the earth: I said not unto the seed of Jacob, Seek you me in vain: I YHUH speak righteousness, I declare things that are right.20 Assemble yourselves and come; draw near together, you that are escaped of the nations: they have no knowledge that set up the wood of their graven image, and pray unto a god that cannot save.21 Tell you, and bring them near; yea, let them take counsel together: who has declared this from ancient time? who has told it from that time? have not I YHUH? and there is no G-d else beside me; a just G-d and a Saviour; there is none beside me.22 Look unto me, and be you saved, all the ends of the earth: for I am G-d, and there is none else.23 I have sworn by myself, the word is gone out of my mouth in righteousness, and shall not return, That unto me every knee shall bow, every tongue shall swear.24 Surely, shall one say, in YHUH have I righteousness and strength: even to him shall men come; and all that are incensed against him shall be ashamed.25 In YHUH shall all the seed of Israel be justified, and shall glory. **Isa** 46:1 Bel bow down, Nebo stoopeth, their idols were upon the beasts, and upon the cattle: your carriages were heavy loaden; they are a burden to the weary beast.2 They stoop, they bow down together; they could not deliver the burden, but themselves are gone into captivity.

משא 4853 ונפשם 5315 בשבי 7628 הלכה 1980: 46:3 שמעו 8085 אלי 413 בית 1004 יעקב 3290 וכל 3605 שארית 7611
masa'; uanapsham bashabiy halakah. shim'au 'aelay beyt ya'aqob, uakal sha'aeriyt
**the burden but themselves into captivity are gone Hearken unto me O house of Jacob and all the remnant of**

בית 1004 ישראל 3478 העמסים 6006 מני 4480 בטן 990 הנשאים 5375 מני 4480 רחם 7356: 46:4 ועד 5704
beyt yisra'ael; ha'amusiym miniy beten, hanasu'aym miniy racham. ua'ad
**the house of Israel which are borne *by me* from the belly which are carried from the womb And even to**

זקנה 2209 אני 589 הוא 1931 ועד 5704 שיבה 7872 אני 589 אסבל 5445 אני 589 עשיתי 6213 ואני 589 אשא 5375 ואני 589 אסבל 5445
ziqnah 'aniy hua', ua'ad sheybah 'aniy 'asbol; 'aniy 'asiytiy ua'aniy 'asa', ua'aniy 'asbol
***your* old age I *am* he and even to hoar hairs *you* I will carry I have made and I will bear even I will carry**

ואמלט 4422: 46:5 למי 4310 תדמיוני 1819 ותשוו 7737 ותמשלוני 4911 ונדמה 1819: 46:6
ua'amalet. lamiy tadamyuniy uatashuu; uatamshiluniy uanidmeh.
**and will deliver *you* To whom will you liken me and make *me* equal and compare me that we may be like?**

הזלים 2107 זהב 2091 מכיס 3599 וכסף 3701 בקנה 7070 ישקלו 8254 ישכרו 7936 צורף 6884 ויעשהו 6213 אל 410
hazaliym zahab mikiys, uakesep baqaneh yishqolu; yiskaru tzourep uaya'asehu 'ael,
**They lavish gold out of the bag and silver in the balance weigh *and* hire a goldsmith and he make it *a* god**

יסגדו 5456 אף 637 ישתחוו 7812: 46:7 ישאהו 5375 על 5921 כתף 3802 יסבלהו 5445 ויניחהו 3240 תחתיו 8478
yisgadu 'ap yishtachauu yisa'ahu 'al katep yisbaluhu uayanychuhu tachtayu
**they fall down yea they worship They bear him upon the shoulder they carry him and set him in his place**

ויעמד 5975 ממקומו 4725 לא 3808 ימיש 4185 אף 637 יצעק 6817 אליו 413 ולא 3808 יענה 6030 מצרתו 6869
uaya'amod, mimaqoumou la' yamiysh; 'ap yitz'aq 'aelayu uala' ya'aneh, mitzaratou
**and he stands from his place not shall he remove yea *one* shall cry unto him yet not can he answer out of his trouble**

לא 3808 יושיענו 3467: 46:8 זכרו 2142 זאת 2063 והתאששו 377 השיבו 7725 פושעים 6586 על 5921 לב 3820: 46:9
la' yoshiy'anu. zichru za't uahit'ashashu; hashiybu pousha'aym 'al leb.
**nor save him Remember this and show yourselves men bring *it* again O you transgressors to mind**

זכרו 2142 ראשנות 7223 מעולם 5769 כי 3588 אנכי 595 אל 410 ואין 369 עוד 5750 אלהים 430 ואפס 657
zikru ra'shonout me'aulam; kiy 'anokiy 'ael ua'aeyn 'aud, 'alohiym ua'apes
**Remember the former things of old for I *am* El and *there is* none else *I am* Elohim and *there is* none**

כמוני 3644: 46:10 מגיד 5046 מראשית 7225 אחרית 319 ומקדם 6924 אשר 834 לא 3808 נעשו 6213 אמר 559
kamouniy. magiyd mere'shiyt 'achariyt, uamiqedem 'asher la' naa'asu; 'amer
**like me Declaring from the beginning the end and from ancient times *the things* that not *yet* are done saying**

עצתי 6098 תקום 6965 וכל 3605 חפצי 2656 אעשה 6213: 46:11 קרא 7121 ממזרח 4217 עיט 5861 מארץ 776 מרחק 7801
'atzatiy taqum, uakal cheptziy 'aaseh. qorea' mimizrach 'ayit, me'aretz merchaq
**My counsel shall stand and all my pleasure I will do Calling from the east a ravenous bird from a country far**

איש 376 עצתו 6098 אף 637 דברתי 1696 אף 637 אביאנה 935 יצרתי 3335 אף 637 אעשנה 6213:
'aysh 'atzatou 'ap dibartiy 'ap 'abiy'anah, yatzartiy 'ap 'aasenah.
**the man *that executes* my counsel yea I have spoken *it* also I will bring it to pass I have purposed *it* also I will do it**

Isa 46:3 Hearken unto me, O house of Jacob, and all the remnant of the house of Israel, which are borne by me from the belly, which are carried from the womb:4 And even to your old age I am he; and even to hoar hairs will I carry you: I have made, and I will bear; even I will carry, and will deliver you.5 To whom will you liken me, and make me equal, and compare me, that we may be like?6 They lavish gold out of the bag, and weigh silver in the balance, and hire a goldsmith; and he make it a god: they fall down, yea, they worship.7 They bear him upon the shoulder, they carry him, and set him in his place, and he stand; from his place shall he not remove: yea, one shall cry unto him, yet can he not answer, nor save him out of his trouble.8 Remember this, and show yourselves men: bring it again to mind, O you transgressors.9 Remember the former things of old: for I am G-d, and there is none else; I am G-d, and there is none like me,10 Declaring the end from the beginning, and from ancient times the things that are not yet done, saying, My counsel shall stand, and I will do all my pleasure:11 Calling a ravenous bird from the east, the man that executeth my counsel from a far country: yea, I have spoken it, I will also bring it to pass; I have purposed it, I will also do it.

**46:12** שמעו 8085 אלי 413 אבירי 47 לב 3820 הרחוקים 7350 מצדקה 6666: **46:13** קרבתי 7126 צדקתי 6666 לא 3808
shim'au 'aelay 'abiyrey leb; harachouqiym mitzdaqah. qerabtiy tzidqatiy la'
**Hearken unto me you stout hearted that *are* far from righteousness I bring near my righteousness not**

תרחק 7368 ותשועתי 8668 לא 3808 תאחר 309 ונתתי 5414 בציון 6726 תשועה 8668 לישראל 3478 תפארתי 8597:
tirchaq, uatshu'atiy la' ta'acher; uanatatiy batziyoun tashu'ah, layisra'ael tip'artiy.
**it shall be far off and my salvation not shall tarry and I will place in Zion salvation for Israel my glory**

**Isa 47:1** רדי 3381 ושבי 3427 על 5921 עפר 6083 בתולת 1330 בת 1323 בבל 894 שבי 3427 לארץ 776 אין 369 כסא 3678
radiy ushbiy 'al 'apar, batulat bat babel, shabiy la'aretz 'aeyn kisea'
**Come down and sit in the dust O virgin daughter of Babylon sit on the ground *there is* no throne**

בת 1323 כשדים 3778 כי 3588 לא 3808 תוסיפי 3254 יקראו 7121 לך 3807a רכה 7390 וענגה 6028: **47:2** קחי 3947 רחים 7347
bat kasdiym; kiy la' tousiypiy yiqra'au lak, rakah ua'anugah. qachiy rechayim
**O daughter of the Chaldeans for no more shall be called to you tender and delicate Take the millstones**

וטחני 2912 קמח 7058 גלי 1540 צמתך 6777 חשפי 2834 שבל 7640 גלי 1540 שוק 7785 עברי 5674 נהרות 5104: **47:3** תגל 1540
uatachaniy qamach; galiy tzamatek chespiy shobel galiy shouq 'abriy naharout. tigal
**and grind meal uncover your locks make bare the leg uncover the thigh pass over the rivers shall be uncovered**

ערותך 6172 גם 1571 תראה 7200 חרפתך 2781 נקם 5359 אקח 3947 ולא 3808 אפגע 6293 אדם 120: **47:4**
'aruatek, gam tera'ah cherpatek; naqam 'aqach, uala' 'apga' 'adam.
**Your nakedness yea shall be seen your shame vengeance I will take and not I will meet *you as* a man**

גאלנו 1350 יהוה 3068 צבאות 6635 שמו 8034 קדוש 6918 ישראל 3478: **47:5** שבי 3427 דומם 1748 ובאי 935
go'alenu Yahuah tzaba'aut shamou; qadoush yisra'ael. shabiy dumam uabo'ay
***As for* our redeemer Yahuah of hosts *is* his name *the* Holy One of Israel Sit you silent and get you**

בחשך 2822 בת 1323 כשדים 3778 כי 3588 לא 3808 תוסיפי 3254 יקראו 7121 לך 3807a גברת 1404 ממלכות 4467: **47:6**
bachoshek bat kasdiym; kiy la' tousiypiy yiqra'au lak, gaberet mamlakout.
**into darkness O daughter of the Chaldeans for no more shall be called to you The lady of kingdoms**

קצפתי 7107 על 5921 עמי 5971 חללתי 2490 נחלתי 5159 ואתנם 5414 בידך 3027 לא 3808 שמת 7760 להם 1992
qatzaptiy 'al 'amiy, chilaltiy nachalatiy, ua'atanem bayadek; la' samt lahem
**I was wroth with my people I have polluted mine inheritance and I gave them into your hand no you did show them**

רחמים 7356 על 5921 זקן 2205 הכבדת 3513 עלך 5923 מאד 3966: **47:7** ותאמרי 559 לעולם 5769 אהיה 1961 גברת 1404 עד 5704
rachamiym, 'al zaqen hikbadt 'alek ma'ad. uata'mariy, la'aulam 'ahayeh gabaret; 'ad
**mercy upon the ancient have you heavily laid your yoke very And you said for ever I shall be a lady for**

לא 3808 שמת 7760 אלה 428 על 5921 לבך 3820 לא 3808 זכרת 2142 אחריתה 319: **47:8** ועתה 6258 שמעי 8085
la' samt 'aeleh 'al libek, la' zakart 'achariytah. ua'atah shim'ay
**not *so* that did lay these *things* to your heart neither did remember the latter end of it Therefore now hear**

זאת 2063 עדינה 5719 היושבת 3427 לבטח 983 האמרה 559 בלבבה 3824 אני 589 ואפסי 657 עוד 5750
za't 'adiynah hayoushebet labetach, ha'amarah bilbabah, *'aniy* ua'apsiy 'aud;
**this *you that are* given to pleasures that dwell carelessly that say in your heart *I am* and none beside me else**

Isa 46:12 Hearken unto me, you stouthearted, that are far from righteousness:13 I bring near my righteousness; it shall not be far off, and my salvation shall not tarry: and I will place salvation in Zion for Israel my glory. **Isa** 47:1 Come down, and sit in the dust, O virgin daughter of Babylon, sit on the ground: there is no throne, O daughter of the Chaldeans: for you shall no more be called tender and delicate.2 Take the millstones, and grind meal: uncover your locks, make bare the leg, uncover the thigh, pass over the rivers.3 Thy nakedness shall be uncovered, yea, your shame shall be seen: I will take vengeance, and I will not meet you as a man.4 As for our redeemer, YHUH of hosts is his name, the Holy One of Israel.5 Sit you silent, and get you into darkness, O daughter of the Chaldeans: for you shall no more be called, The lady of kingdoms.6 I was wroth with my people, I have polluted mine inheritance, and given them into your hand: you did show them no mercy; upon the ancient have you very heavily laid your yoke.7 And you saidst, I shall be a lady forever: so that you did not lay these things to your heart, neither did remember the latter end of it.8 Therefore hear now this, you that are given to pleasures, that dwellest carelessly, that say in your heart, I am, and none else beside me; I shall not sit as a widow, neither shall I know the loss of children:

| | | | | | | | | | |
|---|---|---|---|---|---|---|---|---|---|
| לא 3808 | אשב 3427 | אלמנה 490 | ולא 3808 | אדע 3045 | שכול 7908: | 47:9 ותבאנה 935 | לך 3807a | שתי 8147 | אלה 428 |
| la' | 'aesheb | 'almanah, | uala' | 'aeda | shakoul. | uataba'nah | lak | shatey | 'aeleh |
| **not** | **I shall sit** | ***as* a widow** | **neither** | **shall I know** | **the loss of children** | **But shall come** | **to you** | **two *things*** | **these** |

| | | | | | | | |
|---|---|---|---|---|---|---|---|
| רגע 7281 | ביום 3117 | אחד 259 | שכול 7908 | ואלמן 489 | כתמם 8537 | באו 935 | עליך 5921 |
| rega' | bayoum | 'achad | shakoul | ua'almon; | katumam | ba'au | 'alayik, |
| **in a moment** | **in day** | **one** | **the loss of children** | **and widowhood** | **in their perfection** | **they shall come** | **upon you** |

| | | | | | |
|---|---|---|---|---|---|
| ברב 7230 | כשפיך 3785 | בעצמת 6109 | חבריך 2267 | מאד 3966: | 47:10 ותבטחי 982 |
| barob | kashapayik, | ba'atzamat | chabarayik | ma'ad. | uatibtachiy |
| **for the multitude of** | **your sorceries** | ***and* for abundance of** | **your enchantments** | ***the* great** | **For you have trusted** |

| | | | | | | | |
|---|---|---|---|---|---|---|---|
| ברעתך 7451 | אמרת 559 | אין 369 | ראני 7200 | חכמתך 2451 | ודעתך 1847 | היא 1931 | שובבתך 7725 |
| bara'atek, | 'amart | 'aeyn | ro'aniy, | chakamatek | ada'tek | hiy'a | shoubatek; |
| **in your wickedness** | **you have said** | **None** | **see me** | **Your wisdom** | **and your knowledge** | **it** | **has perverted you** |

| | | | | | | | | |
|---|---|---|---|---|---|---|---|---|
| ותאמרי 559 | בלבך 3820 | אני 589 | ואפסי 657 | עוד 5750: | 47:11 ובא 935 | עליך 5921 | רעה 7451 | לא 3808 |
| uata'mriy | balibek, | 'aniy | ua'apsiy | 'aud. | uaba' | 'alayik | ra'ah, | la' |
| **and you have said** | **in your heart** | **I *am*** | **and none besides me** | **else** | **Therefore shall come** | **upon you** | **evil** | **not** |

| | | | | | | | | |
|---|---|---|---|---|---|---|---|---|
| תדעי 3045 | שחרה 7837 | ותפל 5307 | עליך 5921 | הוה 1943 | לא 3808 | תוכלי 3201 | כפרה 3722 | ותבא 935 |
| teda'ay | shachrah, | uatipol | 'alayik | houah, | la' | tukaliy | kaprah; | uataba' |
| **you shall know** | **from where it rise** | **and shall fall** | **upon you** | **mischief** | **not** | **you shall be able** | **to put it off** | **and shall come** |

| | | | | | | | |
|---|---|---|---|---|---|---|---|
| עליך 5921 | פתאם 6597 | שואה 7722 | לא 3808 | תדעי 3045: | 47:12 עמדי 5975 | נא 4994 | בחבריך 2267 |
| 'alayik | pit'am | shou'ah | la' | teda'ay. | 'amdiy | naa' | bachabarayik |
| **upon you** | **suddenly** | **desolation** | **not** | ***which* you shall know** | **Stand** | **now** | **with your enchantments** |

| | | | | | | | |
|---|---|---|---|---|---|---|---|
| וברב 7230 | כשפיך 3785 | באשר 834 | יגעת 3021 | מנעוריך 5271 | אולי 194 | תוכלי 3201 | הועיל 3276 |
| uabrob | kashapayik, | ba'asher | yaga'at | mina'aurayik; | 'aulay | tukaliy | hou'ayl |
| **and with the multitude of** | **your sorceries** | **wherein** | **you have laboured** | **from your youth** | **if so be** | **you shall be able** | **to profit** |

| | | | | | | | |
|---|---|---|---|---|---|---|---|
| אולי 194 | תערוצי 6206: | 47:13 נלאית 3811 | ברב 7230 | עצתיך 6098 | יעמדו 5975 | נא 4994 | ויושיעך 3467 |
| 'aulay | ta'aroutziy. | nil'aeyt | barob | 'atzatayik; | ya'amdu | naa' | uayoushiy'ak |
| **if so be** | **you may prevail** | **You are wearied** | **in the multitude of** | **your counsels** | **Let stand up** | **now** | **and save you** |

| | | | | | | | |
|---|---|---|---|---|---|---|---|
| הברו 1895 | שמים 8064 | החזים 2374 | בכוכבים 3556 | מודיעם 3045 | לחדשים 2320 | מאשר 834 | יבאו 935 |
| habaru | shamayim, | hachoziym | bakoukabiym, | moudiy'am | lechadashiym, | me'asher | yabo'au |
| **the astrologers,** | **heavens** | **gazers** | **the star** | **prognosticators** | ***the* monthly** | **from *these things* that** | **shall come** |

| | | | | | | | | | |
|---|---|---|---|---|---|---|---|---|---|
| עליך 5921: | 47:14 הנה 2009 | היו 1961 | כקש 7179 | אש 784 | שרפתם 8313 | לא 3808 | יצילו 5337 | את 853 | נפשם 5315 |
| 'alayik. | hineh | hayu | kaqash | 'aesh | sarapatam, | la' | yatziylu | 'at | napsham |
| **upon you** | **Behold** | **they shall be** | **as stubble** | **the fire** | **shall burn them** | **not** | **they shall deliver** | | **themselves** |

| | | | | | | | | | |
|---|---|---|---|---|---|---|---|---|---|
| מיד 3027 | להבה 3852 | אין 369 | גחלת 1513 | לחמם 2552 | אור 217 | לשבת 3427 | נגדו 5048: | 47:15 כן 3651 | היו 1961 |
| miyad | lehabah; | 'aeyn | gachelet | lachmam, | 'aur | lashabet | negdou. | ken | hayu |
| **from the power of** | **the flame** | ***there shall*** **not** | ***be* a coal** | **to warm at** | ***nor* fire** | **to sit** | **before it** | **Thus** | **shall they be** |

Isa 47:9 But these two things shall come to you in a moment in one day, the loss of children, and widowhood: they shall come upon you in their perfection for the multitude of your sorceries, and for the great abundance of your enchantments. 10 For you have trusted in your wickedness: you have said, None see me. Thy wisdom and your knowledge, it has perverted you; and you have said in your heart, I am, and none else beside me. 11 Therefore shall evil come upon you; you shall not know from whence it rise: and mischief shall fall upon you; you shall not be able to put it off: and desolation shall come upon you suddenly, which you shall not know. 12 Stand now with your enchantments, and with the multitude of your sorceries, wherein you have laboured from your youth; if so be you shall be able to profit, if so be you may prevail. 13 Thou are wearied in the multitude of your counsels. Let now the astrologers, the stargazers, the monthly prognosticators, stand up, and save you from these things that shall come upon you. 14 Behold, they shall be as stubble; the fire shall burn them; they shall not deliver themselves from the power of the flame: there shall not be a coal to warm at, nor fire to sit before it.

לך 3807a | אשר 834 | יגעת 3021 | סחריך 5503 | מנעוריך 5271 | איש 376 | לעברו 5676 | תעו 8582
lak | 'asher | yaga'at; | socharayik | mina'aurayik, | 'aysh | la'abrou | ta'au,
**unto you | *with* whom | you have laboured | *even* your merchants | from your youth | every one | to his quarter | they shall wander**

אין 369 | מושיעך 3467:
'aeyn | moushiy'aek.
**none | shall save you**

**Isa 48:1** שמעו 8085 | זאת 2063 | בית 1004 | יעקב 3290 | הנקראים 7121 | בשם 8034 | ישראל 3478 | וממי 4325 | יהודה 3063
shim'au | za't | beyt | ya'aqob, | haniqra'aym | bashem | yisra'ael, | uamimey | yahudah
**Hear you | this | O house of | Jacob | which are called | by the name of | Israel | out of the waters of | Judah**

יצאו 3318 | הנשבעים 7650 | בשם 8034 | יהוה 3068 | ובאלהי 430 | ישראל 3478 | יזכירו 2142 | לא 3808 | באמת 571 | ולא 3808
yatza'au; | hanishba'aym | bashem | Yahuah | uabe'alohey | yisra'ael | yazkiyru, | la' | be'amet | uala'
**are come forth | which swear | by the name of | Yahuah | and of the Elohim of | Israel | make mention | *but* not | in truth | nor**

בצדקה 6666: | **48:2** כי 3588 | מעיר 5892 | הקדש 6944 | נקראו 7121 | ועל 5921 | אלהי 430 | ישראל 3478 | נסמכו 5564
bitzadaqah. | kiy | me'ayr | haqodesh | niqra'u, | ua'al | 'alohey | yisra'ael | nismaku;
**in righteousness | For | of city | the holy | they call themselves | and upon | the Elohim of | Israel | stay themselves**

יהוה 3068 | צבאות 6635 | שמו 8034: | **48:3** הראשנות 7223 | מאז 227 | הגדתי 5046 | ומפי 6310
Yahuah | tzaba'aut | shamou. | hara'shonout | me'az | higadtiy, | uamipiy
**Yahuah | of hosts | *is* his name | the former things | from the beginning | I have declared | and out of my mouth**

יצאו 3318 | ואשמיעם 8085 | פתאם 6597 | עשיתי 6213 | ותבאנה 935: | **48:4** מדעתי 1847 | כי 3588 | קשה 7186
yatza'ua | ua'ashmiy'aem; | pit'am | 'asiytiy | uataba'nah. | mida'tiy | kiy | qasheh
**they went forth | and I showed them | suddenly | I did *them* | and they came to pass | Because I knew | that | *are* obstinate**

אתה 859 | וגיד 1517 | ברזל 1270 | ערפך 6203 | ומצחך 4696 | נחושה 5154: | **48:5** ואגיד 5046 | לך 3807a | מאז 227
'atah; | uagiyd | barzel | 'arapeka, | uamitzchaka | nachushah. | ua'agiyd | laka | me'az,
**you | and sinew | *is* an iron | your neck | and your brow | brass | I have even declared *it* | to you | from the beginning**

בטרם 2962 | תבוא 935 | השמעתיך 8085 | פן 6435 | תאמר 559 | עצבי 6091 | עשם 6213 | ופסלי 6459
baterem | tabou'a | hishma'atiyka; | pen | ta'mar | 'atzabiy | 'asam, | uapisliy
**before | it came to pass | I showed *it* you | lest | you should say | my idol | has done them | and my graven image**

ונסכי 5262 | צום 6680: | **48:6** שמעת 8085 | חזה 2372 | כלה 3605 | ואתם 859 | הלוא 3808 | תגידו 5046
uaniskiy | tziuam. | shama'ata | chazeh | kulah, | ua'atem | halou'a | tagiydu;
**and my molten image | has commanded them | You have heard | see | all this | and you | not | will declare *it*?**

השמעתיך 8085 | חדשות 2319 | מעתה 6258 | ונצרות 5341 | ולא 3808 | ידעתם 3045: | **48:7** עתה 6258 | נבראו 1254
hishma'atiyka | chadashout | me'atah, | uantzurout | uala' | yada'atam. | 'atah | nibra'au
**I have showed you | new things | from this time | even hidden things | and not | you did know them | now | They are created**

ולא 3808 | מאז 227 | ולפני 6440 | יום 3117 | ולא 3808 | שמעתם 8085 | פן 6435 | תאמר 559 | הנה 2009 | ידעתין 3045:
uala' | me'az, | ualipney | youm | uala' | shama'tam; | pen | ta'mar | hineh | yada'atiyn.
**and not | from the beginning | even before the day | when not | you heard them | lest | you should say | Behold | I knew them**

Isa 47:15 Thus shall they be unto you with whom you have laboured, even your merchants, from your youth: they shall wander everyone to his quarter; none shall save you. **Isa** 48:1 Hear you this, O house of Jacob, which are called by the name of Israel, and are come forth out of the waters of Judah, which swear by the name of YHUH, and make mention of the G-d of Israel, but not in truth, nor in righteousness.2 For they call themselves of the holy city, and stay themselves upon the G-d of Israel; YHUH of hosts is his name.3 I have declared the former things from the beginning; and they went forth out of my mouth, and I showed them; I did them suddenly, and they came to pass.4 Because I knew that you are obstinate, and your neck is an iron sinew, and your brow brass;5 I have even from the beginning declared it to you; before it came to pass I showed it you: lest you should say, Mine idol has done them, and my graven image, and my molten image, has commanded them.6 Thou have heard, see all this; and will not you declare it? I have showed you new things from this time, even hidden things, and you did not know them.7 They are created now, and not from the beginning; even before the day when you heardest them not; lest you should say, Behold, I knew them.

**48:8** גם 1571 לא 3808 שמעת 8085 גם 1571 לא 3808 ידעת 3045 גם 1571 מאז 227 לא 3808 פתחה 6605 אזנך 241 כי 3588 ידעתי 3045
gam la' shama'ata, gam la' yada'ta, gam me'az la' pitchah 'azaneka; kiy yada'tiy
**Yea not you heard yea not you knew yea from that time not was opened *that* your ear for I knew**

בגוד 901 תבגוד 898 ופשע 6586 מבטן 990 קרא 7121 לך 3807a: **48:9** למען 4616 שמי 8034
bagoud tibgoud, uaposhea' mibeten qora' lak. lama'an shamiy
**that you would deal treacherous very and a transgressor from the womb were called to you For sake my name's**

אאריך 748 אפי 639 ותהלתי 8416 אחטם 2413 לך 3807a לבלתי 1115 הכריתך 3772: **48:10** הנה 2009 צרפתיך 6884 ולא 3808
'a'ariyk 'apiy, uatahilatiy 'achatam lak; labiltiy hakariyteka. hineh tzaraptiyka uala'
**will I defer mine anger and for my praise will I refrain for you that not I cut you off Behold I have refined but not**

בכסף 3701 בחרתיך 977 בכור 3564 עני 6040: **48:11** למעני 4616 למעני 4616 אעשה 6213 כי 3588
bakasep; bacharatiyka bakour 'aniy. lama'aniy lama'aniy 'aaseh kiy
**with silver I have chosen you in the furnace of affliction For mine own sake *even* for mine own sake will I do *it* for**

איך 349 יחל 2490 וכבודי 3519 לאחר 312 לא 3808 אתן 5414: **48:12** שמע 8085 אלי 413 יעקב 3290 וישראל 3478
'aeyk yechal; uakboudiy la'acher la' 'aten. shama' 'aelay ya'aqob, uayisra'ael
**how should *my name* be polluted? and my glory unto another not I will give Hearken unto me O Jacob and Israel**

מקראי 7121 אני 589 הוא 1931 אני 589 ראשון 7223 אף 637 אני 589 אחרון 314: **48:13** אף 637 ידי 3027 יסדה 3245 ארץ 776
maqora'ay; 'aniy hua' 'aniy ra'shoun, 'ap 'aniy 'acharoun. 'ap yadiy yasadah 'aretz,
**my called I *am* he I *am* the first also I *am* the last also Mine hand has laid the foundation of the earth**

וימיני 3225 טפחה 2946 שמים 8064 קרא 7121 אני 589 אליהם 413 יעמדו 5975 יחדו 3162: **48:14** הקבצו 6908
uiymiyniy tipchah shamayim; qorea' 'aniy 'aleyhem ya'amdu yachdau. hiqabatzu
**and my right hand has spanned the heavens call *when* I unto them they stand up together assemble yourselves**

כלכם 3605 ושמעו 8085 מי 4310 בהם 871a הגיד 5046 את 853 אלה 428 יהוה 3069 אהבו 157 יעשה 6213 חפצו 2656
kulkem uashama'au, miy' bahem higiyd 'at 'aeleh; Yahuah ahebou, ya'aseh chepatzou
**All you and hear which among them has declared these *things*? Yahuah has loved him he will do his pleasure**

בבבל 894 וזרעו 2220 כשדים 3778: **48:15** אני 589 אני 589 דברתי 1696 אף 637 קראתיו 7121
bababel, uazro'au kasdiym. 'aniy 'aniy dibartiy 'ap qara'tiyu;
**on Babylon and his arm *shall be on* the Chaldeans I *even* I have spoken yea I have called him**

הביאתיו 935 והצליח 6743 דרכו 1870: **48:16** קרבו 7126 אלי 413 שמעו 8085 זאת 2063 לא 3808
habiy'atiyu uahitzliyach darkou. qirbu 'aelay shim'au za't, la'
**I have brought him and he shall make prosperous his way Come you near unto me hear you this not**

מראש 2718 בסתר 5643 דברתי 1696 מעת 6256 היותה 1961 שם 8033 אני 589 ועתה 6258 אדני 136 יהוה 3069 שלחני 7971
mera'sh baseter dibartiy, me'aut hayoutah sham 'aniy; ua'atah, 'adonay Yahuah shalachaniy
**from the beginning in secret I have spoken from the time that it was there *am* I and now Adonai Yahuah has sent me**

ורוחו 7307: **48:17** כה 3541 אמר 559 יהוה 3068 גאלך 1350 קדוש 6918 ישראל 3478 אני 589 יהוה 3068 אלהיך 430
uaruchou. koh 'amar Yahuah go'alka qadoush yisra'ael; 'aniy Yahuah 'aloheyka
**and his Spirit Thus saith Yahuah your Redeemer *the* Holy One of Israel I *am* Yahuah your Elohim**

Isa 48:8 Yea, you heardest not; yea, you knew not; yea, from that time that your ear was not opened: for I knew that you would deal very treacherously, and were called a transgressor from the womb.9 For my name's sake will I defer mine anger, and for my praise will I refrain for you, that I cut you not off.10 Behold, I have refined you, but not with silver; I have chosen you in the furnace of affliction.11 For mine own sake, even for mine own sake, will I do it: for how should my name be polluted? and I will not give my glory unto another.12 Hearken unto me, O Jacob and Israel, my called; I am he; I am the first, I also am the last.13 Mine hand also has laid the foundation of the earth, and my right hand has spanned the heavens: when I call unto them, they stand up together.14 All you, assemble yourselves, and hear; which among them has declared these things? YHUH has loved him: he will do his pleasure on Babylon, and his arm shall be on the Chaldeans.15 I, even I, have spoken; yea, I have called him: I have brought him, and he shall make his way prosperous.16 Come you near unto me, hear you this; I have not spoken in secret from the beginning; from the time that it was, there am I: and now YHUH G-D, and his Spirit, has sent me.17 Thus saith YHUH, your Redeemer, the Holy One of Israel;

| | | | | | | | |
|---|---|---|---|---|---|---|---|
| מלמדך 3925 | להועיל 3276 | מדריכך 1869 | בדרך 1870 | תלך 1980: | **48:18** | לוא 3863 | הקשבת 7181 |
| malamedaka | lahou'ayl, | madriykaka | baderek | telek. | | lua' | hiqshabta |
| **which teach you** | **to profit** | **which lead you** | **by the way *that*** | **you should go** | | **O that** | **you had hearkened** |

| | | | | | | | |
|---|---|---|---|---|---|---|---|
| למצותי 4687 | ויהי 1961 | כנהר 5104 | שלומך 7965 | וצדקתך 6666 | כגלי 1530 | הים 3220: | **48:19** |
| lamitzuotay; | uayahiy | kanahar | shaloumeka, | uatzidqataka | kagaley | hayam. | |
| **to my commandments** | **then have been** | **as a river** | **your peace** | **and your righteousness** | **as the waves of** | **the sea** | |

| | | | | | | |
|---|---|---|---|---|---|---|
| ויהי 1961 | כחול 2344 | זרעך 2233 | וצאצאי 6631 | מעיך 4578 | כמעתיו 4579 | לא 3808 |
| uayahiy | kachoul | zar'aka, | uatze'atza'aey | me'ayka | kim'atayu; | la' |
| **also have been** | **as the sand** | **Your seed** | **and the offspring of** | **your bowels** | **like the gravel thereof** | **not** |

| | | | | | | | | |
|---|---|---|---|---|---|---|---|---|
| יכרת 3772 | ולא 3808 | ישמד 8045 | שמו 8034 | מלפני 6440: | **48:20** | צאו 3318 | מבבל 894 | ברחו 1272 |
| yikaret | uala' | yishamed | shamou | milapanay. | | tza'au | mibabel | birchu |
| **should have been cut off** | **nor** | **destroyed** | **his name** | **from before me** | | **Go you forth** | **of Babylon** | **flee you** |

| | | | | | | | | | | |
|---|---|---|---|---|---|---|---|---|---|---|
| מכשדים 3778 | בקול 6963 | רנה 7440 | הגידו 5046 | השמיעו 8085 | זאת 2063 | הוציאוה 3318 | עד 5704 | קצה 7097 | הארץ 776 | אמרו 559 |
| mikasdiym | baqoul | rinah, | hagiydu | hashmiy'au | za't, | houtziy'auha | 'ad | qatzeh | ha'aretz; | 'amru |
| **from the Chaldeans** | **with a voice of** | **singing** | **declare you** | **tell** | **this** | **utter it *even*** | **to** | **the end of** | **the earth** | **say you** |

| | | | | | | | | | |
|---|---|---|---|---|---|---|---|---|---|
| גאל 1350 | יהוה 3068 | עבדו 5650 | יעקב 3290: | **48:21** | ולא 3808 | צמאו 6770 | בחרבות 2723 | הוליכם 1980 | מים 4325 |
| ga'al | Yahuah | abdou | ya'aqob. | | uala' | tzama'au, | bacharabout | houliykam, | mayim |
| **has redeemed** | **Yahuah** | **his servant** | **Jacob** | | **And not** | **they thirsted** | **through the deserts *when*** | **he led them** | **the waters** |

| | | | | | | | | | |
|---|---|---|---|---|---|---|---|---|---|
| מצור 6697 | הזיל 5140 | למו 3807a | ויבקע 1234 | צור 6697 | ויזבו 2100 | מים 4325: | **48:22** | אין 369 | שלום 7965 |
| mitzur | hiziyl | lamou; | uayibqa' | tzur, | uayazubu | mayim. | | 'aeyn | shaloum, |
| **of the rock** | **he caused to flow out** | **for them** | **he clave also** | **the rock** | **and gushed out** | **the waters** | | ***There is* no** | **peace** |

| | | |
|---|---|---|
| אמר 559 | יהוה 3068 | לרשעים 7563: |
| 'amar | Yahuah | larasha'aym. |
| **saith** | **Yahuah** | **unto the wicked** |

| | | | | | | | | | |
|---|---|---|---|---|---|---|---|---|---|
| **Isa 49:1** | שמעו 8085 | איים 339 | אלי 413 | והקשיבו 7181 | לאמים 3816 | מרחוק 7350 | יהוה 3068 | מבטן 990 | קראני 7121 |
| | shim'au | 'ayiym | 'aelay, | uahaqshiybu | la'amiym | merachouq; | Yahuah | mibeten | qara'aniy, |
| | **Listen** | **O isles** | **unto me** | **and listen you** | **people** | **from far** | **Yahuah** | **from the womb** | **has called me** |

| | | | | | | | | |
|---|---|---|---|---|---|---|---|---|
| ממעי 4578 | אמי 517 | הזכיר 2142 | שמי 8034: | **49:2** | וישם 7760 | פי 6310 | כחרב 2719 | חדה 2299 |
| mim'aey | 'amiy | hizkiyr | shamiy. | | uayasem | piy | kachereb | chadah, |
| **from the bowels of** | **my mother** | **has he made mention of** | **my name** | | **And he has made** | **my mouth** | **like a sword** | **sharp** |

| | | | | | | | | | | |
|---|---|---|---|---|---|---|---|---|---|---|
| בצל 6738 | ידו 3027 | החביאני 2244 | וישימני 7760 | לחץ 2671 | ברור 1305 | באשפתו 827 | הסתירני 5641: | **49:3** | ויאמר 559 | לי 3807a |
| batzel | yadou | hechbiy'aniy; | uayasiymeniy | lachetz | barur, | ba'ashpatou | histiyraniy. | | uaya'mer | liy |
| **in the shadow of** | **his hand** | **has he hid me** | **and made me** | **a shaft** | **polished** | **in his quiver** | **has he hid me** | | **And said** | **unto me** |

| | | | | | | | | | | | |
|---|---|---|---|---|---|---|---|---|---|---|---|
| עבדי 5650 | אתה 859 | ישראל 3478 | אשר 834 | בך 871a | אתפאר 6286: | **49:4** | ואני 589 | אמרתי 559 | לריק 7385 | יגעתי 3021 | לתהו 8414 |
| 'abdiy | 'atah; | yisra'ael | 'asher | baka | 'atpa'ar. | | ua'aniy | 'amartiy | lariyq | yaga'atiy, | latohu |
| ***are* my servant** | **You** | **O Israel** | **whom** | **in** | **I will be glorified** | | **Then I** | **said** | **in vain** | **I have laboured** | **for nought** |

Isa 48:17 I am YHUH your G-d which teach you to profit, which leadeth you by the way that you should go.18 O that you had hearkened to my commandments! then had your peace been as a river, and your righteousness as the waves of the sea:19 Thy seed also had been as the sand, and the offspring of your bowels like the gravel thereof; his name should not have been cut off nor destroyed from before me.20 Go you forth of Babylon, flee you from the Chaldeans, with a voice of singing declare you, tell this, utter it even to the end of the earth; say you, YHUH has redeemed his servant Jacob.21 And they thirsted not when he led them through the deserts: he caused the waters to flow out of the rock for them: he clave the rock also, and the waters gushed out.22 There is no peace, saith YHUH, unto the wicked. **Isa** 49:1 Listen, O isles, unto me; and hear, you people, from far; YHUH has called me from the womb; from the bowels of my mother has he made mention of my name.2 And he has made my mouth like a sharp sword; in the shadow of his hand has he hid me, and made me a polished shaft; in his quiver has he hid me;3 And said unto me, Thou are my servant, O Israel, in whom I will be glorified.4 Then I said, I have laboured in vain, I have spent my strength for nought, and in vain: yet surely my judgment is with YHUH, and my work with my G-d.

49:5

והבל 1892 כחי 3581 כליתי 3615 אכן 403 משפטי 4941 את 854 יהוה 3068 ופעלתי 6468 את 854 אלהי 430: ועתה 6258

uahebel kochiy kileytiy; 'aken mishpatiy 'at Yahuah, uap'alatiy 'at 'alohay. ua'atah

**and in vain my strength I have spent *yet* surely my judgment *is with* Yahuah and my work *with* my Elohim And now**

אמר 559 יהוה 3069 יצרי 3335 מבטן 990 לעבד 5650 לו 3807a לשובב 7725 יעקב 3290 אליו 413 וישראל 3478 לא 3808

'amar Yahuah yotzariy mibeten la'abed lou', lashoubeb ya'aqob 'aelayu, uayisra'ael la'

**saith Yahuah that formed me from the womb servant *to be* his to bring again Jacob to him Though Israel not**

49:6

יאסף 622 ואכבד 3513 בעיני 5869 יהוה 3069 ואלהי 430 היה 1961 עזי 5797: ויאמר 559

ye'asep; ua'akabed ba'aeyney Yahuah, ua'alohay hayah 'aziy. uaya'mer,

**be gathered yet shall I be glorious in the eyes of Yahuah and my Elohim shall be my strength And he said**

נקל 7043 מהיותך 1961 לי 3807a עבד 5650 להקים 6965 את 853 שבטי 7626 יעקב 3290 ונצירי 5336 ישראל 3478

naqel mihayoutaka liy 'abed, lahaqiym 'at shibtey ya'aqob, uantzyrey yisra'ael

**It is a light thing that you should be my servant to raise up the tribes of Jacob and the preserved of Israel**

49:7

להשיב 7725 ונתתיך 5414 לאור 216 גוים 1471 להיות 1961 ישועתי 3444 עד 5704 קצה 7097 הארץ 776:

lahashiyb; uantatiyka la'aur gouyim, lihayout yashu'atiy 'ad qatzeh ha'aretz.

**to restore and I will also give you for a light to the Gentiles that you may be my salvation unto the end of the earth**

כה 3541 אמר 559 יהוה 3068 גאל 1350 ישראל 3478 קדושו 6918 לבזה 960 נפש 5315 למתעב 8581

koh 'amar Yahuah go'ael yisra'ael qadoushou, libzoh nepesh limta'aeb

**Thus saith Yahuah the Redeemer of Israel *and* his Holy One to him whom despise man to him whom abhore**

גוי 1471 לעבד 5650 משלים 4910 מלכים 4428 יראו 7200 וקמו 6965 שרים 8269 וישתחוו 7812 למען 4616 יהוה 3068 אשר 834

gouy la'abed moshaliym, melakiym yir'au uaqamu, sariym uayishtachauu; lama'an Yahuah 'asher

**the nation to a servant of rulers Kings shall see and arise princes also shall worship because of Yahuah that**

49:8

נאמן 539 קדש 6918 ישראל 3478 ויבחרך 977: כה 3541 אמר 559 יהוה 3068 בעת 6256 רצון 7522

ne'aman, qadosh yisra'ael uayibchareka. koh 'amar Yahuah ba'aet ratzoun

**is faithful *and* the Holy One of Israel and he shall choose you Thus saith Yahuah In time an acceptable**

עניתיך 6030 וביום 3117 ישועה 3444 עזרתיך 5826 ואצרך 5341 ואתנך 5414 לברית 1285

'aniytiyka, uabyoum yashu'ah 'azartiyka; ua'atzaraka, ua'atenka libriyt

**have I heard you and in a day of salvation have I helped you and I will preserve you and give you for a covenant of**

49:9

עם 5971 להקים 6965 ארץ 776 להנחיל 5157 נחלות 5159 שממות 8074: לאמר 559 לאסורים 631 צאו 3318

'am, lahaqiym 'aretz, lahanachiyl nachalout shomemout. lea'mor la'asuriym tze'au,

**the people to establish the earth to cause to inherit heritages *the* desolate That you may say to the prisoners Go forth**

לאשר 834 בחשך 2822 הגלו 1540 על 5921 דרכים 1870 ירעו 7462 ובכל 3605 שפיים 8205

la'asher bachoshek higalu; 'al darakiym yir'au, uabkal shapayiym

**to them that *are* in darkness Shew yourselves in the ways They shall feed and in all high places**

49:10

מרעיתם 4830: לא 3808 ירעבו 7456 ולא 3808 יצמאו 6770 ולא 3808 יכם 5221 שרב 8273 ושמש 8121 כי 3588

mar'aytam. la' yir'abu uala' yitzma'au, uala' yakem sharab uashamesh; kiy

**their pastures *shall be* not They shall hunger nor thirst neither shall smite them the heat nor sun for**

Isa 49:5 And now, saith YHUH that formed me from the womb to be his servant, to bring Jacob again to him, Though Israel be not gathered, yet shall I be glorious in the eyes of YHUH, and my G-d shall be my strength.6 And he said, It is a light thing that you should be my servant to raise up the tribes of Jacob, and to restore the preserved of Israel: I will also give you for a light to the Gentiles, that you may be my salvation unto the end of the earth.7 Thus saith YHUH, the Redeemer of Israel, and his Holy One, to him whom man despiseth, to him whom the nation abhorreth, to a servant of rulers, Kings shall see and arise, princes also shall worship, because of YHUH that is faithful, and the Holy One of Israel, and he shall choose you.8 Thus saith YHUH, In an acceptable time have I heard you, and in a day of salvation have I helped you: and I will preserve you, and give you for a covenant of the people, to establish the earth, to cause to inherit the desolate heritages;9 That you may say to the prisoners, Go forth; to them that are in darkness, Shew yourselves. They shall feed in the ways, and their pastures shall be in all high places.10 They shall not hunger nor thirst; neither shall the heat nor sun smite them: for he that has mercy on them shall lead them, even by the springs of water shall he guide them.

49:11
מרחמם 7355 ינהגם 5090 ועל 5921 מבועי 4002 מים 4325 ינהלם 5095: ושמתי 7760 כל 3605
marachamam yanahagem, ua'al mabu'aey mayim yanahalem. uasamtiy kal
**he that has mercy on them shall lead them even by the springs of water shall he guide them And I will make all**

49:12
הרי 2022 לדרך 1870 ומסלתי 4546 ירמון 7311: הנה 2009 אלה 428 מרחוק 7350 יבאו 935 והנה 2009 אלה 428
haray ladarek; uamsilotay yarumun. hineh 'aeleh merachouq yabo'au; uahineh 'aeleh
**my mountains a way and my highways shall be exalted Behold these from far shall come and lo these**

49:13
מצפון 6828 ומים 3220 ואלה 428 מארץ 776 סינים 5515: רנו 7442 שמים 8064 וגילי 1523 ארץ 776
mitzapoun uamiyam, ua'aleh me'aretz siyniym. ranu shamayim uagiyliy 'aretz,
**from the north and from the west and these from the land of Sinim Sing O heavens and be joyful O earth**

יפצחו 6476 הרים 2022 רנה 7440 כי 3588 נחם 5162 יהוה 3068 עמו 5971 ועניו 6041
yiptzchu hariym rinah; kiy nicham Yahuah 'amou, ua'aniyau
**and break forth O mountains *into* singing for has comforted Yahuah his people and his afflicted**

49:14 49:15
ירחם 7355: ותאמר 559 ציון 6726 עזבני 5800 יהוה 3068 ואדני 136 שכחני 7911: התשכח 7911
yarachem. uata'mer tziyoun 'azabaniy Yahuah; ua'adonay shakechaniy. hatishkach
**will have mercy upon But said Zion has forsaken me Yahuah and my Adonai has forgotten me Can forget**

אשה 802 עולה 5764 מרחם 7355 בן 1121 בטנה 990 גם 1571 אלה 428 תשכחנה 7911
'ashah 'aulah, marachem ben bitnah; gam 'aeleh tishkachnah,
**a woman her sucking child that she should not have compassion on the son of her womb? yea they may forget**

49:16
ואנכי 595 לא 3808 אשכחך 7911: הן 2005 על 5921 כפים 3709 חקתיך 2710 חומתיך 2346 נגדי 5048
ua'anokiy la' 'ashkachek. hen 'al kapayim chaqotiyk; choumotayik negdiy
**yet will I not forget you Behold upon the palms of *my* hands I have graven you your walls before me**

49:17
תמיד 8548: מהרו 4116 בניך 1121 מהרסיך 2040 ומחרביך 2717 ממך 4480
tamiyd. miharu banayik; maharasayik uamacharibayik mimek
***are* continually shall make haste Your children your destroyers and they that made you waste of you**

49:18
יצאו 3318: שאי 5375 סביב 5439 עיניך 5869 וראי 7200 כלם 3605 נקבצו 6908 באו 935 לך 3807a חי 2416
yetze'au. sa'ay sabiyb 'aeynayik uara'ay, kulam niqbatzu ba'au lak; chay
**shall go forth Lift up round about your eyes and behold all these gather themselves together *and* come to you live**

אני 589 נאם 5002 יהוה 3068 כי 3588 כלם 3605 כעדי 5716 תלבשי 3847 ותקשרים 7194
'aniy na'am Yahuah kiy kulam ka'adiy tilbashiy, uatqashriym
***As* I saith Yahuah surely *with* them all as with an ornament you shall surely clothe yourselfs and bind them**

49:19
ככלה 3618: כי 3588 חרבתיך 2723 ושממתיך 8074 וארץ 776 הרסתיך 2035 כי 3588 עתה 6258
kakalah. kiy charabotayik uashomamotayik, ua'aretz harisuteyk; kiy 'atah
***on you* as a bride *does* For your waste and your desolate places and the land of your destruction even now**

49:20
תצרי 3334 מיושב 3427 ורחקו 7368 מבלעיך 1104: עוד 5750 יאמרו 559
tetzariy miyousheb, uarachaqu mabal'ayik. 'aud ya'maru
**shall be too narrow by reason of the inhabitants and shall be far away they that swallowed you up again shall say**

Isa 49:11 And I will make all my mountains a way, and my highways shall be exalted.12 Behold, these shall come from far: and, lo, these from the north and from the west; and these from the land of Sinim.13 Sing, O heavens; and be joyful, O earth; and break forth into singing, O mountains: for YHUH has comforted his people, and will have mercy upon his afflicted.14 But Zion said, YHUH has forsaken me, and my Adonai has forgotten me.15 Can a woman forget her sucking child, that she should not have compassion on the son of her womb? yea, they may forget, yet will I not forget you.16 Behold, I have graven you upon the palms of my hands; your walls are continually before me.17 Thy children shall make haste; your destroyers and they that made you waste shall go forth of you.18 Lift up your eyes round about, and behold: all these gather themselves together, and come to you. As I live, saith YHUH, you shall surely clothe you with them all, as with an ornament, and bind them on you, as a bride doeth.19 For your waste and your desolate places and the land of your destruction, shall even now be too narrow by reason of the inhabitants and they that swallowed you up shall be far away.

באזניך 241 בני 1121 שכליך 7923 צר 6862 לי 3807a המקום 4725 גשה 5066 לי 3807a
ba'azanayik, baney shikulayik; tzar liy hamaqoum gashah liy
**in your ears The children which you shall have after you have lost the other *is* too strait for me The place give place to me**

ואשבה 3427: **49:21** ואמרת 559 בלבבך 3824 מי 4310 ילד 3205 לי 3807a את 853 אלה 428 ואני 589
ua'aeshebah. ua'amart bilbabek, miy' yalad liy 'at 'aeleh, ua'aniy
**that I may dwell Then shall you say in your heart Who has begotten me these seeing I**

שכולה 7921 וגלמודה 1565 גלה 1473 וסורה 5493 ואלה 428 מי 4310 גדל 1431 הן 2005 אני 589
shakulah uagalmudah; golah uasurah, ua'aeleh miy' gidel, hen 'aniy
**have lost my children and am desolate a captive and removing to and fro? and these? who has brought up Behold I**

נשארתי 7604 לבדי 905 אלה 428 איפה 375 הם 1992: **49:22** כה 3541 אמר 559 אדני 136 יהוה 3069 הנה 2009 אשא 5375 אל 413 גוים 1471
nish'artiy labadiy, 'aeleh 'aeypoh hem. koh 'amar 'adonay Yahuah hineh 'asa' 'al gouyim
**was left alone these where had they *been*? Thus saith Adonai Yahuah Behold I will lift up to the Gentiles**

ידי 3027 ואל 413 עמים 5971 ארים 7311 נסי 5251 והביאו 935 בניך 1121 בחצן 2684 ובנתיך 1323 על 5921
yadiy, ua'al 'amiym 'ariym nisiy; uahebiy'au banayik bachotzen, uabnotayik 'al
**mine hand to the people *and* set up my standard and they shall bring your sons in *their* arms and your daughters upon**

כתף 3802 תנשאנה 5375: **49:23** והיו 1961 מלכים 4428 אמניך 539 ושרותיהם 8282 מיניקתיך 3243
katep tinasa'nah. uahayu malakiym 'amanayik, uasarouteyhem meyniyqotayik,
***their* shoulders shall be carried And shall be kings your nursing fathers and their queens your nursing mothers**

אפים 639 ארץ 776 ישתחוו 7812 לך 3807a ועפר 6083 רגליך 7272 ילחכו 3897 וידעת 3045 כי 3588 אני 589
'apayim, 'aretz yishtachauu lak, ua'apar raglayik yalacheku; uayada'at kiy 'aniy
**with *their* face *toward* the earth they shall bow down to you the dust of your feet lick up and you shall know that I *am***

יהוה 3068 אשר 834 לא 3808 יבשו 954 קוי 6960: **49:24** היקח 3947 מגבור 1368 מלקוח 4455 ואם 518 שבי 7628
Yahuah, 'asher la' yeboshu qouay. hayuqach migibour malqouach; ua'am shabiy
**Yahuah for not they shall be ashamed that wait for me Shall be taken from the mighty the prey or captive**

צדיק 6662 ימלט 4422: **49:25** כי 3588 כה 3541 אמר 559 יהוה 3068 גם 1571 שבי 7628 גבור 1368 יקח 3947
tzadiyq yimalet. kiy koh 'amar Yahuah gam shabiy gibour yuqach,
**the lawful delivered? But thus saith Yahuah Even the captives of the mighty shall be taken away**

ומלקוח 4455 עריץ 6184 ימלט 4422 ואת 854 יריבך 3401 אנכי 595 אריב 7378 ואת 853 בניך 1121
uamalqouach 'ariytz yimalet; ua'at yariybek 'anokiy 'ariyb, ua'at banayik
**and the prey of the terrible shall be delivered *for with* him that contend with you I will contend *and* your children**

אנכי 595 אושיע 3467: **49:26** והאכלתי 398 את 853 מוניך 3238 את 853 בשרם 1320 וכעסיס 6071
'anokiy 'aushiya. uaha'akaltiy 'at mounayik 'at basaram, uake'asiys
**I will save And I will feed them that oppress you with their own flesh and as with sweet wine**

דמם 1818 ישכרון 7937 וידעו 3045 כל 3605 בשר 1320 כי 3588 אני 589 יהוה 3068 מושיעך 3467
damam yishkarun; uayada'aua kal basar, kiy 'aniy Yahuah moushiy'aek,
***with* their own blood they shall be drunken and shall know all flesh that I Yahuah *am* your Saviour**

Isa 49:20 The children which you shall have, after you have lost the other, shall say again in your ears, The place is too strait for me: give place to me that I may dwell.21 Then shall you say in your heart, Who has begotten me these, seeing I have lost my children, and am desolate, a captive, and removing to and fro? and who has brought up these? Behold, I was left alone; these, where had they been?22 Thus saith YHUH G-D, Behold, I will lift up mine hand to the Gentiles, and set up my standard to the people: and they shall bring your sons in their arms, and your daughters shall be carried upon their shoulders.23 And kings shall be your nursing fathers, and their queens your nursing mothers: they shall bow down to you with their face toward the earth, and lick up the dust of your feet; and you shall know that I am YHUH: for they shall not be ashamed that wait for me.24 Shall the prey be taken from the mighty, or the lawful captive delivered?25 But thus saith YHUH, Even the captives of the mighty shall be taken away, and the prey of the terrible shall be delivered: for I will contend with him that contendeth with you, and I will save your children.26 And I will feed them that oppress you with their own flesh; and they shall be drunken with their own blood, as with sweet wine: and all flesh shall know that I YHUH am your Saviour and your Redeemer, the mighty One of Jacob.

וגאלך 1350 אביר 46 יעקב 3290:
uago'alek 'abiyr ya'aqob.
**and your Redeemer the mighty One of Jacob**

**Isa 50:1** כה 3541 אמר 559 יהוה 3068 אי 335 זה 2088 ספר 5612 כריתות 3748 אמכם 517 אשר 834 שלחתיה 7971 או 176 מי 4310
koh 'amar Yahuah 'ay zeh seper kariytut 'amkem 'asher shilachtiyha, 'au miy'
**Thus saith Yahuah Where *is* he the bill of divorcement your mother's whom I have put away or which**

מנושי 5383 אשר 834 מכרתי 4376 אתכם 853 לו 3807a הן 2005 בעונתיכם 5771 נמכרתם 4376
minoushay, 'asher makartiy 'atkem lou'; hen ba'auonoteykem nimkartem,
**of my creditors *is it* to whom I have sold you? to whom Behold for your iniquities have you sold yourselves**

ובפשעיכם 6588 שלחה 7971 אמכם 517: **50:2** מדוע 4069 באתי 935 ואין 369 איש 376 קראתי 7121
uabpish'aeykem shulchah 'amkem. madua' ba'tiy ua'aeyn 'aysh, qara'tiy
**and for your transgressions is put away your mother Wherefore when I came was there no man? when I called**

ואין 369 עונה 6030 הקצור 7114 קצרה 7114 ידי 3027 מפדות 6304 ואם 518 אין 369 בי 871a כח 3581 להציל 5337
ua'aeyn 'auneh haqatzour qatzarah yadiy mipdut, ua'am 'aeyn biy koach lahatziyl;
***was there* none to answer? Is at all shortened my hand that it cannot redeem? or no *have* I power to deliver?**

הן 2005 בגערתי 1606 אחריב 2717 ים 3220 אשים 7760 נהרות 5104 מדבר 4057 תבאש 887 דגתם 1710 מאין 369 מים 4325 ותמת 4191
hen baga'aratiy 'achariyb yam, 'asiym naharout midbar, tib'ash dagatam me'ayn mayim, uatamot
**behold at my rebuke I dry up the sea I make the rivers a wilderness stink their fish because *there is* no water and die**

בצמא 6772: **50:3** אלביש 3847 שמים 8064 קדרות 6940 ושק 8242 אשים 7760 כסותם 3682: **50:4** אדני 136 יהוה 3069 נתן 5414
batzama'. 'albiysh shamayim qadrut; uasaq 'asiym kasutam. 'adonay Yahuah natan
**for thirst I clothe the heavens *with* blackness and sackcloth I make their covering Adonai Yahuah has given**

לי 3807a לשון 3956 למודים 3928 לדעת 3045 לעות 5790 את 853 יעף 3287 דבר 1697 יעיר 5782
liy lashoun limudiym, lada'at la'aut 'at ya'aep dabar; ya'ayr
**me the tongue the learned that I should know *how* to speak in season *to him that is* weary a word he waken**

בבקר 1242 בבקר 1242 יעיר 5782 לי 3807a אזן 241 לשמע 8085 כלמודים 3928: **50:5** אדני 136 יהוה 3068 פתח 6605 לי 3807a אזן 241 ואנכי 595
baboqer baboqer, ya'ayr liy 'azen, lishmoa' kalimudiym. 'adonay Yahuah patach liy 'azen, ua'anokiy
**morning by morning he waken mine ear to hear as the learned Adonai Yahuah has opened mine ear and I**

לא 3808 מריתי 4784 אחור 268 לא 3808 נסוגתי 5472: **50:6** גוי 1460 נתתי 5414 למכים 5221 ולחיי 3895
la' mariytiy; 'achour la' nasugotiy. geuiy natatiy lamakiym, ualchayay
**not was rebellious back neither turned away my back I gave to the smiters and my cheeks**

למרטים 4803 פני 6440 לא 3808 הסתרתי 5641 מכלמות 3639 ורק 7536: **50:7** ואדני 136 יהוה 3069 יעזר 5826
lamoratiym; panay la' histartiy, miklimout uaroq. ua'adonay Yahuah ya'azar
**to them that plucked off the hair my face not I hid from shame and spitting For Adonai Yahuah will help**

לי 3807a על 5921 כן 3651 לא 3808 נכלמתי 3637 על 5921 כן 3651 שמתי 7760 פני 6440 כחלמיש 2496 ואדע 3045 כי 3588
liy, 'al ken la' niklamatiy; 'al ken samtiy panay kachalamiysh, ua'aeda' kiy
**me therefore after not shall I be confounded therefore after have I set my face like a flint and I know that**

**Isa** 50:1 Thus saith YHUH, Where is the bill of your mother's divorcement, whom I have put away? or which of my creditors is it to whom I have sold you? Behold, for your iniquities have you sold yourselves, and for your transgressions is your mother put away.2 Wherfore, when I came, was there no man? when I called, was there none to answer? Is my hand shortened at all, that it cannot redeem? or have I no power to deliver? behold, at my rebuke I dry up the sea, I make the rivers a wilderness: their fish stinketh, because there is no water, and die for thirst.3 I clothe the heavens with blackness, and I make sackcloth their covering.4 The Adonai G-D has given me the tongue of the learned, that I should know how to speak a word in season to him that is weary: he wakeneth morning by morning, he wakeneth mine ear to hear as the learned.5 The Adonai G-D has opened mine ear, and I was not rebellious, neither turned away back.6 I gave my back to the smiters, and my cheeks to them that plucked off the hair: I hid not my face from shame and spitting.7 For YHUH G-D will help me; therefore shall I not be confounded: therefore have I set my face like a flint, and I know that I shall not be ashamed.

| לא 3808 | אבוש 954: | 50:8 | קרוב 7138 | מצדיקי 6663 | מי 4310 | יריב 7378 | אתי 854 | נעמדה 5975 | יחד 3162 | מי 4310 | בעל 1167 |
|---|---|---|---|---|---|---|---|---|---|---|---|
| la' | 'aeboush. | | qaroub | matzdiyqiy, | miy' | yariyb | 'atiy | na'amdah | yachad; | miy' | ba'al |
| **not** | **I shall be ashamed** | | ***He is* near** | **that justifies me** | **who** | **will contend** | **with me?** | **let us stand** | **together** | **who** | ***is* chief** |

| משפטי 4941 | יגש 5066 | אלי 413: | 50:9 | הן 2005 | אדני 136 | יהוה 3069 | יעזר 5826 | לי 3807a | מי 4310 | הוא 1931 | ירשיעני 7561 |
|---|---|---|---|---|---|---|---|---|---|---|---|
| mishpatiy | yigash | 'aelay. | | hen | 'adonay | Yahuah | ya'azar | liy, | miy' | hua' | yarshiy'aeniy; |
| **my adversary?** | **let him come near** | **to me** | | **Behold** | **Adonai** | **Yahuah** | **will help** | **me** | **who *is*** | **he *that*** | **shall condemn me?** |

| הן 2005 | כלם 3605 | כבגד 899 | יבלו 1086 | עש 6211 | יאכלם 398: | 50:10 | מי 4310 | בכם 871a | ירא 3373 | יהוה 3068 |
|---|---|---|---|---|---|---|---|---|---|---|
| hen | kulam | kabeged | yiblu, | 'ash | ya'kalem. | | miy' | bakem | yarea' | Yahuah, |
| **lo** | **they all** | **as a garment** | **shall wax old** | **the moth** | **shall eat them up** | | **Who *is*** | **among you** | **that fear** | **Yahuah** |

| שמע 8085 | בקול 6963 | עבדו 5650 | אשר 834 | הלך 1980 | חשכים 2825 | ואין 369 | נגה 5051 | לו 3807a | יבטח 982 | בשם 8034 | יהוה 3068 |
|---|---|---|---|---|---|---|---|---|---|---|---|
| shomea' | baqoul | abdou; | 'asher | halak | chashekiym, | ua'aeyn | nogah | lou', | yibtach | bashem | Yahuah, |
| **that obeyed** | **the voice of** | **his servant** | **that** | **walk** | ***in* darkness** | **and no** | **light?** | **has** | **let him trust** | **in the name of** | **Yahuah** |

| וישען 8172 | באלהיו 430: | 50:11 | הן 2005 | כלכם 3605 | קדחי 6919 | אש 784 | מאזרי 247 | זיקות 2131 | לכו 1980 |
|---|---|---|---|---|---|---|---|---|---|
| uayisha'aen | be'alohayu. | | hen | kulkem | qodachey | 'aesh | ma'azrey | ziyqout; | laku |
| **and stay** | **upon his Elohim** | | **Behold** | **all you** | **that kindle** | **a fire** | **that compass *yourselves* about** | ***with* sparks** | **walk** |

| באור 217 | אשכם 784 | ובזיקות 2131 | בערתם 1197 | מידי 3027 | היתה 1961 | זאת 2063 | לכם 3807a | למעצבה 4620 |
|---|---|---|---|---|---|---|---|---|
| ba'ur | 'ashkem, | uabziyqout | bi'artem, | miyadiy | hayetah | za't | lakem, | lam'atzebah |
| **in the light of** | **your fire** | **and in the sparks** | ***that* you have kindled** | **of mine hand** | **shall have** | **This** | **to you** | **in sorrow** |

| תשכבון 7901: |
|---|
| tishkabun. |
| **you shall lie down** |

| **Isa 51:1** | שמעו 8085 | אלי 413 | רדפי 7291 | צדק 6664 | מבקשי 1245 | יהוה 3068 | הביטו 5027 | אל 413 | צור 6697 |
|---|---|---|---|---|---|---|---|---|---|
| | shim'au | 'aelay | rodapey | tzedeq | mabaqshey | Yahuah; | habiytu | 'al | tzur |
| | **Hearken** | **to me** | **you that follow after** | **righteousness** | **you that seek** | **Yahuah** | **look** | **unto** | **the rock** |

| חצבתם 2672 | ואל 413 | מקבת 4718 | בור 953 | נקרתם 5365: | 51:2 | הביטו 5027 | אל 413 | אברהם 85 | אביכם 1 | ואל 413 |
|---|---|---|---|---|---|---|---|---|---|---|
| chutzabtem, | ua'al | maqebet | bour | nuqartem. | | habiytu | 'al | 'abraham | 'abiykem, | ua'al |
| ***where* you are hewn** | **and to** | **the hole of** | **the pit** | ***where* you are digged** | | **Look** | **unto** | **Abraham** | **your father** | **and unto** |

| שרה 8283 | תחוללכם 2342 | כי 3588 | אחד 259 | קראתיו 7121 | ואברכהו 1288 | וארבהו 7235: | 51:3 | כי 3588 | נחם 5162 | יהוה 3068 |
|---|---|---|---|---|---|---|---|---|---|---|
| sarah | tachoulelkem; | kiy | 'achad | qara'tiyu, | ua'abarakehu | ua'arbehu. | | kiy | nicham | Yahuah |
| **Sarah** | ***that* bare you** | **for** | **alone** | **I called him** | **and blessed him** | **and increased him** | | **For** | **shall comfort** | **Yahuah** |

| ציון 6726 | נחם 5162 | כל 3605 | חרבתיה 2723 | וישם 7760 | מדברה 4057 | כעדן 5731 | וערבתה 6160 | כגן 1588 |
|---|---|---|---|---|---|---|---|---|
| tziyoun, | nicham | kal | charaboteyha, | uayasem | midbarah | ka'aeden, | ua'arbatah | kagan |
| **Zion** | **he will comfort** | **all** | **her waste places** | **and he will make** | **her wilderness** | **like Eden** | **and her desert** | **like the garden of** |

| יהוה 3068 | ששון 8342 | ושמחה 8057 | ימצא 4672 | בה 871a | תודה 8426 | וקול 6963 | זמרה 2172: | 51:4 | הקשיבו 7181 | אלי 413 |
|---|---|---|---|---|---|---|---|---|---|---|
| Yahuah; | sasoun | uasimchah | yimatzea' | bah, | toudah | uaqoul | zimrah. | | haqashiybu | 'aelay |
| **Yahuah** | **joy** | **and gladness** | **shall be found** | **therein** | **thanksgiving** | **and the voice of** | **melody** | | **Hearken** | **unto me** |

Isa 50:8 He is near that justifieth me; who will contend with me? let us stand together: who is mine adversary? let him come near to me.9 Behold, YHUH G-D will help me; who is he that shall condemn me? lo, they all shall wax old as a garment; the moth shall eat them up.10 Who is among you that fear YHUH, that obeyeth the voice of his servant, that walk in darkness, and has no light? let him trust in the name of YHUH, and stay upon his G-d.11 Behold, all you that kindle a fire, that compass yourselves about with sparks: walk in the light of your fire, and in the sparks that you have kindled. This shall you have of mine hand; you shall lie down in sorrow. **Isa** 51:1 Hearken to me, you that follow after righteousness, you that seek YHUH: look unto the rock whence you are hewn, and to the hole of the pit whence you are digged.2 Look unto Abraham your father, and unto Sarah that bare you: for I called him alone, and blessed him, and increased him.3 For YHUH shall comfort Zion: he will comfort all her waste places; and he will make her wilderness like Eden, and her desert like the garden of YHUH; joy and gladness shall be found therein, thanksgiving, and the voice of melody.

עמי 5971 ולאומי 3816 אלי 413 האזינו 238 כי 3588 תורה 8451 מאתי 853 תצא 3318 ומשפטי 4941 לאור 216 עמים 5971
'amiy, ual'aumiy 'aelay ha'aziynu; kiy tourah me'atiy tetzea', uamishpatiy, la'aur 'amiym
**my people O my nation unto me give ear for a law from me shall proceed and my judgment for a light of the people**

ארגיע 7280: **51:5** קרוב 7138 צדקי 6664 יצא 3318 ישעי 3468 וזרעי 2220 עמים 5971 ישפטו 8199 אלי 413
'argiya'. qaroub tzidqiy yatza' yish'ay, uazro'ay 'amiym yishpotu; 'aelay
**I will make to rest *is* near My righteousness is gone forth my salvation and mine arms the people shall judge upon me**

איים 339 יקוו 6960 ואל 413 זרעי 2220 ייחלון 3176: **51:6** שאו 5375 לשמים 8064 עיניכם 5869 והביטו 5027 אל 413 הארץ 776
'ayiym yaqauu, ua'al zaro'ay yayachelun. sa'au lashamayim 'aeyneykem uahabiytu 'al ha'aretz
**the isles shall wait and on mine arm shall they trust Lift up to the heavens your eyes and look upon the earth**

מתחת 8478 כי 3588 שמים 8064 כעשן 6227 נמלחו 4414 והארץ 776 כבגד 899 תבלה 1086
mitachat, kiy shamayim ke'ashan nimlachu uaha'aretz kabeged tibleh,
**beneath for the heavens like smoke shall vanish away and the earth like a garment shall wax old**

וישביה 3427 כמו 3644 כן 3654 ימותון 4191 וישועתי 3444 לעולם 5769 תהיה 1961 וצדקתי 6666 לא 3808
uayoshabeyha kamou ken yamutun; uiyshu'atiy la'aulam tihayeh, uatzidqatiy la'
**and they that dwell therein in like manner shall die but my salvation for ever shall be and my righteousness not**

תחת 2865: **51:7** שמעו 8085 אלי 413 ידעי 3045 צדק 6664 עם 5971 תורתי 8451 בלבם 3820 אל 408 תיראו 3372
techat. shim'au 'aelay yoda'aey tzedeq, 'am touratiy balibam; 'al tiyra'au
**shall be abolished Hearken unto me you that know righteousness the people *is* my law in whose heart not fear you**

חרפת 2781 אנוש 582 ומגדפתם 1421 אל 408 תחתו 2865: **51:8** כי 3588 כבגד 899 יאכלם 398 עש 6211
cherpat 'anoush, uamigidupotam 'al techatu. kiy kabeged ya'kalem 'ash,
**the reproach of men of their revilings neither be you afraid For like a garment shall eat them up the moth**

וכצמר 6785 יאכלם 398 סס 5580 וצדקתי 6666 לעולם 5769 תהיה 1961 וישועתי 3444 לדור 1755
uakatzemer ya'kalem sas; uatzidqatiy la'aulam tihayeh, uiyshu'atiy ladour
**and like wool shall eat them the worm but my righteousness for ever shall be and my salvation from generation to**

דורים 1755: **51:9** עורי 5782 עורי 5782 לבשי 3847 עז 5797 זרוע 2220 יהוה 3069 עורי 5782 כימי 3117 קדם 6924 דרות 1755
douriym. 'auriy 'auriy libshiy 'az zaroua' Yahuah, 'auriy kiymey qedem, dorout
**generation Awake awake put on strength O arm of Yahuah awake as days *in the* ancient *in* the generations of**

עולמים 5769 הלוא 3808 את 859 היא 1931 המחצבת 2672 רהב 7294 מחוללת 2490 תנין 8577: **51:10** הלוא 3808 את 859 היא 1931
'aulamiym; halou'a 'at hiy'a hamachatzebet rahab machoulelet taniyn. halou'a 'at hiy'a
**old not. *Are You* him that has cut Rahab *and* wounded the dragon? *Are* not *You* him**

המחרבת 2717 ים 3220 מי 4325 תהום 8415 רבה 7227 השמה 7760 מעמקי 4615 ים 3220 דרך 1870 לעבר 5674
hamacharebet yam, mey tahoum rabah; hasamah ma'amaqey yam, derek la'abor
**which has dried the sea the waters of the deep *the* great that has made the depths of the sea a way to pass over?**

גאולים 1350: **51:11** ופדויי 6299 יהוה 3068 ישובון 7725 ובאו 935 ציון 6726 ברנה 7440 ושמחת 8057
ga'uliym. uapduyey Yahuah yashubun, uaba'au tziyoun barinah, uasimchat
***for* the ransomed Therefore the redeemed of Yahuah shall return and come *unto* Zion with singing *shall be* and joy**

Isa 51:4 Hearken unto me, my people; and give ear unto me, O my nation: for a law shall proceed from me, and I will make my judgment to rest for a light of the people.5 My righteousness is near; my salvation is gone forth, and mine arms shall judge the people; the isles shall wait upon me, and on mine arm shall they trust.6 Lift up your eyes to the heavens, and look upon the earth beneath: for the heavens shall vanish away like smoke, and the earth shall wax old like a garment, and they that dwell therein shall die in like manner: but my salvation shall be forever, and my righteousness shall not be abolished.7 Hearken unto me, you that know righteousness, the people in whose heart is my law; fear you not the reproach of men, neither be you afraid of their revilings.8 For the moth shall eat them up like a garment, and the worm shall eat them like wool: but my righteousness shall be forever, and my salvation from generation to generation.9 Awake, awake, put on strength, O arm of YHUH; awake, as in the ancient days, in the generations of old. Art you not it that has cut Rahab, and wounded the dragon?10 Art you not it which has dried the sea, the waters of the great deep; that has made the depths of the sea a way for the ransomed to pass over?11 Therefore the redeemed of YHUH shall return, and come with singing unto Zion;

51:12
עולם 5769 על 5921 ראשם 7218 ששון 8342 ושמחה 8057 ישיגון 5381 נסו 5127 יגון 3015 ואנחה 585: אנכי 595
'aulam 'al ra'sham; sasoun uasimchah yasiygun, nasu yagoun ua'anachah. 'anokiy
**everlasting upon their head gladness and joy they shall obtain shall flee away *and* sorrow and mourning I *even***

אנכי 595 הוא 1931 מנחמכם 5162 מי 4310 את 859 ותיראי 3372 מאנוש 582 ימות 4191 ומבן 1121 אדם 120
'anokiy hua' manachemakem; miy' 'at uatiyra'ay me'anoush yamut, uamiben 'adam
**I *am* he that comforted you who *are* You that you should be afraid of a man *that* shall die and of the son of man**

51:13
חציר 2682 ינתן 5414: ותשכח 7911 יהוה 3068 עשך 6213 נוטה 5186 שמים 8064
chatziyr yinaten. uatishkach Yahuah 'aseka, nouteh shamayim
***as* grass *which* shall be made And forget Yahuah your maker that has stretched forth the heavens**

ויסד 3245 ארץ 776 ותפחד 6342 תמיד 8548 כל 8548 היום 3117 מפני 6440 חמת 2534 המציק 6693
uayosed 'aretz uatapched tamiyd kal hayoum, mipaney chamat hametziyq,
**and laid the foundations of the earth and have feared continually every day because of the fury of the oppressor**

51:14
כאשר 834 כונן 3559 להשחית 7843 ואיה 346 חמת 2534 המציק 6693: מהר 4116 צעה 6808
ka'asher kounen lahashchiyt; ua'ayeh chamat hametziyq. mihar tzo'ah
**as if he were ready to destroy? and where *is* the fury of the oppressor? hasten The captive exile**

51:15
להפתח 6605 ולא 3808 ימות 4191 לשחת 7845 ולא 3808 יחסר 2637 לחמו 3899: ואנכי 595 יהוה 3068
lahipateach; uala' yamut lashachat, uala' yechsar lachmou. ua'anokiy Yahuah
**that he may be loosed and not that he should die in the pit nor that should fail his bread But I *am* Yahuah**

51:16
אלהיך 430 רגע 7280 הים 3220 ויהמו 1993 גליו 1530 יהוה 3068 צבאות 6635 שמו 8034: ואשים 7760 דברי 1697
'aloheyka, roga' hayam, uayehemu galayu; Yahuah tzaba'aut shamou. ua'asiym dabaray
**your Elohim that divided the sea roared whose waves Yahuah of hosts *is* his name And I have put my words**

בפיך 6310 ובצל 6738 ידי 3027 כסיתיך 3680 לנטע 5193 שמים 8064
bapiyka, uabtzel yadiy kisiytiyka; lintoa' shamayim
**in your mouth you in the shadow of mine hand and I have covered you that I may plant the heavens**

51:17
וליסד 3245 ארץ 776 ולאמר 559 לציון 6726 עמי 5971 אתה 859: התעוררי 5782 התעוררי 5782 קומי 6965
ualiysod 'aretz, ualea'mor latziyoun 'amiy 'atah. hit'aurariy hit'aurariy, quamiy
**and lay the foundations of the earth and say unto Zion *are* my people You Awake awake stand up**

ירושלם 3389 אשר 834 שתית 8354 מיד 3027 יהוה 3068 את 853 כוס 3563 חמתו 2534 את 853 קבעת 6907 כוס 3563
yarushalaim, 'asher shatiyt miyad Yahuah 'at kous chamatou; 'at quba'at kous
**O Jerusalem which have drunk at the hand of Yahuah the cup of his fury the dregs of the cup of**

51:18
התרעלה 8653 שתית 8354 מצית 4680: אין 369 מנהל 5059 לה 3807a מכל 3605 בנים 1121
hatar'aelah shatiyt matziyt. 'aeyn manahel lah, mikal baniym
**the trembling you have drunken *and* wrung *them* out *There is* none to guide her among all the sons of**

ילדה 3205 ואין 369 מחזיק 2388 בידה 3027 מכל 3605 בנים 1121 גדלה 1431:
yaladah; ua'aeyn machaziyq bayadah, mikal baniym gadelah.
***whom* she has brought forth neither *is there any* that takes her by the hand of all the sons *that* she has brought up**

Isa 51:11 and everlasting joy shall be upon their head: they shall obtain gladness and joy; and sorrow and mourning shall flee away.12 I, even I, am he that comforteth you: who are you, that you should be afraid of a man that shall die, and of the son of man which shall be made as grass;13 And forgettest YHUH your maker, that has stretched forth the heavens, and laid the foundations of the earth; and have feared continually every day because of the fury of the oppressor, as if he were ready to destroy? and where is the fury of the oppressor?14 The captive exile hasteneth that he may be loosed, and that he should not die in the pit, nor that his bread should fail.15 But I am YHUH your G-d, that divided the sea, whose waves roared: YHUH of hosts is his name.16 And I have put my words in your mouth, and I have covered you in the shadow of mine hand, that I may plant the heavens, and lay the foundations of the earth, and say unto Zion, Thou are my people.17 Awake, awake, stand up, O Jerusalem, which have drunk at the hand of YHUH the cup of his fury; you have drunken the dregs of the cup of trembling, and wrung them out.18 There is none to guide her among all the sons whom she has brought forth; neither is there any that take her by the hand of all the sons that she has brought up.

**51:19**
שתים 8147 הנה 2007 קראתיך 7122 מי 4310 ינוד 5110 לך 3807a השד 7701 והשבר 7667 והרעב 7458
shatayim henah qora'atayik, miy' yanud lak; hashod uahasheber uahara'ab
**two These *things* are come unto you who shall be sorry for you? desolation and destruction and the famine**

והחרב 2719 מי 4310 אנחמך 5162: **51:20** בניך 1121 עלפו 5968 שכבו 7901 בראש 7218 כל 3605 חוצות 2351
uahachereb miy' 'anachamek. banayik 'alpu shakabu bara'sh kal chutzout
**and the sword *by* whom shall I comfort you? Your sons have fainted they lie at the head of all the streets**

כתוא 8377 מכמר 4364 המלאים 4390 חמת 2534 יהוה 3068 גערת 1606 אלהיך 430: **51:21** לכן 3651 שמעי 8085
katob mikmar; hamale'aym chamat Yahuah ga'arat 'alohayik. laken shim'ay
**as a wild bull (*antelope*) in a net they are full of of the fury of Yahuah the rebuke of your Elohim Therefore hear**

נא 4994 זאת 2063 עניה 6041 ושכרת 7937 ולא 3808 מיין 3196: **51:22** כה 3541 אמר 559 אדניך 113 יהוה 3068 ואלהיך 430
naa' za't 'aniyah; uashkurat uala' miyayin. koh 'amar 'adonayik Yahuah ua'alohayik
**now this you afflicted and drunken but not with wine Thus saith your Adonai Yahuah and your Elohim**

יריב 7378 עמו 5971 הנה 2009 לקחתי 3947 מידך 3027 את 853 כוס 3563 התרעלה 8653 את 853 קבעת 6907
yariyb 'amou, hineh laqachtiy miyadek 'at kous hatar'aelah; 'at quba'at
***that* plead *the cause of* his people Behold I have taken out of your hand cup of the trembling *even* the dregs of**

כוס 3563 חמתי 2534 לא 3808 תוסיפי 3254 לשתותה 8354 עוד 5750: **51:23** ושמתיה 7760 ביד 3027 מוגיך 3013
kous chamatiy, la' tousiypiy lishtoutah 'aud. uasamtiyha bayad mougayik,
**the cup of my fury no more you shall drink it again But I will put it into the hand of them that afflict you**

אשר 834 אמרו 559 לנפשך 5315 שחי 7812 ונעברה 5674 ותשימי 7760 כארץ 776 גוך 1460 וכחוץ 2351
'asher 'amaru lanapshek shachiy uana'aborah; uatasiymiy ka'aretz geuek, uakachutz
**which have said to your soul Bow down that we may go over and you have laid as the ground your body and as the street**

לעברים 5674:
la'abariym.
**to them that went over**

**Isa 52:1**
עורי 5782 עורי 5782 לבשי 3847 עזך 5797 ציון 6726 לבשי 3847 בגדי 899 תפארתך 8597 ירושלם 3389 עיר 5892 הקדש 6944
'auriy 'auriy libshiy 'azek tziyoun; libshiy bigdey tip'artek, yarushalaim 'ayr haqodesh,
**Awake awake put on your strength O Zion put on garments your beautiful O Jerusalem city the holy**

כי 3588 לא 3808 יוסיף 3254 יבא 935 בך 871a עוד 5750 ערל 6189 וטמא 2931: **52:2** התנערי 5287
kiy la' yousiyp yaba' bak 'aud 'arel uatamea'. hitna'ariy
**for no more there shall come into you henceforth the uncircumcised and the unclean Shake yourself**

מעפר 6083 קומי 6965 שבי 3427 ירושלם 3389 התפתחו 6605 מוסרי 4147 צוארך 6677 שביה 7628 בת 1323
me'apar quamiy shabiy yarushalaim; hitpatechu mousarey tzaua'rek, shabiyah bat
**from the dust arise *and* sit down O Jerusalem loose yourself from the bands of your neck O captive daughter of**

ציון 6726: **52:3** כי 3588 כה 3541 אמר 559 יהוה 3068 חנם 2600 נמכרתם 4376 ולא 3808 בכסף 3701
tziyoun. kiy koh 'amar Yahuah, chinam nimkartem; uala' uakesep
**Zion For thus saith Yahuah for nought You have sold yourselves and without money**

Isa 51:19 These two things are come unto you; who shall be sorry for you? desolation, and destruction, and the famine, and the sword: by whom shall I comfort you?20 Thy sons have fainted, they lie at the head of all the streets, as a wild bull in a net: they are full of the fury of YHUH, the rebuke of your G-d.21 Therefore hear now this, you afflicted, and drunken, but not with wine:22 Thus saith your Adonai YHUH, and your G-d that pleadeth the cause of his people, Behold, I have taken out of your hand the cup of trembling, even the dregs of the cup of my fury; you shall no more drink it again:23 But I will put it into the hand of them that afflict you; which have said to your soul, Bow down, that we may go over: and you have laid your body as the ground, and as the street, to them that went over. **Isa** 52:1 Awake, awake; put on your strength, O Zion; put on your beautiful garments, O Jerusalem, the holy city: for henceforth there shall no more come into you the uncircumcised and the unclean.2 Shake thyself from the dust; arise, and sit down, O Jerusalem: loose thyself from the bands of your neck, O captive daughter of Zion.3 For thus saith YHUH, You have sold yourselves for nought; and you shall be redeemed without money.

52:4
תגאלו 1350: כי 3588 כה 3541 אמר 559 אדני 136 יהוה 3069 מצרים 4714 ירד 3381 עמי 5971 בראשנה 7223 לגור 1481
tiga'aelu. kiy koh 'amar 'adonay Yahuah, mitzrayim yarad 'amiy bara'shonah lagur
**you shall be redeemed For thus saith Adonai Yahuah *into* Egypt went down My people aforetime to sojourn**

52:5
שם 8033 ואשור 804 באפס 657 עשקו 6231: ועתה 6258 מי 4310 לי 3807a פה 6311 נאם 5002 יהוה 3068 כי 3588
sham; ua'ashur ba'apes 'ashaqou. ua'atah miy' liy poh na'am Yahuah, kiy
**there and the Assyrian without cause oppressed them Now therefore what *have* I here saith Yahuah that**

לקח 3947 עמי 5971 חנם 2600 משלו 4910 יהילילו 3213 נאם 5002 יהוה 3068 ותמיד 8548 כל 3605
luqach 'amiy chinam; moshalou yaheylylu na'am Yahuah, uatamiyd kal
**is taken away my people for nought? they that rule over them make them to howl saith Yahuah and continually every**

52:6
היום 3117 שמי 8034 מנאץ 5006: לכן 3651 ידע 3045 עמי 5971 שמי 8034 לכן 3651 ביום 3117 ההוא 1931
hayoum shamiy mino'atz. laken yeda' 'amiy shamiy; laken bayoum hahua',
**day my name *is* blasphemed Therefore shall know my people my name therefore *they shall know* in day he**

52:7
כי 3588 אני 589 הוא 1931 המדבר 1696 הנני 2005: מה 4100 נאוו 4998 על 5921 ההרים 2022 רגלי 7272
kiy 'aniy hua' hamadaber hineniy. mah na'auu 'al hehariym ragley
**that I *am* he that does speak behold, it is I How beautiful upon the mountains *are* the feet of**

מבשר 1319 משמיע 8085 שלום 7965 מבשר 1319 טוב 2896 משמיע 8085 ישועה 3444 אמר 559
mabaser, mashmiya' shaloum mabaser toub mashmiya' yashu'ah; 'amer
**him that bring good tidings that publisheth peace that bring good tidings of good that publisheth salvation that saith**

52:8
לציון 6726 מלך 4427 אלהיך 430: קול 6963 צפיך 6822 נשאו 5375 קול 6963 יחדו 3162 ירננו 7442 כי 3588 עין 5869
latziyoun malak 'alohayik. qoul tzopayik nasa'au qoul yachdau yaranenu; kiy 'ayin
**unto Zion reigns Your Elohim the voice Your watchmen shall lift up *with* the voice together shall they sing for eye**

52:9
בעין 5869 יראו 7200 בשוב 7725 יהוה 3068 ציון 6726: פצחו 6476 רננו 7442 יחדו 3162 חרבות 2723
ba'ayin yir'au, bashub Yahuah tziyoun. pitzchu rannu yachdau, charabout
**to eye they shall see when shall bring again Yahuah Zion Break forth into joy sing together you waste places of**

52:10
ירושלם 3389 כי 3588 נחם 5162 יהוה 3068 עמו 5971 גאל 1350 ירושלם 3389: חשף 2834 יהוה 3068 את 853
yarushalaim; kiy nicham Yahuah 'amou, ga'al yarushalaim. chasap Yahuah 'at
**Jerusalem for has comforted Yahuah his people he has redeemed Jerusalem has made bare Yahuah**

זרוע 2220 קדשו 6944 לעיני 5869 כל 3605 הגוים 1471 וראו 7200 כל 3605 אפסי 657 ארץ 776 את 853 ישועת 3444
zaroua' qadashou, la'aeyney kal hagouyim; uar'au kal 'apsey 'aretz, 'at yashu'at
**arm his holy in the eyes of all the nations and shall see all the ends of the earth the salvation of**

52:11
אלהינו 430: סורו 5493 סורו 5493 צאו 3318 משם 8033 טמא 2931 אל 408 תגעו 5060 צאו 3318 מתוכה 8432
'aloheynu. suru suru tza'au misham, tamea' 'al tiga'au; tza'au mitoukah,
**our Elohim Depart you depart you go you out from there unclean *thing* no touch go you out of the midst of her**

52:12
הברו 1305 נשאי 5375 כלי 3627 יהוה 3068: כי 3588 לא 3808 בחפזון 2649 תצאו 3318 ובמנוסה 4499 לא 3808 תלכון 1980
hibaru nosa'aey kaley Yahuah. kiy la' bachipazoun tetze'au, uabimnusah la' telekun;
**be you clean that bear the vessels of Yahuah For not with haste you shall go out by flight nor go**

Isa 52:4 For thus saith YHUH G-D, My people went down aforetime into Egypt to sojourn there; and the Assyrian oppressed them without cause.5 Now therefore, what have I here, saith YHUH, that my people is taken away for nought? they that rule over them make them to howl, saith YHUH; and my name continually every day is blasphemed.6 Therefore my people shall know my name: therefore they shall know in that day that I am he that doth speak: behold, it is I.7 How beautiful upon the mountains are the feet of him that bring good tidings, that publisheth peace; that bring good tidings of good, that publisheth salvation; that saith unto Zion, Thy G-d reigned!8 Thy watchmen shall lift up the voice; with the voice together shall they sing: for they shall see eye to eye, when YHUH shall bring again Zion.9 Break forth into joy, sing together, you waste places of Jerusalem: for YHUH has comforted his people, he has redeemed Jerusalem.10 YHUH has made bare his holy arm in the eyes of all the nations; and all the ends of the earth shall see the salvation of our G-d.11 Depart you, depart you, go you out from thence, touch no unclean thing; go you out of the midst of her; be you clean, that bear the vessels of YHUH.12 For you shall not go out with haste, nor go by flight: for YHUH will go before you; and the G-d of Israel will be your rear guard.

| כי 3588 | הלך 1980 | לפניכם 6440 | יהוה 3069 | ומאספכם 622 | אלהי 430 | ישראל 3478: | 52:13 | הנה 2009 | ישכיל 7919 |
|---|---|---|---|---|---|---|---|---|---|
| kiy | holek | lipneykem | Yahuah, | uam'asipkem | 'alohey | yisra'ael. | | hineh | yaskiyl |
| **for** | **will go** | **before you** | **Yahuah** | **and your rearward** | **the Elohim of** | **Israel *will be*** | | **Behold** | **shall deal prudently** |

| עבדי 5650 | ירום 7311 | ונשא 5375 | וגבה 1361 | מאד 3966: | 52:14 | כאשר 834 | שממו 8074 | עליך 5921 | רבים 7227 | כן 3651 |
|---|---|---|---|---|---|---|---|---|---|---|
| 'abdiy; | yarum | uanisa' | uagabah | ma'ad. | | ka'asher | shamamu | 'alayik | rabiym, | ken |
| **my servant** | **he shall be exalted** | **and extolled** | **and be high** | **very** | | **As** | **were astonied** | **at you** | **many** | **so** |

| משחת 7893 | מאיש 376 | מראהו 4758 | ותארו 8389 | מבני 1121 | אדם 120: | 52:15 | כן 3651 | יזה 5137 | גוים 1471 |
|---|---|---|---|---|---|---|---|---|---|
| mishchat | me'aysh | mar'aehu; | uato'arou | mibney | 'adam. | | ken | yazeh | gouyim |
| **was marred** | **more than any man** | **his visage** | **and his form** | **more than the sons of** | **men** | | **So** | **shall he sprinkle** | **nations** |

| רבים 7227 | עליו 5921 | יקפצו 7092 | מלכים 4428 | פיהם 6310 | כי 3588 | אשר 834 | לא 3808 | ספר 5608 | להם 3807a | ראו 7200 | ואשר 834 |
|---|---|---|---|---|---|---|---|---|---|---|---|
| rabiym, | 'alayu | yiqpatzu | malakiym | piyhem; | kiy | 'asher | la' | supar | lahem | ra'au, | ua'asher |
| **many** | **at him** | **shall shut** | **the kings** | **their mouths** | **for *that*** | **which** | **not** | **had been told** | **them** | **shall they see** | **and *that* which** |

| לא 3808 | שמעו 8085 | התבוננו 995: |
|---|---|---|
| la' | shama'au | hitbounanu. |
| **not** | **they had heard** | **shall they consider** |

**Isa 53:1**

| מי 4310 | האמין 539 | לשמעתנו 8052 | וזרוע 2220 | יהוה 3068 | על 5921 | מי 4310 | נגלתה 1540: | 53:2 | ויעל 5927 |
|---|---|---|---|---|---|---|---|---|---|
| miy' | he'amiyn | lishmu'atenu; | uazaoua' | Yahuah | 'al | miy' | niglatah. | | uaya'al |
| **Who** | **has believed** | **our report?** | **and the arm of** | **Yahuah** | **to** | **whom** | **is revealed?** | | **For he shall grow up** |

| כיונק 3126 | לפניו 6440 | וכשרש 8328 | מארץ 776 | ציה 6723 | לא 3808 | תאר 8389 | לו 3807a | ולא 3808 | הדר 1926 |
|---|---|---|---|---|---|---|---|---|---|
| kayouneq | lapanayu, | uakashoresh | me'aretz | tziyah, | la' | to'ar | lou' | uala' | hadar; |
| **as a tender plant** | **before him** | **and as a root** | **out of a ground** | **dry** | **no** | **form** | **he *has*** | **and nor** | **comeliness** |

| ונראהו 7200 | ולא 3808 | מראה 4758 | ונחמדהו 2530: | 53:3 | נבזה 959 | וחדל 2310 | אישים 376 |
|---|---|---|---|---|---|---|---|
| uanir'aehu | uala' | mar'aeh | uanechmadehu. | | nibzeh | uachadal | 'ayshiym, |
| **when we shall see him** | ***there is* no** | **beauty** | **that we should desire him** | | **He is despised** | **and rejected of** | **men** |

| איש 376 | מכאבות 4341 | וידוע 3045 | חלי 2483 | וכמסתר 4564 | פנים 6440 | ממנו 4480 | נבזה 959 | ולא 3808 |
|---|---|---|---|---|---|---|---|---|
| 'aysh | mak'about | uiydua' | chaliy; | uakmaster | paniym | mimenu, | nibzeh | uala' |
| **a man of** | **sorrows** | **and acquainted with** | **grief** | **and we hid as it were** | ***our* faces** | **from him** | **he was despised** | **and not** |

| חשבנהו 2803: | 53:4 | אכן 403 | חלינו 2483 | הוא 1931 | נשא 5375 | ומכאבינו 4341 | סבלם 5445 | ואנחנו 587 | חשבנהו 2803 | נגוע 5060 |
|---|---|---|---|---|---|---|---|---|---|---|
| chashabnuhu. | | 'aken | chalayenu | hua' | nasa', | uamak'abeynu | sabalam; | ua'anachnu | chashabnuhu, | nagua' |
| **we esteemed him** | | **Surely** | **our griefs** | **he** | **has borne** | **and our sorrows** | **carried** | **yet we** | **did esteem him** | **stricken** |

| מכה 5221 | אלהים 430 | ומענה 6031: | 53:5 | והוא 1931 | מחלל 2490 | מפשענו 6588 | מדכא 1792 | מעונתינו 5771 |
|---|---|---|---|---|---|---|---|---|
| mukeh | 'alohiym | uam'aneh. | | uahu'a | macholal | mipasha'aenu, | maduka' | me'auonoteynu; |
| **smitten of** | **Elohim** | **and afflicted** | | **But he** | ***was* wounded** | **for our transgressions** | ***he was* bruised** | **for our iniquities** |

| מוסר 4148 | שלומנו 7965 | עליו 5921 | ובחברתו 2250 | נרפא 7495 | לנו 3807a: | 53:6 | כלנו 3605 | כצאן 6629 |
|---|---|---|---|---|---|---|---|---|
| musar | shaloumenu | 'alayu, | uabachaburatou | nirpa' | lanu. | | kulanu | katza'n |
| **the chastisement of** | **our peace** | ***was* upon him** | **and with his stripes** | **we are healed** | **to us** | | **All** | **like sheep** |

Isa 52:13 Behold, my servant shall deal prudently, he shall be exalted and extolled, and be very high.14 As many were astonied at you; his visage was so marred more than any man, and his form more than the sons of men:15 So shall he sprinkle many nations; the kings shall shut their mouths at him: for that which had not been told them shall they see; and that which they had not heard shall they consider. **Isa** 53:1 Who has believed our report? and to whom is the arm of YHUH revealed?2 For he shall grow up before him as a tender plant, and as a root out of a dry ground: he has no form nor comeliness; and when we shall see him, there is no beauty that we should desire him.3 He is despised and rejected of men; a man of sorrows, and acquainted with grief: and we hid as it were our faces from him; he was despised, and we esteemed him not.4 Surely he has borne our griefs, and carried our sorrows: yet we did esteem him stricken, smitten of G-d, and afflicted.5 But he was wounded for our transgressions, he was bruised for our iniquities: the chastisement of our peace was upon him; and with his stripes we are healed.

תעינו 8582 | איש 376 | לדרכו 1870 | פנינו 6437 | ויהוה 3068 | הפגיע 6293 | בו 871a | את 853 | עון 5771
ta'aynu, | 'aysh | ladarkou | paniynu; | uaYahuah | hipgiya' | bou, | 'at | 'auon
**we have gone astray | every one | to his own way | we have turned | and Yahuah | has laid | in him | the iniquity of**

**53:7**
כלנו 3605: | נגש 5065 | והוא 1931 | נענה 6031 | ולא 3808 | יפתח 6605 | פיו 6310 | כשה 7716 | לטבח 2874 | יובל 2986
kulanu. | nigas | uahu'a | na'aneh | uala' | yiptach | piyu | kaseh | latebach | yubal,
**us all | He was oppressed | and he | was afflicted | yet not | he opened | his mouth | as a lamb | to the slaughter | he is brought**

**53:8**
וכרחל 7353 | לפני 6440 | גזזיה 1494 | נאלמה 481 | ולא 3808 | יפתח 6605 | פיו 6310: | מעצר 6115 | וממשפט 4941 | לקח 3947
uakrachel | lipney | gozazeyha | ne'alamah; | uala' | yiptach | piyu. | me'atzer | uamimishpat | luqach,
**and as a sheep | before | her shearers | is dumb | so not | he open | his mouth | from prison | and from judgment | He was taken**

ואת 853 | דורו 1755 | מי 4310 | ישוחח 7878 | כי 3588 | נגזר 1504 | מארץ 776 | חיים 2416 | מפשע 6588
ua'at | dourou | miy' | yasoucheach; | kiy | nigzar | me'aretz | chayiym, | mipesha'
***and* | his generation? | who | shall declare | for | he was cut off | out of the land of | the living | for the transgression of**

**53:9**
עמי 5971 | נגע 5061 | למו 3807a: | ויתן 5414 | את 854 | רשעים 7563 | קברו 6913 | ואת 854 | עשיר 6223 | במתיו 4194 | על 5921 | לא 3808
'amiy | nega' | lamou. | uayiten | 'at | rasha'aym | qibrou, | ua'at | 'ashiyr | bamotayu; | 'al | la'
**my people | stricken | *was* he | And he made | *with* | the wicked | his grave | *and with* | the rich | in his death | because | no**

**53:10**
חמס 2555 | עשה 6213 | ולא 3808 | מרמה 4820 | בפיו 6310: | ויהוה 3068 | חפץ 2654 | דכאו 1792 | החלי 2470
chamas | 'asah, | uala' | mirmah | bapiyu. | laYahuah | chapetz | dak'au | hechaliy,
**violence | he had done | neither | *was any* deceit | in his mouth | Yet Yahuah | it pleased | to bruise him | he has put *him* to grief**

אם 518 | תשים 7760 | אשם 817 | נפשו 5315 | יראה 7200 | זרע 2233 | יאריך 748 | ימים 3117 | וחפץ 2656 | יהוה 3068
'am | tasiym | 'asham | napshou, | yir'ah | zera' | ya'ariyk | yamiym; | uachepetz | Yahuah
**when | you shall make | an offering for sin | his soul | he shall see | *his* seed | he shall prolong | *his* days | and the pleasure of | Yahuah**

**53:11**
בידו 3027 | יצלח 6743: | מעמל 5999 | נפשו 5315 | יראה 7200 | ישבע 7646 | בדעתו 1847 | יצדיק 6663
bayadou | yitzlach. | me'amal | napshou | yir'ah | yisba', | bada'tou, | yatzdiyq
**in his hand | shall prosper | of the travail of | his soul | He shall see | *and* shall be satisfied | by his knowledge | shall justify**

**53:12**
צדיק 6662 | עבדי 5650 | לרבים 7227 | ועונתם 5771 | הוא 1931 | יסבל 5445: | לכן 3651 | אחלק 2505 | לו 3807a
tzadiyq | 'abdiy | larabiym; | ua'auonotam | hua' | yisbol. | laken | 'achaleq | lou'
**righteous | my servant | many | for their iniquities | he | shall bear | Therefore | will I divide | him**

ברבים 7227 | ואת 854 | עצומים 6099 | יחלק 2505 | שלל 7998 | תחת 8478 | אשר 834 | הערה 6168 | למות 4194 | נפשו 5315
barabiym, | ua'at | 'atzumiym | yachaleq | shalal | tachat, | 'asher | he'arah | lamauet | napshou,
***a portion* with the great | *and with* | the strong | he shall divide | the spoil | because | which | he has poured out | unto death | his soul**

ואת 854 | פשעים 6586 | נמנה 4487 | והוא 1931 | חטא 2399 | רבים 7227 | נשא 5375 | ולפשעים 6586 | יפגיע 6293:
ua'at | posha'aym | nimnah; | uahu'a | cheta' | rabiym | nasa', | ualaposha'aym | yapgiya'.
***and with* | the transgressors | he was numbered | and he | the sin of | many | bare | the transgressors | and made intercession for**

**Isa 54:1**
רני 7442 | עקרה 6135 | לא 3808 | ילדה 3205 | פצחי 6476 | רנה 7440 | וצהלי 6670 | לא 3808
raniy | 'aqarah | la' | yaladah; | pitzchiy | rinah | uatzahaliy | la'
**Sing | O barren | not | you *that* did bear | break forth into | singing | and cry aloud | not**

Isa 53:6 All we like sheep have gone astray; we have turned everyone to his own way; and YHUH has laid on him the iniquity of us all.7 He was oppressed, and he was afflicted, yet he opened not his mouth: he is brought as a lamb to the slaughter, and as a sheep before her shearers is dumb, so he openeth not his mouth.8 He was taken from prison and from judgment: and who shall declare his generation? for he was cut off out of the land of the living: for the transgression of my people was he stricken.9 And he made his grave with the wicked, and with the rich in his death; because he had done no violence, neither was any deceit in his mouth.10 Yet it pleased YHUH to bruise him; he has put him to grief: when you shall make his soul an offering for sin, he shall see his seed, he shall prolong his days, and the pleasure of YHUH shall prosper in his hand.11 He shall see of the travail of his soul, and shall be satisfied: by his knowledge shall my righteous servant justify many; for he shall bear their iniquities.12 Therefore will I divide him a portion with the great, and he shall divide the spoil with the strong; because he has poured out his soul unto death: and he was numbered with the transgressors; and he bare the sin of many, and made intercession for the transgressors. **Isa** 54:1 Sing, O barren, you that did not bear; break forth into singing, and cry aloud,

**Isa 55:1** הוי 1945 כל 3605 צמא 6771 לכו 1980 למים 4325 ואשר 834 אין 369 לו 3807a כסף 3701 לכו 1980 שברו 7666 ואכלו 398
houy kal tzamea' laku lamayim, ua'asher 'aeyn lou' kasep; laku shibru ue'akolu,
**Ho every one that thirst come you to the waters and that *has* no he money come you buy and eat**

ולכו 1980 שברו 7666 בלוא 3808 כסף 3701 ובלוא 3808 מחיר 4242 יין 3196 וחלב 2461: **55:2** למה 4100 תשקלו 8254 כסף 3701
ualku shibru, balou'a kesep uablou'a machiyr yayin uachalab. lamah tishqalu kesep
**yea come buy without money and without price wine and milk Wherefore do you spend money**

בלוא 3808 לחם 3899 ויגיעכם 3018 בלוא 3808 לשבעה 7654 שמעו 8085 שמוע 8085 אלי 413 ואכלו 398
balou'a lachem, uiygiy'akem balou'a lasaba'ah; shim'au shamoua' 'aelay ua'aklu
**for *that which* is not bread? and your wages for not? *that which* satisfies hearken diligently unto me and eat you**

טוב 2896 ותתענג 6026 בדשן 1880 נפשכם 5315: **55:3** הטו 5186 אזנכם 241 ולכו 1980 אלי 413 שמעו 8085 ותחי 2421
toub, uatit'anag badeshen napshakem. hatu 'aznakem ualku 'aelay, shim'au uatchiy
***that which is* good and let delight itself in fatness your soul Incline your ear and come unto me hear and shall live**

נפשכם 5315 ואכרתה 3772 לכם 3807a ברית 1285 עולם 5769 חסדי 2617 דוד 1732 הנאמנים 539: **55:4** הן 2005 עד 5707
napshakem; ua'akratah lakem bariyt 'aulam, chasdey dauid hane'amaniym. hen 'aed
**your soul and I will make with you an covenant everlasting mercies of David *even* the sure Behold *for* a witness**

לאומים 3816 נתתיו 5414 נגיד 5057 ומצוה 6680 לאמים 3816: **55:5** הן 2005 גוי 1471 לא 3808 תדע 3045
la'amiym natatiyu; nagiyd uamtzaueh la'amiym. hen gouy la' teda'
**to the people I have given him a leader and commander to the people Behold a nation not *that* you know**

תקרא 7121 וגוי 1471 לא 3808 ידעוך 3045 אליך 413 ירוצו 7323 למען 4616 יהוה 3068 אלהיך 430
tiqraa', uagouy la' yada'auka 'aeleyka yarutzu; lama'an Yahuah 'aloheyka,
**you shall call and nations not *that* knew you unto you shall run because of Yahuah your Elohim**

ולקדוש 6918 פארך 6286 ישראל 3478 כי 3588 פארך 6286: **55:6** דרשו 1875 יהוה 3068 בהמצאו 4672
ualiqadoush yisra'ael kiy pe'arak. dirshu Yahuah bahimatza'au;
**and for the Holy One of Israel for he has glorified you Seek you Yahuah while he may be found**

קראהו 7121 בהיותו 1961 קרוב 7138: **55:7** יעזב 5800 רשע 7563 דרכו 1870 ואיש 376 און 205 מחשבתיו 4284
qara'ahu bihayotou qaroub. ya'azob rasha' darkou, ua'aysh 'auen machshabotayu;
**call you upon him while he is near Let forsake the wicked his way and man *the* unrighteous his thoughts**

וישב 7725 אל 413 יהוה 3069 וירחמהו 7355 ואל 413 אלהינו 430 כי 3588 ירבה 7235 לסלוח 5545: **55:8**
uayashob 'al Yahuah uiyrachamehu, ua'al 'aloheynu kiy yarbeh lisloach.
**and let him return unto Yahuah and he will have mercy upon him and to our Elohim for abundantly he will pardon**

כי 3588 לא 3808 מחשבותי 4284 מחשבותיכם 4284 ולא 3808 דרכיכם 1870 דרכי 1870 נאם 5002 יהוה 3068: **55:9** כי 3588 גבהו 1361
kiy la' machshaboutay machshabouteykem, uala' darkeykem darakay; na'am Yahuah. kiy gabahu
**For not my thoughts *are* your thoughts neither *are* your ways my ways saith Yahuah For are higher**

שמים 8064 מארץ 776 כן 3651 גבהו 1361 דרכי 1870 מדרכיכם 1870 ומחשבתי 4284 ממחשבתיכם 4284: **55:10** כי 3588
shamayim me'aretz; ken gabahu darakay midarkeykem, uamachshabotay mimachshaboteykem. kiy
***as* the heavens than the earth so are higher my ways than your ways and my thoughts than your thoughts For**

**Isa** 55:1 Ho, everyone that thirsteth, come you to the waters, and he that has no money; come you, buy, and eat; yea, come, buy wine and milk without money and without price.2 Wherefore do you spend money for that which is not bread? and your labour for that which satisfieth not? hear diligently unto me, and eat you that which is good, and let your soul delight itself in fatness.3 Incline your ear, and come unto me: hear, and your soul shall live; and I will make an everlasting covenant with you, even the sure mercies of David.4 Behold, I have given him for a witness to the people, a leader and commander to the people.5 Behold, you shall call a nation that you know not, and nations that knew not you shall run unto you because of YHUH your G-d, and for the Holy One of Israel; for he has glorified you.6 Seek you YHUH while he may be found, call you upon him while he is near:7 Let the wicked forsake his way, and the unrighteous man his thoughts: and let him return unto YHUH, and he will have mercy upon him; and to our G-d, for he will abundantly pardon.8 For my thoughts are not your thoughts, neither are your ways my ways, saith YHUH.9 For as the heavens are higher than the earth, so are my ways higher than your ways, and my thoughts than your thoughts.

כאשר 834 ירד 3381 הגשם 1653 והשלג 7950 מן 4480 השמים 8064 ושמה 8033 לא 3808 ישוב 7725 כי 3588 אם 518 הרוה 7301 את 853
ka'asher yered hageshem uahasheleg min hashamayim, uashamah la' yashub, kiy 'am hiruah 'at
**as comes down the rain and the snow from heaven and there not return but rather watereth**

הארץ 776 והולידה 3205 והצמיחה 6779 ונתן 5414 זרע 2233 לזרע 2232 ולחם 3899 לאכל 398: **55:11** כן 3651
ha'aretz, uahouliydah uahitzmiychah; uanatan zera' lazorea', ua'alechem la'akel. ken
**the earth and make it bring forth and bud that it may give seed to the sower and bread to the eater So**

יהיה 1961 דברי 1697 אשר 834 יצא 3318 מפי 6310 לא 3808 ישוב 7725 אלי 413 ריקם 7387 כי 3588 אם 518 עשה 6213
yihayeh dabariy 'asher yetzea' mipiy, la' yashub 'aelay reyqam; kiy 'am 'asah
**shall be my word that goes forth out of my mouth not it shall return unto me void but rather it shall accomplish**

את 853 אשר 834 חפצתי 2654 והצליח 6743 אשר 834 שלחתיו 7971: **55:12** כי 3588 בשמחה 8057 תצאו 3318
'at 'asher chapatztiy, uahitzliyach 'asher shalachtiyu. kiy basimchah tetze'au,
**that which I please and it shall prosper *in the thing* whereto I sent it For with joy you shall go out**

ובשלום 7965 תובלון 2986 ההרים 2022 והגבעות 1389 יפצחו 6476 לפניכם 6440 רנה 7440 וכל 3605 עצי 6086
uabshaloum tubalun; hehariym uahagaba'aut, yiptzachu lipneykem rinah, uakal 'atzey
**and with peace be led forth the mountains and the hills shall break forth before you *into* singing and all the trees of**

השדה 7704 ימחאו 4222 כף 3709: **55:13** תחת 8478 הנעצוץ 5285 יעלה 5927 ברוש 1265 תחת 8478 הסרפד 5636 יעלה 5927
hasadeh yimcha'au kap. tachat hana'atzutz ya'aleh baroush, tachat hasirpad ya'aleh
**the field shall clap *their* hands Instead of the thorn shall come up the fir tree and instead of the brier shall come up**

הדס 1918 והיה 1961 ליהוה 3068 לשם 8034 לאות 226 עולם 5769 לא 3808 יכרת 3772:
hadas; uahayah laYahuah lashem, la'aut 'aulam la' yikaret.
**the myrtle tree and it shall be to Yahuah for a name for an sign everlasting not *that* shall be cut off**

**Isa 56:1** כה 3541 אמר 559 יהוה 3068 שמרו 8104 משפט 4941 ועשו 6213 צדקה 6666 כי 3588 קרובה 7138 ישועתי 3444 לבוא 935
koh 'amar Yahuah, shimru mishapat ua'asu tzadaqah; kiy qaroubah yashu'atiy labou'a,
**Thus saith Yahuah Keep you judgment and do justice for *is* near my salvation to come**

וצדקתי 6666 להגלות 1540: **56:2** אשרי 835 אנוש 582 יעשה 6213 זאת 2063 ובן 1121 אדם 120 יחזיק 2388 בה 871a
uatzidqatiy lahigalout. 'ashrey 'anoush ya'aseh za't, uaben 'adam yachaziyq bah;
**and my righteousness to be revealed Blessed *is* the man *that* does this and the son of man *that* lay hold on it**

שמר 8104 שבת 7676 מחללו 2490 ושמר 8104 ידו 3027 מעשות 6213 כל 3605 רע 7451: **56:3** ואל 408 יאמר 559 בן 1121
shomer shabat mechalalou, uashomer yadou me'asout kal ra'. ua'al ya'mar ben
**that keep the sabbath from polluting it and keep his hand from doing any evil Neither let saying the son of**

הנכר 5236 הנלוה 3867 אל 413 יהוה 3068 לאמר 559 הבדל 914 יבדילני 914 יהוה 3068 מעל 5921 עמו 5971 ואל 408
hanekar, haniluah 'al Yahuah lea'mor, habdel yabdiylaniy Yahuah me'al 'amou; ua'al
**the stranger that has joined himself to Yahuah saying has utterly separated me Yahuah from his people neither**

יאמר 559 הסריס 5631 הן 2005 אני 589 עץ 6086 יבש 3002: **56:4** כי 3588 כה 3541 אמר 559 יהוה 3068 לסריסים 5631 אשר 834 ישמרו 8104 את 853
ya'mar hasariys, hen 'aniy 'aetz yabesh. kiy koh 'amar Yahuah lasariysiym 'asher yishmaru 'at
**let say the eunuch Behold I *am* a tree dry For thus saith Yahuah unto the eunuchs that keep**

Isa 55:10 For as the rain cometh down, and the snow from heaven, and returneth not thither, but watereth the earth, and make it bring forth and bud, that it may give seed to the sower, and bread to the eater:11 So shall my word be that go forth out of my mouth: it shall not return unto me void, but it shall accomplish that which I please, and it shall prosper in the thing whereto I sent it.12 For you shall go out with joy, and be led forth with peace: the mountains and the hills shall break forth before you into singing, and all the trees of the field shall clap their hands.13 Instead of the thorn shall come up the fir tree, and instead of the brier shall come up the myrtle tree: and it shall be to YHUH for a name, for an everlasting sign that shall not be cut off. **Isa** 56:1 Thus saith YHUH, Keep you judgment, and do justice: for my salvation is near to come, and my righteousness to be revealed.2 Blessed is the man that doeth this, and the son of man that layeth hold on it; that keep the Sabbath from polluting it, and keep his hand from doing any evil.3 Neither let the son of the stranger, that has joined himself to YHUH, speak, saying, YHUH has utterly separated me from his people: neither let the eunuch say, Behold, I am a dry tree.4 For thus saith YHUH unto the eunuchs that keep my sabbaths, and choose the things that please me, and take hold of my covenant;

| 7676 שבתותי | 977 ובחרו | 834 באשר | 2654 חפצתי | 2388 ומחזיקים | 1285: בבריתי | 56:5 | 5414 ונתתי | 3807a להם |
|---|---|---|---|---|---|---|---|---|
| shabtoutay, | ubacharu | ba'asher | chapatzatiy; | uamachaziyqiym | bibriytiy. | | uanatatiy | lahem |
| **my sabbaths** | **and choose *the things*** | **that** | **please me** | **and take hold** | **of my covenant** | | **Even will I give** | **unto them** |

| 1004 בביתי | 2346 ובחומתי | 3027 יד | 8034 ושם | 2896 טוב | 1121 מבנים | 1323 ומבנות | 8034 שם | 5769 עולם |
|---|---|---|---|---|---|---|---|---|
| babeytiy | uabchoumotay | yad | uashem , | toub | mibaniym | uamibanout; | shem | 'aulam |
| **in mine house** | **and within my walls** | **a place** | **and a name** | **better than** | **of sons** | **and of daughters** | **an name** | **everlasting** |

| 5414 אתן | 3807a לו | 834 אשר | 3808 לא | 3772: יכרת | 56:6 | 1121 ובני | 5236 הנכר | 3867 הנלוים | 5921 על | 3068 יהוה |
|---|---|---|---|---|---|---|---|---|---|---|
| 'aten | lou', | 'asher | la' | yikaret. | | uabney | hanekar, | haniluiym | 'al | Yahuah |
| **I will give** | **them** | **that** | **not** | **shall be cut off** | | **Also the sons of** | **the stranger** | **that join themselves** | **to** | **Yahuah** |

| 8334 לשרתו | 157 ולאהבה | 853 את | 8034 שם | 3068 יהוה | 1961 להיות | 3807a לו | 5650 לעבדים | 3605 כל | 8104 שמר | 7676 שבת |
|---|---|---|---|---|---|---|---|---|---|---|
| lasharatou, | uala'ahabah | 'at | shem | Yahuah, | lihayout | lou' | la'abadiym; | kal | shomer | shabat |
| **to serve him** | **and to love** | | **the name of** | **Yahuah** | **to be** | **his** | **servants** | **every one** | **that keep** | **the sabbath** |

| 2490 מחללו | 2388 ומחזיקים | 1285: בבריתי | 56:7 | 935 והביאותים | 413 אל | 2022 הר | 6944 קדשי |
|---|---|---|---|---|---|---|---|
| mechalalou, | uamachaziyqiym | bibriytiy. | | uahabiy'autiym | 'al | har | qadashiy |
| **from polluting it** | **and takes hold** | **of my covenant** | | **Even them will I bring** | **to** | **mountain** | **my holy** |

| 8055 ושמחתים | 1004 בבית | 8605 תפלתי | 5930 עולתיהם | 2077 וזבחיהם | 7522 לרצון | 5921 על | 4196 מזבחי |
|---|---|---|---|---|---|---|---|
| uasimachtiym | babeyt | tapilatiy, | 'auloteyhem | uazibcheyhem | laratzoun | 'al | mizbachiy; |
| **and make them joyful** | **in my house of** | **prayer** | **their burnt offerings** | **and their sacrifices** | ***shall be* accepted** | **upon** | **mine altar** |

| 3588 כי | 1004 ביתי | 1004 בית | 8605 תפלה | 7121 יקרא | 3605 לכל | 5971: העמים | 56:8 | 5002 נאם | 136 אדני | 3068 יהוה | 6908 מקבץ |
|---|---|---|---|---|---|---|---|---|---|---|---|
| kiy | beytiy, | beyt | tapilah | yiqarea' | lakal | ha'amiym. | | na'am | 'adonay | Yahuah, | maqabetz |
| **for** | **mine house** | **an house of** | **prayer** | **shall be called** | **for all** | **people** | | **saith** | **Adonai** | **Yahuah** | **which gathered** |

| 1760 נדחי | 3478 ישראל | 5750 עוד | 6908 אקבץ | 5921 עליו | 6908: לנקבציו | 56:9 | 3605 כל |
|---|---|---|---|---|---|---|---|
| nidchey | yisra'ael; | 'aud | 'aqabetz | 'alayu | laniqbatzayu. | | kal |
| **the outcasts of** | **Israel** | **Yet** | **will I gather *others*** | **to him** | **beside those that are gathered unto him** | | **All** |

| 2416 חיתו | 7704 שדי | 857 אתיו | 398 לאכל | 3605 כל | 2416 חיתו | 3293: ביער | 56:10 | 6822 צפו | 5787 עורים | 3605 כלם | 3808 לא |
|---|---|---|---|---|---|---|---|---|---|---|---|
| chaytou | saday; | 'aetayu | le'akol | kal | chaytou | baya'ar. | | tzopu | 'auriym | kulam | la' |
| **you beasts of** | **the field** | **come you** | **to devour** | ***yea* all** | **you beasts** | **in the forest** | | **His watchmen** | ***are* blind** | **they all** | **not** |

| 3045 ידעו | 3605 כלם | 3611 כלבים | 483 אלמים | 3808 לא | 3201 יוכלו | 5024 לנבח | 1957 הזים | 7901 שכבים | 157 אהבי | 5123: לנום | 56:11 |
|---|---|---|---|---|---|---|---|---|---|---|---|
| yada'au, | kulam | kalabiym | 'almiym, | la' | yukalu | linboach; | hoziym | shokabiym, | 'ahabey | lanum. | |
| **they know** | **they *are* all** | **dogs** | **dumb** | **not** | **they can** | **bark** | **sleeping** | **lying down** | **loving** | **to slumber** | |

| 3611 והכלבים | 5794 עזי | 5315 נפש | 3808 לא | 3045 ידעו | 7646 שבעה | 1992 והמה | 7462 רעים | 3808 לא | 3045 ידעו | 995 הבין |
|---|---|---|---|---|---|---|---|---|---|---|
| uahakalabiym | 'azey | nepesh, | la' | yada'au | saba'ah, | uahemah | ro'aym, | la' | yada'au | habiyn; |
| **Yea, dogs** | **fierce** | ***they are* greedy** | **never** | ***which* can have** | **enough** | **and they** | ***are* shepherds** | ***that* not** | **can** | **understand** |

| 3605 כלם | 1870 לדרכם | 6437 פנו | 376 איש | 1215 לבצעו | 7097: מקצהו | 56:12 | 857 אתיו | 3947 אקחה | 3196 יין |
|---|---|---|---|---|---|---|---|---|---|
| kulam | ladarkam | panu, | 'aysh | labitz'au | miqatzehu. | | 'aetayu | 'aqchah | yayin |
| **have all** | **to their own way** | **look** | **every one** | **for his gain** | **from his quarter** | | **Come you** | ***say they* I will fetch** | **wine** |

Isa 56:5 Even unto them will I give in mine house and within my walls a place and a name better than of sons and of daughters: I will give them an everlasting name, that shall not be cut off.6 Also the sons of the stranger, that join themselves to YHUH, to serve him, and to love the name of YHUH, to be his servants, everyone that keep the Sabbath from polluting it, and take hold of my covenant;7 Even them will I bring to my holy mountain, and make them joyful in my house of prayer: their burnt offerings and their sacrifices shall be accepted upon mine altar; for mine house shall be called an house of prayer for all people.8 The Adonai G-D which gathereth the outcasts of Israel saith, Yet will I gather others to him, beside those that are gathered unto him.9 All you beasts of the field, come to devour, yea, all you beasts in the forest.10 His watchmen are blind: they are all ignorant, they are all dumb dogs, they cannot bark; sleeping, lying down, loving to slumber.11 Yea, they are greedy dogs which can never have enough, and they are shepherds that cannot understand: they all look to their own way, everyone for his gain, from his quarter.12 Come you, say they, I will fetch wine, and we will fill ourselves with strong drink; and tomorrow shall be as this day, and much more abundant.

| | | | | | | | | |
|---|---|---|---|---|---|---|---|---|
| ונסבאה 5433 | שכר 7941 | והיה 1961 | כזה 2088 | יום 3117 | מחר 4279 | גדול 1419 | יתר 3499 | מאד 3966: |
| uanisba'ah | shekar; | uahayah | kazeh | youm | machar, | gadoul | yeter | ma'ad. |
| **and we will fill ourselves with** | **strong drink** | **and shall be** | **as this** | **day** | **to morrow** | **abundant** | **more** | ***and* much** |

| **Isa 57:1** | | | | | | | | | | | |
|---|---|---|---|---|---|---|---|---|---|---|---|
| הצדיק 6662 | אבד 6 | ואין 369 | איש 376 | שם 7760 | על 5921 | לב 3820 | ואנשי 582 | חסד 2617 | נאספים 622 | באין 369 | מבין 995 |
| hatzadiyq | 'abad, | ua'aeyn | 'aysh | sam | 'al | leb; | ua'anshey | chesed | ne'asapiym | ba'aeyn | mebiyn, |
| **The righteous** | **perish** | **and no** | **man** | **lay *it*** | **to** | **heart** | **and men** | **merciful** | ***are* taken away** | **none** | **considering** |

| | | | | | **57:2** | | | |
|---|---|---|---|---|---|---|---|---|
| כי 3588 | מפני 6440 | הרעה 7451 | נאסף 622 | הצדיק 6662: | יבוא 935 | שלום 7965 | ינוחו 5117 | על 5921 |
| kiy | mipaney | hara'ah | ne'asap | hatzadiyq. | yabou'a | shaloum, | yanuchu | 'al |
| **that** | **from** | **the evil** | ***to come* is taken away** | **the righteous** | **He shall enter into** | **peace** | **they shall rest** | **in** |

| | | | **57:3** | | | | | |
|---|---|---|---|---|---|---|---|---|
| משכבותם 4904 | הלך 1980 | נכחו 5228: | ואתם 859 | קרבו 7126 | הנה 2008 | בני 1121 | ענה 6049 | זרע 2233 |
| mishkaboutam; | holek | nakochou. | ua'atem | qirbu | henah | baney | 'ananah; | zera' |
| **their beds** | ***each one* walking** | ***in* his uprightness** | **But you** | **draw near** | **here** | **sons of** | **the sorceress** | **the seed of** |

| | | **57:4** | | | | | | |
|---|---|---|---|---|---|---|---|---|
| מנאף 5003 | ותזנה 2181: | על 5921 | מי 4310 | תתענגו 6026 | על 5921 | מי 4310 | תרחיבו 7337 | פה 6310 |
| mana'aep | uatizneh. | 'al | miy' | tit'anagu, | 'al | miy' | tarchiybu | peh |
| **the adulterer** | **and the whore** | **Against** | **whom** | **do you sport yourselves?** | **against** | **whom** | **make you wide** | **a mouth** |

| | | | | | | | | **57:5** | |
|---|---|---|---|---|---|---|---|---|---|
| תאריכו 748 | לשון 3956 | הלוא 3808 | אתם 859 | ילדי 3206 | פשע 6588 | זרע 2233 | שקר 8267: | הנחמים 2552 | באלים 410 |
| ta'ariyku | lashoun; | halou'a | 'atem | yalidey | pesha' | zera' | shaqer. | hanechamiym | ba'aelim, |
| ***and* draw out the tongue?** | | **not *are*** | **you** | **children of transgression** | | **a seed of** | **falsehood** | **Enflaming yourselves** | **with idols** |

| | | | | | | | | | **57:6** |
|---|---|---|---|---|---|---|---|---|---|
| תחת 8478 | כל 3605 | עץ 6086 | רענן 7488 | שחטי 7819 | הילדים 3206 | בנחלים 5158 | תחת 8478 | סעפי 5585 | הסלעים 5553: |
| tachat | kal | 'aetz | ra'anan; | shochatey | hayladiym | banachaliym, | tachat | sa'apey | hasala'aym. |
| **under** | **every** | **tree** | **green** | **slaying** | **the children** | **in the valleys** | **under** | **the clifts of** | **the rocks?** |

| | | | | | | | | |
|---|---|---|---|---|---|---|---|---|
| בחלקי 2511 | נחל 5158 | חלקך 2506 | הם 1992 | הם 1992 | גורלך 1486 | גם 1571 | להם 1992 | שפכת 8210 |
| bachalqey | nachal | chelqek, | hem | hem | gouralek; | gam | lahem | shapakt |
| **Among the smooth *stones* of** | **the stream** | ***is* your portion** | **they** | **they** | ***are* your lot** | **even** | **to them** | **have you poured** |

| | | | | | | **57:7** | | |
|---|---|---|---|---|---|---|---|---|
| נסך 5262 | העלית 5927 | מנחה 4503 | העל 5921 | אלה 428 | אנחם 5162: | על 5921 | הר 2022 | גבה 1364 |
| nesech | he'aliyt | minchah, | ha'al | 'aeleh | 'anachem. | 'al | har | gaboah |
| **a drink offering** | **you have offered** | **a meat offering** | **in** | **these?** | **Should I receive comfort** | **Upon** | **a mountain** | **lofty** |

| | | | | | | | | **57:8** | | |
|---|---|---|---|---|---|---|---|---|---|---|
| ונשא 5375 | שמת 7760 | משכבך 4904 | גם 1571 | שם 8033 | עלית 5927 | לזבח 2076 | זבח 2077: | ואחר 310 | הדלת 1817 | והמזוזה 4201 |
| uanisa', | samta | mishkabek; | gam | sham | 'aliyt | lizboach | zabach. | ua'achar | hadelet | uahamazuzah, |
| **and high** | **have you set** | **your bed** | **even** | **there** | **went you up** | **to offer** | **sacrifice** | **Behind also** | **the doors** | **and the posts** |

| | | | | | |
|---|---|---|---|---|---|
| שמת 7760 | זכרונך 2146 | כי 3588 | מאתי 853 | גלית 1540 | ותעלי 5927 |
| samt | zikrounek; | kiy | me'atiy | giliyt | uata'aliy, |
| **have you set up** | **your remembrance** | **for** | **than me** | **you have discovered** | ***yourself to another* and are gone up** |

| | | | | | | | | |
|---|---|---|---|---|---|---|---|---|
| הרחבת 7337 | משכבך 4904 | ותכרת 3772 | לך 3807a | מהם 1992 | אהבת 157 | משכבם 4904 | יד 3027 | חזית 2372: |
| hirchabt | mishkabek | uatikrat | lak | mehem, | 'ahabt | mishkabam | yad | chaziyt. |
| **you have enlarged** | **your bed** | **and made to you** | ***a covenant*** | **with them** | **you love** | **their bed** | **where** | **you saw *it*** |

**Isa 57:1** The righteous perisheth, and no man layeth it to heart: and merciful men are taken away, none considering that the righteous is taken away from the evil to come.2 He shall enter into peace: they shall rest in their beds, each one walking in his uprightness.3 But draw near hither, you sons of the sorceress, the seed of the adulterer and the whore.4 Against whom do you sport yourselves? against whom make you a wide mouth, and draw out the tongue? are you not children of transgression, a seed of falsehood,5 Enflaming yourselves with idols under every green tree, slaying the children in the valleys under the clifts of the rocks?6 Among the smooth stones of the stream is your portion; they, they are your lot: even to them have you poured a drink offering, you have offered a meat offering. Should I receive comfort in these?7 Upon a lofty and high mountain have you set your bed: even thither went you up to offer sacrifice.8 Behind the doors also and the posts have you set up your remembrance: for you have discovered thyself to another than me, and are gone up; you have enlarged your bed, and made you a covenant with them; you lovedst their bed where you saw it.

| 57:9 ותשרי 7788 | למלך 4428 | בשמן 8081 | ותרבי 7235 | רקחיך 7547 | ותשלחי 7971 | צריך 6735 | עד 5704 |
|---|---|---|---|---|---|---|---|
| uatashuriy | lamelek | bashemen, | uatarbiy | riquchayik; | uatashalchiy | tzirayik | 'ad |
| **And you went** | **to the king** | **with ointment** | **and did increase** | **your perfumes** | **and did send** | **your messengers** | **unto** |

| מרחק 7350 | ותשפילי 8213 | עד 5704 | שאול 7585: | 57:10 ברב 7230 | דרכך 1870 | יגעת 3021 | לא 3808 |
|---|---|---|---|---|---|---|---|
| merachoq, | uatashpiyliy | 'ad | sha'aul. | barob | darkek | yaga'at, | la' |
| **far off** | **and did debase *yourself even*** | **unto** | **hell (*grave*)** | **in the greatness of** | **your way** | **You are wearied** | **not** |

| אמרת 559 | נואש 2976 | חית 2416 | ידך 3027 | מצאת 4672 | על 5921 | כן 3651 | לא 3808 | חלית 2470: | 57:11 ואת 853 |
|---|---|---|---|---|---|---|---|---|---|
| 'amart | nou'ash; | chayat | yadek | matza't, | 'al | ken | la' | chaliyt. | ua'at |
| ***yet* said you** | **There is no hope** | **the life of** | **your hand** | **you have found** | **therefore** | **after** | **not** | **you were grieved** | ***And*** |

| מי 4310 | דאגת 1672 | ותיראי 3372 | כי 3588 | תכזבי 3576 | ואותי 853 | לא 3808 | זכרת 2142 | לא 3808 | שמת 7760 | על 5921 |
|---|---|---|---|---|---|---|---|---|---|---|
| miy' | da'agt | uatiyra'ay | kiy | tekazebiy, | ua'atiy | la' | zakart, | la' | samt | 'al |
| **of whom** | **have you been afraid** | **or feared** | **that** | **you have lied** | **and me** | **not** | **have remembered** | **nor** | **laid *it*** | **to** |

| לבך 3820 | הלא 3808 | אני 589 | מחשה 2814 | ומעלם 5769 | ואותי 853 | לא 3808 | תיראי 3372: | 57:12 אני 589 | אגיד 5046 |
|---|---|---|---|---|---|---|---|---|---|
| libek; | hala' | 'aniy | machasheh | uame'alam, | ua'atiy | la' | tiyra'ay. | 'aniy | 'agiyd |
| **your heart?** | **not** | **I** | **hvae held my peace** | **even of old** | **and you** | **not** | **fear me** | **I** | **will declare** |

| צדקתך 6666 | ואת 853 | מעשיך 4639 | ולא 3808 | יועילוך 3276: | 57:13 בזעקך 2199 | יצילך 5337 | קבוציך 6899 |
|---|---|---|---|---|---|---|---|
| tzidqatek; | ua'at | ma'asayik | uala' | you'ayluk. | baza'aqek | yatziyluk | qibutzayik, |
| **your righteousness** | ***and*** | **your works** | **for not** | **they shall profit you** | **When you cry** | **let deliver you** | **your companies** |

| ואת 853 | כלם 3605 | ישא 5375 | רוח 7307 | יקח 3947 | הבל 1892 | והחוסה 2620 | בי 871a | ינחל 5157 | ארץ 776 |
|---|---|---|---|---|---|---|---|---|---|
| ua'at | kulam | yisaa' | ruach | yiqach | habel; | uahachouseh | biy | yinchal | 'aretz, |
| ***but*** | **them all** | **shall carry away** | **the wind** | **shall take *them*** | **vanity** | **but he that put his trust** | **in me** | **shall possess** | **the land** |

| ויירש 3423 | הר 2022 | קדשי 6944: | 57:14 ואמר 559 | סלו 5549 | סלו 5549 | פנו 6437 | דרך 1870 | הרימו 7311 |
|---|---|---|---|---|---|---|---|---|
| uayiyrash | har | qadashiy | ua'amar | solu | solu | panu | darek; | hariymu |
| **and shall inherit** | **mountain** | **my holy** | **And shall say** | **Cast you up** | **cast you up** | **prepare** | **the way** | **take up** |

| מכשול 4383 | מדרך 1870 | עמי 5971: | 57:15 כי 3588 | כה 3541 | אמר 559 | רם 7311 | ונשא 5375 | שכן 7931 | עד 5703 |
|---|---|---|---|---|---|---|---|---|---|
| mikshoul | miderek | 'amiy. | kiy | koh | 'amar | ram | uanisa', | shoken | 'ad |
| **the stumblingblock** | **out of the way of** | **my people** | **For** | **thus** | **saith** | ***the* high** | **and lofty One** | **that inhabiteth** | **eternity** |

| וקדוש 6918 | שמו 8034 | מרום 4791 | וקדוש 6918 | אשכון 7931 | ואת 854 | דכא 1793 | ושפל 8217 | רוח 7307 | להחיות 2421 |
|---|---|---|---|---|---|---|---|---|---|
| uaqadoush | shamou, | maroum | uaqadoush | 'ashkoun; | ua'at | daka' | ushpal | ruach, | lahachayout |
| ***is* Holy** | **whose name** | ***the* high** | **and holy *place*** | **I dwell in** | ***and with*** | ***that is* of a contrite** | **and humble** | **spirit** | **to revive** |

| רוח 7307 | שפלים 8217 | ולהחיות 2421 | לב 3820 | נדכאים 1792: | 57:16 כי 3588 | לא 3808 | לעולם 5769 | אריב 7378 | ולא 3808 | לנצח 5331 |
|---|---|---|---|---|---|---|---|---|---|---|
| ruach | shapaliym, | ualhachayout | leb | nidka'aym. | kiy | la' | la'aulam | 'ariyb, | uala' | lanetzach |
| **spirit** | **the humble** | **and to revive** | **the heart of** | **the contrite ones** | **For** | **not** | **for ever** | **I will contend** | **neither** | **always** |

| אקצוף 7107 | כי 3588 | רוח 7307 | מלפני 6440 | יעטוף 5848 | ונשמות 5397 | אני 589 | עשיתי 6213: | 57:17 בעון 5771 |
|---|---|---|---|---|---|---|---|---|
| 'aqtzoup; | kiy | ruach | milapanay | ya'atoup, | uanshamout | 'aniy | 'asiytiy. | ba'auon |
| **will I be wroth for** | **the spirit before me** | | | **should fail and the souls *which* I have made** | | | | **For the iniquity of** |

Isa 57:9 And you went to the king with ointment, and did increase your perfumes, and did send your messengers far off, and did debase thyself even unto hell.10 Thou are wearied in the greatness of your way; yet saidst you not, There is no hope: you have found the life of your hand; therefore you were not grieved.11 And of whom have you been afraid or feared, that you have lied, and have not remembered me, nor laid it to your heart? have not I held my peace even of old, and you fearest me not?12 I will declare your righteousness, and your works; for they shall not profit you.13 When you criest, let your companies deliver you; but the wind shall carry them all away; vanity shall take them: but he that put his trust in me shall possess the land, and shall inherit my holy mountain;14 And shall say, Cast you up, cast you up, prepare the way, take up the stumblingblock out of the way of my people.15 For thus saith the high and lofty One that inhabiteth eternity, whose name is Holy; I dwell in the high and holy place, with him also that is of a contrite and humble spirit, to revive the spirit of the humble, and to revive the heart of the contrite ones.16 For I will not contend forever, neither will I be always wroth: for the spirit should fail before me, and the souls which I have made.

בצעו 1215 קצפתי 7107 ואכהו 5221 הסתר 5641 ואקצף 7107 וילך 1980 שובב 7726 בדרך 1870
bitz'au qatzaptiy ua'akehu hasater ua'aqtzop; uayelek shoubab baderek
**his covetousness was I wroth and smote him I hid me and was wroth and he went on frowardly in the way of**

57:18
לבו 3820: דרכיו 1870 ראיתי 7200 וארפאהו 7495 ואנחהו 5148 ואשלם 7999 נחמים 5150 לו 3807a
libou. darakayu ra'aytiy ua'arpa'aehu; ua'anchehu ua'ashalem nichumiym lou'
**his heart his ways I have seen and will heal him I will lead him also and restore comforts unto him**

57:19
ולאבליו 57: בורא 1254 נוב 5108 שפתים 8193 שלום 7965 שלום 7965 לרחוק 7350 ולקרוב 7138
uala'abelayu. bourea' nub sapatayim; shaloum shaloum larachouq ualaqaroub
**and to his mourners I create the fruit of the lips Peace peace to *him that is* far off and to *him that is* near**

57:20
אמר 559 יהוה 3068 ורפאתיו 7495: והרשעים 7563 כים 3220 נגרש 1644 כי 3588 השקט 8252 לא 3808 יוכל 3201 ויגרשו 1644
'amar Yahuah uarpa'tiyu. uaharasha'aym kayam nigrash; kiy hashqet la' yukal, uayigrashu
**saith Yahuah and I will heal him But the wicked *are* like the sea troubled when rest not it can cast up**

57:21
מימיו 4325 רפש 7516 וטיט 2916: אין 369 שלום 7965 אמר 559 אלהי 430 לרשעים 7563:
meymayu repesh uatiyt. 'aeyn shaloum, 'amar 'alohay larasha'aym.
**whose waters mire and dirt *There is* no peace saith my Elohim to the wicked**

**Isa 58:1**
קרא 7121 בגרון 1627 אל 408 תחשך 2820 כשופר 7782 הרם 7311 קולך 6963 והגד 5046 לעמי 5971 פשעם 6588
qara' bagaroun 'al tachsok, kashoupar harem qouleka; uahaged la'amiy pish'am,
**Cry aloud not spare like a trumpet lift up your voice and show my people their transgression**

58:2
ולבית 1004 יעקב 3290 חטאתם 2403: ואותי 853 יום 3117 יום 3117 ידרשון 1875 ודעת 1847 דרכי 1870 יחפצון 2654 כגוי 1471
ualbeyt ya'aqob chata'tam. ua'atiy, youm youm yidroshun, uada'at darakay yechapatzun; kagouy
**and the house of Jacob their sins Yet me day *to* day they seek and to know my ways delight as a nation**

אשר 834 צדקה 6666 עשה 6213 ומשפט 4941 אלהיו 430 לא 3808 עזב 5800 ישאלוני 7592 משפטי 4941 צדק 6664
'asher tzadaqah 'asah, uamishpat 'alohayu la' 'azab, yish'aluniy mishpatey tzedeq,
**that righteousness did and the ordinance of their Elohim not forsook they ask of me the ordinances of justice**

58:3
קרבת 7132 אלהים 430 יחפצון 2654: למה 4100 צמנו 6684 ולא 3808 ראית 7200
qirbat 'alohiym yechapatzun. lamah tzamnu uala' ra'ayta,
**approaching to Elohim they take delight in Wherefore have we fasted *say they* and not? you see *wherefore***

ענינו 6031 נפשנו 5315 ולא 3808 תדע 3045 הן 2005 ביום 3117 צמכם 6685 תמצאו 4672 חפץ 2656 וכל 3605
'aniynu napshenu uala' teda'; hen bayoum tzomakem timtze'u chepetz, uakal
**have we afflicted our soul and no you take knowledge? Behold in the day of your fast you find pleasure and all**

58:4
עצביכם 6092 תנגשו 5065: הן 2005 לריב 7379 ומצה 4683 תצומו 6684 ולהכות 5221 באגרף 106 רשע 7562 לא 3808
'atzbeykem tingosu. hen lariyb uamatzah tatzumu, ualhakout ba'agrop resha'; la'
**your labours exact Behold for strife and debate you fast and to smite with the fist of wickedness not**

58:5
תצומו 6684 כיום 3117 להשמיע 8085 במרום 4791 קולכם 6963: הכזה 2088 יהיה 1961 צום 6685 אבחרהו 977
tatzumu kayoum, lahashmiya' bamaroum qoulkem. hakazeh, yihayeh tzoum 'abcharehu,
**you shall fast as *you do this* day to make to be heard on high your voice such Is it a fast that I have chosen?**

Isa 57:17 For the iniquity of his covetousness was I wroth, and smote him: I hid me, and was wroth, and he went on frowardly in the way of his heart.18 I have seen his ways, and will heal him: I will lead him also, and restore comforts unto him and to his mourners.19 I create the fruit of the lips; Peace, peace to him that is far off, and to him that is near, saith YHUH; and I will heal him.20 But the wicked are like the troubled sea, when it cannot rest, whose waters cast up mire and dirt.21 There is no peace, saith my G-d, to the wicked. **Isa** 58:1 Cry aloud, spare not, lift up your voice like a trumpet, and show my people their transgression, and the house of Jacob their sins.2 Yet they seek me daily, and delight to know my ways, as a nation that did righteousness, and forsook not the ordinance of their G-d: they ask of me the ordinances of justice; they take delight in approaching to G-d.3 Wherefore have we fasted, say they, and you seest not? wherefore have we afflicted our soul, and you takest no knowledge? Behold, in the day of your fast you find pleasure, and exact all your labours.4 Behold, you fast for strife and debate, and to smite with the fist of wickedness: you shall not fast as you do this day, to make your voice to be heard on high.

| | | | | | | | | | |
|---|---|---|---|---|---|---|---|---|---|
| יום 3117 | ענות 6031 | אדם 120 | נפשו 5315 | הלכף 3721 | כאגמן 100 | ראשו 7218 | ושק 8242 | ואפר 665 | יציע 3331 |
| youm | 'anout | 'adam | napshou; | halakop | ka'agmon | ra'shou, | uasaq | ua'aper | yatziya', |
| **a day** | **to afflict *for* a man** | | **his soul?** | ***is it* to bow down** | **as a bulrush** | **his head** | **and sackcloth** | **and ashes *under him?*** | **to spread** |

| | | | | | | | | | | | |
|---|---|---|---|---|---|---|---|---|---|---|---|
| הלזה 2088 | תקרא 7121 | צום 6685 | ויום 3117 | רצון 7522 | ליהוה 3068: | 58:6 | הלוא 3808 | זה 2088 | צום 6685 | אבחרהו 977 | פתח 6605 |
| halazeh | tiqra' | tzoum, | uayoum | ratzoun | laYahuah. | | halou'a | zeh | tzoum | 'abcharehu | pateach |
| **this** | **will you call** | **a fast** | **and an day** | **acceptable** | **to Yahuah?** | | ***Is* not** | **this** | **the fast** | **that I have chosen?** | **to loose** |

| | | | | | | | | | |
|---|---|---|---|---|---|---|---|---|---|
| חרצבות 2784 | רשע 7562 | התר 5425 | אגדות 92 | מוטה 4133 | ושלח 7971 | רצוצים 7533 | חפשים 2670 | וכל 3605 | מוטה 4133 |
| chartzubout | resha', | hater | agudout | moutah; | uashalach | ratzutziym | chapashiym, | uakal | moutah |
| **the bands of** | **wickedness** | **to undo** | **burdens** | ***the* heavy** | **and to let go** | **the oppressed** | **free** | **and every** | **yoke?** |

| | | | | | | | | | |
|---|---|---|---|---|---|---|---|---|---|
| תנתקו 5423: | 58:7 | הלוא 3808 | פרס 6536 | לרעב 7457 | לחמך 3899 | ועניים 6041 | מרודים 4788 | תביא 935 | בית 1004 |
| tanatequ. | | halou'a | paros | lara'aeb | lachmeka, | ua'aniyiym | marudiym | tabiy'a | bayit; |
| **that you break** | | ***Is it* not** | **to deal** | **to the hungry** | **your bread** | **and the poor** | **that are cast out** | **that you bring** | ***to* the house?** |

| | | | | | | | | |
|---|---|---|---|---|---|---|---|---|
| כי 3588 | תראה 7200 | ערם 6174 | וכסיתו 3680 | ומבשרך 1320 | לא 3808 | תתעלם 5956: | 58:8 | אז 227 |
| kiy | tir'ah | 'arom | uakisiytou, | uamibsaraka | la' | tit'alam. | | 'az |
| **when** | **you see** | **the naked** | **and that you cover him** | **and from your own flesh?** | **not** | **that you hide yourself** | | **Then** |

| | | | | | | | |
|---|---|---|---|---|---|---|---|
| יבקע 1234 | כשחר 7837 | אורך 216 | וארכתך 724 | מהרה 4120 | תצמח 6779 | והלך 1980 | לפניך 6440 |
| yibaqa' | kashachar | 'aureka, | ua'arukataka | maherah | tatzmiach; | uahalak | lapaneyka |
| **shall break forth** | **as the morning** | **your light** | **and your health** | **speedily** | **shall spring forth** | **and shall go** | **before you** |

| | | | | | | | | |
|---|---|---|---|---|---|---|---|---|
| צדקך 6664 | כבוד 3519 | יהוה 3068 | יאספך 622: | 58:9 | אז 227 | תקרא 7121 | ויהוה 3068 | יענה 6030 |
| tzidqeka, | kaboud | Yahuah | ya'asapeka. | | 'az | tiqraa' | uaYahuah | ya'aneh, |
| **your righteousness** | **the glory of** | **Yahuah** | **shall be your rearward** | | **Then** | **shall you call** | **and Yahuah** | **shall answer** |

| | | | | | | | | |
|---|---|---|---|---|---|---|---|---|
| תשוע 7768 | ויאמר 559 | הנני 2005 | אם 518 | תסיר 5493 | מתוכך 8432 | מוטה 4133 | שלח 7971 | אצבע 676 |
| tashaua' | uaya'mar | hineniy; | 'am | tasiyr | mitoukaka | moutah, | shalach | 'atzba |
| **you shall cry** | **and he shall say** | **Here I *am*** | **If** | **you take away** | **from the midst of you** | **the yoke** | **the putting forth of** | **the finger** |

| | | | | | | | | | |
|---|---|---|---|---|---|---|---|---|---|
| ודבר 1696 | און 205: | 58:10 | ותפק 6329 | לרעב 7457 | נפשך 5315 | ונפש 5315 | נענה 6031 | תשביע 7646 | וזרח 2224 |
| uadaber | 'auen. | | uatapeq | lara'aeb | napsheka, | uanepesh | na'anah | tasbiya'; | uazarach |
| **and speaking** | **vanity** | | **And *if* you draw out** | **to the hungry** | **your soul** | **and soul** | ***the* afflicted** | **satisfy** | **then shall rise** |

| | | | | | | | | |
|---|---|---|---|---|---|---|---|---|
| בחשך 2822 | אורך 216 | ואפלתך 653 | כצהרים 6672: | 58:11 | ונחך 5148 | יהוה 3069 | תמיד 8548 | והשביע 7646 |
| bachoshek | 'aureka, | ua'apelataka | katzaharayim. | | uanachaka | Yahuah | tamiyd | uahisbiya' |
| **in obscurity** | **your light** | **and your darkness** | ***be* as the noonday** | | **And shall guide you** | **Yahuah** | **continually** | **and satisfy** |

| | | | | | | | | |
|---|---|---|---|---|---|---|---|---|
| בצחצחות 6710 | נפשך 5315 | ועצמתיך 6106 | יחליץ 2502 | והיית 1961 | כגן 1588 | רוה 7302 | וכמוצא 4161 | מים 4325 |
| batzachtzachout | napsheka, | ua'atzmoteyka | yachaliytz; | uahayiyta | kagan | raueh, | uakmoutza' | mayim, |
| **in drought** | **your soul** | **and your bones** | **make fat** | **and you shall be** | **like a garden** | **watered** | **and like a spring of** | **water** |

| | | | | | | | | |
|---|---|---|---|---|---|---|---|---|
| אשר 834 | לא 3808 | יכזבו 3576 | מימיו 4325: | 58:12 | ובנו 1129 | ממך 4480 | חרבות 2723 | עולם 5769 |
| 'asher | la' | yakazbu | meymayu. | | uabanu | mimaka | charabout | 'aulam, |
| **whose** | **not** | **fail** | **waters** | | **And *they that shall be* of you shall build** | **of you** | **waste places** | ***the* old** |

Isa 58:5 Is it such a fast that I have chosen? a day for a man to afflict his soul? is it to bow down his head as a bulrush, and to spread sackcloth and ashes under him? will you call this a fast, and an acceptable day to YHUH?6 Is not this the fast that I have chosen? to loose the bands of wickedness, to undo the heavy burdens, and to let the oppressed go free, and that you break every yoke?7 Is it not to deal your bread to the hungry, and that you bring the poor that are cast out to your house? when you seest the naked, that you cover him; and that you hide not thyself from your own flesh?8 Then shall your light break forth as the morning, and your health shall spring forth speedily: and your righteousness shall go before you; the glory of YHUH shall be your rear guard.9 Then shall you call, and YHUH shall answer; you shall cry, and he shall say, Here I am. If you take away from the midst of you the yoke, the putting forth of the finger, and speaking vanity;10 And if you draw out your soul to the hungry, and satisfy the afflicted soul; then shall your light rise in obscurity, and your darkness be as the noonday:11 And YHUH shall guide you continually, and satisfy your soul in drought, and make fat your bones: and you shall be like a watered garden, and like a spring of water, whose waters fail not.12 And they that shall be of you shall build the old waste places:

מוסדי 4146 | דור 1755 | ודור 1755 | תקומם 6965 | וקרא 7121 | לך 3807a | גדר 1443 | פרץ 6556
mousadey | dour | uadour | taqoumem; | uaqora' | laka | goder | peretz,
**the foundations of | many | to generations | you shall raise up | and shall be called | to you | The repairer of | the breach**

משבב 7725 | נתיבות 5410 | לשבת 3427: | **58:13** | אם 518 | תשיב 7725 | משבת 7676 | רגלך 7272 | עשות 6213 | חפציך 2656
mashobeb | natiybout | lashabet. | 'am | tashiyb | mishabat | ragleka, | asout | chapatzeyka
**The restorer of | paths | to dwell in | If | you turn away | from the sabbath | your foot | *from* doing | your pleasure**

ביום 3117 | קדשי 6944 | וקראת 7121 | לשבת 7676 | ענג 6027 | לקדוש 6918 | יהוה 3068 | מכבד 3513 | וכבדתו 3513 | מעשות 6213
bayoum | qadashiy | uaqara'ta | lashabat | 'aneg, | liqdoush | Yahuah | maqubad, | uakibadtou | me'asout
**on day | my holy | and call | the sabbath | a delight | the holy of | Yahuah | honorable | and shall honor him | not doing**

דרכיך 1870 | ממצוא 4672 | חפצך 2656 | ודבר 1696 | דבר 1697: | **58:14** | אז 227 | תתענג 6026 | על 5921
darakeyka, | mimtzou'a | chepatzaka | uadaber | dabar. | 'az, | tit'anag | 'al
**your own ways | nor finding | your own pleasure | nor speaking | *your own* words | Then | shall you delight yourself | in**

יהוה 3068 | והרכבתיך 7392 | על 5921 | במותי 1116 | ארץ 776 | והאכלתיך 398 | נחלת 5159 | יעקב 3290
Yahuah, | uahirkabtiyka | 'al | bamutey | 'aretz; | uaha'akaltiyka, | nachalat | ya'aqob
**Yahuah | and I will cause you to ride | upon | the high places of | the earth | and feed you | with the heritage of | Jacob**

אביך 1 | כי 3588 | פי 6310 | יהוה 3068 | דבר 1696:
'abiyka, | kiy | piy | Yahuah | diber.
**your father for | the mouth of | Yahuah has spoken *it***

**Isa 59:1** | **59:2**
הן 2005 | לא 3808 | קצרה 7114 | יד 3027 | יהוה 3068 | מהושיע 3467 | ולא 3808 | כבדה 3513 | אזנו 241 | משמוע 8085:
hen | la' | qatzarah | yad | Yahuah | mehoushiya'; | uala' | kabdah | 'azanou | mishmoua'.
**Behold | not | is shortened | hand | Yahuah's | that it cannot save | neither | heavy | his ear | that it cannot hear**

כי 3588 | אם 518 | עונתיכם 5771 | היו 1961 | מבדלים 914 | בינכם 996 | לבין 996 | אלהיכם 430 | וחטאותיכם 2403 | הסתירו 5641 | פנים 6440
kiy | 'am | 'auonoteykem | hayu | mabdiliym, | beynekem | labeyn | 'aloheykem; | uachata'uteykem, | histiyru | paniym
**But | rather | your iniquities | have | separated | between you | and between | your Elohim | and your sins | have hid | *his* face**

מכם 4480 | משמוע 8085: | **59:3** | כי 3588 | כפיכם 3709 | נגאלו 1351 | בדם 1818 | ואצבעותיכם 676 | בעון 5771 | שפתותיכם 8193
mikem | mishmoua'. | kiy | kapeykem | nago'alu | badam, | ua'atzba'auteykem | be'auoun; | siptouteykem
**from you | that he will not hear | For | your hands | are defiled | with blood | and your fingers | with iniquity | your lips**

דברו 1696 | שקר 8267 | לשונכם 3956 | עולה 5766 | תהגה 1897: | **59:4** | אין 369 | קרא 7121 | בצדק 6664 | ואין 369 | נשפט 8199 | באמונה 530
dibru | sheqer, | lashounakem | 'aulah | tehageh. | 'aeyn | qorea' | batzedeq, | ua'aeyn | nishpat | be'amunah;
**have spoken lies | your tongue | perverseness | has muttered | None | call | for justice nor | *any* will plead | for truth**

בטוח 982 | על 5921 | תהו 8414 | ודבר 1696 | שוא 7723 | הרו 2029 | עמל 5999 | והוליד 3205 | און 205: | **59:5** | ביצי 1000 | צפעוני 6848
batouach | 'al | tohu | uadaber | shau'a, | harou | 'amal | uahouleyd | 'auen. | beytzey | tzip'auniy
**they trust | in | vanity | and speak | lies | *they* conceive | mischief | and bring forth | iniquity | eggs | cockatrice'**

בקעו 1234 | וקורי 6980 | עכביש 5908 | יארגו 707 | האכל 398 | מביציהם 1000 | ימות 4191 | והזורה 2116 | תבקע 1234
biqe'au, | uaqurey | 'akabiysh | ye'arogu; | ha'akel | mibeytzeyhem | yamut, | uahazureh | tibaqa'
**They hatch | and web | *the* spider's | weave | he that eat of their eggs | die | and that which is crushed | break out into**

Isa 58:12 you shall raise up the foundations of many generations; and you shall be called, The repairer of the breach, The restorer of paths to dwell in.13 If you turn away your foot from the Sabbath, from doing your pleasure on my holy day; and call the Sabbath a delight, the holy of YHUH, honourable; and shall honor him, not doing your own ways, nor finding your own pleasure, nor speaking your own words:14 Then shall you delight thyself in YHUH; and I will cause you to ride upon the high places of the earth, and feed you with the heritage of Jacob your father: for the mouth of YHUH has spoken it. **Isa** 59:1 Behold, YHUH's hand is not shortened, that it cannot save; neither his ear heavy, that it cannot hear:2 But your iniquities have separated between you and your G-d, and your sins have hid his face from you, that he will not hear.3 For your hands are defiled with blood, and your fingers with iniquity; your lips have spoken lies, your tongue has muttered perverseness.4 None call for justice, nor any pleadeth for truth: they trust in vanity, and speak lies; they conceive mischief, and bring forth iniquity.5 They hatch cockatrice' eggs, and weave the spider's web: he that eateth of their eggs die, and that which is crushed breaketh out into a viper.

| אפעה 660: | 59:6 קוריהם 6980 | לא 3808 | יהיו 1961 | לבגד 899 | ולא 3808 | יתכסו 3680 | במעשיהם 4639 | מעשיהם 4639 |
|---|---|---|---|---|---|---|---|---|
| 'ap'ah. | qureyhem | la' | yihayu | labeged, | uala' | yitkasu | bama'aseyhem; | ma'aseyhem |
| **a viper** | **Their webs** | **not** | **shall become** | **garments** | **neither** | **shall they cover themselves** | **with their works** | **their works** |

| מעשי 4639 | און 205 | ופעל 6467 | חמס 2555 | בכפיהם 3709: | 59:7 רגליהם 7272 | לרע 7451 | ירצו 7323 | וימהרו 4116 | לשפך 8210 |
|---|---|---|---|---|---|---|---|---|---|
| ma'asey | 'auen, | uapo'al | chamas | bakapeyhem. | ragleyhem | lara' | yarutzu, | uiymaharu, | lishpok |
| ***are*** **works of** | **iniquity** | **and the act of** | **violence** | ***is*** **in their hands** | **Their feet** | **to evil** | **run** | **and they make haste** | **to shed** |

| דם 1818 | נקי 5355 | מחשבותיהם 4284 | מחשבות 4284 | און 205 | שד 7701 | ושבר 7667 | במסלותם 4546: | 59:8 דרך 1870 |
|---|---|---|---|---|---|---|---|---|
| dam | naqiy; | machshabouteyhem | machashabout | 'auen, | shod | uasheber | bimasiloutam. | derek |
| **blood** | **innocent** | **their thoughts** | ***are*** **thoughts of** | **iniquity** | **wasting** | **and destruction** | ***are*** **in their paths** | **The way of** |

| שלום 7965 | לא 3808 | ידעו 3045 | ואין 369 | משפט 4941 | במעגלותם 4570 | נתיבותיהם 5410 | עקשו 6140 | להם 1992 |
|---|---|---|---|---|---|---|---|---|
| shaloum | la' | yada'au, | ua'aeyn | mishapat | bam'agloutam; | natiybouteyhem | 'aqshu | lahem, |
| **peace** | **not** | **they know** | **and** ***there is*** **no** | **judgment** | **in their goings** | **paths** | **they have made crooked** | **them** |

| כל 3605 | דרך 1869 | בה 871a | לא 3808 | ידע 3045 | שלום 7965: | 59:9 על 5921 | כן 3651 | רחק 7368 | משפט 4941 | ממנו 4480 | ולא 3808 |
|---|---|---|---|---|---|---|---|---|---|---|---|
| kal | dorek | bah, | la' | yada' | shaloum. | 'al | ken, | rachaq | mishapat | mimenu, | uala' |
| **whosoever** | **goes** | **therein** | **not** | **shall know** | **peace** | **Therefore** | **after** | **is far** | **judgment** | **from us** | **neither** |

| תשיגנו 5381 | צדקה 6666 | נקוה 6960 | לאור 216 | והנה 2009 | חשך 2822 | לנגהות 5054 | באפלות 653 | נהלך 1980: | 59:10 נגששה 1659 |
|---|---|---|---|---|---|---|---|---|---|
| tasiygenu | tzadaqah; | naqaueh | la'aur | uahineh | choshek, | lingohout | ba'apelout | nahalek. | nagashashah |
| **does overtake us** | **justice** | **we wait** | **for light** | **but behold** | **obscurity** | **for brightness** | **in darkness** | ***but*** **we walk** | **We grope** |

| כעורים 5787 | קיר 7023 | וכאין 369 | עינים 5869 | נגששה 1659 | כשלנו 3782 | בצהרים 6672 | כנשף 5399 |
|---|---|---|---|---|---|---|---|
| ka'auariym | qiyr, | uak'aeyn | 'aeynayim | nagasheshah; | kashalnu | batzaharayim | kaneshep, |
| **like the blind** | ***for*** **the wall** | **and no** | **eyes** | **we grope as if** ***we had*** | **we stumble** | **at noonday** | **as in the night** |

| באשמנים 820 | כמתים 4191: | 59:11 נהמה 1993 | כדבים 1677 | כלנו 3605 | וכיונים 3123 | הגה 1897 | נהגה 1897 | נקוה 6960 |
|---|---|---|---|---|---|---|---|---|
| ba'ashmaniym | kametiym. | nehemeh | kadubiym | kulanu, | uakayouniym | hagoh | nehageh; | naqaueh |
| ***we are*** **in desolate places** | **as dead** ***men*** | **We roar** | **like bears** | **all** | **and like doves** | **mourn** | **sore** | **we look** |

| למשפט 4941 | ואין 369 | לישועה 3444 | רחקה 7368 | ממנו 4480: | 59:12 כי 3588 | רבו 7235 | פשעינו 6588 |
|---|---|---|---|---|---|---|---|
| lamishpat | ua'ayin, | liyshu'ah | rachaqah | mimenu. | kiy | rabu | pasha'aeynu |
| **for judgment** | **but** ***there is*** **none** | **for salvation** | ***but*** **it is far off** | **from us** | **For** | **are multiplied** | **our transgressions** |

| נגדך 5048 | וחטאותינו 2403 | ענתה 6030 | בנו 871a | כי 3588 | פשעינו 6588 | אתנו 854 | ועונתינו 5771 |
|---|---|---|---|---|---|---|---|
| negdeka, | uachata'uteynu | 'anatah | ba'nu; | kiy | pasha'aeynu | 'atanu, | ua'auonoteynu |
| **before you** | **and our sins** | **testify** | **against us** | **for** | **our transgressions** | ***are*** **with us** | **and** ***as for*** **our iniquities** |

| ידענום 3045: | 59:13 פשע 6586 | וכחש 3584 | ביהוה 3068 | ונסוג 5253 | מאחר 310 | אלהינו 430 | דבר 1696 |
|---|---|---|---|---|---|---|---|
| yada'anum. | pashoa' | uakachesh | baYahuah, | uanasoug | me'achar | 'aloheynu; | daber |
| **we know them** | ***In*** **transgressing** | **and lying** | **against Yahuah** | **and departing away** | **from** | **our Elohim** | **speaking** |

| עשק 6233 | וסרה 5627 | הרו 2029 | והגו 1897 | מלב 3820 | דברי 1697 | שקר 8267: | 59:14 והסג 5253 | אחור 268 |
|---|---|---|---|---|---|---|---|---|
| 'asheq | uasarah, | horou | uahogou | mileb | dibrey | shaqer. | uahusag | 'achour |
| **oppression** | **and revolt** | **conceiving** | **and uttering** | **from the heart** | **words of** | **falsehood** | **And is turned away** | **backward** |

Isa 59:6 Their webs shall not become garments, neither shall they cover themselves with their works: their works are works of iniquity, and the act of violence is in their hands.7 Their feet run to evil, and they make have to shed innocent blood: their thoughts are thoughts of iniquity; wasting and destruction are in their paths.8 The way of peace they know not; and there is no judgment in their goings: they have made them crooked paths: whosoever go therein shall not know peace.9 Therefore is judgment far from us, neither doth justice overtake us: we wait for light, but behold obscurity; for brightness, but we walk in darkness.10 We grope for the wall like the blind, and we grope as if we had no eyes: we stumble at noonday as in the night; we are in desolate places as dead men.11 We roar all like bears, and mourn sore like doves: we look for judgment, but there is none; for salvation, but it is far off from us.12 For our transgressions are multiplied before you, and our sins testify against us: for our transgressions are with us; and as for our iniquities, we know them;13 In transgressing and lying against YHUH, and departing away from our G-d, speaking oppression and revolt, conceiving and uttering from the heart words of falsehood.14 And judgment is turned away backward, and justice stand afar off: for truth is fallen in the street, and equity cannot enter.

59:15

משפט 4941 וצדקה 6666 מרחוק 7350 תעמד 5975 כי 3588 כשלה 3782 ברחוב 7339 אמת 571 ונכחה 5229 לא 3808 תוכל 3201 לבוא 935: ותהי 1961
mishapat, uatzdaqah merachouq ta'amod; kiy kashalah barachoub 'amet, uankochah la' tukal labou'a. uatahiy
**judgment and justice afar off stands for is fallen in the street truth and equity not can enter Yea**

האמת 571 נעדרת 5737 וסר 5493 מרע 7451 משתולל 7997 וירא 7200 יהוה 3068 וירע 7489 בעיניו 5869 כי 3588
ha'amet ne'aderet, uasar mera' mishtoulel; uayar'a Yahuah uayera' ba'aeynayu kiy
**the truth fail and he *that* departs from evil make himself a prey and saw *it* Yahuah and it displeased sight of him that**

59:16

אין 369 משפט 4941: וירא 7200 כי 3588 אין 369 איש 376 וישתומם 8074 כי 3588 אין 369 מפגיע 6293
'aeyn mishapat. uayr'a kiy 'aeyn 'aysh, uayishtoumem kiy 'aeyn mapgiya';
***there was* no judgment And he saw that *there was* no man and wondered that *there was* no intercessor**

59:17

ותושע 3467 לו 3807a זרעו 2220 וצדקתו 6666 היא 1931 סמכתהו 5564: וילבש 3847
uatousha' lou' zaro'au, uatzidqatou hiy'a samakatahu. uayilbash
**therefore brought salvation unto him his arm and his righteousness it sustained him For he put on**

צדקה 6666 כשרין 8302 וכובע 3553 ישועה 3444 בראשו 7218 וילבש 3847 בגדי 899 נקם 5359
tzadaqah kashiryan, uakouba' yashu'ah bara'shou; uayilbash bigdey naqam
**righteousness as a breastplate and an helmet of salvation upon his head and he put on the garments of vengeance**

59:18

תלבשת 8516 ויעט 5844 כמעיל 4598 קנאה 7068: כעל 5921 גמלות 1578 כעל 5921 ישלם 7999 חמה 2534
tilboshet, uaya'at kam'ayl qin'ah. ka'al gamulout ka'al yashalem, chemah
***for* clothing and was clad with as a cloke zeal According to *their* deeds accordingly he will repay fury**

59:19

לצריו 6862 גמול 1576 לאיביו 341 לאיים 339 גמול 1576 ישלם 7999: וייראו 3372 ממערב 4628
latzarayu, gamul la'ayabayu; la'ayiym gamul yashalem. uayiyra'au mima'arab
**to his adversaries recompence to his enemies to the islands recompence he will repay So shall they fear from the west**

את 853 שם 8034 יהוה 3068 וממזרח 4217 שמש 8121 את 853 כבודו 3519 כי 3588 יבוא 935 כנהר 5104 צר 6862
'at shem Yahuah, umimizrach shemesh 'at kaboudou; kiy yabou'a kanahar tzar,
**the name of Yahuah and from the rising of the sun his glory When shall come in like a flood the enemy**

59:20

רוח 7307 יהוה 3068 נססה 5127 בו 871a: ובא 935 לציון 6726 גואל 1350
ruach Yahuah nosasah bou. uaba' latziyoun gou'ael,
**the Spirit of Yahuah shall lift up a standard against him And shall come to Zion the Redeemer**

59:21

ולשבי 7725 פשע 6588 ביעקב 3290 נאם 5002 יהוה 3068: ואני 589 זאת 2063 בריתי 1285 אותם 854
ualshabey pesha' baya'aqob; na'am Yahuah. ua'aniy, za't bariytiy 'autam
**and unto them that turn from transgression in Jacob saith Yahuah As for me this *is* my covenant with them**

אמר 559 יהוה 3068 רוחי 7307 אשר 834 עליך 5921 ודברי 1697 אשר 834 שמתי 7760 בפיך 6310 לא 3808 ימושו 4185
'amar Yahuah, ruchiy 'asher 'aleyka, uadbaray 'asher samtiy bapiyka; la' yamushu
**saith Yahuah My spirit that *is* upon you and my words which I have put in your mouth not shall depart**

מפיך 6310 ומפי 6310 זרעך 2233 ומפי 6310 זרע 2233 זרעך 2233 אמר 559 יהוה 3068
mipiyka uamipiy zar'aka uamipiy zera' zar'aka 'amar Yahuah,
**out of your mouth nor out of the mouth of your seed nor out of the mouth of your seed's seed saith Yahuah**

Isa 59:15 Yea, truth faileth; and he that departeth from evil make himself a prey: and YHUH saw it, and it displeased him that there was no judgment.16 And he saw that there was no man, and wondered that there was no intercessor: therefore his arm brought salvation unto him; and his righteousness, it sustained him.17 For he put on righteousness as a breastplate, and an helmet of salvation upon his head; and he put on the garments of vengeance for clothing, and was clad with zeal as a cloke.18 According to their deeds, accordingly he will repay, fury to his adversaries, recompence to his enemies; to the islands he will repay recompence.19 So shall they fear the name of YHUH from the west, and his glory from the rising of the sun. When the enemy shall come in like a flood, the Spirit of YHUH shall lift up a standard against him.20 And the Redeemer shall come to Zion, and unto them that turn from transgression in Jacob, saith YHUH.21 As for me, this is my covenant with them, saith YHUH; My spirit that is upon you, and my words which I have put in your mouth, shall not depart out of your mouth, nor out of the mouth of your seed, nor out of the mouth of your seed's seed, saith YHUH, from henceforth and forever.

מעתה 6258 ועד 5704 עולם 5769:
me'atah ua'ad 'aulam.
**from henceforth and for ever**

**Isa 60:1** קומי 6965 אורי 215 כי 3588 בא 935 אורך 216 וכבוד 3519 יהוה 3068 עליך 5921 זרח 2224: **60:2** כי 3588 הנה 2009 החשך 2822
quamiy 'auriy kiy ba' 'aurek; uakaboud Yahuah 'alayik zarach. kiy hineh hachoshek
**Arise shine for is come your light and the glory of Yahuah upon you is risen For behold the darkness**

יכסה 3680 ארץ 776 וערפל 6205 לאמים 3816 ועליך 5921 יזרח 2224 יהוה 3068 וכבודו 3519 עליך 5921
yechasseh 'aretz, ua'arapel la'amiym; ua'alayik yizrach Yahuah, uakboudou 'alayik
**shall cover the earth and gross darkness the people but upon you shall arise Yahuah and his glory upon you**

יראה 7200: **60:3** והלכו 1980 גוים 1471 לאורך 216 ומלכים 4428 לנגה 5051 זרחך 2225: **60:4** שאי 5375
yera'ah. uahalaku gouyim la'aurek; uamalakiym lanogah zarchek. sa'ay
**shall be seen And shall come the Gentiles to your light and kings to the brightness of your rising Lift up**

סביב 5439 עיניך 5869 וראי 7200 כלם 3605 נקבצו 6908 באו 935 לך 3807a בניך 1121 מרחוק 7350 יבאו 935
sabiyb 'aeynayik uara'ay, kulam niqbatzu ba'au lak; banayik merachouq yabo'au,
**round about your eyes and see all they gather themselves together they come to you your sons from far shall come**

ובנתיך 1323 על 5921 צד 6654 תאמנה 539: **60:5** אז 227 תראי 7200 ונהרת 5102 ופחד 6342 ורחב 7337
uabnotayik 'al tzad ta'amanah. 'az tiyr'ay uanahart, uapachad uarachab
**and your daughters at *your* side shall be nursed Then you will see and flow together and shall fear and be enlarged**

לבבך 3824 כי 3588 יהפך 2015 עליך 5921 המון 1995 ים 3220 חיל 2428 גוים 1471 יבאו 935
lababek; kiy yehapek 'alayik hamoun yam, cheyl gouyim yabo'au
**your heart because shall be converted unto you the abundance of the sea the forces of the Gentiles shall come**

לך 3807a: **60:6** שפעת 8229 גמלים 1581 תכסך 3680 בכרי 1070 מדין 4080 ועיפה 5891 כלם 3605 משבא 7614
lak. ship'at gamaliym takasek, bikrey midyan ua'aeypah, kulam mishaba'
**unto you The multitude of camels shall cover you the dromedaries of Midian and Ephah all they from Sheba**

יבאו 935 זהב 2091 ולבונה 3828 ישאו 5375 ותהלת 8416 יהוה 3068 יבשרו 1319: **60:7** כל 3605 צאן 6629
yabo'au; zahab ualabounah yisa'au, uatahilot Yahuah yabaseru. kal tza'n
**shall come gold and incense they shall bring the praises of Yahuah and they shall show forth All the flocks of**

קדר 6938 יקבצו 6908 לך 3807a אילי 352 נביות 5032 ישרתונך 8334 יעלו 5927 על 5921
qedar yiqabatzu lak, 'aeyley nabayout yasharatunek; ya'alu 'al
**Kedar shall be gathered together unto you the rams of Nebaioth shall minister unto you they shall come up with**

רצון 7522 מזבחי 4196 ובית 1004 תפארתי 8597 אפאר 6286: **60:8** מי 4310 אלה 428 כעב 5645 תעופינה 5774
ratzoun mizbachiy, uabeyt tip'artiy 'apa'aer. miy' 'aeleh ka'ab ta'aupeynah;
**acceptance *on* mine altar and the house of my glory I will glorify Who *are* these as a cloud *that* fly**

וכיונים 3123 אל 413 ארבתיהם 699: **60:9** כי 3588 לי 3807a איים 339 יקוו 6960 ואניות 591 תרשיש 8659 בראשנה 7223
uakayouniym 'al 'aruboteyhem. kiy liy 'ayiym yaqauu, ua'aniyout tarshiysh bara'shonah,
**and as the doves to their windows? Surely for me the isles shall wait and the ships of Tarshish first**

**Isa** 60:1 Arise, shine; for your light is come, and the glory of YHUH is risen upon you.2 For, behold, the darkness shall cover the earth, and gross darkness the people: but YHUH shall arise upon you, and his glory shall be seen upon you.3 And the Gentiles shall come to your light, and kings to the brightness of your rising.4 Lift up your eyes round about, and see: all they gather themselves together, they come to you: your sons shall come from far, and your daughters shall be nursed at your side.5 Then you shall see, and flow together, and your heart shall fear, and be enlarged; because the abundance of the sea shall be converted unto you, the forces of the Gentiles shall come unto you.6 The multitude of camels shall cover you, the dromedaries of Midian and Ephah; all they from Sheba shall come: they shall bring gold and incense; and they shall show forth the praises of YHUH.7 All the flocks of Kedar shall be gathered together unto you, the rams of Nebaioth shall minister unto you: they shall come up with acceptance on mine altar, and I will glorify the house of my glory.8 Who are these that fly as a cloud, and as the doves to their windows?9 Surely the isles shall wait for me, and the ships of Tarshish first, to bring your sons from far, their silver and their gold with them, unto the name of YHUH your G-d, and to the Holy One of Israel, because he has glorified you.

| להביא 935 | בניך 1121 | מרחוק 7350 | כספם 3701 | וזהבם 2091 | אתם 854 | לשם 8034 | יהוה 3068 | אלהיך 430 |
|---|---|---|---|---|---|---|---|---|
| lahabiy'a | banayik | merachouq, | kaspam | uazhabam | 'atam; | lashem | Yahuah | 'alohayik, |
| **to bring** | **your sons** | **from far** | **their silver** | **and their gold** | **with them** | **unto the name of** | **Yahuah** | **your Elohim** |

| ולקדוש 6918 | ישראל 3478 | כי 3588 | פארך 6286: | 60:10 ובנו 1129 | בני 1121 | נכר 5236 | חמתיך 2346 |
|---|---|---|---|---|---|---|---|
| ualiqadoush | yisra'ael | kiy | pe'arak. | uabanu | baney | nekar | chomotayik, |
| **and to the Holy One of** | **Israel** | **because** | **he has glorified you** | **And shall build up** | **the sons of** | **strangers** | **your walls** |

| ומלכיהם 4428 | ישרתונך 8334 | כי 3588 | בקצפי 7110 | הכיתיך 5221 | וברצוני 7522 | רחמתיך 7355: | 60:11 |
|---|---|---|---|---|---|---|---|
| uamalkeyhem | yasharatunek; | kiy | baqitzpiy | hikiytiyk, | uabirtzouniy | richamtiyk. | |
| **and their kings** | **shall minister unto you** | **for** | **in my wrath** | **I smote you** | **but in my favor** | **have I had mercy on you** | |

| ופתחו 6605 | שעריך 8179 | תמיד 8548 | יומם 3119 | ולילה 3915 | לא 3808 | יסגרו 5462 | להביא 935 | אליך 413 |
|---|---|---|---|---|---|---|---|---|
| uapitchu | sha'arayik | tamiyd | youmam | ualayalah | la' | yisageru; | lahabiy'a | 'alayik |
| **Therefore shall be open** | **your gates** | **continually** | **day** | **nor night** | **not** | **they shall be shut** | **that *men* may bring** | **unto you** |

| חיל 2428 | גוים 1471 | ומלכיהם 4428 | נהוגים 5090: | 60:12 | כי 3588 | הגוי 1471 | והממלכה 4467 | אשר 834 | לא 3808 |
|---|---|---|---|---|---|---|---|---|---|
| cheyl | gouyim, | uamalkeyhem | nahugiym. | | kiy | hagouy | uahamamlakah | 'asher | la' |
| **the forces of** | **the Gentiles** | **and *that* their kings** | ***may be* brought** | | **For** | **the nation** | **and kingdom** | **that** | **not** |

| יעבדוך 5647 | יאבדו 6 | והגוים 1471 | חרב 2717 | יחרבו 2717: | 60:13 | כבוד 3519 | הלבנון 3844 | אליך 413 | יבוא 935 |
|---|---|---|---|---|---|---|---|---|---|
| ya'abduk | ya'bedu; | uahagouyim | charob | yecherabu. | | kaboud | halabanoun | 'aelayik | yabou'a, |
| **will serve you** | **shall perish** | **yea *those* nations** | **shall be utterly** | **wasted** | | **glory of** | **The Lebanon** | **unto you** | **shall come** |

| ברוש 1265 | תדהר 8410 | ותאשור 8391 | יחדו 3162 | לפאר 6286 | מקום 4725 | מקדשי 4720 | ומקום 4725 | רגלי 7272 |
|---|---|---|---|---|---|---|---|---|
| baroush | tidhar | uat'ashur | yachdau; | lapa'aer | maqoum | miqadashiy, | uamqoum | raglay |
| **the fir tree** | **the pine** | **and the box tree** | **together** | **to beautify** | **the place of** | **my sanctuary** | **and the place of** | **my feet** |

| אכבד 3513: | 60:14 | והלכו 1980 | אליך 413 | שחוח 7817 | בני 1121 | מעניך 6031 |
|---|---|---|---|---|---|---|
| 'akabed. | | uahalaku | 'aelayik | shachouach | baney | ma'anayik, |
| **I will make glorious** | | **also shall come** | **unto you** | **bending** | **The sons of** | **them that afflicted you** |

| והשתחוו 7812 | על 5921 | כפות 3709 | רגליך 7272 | כל 3605 | מנאציך 5006 | וקראו 7121 | לך 3807a |
|---|---|---|---|---|---|---|---|
| uahishtachauu | 'al | kapout | raglayik | kal | mana'atzayik; | uaqara'au | lak |
| **and shall bow themselves down** | **at** | **the soles of** | **your feet** | **all** | **they that despised you** | **and they shall call** | **to you** |

| עיר 5892 | יהוה 3069 | ציון 6726 | קדוש 6918 | ישראל 3478: | 60:15 | תחת 8478 | היותך 1961 | עזובה 5800 | ושנואה 8130 |
|---|---|---|---|---|---|---|---|---|---|
| 'ayr | Yahuah, | tziyoun | qadoush | yisra'ael. | | tachat | hayoutek | 'azubah | uasnu'ah |
| **The city of** | **Yahuah** | **The Zion of** | ***the* Holy One of** | **Israel** | | **Whereas** | **you have been** | **forsaking** | **and hated** |

| ואין 369 | עובר 5674 | ושמתיך 7760 | לגאון 1347 | עולם 5769 | משוש 4885 | דור 1755 | ודור 1755: | 60:16 |
|---|---|---|---|---|---|---|---|---|
| ua'aeyn | 'auber; | uasamtiyk | lig'aun | 'aulam, | masous | dour | uadour. | |
| **so that no man** | **went through** | ***you,* I will make** | **an excellency** | **eternal** | **a joy of** | **many** | **to generations** | |

| וינקת 3243 | חלב 2461 | גוים 1471 | ושד 7699 | מלכים 4428 | תינקי 3243 | וידעת 3045 | כי 3588 | אני 589 | יהוה 3068 |
|---|---|---|---|---|---|---|---|---|---|
| uayanaqt | chaleb | gouyim, | uashod | malakiym | tiynaqiy; | uayada'at, | kiy | 'aniy | Yahuah |
| **You shall also suck the milk of** | | **the Gentiles** | **the breast of** | **kings** | **shall suck** | **and you shall know that** | | **I** | **Yahuah** |

Isa 60:10 And the sons of strangers shall build up your walls, and their kings shall minister unto you: for in my wrath I smote you, but in my favor have I had mercy on you.11 Therefore your gates shall be open continually; they shall not be shut day nor night; that men may bring unto you the forces of the Gentiles, and that their kings may be brought.12 For the nation and kingdom that will not serve you shall perish; yea, those nations shall be utterly wasted.13 The glory of Lebanon shall come unto you, the fir tree, the pine tree, and the box together, to beautify the place of my sanctuary; and I will make the place of my feet glorious.14 The sons also of them that afflicted you shall come bending unto you; and all they that despised you shall bow themselves down at the soles of your feet; and they shall call you, The city of YHUH, The Zion of the Holy One of Israel.15 Whereas you have been forsaken and hated, so that no man went through you, I will make you an eternal excellency, a joy of many generations.16 Thou shall also suck the milk of the Gentiles, and shall suck the breast of kings: and you shall know that I YHUH am your Saviour and your Redeemer, the mighty One of Jacob.

| | | | | 60:17 | | | | |
|---|---|---|---|---|---|---|---|---|
| מושיעך 3467 | וגאלך 1350 | אביר 46 | יעקב 3290: | תחת 8478 | הנחשת 5178 | אביא 935 | זהב 2091 | ותחת 8478 |
| moushiy'aek, | uago'alek | 'abiyr | ya'aqob. | tachat | hanachoshet | 'abiy'a | zahab, | uatachat |
| ***am* your Saviour** | **and your Redeemer** | **the mighty One of** | **Jacob** | **For** | **brass** | **I will bring** | **gold** | **and for** |

| | | | | | | | | | | |
|---|---|---|---|---|---|---|---|---|---|---|
| הברזל 1270 | אביא 935 | כסף 3701 | ותחת 8478 | העצים 6086 | נחשת 5178 | ותחת 8478 | האבנים 68 | ברזל 1270 | ושמתי 7760 | פקדתך 6486 |
| habarzel | 'abiy'a | kesep, | uatachat | ha'aetziym | nachoshet, | uatachat | ha'abaniym | barzel; | uasamtiy | paqudatek |
| **iron** | **I will bring** | **silver** | **and for** | **wood** | **brass** | **and for** | **the stones** | **iron** | **I will also make** | **your officers** |

| | | | 60:18 | | | | | | |
|---|---|---|---|---|---|---|---|---|---|
| שלום 7965 | ונגשיך 5065 | צדקה 6666: | לא 3808 | ישמע 8085 | עוד 5750 | חמס 2555 | בארצך 776 | שד 7701 | ושבר 7667 |
| shaloum, | uanogasayik | tzadaqah. | la' | yishama' | 'aud | chamas | ba'artzek, | shod | uasheber |
| **peace** | **and your exactors** | **righteousness** | **no** | **shall be heard** | **more** | **Violence** | **in your land** | **wasting** | **nor destruction** |

| | | | | | | 60:19 | | | |
|---|---|---|---|---|---|---|---|---|---|
| בגבוליך 1366 | וקראת 7121 | ישועה 3444 | חומתיך 2346 | ושעריך 8179 | תהלה 8416: | לא 3808 | יהיה 1961 | לך 3807a | עוד 5750 |
| bigabulayik; | uaqara't | yashu'ah | choumotayik, | uash'arayik | tahilah. | la' | yihayeh | lak | 'aud |
| **within your borders** | **but you shall call** | **Salvation** | **your walls** | **and your gates** | **Praise** | **no** | **shall be** | **to your** | **more** |

| | | | | | | | | | | | |
|---|---|---|---|---|---|---|---|---|---|---|---|
| השמש 8121 | לאור 216 | יומם 3119 | ולנגה 5051 | הירח 3394 | לא 3808 | יאיר 215 | לך 3807a | והיה 1961 | לך 3807a | יהוה 3068 | לאור 216 |
| hashemesh | la'aur | youmam, | ualnogah | hayareach | la' | ya'ayr | lak; | uahayah | lak | Yahuah | la'aur |
| **The sun** | **light** | **by day** | **for brightness** | **the moon** | **neither** | **shall give light** | **unto you** | **but shall be** | **unto you** | **Yahuah** | **an light** |

| | | | 60:20 | | | | | |
|---|---|---|---|---|---|---|---|---|
| עולם 5769 | ואלהיך 430 | לתפארתך 8597: | לא 3808 | יבוא 935 | עוד 5750 | שמשך 8121 | וירחך 3391 | לא 3808 |
| 'aulam, | ua'alohayik | latipa'artek. | la' | yabou'a | 'aud | shimshek, | uiyrechek | la' |
| **everlasting** | **and your Elohim** | **your glory** | **no** | **shall go down** | **more** | **Your sun** | **your moon** | **neither** |

| | | | | | | | | | | 60:21 |
|---|---|---|---|---|---|---|---|---|---|---|
| יאסף 622 | כי 3588 | יהוה 3068 | יהיה 1961 | לך 3807a | לאור 216 | עולם 5769 | ושלמו 7999 | ימי 3117 | אבלך 60: | |
| ye'asep; | kiy | Yahuah | yihayeh | lak | la'aur | 'aulam, | uashalamu | yamey | 'ablek. | |
| **shall withdraw itself** | **for** | **Yahuah** | **shall be** | **to you** | **light** | **everlasting** | **and shall be ended** | **the days of** | **your mourning** | |

| | | | | | | | | |
|---|---|---|---|---|---|---|---|---|
| ועמך 5971 | כלם 3605 | צדיקים 6662 | לעולם 5769 | יירשו 3423 | ארץ 776 | נצר 5342 | מטעו 4302 | מעשה 4639 |
| ua'amaka | kulam | tzadiyqiym, | la'aulam | yiyrashu | 'aretz; | netzer | mata'au | ma'aseh |
| **Your people also** | ***shall be* all** | **righteous** | **for ever** | **they shall inherit** | **the land** | **the branch of** | **my planting,** | **the work of** |

| | | 60:22 | | | | | | | |
|---|---|---|---|---|---|---|---|---|---|
| ידי 3027 | להתפאר 6286: | הקטן 6996 | יהיה 1961 | לאלף 505 | והצעיר 6810 | לגוי 1471 | עצום 6099 | אני 589 | יהוה 3068 |
| yaday | lahitpa'aer. | haqaton | yihayeh | la'alep, | uahatza'ayr | lagouy | 'atzum; | 'aniy | Yahuah |
| **my hands** | **that I may be glorified** | **A little one** | **shall become** | **a thousand** | **and a small one** | **a nation** | **strong** | **I** | **Yahuah** |

| | |
|---|---|
| בעתה 6256 | אחישנה 2363: |
| ba'atah | 'achiyshenahah. |
| **in his time** | **will hasten it** |

| Isa 61:1 | | | | | | | | |
|---|---|---|---|---|---|---|---|---|
| רוח 7307 | אדני 136 | יהוה 3069 | עלי 5921 | יען 3282 | משח 4886 | יהוה 3068 | אתי 853 | לבשר 1319 |
| ruach | 'adonay | Yahuah | 'alay; | ya'an | mashach | Yahuah | 'atiy | labaser |
| **The Spirit of** | **Adonai** | **Yahuah** | ***is* upon me** | **because** | **has anointed** | **Yahuah** | **me** | **to preach good tidings unto** |

| | | | | | | | | |
|---|---|---|---|---|---|---|---|---|
| ענוים 6035 | שלחני 7971 | לחבש 2280 | לנשברי 7665 | לב 3820 | לקרא 7121 | לשבוים 7617 | דרור 1865 | ולאסורים 631 |
| 'anauiym, | shalachaniy | lachabosh | lanishbarey | leb, | liqra' | lishbuyim | darour, | uala'asuriym |
| **the meek** | **he has sent me** | **to bind up** | **the broken** | **hearted** | **to proclaim** | **to the captives** | **liberty** | **and to *them that are* bound** |

Isa 60:17 For brass I will bring gold, and for iron I will bring silver, and for wood brass, and for stones iron: I will also make your officers peace, and your exactors righteousness.18 Violence shall no more be heard in your land, wasting nor destruction within your borders; but you shall call your walls Salvation, and your gates Praise.19 The sun shall be no more your light by day; neither for brightness shall the moon give light unto you: but YHUH shall be unto you an everlasting light, and your G-d your glory.20 Thy sun shall no more go down; neither shall your moon withdraw itself: for YHUH shall be your everlasting light, and the days of your mourning shall be ended.21 Thy people also shall be all righteous: they shall inherit the land forever, the branch of my planting, the work of my hands, that I may be glorified.22 A little one shall become a thousand, and a small one a strong nation: I YHUH will hasten it in his time. **Isa** 61:1 The Spirit of YHUH G-D is upon me; because YHUH has anointed me to preach good tidings unto the meek; he has sent me to bind up the brokenhearted, to proclaim liberty to the captives, and the opening of the prison to them that are bound;

| פקח 6495 | קוח 6495: | 61:2 לקרא 7121 | שנת 8141 | רצון 7522 | ליהוה 3068 | ויום 3117 | נקם 5359 | לאלהינו 430 |
|---|---|---|---|---|---|---|---|---|
| paqach | qouach. | liqra' | shenat | ratzoun | laYahuah, | uayoum | naqam | le'aloheynu; |
| **the opening of** | **the prison** | **To proclaim** | **year** | ***the* acceptable** | **of Yahuah** | **and the day of** | **vengeance** | **of our Elohim** |

| לנחם 5162 | כל 3605 | אבלים 57: | 61:3 לשום 7760 | לאבלי 57 | ציון 6726 | לתת 5414 | להם 3807a | פאר 6287 | תחת 8478 | אפר 665 |
|---|---|---|---|---|---|---|---|---|---|---|
| lanachem | kal | 'abeliym. | lasum | la'abeley | tziyoun, | latet | lahem | pa'aer | tachat | 'aeper, |
| **to comfort** | **all** | **that mourn** | **To appoint** | **unto them that mourn in** | **Zion** | **to give** | **unto them** | **beauty** | **for** | **ashes** |

| שמן 8081 | ששון 8342 | תחת 8478 | אבל 60 | מעטה 4594 | תהלה 8416 | תחת 8478 | רוח 7307 | כהה 3544 | וקרא 7121 | להם 3807a |
|---|---|---|---|---|---|---|---|---|---|---|
| shemen | sasoun | tachat | 'abel, | ma'ateh | tahilah, | tachat | ruach | kehah; | uaqora' | lahem |
| **the oil of** | **joy** | **for** | **mourning** | **the garment of** | **praise** | **for** | **the spirit of** | **heaviness** | **that might be called** | **they** |

| אילי 352 | הצדק 6664 | מטע 4302 | יהוה 3068 | להתפאר 6286: | 61:4 ובנו 1129 | חרבות 2723 | עולם 5769 |
|---|---|---|---|---|---|---|---|
| 'aeyley | hatzedeq, | mata' | Yahuah | lahitpa'aer. | uabanu | charabout | 'aulam, |
| **trees of** | **righteousness** | **the planting of** | **Yahuah** | **that he might be glorified** | **And they shall build** | **wastes** | ***the* old** |

| שממות 8074 | ראשנים 7223 | יקוממו 6965 | וחדשו 2318 | ערי 5892 | חרב 2721 | שממות 8074 | דור 1755 |
|---|---|---|---|---|---|---|---|
| shomamout | ra'shoniym | yaqoumemu; | uachidshu | 'arey | choreb, | shomamout | dour |
| **desolations** | ***the* former** | **they shall raise up** | **and they shall repair** | **cities** | ***the* waste** | **the desolations of** | **many** |

| ודור 1755: | 61:5 ועמדו 5975 | זרים 2114 | ורעו 7462 | צאנכם 6629 | ובני 1121 | נכר 5236 | אכריכם 406 |
|---|---|---|---|---|---|---|---|
| uadour. | ua'amadu | zariym, | uar'au | tza'nakem; | uabney | nekar, | 'akareykem |
| **to generations** | **And shall stand** | **strangers** | **and feed** | **your flocks** | **and the sons of** | **the alien** | ***shall be* your plowmen** |

| וכרמיכם 3755: | 61:6 ואתם 859 | כהני 3548 | יהוה 3068 | תקראו 7121 | משרתי 8334 | אלהינו 430 | יאמר 559 |
|---|---|---|---|---|---|---|---|
| uakorameykem. | ua'atem, | kohaney | Yahuah | tikkare'au, | masharatey | 'aloheynu, | ye'amer |
| **and your vinedressers** | **But you** | **the Priests of** | **Yahuah** | **shall be named** | **the Ministers of** | **our Elohim** | ***men* shall call** |

| לכם 3807a | חיל 2428 | גוים 1471 | תאכלו 398 | ובכבודם 3519 | תתימרו 3235: | 61:7 תחת 8478 | בשתכם 1322 |
|---|---|---|---|---|---|---|---|
| lakem; | cheyl | gouyim | ta'kelu, | uabikboudam | tityamaru. | tachat | bashtakem |
| **to you** | **the riches of** | **the Gentiles** | **you shall eat** | **and in their glory** | **shall you boast yourselves** | **For** | **your shame** |

| משנה 4932 | וכלמה 3639 | ירנו 7442 | חלקם 2506 | לכן 3651 | בארצם 776 | משנה 4932 |
|---|---|---|---|---|---|---|
| mishneh, | uaklimah | yaronu | chelaqam; | laken | ba'artzam | mishneh |
| ***you shall have* double** | **and *for* confusion** | **they shall rejoice in** | **their portion** | **therefore** | **in their land** | **the double** |

| יירשו 3423 | שמחת 8057 | עולם 5769 | תהיה 1961 | להם 3807a: | 61:8 כי 3588 | אני 589 | יהוה 3068 | אהב 157 | משפט 4941 | שנא 8130 | גזל 1498 |
|---|---|---|---|---|---|---|---|---|---|---|---|
| yiyrashu, | simchat | 'aulam | tihayeh | lahem. | kiy | 'aniy | Yahuah | 'aheb | mishapat, | sonea' | gazel |
| **they shall possess** | **joy** | **everlasting** | **shall be** | **unto them** | **For** | **I** | **Yahuah** | **love** | **judgment** | **I hate** | **robbery** |

| בעולה 5930 | ונתתי 5414 | פעלתם 6468 | באמת 571 | וברית 1285 | עולם 5769 | אכרות 3772 | להם 3807a: | 61:9 |
|---|---|---|---|---|---|---|---|---|
| be'aulah; | uanatatiy | pa'ulatam | be'amet, | uabriyt | 'aulam | 'akrout | lahem. | |
| **for burnt offering** | **and I will direct** | **their work** | **in truth** | **an covenant** | **everlasting** | **I will make** | **with them** | |

| ונודע 3045 | בגוים 1471 | זרעם 2233 | וצאצאיהם 6631 | בתוך 8432 | העמים 5971 | כל 3605 | ראיהם 7200 |
|---|---|---|---|---|---|---|---|
| uanouda' | bagouyim | zar'am, | uatze'atza'aeyhem | batouk | ha'amiym; | kal | ro'aeyhem |
| **And shall be known** | **among the Gentiles** | **their seed** | **and their offspring** | **among** | **the people** | **all** | **that see them** |

Isa 61:2 To proclaim the acceptable year of YHUH, and the day of vengeance of our G-d; to comfort all that mourn;3 To appoint unto them that mourn in Zion, to give unto them beauty for ashes, the oil of joy for mourning, the garment of praise for the spirit of heaviness; that they might be called trees of righteousness, the planting of YHUH, that he might be glorified.4 And they shall build the old wastes, they shall raise up the former desolations, and they shall repair the waste cities, the desolations of many generations.5 And strangers shall stand and feed your flocks, and the sons of the alien shall be your plowmen and your vinedressers.6 But you shall be named the Priests of YHUH: men shall call you the Ministers of our G-d: you shall eat the riches of the Gentiles, and in their glory shall you boast yourselves.7 For your shame you shall have double; and for confusion they shall rejoice in their portion: therefore in their land they shall possess the double: everlasting joy shall be unto them.8 For I YHUH love judgment, I hate robbery for burnt offering; and I will direct their work in truth, and I will make an everlasting covenant with them.9 And their seed shall be known among the Gentiles, and their offspring among the people: all that see them shall acknowledge them, that they are the seed which YHUH has blessed.

61:10

יכירום 5234 כי 3588 הם 1992 זרע 2233 ברך 1288 יהוה 3068: שוש 7797 אשיש 7797 ביהוה 3068
yakiyrum, kiy hem zera' berak Yahuah. sous 'asiys baYahuah
**shall acknowledge them that they *are* the seed has blessed *which* Yahuah I will greatly rejoice in Yahuah**

תגל 1523 נפשי 5315 באלהי 430 כי 3588 הלבישני 3847 בגדי 899 ישע 3468 מעיל 4598 צדקה 6666
tagel napshiy be'alohay, kiy hilbiyshany bigdey yesha', ma'ayl tzadaqah
**shall be joyful my soul in my Elohim for he has clothed me with the garments of salvation *with* the robe of righteousness**

61:11

יעטני 3271 כחתן 2860 יכהן 3547 פאר 6287 וככלה 3618 תעדה 5710 כליה 3627: כי 3588
ya'ataniy; kechatan yakahen pa'aer, uakakalah ta'adeh keleyha. kiy
**he has covered me as a bridegroom deck *himself* with ornaments and as a bride adorn *herself* with her jewels For**

כארץ 776 תוציא 3318 צמחה 6780 וכגנה 1593 זרועיה 2221 תצמיח 6779 כן 3651 אדני 136
ka'aretz toutziy'a tzimchah, uakganah zeru'ayha tatzmiyach; ken 'adonay
**as the earth you bring forth her bud and as the garden the things that are sown in it cause to spring forth so Adonai**

יהוה 3068 יצמיח 6779 צדקה 6666 ותהלה 8416 נגד 5048 כל 3605 הגוים 1471:
Yahuah yatzmiyach tzadaqah uatahilah, neged kal hagouyim.
**Yahuah will cause to spring forth righteousness and praise before all the nations**

Isa 62:1

למען 4616 ציון 6726 לא 3808 אחשה 2814 ולמען 4616 ירושלם 3389 לא 3808 אשקוט 8252 עד 5704 יצא 3318 כנגה 5051
lama'an tziyoun la' 'achesheh, ualma'an yarushalaim la' 'ashqout; 'ad yetzea' kanogah
**For sake Zion's not will I hold my peace and for sake Jerusalem's not I will rest until go forth as brightness**

62:2

צדקה 6664 וישועתה 3444 כלפיד 3940 יבער 1197: וראו 7200 גוים 1471 צדקך 6664
tzidqah, uiyshu'atah kalapiyd yib'ar. uar'au gouyim tzidqek,
**the righteousness thereof and the salvation thereof as a lamp *that* burn And shall see the Gentiles your righteousness**

62:3

וכל 3605 מלכים 4428 כבודך 3519 וקרא 7121 לך 3807a שם 8034 חדש 2319 אשר 834 פי 6310 יהוה 3068 יקבנו 5344:
uakal melakiym kaboudek; uaqora' lak shem chadash, 'asher piy Yahuah yiqabenu.
**and all kings your glory and shall be called by to you a name new which the mouth of Yahuah shall name**

62:4

והיית 1961 עטרת 5850 תפארת 8597 ביד 3027 יהוה 3068 וצנוף 6797 מלוכה 4410 בכף 3709 אלהיך 430:
uahayiyt ateret tip'aret bayad Yahuah; uatznoup malukah bakap 'alohayik.
**You shall also be a crown of glory in the hand of Yahuah and a diadem royal in the hand of your Elohim**

לא 3808 יאמר 559 לך 3807a עוד 5750 עזובה 5800 ולארצך 776 לא 3808 יאמר 559 עוד 5750 שממה 8077 כי 3588 לך 3807a
la' ye'amer lak 'aud 'azubah, ual'artzek la' ye'amer 'aud shamamah, kiy lak,
**no shall be termed to you more Forsaken shall your land neither be termed any more Desolate but to you**

62:5

יקרא 7121 חפצי 2657 בה 871a ולארצך 776 בעולה 1166 כי 3588 חפץ 2654 יהוה 3068 בך 871a וארצך 776 תבעל 1166:
yiqarea' cheptziy bah, ual'artzek ba'ulah; kiy chapetz Yahuah bak, ua'artzek tiba'ael.
**shall be called Hephzi bah and your land Beulah for delight Yahuah in you and your land shall be married**

כי 3588 יבעל 1166 בחור 970 בתולה 1330 יבעלוך 1166 בניך 1121 ומשוש 4885 חתן 2860
kiy yib'al bachur batulah, yib'aluk banayik; uamsous chatan
**For *as* marrieth a young man a virgin *so* shall marry you your sons and rejoice *as* the bridegroom**

Isa 61:10 I will greatly rejoice in YHUH, my soul shall be joyful in my G-d; for he has clothed me with the garments of salvation, he has covered me with the robe of righteousness, as a bridegroom decketh himself with ornaments, and as a bride adorneth herself with her jewels.11 For as the earth bring forth her bud, and as the garden causeth the things that are sown in it to spring forth; so YHUH G-D will cause righteousness and praise to spring forth before all the nations. **Isa** 62:1 For Zion's sake will I not hold my peace, and for Jerusalem's sake I will not rest, until the righteousness thereof go forth as brightness, and the salvation thereof as a lamp that burneth.2 And the Gentiles shall see your righteousness, and all kings your glory: and you shall be called by a new name, which the mouth of YHUH shall name.3 Thou shall also be a crown of glory in the hand of YHUH, and a royal diadem in the hand of your G-d.4 Thou shall no more be termed Forsaken; neither shall your land anymore be termed Desolate: but you shall be called Hephzi-bah, and your land Beulah: for YHUH delighteth in you, and your land shall be married.5 For as a young man marrieth a virgin, so shall your sons marry you: and as the bridegroom rejoice over the bride, so shall your G-d rejoice over you.

62:6

על 5921 כלה 3618 ישיש 7797 עליך 5921 אלהיך 430: על 5921 חומתיך 2346 ירושלם 3389 הפקדתי 6485 שמרים 8104 כל 3605
'al kalah, yasiys 'alayik 'alohayik. 'al choumotayik yarushalaim, hipqadtiy shomariym, kal
**over the bride *so* shall rejoice over you your Elohim upon your walls O Jerusalem I have set watchmen nor**

היום 3117 וכל 3605 הלילה 3915 תמיד 8548 לא 3808 יחשו 2814 המזכרים 2142 את 853 יהוה 3068 אל 408 דמי 1824
hayoum uakal halayalah tamiyd la' yechashu; hamazkiriym 'at Yahuah, 'al damiy
**day and all night always never *which* shall hold their peace that make mention of Yahuah not keep silence**

62:7 62:8

לכם 3807a: ואל 408 תתנו 5414 דמי 1824 לו 3807a עד 5704 יכונן 3559 ועד 5704 ישים 7760 את 853 ירושלם 3389 תהלה 8416 בארץ 776:
lakem. ua'al titanu damiy lou'; 'ad yakounen ua'ad yasiym 'at yarushalaim tahilah ba'aretz.
**for you And no give rest him till he establish and till he make Jerusalem a praise in the earth**

נשבע 7650 יהוה 3068 בימינו 3225 ובזרוע 2220 עזו 5797 אם 518 אתן 5414 את 853 דגנך 1715 עוד 5750 מאכל 3978
nishba' Yahuah biymiynou uabizroua' 'azou; 'am 'aten 'at daganek 'aud ma'akal
**has sworn Yahuah by his right hand and by the arm of his strength Surely no I will give your corn more *to be* meat**

62:9

לאיביך 341 ואם 518 ישתו 8354 בני 1121 נכר 5236 תירושך 8492 אשר 834 יגעת 3021 בו 871a: כי 3588
la'ayabayik, ua'am yishtu baney nekar tiyroushek, 'asher yaga'at bou. kiy
**for your enemies and not shall drink the sons of the stranger your wine *the* which you have laboured for But**

מאספיו 622 יאכלהו 398 והללו 1984 את 853 יהוה 3068 ומקבציו 6908 ישתהו 8354
ma'aspayu ya'kaluhu, uahillu 'at Yahuah; uamqabtzayu yishtuhu
**they that have gathered it shall eat it and praise Yahuah and they that have brought it together shall drink it**

62:10

בחצרות 2691 קדשי 6944: עברו 5674 עברו 5674 בשערים 8179 פנו 6437 דרך 1870 העם 5971 סלו 5549 סלו 5549
bachatzarout qadashiy 'abru 'abru bash'ariym, panu derek ha'am; solu solu
**in the courts of my holiness Go through go through the gates prepare you the way of the people cast up cast up**

62:11

המסלה 4546 סקלו 5619 מאבן 68 הרימו 7311 נס 5251 על 5921 העמים 5971: הנה 2009 יהוה 3068 השמיע 8085 אל 413
hamasilah saqlu me'aben, hariymu nes 'al ha'amiym. hineh Yahuah hishmiya' 'al
**the highway gather out the stones lift up a standard for the people Behold Yahuah has proclaimed unto**

קצה 7097 הארץ 776 אמרו 559 לבת 1323 ציון 6726 הנה 2009 ישעך 3468 בא 935 הנה 2009 שכרו 7939 אתו 854
qatzeh ha'aretz, 'amru labat tziyoun, hineh yish'aek ba'; hineh sekarou 'atou,
**the end of the world Say you to the daughter of Zion Behold your salvation comes behold his reward *is* with him**

62:12

ופעלתו 6468 לפניו 6440: וקראו 7121 להם 1992 עם 5971 הקדש 6944 גאולי 1350 יהוה 3069 ולך 3807a יקרא 7121
uap'alatou lapanayu. uaqar'au lahem 'am haqodesh ga'auley Yahuah; ualak yiqarea'
**and his work before him And they shall call them people The holy The redeemed of Yahuah and you shall be called**

דרושה 1875 עיר 5892 לא 3808 נעזבה 5800:
darushah, 'ayr la' ne'azabah.
**Sought out A city not forsaken**

**Isa 63:1**

מי 4310 זה 2088 בא 935 מאדום 123 חמוץ 2556 בגדים 899 מבצרה 1224 זה 2088 הדור 1921 בלבושו 3830 צעה 6808
miy' zeh ba' me'adoum, chamutz bagadiym mibatzrah, zeh hadur bilbushou, tzo'ah
**Who *is* this that comes from Edom *with* dyed garments from Bozrah? this *that is* glorious in his apparel travelling**

Isa 62:6 I have set watchmen upon your walls, O Jerusalem, which shall never hold their peace day nor night: you that make mention of YHUH, keep not silence,7 And give him no rest, till he establish, and till he make Jerusalem a praise in the earth.8 YHUH has sworn by his right hand, and by the arm of his strength, Surely I will no more give your corn to be meat for your enemies; and the sons of the stranger shall not drink your wine, for the which you have laboured:9 But they that have gathered it shall eat it, and praise YHUH; and they that have brought it together shall drink it in the courts of my holiness.10 Go through, go through the gates; prepare you the way of the people; cast up, cast up the highway; gather out the stones; lift up a standard for the people.11 Behold, YHUH has proclaimed unto the end of the world, Say you to the daughter of Zion, Behold, your salvation cometh; behold, his reward is with him, and his work before him.12 And they shall call them, The holy people, The redeemed of YHUH: and you shall be called, Sought out, A city not forsaken. **Isa** 63:1 Who is this that cometh from Edom, with dyed garments from Bozrah? this that is glorious in his apparel, travelling in the greatness of his strength? I that speak in righteousness, mighty to save.

| | | | | | | | | | |
|---|---|---|---|---|---|---|---|---|---|
| ברב 7230<br>barob<br>**in the greatness of** | כחו 3581<br>kochou;<br>**his strength?** | אני 589<br>'aniy<br>**I** | מדבר 1696<br>madaber<br>**that speak** | בצדקה 6666<br>bitzadaqah<br>**in righteousness** | רב 7227<br>rab<br>**mighty** | להושיע 3467:<br>lahoushiya'.<br>**to save** | 63:2 | מדוע 4069<br>madua'<br>**Wherefore** | אדם 122<br>'adom<br>***are you* red** |
| ללבושך 3830<br>lilbusheka;<br>**in your apparel** | ובגדיך 899<br>uabgadeyka<br>**and your garments** | כדרך 1869<br>kadorek<br>**like him that tread** | בגת 1660:<br>bagat.<br>**in the winefat?** | 63:3 | פורה 6333<br>pu'rah<br>**the winepress** | דרכתי 1869<br>daraktiy<br>**I have trodden** | לבדי 905<br>labadiy,<br>**alone** | | |
| ומעמים 5971<br>uame'amiym<br>**and of the people** | אין 369<br>'aeyn<br>***there was* no** | איש 376<br>'aysh<br>**man** | אתי 854<br>'atiy,<br>**with me** | ואדרכם 1869<br>ua'adrakem<br>**for I will tread them** | באפי 639<br>ba'apiy,<br>**in mine anger** | וארמסם 7429<br>ua'armasem<br>**and trample them** | בחמתי 2534<br>bachamatiy;<br>**in my fury** | | |
| ויז 5137<br>uayez<br>**and shall be sprinkled** | נצחם 5332<br>nitzcham<br>**their blood** | על 5921<br>'al<br>**upon** | בגדי 899<br>bagaday,<br>**my garments** | וכל 3605<br>uakal<br>**and all** | מלבושי 4403<br>malbushay<br>**my raiment** | אגאלתי 1351:<br>'ag'alatiy.<br>**I will stain** | 63:4 | כי 3588<br>kiy<br>**For** | יום 3117<br>youm<br>**the day of** |
| | | | | | | | | | נקם 5359<br>naqam<br>**vengeance** |
| בלבי 3820<br>balibiy;<br>***is* in mine heart** | ושנת 8141<br>uashnat<br>**and the year of** | גאולי 1350<br>ga'ulay<br>**my redeemed** | באה 935:<br>ba'ah.<br>**is come** | 63:5 | ואביט 5027<br>ua'abiyt<br>**And I looked** | ואין 369<br>ua'aeyn<br>**and *there was* none** | עזר 5826<br>'azer,<br>**to help** | ואשתומם 8074<br>ua'ashtoumem<br>**and I wondered** | |
| ואין 369<br>ua'aeyn<br>**that *there was* none** | סומך 5564<br>soumek;<br>**to uphold** | ותושע 3467<br>uatousha'<br>**therefore brought salvation** | לי 3807a<br>liy<br>**unto me** | זרעי 2220<br>zaro'ay,<br>**mine own arm** | וחמתי 2534<br>uachamatiy<br>**and my fury** | היא 1931<br>hiy'a<br>**it** | סמכתני 5564:<br>samakataniy.<br>**upheld me** | 63:6 | |
| ואבוס 947<br>ua'abus<br>**And I will tread down** | עמים 5971<br>'amiym<br>**the people** | באפי 639<br>ba'apiy,<br>**in mine anger** | ואשכרם 7937<br>ua'ashakrem<br>**and make them drunk** | בחמתי 2534<br>bachamatiy;<br>**in my fury** | ואוריד 3381<br>ua'ariyd<br>**and I will bring down** | לארץ 776<br>la'aretz<br>**to the earth** | | | |
| נצחם 5332:<br>nitzcham.<br>**their strength** | 63:7 | חסדי 2617<br>chasdey<br>**the lovingkindnesses of** | יהוה 3068<br>Yahuah<br>**Yahuah** | אזכיר 2142<br>'azkiyr<br>**I will mention** | תהלת 8416<br>tahilot<br>***and* the praises of** | יהוה 3068<br>Yahuah,<br>**Yahuah** | כעל 5921<br>ka'al<br>**according to** | כל 3605<br>kal<br>**all** | אשר 834<br>'asher<br>**that** |
| גמלנו 1580<br>gamalanu<br>**has bestowed on us** | יהוה 3068<br>Yahuah;<br>**Yahuah** | ורב 7227<br>uarab<br>**and the great** | טוב 2898<br>toub<br>**goodness** | לבית 1004<br>labeyt<br>**toward the house of** | ישראל 3478<br>yisra'ael,<br>**Israel** | אשר 834<br>'asher<br>**which** | גמלם 1580<br>gamalam<br>**he has bestowed on them** | | |
| כרחמיו 7356<br>karachamayu<br>**according to his mercies** | וכרב 7230<br>uakrob<br>**and according to the multitude of** | חסדיו 2617:<br>chasadayu.<br>**his lovingkindnesses** | 63:8 | ויאמר 559<br>uaya'mer<br>**For he said** | אך 389<br>'ak<br>**Surely** | עמי 5971<br>'amiy<br>***are* my people** | | | |
| המה 1992<br>hemah,<br>**they** | בנים 1121<br>baniym<br>**children** | לא 3808<br>la'<br>**not** | ישקרו 8266<br>yashaqeru;<br>***that* will lie** | ויהי 1961<br>uayahiy<br>**so he was** | להם 1992<br>lahem<br>**their** | למושיע 3467:<br>lamoushiya'.<br>**Saviour** | 63:9 | בכל 3605<br>bakal<br>**In all** | צרתם 6869<br>tzaratam<br>**their affliction** |
| | | | | | | | | לא 3808<br>la'<br>**not** | צר 6862<br>tzar,<br>***he was* afflicted** |
| ומלאך 4397<br>uamal'ak<br>**and the angel of** | פניו 6440<br>panayu<br>**his presence** | הושיעם 3467<br>houshiy'am,<br>**saved them** | באהבתו 160<br>ba'ahabatou<br>**in his love** | ובחמלתו 2551<br>uabchemlatou<br>**and in his pity** | הוא 1931<br>hua'<br>**he** | גאלם 1350<br>ga'alam;<br>**redeemed them** | וינטלם 5190<br>uayanatlem<br>**and he bare them** | | |

Isa 63:2 Wherefore are you red in your apparel, and your garments like him that treadeth in the winefat?3 I have trodden the winepress alone; and of the people there was none with me: for I will tread them in mine anger, and trample them in my fury; and their blood shall be sprinkled upon my garments, and I will stain all my raiment.4 For the day of vengeance is in mine heart, and the year of my redeemed is come.5 And I looked, and there was none to help; and I wondered that there was none to uphold: therefore mine own arm brought salvation unto me; and my fury, it upheld me.6 And I will tread down the people in mine anger, and make them drunk in my fury, and I will bring down their strength to the earth.7 I will mention the lovingkindnesses of YHUH, and the praises of YHUH, according to all that YHUH has bestowed on us, and the great goodness toward the house of Israel, which he has bestowed on them according to his mercies, and according to the multitude of his lovingkindnesses.8 For he said, Surely they are my people, children that will not lie: so he was their Saviour.9 In all their affliction he was afflicted, and the angel of his presence saved them: in his love and in his pity he redeemed them; and he bare them, and carried them all the days of old.

| וינשאם 5375 | כל 3605 | ימי 3117 | עולם 5769: | 63:10 והמה 1992 | מרו 4784 | ועצבו 6087 | את 853 | רוח 7307 | קדשו 6944 |
|---|---|---|---|---|---|---|---|---|---|
| uayanas'aem | kal | yamey | 'aulam. | uahemah | maru | ua'atzbu | 'at | ruach | qadashou; |
| **and carried them** | **all** | **the days of** | **old** | **But they** | **rebelled** | **and vexed** | | **Spirit** | **his holy** |

| ויהפך 2015 | להם 3807a | לאויב 341 | הוא 1931 | נלחם 3898 | בם 871a: | 63:11 ויזכר 2142 | ימי 3117 | עולם 5769 |
|---|---|---|---|---|---|---|---|---|
| uayehapek | lahem | la'auyeb | hua' | nilcham | bam. | uayizkor | yamey | 'aulam |
| **therefore he was turned** | ***to be* their** | **enemy** | ***and* he** | **fought** | **against them** | **Then he remembered** | **the days of** | **old** |

| משה 4872 | עמו 5971 | איה 346 | המעלם 5927 | מים 3220 | את 854 | רעי 7462 | צאנו 6629 | איה 346 |
|---|---|---|---|---|---|---|---|---|
| mosheh | 'amou; | 'ayeh | hama'alem | miyam, | 'at | ro'aey | tza'nou, | 'ayeh |
| **Moses** | ***and* his people** | ***saying* Where** | ***is* he that brought them up** | **out of the sea** | ***with*** | **the shepherd of** | **his flock?** | **where *is*** |

| השם 7760 | בקרבו 7130 | את 853 | רוח 7307 | קדשו 6944: | 63:12 מוליך 1980 | לימין 3225 | משה 4872 | זרוע 2220 | תפארתו 8597 |
|---|---|---|---|---|---|---|---|---|---|
| hasam | baqirbou | 'at | ruach | qadashou. | mouliyk | liyamiyn | mosheh, | zaroua' | tip'artou; |
| **he that put** | **within him?** | | **Spirit** | **his holy** | **that led** | ***them* by the right hand of** | **Moses** | **arm** | ***with* his glorious** |

| בוקע 1234 | מים 4325 | מפניהם 6440 | לעשות 6213 | לו 3807a | שם 8034 | עולם 5769: | 63:13 מוליכם 1980 | בתהמות 8415 | כסוס 5483 |
|---|---|---|---|---|---|---|---|---|---|
| bouqea' | mayim | mipaneyhem, | la'asout | lou' | shem | 'aulam. | mouliykam | batahomout; | kasus |
| **dividing** | **the water** | **before them** | **to make** | **himself** | **an name?** | **everlasting** | **That led them** | **through the deep** | **as an horse** |

| במדבר 4057 | לא 3808 | יכשלו 3782: | 63:14 כבהמה 929 | בבקעה 1237 | תרד 3381 | רוח 7307 | יהוה 3068 |
|---|---|---|---|---|---|---|---|
| bamidbar | la' | yikashelu. | kabahemah | babiq'ah | tered, | ruach | Yahuah |
| **in the wilderness** | **not** | ***that* they should stumble?** | **As a beast** | **into the valley** | **goes down** | **the Spirit of** | **Yahuah** |

| תניחנו 5117 | כן 3651 | נהגת 5090 | עמך 5971 | לעשות 6213 | לך 3807a | שם 8034 | תפארת 8597: | 63:15 הבט 5027 | משמים 8064 |
|---|---|---|---|---|---|---|---|---|---|
| taniychenu; | ken | nihagta | 'amaka, | la'asout | laka | shem | tip'aret. | habet | mishamayim |
| **caused him to rest** | **so** | **did you lead** | **your people** | **to make** | **to yourself** | **a name** | **glorious** | **Look down** | **from heaven** |

| וראה 7200 | מזבל 2073 | קדשך 6944 | ותפארתך 8597 | איה 346 | קנאתך 7068 | וגבורתך 1369 | המון 1995 |
|---|---|---|---|---|---|---|---|
| uar'aeh, | mizabul | qadashaka | uatip'arteka; | 'ayeh | qin'ataka | uagaburoteka, | hamoun |
| **and behold** | **from the habitation of** | **your holiness** | **and of your glory** | **where** | ***is* your zeal** | **and your strength** | **the sounding of** |

| מעיך 4578 | ורחמיך 7356 | אלי 413 | התאפקו 662: | 63:16 כי 3588 | אתה 859 | אבינו 1 | כי 3588 | אברהם 85 |
|---|---|---|---|---|---|---|---|---|
| me'ayka | uarachameyka | 'aelay | hit'apaqu. | kiy | 'atah | 'abiynu, | kiy | 'abraham |
| **your bowels** | **and of your mercies** | **toward me?** | **are they restrained?** | **Doubtless** | **you** | ***are* our father** | **though** | **Abraham** |

| לא 3808 | ידענו 3045 | וישראל 3478 | לא 3808 | יכירנו 5234 | אתה 859 | יהוה 3068 | אבינו 1 | גאלנו 1350 | מעולם 5769 |
|---|---|---|---|---|---|---|---|---|---|
| la' | yada'anu, | uayisra'ael | la' | yakiyranu; | 'atah | Yahuah | 'abiynu, | go'alenu | me'aulam |
| **not** | **know of us** | **and Israel** | **not** | **acknowledge us** | **you** | **O Yahuah** | ***are* our father** | **our redeemer** | ***is* from everlasting** |

| שמך 8034: | 63:17 למה 4100 | תתענו 8582 | יהוה 3068 | מדרכיך 1870 | תקשיח 7188 | לבנו 3820 | מיראתך 3374 |
|---|---|---|---|---|---|---|---|
| shameka. | lamah | tat'aenu | Yahuah | midrakeyka, | taqshiyach | libenu | miyir'ateka; |
| **your name** | **why** | **have you made us to err** | **O Yahuah** | **from your ways** | ***and* hardened** | **our heart** | **from your fear?** |

| שוב 7725 | למען 4616 | עבדיך 5650 | שבטי 7626 | נחלתך 5159: | 63:18 למצער 4705 | ירשו 3423 | עם 5971 |
|---|---|---|---|---|---|---|---|
| shub | lama'an | 'abadeyka, | shibtey | nachalateka. | lamitz'ar | yarashu | 'am |
| **Return** | **for sake** | **your servants'** | **the tribes of** | **your inheritance** | ***it* but a little while** | **have possessed** | **The people of** |

Isa 63:10 But they rebelled, and vexed his holy Spirit: therefore he was turned to be their enemy, and he fought against them.11 Then he remembered the days of old, Moses, and his people, saying, Where is he that brought them up out of the sea with the shepherd of his flock? where is he that put his holy Spirit within him?12 That led them by the right hand of Moses with his glorious arm, dividing the water before them, to make himself an everlasting name?13 That led them through the deep, as an horse in the wilderness, that they should not stumble?14 As a beast go down into the valley, the Spirit of YHUH caused him to rest: so did you lead your people, to make thyself a glorious name.15 Look down from heaven, and behold from the habitation of your holiness and of your glory: where is your zeal and your strength, the sounding of your bowels and of your mercies toward me? are they restrained?16 Doubtless you are our father, though Abraham be ignorant of us, and Israel acknowledge us not: you, O YHUH, are our father, our redeemer; your name is from everlasting.17 O YHUH, why have you made us to err from your ways, and hardened our heart from your fear? Return for your servants' sake, the tribes of your inheritance.18 The people of your holiness have possessed it but a little while: our adversaries have trodden down your sanctuary.

| | | | | 63:19 | | | |
|---|---|---|---|---|---|---|---|
| קדשך 6944 | צרינו 6862 | בוססו 947 | מקדשך 4720: | היינו 1961 | מעולם 5769 | לא 3808 | משלת 4910 |
| qadasheka | tzareynu | bousasu | miqadasheka. | hayiynu, | me'aulam | la' | mashalta |
| **your holiness** | **our adversaries** | **have trodden down** | **your sanctuary** | **We are *yours*** | **never** | **not** | **you bare rule** |

| | | | | |
|---|---|---|---|---|
| בם 871a | לא 3808 | נקרא 7121 | שמך 8034 | עליהם 5921 |
| bam, | la' | niqra' | shimka | 'aleyhem |
| **over them** | **not** | **they were called** | **your name** | **by** |

| Isa 64:1 | | | | | | |
|---|---|---|---|---|---|---|
| | לוא 3863 | קרעת 7167 | שמים 8064 | ירדת 3381 | מפניך 6440 | הרים 2022 |
| | lua' | qara'ta | shamayim | yaradta, | mipaneyka | hariym |
| | **Oh that** | **you would rend** | **the heavens** | **that you would come down** | **at your presence** | **the mountains** |

| | 64:2 | | | | | | | |
|---|---|---|---|---|---|---|---|---|
| נזלו 2151: | כקדח 6919 | אש 784 | המסים 2003 | מים 4325 | תבעה 1158 | אש 784 | להודיע 3045 | שמך 8034 |
| nazolu. | kiqdoach | 'aesh | hamasiym, | mayim | tib'ah | 'aesh, | lahoudiya' | shimka |
| **that might flow down** | **As burn** | **fire** | ***when* the melting** | **the waters** | **cause to boil** | **the fire** | **to make known** | **your name** |

| | | | | 64:3 | | |
|---|---|---|---|---|---|---|
| לצריך 6862 | מפניך 6440 | גוים 1471 | ירגזו 7264: | בעשותך 6213 | נוראות 3372 | לא 3808 |
| latzareyka; | mipaneyka | gouyim | yiragazu. | ba'asoutaka | noura'aut | la' |
| **to your adversaries** | **at your presence** | ***that* the nations** | **may tremble** | **When you did** | **terrible things** | **not** |

| | | | | | 64:4 |
|---|---|---|---|---|---|
| נקוה 6960 | ירדת 3381 | מפניך 6440 | הרים 2022 | נזלו 2151: | ומעולם 5769 |
| naqaueh; | yaradta | mipaneyka | hariym | nazolu. | uame'aulam |
| ***which* we looked for** | **you come down** | **at your presence** | **the mountains** | **flowed down** | **For since the beginning of the world** |

| | | | | | | | | | |
|---|---|---|---|---|---|---|---|---|---|
| לא 3808 | שמעו 8085 | לא 3808 | האזינו 238 | עין 5869 | לא 3808 | ראתה 7200 | אלהים 430 | זולתך 2108 | יעשה 6213 |
| la' | shama'au | la' | he'aziynu; | 'ayin | la' | ra'atah, | 'alohiym | zulataka, | ya'aseh |
| **not** | ***men* have heard** | **nor** | **perceived by the ear** | **the eye** | **neither** | **has seen** | **O Elohim** | **beside you** | ***what* he has prepared** |

| | | 64:5 | | | | | |
|---|---|---|---|---|---|---|---|
| למחכה 2442 | לו 3807a: | פגעת 6293 | את 853 | שש 7797 | ועשה 6213 | צדק 6664 | בדרכיך 1870 |
| limchakeh | lou'. | paga'ata | 'at | sas | ua'aseh | tzedeq, | bidarakeyka |
| **for him that wait** | **for him** | **You meetest** | | **him that rejoice** | **and work** | **righteousness** | **in your ways** |

| | | | | | | | | 64:6 |
|---|---|---|---|---|---|---|---|---|
| יזכרוך 2142 | הן 2005 | אתה 859 | קצפת 7107 | ונחטא 2398 | בהם 871a | עולם 5769 | ונושע 3467: | |
| yizkaruka; | hen | 'atah | qatzapta | uanecheta', | bahem | 'aulam | uaniuashea'. | |
| ***those that* remember you** | **behold** | **you** | **are wroth** | **for we have sinned** | **in those** | ***is* continuance** | **and we shall be saved** | |

| | | | | | | | | | |
|---|---|---|---|---|---|---|---|---|---|
| ונהי 1961 | כטמא 2931 | כלנו 3605 | וכבגד 899 | עדים 5708 | כל 3605 | צדקתינו 6666 | ונבל 5034 | כעלה 5929 | כלנו 3605 |
| uanahiy | katamea' | kulanu, | uakbeged | 'adiym | kal | tzidqoteynu; | uanabel | ke'aleh | kulanu, |
| **But we are** | **as an unclean *thing*** | **all** | **and as rags** | **filthy** | **all** | **our righteousnesses *are*** | **and do fade** | **as a leaf** | **we all** |

| | | | 64:7 | | | |
|---|---|---|---|---|---|---|
| ועוננו 5771 | כרוח 7307 | ישאנו 5375: | ואין 369 | קורא 7121 | בשמך 8034 | מתעורר 5782 |
| ua'auonenu | karuach | yisa'anu. | ua'aeyn | qourea' | bashimaka, | mit'auer |
| **and our iniquities** | **like the wind** | **have taken us away** | **And *there is* none** | **that call** | **upon your name** | **that stir up himself** |

| | | | | | | | | | 64:8 |
|---|---|---|---|---|---|---|---|---|---|
| להחזיק 2388 | בך 871a | כי 3588 | הסתרת 5641 | פניך 6440 | ממנו 4480 | ותמוגנו 4127 | ביד 3027 | עוננו 5771: | ועתה 6258 |
| lahachaziyq | bak; | kiy | histarta | paneyka | mimenu, | uatamugenu | bayad | 'auonenu. | ua'atah |
| **to take hold of you** | **for** | **you have hid** | **your face** | **from us** | | **and have consumed us** | **because of** | **our iniquities** | **But now** |

Isa 63:19 We are your: you never barest rule over them; they were not called by your name. **Isa** 64:1 Oh that you would rend the heavens, that you would come down, that the mountains might flow down at your presence,2 As when the melting fire burneth, the fire causeth the waters to boil, to make your name known to your adversaries, that the nations may tremble at your presence!3 When you did terrible things which we looked not for, you came down, the mountains flowed down at your presence.4 For since the beginning of the world men have not heard, nor perceived by the ear, neither has the eye seen, O G-d, beside you, what he has prepared for him that waiteth for him.5 Thou meet him that rejoice and worketh righteousness, those that remember you in your ways: behold, you are wroth; for we have sinned: in those is continuance, and we shall be saved.6 But we are all as an unclean thing, and all our righteousnesses are as filthy rags; and we all do fade as a leaf; and our iniquities, like the wind, have taken us away.7 And there is none that call upon your name, that stirreth up himself to take hold of you: for you have hid your face from us, and have consumed us, because of our iniquities.8 But now, O YHUH, you are our father; we are the clay, and you our potter; and we all are the work of your hand.

| יהוה 3069 | אבינו 1 | אתה 859 | אנחנו 587 | החמר 2563 | ואתה 859 | יצרנו 3335 | ומעשה 4639 | ידך 3027 | כלנו 3605: | 64:9 אל 408 |
|---|---|---|---|---|---|---|---|---|---|---|
| Yahuah | 'abiynu | 'atah; | 'anachnu | hachamor | ua'atah | yotzarenu, | uama'aseh | yadaka | kulanu. | 'al |
| **Yahuah** | ***are* our father** | **you** | **we** | ***are* the clay** | **and you** | **our potter** | **and the work of** | **your hand** | **we all *are*** | **not** |

| תקצף 7107 | יהוה 3068 | עד 5704 | מאד 3966 | ואל 408 | לעד 5703 | תזכר 2142 | עון 5771 | הן 2005 | הבט 5027 | נא 4994 | עמך 5971 |
|---|---|---|---|---|---|---|---|---|---|---|---|
| tiqtzop | Yahuah | 'ad | ma'ad, | ua'al | la'ad | tizkor | 'auon; | hen | habet | naa' | 'ameka |
| **Be wroth** | **O Yahuah** | **very** | **sore** | **neither** | **for ever** | **remember** | **iniquity** | **behold** | **see** | **we beseech you** | **your people** |

| כלנו 3605: | 64:10 ערי 5892 | קדשך 6944 | היו 1961 | מדבר 4057 | ציון 6726 | מדבר 4057 | היתה 1961 | ירושלם 3389 | שממה 8077: | 64:11 בית 1004 |
|---|---|---|---|---|---|---|---|---|---|---|
| kulanu. | 'arey | qadashaka | hayu | midbar; | tziyoun | midbar | hayatah, | yarushalaim | shamamah. | beyt |
| **we *are* all** | **cities** | **Your holy** | **are** | **a wilderness** | **Zion** | **a wilderness** | **is** | **Jerusalem** | **a desolation** | **house** |

| קדשנו 6944 | ותפארתנו 8597 | אשר 834 | הללוך 1984 | אבתינו 1 | היה 1961 | לשרפת 8316 | אש 784 | וכל 3605 | מחמדינו 4261 | היה 1961 |
|---|---|---|---|---|---|---|---|---|---|---|
| qadashenu | uatip'artenu, | 'asher | hilluka | 'aboteynu, | hayah | lisrepat | 'aesh; | uakal | machamadeynu | hayah |
| **Our holy** | **and our beautiful** | **where** | **praised you** | **our fathers** | **is** | **burned up with** | **fire** | **and all** | **our pleasant things** | **are** |

| לחרבה 2723: | 64:12 העל 5921 | אלה 428 | תתאפק 662 | יהוה 3068 | תחשה 2814 | ותעננו 6031 | עד 5704 |
|---|---|---|---|---|---|---|---|
| lacharabah. | ha'al | 'aeleh | tit'apaq | Yahuah; | techesheh | uat'anenu | 'ad |
| **laid waste** | **for** | **these *things*** | **Will you refrain yourself** | **O Yahuah** | **will you hold your peace** | **and afflict us** | **very** |

| מאד 3966: |
|---|
| ma'ad. |
| **sore?** |

| **Isa 65:1** נדרשתי 1875 | ללוא 3808 | שאלו 7592 | נמצאתי 4672 | ללא 3808 | בקשני 1245 | אמרתי 559 | הנני 2005 |
|---|---|---|---|---|---|---|---|
| nidrashtiy | lalou'a | sha'alu, | nimtzea'tiy | lala' | biqshuniy; | 'amartiy | hineniy |
| **I am sought** | **not *for me*** | **of *them that* asked** | **I am found** | **not** | **of *them that* sought me** | **I said** | **Behold me** |

| הנני 2005 | אל 413 | גוי 1471 | לא 3808 | קרא 7121 | בשמי 8034: | 65:2 פרשתי 6566 | ידי 3027 | כל 3605 | היום 3117 | אל 413 | עם 5971 |
|---|---|---|---|---|---|---|---|---|---|---|---|
| hineniy, | 'al | gouy | la' | gara' | bishmiy. | perastiy | yaday | kal | hayoum | 'al | 'am |
| **behold me** | **unto** | **a nation** | **not** | ***that* was called** | **by my name** | **I have spread out** | **my hands** | **all** | **the day** | **unto** | **a people** |

| סורר 5637 | ההלכים 1980 | הדרך 1870 | לא 3808 | טוב 2896 | אחר 310 | מחשבתיהם 4284: | 65:3 העם 5971 | המכעיסים 3707 | אותי 853 |
|---|---|---|---|---|---|---|---|---|---|
| sourer; | haholakiym | haderek | la' | toub, | 'achar | machshaboteyhem. | ha'am, | hamak'aysiym | 'autiy |
| **rebellious** | **which walk in** | **a way** | **not** | ***that was* good** | **after** | **their own thoughts** | **A people** | **that provoke to anger** | **me** |

| על 5921 | פני 6440 | תמיד 8548 | זבחים 2076 | בגנות 1593 | ומקטרים 6999 | על 5921 | הלבנים 3843: | 65:4 הישבים 3427 |
|---|---|---|---|---|---|---|---|---|
| 'al | panay | tamiyd; | zobchiym | baganout, | uamqatriym | 'al | halabeniym. | hayoshabiym |
| **to** | **my face** | **continually** | **that sacrifice** | **in gardens** | **and burn incense** | **upon** | **altars of brick** | **Which remain** |

| בקברים 6913 | ובנצורים 5341 | ילינו 3885 | האכלים 398 | בשר 1320 | החזיר 2386 | ופרק 6564 | פגלים 6292 |
|---|---|---|---|---|---|---|---|
| baqabariym, | uabantzuriym | yaliynu; | ha'akaliym | basar | hachaziyr, | uapraq | piguliym |
| **among the graves** | **and in the monuments** | **lodge** | **which eat** | **flesh** | **swine's** | **and broth of** | **abominable** |

| כליהם 3627: | 65:5 האמרים 559 | קרב 7126 | אליך 413 | אל 408 | תגש 5066 | בי 871a | כי 3588 | קדשתיך 6942 | אלה 428 |
|---|---|---|---|---|---|---|---|---|---|
| kaleyhem. | ha'amariym | qarab | 'aeleyka, | 'al | tigash | biy | kiy | qadashtiyka; | 'aeleh |
| ***things is in* their vessels** | **Which say** | **Stand** | **by yourself** | **not** | **come near** | **to me** | **for** | **I am holier than you** | **These** |

Isa 64:9 Be not wroth very sore, O YHUH, neither remember iniquity forever: behold, see, we beseech you, we are all your people.10 Thy holy cities are a wilderness, Zion is a wilderness, Jerusalem a desolation.11 Our holy and our beautiful house, where our fathers praised you, is burned up with fire: and all our pleasant things are laid waste.12 Wilt you refrain thyself for these things, O YHUH? will you hold your peace, and afflict us very sore? **Isa** 65:1 I am sought of them that asked not for me; I am found of them that sought me not: I said, Behold me, behold me, unto a nation that was not called by my name.2 I have spread out my hands all the day unto a rebellious people, which walk in a way that was not good, after their own thoughts;3 A people that provoketh me to anger continually to my face; that sacrificeth in gardens, and burneth incense upon altars of brick;4 Which remain among the graves, and lodge in the monuments, which eat swine's flesh, and broth of abominable things is in their vessels;5 Which say, Stand by thyself, come not near to me; for I am holier than you. These are a smoke in my nose, a fire that burneth all the day.

65:6
עשן 6227 באפי 639 אש 784 יקדת 3344 כל 3605 היום 3117: הנה 2009 כתובה 3789 לפני 6440 לא 3808 אחשה 2814 כי 3588
'ashan ba'apiy, 'aesh yoqedet kal hayoum. hineh katubah lapanay; la' 'achaseh kiy
***are* a smoke in my nose a fire that burn all the day Behold *it is* written before me not I will keep silence but**

65:7
אם 518 שלמתי 7999 ושלמתי 7999 על 5921 חיקם 2436: עונתיכם 5771 ועונת 5771 אבותיכם 1 יחדו 3162
'am shilamtiy, uashilamtiy 'al cheyqam. 'auonoteykem ua'auonot abouteykem yachdau
**rather will recompense even recompense into their bosom Your iniquities and the iniquities of your fathers together**

אמר 559 יהוה 3068 אשר 834 קטרו 6999 על 5921 ההרים 2022 ועל 5921 הגבעות 1389 חרפוני 2778
'amar Yahuah, 'asher qitru 'al heharîym, ua'al hagaba'aut cherapuniy;
**saith Yahuah which have burned incense upon the mountains and upon the hills blasphemed me**

65:8
ומדתי 4058 פעלתם 6468 ראשנה 7223 על 5921 חיקם 2436: כה 3541 אמר 559 יהוה 3068 כאשר 834 ימצא 4672
uamadotiy pa'ulatam ra'shonah 'al cheyqam. koh 'amar Yahuah ka'asher yimatzea'
**therefore will I measure work their former into their bosom Thus saith Yahuah As is found**

התירוש 8492 באשכול 811 ואמר 559 אל 408 תשחיתהו 7843 כי 3588 ברכה 1293 בו 871a כן 3651 אעשה 6213 למען 4616 עבדי 5650
hatiyroush ba'ashkoul, ua'amar 'al tashchiytehu, kiy barakah bou; ken 'aaseh lama'an 'abaday,
**the new wine in the cluster and *one* saith not Destroy it for a blessing *is* in it so will I do for sakes my servants'**

65:9
לבלתי 1115 השחית 7843 הכל 3605: והוצאתי 3318 מיעקב 3290 זרע 2233 ומיהודה 3063 יורש 3423
labiltiy hashchiyt hakol. uahoutzea'tiy miya'aqob zera', uamiyahudah youresh
**that not I may destroy them all And I will bring forth out of Jacob a seed and out of Judah an inheritor**

65:10
הרי 2022 וירשוה 3423 בחירי 972 ועבדי 5650 ישכנו 7931 שמה 8033: והיה 1961 השרון 8289 לנוה 5116
haray; uiyreshuha bachiyray, ua'abaday yishkanu shamah. uahayah hasharoun linueh
**of my mountains shall inherit and mine elect it and my servants shall dwell there And shall be Sharon a fold of**

65:11
צאן 6629 ועמק 6010 עכור 5911 לרבץ 7258 בקר 1241 לעמי 5971 אשר 834 דרשוני 1875: ואתם 859
tza'n, ua'ameq 'achour larebetz baqar; la'amiy 'asher darashuniy. ua'atem
**flocks and the valley of Achor a place for to lie down in the herds for my people that have sought me But you *are***

עזבי 5800 יהוה 3068 השכחים 7911 את 853 הר 2022 קדשי 6944 הערכים 6186 לגד 1408 שלחן 7979 והממלאים 4390
'azabey Yahuah, hashakechiym 'at har qadashiy ha'arakiym lagad shulchan, uahamamal'aym
**they that forsake Yahuah that forget mountain my holy that prepare for that troop a table and that furnish**

65:12
למני 4507 ממסך 4469: ומניתי 4487 אתכם 853 לחרב 2719 וכלכם 3605 לטבח 2874
lamniy misak. uamaniytiy 'atkem lachereb, uakulkem latebach
**unto that number the drink offering Therefore will I number you to the sword and you all to the slaughter**

תכרעו 3766 יען 3282 קראתי 7121 ולא 3808 עניתם 6030 דברתי 1696 ולא 3808 שמעתם 8085 ותעשו 6213 הרע 7451 בעיני 5869
tikra'au, ya'an qaraa'tiy uala' 'aniytem, dibartiy uala' shama'tem; uata'asu hara' ba'aeynay,
**shall bow down because I called not when you did answer I spoke not you did hear but did evil before mine eyes**

65:13
ובאשר 834 לא 3808 חפצתי 2654 בחרתם 977: לכן 3651 כה 3541 אמר 559 אדני 136 יהוה 3069 הנה 2009
uaba'asher la' chapatztiy bacharatem. laken koh 'amar 'adonay Yahuah hineh
**and wherein not I delighted did choose *that* Therefore thus saith Adonai Yahuah Behold**

Isa 65:6 Behold, it is written before me: I will not keep silence, but will recompense, even recompense into their bosom,7 Your iniquities, and the iniquities of your fathers together, saith YHUH, which have burned incense upon the mountains, and blasphemed me upon the hills: therefore will I measure their former work into their bosom.8 Thus saith YHUH, As the new wine is found in the cluster, and one saith, Destroy it not; for a blessing is in it: so will I do for my servants' sakes, that I may not destroy them all.9 And I will bring forth a seed out of Jacob, and out of Judah an inheritor of my mountains: and mine elect shall inherit it, and my servants shall dwell there.10 And Sharon shall be a fold of flocks, and the valley of Achor a place for the herds to lie down in, for my people that have sought me.11 But you are they that forsake YHUH, that forget my holy mountain, that prepare a table for that troop, and that furnish the drink offering unto that number.12 Therefore will I number you to the sword, and you shall all bow down to the slaughter: because when I called, you did not answer; when I spoke, you did not hear; but did evil before mine eyes, and did choose that wherein I delighted not.13 Therefore thus saith YHUH G-D, Behold, my servants shall eat, but you shall be hungry: behold, my servants shall drink, but you shall be thirsty:

עבדי 5650 יאכלו 398 ואתם 859 תרעבו 7456 הנה 2009 עבדי 5650 ישתו 8354 ואתם 859 תצמאו 6770 הנה 2009 עבדי 5650
'abaday ya'kelu ua'atem tir'abu, hineh 'abaday yishtu ua'atem titzma'au; hineh 'abaday
**my servants shall eat but you shall be hungry behold my servants shall drink but you shall be thirsty behold my servants**

ישמחו 8055 ואתם 859 תבשו 954: **65:14** הנה 2009 עבדי 5650 ירנו 7442 מטוב 2898 לב 3820 ואתם 859 תצעקו 6817 מכאב 3511
yismachu ua'atem teboshu. hineh 'abaday yaronu mitub leb; ua'atem titz'aqu mik'aeb
**shall rejoice but you shall be ashamed Behold my servants shall sing for joy of heart but you shall cry for sorrow of**

לב 3820 ומשבר 7667 רוח 7307 תילילו 3213: **65:15** והנחתם 3240 שמכם 8034 לשבועה 7621 לבחירי 972
leb, uamisheber ruach tayeliylu. uahinachtem shimkem lishu'ah libchiyray,
**heart and for vexation of spirit shall howl And you shall leave your name for a curse unto my chosen**

והמיתך 4191 אדני 136 יהוה 3069 ולעבדיו 5650 יקרא 7121 שם 8034 אחר 312: **65:16** אשר 834 המתברך 1288 בארץ 776
uahemiytaka 'adonay Yahuah; uala'abadayu yiqra' shem 'acher. 'asher hamitbarek ba'aretz,
**for shall slay you Adonai Yahuah and his servants call name *by* another *That he* who bless himself in the earth**

יתברך 1288 באלהי 430 אמן 543 והנשבע 7650 בארץ 776 ישבע 7650 באלהי 430 אמן 543 כי 3588
yitbarek be'alohey 'amen, uahanishba' ba'aretz, yishaba' be'alohey 'amen; kiy
**shall bless himself in the Elohim of truth and he that swears in the earth shall swear by the Elohim of truth because**

נשכחו 7911 הצרות 6869 הראשנות 7223 וכי 3588 נסתרו 5641 מעיני 5869: **65:17** כי 3588 הנני 2005 בורא 1254 שמים 8064
nishkachu, hatzarout hari'shonout, uakiy nistaru me'aeynay. kiy hinniy bourea' shamayim
**are forgotten troubles the former and because they are hid from mine eyes For behold I create heavens**

חדשים 2319 וארץ 776 חדשה 2319 ולא 3808 תזכרנה 2142 הראשנות 7223 ולא 3808 תעלינה 5927 על 5921 לב 3820: **65:18** כי 3588
chadashiym ua'aretz chadashah; uala' tizakarnah hari'shonout, uala' ta'aleynah 'al leb. kiy
**new and a earth new and not shall be remembered the former nor come into mind But**

אם 518 שישו 7797 וגילו 1523 עדי 5703 עד 5704 אשר 834 אני 589 בורא 1254 כי 3588 הנני 2005 בורא 1254 את 853 ירושלם 3389 גילה 1525
'am siysu uagiylu 'adey 'ad, 'asher 'aniy bourea'; kiy hinniy bourea' 'at yarushalaim giylah
**rather be you glad and rejoice ever for *in that* which I create for behold I create Jerusalem a rejoicing**

ועמה 5971 משוש 4885: **65:19** וגלתי 1523 בירושלם 3389 וששתי 7797 בעמי 5971 ולא 3808 ישמע 8085 בה 871a עוד 5750
ua'amah masous. uagaltiy biyarushalaim uasastiy ua'amiy; uala' yishama' bah 'aud,
**and her people a joy And I will rejoice in Jerusalem and joy in my people and no shall be heard in her more**

קול 6963 בכי 1065 וקול 6963 זעקה 2201: **65:20** לא 3808 יהיה 1961 משם 8033 עוד 5750 עול 5764 ימים 3117
qoul bakiy uaqoul za'aqah. la' yihayeh misham 'aud, 'aul yamiym
**the voice of weeping nor the voice of crying no There shall be there more an infant of days**

וזקן 2205 אשר 834 לא 3808 ימלא 4390 את 853 ימיו 3117 כי 3588 הנער 5288 בן 1121 מאה 3967 שנה 8141 ימות 4191 והחוטא 2398 בן 1121
uazaqen, 'asher la' yamalea' 'at yamayu; kiy hana'ar, ben me'ah shanah yamut, uahachouta', ben
**nor an old man that not has filled his days for the child old an hundred years shall die but the sinner old**

מאה 3967 שנה 8141 יקלל 7043: **65:21** ובנו 1129 בתים 1004 וישבו 3427 ונטעו 5193
me'ah shanah yaqulal. uabanu batiym uayashabu; uanata'au
***being* an hundred years shall be accursed And they shall build houses and inhabit *them* and they shall plant**

Isa 65:13 behold, my servants shall rejoice, but you shall be ashamed:14 Behold, my servants shall sing for joy of heart, but you shall cry for sorrow of heart, and shall howl for vexation of spirit.15 And you shall leave your name for a curse unto my chosen: for YHUH G-D shall slay you, and call his servants by another name:16 That he who blesseth himself in the earth shall bless himself in the G-d of truth; and he that sweareth in the earth shall swear by the G-d of truth; because the former troubles are forgotten, and because they are hid from mine eyes.17 For, behold, I create new heavens and a new earth: and the former shall not be remembered, nor come into mind.18 But be you glad and rejoice forever in that which I create: for, behold, I create Jerusalem a rejoicing, and her people a joy.19 And I will rejoice in Jerusalem, and joy in my people: and the voice of weeping shall be no more heard in her, nor the voice of crying.20 There shall be no more thence an infant of days, nor an old man that has not filled his days: for the child shall die an hundred years old; but the sinner being an hundred years old shall be accursed.21 And they shall build houses, and inhabit them; and they shall plant vineyards, and eat the fruit of them.

| | | | | | | | | | | |
|---|---|---|---|---|---|---|---|---|---|---|
| 3754 כרמים | 398 ואכלו | 6529: פרים | 65:22 | 3808 לא | 1129 יבנו | 312 ואחר | 3427 ישב | 3808 לא | 5193 יטעו | 312 ואחר |
| karamiym, | ua'akalu | piryam. | | la' | yibnu | ua'acher | yesheb, | la' | yit'au | ua'acher |
| **vineyards** | **and eat** | **the fruit of them** | | **not** | **They shall build** | **and another** | **inhabit** | **not** | **they shall plant** | **and another** |

| | | | | | | | | | | |
|---|---|---|---|---|---|---|---|---|---|---|
| 398 יאכל | 3588 כי | 3117 כימי | 6086 העץ | 3117 ימי | 5971 עמי | 4639 ומעשה | 3027 ידיהם | 1086 יבלו | 972: בחירי | 65:23 |
| ya'kel; | kiy | kiymey | ha'aetz | yamey | 'amiy, | uama'aseh | yadeyhem | yabalu | bachiyray. | |
| **eat** | **for** | **as the days of** | **a tree** | ***are* the days of** | **my people** | **and the work of** | **their hands** | **shall long enjoy** | **mine elect** | |

| | | | | | | | | | | |
|---|---|---|---|---|---|---|---|---|---|---|
| 3808 לא | 3021 ייגעו | 7385 לריק | 3808 ולא | 3205 ילדו | 928 לבהלה | 3588 כי | 2233 זרע | 1288 ברוכי | 3069 יהוה | 1992 המה |
| la' | yiyga'au | lariyq, | uala' | yeladu | labehalah; | kiy | zera' | barukey | Yahuah | hemah, |
| **not** | **They shall labour** | **in vain** | **nor** | **bring forth** | **for trouble** | **for** | ***are* the seed of** | **the blessed of** | **Yahuah** | **they** |

| | | | | | | | | | |
|---|---|---|---|---|---|---|---|---|---|
| 6631 וצאצאיהם | 854: אתם | 65:24 | 1961 והיה | 2962 טרם | 7121 יקראו | 589 ואני | 6030 אענה | 5750 עוד | 1992 הם |
| uatze'atza'aeyhem | 'atam. | | uahayah | terem | yiqra'au | ua'aniy | 'a'aneh; | 'aud | hem |
| **and their offspring** | **with them** | | **And it shall come to pass** | **before** | **they call** | **that I** | **will answer** | **while yet** | **they** |

| | | | | | | | | | | | |
|---|---|---|---|---|---|---|---|---|---|---|---|
| 1696 מדברים | 589 ואני | 8085: אשמע | 65:25 | 2061 זאב | 2924 וטלה | 7462 ירעו | 259 כאחד | 738 ואריה | 1241 כבקר | 398 יאכל | 8401 תבן |
| madabriym | ua'aniy | 'ashma. | | za'aeb | uataleh | yir'au | ka'achad, | ua'aryeh | kabaqar | ya'kal | teben, |
| **are speaking** | **and I** | **will hear** | | **The wolf** | **and the lamb** | **shall feed** | **together** | **and the lion** | **like the bullock** | **shall eat** | **straw** |

| | | | | | | | | | | | |
|---|---|---|---|---|---|---|---|---|---|---|---|
| 5175 ונחש | 6083 עפר | 3899 לחמו | 3808 לא | 7489 ירעו | 3808 ולא | 7843 ישחיתו | 3605 בכל | 2022 הר | 6944 קדשי | 559 אמר | 3068: יהוה |
| uanachash | 'apar | lachmou; | la' | yare'au | uala' | yashchiytu | bakal | har | qadashiy | 'amar | Yahuah. |
| **and serpent's** | **dust** | ***shall be the* meat** | **not** | **They shall hurt** | **nor** | **destroy** | **in all** | **mountain** | **my holy** | **saith** | **Yahuah** |

| | | | | | | | | | | | | |
|---|---|---|---|---|---|---|---|---|---|---|---|---|
| Isa 66:1 | 3541 כה | 559 אמר | 3068 יהוה | 8064 השמים | 3678 כסאי | 776 והארץ | 1916 הדם | 7272 רגלי | 335 אי | 2088 זה | 1004 בית | 834 אשר |
| | koh | 'amar | Yahuah, | hashamayim | kis'ay, | uaha'aretz | hadom | raglay; | 'aey | zeh | bayit | 'asher |
| | **Thus** | **saith** | **Yahuah** | **The heaven** | ***is* my throne** | **and the earth *is*** | **stool** | **my foot** | **where *is*** | **then** | **the house** | **that** |

| | | | | | | | | | | | |
|---|---|---|---|---|---|---|---|---|---|---|---|
| 1129 תבנו | 3807a לי | 335 ואי | 2088 זה | 4725 מקום | 4496: מנוחתי | 66:2 | 853 ואת | 3605 כל | 428 אלה | 3027 ידי | 6213 עשתה |
| tibnu | liy, | ua'aey | zeh | maqoum | manuchatiy. | | ua'at | kal | 'aeleh | yadiy | 'asatah, |
| **you build** | **unto me?** | **and where *is*** | **then** | **the place of** | **my rest?** | | ***For*** | **all** | **those** | **mine hand** | ***things* has made** |

| | | | | | | | | | | |
|---|---|---|---|---|---|---|---|---|---|---|
| 1961 ויהיו | 3605 כל | 428 אלה | 5002 נאם | 3068 יהוה | 413 ואל | 2088 זה | 5027 אביט | 413 אל | 6041 עני | 5223 ונכה |
| uayihayu | kal | 'aeleh | na'am | Yahuah; | ua'al | zeh | 'abiyt, | 'al | 'aniy | uankeh |
| **and have been** | **all** | **those *things*** | **saith** | **Yahuah** | **but to** | **this** | ***man* will I look** | ***even* to** | ***him that is* poor** | **and of a contrite** |

| | | | | | | | | | | |
|---|---|---|---|---|---|---|---|---|---|---|
| 7307 רוח | 2730 וחרד | 5921 על | 1697: דברי | 66:3 | 7819 שוחט | 7794 השור | 5221 מכה | 376 איש | 2076 זובח | 7716 השה |
| ruach, | uachared | 'al | dabariy. | | shouchet | hashour | makeh | 'aysh, | zoubeach | haseh |
| **spirit** | **and tremble** | **at** | **my word** | | **He that kills** | **an ox** | ***is as if* he slew** | **a man** | **he that sacrifice** | **a lamb *as if*** |

| | | | | | | | | | |
|---|---|---|---|---|---|---|---|---|---|
| 6202 ערף | 3611 כלב | 5927 מעלה | 4503 מנחה | 1818 דם | 2386 חזיר | 2142 מזכיר | 3828 לבנה | 1288 מברך | 205 און |
| 'arep | keleb, | ma'aleh | minchah | dam | chaziyr, | mazkiyr | labonah | mabarek | 'auen; |
| **he cut off a neck** | **dog's** | **he that offer** | **an oblation** | **blood** | ***as if he offered* swine's** | **he that burn** | **incense** | ***as if* he blessed** | **an idol** |

| | | | | | | | | | |
|---|---|---|---|---|---|---|---|---|---|
| 1571 גם | 1992 המה | 977 בחרו | 1870 בדרכיהם | 8251 ובשקוציהם | 5315 נפשם | 2654: חפצה | 66:4 1571 גם | 589 אני | 977 אבחר |
| gam | hemah, | bacharu | badarkeyhem, | uabshiqutzeyhem | napsham | chapetzah. | gam | 'aniy | 'abchar |
| **Yea** | **they** | **have chosen** | **their own ways** | **and in their abominations** | **their soul** | **delight** | **also** | **I** | **will choose** |

Isa 65:22 They shall not build, and another inhabit; they shall not plant, and another eat: for as the days of a tree are the days of my people, and mine elect shall long enjoy the work of their hands.23 They shall not labour in vain, nor bring forth for trouble; for they are the seed of the blessed of YHUH, and their offspring with them.24 And it shall come to pass, that before they call, I will answer; and while they are yet speaking, I will hear.25 The wolf and the lamb shall feed together, and the lion shall eat straw like the bullock: and dust shall be the serpent's meat. They shall not hurt nor destroy in all my holy mountain, saith YHUH. **Isa** 66:1 Thus saith YHUH, The heaven is my throne, and the earth is my footstool: where is the house that you build unto me? and where is the place of my rest?2 For all those things has mine hand made, and those things have been, saith YHUH: but to this man will I look, even to him that is poor and of a contrite spirit, and trembleth at my word.3 He that kill an ox is as if he slew a man; he that sacrificeth a lamb, as if he cut off a dog's neck; he that offereth an oblation, as if he offered swine's blood; he that burneth incense, as if he blessed an idol. Yea, they have chosen their own ways, and their soul delighteth in their abominations.

| 8586 בתעלליהם | 4035 ומגורתם | 935 אביא | 1992 להם | 3282 יען | 7121 קראתי | 369 ואין | 6030 עונה | 1696 דברתי | 3808 ולא |
|---|---|---|---|---|---|---|---|---|---|
| bata'aluleyhem, | uamgurotam | 'abiy'a | lahem, | ya'an | qaraa'tiy | ua'aeyn | 'auneh, | dibartiy | uala' |
| **their delusions** | **and their fears** | **will bring** | **upon them** | **because** | **I called** | **when none** | **did answer** | **I spoke** | **when not** |

| 8085 שמעו | 6213 ויעשו | 7451 הרע | 5869 בעיני | 834 ובאשר | 3808 לא | 2654 חפצתי | 977: בחרו | 66:5 | 8085 שמעו | 1697 דבר |
|---|---|---|---|---|---|---|---|---|---|---|
| shame'au; | uaya'asu | hara' | ba'aeynay, | uaba'asher | la' | chapatztiy | bacharu. | | shim'au | dabar |
| **they did hear** | **but they did** | **evil** | **before mine eyes** | **and in which** | **not** | **I delighted** | **chose *that*** | | **Hear** | **the word of** |

| 3068 יהוה | 2730 החרדים | 413 אל | 1697 דברו | 559 אמרו | 251 אחיכם | 8130 שנאיכם | 5077 מנדיכם | 4616 למען | 8034 שמי |
|---|---|---|---|---|---|---|---|---|---|
| Yahuah, | hacharediym | 'al | dabarou; | 'amaru | 'acheykem | son'aeykem | manadeykem, | lama'an | shamiy |
| **Yahuah** | **you that tremble** | **at** | **his word** | **said** | **your brethren** | **that hated you** | **that cast you out** | **for sake** | **my name's** |

| 3513 יכבד | 3068 יהוה | 7200 ונראה | 8057 בשמחתכם | 1992 והם | 954: יבשו | 66:6 | 6963 קול | 7588 שאון | 5892 מעיר |
|---|---|---|---|---|---|---|---|---|---|
| yikbad | Yahuah, | uanir'ah | basimchatakem | uahem | yeboshu. | | qoul | sha'aun | me'ayr, |
| **Let be glorified** | **Yahuah** | **but he shall appear** | **to your joy** | **and they** | **shall be ashamed** | | **A voice of** | **noise** | **from the city** |

| 6963 קול | 1964 מהיכל | 6963 קול | 3068 יהוה | 7999 משלם | 1576 גמול | 341: לאיביו | 66:7 | 2962 בטרם | 2342 תחיל |
|---|---|---|---|---|---|---|---|---|---|
| qoul | meheykal; | qoul | Yahuah, | mashalem | gamul | la'ayabayu. | | baterem | tachiyl |
| **a voice** | **from the temple** | **a voice of** | **Yahuah** | **that render** | **recompence** | **to his enemies** | | **Before** | **she travailed** |

| 3205 ילדה | 2962 בטרם | 935 יבוא | 2256 חבל | 3807a לה | 4422 והמליטה | 2145: זכר | 66:8 | 4310 מי | 8085 שמע | 2063 כזאת |
|---|---|---|---|---|---|---|---|---|---|---|
| yaladah; | baterem | yabou'a | chebel | lah | uahimliytah | zakar. | | miy' | shama' | kaza't, |
| **she brought forth** | **before** | **came** | **pain** | **her** | **she was delivered of** | **a man child** | | **Who** | **has heard** | **such *a thing*?** |

| 4310 מי | 7200 ראה | 428 כאלה | 2342 היוחל | 776 ארץ | 3117 ביום | 259 אחד | 518 אם | 3205 יולד | 1471 גוי | 6471 פעם |
|---|---|---|---|---|---|---|---|---|---|---|
| miy' | ra'ah | ka'aeleh, | hayukal | 'aretz | bayoum | 'achad, | 'am | yiualed | gouy | pa'am |
| **who** | **has seen** | **such things?** | **Shall be made to bring forth** | **the earth** | **in day?** | **one** | **or** | **shall be born** | **a nation** | **this time** |

| 259 אחת | 3588 כי | 2342 חלה | 1571 גם | 3205 ילדה | 6726 ציון | 853 את | 1121: בניה | 66:9 | 589 האני | 7665 אשביר | 3808 ולא |
|---|---|---|---|---|---|---|---|---|---|---|---|
| 'achat; | kiy | chalah | gam | yaldah | tziyoun | 'at | baneyha. | | ha'aniy | 'ashbiyr | uala' |
| **one?** | **for** | **travailed** | **as soon as** | **she brought forth** | **Zion** | | **her children** | | **Shall I** | **bring to the birth** | **and not** |

| 3205 אוליד | 559 יאמר | 3068 יהוה | 518 אם | 589 אני | 3205 המוליד | 6113 ועצרתי | 559 אמר | 430: אלהיך | 66:10 |
|---|---|---|---|---|---|---|---|---|---|
| 'auliyd | ya'mar | Yahuah; | 'am | 'aniy | hamouliyd | ua'atzartiy | 'amar | 'alohayik. | |
| **cause to bring forth?** | **saith** | **Yahuah** | **or** | **I** | **shall cause to bring forth** | **and shut *the womb*?** | **saith** | **your Elohim** | |

| 8055 שמחו | 854 את | 3389 ירושלם | 1523 וגילו | 871a בה | 3605 כל | 157 אהביה | 7797 שישו | 854 אתה | 4885 משוש | 3605 כל |
|---|---|---|---|---|---|---|---|---|---|---|
| simchu | 'at | yarushalaim | uagiylu | bah | kal | 'ahabeyha; | siysu | 'atah | masous, | kal |
| **Rejoice you** | ***with*** | **Jerusalem** | **and be glad** | **with her** | **all** | **you that love her** | **rejoice** | **with her** | **for joy** | **all** |

| 56 המתאבלים | 5921: עליה | 66:11 | 4616 למען | 3243 תינקו | 7646 ושבעתם | 7699 משד | 8575 תנחמיה | 4616 למען |
|---|---|---|---|---|---|---|---|---|
| hamit'abliym | 'aleyha. | | lama'an | tinaqu | uasba'atem, | mishod | tanchumeyha; | lama'an |
| **you that mourn** | **for her** | | **That** | **you may suck** | **and be satisfied** | **with the breasts of** | **her consolations** | **that** |

| 4711 תמצו | 6026 והתענגתם | 2123 מזיז | 3519: כבודה | 66:12 | 3588 כי | 3541 כה | 559 אמר | 3068 יהוה | 2005 הנני | 5186 נטה |
|---|---|---|---|---|---|---|---|---|---|---|
| tamotzu | uahit'anagtem | miziyz | kaboudah. | | kiy | koh | 'amar | Yahuah | hinniy | noteh |
| **you may milk out** | **and be delighted** | **with the abundance of** | **her glory** | | **For** | **thus** | **saith** | **Yahuah** | **Behold** | **I will extend** |

Isa 66:4 I also will choose their delusions, and will bring their fears upon them; because when I called, none did answer; when I spoke, they did not hear: but they did evil before mine eyes, and chose that in which I delighted not.5 Hear the word of YHUH, you that tremble at his word; your brethren that hated you, that cast you out for my name's sake, said, Let YHUH be glorified: but he shall appear to your joy, and they shall be ashamed.6 A voice of noise from the city, a voice from the temple, a voice of YHUH that rendereth recompence to his enemies.7 Before she travailed, she brought forth; before her pain came, she was delivered of a man child.8 Who has heard such a thing? who has seen such things? Shall the earth be made to bring forth in one day? or shall a nation be born at once? for as soon as Zion travailed, she brought forth her children.9 Shall I bring to the birth, and not cause to bring forth? saith YHUH: shall I cause to bring forth, and shut the womb? saith your G-d.10 Rejoice you with Jerusalem, and be glad with her, all you that love her: rejoice for joy with her, all you that mourn for her:11 That you may suck, and be satisfied with the breasts of her consolations; that you may milk out, and be delighted with the abundance of her glory.12 For thus saith YHUH, Behold, I will extend peace to her like a river, and the glory of the Gentiles like a flowing stream:

אליה 413 כנהר 5104 שלום 7965 וכנחל 5158 שוטף 7857 כבוד 3519 גוים 1471 וינקתם 3243 על 5921 צד 6654
'aeleyha kanahar shaloum uaknachal shoutep kaboud gouyim uiynaqtem; 'al tzad
**to her like a river peace and like a stream flowing the glory of the Gentiles and then shall you suck upon *her* sides**

תנשאו 5375 ועל 5921 ברכים 1290 תשעשעו 8173: **66:13** כאיש 376 אשר 834 אמו 517 תנחמנו 5162 כן 3651 אנכי 595 אנחמכם 5162
tinase'au, ua'al birkayim tasha'asha'au. ka'aysh 'asher 'amou tanachamenu; ken 'anokiy 'anachemkem,
**you shall be borne upon *her* knees be dandled As one whom his mother comforted so will I comfort you**

ובירושלם 3389 תנחמו 5162: **66:14** וראיתם 7200 ושש 7797 לבכם 3820 ועצמותיכם 6106
uabiyarushalaim tanuchamu. uar'aytem uasas libakem, ua'atzmouteykem
**and in Jerusalem you shall be comforted And when you see *this* and shall rejoice your heart and your bones**

כדשא 1877 תפרחנה 6524 ונודעה 3045 יד 3027 יהוה 3068 את 854 עבדיו 5650 וזעם 2194 את 853
kadesha' tiprachnah; uanoud'ah yad Yahuah 'at 'abadayu, uaza'am 'at
**like an herb shall flourish and shall be known the hand of Yahuah *toward* his servants and *his* indignation**

איביו 341: **66:15** כי 3588 הנה 2009 יהוה 3068 באש 784 יבוא 935 וכסופה 5492 מרכבתיו 4818 להשיב 7725 בחמה 2534
'ayabayu. kiy hineh Yahuah ba'aesh yabou'a, uakasupah markabotayu; lahashiyb bachemah
***toward* his enemies For behold Yahuah with fire will come and like a whirlwind *with* his chariots to render with fury**

אפו 639 וגערתו 1606 בלהבי 3851 אש 784: **66:16** כי 3588 באש 784 יהוה 3068 נשפט 8199 ובחרבו 2719 את 854 כל 3605 בשר 1320
'apou, uaga'aratou balahabey 'aesh. kiy ba'aesh Yahuah nishpat, uabcharbou 'at kal basar;
**his anger and his rebuke with flames of fire For by fire Yahuah will plead and by his sword *with* all flesh**

ורבו 7231 חללי 2491 יהוה 3068: **66:17** המתקדשים 6942 והמטהרים 2891 אל 413 הגנות 1593 אחר 310
uarabu challey Yahuah. hamitqadshiym uahamitahariym 'al haganout, 'achar
**and shall be many the slain of Yahuah They that sanctify themselves and purify themselves in the gardens behind**

אחד 259 בתוך 8432 אכלי 398 בשר 1320 החזיר 2386 והשקץ 8263 והעכבר 5909 יחדו 3162 יספו 5486 נאם 5002
'achad batauek, 'akley basar hachaziyr, uahasheqetz uaha'akbar; yachdau yasupu na'am
**one *tree* in the midst eating flesh swine's and the abomination and the mouse together shall be consumed saith**

יהוה 3068: **66:18** ואנכי 595 מעשיהם 4639 ומחשבתיהם 4284 באה 935 לקבץ 6908 את 853 כל 3605 הגוים 1471
Yahuah. ua'anokiy, ma'aseyhem uamachshaboteyhem, ba'ah laqabetz 'at kal hagouyim
**Yahuah For I *know* their works and their thoughts it shall come that I will gather all nations**

והלשנות 3956 ובאו 935 וראו 7200 את 853 כבודי 3519: **66:19** ושמתי 7760 בהם 871a אות 226 ושלחתי 7971 מהם 1992
uahalshonout; uaba'au uar'au 'at kaboudiy. uasamtiy bahem 'aut, uashilachtiy mehem
**and tongues and they shall come and see my glory And I will set among them a sign and I will send those**

פליטים 6412 אל 413 הגוים 1471 תרשיש 8659 פול 6322 ולוד 3865 משכי 4900 קשת 7198 תבל 8422 ויון 3120 האיים 339
paleytiym 'al hagouyim tarshiysh pul ua'lud moshakey qeshet tubal uayauan; ha'ayiym
**that escape of them unto the nations *to* Tarshish Pul and Lud that draw the bow *to* Tubal and Javan *to* the isles**

הרחקים 7350 אשר 834 לא 3808 שמעו 8085 את 853 שמעי 8088 ולא 3808 ראו 7200 את 853 כבודי 3519 והגידו 5046 את 853
harachoqiym, 'asher la' shama'au 'at shim'ay uala' ra'au 'at kaboudiy, uahigiydu 'at
**afar off that not have heard my fame neither have seen my glory and they shall declare**

Isa 66:12 then shall you suck, you shall be borne upon her sides, and be dandled upon her knees.13 As one whom his mother comforteth, so will I comfort you; and you shall be comforted in Jerusalem.14 And when you see this, your heart shall rejoice, and your bones shall flourish like an herb: and the hand of YHUH shall be known toward his servants, and his indignation toward his enemies.15 For, behold, YHUH will come with fire, and with his chariots like a whirlwind, to render his anger with fury, and his rebuke with flames of fire.16 For by fire and by his sword will YHUH plead with all flesh: and the slain of YHUH shall be many.17 They that sanctify themselves, and purify themselves in the gardens behind one tree in the midst, eating swine's flesh, and the abomination, and the mouse, shall be consumed together, saith YHUH.18 For I know their works and their thoughts: it shall come, that I will gather all nations and tongues; and they shall come, and see my glory.19 And I will set a sign among them, and I will send those that escape of them unto the nations, to Tarshish, Pul, and Lud, that draw the bow, to Tubal, and Javan, to the isles afar off, that have not heard my fame, neither have seen my glory; and they shall declare my glory among the Gentiles.

| כבודי 3519 | בגוים 1471: | 66:20 והביאו 935 | את 853 | כל 3605 | אחיכם 251 | מכל 3605 | הגוים 1471 | מנחה 4503 |
|---|---|---|---|---|---|---|---|---|
| kaboudiy | bagouyim. | uahebiy'au | 'at | kal | 'acheykem | mikal | hagouyim | minchah |
| **my glory** | **among the Gentiles** | **And they shall bring** | | **all** | **your brethren** | **out of all** | **nations** | ***for* an offering** |

| ליהוה 3068 | בסוסים 5483 | וברכב 7393 | ובצבים 6632 | ובפרדים 6505 | ובכרכרות 3753 | על 5921 | הר 2022 | קדשי 6944 |
|---|---|---|---|---|---|---|---|---|
| laYahuah | basusiym | uabarekeb | uabatzabiym | uabapradiym | uabakirkarout, | 'al | har | qadashiy |
| **unto Yahuah** | **upon horses** | **and in chariots** | **and in litters** | **and upon mules** | **and upon swift beasts** | **to** | **mountain** | **my holy** |

| ירושלם 3389 | אמר 559 | יהוה 3068 | כאשר 834 | יביאו 935 | בני 1121 | ישראל 3478 | את 853 | המנחה 4503 | בכלי 3627 | טהור 2889 | בית 1004 |
|---|---|---|---|---|---|---|---|---|---|---|---|
| yarushalaim | 'amar | Yahuah; | ka'asher | yabiy'au | baney | yisra'ael | 'at | haminchah | bikliy | tahour | beyt |
| **Jerusalem** | **saith** | **Yahuah** | **as** | **bring** | **the children of** | **Israel** | | **an offering** | **in a vessel** | **clean** | ***into* the house of** |

| יהוה 3068: | 66:21 וגם 1571 | מהם 1992 | אקח 3947 | לכהנים 3548 | ללוים 3881 | אמר 559 | יהוה 3068: | 66:22 כי 3588 | כאשר 834 | השמים 8064 |
|---|---|---|---|---|---|---|---|---|---|---|
| Yahuah. | uagam | mehem | 'aqach | lakohaniym | lalauiyim | 'amar | Yahuah. | kiy | ka'asher | hashamayim |
| **Yahuah** | **And also** | **of them** | **I will take** | **for priests** | ***and* for Levites** | **saith** | **Yahuah** | **For** | **as** | **heavens** |

| החדשים 2319 | והארץ 776 | החדשה 2319 | אשר 834 | אני 589 | עשה 6213 | עמדים 5975 | לפני 6440 | נאם 5002 | יהוה 3068 | כן 3651 | יעמד 5975 |
|---|---|---|---|---|---|---|---|---|---|---|---|
| hachadashiym | uaha'aretz | hachadashah | 'asher | 'aniy | 'aseh | 'amdiym | lapanay | na'am | Yahuah; | ken | ya'amod |
| **the new** | **and earth** | **the new** | **which** | **I** | **will make** | **shall remain** | **before me** | **saith** | **Yahuah** | **so** | **shall remain** |

| זרעכם 2233 | ושמכם 8034: | 66:23 והיה 1961 | מדי 1767 | חדש 2320 | בחדשו 2320 | ומדי 1767 | שבת 7676 |
|---|---|---|---|---|---|---|---|
| zar'akem | uashimkem. | uahayah, | midey | chodesh | bachadashou, | uamidey | shabat |
| **your seed** | **and your name** | **And it shall come to pass** | ***that* from** | ***one* new moon** | **to another** | **and from** | ***one* sabbath** |

| בשבתו 7676 | יבוא 935 | כל 3605 | בשר 1320 | להשתחות 7812 | לפני 6440 | אמר 559 | יהוה 3068: | 66:24 ויצאו 3318 | וראו 7200 |
|---|---|---|---|---|---|---|---|---|---|
| bashabatou; | yabou'a | kal | basar | lahishtachauot | lapanay | 'amar | Yahuah. | uayatza'au | uar'au, |
| **to another** | **shall come** | **all** | **flesh** | **to worship** | **before me** | **saith** | **Yahuah** | **And they shall go forth** | **and look** |

| בפגרי 6297 | האנשים 582 | הפשעים 6586 | בי 871a | כי 3588 | תולעתם 8438 | לא 3808 | תמות 4191 | ואשם 784 | לא 3808 |
|---|---|---|---|---|---|---|---|---|---|
| bapigrey | ha'anashiym, | haposha'aym | biy; | kiy | toula'tam | la' | tamut, | ua'asham | la' |
| **upon the carcases of** | **the men** | **that have transgressed** | **against me** | **for** | **their worm** | **not** | **shall die** | **their fire** | **neither** |

| תכבה 3518 | והיו 1961 | דראון 1860 | לכל 3605 | בשר 1320: |
|---|---|---|---|---|
| tikbeh, | uahayu | dera'aun | lakal | basar. |
| **shall be quenched** | **and they shall be** | **an abhorring** | **unto all** | **flesh** |

Isa 66:20 And they shall bring all your brethren for an offering unto YHUH out of all nations upon horses, and in chariots, and in litters, and upon mules, and upon swift beasts, to my holy mountain Jerusalem, saith YHUH, as the children of Israel bring an offering in a clean vessel into the house of YHUH.21 And I will also take of them for priests and for Levites, saith YHUH.22 For as the new heavens and the new earth, which I will make, shall remain before me, saith YHUH, so shall your seed and your name remain.23 And it shall come to pass, that from one new moon to another, and from one Sabbath to another, shall all flesh come to worship before me, saith YHUH.24 And they shall go forth, and look upon the carcases of the men that have transgressed against me: for their worm shall not die, neither shall their fire be quenched; and they shall be an abhorring unto all flesh.

# JEREMIAH
## (*Yirmayahu*)

The first verse identifies the Prophet Jeremiah as the author of the Book of Jeremiah which was written between 630 and 580 B.C. and records the final prophecies given to the House of Judah, warning of oncoming destruction if the nation did not repent from breaking Torah. Jeremiahs name in Hebrew means *Yah is exalted.* Elohim calls out through His prophet Jeremiah for the nation to turn back and perhaps escape the consequences of destruction if they continue in idolatry and immorality.

| **Jeremiah 1:1** דברי 1697 | ירמיהו 3414 | בן 1121 | חלקיהו 2518 | מן 4480 | הכהנים 3548 | אשר 834 | בענתות 6068 | בארץ 776 |
|---|---|---|---|---|---|---|---|---|
| dibrey | yirmayahu | ben | chilqiyahu; | min | hakohaniym | 'asher | ba'anatout, | ba'aretz |
| **The words of** | **Jeremiah** | **the son of** | **Hilkiah** | **of** | **the priests** | **that** | ***were* in Anathoth** | **in the land of** |

| בנימן 1144: | **1:2** אשר 834 | היה 1961 | דבר 1697 | יהוה 3068 | אליו 413 | בימי 3117 | יאשיהו 2977 | בן 1121 | אמון 526 | מלך 4428 | יהודה 3063 |
|---|---|---|---|---|---|---|---|---|---|---|---|
| binyamin. | 'asher | hayah | dabar | Yahuah | 'aelayu, | biymey | ya'shiyahu | ben | 'amoun | melek | yahudah; |
| **Benjamin** | **whom** | **came** | **the word of** | **Yahuah** | **To** | **in the days of** | **Josiah** | **the son of** | **Amon** | **king of** | **Judah** |

| בשלש 7969 | עשרה 6240 | שנה 8141 | למלכו 4427: | **1:3** ויהי 1961 | בימי 3117 | יהויקים 3079 | בן 1121 | יאשיהו 2977 | מלך 4428 | יהודה 3063 |
|---|---|---|---|---|---|---|---|---|---|---|
| bishlosh | 'asreh | shanah | lamalakou. | uayahiy, | biymey | yahouyaqiym | ben | ya'shiyahu | melek | yahudah, |
| **three** | **ten** | **year** | **of his reign** | **It came also** | **in the days of** | **Jehoiakim** | **the son of** | **Josiah** | **king of** | **Judah** |

| עד 5704 | תם 8552 | עשתי 6249 | עשרה 6240 | שנה 8141 | לצדקיהו 6667 | בן 1121 | יאשיהו 2977 | מלך 4428 | יהודה 3063 | עד 5704 |
|---|---|---|---|---|---|---|---|---|---|---|
| 'ad | tom | 'ashtey | 'asreh | shanah, | latzidqiyahu | ben | ya'shiyahu | melek | yahudah; | 'ad |
| **unto** | ***the* end of** | ***the* one of** | **ten** | **year** | **of Zedekiah** | **the son of** | **Josiah** | **king of** | **Judah** | **unto** |

| גלות 1540 | ירושלם 3389 | בחדש 2320 | החמישי 2549: | **1:4** ויהי 1961 | דבר 1697 | יהוה 3068 | אלי 413 |
|---|---|---|---|---|---|---|---|
| galout | yarushalaim | bachodesh | hachamiyshiy. | uayahiy | dabar | Yahuah | 'aelay |
| ***the* carrying away of captive of** | **Jerusalem** | **in month** | **the fifth** | **Then came** | **the word of** | **Yahuah** | **unto me** |

| לאמר 559: | **1:5** בטרם 2962 | אצורך 3335 | בבטן 990 | ידעתיך 3045 | ובטרם 2962 | תצא 3318 | מרחם 7358 | הקדשתיך 6942 |
|---|---|---|---|---|---|---|---|---|
| lea'mor. | baterem | 'atzuraka | babeten | yada'atiyka, | uabterem | tetzea' | merechem | hiqdashtiyka; |
| **saying** | **Before** | **I formed you** | **in the belly** | **I knew you** | **and before** | **you come forth** | **out of the womb** | **I sanctified you** |

| נביא 5030 | לגוים 1471 | נתתיך 5414: | **1:6** ואמר 559 | אהה 162 | אדני 136 | יהוה 3069 | הנה 2009 | לא 3808 | ידעתי 3045 | דבר 1696 | כי 3588 |
|---|---|---|---|---|---|---|---|---|---|---|---|
| nabiy'a | lagouyim | natatiyka. | ua'amar, | 'ahah | 'adonay | Yahuah, | hineh | la' | yada'tiy | daber; | kiy |
| **a prophet** | **unto the nations** | ***and* I ordained you** | **Then said I** | **Ah** | **Adonai** | **Yahuah** | **behold** | **not** | **I can** | **speak** | **for** |

| נער 5288 | אנכי 595: | **1:7** ויאמר 559 | יהוה 3068 | אלי 413 | אל 408 | תאמר 559 | נער 5288 | אנכי 595 | כי 3588 | על 5921 | כל 3605 | אשר 834 | אשלחך 7971 |
|---|---|---|---|---|---|---|---|---|---|---|---|---|---|
| na'ar | 'anokiy. | uaya'mer | Yahuah | 'aelay, | 'al | ta'mar | na'ar | 'anokiy; | kiy | 'al | kal | 'asher | 'ashlachaka |
| ***am* a child** | **I** | **But said** | **Yahuah** | **unto me** | **not** | **Say *am*** | **a child** | **I** | **for** | **to** | **all** | **that** | **I shall send you** |

| תלך 1980 | ואת 853 | כל 3605 | אשר 834 | אצוך 6680 | תדבר 1696: | **1:8** אל 408 | תירא 3372 | מפניהם 6440 | כי 3588 | אתך 854 |
|---|---|---|---|---|---|---|---|---|---|---|
| telek, | ua'at | kal | 'asher | 'atzaueka | tadaber. | 'al | tiyraa' | mipaneyhem; | kiy | 'ataka |
| **you shall go *and*** | | **all** | **whatsoever** | **I command you** | **you shall speak** | **not** | **Be afraid of** | **their faces** | **for *am*** | **with you** |

| אני 589 | להצלך 5337 | נאם 5002 | יהוה 3069: | **1:9** וישלח 7971 | יהוה 3068 | את 853 | ידו 3027 | ויגע 5060 | על 5921 | פי 6310 | ויאמר 559 |
|---|---|---|---|---|---|---|---|---|---|---|---|
| 'aniy | lahatzileka | na'am | Yahuah. | uayishlach | Yahuah | 'at | yadou, | uayaga' | 'al | piy; | uaya'mer |
| **I** | **to deliver you** | **saith** | **Yahuah** | **Then put forth** | **Yahuah** | | **his hand** | **and touched** | **on** | **my mouth** | **And said** |

**Jeremiah** 1:1 The words of Jeremiah the son of Hilkiah, of the priests that were in Anathoth in the land of Benjamin:2 To whom the word of YHUH came in the days of Josiah the son of Amon king of Judah, in the thirteenth year of his reign.3 It came also in the days of Jehoiakim the son of Josiah king of Judah, unto the end of the eleventh year of Zedekiah the son of Josiah king of Judah, unto the carrying away of Jerusalem captive in the fifth month.4 Then the word of YHUH came unto me, saying,5 Before I formed you in the belly I knew you; and before you came forth out of the womb I sanctified you, and I ordained you a prophet unto the nations.6 Then said I, Ah, Adonai G-D! behold, I cannot speak: for I am a child.7 But YHUH said unto me, Say not, I am a child: for you shall go to all that I shall send you, and whatsoever I command you you shall speak.8 Be not afraid of their faces: for I am with you to deliver you, saith YHUH.9 Then YHUH put forth his hand, and touched my mouth. And YHUH said unto me, Behold, I have put my words in your mouth.

1:10

יהוה 3068 אלי 413 הנה 2009 נתתי 5414 דברי 1697 בפיך 6310: ראה 7200 הפקדתיך 6485 היום 3117 הזה 2088 על 5921 הגוים 1471
Yahuah 'aelay, hineh natatiy dabaray bapiyka. ra'aeh hipqadtiyka hayoum hazeh, 'al hagouyim
**Yahuah unto me Behold I have put my words in your mouth See I have set you day this over the nations**

1:11

ועל 5921 הממלכות 4467 לנתוש 5428 ולנתוץ 5422 ולהאביד 6 ולהרוס 2040 לבנות 1129 ולנטוע 5193:
ua'al hamamlakout, lintoush ualintoutz ualha'abiyd ualaharous; libnout ualintoua'.
**and over the kingdoms to root out and to pull down and to destroy and to throw down to build and to plant**

ויהי 1961 דבר 1697 יהוה 3068 אלי 413 לאמר 559 מה 4100 אתה 859 ראה 7200 ירמיהו 3414 ואמר 559 מקל 4731 שקד 8247
uayahiy dabar Yahuah 'aelay lea'mor, mah 'atah ro'ah yirmayahu; ua'amar maqel shaqed
**Moreover came the word of Yahuah unto me saying what you? see Jeremiah And I said a rod of an almond tree**

1:12

אני 589 ראה 7200: ויאמר 559 יהוה 3068 אלי 413 היטבת 3190 לראות 7200 כי 3588 שקד 8245 אני 589 על 5921 דברי 1697 לעשתו 6213:
'aniy ro'ah. uaya'mer Yahuah 'aelay heytabta lir'aut; kiy shoqed 'aniy 'al dabariy la'asotou.
**I see Then said Yahuah unto me You have well seen for will hasten I on my word to perform it**

1:13

ויהי 1961 דבר 1697 יהוה 3068 אלי 413 שנית 8145 לאמר 559 מה 4100 אתה 859 ראה 7200 ואמר 559 סיר 5518 נפוח 5301 אני 589
uayahiy dabar Yahuah 'aelay sheniyt lea'mor, mah 'atah ro'ah; ua'amar, siyr napuach 'aniy
**And came the word of Yahuah unto me *the* second *time* saying What you? see And I said a pot seething I**

1:14

ראה 7200 ופניו 6440 מפני 6440 צפונה 6828: ויאמר 559 יהוה 3068 אלי 413 מצפון 6828 תפתח 6605 הרעה 7451
ro'ah, uapanayu mipaney tzapounah. uaya'mer Yahuah 'aelay; mitzapoun tipatach hara'ah,
**see and the face thereof *is* toward the north Then said Yahuah unto me Out of the north shall break forth an evil**

1:15

על 5921 כל 3605 ישבי 3427 הארץ 776: כי 3588 הנני 2005 קרא 7121 לכל 3605 משפחות 4940 ממלכות 4467 צפונה 6828
'al kal yoshabey ha'aretz. kiy hinniy qorea', lakal mishpachout mamlakout tzapounah
**upon all the inhabitants of the land For lo, I will call all the families of the kingdoms of the north**

נאם 5002 יהוה 3068 ובאו 935 ונתנו 5414 איש 376 כסאו 3678 פתח 6607 שערי 8179 ירושלם 3389
na'am Yahuah; uaba'au uanatanu 'aysh kis'au petach sha'arey yarushalaim,
**saith Yahuah and they shall come and they shall set every one his throne *at* the entering of the gates of Jerusalem**

1:16

ועל 5921 כל 3605 חומתיה 2346 סביב 5439 ועל 5921 כל 3605 ערי 5892 יהודה 3063: ודברתי 1696
ua'al kal choumoteyha sabiyb, ua'al kal 'arey yahudah. uadibartiy
**and against all the walls thereof round about and against all the cities of Judah And I will utter**

משפטי 4941 אותם 854 על 5921 כל 3605 רעתם 7451 אשר 834 עזבוני 5800 ויקטרו 6999 לאלהים 430
mishpatay 'autam, 'al kal ra'atam; 'asher 'azabuniy, uayqatru le'alohiym
**my judgments against them touching all their wickedness who have forsaken me and have burned incense unto gods**

1:17

אחרים 312 וישתחוו 7812 למעשי 4639 ידיהם 3027: ואתה 859 תאזר 247 מתניך 4975 וקמת 6965 ודברת 1696
'acheriym, uayishtachauu lama'asey yadeyhem. ua'atah te'azor mataneyka, uaqamta uadibarta
**other and worshipped the works of their own hands You therefore gird up your loins and arise and speak**

אליהם 413 את 853 כל 3605 אשר 834 אנכי 595 אצוך 6680 אל 408 תחת 2865 מפניהם 6440 פן 6435 אחתך 2865 לפניהם 6440:
'aleyhem, 'at kal 'asher 'anokiy 'atzaueka; 'al techat mipaneyhem, pen 'achitaka lipneyhem.
**unto them all that I command you not be dismayed at their faces lest I confound you before them**

Jer 1:10 See, I have this day set you over the nations and over the kingdoms, to root out, and to pull down, and to destroy, and to throw down, to build, and to plant.11 Moreover the word of YHUH came unto me, saying, Jeremiah, what seest you? And I said, I see a rod of an almond tree.12 Then said YHUH unto me, Thou have well seen: for I will hasten my word to perform it.13 And the word of YHUH came unto me the second time, saying, What seest you? And I said, I see a seething pot; and the face thereof is toward the north.14 Then YHUH said unto me, Out of the north an evil shall break forth upon all the inhabitants of the land.15 For, lo, I will call all the families of the kingdoms of the north, saith YHUH; and they shall come, and they shall set everyone his throne at the entering of the gates of Jerusalem, and against all the walls thereof round about, and against all the cities of Judah.16 And I will utter my judgments against them touching all their wickedness, who have forsaken me, and have burned incense unto other gods, and worshipped the works of their own hands.17 Thou therefore gird up your loins, and arise, and speak unto them all that I command you: be not dismayed at their faces, lest I confound you before them.

1:18
ואני 589 הנה 2009 נתתיך 5414 היום 3117 לעיר 5892 מבצר 4013 ולעמוד 5982 ברזל 1270 ולחמות 2346 נחשת 5178 על 5921 כל 3605
ua'aniy hineh natatiyka hayoum, la'ayr mibtzar ual'amud barzel ualchomout nachoshet 'al kal
**For I behold have made you this day a city defenced and an pillar iron and walls brasen against the whole**

הארץ 776 למלכי 4428 יהודה 3063 לשריה 8269 לכהניה 3548 ולעם 5971
ha'aretz; lamalkey yahudah lasareyha, lakohaneyha ual'am
**land against the kings of Judah against the princes thereof against the priests thereof and against the people of**

הארץ 776: 1:19 ונלחמו 3898 אליך 413 ולא 3808 יוכלו 3201 לך 3807a כי 3588 אתך 854 אני 589 נאם 5002 יהוה 3068
ha'aretz. uanilchamu 'aeleyka uala' yukalu lak; kiy 'ataka 'aniy na'am Yahuah
**the land And they shall fight against you but not they shall prevail against you for *am* with you I saith Yahuah**

להצילך 5337:
lahatziyleka.
**to deliver you**

Jer 2:1
ויהי 1961 דבר 1697 יהוה 3068 אלי 413 לאמר 559: 2:2 הלך 1980 וקראת 7121 באזני 241 ירושלם 3389 לאמר 559 כה 3541
uayahiy dabar Yahuah 'aelay lea'mor. halok uaqara'ta ua'azaney yarushalaim lea'mor, koh
**Moreover came the word of Yahuah to me saying Go and cry in the ears of Jerusalem saying Thus**

אמר 559 יהוה 3068 זכרתי 2142 לך 3807a חסד 2617 נעוריך 5271 אהבת 160 כלולתיך 3623 לכתך 1980 אחרי 310
'amar Yahuah, zakartiy lak chesed na'aurayik, 'ahabat kalulotayik; lekatek 'acharay
**saith Yahuah I remember to you the kindness of your youth the love of your espousals when you went after me**

במדבר 4057 בארץ 776 לא 3808 זרועה 2232: 2:3 קדש 6944 ישראל 3478 ליהוה 3068 ראשית 7225 תבואתה 8393
bamidbar, ba'aretz la' zaru'ah. qodesh yisra'ael laYahuah, ra'shiyt tabu'atoh;
**in the wilderness in a land *that was* not sown *was* holiness Israel unto Yahuah *and* the firstfruits of his increase**

כל 3605 אכליו 398 יאשמו 816 רעה 7451 תבא 935 אליהם 413 נאם 5002 יהוה 3068: 2:4 שמעו 8085 דבר 1697 יהוה 3068
kal 'aklayu ye'ashamu, ra'ah taba' 'aleyhem na'am Yahuah. shim'au dabar Yahuah
**all that devour him shall offend evil shall come upon them saith Yahuah Hear you the word of Yahuah**

בית 1004 יעקב 3290 וכל 3605 משפחות 4940 בית 1004 ישראל 3478: 2:5 כה 3541 אמר 559 יהוה 3068 מה 4100 מצאו 4672 אבותיכם 1
beyt ya'aqob; uakal mishpachout beyt yisra'ael. koh 'amar Yahuah mah matza'au abouteykem
**O house of Jacob and all the families of the house of Israel Thus saith Yahuah What have found your fathers**

בי 871a עול 5766 כי 3588 רחקו 7368 מעלי 5921 וילכו 1980 אחרי 310 ההבל 1892 ויהבלו 1891: 2:6 ולא 3808
biy 'auel, kiy rachaqu me'alay; uayelaku 'acharey hahebel uayehbalu. uala'
**in me iniquity that they are gone far from me and have walked after vanity and are become vain? Neither**

אמרו 559 איה 346 יהוה 3068 המעלה 5927 אתנו 853 מארץ 776 מצרים 4714 המוליך 1980 אתנו 853 במדבר 4057
'amaru, 'ayeh Yahuah, hama'aleh 'atanu me'aretz mitzrayim; hamouliyk 'atanu bamidbar,
**said they Where *is* Yahuah that brought up us out of the land of Egypt that led us through the wilderness**

בארץ 776 ערבה 6160 ושוחה 7745 בארץ 776 ציה 6723 וצלמות 6757 בארץ 776 . לא 3808
ba'aretz 'arabah uashuchah ba'aretz tziyah uatzalmauet, ba'aretz, la'
**through a land of deserts and of pits through a land of drought and of the shadow of death through a land *that* no**

Jer 1:18 For, behold, I have made you this day a defenced city, and an iron pillar, and brasen walls against the whole land, against the kings of Judah, against the princes thereof, against the priests thereof, and against the people of the land.19 And they shall fight against you; but they shall not prevail against you; for I am with you, saith YHUH, to deliver you. **Jer** 2:1 Moreover the word of YHUH came to me, saying,2 Go and cry in the ears of Jerusalem, saying, Thus saith YHUH; I remember you, the kindness of your youth, the love of your espousals, when you went after me in the wilderness, in a land that was not sown.3 Israel was holiness unto YHUH, and the firstfruits of his increase: all that devour him shall offend; evil shall come upon them, saith YHUH.4 Hear you the word of YHUH, O house of Jacob, and all the families of the house of Israel:5 Thus saith YHUH, What iniquity have your fathers found in me, that they are gone far from me, and have walked after vanity, and are become vain?6 Neither said they, Where is YHUH that brought us up out of the land of Egypt, that led us through the wilderness, through a land of deserts and of pits, through a land of drought, and of the shadow of death, through a land that no man passed through, and where no man dwelt?

עבר 5674 בה 871a איש 376 ולא 3808 ישב 3427 אדם 120 שם 8033: 2:7 ואביא 935 אתכם 853 אל 413 ארץ 776 הכרמל 3759 לאכל 398
'abar bah 'aysh, uala' yashab 'adam sham. ua'abiy 'atkem 'al 'aretz hakarmel, le'akol
**passed through man and no dwelt? man where And I brought you into a country plentiful to eat**

פריה 6529 וטובה 2898 ותבאו 935 ותטמאו 2930 את 853 ארצי 776 ונחלתי 5159 שמתם 7760
piryah uatubah; uatabo'au uatatam'au 'at 'artziy, uanachalatiy samtem
**the fruit thereof and the goodness thereof when you entered you defiled my land and mine heritage made**

לתועבה 8441: 2:8 הכהנים 3548 לא 3808 אמרו 559 איה 346 יהוה 3068 ותפשי 8610 התורה 8451 לא 3808 ידעוני 3045
latou'aebah. hakohaniym, la' 'amaru 'ayeh Yahuah, uatopasey hatourah la' yada'auniy,
**an abomination The priests not said Where *is* Yahuah? and they that handle the law not knew me**

והרעים 7462 פשעו 6586 בי 871a והנביאים 5030 נבאו 5012 בבעל 1168 ואחרי 310 לא 3808 יועלו 3276
uaharo'aym pasha'au biy; uahanabiy'aym niba'au baba'al, ua'acharey la' you'aylu
**the pastors also transgressed against me and the prophets prophesied by Baal and after not *things that* do profit**

הלכו 1980: 2:9 לכן 3651 עד 5750 אריב 7378 אתכם 854 נאם 5002 יהוה 3068 ואת 854 בני 1121 בניכם 1121 אריב 7378: 2:10
halaku. laken, 'aud 'ariyb 'atakem na'am Yahuah; ua'at baney baneykem 'ariyb.
**walked Wherefore yet I will plead with you saith Yahuah *and with* your children's children will I plead**

כי 3588 עברו 5674 איי 339 כתיים 3794 וראו 7200 וקדר 6938 שלחו 7971 והתבוננו 995 מאד 3966 וראו 7200 הן 2005 היתה 1961
kiy 'abru 'ayey kitiyiym uar'au, uaqedar shilchu uahitbounanu ma'ad; uar'au hen hayatah
**For pass over the isles of Chittim and see and Kedar send *unto* and consider diligently and see if there be**

כזאת 2063: 2:11 ההימיר 4171 גוי 1471 אלהים 430 והמה 1992 לא 3808 אלהים 430 ועמי 5971 המיר 4171
kaza't. haheymiyr gouy 'alohiym, uahemah la' 'alohiym; ua'amiy hemiyr
**such as this Has changed a nation *their* gods which are yet no gods? but my people have changed**

כבודו 3519 בלוא 3808 יועיל 3276: 2:12 שמו 8074 שמים 8064 על 5921 זאת 2063 ושערו 8175
kaboudou balou'a you'ayl. shomu shamayim 'al za't; uasa'aru
**their glory *that which* for not does profit Be astonished O you heavens at this and be horribly afraid**

חרבו 2717 מאד 3966 נאם 5002 יהוה 3068: 2:13 כי 3588 שתים 8147 רעות 7451 עשה 6213 עמי 5971 אתי 853 עזבו 5800
charbou ma'ad na'am Yahuah. kiy shatayim ra'aut 'asah 'amiy; 'atiy 'azabu
**be you desolate very saith Yahuah For two evils have committed my people me they have forsaken**

מקור 4726 מים 4325 חיים 2416 לחצב 2672 להם 3807a בארות 877 בארת 877 נשברים 7665 אשר 834 לא 3808 יכלו 3557 המים 4325: 2:14
maqour mayim chayiym, lachtzob lahem bo'arout, ba'rot nishbariym, 'asher la' yakilu hamayim.
**the fountain of waters living *and* hewed out them cisterns cisterns broken that no can hold water**

העבד 5650 ישראל 3478 אם 518 יליד 3211 בית 1004 הוא 1931 מדוע 4069 היה 1961 לבז 957: 2:15 עליו 5921 ישאגו 7580 כפרים 3715
ha'abed yisra'ael, 'am yaliyd bayit hua'; madua' hayah labaz. 'alayu yish'agu kapiriym,
***Is* servant? Israel or born *slave*? a home *is* he why is he spoiled? unto him roared The young lions**

נתנו 5414 קולם 6963 וישיתו 7896 ארצו 776 לשמה 8047 עריו 5892 נצתה 3341 מבלי 1097 ישב 3427: 2:16 גם 1571 בני 1121
natanu qoulam; uayashiytu artzou lashamah, 'arayu nitzetah mibaliy yosheb. gam baney
***and* yelled aloud and they made his land waste his cities are burned without inhabitant Also the children of**

Jer 2:7 And I brought you into a plentiful country, to eat the fruit thereof and the goodness thereof; but when you entered, you defiled my land, and made mine heritage an abomination.8 The priests said not, Where is YHUH? and they that handle the law knew me not: the pastors also transgressed against me, and the prophets prophesied by Baal, and walked after things that do not profit.9 Wherefore I will yet plead with you, saith YHUH, and with your children's children will I plead.10 For pass over the isles of Chittim, and see; and send unto Kedar, and consider diligently, and see if there be such a thing.11 Hath a nation changed their gods, which are yet no gods? but my people have changed their glory for that which doth not profit.12 Be astonished, O you heavens, at this, and be horribly afraid, be you very desolate, saith YHUH.13 For my people have committed two evils; they have forsaken me the fountain of living waters, and hewed them out cisterns, broken cisterns, that can hold no water.14 Is Israel a servant? is he a homeborn slave? why is he spoiled?15 The young lions roared upon him, and yelled, and they made his land waste: his cities are burned without inhabitant.16 Also the children of Noph and Tahapanes have broken the crown of your head.

2:17

נף 5297 ותחפנס 8471 ירעוך 7462 קדקד 6936: הלוא 3808 זאת 2063 תעשה 6213 לך 3807a
nof uatachpanes yir'auk qadaqod. halou'a za't ta'aseh lak;
**of Noph and Tahanites have broken *the* crown of your head not this Have you procured unto yourself**

2:18

עזבך 5800 את 853 יהוה 3068 אלהיך 430 בעת 6256 מוליכך 1980 בדרך 1870: ועתה 6258 מה 4100 לך 3807a
'azabek 'at Yahuah 'alohayik, ba'aet mouliykek badarek. ua'atah, mah lak
**in that you have forsaken Yahuah your Elohim when he led you by the way? And now what have you**

לדרך 1870 מצרים 4714 לשתות 8354 מי 4325 שחור 7883 ומה 4100 לך 3807a לדרך 1870 אשור 804 לשתות 8354
laderek mitzrayim, lishtout mey shichour; uamah lak laderek 'ashur, lishtout
***to do* in the way of Egypt to drink the waters of Shihor? or what have you *to do* in the way of Assyria to drink**

2:19

מי 4325 נהר 5104: תיסרך 3256 רעתך 7451 ומשבותיך 4878 תוכחך 3198
mey nahar. tayasrek ra'atek, uamashuboutayik toukichuk,
**the waters of the river? shall correct you Thine own wickedness and your backslidings shall reprove you**

ודעי 3045 וראי 7200 כי 3588 רע 7451 ומר 4751 עזבך 5800 את 853 יהוה 3068 אלהיך 430 ולא 3808
uda'ay uara'ay kiy ra' uamar, 'azabek 'at Yahuah 'alohayik; uala'
**know therefore and see that *it is* an evil *thing* and bitter that you have forsaken Yahuah your Elohim and not**

2:20

פחדתי 6345 אליך 413 נאם 5002 אדני 136 יהוה 3069 צבאות 6635: כי 3588 מעולם 5769 שברתי 7665 עלך 5923 נתקתי 5423
pachdatiy 'aelayik, na'am 'adonay Yahuah tzaba'aut. kiy me'aulam shabartiy 'alek, nitaqtiy
***that* my fear *is* in you saith Adonai Yahuah of hosts For of old time I have broken your yoke *and* burst**

מוסרתיך 4147 ותאמרי 559 לא 3808 אעבד 5647 כי 3588 על 5921 כל 3605 גבעה 1389 גבהה 1364 ותחת 8478 כל 3605 עץ 6086 רענן 7488
mousarotayik, uata'mariy la' 'a'abod kiy 'al kal gib'ah gabohah, uatachat kal 'aetz ra'anan,
**your bands and you said not I will transgress; when upon every hill high and under every tree green**

2:21

את 859 צעה 6808 זנה 2181: ואנכי 595 נטעתיך 5193 שרק 8321 כלה 3605 זרע 2233 אמת 571 ואיך 349
'at tzo'ah zonah. ua'anokiy nata'tiyk soreq, kuloh zera' 'amet; ua'aeyk
***you* wanderest playing the harlot Yet I had planted you a noble vine wholly a seed right how then**

2:22

נהפכת 2015 לי 3807a סורי 5494 הגפן 1612 נכריה 5237: כי 3588 אם 518 תכבסי 3526 בנתר 5427 ותרבי 7235
nehapakt liy, surey hagapen nakariyah. kiy 'am takabsiy baneter, uatarbiy
**are you turned unto me? *the* degenerate plant of a strange For though you wash youself with nitre and take much**

2:23

לך 3807a ברית 1287 נכתם 3799 עונך 5771 לפני 6440 נאם 5002 אדני 136 יהוה 3069: איך 349 תאמרי 559 לא 3808 נטמאתי 2930
lak boriyt; niktam 'auonek lapanay, na'am 'adonay Yahuah. 'aeyk ta'mariy la' nitmea'tiy,
**to you soap is marked *yet* your iniquity before me saith Adonai Yahuah How can you say not I am polluted**

אחרי 310 הבעלים 1168 לא 3808 הלכתי 1980 ראי 7200 דרכך 1870 בגיא 1516 דעי 3045 מה 4100 עשית 6213 בכרה 1072
'acharey haba'aliym la' halaktiy, ra'ay darkek bagay'a, da'ay meh 'asiyt; bikrah
**after Baalim? not I have gone see your way in the valley know what you have done *you are* a dromedary**

2:24

קלה 7031 משרכת 8308 דרכיה 1870: פרה 6501 למד 3928 מדבר 4057 באות 185 נפשו 5315 שאפה 7602 רוח 7307
qalah masareket darakeyha. pereh limud midbar, ba'auat napshou sha'apah ruach,
**swift traversing her ways A wild ass used to the wilderness at her pleasure his soul *that* snuffeth up the wind**

Jer 2:17 Hast you not procured this unto thyself, in that you have forsaken YHUH your G-d, when he led you by the way?18 And now what have you to do in the way of Egypt, to drink the waters of Sihor? or what have you to do in the way of Assyria, to drink the waters of the river?19 Thine own wickedness shall correct you, and your backslidings shall reprove you: know therefore and see that it is an evil thing and bitter, that you have forsaken YHUH your G-d, and that my fear is not in you, saith YHUH G-D of hosts.20 For of old time I have broken your yoke, and burst your bands; and you saidst, I will not transgress; when upon every high hill and under every green tree you wanderest, playing the harlot.21 Yet I had planted you a noble vine, wholly a right seed: how then are you turned into the degenerate plant of a strange vine unto me?22 For though you wash you with nitre, and take you much soap, yet your iniquity is marked before me, saith YHUH G-D.23 How canst you say, I am not polluted, I have not gone after Baalim? see your way in the valley, know what you have done: you are a swift dromedary traversing her ways;24 A wild ass used to the wilderness, that snuffeth up the wind at her pleasure; in her occasion who can turn her away? all they that seek her will not weary themselves; in her month they shall find her.

| תאנתה 8385 | מי 4310 | ישיבנה 7725 | כל 3605 | מבקשיה 1245 | לא 3808 | ייעפו 3286 | בחדשה 2320 |
|---|---|---|---|---|---|---|---|
| ta'anatah | miy' | yashiybenah; | kal | mabaqsheyha | la' | yiy'apu, | bachadashah |
| ***in* her occasion** | **who** | **can turn her away?** | **all** | **they that seek her** | **not** | **will weary themselves** | **in her month** |

| ימצאונה 4672: | 2:25 מנעי 4513 | רגלך 7272 | מיחף 3182 | וגורנך 1637 | מצמאה 6773 | ותאמרי 559 | נואש 2976 |
|---|---|---|---|---|---|---|---|
| yimtza'aunaha. | mina'ay | raglek | miyachep, | uagouronek | mitzima'ah; | uata'mariy | nou'ash, |
| **they shall find her** | **Withhold** | **your foot** | **from being unshod** | **and your throat** | **from thirst** | **but you said** | **There is hope** |

| לוא 3808 | כי 3588 | אהבתי 157 | זרים 2114 | ואחריהם 310 | אלך 1980: | 2:26 כבשת 1322 | גנב 1590 | כי 3588 | ימצא 4672 | כן 3651 | הבישו 954 |
|---|---|---|---|---|---|---|---|---|---|---|---|
| lua' | kiy | 'ahabtiy | zariym | ua'achareyhem | 'aelek. | kaboshet | ganab | kiy | yimatzea', | ken | hobiyshu |
| **no** | **for** | **I have loved** | **strangers** | **and after them** | **will I go** | **As is ashamed** | **the thief** | **when** | **he is found** | **so** | **ashamed** |

| בית 1004 | ישראל 3478 | המה 1992 | מלכיהם 4428 | שריהם 8269 | וכהניהם 3548 | ונביאיהם 5030: | 2:27 אמרים 559 | לעץ 6086 |
|---|---|---|---|---|---|---|---|---|
| beyt | yisra'ael; | hemah | malkeyhem | sareyhem, | uakohaneyhem | uanbiy'aeyhem. | 'amariym | la'aetz |
| ***is the* house of** | **Israel** | **they** | **their kings** | **their princes** | **and their priests** | **and their prophets** | **Saying** | **to a stock** |

| אבי 1 | אתה 859 | ולאבן 68 | את 859 | ילדתני 3205 | כי 3588 | פנו 6437 | אלי 413 | ערף 6203 | ולא 3808 |
|---|---|---|---|---|---|---|---|---|---|
| 'abiy | 'atah, | uala'aben | 'at | yalidtany | kiy | panu | 'aelay | 'arep | uala' |
| ***are* my father** | **to you** | **and to a stone** | ***you*** | **has brought me forth** | **for** | **they have turned** | **unto me** | ***their* back** | **and not** |

| פנים 6440 | ובעת 6256 | רעתם 7451 | יאמרו 559 | קומה 6965 | והושיענו 3467: | 2:28 ואיה 346 | אלהיך 430 | אשר 834 |
|---|---|---|---|---|---|---|---|---|
| paniym; | uab'aet | ra'atam | ya'maru, | qumah | uahoushiy'aenu. | ua'ayeh | 'aloheyka | 'asher |
| ***their* face** | **but in the time of** | **their trouble** | **they will say** | **Arise** | **and save us** | **But where** | ***are* your gods** | **that** |

| עשית 6213 | לך 3807a | יקומו 6965 | אם 518 | יושיעוך 3467 | בעת 6256 | רעתך 7451 | כי 3588 | מספר 4557 |
|---|---|---|---|---|---|---|---|---|
| 'ashiyta | lak, | yaqumu | 'am | youshiy'auka | ba'aet | ra'ateka; | kiy | mispar |
| **you have made** | **to you?** | **let them arise** | **if** | **they can save you** | **in the time of** | **your trouble** | **for** | ***according to* the number of** |

| עריך 5892 | היו 1961 | אלהיך 430 | יהודה 3063: | 2:29 למה 4100 | תריבו 7378 | אלי 413 | כלכם 3605 | פשעתם 6586 | בי 871a |
|---|---|---|---|---|---|---|---|---|---|
| 'areyka, | hayu | 'aloheyka | yahudah. | lamah | tariybu | 'aelay; | kulkem | pasha'atem | biy |
| **your cities** | **are** | **your gods** | **O Judah** | **Wherefore** | **will you plead** | **with me?** | **you all** | **have transgressed** | **against me** |

| נאם 5002 | יהוה 3068: | 2:30 לשוא 7723 | הכיתי 5221 | את 853 | בניכם 1121 | מוסר 4148 | לא 3808 | לקחו 3947 | אכלה 398 |
|---|---|---|---|---|---|---|---|---|---|
| na'am | Yahuah. | lashau'a | hikeytiy | 'at | baneykem, | musar | la' | laqachu; | 'akalah |
| **saith** | **Yahuah** | **In vain** | **have I smitten** | | **your children** | **correction** | **no** | **they received** | **has devoured** |

| חרבכם 2719 | נביאיכם 5030 | כאריה 738 | משחית 7843: | 2:31 הדור 1755 | אתם 859 | ראו 7200 | דבר 1697 | יהוה 3068 | המדבר 4057 |
|---|---|---|---|---|---|---|---|---|---|
| charbakem | nabiy'aeykem | ka'aryeh | mashchiyt. | hadour, | 'atem | ra'au | dabar | Yahuah, | hamidbar |
| **your own sword** | **your prophets** | **like a lion** | **destroying** | **O generation** | **you** | **see** | **the word of** | **Yahuah** | **a wilderness** |

| הייתי 1961 | לישראל 3478 | אם 518 | ארץ 776 | מאפליה 3991 | מדוע 4069 | אמרו 559 | עמי 5971 | רדנו 7300 | לוא 3808 | נבוא 935 | עוד 5750 |
|---|---|---|---|---|---|---|---|---|---|---|---|
| hayiytiy | layisra'ael, | 'am | 'aretz | ma'apelayah; | madua' | 'amaru | 'amiy | radanu, | lua' | nabua' | 'aud |
| **Have I been** | **unto Israel?** | **or** | **a land of** | **darkness?** | **wherefore** | **say** | **my people** | **We are lords** | **no** | **we will come** | **more** |

| אליך 413: | 2:32 התשכח 7911 | בתולה 1330 | עדיה 5716 | כלה 3618 | קשריה 7196 | ועמי 5971 | שכחוני 7911 | ימים 3117 |
|---|---|---|---|---|---|---|---|---|
| 'aeleyka. | hatishkach | batulah | 'adyah, | kalah | qishureyha; | ua'amiy | shakechuniy, | yamiym |
| **unto you?** | **Can forget** | **a maid (*virgin*)** | **her ornaments** | ***or* a bride** | **her attire?** | **yet my people** | **have forgotten me** | **days** |

Jer 2:25 Withhold your foot from being unshod, and your throat from thirst: but you saidst, There is no hope: no; for I have loved strangers, and after them will I go.26 As the thief is ashamed when he is found, so is the house of Israel ashamed; they, their kings, their princes, and their priests, and their prophets,27 Saying to a stock, Thou are my father; and to a stone, Thou have brought me forth: for they have turned their back unto me, and not their face: but in the time of their trouble they will say, Arise, and save us.28 But where are your gods that you have made you? let them arise, if they can save you in the time of your trouble: for according to the number of your cities are your gods, O Judah.29 Wherefore will you plead with me? you all have transgressed against me, saith YHUH.30 In vain have I smitten your children; they received no correction: your own sword has devoured your prophets, like a destroying lion.31 O generation, see you the word of YHUH. Have I been a wilderness unto Israel? a land of darkness? wherefore say my people, We are lords; we will come no more unto you?32 Can a maid forget her ornaments, or a bride her attire? yet my people have forgotten me days without number.

2:33
אין 369 מספר 4557: מה 4100 תיטבי 3190 דרכך 1870 לבקש 1245 אהבה 160 לכן 3651 גם 1571 את 853 הרעות 7451 למדתי 3925
'aeyn mispar. mah teytibiy darkek labaqesh 'ahabah; laken gam 'at hara'aut, limadtiy
**without number Why trim you your way to seek love? therefore also the wicked ones have you taught**

2:34
את 853 דרכיך 1870: גם 1571 בכנפיך 3671 נמצאו 4672 דם 1818 נפשות 5315 אביונים 34 נקיים 5355 לא 3808 במחתרת 4290
'at darakayik. gam biknapayik nimtza'au, dam napshout 'abyouniym naqiyiym; la' bamachateret
**your ways Also in your skirts is found the blood of the souls of *the* poor innocents not by secret search**

2:35
מצאתים 4672 כי 3588 על 5921 כל 3605 אלה 428: ותאמרי 559 כי 3588 נקיתי 5352 אך 389 שב 7725 אפו 639 ממני 4480
matza'tiym kiy 'al kal 'aeleh. uato'mariy kiy niqeytiy, 'ak shab 'apou mimeniy;
**I have found it but upon all these Yet you say Because I am innocent surely shall turn his anger from me**

2:36
הנני 2005 נשפט 8199 אותך 854 על 5921 אמרך 559 לא 3808 חטאתי 2398: מה 4100 תזלי 235 מאד 3966 לשנות 8138 את 853
hinniy nishpat autak, 'al 'amarek la' chata'tiy. mah tezaliy ma'ad lashanout 'at
**Behold I will plead with you because you say not I have sinned Why gad you about so much to change**

2:37
דרכך 1870 גם 1571 ממצרים 4714 תבושי 954 כאשר 834 בשת 954 מאשור 804: גם 1571 מאת 853 זה 2088
darkek; gam mimitzrayim teboushiy, ka'asher boshet me'ashur. gam me'at zeh
**your way? also of Egypt you shall be ashamed as you were ashamed of Assyria Yea from him**

תצאי 3318 וידיך 3027 על 5921 ראשך 7218 כי 3588 מאס 3988 יהוה 3068 במבטחיך 4009 ולא 3808
tetza'ay, uayadayik 'al ra'shek; kiy ma'as Yahuah bamibtachayik, uala'
**you shall go forth and your hands upon upon your head for has rejected Yahuah your confidences and not**

תצליחי 6743 להם 3807a:
tatzliychiy lahem.
**you shall prosper in them**

**Jer 3:1**
לאמר 559 הן 2005 ישלח 7971 איש 376 את 853 אשתו 802 והלכה 1980 מאתו 853 והיתה 1961 לאיש 376 אחר 312 הישוב 7725
lea'mor hen yashalach 'aysh 'at ashtou uahalakah me'atou uahayatah la'aysh 'acher, hayashub
**They say If put away a man his wife and she go from him and become shall man's another he return**

אליה 413 עוד 5750 הלוא 3808 חנוף 2610 תחנף 2610 הארץ 776 ההיא 1931 ואת 859 זנית 2181 רעים 7453 רבים 7227
'aeleyha 'aud, halou'a chanop techanap ha'aretz hahiy'a; ua'at, zaniyt re'aym rabiym,
**unto her again? not shall polluted? be greatly the land that *but you* have played the harlot with lovers many**

3:2
ושוב 7725 אלי 413 נאם 5002 יהוה 3068: שאי 5375 עיניך 5869 על 5921 שפים 8205 וראי 7200 איפה 375 לא 3808
uashoub 'aelay na'am Yahuah. sa'ay 'aeynayik 'al shapayim uara'ay, 'aeypoh la'
**yet return again to me saith Yahuah Lift up your eyes unto the high places and see where not**

שגלת 7693 על 5921 דרכים 1870 ישבת 3427 להם 3807a כערבי 6163 במדבר 4057 ותחניפי 2610
shugalt 'al darakiym yoshabot lahem, ka'arabiy bamidbar; uatachaniypiy
**you have been lien with. In the ways have you sat for them as the Arabian in the wilderness and you have polluted**

3:3
ארץ 776 בזנותיך 2184 וברעתך 7451: וימנעו 4513 רבבים 7241 ומלקוש 4456
'aretz, biznutayik uabra'atek. uayimana'au rabibiym, uamalqoush
**the land with your whoredoms and with your wickedness Therefore have been withholden the showers and latter rain**

Jer 2:33 Why trimmest you your way to seek love? therefore have you also taught the wicked ones your ways.34 Also in your skirts is found the blood of the souls of the poor innocents: I have not found it by secret search, but upon all these.35 Yet you say, Because I am innocent, surely his anger shall turn from me. Behold, I will plead with you, because you say, I have not sinned.36 Why gaddest you about so much to change your way? you also shall be ashamed of Egypt, as you were ashamed of Assyria.37 Yea, you shall go forth from him, and your hands upon your head: for YHUH has rejected your confidences, and you shall not prosper in them. **Jer** 3:1 They say, If a man put away his wife, and she go from him, and become another man's, shall he return unto her again? shall not that land be greatly polluted? but you have played the harlot with many lovers; yet return again to me, saith YHUH.2 Lift up your eyes unto the high places, and see where you have not been lien with. In the ways have you sat for them, as the Arabian in the wilderness; and you have polluted the land with your whoredoms and with your wickedness.3 Therefore the showers have been withholden, and there has been no latter rain; and you had a whore's forehead, you refusedst to be ashamed.

3:4
לוא 3808 היה 1961 ומצח 4696 אשה 802 זונה 2181 היה 1961 לך 3807a מאנת 3985 הכלם 3637: הלוא 3808
lua' hayah; uametzach 'ashah zounah hayah lak, me'ant hikalem. halou'a
**no there has been and a forehead whore's commit fornication you had to you refused to be ashamed not**

3:5
מעתה 6258 קראתי 7121 לי 3807a אבי 1 אלוף 441 נערי 5271 אתה 859: הינטר 5201 לעולם 5769
me'atah, qara'tiy liy 'abiy; 'alup na'uray 'atah. hayintor la'aulam,
**from this time will you cry unto me My father *are* the guide of my youth? you Will he reserve *his anger* for ever?**

3:6
אם 518 ישמר 8104 לנצח 5331 הנה 2009 דברתי 1696 ותעשי 6213 הרעות 7451 ותוכל 3201: ויאמר 559 יהוה 3069 אלי 413
'am yishmor lanetzach; hineh dibartiy uata'asiy hara'aut uatukal. uaya'mer Yahuah 'aelay,
**or will he keep *it* to the end? Behold you have spoken and done evil things as you could said also Yahuah unto me**

בימי 3117 יאשיהו 2977 המלך 4428 הראית 7200 אשר 834 עשתה 6213 משבה 4878 ישראל 3478 הלכה 1980 היא 1931 על 5921 כל 3605
biymey ya'shiyahu hamelek, hara'ayta, 'asher 'astah mashubah yisra'ael; holakah hiy'a 'al kal
**in the days of Josiah the king Have you seen *that* which has done? backsliding Israel is gone up she upon every**

3:7
הר 2022 גבה 1364 ואל 413 תחת 8478 כל 3605 עץ 6086 רענן 7488 ותזני 2181 שם 8033: ואמר 559 אחרי 310
har gaboah, ua'al tachat kal 'aetz ra'anan uatizniy sham. ua'amar, 'acharey
**mountain high and to under every tree green and there has played the harlot there And I said after**

עשותה 6213 את 853 כל 3605 אלה 428 אלי 413 תשוב 7725 ולא 3808 שבה 7725 ותראה 7200 בגודה 901 אחותה 269
'asoutah 'at kal 'aeleh 'aelay tashub uala' shabah; uaterah bagoudah achoutah
**she had done all these *things* unto me Turn you But not she returned *it* And saw her treacherous sister**

3:8
יהודה 3063: וארא 7200 כי 3588 על 5921 כל 3605 אדות 182 אשר 834 נאפה 5003 משבה 4878 ישראל 3478
yahudah. ua'aera', kiy 'al kal 'adout 'asher ni'apah mashubah yisra'ael,
**Judah And I saw when for all the causes whereby committed adultery backsliding Israel**

שלחתיה 7971 ואתן 5414 את 853 ספר 5612 כריתתיה 3748 אליה 413 ולא 3808 יראה 3372 בגדה 898 יהודה 3063 אחותה 269
shilachtiyha ua'aten 'at seper kariytuteyha 'aeleyha; uala' yara'ah bogedah yahudah achoutah,
**I had put her away and given a bill of divorce unto her yet not feared her treacherous Judah sister**

3:9
ותלך 1980 ותזן 2181 גם 1571 היא 1931: והיה 1961 מקל 6963 זנותה 2184
uatelek uatizen gam hiy'a. uahayah miqol zanutah,
**but went and played the harlot also she And it came to pass through the lightness of her whoredom**

3:10
ותחנף 2610 את 853 הארץ 776 ותנאף 5003 את 854 האבן 68 ואת 854 העץ 6086: וגם 1571 בכל 3605 זאת 2063 לא 3808
uatechanap 'at ha'aretz; uatin'ap 'at ha'aben ua'at ha'aetz. uagam bakal za't, la'
**that she defiled the land and committed adultery *with* stones *and with* stocks And yet for all this not**

3:11
שבה 7725 אלי 413 בגודה 901 אחותה 269 יהודה 3063 בכל 3605 לבה 3820 כי 3588 אם 518 בשקר 8267 נאם 5002 יהוה 3068:
shabah 'aelay bagoudah achoutah yahudah bakal libah; kiy 'am basheqer na'am Yahuah.
**has turned unto me her treacherous sister Judah with whole her heart but ratyher feignedly saith Yahuah**

3:12
ויאמר 559 יהוה 3068 אלי 413 צדקה 6663 נפשה 5315 משבה 4878 ישראל 3478 מבגדה 898 יהודה 3063: הלך 1980
uaya'mer Yahuah 'aelay, tzidqah napshah mashubah yisra'ael; mibogedah yahudah. halok
**And said Yahuah unto me has justified herself *The* backsliding Israel more than treacherous Judah Go**

Jer 3:4 Wilt you not from this time cry unto me, My father, you are the guide of my youth?5 Will he reserve his anger forever? will he keep it to the end? Behold, you have spoken and done evil things as you couldest.6 YHUH said also unto me in the days of Josiah the king, Hast you seen that which backsliding Israel has done? she is gone up upon every high mountain and under every green tree, and there has played the harlot.7 And I said after she had done all these things, Turn you unto me. But she returned not. And her treacherous sister Judah saw it.8 And I saw, when for all the causes whereby backsliding Israel committed adultery I had put her away, and given her a bill of divorce; yet her treacherous sister Judah feared not, but went and played the harlot also.9 And it came to pass through the lightness of her whoredom, that she defiled the land, and committed adultery with stones and with stocks.10 And yet for all this her treacherous sister Judah has not turned unto me with her whole heart, but eignedly, saith YHUH.11 And YHUH said unto me, The backsliding Israel has justified herself more than treacherous Judah.12 Go and proclaim these words toward the north, and say, Return, you backsliding Israel, saith YHUH;

וקראת 7121 את 853 הדברים 1697 האלה 428 צפונה 6828 ואמרת 559 שובה 7725 משבה 4878 ישראל 3478 נאם 5002 יהוה 3068
uaqara'ta 'at hadabariym ha'aeleh tzapounah, ua'amarta shubah mashubah yisra'ael na'am Yahuah,
**and proclaim these words these toward the north and say Return you backsliding Israel saith Yahuah**

לוא 3808 אפיל 5307 פני 6440 בכם 871a כי 3588 חסיד 2623 אני 589 נאם 5002 יהוה 3068 לא 3808 אטור 5201
lua' 'apiyl panay bakem; kiy chasiyd 'aniy na'am Yahuah, la' 'atour
**not *and* I will cause to fall mine anger upon you for *am* merciful I saith Yahuah not *and* I will keep**

3:13
לעולם 5769: אך 389 דעי 3045 עונך 5771 כי 3588 ביהוה 3068 אלהיך 430 פשעת 6586
la'aulam. 'ak da'ay 'auonek, kiy baYahuah 'alohayik pasha'at;
***anger* for ever Only acknowledge your iniquity that against Yahuah your Elohim you have transgressed**

ותפזרי 6340 את 853 דרכיך 1870 לזרים 2114 תחת 8478 כל 3605 עץ 6086 רענן 7488 ובקולי 6963 לא 3808 שמעתם 8085
uatapazriy 'at darakayik lazariym, tachat kal 'aetz ra'anan, uabqouliy la' shama'tem
**and have scattered your ways to the strangers under every tree green and my voice not you have obeyed**

3:14
נאם 5002 יהוה 3068: שובו 7725 בנים 1121 שובבים 7726 נאם 5002 יהוה 3068 כי 3588 אנכי 595 בעלתי 1166 בכם 871a ולקחתי 3947
na'am Yahuah. shubu baniym shoubabiym na'am Yahuah, kiy 'anokiy ba'altiy bakem; ualaqachtiy
**saith Yahuah Turn children O backsliding saith Yahuah for I am married unto you and I will take**

3:15
אתכם 853 אחד 259 מעיר 5892 ושנים 8147 ממשפחה 4940 והבאתי 935 אתכם 853 ציון 6726: ונתתי 5414 לכם 3807a רעים 7462
'atkem 'achad me'ayr, uashnayim mimishpachah, uahebea'tiy 'atkem tziyoun. uanatatiy lakem ro'aym
**you one of a city and two of a family and I will bring you *to* Zion And I will give to you pastors**

3:16
כלבי 3820 ורעו 7462 אתכם 853 דעה 1844 והשכיל 7919: והיה 1961 כי 3588
kalibiy; uar'au 'atkem de'ah uahaskeyl. uahayah kiy
**according to mine heart which shall feed you with knowledge and understanding And it shall come to pass when**

תרבו 7235 ופריתם 6509 בארץ 776 בימים 3117 ההמה 1992 נאם 5002 יהוה 3068 לא 3808 יאמרו 559 עוד 5750 ארון 727
tirbu uapriytem ba'aretz bayamiym hahemah na'am Yahuah, la' ya'maru 'aud, 'aroun
**you be multiplied and increased in the land in days those saith Yahuah no they shall say more The ark of**

ברית 1285 יהוה 3068 ולא 3808 יעלה 5927 על 5921 לב 3820 ולא 3808 יזכרו 2142 בו 871a ולא 3808 יפקדו 6485
bariyt Yahuah, uala' ya'aleh 'al leb; uala' yizkaru bou uala' yipqodu,
**the covenant of Yahuah neither shall it come to mind neither shall they remember it neither shall they visit *it***

3:17
ולא 3808 יעשה 6213 עוד 5750: בעת 6256 ההיא 1931 יקראו 7121 לירושלם 3389 כסא 3678 יהוה 3068
uala' ye'aseh 'aud. ba'aet hahiy'a, yiqra'au liyarushalaim kisea' Yahuah,
**neither shall *that* be done any more At time that they shall call Jerusalem the throne of Yahuah**

ונקוו 6960 אליה 413 כל 3605 הגוים 1471 לשם 8034 יהוה 3068 לירושלם 3389 ולא 3808 ילכו 1980 עוד 5750 אחרי 310
uaniquu 'aeleyha kal hagouyim lashem Yahuah liyarushalaim; uala' yelaku 'aud, 'acharey
**shall be gathered unto it all the nations to the name of Yahuah to Jerusalem neither shall they walk any more after**

3:18
שררות 8307 לבם 3820 הרע 7451: בימים 3117 ההמה 1992 ילכו 1980 בית 1004 יהודה 3063 על 5921 בית 1004 ישראל 3478
sharirut libam hara'. bayamiym hahemah, yelaku beyt yahudah 'al beyt yisra'ael;
**the imagination of heart their evil In days those shall walk the house of Judah with the house of Israel**

Jer 3:12 and I will not cause mine anger to fall upon you: for I am merciful, saith YHUH, and I will not keep anger forever.13 Only acknowledge your iniquity, that you have transgressed against YHUH your G-d, and have scattered your ways to the strangers under every green tree, and you have not obeyed my voice, saith YHUH.14 Turn, O backsliding children, saith YHUH; for I am married unto you: and I will take you one of a city, and two of a family, and I will bring you to Zion:15 And I will give you pastors according to mine heart, which shall feed you with knowledge and understanding.16 And it shall come to pass, when you be multiplied and increased in the land, in those days, saith YHUH, they shall say no more, The ark of the covenant of YHUH: neither shall it come to mind: neither shall they remember it; neither shall they visit it; neither shall that be done anymore.17 At that time they shall call Jerusalem the throne of YHUH; and all the nations shall be gathered unto it, to the name of YHUH, to Jerusalem: neither shall they walk anymore after the imagination of their evil heart.18 In those days the house of Judah shall walk with the house of Israel, and they shall come together out of the land of the north to the land that I have given for an inheritance unto your fathers.

ויבאו 935 יחדו 3162 מארץ 776 צפון 6828 על 5921 הארץ 776 אשר 834 הנחלתי 5157 את 853
uayabo'au yachdau me'aretz tzapoun, 'al ha'aretz 'asher hinchaltiy 'at
**and they shall come together out of the land of the north to the land that I have given for an inheritance unto**

3:19
אבותיכם 1: ואנכי 595 אמרתי 559 איך 349 אשיתך 7896 בבנים 1121 ואתן 5414 לך 3807a ארץ 776 חמדה 2532
abouteykem. ua'anokiy 'amartiy, 'aeyk 'ashiytek babaniym, ua'aten lak 'aretz chemdah,
**your fathers But I said How shall I put you among the children of and give to you a land pleasant**

נחלת 5159 צבי 6643 צבאות 6635 גוים 1471 ואמר 559 אבי 1 תקראו 7121 לי 3807a ומאחרי 310 לא 3808 תשובו 7725:
nachalat tzabiy tzib'aut gouyim; ua'amar, 'abiy tiqra'au liy, uame'acharay la' tashubu
**a heritage of goodly the hosts of nations? and I said My father you shall call to me and from me not shall turn away**

3:20
אכן 403 בגדה 898 אשה 802 מרעה 7453 כן 3651 בגדתם 898 בי 871a בית 1004
'aken bagadah 'ashah mere'ah; ken bagadtem biy beyt
**Surely treacherously depart *as* a wife from her husband so have you dealt treacherously with me O house of**

3:21
ישראל 3478 נאם 5002 יהוה 3068: קול 6963 על 5921 שפיים 8205 נשמע 8085 בכי 1065 תחנוני 8469 בני 1121
yisra'ael na'am Yahuah. qoul 'al shapayiym nishma', bakiy tachanuney baney
**Israel saith Yahuah A voice upon the high places was heard weeping *and* supplications of the children of**

3:22
ישראל 3478 כי 3588 העוו 5753 את 853 דרכם 1870 שכחו 7911 את 853 יהוה 3068 אלהיהם 430: שובו 7725
yisra'ael; kiy he'auu 'at darkam, shakachu 'at Yahuah 'aloheyhem. shubu
**Israel for they have perverted their way *and* they have forgotten Yahuah their Elohim Return**

בנים 1121 שובבים 7726 ארפה 7495 משובתיכם 4878 הננו 2005 אתנו 857 לך 3807a כי 3588 אתה 859 יהוה 3068
baniym shoubabiym, 'arpah mashuboteykem; hinanu 'atanu lak, kiy 'atah Yahuah
**children you backsliding *and* I will heal your backslidings Behold we come unto you for you *are* Yahuah**

3:23
אלהינו 430: אכן 403 לשקר 8267 מגבעות 1389 המון 1995 הרים 2022 אכן 403 ביהוה 3068
'aloheynu. 'aken lasheqer migba'aut hamoun hariym; 'aken baYahuah
**our Elohim Truly in vain *is salvation hoped for* from the hills *and from* the multitude of mountains truly in Yahuah**

3:24
אלהינו 430 תשועת 8668 ישראל 3478: והבשת 1322 אכלה 398 את 853 יגיע 3018 אבותינו 1 מנעורינו 5271 את 853
'aloheynu, tashu'at yisra'ael. uahaboshet, 'akalah 'at yagiya' abouteynu mina'ureynu; 'at
**our Elohim *is* the salvation of Israel For shame has devoured the labour of our fathers from our youth**

3:25
צאנם 6629 ואת 853 בקרם 1241 את 853 בניהם 1121 ואת 853 בנותיהם 1323: נשכבה 7901 בבשתנו 1322 ותכסנו 3680
tzea'nam ua'at baqaram, 'at baneyhem ua'at banouteyhem. nishkabah babashatenu, uatkasenu
**their flocks *and* their herds their sons *and* their daughters We lie down in our shame and cover us**

כלמתנו 3639 כי 3588 ליהוה 3068 אלהינו 430 חטאנו 2398 אנחנו 587 ואבותינו 1 מנעורינו 5271 ועד 5704 היום 3117
kalimatenu kiy laYahuah 'aloheynu chata'nu, 'anachnu ua'abouteynu, mina'ureynu ua'ad hayoum
**our confusion for against Yahuah our Elohim we have sinned we and our fathers from our youth even unto day**

הזה 2088 ולא 3808 שמענו 8085 בקול 6963 יהוה 3068 אלהינו 430:
hazeh; uala' shama'anu, baqoul Yahuah 'aloheynu.
**this and not have obeyed the voice of Yahuah our Elohim**

Jer 3:19 But I said, How shall I put you among the children, and give you a pleasant land, a goodly heritage of the hosts of nations? and I said, Thou shall call me, My father; and shall not turn away from me.20 Surely as a wife treacherously departeth from her husband, so have you dealt treacherously with me, O house of Israel, saith YHUH.21 A voice was heard upon the high places, weeping and supplications of the children of Israel: for they have perverted their way, and they have forgotten YHUH their G-d.22 Return, you backsliding children, and I will heal your backslidings. Behold, we come unto you; for you are YHUH our G-d.23 Truly in vain is salvation hoped for from the hills, and from the multitude of mountains: truly in YHUH our G-d is the salvation of Israel.24 For shame has devoured the labour of our fathers from our youth; their flocks and their herds, their sons and their daughters.25 We lie down in our shame, and our confusion covereth us: for we have sinned against YHUH our G-d, we and our fathers, from our youth even unto this day, and have not obeyed the voice of YHUH our G-d.

**Jer 4:1** אם 518 תשוב 7725 ישראל 3478 נאם 5002 יהוה 3068 אלי 413 תשוב 7725 ואם 518 תסיר 5493 שקוציך 8251
'am tashub yisra'ael na'am Yahuah 'aelay tashub; ua'am tasiyr shiqutzeyka
**If you will return O Israel saith Yahuah unto me return and if you will put away your abominations**

מפני 6440 ולא 3808 תנוד 5110: **4:2** ונשבעת 7650 חי 2416 יהוה 3068 באמת 571 במשפט 4941
mipanay uala' tanud. uanishba'ata chay Yahuah, be'amet bamishpat
**out of my sight and then not shall you remove And you shall swear live Yahuah in truth in judgment**

ובצדקה 6666 והתברכו 1288 בו 871a גוים 1471 ובו 871a יתהללו 1984: **4:3** כי 3588 כה 3541 אמר 559
uabitzdaqah; uahitbaraku bou gouyim uabou yitahalalu. kiy koh 'amar
**and in righteousness and shall bless themselves in him the nations and in him shall they glory For thus saith**

יהוה 3068 לאיש 376 יהודה 3063 ולירושלם 3389 נירו 5214 לכם 3807a ניר 5215 ואל 408 תזרעו 2232 אל 413 קוצים 6975: **4:4**
Yahuah la'aysh yahudah ualiyarushalaim, niyru lakem niyr; ua'al tizra'au 'al qoutziym.
**Yahuah to the men of Judah and Jerusalem Break up to your fallow ground and not sow among thorns**

המלו 4135 ליהוה 3068 והסרו 5493 ערלות 6190 לבבכם 3824 איש 376 יהודה 3063 וישבי 3427
himolu laYahuah uahasiru 'arlout lababkem, 'aysh yahudah uayoushabey
**Circumcise yourselves to Yahuah and take away the foreskins of your heart *you* men of Judah and inhabitants of**

ירושלם 3389 פן 6435 תצא 3318 כאש 784 חמתי 2534 ובערה 1197 ואין 369 מכבה 3518 מפני 6440 רע 7455 מעלליכם 4611: **4:5**
yarushalaim; pen tetzea' ka'aesh chamatiy, uaba'arah ua'aeyn makabeh, mipaney roa' ma'alleykem.
**Jerusalem lest come forth like fire my fury and burn that none can quench *it* because of the evil of your doings**

הגידו 5046 ביהודה 3063 ובירושלם 3389 השמיעו 8085 ואמרו 559 ותקעו 8628 שופר 7782 בארץ 776 קראו 7121 מלאו 4390
hagiydu bayahudah, uabiyarushalaim hashmiy'au, ua'amru utiq'au shoupar ba'aretz; qara'au mala'au
**Declare you in Judah and in Jerusalem publish and say Blow you the trumpet in the land cry gather together**

ואמרו 559 האספו 622 ונבואה 935 אל 413 ערי 5892 המבצר 4013: **4:6** שאו 5375 נס 5251 ציונה 6726 העיזו 5756
ua'amru, he'asapu uanabou'ah 'al 'arey hamibtzar. sa'au nes tziyounah, ha'ayzu
**and say Assemble yourselves and let us go into cities the defenced Set up the standard toward Zion retire**

אל 408 תעמדו 5975 כי 3588 רעה 7451 אנכי 595 מביא 935 מצפון 6828 ושבר 7667 גדול 1419: **4:7** עלה 5927 אריה 738
'al ta'amodu; kiy ra'ah, 'anokiy mebiy'a mitzapoun uasheber gadoul. 'alah 'aryeh
**not stay for evil I will bring from the north and a destruction great is come up The lion**

מסבכו 5441 ומשחית 7843 גוים 1471 נסע 5265 יצא 3318 ממקמו 4725 לשום 7760 ארצך 776 לשמה 8047
misubkou, uamashchiyt gouyim, nasa' yatza' mimaqomou; lasum 'artzek lashamah,
**from his thicket and the destroyer of the Gentiles is on his way he is gone forth from his place to make your land desolate**

עריך 5892 תצינה 5327 מאין 369 יושב 3427: **4:8** על 5921 זאת 2063 חגרו 2296 שקים 8242 ספדו 5594 והילילו 3213 כי 3588
'arayik titzeynah me'ayn yousheb. 'al za't chigru saqiym sipdu uaheyliylu; kiy
***and* your cities shall be laid waste without an inhabitant For this gird you with sackcloth lament and howl for**

לא 3808 שב 7725 חרון 2740 אף 639 יהוה 3068 ממנו 4480: **4:9** והיה 1961 ביום 3117 ההוא 1931 נאם 5002 יהוה 3068
la' shab charoun 'ap Yahuah mimenu. uahayah bayoum hahua' na'am Yahuah,
**not is turned back *the* fierce anger of Yahuah from us And it shall come to pass at day that saith Yahuah**

**Jer** 4:1 If you will return, O Israel, saith YHUH, return unto me: and if you will put away your abominations out of my sight, then shall you not remove.2 And you shall swear, YHUH live, in truth, in judgment, and in righteousness; and the nations shall bless themselves in him, and in him shall they glory.3 For thus saith YHUH to the men of Judah and Jerusalem, Break up your fallow ground, and sow not among thorns.4 Circumcise yourselves to YHUH, and take away the foreskins of your heart, you men of Judah and inhabitants of Jerusalem: lest my fury come forth like fire, and burn that none can quench it, because of the evil of your doings.5 Declare you in Judah, and publish in Jerusalem; and say, Blow you the trumpet in the land: cry, gather together, and say, Assemble yourselves, and let us go into the defenced cities.6 Set up the standard toward Zion: retire, stay not: for I will bring evil from the north, and a great destruction.7 The lion is come up from his thicket, and the destroyer of the Gentiles is on his way; he is gone forth from his place to make your land desolate; and your cities shall be laid waste, without an inhabitant.8 For this gird you with sackcloth, lament and howl: for the fierce anger of YHUH is not turned back from us.9 And it shall come to pass at that day, saith YHUH, that the heart of the king shall perish, and the heart of the princes;

| יאבד 6 | לב 3820 | המלך 4428 | ולב 3820 | השרים 8269 | ונשמו 8074 | הכהנים 3548 | והנביאים 5030 |
|---|---|---|---|---|---|---|---|
| ya'bad | leb | hamelek | ualeb | hasariym; | uanashamu | hakohaniym, | uahanabiy'aym |
| **shall perish** | ***that* the heart of** | **the king** | **and the heart of** | **the princes** | **and shall be astonished** | **the priests** | **and the prophets** |

| יתמהו 8539: | 4:10 | ואמר 559 | אהה 162 | אדני 136 | יהוה 3069 | אכן 403 | השא 5377 | השאת 5377 | לעם 5971 | הזה 2088 | ולירושלם 3389 |
|---|---|---|---|---|---|---|---|---|---|---|---|
| yitmahu. | | ua'amar | 'ahah | 'adonay | Yahuah | 'aken | hashea' | hishea'ta | la'am | hazeh | ualiyarushalaim |
| **shall wonder** | | **Then said I** | **Ah** | **Adonai** | **Yahuah** | **surely** | **you have greatly** | **deceived** | **people** | **this** | **and Jerusalem** |

| לאמר 559 | שלום 7965 | יהיה 1961 | לכם 3807a | ונגעה 5060 | חרב 2719 | עד 5704 | הנפש 5315: | 4:11 | בעת 6256 | ההיא 1931 | יאמר 559 |
|---|---|---|---|---|---|---|---|---|---|---|---|
| lea'mor, | shaloum | yihayeh | lakem; | uanaga'ah | chereb | 'ad | hanapesh. | | ba'aet | hahiy'a, | ye'amer |
| **saying** | **peace** | **shall have** | **to you** | **whereas reached** | **the sword** | **unto** | **the soul** | | **At time** | **that** | **shall it be said** |

| לעם 5971 | הזה 2088 | ולירושלם 3389 | רוח 7307 | צח 6703 | שפיים 8205 | במדבר 4057 | דרך 1870 | בת 1323 | עמי 5971 |
|---|---|---|---|---|---|---|---|---|---|
| la'am | hazeh | ualiyarushalaim, | ruach | tzach | shapayiym | bamidbar, | derek | bat | 'amiy; |
| **to people** | **this** | **and to Jerusalem** | **A wind of** | **dry** | **the high places** | **in the wilderness** | **toward** | **the daughter of** | **my people** |

| לוא 3808 | לזרות 2219 | ולוא 3808 | להבר 1305: | 4:12 | רוח 7307 | מלא 4390 | מאלה 428 | יבוא 935 | לי 3807a | עתה 6258 | גם 1571 | אני 589 |
|---|---|---|---|---|---|---|---|---|---|---|---|---|
| lua' | lizrout | ualou'a | lahabar. | | ruach | malea' | me'aeleh | yabou'a | liy; | 'atah | gam | 'aniy |
| **not** | **to fan** | **and nor** | **to cleanse** | | ***Even* a wind** | **full** | **from those** | ***places* shall come** | **unto me** | **now** | **also** | **I** |

| אדבר 1696 | משפטים 4941 | אותם 854: | 4:13 | הנה 2009 | כעננים 6051 | יעלה 5927 | וכסופה 5492 | מרכבותיו 4818 |
|---|---|---|---|---|---|---|---|---|
| 'adaber | mishpatiym | 'autam. | | hineh | ka'ananiym | ya'aleh, | uakasupah | markaboutayu, |
| **will give** | **sentence** | **against them** | | **Behold** | **as clouds** | **he shall come up** | **and as a whirlwind** | **his chariots *shall be*** |

| קלו 7043 | מנשרים 5404 | סוסיו 5483 | אוי 188 | לנו 3807a | כי 3588 | שדדנו 7703: | 4:14 | כבסי 3526 | מרעה 7451 | לבך 3820 | ירושלם 3389 |
|---|---|---|---|---|---|---|---|---|---|---|---|
| qalu | minshariym | susayu; | 'auy | lanu | kiy | shudadanu. | | kabsiy | mera'ah | libek | yarushalaim, |
| **are swifter** | **than eagles** | **his horses** | **Woe** | **unto us** | **for** | **we are spoiled** | | **wash** | **from wickedness** | **your heart** | **O Jerusalem** |

| למען 4616 | תושעי 3467 | עד 5704 | מתי 4970 | תלין 3885 | בקרבך 7130 | מחשבות 4284 | אונך 205: | 4:15 | כי 3588 | קול 6963 | מגיד 5046 |
|---|---|---|---|---|---|---|---|---|---|---|---|
| lama'an | tiuashe'ay; | 'ad | matay | taliyn | baqirbek | machashabout | 'aunek. | | kiy | qoul | magiyd |
| **that** | **you may be saved** | **How** | **long** | **shall lodge** | **within you?** | **thoughts** | **your vain** | | **For** | **a voice** | **declareth** |

| מדן 1835 | ומשמיע 8085 | און 205 | מהר 2022 | אפרים 669: | 4:16 | הזכירו 2142 | לגוים 1471 | הנה 2009 | השמיעו 8085 | על 5921 |
|---|---|---|---|---|---|---|---|---|---|---|
| midan; | uamashmiya' | 'auen | mehar | 'aprayim. | | hazakiryu | lagouyim, | hineh | hashmiy'au | 'al |
| **from Dan** | **and publisheth** | **affliction** | **from mount** | **Ephraim** | | **Make you mention** | **to the nations** | **behold** | **publish** | **against** |

| ירושלם 3389 | נצרים 5341 | באים 935 | מארץ 776 | המרחק 4801 | ויתנו 5414 | על 5921 | ערי 5892 | יהודה 3063 | קולם 6963: | 4:17 |
|---|---|---|---|---|---|---|---|---|---|---|
| yarushalaim, | notzariym | ba'aym | me'aretz | hamerchaq; | uayitanu | 'al | 'arey | yahudah | qoulam. | |
| **Jerusalem** | ***that* watchers** | **come** | **from a country** | **far** | **and give out** | **against** | **the cities of** | **Judah** | **their voice** | |

| כשמרי 8104 | שדי 7704 | היו 1961 | עליה 5921 | מסביב 5439 | כי 3588 | אתי 853 | מרתה 4784 | נאם 5002 | יהוה 3069: | 4:18 |
|---|---|---|---|---|---|---|---|---|---|---|
| kashomarey | saday, | hayu | 'aleyha | misabiyb; | kiy | 'atiy | maratah | na'am | Yahuah. | |
| **As keepers of** | **a field** | **are they** | **against her** | **round about** | **because** | **against me** | **she has been rebellious** | **saith** | **Yahuah** | |

| דרכך 1870 | ומעלליך 4611 | עשו 6213 | אלה 428 | לך 3807a | זאת 2063 | רעתך 7451 | כי 3588 | מר 4751 | כי 3588 |
|---|---|---|---|---|---|---|---|---|---|
| darkek | uama'alalayik, | asou | 'aeleh | lak; | za't | ra'atek | kiy | mar, | kiy |
| **Your way** | **and your doings** | **have procured** | **these *things*** | **unto you** | **this *is*** | **your wickedness** | **because** | **it is bitter** | **because** |

Jer 4:9 and the priests shall be astonished, and the prophets shall wonder.10 Then said I, Ah, Adonai G-D! surely you have greatly deceived this people and Jerusalem, saying, You shall have peace; whereas the sword reacheth unto the soul.11 At that time shall it be said to this people and to Jerusalem, A dry wind of the high places in the wilderness toward the daughter of my people, not to fan, nor to cleanse,12 Even a full wind from those places shall come unto me: now also will I give sentence against them.13 Behold, he shall come up as clouds, and his chariots shall be as a whirlwind: his horses are swifter than eagles. Woe unto us! for we are spoiled.14 O Jerusalem, wash your heart from wickedness, that you may be saved. How long shall your vain thoughts lodge within you?15 For a voice declareth from Dan, and publisheth affliction from mount Ephraim.16 Make you mention to the nations; behold, publish against Jerusalem, that watchers come from a far country, and give out their voice against the cities of Judah.17 As keepers of a field, are they against her round about; because she has been rebellious against me, saith YHUH.18 Thy way and your doings have procured these things unto you; this is your wickedness, because it is bitter, because it reacheth unto your heart.

4:19

נגע 5060 עד 5704 לבך 3820: מעי 4578 מעי 4578 אחולה 2342 קירות 7023 לבי 3820 המה 1993 לי 3807a לבי 3820 לא 3808

naga' 'ad libek. me'ay me'ay 'achulah qiyrout libiy homeh liy libiy la'

**it reached unto your heart My bowels my bowels I am pained very *at* my heart make a noise in me my heart cannot**

4:20

אחריש 2790 כי 3588 קול 6963 שופר 7782 שמעתי 8085 נפשי 5315 תרועת 8643 מלחמה 4421: שבר 7667

'achariysh; kiy qoul shoupar shama'atiy napshiy, taru'at milchamah. sheber

**I hold my peace because the sound of the trumpet you have heard, O my soul the alarm of war Destruction**

4:21

על 5921 שבר 7667 נקרא 7121 כי 3588 שדדה 7703 כל 3605 הארץ 776 פתאם 6597 שדדו 7703 אהלי 168 רגע 7281 יריעתי 3407:

'al sheber niqra', kiy shuddah kal ha'aretz; pit'am shudadu 'ahalay, rega' yariy'atay.

**upon destruction is cried for is spoiled whole the land suddenly spoiled are my tents *in* a moment *and* my curtains**

4:22

עד 5704 מתי 4970 אראה 7200 נס 5251 אשמעה 8085 קול 6963 שופר 7782: כי 3588 אויל 191 עמי 5971 אותי 853 לא 3808

'ad matay 'ar'ah nes; 'ashma'ah qoul shoupar. kiy 'auiyl 'amiy, 'autiy la'

**How long shall I see the standard *and* hear the sound of the trumpet? For *is* foolish my people me not**

ידעו 3045 בנים 1121 סכלים 5530 המה 1992 ולא 3808 נבונים 995 המה 1992 חכמים 2450 המה 1992 להרע 7489

yada'au, baniym sakaliym hemah, uala' nabouniym hemah; chakamiym hemah lahara',

**they have known children *are* sottish they and none have understanding they *are* wise they to do evil**

4:23

ולהיטיב 3190 לא 3808 ידעו 3045: ראיתי 7200 את 853 הארץ 776 והנה 2009 תהו 8414 ובהו 922 ואל 413

ualheytiyb la' yada'au. ra'aytiy 'at ha'aretz, uahineh tohu uabohu; ua'al

**but to do good no they have knowledge I beheld the earth and lo *it was* without form and void and to**

4:24

השמים 8064 ואין 369 אורם 216: ראיתי 7200 ההרים 2022 והנה 2009 רעשים 7493 וכל 3605 הגבעות 1389

hashamayim ua'aeyn 'auram. ra'aytiy heharim, uahineh ro'ashiym; uakal hagaba'aut

**the heavens and they *had* no light I beheld the mountains and lo they trembled and all the hills**

4:25 4:26

התקלקלו 7043: ראיתי 7200 והנה 2009 אין 369 האדם 120 וכל 3605 עוף 5775 השמים 8064 נדדו 5074: ראיתי 7200 והנה 2009

hitqalqalu. ra'aytiy uahineh 'aeyn ha'adam; uakal 'aup hashamayim nadadu. ra'aytiy uahineh

**moved lightly I beheld and lo *there was* no man and all the birds of the heavens were fled I beheld and lo**

הכרמל 3759 המדבר 4057 וכל 3605 עריו 5892 נתצו 5422 מפני 6440 יהוה 3068 מפני 6440 חרון 2740

hakarmel hamidbar; uakal 'arayu, nittzu mipaney Yahuah, mipaney charoun

**the fruitful place *was* a wilderness and all the cities thereof were broken down at the presence of Yahuah *and* by fierce**

4:27 4:28

אפו 639: כי 3588 כה 3541 אמר 559 יהוה 3068 שממה 8077 תהיה 1961 כל 3605 הארץ 776 וכלה 3617 לא 3808 אעשה 6213: על 5921

'apou. kiy koh 'amar Yahuah, shamamah tihayeh kal ha'aretz; uakalah la' 'aaseh. 'al

**his anger For thus has said Yahuah desolate shall be whole The land yet a full end not will I make For**

זאת 2063 תאבל 56 הארץ 776 וקדרו 6937 השמים 8064 ממעל 4605 על 5921 כי 3588 דברתי 1696 זמתי 2161 ולא 3808

za't te'abal ha'aretz, uaqadaru hashamayim mima'al; 'al kiy dibartiy zamotiy, uala'

**this shall mourn the earth and be black the heavens above because that I have spoken *it* I have purposed *it* and not**

4:29

נחמתי 5162 ולא 3808 אשוב 7725 ממנה 4480: מקול 6963 פרש 6571 ורמה 7411 קשת 7198 ברחת 1272 כל 3605

nichamtiy uala' 'ashub mimenah. miqoul parash uaromeh qeshet, borachat kal

**will repent neither will I turn back from it for the noise of the horsemen and bowmen archers shall flee The whole**

Jer 4:19 My bowels, my bowels! I am pained at my very heart; my heart make a noise in me; I cannot hold my peace, because you have heard, O my soul, the sound of the trumpet, the alarm of war.20 Destruction upon destruction is cried; for the whole land is spoiled: suddenly are my tents spoiled, and my curtains in a moment.21 How long shall I see the standard, and hear the sound of the trumpet?22 For my people is foolish, they have not known me; they are sottish children, and they have none understanding: they are wise to do evil, but to do good they have no knowledge.23 I beheld the earth, and, lo, it was without form, and void; and the heavens, and they had no light.24 I beheld the mountains, and, lo, they trembled, and all the hills moved lightly.25 I beheld, and, lo, there was no man, and all the birds of the heavens were fled.26 I beheld, and, lo, the fruitful place was a wilderness, and all the cities thereof were broken down at the presence of YHUH, and by his fierce anger.27 For thus has YHUH said, The whole land shall be desolate; yet will I not make a full end.28 For this shall the earth mourn, and the heavens above be black: because I have spoken it, I have purposed it, and will not repent, neither will I turn back from it.29 The whole city shall flee for the noise of the horsemen and bowmen; they shall go into thickets, and climb up upon the rocks:

| העיר 5892 | באו 935 | בעבים 5645 | ובכפים 3710 | עלו 5927 | כל 3605 | העיר 5892 | עזובה 5800 | ואין 369 | יושב 3427 | בהן 2004 |
|---|---|---|---|---|---|---|---|---|---|---|
| ha'ayr, | ba'au | ba'abiym, | uabakepiym | 'alu; | kal | ha'ayr | 'azubah, | ua'aeyn | yousheb | bahen |
| **city** | **they shall go** | **into thickets** | **and upon the rocks** | **climb up** | **every** | **city** | ***shall be* forsaken** | **and not** | **dwell** | **therein** |

| איש 376: | 4:30 | ואתי 859 | שדוד 7703 | מה 4100 | תעשי 6213 | כי 3588 | תלבשי 3847 | שני 8147 | כי 3588 |
|---|---|---|---|---|---|---|---|---|---|
| 'aysh. | | ua'atiy | shadud | mah | ta'asiy, | kiy | tilbashiy | shaniy | kiy |
| **a man** | | **And *when* you** | ***are* spoiled** | **what** | **will you do?** | **Though** | **you cloth yourself with** | **crimson** | **though** |

| תעדי 5710 | עדי 5716 | זהב 2091 | כי 3588 | תקרעי 7167 | בפוך 6320 | עיניך 5869 | לשוא 7723 |
|---|---|---|---|---|---|---|---|
| ta'adiy | 'adiy | zahab, | kiy | tiqra'ay | bapuk | 'aeynayik, | lashau'a |
| **you deck youself with** | **ornaments of** | **gold** | **though** | **you rentest** | **with painting** | **your face** | **in vain** |

| תתיפי 3302 | מאסו 3988 | בך 871a | עגבים 5689 | נפשך 5315 | יבקשו 1245: | 4:31 | כי 3588 | קול 6963 |
|---|---|---|---|---|---|---|---|---|
| titayapiy; | ma'asu | bak | 'agabiym | napshek | yabaqeshu. | | kiy | qoul |
| **shall you make yourself fair** | **will despise** | **against you** | ***your* lovers** | **your life** | **they will seek** | | **For** | **a voice** |

| כחולה 2470 | שמעתי 8085 | צרה 6869 | כמבכירה 1069 | קול 6963 | בת 1323 |
|---|---|---|---|---|---|
| kachoulah | shama'atiy, | tzarah | kamabakiyrah, | qoul | bat |
| **as of a woman in travail** | **I have heard** | ***and* the anguish** | **as of her that bring forth her first child** | **the voice of** | **the daughter of** |

| ציון 6726 | תתיפח 3306 | תפרש 6566 | כפיה 3709 | אוי 188 | נא 4994 | לי 3807a | כי 3588 | עיפה 5888 | נפשי 5315 |
|---|---|---|---|---|---|---|---|---|---|
| tziyoun | tityapeach | tapares | kapeyha; | 'auy | naa' | liy, | kiy | 'ayapah | napshiy |
| **Zion** | ***that* bewaileth herself** | ***that* spread** | **her hands** | ***saying* Woe** | **now *is*** | **me** | **for** | **is wearied** | **my soul** |

| להרגים 2026: |
|---|
| lahoragiym. |
| **because of murderers** |

| Jer 5:1 | שוטטו 7751 | בחוצות 2351 | ירושלם 3389 | וראו 7200 | נא 4994 | ודעו 3045 | ובקשו 1245 |
|---|---|---|---|---|---|---|---|
| | shouttu | bachutzout | yarushalaim, | uar'au | naa' | uad'au | uabaqshu |
| | **Run you to and fro** | **through the streets of** | **Jerusalem** | **and see** | **now** | **and know** | **and seek** |

| ברחובותיה 7339 | אם 518 | תמצאו 4672 | איש 376 | אם 518 | יש 3426 | עשה 6213 | משפט 4941 | מבקש 1245 | אמונה 530 |
|---|---|---|---|---|---|---|---|---|---|
| birchoutbouteyha, | 'am | timtza'au | 'aysh, | 'am | yesh | 'aseh | mishapat | mabaqesh | 'amunah; |
| **in the broad places thereof** | **if** | **you can find** | **a man** | **if** | **there be** | ***any* that execute** | **judgment** | **that seek** | **the truth** |

| ואסלח 5545 | לה 3807a: | 5:2 | ואם 518 | חי 2416 | יהוה 3068 | יאמרו 559 | לכן 3651 | לשקר 8267 | ישבעו 7650: | 5:3 | יהוה 3068 | עיניך 5869 |
|---|---|---|---|---|---|---|---|---|---|---|---|---|
| ua'aslach | lah. | | ua'am | chay | Yahuah | ya'meru; | laken | lasheqer | yishabe'au. | | Yahuah | 'aeyneyka |
| **and I will pardon** | **it** | | **And though** | **live** | **Yahuah** | **they say** | **surely** | **falsely** | **they swear** | | **O Yahuah** | **your eyes** |

| הלוא 3808 | לאמונה 530 | הכיתה 5221 | אתם 859 | ולא 3808 | חלו 2342 | כליתם 3615 | מאנו 3985 |
|---|---|---|---|---|---|---|---|
| halou'a | le'amunah | hikiytah | 'atam | uala' | chalu, | kiliytam | me'anu |
| ***are* not** | **upon the truth?** | **you have struck** | **them** | **but not** | **they have grieved** | **you have consumed them** | ***but* they have refused** |

| קחת 3947 | מוסר 4148 | חזקו 2388 | פניהם 6440 | מסלע 5553 | מאנו 3985 | לשוב 7725: | 5:4 | ואני 589 | אמרתי 559 |
|---|---|---|---|---|---|---|---|---|---|
| qachat | musar; | chizqu | paneyhem | misela', | me'anu | lashub. | | ua'aniy | 'amartiy, |
| **to receive** | **correction** | **they have made harder** | **their faces** | **than a rock** | **they have refused** | **to return** | | **Therefore I** | **said** |

Jer 4:29 every city shall be forsaken, and not a man dwell therein.30 And when you are spoiled, what will you do? Though you clothest thyself with crimson, though you deckest you with ornaments of gold, though you rentest your face with painting, in vain shall you make thyself fair; your lovers will despise you, they will seek your life.31 For I have heard a voice as of a woman in travail, and the anguish as of her that bring forth her first child, the voice of the daughter of Zion, that bewaileth herself, that spreadeth her hands, saying, Woe is me now! for my soul is wearied because of murderers. **Jer** 5:1 Run you to and fro through the streets of Jerusalem, and see now, and know, and seek in the broad places thereof, if you can find a man, if there be any that executeth judgment, that seek the truth; and I will pardon it.2 And though they say, YHUH live; surely they swear falsely.3 O YHUH, are not your eyes upon the truth? you have stricken them, but they have not grieved; you have consumed them, but they have refused to receive correction: they have made their faces harder than a rock; they have refused to return.4 Therefore I said, Surely these are poor; they are foolish: for they know not the way of YHUH, nor the judgment of their G-d.

5:5
אך 389 דלים 1800 הם 1992 נואלו 2973 כי 3588 לא 3808 ידעו 3045 דרך 1870 יהוה 3068 משפט 4941 אלהיהם 430:
'ak daliym hem; nou'alu kiy la' yada'au derek Yahuah, mishapat 'aloheyhem.
**Surely *are* poor these they are foolish for not they know the way of Yahuah *nor* the judgment of their Elohim**

אלכה 1980 לי 3807a אל 413 הגדלים 1419 ואדברה 1696 אותם 853 כי 3588 המה 1992 ידעו 3045 דרך 1870 יהוה 3068
'aelakah liy 'al hagadoliym ua'adabarah 'autam, kiy hemah, yada'au derek Yahuah,
**I will get me unto the great men and will speak unto them for they have known the way of Yahuah**

5:6
משפט 4941 אלהיהם 430 אך 389 המה 1992 יחדו 3162 שברו 7665 על 5923 נתקו 5423 מוסרות 4147: על 5921 כן 3651
mishapat 'aloheyhem; 'ak hemah yachdau shabaru 'al, nitqu mouserout. 'al ken
***and* the judgment of their Elohim but these altogether have broken the yoke *and* burst the bonds Wherefore after**

הכם 5221 אריה 738 מיער 3293 זאב 2061 ערבות 6160 ישדדם 7703 נמר 5246 שקד 8245 על 5921 עריהם 5892
hikam 'aryeh miya'ar, za'aeb arabout yashadadem, namer shoqed 'al 'areyhem,
**shall slay them a lion out of the forest *and* a wolf of the evenings shall spoil them a leopard shall watch over their cities**

כל 3605 היוצא 3318 מהנה 2007 יטרף 2963 כי 3588 רבו 7231 פשעיהם 6588 עצמו 6105
kal hayoutzea' mehenah yitarep; kiy rabu pish'aeyhem, 'atzamu
**every one that goes out there shallbe torn in pieces because are many their transgressions are increased**

5:7
משבותיהם 4878 אי 335 לזאת 2063 אסלוח 5545 לך 3807a בניך 1121 עזבוני 5800 וישבעו 7650 בלא 3808
meshubouteyhem 'ay laza't 'aslouch lak, banayik 'azabuniy, uayishaba'au bala'
**their backsliding How for this? shall I pardon to you your children have forsaken me and sworn by *them that are* no**

אלהים 430 ואשבע 7650 אותם 853 וינאפו 5003 ובית 1004 זונה 2181
'alohiym; ua'asbia' 'autam uayin'apu, uabeyt zounah
**gods when I had fed to the full them they then committed adultery and houses *in the* harlots'**

5:8
יתגדדו 1413: סוסים 5483 מיזנים 2109 משכים 7904 היו 1961 איש 376 אל 413 אשת 802 רעהו 7453
yitgodadu. susiym mayuzaniym mashkiym hayu; 'aysh 'al 'aeshet re'aehu
**assembled themselves by troops horses *as* fed in the morning They were every one after wife his neighbour's**

5:9
יצהלו 6670: העל 5921 אלה 428 לוא 3808 אפקד 6485 נאם 5002 יהוה 3068 ואם 518 בגוי 1471 אשר 834 כזה 2088 לא 3808
yitzhalu. ha'al 'aeleh lua' 'apqod na'am Yahuah; ua'am bagouy 'asher kazeh, la'
**neighed for these *things*? not Shall I visit saith Yahuah and on a nation such as this? not**

5:10
תתנקם 5358 נפשי 5315: עלו 5927 בשרותיה 8284 ושחתו 7843 וכלה 3617 אל 408 תעשו 6213 הסירו 5493 נטישותיה 5189
titnaqem napshiy. 'alu basharouteyha uashachetu, uakalah 'al ta'asu; hasiyru natiyshouteyha,
**shall be avenged my soul Go you up upon her walls and destroy but a full end not make take away her battlements**

5:11
כי 3588 לוא 3808 ליהוה 3068 המה 1992: כי 3588 בגוד 898 בגדו 898 בי 871a בית 1004 ישראל 3478
kiy lua' laYahuah hemah. kiy bagoud bagadu biy, beyt yisra'ael
**for not for Yahuah's they *are* For have dealt very treacherously against me the house of Israel**

5:12
ובית 1004 יהודה 3063 נאם 5002 יהוה 3068: כחשו 3584 ביהוה 3068 ויאמרו 559 לא 3808 הוא 1931 ולא 3808 תבוא 935
uabeyt yahudah na'am Yahuah. kichashu baYahuah, uaya'maru la' hua'; uala' tabou'a
**and the house of Judah saith Yahuah They have belied Yahuah and said *It is* not he neither come**

Jer 5:5 I will get me unto the great men, and will speak unto them; for they have known the way of YHUH, and the judgment of their G-d: but these have altogether broken the yoke, and burst the bonds.6 Wherefore a lion out of the forest shall slay them, and a wolf of the evenings shall spoil them, a leopard shall watch over their cities: everyone that go out thence shall be torn in pieces: because their transgressions are many, and their backslidings are increased.7 How shall I pardon you for this? your children have forsaken me, and sworn by them that are no gods: when I had fed them to the full, they then committed adultery, and assembled themselves by troops in the harlots' houses.8 They were as fed horses in the morning: everyone neighed after his neighbor's wife.9 Shall I not visit for these things? saith YHUH: and shall not my soul be avenged on such a nation as this?10 Go you up upon her walls, and destroy; but make not a full end: take away her battlements; for they are not YHUH's.11 For the house of Israel and the house of Judah have dealt very treacherously against me, saith YHUH.12 They have belied YHUH, and said, It is not he; neither shall evil come upon us; neither shall we see sword nor famine:

5:13

עלינו 5921 | רעה 7451 | וחרב 2719 | ורעב 7458 | לוא 3808 | נראה 7200: | והנביאים 5030 | יהיו 1961 | לרוח 7307 | והדבר 1696
'aleynu | ra'ah, | uachereb | uara'ab | lua' | nir'ah. | uahanabiy'aym | yihayu | laruach, | uahadiber
**upon us | shall evil | sword | nor famine | neither | shall we see | And the prophets | shall become | wind | and the word *is***

5:14

אין 369 | בהם 871a | כה 3541 | יעשה 6213 | להם 3807a: | לכן 3651 | כה 3541 | אמר 559 | יהוה 3068 | אלהי 430 | צבאות 6635 | יען 3282 | דברכם 1696
'aeyn | bahem; | koh | ye'aseh | lahem. | laken, | koh | 'amar | Yahuah | 'alohey | tzaba'aut, | ya'an | daberkem,
**not | in them | thus | shall it be done | unto them | Wherefore | thus | saith | Yahuah | Elohim | of hosts | Because | you speak**

את 853 | הדבר 1697 | הזה 2088 | הנני 2005 | נתן 5414 | דברי 1697 | בפיך 6310 | לאש 784 | והעם 5971 | הזה 2088 | עצים 6086
'at | hadabar | hazeh; | hinniy | noten | dabaray | bapiyka | la'aesh, | uaha'am | hazeh | 'aetziym
**| word | this | behold | I will make | my words | in your mouth | fire | and people | this | wood**

5:15

ואכלתם 398: | הנני 2005 | מביא 935 | עליכם 5921 | גוי 1471 | ממרחק 4801 | בית 1004 | ישראל 3478 | נאם 5002 | יהוה 3068
ua'akalatam. | hinniy | mebiy'a | 'aleykem | gouy | mimerchaq | beyt | yisra'ael | na'am | Yahuah;
**and it shall devour them | Lo, I | will bring | upon you | a nation | from far | O house of | Israel | saith | Yahuah**

גוי 1471 | איתן 386 | הוא 1931 | גוי 1471 | מעולם 5769 | הוא 1931 | גוי 1471 | לא 3808 | תדע 3045 | לשנו 3956 | ולא 3808 | תשמע 8085 | מה 4100
gouy | 'aeytan | hua', | gouy | me'aulam | hua', | gouy | la' | teda' | lashonou, | uala' | tishma' | mah
***is* a nation | mighty | it *is* | an nation | ancient | it | a nation | not | you know | whose language | neither | understand | what**

5:16 5:17

ידבר 1696: | אשפתו 827 | כקבר 6913 | פתוח 6605 | כלם 3605 | גבורים 1368: | ואכל 398 | קצירך 7105
yadaber. | 'ashpatou | kaqeber | patuach; | kulam | gibouriym. | ua'akal | qatziyraka
**they say | Their quiver *is* | as an sepulchre | open | they *are* all | mighty men | And they shall eat up | your harvest**

ולחמך 3899 | יאכלו 398 | בניך 1121 | ובנותיך 1323 | יאכל 398 | צאנך 6629 | ובקרך 1241
ualachmeka, | ya'kalu | baneyka | uabnouteyka, | ya'kal | tza'naka | uabqareka,
**and your bread | should eat | *which* your sons | and your daughters | they shall eat up | your flocks | and your herds**

יאכל 398 | גפנך 1612 | ותאנתך 8384 | ירשש 7567 | ערי 5892 | מבצריך 4013 | אשר 834 | אתה 859 | בוטח 982 | בהנה 2007
ya'kal | gapnaka | uat'aenateka; | yaroshesh | 'arey | mibtzareyka, | 'asher | 'atah | bouteach | bahenah
**they shall eat up | your vines | and your fig trees | they shall impoverish | cities | your fenced | wherein | you | trust | in them**

5:18 5:19

בחרב 2719: | וגם 1571 | בימים 3117 | ההמה 1992 | נאם 5002 | יהוה 3068 | לא 3808 | אעשה 6213 | אתכם 854 | כלה 3617:
bechareb. | ua'gam | bayamiym | hahemah | na'am | Yahuah; | la' | 'aaseh | 'atakem | kalah.
**with the sword | Nevertheless | in days | those | saith | Yahuah | not | I will make | with you | a full end**

והיה 1961 | כי 3588 | תאמרו 559 | תחת 8478 | מה 4100 | עשה 6213 | יהוה 3068 | אלהינו 430 | לנו 3807a | את 853 | כל 3605 | אלה 428
uahayah | kiy | ta'maru, | tachat | meh, | 'asah | Yahuah | 'aloheynu | lanu | 'at | kal | 'aeleh;
**And it shall come to pass | when | you shall say | for | where | does | Yahuah | our Elohim | *things* unto us? | | all | these**

ואמרת 559 | אליהם 413 | כאשר 834 | עזבתם 5800 | אותי 853 | ותעבדו 5647 | אלהי 430 | נכר 5236 | בארצכם 776 | כן 3651
ua'amarta | 'aleyhem, | ka'asher | 'azabtem | 'autiy | uata'abdu | 'alohey | nekar | ba'artzakem, | ken
**then shall you answer | them | Like as | you have forsaken | me | and served | gods | strange | in your land | so**

5:20

תעבדו 5647 | זרים 2114 | בארץ 776 | לא 3808 | לכם 3807a: | הגידו 5046 | זאת 2063 | בבית 1004 | יעקב 3290 | והשמיעוה 8085
ta'abdu | zariym, | ba'aretz | la' | lakem. | hagiydu | za't | babeyt | ya'aqob; | uahashamiy'uaha
**shall you serve | strangers | in a land *that is* | not | to yours | Declare | this | in the house of | Jacob | and publish it**

Jer 5:13 And the prophets shall become wind, and the word is not in them: thus shall it be done unto them.14 Wherefore thus saith YHUH G-d of hosts, Because you speak this word, behold, I will make my words in your mouth fire, and this people wood, and it shall devour them.15 Lo, I will bring a nation upon you from far, O house of Israel, saith YHUH: it is a mighty nation, it is an ancient nation, a nation whose language you know not, neither understandest what they say.16 Their quiver is as an open sepulcher, they are all mighty men.17 And they shall eat up your harvest, and your bread, which your sons and your daughters should eat: they shall eat up your flocks and your herds: they shall eat up your vines and your fig trees: they shall impoverish your fenced cities, wherein you trustedst, with the sword.18 Nevertheless in those days, saith YHUH, I will not make a full end with you.19 And it shall come to pass, when you shall say, Wherefore doeth YHUH our G-d all these things unto us? then shall you answer them, Like as you have forsaken me, and served strange gods in your land, so shall you serve strangers in a land that is not yours.20 Declare this in the house of Jacob, and publish it in Judah, saying,

ביהודה 3063 לאמר 559: 5:21 שמעו 8085 נא 4994 זאת 2063 עם 5971 סכל 5530 ואין 369 לב 3820 עינים 5869 להם 3807a ולא 3808
biyahudah lea'mor. shim'au naa' za't, 'am sakal ua'aeyn leb; 'aeynayim lahem uala'
**in Judah saying Hear now this people O foolish and without understanding eyes which have and not**

יראו 7200 אזנים 241 להם 3807a ולא 3808 ישמעו 8085: 5:22 האותי 853 לא 3808 תיראו 3372 נאם 5002 יהוה 3068 אם 518 מפני 6440 לא 3808
yir'au, 'azanayim lahem uala' yishma'au. ha'autiy la' tiyra'au na'am Yahuah 'am mipanay la'
**see ears which have and not hear me? not Fear you saith Yahuah if at my presence not**

תחילו 2342 אשר 834 שמתי 7760 חול 2344 גבול 1366 לים 3220 חק 2706 עולם 5769 ולא 3808 יעברנהו 5674
tachiylu, 'asher samtiy choul gabul layam, chaq 'aulam uala' ya'abrenhu;
**will you tremble which have placed the sand *for* the bound of the sea *by* a decree perpetual that not can pass it**

ויתגעשו 1607 ולא 3808 יוכלו 3201 והמו 1993 גליו 1530 ולא 3808
uayitga'ashu uala' yukalu, uahamu galayu uala'
**and thereof toss themselves yet not can they prevail though they roar though the waves and not**

יעברנהו 5674: 5:23 ולעם 5971 הזה 2088 היה 1961 לב 3820 סורר 5637 ומורה 4784 סרו 5493 5:24 וילכו 1980:
ya'abrunhu. uala'am hazeh hayah, leb sourer uamoureh; saru uayeleku.
**yet can they pass over it? But people this has a heart revolting and a rebellious they are revolted and gone**

ולא 3808 אמרו 559 בלבבם 3824 נירא 3372 נא 4994 את 853 יהוה 3068 אלהינו 430 הנתן 5414 גשם 1653 וירה 3138 ומלקוש 4456
uala' 'amaru bilbabam, niyra' naa' 'at Yahuah 'aloheynu, hanoten, geshem uayoreh uamalqoush
**Neither say they in their heart Let us fear now Yahuah our Elohim that gives rain *both* the former and the latter**

בעתו 6256 שבעות 7620 חקות 2708 קציר 7105 ישמר 8104 לנו 3807a: 5:25 עונותיכם 5771 הטו 5186 אלה 428
ba'atou; shabu'aut chuqout qatziyr yishmor lanu. auonouteykem hitu 'aeleh;
**in his season weeks of *the* appointed the harvest he reserve unto us Your iniquities have turned away these *things***

וחטאותיכם 2403 מנעו 4513 הטוב 2896 מכם 4480: 5:26 כי 3588 נמצאו 4672 בעמי 5971 רשעים 7563 ישור 7789
uachata'uteykem, mana'au hatoub mikem. kiy nimtza'au ua'amiy rasha'aym; yashur
**and your sins have withholden good *things* from you For are found among my people wicked *men* they lay wait**

כשך 7918 יקושים 3353 הציבו 5324 משחית 4889 אנשים 582 ילכדו 3920: 5:27 ככלוב 3619 מלא 4392 עוף 5775 כן 3651 בתיהם 1004
kashak yaqushiym, hitziybu mashchiyt 'anashiym yilkodu. kikalub malea' 'aup, ken bateyhem
**as he that sets snares they set a trap men they catch As a cage is full of birds so *are* their houses**

מלאים 4392 מרמה 4820 על 5921 כן 3651 גדלו 1431 ויעשירו 6238: 5:28 שמנו 8080 עשתו 6245 גם 1571
male'aym mirmah; 'al ken gadalu uaiya'ashiyru. shamanu 'ashatu, gam
**full of deceit therefore so they are become great and waxen rich They are waxen fat they shine yea**

עברו 5674 דברי 1697 רע 7451 דין 1779 לא 3808 דנו 1777 דין 1779 יתום 3490 ויצליחו 6743
'abaru dibrey ra', diyn la' danu, diyn yatoum uayatzliychu;
**they overpass the deeds of the wicked the cause not they judge the cause of the fatherless yet they prosper**

ומשפט 4941 אביונים 34 לא 3808 שפטו 8199: 5:29 העל 5921 אלה 428 לא 3808 אפקד 6485 נאם 5002 יהוה 3068 אם 518 בגוי 1471
uamishpat 'abyouniym la' shapatu. ha'al 'aeleh la' 'apqod na'am Yahuah; 'am bagouy
**and the right of the needy not do they judge for these *things*? not Shall I visit saith Yahuah on a nation**

Jer 5:21 Hear now this, O foolish people, and without understanding; which have eyes, and see not; which have ears, and hear not:22 Fear you not me? saith YHUH: will you not tremble at my presence, which have placed the sand for the bound of the sea by a perpetual decree, that it cannot pass it: and though the waves thereof toss themselves, yet can they not prevail; though they roar, yet can they not pass over it?23 But this people has a revolting and a rebellious heart; they are revolted and gone.24 Neither say they in their heart, Let us now fear YHUH our G-d, that give rain, both the former and the latter, in his season: he reserveth unto us the appointed weeks of the harvest.25 Your iniquities have turned away these things, and your sins have withholden good things from you.26 For among my people are found wicked men: they lay wait, as he that set snares; they set a trap, they catch men.27 As a cage is full of birds, so are their houses full of deceit: therefore they are become great, and waxen rich.28 They are waxen fat, they shine: yea, they overpass the deeds of the wicked: they judge not the cause, the cause of the fatherless, yet they prosper; and the right of the needy do they not judge.29 Shall I not visit for these things? saith YHUH: shall not my soul be avenged on such a nation as this?

5:30 … 5:31

אשר 834 כזה 2088 לא 3808 תתנקם 5358 נפשי 5315: שמה 8047 ושערורה 8186 נהיתה 1961 בארץ 776:
'asher kazeh, la' titnaqem napshiy. shamah uasha'arurah, nihyatah ba'aretz.
**such as this? not shall be avenged my soul A wonderful and horrible thing is committed in the land**

הנביאים 5030 נבאו 5012 בשקר 8267 והכהנים 3548 ירדו 7287 על 5921 ידיהם 3027 ועמי 5971 אהבו 157 כן 3651 ומה 4100
hanabiy'aym niba'au basheqer, uahakohaniym yirdu 'al yadeyhem, ua'amiy 'ahabu ken; uamah
**The prophets prophesy falsely and the priests bear rule by their means and my people love *to have it* so and what**

תעשו 6213 לאחריתה 319:
ta'asu la'achariytah.
**will you do in the end thereof?**

**Jer 6:1**
העזו 5756 בני 1121 בנימן 1144 מקרב 7130 ירושלם 3389 ובתקוע 8620 תקעו 8628
ha'azu baney binyamin, miqereb yarushalaim, uabitqoua' tiq'au
**gather yourselves to flee O you children of Benjamin out of the midst of Jerusalem and in Tekoa blow**

שופר 7782 ועל 5921 בית 1021 הכרם 3754 שאו 5375 משאת 4864 כי 3588 רעה 7451 נשקפה 8259 מצפון 6828 ושבר 7667
shoupar, ua'al beyt hakerem sa'au mas'aet; kiy ra'ah nishqapah mitzapoun uasheber
**the trumpet and in Beth haccerem set up a sign of fire for evil appear out of the north and destruction**

6:2 … 6:3

גדול 1419: הנוה 5116 והמענגה 6026 דמיתי 1819 בת 1323 ציון 6726: אליה 413 יבאו 935 רעים 7462
gadoul. hanauah uahama'unagah, damiytiy bat tziyoun. 'aeleyha yabo'au ro'aym
**great *a* comely and delicate *woman* I have likened to *the* daughter of Zion unto her shall come The shepherds**

6:4

ועדריהם 5739 תקעו 8628 עליה 5921 אהלים 168 סביב 5439 רעו 7462 איש 376 את 853 ידו 3027:
ua'adreyhem; taqa'au 'aleyha 'ahaliym sabiyb, ra'au 'aysh 'at yadou.
**with their flocks they shall pitch against her *their* tents round about they shall feed every one *in* his place**

קדשו 6942 עליה 5921 מלחמה 4421 קומו 6965 ונעלה 5927 בצהרים 6672 אוי 188 לנו 3807a כי 3588 פנה 6437 היום 3117 כי 3588
qadashu 'aleyha milchamah, qumu uana'aleh batzaharayim; 'auy lanu kiy panah hayoum, kiy
**Prepare you against her war arise and let us go up at noon Woe unto us for goes away the day for**

6:5 … 6:6

ינטו 5186 צללי 6752 ערב 6153: קומו 6965 ונעלה 5927 בלילה 3915 ונשחיתה 7843 ארמנותיה 759: כי 3588
yinatu tzilaley 'areb. qumu uana'aleh balayalah, uanashchiytah armanouteyha. kiy
**are stretched out the shadows of the evening Arise and let us go by night and let us destroy her palaces For**

כה 3541 אמר 559 יהוה 3068 צבאות 6635 כרתו 3772 עצה 6097 ושפכו 8210 על 5921 ירושלם 3389 סללה 5550 היא 1931 העיר 5892 הפקד 6485
koh 'amar Yahuah tzaba'aut, kirtu 'aetzah, uashipku 'al yarushalaim solalah; hiy'a ha'ayr hapaqad,
**thus has said Yahuah of hosts Hew you down trees and cast against Jerusalem a mount this *is* the city to be visited**

6:7

כלה 3605 עשק 6233 בקרבה 7130: כהקיר 6979 בור 953 מימיה 4325 כן 3651 הקרה 6979 רעתה 7451 חמס 2555
kulah 'asheq baqirbah. kahaqiyr beuer meymeyha, ken heqerah ra'atah; chamas
**she *is* wholly oppression in the midst of her As cast out a fountain her waters so she cast out her wickedness violence**

6:8

ושד 7701 ישמע 8085 בה 871a על 5921 פני 6440 תמיד 8548 חלי 2483 ומכה 4347: הוסרי 3256 ירושלם 3389 פן 6435 תקע 3363
uashod yishama' bah 'al panay tamiyd chaliy uamakah. hiuasariy yarushalaim, pen teqa'
**and spoil is heard in her before me continually *is* grief and wounds Be you instructed O Jerusalem lest depart**

Jer 5:30 A wonderful and horrible thing is committed in the land;31 The prophets prophesy falsely, and the priests bear rule by their means; and my people love to have it so: and what will you do in the end thereof? **Jer** 6:1 O you children of Benjamin, gather yourselves to flee out of the midst of Jerusalem, and blow the trumpet in Tekoa, and set up a sign of fire in Beth-haccerem: for evil appeareth out of the north, and great destruction.2 I have likened the daughter of Zion to a comely and delicate woman.3 The shepherds with their flocks shall come unto her; they shall pitch their tents against her round about; they shall feed everyone in his place.4 Prepare you war against her; arise, and let us go up at noon. Woe unto us! for the day go away, for the shadows of the evening are stretched out.5 Arise, and let us go by night, and let us destroy her palaces.6 For thus has YHUH of hosts said, Hew you down trees, and cast a mount against Jerusalem: this is the city to be visited; she is wholly oppression in the midst of her.7 As a fountain casteth out her waters, so she casteth out her wickedness: violence and spoil is heard in her; before me continually is grief and wounds.8 Be you instructed, O Jerusalem, lest my soul depart from you; lest I make you desolate, a land not inhabited.

6:9
נפשי 5315 ממך 4480 פן 6435 אשימך 7760 שממה 8077 ארץ 776 לוא 3808 נושבה 3427: כה 3541 אמר 559 יהוה 3068 צבאות 6635
napshiy mimek; pen 'asiymek shamamah, 'aretz lua' noushabah. koh 'amar Yahuah tzaba'aut,
**my soul from you lest I make you desolate a land not inhabited Thus saith Yahuah of hosts**

עולל 5953 יעוללו 5953 כגפן 1612 שארית 7611 ישראל 3478 השב 7725 ידך 3027 כבוצר 1219 על 5921
'aulel ya'aulalu kagepen sha'aeriyt yisra'ael; hasheb yadaka, kaboutzer 'al
**They shall throughly glean as a vine the remnant of Israel turn back your hand as a grapegatherer into**

6:10
סלסלות 5552: על 5921 מי 4310 אדברה 1696 ואעידה 5749 וישמעו 8085 הנה 2009 ערלה 6189 אזנם 241 ולא 3808
salsilout. 'al miy' 'adabrah ua'a'aydah uayishma'u, hineh 'arlah 'azanam, uala'
**the baskets To whom shall I speak and give warning that they may hear? behold *is* uncircumcised their ear and not**

6:11
יוכלו 3201 להקשיב 7181 הנה 2009 דבר 1697 יהוה 3068 היה 1961 להם 3807a לחרפה 2781 לא 3808 יחפצו 2654 בו 871a:
yukalu lahaqshiyb; hineh dabar Yahuah hayah lahem lacherpah la' yachpetzu bou.
**can they listen behold the word of Yahuah is unto them a reproach no they have delight in it**

ואת 854 חמת 2534 יהוה 3068 מלאתי 4392 נלאיתי 3811 הכיל 3557 שפך 8210 על 5921 עולל 5768 בחוץ 2351
ua'at chamat Yahuah malea'tiy nil'aeytiy hakiyl, shapok 'al 'aulal bachutz,
***Therefore with* the fury of Yahuah I am full of I am weary holding in I will pour it out upon the children abroad**

ועל 5921 סוד 5475 בחורים 970 יחדו 3162 כי 3588 גם 1571 איש 376 עם 5973 אשה 802 ילכדו 3920 זקן 2205 עם 5973
ua'al coud bachuriym yachdau; kiy gam 'aysh 'am 'ashah yilakedu, zaqen 'am
**and upon the assembly of young men together for even the husband with the wife shall be taken the aged with**

6:12
מלא 4390 ימים 3117: ונסבו 5437 בתיהם 1004 לאחרים 312 שדות 7704 ונשים 802 יחדו 3162 כי 3588
malea' yamiym. uanasabu bateyhem la'acheriym, sadout uanashiym yachdau; kiy
***him that is* full of days And shall be turned their houses unto others *with* their fields and wives together for**

6:13
אטה 5186 את 853 ידי 3027 על 5921 ישבי 3427 הארץ 776 נאם 5002 יהוה 3068: כי 3588 מקטנם 6996
'ateh 'at yadiy 'al yoshabey ha'aretz na'am Yahuah. kiy miqtanam
**I will stretch out my hand upon the inhabitants of the land saith Yahuah For from the least of them**

ועד 5704 גדולם 1419 כלו 3605 בוצע 1214 בצע 1215 ומנביא 5030 ועד 5704 כהן 3548 כלו 3605
ua'ad gadoulam, kulou boutzea' batza'; uaminabiy'a ua'ad kohen, kulou
**even unto the greatest of them every one *is* given to covetousness and from the prophet even unto the priest every one**

6:14
עשה 6213 שקר 8267: וירפאו 7495 את 853 שבר 7667 עמי 5971 על 5921 נקלה 7043 לאמר 559 שלום 7965
'asheh shaqer. uayarap'au 'at sheber 'amiy 'al naqalah, lea'mor shaloum
**deal falsely They have healed also the hurt *of the daughter* of my people on slightly saying Peace**

6:15
שלום 7965 ואין 369 שלום 7965: הבישו 3001 כי 3588 תועבה 8441 עשו 6213 גם 1571 בוש 954
shaloum; ua'aeyn shaloum. hobiyshu kiy tou'aebah 'asu; gam boush
**peace when *there is* no peace Were they ashamed when abomination? they had committed nay they were at all**

לא 3808 יבושו 954 גם 1571 הכלים 3637 לא 3808 ידעו 3045 לכן 3651 יפלו 5307 בנפלים 5307 בעת 6256
la' yeboushu, gam hakaliym la' yada'au, laken yiplu banopaliym ba'aet
**neither ashamed even blush not could they therefore they shall fall among them that fall at the time**

Jer 6:9 Thus saith YHUH of hosts, They shall throughly glean the remnant of Israel as a vine: turn back your hand as a grapegatherer into the baskets.10 To whom shall I speak, and give warning, that they may hear? behold, their ear is uncircumcised, and they cannot hear: behold, the word of YHUH is unto them a reproach; they have no delight in it.11 Therefore I am full of the fury of YHUH; I am weary with holding in: I will pour it out upon the children abroad, and upon the assembly of young men together: for even the husband with the wife shall be taken, the aged with him that is full of days.12 And their houses shall be turned unto others, with their fields and wives together: for I will stretch out my hand upon the inhabitants of the land, saith YHUH.13 For from the least of them even unto the greatest of them everyone is given to covetousness; and from the prophet even unto the priest everyone deal falsely.14 They have healed also the hurt of the daughter of my people slightly, saying, Peace, peace; when there is no peace.15 Were they ashamed when they had committed abomination? nay, they were not at all ashamed, neither could they blush: therefore they shall fall among them that fall: at the time that I visit them they shall be cast down, saith YHUH.

| פקדתים 6485 | יכשלו 3782 | אמר 559 | יהוה 3068: | 6:16 | כה 3541 | אמר 559 | יהוה 3068 | עמדו 5975 | על 5921 | דרכים 1870 | וראו 7200 |
|---|---|---|---|---|---|---|---|---|---|---|---|
| paqadtiym | yikashalu | 'amar | Yahuah. | | koh | 'amar | Yahuah | 'amadu | 'al | darakiym | uar'au |
| ***that* I visit them** | **they shall be cast down** | **saith** | **Yahuah** | | **Thus** | **saith** | **Yahuah** | **Stand you** | **in** | **the ways** | **and see** |

| ושאלו 7592 | לנתבות 5410 | עולם 5769 | אי 335 | זה 2088 | דרך 1870 | הטוב 2896 | ולכו 1980 | בה 871a | ומצאו 4672 | מרגוע 4771 | לנפשכם 5315 |
|---|---|---|---|---|---|---|---|---|---|---|---|
| uasha'alu | lintibout | 'aulam, | 'aey | zeh | derek | hatoub | ualku | bah, | uamitza'au | margoua' | lanapshakem; |
| **and ask** | **for paths** | ***the* old** | **where** | **this** | **way** | ***is* the good** | **and walk** | **therein** | **and you shall find** | **rest** | **for your souls** |

| ויאמרו 559 | לא 3808 | נלך 1980: | 6:17 | והקמתי 6965 | עליכם 5921 | צפים 6822 | הקשיבו 7181 | לקול 6963 | שופר 7782 |
|---|---|---|---|---|---|---|---|---|---|
| uaya'maru | la' | nelek. | | uahaqimotiy | 'aleykem | tzopiym, | haqashiybu | laqoul | shoupar; |
| **But they said therein** | **not** | **We will walk** | | **Also I set** | **over you** | **watchmen** | ***saying* Hearken** | **to the sound of** | **the trumpet** |

| ויאמרו 559 | לא 3808 | נקשיב 7181: | 6:18 | לכן 3651 | שמעו 8085 | הגוים 1471 | ודעי 3045 | עדה 5712 | את 853 | אשר 834 |
|---|---|---|---|---|---|---|---|---|---|---|
| uaya'maru | la' | naqshiyb. | | laken | shim'au | hagouyim; | uda'ay | 'aedah | 'at | 'asher |
| **But they said** | **not** | **We will listen** | | **Therefore** | **hear** | **you nations** | **and know** | **O congregation** | | **what *is*** |

| בם 871a: | 6:19 | שמעי 8085 | הארץ 776 | הנה 2009 | אנכי 595 | מביא 935 | רעה 7451 | אל 413 | העם 5971 | הזה 2088 | פרי 6529 |
|---|---|---|---|---|---|---|---|---|---|---|---|
| bam. | | shim'ay | ha'aretz, | hineh | 'anokiy | mebiy'a | ra'ah | 'al | ha'am | hazeh | pariy |
| **among them** | | **Hear** | **O earth** | **behold** | **I** | **will bring** | **evil** | **upon** | **the people** | **this** | ***even* the fruit of** |

| מחשבותם 4284 | כי 3588 | על 5921 | דברי 1697 | לא 3808 | הקשיבו 7181 | ותורתי 8451 | וימאסו 3988 | בה 871a: | 6:20 |
|---|---|---|---|---|---|---|---|---|---|
| machshaboutam; | kiy | 'al | dabaray | la' | hiqshiybu, | uatouratiy | uayim'asu | bah. | |
| **their thoughts** | **because** | **unto** | **my words** | **not** | **they have hearkened** | **nor to my law** | **but rejected** | **it** | |

| למה 4100 | זה 2088 | לי 3807a | לבונה 3828 | משבא 7614 | תבוא 935 | וקנה 7070 | הטוב 2896 | מארץ 776 | מרחק 7801 |
|---|---|---|---|---|---|---|---|---|---|
| lamah | zeh | liy | labounah | mishaba' | tabou'a, | uaqaneh | hatoub | me'aretz | merchaq; |
| **To what purpose** | **there** | **to me** | **incense** | **from Sheba** | **comes** | **and cane** | **the sweet** | **from a country?** | **far** |

| עלותיכם 5930 | לא 3808 | לרצון 7522 | וזבחיכם 2077 | לא 3808 | ערבו 6149 | לי 3807a: | 6:21 | לכן 3651 | כה 3541 | אמר 559 | יהוה 3068 |
|---|---|---|---|---|---|---|---|---|---|---|---|
| 'alouteykem | la' | laratzoun, | uazibcheykem | la' | 'arabu | liy. | | laken, | koh | 'amar | Yahuah, |
| **your burnt offerings** | ***are* not** | **acceptable** | **your sacrifices** | **nor** | **sweet** | **unto me** | | **Therefore** | **thus** | **saith** | **Yahuah** |

| הנני 2005 | נתן 5414 | אל 413 | העם 5971 | הזה 2088 | מכשלים 4383 | וכשלו 3782 | בם 871a | אבות 1 | ובנים 1121 | יחדו 3162 |
|---|---|---|---|---|---|---|---|---|---|---|
| hinniy | noten | 'al | ha'am | hazeh | mikasholiym; | uakashlu | bam | about | uabaniym | yachdau |
| **Behold I** | **will lay** | **before** | **the people** | **this** | **stumblingblocks** | **and shall fall** | **upon them** | **the fathers** | **and the sons** | **together** |

| שכן 7934 | ורעו 7453 | יאבדו 6 | 6:22 | כה 3541 | אמר 559 | יהוה 3068 | הנה 2009 | עם 5971 | בא 935 | מארץ 776 | צפון 6828 |
|---|---|---|---|---|---|---|---|---|---|---|---|
| shaken | uarea'au | yabadu | | koh | 'amar | Yahuah, | hineh | 'am | ba' | me'aretz | tzapoun; |
| **the neighbour** | **and his friend** | **shall perish** | | **Thus** | **saith** | **Yahuah** | **Behold** | **a people** | **comes** | **from country** | ***the* north** |

| וגוי 1471 | גדול 1419 | יעור 5782 | מירכתי 3411 | ארץ 776: | 6:23 | קשת 7198 | וכידון 3591 | יחזיקו 2388 | אכזרי 394 |
|---|---|---|---|---|---|---|---|---|---|
| uagouy | gadoul, | ya'aur | miyarkatey | 'aretz. | | qeshet | uakiydoun | yachaziyqu, | 'akzariy |
| **and a nation** | **great** | **shall be raised** | **from the sides of** | ***the* earth** | | **bow** | **and spear** | **They shall lay hold on** | ***are* cruel** |

| הוא 1931 | ולא 3808 | ירחמו 7355 | קולם 6963 | כים 3220 | יהמה 1993 | ועל 5921 | סוסים 5483 | ירכבו 7392 | ערוך 6186 | כאיש 376 | למלחמה 4421 |
|---|---|---|---|---|---|---|---|---|---|---|---|
| hua' | uala' | yarachemu, | qoulam | kayam | yehemeh, | ua'al | susiym | yirkabu; | 'aruk, | ka'aysh | lamilchamah, |
| **they** | **and no** | **have mercy** | **their voice** | **like the sea** | **roar** | **and upon** | **horses** | **they ride** | **set in array** | **as men** | **for war** |

Jer 6:16 Thus saith YHUH, Stand you in the ways, and see, and ask for the old paths, where is the good way, and walk therein, and you shall find rest for your souls. But they said, We will not walk therein.17 Also I set watchmen over you, saying, Hearken to the sound of the trumpet. But they said, We will not hear.18 Therefore hear, you nations, and know, O congregation, what is among them.19 Hear, O earth: behold, I will bring evil upon this people, even the fruit of their thoughts, because they have not hearkened unto my words, nor to my law, but rejected it.20 To what purpose cometh there to me incense from Sheba, and the sweet cane from a far country? your burnt offerings are not acceptable, nor your sacrifices sweet unto me.21 Therefore thus saith YHUH, Behold, I will lay stumblingblocks before this people, and the fathers and the sons together shall fall upon them; the neighbor and his friend shall perish.22 Thus saith YHUH, Behold, a people cometh from the north country, and a great nation shall be raised from the sides of the earth.23 They shall lay hold on bow and spear; they are cruel, and have no mercy; their voice roareth like the sea; and they ride upon horses, set in array as men for war against you, O daughter of Zion.

6:24
עליך 5921 בת 1323 ציון 6726: שמענו 8085 את 853 שמעו 8089 רפו 7503 ידינו 3027 צרה 6869
'alayik bat tziyoun. shama'anu 'at shama'au rapua' yadeynu; tzarah
**against you O daughter of Zion We have heard the fame thereof wax feeble our hands anguish**

6:25
החזיקתנו 2388 חיל 2427 כיולדה 3205: אל 408 תצאי 3318 השדה 7704 ובדרך 1870 אל 408 תלכי 1980 כי 3588
hecheziyqatnu, chiyl kayouledah. 'al tetza'ay hasadeh, uabaderek 'al telekiy kiy
**has taken hold of us *and* pain as of a woman in travail not Go forth into the field by the way nor walk for**

6:26
חרב 2719 לאיב 341 מגור 4032 מסביב 5439: בת 1323 עמי 5971 חגרי 2296 שק 8242 והתפלשי 6428
chereb la'ayeb, magour misabiyb. bat 'amiy chigri saq uahitpalshiy
**the sword of the enemy *and* fear *is* on every side O daughter of my people gird *you* with sackcloth and wallow yourself**

באפר 665 אבל 60 יחיד 3173 עשי 6213 לך 3807a מספד 4553 תמרורים 8563 כי 3588 פתאם 6597 יבא 935 השדד 7703
ba'aper, 'abel yachiyd 'asiy lak, mispad tamaruriym; kiy pit'am, yaba' hashoded
**in ashes mourning *as for* an only son make to you lamentation most bitter for suddenly shall come the spoiler**

6:27 6:28
עלינו 5921: בחון 969 נתתיך 5414 בעמי 5971 מבצר 4013 ותדע 3045 ובחנת 974 את 853 דרכם 1870:
'aleynu. bachoun natatiyka ua'amiy mibtzar; uateda' uabachanta 'at darkam.
**upon us *for* a tower I have set you among my people *and* a fortress that you may know and try their way**

6:29
כלם 3605 סרי 5493 סוררים 5637 הלכי 1980 רכיל 7400 נחשת 5178 וברזל 1270 כלם 3605 משחיתים 7843 המה 1992: נחר 2787
kulam sarey sourariym, holakey rakiyl nachoshet uabarzel; kulam mashchitiym hemah. nachar
**They *are* all grievous revolters walking with slanders *they are* brass and iron *are* all corrupters they are burned**

6:30
מפח 4647 מאשתם 800 עפרת 5777 לשוא 7723 צרף 6884 צרוף 6884 ורעים 7451 לא 3808 נתקו 5423: כסף 3701
mapuach, me'aeshtam 'aparet; lashau'a tzarap tzaroup, uar'aym la' nitaqu. kesep
**The bellows of the fire: the lead in vain the founder melt for the wicked not are plucked away silver**

נמאס 3988 קראו 7121 להם 3807a כי 3588 מאס 3988 יהוה 3068 בהם 871a:
nim'as, qara'au lahem; kiy ma'as Yahuah bahem.
**Reprobate shall *men* call them Because has rejected Yahuah them**

**Jer 7:1** 7:2
הדבר 1697 אשר 834 היה 1961 אל 413 ירמיהו 3414 מאת 853 יהוה 3068 לאמר 559: עמד 5975 בשער 8179 בית 1004 יהוה 3068
hadabar 'asher hayah 'al yirmayahu, me'at Yahuah lea'mor. 'amod, basha'ar beyt Yahuah,
**The word that came to Jeremiah from Yahuah saying Stand in the gate of house Yahuah's**

וקראת 7121 שם 8033 את 853 הדבר 1697 הזה 2088 ואמרת 559 שמעו 8085 דבר 1697 יהוה 3068 כל 3605 יהודה 3063 הבאים 935
uaqara'ta sham, 'at hadabar hazeh; ua'amarta shim'au dabar Yahuah kal yahudah haba'aym
**and proclaim there word this and say Hear the word of Yahuah all *you of* Judah that enter in**

7:3
בשערים 8179 האלה 428 להשתחות 7812 ליהוה 3068: כה 3541 אמר 559 יהוה 3068 צבאות 6635 אלהי 430 ישראל 3478 היטיבו 3190 דרכיכם 1870
bash'ariym ha'aeleh, lahishtachauot laYahuah. koh 'amar Yahuah tzaba'aut 'alohey yisra'ael, heytiybu darkeykem
**at gates these to worship Yahuah Thus saith Yahuah of hosts the Elohim of Israel Amend your ways**

7:4
ומעלליכם 4611 ואשכנה 7931 אתכם 853 במקום 4725 הזה 2088: אל 408 תבטחו 982 לכם 3807a אל 413 דברי 1697 השקר 8267
uama'alleykem; ua'ashaknah 'atkem, bamaqoum hazeh. 'al tibtachu lakem, 'al dibrey hasheqer
**and your doings and I will cause to dwell you in place this not Trust to you in words lying**

Jer 6:24 We have heard the fame thereof: our hands wax feeble: anguish has taken hold of us, and pain, as of a woman in travail.25 Go not forth into the field, nor walk by the way; for the sword of the enemy and fear is on every side.26 O daughter of my people, gird you with sackcloth, and wallow thyself in ashes: make you mourning, as for an only son, most bitter lamentation: for the spoiler shall suddenly come upon us.27 I have set you for a tower and a fortress among my people, that you may know and try their way.28 They are all grievous revolters, walking with slanders: they are brass and iron; they are all corrupters.29 The bellows are burned, the lead is consumed of the fire; the founder melteth in vain: for the wicked are not plucked away.30 Reprobate silver shall men call them, because YHUH has rejected them. **Jer** 7:1 The word that came to Jeremiah from YHUH, saying,2 Stand in the gate of YHUH's house, and proclaim there this word, and say, Hear the word of YHUH, all you of Judah, that enter in at these gates to worship YHUH.3 Thus saith YHUH of hosts, the G-d of Israel, Amend your ways and your doings, and I will cause you to dwell in this place.4 Trust you not in lying words, saying, The temple of YHUH, The temple of YHUH, The temple of YHUH, are these.

לאמר 559 היכל 1964 יהוה 3068 היכל 1964 יהוה 3068 היכל 1964 יהוה 3068 המה 1992: 7:5 כי 3588 אם 518 היטיב 3190
lea'mor; heykal Yahuah heykal Yahuah, heykal Yahuah hemah. kiy 'am heyteyb
**saying The temple of Yahuah The temple of Yahuah The temple of Yahuah These For if you throughly**

תיטיבו 3190 את 853 דרכיכם 1870 ואת 853 מעלליכם 4611 אם 518 עשו 6213 תעשו 6213 משפט 4941 בין 996 איש 376 ובין 996
teytiybu, 'at darkeykem ua'at ma'alleykem; 'am asou ta'asu mishapat, beyn 'aysh uabeyn
**amend your ways *and* your doings if you throughly execute judgment between a man and between**

רעהו 7453: 7:6 גר 1616 יתום 3490 ואלמנה 490 לא 3808 תעשקו 6231 ודם 1818 נקי 5355 אל 408 תשפכו 8210
re'aehu. ger yatoum ua'almanah la' ta'ashoqu, uadam naqiy, 'al tishpaku
**his neighbour *If* the stranger the fatherless and the widow not you oppress and blood innocent not shed**

במקום 4725 הזה 2088 ואחרי 310 אלהים 430 אחרים 312 לא 3808 תלכו 1980 לרע 7451 לכם 3807a: 7:7 ושכנתי 7931 אתכם 853
bamaqoum hazeh; ua'acharey 'alohiym 'acheriym la' telaku lara' lakem. uashikantiy 'atkem
**in place this after gods other neitjher walk to hurt to your Then will I cause to dwell you**

במקום 4725 הזה 2088 בארץ 776 אשר 834 נתתי 5414 לאבותיכם 1 למן 4480 עולם 5769 ועד 5704 עולם 5769: 7:8 הנה 2009 אתם 859 בטחים 982
bamaqoum hazeh, ba'aretz 'asher natatiy la'abouteykem; lamin 'aulam ua'ad 'aulam. hineh 'atem botachiym
**in place this in the land that I gave to your fathers for ever and for ever Behold you trust**

לכם 3807a על 5921 דברי 1697 השקר 8267 לבלתי 1115 הועיל 3276: 7:9 הגנב 1589 רצח 7523 ונאף 5003 והשבע 7650 לשקר 8267
lakem, 'al dibrey hashaqer; labiltiy hou'ayl. haganob ratzoach uana'ap, uahishabea' lasheqer
**for you in words lying that cannot profit Will you steal murder and commit adultery and swear falsely**

וקטר 6999 לבעל 1168 והלך 1980 אחרי 310 אלהים 430 אחרים 312 אשר 834 לא 3808 ידעתם 3045: 7:10 ובאתם 935 ועמדתם 5975
uaqater laba'al; uahalok, 'acharey 'alohiym 'acheriym 'asher la' yada'tem. uaba'tem ua'amadtem
**and burn incense unto Baal and walk after gods other whom not you know And you come and stand**

לפני 6440 בבית 1004 הזה 2088 אשר 834 נקרא 7121 שמי 8034 עליו 5921 ואמרתם 559 נצלנו 5337 למען 4616 עשות 6213 את 853 כל 3605
lapanay, babayit hazeh 'asher niqra' shamiy 'alayu, ua'amartem nitzalnu; lama'an asout, 'at kal
**before me in house this which is called my name by and you say We are delivered to do all**

התועבות 8441 האלה 428: 7:11 המערת 4631 פרצים 6530 היה 1961 הבית 1004 הזה 2088 אשר 834 נקרא 7121 שמי 8034 עליו 5921 בעיניכם 5869
hatou'aebout ha'aeleh. hama'arat paritziym, hayah habayit hazeh 'asher niqra' shamiy 'alayu ba'aeyneykem;
**abominations? these a den of robbers Is become house this which is called my name by in your eyes?**

גם 1571 אנכי 595 הנה 2009 ראיתי 7200 נאם 5002 יהוה 3069: 7:12 כי 3588 לכו 1980 נא 4994 אל 413 מקומי 4725 אשר 834 בשילו 7887 אשר 834
gam 'anokiy hineh ra'aytiy na'am Yahuah. kiy laku na, 'al maqoumiy 'asher bashiylou, 'asher
**even I Behold have seen *it* saith Yahuah But go you now unto my place which *was* in Shiloh where**

שכנתי 7931 שמי 8034 שם 8033 בראשונה 7223 וראו 7200 את 853 אשר 834 עשיתי 6213 לו 3807a מפני 6440 רעת 7451 עמי 5971
shikantiy shamiy sham bara'shounah; uar'au 'at 'asher 'asiytiy lou', mipaney ra'at 'amiy
**I set my name where at the first and see what I did to it for the wickedness of my people**

ישראל 3478: 7:13 ועתה 6258 יען 3282 עשותכם 6213 את 853 כל 3605 המעשים 4639 האלה 428 נאם 5002 יהוה 3068 ואדבר 1696 אליכם 413
yisra'ael. ua'atah, ya'an 'asoutakem 'at kal hama'asiym ha'aeleh na'am Yahuah; ua'adaber 'aleykem
**Israel And now because you have done all works these saith Yahuah and I spoke unto you**

Jer 7:5 For if you throughly amend your ways and your doings; if you throughly execute judgment between a man and his neighbor;6 If you oppress not the stranger, the fatherless, and the widow, and shed not innocent blood in this place, neither walk after other gods to your hurt:7 Then will I cause you to dwell in this place, in the land that I gave to your fathers, forever and ever.8 Behold, you trust in lying words, that cannot profit.9 Will you steal, murder, and commit adultery, and swear falsely, and burn incense unto Baal, and walk after other gods whom you know not;10 And come and stand before me in this house, which is called by my name, and say, We are delivered to do all these abominations?11 Is this house, which is called by my name, become a den of robbers in your eyes? Behold, even I have seen it, saith YHUH.12 But go you now unto my place which was in Shiloh, where I set my name at the first, and see what I did to it for the wickedness of my people Israel.13 And now, because you have done all these works, saith YHUH, and I spoke unto you, rising up early and speaking, but you heard not; and I called you, but you answered not;

השכם 7925 ודבר 1696 ולא 3808 שמעתם 8085 ואקרא 7121 אתכם 853 ולא 3808 עניתם 6030: 7:14 ועשיתי 6213
hashkem uadaber uala' shama'atem, ua'aqra' 'atkem uala' 'aniytem. ua'asiytiy
**rising up early and speaking but not you heard and I called you but not you answered Therefore will I do**

לבית 1004 אשר 834 נקרא 7121 שמי 8034 עליו 5921 אשר 834 אתם 859 בטחים 982 בו 871a ולמקום 4725 אשר 834 נתתי 5414
labayit 'asher niqra' shamiy 'alayu, 'asher 'atem botachiym bou, ualamaqoum, 'asher natatiy
**unto *this* house which is called my name by wherein you trust in him and unto the place which I gave**

לכם 3807a ולאבותיכם 1 כאשר 834 עשיתי 6213 לשלו 7887: 7:15 והשלכתי 7993 אתכם 853 מעל 5921 פני 6440 כאשר 834
lakem uala'abouteykem; ka'asher 'asiytiy lashilou. uahishlachtiy 'atkem me'al panay; ka'asher
**to you and to your fathers as I have done to Shiloh And I will cast out you out of my sight as**

השלכתי 7993 את 853 כל 3605 אחיכם 251 את 853 כל 3605 זרע 2233 אפרים 669: 7:16 ואתה 859 אל 408 תתפלל 6419 בעד 1157
hishlaktiy 'at kal 'acheykem, 'at kal zera' 'aprayim. ua'atah 'al titpalel ba'ad
**I have cast out all your brethren *even* the whole seed of Ephraim Therefore you not pray for**

העם 5971 הזה 2088 ואל 408 תשא 5375 בעדם 1157 רנה 7440 ותפלה 8605 ואל 408 תפגע 6293 בי 871a כי 3588 אינני 369
ha'am hazeh, ua'al tisa' ba'adam rinah uatapilah ua'al tipga' biy; kiy 'aeyneniy
**the people this neither lift up cry nor prayer for them neither make intercession to me for I not**

שמע 8085 אתך 853: 7:17 האינך 369 ראה 7200 מה 4100 המה 1992 עשים 6213 בערי 5892 יהודה 3063 ובחצות 2351
shomea' 'atak. ha'aeynaka ro'ah, mah hemah 'asiym ba'arey yahudah; uabchutzout
**will hear you not See you what they do in the cities of Judah and in the streets of**

ירושלם 3389: 7:18 הבנים 1121 מלקטים 3950 עצים 6086 והאבות 1 מבערים 1197 את 853 האש 784 והנשים 802 לשות 3888
yarushalaim. habaniym malaqtiym 'aetziym, uaha'about maba'ariym 'at ha'aesh, uahanashiym lashout
**Jerusalem The children gather wood and the fathers kindle the fire and the women knead**

בצק 1217 לעשות 6213 כונים 3561 למלכת 4446 השמים 8064 והסך 5258 נסכים 5262 לאלהים 430 אחרים 312 למען 4616
batzeq; la'asout kauaniym limaleket hashamayim, uahasek nasakiym le'alohiym 'acheriym, lama'an
***their* dough to make cakes to the queen of heaven and to pour out drink offerings unto gods other that**

הכעסני 3707: 7:19 האתי 853 הם 1992 מכעסים 3707 נאם 5002 יהוה 3068 הלוא 3808 אתם 853
haka'aseniy. ha'autiy hem mak'aysiym na'am Yahuah; halou'a 'atam,
**they may provoke me to anger me they Do provoke to anger? saith Yahuah *do they* not *provoke* themselves**

למען 4616 בשת 1322 פניהם 6440: 7:20 לכן 3651 כה 3541 אמר 559 אדני 136 יהוה 3069 הנה 2009 אפי 639 וחמתי 2534
lama'an boshet paneyhem. laken koh 'amar 'adonay Yahuah hineh 'apiy uachamatiy
**to the confusion of their own faces? Therefore thus saith Adonai Yahuah Behold mine anger and my fury**

נתכת 5413 אל 413 המקום 4725 הזה 2088 על 5921 האדם 120 ועל 5921 הבהמה 929 ועל 5921 עץ 6086 השדה 7704 ועל 5921
niteket 'al hamaqoum hazeh, 'al ha'adam ua'al habehemah, ua'al 'aetz hasadeh ua'al
**shall be poured out upon place this upon man and upon beast and upon the trees of the field and upon**

פרי 6529 האדמה 127 ובערה 1197 ולא 3808 תכבה 3518: 7:21 כה 3541 אמר 559 יהוה 3068 צבאות 6635 אלהי 430
pariy ha'adamah; uaba'arah uala' tikbeh. koh 'amar Yahuah tzaba'aut 'alohey
**the fruit of the ground and it shall burn and not shall be quenched Thus saith Yahuah of hosts the Elohim of**

Jer 7:14 Therefore will I do unto this house, which is called by my name, wherein you trust, and unto the place which I gave to you and to your fathers, as I have done to Shiloh.15 And I will cast you out of my sight, as I have cast out all your brethren, even the whole seed of Ephraim.16 Therefore pray not you for this people, neither lift up cry nor prayer for them, neither make intercession to me: for I will not hear you.17 See you not what they do in the cities of Judah and in the streets of Jerusalem?18 The children gather wood, and the fathers kindle the fire, and the women knead their dough, to make cakes to the queen of heaven, and to pour out drink offerings unto other gods, that they may provoke me to anger.19 Do they provoke me to anger? saith YHUH: do they not provoke themselves to the confusion of their own faces?20 Therefore thus saith YHUH G-D; Behold, mine anger and my fury shall be poured out upon this place, upon man, and upon beast, and upon the trees of the field, and upon the fruit of the ground; and it shall burn, and shall not be quenched.21 Thus saith YHUH of hosts, the G-d of Israel; Put your burnt offerings unto your sacrifices, and eat flesh.

7:22

ישראל 3478 עלותיכם 5930 ספו 5595 על 5921 זבחיכם 2077 ואכלו 398 בשר 1320: כי 3588 לא 3808 דברתי 1696 את 854 אבותיכם 1

yisra'ael; 'alouteykem sapu 'al zibcheykem ua'aklu basar. kiy la' dibartiy 'at abouteykem

**Israel your burnt offerings Put unto your sacrifices and eat flesh For not I spoke *unto* your fathers**

ולא 3808 צויתים 6680 ביום 3117 הוציא 3318 אותם 853 מארץ 776 מצרים 4714 על 5921 דברי 1697 עולה 5930

uala' tziuiytiym, bayoum houtziy'a 'autam me'aretz mitzrayim; 'al dibrey aulah

**nor commanded them in the day that I brought them out of the land of Egypt on concerning burnt offerings**

7:23

וזבח 2077: כי 3588 אם 518 את 853 הדבר 1697 הזה 2088 צויתי 6680 אותם 853 לאמר 559 שמעו 8085 בקולי 6963 והייתי 1961 לכם 3807a

uazabach. kiy 'am 'at hadabar hazeh tziuiytiy 'autam lea'mor shim'au baqouliy, uahayiytiy lakem

**or sacrifices But rather thing this commanded I them saying Obey my voice and I will be to your**

לאלהים 430 ואתם 859 תהיו 1961 לי 3807a לעם 5971 והלכתם 1980 בכל 3605 הדרך 1870 אשר 834 אצוה 6680 אתכם 853 למען 4616

le'alohiym, ua'atem tihayu liy la'am; uahalaktem, bakal haderek 'asher 'atzaueh 'atkem, lama'an

**to Elohim and you shall be my people and walk you in all the ways that I have commanded you that**

7:24

ייטב 3190 לכם 3807a: ולא 3808 שמעו 8085 ולא 3808 הטו 5186 את 853 אזנם 241 וילכו 1980 במעצות 4156

yiytab lakem. uala' shama'au uala' hitu 'at 'azanam, uayelaku bamo'aetzout,

**it may be well unto you But not they hearkened nor inclined their ear but walked in the counsels**

7:25

בשררות 8307 לבם 3820 הרע 7451 ויהיו 1961 לאחור 268 ולא 3808 לפנים 6440: למן 4480 היום 3117 אשר 834 יצאו 3318

bishrirut libam hara'; uayihayu la'achour uala' lapaniym. lemin hayoum, 'asher yatza'ua

***and* in the imagination of heart their evil and went backward and not forward Since the day that came forth**

אבותיכם 1 מארץ 776 מצרים 4714 עד 5704 היום 3117 הזה 2088 ואשלח 7971 אליכם 413 את 853 כל 3605 עבדי 5650

abouteykem me'aretz mitzrayim, 'ad hayoum hazeh; ua'ashlach 'aleykem 'at kal 'abaday

**your fathers out of the land of Egypt until day this I have even sent unto you all my servants**

7:26

הנביאים 5030 יום 3117 השכם 7925 ושלח 7971: ולוא 3808 שמעו 8085 אלי 413 ולא 3808 הטו 5186 את 853 אזנם 241

hanabiy'aym, youm hashkem uashaloach. ualou'a shama'au 'aelay, uala' hitu 'at 'azanam;

**the prophets daily rising up early and sending *them* Yet not they hearkened unto me nor inclined their ear**

7:27

ויקשו 7185 את 853 ערפם 6203 הרעו 7489 מאבותם 1: ודברת 1696 אליהם 413 את 853 כל 3605

uayaqshu 'at 'arapam, here'au me'aboutam. uadibarta 'aleyhem 'at kal

**but hardened their neck they did worse than their fathers Therefore you shall speak unto them all**

7:28

הדברים 1697 האלה 428 ולא 3808 ישמעו 8085 אליך 413 וקראת 7121 אליהם 413 ולא 3808 יענוכה 6030:

hadabariym ha'aeleh, uala' yishma'au 'aeleyka; uaqara'ta 'aleyhem uala' ya'anukah.

**words these but not they will listen to you you shall also call unto them but not they will answer**

ואמרת 559 אליהם 413 זה 2088 הגוי 1471 אשר 834 לוא 3808 שמעו 8085 בקול 6963 יהוה 3068 אלהיו 430 ולא 3808 לקחו 3947

ua'amarta 'aleyhem, zeh hagouy 'asher lua' shama'au, baqoul Yahuah 'alohayu, uala' laqchu

**But you shall say unto them This This *is* a nation that not obeyed the voice of Yahuah their Elohim nor receive**

7:29

מוסר 4148 אבדה 6 האמונה 530 ונכרתה 3772 מפיהם 6310: גזי 1494 נזרך 5145 והשליכי 7993

musar; 'abadah ha'amunah, uanikratah mipiyhem. gaziy nizrek uahashaliykiy,

**correction is perished truth and is cut off from their mouth Cut off your hair *O Jerusalem* and cast *it* away**

Jer 7:22 For I spoke not unto your fathers, nor commanded them in the day that I brought them out of the land of Egypt, concerning burnt offerings or sacrifices:23 But this thing commanded I them, saying, Obey my voice, and I will be your G-d, and you shall be my people: and walk you in all the ways that I have commanded you, that it may be well unto you.24 But they hearkened not, nor inclined their ear, but walked in the counsels and in the imagination of their evil heart, and went backward, and not forward.25 Since the day that your fathers came forth out of the land of Egypt unto this day I have even sent unto you all my servants the prophets, daily rising up early and sending them:26 Yet they hearkened not unto me, nor inclined their ear, but hardened their neck: they did worse than their fathers.27 Therefore you shall speak all these words unto them; but they will not hear to you: you shall also call unto them; but they will not answer you.28 But you shall say unto them, This is a nation that obeyeth not the voice of YHUH their G-d, nor receive correction: truth is perished, and is cut off from their mouth.

7:30
ושאי 5375 על 5921 שפים 8205 קינה 7015 כי 3588 מאס 3988 יהוה 3068 ויטש 5203 את 853 דור 1755 עברתו 5678:
us'ay 'al shapayim qiynah; kiy ma'as Yahuah, uayitosh 'at dour 'abratou.
**and take up on high places a lamentation for has rejected Yahuah and forsaken the generation of his wrath**

כי 3588 עשו 6213 בני 1121 יהודה 3063 הרע 7451 בעיני 5869 נאום 5002 יהוה 3068 שמו 7760 שקוציהם 8251 בבית 1004
kiy 'asu baney yahudah hara' ba'aeynay na'aum Yahuah; samu shiqutzeyhem, babayit
**For have done the children of Judah evil in my sight saith Yahuah they have set their abominations in the house**

7:31
אשר 834 נקרא 7121 שמי 8034 עליו 5921 לטמאו 2930: ובנו 1129 במות 1116 התפת 8612 אשר 834 בגיא 1516
'asher niqra' shamiy 'alayu latam'au. uabanu bamout hatopet, 'asher bagey'a
**which is called my name by to pollute it And they have built the high places of Tophet which *is* in the valley of**

בן 1121 הנם 2011 לשרף 8313 את 853 בניהם 1323 ואת 853 בנתיהם 1121 באש 784 אשר 834 לא 3808 צויתי 6680 ולא 3808
ben hinom, lisrop 'at baneyhem ua'at banoteyhem ba'aesh; 'asher la' tziuiytiy, uala'
**the son of Hinnom to burn their sons *and* their daughters in the fire which not I commanded *them* neither**

7:32
עלתה 5927 על 5921 לבי 3820: לכן 3651 הנה 2009 ימים 3117 באים 935 נאם 5002 יהוה 3068 ולא 3808 יאמר 559 עוד 5750 התפת 8612
'alatah 'al libiy. laken hineh yamiym ba'aym na'am Yahuah, uala' ye'amer 'aud hatopet
**came it into my heart Therefore behold the days come saith Yahuah that no it shall be called more Tophet**

וגיא 1516 בן 1121 הנם 2011 כי 3588 אם 518 גיא 1516 ההרגה 2028 וקברו 6912 בתפת 8612 מאין 370
uagey'a ben hinom, kiy 'am gey'a haharegah; uaqabaru uatopet me'ayn
**nor the valley of the son of Hinnom but rather valley of the slaughter for they shall bury in Tophet till there be no**

7:33
מקום 4725: והיתה 1961 נבלת 5038 העם 5971 הזה 2088 למאכל 3978 לעוף 5775 השמים 8064 ולבהמת 929
maqoum. uahayatah niblat ha'am hazeh lama'akal, la'oup hashamayim ualbehemat
**place And shall be the carcases of the people this meat for the fowls of the heaven and for the beasts of**

7:34
הארץ 776 ואין 369 מחריד 2729: והשבתי 7673 מערי 5892 יהודה 3063 ומחצות 2351
ha'aretz; ua'aeyn machariyd. uahishbatiy me'arey yahudah, uamechutzout
**the earth and none shall fray *them* away Then will I cause to cease from the cities of Judah and from the streets of**

ירושלם 3389 קול 6963 ששון 8342 וקול 6963 שמחה 8057 קול 6963 חתן 2860 וקול 6963 כלה 3618 כי 3588
yarushalaim, qoul sasoun uaqoul simchah, qoul chatan uaqoul kalah; kiy
**Jerusalem the voice of mirth and the voice of gladness the voice of the bridegroom and the voice of the bride for**

לחרבה 2723 תהיה 1961 הארץ 776:
lacharabah tihayeh ha'aretz.
**desolate shall be the land**

**Jer 8:1**
בעת 6256 ההיא 1931 נאם 5002 יהוה 3068 ויציאו 3318 את 853 עצמות 6106 מלכי 4428 יהודה 3063 ואת 853 עצמות 6106
ba'aet hahiy'a na'am Yahuah uayotziy'au 'at atzmout malkey yahudah ua'at 'atzmout
**At time that saith Yahuah they shall bring out the bones of the kings of Judah *and* the bones of**

שריו 8269 ואת 853 עצמות 6106 הכהנים 3548 ואת 853 עצמות 6106 הנביאים 5030 ואת 853 עצמות 6106 יושבי 3427
sarayu ua'at atzmout hakohaniym ua'at atzmout hanabiy'aym, ua'at atzmout youshabey
**his princes *and* the bones of the priests *and* the bones of the prophets *and* the bones of the inhabitants of**

Jer 7:29 Cut off your hair, O Jerusalem, and cast it away, and take up a lamentation on high places; for YHUH has rejected and forsaken the generation of his wrath.30 For the children of Judah have done evil in my sight, saith YHUH: they have set their abominations in the house which is called by my name, to pollute it.31 And they have built the high places of Tophet, which is in the valley of the son of Hinnom, to burn their sons and their daughters in the fire; which I commanded them not, neither came it into my heart.32 Therefore, behold, the days come, saith YHUH, that it shall no more be called Tophet, nor the valley of the son of Hinnom, but the valley of slaughter: for they shall bury in Tophet, till there be no place.33 And the carcases of this people shall be meat for the fowls of the heaven, and for the beasts of the earth; and none shall fray them away.34 Then will I cause to cease from the cities of Judah, and from the streets of Jerusalem, the voice of mirth, and the voice of gladness, the voice of the bridegroom, and the voice of the bride: for the land shall be desolate. **Jer** 8:1 At that time, saith YHUH, they shall bring out the bones of the kings of Judah, and the bones of his princes, and the bones of the priests, and the bones of the prophets, and the bones of the inhabitants of Jerusalem, out of their graves:

8:2
ירושלם 3389 | מקבריהם 6913: | ושטחום 7849 | לשמש 8121 | ולירח 3394 | ולכל 3605 | צבא 6635
yarushalaim | miqibreyhem. | uashtachum | lashemesh | ualayareach | ualkol | tzaba'
**Jerusalem | out of their graves | And they shall spread them | before the sun | and the moon | and all | the host of**

השמים 8064 | אשר 834 | אהבום 157 | ואשר 834 | עבדום 5647 | ואשר 834 | הלכו 1980 | אחריהם 310 | ואשר 834
hashamayim, | 'asher | 'ahebum | ua'asher | 'abadum | ua'asher | halaku | 'achareyhem, | ua'asher
**heaven | whom | they have loved | and whom | they have served | and whom | they have walked | after | and whom**

דרשום 1875 | ואשר 834 | השתחוו 7812 | להם 3807a | לא 3808 | יאספו 622 | ולא 3808 | יקברו 6912 | לדמן 1828 | על 5921
darashum, | ua'asher | hishtachauu | lahem; | la' | ye'asapu | uala' | yiqaberu, | ladomen | 'al
**they have sought | and whom | they have worshipped | to | not | they shall be gathered | nor | be buried | for dung | upon**

8:3
פני 6440 | האדמה 127 | יהיו 1961: | ונבחר 977 | מות 4194 | מחיים 2416 | לכל 3605 | השארית 7611 | הנשארים 7604
paney | ha'adamah | yihayu. | uanibchar | mauet | mechayiym, | lakol, | hasha'eriyt | hanisha'ariym,
**the face of | the earth | they shall be | And shall be chosen | death | rather than life | by all | the residue of | them that remain**

מן 4480 | המשפחה 4940 | הרעה 7451 | הזאת 2063 | בכל 3605 | המקמות 4725 | הנשארים 7604 | אשר 834 | הדחתים 5080 | שם 8033 | נאם 5002 | יהוה 3068
min | hamishpachah | hara'ah | haza't; | bakal | hamaqomout | hanisha'ariym | 'asher | hidachtiym | sham, | na'am | Yahuah
**of | family | evil | this | in all | the places | which remain | where | I have driven them | there | saith | Yahuah**

8:4
צבאות 6635: | ואמרת 559 | אליהם 413 | כה 3541 | אמר 559 | יהוה 3068 | היפלו 5307 | ולא 3808 | יקומו 6965 | אם 518
tzaba'aut. | ua'amarta | 'aleyhem, | koh | 'amar | Yahuah, | hayiplu | uala' | yaqumu; | 'am
**of hosts | Moreover you shall say | unto them | Thus | saith | Yahuah | Shall they fall | and not | arise? | if**

8:5
ישוב 7725 | ולא 3808 | ישוב 7725: | מדוע 4069 | שובבה 7725 | העם 5971 | הזה 2088 | ירושלם 3389 | משבה 4878
yashub | uala' | yashub. | madua' | shoubah | ha'am | hazeh | yarushalaim | mashubah
**shall he turn away | and not | return? | Why *then* | is slidden back | the people *of* | this | Jerusalem | *by* a backsliding?**

8:6
נצחת 5331 | החזיקו 2388 | בתרמית 8649 | מאנו 3985 | לשוב 7725: | הקשבתי 7181 | ואשמע 8085 | לוא 3808 | כן 3651 | ידברו 1696 | אין 369
nitzachat; | hecheziyqu | batarmiyt, | me'anu | lashub. | hiqshabtiy | ua'ashma' | lua' | ken | yadaberu, | 'aeyn
**perpetual | they hold fast | deceit | they refuse | to return | I hearkened | and heard | not | aright | *but* they spoke | no**

איש 376 | נחם 5162 | על 5921 | רעתו 7451 | לאמר 559 | מה 4100 | עשיתי 6213 | כלה 3605 | שב 7725 | במרצותם 4794 | כסוס 5483
'aysh, | nicham | 'al | ra'atou, | lea'mor | meh | 'asiytiy; | kuloh, | shab | bimarutzoutam | kasus
**man | repented *him* | of | his wickedness | saying | What | have I done? | every one | turned | to his course, | as the horse**

8:7
שוטף 7857 | במלחמה 4421: | גם 1571 | חסידה 2624 | בשמים 8064 | ידעה 3045 | מועדיה 4150 | ותר 8449 | וסוס 5483
shoutep | bamilchamah. | gam | chasiydah | bashamayim, | yada'ah | mou'adeyha, | uator | uasus
**rushes | into the battle | Yea | the stork | in the heaven | knows | her appointed times | and the turtle | and the crane**

8:8
ועגור 5693 | שמרו 8104 | את 853 | עת 6256 | באנה 935 | ועמי 5971 | לא 3808 | ידעו 3045 | את 853 | משפט 4941 | יהוה 3068:
ua'agur, | shamaru | 'at | 'at | bo'anah; | ua'amiy | la' | yada'au, | 'at | mishapat | Yahuah.
**and the swallow | observe | | the time of | their coming | but my people | not | know | | the judgment of | Yahuah**

איכה 349 | תאמרו 559 | חכמים 2450 | אנחנו 587 | ותורת 8451 | יהוה 3068 | אתנו 854 | אכן 403 | הנה 2009 | לשקר 8267 | עשה 6213 | עט 5842
'aeykah | ta'maru | chakamiym | 'anachnu, | uatourat | Yahuah | 'atanu; | 'aken | hineh | lasheqer | 'asah, | 'at
**How | do you say | *are* wise | We | and the law of | Yahuah *is* | with us? | certainly | Lo | in vain | made he *it* | the pen of**

Jer 8:2 And they shall spread them before the sun, and the moon, and all the host of heaven, whom they have loved, and whom they have served, and after whom they have walked, and whom they have sought, and whom they have worshipped: they shall not be gathered, nor be buried; they shall be for dung upon the face of the earth.3 And death shall be chosen rather than life by all the residue of them that remain of this evil family, which remain in all the places whither I have driven them, saith YHUH of hosts.4 Moreover you shall say unto them, Thus saith YHUH; Shall they fall, and not arise? shall he turn away, and not return?5 Why then is this people of Jerusalem slidden back by a perpetual backsliding? they hold fast deceit, they refuse to return.6 I hearkened and heard, but they spoke not aright: no man repented him of his wickedness, saying, What have I done? everyone turned to his course, as the horse rusheth into the battle.7 Yea, the stork in the heaven know her appointed times; and the turtle and the crane and the swallow observe the time of their coming; but my people know not the judgment of YHUH.8 How do you say, We are wise, and the law of YHUH is with us? Lo, certainly in vain made he it; the pen of the scribes is in vain.

| שקר 8267 | 8:9 ספרים 5608: | הבישו 954 | חכמים 2450 | חתו 2865 | וילכדו 3920 | הנה 2009 | בדבר 1697 | יהוה 3068 |
|---|---|---|---|---|---|---|---|---|
| sheqer | sopariym. | hobiyshu | chakamiym, | chatu | uayilakedu; | hineh | bidbar | Yahuah |
| ***is* in vain** | **the scribes** | **are ashamed** | **The wise men** | **they are dismayed** | **and taken** | **lo** | **the word of** | **Yahuah** |

| מאסו 3988 | וחכמת 2451 | מה 4100 | להם 3807a: | 8:10 | לכן 3651 | אתן 5414 | את 853 | נשיהם 802 | לאחרים 312 | שדותיהם 7704 |
|---|---|---|---|---|---|---|---|---|---|---|
| ma'asu, | uachakamat | meh | lahem. | | laken | 'aten | 'at | nasheyhem | la'acheriym, | sadouteyhem |
| **they have rejected** | **and wisdom** | **what *is*** | **in them?** | | **Therefore** | **will I give** | | **their wives** | **unto others** | ***and* their fields** |

| ליורשים 3423 | כי 3588 | מקטן 6996 | ועד 5704 | גדול 1419 | כלה 3605 | בצע 1214 | בצע 1215 |
|---|---|---|---|---|---|---|---|
| layourashiym, | kiy | miqaton | ua'ad | gadoul, | kuloh | botzea' | batza'; |
| **to them that shall inherit *them*** | **for** | **from the least** | **even unto** | **the greatest** | **every one** | **is given to** | **covetousness** |

| מנביא 5030 | ועד 5704 | כהן 3548 | כלה 3605 | עשה 6213 | שקר 8267: | 8:11 | וירפו 7495 | את 853 | שבר 7667 |
|---|---|---|---|---|---|---|---|---|---|
| minabiy'a | ua'ad | kohen, | kuloh | 'asheh | shaqer. | | uayarapu | 'at | sheber |
| **from the prophet** | **even unto** | **the priest** | **every one** | **deal** | **falsely** | | **For they have healed** | | **the hurt of** |

| בת 1323 | עמי 5971 | על 5921 | נקלה 7043 | לאמר 559 | שלום 7965 | שלום 7965 | ואין 369 | שלום 7965: | 8:12 | הבשו 3001 |
|---|---|---|---|---|---|---|---|---|---|---|
| bat | 'amiy | 'al | naqalah, | lea'mor | shaloum | shaloum; | ua'aeyn | shaloum. | | hobishu |
| **the daughter of** | **my people** | **on** | **slightly** | **saying** | **Peace** | **peace** | **when *there is* no** | **peace** | | **Were they ashamed** |

| כי 3588 | תועבה 8441 | עשו 6213 | גם 1571 | בוש 954 | לא 3808 | יבשו 954 | והכלם 3637 | לא 3808 | ידעו 3045 | לכן 3651 |
|---|---|---|---|---|---|---|---|---|---|---|
| kiy | tou'aebah | 'asu; | gam | boush | la' | yeboshu, | uahikalem | la' | yada'au, | laken |
| **when** | **abomination?** | **they had committed** | **nay** | **they were at all** | **not** | **ashamed** | **blush** | **neither** | **could they** | **therefore** |

| יפלו 5307 | בנפלים 5307 | בעת 6256 | פקדתם 6486 | יכשלו 3782 | אמר 559 | יהוה 3068: | 8:13 | אסף 622 |
|---|---|---|---|---|---|---|---|---|
| yiplu | banopaliym, | ba'aet | paqudatam | yikashalu | 'amar | Yahuah. | | 'asoup |
| **shall they fall** | **among them that fall** | **in the time of** | **their visitation** | **they shall be cast down** | **saith** | **Yahuah** | | **surely** |

| אסיפם 5486 | נאם 5002 | יהוה 3069 | אין 369 | ענבים 6025 | בגפן 1612 | ואין 369 | תאנים 8384 | בתאנה 8384 | והעלה 5929 |
|---|---|---|---|---|---|---|---|---|---|
| 'asiypem | na'am | Yahuah; | 'aeyn | 'anabiym | bagepen | ua'aeyn | ta'aeniym | bata'aenah, | uahe'aleh |
| **I will consume them** | **saith** | **Yahuah** | ***there shall be* no** | **grapes** | **on the vine** | **nor** | **figs** | **on the fig tree** | **and the leaf** |

| נבל 5034 | ואתן 5414 | להם 3807a | יעברום 5674: | 8:14 | על 5921 | מה 4100 | אנחנו 587 | ישבים 3427 |
|---|---|---|---|---|---|---|---|---|
| nabel, | ua'aten | lahem | ya'abrum. | | 'al | mah | 'anachnu | yoshbiym, |
| **shall fade** | **and *the things that* I have given** | **them** | **shall pass away from them** | | **on** | **Why** | **we** | **do sit still?** |

| האספו 622 | ונבוא 935 | אל 413 | ערי 5892 | המבצר 4013 | ונדמה 1826 | שם 8033 | כי 3588 | יהוה 3068 | אלהינו 430 |
|---|---|---|---|---|---|---|---|---|---|
| he'asapu, | uanabou'a | 'al | 'arey | hamibtzar | uanidmah | sham; | kiy | Yahuah | 'aloheynu |
| **assemble yourselves** | **and let us enter** | **into** | **cities** | **the defenced** | **and let us be silent** | **there** | **for** | **Yahuah** | **our Elohim** |

| הדמנו 1826 | וישקנו 8248 | מי 4325 | ראש 7219 | כי 3588 | חטאנו 2398 | ליהוה 3068: | 8:15 | קוה 6960 |
|---|---|---|---|---|---|---|---|---|
| hadimanu | uayashqenu | mey | ra'sh, | kiy | chata'nu | laYahuah. | | qaueh |
| **has put us to silence** | **and given us to drink** | **water of** | **gall** | **because** | **we have sinned** | **against Yahuah** | | **We looked** |

| לשלום 7965 | ואין 369 | טוב 2896 | לעת 6256 | מרפה 4832 | והנה 2009 | בעתה 1205: | 8:16 | מדן 1835 | נשמע 8085 | נחרת 5170 |
|---|---|---|---|---|---|---|---|---|---|---|
| lashaloum | ua'aeyn | toub; | la'aet | marpeh | uahineh | ba'atah. | | midan | nishma' | nacharat |
| **for peace** | **but no** | **good** | ***came and* for a time of** | **health** | **and behold** | **trouble** | | **from Dan** | **was heard** | **The snorting of** |

Jer 8:9 The wise men are ashamed, they are dismayed and taken: lo, they have rejected the word of YHUH; and what wisdom is in them?10 Therefore will I give their wives unto others, and their fields to them that shall inherit them: foreveryone from the least even unto the greatest is given to covetousness, from the prophet even unto the priest everyone deal falsely.11 For they have healed the hurt of the daughter of my people slightly, saying, Peace, peace; when there is no peace.12 Were they ashamed when they had committed abomination? nay, they were not at all ashamed, neither could they blush: therefore shall they fall among them that fall: in the time of their visitation they shall be cast down, saith YHUH.13 I will surely consume them, saith YHUH: there shall be no grapes on the vine, nor figs on the fig tree, and the leaf shall fade; and the things that I have given them shall pass away from them.14 Why do we sit still? assemble yourselves, and let us enter into the defenced cities, and let us be silent there: for YHUH our G-d has put us to silence, and given us water of gall to drink, because we have sinned against YHUH.15 We looked for peace, but no good came; and for a time of health, and behold trouble!16 The snorting of his horses was heard from Dan: the whole land trembled at the sound of the neighing of his strong ones;

סוסיו 5483 מקול 6963 מצהלות 4684 אביריו 47 רעשה 7493 כל 3605 הארץ 776 ויבואו 935 ויאכלו 398
susayu, miqoul mitzhalout 'abiyrayu, ra'ashah kal ha'aretz; uayabou'au, uayo'akalu
**his horses at the sound of the neighing of his strong ones trembled whole the land for they are come and have devoured**

ארץ 776 ומלואה 4393 עיר 5892 וישבי 3427 בה 871a: **8:17** כי 3588 הנני 2005 משלח 7971 בכם 871a נחשים 5175
'aretz uamlou'ah, 'ayr uayoshabey bah. kiy hinniy mashaleach bakem, nachashiym
**the land and all that is in it the city and those that dwell therein For behold I will send among you serpents**

צפענים 6848 אשר 834 אין 369 להם 3807a לחש 3908 ונשכו 5391 אתכם 853 נאם 5002 יהוה 3068: **8:18**
tzipa'aniym, 'asher 'aeyn lahem lachash; uanishku 'atkem na'am Yahuah.
**cockatrices which *will* not for them *be* charmed and they shall bite you saith Yahuah**

מבליגיתי 4010 עלי 5921 יגון 3015 עלי 5921 לבי 3820 דוי 1742: **8:19** הנה 2009 קול 6963 שועת 7775 בת 1323
mabliygiytiy 'aley yagoun; 'alay libiy dauay. hineh qoul shau'at bat
***When* I would comfort myself against sorrow in me my heart *is* faint Behold the voice of the cry of the daughter of**

עמי 5971 מארץ 776 מרחקים 4801 היהוה 3068 אין 369 בציון 6726 אם 518 מלכה 4428 אין 369 בה 871a מדוע 4069
'amiy, me'aretz marchaqiym, haYahuah 'aeyn batziyoun, 'am malkah 'aeyn bah; madua',
**my people because of country them that dwell in a far the Yahuah *Is* not in Zion? or her king *is* not in her? Why**

הכעסוני 3707 בפסליהם 6456 בהבלי 1892 נכר 5236: **8:20** עבר 5674 קציר 7105 כלה 3615
hika'asuniy bipasileyhem bahabley nekar. 'abar qatziyr kalah
**have they provoked me to anger with their graven images *and* with vanities? strange is past The harvest is ended**

קיץ 7019 ואנחנו 587 לוא 3808 נושענו 3467: **8:21** על 5921 שבר 7667 בת 1323 עמי 5971 השברתי 7665 קדרתי 6937
qayitz; ua'anachnu lua' nousha'anu. 'al sheber bat 'amiy hashabaratiy; qadartiy
**the summer and we not are saved For the hurt of the daughter of my people am I hurt I am black**

שמה 8047 החזקתני 2388: **8:22** הצרי 6875 אין 369 בגלעד 1568 אם 518 רפא 7495 אין 369 שם 8033 כי 3588 מדוע 4069
shamah hecheziqataniy. hatzariy 'aeyn bagil'ad, 'am ropea' 'aeyn sham; kiy, madua'
**astonishment has taken hold on me balm *Is there* no in Gilead or physician *is there* no there? then why**

לא 3808 עלתה 5927 ארכת 724 בת 1323 עמי 5971:
la' 'alatah, 'arukat bat 'amiy.
**not is recovered? the health of the daughter of my people**

**Jer 9:1** מי 4310 יתן 5414 ראשי 7218 מים 4325 ועיני 5869 מקור 4726 דמעה 1832 ואבכה 1058 יומם 3119 ולילה 3915
miy' yiten ra'shiy mayim, ua'aeynay maqour dim'ah; ua'abkeh youmam ualayalah,
**Oh that were my head waters and mine eyes a fountain of tears that I might weep for day and night**

את 853 חללי 2491 בת 1323 עמי 5971: **9:2** מי 4310 יתנני 5414 במדבר 4057 מלון 4411 ארחים 732
'at challey bat 'amiy. miy' yitaneniy bamidbar, maloun 'arachiym,
**the slain of the daughter of my people Oh that I had in the wilderness a lodging place of wayfaring men**

ואעזבה 5800 את 853 עמי 5971 ואלכה 1980 מאתם 853 כי 3588 כלם 3605 מנאפים 5003 עצרת 6116 בגדים 898:
ua'a'azbah 'at 'amiy, ua'aelakah me'atam; kiy kulam mana'apiym, 'atzeret bogadiym.
**that I might leave my people and go from them for they *be* all adulterers an assembly of treacherous men**

Jer 8:17 For, behold, I will send serpents, cockatrices, among you, which will not be charmed, and they shall bite you, saith YHUH.18 When I would comfort myself against sorrow, my heart is faint in me.19 Behold the voice of the cry of the daughter of my people because of them that dwell in a far country: Is not YHUH in Zion? is not her king in her? Why have they provoked me to anger with their graven images, and with strange vanities?20 The harvest is past, the summer is ended, and we are not saved.21 For the hurt of the daughter of my people am I hurt; I am black; astonishment has taken hold on me.22 Is there no balm in Gilead; is there no physician there? why then is not the health of the daughter of my people recovered? **Jer** 9:1 Oh that my head were waters, and mine eyes a fountain of tears, that I might weep day and night for the slain of the daughter of my people!2 Oh that I had in the wilderness a lodging place of wayfaring men; that I might leave my people, and go from them! for they be all adulterers, an assembly of treacherous men.

9:3
וידרכו 1869 את 853 לשונם 3956 קשתם 7198 שקר 8267 ולא 3808 לאמונה 530 גברו 1396 בארץ 776 כי 3588
uayadraku 'at lashounam qashtam sheqer, uala' le'amunah gabaru ba'aretz; kiy
**And they bend their tongues *like* their bow *for* lies but not for the truth they are valiant upon the earth for**

9:4
מרעה 7451 אל 413 רעה 7451 יצאו 3318 ואתי 853 לא 3808 ידעו 3045 נאם 5002 יהוה 3068: איש 376 מרעהו 7453 השמרו 8104
mera'ah 'al ra'ah yatza'au ua'atiy la' yada'au na'am Yahuah. 'aysh mere'aehu hishameru,
**from evil to evil they proceed and me not they know saith Yahuah every one of his neighbour Take you heed**

ועל 5921 כל 3605 אח 251 אל 408 תבטחו 982 כי 3588 כל 3605 אח 251 עקוב 6117 יעקב 6117 וכל 3605 רע 7453 רכיל 7400
ua'al kal 'ach 'al tibtachu; kiy kal 'ach aqoub ya'aqob, uakal rea' rakiyl
**and in any brother not trust you for every brother will utterly supplant and every neighbour *with* slanders**

9:5
יהלך 1980: ואיש 376 ברעהו 7453 יהתלו 2048 ואמת 571 לא 3808 ידברו 1696 למדו 3925 לשונם 3956
yahalok. ua'aysh bare'aehu yahatelu, ua'amet la' yadaberu; limdu lashounam
**will walk And every one his neighbour they will deceive and the truth not will speak they have taught their tongue**

9:6
דבר 1696 שקר 8267 העוה 5753 נלאו 3811: שבתך 3427 בתוך 8432 מרמה 4820 במרמה 4820
daber sheqer ha'aueh nila'au. shibtaka batouk mirmah; bamirmah
**to speak lies to commit iniquity *and* weary themselves Thine habitation *is* in the midst of deceit through deceit**

9:7
מאנו 3985 דעת 3045 אותי 853 נאם 5002 יהוה 3068: לכן 3651 כה 3541 אמר 559 יהוה 3068 צבאות 6635 הנני 2005 צורפם 6884
me'anu da'at 'autiy na'am Yahuah. laken, koh 'amar Yahuah tzaba'aut, hinniy tzourapam
**they refuse to know me saith Yahuah Therefore thus saith Yahuah of hosts Behold I will melt them**

9:8
ובחנתים 974 כי 3588 איך 349 אעשה 6213 מפני 6440 בת 1323 עמי 5971: חץ 2671 שוחט 7819 לשונם 3956 מרמה 4820
uabchantiym; kiy 'aeyk 'aaseh, mipaney bat 'amiy. chetz shouchet lashounam mirmah
**and try them for how shall I do for the daughter of my people? *is as* an arrow shot out; Their tongue deceit**

9:9
דבר 1696 בפיו 6310 שלום 7965 את 854 רעהו 7453 ידבר 1696 ובקרבו 7130 ישים 7760 ארבו 696: העל 5921 אלה 428
diber; bapiyu, shaloum 'at re'aehu yadaber, uabqirbou yasiym 'arabou. ha'al 'aeleh
**it speak with his mouth peaceably *to* his neighbour *one* speak but in heart he lay his wait for these *things*?**

9:10
לא 3808 אפקד 6485 בם 871a נאם 5002 יהוה 3068 אם 518 בגוי 1471 אשר 834 כזה 2088 לא 3808 תתנקם 5358 נפשי 5315: על 5921
la' 'apqad bam na'am Yahuah; 'am bagouy 'asher kazeh, la' titnaqem napshiy. 'al
**not Shall I visit them saith Yahuah or on a nation such as this? not shall be avenged my soul For**

ההרים 2022 אשא 5375 בכי 1065 ונהי 5092 ועל 5921 נאות 4999 מדבר 4057 קינה 7015 כי 3588
hehariym 'asa' bakiy uanehiy, ua'al na'aut midbar qiynah, kiy
**the mountains will I take up a weeping and wailing and for the habitations of the wilderness a lamentation because**

נצתו 3341 מבלי 1097 איש 376 עבר 5674 ולא 3808 שמעו 8085 קול 6963 מקנה 4735 מעוף 5775
nitztu mibaliy 'aysh 'aber, uala' shama'au qoul miqneh; me'aup
**they are burned up so that no man can pass through *them* neither can *men* hear the voice of the cattle *both* the fowl of**

9:11
השמים 8064 ועד 5704 בהמה 929 נדדו 5074 הלכו 1980: ונתתי 5414 את 853 ירושלם 3389 לגלים 1530 מעון 4583 תנים 8577
hashamayim ua'ad bahemah, nadadu halaku. uanatatiy 'at yarushalaim lagaliym ma'aun taniym;
**the heavens and unto the beast are fled they are gone And I will make Jerusalem heaps *and* a den of dragons**

Jer 9:3 And they bend their tongues like their bow for lies: but they are not valiant for the truth upon the earth; for they proceed from evil to evil, and they know not me, saith YHUH.4 Take you heed everyone of his neighbor, and trust you not in any brother: forevery brother will utterly supplant, and every neighbor will walk with slanders.5 And they will deceive everyone his neighbor, and will not speak the truth: they have taught their tongue to speak lies, and weary themselves to commit iniquity.6 Thine habitation is in the midst of deceit; through deceit they refuse to know me, saith YHUH.7 Therefore thus saith YHUH of hosts, Behold, I will melt them, and try them; for how shall I do for the daughter of my people?8 Their tongue is as an arrow shot out; it speaketh deceit: one speaketh peaceably to his neighbor with his mouth, but in heart he layeth his wait.9 Shall I not visit them for these things? saith YHUH: shall not my soul be avenged on such a nation as this?10 For the mountains will I take up a weeping and wailing, and for the habitations of the wilderness a lamentation, because they are burned up, so that none can pass through them; neither can men hear the voice of the cattle; both the fowl of the heavens and the beast are fled; they are gone.11 And I will make Jerusalem heaps, and a den of dragons; and I will make the cities of Judah desolate, without an inhabitant.

9:12

ואת 853 ערי 5892 יהודה 3063 אתן 5414 שממה 8077 מבלי 1097 יושב 3427: מי 4310 האיש 376 החכם 2450 ויבן 995

ua'at 'arey yahudah 'aten shamamah mibaliy yousheb. miy' ha'aysh hechakam uayaben

***and*** **the cities of Judah I will make desolate without an inhabitant Who man *is* the wise that may understand**

את 853 זאת 2063 ואשר 834 דבר 1696 פי 6310 יהוה 3068 אליו 413 ויגדה 5046 על 5921 מה 4100

'at za't, ua'asher diber piy Yahuah 'aelayu uayagidah; 'al mah

**this? and to whom has spoken the mouth of Yahuah *who is he* to whom that he may declare it for what**

9:13

אבדה 6 הארץ 776 נצתה 3341 כמדבר 4057 מבלי 1097 עבר 5674: ויאמר 559 יהוה 3069 על 5921

'abadah ha'aretz, nitztah kamidbar mibliy 'aber. uaya'mer Yahuah, 'al

**perish the land *and* is burned up like a wilderness that none passed through? And saith Yahuah Because**

9:14

עזבם 5800 את 853 תורתי 8451 אשר 834 נתתי 5414 לפניהם 6440 ולא 3808 שמעו 8085 בקולי 6963 ולא 3808 הלכו 1980 בה 871a:

'azabam 'at touratiy, 'asher natatiy lipneyhem; uala' shama'au baqouliy uala' halaku bah.

**they have forsaken my law which I set before them and not have obeyed my voice neither walked therein;**

9:15

וילכו 1980 אחרי 310 שררות 8307 לבם 3820 ואחרי 310 הבעלים 1168 אשר 834 למדום 3925 אבותם 1:

uayelaku, 'acharey sharirut libam; ua'acharey haba'aliym, 'asher limadum aboutam.

**But have walked after the imagination of their own heart and after Baalim which taught their fathers**

לכן 3651 כה 3541 אמר 559 יהוה 3068 צבאות 6635 אלהי 430 ישראל 3478 הנני 2005 מאכילם 398 את 853 העם 5971 הזה 2088

laken, koh 'amar Yahuah tzaba'aut 'alohey yisra'ael, hinniy ma'akiylam 'at ha'am hazeh

**Therefore thus saith Yahuah of hosts the Elohim of Israel Behold I will feed them the people *even* this**

9:16

לענה 3939 והשקיתים 8248 מי 4325 ראש 7219: והפצותים 6327 בגוים 1471 אשר 834 לא 3808

la'anah; uahishqiytiym mey ra'sh. uahapitzoutiym bagouyim, 'asher la'

**with wormwood and give them to drink water of gall I will scatter them also among the heathen whom neither**

9:17

ידעו 3045 המה 1992 ואבותם 1 ושלחתי 7971 אחריהם 310 את 853 החרב 2719 עד 5704 כלותי 3615 אותם 853:

yada'au, hemah ba'aboutam; uashilachtiy 'achareyhem 'at hachereb, 'ad kaloutiy 'autam.

**have known they nor their fathers and I will send after them a sword till I have consumed them**

כה 3541 אמר 559 יהוה 3068 צבאות 6635 התבוננו 995 וקראו 7121 למקוננות 6969 ותבואינה 935 ואל 413

koh 'amar Yahuah tzaba'aut, hitbounau uaqir'au lamaqounanout uatbou'aynah; ua'al

**Thus saith Yahuah of hosts Consider you and call for the mourning women that they may come and for**

9:18

החכמות 2450 שלחו 7971 ותבואנה 935: ותמהרנה 4116 ותשנה 5375 עלינו 5921 נהי 5092

hachakamout shilchu uatabou'anah. uatmaheranah uatisenah 'aleynu nehiy;

**cunning *women* send that they may come And let them make haste and take up for us a wailing**

9:19

ותרדנה 33181 עינינו 5869 דמעה 1832 ועפעפינו 6079 יזלו 5140 מים 4325: כי 3588 קול 6963 נהי 5092 נשמע 8085

uateradnah 'aeyneynu dim'ah, ua'ap'apeynu yizlu mayim. kiy qoul nahiy nishma'

**that may run down our eyes *with* tears and our eyelids gush out *with* waters For a voice of wailing is heard**

מציון 6726 איך 349 שדדנו 7703 בשנו 954 מאד 3966 כי 3588 עזבנו 5800 ארץ 776 כי 3588 השליכו 7993

mitziyoun 'aeyk shudadanu; boshanu ma'ad kiy 'azabnu 'aretz, kiy hishliyku

**out of Zion How are we spoiled we are confounded greatly because we have forsaken the land because have cast *us* out**

Jer 9:12 Who is the wise man, that may understand this? and who is he to whom the mouth of YHUH has spoken, that he may declare it, for what the land perisheth and is burned up like a wilderness, that none pass through?13 And YHUH saith, Because they have forsaken my law which I set before them, and have not obeyed my voice, neither walked therein;14 But have walked after the imagination of their own heart, and after Baalim, which their fathers taught them:15 Therefore thus saith YHUH of hosts, the G-d of Israel; Behold, I will feed them, even this people, with wormwood, and give them water of gall to drink.16 I will scatter them also among the heathen, whom neither they nor their fathers have known: and I will send a sword after them, till I have consumed them.17 Thus saith YHUH of hosts, Consider you, and call for the mourning women, that they may come; and send for cunning women, that they may come:18 And let them make haste, and take up a wailing for us, that our eyes may run down with tears, and our eyelids gush out with waters.19 For a voice of wailing is heard out of Zion, How are we spoiled! we are greatly confounded, because we have forsaken the land, because our dwellings have cast us out.

| | 9:20 | | | | | | | | |
|---|---|---|---|---|---|---|---|---|---|
| משכנותינו 4908: | כי 3588 | שמענה 8085 | נשים 802 | דבר 1697 | יהוה 3068 | ותקח 3947 | אזנכם 241 | דבר 1697 | פיו 6310 |
| mishkanouteynu. | kiy | shama'anah | nashiym | dabar | Yahuah, | uatiqach | 'aznakem | dabar | piyu; |
| **our dwellings** | **Yet** | **hear** | **O you women** | **the word of** | **Yahuah** | **and let receive** | **your ear** | **the word of** | **his mouth** |

| | | | | | | 9:21 | | |
|---|---|---|---|---|---|---|---|---|
| ולמדנה 3925 | בנותיכם 1323 | נהי 5092 | ואשה 802 | רעותה 7468 | קינה 7015: | כי 3588 | עלה 5927 | מות 4194 |
| ualamedanah | banouteykem | nehiy, | ua'ashah | ra'utah | qiynah. | kiy | 'alah | mauet |
| **and teach** | **your daughters** | **wailing** | **and every one** | **her neighbour** | **lamentation** | **For** | **is come up** | **death** |

| | | | | | | |
|---|---|---|---|---|---|---|
| בחלונינו 2474 | בא 935 | בארמנותינו 759 | להכרית 3772 | עולל 5768 | מחוץ 2351 | בחורים 970 |
| bachalouneynu, | ba' | ba'armanouteynu; | lahakriyt | 'aulal | michutz, | bachuriym |
| **into our windows** | ***and* is entered** | **into our palaces** | **to cut off** | **the children** | **from without** | ***and* the young men** |

| | 9:22 | | | | | | | | | | | |
|---|---|---|---|---|---|---|---|---|---|---|---|---|
| מרחבות 7339: | דבר 1696 | כה 3541 | נאם 5002 | יהוה 3068 | ונפלה 5307 | נבלת 5038 | האדם 120 | כדמן 1828 | על 5921 | פני 6440 | השדה 7704 |
| merachobout. | daber, | koh | na'am | Yahuah, | uanapalah | niblat | ha'adam, | kadomen | 'al | paney | hasadeh; |
| **from the streets** | **Speak** | **Thus** | **saith** | **Yahuah** | **Even shall fall** | **the carcases of** | **men** | **as dung** | **upon** | **open** | **the field** |

| | | | | | 9:23 | | | | |
|---|---|---|---|---|---|---|---|---|---|
| וכעמיר 5995 | מאחרי 310 | הקצר 7114 | ואין 369 | מאסף 622: | כה 3541 | אמר 559 | יהוה 3068 | אל 408 | יתהלל 1984 |
| uak'amiyr | me'acharey | haqotzer | ua'aeyn | ma'asep. | koh | 'amar | Yahuah | 'al | yithalel |
| **and as the handful** | **after** | **the harvestman** | **and none** | **shall gather *them*** | **Thus** | **saith** | **Yahuah** | **not** | **Let *man* glory** |

| | | | | | | | | | | 9:24 |
|---|---|---|---|---|---|---|---|---|---|---|
| חכם 2450 | בחכמתו 2451 | ואל 408 | יתהלל 1984 | הגבור 1368 | בגבורתו 1369 | אל 408 | יתהלל 1984 | עשיר 6223 | בעשרו 6239: | כי 3588 |
| chakam | bachakamatou, | ua'al | yithalel | hagibour | bigaburatou; | 'al | yithalel | 'ashiyr | ba'asharou. | kiy |
| **the wise** | **in his wisdom** | **neither** | ***man* glory** | **let the mighty** | **in his might** | **not** | **let glory** | ***the* rich *man*** | **in his riches** | **But** |

| | | | | | | | | | | |
|---|---|---|---|---|---|---|---|---|---|---|
| אם 518 | בזאת 2063 | יתהלל 1984 | המתהלל 1984 | השכל 7919 | וידע 3045 | אותי 853 | כי 3588 | אני 589 | יהוה 3068 | עשה 6213 |
| 'am | baza't | yithalel | hamithalel, | haskel | uayadoa' | 'autiy | kiy | 'aniy | Yahuah, | 'asheh |
| **rather** | **in this** | **let him that glories** | **glory** | **that he understands** | **and knows** | **me** | **that** | **I *am*** | **Yahuah** | **which exercise** |

| | | | | | | | | | 9:25 |
|---|---|---|---|---|---|---|---|---|---|
| חסד 2617 | משפט 4941 | וצדקה 6666 | בארץ 776 | כי 3588 | באלה 428 | חפצתי 2654 | נאם 5002 | יהוה 3068: | הנה 2009 |
| chesed | mishapat | uatzdaqah | ba'aretz; | kiy | ba'aeleh | chapatztiy | na'am | Yahuah. | hineh |
| **lovingkindness** | **judgment** | **and righteousness** | **in the earth** | **for** | **in these *things*** | **I delight** | **saith** | **Yahuah** | **Behold** |

| | | | | | | | | | 9:26 |
|---|---|---|---|---|---|---|---|---|---|
| ימים 3117 | באים 935 | נאם 5002 | יהוה 3068 | ופקדתי 6485 | על 5921 | כל 3605 | מול 4135 | בערלה 6190: | |
| yamiym | ba'aym | na'am | Yahuah; | uapaqadtiy, | 'al | kal | mul | ba'aralah. | |
| **the days** | **come** | **saith** | **Yahuah** | **that I will punish** | **on** | **all** | ***them which are* circumcised** | **with the uncircumcised** | |

| | | | | | | | | | | | |
|---|---|---|---|---|---|---|---|---|---|---|---|
| על 5921 | מצרים 4714 | ועל 5921 | יהודה 3063 | ועל 5921 | אדום 123 | ועל 5921 | בני 1121 | עמון 5983 | ועל 5921 | מואב 4124 | ועל 5921 | כל 3605 |
| 'al | mitzrayim | ua'al | yahudah, | ua'al | 'adoum | ua'al | baney | 'amoun | ua'al | mou'ab, | ua'al | kal |
| **in** | **Egypt** | **and in** | **Judah** | **and in** | **Edom** | **and in** | **and the children of** | **Ammon** | **and in** | **Moab** | **and in** | **all** |

| | | | | | | | | | |
|---|---|---|---|---|---|---|---|---|---|
| קצוצי 7112 | פאה 6285 | הישבים 3427 | במדבר 4057 | כי 3588 | כל 3605 | הגוים 1471 | ערלים 6189 | וכל 3605 | בית 1004 |
| qatzutzey | pe'ah, | hayoshbiym | bamidbar; | kiy | kal | hagouyim | 'areliym, | uakal | beyt |
| ***that are* in the utmost** | **corners** | **that dwell** | **in the wilderness** | **for** | **all** | ***these* nations *are*** | **uncircumcised** | **and all** | **the house of** |

| | | |
|---|---|---|
| ישראל 3478 | ערלי 6189 | לב 3820: |
| yisra'ael | 'arley | leb. |
| **Israel** | ***are* uncircumcised in** | **the heart** |

Jer 9:20 Yet hear the word of YHUH, O you women, and let your ear receive the word of his mouth, and teach your daughters wailing, and everyone her neighbor lamentation.21 For death is come up into our windows, and is entered into our palaces, to cut off the children from without, and the young men from the streets.22 Speak, Thus saith YHUH, Even the carcases of men shall fall as dung upon the open field, and as the handful after the harvestman, and none shall gather them.23 Thus saith YHUH, Let not the wise man glory in his wisdom, neither let the mighty man glory in his might, let not the rich man glory in his riches:24 But let him that glorieth glory in this, that he understandeth and know me, that I am YHUH which exercise lovingkindness, judgment, and righteousness, in the earth: for in these things I delight, saith YHUH.25 Behold, the days come, saith YHUH, that I will punish all them which are circumcised with the uncircumcised;26 Egypt, and Judah, and Edom, and the children of Ammon, and Moab, and all that are in the utmost corners, that dwell in the wilderness: for all these nations are uncircumcised, and all the house of Israel are uncircumcised in the heart.

**Jer 10:1** … 10:2

שמעו 8085 את 853 הדבר 1697 אשר 834 דבר 1696 יהוה 3068 עליכם 5921 בית 1004 ישראל 3478: כה 3541 אמר 559 יהוה 3068 אל 413
shim'au 'at hadabar, 'asher diber Yahuah 'aleykem beyt yisra'ael. koh 'amar Yahuah 'al
**Hear you the word which speak Yahuah unto you O house of Israel Thus saith Yahuah about**

דרך 1870 הגוים 1471 אל 408 תלמדו 3925 ומאתות 226 השמים 8064 אל 408 תחתו 2865 כי 3588 יחתו 2865 הגוים 1471
derek hagouyim 'al tilmadu, uame'atout hashamayim 'al techatu; kiy yechatu hagouyim
**the way of the heathen not Learn and at the signs of heaven not be dismayed for are dismayed the heathen**

10:3

מהמה 1992: כי 3588 חקות 2708 העמים 5971 הבל 1892 הוא 1931 כי 3588 עץ 6086 מיער 3293 כרתו 3772 מעשה 4639
mehemah. kiy chuqout ha'amiym hebel hua'; kiy 'aetz miya'ar karatou, ma'aseh
**at them For the customs of the people *are* vain he for a tree out of the forest *one* cuts the work of**

10:4

ידי 3027 חרש 2796 במעצד 4621: בכסף 3701 ובזהב 2091 ייפהו 3302 במסמרות 4548 ובמקבות 4717
yadey charash bama'atzad. bakesep uabzahab yayapehu; bamasmarout uabmaqabout
**the hands of the workman with the axe with silver and with gold They deck it with nails and with hammers**

10:5

יחזקום 2388 ולוא 3808 יפיק 6328: כתמר 8560 מקשה 4749 המה 1992 ולא 3808 ידברו 1696 נשוא 5375 ינשוא 5375 כי 3588
yachazqum ualou'a yapiyq. katomer miqshah hemah uala' yadaberu, nasou'a yinasu'a kiy
**they fasten it that not it move as the palm tree *are* upright They but not speak they must needs be borne because**

10:6

לא 3808 יצעדו 6805 אל 408 תיראו 3372 מהם 1992 כי 3588 לא 3808 ירעו 7489 וגם 1571 היטיב 3190 אין 369 אותם 854:
la' yitz'adu; 'al tiyra'au mehem kiy la' yare'au, uagam heyteyb 'aeyn 'autam.
**cannot they go not Be afraid of them for cannot they do evil neither also to do good neither *is it* in them**

10:7

מאין 369 כמוך 3644 יהוה 3068 גדול 1419 אתה 859 וגדול 1419 שמך 8034 בגבורה 1369: מי 4310 לא 3808
me'ayn kamouka Yahuah; gadoul 'atah uagadoul shimka bigburah. miy' la'
**Forasmuch as *there is* none like unto you O Yahuah *are* great you and great *is* your name in might Who not**

יראך 3372 מלך 4428 הגוים 1471 כי 3588 לך 3807a יאתה 2969 כי 3588 בכל 3605 חכמי 2450
yira'aka melek hagouyim, kiy laka ya'atah; kiy bakal chakmey
**would fear you O King of the nations? for to you does he appertain: forasmuch as among all the wise *men* of**

10:8

הגוים 1471 ובכל 3605 מלכותם 4438 מאין 369 כמוך 3644: ובאחת 259 יבערו 1197 ויכסלו 3688
hagouyim uabkal malkutam me'ayn kamouka. uab'achat yib'aru uayikasalu;
**the nations and in all their kingdoms there is none like unto you But altogether they are brutish and foolish**

10:9

מוסר 4148 הבלים 1892 עץ 6086 הוא 1931: כסף 3701 מרקע 7554 מתרשיש 8659 יובא 935 וזהב 2091 מאופז 210
musar habaliym 'aetz hua'. kesep maruqa' mitarshiysh yuba', uazahab me'aupaz,
***is* a doctrine of vanities the stock he Silver spread into plates from Tarshish is brought and gold from Uphaz**

מעשה 4639 חרש 2796 וידי 3027 צורף 6884 תכלת 8504 וארגמן 713 לבושם 3830 מעשה 4639 חכמים 2450
ma'aseh charash uiydey tzourep; takelet ua'argaman labusham, ma'aseh chakamiym
**the work of the workman and of the hands of the founder blue and purple *is* their clothing the work of cunning *men***

10:10

כלם 3605: ויהוה 3068 אלהים 430 אמת 571 הוא 1931 אלהים 430 חיים 2416 ומלך 4428 עולם 5769 מקצפו 97110
kulam. uaYahuah 'alohiym 'amet, hua' 'alohiym chayiym uamelek 'aulam; miqitzpou
**they *are* all But Yahuah Elohim *is* the true he Elohim *is* the living and an king everlasting at his wrath**

**Jer** 10:1 Hear you the word which YHUH speaketh unto you, O house of Israel:2 Thus saith YHUH, Learn not the way of the heathen, and be not dismayed at the signs of heaven; for the heathen are dismayed at them.3 For the customs of the people are vain: for one cutteth a tree out of the forest, the work of the hands of the workman, with the axe.4 They deck it with silver and with gold; they fasten it with nails and with hammers, that it move not.5 They are upright as the palm tree, but speak not: they must needs be borne, because they cannot go. Be not afraid of them; for they cannot do evil, neither also is it in them to do good.6 Forasmuch as there is none like unto you, O YHUH; you are great, and your name is great in might.7 Who would not fear you, O King of nations? for to you doth it appertain: forasmuch as among all the wise men of the nations, and in all their kingdoms, there is none like unto you.8 But they are altogether brutish and foolish: the stock is a doctrine of vanities.9 Silver spread into plates is brought from Tarshish, and gold from Uphaz, the work of the workman, and of the hands of the founder: blue and purple is their clothing: they are all the work of cunning men.10 But YHUH is the true G-d, he is the living G-d, and an everlasting king: at his wrath the earth shall tremble, and the nations shall not be able to abide his indignation.

תרעש 7493 | הארץ 776 | ולא 3808 | יכלו 3557 | גוים 1471 | זעמו 2195: | 10:11 | כדנה 1836 | תאמרון 560 | להום 3807a
tira'ash | ha'aretz, | uala' | yakilu | gouyim | za'amou. | | kidanah | ta'marun | lahoum,
**shall tremble** | **the earth** | **and not** | ***the* shall be able to abide** | **nations** | **his indignation** | | **Thus** | **shall you say** | **unto them**

אלהיא 426 | די 1768 | שמיא 8065 | וארקא 778 | לא 3809 | עבדו 5648 | יאבדו 7 | מארעא 772 | ומן 4481 | תחות 8460 | שמיא 8065
'alahaya', | diy | shamaya' | ua'arqa' | la' | 'abadu; | yea'badu | me'araa' | uamin | tachout | shamaya'
**The gods that** | **the heavens** | **and the earth** | **not** | **have made *even*** | **they shall perish** | **from the earth** | **and from under** | **heavens**

אלה 429: | 10:12 | עשה 6213 | ארץ 776 | בכחו 3581 | מכין 3559 | תבל 8398 | בחכמתו 2451 | ובתבונתו 8394
'aeleh. | | 'aseh | 'aretz | bakochou, | mekiyn | tebel | bachakamatou; | uabitbunatou
**these** | | **He has made** | **the earth** | **by his power** | **he has established** | **the world** | **by his wisdom** | **and by his discretion**

נטה 5186 | שמים 8064: | 10:13 | לקול 6963 | תתו 5414 | המון 1995 | מים 4325 | בשמים 8064
natah | shamayim. | | laqoul | titou | hamoun | mayim | bashamayim,
**has stretched out** | **the heavens** | | **When his voice** | **he utter** | ***there is* a multitude of** | **waters** | **in the heavens**

ויעלה 5927 | נשאים 5387 | מקצה 7097 | ארץ 776 | ברקים 1300 | למטר 4306 | עשה 6213 | ויוצא 3318 | רוח 7307
uaya'aleh | nashi'aym | miqtzeh | 'aretz | baraqiym | lamatar | 'asah, | uayoutzea' | ruach
**and he cause to ascend** | **the vapours** | **from the ends of** | **the earth** | **lightnings** | **with rain** | **he make** | **and bring forth** | **the wind**

מאצרתיו 214: | 10:14 | נבער 1197 | כל 3605 | אדם 120 | מדעת 1847 | הביש 3001 | כל 3605 | צורף 6884 | מפסל 6459 | כי 3588
me'atzarotayu. | | nib'ar | kal | 'adam | mida'at, | hobiysh | kal | tzourep | mipasel; | kiy
**out of his treasures** | | **is brutish** | **Every** | **man** | **in *his* knowledge** | **is confounded** | **every** | **founder** | **by the graven image** | **for**

שקר 8267 | נסכו 5262 | ולא 3808 | רוח 7307 | בם 871a: | 10:15 | הבל 1892 | המה 1992 | מעשה 4639 | תעתעים 8595
sheqer | niskou | uala' | ruach | bam. | | hebel | hemah, | ma'aseh | ta'atu'aym;
***is* falsehood** | **his molten image** | **and *there is* no** | **breath** | **in them** | | ***are* vanity** | **They** | ***and* the work of** | **errors**

בעת 6256 | פקדתם 6486 | יאבדו 6: | 10:16 | לא 3808 | כאלה 428 | חלק 2506 | יעקב 3290 | כי 3588 | יוצר 3335
ba'aet | paqudatam | ya'bedu. | | la' | ka'aeleh | cheleq | ya'aqob, | kiy | youtzer
**in the time of** | **their visitation** | **they shall perish** | | **not** | **like them** | **The portion of** | **Jacob** | ***is* for** | ***is* the former of**

הכל 3605 | הוא 1931 | וישראל 3478 | שבט 7626 | נחלתו 5159 | יהוה 3068 | צבאות 6635 | שמו 8034: | 10:17 | אספי 622 | מארץ 776
hakol | hua', | uayisra'ael, | shebet | nachalatou; | Yahuah | tzaba'aut | shamou. | | 'aspiy | me'aretz
**all *things*** | **he** | **and Israel** | ***is* the rod of** | **his inheritance** | **Yahuah** | **of hosts** | ***is* his name** | | **Gather up** | **out of the land**

כנעתך 3666 | ישבתי 3427 | במצור 4692: | 10:18 | כי 3588 | כה 3541 | אמר 559 | יהוה 3069 | הנני 2005 | קולע 7049 | את 853 | יושבי 3427
kin'atek; | yoshabtiy | bamatzour. | | kiy | koh | 'amar | Yahuah, | hinniy | qoulea' | 'at | youshabey
**your wares** | **O inhabitant** | **of the fortress** | | **For** | **thus** | **saith** | **Yahuah** | **Behold** | **I will sling out** | | **the inhabitants of**

הארץ 776 | בפעם 6471 | הזאת 2063 | והצרותי 6887 | להם 1992 | למען 4616 | ימצאו 4672: | 10:19 | אוי 188 | לי 3807a | על 5921 | שברי 7667 | נחלה 2470
ha'aretz | bapa'am | haza't; | uahatzeroutiy | lahem | lama'an | yimtza'au. | | 'auy | liy | 'al | shibriy, | nachalah
**the land** | **at once** | **this** | **and will distress them** | | **that** | **they may find it so** | | **Woe** | ***is* me** | **for** | **my hurt** | **is grievous**

מכתי 4347 | ואני 589 | אמרתי 559 | אך 389 | זה 2088 | חלי 2483 | ואשאנו 5375: | 10:20 | אהלי 168 | שדד 7703 | וכל 3605 | מיתרי 4340
makatiy; | ua'aniy | 'amartiy, | 'ak | zeh | chaliy | ua'asa'anu. | | 'ahaliy | shudad, | uakal | meytaray
**my wound** | **but I** | **said** | **Truly** | **this** | ***is* a grief** | **and I must bear it** | | **My tabernacle** | **is spoiled** | **and all** | **my cords**

Jer 10:11 Thus shall you say unto them, The gods that have not made the heavens and the earth, even they shall perish from the earth, and from under these heavens.12 He has made the earth by his power, he has established the world by his wisdom, and has stretched out the heavens by his discretion.13 When he uttereth his voice, there is a multitude of waters in the heavens, and he causeth the vapours to ascend from the ends of the earth; he make lightnings with rain, and bring forth the wind out of his treasures.14 Every man is brutish in his knowledge: every founder is confounded by the graven image: for his molten image is falsehood, and there is no breath in them.15 They are vanity, and the work of errors: in the time of their visitation they shall perish.16 The portion of Jacob is not like them: for he is the former of all things; and Israel is the rod of his inheritance: YHUH of hosts is his name.17 Gather up your wares out of the land, O inhabitant of the fortress.18 For thus saith YHUH, Behold, I will sling out the inhabitants of the land at this once, and will distress them, that they may find it so.19 Woe is me for my hurt! my wound is grievous: but I said, Truly this is a grief, and I must bear it.20 My tabernacle is spoiled, and all my cords are broken: my children are gone forth of me, and they are not: there is none to stretch forth my tent anymore, and to set up my curtains.

נתקו 5423 בני 1121 יצאני 3318 ואינם 369 אין 369 נטה 5186 עוד 5750 אהלי 168 ומקים 6965
nitaqu; banay yatza'aniy ua'aeynam, 'aeyn noteh 'aud 'ahaliy, uameqiym
**are broken my children are gone forth of me and they *are* not *there is* none to stretch forth any more my tent and to set up**

10:21
יריעותי 3407: כי 3588 נבערו 1197 הרעים 7462 ואת 853 יהוה 3068 לא 3808 דרשו 1875 על 5921 כן 3651 לא 3808
yariy'atay. kiy nib'aru haro'aym, ua'at Yahuah la' darashu; 'al ken la'
**my curtains For are become brutish the pastors *and* Yahuah not have sought therefore after not**

10:22
השכילו 7919 וכל 3605 מרעיתם 4830 נפוצה 6327: קול 6963 שמועה 8052 הנה 2009 באה 935 ורעש 7494
hiskiylu, uakal mar'aytam napoutzah. qoul shamu'ah hineh ba'ah, uara'ash
**they shall prosper and all their flocks shall be scattered the noise of the bruit Behold is come and a commotion**

10:23
גדול 1419 מארץ 776 צפון 6828 לשום 7760 את 853 ערי 5892 יהודה 3063 שממה 8077 מעון 4583 תנים 8577: ידעתי 3045
gadoul me'aretz tzapoun; lasum 'at 'arey yahudah shamamah ma'aun taniym. yada'tiy
**great out of country *the* north to make the cities of Judah desolate *and* a den of dragons I know**

10:24
יהוה 3068 כי 3588 לא 3808 לאדם 120 דרכו 1870 לא 3808 לאיש 376 הלך 1980 והכין 3559 את 853 צעדו 6806: יסרני 3256
Yahuah, kiy la' la'adam darkou; la' la'aysh holek, uahakiyn 'at tza'adou. yasreniy
**O Yahuah that not of man *is* the way in himself *it is* not in man that walk to direct his steps correct me**

10:25
יהוה 3068 אך 389 במשפט 4941 אל 408 באפך 639 פן 6435 תמעטני 4591: שפך 8210 חמתך 2534 על 5921
Yahuah 'ak bamishpat; 'al ba'apaka pen tam'ateniy. shapok chamataka, 'al
**O Yahuah but with judgment not in your anger lest you bring me to nothing Pour out your fury upon**

הגוים 1471 אשר 834 לא 3808 ידעוך 3045 ועל 5921 משפחות 4940 אשר 834 בשמך 8034 לא 3808 קראו 7121 כי 3588 אכלו 398
hagouyim 'asher la' yada'auka, ua'al mishpachout, 'asher bashimaka la' qara'au; kiy 'akalu
**the heathen that not know you and upon the families that on your name not call for they have eaten up**

את 853 יעקב 3290 ואכלהו 398 ויכלהו 3615 ואת 853 נוהו 5116 השמו 8074:
'at ya'aqob, ua'akaluhu uayakaluhu, ua'at nauehu heshamu.
**Jacob and devoured him and consumed him *and* his habitation have made desolate**

**Jer 11:1** 11:2
הדבר 1697 אשר 834 היה 1961 אל 413 ירמיהו 3414 מאת 853 יהוה 3068 לאמר 559: שמעו 8085 את 853 דברי 1697 הברית 1285
hadabar 'asher hayah 'al yirmayahu, me'at Yahuah lea'mor. shim'au 'at dibrey habariyt
**The word that came to Jeremiah from Yahuah saying Hear you the words of covenant**

11:3
הזאת 2063 ודברתם 1696 אל 413 איש 376 יהודה 3063 ועל 5921 ישבי 3427 ירושלם 3389: ואמרת 559 אליהם 413 כה 3541
haza't; uadibartam 'al 'aysh yahudah, ua'al yoshabey yarushalaim. ua'amarta 'aleyhem, koh
**this and speak unto the men of Judah and to the inhabitants of Jerusalem And say you unto them Thus**

11:4
אמר 559 יהוה 3068 אלהי 430 ישראל 3478 ארור 779 האיש 376 אשר 834 לא 3808 ישמע 8085 את 853 דברי 1697 הברית 1285 הזאת 2063:
'amar Yahuah 'alohey yisra'ael; 'arur ha'aysh, 'asher la' yishma', 'at dibrey habariyt haza't.
**saith Yahuah Elohim of Israel Cursed *be* the man that not obeyed the words of covenant this**

אשר 834 צויתי 6680 את 853 אבותיכם 1 ביום 3117 הוציאי 3318 אותם 853 מארץ 776 מצרים 4714 מכור 3564
'asher tziuiytiy 'at abouteykem bayoum houtziy'ay 'autam me'eretz mitzrayim mikur
**Which I commanded your fathers in the day *that* I brought forth them out of the land of Egypt from furnace**

Jer 10:21 For the pastors are become brutish, and have not sought YHUH: therefore they shall not prosper, and all their flocks shall be scattered.22 Behold, the noise of the bruit is come, and a great commotion out of the north country, to make the cities of Judah desolate, and a den of dragons.23 O YHUH, I know that the way of man is not in himself: it is not in man that walk to direct his steps.24 O YHUH, correct me, but with judgment; not in your anger, lest you bring me to nothing.25 Pour out your fury upon the heathen that know you not, and upon the families that call not on your name: for they have eaten up Jacob, and devoured him, and consumed him, and have made his habitation desolate. **Jer** 11:1 The word that came to Jeremiah from YHUH, saying,2 Hear you the words of this covenant, and speak unto the men of Judah, and to the inhabitants of Jerusalem;3 And say you unto them, Thus saith YHUH G-d of Israel; Cursed be the man that obeyeth not the words of this covenant,4 Which I commanded your fathers in the day that I brought them forth out of the land of Egypt, from the iron furnace, saying, Obey my voice, and do them, according to all which I command you: so shall you be my people, and I will be your G-d:

| | | | | | | | | | | | |
|---|---|---|---|---|---|---|---|---|---|---|---|
| 1270 הברזל | 559 לאמר | 8085 שמעו | 6963 בקולי | 6213 ועשיתם | 853 אותם | 3605 ככל | 834 אשר | 6680 אצוה | 853 אתכם | 1961 והייתם | 3807a לי |
| habarzel | lea'mor, | shim'au | baqouliy | ua'asiytem | 'autam, | kakol | 'asher | 'atzaueh | 'atkem; | uihayiytem | liy |
| **the iron** | **saying** | **Obey** | **my voice** | **and do** | **them** | **according to all** | **which** | **I command** | **you** | **so shall you be** | **my** |

| | | | | | | | | | | | |
|---|---|---|---|---|---|---|---|---|---|---|---|
| 5971 לעם | 595 ואנכי | 1961 אהיה | 3807a לכם | 430: לאלהים | 11:5 | 4616 למען | 6965 הקים | 853 את | 7621 השבועה | 834 אשר | 7650 נשבעתי |
| la'am, | ua'anokiy, | 'ahayeh | lakem | le'alohiym. | | lama'an | haqiym | 'at | hashabu'ah | 'asher | nishba'atiy |
| **people** | **and I** | **will be** | **to your** | **to Elohim** | | **That** | **I may perform** | | **the oath** | **which** | **I have sworn** |

| | | | | | | | | | | | |
|---|---|---|---|---|---|---|---|---|---|---|---|
| 1 לאבותיכם | 5414 לתת | 1992 להם | 776 ארץ | 2100 זבת | 2461 חלב | 1706 ודבש | 3117 כיום | 2088 הזה | 6030 ואען | 559 ואמר | 543 אמן |
| la'abouteykem, | latet | lahem | 'aretz | zabat | chalab | uadbash | kayoum | hazeh; | ua'aan | ua'amar | 'amen |
| **unto your fathers** | **to give** | **them** | **a land** | **flowing** | **with milk** | **and honey** | **as day** | ***it is* this** | **Then answered I** | **and said** | **So be it** |

| | | | | | | | | | | | |
|---|---|---|---|---|---|---|---|---|---|---|---|
| 3069: יהוה | 11:6 | 559 ויאמר | 3068 יהוה | 413 אלי | 7121 קרא | 853 את | 3605 כל | 1697 הדברים | 428 האלה | 5892 בערי | 3063 יהודה |
| Yahuah. | | uaya'mer | Yahuah | 'aelay, | qara' | 'at | kal | hadabariym | ha'aeleh | ba'arey | yahudah, |
| **Yahuah** | | **Then said** | **Yahuah** | **unto me** | **Proclaim** | | **all** | **words** | **these** | **in the cities of** | **Judah** |

| | | | | | | | | | | | |
|---|---|---|---|---|---|---|---|---|---|---|---|
| 2351 ובחצות | 3389 ירושלם | 559 לאמר | 8085 שמעו | 853 את | 1697 דברי | 1285 הברית | 2063 הזאת | 6213 ועשיתם | 853: אותם | 11:7 | 3588 כי |
| uabchutzout | yarushalaim | lea'mor; | shim'au, | 'at | dibrey | habariyt | haza't, | ua'asiytem | 'autam. | | kiy |
| **and in the streets of** | **Jerusalem** | **saying** | **Hear you** | | **the words of** | **covenant** | **this** | **and do** | **them** | | **For** |

| | | | | | | | | | |
|---|---|---|---|---|---|---|---|---|---|
| 5749 העד | 5749 העדתי | 1 באבותיכם | 3117 ביום | 5927 העלותי | 853 אותם | 776 מארץ | 4714 מצרים | 5704 ועד | 3117 היום |
| ha'aed | ha'adotiy | ba'abouteykem, | bayoum | ha'aloutiy | 'autam | me'aretz | mitzrayim | ua'ad | hayoum |
| **I earnestly** | **protested** | **unto your fathers** | **in the day** | ***that* I brought up** | **them** | **out of the land of** | **Egypt** | **even unto** | **day** |

| | | | | | | | | | | | |
|---|---|---|---|---|---|---|---|---|---|---|---|
| 2088 הזה | 7925 השכם | 5749 והעד | 559 לאמר | 8085 שמעו | 6963: בקולי | 11:8 | 3808 ולא | 8085 שמעו | 3808 ולא | 5186 הטו | 853 את | 
| hazeh, | hashkem | uaha'aed | lea'mor; | shim'au | baqouliy. | | uala' | shama'au | uala' | hitu | 'at |
| **this** | **rising early** | **and protesting** | **saying** | **Obey** | **my voice** | | **Yet not** | **they obeyed** | **nor** | **inclined** | |

| |
|---|
| 241 אזנם |
| 'azanam, |
| **their ear** |

| | | | | | | | | | |
|---|---|---|---|---|---|---|---|---|---|
| 1980 וילכו | 376 איש | 8307 בשרירות | 3820 לבם | 7451 הרע | 935 ואביא | 5921 עליהם | 853 את | 3605 כל | 1697 דברי |
| uayelaku, | 'aysh | bishriyrut | libam | hara'; | ua'abiy | 'aleyhem | 'at | kal | dibrey |
| **but walked** | **every one** | **in the imagination of** | **their heart** | **evil** | **therefore I will bring** | **upon them** | | **all** | **the words of** |

| | | | | | | | | | | | |
|---|---|---|---|---|---|---|---|---|---|---|---|
| 1285 הברית | 2063 הזאת | 834 אשר | 6680 צויתי | 6213 לעשות | 3808 ולא | 6213: עשו | 11:9 | 559 ויאמר | 3068 יהוה | 413 אלי | 4672 נמצא |
| habariyt | haza't | 'asher | tziuiytiy | la'asout | uala' | 'asu. | | uaya'mer | Yahuah | 'aelay; | nimtza |
| **covenant** | **this** | **which** | **I commanded** | ***them* to do** | **but not** | **they did *them*** | | **And said** | **Yahuah** | **unto me** | **is found** |

| | | | | | | | |
|---|---|---|---|---|---|---|---|
| 7195 קשר | 376 באיש | 3063 יהודה | 3427 ובישבי | 3389: ירושלם | 11:10 | 7725 שבו | 5921 על |
| qesher | ba'aysh | yahudah, | uabyoshabey | yarushalaim. | | shabu | 'al |
| **A conspiracy** | **among the men of** | **Judah** | **and among the inhabitants of** | **Jerusalem** | | **They are turned back** | **to** |

| | | | | | | | | | | |
|---|---|---|---|---|---|---|---|---|---|---|
| 5771 עונת | 1 אבותם | 7223 הראשנים | 834 אשר | 3985 מאנו | 8085 לשמוע | 853 את | 1697 דברי | 1992 והמה | 1980 הלכו | 310 אחרי |
| 'auonot | aboutam | hara'shoniym, | 'asher | me'anu | lishmoua' | 'at | dabaray, | uahemah | halaku, | 'acharey |
| **the iniquities of** | **with their fathers** | **their ancestors** | **which** | **refused** | **to hear** | | **my words** | **and they** | **went** | **after** |

| | | | | | | | | | | |
|---|---|---|---|---|---|---|---|---|---|---|
| 430 אלהים | 312 אחרים | 5647 לעבדם | 6565 הפרו | 1004 בית | 3478 ישראל | 1004 ובית | 3063 יהודה | 853 את | 1285 בריתי | 834 אשר |
| 'alohiym | 'acheriym | la'abadam; | heperu | beyt | yisra'ael | uabeyt | yahudah, | 'at | bariytiy | 'asher |
| **gods** | **other** | **to serve them** | **have broken** | **the house of** | **Israel** | **and the house of** | **Judah** | | **my covenant** | **which** |

Jer 11:5 That I may perform the oath which I have sworn unto your fathers, to give them a land flowing with milk and honey, as it is this day. Then answered I, and said, So be it, O YHUH.6 Then YHUH said unto me, Proclaim all these words in the cities of Judah, and in the streets of Jerusalem, saying, Hear you the words of this covenant, and do them.7 For I earnestly protested unto your fathers in the day that I brought them up out of the land of Egypt, even unto this day, rising early and protesting, saying, Obey my voice.8 Yet they obeyed not, nor inclined their ear, but walked everyone in the imagination of their evil heart: therefore I will bring upon them all the words of this covenant, which I commanded them to do; but they did them not.9 And YHUH said unto me, A conspiracy is found among the men of Judah, and among the inhabitants of Jerusalem.10 They are turned back to the iniquities of their forefathers, which refused to hear my words; and they went after other gods to serve them: the house of Israel and the house of Judah have broken my covenant which I made with their fathers.

כרתי 3772 את 854 אבותם 1: 11:11 לכן 3651 כה 3541 אמר 559 יהוה 3068 הנני 2005 מביא 935 אליהם 413 רעה 7451 אשר 834 לא 3808
karatiy 'at aboutam. laken, koh 'amar Yahuah, hinniy mebiy'a 'aleyhem ra'ah, 'asher la'
**I made *with* their fathers Therefore thus saith Yahuah Behold I will bring upon them evil which not**

יוכלו 3201 לצאת 3318 ממנה 4480 וזעקו 2199 אלי 413 ולא 3808 אשמע 8085 אליהם 413: 11:12 והלכו 1980
yukalu latzea't mimenah; uaza'aqu 'aelay, uala' 'ashma 'aleyhem. uahalaku
**they shall be able to escape from and though they shall cry unto me not I will listen unto them Then shall go**

ערי 5892 יהודה 3063 וישבי 3427 ירושלם 3389 וזעקו 2199 אל 413 האלהים 430 אשר 834 הם 1992 מקטרים 6999 להם 3807a
'arey yahudah, uayoushabey yarushalaim, uaza'aqu 'al ha'alohiym, 'asher hem maqatriym lahem;
**the cities of Judah and inhabitants of Jerusalem and cry unto the gods whom they offer incense unto**

והושע 3467 לא 3808 יושיעו 3467 להם 3807a בעת 6256 רעתם 7451: 11:13 כי 3588 מספר 4557 עריך 5892
uahoushea' la' youshiy'au lahem ba'aet ra'atam. kiy mispar 'areyka,
**but they shall save not at all them in the time of their trouble For *according to* the number of your cities**

היו 1961 אלהיך 430 יהודה 3063 ומספר 4557 חצות 2351 ירושלם 3389 שמתם 7760 מזבחות 4196
hayu 'aloheyka yahudah; uamispar chutzout yarushalaim, samtem mizbachout
**were your gods O Judah and *according to* the number of the streets of Jerusalem have you set up altars**

לבשת 1322 מזבחות 4196 לקטר 6999 לבעל 1168: 11:14 ואתה 859 אל 408 תתפלל 6419 בעד 1157 העם 5971 הזה 2088
laboshet, mizbachout laqater laba'al. ua'atah, 'al titpalel ba'ad ha'am hazeh,
**to *that* shameful thing *even* altars to burn incense unto Baal Therefore you not pray for the people this**

ואל 408 תשא 5375 בעדם 1157 רנה 7440 ותפלה 8605 כי 3588 אינני 369 שמע 8085 בעת 6256 קראם 7121 אלי 413 בעד 1157
ua'al tisa' ba'adam rinah uatapilah; kiy 'aeyneniy shomea', ba'aet qara'am 'aelay ba'ad
**neither lift up for them a cry or prayer for I not will hear *them* in the time that they cry unto me for**

רעתם 7451: 11:15 מה 4100 לידידי 3039 בביתי 1004 עשותה 6213 המזמתה 4209 הרבים 7227 ובשר 1320
ra'atam. meh liydiydiy babeytiy, 'asoutah hamazimatah harabiym, uabsar
**their trouble What *has* my beloved *to do* in mine house *seeing* she has wrought lewdness with many and flesh**

קדש 6944 יעברו 5674 מעליך 5921 כי 3588 רעתכי 7451 אז 227 תעלזי 5937: 11:16 זית 2132 רענן 7488 יפה 3303 פרי 6529 תאר 8389
qodesh ya'abru me'alayik; kiy ra'atekiy 'az ta'alozy. zayit ra'anan yapeh pary to'ar,
***the* holy is passed from you? when you do evil then you rejoicest A olive tree green fair fruit *and* of goodly**

קרא 7121 יהוה 3068 שמך 8034 לקול 6963 המולה 1999 גדלה 1419 הצית 3341 אש 784 עליה 5921 ורעו 7489
qara' Yahuah shamek; laqoul hamulah gadolah, hitziyt 'aesh 'aeleyha, uar'au
**called Yahuah your name with the noise of a tumult great he has kindled fire upon it and are broken**

דליותיו 1808: 11:17 ויהוה 3068 צבאות 6635 הנוטע 5193 אותך 853 דבר 1696 עליך 5921 רעה 7451 בגלל 1558
daliyoutayu. uaYahuah tzaba'aut hanoutea' autak, diber 'alayik ra'ah; biglal
**the branches of it For Yahuah of hosts that planted you has pronounced against you evil for**

רעת 7451 בית 1004 ישראל 3478 ובית 1004 יהודה 3063 אשר 834 עשו 6213 להם 1992
ra'at beyt yisra'ael uabeyt yahudah, 'asher 'asu lahem
**the evil of the house of Israel and of the house of Judah which they have done against themselves**

Jer 11:11 Therefore thus saith YHUH, Behold, I will bring evil upon them, which they shall not be able to escape; and though they shall cry unto me, I will not hear unto them.12 Then shall the cities of Judah and inhabitants of Jerusalem go, and cry unto the gods unto whom they offer incense: but they shall not save them at all in the time of their trouble.13 For according to the number of your cities were your gods, O Judah; and according to the number of the streets of Jerusalem have you set up altars to that shameful thing, even altars to burn incense unto Baal.14 Therefore pray not you for this people, neither lift up a cry or prayer for them: for I will not hear them in the time that they cry unto me for their trouble.15 What has my beloved to do in mine house, seeing she has wrought lewdness with many, and the holy flesh is passed from you? when you does evil, then you rejoicest.16 YHUH called your name, A green olive tree, fair, and of goodly fruit: with the noise of a great tumult he has kindled fire upon it, and the branches of it are broken.17 For YHUH of hosts, that planted you, has pronounced evil against you, for the evil of the house of Israel and of the house of Judah, which they have done against themselves to provoke me to anger in offering incense unto Baal.

11:18
להכעסני 3707 לקטר 6999 לבעל 1168: ויהוה 3068 הודיעני 3045 ואדעה 3045 אז 227
lahak'ayseniy laqater laba'al. uaYahuah houdiy'aniy ua'aeda'ah; 'az
**to provoke me to anger in offering incense unto Baal And Yahuah has given me knowledge *of it* and I know *it* then**

11:19
הראיתני 7200 מעלליהם 4611: ואני 589 ככבש 3532 אלוף 441 יובל 2986 לטבוח 2873 ולא 3808 ידעתי 3045 כי 3588
hir'aytaniy ma'alleyhem. ua'aniy kakebes 'alup yubal litabouach; uala' yada'tiy kiy
**you showed me their doings But I *was* like a lamb *or* an ox *that* is brought to the slaughter and not I knew that**

עלי 5921 חשבו 2803 מחשבות 4284 נשחיתה 7843 עץ 6086 בלחמו 3899 ונכרתנו 3772
'alay chashabu machashabout, nashchiytah 'aetz balachmou uanikratenu
**against me they had devised devices *saying* Let us destroy the tree with the fruit thereof and let us cut him off**

11:20
מארץ 776 חיים 2416 ושמו 8034 לא 3808 יזכר 2142 עוד 5750: ויהוה 3068 צבאות 6635 שפט 8199
me'aretz chayiym, uashmou la' yizaker 'aud. uaYahuah tzaba'aut shopet
**from the land of the living that his name no may be remembered more But O Yahuah of hosts that judge**

צדק 6664 בחן 974 כליות 3629 ולב 3820 אראה 7200 נקמתך 5360 מהם 1992 כי 3588 אליך 413 גליתי 1540 את 853
tzedeq, bochen kalayout ualeb; 'ar'ah niqmataka mehem, kiy 'aeleyka giliytiy 'at
**righteously that try the reins and the heart let me see your vengeance on them for unto you have I revealed**

11:21
ריבי 7379: לכן 3651 כה 3541 אמר 559 יהוה 3068 על 5921 אנשי 582 ענתות 6068 המבקשים 1245 את 853 נפשך 5315 לאמר 559 לא 3808
riybiy. laken, koh 'amar Yahuah 'al 'anshey 'anatout, hamabaqshiym 'at napshaka lea'mor; la'
**my cause Therefore thus saith Yahuah of the men of Anathoth that seek your life saying not**

11:22
תנבא 5012 בשם 8034 יהוה 3068 ולא 3808 תמות 4191 בידנו 3027: לכן 3651 כה 3541 אמר 559 יהוה 3068 צבאות 6635 הנני 2005
tinabea' bashem Yahuah, uala' tamut bayadenu. laken, koh 'amar Yahuah tzaba'aut, hinniy
**Prophesy in the name of Yahuah that not you die by our hand Therefore thus saith Yahuah of hosts Behold I**

11:23
פקד 6485 עליהם 5921 הבחורים 970 ימתו 4191 בחרב 2719 בניהם 1121 ובנותיהם 1323 ימתו 4191 ברעב 7458:
poqed 'aleyhem; habachuriym yamutu bachereb, baneyhem uabnouteyhem, yamutu bara'ab.
**will punish them the young men shall die by the sword their sons and their daughters shall die by famine**

ושארית 7611 לא 3808 תהיה 1961 להם 3807a כי 3588 אביא 935 רעה 7451 אל 413 אנשי 582 ענתות 6068 שנת 8141
uash'aeriyt la' tihayeh lahem; kiy 'abiy'a ra'ah 'al 'anshey 'anatout shanat
**And remnant no there shall be of them for I will bring evil upon the men of Anathoth *even* the year of**

פקדתם 6486:
paqudatam.
**their visitation**

**Jer 12:1**
צדיק 6662 אתה 859 יהוה 3068 כי 3588 אריב 7378 אליך 413 אך 389 משפטים 4941 אדבר 1696 אותך 854 מדוע 4069
tzadiyq 'atah Yahuah, kiy 'ariyb 'aeleyka; 'ak mishpatiym 'adaber autak, madua',
**Righteous *are* you O Yahuah when I plead with you yet *of your* judgments let me talk with you Wherefore**

דרך 1870 רשעים 7563 צלחה 6743 שלו 7951 כל 3605 בגדי 899 בגד 898:
derek rasha'aym tzalechah, shalu kal bogadey baged.
**the way of the wicked does prosper *wherefore* are they happy all very that deal treacherously?**

Jer 11:18 And YHUH has given me knowledge of it, and I know it: then you shewedst me their doings.19 But I was like a lamb or an ox that is brought to the slaughter; and I knew not that they had devised devices against me, saying, Let us destroy the tree with the fruit thereof, and let us cut him off from the land of the living, that his name may be no more remembered.20 But, O YHUH of hosts, that judgest righteously, that triest the reins and the heart, let me see your vengeance on them: for unto you have I revealed my cause.21 Therefore thus saith YHUH of the men of Anathoth, that seek your life, saying, Prophesy not in the name of YHUH, that you die not by our hand:22 Therefore thus saith YHUH of hosts, Behold, I will punish them: the young men shall die by the sword; their sons and their daughters shall die by famine:23 And there shall be no remnant of them: for I will bring evil upon the men of Anathoth, even the year of their visitation. **Jer** 12:1 Righteous are you, O YHUH, when I plead with you: yet let me talk with you of your judgments: Wherefore doth the way of the wicked prosper? wherefore are all they happy that deal very treacherously?

| 12:2 | | | | | | | | |
|---|---|---|---|---|---|---|---|---|
| נטעתם 5193 | גם 1571 | שרשו 8327 | ילכו 1980 | גם 1571 | עשו 6213 | פרי 6529 | קרוב 7138 | אתה 859 |
| nata'tam | gam | shorashu, | yelaku | gam | 'asu | periy; | qaroub | 'atah |
| **You have planted them** | **yea** | **they have taken root** | **they grow** | **yea** | **they bring forth** | **fruit** | ***are* near** | **you** |

| | | | 12:3 | | | | | |
|---|---|---|---|---|---|---|---|---|
| בפיהם 6310 | ורחוק 7350 | מכליותיהם 3629: | ואתה 859 | יהוה 3068 | ידעתני 3045 | תראני 7200 | ובחנת 974 | לבי 3820 |
| bapiyhem, | uarachouq | mikilyouteyhem. | ua'atah | Yahuah | yada'ataniy, | tir'aeniy | uabachanta | libiy |
| **in their mouth** | **and far** | **from their reins** | **But you** | **O Yahuah** | **know me** | **you have seen me** | **and tried** | **mine heart** |

| | | | | | | | 12:4 | |
|---|---|---|---|---|---|---|---|---|
| אתך 854 | התקם 5423 | כצאן 6629 | לטבחה 2878 | והקדשם 6942 | ליום 3117 | הרגה 2028: | עד 5704 | מתי 4970 |
| 'atak; | hatiqem | katza'n | latibchah, | uahaqadishem | layoum | haregah. | 'ad | matay |
| **toward you** | **pull them out** | **like sheep** | **for the slaughter** | **and prepare them** | **for the day of** | **slaughter** | **How** | **long** |

| | | | | | | | | |
|---|---|---|---|---|---|---|---|---|
| תאבל 56 | הארץ 776 | ועשב 6212 | כל 3605 | השדה 7704 | ייבש 3001 | מרעת 7451 | ישבי 3427 | בה 871a |
| te'abal | ha'aretz, | ua'aeseb | kal | hasadeh | yiybash; | mera'at | yoshabey | bah, |
| **shall mourn** | **the land** | **and the herbs of** | **every** | **field** | **wither** | **for the wickedness of** | **them that dwell** | **therein?** |

| | | | | | | | | 12:5 | | | |
|---|---|---|---|---|---|---|---|---|---|---|---|
| ספתה 5595 | בהמות 929 | ועוף 5775 | כי 3588 | אמרו 559 | לא 3808 | יראה 7200 | את 853 | אחריתנו 319: | כי 3588 | את 854 | רגלים 7273 |
| sapatah | bahemout | ba'aup, | kiy | 'amaru, | la' | yir'ah | 'at | 'achariytenu. | kiy | 'at | ragliym |
| **are consumed** | **the beasts** | **and the birds** | **because** | **they said** | **not** | **He shall see** | | **our last end** | **If** | ***with*** | **the footmen** |

| | | | | | | | | |
|---|---|---|---|---|---|---|---|---|
| רצתה 7323 | וילאוך 3811 | ואיך 349 | תתחרה 8474 | את 854 | הסוסים 5483 | ובארץ 776 | שלום 7965 | אתה 859 |
| ratzatah | uayal'auka, | ua'aeyk | tatachareh | 'at | hasusiym; | uab'aretz | shaloum | 'atah |
| **you have run** | **and they have wearied you** | **then how** | **can you contend** | ***with*** | **horses?** | **and if the land of** | **peace** | ***wherein* you** |

| | | | | | 12:6 | | | |
|---|---|---|---|---|---|---|---|---|
| בוטח 982 | ואיך 349 | תעשה 6213 | בגאון 1347 | הירדן 3383: | כי 3588 | גם 1571 | אחיך 251 | ובית 1004 |
| bouteach, | ua'aeyk | ta'aseh | big'aun | hayarden. | kiy | gam | 'acheyka | uabeyt |
| **trust** | ***they wearied you* then how** | **will you do** | **in swelling of** | **the Jordan?** | **For** | **even** | **your brethren** | **and the house of** |

| | | | | | | | | | | |
|---|---|---|---|---|---|---|---|---|---|---|
| אביך 1 | גם 1571 | המה 1992 | בגדו 898 | בך 871a | גם 1571 | המה 1992 | קראו 7121 | אחריך 310 | מלא 4390 | אל 408 |
| 'abiyka, | gam | hemah | bagadu | bak, | gam | hemah | qara'au | 'achareyka | malea'; | 'al |
| **your father** | **even** | **they** | **have dealt treacherously** | **with you** | **yea** | **they** | **have called** | **after you** | **a multitude** | **not** |

| | | | | | | 12:7 | | | | |
|---|---|---|---|---|---|---|---|---|---|---|
| תאמן 539 | בם 871a | כי 3588 | ידברו 1696 | אליך 413 | טובות 2896: | עזבתי 5800 | את 853 | ביתי 1004 | נטשתי 5203 | את 853 |
| ta'amen | bam, | kiy | yadabru | 'aeleyka | toubout. | 'azabtiy | 'at | beytiy, | natashtiy | 'at |
| **you believe** | **them** | **though** | **they speak** | **unto you** | **fair words** | **I have forsaken** | | **mine house** | **I have left** | |

| | | | | | | | 12:8 | |
|---|---|---|---|---|---|---|---|---|
| נחלתי 5159 | נתתי 5414 | את 853 | ידדות 3033 | נפשי 5315 | בכף 3709 | איביה 341: | היתה 1961 | לי 3807a |
| nachalatiy; | natatiy | 'at | yadidut | napshiy | bakap | 'ayabeyha. | hayatah | liy |
| **mine heritage** | **I have given** | | **the dearly beloved of** | **my soul** | **into the hand of** | **her enemies** | **is become** | **unto me** |

| | | | | | | | | | 12:9 | |
|---|---|---|---|---|---|---|---|---|---|---|
| נחלתי 5159 | כאריה 738 | ביער 3293 | נתנה 5414 | עלי 5921 | בקולה 6963 | על 5921 | כן 3651 | שנאתיה 8130: | העיט 5861 | צבוע 6641 |
| nachalatiy | ka'aryeh | baya'ar; | natanah | 'alay | baqoulah | 'al | ken | sana'tiyha. | ha'ayit | tzabua' |
| **Mine heritage** | **as a lion** | **in the forest** | **it cry out** | **against me** | **it cry out** | **therefore** | **have come** | **I hated it** | ***as* a bird** | **speckled** |

| | | | | | | | | | | |
|---|---|---|---|---|---|---|---|---|---|---|
| נחלתי 5159 | לי 3807a | העיט 5861 | סביב 5439 | עליה 5921 | לכו 1980 | אספו 622 | כל 3605 | חית 2416 | השדה 7704 | התיו 857 |
| nachalatiy | liy, | ha'ayit | sabiyb | 'aleyha; | laku, | 'aspu | kal | chayat | hasadeh | hetayu |
| **Mine heritage *is*** | **unto me** | **the birds** | **round about** | ***are* against her** | **come you** | **assemble** | **all** | **the beasts of** | **the field** | **come** |

Jer 12:2 Thou have planted them, yea, they have taken root: they grow, yea, they bring forth fruit: you are near in their mouth, and far from their reins.3 But you, O YHUH, know me: you have seen me, and tried mine heart toward you: pull them out like sheep for the slaughter, and prepare them for the day of slaughter.4 How long shall the land mourn, and the herbs of every field where, for the wickedness of them that dwell therein? the beasts are consumed, and the birds; because they said, He shall not see our last end.5 If you have run with the footmen, and they have wearied you, then how canst you contend with horses? and if in the land of peace, wherein you trustedst, they wearied you, then how will you do in the swelling of Jordan?6 For even your brethren, and the house of your father, even they have dealt treacherously with you; yea, they have called a multitude after you: believe them not, though they speak fair words unto you.7 I have forsaken mine house, I have left mine heritage; I have given the dearly beloved of my soul into the hand of her enemies.8 Mine heritage is unto me as a lion in the forest; it crieth out against me: therefore have I hated it.9 Mine heritage is unto me as a speckled bird, the birds round about are against her; come you, assemble all the beasts of the field, come to devour.

12:10
לאכלה 402: | רעים 7462 | רבים 7227 | שחתו 7843 | כרמי 3754 | בססו 947 | את 853 | חלקתי 2513
la'akalah | ro'aym | rabiym | shichatu | karmiy, | bosasu | 'at | chelqatiy;
**to devour | pastors | Many | have destroyed | my vineyard | they have trodden under foot | | my portion**

12:11
נתנו 5414 | את 853 | חלקת 2513 | חמדתי 2532 | למדבר 4057 | שממה 8077: | שמה 7760 | לשממה 8076 | אבלה 56 | עלי 5921
natanu | 'at | chelqat | chemdatiy | lamidbar | shamamah. | samah | lishmamah, | 'abalah | 'alay
**they have made | | portion | my pleasant | a wilderness | desolate | They have made it | desolate | it mourns | unto me**

12:12
שממה 8077 | נשמה 8074 | כל 3605 | הארץ 776 | כי 3588 | אין 369 | איש 376 | שם 7760 | על 5921 | לב 3820: | על 5921 | כל 3605 | שפים 8205
shamemah; | nashamah | kal | ha'aretz, | kiy | 'aeyn | 'aysh | sam | 'al | leb. | 'al | kal | shapayim
***and being* desolate | is made desolate | whole | the land | because | no | man | lay *it* | to | heart | upon | all | high places**

במדבר 4057 | באו 935 | שדדים 7703 | כי 3588 | חרב 2719 | ליהוה 3068 | אכלה 398 | מקצה 7097 | ארץ 776 | ועד 5704
bamidbar, | ba'au | shodadiym, | kiy | chereb | laYahuah | 'akalah, | miqtzeh | 'aretz | ua'ad
**through the wilderness | are come | The spoilers | for | the sword | of Yahuah | shall devour | from the *one* end of | the land | even to**

12:13
קצה 7097 | הארץ 776 | אין 369 | שלום 7965 | לכל 3605 | בשר 1320: | זרעו 2232 | חטים 2406 | וקצים 6975 | קצרו 7114
qatzeh | ha'aretz; | 'aeyn | shaloum | lakal | basar. | zara'au | chitiym | uaqotziym | qatzaru,
**the *other* end of | the land | no | peace | shall all have | flesh | They have sown | wheat | but thorns | shall reap**

נחלו 2470 | לא 3808 | יועלו 3276 | ובשו 954 | מתבואתיכם 8393 | מחרון 2740
nechlu | la' | you'aylu; | uaboshu | mitbu'ateykem, | mecharoun
**they have put themselves to pain | not | *but* shall profit | and they shall be ashamed | of your revenues | because of the fierce**

12:14
אף 639 | יהוה 3068: | כה 3541 | אמר 559 | יהוה 3068 | על 5921 | כל 3605 | שכני 7934 | הרעים 7451 | הנגעים 5060 | בנחלה 5159 | אשר 834
'ap | Yahuah. | koh | 'amar | Yahuah | 'al | kal | shakenay | hara'aym, | hanoga'aym | banachalah, | 'asher
**anger of | Yahuah | Thus | saith | Yahuah | against | all | mine neighbours | evil | that touch | the inheritance | which**

הנחלתי 5157 | את 853 | עמי 5971 | את 853 | ישראל 3478 | הנני 2005 | נתשם 5428 | מעל 5921 | אדמתם 127 | ואת 853 | בית 1004
hinchaltiy | 'at | 'amiy | 'at | yisra'ael; | hinniy | notasham | me'al | 'admatam, | ua'at | beyt
**I have caused to inherit | | my people | | Israel | Behold I | will pluck them | out of | their land | *and* | the house of**

12:15
יהודה 3063 | אתוש 5428 | מתוכם 8432: | והיה 1961 | אחרי 310 | נתשי 5428 | אותם 853 | אשוב 7725
yahudah | 'atoush | mitoukam. | uahayah, | 'acharey | natashiy | 'autam, | 'ashub
**Judah | I shall pluck out | from among them | And it shall come to pass | after | I have plucked out | them | I will return**

12:16
ורחמתים 7355 | והשבתים 7725 | איש 376 | לנחלתו 5159 | ואיש 376 | לארצו 776:
uarichamtiym; | uahashibotiym | 'aysh | lanachalatou | ua'aysh | la'artzou.
**and have compassion on them | and will bring them again | every man | to his heritage | and every man | to his land**

והיה 1961 | אם 518 | למד 3925 | ילמדו 3925 | את 853 | דרכי 1870 | עמי 5971 | להשבע 7650 | בשמי 8034 | חי 2416
uahayah | 'am | lamod | yilmadu | 'at | darkey | 'amiy | lahishabea' | bishmiy | chay
**And it shall come to pass | if | they will diligently | learn | | the ways of | my people | to swear | by my name | live**

יהוה 3069 | כאשר 834 | למדו 3925 | את 853 | עמי 5971 | להשבע 7650 | בבעל 1168 | ונבנו 1129 | בתוך 8432
Yahuah, | ka'asher | limdu | 'at | 'amiy, | lahishabea' | baba'al; | uanibnu | batouk
**Yahuah | as | they taught | | my people | to swear | by Baal | then shall they be built | in the midst of**

Jer 12:10 Many pastors have destroyed my vineyard, they have trodden my portion under foot, they have made my pleasant portion a desolate wilderness.11 They have made it desolate, and being desolate it mourn unto me; the whole land is made desolate, because no man layeth it to heart.12 The spoilers are come upon all high places through the wilderness: for the sword of YHUH shall devour from the one end of the land even to the other end of the land: no flesh shall have peace.13 They have sown wheat, but shall reap thorns: they have put themselves to pain, but shall not profit: and they shall be ashamed of your revenues because of the fierce anger of YHUH.14 Thus saith YHUH against all mine evil neighbors, that touch the inheritance which I have caused my people Israel to inherit; Behold, I will pluck them out of their land, and pluck out the house of Judah from among them.15 And it shall come to pass, after that I have plucked them out I will return, and have compassion on them, and will bring them again, every man to his heritage, and every man to his land.16 And it shall come to pass, if they will diligently learn the ways of my people, to swear by my name, YHUH live; as they taught my people to swear by Baal; then shall they be built in the midst of my people.

12:17
עמי 5971: ואם 518 לא 3808 ישמעו 8085 ונתשתי 5428 את 853 הגוי 1471 ההוא 1931 נתוש 5428 ואבד 6 נאם 5002 יהוה 3068:
'amiy. ua'am la' yishma'au; uanatashtiy 'at hagouy hahua' natoush ua'abed na'am Yahuah.
**my people But if not they will obey I will utterly nation that pluck up and destroy saith Yahuah**

**Jer 13:1**
כה 3541 אמר 559 יהוה 3068 אלי 413 הלוך 1980 וקנית 7069 לך 3807a אזור 232 פשתים 6593 ושמתו 7760 על 5921 מתניך 4975
koh 'amar Yahuah 'aelay, halouk uaqaniyta laka 'aezour pishtiym, uasamtou 'al mataneyka;
**Thus saith Yahuah unto me Go and get to you a girdle linen and put it upon your loins**

13:2 13:3
ובמים 4325 לא 3808 תבאהו 935: ואקנה 7069 את 853 האזור 232 כדבר 1697 יהוה 3068 ואשם 7760 על 5921 מתני 4975:
uabamayim la' tabi'aehu. ua'aqneh 'at ha'aezour kidbar Yahuah; ua'asim 'al matanay.
**and in water not put it So I got a girdle according to the word of Yahuah and put *it* on my loins**

13:4
ויהי 1961 דבר 1697 יהוה 3068 אלי 413 שנית 8145 לאמר 559: קח 3947 את 853 האזור 232 אשר 834 קנית 7069 אשר 834
uayahiy dabar Yahuah 'aelay sheniyt lea'mor. qach 'at ha'aezour 'asher qaniyta 'asher
**And came the word of Yahuah unto me *the* second time saying Take the girdle that you have got which**

13:5
על 5921 מתניך 4975 וקום 6965 לך 1980 פרתה 6578 וטמנהו 2934 שם 8033 בנקיק 5357 הסלע 5553: ואלך 1980 ואטמנהו 2934
'al mataneyka; uaqum lek paratah, uatamanehu sham binqiyq hasala'. wa'alek ua'atmanehu
***is* upon your loins and arise go you to Euphrates and hide it there in a hole of the rock So I went and hid it**

13:6
בפרת 6578 כאשר 834 צוה 6680 יהוה 3068 אותי 853: ויהי 1961 מקץ 7093 ימים 3117 רבים 7227 ויאמר 559 יהוה 3068
biparat; ka'asher tziuah Yahuah 'autiy. uayahiy miqetz yamiym rabiym; uaya'mer Yahuah
**by Euphrates as commanded Yahuah me And it came to pass after days many that said Yahuah**

13:7
אלי 413 קום 6965 לך 1980 פרתה 6578 וקח 3947 משם 8033 את 853 האזור 232 אשר 834 צויתיך 6680 לטמנו 2934 שם 8033:
'aelay, qum lek paratah, uaqach misham 'at ha'aezour, 'asher tziuiytiyka latamanou sham.
**unto me Arise go you to Euphrates and take from there the girdle which I commanded you to hide there**

ואלך 1980 פרתה 6578 ואחפר 2658 ואקח 3947 את 853 האזור 232 מן 4480 המקום 4725 אשר 834 טמנתיו 2934 שמה 8033 והנה 2009
wa'alek paratah, ua'achpor, ua'aqach 'at ha'aezour, min hamaqoum 'asher tamanatiyu shamah; uahineh
**Then I went to Euphrates and digged and took the girdle from the place where I had hid it there and behold**

13:8 13:9
נשחת 7843 האזור 232 לא 3808 יצלח 6743 לכל 3605: ויהי 1961 דבר 1697 יהוה 3068 אלי 413 לאמר 559:
nishchat ha'aezour, la' yitzlach lakol. uayahiy dabar Yahuah 'aelay lea'mor.
**was marred it the girdle not it was profitable for nothing Then came the word of Yahuah unto me saying**

13:10
כה 3541 אמר 559 יהוה 3068 ככה 3602 אשחית 7843 את 853 גאון 1347 יהודה 3063 ואת 853 גאון 1347 ירושלם 3389 הרב 7227:
koh 'amar Yahuah; kakah 'ashchiyt 'at ga'aun yahudah ua'at ga'aun yarushalaim harab.
**Thus saith Yahuah After this manner will I mar the pride of Judah *and* pride of Jerusalem the great**

העם 5971 הזה 2088 הרע 7451 המאנים 3987 לשמוע 8085 את 853 דברי 1697 ההלכים 1980 בשררות 8307 לבם 3820 וילכו 1980
ha'am hazeh hara' hame'aniym lishmoua' 'at dabaray, haholakiym bishrirut libam, uayelaku,
**the people This evil which refuse to hear my words which walk in the imagination of their heart and walk**

אחרי 310 אלהים 430 אחרים 312 לעבדם 5647 ולהשתחות 7812 להם 1992 ויהי 1961 כאזור 232 הזה 2088 אשר 834 לא 3808 יצלח 6743
'acharey 'alohiym 'acheriym, la'abadam ualhishtachauot lahem; uiyhiy ka'aezour hazeh, 'asher la' yitzlach
**after gods other to serve them and to worship them shall even be as girdle this which nothing is good**

Jer 12:17 But if they will not obey, I will utterly pluck up and destroy that nation, saith YHUH. **Jer** 13:1 Thus saith YHUH unto me, Go and get you a linen girdle, and put it upon your loins, and put it not in water.2 So I got a girdle according to the word of YHUH, and put it on my loins.3 And the word of YHUH came unto me the second time, saying,4 Take the girdle that you have got, which is upon your loins, and arise, go to Euphrates, and hide it there in a hole of the rock.5 So I went, and hid it by Euphrates, as YHUH commanded me.6 And it came to pass after many days, that YHUH said unto me, Arise, go to Euphrates, and take the girdle from thence, which I commanded you to hide there.7 Then I went to Euphrates, and digged, and took the girdle from the place where I had hid it: and, behold, the girdle was marred, it was profitable for nothing.8 Then the word of YHUH came unto me, saying,9 Thus saith YHUH, After this manner will I mar the pride of Judah, and the great pride of Jerusalem.10 This evil people, which refuse to hear my words, which walk in the imagination of their heart, and walk after other gods, to serve them, and to worship them, shall even be as this girdle, which is good for nothing.

13:11

לכל 3605: כי 3588 כאשר 834 ידבק 1692 האזור 232 אל 413 מתני 4975 איש 376 כן 3651 הדבקתי 1692 אלי 413 את 853
lakol. kiy ka'asher yidbaq ha'aezour 'al mataney 'aysh, ken hidbaqtiy 'aelay 'at
**for nothing For as cleave the girdle to the loins of a man so have I caused to cleave unto me**

כל 3605 בית 1004 ישראל 3478 ואת 853 כל 3605 בית 1004 יהודה 3063 נאם 5002 יהוה 3068 להיות 1961 לי 3807a לעם 5971
kal beyt yisra'ael ua'at kal beyt yahudah na'am Yahuah, lihayout liy la'am,
**the whole house of Israel *and* the whole house of Judah saith Yahuah that they might be unto me for a people**

13:12

ולשם 8034 ולתהלה 8416 ולתפארת 8597 ולא 3808 שמעו 8085: ואמרת 559 אליהם 413 את 853
ualshem ualitahilah ualtip'aret; uala' shame'au. ua'amarta 'aleyhem 'at
**and for a name and for a praise and for a glory but not they would hear Therefore you shall speak unto them**

הדבר 1697 הזה 2088 כה 3541 אמר 559 יהוה 3068 אלהי 430 ישראל 3478 כל 3605 נבל 5035 ימלא 4390 יין 3196 ואמרו 559
hadabar hazeh, koh 'amar Yahuah 'alohey yisra'ael, kal nebel yimalea' yayin; ua'amaru
**word this Thus saith Yahuah Elohim of Israel Every bottle shall be filled with wine and they shall say**

13:13

אליך 413 הידע 3045 לא 3808 נדע 3045 כי 3588 כל 3605 נבל 5035 ימלא 4390 יין 3196: ואמרת 559 אליהם 413
'aeleyka, hayadoa' la' neda', kiy kal nebel yimalea' yayin. ua'amarta 'aleyhem
**unto you Do we certainly not know that every bottle shall be filled with wine? Then shall you say unto them**

כה 3541 אמר 559 יהוה 3068 הנני 2005 ממלא 4390 את 853 כל 3605 ישבי 3427 הארץ 776 הזאת 2063 ואת 853 המלכים 4428 הישבים 3427
koh 'amar Yahuah hinniy mamalea' 'at kal yoshabey ha'aretz haza't ua'at hamalakiym hayoshbiym
**Thus saith Yahuah Behold I will fill all the inhabitants of the land this *even* the kings that sit**

לדוד 1732 על 5921 כסאו 3678 ואת 853 הכהנים 3548 ואת 853 הנביאים 5030 ואת 853 כל 3605 ישבי 3427 ירושלם 3389
ladauid 'al kis'au ua'at hakohaniym ua'at hanabiy'aym, ua'at kal yoshabey yarushalaim
**David's upon throne *and* the priests *and* the prophets *and* all the inhabitants of Jerusalem**

13:14

שכרון 7943: ונפצתים 5310 איש 376 אל 413 אחיו 251 והאבות 1 והבנים 1121 יחדו 3162 נאם 5002 יהוה 3068
shikaroun. uanipatztiym 'aysh 'al 'achiyu uaha'about uahabaniym yachdau na'am Yahuah;
***with* drunkenness And I will dash them one against another even the fathers and the sons together saith Yahuah**

13:15

לא 3808 אחמול 2550 ולא 3808 אחוס 2347 ולא 3808 ארחם 7355 מהשחיתם 7843: שמעו 8085 והאזינו 238 אל 408 תגבהו 1361 כי 3588
la' 'achmoul uala' 'achus uala' 'arachem mehashchiytam. shim'au uaha'aziynu 'al tigbahu; kiy
**not I will pity nor spare nor have mercy but destroy them Hear you and give ear not be proud for**

13:16

יהוה 3068 דבר 1696: תנו 5414 ליהוה 3068 אלהיכם 430 כבוד 3519 בטרם 2962 יחשך 2821 ובטרם 2962 יתנגפו 5062 רגליכם 7272
Yahuah diber. tanu laYahuah 'aloheykem kaboud baterem yachshik, uabterem yitnagpu ragleykem
**Yahuah has spoken Give to Yahuah your Elohim glory before he cause darkness and before stumble your feet**

על 5921 הרי 2022 נשף 5399 וקויתם 6960 לאור 216 ושמה 7760 לצלמות 6757 ישית 7896
'al harey nashep; uaqiuiytem la'aur uasamah latzalmauet, yashiyt
**upon mountains *the* dark and while you look for light and he turn it into the shadow of death *and* make**

13:17

לערפל 6205: ואם 518 לא 3808 תשמעוה 8085 במסתרים 4565 תבכה 1058 נפשי 5315 מפני 6440 גוה 1466 ודמע 1830
la'arapel. ua'am la' tishma'auha, bamistariym tibkeh napshiy mipaney geuah; uadamoa'
***it* gross darkness But if not you will hear it in secret places shall weep my soul for *your* pride and sore**

Jer 13:11 For as the girdle cleaveth to the loins of a man, so have I caused to cleave unto me the whole house of Israel and the whole house of Judah, saith YHUH; that they might be unto me for a people, and for a name, and for a praise, and for a glory: but they would not hear.12 Therefore you shall speak unto them this word; Thus saith YHUH G-d of Israel, Every bottle shall be filled with wine: and they shall say unto you, Do we not certainly know that every bottle shall be filled with wine?13 Then shall you say unto them, Thus saith YHUH, Behold, I will fill all the inhabitants of this land, even the kings that sit upon David's throne, and the priests, and the prophets, and all the inhabitants of Jerusalem, with drunkenness.14 And I will dash them one against another, even the fathers and the sons together, saith YHUH: I will not pity, nor spare, nor have mercy, but destroy them.15 Hear you, and give ear; be not proud: for YHUH has spoken.16 Give glory to YHUH your G-d, before he cause darkness, and before your feet stumble upon the dark mountains, and, while you look for light, he turn it into the shadow of death, and make it gross darkness.17 But if you will not hear it, my soul shall weep in secret places for your pride; and mine eye shall weep sore, and run down with tears, because YHUH's flock is carried away captive.

| | | | | | | | | | | |
|---|---|---|---|---|---|---|---|---|---|---|
| תדמע 1830 | ותרד 3381 | עיני 5869 | דמעה 1832 | כי 3588 | נשבה 7617 | עדר 5739 | יהוה 3068: | 13:18 | אמר 559 | למלך 4428 |
| tidma' | uatered | 'aeyniy | dim'ah, | kiy | nishbah | 'aeder | Yahuah. | | 'amor | lamelek |
| **shall weep** | **and run down** | **mine eye** | ***with* tears** | **because** | **is carried away captive** | **flock** | **Yahuah's** | | **Say** | **unto the king** |

| | | | | | | |
|---|---|---|---|---|---|---|
| ולגבירה 1377 | השפילו 8213 | שבו 3427 | כי 3588 | ירד 3381 | מראשותיכם 4761 | עטרת 5850 |
| ualagabiyrah | hashapiylu | shebu; | kiy | yarad | mar'ashouteykem, | ateret |
| **and to the queen** | **Humble yourselves** | **sit down** | **for** | **shall come down** | **your principalities** | ***even* the crown of** |

| | | | | | | | | |
|---|---|---|---|---|---|---|---|---|
| תפארתכם 8597: | 13:19 | ערי 5892 | הנגב 5045 | סגרו 5462 | ואין 369 | פתח 6605 | הגלת 1540 | יהודה 3063 |
| tip'artakem. | | 'arey | hanegeb | sugru | ua'aeyn | poteach; | hagalat | yahudah |
| **your glory** | | **The cities of** | **the south** | **shall be shut up** | **and none** | **shall open *them*** | **shall be carried away captive** | **Judah** |

| | | | | | | | | |
|---|---|---|---|---|---|---|---|---|
| כלה 3605 | הגלת 1540 | שלומים 7965: | 13:20 | שאי 5375 | עיניכם 5869 | וראי 7200 | הבאים 935 | מצפון 6828 |
| kulah | hagalat | shaloumiym. | | sa'ay | 'aeyneykem | uar'au | haba'aym | mitzapoun; |
| **all of it** | **it shall be carried away captive** | **wholly** | | **Lift up** | **your eyes** | **and behold** | **them that come** | **from the north** |

| | | | | | | | | | | |
|---|---|---|---|---|---|---|---|---|---|---|
| איה 346 | העדר 5739 | נתן 5414 | לך 3807a | צאן 6629 | תפארתך 8597: | 13:21 | מה 4100 | תאמרי 559 | כי 3588 | יפקד 6485 | עליך 5921 |
| 'ayeh, | ha'aeder | nitan | lak, | tza'n | tip'artek. | | mah | ta'mariy | kiy | yipqod | 'alayik, |
| **where** | ***is* the flock** | ***that* was given** | **to you** | **flock?** | **your beautiful** | | **What** | **will you say** | **when** | **he shall punish** | **you?** |

| | | | | | | | | | | |
|---|---|---|---|---|---|---|---|---|---|---|
| ואת 859 | למדת 3925 | אתם 853 | עליך 5921 | אלפים 441 | לראש 7218 | הלוא 3808 | חבלים 2256 | יאחזוך 270 | כמו 3644 | אשת 802 |
| ua'at | limadt | 'atam | 'alayik | 'alupiym | lara'sh; | halou'a | chabaliym | ya'chazuk, | kamou | 'aeshet |
| ***for you*** | **have taught** | **them** | **over you** | ***to be* captains** | ***and* as chief** | **not** | **sorrows** | **shall take you** | **as** | **a woman** |

| | | | | | | | | | |
|---|---|---|---|---|---|---|---|---|---|
| לדה 3205: | 13:22 | וכי 3588 | תאמרי 559 | בלבבך 3824 | מדוע 4069 | קראני 7122 | אלה 428 | ברב 7230 | עונך 5771 |
| ledah. | | uakiy | ta'mariy | bilbabek, | madua' | qara'aniy | 'aeleh; | barob | 'auonek |
| **in travail?** | | **And if** | **you say** | **in your heart** | **Wherefore** | **come upon me?** | **these *things*** | **For the greatness of** | **your iniquity** |

| | | | | | | | | | |
|---|---|---|---|---|---|---|---|---|---|
| נגלו 1540 | שוליך 7757 | נחמסו 2554 | עקביך 6119: | 13:23 | היהפך 2015 | כושי 3569 | עורו 5785 | ונמר 5246 | חברברתיו 2272 |
| niglu | shulayik | nechmasu | 'aqebayik. | | hayahapok | kushiy | 'aurou, | uanamer | chabarburotayu; |
| **are discovered** | **your skirts** | **made bare *and*** | **your heels** | | **Can change** | **the Ethiopian** | **his skin** | **or the leopard** | **his spots?** |

| | | | | | | | | |
|---|---|---|---|---|---|---|---|---|
| גם 1571 | אתם 859 | תוכלו 3201 | להיטיב 3190 | למדי 3928 | הרע 7489: | 13:24 | ואפיצם 6327 | כקש 7179 |
| gam | 'atem | tukalu | laheytiyb, | limudey | harea'. | | ua'apiytzem | kaqash |
| **also** | **you *then*** | **may do** | **good** | **that are accustomed** | **to do evil** | | **Therefore will I scatter them** | **as the stubble** |

| | | | | | | | | | |
|---|---|---|---|---|---|---|---|---|---|
| עובר 5674 | לרוח 7307 | מדבר 4057: | 13:25 | זה 2088 | גורלך 1486 | מנת 4490 | מדיך 4055 | מאתי 853 | נאם 5002 |
| 'auber; | laruach | midbar. | | zeh | gouralek | menot | midayik | me'atiy | na'am |
| **that passed away** | **by the wind of** | **the wilderness** | | **This** | ***is* your lot** | **the portion of** | **your measures** | **from me** | **saith** |

| | | | | | | | | | | | |
|---|---|---|---|---|---|---|---|---|---|---|---|
| יהוה 3068 | אשר 834 | שכחת 7911 | אותי 853 | ותבטחי 982 | בשקר 8267: | 13:26 | וגם 1571 | אני 589 | חשפתי 2834 | שוליך 7757 | על 5921 |
| Yahuah; | 'asher | shakachat | 'autiy, | uatibtachiy | bashaqer. | | uagam | 'aniy | chasaptiy | shulayik | 'al |
| **Yahuah** | **because** | **you have forgotten** | **me** | **and trusted** | **in falsehood** | | **Therefore** | **I** | **will discover** | **your skirts** | **upon** |

| | | | | | | | | |
|---|---|---|---|---|---|---|---|---|
| פניך 6440 | ונראה 7200 | קלונך 7036: | 13:27 | נאפיך 5004 | ומצהלותיך 4684 | זמת 2154 | זנותך 2184 | על 5921 |
| panayik; | uanir'ah | qalounek. | | ni'apayik | uamitzhaloutayik | zimat | zanutek, | 'al |
| **your face** | **that may appear** | **your shame** | | **your adulteries** | **and your neighings** | **the lewdness of** | **your whoredom** | **on** |

Jer 13:18 Say unto the king and to the queen, Humble yourselves, sit down: for your principalities shall come down, even the crown of your glory.19 The cities of the south shall be shut up, and none shall open them: Judah shall be carried away captive all of it, it shall be wholly carried away captive.20 Lift up your eyes, and behold them that come from the north: where is the flock that was given you, your beautiful flock?21 What will you say when he shall punish you? for you have taught them to be captains, and as chief over you: shall not sorrows take you, as a woman in travail?22 And if you say in your heart, Wherefore come these things upon me? For the greatness of your iniquity are your skirts discovered, and your heels made bare.23 Can the Ethiopian change his skin, or the leopard his spots? then may you also do good, that are accustomed to do evil.24 Therefore will I scatter them as the stubble that pass away by the wind of the wilderness.25 This is your lot, the portion of your measures from me, saith YHUH; because you have forgotten me, and trusted in falsehood.26 Therefore will I discover your skirts upon your face, that your shame may appear.27 I have seen your adulteries, and your neighings, the lewdness of your whoredom, and your abominations on the hills in the fields. Woe unto you, O Jerusalem! will you not be made clean? when shall it once be?

גבעות 1389 בשדה 7704 ראיתי 7200 שקוציך 8251 אוי 188 לך 3807a ירושלם 3389 לא 3808 תטהרי 2891
gaba'aut basadeh, ra'aytiy shiqutzayik; 'auy lak yarushalaim, la' titahariy,
**the hills in the fields I have seen *and* your abominations Woe unto you O Jerusalem not will you be made clean?**

אחרי 310 מתי 4970 עד 5750:
'acharey matay 'ad.
**after when *shall it* once be?**

**Jer 14:1** אשר 834 היה 1961 דבר 1697 יהוה 3068 אל 413 ירמיהו 3414 על 5921 דברי 1697 הבצרות 1226: **14:2** אבלה 56 יהודה 3063
'asher hayah dabar Yahuah 'al yirmayahu, 'al dibrey habatzarout. 'abalah yahudah,
**that came The word of Yahuah to Jeremiah in concerning the dearth mourns Judah**

ושעריה 8179 אמללו 535 קדרו 6937 לארץ 776 וצוחת 6682 ירושלם 3389 עלתה 5927: **14:3** ואדריהם 117
uash'areyha 'amlalu qadaru la'aretz; uatziuchat yarushalaim 'alatah. ua'adireyhem,
**and the gates thereof languish they are black unto the ground and the cry of Jerusalem is gone up And their nobles**

שלחו 7971 צעוריהם 6810 למים 4325 באו 935 על 5921 גבים 1356 לא 3808 מצאו 4672 מים 4325 שבו 7725 כליהם 3627
shalachu tza'aureyhem lamayim; ba'au 'al gebiym la' matza'au mayim, shabu kaleyhem
**have sent their little ones to the waters they came to the pits no *and* found water they returned with their vessels**

ריקם 7387 בשו 954 והכלמו 3637 וחפו 2645 ראשם 7218: **14:4** בעבור 5668 האדמה 127 חתה 2865 כי 3588 לא 3808
reyqam, boshu uahaklamu uachapu ra'sham. ba'abur ha'adamah chatah, kiy la'
**empty they were ashamed and confounded and covered their heads Because the ground is chapt for no**

היה 1961 גשם 1653 בארץ 776 בשו 954 אכרים 406 חפו 2645 ראשם 7218: **14:5** כי 3588 גם 1571 אילת 365 בשדה 7704
hayah geshem ba'aretz; boshu 'akariym chapu ra'sham. kiy gam 'ayelet basadeh,
**there was rain in the earth were ashamed the plowmen they covered their heads Yea also the hind in the field**

ילדה 3205 ועזוב 5800 כי 3588 לא 3808 היה 1961 דשא 1877: **14:6** ופראים 6501 עמדו 5975 על 5921 שפים 8205
yaldah ua'azoub; kiy la' hayah desha'. uapra'aym 'amadu 'al shapayim,
**calved and forsook *it* because no there was grass And the wild asses did stand in the high places**

שאפו 7602 רוח 7307 כתנים 8577 כלו 3615 עיניהם 5869 כי 3588 אין 369 עשב 6212: **14:7** אם 518 עונינו 5771 ענו 6030
sha'apu ruach kataniym; kalu 'aeyneyhem kiy 'aeyn 'aeseb. 'am 'auoneynu 'anu
**they snuffed up the wind like dragons did fail their eyes because *there was* no grass though our iniquities testify**

בנו 871a יהוה 3068 עשה 6213 למען 4616 שמך 8034 כי 3588 רבו 7231 משובתינו 4878 לך 3807a חטאנו 2398: **14:8**
ba'nu, Yahuah 'aseh lama'an shameka; kiy rabu mashuboteynu laka chata'nu.
**against us O Yahuah do you *it* for sake your name's for are many our backslidings against you we have sinned**

מקוה 4723 ישראל 3478 מושיעו 3467 בעת 6256 צרה 6869 למה 4100 תהיה 1961 כגר 1616 בארץ 776
miqueh yisra'ael, moushiy'au ba'aet tzarah; lamah tihayeh kager ba'aretz,
**O the hope of Israel the saviour thereof in time of trouble why should you be as a stranger in the land**

וכארח 732 נטה 5186 ללון 3885: **14:9** למה 4100 תהיה 1961 כאיש 376 נדהם 1724
uak'areach natah lalun. lamah tihayeh ka'aysh nidaham,
**and as a wayfaring man *that* turned aside to tarry for a night? Why should you be as a man astonied**

**Jer** 14:1 The word of YHUH that came to Jeremiah concerning the dearth.2 Judah mourn, and the gates thereof languish; they are black unto the ground; and the cry of Jerusalem is gone up.3 And their nobles have sent their little ones to the waters: they came to the pits, and found no water; they returned with their vessels empty; they were ashamed and confounded, and covered their heads.4 Because the ground is chapt, for there was no rain in the earth, the plowmen were ashamed, they covered their heads.5 Yea, the hind also calved in the field, and forsook it, because there was no grass.6 And the wild asses did stand in the high places, they snuffed up the wind like dragons; their eyes did fail, because there was no grass.7 O YHUH, though our iniquities testify against us, do you it for your name's sake: for our backslidings are many; we have sinned against you.8 O the hope of Israel, the savior thereof in time of trouble, why should you be as a stranger in the land, and as a wayfaring man that turneth aside to tarry for a night?9 Why should you be as a man astonied, as a mighty man that cannot save? yet you, O YHUH, are in the midst of us, and we are called by your name; leave us not.

| כגבור 1368 | לא 3808 | יוכל 3201 | להושיע 3467 | ואתה 859 | בקרבנו 7130 | יהוה 3068 | ושמך 8034 | עלינו 5921 |
|---|---|---|---|---|---|---|---|---|
| kagibour | la' | yukal | lahoushiya'; | ua'atah | baqirbenu | Yahuah | uashimaka | 'aleynu |
| **as a mighty man *that*** | **not** | **can** | **save?** | **yet you** | ***are* in the midst of us** | **O Yahuah** | **and your name** | **by** |

| נקרא 7121 | אל 408 | תנחנו 3240: | 14:10 | כה 3541 | אמר 559 | יהוה 3068 | לעם 5971 | הזה 2088 | כן 3651 | אהבו 157 | לנוע 5128 | רגליהם 7272 |
|---|---|---|---|---|---|---|---|---|---|---|---|---|
| niqra' | 'al | tanichenu. | | koh | 'amar | Yahuah | la'am | hazeh, | ken | 'ahabu | lanua', | ragleyhem |
| **we are called** | **not** | **leave us** | | **Thus** | **saith** | **Yahuah** | **unto people** | **this** | **Thus** | **have they loved** | **to wander** | **their feet** |

| לא 3808 | חשכו 2820 | ויהוה 3068 | לא 3808 | רצם 7521 | עתה 6258 | יזכר 2142 | עונם 5771 | ויפקד 6485 |
|---|---|---|---|---|---|---|---|---|
| la' | chasaku; | uaYahuah | la' | ratzam, | 'atah | yizkor | 'auonam, | uayipqod |
| **not** | **they have refrained** | **therefore Yahuah** | **not** | **does accept them** | **now** | **he will remember** | **their iniquity** | **and visit** |

| חטאתם 2403: | 14:11 | ויאמר 559 | יהוה 3068 | אלי 413 | אל 408 | תתפלל 6419 | בעד 1157 | העם 5971 | הזה 2088 | לטובה 2896: | 14:12 | כי 3588 | יצמו 6684 |
|---|---|---|---|---|---|---|---|---|---|---|---|---|---|
| chata'tam. | | uaya'mer | Yahuah | 'aelay; | 'al | titpalel | ba'ad | ha'am | hazeh | latoubah. | | kiy | yatzumu, |
| **their sins** | | **Then said** | **Yahuah** | **unto me** | **not** | **Pray** | **for** | **the people** | **this** | **for *their* good** | | **When** | **they fast** |

| אינני 369 | שמע 8085 | אל 413 | רנתם 7440 | וכי 3588 | יעלו 5927 | עלה 5930 | ומנחה 4503 | אינני 369 | רצם 7521 | כי 3588 |
|---|---|---|---|---|---|---|---|---|---|---|
| 'aeyneniy | shomea' | 'al | rinatam, | uakiy | ya'alu | 'alah | uaminchah | 'aeyneniy | rotzam; | kiy, |
| **I not** | **will hear** | **to** | **their cry** | **and when** | **they offer** | **burnt offering** | **and an oblation** | **I not** | **will accept them** | **but** |

| בחרב 2719 | וברעב 7458 | ובדבר 1698 | אנכי 595 | מכלה 3615 | אותם 853: | 14:13 | ואמר 559 | אהה 162 | אדני 136 |
|---|---|---|---|---|---|---|---|---|---|
| bachereb | uabara'ab | uabadber, | 'anokiy | makaleh | 'autam. | | ua'amar | 'ahah | 'adonay |
| **by the sword** | **and by the famine** | **and by the pestilence** | **I** | **will consume** | **them** | | **Then said I** | **Ah** | **Adonai** |

| יהוה 3069 | הנה 2009 | הנבאים 5030 | אמרים 559 | להם 3807a | לא 3808 | תראו 7200 | חרב 2719 | ורעב 7458 | לא 3808 | יהיה 1961 | לכם 3807a | כי 3588 |
|---|---|---|---|---|---|---|---|---|---|---|---|---|
| Yahuah | hineh | hanabiy'aym | 'amariym | lahem | la' | tir'au | chereb, | uara'ab | la' | yihayeh | lakem; | kiy |
| **Yahuah** | **behold** | **the prophets** | **say** | **unto them** | **not** | **You shall see** | **the sword** | **famine** | **neither** | **shall have** | **to you** | **but** |

| שלום 7965 | אמת 571 | אתן 5414 | לכם 3807a | במקום 4725 | הזה 2088: | 14:14 | ויאמר 559 | יהוה 3068 | אלי 413 | שקר 8267 | הנבאים 5030 | נבאים 5012 |
|---|---|---|---|---|---|---|---|---|---|---|---|---|
| shaloum | 'amet | 'aten | lakem, | bamaqoum | hazeh. | | uaya'mer | Yahuah | 'aelay, | sheqer | hanabiy'aym | nabi'aym |
| **peace** | **assured** | **I will give** | **to you** | **in place** | **this** | | **Then said** | **Yahuah** | **unto me** | **lies** | **The prophets** | **prophesy** |

| בשמי 8034 | לא 3808 | שלחתים 7971 | ולא 3808 | צויתים 6680 | ולא 3808 | דברתי 1696 | אליהם 413 | חזון 2377 | שקר 8267 |
|---|---|---|---|---|---|---|---|---|---|
| bishmiy, | la' | shalachtiym | uala' | tziuiytiym, | uala' | dibartiy | 'aleyhem; | chazoun | sheqer |
| **in my name** | **not** | **I sent them** | **neither** | **have I commanded them** | **neither** | **spoke** | **unto them** | **a vision** | **false** |

| וקסם 7081 | ואלול 457 | ותרמות 8649 | לבם 3820 | המה 1992 | מתנבאים 5012 | לכם 3807a: | 14:15 | לכן 3651 | כה 3541 |
|---|---|---|---|---|---|---|---|---|---|
| uaqesem | ua'alul | uatarmut | libam, | hemah | mitnaba'aym | lakem. | | laken | koh |
| **and divination** | **and the thing of nought,** | **and the deceit of** | **their heart** | **they** | **prophesy** | **unto you** | | **Therefore** | **thus** |

| אמר 559 | יהוה 3068 | על 5921 | הנבאים 5030 | הנבאים 5012 | בשמי 8034 | ואני 589 | לא 3808 | שלחתים 7971 | והמה 1992 | אמרים 559 | חרב 2719 |
|---|---|---|---|---|---|---|---|---|---|---|---|
| 'amar | Yahuah | 'al | hanabiy'aym | hanaba'aym | bishmiy | ua'aniy | la' | shalachtiym | uahemah | 'amariym, | chereb |
| **saith** | **Yahuah** | **concerning** | **the prophets** | **that prophesy** | **in my name** | **and I** | **not** | **sent them** | **yet they** | **say** | **Sword** |

| ורעב 7458 | לא 3808 | יהיה 1961 | בארץ 776 | הזאת 2063 | בחרב 2719 | וברעב 7458 | יתמו 8552 | הנבאים 5012 | ההמה 1992: |
|---|---|---|---|---|---|---|---|---|---|
| uara'ab, | la' | yihayeh | ba'aretz | haza't; | bachereb | uabara'ab | yitamu, | hanabiy'aym | hahemah. |
| **and famine** | **not** | **shall be** | **in land** | **this** | **By sword** | **and famine** | **shall be consumed** | **prophets** | **those** |

Jer 14:10 Thus saith YHUH unto this people, Thus have they loved to wander, they have not refrained their feet, therefore YHUH doth not accept them; he will now remember their iniquity, and visit their sins.11 Then said YHUH unto me, Pray not for this people for their good.12 When they fast, I will not hear their cry; and when they offer burnt offering and an oblation, I will not accept them: but I will consume them by the sword, and by the famine, and by the pestilence.13 Then said I, Ah, Adonai G-D! behold, the prophets say unto them, You shall not see the sword, neither shall you have famine; but I will give you assured peace in this place.14 Then YHUH said unto me, The prophets prophesy lies in my name: I sent them not, neither have I commanded them, neither spoke unto them: they prophesy unto you a false vision and divination, and a thing of nought, and the deceit of their heart.15 Therefore thus saith YHUH concerning the prophets that prophesy in my name, and I sent them not, yet they say, Sword and famine shall not be in this land; By sword and famine shall those prophets be consumed.

| **14:16** והעם 5971 | אשר 834 | המה 1992 | נבאים 5012 | להם 1992 | יהיו 1961 | משלכים 7993 | בחצות 2351 | ירושלם 3389 | מפני 6440 |
|---|---|---|---|---|---|---|---|---|---|
| uaha'am | 'asher | hemah | naba'aym | lahem | yihayu | mushlakiym | bachutzout | yarushalaim | mipaney |
| **And the people** | **whom** | **they** | **prophesy** | **to them** | **shall be** | **cast out** | **in the streets of** | **Jerusalem** | **because of** |

| הרעב 7458 | והחרב 2719 | ואין 369 | מקבר 6912 | להמה 1992 | המה 1992 | נשיהם 802 | ובניהם 1121 | ובנתיהם 1323 |
|---|---|---|---|---|---|---|---|---|
| hara'ab | uahachereb, | ua'aeyn | maqaber | lahemah, | hemah | nasheyhem, | uabneyhem | uabnoteyhem; |
| **the famine** | **and the sword** | **and they shall have none** | **to bury** | **them** | **they** | **their wives** | **nor their sons** | **nor their daughters** |

| ושפכתי 8210 | עליהם 5921 | את 853 | רעתם 7451: | **14:17** | ואמרת 559 | אליהם 413 | את 853 | הדבר 1697 | הזה 2088 |
|---|---|---|---|---|---|---|---|---|---|
| uashapakatiy | 'aleyhem | 'at | ra'atam. | | ua'amarta | 'aleyhem | 'at | hadabar | hazeh, |
| **for I will pour** | **upon them** | | **their wickedness** | | **Therefore you shall say** | **unto them** | | **word** | **this** |

| תרדנה 3381 | עיני 5869 | דמעה 1832 | לילה 3915 | ויומם 3119 | ואל 408 | תדמינה 1820 | כי 3588 | שבר 7665 | גדול 1419 | נשברה 7667 |
|---|---|---|---|---|---|---|---|---|---|---|
| teradnah | 'aeynay | dim'ah | layalah | uayoumam | ua'al | tidmeynah; | kiy | sheber | gadoul | nishbarah, |
| **Let run down with** | **mine eyes** | **tears** | **night** | **and day** | **and not** | **let them cease** | **for** | **is broken** | ***with* a great** | **breach** |

| בתולת 1330 | בת 1323 | עמי 5971 | מכה 4347 | נחלה 2470 | מאד 3966: | **14:18** אם 518 | יצאתי 3318 | השדה 7704 | והנה 2009 | חללי 2491 |
|---|---|---|---|---|---|---|---|---|---|---|
| batulat | bat | 'amiy, | makah | nachalah | ma'ad. | 'am | yatza'tiy | hasadeh, | uahineh | challey |
| **the virgin** | **daughter of** | **my people** | ***with* a blow** | **grievous** | **very** | **If** | **I go forth** | **the field** | **then behold** | **the slain** |

| חרב 2719 | ואם 518 | באתי 935 | העיר 5892 | והנה 2009 | תחלואי 8463 | רעב 7458 | כי 3588 | גם 1571 | נביא 5030 | גם 1571 |
|---|---|---|---|---|---|---|---|---|---|---|
| chereb, | ua'am | ba'tiy | ha'ayr, | uahineh | tachalu'aey | ra'ab; | kiy | gam | nabiy'a | gam |
| **with the sword** | **and if** | **I enter into** | **the city** | **then behold** | **them that are sick** | **with famine** | **yea** | **both** | **the prophet *and*** | **also** |

| כהן 3548 | סחרו 5503 | אל 413 | ארץ 776 | ולא 3808 | ידעו 3045: | **14:19** המאס 3988 | מאסת 3988 | את 853 | יהודה 3063 | אם 518 | בציון 6726 |
|---|---|---|---|---|---|---|---|---|---|---|---|
| kohen | sacharu | 'al | 'aretz | uala' | yada'au. | hama'as | ma'asta | 'at | yahudah, | 'am | batziyoun |
| **the priest** | **go about** | **into** | **a land** | **that not** | **they know** | **Have utterly** | **you rejected** | | **Judah** | **or** | **in Zion?** |

| געלה 1602 | נפשך 5315 | מדוע 4069 | הכיתנו 5221 | ואין 369 | לנו 3807a | מרפא 4832 | קוה 6960 | לשלום 7965 | ואין 369 |
|---|---|---|---|---|---|---|---|---|---|
| ga'alah | napsheka, | madua' | hikiytanu, | ua'aeyn | lanu | marpea'; | qaueh | lashaloum | ua'aeyn |
| **have lothed** | **your soul** | **why** | **have you stricken us** | **and *there is* no** | **for us?** | **healing** | **we looked** | **for peace** | **and *there is* no** |

| טוב 2896 | ולעת 6256 | מרפא 4832 | והנה 2009 | בעתה 1205: | **14:20** ידענו 3045 | יהוה 3068 | רשענו 7562 |
|---|---|---|---|---|---|---|---|
| toub, | ual'aet | marpea' | uahineh | ba'atah. | yada'nu | Yahuah | rish'aenu |
| **good** | **and for the time of** | **healing** | **and behold** | **trouble** | **We acknowledge** | **O Yahuah** | **our wickedness** |

| עון 5771 | אבותינו 1 | כי 3588 | חטאנו 2398 | לך 3807a: | **14:21** אל 408 | תנאץ 5006 | למען 4616 | שמך 8034 | אל 408 |
|---|---|---|---|---|---|---|---|---|---|
| 'auon | abouteynu; | kiy | chata'nu | lak. | 'al | tina'atz | lama'an | shimka, | 'al |
| ***and* the iniquity of** | **our fathers** | **for** | **for we have sinned against you** | | **not** | **Do you abhor *us*** | **for sake** | **your name's** | **not** |

| תנבל 5034 | כסא 3678 | כבודך 3519 | זכר 2142 | אל 408 | תפר 6565 | בריתך 1285 | אתנו 854: | **14:22** היש 3426 |
|---|---|---|---|---|---|---|---|---|
| tanabel | kisea' | kaboudeka; | zakor | 'al | taper | bariytaka | 'atanu. | hayesh |
| **do disgrace** | **the throne of** | **your glory** | **remember** | **not** | **break** | **your covenant** | **with us** | **Are there** |

| בהבלי 1892 | הגוים 1471 | מגשמים 1652 | ואם 518 | השמים 8064 | יתנו 5414 | רבבים 7241 | הלא 3808 | אתה 859 | הוא 1931 |
|---|---|---|---|---|---|---|---|---|---|
| bahabley | hagouyim | magashimiym, | ua'am | hashamayim | yitanu | rabibiym; | hala' | 'atah | hua' |
| ***any* among the vanities of** | **the Gentiles** | **that can cause rain?** | **or** | **the heavens** | **can give** | **shower?** | ***are* not** | **you** | **he** |

Jer 14:16 And the people to whom they prophesy shall be cast out in the streets of Jerusalem because of the famine and the sword; and they shall have none to bury them, them, their wives, nor their sons, nor their daughters: for I will pour their wickedness upon them.17 Therefore you shall say this word unto them; Let mine eyes run down with tears night and day, and let them not cease: for the virgin daughter of my people is broken with a great breach, with a very grievous blow.18 If I go forth into the field, then behold the slain with the sword! and if I enter into the city, then behold them that are sick with famine! yea, both the prophet and the priest go about into a land that they know not.19 Hast you utterly rejected Judah? has your soul lothed Zion? why have you smitten us, and there is no healing for us? we looked for peace, and there is no good; and for the time of healing, and behold trouble!20 We acknowledge, O YHUH, our wickedness, and the iniquity of our fathers: for we have sinned against you.21 Do not abhor us, for your name's sake, do not disgrace the throne of your glory: remember, break not your covenant with us.22 Are there any among the vanities of the Gentiles that can cause rain? or can the heavens give showers? are not you he, O YHUH our G-d? therefore we will wait upon you: for you have made all these things.

יהוה 3068 אלהינו 430 ונקוה 6960 לך 3807a כי 3588 אתה 859 עשית 6213 את 853 כל 3605 אלה 428:
Yahuah 'aloheynu uanqaueh lak, kiy 'atah 'ashiyta 'at kal 'aeleh.
**Yahuah our Elohim? therefore we will wait upon you for you have made all these *things***

**Jer 15:1**
ויאמר 559 יהוה 3068 אלי 413 אם 518 יעמד 5975 משה 4872 ושמואל 8050 לפני 6440 אין 369 נפשי 5315
uaya'mer Yahuah 'aelay, 'am ya'amod mosheh uashamu'ael lapanay, 'aeyn napshiy
**Then said Yahuah unto me though stood Though Moses and Samuel before me *could* not *yet* my mind**

אל 413 העם 5971 הזה 2088 שלח 7971 מעל 5921 פני 6440 ויצאו 3318: **15:2** והיה 1961 כי 3588
'al ha'am hazeh; shalach me'al panay uayetze'au. uahayah kiy
***be* toward the people this cast *them* out of my sight and let them go forth And it shall come to pass if**

יאמרו 559 אליך 413 אנה 575 נצא 3318 ואמרת 559 אליהם 413 כה 3541 אמר 559 יהוה 3068 אשר 834 למות 4194
ya'maru 'aeleyka 'anah netzea'; ua'amarta 'aleyhem koh 'amar Yahuah 'asher lamauet
**they say unto you Where shall we go forth? then you shall tell them Thus saith Yahuah Such as *are* for death**

למות 4194 ואשר 834 לחרב 2719 לחרב 2719 ואשר 834 לרעב 7458 לרעב 7458 ואשר 834
lamauet ua'asher lachereb lachereb, ua'asher lara'ab lara'ab, ua'asher
**to death and such as *are* for the sword to the sword and such as *are* for the famine to the famine and such as**

לשבי 7628 לשבי 7628: **15:3** ופקדתי 6485 עליהם 5921 ארבע 702 משפחות 4940 נאם 5002 יהוה 3068 את 853 החרב 2719
lashbiy lashebiy. uapaqadtiy 'aleyhem 'arba mishpachout na'am Yahuah, 'at hachereb
***are* for the captivity to the captivity And I will appoint over them four kinds saith Yahuah the sword**

להרג 2026 ואת 853 הכלבים 3611 לסחב 5498 ואת 853 עוף 5775 השמים 8064 ואת 853 בהמת 929 הארץ 776 לאכל 398
laharog, ua'at hakalabiym lisachob; ua'at 'aup hashamayim ua'at behemat ha'aretz le'akol
**to slay *and* the dogs to tear *and* the fowls of the heaven *and* the beasts of the earth to devour**

ולהשחית 7843: **15:4** ונתתים 5414 לזועה 2113 לכל 3605 ממלכות 4467 הארץ 776 בגלל 1558 מנשה 4519 בן 1121
ualhashachiyt. uantatiym lazua'ah lakol mamlakout ha'aretz; biglal manasheh ben
**and destroy And I will cause to be removed into all kingdoms of the earth because of Manasseh the son of**

יחזקיהו 2396 מלך 4428 יהודה 3063 על 5921 אשר 834 עשה 6213 בירושלם 3389: **15:5** כי 3588 מי 4310 יחמל 2550 עליך 5921
yachizqiyahu melek yahudah, 'al 'asher 'asah biyarushalaim. kiy miy' yachmol 'alayik
**Hezekiah king of Judah for *that* which he did in Jerusalem For who shall have pity upon you**

ירושלם 3389 ומי 4310 ינוד 5110 לך 3807a ומי 4310 יסור 5493 לשאל 7592 לשלם 7965 לך 3807a: **15:6** את 859 נטשת 5203 אתי 853
yarushalaim, uamiy yanud lak; uamiy yasur, lisha'al lashalom lak. 'at natasht 'atiy
**Jerusalem? or who shall mourn to you? or who shall go aside to ask how doing? to you *You* have forsaken me**

נאם 5002 יהוה 3068 אחור 268 תלכי 1980 ואט 5186 את 853 ידי 3027 עליך 5921 ואשחיתך 7843
na'am Yahuah 'achour telekiy; ua'at 'at yadiy 'alayik ua'ashchiytek,
**saith Yahuah backward you are gone therefore will I stretch out my hand against you and I shall destroy you**

נלאיתי 3811 הנחם 5162: **15:7** ואזרם 2219 במזרה 4214 בשערי 8179 הארץ 776 שכלתי 7921
nil'aeytiy hinachem. ua'azrem bamizreh basha'arey ha'aretz; shikaltiy
**I am weary with repenting And I will fan them with a fan in the gates of the land I will bereave *them* of children**

**Jer** 15:1 Then said YHUH unto me, Though Moses and Samuel stood before me, yet my mind could not be toward this people: cast them out of my sight, and let them go forth.2 And it shall come to pass, if they say unto you, Whither shall we go forth? then you shall tell them, Thus saith YHUH; Such as are for death, to death; and such as are for the sword, to the sword; and such as are for the famine, to the famine; and such as are for the captivity, to the captivity.3 And I will appoint over them four kinds, saith YHUH: the sword to slay, and the dogs to tear, and the fowls of the heaven, and the beasts of the earth, to devour and destroy.4 And I will cause them to be removed into all kingdoms of the earth, because of Manasseh the son of Hezekiah king of Judah, for that which he did in Jerusalem.5 For who shall have pity upon you, O Jerusalem? or who shall bemoan you? or who shall go aside to ask how you does?6 Thou have forsaken me, saith YHUH, you are gone backward: therefore will I stretch out my hand against you, and destroy you; I am weary with repenting.7 And I will fan them with a fan in the gates of the land; I will bereave them of children, I will destroy my people, since they return not from their ways.

| אבדתי 6 | את 853 | עמי 5971 | מדרכיהם 1870 | לוא 3808 | שבו 7725: | 15:8 | עצמו 6105 | לי 3807a | אלמנתו 490 |
|---|---|---|---|---|---|---|---|---|---|
| 'abadtiy | 'at | 'amiy, | midarkeyhem | lua' | shabu. | | 'atzamu | liy | 'almanotau |
| **I will destroy** | | **my people** | **from their ways** | **not** | ***since* they return** | | **are increased** | **to me** | **Their widows** |

| מחול 2344 | ימים 3220 | הבאתי 935 | להם 3807a | על 5921 | אם 517 | בחור 970 | שדד 7703 | בצהרים 6672 |
|---|---|---|---|---|---|---|---|---|
| mechoul | yamiym, | hebea'tiy | lahem | 'al | 'am | bachur | shoded | batzaharayim; |
| **above the sand of** | **the seas** | **I have brought** | **upon them** | **against** | **the mother of** | **the young men** | **a spoiler** | **at noonday** |

| הפלתי 5307 | עליה 5921 | פתאם 6597 | עיר 5892 | ובהלות 928: | 15:9 | אמללה 535 | ילדת 3205 | השבעה 7651 |
|---|---|---|---|---|---|---|---|---|
| hipaltiy | 'aleyha | pit'am, | 'ayr | uabehalout. | | 'amlalah | yoledet | hashib'ah, |
| **I have caused *him* to fall** | **upon it** | **suddenly** | ***upon* the city** | **and terrors** | | **languish** | **She that has borne** | **seven** |

| נפחה 5301 | נפשה 5315 | באה 935 | שמשה 8121 | בעד 5750 | יומם 3119 | בושה 954 | וחפרה 2659 |
|---|---|---|---|---|---|---|---|
| napachah | napshah | ba'ah | shimshah | ba'aud | youmam | boushah | uachaperah; |
| **she has given up** | **the ghost** | **is gone down** | **her sun** | **while it was yet** | **day** | **she has been ashamed** | **and confounded** |

| ושאריתם 7611 | לחרב 2719 | אתן 5414 | לפני 6440 | איביהם 341 | נאם 5002 | יהוה 3068: | 15:10 | אוי 188 | לי 3807a | אמי 517 |
|---|---|---|---|---|---|---|---|---|---|---|
| uash'aeriytam, | lachereb | 'aten | lipney | 'ayabeyhem | na'am | Yahuah. | | 'auy | liy | 'amiy, |
| **and the residue of them** | **to the sword** | **will I deliver** | **before** | **their enemies** | **saith** | **Yahuah** | | **Woe** | ***is* me** | **my mother** |

| כי 3588 | ילדתני 3205 | איש 376 | ריב 7379 | ואיש 376 | מדון 4066 | לכל 3605 | הארץ 776 | לא 3808 | נשיתי 5383 | ולא 3808 |
|---|---|---|---|---|---|---|---|---|---|---|
| kiy | yalidtiniy, | 'aysh | riyb | ua'aysh | madoun | lakal | ha'aretz; | la' | nashiytiy | uala' |
| **that** | **you have borne me** | **a man of** | **strife** | **and a man of** | **contention** | **to whole** | **the earth** | **neither** | **I have lent on usury** | **nor** |

| נשו 5383 | בי 871a | כלה 3605 | מקללוני 7043: | 15:11 | אמר 559 | יהוה 3068 | אם 518 | לא 3808 | שרותך 8293 |
|---|---|---|---|---|---|---|---|---|---|
| nashu | biy | kuloh | maqallauniy. | | 'amar | Yahuah, | 'am | la' | sharoticha |
| ***men* have lent on usury** | **to me** | ***yet* every one of them** | **does curse me** | | **said** | **Yahuah** | **verily** | ***with* not** | **your remnant;** |

| לטוב 2896 | אם 518 | לוא 3808 | הפגעתי 6293 | בך 871a | בעת 6256 | רעה 7451 | ובעת 6256 | צרה 6869 | את 853 |
|---|---|---|---|---|---|---|---|---|---|
| latoub; | 'am | lua' | hipga'atiy | baka, | ba'aet | ra'ah | uab'aet | tzarah | 'at |
| **it shall be well** | **verily** | **not** | **I will cause entreat** | **to you** | ***well* in the time of** | **evil** | **and in the time of** | **affliction** | |

| האיב 341: | 15:12 | הירע 7489 | ברזל 1270 | ברזל 1270 | מצפון 6828 | ונחשת 5178: | 15:13 | חילך 2428 | ואוצרותיך 214 |
|---|---|---|---|---|---|---|---|---|---|
| ha'auyeb. | | hayaroa' | barzel | barzel | mitzapoun | uanchoshet. | | cheylaka | ua'autzarouteyka |
| **the enemy** | | **Shall break** | **iron** | **iron** | ***the* northern** | **and the steel?** | | **Your substance** | **and your treasures** |

| לבז 957 | אתן 5414 | לא 3808 | במחיר 4242 | ובכל 3605 | חטאותיך 2403 | ובכל 3605 | גבוליך 1366: | 15:14 |
|---|---|---|---|---|---|---|---|---|
| labaz | 'aten | la' | bimachiyr; | uabkal | chata'uteyka | uabkal | gabuleyka. | |
| **to the spoil** | **will I give** | **without** | **price** | **and *that* for all** | **your sins** | **even in all** | **your borders** | |

| והעברתי 5674 | את 854 | איביך 341 | בארץ 776 | לא 3808 | ידעת 3045 | כי 3588 | אש 784 | קדחה 6919 | באפי 639 |
|---|---|---|---|---|---|---|---|---|---|
| uaha'abartiy | 'at | 'ayabeyka, | ba'aretz | la' | yada'ta; | kiy | 'aesh | qadachah | ba'apiy |
| **And I will make *you* to pass** | ***with*** | **your enemies** | **into a land** | **not** | ***which* you know** | **for** | **a fire** | **is kindled** | **in mine anger** |

| עליכם 5921 | תוקד 3344: | 15:15 | אתה 859 | ידעת 3045 | יהוה 3068 | זכרני 2142 | ופקדני 6485 | והנקם 5358 | לי 3807a |
|---|---|---|---|---|---|---|---|---|---|
| 'aleykem | tuqad. | | 'atah | yada'ta | Yahuah | zakareniy | uapaqadeniy | uahinaqem | liy |
| **upon you** | ***which* shall burn** | | **you** | **know** | **O Yahuah** | **remember me** | **and visit me** | **and revenge me** | |

Jer 15:8 Their widows are increased to me above the sand of the seas: I have brought upon them against the mother of the young men a spoiler at noonday: I have caused him to fall upon it suddenly, and terrors upon the city.9 She that has borne seven languisheth: she has given up the ghost; her sun is gone down while it was yet day: she has been ashamed and confounded: and the residue of them will I deliver to the sword before their enemies, saith YHUH.10 Woe is me, my mother, that you have borne me a man of strife and a man of contention to the whole earth! I have neither lent on usury, nor men have lent to me on usury; yet everyone of them doth curse me.11 YHUH said, Verily it shall be well with your remnant; verily I will cause the enemy to entreat you well in the time of evil and in the time of affliction.12 Shall iron break the northern iron and the steel?13 Thy substance and your treasures will I give to the spoil without price, and that for all your sins, even in all your borders.14 And I will make you to pass with your enemies into a land which you know not: for a fire is kindled in mine anger, which shall burn upon you.15 O YHUH, you know: remember me, and visit me, and revenge me of my persecutors; take me not away in your longsuffering: know that for your sake I have suffered rebuke.

7291 מרדפי 408 אל 750 לארך 639 אפך 3947 תקחני 3045 דע 5375 שאתי 5921 עליך 2781: חרפה **15:16**
merodapay, 'al la'arek 'apaka tiqacheniy; da' sa'aetiy 'aleyka cherpah.
**of my persecutors not of your long suffering take me away know *that* I have suffered for your sake rebuke**

4672 נמצאו 1697 דבריך 398 ואכלם 1961 ויהי 1697 דבריך 3807a לי 8342 לששון 8057 ולשמחת 3824 לבבי 3588 כי
nimtza'au dabareyka ua'akalem, uayahiy dabarayka liy, lasasoun ualsimchat lababiy; kiy
**were found Your words and I did eat them and was your word unto me the joy and rejoicing of mine heart for**

7121 נקרא 8034 שמך 5921 עלי 3068 יהוה 430 אלהי 6635: צבאות **15:17** 3808 לא 3427 ישבתי 5475 בסוד 7832 משחקים
niqra' shimka 'alay, Yahuah 'alohey tzaba'aut. la' yashabtiy basoud masachaqiym
**I am called your name by O Yahuah Elohim of hosts not I sat in the assembly of the mockers**

5937 ואעלז 6440 מפני 3027 ידך 910 בדד 3427 ישבתי 3588 כי 2195 זעם 4390: מלאתני **15:18** 4100 למה 1961 היה 3511 כאבי
ua'a'loz; mipaney yadaka badad yashabtiy, kiy za'am milea'taniy. lamah hayah ka'aebiy
**nor rejoiced because of your hand alone I sat for indignation you have filled me with Why is my pain**

5331 נצח 4347 ומכתי 605 אנושה 3985 מאנה 7495 הרפא 1961 היו 1961 תהיה 3807a לי 3644 כמו 391 אכזב 4325 מים
netzach, uamakatiy 'anushah me'anah herapea', hayou tihayeh liy kamou 'akzab, mayim
**perpetual and my wound incurable *which* refuse to be healed? will you be altogether unto me as a liar *and as* waters**

3808 לא 539: נאמנו **15:19** 3651 לכן 3541 כה 559 אמר 3068 יהוה 518 אם 7725 תשוב 7725 ואשיבך 6440 לפני
la' ne'amanu. laken koh 'amar Yahuah 'am tashub ua'ashiybaka lapanay
**not *that* fail? Therefore thus saith Yahuah If you return then will I bring you again before me**

5975 תעמד 518 ואם 3318 תוציא 3368 יקר 2151 מזולל 6310 כפי 1961 תהיה 3427 ישבו 1992 המה 413 אליך
ta'amod, ua'am toutziy'a yaqar mizoulel kapiy tihayeh; yashubu hemah 'aeleyka,
***and* you shall stand and if you take forth *the* precious from the vile as my mouth you shall be let return them unto you**

859 ואתה 3808 לא 7725 תשוב 413: אליהם **15:20** 5414 ונתתיך 5971 לעם 2088 הזה 2346 לחומת 5178 נחשת 1219 בצורה
ua'atah la' tashub 'aleyhem. uantatiyka la'am hazeh, lachoumat nachoshet batzurah,
**but you not return unto them And I will make you unto people this a wall brasen fenced**

3898 ונלחמו 413 אליך 3808 ולא 3201 יוכלו 3807a לך 3588 כי 854 אתך 589 אני 3467 להושיעך
uanilchamu 'aeleyka uala' yukalu lak; kiy 'ataka 'aniy lahoushiy'aka
**and they shall fight against you but not they shall prevail against you for *am* with you I to save you**

5337 ולהצילך 5002 נאם 3068: יהוה **15:21** 5337 והצלתיך 3027 מיד 7451 רעים 6299 ופדתיך
ualhatziyleka na'am Yahuah. uahitzaltiyka miyad ra'aym; uapditiyka
**and to deliver you saith Yahuah And I will deliver you out of the hand of the wicked and I will redeem you**

3709 מכף 6184: ערצים
mikap 'aritziym.
**out of the hand of the terrible**

**Jer 16:1** 1961 ויהי 1697 דבר 3068 יהוה 413 אלי 559: לאמר **16:2** 3808 לא 3947 תקח 3807a לך 802 אשה 3808 ולא 1961 יהיו
uayahiy dabar Yahuah 'aelay lea'mor. la' tiqach laka 'ashah; uala' yihayu
**came also The word of Yahuah unto me saying not You shall take to you a wife neither shall have**

Jer 15:16 Thy words were found, and I did eat them; and your word was unto me the joy and rejoicing of mine heart: for I am called by your name, O YHUH G-d of hosts.17 I sat not in the assembly of the mockers, nor rejoiced; I sat alone because of your hand: for you have filled me with indignation.18 Why is my pain perpetual, and my wound incurable, which refuseth to be healed? will you be altogether unto me as a liar, and as waters that fail?19 Therefore thus saith YHUH, If you return, then will I bring you again, and you shall stand before me: and if you take forth the precious from the vile, you shall be as my mouth: let them return unto you; but return not you unto them.20 And I will make you unto this people a fenced brasen wall: and they shall fight against you, but they shall not prevail against you: for I am with you to save you and to deliver you, saith YHUH.21 And I will deliver you out of the hand of the wicked, and I will redeem you out of the hand of the terrible. **Jer** 16:1 The word of YHUH came also unto me, saying,2 Thou shall not take you a wife, neither shall you have sons or daughters in this place.

לך 3807a בנים 1121 ובנות 1323 במקום 4725 הזה 2088: 16:3 כי 3588 כה 3541 אמר 559 יהוה 3068 על 5921 הבנים 1121 ועל 5921
laka baniym uabanout, bamaqoum hazeh. kiy koh 'amar Yahuah 'al habaniym ua'al
**to you sons or daughters in place this For thus saith Yahuah concerning the sons and concerning**

הבנות 1323 הילודים 3209 במקום 4725 הזה 2088 ועל 5921 אמתם 517 הילדות 3205 אותם 853 ועל 5921 אבותם 1
habanout, hayilodiym bamaqoum hazeh; ua'al 'amotam hayoladout 'autam, ua'al aboutam
**the daughters that are born in place this and concerning their mothers that bare them and concerning their fathers**

המולדים 3205 אותם 853 בארץ 776 הזאת 2063: 16:4 ממותי 4463 תחלאים 8463 ימתו 4191 לא 3808 יספדו 5594 ולא 3808
hamoulidiym 'autam ba'aretz haza't. mamoutey tachalu'aym yamutu, la' yisapadu uala'
**that beget them in land this deaths** ***of*** **grievous They shall die not they shall be lamented neither**

יקברו 6912 לדמן 1828 על 5921 פני 6440 האדמה 127 יהיו 1961 ובחרב 2719 וברעב 7458
yiqaberu, ladomen 'al paney ha'adamah yihayu; uabachereb uabara'ab
**shall they be buried as dung upon the face of the earth** ***but*** **they shall be and by the sword and by famine**

יכלו 3615 והיתה 1961 נבלתם 5038 למאכל 3978 לעוף 5775 השמים 8064 ולבהמת 929
yiklu, uahayatah niblatam lama'akal, la'oup hashamayim ualbehemat
**they shall be consumed and shall be their carcases meat for the fowls of heaven and for the beasts of**

הארץ 776: 16:5 כי 3588 כה 3541 אמר 559 יהוה 3068 אל 408 תבוא 935 בית 1004 מרזח 4798 ואל 408 תלך 1980 לספוד 5594 ואל 408 תנד 5110
ha'aretz. kiy koh 'amar Yahuah 'al tabou'a beyt marzeach, ua'al telek lispoud, ua'al tanod
**the earth For thus saith Yahuah not Enter into the house of mourning neither go to lament nor bemoan**

להם 3807a כי 3588 אספתי 622 את 853 שלומי 7965 מאת 853 העם 5971 הזה 2088 נאם 5002 יהוה 3068 את 853 החסד 2617 ואת 853
lahem; kiy 'asaptiy 'at shaloumiy me'at ha'am hazeh na'am Yahuah, 'at hachesed ua'at
**them for I have taken away my peace from the people this saith Yahuah** ***even*** **lovingkindness** ***and***

הרחמים 7356: 16:6 ומתו 4191 גדלים 1419 וקטנים 6996 בארץ 776 הזאת 2063 לא 3808 יקברו 6912 ולא 3808
harachamiym. uametu gadoliym uaqtaniym ba'aretz haza't la' yiqaberu; uala'
**mercies Both shall die the great and the small in land this not they shall be buried neither**

יספדו 5594 להם 1992 ולא 3808 יתגדד 1413 ולא 3808 יקרח 7139 להם 1992: 16:7 ולא 3808 יפרסו 6536
yispadu lahem, uala' yitgodad, uala' yiqareach lahem. uala' yiparasu
**shall** ***men*** **lament for them nor cut themselves nor make themselves bald for them Neither shall** ***men*** **tear**

להם 3807a על 5921 אבל 60 לנחמו 5162 על 5921 מת 4191 ולא 3808 ישקו 8248 אותם 853 כוס 3563
lahem 'al 'abel lanachamou 'al met; uala' yashqu 'autam kous
***themselves*** **for them in mourning to comfort them for the dead neither shall** ***men*** **give to drink them the cup of**

תנחומים 8575 על 5921 אביו 1 ועל 5921 אמו 517: 16:8 ובית 1004 משתה 4960 לא 3808 תבוא 935 לשבת 3427
tanchumiym, 'al 'abiyu ua'al 'amou. uabeyt mishteh la' tabou'a lashabet
**consolation for their father or for their mother also the house of feasting not You shall go** ***into*** **to sit**

אותם 854 לאכל 398 ולשתות 8354: 16:9 כי 3588 כה 3541 אמר 559 יהוה 3068 צבאות 6635 אלהי 430 ישראל 3478 הנני 2005
'autam; le'akol ualishtout. kiy koh 'amar Yahuah tzaba'aut 'alohey yisra'ael, hinniy
**with them to eat and to drink For thus saith Yahuah of hosts the Elohim of Israel Behold I**

Jer 16:3 For thus saith YHUH concerning the sons and concerning the daughters that are born in this place, and concerning their mothers that bare them, and concerning their fathers that begat them in this land;4 They shall die of grievous deaths; they shall not be lamented; neither shall they be buried; but they shall be as dung upon the face of the earth: and they shall be consumed by the sword, and by famine; and their carcases shall be meat for the fowls of heaven, and for the beasts of the earth.5 For thus saith YHUH, Enter not into the house of mourning, neither go to lament nor bemoan them: for I have taken away my peace from this people, saith YHUH, even lovingkindness and mercies.6 Both the great and the small shall die in this land: they shall not be buried, neither shall men lament for them, nor cut themselves, nor make themselves bald for them:7 Neither shall men tear themselves for them in mourning, to comfort them for the dead; neither shall men give them the cup of consolation to drink for their father or for their mother.8 Thou shall not also go into the house of feasting, to sit with them to eat and to drink.9 For thus saith YHUH of hosts, the G-d of Israel; Behold, I will cause to cease out of this place in your eyes, and in your days, the voice of mirth, and the voice of gladness, the voice of the bridegroom, and the voice of the bride.

7673 משבית 4480 מן 4725 המקום 2088 הזה 5869 לעיניכם 3117 ובימיכם 6963 קול 8342 ששון 6963 וקול 8057 שמחה
mashbiyt min hamaqoum hazeh la'aeyneykem uabiymeykem; qoul sasoun uaqoul simchah,
**will cause to cease out of place this in your eyes and in your days the voice of mirth and the voice of gladness**

16:10
6963 קול 2860 חתן 6963 וקול 3618: כלה 1961 והיה 3588 כי 5046 תגיד 5971 לעם 2088 הזה
qoul chatan uaqoul kalah. uahayah, kiy tagiyd la'am hazeh,
**the voice of the bridegroom and the voice of the bride And it shall come to pass when you shall show people this**

853 את 3605 כל 1697 הדברים 428 האלה 559 ואמרו 413 אליך 5921 על 4100 מה 1696 דבר 3068 יהוה 5921 עלינו 853 את
'at kal hadabariym ha'aeleh; ua'amaru 'aeleyka, 'al meh diber Yahuah 'aleynu 'at
**all words these and they shall say unto you Wherefore what has pronounced Yahuah against us?**

3605 כל 7451 הרעה 1419 הגדולה 2063 הזאת 4100 ומה 5771 עוננו 4100 ומה 2403 חטאתנו 834 אשר 2398 חטאנו 3068 ליהוה
kal hara'ah hagadoulah haza't, uameh 'auonenu uameh chata'tenu, 'asher chata'nu laYahuah
**all evil great this or what *is* our iniquity? or what *is* our sin that we have committed against Yahuah**

16:11
430: אלהינו 559 ואמרת 413 אליהם 5921 על 834 אשר 5800 עזבו 1 אבותיכם 853 אותי 5002 נאם 3068 יהוה
'aloheynu. ua'amarta 'aleyhem, 'al 'asher 'azabu abouteykem 'autiy na'am Yahuah,
**our Elohim? Then shall you say unto them Because which have forsaken your fathers me saith Yahuah**

1980 וילכו 310 אחרי 430 אלהים 312 אחרים 5647 ויעבדום 7812 וישתחוו 3807a להם 853 ואתי 5800 עזבו
uayelaku, 'acharey 'alohiym 'acheriym, uaya'abdum uayishtachauu lahem; ua'atiy 'azabu,
**and have walked after gods other and have served them and have worshipped them and me have forsaken**

16:12
853 ואת 8451 תורתי 3808 לא 8104: שמרו 859 ואתם 7489 הרעתם 6213 לעשות 1 מאבותיכם 2005 והנכם 1980 הלכים 376 איש
ua'at touratiy la' shamaru. ua'atem hare'atem la'asout me'abouteykem; uahinakem holakiym, 'aysh
***and* my law not have kept And you worse have done than your fathers for behold you walk every one**

16:13
310 אחרי 8307 שררות 3820 לבו 7451 הרע 1115 לבלתי 8085 שמע 413: אלי 2904 והטלתי 853 אתכם 5921 מעל
'acharey sharirut libou hara', labiltiy shamoa' 'aelay. uahetaltiy 'atkem, me'al
**after the imagination of his heart evil that not they may listen unto me Therefore will I cast you out of**

776 הארץ 2063 הזאת 5921 על 776 הארץ 834 אשר 3808 לא 3045 ידעתם 859 אתם 1 ואבותיכם 5647 ועבדתם 8033 שם 853 את
ha'aretz haza't, 'al ha'aretz 'asher la' yada'tem, 'atem ua'abouteykem; ua'abadtem sham 'at
**the land this into a land that not you know *neither* you nor your fathers and shall you serve there**

16:14
430 אלהים 312 אחרים 3119 יומם 3915 ולילה 834 אשר 3808 לא 5414 אתן 3807a לכם 2594: חנינה 3651 לכן 2009 הנה 3117 ימים 935 באים
'alohiym 'acheriym youmam ualayalah, 'asher la' 'aten lakem chaniynah. laken hineh yamiym ba'aym
**gods other day and night where not I will show to you favor Therefore behold the days come**

5002 נאם 3068 יהוה 3808 ולא 559 יאמר 5750 עוד 2416 חי 3068 יהוה 834 אשר 5927 העלה 853 את 1121 בני 3478 ישראל
na'am Yahuah; uala' ye'amer 'aud chay Yahuah, 'asher he'alah 'at baney yisra'ael
**saith Yahuah that no it shall be said more live Yahuah that brought up the children of Israel**

16:15
776 מארץ 4714: מצרים 3588 כי 518 אם 2416 חי 3068 יהוה 834 אשר 5927 העלה 853 את 1121 בני 3478 ישראל
me'aretz mitzrayim. kiy 'am chay Yahuah 'asher he'alah 'at baney yisra'ael
**out of the land of Egypt But rather live Yahuah that brought up the children of Israel**

Jer 16:10 And it shall come to pass, when you shall show this people all these words, and they shall say unto you, Wherefore has YHUH pronounced all this great evil against us? or what is our iniquity? or what is our sin that we have committed against YHUH our G-d?11 Then shall you say unto them, Because your fathers have forsaken me, saith YHUH, and have walked after other gods, and have served them, and have worshipped them, and have forsaken me, and have not kept my law;12 And you have done worse than your fathers; for, behold, you walk everyone after the imagination of his evil heart, that they may not hear unto me:13 Therefore will I cast you out of this land into a land that you know not, neither you nor your fathers; and there shall you serve other gods day and night; where I will not show you favor.14 Therefore, behold, the days come, saith YHUH, that it shall no more be said, YHUH live, that brought up the children of Israel out of the land of Egypt;15 But, YHUH live, that brought up the children of Israel from the land of the north, and from all the lands whither he had driven them: and I will bring them again into their land that I gave unto their fathers.

מארץ 776 צפון 6828 ומכל 3605 הארצות 776 אשר 834 הדיחם 5080 שמה 8033 והשבתים 7725 על 5921
me'aretz tzapoun, uamikol ha'aratzout, 'asher hidiycham shamah; uahashibotiym 'al
**from the land of the north and from all the lands where he had driven them their and I will bring them again into**

אדמתם 127 אשר 834 נתתי 5414 לאבותם 1: 16:16 הנני 2005 שלח 7971 לדוגים 1728 רבים 7227 נאם 5002 יהוה 3068
'admatam, 'asher natatiy la'aboutam. hinniy sholeach ladayagiym rabiym na'am Yahuah
**their land that I gave unto their fathers Behold I will send for fishers, many saith Yahuah**

ודיגום 1770 ואחרי 310 כן 3651 אשלח 7971 לרבים 7227 צידים 6719 וצדום 6679 מעל 5921 כל 3605 הר 2022
uadiygum; ua'acharey ken, 'ashlach larabiym tzayadiym, uatzadum me'al kal har
**and they shall fish them and after this will I send for many hunters and they shall hunt from every mountain**

ומעל 5921 כל 3605 גבעה 1389 ומנקיקי 5357 הסלעים 5553: 16:17 כי 3588 עיני 5869 על 5921 כל 3605 דרכיהם 1870 לא 3808
uame'al kal gib'ah, uaminqiyqey hasala'aym. kiy 'aeynay 'al kal darkeyhem, la'
**and from every hill and out of the holes of the rocks For mine eyes *are* upon all their ways not**

נסתרו 5641 מלפני 6440 ולא 3808 נצפן 6845 עונם 5771 מנגד 5048 עיני 5869: 16:18 ושלמתי 7999 ראשונה 7223 משנה 4932
nistaru milapanay; uala' nitzpan 'auonam mineged 'aeynay. uashilamtiy ra'shounah, mishneh
**they are hid from my face neither is hid their iniquity from mine eyes And I will recompense first double**

עונם 5771 וחטאתם 2403 על 5921 חללם 2490 את 853 ארצי 776 בנבלת 5038 שקוציהם 8251
'auonam uachata'tam, 'al challam 'at 'artziy; baniblat shiqutzeyhem
**their iniquity and their sin because they have defiled my land with the carcases of their detestable**

ותועבותיהם 8441 מלאו 4390 את 853 נחלתי 5159: 16:19 יהוה 3068 עזי 5797 ומעזי 4581 ומנוסי 4498
uatou'abouteyhem, mala'au 'at nachalatiy. Yahuah 'aziy uama'aziy uamnusiy
**and abominable things they have filled mine inheritance O Yahuah my strength and my fortress and my refuge**

ביום 3117 צרה 6869 אליך 413 גוים 1471 יבאו 935 מאפסי 657 ארץ 776 ויאמרו 559 אך 389 שקר 8267
bayoum tzarah; 'aeleyka, gouyim yabo'au me'apsey 'aretz, uaya'maru, 'ak sheqer
**in the day of affliction unto you the Gentiles shall come from the ends of the earth and shall say Surely lies**

נחלו 5157 אבותינו 1 הבל 1892 ואין 369 בם 871a מועיל 3276: 16:20 היעשה 6213 לו 3807a אדם 120 אלהים 430
nachalu abouteynu, hebel ua'aeyn bam mou'ayl. haya'aseh lou' 'adam 'alohiym;
**have inherited our fathers vanity and *there is* no *things* wherein profit Shall make unto himself a man gods**

והמה 1992 לא 3808 אלהים 430: 16:21 לכן 3651 הנני 2005 מודיעם 3045 בפעם 6471 הזאת 2063 אודיעם 3045 את 853
uahemah la' 'alohiym. laken hinniy moudiy'am, bapa'am haza't, 'audiy'aem 'at
**and they *are* no gods? Therefore behold cause them to know once this I will cause them to know**

ידי 3027 ואת 853 גבורתי 1369 וידעו 3045 כי 3588 שמי 8034 יהוה 3068:
yadiy ua'at gaburatiy; uayada'aua kiy shamiy Yahuah.
**mine hand *and* my might and they shall know that my name *is* Yahuah**

**Jer 17:1** חטאת 2403 יהודה 3063 כתובה 3789 בעט 5842 ברזל 1270 בצפרן 6856 שמיר 8068 חרושה 2790 על 5921
chata't yahudah, katubah ba'aet barzel batziporen shamiyr; charushah 'al
**The sin of Judah *is* written with a pen of iron *and* with the point of a diamond *it is* graven upon**

Jer 16:16 Behold, I will send for many fishers, saith YHUH, and they shall fish them; and after will I send for many hunters, and they shall hunt them from every mountain, and from every hill, and out of the holes of the rocks.17 For mine eyes are upon all their ways: they are not hid from my face, neither is their iniquity hid from mine eyes.18 And first I will recompense their iniquity and their sin double; because they have defiled my land, they have filled mine inheritance with the carcases of their detestable and abominable things.19 O YHUH, my strength, and my fortress, and my refuge in the day of affliction, the Gentiles shall come unto you from the ends of the earth, and shall say, Surely our fathers have inherited lies, vanity, and things wherein there is no profit.20 Shall a man make gods unto himself, and they are no gods?21 Therefore, behold, I will this once cause them to know, I will cause them to know mine hand and my might; and they shall know that my name is The YHUH. **Jer** 17:1 The sin of Judah is written with a pen of iron, and with the point of a diamond: it is graven upon the table of their heart, and upon the horns of your altars;

17:2
לוח 3871 לבם 3820 ולקרנות 7161 מזבחותיכם 4196: כזכר 2142 בניהם 1121 מזבחותם 4196
luach libam, ualqarnout mizbachouteykem. kizkor baneyhem mizbachoutam,
**the table of their heart and upon the horns of your altars While remember their children their altars**

17:3
ואשריהם 842 על 5921 עץ 6086 רענן 7488 על 5921 גבעות 1389 הגבהות 1364: הררי 2042 בשדה 7704 חילך 2428 כל 3605
ua'ashereyhem 'al 'aetz ra'anan; 'al gaba'aut hagabohout. harariy basadeh, cheylaka kal
**and their groves by trees green upon hills the high O my mountain in the field your substance *and* all**

17:4
אוצרותיך 214 לבז 957 אתן 5414 במתיך 1116 בחטאת 2403 בכל 3605 גבוליך 1366:
'autzarouteyka labaz 'aten; bamoteyka bachata't bakal gabuleyka.
**your treasures to the spoil I will give *and* your high places for sin throughout all your borders**

ושמטתה 8058 ובך 871a מנחלתך 5159 אשר 834 נתתי 5414 לך 3807a והעבדתיך 5647 את 853
uashamatah, uabka minachalataka 'asher natatiy lak, uaha'abadtiyka 'at
**And you shall discontinue even yourself from your heritage that I gave to you and I will cause you to serve**

איביך 341 בארץ 776 אשר 834 לא 3808 ידעת 3045 כי 3588 אש 784 קדחתם 6919 באפי 639 עד 5704 עולם 5769
'ayabeyka, ba'aretz 'asher la' yada'ta; kiy 'aesh qadachtem ba'apiy 'ad 'aulam
**your enemies in the land which not you know for a fire you have kindled in mine anger for ever**

17:5
תוקד 3344: כה 3541 אמר 559 יהוה 3068 ארור 779 הגבר 1397 אשר 834 יבטח 982 באדם 120 ושם 7760 בשר 1320 זרעו 2220 ומן 4480
tuqad. koh 'amar Yahuah 'arur hageber 'asher yibtach ba'adam, uasam basar zaro'au; uamin
***which* shall burn Thus saith Yahuah Cursed *be* the man that trust in man and make flesh his arm and from**

17:6
יהוה 3068 יסור 5493 לבו 3820: והיה 1961 כערער 6176 בערבה 6160 ולא 3808 יראה 7200 כי 3588 יבוא 935 טוב 2896
Yahuah yasur libou. uahayah ka'ara'ar ba'arabah, uala' yir'ah kiy yabou'a toub;
**Yahuah depart whose heart For he shall be like the heath in the desert and not shall see when comes good**

17:7
ושכן 7931 חררים 2788 במדבר 4057 ארץ 776 מלחה 4420 ולא 3808 תשב 3427: ברוך 1288 הגבר 1397 אשר 834
uashakan chareriym bamidbar, 'aretz malechah uala' tesheb. baruk hageber, 'asher
**but shall inhabit the parched places in the wilderness land *in* a salt and not inhabited Blessed *is* the man that**

17:8
יבטח 982 ביהוה 3068 והיה 1961 יהוה 3068 מבטחו 4009: והיה 1961 כעץ 6086 שתול 8362 על 5921 מים 4325 ועל 5921 יובל 3105
yibtach baYahuah; uahayah Yahuah mibatachou. uahayah ka'aetz shatul 'al mayim, ua'al yubal
**trust in Yahuah and is Yahuah whose hope For he shall be as a tree planted by the waters and by the river**

ישלח 7971 שרשיו 8328 ולא 3808 ירא 7200 כי 3588 יבא 935 חם 2527 והיה 1961 עלהו 5929 רענן 7488 ובשנת 8141 בצרת 1226
yashalach sharashayu, uala' yira kiy yaba' chom, uahayah 'alehu ra'anan; uabishnat batzoret
***that* spread out her roots and not shall see when comes heat but shall be her leaf green and in the year of drought**

17:9
לא 3808 ידאג 1672 ולא 3808 ימיש 4185 מעשות 6213 פרי 6529: עקב 6121 הלב 3820 מכל 3605
la' yida'ag, uala' yamiysh me'asout periy. 'aqob haleb mikol
**not shall be careful neither shall cease from yielding fruit *is* deceitful The heart above all**

17:10
ואנש 605 הוא 1931 מי 4310 ידענו 3045: אני 589 יהוה 3068 חקר 2713 לב 3820 בחן 974 כליות 3629 ולתת 5414
ua'anush hua'; miy' yeda'anu. 'aniy Yahuah choqer leb bochen kalayout; ualatet
***things* and desperately wicked it? who can know I Yahuah search the heart *I* try the reins even to give**

Jer 17:2 Whilst their children remember their altars and their groves by the green trees upon the high hills.3 O my mountain in the field, I will give your substance and all your treasures to the spoil, and your high places for sin, throughout all your borders.4 And you, even thyself, shall discontinue from your heritage that I gave you; and I will cause you to serve your enemies in the land which you know not: for you have kindled a fire in mine anger, which shall burn forever.5 Thus saith YHUH; Cursed be the man that trusteth in man, and make flesh his arm, and whose heart departeth from YHUH.6 For he shall be like the heath in the desert, and shall not see when good cometh; but shall inhabit the parched places in the wilderness, in a salt land and not inhabited.7 Blessed is the man that trusteth in YHUH, and whose hope YHUH is.8 For he shall be as a tree planted by the waters, and that spreadeth out her roots by the river, and shall not see when heat cometh, but her leaf shall be green; and shall not be careful in the year of drought, neither shall cease from yielding fruit.9 The heart is deceitful above all things, and desperately wicked: who can know it?10 I YHUH search the heart, I try the reins, even to give every man according to his ways, and according to the fruit of his doings.

| לאיש 376 | כדרכו 1870 | כפרי 6529 | מעלליו 4611: | 17:11 | קרא 7124 | דגר 1716 | ולא 3808 |
|---|---|---|---|---|---|---|---|
| la'aysh | kedarkou | kipariy | ma'alalayu. | | qorea' | dagar | uala' |
| **every man** | **according to his ways,** | ***and* according to the fruit of** | **his doings** | | ***As* the partridge** | **sit** | ***on eggs* and not** |

| ילד 3205 | עשה 6213 | עשר 6239 | ולא 3808 | במשפט 4941 | בחצי 2677 | ימו 3117 | יעזבנו 5800 | ובאחריתו 319 | יהיה 1961 |
|---|---|---|---|---|---|---|---|---|---|
| yalad, | 'asheh | 'asher | uala' | bamishpat; | bachatziy | yamou | ya'azbenu, | uab'achariytou | yihayeh |
| **hatcheth** | ***them so*** | **he that get riches** | **and not** | **by right** | **in the midst of** | **his days** | **shall leave them** | **and at his end** | **shall be** |

| נבל 5036: | 17:12 | כסא 3678 | כבוד 3519 | מרום 4791 | מראשון 7223 | מקום 4725 | מקדשנו 4720: | 17:13 | מקוה 4723 | ישראל 3478 |
|---|---|---|---|---|---|---|---|---|---|---|
| nabal. | | kisea' | kaboud, | maroum | mera'shoun; | maqoum | miqadashenu. | | miqueh | yisra'ael |
| **a fool** | | **A throne** | **glorious** | **high** | **from the beginning** | ***is* the place of** | **our sanctuary** | | **the hope of** | **Israel** |

| יהוה 3068 | כל 3605 | עזביך 5800 | יבשו 954 | יסורי 3249 | בארץ 776 | יכתבו 3789 | כי 3588 |
|---|---|---|---|---|---|---|---|
| Yahuah, | kal | 'azabeyka | yeboshu; | yisouray | ba'aretz | yikatebu, | kiy |
| **O Yahuah** | **all** | **that forsake you** | **shall be ashamed** | **and they that depart from me** | **in the earth** | **shall be written** | **because** |

| עזבו 5800 | מקור 4726 | מים 4325 | חיים 2416 | את 853 | יהוה 3068: | 17:14 | רפאני 7495 | יהוה 3068 | וארפא 7495 |
|---|---|---|---|---|---|---|---|---|---|
| 'azabu | maqour | mayim | chayiym | 'at | Yahuah. | | rapa'aeniy | Yahuah | ua'aerapea', |
| **they have forsaken** | **the fountain of** | **waters** | **living** | | **Yahuah** | | **Heal me** | **O Yahuah** | **and I shall be healed** |

| הושיעני 3467 | ואושעה 3467 | כי 3588 | תהלתי 8416 | אתה 859: | 17:15 | הנה 2009 | המה 1992 | אמרים 559 | אלי 413 | איה 346 | דבר 1697 |
|---|---|---|---|---|---|---|---|---|---|---|---|
| houshiy'aeniy | ua'auashe'ah; | kiy | tahilatiy | 'atah. | | hineh | hemah | 'amariym | 'aelay; | 'ayeh | dabar |
| **save me** | **and I shall be saved** | **for** | ***are* my praise** | **you** | | **Behold** | **they** | **say** | **unto me** | **Where *is*** | **the word of** |

| יהוה 3068 | יבוא 935 | נא 4994: | 17:16 | ואני 589 | לא 3808 | אצתי 213 | מרעה 7462 | אחריך 310 | ויום 3117 | אנוש 605 |
|---|---|---|---|---|---|---|---|---|---|---|
| Yahuah | yabou'a | na. | | ua'aniy | la' | 'atztiy | mero'ah | 'achareyka, | uayoum | 'anush |
| **Yahuah?** | **let it come** | **now** | | **As for me** | **not** | **I have hastened** | **from *being* a pastor** | **to follow you** | **day** | ***the* woeful** |

| לא 3808 | התאויתי 183 | אתה 859 | ידעת 3045 | מוצא 4161 | שפתי 8193 | נכח 5227 | פניך 6440 | היה 1961: | 17:17 | אל 408 | תהיה 1961 |
|---|---|---|---|---|---|---|---|---|---|---|---|
| la' | hit'aueytiy | 'atah | yada'ta; | moutza' | sapatay, | nokach | paneyka | hayah. | | 'al | tihayeh |
| **neither** | **have I desired** | **you** | **know** | **that which came out of** | **my lips** | **was *right*** | **before of you** | **he** | | **not** | **Be** |

| לי 3807a | למחתה 4288 | מחסי 4268 | אתה 859 | ביום 3117 | רעה 7451: | 17:18 | יבשו 954 | רדפי 7291 | ואל 408 |
|---|---|---|---|---|---|---|---|---|---|
| liy | limachitah; | machasiy | 'atah | bayoum | ra'ah. | | yeboshu | rodapay | ua'al |
| **unto me** | **a terror** | ***are* my hope** | **you** | **in the day of** | **evil** | | **Let them be confounded** | **that persecute me** | **but not** |

| אבשה 954 | אני 589 | יחתו 2865 | המה 1992 | ואל 408 | אחתה 2865 | אני 589 | הביא 935 | עליהם 5921 | יום 3117 | רעה 7451 |
|---|---|---|---|---|---|---|---|---|---|---|
| 'aeboshah | 'aniy, | yechatu | hemah, | ua'al | 'aechatah | 'aniy; | habiy'a | 'aleyhem | youm | ra'ah, |
| **let be confounded** | **me** | **let be dismayed** | **them** | **but not** | **let be dismayed** | **me** | **bring** | **upon them** | **the day of** | **evil** |

| ומשנה 4932 | שברון 7670 | שברם 7665: | 17:19 | כה 3541 | אמר 559 | יהוה 3068 | אלי 413 | הלך 1980 | ועמדת 5975 | בשער 8179 |
|---|---|---|---|---|---|---|---|---|---|---|
| uamishneh | shibaroun | shabarem. | | koh | 'amar | Yahuah | 'aelay, | halok | ua'amadta | basha'ar |
| **and double** | **destruction** | **destroy them *with*** | | **Thus** | **said** | **Yahuah** | **unto me** | **Go** | **and stand** | **in the gate of** |

| בני 1121 | עם 5971 | אשר 834 | יבאו 935 | בו 871a | מלכי 4428 | יהודה 3063 | ואשר 834 | יצאו 3318 | בו 871a | ובכל 3605 |
|---|---|---|---|---|---|---|---|---|---|---|
| baney | 'am | 'asher | yabo'au | bou | malkey | yahudah, | ua'asher | yetz'au | bou; | uabkol |
| **the children of** | **the people** | **whereby** | **come in** | **in him** | **the kings of** | **Judah** | **and by the which** | **they go out** | **in him** | **and in all** |

Jer 17:11 As the partridge sitteth on eggs, and hatcheth them not; so he that get riches, and not by right, shall leave them in the midst of his days, and at his end shall be a fool.12 A glorious high throne from the beginning is the place of our sanctuary.13 O YHUH, the hope of Israel, all that forsake you shall be ashamed, and they that depart from me shall be written in the earth, because they have forsaken YHUH, the fountain of living waters.14 Heal me, O YHUH, and I shall be healed; save me, and I shall be saved: for you are my praise.15 Behold, they say unto me, Where is the word of YHUH? let it come now.16 As for me, I have not hastened from being a pastor to follow you: neither have I desired the woeful day; you know: that which came out of my lips was right before you.17 Be not a terror unto me: you are my hope in the day of evil.18 Let them be confounded that persecute me, but let not me be confounded: let them be dismayed, but let not me be dismayed: bring upon them the day of evil, and destroy them with double destruction.19 Thus said YHUH unto me; Go and stand in the gate of the children of the people, whereby the kings of Judah come in, and by the which they go out, and in all the gates of Jerusalem;

17:20

שערי 8179 ירושלם 3389: ואמרת 559 אליהם 413 שמעו 8085 דבר 1697 יהוה 3068 מלכי 4428 יהודה 3063 וכל 3605 יהודה 3063
sha'arey yarushalaim. ua'amarta 'aleyhem shim'au dabar Yahuah malkey yahudah uakal yahudah,
**the gates of Jerusalem And say unto them Hear you the word of Yahuah you kings of Judah and all Judah**

17:21

וכל 3605 ישבי 3427 ירושלם 3389 הבאים 935 בשערים 8179 האלה 428: כה 3541 אמר 559 יהוה 3068 השמרו 8104
uakol yoshabey yarushalaim; haba'aym bash'ariym ha'aeleh. koh 'amar Yahuah, hishamaru
**and all the inhabitants of Jerusalem that enter in by gates these Thus saith Yahuah Take heed**

17:22

בנפשותיכם 5315 ואל 408 תשאו 5375 משא 4853 ביום 3117 השבת 7676 והבאתם 935 בשערי 8179 ירושלם 3389: ולא 3808
banapshouteykem; ua'al tis'au masa' bayoum hashabat, uahabea'tem basha'arey yarushalaim. uala'
**to yourselves and no bear burden on day the sabbath nor bring *it* in by the gates of Jerusalem Neither**

תוציאו 3318 משא 4853 מבתיכם 1004 ביום 3117 השבת 7676 וכל 3605 מלאכה 4399 לא 3808 תעשו 6213 וקדשתם 6942 את 853 יום 3117
toutziy'au masa' mibateykem bayoum hashabat, uakal mala'kah la' ta'asu; uaqidashtem 'at youm
**carry forth a burden out of your houses on day the sabbath any work neither do you but hallow you day**

17:23

השבת 7676 כאשר 834 צויתי 6680 את 853 אבותיכם 1: ולא 3808 שמעו 8085 ולא 3808 הטו 5186 את 853 אזנם 241
hashabat, ka'asher tziuiytiy 'at abouteykem. uala' shama'au, uala' hitu 'at 'azanam;
**the sabbath as I commanded your fathers But not they obeyed neither inclined their ear**

17:24

ויקשו 7185 את 853 ערפם 6203 לבלתי 1115 שומע 8085 ולבלתי 1115 קחת 3947 מוסר 4148: והיה 1961
uayaqshu 'at 'arapam, labiltiy shouma' ualbiltiy qachat musar. uahayah
**but made stiff their neck that not they might hear, nor receive instruction And it shall come to pass**

אם 518 שמע 8085 תשמעון 8085 אלי 413 נאם 5002 יהוה 3068 לבלתי 1115 הביא 935 משא 4853 בשערי 8179 העיר 5892 הזאת 2063
'am shamoa' tishma'aun 'aelay na'am Yahuah, labiltiy habiy'a masa', basha'arey ha'ayr haza't
**if you diligently listen unto me saith Yahuah to no bring in burden through the gates of city this**

17:25

ביום 3117 השבת 7676 ולקדש 6942 את 853 יום 3117 השבת 7676 לבלתי 1115 עשות 6213 בה 871a כל 3605 מלאכה 4399:
bayoum hashabat; ualqadesh 'at youm hashabat, labiltiy asout boh kal mala'kah.
**on day the sabbath but hallow day the sabbath no to do therein; no work**

ובאו 935 בשערי 8179 העיר 5892 הזאת 2063 מלכים 4428 ושרים 8269 ישבים 3427 על 5921 כסא 3678 דוד 1732
uaba'au uasha'arey ha'ayr haza't malakiym uasariym yoshbiym 'al kisea' dauid
**Then shall there enter into the gates of city this kings and princes sitting upon the throne of David**

רכבים 7392 ברכב 7393 ובסוסים 5483 המה 1992 ושריהם 8269 איש 376 יהודה 3063 וישבי 3427 ירושלם 3389
rokabiym barekeb uabasusiym, hemah uasareyhem, 'aysh yahudah uayoushabey yarushalaim;
**riding in chariots and on horses they and their princes the men of Judah and the inhabitants of Jerusalem**

17:26

וישבה 3427 העיר 5892 הזאת 2063 לעולם 5769: ובאו 935 מערי 5892 יהודה 3063 ומסביבות 5439
uayashabah ha'ayr haza't la'aulam. uaba'au me'arei yahudah uamisbiybout
**and shall remain city this for ever And they shall come from the cities of Judah and from the places about**

ירושלם 3389 ומארץ 776 בנימן 1144 ומן 4480 השפלה 8219 ומן 4480 ההר 2022 ומן 4480 הנגב 5045 מבאים 935
yarushalaim uame'aretz binyamin, uamin hashapelah uamin hahar uamin hanegeb, mabi'aym
**Jerusalem and from the land of Benjamin and from the plain and from the mountains and from the south bringing**

Jer 17:20 And say unto them, Hear you the word of YHUH, you kings of Judah, and all Judah, and all the inhabitants of Jerusalem, that enter in by these gates:21 Thus saith YHUH; Take heed to yourselves, and bear no burden on the Sabbath day, nor bring it in by the gates of Jerusalem;22 Neither carry forth a burden out of your houses on the Sabbath day, neither do you any work, but hallow you the Sabbath day, as I commanded your fathers.23 But they obeyed not, neither inclined their ear, but made their neck stiff, that they might not hear, nor receive instruction.24 And it shall come to pass, if you diligently hear unto me, saith YHUH, to bring in no burden through the gates of this city on the Sabbath day, but hallow the Sabbath day, to do no work therein;25 Then shall there enter into the gates of this city kings and princes sitting upon the throne of David, riding in chariots and on horses, they, and their princes, the men of Judah, and the inhabitants of Jerusalem: and this city shall remain forever.26 And they shall come from the cities of Judah, and from the places about Jerusalem, and from the land of Benjamin, and from the plain, and from the mountains, and from the south, bringing burnt offerings, and sacrifices, and meat offerings, and incense, and bringing sacrifices of praise, unto the house of YHUH.

| עולה 5930 | וזבח 2077 | ומנחה 4503 | ולבונה 3828 | ומבאי 935 | תודה 8426 | בית 1004 |
|---|---|---|---|---|---|---|
| aulah | uazebach | uaminchah | ualabounah; | uambi'aey | toudah | beyt |
| **burnt offerings** | **and sacrifices** | **and meat offerings** | **and incense** | **and bringing** | **sacrifices of praise** | ***unto* the house of** |

| יהוה 3068: | 17:27 | ואם 518 | לא 3808 | תשמעו 8085 | אלי 413 | לקדש 6942 | את 853 | יום 3117 | השבת 7676 | ולבלתי 1115 | שאת 5375 | משא 4853 |
|---|---|---|---|---|---|---|---|---|---|---|---|---|
| Yahuah. | | ua'am | la' | tishma'au | 'aelay, | laqadesh | 'at | youm | hashabat, | ualbiltiy | sa'aet | masa', |
| **Yahuah** | | **But if** | **not** | **you will listen** | **unto me** | **to hallow** | | **day** | **the sabbath** | **and not** | **you to bear** | **a burden** |

| ובא 935 | בשערי 8179 | ירושלם 3389 | ביום 3117 | השבת 7676 | והצתי 3341 | אש 784 | בשעריה 8179 |
|---|---|---|---|---|---|---|---|
| uaba' | basha'arey | yarushalaim | bayoum | hashabat; | uahitzatiy | 'aesh | bish'areyha, |
| **even entering in** | **at the gates of** | **Jerusalem** | **on day** | **the sabbath** | **then will I kindle** | **a fire** | **in the gates thereof** |

| ואכלה 398 | ארמנות 759 | ירושלם 3389 | ולא 3808 | תכבה 3518: |
|---|---|---|---|---|
| ua'akalah | 'armanout | yarushalaim | uala' | tikbeh. |
| **and it shall devour** | **the palaces of** | **Jerusalem** | **and not** | **it shall be quenched** |

| **Jer 18:1** | הדבר 1697 | אשר 834 | היה 1961 | אל 413 | ירמיהו 3414 | מאת 853 | יהוה 3068 | לאמר 559: | **18:2** | קום 6965 | וירדת 3381 | בית 1004 | היוצר 3335 |
|---|---|---|---|---|---|---|---|---|---|---|---|---|---|
| | hadabar | 'asher | hayah | 'al | yirmayahu, | me'at | Yahuah | lea'mor. | | qum | uayaradta | beyt | hayoutzer; |
| | **The word** | **which** | **came** | **to** | **Jeremiah** | **from** | **Yahuah** | **saying** | | **Arise** | **and go down to** | **house** | **the potter's** |

| ושמה 8034 | אשמיעך 8085 | את 853 | דברי 1697: | **18:3** | וארד 3381 | בית 1004 | היוצר 3335 | והנהו 2009 | עשה 6213 |
|---|---|---|---|---|---|---|---|---|---|
| uashamah | 'ashmiy'aka | 'at | dabaray. | | ua'ared | beyt | hayoutzer; | uahinehu | 'aseh |
| **and there** | **I will cause you to hear** | | **my words** | | **Then I went down to** | **house** | **the potter's** | **and behold,** | **he wrought** |

| מלאכה 4399 | על 5921 | האבנים 70: | **18:4** | ונשחת 7843 | הכלי 3627 | אשר 834 | הוא 1931 | עשה 6213 | בחמר 2563 | ביד 3027 | היוצר 3335 |
|---|---|---|---|---|---|---|---|---|---|---|---|
| mala'kah | 'al | ha'abanayim. | | uanishchat | hakaliy, | 'asher | hua' | 'aseh | bachomer | bayad | hayoutzer; |
| **a work** | **on** | **the wheels** | | **And was marred** | **the vessel** | **that** | **he** | **made** | **of clay** | **in the hand of** | **the potter** |

| ושב 7725 | ויעשהו 6213 | כלי 3627 | אחר 312 | כאשר 834 | ישר 3474 | בעיני 5869 | היוצר 3335 | לעשות 6213: | **18:5** | ויהי 1961 | דבר 1697 | יהוה 3068 |
|---|---|---|---|---|---|---|---|---|---|---|---|---|
| uashab, | uay'asehu | kaliy | 'acher, | ka'asher | yashar | ba'aeyney | hayoutzer | la'asout. | | uayahiy | dabar | Yahuah |
| **so again** | **he made it** | **vessel** | **another** | **as** | **good** | **to seemed** | **the potter** | **to make *it*** | | **Then came** | **the word of** | **Yahuah** |

| אלי 413 | לאמור 559: | **18:6** | הכיוצר 3335 | הזה 2088 | לא 3808 | אוכל 3201 | לעשות 6213 | לכם 3807a | בית 1004 | ישראל 3478 | נאם 5002 | יהוה 3068 | הנה 2009 |
|---|---|---|---|---|---|---|---|---|---|---|---|---|---|
| 'aelay | lea'mour. | | hakayoutzer | hazeh | la' | 'aukal | la'asout | lakem | beyt | yisra'ael | na'am | Yahuah; | hineh |
| **to me** | **saying** | | **as potter?** | **this** | **not** | **can** | **I do** | **with you** | **O house of** | **Israel** | **saith** | **Yahuah** | **Behold** |

| כחמר 2563 | ביד 3027 | היוצר 3335 | כן 3651 | אתם 859 | בידי 3027 | בית 1004 | ישראל 3478: | **18:7** | רגע 7281 | אדבר 1696 |
|---|---|---|---|---|---|---|---|---|---|---|
| kachomer | bayad | hayoutzer, | ken | 'atem | biydey | beyt | yisra'ael. | | rega' | 'adaber, |
| **as the clay** | ***is* in hand** | **the potter's** | **so** | ***are* you** | **in mine hand** | **O house of** | **Israel** | | ***At what* instant** | **I shall speak** |

| על 5921 | גוי 1471 | ועל 5921 | ממלכה 4467 | לנתוש 5428 | ולנתוץ 5422 | ולהאביד 6: | **18:8** | ושב 7725 | הגוי 1471 | ההוא 1931 |
|---|---|---|---|---|---|---|---|---|---|---|
| 'al | gouy | ua'al | mamlakah; | lintoush | ualintoutz | ualha'abiyd. | | uashab | hagouy | hahua', |
| **concerning** | **a nation** | **and concerning** | **a kingdom** | **to pluck up** | **and to pull down** | **and to destroy *it*** | | **If turn** | **nation** | **that** |

| מרעתו 7451 | אשר 834 | דברתי 1696 | עליו 5921 | ונחמתי 5162 | על 5921 | הרעה 7451 | אשר 834 | חשבתי 2803 | לעשות 6213 | לו 3807a: |
|---|---|---|---|---|---|---|---|---|---|---|
| mera'atou, | 'asher | dibartiy | 'alayu; | uanichamtiy | 'al | hara'ah, | 'asher | chashabtiy | la'asout | lou'. |
| **from their evil** | **whom** | **I have pronounced** | **against** | **I will repent of** | | **the evil** | **that** | **I thought** | **to do** | **unto them** |

Jer 17:27 But if you will not hear unto me to hallow the Sabbath day, and not to bear a burden, even entering in at the gates of Jerusalem on the Sabbath day; then will I kindle
a fire in the gates thereof, and it shall devour the palaces of Jerusalem, and it shall not be quenched. **Jer** 18:1 The word which came to Jeremiah from YHUH, saying,2 Arise,
and go down to the potter's house, and there I will cause you to hear my words.3 Then I went down to the potter's house, and, behold, he wrought a work on the wheels.4 And
the vessel that he made of clay was marred in the hand of the potter: so he made it again another vessel, as seemed good to the potter to make it.5 Then the word of YHUH
came to me, saying,6 O house of Israel, cannot I do with you as this potter? saith YHUH. Behold, as the clay is in the potter's hand, so are you in mine hand, O house of Israel.7
At what instant I shall speak concerning a nation, and concerning a kingdom, to pluck up, and to pull down, and to destroy it;8 If that nation, against whom I have pronounced,
turn from their evil, I will repent of the evil that I thought to do unto them.

**18:9** ... **18:10**

ורגע 7281 אדבר 1696 על 5921 גוי 1471 ועל 5921 ממלכה 4467 לבנת 1129 ולנטע 5193: ועשה 6213
uarega' 'adaber, 'al gouy ua'al mamlakah; libnat ualintoa'. ua'asah
**And *at what* instant I shall speak concerning a nation and concerning a kingdom to build and to plant *it* If it do**

הרעה 7451 בעיני 5869 לבלתי 1115 שמע 8085 בקולי 6963 ונחמתי 5162 על 5921 הטובה 2896 אשר 834 אמרתי 559 להיטיב 3190
hara'ah ba'aeynay, labiltiy shamoa' baqouliy; uanichamtiy 'al hatoubah, 'asher 'amartiy laheytiyb
**evil in my sight that not it obey my voice then I will repent of the good wherewith I said I would benefit**

**18:11**

אותו 853: ועתה 6258 אמר 559 נא 4994 אל 413 איש 376 יהודה 3063 ועל 5921 יושבי 3427 ירושלם 3389 לאמר 559 כה 3541
'autou. ua'atah 'amar naa' 'al 'aysh yahudah ua'al youshabey yarushalaim lea'mor, koh
**them Now therefore speak go to to the men of Judah and to the inhabitants of Jerusalem saying Thus**

אמר 559 יהוה 3068 הנה 2009 אנכי 595 יוצר 3335 עליכם 5921 רעה 7451 וחשב 2803 עליכם 5921 מחשבה 4284 שובו 7725 נא 4994 איש 376
'amar Yahuah, hineh 'anokiy youtzer 'aleykem ra'ah, uachosheb 'aleykem machashabah; shubu na, 'aysh
**saith Yahuah Behold I frame against you evil and devise against you a device return you now every one**

**18:12**

מדרכו 1870 הרעה 7451 והיטיבו 3190 דרכיכם 1870 ומעלליכם 4611: ואמרו 559 נואש 2976 כי 3588 אחרי 310
midarkou hara'ah, uaheytiybu darkeykem uama'alleykem. ua'amaru nou'ash; kiy 'acharey
**from his way evil and make good your ways and your doings And they said There is no hope but after**

**18:13**

מחשבותינו 4284 נלך 1980 ואיש 376 שררות 8307 לבו 3820 הרע 7451 נעשה 6213: לכן 3651 כה 3541 אמר 559
machshabouteynu nelek, ua'aysh sharirut libou hara' na'aseh. laken, koh 'amar
**our own devices we will walk and every one the imagination of his heart evil we will do Therefore thus saith**

יהוה 3068 שאלו 7592 נא 4994 בגוים 1471 מי 4310 שמע 8085 כאלה 428 שעררת 8186 עשתה 6213 מאד 3966 בתולת 1330
Yahuah, sha'alu naa' bagouyim, miy' shama' ka'aeleh; sha'arurit 'astah ma'ad, batulat
**Yahuah Ask you now among the heathen who has heard such *things* a horrible thing has done very the virgin of**

**18:14**

ישראל 3478: היעזב 5800 מצור 6697 שדי 7704 שלג 7950 לבנון 3844 אם 518 ינתשו 5428
yisra'ael. haya'azob mitzur saday sheleg labanoun; 'am yinatashu,
**Israel Will *a man* leave *which comes* from the rock of the field? the snow of Lebanon or shall be forsaken?**

**18:15**

מים 4325 זרים 2114 קרים 7119 נוזלים 5140: כי 3588 שכחני 7911 עמי 5971 לשוא 7723
mayim zariym qariym nouzaliym. kiy shakechuniy 'amiy lashau'a
**waters that come from another place the cold flowing Because has forgotten me my people to vanity**

יקטרו 6999 ויכשלום 3782 בדרכיהם 1870 שבילי 7635 עולם 5769 ללכת 1980
yaqateru; uayakshilum badarkeyhem shabiyley 'aulam, laleket
**they have burned incense and they have caused them to stumble in their ways paths *from* the ancient to walk in**

**18:16**

נתיבות 5410 דרך 1870 לא 3808 סלולה 5549: לשום 7760 ארצם 776 לשמה 8047 שרוקת 8292 עולם 5769 כל 3605 עובר 5674
natiybout, derek la' salulah. lasum 'artzam lashamah sharuqat 'aulam; kal 'auber
**paths *in* a way not cast up To make their land desolate *and* a hissing; perpetual every one that passed**

**18:17**

עליה 5921 ישם 8074 ויניד 5110 בראשו 7218: כרוח 7307 קדים 6921 אפיצם 6327 לפני 6440 אויב 341
'aleyha, yishom uayaniyd bara'shou. karuach qadiym 'apiytzem lipney auyeb;
**thereby shall be astonished and wag his head as with an wind east I will scatter them before the enemy**

Jer 18:9 And at what instant I shall speak concerning a nation, and concerning a kingdom, to build and to plant it;10 If it do evil in my sight, that it obey not my voice, then I will repent of the good, wherewith I said I would benefit them.11 Now therefore go to, speak to the men of Judah, and to the inhabitants of Jerusalem, saying, Thus saith YHUH; Behold, I frame evil against you, and devise a device against you: return you now everyone from his evil way, and make your ways and your doings good.12 And they said, There is no hope: but we will walk after our own devices, and we will everyone do the imagination of his evil heart.13 Therefore thus saith YHUH; Ask you now among the heathen, who has heard such things: the virgin of Israel has done a very horrible thing.14 Will a man leave the snow of Lebanon which cometh from the rock of the field? or shall the cold flowing waters that come from another place be forsaken?15 Because my people has forgotten me, they have burned incense to vanity, and they have caused them to stumble in their ways from the ancient paths, to walk in paths, in a way not cast up;16 To make their land desolate, and a perpetual hissing; everyone that pass thereby shall be astonished, and wag his head.17 I will scatter them as with an east wind before the enemy; I will show them the back, and not the face, in the day of their calamity.

| ערף 6203 | ולא 3808 | פנים 6440 | אראם 7200 | ביום 3117 | אידם 343: | 18:18 | ויאמרו 559 | לכו 1980 | ונחשבה 2803 |
|---|---|---|---|---|---|---|---|---|---|
| 'arep | uala' | paniym | 'ar'aem | bayoum | 'aeydam. | | uaya'maru, | laku | uanachshabah |
| **the back** | **and not** | **the face** | **I will show them** | **in the day of** | **their calamity** | | **Then said they** | **Come** | **and let us devise** |

| על 5921 | ירמיהו 3414 | מחשבות 4284 | כי 3588 | לא 3808 | תאבד 6 | תורה 8451 | מכהן 3548 | ועצה 6098 | מחכם 2450 | ודבר 1697 |
|---|---|---|---|---|---|---|---|---|---|---|
| 'al | yirmayahu | machashabout | kiy | la' | ta'bad | tourah | mikohen, | ua'aetzah | mechakam, | uadabar |
| **against** | **Jeremiah** | **devices** | **for** | **not** | **shall perish** | **the law** | **from the priest** | **nor counsel** | **from the wise** | **nor the word** |

| מנביא 5030 | לכו 1980 | ונכהו 5221 | בלשון 3956 | ואל 408 | נקשיבה 7181 | אל 413 | כל 3605 | דבריו 1697: | 18:19 |
|---|---|---|---|---|---|---|---|---|---|
| minabiy'a; | laku | uanakehu | balashoun, | ua'al | naqshiybah | 'al | kal | dabarayu. | |
| **from the prophet** | **Come** | **and let us smite him** | **with the tongue** | **and not** | **let us give heed** | **to** | **any of** | **his words** | |

| הקשיבה 7181 | יהוה 3068 | אלי 413 | ושמע 8085 | לקול 6963 | יריבי 3401: | 18:20 | הישלם 7999 | תחת 8478 | טובה 2896 |
|---|---|---|---|---|---|---|---|---|---|
| haqashiybah | Yahuah | 'aelay; | uashma' | laqoul | yariybay. | | hayashulam | tachat | toubah |
| **Give heed** | **O Yahuah** | **to me** | **and listen** | **to the voice of** | **them that contend** | | **Shall be recompensed** | **for** | **good?** |

| רעה 7451 | כי 3588 | כרו 3738 | שוחה 7745 | לנפשי 5315 | זכר 2142 | עמדי 5975 | לפניך 6440 | לדבר 1696 | עליהם 5921 | טובה 2896 |
|---|---|---|---|---|---|---|---|---|---|---|
| ra'ah, | kiy | karu | shuchah | lanapshiy; | zakor | 'amadiy | lapaneyka, | ladaber | 'aleyhem | toubah, |
| **evil** | **for** | **they have digged** | **a pit** | **for my soul** | **Remember** | **that I stood** | **before you** | **to speak** | **for them** | **good** |

| להשיב 7725 | את 853 | חמתך 2534 | מהם 1992: | 18:21 | לכן 3651 | תן 5414 | את 853 | בניהם 1121 | לרעב 7458 |
|---|---|---|---|---|---|---|---|---|---|
| lahashiyb | 'at | chamataka | mehem. | | laken | ten | 'at | baneyhem | lara'ab, |
| ***and* to turn away** | | **your wrath** | **from them** | | **Therefore** | **deliver up** | | **their children** | **to the famine** |

| והגרם 5064 | על 5921 | ידי 3027 | חרב 2719 | ותהינה 1961 | נשיהם 802 | שכלות 7909 | ואלמנות 490 |
|---|---|---|---|---|---|---|---|
| uahagirem | 'al | yadey | chereb | uatihayenah | nasheyhem | shakulout | ua'almanout, |
| **and pour out their *blood*** | **by** | **the force of** | **the sword** | **and let be** | **their wives** | **bereaved of their children** | **and *be* widows** |

| ואנשיהם 582 | יהיו 1961 | הרגי 2026 | מות 4194 | בחוריהם 970 | מכי 5221 | חרב 2719 | במלחמה 4421: | 18:22 | תשמע 8085 | זעקה 2201 |
|---|---|---|---|---|---|---|---|---|---|---|
| ua'ansheyhem, | yihayu | harugey | mauet; | bachureyhem, | mukey | chereb | bamilchamah. | | tishama' | za'aqah |
| **and their men** | **let be** | **put to** | **death** | ***let* their young men** | ***be* slain by** | **the sword** | **in battle** | | **Let be heard** | **a cry** |

| מבתיהם 1004 | כי 3588 | תביא 935 | עליהם 5921 | גדוד 1416 | פתאם 6597 | כי 3588 | כרו 3738 | שיחה 7882 | ללכדני 3920 |
|---|---|---|---|---|---|---|---|---|---|
| mibateyhem, | kiy | tabiy'a | 'aleyhem | gadud | pit'am; | kiy | karu | shiychah | lalakadeniy, |
| **from their houses** | **when** | **you shall bring** | **upon them** | **a troop** | **suddenly** | **for** | **they have digged** | **a pit** | **to take me** |

| ופחים 6341 | טמנו 2934 | לרגלי 7272: | 18:23 | ואתה 859 | יהוה 3068 | ידעת 3045 | את 853 | כל 3605 | עצתם 6098 | עלי 5921 | למות 4194 | אל 408 | תכפר 3722 |
|---|---|---|---|---|---|---|---|---|---|---|---|---|---|
| uapachiym | tamanu | laraglay. | | ua'atah | Yahuah | yada'ta | 'at | kal | 'atzatam | 'alay | lamauet, | 'al | takaper |
| **and snares hid** | | **for my feet** | | **Yet you** | **Yahuah** | **know** | | **all** | **their counsel against me** | | **to slay *me*** | **not** | **forgive** |

| על 5921 | עונם 5771 | וחטאתם 2403 | מלפניך 6440 | אל 408 | תמחי 4229 | והיו 1961 | מכשלים 3782 | לפניך 6440 | בעת 6256 |
|---|---|---|---|---|---|---|---|---|---|
| 'al | 'auonam, | uachata'tam | milpaneyka | 'al | temchiy; | uahayu | mukshaliym | lapaneyka, | ba'aet |
| **against** | **their iniquity** | **their sin** | **from your sight** | **neither** | **blot out** | **but let them be** | **overthrown** | **before you** | **in the time of** |

| אפך 639 | עשה 6213 | בהם 871a: |
|---|---|---|
| 'apaka | 'aseh | bahem. |
| **your anger** | **deal *thus*** | **with them** |

Jer 18:18 Then said they, Come, and let us devise devices against Jeremiah; for the law shall not perish from the priest, nor counsel from the wise, nor the word from the prophet. Come, and let us smite him with the tongue, and let us not give heed to any of his words.19 Give heed to me, O YHUH, and hear to the voice of them that contend with me.20 Shall evil be recompensed for good? for they have digged a pit for my soul. Remember that I stood before you to speak good for them, and to turn away your wrath from them.21 Therefore deliver up their children to the famine, and pour out their blood by the force of the sword; and let their wives be bereaved of their children, and be widows; and let their men be put to death; let their young men be slain by the sword in battle.22 Let a cry be heard from their houses, when you shall bring a troop suddenly upon them: for they have digged a pit to take me, and hid snares for my feet.23 Yet, YHUH, you know all their counsel against me to slay me: forgive not their iniquity, neither blot out their sin from your sight, but let them be overthrown before you; deal thus with them in the time of your anger. **Jer** 19:1 Thus saith YHUH, Go and get a potter's earthen bottle, and take of the ancients of the people, and of the ancients of the priests;

**Jer 19:1** כה 3541 אמר 559 יהוה 3068 הלוך 1980 וקנית 7069 בקבק 1228 יוצר 3335 חרש 2789 ומזקני 2205 העם 5971
koh 'amar Yahuah, halouk uaqaniyta baqbuq youtzer chares; uamiziqney ha'am,
**Thus saith Yahuah Go and get a bottle potter's earthen and *take* of the ancients of the people**

ומזקני 2205 הכהנים 3548: **19:2** ויצאת 3318 אל 413 גיא 1516 בן 1121 הנם 2011 אשר 834 פתח 6607 שער 8179
uamiziqney hakohaniym. uayatza'ta 'al gey'a ben hinom, 'asher petach sha'ar
**and of the ancients of the priests And go forth unto the valley of the son of Hinnom which *is* by the entry of gate**

החרסות 2777 וקראת 7121 שם 8033 את 853 הדברים 1697 אשר 834 אדבר 1696 אליך 413: **19:3** ואמרת 559 שמעו 8085 דבר 1697 יהוה 3068
hacharasut uaqara'ta sham, 'at hadabariym 'asher 'adaber 'aeleyka. ua'amarta shim'au dabar Yahuah,
**the east and proclaim there the words that I shall tell you And say Hear you the word of Yahuah**

מלכי 4428 יהודה 3063 וישבי 3427 ירושלם 3389 כה 3541 אמר 559 יהוה 3068 צבאות 6635 אלהי 430 ישראל 3478 הנני 2005
malkey yahudah, uayoushabey yarushalaim; koh 'amar Yahuah tzaba'aut 'alohey yisra'ael, hinniy
**O kings of Judah and inhabitants of Jerusalem Thus saith Yahuah of hosts the Elohim of Israel Behold I**

מביא 935 רעה 7451 על 5921 המקום 4725 הזה 2088 אשר 834 כל 3605 שמעה 8085 תצלנה 6750 אזניו 241: **19:4** יען 3282 אשר 834
mebiy'a ra'ah 'al hamaqoum hazeh, 'asher kal shoma'ah titzalnah 'azanayu. ya'an 'asher
**will bring evil upon place this *the* which whosoever hear shall tingle his ears Because which**

עזבני 5800 וינכרו 5234 את 853 המקום 4725 הזה 2088 ויקטרו 6999 בו 871a לאלהים 430 אחרים 312
'azabuniy, uayanakru 'at hamaqoum hazeh uayaqatru bou le'alohiym 'acheriym,
**they have forsaken me and have estranged place this and have burned incense in it unto gods other**

אשר 834 לא 3808 ידעום 3045 המה 1992 ואבותיהם 1 ומלכי 4428 יהודה 3063 ומלאו 4390 את 853 המקום 4725 הזה 2088
'asher la' yada'aum hemah ua'abouteyhem uamalkey yahudah; uamal'au 'at hamaqoum hazeh
**whom neither have known they nor their fathers nor the kings of Judah and have filled with place this**

דם 1818 נקים 5355: **19:5** ובנו 1129 את 853 במות 1116 הבעל 1168 לשרף 8313 את 853 בניהם 1121 באש 784
dam naqiyim. uabanu 'at bamout haba'al, lisrop 'at baneyhem ba'aesh
**the blood of innocents They have built also the high places of Baal to burn their sons with fire**

עלות 5930 לבעל 1168 אשר 834 לא 3808 צויתי 6680 ולא 3808 דברתי 1696 ולא 3808 עלתה 5927 על 5921 לבי 3820: **19:6** לכן 3651
'alout laba'al; 'asher la' tziuiytiy uala' dibartiy, uala' 'alatah 'al libiy. laken
***for* burnt offerings unto Baal which not I commanded nor spoke *it* neither came *it* into my mind Therefore**

הנה 2009 ימים 3117 באים 935 נאם 5002 יהוה 3068 ולא 3808 יקרא 7121 למקום 4725 הזה 2088 עוד 5750 התפת 8612 וגיא 1516 בן 1121
hineh yamiym ba'aym na'am Yahuah, uala' yiqarea' lamaqoum hazeh 'aud hatopet uagey'a ben
**behold the days come saith Yahuah that no shall be called place this more Tophet nor the valley of the son of**

הנם 2011 כי 3588 אם 518 גיא 1516 ההרגה 2028: **19:7** ובקתי 1238 את 853 עצת 6098 יהודה 3063 וירושלם 3389
hinom; kiy 'am gey'a haharegah. uabaqotiy 'at 'atzat yahudah uiyarushalaim
**Hinnom but rather The valley of slaughter And I will make void the counsel of Judah and Jerusalem**

במקום 4725 הזה 2088 והפלתים 5307 בחרב 2719 לפני 6440 איביהם 341 וביד 3027 מבקשי 1245
bamaqoum hazeh, uahipaltiym bachereb lipney 'ayabeyhem, uabyad mabaqshey
**in place this and I will cause them to fall by the sword before their enemies and by the hands of them that seek**

Jer 19:2 And go forth unto the valley of the son of Hinnom, which is by the entry of the east gate, and proclaim there the words that I shall tell you,3 And say, Hear you the word of YHUH, O kings of Judah, and inhabitants of Jerusalem; Thus saith YHUH of hosts, the G-d of Israel; Behold, I will bring evil upon this place, the which whosoever hear, his ears shall tingle.4 Because they have forsaken me, and have estranged this place, and have burned incense in it unto other gods, whom neither they nor their fathers have known, nor the kings of Judah, and have filled this place with the blood of innocents;5 They have built also the high places of Baal, to burn their sons with fire for burnt offerings unto Baal, which I commanded not, nor spoke it, neither came it into my mind:6 Therefore, behold, the days come, saith YHUH, that this place shall no more be called Tophet, nor The valley of the son of Hinnom, but The valley of slaughter.7 And I will make void the counsel of Judah and Jerusalem in this place; and I will cause them to fall by the sword before their enemies, and by the hands of them that seek their lives: and their carcases will I give to be meat for the fowls of the heaven, and for the beasts of the earth.

| 5315 נפשם | 5414 ונתתי | 853 את | 5038 נבלתם | 3978 למאכל | 5775 לעוף | 8064 השמים | 929 ולבהמת | 776: הארץ | 19:8 |
|---|---|---|---|---|---|---|---|---|---|
| napsham; | uanatatiy | 'at | niblatam | lama'akal, | la'oup | hashamayim | ualbehemat | ha'aretz. | |
| **their lives** | **and will I give** | | **their carcases** | ***to be* meat** | **for the fowls of** | **the heaven** | **and for the beasts of** | **the earth** | |

| 7760 ושמתי | 853 את | 5892 העיר | 2063 הזאת | 8047 לשמה | 8322 ולשרקה | 3605 כל | 5674 עבר | 5921 עליה | 8074 ישם | 8319 וישרק |
|---|---|---|---|---|---|---|---|---|---|---|
| uasamtiy | 'at | ha'ayr | haza't, | lashamah | ualishreqah; | kal | 'aber | 'aleyha, | yishom | uayishroq |
| **And I will make** | | **city** | **this** | **desolate** | **and an hissing** | **every one** | **that passed** | **thereby** | **shall be astonished** | **and hiss** |

| 5921 על | 3605 כל | 4347: מכתה | 19:9 | 398 והאכלתים | 853 את | 1320 בשר | 1121 בניהם | 853 ואת | 1320 בשר |
|---|---|---|---|---|---|---|---|---|---|
| 'al | kal | makoteha. | | uaha'akaltiym | 'at | basar | baneyhem, | ua'at | basar |
| **because of** | **all** | **the plagues thereof** | | **And I will cause them to eat** | | **the flesh of** | **their sons** | ***and*** | **the flesh of** |

| 1323 בנתיהם | 376 ואיש | 1320 בשר | 7453 רעהו | 398 יאכלו | 4692 במצור | 4689 ובמצוק | 834 אשר | 6693 יציקו | 3807a להם |
|---|---|---|---|---|---|---|---|---|---|
| banoteyhem, | ua'aysh | basar | re'aehu | ya'kelu; | bamatzour | uabmatzouq, | 'asher | yatziyqu | lahem |
| **their daughters** | **of every one** | **the flesh of** | **his friend** | **they shall eat** | **in the siege** | **and straitness** | **wherewith** | **shall straiten** | **them** |

| 341 איביהם | 1245 ומבקשי | 5315: נפשם | 19:10 | 7665 ושברת | 1228 הבקבק | 5869 לעיני | 582 האנשים | 1980 ההלכים |
|---|---|---|---|---|---|---|---|---|
| 'ayabeyhem | uamabaqshey | napsham. | | uashabarta | habaqbuq; | la'aeyney | ha'anashiym, | haholakiym |
| **their enemies** | **and they that seek** | **their lives** | | **Then shall you break** | **the bottle** | **in the sight of** | **the men** | **that go** |

| 854: אותך | 19:11 | 559 ואמרת | 413 אליהם | 3541 כה | 559 אמר | 3068 יהוה | 6635 צבאות | 3602 ככה | 7665 אשבר | 853 את | 5971 העם | 2088 הזה | 853 ואת |
|---|---|---|---|---|---|---|---|---|---|---|---|---|---|
| autak. | | ua'amarta | 'aleyhem | koh | 'amar | Yahuah | tzaba'aut, | kakah | 'ashbor | 'at | ha'am | hazeh | ua'at |
| **with you,** | | **And shall say** | **unto them** | **Thus** | **saith** | **Yahuah** | **of hosts** | **Even so** | **will I break** | | **the people** | **this** | ***and*** |

| 5892 העיר | 2063 הזאת | 834 כאשר | 7665 ישבר | 853 את | 3627 כלי | 3335 היוצר | 834 אשר | 3808 לא | 3201 יוכל | 7495 להרפה | 5750 עוד | 8612 ובתפת |
|---|---|---|---|---|---|---|---|---|---|---|---|---|
| ha'ayr | haza't, | ka'asher | yishbor | 'at | kaliy | hayoutzer, | 'asher | la' | yukal | laherapeh | 'aud; | uabtopet |
| **city** | **this** | **as** | ***one* break** | | **a vessel** | **potter's** | **that** | **not** | **can** | **be made whole** | **again** | **and in Tophet** |

| 6912 יקברו | 369 מאין | 4725 מקום | 6912: לקבור | 19:12 | 3651 כן | 6213 אעשה | 4725 למקום | 2088 הזה | 5002 נאם | 3068 יהוה |
|---|---|---|---|---|---|---|---|---|---|---|
| yiqbaru, | me'ayn | maqoum | liqbour. | | ken | 'aaseh | lamaqoum | hazeh | na'am | Yahuah |
| **they shall bury *them*** | **till *there be* no** | **place** | **to bury** | | **Thus** | **will I do** | **unto place** | **this** | **saith** | **Yahuah** |

| 3427 ולישביו | 5414 ולתת | 853 את | 5892 העיר | 2063 הזאת | 8612: כתפת | 19:13 | 1961 והיו | 1004 בתי |
|---|---|---|---|---|---|---|---|---|
| ualyoushabayu; | ualatet | 'at | ha'ayr | haza't | katopet. | | uahayu | batey |
| **and to the inhabitants thereof** | **and *even* make** | | **city** | **this** | **as Tophet** | | **And shall be** | **the houses of** |

| 3389 ירושלם | 1004 ובתי | 4428 מלכי | 3063 יהודה | 4725 כמקום | 8612 התפת | 2931 הטמאים | 3605 לכל | 1004 הבתים | 834 אשר |
|---|---|---|---|---|---|---|---|---|---|
| yarushalaim, | uabatey | malkey | yahudah, | kimaqoum | hatopet | hatame'aym; | lakol | habatiym, | 'asher |
| **Jerusalem** | **and the houses of** | **the kings of** | **Judah** | **as the place of** | **Tophet** | **defiled** | **because of all** | **the houses** | **whose** |

| 6999 קטרו | 5921 על | 1406 גגתיהם | 3605 לכל | 6635 צבא | 8064 השמים | 5258 והסך | 5262 נסכים |
|---|---|---|---|---|---|---|---|
| qitru | 'al | gagoteyhem | lakol | tzaba' | hashamayim, | uahasek | nasakiym |
| **they have burned incense** | **upon** | **roofs** | **unto all** | **the host of** | **heaven** | **and have poured out** | **drink offerings** |

| 430 לאלהים | 312: אחרים | 19:14 | 935 ויבא | 3414 ירמיהו | 8612 מהתפת | 834 אשר | 7971 שלחו | 3068 יהוה | 8033 שם | 5012 להנבא | 5975 ויעמד |
|---|---|---|---|---|---|---|---|---|---|---|---|
| le'alohiym | 'acheriym. | | uayaba' | yirmayahu | mehatopet, | 'asher | shalachou | Yahuah | sham | lahinabea'; | uaya'amod |
| **unto gods** | **other** | | **Then came** | **Jeremiah** | **from Tophet** | **where** | **had sent him** | **Yahuah** | **there** | **to prophesy** | **and he stood** |

Jer 19:8 And I will make this city desolate, and an hissing; everyone that pass thereby shall be astonished and hiss because of all the plagues thereof.9 And I will cause them to eat the flesh of their sons and the flesh of their daughters, and they shall eat everyone the flesh of his friend in the siege and straitness, wherewith their enemies, and they that seek their lives, shall straiten them.10 Then shall you break the bottle in the sight of the men that go with you,11 And shall say unto them, Thus saith YHUH of hosts; Even so will I break this people and this city, as one breaketh a potter's vessel, that cannot be made whole again: and they shall bury them in Tophet, till there be no place to bury.12 Thus will I do unto this place, saith YHUH, and to the inhabitants thereof, and even make this city as Tophet:13 And the houses of Jerusalem, and the houses of the kings of Judah, shall be defiled as the place of Tophet, because of all the houses upon whose roofs they have burned incense unto all the host of heaven, and have poured out drink offerings unto other gods.14 Then came Jeremiah from Tophet, whither YHUH had sent him to prophesy; and he stood in the court of YHUH's house and said to all the people,

**19:15**

בחצר 2691 | בית 1004 | יהוה 3068 | ויאמר 559 | אל 413 | כל 3605 | העם 5971: | כה 3541 | אמר 559 | יהוה 3068 | צבאות 6635 | אלהי 430
bachatzar | beyt | Yahuah, | uaya'mer | 'al | kal | ha'am. | koh | 'amar | Yahuah | tzaba'aut | 'alohey
**in the court of | house | Yahuah's | and said | to | all | the people | Thus | saith | Yahuah | of hosts | the Elohim of**

ישראל 3478 | הנני 2005 | מבי 935 | אל 413 | העיר 5892 | הזאת 2063 | ועל 5921 | כל 3605 | עריה 5892 | את 853 | כל 3605 | הרעה 7451 | אשר 834
yisra'ael, | hinniy | mebiy' | 'al | ha'ayr | haza't | ua'al | kal | 'areyha, | 'at | kal | hara'ah, | 'asher
**Israel | behold I | will bring | upon | city | this | and upon | all | her towns | | all | the evil | that**

דברתי 1696 | עליה 5921 | כי 3588 | הקשו 7185 | את 853 | ערפם 6203 | לבלתי 1115 | שמוע 8085 | את 853 | דברי 1697:
dibartiy | 'aleyha; | kiy | hiqshu | 'at | 'arapam, | labiltiy | shamoua' | 'at | dabaray.
**I have pronounced against it | because they have hardened | their necks | that not | they might hear | my words**

**Jer 20:1**

וישמע 8085 | פשחור 6583 | בן 1121 | אמר 564 | הכהן 3548 | והוא 1931 | פקיד 6496 | נגיד 5057 | בבית 1004 | יהוה 3068 | את 853
uayishma' | pashchur | ben | 'amer | hakohen, | uahu'a | paqiyd | nagiyd | babeyt | Yahuah; | 'at
**Now heard | Pashur | the son of | Immer | the priest | who *was* also | governor | chief | in the house of | Yahuah**

**20:2**

ירמיהו 3414 | נבא 5012 | את 853 | הדברים 1697 | האלה 428: | ויכה 5221 | פשחור 6583 | את 853 | ירמיהו 3414 | הנביא 5030 | ויתן 5414 | אתו 853
yirmayahu, | niba' | 'at | hadabariym | ha'aeleh. | uayakeh | pashchur, | 'at | yirmayahu | hanabiy'a; | uayiten | 'atou
***that* Jeremiah | prophesied | | things | these | Then smote | Pashur | | Jeremiah | the prophet | and put | him**

**20:3**

על 5921 | המהפכת 4115 | אשר 834 | בשער 8179 | בנימן 1144 | העליון 5945 | אשר 834 | בבית 1004 | יהוה 3068: | ויהי 1961
'al | hamahpeket, | 'asher | basha'ar | binyamin | ha'alyoun, | 'asher | babeyt | Yahuah. | uayahiy
**in | the stocks | that *were* | in gate of | Benjamin | the high | which | *was* by the house of | Yahuah | And it came to pass**

ממחרת 4283 | ויצא 3318 | פשחור 6583 | את 853 | ירמיהו 3414 | מן 4480 | המהפכת 4115 | ויאמר 559 | אליו 413 | ירמיהו 3414 | לא 3808
mimacharat, | uayotzea' | pashchur | 'at | yirmayahu | min | hamahpaket; | uaya'mer | 'aelayu | yirmayahu, | la'
**on the morrow | that brought forth | Pashur | | Jeremiah | out of | the stocks | Then said | unto him | Jeremiah | not**

**20:4**

פשחור 6583 | קרא 7121 | יהוה 3068 | שמך 8034 | כי 3588 | אם 518 | מגור 4036 | מסביב 4036: | כי 3588 | כה 3541 | אמר 559 | יהוה 3068 | הנני 2005
pashchur | qara' | Yahuah | shameka, | kiy | 'am | magour | misabiyb. | kiy | koh | 'amar | Yahuah | hinniy
**Pashur | has called | Yahuah | your name | but | rather | Magor | missabib | For | thus | saith | Yahuah | Behold I**

נתנך 5414 | למגור 4032 | לך 3807a | ולכל 3605 | אהביך 157 | ונפלו 5307 | בחרב 2719 | איביהם 341 | ועיניך 5869
notenaka | lamagour | laka | ualkal | 'ahabeyka, | uanapalu | bachereb | 'ayabeyhem | ua'aeyneyka
**will make you | a terror | to yourself | and to all | your friends | and they shall fall | by the sword of | their enemies | and your eyes**

ראות 7200 | ואת 853 | כל 3605 | יהודה 3063 | אתן 5414 | ביד 3027 | מלך 4428 | בבל 894 | והגלם 1540
ro'aut; | ua'at | kal | yahudah, | 'aten | bayad | melek | babel, | uahiglam
**shall behold *it* | *and* | all | Judah | I will give | into the hand of | the king of | Babylon | and he shall carry them captive**

**20:5**

בבלה 894 | והכם 5221 | בחרב 2719: | ונתתי 5414 | את 853 | כל 3605 | חסן 2633 | העיר 5892 | הזאת 2063
babelah | uahikam | bechareb. | uanatatiy, | 'at | kal | chosen | ha'ayr | haza't,
**into Babylon | and shall slay them | with the sword | Moreover I will deliver | | all | the strength of | city | this**

ואת 853 | כל 3605 | יגיעה 3018 | ואת 853 | כל 3605 | יקרה 3366 | ואת 853 | כל 3605 | אוצרות 214 | מלכי 4428
ua'at | kal | yagiy'ah | ua'at | kal | yaqarah; | ua'at | kal | 'autzarout | malkey
***and* | all | the labours thereof | *and* | all | the precious things thereof | *and* | all | the treasures of | the kings of**

Jer 19:15 Thus saith YHUH of hosts, the G-d of Israel; Behold, I will bring upon this city and upon all her towns all the evil that I have pronounced against it, because they have hardened their necks, that they might not hear my words. **Jer** 20:1 Now Pashur the son of Immer the priest, who was also chief governor in the house of YHUH, heard that Jeremiah prophesied these things.2 Then Pashur smote Jeremiah the prophet, and put him in the stocks that were in the high gate of Benjamin, which was by the house of YHUH.3 And it came to pass on the morrow, that Pashur brought forth Jeremiah out of the stocks. Then said Jeremiah unto him, YHUH has not called your name Pashur, but Magor-missabib.4 For thus saith YHUH, Behold, I will make you a terror to thyself, and to all your friends: and they shall fall by the sword of their enemies, and your eyes shall behold it: and I will give all Judah into the hand of the king of Babylon, and he shall carry them captive into Babylon, and shall slay them with the sword.5 Moreover I will deliver all the strength of this city, and all the labours thereof, and all the precious things thereof, and all the treasures of the kings of Judah will I give into the hand of their enemies, which shall spoil them, and take them, and carry them to Babylon.

| יהודה 3063 | אתן 5414 | ביד 3027 | איביהם 341 | ובזזום 962 | ולקחום 3947 | והביאום 935 | בבלה 894: | 20:6 |
|---|---|---|---|---|---|---|---|---|
| yahudah, | 'aten | bayad | 'ayabeyhem, | uabzazum | ualqachum, | uahebiy'am | babelah. | |
| **Judah** | **will I give** | **into the hand of** | **their enemies** | **which shall spoil them** | **and take them** | **and carry them** | **to Babylon** | |

| ואתה 859 | פשחור 6583 | וכל 3605 | ישבי 3427 | ביתך 1004 | תלכו 1980 | בשבי 7628 | ובבל 894 | תבוא 935 | ושם 8033 |
|---|---|---|---|---|---|---|---|---|---|
| ua'atah | pashchur, | uakol | yoshabey | beytaka, | telaku | bashebiy; | uababel | tabou'a, | uasham |
| **And you** | **Pashur** | **and all** | **that dwell** | **in your house** | **shall go** | **into captivity** | **and Babylon** | **you shall come to** | **and there** |

| תמות 4191 | ושם 8033 | תקבר 6912 | אתה 859 | וכל 3605 | אהביך 157 | אשר 834 | נבאת 5012 | להם 1992 | בשקר 8267: | 20:7 |
|---|---|---|---|---|---|---|---|---|---|---|
| tamut | uasham | tiqaber, | 'atah | uakal | 'ahabeyka, | 'asher | nibea'ta | lahem | bashaqer. | |
| **you shall die** | **and there** | **shall be buried** | **you** | **and all** | **your friends** | ***to* whom** | **you have prophesied** | **to them** | **lies** | |

| פתיתני 6601 | יהוה 3068 | ואפת 6601 | חזקתני 2388 | ותוכל 3201 | הייתי 1961 | לשחוק 7814 | כל 3605 |
|---|---|---|---|---|---|---|---|
| pitiytaniy | Yahuah | ua'apat, | chazaqtaniy | uatukal; | hayiytiy | lischouq | kal |
| **you have deceived me** | **O Yahuah** | **and I was deceived** | **you are stronger than I** | **and have prevailed** | **I am** | **in derision** | **all** |

| היום 3117 | כלה 3605 | לעג 3932 | לי 3807a: | 20:8 | כי 3588 | מדי 1767 | אדבר 1696 | אזעק 2199 | חמס 2555 | ושד 7701 | אקרא 7121 | כי 3588 | היה 1961 |
|---|---|---|---|---|---|---|---|---|---|---|---|---|---|
| hayoum, | kuloh | la'aeg | liy. | | kiy | midey | 'adaber | 'az'aq, | chamas | uashod | 'aqraa'; | kiy | hayah |
| **daily** | **every one** | **mock** | **me** | | **For** | **since** | **I spoke** | **I cried out** | **violence** | **and spoil** | **I cried** | **because** | **was made** |

| דבר 1697 | יהוה 3068 | לי 3807a | לחרפה 2781 | ולקלס 7047 | כל 3605 | היום 3117: | 20:9 | ואמרתי 559 | לא 3808 | אזכרנו 2142 |
|---|---|---|---|---|---|---|---|---|---|---|
| dabar | Yahuah | liy | lacherpah | ualqeles | kal | hayoum. | | ua'amartiy | la' | 'azkarenu, |
| **the word of** | **Yahuah** | **unto me** | **a reproach** | **and a derision** | **all** | **daily** | | **Then I said** | **not** | **I will make mention of him** |

| ולא 3808 | אדבר 1696 | עוד 5750 | בשמו 8034 | והיה 1961 | בלבי 3820 | כאש 784 | בערת 1197 | עצר 6113 | בעצמתי 6106 | ונלאיתי 3811 |
|---|---|---|---|---|---|---|---|---|---|---|
| uala' | 'adaber | 'aud | bishmou, | uahayah | balibiy | ka'aesh | bo'aret, | 'atzur | ba'atzmotay; | uanil'aeytiy |
| **nor** | **speak** | **anymore** | **in his name** | **But *his word* was** | **in mine heart** | **as a fire** | **burning** | **shut up** | **in my bones** | **and I was weary** |

| כלכל 3557 | ולא 3808 | אוכל 3201: | 20:10 | כי 3588 | שמעתי 8085 | דבת 1681 | רבים 7227 | מגור 4032 | מסביב 5439 | הגידו 5046 |
|---|---|---|---|---|---|---|---|---|---|---|
| kalakel | uala' | 'aukal. | | kiy | shama'atiy | dibat | rabiym | magour | misabiyb | hagiydu |
| **with forbearing** | **and not** | ***stay* I could** | | **For** | **I heard** | **the defaming of** | **many** | **fear** | **on every side** | **Report** |

| ונגידנו 5046 | כל 3605 | אנוש 582 | שלומי 7965 | שמרי 8104 | צלעי 6761 | אולי 194 | יפתה 6601 |
|---|---|---|---|---|---|---|---|
| uanagiydenu, | kal | 'anoush | shaloumiy, | shomrey | tzal'ay; | 'aulay | yaputeh |
| ***say they* and we will report it** | **All** | **those** | **my familiars** | **watched for** | **my halting *saying*** | **Peradventure** | **he will be enticed** |

| ונוכלה 3201 | לו 3807a | ונקחה 3947 | נקמתנו 5360 | ממנו 4480: | 20:11 | ויהוה 3068 | אותי 854 | כגבור 1368 |
|---|---|---|---|---|---|---|---|---|
| uanukalah | lou', | uaniqchah | niqmatenu | mimenu. | | uaYahuah | 'autiy | kagibour |
| **and we shall prevail** | **against him** | **and we shall take** | **our revenge** | **on him** | | **But Yahuah** | ***is* with me** | **as a mighty one** |

| עריץ 6184 | על 5921 | כן 3651 | רדפי 7291 | יכשלו 3782 | ולא 3808 | יכלו 3201 | בשו 954 | מאד 3966 | כי 3588 | לא 3808 |
|---|---|---|---|---|---|---|---|---|---|---|
| 'ariytz, | 'al | ken | rodapay | yikashalu | uala' | yukalu; | boshu | ma'ad | kiy | la' |
| **terrible** | **therefore** | **after** | **my persecutors** | **shall stumble** | **and not** | **they shall prevail** | **they shall be ashamed** | **greatly** | **for** | **not** |

| השכילו 7919 | כלמת 3639 | עולם 5769 | לא 3808 | תשכח 7911: | 20:12 | ויהוה 3068 | צבאות 6635 | בחן 974 | צדיק 6662 |
|---|---|---|---|---|---|---|---|---|---|
| hiskiylu, | kalimat | 'aulam | la' | tishakeach. | | uaYahuah | tzaba'aut | bochen | tzadiyq, |
| **they shall prosper** | **confusion *their*** | **everlasting** | **never** | **shall be forgotten** | | **But O Yahuah** | **of hosts** | **that try** | **the righteous** |

Jer 20:6 And you, Pashur, and all that dwell in your house shall go into captivity: and you shall come to Babylon, and there you shall die, and shall be buried there, you, and all your friends, to whom you have prophesied lies.7 O YHUH, you have deceived me, and I was deceived: you are stronger than I, and have prevailed: I am in derision daily, everyone mocketh me.8 For since I spoke, I cried out, I cried violence and spoil; because the word of YHUH was made a reproach unto me, and a derision, daily.9 Then I said, I will not make mention of him, nor speak anymore in his name. But his word was in mine heart as a burning fire shut up in my bones, and I was weary with forbearing, and I could not stay.10 For I heard the defaming of many, fear on every side. Report, say they, and we will report it. All my familiars watched for my halting, saying, Peradventure he will be enticed, and we shall prevail against him, and we shall take our revenge on him.11 But YHUH is with me as a mighty terrible one: therefore my persecutors shall stumble, and they shall not prevail: they shall be greatly ashamed; for they shall not prosper: their everlasting confusion shall never be forgotten.12 But, O YHUH of hosts, that triest the righteous, and seest the reins and the heart, let me see your vengeance on them: for unto you have I opened my cause.

| 7200 ראה | 3629 כליות | 3820 ולב | 7200 אראה | 5360 נקמתך | 1992 מהם | 3588 כי | 413 אליך | 1540 גליתי | 853 את | 7379: ריבי | 20:13 |
|---|---|---|---|---|---|---|---|---|---|---|---|
| ro'ah | kalayout | ualeb; | 'ar'ah | niqmataka | mehem, | kiy | 'aeleyka | giliytiy | 'at | riybiy. | |
| ***and* see** | **the reins** | **and the heart** | **let me see** | **your vengeance** | **on them** | **for** | **unto you** | **have I opened** | | **my cause** | |

| 7891 שירו | 3068 ליהוה | 1984 הללו | 853 את | 3068 יהוה | 3588 כי | 5337 הציל | 853 את | 5315 נפש | 34 אביון | 3027 מיד |
|---|---|---|---|---|---|---|---|---|---|---|
| shiyru | laYahuah, | halalu | 'at | Yahuah; | kiy | hitziyl | 'at | nepesh | abyoun | miyad |
| **Sing** | **unto Yahuah** | **praise you** | | **Yahuah** | **for** | **he has delivered** | | **the soul of** | **the poor** | **from the hand of** |

| 7489: מרעים | 20:14 | 779 ארור | 3117 היום | 834 אשר | 3205 ילדתי | 871a בו | 3117 יום | 834 אשר | 3205 ילדתני | 517 אמי | 408 אל | 1961 יהי |
|---|---|---|---|---|---|---|---|---|---|---|---|---|
| mare'aym. | | 'arur | hayoum, | 'asher | yuladtiy | bou; | youm | 'asher | yaladatniy | 'amiy | 'al | yahiy |
| **evildoers** | | **Cursed** | ***be* the day** | **wherein** | **I was born** | **in him** | **the day** | **wherein** | **bare me** | **my mother** | **not** | **let be** |

| 1288: ברוך | 20:15 | 779 ארור | 376 האיש | 834 אשר | 1319 בשר | 853 את | 1 אבי | 559 לאמר | 3205 ילד | 3807a לך | 1121 בן | 2145 זכר |
|---|---|---|---|---|---|---|---|---|---|---|---|---|
| baruk. | | 'arur | ha'aysh, | 'asher | bisar | 'at | 'abiy | lea'mor, | yulad | laka | ben | zakar; |
| **blessed** | | **Cursed** | ***be* the man** | **who** | **brought tidings to** | | **my father** | **saying** | **is born** | **unto you** | **A child** | **man** |

| 8056 שמח | 8056: שמחהו | 20:16 | 1961 והיה | 376 האיש | 1931 ההוא | 5892 כערים | 834 אשר | 2015 הפך | 3069 יהוה | 3808 ולא | 5162 נחם |
|---|---|---|---|---|---|---|---|---|---|---|---|
| sameach | simachahu. | | uahayah | ha'aysh | hahua', | ke'ariym | 'asher | hapak | Yahuah | uala' | nicham; |
| **very glad** | **making him** | | **And let be** | **man** | **that** | **as the cities** | **which** | **overthrew** | **Yahuah** | **and not** | **repented** |

| 8085 ושמע | 2201 זעקה | 1242 בבקר | 8643 ותרועה | 6256 בעת | 6672: צהרים | 20:17 | 834 אשר | 3808 לא | 4191 מותתני |
|---|---|---|---|---|---|---|---|---|---|
| uashama' | za'aqah | baboqer, | uatru'ah | ba'aet | tzaharayim. | | 'asher | la' | moutaniy |
| **and let him hear** | **the cry** | **in the morning** | **and the shouting** | **at tide** | **noon** | | **Because** | **not** | **he slew me** |

| 7358 מרחם | 1961 ותהי | 3807a לי | 517 אמי | 6913 קברי | 7358 ורחמה | 2030 הרת | 5769: עולם | 20:18 |
|---|---|---|---|---|---|---|---|---|
| merachem; | uatahiy | liy | 'amiy | qibriy, | uarachmah | harat | 'aulam. | |
| **from the womb** | **or might have been** | ***that* for me** | **my mother** | **my grave** | **and her womb** | **great *with me*** | ***to be* always** | |

| 4100 למה | 2088 זה | 7358 מרחם | 3318 יצאתי | 7200 לראות | 5999 עמל | 3015 ויגון | 3615 ויכלו | 1322 בבשת | 3117: ימי |
|---|---|---|---|---|---|---|---|---|---|
| lamah | zeh | merechem | yatza'tiy, | lera'aut | 'amal | uayagoun; | uayiklu | baboshet | yamay. |
| **Wherefore** | **this** | **out of the womb** | **came I forth** | **to see** | **labour** | **and sorrow** | **that should be consumed** | **with shame?** | **my days** |

| Jer 21:1 | 1697 הדבר | 834 אשר | 1961 היה | 413 אל | 3414 ירמיהו | 853 מאת | 3068 יהוה | 7971 בשלח | 413 אליו | 4428 המלך | 6667 צדקיהו | 853 את | 6583 פשחור |
|---|---|---|---|---|---|---|---|---|---|---|---|---|---|
| | hadabar | 'asher | hayah | 'al | yirmayahu | me'at | Yahuah; | bishloach | 'aelayu | hamelek | tzidqiyahu, | 'at | pashchur |
| | **The word** | **which** | **came** | **unto** | **Jeremiah** | **from** | **Yahuah** | **when sent** | **unto him** | **king** | **Zedekiah** | | **Pashur** |

| 1121 בן | 4441 מלכיה | 853 ואת | 6846 צפניה | 1121 בן | 4641 מעשיה | 3548 הכהן | 559: לאמר | 21:2 | 1875 דרש | 4994 נא | 1157 בעדנו | 853 את |
|---|---|---|---|---|---|---|---|---|---|---|---|---|
| ben | malkiyah, | ua'at | tzapanyah | ben | ma'aseyah | hakohen | lea'mor. | | darash | naa' | ba'adenu | 'at |
| **the son of** | **Melchiah** | ***and*** | **Zephaniah** | **the son of** | **Maaseiah** | **the priest** | **saying** | | **Inquire of** | **I pray you** | **for us** | |

| 3068 יהוה | 3588 כי | 5019 נבוכדראצר | 4428 מלך | 894 בבל | 3898 נלחם | 5921 עלינו | 194 אולי | 6213 יעשה | 3068 יהוה | 854 אותנו |
|---|---|---|---|---|---|---|---|---|---|---|
| Yahuah, | kiy | nabukadra'tzar | melek | babel | nilcham | 'aleynu; | 'aulay | ya'aseh | Yahuah | autanu |
| **Yahuah** | **for** | **Nebuchadrezzar** | **king of** | **Babylon** | **make war** | **against us** | **if so be** | **will deal** | ***that* Yahuah** | **with us** |

| 3605 ככל | 6381 נפלאתיו | 5927 ויעלה | 5921: מעלינו | 21:3 | 559 ויאמר | 3414 ירמיהו | 413 אליהם | 3541 כה | 559 תאמרון |
|---|---|---|---|---|---|---|---|---|---|
| kakal | nipla'atayu, | uaya'aleh | me'aleynu. | | uaya'mer | yirmayahu | 'aleyhem; | koh | ta'marun |
| **according to all** | **his wondrous works** | **that he may go up** | **from us** | | **Then said** | **Jeremiah** | **unto them** | **Thus** | **shall you say** |

Jer 20:13 Sing unto YHUH, praise you YHUH: for he has delivered the soul of the poor from the hand of evildoers.14 Cursed be the day wherein I was born: let not the day wherein my mother bare me be blessed.15 Cursed be the man who brought tidings to my father, saying, A man child is born unto you; making him very glad.16 And let that man be as the cities which YHUH overthrew, and repented not: and let him hear the cry in the morning, and the shouting at noontide;17 Because he slew me not from the womb; or that my mother might have been my grave, and her womb to be always great with me.18 Wherefore came I forth out of the womb to see labour and sorrow, that my days should be consumed with shame? **Jer** 21:1 The word which came unto Jeremiah from YHUH, when king Zedekiah sent unto him Pashur the son of Melchiah, and Zephaniah the son of Maaseiah the priest, saying,2 Inquire, I pray you, of YHUH for us; for Nebuchadrezzar king of Babylon make war against us; if so be that YHUH will deal with us according to all his wondrous works, that he may go up from us.3 Then said Jeremiah unto them, Thus shall you say to Zedekiah:

אל 413 צדקיהו 6667: 21:4 כה 3541 אמר 559 יהוה 3068 אלהי 430 ישראל 3478 הנני 2005 מסב 5437 את 853 כלי 3627 המלחמה 4421
'al tzidqiyahu. koh 'amar Yahuah 'alohey yisra'ael, hinniy meseb 'at kaley hamilchamah
**to Zedekiah Thus saith Yahuah Elohim of Israel Behold I will turn back the weapons of war**

אשר 834 בידכם 3027 אשר 834 אתם 859 נלחמים 3898 בם 871a את 853 מלך 4428 בבל 894 ואת 853 הכשדים 3778
'asher bayedkem 'asher 'atem nilchamiym bam, 'at melek babel ua'at hakasdiym,
**that *are* in your hands wherewith you fight against in them the king of Babylon *and* *against* the Chaldeans**

הצרים 6696 עליכם 5921 מחוץ 2351 לחומה 2346 ואספתי 622 אותם 853 אל 413 תוך 8432 העיר 5892 הזאת 2063: 21:5
hatzariym 'aleykem, michutz lachoumah; ua'asaptiy 'autam, 'al touk ha'ayr haza't.
**which besiege you without the walls and I will assemble them into the midst of city this**

ונלחמתי 3898 אני 589 אתכם 854 ביד 3027 נטויה 5186 ובזרוע 2220 חזקה 2389 ובאף 639 ובחמה 2534
uanilchamtiy 'aniy 'atakem, bayad netuyah uabizroua' chazaqah; uab'ap uabchemah
**And I will fight myself against you with an hand outstretched and with a arm strong even in anger and in fury**

ובקצף 7110 גדול 1419: 21:6 והכיתי 5221 את 853 יושבי 3427 העיר 5892 הזאת 2063 ואת 853 האדם 120 ואת 853 הבהמה 929
uabqetzep gadoul. uahikeytiy, 'at youshabey ha'ayr haza't, ua'at ha'adam ua'at habehemah;
**and in wrath great And I will smite the inhabitants of city this *both* man *and* beast**

בדבר 1698 גדול 1419 ימתו 4191: 21:7 ואחרי 310 כן 3651 נאם 5002 יהוה 3068 אתן 5414 את 853 צדקיהו 6667 מלך 4428
badeber gadoul yamutu. ua'acharey ken na'am Yahuah 'aten 'at tzidqiyahu melek
**of a pestilence great they shall die And afterward so saith Yahuah I will deliver Zedekiah king of**

יהודה 3063 ואת 853 עבדיו 5650 ואת 853 העם 5971 ואת 853 הנשארים 7604 בעיר 5892 הזאת 2063 מן 4480 הדבר 1698 מן 4480 החרב 2719
yahudah ua'at 'abadayu ua'at ha'am ua'at hanisha'ariym ba'ayr haza't min hadeber min hachereb
**Judah *and* his servants *and* the people *and* such as are left in city this from the pestilence from the sword**

ומן 4480 הרעב 7458 ביד 3027 נבוכדראצר 5019 מלך 4428 בבל 894 וביד 3027 איביהם 341
uamin hara'ab, bayad nabukadra'tzar melek babel, uabyad 'ayabeyhem,
**and from the famine into the hand of Nebuchadrezzar king of Babylon and into the hand of their enemies**

וביד 3027 מבקשי 1245 נפשם 5315 והכם 5221 לפי 6310 חרב 2719 לא 3808 יחוס 2347
uabyad mabaqshey napsham; uahikam lapiy chereb, la' yachus
**and into the hand of those that seek their life and he shall smite them with the edge of the sword not he shall spare**

עליהם 5921 ולא 3808 יחמל 2550 ולא 3808 ירחם 7355: 21:8 ואל 413 העם 5971 הזה 2088 תאמר 559 כה 3541 אמר 559 יהוה 3069
'aleyhem, uala' yachmol uala' yarachem. ua'al ha'am hazeh ta'mar, koh 'amar Yahuah;
**them neither have pity nor have mercy And unto the people this you shall say Thus saith Yahuah**

הנני 2005 נתן 5414 לפניכם 6440 את 853 דרך 1870 החיים 2416 ואת 853 דרך 1870 המות 4194: 21:9 הישב 3427 בעיר 5892 הזאת 2063
hinniy noten lipneykem, 'at derek hachayiym ua'at derek hamauet. hayosheb ba'ayr haza't,
**Behold I set before you the way of life *and* the way of death He that abide in city this**

ימות 4191 בחרב 2719 וברעב 7458 ובדבר 1698 והיוצא 3318 ונפל 5307 על 5921 הכשדים 3778 הצרים 6696
yamut bachereb uabara'ab uabadaber; uahayotzea' uanapal 'al hakasdiym hatzariym
**shall die by the sword and by the famine and by the pestilence but he that goes out and fall to the Chaldeans that besiege**

Jer 21:4 Thus saith YHUH G-d of Israel; Behold, I will turn back the weapons of war that are in your hands, wherewith you fight against the king of Babylon, and against the Chaldeans, which besiege you without the walls, and I will assemble them into the midst of this city.5 And I myself will fight against you with an outstretched hand and with a strong arm, even in anger, and in fury, and in great wrath.6 And I will smite the inhabitants of this city, both man and beast: they shall die of a great pestilence.7 And afterward, saith YHUH, I will deliver Zedekiah king of Judah, and his servants, and the people, and such as are left in this city from the pestilence, from the sword, and from the famine, into the hand of Nebuchadrezzar king of Babylon, and into the hand of their enemies, and into the hand of those that seek their life: and he shall smite them with the edge of the sword; he shall not spare them, neither have pity, nor have mercy.8 And unto this people you shall say, Thus saith YHUH; Behold, I set before you the way of life, and the way of death.9 He that abideth in this city shall die by the sword, and by the famine, and by the pestilence: but he that go out, and fall to the Chaldeans that besiege you, he shall live, and his life shall be unto him for a prey.

21:10

עליכם 5921 יחיה 2421 והיתה 1961 לו 3807a נפשו 5315 לשלל 7998: כי 3588 שמתי 7760 פני 6440 בעיר 5892 הזאת 2063 לרעה 7451
'aleykem yichayeh uahayatah lou' napshou lashalal. kiy samtiy panay ba'ayr haza't lara'ah
**on you he shall live and shall be unto him his life for a prey For I have set my face against city this for evil**

21:11

ולא 3808 לטובה 2896 נאם 5002 יהוה 3068 ביד 3027 מלך 4428 בבל 894 תנתן 5414 ושרפה 8313 באש 784:
uala' latoubah na'am Yahuah; bayad melek babel tinaten, uasrapah ba'aesh.
**and not for good saith Yahuah into the hand of the king of Babylon it shall be given and he shall burn it with fire**

21:12

ולבית 1004 מלך 4428 יהודה 3063 שמעו 8085 דבר 1697 יהוה 3068: בית 1004 דוד 1732 כה 3541 אמר 559
ualbeyt melek yahudah, shim'au dabar Yahuah. beyt dauid, koh 'amar
**And touching the house of the king of Judah *say* Hear you the word of Yahuah O house of David thus saith**

יהוה 3068 דינו 1777 לבקר 1242 משפט 4941 והצילו 5337 גזול 1497 מיד 3027 עושק 6231 פן 6435 תצא 3318
Yahuah, diynu laboqer mishapat, uahatziylu gazul miyad 'ausheq; pen tetzea'
**Yahuah Execute in the morning judgment and deliver *him that is* spoiled out of the hand of the oppressor lest go out**

21:13

כאש 784 חמתי 2534 ובערה 1197 ואין 369 מכבה 3518 מפני 6440 רע 7455 מעלליהם 4611 הנני 2005 אליך 413
ka'aesh chamatiy, uaba'arah ua'aeyn makabeh, mipaney roa' ma'alleyhem hinniy 'aleyka
**like fire my fury and burn that none can quench *it* because of the evil of your doings Behold I *am* against you**

ישבת 3427 העמק 6010 צור 6697 המישר 4334 נאם 5002 יהוה 3068 האמרים 559 מי 4310 יחת 5181 עלינו 5921 ומי 4310
yoshebet ha'aemeq tzur hamiyshor na'am Yahuah; ha'amariym miy' yechat 'aleynu, uamiy
**O inhabitant of the valley *and* rock of the plain saith Yahuah which say Who shall come down against us? or who**

21:14

יבוא 935 במעונותינו 4585: ופקדתי 6485 עליכם 5921 כפרי 6529 מעלליכם 4611 נאם 5002 יהוה 3068
yabou'a bima'aunouteynu. uapaqadtiy 'aleykem kipariy ma'alleykem na'am Yahuah;
**shall enter into our habitations? But I will punish you according to the fruit of your doings saith Yahuah**

והצתי 3341 אש 784 ביערה 3293 ואכלה 398 כל 3605 סביביה 5439:
uahitzatiy 'aesh baya'arah, ua'akalah kal sabiybeyha.
**and I will kindle a fire in the forest thereof and it shall devour all *things* round about it**

**Jer 22:1**

כה 3541 אמר 559 יהוה 3068 רד 3381 בית 1004 מלך 4428 יהודה 3063 ודברת 1696 שם 8033 את 853 הדבר 1697 הזה 2088:
koh 'amar Yahuah, reed beyt melek yahudah; uadibarta sham, 'at hadabar hazeh.
**Thus saith Yahuah Go down to the house of the king of Judah and speak there word this**

22:2

ואמרת 559 שמע 8085 דבר 1697 יהוה 3068 מלך 4428 יהודה 3063 הישב 3427 על 5921 כסא 3678 דוד 1732 אתה 859 ועבדיך 5650
ua'amarta shama' dabar Yahuah, melek yahudah, hayosheb 'al kisea' dauid; 'atah ua'abadeyka
**And say Hear the word of Yahuah O king of Judah that sit upon the throne of David you and your servants**

22:3

ועמך 5971 הבאים 935 בשערים 8179 האלה 428: כה 3541 אמר 559 יהוה 3068 עשו 6213 משפט 4941 וצדקה 6666
ua'amaka, haba'aym bash'ariym ha'aeleh. koh 'amar Yahuah 'asu mishapat uatzdaqah,
**and your people that enter in by gates these Thus saith Yahuah Execute you judgment and righteousness**

והצילו 5337 גזול 1497 מיד 3027 עשוק 6216 וגר 1616 יתום 3490 ואלמנה 490 אל 408 תנו 3238 אל 408
uahatziylu gazul miyad 'ashouq; uager yatoum ua'almanah 'al tonu 'al
**and deliver the spoiled out of the hand of the oppressor and the stranger the fatherless nor the widow no do wrong no**

Jer 21:10 For I have set my face against this city for evil, and not for good, saith YHUH: it shall be given into the hand of the king of Babylon, and he shall burn it with fire.11
And touching the house of the king of Judah, say, Hear you the word of YHUH;12 O house of David, thus saith YHUH; Execute judgment in the morning, and deliver him that is spoiled out of the hand of the oppressor, lest my fury go out like fire, and burn that none can quench it, because of the evil of your doings.13 Behold, I am against you, O inhabitant of the valley, and rock of the plain, saith YHUH; which say, Who shall come down against us? or who shall enter into our habitations?14 But I will punish you according to the fruit of your doings, saith YHUH: and I will kindle a fire in the forest thereof, and it shall devour all things round about it. **Jer** 22:1 Thus saith YHUH; Go down to the house of the king of Judah, and speak there this word,2 And say, Hear the word of YHUH, O king of Judah, that sittest upon the throne of David, you, and your servants, and your people that enter in by these gates:3 Thus saith YHUH; Execute you judgment and righteousness, and deliver the spoiled out of the hand of the oppressor: and do no wrong, do no violence to the stranger, the fatherless, nor the widow, neither shed innocent blood in this place.

22:4

תחמסו 2554 ודם 1818 נקי 5355 אל 408 תשפכו 8210 במקום 4725 הזה 2088: כי 3588 אם 518 עשו 6213 תעשו 6213 את 853 הדבר 1697 הזה 2088
tachmosu, uadam naqiy, 'al tishpaku bamaqoum hazeh. kiy 'am asou ta'asu, 'at hadabar hazeh;
**do violence *to* blood innocent neither shed in place this For if you do indeed thing this**

ובאו 935 בשערי 8179 הבית 1004 הזה 2088 מלכים 4428 ישבים 3427 לדוד 1732 על 5921 כסאו 3678 רכבים 7392 ברכב 7393
uaba'au uasha'arey habayit hazeh malakiym yoshbiym ladauid 'al kis'au, rokabiym barekeb
**then shall there enter in by the gates of house this kings sitting of David upon the throne riding in chariots**

22:5

ובסוסים 5483 הוא 1931 ועבדו 5650 ועמו 5971: ואם 518 לא 3808 תשמעו 8085 את 853 הדברים 1697 האלה 428 בי 871a
uabasusiym, hua' ua'abdau ua'amou. ua'am la' tishma'au, 'at hadabariym ha'aeleh; biy
**and on horses he and his servants and his people But if not you will hear words these by myself**

22:6

נשבעתי 7650 נאם 5002 יהוה 3068 כי 3588 לחרבה 2723 יהיה 1961 הבית 1004 הזה 2088: כי 3588 כה 3541 אמר 559 יהוה 3068 על 5921 בית 1004
nishba'atiy na'am Yahuah, kiy lacharabah yihayeh habayit hazeh. kiy koh 'amar Yahuah 'al beyt
**I swear saith Yahuah that a desolation shall become house this For thus saith Yahuah unto house of**

מלך 4428 יהודה 3063 גלעד 1568 אתה 859 לי 3807a ראש 7218 הלבנון 3844 אם 518 לא 3808 אשיתך 7896 מדבר 4057
melek yahudah, gil'ad 'atah liy ra'sh halabanoun; 'am la' 'ashiytaka midbar,
***the* king's Judah *are* Gilead You unto me *and* the head of Lebanon *yet* surely not I will make a wilderness**

22:7

ערים 5892 לא 3808 נושבה 3427 וקדשתי 6942 עליך 5921 משחתים 7843 איש 376 וכליו 3627
'ariym la' noushabah uaqidashtiy 'aleyka mashchitiym 'aysh uakelayu;
***and* cities not *which* are inhabited And I will prepare against you destroyers every one with his weapons**

22:8

וכרתו 3772 מבחר 4005 ארזיך 730 והפילו 5307 על 5921 האש 784: ועברו 5674 גוים 1471 רבים 7227 על 5921 העיר 5892
uakaratu mibchar 'arazeyka, uahipiylu 'al ha'aesh. ua'abaru gouyim rabiym, 'al ha'ayr
**and they shall cut down choice your cedars and cast *them* into the fire And shall pass nations many by city**

הזאת 2063 ואמרו 559 איש 376 אל 413 רעהו 7453 על 5921 מה 4100 עשה 6213 יהוה 3068 ככה 3602 לעיר 5892
haza't; ua'amaru 'aysh 'al re'aehu, 'al meh 'asah Yahuah kakah, la'ayr
**this and they shall say every man to his neighbour Wherefore how long has done Yahuah thus unto city?**

22:9

הגדולה 1419 הזאת 2063: ואמרו 559 על 5921 אשר 834 עזבו 5800 את 853 ברית 1285 יהוה 3068
hagadoulah haza't. ua'amaru, 'al 'asher 'azabu, 'at bariyt Yahuah
**great this Then they shall answer Because which they have forsaken the covenant of Yahuah**

22:10

אלהיהם 430 וישתחוו 7812 לאלהים 430 אחרים 312 ויעבדום 5647: אל 408 תבכו 1058 למת 4191 ואל 408 תנדו 5110
'aloheyhem; uayishtachauu le'alohiym 'acheriym uaya'abdum. 'al tibku lamet, ua'al tanudu
**their Elohim and worshipped to gods other and served them not Weep you for the dead neither bemoan**

22:11

לו 3807a בכו 1058 בכו 1058 להלך 1980 כי 3588 לא 3808 ישוב 7725 עוד 5750 וראה 7200 את 853 ארץ 776 מולדתו 4138:
lou'; baku bakou laholek, kiy la' yashub 'aud, uara'ah 'at 'aretz mouladtou.
**him *but* weep sore for him that goes away for no he shall return more nor see country his native**

כי 3588 כה 3541 אמר 559 יהוה 3068 אל 413 שלם 7967 בן 1121 יאשיהו 2977 מלך 4428 יהודה 3063 המלך 4427 תחת 8478 יאשיהו 2977
kiy koh 'amar Yahuah 'al shalum ben ya'shiyahu melek yahudah, hamolek tachat ya'shiyahu
**For thus saith Yahuah touching Shallum the son of Josiah king of Judah which reigned instead of Josiah**

Jer 22:4 For if you do this thing indeed, then shall there enter in by the gates of this house kings sitting upon the throne of David, riding in chariots and on horses, he, and his servants, and his people.5 But if you will not hear these words, I swear by myself, saith YHUH, that this house shall become a desolation.6 For thus saith YHUH unto the king's house of Judah; Thou are Gilead unto me, and the head of Lebanon: yet surely I will make you a wilderness, and cities which are not inhabited.7 And I will prepare destroyers against you, everyone with his weapons: and they shall cut down your choice cedars, and cast them into the fire.8 And many nations shall pass by this city, and they shall say every man to his neighbor, Wherefore has YHUH done thus unto this great city?9 Then they shall answer, Because they have forsaken the covenant of YHUH their G-d, and worshipped other gods, and served them.10 Weep you not for the dead, neither bemoan him: but weep sore for him that go away: for he shall return no more, nor see his native country.11 For thus saith YHUH touching Shallum the son of Josiah king of Judah, which reigned instead of Josiah his father, which went forth out of this place; He shall not return thither anymore:

1 אביו 834 אשר 3318 יצא 4480 מן 4725 המקום 2088 הזה 3808 לא 7725 ישוב 8033 שם 5750 עוד: 22:12 3588 כי 4725 במקום 834 אשר
'abiyu, 'asher yatza' min hamaqoum hazeh; la' yashub sham 'aud. kiy, bimaqoum 'asher
**his father which went forth out of place this not He shall return there any more But in the place where**

1540 הגלו 853 אתו 8033 שם 4191 ימות 853 ואת 776 הארץ 2063 הזאת 3808 לא 7200 יראה 5750 עוד: 22:13 1945 הוי
higlu 'atou sham yamut; ua'at ha'aretz haza't la' yir'ah 'aud. houy
**they have led captive him there he shall die *and* the land this no shall see more Woe**

1129 בנה 1004 ביתו 3808 בלא 6664 צדק 5944 ועליותיו 3808 בלא 4941 משפט 7453 ברעהו 5647 יעבד
boneh beytou bala' tzedeq, ba'aliyoutayu bala' mishapat; bare'aehu ya'abod
***unto* him that builds his house by unrighteousness and his chambers by wrong his neighbour's *that* use service**

2600 חנם 6467 ופעלו 3808 לא 5414 יתן 3807a לו: 22:14 559 האמר 1129 אבנה 3807a לי 1004 בית 4060 מדות 5944 ועליות
chinam, uapo'alou la' yiten lou'. ha'amer, 'abneh liy beyt midout, ua'aliyout
**without wages and his work not *for* gives him That saith I will build me a house wide and chambers**

7304 מרוחים 7167 וקרע 3807a לו 2474 חלוני 5603 וספון 730 בארז 4886 ומשוח 8350 בששר: 22:15 4427 התמלך
maruachiym; uaqara' lou' chalounay, uasapun ba'arez, uamashouach bashashar. hatimlok,
**large and cuts out him windows and *it is* cieled with cedar and painted with vermilion Shall you reign**

3588 כי 859 אתה 8474 מתחרה 730 בארז 1 אביך 3808 הלוא 398 אכל 8354 ושתה 6213 ועשה 4941 משפט 6666 וצדקה 227 אז
kiy 'atah matachareh ba'arez; 'abiyka halou'a 'akal uashatah, ua'asah mishapat uatzdaqah, 'az
**because you close *yourself* in cedar? your fathers not did eat and drink and do judgment and justice *and* then**

2896 טוב 3807a לו: 22:16 1777 דן 1779 דין 6041 עני 34 ואביון 227 אז 2896 טוב 3808 הלוא 1931 היא 1847 הדעת
toub lou'. dan diyn 'aniy ua'abyoun 'az toub; halou'a hiy'a hada'at
***it was* well with him? He judged the cause of the poor and needy then *it was* well *with him: was* not this to know**

853 אתי 5002 נאם 3068 יהוה: 22:17 3588 כי 369 אין 5869 עיניך 3820 ולבך 3588 כי 518 אם 5921 על 1215 בצעך 5921 ועל 1818 דם
'atiy na'am Yahuah. kiy 'aeyn 'aeyneyka ualibaka, kiy 'am 'al bitz'aka; ua'al dam
**me? saith Yahuah But *are*not your eyes and your heart but rather for your covetousness and for blood**

5355 הנקי 8210 לשפוך 5921 ועל 6233 העשק 5921 ועל 4835 המרוצה 6213 לעשות: 22:18 3651 לכן 3541 כה 559 אמר 3068 יהוה 413 אל
hanaqiy lishpouk, ua'al ha'asheq ua'al hamarutzah la'asout. laken koh 'amar Yahuah 'al
**innocent to shed and for oppression and for violence to do it Therefore thus saith Yahuah concerning**

3079 יהויקים 1121 בן 2977 יאשיהו 4428 מלך 3063 יהודה 3808 לא 5594 יספדו 3807a לו 1945 הוי 251 אחי 1945 והוי 269 אחות
yahouyaqiym ben ya'shiyahu melek yahudah, la' yispadu lou', houy 'achiy uahouy achout;
**Jehoiakim the son of Josiah king of Judah not They shall lament for him *saying* Ah my brother or, Ah sister**

3808 לא 5594 יספדו 3807a לו 1945 הוי 113 אדון 1945 והוי 1935 הדה: 22:19 6900 קבורת 2543 חמור 6912 יקבר
la' yispadu lou', houy 'adoun uahouy hodoh qaburat chamour yiqaber;
**not they shall lament for him *saying* Ah adonai or, Ah his glory *with* the burial of an ass He shall be buried**

5498 סחוב 7993 והשלך 1973 מהלאה 8179 לשערי 3389 ירושלם: 22:20 5927 עלי 3844 הלבנון 6817 וצעקי 1316 ובבשן 5414 תני
sachoub uahashalek, mehala'ah lasha'arey yarushalaim. 'aliy halabanoun utz'aqiy, uababashan taniy
**drawn and cast forth beyond the gates of Jerusalem Go up to Lebanon and cry and in Bashan lift up**

Jer 22:12 But he shall die in the place whither they have led him captive, and shall see this land no more.13 Woe unto him that buildeth his house by unrighteousness, and his chambers by wrong; that useth his neighbor's service without wages, and give him not for his work;14 That saith, I will build me a wide house and large chambers, and cutteth him out windows; and it is cieled with cedar, and painted with vermilion.15 Shalt you reign, because you closest thyself in cedar? did not your father eat and drink, and do judgment and justice, and then it was well with him?16 He judged the cause of the poor and needy; then it was well with him: was not this to know me? saith YHUH.17 But your eyes and your heart are not but for your covetousness, and for to shed innocent blood, and for oppression, and for violence, to do it.18 Therefore thus saith YHUH concerning Jehoiakim the son of Josiah king of Judah; They shall not lament for him, saying, Ah my brother! or, Ah sister! they shall not lament for him, saying, Ah lord! or, Ah his glory!19 He shall be buried with the burial of an ass, drawn and cast forth beyond the gates of Jerusalem.20 Go up to Lebanon, and cry; and lift up your voice in Bashan, and cry from the passages: for all your lovers are destroyed.

22:21

קולך 6963 וצעקי 6817 מעברים 5676 כי 3588 נשברו 7665 כל 3605 מאהביך 157: דברתי 1696 אליך 413 בשלותיך 7962
qoulek; uatza'aqiy me'abariym, kiy nishbaru kal ma'ahabayik. dibartiy 'aelayik bashaluotayik,
**your voice and cry from the passages for are destroyed all your lovers I spoke unto you in your prosperity**

22:22

אמרת 559 לא 3808 אשמע 8085 זה 2088 דרכך 1870 מנעוריך 5271 כי 3588 לא 3808 שמעת 8085 בקולי 6963: כל 3605
'amart la' 'ashma; zeh darkek mina'aurayik, kiy la' shama'at baqouliy. kal
***but* you said not I will hear This *has been* your manner from your youth that not you obeyed my voice all**

רעיך 7462 תרעה 7462 רוח 7307 ומאהביך 157 בשבי 7628 ילכו 1980 כי 3588 אז 227 תבשי 954 ונכלמת 3637
ro'ayik tir'eh ruach, uam'ahabayik bashabiy yeleku; kiy 'az teboshiy uaniklamt,
**shall eat up your pastors The wind and your lovers into captivity shall go surely then shall you be ashamed and confounded**

22:23

מכל 3605 רעתך 7451: ישבתי 3427 בלבנון 3844 מקננתי 7077 בארזים 730 מה 4100 נחנת 2603
mikol ra'atek. yoshabtiy balabanoun, maqunantiy ba'araziym; mah nechant
**for all your wickedness O inhabitant of Lebanon that makes your nest in the cedars how gracious shall you be**

22:24

בבא 935 לך 3807a חבלים 2256 חיל 2427 כילדה 3205: חי 2416 אני 589 נאם 5002 יהוה 3068 כי 3588 אם 518 יהיה 1961
baba' lak chabaliym, chiyl kayoledah chay 'aniy na'am Yahuah kiy 'am yihayeh
**when come upon you pangs the pain as of a woman in travail *As* live I saith Yahuah even though were**

22:25

כניהו 3659 בן 1121 יהויקים 3079 מלך 4428 יהודה 3063 חותם 2368 על 5921 יד 3027 ימיני 3225 כי 3588 משם 8033 אתקנך 5423:
kanyahu ben yahouyaqiym melek yahudah, choutam 'al yad yamiyniy; kiy misham 'atqenaka.
**Coniah the son of Jehoiakim king of Judah the signet upon hand my right yet from there would I pluck you**

ונתתיך 5414 ביד 3027 מבקשי 1245 נפשך 5315 וביד 3027 אשר 834 אתה 859 יגור 3016 מפניהם 6440
uantatiyka, bayad mabaqshey napsheka, uabyad 'asher 'atah yagour mipaneyhem;
**And I will give you into the hand of them that seek your life and into the hand *of them* whose you fear face**

22:26

וביד 3027 נבוכדראצר 5019 מלך 4428 בבל 894 וביד 3027 הכשדים 3778: והטלתי 2904 אתך 853
uabyad nabukadra'tzar melek babel uabyad hakasdiym. uahetaltiy 'ataka,
**even into the hand of Nebuchadrezzar king of Babylon and into the hand of the Chaldeans And I will cast out you**

ואת 853 אמך 517 אשר 834 ילדתך 3205 על 5921 הארץ 776 אחרת 312 אשר 834 לא 3808 ילדתם 3205 שם 8033 ושם 8033
ua'at 'amaka 'asher yaladataka, 'al ha'aretz 'acheret, 'asher la' yuladtem sham; uasham
***and* your mother that bare you into country another where not you were born where and there**

22:27

תמותו 4191: ועל 5921 הארץ 776 אשר 834 הם 1992 מנשאים 5375 את 853 נפשם 5315 לשוב 7725 שם 8033 שמה 8033 לא 3808
tamutu. ua'al ha'aretz, 'asher hem manas'aym 'at napsham lashub sham; shamah la'
**shall you die But to the land whereunto they desire any to return in it there not**

22:28

ישובו 7725: העצב 6089 נבזה 959 נפוץ 5310 האיש 376 הזה 2088 כניהו 3659 אם 518 כלי 3627 אין 369 חפץ 2656 בו 871a
yashubu. ha'atzeb nibzeh naputz, ha'aysh hazeh kanyahu, 'am kaliy, 'aeyn chepetz bou;
**shall they return *Is* a idol? despised broken man this Coniah or *is he* a vessel is no pleasure? wherein**

22:29

מדוע 4069 הוטלו 2904 הוא 1931 וזרעו 2233 והשלכו 7993 על 5921 הארץ 776 אשר 834 לא 3808 ידעו 3045: ארץ 776 ארץ 776
madua' hutalu hua' uazar'au, uahushlaku, 'al ha'aretz 'asher la' yada'au. 'aretz 'aretz
**wherefore and are cast out he and his seed and are cast into a land which not? they know O earth earth**

Jer 22:21 I spoke unto you in your prosperity; but you saidst, I will not hear. This has been your manner from your youth, that you obeyed not my voice.22 The wind shall eat up all your pastors, and your lovers shall go into captivity: surely then shall you be ashamed and confounded for all your wickedness.23 O inhabitant of Lebanon, that make your nest in the cedars, how gracious shall you be when pangs come upon you, the pain as of a woman in travail!24 As I live, saith YHUH, though Coniah the son of Jehoiakim king of Judah were the signet upon my right hand, yet would I pluck you thence;25 And I will give you into the hand of them that seek your life, and into the hand of them whose face you fearest, even into the hand of Nebuchadrezzar king of Babylon, and into the hand of the Chaldeans.26 And I will cast you out, and your mother that bare you, into another country, where you were not born; and there shall you die.27 But to the land whereunto they desire to return, thither shall they not return.28 Is this man Coniah a despised broken idol? is he a vessel wherein is no pleasure? wherefore are they cast out, he and his seed, and are cast into a land which they know not?

776 ארץ 8085 שמעי 1697 דבר 3069: יהוה **22:30** 3541 כה 559 אמר 3068 יהוה 3789 כתבו 853 את 376 האיש 2088 הזה 6185 עריריי 1397 גבר 3808 לא
'aretz; shim'ay dabar Yahuah. koh 'amar Yahuah kitbu 'at ha'aysh hazeh 'ariyriy, geber la'
**earth hear the word of Yahuah Thus saith Yahuah Write you man this childless a man not**

6743 יצלח 3117 בימיו 3588 כי 3808 לא 6743 יצלח 2233 מזרעו 376 איש 3427 ישב 5921 על 3678 כסא 1732 דוד 4910 ומשל
yitzlach bayamayu; kiy la' yitzlach mizar'au, 'aysh yosheb 'al kisea' dauid, uamoshel
***that* shall prosper in his days for no shall prosper of his seed man sitting upon the throne of David and ruling**

5750 עוד 3063: ביהודה
'aud biyahudah.
**any more in Judah**

**Jer 23:1** 1945 הוי 7462 רעים 6 מאבדים 6327 ומפצים 853 את 6629 צאן 4830 מרעיתי 5002 נאם 3068: יהוה **23:2** 3651 לכן
houy ro'aym, ma'abdiym uamapitziym 'at tza'n mara'aytiy na'am Yahuah. laken
**Woe *be unto* the pastors that destroy and scatter the sheep of my pasture saith Yahuah Therefore**

3541 כה 559 אמר 3068 יהוה 430 אלהי 3478 ישראל 5921 על 7462 הרעים 7462 הרעים 853 את 5971 עמי 859 אתם 6327 הפצתם 853 את
koh 'amar Yahuah 'alohey yisra'ael, 'al haro'aym haro'aym 'at 'amiy 'atem hapitzotem 'at
**thus saith Yahuah Elohim of Israel against the pastors that feed my people You have scattered**

6629 צאני 5080 ותדחום 3808 ולא 6485 פקדתם 853 אתם 2005 הנני 6485 פקד 5921 עליכם 853 את 7455 רע 4611 מעלליכם
tza'niy uatadichum, uala' paqadtem 'atam; hinniy poqed 'aleykem 'at roa' ma'alleykem
**my flock and driven them away and not have visited them behold I will visit upon you the evil of your doings**

5002 נאם 3068: יהוה **23:3** 589 ואני 6908 אקבץ 853 את 7611 שארית 6629 צאני 3605 מכל 776 הארצות 834 אשר 5080 הדחתי 853 אתם
na'am Yahuah. ua'aniy, 'aqabetz 'at sha'aeriyt tza'niy, mikol ha'aratzout, 'asher hidachtiy 'atam
**saith Yahuah And I will gather the remnant of my flock out of all countries where I have driven them**

8033 שם 7725 והשבתי 853 אתהן 5921 על 5116 נוהן 6509 ופרו 7235: ורבו **23:4** 6965 והקמתי 5921 עליהם
sham; uahashibotiy 'athen 'al nauehen uaparu uarabu. uahaqimotiy 'aleyhem
**there and will bring again them to their folds and they shall be fruitful and increase And I will set up over them**

7462 רעים 7462 ורעום 3808 ולא 3372 ייראו 5750 עוד 3808 ולא 2865 יחתו 3808 ולא 6485 יפקדו 5002 נאם
ro'aym uara'aum; uala' yiyra'au 'aud uala' yechatu uala' yipaqedu na'am
**shepherds which shall feed them and no they shall fear more nor be dismayed neither shall they be lacking saith**

3068: יהוה **23:5** 2009 הנה 3117 ימים 935 באים 5002 נאם 3068 יהוה 6965 והקמתי 1732 לדוד 6780 צמח 6662 צדיק 4427 ומלך 4428 מלך
Yahuah. hineh yamiym ba'aym na'am Yahuah, uahaqimotiy ladauid tzemach tzadiyq; uamalak melek
**Yahuah Behold the days come saith Yahuah that I will raise unto David a Branch righteous and shall reign a King**

7919 והשכיל 6213 ועשה 4941 משפט 6666 וצדקה 776: בארץ **23:6** 3117 בימיו 3467 תושע 3063 יהודה 3478 וישראל
uahiskiyl, ua'asah mishapat uatzdaqah ba'aretz. bayamayu tiuasha' yahudah, uayisra'ael
**and prosper and shall execute judgment and justice in the earth In his days shall be saved Judah and Israel**

7931 ישכן 983 לבטח 2088 וזה 8034 שמו 834 אשר 7121 יקראו 3072 יהוה 3072: צדקנו **23:7** 3651 לכן
yishkan labetach; uazeh shamou 'asher yiqra'au Yahuah tzidqenu. laken
**shall dwell safely and this *is* his name whereby he shall be called YAHUAH OUR RIGHTEOUSNESS Therefore**

Jer 22:29 O earth, earth, earth, hear the word of YHUH.30 Thus saith YHUH, Write you this man childless, a man that shall not prosper in his days: for no man of his seed shall prosper, sitting upon the throne of David, and ruling anymore in Judah. **Jer** 23:1 Woe be unto the pastors that destroy and scatter the sheep of my pasture! saith YHUH.2 Therefore thus saith YHUH G-d of Israel against the pastors that feed my people; You have scattered my flock, and driven them away, and have not visited them: behold, I will visit upon you the evil of your doings, saith YHUH.3 And I will gather the remnant of my flock out of all countries whither I have driven them, and will bring them again to their folds; and they shall be fruitful and increase.4 And I will set up shepherds over them which shall feed them: and they shall fear no more, nor be dismayed, neither shall they be lacking, saith YHUH.5 Behold, the days come, saith YHUH, that I will raise unto David a righteous Branch, and a King shall reign and prosper, and shall execute judgment and justice in the earth.6 In his days Judah shall be saved, and Israel shall dwell safely: and this is his name whereby he shall be called, THE YHUH OUR RIGHTEOUSNESS.

הנה 2009 ימים 3117 באים 935 נאם 5002 יהוה 3068 ולא 3808 יאמרו 559 עוד 5750 חי 2416 יהוה 3068 אשר 834 העלה 5927 את 853 בני 1121
hineh yamiym ba'aym na'am Yahuah; uala' ya'maru 'aud chay Yahuah, 'asher he'alah 'at baney
**behold the days come saith Yahuah that no they shall say more live Yahuah which brought up the children of**

23:8
ישראל 3478 מארץ 776 מצרים 4714: כי 3588 אם 518 חי 2416 יהוה 3068 אשר 834 העלה 5927 ואשר 834 הביא 935 את 853
yisra'ael me'aretz mitzrayim. kiy 'am chay Yahuah 'asher he'alah ua'asher habiy'a 'at
**Israel out of the land of Egypt But rather live Yahuah which brought up and which led**

זרע 2233 בית 1004 ישראל 3478 מארץ 776 צפונה 6828 ומכל 3605 הארצות 776 אשר 834 הדחתים 5080 שם 8033
zera' beyt yisra'ael me'aretz tzapounah, uamikol ha'aratzout, 'asher hidachtiym sham;
**the seed of the house of Israel country out of *the* north and from all countries where I had driven them their**

23:9
וישבו 3427 על 5921 אדמתם 127: לנבאים 5030 נשבר 7665 לבי 3820 בקרבי 7130 רחפו 7363 כל 3605
uayashabu 'al 'admatam. lanabi'aym nishbar libiy uaqirbiy, rachapu kal
**and they shall dwell in their own land because of the prophets is broken Mine heart within me shake all**

עצמותי 6106 הייתי 1961 כאיש 376 שכור 7910 וכגבר 1397 עברו 5674 יין 3196 מפני 6440 יהוה 3068 ומפני 6440
atzmoutay, hayiytiy ka'aysh shikour, uakgeber 'abarou yayin; mipaney Yahuah, uamipaney
**my bones I am like a man drunken and like a man whom has overcome wine because of Yahuah and because of**

23:10
דברי 1697 קדשו 6944: כי 3588 מנאפים 5003 מלאה 4390 הארץ 776 כי 3588 מפני 6440 אלה 423 אבלה 56 הארץ 776 יבשו 3001
dibrey qadashou. kiy mana'apiym mal'ah ha'aretz, kiy mipaney 'alah 'abalah ha'aretz, yabashu
**the words of his holiness For adulterers is full of the land for because of swearing mourns the land are dried up**

23:11
נאות 4999 מדבר 4057 ותהי 1961 מרוצתם 4794 רעה 7451 וגבורתם 1369 לא 3808 כן 3651: כי 3588 גם 1571 נביא 5030
na'aut midbar; uatahiy marutzatam ra'ah, uagaburatam la' ken. kiy gam nabiy'a
**the pleasant places of the wilderness and is their course evil and their force *is* not right For both prophet**

23:12
גם 1571 כהן 3548 חנפו 2610 גם 1571 בביתי 1004 מצאתי 4672 רעתם 7451 נאם 5002 יהוה 3068: לכן 3651 יהיה 1961
gam kohen chanepu; gam babeytiy matza'tiy ra'atam na'am Yahuah. laken yihayeh
**and also priest are profane yea in my house have I found their wickedness saith Yahuah Wherefore shall be**

דרכם 1870 להם 1992 כחלקלקות 2519 באפלה 653 ידחו 1760 ונפלו 5307 בה 871a כי 3588 אביא 935
darkam lahem, kachalaqlaqout ba'apelah, yidachu uanapalu bah; kiy 'abiy'a
**their way unto them as slippery *ways* in the darkness they shall be driven on and fall therein for I will bring**

23:13
עליהם 5921 רעה 7451 שנת 8141 פקדתם 6486 נאם 5002 יהוה 3069: ובנביאי 5030 שמרון 8111 ראיתי 7200
'aleyhem ra'ah shanat paqudatam na'am Yahuah. uabinbiy'aey shomaroun ra'aytiy
**upon them evil *even* the year of their visitation saith Yahuah And in the prophets of Samaria I have seen**

23:14
תפלה 8604 הנבאו 5012 בבעל 1168 ויתעו 8582 את 853 עמי 5971 את 853 ישראל 3478: ובנבאי 5030
tiplah; hinaba'au baba'al, uayata'au 'at 'amiy 'at yisra'ael. uabinbi'aey
**folly they prophesied in Baal and caused to err my people Israel also in the prophets of**

ירושלם 3389 ראיתי 7200 שערורה 8186 נאוף 5003 והלך 1980 בשקר 8267 וחזקו 2388 ידי 3027
yarushalaim ra'aytiy sha'arurah, na'aup uahalok basheqer uachizqu yadey
**Jerusalem I have seen an horrible thing they commit adultery and walk in lies they strengthen also the hands of**

Jer 23:7 Therefore, behold, the days come, saith YHUH, that they shall no more say, YHUH live, which brought up the children of Israel out of the land of Egypt;8 But, YHUH live, which brought up and which led the seed of the house of Israel out of the north country, and from all countries whither I had driven them; and they shall dwell in their own land.9 Mine heart within me is broken because of the prophets; all my bones shake; I am like a drunken man, and like a man whom wine has overcome, because of YHUH, and because of the words of his holiness.10 For the land is full of adulterers; for because of swearing the land mourn; the pleasant places of the wilderness are dried up, and their course is evil, and their force is not right.11 For both prophet and priest are profane; yea, in my house have I found their wickedness, saith YHUH.12 Wherefore their way shall be unto them as slippery ways in the darkness: they shall be driven on, and fall therein: for I will bring evil upon them, even the year of their visitation, saith YHUH.13 And I have seen folly in the prophets of Samaria; they prophesied in Baal, and caused my people Israel to err.14 I have seen also in the prophets of Jerusalem an horrible thing: they commit adultery, and walk in lies: they strengthen also the hands of evildoers, that none doth return from his wickedness:

מרעים 7489 לבלתי 1115 שבו 7725 איש 376 מרעתו 7451 היו 1961 לי 3807a כלם 3605 כסדם 5467
mere'aym, labiltiy shabu, 'aysh mera'atou; hayu liy kulam kisadom,
**evildoers that none does return man from his wickedness they are unto me all of them as Sodom**

וישביה 3427 כעמרה 6017: 23:15 לכן 3651 כה 3541 אמר 559 יהוה 3068 צבאות 6635 על 5921 הנבאים 5030 הנני 2005
uayoshabeyha ka'amorah. laken koh 'amar Yahuah tzaba'aut 'al hanabiy'aym, hinniy
**and the inhabitants thereof as Gomorrah Therefore thus saith Yahuah of hosts concerning the prophets Behold I**

מאכיל 398 אותם 853 לענה 3939 והשקתים 8248 מי 4325 ראש 7219 כי 3588 מאת 853 נביאי 5030 ירושלם 3389
ma'akiyl 'autam la'anah, uahishqitiym mey ra'sh; kiy, me'at nabiy'aey yarushalaim,
**will feed them with wormwood and make them drink the water of gall for from the prophets of Jerusalem**

יצאה 3318 חנפה 2613 לכל 3605 הארץ 776: 23:16 כה 3541 אמר 559 יהוה 3068 צבאות 6635 אל 408 תשמעו 8085 על 5921 דברי 1697
yatz'ah chanupah lakal ha'aretz. koh 'amar Yahuah tzaba'aut, 'al tishma'au 'al dibrey
**is gone forth profaneness into all the land Thus saith Yahuah of hosts not Hearken unto the words of**

הנבאים 5030 הנבאים 5012 לכם 3807a מהבלים 1891 המה 1992 אתכם 853 חזון 2377 לבם 3820 ידברו 1696 לא 3808
hanabiy'aym hanaba'aym lakem, mahabiliym hemah 'atkem; chazoun libam yadaberu, la'
**the prophets that prophesy unto you make vain they you a vision of their own heart they speak *and* not**

מפי 6310 יהוה 3068: 23:17 אמרים 559 אמור 559 למנאצי 5006 דבר 1696 יהוה 3068 שלום 7965 יהיה 1961 לכם 3807a
mipiy Yahuah. 'amariym 'amour limana'atzay, diber Yahuah, shaloum yihayeh lakem;
**out of the mouth of Yahuah They say still unto them that despise me has said Yahuah peace shall have to you**

וכל 3605 הלך 1980 בשררות 8307 לבו 3820 אמרו 559 לא 3808 תבוא 935 עליכם 5921 רעה 7451: 23:18 כי 3588
uakol halok bishrirut libou 'amaru, la' tabou'a 'aleykem ra'ah. kiy
**and every one that walk after the imagination of his own heart they say *unto* No shall come upon you evil For**

מי 4310 עמד 5975 בסוד 5475 יהוה 3068 וירא 7200 וישמע 8085 את 853 דברו 1697 מי 4310 הקשיב 7181 דברי 1697
miy' 'amad basoud Yahuah, uayera' uayishma' 'at debarou; miy' hiqshiyb dabariy
**who has stood in the counsel of Yahuah and has perceived and heard his word? who has marked his word**

וישמע 8085: 23:19 הנה 2009 סערת 5591 יהוה 3068 חמה 2534 יצאה 3318 וסער 5591 מתחולל 2342 על 5921 ראש 7218
uayishma'. hineh sa'arat Yahuah chemah yatz'ah, uasa'ar mitchoulel; 'al ra'sh
**and heard *it*? Behold a whirlwind of Yahuah *in* fury is gone forth even a whirlwind grievous upon the head of**

רשעים 7563 יחול 2342: 23:20 לא 3808 ישוב 7725 אף 639 יהוה 3068 עד 5704 עשתו 6213 ועד 5704
rasha'aym yachul. la' yashub 'ap Yahuah, 'ad 'asotou ua'ad
**the wicked it shall fall grievously not shall return The anger of Yahuah until he have executed and till**

הקימו 6965 מזמות 4209 לבו 3820 באחרית 319 הימים 3117 תתבוננו 995 בה 871a בינה 998: 23:21 לא 3808
haqiymou mazimout libou; ba'achariyt hayamiym, titbounnu bah biynah. la'
**he have performed the thoughts of his heart in latter the days you shall consider it perfectly not**

שלחתי 7971 את 853 הנבאים 5030 והם 1992 רצו 7323 לא 3808 דברתי 1696 אליהם 413 והם 1992 נבאו 5012: 23:22 ואם 518
shalachtiy 'at hanabiy'aym uahem ratzu; la' dibartiy 'aleyhem uahem niba'au. ua'am
**I have sent these prophets yet they ran not I have spoken to them yet they prophesied But if**

Jer 23:14 they are all of them unto me as Sodom, and the inhabitants thereof as Gomorrah.15 Therefore thus saith YHUH of hosts concerning the prophets; Behold, I will feed them with wormwood, and make them drink the water of gall: for from the prophets of Jerusalem is profaneness gone forth into all the land.16 Thus saith YHUH of hosts, Hearken not unto the words of the prophets that prophesy unto you: they make you vain: they speak a vision of their own heart, and not out of the mouth of YHUH.17 They say still unto them that despise me, YHUH has said, You shall have peace; and they say unto everyone that walk after the imagination of his own heart, No evil shall come upon you.18 For who has stood in the counsel of YHUH, and has perceived and heard his word? who has marked his word, and heard it?19 Behold, a whirlwind of YHUH is gone forth in fury, even a grievous whirlwind: it shall fall grievously upon the head of the wicked.20 The anger of YHUH shall not return, until he have executed, and till he have performed the thoughts of his heart: in the latter days you shall consider it perfectly.21 I have not sent these prophets, yet they ran: I have not spoken to them, yet they prophesied.

| עמדו 5975 | בסודי 5475 | וישמעו 8085 | דברי 1697 | את 853 | עמי 5971 | וישבום 7725 |
|---|---|---|---|---|---|---|
| 'amadu | basoudiy; | uayashmi'au | dabaray | 'at | 'amiy, | uiyshibum |
| **they had stood** | **in my counsel** | **and had caused to hear** | **my words** | | **my people** | **then they should have turned them** |

| מדרכם 1870 | הרע 7451 | ומרע 7455 | מעלליהם 4611: | 23:23 | האלהי 430 | מקרב 7128 | אני 589 | נאם 5002 | יהוה 3068 | ולא 3808 | אלהי 430 |
|---|---|---|---|---|---|---|---|---|---|---|---|
| midarkam | hara', | uameroa' | ma'alleyhem. | | ha'alohey | miqarob | 'aniy | na'am | Yahuah; | uala' | 'alohey |
| **from way** | **their evil** | **and from the evil of** | **their doings** | | ***Am* a Elohim** | **at hand** | **I** | **saith** | **Yahuah** | **and not** | **a Elohim** |

| מרחק 7350: | 23:24 | אם 518 | יסתר 5641 | איש 376 | במסתרים 4565 | ואני 589 | לא 3808 | אראנו 7200 | נאם 5002 | יהוה 3068 | הלוא 3808 | את 853 |
|---|---|---|---|---|---|---|---|---|---|---|---|---|
| merachoq. | | 'am | yisater | 'aysh | bamistariym | ua'aniy | la' | 'ar'anu | na'am | Yahuah; | halou'a | 'at |
| **far off?** | | **if** | **Can hide himself** | **any** | **in secret places** | **that I** | **not** | **shall see him?** | **saith** | **Yahuah** | **not** | |

| השמים 8064 | ואת 853 | הארץ 776 | אני 589 | מלא 4390 | נאם 5002 | יהוה 3068: | 23:25 | שמעתי 8085 | את 853 | אשר 834 | אמרו 559 | הנבאים 5030 |
|---|---|---|---|---|---|---|---|---|---|---|---|---|
| hashamayim | ua'at | ha'aretz | 'aniy | malea' | na'am | Yahuah. | | shama'atiy, | 'at | 'asher | 'amaru | hanabiy'aym, |
| **heaven** | ***and*** | **the earth?** | **I** | **Do fill** | **saith** | **Yahuah** | | **I have heard** | | **what** | **said** | **the prophets** |

| הנבאים 5012 | בשמי 8034 | שקר 8267 | לאמר 559 | חלמתי 2492 | חלמתי 2492: | 23:26 | עד 5704 | מתי 4970 | היש 3426 | בלב 3820 |
|---|---|---|---|---|---|---|---|---|---|---|
| hanaba'aym | bishmiy | sheqer | lea'mor; | chalamtiy | chalamatiy. | | 'ad | matay, | hayesh | baleb |
| ***that* prophesy** | **in my name** | **lies** | **saying** | **I have dreamed** | **I have dreamed** | | **How** | **long** | **shall *this* be** | **in the heart of** |

| הנבאים 5030 | נבאי 5012 | השקר 8267 | ונביאי 5030 | תרמת 8649 | לבם 3820: | 23:27 | החשבים 2803 |
|---|---|---|---|---|---|---|---|
| hanabiy'aym | niba'aey | hashaqer; | uanbiy'aey | tarmit | libam. | | hachoshabiym, |
| **the prophets** | **that prophesy** | **lies?** | **yes, they are prophets of** | **the deceit of** | **their own heart** | | ***Which* think** |

| להשכיח 7911 | את 853 | עמי 5971 | שמי 8034 | בחלומתם 2472 | אשר 834 | יספרו 5608 | איש 376 | לרעהו 7453 | כאשר 834 |
|---|---|---|---|---|---|---|---|---|---|
| lahashkiyach | 'at | 'amiy | shamiy, | bachaloumotam, | 'asher | yasapru | 'aysh | lare'aehu; | ka'asher |
| **to cause to forget** | | **my people** | **my name** | **by their dreams** | **which** | **they tell** | **every man** | **to his neighbour** | **as** |

| שכחו 7911 | אבותם 1 | את 853 | שמי 8034 | בבעל 1168: | 23:28 | הנביא 5030 | אשר 834 | אתו 854 | חלום 2472 | יספר 5608 | חלום 2472 |
|---|---|---|---|---|---|---|---|---|---|---|---|
| shakachu | aboutam | 'at | shamiy | baba'al. | | hanabiy'a | 'asher | 'atou | chaloum | yasaper | chaloum, |
| **have forgotten** | **their fathers** | | **my name** | **for Baal** | | **The prophet** | **that** | **he *has*** | **a dream** | **let him tell** | **a dream** |

| ואשר 834 | דברי 1697 | אתו 854 | ידבר 1696 | דברי 1697 | אמת 571 | מה 4100 | לתבן 8401 | את 854 | הבר 1250 | נאם 5002 |
|---|---|---|---|---|---|---|---|---|---|---|
| ua'asher | dabariy | 'atou, | yadaber | dabariy | 'amet; | mah | lateben | 'at | habar | na'am |
| **and he that** | ***has* my word** | **and he that** | **let him speak** | **my word** | **faithfully** | **What** | ***is* the chaff** | ***to*** | **the wheat?** | **said** |

| יהוה 3068: | 23:29 | הלוא 3808 | כה 3541 | דברי 1697 | כאש 784 | נאם 5002 | יהוה 3068 | וכפטיש 6360 | יפצץ 6327 | סלע 5553: | 23:30 |
|---|---|---|---|---|---|---|---|---|---|---|---|
| Yahuah. | | halou'a | koh | dabariy | ka'aesh | na'am | Yahuah; | uakpatiysh | yapotzetz | sala'. | |
| **Yahuah** | | ***Is* not** | **like** | **my word** | **as a fire?** | **said** | **Yahuah** | **and like a hammer** | ***that* break in pieces?** | **the rock** | |

| לכן 3651 | הנני 2005 | על 5921 | הנבאים 5030 | נאם 5002 | יהוה 3068 | מגנבי 1589 | דברי 1697 | איש 376 | מאת 853 | רעהו 7453: | 23:31 |
|---|---|---|---|---|---|---|---|---|---|---|---|
| laken | hinniy | 'al | hanabiy'aym | na'am | Yahuah; | maganbey | dabaray, | 'aysh | me'at | re'aehu. | |
| **Therefore** | **behold I *am*** | **against** | **the prophets** | **saith** | **Yahuah** | **that steal** | **my words** | **every one** | **from** | **his neighbour** | |

| הנני 2005 | על 5921 | הנביאם 5030 | נאם 5002 | יהוה 3068 | הלקחים 3947 | לשונם 3956 | וינאמו 5001 | נאם 5002: | 23:32 | הנני 2005 | על 5921 |
|---|---|---|---|---|---|---|---|---|---|---|---|
| hinniy | 'al | hanabiy'am | na'am | Yahuah; | haloqachiym | lashounam, | uayin'amu | na'am. | | hinniy | 'al |
| **Behold I *am*** | **against** | **the prophets** | **saith** | **Yahuah** | **that use** | **their tongues** | **and say** | **He saith** | | **Behold I *am*** | **against** |

Jer 23:22 But if they had stood in my counsel, and had caused my people to hear my words, then they should have turned them from their evil way, and from the evil of their doings.23 Am I a G-d at hand, saith YHUH, and not a G-d afar off?24 Can any hide himself in secret places that I shall not see him? saith YHUH. Do not I fill heaven and earth? saith YHUH.25 I have heard what the prophets said, that prophesy lies in my name, saying, I have dreamed, I have dreamed.26 How long shall this be in the heart of the prophets that prophesy lies? yea, they are prophets of the deceit of their own heart;27 Which think to cause my people to forget my name by their dreams which they tell every man to his neighbor, as their fathers have forgotten my name for Baal.28 The prophet that has a dream, let him tell a dream; and he that has my word, let him speak my word faithfully. What is the chaff to the wheat? saith YHUH.29 Is not my word like as a fire? saith YHUH; and like a hammer that breaketh the rock in pieces?30 Therefore, behold, I am against the prophets, saith YHUH, that steal my words everyone from his neighbor.31 Behold, I am against the prophets, saith YHUH, that use their tongues, and say, He saith.

5012 נבאי 2472 חלמות 8267 שקר 5002 נאם 3068 יהוה 5608 ויספרום 8582 ויתעו 853 את 5971 עמי 8267 בשקריהם
niba'aey chalomout sheqer na'am Yahuah, uayasaprum uayata'au 'at 'amiy, bashiqreyhem
**them that prophesy dreams false saith Yahuah and do tell them and cause to err my people by their lies**

6350 ובפחזותם 595 ואנכי 3808 לא 7971 שלחתים 3808 ולא 6680 צויתים 3276 והועיל 3808 לא 3276 יועילו
uabpachazutam; ua'anokiy la' shalachtiym uala' tziuiytiym, uahou'aeyl la' you'aylu
**and by their lightness yet I not sent them nor commanded them therefore they shall profit not at all**

5971 לעם 2088 הזה 5002 נאם 3068 יהוה: **23:33** 3588 וכי 7592 ישאלך 5971 העם 2088 הזה 176 או 5030 הנביא 176 או 3548 כהן 559 לאמר
la'am hazeh na'am Yahuah. uakiy yish'alaka ha'am hazeh 'au hanabiy'a 'au kohen lea'mor,
**people this saith Yahuah And when shall ask you the people this or the prophet or a priest saying**

4100 מה 4853 משא 3068 יהוה 559 ואמרת 413 אליהם 853 את 4100 מה 4853 משא 5203 ונטשתי 853 אתכם 5002 נאם
mah masa' Yahuah; ua'amarta 'aleyhem 'at mah masa', uanatashatiy 'atkem na'am
**What *is* the burden of Yahuah? and you shall then say unto them What burden? I will even forsake you saith**

3068 יהוה: **23:34** 5030 והנביא 3548 והכהן 5971 והעם 834 אשר 559 יאמר 4853 משא 3068 יהוה
Yahuah. uahanabiy'a uahakohen uaha'am, 'asher ya'mar masa' Yahuah;
**Yahuah And *as for* the prophet and the priest and the people that shall say The burden of Yahuah**

6485 ופקדתי 5921 על 376 האיש 1931 ההוא 5921 ועל 1004 ביתו: **23:35** 3541 כה 559 תאמרו 376 איש 5921 על 7453 רעהו
uapaqadtiy 'al ha'aysh hahua' ua'al beytou. koh ta'maru 'aysh 'al re'aehu
**I will even punish on man that and on his house Thus shall you say every one to his neighbour**

376 ואיש 413 אל 251 אחיו 4100 מה 6030 ענה 3068 יהוה 4100 ומה 1696 דבר 3068 יהוה: **23:36** 4853 ומשא
ua'aysh 'al 'achiyu; meh 'anah Yahuah, uamah diber Yahuah. uamasa'
**and every one to his brother What has answered? Yahuah and what has spoken? Yahuah And the burden of**

3068 יהוה 3808 לא 2142 תזכרו 5750 עוד 3588 כי 4853 המשא 1961 יהיה 376 לאיש 1697 דברו 2015 והפכתם 853 את
Yahuah la' tizkaru 'aud; kiy hamasa', yihayeh la'aysh dabarou, uahapaktem, 'at
**Yahuah no shall you mention more for his burden shall be every man's word for you have perverted**

1697 דברי 430 אלהים 2416 חיים 3068 יהוה 6635 צבאות 430 אלהינו: **23:37** 3541 כה 559 תאמר 413 אל 5030 הנביא 4100 מה
dibrey 'alohiym chayiym, Yahuah tzaba'aut 'aloheynu. koh ta'mar 'al hanabiy'a; meh
**the words of Elohim *the* living *of* Yahuah of hosts our Elohim Thus shall you say to the prophet What**

6030 ענך 3068 יהוה 4100 ומה 1696 דבר 3068 יהוה: **23:38** 518 ואם 4853 משא 3068 יהוה 559 תאמרו 3651 לכן
'anak Yahuah, uamah diber Yahuah. ua'am masa' Yahuah ta'maru laken,
**has answered you? Yahuah and What has spoken? Yahuah But since The burden of Yahuah you say therefore**

3541 כה 559 אמר 3068 יהוה 3282 יען 559 אמרכם 853 את 1697 הדבר 2088 הזה 4853 משא 3068 יהוה 7971 ואשלח 413 אליכם 559 לאמר
koh 'amar Yahuah, ya'an 'amarakem 'at hadabar hazeh masa' Yahuah; ua'ashlach 'aleykem lea'mor,
**thus saith Yahuah Because you say word this The burden of Yahuah and I have sent unto you saying**

3808 לא 559 תאמרו 4853 משא 3068 יהוה: **23:39** 3651 לכן 2005 הנני 5382 ונשיתי 853 אתכם 5377 נשא 5203 ונטשתי
la' ta'maru masa' Yahuah. laken hinniy, uanashiytiy 'atkem nasha'; uanatashtiy
**not You shall say The burden of Yahuah Therefore behold I even I will forget you utterly and I will forsake**

Jer 23:32 Behold, I am against them that prophesy false dreams, saith YHUH, and do tell them, and cause my people to err by their lies, and by their lightness; yet I sent them not, nor commanded them: therefore they shall not profit this people at all, saith YHUH.33 And when this people, or the prophet, or a priest, shall ask you, saying, What is the burden of YHUH? you shall then say unto them, What burden? I will even forsake you, saith YHUH.34 And as for the prophet, and the priest, and the people, that shall say, The burden of YHUH, I will even punish that man and his house.35 Thus shall you say everyone to his neighbor, and everyone to his brother, What has YHUH answered? and, What has YHUH spoken?36 And the burden of YHUH shall you mention no more: forevery man's word shall be his burden; for you have perverted the words of the living G-d, of YHUH of hosts our G-d.37 Thus shall you say to the prophet, What has YHUH answered you? and, What has YHUH spoken?38 But since you say, The burden of YHUH; therefore thus saith YHUH; Because you say this word, The burden of YHUH, and I have sent unto you, saying, You shall not say, The burden of YHUH;39 Therefore, behold, I, even I, will utterly forget you, and I will forsake you, and the city that I gave you and your fathers, and cast you out of my presence:

**23:40**
853 אתכם 853 ואת 5892 העיר 834 אשר 5414 נתתי 3807a לכם 1 ולאבותיכם 5921 מעל 6440 פני: 5414 ונתתי
'atkem, ua'at ha'ayr 'asher natatiy lakem uala'abouteykem me'al panay. uanatatiy
**you *and* the city that I gave to you and your fathers *and cast you* out of my presence And I will bring**

5921 עליכם 2781 חרפת 5769 עולם 3640 וכלמות 5769 עולם 834 אשר 3808 לא 7911 תשכח:
'aleykem cherpat 'aulam; uaklimut 'aulam, 'asher la' tishakeach.
**upon you an reproach everlasting and a shame perpetual which not shall be forgotten**

**Jer 24:1**
7200 הראני 3068 יהוה 2009 והנה 8147 שני 1736 דודאי 8384 תאנים 3259 מועדים 6440 לפני 1964 היכל 3068 יהוה 310 אחרי
hir'aniy Yahuah uahineh, shaney duda'aey ta'aeniym, mu'adiym lipney heykal Yahuah; 'acharey
**showed me Yahuah and behold two baskets of figs *were* set before the temple of Yahuah after that**

1540 הגלות 5019 נבוכדראצר 4428 מלך 894 בבל 853 את 3204 יכניהו 1121 בן 3079 יהויקים 4428 מלך 3063 יהודה 853 ואת
hagalout nabukadra'tzar melek babel 'at yakanyahu ben yahouyaqiym melek yahudah ua'at
**had carried away captive Nebuchadrezzar king of Babylon Jeconiah the son of Jehoiakim king of Judah *and***

8269 שרי 3063 יהודה 854 ואת 2796 החרש 854 ואת 4525 המסגר 3389 מירושלם 935 ויבאם 894 בבל:
sarey yahudah ua'at hecharash ua'at hamasger miyarushalaim, uayabiy'aem babel.
**the princes of Judah *with* the carpenters *and* smiths from Jerusalem and had brought them to Babylon**

**24:2**
1731 הדוד 259 אחד 8384 תאנים 2896 טבות 3966 מאד 8384 כתאני 1073 הבכרות 1731 והדוד 259 אחד 8384 תאנים 7451 רעות
hadud 'achad, ta'aeniym tobout ma'ad, kita'aeney habakurout; uahadud 'achad, ta'aeniym ra'aut
**basket One figs good *had* very *even* like the figs *that are* first ripe and the basket other figs naughty**

3966 מאד 834 אשר 3808 לא 398 תאכלנה 7455 מרע:
ma'ad, 'asher la' te'akalnah meroa'.
***had* very which not could be eaten they were so bad**

**24:3**
559 ויאמר 3068 יהוה 413 אלי 4100 מה 859 אתה 7200 ראה 3414 ירמיהו
uaya'mer Yahuah 'aelay, mah 'atah ro'ah yirmayahu,
**Then said Yahuah unto me What you see Jeremiah?**

559 ואמר 8384 תאנים 8384 התאנים 2896 הטבות 2896 טבות 3966 מאד 7451 והרעות 7451 רעות 3966 מאד 834 אשר 3808 לא 398 תאכלנה
ua'amar ta'aeniym; hata'aeniym hatobout tobout ma'ad, uahara'at ra'aut ma'ad, 'asher la' te'akalnah
**And I said Figs figs the good good very and the evil evil very that cannot be eaten**

7455 מרע:
meroa'.
**they are so evil**

**24:4**
1961 ויהי 1697 דבר 3068 יהוה 413 אלי 559 לאמר:
uayahiy dabar Yahuah 'aelay lea'mor.
**Again came the word of Yahuah unto me saying**

**24:5**
3541 כה 559 אמר 3068 יהוה 430 אלהי 3478 ישראל
koh 'amar Yahuah 'alohey yisra'ael,
**Thus saith Yahuah the Elohim of Israel**

8384 כתאנים 2896 הטבות 428 האלה 3651 כן 5234 אכיר 853 את 1546 גלות 3063 יהודה 834 אשר
kata'aeniym hatobout ha'aeleh; ken 'akiyr 'at galut yahudah, 'asher
**Like figs good these so will I acknowledge them that are carried away captive of Judah whom**

7971 שלחתי 4480 מן 4725 המקום 2088 הזה 776 ארץ 3778 כשדים 2896 לטובה:
shilachtiy min hamaqoum hazeh 'aretz kasdiym latoubah.
**I have sent out of place this *into* the land of the Chaldeans for *their* good**

**24:6**
7760 ושמתי 5869 עיני 5921 עליהם
uasamtiy 'aeyniy 'aleyhem
**For I will set mine eyes upon them**

2896 לטובה 7725 והשבתים 5921 על 776 הארץ 2063 הזאת 1129 ובניתים 3808 ולא 2040 אהרס
latoubah, uahashibotiym 'al ha'aretz haza't; uabniytiym uala' 'aharos,
**for good and I will bring them again to the land this and I will build them and not pull *them* down**

Jer 23:40 And I will bring an everlasting reproach upon you, and a perpetual shame, which shall not be forgotten. **Jer** 24:1 YHUH showed me, and, behold, two baskets of figs were set before the temple of YHUH, after that Nebuchadrezzar king of Babylon had carried away captive Jeconiah the son of Jehoiakim king of Judah, and the princes of Judah, with the carpenters and smiths, from Jerusalem, and had brought them to Babylon.2 One basket had very good figs, even like the figs that are first ripe: and the other basket had very naughty figs, which could not be eaten, they were so bad.3 Then said YHUH unto me, What seest you, Jeremiah? And I said, Figs; the good figs, very good; and the evil, very evil, that cannot be eaten, they are so evil.4 Again the word of YHUH came unto me, saying,5 Thus saith YHUH, the G-d of Israel; Like these good figs, so will I acknowledge them that are carried away captive of Judah, whom I have sent out of this place into the land of the Chaldeans for their good.6 For I will set mine eyes upon them for good, and I will bring them again to this land: and I will build them, and not pull them down; and I will plant them, and not pluck them up.

ונטעתים 5193 ולא 3808 אתוש 5428: 24:7 ונתתי 5414 להם 3807a לב 3820 לדעת 3045 אתי 853 כי 3588 אני 589 יהוה 3068
uanta'atiym uala' 'atoush. uanatatiy lahem leb lada'at 'atiy, kiy 'aniy Yahuah,
**and I will plant them and not I shall pluck *them* up And I will give them an heart to know me that I *am* Yahuah**

והיו 1961 לי 3807a לעם 5971 ואנכי 595 אהיה 1961 להם 3807a לאלהים 430 כי 3588 ישבו 7725 אלי 413 בכל 3605
uahayu liy la'am, ua'anokiy, 'ahayeh lahem le'alohiym; kiy yashubu 'aelay bakal
**and they shall be my people and I will be their to Elohim for they shall return unto me their whole**

לבם 3820: 24:8 וכתאנים 8384 הרעות 7451 אשר 834 לא 3808 תאכלנה 398 מרע 7455 כי 3588 כה 3541 אמר 559 יהוה 3068 כן 3651 אתן 5414
libam. uakat'aeniym hara'aut, 'asher la' te'akalnah meroa'; kiy koh 'amar Yahuah ken 'aten
**their heart And as figs the evil which cannot be eaten they are so evil surely thus saith Yahuah So will I give**

את 853 צדקיהו 6667 מלך 4428 יהודה 3063 ואת 853 שריו 8269 ואת 853 שארית 7611 ירושלם 3389 הנשארים 7604 בארץ 776 הזאת 2063
'at tzidqiyahu melek yahudah ua'at sarayu ua'at sha'aeriyt yarushalaim, hanisha'ariym ba'aretz haza't,
**Zedekiah the king of Judah *and* his princes *and* the residue of Jerusalem that remain in land this**

והישבים 3427 בארץ 776 מצרים 4714: 24:9 ונתתים 5414 לזועה 2113 לרעה 7451 לכל 3605
uahayoushabiym ba'aretz mitzrayim. uantatiym lazua'ah lara'ah, lakol
**and them that dwell in the land of Egypt And I will deliver them to be removed for *their* hurt into all**

ממלכות 4467 הארץ 776 לחרפה 2781 ולמשל 4912 לשנינה 8148 ולקללה 7045 בכל 3605 המקמות 4725 אשר 834
mamlakout ha'aretz; lacherpah ualmashal lishniynah ualiqlalah, bakal hamaqomout 'asher
**the kingdoms of the earth *to be* a reproach and a proverb a taunt and a curse in all places where**

אדיחם 5080 שם 8033: 24:10 ושלחתי 7971 בם 871a את 853 החרב 2719 את 853 הרעב 7458 ואת 853 הדבר 1698 עד 5704
'adiychem sham. uashilachtiy bam, 'at hachereb 'at hara'ab ua'at hadaber; 'ad
**I shall drive them there And I will send among them the sword the famine *and* the pestilence till**

תמם 8552 מעל 5921 האדמה 127 אשר 834 נתתי 5414 להם 1992 ולאבותיהם 1:
tumam me'al ha'adamah, 'asher natatiy lahem uala'abouteyhem.
**they be consumed from off the land that I gave unto them and to their fathers**

**Jer 25:1** הדבר 1697 אשר 834 היה 1961 על 5921 ירמיהו 3414 על 5921 כל 3605 עם 5971 יהודה 3063 בשנה 8141 הרבעית 7243
hadabar 'asher hayah 'al yirmayahu 'al kal 'am yahudah, bashanah harabi'ayt,
**The word that came to Jeremiah concerning all the people of Judah in year the fourth**

ליהויקים 3079 בן 1121 יאשיהו 2977 מלך 4428 יהודה 3063 היא 1931 השנה 8141 הראשנית 7224 לנבוכדראצר 5019 מלך 4428 בבל 894: 25:2
liyahouyaqiym ben ya'shiyahu melek yahudah; hiy'a, hashanah hara'shoniyt, linabukadra'tzar melek babel.
**of Jehoiakim the son of Josiah king of Judah that year *was* the first of Nebuchadrezzar king of Babylon**

אשר 834 דבר 1696 ירמיהו 3414 הנביא 5030 על 5921 כל 3605 עם 5971 יהודה 3063 ואל 413 כל 3605 ישבי 3427 ירושלם 3389
'asher diber yirmayahu hanabiy'a 'al kal 'am yahudah, ua'ael kal yoshabey yarushalaim
***The* which spoke Jeremiah the prophet unto all the people of Judah and to all the inhabitants of Jerusalem**

לאמר 559: 25:3 מן 4480 שלש 7969 עשרה 6240 שנה 8141 ליאשיהו 2977 בן 1121 אמון 526 מלך 4428 יהודה 3063 ועד 5704 היום 3117 הזה 2088
lea'mor. min shalosh 'asreh shanah laya'shiyahu ben 'amoun melek yahudah ua'ad hayoum hazeh,
**saying From *the* three ten year of Josiah the son of Amon king of Judah even unto day this**

Jer 24:7 And I will give them an heart to know me, that I am YHUH: and they shall be my people, and I will be their G-d: for they shall return unto me with their whole heart.8 And as the evil figs, which cannot be eaten, they are so evil; surely thus saith YHUH, So will I give Zedekiah the king of Judah, and his princes, and the residue of Jerusalem, that remain in this land, and them that dwell in the land of Egypt:9 And I will deliver them to be removed into all the kingdoms of the earth for their hurt, to be a reproach and a proverb, a taunt and a curse, in all places whither I shall drive them.10 And I will send the sword, the famine, and the pestilence, among them, till they be consumed from off the land that I gave unto them and to their fathers. **Jer** 25:1 The word that came to Jeremiah concerning all the people of Judah in the fourth year of Jehoiakim the son of Josiah king of Judah, that was the first year of Nebuchadrezzar king of Babylon;2 The which Jeremiah the prophet spoke unto all the people of Judah, and to all the inhabitants of Jerusalem, saying,3 From the thirteenth year of Josiah the son of Amon king of Judah, even unto this day, that is the three and twentieth year, the word of YHUH has come unto me, and I have spoken unto you, rising early and speaking; but you have not hearkened.

זה 2088 שלש 7969 ועשרים 6242 שנה 8141 היה 1961 דבר 1697 יהוה 3068 אלי 413 ואדבר 1696 אליכם 413 אשכים 7925
zeh shalosh ua'asriym shanah, hayah dabar Yahuah 'aelay; ua'adaber 'aleykem 'ashkeym
**that *is the* three and twentieth year has come the word of Yahuah unto me and I have spoken unto you rising early**

ודבר 1696 ולא 3808 שמעתם 8085: **25:4** ושלח 7971 יהוה 3068 אליכם 413 את 853 כל 3605 עבדיו 5650 הנבאים 5030
uadaber uala' shama'tem. uashalach Yahuah 'aleykem 'at kal 'abadayu hanabiy'aym
**and speaking but not you have hearkened And has sent Yahuah unto you all his servants the prophets**

השכם 7925 ושלח 7971 ולא 3808 שמעתם 8085 ולא 3808 הטיתם 5186 את 853 אזנכם 241 לשמע 8085: **25:5** לאמר 559
hashkem uashaloach uala' shama'tem; uala' hitiytem 'at 'aznakem lishmoa'. lea'mor,
**rising early and sending *them* but not you have hearkened nor inclined your ear to hear They said**

שובו 7725 נא 4994 איש 376 מדרכו 1870 הרעה 7451 ומרע 7455 מעלליכם 4611 ושבו 3427 על 5921 האדמה 127 אשר 834
shubu naa' 'aysh midarkou hara'ah uameroa' ma'alleykem, uashbu 'al ha'adamah, 'asher
**Turn you again now every one from his way evil and from the evil of your doings and dwell in the land that**

נתן 5414 יהוה 3069 לכם 3807a ולאבותיכם 1 למן 4480 עולם 5769 ועד 5704 עולם 5769: **25:6** ואל 408 תלכו 1980 אחרי 310 אלהים 430
natan Yahuah lakem uala'abouteykem; lemin 'aulam ua'ad 'aulam. ua'al telaku, 'acharey 'alohiym
**has given Yahuah unto you and to your fathers for ever and for ever And not go after gods**

אחרים 312 לעבדם 5647 ולהשתחות 7812 להם 3807a ולא 3808 תכעיסו 3707 אותי 854 במעשה 4639 ידיכם 3027 ולא 3808
'acheriym, la'abadam ualhishtachauot lahem; uala' tak'aysu 'autiy bama'aseh yadeykem, uala'
**other to serve them and to worship them and not provoke to anger me with the works of your hands and no**

ארע 7489 לכם 3807a: **25:7** ולא 3808 שמעתם 8085 אלי 413 נאם 5002 יהוה 3068 למען 4616 הכעסוני 3707
'ara lakem. uala' shama'tem 'aelay na'am Yahuah; lama'an hika'asuniy
**I will do hurt to you Yet not you have hearkened unto me saith Yahuah that you might provoke me to anger**

במעשה 4639 ידיכם 3027 לרע 7451 לכם 3807a: **25:8** לכן 3651 כה 3541 אמר 559 יהוה 3068 צבאות 6635 יען 3282 אשר 834 לא 3808
bama'aseh yadeykem lara' lakem. laken koh 'amar Yahuah tzaba'aut; ya'an 'asher la'
**with the works of your hands to hurt to your own Therefore thus saith Yahuah of hosts Because after not**

שמעתם 8085 את 853 דברי 1697: **25:9** הנני 2005 שלח 7971 ולקחתי 3947 את 853 כל 3605 משפחות 4940 צפון 6828 נאם 5002 יהוה 3068
shama'tem 'at dabaray. hinniy sholeach ualaqachtiy 'at kal mishpachout tzapoun na'am Yahuah
**you have heard my words Behold I will send and take all the families of the north saith Yahuah**

ואל 413 נבוכדראצר 5019 מלך 4428 בבל 894 עבדי 5650 והבאתים 935 על 5921 הארץ 776 הזאת 2063 ועל 5921
ua'al nabukadra'tzar melek babel 'abdiy uahabi'atiym 'al ha'aretz haza't ua'al
**and to Nebuchadrezzar the king of Babylon my servant and will bring them against the land this and against**

ישביה 3427 ועל 5921 כל 3605 הגוים 1471 האלה 428 סביב 5439 והחרמתים 2763 ושמתים 7760
yoshabeyha, ua'al kal hagouyim ha'aeleh sabiyb; uahacharamtiym, uasamatiym
**the inhabitants thereof and against all nations these round about and will utterly destroy them and make them**

לשמה 8047 ולשרקה 8322 ולחרבות 2723 עולם 5769: **25:10** והאבדתי 6 מהם 1992 קול 6963 ששון 8342
lashamah ualishreqah, ualcharabout 'aulam. uaha'abadatiy mehem, qoul sasoun
**an astonishment and an hissing and desolations perpetual Moreover I will take from them the voice of mirth**

Jer 25:4 And YHUH has sent unto you all his servants the prophets, rising early and sending them; but you have not hearkened, nor inclined your ear to hear.5 They said, Turn you again now everyone from his evil way, and from the evil of your doings, and dwell in the land that YHUH has given unto you and to your fathers forever and ever:6 And go not after other gods to serve them, and to worship them, and provoke me not to anger with the works of your hands; and I will do you no hurt.7 Yet you have not hearkened unto me, saith YHUH; that you might provoke me to anger with the works of your hands to your own hurt.8 Therefore thus saith YHUH of hosts; Because you have not heard my words,9 Behold, I will send and take all the families of the north, saith YHUH, and Nebuchadrezzar the king of Babylon, my servant, and will bring them against this land, and against the inhabitants thereof, and against all these nations round about, and will utterly destroy them, and make them an astonishment, and an hissing, and perpetual desolations.10 Moreover I will take from them the voice of mirth, and the voice of gladness, the voice of the bridegroom, and the voice of the bride, the sound of the millstones, and the light of the candle.

| וקול 6963 | שמחה 8057 | קול 6963 | חתן 2860 | וקול 6963 | כלה 3618 | קול 6963 | רחים 7347 |
|---|---|---|---|---|---|---|---|
| uaqoul | simchah, | qoul | chatan | uaqoul | kalah; | qoul | rechayim |
| **and the voice of** | **gladness** | **the voice of** | **the bridegroom** | **and the voice of** | **the bride** | **the sound of** | **the millstones** |

| ואור 216 | נר 5216: | 25:11 | והיתה 1961 | כל 3605 | הארץ 776 | הזאת 2063 | לחרבה 2723 | לשמה 8047 | ועבדו 5647 |
|---|---|---|---|---|---|---|---|---|---|
| ua'aur | ner. | | uahayatah | kal | ha'aretz | haza't, | lacharabah | lashamah; | ua'abadu |
| **and the light of** | **the candle** | | **And shall be** | **whole** | **the land** | **this** | **a desolation** | ***and* an astonishment** | **and shall serve** |

| הגוים 1471 | האלה 428 | את 853 | מלך 4428 | בבל 894 | שבעים 7657 | שנה 8141: | 25:12 | והיה 1961 | כמלאות 4390 |
|---|---|---|---|---|---|---|---|---|---|
| hagouyim | ha'aeleh | 'at | melek | babel | shib'aym | shanah. | | uahayah | kimala'ut |
| **nations** | **these** | | **the king of** | **Babylon** | **seventy** | **years** | | **And it shall come to pass** | **when are accomplished** |

| שבעים 7657 | שנה 8141 | אפקד 6485 | על 5921 | מלך 4428 | בבל 894 | ועל 5921 | הגוי 1471 | ההוא 1931 | נאם 5002 | יהוה 3068 | את 853 | עונם 5771 |
|---|---|---|---|---|---|---|---|---|---|---|---|---|
| shib'aym | shanah | 'apqod | 'al | melek | babel | ua'al | hagouy | hahua' | na'am | Yahuah | 'at | 'auonam |
| **seventy** | **years** | ***that* I will punish** | **on** | **the king of** | **Babylon** | **and on** | **nation** | **that** | **saith** | **Yahuah** | | ***for* their iniquity** |

| ועל 5921 | ארץ 776 | כשדים 3778 | ושמתי 7760 | אתו 853 | לשממות 8077 | עולם 5769: | 25:13 | והבאיתי 935 | על 5921 | הארץ 776 | ההיא 1931 |
|---|---|---|---|---|---|---|---|---|---|---|---|
| ua'al | 'aretz | kasdiym; | uasamtiy | 'atou | lashimamout | 'aulam. | | uahebay'tiy | 'al | ha'aretz | hahiy'a, |
| **and on** | **the land of** | **the Chaldeans** | **and will make** | **it** | **desolations** | **perpetual** | | **And I will bring** | **upon** | **land** | **that** |

| את 853 | כל 3605 | דברי 1697 | אשר 834 | דברתי 1696 | עליה 5921 | את 853 | כל 3605 | הכתוב 3789 | בספר 5612 | הזה 2088 | אשר 834 |
|---|---|---|---|---|---|---|---|---|---|---|---|
| 'at | kal | dabaray | 'asher | dibartiy | 'aleyha; | 'at | kal | hakatub | baseper | hazeh, | 'asher |
| | **all** | **my words** | **which** | **I have pronounced** | **against it, *even*** | | **all** | **that is written** | **in book** | **this** | **which** |

| נבא 5012 | ירמיהו 3414 | על 5921 | כל 3605 | הגוים 1471: | 25:14 | כי 3588 | עבדו 5647 | בם 871a | גם 1571 | המה 1992 | גוים 1471 | רבים 7227 |
|---|---|---|---|---|---|---|---|---|---|---|---|---|
| niba' | yirmayahu | 'al | kal | hagouyim. | | kiy | 'abadu | bam | gam | hemah | gouyim | rabiym, |
| **has prophesied** | **Jeremiah** | **against** | **all** | **the nations** | | **For** | **shall serve** | **themselves** | **also** | **of them** | **nations** | **many** |

| ומלכים 4428 | גדולים 1419 | ושלמתי 7999 | להם 3807a | כפעלם 6467 | וכמעשה 4639 |
|---|---|---|---|---|---|
| uamalakiym | gadouliym; | uashilamtiy | lahem | kapa'alam | uakma'aseh |
| **and kings** | **great** | **and I will recompense** | **them** | **according to their deeds** | **and according to the works of** |

| ידיהם 3027: | 25:15 | כי 3588 | כה 3541 | אמר 559 | יהוה 3068 | אלהי 430 | ישראל 3478 | אלי 413 | קח 3947 | את 853 | כוס 3563 | היין 3196 | החמה 2534 |
|---|---|---|---|---|---|---|---|---|---|---|---|---|---|
| yadeyhem. | | kiy | koh | 'amar | Yahuah | 'alohey | yisra'ael | 'aelay, | qach | 'at | kous | hayayin | hachomah |
| **their own hands** | | **For** | **thus** | **saith** | **Yahuah** | **Elohim of** | **Israel** | **unto me** | **Take** | | **cup of** | **the wine** | **fury** |

| הזאת 2063 | מידי 3027 | והשקיתה 8248 | אתו 853 | את 853 | כל 3605 | הגוים 1471 | אשר 834 | אנכי 595 | שלח 7971 | אותך 853 | אליהם 413: | 25:16 |
|---|---|---|---|---|---|---|---|---|---|---|---|---|
| haza't | miyadiy; | uahishqiytah | 'atou | 'at | kal | hagouyim, | 'asher | 'anokiy | sholeach | 'autaka | 'aleyhem. | |
| **this** | **at my hand** | **and cause to drink** | **it** | | **all** | **the nations** | ***to* whom** | **I** | **send** | **you** | **whom** | |

| ושתו 8354 | והתגעשו 1607 | והתהללו 1984 | מפני 6440 | החרב 2719 | אשר 834 | אנכי 595 | שלח 7971 | בינתם 996: | 25:17 |
|---|---|---|---|---|---|---|---|---|---|
| uashatu | uahitgo'ashu | uahitholalu; | mipaney | hachereb, | 'asher | 'anokiy | sholeach | beynotam. | |
| **And they shall drink** | **and be moved** | **and be mad** | **because of** | **the sword** | **that** | **I** | **will send** | **among them** | |

| ואקח 3947 | את 853 | הכוס 3563 | מיד 3027 | יהוה 3068 | ואשקה 8248 | את 853 | כל 3605 | הגוים 1471 | אשר 834 | שלחני 7971 | יהוה 3068 |
|---|---|---|---|---|---|---|---|---|---|---|---|
| ua'aqach | 'at | hakous | miyad | Yahuah; | ua'ashqeh | 'at | kal | hagouyim, | 'asher | shalachaniy | Yahuah |
| **Then took I** | | **the cup** | **at hand** | **Yahuah's** | **and made to drink** | | **all** | **the nations** | ***unto* whom** | **had sent me** | **Yahuah** |

Jer 25:11 And this whole land shall be a desolation, and an astonishment; and these nations shall serve the king of Babylon seventy years.12 And it shall come to pass, when seventy years are accomplished, that I will punish the king of Babylon, and that nation, saith YHUH, for their iniquity, and the land of the Chaldeans, and will make it perpetual desolations.13 And I will bring upon that land all my words which I have pronounced against it, even all that is written in this book, which Jeremiah has prophesied against all the nations.14 For many nations and great kings shall serve themselves of them also: and I will recompense them according to their deeds, and according to the works of their own hands.15 For thus saith YHUH G-d of Israel unto me; Take the wine cup of this fury at my hand, and cause all the nations, to whom I send you, to drink it.16 And they shall drink, and be moved, and be mad, because of the sword that I will send among them.17 Then took I the cup at YHUH's hand, and made all the nations to drink, unto whom YHUH had sent me:

25:18

אליהם 413: את 853 ירושלם 3389 ואת 853 ערי 5892 יהודה 3063 ואת 853 מלכיה 4428 את 853 שריה 8269
'aleyhem. 'at yarushalaim ua'at 'arey yahudah, ua'at malakeyha 'at sareyha;
**whom** ***To wit*** **Jerusalem** ***and*** **the cities of Judah** ***and*** **the kings thereof** ***and*** **the princes thereof**

25:19

לתת 5414 אתם 859 לחרבה 2723 לשמה 8047 לשרקה 8322 ולקללה 7045 כיום 3117 הזה 2088: את 853 פרעה 6547 מלך 4428
latet 'atam lacharabah lashamah lishreqah ualiqlalah kayoum hazeh. 'at par'ah melek
**to make them a desolation an astonishment an hissing and a curse as day** ***it is*** **this Pharaoh king of**

25:20

מצרים 4714 ואת 853 עבדיו 5650 ואת 853 שריו 8269 ואת 853 כל 3605 עמו 5971: ואת 853 כל 3605 הערב 6154 ואת 853 כל 3605
mitzrayim ua'at 'abadayu ua'at sarayu ua'at kal 'amou. ua'at kal ha'areb, ua'at kal
**Egypt** ***and*** **his servants** ***and*** **his princes** ***and*** **all his people** ***And*** **all the mingled people** ***and*** **all**

מלכי 4428 ארץ 776 העוץ 5780 ואת 853 כל 3605 מלכי 4428 ארץ 776 פלשתים 6430 ואת 853 אשקלון 831 ואת 853 עזה 5804 ואת 853
malkey 'aretz ha'autz; ua'at, kal malkey 'aretz palishtiym, ua'at 'ashqaloun ua'at 'azah ua'at
**the kings of the land of Uz** ***and*** **all the kings of the land of the Philistines** ***and*** **Ashkelon** ***and*** **Azzah** ***and***

25:21 25:22

עקרון 6138 ואת 853 שארית 7611 אשדוד 795: את 853 אדום 123 ואת 853 מואב 4124 ואת 853 בני 1121 עמון 5983: ואת 853
aqroun, ua'at sha'aeriyt 'ashdoud. 'at 'adoum ua'at mou'ab ua'at baney 'amoun. ua'at
**Ekron** ***and*** **the remnant of Ashdod Edom** ***and*** **Moab** ***and*** **the children of Ammon** ***And***

25:23

כל 3605 מלכי 4428 צר 6865 ואת 853 כל 3605 מלכי 4428 צידון 6721 ואת 853 מלכי 4428 האי 339 אשר 834 בעבר 5676 הים 3220:
kal malkey tzor, ua'at kal malkey tziydoun; ua'at malkey ha'ay, 'asher ba'aeber hayam.
**all the kings of Tyrus** ***and*** **all the kings of Zidon** ***and*** **the kings of the isles which** ***are*** **beyond the sea**

25:24

ואת 853 דדן 1719 ואת 853 תימא 8485 ואת 853 בוז 938 ואת 853 כל 3605 קצוצי 7112 פאה 6285: ואת 853 כל 3605 מלכי 4428 ערב 6152
ua'at dadan ua'at teymaa' ua'at buz, ua'at kal qatzutzey pe'ah. ua'at kal malkey 'arab;
***And*** **Dedan** ***and*** **Tema** ***and*** **Buz** ***and*** **all** ***that are*** **in the utmost corners** ***And*** **all the kings of Arabia**

25:25

ואת 853 כל 3605 מלכי 4428 הערב 6154 השכנים 7931 במדבר 4057: ואת 853 כל 3605 מלכי 4428 זמרי 2174 ואת 853 כל 3605
ua'at kal malkey ha'areb, hashokaniym bamidbar. ua'at kal malkey zimriy, ua'at kal
***and*** **all the kings of the mingled people that dwell in the desert** ***And*** **all the kings of Zimri** ***and*** **all**

25:26

מלכי 4428 עילם 5867 ואת 853 כל 3605 מלכי 4428 מדי 4074: ואת 853 כל 3605 מלכי 4428 הצפון 6828 הקרבים 7138
malkey 'aeylam, ua'at kal malkey maday. ua'at kal malkey hatzapoun, haqarobiym
**the kings of Elam** ***and*** **all the kings of the Medes** ***And*** **all the kings of the north near**

והרחקים 7350 איש 376 אל 413 אחיו 251 ואת 853 כל 3605 הממלכות 4467 הארץ 776 אשר 834 על 5921 פני 6440 האדמה 127
uaharachoqiym 'aysh 'al 'achiyu, ua'at kal hamamlakout ha'aretz, 'asher 'al paney ha'adamah;
**and far one with another** ***and*** **all the kingdoms of the world which** ***are*** **upon the face of the earth**

25:27

ומלך 4428 ששך 8347 ישתה 8354 אחריהם 310: ואמרת 559 אליהם 413 כה 3541 אמר 559 יהוה 3068 צבאות 6635
uamelek sheshak yishteh 'achareyhem. ua'amarta 'aleyhem koh 'amar Yahuah tzaba'aut
**and the king of Sheshach shall drink after them Therefore you shall say unto them Thus saith Yahuah of hosts**

אלהי 430 ישראל 3478 שתו 8354 ושכרו 7937 וקיו 7006 ונפלו 5307 ולא 3808 תקומו 6965 מפני 6440 החרב 2719 אשר 834 אנכי 595
'alohey yisra'ael, shatu uashikaru uaqyu, uanipalu uala' taqumu; mipaney hachereb, 'asher 'anokiy
**the Elohim of Israel Drink you and be drunken and spue and fall and no** ***more*** **rise because of the sword which I**

Jer 25:18 To wit, Jerusalem, and the cities of Judah, and the kings thereof, and the princes thereof, to make them a desolation, an astonishment, an hissing, and a curse; as it is this day;19 Pharaoh king of Egypt, and his servants, and his princes, and all his people;20 And all the mingled people, and all the kings of the land of Uz, and all the kings of the land of the Philistines, and Ashkelon, and Azzah, and Ekron, and the remnant of Ashdod,21 Edom, and Moab, and the children of Ammon,22 And all the kings of Tyrus, and all the kings of Zidon, and the kings of the isles which are beyond the sea,23 Dedan, and Tema, and Buz, and all that are in the utmost corners,24 And all the kings of Arabia, and all the kings of the mingled people that dwell in the desert,25 And all the kings of Zimri, and all the kings of Elam, and all the kings of the Medes,26 And all the kings of the north, far and near, one with another, and all the kingdoms of the world, which are upon the face of the earth: and the king of Sheshach shall drink after them.27 Therefore you shall say unto them, Thus saith YHUH of hosts, the G-d of Israel; Drink you, and be drunken, and spue, and fall, and rise no more, because of the sword which I will send among you.

| שלח 7971 | ביניכם 996: | 25:28 | והיה 1961 | כי 3588 | ימאנו 3985 | לקחת 3947 | הכוס 3563 | מידך 3027 | לשתות 8354 | ואמרת 559 |
|---|---|---|---|---|---|---|---|---|---|---|
| sholeach | beyneykem. | | uahayah, | kiy | yama'anu | lakachat | hakous | miyadaka | lishtout; | ua'amarta |
| **will send** | **among you** | | **And it shall be** | **if** | **they refuse** | **to take** | **the cup** | **at your hand** | **to drink** | **then shall you say** |

| אליהם 413 | כה 3541 | אמר 559 | יהוה 3068 | צבאות 6635 | שתו 8354 | תשתו 8354: | 25:29 | כי 3588 | הנה 2009 | בעיר 5892 | אשר 834 | נקרא 7121 | שמי 8034 |
|---|---|---|---|---|---|---|---|---|---|---|---|---|---|
| 'aleyhem, | koh | 'amar | Yahuah | tzaba'aut | shatou | tishtu. | | kiy | hineh | ba'ayr | 'asher | niqra' | shamiy |
| **unto them** | **Thus** | **saith** | **Yahuah** | **of hosts** | **shall certainly** | **You drink** | | **For** | **lo** | **on the city** | **which** | **is called** | **my name** |

| עליה 5921 | אנכי 595 | מחל 2490 | להרע 7489 | ואתם 859 | הנקה 5352 | תנקו 5352 | לא 3808 | תנקו 5352 |
|---|---|---|---|---|---|---|---|---|
| 'aleyha, | 'anokiy | mechel | lahara', | ua'atem | hinaqeh | tinaqu; | la' | tinaqu, |
| **by** | **I** | **begin** | **to bring evil** | **and you** | **should be utterly** | **you shall be unpunished?** | **not** | **you shall be unpunished** |

| כי 3588 | חרב 2719 | אני 589 | קרא 7121 | על 5921 | כל 3605 | ישבי 3427 | הארץ 776 | נאם 5002 | יהוה 3068 | צבאות 6635: | 25:30 | ואתה 859 |
|---|---|---|---|---|---|---|---|---|---|---|---|---|
| kiy | chereb, | 'aniy | qorea' | 'al | kal | yoshabey | ha'aretz, | na'am | Yahuah | tzaba'aut. | | ua'atah |
| **for** | **a sword** | **I** | **will call** | **upon** | **all** | **the inhabitants of** | **the earth** | **saith** | **Yahuah** | **of hosts** | | **Therefore you** |

| תנבא 5012 | אליהם 413 | את 853 | כל 3605 | הדברים 1697 | האלה 428 | ואמרת 559 | אליהם 413 | יהוה 3068 | ממרום 4791 | ישאג 7580 |
|---|---|---|---|---|---|---|---|---|---|---|
| tinabea' | 'aleyhem, | 'at | kal | hadabariym | ha'aeleh; | ua'amarta | 'aleyhem, | Yahuah | mimaroum | yish'ag |
| **prophesy** | **against them** | | **all** | **words** | **these** | **and say** | **unto them** | **Yahuah** | **from on high** | **shall roar** |

| וממעון 4583 | קדשו 6944 | יתן 5414 | קולו 6963 | שאג 7580 | ישאג 7580 | על 5921 | נוהו 5116 | הידד 1959 |
|---|---|---|---|---|---|---|---|---|
| uamima'aun | qadashou | yiten | qoulou, | sha'ag | yish'ag | 'al | nauehu, | heydad |
| **and from habitation** | **his holy** | **utter** | **his voice** | **he shall mightily** | **roar** | **upon** | **his habitation** | **a shout** |

| כדרכים 1869 | יענה 6030 | אל 413 | כל 3605 | ישבי 3427 | הארץ 776: | 25:31 | בא 935 | שאון 7588 | עד 5704 |
|---|---|---|---|---|---|---|---|---|---|
| kadorakiym | ya'aneh, | 'al | kal | yoshabey | ha'aretz. | | ba' | sha'aun | 'ad |
| **as they that tread *the grapes*** | **he shall give** | **against** | **all** | **the inhabitants of** | **the earth** | | **shall come *even*** | **A noise** | **to** |

| קצה 7097 | הארץ 776 | כי 3588 | ריב 7379 | ליהוה 3068 | בגוים 1471 | נשפט 8199 | הוא 1931 | לכל 3605 | בשר 1320 | הרשעים 7563 |
|---|---|---|---|---|---|---|---|---|---|---|
| qatzeh | ha'aretz, | kiy | riyb | laYahuah | bagouyim, | nishpat | hua' | lakal | basar; | harasha'aym |
| **the ends of** | **the earth** | **for *has*** | **a controversy** | **for Yahuah** | **with the nations** | **will plead** | **he** | **with all** | **flesh** | ***that are* wicked** |

| נתנם 5414 | לחרב 2719 | נאם 5002 | יהוה 3068: | 25:32 | כה 3541 | אמר 559 | יהוה 3068 | צבאות 6635 | הנה 2009 | רעה 7451 | יצאת 3318 |
|---|---|---|---|---|---|---|---|---|---|---|---|
| natanam | lachereb | na'am | Yahuah. | | koh | 'amar | Yahuah | tzaba'aut, | hineh | ra'ah | yatzea't |
| **he will give them** | **to the sword** | **saith** | **Yahuah** | | **Thus** | **saith** | **Yahuah** | **of hosts** | **Behold** | **evil** | **shall go forth** |

| מגוי 1471 | אל 413 | גוי 1471 | וסער 5591 | גדול 1419 | יעור 5782 | מירכתי 3411 | ארץ 776: | 25:33 | והיו 1961 |
|---|---|---|---|---|---|---|---|---|---|
| migouy | 'al | gouy; | uasa'ar | gadoul, | ya'aur | miyarkatey | 'aretz. | | uahayu |
| **from nation** | **to** | **nation** | **and a whirlwind** | **great** | **shall be raised up** | **from the coasts of** | **the earth** | | **And shall be** |

| חללי 2491 | יהוה 3068 | ביום 3117 | ההוא 1931 | מקצה 7097 | הארץ 776 | ועד 5704 | קצה 7097 | הארץ 776 | לא 3808 |
|---|---|---|---|---|---|---|---|---|---|
| challey | Yahuah | bayoum | hahua', | miqtzeh | ha'aretz | ua'ad | qatzeh | ha'aretz; | la' |
| **the slain of** | **Yahuah** | **at day** | **that** | **from *one* end of** | **the earth** | **even unto** | ***the other* end of** | **the earth** | **not** |

| יספדו 5594 | ולא 3808 | יאספו 622 | ולא 3808 | יקברו 6912 | לדמן 1828 | על 5921 | פני 6440 | האדמה 127 | יהיו 1961: | 25:34 | הילילו 3213 |
|---|---|---|---|---|---|---|---|---|---|---|---|
| yisapadu, | uala' | ye'asapu | uala' | yiqaberu, | ladomen | 'al | paney | ha'adamah | yihayu. | | heyliylu |
| **they shall be lamented** | **neither** | **gathered** | **nor** | **buried** | **dung** | **upon** | **suffaces of** | **the ground** | **they shall be** | | **Howl** |

Jer 25:28 And it shall be, if they refuse to take the cup at your hand to drink, then shall you say unto them, Thus saith YHUH of hosts; You shall certainly drink.29 For, lo, I begin to bring evil on the city which is called by my name, and should you be utterly unpunished? You shall not be unpunished: for I will call for a sword upon all the inhabitants of the earth, saith YHUH of hosts.30 Therefore prophesy you against them all these words, and say unto them, YHUH shall roar from on high, and utter his voice from his holy habitation; he shall mightily roar upon his habitation; he shall give a shout, as they that tread the grapes, against all the inhabitants of the earth.31 A noise shall come even to the ends of the earth; for YHUH has a controversy with the nations, he will plead with all flesh; he will give them that are wicked to the sword, saith YHUH.32 Thus saith YHUH of hosts, Behold, evil shall go forth from nation to nation, and a great whirlwind shall be raised up from the coasts of the earth.33 And the slain of YHUH shall be at that day from one end of the earth even unto the other end of the earth: they shall not be lamented, neither gathered, nor buried; they shall be dung upon the ground.

הרעים 7462 וזעקו 2199 והתפלשו 6428 אדירי 117 הצאן 6629 כי 3588 מלאו 4390 ימיכם 3117
haro'aym uaza'aqu, uahitpalshu 'adiyrey hatza'an, kiy mala'au yameykem
**you shepherds and cry and wallow yourselves *in the ashes* you principal of the flock for are accomplished the days of**

לטבוח 2873 ותפוצותיכם 8600 ונפלתם 5307 ככלי 3627 חמדה 2532: **25:35** ואבד 6 מנוס 4498 מן 4480
litabouach; uatapoutzoutiykem, uanpaltem kikliy chemdah. ua'abad manous min
**your slaughter and of your dispersions and you shall fall like a vessel pleasant And to flee shall have no way from**

הרעים 7462 ופליטה 6413 מאדירי 117 הצאן 6629: **25:36** קול 6963 צעקת 6818 הרעים 7462 ויללת 3215
haro'aym; uapleytah me'adiyrey hatza'an. qoul tza'aqat haro'aym, uiylalat
**the shepherds nor to escape the principal of the flock A voice of the cry of the shepherds and an howling of**

אדירי 117 הצאן 6629 כי 3588 שדד 7703 יהוה 3068 את 853 מרעיתם 4830: **25:37** ונדמו 1826 נאות 4999
'adiyrey hatza'an; kiy shoded Yahuah 'at mar'aytam. uanadamu na'aut
**the principal of the flock *shall be heard* for has spoiled Yahuah their pasture And are cut down habitations**

השלום 7965 מפני 6440 חרון 2740 אף 639 יהוה 3068: **25:38** עזב 5800 ככפיר 3715 סכו 5520 כי 3588 היתה 1961 ארצם 776
hashaloum; mipaney charoun 'ap Yahuah. 'azab kakapiyr sukou; kiy hayatah 'artzam
***the* peaceable because of *the* fierce anger of Yahuah He has forsaken as the lion his covert for is their land**

לשמה 8047 מפני 6440 חרון 2740 היונה 3238 ומפני 6440 חרון 2740 אפו 639:
lashamah, mipaney charoun hayounah, uamipaney charoun 'apou.
**desolate because of the fierceness of the oppressor and because of fierce his anger**

**Jer 26:1** בראשית 7225 ממלכות 4468 יהויקים 3079 בן 1121 יאשיהו 2977 מלך 4428 יהודה 3063 היה 1961 הדבר 1697 הזה 2088 מאת 853
bara'shiyt, mamlakut yahouyaqiym ben ya'shiyahu melek yahudah; hayah hadabar hazeh, me'at
**In the beginning of the reign of Jehoiakim the son of Josiah king of Judah came word this from**

יהוה 3068 לאמר 559: **26:2** כה 3541 אמר 559 יהוה 3068 עמד 5975 בחצר 2691 בית 1004 יהוה 3068 ודברת 1696 על 5921 כל 3605 ערי 5892
Yahuah lea'mor. koh 'amar Yahuah 'amod bachatzar beyt Yahuah uadibarta 'al kal 'arey
**Yahuah saying Thus saith Yahuah Stand in the court of house Yahuah's and speak unto all the cities of**

יהודה 3063 הבאים 935 להשתחות 7812 בית 1004 יהוה 3068 את 853 כל 3605 הדברים 1697 אשר 834 צויתיך 6680 לדבר 1696 אליהם 413
yahudah, haba'aym lahishtachauot beyt Yahuah, 'at kal hadabariym, 'asher tziuiytiyka ladaber 'aleyhem;
**Judah which come to worship in house Yahuah's all the words that I command you to speak unto them**

אל 408 תגרע 1639 דבר 1697: **26:3** אולי 194 ישמעו 8085 וישבו 7725 איש 376 מדרכו 1870 הרעה 7451 ונחמתי 5162 אל 413
'al tigra' dabar. 'aulay yishma'au, uayashubu 'aysh midarkou hara'ah; uanichamtiy 'al
**not diminish a word If so be they will listen and turn every man from way his evil way that I may repent me to**

הרעה 7451 אשר 834 אנכי 595 חשב 2803 לעשות 6213 להם 3807a מפני 6440 רע 7455 מעלליהם 4611: **26:4** ואמרת 559
hara'ah, 'asher 'anokiy chosheb la'asout lahem, mipaney roa' ma'alleyhem. ua'amarta
**of the evil which I purpose to do unto them because of the evil of their doings And you shall say**

אליהם 413 כה 3541 אמר 559 יהוה 3068 אם 518 לא 3808 תשמעו 8085 אלי 413 ללכת 1980 בתורתי 8451 אשר 834 נתתי 5414 לפניכם 6440:
'aleyhem, koh 'amar Yahuah; 'am la' tishma'au 'aelay, laleket batouratiy, 'asher natatiy lipneykem.
**unto them Thus saith Yahuah If not you will listen to me to walk in my law which I have set before you**

Jer 25:34 Howl, you shepherds, and cry; and wallow yourselves in the ashes, you principal of the flock: for the days of your slaughter and of your dispersions are accomplished; and you shall fall like a pleasant vessel.35 And the shepherds shall have no way to flee, nor the principal of the flock to escape.36 A voice of the cry of the shepherds, and an howling of the principal of the flock, shall be heard: for YHUH has spoiled their pasture.37 And the peaceable habitations are cut down because of the fierce anger of YHUH.38 He has forsaken his covert, as the lion: for their land is desolate because of the fierceness of the oppressor, and because of his fierce anger. **Jer** 26:1 In the beginning of the reign of Jehoiakim the son of Josiah king of Judah came this word from YHUH, saying,2 Thus saith YHUH; Stand in the court of YHUH's house, and speak unto all the cities of Judah, which come to worship in YHUH's house, all the words that I command you to speak unto them; diminish not a word:3 If so be they will hear, and turn every man from his evil way, that I may repent me of the evil, which I purpose to do unto them because of the evil of their doings.4 And you shall say unto them, Thus saith YHUH; If you will not hear to me, to walk in my law, which I have set before you,

**26:5**
לשמע 8085 על 5921 דברי 1697 עבדי 5650 הנבאים 5030 אשר 834 אנכי 595 שלח 7971 אליכם 413 והשכם 7925
lishmoa', 'al dibrey 'abaday hanabiy'aym, 'asher 'anokiy sholeach 'aleykem; uahashakem
**To listen to the words of my servants the prophets whom I sent unto you both rising up early**

ושלח 7971 ולא 3808 שמעתם 8085: **26:6** ונתתי 5414 את 853 הבית 1004 הזה 2088 כשלה 7887 ואת 853 העיר 5892
uashaloach uala' shama'tem. uanatatiy 'at habayit hazeh kashiloh; ua'at ha'ayr
**and sending *them* but not you have hearkened Then will I make house this like Shiloh *and* city**

הזאתה 2063 אתן 5414 לקללה 7045 לכל 3605 גויי 1471 הארץ 776: **26:7** וישמעו 8085 הכהנים 3548 והנבאים 5030 וכל 3605
haza'tah 'aten liqlalah, lakol gouyey ha'aretz. uayishma'au hakohaniym uahanabiy'aym uakal
**this will make a curse to all the nations of the earth So heard the priests and the prophets and all**

העם 5971 את 853 ירמיהו 3414 מדבר 1696 את 853 הדברים 1697 האלה 428 בבית 1004 יהוה 3068: **26:8** ויהי 1961
ha'am; 'at yirmayahu, madaber 'at hadabariym ha'aeleh babeyt Yahuah. uayahiy
**the people Jeremiah speaking words these in the house of Yahuah Now it came to pass**

ככלות 3615 ירמיהו 3414 לדבר 1696 את 853 כל 3605 אשר 834 צוה 6680 יהוה 3068 לדבר 1696 אל 413 כל 3605
kakalout yirmayahu, ladaber 'at kal 'asher tziuah Yahuah, ladaber 'al kal
**when had made an end Jeremiah of speaking all that had commanded Yahuah *him* to speak unto all**

העם 5971 ויתפשו 8610 אתו 853 הכהנים 3548 והנבאים 5030 וכל 3605 העם 5971 לאמר 559 מות 4191 תמות 4191: **26:9** מדוע 4069
ha'am; uayitpasu 'atou hakohaniym uahanabiy'aym uakal ha'am lea'mor mout tamut. madua'
**the people that took him the priests and the prophets and all the people saying You shall surely die Why**

נבית 5012 בשם 8034 יהוה 3068 לאמר 559 כשלו 7887 יהיה 1961 הבית 1004 הזה 2088 והעיר 5892 הזאת 2063 תחרב 2717
nibeyta bashem Yahuah lea'mor, kashilou yihayeh habayit hazeh, uaha'ayr haza't techarab
**have you prophesied in the name of Yahuah saying like Shiloh shall be house This and city this shall be desolate**

מאין 369 יושב 3427 ויקהל 6950 כל 3605 העם 5971 אל 413 ירמיהו 3414 בבית 1004 יהוה 3068: **26:10** וישמעו 8085
me'ayn yousheb; uayiqahel kal ha'am 'al yirmayahu babeyt Yahuah. uayishma'au
**without an inhabitant? And were gathered all the people against Jeremiah in the house of Yahuah When heard**

שרי 8269 יהודה 3063 את 853 הדברים 1697 האלה 428 ויעלו 5927 מבית 1004 המלך 4428 בית 1004 יהוה 3068
sarey yahudah, 'at hadabariym ha'aeleh, uaya'alu mibeyt hamelek beyt Yahuah;
**the princes of Judah things these then they came up from house of the king's unto the house of Yahuah**

וישבו 3427 בפתח 6607 שער 8179 יהוה 3068 החדש 2319: **26:11** ויאמרו 559 הכהנים 3548 והנבאים 5030 אל 413
uayeshabu bapetach sha'ar Yahuah hechadash. uaya'maru hakohaniym uahanabiy'aym 'al
**and sat down in the entry of gate of Yahuah's *house* the new Then spoke the priests and the prophets unto**

השרים 8269 ואל 413 כל 3605 העם 5971 לאמר 559 משפט 4941 מות 4194 לאיש 376 הזה 2088 כי 3588 נבא 5012 אל 413 העיר 5892
hasariym, ua'al kal ha'am lea'mor; mishapat mauet la'aysh hazeh, kiy niba' 'al ha'ayr
**the princes and to all the people saying *is* worthy to die man This for he has prophesied against city**

הזאת 2063 כאשר 834 שמעתם 8085 באזניכם 241: **26:12** ויאמר 559 ירמיהו 3414 אל 413 כל 3605 השרים 8269 ואל 413 כל 3605
haza't, ka'asher shama'tem ba'azaneykem. uaya'mer yirmayahu 'al kal hasariym, ua'al kal
**this as you have heard with your ears Then spoke Jeremiah unto to all the princes and to all**

Jer 26:5 To hear to the words of my servants the prophets, whom I sent unto you, both rising up early, and sending them, but you have not hearkened;6 Then will I make this house like Shiloh, and will make this city a curse to all the nations of the earth.7 So the priests and the prophets and all the people heard Jeremiah speaking these words in the house of YHUH.8 Now it came to pass, when Jeremiah had made an end of speaking all that YHUH had commanded him to speak unto all the people, that the priests and the prophets and all the people took him, saying, Thou shall surely die.9 Why have you prophesied in the name of YHUH, saying, This house shall be like Shiloh, and this city shall be desolate without an inhabitant? And all the people were gathered against Jeremiah in the house of YHUH.10 When the princes of Judah heard these things, then they came up from the king's house unto the house of YHUH, and sat down in the entry of the new gate of YHUH's house.11 Then spoke the priests and the prophets unto the princes and to all the people, saying, This man is worthy to die; for he has prophesied against this city, as you have heard with your ears.12 Then spoke Jeremiah unto all the princes and to all the people, saying, YHUH sent me to prophesy against this house and against this city all the words that you have heard.

העם 5971 לאמר 559 יהוה 3068 שלחני 7971 להנבא 5012 אל 413 הבית 1004 הזה 2088 ואל 413 העיר 5892 הזאת 2063 את 853 כל 3605
ha'am lea'mor; Yahuah shalachaniy, lahinabea' 'al habayit hazeh ua'al ha'ayr haza't, 'at kal
**the people saying Yahuah sent me to prophesy against house this and against city this all**

26:13
הדברים 1697 אשר 834 שמעתם 8085: ועתה 6258 היטיבו 3190 דרכיכם 1870 ומעלליכם 4611 ושמעו 8085 בקול 6963
hadabariym 'asher shama'tem. ua'atah, heytiybu darkeykem uama'alleykem, uashim'au baqoul
**the words that you have heard Therefore now amend your ways and your doings and obey the voice of**

26:14
יהוה 3068 אלהיכם 430 וינחם 5162 יהוה 3068 אל 413 הרעה 7451 אשר 834 דבר 1697 עליכם 5921: ואני 589
Yahuah 'aloheykem; uayinachem Yahuah, 'al hara'ah, 'asher diber 'aleykem. ua'aniy
**Yahuah your Elohim and will repent him Yahuah of the evil that he has pronounced against you As for me**

26:15
הנני 2005 בידכם 3027 עשו 6213 לי 3807a כטוב 2896 וכישר 3477 בעיניכם 5869: אך 389 ידע 3045 תדעו 3045 כי 3588
hinniy bayedkem; 'asu liy katoub uakayashar ba'aeyneykem. 'ak yadoa' teda'au, kiy
**behold I *am* in your hand do with me as seems good and meet unto you But know you for certain that**

אם 518 ממתים 4191 אתם 859 אתי 853 כי 3588 דם 1818 נקי 5355 אתם 859 נתנים 5414 עליכם 5921 ואל 413 העיר 5892 הזאת 2063
'am mamiytiym 'atem 'atiy kiy dam naqiy, 'atem notaniym 'aleykem, ua'al ha'ayr haza't
**if put to death you me surely blood innocent you shall bring upon yourselves and upon city this**

ואל 413 ישביה 3427 כי 3588 באמת 571 שלחני 7971 יהוה 3068 עליכם 5921 לדבר 1696 באזניכם 241 את 853 כל 3605
ua'al yoshabeyha; kiy be'amet, shalachaniy Yahuah 'aleykem, ladaber ba'azaneykem, 'at kal
**and upon the inhabitants thereof for of a truth has sent me Yahuah unto you to speak in your ears all**

26:16
הדברים 1697 האלה 428: ויאמרו 559 השרים 8269 וכל 3605 העם 5971 אל 413 הכהנים 3548 ואל 413 הנביאים 5030 אין 369 לאיש 376
hadabariym ha'aeleh. uaya'maru hasariym uakal ha'am, 'al hakohaniym ua'al hanabiy'aym; 'aeyn la'aysh
**words these Then said the princes and all the people unto the priests and to the prophets *is* not man**

26:17
הזה 2088 משפט 4941 מות 4194 כי 3588 בשם 8034 יהוה 3069 אלהינו 430 דבר 1696 אלינו 413: ויקמו 6965 אנשים 582
hazeh mishapat mauet, kiy, bashem Yahuah 'aloheynu diber 'aleynu. uayaqumu 'anashiym,
**This worthy to die for in the name of Yahuah our Elohim he has spoken to us Then rose up certain**

26:18
מזקני 2205 הארץ 776 ויאמרו 559 אל 413 כל 3605 קהל 6951 העם 5971 לאמר 559: מיכיה 4320 המורשתי 4183 היה 1961
miziqney ha'aretz; uaya'maru, 'al kal qahal ha'am lea'mor. miykayah hamourashtiy, hayah
**of the elders of the land and spoke to all the assembly of the people saying Micah the Morasthite will be**

נבא 5012 בימי 3117 חזקיהו 2396 מלך 4428 יהודה 3063 ויאמר 559 אל 413 כל 3605 עם 5971 יהודה 3063 לאמר 559 כה 3541 אמר 559
niba', biymey chizqiyahu melek yahudah; uaya'mer 'al kal 'am yahudah lea'mor koh 'amar
**prophesied in the days of Hezekiah king of Judah and spoke to all the people of Judah saying Thus saith**

יהוה 3068 צבאות 6635 ציון 6726 שדה 7704 תחרש 2790 וירושלים 3389 עיים 5856 תהיה 1961 והר 2022 הבית 1004
Yahuah tzaba'aut, tziyoun sadeh techaresh uiyarushalayim 'ayiym tihayeh, uahar habayit
**Yahuah of hosts Zion *like* a field shall be plowed and Jerusalem heaps shall become and the mountain of the house**

26:19
לבמות 1116 יער 3293: ההמת 4191 המתהו 4191 חזקיהו 2396 מלך 4428 יהודה 3063 וכל 3605 יהודה 3063 הלא 3808
labamout ya'ar. hehamet hemituhu chizqiyahu melek yahudah uakal yahudah, hala'
**as the high places of a forest Did to death? put him at all Hezekiah king of Judah and all Judah not**

Jer 26:13 Therefore now amend your ways and your doings, and obey the voice of YHUH your G-d; and YHUH will repent him of the evil that he has pronounced against you.14 As for me, behold, I am in your hand: do with me as seem good and meet unto you.15 But know you for certain, that if you put me to death, you shall surely bring innocent blood upon yourselves, and upon this city, and upon the inhabitants thereof: for of a truth YHUH has sent me unto you to speak all these words in your ears.16 Then said the princes and all the people unto the priests and to the prophets; This man is not worthy to die: for he has spoken to us in the name of YHUH our G-d.17 Then rose up certain of the elders of the land, and spoke to all the assembly of the people, saying,18 Micah the Morasthite prophesied in the days of Hezekiah king of Judah, and spoke to all the people of Judah, saying, Thus saith YHUH of hosts; Zion shall be plowed like a field, and Jerusalem shall become heaps, and the mountains of the house as the high places of a forest.19 Did Hezekiah king of Judah and all Judah put him at all to death? did he not fear YHUH, and besought YHUH, and YHUH repented him of the evil which he had pronounced against them? Thus might we procure great evil against our souls.

| ירא 3373 | את 853 | יהוה 3068 | ויחל 2470 | את 853 | פני 6440 | יהוה 3068 | וינחם 5162 | יהוה 3068 | אל 413 | הרעה 7451 | אשר 834 |
|---|---|---|---|---|---|---|---|---|---|---|---|
| yarea' | 'at | Yahuah | uayachal | 'at | paney | Yahuah, | uayinachem | Yahuah, | 'al | hara'ah | 'asher |
| **did he fear** | | **Yahuah** | **and besought** | | **the favor** | **Yahuah** | **and repented him** | **Yahuah** | **of** | **the evil** | **which** |

| דבר 1696 | עליהם 5921 | ואנחנו 587 | עשים 6213 | רעה 7451 | גדולה 1419 | על 5921 | נפשותינו 5315: | **26:20** | וגם 1571 | איש 376 |
|---|---|---|---|---|---|---|---|---|---|---|
| diber | 'aleyhem; | ua'anachnu, | 'asiym | ra'ah | gadoulah | 'al | napshouteynu. | | uagam | 'aysh, |
| **he had pronounced** | **against them?** | **Thus we** | **might procure** | **evil** | **great** | **against** | **our souls** | | **And also** | **a man** |

| היה 1961 | מתנבא 5012 | בשם 8034 | יהוה 3068 | אוריהו 223 | בן 1121 | שמעיהו 8089 | מקרית 7157 | היערים 3293 | ויבנא 5012 |
|---|---|---|---|---|---|---|---|---|---|
| hayah | mitnabea' | bashem | Yahuah, | 'auriyahu | ben | shama'yahu, | miqiryat | haya'ariym; | uayinabea' |
| **there was** | **that prophesied** | **in the name of** | **Yahuah** | **Urijah** | **the son of** | **Shemaiah** | **of Kirjath** | **jearim** | **who prophesied** |

| על 5921 | העיר 5892 | הזאת 2063 | ועל 5921 | הארץ 776 | הזאת 2063 | ככל 3605 | דברי 1697 | ירמיהו 3414: | **26:21** | וישמע 8085 |
|---|---|---|---|---|---|---|---|---|---|---|
| 'al | ha'ayr | haza't | ua'al | ha'aretz | haza't, | kakol | dibrey | yirmayahu. | | uayishma' |
| **against** | **city** | **this** | **and against** | **the land** | **this** | **according to all** | **the words of** | **Jeremiah** | | **And when heard** |

| המלך 4428 | יהויקים 3079 | וכל 3605 | גבוריו 1368 | וכל 3605 | השרים 8269 | את 853 | דבריו 1697 | ויבקש 1245 | המלך 4428 | המיתו 4191 |
|---|---|---|---|---|---|---|---|---|---|---|
| hamelek | yahouyaqiym | uakal | gibourayu | uakal | hasariym | 'at | dabarayu, | uaybaqesh | hamelek | hamiytou; |
| **the king** | **Jehoiakim** | **with all** | **his mighty men** | **and all** | **the princes** | | **his words** | **and sought** | **the king** | **to put him to death** |

| וישמע 8085 | אוריהו 223 | וירא 3372 | ויברח 1272 | ויבא 935 | מצרים 4714: | **26:22** | וישלח 7971 | המלך 4428 | יהויקים 3079 |
|---|---|---|---|---|---|---|---|---|---|
| uayishma' | 'auriyahu | uayira', | uayibrach | uayaba' | mitzrayim. | | uayishlach | hamelek | yahouyaqiym |
| **when heard *it*** | **Urijah** | **but he was afraid** | **and fled** | **and went into** | **Egypt** | | **And sent into** | **the king** | **Jehoiakim** |

| אנשים 582 | מצרים 4714 | את 853 | אלנתן 494 | בן 1121 | עכבור 5907 | ואנשים 582 | אתו 854 | אל 413 | מצרים 4714: | **26:23** |
|---|---|---|---|---|---|---|---|---|---|---|
| 'anashiym | mitzrayim; | 'at | 'alnatan | ben | akbour | ua'anashiym | 'atou | 'al | mitzrayim. | |
| **men** | **Egypt** | | ***namely* Elnathan** | **the son of** | **Achbor** | **and certain men** | **with him** | **into** | **Egypt** | |

| ויוציאו 3318 | את 853 | אוריהו 223 | ממצרים 4714 | ויבאהו 935 | אל 413 | המלך 4428 | יהויקים 3079 | ויכהו 5221 |
|---|---|---|---|---|---|---|---|---|
| uayoutziy'au | 'at | 'auriyahu | mimitzrayim, | uayabi'ahu | 'al | hamelek | yahouyaqiym, | uayakehu |
| **And they fetched forth** | | **Urijah** | **out of Egypt** | **and brought him** | **unto** | **the king** | **Jehoiakim** | **who slew him** |

| בחרב 2719 | וישלך 7993 | את 853 | נבלתו 5038 | אל 413 | קברי 6913 | בני 1121 | העם 5971: | **26:24** | אך 389 | יד 3027 |
|---|---|---|---|---|---|---|---|---|---|---|
| bechareb; | uayashlek | 'at | niblatou, | 'al | qibrey | baney | ha'am. | | 'ach, | yad |
| **with the sword** | **and cast** | | **his dead body** | **into** | **the graves of** | **common** | **the people** | | **Nevertheless** | **the hand of** |

| אחיקם 296 | בן 1121 | שפן 8227 | היתה 1961 | את 854 | ירמיהו 3414 | לבלתי 1115 | תת 5414 | אתו 853 | ביד 3027 | העם 5971 |
|---|---|---|---|---|---|---|---|---|---|---|
| 'achiyqam | ben | shapan, | hayatah | 'at | yirmayahu; | labiltiy | tet | 'atou | bayad | ha'am |
| **Ahikam** | **the son of** | **Shaphan** | **was *with*** | | **Jeremiah** | **that not** | **they should give** | **him** | **into the hand of** | **the people** |

| להמיתו 4191: |
|---|
| lahamiytou. |
| **to put him to death** |

| **Jer 27:1** | בראשית 7225 | ממלכת 4467 | יהויקים 3079 | בן 1121 | יאושיהו 2977 | מלך 4428 | יהודה 3063 | היה 1961 | הדבר 1697 | הזה 2088 | אל 413 |
|---|---|---|---|---|---|---|---|---|---|---|---|
| | bara'shiyt, | mamleket | yahouyaqiym | ben | ya'shiyahu | melek | yahudah; | hayah | hadabar | hazeh | 'al |
| | **In the beginning of** | **the reign of** | **Jehoiakim** | **the son of** | **Josiah** | **king of** | **Judah** | **came** | **word** | **this** | **unto** |

Jer 26:20 And there was also a man that prophesied in the name of YHUH, Urijah the son of Shemaiah of Kirjath-jearim, who prophesied against this city and against this land
according to all the words of Jeremiah:21 And when Jehoiakim the king, with all his mighty men, and all the princes, heard his words, the king sought to put him to death: but
when Urijah heard it, he was afraid, and fled, and went into Egypt;22 And Jehoiakim the king sent men into Egypt, namely, Elnathan the son of Achbor, and certain men with
him into Egypt.23 And they fetched forth Urijah out of Egypt, and brought him unto Jehoiakim the king; who slew him with the sword, and cast his dead body into the graves
of the common people.24 Nevertheless the hand of Ahikam the son of Shaphan was with Jeremiah, that they should not give him into the hand of the people to put him to
death. **Jer** 27:1 In the beginning of the reign of Jehoiakim the son of Josiah king of Judah came this word unto Jeremiah from YHUH, saying,

ירמיה 3414 מאת 853 יהוה 3069 לאמר 559: 27:2 כה 3541 אמר 559 יהוה 3068 אלי 413 עשה 6213 לך 3807a מוסרות 4147 ומטות 4133 ונתתם 5414 על 5921
yirmayah, me'at Yahuah lea'mor. koh 'amar Yahuah 'aelay, 'aseh laka, mouserout uamotout; uantatam 'al
**Jeremiah from Yahuah saying Thus saith Yahuah to me Make to you bonds and yokes and put them upon**

צוארך 6677: 27:3 ושלחתם 7971 אל 413 מלך 4428 אדום 123 ואל 413 מלך 4428 מואב 4124 ואל 413 מלך 4428 בני 1121 עמון 5983
tzaua'reka. uashilachtam 'al melek 'adoum ua'al melek mou'ab, ua'al melek baney 'amoun,
**your neck And send them to the king of Edom and to the king of Moab and to the king of the sons of Ammon**

ואל 413 מלך 4428 צר 6865 ואל 413 מלך 4428 צידון 6721 ביד 3027 מלאכים 4397 הבאים 935 ירושלם 3389 אל 413
ua'al melek tzor ua'al melek tziydoun; bayad mal'akiym haba'aym yarushalaim, 'al
**and to the king of Tyrus and to the king of Zidon by the hand of the messengers which come to Jerusalem unto**

צדקיהו 6667 מלך 4428 יהודה 3063: 27:4 וצוית 6680 אתם 853 אל 413 אדניהם 113 לאמר 559 כה 3541 אמר 559 יהוה 3068 צבאות 6635
tzidqiyahu melek yahudah. uatziuiyta 'atam, 'al 'adoneyhem lea'mor; koh 'amar Yahuah tzaba'aut
**Zedekiah king of Judah And command them unto their masters to say Thus saith Yahuah of hosts**

אלהי 430 ישראל 3478 כה 3541 תאמרו 559 אל 413 אדניכם 113: 27:5 אנכי 595 עשיתי 6213 את 853 הארץ 776 את 853 האדם 120 ואת 853
'alohey yisra'ael, koh ta'maru 'al 'adoneykem. 'anokiy 'asiytiy 'at ha'aretz, 'at ha'adam ua'at
**the Elohim of Israel Thus shall you say unto your masters I have made the earth the man *and***

הבהמה 929 אשר 834 על 5921 פני 6440 הארץ 776 בכחי 3581 הגדול 1419 ובזרועי 2220 הנטויה 5186 ונתתיה 5414
habehemah 'asher 'al paney ha'aretz, bakochiy hagadoul, uabizrou'ay hanatuyah; uantatiyha
**the beast that *are* upon suffaces of the ground by my power great and by my arm outstretched and have given it**

לאשר 834 ישר 3474 בעיני 5869: 27:6 ועתה 6258 אנכי 595 נתתי 5414 את 853 כל 3605 הארצות 776 האלה 428 ביד 3027
la'asher yashar ba'aeynay. ua'atah, 'anokiy natatiy 'at kal ha'aratzout ha'aeleh, bayad
**unto whom meet it seemed unto me And now I have given all lands these into the hand of**

נבוכדנאצר 5019 מלך 4428 בבל 894 עבדי 5650 וגם 1571 את 853 חית 2416 השדה 7704 נתתי 5414 לו 3807a
unabukadra'tzar melek babel 'abdiy; ua'gam 'at chayat hasadeh, natatiy lou'
**Nebuchadnezzar the king of Babylon my servant and also the beasts of the field have I given him**

לעבדו 5647: 27:7 ועבדו 5647 אתו 853 כל 3605 הגוים 1471 ואת 853 בנו 1121 ואת 853 בן 1121 בנו 1121 עד 5704 בא 935
la'abadou. ua'abadu 'atou kal hagouyim, ua'at banou ua'at ben banou; 'ad ba'
**to serve him And shall serve him all nations *and* his son *and* his son's son until come**

עת 6256 ארצו 776 גם 1571 הוא 1931 ועבדו 5647 בו 871a גוים 1471 רבים 7227 ומלכים 4428 גדלים 1419: 27:8
'at artzou gam hua', ua'abadu bou gouyim rabiym, uamalakiym gadoliym.
***the very* time of his land then he and shall serve themselves of him nations many and kings great**

והיה 1961 הגוי 1471 והממלכה 4467 אשר 834 לא 3808 יעבדו 5647 אתו 853 את 853 נבוכדנאצר 5019
uahayah hagouy uahamamlakah, 'asher la' ya'abadu 'atou 'at unabukadra'tzar
**And it shall come to pass *that* the nation and kingdom which not will serve the same Nebuchadnezzar**

מלך 4428 בבל 894 ואת 853 אשר 834 לא 3808 יתן 5414 את 853 צוארו 6677 בעל 5923 מלך 4428 בבל 894 בחרב 2719
melek babel, ua'at 'asher la' yiten 'at tzaua'rou, ba'al melek babel; bachereb
**the king of Babylon *and* that not will put their neck under the yoke of the king of Babylon with the sword**

Jer 27:2 Thus saith YHUH to me; Make you bonds and yokes, and put them upon your neck,3 And send them to the king of Edom, and to the king of Moab, and to the king of the Ammonites, and to the king of Tyrus, and to the king of Zidon, by the hand of the messengers which come to Jerusalem unto Zedekiah king of Judah;4 And command them to say unto their masters, Thus saith YHUH of hosts, the G-d of Israel; Thus shall you say unto your masters;5 I have made the earth, the man and the beast that are upon the ground, by my great power and by my outstretched arm, and have given it unto whom it seemed meet unto me.6 And now have I given all these lands unto the hand of Nebuchadnezzar the king of Babylon, my servant; and the beasts of the field have I given him also to serve him.7 And all nations shall serve him, and his son, and his son's son, until the very time of his land come: and then many nations and great kings shall serve themselves of him.8 And it shall come to pass, that the nation and kingdom which will not serve the same Nebuchadnezzar the king of Babylon, and that will not put their neck under the yoke of the king of Babylon, that nation will I punish, saith YHUH, with the sword, and with the famine, and with the pestilence, until I have consumed them by his hand.

| ובערב 7458 | ובדבר 1698 | אפקד 6485 | על 5921 | הגוי 1471 | ההוא 1931 | נאם 5002 | יהוה 3068 | עד 5704 | תמי 8552 |
|---|---|---|---|---|---|---|---|---|---|
| uabara'ab | uabadber | 'apqod | 'al | hagouy | hahua' | na'am | Yahuah, | 'ad | tumiy |
| **and with the famine** | **and with the pestilence** | **will I punish** | **on** | **nation** | **that** | **saith** | **Yahuah** | **until** | **I have consumed** |

| אתם 853 | בידו 3027: | 27:9 ואתם 859 | אל 408 | תשמעו 8085 | אל 413 | נביאיכם 5030 | ואל 413 | קסמיכם 7080 | ואל 413 | חלמתיכם 2472 |
|---|---|---|---|---|---|---|---|---|---|---|
| 'atam | bayadou. | ua'atem | 'al | tishma'au | 'al | nabiy'aeykem | ua'al | qosameykem, | ua'ael | chalomoteykem, |
| **them** | **by his hand** | **Therefore you** | **not** | **listen** | **to** | **your prophets** | **nor to** | **your diviners** | **nor to** | **your dreamers** |

| ואל 413 | ענניכם 6049 | ואל 413 | כשפיכם 3786 | אשר 834 | הם 1992 | אמרים 559 | אליכם 413 | לאמר 559 | לא 3808 | תעבדו 5647 | את 853 |
|---|---|---|---|---|---|---|---|---|---|---|---|
| ua'al | 'ananeykem | ua'al | kashapeykem; | 'asher | hem | 'amariym | 'aleykem | lea'mor, | la' | ta'abdu | 'at |
| **nor to** | **your enchanters** | **nor to** | **your sorcerers** | **which** | **they** | **speak** | **unto you** | **saying** | **not** | **You shall serve** | |

| מלך 4428 | בבל 894: | 27:10 כי 3588 | שקר 8267 | הם 1992 | נבאים 5012 | לכם 3807a | למען 4616 | הרחיק 7368 | אתכם 853 | מעל 5921 | אדמתכם 127 |
|---|---|---|---|---|---|---|---|---|---|---|---|
| melek | babel. | kiy | sheqer, | hem | nabi'aym | lakem; | lama'an | harchiyq | 'atkem | me'al | 'admatkem, |
| **the king of** | **Babylon** | **For** | **a lie** | **they** | **prophesy** | **unto you** | **to** | **remove far** | **you** | **from** | **your land** |

| והדחתי 5080 | אתכם 853 | ואבדתם 6: | 27:11 והגוי 1471 | אשר 834 | יביא 935 | את 853 | צוארו 6677 |
|---|---|---|---|---|---|---|---|
| uahidachtiy | 'atkem | ua'abadtem. | uahagouy, | 'asher | yabiy'a | 'at | tzaua'rou |
| **and that I should drive out** | **you** | **and you should perish** | **But the nations** | **that** | **bring** | | **their neck** |

| בעל 5923 | מלך 4428 | בבל 894 | ועבדו 5647 | והנחתיו 3240 | על 5921 | אדמתו 127 | נאם 5002 | יהוה 3068 |
|---|---|---|---|---|---|---|---|---|
| ba'al | melek | babel | ua'abadou; | uahinachtiyu | 'al | 'admatou | na'am | Yahuah, |
| **under the yoke of** | **the king of** | **Babylon** | **and serve him** | **those will I let remain still** | **in** | **their own land** | **saith** | **Yahuah** |

| ועבדה 5647 | וישב 3427 | בה 871a: | 27:12 ואל 413 | צדקיה 6667 | מלך 4428 | יהודה 3063 | דברתי 1696 | ככל 3605 | הדברים 1697 |
|---|---|---|---|---|---|---|---|---|---|
| ua'abadah | uayashab | bah. | ua'al | tzidqiyah | melek | yahudah | dibartiy, | kakal | hadabariym |
| **and they shall till it** | **and dwell** | **therein** | **also to** | **Zedekiah** | **king of** | **Judah** | **I spoke** | **according to all** | **words** |

| האלה 428 | לאמר 559 | הביאו 935 | את 853 | צואריכם 6677 | בעל 5923 | מלך 4428 | בבל 894 | ועבדו 5647 | אתו 853 | ועמו 5971 |
|---|---|---|---|---|---|---|---|---|---|---|
| ha'aeleh | lea'mor; | habiy'au | 'at | tzaua'reykem | ba'al | melek | babel, | ua'abdu | 'atou | ua'amou |
| **these** | **saying** | **Bring** | | **your necks** | **under the yoke of** | **the king of** | **Babylon** | **and serve** | **him** | **and his people** |

| וחיו 2421: | 27:13 למה 4100 | תמותו 4191 | אתה 859 | ועמך 5971 | בחרב 2719 | ברעב 7458 | ובדבר 1698 | כאשר 834 |
|---|---|---|---|---|---|---|---|---|
| uichayu. | lamah | tamutu | 'atah | ua'ameka, | bachereb | bara'ab | uabadaber | ka'asher |
| **and live** | **Why** | **will you die** | **you** | **and your people** | **by the sword** | **by the famine** | **and by the pestilence** | **as** |

| דבר 1696 | יהוה 3068 | אל 413 | הגוי 1471 | אשר 834 | לא 3808 | יעבד 5647 | את 853 | מלך 4428 | בבל 894: | 27:14 ואל 408 | תשמעו 8085 | אל 413 |
|---|---|---|---|---|---|---|---|---|---|---|---|---|
| diber | Yahuah, | 'al | hagouy | 'asher | la' | ya'abod | 'at | melek | babel. | ua'al | tishma'au | 'al |
| **has spoken** | **Yahuah** | **against** | **the nation** | **that** | **not** | **will serve** | | **the king of** | **Babel?** | **Therefore not** | **listen** | **unto** |

| דברי 1697 | הנבאים 5030 | האמרים 559 | אליכם 413 | לאמר 559 | לא 3808 | תעבדו 5647 | את 853 | מלך 4428 | בבל 894 | כי 3588 | שקר 8267 |
|---|---|---|---|---|---|---|---|---|---|---|---|
| dibrey | hanabiy'aym, | ha'amariym | 'aleykem | lea'mor, | la' | ta'abdu | 'at | melek | babel; | kiy | sheqer, |
| **the words of** | **the prophets** | **that speak** | **unto you** | **saying** | **not** | **You shall serve** | | **the king of** | **Babylon** | **for** | **a lie** |

| הם 1992 | נבאים 5012 | לכם 3807a: | 27:15 כי 3588 | לא 3808 | שלחתים 7971 | נאם 5002 | יהוה 3068 | והם 1992 | נבאים 5012 | בשמי 8034 |
|---|---|---|---|---|---|---|---|---|---|---|
| hem | nabi'aym | lakem. | kiy | la' | shalachtiym | na'am | Yahuah, | uahem | nabi'aym | bishmiy |
| **they** | **prophesy** | **unto you** | **For** | **not** | **I have sent them** | **saith** | **Yahuah** | **yet they** | **prophesy** | **in my name** |

Jer 27:9 Therefore hear not you to your prophets, nor to your diviners, nor to your dreamers, nor to your enchanters, nor to your sorcerers, which speak unto you, saying, You shall not serve the king of Babylon:10 For they prophesy a lie unto you, to remove you far from your land; and that I should drive you out, and you should perish.11 But the nations that bring their neck under the yoke of the king of Babylon, and serve him, those will I let remain still in their own land, saith YHUH; and they shall till it, and dwell therein.12 I spoke also to Zedekiah king of Judah according to all these words, saying, Bring your necks under the yoke of the king of Babylon, and serve him and his people, and live.13 Why will you die, you and your people, by the sword, by the famine, and by the pestilence, as YHUH has spoken against the nation that will not serve the king of Babylon?14 Therefore hear not unto the words of the prophets that speak unto you, saying, You shall not serve the king of Babylon: for they prophesy a lie unto you.15 For I have not sent them, saith YHUH, yet they prophesy a lie in my name; that I might drive you out, and that you might perish, you, and the prophets that prophesy unto you.

לשקר 8267 למען 4616 הדיחי 5080 אתכם 853 ואבדתם 6 אתם 859 והנבאים 5030 הנבאים 5012 לכם 3807a: 27:16
lashaqer; lama'an hadiychiy 'atkem ua'abadtem, 'atem uahanabiy'aym hanaba'aym lakem.
**a lie that I might drive out you and that might you perish you and the prophets that prophesy unto you**

ואל 413 הכהנים 3548 ואל 413 כל 3605 העם 5971 הזה 2088 דברתי 1696 לאמר 559 כה 3541 אמר 559 יהוה 3068 אל 408 תשמעו 8085 אל 413
ua'al hakohaniym ua'al kal ha'am hazeh dibartiy lea'mor, koh 'amar Yahuah 'al tishma'au 'al
**Also to the priests and to all the people this I spoke saying Thus saith Yahuah not Hearken to**

דברי 1697 נביאיכם 5030 הנבאים 5012 לכם 3807a לאמר 559 הנה 2009 כלי 3627 בית 1004 יהוה 3068 מושבים 7725
dibrey nabiy'aeykem, hanaba'aym lakem lea'mor, hineh kaley beyt Yahuah mushabiym
**the words of your prophets that prophesy unto you saying Behold the vessels of house Yahuah's shall be brought again**

מבבלה 894 עתה 6258 מהרה 4120 כי 3588 שקר 8267 המה 1992 נבאים 5012 לכם 3807a: 27:17 אל 408 תשמעו 8085 אליהם 413 עבדו 5647 את 853
mibabelah 'atah maherah; kiy sheqer, hemah naba'aym lakem. 'al tishma'au 'aleyhem, 'abdu 'at
**from Babylon now shortly for a lie they prophesy unto you not Hearken unto them serve**

מלך 4428 בבל 894 וחיו 2421 למה 4100 תהיה 1961 העיר 5892 הזאת 2063 חרבה 2723: 27:18 ואם 518 נבאים 5030 הם 1992 ואם 518 יש 3426
melek babel uachyu; lamah tihayeh ha'ayr haza't charabah. ua'am nabi'aym hem, ua'am yesh
**the king of Babylon and live wherefore should be city this laid waste? But if *be* prophets they and if be**

דבר 1697 יהוה 3068 אתם 854 יפגעו 6293 נא 4994 ביהוה 3068 צבאות 6635 לבלתי 1115 באו 935 הכלים 3627
dabar Yahuah 'atam; yipga'au naa' baYahuah tzaba'aut, labiltiy bo'au hakeliym
**the word of Yahuah with them let them make intercession now to Yahuah of hosts that not go the vessels**

הנותרים 3498 בבית 1004 יהוה 3068 ובית 1004 מלך 4428 יהודה 3063 ובירושלם 3389 בבלה 894: 27:19 כי 3588
hanoutariym babeyt Yahuah uabeyt melek yahudah uabiyarushalaim babelah. kiy
**which are left in the house of Yahuah and *in* the house of the king of Judah and at Jerusalem to Babylon For**

כה 3541 אמר 559 יהוה 3068 צבאות 6635 אל 413 העמדים 5982 ועל 5921 הים 3220 ועל 5921 המכנות 4350
koh 'amar Yahuah tzaba'aut, 'al ha'amudiym, ua'al hayam ua'al hamakonout;
**thus saith Yahuah of hosts concerning the pillars and concerning the sea and concerning the bases**

ועל 5921 יתר 3499 הכלים 3627 הנותרים 3498 בעיר 5892 הזאת 2063: 27:20 אשר 834 לא 3808 לקחם 3947 נבוכדנאצר 5019
ua'al yeter hakeliym, hanoutariym ba'ayr haza't. 'asher la' laqacham, unabukadra'tzar
**and concerning the residue of the vessels that remain in city this Which not took Nebuchadnezzar**

מלך 4428 בבל 894 בגלותו 1540 את 853 יכוניה 3204 בן 1121 יהויקים 3079 מלך 4428 יהודה 3063 מירושלם 3389
melek babel, bagaloutou 'at yakaunyah ben yahouyaqiym melek yahudah miyarushalaim
**king of Babylon when he carried away captive Jeconiah the son of Jehoiakim king of Judah from Jerusalem**

בבלה 894 ואת 853 כל 3605 חרי 2715 יהודה 3063 וירושלם 3389: 27:21 כי 3588 כה 3541 אמר 559 יהוה 3068 צבאות 6635 אלהי 430
babelah; ua'at kal chorey yahudah uiyarushalaim. kiy koh 'amar Yahuah tzaba'aut 'alohey
**to Babylon *and* all the nobles of Judah and Jerusalem Yea thus saith Yahuah of hosts the Elohim of**

ישראל 3478 על 5921 הכלים 3627 הנותרים 3498 בית 1004 יהוה 3068 ובית 1004 מלך 4428 יהודה 3063
yisra'ael; 'al hakeliym, hanoutariym beyt Yahuah, uabeyt melek yahudah
**Israel concerning the vessels that remain *in* the house of Yahuah and *in* the house of the king of Judah**

Jer 27:16 Also I spoke to the priests and to all this people, saying, Thus saith YHUH; Hearken not to the words of your prophets that prophesy unto you, saying, Behold, the vessels of YHUH's house shall now shortly be brought again from Babylon: for they prophesy a lie unto you.17 Hearken not unto them; serve the king of Babylon, and live: wherefore should this city be laid waste?18 But if they be prophets, and if the word of YHUH be with them, let them now make intercession to YHUH of hosts, that the vessels which are left in the house of YHUH, and in the house of the king of Judah, and at Jerusalem, go not to Babylon.19 For thus saith YHUH of hosts concerning the pillars, and concerning the sea, and concerning the bases, and concerning the residue of the vessels that remain in this city,20 Which Nebuchadnezzar king of Babylon took not, when he carried away captive Jeconiah the son of Jehoiakim king of Judah from Jerusalem to Babylon, and all the nobles of Judah and Jerusalem;21 Yea, thus saith YHUH of hosts, the G-d of Israel, concerning the vessels that remain in the house of YHUH, and in the house of the king of Judah and of Jerusalem;

27:22

וירושלם 3389: בבלה 894 יובאו 935 ושמה 8033 יהיו 1961 עד 5704 יום 3117 פקדי 6485 אתם 853 נאם 5002
uiyarushalaim. babelah yuba'au uashamah yihayu; 'ad youm paqadiy 'atam na'am
**and of Jerusalem to Babylon They shall be carried and there shall they be until the day that I visit them saith**

יהוה 3068 והעליתים 5927 והשיבתים 7725 אל 413 המקום 4725 הזה 2088:
Yahuah, uaha'aliytiym uahashiybotiym, 'al hamaqoum hazeh.
**Yahuah then will I bring them up and restore them to place this**

**Jer 28:1**
ויהי 1961 בשנה 8141 ההיא 1931 בראשית 7225 ממלכת 4467 צדקיה 6667 מלך 4428 יהודה 3063 בשנת 8141
uayahiy bashanah hahiy'a, bara'shiyt mamleket tzidqiyah melek yahudah, bashnat
**And it came to pass year the same in the beginning of the reign of Zedekiah king of Judah in year**

הרבעית 7243 בחדש 2320 החמישי 2549 אמר 559 אלי 413 חנניה 2608 בן 1121 עזור 5809 הנביא 5030 אשר 834 מגבעון 1391
harabi'ayt, bachodesh hachamiyshiy; 'amar 'aelay chananyah ben 'azur hanabiy'a 'asher migib'aun
**the fourth *and* in month the fifth spoke unto me *that* Hananiah the son of Azur the prophet which *was* of Gibeon**

28:2
בבית 1004 יהוה 3068 לעיני 5869 הכהנים 3548 וכל 3605 העם 5971 לאמר 559: כה 3541 אמר 559 יהוה 3068 צבאות 6635
babeyt Yahuah, la'aeyney hakohaniym uakal ha'am lea'mor. koh 'amar Yahuah tzaba'aut
**in the house of Yahuah in the presence of the priests and of all the people saying Thus speak Yahuah of hosts**

28:3
אלהי 430 ישראל 3478 לאמר 559 שברתי 7665 את 853 על 5921 מלך 4428 בבל 894: בעוד 5750 שנתים 8141 ימים 3117
'alohey yisra'ael lea'mor; shabartiy 'at 'al melek babel. be'aud shanatayim yamiym,
**the Elohim of Israel saying I have broken the yoke of the king of Babylon Within two years full**

אני 589 משיב 7725 אל 413 המקום 4725 הזה 2088 את 853 כל 3605 כלי 3627 בית 1004 יהוה 3068 אשר 834 לקח 3947
'aniy meshiyb 'al hamaqoum hazeh, 'at kal kaley beyt Yahuah; 'asher laqach
**I will bring again into place this all the vessels of house Yahuah's that took away**

28:4
נבוכדנאצר 5019 מלך 4428 בבל 894 מן 4480 המקום 4725 הזה 2088 ויביאם 935 בבל 894: ואת 853 יכניה 3204 בן 1121
unabukadra'tzar melek babel min hamaqoum hazeh, uayabiy'aem babel. ua'at yakanyah ben
**Nebuchadnezzar king of Babylon from place this and carried them to Babylon *And* Jeconiah the son of**

יהויקים 3079 מלך 4428 יהודה 3063 ואת 854 כל 3605 גלות 1546 יהודה 3063 הבאים 935 בבלה 894 אני 589 משיב 7725 אל 413
yahouyaqiym melek yahudah ua'at kal galut yahudah haba'aym babelah, 'aniy meshiyb 'al
**Jehoiakim king of Judah *with* all the captives of Judah that went into Babylon I will bring again to**

28:5
המקום 4725 הזה 2088 נאם 5002 יהוה 3068 כי 3588 אשבר 7665 את 853 על 5923 מלך 4428 בבל 894: ויאמר 559 ירמיה 3414
hamaqoum hazeh na'am Yahuah; kiy 'ashbor, 'at 'al melek babel. uaya'mer yirmayah
**place this saith Yahuah for I will break the yoke of the king of Babylon Then said Jeremiah**

הנביא 5030 אל 413 חנניה 2608 הנביא 5030 לעיני 5869 הכהנים 3548 ולעיני 5869 כל 3605 העם 5971 העמדים 5975
hanabiy'a, 'al chananyah hanabiy'a; la'aeyney hakohaniym ual'aeyney kal ha'am, ha'amadiym
**the prophet unto Hananiah the prophet in the presence of the priests and in the presence of all the people that stood**

28:6
בבית 1004 יהוה 3068: ויאמר 559 ירמיה 3414 הנביא 5030 אמן 543 כן 3651 יעשה 6213 יהוה 3069 יקם 6965 יהוה 3069 את 853
babeyt Yahuah. uaya'mer yirmayah hanabiy'a, 'amen ken ya'aseh Yahuah; yaqem Yahuah 'at
**in the house of Yahuah Even said Jeremiah the prophet Amen so do Yahuah perform Yahuah**

Jer 27:22 They shall be carried to Babylon, and there shall they be until the day that I visit them, saith YHUH; then will I bring them up, and restore them to this place. **Jer** 28:1 And it came to pass the same year, in the beginning of the reign of Zedekiah king of Judah, in the fourth year, and in the fifth month, that Hananiah the son of Azur the prophet, which was of Gibeon, spoke unto me in the house of YHUH, in the presence of the priests and of all the people, saying,2 Thus speaketh YHUH of hosts, the G-d of Israel, saying, I have broken the yoke of the king of Babylon.3 Within two full years will I bring again into this place all the vessels of YHUH's house, that Nebuchadnezzar king of Babylon took away from this place, and carried them to Babylon:4 And I will bring again to this place Jeconiah the son of Jehoiakim king of Judah, with all the captives of Judah, that went into Babylon, saith YHUH: for I will break the yoke of the king of Babylon.5 Then the prophet Jeremiah said unto the prophet Hananiah in the presence of the priests, and in the presence of all the people that stood in the house of YHUH,6 Even the prophet Jeremiah said, Amen: YHUH do so: YHUH perform your words which you have prophesied, to bring again the vessels of YHUH's house, and all that is carried away captive, from Babylon into this place.

דבריך 1697 אשר 834 נבאת 5012 להשיב 7725 כלי 3627 בית 1004 יהוה 3069 וכל 3605 הגולה 1473
debareyka, 'asher nibea'ta, lahashiyb kaley beyt Yahuah uakal hagoulah,
**your words which you have prophesied to bring again the vessels of house Yahuah and all that is carried away captive**

מבבל 894 אל 413 המקום 4725 הזה 2088: 28:7 אך 389 שמע 8085 נא 4994 הדבר 1697 הזה 2088 אשר 834 אנכי 595 דבר 1696
mibabel 'al hamaqoum hazeh. 'ak shama' naa' hadabar hazeh, 'asher 'anokiy dober
**from Babylon into place this Nevertheless listen you now this word this that I speak**

באזניך 241 ובאזני 241 כל 3605 העם 5971: 28:8 הנביאים 5030 אשר 834 היו 1961 לפני 6440 ולפניך 6440 מן 4480
ba'azaneyka; uab'azaney kal ha'am. hanabiy'aym, 'asher hayu lapanay ualpaneyka min
**in your ears and in the ears of all the people The prophets that have been before me and before you of**

העולם 5769 וינבאו 5012 אל 413 ארצות 776 רבות 7227 ועל 5921 ממלכות 4467 גדלות 1419 למלחמה 4421 ולרעה 7451
ha'aulam; uayinaba'au 'al 'aratzout rabout ua'al mamlakout gadolout, lamilchamah ualra'ah
**old prophesied *both* against countries many and against kingdoms great of war and of evil**

ולדבר 1698: 28:9 הנביא 5030 אשר 834 ינבא 5012 לשלום 7965 בבא 935 דבר 1697 הנביא 5030
ualdaber. hanabiy'a 'asher yinabea' lashaloum; baba' dabar hanabiy'a,
**and of pestilence The prophet which prophesieth of peace when shall come to pass the word of the prophet**

יודע 3045 הנביא 5030 אשר 834 שלחו 7971 יהוה 3068 באמת 571: 28:10 ויקח 3947 חנניה 2608 הנביא 5030 את 853
yiuada' hanabiy'a, 'asher shalachou Yahuah be'amet. uayiqach chananyah hanabiy'a 'at
**then shall be known the prophet that has sent him Yahuah truly Then took Hananiah the prophet**

המוטה 4133 מעל 5921 צואר 6677 ירמיה 3414 הנביא 5030 וישברהו 7665: 28:11 ויאמר 559 חנניה 2608 לעיני 5869 כל 3605
hamoutah, me'al tzaua'ar yirmayah hanabiy'a; uayishbarehu. uaya'mer chananyah la'aeyney kal
**the yoke from off neck Jeremiah's the prophet and brake it And spoke Hananiah in the presence of all**

העם 5971 לאמר 559 כה 3541 אמר 559 יהוה 3068 ככה 3602 אשבר 7665 את 853 על 5923 נבכדנאצר 5019 מלך 4428 בבל 894
ha'am lea'mor, koh 'amar Yahuah kakah 'ashbor 'at 'al unabukadra'tzar melek babel,
**the people saying Thus saith Yahuah Even so will I break the yoke of Nebuchadnezzar king of Babylon**

בעוד 5750 שנתים 8141 ימים 3117 מעל 5921 צואר 6677 כל 3605 הגוים 1471 וילך 1980 ירמיה 3414 הנביא 5030 לדרכו 1870:
ba'aud shanatayim yamiym, me'al tzaua'ar kal hagouyim; uayelek yirmayah hanabiy'a ladarkou.
**within *the space of* two years full from the neck of all nations And went Jeremiah the prophet his way**

28:12 ויהי 1961 דבר 1697 יהוה 3068 אל 413 ירמיה 3414 אחרי 310 שבור 7665 חנניה 2608 הנביא 5030 את 853
uayahiy dabar Yahuah 'al yirmayah; 'acharey shabour chananyah hanabiy'a 'at
**Then came the word of Yahuah unto Jeremiah *the prophet* after that had broken Hananiah the prophet**

המוטה 4133 מעל 5921 צואר 6677 ירמיה 3414 הנביא 5030 לאמר 559: 28:13 הלוך 1980 ואמרת 559 אל 413 חנניה 2608 לאמר 559 כה 3541 אמר 559
hamoutah, me'al, tzaua'ar yirmayah hanabiy'a lea'mor. halouk ua'amarta 'al chananyah lea'mor, koh 'amar
**the yoke from off the neck of Jeremiah the prophet saying Go and tell to Hananiah saying Thus saith**

יהוה 3068 מוטת 4133 עץ 6086 שברת 7665 ועשית 6213 תחתיהן 8478 מטות 4133 ברזל 1270: 28:14 כי 3588 כה 3541 אמר 559
Yahuah, moutot 'aetz shabarata; ua'asiyta tachateyhen motout barzel. kiy koh 'amar
**Yahuah the yokes of wood You have broken but you shall make for them yokes of iron For thus saith**

Jer 28:7 Nevertheless hear you now this word that I speak in your ears, and in the ears of all the people;8 The prophets that have been before me and before you of old prophesied both against many countries, and against great kingdoms, of war, and of evil, and of pestilence.9 The prophet which prophesieth of peace, when the word of the prophet shall come to pass, then shall the prophet be known, that YHUH has truly sent him.10 Then Hananiah the prophet took the yoke from off the prophet Jeremiah's neck, and break it.11 And Hananiah spoke in the presence of all the people, saying, Thus saith YHUH; Even so will I break the yoke of Nebuchadnezzar king of Babylon from the neck of all nations within the space of two full years. And the prophet Jeremiah went his way.12 Then the word of YHUH came unto Jeremiah the prophet, after that Hananiah the prophet had broken the yoke from off the neck of the prophet Jeremiah, saying,13 Go and tell Hananiah, saying, Thus saith YHUH; Thou have broken the yokes of wood; but you shall make for them yokes of iron.

| יהוה 3068 | צבאות 6635 | אלהי 430 | ישראל 3478 | על 5923 | ברזל 1270 | נתתי 5414 | על 5921 | צואר 6677 | כל 3605 | הגוים 1471 | האלה 428 |
|---|---|---|---|---|---|---|---|---|---|---|---|
| Yahuah | tzaba'aut | 'alohey | yisra'ael, | 'al | barzel | natatiy | 'al | tzaua'ar | kal | hagouyim | ha'aeleh, |
| **Yahuah** | **of hosts** | **the Elohim of** | **Israel** | **a yoke of** | **iron** | **I have put** | **upon** | **the neck of** | **all** | **these nations** | **these** |

| לעבד 5647 | את 853 | נבכדנאצר 5019 | מלך 4428 | בבל 894 | ועבדהו 5647 | וגם 1571 | את 853 | חית 2416 | השדה 7704 |
|---|---|---|---|---|---|---|---|---|---|
| la'abod | 'at | unabukadra'tzar | melek | babel | ua'abaduhu; | ua'gam | 'at | chayat | hasadeh |
| **that they may serve** | | **Nebuchadnezzar** | **king of** | **Babylon** | **and they shall serve him** | **and also** | | **the beasts of** | **the field** |

| נתתי 5414 | לו 3807a: | **28:15** | ויאמר 559 | ירמיה 3414 | הנביא 5030 | אל 413 | חנניה 2608 | הנביא 5030 | שמע 8085 | נא 4994 | חנניה 2608 | לא 3808 |
|---|---|---|---|---|---|---|---|---|---|---|---|---|
| natatiy | lou'. | | uaya'mer | yirmayah | hanabiy'a | 'al | chananyah | hanabiy'a | shama' | naa' | chananyah; | la' |
| **I have given** | **him** | | **Then said** | **Jeremiah** | **the prophet** | **unto** | **Hananiah** | **the prophet** | **Hear** | **now** | **Hananiah** | **not** |

| שלחך 7971 | יהוה 3068 | ואתה 859 | הבטחת 982 | את 853 | העם 5971 | הזה 2088 | על 5921 | שקר 8267: | **28:16** | לכן 3651 | כה 3541 | אמר 559 | יהוה 3068 |
|---|---|---|---|---|---|---|---|---|---|---|---|---|---|
| shalachaka | Yahuah, | ua'atah, | hibtachta | 'at | ha'am | hazeh | 'al | shaqer. | | laken, | koh | 'amar | Yahuah, |
| **has sent you** | **Yahuah** | **but you** | **make to trust** | | **the people** | **this** | **in** | **a lie** | | **Therefore** | **thus** | **saith** | **Yahuah** |

| הנני 2005 | משלחך 7971 | מעל 5921 | פני 6440 | האדמה 127 | השנה 8141 | אתה 859 | מת 4191 | כי 3588 | סרה 5627 | דברת 1696 | אל 413 |
|---|---|---|---|---|---|---|---|---|---|---|---|
| hinniy | mashalechaka, | me'al | paney | ha'adamah; | hashanah | 'atah | met, | kiy | sarah | dibarta | 'al |
| **Behold I** | **will cast you** | **from off** | **the face of** | **the earth** | ***this* year** | **you** | **shall die** | **because** | **rebellion** | **you have taught** | **against** |

| יהוה 3068: | **28:17** | וימת 4191 | חנניה 2608 | הנביא 5030 | בשנה 8141 | ההיא 1931 | בחדש 2320 | השביעי 7637: |
|---|---|---|---|---|---|---|---|---|
| Yahuah. | | uayamat | chananyah | hanabiy'a | bashanah | hahiy'a; | bachodesh | hashabiy'ay. |
| **Yahuah** | | **So died** | **Hananiah** | **the prophet** | **year** | **the same** | **in month** | **the seventh** |

| **Jer 29:1** | ואלה 428 | דברי 1697 | הספר 5612 | אשר 834 | שלח 7971 | ירמיה 3414 | הנביא 5030 | מירושלם 3389 | אל 413 | יתר 3499 |
|---|---|---|---|---|---|---|---|---|---|---|
| | ua'aleh | dibrey | haseper, | 'asher | shalach | yirmayah | hanabiy'a | miyarushalaim; | 'al | yeter |
| | **Now these *are*** | **the words of** | **the letter** | **that** | **sent** | **Jeremiah** | **the prophet** | **from Jerusalem** | **unto** | **the residue of** |

| זקני 2205 | הגולה 1473 | ואל 413 | הכהנים 3548 | ואל 413 | הנביאים 5030 | ואל 413 | כל 3605 | העם 5971 | אשר 834 |
|---|---|---|---|---|---|---|---|---|---|
| ziqney | hagoulah, | ua'al | hakohaniym | ua'al | hanabiy'aym | ua'al | kal | ha'am, | 'asher |
| **the elders** | **which were carried away captives** | **and to** | **the priests** | **and to** | **the prophets** | **and to** | **all** | **the people** | **whom** |

| הגלה 1540 | נבוכדנאצר 5019 | מירושלם 3389 | בבלה 894: | **29:2** | אחרי 310 | צאת 3318 | יכניה 3204 | המלך 4428 |
|---|---|---|---|---|---|---|---|---|
| hegalah | unabukadra'tzar | miyarushalaim | babelah. | | 'acharey | tzea't | yechaneyah | hamelek |
| **had carried away captive** | **Nebuchadnezzar** | **from Jerusalem** | **to Babylon** | | **After that** | **were departed** | **Jeconiah** | **the king** |

| והגבירה 1377 | והסריסים 5631 | שרי 8269 | יהודה 3063 | וירושלם 3389 | והחרש 2796 | והמסגר 4525 |
|---|---|---|---|---|---|---|
| uahagabiyrah | uahasariysiym | sarey | yahudah | uiyarushalaim | uahecharish | uahamasger |
| **and the queen** | **and the eunuchs** | **the princes of** | **Judah** | **and Jerusalem** | **and the carpenters** | **and the smiths** |

| מירושלם 3389: | **29:3** | ביד 3027 | אלעשה 501 | בן 1121 | שפן 8227 | וגמריה 1587 | בן 1121 | חלקיה 2518 | אשר 834 | שלח 7971 |
|---|---|---|---|---|---|---|---|---|---|---|
| miyarushalaim. | | bayad | 'alasah | ben | shapan, | uagamaryah | ben | chilqiyah; | 'asher | shalach |
| **from Jerusalem** | | **By the hand of** | **Elasah** | **the son of** | **Shaphan** | **and Gemariah** | **the son of** | **Hilkiah** | **whom** | **sent unto** |

| צדקיה 6667 | מלך 4428 | יהודה 3063 | אל 413 | נבוכדנאצר 5019 | מלך 4428 | בבל 894 | בבלה 894 | לאמר 559: | **29:4** | כה 3541 | אמר 559 | יהוה 3068 | צבאות 6635 |
|---|---|---|---|---|---|---|---|---|---|---|---|---|---|
| tzidqiyah | melek | yahudah, | 'al | unabukadra'tzar | melek | babel | babelah | lea'mor. | | koh | 'amar | Yahuah | tzaba'aut |
| **Zedekiah** | **king of** | **Judah** | **to** | **Nebuchadnezzar** | **king of** | **Babylon** | **in Babylon** | **saying** | | **Thus** | **saith** | **Yahuah** | **of hosts** |

Jer 28:14 For thus saith YHUH of hosts, the G-d of Israel; I have put a yoke of iron upon the neck of all these nations, that they may serve Nebuchadnezzar king of Babylon; and they shall serve him: and I have given him the beasts of the field also.15 Then said the prophet Jeremiah unto Hananiah the prophet, Hear now, Hananiah; YHUH has not sent you; but you make this people to trust in a lie.16 Therefore thus saith YHUH; Behold, I will cast you from off the face of the earth: this year you shall die, because you have taught rebellion against YHUH.17 So Hananiah the prophet died the same year in the seventh month. **Jer** 29:1 Now these are the words of the letter that Jeremiah the prophet sent from Jerusalem unto the residue of the elders which were carried away captives, and to the priests, and to the prophets, and to all the people whom Nebuchadnezzar had carried away captive from Jerusalem to Babylon;2(After that Jeconiah the king, and the queen, and the eunuchs, the princes of Judah and Jerusalem, and the carpenters, and the smiths, were departed from Jerusalem;)3 By the hand of Elasah the son of Shaphan, and Gemariah the son of Hilkiah, (whom Zedekiah king of Judah sent unto Babylon to Nebuchadnezzar king of Babylon) saying,

אלהי 430 ישראל 3478 לכל 3605 הגולה 1473 אשר 834 הגליתי 1540 מירושלם 3389
'alohey yisra'ael; lakal hagoulah, 'asher higleytiy miyarushalaim
**the Elohim of Israel unto all that are carried away captives whom I have caused to be carried away from Jerusalem**

בבלה 894: 29:5 בנו 1129 בתים 1004 ושבו 3427 ונטעו 5193 גנות 1593 ואכלו 398 את 853 פרין 6529: 29:6 קחו 3947
babelah. banu batiym uashebu; uanit'au ganout, ua'aklu 'at piryan. qachu
**unto Babylon Build you houses and dwell *in them* and plant gardens and eat the fruit of them Take you**

נשים 802 והולידו 3205 בנים 1121 ובנות 1323 וקחו 3947 לבניכם 1121 נשים 802 ואת 853 בנותיכם 1323 תנו 5414 לאנשים 582
nashiym, uahouliydu baniym uabanout uaqchu libneykem nashiym, ua'at banouteykem tanu la'anashiym,
**wives and beget sons and daughters and take for your sons wives *and* your daughters give to husbands**

ותלדנה 3205 בנים 1121 ובנות 1323 ורבו 7235 שם 8033 ואל 408 תמעטו 4591: 29:7 ודרשו 1875 את 853
uateladnah baniym uabanout; uarbu sham ua'al tima'atu. uadirshu 'at
**that they may bear sons and daughters that you may be increased there and not diminished And seek**

שלום 7965 העיר 5892 אשר 834 הגליתי 1540 אתכם 853 שמה 8033 והתפללו 6419 בעדה 1157 אל 413 יהוה 3068
shaloum ha'ayr, 'asher higleytiy 'atkem shamah, uahitpallu ba'adah 'al Yahuah;
**the peace of the city where I have caused to be carried away captives you where and pray for it unto Yahuah**

כי 3588 בשלומה 7965 יהיה 1961 לכם 3807a שלום 7965: 29:8 כי 3588 כה 3541 אמר 559 יהוה 3068 צבאות 6635 אלהי 430
kiy bishloumah, yihayeh lakem shaloum. kiy koh 'amar Yahuah tzaba'aut 'alohey
**for in the peace thereof shall you have to you peace For thus saith Yahuah of hosts the Elohim of**

ישראל 3478 אל 408 ישיאו 5377 לכם 3807a נביאיכם 5030 אשר 834 בקרבכם 7130 וקסמיכם 7080 ואל 408 תשמעו 8085 אל 413
yisra'ael, 'al yashiy'u lakem nabiy'aeykem 'asher baqirbakem uaqosameykem; ua'al tishma'au 'al
**Israel not Let deceive to you your prophets that *be* in the midst of you and your diviners neither listen to**

חלמתיכם 2472 אשר 834 אתם 859 מחלמים 2492: 29:9 כי 3588 בשקר 8267 הם 1992 נבאים 5012 לכם 3807a בשמי 8034 לא 3808
chalomoteykem, 'asher 'atem machlamiym. kiy basheqer, hem naba'aym lakem bishmiy; la'
**your dreams which you cause to be dreamed For falsely they prophesy unto you in my name not**

שלחתים 7971 נאם 5002 יהוה 3068: 29:10 כי 3588 כה 3541 אמר 559 יהוה 3068 כי 3588 לפי 6310 מלאת 4390 לבבל 894 שבעים 7657
shalachtiym na'am Yahuah. kiy koh 'amar Yahuah, kiy lapiy mala't lababel shib'aym
**I have sent them saith Yahuah For thus saith Yahuah That after be accomplished at Babylon seventy**

שנה 8141 אפקד 6485 אתכם 853 והקמתי 6965 עליכם 5921 את 853 דברי 1697 הטוב 2896 להשיב 7725 אתכם 853 אל 413 המקום 4725
shanah 'apqod 'atkem; uahaqimotiy 'aleykem 'at dabariy hatoub, lahashiyb 'atkem, 'al hamaqoum
**years I will visit you and perform toward you my word good in causing to return you to place**

הזה 2088: 29:11 כי 3588 אנכי 595 ידעתי 3045 את 853 המחשבת 4284 אשר 834 אנכי 595 חשב 2803 עליכם 5921 נאם 5002 יהוה 3068 מחשבות 4284
hazeh. kiy 'anokiy yada'tiy 'at hamachashabot, 'asher 'anokiy chosheb 'aleykem na'am Yahuah; machashabout
**this For I know the thoughts that I think toward you saith Yahuah thoughts of**

שלום 7965 ולא 3808 לרעה 7451 לתת 5414 לכם 3807a אחרית 319 ותקוה 8615: 29:12 וקראתם 7121 אתי 853 והלכתם 1980
shaloum uala' lara'ah, latet lakem 'achariyt uatiquah. uaqara'tem 'atiy uahalakatem,
**peace and not of evil to give to you an end expected Then shall you call upon me and you shall go**

Jer 29:4 Thus saith YHUH of hosts, the G-d of Israel, unto all that are carried away captives, whom I have caused to be carried away from Jerusalem unto Babylon;5 Build you houses, and dwell in them; and plant gardens, and eat the fruit of them;6 Take you wives, and beget sons and daughters; and take wives for your sons, and give your daughters to husbands, that they may bear sons and daughters; that you may be increased there, and not diminished.7 And seek the peace of the city whither I have caused you to be carried away captives, and pray unto YHUH for it: for in the peace thereof shall you have peace.8 For thus saith YHUH of hosts, the G-d of Israel; Let not your prophets and your diviners, that be in the midst of you, deceive you, neither hear to your dreams which you cause to be dreamed.9 For they prophesy falsely unto you in my name: I have not sent them, saith YHUH.10 For thus saith YHUH, That after seventy years be accomplished at Babylon I will visit you, and perform my good word toward you, in causing you to return to this place.11 For I know the thoughts that I think toward you, saith YHUH, thoughts of peace, and not of evil, to give you an expected end.12 Then shall you call upon me, and you shall go and pray unto me, and I will hear unto you.

29:13

והתפללתם 6419 אלי 413 ושמעתי 8085 אליכם 413: ובקשתם 1245 אתי 853 ומצאתם 4672 כי 3588 תדרשני 1875
uahitpalaltem 'aelay; uashama'tiy 'aleykem. uabiqashtem 'atiy uamatza'tem; kiy tidrashuny
**and pray unto me and I will listen unto you And you shall seek me and find *me* when you shall search for me**

29:14

בכל 3605 לבבכם 3824: ונמצאתי 4672 לכם 3807a נאם 5002 יהוה 3068 ושבתי 7725 את 853 שביתכם 7622
bakal lababkem. uanimtzea'tiy lakem na'am Yahuah uashabtiy 'at shebiytakem
**with all your heart And I will be found of you saith Yahuah and I will turn away your captivity**

וקבצתי 6908 אתכם 853 מכל 3605 הגוים 1471 ומכל 3605 המקומות 4725 אשר 834 הדחתי 5080 אתכם 853 שם 8033 נאם 5002
uaqibatztiy 'atkem mikal hagouyim uamikal hamaqoumout, 'asher hidachtiy 'atkem sham na'am
**and I will gather you from all the nations and from all the places where I have driven you there saith**

29:15

יהוה 3068 והשבתי 7725 אתכם 853 אל 413 המקום 4725 אשר 834 הגליתי 1540 אתכם 853 משם 8033:
Yahuah; uahashibotiy 'atkem, 'al hamaqoum, 'asher higleytiy 'atkem misham.
**Yahuah and I will bring again you into the place where I caused to be carried away captive you there**

29:16

כי 3588 אמרתם 559 הקים 6965 לנו 3807a יהוה 3068 נבאים 5030 בבלה 894: כי 3588 כה 3541 אמר 559 יהוה 3068 אל 413
kiy 'amartem; heqiym lanu Yahuah nabi'aym babelah. kiy koh 'amar Yahuah 'al
**Because you have said has raised up us Yahuah prophets in Babylon *Know* that thus saith Yahuah of**

המלך 4428 היושב 3427 אל 413 כסא 3678 דוד 1732 ואל 413 כל 3605 העם 5971 היושב 3427 בעיר 5892 הזאת 2063 אחיכם 251
hamelek hayousheb 'al kisea' dauid, ua'al kal ha'am, hayousheb ba'ayr haza't; 'acheykem
**the king that sit upon the throne of David and of all the people that dwell in city this *and of* your brethren**

29:17

אשר 834 לא 3808 יצאו 3318 אתכם 854 בגולה 1473: כה 3541 אמר 559 יהוה 3068 צבאות 6635 הנני 2005 משלח 7971 בם 871a
'asher la' yatza'ua 'atakem bagoulah. koh 'amar Yahuah tzaba'aut, hinniy mashaleach bam,
**that not are gone forth with you into captivity Thus saith Yahuah of hosts Behold I will send upon them**

את 853 החרב 2719 את 853 הרעב 7458 ואת 853 הדבר 1698 ונתתי 5414 אותם 853 כתאנים 8384 השערים 8182 אשר 834 לא 3808
'at hachereb 'at hara'ab ua'at hadaber; uanatatiy 'autam, kata'aeniym hasho'ariym, 'asher la'
**the sword the famine *and* the pestilence and will make them figs like vile that cannot**

29:18

תאכלנה 398 מרע 7455: ורדפתי 7291 אחריהם 310 בחרב 2719 ברעב 7458 ובדבר 1698
te'akalnah meroa'. uaradaptiy 'achareyhem, bachereb bara'ab uabadaber;
**be eaten they are so evil And I will persecute them with the sword with the famine and with the pestilence**

ונתתים 5414 לזועה 2113 לכל 3605 ממלכות 4467 הארץ 776 לאלה 423 ולשמה 8047 ולשרקה 8322
uantatiym lazua'ah lakol mamlakout ha'aretz, la'alah ualshamah ualishreqah
**and will deliver them to be removed to all the kingdoms of the earth to be a curse and an astonishment and an hissing**

29:19

ולחרפה 2781 בכל 3605 הגוים 1471 אשר 834 הדחתים 5080 שם 8033: תחת 8478 אשר 834 לא 3808 שמעו 8085
ualcherpah, bakal hagouyim 'asher hidachtiym sham. tachat 'asher la' shama'au
**and a reproach among all the nations where I have driven them there Because which not they have hearkened**

אל 413 דברי 1697 נאם 5002 יהוה 3068 אשר 834 שלחתי 7971 אליהם 413 את 854 עבדי 5650 הנבאים 5030 השכם 7925
'al dabaray na'am Yahuah; 'asher shalachtiy 'aleyhem 'at 'abaday hanabiy'aym hashkem
**to my words saith Yahuah which I sent unto them *by* my servants the prophets rising up early**

Jer 29:13 And you shall seek me, and find me, when you shall search for me with all your heart.14 And I will be found of you, saith YHUH: and I will turn away your captivity, and I will gather you from all the nations, and from all the places whither I have driven you, saith YHUH; and I will bring you again into the place whence I caused you to be carried away captive.15 Because you have said, YHUH has raised us up prophets in Babylon;16 Know that thus saith YHUH of the king that sitteth upon the throne of David, and of all the people that dwell in this city, and of your brethren that are not gone forth with you into captivity;17 Thus saith YHUH of hosts; Behold, I will send upon them the sword, the famine, and the pestilence, and will make them like vile figs, that cannot be eaten, they are so evil.18 And I will persecute them with the sword, with the famine, and with the pestilence, and will deliver them to be removed to all the kingdoms of the earth, to be a curse, and an astonishment, and an hissing, and a reproach, among all the nations whither I have driven them:19 Because they have not hearkened to my words, saith YHUH, which I sent unto them by my servants the prophets, rising up early and sending them; but you would not hear, saith YHUH.

| ושלח 7971 | ולא 3808 | שמעתם 8085 | נאם 5002 | יהוה 3068: | 29:20 | ואתם 859 | שמעו 8085 | דבר 1697 | יהוה 3068 | כל 3605 |
|---|---|---|---|---|---|---|---|---|---|---|
| uashaloach, | uala' | shama'tem | na'am | Yahuah. | | ua'atem | shim'au | dabar | Yahuah; | kal |
| **and sending *them*** | **but not** | **you would hear** | **saith** | **Yahuah** | | **you therefore** | **Hear** | **the word of** | **Yahuah** | **all** |

| הגולה 1473 | אשר 834 | שלחתי 7971 | מירושלם 3389 | בבלה 894: | 29:21 | כה 3541 | אמר 559 | יהוה 3068 | צבאות 6635 | אלהי 430 |
|---|---|---|---|---|---|---|---|---|---|---|
| hagoulah, | 'asher | shilachtiy | miyarushalaim | babelah. | | koh | 'amar | Yahuah | tzaba'aut | 'alohey |
| ***you of* the captivity** | **whom** | **I have sent** | **from Jerusalem** | **to Babylon** | | **Thus** | **saith** | **Yahuah** | **of hosts** | **the Elohim of** |

| ישראל 3478 | אל 413 | אחאב 256 | בן 1121 | קוליה 6964 | ואל 413 | צדקיהו 6667 | בן 1121 | מעשיה 4641 | הנבאים 5012 | לכם 3807a | בשמי 8034 |
|---|---|---|---|---|---|---|---|---|---|---|---|
| yisra'ael, | 'al | 'ach'ab | ben | qoulayah | ua'al | tzidqiyahu | ben | ma'aseyah, | hanaba'aym | lakem | bishmiy |
| **Israel** | **of** | **Ahab** | **the son of** | **Kolaiah** | **and of** | **Zedekiah** | **the son of** | **Maaseiah** | **which prophesy** | **unto you** | **in my name** |

| שקר 8267 | הנני 2005 | נתן 5414 | אתם 853 | ביד 3027 | נבוכדראצר 5019 | מלך 4428 | בבל 894 | והכם 5221 |
|---|---|---|---|---|---|---|---|---|
| shaqer; | hinniy | noten | 'atam, | bayad | nabukadre'tzar | melek | babel, | uahikam |
| **a lie** | **Behold** | **I will deliver** | **them** | **into the hand of** | **Nebuchadrezzar** | **king of** | **Babylon** | **and he shall slay them** |

| לעיניכם 5869: | 29:22 | ולקח 3947 | מהם 1992 | קללה 7045 | לכל 3605 | גלות 1546 | יהודה 3063 | אשר 834 | בבבל 894 |
|---|---|---|---|---|---|---|---|---|---|
| la'ayneykem. | | ualuqach | mehem | qalalah, | lakol | galut | yahudah, | 'asher | bababel |
| **before your eyes** | | **And shall be taken up** | **of them** | **a curse** | **by all** | **the captivity of** | **Judah** | **which** | ***are* in Babylon** |

| לאמר 559 | ישמך 7760 | יהוה 3068 | כצדקיהו 6667 | וכאחב 256 | אשר 834 | קלם 7033 | מלך 4428 | בבל 894 | באש 784: | 29:23 | יען 3282 |
|---|---|---|---|---|---|---|---|---|---|---|---|
| lea'mor; | yasimaka | Yahuah | katzidqiyahu | uak'achab, | 'asher | qalam | melek | babel | ba'aesh. | | ya'an |
| **saying** | **make you** | **Yahuah** | **like Zedekiah** | **and like Ahab** | **whom** | **roasted** | **the king of** | **Babylon** | **in the fire** | | **Because** |

| אשר 834 | עשו 6213 | נבלה 5039 | בישראל 3478 | וינאפו 5003 | את 854 | נשי 802 | רעיהם 7453 |
|---|---|---|---|---|---|---|---|
| 'asher | 'asu | nabalah | bayisra'ael, | uayana'apu | 'at | nashey | re'aeyhem, |
| **which** | **they have committed** | **villany** | **in Israel** | **and have committed adultery** | ***with*** | **wives** | **their neighbours'** |

| וידברו 1696 | דבר 1697 | בשמי 8034 | שקר 8267 | אשר 834 | לוא 3808 | צויתים 6680 | ואנכי 595 | הוידע 3045 | ועד 5707 | נאם 5002 |
|---|---|---|---|---|---|---|---|---|---|---|
| uayadabru | dabar | bishmiy | sheqer, | 'asher | lua' | tziuiytim; | ua'anokiy | huyodea' | ua'ad | na'am |
| **and have spoken** | **words** | **in my name** | **lying** | **which** | **not** | **I have commanded** | **even I** | **know** | **and *am* a witness** | **saith** |

| יהוה 3068: | 29:24 | ואל 413 | שמעיהו 8089 | הנחלמי 5161 | תאמר 559 | לאמר 559: | 29:25 | כה 3541 | אמר 559 | יהוה 3068 | צבאות 6635 |
|---|---|---|---|---|---|---|---|---|---|---|---|
| Yahuah. | | ua'al | shama'yahu | hanechelamiy | ta'mar | lea'mor. | | koh | 'amar | Yahuah | tzaba'aut |
| **Yahuah** | | ***Thus* also to** | **Shemaiah** | **the Nehelamite** | **shall you speak** | **saying** | | **Thus** | **speak** | **Yahuah** | **of hosts** |

| אלהי 430 | ישראל 3478 | לאמר 559 | יען 3282 | אשר 834 | אתה 859 | שלחת 7971 | בשמכה 8034 | ספרים 5612 | אל 413 | כל 3605 | העם 5971 | אשר 834 |
|---|---|---|---|---|---|---|---|---|---|---|---|---|
| 'alohey | yisra'ael | lea'mor; | ya'an | 'asher | 'atah | shalachta | bashimakah | sapariym, | 'al | kal | ha'am | 'asher |
| **the Elohim of** | **Israel** | **saying** | **Because** | **which** | **you** | **have sent** | **in your name** | **letters** | **unto** | **all** | **the people** | **that** |

| בירושלם 3389 | ואל 413 | צפניה 6846 | בן 1121 | מעשיה 4641 | הכהן 3548 | ואל 413 | כל 3605 | הכהנים 3548 | לאמר 559: | 29:26 | יהוה 3068 |
|---|---|---|---|---|---|---|---|---|---|---|---|
| biyarushalaim, | ua'al | tzapanyah | ben | ma'aseyah | hakohen, | ua'ael | kal | hakohaniym | lea'mor. | | Yahuah |
| ***are* at Jerusalem** | **and to** | **Zephaniah** | **the son of** | **Maaseiah** | **the priest** | **and to** | **all** | **the priests** | **saying** | | **Yahuah** |

| נתנך 5414 | כהן 3548 | תחת 8478 | יהוידע 3077 | הכהן 3548 | להיות 1961 | פקדים 6496 | בית 1004 | יהוה 3068 | לכל 3605 |
|---|---|---|---|---|---|---|---|---|---|
| natanaka | kohen, | tachat | yahouyada' | hakohen, | lihayout | paqidiym | beyt | Yahuah, | lakal |
| **has made you** | **priest** | **in the stead of** | **Jehoiada** | **the priest** | **that you should be** | **officers** | ***in* the house of** | **Yahuah** | **for every** |

Jer 29:20 Hear you therefore the word of YHUH, all you of the captivity, whom I have sent from Jerusalem to Babylon:21 Thus saith YHUH of hosts, the G-d of Israel, of Ahab the son of Kolaiah, and of Zedekiah the son of Maaseiah, which prophesy a lie unto you in my name; Behold, I will deliver them into the hand of Nebuchadrezzar king of Babylon; and he shall slay them before your eyes;22 And of them shall be taken up a curse by all the captivity of Judah which are in Babylon, saying, YHUH make you like Zedekiah and like Ahab, whom the king of Babylon roasted in the fire;23 Because they have committed villany in Israel, and have committed adultery with their neighbors' wives, and have spoken lying words in my name, which I have not commanded them; even I know, and am a witness, saith YHUH.24 Thus shall you also speak to Shemaiah the Nehelamite, saying,25 Thus speaketh YHUH of hosts, the G-d of Israel, saying, Because you have sent letters in your name unto all the people that are at Jerusalem, and to Zephaniah the son of Maaseiah the priest, and to all the priests, saying,26 YHUH has made you priest in the stead of Jehoiada the priest, that you should be officers in the house of YHUH, forevery man that is mad, and make himself a prophet, that you should put him in prison, and in the stocks.

29:27
איש 376 משגע 7696 ומתנבא 5012 ונתתה 5414 אתו 853 אל 413 המהפכת 4115 ואל 413 הצינק 6729:
'aysh mashuga' uamitnabea'; uanatatah 'atou 'al hamahpeket ua'al hatziynoq.
**man *that is* mad and make himself a prophet that you should put him in prison and in the stocks**

29:28
ועתה 6258 למה 4100 לא 3808 גערת 1605 בירמיהו 3414 הענתתי 6069 המתנבא 5012 לכם 3807a: כי 3588
ua'atah, lamah la' ga'arta, bayirmayahu ha'antotiy; hamitnabea' lakem. kiy
**Now therefore why not have you reproved Jeremiah of Anathoth which make himself a prophet to you? For**

על 5921 כן 3651 שלח 7971 אלינו 413 בבל 894 לאמר 559 ארכה 752 היא 1931 בנו 1129 בתים 1004 ושבו 3427
'al ken shalach 'aeleynu babel lea'mor 'arukah hiy'a; banu batiym uashebu,
**therefore after that he sent unto us *in* Babylon saying *captivity is* long This build you houses and dwell**

29:29
ונטעו 5193 גנות 1593 ואכלו 398 את 853 פריהן 6529: ויקרא 7121 צפניה 6846 הכהן 3548 את 853 הספר 5612 הזה 2088
uanit'au ganout, ua'aklu 'at pariyhen. uayiqra' tzapanyah hakohen 'at haseper hazeh;
***in them* and plant gardens and eat the fruit of them And read Zephaniah the priest letter this**

29:30
29:31
באזני 241 ירמיהו 3414 הנביא 5030: ויהי 1961 דבר 1697 יהוה 3068 אל 413 ירמיהו 3414 לאמר 559: שלח 7971 על 5921
ba'azaney yirmayahu hanabiy'a. uayahiy dabar Yahuah, 'al yirmayahu lea'mor. shalach 'al
**in the ears of Jeremiah the prophet Then came the word of Yahuah unto Jeremiah saying Send to**

כל 3605 הגולה 1473 לאמר 559 כה 3541 אמר 559 יהוה 3068 אל 413 שמעיה 8098 הנחלמי 5161 יען 3282 אשר 834
kal hagoulah lea'mor, koh 'amar Yahuah, 'al shama'yah hanechelamiy; ya'an 'asher
**all them of the captivity saying Thus saith Yahuah concerning Shemaiah the Nehelamite Because after**

29:32
נבא 5012 לכם 3807a שמעיה 8098 ואני 589 לא 3808 שלחתיו 7971 ויבטח 982 אתכם 853 על 5921 שקר 8267:
niba' lakem shama'yah, ua'aniy la' shalachtiyu, uayabtach 'atkem 'al shaqer.
**has prophesied unto you *that* Shemaiah and I not sent him and he caused to trust you in a lie**

לכן 3651 כה 3541 אמר 559 יהוה 3069 הנני 2005 פקד 6485 על 5921 שמעיה 8098 הנחלמי 5161 ועל 5921 זרעו 2233 לא 3808 יהיה 1961
laken koh 'amar Yahuah hinniy poqed 'al shama'yah hanechelamiy ua'al zar'au la' yihayeh
**Therefore thus saith Yahuah Behold I will punish on Shemaiah the Nehelamite and on his seed not he shall have**

לו 3807a איש 376 יושב 3427 בתוך 8432 העם 5971 הזה 2088 ולא 3808 יראה 7200 בטוב 2896 אשר 834 אני 589 עשה 6213 לעמי 5971
lou' 'aysh yousheb batouk ha'am hazeh, uala' yir'ah batoub 'asher 'aniy 'aseh la'amiy
**to him a man to dwell among the people this neither shall he behold the good that I will do for my people**

נאם 5002 יהוה 3069 כי 3588 סרה 5627 דבר 1696 על 5921 יהוה 3069:
na'am Yahuah; kiy sarah diber 'al Yahuah.
**saith Yahuah because rebellion he has taught against Yahuah**

**Jer 30:1**
30:2
הדבר 1697 אשר 834 היה 1961 אל 413 ירמיהו 3414 מאת 853 יהוה 3068 לאמר 559: כה 3541 אמר 559 יהוה 3068 אלהי 430 ישראל 3478
hadabar 'asher hayah 'al yirmayahu, me'at Yahuah lea'mor. koh 'amar Yahuah 'alohey yisra'ael
**The word which came to Jeremiah from Yahuah saying Thus speak Yahuah Elohim of Israel**

30:3
לאמר 559 כתב 3789 לך 3807a את 853 כל 3605 הדברים 1697 אשר 834 דברתי 1696 אליך 413 אל 413 ספר 5612: כי 3588 הנה 2009 ימים 3117
lea'mor; katab laka, 'at kal hadabariym 'asher dibartiy 'aeleyka 'al seper. kiy hineh yamiym
**saying Write for you all the words that I have spoken unto you in a book For lo the days**

Jer 29:27 Now therefore why have you not reproved Jeremiah of Anathoth, which make himself a prophet to you?28 For therefore he sent unto us in Babylon, saying, This captivity is long: build you houses, and dwell in them; and plant gardens, and eat the fruit of them.29 And Zephaniah the priest read this letter in the ears of Jeremiah the prophet.30 Then came the word of YHUH unto Jeremiah, saying,31 Send to all them of the captivity, saying, Thus saith YHUH concerning Shemaiah the Nehelamite, Because that Shemaiah has prophesied unto you, and I sent him not, and he caused you to trust in a lie:32 Therefore thus saith YHUH; Behold, I will punish Shemaiah the Nehelamite, and his seed: he shall not have a man to dwell among this people; neither shall he behold the good that I will do for my people, saith YHUH; because he has taught rebellion against YHUH. **Jer** 30:1 The word that came to Jeremiah from YHUH, saying,2 Thus speaketh YHUH G-d of Israel, saying, Write you all the words that I have spoken unto you in a book. 3 For, lo, the days come, saith YHUH, that I will bring again the captivity of my people Israel and Judah, saith YHUH:

| באים 935 | נאם 5002 | יהוה 3068 | ושבתי 7725 | את 853 | שבות 7622 | עמי 5971 | ישראל 3478 | ויהודה 3063 | אמר 559 | יהוה 3068 |
|---|---|---|---|---|---|---|---|---|---|---|
| ba'aym | na'am | Yahuah, | uashabatiy | 'at | shabut | 'amiy | yisra'ael | uayahudah | 'amar | Yahuah; |
| **come** | **saith** | **Yahuah** | **that I will bring again** | | **the captivity of** | **my people** | **Israel** | **and Judah** | **saith** | **Yahuah** |

| והשבתים 7725 | אל 413 | הארץ 776 | אשר 834 | נתתי 5414 | לאבותם 1 | וירשוה 3423: | 30:4 | ואלה 428 |
|---|---|---|---|---|---|---|---|---|
| uahashibotiym, | 'al | ha'aretz | 'asher | natatiy | la'aboutam | uiyreshuha. | | ua'aleh |
| **and I will cause them to return** | **to** | **the land** | **that** | **I gave** | **to their fathers** | **and they shall possess it** | | **And these** |

| הדברים 1697 | אשר 834 | דבר 1696 | יהוה 3068 | אל 413 | ישראל 3478 | ואל 413 | יהודה 3063: | 30:5 | כי 3588 | כה 3541 | אמר 559 | יהוה 3068 |
|---|---|---|---|---|---|---|---|---|---|---|---|---|
| hadabariym, | 'asher | diber | Yahuah | 'al | yisra'ael | ua'al | yahudah. | | kiy | koh | 'amar | Yahuah, |
| ***are* the words** | **that** | **spoke** | **Yahuah** | **concerning** | **Israel** | **and concerning** | **Judah** | | **For** | **thus** | **saith** | **Yahuah** |

| קול 6963 | חרדה 2731 | שמענו 8085 | פחד 6343 | ואין 369 | שלום 7965: | 30:6 | שאלו 7592 | נא 4994 | וראו 7200 | אם 518 | ילד 3205 |
|---|---|---|---|---|---|---|---|---|---|---|---|
| qoul | charadah | shama'anu; | pachad | ua'aeyn | shaloum. | | sha'alu | naa' | uar'au, | 'am | yoled |
| **a voice of** | **trembling** | **We have heard** | ***of* fear** | **and not** | ***of* peace** | | **Ask you** | **now** | **and see** | **whether** | **does travail with child?** |

| זכר 2145 | מדוע 4069 | ראיתי 7200 | כל 3605 | גבר 1397 | ידיו 3027 | על 5921 | חלציו 2504 | כיולדה 3205 | ונהפכו 2015 | כל 3605 |
|---|---|---|---|---|---|---|---|---|---|---|
| zakar; | madua' | ra'aytiy | kal | geber | yadayu | 'al | chalatzayu | kayouledah, | uanehepaku | kal |
| **a man** | **wherefore** | **do I see** | **every** | **man** | ***with* his hands** | **on** | **his loins** | **as a woman in travail** | **and are turned** | **all** |

| פנים 6440 | לירקון 3420: | 30:7 | הוי 1945 | כי 3588 | גדול 1419 | היום 3117 | ההוא 1931 | מאין 369 | כמהו 3644 | ועת 6256 | צרה 6869 | היא 1931 |
|---|---|---|---|---|---|---|---|---|---|---|---|---|
| paniym | layeraqoun. | | houy, | kiy | gadoul | hayoum | hahua' | me'ayin | kamohu; | ua'at | tzarah | hiy'a |
| **faces** | **into paleness?** | | **Alas** | **for** | ***is* great** | **day** | **that** | **so that none** | ***is* like it** | ***is* even the time** | **trouble** | **it** |

| ליעקב 3290 | וממנה 4480 | יושע 3467: | 30:8 | והיה 1961 | ביום 3117 | ההוא 1931 | נאם 5002 | יהוה 3068 | צבאות 6635 |
|---|---|---|---|---|---|---|---|---|---|
| laya'aqob, | uamimenah | yiuashea'. | | uahayah | bayoum | hahua' | na'am | Yahuah | tzaba'aut, |
| **of Jacob's** | **but out of it** | **he shall be saved** | | **For it shall come to pass** | **in day** | **that** | **saith** | **Yahuah** | **of hosts** |

| אשבר 7665 | עלו 5923 | מעל 5921 | צוארך 6677 | ומוסרותיך 4147 | אנתק 5423 | ולא 3808 | יעבדו 5647 | בו 871a | עוד 5750 |
|---|---|---|---|---|---|---|---|---|---|
| 'ashbor | 'alou | me'al | tzaua'reka, | uamousarouteyka | 'anateq; | uala' | ya'abdu | bou | 'aud |
| ***that* I will break** | **his yoke** | **from off** | **your neck** | **and your bonds** | **I will burst** | **and no** | **shall serve themselves** | **of him** | **more** |

| זרים 2114: | 30:9 | ועבדו 5647 | את 853 | יהוה 3069 | אלהיהם 430 | ואת 853 | דוד 1732 | מלכם 4428 | אשר 834 | אקים 6965 |
|---|---|---|---|---|---|---|---|---|---|---|
| zariym. | | ua'abadu, | 'at | Yahuah | 'aloheyhem; | ua'at | dauid | malkam, | 'asher | 'aqiym |
| **strangers** | | **But they shall serve** | | **Yahuah** | **their Elohim** | ***and*** | **David** | **their king** | **whom** | **I will raise up** |

| להם 1992: | 30:10 | ואתה 859 | אל 408 | תירא 3372 | עבדי 5650 | יעקב 3290 | נאם 5002 | יהוה 3068 | ואל 408 | תחת 2865 | ישראל 3478 | כי 3588 |
|---|---|---|---|---|---|---|---|---|---|---|---|---|
| lahem. | | ua'atah | 'al | tiyraa' | 'abdiy | ya'aqob | na'am | Yahuah | ua'al | techat | yisra'ael, | kiy |
| **unto them** | | **Therefore you** | **not** | **fear** | **O my servant** | **Jacob** | **saith** | **Yahuah** | **neither** | **be dismayed** | **O Israel** | **for** |

| הנני 2005 | מושיעך 3467 | מרחוק 7350 | ואת 853 | זרעך 2233 | מארץ 776 | שבים 7628 | ושב 7725 | יעקב 3290 |
|---|---|---|---|---|---|---|---|---|
| hinniy | moushiy'aka | merachouq, | ua'at | zar'aka | me'aretz | shibyam; | uashab | ya'aqob |
| **lo I** | **will save you** | **from afar** | ***and*** | **your seed** | **from the land of** | **their captivity** | **and shall return** | **Jacob** |

| ושקט 8252 | ושאנן 7599 | ואין 369 | מחריד 2729: | 30:11 | כי 3588 | אתך 854 | אני 589 | נאם 5002 | יהוה 3068 |
|---|---|---|---|---|---|---|---|---|---|
| uashaqat | uasha'anan | ua'aeyn | machariyd. | | kiy | 'ataka | 'aniy | na'am | Yahuah |
| **and shall be in rest** | **and be quiet** | **and none** | **shall make *him* afraid** | | **For** | ***am* with you** | **I** | **saith** | **Yahuah** |

Jer 30:3 and I will cause them to return to the land that I gave to their fathers, and they shall possess it.4 And these are the words that YHUH spoke concerning Israel and concerning Judah.5 For thus saith YHUH; We have heard a voice of trembling, of fear, and not of peace.6 Ask you now, and see whether a man doth travail with child? wherefore do I see every man with his hands on his loins, as a woman in travail, and all faces are turned into paleness?7 Alas! for that day is great, so that none is like it: it is even the time of Jacob's trouble; but he shall be saved out of it.8 For it shall come to pass in that day, saith YHUH of hosts, that I will break his yoke from off your neck, and will burst your bonds, and strangers shall no more serve themselves of him:9 But they shall serve YHUH their G-d, and David their king, whom I will raise up unto them.10 Therefore fear you not, O my servant Jacob, saith YHUH; neither be dismayed, O Israel: for, lo, I will save you from afar, and your seed from the land of their captivity; and Jacob shall return, and shall be in rest, and be quiet, and none shall make him afraid.

להושיעך 3467 כי 3588 עשה 6213 כלה 3617 בכל 3605 הגוים 1471 אשר 834 הפצותיך 6327 שם 8033 אך 389 אתך 854 לא 3808
lahoushiy'aka; kiy 'aaseh kalah bakal hagouyim 'asher hapitzoutiyka sham, 'ak 'atka la'
**to save you though I make a full end of all nations where I have scattered you there yet of you not**

30:12
עשה 6213 כלה 3617 ויסרתיך 3256 למשפט 4941 ונקה 5352 לא 3808 אנקך 5352: כי 3588 כה 3541
'aaseh kalah, uayisartiyka lamishpat, uanaqeh la' 'anaqeka. kiy koh
**will I make a full end but I will correct you in measure and will leave you altogether not unpunished For thus**

30:13
אמר 559 יהוה 3068 אנוש 605 לשברך 7667 נחלה 2470 מכתך 4347: אין 369 דן 1777 דינך 1779
'amar Yahuah 'anush lashibrek; nachalah makatek. 'aeyn dan diynek
**saith Yahuah *is* incurable Your bruise *is* grievous *and* your wound *There is* none to plead your cause**

30:14
למזור 4205 רפאות 7499 תעלה 8585 אין 369 לך 3807a: כל 3605 מאהביך 157 שכחוך 7911 אותך 853 לא 3808
lamazour; rapu'aut ta'alah 'aeyn lak. kal ma'ahabayik shakechuk, autak la'
**that you may be bound up medicines healing have no to you All your lovers have forgotten you; you not**

ידרשו 1875 כי 3588 מכת 4347 אויב 341 הכיתיך 5221 מוסר 4148 אכזרי 394 על 5921
yidroshu; kiy makat auyeb hikiytiyk musar 'akzariy, 'al
**they seek for *with* the wound of an enemy I have wounded you *with* the chastisement of a cruel one for**

30:15
רב 7230 עונך 5771 עצמו 6105 חטאתיך 2403: מה 4100 תזעק 2199 על 5921 שברך 7667 אנוש 605
rob 'auonek, 'atzamu chata'tayik. mah tiz'aq 'al shibrek, 'anush
**the multitude of your iniquity were increased *because* your sins Why cry you for your affliction? *is* incurable**

30:16
מכאבך 4341 על 5921 רב 7230 עונך 5771 עצמו 6105 חטאתיך 2403 עשיתי 6213 אלה 428 לך 3807a:
maka'abek; 'al rob 'auonek, 'atzamu chata'tayik, 'asiytiy 'aeleh lak.
**your sorrow for the multitude of your iniquity were increased *because* your sins I have done these *things* unto you**

לכן 3651 כל 3605 אכליך 398 יאכלו 398 וכל 3605 צריך 6862 כלם 3605 בשבי 7628 ילכו 1980
laken kal 'akalayik ye'akelu, uakal tzarayik kulam bashabiy yeleku;
**Therefore all they that devour you shall be devoured and all your adversaries every one of them into captivity shall go**

30:17
והיו 1961 שאסיך 7601 למשסה 4933 וכל 3605 בזזיך 962 אתן 5414 לבז 957: כי 3588 אעלה 5927 ארכה 724
uahayu sha'sayik limshisah, uakal bozazayik 'aten labaz. kiy 'a'aleh 'arukah
**and they shall be that spoil you a spoil and all that prey upon you will I give for a prey For I will restore health**

לך 3807a וממכותיך 4347 ארפאך 7495 נאם 5002 יהוה 3068 כי 3588 נדחה 5080 קראו 7121 לך 3807a ציון 6726 היא 1931
lak uamimakoutayik 'arpa'aek na'am Yahuah; kiy nidachah qara'au lak, tziyoun hiy'a,
**unto you and of your wounds I will heal you saith Yahuah because an Outcast they called to you *saying* Zion This *is***

30:18
דרש 1875 אין 369 לה 3807a: כה 3541 אמר 559 יהוה 3068 הנני 2005 שב 7725 שבות 7622 אהלי 168 יעקוב 3290
doresh 'aeyn lah. koh 'amar Yahuah hinniy shab shabut 'ahaley ya'aqoub,
**seek after no man whom Thus saith Yahuah Behold I will bring again the captivity of tents Jacob's**

ומשכנתיו 4908 ארחם 7355 ונבנתה 1129 עיר 5892 על 5921 תלה 8510 וארמון 759 על 5921
uamishkanotayu 'arachem; uanibnatah 'ayr 'al tilah, ua'armoun 'al
**and on his dwellingplaces have mercy and shall be builded the city upon her own heap and the palace after**

Jer 30:11 For I am with you, saith YHUH, to save you: though I make a full end of all nations whither I have scattered you, yet will I not make a full end of you: but I will correct you in measure, and will not leave you altogether unpunished.12 For thus saith YHUH, Thy bruise is incurable, and your wound is grievous.13 There is none to plead your cause, that you may be bound up: you have no healing medicines.14 All your lovers have forgotten you; they seek you not; for I have wounded you with the wound of an enemy, with the chastisement of a cruel one, for the multitude of your iniquity; because your sins were increased.15 Why criest you for your affliction? your sorrow is incurable for the multitude of your iniquity: because your sins were increased, I have done these things unto you.16 Therefore all they that devour you shall be devoured; and all your adversaries, everyone of them, shall go into captivity; and they that spoil you shall be a spoil, and all that prey upon you will I give for a prey.17 For I will restore health unto you, and I will heal you of your wounds, saith YHUH; because they called you an Outcast, saying, This is Zion, whom no man seek after.18 Thus saith YHUH; Behold, I will bring again the captivity of Jacob's tents, and have mercy on his dwellingplaces;

| משפטו 4941 | ישב 3427: | 30:19 ויצא 3318 | מהם 1992 | תודה 8426 | וקול 6963 | משחקים 7832 |
|---|---|---|---|---|---|---|
| mishpatou | yesheb. | uayatza' | mehem | toudah | uaqoul | masachaqiym; |
| **the manner thereof shall remain** | | **And shall proceed** | **out of them** | **thanksgiving** | **and the voice of** | **them that make merry** |

| והרבתים 7235 | ולא 3808 | ימעטו 4591 | והכבדתים 3513 | ולא 3808 | יצערו 6819: | 30:20 והיו 1961 |
|---|---|---|---|---|---|---|
| uahirbitiym | uala' | yim'atu, | uahikbadtiym | uala' | yitz'aru. | uahayu |
| **and I will multiply them** | **and not** | **they shall be few** | **I will also glorify them** | **and not** | **they shall be small** | **also shall be** |

| בניו 1121 | כקדם 6924 | ועדתו 5712 | לפני 6440 | תכון 3559 | ופקדתי 6485 | על 5921 | כל 3605 |
|---|---|---|---|---|---|---|---|
| banayu | kaqedem, | ba'adatou | lapanay | tikoun; | uapaqadtiy, | 'al | kal |
| **Their children** | **as aforetime** | **and their congregation** | **before me** | **shall be established** | **and I will punish** | **on** | **all** |

| לחציו 3905: | 30:21 והיה 1961 | אדירו 117 | ממנו 4480 | ומשלו 4910 | מקרבו 7130 | יצא 3318 |
|---|---|---|---|---|---|---|
| lochatzayu. | uahayah | 'adiyrou | mimenu, | uamoshalou | miqirbou | yetzea', |
| **that oppress them** | **And shall be** | **their nobles** | **of themselves** | **and their governor** | **from the midst of them** | **shall proceed** |

| והקרבתיו 7126 | ונגש 5066 | אלי 413 | כי 3588 | מי 4310 | הוא 1931 | זה 2088 | ערב 6148 | את 853 | לבו 3820 |
|---|---|---|---|---|---|---|---|---|---|
| uahiqrabtiyu | uanigash | 'aelay; | kiy | miy' | hua' | zeh | 'arab | 'at | libou |
| **and I will cause him to draw near** | **and he shall approach** | **unto me** | **for** | **who *is*** | **this** | **he** | **that engaged** | | **his heart** |

| לגשת 5066 | אלי 413 | נאם 5002 | יהוה 3068: | 30:22 והייתם 1961 | לי 3807a | לעם 5971 | ואנכי 595 | אהיה 1961 | לכם 3807a | לאלהים 430: | 30:23 |
|---|---|---|---|---|---|---|---|---|---|---|---|
| lageshet | 'aelay | na'am | Yahuah. | uihyiytem | liy | la'am; | ua'anokiy, | 'ahayeh | lakem | le'alohiym. | |
| **to approach** | **unto me?** | **saith** | **Yahuah** | **And you shall be** | **my** | **people** | **and I** | **will be** | **to your** | **unto Elohim** | |

| הנה 2009 | סערת 5591 | יהוה 3068 | חמה 2534 | יצאה 3318 | סער 5591 | מתגורר 1641 | על 5921 | ראש 7218 | רשעים 7563 |
|---|---|---|---|---|---|---|---|---|---|
| hineh | sa'arat | Yahuah | chemah | yatz'ah, | sa'ar | mitgourer; | 'al | ra'sh | rasha'aym |
| **Behold** | **the whirlwind of** | **Yahuah** | ***with* fury** | **goes forth** | **a whirlwind** | **continuing** | **upon** | ***the* head of** | ***the* wicked** |

| יחול 2342: | 30:24 לא 3808 | ישוב 7725 | חרון 2740 | אף 639 | יהוה 3068 | עד 5704 | עשתו 6213 | ועד 5704 |
|---|---|---|---|---|---|---|---|---|
| yachul. | la' | yashub, | choroun | 'ap | Yahuah, | 'ad | 'asotou | ua'ad |
| **it shall fall with pain** | ***The* not** | **shall return** | **fierce** | **anger of** | **Yahuah** | **until** | **he have done *it*** | **and until** |

| הקימו 6965 | מזמות 4209 | לבו 3820 | באחרית 319 | הימים 3117 | תתבוננו 995 | בה 871a: |
|---|---|---|---|---|---|---|
| haqiymou | mazimout | libou; | ba'achariyt | hayamiym | titbounanu | bah. |
| **he have performed** | **the intents of** | **his heart** | **in latter** | **the days** | **you shall consider** | **it** |

| Jer 31:1 בעת 6256 | ההיא 1931 | נאם 5002 | יהוה 3068 | אהיה 1961 | לאלהים 430 | לכל 3605 | משפחות 4940 | ישראל 3478 | והמה 1992 | יהיו 1961 | לי 3807a |
|---|---|---|---|---|---|---|---|---|---|---|---|
| ba'aet | hahiy'a | na'am | Yahuah, | 'ahayeh | le'alohiym, | lakol | mishpachout | yisra'ael; | uahemah | yihayu | liy |
| **At time** | **the same** | **saith** | **Yahuah** | **will I be** | **the Elohim** | **of all** | **the families of** | **Israel** | **and they** | **shall be** | **my** |

| לעם 5971: | 31:2 כה 3541 | אמר 559 | יהוה 3068 | מצא 4672 | חן 2580 | במדבר 4057 | עם 5971 | שרידי 8300 | חרב 2719 | הלוך 1980 |
|---|---|---|---|---|---|---|---|---|---|---|
| la'am. | koh | 'amar | Yahuah, | matza' | chen | bamidbar, | 'am | sariydey | chareb; | halouk |
| **people** | **Thus** | **saith** | **Yahuah** | **found** | **grace** | **in the wilderness** | **The people** | ***which were* left of** | **the sword** | **when I went** |

| להרגיעו 7280 | ישראל 3478: | 31:3 מרחוק 7350 | יהוה 3068 | נראה 7200 | לי 3807a | ואהבת 160 | עולם 5769 |
|---|---|---|---|---|---|---|---|
| lahargiy'au | yisra'ael. | merachouq | Yahuah | nir'ah | liy; | ua'ahabat | 'aulam |
| **to cause him to rest *even*** | **Israel** | **of old** | **Yahuah** | **has appeared** | **unto me *saying*** | **Yea an love** | **everlasting** |

Jer 30:18 and the city shall be built upon her own heap, and the palace shall remain after the manner thereof.19 And out of them shall proceed thanksgiving and the voice of them that make merry: and I will multiply them, and they shall not be few; I will also glorify them, and they shall not be small.20 Their children also shall be as aforetime, and their congregation shall be established before me, and I will punish all that oppress them.21 And their nobles shall be of themselves, and their governor shall proceed from the midst of them; and I will cause him to draw near, and he shall approach unto me: for who is this that engaged his heart to approach unto me? saith YHUH.22 And you shall be my people, and I will be your G-d.23 Behold, the whirlwind of YHUH go forth with fury, a continuing whirlwind: it shall fall with pain upon the head of the wicked.24 The fierce anger of YHUH shall not return, until he have done it, and until he have performed the intents of his heart: in the latter days you shall consider it. **Jer** 31:1 At the same time, saith YHUH, will I be the G-d of all the families of Israel, and they shall be my people.2 Thus saith YHUH, The people which were left of the sword found grace in the wilderness; even Israel, when I went to cause him to rest.3 YHUH has appeared of old unto me, saying, Yea, I have loved you with an everlasting love:

| | | | | | | | |
|---|---|---|---|---|---|---|---|
| אהבתיך 157 | על 5921 | כן 3651 | משכתיך 4900 | חסד 2617: | 31:4 | עוד 5750 | אבנך 1129 |
| 'ahabtiyk, | 'al | ken | mashaktiyk | chased. | | 'aud | 'abnek |
| **I have loved you *with*** | **on** | **therefore** | **have I drawn you** | ***with* lovingkindness** | | **Again** | **I will build you** |

| | | | | | | |
|---|---|---|---|---|---|---|
| ונבנית 1129 | בתולת 1330 | ישראל 3478 | עוד 5750 | תעדי 5710 | תפיך 8596 | ויצאת 3318 |
| uanibneyt, | batulat | yisra'ael; | 'aud | ta'adiy | tupayik, | uayatza't |
| **and you shall be built** | **O virgin of** | **Israel** | **again** | **you shall be adorned with** | **your tabrets** | **and shall go forth** |

| | | | | | | | |
|---|---|---|---|---|---|---|---|
| במחול 4234 | משחקים 7832: | 31:5 | עוד 5750 | תטעי 5193 | כרמים 3754 | בהרי 2022 | שמרון 8111 |
| bimachoul | masachaqiym. | | 'aud | tit'ay | karamiym, | baharey | shomaroun; |
| **in the dances of** | **them that make merry** | | **yet** | **You shall plant** | **vines** | **upon the mountains of** | **Samaria** |

| | | | | | | | | | |
|---|---|---|---|---|---|---|---|---|---|
| נטעו 5193 | נטעים 5193 | וחללו 2490: | 31:6 | כי 3588 | יש 3426 | יום 3117 | קראו 7121 | נצרים 5341 |
| nata'au | nota'aym | uachilelu. | | kiy | yesh | youm, | qara'au | notzariym |
| **the planters** | **shall plant** | **and shall eat *them* as common things** | | **For** | **there shall be** | **a day** | **shall cry** | ***that* the watchmen** |

| | | | | | | | | | | | |
|---|---|---|---|---|---|---|---|---|---|---|---|
| בהר 2022 | אפרים 669 | קומו 6965 | ונעלה 5927 | ציון 6726 | אל 413 | יהוה 3068 | אלהינו 430: | 31:7 | כי 3588 | כה 3541 | אמר 559 | יהוה 3068 |
| bahar | 'aprayim; | qumu | uana'aleh | tziyoun, | 'al | Yahuah | 'aloheynu. | | kiy | koh | 'amar | Yahuah |
| **upon the mount** | **Ephraim** | **Arise you** | **and let us go up to** | **Zion** | **unto** | **Yahuah** | **our Elohim** | | **For** | **thus** | **saith** | **Yahuah** |

| | | | | | | | | | | |
|---|---|---|---|---|---|---|---|---|---|---|
| רנו 7442 | ליעקב 3290 | שמחה 8057 | וצהלו 6670 | בראש 7218 | הגוים 1471 | השמיעו 8085 | הללו 1984 | ואמרו 559 | הושע 3467 | יהוה 3068 |
| ranu | laya'aqob | simchah, | uatzahalu | bara'sh | hagouyim; | hashmiy'au | halalu | ua'amru, | housha' | Yahuah |
| **Sing** | **for Jacob *with*** | **gladness** | **and shout** | **among the chief of** | **the nations** | **publish you** | **praise you** | **and say** | **save** | **O Yahuah** |

| | | | | | | | | | | |
|---|---|---|---|---|---|---|---|---|---|---|
| את 853 | עמך 5971 | את 853 | שארית 7611 | ישראל 3478: | 31:8 | הנני 2005 | מביא 935 | אותם 853 | מארץ 776 | צפון 6828 |
| 'at | 'amaka, | 'at | sha'aeriyt | yisra'ael. | | hinniy | mebiy'a | 'autam | me'aretz | tzapoun, |
| | **your people** | | **the remnant of** | **Israel** | | **Behold I** | **will bring** | **them** | **from country** | **the north** |

| | | | | | | |
|---|---|---|---|---|---|---|
| וקבצתים 6908 | מירכתי 3411 | ארץ 776 | בם 871a | עור 5787 | ופסח 6455 | הרה 2030 |
| uaqibatztiym | miyarkatey | 'aretz | bam | 'aur | uapiseach, | harah |
| **and gather them** | **from the coasts of** | **the earth** | ***and* with them** | **the blind** | **and the lame** | **the woman with child** |

| | | | | | | | | |
|---|---|---|---|---|---|---|---|---|
| וילדת 3205 | יחדו 3162 | קהל 6951 | גדול 1419 | ישובו 7725 | הנה 2008: | 31:9 | בבכי 1065 | יבאו 935 |
| uayoledet | yachdau; | qahal | gadoul | yashubu | henah. | | bibkiy | yabo'au, |
| **and her that travail with child** | **together** | **a company** | **great** | **shall return** | **here** | | **with weeping** | **They shall come** |

| | | | | | | | | | |
|---|---|---|---|---|---|---|---|---|---|
| ובתחנונים 8469 | אובילם 2986 | אוליכם 1980 | אל 413 | נחלי 5158 | מים 4325 | בדרך 1870 | ישר 3477 | לא 3808 |
| uabtachanuniym | 'aubiylem | 'auliykem | 'al | nachaley | mayim, | baderek | yashar, | la' |
| **and with supplications** | **will I lead them** | **I will cause them to walk** | **by** | **the rivers of** | **waters** | **in a way** | **straight** | **not** |

| | | | | | | | | | | |
|---|---|---|---|---|---|---|---|---|---|---|
| יכשלו 3782 | בה 871a | כי 3588 | הייתי 1961 | לישראל 3478 | לאב 1 | ואפרים 669 | בכרי 1060 | הוא 1931: | 31:10 | שמעו 8085 |
| yikashalu | bah; | kiy | hayiytiy | layisra'ael | la'ab, | ua'aprayim | bakoriy | hua'. | | shim'au |
| **they shall stumble** | **wherein** | **for** | **I am** | **to Israel** | **a father** | **and Ephraim** | ***is* my firstborn** | **he** | | **Hear** |

| | | | | | | | | |
|---|---|---|---|---|---|---|---|---|
| דבר 1697 | יהוה 3068 | גוים 1471 | והגידו 5046 | באיים 339 | ממרחק 4801 | ואמרו 559 | מזרה 2219 | ישראל 3478 |
| dabar | Yahuah | gouyim, | uahagiydu | ba'ayiym | mimerchaq; | ua'amru, | mazareh | yisra'ael |
| **the word of** | **Yahuah** | **O you nations** | **and declare *it*** | **in the isles** | **afar off** | **and say** | **He that scattered** | **Israel** |

Jer 31:3 therefore with lovingkindness have I drawn you.4 Again I will build you, and you shall be built, O virgin of Israel: you shall again be adorned with your tabrets, and shall go forth in the dances of them that make merry.5 Thou shall yet plant vines upon the mountains of Samaria: the planters shall plant, and shall eat them as common things.6 For there shall be a day, that the watchmen upon the mount Ephraim shall cry, Arise you, and let us go up to Zion unto YHUH our G-d.7 For thus saith YHUH; Sing with gladness for Jacob, and shout among the chief of the nations: publish you, praise you, and say, O YHUH, save your people, the remnant of Israel.8 Behold, I will bring them from the north country, and gather them from the coasts of the earth, and with them the blind and the lame, the woman with child and her that travaileth with child together: a great company shall return thither.9 They shall come with weeping, and with supplications will I lead them: I will cause them to walk by the rivers of waters in a straight way, wherein they shall not stumble: for I am a father to Israel, and Ephraim is my firstborn.10 Hear the word of YHUH, O you nations, and declare it in the isles afar off, and say, He that scattered Israel will gather him, and keep him, as a shepherd doth his flock.

| יקבצנו 6908 | ושמרו 8104 | כרעה 7462 | עדרו 5739: | 31:11 | כי 3588 | פדה 6299 | יהוה 3068 | את 853 | יעקב 3290 |
|---|---|---|---|---|---|---|---|---|---|
| yaqabtzenu, | uashmarou | kara'ah | 'adrou. | | kiy | padah | Yahuah | 'at | ya'aqob; |
| **will gather him** | **and keep him** | **as a shepherd** | ***does* his flock** | | **For** | **has redeemed** | **Yahuah** | | **Jacob** |

| וגאלו 1350 | מיד 3027 | חזק 2389 | ממנו 4480: | 31:12 | ובאו 935 | ורננו 7442 |
|---|---|---|---|---|---|---|
| uag'alou | miyad | chazaq | mimenu. | | uaba'au | uarinnu |
| **and ransomed him** | **from the hand of** | ***him that was* stronger** | **than he** | | **Therefore they shall come** | **and sing** |

| במרום 4791 | ציון 6726 | ונהרו 5102 | אל 413 | טוב 2898 | יהוה 3068 | על 5921 | דגן 1715 | ועל 5921 | תירש 3492 | ועל 5921 |
|---|---|---|---|---|---|---|---|---|---|---|
| bimaroum | tziyoun | uanaharu | 'al | toub | Yahuah | 'al | dagan | ua'al | tiyrosh | ua'al |
| **in the height of** | **Zion** | **and shall flow together** | **to** | **the goodness of** | **Yahuah** | **for** | **wheat** | **and for** | **wine** | **and for** |

| יצהר 3323 | ועל 5921 | בני 1121 | צאן 6629 | ובקר 1241 | והיתה 1961 | נפשם 5315 | כגן 1588 | רוה 7302 | ולא 3808 |
|---|---|---|---|---|---|---|---|---|---|
| yitzhar, | ua'al | baney | tza'n | uabaqar; | uahayatah | napsham | kagan | raueh, | uala' |
| **oil** | **and for** | **the young of** | **the flock** | **and of the herd** | **and shall be** | **their soul** | **as a garden** | **watered** | **and not** |

| יוסיפו 3254 | לדאבה 1669 | עוד 5750: | 31:13 | אז 227 | תשמח 8055 | בתולה 1330 | במחול 4234 | ובחרים 970 | וזקנים 2205 | יחדו 3162 |
|---|---|---|---|---|---|---|---|---|---|---|
| yousiypu | lada'abah | 'aud. | | 'az | tismach | batulah | bamachoul, | uabachriym | uazqeniym | yachdau; |
| **they shall any more** | **sorrow** | **at all** | | **Then** | **shall rejoice** | **the virgin** | **in the dance** | **both young men** | **and old** | **together** |

| והפכתי 2015 | אבלם 60 | לששון 8342 | ונחמתים 5162 | ושמחתים 8055 | מיגונם 3015: | 31:14 |
|---|---|---|---|---|---|---|
| uahapaktiy | 'ablam | lasasoun | uanichamtiym, | uasimachtiym | miygounam. | |
| **for I will turn** | **their mourning** | **into joy** | **and will comfort them** | **and make them rejoice** | **from their sorrow** | |

| ורויתי 7301 | נפש 5315 | הכהנים 3548 | דשן 1880 | ועמי 5971 | את 854 | טובי 2898 | ישבעו 7646 | נאם 5002 |
|---|---|---|---|---|---|---|---|---|
| uariueytiy | nepesh | hakohaniym | dashen; | ua'amiy | 'at | tubiy | yisba'au | na'am |
| **And I will satiate with** | **the soul of** | **the priests** | **fatness** | **and my people** | ***with*** | **my goodness** | **shall be satisfied** | **saith** |

| יהוה 3068: | 31:15 | כה 3541 | אמר 559 | יהוה 3068 | קול 6963 | ברמה 7414 | נשמע 8085 | נהי 5092 | בכי 1065 | תמרורים 8563 | רחל 7354 | מבכה 1058 | על 5921 |
|---|---|---|---|---|---|---|---|---|---|---|---|---|---|
| Yahuah. | | koh | 'amar | Yahuah | qoul | baramah | nishma' | nahiy | bakiy | tamaruriym, | rachel | mabakah | 'al |
| **Yahuah** | | **Thus** | **saith** | **Yahuah** | **A voice** | **in Ramah** | **was heard** | **lamentation** | **weeping** | ***and* bitter** | **Rahel** | **weeping** | **for** |

| בניה 1121 | מאנה 3985 | להנחם 5162 | על 5921 | בניה 1121 | כי 3588 | איננו 369: | 31:16 | כה 3541 | אמר 559 | יהוה 3068 | מנעי 4513 |
|---|---|---|---|---|---|---|---|---|---|---|---|
| baneyha; | me'anah | lahinachem | 'al | baneyha | kiy | 'aeynenu. | | koh | 'amar | Yahuah | mina'ay |
| **her children** | **refused** | **to be comforted** | **for** | **her children** | **because** | **they were not** | | **Thus** | **saith** | **Yahuah** | **Refrain** |

| קולך 6963 | מבכי 1065 | ועיניך 5869 | מדמעה 1832 | כי 3588 | יש 3426 | שכר 7939 | לפעלתך 6468 | נאם 5002 | יהוה 3068 |
|---|---|---|---|---|---|---|---|---|---|
| qoulek | mibekiy, | ua'aeynayika | midim'ah; | kiy | yesh | sakar | lip'alatek | na'am | Yahuah, |
| **your voice** | **from weeping** | **and your eyes** | **from tears** | **for** | **shall be** | **rewarded** | **your work** | **saith** | **Yahuah** |

| ושבו 7725 | מארץ 776 | אויב 341: | 31:17 | ויש 3426 | תקוה 8615 | לאחריתך 319 | נאם 5002 | יהוה 3068 |
|---|---|---|---|---|---|---|---|---|
| uashabu | me'aretz | auyeb. | | uayesh | tiquah | la'achariytek | na'am | Yahuah; |
| **and they shall come again** | **from the land of** | **the enemy** | | **And there is** | **hope** | **in your end** | **saith** | **Yahuah** |

| ושבו 7725 | בנים 1121 | לגבולם 1366: | 31:18 | שמוע 8085 | שמעתי 8085 | אפרים 669 | מתנודד 5110 |
|---|---|---|---|---|---|---|---|
| uashabu | baniym | ligabulam. | | shamoua' | shama'atiy, | 'aprayim | mitnouded, |
| **that shall come again** | **your children** | **to their own border** | | **I have surely heard** | | **Ephraim bemoaning himself** | |

Jer 11:11 For YHUH has redeemed Jacob, and ransomed him from the hand of him that was stronger than he.12 Therefore they shall come and sing in the height of Zion, and shall flow together to the goodness of YHUH, for wheat, and for wine, and for oil, and for the young of the flock and of the herd: and their soul shall be as a watered garden; and they shall not sorrow anymore at all.13 Then shall the virgin rejoice in the dance, both young men and old together: for I will turn their mourning into joy, and will comfort them, and make them rejoice from their sorrow.14 And I will satiate the soul of the priests with fatness, and my people shall be satisfied with my goodness, saith YHUH.15 Thus saith YHUH; A voice was heard in Ramah, lamentation, and bitter weeping; Rahel weeping for her children refused to be comforted for her children, because they were not.16 Thus saith YHUH; Refrain your voice from weeping, and your eyes from tears: for your work shall be rewarded, saith YHUH; and they shall come again from the land of the enemy.17 And there is hope in your end, saith YHUH, that your children shall come again to their own border.18 I have surely heard Ephraim bemoaning himself thus; Thou have chastised me, and I was chastised, as a bullock unaccustomed to the yoke: turn you me, and I shall be turned; for you are YHUH my G-d.

יסרתני 3256 ואוסר 3256 כעגל 5695 לא 3808 למד 3925 השיבני 7725
yisartaniy ua'auaser, ka'aegel la' lumad; hashiybeniy
***thus* You have chastised me and I was chastised as a bullock not accustomed *to the yoke* turn you me**

ואשובה 7725 כי 3588 אתה 859 יהוה 3068 אלהי 430: 31:19 כי 3588 אחרי 310 שובי 7725 נחמתי 5162 ואחרי 310
ua'ashubah, kiy 'atah Yahuah 'alohay. kiy 'acharey shubiy nichamatiy, ua'acharey
**and I shall be turned for you *are* Yahuah my Elohim Surely after that I was turned I repented and after that**

הודעי 3045 ספקתי 5606 על 5921 ירך 3409 בשתי 954 וגם 1571 נכלמתי 3637 כי 3588 נשאתי 5375 חרפת 2781
hiuada'ay, sapaqtiy 'al yarek; boshatiy uagam niklamtiy, kiy nasa'tiy cherpat
**I was instructed I smote upon *my* thigh I was ashamed yea even confounded because I did bear the reproach of**

נעורי 5271: 31:20 הבן 1121 יקיר 3357 לי 3807a אפרים 669 אם 518 ילד 3206 שעשעים 8191 כי 3588 מדי 1767 דברי 1697 בו 871a
na'auray. haben yakiyr liy 'aprayim, 'am yeled sha'ashu'aym, kiy midey dabriy bou,
**my youth *Is* son? dear my Ephraim *is he* or a child? pleasant for since I spoke against him**

זכר 2142 אזכרנו 2142 עוד 5750 על 5921 כן 3651 המו 1993 מעי 4578 לו 3807a רחם 7355
zakor 'azkarenu 'aud; 'al ken, hamu me'ay lou', rachem
**I do remember earnestly him still therefore after that are troubled my bowels for him I will surely**

ארחמנו 7355 נאם 5002 יהוה 3068: 31:21 הציבי 5324 לך 3807a צינים 6725 שמי 7760 לך 3807a תמרורים 8564 שתי 7896 לבך 3820
'arachamenu na'am Yahuah. hatziybiy lak tziyuniym, simiy lak tamaruriym, shitiy libek,
**have mercy upon him saith Yahuah Set up to you waymarks make for you high heaps set your heart**

למסלה 4546 דרך 1870 הלכתי 1980 שובי 7725 בתולת 1330 ישראל 3478 שבי 7725 אל 413 עריך 5892 אלה 428:
lamasilah derek halaktiy shubiy batulat yisra'ael, shubiy 'al 'arayik 'aeleh.
**toward the highway *even* the way *which* you went turn again O virgin of Israel turn again to your cities these**

31:22 עד 5704 מתי 4970 תתחמקין 2559 הבת 1323 השובבה 7728 כי 3588 ברא 1254 יהוה 3068 חדשה 2319
'ad matay titchamaqiyn, habat hashoubebah; kiy bara' Yahuah chadashah
**How long will you go about O you daughter? backsliding for has created Yahuah a new thing**

בארץ 776 נקבה 5347 תסובב 5437 גבר 1397: 31:23 כה 3541 אמר 559 יהוה 3068 צבאות 6635 אלהי 430 ישראל 3478 עוד 5750
ba'aretz, naqebah tasoubeb gaber. koh 'amar Yahuah tzaba'aut 'alohey yisra'ael, 'aud
**in the earth A woman shall compass a man Thus saith Yahuah of hosts the Elohim of Israel As yet**

יאמרו 559 את 853 הדבר 1697 הזה 2088 בארץ 776 יהודה 3063 ובעריו 5892 בשובי 7725 את 853
ya'maru 'at hadabar hazeh, ba'aretz yahudah uab'arayu, bashubiy 'at
**they shall use speech this in the land of Judah and in the cities thereof when I shall bring again**

שבותם 7622 יברכך 1288 יהוה 3068 נוה 5116 צדק 6664 הר 2022 הקדש 6944: 31:24 וישבו 3427 בה 871a
shabutam; yabarekka Yahuah naueh tzedeq har haqodesh. uayashabu bah
**their captivity bless you Yahuah O habitation of justice *and* mountain of holiness And there shall dwell in itself**

יהודה 3063 וכל 3605 עריו 5892 יחדו 3162 אכרים 406 ונסעו 5265 בעדר 5739: 31:25 כי 3588 הרויתי 7301
yahudah uakal 'arayu yachdau; 'akariym uanasa'au ba'aeder. kiy hirueytiy
**Judah and in all the cities thereof together husbandmen and they *that* go forth with flocks For I have satiated**

Jer 31:19 Surely after that I was turned, I repented; and after that I was instructed, I smote upon my thigh: I was ashamed, yea, even confounded, because I did bear the reproach of my youth.20 Is Ephraim my dear son? is he a pleasant child? for since I spoke against him, I do earnestly remember him still: therefore my bowels are troubled for him; I will surely have mercy upon him, saith YHUH.21 Set you up waymarks, make you high heaps: set your heart toward the highway, even the way which you went: turn again, O virgin of Israel, turn again to these your cities.22 How long will you go about, O you backsliding daughter? for YHUH has created a new thing in the earth, A woman shall compass a man.23 Thus saith YHUH of hosts, the G-d of Israel; As yet they shall use this speech in the land of Judah and in the cities thereof, when I shall bring again their captivity; YHUH bless you, O habitation of justice, and mountain of holiness.24 And there shall dwell in Judah itself, and in all the cities thereof together, husbandmen, and they that go forth with flocks. 25 For I have satiated the weary soul, and I have replenished every sorrowful soul.

31:26

5315 נפש 5889 עיפה 3605 וכל 5315 נפש 1669 דאבה 4390 מלאתי: 5921 על 2063 זאת 6974 הקיצתי 7200 וראה 8142 ושנתי
nepesh 'ayepah; uakal nepesh da'abah milea'tiy. 'al za't heqiytzotiy ua'ar'ah; uashnatiy
**soul *the* weary and every soul sorrowful I have replenished Upon this I awaked and beheld and my sleep**

31:27

6149 ערבה 3807a לי: 2009 הנה 3117 ימים 935 באים 5002 נאם 3068 יהוה 2232 וזרעתי 853 את 1004 בית 3478 ישראל 853 ואת
'arabah liy. hineh yamiym ba'aym na'am Yahuah; uazara'atiy, 'at beyt yisra'ael ua'at
**was sweet unto me Behold the days come saith Yahuah that I will sow the house of Israel *and***

31:28

1004 בית 3063 יהודה 2233 זרע 120 אדם 2233 וזרע 929 בהמה: 1961 והיה 834 כאשר
beyt yahudah, zera' 'adam uazera' bahemah. uahayah ka'asher
**the house of Judah *with* the seed of man and with the seed of beast And it shall come to pass *that* like as**

8245 שקדתי 5921 עליהם 5428 לנתוש 5422 ולנתוץ 2040 ולהרס 6 ולהאביד 7489 ולהרע 3651 כן
shaqadtiy 'aleyhem, lintoush ualintoutz ualharos ualha'abiyd ualharea'; ken
**I have watched over them to pluck up and to break down and to throw down and to destroy and to afflict so**

31:29

8245 אשקד 5921 עליהם 1129 לבנות 5193 ולנטוע 5002 נאם 3068 יהוה: 3117 בימים 1992 ההם 3808 לא 559 יאמרו 5750 עוד
'ashqod 'aleyhem libnout ualintoua' na'am Yahuah. bayamiym hahem, la' ya'maru 'aud,
**will I watch over them to build and to plant saith Yahuah In days those no they shall say more**

31:30

1 אבות 398 אכלו 1155 בסר 8127 ושני 1121 בנים 6949 תקהינה: 3588 כי 518 אם 376 איש
'about 'akalu boser; uashiney baniym tiqheynah. kiy 'am 'aysh
**The fathers have eaten a sour grape and teeth *the* children's are set on edge But rather every one**

31:31

5771 בעונו 4191 ימות 3605 כל 120 האדם 398 האכל 1155 הבסר 6949 תקהינה 8127 שניו: 2009 הנה 3117 ימים
ba'auonou yamut; kal ha'adam ha'akel haboser tiqheynah shinayu. hineh yamiym
**for his own iniquity shall die every man that eat the sour grape shall be set on edge his teeth Behold the days**

935 באים 5002 נאם 3068 יהוה 3772 וכרתי 854 את 1004 בית 3478 ישראל 854 ואת 1004 בית 3063 יהודה 1285 ברית
ba'aym na'am Yahuah; uakaratiy, 'at beyt yisra'ael ua'at beyt yahudah bariyt
**come saith Yahuah that I will make *with* the house of Israel *and with* the house of Judah a covenant**

31:32

2319 חדשה: 3808 לא 1285 כברית 834 אשר 3772 כרתי 854 את 1 אבותם 3117 ביום 2388 החזיקי 3027 בידם
chadashah. la' kabriyt, 'asher karatiy 'at aboutam, bayoum hechaziyqiy bayadam,
**new Not according to the covenant that I made *with* their fathers in the day *that* I took them by the hand**

3318 להוציאם 776 מארץ 4714 מצרים 834 אשר 1992 המה 6565 הפרו 853 את 1285 בריתי 595 ואנכי 1166 בעלתי
lahoutziy'am me'aretz mitzrayim; 'asher hemah heperu 'at bariytiy, ua'anokiy ba'altiy
**to bring them out of the land of Egypt which they brake my covenant although I was an husband**

31:33

871a בם 5002 נאם 3068 יהוה: 3588 כי 2063 זאת 1285 הברית 834 אשר 3772 אכרת 854 את 1004 בית 3478 ישראל 310 אחרי
bam na'am Yahuah. kiy za't habariyt 'asher 'akrot 'at beyt yisra'ael 'acharey
**unto them saith Yahuah But this *shall be* the covenant that I will make *with* the house of Israel After**

3117 הימים 1992 ההם 5002 נאם 3068 יהוה 5414 נתתי 853 את 8451 תורתי 7130 בקרבם 5921 ועל 3820 לבם 3789 אכתבנה 1961 והייתי
hayamiym hahem na'am Yahuah, natatiy 'at touratiy baqirbam, ua'al libam 'aktabenah; uahayiytiy
**days those saith Yahuah I will put my law in their inward parts and in their hearts write it and will be**

Jer 31:26 Upon this I awaked, and beheld; and my sleep was sweet unto me.27 Behold, the days come, saith YHUH, that I will sow the house of Israel and the house of Judah with the seed of man, and with the seed of beast.28 And it shall come to pass, that like as I have watched over them, to pluck up, and to break down, and to throw down, and to destroy, and to afflict; so will I watch over them, to build, and to plant, saith YHUH.29 In those days they shall say no more, The fathers have eaten a sour grape, and the children's teeth are set on edge.30 But everyone shall die for his own iniquity: every man that eateth the sour grape, his teeth shall be set on edge.31 Behold, the days come, saith YHUH, that I will make a new covenant with the house of Israel, and with the house of Judah:32 Not according to the covenant that I made with their fathers in the day that I took them by the hand to bring them out of the land of Egypt; which my covenant they break, although I was an husband unto them, saith YHUH:33 But this shall be the covenant that I will make with the house of Israel; After those days, saith YHUH, I will put my law in their inward parts, and write it in their hearts; and will be their G-d, and they shall be my people.

להם 3807a לאלהים 430 והמה 1992 יהיו 1961 לי 3807a לעם 5971: 31:34 ולא 3808 ילמדו 3925 עוד 5750 איש 376 את 853 רעהו 7453
lahem le'alohiym, uahemah yihayu liy la'am. uala' yalamdu 'aud, 'aysh 'at re'aehu
**their to Elohim and they shall be my people And no they shall teach more every man his neighbour**

ואיש 376 את 853 אחיו 251 לאמר 559 דעו 3045 את 853 יהוה 3068 כי 3588 כולם 3605 ידעו 3045 אותי 853 למקטנם 6996
ua'aysh 'at 'achiyu lea'mor, da'au 'at Yahuah; kiy kulam yeda'au 'autiy lamiqtanam
**and every man his brother saying Know Yahuah for all they shall know me from the least of them**

ועד 5704 גדולם 1419 נאם 5002 יהוה 3068 כי 3588 אסלח 5545 לעונם 5771 ולחטאתם 2403 לא 3808 אזכר 2142
ua'ad gadoulam na'am Yahuah, kiy 'aslach la'auonam, ualchata'tam la' 'azkar
**and unto the greatest of them saith Yahuah for I will forgive their iniquity their sin no and I will remember**

עוד 5750: 31:35 כה 3541 אמר 559 יהוה 3068 נתן 5414 שמש 8121 לאור 216 יומם 3119 חקת 2708 ירח 3394
'aud. koh 'amar Yahuah noten shemesh la'aur youmam, chuqot yareach
**more Thus saith Yahuah which gives the sun for a light by day *and* the ordinances of the moon**

וכוכבים 3556 לאור 216 לילה 3915 רגע 7280 הים 3220 ויהמו 1993 גליו 1530 יהוה 3068 צבאות 6635 שמו 8034: 31:36
uakoukabiym la'aur layalah; roga' hayam uayehemu galayu, Yahuah tzaba'aut shamou.
**and of the stars for a light by night which divides the sea when roar the waves thereof Yahuah of hosts *is* his name**

אם 518 ימשו 4185 החקים 2706 האלה 428 מלפני 6440 נאם 5002 יהוה 3068 גם 1571 זרע 2233 ישראל 3478 ישבתו 7673 מהיות 1961
'am yamushu hachuqiym ha'aeleh milapanay na'am Yahuah; gam zera' yisra'ael yishbatu, mihyout
**If depart ordinances those from before me saith Yahuah also *then* the seed of Israel shall cease from being**

גוי 1471 לפני 6440 כל 3605 הימים 3117: 31:37 כה 3541 אמר 559 יהוה 3068 אם 518 ימדו 4058 שמים 8064 מלמעלה 4605
gouy lapanay kal hayamiym. koh 'amar Yahuah 'am yimadu shamayim milma'alah,
**a nation before me for ever Thus saith Yahuah If can be measured heaven above**

ויחקרו 2713 מוסדי 4146 ארץ 776 למטה 4295 גם 1571 אני 589 אמאס 3988 בכל 3605 זרע 2233 ישראל 3478 על 5921 כל 3605
uayechaqaru mousadey 'aretz lamatah; gam 'aniy 'am'as bakal zera' yisra'ael 'al kal
**and searched out the foundations of the earth beneath also I will cast off all the seed of Israel for all**

אשר 834 עשו 6213 נאם 5002 יהוה 3068: 31:38 הנה 2009 ימים 3117 כך באים Q935 נאם 5002 יהוה 3068 ונבנתה 1129 העיר 5892
'asher 'asu na'am Yahuah. hineh yamiym kak ba'aym na'am Yahuah; uanibnatah ha'ayr
**that they have done saith Yahuah Behold the days (to come) saith Yahuah that shall be built the city**

ליהוה 3068 ממגדל 4026 חננאל 2606 שער 8179 הפנה 6438: 31:39 ויצא 3318 עוד 5750 קוה 6961 המדה 4060
laYahuah, mimigdal chanan'ael sha'ar hapinah. uayatza' 'aud qauah hamidah
**to Yahuah from the tower of Hananeel *unto* the gate of the corner And shall go forth yet line the measuring**

נגדו 5048 על 5921 גבעת 1389 גרב 1619 ונסב 5437 געתה 1601: 31:40 וכל 3605 העמק 6010 הפגרים 6297
negdou, 'al gib'at gareb; uanasab go'atah. uakal ha'aemeq hapagariym
**over against it unto the hill Gareb and shall compass about to Goath And the whole valley of the dead bodies**

והדשן 1880 וכל 3605 השרמות 8309 עד 5704 נחל 5158 קדרון 6939 עד 5704 פנת 6438 שער 8179 הסוסים 5483
uahadeshen uakal hasharemout 'ad nachal qidroun 'ad pinat sha'ar hasusiym
**and of the ashes and all the fields unto the brook of Kidron unto *the* corner of gate the horse**

Jer 31:34 And they shall teach no more every man his neighbor, and every man his brother, saying, Know YHUH: for they shall all know me, from the least of them unto the greatest of them, saith YHUH; for I will forgive their iniquity, and I will remember their sin no more.35 Thus saith YHUH, which give the sun for a light by day, and the ordinances of the moon and of the stars for a light by night, which divideth the sea when the waves thereof roar; YHUH of hosts is his name:36 If those ordinances depart from before me, saith YHUH, then the seed of Israel also shall cease from being a nation before me forever.37 Thus saith YHUH; If heaven above can be measured, and the foundations of the earth searched out beneath, I will also cast off all the seed of Israel for all that they have done, saith YHUH.38 Behold, the days come, saith YHUH, that the city shall be built to YHUH from the tower of Hananeel unto the gate of the corner.39 And the measuring line shall yet go forth over against it upon the hill Gareb, and shall compass about to Goath.40 And the whole valley of the dead bodies, and of the ashes, and all the fields unto the brook of Kidron, unto the corner of the horse gate toward the east, shall be holy unto YHUH; it shall not be plucked up, nor thrown down anymore forever.

מזרחה 4217 קדש 6944 ליהוה 3068 לא 3808 ינתש 5428 ולא 3808 יהרס 2040 עוד 5750 לעולם 5769:
mizrachah, qodesh laYahuah; la' yinatesh uala' yehares 'aud la'aulam.
**toward the east *shall be* holy unto Yahuah not it shall be plucked up nor thrown down any more for ever**

**Jer 32:1** הדבר 1697 אשר 834 היה 1961 אל 413 ירמיהו 3414 מאת 853 יהוה 3068 בשנת 8141 העשרית 6224 לצדקיהו 6667 מלך 4428 יהודה 3063
hadabar 'asher hayah 'al yirmayahu me'at Yahuah, bishnat ha'asiriyt, latzidqiyahu melek yahudah;
**The word that came to Jeremiah from Yahuah in year the tenth of Zedekiah king of Judah**

היא 1931 השנה 8141 שמנה 8083 עשרה 6240 שנה 8141 לנבוכדראצר 5019: **32:2** ואז 227 חיל 2428 מלך 4428 בבל 894 צרים 6696
hiy'a hashanah shamonah 'asreh shanah linabukadra'tzar. ua'az, cheyl melek babel, tzariym
**which *was* the year eight ten year of Nebuchadrezzar For then army the king of Babylon's besieged**

על 5921 ירושלם 3389 וירמיהו 3414 הנביא 5030 היה 1961 כלוא 3607 בחצר 2691 המטרה 4307 אשר 834 בית 1004 מלך 4428
'al yarushalaim; uayirmayahu hanabiy'a, hayah kalua' bachatzar hamatarah, 'asher beyt melek
**on Jerusalem and Jeremiah the prophet was shut up in the court of the prison which house *was* in the king of**

יהודה 3063: **32:3** אשר 834 כלאו 3607 צדקיהו 6667 מלך 4428 יהודה 3063 לאמר 559 מדוע 4069 אתה 859 נבא 5012 לאמר 559 כה 3541
yahudah. 'asher kala'au, tzidqiyahu melek yahudah lea'mor; madua' 'atah niba' lea'mor, koh
**Judah's For had shut him up Zedekiah king of Judah saying Wherefore you do prophesy and say Thus**

אמר 559 יהוה 3068 הנני 2005 נתן 5414 את 853 העיר 5892 הזאת 2063 ביד 3027 מלך 4428 בבל 894 ולכדה 3920: **32:4**
'amar Yahuah, hinniy noten 'at ha'ayr haza't bayad melek babel ualkadah.
**saith Yahuah Behold I will give city this into the hand of the king of Babylon and he shall take it**

וצדקיהו 6667 מלך 4428 יהודה 3063 לא 3808 ימלט 4422 מיד 3027 הכשדים 3778 כי 3588 הנתן 5414 ינתן 5414
uatzidqiyahu melek yahudah, la' yimalet miyad hakasdiym; kiy hinaton yinaten
**And Zedekiah king of Judah not shall escape out of the hand of the Chaldeans but shall surely be delivered**

ביד 3027 מלך 4428 בבל 894 ודבר 1696 פיו 6310 עם 5973 פיו 6310 ועיניו 5869 את 853 עינו 5869
bayad melek babel, uadiber piyu 'am piyu, ua'aeynayu 'at 'aeynou
**into the hand of the king of Babylon and shall speak *with him* mouth to mouth and his eyes his eyes**

תראינה 7200: **32:5** ובבל 894 יולך 1980 את 853 צדקיהו 6667 ושם 8033 יהיה 1961 עד 5704 פקדי 6485 אתו 853 נאם 5002 יהוה 3068
tir'aynah. uababel youlik 'at tzidqiyahu uasham yihayeh, 'ad paqadiy 'atou na'am Yahuah;
**shall behold And Babylon he shall take Zedekiah *to* and there shall he be until I visit him saith Yahuah**

כי 3588 תלחמו 3898 את 854 הכשדים 3778 לא 3808 תצליחו 6743: **32:6** ויאמר 559 ירמיהו 3414 היה 1961 דבר 1697 יהוה 3068
kiy tilachamu 'at hakasdiym la' tatzliychu. uaya'mer yirmayahu; hayah dabar Yahuah
**though you fight *with* the Chaldeans not you shall prosper? And said Jeremiah came The word of Yahuah**

אלי 413 לאמר 559: **32:7** הנה 2009 חנמאל 2601 בן 1121 שלם 7967 דדך 1730 בא 935 אליך 413 לאמר 559 קנה 7069 לך 3807a את 853
'aelay lea'mor. hineh chanam'ael, ben shalum dodaka, ba' 'aeleyka lea'mor; qaneh laka, 'at
**unto me saying Behold Hanameel the son of Shallum your uncle shall come unto you saying Buy for you**

שדי 7704 אשר 834 בענתות 6068 כי 3588 לך 3807a משפט 4941 הגאלה 1353 לקנות 7069: **32:8** ויבא 935 אלי 413 חנמאל 2601 בן 1121
sadiy 'asher ba'anatout, kiy laka mishapat haga'ulah liqnout. uayaba' 'aelay chanam'ael ben
**my field that *is* in Anathoth for *is* to you the right of redemption to buy *it* So came to me Hanameel son**

**Jer** 32:1 The word that came to Jeremiah from YHUH in the tenth year of Zedekiah king of Judah, which was the eighteenth year of Nebuchadrezzar.2 For then the king of Babylon's army besieged Jerusalem: and Jeremiah the prophet was shut up in the court of the prison, which was in the king of Judah's house.3 For Zedekiah king of Judah had shut him up, saying, Wherefore dost you prophesy, and say, Thus saith YHUH, Behold, I will give this city into the hand of the king of Babylon, and he shall take it;4 And Zedekiah king of Judah shall not escape out of the hand of the Chaldeans, but shall surely be delivered into the hand of the king of Babylon, and shall speak with him mouth to mouth, and his eyes shall behold his eyes;5 And he shall lead Zedekiah to Babylon, and there shall he be until I visit him, saith YHUH: though you fight with the Chaldeans, you shall not prosper?6 And Jeremiah said, The word of YHUH came unto me, saying,7 Behold, Hanameel the son of Shallum your uncle shall come unto you, saying, Buy you my field that is in Anathoth: for the right of redemption is your to buy it.

| דדי 1730 | כדבר 1697 | יהוה 3068 | אל 413 | חצר 2691 | המטרה 4307 | ויאמר 559 | אלי 413 | קנה 7069 | נא 4994 | את 853 |
|---|---|---|---|---|---|---|---|---|---|---|
| dodiy | kidbar | Yahuah | 'al | chatzar | hamatarah | uaya'mer | 'aelay | qaneh | naa' | 'at |
| **mine uncle's** | **according to the word of** | **Yahuah** | **in** | **the court of** | **the prison** | **and said** | **unto me** | **Buy** | **I pray you** | |

| שדי 7704 | אשר 834 | בענתות 6068 | אשר 834 | בארץ 776 | בנימין 1144 | כי 3588 | לך 3807a | משפט 4941 | הירשה 3425 | ולך 3807a |
|---|---|---|---|---|---|---|---|---|---|---|
| sadiy | 'asher | ba'anatout | 'asher | ba'aretz | binyamiyn, | kiy | laka | mishapat | hayarushah | ualaka |
| **my field** | **that** | ***is* in Anathoth** | **which** | ***is* in the country of** | **Benjamin** | **for *is*** | **to your** | **the right of** | **inheritance** | **and your** |

| הגאלה 1353 | קנה 7069 | לך 3807a | ואדע 3045 | כי 3588 | דבר 1697 | יהוה 3068 | הוא 1931: | 32:9 | ואקנה 7069 | את 853 |
|---|---|---|---|---|---|---|---|---|---|---|
| haga'ulah | qaneh | lak; | ua'aeda' | kiy | dabar | Yahuah | hua'. | | ua'aqneh | 'at |
| **the redemption *is*** | **buy** | ***it* for yourself** | **Then I knew** | **that** | ***was* the word of** | **Yahuah** | **this** | | **And I bought** | |

| השדה 7704 | מאת 853 | חנמאל 2601 | בן 1121 | דדי 1730 | אשר 834 | בענתות 6068 | ואשקלה 8254 | לו 3807a | את 853 | הכסף 3701 | שבעה 7651 |
|---|---|---|---|---|---|---|---|---|---|---|---|
| hasadeh, | me'at | chanam'ael | ben | dodiy | 'asher | ba'anatout; | ua'ashqalah | lou' | 'at | hakesep, | shib'ah |
| **the field** | **of** | **Hanameel** | **son** | **my uncle's** | **that** | ***was* in Anathoth** | **and weighed** | **him** | | **the money** | ***even* seven** |

| שקלים 8255 | ועשרה 6235 | הכסף 3701: | 32:10 | ואכתב 3789 | בספר 5612 | ואחתם 2856 | ואעד 5749 | עדים 5707 | ואשקל 8254 |
|---|---|---|---|---|---|---|---|---|---|
| shaqaliym | ua'asarah | hakasep. | | ua'aktob | baseper | ua'achtom, | ua'a'aed | 'aediym; | ua'ashqol |
| **shekels** | **and ten** | ***of* silver** | | **And I subscribed** | **the evidence** | **and sealed** | ***it* and took** | **witnesses** | **and weighed** |

| הכסף 3701 | במאזנים 3976: | 32:11 | ואקח 3947 | את 853 | ספר 5612 | המקנה 4736 | את 853 | החתום 2856 |
|---|---|---|---|---|---|---|---|---|
| hakesep | bama'zanayim. | | ua'aqach | 'at | seper | hamiqnah; | 'at | hechatum |
| ***him* the money** | **in the balances** | | **So I took** | | **the evidence of** | **the purchase** | | ***both* that which was sealed** |

| המצוה 4687 | והחקים 2706 | ואת 853 | הגלוי 1540: | 32:12 | ואתן 5414 | את 853 | הספר 5612 | המקנה 4736 | אל 413 |
|---|---|---|---|---|---|---|---|---|---|
| hamitzuah | uahachuqiym | ua'at | hagaluy. | | ua'aten | 'at | haseper | hamiqnah, | 'al |
| ***according* to the law** | **and custom** | ***and*** | **that which was open** | | **And I gave** | | **the evidence of** | **the purchase** | **unto** |

| ברוך 1263 | בן 1121 | נריה 5374 | בן 1121 | מחסיה 4271 | לעיני 5869 | חנמאל 2601 | דדי 1730 | ולעיני 5869 |
|---|---|---|---|---|---|---|---|---|
| baruk | ben | neriyah | ben | machseyah | la'aeyney | chanam'ael | dodiy, | ual'aeyney |
| **Baruch** | **the son of** | **Neriah** | **the son of** | **Maaseiah** | **in the sight of** | **Hanameel** | **mine uncle's** | ***son* and in the presence of** |

| העדים 5707 | הכתבים 3789 | בספר 5612 | המקנה 4736 | לעיני 5869 | כל 3605 | היהודים 3064 | הישבים 3427 | בחצר 2691 |
|---|---|---|---|---|---|---|---|---|
| ha'aediym, | hakotabiym | baseper | hamiqnah; | la'aeyney | kal | hayahudiym, | hayoshabiym | bachatzar |
| **the witnesses** | **that subscribed** | **the book of** | **the purchase** | **before** | **all** | **the Jews** | **that sat** | **in the court of** |

| המטרה 4307: | 32:13 | ואצוה 6680 | את 853 | ברוך 1263 | לעיניהם 5869 | לאמר 559: | 32:14 | כה 3541 | אמר 559 | יהוה 3068 | צבאות 6635 | אלהי 430 |
|---|---|---|---|---|---|---|---|---|---|---|---|---|
| hamatarah. | | ua'atzaueh | 'at | baruk, | la'aeyneyhem | lea'mor. | | koh | 'amar | Yahuah | tzaba'aut | 'alohey |
| **the prison** | | **And I charged** | | **Baruch** | **before them** | **saying** | | **Thus** | **saith** | **Yahuah** | **of hosts** | **the Elohim of** |

| ישראל 3478 | לקוח 3947 | את 853 | הספרים 5612 | האלה 428 | את 853 | ספר 5612 | המקנה 4736 | הזה 2088 | ואת 853 | החתום 2856 | ואת 853 | ספר 5612 |
|---|---|---|---|---|---|---|---|---|---|---|---|---|
| yisra'ael, | laqouach | 'at | hasapariym | ha'aeleh | 'at | seper | hamiqnah | hazeh | ua'at | hechatum, | ua'at | seper |
| **Israel** | **Take** | | **evidences** | **these** | | **evidence of** | **the purchase** | **this** | ***both*** | **which is sealed** | ***and*** | **evidence** |

| הגלוי 1540 | הזה 2088 | ונתתם 5414 | בכלי 3627 | חרש 2789 | למען 4616 | יעמדו 5975 | ימים 3117 | רבים 7227: | 32:15 | כי 3588 | כה 3541 |
|---|---|---|---|---|---|---|---|---|---|---|---|
| hagaluy | hazeh, | uantatam | bikley | chares; | lama'an | ya'amdu | yamiym | rabiym. | | kiy | koh |
| **which is open** | **this** | **and put them** | **in an vessel** | **earthen** | **that** | **they may continue** | **days** | **many** | | **For** | **thus** |

Jer 32:8 So Hanameel mine uncle's son came to me in the court of the prison according to the word of YHUH, and said unto me, Buy my field, I pray you, that is in Anathoth, which is in the country of Benjamin: for the right of inheritance is your, and the redemption is your; buy it for thyself. Then I knew that this was the word of YHUH.9 And I bought the field of Hanameel my uncle's son, that was in Anathoth, and weighed him the money, even seventeen shekels of silver.10 And I subscribed the evidence, and sealed it, and took witnesses, and weighed him the money in the balances.11 So I took the evidence of the purchase, both that which was sealed according to the law and custom, and that which was open:12 And I gave the evidence of the purchase unto Baruch the son of Neriah, the son of Maaseiah, in the sight of Hanameel mine uncle's son, and in the presence of the witnesses that subscribed the book of the purchase, before all the Jews that sat in the court of the prison.13 And I charged Baruch before them, saying,14 Thus saith YHUH of hosts, the G-d of Israel; Take these evidences, this evidence of the purchase, both which is sealed, and this evidence which is open; and put them in an earthen vessel, that they may continue many days.

אמר 559 יהוה 3068 צבאות 6635 אלהי 430 ישראל 3478 עוד 5750 יקנו 7069 בתים 1004 ושדות 7704 וכרמים 3754 בארץ 776
'amar Yahuah tzaba'aut 'alohey yisra'ael; 'aud yiqanu batiym uasadout uakramiym ba'aretz
**saith Yahuah of hosts the Elohim of Israel again shall be possessed Houses and fields and vineyards in land**

הזאת 2063: **32:16** ואתפלל 6419 אל 413 יהוה 3068 אחרי 310 תתי 5414 את 853 ספר 5612 המקנה 4736 אל 413 ברוך 1263
haza't. ua'atpalel 'al Yahuah; 'acharey titiy 'at seper hamiqnah, 'al baruk
**this Now I prayed unto Yahuah when I had delivered the evidence of the purchase unto Baruch**

בן 1121 נריה 5374 לאמר 559: **32:17** אהה 162 אדני 136 יהוה 3068 הנה 2009 אתה 859 עשית 6213 את 853 השמים 8064 ואת 853 הארץ 776
ben neriyah lea'mor. 'ahah 'adonay Yahuah hineh 'atah 'ashiyta, 'at hashamayim ua'at ha'aretz,
**the son of Neriah saying Ah Adonai Yahuah behold you have made the heaven *and* the earth**

בכחך 3581 הגדול 1419 ובזרעך 2220 הנטויה 5186 לא 3808 יפלא 6381 ממך 4480 כל 3605 דבר 1697: **32:18** עשה 6213
bakochaka hagadoul, uabizro'aka hanatuyah; la' yipalea' mimaka kal dabar. 'asheh
**by your power great and arm stretched out nothing *and* there is too hard for you any of nothing You show**

חסד 2617 לאלפים 505 ומשלם 7999 עון 5771 אבות 1 אל 413 חיק 2436 בניהם 1121 אחריהם 310
chesed la'alapiym, uamashalem 'auon about, 'al cheyq baneyhem 'achareyhem;
**lovingkindness unto thousands and recompensest the iniquity of the fathers into the bosom of their children after them**

האל 410 הגדול 1419 הגבור 1368 יהוה 3068 צבאות 6635 שמו 8034: **32:19** גדל 1419 העצה 6098 ורב 7227 העליליה 5950 אשר 834
ha'ael hagadoul hagibour, Yahuah tzaba'aut shamou. gagol ha'aetzah, uarab ha'aliyliyah; 'asher
**the El the Great the Mighty Yahuah of hosts *is* his name Great in counsel and mighty in work for**

עיניך 5869 פקחות 6491 על 5921 כל 3605 דרכי 1870 בני 1121 אדם 120 לתת 5414 לאיש 376 כדרכיו 1870
'aeyneyka paquchout, 'al kal darkey baney 'adam, latet la'aysh kidrakayu,
**your eyes *are* open unto all the ways of the sons of men to give every one according to his ways**

וכפרי 6529 מעלליו 4611: **32:20** אשר 834 שמת 7760 אתות 226 ומפתים 4159 בארץ 776 מצרים 4714 עד 5704
uakipriy ma'alalayu. 'asher samta 'autot uamopatiym ba'aretz mitzrayim 'ad
**and according to the fruit of his doings Which have set signs and wonders in the land of Egypt *even* unto**

היום 3117 הזה 2088 ובישראל 3478 ובאדם 120 ותעשה 6213 לך 3807a שם 8034 כיום 3117 הזה 2088: **32:21**
hayoum hazeh, uabyisra'ael uaba'adam; uata'aseh laka shem kayoum hazeh.
**day this and in Israel and among *other* men and have made to you a name as day *at* this**

ותצא 3318 את 853 עמך 5971 את 853 ישראל 3478 מארץ 776 מצרים 4714 באתות 226 ובמופתים 4159
uatoutzea' 'at 'ameka 'at yisra'ael me'aretz mitzrayim; ba'atot uabmouptiym,
**And have brought forth your people Israel out of the land of Egypt with signs and with wonders**

וביד 3027 חזקה 2389 ובאזרוע 248 נטויה 5186 ובמורא 4172 גדול 1419: **32:22** ותתן 5414 להם 3807a את 853
uabyad chazaqah uab'azroua' netuyah, uabmoura' gadoul. uatiten lahem 'at
**and with a hand strong and with a arm stretched out and with terror great And have given them**

הארץ 776 הזאת 2063 אשר 834 נשבעת 7650 לאבותם 1 לתת 5414 להם 3807a ארץ 776 זבת 2100 חלב 2461 ודבש 1706:
ha'aretz haza't, 'asher nishba'ta la'aboutam latet lahem; 'aretz zabat chalab uadbash.
**the land this which you did swear to their fathers to give them a land flowing with milk and honey**

Jer 32:15 For thus saith YHUH of hosts, the G-d of Israel; Houses and fields and vineyards shall be possessed again in this land.16 Now when I had delivered the evidence of
the purchase unto Baruch the son of Neriah, I prayed unto YHUH, saying,17 Ah Adonai G-D! behold, you have made the heaven and the earth by your great power and
stretched out arm, and there is nothing too hard for you:18 Thou shewest lovingkindness unto thousands, and recompensest the iniquity of the fathers into the bosom of their
children after them: the Great, the Mighty G-d, YHUH of hosts, is his name,19 Great in counsel, and mighty in work: for your eyes are open upon all the ways of the sons of
men: to give everyone according to his ways, and according to the fruit of his doings:20 Which have set signs and wonders in the land of Egypt, even unto this day, and in
Israel, and among other men; and have made you a name, as at this day;21 And have brought forth your people Israel out of the land of Egypt with signs, and with wonders,
and with a strong hand, and with a stretched out arm, and with great terror;22 And have given them this land, which you did swear to their fathers to give them, a land flowing
with milk and honey;

32:23
ויבאו 935 וירשו 3423 אתה 853 ולא 3808 שמעו 8085 בקולך 6963 ובתרותך 8451 לא 3808 הלכו 1980 את 853 כל 3605
uayabo'au uayirshu 'atah, uala' shama'au uaqouleka uabtoroutaka la' halaku, 'at kal
**And they came in and possessed it but not they obeyed your voice in your law neither walked *of* all**

אשר 834 צויתה 6680 להם 3807a לעשות 6213 לא 3808 עשו 6213 ותקרא 7122 אתם 853 את 853 כל 3605
'asher tziuiytah lahem la'asout la' 'asu; uataqrea' 'atam, 'at kal
**that you commanded them they have done nothing to do therefore you have caused to come upon them all**

32:24
הרעה 7451 הזאת 2063: הנה 2009 הסללות 5550 באו 935 העיר 5892 ללכדה 3920 והעיר 5892 נתנה 5414 ביד 3027
hara'ah haza't. hineh hasolalout, ba'au ha'ayr lalakadah uaha'ayr nitnah, bayad
**evil this Behold the mounts they are come unto the city to take it and the city is given into the hand of**

הכשדים 3778 הנלחמים 3898 עליה 5921 מפני 6440 החרב 2719 והרעב 7458 והדבר 1698 ואשר 834
hakasdiym hanilchamiym 'aleyha, mipaney hachereb uahara'ab uahadaber; ua'asher
**the Chaldeans that fight against it because of the sword and of the famine and of the pestilence and what**

32:25
דברת 1696 היה 1961 והנך 2005 ראה 7200: ואתה 859 אמרת 559 אלי 413 אדני 136 יהוה 3069 קנה 7069
dibarta hayah uahinaka ro'ah. ua'atah 'amarta 'aelay 'adonay Yahuah, qaneh
**you have spoken is come to pass and behold you see *it* And you have said unto me O Adonai Yahuah Buy**

32:26
לך 3807a השדה 7704 בכסף 3701 והעד 5749 עדים 5707 והעיר 5892 נתנה 5414 ביד 3027 הכשדים 3778: ויהי 1961
laka hasadeh bakesep uaha'aed 'aediym; uaha'ayr nitnah bayad hakasdiym. uayahiy
**for you the field for money and take witnesses for the city is given into the hand of the Chaldeans Then came**

32:27
דבר 1697 יהוה 3068 אל 413 ירמיהו 3414 לאמר 559: הנה 2009 אני 589 יהוה 3068 אלהי 430 כל 3605 בשר 1320 הממני 4480
dabar Yahuah, 'al yirmayahu lea'mor. hineh 'aniy Yahuah, 'alohey kal basar; hamimeniy,
**the word of Yahuah unto Jeremiah saying Behold I *am* Yahuah the Elohim of all flesh for me?**

32:28
יפלא 6381 כל 3605 דבר 1697: לכן 3651 כה 3541 אמר 559 יהוה 3068 הנני 2005 נתן 5414 את 853 העיר 5892 הזאת 2063
yipalea' kal dabar. laken koh 'amar Yahuah; hinniy noten 'at ha'ayr haza't
**is there too hard any thing Therefore thus saith Yahuah Behold I will give city this**

32:29
ביד 3027 הכשדים 3778 וביד 3027 נבוכדראצר 5019 מלך 4428 בבל 894 ולכדה 3920:
bayad hakasdiym, uabyad nabukadra'tzar melek babel ualkadah.
**into the hand of the Chaldeans and into the hand of Nebuchadrezzar king of Babylon and he shall take it**

ובאו 935 הכשדים 3778 הנלחמים 3898 על 5921 העיר 5892 הזאת 2063 והציתו 3341 את 853 העיר 5892 הזאת 2063 באש 784 ושרפוה 8313
uaba'au hakasdiym, hanilchamiym 'al ha'ayr haza't, uahitziytu 'at ha'ayr haza't ba'aesh uasrapuha;
**And shall come the Chaldeans that fight against city this and set on city this fire and burn it**

ואת 854 הבתים 1004 אשר 834 קטרו 6999 על 5921 גגותיהם 1406 לבעל 1168 והסכו 5258 נסכים 5262 לאלהים 430
ua'at habatiym 'asher qitru 'al gagouteyhem laba'al, uahisiku nasakiym le'alohiym
***with* the houses whose they have offered incense upon roofs unto Baal and poured out drink offerings unto gods**

32:30
אחרים 312 למען 4616 הכעסני 3707: כי 3588 היו 1961 בני 1121 ישראל 3478 ובני 1121 יהודה 3063 אך 389
'acheriym, lama'an haka'aseniy. kiy hayu baney yisra'ael uabney yahudah, 'ak
**other to provoke me to anger For have the children of Israel and the children of Judah only**

Jer 32:23 And they came in, and possessed it; but they obeyed not your voice, neither walked in your law; they have done nothing of all that you commanded them to do: therefore you have caused all this evil to come upon them:24 Behold the mounts, they are come unto the city to take it; and the city is given into the hand of the Chaldeans, that fight against it, because of the sword, and of the famine, and of the pestilence: and what you have spoken is come to pass; and, behold, you seest it.25 And you have said unto me, O Adonai G-D, Buy you the field for money, and take witnesses; for the city is given into the hand of the Chaldeans.26 Then came the word of YHUH unto Jeremiah, saying,27 Behold, I am YHUH, the G-d of all flesh: is there anything too hard for me?28 Therefore thus saith YHUH; Behold, I will give this city into the hand of the Chaldeans, and into the hand of Nebuchadrezzar king of Babylon, and he shall take it:29 And the Chaldeans, that fight against this city, shall come and set fire on this city and burn it with the houses, upon whose roofs they have offered incense unto Baal and poured out drink offerings unto other gods, to provoke me to anger.30 For the children of Israel and the children of Judah have only done evil before me from their youth:

עשים 6213 הרע 7451 בעיני 5869 מנערתיהם 5271 כי 3588 בני 1121 ישראל 3478 אך 389 מכעסים 3707 אתי 854
'asiym hara' ba'aeynay mina'aroteyhem; kiy baney yisra'ael, 'ak mak'aysiym 'atiy
**done evil before me from their youth for the children of Israel only have provoked me to anger with**

במעשה 4639 ידיהם 3027 נאם 5002 יהוה 3068: 32:31 כי 3588 על 5921 אפי 639 ועל 5921 חמתי 2534 היתה 1961 לי 3807a
bama'aseh yadeyhem na'am Yahuah. kiy 'al 'apiy ua'al chamatiy, hayatah liy
**the work of their hands saith Yahuah For a provocation of mine anger and of my fury has been to me *as***

העיר 5892 הזאת 2063 למן 4480 היום 3117 אשר 834 בנו 1129 אותה 853 ועד 5704 היום 3117 הזה 2088 להסירה 5493 מעל 5921
ha'ayr haza't, lamin hayoum 'asher banu 'autah, ua'ad hayoum hazeh; lahasiyrah me'al
**city this from the day that they built it even unto day this that I should remove it from before**

פני 6440: 32:32 על 5921 כל 3605 רעת 7451 בני 1121 ישראל 3478 ובני 1121 יהודה 3063 אשר 834 עשו 6213
panay. 'al kal ra'at baney yisra'ael uabney yahudah, 'asher 'asu
**my face Because of all the evil of the children of Israel and of the children of Judah which they have done**

להכעסני 3707 המה 1992 מלכיהם 4428 שריהם 8269 כהניהם 3548 ונביאיהם 5030 ואיש 376 יהודה 3063
lahak'ayseniy, hemah malkeyhem sareyhem, kohaneyhem uanbiy'aeyhem; ua'aysh yahudah,
**to provoke me to anger they their kings their princes their priests and their prophets and the men of Judah**

וישבי 3427 ירושלם 3389: 32:33 ויפנו 6437 אלי 413 ערף 6203 ולא 3808 פנים 6440 ולמד 3925 אתם 859
uayoushabey yarushalaim. uayipnu 'aelay 'arep uala' paniym; ualamed 'atam
**and the inhabitants of Jerusalem And they have turned unto me the back and not the face though I taught them**

השכם 7925 ולמד 3925 ואינם 369 שמעים 8085 לקחת 3947 מוסר 4148: 32:34 וישימו 7760
hashkem ualamed, ua'aeynam shoma'aym laqachat musar. uayasiymu
**rising up early and teaching *them* yet not they have hearkened to receive instruction But they set**

שקוציהם 8251 בבית 1004 אשר 834 נקרא 7121 שמי 8034 עליו 5921 לטמאו 2930: 32:35 ויבנו 1129 את 853 במות 1116
shiqutzeyhem, babayit 'asher niqra' shamiy 'alayu latam'au. uayibnu 'at bamout
**their abominations in the house which is called by my name it to defile And they built the high places of**

הבעל 1168 אשר 834 בגיא 1516 בן 1121 הנם 2011 להעביר 5674 את 853 בניהם 1121 ואת 853 בנותיהם 1323
haba'al 'asher bagey'a ben hinom, laha'abiyr 'at baneyhem ua'at banouteyhem
**Baal which *are* in the valley of the son of Hinnom to cause to pass through their sons *and* their daughters**

למלך 4432 אשר 834 לא 3808 צויתים 6680 ולא 3808 עלתה 5927 על 5921 לבי 3820 לעשות 6213 התועבה 8441
lamolek 'asher la' tziuiytiym, uala' 'alatah 'al libiy, la'asout hatou'aebah
***the fire* unto Molek which not I commanded them neither came it into my mind that they should do abomination**

הזאת 2063 למען 4616 החטי 2398 את 853 יהודה 3063: 32:36 ועתה 6258 לכן 3651 כה 3541 אמר 559 יהוה 3068 אלהי 430 ישראל 3478
haza't; lama'an hachatiy 'at yahudah. ua'atah laken koh 'amar Yahuah 'alohey yisra'ael;
**this to cause to sin Judah And now therefore thus saith Yahuah the Elohim of Israel**

אל 413 העיר 5892 הזאת 2063 אשר 834 אתם 859 אמרים 559 נתנה 5414 ביד 3027 מלך 4428 בבל 894
'al ha'ayr haza't 'asher 'atem 'amariym, nitnah bayad melek babel,
**concerning city this whereof you say It shall be delivered into the hand of the king of Babylon**

Jer 32:30 for the children of Israel have only provoked me to anger with the work of their hands, saith YHUH.31 For this city has been to me as a provocation of mine anger and of my fury from the day that they built it even unto this day; that I should remove it from before my face,32 Because of all the evil of the children of Israel and of the children of Judah, which they have done to provoke me to anger, they, their kings, their princes, their priests, and their prophets, and the men of Judah, and the inhabitants of Jerusalem.33 And they have turned unto me the back, and not the face: though I taught them, rising up early and teaching them, yet they have not hearkened to receive instruction.34 But they set their abominations in the house, which is called by my name, to defile it.35 And they built the high places of Baal, which are in the valley of the son of Hinnom, to cause their sons and their daughters to pass through the fire unto Molech; which I commanded them not, neither came it into my mind, that they should do this abomination, to cause Judah to sin.36 And now therefore thus saith YHUH, the G-d of Israel, concerning this city, whereof you say, It shall be delivered into the hand of the king of Babylon by the sword, and by the famine, and by the pestilence;

| בחרב 2719 | ובערב 7458 | ובדבר 1698: | 32:37 | הנני 2005 | מקבצם 6908 | מכל 3605 | הארצות 776 | אשר 834 |
|---|---|---|---|---|---|---|---|---|
| bachereb | uabara'ab | uabadaber. | | hinniy | maqabtzam | mikal | ha'aratzout, | 'asher |
| **by the sword** | **and by the famine** | **and by the pestilence** | | **Behold I** | **will gather them** | **outof all** | **countries** | **where** |

| הדחתים 5080 | שם 8033 | באפי 639 | ובחמתי 2534 | ובקצף 7110 | גדול 1419 | והשבתים 7725 | אל 413 | המקום 4725 |
|---|---|---|---|---|---|---|---|---|
| hidachtiym | sham | ba'apiy | uabachamatiy | uabqetzep | gadoul; | uahashibotiym | 'al | hamaqoum |
| **I have driven them** | **there** | **in mine anger** | **and in my fury** | **and in wrath** | **great** | **and I will bring them again** | **unto** | **place** |

| הזה 2088 | והשבתים 3427 | לבטח 983: | 32:38 | והיו 1961 | לי 3807a | לעם 5971 | ואני 589 | אהיה 1961 | להם 3807a |
|---|---|---|---|---|---|---|---|---|---|
| hazeh, | uahoshabtiym | labetach. | | uahayu | liy | la'am; | ua'aniy | 'ahayeh | lahem |
| **this** | **and I will cause them to dwell** | **safely** | | **And they shall be** | **my** | **people** | **and I** | **will be** | **their** |

| לאלהים 430: | 32:39 | ונתתי 5414 | להם 3807a | לב 3820 | אחד 259 | ודרך 1870 | אחד 259 | ליראה 3372 | אותי 853 | כל 3605 | הימים 3117 |
|---|---|---|---|---|---|---|---|---|---|---|---|
| le'alohiym. | | uanatatiy | lahem | leb | 'achad | uaderek | 'achad, | layir'ah | 'autiy | kal | hayamiym; |
| **to Elohim** | | **And I will give** | **them** | **heart** | **one** | **and way** | **one** | **that they may fear** | **me** | **for** | **ever** |

| לטוב 2896 | להם 3807a | ולבניהם 1121 | אחריהם 310: | 32:40 | וכרתי 3772 | להם 3807a | ברית 1285 | עולם 5769 | אשר 834 |
|---|---|---|---|---|---|---|---|---|---|
| latoub | lahem, | ualibneyhem | 'achareyhem. | | uakaratiy | lahem | bariyt | 'aulam, | 'asher |
| **for the good** | **of them** | **and of their children** | **after them** | | **And I will make** | **with them** | **an covenant** | **everlasting** | **that** |

| לא 3808 | אשוב 7725 | מאחריהם 310 | להיטיבי 3190 | אותם 853 | ואת 853 | יראתי 3374 | אתן 5414 | בלבבם 3824 | לבלתי 1115 |
|---|---|---|---|---|---|---|---|---|---|
| la' | 'ashub | me'achareyhem, | laheytiybiy | 'autam; | ua'at | yira'atiy | 'aten | bilbabam, | labiltiy |
| **not** | **I will turn away** | **from them** | **to do good** | **them** | ***but*** | **my fear** | **I will put** | **in their hearts** | **that not** |

| סור 5493 | מעלי 5921: | 32:41 | וששתי 7797 | עליהם 5921 | להטיב 2895 | אותם 853 | ונטעתים 5193 | בארץ 776 | הזאת 2063 |
|---|---|---|---|---|---|---|---|---|---|
| sur | me'alay. | | uasastiy | 'aleyhem | lahetiyb | 'autam; | uanta'atiym | ba'aretz | haza't |
| **they shall depart** | **from me** | | **Yea I will rejoice** | **over them** | **to do good** | **them** | **and I will plant them** | **in land** | **this** |

| באמת 571 | בכל 3605 | לבי 3820 | ובכל 3605 | נפשי 5315: | 32:42 | כי 3588 | כה 3541 | אמר 559 | יהוה 3068 | כאשר 834 | הבאתי 935 | אל 413 |
|---|---|---|---|---|---|---|---|---|---|---|---|---|
| be'amet, | bakal | libiy | uabkal | napshiy. | | kiy | koh | 'amar | Yahuah, | ka'asher | hebea'tiy | 'al |
| **assuredly** | **with whole** | **my heart** | **and with whole** | **my soul** | | **For** | **thus** | **saith** | **Yahuah** | **Like as** | **I have brought** | **upon** |

| העם 5971 | הזה 2088 | את 853 | כל 3605 | הרעה 7451 | הגדולה 1419 | הזאת 2063 | כן 3651 | אנכי 595 | מביא 935 | עליהם 5921 | את 853 | כל 3605 | הטובה 2896 | אשר 834 |
|---|---|---|---|---|---|---|---|---|---|---|---|---|---|---|
| ha'am | hazeh, | 'at | kal | hara'ah | hagadoulah | haza't; | ken | 'anokiy | mebiy'a | 'aleyhem | 'at | kal | hatoubah, | 'asher |
| **the people** | **this** | | **all** | **evil** | **great** | **this** | **so** | **I** | **will bring upon them** | | | **all** | **the good** | **that** |

| אנכי 595 | דבר 1697 | עליהם 5921: | 32:43 | ונקנה 7069 | השדה 7704 | בארץ 776 | הזאת 2063 | אשר 834 | אתם 859 | אמרים 559 | שממה 8077 |
|---|---|---|---|---|---|---|---|---|---|---|---|
| 'anokiy | dober | 'aleyhem. | | uaniqnah | hasadeh | ba'aretz | haza't; | 'asher | 'atem | 'amariym, | shamamah |
| **I** | **have promised them** | | | **And shall be bought** | **fields** | **in land** | **this** | **whereof** | **you** | **say** | ***is* desolate** |

| היא 1931 | מאין 369 | אדם 120 | ובהמה 929 | נתנה 5414 | ביד 3027 | הכשדים 3778: | 32:44 | שדות 7704 | בכסף 3701 | יקנו 7069 |
|---|---|---|---|---|---|---|---|---|---|---|
| hiy'a | me'ayn | 'adam | uabahemah, | nitnah | bayad | hakasdiym. | | sadout | bakesep | yiqnu, |
| **It** | **without** | **man** | **or beast** | **it is given** | **into the hand of** | **the Chaldeans** | | ***Men* fields** | **for money** | **shall buy** |

| וכתוב 3789 | בספר 5612 | וחתום 2856 | והעד 5749 | עדים 5707 | בארץ 776 | בנימן 1144 | ובסביבי 5439 | ירושלם 3389 |
|---|---|---|---|---|---|---|---|---|
| uakatoub | baseper | uachatoum | uaha'aed | 'aediym | ba'aretz | binyamin | uabisbiybey | yarushalaim, |
| **and subscribe** | **evidences** | **and seal *them*** | **and take** | **witnesses** | **in the land of** | **Benjamin** | **and in the places about** | **Jerusalem** |

Jer 32:37 Behold, I will gather them out of all countries, whither I have driven them in mine anger, and in my fury, and in great wrath; and I will bring them again unto this place, and I will cause them to dwell safely:38 And they shall be my people, and I will be their G-d:39 And I will give them one heart, and one way, that they may fear me forever, for the good of them, and of their children after them:40 And I will make an everlasting covenant with them, that I will not turn away from them, to do them good; but I will put my fear in their hearts, that they shall not depart from me.41 Yea, I will rejoice over them to do them good, and I will plant them in this land assuredly with my whole heart and with my whole soul.42 For thus saith YHUH; Like as I have brought all this great evil upon this people, so will I bring upon them all the good that I have promised them.43 And fields shall be bought in this land, whereof you say, It is desolate without man or beast; it is given into the hand of the Chaldeans.44 Men shall buy fields for money, and subscribe evidences, and seal them, and take witnesses in the land of Benjamin, and in the places about Jerusalem, and in the cities of Judah, and in the cities of the mountains, and in the cities of the valley, and in the cities of the south: for I will cause their captivity to return, saith YHUH.

| ובערי 5892 | יהודה 3063 | ובערי 5892 | ההר 2022 | ובערי 5892 | השפלה 8219 | ובערי 5892 | הנגב 5045 |
|---|---|---|---|---|---|---|---|
| uab'arey | yahudah | uab'arey | hahar, | uab'arey | hashapelah | uab'arey | hanegeb; |
| **and in the cities of** | **Judah** | **and in the cities of** | **the mountains** | **and in the cities of** | **the valley** | **and in the cities of** | **the south** |

| כי 3588 | אשיב 7725 | את 853 | שבותם 7622 | נאם 5002 | יהוה 3068: |
|---|---|---|---|---|---|
| kiy | 'ashiyb | 'at | shabutam | na'am | Yahuah. |
| **for** | **I will cause to return** | | **their captivity** | **saith** | **Yahuah** |

| **Jer 33:1** | ויהי 1961 | דבר 1697 | יהוה 3068 | אל 413 | ירמיהו 3414 | שנית 8145 | והוא 1931 | עודנו 5750 | עצור 6113 |
|---|---|---|---|---|---|---|---|---|---|
| | uayahiy | dabar | Yahuah | 'al | yirmayahu | sheniyt; | uahu'a | audenu | 'atzur, |
| | **Moreover came** | **the word of** | **Yahuah** | **unto** | **Jeremiah** | ***the* second time** | **while he** | **yet** | **was shut up** |

| בחצר 2691 | המטרה 4307 | לאמר 559: | **33:2** | כה 3541 | אמר 559 | יהוה 3068 | עשה 6213 | יהוה 3068 | יוצר 3335 | אותה 853 | להכינה 3559 |
|---|---|---|---|---|---|---|---|---|---|---|---|
| bachatzar | hamatarah | lea'mor. | | koh | 'amar | Yahuah | 'asah; | Yahuah | youtzer | 'autah | lahakiynah |
| **in the court of** | **the prison** | **saying** | | **Thus** | **saith** | **Yahuah** | **the maker thereof** | **Yahuah** | **that formed** | **it** | **to establish it** |

| יהוה 3068 | שמו 8034: | **33:3** | קרא 7121 | אלי 413 | ואענך 6030 | ואגידה 5046 | לך 3807a | גדלות 1419 | ובצרות 1219 | לא 3808 |
|---|---|---|---|---|---|---|---|---|---|---|
| Yahuah | shamou. | | qara' | 'aelay | ua'a'aneka; | ua'agiydah | laka | gadolout | uabtzurout | la' |
| **Yahuah** | ***is* his name** | | **Call** | **unto me** | **and I will answer you** | **and show** | **to you** | **great** | **and mighty things** | **not** |

| ידעתם 3045: | **33:4** | כי 3588 | כה 3541 | אמר 559 | יהוה 3068 | אלהי 430 | ישראל 3478 | על 5921 | בתי 1004 | העיר 5892 | הזאת 2063 |
|---|---|---|---|---|---|---|---|---|---|---|---|
| yada'atam. | | kiy | koh | 'amar | Yahuah | 'alohey | yisra'ael, | 'al | batey | ha'ayr | haza't, |
| **which you know** | | **For** | **thus** | **saith** | **Yahuah** | **the Elohim of** | **Israel** | **concerning** | **the houses of** | **city** | **this** |

| ועל 5921 | בתי 1004 | מלכי 4428 | יהודה 3063 | הנתצים 5422 | אל 413 | הסללות 5550 | ואל 413 | החרב 2719: | **33:5** |
|---|---|---|---|---|---|---|---|---|---|
| ua'al | batey | malkey | yahudah; | hanatutziym | 'al | hasolalout | ua'al | hechareb. | |
| **and concerning** | **the houses of** | **the kings of** | **Judah** | **which are thrown down** | **by** | **the mounts** | **and by** | **the sword** | |

| באים 935 | להלחם 3898 | את 854 | הכשדים 3778 | ולמלאם 4390 | את 854 | פגרי 6297 | האדם 120 | אשר 834 | הכיתי 5221 |
|---|---|---|---|---|---|---|---|---|---|
| ba'aym, | lahilachem | 'at | hakasdiym, | ualmal'am | 'at | pigrey | ha'adam, | 'asher | hikeytiy |
| **They come** | **to fight** | ***with*** | **the Chaldeans** | **but *it is* to fill them** | ***with*** | **dead bodies of** | **the men** | **whom** | **I have slain** |

| באפי 639 | ובחמתי 2534 | ואשר 834 | הסתרתי 5641 | פני 6440 | מהעיר 5892 | הזאת 2063 | על 5921 | כל 3605 | רעתם 7451: | **33:6** | הנני 2005 |
|---|---|---|---|---|---|---|---|---|---|---|---|
| ba'apiy | uabachamatiy; | ua'asher | histartiy | panay | meha'ayr | haza't, | 'al | kal | ra'atam. | | hinniy |
| **in mine anger** | **and in my fury** | **and whose** | **I have hid** | **my face** | **from city** | **this** | **for** | **all** | **wickedness** | | **Behold** |

| מעלה 5927 | לה 3807a | ארכה 724 | ומרפא 4832 | ורפאתים 7495 | וגליתי 1540 | להם 1992 | עתרת 6283 | שלום 7965 |
|---|---|---|---|---|---|---|---|---|
| ma'aleh | lah | 'arukah | uamarpea' | uarpa'tiym; | uagileytiy | lahem, | ateret | shaloum |
| **I will bring** | **it** | **health** | **and cure** | **and I will cure them** | **and will reveal** | **unto them** | **the abundance of** | **peace** |

| ואמת 571: | **33:7** | והשבתי 7725 | את 853 | שבות 7622 | יהודה 3063 | ואת 853 | שבות 7622 | ישראל 3478 |
|---|---|---|---|---|---|---|---|---|
| ua'amet. | | uahashibotiy | 'at | shabut | yahudah, | ua'at | shabut | yisra'ael; |
| **and truth** | | **And I will cause to return** | | **the captivity of** | **Judah** | ***and*** | **the captivity of** | **Israel** |

| ובנתים 1129 | כבראשנה 7223: | **33:8** | וטהרתים 2891 | מכל 3605 | עונם 5771 | אשר 834 | חטאו 2398 |
|---|---|---|---|---|---|---|---|
| uabnitiym | kabara'shonah. | | uatihartiym, | mikal | 'auonam | 'asher | chata'au |
| **and will build them** | **as at the first** | | **And I will cleanse them** | **from all** | **their iniquity** | **whereby** | **they have sinned** |

**Jer** 33:1 Moreover the word of YHUH came unto Jeremiah the second time, while he was yet shut up in the court of the prison, saying,2 Thus saith YHUH the maker thereof, YHUH that formed it, to establish it; YHUH is his name;3 Call unto me, and I will answer you, and show you great and mighty things, which you know not.4 For thus saith YHUH, the G-d of Israel, concerning the houses of this city, and concerning the houses of the kings of Judah, which are thrown down by the mounts, and by the sword;5 They come to fight with the Chaldeans, but it is to fill them with the dead bodies of men, whom I have slain in mine anger and in my fury, and for all whose wickedness I have hid my face from this city.6 Behold, I will bring it health and cure, and I will cure them, and will reveal unto them the abundance of peace and truth.7 And I will cause the captivity of Judah and the captivity of Israel to return, and will build them, as at the first.8 And I will cleanse them from all their iniquity, whereby they have sinned against me; and I will pardon all their iniquities, whereby they have sinned, and whereby they have transgressed against me.

| לי 3807a | וסלחתי 5545 | לכול 3605 | עונותיהם 5771 | אשר 834 | חטאו 2398 | לי 3807a | ואשר 834 |
|---|---|---|---|---|---|---|---|
| liy; | uasalachtiy, | lakul | 'auonouteyhem | 'asher | chata'au | liy, | ua'asher |
| **against me** | **and I will pardon** | **all** | **their iniquities** | **whereby** | **they have sinned** | **to me** | **and whereby** |

| פשעו 6586 | בי 871a: | 33:9 והיתה 1961 | לי 3807a | לשם 8034 | ששון 8342 | לתהלה 8416 | ולתפארת 8597 | לכל 3605 |
|---|---|---|---|---|---|---|---|---|
| pasha'au | biy. | uahayatah | liy, | lashem | sasoun | litahilah | ualtip'aret, | lakol |
| **they have transgressed** | **against me** | **And it shall be** | **to me** | **a name of** | **joy** | **a praise** | **and an honor** | **before all** |

| גויי 1471 | הארץ 776 | אשר 834 | ישמעו 8085 | את 853 | כל 3605 | הטובה 2896 | אשר 834 | אנכי 595 | עשה 6213 | אתם 853 | ופחדו 6342 |
|---|---|---|---|---|---|---|---|---|---|---|---|
| gouyey | ha'aretz; | 'asher | yishma'au | 'at | kal | hatoubah, | 'asher | 'anokiy | 'aseh | 'atam, | uapachadu |
| **the nations of** | **the earth** | **which** | **shall hear** | | **all** | **the good** | **that** | **I** | **do unto** | **them** | **and they shall fear** |

| ורגזו 7264 | על 5921 | כל 3605 | הטובה 2896 | ועל 5921 | כל 3605 | השלום 7965 | אשר 834 | אנכי 595 | עשה 6213 | לה 3807a: | 33:10 כה 3541 | אמר 559 |
|---|---|---|---|---|---|---|---|---|---|---|---|---|
| uaragazu, | 'al | kal | hatoubah | ua'al | kal | hashaloum, | 'asher | 'anokiy | 'asheh | lah. | koh | 'amar |
| **and tremble** | **for** | **all** | **the goodness** | **and for** | **all** | **the prosperity** | **that** | **I** | **procure** | **unto it** | **Thus** | **saith** |

| יהוה 3068 | עוד 5750 | ישמע 8085 | במקום 4725 | הזה 2088 | אשר 834 | אתם 859 | אמרים 559 | חרב 2720 | הוא 1931 | מאין 369 | אדם 120 |
|---|---|---|---|---|---|---|---|---|---|---|---|
| Yahuah | 'aud | yishama' | bammakom | hazeh | 'asher | 'atem | 'amariym, | chareb | hua', | me'ayn | 'adam |
| **Yahuah** | **Again** | **there shall be heard** | **in place** | **this** | **which** | **you** | **say** | ***shall be* desolate** | **he** | **without** | **man** |

| ומאין 369 | בהמה 929 | בערי 5892 | יהודה 3063 | ובחצות 2351 | ירושלם 3389 | הנשמות 8074 | מאין 369 | אדם 120 |
|---|---|---|---|---|---|---|---|---|
| uame'aeyn | bahemah; | ba'arey | yahudah | uabchutzout | yarushalaim, | hanashamout, | me'ayn | 'adam |
| **and without** | **beast** | ***even* in the cities of** | **Judah** | **and in the streets of** | **Jerusalem** | **that are desolate** | **without** | **man** |

| ומאין 369 | יושב 3427 | ומאין 369 | בהמה 929: | 33:11 קול 6963 | ששון 8342 | וקול 6963 | שמחה 8057 | קול 6963 |
|---|---|---|---|---|---|---|---|---|
| uame'aeyn | yousheb | uame'aeyn | bahemah. | qoul | sasoun | uaqoul | simchah, | qoul |
| **and without** | **inhabitant** | **and without** | **beast** | **The voice of** | **joy** | **and the voice of** | **gladness** | **the voice of** |

| חתן 2860 | וקול 6963 | כלה 3618 | קול 6963 | אמרים 559 | הודו 3034 | את 853 | יהוה 3068 | צבאות 6635 | כי 3588 | טוב 2896 |
|---|---|---|---|---|---|---|---|---|---|---|
| chatan | uaqoul | kalah | qoul | 'amariym | houdu | 'at | Yahuah | tzaba'aut | kiy | toub |
| **the bridegroom** | **and the voice of** | **the bride** | **the voice of** | **them that shall say** | **Praise** | | **Yahuah** | **of hosts** | **for** | ***is* good** |

| יהוה 3068 | כי 3588 | לעולם 5769 | חסדו 2617 | מבאים 935 | תודה 8426 | בית 1004 | יהוה 3068 |
|---|---|---|---|---|---|---|---|
| Yahuah | kiy | la'aulam | chasdou, | mabi'aym | toudah | beyt | Yahuah; |
| **for Yahuah** | **for** | ***endures* for ever** | **his mercy** | ***and* of them that shall bring** | **the sacrifice of praise into** | **the house of** | **Yahuah** |

| כי 3588 | אשיב 7725 | את 853 | שבות 7622 | הארץ 776 | כבראשנה 7223 | אמר 559 | יהוה 3068: | 33:12 כה 3541 | אמר 559 | יהוה 3068 | צבאות 6635 |
|---|---|---|---|---|---|---|---|---|---|---|---|
| kiy | 'ashiyb | 'at | shabut | ha'aretz | kabara'shonah | 'amar | Yahuah. | koh | 'amar | Yahuah | tzaba'aut |
| **For** | **I will cause to return** | | **the captivity of** | **the land** | **as at the first** | **saith** | **Yahuah** | **Thus** | **saith** | **Yahuah** | **of hosts** |

| עוד 5750 | יהיה 1961 | במקום 4725 | הזה 2088 | החרב 2720 | מאין 369 | אדם 120 | ועד 5704 | בהמה 929 | ובכל 3605 | עריו 5892 |
|---|---|---|---|---|---|---|---|---|---|---|
| 'aud | yihayeh | bamaqoum | hazeh, | hechareb | me'ayn | 'adam | ua'ad | bahemah | uabkol | 'arayu; |
| **Again** | **which is** | **in place** | **this** | **desolate** | **without** | **man** | **and without** | **beast** | **and in all** | **the cities thereof** |

| נוה 5116 | רעים 7462 | מרבצים 7257 | צאן 6629: | 33:13 בערי 5892 | ההר 2022 | בערי 5892 |
|---|---|---|---|---|---|---|
| naueh | ro'aym, | marbitziym | tza'n. | ba'arey | hahar | ba'arey |
| ***shall be* an habitation of** | **shepherds** | **causing to lie down *their*** | **flocks** | **In the cities of** | **the mountains** | **in the cities of** |

Jer 33:9 And it shall be to me a name of joy, a praise and an honor before all the nations of the earth, which shall hear all the good that I do unto them: and they shall fear and tremble for all the goodness and for all the prosperity that I procure unto it.10 Thus saith YHUH; Again there shall be heard in this place, which you say shall be desolate without man and without beast, even in the cities of Judah, and in the streets of Jerusalem, that are desolate, without man, and without inhabitant, and without beast,11 The voice of joy, and the voice of gladness, the voice of the bridegroom, and the voice of the bride, the voice of them that shall say, Praise YHUH of hosts: for YHUH is good; for his mercy endureth forever: and of them that shall bring the sacrifice of praise into the house of YHUH. For I will cause to return the captivity of the land, as at the first, saith YHUH.12 Thus saith YHUH of hosts; Again in this place, which is desolate without man and without beast, and in all the cities thereof, shall be an habitation of shepherds causing their flocks to lie down.

השפלה 8219 ובערי 5892 הנגב 5045 ובארץ 776 בנימן 1144 ובסביבי 5439 ירושלם 3389 ובערי 5892
hashapelah uab'arey hanegeb, uab'aretz binyamin uabisbiybey yarushalaim uab'arey
**the vale and in the cities of the south and in the land of Benjamin and in the places about Jerusalem and in the cities of**

יהודה 3063 עד 5704 תעברנה 5674 הצאן 6629 על 5921 ידי 3027 מונה 4487 אמר 559 יהוה 3068: 33:14 הנה 2009 ימים 3117 באים 935
yahudah; 'aud ta'aboranah hatza'an 'al yadey mouneh 'amar Yahuah. hineh yamiym ba'aym
**Judah again shall pass the flocks under the hands of him that tell *them* saith Yahuah Behold the days come**

נאם 5002 יהוה 3068 והקמתי 6965 את 853 הדבר 1697 הטוב 2896 אשר 834 דברתי 1696 אל 413 בית 1004 ישראל 3478 ועל 5921
na'am Yahuah; uahaqimotiy 'at hadabar hatoub, 'asher dibartiy 'al beyt yisra'ael ua'al
**saith Yahuah that I will perform that thing good which I have promised unto the house of Israel and to**

בית 1004 יהודה 3063: 33:15 בימים 3117 ההם 1992 ובעת 6256 ההיא 1931 אצמיח 6779 לדוד 1732 צמח 6780
beyt yahudah. bayamiym hahem uaba'aet hahiy'a, 'atzmiyach ladauid tzemach
**the house of Judah In days those and at time that will I cause to grow up unto David the Branch of**

צדקה 6666 ועשה 6213 משפט 4941 וצדקה 6666 בארץ 776: 33:16 בימים 3117 ההם 1992 תושע 3467 יהודה 3063
tzadaqah; ua'asah mishapat uatzdaqah ba'aretz. bayamiym hahem tiuasha' yahudah,
**righteousness and he shall execute judgment and righteousness in the land In days those shall be saved Judah**

וירושלם 3389 תשכון 7931 לבטח 983 וזה 2088 אשר 834 יקרא 7121 לה 3807a יהוה 3072 צדקנו 3072: 33:17
uiyarushalaim tishkoun labetach; uazeh 'asher yiqra' lah Yahuah tzidqenu.
**and Jerusalem shall dwell safely and this *is the name* wherewith shall be called she Yahuah our righteousness**

כי 3588 כה 3541 אמר 559 יהוה 3068 לא 3808 יכרת 3772 לדוד 1732 איש 376 ישב 3427 על 5921 כסא 3678 בית 1004 ישראל 3478: 33:18
kiy koh 'amar Yahuah; la' yikaret ladauid, 'aysh yosheb 'al kisea' beyt yisra'ael.
**For thus saith Yahuah never shall want David a man to sit upon the throne of the house of Israel**

ולכהנים 3548 הלוים 3881 לא 3808 יכרת 3772 איש 376 מלפני 6440 מעלה 5927 עולה 5930 ומקטיר 6999 מנחה 4503
ualakohaniym halauiyim, la' yikaret 'aysh milapanay; ma'aleh aulah uamaqtiyr minchah
**the priests the Levites Neither shall want a man before me to offer burnt offerings and to kindle meat offerings**

ועשה 6213 זבח 2077 כל 3605 הימים 3117: 33:19 ויהי 1961 דבר 1697 יהוה 3068 אל 413 ירמיהו 3414 לאמור 559: 33:20 כה 3541 אמר 559
ua'aseh zebach kal hayamiym. uayahiy dabar Yahuah, 'al yirmayahu lea'mour. koh 'amar
**and to do sacrifice all of continually And came the word of Yahuah unto Jeremiah saying Thus saith**

יהוה 3068 אם 518 תפרו 6565 את 853 בריתי 1285 היום 3117 ואת 853 בריתי 1285 הלילה 3915 ולבלתי 1115 היות 1961
Yahuah, 'am taperu 'at bariytiy hayoum, ua'at bariytiy halayalah; ualbiltiy hayout
**Yahuah If you can break my covenant of the day *and* my covenant of the night and that not there should be**

יומם 3119 ולילה 3915 בעתם 6256: 33:21 גם 1571 בריתי 1285 תפר 6565 את 854 דוד 1732 עבדי 5650
yomam ualayalah ba'atam. gam bariytiy tupar 'at dauid 'abdiy,
**day and night in their season *Then* also my covenant may be broken *with* David my servant *that***

מהיות 1961 לו 3807a בן 1121 מלך 4427 על 5921 כסאו 3678 ואת 854 הלוים 3881 הכהנים 3548 משרתי 8334: 33:22 אשר 834
mihyout lou' ben molek 'al kis'au; ua'at halauiyim hakohaniym masharatay. 'asher
**he should not have to him a son to reign upon his throne *and with* the Levites the priests my ministers As**

Jer 33:13 In the cities of the mountains, in the cities of the vale, and in the cities of the south, and in the land of Benjamin, and in the places about Jerusalem, and in the cities of Judah, shall the flocks pass again under the hands of him that tell them, saith YHUH.14 Behold, the days come, saith YHUH, that I will perform that good thing which I have promised unto the house of Israel and to the house of Judah.15 In those days, and at that time, will I cause the Branch of righteousness to grow up unto David; and he shall execute judgment and righteousness in the land.16 In those days shall Judah be saved, and Jerusalem shall dwell safely: and this is the name wherewith she shall be called, YHUH our righteousness.17 For thus saith YHUH; David shall never want a man to sit upon the throne of the house of Israel;18 Neither shall the priests the Levites want a man before me to offer burnt offerings, and to kindle meat offerings, and to do sacrifice continually.19 And the word of YHUH came unto Jeremiah, saying,20 Thus saith YHUH; If you can break my covenant of the day, and my covenant of the night, and that there should not be day and night in their season;21 Then may also my covenant be broken with David my servant, that he should not have a son to reign upon his throne; and with the Levites the priests, my ministers.

לא 3808 יספר 5608 צבא 6635 השמים 8064 ולא 3808 ימד 4058 חול 2344 הים 3220 כן 3651 ארבה 7235 את 853 זרע 2233
la' yisaper tzaba' hashamayim, uala' yimad choul hayam; ken 'arbeh, 'at zera'
**cannot be numbered host of the heaven neither measured the sand of the sea so will I multiply the seed of**

דוד 1732 עבדי 5650 ואת 853 הלוים 3881 משרתי 8334 אתי 853: **33:23** ויהי 1961 דבר 1697 יהוה 3068 אל 413 ירמיהו 3414
dauid 'abdiy, ua'at halauiyim masharatey 'atiy. uayahiy dabar Yahuah, 'al yirmayahu
**David my servant *and* the Levites that minister unto me Moreover came the word of Yahuah to Jeremiah**

לאמר 559: **33:24** הלוא 3808 ראית 7200 מה 4100 העם 5971 הזה 2088 דברו 1696 לאמר 559 שתי 8147 המשפחות 4940 אשר 834
lea'mor. halou'a ra'ayta, mah ha'am hazeh dibru lea'mor, shatey hamishpachout, 'asher
**saying not Considerest you what the people this have spoken saying two The families which**

בחר 977 יהוה 3068 בהם 871a וימאסם 3988 ואת 853 עמי 5971 ינאצון 5006 מהיות 1961 עוד 5750
bachar Yahuah bahem uayim'asem; ua'at 'amiy yin'atzun, mihyout 'aud
**has chosen Yahuah which he has even cast them off? *thus* my people they have despised that they should be *no* more**

גוי 1471 לפניהם 6440: **33:25** כה 3541 אמר 559 יהוה 3068 אם 518 לא 3808 בריתי 1285 יומם 3119 ולילה 3915 חקות 2708
gouy lipneyhem. koh 'amar Yahuah, 'am la' bariytiy youmam ualayalah; chuqout
**a nation before them Thus saith Yahuah If not my covenant *be with* day and night the ordinances of**

שמים 8064 וארץ 776 לא 3808 שמתי 7760: **33:26** גם 1571 זרע 2233 יעקוב 3290 ודוד 1732 עבדי 5650 אמאס 3988
shamayim ua'aretz la' samatiy. gam zera' ya'aqoub uadauid 'abdiy 'am'as,
**heaven and earth not *and if* I have appointed Then the seed of Jacob and David my servant will I cast away**

מקחת 3947 מזרעו 2233 משלים 4910 אל 413 זרע 2233 אברהם 85 ישחק 3446 ויעקב 3290 כי 3588 אשוב 7725
miqachat mizar'au moshaliym, 'al zera' 'abraham yischaq uaya'aqob; kiy 'ashub
***so* that I will not take *any* of his seed *to be* rulers over the seed of Abraham Isaac and Jacob for I will cause to return**

את 853 שבותם 7622 ורחמתים 7355:
'at shabutam uarichamtiym.
**their captivity and have mercy on them**

**Jer 34:1** הדבר 1697 אשר 834 היה 1961 אל 413 ירמיהו 3414 מאת 853 יהוה 3068 ונבוכדראצר 5019 מלך 4428 בבל 894 וכל 3605 חילו 2428
hadabar 'asher hayah 'al yirmayahu me'at Yahuah; unabukadra'tzar melek babel uakal cheylou
**The word which came unto Jeremiah from Yahuah when Nebuchadnezzar king of Babylon and all his army**

וכל 3605 ממלכות 4467 ארץ 776 ממשלת 4475 ידו 3027 וכל 3605 העמים 5971 נלחמים 3898 על 5921 ירושלם 3389 ועל 5921 כל 3605
uakal mamlakout 'aretz memShelet yadou uakal ha'amiym, nilchamiym 'al yarushalaim ua'al kal
**and all the kingdoms of the earth of dominion his and all the people fought against Jerusalem and against all**

עריה 5892 לאמר 559: **34:2** כה 3541 אמר 559 יהוה 3068 אלהי 430 ישראל 3478 הלך 1980 ואמרת 559 אל 413 צדקיהו 6667 מלך 4428
'areyha lea'mor. koh 'amar Yahuah 'alohey yisra'ael, halok ua'amarta, 'al tzidqiyahu melek
**the cities thereof saying Thus saith Yahuah the Elohim of Israel Go and speak to Zedekiah king of**

יהודה 3063 ואמרת 559 אליו 413 כה 3541 אמר 559 יהוה 3068 הנני 2005 נתן 5414 את 853 העיר 5892 הזאת 2063 ביד 3027 מלך 4428
yahudah; ua'amarta 'aelayu, koh 'amar Yahuah, hinniy noten 'at ha'ayr haza't bayad melek
**Judah and tell him Thus saith Yahuah Behold I will give city this into the hand of the king of**

Jer 33:22 As the host of heaven cannot be numbered, neither the sand of the sea measured: so will I multiply the seed of David my servant, and the Levites that minister unto me.23 Moreover the word of YHUH came to Jeremiah, saying,24 Considerest you not what this people have spoken, saying, The two families which YHUH has chosen, he has even cast them off? thus they have despised my people, that they should be no more a nation before them.25 Thus saith YHUH; If my covenant be not with day and night, and if I have not appointed the ordinances of heaven and earth;26 Then will I cast away the seed of Jacob, and David my servant, so that I will not take any of his seed to be rulers over the seed of Abraham, Isaac, and Jacob: for I will cause their captivity to return, and have mercy on them. **Jer** 34:1 The word which came unto Jeremiah from YHUH, when Nebuchadnezzar king of Babylon, and all his army, and all the kingdoms of the earth of his dominion, and all the people, fought against Jerusalem, and against all the cities thereof, saying,2 Thus saith YHUH, the G-d of Israel; Go and speak to Zedekiah king of Judah, and tell him, Thus saith YHUH; Behold, I will give this city into the hand of the king of Babylon, and he shall burn it with fire:

34:3

בבל 894 ושרפה 8313 באש 784: ואתה 859 לא 3808 תמלט 4422 מידו 3027 כי 3588 תפש 8610 תתפש 8610

babel, uasrapah ba'aesh. ua'atah, la' timalet miyadou, kiy tapos titapes,

**Babylon and he shall burn it with fire And you not shall escape out of his hand but shall surely be taken**

ובידו 3027 תנתן 5414 ועיניך 5869 את 853 עיני 5869 מלך 4428 בבל 894 תראינה 7200 ופיהו 6310 את 854 פיך 6310

uabyadou tinaten; ua'aeyneyka 'at 'aeyney melek babel tir'aynah, uapiyhu 'at piyka

**and into his hand delivered and your eyes the eyes of the king of Babylon shall behold *with you* mouth *to* mouth**

34:4

ידבר 1696 ובבל 894 תבוא 935: אך 389 שמע 8085 דבר 1697 יהוה 3068 צדקיהו 6667 מלך 4428 יהודה 3063 כה 3541

yadaber uababel tabou'a. 'ak shama' dabar Yahuah, tzidqiyahu melek yahudah; koh

**he shall speak and Babylon you shall go to Yet hear the word of Yahuah O Zedekiah king of Judah Thus**

34:5

אמר 559 יהוה 3068 עליך 5921 לא 3808 תמות 4191 בחרב 2719: בשלום 7965 תמות 4191 וכמשרפות 4955

'amar Yahuah 'aleyka, la' tamut bechareb. bashaloum tamut, uakmisrapout

**saith Yahuah of you not You shall die by the sword *But* in peace you shall die and with the burnings of**

אבותיך 1 המלכים 4428 הראשנים 7223 אשר 834 היו 1961 לפניך 6440 כן 3651 ישרפו 8313 לך 3807a והוי 1945 אדון 113

abouteyka hamalakiym hara'shoniym 'asher hayu lapaneyka, ken yisrapu lak, uahouy 'adoun

**your fathers kings the former which were before you so shall they burn *odours* for you *saying* and Ah adonai**

34:6

יספדו 5594 לך 3807a כי 3588 דבר 1697 אני 589 דברתי 1696 נאם 5002 יהוה 3068: וידבר 1696 ירמיהו 3414 הנביא 5030

yispedu lak; kiy dabar 'aniy dibartiy na'am Yahuah. uaydaber yirmayahu hanabiy'a,

**they will lament to you for the word I have pronounced saith Yahuah Then spoke Jeremiah the prophet**

34:7

אל 413 צדקיהו 6667 מלך 4428 יהודה 3063 את 853 כל 3605 הדברים 1697 האלה 428 בירושלם 3389: וחיל 2428 מלך 4428 בבל 894

'al tzidqiyahu melek yahudah; 'at kal hadabariym ha'aeleh biyarushalaim. uachayil melek babel,

**unto Zedekiah king of Judah all words these in Jerusalem When army the king of Babylon's**

נלחמים 3898 על 5921 ירושלם 3389 ועל 5921 כל 3605 ערי 5892 יהודה 3063 הנותרות 3498 אל 413 לכיש 3923 ואל 413 עזקה 5825

nilchamiym 'al yarushalaim, ua'al kal 'arey yahudah hanoutarout; 'al lakiysh ua'al 'azeqah,

**fought against Jerusalem and against all the cities of Judah that were left against Lachish and against Azekah**

34:8

כי 3588 הנה 2007 נשארו 7604 בערי 5892 יהודה 3063 ערי 5892 מבצר 4013: הדבר 1697 אשר 834 היה 1961 אל 413 ירמיהו 3414

kiy henah, nish'aru ba'arey yahudah 'arey mibtzar. hadabar 'asher hayah 'al yirmayahu

**for these remained in cities Judah of the cities of defenced *This is* the word that came unto Jeremiah**

מאת 853 יהוה 3069 אחרי 310 כרת 3772 המלך 4428 צדקיהו 6667 ברית 1285 את 854 כל 3605 העם 5971 אשר 834 בירושלם 3389

me'at Yahuah; 'acharey qara'ut hamelek tzidqiyahu bariyt, 'at kal ha'am 'asher biyarushalaim,

**from Yahuah after that had made the king Zedekiah a covenant *with* all the people which *were* at Jerusalem**

34:9

לקרא 7121 להם 1992 דרור 1865: לשלח 7971 איש 376 את 853 עבדו 5650 ואיש 376 את 853

liqra' lahem darour. lashalach 'aysh 'at abdou ua'aysh 'at

**to proclaim unto them liberty That should let go every man his manservant and every man**

שפחתו 8198 העברי 5680 והעבריה 5680 חפשים 2670 לבלתי 1115 עבד 5647 בם 871a ביהודי 3064

shipchatou ha'abriy uaha'abriyah chapashiym; labiltiy 'abad bam biyahudiy

**his maidservant *being* an Hebrew or an Hebrewess free that none should serve *himself* of them *to wit* of a Jew**

Jer 34:3 And you shall not escape out of his hand, but shall surely be taken, and delivered into his hand; and your eyes shall behold the eyes of the king of Babylon, and he shall speak with you mouth to mouth, and you shall go to Babylon.4 Yet hear the word of YHUH, O Zedekiah king of Judah; Thus saith YHUH of you, Thou shall not die by the sword:5 But you shall die in peace: and with the burnings of your fathers, the former kings which were before you, so shall they burn odours for you; and they will lament you, saying, Ah lord! for I have pronounced the word, saith YHUH.6 Then Jeremiah the prophet spoke all these words unto Zedekiah king of Judah in Jerusalem,7 When the king of Babylon's army fought against Jerusalem, and against all the cities of Judah that were left, against Lachish, and against Azekah: for these defenced cities remained of the cities of Judah.8 This is the word that came unto Jeremiah from YHUH, after that the king Zedekiah had made a covenant with all the people which were at Jerusalem, to proclaim liberty unto them;9 That every man should let his manservant, and every man his maidservant, being an Hebrew or an Hebrewess, go free; that none should serve himself of them, to wit, of a Jew his brother.

אחיהו 251 | איש 376: | **34:10** | וישמעו 8085 | כל 3605 | השרים 8269 | וכל 3605 | העם 5971 | אשר 834 | באו 935 | בברית 1285
'achiyhu 'aysh. uayishma'au kal hasariym uakal ha'am 'asher ba'au babariyt,
**his brother man *Now* when heard all the princes and all the people which had entered into the covenant**

לשלח 7971 | איש 376 | את 853 | עבדו 5650 | ואיש 376 | את 853 | שפחתו 8198 | חפשים 2670 | לבלתי 1115
lashalach 'aysh 'at 'abdou ua'aysh 'at shipchatou chapashiym, labiltiy
**that should let go every one his manservant and every one his maidservant free that none**

עבד 5647 | בם 871a | עוד 5750 | וישמעו 8085 | וישלחו 7971: | **34:11** | וישובו 7725 | אחרי 310 | כן 3651
'abad bam 'aud; uayishma'au uayashalechu. uayashubu 'acharey ken,
**should serve *themselves* of them any more then they obeyed and let *them* go But and caused after ward**

וישבו 7725 | את 853 | העבדים 5650 | ואת 853 | השפחות 8198 | אשר 834 | שלחו 7971 | חפשים 2670
uayashibu, 'at ha'abadiym ua'at hashapachout, 'asher shilchu chapashiym;
**they turned to return the servants *and* the handmaids whom they had let go free**

ויכבישום 3533 | לעבדים 5650 | ולשפחות 8198: | **34:12** | ויהי 1961 | דבר 1697 | יהוה 3068 | אל 413
uayakbayshum la'abadiym ualishpachout. uayahiy dabar Yahuah 'al
**and brought them into subjection for servants and for handmaids Therefore came the word of Yahuah to**

ירמיהו 3414 | מאת 853 | יהוה 3068 | לאמר 559: | **34:13** | כה 3541 | אמר 559 | יהוה 3068 | אלהי 430 | ישראל 3478 | אנכי 595 | כרתי 3772 | ברית 1285 | את 854
yirmayahu, me'at Yahuah lea'mor. koh 'amar Yahuah 'alohey yisra'ael; 'anokiy, karatiy bariyt 'at
**Jeremiah from Yahuah saying Thus saith Yahuah the Elohim of Israel I made a covenant *with***

אבותיכם 1 | ביום 3117 | הוצאי 3318 | אותם 853 | מארץ 776 | מצרים 4714 | מבית 1004 | עבדים 5650 | לאמר 559:
abouteykem, bayoum houtzi'ay 'autam me'aretz mitzrayim, mibeyt 'abadiym lea'mor.
**your fathers in the day that I brought forth them out of the land of Egypt out of the house of bondmen saying**

**34:14** | מקץ 7093 | שבע 7651 | שנים 8141 | תשלחו 7971 | איש 376 | את 853 | אחיו 251 | העברי 5680 | אשר 834 | ימכר 4376 | לך 3807a
miqetz sheba' shaniym tashalachu 'aysh 'at 'achiyu ha'abriy 'asher yimaker laka,
**At the end of seven years let you go every man his brother an Hebrew which has been sold unto you**

ועבדך 5647 | שש 8337 | שנים 8141 | ושלחתו 7971 | חפשי 2670 | מעמך 5973 | ולא 3808 | שמעו 8085 | אבותיכם 1
ua'abadaka shesh shaniym, uashilachtou chapashiy me'amak; uala' shama'au abouteykem
**and when he has served you six years you shall let him go free from you but not hearkened your fathers**

אלי 413 | ולא 3808 | הטו 5186 | את 853 | אזנם 241: | **34:15** | ותשבו 7725 | אתם 859 | היום 3117 | ותעשו 6213 | את 853 | הישר 3477 | בעיני 5869
'aelay, uala' hitu 'at 'azanam. uatashubu 'atem hayoum, uata'asu 'at hayashar ba'aeynay,
**unto me neither inclined their ear And were turned you now and had done right in my sight**

לקרא 7121 | דרור 1865 | איש 376 | לרעהו 7453 | ותכרתו 3772 | ברית 1285 | לפני 6440 | בבית 1004 | אשר 834 | נקרא 7121
liqra' darour 'aysh lare'aehu; uatikratu bariyt lapanay, babayit 'asher niqra'
**in proclaiming liberty every man to his neighbour and you had made a covenant before me in the house which is called**

שמי 8034 | עליו 5921: | **34:16** | ותשבו 7725 | ותחללו 2490 | את 853 | שמי 8034 | ותשבו 7725 | איש 376 | את 853
shamiy 'alayu. uatashubu uatachalalu 'at shamiy, uatashibu, 'aysh 'at
**my name by But you turned and polluted my name and caused to return every man**

Jer 34:10 Now when all the princes, and all the people, which had entered into the covenant, heard that everyone should let his manservant, and everyone his maidservant, go free, that none should serve themselves of them anymore, then they obeyed, and let them go.11 But afterward they turned, and caused the servants and the handmaids, whom they had let go free, to return, and brought them into subjection for servants and for handmaids.12 Therefore the word of YHUH came to Jeremiah from YHUH, saying,13 Thus saith YHUH, the G-d of Israel; I made a covenant with your fathers in the day that I brought them forth out of the land of Egypt, out of the house of bondmen, saying,14 At the end of seven years let you go every man his brother an Hebrew, which has been sold unto you; and when he has served you six years, you shall let him go free from you: but your fathers hearkened not unto me, neither inclined their ear.15 And you were now turned, and had done right in my sight, in proclaiming liberty every man to his neighbor; and you had made a covenant before me in the house which is called by my name:16 But you turned and polluted my name, and caused every man his servant, and every man his handmaid, whom you had set at liberty at their pleasure, to return, and brought them into subjection, to be unto you for servants and for handmaids.

5650 עבדו 376 ואיש 853 את 8198 שפחתו 834 אשר 7971 שלחתם 2670 חפשים 5315 לנפשם
abdou ua'aysh 'at shipchatou, 'asher shilachtem chapashiym lanapsham;
**his servant and every man his handmaid whom you had set at liberty at their pleasure**

3533 ותכבשו 853 אתם 1961 להיות 3807a לכם 5650 לעבדים 8198 ולשפחות: **34:17** 3651 לכן 3541 כה 559 אמר 3068 יהוה
yatikbashu 'atam, lihayout lakem, la'abadiym ualishpachout. laken koh 'amar Yahuah
**and brought into subjection them to be unto you for servants and for handmaids Therefore thus saith Yahuah**

859 אתם 3808 לא 8085 שמעתם 413 אלי 7121 לקרא 1865 דרור 376 איש 251 לאחיו 376 ואיש 7453 לרעהו
'atem la' shama'tem 'aelay, liqra' darour, 'aysh la'achiyu ua'aysh lare'aehu;
**you not have hearkened unto me in proclaiming liberty every one to his brother and every man to his neighbour**

2005 הנני 7121 קרא 3807a לכם 1865 דרור 5002 נאם 3068 יהוה 413 אל 2719 החרב 413 אל 1698 הדבר 413 ואל 7458 הרעב 5414 ונתתי
hinniy qorea' lakem darour na'am Yahuah 'al hachereb 'al hadeber ua'al hara'ab, uanatatiy
**behold I proclaim for you a liberty saith Yahuah to the sword to the pestilence and to the famine and I will make**

853 אתכם 2113 לזועה 3605 לכל 4467 ממלכות 776 הארץ: **34:18** 5414 ונתתי 853 את 582 האנשים 5674 העברים
'atkem lazua'ah lakol mamlakout ha'aretz. uanatatiy 'at ha'anashiym, ha'abariym
**you to be removed into all the kingdoms of the earth And I will give the men that have transgressed**

853 את 1285 ברתי 834 אשר 3808 לא 6965 הקימו 853 את 1697 דברי 1285 הברית 834 אשר 3772 כרתו 6440 לפני 5695 העגל
'at bariytiy, 'asher la' heqiymu 'at dibrey habariyt, 'asher karatu lapanay; ha'aegel
**my covenant which not have performed the words of the covenant which they had made before me the calf**

834 אשר 3772 כרתו 8147 לשנים 5674 ויעברו 996 בין 1335 בתריו: **34:19** 8269 שרי 3063 יהודה 8269 ושרי
'asher karatu lishnayim, uaya'abru beyn batarayu. sarey yahudah uasarey
**when they cut in twain and passed between the parts thereof The princes of Judah and the princes of**

3389 ירושלם 5631 הסרסים 3548 והכהנים 3605 וכל 5971 עם 776 הארץ 5674 העברים 996 בין 1335 בתרי 5695 העגל: **34:20**
yarushalaim, hasarisiym uahakohaniym, uakol 'am ha'aretz; ha'abariym, beyn bitrey ha'aegel.
**Jerusalem the eunuchs and the priests and all the people of the land which passed between the parts of the calf**

5414 ונתתי 853 אותם 3027 ביד 341 איביהם 3027 וביד 1245 מבקשי 5315 נפשם 1961 והיתה
uanatatiy 'autam bayad 'ayabeyhem, uabyad mabaqshey napsham; uahayatah
**I will even give them into the hand of their enemies and into the hand of them that seek their life and shall be**

5038 נבלתם 3978 למאכל 5775 לעוף 8064 השמים 929 ולבהמת 776 הארץ: **34:21** 853 ואת 6667 צדקיהו 4428 מלך
niblatam lama'akal, la'oup hashamayim ualbehemat ha'aretz. ua'at tzidqiyahu melek
**their dead bodies for meat unto the fowls of the heaven and to the beasts of the earth *And* Zedekiah king of**

3063 יהודה 853 ואת 8269 שריו 5414 אתן 3027 ביד 341 איביהם 3027 וביד 1245 מבקשי 5315 נפשם
yahudah ua'at sarayu, 'aten bayad 'ayabeyhem, uabyad mabaqshey napsham;
**Judah *and* his princes will I give into the hand of their enemies and into the hand of them that seek their life**

3027 וביד 2428 חיל 4428 מלך 894 בבל 5927 העלים 5921 מעליכם: **34:22** 2005 הנני 6680 מצוה
uabyad cheyl melek babel, ha'aliym me'aleykem. hinniy matzaueh
**and into the hand of army the king of Babylon's which are gone up from you Behold I will command**

Jer 34:17 Therefore thus saith YHUH; You have not hearkened unto me, in proclaiming liberty, everyone to his brother, and every man to his neighbor: behold, I proclaim a liberty for you, saith YHUH, to the sword, to the pestilence, and to the famine; and I will make you to be removed into all the kingdoms of the earth.18 And I will give the men that have transgressed my covenant, which have not performed the words of the covenant which they had made before me, when they cut the calf in twain, and passed between the parts thereof,19 The princes of Judah, and the princes of Jerusalem, the eunuchs, and the priests, and all the people of the land, which passed between the parts of the calf;20 I will even give them into the hand of their enemies, and into the hand of them that seek their life: and their dead bodies shall be for meat unto the fowls of the heaven, and to the beasts of the earth.21 And Zedekiah king of Judah and his princes will I give into the hand of their enemies, and into the hand of them that seek their life, and into the hand of the king of Babylon's army, which are gone up from you.

נאם 5002 יהוה 3068 והשבתים 7725 אל 413 העיר 5892 הזאת 2063 ונלחמו 3898 עליה 5921 ולכדוה 3920 ושרפה 8313
na'am Yahuah uahashibotiym 'al ha'ayr haza't uanilchamu 'aleyha, ualkaduha uasrapuha
**saith Yahuah and cause them to return to city this and they shall fight against it and take it and burn it**

באש 784 ואת 853 ערי 5892 יהודה 3063 אתן 5414 שממה 8077 מאין 369 ישב 3427:
ba'ash; ua'at 'arey yahudah 'aten shamamah me'ayn yosheb.
**with fire *and* the cities of Judah I will make a desolation without an inhabitant**

**Jer 35:1** הדבר 1697 אשר 834 היה 1961 אל 413 ירמיהו 3414 מאת 853 יהוה 3068 בימי 3117 יהויקים 3079 בן 1121 יאשיהו 2977 מלך 4428
hadabar 'asher hayah 'al yirmayahu me'at Yahuah; biymey yahouyaqiym ben ya'shiyahu melek
**The word which came unto Jeremiah from Yahuah in the days of Jehoiakim the son of Josiah king of**

יהודה 3063 לאמר 559: **35:2** הלוך 1980 אל 413 בית 1004 הרכבים 7397 ודברת 1696 אותם 853 והבאותם 935 בית 1004
yahudah lea'mor. halouk 'al beyt harekabiym uadibarta 'autam, uahabi'autam beyt
**Judah saying Go unto the house of the Rechabites and speak unto them and bring them into the house of**

יהוה 3068 אל 413 אחת 259 הלשכות 3957 והשקית 8248 אותם 853 יין 3196: **35:3** ואקח 3947 את 853 יאזניה 2970 בן 1121 ירמיהו 3414
Yahuah, 'al 'achat halashakout; uahishqiyta 'autam yayin. ua'aqach 'at ya'azanyah ben yirmayahu
**Yahuah into one of the chambers and give to drink them wine Then I took Jaazaniah the son of Jeremiah**

בן 1121 חבצניה 2262 ואת 853 אחיו 251 ואת 853 כל 3605 בניו 1121 ואת 853 כל 3605 בית 1004 הרכבים 7397: **35:4**
ben chabatzinyah, ua'at 'achiyu ua'at kal banayu; ua'at kal beyt harekabiym.
**the son of Habaziniah *and* his brethren *and* all his sons *and* the whole house of the Rechabites**

ואבא 935 אתם 853 בית 1004 יהוה 3068 אל 413 לשכת 3957 בני 1121 חנן 2605 בן 1121 יגדליהו 3012 איש 376
ua'abiy 'atam beyt Yahuah, 'al lishkat, baney chanan ben yigdalyahu 'aysh
**And I brought into them the house of Yahuah into the chamber of the sons of Hanan the son of Igdaliah a man of**

האלהים 430 אשר 834 אצל 681 לשכת 3957 השרים 8269 אשר 834 ממעל 4605 ללשכת 3957 מעשיהו 4641 בן 1121 שלם 7967
ha'alohiym; 'asher 'aetzel lishkat hasariym, 'asher mima'al, lalishkat ma'aseyahu ben shalum
**Elohim which *was* by the chamber of the princes which *was* above the chamber of Maaseiah the son of Shallum**

שמר 8104 הסף 5592: **35:5** ואתן 5414 לפני 6440 בני 1121 בית 1004 הרכבים 7397 גבעים 1375 מלאים 4392 יין 3196 וכסות 3563
shomer hasap. ua'aten lipney baney beyt harekabiym, gabi'aym male'aym yayin uakosout;
**the keeper of the door And I set before the sons of the house of the Rechabites pots full of wine and cups**

ואמר 559 אליהם 413 שתו 8354 יין 3196: **35:6** ויאמרו 559 לא 3808 נשתה 8354 יין 3196 כי 3588 יונדב 3122 בן 1121 רכב 7394
ua'amar 'aleyhem shatu yayin. uaya'maru la' nishteh yayin; kiy younadab ben rekab
**and I said unto them Drink you wine But they said no We will drink wine for Jonadab the son of Rechab**

אבינו 1 צוה 6680 עלינו 5921 לאמר 559 לא 3808 תשתו 8354 יין 3196 אתם 859 ובניכם 1121 עד 5704 עולם 5769: **35:7** ובית 1004
'abiynu, tziuah 'aleynu lea'mor, la' tishtu yayin 'atem uabneykem 'ad 'aulam. uabayit
**our father commanded us saying no You shall drink wine *neither* you nor your sons for ever house**

לא 3808 תבנו 1129 וזרע 2233 לא 3808 תזרעו 2232 וכרם 3754 לא 3808 תטעו 5193 ולא 3808 יהיה 1961 לכם 3807a כי 3588 באהלים 168
la' tibnu, uazera' la' tizra'au uakerem la' tita'au, uala' yihayeh lakem; kiy ba'ahaliym
**Neither shall you build seed nor sow vineyard nor plant nor he have to you *any* but in tents**

Jer 34:22 Behold, I will command, saith YHUH, and cause them to return to this city; and they shall fight against it, and take it, and burn it with fire: and I will make the cities of Judah a desolation without an inhabitant. **Jer** 35:1 The word which came unto Jeremiah from YHUH in the days of Jehoiakim the son of Josiah king of Judah, saying,2 Go unto the house of the Rechabites, and speak unto them, and bring them into the house of YHUH, into one of the chambers, and give them wine to drink.3 Then I took Jaazaniah the son of Jeremiah, the son of Habaziniah, and his brethren, and all his sons, and the whole house of the Rechabites;4 And I brought them into the house of YHUH, into the chamber of the sons of Hanan, the son of Igdaliah, a man of G-d, which was by the chamber of the princes, which was above the chamber of Maaseiah the son of Shallum, the keeper of the door:5 And I set before the sons of the house of the Rechabites pots full of wine, and cups, and I said unto them, Drink you wine.6 But they said, We will drink no wine: for Jonadab the son of Rechab our father commanded us, saying, You shall drink no wine, neither you, nor your sons forever:7 Neither shall you build house, nor sow seed, nor plant vineyard, nor have any: but all your days you shall dwell in tents; that you may live many days in the land where you be strangers.

| תשבו 3427 | כל 3605 | ימיכם 3117 | למען 4616 | תחיו 2421 | ימים 3117 | רבים 7227 | על 5921 | פני 6440 | האדמה 127 | אשר 834 | אתם 859 |
|---|---|---|---|---|---|---|---|---|---|---|---|
| teshabu | kal | yameykem, | lama'an | tichayu | yamiym | rabiym | 'al | paney | ha'adamah, | 'asher | 'atem |
| **you shall dwell** | **all** | **your days** | **that** | **you may live** | **days** | **many** | **in** | **surfaces of** | **the land** | **where** | **you** |

| גרים 1481 | שם 8033: | **35:8** ונשמע 8085 | בקול 6963 | יהונדב 3082 | בן 1121 | רכב 7394 | אבינו 1 | לכל 3605 | אשר 834 |
|---|---|---|---|---|---|---|---|---|---|
| gariym | sham. | uanishma', | baqoul | yahounadab | ben | rekab | 'abiynu, | lakol | 'asher |
| ***be* strangers** | **there** | **Thus have we obeyed** | **the voice of** | **Jonadab** | **the son of** | **Rechab** | **our father** | **in all** | **that** |

| צונו 6680 | לבלתי 1115 | שתות 8354 | יין 3196 | כל 3605 | ימינו 3117 | אנחנו 587 | נשינו 802 | בנינו 1121 | ובנתינו 1323: | **35:9** ולבלתי 1115 |
|---|---|---|---|---|---|---|---|---|---|---|
| tziuanu; | labiltiy | shatout | yayin | kal | yameynu, | 'anachnu | nasheynu, | baneynu | uabnoteynu. | ualbiltiy |
| **he has charged us** | **to no** | **drink** | **wine** | **all** | **our days** | **we** | **our wives** | **our sons** | **nor our daughters** | **Nor** |

| בנות 1129 | בתים 1004 | לשבתנו 3427 | וכרם 3754 | ושדה 7704 | וזרע 2233 | לא 3808 | יהיה 1961 | לנו 3807a: | **35:10** ונשב 3427 | באהלים 168 |
|---|---|---|---|---|---|---|---|---|---|---|
| banout | batiym | lashibtenu; | uakerem | uasadeh | uazera' | la' | yihayeh | lanu. | uanesheb | ba'ahaliym; |
| **to build** | **houses** | **for us to dwell in** | **vineyard** | **nor field** | **nor seed** | **neither** | **have** | **we** | **But we have dwelt** | **in tents** |

| ונשמע 8085 | ונעש 6213 | ככל 3605 | אשר 834 | צונו 6680 | יונדב 3122 | אבינו 1: | **35:11** ויהי 1961 |
|---|---|---|---|---|---|---|---|
| uanishma' | uana'as, | kakol | 'asher | tziuanu | younadab | 'abiynu. | uayahiy, |
| **and have obeyed** | **and done** | **according to all** | **that** | **commanded us** | **Jonadab** | **our father** | **But it came to pass** |

| בעלות 5927 | נבוכדראצר 5019 | מלך 4428 | בבל 894 | אל 413 | הארץ 776 | ונאמר 559 | באו 935 | ונבוא 935 | ירושלם 3389 | מפני 6440 |
|---|---|---|---|---|---|---|---|---|---|---|
| ba'alout | nabukadra'tzar | melek | babel | 'al | ha'aretz | uana'mer, | bo'au | uanabou'a | yarushalaim, | mipaney |
| **when came up** | **Nebuchadrezzar** | **king of** | **Babylon** | **into** | **the land** | **that we said** | **Come** | **and let us go to** | **Jerusalem** | **for fear of** |

| חיל 2428 | הכשדים 3778 | ומפני 6440 | חיל 2428 | ארם 758 | ונשב 3427 | בירושלם 3389: | **35:12** ויהי 1961 |
|---|---|---|---|---|---|---|---|
| cheyl | hakasdiym, | uamipaney | cheyl | 'aram; | uanesheb | biyarushalaim. | uayahiy |
| **the army of** | **the Chaldeans** | **and for fear of** | **the army of** | **the Syrians** | **so we dwell** | **at Jerusalem** | **Then came** |

| דבר 1697 | יהוה 3068 | אל 413 | ירמיהו 3414 | לאמר 559: | **35:13** כה 3541 | אמר 559 | יהוה 3069 | צבאות 6635 | אלהי 430 | ישראל 3478 | הלך 1980 | ואמרת 559 |
|---|---|---|---|---|---|---|---|---|---|---|---|---|
| dabar | Yahuah, | 'al | yirmayahu | lea'mor. | koh | 'amar | Yahuah | tzaba'aut | 'alohey | yisra'ael, | halok | ua'amarta |
| **the word of** | **Yahuah** | **unto** | **Jeremiah** | **saying** | **Thus** | **saith** | **Yahuah** | **of hosts** | **the Elohim of** | **Israel** | **Go** | **and tell** |

| לאיש 376 | יהודה 3063 | ולי ושבי 3427 | ירושלם 3389 | הלוא 3808 | תקחו 3947 | מוסר 4148 | לשמע 8085 | אל 413 | דברי 1697 |
|---|---|---|---|---|---|---|---|---|---|
| la'aysh | yahudah, | ualyoushabey | yarushalaim; | halou'a | tiqchu | musar | lishmoa' | 'al | dabaray |
| **the men of** | **Judah** | **and the inhabitants of** | **Jerusalem** | **not** | **Will you receive** | **instruction** | **to listen** | **to** | **my words?** |

| נאם 5002 | יהוה 3069: | **35:14** הוקם 6965 | את 853 | דברי 1697 | יהונדב 3082 | בן 1121 | רכב 7394 | אשר 834 | צוה 6680 | את 853 | בניו 1121 |
|---|---|---|---|---|---|---|---|---|---|---|---|
| na'am | Yahuah. | huqam | 'at | dibrey | yahounadab | ben | rekab | 'asher | tziuah | 'at | banayu |
| **said** | **Yahuah** | ***The* are performed** | | **words of** | **Jonadab** | **the son of** | **Rechab** | **that** | **he commanded** | | **his sons** |

| לבלתי 1115 | שתות 8354 | יין 3196 | ולא 3808 | שתו 8354 | עד 5704 | היום 3117 | הזה 2088 | כי 3588 | שמעו 8085 | את 853 | מצות 4687 | אביהם 1 |
|---|---|---|---|---|---|---|---|---|---|---|---|---|
| labiltiy | shatout | yayin, | uala' | shatu | 'ad | hayoum | hazeh, | kiy | shama'au, | 'at | mitzuat | 'abiyhem; |
| **not** | **to drink** | **wine** | **for none** | **they drink** | **unto** | **day** | **this** | **but** | **obey** | | **commandment** | **their father's** |

| ואנכי 595 | דברתי 1696 | אליכם 413 | השכם 7925 | ודבר 1696 | ולא 3808 | שמעתם 8085 | אלי 413: |
|---|---|---|---|---|---|---|---|
| ua'anokiy | dibartiy | 'aleykem | hashkem | uadaber, | uala' | shama'tem | 'aelay. |
| **notwithstanding I** | **have spoken** | **unto you** | **rising early** | **and speaking** | **but not** | **you hearkened** | **unto me** |

Jer 35:8 Thus have we obeyed the voice of Jonadab the son of Rechab our father in all that he has charged us, to drink no wine all our days, we, our wives, our sons, nor our daughters;9 Nor to build houses for us to dwell in: neither have we vineyard, nor field, nor seed:10 But we have dwelt in tents, and have obeyed, and done according to all that Jonadab our father commanded us.11 But it came to pass, when Nebuchadrezzar king of Babylon came up into the land, that we said, Come, and let us go to Jerusalem for fear of the army of the Chaldeans, and for fear of the army of the Syrians: so we dwell at Jerusalem.12 Then came the word of YHUH unto Jeremiah, saying,13 Thus saith YHUH of hosts, the G-d of Israel; Go and tell the men of Judah and the inhabitants of Jerusalem, Will you not receive instruction to hear to my words? saith YHUH.14 The words of Jonadab the son of Rechab, that he commanded his sons not to drink wine, are performed; for unto this day they drink none, but obey their father's commandment: notwithstanding I have spoken unto you, rising early and speaking; but you hearkened not unto me.

**35:15**
ואשלח 7971 אליכם 413 את 853 כל 3605 עבדי 5650 הנבאים 5030 השכים 7925 ושלח 7971 לאמר 559 שבו 7725
ua'ashlach 'aleykem 'at kal 'abaday hanabiy'aym hashkeym uashaloach lea'mor shubu
**I have sent also unto you all my servants the prophets rising up early and sending *them* saying Return you**

נא 4994 איש 376 מדרכו 1870 הרעה 7451 והיטבו 3190 מעלליכם 4611 ואל 408 תלכו 1980 אחרי 310 אלהים 430 אחרים 312 לעבדם 5647
naa' 'aysh midarkou hara'ah uaheytiybu ma'alleykem, ua'al teleku 'acharey 'alohiym 'acheriym la'abadam,
**now every man from his way evil and amend your doings and not go after gods other to serve them**

ושבו 3427 אל 413 האדמה 127 אשר 834 נתתי 5414 לכם 3807a ולאבתיכם 1 ולא 3808 הטיתם 5186 את 853
uashbu 'al ha'adamah, 'asher natatiy lakem uala'aboteykem; uala' hitiytem 'at
**and you shall dwell in the land which I have given to you and to your fathers but not you have inclined**

אזנכם 241 ולא 3808 שמעתם 8085 אלי 413: **35:16** כי 3588 הקימו 6965 בני 1121 יהונדב 3082 בן 1121 רכב 7394 את 853
'aznakem, uala' shama'tem 'aelay. kiy heqiymu, baney yahounadab ben rekab, 'at
**your ear nor hearkened unto me Because have performed the sons of Jonadab the son of Rechab**

מצות 4687 אביהם 1 אשר 834 צום 6680 והעם 5971 הזה 2088 לא 3808 שמעו 8085 אלי 413: **35:17**
mitzuat 'abiyhem 'asher tziuam; uaha'am hazeh, la' shama'au 'aelay.
**the commandment of their father which he commanded them but people this not has hearkened unto me**

לכן 3651 כה 3541 אמר 559 יהוה 3068 אלהי 430 צבאות 6635 אלהי 430 ישראל 3478 הנני 2005 מביא 935 אל 413 יהודה 3063 ואל 413
laken koh 'amar Yahuah 'alohey tzaba'aut 'alohey yisra'ael, hinniy mebiy'a 'al yahudah, ua'ael
**Therefore thus saith Yahuah Elohim of hosts the Elohim of Israel Behold I will bring upon Judah and upon**

כל 3605 יושבי 3427 ירושלם 3389 את 853 כל 3605 הרעה 7451 אשר 834 דברתי 1696 עליהם 5921 יען 3282 דברתי 1696
kal youshabey yarushalaim, 'at kal hara'ah, 'asher dibartiy 'aleyhem; ya'an dibartiy
**all the inhabitants of Jerusalem all the evil that I have pronounced against them because I have spoken**

אליהם 413 ולא 3808 שמעו 8085 ואקרא 7121 להם 3807a ולא 3808 ענו 6030: **35:18** ולבית 1004
'aleyhem uala' shame'au, ua'aqra' lahem uala' 'anu. ualbeyt
**unto them but not they have heard and I have called unto them but not they have answered And unto the house of**

הרכבים 7397 אמר 559 ירמיהו 3414 כה 3541 אמר 559 יהוה 3068 צבאות 6635 אלהי 430 ישראל 3478 יען 3282 אשר 834 שמעתם 8085
harekabiym 'amar yirmayahu, koh 'amar Yahuah tzaba'aut 'alohey yisra'ael, ya'an 'asher shama'tem,
**the Rechabites said Jeremiah Thus saith Yahuah of hosts the Elohim of Israel Because which you have obeyed**

על 5921 מצות 4687 יהונדב 3082 אביכם 1 ותשמרו 8104 את 853 כל 3605 מצותיו 4687 ותעשו 6213 ככל 3605 אשר 834
'al mitzuat yahounadab 'abiykem; uatishmaru 'at kal mitzuotayu, uata'asu, kakol 'asher
**on the commandment of Jonadab your father and kept all his precepts and done according unto all that**

צוה 6680 אתכם 853: **35:19** לכן 3651 כה 3541 אמר 559 יהוה 3068 צבאות 6635 אלהי 430 ישראל 3478 לא 3808 יכרת 3772
tziuah 'atkem. laken, koh 'amar Yahuah tzaba'aut 'alohey yisra'ael; la' yikaret
**he has commanded you Therefore thus saith Yahuah of hosts the Elohim of Israel not shall want**

איש 376 ליונדב 3122 בן 1121 רכב 7394 עמד 5975 לפני 6440 כל 3605 הימים 3117:
'aysh layounadab ben rekab 'amed lapanay kal hayamiym.
**a man Jonadab the son of Rechab to stand before me for ever**

Jer 35:15 I have sent also unto you all my servants the prophets, rising up early and sending them, saying, Return you now every man from his evil way, and amend your
doings, and go not after other gods to serve them, and you shall dwell in the land which I have given to you and to your fathers: but you have not inclined your ear, nor
hearkened unto me.16 Because the sons of Jonadab the son of Rechab have performed the commandment of their father, which he commanded them; but this people has not
hearkened unto me:17 Therefore thus saith YHUH G-d of hosts, the G-d of Israel; Behold, I will bring upon Judah and upon all the inhabitants of Jerusalem all the evil that I
have pronounced against them: because I have spoken unto them, but they have not heard; and I have called unto them, but they have not answered.18 And Jeremiah said unto
the house of the Rechabites, Thus saith YHUH of hosts, the G-d of Israel; Because you have obeyed the commandment of Jonadab your father, and kept all his precepts, and
done according unto all that he has commanded you:19 Therefore thus saith YHUH of hosts, the G-d of Israel; Jonadab the son of Rechab shall not want a man to stand before
me forever.

**Jer 36:1**
ויהי 1961 בשנה 8141 הרביעית 7243 ליהויקים 3079 בן 1121 יאשיהו 2977 מלך 4428 יהודה 3063 היה 1961 הדבר 1697
uayahiy bashanah harabiy'at, liyahouyaqiym ben ya'shiyahu melek yahudah; hayah hadabar
**And it came to pass in year the fourth of Jehoiakim the son of Josiah king of Judah came *that* word**

36:2
הזה 2088 אל 413 ירמיהו 3414 מאת 853 יהוה 3068 לאמר 559: קח 3947 לך 3807a מגלת 4039 ספר 5612 וכתבת 3789 אליה 413 את 853 כל 3605
hazeh 'al yirmayahu, me'at Yahuah lea'mor. qach laka magilat seper uakatabta 'aeleyha, 'at kal
**this unto Jeremiah from Yahuah saying Take to you a roll of a book and write therein all**

הדברים 1697 אשר 834 דברתי 1696 אליך 413 על 5921 ישראל 3478 ועל 5921 יהודה 3063 ועל 5921 כל 3605 הגוים 1471
hadabariym 'asher dibartiy 'aeleyka 'al yisra'ael ua'al yahudah ua'al kal hagouyim;
**the words that I have spoken unto you against Israel and against Judah and against all the nations**

36:3
מיום 3117 דברתי 1696 אליך 413 מימי 3117 יאשיהו 2977 ועד 5704 היום 3117 הזה 2088: אולי 194 ישמעו 8085
miyoum dibartiy 'aeleyka miymey ya'shiyahu, ua'ad hayoum hazeh. 'aulay yishma'au
**from the day I spoke unto you from the days of Josiah even unto day this It may be will hear**

בית 1004 יהודה 3063 את 853 כל 3605 הרעה 7451 אשר 834 אנכי 595 חשב 2803 לעשות 6213 להם 3807a למען 4616 ישובו 7725
beyt yahudah, 'at kal hara'ah, 'asher 'anokiy chosheb la'asout lahem; lama'an yashubu,
***that* the house of Judah all the evil which I purpose to do unto them that they may return**

36:4
איש 376 מדרכו 1870 הרעה 7451 וסלחתי 5545 לעונם 5771 ולחטאתם 2403: ויקרא 7121 ירמיהו 3414 את 853 ברוך 1263
'aysh midarkou hara'ah, uasalachtiy la'auonam ualchata'tam. uayiqra' yirmayahu, 'at baruk
**every man from his way evil that I may forgive their iniquity and their sin Then called Jeremiah Baruch**

בן 1121 נריה 5374 ויכתב 3789 ברוך 1263 מפי 6310 ירמיהו 3414 את 853 כל 3605 דברי 1697 יהוה 3068 אשר 834 דבר 1696
ben neriyah; uayiktob baruk mipiy yirmayahu, 'at kal dibrey Yahuah 'asher diber
**the son of Neriah and wrote Baruch from the mouth of Jeremiah all the words of Yahuah which he had spoken**

36:5
אליו 413 על 5921 מגלת 4039 ספר 5612: ויצוה 6680 ירמיהו 3414 את 853 ברוך 1263 לאמר 559 אני 589 עצור 6113 לא 3808 אוכל 3201
'aelayu 'al magilat seper. uayatzaueh yirmayahu, 'at baruk lea'mor; 'aniy 'atzur, la' 'aukal,
**unto him upon a roll of a book And commanded Jeremiah Baruch saying I *am* shut up not I can**

36:6
לבוא 935 בית 1004 יהוה 3068: ובאת 935 אתה 859 וקראת 7121 במגלה 4039 אשר 834 כתבת 3789 מפי 6310 את 853
labou'a beyt Yahuah. uaba'ta 'atah uaqara'ta bamagilah 'asher katabta mipiy 'at
**go into the house of Yahuah Therefore go you and read in the roll which you have written from my mouth**

דברי 1697 יהוה 3068 באזני 241 העם 5971 בית 1004 יהוה 3068 ביום 3117 צום 6685 וגם 1571 באזני 241 כל 3605
dibrey Yahuah ba'azaney ha'am beyt Yahuah bayoum tzoum; ua'gam ba'azaney kal
**the words of Yahuah in the ears of the people house *in* Yahuah's upon day *the* fasting and also in the ears of all**

36:7
יהודה 3063 הבאים 935 מעריהם 5892 תקראם 7121: אולי 194 תפל 5307 תחנתם 8467 לפני 6440
yahudah haba'aym me'areyhem tiqra'aem. 'aulay tipol tachinatam lipney
**Judah that come out of their cities you shall read them It may be they will present their supplication before**

יהוה 3069 וישבו 7725 איש 376 מדרכו 1870 הרעה 7451 כי 3588 גדול 1419 האף 639 והחמה 2534 אשר 834 דבר 1696
Yahuah, uayashubu 'aysh midarkou hara'ah; kiy gadoul ha'ap uahachemah, 'asher diber
**Yahuah and will return every one from his way evil for great *is* the anger and the fury that has pronounced**

**Jer** 36:1 And it came to pass in the fourth year of Jehoiakim the son of Josiah king of Judah, that this word came unto Jeremiah from YHUH, saying,2 Take you a roll of a book, and write therein all the words that I have spoken unto you against Israel, and against Judah, and against all the nations, from the day I spoke unto you, from the days of Josiah, even unto this day.3 It may be that the house of Judah will hear all the evil which I purpose to do unto them; that they may return every man from his evil way; that I may forgive their iniquity and their sin.4 Then Jeremiah called Baruch the son of Neriah: and Baruch wrote from the mouth of Jeremiah all the words of YHUH, which he had spoken unto him, upon a roll of a book.5 And Jeremiah commanded Baruch, saying, I am shut up; I cannot go into the house of YHUH:6 Therefore go you, and read in the roll, which you have written from my mouth, the words of YHUH in the ears of the people in YHUH's house upon the fasting day: and also you shall read them in the ears of all Judah that come out of their cities.7 It may be they will present their supplication before YHUH, and will return everyone from his evil way: for great is the anger and the fury that YHUH has pronounced against this people.

| | | | | 36:8 | | | | | | |
|---|---|---|---|---|---|---|---|---|---|---|
| יהוה 3069 | אל 413 | העם 5971 | הזה 2088: | ויעש 6213 | ברוך 1263 | בן 1121 | נריה 5374 | ככל 3605 | אשר 834 | צוהו 6680 |
| Yahuah | 'al | ha'am | hazeh. | uaya'as, | baruk | ben | neriyah, | kakol | 'asher | tziuahu |
| **Yahuah** | **against** | **the people** | **this** | **And did** | **Baruch** | **the son of** | **Neriah** | **according to all** | **that** | **commanded him** |

| | | | | | | | | 36:9 | |
|---|---|---|---|---|---|---|---|---|---|
| ירמיהו 3414 | הנביא 5030 | לקרא 7121 | בספר 5612 | דברי 1697 | יהוה 3068 | בית 1004 | יהוה 3068: | ויהי 1961 | בשנה 8141 |
| yirmayahu | hanabiy'a; | liqra' | baseper | dibrey | Yahuah | beyt | Yahuah. | uayahiy | bashanah |
| **Jeremiah** | **the prophet** | **reading** | **in the book** | **the words of** | **Yahuah** | **house** | ***in* Yahuah's** | **And it came to pass** | **in year** |

| | | | | | | | | | | |
|---|---|---|---|---|---|---|---|---|---|---|
| החמשית 2549 | ליהויקים 3079 | בן 1121 | יאשיהו 2977 | מלך 4428 | יהודה 3063 | בחדש 2320 | התשעי 8671 | קראו 7121 | צום 6685 | לפני 6440 |
| hachamishiyt | liyahouyaqiym | ben | ya'shiyahu | melek | yahudah | bachodesh | hatashi'ay, | qara'au | tzoum | lipney |
| **the fifth** | **of Jehoiakim** | **the son of** | **Josiah** | **king of** | **Judah** | **in month** | **the ninth** | ***that* they proclaimed** | **a fast** | **before** |

| | | | | | | | | | | 36:10 |
|---|---|---|---|---|---|---|---|---|---|---|
| יהוה 3068 | כל 3605 | העם 5971 | בירושלם 3389 | וכל 3605 | העם 5971 | הבאים 935 | מערי 5892 | יהודה 3063 | בירושלם 3389: | |
| Yahuah | kal | ha'am | biyarushalaim; | uakal | ha'am, | haba'aym | me'arey | yahudah | biyarushalaim. | |
| **Yahuah** | ***to* all** | **the people** | **in Jerusalem** | **and to all** | **the people** | **that came** | **from the cities of** | **Judah** | **unto Jerusalem** | |

| | | | | | | | | | |
|---|---|---|---|---|---|---|---|---|---|
| ויקרא 7121 | ברוך 1263 | בספר 5612 | את 853 | דברי 1697 | ירמיהו 3414 | בית 1004 | יהוה 3068 | בלשכת 3957 | גמריהו 1587 |
| uayiqra' | baruk | baseper | 'at | dibrey | yirmayahu | beyt | Yahuah; | balishkat | gamaryahu |
| **Then read** | **Baruch** | **in the book** | | **the words of** | **Jeremiah** | **in the house of** | **Yahuah** | **in the chamber of** | **Gemariah** |

| | | | | | | | | | | | |
|---|---|---|---|---|---|---|---|---|---|---|---|
| בן 1121 | שפן 8227 | הספר 5608 | בחצר 2691 | העליון 5945 | פתח 6607 | שער 8179 | בית 1004 | יהוה 3068 | החדש 2319 | באזני 241 | כל 3605 |
| ben | shapan | hasoper | bechatzer | ha'alyoun, | petach | sha'ar | beyt | Yahuah | hechadash, | ba'azaney | kal |
| **the son of** | **Shaphan** | **the scribe** | **in court** | **the higher** | ***at* the entry of** | **gate of** | **house** | **Yahuah's** | **the new** | **in the ears of** | **all** |

| | 36:11 | | | | | | | | | |
|---|---|---|---|---|---|---|---|---|---|---|
| העם 5971: | וישמע 8085 | מכיהו 4321 | בן 1121 | גמריהו 1587 | בן 1121 | שפן 8227 | את 853 | כל 3605 | דברי 1697 | יהוה 3068 |
| ha'am. | uayishma', | miykayahu | ben | gamaryahu | ben | shapan | 'at | kal | dibrey | Yahuah |
| **the people** | **When had heard** | **Michaiah** | **the son of** | **Gemariah** | **the son of** | **Shaphan** | | **all** | **the words of** | **Yahuah** |

| | | 36:12 | | | | | | | | |
|---|---|---|---|---|---|---|---|---|---|---|
| מעל 5921 | הספר 5612: | וירד 3381 | בית 1004 | המלך 4428 | על 5921 | לשכת 3957 | הספר 5608 | והנה 2009 | שם 8033 | כל 3605 |
| me'al | haseper. | uayered | beyt | hamelek | 'al | lishkat | hasoper, | uahineh | sham, | kal |
| **out of** | **the book** | **Then he went down into** | **house** | **the king's** | **into** | **chamber** | **the scribe's** | **and lo** | **there** | **all** |

| | | | | | | | | | |
|---|---|---|---|---|---|---|---|---|---|
| השרים 8269 | יושבים 3427 | אלישמע 476 | הספר 5608 | ודליהו 1806 | בן 1121 | שמעיהו 8089 | ואלנתן 494 | בן 1121 | עכבור 5907 |
| hasariym | youshabiym; | 'aliyshama' | hasoper | uadalayahu | ben | shama'yahu | ua'alnatan | ben | 'akbour |
| **the princes** | **sat *even*** | **Elishama** | **the scribe** | **and Delaiah** | **the son of** | **Shemaiah** | **and Elnathan** | **the son of** | **Achbor** |

| | | | | | | | | 36:13 | |
|---|---|---|---|---|---|---|---|---|---|
| וגמריהו 1587 | בן 1121 | שפן 8227 | וצדקיהו 6667 | בן 1121 | חנניהו 2608 | וכל 3605 | השרים 8269: | ויגד 5046 | להם 3807a |
| uagamaryahu | ben | shapan | uatzidqiyahu | ben | chananyahu | uakal | hasariym. | uayaged | lahem |
| **and Gemariah** | **the son of** | **Shaphan** | **and Zedekiah** | **the son of** | **Hananiah** | **and all** | **the princes** | **Then declared** | **unto them** |

| | | | | | | | | | | | 36:14 |
|---|---|---|---|---|---|---|---|---|---|---|---|
| מכיהו 4321 | את 853 | כל 3605 | הדברים 1697 | אשר 834 | שמע 8085 | בקרא 7121 | ברוך 1263 | בספר 5612 | באזני 241 | העם 5971: | |
| miykayahu, | 'at | kal | hadabariym | 'asher | shamea'; | biqra' | baruk | baseper | ba'azaney | ha'am. | |
| **Michaiah** | | **all** | **the words** | **that** | **he had heard** | **when read** | **Baruch** | **the book** | **in the ears of** | **the people** | |

| | | | | | | | | | | | | |
|---|---|---|---|---|---|---|---|---|---|---|---|---|
| וישלחו 7971 | כל 3605 | השרים 8269 | אל 413 | ברוך 1263 | את 853 | יהודי 3065 | בן 1121 | נתניהו 5418 | בן 1121 | שלמיהו 8018 | בן 1121 | כושי 3570 |
| uayishlachu | kal | hasariym | 'al | baruk, | 'at | yahudiy | ben | natanyahu | ben | shelemyahu | ben | kushiy |
| **Therefore sent** | **all** | **the princes** | **unto** | **Baruch** | | **Jehudi** | **the son of** | **Nethaniah** | **the son of** | **Shelemiah** | **the son of** | **Cushi** |

Jer 36:8 And Baruch the son of Neriah did according to all that Jeremiah the prophet commanded him, reading in the book the words of YHUH in YHUH's house.9 And it came to pass in the fifth year of Jehoiakim the son of Josiah king of Judah, in the ninth month, that they proclaimed a fast before YHUH to all the people in Jerusalem, and to all the people that came from the cities of Judah unto Jerusalem.10 Then read Baruch in the book the words of Jeremiah in the house of YHUH, in the chamber of Gemariah the son of Shaphan the scribe, in the higher court, at the entry of the new gate of YHUH's house, in the ears of all the people.11 When Michaiah the son of Gemariah, the son of Shaphan, had heard out of the book all the words of YHUH,12 Then he went down into the king's house, into the scribe's chamber: and, lo, all the princes sat there, even Elishama the scribe, and Delaiah the son of Shemaiah, and Elnathan the son of Achbor, and Gemariah the son of Shaphan, and Zedekiah the son of Hananiah, and all the princes.13 Then Michaiah declared unto them all the words that he had heard, when Baruch read the book in the ears of the people.14 Therefore all the princes sent Jehudi the son of Nethaniah, the son of Shelemiah, the son of Cushi, unto Baruch, saying, Take in your hand the roll wherein you have read in the ears of the people, and come.

לאמר 559 המגלה 4039 אשר 834 קראת 7121 בה 871a באזני 241 העם 5971 קחנה 3947 בידך 3027 ולך 1980 ויקח 3947 ברוך 1263
lea'mor hamagilah, 'asher qara'ta bah ba'azaney ha'am, qachenah bayadaka ualek; uayiqach baruk
**saying the roll wherein you have read when in the ears of the people Take in your hand and come So took Baruch**

36:15
בן 1121 נריהו 5374 את 853 המגלה 4039 בידו 3027 ויבא 935 אליהם 413: ויאמרו 559 אליו 413 שב 3427 נא 4994
ben neriyahu 'at hamagilah bayadou, uayaba' 'aleyhem. uaya'maru 'aelayu, shab na,
**the son of Neriah the roll in his hand and came unto them And they said unto him Sit down now**

36:16
וקראנה 7121 באזנינו 241 ויקרא 7121 ברוך 1263 באזניהם 241: ויהי 1961 כשמעם 8085 את 853 כל 3605
uaqra'anah ba'azaneynu; uayiqra' baruk ba'azeneyhem. uayahiy, kasham'am 'at kal
**and read it in our ears read So Baruch *it* in their ears Now it came to pass when they had heard all**

הדברים 1697 פחדו 6342 איש 376 אל 413 רעהו 7453 ויאמרו 559 אל 413 ברוך 1263 הגיד 5046 נגיד 5046 למלך 4428 את 853 כל 3605
hadabariym, pachadu 'aysh 'al re'aehu; uaya'maru 'al baruk, hageyd nagiyd lamelek, 'at kal
**the words they were afraid one both *and* other and said unto Baruch We will surely tell the king of all**

36:17
הדברים 1697 האלה 428: ואת 853 ברוך 1263 שאלו 7592 לאמר 559 הגד 5046 נא 4994 לנו 3807a איך 349 כתבת 3789 את 853 כל 3605
hadabariym ha'aeleh. ua'at baruk, sha'alu lea'mor; haged naa' lanu, 'aeyk, katabta 'at kal
**words these *And* Baruch they asked saying Tell now us How did you write all**

36:18
הדברים 1697 האלה 428 מפיו 6310: ויאמר 559 להם 3807a ברוך 1263 מפיו 6310 יקרא 7121 אלי 413 את 853
hadabariym ha'aeleh mipiyu. uaya'mer lahem baruk, mipiyu yiqra' 'aelay, 'at
**words these at his mouth? Then answered them Baruch with his mouth He pronounced unto me**

36:19
כל 3605 הדברים 1697 האלה 428 ואני 589 כתב 3789 על 5921 הספר 5612 בדיו 1773: ויאמרו 559 השרים 8269 אל 413 ברוך 1263 לך 1980
kal hadabariym ha'aeleh; ua'aniy koteb 'al haseper badayou. uaya'maru hasariym 'al baruk, lek
**all words these and I wrote in the book *them* with ink Then said the princes unto Baruch Go you**

36:20
הסתר 5641 אתה 859 וירמיהו 3414 ואיש 376 אל 408 ידע 3045 איפה 375 אתם 859: ויבאו 935 אל 413 המלך 4428 חצרה 2691
hisater 'atah uayirmayahu; ua'aysh 'al yeda' 'aeypoh 'atem. uayabo'au 'al hamelek chatzerah,
**hide you and Jeremiah and man no let no where you *be* And they went in to the king *into* the court**

ואת 853 המגלה 4039 הפקדו 6485 בלשכת 3957 אלישמע 476 הספר 5608 ויגידו 5046 באזני 241 המלך 4428 את 853 כל 3605
ua'at hamagilah hipqidu, balishkat 'aliyshama' hasoper; uayagiydu ba'azaney hamelek, 'at kal
***but* the roll they laid up in the chamber of Elishama the scribe and told in the ears of the king all**

36:21
הדברים 1697: וישלח 7971 המלך 4428 את 853 יהודי 3065 לקחת 3947 את 853 המגלה 4039 ויקחה 3947 מלשכת 3957 אלישמע 476
hadabariym. uayishlach hamelek 'at yahudiy, laqachat 'at hamagilah, uayiqacheha, milishkat 'aliyshama'
**the words So sent the king Jehudi to fetch the roll and he took it out of chamber Elishama**

הספר 5608 ויקראה 7121 יהודי 3065 באזני 241 המלך 4428 ובאזני 241 כל 3605 השרים 8269 העמדים 5975 מעל 5921
hasoper; uayiqra'aha yahudiy ba'azaney hamelek, uab'azaney kal hasariym, ha'amadiym me'al
**the scribe's And read it Jehudi in the ears of the king and in the ears of all the princes which stood beside**

36:22
המלך 4428: והמלך 4428 יושב 3427 בית 1004 החרף 2779 בחדש 2320 התשיעי 8671 ואת 853 האח 254
hamelek. uahamelek, yousheb beyt hachorep, bachodesh hatashiy'ay; ua'at ha'ach
**the king Now the king sat *in* house the winter in month the ninth *and* *there was a fire* on the hearth**

Jer 36:14 So Baruch the son of Neriah took the roll in his hand, and came unto them.15 And they said unto him, Sit down now, and read it in our ears. So Baruch read it in their ears.16 Now it came to pass, when they had heard all the words, they were afraid both one and other, and said unto Baruch, We will surely tell the king of all these words.17 And they asked Baruch, saying, Tell us now, How did you write all these words at his mouth?18 Then Baruch answered them, He pronounced all these words unto me with his mouth, and I wrote them with ink in the book.19 Then said the princes unto Baruch, Go, hide you, you and Jeremiah; and let no man know where you be.20 And they went in to the king into the court, but they laid up the roll in the chamber of Elishama the scribe, and told all the words in the ears of the king.21 So the king sent Jehudi to fetch the roll: and he took it out of Elishama the scribe's chamber. And Jehudi read it in the ears of the king, and in the ears of all the princes which stood beside the king.22 Now the king sat in the winterhouse in the ninth month: and there was a fire on the hearth burning before him.

36:23

לפניו 6440 מבערת 1197: ויהי 1961 כקרוא 7121 יהודי 3065 שלש 7969 דלתות 1817 וארבעה 702 יקרעה 7167 בתער 8593

lapanayu mabo'aret. uayahiy kiqarou'a yahudiy, shalosh dalatout ua'arbah yiqra'aha bata'ar

**before him burning And it came to pass *that* when had read Jehudi three leaves or four he cut it with knife**

הספר 5608 והשלך 7993 אל 413 האש 784 אשר 834 אל 413 האח 254 עד 5704 תם 8552 כל 3605 המגלה 4039 על 5921 האש 784 אשר 834

hasoper, uahashalek 'al ha'aesh 'asher 'al ha'ach; 'ad tom kal hamagilah, 'al ha'aesh 'asher

**the pin and cast *it* into the fire that *was* on the hearth until was consumed all the roll in the fire that**

36:24

על 5921 האח 254: ולא 3808 פחדו 6342 ולא 3808 קרעו 7167 את 853 בגדיהם 899 המלך 4428 וכל 3605

'al ha'ach. uala' pachadu, uala' qara'au 'at bigadeyhem; hamelek uakal

***was* on the hearth Yet nor they were afraid nor rent their garments *neither* the king nor any of**

36:25

עבדיו 5650 השמעים 8085 את 853 כל 3605 הדברים 1697 האלה 428: וגם 1571 אלנתן 494 ודליהו 1806 וגמריהו 1587

'abadayu, hashom'aym, 'at kal hadabariym ha'aeleh. ua'gam 'alnatan uadalayahu uagamaryahu

**his servants that heard all words these Nevertheless Elnathan and Delaiah and Gemariah**

36:26

הפגעו 6293 במלך 4428 לבלתי 1115 שרף 8313 את 853 המגלה 4039 ולא 3808 שמע 8085 אליהם 413:

hipgi'au bamelek, labiltiy sarop 'at hamagilah; uala' shama' 'aleyhem.

**had made intercession to the king that not he would burn the roll but not he would hear them**

ויצוה 6680 המלך 4428 את 853 ירחמאל 3396 בן 1121 המלך 4428 ואת 853 שריהו 8304 בן 1121 עזריאל 5837 ואת 853 שלמיהו 8018

uayatzaueh hamelek 'at yarachma'ael ben hamelek ua'at sarayahu ben 'azriy'ael, ua'at shelemyahu

**But commanded the king Jerahmeel the son of Hammelek *and* Seraiah the son of Azriel *and* Shelemiah**

36:27

בן 1121 עבדאל 5655 לקחת 3947 את 853 ברוך 1263 הספר 5608 ואת 853 ירמיהו 3414 הנביא 5030 ויסתרם 5641 יהוה 3068: ויהי 1961

ben 'abda'ael, laqachat 'at baruk hasoper, ua'at yirmayahu hanabiy'a; uayastirem Yahuah. uayahiy

**the son of Abdeel to take Baruch the scribe *and* Jeremiah the prophet but hid them Yahuah Then came**

דבר 1697 יהוה 3068 אל 413 ירמיהו 3414 אחרי 310 שרף 8313 המלך 4428 את 853 המגלה 4039 ואת 853 הדברים 1697 אשר 834 כתב 3789

dabar Yahuah 'al yirmayahu; 'acharey sarop hamelek, 'at hamagilah ua'at hadabariym, 'asher katab

**the word of Yahuah to Jeremiah after that had burned the king the roll *and* the words which wrote**

36:28

ברוך 1263 מפי 6310 ירמיהו 3414 לאמר 559: שוב 7725 קח 3947 לך 3807a מגלה 4039 אחרת 312 וכתב 3789 עליה 5921 את 853 כל 3605

baruk mipiy yirmayahu lea'mor. shub qach laka magilah 'acheret; uaktob 'aeleyha, 'at kal

**Baruch at the mouth of Jeremiah saying again Take to you roll another and write in it all**

הדברים 1697 הראשנים 7223 אשר 834 היו 1961 על 5921 המגלה 4039 הראשנה 7223 אשר 834 שרף 8313 יהויקים 3079 מלך 4428

hadabariym hara'shoniym, 'asher hayu, 'al hamagilah hara'shonah, 'asher sarap yahouyaqiym melek

**words the former that were in roll the first which has burned Jehoiakim the king of**

36:29

יהודה 3063: ועל 5921 יהויקים 3079 מלך 4428 יהודה 3063 תאמר 559 כה 3541 אמר 559 יהוה 3068 אתה 859 שרפת 8313 את 853

yahudah. ua'al yahouyaqiym melek yahudah ta'mar, koh 'amar Yahuah; 'atah sarapta 'at

**Judah And to Jehoiakim king of Judah you shall say Thus saith Yahuah You have burned**

המגלה 4039 הזאת 2063 לאמר 559 מדוע 4069 כתבת 3789 עליה 5921 לאמר 559 בא 935 יבוא 935 מלך 4428 בבל 894

hamagilah haza't lea'mor, madua' katabta 'aleyha lea'mor, ba' yabou'a melek babel

**roll this saying Why have you written therein saying shall certainly come The king of Babylon**

Jer 36:23 And it came to pass, that when Jehudi had read three or four leaves, he cut it with the penknife, and cast it into the fire that was on the hearth, until all the roll was consumed in the fire that was on the hearth.24 Yet they were not afraid, nor rent their garments, neither the king, nor any of his servants that heard all these words.25 Nevertheless Elnathan and Delaiah and Gemariah had made intercession to the king that he would not burn the roll: but he would not hear them.26 But the king commanded Jerahmeel the son of Hammelech, and Seraiah the son of Azriel, and Shelemiah the son of Abdeel, to take Baruch the scribe and Jeremiah the prophet: but YHUH hid them.27 Then the word of YHUH came to Jeremiah, after that the king had burned the roll, and the words which Baruch wrote at the mouth of Jeremiah, saying,28 Take you again another roll, and write in it all the former words that were in the first roll, which Jehoiakim the king of Judah has burned.29 And you shall say to Jehoiakim the king of Judah, Thus saith YHUH; Thou have burned this roll, saying, Why have you written therein, saying, The king of Babylon shall certainly come and destroy this land, and shall cause to cease from thence man and beast?

36:30
7843 והשחית 853 את 776 הארץ 2063 הזאת 7673 והשבית 4480 ממנה 120 אדם 929: ובהמה 3651 לכן 3541 כה 559 אמר
uahishchiyt 'at ha'aretz haza't, uahishbiyt mimenah 'adam uabahemah. laken koh 'amar
**and destroy the land this and shall cause to cease from there man and beast Therefore thus saith**

3068 יהוה 5921 על 3079 יהויקים 4428 מלך 3063 יהודה 3808 לא 1961 יהיה 3807a לו 3427 יושב 5921 על 3678 כסא 1732 דוד 5038 ונבלתו
Yahuah 'al yahouyaqiym melek yahudah, la' yihayeh lou' yousheb 'al kisea' dauid; uaniblatou
**Yahuah of Jehoiakim king of Judah none He shall have to sit upon the throne of David and his dead body**

36:31
1961 תהיה 7993 משלכת 2721 לחרב 3117 ביום 7140 ולקרח 3915: בלילה 6485 ופקדתי 5921 עליו 5921 ועל 2233 זרעו 5921 ועל
tihayeh mushleket, lachoreb bayoum ualaqerach balayalah. uapaqadtiy 'alayu ua'al zar'au ua'al
**shall be cast out to the heat in the day and to the frost in the night And I will punish him and on his seed and on**

5650 עבדיו 853 את 5771 עונם 935 והבאתי 5921 עליהם 5921 ועל 3427 ישבי 3389 ירושלם 413 ואל
'abadayu 'at 'auonam; uahebea'tiy 'aleyhem ua'al yoshabey yarushalaim ua'al
**his servants *for* their iniquity and I will bring upon them and upon the inhabitants of Jerusalem and upon**

36:32
376 איש 3063 יהודה 853 את 3605 כל 7451 הרעה 834 אשר 1696 דברתי 413 אליהם 3808 ולא 8085: שמעו
'aysh yahudah, 'at kal hara'ah 'asher dibartiy 'aleyhem uala' shame'au.
**the men of Judah all the evil that I have pronounced against them but not they hearkened**

3414 וירמיהו 3947 לקח 4039 מגלה 312 אחרת 5414 ויתנה 413 אל 1263 ברוך 1121 בן 5374 נריהו 5608 הספר 3789 ויכתב 5921 עליה
uayirmayahu laqach magilah 'acheret, uayitnah 'al baruk ben neriyahu hasoper uayiktob 'aleyha
**Then Jeremiah took roll another and gave it to Baruch the son of Neriah the scribe who wrote therein**

6310 מפי 3414 ירמיהו 853 את 3605 כל 1697 דברי 5612 הספר 834 אשר 8313 שרף 3079 יהויקים 4428 מלך 3063 יהודה
mipiy yirmayahu, 'at kal dibrey haseper, 'asher sarap yahouyaqiym melek yahudah
**from the mouth of Jeremiah all the words of the book which had burned Jehoiakim king of Judah**

784 באש 5750 ועוד 3254 נוסף 5921 עליהם 1697 דברים 7227 רבים 1992: כהמה
ba'aesh; ua'aud nousap 'aleyhem dabariym rabiym kahemah.
**in the fire and besides there were added unto them words many like**

Jer 37:1
4427 וימלך 4428 מלך 6667 צדקיהו 1121 בן 2977 יאשיהו 8478 תחת 3659 כניהו 1121 בן 3079 יהויקים 834 אשר 4427 המליך
uayimlak melek, tzidqiyahu ben ya'shiyahu; tachat, kanyahu ben yahouyaqiym, 'asher himliyk
**And reigned king Zedekiah the son of Josiah instead of Coniah the son of Jehoiakim whom made king**

37:2
5019 נבוכדראצר 4428 מלך 894 בבל 776 בארץ 3063: יהודה 3808 ולא 8085 שמע 1931 הוא 5650 ועבדיו
nabukadra'tzar melek babel ba'aretz yahudah. uala' shama' hua' ua'abadayu
**Nebuchadrezzar king of Babylon in the land of Judah But neither did listen he nor his servants**

37:3
5971 ועם 776 הארץ 413 אל 1697 דברי 3068 יהוה 834 אשר 1696 דבר 3027 ביד 3414 ירמיהו 5030: הנביא 7971 וישלח 4428 המלך
ua'am ha'aretz; 'al dibrey Yahuah, 'asher diber, bayad yirmayahu hanabiy'a. uayishlach hamelek
**nor the people of the land unto the words of Yahuah which he spoke by Jeremiah the prophet And sent the king**

6667 צדקיהו 853 את 3081 יהוכל 1121 בן 8018 שלמיה 853 ואת 6846 צפניהו 1121 בן 4641 מעשיה 3548 הכהן 413 אל 3414 ירמיהו
tzidqiyahu 'at yahukal ben shelemyah, ua'at tzapanyahu ben ma'aseyah hakohen, 'al yirmayahu
**Zedekiah Jehucal the son of Shelemiah *and* Zephaniah the son of Maaseiah the priest to Jeremiah**

Jer 37:30 Therefore thus saith YHUH of Jehoiakim king of Judah; He shall have none to sit upon the throne of David: and his dead body shall be cast out in the day to the heat, and in the night to the frost.31 And I will punish him and his seed and his servants for their iniquity; and I will bring upon them, and upon the inhabitants of Jerusalem, and upon the men of Judah, all the evil that I have pronounced against them; but they hearkened not.32 Then took Jeremiah another roll, and gave it to Baruch the scribe, the son of Neriah; who wrote therein from the mouth of Jeremiah all the words of the book which Jehoiakim king of Judah had burned in the fire: and there were added besides unto them many like words. **Jer** 37:1 And king Zedekiah the son of Josiah reigned instead of Coniah the son of Jehoiakim, whom Nebuchadrezzar king of Babylon made king in the land of Judah.2 But neither he, nor his servants, nor the people of the land, did hear unto the words of YHUH, which he spoke by the prophet Jeremiah.3 And Zedekiah the king sent Jehucal the son of Shelemiah and Zephaniah the son of Maaseiah the priest to the prophet Jeremiah, saying, Pray now unto YHUH our G-d for us.

37:4

הנביא 5030 לאמר 559 התפלל 6419 נא 4994 בעדנו 1157 אל 413 יהוה 3068 אלהינו 430: וירמיהו 3414 בא 935 ויצא 3318 בתוך 8432

hanabiy'a lea'mor; hitpallel naa' ba'adenu, 'al Yahuah 'aloheynu. uayirmayahu ba' uayotzea' batouk

**the prophet saying Pray now for us unto Yahuah our Elohim Now Jeremiah came in and went out among**

37:5

העם 5971 ולא 3808 נתנו 5414 אתו 853 בית 1004 הכליא 3628: וחיל 2428 פרעה 6547 יצא 3318 ממצרים 4714

ha'am; uala' natanu 'atou beyt hakaliya' uachayil par'ah yatza' mimitzrayim;

**the people for not they had put him *into* house of prison Then army Pharaoh's was come forth out of Egypt**

וישמעו 8085 הכשדים 3778 הצרים 6696 על 5921 ירושלם 3389 את 853 שמעם 8088 ויעלו 5927 מעל 5921

uayishma'au hakasdiym hatzariym 'al yarushalaim 'at shima'am, uayea'alu, me'al

**and when heard the Chaldeans that besieged on Jerusalem tidings of them and they departed from**

37:6 37:7

ירושלם 3389: ויהי 1961 דבר 1697 יהוה 3068 אל 413 ירמיהו 3414 הנביא 5030 לאמר 559: כה 3541 אמר 559 יהוה 3068

yarushalaim. uayahiy dabar Yahuah, 'al yirmayahu hanabiy'a lea'mor. koh 'amar Yahuah

**Jerusalem Then came the word of Yahuah unto Jeremiah the prophet saying Thus saith Yahuah**

אלהי 430 ישראל 3478 כה 3541 תאמרו 559 אל 413 מלך 4428 יהודה 3063 השלח 7971 אתכם 853 אלי 413 לדרשני 1875 הנה 2009

'alohey yisra'ael, koh ta'maru 'al melek yahudah, hasholeach 'atkem 'aelay ladarasheniy; hineh

**the Elohim of Israel Thus shall you say to the king of Judah that sent you unto me to inquire of me Behold**

37:8

חיל 2428 פרעה 6547 היצא 3318 לכם 3807a לעזרה 5833 שב 7725 לארצו 776 מצרים 4714:

cheyl par'ah, hayotzea' lakem la'azrah, shab la'artzou mitzrayim.

**army Pharaoh's which is come forth to you to help shall return into their own land *to* Egypt**

37:9

ושבו 7725 הכשדים 3778 ונלחמו 3898 על 5921 העיר 5892 הזאת 2063 ולכדה 3920 ושרפה 8313 באש 784: כה 3541

uashabu hakasdiym, uanilchamu 'al ha'ayr haza't; ualkaduha uasrapuha ba'aesh. koh

**And shall come again the Chaldeans and fight against city this and take it and burn it with fire Thus**

אמר 559 יהוה 3068 אל 408 תשאו 5377 נפשתיכם 5315 לאמר 559 הלך 1980 ילכו 1980 מעלינו 5921 הכשדים 3778 כי 3588 לא 3808

'amar Yahuah 'al tashshi'au napshoteykem lea'mor, halok yelaku me'aleynu hakasdiym; kiy la'

**saith Yahuah not Deceive yourselves saying shall depart surely from us The Chaldeans for not**

37:10

ילכו 1980: כי 3588 אם 518 הכיתם 5221 כל 3605 חיל 2428 כשדים 3778 הנלחמים 3898 אתכם 854

yeleku. kiy 'am hikiytem kal cheyl kasdiym hanilchamiym 'atakem,

**they shall depart For though you had smitten the whole army of the Chaldeans that fight against you**

ונשארו 7604 בם 871a אנשים 582 מדקרים 1856 איש 376 באהלו 168 יקומו 6965 ושרפו 8313 את 853

uanish'aru bam, 'anashiym maduqariym; 'aysh ba'ahalou yaqumu, uasarapu 'at

**and there remained among them men *but* wounded every man in his tent *yet* should they rise up and burn**

37:11

העיר 5892 הזאת 2063 באש 784: והיה 1961 בהעלות 5927 חיל 2428 הכשדים 3778 מעל 5921

ha'ayr haza't ba'aesh. uahayah, bahea'alout cheyl hakasdiym, me'al

**city this with fire And it came to pass *that* when was broken up the army of the Chaldeans from**

37:12

ירושלם 3389 מפני 6440 חיל 2428 פרעה 6547: ויצא 3318 ירמיהו 3414 מירושלם 3389 ללכת 1980 ארץ 776

yarushalaim; mipaney cheyl par'ah. uayetzea' yirmayahu miyarushalaim, laleket 'aretz

**Jerusalem for fear of army Pharaoh's Then went forth Jeremiah out of Jerusalem to go into the land of**

Jer 37:4 Now Jeremiah came in and went out among the people: for they had not put him into prison.5 Then Pharoah's army was come forth out of Egypt: and when the Chaldeans that besieged Jerusalem heard tidings of them, they departed from Jerusalem.6 Then came the word of YHUH unto the prophet Jeremiah, saying,7 Thus saith YHUH, the G-d of Israel; Thus shall you say to the king of Judah, that sent you unto me to inquire of me; Behold, Pharaoh's army, which is come forth to help you, shall return to Egypt into their own land.8 And the Chaldeans shall come again, and fight against this city, and take it, and burn it with fire.9 Thus saith YHUH; Deceive not yourselves, saying, The Chaldeans shall surely depart from us: for they shall not depart.10 For though you had smitten the whole army of the Chaldeans that fight against you, and there remained but wounded men among them, yet should they rise up every man in his tent, and burn this city with fire.11 And it came to pass, that when the army of the Chaldeans was broken up from Jerusalem for fear of Pharaoh's army,12 Then Jeremiah went forth out of Jerusalem to go into the land of Benjamin, to separate himself thence in the midst of the people.

| בנימן 1144 | לחלק 2505 | משם 8033 | בתוך 8432 | העם 5971: | 37:13 ויהי 1961 | הוא 1931 | בשער 8179 | בנימן 1144 |
|---|---|---|---|---|---|---|---|---|
| binyamin; | lachaliq | misham | batouk | ha'am. | uayahiy | hua' | basha'ar | binyamin, |
| **Benjamin** | **to separate *himself*** | **there** | **in the midst of** | **the people** | **And when was** | **he** | **in the gate of** | **Benjamin** |

| ושם 8033 | בעל 1167 | פקדת 6488 | ושמו 8034 | יראייה 3376 | בן 1121 | שלמיה 8018 | בן 1121 | חנניה 2608 | ויתפש 8610 | את 853 |
|---|---|---|---|---|---|---|---|---|---|---|
| uasham | ba'al | paqidut, | uashmou | yir'ayayh, | ben | shelemyah | ben | chananyah; | uayitpos | 'at |
| **and there** | **a captain of** | **the ward** | ***was* whose name** | ***was* Irijah** | **the son of** | **Shelemiah** | **the son of** | **Hananiah** | **and he took** | |

| ירמיהו 3414 | הנביא 5030 | לאמר 559 | אל 413 | הכשדים 3778 | אתה 859 | נפל 5307: | 37:14 ויאמר 559 | ירמיהו 3414 | שקר 8267 | אינני 369 | נפל 5307 |
|---|---|---|---|---|---|---|---|---|---|---|---|
| yirmayahu | hanabiy'a | lea'mor, | 'al | hakasdiym | 'atah | nopel. | uaya'mer | yirmayahu | sheqer, | 'aeyneniy | nopel |
| **Jeremiah** | **the prophet** | **saying** | **to** | **the Chaldeans** | **You** | **fall away** | **Then said** | **Jeremiah** | ***It is* false** | **I not** | **fall away** |

| על 5921 | הכשדים 3778 | ולא 3808 | שמע 8085 | אליו 413 | ויתפש 8610 | יראייה 3376 | בירמיהו 3414 | ויבאהו 935 | אל 413 |
|---|---|---|---|---|---|---|---|---|---|
| 'al | hakasdiym, | uala' | shama' | 'aelayu; | uayitpos | yir'ayayh | bayirmayahu, | uayabi'ahu | 'al |
| **to** | **the Chaldeans** | **But not** | **he hearkened** | **to him** | **so took** | **Irijah** | **Jeremiah** | **and brought him** | **to** |

| השרים 8269: | 37:15 ויקצפו 7107 | השרים 8269 | על 5921 | ירמיהו 3414 | והכו 5221 | אתו 853 | ונתנו 5414 | אותו 853 | בית 1004 | האסור 612 |
|---|---|---|---|---|---|---|---|---|---|---|
| hasariym. | uayiqtzapu | hasariym | 'al | yirmayahu | uahiku | 'atou; | uanatanu | 'autou | beyt | ha'aesur, |
| **the princes** | **Wherefore were wroth** | **the princes** | **with** | **Jeremiah** | **and smote** | **him** | **and put** | **him** | **in house** | **the prison** |

| בית 1004 | יהונתן 3083 | הספר 5608 | כי 3588 | אתו 853 | עשו 6213 | לבית 1004 | הכלא 3608: | 37:16 כי 3588 | בא 935 | ירמיהו 3414 |
|---|---|---|---|---|---|---|---|---|---|---|
| beyt | yahounatan | hasoper, | kiy | 'atou | 'asu | labeyt | hakela'. | kiy | ba' | yirmayahu |
| **in the house of** | **Jonathan** | **the scribe** | **for** | **that** | **they had made** | **to house** | **the prison** | **When** | **was entered** | **Jeremiah** |

| אל 413 | בית 1004 | הבור 953 | ואל 413 | החניות 2588 | וישב 3427 | שם 8033 | ירמיהו 3414 | ימים 3117 | רבים 7227: | 37:17 וישלח 7971 |
|---|---|---|---|---|---|---|---|---|---|---|
| 'al | beyt | habour | ua'al | hachanuyout; | uayesheb | sham | yirmayahu | yamiym | rabiym. | uayishlach |
| **to** | **in house** | **the dungeon** | **and into** | **the cabins** | **and had remained** | **there** | **Jeremiah** | **days** | **many** | **Then sent** |

| המלך 4428 | צדקיהו 6667 | ויקחהו 3947 | וישאלהו 7592 | המלך 4428 | בביתו 1004 | בסתר 5643 | ויאמר 559 | היש 3426 | דבר 1697 | מאת 853 |
|---|---|---|---|---|---|---|---|---|---|---|
| hamelek | tzidqiyahu | uayiqachehu, | uayish'alehu | hamelek | babeytou | baseter, | uaya'mer | hayesh | dabar | me'at |
| **the king** | **Zedekiah** | **and took him out** | **and asked him** | **the king** | **in his house** | **secretly** | **and said** | **Is there** | ***any* word** | **from** |

| יהוה 3068 | ויאמר 559 | ירמיהו 3414 | יש 3426 | ויאמר 559 | ביד 3027 | מלך 4428 | בבל 894 | תנתן 5414: | 37:18 |
|---|---|---|---|---|---|---|---|---|---|
| Yahuah; | uaya'mer | yirmayahu | yesh, | uaya'mer | bayad | melek | babel | tinaten. | |
| **Yahuah?** | **And said** | **Jeremiah** | **There is** | **for said he** | **into the hand of** | **the king of** | **Babylon** | **you shall be delivered** | |

| ויאמר 559 | ירמיהו 3414 | אל 413 | המלך 4428 | צדקיהו 6667 | מה 4100 | חטאתי 2398 | לך 3807a | ולעבדיך 5650 |
|---|---|---|---|---|---|---|---|---|
| uaya'mer | yirmayahu, | 'al | hamelek | tzidqiyahu; | meh | chata'tiy | laka | uala'abadeyka |
| **Moreover said** | **Jeremiah** | **unto** | **king** | **Zedekiah** | **What** | **have I offended** | **against you** | **or against your servants** |

| ולעם 5971 | הזה 2088 | כי 3588 | נתתם 5414 | אותי 853 | אל 413 | בית 1004 | הכלא 3608: | 37:19 ואיו 335 | נביאיכם 5030 |
|---|---|---|---|---|---|---|---|---|---|
| uala'am | hazeh, | kiy | natatem | 'autiy | 'al | beyt | hakela'. | ua'ayou | nabiy'aeykem, |
| **or against this people** | **this** | **that** | **you have put** | **me** | **in** | **house of** | **the prison** | **Where are now** | **your prophets** |

| אשר 834 | נבאו 5012 | לכם 3807a | לאמר 559 | לא 3808 | יבא 935 | מלך 4428 | בבל 894 | עליכם 5921 | ועל 5921 | הארץ 776 |
|---|---|---|---|---|---|---|---|---|---|---|
| 'asher | niba'au | lakem | lea'mor; | la' | yaba' | melek | babel | 'aleykem, | ua'al | ha'aretz |
| **which** | **prophesied** | **unto you** | **saying** | **not** | **shall come** | **The king of** | **Babylon** | **against you** | **nor against** | **the land?** |

Jer 37:13 And when he was in the gate of Benjamin, a captain of the ward was there, whose name was Irijah, the son of Shelemiah, the son of Hananiah; and he took Jeremiah the prophet, saying, Thou fallest away to the Chaldeans.14 Then said Jeremiah, It is false; I fall not away to the Chaldeans. But he hearkened not to him: so Irijah took Jeremiah, and brought him to the princes.15 Wherefore the princes were wroth with Jeremiah, and smote him, and put him in prison in the house of Jonathan the scribe: for they had made that the prison.16 When Jeremiah was entered into the dungeon, and into the cabins, and Jeremiah had remained there many days;17 Then Zedekiah the king sent, and took him out: and the king asked him secretly in his house, and said, Is there any word from YHUH? And Jeremiah said, There is: for, said he, you shall be delivered into the hand of the king of Babylon.18 Moreover Jeremiah said unto king Zedekiah, What have I offended against you, or against your servants, or against this people, that you have put me in prison?19 Where are now your prophets which prophesied unto you, saying, The king of Babylon shall not come against you, nor against this land?

| | 37:20 | | | | | | | |
|---|---|---|---|---|---|---|---|---|
| הזאת 2063: | ועתה 6258 | שמע 8085 | נא 4994 | אדני 113 | המלך 4428 | תפל 5307 | נא 4994 | תחנתי 8467 |
| haza't. | ua'atah | shama' | naa' | 'adoniy | hamelek; | tipal | naa' | tachinatiy |
| **this** | **Therefore now** | **hear** | **I pray you** | **O my adonai** | **the king** | **let be accepted** | **I pray you** | **my supplication** |

| | | | | | | | | 37:21 |
|---|---|---|---|---|---|---|---|---|
| לפניך 6440 | ואל 408 | תשבני 7725 | בית 1004 | יהונתן 3083 | הספר 5608 | ולא 3808 | אמות 4191 | שם 8033: |
| lapaneyka, | ua'al | tashibeniy, | beyt | yahounatan | hasoper, | uala' | 'amut | sham. |
| **before you** | **that not** | **you cause me to return to** | **the house of** | **Jonathan** | **the scribe** | **lest** | **I die** | **there** |

| | | | | | | | |
|---|---|---|---|---|---|---|---|
| ויצוה 6680 | המלך 4428 | צדקיהו 6667 | ויפקדו 6485 | את 853 | ירמיהו 3414 | בחצר 2691 | המטרה 4307 |
| uayatzaueh | hamelek | tzidqiyahu, | uayapqidu | 'at | yirmayahu | bachatzar | hamatarah |
| **Then commanded** | **the king** | **Zedekiah** | **that they should commit** | | **Jeremiah** | **into the court of** | **the prison** |

| | | | | | | | | | | | |
|---|---|---|---|---|---|---|---|---|---|---|---|
| ונתן 5414 | לו 3807a | ככר 3603 | לחם 3899 | ליום 3117 | מחוץ 2351 | האפים 644 | עד 5704 | תם 8552 | כל 3605 | הלחם 3899 | מן 4480 |
| uanaton | lou' | kikar | lachem | layoum | michutz | ha'apiym, | 'ad | tom | kal | halechem | min |
| **and that they should give him** | | **a piece of** | **bread** | **daily** | **out of street** | **the bakers'** | **until** | **were spent** | **all** | **the bread** | **in** |

| | | | | |
|---|---|---|---|---|
| העיר 5892 | וישב 3427 | ירמיהו 3414 | בחצר 2691 | המטרה 4307: |
| ha'ayr; | uayesheb | yirmayahu, | bachatzar | hamatarah. |
| **the city** | **Thus remained** | **Jeremiah** | **in the court of** | **the prison** |

| **Jer 38:1** | | | | | | | | | | |
|---|---|---|---|---|---|---|---|---|---|---|
| | וישמע 8085 | שפטיה 8203 | בן 1121 | מתן 4977 | וגדליהו 1436 | בן 1121 | פשחור 6583 | ויוכל 3116 | בן 1121 | שלמיהו 8018 |
| | uayishma' | shapatyah | ben | matan, | uagadalyahu | ben | pashchur, | uayukal | ben | shelemyahu, |
| | **Then heard** | **Shephatiah** | **the son of** | **Mattan** | **and Gedaliah** | **the son of** | **Pashur** | **and Jucal** | **the son of** | **Shelemiah** |

| | | | | | | | | | | | | 38:2 | |
|---|---|---|---|---|---|---|---|---|---|---|---|---|---|
| ופשחור 6583 | בן 1121 | מלכיה 4441 | את 853 | הדברים 1697 | אשר 834 | ירמיהו 3414 | מדבר 1696 | אל 413 | כל 3605 | העם 5971 | לאמר 559: | | כה 3541 |
| uapashchur | ben | malkiyah; | 'aet | hadabariym, | 'asher | yirmayahu | madaber | 'al | kal | ha'am | lea'mor. | | koh |
| **and Pashur** | **the son of** | **Malchiah** | | **the words** | **that** | **Jeremiah** | **had spoken** | **unto** | **all** | **the people** | **saying** | | **Thus** |

| | | | | | | | | |
|---|---|---|---|---|---|---|---|---|
| אמר 559 | יהוה 3068 | הישב 3427 | בעיר 5892 | הזאת 2063 | ימות 4191 | בחרב 2719 | ברעב 7458 | ובדבר 1698 |
| 'amar | Yahuah | hayosheb | ba'ayr | haza't, | yamut | bachereb | bara'ab | uabadaber; |
| **saith** | **Yahuah** | **He that remains** | **in city** | **this** | **shall die** | **by the sword** | **by the famine** | **and by the pestilence** |

| | | | | | | | | | 38:3 | |
|---|---|---|---|---|---|---|---|---|---|---|
| והיצא 3318 | אל 413 | הכשדים 3778 | יחיה 2421 | והיתה 1961 | לו 3807a | נפשו 5315 | לשלל 7998 | וחי 2421: | | כה 3541 |
| uahayotzea' | 'al | hakasdiym | yichayeh | uahayatah | lou' | napshou | lashalal | uachay. | | koh |
| **but he that goes forth** | **to** | **the Chaldeans** | **shall live** | **for he shall have** | **his** | **life** | **for a prey** | **and shall live** | | **Thus** |

| | | | | | | | | | | | 38:4 |
|---|---|---|---|---|---|---|---|---|---|---|---|
| אמר 559 | יהוה 3068 | הנתן 5414 | תנתן 5414 | העיר 5892 | הזאת 2063 | ביד 3027 | חיל 2428 | מלך 4428 | בבל 894 | ולכדה 3920: | |
| 'amar | Yahuah; | hinaton | tinaten | ha'ayr | haza't, | bayad | cheyl | melek | babel | ualkadah. | |
| **saith** | **Yahuah** | **shall surely** | **be given** | **city** | **This** | **into the hand of** | **army** | **the king of** | **Babylon's** | **which shall take it** | |

| | | | | | | | | | | | | |
|---|---|---|---|---|---|---|---|---|---|---|---|---|
| ויאמרו 559 | השרים 8269 | אל 413 | המלך 4428 | יומת 4191 | נא 4994 | את 853 | האיש 376 | הזה 2088 | כי 3588 | על 5921 | כן 3651 | הוא 1931 |
| uaya'maru | hasariym | 'al | hamelek, | yumat | naa' | 'at | ha'aysh | hazeh | kiy | 'al | ken | hua' |
| **Therefore said** | **the princes** | **unto** | **the king** | **let be put to death** | **We beseech you** | | **man** | **this** | **for** | **on** | **thus** | **he** |

| | | | | | | | | | | | |
|---|---|---|---|---|---|---|---|---|---|---|---|
| מרפא 7503 | את 853 | ידי 3027 | אנשי 582 | המלחמה 4421 | הנשארים 7604 | בעיר 5892 | הזאת 2063 | ואת 853 | ידי 3027 | כל 3605 | העם 5971 |
| marapea' | 'at | yadey | 'anshey | hamilchamah | hanisha'ariym | ba'ayr | haza't, | ua'at | yadey | kal | ha'am, |
| **weaken** | | **the hands of** | **the man of** | **war** | **that remain** | **in city** | **this** | ***and*** | **the hands of** | **all** | **the people** |

Jer 37:20 Therefore hear now, I pray you, O my lord the king: let my supplication, I pray you, be accepted before you; that you cause me not to return to the house of Jonathan the scribe, lest I die there.21 Then Zedekiah the king commanded that they should commit Jeremiah into the court of the prison, and that they should give him daily a piece of bread out of the bakers' street, until all the bread in the city were spent. Thus Jeremiah remained in the court of the prison. **Jer** 38:1 Then Shephatiah the son of Mattan, and Gedaliah the son of Pashur, and Jucal the son of Shelemiah, and Pashur the son of Malchiah, heard the words that Jeremiah had spoken unto all the people, saying,2 Thus saith YHUH, He that remain in this city shall die by the sword, by the famine, and by the pestilence: but he that go forth to the Chaldeans shall live; for he shall have his life for a prey, and shall live.3 Thus saith YHUH, This city shall surely be given into the hand of the king of Babylon's army, which shall take it.4 Therefore the princes said unto the king, We beseech you, let this man be put to death: for thus he weakeneth the hands of the men of war that remain in this city, and the hands of all the people, in speaking such words unto them: for this man seek not the welfare of this people, but the hurt.

לדבר 1696 אליהם 413 כדברים 1697 האלה 428 כי 3588 האיש 376 הזה 2088 איננו 369 דרש 1875 לשלום 7965 לעם 5971 הזה 2088 כי 3588 אם 518
ladaber 'aleyhem, kadbariym ha'aeleh; kiy ha'aysh hazeh, 'aeynenu doresh lashaloum la'am hazeh kiy 'am
**in speaking unto them words such for man this not seek the welfare of people this for but**

38:5
לרעה 7451: ויאמר 559 המלך 4428 צדקיהו 6667 הנה 2009 הוא 1931 בידכם 3027 כי 3588 אין 369 המלך 4428 יוכל 3201
lara'ah. uaya'mer hamelek tzidqiyahu, hineh hua' bayedkem; kiy 'aeyn hamelek, yukal
**the hurt Then said the king Zedekiah Behold he *is* in your hand for *is* not the king *he that* can do**

38:6
אתכם 853 דבר 1697: ויקחו 3947 את 853 ירמיהו 3414 וישלכו 7993 אתו 853 אל 413 הבור 953 מלכיהו 4441 בן 1121
'atkem dabar. uayiqchu 'at yirmayahu, uayashliku 'atou 'al habour malkiyahu ben
**against you *any* thing Then took they Jeremiah and cast him into the dungeon of Malchiah the son of**

המלך 4428 אשר 834 בחצר 2691 המטרה 4307 וישלחו 7971 את 853 ירמיהו 3414 בחבלים 2256
hamelek, 'asher bachatzar hamatarah, uayshalachu 'at yirmayahu bachabaliym;
**Hammelech that *was* in the court of the prison and they let down Jeremiah with cords**

38:7
ובבור 953 אין 369 מים 4325 כי 3588 אם 518 טיט 2916 ויטבע 2883 ירמיהו 3414 בטיט 2916: וישמע 8085 עבד 5663
uababour 'aeyn mayim kiy 'am tiyt, uayitba' yirmayahu batiyt. uayishma' 'abed
**And in the dungeon *there was* no water but only mire so sunk Jeremiah in the mire Now when heard Ebed**

מלך 4428 הכושי 3569 איש 376 סריס 5631 והוא 1931 בבית 1004 המלך 4428 כי 3588 נתנו 5414 את 853 ירמיהו 3414 אל 413
melek hakushiy 'aysh sariys, uahu'a babeyt hamelek, kiy natanu 'at yirmayahu 'al
**melek the Ethiopian one of the eunuchs which *was* in house the king's that they had put Jeremiah into**

38:8
הבור 953 והמלך 4428 יושב 3427 בשער 8179 בנימן 1144: ויצא 3318 עבד 5663 מלך 4428 מבית 1004 המלך 4428 וידבר 1696
habour; uahamelek yousheb basha'ar binyamin. uayetzea' 'abed melek mibeyt hamelek; uaydaber
**the dungeon the king then sitting in the gate of Benjamin went forth Ebed melek out of house the king's and spoke**

38:9
אל 413 המלך 4428 לאמר 559: אדני 113 המלך 4428 הרעו 7489 האנשים 582 האלה 428 את 853 כל 3605 אשר 834 עשו 6213
'al hamelek lea'mor. 'adoniy hamelek, here'au ha'anashiym ha'aeleh 'at kal 'asher 'asu
**to the king saying My adonai the king have done evil men these *in* all that they have done**

לירמיהו 3414 הנביא 5030 את 853 אשר 834 השליכו 7993 אל 413 הבור 953 וימת 4191 תחתיו 8478 מפני 6440
layirmayahu hanabiy'a, 'at 'asher hishliyku 'al habour; uayamat tachtayu mipaney
**to Jeremiah the prophet whom they have cast into the dungeon and he is like to die in the place where he is for**

38:10
הרעב 7458 כי 3588 אין 369 הלחם 3899 עוד 5750 בעיר 5892: ויצוה 6680 המלך 4428 את 853 עבד 5663 מלך 4428 הכושי 3569
hara'ab, kiy 'aeyn halechem 'aud ba'ayr. uayatzaueh hamelek, 'at 'abed melek hakushiy
**hunger for *there is* no bread more in the city Then commanded the king Ebed melek the Ethiopian**

לאמר 559 קח 3947 בידך 3027 מזה 2088 שלשים 7970 אנשים 582 והעלית 5927 את 853 ירמיהו 3414 הנביא 5030 מן 4480 הבור 953
lea'mor; qach bayadaka mizeh shaloshiym 'anashiym, uaha'aliyta 'at yirmayahu hanabiy'a min habour
**saying Take with you from here thirty men and take up Jeremiah the prophet out of the dungeon**

38:11
בטרם 2962 ימות 4191: ויקח 3947 עבד 5663 מלך 4428 את 853 האנשים 582 בידו 3027 ויבא 935 בית 1004 המלך 4428 אל 413
baterem yamut. uayiqach 'abed melek 'at ha'anashiym bayadou, uayaba' beyt hamelek 'al
**before he die So took Ebed melek the men with him and went into the house of the king to**

Jer 38:5 Then Zedekiah the king said, Behold, he is in your hand: for the king is not he that can do anything against you.6 Then took they Jeremiah, and cast him into the dungeon of Malchiah the son of Hammelech, that was in the court of the prison: and they let down Jeremiah with cords. And in the dungeon there was no water, but mire: so Jeremiah sunk in the mire.7 Now when Ebed-melech the Ethiopian, one of the eunuchs which was in the king's house, heard that they had put Jeremiah in the dungeon; the king then sitting in the gate of Benjamin;8 Ebed-melech went forth out of the king's house, and spoke to the king, saying,9 My lord the king, these men have done evil in all that they have done to Jeremiah the prophet, whom they have cast into the dungeon; and he is like to die for hunger in the place where he is: for there is no more bread in the city.10 Then the king commanded Ebed-melech the Ethiopian, saying, Take from hence thirty men with you, and take up Jeremiah the prophet out of the dungeon, before he die.11 So Ebed-melech took the men with him, and went into the house of the king under the treasury, and took thence old cast clouts and old rotten rags, and let them down by cords into the dungeon to Jeremiah.

8478 תחת 214 האוצר 3947 ויקח 8033 משם 1094 בלוי 5499 הסחבות 1094 ובלוי 4418 מלחים 7971 וישלחם 413 אל 3414 ירמיהו 413 אל
tachat ha'autzar, uayiqach misham balouye hasechabout uablouye malachiym; uayashalchem 'al yirmayahu 'al
**under the treasury and took there old cast clouts and old rotten rags and let them down to Jeremiah into**

38:12
953 הבור 2256 בחבלים: 559 ויאמר 5663 עבד 4428 מלך 3569 הכושי 413 אל 3414 ירמיהו 7760 שים 4994 נא 1094 בלואי 5499 הסחבות
habour bachabaliym. uaya'mer 'abed melek hakushiy 'al yirmayahu, siym naa' balou'aey hasechabout
**the dungeon by cords And said Ebed melek the Ethiopian unto Jeremiah Put now *these* old cast clouts**

38:13
4418 והמלחים 8478 תחת 679 אצלות 3027 ידיך 8478 מתחת 2256 לחבלים 6213 ויעש 3414 ירמיהו 3651 כן: 4900 וימשכו
uahamalachiym tachat atzilout yadeyka, mitachat lachabaliym; uaya'as yirmayahu ken. uayimshaku
**and rotten rags under your armholds his sides from under the cords And did Jeremiah so So they drew up**

853 את 3414 ירמיהו 2256 בחבלים 5927 ויעלו 853 אתו 4480 מן 953 הבור 3427 וישב 3414 ירמיהו 2691 בחצר
'at yirmayahu bachabaliym, uaya'alu 'atou min habour; uayesheb yirmayahu, bachatzar
**Jeremiah with cords and took up him out of the dungeon and remained Jeremiah in the court of**

38:14
4307 המטרה: 7971 וישלח 4428 המלך 6667 צדקיהו 3947 ויקח 853 את 3414 ירמיהו 5030 הנביא 413 אליו 413 אל 3996 מבוא 7992 השלישי
hamatarah. uayishlach hamelek tzidqiyahu, uayiqach 'at yirmayahu hanabiy'a 'aelayu, 'al mabou'a hashaliyshiy,
**the prison Then sent the king Zedekiah and took Jeremiah the prophet unto him into entry the third**

834 אשר 1004 בבית 3068 יהוה 559 ויאמר 4428 המלך 413 אל 3414 ירמיהו 7592 שאל 589 אני 853 אתך 1697 דבר 408 אל 3582 תכחד 4480 ממני
'asher babeyt Yahuah; uaya'mer hamelek 'al yirmayahu, sho'ael 'aniy 'atka dabar, 'al takached mimeniy
**that *is* in the house of Yahuah and said the king unto Jeremiah will ask I you a thing not hide from me**

38:15
1697 דבר: 559 ויאמר 3414 ירמיהו 413 אל 6667 צדקיהו 3588 כי 5046 אגיד 3807a לך 3808 הלוא 4191 המת 4191 תמיתני
dabar. uaya'mer yirmayahu 'al tzidqiyahu, kiy 'agiyd laka, halou'a hamet tamiyteniy;
**anything Then said Jeremiah unto Zedekiah If I declare *it* unto you will not you surely put me to death?**

38:16
3588 וכי 3289 איעצך 3808 לא 8085 תשמע 413 אלי: 7650 וישבע 4428 המלך 6667 צדקיהו 413 אל 3414 ירמיהו 5643 בסתר
uakiy 'ay'atzaka, la' tishma' 'aelay. uayishaba' hamelek tzidqiyahu 'al yirmayahu baseter
**and if I give you counsel not will you listen unto me? So sware the king Zedekiah unto Jeremiah secretly**

559 לאמר 2416 חי 3068 יהוה 853 את 834 אשר 6213 עשה 3807a לנו 853 את 5315 הנפש 2063 הזאת 518 אם 4191 אמיתך 518 ואם
lea'mor; chay Yahuah 'at 'asher 'asah lanu 'at hanepesh haza't 'am 'amiyteka, ua'am
**saying live *As* Yahuah that made us soul this surely not I will put you to death neither**

38:17
5414 אתנך 3027 ביד 582 האנשים 428 האלה 834 אשר 1245 מבקשים 853 את 5315 נפשך: 559 ויאמר 3414 ירמיהו 413 אל
'atenaka, bayad ha'anashiym ha'aeleh, 'asher mabaqshiym 'at napsheka. uaya'mer yirmayahu 'al
**will I give you into the hand of men these that seek your life Then said Jeremiah unto**

6667 צדקיהו 3541 כה 559 אמר 3068 יהוה 430 אלהי 6635 צבאות 430 אלהי 3478 ישראל 518 אם 3318 יצא 3318 תצא 413 אל 8269 שרי
tzidqiyahu koh 'amar Yahuah 'alohey tzaba'aut 'alohey yisra'ael, 'am yatza' tetzea' 'al sarey
**Zedekiah Thus saith Yahuah the Elohim of hosts the Elohim of Israel If you will assuredly go forth unto princes**

4428 מלך 894 בבל 2421 וחיתה 5315 נפשך 5892 והעיר 2063 הזאת 3808 לא 8313 תשרף 784 באש 2421 וחיתה 859 אתה
melek babel uachayatah napsheka, uaha'ayr haza't, la' tisarep ba'aesh; uachayitah 'atah
**the king of Babylon's then shall live your soul and city this not shall be burned with fire and shall live you**

Jer 38:12 And Ebed-melech the Ethiopian said unto Jeremiah, Put now these old cast clouts and rotten rags under your armholes under the cords. And Jeremiah did so.13 So they drew up Jeremiah with cords, and took him up out of the dungeon: and Jeremiah remained in the court of the prison.14 Then Zedekiah the king sent, and took Jeremiah the prophet unto him into the third entry that is in the house of YHUH: and the king said unto Jeremiah, I will ask you a thing; hide nothing from me.15 Then Jeremiah said unto Zedekiah, If I declare it unto you, will you not surely put me to death? and if I give you counsel, will you not hear unto me?16 So Zedekiah the king sware secretly unto Jeremiah, saying, As YHUH live, that made us this soul, I will not put you to death, neither will I give you into the hand of these men that seek your life.17 Then said Jeremiah unto Zedekiah, Thus saith YHUH, the G-d of hosts, the G-d of Israel; If you will assuredly go forth unto the king of Babylon's princes, then your soul shall live, and this city shall not be burned with fire; and you shall live, and your house:

וביתך 1004: 38:18 ואם 518 לא 3808 תצא 3318 אל 413 שרי 8269 מלך 4428 בבל 894 ונתנה 5414 העיר 5892 הזאת 2063
uabeyteka. ua'am la' tetzea', 'al sarey melek babel, uanitanah ha'ayr haza't
**and your house But if not you will go forth to princes the king of Babylon's then shall be given city this**

ביד 3027 הכשדים 3778 ושרפוה 8313 באש 784 ואתה 859 לא 3808 תמלט 4422 מידם 3027: 38:19
bayad hakasdiym, uasrapuha ba'aesh; ua'atah la' timalet miyadam.
**into the hand of the Chaldeans and they shall burn it with fire and you not shall escape out of their hand**

ויאמר 559 המלך 4428 צדקיהו 6667 אל 413 ירמיהו 3414 אני 589 דאג 1672 את 853 היהודים 3064 אשר 834 נפלו 5307 אל 413 הכשדים 3778
uaya'mer hamelek tzidqiyahu 'al yirmayahu; 'aniy do'aeg 'at hayahudiym, 'asher naplu 'al hakasdiym,
**And said the king Zedekiah unto Jeremiah I *am* afraid of the Jews that are fallen to the Chaldeans**

פן 6435 יתנו 5414 אתי 853 בידם 3027 והתעללו 5953 בי 871a: 38:20 ויאמר 559 ירמיהו 3414 לא 3808 יתנו 5414
pen yitanu 'atiy bayadam uahit'alalu biy. uaya'mer yirmayahu la' yitenu;
**lest they deliver me into their hand and they mock me But said Jeremiah not They shall deliver *you.***

שמע 8085 נא 4994 בקול 6963 יהוה 3068 לאשר 834 אני 589 דבר 1696 אליך 413 וייטב 3190 לך 3807a ותחי 2421
shama' naa' baqoul Yahuah la'asher 'aniy dober 'aeleyka, uayiytab laka uatchiy
**Obey I beseech you the voice of Yahuah which I speak unto you so it shall be well unto you and shall live**

נפשך 5315: 38:21 ואם 518 מאן 3986 אתה 859 לצאת 3318 זה 2088 הדבר 1697 אשר 834 הראני 7200 יהוה 3068: 38:22 והנה 2009 כל 3605
napsheka. ua'am ma'aen 'atah latzea't; zeh hadabar, 'asher hir'aniy Yahuah. uahineh kal
**your soul But if refuse you to go forth this *is* the word that has showed me Yahuah And behold all**

הנשים 802 אשר 834 נשארו 7604 בבית 1004 מלך 4428 יהודה 3063 מוצאות 3318 אל 413 שרי 8269 מלך 4428 בבל 894
hanashiym, 'asher nish'aru babeyt melek yahudah, mutza'aut 'al sarey melek babel;
**the women that are left in house the king of Judah's *shall be* brought forth to princes the king of Babylon's**

והנה 2007 אמרות 559 הסיתוך 5496 ויכלו 3201 לך 3807a אנשי 582 שלמך 7965 הטבעו 2883 בבץ 1206
uahenah 'amarout, hisiytuka uayakalu laka 'anshey shalomeka, hatab'au babotz
**and those *women* shall say have set you on and have prevailed against you your close friends are sunk in the mire**

רגלך 7272 נסגו 5472 אחור 268: 38:23 ואת 853 כל 3605 נשיך 802 ואת 853 בניך 1121 מוצאים 3318 אל 413
ragleka nasougu 'achour. ua'at kal nasheyka ua'at baneyka, moutzi'aym 'al
**your feet *and* they are turned away back *So* all your wives *and* your children they shall bring out to**

הכשדים 3778 ואתה 859 לא 3808 תמלט 4422 מידם 3027 כי 3588 ביד 3027 מלך 4428 בבל 894 תתפש 8610 ואת 853
hakasdiym, ua'atah la' timalet miyadam; kiy bayad melek babel titapes, ua'at
**the Chaldeans and you not shall escape outof their hand but by the hand of the king of Babylon shall be taken *and***

העיר 5892 הזאת 2063 תשרף 8313 באש 784: 38:24 ויאמר 559 צדקיהו 6667 אל 413 ירמיהו 3414 איש 376 אל 408 ידע 3045
ha'ayr haza't tisrop ba'aesh. uaya'mer tzidqiyahu 'al yirmayahu, 'aysh 'al yeda'
**city this you shall cause to be burned with fire Then said Zedekiah unto Jeremiah man no Let know**

בדברים 1697 האלה 428 ולא 3808 תמות 4191: 38:25 וכי 3588 ישמעו 8085 השרים 8269 כי 3588 דברתי 1696 אתך 854 ובאו 935
badbariym ha'aeleh uala' tamut. uakiy yishma'au hasariym kiy dibartiy 'atak uaba'au
**of words these and not you shall die But if hear the princes that I have talked with you and they come**

Jer 38:18 But if you will not go forth to the king of Babylon's princes, then shall this city be given into the hand of the Chaldeans, and they shall burn it with fire, and you shall not escape out of their hand.19 And Zedekiah the king said unto Jeremiah, I am afraid of the Jews that are fallen to the Chaldeans, lest they deliver me into their hand, and they mock me.20 But Jeremiah said, They shall not deliver you. Obey, I beseech you, the voice of YHUH, which I speak unto you: so it shall be well unto you, and your soul shall live.21 But if you refuse to go forth, this is the word that YHUH has showed me:22 And, behold, all the women that are left in the king of Judah's house shall be brought forth to the king of Babylon's princes, and those women shall say, Thy friends have set you on, and have prevailed against you: your feet are sunk in the mire, and they are turned away back.23 So they shall bring out all your wives and your children to the Chaldeans: and you shall not escape out of their hand, but shall be taken by the hand of the king of Babylon: and you shall cause this city to be burned with fire.24 Then said Zedekiah unto Jeremiah, Let no man know of these words, and you shall not die.25 But if the princes hear that I have talked with you, and they come unto you, and say unto you, Declare unto us now what you have said unto the king, hide it not from us,

אליך 413 ואמרו 559 אליך 413 הגידה 5046 נא 4994 לנו 3807a מה 4100 דברת 1696 אל 413 המלך 4428 אל 408 תכחד 3582 ממנו 4480 ולא 3808
'aeleyka ua'amaru 'aeleyka hagiydah naa' lanu mah dibarta 'al hamelek 'al takached mimenu uala'
**unto you and say unto you Declare now unto us what you have said unto the king not hide it from us and not**

38:26
נמיתך 4191 ומה 4100 דבר 1696 אליך 413 המלך 4428: ואמרת 559 אליהם 413 מפיל 5307 אני 589
namiyteka; uamah diber 'aeleyka hamelek. ua'amarta 'aleyhem, mapiyl 'aniy
**we will put you to death and what said unto you the king Then you shall say unto them I presented I**

38:27
תחנתי 8467 לפני 6440 המלך 4428 לבלתי 1115 השיבני 7725 בית 1004 יהונתן 3083 למות 4191 שם 8033:
tachinatiy lipney hamelek; labiltiy hashiybeniy beyt yahounatan lamut sham.
**my supplication before the king that not he would cause me to return to house Jonathan's to die there**

ויבאו 935 כל 3605 השרים 8269 אל 413 ירמיהו 3414 וישאלו 7592 אתו 853 ויגד 5046 להם 1992 ככל 3605 הדברים 1697 האלה 428
uayabo'au kal hasariym 'al yirmayahu uayish'alu 'atou, uayaged lahem kakal hadabariym ha'aeleh,
**Then came all the princes unto Jeremiah and asked him and he told them according to all words these**

38:28
אשר 834 צוה 6680 המלך 4428 ויחרשו 2790 ממנו 4480 כי 3588 לא 3808 נשמע 8085 הדבר 1697: וישב 3427
'asher tziuah hamelek; uayacharishu mimenu, kiy la' nishma' hadabar. uayesheb
**that had commanded the king So they left off speaking with him for not was perceived the matter So abode**

ירמיהו 3414 בחצר 2691 המטרה 4307 עד 5704 יום 3117 אשר 834 נלכדה 3920 ירושלם 3389 והיה 1961 כאשר 834 נלכדה 3920
yirmayahu bachatzar hamatarah, 'ad youm 'asher nilkadah yarushalaim; uahayah ka'asher nilkadah
**Jeremiah in the court of the prison until the day that was taken Jerusalem and he was *there* when was taken**

ירושלם 3389:
yarushalaim.
**Jerusalem**

**Jer 39:1**
בשנה 8141 התשעית 8671 לצדקיהו 6667 מלך 4428 יהודה 3063 בחדש 2320 העשרי 6224 בא 935 נבוכדראצר 5019 מלך 4428 בבל 894
bashanah hatashi'ayt latzidqiyahu melek yahudah bachodesh ha'asiyriy, ba' nabukadra'tzar melek babel
**In year the ninth of Zedekiah king of Judah in month the tenth came Nebuchadrezzar king of Babylon**

39:2
וכל 3605 חילו 2428 אל 413 ירושלם 3389 ויצרו 6696 עליה 5921: בעשתי 6249 עשרה 6240 שנה 8141 לצדקיהו 6667
uakal cheylou 'al yarushalaim, uayatzuru 'aleyha. ba'ashtey 'asreh shanah latzidqiyahu,
**and all his army against Jerusalem and they besieged it And in the one of ten year of Zedekiah**

39:3
בחדש 2320 הרביעי 7243 בתשעה 8672 לחדש 2320 הבקעה 1234 העיר 5892: ויבאו 935 כל 3605 שרי 8269 מלך 4428
bachodesh harbiy'ay batish'ah lachodesh; habqa'ah ha'ayr. uayabo'au, kal sarey melek
**in month the fourth the ninth *day* of the month was broken up the city And came in all the princes of the king of**

בבל 894 וישבו 3427 בשער 8179 התוך 8432 נרגל 5371 שר 8269 אצר 687 סמגר 8310 נבו 5015 שר 8269 סכים 8269 רב 7249 סריס 7949 נרגל 5371
babel, uayeshabu basha'ar hatauek; nergal sar 'atzer samgar nabu sar sakiym rab sariys, nergal
**Babylon and sat in gate the middle *even* Nergal -shar- ezer Samgar nebo Sar sechim Rab saris Nergal**

39:4
שר 8269 אצר 687 רב 7248 מג 7248 וכל 3605 שארית 7611 שרי 8269 מלך 4428 בבל 894: ויהי 1961
sar 'atzer rab mag, uakal sha'aeriyt, sarey melek babel. uayahiy
**-shar- ezer Rab mag and all with the residue of the princes of the king of Babylon And it came to pass *that***

Jer 38:25 and we will not put you to death; also what the king said unto you:26 Then you shall say unto them, I presented my supplication before the king, that he would not cause me to return to Jonathan's house, to die there.27 Then came all the princes unto Jeremiah, and asked him: and he told them according to all these words that the king had commanded. So they left off speaking with him; for the matter was not perceived.28 So Jeremiah abode in the court of the prison until the day that Jerusalem was taken: and he was there when Jerusalem was taken. **Jer** 39:1 In the ninth year of Zedekiah king of Judah, in the tenth month, came Nebuchadrezzar king of Babylon and all his army against Jerusalem, and they besieged it.2 And in the eleventh year of Zedekiah, in the fourth month, the ninth day of the month, the city was broken up.3 And all the princes of the king of Babylon came in, and sat in the middle gate, even Nergal-sharezer, Samgar-nebo, Sarsechim, Rab-saris, Nergal-sharezer, Rabmag, with all the residue of the princes of the king of Babylon. 4 And it came to pass, that when Zedekiah the king of Judah saw them, and all the men of war, then they fled, and went forth out of the city by night, by the way of the king's garden, by the gate betwixt the two walls: and he went out the way of the plain.

| כאשר 834 | ראם 7200 | צדקיהו 6667 | מלך 4428 | יהודה 3063 | וכל 3605 | אנשי 582 | המלחמה 4421 | ויברחו 1272 | ויצאו 3318 | לילה 3915 |
|---|---|---|---|---|---|---|---|---|---|---|
| ka'asher | ra'am | tzidqiyahu | melek | yahudah | uakol | 'anshey | hamilchamah, | uayibrachu | uayetza'au | layalah |
| **when** | **saw them** | **Zedekiah** | **the king of** | **Judah** | **and all** | **the men of** | **war** | **then they fled** | **and went forth** | ***by* night** |

| מן 4480 | העיר 5892 | דרך 1870 | גן 1588 | המלך 4428 | בשער 8179 | בין 996 | החמתים 2346 | ויצא 3318 | דרך 1870 |
|---|---|---|---|---|---|---|---|---|---|
| min | ha'ayr | derek | gan | hamelek, | basha'ar | beyn | hachomotayim; | uayetzea' | derek |
| **out of** | **the city** | ***by* the way of** | **garden** | **the king's** | **by the gate** | **between** | **the two walls** | **and he went out** | **the way of** |

| הערבה 6160: | 39:5 וירדפו 7291 | חיל 2428 | כשדים 3778 | אחריהם 310 | וישגו 5381 | את 853 | צדקיהו 6667 | בערבות 6160 | ירחו 3405 |
|---|---|---|---|---|---|---|---|---|---|
| ha'arabah. | uayirdapu | cheyl | kasdiym | 'achareyhem, | uayasiygu | 'at | tzidqiyahu | ba'arbout | yarechou |
| **the plain** | **But pursued** | **army** | ***the* Chaldeans'** | **after them** | **and overtook** | | **Zedekiah** | **in the plains of** | **Jericho** |

| ויקחו 3947 | אתו 853 | ויעלהו 5927 | אל 413 | נבוכדראצר 5019 | מלך 4428 | בבל 894 | רבלתה 7247 | בארץ 776 |
|---|---|---|---|---|---|---|---|---|
| uayiqchu | 'atou, | uaya'aluhu | 'al | nabukadra'tzar | melek | babel | riblatah | ba'aretz |
| **and when they had taken** | **him** | **they brought him up** | **to** | **Nebuchadnezzar** | **king of** | **Babylon** | ***to* Riblah** | **in the land of** |

| חמת 2574 | וידבר 1696 | אתו 853 | משפטים 4941: | 39:6 וישחט 7819 | מלך 4428 | בבל 894 | את 853 | בני 1121 | צדקיהו 6667 | ברבלה 7247 |
|---|---|---|---|---|---|---|---|---|---|---|
| chamat; | uaydaber | 'atou | mishpatiym. | uayishchat | melek | babel | 'at | baney | tzidqiyahu | bariblah |
| **Hamath** | **where he gave** | **upon him** | **judgment** | **Then slew** | **the king of** | **Babylon** | | **the sons of** | **Zedekiah** | **in Riblah** |

| לעיניו 5869 | ואת 853 | כל 3605 | חרי 2715 | יהודה 3063 | שחט 7819 | מלך 4428 | בבל 894: | 39:7 ואת 853 | עיני 5869 | צדקיהו 6667 |
|---|---|---|---|---|---|---|---|---|---|---|
| la'aeynayu; | ua'at | kal | chorey | yahudah, | shachat | melek | babel. | ua'at | 'aeyney | tzidqiyahu |
| **before his eyes** | ***also*** | **all** | **the nobles of** | **Judah** | **slew** | **the king of** | **Babylon** | ***Moreover*** | **eyes** | **Zedekiah's** |

| עור 5786 | ויאסרהו 631 | בנחשתים 5178 | לביא 935 | אתו 853 | בבלה 894: | 39:8 ואת 853 | בית 1004 | המלך 4428 | ואת 853 | בית 1004 |
|---|---|---|---|---|---|---|---|---|---|---|
| 'aur; | uaya'asrehu | banachushatayim, | labiy'a | 'atou | babelah. | ua'at | beyt | hamelek | ua'at | beyt |
| **he put out** | **and bound him** | **with chains** | **to carry** | **him** | **to Babylon** | ***And*** | **house** | **the king's** | ***and*** | **the houses of** |

| העם 5971 | שרפו 8313 | הכשדים 3778 | באש 784 | ואת 853 | חמות 2346 | ירושלם 3389 | נתצו 5422: | 39:9 ואת 853 | יתר 3499 |
|---|---|---|---|---|---|---|---|---|---|
| ha'am, | sarapu | hakasdiym | ba'aesh; | ua'at | choumot | yarushalaim | natatzu. | ua'at | yeter |
| **the people** | **burned** | **the Chaldeans** | **with fire** | ***and*** | **the walls of** | **Jerusalem** | **brake down** | ***Then*** | **the remnant of** |

| העם 5971 | הנשארים 7604 | בעיר 5892 | ואת 853 | הנפלים 5307 | אשר 834 | נפלו 5307 | עליו 5921 | ואת 853 | יתר 3499 | העם 5971 |
|---|---|---|---|---|---|---|---|---|---|---|
| ha'am | hanisha'ariym | ba'ayr, | ua'at | hanopliym | 'asher | naplu | 'aelayu, | ua'at | yeter | ha'am |
| **the people** | **that remained** | **in the city** | ***and*** | **those that fell away** | **that** | **fell** | **to him** | ***with*** | **the rest of** | **the people** |

| הנשארים 7604 | הגלה 1540 | נבוזר 5018 | אדן 135 | רב 7227 | טבחים 2876 | בבל 894: | 39:10 ומן 4480 | העם 5971 |
|---|---|---|---|---|---|---|---|---|
| hanisha'ariym; | hegalah | nabuzar | 'adan | rab | tabachiym | babel. | uamin | ha'am |
| **that remained** | **carried away captive into** | **Nebuzar** | **adan** | **the captain of** | **the guard** | **Babylon** | **But of** | **the people** |

| הדלים 1800 | אשר 834 | אין 369 | להם 3807a | מאומה 3972 | השאיר 7604 | נבוזראדן 5018 | רב 7227 | טבחים 2876 | בארץ 776 | יהודה 3063 |
|---|---|---|---|---|---|---|---|---|---|---|
| hadaliym, | 'asher | 'aeyn | lahem | ma'aumah, | hish'ayr | nabuzar'adan | rab | tabachiym | ba'aretz | yahudah; |
| **the poor of** | **which** | **had no** | **to them** | **thing** | **left** | **Nebuzaradan** | **the captain of** | **the guard** | **in the land of** | **Judah** |

| ויתן 5414 | להם 3807a | כרמים 3754 | ויגבים 3010 | ביום 3117 | ההוא 1931: | 39:11 ויצו 6680 | נבוכדראצר 5019 | מלך 4428 | בבל 894 |
|---|---|---|---|---|---|---|---|---|---|
| uayiten | lahem | karamiym | uiygebiym | bayoum | hahua'. | uayatzau | nabukadra'tzar | melek | babel |
| **and gave them** | | **vineyards** | **and fields** | **at time** | **the same** | **Now gave charge** | **Nebuchadrezzar** | **king of** | **Babylon** |

Jer 39:5 But the Chaldeans' army pursued after them, and overtook Zedekiah in the plains of Jericho: and when they had taken him, they brought him up to Nebuchadnezzar king of Babylon to Riblah in the land of Hamath, where he gave judgment upon him.6 Then the king of Babylon slew the sons of Zedekiah in Riblah before his eyes: also the king of Babylon slew all the nobles of Judah.7 Moreover he put out Zedekiah's eyes, and bound him with chains, to carry him to Babylon.8 And the Chaldeans burned the king's house, and the houses of the people, with fire, and break down the walls of Jerusalem.9 Then Nebuzar-adan the captain of the guard carried away captive into Babylon the remnant of the people that remained in the city, and those that fell away, that fell to him, with the rest of the people that remained.10 But Nebuzar-adan the captain of the guard left of the poor of the people, which had nothing, in the land of Judah, and gave them vineyards and fields at the same time.11 Now Nebuchadrezzar king of Babylon gave charge concerning Jeremiah to Nebuzar-adan the captain of the guard, saying,

| על 5921 | ירמיהו 3414 | ביד 3027 | נבוזראדן 5018 | רב 7227 | טבחים 2876 | לאמר 559: | 39:12 קחנו 3947 | ועיניך 5869 | שים 7760 | עליו 5921 |
|---|---|---|---|---|---|---|---|---|---|---|
| 'al | yirmayahu; | bayad | nabuzar'adan | rab | tabachiym | lea'mor. | qachenu, | ua'aeyneyka | siym | 'alayu, |
| **concerning** | **Jeremiah** | **to** | **Nebuzaradan** | **the captain of** | **the guard** | **saying** | **Take him** | **and well** | **look** | **to him** |

| ואל 408 | תעש 6213 | לו 3807a | מאומה 3972 | רע 7451 | כי 3588 | אם 518 | כאשר 834 | ידבר 1696 | אליך 413 | כן 3651 | עשה 6213 | עמו 5973: |
|---|---|---|---|---|---|---|---|---|---|---|---|---|
| ua'al | ta'as | lou' | ma'aumah | ra'; | kiy, | 'am | ka'asher | yadaber | 'aleyka, | ken | 'aseh | 'amou. |
| **and no** | **do** | **him** | **no** | **harm** | **but** | **rather** | **as which** | **he shall say** | **unto him** | **even as** | **do** | **unto him** |

| 39:13 וישלח 7971 | נבוזראדן 5018 | רב 7227 | טבחים 2876 | ונבושזבן 5021 | רב 7249 | סריס 7249 | ונרגל 5371 | שר 8269 | אצר 687 | רב 7248 | מג 7248 |
|---|---|---|---|---|---|---|---|---|---|---|---|
| uayishlach | nabuzar'adan | rab | tabachiym, | uanabushazban | rab | sariys, | uaneragal | sar | 'atzer | rab | mag; |
| **So sent** | **Nebuzaradan** | **the captain of** | **the guard** | **and Nebushasban** | **Rab** | **saris** | **and Nergal** | **-shar-** | **ezer** | **Rab** | **mag** |

| וכל 3605 | רבי 7227 | מלך 4428 | בבל 894: | 39:14 וישלחו 7971 | ויקחו 3947 | את 853 | ירמיהו 3414 | מחצר 2691 | המטרה 4307 |
|---|---|---|---|---|---|---|---|---|---|
| uakol | rabey | melek | babel. | uayishlachu | uayiqchu | 'at | yirmayahu | mechatzar | hamatarah, |
| **and all** | **princes** | **the king of** | **Babylon's** | **Even they sent** | **and took** | | **Jeremiah** | **out of the court of** | **the prison** |

| ויתנו 5414 | אתו 853 | אל 413 | גדליהו 1436 | בן 1121 | אחיקם 296 | בן 1121 | שפן 8227 | להוצאהו 3318 | אל 413 | הבית 1004 |
|---|---|---|---|---|---|---|---|---|---|---|
| uayitanu | 'atou | 'al | gadalyahu | ben | 'achiyqam | ben | shapan, | lahoutzi'aehu | 'al | habayit; |
| **and committed** | **him** | **unto** | **Gedaliah** | **the son of** | **Ahikam** | **the son of** | **Shaphan** | **that he should carry him** | **to** | **home** |

| וישב 3427 | בתוך 8432 | העם 5971: | 39:15 ואל 413 | ירמיהו 3414 | היה 1961 | דבר 1697 | יהוה 3068 | בהיתו 1961 | עצור 6113 | בחצר 2691 |
|---|---|---|---|---|---|---|---|---|---|---|
| uayesheb | batouk | ha'am. | ua'al | yirmayahu | hayah | dabar | Yahuah; | bihayotou | 'atzur, | bachatzar |
| **so he dwelt** | **among** | **the people** | **Now unto** | **Jeremiah** | **came** | **the word of** | **Yahuah** | **while he was** | **shut up** | **in the court of** |

| המטרה 4307 | לאמר 559: | 39:16 הלוך 1980 | ואמרת 559 | לעבד 5663 | מלך 4428 | הכושי 3569 | לאמר 559 | כה 3541 | אמר 559 | יהוה 3068 | צבאות 6635 |
|---|---|---|---|---|---|---|---|---|---|---|---|
| hamatarah | lea'mor. | halouk | ua'amarta | la'abed | melek | hakushiy | lea'mor, | koh | 'amar | Yahuah | tzaba'aut |
| **the prison** | **saying** | **Go** | **and speak** | **to Ebed** | **melek** | **the Ethiopian** | **saying** | **Thus** | **saith** | **Yahuah** | **of hosts** |

| אלהי 430 | ישראל 3478 | הנני 2005 | מבי 935 | את 853 | דברי 1697 | אל 413 | העיר 5892 | הזאת 2063 | לרעה 7451 | ולא 3808 | לטובה 2896 |
|---|---|---|---|---|---|---|---|---|---|---|---|
| 'alohey | yisra'ael, | hinniy | mebiy' | 'at | dabaray | 'al | ha'ayr | haza't | lara'ah | uala' | latoubah; |
| **the Elohim of** | **Israel** | **Behold I** | **will bring** | | **my words** | **upon** | **city** | **this** | **for evil** | **and not** | **for good** |

| והיו 1961 | לפניך 6440 | ביום 3117 | ההוא 1931: | 39:17 והצלתיך 5337 | ביום 3117 | ההוא 1931 | נאם 5002 | יהוה 3068 |
|---|---|---|---|---|---|---|---|---|
| uahayu | lapaneyka | bayoum | hahua'. | uahitzaltiyka | bayoum | hahua' | na'am | Yahuah; |
| **and they shall be** | **before you** | ***accomplished* in day** | **that** | **But I will deliver you** | **in day** | **that** | **saith** | **Yahuah** |

| ולא 3808 | תנתן 5414 | ביד 3027 | האנשים 582 | אשר 834 | אתה 859 | יגור 3016 | מפניהם 6440: | 39:18 כי 3588 | מלט 4422 |
|---|---|---|---|---|---|---|---|---|---|
| uala' | tinaten | bayad | ha'anashiym, | 'asher | 'atah | yagour | mipaneyhem. | kiy | malet |
| **and not** | **you shall be given** | **into the hand of** | **the men of** | **whom** | **you** | ***are* afraid** | **whom** | **For** | **I will surely** |

| אמלטך 4422 | ובחרב 2719 | לא 3808 | תפל 5307 | והיתה 1961 | לך 3807a | נפשך 5315 | לשלל 7998 | כי 3588 |
|---|---|---|---|---|---|---|---|---|
| 'amaletaka, | uabachereb | la' | tipol; | uahayatah | laka | napshaka | lashalal, | kiy |
| **deliver you** | **and by the sword** | **not** | **you shall fall** | **but shall be** | **unto you** | **your life** | **for a prey** | **because** |

| בטחת 982 | בי 871a | נאם 5002 | יהוה 3068: |
|---|---|---|---|
| batachta | biy | na'am | Yahuah. |
| **you have put your trust in me** | | **saith** | **Yahuah** |

Jer 39:12 Take him, and look well to him, and do him no harm; but do unto him even as he shall say unto you.13 So Nebuzar-adan the captain of the guard sent, and Nebushasban, Rab-saris, and Nergal-sharezer, Rabmag, and all the king of Babylon's princes;14 Even they sent, and took Jeremiah out of the court of the prison, and committed him unto Gedaliah the son of Ahikam the son of Shaphan, that he should carry him home: so he dwelt among the people.15 Now the word of YHUH came unto Jeremiah, while he was shut up in the court of the prison, saying,16 Go and speak to Ebed-melech the Ethiopian, saying, Thus saith YHUH of hosts, the G-d of Israel; Behold, I will bring my words upon this city for evil, and not for good; and they shall be accomplished in that day before you.17 But I will deliver you in that day, saith YHUH: and you shall not be given into the hand of the men of whom you are afraid.18 For I will surely deliver you, and you shall not fall by the sword, but your life shall be for a prey unto you: because you have put your trust in me, saith YHUH.

**Jer 40:1**
הדבר 1697 אשר 834 היה 1961 אל 413 ירמיהו 3414 מאת 853 יהוה 3068 אחר 310 שלח 7971 אתו 853 נבוזראדן 5018 רב 7227
hadabar 'asher hayah 'al yirmayahu me'at Yahuah, 'achar shalach 'atou, nabuzar'adan rab
**The word that came to Jeremiah from Yahuah after that had let go him Nebuzaradan the captain of**

טבחים 2876 מן 4480 הרמה 7414 בקחתו 3947 אתו 853 והוא 1931 אסור 631 באזקים 246 בתוך 8432 כל 3605
tabachiym min haramah; baqachtou 'atou, uahu'a 'asur ba'ziqiym batouk kal
**the guard from Ramah when he had taken him and he being bound in chains among all**

גלות 1546 ירושלם 3389 ויהודה 3063 המגלים 1540 בבלה 894: **40:2** ויקח 3947
galut yarushalaim uayahudah, hamugliym babelah. uayiqach
**that were carried away captive of Jerusalem and Judah which were carried away captive unto Babylon And took**

רב 7227 טבחים 2876 לירמיהו 3414 ויאמר 559 אליו 413 יהוה 3068 אלהיך 430 דבר 1696 את 853 הרעה 7451 הזאת 2063 אל 413
rab tabachiym layirmayahu; uaya'mer 'aelayu, Yahuah 'aloheyka, diber 'at hara'ah haza't, 'al
**the captain of the guard to Jeremiah and said unto him Yahuah your Elohim has pronounced evil this upon**

המקום 4725 הזה 2088: **40:3** ויבא 935 ויעש 6213 יהוה 3068 כאשר 834 דבר 1696 כי 3588 חטאתם 2398
hamaqoum hazeh. uayabea' uaya'as Yahuah ka'asher diber; kiy chata'tem
**place this Now has brought *it* and done Yahuah according as he has said because you have sinned**

ליהוה 3068 ולא 3808 שמעתם 8085 בקולו 6963 והיה 1961 לכם 3807a דבר 1697 הזה 2088: **40:4** ועתה 6258 הנה 2009 פתחתיך 6605
laYahuah uala' shama'tem baqoulou, uahayah lakem dabar hazeh. ua'atah hineh pitachtiyka
**against Yahuah and not have obeyed his voice therefore is come upon you thing this And now behold I loose you**

היום 3117 מן 4480 האזקים 246 אשר 834 על 5921 ידך 3027 אם 518 טוב 2896 בעיניך 5869 לבוא 935 אתי 854 בבל 894 בא 935
hayoum, min ha'ziqiym 'asher 'al yadeka 'am toub ba'aeyneyka labou'a 'atiy babel, ba'
***this* day from the chains which *were* upon your hand If good it seemed unto you to come with me *into* Babylon come**

ואשים 7760 את 853 עיני 5869 עליך 5921 ואם 518 רע 7489 בעיניך 5869 לבוא 935 אתי 854 בבל 894 חדל 2308 ראה 7200 כל 3605
ua'asiym 'at 'aeyniy 'aleyka, ua'am ra' ba'aeyneyka labou'a 'atiy babel chadal; ra'aeh kal
**and I will look well unto you but if ill it seem unto you to come with me *into* Babylon forbear behold all**

הארץ 776 לפניך 6440 אל 413 טוב 2896 ואל 413 הישר 3477 בעיניך 5869 ללכת 1980 שמה 8033 לך 1980: **40:5** ועודנו 5750 לא 3808
ha'aretz lapaneyka, 'al toub ua'al hayashar ba'aeyneyka laleket shamah lek. ua'audenu la'
**the land *is* before you where good and to convenient it seems for you to go where to go you Now while yet not**

ישוב 7725 ושבה 7725 אל 413 גדליה 1436 בן 1121 אחיקם 296 בן 1121 שפן 8227 אשר 834 הפקיד 6485
yashub, yashubah 'al gadalyah ben 'achiyqam ben shapan 'asher hipqiyd
**he was gone back *he said,* Go back also to Gedaliah the son of Ahikam the son of Shaphan whom has made governor**

מלך 4428 בבל 894 בערי 5892 יהודה 3063 ושב 3427 אתו 854 בתוך 8432 העם 5971 או 176 אל 413 כל 3605 הישר 3477
melek babel ba'arey yahudah, uasheb 'atou batouk ha'am, 'au 'al kal hayashar
**the king of Babylon over the cities of Judah and dwell with him among the people or where soever convenient**

בעיניך 5869 ללכת 1980 לך 1980 ויתן 5414 לו 3807a רב 7227 טבחים 2876 ארחה 737 ומשאת 4864 וישלחהו 7971:
ba'aeyneyka laleket lek; uayiten lou' rab tabachiym 'arukah uamas'aet uayashalchehu.
**it seems unto you go to go you So gave him the captain of the guard victuals and a reward and let him go**

**Jer** 40:1 The word that came to Jeremiah from YHUH, after that Nebuzar-adan the captain of the guard had let him go from Ramah, when he had taken him being bound in chains among all that were carried away captive of Jerusalem and Judah, which were carried away captive unto Babylon.2 And the captain of the guard took Jeremiah, and said unto him, YHUH your G-d has pronounced this evil upon this place.3 Now YHUH has brought it, and done according as he has said: because you have sinned against YHUH, and have not obeyed his voice, therefore this thing is come upon you.4 And now, behold, I loose you this day from the chains which were upon your hand. If it seem good unto you to come with me into Babylon, come; and I will look well unto you: but if it seem ill unto you to come with me into Babylon, forbear: behold, all the land is before you: whither it seem good and convenient for you to go, thither go.5 Now while he was not yet gone back, he said, Go back also to Gedaliah the son of Ahikam the son of Shaphan, whom the king of Babylon has made governor over the cities of Judah, and dwell with him among the people: or go wheresoever it seem convenient unto you to go. So the captain of the guard gave him victuals and a reward, and let him go.

| 40:6 ויבא 935 | ירמיהו 3414 | אל 413 | גדליה 1436 | בן 1121 | אחיקם 296 | המצפתה 4708 | וישב 3427 | אתו 854 | בתוך 8432 | העם 5971 |
|---|---|---|---|---|---|---|---|---|---|---|
| uayaba' | yirmayahu | 'al | gadalyah | ben | 'achiyqam | hamitzpatah; | uayesheb | 'atou | batouk | ha'am, |
| **Then went** | **Jeremiah** | **unto** | **Gedaliah** | **the son of** | **Ahikam** | **to Mizpah** | **and dwelt** | **with him** | **among** | **the people** |

| הנשארים 7604 | בארץ 776: | 40:7 וישמעו 8085 | כל 3605 | שרי 8269 | החילים 2428 | אשר 834 | בשדה 7704 | המה 1992 |
|---|---|---|---|---|---|---|---|---|
| hanisha'ariym | ba'aretz. | uayishma'au | kal | sarey | hachayaliym | 'asher | basadeh, | hemah |
| **that were left** | **in the land** | **Now when heard** | **all** | **the captains of** | **the forces** | **which *were*** | **in the fields *even*** | **they** |

| ואנשיהם 582 | כי 3588 | הפקיד 6485 | מלך 4428 | בבל 894 | את 853 | גדליהו 1436 | בן 1121 | אחיקם 296 | בארץ 776 | וכי 3588 |
|---|---|---|---|---|---|---|---|---|---|---|
| ua'ansheyhem, | kiy | hipqiyd | melek | babel | 'at | gadalyahu | ben | 'achiyqam | ba'aretz; | uakiy |
| **and their men** | **that** | **had made governor** | **the king of** | **Babylon** | | **Gedaliah** | **the son of** | **Ahikam** | **in the land** | **and for** |

| הפקיד 6485 | אתו 854 | אנשים 582 | ונשים 802 | וטף 2945 | ומדלת 1803 | הארץ 776 | מאשר 834 | לא 3808 |
|---|---|---|---|---|---|---|---|---|
| hipqiyd | 'atou, | 'anashiym | uanashiym | uatap, | uamidalat | ha'aretz, | me'asher | la' |
| **had committed** | **unto him** | **of the men** | **and women** | **and children** | **and of the poor of** | **the land** | **of** | **not** |

| הגלו 1540 | בבלה 894: | 40:8 ויבאו 935 | אל 413 | גדליה 1436 | המצפתה 4708 | וישמעאל 3458 |
|---|---|---|---|---|---|---|
| hagalu | babelah. | uayabo'au | 'al | gadalyah | hamitzpatah; | uayishma'ae'l |
| **them that were carried away captive** | **to Babylon** | **Then they came** | **to** | **Gedaliah to** | **the Mizpah** | **even Ishmael** |

| בן 1121 | נתניהו 5418 | ויוחנן 3110 | ויונתן 3129 | בני 1121 | קרח 7143 | ושריה 8304 | בן 1121 | תנחמת 8576 | ובני 1121 |
|---|---|---|---|---|---|---|---|---|---|
| ben | natanyahu | uayouchanan | uayounatan | baney | qareach | uasarayah | ben | tanchumet | uabney |
| **the son of** | **Nethaniah** | **and Johanan** | **and Jonathan** | **the sons of** | **Kareah** | **and Seraiah** | **the son of** | **Tanhumeth** | **and the sons of** |

| עופי 5778 | הנטפתי 5200 | ויזניהו 3153 | בן 1121 | המעכתי 4602 | המה 1992 | ואנשיהם 582: | 40:9 וישבע 7650 | להם 3807a | גדליהו 1436 |
|---|---|---|---|---|---|---|---|---|---|
| 'aupay | hanatopatiy, | uiyazanyahu | ben | hama'akatiy, | hemah | ua'ansheyhem. | uayishaba' | lahem | gadalyahu |
| **Ephai** | **the Netophathite** | **and Jezaniah** | **the son of** | **a Maachathite** | **they** | **and their men** | **And sware** | **unto them** | **Gedaliah** |

| בן 1121 | אחיקם 296 | בן 1121 | שפן 8227 | ולאנשיהם 582 | לאמר 559 | אל 408 | תיראו 3372 | מעבוד 5647 | הכשדים 3778 | שבו 3427 | בארץ 776 |
|---|---|---|---|---|---|---|---|---|---|---|---|
| ben | 'achiyqam | ben | shapan | ual'ansheyhem | lea'mor, | 'al | tiyra'au | me'aboud | hakasdiym; | shabu | ba'aretz, |
| **the son of** | **Ahikam** | **the son of** | **Shaphan** | **and to their men** | **saying** | **not** | **Fear** | **to serve** | **the Chaldeans** | **dwell** | **in the land** |

| ועבדו 5647 | את 853 | מלך 4428 | בבל 894 | וייטב 3190 | לכם 3807a: | 40:10 ואני 589 | הנני 2005 | ישב 3427 | במצפה 4709 | לעמד 5975 |
|---|---|---|---|---|---|---|---|---|---|---|
| ua'abdu | 'at | melek | babel | uayiytab | lakem. | ua'aniy, | hinniy | yosheb | bamitzpah, | la'amod |
| **and serve** | | **the king of** | **Babylon** | **and it shall be well** | **with you** | **As for me** | **behold I** | **will dwell** | **at Mizpah** | **to serve** |

| לפני 6440 | הכשדים 3778 | אשר 834 | יבאו 935 | אלינו 413 | ואתם 859 | אספו 622 | יין 3196 | וקיץ 7019 | ושמן 8081 | ושמו 7760 |
|---|---|---|---|---|---|---|---|---|---|---|
| lipney | hakasdiym, | 'asher | yabo'au | 'aeleynu; | ua'atem | 'aspu | yayin | uaqayitz | uashemen, | uasiymu |
| **before** | **the Chaldeans** | **which** | **will come** | **unto us** | **but you** | **gather you** | **wine** | **and summer fruits** | **and oil** | **and put** |

| בכליכם 3627 | ושבו 3427 | בעריכם 5892 | אשר 834 | תפשתם 8610: | 40:11 וגם 1571 | כל 3605 | היהודים 3064 | אשר 834 |
|---|---|---|---|---|---|---|---|---|
| bikleykem, | uashbu | ba'areykem | 'asher | tapastem. | ua'gam | kal | hayahudiym | 'asher |
| ***them* in your vessels** | **and dwell** | **in your cities** | **that** | **you have taken** | **Likewise when** | **all** | **the Jews** | **that** |

| במואב 4124 | ובבני 1121 | עמון 5983 | ובאדום 123 | ואשר 834 | בכל 3605 | הארצות 776 | שמעו 8085 | כי 3588 | נתן 5414 |
|---|---|---|---|---|---|---|---|---|---|
| bamou'ab | uabibney | 'amoun | uabe'adoum | ua'asher | bakal | ha'aratzout | shama'au, | kiy | natan |
| ***were* in Moab** | **and among** | **the Ammonites** | **and in Edom** | **and that *were*** | **in all** | **the countries** | **heard** | **that** | **had left** |

Jer 40:6 Then went Jeremiah unto Gedaliah the son of Ahikam to Mizpah; and dwelt with him among the people that were left in the land.7 Now when all the captains of the forces which were in the fields, even they and their men, heard that the king of Babylon had made Gedaliah the son of Ahikam governor in the land, and had committed unto him men, and women, and children, and of the poor of the land, of them that were not carried away captive to Babylon;8 Then they came to Gedaliah to Mizpah, even Ishmael the son of Nethaniah, and Johanan and Jonathan the sons of Kareah, and Seraiah the son of Tanhumeth, and the sons of Ephai the Netophathite, and Jezaniah the son of a Maachathite, they and their men.9 And Gedaliah the son of Ahikam the son of Shaphan sware unto them and to their men, saying, Fear not to serve the Chaldeans: dwell in the land, and serve the king of Babylon, and it shall be well with you.10 As for me, behold, I will dwell at Mizpah to serve the Chaldeans, which will come unto us: but you, gather you wine, and summer fruits, and oil, and put them in your vessels, and dwell in your cities that you have taken.11 Likewise when all the Jews that were in Moab, and among the Ammonites, and in Edom, and that were in all the countries, heard that the king of Babylon had left a remnant of Judah,

| מלך 4428 | בבל 894 | שארית 7611 | ליהודה 3063 | וכי 3588 | הפקיד 6485 | עליהם 5921 | את 853 | גדליהו 1436 | בן 1121 | אחיקם 296 | בן 1121 |
|---|---|---|---|---|---|---|---|---|---|---|---|
| melek | babel | sha'aeriyt | liyahudah; | uakiy | hipqiyd | 'aleyhem, | 'at | gadalyahu | ben | 'achiyqam | ben |
| **the king of** | **Babylon** | **a remnant** | **of Judah** | **and that** | **he had set** | **over them** | | **Gedaliah** | **the son of** | **Ahikam** | **the son of** |

| שפן 8227: | 40:12 | וישבו 3427 | כל 3605 | היהודים 3064 | מכל 3605 | המקמות 4725 | אשר 834 | נדחו 5080 | שם 8033 | ויבאו 935 |
|---|---|---|---|---|---|---|---|---|---|---|
| shapan. | | uayashubu | kal | hayahudiym, | mikal | hamaqomout | 'asher | nidachu | sham, | uayabo'au |
| **Shaphan** | | **Even returned** | **all** | **the Jews** | **out of all** | **places** | **where** | **they were driven** | **there** | **and came to** |

| ארץ 776 | יהודה 3063 | אל 413 | גדליהו 1436 | המצפתה 4708 | ויאספו 622 | יין 3196 | וקיץ 7019 | הרבה 7235 | מאד 3966: | 40:13 |
|---|---|---|---|---|---|---|---|---|---|---|
| 'aretz | yahudah | 'al | gadalyahu | hamitzpatah; | uaya'aspu | yayin | uaqayitz | harbeh | ma'ad. | |
| **the land of** | **Judah** | **to** | **Gedaliah** | **unto Mizpah** | **and gathered** | **wine** | **and summer fruits** | **much** | **very** | |

| ויוחנן 3110 | בן 1121 | קרח 7143 | וכל 3605 | שרי 8269 | החילים 2428 | אשר 834 | בשדה 7704 | באו 935 | אל 413 | גדליהו 1436 |
|---|---|---|---|---|---|---|---|---|---|---|
| uayouchanan | ben | qareach, | uakal | sarey | hachayaliym | 'asher | basadeh; | ba'au | 'al | gadalyahu |
| **Moreover Johanan** | **the son of** | **Kareah** | **and all** | **the captains of** | **the forces** | **that** | ***were* in the fields** | **came** | **to** | **Gedaliah *to*** |

| המצפתה 4708: | 40:14 | ויאמרו 559 | אליו 413 | הידע 3045 | תדע 3045 | כי 3588 | בעליס 1185 | מלך 4428 | בני 1121 | עמון 5983 |
|---|---|---|---|---|---|---|---|---|---|---|
| hamitzpatah. | | uaya'maru | 'aelayu, | hayadoa' | teda' | kiy | ba'aliys | melek | baney | 'amoun, |
| **Mizpah** | | **And said** | **unto him** | **Do you certainly** | **know** | **that** | **Baalis** | **the king of** | **the son of** | **the Ammonites** |

| שלח 7971 | את 853 | ישמעאל 3458 | בן 1121 | נתניה 5418 | להכתך 5221 | נפש 5315 | ולא 3808 | האמין 539 | להם 3807a | גדליהו 1436 | בן 1121 |
|---|---|---|---|---|---|---|---|---|---|---|---|
| shalach | 'at | yishma'ael | ben | natanyah, | lahakotaka | napesh; | uala' | he'amiyn | lahem, | gadalyahu | ben |
| **has sent** | | **Ishmael** | **the son of** | **Nethaniah** | **to slay you?** | **to slay** | **did not** | **believed** | **them** | **Gedaliah** | **the son of** |

| אחיקם 296: | 40:15 | ויוחנן 3110 | בן 1121 | קרח 7143 | אמר 559 | אל 413 | גדליהו 1436 | בסתר 5643 | במצפה 4709 | לאמר 559 | אלכה 1980 | נא 4994 |
|---|---|---|---|---|---|---|---|---|---|---|---|---|
| 'achiyqam. | | uayouchanan | ben | qareach | 'amar | 'al | gadalyahu | baseter | bamitzpah | lea'mor, | 'aelakah | naa' |
| **Ahikam** | | **Then Johanan** | **the son of** | **Kareah** | **spoke** | **to** | **Gedaliah** | **secretly** | **in Mizpah** | **saying** | **Let me go** | **I pray you** |

| ואכה 5221 | את 853 | ישמעאל 3458 | בן 1121 | נתניה 5418 | ואיש 376 | לא 3808 | ידע 3045 | למה 4100 | יככה 5221 | נפש 5315 |
|---|---|---|---|---|---|---|---|---|---|---|
| ua'akeh | 'at | yishma'ael | ben | natanyah, | ua'aysh | la' | yeda'; | lamah | yakekah | nepesh, |
| **and I will slay** | | **Ishmael** | **the son of** | **Nethaniah** | **and man** | **no** | **shall know *it*** | **wherefore** | **should he** | **slay you** |

| ונפצו 6327 | כל 3605 | יהודה 3064 | הנקבצים 6908 | אליך 413 | ואבדה 6 | שארית 7611 | יהודה 3063: | 40:16 | ויאמר 559 |
|---|---|---|---|---|---|---|---|---|---|
| uanapotzu | kal | yahudah, | haniqbatziym | 'aeleyka, | ua'abadah | sha'aeriyt | yahudah. | | uaya'mer |
| **that should be scattered** | **all** | **the Jews** | **which are gathered** | **unto you** | **and perish** | **the remnant in** | **Judah** | | **But said** |

| גדליהו 1436 | בן 1121 | אחיקם 296 | אל 413 | יוחנן 3110 | בן 1121 | קרח 7143 | אל 408 | תעש 6213 | את 853 | הדבר 1697 | הזה 2088 | כי 3588 | שקר 8267 |
|---|---|---|---|---|---|---|---|---|---|---|---|---|---|
| gadalyahu | ben | 'achiyqam | 'al | youchanan | ben | qareach, | 'al | ta'as | 'at | hadabar | hazeh; | kiy | sheqer |
| **Gedaliah** | **the son of** | **Ahikam** | **unto** | **Johanan** | **the son of** | **Kareah** | **not** | **you shall do** | | **thing** | **this** | **for** | **falsely** |

| אתה 859 | דבר 1696 | אל 413 | ישמעאל 3458: |
|---|---|---|---|
| 'atah | dober | 'al | yishma'ael. |
| **you** | **speak** | **of** | **Ishmael** |

| Jer 41:1 | ויהי 1961 | בחדש 2320 | השביעי 7637 | בא 935 | ישמעאל 3458 | בן 1121 | נתניה 5418 | בן 1121 | אלישמע 476 |
|---|---|---|---|---|---|---|---|---|---|
| | uayahiy | bachodesh | hashabiy'ay, | ba' | yishma'ael | ben | natanyah | ben | 'aliyshama' |
| | **Now it came to pass** | **in month** | **the seventh** | **came *that*** | **Ishmael** | **the son of** | **Nethaniah** | **the son of** | **Elishama** |

Jer 40:11 and that he had set over them Gedaliah the son of Ahikam the son of Shaphan;12 Even all the Jews returned out of all places whither they were driven, and came to the land of Judah, to Gedaliah, unto Mizpah, and gathered wine and summer fruits very much.13 Moreover Johanan the son of Kareah, and all the captains of the forces that were in the fields, came to Gedaliah to Mizpah,14 And said unto him, Dost you certainly know that Baalis the king of the Ammonites has sent Ishmael the son of Nethaniah to slay you? But Gedaliah the son of Ahikam believed them not.15 Then Johanan the son of Kareah spoke to Gedaliah in Mizpah secretly, saying, Let me go, I pray you, and I will slay Ishmael the son of Nethaniah, and no man shall know it: wherefore should he slay you, that all the Jews which are gathered unto you should be scattered, and the remnant in Judah perish?16 But Gedaliah the son of Ahikam said unto Johanan the son of Kareah, Thou shall not do this thing: for you speak falsely of Ishmael. **Jer** 41:1 Now it came to pass in the seventh month, that Ishmael the son of Nethaniah the son of Elishama, of the seed royal, and the princes of the king, even ten men with him, came unto Gedaliah the son of Ahikam to Mizpah; and there they did eat bread together in Mizpah.

מזרע 2233 | המלוכה 4410 | ורבי 7227 | המלך 4428 | ועשרה 6235 | אנשים 582 | אתו 854 | אל 413 | גדליהו 1436 | בן 1121 | אחיקם 296
mizera' hamalukah uarabey hamelek ua'asarah 'anashiym 'atou 'al gadalyahu ben 'achiyqam
**of the seed the royal and the princes of the king even ten men with him unto Gedaliah the son of Ahikam**

המצפתה 4709 | ויאכלו 398 | שם 8033 | לחם 3899 | יחדו 3162 | במצפה 4709: | 41:2 | ויקם 6965 | ישמעאל 3458 | בן 1121 | נתניה 5418
hamitzpatah; uayo'akalu sham lachem yachdau bamitzpah. uayaqam yishma'ael ben natanyah
**to Mizpah and there they did eat there bread together in Mizpah Then arose Ishmael the son of Nethaniah**

ועשרת 6235 | האנשים 582 | אשר 834 | היו 1961 | אתו 854 | ויכו 5221 | את 853 | גדליהו 1436 | בן 1121 | אחיקם 296 | בן 1121 | שפן 8227
ua'aseret ha'anashiym 'asher hayu 'atou, uayaku 'at gadalyahu ben 'achiyqam ben shapan
**and the ten men that were with him and smote Gedaliah the son of Ahikam the son of Shaphan**

בחרב 2719 | וימת 4191 | אתו 853 | אשר 834 | הפקיד 6485 | מלך 4428 | בבל 894 | בארץ 776: | 41:3 | ואת 853 | כל 3605 | היהודים 3064
bachereb uayamet 'atou; 'asher hipqiyd melek babel ba'aretz. ua'at kal hayahudiym,
**with the sword and slew him whom had made governor the king of Babylon over the land *And* all the Jews**

אשר 834 | היו 1961 | אתו 854 | את 854 | גדליהו 1436 | במצפה 4709 | ואת 853 | הכשדים 3778 | אשר 834 | נמצאו 4672 | שם 8033 | את 853 | אנשי 582
'asher hayu 'atou 'at gadalyahu bamitzpah, ua'at hakasdiym 'asher nimtza'au sham; 'at 'anshey
**that were with him *even with* Gedaliah at Mizpah *and* the Chaldeans that were found there *also* men of**

המלחמה 4421 | הכה 5221 | ישמעאל 3458: | 41:4 | ויהי 1961 | ביום 3117 | השני 8145 | להמית 4191 | את 853 | גדליהו 1436 | ואיש 376
hamilchamah, hikah yishma'ael. uayahiy bayoum hasheniy lahamiyt 'at gadalyahu; ua'aysh
***and* the war slew Ishmael And it came to pass day the second after he had slain Gedaliah and man**

לא 3808 | ידע 3045: | 41:5 | ויבאו 935 | אנשים 582 | משכם 7927 | משלו 7887 | ומשמרון 8111 | שמנים 8084 | איש 376
la' yada'. uayabo'au 'anashiym mishakem mishilou uamishomaroun shamoniym 'aysh,
**no knew *it* That there came certain men from shekem from Shiloh and from Samaria *even* fourscore men**

מגלחי 1548 | זקן 2206 | וקרעי 07167 | בגדים 899 | ומתגדדים 1413 | ומנחה 4503 | ולבונה 3828 | בידם 3027
magulchey zaqan uaqru'aey bagadiym uamitgodadiym; uaminchah ualabounah bayadam,
**shaven *having their* beards and rent their clothes and having cut themselves with offerings and incense in their hand**

להביא 935 | בית 1004 | יהוה 3068: | 41:6 | ויצא 3318 | ישמעאל 3458 | בן 1121 | נתניה 5418 | לקראתם 7125 | מן 4480 | המצפה 4709
lahabiy'a beyt Yahuah. uayetzea' yishma'ael ben natanyah liqra'tam min hamitzpah,
**to bring *them* to the house of Yahuah And went forth Ishmael the son of Nethaniah to meet them from Mizpah**

הלך 1980 | הלך 1980 | ובכה 1058 | ויהי 1961 | כפגש 6298 | אתם 853 | ויאמר 559 | אליהם 413 | באו 935 | אל 413 | גדליהו 1436 | בן 1121
halok halok uabokeh; uayahiy kipgosh 'atam, uaya'mer 'aleyhem, bo'au 'al gadalyahu ben
**all along as he went weeping and it came to pass as he met them he said unto them Come to Gedaliah the son of**

אחיקם 296: | 41:7 | ויהי 1961 | כבואם 935 | אל 413 | תוך 8432 | העיר 5892 | וישחטם 7819 | ישמעאל 3458 | בן 1121
'achiyqam. uayahiy kabo'am 'al touk ha'ayr; uayishchatem yishma'ael ben
**Ahikam And it was *so* when they came into the midst of the city that slew them Ishmael the son of**

נתניה 5418 | אל 413 | תוך 8432 | הבור 953 | הוא 1931 | והאנשים 582 | אשר 834 | אתו 854: | 41:8 | ועשרה 6235 | אנשים 582
natanyah 'al touk habour, hua' uaha'anashiym 'asher 'atou. ua'asarah 'anashiym
**Nethaniah *and cast them* into the midst of the pit he and the men that *were* with him But ten men**

Jer 41:2 Then arose Ishmael the son of Nethaniah, and the ten men that were with him, and smote Gedaliah the son of Ahikam the son of Shaphan with the sword, and slew him, whom the king of Babylon had made governor over the land.3 Ishmael also slew all the Jews that were with him, even with Gedaliah, at Mizpah, and the Chaldeans that were found there, and the men of war.4 And it came to pass the second day after he had slain Gedaliah, and no man knew it,5 That there came certain from Shechem, from Shiloh, and from Samaria, even fourscore men, having their beards shaven, and their clothes rent, and having cut themselves, with offerings and incense in their hand, to bring them to the house of YHUH.6 And Ishmael the son of Nethaniah went forth from Mizpah to meet them, weeping all along as he went: and it came to pass, as he met them, he said unto them, Come to Gedaliah the son of Ahikam.7 And it was so, when they came into the midst of the city, that Ishmael the son of Nethaniah slew them, and cast them into the midst of the pit, he, and the men that were with him.8 But ten men were found among them that said unto Ishmael, Slay us not: for we have treasures in the field, of wheat, and of barley, and of oil, and of honey. So he forbare, and slew them not among their brethren.

| נמצאו 4672 | בם 871a | ויאמרו 559 | אל 413 | ישמעאל 3458 | אל 408 | תמתנו 4191 | כי 3588 | יש 3426 | לנו 3807a | מטמנים 4301 | בשדה 7704 | חטים 2406 |
|---|---|---|---|---|---|---|---|---|---|---|---|---|
| nimtza'au | bam, | uaya'maru | 'al | yishma'ael | 'al | tamitenu, | kiy | yesh | lanu | matmoniym | basadeh, | chitiym |
| **were found** | **among them** | **that said** | **unto** | **Ishmael** | **not** | **Slay us** | **for** | **have** | **we** | **treasures** | **in the field** | ***of* wheat** |

| ושערים 8184 | ושמן 8081 | ודבש 1706 | ויחדל 2308 | ולא 3808 | המיתם 4191 | בתוך 8432 | אחיהם 251: | 41:9 | והבור 953 | אשר 834 |
|---|---|---|---|---|---|---|---|---|---|---|
| usa'ariym | uashemen | uadbash; | uayechdal | uala' | hemiytam | batouk | 'acheyhem. | | uahabour, | 'asher |
| **and of barley** | **and of oil** | **and of honey** | **So he forbare** | **and not** | **slew them** | **among** | **their brethren** | | **Now the pit** | **wherein** |

| השליך 7993 | שם 8033 | ישמעאל 3458 | את 853 | כל 3605 | פגרי 6297 | האנשים 582 | אשר 834 | הכה 5221 | ביד 3027 | גדליהו 1436 |
|---|---|---|---|---|---|---|---|---|---|---|
| hishliyk | sham | yishma'ael | 'at | kal | pigrey | ha'anashiym, | 'asher | hikah | bayad | gadalyahu, |
| **had cast** | **there** | **Ishmael** | | **all** | **the dead bodies of** | **the men** | **whom** | **he had slain** | **because of** | **Gedaliah *was*** |

| הוא 1931 | אשר 834 | עשה 6213 | המלך 4428 | אסא 609 | מפני 6440 | בעשא 1201 | מלך 4428 | ישראל 3478 | אתו 853 | מלא 4390 | ישמעאל 3458 | בן 1121 |
|---|---|---|---|---|---|---|---|---|---|---|---|---|
| hua', | 'asher | 'asah | hamelek | 'asa', | mipaney | ba'sha' | melek | yisra'ael; | 'atou, | milea' | yishma'ael | ben |
| **it** | **which** | **had made** | **the king** | **Asa** | **for fear of** | **Baasha** | **king of** | **Israel** | **it** | **filled** | ***and* Ishmael** | **the son of** |

| נתניהו 5418 | חללים 2491: | 41:10 וישב 7617 | ישמעאל 3458 | את 853 | כל 3605 | שארית 7611 | העם 5971 |
|---|---|---|---|---|---|---|---|
| natanyahu | chalaliym. | uayishba | Yishma'el | 'at | kal | sha'aeriyt | ha'am |
| **Nethaniah** | **with *them that were* slain** | **Then carried away captive** | **Ishmael** | | **all** | **the residue of** | **the people** |

| אשר 834 | במצפה 4709 | את 853 | בנות 1323 | המלך 4428 | ואת 853 | כל 3605 | העם 5971 | הנשארים 7604 | במצפה 4709 | אשר 834 |
|---|---|---|---|---|---|---|---|---|---|---|
| 'asher | bamitzpah, | 'at | banout | hamelek | ua'at | kal | ha'am | hanisha'ariym | bamitzpah, | 'asher |
| **that** | ***were* in Mizpah** | | ***even* daughters** | **the king's** | ***and*** | **all** | **the people** | **that remained** | **in Mizpah** | **whom** |

| הפקיד 6485 | נבוזראדן 5018 | רב 7227 | טבחים 2876 | את 853 | גדליהו 1436 | בן 1121 | אחיקם 296 |
|---|---|---|---|---|---|---|---|
| hipqiyd, | nabuzar'adan | rab | tabachiym, | 'at | gadalyahu | ben | 'achiyqam; |
| **had committed to** | **Nebuzaradan** | **the captain of** | **the guard** | | **Gedaliah** | **the son of** | **Ahikam** |

| וישבם 7617 | ישמעאל 3458 | בן 1121 | נתניה 5418 | וילך 1980 | לעבר 5674 | אל 413 | בני 1121 |
|---|---|---|---|---|---|---|---|
| uayishbem | yishma'ael | ben | natanyah, | uayelek | la'abor | 'al | baney |
| **and carried them away captive** | **Ishmael** | **the son of** | **Nethaniah** | **and departed** | **to go over** | **to** | **the sons of** |

| עמון 5983: | 41:11 וישמע 8085 | יוחנן 3110 | בן 1121 | קרח 7143 | וכל 3605 | שרי 8269 | החילים 2428 | אשר 834 | אתו 854 |
|---|---|---|---|---|---|---|---|---|---|
| 'amoun. | uayishma' | youchanan | ben | qareach, | uakal | sarey | hachayaliym | 'asher | 'atou; |
| **the Ammonites** | **But when heard** | **Johanan** | **the son of** | **Kareah** | **and all** | **the captains of** | **the forces** | **that *were*** | **with him** |

| את 853 | כל 3605 | הרעה 7451 | אשר 834 | עשה 6213 | ישמעאל 3458 | בן 1121 | נתניה 5418: | 41:12 ויקחו 3947 | את 853 | כל 3605 | האנשים 582 |
|---|---|---|---|---|---|---|---|---|---|---|---|
| 'at | kal | hara'ah | 'asher | 'asah, | yishma'ael | ben | natanyah. | uayiqchu | 'at | kal | ha'anashiym, |
| | ***of* all** | **the evil** | **that** | **had done** | **Ishmael** | **the son of** | **Nethaniah** | **Then they took** | | **all** | **the men** |

| וילכו 1980 | להלחם 3898 | עם 5973 | ישמעאל 3458 | בן 1121 | נתניה 5418 | וימצאו 4672 | אתו 853 | אל 413 | מים 4325 | רבים 7227 | אשר 834 |
|---|---|---|---|---|---|---|---|---|---|---|---|
| uayelaku, | lahilachem | 'am | yishma'ael | ben | natanyah; | uayimtza'au | 'atou, | 'al | mayim | rabiym | 'asher |
| **and went** | **to fight** | **with** | **Ishmael** | **the son of** | **Nethaniah** | **and found** | **him** | **by** | **waters** | ***the* great** | **that** |

| בגבעון 1391: | 41:13 ויהי 1961 | כראות 7200 | כל 3605 | העם 5971 | אשר 834 | את 854 | ישמעאל 3458 | את 853 | יוחנן 3110 |
|---|---|---|---|---|---|---|---|---|---|
| bagib'aun. | uayahiy, | kir'aut | kal | ha'am | 'asher | 'at | yishma'ael, | 'at | youchanan |
| ***are* in Gibeon** | **Now it came to pass *that*** | **when saw** | **all** | **the people** | **which *were*** | ***with*** | **Ishmael** | | **Johanan** |

Jer 41:9 Now the pit wherein Ishmael had cast all the dead bodies of the men, whom he had slain because of Gedaliah, was it which Asa the king had made for fear of Baasha king of Israel: and Ishmael the son of Nethaniah filled it with them that were slain.10 Then Ishmael carried away captive all the residue of the people that were in Mizpah, even the king's daughters, and all the people that remained in Mizpah, whom Nebuzar-adan the captain of the guard had committed to Gedaliah the son of Ahikam: and Ishmael the son of Nethaniah carried them away captive, and departed to go over to the Ammonites.11 But when Johanan the son of Kareah, and all the captains of the forces that were with him, heard of all the evil that Ishmael the son of Nethaniah had done,12 Then they took all the men, and went to fight with Ishmael the son of Nethaniah, and found him by the great waters that are in Gibeon.13 Now it came to pass, that when all the people which were with Ishmael saw Johanan the son of Kareah, and all the captains of the forces that were with him, then they were glad.

41:14
בן 1121 קרח 7143 ואת 853 כל 3605 שרי 8269 החילים 2428 אשר 834 אתו 854 וישמחו 8055: וישבו 5437
ben qareach, ua'at kal sarey hachayaliym 'asher 'atou; uayismachu. uayasobu
**the son of Kareah *and* all the captains of the forces that *were* with him then they were glad So cast about**

כל 3605 העם 5971 אשר 834 שבה 7617 ישמעאל 3458 מן 4480 המצפה 4709 וישבו 7725 וילכו 1980 אל 413 יוחנן 3110
kal ha'am, 'asher shabah yishma'ael min hamitzpah; uayashubu uayelaku, 'al youchanan
**all the people that had carried away captive Ishmael from Mizpah and returned and went unto Johanan**

41:15
בן 1121 קרח 7143: וישמעאל 3458 בן 1121 נתניה 5418 נמלט 4422 בשמנה 8083 אנשים 582 מפני 6440 יוחנן 3110 וילך 1980 אל 413
ben qareach. uayishma'ae'l ben natanyah, nimlat bishmonah 'anashiym, mipaney youchanan; uayelek 'al
**the son of Kareah But Ishmael the son of Nethaniah escaped with eight men from Johanan and went to**

41:16
בני 1121 עמון 5983: ויקח 3947 יוחנן 3110 בן 1121 קרח 7143 וכל 3605 שרי 8269 החילים 2428 אשר 834
baney 'amoun. uayiqach youchanan ben qareach uakal sarey hachayaliym 'asher
**the sons of the Ammonites Then took Johanan the son of Kareah and all the captains of the forces that *were***

אתו 854 את 853 כל 3605 שארית 7611 העם 5971 אשר 834 השיב 7725 מאת 853 ישמעאל 3458 בן 1121 נתניה 5418 מן 4480
'atou, 'at kal sha'aeriyt ha'am 'asher heshiyb me'at yishma'ael ben natanyah min
**with him all the remnant of the people whom he had recovered from Ishmael the son of Nethaniah from**

המצפה 4709 אחר 310 הכה 5221 את 853 גדליה 1436 בן 1121 אחיקם 296 גברים 1397 אנשי 582 המלחמה 4421
hamitzpah, 'achar hikah, 'at gadalyah ben 'achiyqam; gabariym 'anshey hamilchamah,
**Mizpah after *that* he had slain Gedaliah the son of Ahikam *even* mighty the men of war**

41:17
ונשים 802 וטף 2945 וסרסים 5631 אשר 834 השיב 7725 מגבעון 1391: וילכו 1980
uanashiym uatap uasarisiym, 'asher heshiyb migib'aun. uayelaku,
**and the women and the children and the eunuchs whom he had brought again from Gibeon And they departed**

41:18
וישבו 3427 בגרות 1628 כמוהם 3644 אשר 834 אצל 681 בית 1035 לחם 3899 ללכת 1980 לבוא 935 מצרים 4714: מפני 6440
uayeshabu bagerut kimuham 'asher 'aetzel beyt lachem; laleket labou'a mitzrayim. mipaney
**and dwelt in the habitation of Chimham which *is* by Beth lehem to go to enter into Egypt Because of**

הכשדים 3778 כי 3588 יראו 3372 מפניהם 6440 כי 3588 הכה 5221 ישמעאל 3458 בן 1121 נתניה 5418 את 853 גדליהו 1436
hakasdiym, kiy yara'au mipaneyhem; kiy hikah yishma'ael ben natanyah, 'at gadalyahu
**the Chaldeans for they were afraid of them because had slain Ishmael the son of Nethaniah Gedaliah**

בן 1121 אחיקם 296 אשר 834 הפקיד 6485 מלך 4428 בבל 894 בארץ 776:
ben 'achiyqam, 'asher hipqiyd melek babel ba'aretz.
**the son of Ahikam whom made governor the king of Babylon in the land**

**Jer 42:1**
ויגשו 5066 כל 3605 שרי 8269 החילים 2428 ויוחנן 3110 בן 1121 קרח 7143 ויזניה 3153 בן 1121
uayigashu kal sarey hachayaliym, uayouchanan ben qareach, uiyazanyah ben
**Then came near all the captains of the forces and Johanan the son of Kareah and Jezaniah the son of**

42:2
הושעיה 1955 וכל 3605 העם 5971 מקטן 6996 ועד 5704 גדול 1419: ויאמרו 559 אל 413 ירמיהו 3414 הנביא 5030
housha'yah; uakal ha'am miqaton ua'ad gadoul. uaya'maru 'al yirmayahu hanabiy'a,
**Hoshaiah and all the people from the least even unto the greatest And said unto Jeremiah the prophet**

Jer 41:14 So all the people that Ishmael had carried away captive from Mizpah cast about and returned, and went unto Johanan the son of Kareah.15 But Ishmael the son of Nethaniah escaped from Johanan with eight men, and went to the Ammonites.16 Then took Johanan the son of Kareah, and all the captains of the forces that were with him, all the remnant of the people whom he had recovered from Ishmael the son of Nethaniah, from Mizpah, after that he had slain Gedaliah the son of Ahikam, even mighty men of war, and the women, and the children, and the eunuchs, whom he had brought again from Gibeon:17 And they departed, and dwelt in the habitation of Chimham, which is by Bethlehem, to go to enter into Egypt,18 Because of the Chaldeans: for they were afraid of them, because Ishmael the son of Nethaniah had slain Gedaliah the son of Ahikam, whom the king of Babylon made governor in the land. **Jer** 42:1 Then all the captains of the forces, and Johanan the son of Kareah, and Jezaniah the son of Hoshaiah, and all the people from the least even unto the greatest, came near,2 And said unto Jeremiah the prophet, Let, we beseech you, our supplication be accepted before you, and pray for us unto YHUH your G-d, even for all this remnant; (for we are left but a few of many, as your eyes do behold us:)

תפל 5307 נא 4994 תחנתנו 8467 לפניך 6440 והתפלל 6419 בעדנו 1157 אל 413 יהוה 3068 אלהיך 430 בעד 1157
tipal naa' tachinatenu lapaneyka, uahitpalel ba'adenu 'al Yahuah 'aloheyka, ba'ad
**Let be accepted we beseech you our supplication before you and pray for us unto Yahuah your Elohim *even* for**

כל 3605 השארית 7611 הזאת 2063 כי 3588 נשארנו 7604 מעט 4592 מהרבה 7235 כאשר 834 עיניך 5869 ראות 7200 אתנו 853: 42:3 ויגד 5046
kal hasha'aeriyt haza't; kiy nish'arnu ma'at meharbeh, ka'asher 'ayneyka ro'aut 'atanu. uayaged
**all the remnant this for we are left *but* a few of many as your eyes do behold us That may show**

לנו 3807a יהוה 3069 אלהיך 430 את 853 הדרך 1870 אשר 834 נלך 1980 בה 871a ואת 853 הדבר 1697 אשר 834 נעשה 6213: 42:4 ויאמר 559
lanu Yahuah 'aloheyka, 'at haderek 'asher nelek bah; ua'at hadabar 'asher na'aseh. uaya'mer
**us Yahuah your Elohim the way wherein we may walk in *and* the thing that we may do Then said**

אליהם 413 ירמיהו 3414 הנביא 5030 שמעתי 8085 הנני 2005 מתפלל 6419 אל 413 יהוה 3068 אלהיכם 430 כדבריכם 1697
'aleyhem yirmayahu hanabiy'a shama'atiy, hinniy mitpalel 'al Yahuah 'aloheykem kadibreykem;
**unto them Jeremiah the prophet I have heard *you* behold I will pray unto Yahuah your Elohim according to your words**

והיה 1961 כל 3605 הדבר 1697 אשר 834 יענה 6030 יהוה 3068 אתכם 853 אגיד 5046 לכם 3807a לא 3808
uahayah kal hadabar 'asher ya'aneh Yahuah 'atkem 'agiyd lakem, la'
**and it shall come to pass *that* whatsoever thing which shall answer Yahuah you I will declare *it* unto you I not**

אמנע 4513 מכם 4480 דבר 1697: 42:5 והמה 1992 אמרו 559 אל 413 ירמיהו 3414 יהי 1961 יהוה 3068 בנו 871a לעד 5707 אמת 571
'amna' mikem dabar. uahemah 'amaru 'al yirmayahu, yahiy Yahuah ba'nu, la'aed 'amet
**will keep back from you nothing Then they said to Jeremiah be Yahuah between us witness a true**

ונאמן 539 אם 518 לא 3808 ככל 3605 הדבר 1697 אשר 834 ישלחך 7971 יהוה 3068 אלהיך 430 אלינו 413 כן 3651
uane'aman; 'am la' kakal hadabar 'asher yishlachaka Yahuah 'aloheyka 'aleynu ken
**and faithful if not according to all things *for* the which shall send you Yahuah your Elohim to us even**

נעשה 6213: 42:6 אם 518 טוב 2896 ואם 518 רע 7451 בקול 6963 יהוה 3068 אלהינו 430 אשר 834 אנו 580 שלחים 7971 אתך 853
na'aseh. 'am toub ua'am ra', baqoul Yahuah 'aloheynu, 'asher 'anu sholachiym 'atka
**we do Whether *it be* good or whether *it be* evil the voice of Yahuah our Elohim *to* whom we send you**

אליו 413 נשמע 8085 למען 4616 אשר 834 ייטב 3190 לנו 3807a כי 3588 נשמע 8085 בקול 6963 יהוה 3068 אלהינו 430: 42:7
'aelayu nishma'; lama'an 'asher yiytab lanu, kiy nishma', baqoul Yahuah 'aloheynu.
**to him we will obey so that it may be well with us when we obey the voice of Yahuah our Elohim**

ויהי 1961 מקץ 7093 עשרת 6235 ימים 3117 ויהי 1961 דבר 1697 יהוה 3068 אל 413 ירמיהו 3414: 42:8 ויקרא 7121 אל 413
uayahiy miqetz 'aseret yamiym; uayahiy dabar Yahuah 'al yirmayahu. uayiqra', 'al
**And it came to pass after ten days that came the word of Yahuah unto Jeremiah Then called he to**

יוחנן 3110 בן 1121 קרח 7143 ואל 413 כל 3605 שרי 8269 החילים 2428 אשר 834 אתו 854 ולכל 3605 העם 5971
youchanan ben qareach, ua'ael kal sarey hachayaliym 'asher 'atou; ualkal ha'am,
**Johanan the son of Kareah and to all the captains of the forces which *were* with him and all the people**

למקטן 6996 ועד 5704 גדול 1419: 42:9 ויאמר 559 אליהם 413 כה 3541 אמר 559 יהוה 3068 אלהי 430 ישראל 3478 אשר 834
lamiqaton ua'ad gadoul. uaya'mer 'aleyhem, koh 'amar Yahuah 'alohey yisra'ael; 'asher
**from the least even to the greatest And said unto them Thus saith Yahuah the Elohim of Israel whom**

Jer 42:3 That YHUH your G-d may show us the way wherein we may walk, and the thing that we may do.4 Then Jeremiah the prophet said unto them, I have heard you; behold, I will pray unto YHUH your G-d according to your words; and it shall come to pass, that whatsoever thing YHUH shall answer you, I will declare it unto you; I will keep nothing back from you.5 Then they said to Jeremiah, YHUH be a true and faithful witness between us, if we do not even according to all things for the which YHUH your G-d shall send you to us.6 Whether it be good, or whether it be evil, we will obey the voice of YHUH our G-d, to whom we send you; that it may be well with us, when we obey the voice of YHUH our G-d.7 And it came to pass after ten days, that the word of YHUH came unto Jeremiah.8 Then called he Johanan the son of Kareah, and all the captains of the forces which were with him, and all the people from the least even to the greatest,9 And said unto them, Thus saith YHUH, the G-d of Israel, unto whom you sent me to present your supplication before him;

42:10

7971 שלחתם 853 אתי 413 אליו 5307 להפיל 8467 תחנתכם 6440 לפניו: 518 אם 7725 שוב 3427 תשבו 776 בארץ 2063 הזאת

shalachtem 'atiy 'aelayu, lahapiyl tachinatakem lapanayu. 'am shoub teshabu ba'aretz haza't,

**you sent me unto whom to present your supplication before him If still you will abide in land this**

1129 ובניתי 853 אתכם 3808 ולא 2040 אהרס 5193 ונטעתי 853 אתכם 3808 ולא 5428 אתוש 3588 כי 5162 נחמתי 413 אל

uabaniytiy 'atkem uala' 'aharos, uanata'atiy 'atkem uala' 'atoush; kiy nichamatiy 'al

**then will I build you and not pull *you* down and I will plant you and not I shall pluck *you* up for I repent me of**

42:11

7451 הרעה 834 אשר 6213 עשיתי 3807a לכם: 408 אל 3372 תיראו 6440 מפני 4428 מלך 894 בבל 834 אשר 859 אתם 3373 יראים 6440 מפניו

hara'ah, 'asher 'asiytiy lakem. 'al tiyra'au, mipaney melek babel, 'asher 'atem yare'aym mipanayu;

**the evil that I have done unto you not Be afraid of the king of Babylon whom you are afraid of whom**

42:12

408 אל 3372 תיראו 4480 ממנו 5002 נאם 3068 יהוה 3588 כי 854 אתכם 589 אני 3467 להושיע 853 אתכם 5337 ולהציל 853 אתכם 3027 מידו:

'al tiyra'au mimenu na'am Yahuah, kiy 'atakem 'aniy, lahoushiya' 'atkem ualhatziyl 'atkem miyadou.

**not be afraid of him' saith Yahuah for *am* with you I to save you and to deliver you from his hand**

5414 ואתן 3807a לכם 7356 רחמים 7355 ורחם 853 אתכם 7725 והשיב 853 אתכם 413 אל

ua'aten lakem rachamiym uaricham 'atkem; uaheshiyb 'atkem 'al

**And I will show unto you mercies that he may have mercy upon you and cause to return you to**

42:13

127 אדמתכם: 518 ואם 559 אמרים 859 אתם 3808 לא 3427 נשב 776 בארץ 2063 הזאת 1115 לבלתי 8085 שמע 6963 בקול 3068 יהוה

'admatkem. ua'am 'amariym 'atem, la' nesheb ba'aretz haza't; labiltiy shamoa', baqoul Yahuah

**your own land But if say you not We will dwell in land this neither obey the voice of Yahuah**

42:14

430 אלהיכם: 559 לאמר 3808 לא 3588 כי 776 ארץ 4714 מצרים 935 נבוא 834 אשר 3808 לא 7200 נראה 4421 מלחמה

'aloheykem. lea'mor, la' kiy 'aretz mitzrayim nabua', 'asher la' nir'ah milchamah,

**your Elohim Saying No but *into* the land of Egypt we will go where no we shall see war**

42:15

6963 וקול 7782 שופר 3808 לא 8085 נשמע 3899 וללחם 3808 לא 7456 נרעב 8033 ושם 3427 נשב: 6258 ועתה 3651 לכן

uaqoul shoupar la' nishma'; ualalechem la' nir'ab uasham nesheb. ua'atah laken

**the sound of the trumpet nor hear of bread nor have hunger and there will we dwell And now therefore**

8085 שמעו 1697 דבר 3068 יהוה 7611 שארית 3063 יהודה 3541 כה 559 אמר 3068 יהוה 6635 צבאות 430 אלהי 3478 ישראל 518 אם 859 אתם

shim'au dabar Yahuah sha'aeriyt yahudah; koh 'amar Yahuah tzaba'aut 'alohey yisra'ael, 'am 'atem

**hear the word of Yahuah you remnant of Judah Thus saith Yahuah of hosts the Elohim of Israel If you**

42:16

7760 שום 7760 תשמון 6440 פניכם 935 לבא 4714 מצרים 935 ובאתם 1481 לגור 8033 שם: 1961 והיתה

soum tasimun paneykem laba' mitzrayim, uaba'tem lagur sham. uahayatah

**wholly set your faces to enter into Egypt and you go to sojourn there Then it shall come to pass *that***

2719 החרב 834 אשר 859 אתם 3372 יראים 4480 ממנה 8033 שם 5381 תשיג 853 אתכם 776 בארץ 4714 מצרים 7458 והרעב 834 אשר

hachereb, 'asher 'atem yare'aym mimenah, sham tasiyg 'atkem ba'aretz mitzrayim; uahara'ab 'asher

**the sword which you feared from there shall overtake you in the land of Egypt and the famine whereof**

42:17

859 אתם 1672 דאגים 4480 ממנו 8033 שם 1692 ידבק 310 אחריכם 4714 מצרים 8033 ושם 4191 תמתו: 1961 ויהיו

'atem do'agiym mimenu, sham yidbaq 'achareykem mitzrayim uasham tamutu. uayihayu

**you were afraid whereof there shall follow close after you *in* Egypt and there you shall die So shall it be *with***

Jer 42:10 If you will still abide in this land, then will I build you, and not pull you down, and I will plant you, and not pluck you up: for I repent me of the evil that I have done unto you.11 Be not afraid of the king of Babylon, of whom you are afraid; be not afraid of him, saith YHUH: for I am with you to save you, and to deliver you from his hand.12 And I will show mercies unto you, that he may have mercy upon you, and cause you to return to your own land.13 But if you say, We will not dwell in this land, neither obey the voice of YHUH your G-d,14 Saying, No; but we will go into the land of Egypt, where we shall see no war, nor hear the sound of the trumpet, nor have hunger of bread; and there will we dwell:15 And now therefore hear the word of YHUH, you remnant of Judah; Thus saith YHUH of hosts, the G-d of Israel; If you wholly set your faces to enter into Egypt, and go to sojourn there;16 Then it shall come to pass, that the sword, which you feared, shall overtake you there in the land of Egypt, and the famine, whereof you were afraid, shall follow close after you there in Egypt; and there you shall die.17 So shall it be with all the men that set their faces to go into Egypt to sojourn there; they shall die by the sword, by the famine, and by the pestilence: and none of them shall remain or escape from the evil that I will bring upon them.

כל 3605 האנשים 582 אשר 834 שמו 7760 את 853 פניהם 6440 לבוא 935 מצרים 4714 לגור 1481 שם 8033 ימותו 4191 בחרב 2719
kal ha'anashiym, 'asher samu 'at paneyhem labou'a mitzrayim lagur sham, yamutu bachereb
**all the men that set their faces to go into Egypt to sojourn there they shall die by the sword**

ברעב 7458 ובדבר 1698 ולא 3808 יהיה 1961 להם 3807a שריד 8300 ופליט 6412 מפני 6440 הרעה 7451 אשר 834 אני 589 מביא 935
bara'ab uabadaber; uala' yihayeh lahem sariyd uapaliyt, mipaney hara'ah, 'asher 'aniy mebiy'a
**by the famine and by the pestilence and none shall of them remain or escape from the evil that I will bring**

עליהם 5921: 42:18 כי 3588 כה 3541 אמר 559 יהוה 3068 צבאות 6635 אלהי 430 ישראל 3478 כאשר 834 נתך 5413 אפי 639
'aleyhem. kiy koh 'amar Yahuah tzaba'aut 'alohey yisra'ael ka'asher nitak 'apiy
**upon them For thus saith Yahuah of hosts the Elohim of Israel As has been poured forth mine anger**

וחמתי 2534 על 5921 ישבי 3427 ירושלם 3389 כן 3651 תתך 5413 חמתי 2534 עליכם 5921 בבאכם 935
uachamatiy, 'al yoshabey yarushalaim, ken titak chamatiy 'aleykem, babo'akem
**and my fury upon the inhabitants of Jerusalem so shall be poured forth my fury upon you when you shall enter into**

מצרים 4714 והייתם 1961 לאלה 423 ולשמה 8047 ולקללה 7045 ולחרפה 2781 ולא 3808 תראו 7200 עוד 5750
mitzrayim; uihayiytem la'alah ualshamah ualiqlalah ualcherpah, uala' tir'au 'aud,
**Egypt and you shall be an execration and an astonishment and a curse and a reproach and no you shall see more**

את 853 המקום 4725 הזה 2088: 42:19 דבר 1696 יהוה 3068 עליכם 5921 שארית 7611 יהודה 3063 אל 408 תבאו 935 מצרים 4714
'at hamaqoum hazeh. diber Yahuah 'aleykem sha'aeriyt yahudah, 'al tabo'au mitzrayim;
**place this has said Yahuah concerning you O you remnant of Judah not Go you into Egypt**

ידע 3045 תדעו 3045 כי 3588 העידתי 5749 בכם 871a היום 3117: 42:20 כי 3588 התעתים 8582 בנפשותיכם 5315 כי 3588 אתם 859
yadoa' teda'au, kiy ha'adotiy bakem hayoum. kiy hit'ateiym banapshouteykem kiy 'atem
**know certainly that I have admonished you this day For you dissembled in your hearts when you**

שלחתם 7971 אתי 853 אל 413 יהוה 3068 אלהיכם 430 לאמר 559 התפלל 6419 בעדנו 1157 אל 413 יהוה 3068 אלהינו 430 וככל 3605
shalachtem 'atiy, 'al Yahuah 'aloheykem lea'mor, hitpalel ba'adenu, 'al Yahuah 'aloheynu; uakkol
**sent me unto Yahuah your Elohim saying Pray for us unto Yahuah our Elohim and according unto all**

אשר 834 יאמר 559 יהוה 3068 אלהינו 430 כן 3651 הגד 5046 לנו 3807a ועשינו 6213: 42:21 ואגד 5046 לכם 3807a
'asher ya'mar Yahuah 'aloheynu ken haged lanu ua'asiynu. ua'agid lakem
**that shall say Yahuah our Elohim so declare unto us and we will do *it* And *now* I have declared *it* to you**

היום 3117 ולא 3808 שמעתם 8085 בקול 6963 יהוה 3068 אלהיכם 430 ולכל 3605 אשר 834 שלחני 7971
hayoum; uala' shama'tem, baqoul Yahuah 'aloheykem, ualkal 'asher shalachaniy
**this day but not you have obeyed the voice of Yahuah your Elohim nor any *thing* for the which he has sent me**

אליכם 413: 42:22 ועתה 6258 ידע 3045 תדעו 3045 כי 3588 בחרב 2719 ברעב 7458 ובדבר 1698 תמותו 4191
'aleykem. ua'atah yadoa' teda'au, kiy, bachereb bara'ab uabadber tamutu;
**unto you Now therefore know certainly that by the sword by the famine and by the pestilence you shall die**

במקום 4725 אשר 834 חפצתם 2654 לבוא 935 לגור 1481 שם 8033:
bamaqoum 'asher chapatzatem, labou'a lagur sham.
**in the place where you desire to go *and* to sojourn there**

Jer 42:18 For thus saith YHUH of hosts, the G-d of Israel; As mine anger and my fury has been poured forth upon the inhabitants of Jerusalem; so shall my fury be poured forth upon you, when you shall enter into Egypt: and you shall be an execration, and an astonishment, and a curse, and a reproach; and you shall see this place no more.19 YHUH has said concerning you, O you remnant of Judah; Go you not into Egypt: know certainly that I have admonished you this day.20 For you dissembled in your hearts, when you sent me unto YHUH your G-d, saying, Pray for us unto YHUH our G-d; and according unto all that YHUH our G-d shall say, so declare unto us, and we will do it.21 And now I have this day declared it to you; but you have not obeyed the voice of YHUH your G-d, nor anything for the which he has sent me unto you.22 Now therefore know certainly that you shall die by the sword, by the famine, and by the pestilence, in the place whither you desire to go and to sojourn.

**Jer 43:1** ויהי 1961 ככלות 3615 ירמיהו 3414 לדבר 1696 אל 413 כל 3605 העם 5971 את 853 כל 3605
uayahiy kakalout yirmayahu ladaber 'al kal ha'am, 'at kal
**And it came to pass *that* when had made an end Jeremiah of speaking unto all the people all**

דברי 1697 יהוה 3068 אלהיהם 430 אשר 834 שלחו 7971 יהוה 3068 אלהיהם 430 אליהם 413 את 853 כל 3605 הדברים 1697
dibrey Yahuah 'aloheyhem, 'asher shalachou Yahuah 'aloheyhem 'aleyhem; 'at kal hadabariym
**the words of Yahuah their Elohim *for* which had sent him Yahuah their Elohim to them *even* all words**

האלה 428: **43:2** ויאמר 559 עזריה 5838 בן 1121 הושעיה 1955 ויוחנן 3110 בן 1121 קרח 7143 וכל 3605 האנשים 582 הזדים 2086
ha'aeleh. uaya'mer 'azaryah ben housha'yah uayouchanan ben qareach, uakal ha'anashiym hazediym;
**these Then spoke Azariah the son of Hoshaiah and Johanan the son of Kareah and all the men proud**

אמרים 559 אל 413 ירמיהו 3414 שקר 8267 אתה 859 מדבר 1696 לא 3808 שלחך 7971 יהוה 3068 אלהינו 430 לאמר 559 לא 3808 תבאו 935 מצרים 4714
'amariym 'al yirmayahu, sheqer 'atah madaber, la' shalachaka Yahuah 'aloheynu lea'mor, la' tabo'au mitzrayim
**saying unto Jeremiah falsely You speak not has sent you Yahuah our Elohim to say not Go into Egypt**

לגור 1481 שם 8033: **43:3** כי 3588 ברוך 1263 בן 1121 נריה 5374 מסית 5496 אתך 853 בנו 871a למען 4616 תת 5414 אתנו 853
lagur sham. kiy, baruk ben neriyah, masiyt 'atka ba'nu; lama'an tet 'atanu
**to sojourn there But Baruch the son of Neriah set on you against us for to deliver us**

ביד 3027 הכשדים 3778 להמית 4191 אתנו 853 ולהגלות 1540 אתנו 853 בבל 894: **43:4**
bayad hakasdiym lahamiyt 'atanu, ualhaglout 'atanu babel.
**into the hand of the Chaldeans that they might put us to death us and carry away captives into us Babylon**

ולא 3808 שמע 8085 יוחנן 3110 בן 1121 קרח 7143 וכל 3605 שרי 8269 החילים 2428 וכל 3605 העם 5971 בקול 6963 יהוה 3068
uala' shama' youchanan ben qareach uakal sarey hachayaliym uakal ha'am baqoul Yahuah;
**So not obeyed Johanan the son of Kareah and all the captains of the forces and all the people the voice of Yahuah**

לשבת 3427 בארץ 776 יהודה 3063: **43:5** ויקח 3947 יוחנן 3110 בן 1121 קרח 7143 וכל 3605 שרי 8269 החילים 2428 את 853 כל 3605
lashabet ba'aretz yahudah. uayiqach youchanan ben qareach uakal sarey hachayaliym, 'at kal
**to dwell in the land of Judah But took Johanan the son of Kareah and all the captains of the forces all**

שארית 7611 יהודה 3063 אשר 834 שבו 7725 מכל 3605 הגוים 1471 אשר 834 נדחו 5080 שם 8033 לגור 1481
sha'aeriyt yahudah; 'asher shabu, mikal hagouyim 'asher nidachu sham, lagur
**the remnant of Judah that were returned from all nations where they had been driven there to dwell**

בארץ 776 יהודה 3063: **43:6** את 853 הגברים 1397 ואת 853 הנשים 802 ואת 853 הטף 2945 ואת 853 בנות 1323 המלך 4428 ואת 853 כל 3605
ba'aretz yahudah. 'at hagabariym ua'at hanashiym ua'at hatap ua'at banout hamelek ua'at kal
**in the land of Judah *Even* men *and* women *and* children *and* daughters the king's *and* every**

הנפש 5315 אשר 834 הניח 3240 נבוזראדן 5018 רב 7227 טבחים 2876 את 854 גדליהו 1436 בן 1121 אחיקם 296 בן 1121 שפן 8227
hanepesh, 'asher hiniyach nabuzar'adan rab tabachiym, 'at gadalyahu ben 'achiyqam ben shapan;
**person that had left Nebuzaradan the captain of the guard *with* Gedaliah the son of Ahikam *the* son of Shaphan**

ואת 853 ירמיהו 3414 הנביא 5030 ואת 853 ברוך 1263 בן 1121 נריהו 5374: **43:7** ויבאו 935 ארץ 776 מצרים 4714 כי 3588 לא 3808
ua'at yirmayahu hanabiy'a, ua'at baruk ben neriyahu. uayabo'au 'aretz mitzrayim, kiy la'
***and* Jeremiah the prophet *and* Baruch *the* son of Neriah So they came into the land of Egypt for not**

**Jer** 43:1 And it came to pass, that when Jeremiah had made an end of speaking unto all the people all the words of YHUH their G-d, for which YHUH their G-d had sent him to them, even all these words,2 Then spoke Azariah the son of Hoshaiah, and Johanan the son of Kareah, and all the proud men, saying unto Jeremiah, Thou speak falsely: YHUH our G-d has not sent you to say, Go not into Egypt to sojourn there:3 But Baruch the son of Neriah set you on against us, for to deliver us into the hand of the Chaldeans, that they might put us to death, and carry us away captives into Babylon.4 So Johanan the son of Kareah, and all the captains of the forces, and all the people, obeyed not the voice of YHUH, to dwell in the land of Judah.5 But Johanan the son of Kareah, and all the captains of the forces, took all the remnant of Judah, that were returned from all nations, whither they had been driven, to dwell in the land of Judah;6 Even men, and women, and children, and the king's daughters, and every person that Nebuzar-adan the captain of the guard had left with Gedaliah the son of Ahikam the son of Shaphan, and Jeremiah the prophet, and Baruch the son of Neriah.7 So they came into the land of Egypt: for they obeyed not the voice of YHUH: thus came they even to Tahpanhes.

שמעו 8085 בקול 6963 יהוה 3068 ויבאו 935 עד 5704 תחפנחס 8471: **43:8** ויהי 1961 דבר 1697 יהוה 3068 אל 413
shama'au baqoul Yahuah; uayabo'au 'ad tachpanches. uayahiy dabar Yahuah 'al
**they obeyed the voice of Yahuah thus came they *even* to Tahpanhes Then came the word of Yahuah unto**

ירמיהו 3414 בתחפנחס 8471 לאמר 559: **43:9** קח 3947 בידך 3027 אבנים 68 גדלות 1419 וטמנתם 2934 במלט 4423 במלבן 4404
yirmayahu, batachpanches lea'mor. qach bayadaka 'abaniym gadolout, uatmantam bamelet bamalben,
**Jeremiah in Tahpanhes saying Take in your hand stones great and hide them in the clay in the brickkiln**

אשר 834 בפתח 6607 בית 1004 פרעה 6547 בתחפנחס 8471 לעיני 5869 אנשים 582 יהודים 3064: **43:10** ואמרת 559 אליהם 413
'asher bapetach beyt par'ah batachpanches; la'aeyney 'anashiym yahudiym. ua'amarta 'aleyhem
**which *is* at the entry of house Pharaoh's in Tahpanhes in the sight of the men of Judah And say unto them**

כה 3541 אמר 559 יהוה 3068 צבאות 6635 אלהי 430 ישראל 3478 הנני 2005 שלח 7971 ולקחתי 3947 את 853 נבוכדראצר 5019 מלך 4428
koh 'amar Yahuah tzaba'aut 'alohey yisra'ael, hinniy sholeach ualaqachtiy 'at nabukadra'tzar melek
**Thus saith Yahuah of hosts the Elohim of Israel Behold I will send and take Nebuchadrezzar the king of**

בבל 894 עבדי 5650 ושמתי 7760 כסאו 3678 ממעל 4605 לאבנים 68 האלה 428 אשר 834 טמנתי 2934 ונטה 5186 את 853
babel 'abdiy, uasamtiy kis'au, mima'al la'abaniym ha'aeleh 'asher tamanatiy; uanatah 'at
**Babylon my servant and will set his throne upon stones these that I have hid and he shall spread**

שפרורו 8237 עליהם 5921: **43:11** ובאה 935 והכה 5221 את 853 ארץ 776 מצרים 4714 אשר 834
shaprurou 'aleyhem. uaba'ah uahikah 'at 'aretz mitzrayim; 'asher
**his royal pavilion over them when he comes And he shall smite the land of Egypt *and deliver* such**

למות 4194 למות 4194 ואשר 834 לשבי 7628 לשבי 7628 ואשר 834 לחרב 2719 לחרב 2719: **43:12**
lamauet lamauet, ua'asher lashbiy lashebiy, ua'asher lachereb lechareb.
***as are* for death to death and such *as are* for captivity to captivity and such *as are* for the sword to the sword**

והצתי 3341 אש 784 בבתי 1004 אלהי 430 מצרים 4714 ושרפם 8313 ושבם 7617
uahitzatiy 'aesh, babatey 'alohey mitzrayim, uasrapam uashabam;
**And I will kindle a fire in the houses of the gods of Egypt and he shall burn them and carry them away captives**

ועטה 5844 את 854 ארץ 776 מצרים 4714 כאשר 834 יעטה 5844 הרעה 7462 את 853 בגדו 899 ויצא 3318
ua'atah 'at 'aretz mitzrayim ka'asher ya'ateh hara'ah 'at bigdou, uayatza'
**and he shall array himself *with* the land of Egypt as put on a shepherd his garment and he shall go forth**

משם 8033 בשלום 7965: **43:13** ושבר 7665 את 853 מצבות 4676 בית 1053 שמש 8121 אשר 834 בארץ 776 מצרים 4714
misham bashaloum. uashibar, 'at matzabout beyt shemesh, 'asher ba'aretz mitzrayim;
**from there in peace He shall break also the images of Beth shemesh that *is* in the land of Egypt**

ואת 853 בתי 1004 אלהי 430 מצרים 4714 ישרף 8313 באש 784:
ua'at batey 'alohey mitzrayim yisrop ba'aesh.
***and* the houses of the gods of the Egyptians shall he burn with fire**

**Jer 44:1** הדבר 1697 אשר 834 היה 1961 אל 413 ירמיהו 3414 אל 413 כל 3605 היהודים 3064 הישבים 3427 בארץ 776 מצרים 4714
hadabar 'asher hayah 'al yirmayahu, 'al kal hayahudiym, hayoshbiym ba'aretz mitzrayim;
**The word that came to Jeremiah concerning all the Jews which dwell in the land of Egypt**

Jer 43:8 Then came the word of YHUH unto Jeremiah in Tahpanhes, saying,9 Take great stones in your hand, and hide them in the clay in the brickkiln, which is at the entry of Pharaoh's house in Tahpanhes, in the sight of the men of Judah;10 And say unto them, Thus saith YHUH of hosts, the G-d of Israel; Behold, I will send and take Nebuchadrezzar the king of Babylon, my servant, and will set his throne upon these stones that I have hid; and he shall spread his royal pavilion over them.11 And when he cometh, he shall smite the land of Egypt, and deliver such as are for death to death; and such as are for captivity to captivity; and such as are for the sword to the sword.12 And I will kindle a fire in the houses of the gods of Egypt; and he shall burn them, and carry them away captives: and he shall array himself with the land of Egypt, as a shepherd put on his garment; and he shall go forth from thence in peace.13 He shall break also the images of Beth-shemesh, that is in the land of Egypt; and the houses of the gods of the Egyptians shall he burn with fire. **Jer** 44:1 The word that came to Jeremiah concerning all the Jews which dwell in the land of Egypt, which dwell at Migdol, and at Tahpanhes, and at Noph, and in the country of Pathros, saying,

הישבים 3427 במגדל 4024 ובתחפנחס 8471 ובנף 5297 ובארץ 776 פתרוס 6624 לאמר 559: **44:2** כה 3541 אמר 559 יהוה 3068
hayoshbiym bamigdol uabtachpanches uabnop, uab'aretz patrous lea'mor. koh 'amar Yahuah
**which dwell at Migdol and at Tahpanhes and at Noph and in the country of Pathros saying Thus saith Yahuah**

צבאות 6635 אלהי 430 ישראל 3478 אתם 859 ראיתם 7200 את 853 כל 3605 הרעה 7451 אשר 834 הבאתי 935 על 5921 ירושלם 3389
tzaba'aut 'alohey yisra'ael, 'atem ra'aytem, 'at kal hara'ah 'asher hebea'tiy 'al yarushalaim,
**of hosts the Elohim of Israel You have seen all the evil that I have brought upon Jerusalem**

ועל 5921 כל 3605 ערי 5892 יהודה 3063 והנם 2005 חרבה 2723 היום 3117 הזה 2088 ואין 369 בהם 871a יושב 3427: **44:3**
ua'al kal 'arey yahudah; uahinam charabah hayoum hazeh, ua'aeyn bahem yousheb.
**and upon all the cities of Judah and behold they *are* a desolation day this and no therein *man* dwell**

מפני 6440 רעתם 7451 אשר 834 עשו 6213 להכעסני 3707 ללכת 1980 לקטר 6999
mipaney ra'atam, 'asher 'asu lahak'ayseniy, laleket laqater,
**Because of their wickedness which they have committed to provoke me to anger in that they went to burn incense**

לעבד 5647 לאלהים 430 אחרים 312 אשר 834 לא 3808 ידעום 3045 המה 1992 אתם 859 ואבתיכם 1: **44:4** ואשלח 7971
la'abod le'alohiym 'acheriym; 'asher la' yada'aum, hemah 'atem ua'aboteykem. ua'ashlach
***and* to serve to gods other whom not they knew *neither* they you nor your fathers Howbeit I sent**

אליכם 413 את 853 כל 3605 עבדי 5650 הנביאים 5030 השכים 7925 ושלח 7971 לאמר 559 אל 408 נא 4994 תעשו 6213 את 853 דבר 1697
'aleykem 'at kal 'abaday hanabiy'aym, hashkeym uashaloach lea'mor; 'al naa' ta'asu, 'at dabar
**unto you all my servants the prophets rising early and sending *them* saying not Oh do thing**

התעבה 8441 הזאת 2063 אשר 834 שנאתי 8130: **44:5** ולא 3808 שמעו 8085 ולא 3808 הטו 5186 את 853 אזנם 241 לשוב 7725
hato'aebah haza't 'asher sanea'tiy. uala' shama'au uala' hitu 'at 'azanam, lashub
**abominable this that I hate But not they hearkened nor inclined their ear to turn**

מרעתם 7451 לבלתי 1115 קטר 6999 לאלהים 430 אחרים 312: **44:6** ותתך 5413 חמתי 2534
mera'atam; labiltiy qater le'alohiym 'acheriym. uatitak chamatiy
**from their wickedness to no burn incense unto gods other Wherefore was poured forth my fury**

ואפי 639 ותבער 1197 בערי 5892 יהודה 3063 ובחצות 2351 ירושלם 3389 ותהיינה 1961 לחרבה 2723
ua'apiy, uatib'ar ba'arey yahudah, uabchutzout yarushalaim; uatihayeynah lacharabah
**and mine anger and was kindled in the cities of Judah and in the streets of Jerusalem and they are wasted**

לשממה 8077 כיום 3117 הזה 2088: **44:7** ועתה 6258 כה 3541 אמר 559 יהוה 3068 אלהי 430 צבאות 6635 אלהי 430 ישראל 3478
lishmamah kayoum hazeh. ua'atah koh 'amar Yahuah 'alohey tzaba'aut 'alohey yisra'ael,
***and* desolate as day *at* this Therefore now thus saith Yahuah the Elohim of hosts the Elohim of Israel**

למה 4100 אתם 859 עשים 6213 רעה 7451 גדולה 1419 אל 413 נפשתכם 5315 להכרית 3772 לכם 3807a איש 376 ואשה 802 עולל 5768
lamah 'atem 'asiym ra'ah gadoulah 'al napshotekem, lahakriyt lakem 'aysh ua'ashah 'aulel
**Wherefore you commit evil *this* great against your souls to cut off from you man and woman child**

ויונק 3243 מתוך 8432 יהודה 3063 לבלתי 1115 הותיר 3498 לכם 3807a שארית 7611: **44:8** להכעסני 3707
uayouneq mitouk yahudah; labiltiy houtiyr lakem sha'aeriyt. lahak'ayseniy
**and suckling out of Judah to none leave to you to remain In that you provoke me unto wrath**

Jer 44:2 Thus saith YHUH of hosts, the G-d of Israel; You have seen all the evil that I have brought upon Jerusalem, and upon all the cities of Judah; and, behold, this day they are a desolation, and no man dwell therein,3 Because of their wickedness which they have committed to provoke me to anger, in that they went to burn incense, and to serve other gods, whom they knew not, neither they, you, nor your fathers.4 Howbeit I sent unto you all my servants the prophets, rising early and sending them, saying, Oh, do not this abominable thing that I hate.5 But they hearkened not, nor inclined their ear to turn from their wickedness, to burn no incense unto other gods.6 Wherefore my fury and mine anger was poured forth, and was kindled in the cities of Judah and in the streets of Jerusalem; and they are wasted and desolate, as at this day.7 Therefore now this saith YHUH, the G-d of hosts, the G-d of Israel; Wherefore commit you this great evil against your souls, to cut off from you man and woman, child and suckling, out of Judah, to leave you none to remain;8 In that you provoke me unto wrath with the works of your hands, burning incense unto other gods in the land of Egypt, whither you be gone to dwell, that you might cut yourselves off, and that you might be a curse and a reproach among all the nations of the earth?

| במעשי 4639 | ידיכם 3027 | לקטר 6999 | לאלהים 430 | אחרים 312 | בארץ 776 | מצרים 4714 | אשר 834 | אתם 859 | באים 935 | לגור 1481 |
|---|---|---|---|---|---|---|---|---|---|---|
| bam'asey | yadeykem, | laqater | le'alohiym | 'acheriym | ba'aretz | mitzrayim, | 'asher | 'atem | ba'aym | lagur |
| **with the works of** | **your hands** | **burning incense** | **unto gods** | **other** | **in the land of** | **Egypt** | **where** | **you** | **be gone** | **to dwell** |

| שם 8033 | למען 4616 | הכרית 3772 | לכם 3807a | ולמען 4616 | היותכם 1961 | לקללה 7045 | ולחרפה 2781 | בכל 3605 | גויי 1471 |
|---|---|---|---|---|---|---|---|---|---|
| sham; | lama'an | hakriyt | lakem, | ualma'an | hayoutakem | liqlalah | ualcherpah, | bakal | gouyey |
| **there** | **that** | **you might cut off** | **to yourselves** | **and that** | **you might be** | **a curse** | **and a reproach** | **among all** | **the nations of** |

| הארץ 776: | 44:9 | השכחתם 7911 | את 853 | רעות 7451 | אבותיכם 1 | ואת 853 | רעות 7451 | מלכי 4428 | יהודה 3063 |
|---|---|---|---|---|---|---|---|---|---|
| ha'aretz. | | hashakachtem | 'at | ra'aut | abouteykem | ua'at | ra'aut | malkey | yahudah, |
| **the earth?** | | **Have you forgotten** | | **the wickedness of** | **your fathers** | ***and*** | **the wickedness of** | **the kings of** | **Judah** |

| ואת 853 | רעות 7451 | נשיו 802 | ואת 853 | רעתכם 7451 | ואת 853 | רעת 7451 | נשיכם 802 | אשר 834 |
|---|---|---|---|---|---|---|---|---|
| ua'at | ra'aut | nashayu, | ua'at | ra'atekem, | ua'at | ra'at | nasheykem; | 'asher |
| ***and*** | **the wickedness of** | **their wives** | ***and*** | **your own wickedness** | ***and*** | **the wickedness of** | **your wives** | **which** |

| עשו 6213 | בארץ 776 | יהודה 3063 | ובחצות 2351 | ירושלם 3389: | 44:10 | לא 3808 | דכאו 1792 | עד 5704 |
|---|---|---|---|---|---|---|---|---|
| 'asu | ba'aretz | yahudah, | uabchutzout | yarushalaim. | | la' | duka'au, | 'ad |
| **they have committed** | **in the land of** | **Judah** | **and in the streets of** | **Jerusalem?** | | **not** | **They are humbled *even*** | **unto** |

| היום 3117 | הזה 2088 | ולא 3808 | יראו 3372 | ולא 3808 | הלכו 1980 | בתורתי 8451 | ובחקתי 2708 | אשר 834 | נתתי 5414 | לפניכם 6440 | ולפני 6440 |
|---|---|---|---|---|---|---|---|---|---|---|---|
| hayoum | hazeh; | uala' | yara'au, | uala' | halaku | batouratiy | uabchuqotay, | 'asher | natatiy | lipneykem | ualipaney |
| **day** | **this** | **neither** | **have they feared** | **nor** | **walked** | **in my law** | **nor in my statutes** | **that** | **I set** | **before you** | **and before** |

| אבותיכם 1: | 44:11 | לכן 3651 | כה 3541 | אמר 559 | יהוה 3068 | צבאות 6635 | אלהי 430 | ישראל 3478 | הנני 2005 | שם 7760 | פני 6440 | בכם 871a |
|---|---|---|---|---|---|---|---|---|---|---|---|---|
| abouteykem. | | laken, | koh | 'amar | Yahuah | tzaba'aut | 'alohey | yisra'ael, | hinniy | sam | panay | bakem |
| **your fathers** | | **Therefore** | **thus** | **saith** | **Yahuah** | **of hosts** | **the Elohim of** | **Israel** | **Behold I** | **will set** | **my face** | **against you** |

| לרעה 7451 | ולהכרית 3772 | את 853 | כל 3605 | יהודה 3063: | 44:12 | ולקחתי 3947 | את 853 | שארית 7611 | יהודה 3063 | אשר 834 | שמו 7760 | פניהם 6440 |
|---|---|---|---|---|---|---|---|---|---|---|---|---|
| lara'ah; | ualhakriyt | 'at | kal | yahudah. | | ualaqachtiy | 'at | sha'aeriyt | yahudah, | 'asher | samu | paneyhem |
| **for evil** | **and to cut off** | | **all** | **Judah** | | **And I will take** | | **the remnant of** | **Judah** | **that** | **have set** | **their faces** |

| לבוא 935 | ארץ 776 | מצרים 4714 | לגור 1481 | שם 8033 | ותמו 8552 | כל 3605 | בארץ 776 | מצרים 4714 | יפלו 5307 |
|---|---|---|---|---|---|---|---|---|---|
| labou'a | 'aretz | mitzrayim | lagur | sham | uatamu | kal | ba'aretz | mitzrayim | yipolu, |
| **to go into** | **the land of** | **Egypt** | **to sojourn** | **there** | **and they shall be consumed** | **all** | **in the land of** | **Egypt** | ***and* fall** |

| בחרב 2719 | ברעב 7458 | יתמו 8552 | מקטן 6996 | ועד 5704 | גדול 1419 | בחרב 2719 |
|---|---|---|---|---|---|---|
| bachereb | bara'ab | yitamu, | miqaton | ua'ad | gadoul, | bachereb |
| **by the sword** | ***and* by the famine** | **they shall *even* be consumed** | **from the least** | **even unto** | **the greatest** | **by the sword** |

| וברעב 7458 | ימתו 4191 | והיו 1961 | לאלה 423 | לשמה 8047 | ולקללה 7045 | ולחרפה 2781: | 44:13 |
|---|---|---|---|---|---|---|---|
| uabara'ab | yamutu; | uahayu | la'alah | lashamah, | ualiqlalah | ualcherpah. | |
| **and by the famine** | **they shall die** | **and they shall be** | **an execration** | ***and* an astonishment** | **and a curse** | **and a reproach** | |

| ופקדתי 6485 | על 5921 | היושבים 3427 | בארץ 776 | מצרים 4714 | כאשר 834 | פקדתי 6485 | על 5921 | ירושלם 3389 |
|---|---|---|---|---|---|---|---|---|
| uapaqadtiy, | 'al | hayoushabiym | ba'aretz | mitzrayim, | ka'asher | paqadtiy | 'al | yarushalaim; |
| **For I will punish them** | **that** | **dwell** | **in the land of** | **Egypt** | **as** | **I have punished** | **on** | **Jerusalem** |

Jer 44:9 Have you forgotten the wickedness of your fathers, and the wickedness of the kings of Judah, and the wickedness of their wives, and your own wickedness, and the wickedness of your wives, which they have committed in the land of Judah, and in the streets of Jerusalem?10 They are not humbled even unto this day, neither have they feared, nor walked in my law, nor in my statutes, that I set before you and before your fathers.11 Therefore thus saith YHUH of hosts, the G-d of Israel; Behold, I will set my face against you for evil, and to cut off all Judah.12 And I will take the remnant of Judah, that have set their faces to go into the land of Egypt to sojourn there, and they shall all be consumed, and fall in the land of Egypt; they shall even be consumed by the sword and by the famine: they shall die, from the least even unto the greatest, by the sword and by the famine: and they shall be an execration, and an astonishment, and a curse, and a reproach.13 For I will punish them that dwell in the land of Egypt, as I have punished Jerusalem, by the sword, by the famine, and by the pestilence:

בחרב 2719 ברעב 7458 ובדבר 1698: 44:14 ולא 3808 יהיה 1961 פליט 6412 ושריד 8300 לשארית 7611 יהודה 3063
bachereb bara'ab uabadaber. uala' yihayeh paliyt uasariyd lish'aeriyt yahudah,
**by the sword by the famine and by the pestilence So that none shall escape or remain of the remnant of Judah**

הבאים 935 לגור 1481 שם 8033 בארץ 776 מצרים 4714 ולשוב 7725 ארץ 776 יהודה 3063 אשר 834
haba'aym lagur sham ba'aretz mitzrayim; ualashub 'aretz yahudah, 'asher
**which are gone to sojourn there into the land of Egypt that they should return into the land of Judah *to the* which**

המה 1992 מנשאים 5375 את 853 נפשם 5315 לשוב 7725 לשבת 3427 שם 8033 כי 3588 לא 3808 ישובו 7725 כי 3588 אם 518 פלטים 6412: 44:15
hemah manas'aym 'at napsham lashub lashabet sham, kiy la' yashubu kiy 'am paletiym.
**they have a desire of them to return to dwell there for none shall return but such as shall escape**

ויענו 6030 את 853 ירמיהו 3414 כל 3605 האנשים 582 הידעים 3045 כי 3588 מקטרות 6999 נשיהם 802 לאלהים 430 אחרים 312
uaya'anu 'at yirmayahu, kal ha'anashiym hayoda'aym kiy maqatrout nasheyhem le'alohiym 'acheriym,
**Then answered Jeremiah all the men which knew that had burned incense their wives unto gods other**

וכל 3605 הנשים 802 העמדות 5975 קהל 6951 גדול 1419 וכל 3605 העם 5971 הישבים 3427 בארץ 776 מצרים 4714 בפתרוס 6624
uakal hanashiym ha'amadout qahal gadoul; uakal ha'am hayoshbiym ba'aretz mitzrayim bapatrous
**and all the women that stood by a multitude great even all the people that dwelt in the land of Egypt in Pathros**

לאמר 559: 44:16 הדבר 1697 אשר 834 דברת 1696 אלינו 413 בשם 8034 יהוה 3068 איננו 369 שמעים 8085
lea'mor. hadabar 'asher dibarta 'aleynu bashem Yahuah; 'aeynenu shoma'aym
**saying *As for* the word that you have spoken unto us in the name of Yahuah not we will listen**

אליך 413: 44:17 כי 3588 עשה 6213 נעשה 6213 את 853 כל 3605 הדבר 1697 אשר 834 יצא 3318 מפינו 6310
'aeleyka. kiy 'asoh na'aseh 'at kal hadabar 'asher yatza' mipiynu,
**unto you But we will certainly do whatsoever thing that goes forth out of our own mouth**

לקטר 6999 למלכת 4446 השמים 8064 והסיך 5258 לה 3807a נסכים 5262 כאשר 834 עשינו 6213 אנחנו 587
laqater limaleket hashamayim uahaseyk lah nasakiym ka'asher 'asiynu 'anachnu
**to burn incense unto the queen of heaven and to pour out unto her drink offerings as we have done we**

ואבתינו 1 מלכינו 4428 ושרינו 8269 בערי 5892 יהודה 3063 ובחצות 2351 ירושלם 3389
ua'aboteynu malakeynu uasareynu, ba'arey yahudah, uabchutzout yarushalaim;
**and our fathers our kings and our princes in the cities of Judah and in the streets of Jerusalem**

ונשבע 7646 לחם 3899 ונהיה 1961 טובים 2896 ורעה 7451 לא 3808 ראינו 7200: 44:18 ומן 4480 אז 227 חדלנו 2308 לקטר 6999
uanisba' lechem uanihayeh toubiym, uara'ah la' ra'aynu. uamin 'az chadalnu laqater
**for *then* had we plenty of victuals and were well and evil no saw But since we left off to burn incense**

למלכת 4446 השמים 8064 והסך 5258 לה 3807a נסכים 5262 חסרנו 2637 כל 3605 ובחרב 2719
limaleket hashamayim uahasek lah nasakiym chasarnu kol; uabachereb
**to the queen of heaven and to pour out unto her drink offerings we have wanted all *things* and by the sword**

וברעב 7458 תמנו 8552: 44:19 וכי 3588 אנחנו 587 מקטרים 6999 למלכת 4446 השמים 8064
uabara'ab tamanu. uakiy 'anachnu maqatriym limaleket hashamayim,
**and by the famine have been consumed And when we burned incense to the queen of heaven**

Jer 44:14 So that none of the remnant of Judah, which are gone into the land of Egypt to sojourn there, shall escape or remain, that they should return into the land of Judah, to the which they have a desire to return to dwell there: for none shall return but such as shall escape.15 Then all the men which knew that their wives had burned incense unto other gods, and all the women that stood by, a great multitude, even all the people that dwelt in the land of Egypt, in Pathros, answered Jeremiah, saying,16 As for the word that you have spoken unto us in the name of YHUH, we will not hear unto you.17 But we will certainly do whatsoever thing go forth out of our own mouth, to burn incense unto the queen of heaven, and to pour out drink offerings unto her, as we have done, we, and our fathers, our kings, and our princes, in the cities of Judah, and in the streets of Jerusalem: for then had we plenty of victuals, and were well, and saw no evil.18 But since we left off to burn incense to the queen of heaven, and to pour out drink offerings unto her, we have wanted all things, and have been consumed by the sword and by the famine.19 And when we burned incense to the queen of heaven, and poured out drink offerings unto her, did we make her cakes to worship her, and pour out drink offerings unto her, without our men?

ולהסך 5258 לה 3807a נסכים 5262 המבלעדי 1107 אנשינו 582 עשינו 6213 לה 3807a כונים 3561 להעצבה 6087
ualahasek lah nasakiym; hamibal'adey 'anasheynu, 'asiynu lah kauaniym laha'atzibah,
**and poured out unto her drink offerings without our men? did we make her cakes to worship her**

והסך 5258 לה 3807a נסכים 5262: 44:20 ויאמר 559 ירמיהו 3414 אל 413 כל 3605 העם 5971 על 5921 הגברים 1397 ועל 5921
uahasek lah nasakiym. uaya'mer yirmayahu 'al kal ha'am; 'al hagabariym ua'al
**and pour out unto her drink offerings Then said Jeremiah unto all the people to the men and to**

הנשים 802 ועל 5921 כל 3605 העם 5971 הענים 6030 אתו 853 דבר 1697 לאמר 559: 44:21 הלוא 3808 את 853 הקטר 6999 אשר 834
hanashiym ua'al kal ha'am, ha'aniym 'atou dabar lea'mor. halou'a 'at haqiter, 'asher
**the women and to all the people which were given him *that* answer saying not you burned that**

קטרתם 7002 בערי 5892 יהודה 3063 ובחצות 2351 ירושלם 3389 אתם 859 ואבותיכם 1 מלכיכם 4428 ושריכם 8269
qitartem ba'arey yahudah uabchutzout yarushalaim, 'atem ua'abouteykem malkeykem uasareykem
**The incense in the cities of Judah and in the streets of Jerusalem you and your fathers your kings and your princes**

ועם 5971 הארץ 776 אתם 853 זכר 2142 יהוה 3068 ותעלה 5927 על 5921 לבו 3820: 44:22 ולא 3808 יוכל 3201 יהוה 3068
ua'am ha'aretz; 'atam zakar Yahuah, uata'aleh 'al libou. uala' yukal Yahuah
**and the people of the land them did remember Yahuah and came it *not* into his mind? So that no could Yahuah**

עוד 5750 לשאת 5375 מפני 6440 רע 7455 מעלליכם 4611 מפני 6440 התועבת 8441 אשר 834 עשיתם 6213
'aud lasea't, mipaney roa' ma'alleykem, mipaney hatou'aebot 'asher 'asiytem;
**longer bear because of the evil of your doings *and* because of the abominations which you have committed**

ותהי 1961 ארצכם 776 לחרבה 2723 ולשמה 8047 ולקללה 7045 מאין 369 יושב 3427 כהיום 3117 הזה 2088: 44:23 מפני 6440
uatahiy 'artzakem lacharabah ualshamah ualiqlalah me'ayn yousheb kahayoum hazeh. mipaney
**therefore is your land a desolation and an astonishment and a curse without an inhabitant as day *at* this Because**

אשר 834 קטרתם 6999 ואשר 834 חטאתם 2398 ליהוה 3069 ולא 3808 שמעתם 8085 בקול 6963 יהוה 3069
'asher qitartem ua'asher chata'tem laYahuah uala' shama'tem baqoul Yahuah,
**which you have burned incense and because you have sinned against Yahuah and not have obeyed the voice of Yahuah**

ובתרתו 8451 ובחקתיו 2708 ובעדותיו 5715 לא 3808 הלכתם 1980 על 5921 כן 3651 קראת 7122 אתכם 853 הרעה 7451
uabtoratou uabchuqotayu uab'aedauotayu la' halaktem; 'al ken karat 'atkem hara'ah
**in his law nor in his statutes nor in his testimonies nor walked therefore after is happened unto you evil**

הזאת 2063 כיום 3117 הזה 2088: 44:24 ויאמר 559 ירמיהו 3414 אל 413 כל 3605 העם 5971 ואל 413 כל 3605 הנשים 802 שמעו 8085
haza't kayoum hazeh. uaya'mer yirmayahu 'al kal ha'am, ua'ael kal hanashiym; shim'au
**this as day *at* this Moreover said Jeremiah unto all the people and to all the women Hear**

דבר 1697 יהוה 3068 כל 3605 יהודה 3063 אשר 834 בארץ 776 מצרים 4714: 44:25 כה 3541 אמר 559 יהוה 3068 צבאות 6635 אלהי 430
dabar Yahuah, kal yahudah 'asher ba'aretz mitzrayim. koh 'amar Yahuah tzaba'aut 'alohey
**the word of Yahuah all Judah that *are* in the land of Egypt Thus saith Yahuah of hosts the Elohim of**

ישראל 3478 לאמר 559 אתם 859 ונשיכם 802 ותדברנה 1696 בפיכם 6310 ובידיכם 3027 מלאתם 4390 לאמר 559
yisra'ael lea'mor, 'atem uansheykem uatadaberanah bapiykem uabiydeykem milea'tem lea'mor
**Israel saying You and your wives have both spoken with your mouths and with your hand fulfilled saying**

Jer 44:20 Then Jeremiah said unto all the people, to the men, and to the women, and to all the people which had given him that answer, saying,21 The incense that you burned in the cities of Judah, and in the streets of Jerusalem, you, and your fathers, your kings, and your princes, and the people of the land, did not YHUH remember them, and came it not into his mind?22 So that YHUH could no longer bear, because of the evil of your doings, and because of the abominations which you have committed; therefore is your land a desolation, and an astonishment, and a curse, without an inhabitant, as at this day.23 Because you have burned incense, and because you have sinned against YHUH, and have not obeyed the voice of YHUH, nor walked in his law, nor in his statutes, nor in his testimonies; therefore this evil is happened unto you, as at this day.24 Moreover Jeremiah said unto all the people, and to all the women, Hear the word of YHUH, all Judah that are in the land of Egypt:25 Thus saith YHUH of hosts, the G-d of Israel, saying; You and your wives have both spoken with your mouths, and fulfilled with your hand, saying, We will surely perform our vows that we have vowed, to burn incense to the queen of heaven, and to pour out drink offerings unto her: you will surely accomplish your vows, and surely perform your vows.

עשה 6213 נעשה 6213 את 853 נדרינו 5088 אשר 834 נדרנו 5087 לקטר 6999 למלכת 4446 השמים 8064 ולהסך 5258
'asoh na'aseh 'at nadareynu, 'asher nadarnu laqater limaleket hashamayim, ualahasek
**We will surely perform our vows that we have vowed to burn incense to the queen of heaven and to pour out**

לה 3807a נסכים 5262 הקים 6965 תקימנה 6965 את 853 נדריכם 5088 ועשה 6213 תעשינה 6213 את 853 נדריכם 5088: 44:26
lah nasakiym; haqiym taqiymnah 'at nidreykem, ua'asoh ta'aseynah 'at nidreykem.
**unto her drink offerings you will surely accomplish your vows and surely perform your vows**

לכן 3651 שמעו 8085 דבר 1697 יהוה 3068 כל 3605 יהודה 3063 הישבים 3427 בארץ 776 מצרים 4714 הנני 2005 נשבעתי 7650
laken shim'au dabar Yahuah, kal yahudah hayoshabiym ba'aretz mitzrayim; hinniy nishba'atiy
**Therefore hear you the word of Yahuah all Judah that dwell in the land of Egypt Behold I have sworn**

בשמי 8034 הגדול 1419 אמר 559 יהוה 3068 אם 518 יהיה 1961 עוד 5750 שמי 8034 נקרא 7121 בפי 6310 כל 3605 איש 376 יהודה 3063
bishmiy hagadoul 'amar Yahuah, 'am yihayeh 'aud shamiy niqra' bapiy kal 'aysh yahudah,
**by my name great saith Yahuah no shall be more *that* my name named in the mouth of any man of Judah**

אמר 559 חי 2416 אדני 136 יהוה 3069 בכל 3605 ארץ 776 מצרים 4714: 44:27 הנני 2005 שקד 8245 עליהם 5921 לרעה 7451 ולא 3808 לטובה 2896
'amer chay 'adonay Yahuah bakal 'aretz mitzrayim. hinniy shoqed 'aleyhem lara'ah uala' latoubah;
**saying live Adonai Yahuah in all *the* land of Egypt Behold I will watch over them for evil and not for good**

ותמו 8552 כל 3605 איש 376 יהודה 3063 אשר 834 בארץ 776 מצרים 4714 בחרב 2719 וברעב 7458 עד 5704
uatamu kal 'aysh yahudah 'asher ba'aretz mitzrayim bachereb uabara'ab 'ad
**and shall be consumed all the men of Judah that *are* in the land of Egypt by the sword and by the famine until**

כלותם 3615: 44:28 ופליטי 6412 חרב 2719 ישבון 7725 מן 4480 ארץ 776 מצרים 4714 ארץ 776 יהודה 3063
kaloutam. uapliytey chereb yashubun min 'aretz mitzrayim 'aretz yahudah
**there be an end of them Yet that escape the sword shall return out of the land of Egypt *into* the land of Judah**

מתי 4962 מספר 4557 וידעו 3045 כל 3605 שארית 7611 יהודה 3063 הבאים 935 לארץ 776 מצרים 4714 לגור 1481 שם 8033
matey mispar; uayada'aua kal sha'aeriyt yahudah, haba'aym la'aretz mitzrayim lagur sham,
**a small number and shall know all the remnant of Judah that are gone into the land of Egypt to sojourn there**

דבר 1697 מי 4310 יקום 6965 ממני 4480 ומהם 1992: 44:29 וזאת 2063 לכם 3807a האות 226 נאם 5002 יהוה 3068 כי 3588 פקד 6485
dabar miy' yaqum mimeniy uamehem. uaza't lakem ha'aut na'am Yahuah, kiy poqed
**words whose shall stand mine or theirs And this unto you *shall be* a sign saith Yahuah that I will punish**

אני 589 עליכם 5921 במקום 4725 הזה 2088 למען 4616 תדעו 3045 כי 3588 קום 6965 יקומו 6965 דברי 1697 עליכם 5921 לרעה 7451: 44:30
'aniy 'aleykem bamaqoum hazeh; lama'an teda'au, kiy qoum yaqumu dabaray 'aleykem lara'ah.
**I you in place this that you may know that shall surely stand my words against you for evil**

כה 3541 אמר 559 יהוה 3068 הנני 2005 נתן 5414 את 853 פרעה 6548 חפרע 6548 מלך 4428 מצרים 4714 ביד 3027 איביו 341
koh 'amar Yahuah hinniy noten 'at par'ah chapara' melek mitzrayim bayad 'ayabayu,
**Thus saith Yahuah Behold I will give Pharaoh hophra king of Egypt into the hand of his enemies**

וביד 3027 מבקשי 1245 נפשו 5315 כאשר 834 נתתי 5414 את 853 צדקיהו 6667 מלך 4428 יהודה 3063 ביד 3027
uabyad mabaqshey napshou; ka'asher natatiy 'at tzidqiyahu melek yahudah, bayad
**and into the hand of them that seek his life as I gave Zedekiah king of Judah into the hand of**

Jer 44:26 Therefore hear you the word of YHUH, all Judah that dwell in the land of Egypt; Behold, I have sworn by my great name, saith YHUH, that my name shall no more be named in the mouth of any man of Judah in all the land of Egypt, saying, The Adonai G-D live.27 Behold, I will watch over them for evil, and not for good: and all the men of Judah that are in the land of Egypt shall be consumed by the sword and by the famine, until there be an end of them.28 Yet a small number that escape the sword shall return out of the land of Egypt into the land of Judah, and all the remnant of Judah, that are gone into the land of Egypt to sojourn there, shall know whose words shall stand, mine, or theirs.29 And this shall be a sign unto you, saith YHUH, that I will punish you in this place, that you may know that my words shall surely stand against you for evil:30 Thus saith YHUH; Behold, I will give Pharaoh-hophra king of Egypt into the hand of his enemies, and into the hand of them that seek his life; as I gave Zedekiah king of Judah into the hand of Nebuchadrezzar king of Babylon, his enemy, and that sought his life.

נבוכדראצר 5019 מלך 4428 בבל 894 איבו 341 ומבקש 1245 נפשו 5315:
nabukadra'tzar melek babel 'ayabou uambaqesh napshou.
**Nebuchadrezzar king of Babylon his enemy and that sought his life**

**Jer 45:1**
הדבר 1697 אשר 834 דבר 1696 ירמיהו 3414 הנביא 5030 אל 413 ברוך 1263 בן 1121 נריה 5374 בכתבו 3789 את 853
hadabar, 'asher diber yirmayahu hanabiy'a, 'al baruk ben neriyah; bakatabou 'at
**The word that spoke Jeremiah the prophet unto Baruch the son of Neriah when he had written**

הדברים 1697 האלה 428 על 5921 ספר 5612 מפי 6310 ירמיהו 3414 בשנה 8141 הרבעית 7243 ליהויקים 3079 בן 1121 יאשיהו 2977
hadabariym ha'aeleh 'al sefer mipiy yirmayahu, bashanah harabi'ayt, liyahouyaqiym ben ya'shiyahu
**words these in a book at the mouth of Jeremiah in year the fourth of Jehoiakim the son of Josiah**

מלך 4428 יהודה 3063 לאמר 559: **45:2** כה 3541 אמר 559 יהוה 3068 אלהי 430 ישראל 3478 עליך 5921 ברוך 1263: **45:3** אמרת 559 אוי 188
melek yahudah lea'mor. koh 'amar Yahuah 'alohey yisra'ael; 'aleyka baruk. 'amarta 'auy
**king of Judah saying Thus saith Yahuah the Elohim of Israel unto you O Baruch You did say Woe**

נא 4994 לי 3807a כי 3588 יסף 3254 יהוה 3068 יגון 3015 על 5921 מכאבי 4341 יגעתי 3021 באנחתי 585 ומנוחה 4496 לא 3808 מצאתי 4672: **45:4**
naa' liy, kiy yasap Yahuah yagoun 'al mak'abiy; yaga'atiy ba'anchatiy, uamanuchah la' matza'tiy.
**now! *is* me for has added Yahuah grief to my sorrow I fainted in my sighing rest no and I find**

כה 3541 תאמר 559 אליו 413 כה 3541 אמר 559 יהוה 3068 הנה 2009 אשר 834 בניתי 1129 אני 589 הרס 2040 ואת 853
koh ta'mar 'aelayu, koh 'amar Yahuah, hineh 'asher baniytiy 'aniy hores, ua'at
**Thus shall you say unto him thus saith Yahuah Behold *that* which I have built I will I break down *and***

אשר 834 נטעתי 5193 אני 589 נתש 5428 ואת 853 כל 3605 הארץ 776 היא 1931: **45:5** ואתה 859 תבקש 1245 לך 3807a
'asher nata'atiy 'aniy notesh; ua'at kal ha'aretz hiy'a. ua'atah tabaqesh laka
**that which I have planted I will pluck up *even* whole the land this And you you seek for yourself?**

גדלות 1419 אל 408 תבקש 1245 כי 3588 הנני 2005 מביא 935 רעה 7451 על 5921 כל 3605 בשר 1320 נאם 5002 יהוה 3069 ונתתי 5414
gadolout 'al tabaqesh; kiy hinniy mebiy'a ra'ah 'al kal basar na'am Yahuah, uanatatiy
**great things *them* not seek for behold I will bring evil upon all flesh saith Yahuah but will I give**

לך 3807a את 853 נפשך 5315 לשלל 7998 על 5921 כל 3605 המקמות 4725 אשר 834 תלך 1980 שם 8033:
laka 'at napshaka lashalal, 'al kal hamaqomout 'asher telek sham.
**unto you your life for a prey in all places where you go there**

**Jer 46:1**
אשר 834 היה 1961 דבר 1697 יהוה 3068 אל 413 ירמיהו 3414 הנביא 5030 על 5921 הגוים 1471: **46:2** למצרים 4714 על 5921
'asher hayah dabar Yahuah 'al yirmayahu hanabiy'a 'al hagouyim. lamitzrayim, 'al
**which came The word of Yahuah to Jeremiah the prophet against the gentiles Against Egypt against**

חיל 2428 פרעה 6549 נכו 6549 מלך 4428 מצרים 4714 אשר 834 היה 1961 על 5921 נהר 5104 פרת 6578 בכרכמש 3751 אשר 834 הכה 5221
cheyl par'ah nakou melek mitzrayim, 'asher hayah 'al nahar parat bakarkamish; 'asher hikah,
**the army of Pharaoh necho king of Egypt which was by the river Euphrates in Carchemish which smote**

נבוכדראצר 5019 מלך 4428 בבל 894 בשנת 8141 הרביעית 7243 ליהויקים 3079 בן 1121 יאשיהו 2977 מלך 4428 יהודה 3063: **46:3** ערכו 6186
nabukadra'tzar melek babel, bishnat harabiy'ayt, liyahouyaqiym ben ya'shiyahu melek yahudah. 'arku
**Nebuchadrezzar king of Babylon in year the fourth of Jehoiakim the son of Josiah king of Judah Order you**

**Jer** 45:1 The word that Jeremiah the prophet spoke unto Baruch the son of Neriah, when he had written these words in a book at the mouth of Jeremiah, in the fourth year of Jehoiakim the son of Josiah king of Judah, saying,2 Thus saith YHUH, the G-d of Israel, unto you, O Baruch;3 Thou did say, Woe is me now! for YHUH has added grief to my sorrow; I fainted in my sighing, and I find no rest.4 Thus shall you say unto him, YHUH saith thus; Behold, that which I have built will I break down, and that which I have planted I will pluck up, even this whole land.5 And seek you great things for thyself? seek them not: for, behold, I will bring evil upon all flesh, saith YHUH: but your life will I give unto you for a prey in all places whither you go. **Jer** 46:1 The word of YHUH which came to Jeremiah the prophet against the Gentiles;2 Against Egypt, against the army of Pharaoh-necho king of Egypt, which was by the river Euphrates in Carchemish, which Nebuchadrezzar king of Babylon smote in the fourth year of Jehoiakim the son of Josiah king of Judah.3 Order you the buckler and shield, and draw near to battle.

| מגן 4043 | וצנה 6793 | וגשו 5066 | למלחמה 4421: | 46:4 | אסרו 631 | הסוסים 5483 | ועלו 5927 | הפרשים 6571 | והתיצבו 3320 |
|---|---|---|---|---|---|---|---|---|---|
| magen | uatzinah, | uagshu | lamilchamah. | | 'asaru | hasusiym, | ua'alu | haparashiym, | uahityatzbu |
| **the buckler** | **and shield** | **and draw near** | **to battle** | | **Harness** | **the horses** | **and get up** | **you horsemen** | **and stand forth** |

| בכובעים 3553 | מרקו 4838 | הרמחים 7420 | לבשו 3847 | הסרינת 5630: | 46:5 | מדוע 4069 | ראיתי 7200 | המה 1992 | חתים 2844 |
|---|---|---|---|---|---|---|---|---|---|
| bakoua'aym; | mirqu | haramachiym, | libshu | hasiryonot. | | madua' | ra'aytiy, | hemah | chatiym |
| **with *your* helmets** | **furbish** | **the spears** | ***and* put on** | **the brigandines** | | **Wherefore** | **have I seen** | **them** | **dismayed** |

| נסגים 5472 | אחור 268 | וגבוריהם 1368 | יכתו 3807 | ומנוס 4498 | נסו 5127 | ולא 3808 | הפנו 6437 | מגור 4032 |
|---|---|---|---|---|---|---|---|---|
| nasogiym | 'achour | uagiboureyhem | yukatu, | uamanous | nasu | uala' | hipnu; | magour |
| ***and* turned away** | **back?** | **and their mighty one** | **are beaten down** | **and apace** | **are fled** | **and not** | **look back** | ***for* fear** |

| מסביב 5439 | נאם 5002 | יהוה 3068: | 46:6 | אל 408 | ינוס 5127 | הקל 7031 | ואל 408 | ימלט 4422 | הגבור 1368 | צפונה 6828 | על 5921 |
|---|---|---|---|---|---|---|---|---|---|---|---|
| misabiyb | na'am | Yahuah. | | 'al | yanus | haqal, | ua'al | yimalet | hagibour; | tzapounah | 'al |
| ***was* round about** | **saith** | **Yahuah** | | **not** | **Let flee away** | **the swift** | **nor** | **escape** | **the mighty man** | **toward the north** | **on** |

| יד 3027 | נהר 5104 | פרת 6578 | כשלו 3782 | ונפלו 5307: | 46:7 | מי 4310 | זה 2088 | כיאר 2975 | יעלה 5927 | כנהרות 5104 | יתגעשו 1607 |
|---|---|---|---|---|---|---|---|---|---|---|---|
| yad | nahar | parat, | kashalu | uanapalu. | | miy' | zeh | kaya'ar | ya'aleh; | kanaharout | yitga'ashu |
| **by** | **the river** | **Euphrates** | **they shall stumble** | **and fall** | | **Who** | ***is* this** | **as a flood** | ***that* comes up** | **as the rivers?** | **are moved** |

| מימיו 4325: | 46:8 | מצרים 4714 | כיאר 2975 | יעלה 5927 | וכנהרות 5104 | יתגעשו 1607 | מים 4325 | ויאמר 559 | אעלה 5927 |
|---|---|---|---|---|---|---|---|---|---|
| meymayu. | | mitzrayim | kaya'ar | ya'aleh, | uakanharout | yitgo'ashu | mayim; | uaya'mer, | 'a'aleh |
| **whose waters** | | **Egypt** | **like a flood** | **rise up** | **and like the rivers** | **are moved** | ***his* waters** | **and he saith** | **I will go up** |

| אכסה 3680 | ארץ 776 | אבידה 6 | עיר 5892 | וישבי 3427 | בה 871a: | 46:9 | עלו 5927 | הסוסים 5483 | והתהללו 1984 | הרכב 7393 |
|---|---|---|---|---|---|---|---|---|---|---|
| 'akaseh | 'aretz, | 'abiydah | 'ayr | uayoshabey | bah. | | 'alu | hasusiym | uahitholalu | harekeb, |
| ***and* will cover** | **the earth** | **I will destroy** | **the city** | **and the inhabitants thereof** | | | **Come up** | **you horses** | **and rage** | **you chariots** |

| ויצאו 3318 | הגבורים 1368 | כוש 3568 | ופוט 6316 | תפשי 8610 | מגן 4043 | ולודים 3866 | תפשי 8610 |
|---|---|---|---|---|---|---|---|
| uayetza'au | hagibouriym; | kush | uaput | topsey | magen, | ualudiym | topsey |
| **and let come forth** | **the mighty men** | ***the* Ethiopians** | **and the Libyans** | **that handle** | **the shield** | **and the Lydians** | **that handle** |

| דרכי 1869 | קשת 7198: | 46:10 | והיום 3117 | ההוא 1931 | לאדני 136 | יהוה 3069 | צבאות 6635 | יום 3117 | נקמה 5360 | להנקם 5358 |
|---|---|---|---|---|---|---|---|---|---|---|
| dorakey | qashet. | | uahayoum | hahua' | la'adonay | Yahuah | tzaba'aut, | youm | naqamah | lahinaqem |
| ***and* bend** | **the bow** | | **For the day** | **this *is*** | **of Adonai** | **Yahuah** | **of hosts** | **a day of** | **vengeance** | **that he may avenge him** |

| מצריו 6862 | ואכלה 398 | חרב 2719 | ושבעה 7646 | ורותה 7301 | מדמם 1818 | כי 3588 | זבח 2077 |
|---|---|---|---|---|---|---|---|
| mitzarayu, | ua'akalah | chereb | uasaba'ah, | uarauatah | midamam; | kiy | zebach |
| **of his adversaries** | **and shall devour** | **the sword** | **and it shall be satiate** | **and made drunk** | **with their blood** | **for** | **has a sacrifice** |

| לאדני 136 | יהוה 3069 | צבאות 6635 | בארץ 776 | צפון 6828 | אל 413 | נהר 5104 | פרת 6578: | 46:11 | עלי 5927 | גלעד 1568 | וקחי 3947 | צרי 6875 |
|---|---|---|---|---|---|---|---|---|---|---|---|---|
| la'adonay | Yahuah | tzaba'aut | ba'aretz | tzapoun | 'al | nahar | parat. | | 'aliy | gil'ad | uaqchiy | tzariy, |
| **for Adonai** | **Yahuah** | **of hosts** | **in country** | ***the* north** | **by** | **the river** | **Euphrates** | | **Go up into** | **Gilead** | **and take** | **balm** |

| בתולת 1330 | בת 1323 | מצרים 4714 | לשוא 7723 | הרביתי 7235 | רפאות 7499 | תעלה 8585 | אין 369 | לך 3807a: | 46:12 | שמעו 8085 |
|---|---|---|---|---|---|---|---|---|---|---|
| batulat | bat | mitzrayim; | lashau'a | hirbeytiy | rapu'aut, | ta'alah | 'aeyn | lak. | | shama'au |
| **O virgin** | **the daughter of** | **Egypt** | **in vain** | **shall you use many** | **medicines** | **shall be cured** | **not** | **for you** | | **have heard** |

Jer 46:4 Harness the horses; and get up, you horsemen, and stand forth with your helmets; furbish the spears, and put on the brigandines.5 Wherefore have I seen them dismayed and turned away back? and their mighty ones are beaten down, and are fled apace, and look not back: for fear was round about, saith YHUH.6 Let not the swift flee away, nor the mighty man escape; they shall stumble, and fall toward the north by the river Euphrates.7 Who is this that cometh up as a flood, whose waters are moved as the rivers?8 Egypt rise up like a flood, and his waters are moved like the rivers; and he saith, I will go up, and will cover the earth; I will destroy the city and the inhabitants thereof.9 Come up, you horses; and rage, you chariots; and let the mighty men come forth; the Ethiopians and the Libyans, that handle the shield; and the Lydians, that handle and bend the bow.10 For this is the day of YHUH G-D of hosts, a day of vengeance, that he may avenge him of his adversaries: and the sword shall devour, and it shall be satiate and made drunk with their blood: for YHUH G-D of hosts has a sacrifice in the north country by the river Euphrates.11 Go up into Gilead, and take balm, O virgin, the daughter of Egypt: in vain shall you use many medicines; for you shall not be cured.

1471 גוים 7036 קלונך 6682 וצוחתך 4390 מלאה 776 הארץ 3588 כי 1368 גבור 1368 בגבור 3782 כשלו 3162 יחדיו
gouyim qalounek, uatziuachatek mal'ah ha'aretz; kiy gibour bagibour kashalu, yachdayu
**The nations *of* your shame and your cry has filled the land for the mighty man against the mighty has stumbled together**

5307 נפלו 8147 שניהם: 46:13 1697 הדבר 834 אשר 1696 דבר 3068 יהוה 413 אל 3414 ירמיהו 5030 הנביא 935 לבוא
naplu shaneyhem. hadabar 'asher diber Yahuah, 'al yirmayahu hanabiy'a; labou'a,
***and* they are fallen both The word that spoke Yahuah to Jeremiah the prophet how should come**

5019 נבוכדראצר 4428 מלך 894 בבל 5221 להכות 853 את 776 ארץ 4714 מצרים: 46:14 5046 הגידו 4714 במצרים 8085 והשמיעו
nabukadra'tzar melek babel, lahakout 'at 'aretz mitzrayim. hagiydu bamitzrayim uahashamiy'au
**Nebuchadrezzar king of Babylon *and* smite the land of Egypt Declare you in Egypt and publish**

4024 במגדול 8085 והשמיעו 5297 בנף 8471 ובתחפנחס 559 אמרו 3320 התיצב 3559 והכן 3807a לך 3588 כי 398 אכלה 2719 חרב
bamigdoul, uahashamiy'au banop uabtachpanches; 'amru, hityatzeb uahaken lak, kiy 'aklah chereb
**in Migdol and publish in Noph and in Tahpanhes say you Stand fast and prepare to you for shall devour the sword**

5439 סביביך: 46:15 4069 מדוע 5502 נסחף 47 אביריך 3808 לא 5975 עמד 3588 כי 3068 יהוה 1920 הדפו: 46:16
sabiybeyka. madua' nisachap 'abiyreyka; la' 'amad, kiy Yahuah hadapou.
**round about you Why are swept away? your valiant *men* not they stood because Yahuah did drive them**

7235 הרבה 3782 כושל 1571 גם 5307 נפל 376 איש 413 אל 7453 רעהו 559 ויאמרו 6965 קומה 7725 ונשבה 413 אל 5971 עמנו
hirbah koushel; gam napal 'aysh 'al re'aehu, uaya'maru qumah uanashubah 'al 'amenu,
**He made many to fall yea fell one upon another and they said Arise and let us go again to our own people**

413 ואל 776 ארץ 4138 מולדתנו 6440 מפני 2719 חרב 3238 היונה: 46:17 7121 קראו 8033 שם 6547 פרעה 4428 מלך 4714 מצרים
ua'al 'aretz mouladtenu, mipaney chereb hayounah. qara'au sham; par'ah melek mitzrayim
**and to the land of our nativity from sword the oppressing They did cry there Pharaoh king of Egypt**

7588 שאון 5674 העביר 4150 המועד: 46:18 2416 חי 589 אני 5002 נאם 4428 המלך 3068 יהוה 6635 צבאות 8034 שמו 3588 כי
sha'aun, he'abiyr hamou'aed. chay 'aniy na'am hamelek, Yahuah tzaba'aut shamou; kiy
***is but* a noise he has passed the time appointed *As* live I saith the King *is* Yahuah of hosts whose name Surely**

8396 כתבור 2022 בהרים 3760 וככרמל 3220 בים 935 יבוא: 46:19 3627 כלי 1473 גולה 6213 עשי
katabour behariym, uakkarmel bayam yabou'a. kaley gouleh 'asiy
**as Tabor *is* among the mountains and as Carmel by the sea *so* shall he come furnish *to go into* captivity make**

3807a לך 3427 יושבת 1323 בת 4714 מצרים 3588 כי 5297 נף 8047 לשמה 1961 תהיה 3341 ונצתה 369 מאין 3427 יושב: 46:20
lak, youshebet bat mitzrayim; kiy nop lashamah tihayeh, uanitztah me'ayn yousheb.
**for yourself dwelling in O you daughter Egypt for Noph waste shall be and desolate without an inhabitant**

5697 עגלה 3304 יפה 6310 פיה 4714 מצרים 7171 קרץ 6828 מצפון 935 בא 935 בא: 46:21 1571 גם 7916 שכריה
'aglah yapeh piyah mitzrayim; qeretz mitzapoun ba' ba'. gam sakireyha
**heifer *is like* a very fair Egypt *but* destruction out of the north comes it comes Also her hired men**

7130 בקרבה 5695 כעגלי 4770 מרבק 3588 כי 1571 גם 1992 המה 6437 הפנו 5127 נסו 3162 יחדיו 3808 לא
baqirbah ka'agley marbeq, kiy gam hemah hipnu nasu yachdayu la'
***are* in the midst of her like bullocks fatted for also they are turned back *and* are fled away together not**

Jer 46:12 The nations have heard of your shame, and your cry has filled the land: for the mighty man has stumbled against the mighty, and they are fallen both together.13 The word that YHUH spoke to Jeremiah the prophet, how Nebuchadrezzar king of Babylon should come and smite the land of Egypt.14 Declare you in Egypt, and publish in Migdol, and publish in Noph and in Tahpanhes: say you, Stand fast, and prepare you; for the sword shall devour round about you.15 Why are your valiant men swept away? they stood not, because YHUH did drive them.16 He made many to fall, yea, one fell upon another: and they said, Arise, and let us go again to our own people, and to the land of our nativity, from the oppressing sword.17 They did cry there, Pharaoh king of Egypt is but a noise; he has passed the time appointed.18 As I live, saith the King, whose name is YHUH of hosts, Surely as Tabor is among the mountains, and as Carmel by the sea, so shall he come.19 O you daughter dwelling in Egypt, furnish thyself to go into captivity: for Noph shall be waste and desolate without an inhabitant.20 Egypt is like a very fair heifer, but destruction cometh; it cometh out of the north.21 Also her hired men are in the midst of her like fatted bullocks; for they also are turned back, and are fled away together: they did not stand,

עמדו 5975 כי 3588 יום 3117 אידם 343 בא 935 עליהם 5921 עת 6256 פקדתם 6486: 46:22
'amadu; kiy youm 'aeydam ba' 'aleyhem 'at paqudatam.
**they did stand because the day of their calamity was come upon them *and* the time of their visitation**

קולה 6963 כנחש 5175 ילך 1980 כי 3588 בחיל 2428 ילכו 1980 ובקרדמות 7134 באו 935 לה 3807a כחטבי 2404
qoulah kanachash yelek; kiy bachayil yeleku, uabqardumout ba'au lah, kachotabey
**The voice thereof like a serpent shall go for with an army they shall march and with axes come against her as hewers of**

עצים 6086: 46:23 כרתו 3772 יערה 3293 נאם 5002 יהוה 3068 כי 3588 לא 3808 יחקר 2713 כי 3588 רבו 7231
'aetziym. karatu ya'arah na'am Yahuah, kiy la' yechaqer; kiy rabu
**wood They shall cut down her forest saith Yahuah though cannot it be searched because they are more**

מארבה 697 ואין 369 להם 1992 מספר 4557: 46:24 הבישה 3001 בת 1323 מצרים 4714
me'arbeh, ua'aeyn lahem mispar. hobiyshah bat mitzrayim;
**than the grasshoppers and is without to them number shall be confounded The daughter of Egypt**

נתנה 5414 ביד 3027 עם 5971 צפון 6828: 46:25 אמר 559 יהוה 3068 צבאות 6635 אלהי 430 ישראל 3478
nitanah bayad 'am tzapoun. 'amar Yahuah tzaba'aut 'alohey yisra'ael,
**she shall be delivered into the hand of the people of the north saith Yahuah of hosts the Elohim of Israel**

הנני 2005 פוקד 6485 אל 413 אמון 527 מנא 4996 ועל 5921 פרעה 6547 ועל 5921 מצרים 4714 ועל 5921 אלהיה 430 ועל 5921 מלכיה 4428
hinniy pouqed 'al 'amoun mina', ua'al par'ah ua'al mitzrayim, ua'al 'aloheyha ua'al malakeyha;
**Behold I will punish to the multitude of No and on Pharaoh and on Egypt with their gods and on their kings**

ועל 5921 פרעה 6547 ועל 5921 הבטחים 982 בו 871a: 46:26 ונתתים 5414 ביד 3027 מבקשי 1245 נפשם 5315
ua'al par'ah, ua'al habotachiym bou. uantatiym, bayad mabaqshey napsham,
**even Pharaoh and *all* them that trust in him And I will deliver them into the hand of those that seek their lives**

וביד 3027 נבוכדראצר 5019 מלך 4428 בבל 894 וביד 3027 עבדיו 5650 ואחרי 310 כן 3651
uabyad nabukadra'tzar melek babel uabyad 'abadayu; ua'acharey ken
**and into the hand of Nebuchadrezzar king of Babylon and into the hand his servants and afterward so**

תשכן 7931 כימי 3117 קדם 6924 נאם 5002 יהוה 3068: 46:27 ואתה 859 אל 408 תירא 3372 עבדי 5650 יעקב 3290 ואל 408
tishkon kiymey qedem na'am Yahuah. ua'atah 'al tiyraa' 'abdiy ya'aqob ua'al
**it shall be inhabited as in the days of old saith Yahuah But you not fear O my servant Jacob and not**

תחת 2865 ישראל 3478 כי 3588 הנני 2005 מושעך 3467 מרחוק 7350 ואת 853 זרעך 2233 מארץ 776 שבים 7628
techat yisra'ael, kiy hinniy moushi'aka merachouq, ua'at zar'aka me'aretz shibyam;
**be dismayed O Israel for behold I will save you from afar off *and* your seed from the land of their captivity**

ושב 7725 יעקוב 3290 ושקט 8252 ושאנן 7599 ואין 369 מחריד 2729: 46:28 אתה 859 אל 408 תירא 3372 עבדי 5650
uashab ya'aqoub uashaqat uasha'anan ua'aeyn machariyd. 'atah 'al tiyraa' 'abdiy
**and shall return Jacob and be in rest and at ease and none shall make *him* afraid you not Fear my servant**

יעקב 3290 נאם 5002 יהוה 3068 כי 3588 אתך 854 אני 589 כי 3588 אעשה 6213 כלה 3617 בכל 3605 הגוים 1471 אשר 834 הדחתיך 5080
ya'aqob na'am Yahuah, kiy 'ataka 'aniy; kiy 'aaseh kalah bakal hagouyim 'asher hidachtiyka
**O Jacob saith Yahuah for *am* with you I for I will make a full end of all the nations where I have driven you**

Jer 46:21 because the day of their calamity was come upon them, and the time of their visitation.22 The voice thereof shall go like a serpent; for they shall march with an army, and come against her with axes, as hewers of wood.23 They shall cut down her forest, saith YHUH, though it cannot be searched; because they are more than the grasshoppers, and are innumerable.24 The daughter of Egypt shall be confounded; she shall be delivered into the hand of the people of the north.25 YHUH of hosts, the G-d of Israel, saith; Behold, I will punish the multitude of No, and Pharaoh, and Egypt, with their gods, and their kings; even Pharaoh, and all them that trust in him:26 And I will deliver them into the hand of those that seek their lives, and into the hand of Nebuchadrezzar king of Babylon, and into the hand of his servants: and afterward it shall be inhabited, as in the days of old, saith YHUH.27 But fear not you, O my servant Jacob, and be not dismayed, O Israel: for, behold, I will save you from afar off, and your seed from the land of their captivity; and Jacob shall return, and be in rest and at ease, and none shall make him afraid.28 Fear you not, O Jacob my servant, saith YHUH: for I am with you; for I will make a full end of all the nations whither I have driven you: but I will not make a full end of you, but correct you in measure; yet will I not leave you wholly unpunished.

שמה 8033 ואתך 853 לא 3808 אעשה 6213 כלה 3617 ויסרתיך 3256 למשפט 4941 ונקה 5352 לא 3808
shamah, ua'ataka la' 'aaseh kalah, uayisartiyka lamishpat, uanaqeh la'
**there but you not I will make a full end *of* but correct you in measure yet will I not leave you wholly not**

אנקך 5352:
'anaqeka.
**unpunished**

**Jer 47:1**
אשר 834 היה 1961 דבר 1697 יהוה 3068 אל 413 ירמיהו 3414 הנביא 5030 אל 413 פלשתים 6430 בטרם 2962 יכה 5221
'asher hayah dabar Yahuah 'al yirmayahu hanabiy'a 'al palishtiym; baterem yakeh
**that came The word of Yahuah to Jeremiah the prophet against the Philistines before that smote**

**47:2**
פרעה 6547 את 853 עזה 5804: כה 3541 אמר 559 יהוה 3068 הנה 2009 מים 4325 עלים 5927 מצפון 6828 והיו 1961 לנחל 5158 שוטף 7857
par'ah 'at 'azah. koh 'amar Yahuah hineh mayim 'aliym mitzapoun uahayu lanachal shoutep,
**Pharaoh Gaza Thus saith Yahuah Behold waters rise up out of the north and shall be an flood overflowing**

וישטפו 7857 ארץ 776 ומלואה 4393 עיר 5892 וישבי 3427 בה 871a וזעקו 2199 האדם 120 והילל 3213
uayishtapu 'aretz uamlou'ah, 'ayr uayoshabey bah; uaza'aqu ha'adam, uaheylil
**and shall overflow the land and all that is therein the city and them that dwell therein then shall cry the men and shall howl**

**47:3**
כל 3605 יושב 3427 הארץ 776: מקול 6963 שעטת 8161 פרסות 6541 אביריו 47 מרעש 7494
kal yousheb ha'aretz. miqoul, sha'atat parsout 'abiyrayu, mera'ash
**all the inhabitants of the land At the noise of *the* stamping of the hoofs of his strong *horses* at the rushing of**

לרכבו 7393 המון 1995 גלגליו 1534 לא 3808 הפנו 6437 אבות 1 אל 413 בנים 1121 מרפיון 7510
larikbou, hamoun galgilayu; la' hipnu about 'al baniym, meripyoun
**his chariots *and at* the rumbling of his wheels not shall look back the fathers to *their* children for feebleness of**

**47:4**
ידים 3027: על 5921 היום 3117 הבא 935 לשדוד 7703 את 853 כל 3605 פלשתים 6430 להכרית 3772 לצר 6865 ולצידון 6721
yadayim. 'al hayoum, haba' lishdoud 'at kal palishtiym, lahakriyt latzor ualtziydoun,
**hands Because of the day that comes to spoil all the Philistines *and* to cut off from Tyrus and Zidon**

**47:5**
כל 3605 שריד 8300 עזר 5826 כי 3588 שדד 7703 יהוה 3068 את 853 פלשתים 6430 שארית 7611 אי 339 כפתור 3731:
kal sariyd 'azer; kiy shoded Yahuah 'at palishtiym, sha'aeriyt 'ay kaptour.
**every that remains helper for will spoil Yahuah the Philistines the remnant of the country of Caphtor**

**47:6**
באה 935 קרחה 7144 אל 413 עזה 5804 נדמתה 1820 אשקלון 831 שארית 7611 עמקם 6010 עד 5704 מתי 4970 תתגודדי 1413:
ba'ah qarachah 'al 'azah, nidmatah 'ashqaloun sha'aeriyt 'amqam; 'ad matay titgoudadiy.
**is come Baldness upon Gaza is cut off Ashkelon *with* the remnant of their valley how long will you cut yourself?**

הוי 1945 חרב 2719 ליהוה 3069 עד 5704 אנה 575 לא 3808 תשקטי 8252 האספי 622 אל 413 תערך 8593 הרגעי 7280
houy, chereb laYahuah, 'ad 'anah la' tishqotiy; he'asapiy 'al ta'arek, heraga'ay
**O you sword Yahuah how long *will it be* ere you be quiet? put up yourself into your scabbard rest**

**47:7**
ודמי 1826: איך 349 תשקטי 8252 ויהוה 3068 צוה 6680 לה 3807a אל 413 אשקלון 831 ואל 413 חוף 2348
uadomiy. 'aeyk tishqotiy, uaYahuah tziuah lah; 'al 'ashqaloun ua'al choup
**and be still How can it be quiet seeing Yahuah has given a charge it against Ashkelon and against shore?**

**Jer** 47:1 The word of YHUH that came to Jeremiah the prophet against the Philistines, before that Pharaoh smote Gaza.2 Thus saith YHUH; Behold, waters rise up out of the
north, and shall be an overflowing flood, and shall overflow the land, and all that is therein; the city, and them that dwell therein: then the men shall cry, and all the inhabitants
of the land shall howl.3 At the noise of the stamping of the hoofs of his strong horses, at the rushing of his chariots, and at the rumbling of his wheels, the fathers shall not look
back to their children for feebleness of hands;4 Because of the day that cometh to spoil all the Philistines, and to cut off from Tyrus and Zidon every helper that remain: for
YHUH will spoil the Philistines, the remnant of the country of Caphtor.5 Baldness is come upon Gaza; Ashkelon is cut off with the remnant of their valley: how long will you
cut thyself?6 O you sword of YHUH, how long will it be ere you be quiet? put up thyself into your scabbard, rest, and be still.7 How can it be quiet, seeing YHUH has given it
a charge against Ashkelon, and against the sea shore? there has he appointed it.

הים 3220 שם 8033 יעדה 3259:
hayam sham ya'adah.
**and sea there has he appointed it**

**Jer 48:1**
למואב 4124 כה 3541 אמר 559 יהוה 3068 צבאות 6635 אלהי 430 ישראל 3478 הוי 1945 אל 413 נבו 5015 כי 3588 שדדה 7703
lamou'ab koh 'amar Yahuah tzaba'aut 'alohey yisra'ael, houy 'al nabou' kiy shudadah,
**Against Moab Thus saith Yahuah of hosts the Elohim of Israel Woe unto Nebo for it is spoiled**

הבישה 3001 נלכדה 3920 קריתים 7156 הבישה 3001 המשגב 4869 וחתה 2865: **48:2** אין 369 עוד 5750 תהלת 8416 מואב 4124
hobiyshah nilkadah qiryatayim; hobiyshah hamisgab uachatah. 'aeyn 'aud tahilat mou'ab
**is confounded *and* taken Kiriathaim is confounded Misgab and dismayed *There shall be* no more praise of Moab**

בחשבון 2809 חשבו 2803 עליה 5921 רעה 7451 לכו 1980 ונכריתנה 3772 מגוי 1471 גם 1571 מדמן 4086
bacheshboun, chashabu 'aleyha ra'ah, laku uanakriytenah migouy; gam madmen
**in Heshbon they have devised against it evil come and let us cut it off from *being* a nation Also O Madmen**

תדמי 1826 אחריך 310 תלך 1980 חרב 2719: **48:3** קול 6963 צעקה 6818 מחרונים 2773 שד 7701
tidomiy, 'acharayik telek chareb. qoul tzea'aqah mechorounayim; shod
**you shall be cut down you shall pursue the sword A voice of crying *shall be* from Horonaim spoiling**

ושבר 7667 גדול 1419: **48:4** נשברה 7665 מואב 4124 השמיעו 8085 זעקה 2201 צעוריה 6810 **48:5** כי 3588
uasheber gadoul. nishbarah mou'ab; hishmiy'au za'aqah tza'aureyha kiy
**and destruction great is destroyed Moab have caused to be heard a cry her little ones For**

מעלה 4608 הלחות 3872 בבכי 1065 יעלה 5927 בכי 1065 כי 3588 במורד 4174 חורנים 2773 צרי 6862 צעקת 6818
ma'aleh halchout bibkiy ya'aleh bekiy; kiy bamourad chouronayim, tzarey tza'aqat
**the going up *in* the Luhith continual shall go up weeping for in the going down of Horonaim the enemies a cry of**

שבר 7667 שמעו 8085: **48:6** נסו 5127 מלטו 4422 נפשכם 5315 ותהיינה 1961 כערוער 6176 במדבר 4057: **48:7** כי 3588 יען 3282
sheber shame'au. nusu maltu napshakem; uatihayeynah ka'arou'aer bamidbar. kiy ya'an
**destruction have heard Flee save your lives and be like the heath in the wilderness For because**

בטחך 982 במעשיך 4639 ובאוצרותיך 214 גם 1571 את 859 תלכדי 3920 ויצא 3318 כמיש 3645 בגולה 1473
bitachek bama'asayik uab'autzaroutayik, gam 'at tilakediy; uayatza' kamiysh bagoulah,
**you have trusted in your works and in your treasures also *you* shall be taken and shall go forth Chemosh into captivity**

כהניו 3548 ושריו 8269 יחד 3162 **8:8** ויבא 935 שדד 7703 אל 413 כל 3605 עיר 5892 ועיר 5892 לא 3808 תמלט 4422
kohanayu uasarayu yachad uayaba' shoded 'al kal 'ayr, ua'ayr la' timalet,
***with* his priests and his princes together And shall come the spoiler upon every city and city no shall escape**

ואבד 6 העמק 6010 ונשמד 8045 המישר 4334 אשר 834 אמר 559 יהוה 3068: **48:9** תנו 5414 ציץ 6731 למואב 4124 כי 3588
ua'abad ha'aemeq uanishmad hamiyshor; 'asher 'amar Yahuah. tanu tziytz lamou'ab, kiy
**also shall perish the valley and shall be destroyed the plain as has spoken Yahuah Give wings unto Moab that**

נצא 5323 תצא 3318 ועריה 5892 לשמה 8047 תהיינה 1961 מאין 369 יושב 3427 בהן 2004: **48:10** ארור 779
natza' tetzea'; ua'areyha lashamah tihayeynah, me'ayn yousheb bahen. 'arur,
**it may flee *and* get away for the cities thereof desolate shall be without *any* to dwell therein Cursed**

**Jer** 48:1 Against Moab thus saith YHUH of hosts, the G-d of Israel; Woe unto Nebo! for it is spoiled: Kiriathaim is confounded and taken: Misgab is confounded and dismayed.2 There shall be no more praise of Moab: in Heshbon they have devised evil against it; come, and let us cut it off from being a nation. Also you shall be cut down, O Madmen; the sword shall pursue you.3 A voice of crying shall be from Horonaim, spoiling and great destruction.4 Moab is destroyed; her little ones have caused a cry to be heard.5 For in the going up of Luhith continual weeping shall go up; for in the going down of Horonaim the enemies have heard a cry of destruction.6 Flee, save your lives, and be like the heath in the wilderness.7 For because you have trusted in your works and in your treasures, you shall also be taken: and Chemosh shall go forth into captivity with his priests and his princes together.8 And the spoiler shall come upon every city, and no city shall escape: the valley also shall perish, and the plain shall be destroyed, as YHUH has spoken.9 Give wings unto Moab, that it may flee and get away: for the cities thereof shall be desolate, without any to dwell therein.

48:11

עשה 6213 מלאכת 4399 יהוה 3068 רמיה 7423 וארור 779 מנע 4513 חרבו 2719 מדם 1818: שאנן 7599
'aseh mala'ket Yahuah ramiyah; ua'arur monea' charbou midam. sha'anan
***be* he that does the work of Yahuah deceitfully and cursed *be* he that keep back his sword from blood has been at ease**

מואב 4124 מנעוריו 5271 ושקט 8252 הוא 1931 אל 413 שמריו 8105 ולא 3808 הורק 7324 מכלי 3627 אל 413 כלי 3627
mou'ab mina'urayu, uashoqet hua' 'al shamarayu, uala' huraq mikaliy 'al keliy,
**Moab from his youth and he has settled he on his lees and not has been emptied from vessel to vessel**

48:12

ובגולה 1473 לא 3808 הלך 1980 על 5921 כן 3651 עמד 5975 טעמו 2940 בו 871a וריחו 7381 לא 3808 נמר 4171:
uabagoulah la' halak; 'al ken, 'amad ta'amou bou, uareychou la' namar.
**into captivity neither has he gone therefore after that remained his taste in him and his scent not is changed**

לכן 3651 הנה 2009 ימים 3117 באים 935 נאם 5002 יהוה 3068 ושלחתי 7971 לו 3807a צעים 6808 וצעהו 6808
laken hineh yamiym ba'aym na'am Yahuah, uashilachtiy lou' tzo'aym uatze'ahu;
**Therefore behold the days come saith Yahuah that I will send unto him wanderers that shall cause him to wander**

48:13

וכליו 3627 יריקו 7324 ונבליהם 5035 ינפצו 5310: ובש 954 מואב 4124 מכמוש 3645 כאשר 834 בשו 954
uakelayu yariyqu, uanibleyhem yanapetzu. uabosh mou'ab mikamoush; ka'asher boshu
**and his vessels shall empty their bottles and break And shall be ashamed Moab of Chemosh as was ashamed**

48:14

בית 1004 ישראל 3478 מבית 1008 אל 413 מבטחם 4009: איך 349 תאמרו 559 גבורים 1368 אנחנו 587 ואנשי 582 חיל 2428
beyt yisra'ael, mibeyt 'ael mibatecham. 'aeyk ta'maru, gibouriym 'anachanu; ua'anshey chayil
**the house of Israel of Beth el their confidence How say you *are* mighty We and men strong**

48:15

למלחמה 4421: שדד 7703 מואב 4124 ועריה 5892 עלה 5927 ומבחר 4005 בחוריו 970 ירדו 3381 לטבח 2874
lamilchamah. shudad mou'ab ua'areyha 'alah, uamibchar bachurayu yaradu latabach;
**for the war? is spoiled Moab and her cities gone up *out of* and chosen his young men are gone down to the slaughter**

48:16

נאם 5002 המלך 4428 יהוה 3068 צבאות 6635 שמו 8034: קרוב 7138 איד 343 מואב 4124 לבוא 935 ורעתו 7451 מהרה 4116
na'am hamelek, Yahuah tzaba'aut shamou. qaroub 'aeyd mou'ab labou'a; uara'atou, miharah
**saith the King *is* Yahuah of hosts whose name *is* near The calamity of Moab to come and his affliction hasten**

48:17

מאד 3966: נדו 5110 לו 3807a כל 3605 סביביו 5439 וכל 3605 ידעי 3045 שמו 8034 אמרו 559 איכה 349 נשבר 7665
ma'ad. nudu lou' kal sabiybayu, uakol yod'aey shamou; 'amru, 'aeykah nishbar
**fast bemoan him All you that are about him and all you that know his name say How is broken**

48:18

מטה 4294 עז 5797 מקל 4731 תפארה 8597: רדי 3381 מכבוד 3519 ישבי 3427 בצמא 6772 ישבת 3427 בת 1323
mateh 'az, maqel tip'arah. radiy mikaboud yoshabey uatzama', yoshebet bat
**staff *the* strong rod *and* the beautiful come down from *your* glory that does inhabit in thirst sit you daughter**

48:19

דיבון 1769 כי 3588 שדד 7703 מואב 4124 עלה 5927 בך 871a שחת 7843 מבצריך 4013: אל 413 דרך 1870
diyboun; kiy shoded mou'ab 'alah bak, shichet mibtzarayik. 'al derek
**Dibon for the spoiler of Moab shall come upon you *and* he shall destroy your strong holds by the way**

עמדי 5975 וצפי 6822 יושבת 3427 ערוער 6177 שאלי 7592 נס 5127 ונמלטה 4422 אמרי 559 מה 4100 נהיתה 1961:
'amdiy uatzapiy youshebet arou'aer; sha'aliy nas uanimlatah, 'amriy mah nihayatah.
**stand and espy O inhabitant of Aroer ask him that flee and her that escape *and* say What is done?**

Jer 48:10 Cursed be he that doeth the work of YHUH deceitfully, and cursed be he that keep back his sword from blood.11 Moab has been at ease from his youth, and he has settled on his lees, and has not been emptied from vessel to vessel, neither has he gone into captivity: therefore his taste remained in him, and his scent is not changed.12 Therefore, behold, the days come, saith YHUH, that I will send unto him wanderers, that shall cause him to wander, and shall empty his vessels, and break their bottles.13 And Moab shall be ashamed of Chemosh, as the house of Israel was ashamed of Bethel their confidence.14 How say you, We are mighty and strong men for the war?15 Moab is spoiled, and gone up out of her cities, and his chosen young men are gone down to the slaughter, saith the King, whose name is YHUH of hosts.16 The calamity of Moab is near to come, and his affliction hasteth fast.17 All you that are about him, bemoan him; and all you that know his name, say, How is the strong staff broken, and the beautiful rod!18 Thou daughter that dost inhabit Dibon, come down from your glory, and sit in thirst; for the spoiler of Moab shall come upon you, and he shall destroy your strong holds.19 O inhabitant of Aroer, stand by the way, and espy; ask him that fleeth, and her that escapeth, and say, What is done?

**48:20** **48:21**

הביש 3001 מואב 4124 כי 3588 חתה 2865 הילילי 3213 וזעקי 2199 הגידו 5046 בארנון 769 כי 3588 שדד 7703 מואב 4124:
hobiysh mou'ab kiy chatah heyliyliy uaz'aqiy hagiydu ba'arnoun, kiy shudad mou'ab.
**is confounded Moab for it is broken down howl and cry tell you it in Arnon that is spoiled Moab**

**8:22**

ומשפט 4941 בא 935 אל 413 ארץ 776 המישר 4334 אל 413 חלון 2473 ואל 413 יהצה 3096 ועל 5921 מופעת 4158: ועל 5921
uamishpat ba' 'al 'aretz hamiyshor; 'al choloun ua'al yahtzah ua'al moupa'at ua'al
**And judgment is come upon country the plain upon Holon and upon Jahazah and upon Mephaath And upon**

**48:23**

דיבון 1769 ועל 5921 נבו 5015 ועל 5921 בית 1015 דבלתים 1690: ועל 5921 קריתים 7156 ועל 5921 בית 1014 גמול 1576 ועל 5921
diyboun ua'al nabou', ua'al beyt diblatayim. ua'al qiryatayim ua'al beyt gamul ua'al
**Dibon and upon Nebo and upon Beth diblathaim And upon Kiriathaim and upon Beth gamul and upon**

**48:24**

בית 1010 מעון 4583: ועל 5921 קריות 7152 ועל 5921 בצרה 1224 ועל 5921 כל 3605 ערי 5892 ארץ 776 מואב 4124 הרחקות 7350
beyt ma'aun. ua'al qariyout ua'al batzrah ua'al, kal 'arey 'aretz mou'ab, harachoqout
**Beth meon And upon Kerioth and upon Bozrah and upon all the cities of the land of Moab far**

**48:25** **48:26**

והקרבות 7138: נגדעה 1438 קרן 7161 מואב 4124 וזרעו 2220 נשברה 7665 נאם 5002 יהוה 3068: השכירהו 7937
uahaqarobout. nigda'ah qeren mou'ab, uazero'au nishbarah; na'am Yahuah. hashakiyruhu
**or near is cut off The horn of Moab and his arm is broken saith Yahuah Make you him drunken**

כי 3588 על 5921 יהוה 3068 הגדיל 1431 וספק 5606 מואב 4124 בקיאו 6892 והיה 1961 לשחק 7814 גם 1571
kiy 'al Yahuah higdiyl; uasapaq mou'ab baqiy'au, uahayah lischoq gam
**for against Yahuah he magnified *himself* also shall wallow Moab in his vomit and shall be in derision also**

**48:27**

הוא 1931: ואם 518 לוא 3808 השחק 7814 היה 1961 לך 3807a ישראל 3478 אם 518 בגנבים 1590 נמצאה 4672 כי 3588 מדי 1767
hua'. ua'am lua' haschoq, hayah laka yisra'ael, 'am baganabiym nimtza'ah kiy midey
**he For not a derision was unto you? Israel if since was he found for among thieves?**

**48:28**

דבריך 1697 בו 871a תתנודד 5110: עזבו 5800 ערים 5892 ושכנו 7931 בסלע 5553 ישבי 3427 מואב 4124 והיו 1961
debareyka bou titnoudad. 'azbu 'ariym uashiknu basela', yoshabey mou'ab; uihayu
**you spoke of him you skip for joy leave the cities and dwell in the rock O you that dwell in Moab and be like**

**48:29**

כיונה 3123 תקנן 7077 בעברי 5676 פי 6310 פחת 6354: שמענו 8085 גאון 1347 מואב 4124 גאה 1343
kayounah, taqanen ba'abrey piy pachat. shama'anu ga'aun mou'ab ge'ah
**the dove *that* make her nest in the sides of mouth *the* hole's We have heard the pride of Moab proud**

**48:30**

מאד 3966 גבהו 1363 וגאונו 1347 וגאותו 1346 ורם 7312 לבו 3820: אני 589 ידעתי 3045 נאם 5002
ma'ad; gabahou uag'aunou uaga'auatou uarum libou. 'aniy yada'tiy na'am
***he is* exceeding his loftiness and his arrogancy and his pride and the haughtiness of his heart I know saith**

**48:31**

יהוה 3068 עברתו 5678 ולא 3808 כן 3651 בדיו 907 לא 3808 כן 3651 עשו 6213: על 5921 כן 3651 על 5921 מואב 4124 איליל 3213
Yahuah, 'abratou uala' ken; badayu la' ken 'asu. 'al ken 'al mou'ab 'ayeliyl,
**Yahuah his wrath but *it shall* not *be* so his lies not so *it* shall effect Therefore after that for Moab will I howl**

**48:32**

ולמואב 4124 כלה 3605 אזעק 2199 אל 413 אנשי 582 קיר 7025 חרש 2792 יהגה 1897: מבכי 1065
ualmou'ab kuloh 'az'aq; 'al 'anshey qiyr cheres yehageh. mibakiy
**and for Moab all I will cry out for the men of Kir heres *mine heart* shall mourn with the weeping of**

Jer 48:20 Moab is confounded; for it is broken down: howl and cry; and tell you it in Arnon, that Moab is spoiled,21 And judgment is come upon the plain country; upon Holon, and upon Jahazah, and upon Mephaath,22 And upon Dibon, and upon Nebo, and upon Beth-diblathaim,23 And upon Kiriathaim, and upon Beth-gamul, and upon Beth-meon,24 And upon Kerioth, and upon Bozrah, and upon all the cities of the land of Moab, far or near.25 The horn of Moab is cut off, and his arm is broken, saith YHUH.26 Make you him drunken: for he magnified himself against YHUH: Moab also shall wallow in his vomit, and he also shall be in derision.27 For was not Israel a derision unto you? was he found among thieves? for since you spoke of him, you skippedst for joy.28 O you that dwell in Moab, leave the cities, and dwell in the rock, and be like the dove that make her nest in the sides of the hole's mouth.29 We have heard the pride of Moab, (he is exceeding proud) his loftiness, and his arrogance, and his pride, and the haughtiness of his heart.30 I know his wrath, saith YHUH; but it shall not be so; his lies shall not so effect it.31 Therefore will I howl for Moab, and I will cry out for all Moab; mine heart shall mourn for the men of Kir-heres.

יעזר 3270 אבכה 1058 לך 3807a הגפן 1612 שבמה 7643 נטישתיך 5189 עברו 5674 ים 3220 עד 5704 ים 3220 יעזר 3270 נגעו 5060
ya'azer 'abkeh lak hagapen sibmah, natiyshotayik 'abaru yam, 'ad yam ya'azer naga'au;
**Jazer I will weep for you O vine of Sibmah your plants are gone over the sea to the sea of Jazer they reach *even***

**48:33**
על 5921 קיצך 7019 ועל 5921 בצירך 1210 שדד 7703 נפל 5307: ונאספה 622 שמחה 8057 וגיל 1524
'al qeytzek ua'al batziyrek shoded napal. uane'aspah simchah uagiyl
**upon your summer fruits and upon your vintage the spoiler is fallen And is taken joy and gladness**

מכרמל 3759 ומארץ 776 מואב 4124 ויין 3196 מיקבים 3342 השבתי 7673 לא 3808
mikarmel uame'aretz mou'ab; uayayin miyqabiym hishbatiy, la'
**from the plentiful field and from the land of Moab and wine from the winepresses I have caused to fail none**

**48:34**
ידרך 1869 הידד 1959 הידד 1959 לא 3808 הידד 1959: מזעקת 2201 חשבון 2809 עד 5704 אלעלה 500
yidrok heydad, heydad la' heydad. miza'aqat cheshboun 'ad 'ala'aleh,
**shall tread with shouting *their* shouting *shall be* no shouting From the cry of Heshbon *even* unto Elealeh**

עד 5704 יהץ 3096 נתנו 5414 קולם 6963 מצער 6820 עד 5704 חרנים 2773 עגלת 5697 שלשיה 7992 כי 3588
'ad yahatz natanu qoulam, mitzou'ar 'ad choronayim, 'aglat shalishiyah; kiy
***and even* unto Jahaz have they uttered their voice from Zoar *even* unto Horonaim *as* an heifer of three years old for**

**48:35**
גם 1571 מי 4325 נמרים 5249 למשמות 4923 יהיו 1961: והשבתי 7673 למואב 4124 נאם 5002 יהוה 3068
gam mey nimriym, limashamout yihayu. uahishbatiy lamou'ab na'am Yahuah;
**also the waters of Nimrim desolate shall be Moreover I will cause to cease in Moab saith Yahuah**

**48:36**
מעלה 5927 במה 1116 ומקטיר 6999 לאלהיו 430: על 5921 כן 3651 לבי 3820 למואב 4124
ma'aleh bamah, uamaqtiyr le'alohayu. 'al ken libiy lamou'ab
**him that offer up in the high places and him that burn incense to his gods Therefore after that mine heart for Moab**

כחללים 2485 יהמה 1993 ולבי 3820 אל 413 אנשי 582 קיר 7025 חרש 2792 כחלילים 2485 יהמה 1993 על 5921 כן 3651
kachaliliym yehemeh, ualibiy 'al 'anshey qiyr cheres, kachaliyliym yehemeh; 'al ken
**like pipes shall sound and mine heart for the men of Kir heres like pipes shall sound because after that**

**48:37**
יתרת 3502 עשה 6213 אבדו 6: כי 3588 כל 3605 ראש 7218 קרחה 7144 וכל 3605 זקן 2206 גרעה 1639 על 5921 כל 3605
yitarat 'asah 'abadu. kiy kal ra'sh qarachah, uakal zaqan garu'ah; 'al kal
**the riches *that* he has gotten are perished For every head *shall be* bald and every beard clipped upon all**

**48:38**
ידים 3027 גדדת 1417 ועל 5921 מתנים 4975 שק 8242: על 5921 כל 3605 גגות 1406 מואב 4124
yadayim gadudot, ua'al matanayim saq. 'al kal gagout mou'ab
**the hands *shall be* cuttings and upon the loins sackcloth *There shall be* upon generally the housetops of Moab**

וברחבתיה 7339 כלה 3605 מספד 4553 כי 3588 שברתי 7665 את 853 מואב 4124 ככלי 3627 אין 369 חפץ 2656 בו 871a נאם 5002
uabirchoboteyha kuloh misped; kiy shabartiy 'at mou'ab, kikliy 'aeyn chepetz bou na'am
**and in the streets thereof all lamentation for I have broken Moab like a vessel *is* no pleasure wherein saith**

**48:39**
יהוה 3068: איך 349 חתה 2865 הילילו 3213 איך 349 הפנה 6437 ערף 6203 מואב 4124 בוש 954
Yahuah. 'aeyk chatah heyliylu, 'aeyk hipnah 'arep mou'ab boush;
**Yahuah *saying* How is it broken down They shall howl how has turned the back Moab *with* shame**

Jer 48:32 O vine of Sibmah, I will weep for you with the weeping of Jazer: your plants are gone over the sea, they reach even to the sea of Jazer: the spoiler is fallen upon your summer fruits and upon your vintage.33 And joy and gladness is taken from the plentiful field, and from the land of Moab; and I have caused wine to fail from the winepresses: none shall tread with shouting; their shouting shall be no shouting.34 From the cry of Heshbon even unto Elealeh, and even unto Jahaz, have they uttered their voice, from Zoar even unto Horonaim, as an heifer of three years old: for the waters also of Nimrim shall be desolate.35 Moreover I will cause to cease in Moab, saith YHUH, him that offereth in the high places, and him that burneth incense to his gods.36 Therefore mine heart shall sound for Moab like pipes, and mine heart shall sound like pipes for the men of Kir-heres: because the riches that he has gotten are perished.37 For every head shall be bald, and every beard clipped: upon all the hands shall be cuttings, and upon the loins sackcloth.38 There shall be lamentation generally upon all the housetops of Moab, and in the streets thereof: for I have broken Moab like a vessel wherein is no pleasure, saith YHUH.39 They shall howl, saying, How is it broken down! how has Moab turned the back with shame! so shall Moab be a derision and a dismaying to all them about him.

**48:40**

והיה 1961 מואב 4124 לשחק 7814 ולמחתה 4288 לכל 3605 סביביו 5439: כי 3588 כה 3541 אמר 559 יהוה 3068 הנה 2009 כנשר 5404
uahayah mou'ab lischoq ualimchitah lakal sabiybayu. kiy koh 'amar Yahuah, hineh kanesher
**so shall be Moab a derision and a dismaying to all them about him For thus saith Yahuah Behold as an eagle**

**48:41**

ידאה 1675 ופרש 6566 כנפיו 3671 אל 413 מואב 4124: נלכדה 3920 הקריות 7152 והמצדות 4679 נתפשה 8610
yid'ah; uaparas kanapayu 'al mou'ab. nilkadah haqariyout, uahamatzadout nitpasah;
**he shall fly and shall spread his wings over Moab is taken Kerioth and the strong holds are surprised**

**48:42**

והיה 1961 לב 3820 גבורי 1368 מואב 4124 ביום 3117 ההוא 1931 כלב 3820 אשה 802 מצרה 6887:
uahayah leb gibourey mou'ab bayoum hahua', kaleb 'ashah matzerah.
**and shall be hearts the mighty men's in Moab at day that as the heart of a woman in her pangs**

**48:43**

ונשמד 8045 מואב 4124 מעם 5971 כי 3588 על 5921 יהוה 3068 הגדיל 1431: פחד 6343
uanishmad mou'ab me'am; kiy 'al Yahuah higdiyl. pachad
**And shall be destroyed Moab from *being* a people because against Yahuah he has magnified *himself* Fear**

**48:44**

ופחת 6354 ופח 6341 עליך 5921 יושב 3427 מואב 4124 נאם 5002 יהוה 3068: הניס 5211 מפני 6440 הפחד 6343
uapachat uapach; 'aleyka yousheb mou'ab na'am Yahuah. haniys mipaney hapachad
**and the pit and the snare *shall be* upon you O inhabitant of Moab saith Yahuah He that flees from the fear**

יפל 5307 אל 413 הפחת 6354 והעלה 5927 מן 4480 הפחת 6354 ילכד 3920 בפח 6341 כי 3588 אביא 935 אליה 413 אל 413
yipol 'al hapachat, uaha'aleh min hapachat, yilaked bapach; kiy 'abiy'a 'aeleyha 'al
**shall fall into the pit and he that get up out of the pit shall be taken in the snare for I will bring upon it *even* upon**

**48:45**

מואב 4124 שנת 8141 פקדתם 6486 נאם 5002 יהוה 3068: בצל 6738 חשבון 2809 עמדו 5975 מכח 3581
mou'ab shanat paqudatam na'am Yahuah. batzel cheshboun 'amadu mikoach
**Moab the year of their visitation saith Yahuah under the shadow of Heshbon stood because of the force**

נסים 5127 כי 3588 אש 784 יצא 3318 מחשבון 2809 ולהבה 3852 מבין 996 סיחון 5511 ותאכל 398
nasiym; kiy 'aesh yatza' mecheshboun, ualehabah mibeyn siychoun, uata'kal
**They that fled but a fire shall come forth out of Heshbon and a flame from the midst of Sihon and shall devour**

**48:46**

פאת 6285 מואב 4124 וקדקד 6936 בני 1121 שאון 7588: אוי 188 לך 3807a מואב 4124 אבד 6
pa'at mou'ab, uaqadaqod baney sha'aun. 'auy laka mou'ab, 'abad
**the corner of Moab and the crown of the head of ones *the* tumultuous Woe *be* unto you O Moab perish**

**48:47**

עם 5971 כמוש 3645 כי 3588 לקחו 3947 בניך 1121 בשבי 7628 ובנתיך 1323 בשביה 7633: ושבתי 7725
'am kamoush; kiy luqachu baneyka bashebiy, uabnoteyka bashibyah. uashabatiy
**the people of Chemosh for are taken your sons captives and your daughters captives Yet will I bring again**

שבות 7622 מואב 4124 באחרית 319 הימים 3117 נאם 5002 יהוה 3068 עד 5704 הנה 2008 משפט 4941 מואב 4124:
shabut mou'ab ba'achariyt hayamiym na'am Yahuah; 'ad henah mishpat mou'ab.
**the captivity of Moab in latter the days saith Yahuah far Thus *is* the judgment of Moab**

**Jer 49:1**

לבני 1121 עמון 5983 כה 3541 אמר 559 יהוה 3068 הבנים 1121 אין 369 לישראל 3478 אם 518 יורש 3423 אין 369 לו 3807a
libney 'amoun, koh 'amar Yahuah, habaniym 'aeyn layisra'ael, 'am youresh 'aeyn lou';
**Concerning sons of the Ammonites thus saith Yahuah the sons? Has no for Israel if heir? no has he**

Jer 48:40 For thus saith YHUH; Behold, he shall fly as an eagle, and shall spread his wings over Moab.41 Kerioth is taken, and the strong holds are surprised, and the mighty men's hearts in Moab at that day shall be as the heart of a woman in her pangs.42 And Moab shall be destroyed from being a people, because he has magnified himself against YHUH.43 Fear, and the pit, and the snare, shall be upon you, O inhabitant of Moab, saith YHUH.44 He that fleeth from the fear shall fall into the pit; and he that get up out of the pit shall be taken in the snare: for I will bring upon it, even upon Moab, the year of their visitation, saith YHUH.45 They that fled stood under the shadow of Heshbon because of the force: but a fire shall come forth out of Heshbon, and a flame from the midst of Sihon, and shall devour the corner of Moab, and the crown of the head of the tumultuous ones.46 Woe be unto you, O Moab! the people of Chemosh perisheth: for your sons are taken captives, and your daughters captives.47 Yet will I bring again the captivity of Moab in the latter days, saith YHUH. Thus far is the judgment of Moab. **Jer** 49:1 Concerning the Ammonites, thus saith YHUH; Hath Israel no sons? has he no heir? why then doth their king inherit Gad, and his people dwell in his cities?

49:2

מדוע 4069 ירש 3423 מלכם 4428 את 853 גד 1410 ועמו 5971 בעריו 5892 ישב 3427: לכן 3651 הנה 2009 ימים 3117 באים 935
madua', yarash malkam 'at gad, ua'amou ba'arayu yashab. laken hineh yamiym ba'aym
**why *then* does inherit their king Gad and his people in his cities? dwell Therefore behold the days come**

נאם 5002 יהוה 3068 והשמעתי 8085 אל 413 רבת 7237 בני 1121 עמון 5983 תרועת 8643 מלחמה 4421
na'am Yahuah uahishma'atiy 'al rabat baney 'amoun taru'at milchamah,
**saith Yahuah that I will cause to be heard in Rabbah of the sons of the Ammonites an alarm of war**

והיתה 1961 לתל 8510 שממה 8077 ובנתיה 1323 באש 784 תצתנה 3341 וירש 3423 ישראל 3478 את 853
uahayatah latel shamamah, uabnoteyha ba'aesh titzatnah; uayarash yisra'ael 'at
**and it shall be a heap desolate and her daughters with fire shall be burned then shall be heir Israel**

49:3

ירשיו 3423 אמר 559 יהוה 3068: הילילי 3213 חשבון 2809 כי 3588 שדדה 7703 עי 5857 צעקנה 6817 בנות 1323
yorashayu 'amar Yahuah. heyliyliy cheshboun kiy shudadah 'ay, tza'aqnah banout
**unto them that were his heirs saith Yahuah Howl O Heshbon for is spoiled Ai cry you daughters of**

רבה 7237 חגרנה 2296 שקים 8242 ספדנה 5594 והתשוטטנה 7751 בגדרות 1448 כי 3588 מלכם 4428 בגולה 1473 ילך 1980
rabah chagoranah saqiym, sapodanah uahitshoutatnah bagaderout; kiy malkam bagoulah yelek,
**Rabbah gird you with sackcloth lament and run to and fro by the hedges for their king into captivity shall go**

49:4

כהניו 3548 ושריו 8269 יחדיו 3162: מה 4100 תתהללי 1984 בעמקים 6010 זב 2100 עמקך 6010 הבת 1323
kohanayu uasarayu yachdayu. mah tithalaliy ba'amaqiym, zab 'amqek, habat
***and* his priests and his princes together Wherefore glory you in the valleys flowing your valley O daughter?**

49:5

השובבה 7728 הבטחה 982 באצרתיה 214 מי 4310 יבוא 935 אלי 413: הנני 2005 מביא 935 עליך 5921 פחד 6343 נאם 5002
hashoubebah; habotachah ba'atzaroteyha, miy' yabou'a 'aelay. hinniy mebiy'a 'aleyka pachad, na'am
**backsliding that trusts in her treasures *saying* Who shall come unto me? Behold I will bring upon you a fear saith**

אדני 136 יהוה 3069 צבאות 6635 מכל 3605 סביביך 5439 ונדחתם 5080 איש 376 לפניו 6440 ואין 369
'adonay Yahuah tzaba'aut mikal sabiybayik; uanidachtem 'aysh lapanayu, ua'aeyn
**Adonai Yahuah of hosts from all those that be about you and you shall be driven out every man right forth and none**

49:6

מקבץ 6908 לנדד 5074: ואחרי 310 כן 3651 אשיב 7725 את 853 שבות 7622 בני 1121 עמון 5983
maqabetz lanoded. ua'acharey ken, 'ashiyb 'at shabut baney 'amoun
**shall gather up him that wander And after ward I will bring again the captivity of the children of Ammon**

49:7

נאם 5002 יהוה 3068: לאדום 123 כה 3541 אמר 559 יהוה 3068 צבאות 6635 האין 369 עוד 5750 חכמה 2451 בתימן 8487 אבדה 6
na'am Yahuah. le'adoum, koh 'amar Yahuah tzaba'aut, ha'aeyn 'aud chakamah bateyman; 'abadah
**saith Yahuah Concerning Edom thus saith Yahuah of hosts there is no more *Is* wisdom in Teman? is perished**

49:8

עצה 6098 מבנים 995 נסרחה 5628 חכמתם 2451: נסו 5127 הפנו 6437 העמיקו 6009 לשבת 3427 ישבי 3427 דדן 1719
'aetzah mibaniym, nisrachah chakamatam. nusu hapanu he'miyqu lashabet, yoshabey dadan;
**counsel from the prudent? is vanished? their wisdom Flee you turn back deep dwell O inhabitants of Dedan**

49:9

כי 3588 איד 343 עשו 6215 הבאתי 935 עליו 5921 עת 6256 פקדתיו 6485: אם 518 בצרים 1219 באו 935 לך 3807a
kiy 'aeyd 'aesau hebea'tiy 'alayu 'at paqadtiyu. 'am botzriym ba'au lak,
**for the calamity of Esau I will bring upon him the time *that* I will visit him If grapegatherers come to you**

Jer 49:2 Therefore, behold, the days come, saith YHUH, that I will cause an alarm of war to be heard in Rabbah of the Ammonites; and it shall be a desolate heap, and her daughters shall be burned with fire: then shall Israel be heir unto them that were his heirs, saith YHUH.3 Howl, O Heshbon, for Ai is spoiled: cry, you daughters of Rabbah, gird you with sackcloth; lament, and run to and fro by the hedges; for their king shall go into captivity, and his priests and his princes together.4 Wherefore gloriest you in the valleys, your flowing valley, O backsliding daughter? that trusted in her treasures, saying, Who shall come unto me?5 Behold, I will bring a fear upon you, saith YHUH G-D of hosts, from all those that be about you; and you shall be driven out every man right forth; and none shall gather up him that wandereth.6 And afterward I will bring again the captivity of the children of Ammon, saith YHUH.7 Concerning Edom, thus saith YHUH of hosts; Is wisdom no more in Teman? is counsel perished from the prudent? is their wisdom vanished?8 Flee you, turn back, dwell deep, O inhabitants of Dedan; for I will bring the calamity of Esau upon him, the time that I will visit him.9 If grapegatherers come to you, would they not leave some gleaning grapes? if thieves by night, they will destroy till they have enough.

| לא 3808 | ישארו 7604 | עוללות 5955 | אם 518 | גנבים 1590 | בלילה 3915 | השחיתו 7843 | דים 1767: | 49:10 כי 3588 |
|---|---|---|---|---|---|---|---|---|
| la' | yash'ayru | 'aulelout; | 'am | ganabiym | balayalah | hishchiytu | dayam. | kiy |
| not | would they leave *some* | gleaning grapes? | if | thieves | by night | they will destroy | *till* they have enough | But |

| אני 589 | חשפתי 2834 | את 853 | עשו 6215 | גליתי 1540 | את 853 | מסתריו 4565 | ונחבה 2247 | לא 3808 | יוכל 3201 |
|---|---|---|---|---|---|---|---|---|---|
| 'aniy | chasaptiy | 'at | 'aesau, | gileytiy | 'at | mistarayu, | uanechbah | la' | yukal; |
| I | have made bare | | Esau | I have uncovered | | his secret places | and to hide himself | not | he shall be able |

| שדד 7703 | זרעו 2233 | ואחיו 251 | ושכניו 7934 | ואיננו 369: | 49:11 עזבה 5800 | יתמיך 3490 | אני 589 |
|---|---|---|---|---|---|---|---|
| shudad | zar'au | ua'achayu | uashkenayu | ua'aeynenu. | 'azabah | yatomeyka | 'aniy |
| is spoiled | his seed | and his brethren | and his neighbours | and he is not | Leave | your fatherless children | I |

| אחיה 2421 | ואלמנתיך 490 | עלי 5921 | תבטחו 982: | 49:12 כי 3588 | כה 3541 | אמר 559 | יהוה 3068 | הנה 2009 | אשר 834 | אין 369 |
|---|---|---|---|---|---|---|---|---|---|---|
| 'achayeh; | ua'almanoteyka | 'alay | tibtachu. | kiy | koh | 'amar | Yahuah | hineh | 'asher | 'aeyn |
| will preserve *them* alive | and let your widows | in me | let trust | For | thus | saith | Yahuah | Behold *they* | whose | *was* not |

| משפטם 4941 | לשתות 8354 | הכוס 3563 | שתו 8354 | ישתו 8354 | ואתה 859 | הוא 1931 | נקה 5352 | תנקה 5352 | לא 3808 |
|---|---|---|---|---|---|---|---|---|---|
| mishpatam | lishtout | hakous | shatou | yishtu, | ua'atah | hua', | naqoh | tinaqeh; | la' |
| judgment | to drink of | the cup | have assuredly | drunken | and *are* you | he | *that* shall altogether | go unpunished? | not |

| תנקה 5352 | כי 3588 | שתה 8354 | תשתה 8354: | 49:13 כי 3588 | בי 871a | נשבעתי 7650 | נאם 5002 | יהוה 3068 | כי 3588 |
|---|---|---|---|---|---|---|---|---|---|
| tinaqeh, | kiy | shatoh | tishteh. | kiy | biy | nishba'atiy | na'am | Yahuah, | kiy |
| you shall go unpunished | but | you shall surely | drink *of it* | For | by myself | I have sworn | saith | Yahuah | that |

| לשמה 8047 | לחרפה 2781 | לחרב 2721 | ולקללה 7045 | תהיה 1961 | בצרה 1224 | וכל 3605 | עריה 5892 | תהיינה 1961 | לחרבות 2723 |
|---|---|---|---|---|---|---|---|---|---|
| lashamah | lacherpah | lachoreb | ualiqlalah | tihayeh | batzrah; | uakal | 'areyha | tihayeynah | lacharabout |
| a desolation | a reproach | a waste | and a curse | shall become | Bozrah | and all | the cities thereof | shall be | wastes |

| עולם 5769: | 49:14 שמועה 8052 | שמעתי 8085 | מאת 853 | יהוה 3068 | וציר 6735 | בגוים 1471 | שלוח 7971 |
|---|---|---|---|---|---|---|---|
| 'aulam. | shamu'ah | shama'atiy | me'at | Yahuah, | uatziyr | bagouyim | shaluach; |
| perpetual | a rumour | I have heard | from | Yahuah | and an ambassador | unto the heathen | is sent |

| התקבצו 6908 | ובאו 935 | עליה 5921 | וקומו 6965 | למלחמה 4421: | 49:15 כי 3588 | הנה 2009 | קטן 6996 | נתתיך 5414 |
|---|---|---|---|---|---|---|---|---|
| hitqabtzu | uabo'au | 'aleyha, | uaqumu | lamilchamah. | kiy | hineh | qaton | natatiyka |
| *saying* Gather you together | and come | against her | and rise up | to the battle | For | lo | small | I will make you |

| בגוים 1471 | בזוי 959 | באדם 120: | 49:16 תפלצתך 8606 | השיא 5377 | אתך 853 | זדון 2087 | לבך 3820 |
|---|---|---|---|---|---|---|---|
| bagouyim; | bazuy | ba'adam. | tiplatztaka | hishiy'a | 'atak | zadoun | libeka, |
| among the heathen | *and* despised | among men | Your terribleness | has deceived | you | *and* the pride of | your heart |

| שכני 7931 | בחגוי 2288 | הסלע 5553 | תפשי 8610 | מרום 4791 | גבעה 1389 | כי 3588 | תגביה 1361 | כנשר 5404 |
|---|---|---|---|---|---|---|---|---|
| shokaniy | bachaguey | hasela', | topasiy | maroum | gib'ah; | kiy | tagbiyha | kanesher |
| O you that dwell | in the clefts of | the rock | that hold | the height of | the hill | though | you should make high | as the eagle |

| קנך 7064 | משם 8033 | אורידך 3381 | נאם 5002 | יהוה 3068: | 49:17 והיתה 1961 | אדום 123 | לשמה 8047 | כל 3605 |
|---|---|---|---|---|---|---|---|---|
| qineka, | misham | 'auriydaka | na'am | Yahuah. | uahayatah | 'adoum | lashamah; | kal |
| your nest *as* | from there | I will bring you down | saith | Yahuah | Also will become | Edom | a desolation | every one |

Jer 49:10 But I have made Esau bare, I have uncovered his secret places, and he shall not be able to hide himself: his seed is spoiled, and his brethren, and his neighbors, and he is not.11 Leave your fatherless children, I will preserve them alive; and let your widows trust in me.12 For thus saith YHUH; Behold, they whose judgment was not to drink of the cup have assuredly drunken; and are you he that shall altogether go unpunished? you shall not go unpunished, but you shall surely drink of it.13 For I have sworn by myself, saith YHUH, that Bozrah shall become a desolation, a reproach, a waste, and a curse; and all the cities thereof shall be perpetual wastes.14 I have heard a rumour from YHUH, and an ambassador is sent unto the heathen, saying, Gather you together, and come against her, and rise up to the battle.15 For, lo, I will make you small among the heathen, and despised among men.16 Thy terribleness has deceived you, and the pride of your heart, O you that dwellest in the clefts of the rock, that holdest the height of the hill: though you should make your nest as high as the eagle, I will bring you down from thence, saith YHUH.17 Also Edom shall be a desolation: everyone that go by it shall be astonished, and shall hiss at all the plagues thereof.

49:18

עבר 5674 עליה 5921 ישם 8074 וישרק 8319 על 5921 כל 3605 מכותה 4347: כמהפכת 4114 סדם 5467
'aber 'aleyha, yishom uayishroq 'al kal makouteha. kamahpekat sadom
**that goes by it shall be astonished and shall hiss at all the plagues thereof As in the overthrow of Sodom**

ועמרה 6017 ושכניה 7934 אמר 559 יהוה 3068 לא 3808 ישב 3427 שם 8033 איש 376 ולא 3808 יגור 1481 בה 871a
ua'amorah uashkeneyha 'amar Yahuah; la' yesheb sham 'aysh, uala' yagur bah
**and Gomorrah and the neighbour *cities* thereof saith Yahuah no shall abide there man neither shall dwell in it**

49:19

בן 1121 אדם 120: הנה 2009 כאריה 738 יעלה 5927 מגאון 1347 הירדן 3383 אל 413 נוה 5116
ben 'adam. hineh ka'aryeh ya'aleh miga'aun hayarden 'al naueh
**a son of man Behold like a lion he shall come up from the swelling of the Jordan against the habitation of**

איתן 386 כי 3588 ארגיעה 7280 אריצנו 7323 מעליה 5921 ומי 4310 בחור 970 אליה 413 אפקד 6485 כי 3588
'aeytan kiy 'argiy'ah 'ariytzenu me'aleyha, uamiy bachur 'aeleyha 'apqod; kiy
**the strong but I will suddenly make him run away from her and who *is* a chosen *man that* over her? I may appoint for**

49:20

מי 4310 כמוני 3644 ומי 4310 יעידני 3259 ומי 4310 זה 2088 רעה 7462 אשר 834 יעמד 5975 לפני 6440: לכן 3651
miy' kamouniy uamiy yo'aydeniy, uamiy zeh ro'ah, 'asher ya'amod lapanay. laken
**who *is* like me? and who will appoint me the time? and who *is* that shepherd that will stand before me? Therefore**

שמעו 8085 עצת 6098 יהוה 3068 אשר 834 יעץ 3289 אל 413 אדום 123 ומחשבותיו 4284 אשר 834 חשב 2803 אל 413
shim'au 'atzat Yahuah 'asher ya'atz 'al 'adoum, uamachshaboutayu, 'asher chashab 'al
**hear the counsel of Yahuah that he has taken against Edom and his purposes that he has purposed against**

ישבי 3427 תימן 8487 אם 518 לא 3808 יסחבום 5498 צעירי 6810 הצאן 6629 אם 518 לא 3808 ישים 8074
yoshabey teyman; 'am la' yisachabum tza'ayrey hatza'an, 'am la' yashiym
**the inhabitants of Teman Surely not shall draw them out the least of the flock surely not he shall make desolate**

49:21

עליהם 5921 נוהם 5116: מקול 6963 נפלם 5307 רעשה 7493 הארץ 776 צעקה 6818 בים 3220 סוף 5488 נשמע 8085
'aleyhem nauehem. miqoul niplam, ra'ashah ha'aretz; tza'aqah bayam sup nishma'
**with them their habitations at the noise of their fall is moved The earth *at* the cry sea in the Red was heard**

49:22

קולה 6963: הנה 2009 כנשר 5404 יעלה 5927 וידאה 1675 ויפרש 6566 כנפיו 3671 על 5921 בצרה 1224 והיה 1961
qoulah. hineh kanesher ya'aleh uayid'ah, uayipros kanapayu 'al batzrah uahayah
**the noise thereof Behold as the eagle he shall come up and fly and spread his wings over Bozrah and shall**

49:23

לב 3820 גבורי 1368 אדום 123 ביום 3117 ההוא 1931 כלב 3820 אשה 802 מצרה 6887: לדמשק 1834
leb gibourey 'adoum bayoum hahua', kaleb 'ashah matzerah. ladameseq,
**the heart of the mighty men of Edom at day that be as the heart of a woman in her pangs Concerning Damascus**

בושה 954 חמת 2574 וארפד 774 כי 3588 שמעה 8052 רעה 7451 שמעו 8085 נמגו 4127 בים 3220 דאגה 1674
boushah chamat ua'arpad, kiy shamu'ah ra'ah shama'au namogu; bayam da'agah,
**is confounded Hamath and Arpad for tidings evil they have heard they are fainthearted on the sea *there is* sorrow**

49:24

השקט 8252 לא 3808 יוכל 3201: רפתה 7503 דמשק 1834 הפנתה 6437 לנוס 5127 ורטט 7374 החזיקה 2388 צרה 6869
hashqet la' yukal. rapatah dameseq hipnatah lanus uaretet hechaziyqah; tzarah
**quiet not it can be is waxed feeble Damascus *and* turned herself to flee and fear has seized on *her* anguish**

Jer 49:18 As in the overthrow of Sodom and Gomorrah and the neighbor cities thereof, saith YHUH, no man shall abide there, neither shall a son of man dwell in it.19 Behold, he shall come up like a lion from the swelling of Jordan against the habitation of the strong: but I will suddenly make him run away from her: and who is a chosen man, that I may appoint over her? for who is like me? and who will appoint me the time? and who is that shepherd that will stand before me?20 Therefore hear the counsel of YHUH, that he has taken against Edom; and his purposes, that he has purposed against the inhabitants of Teman: Surely the least of the flock shall draw them out: surely he shall make their habitations desolate with them.21 The earth is moved at the noise of their fall, at the cry the noise thereof was heard in the Red sea.22 Behold, he shall come up and fly as the eagle, and spread his wings over Bozrah: and at that day shall the heart of the mighty men of Edom be as the heart of a woman in her pangs.23 Concerning Damascus. Hamath is confounded, and Arpad: for they have heard evil tidings: they are fainthearted; there is sorrow on the sea; it cannot be quiet.24 Damascus is waxed feeble, and turneth herself to flee, and fear has seized on her: anguish and sorrows have taken her, as a woman in travail.

| | | | 49:25 | | | | | |
|---|---|---|---|---|---|---|---|---|
| 2256 וחבלים | 270 אחזתה | 3205: כיולדה | 349 איך | 3808 לא | 5800 עזבה | 5892 עיר | 8416 תהלה | 7151 קרית |
| uachabaliym | 'achazatah | kayouledah. | 'aeyk | la' | 'azbah | 'ayr | tahilah | qiryat |
| **and sorrows** | **have taken her** | **as a woman in travail** | **How** | **not** | **is left** | **the city of** | **praise** | **the city of** |

| | 49:26 | | | | | | | | |
|---|---|---|---|---|---|---|---|---|---|
| 4885: משושי | 3651 לכן | 5307 יפלו | 970 בחוריה | 7339 ברחבתיה | 3605 וכל | 582 אנשי | 4421 המלחמה | 1826 ידמו | 3117 ביום |
| masousiy. | laken | yiplu | bachureyha | birchoteyha; | uakal | 'anshey | hamilchamah | yidamu | bayoum |
| **my joy** | **Therefore** | **shall fall** | **her young men** | **in her streets** | **and all** | **the men of** | **war** | **shall be cut off** | **in day** |

| | | | | 49:27 | | | | |
|---|---|---|---|---|---|---|---|---|
| 1931 ההוא | 5002 נאם | 3068 יהוה | 6635: צבאות | 3341 והצתי | 784 אש | 2346 בחומת | 1834 דמשק | 398 ואכלה |
| hahua', | na'am | Yahuah | tzaba'aut. | uahitzatiy | 'aesh | bachoumat | damaseq; | ua'akalah |
| **that** | **saith** | **Yahuah** | **of hosts** | **And I will kindle** | **a fire** | **in the wall of** | **Damascus** | **and it shall consume** |

| | | | 49:28 | | | | |
|---|---|---|---|---|---|---|---|
| 759 ארמנות | 1130 בן | 1908: הדד | 6938 לקדר | 4467 ולממלכות | 2674 חצור | 834 אשר | 5221 הכה |
| 'armanout | ben | hadad. | laqedar | ualmamlakout | chatzour, | 'asher | hikah |
| **the palaces of** | **Ben** | **hadad** | **Concerning Kedar** | **and concerning the kingdoms of** | **Hazor** | **which** | **shall smite** |

| | | | | | | | | | | | | |
|---|---|---|---|---|---|---|---|---|---|---|---|---|
| 5020 נבוכדראצור | 4428 מלך | 894 בבל | 3541 כה | 559 אמר | 3068 יהוה | 6965 קומו | 5927 עלו | 413 אל | 6938 קדר | 7703 ושדדו | 853 את | 1121 בני |
| nabukadratzour | melek | babel, | koh | 'amar | Yahuah; | qumu | 'alu | 'al | qedar, | uashadadu | 'at | baney |
| **Nebuchadnezzar** | **king of** | **Babylon** | **thus** | **saith** | **Yahuah** | **Arise you** | **go up** | **to** | **Kedar** | **and spoil** | | **the men of** |

| | 49:29 | | | | | | |
|---|---|---|---|---|---|---|---|
| 6924: קדם | 168 אהליהם | 6629 וצאנם | 3947 יקחו | 3407 יריעותיהם | 3605 וכל | 3627 כליהם | 1581 וגמליהם |
| qedem. | 'ahaleyhem | uatza'nam | yiqachu, | yariy'auteyhem | uakal | kaleyhem | uagamaleyhem |
| **the east** | **Their tents** | **and their flocks** | **shall they take away** | **their curtains** | **and all** | **their vessels** | **and their camels** |

| | | | | | | 49:30 | | | |
|---|---|---|---|---|---|---|---|---|---|
| 5375 ישאו | 1992 להם | 7121 וקראו | 5921 עליהם | 4032 מגור | 5439: מסביב | 5127 נסו | 5110 נדו | 3966 מאד | 6009 העמיקו |
| yis'au | lahem; | uaqar'au | 'aleyhem | magour | misabiyb. | nusu | nudu | ma'ad | he'amiyqu |
| **they shall take** | **to themselves** | **and they shall cry** | **unto them** | **Fear** | ***is* on every side** | **Flee** | **get you** | **far *off*** | **deep** |

| | | | | | | | | | | |
|---|---|---|---|---|---|---|---|---|---|---|
| 3427 לשבת | 3427 ישבי | 2674 חצור | 5002 נאם | 3068 יהוה | 3588 כי | 3289 יעץ | 5921 עליכם | 5019 נבוכדראצר | 4428 מלך | 894 בבל |
| lashabet | yoshabey | chatzour | na'am | Yahuah; | kiy | ya'atz | 'aleykem | nabukadra'tzar | melek | babel |
| **dwell** | **O you inhabitants of** | **Hazor** | **saith** | **Yahuah** | **for** | **has taken** | **against you** | **Nebuchadrezzar** | **king of** | **Babylon** |

| | | | | 49:31 | | | | | |
|---|---|---|---|---|---|---|---|---|---|
| 6098 עצה | 2803 וחשב | 5921 עליהם | 4284: מחשבה | 6965 קומו | 5927 עלו | 413 אל | 1471 גוי | 7961 שליו | 3427 יושב |
| 'aetzah, | uachashab | 'aleyhem | machashabah. | qumu | 'alu, | 'al | gouy | shaleyu | yousheb |
| **counsel** | **and has conceived** | **against you** | **a purpose** | **Arise** | **get you up** | **unto** | **nation** | ***the* wealthy** | **that dwell** |

| | | | | | | | | | | 49:32 |
|---|---|---|---|---|---|---|---|---|---|---|
| 983 לבטח | 5002 נאם | 3068 יהוה | 3808 לא | 1817 דלתים | 3808 ולא | 1280 בריח | 3807a לו | 910 בדד | 7931: ישכנו | 1961 והיו |
| labetach | na'am | Yahuah; | la' | dalatayim | uala' | bariyach | lou' | badad | yishkonu. | uahayu |
| **without care** | **saith** | **Yahuah** | ***which have* neither** | **gates** | **nor** | **bars** | **to him** | **alone** | ***which* dwell** | **And shall be** |

| | | | | | | | | |
|---|---|---|---|---|---|---|---|---|
| 1581 גמליהם | 957 לבז | 1995 והמון | 4735 מקניהם | 7998 לשלל | 2219 וזרתים | 3605 לכל | 7307 רוח | 7112 קצוצי |
| gamaleyhem | labaz, | uahamoun | miqneyhem | lashalal, | uazeritiym | lakal | ruach | qatzutzey |
| **their camels** | **a booty** | **and the multitude of** | **their cattle** | **a spoil** | **and I will scatter** | **into all** | **winds** | **them *that are* in the utmost** |

| | | | | | | | | 49:33 | |
|---|---|---|---|---|---|---|---|---|---|
| 6285 פאה | 3605 ומכל | 5676 עבריו | 935 אביא | 853 את | 343 אידם | 5002 נאם | 3068: יהוה | 1961 והיתה | 2674 חצור |
| pe'ah; | uamikal | 'abarayu | 'abiy'a | 'at | 'aeydam | na'am | Yahuah. | uahayatah | chatzour |
| **corners** | **and from all** | **sides thereof** | **I will bring** | | **their calamity** | **saith** | **Yahuah** | **And shall be** | **Hazor** |

Jer 49:25 How is the city of praise not left, the city of my joy!26 Therefore her young men shall fall in her streets, and all the men of war shall be cut off in that day, saith YHUH of hosts.27 And I will kindle a fire in the wall of Damascus, and it shall consume the palaces of Ben-hadad.28 Concerning Kedar, and concerning the kingdoms of Hazor, which Nebuchadrezzar king of Babylon shall smite, thus saith YHUH; Arise you, go up to Kedar, and spoil the men of the east.29 Their tents and their flocks shall they take away: they shall take to themselves their curtains, and all their vessels, and their camels; and they shall cry unto them, Fear is on every side.30 Flee, get you far off, dwell deep, O you inhabitants of Hazor, saith YHUH; for Nebuchadrezzar king of Babylon has taken counsel against you, and has conceived a purpose against you.31 Arise, get you up unto the wealthy nation, that dwell without care, saith YHUH, which have neither gates nor bars, which dwell alone.32 And their camels shall be a booty, and the multitude of their cattle a spoil: and I will scatter into all winds them that are in the utmost corners; and I will bring their calamity from all sides thereof, saith YHUH.33 And Hazor shall be a dwelling for dragons, and a desolation forever: there shall no man abide there, nor any son of man dwell in it.

למעון 4583 תנים 8577 שממה 8077 עד 5704 עולם 5769 לא 3808 ישב 3427 שם 8033 איש 376 ולא 3808 יגור 1481 בה 871a
lima'aun taniym shamamah 'ad 'aulam; la' yesheb sham 'aysh, uala' yagur bah
**a dwelling for dragons *and* a desolation for ever no there shall abide there man nor dwell in it**

בן 1121 אדם 120: **49:34** אשר 834 היה 1961 דבר 1697 יהוה 3068 אל 413 ירמיהו 3414 הנביא 5030 אל 413 עילם 5867
ben 'adam. 'asher hayah dabar Yahuah 'al yirmayahu hanabiy'a 'al 'aeylam;
***any* son of man that came The word of Yahuah to Jeremiah the prophet against Elam**

בראשית 7225 מלכות 4438 צדקיה 6667 מלך 4428 יהודה 3063 לאמר 559: **49:35** כה 3541 אמר 559 יהוה 3068 צבאות 6635 הנני 2005
bara'shiyt, malkut tzidqiyah melek yahudah lea'mor. koh 'amar Yahuah tzaba'aut, hinniy
**in the beginning of the reign of Zedekiah king of Judah saying Thus saith Yahuah of hosts Behold I**

שבר 7665 את 853 קשת 7198 עילם 5867 ראשית 7225 גבורתם 1369: **49:36** והבאתי 935 אל 413 עילם 5867 ארבע 702 רוחות 7307
shober 'at qeshet 'aeylam; ra'shiyt gaburatam. uahebea'tiy 'al 'aeylam 'arba ruchout,
**will break the bow of Elam the chief of their might And will I bring upon Elam *the* four winds**

מארבע 702 קצות 7098 השמים 8064 וזרתים 2219 לכל 3605 הרחות 7307 האלה 428 ולא 3808 יהיה 1961 הגוי 1471
me'arba' qatzout hashamayim, uazeritiym, lakol haruchout ha'aeleh; uala' yihayeh hagouy,
**from the four quarters of heaven and will scatter them toward all winds those and no there shall be nation**

אשר 834 לא 3808 יבוא 935 שם 8033 נדחי 5080 עולם 5867 **49:37** והחתתי 2865 את 853 עילם 5867 לפני 6440
'asher la' yabou'a sham nidachey 'aulam uahachatatiy 'at 'aeylam lipney
**which not shall come where the outcasts of Elam For I will cause to be dismayed Elam before**

איביהם 341 ולפני 6440 מבקשי 1245 נפשם 5315 והבאתי 935 עליהם 5921 רעה 7451 את 853 חרון 2740 אפי 639 נאם 5002
'ayabeyhem ualipaney mabaqshey napsham, uahebea'tiy 'aleyhem ra'ah 'at charoun 'apiy na'am
**their enemies and before them that seek their life and I will bring upon them evil fierce *even* my anger saith**

יהוה 3068 ושלחתי 7971 אחריהם 310 את 853 החרב 2719 עד 5704 כלותי 3615 אותם 853: **49:38** ושמתי 7760 כסאי 3678
Yahuah; uashilachtiy 'achareyhem 'at hachereb, 'ad kaloutiy 'autam. uasamtiy kis'ay
**Yahuah and I will send after them the sword till I have consumed them And I will set my throne**

בעילם 5867 והאבדתי 6 משם 8033 מלך 4428 ושרים 8269 נאם 5002 יהוה 3068: **49:39** והיה 1961 באחרית 319
ba'aeylam; uaha'abadatiy misham melek uasariym na'am Yahuah. uahayah ba'achariyt
**in Elam and I will destroy from there the king and the princes saith Yahuah But it shall come to pass in latter**

הימים 3117 אשוב 7725 את 853 שבית 7622 עילם 5867 נאם 5002 יהוה 3068:
hayamiym, 'ashub 'at shabyt 'aeylam na'am Yahuah.
**the days *that* I will bring again the captivity of Elam saith Yahuah**

**Jer 50:1** הדבר 1697 אשר 834 דבר 1696 יהוה 3068 אל 413 בבל 894 אל 413 ארץ 776 כשדים 3778 ביד 3027 ירמיהו 3414
hadabar, 'asher diber Yahuah 'al babel 'al 'aretz kasdiym; bayad yirmayahu
**The word that spoke Yahuah against Babylon *and* against the land of the Chaldeans by Jeremiah**

הנביא 5030: **50:2** הגידו 5046 בגוים 1471 והשמיעו 8085 ושאו 5375 נס 5251 השמיעו 8085 אל 408 תכחדו 3582 אמרו 559
hanabiy'a. hagiydu bagouyim uahashamiy'au uas'au nes, hashmiy'au 'al takachedu; 'amru
**the prophet Declare you among the nations and publish and set up a standard publish not *and* conceal say**

Jer 49:34 The word of YHUH that came to Jeremiah the prophet against Elam in the beginning of the reign of Zedekiah king of Judah, saying,35 Thus saith YHUH of hosts; Behold, I will break the bow of Elam, the chief of their might.36 And upon Elam will I bring the four winds from the four quarters of heaven, and will scatter them toward all those winds; and there shall be no nation whither the outcasts of Elam shall not come.37 For I will cause Elam to be dismayed before their enemies, and before them that seek their life: and I will bring evil upon them even my fierce anger, saith YHUH; and I will send the sword after them, till I have consumed them:38 And I will set my throne in Elam, and will destroy from thence the king and the princes, saith YHUH.39 But it shall come to pass in the latter days, that I will bring again the captivity of Elam, saith YHUH. **Jer** 50:1 The word that YHUH spoke against Babylon and against the land of the Chaldeans by Jeremiah the prophet.2 Declare you among the nations, and publish, and set up a standard; publish, and conceal not: say, Babylon is taken, Bel is confounded, Merodach is broken in pieces; her idols are confounded, her images are broken in pieces.

| 3920 נלכדה | 894 בבל | 3001 הביש | 1078 בל | 2865 חת | 4781 מרדך | 3001 הבישו | 6091 עצביה | 2865 חתו |
|---|---|---|---|---|---|---|---|---|
| nilkadah | babel | hobiysh | bel | chat | marodak, | hobiyshu | 'atzabeyha, | chatu |
| **is taken** | **Babylon** | **is confounded** | **Bel** | **is broken in pieces** | **Merodach** | **are confounded** | **her idols** | **are broken in pieces** |

| 1544: גלוליה | 50:3 | 3588 כי | 5927 עלה | 5921 עליה | 1471 גוי | 6828 מצפון | 1931 הוא | 7896 ישית | 853 את | 776 ארצה | 8047 לשמה |
|---|---|---|---|---|---|---|---|---|---|---|---|
| giluleyha. | | kiy | 'alah | 'aleyha | gouy | mitzapoun, | hua' | yashiyt | 'at | 'artzah | lashamah, |
| **her images** | | **For** | **there comes up** | **against her** | **a nation** | **out of the north** | **which** | **shall make** | | **her land** | **desolate** |

| 3808 ולא | 1961 יהיה | 3427 יושב | 871a בה | 120 מאדם | 5704 ועד | 929 בהמה | 5110 נדו | 1980: הלכו | 50:4 | 3117 בימים | 1992 ההמה |
|---|---|---|---|---|---|---|---|---|---|---|---|
| uala' | yihayeh | yousheb | bah; | me'adam | ua'ad | bahemah | nadu | halaku. | | bayamiym | hahemah |
| **and none** | **shall** | **dwell** | **therein** | **both man** | **and unto** | **beast** | **they shall remove** | **they shall depart** | | **In days** | **those** |

| 6256 ובעת | 1931 ההיא | 5002 נאם | 3069 יהוה | 935 יבאו | 1121 בני | 3478 ישראל | 1992 המה | 1121 ובני | 3063 יהודה | 3162 יחדו |
|---|---|---|---|---|---|---|---|---|---|---|
| uaba'aet | hahiy'a | na'am | Yahuah, | yabo'au | baney | yisra'ael | hemah | uabney | yahudah | yachdau; |
| **and in time** | **that** | **saith** | **Yahuah** | **shall come** | **the children of** | **Israel** | **they** | **and the children of** | **Judah** | **together** |

| 1980 הלוך | 1058 ובכו | 1980 ילכו | 853 ואת | 3069 יהוה | 430 אלהיהם | 1245: יבקשו | 50:5 | 6726 ציון | 7592 ישאלו | 1870 דרך | 2008 הנה |
|---|---|---|---|---|---|---|---|---|---|---|---|
| halouk | uabakou | yeleku, | ua'at | Yahuah | 'aloheyhem | yabaqeshu. | | tziyoun | yish'alu, | derek | henah |
| **going** | **and weeping** | **they shall go** | ***and*** | **Yahuah** | **their Elohim** | **seek** | | ***to* Zion** | **They shall ask** | **the way** | **thitherward** |

| 6440 פניהם | 935 באו | 3867 ונלוו | 413 אל | 3068 יהוה | 1285 ברית | 5769 עולם | 3808 לא |
|---|---|---|---|---|---|---|---|
| paneyhem; | bo'au | uaniluu | 'al | Yahuah, | bariyt | 'aulam | la' |
| ***with* their faces** | ***saying* Come** | **and let us join ourselves** | **to** | **Yahuah** | ***in* a covenant** | **perpetual** | **not** |

| 7911: תשכח | 50:6 | 6629 צאן | 6 אבדות | 1961 היה | 5971 עמי | 7462 רעיהם | 8582 התעום |
|---|---|---|---|---|---|---|---|
| tishakeach. | | tza'n | 'abadout | hayah | 'amiy, | ro'aeyhem | hita'aum, |
| ***that* shall be forgotten** | | **sheep** | **ones lost** | **has been** | **My people** | **their shepherds** | **have caused them to go astray** |

| 2022 הרים | 7726 שובבים | 2022 מהר | 413 אל | 1389 גבעה | 1980 הלכו | 7911 שכחו |
|---|---|---|---|---|---|---|
| hariym | shoubabiym | mehar | 'al | gib'ah | halaku, | shakachu |
| ***on* the mountains** | **they have turned away** | **from mountain** | **to** | **hill** | **they have gone** | **they have forgotten** |

| 7258: רבצם | 50:7 | 3605 כל | 4672 מוצאיהם | 398 אכלום | 6862 וצריהם | 559 אמרו | 3808 לא | 816 נאשם | 8478 תחת |
|---|---|---|---|---|---|---|---|---|---|
| ribtzam. | | kal | moutza'aeyhem | 'akalum, | uatzareyhem | 'amaru | la' | ne'asham; | tachat, |
| **their restingplace** | | **All** | **that found them** | **have devoured them** | **and their adversaries** | **said** | **not** | **We offend** | **because** |

| 834 אשר | 2398 חטאו | 3068 ליהוה | 5116 נוה | 6664 צדק | 4723 ומקוה | 1 אבותיהם | 3068: יהוה | 50:8 | 5110 נדו |
|---|---|---|---|---|---|---|---|---|---|
| 'asher | chata'au | laYahuah | naueh | tzedeq, | uamiqaueh | abouteyhem | Yahuah. | | nudu |
| **which** | **they have sinned** | **against Yahuah** | **the habitation of** | **justice** | **even the hope of** | **their fathers** | **Yahuah** | | **Remove** |

| 8432 מתוך | 894 בבל | 776 ומארץ | 3778 כשדים | 3318 יצאו | 1961 והיו | 6260 כעתודים | 6440 לפני | 6629: צאן | 50:9 | 3588 כי |
|---|---|---|---|---|---|---|---|---|---|---|
| mitouk | babel, | uame'aretz | kasdiym | yatze'au | uihayu | ka'atudiym | lipney | tza'n. | | kiy |
| **out of the midst of** | **Babylon** | **out of the land of** | **the Chaldeans** | **go forth** | **and be** | **as the he goats** | **before** | **the flocks** | | **For** |

| 2009 הנה | 595 אנכי | 5782 מעיר | 5927 ומעלה | 5921 על | 894 בבל | 6951 קהל | 1471 גוים | 1419 גדלים | 776 מארץ | 6828 צפון |
|---|---|---|---|---|---|---|---|---|---|---|
| hineh | 'anokiy | me'ayr | uama'aleh | 'al | babel | qahal | gouyim | gadoliym | me'aretz | tzapoun, |
| **lo** | **I** | **will raise** | **and cause to come up** | **against** | **Babylon** | **an assembly of** | **nations** | **great** | **from country** | ***the* north** |

Jer 50:3 For out of the north there cometh up a nation against her, which shall make her land desolate, and none shall dwell therein: they shall remove, they shall depart, both man and beast.4 In those days, and in that time, saith YHUH, the children of Israel shall come, they and the children of Judah together, going and weeping: they shall go, and seek YHUH their G-d.5 They shall ask the way to Zion with their faces thitherward, saying, Come, and let us join ourselves to YHUH in a perpetual covenant that shall not be forgotten.6 My people has been lost sheep: their shepherds have caused them to go astray, they have turned them away on the mountains: they have gone from mountain to hill, they have forgotten their restingplace.7 All that found them have devoured them: and their adversaries said, We offend not, because they have sinned against YHUH, the habitation of justice, even YHUH, the hope of their fathers.8 Remove out of the midst of Babylon, and go forth out of the land of the Chaldeans, and be as the he goats before the flocks.9 For, lo, I will raise and cause to come up against Babylon an assembly of great nations from the north country: and they shall set themselves in array against her; from thence she shall be taken: their arrows shall be as of a mighty expert man; none shall return in vain.

ערכו 6186 לה 3807a משם 8033 תלכד 3920 חציו 2671 כגבור 1368
ua'araku lah, misham tilaked; chitzayu kagibour
**and they shall set themselves in array against her from there she shall be taken their arrows *shall be* as of a mighty man**

משכיל 7919 לא 3808 ישוב 7725 ריקם 7387: 50:10 והיתה 1961 כשדים 3778 לשלל 7998 כל 3605 שלליה 7997 ישבעו 7646 נאם 5002
mashkiyl, la' yashub reyqam. uahayatah kasdiym lashalal; kal sholaleyha yisba'au na'am
**expert none shall return in vain And shall be Chaldea a spoil all that spoil her shall be satisfied saith**

יהוה 3068: 50:11 כי 3588 תשמחי 8055 כי 3588 תעלזי 5937 שסי 8154 נחלתי 5159 כי 3588 תפושי 6335
Yahuah. kiy tismachiy kiy ta'alziy shosey nachalatiy; kiy tapushiy
**Yahuah Because you were glad because you rejoiced O you destroyers of mine heritage because you are grown fat**

כעגלה 5697 דשה 1877 ותצהלי 6670 כאברים 47: 50:12 בושה 954 אמכם 517 מאד 3966 חפרה 2659
ka'agalah daShah, uatitzhaliy ka'abiriym. boushah 'amkem ma'ad, chaparah
**as the heifer *at* grass and bellow as bulls shall be confounded Your mother sore shall be ashamed**

יולדתכם 3205 הנה 2009 אחרית 319 גוים 1471 מדבר 4057 ציה 6723 וערבה 6160: 50:13
youladtakem; hineh 'achariyt gouyim, midbar tziyah ua'arabah.
**she that bare you behold the hindermost of the nations *shall be* a wilderness a dry land and a desert**

מקצף 7110 יהוה 3068 לא 3808 תשב 3427 והיתה 1961 שממה 8077 כלה 3605 כל 3605 עבר 5674 על 5921
miqetzep Yahuah la' tesheb, uahayatah shamamah kulah; kal 'aber 'al
**Because of the wrath of Yahuah not it shall be inhabited but it shall be desolate wholly every one that goes by**

בבל 894 ישם 8074 וישרק 8319 על 5921 כל 3605 מכותיה 4347: 50:14 ערכו 6186 על 5921 בבל 894 סביב 5439
babel, yishom uayishroq 'al kal makouteyha. 'arku 'al babel sabiyb
**Babylon shall be astonished and hiss at all her plagues Put yourselves in array against Babylon round about**

כל 3605 דרכי 1869 קשת 7198 ידו 3034 אליה 413 אל 408 תחמלו 2550 אל 413 חץ 2671 כי 3588 ליהוה 3068 חטאה 2398: 50:15
kal dorakey qeshet, yadu 'aeleyha, 'al tachmalu 'al chetz; kiy laYahuah chata'ah.
**all you that bend the bow shoot at her no spare of arrows for against Yahuah she has sinned**

הריעו 7321 עליה 5921 סביב 5439 נתנה 5414 ידה 3027 נפלו 5307 אשויתיה 803 נהרסו 2040 חומותיה 2346 כי 3588
hariy'au 'aleyha sabiyb natanah yadah, naplu 'ashuyoteyha nehersu choumouteyha; kiy
**Shout against her round about she has given her hand are fallen her foundation are thrown down her walls for**

נקמת 5360 יהוה 3068 היא 1931 הנקמו 5358 בה 871a כאשר 834 עשתה 6213 עשו 6213 לה 3807a: 50:16 כרתו 3772 זורע 2232
niqmat Yahuah hiy'a hinaqamu bah, ka'asher 'astah 'asu lah. kirtu zourea'
***is* the vengeance of Yahuah it take vengeance upon her as she has done do unto her Cut off the sower**

מבבל 894 ותפש 8610 מגל 4038 בעת 6256 קציר 7105 מפני 6440 חרב 2719 היונה 3238 איש 376 אל 413
mibabel, uatopes magal ba'aet qatziyr; mipaney chereb hayounah, 'aysh 'al
**from Babylon and him that handle the sickle in the time of harvest for fear of sword the oppressing every one to**

עמו 5971 יפנו 6437 ואיש 376 לארצו 776 ינסו 5127: 50:17 שה 7716 פזורה 6340 ישראל 3478 אריות 738
'amou yipnu, ua'aysh la'artzou yanusu. seh pazurah yisra'ael arayout
**his people they shall turn and every one to his own land they shall flee *is* a sheep scattered Israel the lions**

Jer 50:10 And Chaldea shall be a spoil: all that spoil her shall be satisfied, saith YHUH.11 Because you were glad, because you rejoiced, O you destroyers of mine heritage, because you are grown fat as the heifer at grass, and bellow as bulls;12 Your mother shall be sore confounded; she that bare you shall be ashamed: behold, the hindermost of the nations shall be a wilderness, a dry land, and a desert.13 Because of the wrath of YHUH it shall not be inhabited, but it shall be wholly desolate: everyone that go by Babylon shall be astonished, and hiss at all her plagues.14 Put yourselves in array against Babylon round about: all you that bend the bow, shoot at her, spare no arrows: for she has sinned against YHUH.15 Shout against her round about: she has given her hand: her foundations are fallen, her walls are thrown down: for it is the vengeance of YHUH: take vengeance upon her; as she has done, do unto her.16 Cut off the sower from Babylon, and him that handleth the sickle in the time of harvest: for fear of the oppressing sword they shall turn everyone to his people, and they shall flee everyone to his own land.17 Israel is a scattered sheep; the lions have driven him away: first the king of Assyria has devoured him; and last this Nebuchadrezzar king of Babylon has broken his bones.

| הדיחו 5080 | הראשון 7223 | אכלו 398 | מלך 4428 | אשור 804 | וזה 2088 | האחרון 314 | עצמו 6105 |
|---|---|---|---|---|---|---|---|
| hidiychu; | hara'shoun | 'akalou | melek | 'ashur, | uazeh | ha'acharoun | 'atzmou, |
| **have driven *him* away** | **first** | **has devoured him** | **the king of** | **Assyria** | **and this** | **the last** | **has broken his bones** |

| נבוכדראצר 5019 | מלך 4428 | בבל 894: | 50:18 | לכן 3651 | כה 3541 | אמר 559 | יהוה 3068 | צבאות 6635 | אלהי 430 | ישראל 3478 | הנני 2005 |
|---|---|---|---|---|---|---|---|---|---|---|---|
| nabukadra'tzar | melek | babel. | | laken, | koh | 'amar | Yahuah | tzaba'aut | 'alohey | yisra'ael, | hinniy |
| **Nebuchadrezzar** | **king of** | **Babylon** | | **Therefore** | **thus** | **saith** | **Yahuah** | **of hosts** | **the Elohim of** | **Israel** | **Behold I** |

| פקד 6485 | אל 413 | מלך 4428 | בבל 894 | ואל 413 | ארצו 776 | כאשר 834 | פקדתי 6485 | אל 413 | מלך 4428 | אשור 804: | 50:19 |
|---|---|---|---|---|---|---|---|---|---|---|---|
| poqed | 'al | melek | babel | ua'al | artzou; | ka'asher | paqadtiy | 'al | melek | 'ashur. | |
| **will punish** | **to** | **the king of** | **Babylon** | **and to** | **his land** | **as** | **I have punished** | **to** | **the king of** | **Assyria** | |

| ושבבתי 7725 | את 853 | ישראל 3478 | אל 413 | נוהו 5116 | ורעה 7462 | הכרמל 3760 | והבשן 1316 | ובהר 2022 |
|---|---|---|---|---|---|---|---|---|
| uashoabtiy | 'at | yisra'ael | 'al | nauehu, | uara'ah | hakarmel | uahabashan; | uabhar |
| **And I will bring again** | | **Israel** | **to** | **his habitation** | **and he shall feed on** | **Carmel** | **and Bashan** | **and upon mount** |

| אפרים 669 | והגלעד 1568 | תשבע 7646 | נפשו 5315: | 50:20 | בימים 3117 | ההם 1992 | ובעת 6256 | ההיא 1931 | נאם 5002 | יהוה 3068 |
|---|---|---|---|---|---|---|---|---|---|---|
| 'aprayim | uahagil'ad | tisba' | napshou. | | bayamiym | hahem | uaba'aet | hahiy'a | na'am | Yahuah |
| **Ephraim** | **and Gilead** | **shall be satisfied** | **his soul** | | **In days** | **those** | **and in time** | **that** | **saith** | **Yahuah** |

| יבקש 1245 | את 853 | עון 5771 | ישראל 3478 | ואיננו 369 | ואת 853 | חטאת 2403 | יהודה 3063 | ולא 3808 | תמצאינה 4672 |
|---|---|---|---|---|---|---|---|---|---|
| yabuqash | 'at | 'auon | yisra'ael | ua'aeynenu, | ua'at | chata't | yahudah | uala' | timatza'ynah; |
| **shall be sought for** | | **the iniquity of** | **Israel** | ***there shall be* none** | ***and*** | **the sins of** | **Judah** | **and not** | **they shall be found** |

| כי 3588 | אסלח 5545 | לאשר 834 | אשאיר 7604: | 50:21 | על 5921 | הארץ 776 | מרתים 4850 | עלה 5927 | עליה 5921 | ואל 413 |
|---|---|---|---|---|---|---|---|---|---|---|
| kiy | 'aslach | la'asher | 'ash'ayr. | | 'al | ha'aretz | maratayim | 'aleh | 'aeleyha, | ua'al |
| **for** | **I will pardon them** | **whom** | **I reserve** | | **against** | **the land *of*** | **Merathaim** | **Go up *even*** | **against it** | **and against** |

| יושבי 3427 | פקוד 6489 | חרב 2717 | והחרם 2763 | אחריהם 310 | נאם 5002 | יהוה 3068 | ועשה 6213 | ככל 3605 | אשר 834 |
|---|---|---|---|---|---|---|---|---|---|
| youshabey | paqoud; | charob | uahacharem | 'achareyhem | na'am | Yahuah, | ua'aseh | kakol | 'asher |
| **the inhabitants of** | **Pekod** | **waste** | **and utterly destroy** | **after them** | **saith** | **Yahuah** | **and do** | **according to all** | **that** |

| צויתיך 6680: | 50:22 | קול 6963 | מלחמה 4421 | בארץ 776 | ושבר 7667 | גדול 1419: | 50:23 | איך 349 | נגדע 1438 |
|---|---|---|---|---|---|---|---|---|---|
| tziuiytiyka. | | qoul | milchamah | ba'aretz; | uasheber | gadoul. | | 'aeyk | nigda' |
| **I have commanded you** | | **A sound of** | **battle** | ***is* in the land** | **and destruction** | ***of* great** | | **How** | **is cut asunder** |

| וישבר 7665 | פטיש 6360 | כל 3605 | הארץ 776 | איך 349 | היתה 1961 | לשמה 8047 | בבל 894 | בגוים 1471: | 50:24 |
|---|---|---|---|---|---|---|---|---|---|
| uayishaber, | patiysh | kal | ha'aretz; | 'aeyk | hayatah | lashamah | babel | bagouyim. | |
| **and broken** | **the hammer of** | **whole** | **the earth** | **how** | **is become** | **a desolation** | **Babylon** | **among the nations** | |

| יקשתי 3369 | לך 3807a | וגם 1571 | נלכדת 3920 | בבל 894 | ואת 859 | לא 3808 | ידעת 3045 | נמצאת 4672 | וגם 1571 | נתפשת 8610 |
|---|---|---|---|---|---|---|---|---|---|---|
| yaqoshatiy | lak | uagam | nilkadt | babel, | ua'at | la' | yada'at; | nimtzea't | uagam | nitpast, |
| **I have laid a snare** | **for you** | **and also** | **you are taken** | **O Babylon** | ***and you*** | **not** | **were aware** | **you are found** | **and also** | **caught** |

| כי 3588 | ביהוה 3068 | התגרית 1624: | 50:25 | פתח 6605 | יהוה 3068 | את 853 | אוצרו 214 | ויוצא 3318 | את 853 |
|---|---|---|---|---|---|---|---|---|---|
| kiy | baYahuah | hitgariyt. | | patach | Yahuah | 'at | uatzarou, | uayoutzea' | 'at |
| **because** | **against Yahuah** | **you have striven** | | **has opened** | **Yahuah** | | **his armoury** | **and has brought forth** | |

Jer 50:18 Therefore thus saith YHUH of hosts, the G-d of Israel; Behold, I will punish the king of Babylon and his land, as I have punished the king of Assyria.19 And I will bring Israel again to his habitation, and he shall feed on Carmel and Bashan, and his soul shall be satisfied upon mount Ephraim and Gilead.20 In those days, and in that time, saith YHUH, the iniquity of Israel shall be sought for, and there shall be none; and the sins of Judah, and they shall not be found: for I will pardon them whom I reserve.21 Go up against the land of Merathaim, even against it, and against the inhabitants of Pekod: waste and utterly destroy after them, saith YHUH, and do according to all that I have commanded you.22 A sound of battle is in the land, and of great destruction.23 How is the hammer of the whole earth cut asunder and broken! how is Babylon become a desolation among the nations!24 I have laid a snare for you, and you are also taken, O Babylon, and you were not aware: you are found, and also caught, because you have striven against YHUH.25 YHUH has opened his armoury, and has brought forth the weapons of his indignation: for this is the work of YHUH G-D of hosts in the land of the Chaldeans.

50:26

כלי 3627 | זעמו 2195 | כי 3588 | מלאכה 4399 | היא 1931 | לאדני 136 | יהוה 3069 | צבאות 6635 | בארץ 776 | כשדים 3778:
kaley za'amou; kiy mala'kah hiy'a, la'adonay Yahuah tzaba'aut ba'aretz kasdiym.
**the weapons of | his indignation | for | *is* the work | this | of Adonai | Yahuah | of hosts | in the land of | the Chaldeans**

באו 935 | לה 3807a | מקץ 7093 | פתחו 6605 | מאבסיה 3965 | סלוה 5549 | כמו 3644 | ערמים 6194 | והחרימוה 2763
bo'au lah miqetz pitchu ma'abuseyha, saluha kamou 'aremiym uahachariymuha;
**Come | against her | from the utmost border | open | her storehouses | cast her up | as | heaps | and destroy her utterly**

50:27

אל 408 | תהי 1961 | לה 3807a | שארית 7611: | חרבו 2717 | כל 3605 | פריה 6499 | ירדו 3381 | לטבח 2874 | הוי 1945 | עליהם 5921
'al tahiy lah sha'aeriyt. chirbu kal pareyha, yeradu latabach; houy 'aleyhem,
**nothing | let be | of her | left | Slay | all | her bullocks | let them go down | to the slaughter | woe | unto them**

50:28

כי 3588 | בא 935 | יומם 3117 | עת 6256 | פקדתם 6486: | קול 6963 | נסים 5127 | ופלטים 6412 | מארץ 776 | בבל 894
kiy ba' youmam 'at paqudatam. qoul nasiym uapletiym me'aretz babel;
**for | is come | their day | the time of | their visitation | The voice of | them that flee | and escape | out of the land of | Babylon**

50:29

להגיד 5046 | בציון 6726 | את 853 | נקמת 5360 | יהוה 3068 | אלהינו 430 | נקמת 5360 | היכלו 1964: | השמיעו 8085 | אל 413
lahagiyd batziyoun, 'at niqmat Yahuah 'aloheynu, niqmat heykalou. hashmiy'au 'al
**to declare | in Zion | the vengeance of | Yahuah | our Elohim | the vengeance of | his temple | Call together | against**

בבל 894 | רבים 7228 | כל 3605 | דרכי 1869 | קשת 7198 | חנו 2583 | עליה 5921 | סביב 5439 | אל 408 | יהי 1961 | כך | לה Q3807a | פלטה 6413
babel rabiym kal dorakey qeshet chanu 'aleyha sabiyb, 'al yahiy kak lah paletah,
**Babylon | the archers | all | you that bend | the bow | camp | against it | round about | none | let | (to | thereof) | escape**

שלמו 7999 | לה 3807a | כפעלה 6467 | ככל 3605 | אשר 834 | עשתה 6213 | עשו 6213 | לה 3807a | כי 3588 | אל 413 | יהוה 3068
shalmu lah kapa'alah, kakol 'asher 'astah 'asu lah; kiy 'al Yahuah
**recompense | her | according to her work | according to all | that | she has done | do | unto her | for | against | Yahuah**

50:30

זדה 2102 | אל 413 | קדוש 6918 | ישראל 3478: | לכן 3651 | יפלו 5307 | בחוריה 970 | ברחבתיה 7339 | וכל 3605
zadah 'al qadoush yisra'ael. laken yiplu bachureyha birchoteyha; uakal
**she has been proud | against | *the* Holy One of | Israel | Therefore | shall fall | her young men | in the streets | and all**

50:31

אנשי 582 | מלחמתה 4421 | ידמו 1826 | ביום 3117 | ההוא 1931 | נאם 5002 | יהוה 3068: | הנני 2005 | אליך 413 | זדון 2087
'anshey milchamtah yidamu bayoum hahua' na'am Yahuah. hinniy 'aeleyka zadoun,
**her men of | war | shall be cut off | in day | that | saith | Yahuah | Behold I *am* | against you | *O you* most proud**

50:32

נאם 5002 | אדני 136 | יהוה 3069 | צבאות 6635 | כי 3588 | בא 935 | יומך 3117 | עת 6256 | פקדתיך 6485: | וכשל 3782
na'am 'adonay Yahuah tzaba'aut; kiy ba' youmaka 'at paqadtiyka. uakashal
**saith | Adonai | Yahuah | of hosts | for | is come | your day | the time | *that* I will visit you | And shall stumble**

זדון 2087 | ונפל 5307 | ואין 369 | לו 3807a | מקים 6965 | והצתי 3341 | אש 784 | בעריו 5892 | ואכלה 398 | כל 3605
zadoun uanapal, ua'aeyn lou' meqym; uahitzatiy 'aesh ba'arayu, ua'akalah kal
***the* most proud | and fall | and none | him | shall raise up | and I will kindle | a fire | in his cities | and it shall devour | all**

50:33

סביבתיו 5439: | כה 3541 | אמר 559 | יהוה 3068 | צבאות 6635 | עשוקים 6231 | בני 1121 | ישראל 3478 | ובני 1121
sabiybotayu. koh 'amar Yahuah tzaba'aut, 'ashuqiym baney yisra'ael uabney
**round about him | Thus | saith | Yahuah of hosts | *were* oppressed | The children of Israel | and the children of**

Jer 50:26 Come against her from the utmost border, open her storehouses: cast her up as heaps, and destroy her utterly: let nothing of her be left.27 Slay all her bullocks; let them go down to the slaughter: woe unto them! for their day is come, the time of their visitation.28 The voice of them that flee and escape out of the land of Babylon, to declare in Zion the vengeance of YHUH our G-d, the vengeance of his temple.29 Call together the archers against Babylon: all you that bend the bow, camp against it round about; let none thereof escape: recompense her according to her work; according to all that she has done, do unto her: for she has been proud against YHUH, against the Holy One of Israel.30 Therefore shall her young men fall in the streets, and all her men of war shall be cut off in that day, saith YHUH.31 Behold, I am against you, O you most proud, saith YHUH G-D of hosts: for your day is come, the time that I will visit you.32 And the most proud shall stumble and fall, and none shall raise him up: and I will kindle a fire in his cities, and it shall devour all round about him.33 Thus saith YHUH of hosts; The children of Israel and the children of Judah were oppressed together: and all that took them captives held them fast; they refused to let them go.

יהודה 3063 יחדו 3162 וכל 3605 שביהם 7617 החזיקו 2388 בם 871a מאנו 3985 שלחם 7971: **50:34** גאלם 1350
yahudah yachdau; uakal shoeyhem hecheziyqu bam, me'anu shalcham. go'alam
**Judah together and all that took them captives held fast them they refused to let them go Their Redeemer**

חזק 2388 יהוה 3068 צבאות 6635 שמו 8034 ריב 7378 יריב 7378 את 853 ריבם 7379 למען 4616 הרגיע 7280 את 853
chazaq, Yahuah tzaba'aut shamou, riyb yariyb 'at riybam; lama'an hirgiya' 'at
***is* strong Yahuah of hosts *is* his name he shall throughly plead their cause that he may give rest to**

הארץ 776 והרגיז 7264 לישבי 3427 בבל 894: **50:35** חרב 2719 על 5921 כשדים 3778 נאם 5002 יהוה 3068 ואל 413
ha'aretz, uahirgiyz layoushabey babel. chereb 'al kasdiym na'am Yahuah; ua'al
**the land and disquiet the inhabitants of Babylon A sword *is* upon the Chaldeans saith Yahuah and upon**

ישבי 3427 בבל 894 ואל 413 שריה 8269 ואל 413 חכמיה 2450: **50:36** חרב 2719 אל 413 הבדים 907
yoshabey babel, ua'al sareyha ua'al chakmeyha. chereb 'al habadiym
**the inhabitants of Babylon and upon her princes and upon her wise *men* A sword *is* upon the liars**

ונאלו 2973 חרב 2719 אל 413 גבוריה 1368 וחתו 2865: **50:37** חרב 2719 אל 413 סוסיו 5483
uano'alu; chereb 'al giboureyha uachatu. chereb 'al susayu
**and they shall dote a sword *is* upon her mighty men and they shall be dismayed A sword *is* upon their horses**

ואל 413 רכבו 7393 ואל 413 כל 3605 הערב 6154 אשר 834 בתוכה 8432 והיו 1961 לנשים 802
ua'al rikbou, ua'al kal ha'areb 'asher batoukah uahayu lanashiym;
**and upon their chariots and upon all the mingled people that *are* in the midst of her and they shall become as women**

חרב 2719 אל 413 אוצרתיה 214 ובזזו 962: **50:38** חרב 2721 אל 413 מימיה 4325 ויבשו 3001
chereb 'al 'autzaroteyha uabuzazu. choreb 'al meymeyha uayabeshu;
**a sword *is* upon her treasures and they shall be robbed A drought *is* upon her waters and they shall be dried up**

כי 3588 ארץ 776 פסלים 6456 היא 1931 ובאימים 367 יתהללו 1984: **50:39** לכן 3651 ישבו 3427
kiy 'aretz pasiliym hiy'a, uaba'aeymiym yitholalu. laken, yeshabu
**for *is* the land of graven images it and upon *their* idols they are mad Therefore shall dwell *there* and**

ציים 6728 את 854 איים 338 וישבו 3427 בה 871a בנות 1323 יענה 3284 ולא 3808
tziyiym 'at 'ayiym, uayashabu bah banout ya'anah; uala'
***the* wild beasts of the desert *with* *the* wild beasts of the islands shall dwell therein first the owls and no**

תשב 3427 עוד 5750 לנצח 5331 ולא 3808 תשכון 7931 עד 5704 דור 1755 ודור 1755: **50:40** כמהפכת 4114
tesheb 'aud lanetzach, uala' tishkoun 'ad dour uadour. kamahpekat
**it shall be inhabited more for ever neither shall it be dwelt in from generation to generation As overthrew**

אלהים 430 את 853 סדם 5467 ואת 853 עמרה 6017 ואת 853 שכניה 7934 נאם 5002 יהוה 3068 לא 3808 ישב 3427 שם 8033
'alohiym 'at sadom ua'at 'amorah ua'at shakeneyha na'am Yahuah; la' yesheb sham
**Elohim Sodom *and* Gomorrah *and* the neighbour *cities* thereof saith Yahuah no *so* shall abide there**

איש 376 ולא 3808 יגור 1481 בה 871a בן 1121 אדם 120: **50:41** הנה 2009 עם 5971 בא 935 מצפון 6828 וגוי 1471 גדול 1419
'aysh, uala' yagur bah ben 'adam. hineh 'am ba' mitzapoun; uagouy gadoul
**man neither shall dwell therein *any* son of man Behold a people shall come from the north and a nation great**

Jer 50:34 Their Redeemer is strong; YHUH of hosts is his name: he shall throughly plead their cause, that he may give rest to the land, and disquiet the inhabitants of Babylon.35 A sword is upon the Chaldeans, saith YHUH, and upon the inhabitants of Babylon, and upon her princes, and upon her wise men.36 A sword is upon the liars; and they shall dote: a sword is upon her mighty men; and they shall be dismayed.37 A sword is upon their horses, and upon their chariots, and upon all the mingled people that are in the midst of her; and they shall become as women: a sword is upon her treasures; and they shall be robbed.38 A drought is upon her waters; and they shall be dried up: for it is the land of graven images, and they are mad upon their idols.39 Therefore the wild beasts of the desert with the wild beasts of the islands shall dwell there, and the owls shall dwell therein: and it shall be no more inhabited forever; neither shall it be dwelt in from generation to generation.40 As G-d overthrew Sodom and Gomorrah and the neighbor cities thereof, saith YHUH; so shall no man abide there, neither shall any son of man dwell therein.41 Behold, a people shall come from the north, and a great nation, and many kings shall be raised up from the coasts of the earth.

50:42

ומלכים 4428 רבים 7227 יערו 5782 מירכתי 3411 ארץ 776: קשת 7198 וכידן 3591 יחזיקו 2388 אכזרי 394

uamalakiym rabiym, ye'aru miyarkatey 'aretz. qeshet uakiydoun yachaziyqu, 'akzariy

**and kings many shall be raised up from the coasts of the earth the bow and the lance They shall hold *are* cruel**

המה 1992 ולא 3808 ירחמו 7355 קולם 6963 כים 3220 יהמה 1993 ועל 5921 סוסים 5483 ירכבו 7392 ערוך 6186

hemah uala' yarachemu, qoulam kayam yehemeh, ua'al susiym yirkabu; 'aruk,

**they and not will show mercy their voice like the sea shall roar and upon horses they shall ride *every one* put in array**

50:43

כאיש 376 למלחמה 4421 עליך 5921 בת 1323 בבל 894: שמע 8085 מלך 4428 בבל 894 את 853 שמעם 8088

ka'aysh lamilchamah, 'aleyka bat babel. shama' melek babel 'at shima'am

**like a man to the battle against you O daughter of Babylon has heard The king of Babylon the report of them**

50:44

ורפו 7503 ידיו 3027 צרה 6869 החזיקתהו 2388 חיל 2427 כיולדה 3205: הנה 2009 כאריה 738

uarapu yadayu; tzarah hechaziyqathu, chiyl kayouledah. hineh ka'aryeh

**and waxed feeble his hands anguish took hold of him *and* pangs as of a woman in travail Behold like a lion**

יעלה 5927 מגאון 1347 הירדן 3383 אל 413 נוה 5116 איתן 386 כי 3588 ארגעה 7280

ya'aleh miga'aun hayarden 'al naueh 'aeytan kiy 'argi'ah

**he shall come up from the swelling of the Jordan unto the habitation of the strong but I will suddenly**

ארוצם 7323 מעליה 5921 ומי 4310 בחור 970 אליה 413 אפקד 6485 כי 3588 מי 4310 כמוני 3644 ומי 4310

'arutzem me'aleyha, uamiy bachur 'aeleyha 'apqod; kiy miy' kamouniy uamiy

**make them run away from her and who *is* a chosen *man that* over her? I may appoint for who *is* like me? and who**

50:45

יועדני 3259 ומי 4310 זה 2088 רעה 7462 אשר 834 יעמד 5975 לפני 6440: לכן 3651 שמעו 8085 עצת 6098

yo'adeniy, uamiy zeh ro'ah, 'asher ya'amod lapanay. laken shim'au 'atzat

**will appoint me the time? and who *is* that shepherd that will stand before me? Therefore hear you the counsel of**

יהוה 3068 אשר 834 יעץ 3289 אל 413 בבל 894 ומחשבותיו 4284 אשר 834 חשב 2803 אל 413 ארץ 776 כשדים 3778

Yahuah 'asher ya'atz 'al babel, uamachshaboutayu, 'asher chashab 'al 'aretz kasdiym;

**Yahuah that he has taken against Babylon and his purposes that he has purposed against the land of the Chaldeans**

אם 518 לא 3808 יסחבום 5498 צעירי 6810 הצאן 6629 אם 518 לא 3808 ישים 8074 עליהם 5921

'am la' yisachabum tza'ayrey hatza'an, 'am la' yashiym 'aleyhem

**Surely not shall draw them out the least of the flock surely not he shall make desolate with them *their***

50:46

נוה 5116: מקול 6963 נתפשה 8610 בבל 894 נרעשה 7493 הארץ 776 וזעקה 2201 בגוים 1471 נשמע 8085:

naueh. miqoul nitpasah babel, nir'ashah ha'aretz; uaz'aqah bagouyim nishma'.

**habitation At the noise of the taking of Babylon is moved the earth and the cry among the nations is heard**

**Jer 51:1**

כה 3541 אמר 559 יהוה 3068 הנני 2005 מעיר 5782 על 5921 בבל 894 ואל 413 ישבי 3427 לב 3820

koh 'amar Yahuah, hinniy me'ayr 'al babel, ua'al yoshabey leb

**Thus saith Yahuah Behold I will raise up against Babylon and against them that dwell in the midst of**

51:2

קמי 6965 רוח 7307 משחית 7843: ושלחתי 7971 לבבל 894 זרים 2114 וזרוה 2219 ויבקקו 1238

qamay; ruach mashchiyt. uashilachtiy lababel zariym uazeruha, uiyboqaqu

**them that rise up against me a wind destroying And will send unto Babylon fanners that shall fan her and shall empty**

Jer 51:42 They shall hold the bow and the lance: they are cruel, and will not show mercy: their voice shall roar like the sea, and they shall ride upon horses, everyone put in array, like a man to the battle, against you, O daughter of Babylon.43 The king of Babylon has heard the report of them, and his hands waxed feeble: anguish took hold of him, and pangs as of a woman in travail.44 Behold, he shall come up like a lion from the swelling of Jordan unto the habitation of the strong: but I will make them suddenly run away from her: and who is a chosen man, that I may appoint over her? for who is like me? and who will appoint me the time? and who is that shepherd that will stand before me?45 Therefore hear you the counsel of YHUH, that he has taken against Babylon; and his purposes, that he has purposed against the land of the Chaldeans: Surely the least of the flock shall draw them out: surely he shall make their habitation desolate with them.46 At the noise of the taking of Babylon the earth is moved, and the cry is heard among the nations. **Jer** 51:1 Thus saith YHUH; Behold, I will raise up against Babylon, and against them that dwell in the midst of them that rise up against me, a destroying wind;2 And will send unto Babylon fanners, that shall fan her, and shall empty her land: for in the day of trouble they shall be against her round about.

| את 853 | ארצה 776 | כי 3588 | היו 1961 | עליה 5921 | מסביב 5439 | ביום 3117 | רעה 7451: | 51:3 | אל 408 | ידרך 1869 |
|---|---|---|---|---|---|---|---|---|---|---|
| 'at | 'artzah; | kiy | hayu | 'aleyha | misabiyb | bayoum | ra'ah. | | 'al | yidrok |
| | **her land** | **for** | **they shall be** | **against her** | **round about** | **in the day of** | **trouble** | | **Against *him that*** | **bend** |

| ידרך 1869 | הדרך 1869 | קשתו 7198 | ואל 408 | יתעל 5927 | בסריונו 5630 | ואל 408 | תחמלו 2550 | אל 413 |
|---|---|---|---|---|---|---|---|---|
| yidrok | hadorek | qashtou, | ua'al | yita'al | basiryonou; | ua'al | tachmalu | 'al |
| **let the archer** | **bend** | **his bow** | **and against *him that*** | **lift himself up** | **in his brigandine** | **and not** | **spare you** | **Nor** |

| בחריה 970 | החרימו 2763 | כל 3605 | צבאה 6635: | 51:4 | ונפלו 5307 | חללים 2491 | בארץ 776 | כשדים 3778 |
|---|---|---|---|---|---|---|---|---|
| bachureyha, | hachariymu | kal | tzaba'ah. | | uanapalu | chalaliym | ba'aretz | kasdiym; |
| **her young men** | **destroy you utterly** | **all** | **her host** | | **Thus shall fall** | **the slain** | **in the land of** | **the Chaldeans** |

| ומדקרים 1856 | בחוצותיה 2351: | 51:5 | כי 3588 | לא 3808 | אלמן 488 | ישראל 3478 | ויהודה 3063 | מאלהיו 430 |
|---|---|---|---|---|---|---|---|---|
| uamaduqariym | bachutzouteyha. | | kiy | la' | 'alman | yisra'ael | uayahudah | me'alohayu, |
| **and *they that are* thrust through** | **in her streets** | | **For** | **not** | ***been* forsaken** | **Israel *has*** | **nor Judah** | **of his Elohim** |

| מיהוה 3068 | צבאות 6635 | כי 3588 | ארצם 776 | מלאה 4390 | אשם 817 | מקדוש 6918 | ישראל 3478: | 51:6 | נסו 5127 |
|---|---|---|---|---|---|---|---|---|---|
| meYahuah | tzaba'aut; | kiy | 'artzam | mal'ah | 'asham, | miqdoush | yisra'ael. | | nusu |
| **of Yahuah** | **of hosts** | **though** | **their land** | **was filled with** | **sin** | **against the Holy One of** | **Israel** | | **Flee** |

| מתוך 8432 | בבל 894 | ומלטו 4422 | איש 376 | נפשו 5315 | אל 408 | תדמו 1826 | בעונה 5771 | כי 3588 | עת 6256 | נקמה 5360 |
|---|---|---|---|---|---|---|---|---|---|---|
| mitouk | babel, | uamalatu | 'aysh | napshou, | 'al | tidamu | ba'auonah; | kiy | 'at | naqamah |
| **out of the midst of** | **Babylon** | **and deliver** | **every man** | **his soul** | **not** | **be cut off** | **in her iniquity** | **for** | ***is* the time** | **vengeance** |

| היא 1931 | ליהוה 3068 | גמול 1576 | הוא 1931 | משלם 7999 | לה 3807a: | 51:7 | כוס 3563 | זהב 2091 | בבל 894 | ביד 3027 | יהוה 3068 |
|---|---|---|---|---|---|---|---|---|---|---|---|
| hiy'a | laYahuah, | gamul | hua' | mashalem | lah. | | kos | zahab | babel | bayad | Yahuah, |
| **this** | **of Yahuah's** | **a recompence** | **he** | **will render** | **unto her** | | ***has been* a cup** | **golden** | **Babylon** | **in hand** | **Yahuah's** |

| משכרת 7937 | כל 3605 | הארץ 776 | מיינה 3196 | שתו 8354 | גוים 1471 | על 5921 | כן 3651 | יתהללו 1984 | גוים 1471: | 51:8 |
|---|---|---|---|---|---|---|---|---|---|---|
| mashakeret | kal | ha'aretz; | miyeynah | shatu | gouyim, | 'al | ken | yitholalu | gouyim. | |
| **that made drunken** | **all** | **the earth** | **of her wine** | **have drunken** | **the nations** | **therefore** | **after that** | **are mad** | **the nations** | |

| פתאם 6597 | נפלה 5307 | בבל 894 | ותשבר 7665 | הילילו 3213 | עליה 5921 | קחו 3947 | צרי 6875 | למכאובה 4341 | אולי 194 | תרפא 7495: | 51:9 |
|---|---|---|---|---|---|---|---|---|---|---|---|
| pit'am | naplah | babel | uatishaber; | heyliylu | 'aeleyha, | qachu | tzariy | lamaka'aubah, | 'aulay | terapea'. | |
| **suddenly** | **is fallen** | **Babylon** | **and destroyed** | **howl** | **for her** | **take** | **balm** | **for her pain** | **if so she** | **may be healed** | |

| רפאנו 7495 | את 853 | בבל 894 | ולא 3808 | נרפתה 7495 | עזבוה 5800 | ונלך 1980 | איש 376 | לארצו 776 | כי 3588 |
|---|---|---|---|---|---|---|---|---|---|
| ripanu | 'at | babel | uala' | nirpatah, | 'azbuha | uanelek | 'aysh | la'artzou; | kiy |
| **We would have healed** | | **Babylon** | **but not** | **she is healed** | **forsake her** | **and let us go** | **every one** | **into his own country** | **for** |

| נגע 5060 | אל 413 | השמים 8064 | משפטה 4941 | ונשא 5375 | עד 5704 | שחקים 7834: | 51:10 | הוציא 3318 | יהוה 3069 | את 853 |
|---|---|---|---|---|---|---|---|---|---|---|
| naga' | 'al | hashamayim | mishpatah, | uanisa' | 'ad | shachaqiym. | | houtziy'a | Yahuah | 'at |
| **reached** | **unto** | **heaven** | **her judgment** | **and is lifted up *even*** | **to** | **the skies** | | **has brought forth** | **Yahuah** | |

| צדקתינו 6666 | באו 935 | ונספרה 5608 | בציון 6726 | את 853 | מעשה 4639 | יהוה 3069 | אלהינו 430: | 51:11 | הברו 1305 | החצים 2671 |
|---|---|---|---|---|---|---|---|---|---|---|
| tzidqoteynu; | bo'au | uansaprah | batziyoun, | 'at | ma'aseh | Yahuah | 'aloheynu. | | haberu | hachitziym |
| **our righteousness** | **come** | **and let us declare** | **in Zion** | | **the work of** | **Yahuah** | **our Elohim** | | **Make bright** | **the arrows** |

Jer 51:3 Against him that bendeth let the archer bend his bow, and against him that lift himself up in his brigandine: and spare you not her young men; destroy you utterly all her host.4 Thus the slain shall fall in the land of the Chaldeans, and they that are thrust through in her streets.5 For Israel has not been forsaken, nor Judah of his G-d, of YHUH of hosts; though their land was filled with sin against the Holy One of Israel.6 Flee out of the midst of Babylon, and deliver every man his soul: be not cut off in her iniquity; for this is the time of YHUH's vengeance; he will render unto her a recompence.7 Babylon has been a golden cup in YHUH's hand, that made all the earth drunken: the nations have drunken of her wine; therefore the nations are mad.8 Babylon is suddenly fallen and destroyed: howl for her; take balm for her pain, if so she may be healed.9 We would have healed Babylon, but she is not healed: forsake her, and let us go everyone into his own country: for her judgment reacheth unto heaven, and is lifted up even to the skies.10 YHUH has brought forth our righteousness: come, and let us declare in Zion the work of YHUH our G-d.11 Make bright the arrows; gather the shields: YHUH has raised up the spirit of the kings of the Medes: for his device is against Babylon, to destroy it; because it is the vengeance of YHUH, the vengeance of his temple.

| מלאו 4390 | השלטים 7982 | העיר 5782 | יהוה 3068 | את 853 | רוח 7307 | מלכי 4428 | מדי 4074 | כי 3588 | על 5921 | בבל 894 | מזמתו 4209 |
|---|---|---|---|---|---|---|---|---|---|---|---|
| mil'au | hashalatiym | he'ayr | Yahuah | 'at | ruach | malkey | maday, | kiy | 'al | babel | mazimatou |
| **gather** | **the shields** | **has raised up** | **Yahuah** | | **the spirit of** | **the kings of** | **the Medes** | **for** | **against** | **Babylon** | **his device *is*** |

| להשחיתה 7843 | כי 3588 | נקמת 5360 | יהוה 3068 | היא 1931 | נקמת 5360 | היכלו 1964: | 51:12 | אל 413 | חומת 2346 | בבל 894 |
|---|---|---|---|---|---|---|---|---|---|---|
| lahashchiytah; | kiy | niqmat | Yahuah | hiy'a, | niqmat | heykalou. | | 'al | choumot | babel |
| **to destroy it** | **because** | ***is* the vengeance of** | **Yahuah** | **it** | **the vengeance of** | **his temple** | | **upon** | **the walls of** | **Babylon** |

| שאו 5375 | נס 5251 | החזיקו 2388 | המשמר 4929 | הקימו 6965 | שמרים 8104 | הכינו 3559 | הארבים 693 | כי 3588 | גם 1571 | זמם 2161 | יהוה 3068 |
|---|---|---|---|---|---|---|---|---|---|---|---|
| sa'au | nes, | hachaziyqu | hamishmar, | haqiymu | shomariym, | hakiynu | ha'arabiym; | kiy | gam | zamam | Yahuah, |
| **Set up** | **the standard** | **make strong** | **the watch** | **set up** | **the watchmen** | **prepare** | **the ambushes** | **for** | **both** | **has devised** | **Yahuah** |

| גם 1571 | עשה 6213 | את 853 | אשר 834 | דבר 1696 | אל 413 | ישבי 3427 | בבל 894: | 51:13 | שכנתי 7931 | על 5921 | מים 4325 | רבים 7227 |
|---|---|---|---|---|---|---|---|---|---|---|---|---|
| gam | 'asah | 'at | 'asher | diber | 'al | yoshabey | babel. | | shokantiy | 'al | mayim | rabiym, |
| **both** | **has done** | | **that which** | **he spoke** | **against** | **the inhabitants of** | **Babylon** | | **O you that dwell** | **upon** | **waters** | **many** |

| רבת 7227 | אוצרת 214 | בא 935 | קצך 7093 | אמת 520 | בצעך 1215: | 51:14 | נשבע 7650 | יהוה 3068 | צבאות 6635 |
|---|---|---|---|---|---|---|---|---|---|
| rabat | 'autzarot; | ba' | qitzek | 'amat | bitz'aek. | | nishba' | Yahuah | tzaba'aut |
| **abundant in** | **treasures** | **is come** | **your end** | ***and* the measure of** | **your covetousness** | | **has sworn** | **Yahuah** | **of hosts** |

| בנפשו 5315 | כי 3588 | אם 518 | מלאתיך 4390 | אדם 120 | כילק 3218 | וענו 6030 | עליך 5921 | הידד 1959: | 51:15 |
|---|---|---|---|---|---|---|---|---|---|
| banapshou; | kiy | 'am | mila'tiyk | 'adam | kayeleq, | ua'anu | 'aleyka | heydad. | |
| **by himself *saying*** | **Surely** | **lo** | **I will fill you with** | **men** | **as with caterpillers** | **and they shall lift up** | **against you** | **a shout** | |

| עשה 6213 | ארץ 776 | בכחו 3581 | מכין 3559 | תבל 8398 | בחכמתו 2451 | ובתבונתו 8394 | נטה 5186 |
|---|---|---|---|---|---|---|---|
| 'aseh | 'aretz | bakochou, | mekiyn | tebel | bachakamatou; | uabitbunatou | natah |
| **He has made** | **the earth** | **by his power** | **he has established** | **the world** | **by his wisdom** | **by his understanding** | **and has stretched out** |

| שמים 8064: | 51:16 | לקול 6963 | תתו 5414 | המון 1995 | מים 4325 | בשמים 8064 | ויעל 5927 | נשאים 5387 |
|---|---|---|---|---|---|---|---|---|
| shamayim. | | laqoul | titou | hamoun | mayim | bashamayim, | uaya'al | nashi'aym |
| **the heaven** | | **When voice** | **he utter *his*** | ***there is* a multitude of** | **waters** | **in the heavens** | **and he cause to ascend** | **the vapours** |

| מקצה 7097 | ארץ 776 | ברקים 1300 | למטר 4306 | עשה 6213 | ויצא 3318 | רוח 7307 | מאצרתיו 214: | 51:17 | נבער 1197 | כל 3605 |
|---|---|---|---|---|---|---|---|---|---|---|
| miqtzeh | 'aretz; | baraqiym | lamatar | 'asah, | uayotzea' | ruach | me'atzarotayu. | | nib'ar | kal |
| **from the ends of** | **the earth** | **lightnings** | **with rain** | **he make** | **and bring forth** | **the wind** | **out of his treasures** | | **is brutish** | **Every** |

| אדם 120 | מדעת 1847 | הביש 3001 | כל 3605 | צרף 6884 | מפסל 6459 | כי 3588 | שקר 8267 | נסכו 5262 |
|---|---|---|---|---|---|---|---|---|
| 'adam | mida'at, | hobiysh | kal | tzorep | mipasel; | kiy | sheqer | niskou |
| **man** | **by *his* knowledge** | **is confounded** | **every** | **founder** | **by the graven image** | **for** | ***is* falsehood** | **his molten image** |

| ולא 3808 | רוח 7307 | בם 871a: | 51:18 | הבל 1892 | המה 1992 | מעשה 4639 | תעתעים 8595 | בעת 6256 | פקדתם 6486 |
|---|---|---|---|---|---|---|---|---|---|
| uala' | ruach | bam. | | hebel | hemah, | ma'aseh | ta'atu'aym; | ba'aet | paqudatam |
| **and *there is* no** | **breath** | **in them** | | ***are* vanity** | **They** | **the work of** | **errors** | **in the time of** | **their visitation** |

| יאבדו 6: | 51:19 | לא 3808 | כאלה 428 | חלק 2506 | יעקוב 3290 | כי 3588 | יוצר 3335 | הכל 3605 | הוא 1931 |
|---|---|---|---|---|---|---|---|---|---|
| ya'bedu. | | la' | ka'aeleh | cheleq | ya'aqoub, | kiy | youtzer | hakol | hua', |
| **they shall perish** | | **not** | **like them** | **The portion of** | **Jacob *is*** | **for** | ***is* the former of** | **all *things*** | **he** |

Jer 51:12 Set up the standard upon the walls of Babylon, make the watch strong, set up the watchmen, prepare the ambushes: for YHUH has both devised and done that which he spoke against the inhabitants of Babylon.13 O you that dwellest upon many waters, abundant in treasures, your end is come, and the measure of your covetousness.14 YHUH of hosts has sworn by himself, saying, Surely I will fill you with men, as with caterpillers; and they shall lift up a shout against you.15 He has made the earth by his power, he has established the world by his wisdom, and has stretched out the heaven by his understanding.16 When he uttereth his voice, there is a multitude of waters in the heavens; and he causeth the vapours to ascend from the ends of the earth: he make lightnings with rain, and bring forth the wind out of his treasures.17 Every man is brutish by his knowledge; every founder is confounded by the graven image: for his molten image is falsehood, and there is no breath in them.18 They are vanity, the work of errors: in the time of their visitation they shall perish.19 The portion of Jacob is not like them; for he is the former of all things: and Israel is the rod of his inheritance: YHUH of hosts is his name.

| ושבט 7626 | נחלתו 5159 | יהוה 3068 | צבאות 6635 | שמו 8034: | 51:20 | מפץ 4661 | אתה 859 | לי 3807a | כלי 3627 |
|---|---|---|---|---|---|---|---|---|---|
| uashebet | nachalatou; | Yahuah | tzaba'aut | shamou. | | mapetz | 'atah | liy, | kaley |
| **and *Israel is* the rod of** | **his inheritance** | **Yahuah** | **of hosts** | ***is* his name** | | **battle axe** | **You *are*** | **my** | ***and* weapons of** |

| מלחמה 4421 | ונפצתי 5310 | בך 871a | גוים 1471 | והשחתי 7843 | בך 871a | ממלכות 4467: | 51:21 |
|---|---|---|---|---|---|---|---|
| milchamah; | uanipatztiy | baka | gouyim, | uahishchatiy | baka | mamlakout. | |
| **war** | **for will I break in pieces** | **with you** | **the nations** | **and will I destroy** | **with you** | **kingdoms** | |

| ונפצתי 5310 | בך 871a | סוס 5483 | ורכבו 7392 | ונפצתי 5310 | בך 871a | רכב 7393 |
|---|---|---|---|---|---|---|
| uanipatztiy | baka, | sus | uarokabou; | uanipatztiy | baka, | rekeb |
| **And will I break in pieces** | **with you** | **the horse** | **and his rider** | **and will I break in pieces** | **with you** | **the chariot** |

| ורכבו 7392: | 51:22 | ונפצתי 5310 | בך 871a | איש 376 | ואשה 802 | ונפצתי 5310 | בך 871a | זקן 2205 |
|---|---|---|---|---|---|---|---|---|
| uarokabou. | | uanipatztiy | baka | 'aysh | ua'ashah, | uanipatztiy | baka | zaqen |
| **and his rider** | | **also will I break in pieces** | **With you** | **man** | **and woman** | **and will I break in pieces** | **with you** | **old** |

| ונער 5288 | ונפצתי 5310 | בך 871a | בחור 970 | ובתולה 1330: | 51:23 | ונפצתי 5310 | בך 871a |
|---|---|---|---|---|---|---|---|
| uana'ar; | uanipatztiy | baka, | bachur | uabtulah. | | uanipatztiy | baka |
| **and young** | **and will I break in pieces** | **with you** | ***the* young man** | **and the maid** | | **I will also break in pieces** | **with you** |

| רעה 7462 | ועדרו 5739 | ונפצתי 5310 | בך 871a | אכר 406 | וצמדו 6776 |
|---|---|---|---|---|---|
| ro'ah | ua'adrou, | uanipatztiy | baka | 'akar | uatzimdou; |
| **the shepherd** | **and his flock** | **and will I break in pieces** | **with you** | **the husbandman** | **and his yoke of oxen** |

| ונפצתי 5310 | בך 871a | פחות 6346 | וסגנים 5461: | 51:24 | ושלמתי 7999 | לבבל 894 | ולכל 3605 | יושבי 3427 |
|---|---|---|---|---|---|---|---|---|
| uanipatztiy | baka, | pachout | uasganiym. | | uashilamtiy | lababel | ualkal | youshabey |
| **and will I break in pieces** | **with you** | **captains** | **and rulers** | | **And I will render** | **unto Babylon** | **and to all** | **the inhabitants of** |

| כשדים 3778 | את 853 | כל 3605 | רעתם 7451 | אשר 834 | עשו 6213 | בציון 6726 | לעיניכם 5869 | נאם 5002 | יהוה 3068: | 51:25 | הנני 2005 |
|---|---|---|---|---|---|---|---|---|---|---|---|
| kasdiym, | 'at | kal | ra'atam | 'asher | 'asu | batziyoun | la'ayneykem; | na'am | Yahuah. | | hinniy |
| **Chaldea** | | **all** | **their evil** | **that** | **they have done** | **in Zion** | **in your sight** | **saith** | **Yahuah** | | **Behold I *am*** |

| אליך 413 | הר 2022 | המשחית 4889 | נאם 5002 | יהוה 3068 | המשחית 7843 | את 853 | כל 3605 | הארץ 776 | ונטיתי 5186 | את 853 |
|---|---|---|---|---|---|---|---|---|---|---|
| 'aeleyka | har | hamashchiyt | na'am | Yahuah, | hamashchiyt | 'at | kal | ha'aretz; | uanatiytiy | 'at |
| **against you** | **O mountain** | **destroying** | **saith** | **Yahuah** | **which destroy** | | **all** | **the earth** | **and I will stretch out** | |

| ידי 3027 | עליך 5921 | וגלגלתיך 1556 | מן 4480 | הסלעים 5553 | ונתתיך 5414 | להר 2022 | שרפה 8316: | 51:26 | ולא 3808 |
|---|---|---|---|---|---|---|---|---|---|
| yadiy | 'aleyka, | uagilgaltiyka | min | hasala'aym, | uantatiyka | lahar | sarepah. | | uala' |
| **mine hand** | **upon you** | **and roll you down** | **from** | **the rocks** | **and will make you** | **a mountain** | **burnt** | | **And not** |

| יקחו 3947 | ממך 4480 | אבן 68 | לפנה 6438 | ואבן 68 | למוסדות 4146 | כי 3588 | שממות 8077 | עולם 5769 | תהיה 1961 | נאם 5002 |
|---|---|---|---|---|---|---|---|---|---|---|
| yiqchu | mimaka | 'aben | lapinah, | ua'aben | lamousadout; | kiy | shimamout | 'aulam | tihayeh | na'am |
| **they shall take** | **of you** | **a stone** | **for a corner** | **nor a stone** | **for foundations** | **but** | **desolate** | **for ever** | **you shall be** | **saith** |

| יהוה 3068: | 51:27 | שאו 5375 | נס 5251 | בארץ 776 | תקעו 8628 | שופר 7782 | בגוים 1471 | קדשו 6942 | עליה 5921 | גוים 1471 |
|---|---|---|---|---|---|---|---|---|---|---|
| Yahuah. | | sa'au | nes | ba'aretz, | tiq'au | shoupar | bagouyim | qadashu | 'aleyha | gouyim, |
| **Yahuah** | | **Set you up** | **a standard** | **in the land** | **blow** | **the trumpet** | **among the nations** | **prepare** | **against her** | **the nations** |

Jer 51:20 Thou are my battle axe and weapons of war: for with you will I break in pieces the nations, and with you will I destroy kingdoms;21 And with you will I break in pieces the horse and his rider; and with you will I break in pieces the chariot and his rider;22 With you also will I break in pieces man and woman; and with you will I break in pieces old and young; and with you will I break in pieces the young man and the maid;23 I will also break in pieces with you the shepherd and his flock; and with you will I break in pieces the husbandman and his yoke of oxen; and with you will I break in pieces captains and rulers.24 And I will render unto Babylon and to all the inhabitants of Chaldea all their evil that they have done in Zion in your sight, saith YHUH.25 Behold, I am against you, O destroying mountain, saith YHUH, which destroyest all the earth: and I will stretch out mine hand upon you, and roll you down from the rocks, and will make you a burnt mountain.26 And they shall not take of you a stone for a corner, nor a stone for foundations; but you shall be desolate forever, saith YHUH.27 Set you up a standard in the land, blow the trumpet among the nations, prepare the nations against her, call together against her the kingdoms of Ararat, Minni, and Ashchenaz; appoint a captain against her; cause the horses to come up as the rough caterpillers.

השמיעו 8085 עליה 5921 ממלכות 4467 אררט 780 מני 4508 ואשכנז 813 פקדו 6485 עליה 5921 טפסר 2951 העלו 5927
hashmiy'au 'aleyha mamlakout 'ararat miniy ua'ashkanaz; piqdu 'aleyha tipsar, ha'alu
**call together against her the kingdoms of Ararat Minni and Ashchenaz appoint against her a captain cause to come up**

סוס 5483 כילק 3218 סמר 5569: **51:28** קדשו 6942 עליה 5921 גוים 1471 את 854 מלכי 4428 מדי 4074 את 853
sus kayeleq samar. qadashu 'aleyha gouyim 'at malkey maday, 'at
**the horses as caterpillers the rough Prepare against her the nations *with* the kings of the Medes**

פחותיה 6346 ואת 853 כל 3605 סגניה 5461 ואת 853 כל 3605 ארץ 776 ממשלתו 4475: **51:29** ותרעש 7493 הארץ 776
pachouteyha ua'at kal saganeyha; ua'at kal 'aretz memshaltou. uatir'ash ha'aretz
**the captains thereof *and* all the rulers thereof *and* all the land of his dominion And shall tremble the land**

ותחל 2342 כי 3588 קמה 6965 על 5921 בבל 894 מחשבות 4284 יהוה 3068 לשום 7760 את 853 ארץ 776 בבל 894
uatachol; kiy qamah 'al babel machashabout Yahuah, lasum 'at 'aretz babel
**and sorrow for shall be performed against Babylon every purpose of Yahuah to make the land of Babylon**

לשמה 8047 מאין 369 יושב 3427: **51:30** חדלו 2308 גבורי 1368 בבל 894 להלחם 3898 ישבו 3427
lashamah me'ayn yousheb. chadalu gibourey babel lahilachem, yashabu
**a desolation without an inhabitant have forborn The mighty men of Babylon to fight they have remained**

במצדות 4679 נשתה 5405 גבורתם 1369 היו 1961 לנשים 802 הציתו 3341 משכנתיה 4908 נשברו 7665
bamatzadout, nashatah gaburatam hayu lanashiym; hitziytu mishkanoteyha nishbaru
**in *their* holds has failed their might they became as women they have burned her dwellingplaces are broken**

בריחיה 1280: **51:31** רץ 7323 לקראת 7125 רץ 7323 ירוץ 7323 ומגיד 5046 לקראת 7125 מגיד 5046 להגיד 5046 למלך 4428
bariycheyha. ratz liqra't ratz yarutz, uamagiyd liqra't magiyd; lahagiyd lamelek
**her bars *One* post to meet shall another run and one messenger to meet another to show the king of**

בבל 894 כי 3588 נלכדה 3920 עירו 5892 מקצה 7097: **51:32** והמעברות 4569 נתפשו 8610 ואת 853 האגמים 98 שרפו 8313
babel, kiy nilkadah ayrou miqatzeh. uahama'abarout nitpasu, ua'at ha'agamiym sarapu
**Babylon that is taken his city at *one* end And that the passages are stopped *and* the reeds they have burned**

באש 784 ואנשי 582 המלחמה 4421 נבהלו 926: **51:33** כי 3588 כה 3541 אמר 559 יהוה 3068 צבאות 6635 אלהי 430 ישראל 3478
ba'ash; ua'anshey hamilchamah nibahalu. kiy koh 'amar Yahuah tzaba'aut 'alohey yisra'ael,
**with fire and the men of war are affrighted For thus saith Yahuah of hosts the Elohim of Israel**

בת 1323 בבל 894 כגרן 1637 עת 6256 הדריכה 1869 עוד 5750 מעט 4592 ובאה 935 עת 6256
bat babel kagoren 'at hidariykah; 'aud ma'at, uba'ah 'at
**The daughter of Babylon *is* like a threshingfloor *it is* time to thresh her yet a little while and shall come the time of**

הקציר 7105 לה 3807a: **51:34** אכלנו 398 הממנו 2000 נבוכדראצר 5019 מלך 4428 בבל 894 הציגנו 3322
haqatziyr lah. 'akalanu hamamanu nabukadra'tzar melek babel hitziyganu
**harvest her has devoured me he has crushed me Nebuchadrezzar the king of Babylon he has made me**

כלי 3627 ריק 7385 בלענו 1104 כתנין 8577 מלא 4390 כרשו 3770 מעדני 5730 הדיחנו 1740
kaliy riyq, bala'anu kataniyn, mila' karesou me'adanay; hediychanu
**an vessel empty he has swallowed me up like a dragon he has filled his belly with my delicates he has cast me out**

Jer 51:28 Prepare against her the nations with the kings of the Medes, the captains thereof, and all the rulers thereof, and all the land of his dominion.29 And the land shall tremble and sorrow: forevery purpose of YHUH shall be performed against Babylon, to make the land of Babylon a desolation without an inhabitant.30 The mighty men of Babylon have forborn to fight, they have remained in their holds: their might has failed; they became as women: they have burned her dwellingplaces; her bars are broken.31 One post shall run to meet another, and one messenger to meet another, to show the king of Babylon that his city is taken at one end,32 And that the passages are stopped, and the reeds they have burned with fire, and the men of war are affrighted.33 For thus saith YHUH of hosts, the G-d of Israel; The daughter of Babylon is like a threshingfloor, it is time to thresh her: yet a little while, and the time of her harvest shall come.34 Nebuchadrezzar the king of Babylon has devoured me, he has crushed me, he has made me an empty vessel, he has swallowed me up like a dragon, he has filled his belly with my delicates, he has cast me out.

**51:35**
חמסי 2555 ושארי 7607 על 5921 בבל 894 תאמר 559 ישבת 3427 ציון 6726 ודמי 1818 אל 413
chamasiy uash'aeriy 'al babel, ta'mar yoshebet tziyoun; uadamiy 'al
**The violence done to me and to my flesh *be* upon Babylon shall say the inhabitant of Zion and my blood upon**

ישבי 3427 כשדים 3778 תאמר 559 ירושלם 3389: **51:36** לכן 3651 כה 3541 אמר 559 יהוה 3068 הנני 2005 רב 7378 את 853
yoshabey kasdiym, ta'mar yarushalaim. laken, koh 'amar Yahuah, hinniy rab 'at
**the inhabitants of Chaldea shall say Jerusalem Therefore thus saith Yahuah Behold I will plead**

ריבך 7379 ונקמתי 5358 את 853 נקמתך 5360 והחרבתי 2717 את 853 ימה 3220 והבשתי 3001 את 853
riybek, uaniqamtiy 'at niqmatek; uahacharabtiy 'at yamah, uahobashtiy 'at
**your cause and I will take for you vengeance for you and I will dry up her sea and make dry**

מקורה 4726: **51:37** והיתה 1961 בבל 894 לגלים 1530 מעון 4583 תנים 8577 שמה 8047 ושרקה 8322 מאין 369
maqourah. uahayatah babel lagaliym ma'aun taniym shamah uashreqah me'ayn
**her springs And will become Babylon heaps a dwellingplace for dragons an astonishment and an hissing without**

יושב 3427: **51:38** יחדו 3162 ככפרים 3715 ישאגו 7580 נערו 5286 כגורי 1484 אריות 738: **51:39** בחמם 2527 אשית 7896
yousheb. yachdau kakapiriym yish'agu; naa'aru kagourey arayout. bachumam 'ashiyt
**an inhabitant together like lions They shall roar they shall yell as whelps lions' In their heat I will make**

את 853 משתיהם 4960 והשכרתים 7937 למען 4616 יעלזו 5937 וישנו 3462 שנת 8142 עולם 5769 ולא 3808 יקיצו 6974
'at mishteyhem, uahishkartiym lama'an ya'alozu, uayashanu shanat 'aulam uala' yaqiytzu;
**their feasts and I will make them drunken that they may rejoice and sleep a sleep perpetual and not wake**

נאם 5002 יהוה 3068: **51:40** אורידם 3381 ככרים 3733 לטבוח 2873 כאילים 352 עם 5973 עתודים 6260: **51:41** איך 349 נלכדה 3920
na'am Yahuah. 'auriydem kakariym litabouach; ka'aeyliym 'am 'atudiym. 'aeyk nilkadah
**saith Yahuah I will bring them down like lambs to the slaughter like rams with he goats How is taken**

ששך 8347 ותתפש 8610 תהלת 8416 כל 3605 הארץ 776 איך 349 היתה 1961 לשמה 8047 בבל 894
sheshak, uatitapes tahilat kal ha'aretz; 'aeyk hayatah lashamah babel
**Sheshach and how is surprised the praise of whole the earth how is become an astonishment Babylon**

בגוים 1471: **51:42** עלה 5927 על 5921 בבל 894 הים 3220 בהמון 1995 גליו 1530 נכסתה 3680: **51:43**
bagouyim. 'alah 'al babel hayam; bahamoun galayu nikasatah.
**among the nations is come up upon Babylon The sea with the multitude of the waves thereof she is covered**

היו 1961 עריה 5892 לשמה 8047 ארץ 776 ציה 6723 וערבה 6160 ארץ 776 לא 3808 ישב 3427 בהן 871a כל 3605 איש 376 ולא 3808 יעבר 5674
hayu 'areyha lashamah, 'aretz tziyah ua'arabah; 'aretz, la' yesheb bahen kal 'aysh, uala' ya'abor
**are Her cities a desolation a land dry and a wilderness a land no dwell wherein no man neither does pass**

בהן 2004 בן 1121 אדם 120: **51:44** ופקדתי 6485 על 5921 בל 1078 בבבל 894 והצאתי 3318 את 853
bahen ben 'adam. uapaqadtiy 'al bel bababel, uahotzea'tiy 'at
**thereby *any* son of man And I will punish on Bel in Babylon and I will bring forth**

בלעו 1105 מפיו 6310 ולא 3808 ינהרו 5102 אליו 413 עוד 5750 גוים 1471 גם 1571
bil'au mipiyu, uala' yinharu 'aelayu 'aud gouyim; gam
**that which he has swallowed up out of his mouth and not shall flow together unto him any more the nations yea**

Jer 51:35 The violence done to me and to my flesh be upon Babylon, shall the inhabitant of Zion say; and my blood upon the inhabitants of Chaldea, shall Jerusalem say.36 Therefore thus saith YHUH; Behold, I will plead your cause, and take vengeance for you; and I will dry up her sea, and make her springs dry.37 And Babylon shall become heaps, a dwellingplace for dragons, an astonishment, and an hissing, without an inhabitant.38 They shall roar together like lions: they shall yell as lion's whelps.39 In their heat I will make their feasts, and I will make them drunken, that they may rejoice, and sleep a perpetual sleep, and not wake, saith YHUH.40 I will bring them down like lambs to the slaughter, like rams with he goats.41 How is Sheshach taken! and how is the praise of the whole earth surprised! how is Babylon become an astonishment among the nations!42 The sea is come up upon Babylon: she is covered with the multitude of the waves thereof.43 Her cities are a desolation, a dry land, and a wilderness, a land wherein no man dwell, neither doth any son of man pass thereby.44 And I will punish Bel in Babylon, and I will bring forth out of his mouth that which he has swallowed up: and the nations shall not flow together anymore unto him: yea, the wall of Babylon shall fall.

חומת 2346 בבל 894 נפלה 5307: **51:45** צאו 3318 מתוכה 8432 עמי 5971 ומלטו 4422 איש 376 את 853 נפשו 5315
choumat babel napalah. tzea'au mitoukah 'amiy, uamalatu 'aysh 'at napshou;
**the wall of Babylon shall fall go you out of the midst of her My people and deliver you every man his soul**

מחרון 2740 אף 639 יהוה 3068: **51:46** ופן 6435 ירך 7401 לבבכם 3824 ותיראו 3372 בשמועה 8052 הנשמעת 8085
mecharoun 'ap Yahuah. uapen yerak lababkem uatiyra'au, bashamu'ah hanishma'at
**from the fierce anger of Yahuah And lest faint your heart and you fear for the rumour that shall be heard**

בארץ 776 ובא 935 בשנה 8141 השמועה 8052 ואחריו 310 בשנה 8141 השמועה 8052 וחמס 2555
ba'aretz; uaba' bashanah hashamu'ah, ua'acharayu bashanah hashamu'ah, uachamas
**in the land shall both come *one* year a rumour and after that in *another* year *shall come* a rumour and violence**

בארץ 776 ומשל 4910 על 5921 משל 4910: **51:47** לכן 3651 הנה 2009 ימים 3117 באים 935 ופקדתי 6485 על 5921
ba'aretz, uamoshel 'al moshel. laken hineh yamiym ba'aym, uapaqadtiy 'al
**in the land ruler against ruler Therefore behold the days come that I will do judgment upon**

פסילי 6456 בבל 894 וכל 3605 ארצה 776 תבוש 954 וכל 3605 חלליה 2491 יפלו 5307 בתוכה 8432: **51:48**
pasiyley babel, uakal 'artzah teboush; uakal chalaleyha yiplu batoukah.
**the graven images of Babylon and whole her land shall be confounded and all her slain shall fall in the midst of her**

ורננו 7442 על 5921 בבל 894 שמים 8064 וארץ 776 וכל 3605 אשר 834 בהם 871a כי 3588 מצפון 6828 יבוא 935 לה 3807a
uarinnu 'al babel shamayim ua'aretz, uakol 'asher bahem; kiy mitzapoun yabou'a lah
**Then shall sing for Babylon the heaven and the earth and all that *is* therein for from the north shall come unto her**

השודדים 7703 נאם 5002 יהוה 3068: **51:49** גם 1571 בבל 894 לנפל 5307 חללי 2491 ישראל 3478 גם 1571 לבבל 894 נפלו 5307
hashoudadiym na'am Yahuah. gam babel linpol challey yisra'ael; gam lababel naplu
**the spoilers saith Yahuah As Babylon to fall *has caused* the slain of Israel so at Babylon shall fall**

חללי 2491 כל 3605 הארץ 776: **51:50** פלטים 6412 מחרב 2719 הלכו 1980 אל 408 תעמדו 5975 זכרו 2142 מרחוק 7350 את 853
challey kal ha'aretz. paletiym mechereb, halaku 'al ta'amodu; zikru merachouq 'at
**the slain of all the earth You that have escaped the sword go away not stand still remember afar off**

יהוה 3068 וירושלם 3389 תעלה 5927 על 5921 לבבכם 3824: **51:51** בשנו 954 כי 3588 שמענו 8085 חרפה 2781 כסתה 3680
Yahuah, uiyarushalaim ta'aleh 'al lababkem. boshanu kiy shama'anu cherpah, kistah
**Yahuah and Jerusalem let come into your mind We are confounded because we have heard reproach has covered**

כלמה 3639 פנינו 6440 כי 3588 באו 935 זרים 2114 על 5921 מקדשי 4720 בית 1004 יהוה 3068: **51:52** לכן 3651 הנה 2009 ימים 3117
kalimah paneynu; kiy ba'au zariym, 'al miqdashey beyt Yahuah. laken hineh yamiym
**shame our faces for are come strangers into the sanctuaries of house Yahuah's Wherefore behold the days**

באים 935 נאם 5002 יהוה 3068 ופקדתי 6485 על 5921 פסיליה 6456 ובכל 3605 ארצה 776 יאנק 602
ba'aym na'am Yahuah, uapaqadtiy 'al pasiyleyha; uabkal 'artzah ye'anoq
**come saith Yahuah that I will do judgment upon her graven images and through all her land shall groan**

חלל 2491: **51:53** כי 3588 תעלה 5927 בבל 894 השמים 8064 וכי 3588 תבצר 1219 מרום 4791
chalal. kiy ta'aleh babel hashamayim, uakiy tabatzer maroum
**the wounded Though should mount up to Babylon heaven and though she should fortify the height of**

Jer 51:45 My people, go you out of the midst of her, and deliver you every man his soul from the fierce anger of YHUH.46 And lest your heart faint, and you fear for the rumour that shall be heard in the land; a rumour shall both come one year, and after that in another year shall come a rumour, and violence in the land, ruler against ruler.47 Therefore, behold, the days come, that I will do judgment upon the graven images of Babylon: and her whole land shall be confounded, and all her slain shall fall in the midst of her.48 Then the heaven and the earth, and all that is therein, shall sing for Babylon: for the spoilers shall come unto her from the north, saith YHUH.49 As Babylon has caused the slain of Israel to fall, so at Babylon shall fall the slain of all the earth.50 You that have escaped the sword, go away, stand not still: remember YHUH afar off, and let Jerusalem come into your mind.51 We are confounded, because we have heard reproach: shame has covered our faces: for strangers are come into the sanctuaries of YHUH's house.52 Wherefore, behold, the days come, saith YHUH, that I will do judgment upon her graven images: and through all her land the wounded shall groan.53 Though Babylon should mount up to heaven, and though she should fortify the height of her strength, yet from me shall spoilers come unto her, saith YHUH.

51:54

עזה 5797 מאתי 854 יבאו 935 שדדים 7703 לה 3807a נאם 5002 יהוה 3068: קול 6963 זעקה 2201 מבבל 894

'azah; me'atiy, yabo'au shodadiym lah na'am Yahuah. qoul za'aqah mibabel;

**her strength *yet* from me shall come spoilers unto her saith Yahuah A sound of a cry *comes* from Babylon**

51:55

ושבר 7667 גדול 1419 מארץ 776 כשדים 3778: כי 3588 שדד 7703 יהוה 3068 את 853 בבל 894 ואבד 6

uasheber gadoul me'aretz kasdiym. kiy shoded Yahuah 'at babel, ua'abad

**and destruction great from the land of the Chaldeans Because has spoiled Yahuah Babylon and destroyed**

51:56

ממנה 4480 קול 6963 גדול 1419 והמו 1993 גליהם 1530 כמים 4325 רבים 7227 נתן 5414 שאון 7588 קולם 6963: כי 3588

mimenah qoul gadoul; uahamu galeyhem kamayim rabiym, nitan sha'aun qoulam. kiy

**out of her voice *the* great when do roar her waves like waters great is uttered a noise of their voice Because**

בא 935 עליה 5921 על 5921 בבל 894 שודד 7703 ונלכדו 3920 גבוריה 1368 חתתה 2865 קשתותם 7198 כי 3588

ba' 'aleyha 'al babel shouded, uanilkadu giboureyha, chittah qashtoutam; kiy

**is come upon her *even* upon Babylon the spoiler and are taken her mighty men is broken *every one of* their bows for**

51:57

אל 410 גמלות 1578 יהוה 3068 שלם 7999 ישלם 7999: והשכרתי 7937 שריה 8269 וחכמיה 2450 פחותיה 6346

'ael gamulout Yahuah shalem yashalem. uahishkartiy sareyha uachakameyha pachouteyha

**El *of* recompences Yahuah shall surely requite And I will make drunk her princes and her wise *men* her captains**

וסגניה 5461 וגבוריה 1368 וישנו 3462 שנת 8142 עולם 5769 ולא 3808 יקיצו 6974 נאם 5002 המלך 4428 יהוה 3068

uasganeyha uagiboureyha, uayashanu shanat 'aulam uala' yaqiytzu; na'am hamelek, Yahuah

**and her rulers and her mighty men and they shall sleep a sleep perpetual and not wake saith the King *is* Yahuah**

51:58

צבאות 6635 שמו 8034: כה 3541 אמר 559 יהוה 3068 צבאות 6635 חמות 2346 בבל 894 הרחבה 7342 ערער 6209 תתערער 6209

tzaba'aut shamou. koh 'amar Yahuah tzaba'aut, chomout babel harachabah 'ar'aer tit'ar'ar,

**of hosts whose name Thus saith Yahuah of hosts The walls of Babylon broad shall be utterly broken**

ושעריה 8179 הגבהים 1364 באש 784 יצתו 3341 ויגעו 3021 עמים 5971 בדי 1767 ריק 7385 ולאמים 3816 בדי 1767 אש 784

uash'areyha hagabohiym ba'aesh yitzatu; uayig'au 'amiym badey riyq uala'amiym badey 'aesh

**and her gates high with fire shall be burned and shall labour the people in vain and the folk in the fire**

51:59

ויעפו 3286: הדבר 1697 אשר 834 צוה 6680 ירמיהו 3414 הנביא 5030 את 853 שריה 8304 בן 1121 נריה 5374

uaya'aepu. hadabar 'asher tziuah yirmayahu hanabiy'a, 'at sarayah ben neriyah

**and they shall be weary The word which commanded Jeremiah the prophet Seraiah the son of Neriah**

בן 1121 מחסיה 4271 בלכתו 1980 את 854 צדקיהו 6667 מלך 4428 יהודה 3063 בבל 894 בשנת 8141 הרביעית 7243 למלכו 4427

ben machseyah balektou 'at tzidqiyahu melek yahudah babel, bishnat harabi'ayt lamalakou;

**the son of Maaseiah when he went *with* Zedekiah the king of Judah *into* Babylon in year in the fourth of his reign**

51:60

ושריה 8304 שר 8269 מנוחה 4496: ויכתב 3789 ירמיהו 3414 את 853 כל 3605 הרעה 7451 אשר 834 תבוא 935 אל 413 בבל 894

uasarayah sar manuchah. uayiktob yirmayahu, 'at kal hara'ah 'asher tabou'a 'al babel

**And *this* Seraiah *was* a prince quiet So wrote Jeremiah all the evil that should come in Babylon**

51:61

אל 413 ספר 5612 אחד 259 את 853 כל 3605 הדברים 1697 האלה 428 הכתבים 3789 אל 413 בבל 894: ויאמר 559 ירמיהו 3414 אל 413

'al seper 'achad; 'at kal hadabariym ha'aeleh, hakatubiym 'al babel. uaya'mer yirmayahu 'al

**upon book a *even* all words these that are written against Babylon And said Jeremiah to**

Jer 51:54 A sound of a cry cometh from Babylon, and great destruction from the land of the Chaldeans:55 Because YHUH has spoiled Babylon, and destroyed out of her the great voice; when her waves do roar like great waters, a noise of their voice is uttered:56 Because the spoiler is come upon her, even upon Babylon, and her mighty men are taken, everyone of their bows is broken: for YHUH G-d of recompences shall surely requite.57 And I will make drunk her princes, and her wise men, her captains, and her rulers, and her mighty men: and they shall sleep a perpetual sleep, and not wake, saith the King, whose name is YHUH of hosts.58 Thus saith YHUH of hosts; The broad walls of Babylon shall be utterly broken, and her high gates shall be burned with fire; and the people shall labour in vain, and the folk in the fire, and they shall be weary.59 The word which Jeremiah the prophet commanded Seraiah the son of Neriah, the son of Maaseiah, when he went with Zedekiah the king of Judah into Babylon in the fourth year of his reign. And this Seraiah was a quiet prince.60 So Jeremiah wrote in a book all the evil that should come upon Babylon, even all these words that are written against Babylon.61 And Jeremiah said to Seraiah, When you come to Babylon, and shall see, and shall read all these words;

| 8304 שריה | 935 כבאך | 894 בבל | 7200 וראית | 7121 וקראת | 853 את | 3605 כל | 1697 הדברים | 428: האלה | 51:62 |
|---|---|---|---|---|---|---|---|---|---|
| sarayah; | kabo'aka | babel, | uara'ayta, | uaqara'ta, | 'at | kal | hadabariym | ha'aeleh. | |
| **to Seraiah** | **When you come to** | **Babylon** | **and you shall see** | **and shall read** | | **all** | **words** | **these** | |

| 559 ואמרת | 3068 יהוה | 859 אתה | 1696 דברת | 413 אל | 4725 המקום | 2088 הזה | 3772 להכריתו | 1115 לבלתי | 1961 היות | 871a בו | 3427 יושב |
|---|---|---|---|---|---|---|---|---|---|---|---|
| ua'amarta, | Yahuah | 'atah | dibarta | 'al | hamaqoum | hazeh | lahakariytou, | labiltiy | heyout | bou | yousheb, |
| **Then shall you say** | **O Yahuah** | **you** | **have spoken** | **against** | **place** | **this** | **to cut it off** | **that none** | **shall** | **in it** | **remain** |

| 120 למאדם | 5704 ועד | 929 בהמה | 3588 כי | 8077 שממות | 5769 עולם | 1961: תהיה | 51:63 | 1961 והיה | 1961 ככלתך |
|---|---|---|---|---|---|---|---|---|---|
| lame'adam | ua'ad | bahemah; | kiy | shimamout | 'aulam | tihayeh. | | uahayah | kakalotaka, |
| ***neither* man** | **nor** | **beast** | **but** | **desolate** | **for ever** | ***that* it shall be** | | **And it shall be** | **when you have made an end** |

| 7121 לקרא | 853 את | 5612 הספר | 2088 הזה | 7194 תקשר | 5921 עליו | 68 אבן | 7993 והשלכתו | 413 אל | 8432 תוך | 6578: פרת | 51:64 |
|---|---|---|---|---|---|---|---|---|---|---|---|
| liqra' | 'at | haseper | hazeh; | tiqshor | 'alayu | 'aben, | uahishlaktou | 'al | touk | parat. | |
| **of reading** | | **book** | **this** | ***that* you shall bind** | **to it** | **a stone** | **and cast it** | **into** | **the midst of** | **Euphrates** | |

| 559 ואמרת | 3602 ככה | 8257 תשקע | 894 בבל | 3808 ולא | 6965 תקום | 6440 מפני | 7451 הרעה | 834 אשר | 595 אנכי | 935 מביא | 5921 עליה |
|---|---|---|---|---|---|---|---|---|---|---|---|
| ua'amarta, | kakah | tishqa' | babel | uala' | taqum | mipaney | hara'ah, | 'asher | 'anokiy | mebiy'a | 'aleyha |
| **And you shall say** | **Thus** | **shall sink** | **Babylon** | **and not** | **and shall rise** | **from** | **the evil** | **that** | **I** | **will bring** | **upon her** |

| 3286 ויעפו | 5704 עד | 2008 הנה | 1697 דברי | 3414: ירמיהו |
|---|---|---|---|---|
| uaya'aepu; | 'ad | henah | dibrey | yirmayahu. |
| **and they shall be weary** | **Thus** | **far** | ***are* the words of** | **Jeremiah** |

| Jer 52:1 | 1121 בן | 6242 עשרים | 259 ואחת | 8141 שנה | 6667 צדקיהו | 4427 במלכו | 259 ואחת | 6240 עשרה | 8141 שנה | 4427 מלך |
|---|---|---|---|---|---|---|---|---|---|---|
| | ben | 'asriym | ua'achat | shanah | tzidqiyahu | bamalakou, | ua'achat | 'asreh | shanah, | malak |
| | **old** | **twenty** | ***was* and one** | **years** | **Zedekiah** | **when he began to reign** | **and one** | **ten** | **years** | **he reigned** |

| 3389 בירושלם | 8034 ושם | 517 אמו | 2537 חמיטל | 1323 בת | 3414 ירמיהו | 3841: מלבנה | 52:2 | 6213 ויעש |
|---|---|---|---|---|---|---|---|---|
| biyarushalaim; | uashem | 'amou, | chamiytal | bat | yirmayahu | milibnah. | | uaya'as |
| **in Jerusalem** | **And name** | **his mother's *was*** | **Hamutal** | **the daughter of** | **Jeremiah** | **of Libnah** | | **And he did** |

| 7451 הרע | 5869 בעיני | 3068 יהוה | 3605 ככל | 834 אשר | 6213 עשה | 3079: יהויקים | 52:3 | 3588 כי | 5921 על | 639 אף |
|---|---|---|---|---|---|---|---|---|---|---|
| hara' | ba'aeyney | Yahuah; | kakol | 'asher | 'asah | yahouyaqiym. | | kiy | 'al | 'ap |
| ***that which was* evil** | **in the eyes of** | **Yahuah** | **according to all** | **that** | **had done** | **Jehoiakim** | | **For** | **through** | **the anger of** |

| 3068 יהוה | 1961 היתה | 3389 בירושלם | 3063 ויהודה | 5704 עד | 7993 השליכו | 853 אותם | 5921 מעל | 6440 פניו | 4775 וימרד | 6667 צדקיהו |
|---|---|---|---|---|---|---|---|---|---|---|
| Yahuah | hayatah | biyarushalaim | uayahudah, | 'ad | hishlikou | 'autam | me'al | panayu; | uayimrod | tzidqiyahu |
| **Yahuah** | **it came to pass** | **in Jerusalem** | **and Judah** | **till** | **he had cast out them** | | **from** | **his presence** | **that rebelled** | **Zedekiah** |

| 4428 במלך | 894: בבל | 52:4 | 1961 ויהי | 8141 בשנה | 8671 התשעית | 4427 למלכו | 2320 בחדש | 6224 העשירי | 6218 בעשור |
|---|---|---|---|---|---|---|---|---|---|
| bamelek | babel. | | uayahiy | bashanah | hatashi'ayt | lamalakou, | bachodesh | ha'asiyriy | be'asour |
| **against the king of** | **Babylon** | | **And it came to pass** | **in year of** | **the ninth** | **his reign** | **in month** | **the tenth** | **in the tenth** |

| 2320 לחדש | 935 בא | 5019 נבוכדראצר | 4428 מלך | 894 בבל | 1931 הוא | 3605 וכל | 2428 חילו | 5921 על | 3389 ירושלם | 2583 ויחנו |
|---|---|---|---|---|---|---|---|---|---|---|
| lachodesh | ba' | nabukadra'tzar | melek | babel | hua' | uakal | cheylou | 'al | yarushalaim, | uayachanu |
| ***day* of the month** | **came *that*** | **Nebuchadrezzar** | **king of** | **Babylon** | **he** | **and all** | **his army** | **against** | **Jerusalem** | **and pitched** |

Jer 51:62 Then shall you say, O YHUH, you have spoken against this place, to cut it off, that none shall remain in it, neither man nor beast, but that it shall be desolate forever.63 And it shall be, when you have made an end of reading this book, that you shall bind a stone to it, and cast it into the midst of Euphrates:64 And you shall say, Thus shall Babylon sink, and shall not rise from the evil that I will bring upon her: and they shall be weary. Thus far are the words of Jeremiah. **Jer** 52:1 Zedekiah was one and twenty years old when he began to reign, and he reigned eleven years in Jerusalem. And his mother's name was Hamutal the daughter of Jeremiah of Libnah.2 And he did that which was evil in the eyes of YHUH, according to all that Jehoiakim had done.3 For through the anger of YHUH it came to pass in Jerusalem and Judah, till he had cast them out from his presence, that Zedekiah rebelled against the king of Babylon.4 And it came to pass in the ninth year of his reign, in the tenth month, in the tenth day of the month, that Nebuchadrezzar king of Babylon came, he and all his army, against Jerusalem, and pitched against it, and built forts against it round about.

52:5

עליה 5921 ויבנו 1129 עליה 5921 דיק 1785 סביב 5439: ותבא 935 העיר 5892 במצור 4692 עד 5704 עשתי 6249 עשרה 6240 שנה 8141
'aleyha; uayibnu 'aleyha dayeq sabiyb. uataba' ha'ayr bamatzour; 'ad 'ashtey 'asreh shanah,
**against it and built against it forts round about So she was the city besieged unto *the* one of ten year**

52:6

למלך 4428 צדקיהו 6667: בחדש 2320 הרביעי 7243 בתשעה 8672 לחדש 2320 ויחזק 2388 הרעב 7458 בעיר 5892 ולא 3808
lamelek tzidqiyahu. bachodesh harbiy'ay batish'ah lachodesh, uayechazaq hara'ab ba'ayr; uala'
**of king Zedekiah in month the fourth in the ninth *day* of the month And was sore the famine in the city so that no**

52:7

היה 1961 לחם 3899 לעם 5971 הארץ 776: ותבקע 1234 העיר 5892 וכל 3605 אנשי 582 המלחמה 4421 יברחו 1272
hayah lechem la'am ha'aretz. uatibaqa' ha'ayr, uakal 'anshey hamilchamah yibrachu
**there was bread for the people of the land Then was broken up the city and all the men of war fled**

ויצאו 3318 מהעיר 5892 לילה 3915 דרך 1870 שער 8179 בין 996 החמתים 2346 אשר 834 על 5921 גן 1588 המלך 4428
uayetza'au meha'ayr layalah, derek sha'ar beyn hachomotayim 'asher 'al gan hamelek,
**and went forth out of the city by night by the way of the gate between the two walls which *was* by garden the king's**

52:8

וכשדים 3778 על 5921 העיר 5892 סביב 5439 וילכו 1980 דרך 1870 הערבה 6160: וירדפו 7291 חיל 2428
uakasdiym 'al ha'ayr sabiyb; uayelaku derek ha'arabah. uayirdapu cheyl
**now the Chaldeans *were* by the city round about: and they went by the way of the plain But pursued *the* army of**

כשדים 3778 אחרי 310 המלך 4428 וישיגו 5381 את 853 צדקיהו 6667 בערבת 6160 ירחו 3405 וכל 3605 חילו 2428 נפצו 6327
kasdiym 'acharey hamelek, uayasiygu 'at tzidqiyahu ba'arbot yarechou; uakal cheylou, napotzu
***the* Chaldeans after the king and overtook Zedekiah in the plains of Jericho and all his army was scattered**

52:9

מעליו 5921: ויתפשו 8610 את 853 המלך 4428 ויעלו 5927 אתו 853 אל 413 מלך 4428 בבל 894 רבלתה 7247 בארץ 776
me'alayu. uayitpasu 'at hamelek, uaya'alu 'atou 'al melek babel riblatah ba'aretz
**from him Then they took the king and carried up him unto the king of Babylon to Riblah in the land of**

52:10

חמת 2574 וידבר 1696 אתו 854 משפטים 4941: וישחט 7819 מלך 4428 בבל 894 את 853 בני 1121 צדקיהו 6667
chamat; uaydaber 'atou mishpatiym. uayishchat melek babel 'at baney tzidqiyahu
**Hamath where he gave upon him judgment And slew the king of Babylon the sons of Zedekiah**

52:11

לעיניו 5869 וגם 1571 את 853 כל 3605 שרי 8269 יהודה 3063 שחט 7819 ברבלתה 7247: ואת 853 עיני 5869 צדקיהו 6667 עור 5786
la'aeynayu; ua'gam 'at kal sarey yahudah shachat bariblatah. ua'at 'aeyney tzidqiyahu 'aur;
**before his eyes also all the princes of Judah he slew in Riblah *Then* the eyes of Zedekiah he put out**

ויאסרהו 631 בנחשתים 5178 ויבאהו 935 מלך 4428 בבל 894 בבלה 894 ויתנהו 5414 בבית 1004 הפקדת 6486 עד 5704
uaya'asrehu banachushtayim, uayabi'ahu melek babel babelah, uayitanehu bebeiyt hapaqudot 'ad
**and bound him in chains and carried him the king of Babylon to Babylon and put him in house the prison till**

52:12

יום 3117 מותו 4194: ובחדש 2320 החמישי 2549 בעשור 6218 לחדש 2320 היא 1931 שנת 8141 תשע 8672 עשרה 6240
youm moutou. uabachodesh hachamiyshiy be'asour lachodesh, hiy'a, shanat tesha' 'asreh
**the day of his death Now in month the fifth in the tenth *day* of the month which *was the* year of nine ten**

שנה 8141 למלך 4428 נבוכדראצר 5019 מלך 4428 בבל 894 בא 935 נבוזראדן 5018 רב 7227 טבחים 2876 עמד 5975 לפני 6440
shanah, lamelek nabukadra'tzar melek babel; ba', nabuzar'adan rab tabachiym, 'amad lipney
**year king of Nebuchadrezzar the king of Babylon came Nebuzaradan captain of the guard *which* abide served**

Jer 52:5 So the city was besieged unto the eleventh year of king Zedekiah.6 And in the fourth month, in the ninth day of the month, the famine was sore in the city, so that there was no bread for the people of the land.7 Then the city was broken up, and all the men of war fled, and went forth out of the city by night by the way of the gate between the two walls, which was by the king's garden; (now the Chaldeans were by the city round about:) and they went by the way of the plain.8 But the army of the Chaldeans pursued after the king, and overtook Zedekiah in the plains of Jericho; and all his army was scattered from him.9 Then they took the king, and carried him up unto the king of Babylon to Riblah in the land of Hamath; where he gave judgment upon him.10 And the king of Babylon slew the sons of Zedekiah before his eyes: he slew also all the princes of Judah in Riblah.11 Then he put out the eyes of Zedekiah; and the king of Babylon bound him in chains, and carried him to Babylon, and put him in prison till the day of his death.12 Now in the fifth month, in the tenth day of the month, which was the nineteenth year of Nebuchadrezzar king of Babylon, came Nebuzar-adan, captain of the guard, which served the king of Babylon, into Jerusalem,13 And burned the house of YHUH, and the king's house; and all the houses of Jerusalem,

52:13

מלך 4428 בבל 894 בירושלם 3389: וישרף 8313 את 853 בית 1004 יהוה 3068 ואת 853 בית 1004 המלך 4428 ואת 853 כל 3605
melek babel biyarushalaim. uayisrop 'at beyt Yahuah ua'at beyt hamelek; ua'at kal
**the king of Babylon into Jerusalem And burned the house of Yahuah *and* house the king's *and* all**

52:14

בתי 1004 ירושלם 3389 ואת 853 כל 3605 בית 1004 הגדול 1419 שרף 8313 באש 784: ואת 853 כל 3605 חמות 2346
batey yarushalaim ua'at kal beyt hagadoul sarap ba'aesh. ua'at kal choumot
**the houses of Jerusalem *and* all the houses of the great *men* burned he with fire *And* all the walls of**

52:15

ירושלם 3389 סביב 5439 נתצו 5422 כל 3605 חיל 2428 כשדים 3778 אשר 834 את 854 רב 7227 טבחים 2876:
yarushalaim sabiyb; natatzu kal cheyl kasdiym, 'asher 'at rab tabachiym.
**Jerusalem round about brake down all the army of the Chaldeans that *were* *with* the captain of the guard**

ומדלות 1803 העם 5971 ואת 853 יתר 3499 העם 5971 הנשארים 7604 בעיר 5892 ואת 853 הנפלים 5307 אשר 834
uamidalout ha'am ua'at yeter ha'am hanisha'ariym ba'ayr, ua'at hanopliym 'asher
**Then of the poor of the people *and* the residue of the people that remained in the city *and* those that fell away that**

נפלו 5307 אל 413 מלך 4428 בבל 894 ואת 853 יתר 3499 האמון 527 הגלה 1540 נבוזראדן 5018 רב 7227
naplu 'al melek babel, ua'at yeter ha'amoun; hegalah nabuzar'adan rab
**fell to the king of Babylon *and* the rest of the multitude carried away captive *certain* Nebuzaradan the captain of**

52:16

טבחים 2876: ומדלות 1803 הארץ 776 השאיר 7604 נבוזראדן 5018 רב 7227 טבחים 2876 לכרמים 3755
tabachiym. uamidalout ha'aretz, hish'ayr nabuzar'adan rab tabachiym; lakoramiym
**the guard But of the poor of the land left *certain* Nebuzaradan the captain of the guard for vinedressers**

52:17

וליגבים 3009: ואת 853 עמודי 5982 הנחשת 5178 אשר 834 לבית 1004 יהוה 3068 ואת 853 המכנות 4350 ואת 853
ualyogabiym. ua'at 'amudey hanachoshet 'asher labeyt Yahuah ua'at hamakonout ua'at
**and for husbandmen *Also* the pillars of brass that *were* in the house of Yahuah *and* the bases *and***

ים 3220 הנחשת 5178 אשר 834 בבית 1004 יהוה 3068 שברו 7665 כשדים 3778 וישאו 5375 את 853 כל 3605 נחשתם 5178
yam hanachoshet 'asher babeyt Yahuah shibru kasdiym; uayis'au 'at kal nachushtam
**sea the brasen that *was* in the house of Yahuah brake the Chaldeans and carried all the brass of them**

52:18

בבלה 894: ואת 853 הסרות 5518 ואת 853 היעים 3257 ואת 853 המזמרות 4212 ואת 853 המזרקת 4219 ואת 853 הכפות 3709 ואת 853
babelah. ua'at hasirout ua'at haya'aym ua'at hamazamarout ua'at hamizraqot ua'at hakapout, ua'at
**to Babylon *also* The caldrons *and* the shovels *and* the snuffers *and* the bowls *and* and the spoons *and***

52:19

כל 3605 כלי 3627 הנחשת 5178 אשר 834 ישרתו 8334 בהם 871a לקחו 3947: ואת 853 הספים 5592 ואת 853
kal kaley hanachoshet 'asher yasharatu bahem laqachu. ua'at Hassippim ua'at
**all the vessels of brass wherewith they ministered in them took they away *And* the basons *and***

המחתות 4289 ואת 853 המזרקות 4219 ואת 853 הסירות 5518 ואת 853 המנרות 4501 ואת 853 הכפות 3709 ואת 853 המנקיות 4518 אשר 834
hamachtot ua'at hamizraqout ua'at hasiyrout ua'at hamanaorout, ua'at hakapout ua'at hamanaqiyout, 'asher
**the firepans *and* the bowls *and* the caldrons *and* the candlesticks *and* the spoons *and* the cups *that* which**

52:20

זהב 2091 זהב 2091 ואשר 834 כסף 3701 כסף 3701 לקח 3947 רב 7227 טבחים 2876: העמודים 5982
zahab zahab, ua'asher kesep kasep; laqach rab tabachiym. ha'amudiym
***was* of gold *in* gold and *that* which *was* of silver *in* silver and took away the captain of the guard The pillars**

Jer 52:13 and all the houses of the great men, burned he with fire:14 And all the army of the Chaldeans, that were with the captain of the guard, break down all the walls of Jerusalem round about.15 Then Nebuzar-adan the captain of the guard carried away captive certain of the poor of the people, and the residue of the people that remained in the city, and those that fell away, that fell to the king of Babylon, and the rest of the multitude.16 But Nebuzar-adan the captain of the guard left certain of the poor of the land for vinedressers and for husbandmen.17 Also the pillars of brass that were in the house of YHUH, and the bases, and the brasen sea that was in the house of YHUH, the Chaldeans break, and carried all the brass of them to Babylon.18 The caldrons also, and the shovels, and the snuffers, and the bowls, and the spoons, and all the vessels of brass wherewith they ministered, took they away.19 And the basons, and the firepans, and the bowls, and the caldrons, and the candlesticks, and the spoons, and the cups; that which was of gold in gold, and that which was of silver in silver, took the captain of the guard away.20 The two pillars, one sea, and twelve brasen bulls that were under the bases, which king Solomon had made in the house of YHUH: the brass of all these vessels was without weight.

שנים 8147 הים 3220 אחד 259 והבקר 1241 שנים 8147 עשר 6240 נחשת 5178 אשר 834 תחת 8478 המכנות 4350 אשר 834 עשה 6213 המלך 4428
shanayim, hayam 'achad uahabaqar shaneym 'asar nachoshet 'asher tachat hamakonout, 'asher 'asah hamelek
**two the sea one and bulls the two ten brasen that *were* under the bases which had made king**

52:21
שלמה 8010 לבית 1004 יהוה 3068 לא 3808 היה 1961 משקל 4948 לנחשתם 5178 כל 3605 הכלים 3627 האלה 428:
shalomoh labeyt Yahuah; la' hayah mishqal, linchushtam kal hakeliym ha'aeleh.
**Solomon in the house of Yahuah without was weight the brass of all vessels these**

והעמודים 5982 שמנה 8083 עשרה 6240 אמה 520 קומה 6967 העמד 5982 האחד 259 וחוט 2339 שתים 8147 עשרה 6240
uaha'amudiym, shamoneh 'asreh 'amah qoumah ha'amud ha'achad, uachut shateym 'asreh
**And *concerning* the pillars eight ten cubits the height of pillar *was* one and a fillet of two ten**

52:22
אמה 520 יסבנו 5437 ועביו 5672 ארבע 702 אצבעות 676 נבוב 5014: וכתרת 3805 עליו 5921 נחשת 5178
'amah yasubenu; ua'abayou 'arba atzba'aut nabub. uachoteret 'alayu nachoshet,
**cubits did compass it and the thickness thereof *was* four fingers *it was* hollow And a chapiter of upon it brass**

וקומת 6967 הכתרת 3805 האחת 259 חמש 2568 אמות 520 ושבכה 7639 ורמונים 7416 על 5921 הכותרת 3805 סביב 5439
uaqoumat hakoteret ha'achat chamesh 'amout uasbakah uarimouniym 'al hakouteret sabiyb
***was* and the height of chapiter one *was* five cubits with network and pomegranates upon the chapiters round about**

52:23
הכל 3605 נחשת 5178 וכאלה 428 לעמוד 5982 השני 8145 ורמונים 7416: ויהיו 1961 הרמנים 7416
hakol nachoshet; uaka'aeleh la'amud hasheniy uarimouniym. uayihayu harimoniym,
**all *of* brass also like unto these pillar The second and the pomegranates *were* And there were pomegranates**

52:24
תשעים 8673 וששה 8337 רוחה 7307 כל 3605 הרמונים 7416 מאה 3967 על 5921 השבכה 7639 סביב 5439: ויקח 3947
tish'aym uashishah ruchah; kal harimouniym me'ah 'al hasabakah sabiyb. uayiqach
**ninety and six *on* a side *and* all the pomegranates *were* an hundred upon the network round about And took**

רב 7227 טבחים 2876 את 853 שריה 8304 כהן 3548 הראש 7218 ואת 853 צפניה 6846 כהן 3548 המשנה 4932 ואת 853 שלשת 7969 שמרי 8104
rab tabachiym, 'at sarayah kohen hara'sh, ua'at tzapanyah kohen hamishneh; ua'at shaloshet shomrey
**the captain of the guard Seraiah priest the chief *and* Zephaniah priest the second *and* *the* three keepers of**

52:25
הסף 5592: ומן 4480 העיר 5892 לקח 3947 סריס 5631 אחד 259 אשר 834 היה 1961 פקיד 6496 על 5921 אנשי 582 המלחמה 4421
hasap. uamin ha'ayr laqach sariys 'achad 'asher hayah paqiyd 'al 'anshey hamilchamah,
**the door also out of the city He took eunuch an which had the charge of the men of war**

ושבעה 7651 אנשים 582 מראי 7200 פני 6440 המלך 4428 אשר 834 נמצאו 4672 בעיר 5892 ואת 853 ספר 5608 שר 8269
uashib'ah 'anashiym mero'aey paney hamelek 'asher nimtza'au ba'ayr, ua'at, soper sar
**and seven men of them that were near person the king's which were found in the city *and* scribe of *the* principal**

הצבא 6635 המצבא 6633 את 853 עם 5971 הארץ 776 וששים 8346 איש 376 מעם 5971 הארץ 776 הנמצאים 4672
hatzaba', hamatzba' 'at 'am ha'aretz; uashishiym 'aysh me'am ha'aretz, hanimtza'aym
**the host who mustered the people of the land and threescore men of the people of the land that were found**

52:26
בתוך 8432 העיר 5892: ויקח 3947 אותם 853 נבוזראדן 5018 רב 7227 טבחים 2876 וילך 1980 אותם 853 אל 413
batouk ha'ayr. uayiqach 'autam, nabuzar'adan rab tabachiym; uayolek 'autam 'al
**in the midst of the city So took them Nebuzaradan the captain of the guard and brought them to**

Jer 52:21 And concerning the pillars, the height of one pillar was eighteen cubits; and a fillet of twelve cubits did compass it; and the thickness thereof was four fingers: it was hollow.22 And a chapiter of brass was upon it; and the height of one chapiter was five cubits, with network and pomegranates upon the chapiters round about, all of brass. The second pillar also and the pomegranates were like unto these.23 And there were ninety and six pomegranates on a side; and all the pomegranates upon the network were an hundred round about.24 And the captain of the guard took Seraiah the chief priest, and Zephaniah the second priest, and the three keepers of the door:25 He took also out of the city an eunuch, which had the charge of the men of war; and seven men of them that were near the king's person, which were found in the city; and the principal scribe of the host, who mustered the people of the land; and threescore men of the people of the land, that were found in the midst of the city.26 So Nebuzar-adan the captain of the guard took them, and brought them to the king of Babylon to Riblah.

52:27

מלך 4428 בבל 894 רבלתה 7247: ויכה 5221 אותם 853 מלך 4428 בבל 894 וימתם 4191 ברבלה 7247 בארץ 776

melek babel riblatah. uayakeh 'autam melek babel uayamiytem bariblah ba'aretz

**the king of Babylon to Riblah And smote them the king of Babylon and put them to death in Riblah in the land of**

52:28

חמת 2574 ויגל 1540 יהודה 3063 מעל 5921 אדמתו 127: זה 2088 העם 5971 אשר 834 הגלה 1540

chamat; uayigel yahudah me'al 'admatou. zeh ha'am, 'asher hegalah

**Hamath Thus was carried away captive Judah out of his own land This *is* the people whom carried away captive**

52:29

נבוכדראצר 5019 בשנת 8141 שבע 7651 יהודים 3064 שלשת 7969 אלפים 505 ועשרים 6242 ושלשה 7969: בשנת 8141 שמונה 8083

nabukadra'tzar; bishnat sheba' yahudiym shaloshet 'alapiym ua'asriym uashloshah. bishnat shamouneh

**Nebuchadrezzar in year *the* seventh Jews three thousand and twenty and three In year *the* eight**

עשרה 6240 לנבוכדראצר 5019 מירושלם 3389 נפש 5315 שמנה 8083 מאות 3967 שלשים 7970

'asreh linabukadra'tzar; miyarushalaim, nepesh shamoneh me'aut shaloshiym

**ten of Nebuchadrezzar *he carried away captive* from Jerusalem persons eight hundred thirty**

52:30

ושנים 8147: בשנת 8141 שלש 7969 ועשרים 6242 לנבוכדראצר 5019 הגלה 1540 נבוזראדן 5018 רב 7227

uashnayim. bishnat shalosh ua'asriym linabukadra'tzar hegalah, nabuzar'adan rab

**and two In year *the* three and twentieth of Nebuchadrezzar carried away captive Nebuzaradan the captain of**

טבחים 2876 יהודים 3064 נפש 5315 שבע 7651 מאות 3967 ארבעים 705 וחמשה 2568 כל 3605 נפש 5315 ארבעת 702 אלפים 505 ושש 8337

tabachiym, yahudiym nepesh sheba' me'aut 'arba'aym uachamishah; kal nepesh 'arba'at 'alapiym uashesh

**the guard of the Jews persons seven hundred forty and five all the persons *were* four thousand and six**

52:31

מאות 3967: ויהי 1961 בשלשים 7970 ושבע 7651 שנה 8141 לגלות 1546 יהויכן 3078 מלך 4428 יהודה 3063

me'aut. uayahiy bishloshiym uasheba' shanah, lagalut yahouyakiyn melek yahudah,

**hundred And it came to pass in thirtieth and the seven year of the captivity of Jehoiachin king of Judah**

בשנים 8147 עשר 6240 חדש 2320 בעשרים 6242 וחמשה 2568 לחדש 2320 נשא 5375 אויל 192 מרדך 4428 מלך 4428 בבל 894

bishneym 'asar chodesh, ba'asriym uachamishah lachodesh; nasa' 'auiyl marodak melek babel

**in two ten month in twentieth and the five *day* of the month lifted up *that* Evil merodach king of Babylon**

בשנת 8141 מלכתו 4438 את 853 ראש 7218 יהויכין 3078 מלך 4428 יהודה 3063 ויצא 3318 אותו 853 מבית 1004

bishnat malkutou, 'at ra'sh yahouyakiyn melek yahudah, uayotzea' 'autou mibeyt

**in the *first* year of his reign the head of Jehoiachin king of Judah and brought forth him out of house**

52:32

הכליא 3628: וידבר 1696 אתו 853 טבות 2896 ויתן 5414 את 853 כסאו 3678 ממעל 4605 לכסא 3678 מלכים 4428 אשר 834

hakaliya' uaydaber 'atou tobout; uayiten 'at kis'au, mima'al, lakisea' melakiym 'asher

**out of prison And spoke unto him kindly and set his throne above the throne of the kings that**

52:33

אתו 854 בבבל 894: ושנה 8138 את 853 בגדי 899 כלאו 3608 ואכל 398 לחם 3899 לפניו 6440 תמיד 8548

'atou bababel. uashanah 'at bigdey kil'au; ua'akol lechem lapanayu tamiyd

***were* with him in Babylon And changed garments his prison and he did eat bread before him continually**

52:34

כל 3605 ימי 3117 חיו 2416: וארחתו 737 ארחת 737 תמיד 8548 נתנה 5414 לו 3807a מאת 853 מלך 4428 בבל 894

kal yamey chayau. ua'aruchatou, 'aruchat tamiyd nitanah lou' me'at melek babel

**all the days of his life And *for* his diet a diet continual there was given him of the king of Babylon**

Jer 52:27 And the king of Babylon smote them, and put them to death in Riblah in the land of Hamath. Thus Judah was carried away captive out of his own land.28 This is the people whom Nebuchadrezzar carried away captive: in the seventh year three thousand Jews and three and twenty:29 In the eighteenth year of Nebuchadrezzar he carried away captive from Jerusalem eight hundred thirty and two persons:30 In the three and twentieth year of Nebuchadrezzar Nebuzar-adan the captain of the guard carried away captive of the Jews seven hundred forty and five persons: all the persons were four thousand and six hundred.31 And it came to pass in the seven and thirtieth year of the captivity of Jehoiachin king of Judah, in the twelfth month, in the five and twentieth day of the month, that Evil-merodach king of Babylon in the first year of his reign lifted up the head of Jehoiachin king of Judah, and brought him forth out of prison,32 And spoke kindly unto him, and set his throne above the throne of the kings that were with him in Babylon,33 And changed his prison garments: and he did continually eat bread before him all the days of his life.34 And for his diet, there was a continual diet given him of the king of Babylon,

Jeremiah 52:34

| 𐤃𐤁𐤓 | 𐤉𐤅𐤌 | 𐤁𐤉𐤅𐤌𐤅 | 𐤏𐤃 | 𐤉𐤅𐤌 | 𐤌𐤅𐤕𐤅 | 𐤊𐤋 | 𐤉𐤌𐤉 | 𐤇𐤉𐤉𐤅 |
|---|---|---|---|---|---|---|---|---|
| דבר 1697 | יום 3117 | ביומו 3117 | עד 5704 | יום 3117 | מותו 4194 | כל 3605 | ימי 3117 | חייו 2416: |
| dabar | youm | bayoumou | 'ad | youm | moutou; | kal | yamey | chayayu. |
| **a portion** | **every** | **day** | **until** | **the day of** | **his death** | **all** | **the days of** | **his life** |

every day a portion until the day of his death, all the days of his life.

# LAMENTATIONS
## (*Eikhah*)

The Book of Lamentations does not explicitly identify its author but tradition is that the Prophet Jeremiah is the author and this is highly possible since Jeremiah witnessed the Babylonians destroying Jerusalem. The book was written approximately between 586 and 575 B.C., during or soon after Jerusalem's destruction by the Babylonians who burned, plundered and destroyed the city of Jerusalem along with Solomon's Temple, which had stood for approximately 400 years. Jeremiah was an eyewitness to all these events caused by Yahuah's wrath being poured out through the invasion, which lead to their captivity for 70 years. Jeremiah was also known as the "*weeping prophet*" because of his deep passion for his people and the city of Jerusalem, Lamentations 3:48-49.

**Lamentations 1:1** איכה 349 ישבה 3427 בדד 910 העיר 5892 רבתי 7227 עם 5971 היתה 1961 כאלמנה 490
'aeykah yashabah badad, ha'ayr rabatiy 'am, hayatah ka'almanah;
**How does sit solitary the city *that was* full of people *how* is she become as a widow she**

רבתי 7227 בגוים 1471 שרתי 8282 במדינות 4082 היתה 1961 למס 4522: **1:2** בכו 1058 תבכה 1058
rabatiy bagouyim, saratiy bamadiynout, hayatah lamas. bakou tibkeh
***that was* great among the nations *and* princess among the provinces *how* she is become tributary weeps She sore**

בלילה 3915 ודמעתה 1832 על 5921 לחיה 3895 אין 369 לה 3807a מנחם 5162 מכל 3605 אהביה 157 כל 3605 רעיה 7453
balayalah, uadim'atah 'al lechayah, 'aeyn lah manachem mikal 'ahabeyha; kal re'ayha
**in the night and her tears *are* on her cheeks has none she to comfort *her* among all her lovers all her friends**

בגדו 898 בה 871a היו 1961 לה 3807a לאיבים 341: **1:3** גלתה 1540 יהודה 3063
bagadu bah, hayu lah la'ayabiym. galatah yahudah
**have dealt treacherously with her they are become her enemies she is gone into captivity Judah**

מעני 6040 ומרב 7230 עבדה 5656 היא 1931 ישבה 3427 בגוים 1471 לא 3808 מצאה 4672 מנוח 4494 כל 3605
me'aniy uamerob 'abodah, hiy'a yashabah bagouyim, la' matz'ah manouach; kal
**because of affliction and because of great servitude she dwell among the heathen no she finds rest all**

רדפיה 7291 השיגוה 5381 בין 996 המצרים 4712: **1:4** דרכי 1870 ציון 6726 אבלות 57 מבלי 1097 באי 935
rodapeyha hisiyguha beyn hamatzariym. darkey tziyoun abelout, mibliy ba'aey
**her persecutors overtook her between the straits The ways of Zion do mourn because none come to**

מועד 4150 כל 3605 שעריה 8179 שוממין 8074 כהניה 3548 נאנחים 584 בתולתיה 1330 נוגות 3013 והיא 1931 מר 4751
mou'aed, kal sha'areyha shoumemiyn, kohaneyha ne'anachiym; batuloteyha nugout uahiy'a mar
**the solemn feasts all her gates are desolate her priests sigh her virgins are afflicted and she *is in* bitterness**

לה 3807a: **1:5** היו 1961 צריה 6862 לראש 7218 איביה 341 שלו 7951 כי 3588 יהוה 3068 הוגה 3013 על 5921
lah. hayu tzareyha lara'sh 'ayabeyha shalu, kiy Yahuah hougah 'al
**to her are become Her adversaries the chief her enemies prosper for Yahuah has afflicted her for**

רב 7230 פשעיה 6588 עולליה 5768 הלכו 1980 שבי 7628 לפני 6440 צר 6862: **1:6** ויצא 3318 מן 4480
rab pasha'ayha; 'aulaleyha halaku shabiy lipney tzar. uayetzea' min
**the multitude of her transgressions her children are gone into captivity before the enemy And is departed from**

בת 1323 ציון 6726 כל 3605 הדרה 1926 היו 1961 שריה 8269 כאילים 354 לא 3808 מצאו 4672 מרעה 4829 וילכו 1980 בלא 3808
bat tziyoun kal hadarah; hayu sareyha, ke'aeyliym la' matza'au mira'ah, uayelaku uala'
**daughter of Zion all her beauty are become her princes like harts no *that* find pasture and they are gone without**

**Lamentations** 1:1 How doth the city sit solitary, that was full of people how is she become as a widow she that was was great among the nations, and princess among the provinces, how is she become tributary 2 She weep sore in the night, and her tears are on her cheeks: among all her lovers she has none to comfort her: all her friends have dealt treacherously with her, they are become her enemies.3 Judah is gone into captivity because of affliction, and because of great servitude: she dwell among the heathen, she findeth no rest: all her persecutors overtook her between the straits.4 The ways of Zion do mourn, because none come to the solemn feasts: all her gates are desolate: her priests sigh, her virgins are afflicted, and she is in bitterness.5 Her adversaries are the chief, her enemies prosper; for YHUH has afflicted her for the multitude of her transgressions: her children are gone into captivity before the enemy.6 And from the daughter of Zion all her beauty is departed: her princes are become like harts that find no pasture, and they are gone without strength before the pursuer.

| | | | 1:7 | | | | | | |
|---|---|---|---|---|---|---|---|---|---|
| כח 3581 | לפני 6440 | רודף 7291: | | זכרה 2142 | ירושלם 3389 | ימי 3117 | עניה 6040 | ומרודיה 4788 | כל 3605 |
| koach | lipney | roudep. | | zakarah | yarushalaim, | yamey | 'anayah | uamrudeyha, | kal |
| **strength** | **before** | **the pursuer** | | **remembered** | **Jerusalem** | ***in* the days of** | **her affliction** | **and of her miseries** | **all** |

| | | | | | | | | | |
|---|---|---|---|---|---|---|---|---|---|
| מחמדיה 4262 | אשר 834 | היו 1961 | מימי 3117 | קדם 6924 | בנפל 5307 | עמה 5971 | ביד 3027 | צר 6862 | ואין 369 |
| machamudeyha, | 'asher | hayu | miymey | qedem; | binpol | 'amah | bayad | tzar, | ua'aeyn |
| **her pleasant things** | **that** | **she had** | **in the days of** | **old** | **when fell** | **her people** | **into the hand of** | **the enemy** | **and none** |

| | | | | | | | 1:8 | | | | |
|---|---|---|---|---|---|---|---|---|---|---|---|
| עוזר 5826 | לה 3807a | ראוה 7200 | צרים 6862 | שחקו 7832 | על 5921 | משבתה 4868: | | חטא 2399 | חטאה 2398 | ירושלם 3389 | על 5921 |
| 'auzer | lah, | ra'auha | tzariym, | sachaqu | 'al | mishbateha. | | chet'a | chata'ah | yarushalaim, | 'al |
| **did help** | **her** | **saw her** | **the adversaries** | ***and* did mock** | **at** | **her sabbaths** | | **grievously** | **has sinned** | **Jerusalem** | **therefore** |

| | | | | | | | | | | |
|---|---|---|---|---|---|---|---|---|---|---|
| כן 3651 | לנידה 5206 | היתה 1961 | כל 3605 | מכבדיה 3513 | הזילוה 2107 | כי 3588 | ראו 7200 | ערותה 6172 | גם 1571 | היא 1931 |
| ken | lanydah | hayatah; | kal | makabdeyha | hiziyluha | kiy | ra'au | 'aruatah, | gam | hiy'a |
| **after that** | **removed** | **she is** | **all** | **that honoured her** | **despise her** | **because** | **they have seen** | **her nakedness** | **yea** | **she** |

| | | | 1:9 | | | | | | |
|---|---|---|---|---|---|---|---|---|---|
| נאנחה 584 | ותשב 7725 | אחור 268: | | טמאתה 2932 | בשוליה 7757 | לא 3808 | זכרה 2142 | אחריתה 319 | ותרד 3381 |
| ne'anchah | uatashab | 'achour. | | tum'atah | bashuleyha, | la' | zakarah | 'achariytah, | uatered |
| **sigheth** | **and turned** | **backward** | | **Her filthiness *is*** | **in her skirts** | **not** | **she remembers** | **her last end** | **therefore she came down** |

| | | | | | | | | | | | 1:10 |
|---|---|---|---|---|---|---|---|---|---|---|---|
| פלאים 6382 | אין 369 | מנחם 5162 | לה 3807a | ראה 7200 | יהוה 3068 | את 853 | עניי 6040 | כי 3588 | הגדיל 1431 | אויב 341: | |
| pala'aym, | 'aeyn | manachem | lah; | ra'aeh | Yahuah | 'at | 'anyiy, | kiy | higdiyl | auyeb. | |
| **wonderfully** | **had no** | **comforter** | **she** | **behold** | **O Yahuah** | | **my affliction** | **for** | **has magnified *himself*** | **the enemy** | |

| | | | | | | | | | |
|---|---|---|---|---|---|---|---|---|---|
| ידו 3027 | פרש 6566 | צר 6862 | על 5921 | כל 3605 | מחמדיה 4261 | כי 3588 | ראתה 7200 | גוים 1471 | באו 935 |
| yadou | paras | tzar, | 'al | kal | machamadeyha; | kiy | ra'atah | gouyim | ba'au |
| **his hand** | **has spread out** | **The adversary** | **upon** | **all** | **her pleasant things** | **for** | **she has seen *that*** | **the heathen** | **entered into** |

| | | | | | | | 1:11 | | |
|---|---|---|---|---|---|---|---|---|---|
| מקדשה 4720 | אשר 834 | צויתה 6680 | לא 3808 | יבאו 935 | בקהל 6951 | לך 3807a: | | כל 3605 | עמה 5971 |
| miqadashah, | 'asher | tziuiytah, | la' | yabo'au | baqahal | lak. | | kal | 'amah |
| **her sanctuary** | **whom** | **you did command** | **not** | ***that* they should enter** | **into congregation** | **to your** | | **All** | **her people** |

| | | | | | | | | | |
|---|---|---|---|---|---|---|---|---|---|
| נאנחים 584 | מבקשים 1245 | לחם 3899 | נתנו 5414 | מחמודיהם 4262 | באכל 400 | להשיב 7725 | נפש 5315 | ראה 7200 | יהוה 3068 |
| ne'anachiym | mabaqshiym | lachem, | natanu | machamoudeyhem | ba'akel | lahashiyb | napesh; | ra'aeh | Yahuah |
| **sigh** | **they seek** | **bread** | **they have given** | **their pleasant things** | **for meat** | **to relieve** | **the soul** | **see** | **O Yahuah** |

| | | | | 1:12 | | | | | | | | |
|---|---|---|---|---|---|---|---|---|---|---|---|---|
| והביטה 5027 | כי 3588 | הייתי 1961 | זוללה 2151: | | לוא 3808 | אליכם 413 | כל 3605 | עברי 5674 | דרך 1870 | הביטו 5027 | וראו 7200 | אם 518 |
| uahabiytah, | kiy | hayiytiy | zoulelah. | | lua' | 'aleykem | kal | 'abarey | derek | habiytu | uar'au, | 'am |
| **and consider** | **for** | **I am become** | **vile** | | ***Is it* nothing** | **to you** | **all** | **you that pass** | **by?** | **behold** | **and see** | **if** |

| | | | | | | | | | | |
|---|---|---|---|---|---|---|---|---|---|---|
| יש 3426 | מכאוב 4341 | כמכאבי 4341 | אשר 834 | עולל 5953 | לי 3807a | אשר 834 | הוגה 3013 | יהוה 3068 | ביום 3117 | חרון 2740 |
| yesh | mak'aub | kamak'abiy, | 'asher | 'aulal | liy; | 'asher | hougah | Yahuah, | bayoum | charoun |
| **there be any** | **sorrow** | **like unto my sorrow** | **which** | **is done** | **unto me** | **wherewith** | **has afflicted** | **Yahuah *me*** | **in the day of** | **fierce** |

| | 1:13 | | | | | | | | |
|---|---|---|---|---|---|---|---|---|---|
| אפו 639: | | ממרום 4791 | שלח 7971 | אש 784 | בעצמתי 6106 | וירדנה 7287 | פרש 6566 | רשת 7568 | לרגלי 7272 |
| 'apou. | | mimaroum | shalach | 'aesh | ba'atzmotay | uayirdenah; | paras | reshet | laraglay |
| **his anger** | | **From above** | **has he sent** | **fire** | **into my bones** | **and it prevailed against them** | **he has spread** | **a net** | **for my feet** |

Lam 1:7 Jerusalem remembered in the days of her affliction and of her miseries all her pleasant things that she had in the days of old, when her people fell into the hand of the enemy, and none did help her: the adversaries saw her, and did mock at her sabbaths.8 Jerusalem has grievously sinned; therefore she is removed: all that honoured her despise her, because they have seen her nakedness: yea, she sigheth, and turneth backward.9 Her filthiness is in her skirts; she remembereth not her last end; therefore she came down wonderfully: she had no comforter. O YHUH, behold my affliction: for the enemy has magnified himself.10 The adversary has spread out his hand upon all her pleasant things: for she has seen that the heathen entered into her sanctuary, whom you did command that they should not enter into your congregation.11 All her people sigh, they seek bread; they have given their pleasant things for meat to relieve the soul: see, O YHUH, and consider; for I am become vile.12 Is it nothing to you, all you that pass by? behold, and see if there be any sorrow like unto my sorrow, which is done unto me, wherewith YHUH has afflicted me in the day of his fierce anger.13 From above has he sent fire into my bones, and it prevaileth against them: he has spread a net for my feet, he has turned me back: he has made me desolate and faint all the day.

1:14
השיבני 7725 אחור 268 נתנני 5414 שממה 8076 כל 3605 היום 3117 דוה 1739: נשקד 8244 על 5923 פשעי 6588
hashiybaniy 'achour, natananiy shomemah, kal hayoum dauah. nisqad 'al pasha'ay
**he has turned me back he has made me desolate all the day *and* faint is bound The yoke of my transgressions**

בידו 3027 ישתרגו 8276 עלו 5927 על 5921 צוארי 6677 הכשיל 3782 כחי 3581 נתנני 5414 אדני 136
bayadou, yistaragu 'alu 'al tzaua'ariy hikshiyl kochiy; natananiy 'adonay,
**by his hand they are wreathed *and* come up upon my neck he has made to fall my strength has delivered me Adonai**

1:15
בידי 3027 לא 3808 אוכל 3201 קום 6965: סלה 5541 כל 3605 אבירי 47 אדני 136
biydey la' 'aukal qum. silah kal 'abiyray 'adonay
**into *their* hands not *from whom* I am able to rise up has trodden under foot all my mighty Adonai**

בקרבי 7130 קרא 7121 עלי 5921 מועד 4150 לשבר 7665 בחורי 970 גת 1660 דרך 1869 אדני 136
baqirbiy, qara' 'alay mou'aed lishbor bachuray; gat darak 'adonay,
***men* in the midst of me he has called against me an assembly to crush my young men *as in* a winepress has trodden Adonai**

1:16
לבתולת 1330 בת 1323 יהודה 3063: על 5921 אלה 428 אני 589 בוכיה 1058 עיני 5869 עיני 5869 ירדה 3381 מים 4325
libatulat bat yahudah. 'al 'aeleh 'aniy boukiyah, 'aeyniy 'aeyniy yoradah mayim,
**the virgin the daughter of Judah For these *things* I weep mine eye mine eye run down with water**

כי 3588 רחק 7368 ממני 4480 מנחם 5162 משיב 7725 נפשי 5315 היו 1961 בני 1121 שוממים 8074 כי 3588 גבר 1396
kiy rachaq mimeniy manachem meshiyb napshiy; hayu banay shoumemiym, kiy gabar
**because is far from me the comforter that should relieve my soul are my children desolate because prevailed**

1:17
אויב 341: פרשה 6566 ציון 6726 בידיה 3027 אין 369 מנחם 5162 לה 3807a צוה 6680 יהוה 3068
auyeb. perasah tziyoun bayadeyha, 'aeyn manachem lah, tziuah Yahuah
**the enemy spread forth Zion her hands *and there is* none to comfort her has commanded Yahuah**

ליעקב 3290 סביביו 5439 צריו 6862 היתה 1961 ירושלם 3389 לנדה 5079
laya'aqob sabiybayu tzarayu; hayatah yarushalaim lanidah
**concerning Jacob *should be* round about him *that* his adversaries she became Jerusalem *is* as a menstruous woman**

1:18
ביניהם 996: צדיק 6662 הוא 1931 יהוה 3069 כי 3588 פיהו 6310 מריתי 4784 שמעו 8085 נא 4994 כל 3605
beyneyhem. tzadiyq hua' Yahuah kiy piyhu mariytiy; shim'au naa' kal
**among them *is* righteous he Yahuah for his commandment I have rebelled against hear I pray you all**

1:19
עמים 5971 וראו 7200 מכאבי 4341 בתולתי 1330 ובחורי 970 הלכו 1980 בשבי 7628: קראתי 7121 למאהבי 157 המה 1992
'amiym uar'au mak'abiy, batulotay uabachuray halaku bashebiy. qaraa'tiy lama'ahabay hemah
**people and behold my sorrow my virgins and my young men are gone into captivity I called for my lovers *but* they**

רמוני 7411 כהני 3548 וזקני 2205 בעיר 5892 גועו 1478 כי 3588 בקשו 1245 אכל 400 למו 3807a וישיבו 7725 את 853
rimuniy, kohanay uazqenay ba'ayr gaua'au; kiy biqshu 'akel lamou, uayashiybu 'at
**deceived me my priests and mine elders in the city gave up the ghost while they sought meat their to relieve**

1:20
נפשם 5315: ראה 7200 יהוה 3068 כי 3588 צר 6862 לי 3807a מעי 4578 חמרמרו 2560 נהפך 2015 לבי 3820 בקרבי 7130
napsham. ra'aeh Yahuah kiy tzar liy me'ay chamarmaru, nehpak libiy baqirbiy,
**their souls Behold O Yahuah for *am in* distress my bowels are troubled is turned mine heart within me**

Lam 1:14 The yoke of my transgressions is bound by his hand: they are wreathed, and come up upon my neck: he has made my strength to fall, YHUH has delivered me into their hands, from whom I am not able to rise up.15 The Adonai has trodden under foot all my mighty men in the midst of me: he has called an assembly against me to crush my young men: YHUH has trodden the virgin, the daughter of Judah, as in a winepress.16 For these things I weep; mine eye, mine eye runneth down with water, because the comforter that should relieve my soul is far from me: my children are desolate, because the enemy prevailed.17 Zion spreadeth forth her hands, and there is none to comfort her: YHUH has commanded concerning Jacob, that his adversaries should be round about him: Jerusalem is as a menstruous woman among them.18 YHUH is righteous; for I have rebelled against his commandment: hear, I pray you, all people, and behold my sorrow: my virgins and my young men are gone into captivity.19 I called for my lovers, but they deceived me: my priests and mine elders gave up the ghost in the city, while they sought their meat to relieve their souls.20 Behold, O YHUH; for I am in distress: my bowels are troubled; mine heart is turned within me; for I have grievously rebelled: abroad the sword bereaveth, at home there is as death.

| | | | | | | | | | | |
|---|---|---|---|---|---|---|---|---|---|---|
| כי 3588 | מרו 4784 | מריתי 4784 | מחוץ 2351 | שכלה 7921 | חרב 2719 | בבית 1004 | כמות 4194: | 1:21 | שמעו 8085 | כי 3588 |
| kiy | marou | mariytiy; | michutz | shiklah | chereb | babayit | kamauet. | | shama'au | kiy |
| **for** | **I have grievously** | **rebelled** | **abroad** | **bereaved** | **the sword** | **at home** | ***there is* as death** | | **They have heard** | **that** |

| | | | | | | | | | | | |
|---|---|---|---|---|---|---|---|---|---|---|---|
| נאנחה 584 | אני 589 | אין 369 | מנחם 5162 | לי 3807a | כל 3605 | איבי 341 | שמעו 8085 | רעתי 7451 | ששו 7797 | כי 3588 | אתה 859 |
| ne'anachah | 'aniy, | 'aeyn | manachem | liy, | kal | 'ayabay | shama'au | ra'atiy | sasu, | kiy | 'atah |
| **I sigh** | **I** | ***there is* none** | **to comfort** | **me** | **all** | **mine enemies** | **have heard of** | **my trouble** | **they are glad** | **that** | **you** |

| | | | | | | | | | |
|---|---|---|---|---|---|---|---|---|---|
| עשית 6213 | הבאת 935 | יום 3117 | קראת 7121 | ויהיו 1961 | כמוני 3644: | 1:22 | תבא 935 | כל 3605 | רעתם 7451 |
| 'ashiyta; | hebe'ta | youm | qara'ta | uayihayu | kamouniy. | | taba' | kal | ra'atam |
| **have done *it*** | **you will bring** | **the day *that*** | **you have called** | **and they shall be** | **like unto me** | | **Let come** | **all** | **their wickedness** |

| | | | | | | | | | | | |
|---|---|---|---|---|---|---|---|---|---|---|---|
| לפניך 6440 | ועולל 5953 | למו 3807a | כאשר 834 | עוללת 5953 | לי 3807a | על 5921 | כל 3605 | פשעי 6588 | כי 3588 | רבות 7227 | אנחתי 585 |
| lapaneyka | ua'aulel | lamou, | ka'asher | 'aulalta | liy | 'al | kal | pasha'ay; | kiy | rabout | 'anchotay |
| **before you** | **and do** | **unto them** | **as** | **you have done** | **unto me** | **for** | **all** | **my transgressions** | **for** | ***are* many** | **my sighs** |

| | |
|---|---|
| ולבי 3820 | דוי 1742: |
| ualibiy | dauay. |
| **and my heart *is* faint** | |

| | | | | | | | | |
|---|---|---|---|---|---|---|---|---|
| **Lam 2:1** | איכה 349 | יעיב 5743 | באפו 639 | אדני 136 | את 853 | בת 1323 | ציון 6726 | השליך 7993 |
| | 'aeykah | ya'ayb | ba'apou | 'adonay | 'at | bat | tziyoun, | hishliyk |
| | **How** | **has covered with a cloud** | **in his anger** | **Adonai** | | **the daughter of** | **Zion** | ***and* cast down** |

| | | | | | | | | | | |
|---|---|---|---|---|---|---|---|---|---|---|
| משמים 8064 | ארץ 776 | תפארת 8597 | ישראל 3478 | ולא 3808 | זכר 2142 | הדם 1916 | רגליו 7272 | ביום 3117 | אפו 639: | 2:2 |
| mishamayim | 'aretz, | tip'aret | yisra'ael; | uala' | zakar | hadom | raglayu | bayoum | 'apou. | |
| **from heaven unto** | **the earth** | **the beauty of** | **Israel** | **and not** | **remembered** | **stool** | **his foot** | **in the day of** | **his anger** | |

| | | | | | | | | | |
|---|---|---|---|---|---|---|---|---|---|
| בלע 1104 | אדני 136 | לא 3808 | חמל 2550 | את 853 | כל 3605 | נאות 4999 | יעקב 3290 | הרס 2040 | בעברתו 5678 |
| bila' | 'adonay | la' | chamal, | 'at | kal | ne'aut | ya'aqob, | haras | be'abratou |
| **has swallowed up** | **Adonai** | **not** | **has pitied** | | **all** | **the habitations of** | **Jacob** | **he has thrown down** | **in his wrath** |

| | | | | | | |
|---|---|---|---|---|---|---|
| מבצרי 4013 | בת 1323 | יהודה 3063 | הגיע 5060 | לארץ 776 | חלל 2490 | ממלכה 4467 |
| mibtzarey | bat | yahudah | higiya' | la'aretz; | chilel | mamlakah |
| **the strong holds of** | **the daughter of** | **Judah** | **he has brought *them* down** | **to the ground** | **he has polluted** | **the kingdom** |

| | | | | | | | | | |
|---|---|---|---|---|---|---|---|---|---|
| ושריה 8269: | 2:3 | גדע 1438 | בחרי 2750 | אף 639 | כל 3605 | קרן 7161 | ישראל 3478 | השיב 7725 | אחור 268 |
| uasareyha. | | gada' | bachariy | 'aap, | kal | qeren | yisra'ael, | heshiyb | 'achour |
| **and the princes thereof** | | **He has cut off** | **in *his* fierce** | **anger** | **all** | **the horn of** | **Israel** | **he has drawn** | **back** |

| | | | | | | | | | |
|---|---|---|---|---|---|---|---|---|---|
| ימינו 3225 | מפני 6440 | אויב 341 | ויבער 1197 | ביעקב 3290 | כאש 784 | להבה 3852 | אכלה 398 | סביב 5439: | 2:4 |
| yamiynou | mipaney | auyeb; | uayib'ar | baya'aqob | ka'aesh | lehabah, | 'aklah | sabiyb. | |
| **his right hand** | **from before** | **the enemy** | **and he burned** | **against Jacob** | **like a fire** | **the flaming** | ***which* devour** | **round about** | |

| | | | | | | | | |
|---|---|---|---|---|---|---|---|---|
| דרך 1869 | קשתו 7198 | כאויב 341 | נצב 5324 | ימינו 3225 | כצר 6862 | ויהרג 2026 | כל 3605 | מחמדי 4261 |
| darak | qashtou | ka'auyeb, | nitzab | yamiynou | katzar, | uayaharog, | kal | machmadey |
| **He has bent** | **his bow** | **like an enemy** | **he stood** | **with his right hand** | **as an adversary** | **and slew** | **all** | ***that were* pleasant to** |

Lam 1:21 They have heard that I sigh: there is none to comfort me: all mine enemies have heard of my trouble; they are glad that you have done it: you will bring the day that you have called, and they shall be like unto me.22 Let all their wickedness come before you; and do unto them, as you have done unto me for all my transgressions: for my sighs are many, and my heart is faint. **Lam** 2:1 How has YHUH covered the daughter of Zion with a cloud in his anger, and cast down from heaven unto the earth the beauty of Israel, and remembered not his footstool in the day of his anger!2 The Adonai has swallowed up all the habitations of Jacob, and has not pitied: he has thrown down in his wrath the strong holds of the daughter of Judah; he has brought them down to the ground: he has polluted the kingdom and the princes thereof.3 He has cut off in his fierce anger all the horn of Israel: he has drawn back his right hand from before the enemy, and he burned against Jacob like a flaming fire, which devour round about.4 He has bent his bow like an enemy: he stood with his right hand as an adversary, and slew all that were pleasant to the eye in the tabernacle of the daughter of Zion: he poured out his fury like fire.

| עין 5869 | באהל 168 | בת 1323 | ציון 6726 | שפך 8210 | כאש 784 | חמתו 2534: | 2:5 היה 1961 | אדני 136 | כאויב 341 |
|---|---|---|---|---|---|---|---|---|---|
| 'ayin; | ba'ahel | bat | tziyoun, | shapak | ka'aesh | chamatou. | hayah | 'adonay | ke'auyeb |
| **the eye** | **in the tabernacle of** | **the daughter of** | **Zion** | **he poured out** | **like fire** | **his fury** | **was** | **Adonai** | **as an enemy** |

| בלע 1104 | ישראל 3478 | בלע 1104 | כל 3605 | ארמנותיה 759 | שחת 7843 | מבצריו 4013 | וירב 7235 |
|---|---|---|---|---|---|---|---|
| bila' | yisra'ael, | bila' | kal | armanouteyha, | shichet | mibtzarayu; | uayereb |
| **he has swallowed up** | **Israel** | **he has swallowed up** | **all** | **her palaces** | **he has destroyed** | **his strong holds** | **and has increased** |

| בבת 1323 | יהודה 3063 | תאניה 8386 | ואניה 592: | 2:6 ויחמס 2554 | כגן 1588 |
|---|---|---|---|---|---|
| babat | yahudah, | ta'aniyah | ua'aniyah. | uayachmos | kagan |
| **in the daughter of** | **Judah** | **mourning** | **and lamentation** | **And he has violently taken away** | **as *if it were of* a garden** |

| שכו 7900 | שחת 7843 | מועדו 4150 | שכח 7911 | יהוה 3068 | בציון 6726 | מועד 4150 |
|---|---|---|---|---|---|---|
| sukou, | shichet | mou'adou; | shikach | Yahuah | batziyoun | mou'aed |
| **his tabernacle** | **he has destroyed** | **his places of the assembly** | **has caused to be forgotten** | **Yahuah** | **in Zion** | **the solemn feasts** |

| ושבת 7676 | וינאץ 5006 | בזעם 2195 | אפו 639 | מלך 4428 | וכהן 3548: | 2:7 זנח 2186 | אדני 136 | מזבחו 4196 |
|---|---|---|---|---|---|---|---|---|
| uashabat, | uayin'atz | baza'am | 'apou | melek | uakohen. | zanach | 'adonay | mizbachou |
| **and sabbaths** | **and has despised** | **in the indignation of** | **his anger** | **the king** | **and the priest** | **has cast off** | **Adonai** | **his altar** |

| נאר 5010 | מקדשו 4720 | הסגיר 5462 | ביד 3027 | אויב 341 | חומת 2346 | ארמנותיה 759 | קול 6963 |
|---|---|---|---|---|---|---|---|
| ni'aer | miqadashou, | hisgiyr | bayad | auyeb, | choumot | armanouteyha; | qoul |
| **he has abhorred** | **his sanctuary** | **he has given up** | **into the hand of** | **the enemy** | **the walls of** | **her palaces** | **a noise** |

| נתנו 5414 | בבית 1004 | יהוה 3068 | כיום 3117 | מועד 4150: | 2:8 חשב 2803 | יהוה 3068 | להשחית 7843 | חומת 2346 |
|---|---|---|---|---|---|---|---|---|
| natanu | babeyt | Yahuah | kayoum | mou'aed. | chashab | Yahuah | lahashchiyt | choumat |
| **they have made** | **in the house of** | **Yahuah** | **as in the day of** | **a solemn feast** | **has purposed** | **Yahuah** | **to destroy** | **the wall of** |

| בת 1323 | ציון 6726 | נטה 5186 | קו 6957 | לא 3808 | השיב 7725 | ידו 3027 | מבלע 1104 |
|---|---|---|---|---|---|---|---|
| bat | tziyoun, | natah | qau, | la' | heshiyb | yadou | mibalea'; |
| **the daughter of** | **Zion** | **he has stretched out** | **a line** | **not** | **he has withdrawn** | **his hand** | **from destroying** |

| ויאבל 56 | חל 2426 | וחומה 2346 | יחדו 3162 | אמללו 535: | 2:9 טבעו 2883 | בארץ 776 | שעריה 8179 |
|---|---|---|---|---|---|---|---|
| uaya'abel | chel | uachoumah | yachdau | 'uamlalu. | taba'au | ba'aretz | sha'areyha, |
| **therefore he made to lament** | **the rampart** | **and the wall** | **together** | **they languished** | **are sunk** | **into the ground** | **Her gates** |

| אבד 6 | ושבר 7665 | בריחיה 1280 | מלכה 4428 | ושריה 8269 | בגוים 1471 | אין 369 | תורה 8451 | גם 1571 |
|---|---|---|---|---|---|---|---|---|
| 'abad | uashibar | barycheyha; | malkah | uasareyha | bagouyim | 'aeyn | tourah, | gam |
| **he has destroyed** | **and broken** | **her bars** | **her king** | **and her princes** | ***are* among the Gentiles** | ***is* no** | ***more* the law** | **also** |

| נביאיה 5030 | לא 3808 | מצאו 4672 | חזון 2377 | מיהוה 3068: | 2:10 ישבו 3427 | לארץ 776 | ידמו 1826 | זקני 2205 |
|---|---|---|---|---|---|---|---|---|
| nabiy'ayha | la' | matza'au | chazoun | meYahuah. | yeshabu | la'aretz | yidamu | ziqney |
| **her prophets** | **no** | **find** | **vision** | **from Yahuah** | **sit** | **upon the ground** | ***and* keep silence** | **The elders of** |

| בת 1323 | ציון 6726 | העלו 5927 | עפר 6083 | על 5921 | ראשם 7218 | חגרו 2296 | שקים 8242 | הורידו 3381 |
|---|---|---|---|---|---|---|---|---|
| bat | tziyoun, | he'alu | 'apar | 'al | ra'sham, | chagaru | saqiym; | houriydu |
| **the daughter of** | **Zion** | **they have cast up** | **dust** | **upon** | **their heads** | **they have girded themselves with** | **sackcloth** | **hang down** |

Lam 2:5 The Adonai was as an enemy: he has swallowed up Israel, he has swallowed up all her palaces: he has destroyed his strong holds, and has increased in the daughter of Judah mourning and lamentation.6 And he has violently taken away his tabernacle, as if it were of a garden: he has destroyed his places of the assembly: YHUH has caused the solemn feasts and sabbaths to be forgotten in Zion, and has despised in the indignation of his anger the king and the priest.7 The Adonai has cast off his altar, he has abhorred his sanctuary, he has given up into the hand of the enemy the walls of her palaces; they have made a noise in the house of YHUH, as in the day of a solemn feast.8 YHUH has purposed to destroy the wall of the daughter of Zion: he has stretched out a line, he has not withdrawn his hand from destroying: therefore he made the rampart and the wall to lament; they languished together.9 Her gates are sunk into the ground; he has destroyed and broken her bars: her king and her princes are among the Gentiles: the law is no more; her prophets also find no vision from YHUH.10 The elders of the daughter of Zion sit upon the ground, and keep silence: they have cast up dust upon their heads; they have girded themselves with sackcloth: the virgins of Jerusalem hang down their heads to the ground.

2:11
776 לארץ 7218 ראשן 1330 בתולת 3389: ירושלם 3615 כלו 1832 בדמעות 5869 עיני 2560 חמרמרו 4578 מעי 8210 נשפך
la'aretz ra'shan, batulot yarushalaim. kalu uadma'aut 'aeynay chamarmaru me'ay, nishpak
**to the ground their heads the virgins of Jerusalem do fail with tears Mine eyes are troubled my bowels is poured**

776 לארץ 3516 כבדי 5921 על 7667 שבר 1323 בת 5971 עמי 5848 בעטף 5768 עולל 3243 ויונק
la'aretz kabediy, 'al sheber bat 'amiy; be'atep 'aulel uayouneq,
**upon the earth my liver for the destruction of the daughter of my people because swoon the children and the sucklings**

2:12
7339 ברחבות 7151: קריה 517 לאמתם 559 יאמרו 346 איה 1715 דגן 3196 ויין 5848 בהתעטפם 2491 כחלל
birchobout qiryah. la'amotam ya'maru, 'ayeh dagan uayayin; bahit'atapam kechalal
**in the streets of the city to their mothers They say Where *is* corn and wine? when they swooned as the wounded**

2:13
7339 ברחבות 5892 עיר 8210 בהשתפך 5315 נפשם 413 אל 2436 חיק 517: אמתם 4100 מה
birchobout 'ayr, bahishtapek napsham, 'al cheyq 'amotam. mah
**in the streets of the city when was poured out their soul into bosom their mothers' What thing**

5749 אעידך 4100 מה 1819 אדמה 3807a לך 1323 הבת 3389 ירושלם 4100 מה 7737 אשוה 3807a לך
'a'aydek mah 'adammeh lak, habat yarushalaim, mah 'ashueh lak
**shall I take to witness for you? what thing shall I liken to you O daughter of Jerusalem? what shall I equal to you**

2:14
5162 ואנחמך 1330 בתולת 1323 בת 6726 ציון 3588 כי 1419 גדול 3220 כים 7667 שברך 4310 מי 7495 ירפא 3807a: לך
ua'anachamek, batulat bat tziyoun; kiy gadoul kayam shibrek miy' yirpa lak.
**that I may comfort O virgin daughter of Zion for *is* great like the sea your breach who can heal for you?**

5030 נביאיך 2372 חזו 3807a לך 7723 שוא 8602 ותפל 3808 ולא 1540 גלו 5921 על 5771 עונך 7725 להשיב
nabiy'ayik, chazu lak shau'a uatapel, uala' gilu 'al 'auonek lahashiyb
**Your prophets have seen for you vain and foolish things and not they have discovered on your iniquity to turn away**

2:15
7622 שביתך 2372 ויחזו 3807a לך 4864 משאות 7723 שוא 4065: ומדוחים 5606 ספקו 5921 עליך 3709 כפים 3605 כל
shabiytek uayechazu lak, mas'aut shau'a uamaduchiym. sapaqu 'aleyka kapayim kal
**your captivity but have seen for you burdens false and causes of banishment clap at you *their* hands All**

5674 עברי 1870 דרך 8319 שרקו 5128 וינעו 7218 ראשם 5921 על 1323 בת 3389 ירושלם 2063 הזאת 5892 העיר 559 שיאמרו
'abarey derek, sharaqu uayaniy'au ra'sham, 'al bat yarushalaim; haza't ha'ayr, sheya'maru
**that pass by they hiss and wag their head at the daughter of Jerusalem *saying, Is* this the city that *men* call**

2:16
3632 כלילת 3308 יפי 4885 משוש 3605 לכל 776: הארץ 6475 פצו 5921 עליך 6310 פיהם 3605 כל 341 אויביך
kaliylat yopiy, masous lakal ha'aretz. patzu 'aleyka piyhem kal 'auyabayik,
**The perfection of beauty The joy of the whole the earth? have opened against you their mouth All your enemies**

8319 שרקו 2786 ויחרקו 8127 שן 559 אמרו 1104 בלענו 389 אך 2088 זה 3117 היום 6960 שקוינהו
sharaqu uayacharqu shen, 'amaru bila'anu; 'ak zeh hayoum sheqiuiynuhu
**they hiss and gnash the teeth they say We have swallowed *her* up certainly this *is* the day that we looked for**

2:17
4672 מצאנו 7200: ראינו 6213 עשה 3068 יהוה 834 אשר 2161 זמם 1214 בצע 565 אמרתו 834 אשר
matza'nu ra'aynu. 'asah Yahuah 'asher zamam, bitza' 'amratou 'asher
**we have found we have seen *it* has done Yahuah *that* which he had devised he has fulfilled his word that**

Lam 2:11 Mine eyes do fail with tears, my bowels are troubled, my liver is poured upon the earth, for the destruction of the daughter of my people; because the children and the sucklings swoon in the streets of the city.12 They say to their mothers, Where is corn and wine? when they swooned as the wounded in the streets of the city, when their soul was poured out into their mothers' bosom.13 What thing shall I take to witness for you? what thing shall I liken to you, O daughter of Jerusalem? what shall I equal to you, that I may comfort you, O virgin daughter of Zion? for your breach is great like the sea: who can heal you?14 Thy prophets have seen vain and foolish things for you: and they have not discovered your iniquity, to turn away your captivity; but have seen for you false burdens and causes of banishment.15 All that pass by clap their hands at you; they hiss and wag their head at the daughter of Jerusalem, saying, Is this the city that men call The perfection of beauty, The joy of the whole earth?16 All your enemies have opened their mouth against you: they hiss and gnash the teeth: they say, We have swallowed her up: certainly this is the day that we looked for; we have found, we have seen it.17 YHUH has done that which he had devised; he has fulfilled his word that he had commanded in the days of old: he has thrown down, and has not pitied:

צוה 6680 | מימי 3117 | קדם 6924 | הרס 2040 | ולא 3808 | חמל 2550 | וישמח 8055 | עליך 5921
tziuah | miymey | qedem, | haras | uala' | chamal; | uayasamch | 'aleyka
**he had commanded | in the days of | old | he has thrown down | and not | has pitied | and he has caused to rejoice | over you**

אויב 341 | הרים 7311 | קרן 7161 | צריך 6862: | 2:18 | צעק 6817 | לבם 3820 | אל 413 | אדני 136 | חומת 2346 | בת 1323
auyeb, | heriym | qeren | tzarayik. | | tzea'aq | libam | 'al | 'adonay; | choumat | bat
***your* enemy | he has set up | the horn of | your adversaries | | cried | Their heart | unto | Adonai | O wall of | the daughter of**

ציון 6726 | הורידי 3381 | כנחל 5158 | דמעה 1832 | יומם 3119 | ולילה 3915 | אל 408 | תתני 5414 | פוגת 6314 | לך 3807a | אל 408 | תדם 1826
tziyoun | houriydiy | kanachal | dim'ah | youmam | ualayalah, | 'al | titaniy | pugat | lak, | 'al | tidom
**Zion | let run down | like a river | tears | day | and night | no | give | rest | to yourself | not | let cease**

בת 1323 | עינך 5869: | 2:19 | קומי 6965 | רני 7442 | בליל 3915 | לראש 7218 | אשמרות 821 | שפכי 8210 | כמים 4325
bat | 'aeynek. | | quamiy | roniy | balayal | lara'sh | 'ashmurout, | shipkiy | kamayim
**the apple of (*daughter*) | your eye | | Arise | cry out | in the night | in the beginning of | the watches | pour out | like water**

לבך 3820 | נכח 5227 | פני 6440 | אדני 136 | שאי 5375 | אליו 413 | כפיך 3709 | על 5921 | נפש 5315 | עולליך 5768 | העטופים 5848
libek, | nokach | paney | 'adonay; | sa'ay | 'aelayu | kapayik, | 'al | nepesh | 'aulalayik, | ha'tupiym
**your heart | before | the face of | Adonai | lift up | toward him | your hands | for | the life of | your young children | that faint**

ברעב 7458 | בראש 7218 | כל 3605 | חוצות 2351: | 2:20 | ראה 7200 | יהוה 3068 | והביטה 5027 | למי 4310 | עוללת 5953 | כה 3541 | אם 518
bara'ab | bara'sh | kal | chutzout. | | ra'aeh | Yahuah | uahabiytah, | lamiy | 'aulalta | koh; | 'am
**for hunger | in the top of | every | street | | Behold | O Yahuah | and consider | to whom | you have done | this | surely**

תאכלנה 398 | נשים 802 | פרים 6529 | עללי 5768 | טפחים 2949 | אם 518 | יהרג 2026 | במקדש 4720 | אדני 136 | כהן 3548
ta'kalnah | nashiym | piryam | 'alaley | tipuchiym, | 'am | yehareg | bamiqdash | 'adonay | kohen
**Shall eat | the women | their fruit | *and* children of | a span long? | surely | shall be slain | in the sanctuary of | Adonai? | the priest**

ונביא 5030: | 2:21 | שכבו 7901 | לארץ 776 | חוצות 2351 | נער 5288 | וזקן 2205 | בתולתי 1330 | ובחורי 970 | נפלו 5307
uanabiy'a. | | shakabu | la'aretz | chutzout | na'ar | uazaqen, | batulotay | uabachuray | naplu
**and the prophet | | *The* lie | on the ground in | the streets | young | and the old | my virgins | and my young men | are fallen**

בחרב 2719 | הרגת 2026 | ביום 3117 | אפך 639 | טבחת 2873 | לא 3808 | חמלת 2550: | 2:22 | תקרא 7121
bachareb; | haragta | bayoum | 'apeka, | tabachta | la' | chamalata. | | tiqraa'
**by the sword | you have slain | *them* in the day of | your anger | you have killed | *and* not | pitied | | You have called**

כיום 3117 | מועד 4150 | מגורי 4032 | מסביב 5439 | ולא 3808 | היה 1961 | ביום 3117 | אף 639 | יהוה 3068 | פליט 6412 | ושריד 8300
kayoum | mou'aed | maguray | misabiyb, | uala' | hayah | bayoum | 'ap | Yahuah | paliyt | uasariyd;
**as in a day | solemn | my terrors | round about | so that none | was | in the day | anger of | Yahuah's | escaped | nor remained**

אשר 834 | טפחתי 2946 | ורביתי 7235 | איבי 341 | כלם 3615:
'asher | tipachtiy | uaribiytiy | 'ayabiy | kilam.
**those that | I have swaddled | and brought up | mine enemy | has consumed**

**Lam 3:1** אני 589 | הגבר 1397 | ראה 7200 | עני 6040 | בשבט 7626 | עברתו 5678: | 3:2 | אותי 853 | נהג 5090 | וילך 1980 | חשך 2822
'aniy | hageber | ra'ah | 'aniy, | bashebet | 'abratou. | | 'autiy | nahag | uayolak | choshek
**I *am* | the man *that* | has seen | affliction | by the rod of | his wrath | | me | He has led | and brought *me into* | darkness**

Lam 2:17 and he has caused your enemy to rejoice over you, he has set up the horn of your adversaries.18 Their heart cried unto the Adonai, O wall of the daughter of Zion, let tears run down like a river day and night: give thyself no rest; let not the apple of your eye cease.19 Arise, cry out in the night: in the beginning of the watches pour out your heart like water before the face of the Adonai: lift up your hands toward him for the life of your young children, that faint for hunger in the top of every street.20 Behold, O YHUH, and consider to whom you have done this. Shall the women eat their fruit, and children of a span long? shall the priest and the prophet be slain in the sanctuary of the Adonai?21 The young and the old lie on the ground in the streets: my virgins and my young men are fallen by the sword; you have slain them in the day of your anger; you have killed, and not pitied.22 Thou have called as in a solemn day my terrors round about, so that in the day of YHUH's anger none escaped nor remained: those that I have swaddled and brought up has mine enemy consumed. **Lam** 3:1 I am the man that has seen affliction by the rod of his wrath.2 He has led me, and brought me into darkness, but not into light.

| ולא 3808 | אור 216: | 3:3 אך 389 | בי 871a | ישב 7725 | יהפך 2015 | ידו 3027 | כל 3605 | היום 3117: | 3:4 בלה 1086 |
|---|---|---|---|---|---|---|---|---|---|
| uala' | 'aur. | 'ak | biy | yashub | yahapok | yadou | kal | hayoum. | bilah |
| **but not** | ***into* light** | **Surely** | **against me** | **is he turned** | **he turned** | **his hand** | ***against me* all** | **the day** | **has he made old** |

| בשרי 1320 | ועורי 5785 | שבר 7665 | עצמותי 6106: | 3:5 בנה 1129 | עלי 5921 | ויקף 5362 | ראש 7219 |
|---|---|---|---|---|---|---|---|
| basariy | ua'auriy, | shibar | atzmoutay. | banah | 'alay | uayaqap | ra'sh |
| **My flesh** | **and my skin** | **he has broken** | **my bones** | **He has builded** | **against me** | **and compassed *me* with** | **gall** |

| ותלאה 8513: | 3:6 במחשכים 4285 | הושיבני 3427 | כמתי 4191 | עולם 5769: | 3:7 גדר 1443 | בעדי 1157 | ולא 3808 |
|---|---|---|---|---|---|---|---|
| uatla'ah. | bamachashakiym | houshiybaniy | kametey | 'aulam. | gadar | ba'adiy | uala' |
| **and travail** | **in dark places** | **He has set me** | **as *they that be* dead of** | **old** | **He has hedged** | **about** | **that cannot** |

| אצא 3318 | הכביד 3513 | נחשתי 5178: | 3:8 גם 1571 | כי 3588 | אזעק 2199 | ואשוע 7768 | שתם 5640 | תפלתי 8605: | 3:9 גדר 1443 |
|---|---|---|---|---|---|---|---|---|---|
| 'aetzea' | hikbiyd | nachashatiy. | gam | kiy | 'az'aq | ua'ashauea', | satam | tapilatiy. | gadar |
| **I get out** | **he has made heavy** | **my chain** | **Also** | **when** | **I cry** | **and shout** | **he shut out** | **my prayer** | **He has inclosed** |

| דרכי 1870 | בגזית 1496 | נתיבתי 5410 | עוה 5753: | 3:10 דב 1677 | ארב 693 | הוא 1931 | לי 3807a | אריה 738 |
|---|---|---|---|---|---|---|---|---|
| darakay | bagaziyt, | natiybotay | 'auah. | dob | 'areb | hua' | liy, | 'aryeh |
| **my ways** | **with hewn stone** | **my paths** | **he has made crooked** | ***as* a bear** | **lying in wait** | **He** | ***was* unto me** | ***and as* a lion** |

| במסתרים 4565: | 3:11 דרכי 1870 | סורר 5493 | ויפשחני 6582 | שמני 7760 | שמם 8076: | 3:12 דרך 1869 |
|---|---|---|---|---|---|---|
| bamistariym. | darakay | sourer | uayapashcheniy | samaniy | shomem. | darak |
| **in secret places** | **my ways** | **He has turned aside** | **and pulled me in pieces** | **he has made me** | **desolate** | **He has bent** |

| קשתו 7198 | ויציבני 5324 | כמטרא 4307 | לחץ 2671: | 3:13 הביא 935 | בכליותי 3629 | בני 1121 | אשפתו 827: | 3:14 |
|---|---|---|---|---|---|---|---|---|
| qashtou | uayatziybeniy, | kamatara' | lachetz. | habiy'a | bakilyoutay, | baney | 'ashpatou. | |
| **his bow** | **and set me** | **as a mark** | **for the arrow** | **He has caused to enter** | **into my reins** | **the arrows of** | **his quiver** | |

| הייתי 1961 | שחק 7814 | לכל 3605 | עמי 5971 | נגינתם 5058 | כל 3605 | היום 3117: | 3:15 השביעני 7646 | במרורים 4844 |
|---|---|---|---|---|---|---|---|---|
| hayiytiy | sachoq | lakal | 'amiy, | nagiynatam | kal | hayoum. | hisbiy'aniy | bamarouriym |
| **I was** | **a derision** | **to all** | **my people** | ***and* their song** | **all** | **the day** | **He has filled me** | **with bitterness** |

| הרוני 7301 | לענה 3939: | 3:16 ויגרס 1638 | בחצץ 2687 | שני 8127 | הכפישני 3728 |
|---|---|---|---|---|---|
| hiruaniy | la'anah. | uayagres | bechatzatz | shinay, | hikpiyshaniy |
| **he has made me drunken** | ***with* wormwood** | **He has also broken** | **with gravel stones** | **my teeth** | **he has covered me** |

| באפר 665: | 3:17 ותזנח 2186 | משלום 7965 | נפשי 5315 | נשיתי 5382 | טובה 2896: | 3:18 ואמר 559 | אבד 6 |
|---|---|---|---|---|---|---|---|
| ba'aeper. | uatiznach | mishaloum | napshiy | nashiytiy | toubah. | ua'amar | 'abad |
| **with ashes** | **And you have removed far off** | **from peace** | **my soul** | **I forgot** | **prosperity** | **And I said** | **is perished** |

| נצחי 5331 | ותוחלתי 8431 | מיהוה 3068: | 3:19 זכר 2142 | עניי 6040 | ומרודי 4788 | לענה 3939 | וראש 7219: | 3:20 |
|---|---|---|---|---|---|---|---|---|
| nitzchiy, | uatouchaltiy | meYahuah. | zakar | 'anyiy | uamrudiy | la'anah | uara'sh. | |
| **My strength** | **and my hope** | **from Yahuah** | **Remembering** | **mine affliction** | **and my misery** | **the wormwood** | **and the gall** | |

| זכור 2142 | תזכור 2142 | ותשיח 7743 | עלי 5921 | נפשי 5315: | 3:21 זאת 2063 | אשיב 7725 | אל 413 | לבי 3820 | על 5921 | כן 3651 |
|---|---|---|---|---|---|---|---|---|---|---|
| zakour | tizkour, | uatashiyach | 'aelay | napshiy. | za't | 'ashiyb | 'al | libiy | 'al | ken |
| **has *them* still in remembrance** | | **and his humbled** | **in me** | **My soul** | **This** | **I recall** | **to** | **my mind** | **therefore** | **after that** |

Lam 3:3 Surely against me is he turned; he turneth his hand against me all the day.4 My flesh and my skin has he made old; he has broken my bones.5 He has built against me, and compassed me with gall and travail.6 He has set me in dark places, as they that be dead of old.7 He has hedged me about, that I cannot get out: he has made my chain heavy.8 Also when I cry and shout, he shutteth out my prayer.9 He has enclosed my ways with hewn stone, he has made my paths crooked.10 He was unto me as a bear lying in wait, and as a lion in secret places.11 He has turned aside my ways, and pulled me in pieces: he has made me desolate.12 He has bent his bow, and set me as a mark for the arrow.13 He has caused the arrows of his quiver to enter into my reins.14 I was a derision to all my people; and their song all the day.15 He has filled me with bitterness, he has made me drunken with wormwood.16 He has also broken my teeth with gravel stones, he has covered me with ashes.17 And you have removed my soul far off from peace: I forgot prosperity.18 And I said, My strength and my hope is perished from YHUH:19 Remembering mine affliction and my misery, the wormwood and the gall.20 My soul has them still in remembrance, and is humbled in me.21 This I recall to my mind, therefore have I hope.

3:22 … 3:23

אוחיל 3176: | חסדי 2617 | יהוה 3068 | כי 3588 | לא 3808 | תמנו 8552 | כי 3588 | לא 3808 | כלו 3615 | רחמיו 7356:

'auchiyl. chasdey Yahuah kiy la' tamanu, kiy la' kalu rachamayu.

**have I hope *It is of* mercies Yahuah's that not we are consumed because not fail his compassions**

3:24

חדשים 2319 | לבקרים 1242 | רבה 7227 | אמונתך 530: | חלקי 2506 | יהוה 3068 | אמרה 559 | נפשי 5315 | על 5921 | כן 3651

chadashiym labaqariym, rabah 'amunateka. chelqiy Yahuah 'amarah napshiy, 'al ken

***They are* new every morning great *is* your faithfulness *is* my portion Yahuah saith my soul therefore after that**

3:25 … 3:26

אוחיל 3176 | לו 3807a: | טוב 2896 | יהוה 3068 | לקוו 6960 | לנפש 5315 | תדרשנו 1875: | טוב 2896

'auchiyl lou'. toub Yahuah laqouau, lanepesh tidrashenu. toub

**will I hope in him *is* good Yahuah unto them that wait for him to the soul *that* seek him *It is* good**

3:27

ויחיל 2342 | ודומם 1748 | לתשועת 8668 | יהוה 3068: | טוב 2896 | לגבר 1397 | כי 3588 | ישא 5375 | על 5923

uayachiyl uadumam, litashu'at Yahuah. toub lageber, kiy yisa' 'al

**that a man should both hope and quietly wait for the salvation of Yahuah *It is* good for a man that he bear the yoke**

3:28 … 3:29

בנעוריו 5271: | ישב 3427 | בדד 910 | וידם 1826 | כי 3588 | נטל 5190 | עליו 5921: | יתן 5414 | בעפר 6083 | פיהו 6310 | אולי 194

bin'urayu. yesheb badad uayidom, kiy natal 'alayu. yiten be'apar piyhu, 'aulay

**in his youth He sit alone and keep silence because he has borne *it* upon him He put in the dust his mouth if so be**

3:30 … 3:31

יש 3426 | תקוה 8615: | יתן 5414 | למכהו 5221 | לחי 3895 | ישבע 7646 | בחרפה 2781: | כי 3588 | לא 3808

yesh tiquah. yiten lamakehu lechiy yisba' bacherpah. kiy la'

**there may be hope He gives to him that smite him *his* cheek he is filled full with reproach For not**

3:32

יזנח 2186 | לעולם 5769 | אדני 136: | כי 3588 | אם 518 | הוגה 3013 | ורחם 7355 | כרב 7230

yiznach la'aulam 'adonay. kiy 'am hougah, uaricham karob

**will cast off for ever Adonai But though he cause grief yet will he have compassion according to the multitude of**

3:33 … 3:34

חסדו 2617 | כי 3588 | לא 3808 | ענה 6031 | מלבו 3820 | ויגה 3013 | בני 1121 | איש 376: | לדכא 1792 | תחת 8478 | רגליו 7272 | כל 3605

chasdou kiy la' 'anah milibou, uayageh baney 'aysh. ladakea' tachat raglayu, kal

**his mercies For not he does afflict willingly nor grieve the children of men To crush under his feet all**

3:35 … 3:36

אסירי 615 | ארץ 776: | להטות 5186 | משפט 4941 | גבר 1397 | נגד 5048 | פני 6440 | עליון 5945: | לעות 5791 | אדם 120

'asiyrey 'aretz. lahatout mishapat gaber, neged paney 'alyoun. la'auet 'adam

**the prisoners of the earth To turn aside the right of a man before the face of the most High To subvert a man**

3:37 … 3:38

בריבו 7379 | אדני 136 | לא 3808 | ראה 7200: | מי 4310 | זה 2088 | אמר 559 | ותהי 1961 | אדני 136 | לא 3808 | צוה 6680:

bariybou, 'adonay la' ra'ah. miy' zeh 'amar uatehiy, 'adonay la' tziuah.

**in his cause Adonai not approve Who *is* he *that* saith and it comes to pass *when* Adonai not? command *it***

3:39

מפי 6310 | עליון 5945 | לא 3808 | תצא 3318 | הרעות 7451 | והטוב 2896: | מה 4100 | יתאונן 596 | אדם 120 | חי 2416 | גבר 1397

mipiy 'alyoun la' tetzea', hara'aut uahatoub. mah yit'aunen 'adam chay, geber

**Out of the mouth of the most High not proceed evil and good? Wherefore does complain a man living a man**

3:40

על 5921 | חטאו 2399 | נחפשה 2664 | דרכינו 1870 | ונחקרה 2713 | ונשובה 7725 | עד 5704 | יהוה 3068:

'al chat'au nachpasah darakeynu uanachqorah, uanashubah 'ad Yahuah.

**for the punishment of his sins? Let us search our ways and try and turn again to Yahuah**

Lam 3:22 It is of YHUH's mercies that we are not consumed, because his compassions fail not.23 They are new every morning: great is your faithfulness.24 YHUH is my portion, saith my soul; therefore will I hope in him.25 YHUH is good unto them that wait for him, to the soul that seek him.26 It is good that a man should both hope and quietly wait for the salvation of YHUH.27 It is good for a man that he bear the yoke in his youth.28 He sitteth alone and keep silence, because he has borne it upon him.29 He put his mouth in the dust; if so be there may be hope.30 He give his cheek to him that smite him: he is filled full with reproach.31 For YHUH will not cast off forever:32 But though he cause grief, yet will he have compassion according to the multitude of his mercies.33 For he doth not afflict willingly nor grieve the children of men.34 To crush under his feet all the prisoners of the earth,35 To turn aside the right of a man before the face of the most High,36 To subvert a man in his cause, YHUH approveth not.37 Who is he that saith, and it cometh to pass, when YHUH commandeth it not?38 Out of the mouth of the most High proceed not evil and good?39 Wherefore doth a living man complain, a man for the punishment of his sins?40 Let us search and try our ways, and turn again to YHUH.

**3:41** **3:42**

נשא 5375 לבבנו 3824 אל 413 כפים 3709 אל 413 אל 410 בשמים 8064: נחנו 5168 פשענו 6586 ומרינו 4784

nisa' lababenu 'al kapayim, 'al 'ael bashamayim. nachanu pasha'anu uamariynu,

**Let us lift up our heart with *our* hands unto El in the heavens We have transgressed and have rebelled**

**3:43** **3:44**

אתה 859 לא 3808 סלחת 5545: סכתה 5526 באף 639 ותרדפנו 7291 הרגת 2026 לא 3808 חמלת 2550:

'atah la' salachata. sakotah ba'ap uatirdapenu, haragta la' chamalata.

**you not have pardoned You have covered with anger and persecuted us you have slain not you have pitied**

**3:45**

סכותה 5526 בענן 6051 לך 3807a מעבור 5674 תפלה 8605: סחי 5501 ומאוס 3973

sakoutah ba'anan lak, me'abour tapilah. sachiy uama'aus

**You have covered with a cloud to yourself should not pass through that *our* prayer *as* the offscouring and refuse**

**3:46** **3:47**

תשימנו 7760 בקרב 7130 העמים 5971: פצו 6475 עלינו 5921 פיהם 6310 כל 3605 איבינו 341: פחד 6343

tasiymenu baqereb ha'amiym. patzu 'aleynu piyhem kal 'ayabeynu. pachad

**You have made us in the midst of the people have opened against us their mouths All our enemies Fear**

**3:48**

ופחת 6354 היה 1961 לנו 3807a השאת 7612 והשבר 7667: פלגי 6388 מים 4325 תרד 3381 עיני 5869 על 5921

uapachat hayah lanu hashea't uahashaber. palgey mayim terad 'aeyniy, 'al

**and a snare is come upon us desolation and destruction *with* rivers of water run down Mine eye for**

**3:49** **3:50**

שבר 7667 בת 1323 עמי 5971: עיני 5869 נגרה 5064 ולא 3808 תדמה 1820 מאין 369 הפגות 2014:

sheber bat 'amiy. 'aeyniy nigrah uala' tidmeh me'ayn hapugout.

**the destruction of the daughter of my people Mine eye trickleth down and not cease without *any* intermission**

**3:51**

עד 5704 ישקיף 8259 וירא 7200 יהוה 3068 משמים 8064: עיני 5869 עוללה 5953 לנפשי 5315 מכל 3605 בנות 1323

'ad yashqiyp uayera', Yahuah mishamayim. 'aeyniy 'aulalah lanapshiy, mikol banout

**Till look down and behold Yahuah from heaven Mine eye affecteth mine heart because of all the daughters of**

**3:52** **3:53**

עירי 5892: צוד 6679 צדוני 6679 כצפור 6833 איבי 341 חנם 2600: צמתו 6789 בבור 953 חיי 2416

'ayriy. tzoud tzaduniy katzipour 'ayabay chinam. tzamatu babour chayay,

**my city chased me sore like a bird Mine enemies without cause They have cut off in the dungeon my life**

**3:54** **3:55**

וידו 3034 אבן 68 בי 871a: צפו 6687 מים 4325 על 5921 ראשי 7218 אמרתי 559 נגזרתי 1504: קראתי 7121 שמך 8034

uayadu 'aben biy. tzapu mayim 'al ra'shiy 'amartiy nigzaratiy. qaraa'tiy shimka

**and cast a stone upojn me flowed Waters over mine head *then* I said I am cut off I called upon your name**

**3:56**

יהוה 3068 מבור 953 תחתיות 8482: קולי 6963 שמעת 8085 אל 408 תעלם 5956 אזנך 241 לרוחתי 7309

Yahuah, mibour tachtiyout. qouliy shama'ata; 'al ta'alem 'aznaka larauachatiy

**O Yahuah out of dungeon *the* low my voice You have heard not hide your ear at my breathing**

**3:57** **3:58**

לשועתי 7775: קרבת 7126 ביום 3117 אקראך 7121 אמרת 559 אל 408 תירא 3372: רבת 7378

lashaua'atiy. qarabta bayoum 'aqra'aka, 'amarta 'al tiyraa'. rabta

**at my cry You drewest near in the day *that* I called upon you you said not Fear you have pleaded**

**3:59**

אדני 136 ריבי 7379 נפשי 5315 גאלת 1350 חיי 2416: ראיתה 7200 יהוה 3068 עותתי 5792 שפטה 8199

'adonay riybey napshiy ga'alta chayay. ra'aytah Yahuah 'auatatiy, shapatah

**O Adonai the causes of my soul you have redeemed my life you have seen O Yahuah my wrong judge you**

Lam 3:41 Let us lift up our heart with our hands unto G-d in the heavens.42 We have transgressed and have rebelled: you have not pardoned.43 Thou have covered with anger, and persecuted us: you have slain, you have not pitied.44 Thou have covered thyself with a cloud, that our prayer should not pass through.45 Thou have made us as the offscouring and refuse in the midst of the people.46 All our enemies have opened their mouths against us.47 Fear and a snare is come upon us, desolation and destruction.48 Mine eye runneth down with rivers of water for the destruction of the daughter of my people.49 Mine eye trickleth down, and ceaseth not, without any intermission,50 Till YHUH look down, and behold from heaven.51 Mine eye affecteth mine heart because of all the daughters of my city.52 Mine enemies chased me sore, like a bird, without cause.53 They have cut off my life in the dungeon, and cast a stone upon me.54 Waters flowed over mine head; then I said, I am cut off.55 I called upon your name, O YHUH, out of the low dungeon.56 Thou have heard my voice: hide not your ear at my breathing, at my cry.57 Thou drewest near in the day that I called upon you: you saidst, Fear not.58 O Adonai, you have pleaded the causes of my soul; you have redeemed my life. 59 O YHUH, you have seen my wrong: judge you my cause.

3:60 | 3:61

משפטי 4941: | ראיתה 7200 | כל 3605 | נקמתם 5360 | כל 3605 | מחשבתם 4284 | לי 3807a: | שמעת 8085
mishpatiy. | ra'aytah | kal | niqmatam, | kal | machshabotam | liy. | shama'ata
**my cause | You have seen | all | their vengeance | *and* all | their imaginations | against me | You have heard**

3:62

חרפתם 2781 | יהוה 3068 | כל 3605 | מחשבתם 4284 | עלי 5921: | שפתי 8193 | קמי 6965
cherpatam | Yahuah, | kal | machshabotam | 'alay. | siptey | qamay
**their reproach | O Yahuah | *and* all | their imaginations | against me | The lips of | those that rose up against me**

3:63 | 3:64

והגיונם 1902 | עלי 5921 | כל 3605 | היום 3117: | שבתם 3427 | וקימתם 7012 | הביטה 5027 | אני 589 | מנגינתם 4485:
uahegyounam, | 'alay | kal | hayoum. | shibtam | uaqiymatam | habiytah, | 'aniy | mangiynatam.
**and their device | against me | all | the day | their sitting down | and their rising up | Behold | I *am* | their music**

3:65

תשיב 7725 | להם 3807a | גמול 1576 | יהוה 3068 | כמעשה 4639 | ידיהם 3027: | תתן 5414 | להם 1992 | מגנת 4044 | לב 3820
tashiyb | lahem | gamul | Yahuah | kama'aseh | yadeyhem. | titen | lahem | maginat | leb,
**Render | unto them | a recompence | O Yahuah | according to the work of | their hands | Give | them | sorrow of | heart**

3:66

תאלתך 8381 | להם 1992: | תרדף 7291 | באף 639 | ותשמידם 8045 | מתחת 8478 | שמי 8064 | יהוה 3068:
ta'alataka | lahem. | tirdop | ba'ap | uatashmiydem, | mitachat | shamey | Yahuah.
**your curse unto them | Persecute in anger and destroy them | from under | the heavens of | Yahuah**

**Lam 4:1**

איכה 349 | יועם 6004 | זהב 2091 | ישנא 8132 | הכתם 3800 | הטוב 2896 | תשתפכנה 8210 | אבני 68 | קדש 6944
'aeykah | yu'am | zahab, | yishna' | haketem | hatoub; | tishtapekanah | 'abney | qodesh,
**How | is become dim | the gold | *how* is changed | fine gold | the most | are poured out | the stones of | the sanctuary**

4:2

בראש 7218 | כל 3605 | חוצות 2351: | בני 1121 | ציון 6726 | היקרים 3368 | המסלאים 5537 | בפז 6337 | איכה 349 | נחשבו 2803
bara'sh | kal | chutzout. | baney | tziyoun | hayaqariym, | hamasula'aym | bapaz; | 'aeykah | nechshabu
**in the top of | every | street | sons of | Zion | The precious | comparable | to fine gold | how | are they esteemed**

4:3

לנבלי 5035 | חרש 2789 | מעשה 4639 | ידי 3027 | יוצר 3335: | גם 1571 | תנין 8577 | חלצו 2502 | שד 7699 | היניקו 3243
lanibley | cheres, | ma'aseh | yadey | youtzer. | gam | taniyn | chalatzu | shad, | heyniyqu
**as pitchers | earthen | the work of | the hands of | the potter | Even | the sea monsters | draw out | the breast | they give suck to**

4:4

גוריהן 1482 | בת 1323 | עמי 5971 | לאכזר 393 | כי 3588 | ענים 3283 | במדבר 4057 | דבק 1692 | לשון 3956
gureyhen; | bat | 'amiy | la'akzar, | kaya | 'aeniym | bamidbar. | dabaq | lashoun
**their young ones | the daughter of | my people | *is become* cruel | like | the ostriches | in the wilderness | cleave | The tongue of**

יונק 3243 | אל 413 | חכו 2441 | בצמא 6772 | עוללים 5768 | שאלו 7592 | לחם 3899 | פרש 6566 | אין 369
youneq | 'al | chikou | batzama'; | 'aulaliym | sha'alu | lechem, | pores | 'aeyn
**the sucking child | to | the roof of his mouth | for thirst | the young children | ask | bread | break | *and* no man**

4:5

להם 1992: | האכלים 398 | למעדנים 4574 | נשמו 8074 | בחוצות 2351 | האמנים 539 | עלי 5921 | תולע 8438
lahem. | ha'akaliym | lama'adaniym, | nashamu | bachutzout; | ha'amuniym | 'aley | toula',
***it* unto them | They that did feed | delicately | are desolate | in the streets | they that were brought up | in | scarlet**

4:6

חבקו 2263 | אשפתות 830: | ויגדל 1431 | עון 5771 | בת 1323 | עמי 5971
chibqu | ashpatout. | uayigdal | 'auon | bat | 'amiy,
**embrace dunghills (*hearth*) | For is greater the punishment of the iniquity of | the daughter of | my people**

Lam 3:60 Thou have seen all their vengeance and all their imaginations against me.61 Thou have heard their reproach, O YHUH, and all their imaginations against me;62 The lips of those that rose up against me, and their device against me all the day.63 Behold their sitting down, and their rising up; I am their musick.64 Render unto them a recompence, O YHUH, according to the work of their hands.65 Give them sorrow of heart, your curse unto them.66 Persecute and destroy them in anger from under the heavens of YHUH. **Lam** 4:1 How is the gold become dim! how is the most fine gold changed! the stones of the sanctuary are poured out in the top of every street.2 The precious sons of Zion, comparable to fine gold, how are they esteemed as earthen pitchers, the work of the hands of the potter!3 Even the sea monsters draw out the breast, they give suck to their young ones: the daughter of my people is become cruel, like the ostriches in the wilderness.4 The tongue of the sucking child cleaveth to the roof of his mouth for thirst: the young children ask bread, and no man breaketh it unto them.5 They that did feed delicately are desolate in the streets: they that were brought up in scarlet embrace dunghills.6 For the punishment of the iniquity of the daughter of my people is greater than the punishment of the sin of Sodom, that was overthrown as in a moment,

| מחטאת 2403 | סדם 5467 | ההפוכה 2015 | כמו 3644 | רגע 7281 | ולא 3808 | חלו 2342 | בה 871a | ידים 3027: | 4:7 |
|---|---|---|---|---|---|---|---|---|---|
| mechata't | sadom; | hahapukah | kamou | raga', | uala' | chalu | bah | yadayim. | |
| **than the punishment of the sin of** | **Sodom** | **that was overthrown** | **as** | ***in* a moment** | **and no** | **stayed** | **on her** | **hands** | |

| זכו 2141 | נזיריה 5139 | משלג 7950 | צחו 6705 | מחלב 2461 | אדמו 119 | עצם 6106 | מפנינים 6443 | ספיר 5601 |
|---|---|---|---|---|---|---|---|---|
| zaku | naziyreyha | misheleg, | tzachu | mechalab; | 'adamu | 'atzem | mipniyniym, | sapiyr |
| **were purer** | **Her Nazarites** | **than snow** | **they were whiter** | **than milk** | **they were more ruddy** | ***in* body** | **than rubies** | ***was* of sapphire** |

| גזרתם 1508: | 4:8 | חשך 2821 | משחור 7815 | תארם 8389 | לא 3808 | נכרו 5234 | בחוצות 2351 | צפד 6821 | עורם 5785 | על 5921 |
|---|---|---|---|---|---|---|---|---|---|---|
| gizratam. | | chashak | mishchour | ta'aram, | la' | nikru | bachutzout; | tzapad | auram | 'al |
| **their polishing** | | **is blacker** | **than a coal** | **Their visage** | **not** | **they are known** | **in the streets** | **cleave** | **their skin** | **to** |

| עצמם 6106 | יבש 3001 | היה 1961 | כעץ 6086: | 4:9 | טובים 2896 | היו 1961 | חללי 2491 | חרב 2719 |
|---|---|---|---|---|---|---|---|---|
| 'atzmam, | yabesh | hayah | ka'aetz. | | toubiym | hayu | challey | chereb, |
| **their bones** | **it is withered** | **it is become** | **like a stick** | | ***They that be* better** | **are those** | **slain with** | **the sword** |

| מחללי 2491 | רעב 7458 | שהם 1992 | יזובו 2100 | מדקרים 1856 | מתנובת 8570 | שדי 7704: | 4:10 |
|---|---|---|---|---|---|---|---|
| mechalaley | ra'ab; | shehem | yazubu | maduqariym, | mitnubot | saday. | |
| **than *they that be* slain with** | **hunger** | **for these** | **pine away** | **stricken through** | **for *want of* the fruits of** | **the field** | |

| ידי 3027 | נשים 802 | רחמניות 7362 | בשלו 1310 | ילדיהן 3206 | היו 1961 | לברות 1262 | למו 3807a | בשבר 7667 |
|---|---|---|---|---|---|---|---|---|
| yadey, | nashiym | rachamaniyout, | bishlu | yaldeyhen; | hayu | labarout | lamou, | basheber |
| **The hands of** | **women** | ***the* pitiful** | **have sodden** | **their own children** | **they were** | **meat** | **their** | **in the destruction of** |

| בת 1323 | עמי 5971: | 4:11 | כלה 3615 | יהוה 3068 | את 853 | חמתו 2534 | שפך 8210 | חרון 2740 | אפו 639 |
|---|---|---|---|---|---|---|---|---|---|
| bat | 'amiy. | | kilah | Yahuah | 'at | chamatou, | shapak | charoun | 'apou; |
| **the daughter of** | **my people** | | **has accomplished** | **Yahuah** | | **his fury** | **he has poured out** | **fierce** | **his anger** |

| ויצת 3341 | אש 784 | בציון 6726 | ותאכל 398 | יסודתיה 3247: | 4:12 | לא 3808 | האמינו 539 | מלכי 4428 |
|---|---|---|---|---|---|---|---|---|
| uayatzet | 'aesh | batziyoun, | uata'kal | yasoudoteyha. | | la' | he'amiynu | malkey |
| **and has kindled** | **a fire** | **in Zion** | **and it has devoured** | **the foundations thereof** | | **not** | **would have believed** | **The kings of** |

| ארץ 776 | וכל 3605 | ישבי 3427 | תבל 8398 | כי 3588 | יבא 935 | צר 6862 | ואויב 341 | בשערי 8179 |
|---|---|---|---|---|---|---|---|---|
| 'aretz, | uakal | yoshabey | tebel; | kiy | yaba' | tzar | ua'auyeb, | basha'arey |
| **the earth** | **and all** | **the inhabitants of** | **the world** | **that** | **should have entered** | **the adversary** | **and the enemy** | **into the gates of** |

| ירושלם 3389: | 4:13 | מחטאת 2403 | נביאיה 5030 | עונות 5771 | כהניה 3548 | השפכים 8210 | בקרבה 7130 |
|---|---|---|---|---|---|---|---|
| yarushalaim. | | mechata't | nabiy'ayha, | 'auonout | kohaneyha; | hashopakiym | baqirbah |
| **Jerusalem** | | **For the sins of** | **her prophets** | ***and* the iniquities of** | **her priests** | **that have shed** | **in the midst of her** |

| דם 1818 | צדיקים 6662: | 4:14 | נעו 5128 | עורים 5787 | בחוצות 2351 | נגאלו 1351 | בדם 1818 |
|---|---|---|---|---|---|---|---|
| dam | tzadiyqiym. | | na'au | 'auriym | bachutzout, | nago'alu | badam; |
| **the blood of** | **the just** | | **They have wandered** | ***as* blind** | ***men* in the streets** | **they have polluted themselves** | **with blood** |

| בלא 3808 | יוכלו 3201 | יגעו 5060 | בלבשיהם 3830: | 4:15 | סורו 5493 | טמא 2931 | קראו 7121 | למו 3807a | סורו 5493 | סורו 5493 | אל 408 |
|---|---|---|---|---|---|---|---|---|---|---|---|
| bala' | yukalu, | yig'au | bilabusheyhem. | | suru | tamea' | qara'au | lamou, | suru | suru | 'al |
| **so that not *men* could touch** | | | **their garments** | | **Depart you** | ***it is* unclean** | **They cried** | **unto them** | **depart** | **depart** | **not** |

Lam 4:6 and no hands stayed on her.7 Her Nazarites were purer than snow, they were whiter than milk, they were more ruddy in body than rubies, their polishing was of sapphire:8 Their visage is blacker than a coal; they are not known in the streets: their skin cleaveth to their bones; it is withered, it is become like a stick.9 They that be slain with the sword are better than they that be slain with hunger: for these pine away, stricken through for want of the fruits of the field.10 The hands of the pitiful women have sodden their own children: they were their meat in the destruction of the daughter of my people.11 YHUH has accomplished his fury; he has poured out his fierce anger, and has kindled a fire in Zion, and it has devoured the foundations thereof.12 The kings of the earth, and all the inhabitants of the world, would not have believed that the adversary and the enemy should have entered into the gates of Jerusalem.13 For the sins of her prophets, and the iniquities of her priests, that have shed the blood of the just in the midst of her,14 They have wandered as blind men in the streets, they have polluted themselves with blood, so that men could not touch their garments.15 They cried unto them, Depart you; it is unclean; depart, depart, touch not: when they fled away and wandered, they said among the heathen, They shall no more sojourn there.

| תגעו 5060 | כי 3588 | נצו 5132 | גם 1571 | נעו 5128 | אמרו 559 | בגוים 1471 | לא 3808 | יוסיפו 3254 |
|---|---|---|---|---|---|---|---|---|
| tiga'au, | kiy | natzu | gam | na'au; | 'amaru | bagouyim, | la' | yousiypu |
| **touch** | **when** | **they fled away** | **moreover** | ***and* wandered** | **they said** | **among the heathen** | **no** | **They shall more** |

| לגור 1481: | 4:16 | פני 6440 | יהוה 3068 | חלקם 2505 | לא 3808 | יוסיף 3254 | להביטם 5027 | פני 6440 | כהנים 3548 | לא 3808 |
|---|---|---|---|---|---|---|---|---|---|---|
| lagur. | | paney | Yahuah | chilqam, | la' | yousiyp | lahabiytam; | paney | kohaniym | la' |
| **sojourn *there*** | | **The anger of** | **Yahuah** | **has divided them** | **no** | **he will more** | **regard them** | **the persons of** | **the priests** | **not** |

| נשאו 5375 | זקנים 2205 | לא 3808 | חננו 2603: | 4:17 | עודינה 5750 | תכלינה 3615 | עינינו 5869 | אל 413 | עזרתנו 5833 | הבל 1892 |
|---|---|---|---|---|---|---|---|---|---|---|
| nasa'au, | zaqeniym | la' | chananu. | | 'audeynah | tikleynah | 'aeyneynu, | 'al | 'azratenu | habel; |
| **they respected** | **the elders** | **not** | **they favoured** | | ***As for us*, as yet** | **failed** | **our eyes** | **for** | **our help** | **vain** |

| בצפיתנו 6822 | צפינו 6822 | אל 413 | גוי 1471 | לא 3808 | יושע 3467: | 4:18 | צדו 6679 | צעדינו 6806 | מלכת 1980 |
|---|---|---|---|---|---|---|---|---|---|
| batzipiyatenu | tzipiynu, | 'al | gouy | la' | youshia'. | | tzadu | tza'adeynu, | mileket |
| **in our watching** | **we have watched** | **for** | **a nation** | **not *us*** | ***that* could save** | | **They hunt** | **our steps *that we cannot*** | **go** |

| ברחבתינו 7339 | קרב 7126 | קצינו 7093 | מלאו 4390 | ימינו 3117 | כי 3588 | בא 935 | קצינו 7093: | 4:19 | קלים 7031 | היו 1961 | רדפינו 7291 |
|---|---|---|---|---|---|---|---|---|---|---|---|
| birchoboteynu; | qarab | qitzeynu | mala'au | yameynu | kiy | ba' | qitzeynu. | | qaliym | hayu | rodapeynu, |
| **in our streets** | **is near** | **our end** | **are fulfilled** | **our days** | **for** | **is come** | **our end** | | **swifter** | **are** | **Our persecutors** |

| מנשרי 5404 | שמים 8064 | על 5921 | ההרים 2022 | דלקנו 1814 | במדבר 4057 | ארבו 693 | לנו 3807a: | 4:20 |
|---|---|---|---|---|---|---|---|---|
| minishrey | shamayim; | 'al | hehariym | dalaqunu, | bamidbar | 'arabu | lanu. | |
| **than the eagles of** | **the heaven** | **upon** | **the mountains** | **they pursued us** | **in the wilderness** | **they laid wait** | **for us** | |

| רוח 7307 | אפינו 639 | משיח 4899 | יהוה 3068 | נלכד 3920 | בשחיתותם 7825 | אשר 834 | אמרנו 559 | בצלו 6738 |
|---|---|---|---|---|---|---|---|---|
| ruach | 'apeynu | mashiyach | Yahuah, | nilkad | bishchiytoutam; | 'asher | 'amarnu, | batzilou |
| **The breath of** | **our nostrils** | **the anointed of** | **Yahuah** | **was taken** | **in their pits** | **of whom** | **we said** | **Under his shadow** |

| נחיה 2421 | בגוים 1471: | 4:21 | שישי 7797 | ושמחי 2056 | בת 1323 | אדום 123 | יושבתי 3427 | בארץ 776 | עוץ 5780 | גם 1571 |
|---|---|---|---|---|---|---|---|---|---|---|
| nichayeh | bagouyim. | | siysiy | uasimchiy | bat | 'adoum, | youshabtiy | ba'aretz | 'autz; | gam |
| **we shall live** | **among the heathen** | | **Rejoice** | **and be glad** | **O daughter of** | **Edom** | **that dwell** | **in the land of** | **Uz** | **also** |

| עליך 5921 | תעבר 5674 | כוס 3563 | תשכרי 7937 | ותתערי 6168: | 4:22 | תם 8552 |
|---|---|---|---|---|---|---|
| 'aleyka | ta'abar | kous, | tishkariy | uatit'ariy. | | tam |
| **unto you** | **shall pass through** | **the cup** | **you shall be drunken** | **and shall make yourself naked** | | ***The* is accomplished** |

| עונך 5771 | בת 1323 | ציון 6726 | לא 3808 | יוסיף 3254 | להגלותך 1540 | פקד 6485 |
|---|---|---|---|---|---|---|
| 'auonek | bat | tziyoun, | la' | yousiyp | lahagloutek; | paqad |
| **punishment of your iniquity** | **O daughter of** | **Zion** | **no** | **he will more** | **carry you away into captivity** | **he will visit** |

| עונך 5771 | בת 1323 | אדום 123 | גלה 1540 | על 5921 | חטאתיך 2403: |
|---|---|---|---|---|---|
| 'auonek | bat | 'adoum, | gilah | 'al | chata'tayik. |
| **your iniquity** | **O daughter of** | **Edom** | **he will discover** | **on** | **your sins** |

| **Lam 5:1** | זכר 2142 | יהוה 3068 | מה 4100 | היה 1961 | לנו 3807a | הביט 5027 | וראה 7200 | את 853 | חרפתנו 2781: | 5:2 | נחלתנו 5159 |
|---|---|---|---|---|---|---|---|---|---|---|---|
| | zakor | Yahuah | meh | hayah | lanu, | habiyt | uar'aeh | 'at | cherpatenu. | | nachalatenu |
| | **Remember** | **O Yahuah** | **what** | **is come** | **upon us** | **consider** | **and behold** | | **our reproach** | | **Our inheritance** |

Lam 4:16 The anger of YHUH has divided them; he will no more regard them: they respected not the persons of the priests, they favoured not the elders.17 As for us, our eyes as yet failed for our vain help: in our watching we have watched for a nation that could not save us.18 They hunt our steps, that we cannot go in our streets: our end is near, our days are fulfilled; for our end is come.19 Our persecutors are swifter than the eagles of the heaven: they pursued us upon the mountains, they laid wait for us in the wilderness.20 The breath of our nostrils, the anointed of YHUH, was taken in their pits, of whom we said, Under his shadow we shall live among the heathen.21 Rejoice and be glad, O daughter of Edom, that dwellest in the land of Uz; the cup also shall pass through unto you: you shall be drunken, and shall make thyself naked.22 The punishment of your iniquity is accomplished, O daughter of Zion; he will no more carry you away into captivity: he will visit your iniquity, O daughter of Edom; he will discover your sins. **Lam** 5:1 Remember, O YHUH, what is come upon us: consider, and behold our reproach.2 Our inheritance is turned to strangers, our houses to aliens.

5:3 5:4
נהפכה 2015 לזרים 2114 בתינו 1004 לנכרים 5237: יתומים 3490 היינו 1961 אין 369 אב 1 אמתינו 517 כאלמנות 490:
nehepkah lazariym, bateynu lanakariym. yatoumiym hayiynu 'aeyn 'ab, 'amoteynu ka'almanout.
**is turned to strangers our houses to aliens orphans We are there is no father our mothers *are* as widows**

5:5
מימינו 4325 בכסף 3701 שתינו 8354 עצינו 6086 במחיר 4242 יבאו 935: על 5921 צוארנו 6677 נרדפנו 7291 יגענו 3021
meymeynu bakesep shatiynu, 'aetzeynu bimachiyr yabo'au. 'al tzaua'renu nirdapanu, yaga'anu
**our water for money We have drunken our wood is sold *unto us* they come under Our necks *are* persecution we labour**

5:6 5:7
לא 3808 הונח 5117 לנו 3807a: מצרים 4713 נתנו 5414 יד 3027 אשור 804 לשבע 7646 לחם 3899:
la' hunach lanu. mitzrayim natanu yad, 'ashur lisboa' lachem.
**no rest *and* have *to* the Egyptian We have given the hand *and to* the Assyrians to be satisfied with bread**

5:8
אבתינו 1 חטאו 2398 אינם 369 אנחנו 587 עונתיהם 5771 סבלנו 5445: עבדים 5650 משלו 4910 בנו 871a
'aboteynu chata'au 'aeynam 'anachnu 'auonouteyhem sabalanu. 'abadiym mashalu ba'nu,
**Our fathers have sinned and are not and we their iniquities have borne Servants have ruled over us**

5:9
פרק 6561 אין 369 מידם 3027: בנפשנו 5315 נביא 935 לחמנו 3899 מפני 6440 חרב 2719
poreq 'aeyn miyadam. banapshenu nabiy'a lachamenu, mipaney chereb
**that does deliver *there is* none *us* out of their hand with *the peril of* our lives We got our bread because of the sword of**

5:10 5:11
המדבר 4057: עורנו 5785 כתנור 8574 נכמרו 3648 מפני 6440 זלעפות 2152 רעב 7458: נשים 802 בציון 6726 ענו 6031
hamidbar. 'aurenu katanur nikmaru, mipney zal'apout ra'ab. nashiym batziyoun 'anu,
**the wilderness Our skin like an oven was black because of *the* terrible famine the women in Zion They ravished**

5:12
בתלת 1330 בערי 5892 יהודה 3063: שרים 8269 בידם 3027 נתלו 8518 פני 6440 זקנים 2205 לא 3808
batlot ba'arey yahudah. sariym bayadam nitlu, paney zaqeniym la'
***and* the maids in the cities of Judah Princes by their hand are hanged up the faces of elders not**

5:13 5:14
נהדרו 1921: בחורים 970 טחון 2911 נשאו 5375 ונערים 5288 בעץ 6086 כשלו 3782: זקנים 2205
nehdaru. bachuriym tachoun nasa'au, uan'ariym ba'aetz kashalu. zaqeniym
**were honoured the young men to grind They took and the children of under the wood fell The elders**

5:15
משער 8179 שבתו 7673 בחורים 970 מנגינתם 5058: שבת 7674 משוש 4885 לבנו 3820 נהפך 2015 לאבל 60
misha'ar shabatu, bachuriym minagiynatam. shabat masous libenu, nehapak la'aebel
**from the gate have ceased the young men from their music is ceased The joy of our heart is turned into mourning**

5:16 5:17
מחלנו 4234: נפלה 5307 עטרת 5850 ראשנו 7218 אוי 188 נא 4994 לנו 3807a כי 3588 חטאנו 2398: על 5921 זה 2088
macholenu. naplah ateret ra'shenu, 'auy naa' lanu kiy chata'nu. 'al zeh,
**our dance is fallen The crown *from* our head woe I beseech you unto us that we have sinned For this**

5:18
היה 1961 דוה 1739 לבנו 3820 על 5921 אלה 428 חשכו 2821 עינינו 5869: על 5921 הר 2022 ציון 6726 ששמם 8074
hayah daueh libenu, 'al 'aeleh chashaku 'aeyneynu. 'al har tziyoun sheshamem,
**is faint our heart for these are dim *things* our eyes Because of the mountain of Zion which is desolate**

5:19 5:20
שועלים 7776 הלכו 1980 בו 871a: אתה 859 יהוה 3069 לעולם 5769 תשב 3427 כסאך 3678 לדר 1755 ודור 1755: למה 4100
shu'aliym halaku bou. 'atah Yahuah la'aulam tesheb, kis'aka lador uadour. lamah
**the foxes walk upon it You Yahuah for ever remain your throne from generation to generation Wherefore**

Lam 5:3 We are orphans and fatherless, our mothers are as widows.4 We have drunken our water for money; our wood is sold unto us.5 Our necks are under persecution: we labour, and have no rest.6 We have given the hand to the Egyptians, and to the Assyrians, to be satisfied with bread.7 Our fathers have sinned, and are not; and we have borne their iniquities.8 Servants have ruled over us: there is none that doth deliver us out of their hand.9 We got our bread with the peril of our lives because of the sword of the wilderness.10 Our skin was black like an oven because of the terrible famine.11 They ravished the women in Zion, and the maids in the cities of Judah.12 Princes are hanged up by their hand: the faces of elders were not honoured.13 They took the young men to grind, and the children fell under the wood.14 The elders have ceased from the gate, the young men from their musick.15 The joy of our heart is ceased; our dance is turned into mourning.16 The crown is fallen from our head: woe unto us, that we have sinned!17 For this our heart is faint; for these things our eyes are dim.18 Because of the mountain of Zion, which is desolate, the foxes walk upon it.19 Thou, O YHUH, remainest forever; your throne from generation to generation.

| 𐤋𐤍𐤑𐤇 | 𐤕𐤔𐤊𐤇𐤍𐤅 | 𐤕𐤏𐤆𐤁𐤍𐤅 | 𐤋𐤀𐤓𐤊 | 𐤉𐤌𐤉𐤌 | **5:21** 𐤄𐤔𐤉𐤁𐤍𐤅 | 𐤉𐤄𐤅𐤄 | 𐤀𐤋𐤉𐤊 | 𐤅𐤍𐤔𐤅𐤁 |
|---|---|---|---|---|---|---|---|---|
| לנצח 5331 | תשכחנו 7911 | תעזבנו 5800 | לארך 753 | ימים 3117: | השיבנו 7725 | יהוה 3068 | אליך 413 | ונשוב 7725 |
| lanetzach | tishkachenu, | ta'azbenu | la'arek | yamiym. | hashiybenu | Yahuah | 'aeleyka | uanashub |
| **for ever** | **do you forget us** | ***and* forsake us** | **so long** | **time?** | **Turn you us** | **O Yahuah** | **unto you** | **and we shall be turned** |

| 𐤇𐤃𐤔 | 𐤉𐤌𐤉𐤍𐤅 | 𐤊𐤒𐤃𐤌 | **5:22** 𐤊𐤉 | 𐤀𐤌 | 𐤌𐤀𐤎 | 𐤌𐤀𐤎𐤕𐤍𐤅 | 𐤒𐤑𐤐𐤕 | 𐤏𐤋𐤉𐤍𐤅 | 𐤏𐤃 | 𐤌𐤀𐤃 |
|---|---|---|---|---|---|---|---|---|---|---|
| חדש 2318 | ימינו 3117 | כקדם 6924: | כי 3588 | אם 518 | מאס 3988 | מאסתנו 3973 | קצפת 7107 | עלינו 5921 | עד 5704 | מאד 3966: |
| chadesh | yameynu | kaqedem. | kiy | 'am | ma'as | ma'astanu, | qatzapta | 'aleynu | 'ad | ma'ad. |
| **renew** | **our days** | **as of old** | **But** | **if** | **utterly** | **you have rejected us** | **you are wroth** | **agaianst us** | **are** | **very** |

Lam 5:20 Wherefore dost you forget us forever, and forsake us so long time?21 Turn you us unto you, O YHUH, and we shall be turned; renew our days as of old.22 But you have utterly rejected us; you are very wroth against us.

# EZEKIEL
## (*Yachezqeal*)

Ezekiel 1:3 identifies the Prophet Ezekiel as the author which was likely written between 593 and 565 B.C. during the Babylonian captivity of the House of Judah. The name Ezekiel means *El is my strength.* He was also a contemporary of both Jeremiah and Daniel and begin his life's ministry as a priest at age thirty, when he had a majestic vision and attempted to bring his people to repentance and obedience to Torah if they expected to avoid judgment and receive blessings. His book can be divided into four sections: Chapters 1-24: warning prophecies on the ruin of Jerusalem; chapters 25-32: prophecies of Elohim's judgment on nearby nations; chapter 33: a last call for repentance to Israel; and chapters 34-48: prophecies concerning the future restoration of Israel.

| **Ezekiel 1:1** ויהי 1961 | בשלשים 7970 | שנה 8141 | ברביעי 7243 | בחמשה 2568 | לחדש 2320 | ואני 589 | בתוך 8432 |
|---|---|---|---|---|---|---|---|
| uayahiy | bishloshiym | shanah, | barabiy'ay | bachamishah | lachodesh, | ua'aniy | batouk |
| **Now it came to pass** | **in the thirtieth** | **year** | **in the fourth *month*** | **in the fifth *day*** | **of the month** | **as I *was*** | **among** |

| הגולה 1473 | על 5921 | נהר 5104 | כבר 3529 | נפתחו 6605 | השמים 8064 | ואראה 7200 | מראות 4759 | אלהים 430: | **1:2** | בחמשה 2568 |
|---|---|---|---|---|---|---|---|---|---|---|
| hagoulah | 'al | nahar | kabar; | niptachu | hashamayim, | ua'ar'ah | mar'aut | 'alohiym. | | bachamishah |
| **the captives** | **by** | **the river of** | **Chebar** | **were opened** | ***that* the heavens** | **and I saw** | **visions of** | **Elohim** | | **In the fifth** |

| לחדש 2320 | היא 1931 | השנה 8141 | החמישית 2549 | לגלות 1546 | המלך 4428 | יויכין 3112: | **1:3** | היה 1961 | היה 1961 | דבר 1697 | יהוה 3068 |
|---|---|---|---|---|---|---|---|---|---|---|---|
| lachodesh; | hiy'a | hashanah | hachamiyshiyt, | lagalut | hamelek | youyakiyn. | | hayoh | hayah | dabar | Yahuah |
| ***day* of the month** | **which** | **year of** | ***was* the fifth** | **captivity** | **king** | **Jehoiachin's** | | **came** | **expressly** | **The word of** | **Yahuah** |

| אל 413 | יחזקאל 3168 | בן 1121 | בוזי 941 | הכהן 3548 | בארץ 776 | כשדים 3778 | על 5921 | נהר 5104 | כבר 3529 | ותהי 1961 | עליו 5921 | שם 8033 |
|---|---|---|---|---|---|---|---|---|---|---|---|---|
| 'al | yachezqea'l | ben | buziy | hakohen | ba'aretz | kasdiym | 'al | nahar | kabar; | uatahiy | 'alayu | sham |
| **unto** | **Ezekiel** | **the son of** | **Buzi** | **the priest** | **in the land of** | **the Chaldeans** | **by** | ***the* river** | **Chebar** | **and was** | **upon him** | **there** |

| יד 3027 | יהוה 3068: | **1:4** | וארא 7200 | והנה 2009 | רוח 7307 | סערה 5591 | באה 935 | מן 4480 | הצפון 6828 | ענן 6051 | גדול 1419 | ואש 784 |
|---|---|---|---|---|---|---|---|---|---|---|---|---|
| yad | Yahuah. | | ua'aera' | uahineh | ruach | sa'arah | ba'ah | min | hatzapoun, | 'anan | gadoul | ua'aesh |
| **the hand of** | **Yahuah** | | **And I looked** | **and behold** | **wind** | **a whirl** | **came** | **out of** | **the north** | **a cloud** | **great** | **and a fire** |

| מתלקחת 3947 | ונגה 5051 | לו 3807a | סביב 5439 | ומתוכה 8432 | כעין 5869 | החשמל 2830 |
|---|---|---|---|---|---|---|
| mitlaqachat, | uanogah | lou' | sabiyb; | uamitoukah, | ka'aeyn | hachashmal |
| **infolding itself** | **and a brightness** | **it** | ***was* about** | **and out of the midst thereof** | **as the colour of** | **amber** |

| מתוך 8432 | האש 784: | **1:5** | ומתוכה 8432 | דמות 1823 | ארבע 702 | חיות 2416 | וזה 2088 |
|---|---|---|---|---|---|---|---|
| mitouk | ha'aesh. | | uamitoukah, | damut | 'arba | chayout; | uazeh |
| **out of the midst of** | **the fire** | | **Also out of the midst thereof** | ***came* the likeness of** | **four** | **living creatures** | **And this** |

| מראיהן 4758 | דמות 1823 | אדם 120 | להנה 2007: | **1:6** | וארבעה 702 | פנים 6440 | לאחת 259 | וארבע 702 | כנפים 3671 | לאחת 259 |
|---|---|---|---|---|---|---|---|---|---|---|
| mar'aeyhen, | damut | 'adam | lahenah. | | ua'arbah | paniym | la'aechat; | ua'arba' | kanapayim | la'achat |
| ***was* their appearance** | **the likeness of** | **a man** | **they had** | | **And four** | **faces** | **every one** | ***had* and four** | **wings** | **every one** |

| להם 3807a: | **1:7** | ורגליהם 7272 | רגל 7272 | ישרה 3477 | וכף 3709 | רגליהם 7272 | ככף 3709 | רגל 7272 | עגל 5695 |
|---|---|---|---|---|---|---|---|---|---|
| lahem. | | uaragleyhem | regel | yasharah; | uakap | ragleyhem, | kakap | regel | 'aegel, |
| **had them** | | **And their feet** | **feet** | ***were* straight** | **and the sole of** | **their feet** | ***was* like the sole of** | **a foot** | **calf's** |

| ונצצים 5340 | כעין 5869 | נחשת 5178 | קלל 7044: | **1:8** | וידו 3027 | אדם 120 | מתחת 8478 | כנפיהם 3671 | על 5921 |
|---|---|---|---|---|---|---|---|---|---|
| uanotzatziym, | ka'aeyn | nachoshet | qalal. | | uayadou | 'adam, | mitachat | kanapeyhem, | 'al |
| **and they sparkled** | **like the colour of** | **brass** | **burnished** | | **And they had the hands of** | **a man** | **under** | **their wings** | **on** |

**Ezekiel** 1:1 Now it came to pass in the thirtieth year, in the fourth month, in the fifth day of the month, as I was among the captives by the river of Chebar, that the heavens were opened, and I saw visions of G-d.2 In the fifth day of the month, which was the fifth year of king Jehoiachin's captivity,3 The word of YHUH came expressly unto Ezekiel the priest, the son of Buzi, in the land of the Chaldeans by the river Chebar; and the hand of YHUH was there upon him.4 And I looked, and, behold, a whirlwind came out of the north, a great cloud, and a fire infolding itself, and a brightness was about it, and out of the midst thereof as the colour of amber, out of the midst of the fire.5 Also out of the midst thereof came the likeness of four living creatures. And this was their appearance; they had the likeness of a man.6 And everyone had four faces, and everyone had four wings.7 And their feet were straight feet; and the sole of their feet was like the sole of a calf's foot: and they sparkled like the colour of burnished brass.8 And they had the hands of a man under their wings on their four sides; and they four had their faces and their wings.

| | | | | | 1:9 | | | | |
|---|---|---|---|---|---|---|---|---|---|
| ארבעת 702 | רבעיהם 7253 | ופניהם 6440 | וכנפיהם 3671 | לארבעתם 702: | חברת 2266 | אשה 802 | אל 413 | אחותה 269 | כנפיהם 3671 |
| 'arba'at | riba'aeyhem; | uapneyhem | uakanpeyhem | la'arba'atam. | chobrot | 'ashah | 'al | achoutah | kanapeyhem; |
| **four** | **their sides** | **had their faces** | **and their wings** | **they four had** | ***were* joined** | **one** | **to** | **another of her** | **Their wings** |

| | | | | | | | | 1:10 | |
|---|---|---|---|---|---|---|---|---|---|
| לא 3808 | יסבו 5437 | בלכתן 1980 | איש 376 | אל 413 | עבר 5674 | פניו 6440 | ילכו 1980: | ודמות 1823 | פניהם 6440 |
| la' | yisabu | balektan, | 'aysh | 'al | 'aeber | panayu | yeleku. | uadmut | paneyhem |
| **not** | **they turned** | **when they went** | **every one** | **to** | **straight** | **forward** | **they went** | **As for the likeness of** | **their faces** |

| | | | | | | | | | |
|---|---|---|---|---|---|---|---|---|---|
| פני 6440 | אדם 120 | ופני 6440 | אריה 738 | אל 413 | הימין 3225 | לארבעתם 702 | ופני 6440 | שור 7794 | מהשמאול 8040 |
| paney | 'adam | uapaney | 'aryeh | 'al | hayamiyn | la'arba'atam, | uapaniy | shour | mehasama'ul |
| **the face of** | **a man** | **and the face of** | **a lion** | **on** | **the right side** | **they four had** | **and the face of** | **an ox** | **on the left side** |

| | | | | 1:11 | | | |
|---|---|---|---|---|---|---|---|
| לארבעתן 702 | ופני 6440 | נשר 5404 | לארבעתן 702: | ופניהם 6440 | וכנפיהם 3671 | פרדות 6504 | מלמעלה 4605 |
| la'arba'atan; | uapaniy | nesher | la'arba'atan. | uapneyhem | uakanpeyhem | parudout | milma'alah; |
| **they four had** | **also the face of** | **an eagle** | **they four had** | **Thus *were* their faces** | **and their wings *were*** | **stretched** | **upward** |

| | | | | | | | | 1:12 | |
|---|---|---|---|---|---|---|---|---|---|
| לאיש 376 | שתים 8147 | חברות 2266 | איש 376 | ושתים 8147 | מכסות 3680 | את 853 | גויתיהנה 1472: | ואיש 376 | אל 413 |
| la'aysh, | shatayim | chobarout | 'aysh, | uashtayim | makasout, | 'at | gauiyoteyhenah | ua'aysh | 'al |
| ***wings* of every one** | **two** | ***were* joined** | **one *to another*** | **and two** | **covered** | | **their bodies** | **And every one** | **to** |

| | | | | | | | | | | | |
|---|---|---|---|---|---|---|---|---|---|---|---|
| עבר 5676 | פניו 6440 | ילכו 1980 | אל 413 | אשר 834 | יהיה 1961 | שמה 8033 | הרוח 7307 | ללכת 1980 | ילכו 1980 | לא 3808 | יסבו 5437 |
| 'aeber | panayu | yeleku; | 'al | 'asher | yihayeh | shamah | haruach | laleket | yeleku, | la' | yisabu |
| **straight** | **forward** | **they went** | **to** | **where** | **was** | **there** | **the spirit** | **to go** | **they went** | **not** | ***and* they turned** |

| | 1:13 | | | | | |
|---|---|---|---|---|---|---|
| בלכתן 1980: | ודמות 1823 | החיות 2416 | מראיהם 4758 | כגחלי 1513 | אש 784 | בערות 1197 |
| balektan. | uadmut | hachayout | mar'aeyhem | kagachaley | 'aesh, | bu'arout |
| **when they went** | **As for the likeness of** | **the living creatures** | **their appearance *was*** | **like coals of** | **fire** | **burning** |

| | | | | | | | |
|---|---|---|---|---|---|---|---|
| כמראה 4758 | הלפדים 3940 | היא 1931 | מתהלכת 1980 | בין 996 | החיות 2416 | ונגה 5051 | לאש 784 |
| kamar'aeh | halapiydim, | hiy'a | mithaleket | beyn | hachayout; | uanogah | la'aesh, |
| ***and* like the appearance of** | **lamps** | **it** | **went up and down** | **among** | **the living creatures** | **and bright** | **the fire** |

| | | | | 1:14 | | | |
|---|---|---|---|---|---|---|---|
| ומן 4480 | האש 784 | יוצא 3318 | ברק 1300: | והחיות 2416 | רצוא 7519 | ושוב 7725 | כמראה 4758 |
| uamin | ha'aesh | youtzea' | baraq. | uahachayout | ratzou'a | uashoub; | kamar'aeh |
| ***was* and out of** | **the fire** | **went forth** | **lightning** | **And the living creatures** | **ran** | **and returned** | **as the appearance of** |

| | 1:15 | | | | | | | |
|---|---|---|---|---|---|---|---|---|
| הבזק 965: | וארא 7200 | החיות 2416 | והנה 2009 | אופן 212 | אחד 259 | בארץ 776 | אצל 681 | החיות 2416 |
| habazaq. | ua'aera' | hachayout; | uahineh | 'aupan | 'achad | ba'aretz | 'aetzel | hachayout |
| **a flash of lightning** | **as I beheld** | **the living creatures** | **Now behold** | **wheel** | **one** | **upon the earth** | **by** | **the living creatures** |

| | | 1:16 | | | | | |
|---|---|---|---|---|---|---|---|
| לארבעת 702 | פניו 6440: | מראה 4758 | האופנים 212 | ומעשיהם 4639 | כעין 5869 | תרשיש 8658 | ודמות 1823 |
| la'arba'at | panayu. | mar'aeh | ha'aupaniym | uama'aseyhem | ka'aeyn | tarshiysh, | uadmut |
| **with four** | **his faces** | **The appearance of** | **the wheels** | **and their work** | ***was* like unto the colour of** | **a beryl** | **and likeness** |

| | | | | | | | | |
|---|---|---|---|---|---|---|---|---|
| אחד 259 | לארבעתן 702 | ומראיהם 4758 | ומעשיהם 4639 | כאשר 834 | יהיה 1961 | האופן 212 | בתוך 8432 | האופן 212: |
| 'achad | la'arba'atan; | uamar'aeyhem | uama'aseyhem, | ka'asher | yihayeh | ha'aupan | batouk | ha'aupan. |
| **one** | **they four had** | **and their appearance** | **and their work *was*** | **as** | **it were** | **a wheel** | **in the middle of** | **a wheel** |

Eze 1:9 Their wings were joined one to another; they turned not when they went; they went everyone straight forward.10 As for the likeness of their faces, they four had the face of a man, and the face of a lion, on the right side: and they four had the face of an ox on the left side; they four also had the face of an eagle.11 Thus were their faces: and their wings were stretched upward; two wings of everyone were joined one to another, and two covered their bodies.12 And they went everyone straight forward: whither the spirit was to go, they went; and they turned not when they went.13 As for the likeness of the living creatures, their appearance was like burning coals of fire, and like the appearance of lamps: it went up and down among the living creatures; and the fire was bright, and out of the fire went forth lightning.14 And the living creatures ran and returned as the appearance of a flash of lightning.15 Now as I beheld the living creatures, behold one wheel upon the earth by the living creatures, with his four faces.16 The appearance of the wheels and their work was like unto the colour of a beryl: and they four had one likeness: and their appearance and their work was as it were a wheel in the middle of a wheel.

**1:17** על 5921 | ארבעת 702 | רבעיהן 7253 | בלכתם 1980 | ילכו 1980 | לא 3808 | יסבו 5437 | בלכתן 1980: **1:18**

'al 'arba'at riba'aeyhen balektam yeleku; la' yisabu balektan.

**upon four their sides When they went they went not *and* they turned when they went**

וגביהן 1354 | וגבה 1363 | להם 1992 | ויראה 3374 | להם 1992 | וגבתם 1354 | מלאת 4392 | עינים 5869 | סביב 5439

uagabeyhen, uagobah lahem uayir'ah lahem; uagabotam, male'at 'aeynayim sabiyb

**As for their rings *were* so high they that dreadful they *were* and their rings *were* full of eyes round about**

לארבעתן 702: | **1:19** ובלכת 1980 | החיות 2416 | ילכו 1980 | האופנים 212 | אצלם 681 | ובהנשא 5375

la'arba'atan. uableket hachayout, yelaku ha'aupaniym 'atzlam; uabahinasea'

**them four And when went the living creatures went the wheels by them and when were lifted up**

החיות 2416 | מעל 5921 | הארץ 776 | ינשאו 5375 | האופנים 212: | **1:20** על 5921 | אשר 834 | יהיה 1961 | שם 8033 | הרוח 7307 | ללכת 1980

hachayout me'al ha'aretz, yinasa'au ha'aupaniym. 'al 'asher yihayeh sham haruach laleket

**the living creatures from the earth were lifted up the wheels Whither soever was there the spirit to go**

ילכו 1980 | שמה 8033 | הרוח 7307 | ללכת 1980 | והאופנים 212 | ינשאו 5375 | לעמתם 5980 | כי 3588 | רוח 7307

yeleku, shamah haruach laleket; uaha'aupaniym, yinasa'au la'amatam, kiy ruach

**they went there *was their* spirit to go and the wheels were lifted up over against them for the spirit of**

החיה 2416 | באופנים 212: | **1:21** בלכתם 1980 | ילכו 1980 | ובעמדם 5975 | יעמדו 5975

hachayah ba'aupaniym. balektam yeleku, uab'amadam ya'amodu;

**the living creature *was* in the wheels When those went *these* went and when those stood *these* stood**

ובהנשאם 5375 | מעל 5921 | הארץ 776 | ינשאו 5375 | האופנים 212 | לעמתם 5980 | כי 3588 | רוח 7307

uabhinasa'am me'al ha'aretz, yinasa'au ha'aupaniym la'amatam, kiy ruach

**and when those were lifted up from the earth were lifted up the wheels over against them for the spirit of**

החיה 2416 | באופנים 212: | **1:22** ודמות 1823 | על 5921 | ראשי 7218 | החיה 2416 | רקיע 7549

hachayah ba'aupaniym. uadmut 'al ra'shey hachayah raqiya',

**the living creature *was* in the wheels And the likeness of upon the heads of the living creature the firmament**

כעין 5869 | הקרח 7140 | הנורא 3372 | נטוי 5186 | על 5921 | ראשיהם 7218 | מלמעלה 4605: | **1:23** ותחת 8478 | הרקיע 7549

ka'aeyn haqerach hanoura'; natuy 'al ra'sheyhem milma'alah. uatachat haraqiya',

***was* as the colour of crystal the terrible stretched forth over their heads above And under the firmament**

כנפיהם 3671 | ישרות 3477 | אשה 802 | אל 413 | אחותה 269 | לאיש 376 | שתים 8147 | מכסות 3680 | להנה 2007

kanapeyhem yasharout, 'ashah 'al achoutah; la'aysh, shatayim makasout lahenah,

***were* their wings straight the one toward the other of her every one had two which covered on this side**

ולאיש 376 | שתים 8147 | מכסות 3680 | להנה 2007 | את 853 | גויתיהם 1472: | **1:24** ואשמע 8085 | את 853 | קול 6963 | כנפיהם 3671

ual'aysh, shatayim makasout lahenah, 'at gauiyoteyhem. ua'ashma' 'at qoul kanapeyhem

**and every one had two which covered on that side their bodies And I heard the noise of their wings**

כקול 6963 | מים 4325 | רבים 7227 | כקול 6963 | שדי 7706 | בלכתם 1980 | קול 6963 | המלה 1999 | כקול 6963 | מחנה 4264

kaqoul mayim rabiym kaqoul shaday balektam, qoul hamulah kaqoul machaneh;

**like the noise of waters great as the voice of the Almighty when they went the voice of speech as the noise of an host**

Eze 1:17 When they went, they went upon their four sides: and they turned not when they went.18 As for their rings, they were so high that they were dreadful; and their rings were full of eyes round about them four.19 And when the living creatures went, the wheels went by them: and when the living creatures were lifted up from the earth, the wheels were lifted up.20 Whithersoever the spirit was to go, they went, thither was their spirit to go; and the wheels were lifted up over against them: for the spirit of the living creature was in the wheels.21 When those went, these went; and when those stood, these stood; and when those were lifted up from the earth, the wheels were lifted up over against them: for the spirit of the living creature was in the wheels.22 And the likeness of the firmament upon the heads of the living creature was as the colour of the terrible crystal, stretched forth over their heads above.23 And under the firmament were their wings straight, the one toward the other: everyone had two, which covered on this side, and everyone had two, which covered on that side, their bodies.24 And when they went, I heard the noise of their wings, like the noise of great waters, as the voice of the Almighty, the voice of speech, as the noise of an host: when they stood, they let down their wings.

בעמדם 5975 תרפינה 7503 כנפיהן 3671: **1:25** ויהי 1961 קול 6963 מעל 5921 לרקיע 7549 אשר 834 על 5921 ראשם 7218
ba'amadam tarapeynah kanapeyhen. uayahiy qoul me'al laraqiya' 'asher 'al ra'sham;
**when they stood they let down their wings And there was a voice from the firmament that *was* over their heads**

בעמדם 5975 תרפינה 7503 כנפיהן 3671: **1:26** וממעל 4605 לרקיע 7549 אשר 834 על 5921 ראשם 7218
ba'amadam tarapeynah kanapeyhen. uamima'al, laraqiya' 'asher 'al ra'sham,
**when they stood *and* had let down their wings And above the firmament that *was* over their heads**

כמראה 4758 אבן 68 ספיר 5601 דמות 1823 כסא 3678 ועל 5921 דמות 1823 הכסא 3678 דמות 1823
kamar'aeh 'aben sapiyr damut kisea'; ua'al damut hakisea', damut
**as the appearance of a stone sapphire *was* the likeness of a throne and upon the likeness of the throne *was* the likeness**

כמראה 4758 אדם 120 עליו 5921 מלמעלה 4605: **1:27** וארא 7200 כעין 5869 חשמל 2830 כמראה 4758 אש 784 בית 1004
kamar'aeh 'adam 'alayu milma'alah. ua'aera' ka'aeyn chashmal, kamar'aeh 'aesh beyt
**as the appearance a man upon it above And I saw as the colour of amber as the appearance of fire within**

לה 3807a סביב 5439 ממראה 4758 מתניו 4975 ולמעלה 4605 וממראה 4758 מתניו 4975 ולמטה 4295
lah sabiyb, mimar'aeh matanayu ualma'alah; uamimar'aeh matanayu ualmatah,
**it round about from the appearance of his loins even upward and from the appearance of his loins even downward**

ראיתי 7200 כמראה 4758 אש 784 ונגה 5051 לו 3807a סביב 5439: **1:28** כמראה 4758 הקשת 7198 אשר 834
ra'aytiy kamar'aeh 'aesh, uanogah lou' sabiyb. kamar'aeh haqeshet 'asher
**I saw as it were the appearance of fire and brightness it had round about As the appearance of the bow that**

יהיה 1961 בענן 6051 ביום 3117 הגשם 1653 כן 3651 מראה 4758 הנגה 5051 סביב 5439 הוא 1931
yihayeh ba'anan bayoum hageshem, ken mar'aeh hanogah sabiyb, hua'
**is in the cloud in the day of rain so *was* the appearance of the brightness round about This**

מראה 4758 דמות 1823 כבוד 3519 יהוה 3068 ואראה 7200 ואפל 5307 על 5921 פני 6440 ואשמע 8085 קול 6963
mar'aeh damut kaboud Yahuah; ua'ar'ah ua'apol 'al panay, ua'ashma' qoul
***was* the appearance of the likeness of the glory of Yahuah when I saw *it* And I fell upon my face and I heard a voice of**

מדבר 1696:
madaber.
**one that spoke**

**Ezek 2:1** ויאמר 559 אלי 413 בן 1121 אדם 120 עמד 5975 על 5921 רגליך 7272 ואדבר 1696 אתך 853: **2:2** ותבא 935 בי 871a
uaya'mer 'aelay; ben 'adam 'amod 'al ragleyka, ua'adaber 'atak. uataba' biy
**And he said unto me Son of man stand upon your feet and I will speak unto you And entered into me**

רוח 7307 כאשר 834 דבר 1696 אלי 413 ותעמדני 5975 על 5921 רגלי 7272 ואשמע 8085 את 853 מדבר 1696 אלי 413: **2:3** ויאמר 559
ruach, ka'asher diber 'aelay, uata'amideniy 'al raglay; ua'ashma' 'at midaber 'aelay. uaya'mer
**the spirit when he spoke unto me and set me upon my feet that I heard him that spoke unto me And he said**

אלי 413 בן 1121 אדם 120 שולח 7971 אני 589 אותך 853 אל 413 בני 1121 ישראל 3478 אל 413 גוים 1471 המורדים 4775 אשר 834
'aelay, ben 'adam shouleach 'aniy 'autaka 'al baney yisra'ael, 'al gouyim hamourdiym 'asher
**unto me Son of man send I you to the children of Israel to a nation rebellious that**

Eze 1:25 And there was a voice from the firmament that was over their heads, when they stood, and had let down their wings.26 And above the firmament that was over their heads was the likeness of a throne, as the appearance of a sapphire stone: and upon the likeness of the throne was the likeness as the appearance of a man above upon it.27 And I saw as the colour of amber, as the appearance of fire round about within it, from the appearance of his loins even upward, and from the appearance of his loins even downward, I saw as it were the appearance of fire, and it had brightness round about.28 As the appearance of the bow that is in the cloud in the day of rain, so was the appearance of the brightness round about. This was the appearance of the likeness of the glory of YHUH. And when I saw it, I fell upon my face, and I heard a voice of one that spoke. **Eze** 2:1 And he said unto me, Son of man, stand upon your feet, and I will speak unto you.2 And the spirit entered into me when he spoke unto me, and set me upon my feet, that I heard him that spoke unto me.3 And he said unto me, Son of man, I send you to the children of Israel, to a rebellious nation that has rebelled against me: they and their fathers have transgressed against me, even unto this very day.

**2:4**
מרדו 4775 | בי 871a | המה 1992 | ואבותם 1 | פשעו 6586 | בי 871a | עד 5704 | עצם 6106 | היום 3117 | הזה 2088:
maredu | biy; | hemah | ba'aboutam | pasha'au | biy, | 'ad | 'atzem | hayoum | hazeh.
**has rebelled | against me | they | and their fathers | have transgressed | against me | *even* unto | very | day | this**

והבנים 1121 | קשי 7186 | פנים 6440 | וחזקי 2389 | לב 3820 | אני 589 | שולח 7971 | אותך 853 | אליהם 413 | ואמרת 559 | אליהם 413
uahabaniym, | qashey | paniym | uachizqey | leb, | 'aniy | shouleach | 'autaka | 'aleyhem; | ua'amarta | 'aleyhem,
**For children *they are* | impudent | against | and stiff | hearted | I | I do send | you | unto them | and you shall say | unto them**

**2:5**
כה 3541 | אמר 559 | אדני 136 | יהוה 3069: | והמה 1992 | אם 518 | ישמעו 8085 | ואם 518 | יחדלו 2308 | כי 3588 | בית 1004 | מרי 4805
koh | 'amar | 'adonay | Yahuah. | uahemah | 'am | yishma'au | ua'am | yechdalu, | kiy | beyt | mariy
**Thus | saith | Adonai | Yahuah | And they | whether | they will hear | or whether | they will forbear | for *are* | a house | rebellious**

**2:6**
המה 1992 | וידעו 3045 | כי 3588 | נביא 5030 | היה 1961 | בתוכם 8432: | ואתה 859 | בן 1121 | אדם 120 | אל 408 | תירא 3372 | מהם 1992
hemah; | uayada'au, | kiy | nabiy'a | hayah | batoukam. | ua'atah | ben | 'adam | 'al | tiyraa' | mehem
**they | yet shall know | that | a prophet | there has been | among them | And you | son of | man | not | be afraid | of them**

ומדבריהם 1697 | אל 408 | תירא 3372 | כי 3588 | סרבים 5621 | וסלונים 5544 | אותך 854 | ואל 413 | עקרבים 6137 | אתה 859 | יושב 3427
uamidibreyhem | 'al | tiyraa', | kiy | sarabiym | uasalouniym | autak, | ua'al | 'aqrabiym | 'atah | yousheb;
**of their words | neither | be afraid | though | briers | and thorns *be* | with you | and among | scorpions | you | do dwell**

**2:7**
מדבריהם 1697 | אל 408 | תירא 3372 | ומפניהם 6440 | אל 408 | תחת 2865 | כי 3588 | בית 1004 | מרי 4805 | המה 1992:
midibareyhem | 'al | tiyraa' | uamipaneyhem | 'al | techat, | kiy | beyt | mariy | hemah.
**of their words | not | be afraid | at their looks | nor | be dismayed | though *be* | a house | rebellious | they**

ודברת 1696 | את 853 | דברי 1697 | אליהם 413 | אם 518 | ישמעו 8085 | ואם 518 | יחדלו 2308 | כי 3588
uadibarta | 'at | dabaray | 'aleyhem, | 'am | yishma'au | ua'am | yechdalu; | kiy
**And you shall speak | | my words | unto them | whether | they will hear | or whether | they will forbear | for**

**2:8**
מרי 4805 | המה 1992: | ואתה 859 | בן 1121 | אדם 120 | שמע 8085 | את 853 | אשר 834 | אני 589 | מדבר 1696 | אליך 413 | אל 408 | תהי 1961 | מרי 4805
mariy | hemah. | ua'atah | ben | 'adam, | shama' | 'at | 'asher | 'aniy | madaber | 'aeleyka, | 'al | tahiy | meriy
***are* most rebellious | they | But you | son of | man | hear | | what | I | say | unto you | not | Be you | rebellious**

**2:9**
כבית 1004 | המרי 4805 | פצה 6475 | פיך 6310 | ואכל 398 | את 853 | אשר 834 | אני 589 | נתן 5414 | אליך 413: | ואראה 7200 | והנה 2009
kabeyt | hameriy; | patzeh | piyka, | ua'akol | 'at | 'asher | 'aniy | noten | 'aeleyka. | ua'ar'ah | uahineh
**like house that | rebellious | open | your mouth | and eat | | that | I | give | you | And when I looked | and behold**

**2:10**
יד 3027 | שלוחה 7971 | אלי 413 | והנה 2009 | בו 871a | מגלת 4039 | ספר 5612: | ויפרש 6566 | אותה 853 | לפני 6440 | והיא 1931 | כתובה 3789
yad | shaluchah | 'aelay; | uahineh | bou | magilat | seper. | uayipros | 'autah | lapanay, | uahiy'a | katubah
**an hand | *was* sent | unto me | and lo *was* | therein | a roll of | a book | And he spread | it | before me | and it | *was* written**

פנים 6440 | ואחור 268 | וכתוב 3789 | אליה 413 | קנים 7015 | והגה 1899 | והי 1958:
paniym | ua'achour; | uakatub | 'aeleyha, | qiniym | uahegeh | uahiy.
**within | and without | and *there was* written | therein | lamentations | and mourning | and woe**

**Ezek 3:1**
ויאמר 559 | אלי 413 | בן 1121 | אדם 120 | את 853 | אשר 834 | תמצא 4672 | אכול 398 | אכול 398 | את 853 | המגלה 4039 | הזאת 2063 | ולך 1980
uaya'mer | 'aelay, | ben | 'adam | 'at | 'asher | timtzaa' | 'akoul; | 'akoul | 'at | hamagilah | haza't, | ualek
**Moreover he said | unto me | Son of | man | | that | you find | eat | eat | | roll | this | and go**

Eze 2:4 For they are impudent children and stiffhearted. I do send you unto them; and you shall say unto them, Thus saith YHUH G-D.5 And they, whether they will hear, or whether they will forbear, (for they are a rebellious house,) yet shall know that there has been a prophet among them.6 And you, son of man, be not afraid of them, neither be afraid of their words, though briers and thorns be with you, and you dost dwell among scorpions: be not afraid of their words, nor be dismayed at their looks, though they be a rebellious house.7 And you shall speak my words unto them, whether they will hear, or whether they will forbear: for they are most rebellious.8 But you, son of man, hear what I say unto you; Be not you rebellious like that rebellious house: open your mouth, and eat that I give you.9 And when I looked, behold, an hand was sent unto me; and, lo, a roll of a book was therein;10 And he spread it before me; and it was written within and without: and there was written therein lamentations, and mourning, and woe. **Eze** 3:1 Moreover he said unto me, Son of man, eat that you findest; eat this roll, and go speak unto the house of Israel.

דבר 1696 אל 413 בית 1004 ישראל 3478: 3:2 ואפתח 6605 את 853 פי 6310 ויאכלני 398 את 853 המגלה 4039 הזאת 2063: 3:3
daber 'al beyt yisra'ael. ua'aptach 'at piy; uaya'akileniy, 'at hamagilah haza't.
**speak unto the house of Israel So I opened my mouth and he caused me to eat roll this**

ויאמר 559 אלי 413 בן 1121 אדם 120 בטנך 990 תאכל 398 ומעיך 4578 תמלא 4390 את 854 המגלה 4039 הזאת 2063 אשר 834 אני 589
uaya'mer 'aelay, ben 'adam bitnaka ta'akel uame'ayka tamalea', 'at hamagilah haza't, 'asher 'aniy
**And he said unto me Son of man your belly cause to eat and your bowels fill *with* roll this that I**

נתן 5414 אליך 413 ואכלה 398 ותהי 1961 בפי 6310 כדבש 1706 למתוק 4966: 3:4 ויאמר 559 אלי 413 בן 1121 אדם 120
noten 'aeleyka; ua'akalah, uatahiy bapiy kidbash lamatouq. uaya'mer 'aelay; ben 'adam,
**give to you Then did I eat *it* and it was in my mouth as honey for sweetness And he said unto me Son of man**

לך 1980 בא 935 אל 413 בית 1004 ישראל 3478 ודברת 1696 בדברי 1697 אליהם 413: 3:5 כי 3588 לא 3808 אל 413 עם 5971 עמקי 6012
lek ba' 'al beyt yisra'ael, uadibarta bidbaray 'aleyhem. kiy la' 'al 'am 'amqey
**go you get you unto the house of Israel and speak with my words unto them For not to a people of a strange**

שפה 8193 וכבדי 3515 לשון 3956 אתה 859 שלוח 7971 אל 413 בית 1004 ישראל 3478: 3:6 לא 3808 אל 413 עמים 5971 רבים 7227 עמקי 6012
sapah uakibdey lashoun 'atah shaluach; 'al beyt yisra'ael. la' 'al 'amiym rabiym, 'amqey
**speech and an hard of language you *are* sent *but* to the house of Israel Not to people of many a strange**

שפה 8193 וכבדי 3515 לשון 3956 אשר 834 לא 3808 תשמע 8085 דבריהם 1697 אם 518 לא 3808 אליהם 413 שלחתיך 7971 המה 1992
sapah uakibdey lashoun, 'asher la' tishma' dibreyhem; 'am la' 'aleyhem shalachtiyka, hemah
**speech and an hard of language whose not you can understand words Surely not to them had I sent they**

ישמעו 8085 אליך 413: 3:7 ובית 1004 ישראל 3478 לא 3808 יאבו 14 לשמע 8085 אליך 413 כי 3588 אינם 369 אבים 14
yishma'au 'aeleyka. uabeyt yisra'ael, la' ya'bu lishmoa' 'aeleyka, kiy 'aeynam 'abiym
**would have hearkened unto you But the house of Israel not will listen unto you for not they will**

לשמע 8085 אלי 413 כי 3588 כל 3605 בית 1004 ישראל 3478 חזקי 2389 מצח 4696 וקשי 7186 לב 3820 המה 1992: 3:8 הנה 2009
lishmoa' 'aelay; kiy kal beyt yisra'ael, chizaqey metzach uaqshey leb hemah. hineh
**listen unto me for all the house of Israel *are* impudent brow and hard hearted they Behold**

נתתי 5414 את 853 פניך 6440 חזקים 2389 לעמת 5980 פניהם 6440 ואת 853 מצחך 4696 חזק 2389 לעמת 5980 מצחם 4696: 3:9
natatiy 'at paneyka chazaqiym la'amat paneyhem; ua'at mitzachaka chazaq la'amat mitzacham.
**I have made your face strong against their faces *and* your forehead strong against their foreheads**

כשמיר 8068 חזק 2389 מצר 6864 נתתי 5414 מצחך 4696 לא 3808 תירא 3372 אותם 853 ולא 3808 תחת 2865 מפניהם 6440
kashamiyr chazaq mitzor natatiy mitzacheka; la' tiyraa' 'autam uala' techat mipaneyhem,
**As an adamant harder than flint have I made your forehead not fear them neither be dismayed at their looks**

כי 3588 בית 1004 מרי 4805 המה 1992: 3:10 ויאמר 559 אלי 413 בן 1121 אדם 120 את 853 כל 3605 דברי 1697 אשר 834
kiy beyt mariy hemah. uaya'mer 'aelay; ben 'adam 'at kal dabaray 'asher
**though *be* a house rebellious they Moreover he said unto me Son of man all my words that**

אדבר 1696 אליך 413 קח 3947 בלבבך 3824 ובאזניך 241 שמע 8085: 3:11 ולך 1980 בא 935 אל 413 הגולה 1473
'adaber 'aeleyka, qach bilbabaka uab'azaneyka shama'. ualek ba' 'al hagoulah
**I shall speak unto you receive in your heart and with your ears hear And go get you to them of the captivity**

Eze 3:2 So I opened my mouth, and he caused me to eat that roll.3 And he said unto me, Son of man, cause your belly to eat, and fill your bowels with this roll that I give you. Then did I eat it; and it was in my mouth as honey for sweetness.4 And he said unto me, Son of man, go, get you unto the house of Israel, and speak with my words unto them.5 For you are not sent to a people of a strange speech and of an hard language, but to the house of Israel;6 Not to many people of a strange speech and of an hard language, whose words you canst not understand. Surely, had I sent you to them, they would have hearkened unto you.7 But the house of Israel will not hear unto you; for they will not hear unto me: for all the house of Israel are impudent and hardhearted.8 Behold, I have made your face strong against their faces, and your forehead strong against their foreheads.9 As an adamant harder than flint have I made your forehead: fear them not, neither be dismayed at their looks, though they be a rebellious house.10 Moreover he said unto me, Son of man, all my words that I shall speak unto you receive in your heart, and hear with your ears.11 And go, get you to them of the captivity, unto the children of your people, and speak unto them, and tell them, Thus saith YHUH G-D; whether they will hear, or whether they will forbear.

| אל 413 | בני 1121 | עמך 5971 | ודברת 1696 | אליהם 413 | ואמרת 559 | אליהם 413 | כה 3541 | אמר 559 | אדני 136 | יהוה 3069 | אם 518 |
|---|---|---|---|---|---|---|---|---|---|---|---|
| 'al | baney | 'ameka, | uadibarta | 'aleyhem | ua'amarta | 'aleyhem, | koh | 'amar | 'adonay | Yahuah; | 'am |
| **unto** | **the children of** | **your people** | **and speak** | **unto them** | **and tell** | **them** | **Thus** | **saith** | **Adonai** | **Yahuah** | **whether** |

| ישמעו 8085 | ואם 518 | יחדלו 2308: | 3:12 ותשאני 5375 | רוח 7307 | ואשמע 8085 | אחרי 310 | קול 6963 | רעש 7494 |
|---|---|---|---|---|---|---|---|---|
| yishma'au | ua'am | yechdalu. | uatisa'aeniy | ruach, | ua'ashma' | 'acharay, | qoul | ra'ash |
| **they will hear** | **or whether** | **they will forbear** | **Then took me up** | **the spirit** | **and I heard** | **behind me** | **a voice of** | **a rushing** |

| גדול 1419 | ברוך 1288 | כבוד 3519 | יהוה 3068 | ממקומו 4725: | 3:13 וקול 6963 | כנפי 3671 | החיות 2416 |
|---|---|---|---|---|---|---|---|
| gadoul; | baruk | kaboud | Yahuah | mimaqoumou. | uaqoul | kanpey | hachayout, |
| **great *saying*** | **Blessed *be*** | **the glory of** | **Yahuah** | **from his place** | ***I heard* also the noise of** | **the wings of** | **the living creatures** |

| משיקות 5401 | אשה 802 | אל 413 | אחותה 269 | וקול 6963 | האופנים 212 | לעמתם 5980 | וקול 6963 | רעש 7494 |
|---|---|---|---|---|---|---|---|---|
| mashiyqout | 'ashah | 'al | achoutah, | uaqoul | ha'aupaniym | la'amatam; | uaqoul | ra'ash |
| **that touched** | **one** | **to** | **another of her** | **and the noise of** | **the wheels** | **over against them** | **and a noise of** | **a rushing** |

| גדול 1419: | 3:14 ורוח 7307 | נשאתני 5375 | ותקחני 3947 | ואלך 1980 | מר 4751 | בחמת 2534 | רוחי 7307 | ויד 3027 |
|---|---|---|---|---|---|---|---|---|
| gadoul. | uaruach | nasa'atniy | uatiqacheniy; | ua'aelek | mar | bachamat | ruchiy, | uayad |
| **great** | **So the spirit** | **lifted me up** | **and took me away** | **and I went in** | **bitterness** | **in the heat of** | **my spirit** | **but the hand of** |

| יהוה 3068 | עלי 5921 | חזקה 2389: | 3:15 ואבוא 935 | אל 413 | הגולה 1473 | תל 8512 | אביב 24 | הישבים 3427 | אל 413 | נהר 5104 |
|---|---|---|---|---|---|---|---|---|---|---|
| Yahuah | 'alay | chazaqah. | ua'abou'a | 'al | hagoulah | tel | 'abiyb | hayoshbiym | 'al | nahar |
| **Yahuah** | **upon me** | **was strong** | **Then I came** | **to** | **them of the captivity at** | **Tel** | **abib** | **that dwelt** | **by** | **the river of** |

| כבר 3529 | ואשר 834 | המה 1992 | יושבים 3427 | שם 8033 | ואשב 3427 | שם 8033 | שבעת 7651 | ימים 3117 | משמים 8074 | בתוכם 8432: | 3:16 |
|---|---|---|---|---|---|---|---|---|---|---|---|
| kabar | ua'asher | hemah | youshabiym | sham; | ua'aesheb | sham | shib'at | yamiym | mashmiym | batoukam. | |
| **Chebar** | **and I sat** | **they** | **sat** | **where** | **and remained** | **there** | **seven** | **days** | **astonished** | **among them** | |

| ויהי 1961 | מקצה 7097 | שבעת 7651 | ימים 3117 | ויהי 1961 | דבר 1697 | יהוה 3068 | אלי 413 | לאמר 559: | 3:17 בן 1121 | אדם 120 |
|---|---|---|---|---|---|---|---|---|---|---|
| uayahiy | miqtzeh | shib'at | yamiym; | uayahiy | dabar | Yahuah | 'aelay | lea'mor. | ben | 'adam |
| **And it came to pass** | **at the end of** | **seven** | **days** | **that came** | **the word of** | **Yahuah** | **unto me** | **saying** | **Son of** | **man** |

| צפה 6822 | נתתיך 5414 | לבית 1004 | ישראל 3478 | ושמעת 8085 | מפי 6310 | דבר 1697 | והזהרת 2094 | אותם 853 |
|---|---|---|---|---|---|---|---|---|
| tzopeh | natatiyka | labeyt | yisra'ael; | uashama'ta | mipiy | dabar, | uahizharta | 'autam |
| **a watchman** | **I have made you** | **unto the house of** | **Israel** | **therefore hear** | **at my mouth** | **the word** | **and give warning** | **them** |

| ממני 4480: | 3:18 באמרי 559 | לרשע 7563 | מות 4194 | תמות 4191 | ולא 3808 | הזהרתו 2094 | ולא 3808 | דברת 1696 |
|---|---|---|---|---|---|---|---|---|
| mimeniy. | ba'amariy | larasha' | mout | tamut, | uala' | hizhartou, | uala' | dibarta |
| **from me** | **When I say** | **unto the wicked** | **You shall surely** | **die** | **and not** | **you give him warning** | **nor** | **speak** |

| להזהיר 2094 | רשע 7563 | מדרכו 1870 | הרשעה 7563 | לחיתו 2421 | הוא 1931 | רשע 7563 | בעונו 5771 | ימות 4191 | ודמו 1818 |
|---|---|---|---|---|---|---|---|---|---|
| lahazhiyr | rasha' | midarkou | harasha'ah | lachayotou; | hua' | rasha' | ba'auonou | yamut, | uadamou |
| **to warn** | **the wicked** | **from his way** | **wicked** | **to save his life** | **the same** | **wicked** | **in his iniquity** | ***man* shall die** | **but his blood** |

| מידך 3027 | אבקש 1245: | 3:19 ואתה 859 | כי 3588 | הזהרת 2094 | רשע 7563 | ולא 3808 | שב 7725 | מרשעו 7562 |
|---|---|---|---|---|---|---|---|---|
| miyadaka | 'abaqesh. | ua'atah | kiy | hizharta | rasha', | uala' | shab | merish'au, |
| **at your hand** | **will I require** | **Yet you** | **if** | **warn** | **the wicked** | **does not** | **and he turn not** | **from his wickedness** |

Eze 3:12 Then the spirit took me up, and I heard behind me a voice of a great rushing, saying, Blessed be the glory of YHUH from his place.13 I heard also the noise of the wings of the living creatures that touched one another, and the noise of the wheels over against them, and a noise of a great rushing.14 So the spirit lifted me up, and took me away, and I went in bitterness, in the heat of my spirit; but the hand of YHUH was strong upon me.15 Then I came to them of the captivity at Tel-abib, that dwelt by the river of Chebar, and I sat where they sat, and remained there astonished among them seven days.16 And it came to pass at the end of seven days, that the word of YHUH came unto me, saying,17 Son of man, I have made you a watchman unto the house of Israel: therefore hear the word at my mouth, and give them warning from me.18 When I say unto the wicked, Thou shall surely die; and you givest him not warning, nor speak to warn the wicked from his wicked way, to save his life; the same wicked man shall die in his iniquity; but his blood will I require at your hand.19 Yet if you warn the wicked, and he turn not from his wickedness, nor from his wicked way, he shall die in his iniquity; but you have delivered your soul.

| ומדרכו 1870 | הרשעה 7563 | הוא 1931 | בעונו 5771 | ימות 4191 | ואתה 859 | את 853 | נפשך 5315 | הצלת 5337: | 3:20 |
|---|---|---|---|---|---|---|---|---|---|
| uamidarkou | harasha'ah; | hua' | ba'auonou | yamut, | ua'atah | 'at | napshaka | hitzalta. | |
| **way** | **nor from his wicked** | **he** | **in his iniquity** | **shall die** | **but you** | | **your soul** | **have delivered** | |

| ובשוב 7725 | צדיק 6662 | מצדקו 6664 | ועשה 6213 | עול 5766 | ונתתי 5414 | מכשול 4383 | לפניו 6440 |
|---|---|---|---|---|---|---|---|
| uabshub | tzadiyq | mitzidqou | ua'asah | 'auel, | uanatatiy | mikshoul | lapanayu |
| **Again, When does turn** | **a righteous *man*** | **from his righteousness** | **and commit** | **iniquity** | **and I lay** | **a stumblingblock** | **before him** |

| הוא 1931 | ימות 4191 | כי 3588 | לא 3808 | הזהרתו 2094 | בחטאתו 2403 | ימות 4191 | ולא 3808 | תזכרן 2142 |
|---|---|---|---|---|---|---|---|---|
| hua' | yamut; | kiy | la' | hizhartou | bachata'tou | yamut, | uala' | tizakarna, |
| **he** | **shall die** | **because** | **not** | **you have given him warning** | **in his sin** | **he shall die** | **and not** | **shall be remembered** |

| צדקתו 6666 | אשר 834 | עשה 6213 | ודמו 1818 | מידך 3027 | אבקש 1245: | 3:21 | ואתה 859 | כי 3588 | הזהרתו 2094 |
|---|---|---|---|---|---|---|---|---|---|
| tzidqotau | 'asher | 'asah, | uadamou | miyadaka | 'abaqesh. | | ua'atah | kiy | hizhartou |
| **his righteousness** | **which** | **he has done** | **but his blood** | **at your hand** | **will I require** | | **Nevertheless you** | **if** | **warn** |

| צדיק 6662 | לבלתי 1115 | חטא 2398 | צדיק 6662 | והוא 1931 | לא 3808 | חטא 2398 | חיו 2421 | יחיה 2421 | כי 3588 | נזהר 2094 |
|---|---|---|---|---|---|---|---|---|---|---|
| tzadiyq, | labiltiy | chata' | tzadiyq | uahu'a | la' | chata'; | chayou | yichayeh | kiy | nizhar, |
| ***the* righteous *man*** | **that not** | **sin** | **the righteous** | **and he** | **not** | **does sin** | **he shall surely** | **live** | **because** | **he is warned** |

| ואתה 859 | את 853 | נפשך 5315 | הצלת 5337: | 3:22 | ותהי 1961 | עלי 5921 | שם 8033 | יד 3027 | יהוה 3068 | ויאמר 559 | אלי 413 | קום 6965 |
|---|---|---|---|---|---|---|---|---|---|---|---|---|
| ua'atah | 'at | napshaka | hitzalta. | | uatahiy | 'alay | sham | yad | Yahuah; | uaya'mer | 'aelay, | qum |
| **also you** | | **your soul** | **have delivered** | | **And was** | **upon me** | **there** | **the hand of** | **Yahuah** | **and he said** | **unto me** | **Arise** |

| צא 3318 | אל 413 | הבקעה 1237 | ושם 8033 | אדבר 1696 | אותך 854: | 3:23 | ואקום 6965 | ואצא 3318 | אל 413 | הבקעה 1237 | והנה 2009 | שם 8033 |
|---|---|---|---|---|---|---|---|---|---|---|---|---|
| tzea' | 'al | habiq'ah, | uasham | 'adaber | autak. | | ua'aqum | ua'aetzea' | 'al | habiq'ah | uahineh | sham |
| **go forth** | **into** | **the plain** | **and there** | **I will talk** | **with you** | | **Then I arose** | **and went forth** | **into** | **the plain** | **and behold** | **there** |

| כבוד 3519 | יהוה 3068 | עמד 5975 | ככבוד 3519 | אשר 834 | ראיתי 7200 | על 5921 | נהר 5104 | כבר 3529 | ואפל 5307 | על 5921 | פני 6440: | 3:24 |
|---|---|---|---|---|---|---|---|---|---|---|---|---|
| kaboud | Yahuah | 'amed, | kakaboud | 'asher | ra'aytiy | 'al | nahar | kabar; | ua'apol | 'al | panay. | |
| **the glory of** | **Yahuah** | **stood** | **as the glory** | **which** | **I saw** | **by** | **the river of** | **Chebar** | **and I fell** | **on** | **my face** | |

| ותבא 935 | בי 871a | רוח 7307 | ותעמדני 5975 | על 5921 | רגלי 7272 | וידבר 1696 | אתי 854 | ויאמר 559 | אלי 413 | בא 935 | הסגר 5462 |
|---|---|---|---|---|---|---|---|---|---|---|---|
| uataba' | biy | ruach, | uata'amideniy | 'al | raglay; | uaydaber | 'atiy | uaya'mer | 'aelay, | ba' | hisager |
| **Then entered** | **into me** | **the spirit** | **and set me** | **upon** | **my feet** | **and spoke** | **with me** | **and said** | **unto me** | **Go** | **shut yourself** |

| בתוך 8432 | ביתך 1004: | 3:25 | ואתה 859 | בן 1121 | אדם 120 | הנה 2009 | נתנו 5414 | עליך 5921 | עבותים 5688 | ואסרוך 631 | בהם 871a |
|---|---|---|---|---|---|---|---|---|---|---|---|
| batouk | beytaka. | | ua'atah | ben | 'adam, | hineh | natanu | 'aleyka | aboutiym, | ua'asaruka | bahem; |
| **within** | **your house** | | **But you** | **O son of** | **man** | **behold** | **they shall put** | **upon you** | **bands** | **and shall bind you** | **with them** |

| ולא 3808 | תצא 3318 | בתוכם 8432: | 3:26 | ולשונך 3956 | אדביק 1692 | אל 413 | חכך 2441 |
|---|---|---|---|---|---|---|---|
| uala' | tetzea' | batoukam. | | ualshounaka | 'adbiyq | 'al | chikeka, |
| **and not** | **you shall go out** | **among them** | | **And your tongue** | **I will make cleave** | **to** | ***the* roof of your mouth** |

| ונאלמת 481 | ולא 3808 | תהיה 1961 | להם 3807a | לאיש 376 | מוכיח 3198 | כי 3588 | בית 1004 | מרי 4805 | המה 1992: |
|---|---|---|---|---|---|---|---|---|---|
| uane'alamta, | uala' | tihayeh | lahem | la'aysh | moukiyach; | kiy | beyt | mariy | hemah. |
| **that you shall be dumb** | **and not** | **shall be** | **to them** | **man** | **reprover** | **for *are*** | **a house** | **rebellious** | **they** |

Eze 3:20 Again, When a righteous man doth turn from his righteousness, and commit iniquity, and I lay a stumblingblock before him, he shall die: because you have not given him warning, he shall die in his sin, and his righteousness which he has done shall not be remembered; but his blood will I require at your hand.21 Nevertheless if you warn the righteous man, that the righteous sin not, and he doth not sin, he shall surely live, because he is warned; also you have delivered your soul.22 And the hand of YHUH was there upon me; and he said unto me, Arise, go forth into the plain, and I will there talk with you.23 Then I arose, and went forth into the plain: and, behold, the glory of YHUH stood there, as the glory which I saw by the river of Chebar: and I fell on my face.24 Then the spirit entered into me, and set me upon my feet, and spoke with me, and said unto me, Go, shut thyself within your house.25 But you, O son of man, behold, they shall put bands upon you, and shall bind you with them, and you shall not go out among them:26 And I will make your tongue cleave to the roof of your mouth, that you shall be dumb, and shall not be to them a reprover: for they are a rebellious house.

**3:27**
ובדברי 1696 אותך 854 אפתח 6605 את 853 פיך 6310 ואמרת 559 אליהם 413 כה 3541 אמר 559 אדני 136 יהוה 3068
uabdabariy 'autaka 'aptach 'at piyka, ua'amarta 'aleyhem, koh 'amar 'adonay Yahuah;
**But when I speak with you I will open your mouth and you shall say unto them Thus saith Adonai Yahuah**

השמע 8085 ישמע 8085 והחדל 2310 יחדל 2308 כי 3588 בית 1004 מרי 4805 המה 1992:
hashomea' yishma' uahechadel yechdal, kiy beyt mariy hemah.
**He that hear let him hear and he that forbeareth let him forbear for *are* a house rebellious they**

**Ezek 4:1**
ואתה 859 בן 1121 אדם 120 קח 3947 לך 3807a לבנה 3843 ונתתה 5414 אותה 853 לפניך 6440 וחקות 2710 עליה 5921 עיר 5892 את 853
ua'atah ben 'adam qach laka labenah, uanatatah 'autah lapaneyka; uachaqouta 'aleyha 'ayr 'at
**You also son of man take to you a tile and lay it before you and pourtray upon it the city**

ירושלם 3389: **4:2** ונתתה 5414 עליה 5921 מצור 4692 ובנית 1129 עליה 5921 דיק 1785 ושפכת 8210 עליה 5921 סללה 5550 ונתתה 5414
yarushalaim. uanatatah 'aeleyha matzour, uabaniyta 'aeleyha dayeq, uashapakta 'aeleyha solalah; uanatatah
***even* Jerusalem And lay against it siege and build against it a fort and cast against it a mount set also**

עליה 5921 מחנות 4264 ושים 7760 עליה 5921 כרים 3733 סביב 5439: **4:3** ואתה 859 קח 3947 לך 3807a מחבת 4227 ברזל 1270
'aeleyha machanout vesim 'aleyha kariym sabiyb. ua'atah qach laka machabat barzel,
**against it the camp and set against it *battering* rams round about Moreover you take you unto an pan iron**

ונתתה 5414 אותה 853 קיר 7023 ברזל 1270 בינך 996 ובין 996 העיר 5892 והכינתה 3559 את 853 פניך 6440 אליה 413
uanatatah 'autah qiyr barzel, beynaka uabeyn ha'ayr; uahakiynotah 'at paneyka 'aeleyha
**and set it *for* a wall of iron between you and between the city and set your face against it**

והיתה 1961 במצור 4692 וצרת 6696 עליה 5921 אות 226 היא 1931 לבית 1004 ישראל 3478: **4:4** ואתה 859
uahayatah bamatzour uatzarta 'aleyha, 'aut hiy'a labeyt yisra'ael. ua'atah
**and it shall be besieged and you shall lay siege against it *shall be* a sign This to the house of Israel you also**

שכב 7901 על 5921 צדך 6654 השמאלי 8042 ושמת 7760 את 853 עון 5771 בית 1004 ישראל 3478 עליו 5921 מספר 4557
shakab 'al tzidaka hasama'liy, uasamta 'at 'auon beyt yisra'ael 'alayu; mispar
**Lie upon side your left and lay the iniquity of the house of Israel upon it *according* to the number of**

הימים 3117 אשר 834 תשכב 7901 עליו 5921 תשא 5375 את 853 עונם 5771: **4:5** ואני 589 נתתי 5414 לך 3807a את 853 שני 8147
hayamiym 'asher tishkab 'aelayu, tisa' 'at 'auonam. ua'aniy, natatiy laka 'at shaney
**the days that you shall lie upon it you shall bear their iniquity For I have laid upon you the years of**

עונם 5771 למספר 4557 ימים 3117 שלש 7969 מאות 3967 ותשעים 8673 יום 3117 ונשאת 5375 עון 5771
'auonam, lamispar yamiym, shalosh me'aut uatish'aym youm; uanasa'ta 'auon
**their iniquity according to the number of the days three hundred and ninety days so shall you bear the iniquity of**

בית 1004 ישראל 3478: **4:6** וכלית 3615 את 853 אלה 428 ושכבת 7901 על 5921 צדך 6654 הימוני 3227 שנית 8145
beyt yisra'ael. uakiliyta 'at 'aeleh, uashakabta 'al tzidaka hayamouniy sheniyt,
**the house of Israel And when you have accomplished them lie on side your right again**

ונשאת 5375 את 853 עון 5771 בית 1004 יהודה 3063 ארבעים 705 יום 3117 יום 3117 לשנה 8141 יום 3117 לשנה 8141
uanasa'ta 'at 'auon beyt yahudah; 'arba'aym youm, youm lashanah youm lashanah
**and you shall bear the iniquity of the house of Judah forty days each for day a year**

Eze 3:27 But when I speak with you, I will open your mouth, and you shall say unto them, Thus saith YHUH G-D; He that hear, let him hear; and he that forbeareth, let him forbear: for they are a rebellious house. **Eze** 4:1 Thou also, son of man, take you a tile, and lay it before you, and pourtray upon it the city, even Jerusalem:2 And lay siege against it, and build a fort against it, and cast a mount against it; set the camp also against it, and set battering rams against it round about.3 Moreover take you unto you an iron pan, and set it for a wall of iron between you and the city: and set your face against it, and it shall be besieged, and you shall lay siege against it. This shall be a sign to the house of Israel.4 Lie you also upon your left side, and lay the iniquity of the house of Israel upon it: according to the number of the days that you shall lie upon it you shall bear their iniquity.5 For I have laid upon you the years of their iniquity, according to the number of the days, three hundred and ninety days: so shall you bear the iniquity of the house of Israel.6 And when you have accomplished them, lie again on your right side, and you shall bear the iniquity of the house of Judah forty days: I have appointed you each day for a year.

| נתתיו 5414 | לך 3807a: | 4:7 ואל 413 | מצור 4692 | ירושלם 3389 | תכין 3559 | פניך 6440 | וזרעך 2220 |
|---|---|---|---|---|---|---|---|
| natatiyu | lak. | ua'al | matzour | yarushalaim | takiyn | paneyka, | uazro'aka |
| **I have appointed** | **to you** | **Therefore toward** | **the siege of** | **Jerusalem** | **you shall set** | **your face** | **and your arm** |

| חשופה 2834 | ונבאת 5012 | עליה 5921: | 4:8 והנה 2009 | נתתי 5414 | עליך 5921 | עבותים 5688 | ולא 3808 | תהפך 2015 |
|---|---|---|---|---|---|---|---|---|
| chasupah; | uanibea'ta | 'aleyha. | uahineh | natatiy | 'aleyka | aboutiym; | uala' | tehapek |
| ***shall be* uncovered** | **and you shall prophesy** | **against it** | **And behold** | **I will lay** | **upon you** | **bands** | **and not** | **you shall turn** |

| מצדך 6654 | אל 413 | צדך 6654 | עד 5704 | כלותך 3615 | ימי 3117 | מצורך 4692: | 4:9 ואתה 859 | קח 3947 | לך 3807a | חטין 2406 |
|---|---|---|---|---|---|---|---|---|---|---|
| mitzidaka | 'al | tzideka, | 'ad | kaloutaka | yamey | matzureka. | ua'atah | qach | laka | chitiyn |
| **you from one side** | **to** | **another** | **till** | **you have ended** | **the days of** | **your siege** | **you also** | **Take** | **unto you** | **wheat** |

| ושערים 8184 | ופול 6321 | ועדשים 5742 | ודחן 1764 | וכסמים 3698 | ונתתה 5414 | אותם 853 | בכלי 3627 | אחד 259 | ועשית 6213 | אותם 853 | לך 3807a |
|---|---|---|---|---|---|---|---|---|---|---|---|
| uasa'ariym | uapoul | ua'adashiym | uadochan | uakusmiym, | uanatatah | 'autam | bikliy | 'achad, | ua'asiyta | 'autam | laka |
| **and barley** | **and beans** | **and lentiles** | **and millet** | **and fitches** | **and put** | **them** | **in vessel** | **one** | **and make** | **you** | **thereof** |

| ללחם 3899 | מספר 4557 | הימים 3117 | אשר 834 | אתה 859 | שוכב 7901 | על 5921 | צדך 6654 | שלש 7969 | מאות 3967 | ותשעים 8673 | יום 3117 |
|---|---|---|---|---|---|---|---|---|---|---|---|
| lalachem; | mispar | hayamiym | 'asher | 'atah | shoukeb | 'al | tzidaka, | shalosh | me'aut | uatish'aym | youm |
| **bread** | ***according* to the number of** | **the days** | **that** | **you** | **shall lie** | **upon** | **your side** | **three** | **hundred** | **and ninety** | **days** |

| תאכלנו 398: | 4:10 ומאכלך 3978 | אשר 834 | תאכלנו 398 | במשקול 4946 | עשרים 6242 | שקל 8255 | ליום 3117 | מעת 6256 | עד 5704 |
|---|---|---|---|---|---|---|---|---|---|
| ta'kalenu. | uama'akalaka | 'asher | ta'kalenu, | bamishqoul | 'asriym | sheqel | layoum; | me'aut | 'ad |
| **shall you eat thereof** | **And your meat** | **which** | **you shall eat** | ***shall be* by weight** | **twenty** | **shekels** | **a day** | **from time** | **to** |

| עת 6256 | תאכלנו 398: | 4:11 ומים 4325 | במשורה 4884 | תשתה 8354 | ששית 8345 | ההין 1969 | מעת 6256 | עד 5704 | עת 6256 |
|---|---|---|---|---|---|---|---|---|---|
| 'at | ta'kalenu. | uamayim | bimsurah | tishteh | shishiyt | hahiyn; | me'aut | 'ad | 'at |
| **time** | **shall you eat it** | **also water** | **by measure** | **You shall drink** | **the sixth part of** | **an hin** | **from time** | **to** | **time** |

| תשתה 8354: | 4:12 ועגת 5692 | שערים 8184 | תאכלנה 398 | והיא 1931 | בגללי 1561 | צאת 6627 | האדם 120 | תעגנה 5746 |
|---|---|---|---|---|---|---|---|---|
| tishteh. | ua'agat | sa'ariym | ta'kalenah; | uahiy'a, | bagelaley | tzea't | ha'adam, | ta'agenah |
| **shall you drink** | **And cakes** | ***as* barley** | **you shall eat it** | **and it** | **with dung** | **that comes out of** | **man** | **you shall bake** |

| לעיניהם 5869: | 4:13 ויאמר 559 | יהוה 3068 | ככה 3602 | יאכלו 398 | בני 1121 | ישראל 3478 | את 853 | לחמם 3899 | טמא 2931 |
|---|---|---|---|---|---|---|---|---|---|
| la'aeyneyhem. | uaya'mer | Yahuah, | kakah | ya'kalu | baney | yisra'ael | 'at | lachmam | tamea'; |
| **in their sight** | **And said** | **Yahuah** | **Even thus** | **shall eat** | **the children of** | **Israel** | | **their bread** | **defiled** |

| בגוים 1471 | אשר 834 | אדיחם 5080 | שם 8033: | 4:14 ואמר 559 | אהה 162 | אדני 136 | יהוה 3068 | הנה 2009 | נפשי 5315 | לא 3808 |
|---|---|---|---|---|---|---|---|---|---|---|
| bagouyim | 'asher | 'adiychem | sham. | ua'amar, | 'ahah | 'adonay | Yahuah, | hineh | napshiy | la' |
| **among the Gentiles** | **where** | **I will drive them** | **there** | **Then said I** | **Ah** | **Adonai** | **Yahuah** | **behold** | **my soul** | **not** |

| מטמאה 2930 | ונבלה 5038 | וטרפה 2966 | לא 3808 | אכלתי 398 | מנעורי 5271 | ועד 5704 | עתה 6258 |
|---|---|---|---|---|---|---|---|
| matuma'ah; | uanbelah | uatrepah | la' | 'akaltiy | mina'auray | ua'ad | 'atah, |
| **has been polluted** | **for of that which die of itself** | **or is torn in pieces** | **not** | **have I eaten** | **from my youth up** | **even till** | **now** |

| ולא 3808 | בא 935 | בפי 6310 | בשר 1320 | פגול 6292: | 4:15 ויאמר 559 | אלי 413 | ראה 7200 | נתתי 5414 | לך 3807a | את 853 |
|---|---|---|---|---|---|---|---|---|---|---|
| uala' | ba' | bapiy | basar | pigul. | uaya'mer | 'aelay, | ra'aeh, | natatiy | laka | 'at |
| **neither** | **came there** | **into my mouth** | **flesh** | **abominable** | **Then he said** | **unto me** | **lo (*see*)** | **I have given** | **to you** | |

Eze 4:7 Therefore you shall set your face toward the siege of Jerusalem, and your arm shall be uncovered, and you shall prophesy against it.8 And, behold, I will lay bands upon you, and you shall not turn you from one side to another, till you have ended the days of your siege.9 Take you also unto you wheat, and barley, and beans, and lentiles, and millet, and fitches, and put them in one vessel, and make you bread thereof, according to the number of the days that you shall lie upon your side, three hundred and ninety days shall you eat thereof.10 And your meat which you shall eat shall be by weight, twenty shekels a day: from time to time shall you eat it.11 Thou shall drink also water by measure, the sixth part of an hin: from time to time shall you drink.12 And you shall eat it as barley cakes, and you shall bake it with dung that cometh out of man, in their sight.13 And YHUH said, Even thus shall the children of Israel eat their defiled bread among the Gentiles, whither I will drive them.14 Then said I, Ah Adonai G-D! behold, my soul has not been polluted: for from my youth up even till now have I not eaten of that which die of itself, or is torn in pieces; neither came there abominable flesh into my mouth.15 Then he said unto me, Lo, I have given you cow's dung for man's dung, and you shall prepare your bread therewith.

4:16

צפועי 6832 הבקר 1241 תחת 8478 גללי 1561 האדם 120 ועשית 6213 את 853 לחמך 3899 עליהם 5921: ויאמר 559 אלי 413
tzapu'ay habaqar, tachat gelley ha'adam; ua'asiyta 'at lachmaka 'aleyhem. uaya'mer 'aelay,
**dung cow's for dung man's and you shall prepare your bread therewith Moreover he said unto me**

בן 1121 אדם 120 הנני 2005 שבר 7665 מטה 4294 לחם 3899 בירושלם 3389 ואכלו 398 לחם 3899 במשקל 4948 ובדאגה 1674
ben 'adam hinniy shober mateh lechem biyarushalaim, ua'akalu lechem bamishqal uabida'agah;
**Son of man behold I will break the staff of bread in Jerusalem and they shall eat bread by weight and with care**

4:17

ומים 4325 במשורה 4884 ובשממון 8078 ישתו 8354: למען 4616 יחסרו 2637 לחם 3899 ומים 4325
uamayim bimsurah uabshimamoun yishtu. lama'an yachsaru lechem uamayim;
**and water by measure and with astonishment they shall drink That they may want bread and water**

ונשמו 8074 איש 376 ואחיו 251 ונמקו 4743 בעונם 5771:
uanashamu 'aysh ua'achiyu, uanamaqu ba'auonam.
**and be astonied one with another and consume away for their iniquity**

**Ezek 5:1**

ואתה 859 בן 1121 אדם 120 קח 3947 לך 3807a חרב 2719 חדה 2299 תער 8593 הגלבים 1532 תקחנה 3947 לך 3807a והעברת 5674
ua'atah ben 'adam qach laka chereb chadah, ta'ar hagalabiym tiqachenah lak, uaha'abarta
**And you son of man take for you a knife sharp a razor barber's take for you and cause *it* to pass**

5:2

על 5921 ראשך 7218 ועל 5921 זקנך 2206 ולקחת 3947 לך 3807a מאזני 3976 משקל 4948 וחלקתם 2505: שלשית 7992 באור 217
'al ra'shaka ua'al zaqaneka; ualaqachta laka ma'zaney mishqal uachilaqtam. shalishiyt, ba'ur
**upon your head and upon your beard then take for you balances to weigh and divide *the hair* a third part with fire**

תבעיר 1197 בתוך 8432 העיר 5892 כמלאת 4390 ימי 3117 המצור 4692 ולקחת 3947 את 853 השלשית 7992
taba'ayr batouk ha'ayr, kimla't yamey hamatzour; ualaqachta 'at hashalishiyt,
**You shall burn in the midst of the city when are fulfilled the days of the siege and you shall take a third part**

תכה 5221 בחרב 2719 סביבותיה 5439 והשלשית 7992 תזרה 2219 לרוח 7307 וחרב 2719 אריק 7324
takeh bachereb sabiybouteyha, uahashalishiyt tizreh laruach, uachereb 'ariyq
***and* smite with a knife about it and a third part you shall scatter in the wind and a sword I will draw out**

5:3 5:4

אחריהם 310: ולקחת 3947 משם 8033 מעט 4592 במספר 4557 וצרת 6696 אותם 853 בכנפיך 3671: ומהם 1992 עוד 5750
'achareyhem. ualaqachta misham ma'at bamispar; uatzarta 'autam biknapeyka. uamehem 'aud
**after them You shall also take thereof a few in number and bind them in your skirts Then of them again**

תקח 3947 והשלכת 7993 אותם 853 אל 413 תוך 8432 האש 784 ושרפת 8313 אתם 853 באש 784 ממנו 4480 תצא 3318 אש 784 אל 413
tiqach, uahishlakta 'autam 'al touk ha'aesh, uasarapta 'atam ba'aesh; mimenu tetzea' 'aesh 'al
**take and cast them into the midst of the fire and burn them in the fire *for* thereof shall come forth a fire into**

5:5

כל 3605 בית 1004 ישראל 3478: כה 3541 אמר 559 אדני 136 יהוה 3069 זאת 2063 ירושלם 3389 בתוך 8432 הגוים 1471 שמתיה 7760
kal beyt yisra'ael. koh 'amar 'adonay Yahuah, za't yarushalaim, batouk hagouyim samtiyha;
**all the house of Israel Thus saith Adonai Yahuah This *is* Jerusalem in the midst of the nations I have set it**

5:6

וסביבותיה 5439 ארצות 776: ותמר 4784 את 853 משפטי 4941 לרשעה 7564 מן 4480
uasbiybouteyha 'aratzout. uatemer 'at mishpatay larish'ah min
**and round about her countries *that are* And she has changed my judgments into wickedness more than**

Eze 4:16 Moreover he said unto me, Son of man, behold, I will break the staff of bread in Jerusalem: and they shall eat bread by weight, and with care; and they shall drink water by measure, and with astonishment:17 That they may want bread and water, and be astonied one with another, and consume away for their iniquity. **Eze** 5:1 And you, son of man, take you a sharp knife, take you a barber's razor, and cause it to pass upon your head and upon your beard: then take you balances to weight, and divide the hair.2 Thou shall burn with fire a third part in the midst of the city, when the days of the siege are fulfilled: and you shall take a third part, and smite about it with a knife: and a third part you shall scatter in the wind; and I will draw out a sword after them.3 Thou shall also take thereof a few in number, and bind them in your skirts.4 Then take of them again, and cast them into the midst of the fire, and burn them in the fire; for thereof shall a fire come forth into all the house of Israel.5 Thus saith YHUH G-D; This is Jerusalem: I have set it in the midst of the nations and countries that are round about her.6 And she has changed my judgments into wickedness more than the nations, and my statutes more than the countries that are round about her: for they have refused my judgments and my statutes, they have not walked in them.

הגוים 1471 ואת 853 חקותי 2708 מן 4480 הארצות 776 אשר 834 סביבותיה 5439 כי 3588 במשפטי 4941 מאסו 3988
hagouyim, ua'at chuquotay, min ha'aratzout 'asher sabiybouteyha; kiy bamishpatay ma'asu,
**the nations *and* my statutes more than the countries that *are* round about her for my judgments they have refused**

וחקותי 2708 לא 3808 הלכו 1980 בהם 871a: 5:7 לכן 3651 כה 3541 אמר 559 אדני 136 יהוה 3068 יען 3282 המנכם 1995
uachuqoutay la' halaku bahem. laken koh 'amar 'adonay Yahuah ya'an hamanakem
**and my statutes not they have walked in them Therefore thus saith Adonai Yahuah Because you multiplied**

מן 4480 הגוים 1471 אשר 834 סביבותיכם 5439 בחקותי 2708 לא 3808 הלכתם 1980 ואת 853 משפטי 4941 לא 3808
min hagouyim 'asher sabiybouteykem, bachuqoutay la' halaktem, ua'at mishpatay la'
**more than the nations that *are* round about you in my statutes not *and* have walked *neither* my judgments neither**

עשיתם 6213 וכמשפטי 4941 הגוים 1471 אשר 834 סביבותיכם 5439 לא 3808 עשיתם 6213: 5:8 לכן 3651 כה 3541
'asiytem; uakmishpatey hagouyim 'asher sabiybouteykem la' 'asiytem. laken, koh
**have kept according to the judgments of the nations that *are* round about you neither have done Therefore thus**

אמר 559 אדני 136 יהוה 3069 הנני 2005 עליך 5921 גם 1571 אני 589 ועשיתי 6213 בתוכך 8432 משפטים 4941 לעיני 5869
'amar 'adonay Yahuah, hinniy 'alayik gam 'aniy; ua'asiytiy batoukek mishpatiym la'aeyney
**saith Adonai Yahuah behold I *am* against you even I and will execute in the midst of you judgments in the sight of**

הגוים 1471: 5:9 ועשיתי 6213 בך 871a את 853 אשר 834 לא 3808 עשיתי 6213 ואת 853 אשר 834 לא 3808 אעשה 6213 כמהו 3644
hagouyim. ua'asiytiy bak, 'at 'asher la' 'asiytiy, ua'at 'asher la' 'aaseh kamohu
**the nations And I will do I have in you that which not done *and* whereunto not I will do the like**

עוד 5750 יען 3282 כל 3605 תועבתיך 8441: 5:10 לכן 3651 אבות 1 יאכלו 398 בנים 1121 בתוכך 8432
'aud; ya'an kal tou'abotayik. laken, about ya'kalu baniym batoukek,
**any more because of all your abominations Therefore the fathers shall eat the sons of in the midst of you**

ובנים 1121 יאכלו 398 אבותם 1 ועשיתי 6213 בך 871a שפטים 8201 וזריתי 2219 את 853 כל 3605 שאריתך 7611
uabaniym ya'kalu aboutam; ua'asiytiy bak shapatiym, uazeriytiy 'at kal sha'aeriytek
**and the sons of shall eat their fathers and I will execute in you judgments and will I scatter the whole remnant of you**

לכל 3605 רוח 7307: 5:11 לכן 3651 חי 2416 אני 589 נאם 5002 אדני 136 יהוה 3069 אם 518 לא 3808 יען 3282 את 853 מקדשי 4720
lakal ruach. laken chay 'aniy, na'am 'adonay Yahuah 'am la', ya'an 'at miqadashiy
**into all the winds Wherefore live *as* I saith Adonai Yahuah Surely no because my sanctuary**

טמאת 2930 בכל 3605 שקוציך 8251 ובכל 3605 תועבתיך 8441 וגם 1571 אני 589 אגרע 1639
timea't, bakal shiqutzayik uabkal tou'abotayik; uagam 'aniy 'agra'
**you have defiled with all your detestable things and with all your abominations therefore also I will diminish *you***

ולא 3808 תחוס 2347 עיני 5869 וגם 1571 אני 589 לא 3808 אחמול 2550: 5:12 שלשתיך 7992 בדבר 1698 ימותו 4191
uala' tachous 'aeyniy, uagam 'aniy la' 'achmoul. shalishiteiyk badeber yamutu,
**neither shall spare mine eye neither I neither will I have any pity A third part of you with the pestilence shall die**

וברעב 7458 יכלו 3615 בתוכך 8432 והשלשית 7992 בחרב 2719 יפלו 5307 סביבותיך 5439
uabara'ab yiklu batoukek, uahashalishiyt, bachereb yiplu sabiyboutayik;
**and with famine shall they be consumed in the midst of you and a third part by the sword shall fall round about you**

Eze 5:7 Therefore thus saith YHUH G-D; Because you multiplied more than the nations that are round about you, and have not walked in my statutes, neither have kept my judgments, neither have done according to the judgments of the nations that are round about you;8 Therefore thus saith YHUH G-D; Behold, I, even I, am against you, and will execute judgments in the midst of you in the sight of the nations.9 And I will do in you that which I have not done, and whereunto I will not do anymore the like, because of all your abominations.10 Therefore the fathers shall eat the sons in the midst of you, and the sons shall eat their fathers; and I will execute judgments in you, and the whole remnant of you will I scatter into all the winds.11 Wherefore, as I live, saith YHUH G-D; Surely, because you have defiled my sanctuary with all your detestable things, and with all your abominations, therefore will I also diminish you; neither shall mine eye spare, neither will I have any pity.12 A third part of you shall die with the pestilence, and with famine shall they be consumed in the midst of you: and a third part shall fall by the sword round about you and I will scatter a third part into all the winds, and I will draw out a sword after them.

7992 והשלישית | 3605 לכל | 7307 רוח | 2219 אזרה | 2719 וחרב | 7324 אריק | 310 אחריהם: | **5:13** 3615 וכלה
uahashaliyshiyt lakal ruach 'azareh, uachereb 'ariyq 'achareyhem. uakalah
**and a third part into all the winds I will scatter and a sword I will draw out after them Thus shall be accomplished**

639 אפי | 5117 והנחותי | 2534 חמתי | 871a בם | 5162 והנחמתי | 3045 וידעו | 3588 כי | 589 אני | 3068 יהוה
'apiy, uahanichoutiy chamatiy bam uahinechamatiy; uayada'aua kiy 'aniy Yahuah
**mine anger and I will cause to rest my fury upon them and I will be comforted and they shall know that I Yahuah**

1696 דברתי | 7068 בקנאתי | 3615 בכלותי | 2534 חמתי | 871a בם: | **5:14** 5414 ואתנך | 2723 לחרבה
dibartiy baqin'atiy, bakaloutiy chamatiy bam. ua'atanek lacharabah
**have spoken *it* in my zeal when I have accomplished my fury in them Moreover I will make you waste**

2781 ולחרפה | 1471 בגוים | 834 אשר | 5439 סביבותיך | 5869 לעיני | 3605 כל | 5674 עובר: | **5:15** 1961 והיתה
ualcherpah, bagouyim 'asher sabiyboutayik; la'aeyney kal 'auber. uahayatah
**and a reproach among the nations that *are* round about you in the sight of all that pass by So it shall be**

2781 חרפה | 1422 וגדופה | 4148 מוסר | 4923 ומשמה | 1471 לגוים | 834 אשר | 5439 סביבותיך
cherpah uagdupah musar uamshamah, lagouyim 'asher sabiyboutayik;
**a reproach and a taunt an instruction and an astonishment unto the nations that *are* round about you**

6213 בעשותי | 871a בך | 8201 שפטים | 639 באף | 2534 ובחמה | 8433 ובתכחות | 2534 חמה | 589 אני | 3068 יהוה | 1696 דברתי: | **5:16**
ba'asoutiy bak shapatiym ba'ap uabchemah uabtokachout chemah, 'aniy Yahuah dibartiy.
**when I shall execute in you judgments in anger and in fury and in rebukes furious I Yahuah have spoken *it***

7971 בשלחי | 853 את | 2671 חצי | 7458 הרעב | 7451 הרעים | 871a בהם | 834 אשר | 1961 היו | 4889 למשחית | 834 אשר | 7971 אשלח
bashalchiy 'at chitzey hara'ab hara'aym bahem 'asher hayu lamashchiyt, 'asher 'ashalach
**When I shall send arrows of famine the evil upon them which shall be for *their* destruction *and* which I will send**

853 אותם | 7843 לשחתכם | 7458 ורעב | 3254 אסף | 5921 עליכם | 7665 ושברתי | 3807a לכם | 4294 מטה | 3899 לחם: | **5:17** 7971 ושלחתי
'autam lashachetakem; uara'ab 'asep 'aleykem, uashabartiy lakem mateh lachem. uashilachtiy
**you to destroy and the famine I will increase upon you and will break to your staff of bread So will I send**

5921 עליכם | 7458 רעב | 2416 וחיה | 7451 רעה | 7921 ושכלך | 1698 ודבר | 1818 ודם | 5674 יעבר | 871a בך
'aleykem ra'ab uachayah ra'ah uashikluk, uadeber uadam ya'abar bak;
**upon you famine and beasts evil and they shall bereave you and pestilence and blood shall pass through against you**

2719 וחרב | 935 אביא | 5921 עליך | 589 אני | 3068 יהוה | 1696 דברתי:
uachereb 'abiy'a 'alayik, 'aniy Yahuah dibartiy.
**and the sword I will bring upon you I Yahuah have spoken *it***

**Ezek 6:1** 1961 ויהי | 1697 דבר | 3068 יהוה | 413 אלי | 559 לאמר: | **6:2** 1121 בן | 120 אדם | 7760 שים | 6440 פניך | 413 אל | 2022 הרי
uayahiy dabar Yahuah 'aelay lea'mor. ben 'adam siym paneyka 'al harey
**And came the word of Yahuah unto me saying Son of man set your face toward the mountains of**

3478 ישראל | 5012 והנבא | 413 אליהם: | **6:3** 559 ואמרת | 2022 הרי | 3478 ישראל | 8085 שמעו | 1697 דבר | 136 אדני | 3069 יהוה | 3541 כה
yisra'ael; uahinabea' 'aleyhem. ua'amarta, harey yisra'ael, shim'au dabar 'adonay Yahuah; koh
**Israel and prophesy against them And say You mountains of Israel hear the word of Adonai Yahuah Thus**

Eze 5:13 Thus shall mine anger be accomplished, and I will cause my fury to rest upon them, and I will be comforted: and they shall know that I YHUH have spoken it in my zeal, when I have accomplished my fury in them.14 Moreover I will make you waste, and a reproach among the nations that are round about you, in the sight of all that pass by.15 So it shall be a reproach and a taunt, an instruction and an astonishment unto the nations that are round about you, when I shall execute judgments in you in anger and in fury and in furious rebukes. I YHUH have spoken it.16 When I shall send upon them the evil arrows of famine, which shall be for their destruction, and which I will send to destroy you: and I will increase the famine upon you, and will break your staff of bread:17 So will I send upon you famine and evil beasts, and they shall bereave you; and pestilence and blood shall pass through you; and I will bring the sword upon you. I YHUH have spoken it. **Eze** 6:1 And the word of YHUH came unto me, saying,2 Son of man, set your face toward the mountains of Israel, and prophesy against them,3 And say, You mountains of Israel, hear the word of YHUH G-D; Thus saith YHUH G-D to the mountains, and to the hills, to the rivers, and to the valleys; Behold, I, even I, will bring a sword upon you, and I will destroy your high places.

| אמר 559 | אדני 136 | יהוה 3069 | להרים 2022 | ולגבעות 1389 | לאפיקים 650 | ולגאית 1516 | הנני 2009 | אני 589 | מביא 935 |
|---|---|---|---|---|---|---|---|---|---|
| 'amar | 'adonay | Yahuah | lahariym | ualagaba'aut | la'apiyqiym | ualaga'ayot | hinniy | 'aniy | mebiy'a |
| **saith** | **Adonai** | **Yahuah** | **to the mountains** | **and to the hills** | **to the rivers** | **and to the valleys** | **Behold I** | ***even* I** | **will bring** |

| עליכם 5921 | חרב 2719 | ואבדתי 6 | במותיכם 1116: | 6:4 | ונשמו 8074 | מזבחותיכם 4196 | ונשברו 7665 |
|---|---|---|---|---|---|---|---|
| 'aleykem | chereb, | ua'abadtiy | bamouteykem. | | uanashamu | mizbachouteykem, | uanishbaru |
| **upon you** | **a sword** | **and I will destroy** | **your high places** | | **And shall be desolate** | **your altars** | **and shall be broken** |

| חמניכם 2553 | והפלתי 5307 | חלליכם 2491 | לפני 6440 | גלוליכם 1544: | 6:5 | ונתתי 5414 | את 853 | פגרי 6297 |
|---|---|---|---|---|---|---|---|---|
| chamaneykem; | uahipaltiy | challeykem, | lipney | giluleykem. | | uanatatiy, | 'at | pigrey |
| **your images** | **and I will cast down** | **your slain** | ***men* before** | **your idols** | | **And I will lay** | | **the dead carcases of** |

| בני 1121 | ישראל 3478 | לפני 6440 | גלוליהם 1544 | וזריתי 2219 | את 853 | עצמותיכם 6106 | סביבות 5439 | מזבחותיכם 4196: | 6:6 |
|---|---|---|---|---|---|---|---|---|---|
| baney | yisra'ael, | lipney | giluleyhem; | uazeriytiy | 'at | atzmouteykem, | sabiybout | mizbachouteykem. | |
| **the children of** | **Israel** | **before** | **their idols** | **and I will scatter** | | **your bones** | **round about** | **your altars** | |

| בכל 3605 | מושבותיכם 4186 | הערים 5892 | תחרבנה 2717 | והבמות 1116 | תישמנה 3456 | למען 4616 | יחרבו 2717 |
|---|---|---|---|---|---|---|---|
| bakal | moushabouteykem, | he'ariym | techerabnah, | uahabamout | tiyshamanah; | lama'an | yecherbu |
| **In all** | **your dwellingplaces** | **the cities** | **shall be laid waste** | **and the high places** | **shall be desolate** | **that** | **may be laid waste** |

| ויאשמו 816 | מזבחותיכם 4196 | ונשברו 7665 | ונשבתו 7673 | גלוליכם 1544 | ונגדעו 1438 | חמניכם 2553 |
|---|---|---|---|---|---|---|
| uaye'ashamou | mizbachouteykem, | uanishbaru | uanishbatu | giluleykem, | uanigda'au | chamaneykem, |
| **and made desolate** | **your altars** | **and may be broken** | **and cease** | **your idols** | **and may be cut down** | **your images** |

| ונמחו 4229 | מעשיכם 4639: | 6:7 | ונפל 5307 | חלל 2491 | בתוככם 8432 | וידעתם 3045 | כי 3588 | אני 589 |
|---|---|---|---|---|---|---|---|---|
| uanimchu | ma'aseykem. | | uanapal | chalal | batoukakem; | uiyda'tem | kiy | 'aniy |
| **and may be abolished** | **your works** | | **And shall fall** | **the slain** | **in the midst of you** | **and you shall know** | **that** | **I *am*** |

| יהוה 3068: | 6:8 | והותרתי 3498 | בהיות 1961 | לכם 3807a | פליטי 6412 | חרב 2719 | בגוים 1471 |
|---|---|---|---|---|---|---|---|
| Yahuah. | | uahoutartiy, | bihayout | lakem | paliytey | chereb | bagouyim; |
| **Yahuah** | | **Yet will I leave a remnant** | **that may have** | **to you** | ***some* that shall escape** | **the sword** | **among the nations** |

| בהזרותיכם 2219 | בארצות 776: | 6:9 | וזכרו 2142 | פליטיכם 6412 | אותי 853 |
|---|---|---|---|---|---|
| bahizarouteykem | ba'aratzout. | | uazakaru | paliyteykem | 'autiy, |
| **when you shall be scattered** | **through the countries** | | **And shall remember** | **they that escape of you** | **me** |

| בגוים 1471 | אשר 834 | נשבו 7617 | שם 8033 | אשר 834 | נשברתי 7665 | את 853 | לבם 3820 | הזונה 2181 | אשר 834 |
|---|---|---|---|---|---|---|---|---|---|
| bagouyim | 'asher | nishbu | sham | 'asher | nishbartiy | 'at | libam | hazouneh, | 'asher |
| **among the nations** | **where** | **they shall be carried captives** | **there** | **because** | **I am broken *with*** | | **their heart** | **whorish** | **which** |

| סר 5493 | מעלי 5921 | ואת 854 | עיניהם 5869 | הזנות 2181 | אחרי 310 | גלוליהם 1544 | ונקטו 6962 | בפניהם 6440 | אל 413 |
|---|---|---|---|---|---|---|---|---|---|
| sar | me'alay, | ua'at | 'aeyneyhem, | hazonout | 'acharey | giluleyhem; | uanaqotu | bipneyhem, | 'al |
| **has departed** | **from me** | ***and with*** | **their eyes** | ***which* go a whoring** | **after** | **their idols** | **and they shall lothe** | **themselves** | **for** |

| הרעות 7451 | אשר 834 | עשו 6213 | לכל 3605 | תועבתיהם 8441: | 6:10 | וידעו 3045 | כי 3588 | אני 589 | יהוה 3068 | לא 3808 |
|---|---|---|---|---|---|---|---|---|---|---|
| hare'auta | 'asher | 'asu, | lakol | tou'aboteyhem. | | uayada'aua | kiy | 'aniy | Yahuah; | la' |
| **the evils** | **which** | **they have committed** | **in all** | **their abominations** | | **And they shall know** | **that** | **I *am*** | **Yahuah** | **not** |

Eze 6:4 And your altars shall be desolate, and your images shall be broken: and I will cast down your slain men before your idols.5 And I will lay the dead carcases of the children of Israel before their idols; and I will scatter your bones round about your altars.6 In all your dwellingplaces the cities shall be laid waste, and the high places shall be desolate; that your altars may be laid waste and made desolate, and your idols may be broken and cease, and your images may be cut down, and your works may be abolished.7 And the slain shall fall in the midst of you, and you shall know that I am YHUH.8 Yet will I leave a remnant, that you may have some that shall escape the sword among the nations, when you shall be scattered through the countries.9 And they that escape of you shall remember me among the nations whither they shall be carried captives, because I am broken with their whorish heart, which has departed from me, and with their eyes, which go a whoring after their idols: and they shall lothe themselves for the evils which they have committed in all their abominations.10 And they shall know that I am YHUH, and that I have not said in vain that I would do this evil unto them.

אל 413 חנם 2600 דברתי 1696 לעשות 6213 להם 3807a הרעה 7451 הזאת 2063: 6:11 כה 3541 אמר 559 אדני 136 יהוה 3068 הכה 5221
'al chinam dibartiy, la'asout lahem hara'ah haza't. koh 'amar 'adonay Yahuah hakeh
**in vain *and that* I have said that I would do unto them evil this Thus saith Adonai Yahuah Smite**

בכפך 3709 ורקע 7554 ברגלך 7272 ואמר 559 אח 253 אל 413 כל 3605 תועבות 8441 רעות 7451 בית 1004 ישראל 3478 אשר 834
bakapaka uarqa' baraglaka ue'amar 'ach, 'al kal tou'about ra'aut beyt yisra'ael; 'asher,
**with your hand and stamp with your foot and say Alas for all abominations of *the* evil the house of Israel for**

בחרב 2719 ברעב 7458 ובדבר 1698 יפלו 5307: 6:12 הרחוק 7350 בדבר 1698 ימות 4191
bachereb bara'ab uabadber yipolu. harachouq badeber yamut,
**by the sword by the famine and by the pestilence they shall fall He that is far off of the pestilence shall die**

והקרוב 7138 בחרב 2719 יפול 5307 והנשאר 7604 והנצור 5341 ברעב 7458 ימות 4191 וכליתי 3615
uahaqaroub bachereb yipoul, uahanish'ar uahanatzur, bara'ab yamut; uakileytiy
**and he that is near by the sword shall fall and he that remains and is besieged by the famine shall die thus will I accomplish**

חמתי 2534 בם 871a: 6:13 וידעתם 3045 כי 3588 אני 589 יהוה 3068 בהיות 1961 חלליהם 2491 בתוך 8432 גלוליהם 1544
chamatiy bam. uiyda'tem kiy 'aniy Yahuah, bihayout chalayhem, batouk giluleyhem,
**my fury upon them Then shall you know that I *am* Yahuah when shall be their slain *men* among their idols**

סביבות 5439 מזבחותיהם 4196 אל 413 כל 3605 גבעה 1389 רמה 7311 בכל 3605 ראשי 7218 ההרים 2022 ותחת 8478 כל 3605 עץ 6086
sabiybout mizbachouteyhem; 'al kal gib'ah ramah bakal ra'shey hehariym, uatachat kal 'aetz
**round about their altars upon every hill high in all the tops of the mountains and under every tree**

רענן 7488 ותחת 8478 כל 3605 אלה 424 עבתה 5687 מקום 4725 אשר 834 נתנו 5414 שם 8033 ריח 7381 ניחח 5207 לכל 3605 גלוליהם 1544: 6:14
ra'anan uatachat kal 'alah 'abutah, maqoum, 'asher natanu sham reyach niychoach, lakol giluleyhem.
**green and under every oak thick the place where they did offer where savour sweet to all their idols**

ונטיתי 5186 את 853 ידי 3027 עליהם 5921 ונתתי 5414 את 853 הארץ 776 שממה 8077 ומשמה 4923
uanatiytiy 'at yadiy 'aleyhem, uanatatiy 'at ha'aretz shamamah uamshamah
**So will I stretch out my hand upon them and make the land desolate yea desolate**

ממדבר 4057 דבלתה 1689 בכל 3605 מושבותיהם 4186 וידעו 3045 כי 3588 אני 589 יהוה 3068:
mimidbar diblatah, bakol moushabouteyhem; uayada'aua kiy 'aniy Yahuah.
**more than the wilderness toward Diblath in all their habitations and they shall know that I *am* Yahuah**

**Ezek 7:1** ויהי 1961 דבר 1697 יהוה 3068 אלי 413 לאמר 559: 7:2 ואתה 859 בן 1121 אדם 120 כה 3541 אמר 559 אדני 136 יהוה 3069
uayahiy dabar Yahuah 'aelay lea'mor. ua'atah ben 'adam, koh 'amar 'adonay Yahuah
**Moreover came the word of Yahuah unto me saying Also you son of man thus saith Adonai Yahuah**

לאדמת 127 ישראל 3478 קץ 7093 בא 935 הקץ 7093 על 5921 ארבעת 702 כנפות 3671 הארץ 776: 7:3 עתה 6258 הקץ 7093
la'admat yisra'ael qetz; ba' haqetz, 'al 'arba'at kanapout ha'aretz. 'atah haqetz
**unto the land of Israel An end is come the end upon *the* four corners of the land Now *is* the end *come***

עליך 5921 ושלחתי 7971 אפי 639 בך 871a ושפטתיך 8199 כדרכיך 1870 ונתתי 5414 עליך 5921
'aleyka, uashilachtiy 'apiy bak, uashpatatiyk kidrakayik; uanatatiy 'alayik,
**upon you and I will send mine anger upon you and will judge you according to your ways and will recompense upon you**

Eze 6:11 Thus saith YHUH G-D; Smite with your hand, and stamp with your foot, and say, Alas for all the evil abominations of the house of Israel! for they shall fall by the sword, by the famine, and by the pestilence.12 He that is far off shall die of the pestilence; and he that is near shall fall by the sword; and he that remain and is besieged shall die by the famine: thus will I accomplish my fury upon them.13 Then shall you know that I am YHUH, when their slain men shall be among their idols round about their altars, upon every high hill, in all the tops of the mountains, and under every green tree, and under every thick oak, the place where they did offer sweet savour to all their idols.14 So will I stretch out my hand upon them, and make the land desolate, yea, more desolate than the wilderness toward Diblath, in all their habitations: and they shall know that I am YHUH. **Eze** 7:1 Moreover the word of YHUH came unto me, saying,2 Also, you son of man, thus saith YHUH G-D unto the land of Israel; An end, the end is come upon the four corners of the land.3 Now is the end come upon you, and I will send mine anger upon you, and will judge you according to your ways, and will recompense upon you all your abominations.

את 853 כל 3605 תועבתיך 8441: 7:4 ולא 3808 תחוס 2347 עיני 5869 עליך 5921 ולא 3808 אחמול 2550 כי 3588 דרכיך 1870 עליך 5921
'at kal tou'abotayik. uala' tachous 'aeyniy 'aleyka uala' 'achmoul; kiy darakayik 'aleyka
**all your abominations And not shall spare mine eye you neither will I have pity but your ways upon you**

אתן 5414 ותועבותיך 8441 בתוכך 8432 תהיין 1961 וידעתם 3045 כי 3588 אני 589 יהוה 3068: 7:5 כה 3541
'aten, uatou'aboutayik batoukek tihayeyna, uiyda'tem kiy 'aniy Yahuah. koh
**I will recompense and your abominations in the midst of you shall be and you shall know that I *am* Yahuah Thus**

אמר 559 אדני 136 יהוה 3068 רעה 7451 אחת 259 רעה 7451 הנה 2009 באה 935: 7:6 קץ 7093 בא 935 בא 935 הקץ 7093 הקיץ 6974 אליך 413 הנה 2009
'amar 'adonay Yahuah; ra'ah 'achat ra'ah hineh ba'ah. qetz ba', ba' haqetz heqiytz 'aeleyka; hineh
**saith Adonai Yahuah An evil an only evil behold is come An end is come is come the end it watch for you behold**

באה 935: 7:7 באה 935 הצפירה 6843 אליך 413 יושב 3427 הארץ 776 בא 935 העת 6256 קרוב 7138 היום 3117 מהומה 4103
ba'ah. ba'ah hatzapiyrah 'aeleyka yousheb ha'aretz; ba' ha'aet, qaroub hayoum mahumah
**it is come is come The morning unto you O you that dwell in the land iscome the time *is* near the day of trouble**

ולא 3808 הד 1906 הרים 2022: 7:8 עתה 6258 מקרוב 7138 אשפוך 8210 חמתי 2534 עליך 5921 וכליתי 3615
uala' hed hariym. 'atah miqaroub, 'ashpouk chamatiy 'aleyka, uakileytiy
**and not the sounding again of the mountains Now shortly will I pour out my fury upon you and accomplish**

אפי 639 בך 871a ושפטתיך 8199 כדרכיך 1870 ונתתי 5414 עליך 5921 את 853 כל 3605
'apiy bak, uashpatatiyk kidrakayik; uanatatiy 'aleyka, 'at kal
**mine anger upon you and I will judge you according to your ways and will recompense to you *for* all**

תועבותיך 8441: 7:9 ולא 3808 תחוס 2347 עיני 5869 ולא 3808 אחמול 2550 כדרכיך 1870 עליך 5921
tou'aboutayik. uala' tachous 'aeyniy uala' 'achmoul; kidrakayik 'alayik
**your abominations And not shall spare mine eye neither will I have pity according to your ways to you**

אתן 5414 ותועבותיך 8441 בתוכך 8432 תהיין 1961 וידעתם 3045 כי 3588 אני 589 יהוה 3068
'aten, uatou'aboutayik batoukek tihayeyna, uiyda'tem kiy 'aniy Yahuah
**I will recompense and your abominations *that* are in the midst of you they are and you shall know that I *am* Yahuah**

מכה 5221: 7:10 הנה 2009 היום 3117 הנה 2009 באה 935 יצאה 3318 הצפרה 6843 צץ 6692 המטה 4294 פרח 6524
makeh. hineh hayoum hineh ba'ah; yatz'ah hatzapirah, tzatz hamateh, parach
**that smite Behold the day behold it is come is gone forth the morning has blossomed the rod has budded**

הזדון 2087: 7:11 החמס 2555 קם 6965 למטה 4294 רשע 7562 לא 3808 מהם 1992 ולא 3808 מהמונם 1995 ולא 3808
hazadoun. hechamas qam lamateh resha'; la' mehem uala' mehamounam uala'
**pride Violence is risen up into a rod of wickedness none of them *shall remain* nor of their multitude nor**

מהמהם 1991 ולא 3808 נה 5089 בהם 871a: 7:12 בא 935 העת 6256 הגיע 5060 היום 3117 הקונה 7069 אל 408 ישמח 8055
mehemehem uala' noah bahem. ba' ha'aet higiya' hayoum, haqouneh 'al yismach,
**of any of theirs neither *shall there be* wailing of them is come The time draw near the day the buyer not let rejoice**

והמוכר 4376 אל 408 יתאבל 56 כי 3588 חרון 2740 אל 413 כל 3605 המונה 1995: 7:13 כי 3588 המוכר 4376 אל 413 הממכר 4465
uahamouker 'al yit'abal; kiy charoun 'al kal hamounah. kiy hamouker, 'al hamimkar
**the seller nor mourn for wrath *is* upon all the multitude thereof For the seller to that which is sold**

Eze 7:4 And mine eye shall not spare you, neither will I have pity: but I will recompense your ways upon you, and your abominations shall be in the midst of you: and you shall know that I am YHUH.5 Thus saith YHUH G-D; An evil, an only evil, behold, is come.6 An end is come, the end is come: it watcheth for you; behold, it is come.7 The morning is come unto you, O you that dwellest in the land: the time is come, the day of trouble is near, and not the sounding again of the mountains.8 Now will I shortly pour out my fury upon you, and accomplish mine anger upon you: and I will judge you according to your ways, and will recompense you for all your abominations.9 And mine eye shall not spare, neither will I have pity: I will recompense you according to your ways and your abominations that are in the midst of you; and you shall know that I am YHUH that smite.10 Behold the day, behold, it is come: the morning is gone forth; the rod has blossomed, pride has budded.11 Violence is risen up into a rod of wickedness: none of them shall remain, nor of their multitude, nor of any of theirs: neither shall there be wailing for them.12 The time is come, the day draweth near: let not the buyer rejoice, nor the seller mourn: for wrath is upon all the multitude thereof.13 For the seller shall not return to that which is sold, although they were yet alive:

לא 3808 ישוב 7725 ועוד 5750 בחיים 2416 חיתם 2416 כי 3588 חזון 2377 אל 413 כל 3605 המונה 1995 לא 3808
la' yashub, ua'aud bachayiym chayatam; kiy chazoun 'al kal hamounah la'
**not shall return although yet they were alive for the vision *is* touching the whole multitude thereof not**

ישוב 7725 ואיש 376 בעונו 5771 חיתו 2416 לא 3808 יתחזקו 2388: 7:14 תקעו 8628 בתקוע 8619
yashub, ua'aysh ba'auonou chayatou la' yitchazaqu. taqa'au bataqoua'
***which* shall return any in the iniquity of his life neither shall strengthen himself They have blown the trumpet**

והכין 3559 הכל 3605 ואין 369 הלך 1980 למלחמה 4421 כי 3588 חרוני 2740 אל 413 כל 3605 המונה 1995: 7:15
uahakiyn hakol, ua'aeyn halok lamilchamah; kiy charouniy 'al kal hamounah.
**even to make ready all but none goes to the battle for my wrath *is* upon all the multitude thereof**

החרב 2719 בחוץ 2351 והדבר 1698 והרעב 7458 מבית 1004 אשר 834 בשדה 7704 בחרב 2719 ימות 4191 ואשר 834
hachereb bachutz, uahadeber uahara'ab mibayit; 'asher basadeh bachereb yamut, ua'asher
**The sword *is* without and the pestilence and the famine within *he* that *is* in the field with the sword shall die and he that**

בעיר 5892 רעב 7458 ודבר 1698 יאכלנו 398: 7:16 ופלטו 6403 פליטיהם 6412 והיו 1961 אל 413
ba'ayr, ra'ab uadeber ya'kalenu. uapalatu paliyteyhem, uahayu 'al
***is* in the city famine and pestilence shall devour him But they that escape of them shall escape and shall be on**

ההרים 2022 כיוני 3123 הגאיות 1516 כלם 3605 המות 1993 איש 376 בעונו 5771: 7:17 כל 3605 הידים 3027 תרפינה 7503
heharym, kayouney hage'ayout kulam homout; 'aysh ba'auonou. kal hayadayim tirpeynah;
**the mountains like doves of the valleys all of them mourning every one for his iniquity All hands shall be feeble**

וכל 3605 ברכים 1290 תלכנה 1980 מים 4325: 7:18 וחגרו 2296 שקים 8242 וכסתה 3680 אותם 853
uakal birkayim telaknah mayim. uachagaru saqiym, uakistah 'autam
**and all knees shall be weak *as* water They shall also gird *themselves* with sackcloth and shall cover them**

פלצות 6427 ואל 413 כל 3605 פנים 6440 בושה 955 ובכל 3605 ראשיהם 7218 קרחה 7144: 7:19 כספם 3701 בחוצות 2351
palatzut; ua'ael kal paniym bushah, uabkal ra'sheyhem qarachah. kaspam bachutzout
**horror and upon all faces shame *shall be* upon all their heads baldness their silver in the streets**

ישליכו 7993 וזהבם 2091 לנדה 5079 יהיה 1961 כספם 3701 וזהבם 2091 לא 3808 יוכל 3201 להצילם 5337
yashliyku, uazhabam lanidah yihayeh kaspam uazhabam la' yukal lahatziylam,
**They shall cast and their gold shall be removed shall be their silver and their gold not able to deliver them**

ביום 3117 עברת 5678 יהוה 3068 נפשם 5315 לא 3808 ישבעו 7646 ומעיהם 4578 לא 3808 ימלאו 4390 כי 3588
bayoum 'abrat Yahuah, napsham la' yasabe'au, uame'ayhem la' yamalea'u; kiy
**in the day of the wrath of Yahuah their souls not they shall satisfy their bowels neither fill because**

מכשול 4383 עונם 5771 היה 1961: 7:20 וצבי 6643 עדיו 5716 לגאון 1347 שמהו 7760 וצלמי 6754
mikshoul 'auonam hayah. uatzbiy 'adyou laga'aun samahu, uatzalmey
**the stumblingblock of their iniquity it is As for the beauty of his ornament in majesty he set it but the images of**

תועבתם 8441 שקוציהם 8251 עשו 6213 בו 871a על 5921 כן 3651 נתתיו 5414 להם 3807a
tou'abotam shiqutzeyhem 'asu bou; 'al ken natatiyu lahem
**their abominations *and* of their detestable things they made therein therefore after that have I set it from them**

Eze 7:13 for the vision is touching the whole multitude thereof, which shall not return; neither shall any strengthen himself in the iniquity of his life.14 They have blown the trumpet, even to make all ready; but none go to the battle: for my wrath is upon all the multitude thereof.15 The sword is without, and the pestilence and the famine within: he that is in the field shall die with the sword; and he that is in the city, famine and pestilence shall devour him.16 But they that escape of them shall escape, and shall be on the mountains like doves of the valleys, all of them mourning, everyone for his iniquity.17 All hands shall be feeble, and all knees shall be weak as water.18 They shall also gird themselves with sackcloth, and horror shall cover them; and shame shall be upon all faces, and baldness upon all their heads.19 They shall cast their silver in the streets, and their gold shall be removed: their silver and their gold shall not be able to deliver them in the day of the wrath of YHUH: they shall not satisfy their souls, neither fill their bowels: because it is the stumblingblock of their iniquity.20 As for the beauty of his ornament, he set it in majesty: but they made the images of their abominations and of their detestable things therein: therefore have I set it far from them.

7:21

לנדה 5079: ונתתיו 5414 ביד 3027 הזרים 2114 לבז 957 ולרשעי 7563 הארץ 776 לשלל 7998
lanidah. uantatiyu bayad hazariym labaz, ualrish'aey ha'aretz lashalal;
**far And I will give it into the hands of the strangers for a prey and to the wicked of the earth for a spoil**

7:22

וחללה 2490 והסבותי 5437 פני 6440 מהם 1992 וחללו 2490 את 853 צפוני 6845 ובאו 935
uachileluh uahasiboutiy panay mehem, uachillu 'at tzapuniy; uaba'au
**and they shall pollute it will I turn also My face from them and they shall pollute my secret *place* for shall enter**

7:23

בה 871a פריצים 6530 וחללוה 2490: עשה 6213 הרתוק 7569 כי 3588 הארץ 776 מלאה 4390 משפט 4941 דמים 1818 והעיר 5892 מלאה 4390
bah pariytziym uachilluha. 'aseh haratouq; kiy ha'aretz, mal'ah mishapat damiym, uaha'ayr mal'ah
**into it the robbers and defile *it* Make a chain for the land is full of crimes bloody and the city is full of**

7:24

חמס 2555: והבאתי 935 רעי 7451 גוים 1471 וירשו 3423 את 853 בתיהם 1004
chamas. uahebea'tiy ra'aey gouyim, uayarashu 'at bateyhem;
**violence Wherefore I will bring the worst of the heathen and they shall possess their houses**

7:25

והשבתי 7673 גאון 1347 עזים 5794 ונחלו 2490 מקדשיהם 6942: קפדה 7089 בא 935
uahishbatiy ga'aun 'aziym, uanichalu maqadsheyhem. qapadah ba';
**I will also make to cease the pomp of the strong and shall be defile their holy places Destruction comes**

7:26

ובקשו 1245 שלום 7965 ואין 369: הוה 1943 על 5921 הוה 1943 תבוא 935 ושמעה 8052 אל 413 שמועה 8052
uabiqshu shaloum ua'ayin. houah 'al houah tabou'a, uashmu'ah 'al shamu'ah
**and they shall seek peace and there shall be none Mischief upon mischief shall come and rumour upon rumour**

תהיה 1961 ובקשו 1245 חזון 2377 מנביא 5030 ותורה 8451 תאבד 6 מכהן 3548 ועצה 6098
tihayeh; uabiqshu chazoun minabiy'a, uatourah ta'bad mikohen, ua'aetzah
**shall be then shall they seek a vision of the prophet but the law shall perish from the priest and counsel**

7:27

מזקנים 2205: המלך 4428 יתאבל 56 ונשיא 5387 ילבש 3847 שממה 8077 וידי 3027 עם 5971
mizqeniym. hamelek yit'abal, uanasiy'a yilbash shamamah, uaydey 'am
**from the ancients The king shall mourn and the prince shall be clothed with desolation and the hands of the people of**

הארץ 776 תבהלנה 926 מדרכם 1870 אעשה 6213 אותם 853 ובמשפטיהם 4941 אשפטם 8199
ha'aretz tibahalnah; midarkam 'aaseh 'autam uabmishpateyhem 'ashpatem,
**the land shall be troubled after their way I will do unto them and according to their deserts will I judge them**

וידעו 3045 כי 3588 אני 589 יהוה 3068:
uayada'aua kiy 'aniy Yahuah.
**and they shall know that I *am* Yahuah**

**Ezek 8:1**

ויהי 1961 בשנה 8141 הששית 8345 בששי 8345 בחמשה 2568 לחדש 2320 אני 589 יושב 3427
uayahiy bashanah hashishiyt, bashishiy bachamishah lachodesh, 'aniy yousheb
**And it came to pass in year the sixth in the sixth *month* in the fifth *day* of the month as I sat**

בביתי 1004 וזקני 2205 יהודה 3063 יושבים 3427 לפני 6440 ותפל 5307 עלי 5921 שם 8033 יד 3027 אדני 136 יהוה 3069:
babeytiy, uaziqney yahudah youshabiym lapanay; uatipol 'alay sham, yad 'adonay Yahuah.
**in mine house and the elders of Judah sat before me that fell upon me there the hand of Adonai Yahuah**

Eze 7:21 And I will give it into the hands of the strangers for a prey, and to the wicked of the earth for a spoil; and they shall pollute it.22 My face will I turn also from them, and they shall pollute my secret place: for the robbers shall enter into it, and defile it.23 Make a chain: for the land is full of bloody crimes, and the city is full of violence.24 Wherefore I will bring the worst of the heathen, and they shall possess their houses: I will also make the pomp of the strong to cease; and their holy places shall be defiled.25 Destruction cometh; and they shall seek peace, and there shall be none.26 Mischief shall come upon mischief, and rumour shall be upon rumour; then shall they seek a vision of the prophet; but the law shall perish from the priest, and counsel from the ancients.27 The king shall mourn, and the prince shall be clothed with desolation, and the hands of the people of the land shall be troubled: I will do unto them after their way, and according to their deserts will I judge them; and they shall know that I am YHUH. **Eze 8:1** And it came to pass in the sixth year, in the sixth month, in the fifth day of the month, as I sat in mine house, and the elders of Judah sat before me, that the hand of YHUH G-D fell there upon me.

| 8:2 | | | | | | | | |
|---|---|---|---|---|---|---|---|---|
| וארא 7200 | והנה 2009 | דמות 1823 | כמראה 4758 | אש 784 | ממראה 4758 | מתניו 4975 | ולמטה 4295 | אש 784 |
| ua'ar'ah, | uahineh | damut | kamar'aeh | 'aesh, | mimar'aeh | matanayu | ualmatah | 'aesh; |
| **Then I beheld** | **and lo** | **a likeness** | **as the appearance of** | **fire** | **from the appearance of** | **his loins** | **even downward** | **fire** |

| | | | | | | 8:3 |
|---|---|---|---|---|---|---|
| וממתניו 4975 | ולמעלה 4605 | כמראה 4758 | זהר 2096 | כעין 5869 | החשמלה 2830: | וישלח 7971 |
| uamimatanayu | ualma'alah, | kamar'aeh | zohar | ka'aeyn | hachashmalah. | uayishlach |
| **and from his loins** | **even upward** | **as the appearance of** | **brightness** | **as the colour of** | **amber** | **And he put forth** |

| | | | | | | | | | | |
|---|---|---|---|---|---|---|---|---|---|---|
| תבנית 8403 | יד 3027 | ויקחני 3947 | בציצת 6734 | ראשי 7218 | ותשא 5375 | אתי 853 | רוח 7307 | בין 996 | הארץ 776 | ובין 996 |
| tabaniyt | yad, | uayiqacheniy | batziytzit | ra'shiy; | uatisa' | 'atiy | ruach | beyn | ha'aretz | uabeyn |
| **the form of** | **an hand** | **and took me** | **by a lock of** | **mine head** | **and lifted up** | **me** | **the spirit** | **between** | **the earth** | **and between** |

| | | | | | | | | | |
|---|---|---|---|---|---|---|---|---|---|
| השמים 8064 | ותבא 935 | אתי 853 | ירושלמה 3389 | במראות 4759 | אלהים 430 | אל 413 | פתח 6607 | שער 8179 | הפנימית 6442 |
| hashamayim | uatabea' | 'atiy | yarushalamah | bemar'aut | 'alohiym, | 'al | petach | sha'ar | hapaniymiyt |
| **the heaven** | **and brought** | **me** | **to Jerusalem** | **in the visions of** | **Elohim** | **to** | **the door of** | **gate** | **the inner** |

| | | | | | | | | 8:4 |
|---|---|---|---|---|---|---|---|---|
| הפונה 6437 | צפונה 6828 | אשר 834 | שם 8033 | מושב 4186 | סמל 5566 | הקנאה 7068 | המקנה 7069: | |
| hapouneh | tzapounah, | 'asher | sham | moushab, | semel | haqin'ah | hamaqneh. | |
| **that looks toward** | **the north** | **where** | **there** | ***was* the seat of** | **the image of** | **jealousy** | **which provoke to jealousy** | |

| | | | | | | | | | 8:5 |
|---|---|---|---|---|---|---|---|---|---|
| והנה 2009 | שם 8033 | כבוד 3519 | אלהי 430 | ישראל 3478 | כמראה 4758 | אשר 834 | ראיתי 7200 | בבקעה 1237: | |
| uahineh | sham, | kaboud | 'alohey | yisra'ael; | kamara'ah | 'asher | ra'aytiy | babiq'ah. | |
| **And behold *was*** | **there** | **the glory of** | **the Elohim of** | **Israel** | **according to the vision** | **that** | **I saw** | **in the plain** | |

| | | | | | | | | | | | |
|---|---|---|---|---|---|---|---|---|---|---|---|
| ויאמר 559 | אלי 413 | בן 1121 | אדם 120 | שא 5375 | נא 4994 | עיניך 5869 | דרך 1870 | צפונה 6828 | ואשא 5375 | עיני 5869 |
| uaya'mer | 'aelay, | ben | 'adam | sa | naa' | 'aeyneyka | derek | tzapounah; | ua'asa' | 'aeynay |
| **Then said he** | **unto me** | **Son of** | **man** | **lift up** | **now** | **your eyes** | **the way toward** | **the north** | **So I lifted up** | **mine eyes** |

| | | | | | | | | | | 8:6 |
|---|---|---|---|---|---|---|---|---|---|---|
| דרך 1870 | צפונה 6828 | והנה 2009 | מצפון 6828 | לשער 8179 | המזבח 4196 | סמל 5566 | הקנאה 7068 | הזה 2088 | בבאה 872: | |
| derek | tzapounah, | uahineh | mitzapoun | lasha'ar | hamizbeach, | semel | haqin'ah | hazeh | babo'ah. | |
| **the way toward** | **the north** | **and behold** | **northward** | **at the gate of** | **the altar** | **image of** | **jealousy** | **this** | **in the entry** | |

| | | | | | | | | | | |
|---|---|---|---|---|---|---|---|---|---|---|
| ויאמר 559 | אלי 413 | בן 1121 | אדם 120 | הראה 7200 | אתה 859 | מהם 1992 | עשים 6213 | תועבות 8441 | גדלות 1419 | אשר 834 |
| uaya'mer | 'aelay, | ben | 'adam | hara'ah | 'atah | mehem | 'asiym; | tou'aebout | gadolout | 'asher |
| **He said furthermore** | **unto me** | **Son of** | **man** | **see** | **you** | **what** | **they do?** | **abominations** | ***even* the great** | **that** |

| | | | | | | | | |
|---|---|---|---|---|---|---|---|---|
| בית 1004 | ישראל 3478 | עשים 6213 | פה 6311 | לרחקה 7368 | מעל 5921 | מקדשי 4720 | ועוד 5750 | תשוב 7725 |
| beyt | yisra'ael | 'asiym | poh, | larachaqah | me'al | miqadashiy, | ua'aud | tashub |
| **the house of** | **Israel** | **commit** | **here** | **that I should go far off** | **from** | **my sanctuary?** | **but yet** | **turn you again** |

| | | | 8:7 | | | | | |
|---|---|---|---|---|---|---|---|---|
| תראה 7200 | תועבות 8441 | גדלות 1419: | ויבא 935 | אתי 853 | אל 413 | פתח 6607 | החצר 2691 | ואראה 7200 |
| tir'ah, | tou'aebout | gadolout. | uayabea' | 'atiy | 'al | petach | hechatzer; | ua'ar'ah |
| ***and* you shall see** | **abominations** | **greater** | **And he brought** | **me** | **to** | **the door of** | **the court** | **and when I looked** |

| | | | | 8:8 | | | | | | |
|---|---|---|---|---|---|---|---|---|---|---|
| והנה 2009 | חר 2356 | אחד 259 | בקיר 7023: | ויאמר 559 | אלי 413 | בן 1121 | אדם 120 | חתר 2864 | נא 4994 | בקיר 7023 |
| uahineh | chor | 'achad | baqiyr. | uaya'mer | 'aelay, | ben | 'adam | chatar | naa' | baqiyr; |
| **and behold** | **hole** | **a** | **in the wall** | **Then said he** | **unto me** | **Son of** | **man** | **dig** | **now** | **in the wall** |

Eze 8:2 Then I beheld, and lo a likeness as the appearance of fire: from the appearance of his loins even downward, fire; and from his loins even upward, as the appearance of brightness, as the colour of amber.3 And he put forth the form of an hand, and took me by a lock of mine head; and the spirit lifted me up between the earth and the heaven, and brought me in the visions of G-d to Jerusalem, to the door of the inner gate that look toward the north; where was the seat of the image of jealousy, which provoketh to jealousy.4 And, behold, the glory of the G-d of Israel was there, according to the vision that I saw in the plain.5 Then said he unto me, Son of man, lift up your eyes now the way toward the north. So I lifted up mine eyes the way toward the north, and behold northward at the gate of the altar this image of jealousy in the entry.6 He said furthermore unto me, Son of man, seest you what they do? even the great abominations that the house of Israel committeth here, that I should go far off from my sanctuary? but turn you yet again, and you shall see greater abominations.7 And he brought me to the door of the court; and when I looked, behold a hole in the wall.8 Then said he unto me, Son of man, dig now in the wall: and when I had digged in the wall, behold a door.

| ואחתר 2864 | בקיר 7023 | והנה 2009 | פתח 6607 | אחד 259: | 8:9 ויאמר 559 | אלי 413 | בא 935 | וראה 7200 | את 853 | התועבות 8441 |
|---|---|---|---|---|---|---|---|---|---|---|
| ua'achtor | baqiyr, | uahineh | petach | 'achad. | uaya'mer | 'aelay; | ba' | uar'aeh | 'at | hatou'aebout |
| **and when I had digged** | **in the wall** | **and behold** | **door** | **a** | **And he said** | **unto me** | **Go in** | **and behold** | | **abominations** |

| הרעות 7451 | אשר 834 | הם 1992 | עשים 6213 | פה 6311: | 8:10 ואבוא 935 | ואראה 7200 | והנה 2009 | כל 3605 | תבנית 8403 | רמש 7431 | ובהמה 929 |
|---|---|---|---|---|---|---|---|---|---|---|---|
| hara'aut, | 'asher | hem | 'asiym | poh. | ua'abou'a | ua'ar'ah | uahineh | kal | tabaniyt | remes | uabahemah |
| **the wicked** | **that** | **they** | **do** | **here** | **So I went in** | **and saw** | **and behold** | **every** | **form of** | **creeping things** | **and beasts** |

| שקץ 8263 | וכל 3605 | גלולי 1544 | בית 1004 | ישראל 3478 | מחקה 4207 | על 5921 | הקיר 7023 | סביב 5439 | סביב 5439: | 8:11 ושבעים 7657 |
|---|---|---|---|---|---|---|---|---|---|---|
| sheqetz, | uakal | giluley | beyt | yisra'ael; | machuqeh | 'al | haqiyr | sabiyb | sabiyb. | uashib'aym |
| **abominable** | **and all** | **the idols of** | **the house of** | **Israel** | **pourtrayed** | **upon** | **the wall** | **round** | **about** | **And seventy** |

| איש 376 | מזקני 2205 | בית 1004 | ישראל 3478 | ויאזניהו 2970 | בן 1121 | שפן 8227 | עמד 5975 | בתוכם 8432 | עמדים 5975 |
|---|---|---|---|---|---|---|---|---|---|
| 'aysh | miziqney | beyt | yisra'ael | uaya'azanyahu | ben | shapan | 'amed | batoukam | 'amdiym |
| **men of** | **the ancients of** | **the house of** | **Israel** | **and Jaazaniah** | **the son of** | **Shaphan** | **there stood** | **in the midst of them** | **stood** |

| לפניהם 6440 | ואיש 376 | מקטרתו 4730 | בידו 3027 | ועתר 6282 | ענן 6051 | הקטרת 7004 | עלה 5927: | 8:12 ויאמר 559 | אלי 413 |
|---|---|---|---|---|---|---|---|---|---|
| lipneyhem, | ua'aysh | miqtartou | bayadou; | ua'atar | 'anan | haqatoret | 'aleh. | uaya'mer | 'aelay |
| **before them** | **with every man** | **his censer** | **in his hand** | **and a thick** | **cloud of** | **incense** | **went up** | **Then said he** | **unto me** |

| הראית 7200 | בן 1121 | אדם 120 | אשר 834 | זקני 2205 | בית 1004 | ישראל 3478 | עשים 6213 | בחשך 2822 | איש 376 |
|---|---|---|---|---|---|---|---|---|---|
| hara'ayta | ben | 'adam | 'asher | ziqney | beyt | yisra'ael | 'asiym | bachoshek, | 'aysh |
| **have you seen** | **Son of** | **man** | **what** | **the ancients of** | **the house of** | **Israel** | **do** | **in the dark** | **every man** |

| בחדרי 2315 | משכיתו 4906 | כי 3588 | אמרים 559 | אין 369 | יהוה 3069 | ראה 7200 | אתנו 853 | עזב 5800 | יהוה 3069 | את 853 | הארץ 776: | 8:13 |
|---|---|---|---|---|---|---|---|---|---|---|---|---|
| bachadrey | maskiytou; | kiy | 'amariym, | 'aeyn | Yahuah | ro'ah | 'atanu, | 'azab | Yahuah | 'at | ha'aretz. | |
| **in the chambers of** | **his imagery?** | **for** | **they say** | **not** | **Yahuah** | **see** | **us** | **has forsaken** | **Yahuah** | | **the earth** | |

| ויאמר 559 | אלי 413 | עוד 5750 | תשוב 7725 | תראה 7200 | תועבות 8441 | גדלות 1419 | אשר 834 | המה 1992 | עשים 6213: | 8:14 |
|---|---|---|---|---|---|---|---|---|---|---|
| uaya'mer | 'aelay; | 'aud | tashub | tir'ah | tou'aebout | gadolout | 'asher | hemah | 'asiym. | |
| **He said also** | **unto me** | **Yet** | **Turn you again** | ***and* you shall see** | **abominations** | **greater** | **that** | **they** | **do** | |

| ויבא 935 | אתי 853 | אל 413 | פתח 6607 | שער 8179 | בית 1004 | יהוה 3068 | אשר 834 | אל 413 | הצפונה 6828 | והנה 2009 | שם 8033 |
|---|---|---|---|---|---|---|---|---|---|---|---|
| uayabea' | 'atiy, | 'al | petach | sha'ar | beyt | Yahuah, | 'asher | 'al | hatzapounah; | uahineh | sham |
| **Then he brought me** | | **to** | **the door of** | **the gate of** | **house** | **Yahuah's** | **which *was*** | **toward** | **the north** | **and behold** | **there** |

| הנשים 802 | ישבות 3327 | מבכות 1058 | את 853 | התמוז 8542: | 8:15 ויאמר 559 | אלי 413 | הראית 7200 | בן 1121 | אדם 120 | עוד 5750 |
|---|---|---|---|---|---|---|---|---|---|---|
| hanashiym | yoshabout, | mabakout | 'at | hatamuz. | uaya'mer | 'aelay | hara'ayta | ben | 'adam; | 'aud |
| **women** | **sat** | **weeping for** | | **Tammuz** | **Then said he** | **unto me** | **Have you seen *this*** | **O son of** | **man?** | **yet** |

| תשוב 7725 | תראה 7200 | תועבות 8441 | גדלות 1419 | מאלה 428: | 8:16 ויבא 935 | אתי 853 | אל 413 | חצר 2691 | בית 1004 |
|---|---|---|---|---|---|---|---|---|---|
| tashub | tir'ah | tou'aebout | gadolout | me'aeleh. | uayabea' | 'atiy, | 'al | chatzar | beyt |
| **turn you again** | ***and* you shall see** | **abominations** | **greater** | **than these** | **And he brought** | **me** | **into** | **court of** | **house** |

| יהוה 3068 | הפנימית 6442 | והנה 2009 | פתח 6607 | היכל 1964 | יהוה 3068 | בין 996 | האולם 197 | ובין 996 | המזבח 4196 |
|---|---|---|---|---|---|---|---|---|---|
| Yahuah | hapaniymiyt | uahineh | petach | heykal | Yahuah | beyn | ha'aulam | uabeyn | hamizbeach, |
| **Yahuah's** | **the inner** | **and behold *at*** | **the door of** | **the temple of** | **Yahuah** | **between** | **the porch** | **and between** | **the altar *were*** |

Eze 8:9 And he said unto me, Go in, and behold the wicked abominations that they do here.10 So I went in and saw; and behold every form of creeping things, and abominable beasts, and all the idols of the house of Israel, pourtrayed upon the wall round about.11 And there stood before them seventy men of the ancients of the house of Israel, and in the midst of them stood Jaazaniah the son of Shaphan, with every man his censer in his hand; and a thick cloud of incense went up.12 Then said he unto me, Son of man, have you seen what the ancients of the house of Israel do in the dark, every man in the chambers of his imagery? for they say, YHUH see us not; YHUH has forsaken the earth.13 He said also unto me, Turn you yet again, and you shall see greater abominations that they do.14 Then he brought me to the door of the gate of YHUH's house which was toward the north; and, behold, there sat women weeping for Tammuz.15 Then said he unto me, Hast you seen this, O son of man? turn you yet again, and you shall see greater abominations than these.16 And he brought me into the inner court of YHUH's house, and, behold, at the door of the temple of YHUH, between the porch and the altar, were about five and twenty men, with their backs toward the temple of YHUH, and their faces toward the east; and they worshipped the sun toward the east.

| כעשרים 6242 | וחמשה 2568 | איש 376 | אחריהם 268 | אל 413 | היכל 1964 | יהוה 3068 | ופניהם 6440 | קדמה 6924 | והמה 1992 |
|---|---|---|---|---|---|---|---|---|---|
| ka'asriym | uachamishah | 'aysh; | 'achoreyhem | 'al | heykal | Yahuah | uapneyhem | qedamah, | uahemah |
| about twenty | and five | men | *with* their backs | toward | the temple of | Yahuah | and their faces | toward the east | and they |

| משתחויתם 7812 | קדמה 6924 | לשמש 8121: | 8:17 ויאמר 559 | אלי 413 | הראית 7200 | בן 1121 | אדם 120 | הנקל 7043 |
|---|---|---|---|---|---|---|---|---|
| mishtachauiytem | qedamah | lashamesh. | uaya'mer | 'aelay | hara'ayta | ben | 'adam | hanaqel |
| worshipped | toward the east | the sun | Then he said | unto me | Have you seen *this* | O son of | man? | Is it a light thing |

| לבית 1004 | יהודה 3063 | מעשות 6213 | את 853 | התועבות 8441 | אשר 834 | עשו 6213 | פה 6311 | כי 3588 | מלאו 4390 | את 853 |
|---|---|---|---|---|---|---|---|---|---|---|
| labeyt | yahudah, | me'asout | 'at | hatou'aebout | 'asher | 'asu | poh; | kiy | mala'au | 'at |
| to the house of | Judah | that they commit | | the abominations | which | they commit | here? | for | they have filled | |

| הארץ 776 | חמס 2555 | וישבו 3427 | להכעיסני 3707 | והנם 2005 | שלחים 7971 | את 853 | הזמורה 2156 | אל 413 |
|---|---|---|---|---|---|---|---|---|
| ha'aretz | chamas, | uayashubu | lahak'ayseniy, | uahinam | sholachiym | 'at | hazamourah | 'al |
| the land | *with* violence | and have returned | to provoke me to anger | and lo they | put | | the branch | to |

| אפם 639: | 8:18 וגם 1571 | אני 589 | אעשה 6213 | בחמה 2534 | לא 3808 | תחוס 2347 | עיני 5869 | ולא 3808 | אחמל 2550 |
|---|---|---|---|---|---|---|---|---|---|
| 'apam. | uagam | 'aniy | 'aaseh | bachemah, | la' | tachous | 'aeyniy | uala' | 'achmol; |
| their nose | Therefore also | I | I will deal | in fury | not | shall spare | mine eye | neither | will I have pity |

| וקראו 7121 | באזני 241 | קול 6963 | גדול 1419 | ולא 3808 | אשמע 8085 | אותם 853: |
|---|---|---|---|---|---|---|
| uaqar'au | ba'azanay | qoul | gadoul, | uala' | 'ashma | 'autam. |
| and though they cry | in mine ears | *with* a voice | loud | not | *yet* will I hear | them |

| Ezek 9:1 ויקרא 7121 | באזני 241 | קול 6963 | גדול 1419 | לאמר 559 | קרבו 7126 | פקדות 6486 | העיר 5892 |
|---|---|---|---|---|---|---|---|
| uayiqra' | ba'azanay, | qoul | gadoul | lea'mor, | qarabu | paqudout | ha'ayr; |
| He cried also | in mine ears | *with* a voice | loud | saying | Cause to draw near | them that have charge over | the city |

| ואיש 376 | כלי 3627 | משחתו 4892 | בידו 3027: | 9:2 והנה 2009 | ששה 8337 | אנשים 582 | באים 935 | מדרך 1870 | שער 8179 |
|---|---|---|---|---|---|---|---|---|---|
| ua'aysh | kaliy | mashchetou | bayadou. | uahineh | shishah | 'anashiym | ba'aym | miderek | sha'ar |
| even every man | weapon | *with* his destroying | in his hand | And behold | six | man | came | from the way of | gate |

| העליון 5945 | אשר 834 | מפנה 6437 | צפונה 6828 | ואיש 376 | כלי 3627 | מפצו 4660 | בידו 3027 | ואיש 376 | אחד 259 | בתוכם 8432 |
|---|---|---|---|---|---|---|---|---|---|---|
| ha'alyoun | 'asher | mapaneh | tzapounah, | ua'aysh | kaliy | mapatzou | bayadou, | ua'aysh | 'achad | batoukam |
| the higher | which | lies toward | the north | and every man | a weapon | slaughter | in his hand | and man | one | among them |

| לבש 3847 | בדים 906 | וקסת 7083 | הספר 5608 | במתניו 4975 | ויבאו 935 | ויעמדו 5975 | אצל 681 | מזבח 4196 | הנחשת 5178: 9:3 |
|---|---|---|---|---|---|---|---|---|---|
| labush | badiym, | uaqeset | hasoper | bamatnayu; | uayabo'au | uaya'amdu, | 'aetzel | mizbach | hanachoshet. |
| *was* clothed | *with* linen | with a inkhorn | writer's | by his side | and they went in | and stood | beside | altar | the brasen |

| וכבוד 3519 | אלהי 430 | ישראל 3478 | נעלה 5927 | מעל 5921 | הכרוב 3742 | אשר 834 | היה 1961 | עליו 5921 | אל 413 | מפתן 4670 |
|---|---|---|---|---|---|---|---|---|---|---|
| uakaboud | 'alohey | yisra'ael, | na'alah | me'al | hakarub | 'asher | hayah | 'alayu, | 'al | miptan |
| And the glory of | the Elohim of | Israel | was gone up | from | the cherub | whereupon | he was | on him | to | the threshold of |

| הבית 1004 | ויקרא 7121 | אל 413 | האיש 376 | הלבש 3847 | הבדים 906 | אשר 834 | קסת 7083 | הספר 5608 | במתניו 4975: | 9:4 ויאמר 559 |
|---|---|---|---|---|---|---|---|---|---|---|
| habayit; | uayiqra', | 'al | ha'aysh | halabush | habadiym, | 'asher | qeset | hasoper | bamatnayu. | uaya'mer |
| the house | And he called | to | the man | clothed with | linen | which | inkhorn | *had* the writer's | by his side | And said |

Eze 8:17 Then he said unto me, Hast you seen this, O son of man? Is it a light thing to the house of Judah that they commit the abominations which they commit here? for they have filled the land with violence, and have returned to provoke me to anger: and, lo, they put the branch to their nose.18 Therefore will I also deal in fury: mine eye shall not spare, neither will I have pity: and though they cry in mine ears with a loud voice, yet will I not hear them. **Eze** 9:1 He cried also in mine ears with a loud voice, saying, Cause them that have charge over the city to draw near, even every man with his destroying weapon in his hand.2 And, behold, six men came from the way of the higher gate, which lie toward the north, and every man a slaughter weapon in his hand; and one man among them was clothed with linen, with a writer's inkhorn by his side: and they went in, and stood beside the brasen altar.3 And the glory of the G-d of Israel was gone up from the cherub, whereupon he was, to the threshold of the house. And he called to the man clothed with linen, which had the writer's inkhorn by his side;

| 3069 יהוה | 413 אלו | 5674 עבר | 8432 בתוך | 5892 העיר | 8432 בתוך | 3389 ירושלם | 8427 והתוית | 8420 תו | 5921 על |
|---|---|---|---|---|---|---|---|---|---|
| Yahuah | 'aelou | 'abor | batouk | ha'ayr, | batouk | yarushalaim; | uahituiyta | tau | 'al |
| **Yahuah** | **unto him** | **Go** | **through the midst of** | **the city** | **through the midst of** | **Jerusalem** | **and set** | **a mark** | **upon** |

| 4696 מצחות | 582 האנשים | 584 הנאנחים | 602 והנאנקים | 5921 על | 3605 כל | 8441 התועבות | 6213 הנעשות |
|---|---|---|---|---|---|---|---|
| mitzchout | ha'anashiym, | hane'anachiym | uahane'anaqiym, | 'al | kal | hatou'about, | hana'asout |
| **the foreheads of** | **the men** | **that sigh** | **and that cry** | **for** | **all** | **the abominations** | **that be done** |

| 8432 בתוכה: | 9:5 | 428 ולאלה | 559 אמר | 241 באזני | 5674 עברו | 5892 בעיר | 310 אחריו | 5221 והכו | 5921 על |
|---|---|---|---|---|---|---|---|---|---|
| batoukah. | | ual'aeleh | 'amar | ba'azanay, | 'abru | ba'ayr | 'acharayu | uahaku; | 'al |
| **in the midst thereof** | | **And to the others** | **he said** | **in mine hearing** | **Go you** | **through the city** | **after him** | **and smite** | **not** |

| 2347 תחס | 5869 עיניכם | 408 ואל | 2550 תחמלו: | 9:6 | 2205 זקן | 970 בחור | 1330 ובתולה | 2945 וטף | 802 ונשים | 2026 תהרגו |
|---|---|---|---|---|---|---|---|---|---|---|
| tachos | 'aeyneykem | ua'al | tachamolu. | | zaqen | bachur | uabtulah | uatap | uanashiym | tahargu |
| **let spare** | **your eye** | **neither** | **have you pity** | | **old** | ***and* young** | **both maids** | **and little children** | **and women** | **Slay** |

| 4889 למשחית | 5921 ועל | 3605 כל | 376 איש | 834 אשר | 5921 עליו | 8420 התו | 408 אל | 5066 תגשו | 4720 וממקדשי | 2490 תחלו | 2490 ויחלו |
|---|---|---|---|---|---|---|---|---|---|---|---|
| lamashchiyt, | ua'al | kal | 'aysh | 'asher | 'alayu | hatau | 'al | tigashu, | uamimiqdashiy | tachelu; | uayachelu |
| **utterly** | **but** | **any** | **man** | **whom** | **upon** | ***is* the mark** | **not** | **come near** | **and at my sanctuary** | **begin** | **Then they began** |

| 582 באנשים | 2205 הזקנים | 834 אשר | 6440 לפני | 1004 הבית: | 9:7 | 559 ויאמר | 413 אליהם | 2930 טמאו | 853 את | 1004 הבית | 4390 ומלאו | 853 את |
|---|---|---|---|---|---|---|---|---|---|---|---|---|
| ba'anashiym | hazaqeniym, | 'asher | lipney | habayit. | | uaya'mer | 'aleyhem | tama'au | 'at | habayit, | uamal'au | 'at |
| **at men** | **the ancient** | **which** | ***were* before** | **the house** | | **And he said** | **unto them** | **Defile** | | **the house** | **and fill** | |

| 2691 החצרות | 2491 חללים | 3318 צאו | 3318 ויצאו | 5221 והכו | 5892 בעיר: | 9:8 | 1961 ויהי |
|---|---|---|---|---|---|---|---|
| hachatzerout | chalaliym | tze'au; | uayatza'au | uahiku | ba'ayr. | | uayahiy |
| **the courts** | ***with* the slain** | **go you forth** | **And they went forth** | **and slew** | **in the city** | | **And it came to pass** |

| 5221 כהכותם | 7604 ונאשאר | 589 אני | 5307 ואפלה | 5921 על | 6440 פני | 2199 ואזעק | 559 ואמר | 162 אהה | 136 אדני | 3069 יהוה |
|---|---|---|---|---|---|---|---|---|---|---|
| kahakoutam, | uana'sha'ar | 'aniy; | ua'apalah | 'al | panay | ua'azaq, | ua'amar | 'ahah | 'adonay | Yahuah, |
| **while they were slaying them** | **and was left** | **I** | **that I fell** | **upon** | **my face** | **and cried** | **and said I** | **Ah** | **Adonai** | **Yahuah** |

| 7843 המשחית | 859 אתה | 853 את | 3605 כל | 7611 שארית | 3478 ישראל | 8210 בשפכך | 853 את | 2534 חמתך | 5921 על | 3389 ירושלם: | 9:9 |
|---|---|---|---|---|---|---|---|---|---|---|---|
| hamashchiyt | 'atah, | 'at | kal | sha'aeriyt | yisra'ael, | bashapakaka | 'at | chamataka | 'al | yarushalaim. | |
| **will destroy** | **you** | | **all** | **the residue of** | **Israel** | **in your pouring out of** | | **your fury** | **upon** | **Jerusalem?** | |

| 559 ויאמר | 413 אלי | 5771 עון | 1004 בית | 3478 ישראל | 3063 ויהודה | 1419 גדול | 3966 במאד | 3966 מאד | 4390 ותמלא | 776 הארץ |
|---|---|---|---|---|---|---|---|---|---|---|
| uaya'mer | 'aelay, | 'auon | beyt | yisra'ael | uayahudah | gadoul | bim'ad | ma'ad, | uatimalea' | ha'aretz |
| **Then said he** | **unto me** | **The iniquity of** | **the house of** | **Israel** | **and Judah** | **great** | ***is* exceeding** | **very** | **and is full of** | **the land** |

| 1818 דמים | 5892 והעיר | 4390 מלאה | 4297 מטה | 3588 כי | 559 אמרו | 5800 עזב | 3068 יהוה | 853 את | 776 הארץ | 369 ואין | 3068 יהוה |
|---|---|---|---|---|---|---|---|---|---|---|---|
| damiym, | uaha'ayr | mal'ah | muteh; | kiy | 'amaru, | 'azab | Yahuah | 'at | ha'aretz, | ua'aeyn | Yahuah |
| **blood** | **and the city** | **full of** | **perverseness** | **for** | **they say** | **has forsaken** | **Yahuah** | | **the earth** | **and not** | **Yahuah** |

| 7200 ראה: | 9:10 | 1571 וגם | 589 אני | 3808 לא | 2347 תחוס | 5869 עיני | 3808 ולא | 2550 אחמל | 1870 דרכם | 7218 בראשם |
|---|---|---|---|---|---|---|---|---|---|---|
| ro'ah. | | ua'gam | 'aniy, | la' | tachous | 'aeyniy | uala' | 'achmol; | darkam | bara'sham |
| **see** | | **And as for also** | **me** | **not** | **shall spare** | **mine eye** | **neither** | **will I have pity** | **their way** | **upon their head** |

Eze 9:4 And YHUH said unto him, Go through the midst of the city, through the midst of Jerusalem, and set a mark upon the foreheads of the men that sigh and that cry for all the abominations that be done in the midst thereof.5 And to the others he said in mine hearing, Go you after him through the city, and smite: let not your eye spare, neither have you pity:6 Slay utterly old and young, both maids, and little children, and women: but come not near any man upon whom is the mark; and begin at my sanctuary. Then they began at the ancient men which were before the house.7 And he said unto them, Defile the house, and fill the courts with the slain: go you forth. And they went forth, and slew in the city.8 And it came to pass, while they were slaying them, and I was left, that I fell upon my face, and cried, and said, Ah Adonai G-D! will you destroy all the residue of Israel in your pouring out of your fury upon Jerusalem?9 Then said he unto me, The iniquity of the house of Israel and Judah is exceeding great, and the land is full of blood, and the city full of perverseness: for they say, YHUH has forsaken the earth, and YHUH see not.10 And as for me also, mine eye shall not spare, neither will I have pity, but I will recompense their way upon their head.

9:11

נתתי 5414: והנה 2009 האיש 376 לבש 3830 הבדים 906 אשר 834 הקסת 7083 במתניו 4975 משיב 7725
natatiy. uahineh ha'aysh labush habadiym, 'asher haqeset bamatnayu, meshiyb
***but*** **I will recompense And behold the man clothed with the linen which *had* the inkhorn by his side reported**

דבר 1697 לאמר 559 עשיתי 6213 כאשר 834 צויתני 6680:
dabar lea'mor; 'asiytiy ka'asher tziuiytaniy.
**the matter saying I have done as you have commanded me**

**Ezek 10:1** וארא 7200 והנה 2009 אל 413 הרקיע 7549 אשר 834 על 5921 ראש 7218 הכרבים 3742 כאבן 68
ua'ar'ah, uahineh 'al haraqiya' 'asher 'al ra'sh hakarubiym, ka'aben
**Then I looked and behold in the firmament that *was* above the head of the cherubims as it were stone**

ספיר 5601 כמראה 4758 דמות 1823 כסא 3678 נראה 7200 עליהם 5921: 10:2 ויאמר 559 אל 413 האיש 376 לבש 3847
sapiyr, kamar'aeh damut kisea'; nir'ah 'aleyhem. uaya'mer 'al ha'aysh labush
**sapphire as the appearance of the likeness of a throne there appeared over them And he spoke unto the man clothed**

הבדים 906 ויאמר 559 בא 935 אל 413 בינות 996 לגלגל 1534 אל 413 תחת 8478 לכרוב 3742 ומלא 4390 חפניך 2651 גחלי 1513 אש 784
habadiym, uaya'mer ba' 'al beynout lagalgal 'al tachat lakrub, uamalea' chapaneyka gachaley 'aesh
***with*** **linen and said Go in between *even* the wheels to under the cherub and fill your hand with coals of fire**

מבינות 996 לכרבים 3742 וזרק 2236 על 5921 העיר 5892 ויבא 935 לעיני 5869: 10:3 והכרבים 3742 עמדים 5975
mibeynout lakrubiym, uazroq 'al ha'ayr; uayaba' la'aeynay. uahakarubiym, 'amdiym
**from between the cherubims and scatter *them* over the city And he entered in my sight Now the cherubims stood**

מימין 3225 לבית 1004 בבאו 935 האיש 376 והענן 6051 מלא 4390 את 853 החצר 2691 הפנימית 6442: 10:4 וירם 7311
miymiyn labayit babo'au ha'aysh; uahe'anan malea', 'at hechatzer hapaniymiyt. uayaram
**on the right side of the house when went in the man and the cloud filled court the inner Then went up**

כבוד 3519 יהוה 3069 מעל 5921 הכרוב 3742 על 5921 מפתן 4670 הבית 1004 וימלא 4390 הבית 1004 את 854 הענן 6051
kaboud Yahuah me'al hakarub, 'al miptan habayit; uayimalea' habayit 'at he'anan,
***the*** **glory Yahuah from the cherub *and stood* over the threshold of the house and was filled the house *with* the cloud**

והחצר 2691 מלאה 4390 את 854 נגה 5051 כבוד 3519 יהוה 3069: 10:5 וקול 6963 כנפי 3671 הכרובים 3742 נשמע 8085
uahechatzer mal'ah, 'at nogah kaboud Yahuah. uaqoul kanpey hakarubiym, nishma'
**and the court was full *of* the brightness of glory Yahuah And the sound of wings the cherubims' was heard**

עד 5704 החצר 2691 החיצנה 2435 כקול 6963 אל 410 שדי 7706 בדברו 1696: 10:6 ויהי 1961
'ad hechatzer hachiytzonah; kaqoul 'ael shaday badabrou. uayahiy,
***even*** **to court the outer as the voice of El the Almighty when he speak And it came to pass**

בצותו 6680 את 853 האיש 376 לבש 3847 הבדים 906 לאמר 559 קח 3947 אש 784 מבינות 996 לגלגל 1534
batzauotou 'at ha'aysh labush habadiym lea'mor, qach 'aesh mibeynout lagalgal,
***that*** **when he had commanded the man clothed with the linen saying Take fire from between the wheels**

מבינות 996 לכרובים 3742 ויבא 935 ויעמד 5975 אצל 681 האופן 212: 10:7 וישלח 7971 הכרוב 3742 את 853
mibeynout lakrubiym; uayaba' uaya'amod, 'aetzel ha'aupan. uayishlach hakarub 'at
**from between the cherubims then he went in and stood beside the wheels And stretched forth *one* cherub**

Eze 10:11 And, behold, the man clothed with linen, which had the inkhorn by his side, reported the matter, saying, I have done as you have commanded me. **Eze** 10:1 Then I looked, and, behold, in the firmament that was above the head of the cherubims there appeared over them as it were a sapphire stone, as the appearance of the likeness of a throne.2 And he spoke unto the man clothed with linen, and said, Go in between the wheels, even under the cherub, and fill your hand with coals of fire from between the cherubims, and scatter them over the city. And he went in in my sight.3 Now the cherubims stood on the right side of the house, when the man went in; and the cloud filled the inner court.4 Then the glory of YHUH went up from the cherub, and stood over the threshold of the house; and the house was filled with the cloud, and the court was full of the brightness of YHUH's glory.5 And the sound of the cherubims' wings was heard even to the outer court, as the voice of the Almighty G-d when he speaketh.6 And it came to pass, that when he had commanded the man clothed with linen, saying, Take fire from between the wheels, from between the cherubims; then he went in, and stood beside the wheels.7 And one cherub stretched forth his hand from between the cherubims unto the fire that was between the cherubims, and took thereof,

ידו 3027 מבינות 996 לכרובים 3742 אל 413 האש 784 אשר 834 בינות 996 הכרבים 3742 וישא 5375 ויתן 5414 אל 413
yadou mibeynout lakrubiym, 'al ha'aesh 'asher beynout hakarubiym, uayisaa' uayiten, 'al
**his hand from between the cherubims unto the fire that *was* between the cherubims and took *thereof* and put *it* into**

חפני 2651 לבש 3847 הבדים 906 ויקח 3947 ויצא 3318: 10:8 וירא 7200 לכרבים 3742
chapaney labush habadiym; uayiqach uayetzea'. uayera' lakrubiym;
**the hands of *him that was* clothed with the linen who took *it* and went out And there appeared in the cherubims**

תבנית 8403 יד 3027 אדם 120 תחת 8478 כנפיהם 3671: 10:9 ואראה 7200 והנה 2009 ארבעה 702 אופנים 212 אצל 681
tabaniyt yad 'adam, tachat kanapeyhem. ua'ar'ah, uahineh 'arba'ah 'aupaniym 'aetzel
**the form of a hand man's under their wings And when I looked and behold *the* four wheels by**

הכרובים 3742 אופן 212 אחד 259 אצל 681 הכרוב 3742 אחד 259 ואופן 212 אחד 259 אצל 681 הכרוב 3742 אחד 259 ומראה 4758
hakarubiym 'aupan 'achad, 'aetzel hakarub 'achad, ua'aupan 'achad, 'aetzel hakarub 'achad; uamara'aeh
**the cherubims wheel one by cherub one and wheel another by cherub another and the appearance of**

האופנים 212 כעין 5869 אבן 68 תרשיש 8658: 10:10 ומראיהם 4758 דמות 1823 אחד 259 לארבעתם 702
ha'aupaniym, ka'aeyn 'aben tarshiysh. uamar'aeyhem, damut 'achad la'arba'atam;
**the wheels *was* as the colour of a stone beryl And *as for* their appearances likeness one they four had**

כאשר 834 יהיה 1961 האופן 212 בתוך 8432 האופן 212: 10:11 בלכתם 1980 אל 413 ארבעת 702 רבעיהם 7253 ילכו 1980 לא 3808
ka'asher yihayeh ha'aupan batouk ha'aupan. balektam, 'al 'arba'at riba'aeyhem yeleku, la'
**as if had been a wheel in the midst of a wheel When they went upon four their sides they went not**

יסבו 5437 בלכתם 1980 כי 3588 המקום 4725 אשר 834 יפנה 6437 הראש 7218 אחריו 310 ילכו 1980 לא 3808 יסבו 5437
yisabu balektam; kiy hamaqoum 'asher yipneh hara'sh 'acharayu yeleku, la' yisabu
**they turned as they went but *to* the place which looked the head they followed it not they turned**

בלכתם 1980: 10:12 וכל 3605 בשרם 1320 וגבהם 1354 וידיהם 3027 וכנפיהם 3671 והאופנים 212 מלאים 4392
balektam. uakal basaram uagabehm, uiydeyhem uakanpeyhem; uaha'aupaniym, male'aym
**as they went And whole their body and their backs and their hands and their wings and the wheels *were* full of**

עינים 5869 סביב 5439 לארבעתם 702 אופניהם 212: 10:13 לאופנים 212 להם 3807a קורא 7121 הגלגל 1534
'aeynayim sabiyb, la'arba'atam 'aupaneyhem. la'aupaniym; lahem goura' hagalgal
**eyes round about that they four had *even* the wheels As for the wheels unto them it was cried O wheel**

באזני 241: 10:14 וארבעה 702 פנים 6440 לאחד 259 פני 6440 האחד 259 פני 6440 הכרוב 3742 ופני 6440 השני 8145
ba'azanay. ua'arbah paniym la'achad; paney ha'achad paney hakarub, uapaney hasheniy
**in my hearing And four faces every one had face the first *was* the face of a cherub and face the second**

פני 6440 אדם 120 והשלישי 7992 פני 6440 אריה 738 והרביעי 7243 פני 6440 נשר 5404: 10:15 וירמו 7426
paney 'adam, uahashlishiy paney 'aryeh, uaharabiy'ay paney nasher. uayeromu
***was* the face of a man and the third the face of a lion and the fourth the face of an eagle And were lifted up**

הכרובים 3742 היא 1931 החיה 2416 אשר 834 ראיתי 7200 בנהר 5104 כבר 3529: 10:16 ובלכת 1980 הכרובים 3742
hakarubiym; hiy'a hachayah, 'asher ra'aytiy binhar kabar. uableket hakarubiym,
**the cherubims This *is* the living creature that I saw by the river of Chebar And when went the cherubims**

Eze 10:7 and put it into the hands of him that was clothed with linen: who took it, and went out.8 And there appeared in the cherubims the form of a man's hand under their wings.9 And when I looked, behold the four wheels by the cherubims, one wheel by one cherub, and another wheel by another cherub: and the appearance of the wheels was as the colour of a beryl stone.10 And as for their appearances, they four had one likeness, as if a wheel had been in the midst of a wheel.11 When they went, they went upon their four sides; they turned not as they went, but to the place whither the head looked they followed it; they turned not as they went.12 And their whole body, and their backs, and their hands, and their wings, and the wheels, were full of eyes round about, even the wheels that they four had.13 As for the wheels, it was cried unto them in my hearing, O wheel.14 And everyone had four faces: the first face was the face of a cherub, and the second face was the face of a man, and the third the face of a lion, and the fourth the face of an eagle.15 And the cherubims were lifted up. This is the living creature that I saw by the river of Chebar.16 And when the cherubims went, the wheels went by them: and when the cherubims lifted up their wings to mount up from the earth, the same wheels also turned not from beside them.

ילכו 1980 האופנים 212 אצלם 681 ובשאת 5375 הכרובים 3742 את 853 כנפיהם 3671 לרום 7311 מעל 5921 הארץ 776 לא 3808
yelaku ha'aupaniym 'atzlam; uabis'aet hakarubiym 'at kanapeyhem, larum me'al ha'aretz, la'
**went the wheels by them and when lifted up the cherubims their wings to mount up from the earth not**

יסבו 5437 האופנים 212 גם 1571 הם 1992 מאצלם 681: **10:17** בעמדם 5975 יעמדו 5975 וברומם 7311
yisabu ha'aupaniym gam hem me'atzslam. ba'amadam ya'amodu, uabroumam
**turned wheels also the same from beside them When they stood *these* stood and when they were lifted up**

ירומו 7426 אותם 853 כי 3588 רוח 7307 החיה 2416 בהם 871a: **10:18** ויצא 3318 כבוד 3519 יהוה 3068
yeroumu 'autam; kiy ruach hachayah bahem. uayetzea' kaboud Yahuah,
***these* lifted up themselves *also* for the spirit of the living creature *was* in them Then departed the glory of Yahuah**

מעל 5921 מפתן 4670 הבית 1004 ויעמד 5975 על 5921 הכרובים 3742: **10:19** וישאו 5375 הכרובים 3742 את 853 כנפיהם 3671
me'al miptan habayit; uaya'amod 'al hakarubiym. uayis'au hakarubiym 'at kanapeyhem
**from off the threshold of the house and stood over the cherubims And lifted up the cherubims their wings**

וירומו 7426 מן 4480 הארץ 776 לעיני 5869 בצאתם 3318 והאופנים 212 לעמתם 5980
uayeroumu min ha'aretz la'aeynay batzea'tam, uaha'aupaniym la'amatam;
**and mounted up from the earth in my sight when they went out and the wheels also *were* beside them**

ויעמד 5975 פתח 6607 שער 8179 בית 1004 יהוה 3068 הקדמוני 6931 וכבוד 3519 אלהי 430 ישראל 3478
uaya'amod, petach sha'ar beyt Yahuah haqadmouniy, uakaboud 'alohey yisra'ael
**and *every one* stood at the door of gate of house Yahuah's the east and the glory of the Elohim of Israel**

עליהם 5921 מלמעלה 4605: **10:20** היא 1931 החיה 2416 אשר 834 ראיתי 7200 תחת 8478 אלהי 430 ישראל 3478
'aleyhem milma'alah. hiy'a hachayah, 'asher ra'aytiy tachat 'alohey yisra'ael
***was* over them above This *is* the living creature that I saw under the Elohim of Israel**

בנהר 5104 כבר 3529 ואדע 3045 כי 3588 כרובים 3742 המה 1992: **10:21** ארבעה 702 ארבעה 702 פנים 6440 לאחד 259
binahar kabar; ua'aeda' kiy karubiym hemah. 'arba'ah 'arba'ah paniym la'achad,
**by the river of Chebar and I knew that *were* the cherubims they four apiece faces Every one had**

וארבע 702 כנפים 3671 לאחד 259 ודמות 1823 ידי 3027 אדם 120 תחת 8478 כנפיהם 3671: **10:22** ודמות 1823
ua'arba' kanapayim la'achad; uadmut yadey 'adam, tachat kanapeyhem. uadmut
**had four wings every one and the likeness of the hands of a man *was* under their wings And the likeness of**

פניהם 6440 המה 1992 הפנים 6440 אשר 834 ראיתי 7200 על 5921 נהר 5104 כבר 3529 מראיהם 4758 ואותם 853 איש 376
paneyhem, hemah hapaniym, 'asher ra'aytiy 'al nahar kabar, mar'aeyhem ua'atam; 'aysh
**their faces *was* the same faces which I saw by the river of Chebar their appearances and themselves every one**

אל 413 עבר 5676 פניו 6440 ילכו 1980:
'al 'aeber panayu yeleku.
**to straight forward they went**

**Ezek 11:1** ותשא 5375 אתי 853 רוח 7307 ותבא 935 אתי 853 אל 413 שער 8179 בית 1004 יהוה 3068 הקדמוני 6931 הפונה 6437
uatisa' 'atiy ruach, uatabea' 'atiy 'al sha'ar beyt Yahuah haqadmouniy hapouneh
**Moreover lifted up me the spirit and brought me unto gate of house Yahuah's the east which looks**

Eze 10:17 When they stood, these stood; and when they were lifted up, these lifted up themselves also: for the spirit of the living creature was in them.18 Then the glory of YHUH departed from off the threshold of the house, and stood over the cherubims.19 And the cherubims lifted up their wings, and mounted up from the earth in my sight: when they went out, the wheels also were beside them, and everyone stood at the door of the east gate of YHUH's house; and the glory of the G-d of Israel was over them above.20 This is the living creature that I saw under the G-d of Israel by the river of Chebar; and I knew that they were the cherubims.21 Every one had four faces apiece, and everyone four wings; and the likeness of the hands of a man was under their wings.22 And the likeness of their faces was the same faces which I saw by the river of Chebar, their appearances and themselves: they went everyone straight forward. **Eze** 11:1 Moreover the spirit lifted me up, and brought me unto the east gate of YHUH's house, which look eastward: and behold at the door of the gate five and twenty men; among whom I saw Jaazaniah the son of Azur, and Pelatiah the son of Benaiah, the princes of the people.

קדימה 6921 והנה 2009 בפתח 6607 השער 8179 עשרים 6242 וחמשה 2568 איש 376 ואראה 7200 בתוכם 8432 את 853 יאזניה 2970
qadiymah, uahineh bapetach hasha'ar, 'asriym uachamishah 'aysh; ua'ar'ah batoukam 'at ya'azanyah
**eastward and behold at the door of the gate and twenty five and men I saw among whom Jaazaniah**

בן 1121 עזר 5809 ואת 853 פלטיהו 6410 בן 1121 בניהו 1141 שרי 8269 העם 5971: 11:2 ויאמר 559 אלי 413 בן 1121 אדם 120 אלה 428
ben 'azur ua'at palatyahu ben banayahu sarey ha'am. uaya'mer 'aelay; ben 'adam 'aeleh
**the son of Azur *and* Pelatiah the son of Benaiah princes of the people Then said he unto me Son of man these**

האנשים 582 החשבים 2803 און 205 והיעצים 3289 עצת 6098 רע 7451 בעיר 5892 הזאת 2063: 11:3 האמרים 559 לא 3808 בקרוב 7138
ha'anashiym hachoshabiym 'auen uahayo'atziym 'atzat ra' ba'ayr haza't. ha'amariym, la' uaqaroub
***are* the men that devise mischief and give counsel wicked in city this Which say *It is* not near**

בנות 1129 בתים 1004 היא 1931 הסיר 5518 ואנחנו 587 הבשר 1320: 11:4 לכן 3651 הנבא 5012 עליהם 5921 הנבא 5012
banout batiym; hiy'a hasiyr, ua'anachnu habasar. laken hinabea' 'aleyhem; hinabea'
**let us build houses this *city is* the caldron and we *be* the flesh Therefore prophesy against them prophesy**

בן 1121 אדם 120: 11:5 ותפל 5307 עלי 5921 רוח 7307 יהוה 3068 ויאמר 559 אלי 413 אמר 559 כה 3541 אמר 559 יהוה 3068 כן 3651
ben 'adam. uatipol 'alay ruach Yahuah uaya'mer 'aelay, 'amor koh 'amar Yahuah, ken
**O son of man And fell upon me the Spirit of Yahuah and said unto me Speak Thus saith Yahuah Thus**

אמרתם 559 בית 1004 ישראל 3478 ומעלות 4609 רוחכם 7307 אני 589 ידעתיה 3045: 11:6
'amartem beyt yisra'ael; uama'alout ruchakem 'aniy yada'atiyha.
**have you said O house of Israel for the things that come into your mind *every one of them* I know**

הרביתם 7235 חלליכם 2491 בעיר 5892 הזאת 2063 ומלאתם 4390 חוצתיה 2351 חלל 2491: 11:7 לכן 3651 כה 3541
hirbeyhem challeykem ba'ayr haza't; uamilea'tem chutzoteyha chalal. laken, koh
**You have multiplied your slain in city this and you have filled the streets thereof *with* the slain Therefore thus**

אמר 559 אדני 136 יהוה 3069 חלליכם 2491 אשר 834 שמתם 7760 בתוכה 8432 המה 1992 הבשר 1320 והיא 1931 הסיר 5518
'amar 'adonay Yahuah challeykem 'asher samtem batoukah, hemah habasar uahiy'a hasiyr;
**saith Adonai Yahuah Your slain whom you have laid in the midst of it they *are* the flesh and this *city is* the caldron**

ואתכם 853 הוציא 3318 מתוכה 8432: 11:8 חרב 2719 יראתם 3372 וחרב 2719 אביא 935 עליכם 5921 נאם 5002
ua'atkem houtziy'a mitoukah. chereb yarea'tem; uachereb 'abiy'a 'aleykem, na'am
**but you I will bring forth out of the midst of it the sword You have feared and a sword I will bring upon you saith**

אדני 136 יהוה 3069: 11:9 והוצאתי 3318 אתכם 853 מתוכה 8432 ונתתי 5414 אתכם 853 ביד 3027 זרים 2114
'adonay Yahuah. uahoutzea'tiy 'atkem mitoukah, uanatatiy 'atkem bayad zariym;
**Adonai Yahuah And I will bring out you of the midst thereof and deliver you into the hands of strangers**

ועשיתי 6213 בכם 871a שפטים 8201: 11:10 בחרב 2719 תפלו 5307 על 5921 גבול 1366 ישראל 3478 אשפוט 8199 אתכם 853
ua'asiytiy bakem shapatiym. bachereb tipolu, 'al gabul yisra'ael 'ashpout 'atkem;
**and will execute among you judgments by the sword You shall fall in the border of Israel I will judge you**

וידעתם 3045 כי 3588 אני 589 יהוה 3068: 11:11 היא 1931 לא 3808 תהיה 1961 לכם 3807a לסיר 5518 ואתם 859 תהיו 1961
uiyda'tem kiy 'aniy Yahuah. hiy'a, la' tihayeh lakem lasiyr, ua'atem tihayu
**and shall know that I *am* Yahuah This not *city* shall be to your caldron neither you shall be**

Eze 11:2 Then said he unto me, Son of man, these are the men that devise mischief, and give wicked counsel in this city:3 Which say, It is not near; let us build houses: this city is the caldron, and we be the flesh.4 Therefore prophesy against them, prophesy, O son of man.5 And the Spirit of YHUH fell upon me, and said unto me, Speak; Thus saith YHUH; Thus have you said, O house of Israel: for I know the things that come into your mind, everyone of them.6 You have multiplied your slain in this city, and you have filled the streets thereof with the slain.7 Therefore thus saith YHUH G-D; Your slain whom you have laid in the midst of it, they are the flesh, and this city is the caldron: but I will bring you forth out of the midst of it.8 You have feared the sword; and I will bring a sword upon you, saith YHUH G-D.9 And I will bring you out of the midst thereof, and deliver you into the hands of strangers, and will execute judgments among you.10 You shall fall by the sword; I will judge you in the border of Israel; and you shall know that I am YHUH.11 This city shall not be your caldron, neither shall you be the flesh in the midst thereof; but I will judge you in the border of Israel:

11:12

בתוכה 8432 לבשר 1320 אל 413 גבול 1366 ישראל 3478 אשפט 8199 אתכם 853: וידעתם 3045 כי 3588 אני 589
batoukah labasar; 'al gabul yisra'ael 'ashpot 'atkem. uiyda'tem kiy 'aniy
**in the midst thereof the flesh in the border of Israel *but* I will judge you And you shall know that I *am***

יהוה 3068 אשר 834 בחקי 2706 לא 3808 הלכתם 1980 ומשפטי 4941 לא 3808 עשיתם 6213 וכמשפטי 4941
Yahuah, 'asher bachuqay la' halaktem, uamishpatay la' 'asiytem; uakmishapatey
**Yahuah for in my statutes not you have walked my judgments neither executed but after the manners of**

11:13

הגוים 1471 אשר 834 סביבותיכם 5439 עשיתם 6213: ויהי 1961 כהנבאי 5012 ופלטיהו 6410 בן 1121
hagouyim 'asher sabiybouteykem 'asiytem. uayahiy kahinaba'ay, uaplatyahu ben
**the heathen that *are* round about you have done And it came to pass when I prophesied that Pelatiah the son of**

בניה 1141 מת 4191 ואפל 5307 על 5921 פני 6440 ואזעק 2199 קול 6963 גדול 1419 ואמר 559 אהה 162 אדני 136 יהוה 3069 כלה 3617
banayah met; ua'apol 'al panay ua'azaq qoul gadoul, ua'amar 'ahah 'adonay Yahuah, kalah
**Benaiah died Then fell I down upon my face and cried with a voice loud and said Ah Adonai Yahuah a full end of**

11:14 11:15

אתה 859 עשה 6213 את 853 שארית 7611 ישראל 3478: ויהי 1961 דבר 1697 יהוה 3068 אלי 413 לאמר 559: בן 1121
'atah 'aseh, 'at sha'aeriyt yisra'ael. uayahiy dabar Yahuah 'aelay lea'mor. ben
**you will make the remnant of Israel? Again came the word of Yahuah unto me saying Son of**

אדם 120 אחיך 251 אחיך 251 אנשי 582 גאלתך 1353 וכל 3605 בית 1004 ישראל 3478 כלה 3605 אשר 834
'adam, 'acheyka 'acheyka 'anshey ga'alateka, uakal beyt yisra'ael kuloh; 'asher
**man your brethren *even* your brethren the men of your kindred and all the house of Israel wholly whom**

אמרו 559 להם 3807a ישבי 3427 ירושלם 3389 רחקו 7368 מעל 5921 יהוה 3068 לנו 3807a היא 1931 נתנה 5414 הארץ 776
'amaru lahem yoshabey yarushalaim, rachaqu me'al Yahuah, lanu hiy'a nitnah ha'aretz
**have said *are* they unto the inhabitants of Jerusalem Get you far from Yahuah unto us this is given the land**

11:16

למורשה 4181: לכן 3651 אמר 559 כה 3541 אמר 559 אדני 136 יהוה 3069 כי 3588 הרחקתים 7368 בגוים 1471
lamourashah. laken 'amor, koh 'amar 'adonay Yahuah kiy hirchaqtiym bagouyim,
**in possession Therefore say Thus saith Adonai Yahuah Although I have cast them far off among the heathen**

וכי 3588 הפיצותים 6327 בארצות 776 ואהי 1961 להם 3807a למקדש 4720 מעט 4592 בארצות 776
uakiy hapiytzoutiym ba'aratzout; ua'ahiy lahem lamiqdash ma'at, ba'aratzout
**and although I have scattered them among the countries yet will I be to them as a sanctuary little in the countries**

11:17

אשר 834 באו 935 שם 8033: לכן 3651 אמר 559 כה 3541 אמר 559 אדני 136 יהוה 3068 וקבצתי 6908 אתכם 853 מן 4480
'asher ba'au sham. laken 'amor, koh 'amar 'adonay Yahuah uaqibatztiy 'atkem min
**where they shall come there Therefore say Thus saith Adonai Yahuah I will even gather you from**

העמים 5971 ואספתי 622 אתכם 853 מן 4480 הארצות 776 אשר 834 נפצותם 6327 בהם 871a ונתתי 5414 לכם 3807a
ha'amiym, ua'asaptiy 'atkem, min ha'aratzout, 'asher napotzoutem bahem; uanatatiy lakem
**the people and I will assemble you out of the countries where you have been scattered in them and I will give to you**

11:18

את 853 אדמת 127 ישראל 3478: ובאו 935 שמה 8033 והסירו 5493 את 853 כל 3605
'at 'admat yisra'ael. uaba'au shamah; uahesiyru 'at kal
**the land of Israel And they shall come there and they shall take away all**

Eze 11:12 And you shall know that I am YHUH: for you have not walked in my statutes, neither executed my judgments, but have done after the manners of the heathen that are round about you.13 And it came to pass, when I prophesied, that Pelatiah the son of Benaiah died. Then fell I down upon my face, and cried with a loud voice, and said, Ah Adonai G-D! will you make a full end of the remnant of Israel?14 Again the word of YHUH came unto me, saying,15 Son of man, your brethren, even your brethren, the men of your kindred, and all the house of Israel wholly, are they unto whom the inhabitants of Jerusalem have said, Get you far from YHUH: unto us is this land given in possession.16 Therefore say, Thus saith YHUH G-D; Although I have cast them far off among the heathen, and although I have scattered them among the countries, yet will I be to them as a little sanctuary in the countries where they shall come.17 Therefore say, Thus saith YHUH G-D; I will even gather you from the people, and assemble you out of the countries where you have been scattered, and I will give you the land of Israel.18 And they shall come thither, and they shall take away all the detestable things thereof and all the abominations thereof from thence.

11:19
שקוציה 8251 ואת 853 כל 3605 תועבותיה 8441 ממנה 4480: ונתתי 5414 להם 3807a לב 3820 אחד 259
shiqutzeyha ua'at kal tou'abouteyha mimenah. uanatatiy lahem leb 'achad,
**the detestable things thereof *and* all the abominations thereof from there And I will give them heart one**

ורוח 7307 חדשה 2319 אתן 5414 בקרבכם 7130 והסרתי 5493 לב 3820 האבן 68 מבשרם 1320 ונתתי 5414 להם 3807a
uaruach chadashah 'aten baqirbakem; uahasirotiy leb ha'aben mibasaram, uanatatiy lahem
**and a spirit new I will put within you and I will take heart the stony out of their flesh and will give them**

11:20
לב 3820 בשר 1320: למען 4616 בחקתי 2708 ילכו 1980 ואת 853 משפטי 4941 ישמרו 8104 ועשו 6213 אתם 853
leb basar. lama'an bachuqotay yeleku, ua'at mishpatay yishmaru ua'asu 'atam;
**an heart of flesh That in my statutes they may walk *and* mine ordinances keep and do them**

11:21
והיו 1961 לי 3807a לעם 5971 ואני 589 אהיה 1961 להם 3807a לאלהים 430: ואל 413 לב 3820
uahayu liy la'am, ua'aniy 'ahayeh lahem le'alohiym. ua'al leb
**and they shall be my people and I will be their to Elohim But after *as for them* whose heart**

שקוציהם 8251 ותועבותיהם 8441 לבם 3820 הלך 1980 דרכם 1870 בראשם 7218 נתתי 5414 נאם 5002
shiqutzeyhem uatou'abouteyhem libam halok; darkam bara'sham natatiy, na'am
**their detestable things and their abominations the heart of walk their way upon their own heads I will recompense saith**

11:22
אדני 136 יהוה 3068: וישאו 5375 הכרובים 3742 את 853 כנפיהם 3671 והאופנים 212 לעמתם 5980 וכבוד 3519
'adonay Yahuah. uayis'au hakarubiym 'at kanapeyhem, uaha'aupaniym la'amatam; uakaboud
**Adonai Yahuah Then did lift up the cherubims their wings and the wheels beside them and the glory of**

11:23
אלהי 430 ישראל 3478 עליהם 5921 מלמעלה 4605: ויעל 5927 כבוד 3519 יהוה 3068 מעל 5921 תוך 8432 העיר 5892
'alohey yisra'ael 'aleyhem milma'alah. uaya'al kaboud Yahuah, me'al touk ha'ayr;
**the Elohim of Israel *was* over them above And went up the glory of Yahuah from the midst of the city**

11:24
ויעמד 5975 על 5921 ההר 2022 אשר 834 מקדם 6924 לעיר 5892: ורוח 7307 נשאתני 5375 ותביאני 935
uaya'amod 'al hahar, 'asher miqedem la'ayr. uaruach nasa'atniy, uatabiy'aeniy
**and stood upon the mountain which *is* on the east side of the city Afterwards the spirit took me up and brought me**

כשדימה 3778 אל 413 הגולה 1473 במראה 4758 ברוח 7307 אלהים 430 ויעל 5927 מעלי 5921 המראה 4758 אשר 834
kasdiymah 'al hagoulah, bamar'ah baruach 'alohiym; uaya'al me'alay, hamar'ah 'asher
**into Chaldea to them of the captivity in a vision by the Spirit of Elohim So went up from me the vision that**

11:25
ראיתי 7200: ואדבר 1696 אל 413 הגולה 1473 את 853 כל 3605 דברי 1697 יהוה 3068 אשר 834 הראני 7200:
ra'aytiy. ua'adaber 'al hagoulah; 'at kal dibrey Yahuah 'asher her'aniy.
**I had seen Then I spoke unto them of the captivity all the things Yahuah that had showed me**

**Ezek 12:1** 12:2
ויהי 1961 דבר 1697 יהוה 3068 אלי 413 לאמר 559: בן 1121 אדם 120 בתוך 8432 בית 1004 המרי 4805 אתה 859
uayahiy dabar Yahuah 'aelay lea'mor. ben 'adam batouk beyt hameriy 'atah
**also came The word of Yahuah unto me saying Son of man in the midst of a house rebellious you**

ישב 3427 אשר 834 עינים 5869 להם 3807a לראות 7200 ולא 3808 ראו 7200 אזנים 241 להם 3807a לשמע 8085 ולא 3808 שמעו 8085 כי 3588 בית 1004
yosheb; 'asher 'aeynayim lahem lir'aut uala' ra'au, 'azanayim lahem lishmoa' uala' shame'au, kiy beyt
**dwell which eyes have to see and not see *have* ears they to hear and not hear for *are* a house**

Eze 11:19 And I will give them one heart, and I will put a new spirit within you; and I will take the stony heart out of their flesh, and will give them an heart of flesh:20 That they may walk in my statutes, and keep mine ordinances, and do them: and they shall be my people, and I will be their G-d.21 But as for them whose heart walk after the heart of their detestable things and their abominations, I will recompense their way upon their own heads, saith YHUH G-D.22 Then did the cherubims lift up their wings, and the wheels beside them; and the glory of the G-d of Israel was over them above.23 And the glory of YHUH went up from the midst of the city, and stood upon the mountain which is on the east side of the city.24 Afterwards the spirit took me up, and brought me in a vision by the Spirit of G-d into Chaldea, to them of the captivity. So the vision that I had seen went up from me.25 Then I spoke unto them of the captivity all the things that YHUH had showed me. **Eze** 12:1 The word of YHUH also came unto me, saying,2 Son of man, you dwellest in the midst of a rebellious house, which have eyes to see, and see not; they have ears to hear, and hear not: for they are a rebellious house.

12:3
מרי 4805 הם 1992: ואתה 859 בן 1121 אדם 120 עשה 6213 לך 3807a כלי 3627 גולה 1473 וגלה 1540 יומם 3119 לעיניהם 5869
mariy hem. ua'atah ben 'adam, 'aseh laka kaley gouleh, uagleh youmam la'aeyneyhem;
**rebellious they Therefore you son of man prepare for you stuff for removing and remove by day in their sight**

וגלית 1540 ממקומך 4725 אל 413 מקום 4725 אחר 312 לעיניהם 5869 אולי 194 יראו 7200 כי 3588 בית 1004
uagaliyta mimaqoumaka 'al maqoum 'acher la'aeyneyhem, 'aulay yir'au, kiy beyt
**and you shall remove from your place to place another in their sight it may be they will consider though *be* a house**

12:4
מרי 4805 המה 1992: והוצאת 3318 כליך 3627 ככלי 3627 גולה 1473 יומם 3119 לעיניהם 5869 ואתה 859
mariy hemah. uahotzea'ta keleyka kikley gouleh youmam la'aeyneyhem; ua'atah,
**rebellious they Then shall you bring forth your stuff as stuff for removing by day in their sight and you**

12:5
תצא 3318 בערב 6153 לעיניהם 5869 כמוצאי 4161 גולה 1473: לעיניהם 5869 חתר 2864 לך 3807a בקיר 7023
tetzea' ba'areb la'aeyneyhem, kamoutza'aey goulah. la'aeyneyhem chator laka baqiyr;
**shall go forth at even in their sight as they that go forth into captivity in their sight Dig for you through the wall**

12:6
והוצאת 3318 בו 871a: לעיניהם 5869 על 5921 כתף 3802 תשא 5375 בעלטה 5939 תוציא 3318
uahoutzea'ta bou. la'aeyneyhem 'al katep tisa' ba'alatah toutziy'a,
**and you carry out thereby In their sight upon *your* shoulders shall you bear *it* in the twilight *and* you carry *it* forth**

12:7
פניך 6440 תכסה 3680 ולא 3808 תראה 7200 את 853 הארץ 776 כי 3588 מופת 4159 נתתיך 5414 לבית 1004 ישראל 3478:
paneyka takaseh, uala' tir'ah 'at ha'aretz; kiy moupet natatiyka labeyt yisra'ael.
**your face you shall cover that not you see the ground for *for* a sign I have set you unto the house of Israel**

ואעש 6213 כן 3651 כאשר 834 צויתי 6680 כלי 3627 הוצאתי 3318 ככלי 3627 גולה 1473 יומם 3119 ובערב 6153 חתרתי 2864
ua'aas ken ka'asher tzueytiy kelay houtzea'tiy kikley gouleh youmam, uaba'areb chatartiy
**And I did so as I was commanded my stuff I brought forth as stuff for captivity by day and in the even I digged**

12:8
לי 3807a בקיר 7023 ביד 3027 בעלטה 5939 הוצאתי 3318 על 5921 כתף 3802 נשאתי 5375 לעיניהם 5869:
liy baqiyr bayad; ba'alatah houtzea'tiy 'al katep nasa'tiy la'aeyneyhem.
**mine through the wall with hand in the twilight I brought *it* forth upon *my* shoulder *and* I bare *it* in their sight**

12:9
ויהי 1961 דבר 1697 יהוה 3068 אלי 413 בבקר 1242 לאמר 559: בן 1121 אדם 120 הלא 3808 אמרו 559 אליך 413 בית 1004
uayahiy dabar Yahuah 'aelay baboqer lea'mor. ben 'adam hala' 'amaru 'aeleyka beyt
**And came the word of Yahuah unto me in the morning saying Son of man not has said unto you the house of**

12:10
ישראל 3478 בית 1004 המרי 4805 מה 4100 אתה 859 עשה 6213: אמר 559 אליהם 413 כה 3541 אמר 559 אדני 136 יהוה 3069
yisra'ael beyt hameriy; mah 'atah 'aseh. 'amor 'aleyhem, koh 'amar 'adonay Yahuah;
**Israel house the rebellious What you? do Say you unto them Thus saith Adonai Yahuah**

12:11
הנשיא 5387 המשא 4853 הזה 2088 בירושלם 3389 וכל 3605 בית 1004 ישראל 3478 אשר 834 המה 1992 בתוכם 8432: אמר 559
hanasiy'a hamasa' hazeh biyarushalam, uakal beyt yisra'ael 'asher hemah batoukam. 'amor
***concern* the prince burden This in Jerusalem and all the house of Israel that them *are* among Say**

אני 589 מופתכם 4159 כאשר 834 עשיתי 6213 כן 3651 יעשה 6213 להם 3807a בגולה 1473 בשבי 7628 ילכו 1980:
'aniy moupetakem; ka'asher 'asiytiy, ken ye'aseh lahem, bagoulah bashabiy yeleku.
**I *am* your sign like as I have done so shall it be done unto them they shall remove into captivity *and* go**

Eze 12:3 Therefore, you son of man, prepare you stuff for removing, and remove by day in their sight; and you shall remove from your place to another place in their sight: it may be they will consider, though they be a rebellious house.4 Then shall you bring forth your stuff by day in their sight, as stuff for removing: and you shall go forth at even in their sight, as they that go forth into captivity.5 Dig you through the wall in their sight, and carry out thereby.6 In their sight shall you bear it upon your shoulders, and carry it forth in the twilight: you shall cover your face, that you see not the ground: for I have set you for a sign unto the house of Israel.7 And I did so as I was commanded: I brought forth my stuff by day, as stuff for captivity, and in the even I digged through the wall with mine hand; I brought it forth in the twilight, and I bare it upon my shoulder in their sight.8 And in the morning came the word of YHUH unto me, saying,9 Son of man, has not the house of Israel, the rebellious house, said unto you, What does you?10 Say you unto them, Thus saith YHUH G-D; This burden concerneth the prince in Jerusalem, and all the house of Israel that are among them.11 Say, I am your sign: like as I have done, so shall it be done unto them: they shall remove and go into captivity.

12:12
והנשיא 5387 אשר 834 בתוכם 8432 אל 413 כתף 3802 ישא 5375 בעלטה 5939 ויצא 3318 בקיר 7023
uahanasiy'a 'asher batoukam 'al katep yisa' ba'alatah uayetzea', baqiyr
**And the prince that *is* among them upon *his* shoulder shall bear in the twilight and shall go forth through the wall**

יחתרו 2864 להוציא 3318 בו 871a פניו 6440 יכסה 3680 יען 3282 אשר 834 לא 3808 יראה 7200 לעין 5869 הוא 1931 את 853
yachtaru lahoutziy'a bou; panayu yakaseh, ya'an, 'asher la' yir'ah la'ayin hua' 'at
**they shall dig to carry out thereby his face he shall cover because that not see with *his* eyes he**

12:13
הארץ 776: ופרשתי 6566 את 853 רשתי 7568 עליו 5921 ונתפש 8610 במצודתי 4686 והבאתי 935 אתו 853
ha'aretz. uaparastiy 'at rishtiy 'alayu, uanitpas bimtzudatiy; uahebea'tiy 'atou
**the ground also will I spread My net upon him and he shall be taken in my snare and I will bring him**

12:14
בבלה 894 ארץ 776 כשדים 3778 ואותה 853 לא 3808 יראה 7200 ושם 8033 ימות 4191: וכל 3605
babelah 'aretz kasdiym, ua'atah la' yir'ah uasham yamut. uakol
**to Babylon the land of the Chaldeans yet it (*her*) not shall he see though there he shall die And toward every**

אשר 834 סביבתיו 5439 עזרה 5828 וכל 3605 אגפיו 102 אזרה 2219 לכל 3605 רוח 7307 וחרב 2719 אריק 7324
'asher sabiybotayu 'azroh uakal 'agapayu 'azareh lakal ruach; uachereb 'ariyq
**that *are* about him to help him all his bands I will scatter and all wind and the sword I will draw out**

12:15
אחריהם 310: וידעו 3045 כי 3588 אני 589 יהוה 3068 בהפיצי 6327 אותם 853 בגוים 1471 וזריתי 2219
'achareyhem. uayada'aua kiy 'aniy Yahuah; bahapiytziy 'autam bagouyim, uazeriytiy
**after them And they shall know that I *am* Yahuah when I shall scatter them among the nations and disperse**

12:16
אותם 853 בארצות 776: והותרתי 3498 מהם 1992 אנשי 582 מספר 4557 מחרב 2719 מרעב 7458
'autam ba'aratzout. uahoutartiy mehem 'anshey mispar, mechereb mera'ab
**them in the countries But I will leave of them a men few from the sword from the famine**

ומדבר 1698 למען 4616 יספרו 5608 את 853 כל 3605 תועבותיהם 8441 בגוים 1471 אשר 834 באו 935
uamidaber; lama'an yasapru 'at kal tou'abouteyhem, bagouyim 'asher ba'au
**and from the pestilence that they may declare all their abominations among the heathen where they come**

12:17 12:18
שם 8033 וידעו 3045 כי 3588 אני 589 יהוה 3068: ויהי 1961 דבר 1697 יהוה 3068 אלי 413 לאמר 559: בן 1121
sham, uayada'aua kiy 'aniy Yahuah. uayahiy dabar Yahuah 'aelay lea'mor. ben
**there and they shall know that I *am* Yahuah Moreover came the word of Yahuah to me saying Son of**

12:19
אדם 120 לחמך 3899 ברעש 7494 תאכל 398 ומימיך 4325 ברגזה 7269 ובדאגה 1674 תשתה 8354: ואמרת 559 אל 413
'adam lachmaka bara'ash ta'kel; uameymeyka baragazah uabida'agah tishteh. ua'amarta 'al
**man your bread with quaking eat and your water with trembling and with carefulness drink And say unto**

עם 5971 הארץ 776 כה 3541 אמר 559 אדני 136 יהוה 3069 ליושבי 3427 ירושלם 3389 אל 413 אדמת 127 ישראל 3478
'am ha'aretz koh 'amar 'adonay Yahuah layoushabey yarushalaim 'al 'admat yisra'ael,
**the people of the land *of* Thus saith Adonai Yahuah of the inhabitants of Jerusalem *and* of the land Israel**

לחמם 3899 בדאגה 1674 יאכלו 398 ומימיהם 4325 בשממון 8078 ישתו 8354 למען 4616 תשם 3456 ארצה 776
lachmam bida'agah ya'kelu, uameymeyhem bashimamoun yishtu; lama'an tesham 'artzah
**their bread with carefulness They shall eat and their water with astonishment drink that may be desolate her land**

Eze 12:12 And the prince that is among them shall bear upon his shoulder in the twilight, and shall go forth: they shall dig through the wall to carry out thereby: he shall cover his face, that he see not the ground with his eyes.13 My net also will I spread upon him, and he shall be taken in my snare: and I will bring him to Babylon to the land of the Chaldeans; yet shall he not see it, though he shall die there.14 And I will scatter toward every wind all that are about him to help him, and all his bands; and I will draw out the sword after them.15 And they shall know that I am YHUH, when I shall scatter them among the nations, and disperse them in the countries.16 But I will leave a few men of them from the sword, from the famine, and from the pestilence; that they may declare all their abominations among the heathen whither they come; and they shall know that I am YHUH.17 Moreover the word of YHUH came to me, saying,18 Son of man, eat your bread with quaking, and drink your water with trembling and with carefulness;19 And say unto the people of the land, Thus saith YHUH G-D of the inhabitants of Jerusalem, and of the land of Israel; They shall eat their bread with carefulness, and drink their water with astonishment, that her land may be desolate from all that is therein, because of the violence of all them that dwell therein.

12:20
ממלאה 4393 מחמס 2555 כל 3605 הישבים 3427 בה 871a: והערים 5892 הנושבות 3427
mimalo'ah, mechamas kal hayoshabiym bah. uahe'ariym hanoushabout
**from all that is therein because of the violence of all them that dwell therein And the cities that are inhabited**

12:21
תחרבנה 2717 והארץ 776 שממה 8077 תהיה 1961 וידעתם 3045 כי 3588 אני 589 יהוה 3068: ויהי 1961 דבר 1697
techerabnah, uaha'aretz shamamah tihayeh; uiyda'tem kiy 'aniy Yahuah. uayahiy dabar
**shall be laid waste and the land desolate shall be and you shall know that I *am* Yahuah And came the word of**

12:22
יהוה 3068 אלי 413 לאמר 559: בן 1121 אדם 120 מה 4100 המשל 4912 הזה 2088 לכם 3807a על 5921 אדמת 127 ישראל 3478 לאמר 559
Yahuah 'aelay lea'mor. ben 'adam, mah hamashal hazeh lakem, 'al 'admat yisra'ael lea'mor;
**Yahuah unto me saying Son of man what proverb *is* this *that* to you *have* in the land of Israel saying**

12:23
יארכו 748 הימים 3117 ואבד 6 כל 3605 חזון 2377: לכן 3651 אמר 559 אליהם 413 כה 3541 אמר 559 אדני 136 יהוה 3068
ya'arku hayamiym, ua'abad kal chazoun. laken 'amor 'aleyhem, koh 'amar 'adonay Yahuah
**are prolonged The days and fail? every vision therefore Tell them Thus saith Adonai Yahuah**

השבתי 7673 את 853 המשל 4912 הזה 2088 ולא 3808 ימשלו 4911 אתו 853 עוד 5750 בישראל 3478 כי 3588 אם 518 דבר 1696
hishbatiy 'at hamashal hazeh, uala' yimshalu 'atou 'aud bayisra'ael; kiy 'am daber
**I will make to cease proverb this and no they shall use as a proverb it more in Israel for but say**

12:24
אליהם 413 קרבו 7126 הימים 3117 ודבר 1697 כל 3605 חזון 2377: כי 3588 לא 3808 יהיה 1961 עוד 5750 כל 3605 חזון 2377
'aleyhem, qarabu hayamiym, uadbar kal chazoun. kiy la' yihayeh 'aud kal chazoun
**unto them are at hand The days and the effect of every vision For no there shall be more any vision**

12:25
שוא 7723 ומקסם 4738 חלק 2509 בתוך 8432 בית 1004 ישראל 3478: כי 3588 אני 589 יהוה 3068 אדבר 1696 את 853 אשר 834
shau'a uamiqsam chalaq; batouk beyt yisra'ael. kiy 'aniy Yahuah 'adaber 'at 'asher
**vain nor divination flattering within the house of Israel For I *am* Yahuah I will speak that**

אדבר 1696 דבר 1697 ויעשה 6213 לא 3808 תמשך 4900 עוד 5750 כי 3588 בימיכם 3117 בית 1004 המרי 4805
'adaber dabar uaye'aseh, la' timashek 'aud; kiy biymeykem beyt hameriy,
**I shall speak the word and shall come to pass no it shall be prolonged more for in your days O house rebellious**

12:26
אדבר 1696 דבר 1697 ועשיתיו 6213 נאם 5002 אדני 136 יהוה 3069: ויהי 1961 דבר 1697 יהוה 3068 אלי 413
'adaber dabar ua'asiytiyu, na'am 'adonay Yahuah. uayahiy dabar Yahuah 'aelay
**will I say the word and will perform it saith *the* Adonai Yahuah Again came the word of Yahuah to me**

12:27
לאמר 559: בן 1121 אדם 120 הנה 2009 בית 1004 ישראל 3478 אמרים 559 החזון 2377 אשר 834 הוא 1931 חזה 2374 לימים 3117
lea'mor. ben 'adam, hineh beyt yisra'ael 'amariym, hechazoun 'asher hua' chozeh layamiym
**saying Son of man behold *they of* the house of Israel say The vision that he see *to come is* for days**

12:28
רבים 7227 ולעתים 6256 רחוקות 7350 הוא 1931 נבא 5012: לכן 3651 אמר 559 אליהם 413 כה 3541 אמר 559 אדני 136 יהוה 3069
rabiym; ual'atiym rachouqout hua' niba'. laken 'amor 'aleyhem, koh 'amar 'adonay Yahuah,
**many and of the times *that are* far off he prophesieth Therefore say unto them Thus saith Adonai Yahuah**

לא 3808 תמשך 4900 עוד 5750 כל 3605 דברי 1697 אשר 834 אדבר 1696 דבר 1697 ויעשה 6213 נאם 5002
la' timashek 'aud kal dabaray; 'asher 'adaber dabar uaye'aseh, na'am
**none of There shall be prolonged any more none of my words which I have spoken the word but shall be done saith**

Eze 12:20 And the cities that are inhabited shall be laid waste, and the land shall be desolate; and you shall know that I am YHUH.21 And the word of YHUH came unto me, saying,22 Son of man, what is that proverb that you have in the land of Israel, saying, The days are prolonged, and every vision faileth?23 Tell them therefore, Thus saith YHUH G-D; I will make this proverb to cease, and they shall no more use it as a proverb in Israel; but say unto them, The days are at hand, and the effect of every vision.24 For there shall be no more any vain vision nor flattering divination within the house of Israel.25 For I am YHUH: I will speak, and the word that I shall speak shall come to pass; it shall be no more prolonged: for in your days, O rebellious house, will I say the word, and will perform it, saith YHUH G-D.26 Again the word of YHUH came to me, saying,27 Son of man, behold, they of the house of Israel say, The vision that he see is for many days to come, and he prophesieth of the times that are far off.28 Therefore say unto them, Thus saith YHUH G-D; There shall none of my words be prolonged anymore, but the word which I have spoken shall be done, saith YHUH G-D.

אדני 136 יהוה 3069:
'adonay Yahuah.
**Adonai Yahuah**

**Ezek 13:1**
ויהי 1961 דבר 1697 יהוה 3068 אלי 413 לאמר 559: **13:2** בן 1121 אדם 120 הנבא 5012 אל 413 נביאי 5030 ישראל 3478
uayahiy dabar Yahuah 'aelay lea'mor. ben 'adam hinabea' 'al nabiy'aey yisra'ael
**And came the word of Yahuah unto me saying Son of man prophesy against the prophets of Israel**

הנבאים 5012 ואמרת 559 לנביאי 5030 מלבם 3820 שמעו 8085 דבר 1697 יהוה 3068: **13:3** כה 3541
haniba'aym; ua'amarta linabiy'aey milibam, shim'au dabar Yahuah. koh
**that prophesy and say you unto them that prophesy out of their own hearts Hear you the word of Yahuah Thus**

אמר 559 אדני 136 יהוה 3069 הוי 1945 על 5921 הנביאים 5030 הנבלים 5036 אשר 834 הלכים 1980 אחר 310 רוחם 7307 ולבלתי 1115
'amar 'adonay Yahuah, houy 'al hanabiy'aym hanabaliym; 'asher holakiym 'achar rucham ualbiltiy
**saith Adonai Yahuah Woe unto prophets the foolish that follow after their own spirit and nothing**

ראו 7200: **13:4** כשעלים 7776 בחרבות 2723 נביאיך 5030 ישראל 3478 היו 1961: **13:5** לא 3808 עליתם 5927 בפרצות 6556
ra'au. kashu'aliym bacharabout; nabiy'ayka yisra'ael hayu. la' 'aliytem baparatzout,
**have seen like the foxes in the deserts your prophets O Israel are nor You have gone up into the gaps**

ותגדרו 1443 גדר 1447 על 5921 בית 1004 ישראל 3478 לעמד 5975 במלחמה 4421 ביום 3117 יהוה 3068: **13:6** חזו 2372
uatigdaru gader 'al beyt yisra'ael; la'amod bamilchamah bayoum Yahuah. chazu
**neither made up the hedge for the house of Israel to stand in the battle in the day of Yahuah They have seen**

שוא 7723 וקסם 7081 כזב 3577 האמרים 559 נאם 5002 יהוה 3068 ויהוה 3068 לא 3808 שלחם 7971
shau'a uaqesem kazab, ha'amariym na'am Yahuah, uaYahuah la' shalacham;
**vanity and divination lying saying saith Yahuah and Yahuah not has sent them**

ויחלו 3176 לקים 6965 דבר 1697: **13:7** הלוא 3808 מחזה 4236 שוא 7723 חזיתם 2372
uayichalu laqayem dabar. halou'a machazeh shau'a chaziytem,
**and they have made *others* to hope that they would confirm the word not a vision vain Have you seen**

ומקסם 4738 כזב 3577 אמרתם 559 ואמרים 559 נאם 5002 יהוה 3068 ואני 589 לא 3808 דברתי 1696: **13:8** לכן 3651
uamiqsam kazab 'amartem; ua'amariym na'am Yahuah, ua'aniy la' dibartiy. laken,
**and a divination lying have you not spoken whereas you say saith Yahuah *it*: albeit I not have spoken? Therefore**

כה 3541 אמר 559 אדני 136 יהוה 3069 יען 3282 דברכם 1696 שוא 7723 וחזיתם 2372 כזב 3577 לכן 3651 הנני 2005 אליכם 413
koh 'amar 'adonay Yahuah, ya'an daberkem shau'a, uachaziytem kazab; laken hinniy 'aleykem,
**thus saith Adonai Yahuah Because you have spoken vanity and seen lies therefore behold I *am* against you**

נאם 5002 אדני 136 יהוה 3069: **13:9** והיתה 1961 ידי 3027 אל 413 הנביאים 5030 החזים 2374 שוא 7723 והקסמים 7080 כזב 3577
na'am 'adonay Yahuah. uahayatah yadiy, 'al hanabiy'aym hachoziym shau'a uahaqosamiym kazab
**saith Adonai Yahuah And shall be mine hand upon the prophets that see vanity and that divine lies**

בסוד 5475 עמי 5971 לא 3808 יהיו 1961 ובכתב 3791 בית 1004 ישראל 3478 לא 3808 יכתבו 3789
basoud 'amiy la' yihayu, uabikatab beyt yisra'ael la' yikatebu,
**in the assembly of my people not they shall be in the writing of the house of Israel neither shall they be written**

**Eze** 13:1 And the word of YHUH came unto me, saying,2 Son of man, prophesy against the prophets of Israel that prophesy, and say you unto them that prophesy out of their own hearts, Hear you the word of YHUH;3 Thus saith YHUH G-D; Woe unto the foolish prophets, that follow their own spirit, and have seen nothing!4 O Israel, your prophets are like the foxes in the deserts.5 You have not gone up into the gaps, neither made up the hedge for the house of Israel to stand in the battle in the day of YHUH.6 They have seen vanity and lying divination, saying, YHUH saith: and YHUH has not sent them: and they have made others to hope that they would confirm the word.7 Have you not seen a vain vision, and have you not spoken a lying divination, whereas you say, YHUH saith it; albeit I have not spoken?8 Therefore thus saith YHUH G-D; Because you have spoken vanity, and seen lies, therefore, behold, I am against you, saith YHUH G-D.9 And mine hand shall be upon the prophets that see vanity, and that divine lies: they shall not be in the assembly of my people, neither shall they be written in the writing of the house of Israel, neither shall they enter into the land of Israel; and you shall know that I am YHUH G-D.

| ואל 413 | אדמת 127 | ישראל 3478 | לא 3808 | יבאו 935 | וידעתם 3045 | כי 3588 | אני 589 | אדני 136 | יהוה 3068: | 13:10 | יען 3282 |
|---|---|---|---|---|---|---|---|---|---|---|---|
| ua'al | 'admat | yisra'ael | la' | yabo'au; | uiyda'tem | kiy | 'aniy | 'adonay | Yahuah. | | ya'an |
| **into** | **the land of** | **Israel** | **neither** | **shall they enter** | **and you shall know** | **that** | **I *am*** | **Adonai** | **Yahuah** | | **Because** |

| וביען 3282 | הטעו 2937 | את 853 | עמי 5971 | לאמר 559 | שלום 7965 | ואין 369 | שלום 7965 | והוא 1931 | בנה 1129 | חיץ 2434 |
|---|---|---|---|---|---|---|---|---|---|---|
| uabya'an | hita'au | 'at | 'amiy | lea'mor | shaloum | ua'aeyn | shaloum; | uahu'a | boneh | chayitz, |
| **even because** | **they have seduced** | | **my people** | **saying** | **Peace** | **and *there was* no** | **peace** | **and one** | **built up** | **a wall** |

| והנם 2009 | טחים 2902 | אתו 853 | תפל 8602: | 13:11 | אמר 559 | אל 413 | טחי 2902 | תפל 8602 |
|---|---|---|---|---|---|---|---|---|
| uahinam | tachiym | 'atou | tapel. | | 'amor | 'al | tachey | tapel |
| **and lo** | ***others* daubed** | **it** | ***with* untempered *morter*** | | **Say them** | **unto** | **which daub** | ***it with* untempered** |

| ויפל 5307 | היה 1961 | גשם 1653 | שוטף 7857 | ואתנה 859 | אבני 68 | אלגביש 417 | תפלנה 5307 | ורוח 7307 | סערות 5591 |
|---|---|---|---|---|---|---|---|---|---|
| uayipol; | hayah | geshem | shoutep, | ua'atenah | 'abney | 'algabiysh | tipolanah, | uaruach | sa'arout |
| ***morter* that it shall fall** | **there shall be** | **an shower** | **overflowing** | **and you** | **stones** | **O great hail** | **shall fall** | **and a wind** | **stormy** |

| תבקע 1234: | 13:12 | והנה 2009 | נפל 5307 | הקיר 7023 | הלוא 3808 | יאמר 559 | אליכם 413 | איה 346 | הטיח 2915 | אשר 834 |
|---|---|---|---|---|---|---|---|---|---|---|
| tabaqea'. | | uahineh | napal | haqiyr; | halou'a | ye'amer | 'aleykem, | 'ayeh | hatiyacha | 'asher |
| **shall rend *it*** | | **Lo when** | **is fallen** | **the wall** | **not** | **shall it be said** | **unto you** | **Where** | ***is* the daubing** | **wherewith** |

| טחתם 2902: | 13:13 | לכן 3651 | כה 3541 | אמר 559 | אדני 136 | יהוה 3069 | ובקעתי 1234 | רוח 7307 | סערות 5591 | בחמתי 2534 |
|---|---|---|---|---|---|---|---|---|---|---|
| tachtem. | | laken, | koh | 'amar | 'adonay | Yahuah, | uabiqa'atiy | ruach | sa'arout | bachamatiy; |
| **you have daubed *it*?** | | **Therefore** | **thus** | **saith** | **Adonai** | **Yahuah** | **I will even rend** | ***it* with a wind** | **stormy** | **in my fury** |

| וגשם 1653 | שטף 7857 | באפי 639 | יהיה 1961 | ואבני 68 | אלגביש 417 | בחמה 2534 | לכלה 3617: | 13:14 |
|---|---|---|---|---|---|---|---|---|
| uageshem | shotep | ba'apiy | yihayeh, | ua'abney | 'algabiysh | bachemah | lakalah. | |
| **an shower** | **overflowing** | **in mine anger** | **there shall be** | **and stones** | **great hail** | **in *my* fury** | **to consume it** | |

| והרסתי 2040 | את 853 | הקיר 7023 | אשר 834 | טחתם 2902 | תפל 8602 | והגעתיהו 5060 | אל 413 | הארץ 776 |
|---|---|---|---|---|---|---|---|---|
| uaharasatiy | 'at | haqiyr | 'asher | tachtem | tapel | uahiga'atiyhu | 'al | ha'aretz |
| **So will I break down** | | **the wall** | **that** | **you have daubed** | ***with* untempered** | ***morter* and bring it down** | **to** | **the ground** |

| ונגלה 1540 | יסדו 3247 | ונפלה 5307 | וכליתם 3615 | בתוכה 8432 |
|---|---|---|---|---|
| uaniglah | yasodou; | uanapalah | uakliytem | batoukah, |
| **so that shall be discovered** | **the foundation thereof** | **and it shall fall** | **and you shall be consumed** | **in the midst thereof** |

| וידעתם 3045 | כי 3588 | אני 589 | יהוה 3068: | 13:15 | וכליתי 3615 | את 853 | חמתי 2534 | בקיר 7023 |
|---|---|---|---|---|---|---|---|---|
| uiyda'tem | kiy | 'aniy | Yahuah. | | uakileytiy | 'at | chamatiy | baqiyr, |
| **and you shall know** | **that** | **I *am*** | **Yahuah** | | **Thus will I accomplish** | | **my wrath** | **upon the wall** |

| ובטחים 2902 | אתו 853 | תפל 8602 | ואמר 559 | לכם 3807a | אין 369 | הקיר 7023 |
|---|---|---|---|---|---|---|
| uabatachiym | 'atou | tapel; | ua'aumar | lakem | 'aeyn | haqiyr, |
| **and upon them that have daubed** | **it** | ***with* untempered** | ***morter* and will say** | **unto you** | ***is* no *more,* neither** | **The wall** |

| ואין 369 | הטחים 2902 | אתו 853: | 13:16 | נביאי 5030 | ישראל 3478 | הנבאים 5012 | אל 413 | ירושלם 3389 |
|---|---|---|---|---|---|---|---|---|
| ua'aeyn | hatachiym | 'atou. | | nabiy'aey | yisra'ael, | haniba'aym | 'al | yarushalaim, |
| **are gone** | **they that daubed** | **it** | | ***To wit* the prophets of** | **Israel** | **which prophesy** | **concerning** | **Jerusalem** |

Eze 13:10 Because, even because they have seduced my people, saying, Peace; and there was no peace; and one built up a wall, and, lo, others daubed it with untempered morter:11 Say unto them which daub it with untempered morter, that it shall fall: there shall be an overflowing shower; and you, O great hailstones, shall fall; and a stormy wind shall rend it.12 Lo, when the wall is fallen, shall it not be said unto you, Where is the daubing wherewith you have daubed it?13 Therefore thus saith YHUH G-D; I will even rend it with a stormy wind in my fury; and there shall be an overflowing shower in mine anger, and great hailstones in my fury to consume it.14 So will I break down the wall that you have daubed with untempered morter, and bring it down to the ground, so that the foundation thereof shall be discovered, and it shall fall, and you shall be consumed in the midst thereof: and you shall know that I am YHUH.15 Thus will I accomplish my wrath upon the wall, and upon them that have daubed it with untempered morter, and will say unto you, The wall is no more, neither they that daubed it;

ומכשול 4383 עונו 5771 ישים 7760 נכח 5227 פניו 6440 ובא 935 אל 413 הנביא 5030 לדרש 1875 לו 3807a בי 871a
uamikshoul auonou, yasiym nokach panayu; uaba' 'al hanabiy'a lidrash lou' biy,
**and the stumblingblock of his iniquity put before his face and comes to a prophet to inquire of him concerning me**

אני 589 יהוה 3068 נענה 6030 לו 3807a בי 871a: 14:8 ונתתי 5414 פני 6440 באיש 376 ההוא 1931 והשמתיהו 8074 לאות 226
'aniy Yahuah, naa'aneh lou' biy. uanatatiy panay ba'aysh hahua', uahasimotiyhu la'aut
**I Yahuah will answer him by myself And I will set my face against man that and will make him a sign**

ולמשלים 4912 והכרתיו 3772 מתוך 8432 עמי 5971 וידעתם 3045 כי 3588 אני 589 יהוה 3068: 14:9
ualimshaliym, uahikratiyu mitouk 'amiy; uiyda'tem kiy 'aniy Yahuah.
**and a proverb and I will cut him off from the midst of my people and you shall know that I *am* Yahuah**

והנביא 5030 כי 3588 יפתה 6601 ודבר 1696 דבר 1697 אני 589 יהוה 3068 פתיתי 6601 את 853 הנביא 5030 ההוא 1931
uahanabiy'a kiy yaputeh uadiber dabar, 'aniy Yahuah piteytiy, 'at hanabiy'a hahua';
**And the prophet if be deceived when he has spoken a thing I Yahuah have deceived prophet that**

ונטיתי 5186 את 853 ידי 3027 עליו 5921 והשמדתיו 8045 מתוך 8432 עמי 5971 ישראל 3478: 14:10
uanatiytiy 'at yadiy 'alayu, uahishmadtiyu, mitouk 'amiy yisra'ael.
**and I will stretch out my hand upon him and will destroy him from the midst of my people Israel**

ונשאו 5375 עונם 5771 כעון 5771 הדרש 1875 כעון 5771
uanasa'au 'auonam; ka'auon hadoresh, ka'auon
**And they shall bear *the* punishment of their iniquity the punishment of him that seek *unto him; even* as the punishment of**

הנביא 5030 יהיה 1961: 14:11 למען 4616 לא 3808 יתעו 8582 עוד 5750 בית 1004 ישראל 3478 מאחרי 310 ולא 3808 יטמאו 2930
hanabiy'a yihayeh. lama'an la' yit'au 'aud beyt yisra'ael me'acharay, uala' yitam'au
**the prophet shall be That no may go astray more the house of Israel from me neither be polluted**

עוד 5750 בכל 3605 פשעיהם 6588 והיו 1961 לי 3807a לעם 5971 ואני 589 אהיה 1961 להם 3807a לאלהים 430 נאם 5002
'aud bakal pish'aeyhem; uahayu liy la'am, ua'aniy 'ahayeh lahem le'alohiym, na'am
**any more with all their transgressions but that they may be my people and I may be their to Elohim saith**

אדני 136 יהוה 3069: 14:12 ויהי 1961 דבר 1697 יהוה 3068 אלי 413 לאמר 559: 14:13 בן 1121 אדם 120 ארץ 776 כי 3588 תחטא 2398
'adonay Yahuah. uayahiy dabar Yahuah 'aelay lea'mor. ben 'adam, 'aretz kiy techeta'
**Adonai Yahuah came again The word of Yahuah to me saying Son of man the land when sin**

לי 3807a למעל 4603 מעל 4604 ונטיתי 5186 ידי 3027 עליה 5921 ושברתי 7665 לה 3807a מטה 4294
liy lim'al ma'al, uanatiytiy yadiy 'aeleyha, uashabartiy lah mateh
**against me by trespassing grievously then will I stretch out mine hand upon it and will break thereof the staff of**

לחם 3899 והשלחתי 7971 בה 871a רעב 7458 והכרתי 3772 ממנה 4480 אדם 120 ובהמה 929: 14:14 והיו 1961 שלשת 7969
lachem; uahishlachtiy bah ra'ab, uahikratiy mimenah 'adam uabahemah. uahayu shaloshet
**the bread and will send upon it famine and will cut off from it man and beast Though were three**

האנשים 582 האלה 428 בתוכה 8432 נח 5146 דנאל 1840 ואיוב 347 המה 1992 בצדקתם 6666 ינצלו 5337 נפשם 5315
ha'anashiym ha'aeleh batoukah, noach dani'al la'ayoub; hemah batzidqatam yanatzalu napsham,
**men these in it Noah Daniel and Job they by their righteousness should deliver *but* their own souls**

Eze 14:8 And I will set my face against that man, and will make him a sign and a proverb, and I will cut him off from the midst of my people; and you shall know that I am YHUH.9 And if the prophet be deceived when he has spoken a thing, I YHUH have deceived that prophet, and I will stretch out my hand upon him, and will destroy him from the midst of my people Israel.10 And they shall bear the punishment of their iniquity: the punishment of the prophet shall be even as the punishment of him that seek unto him;11 That the house of Israel may go no more astray from me, neither be polluted anymore with all their transgressions; but that they may be my people, and I may be their G-d, saith YHUH G-D.12 The word of YHUH came again to me, saying,13 Son of man, when the land sin against me by trespassing grievously, then will I stretch out mine hand upon it, and will break the staff of the bread thereof, and will send famine upon it, and will cut off man and beast from it:14 Though these three men, Noah, Daniel, and Job, were in it, they should deliver but their own souls by their righteousness, saith YHUH G-D.

14:15
נאם 5002 אדני 136 יהוה 3068: לו 3863 חיה 2416 רעה 7451 אעביר 5674 בארץ 776 ושכלתה 7921 והיתה 1961
na'am 'adonay Yahuah. lou' chayah ra'ah 'aabiyr ba'aretz uashiklatah; uahayatah
**saith Adonai Yahuah If beasts noisome I cause to pass through the land and they spoil it so that it be**

14:16
שממה 8077 מבלי 1097 עובר 5674 מפני 6440 החיה 2416: שלשת 7969 האנשים 582 האלה 428 בתוכה 8432 חי 2416
shamamah mibliy 'auber, mipaney hachayah. shaloshet ha'anashiym ha'aeleh batoukah chay
**desolate that no man may pass through because of the beasts *Though* three men these *were* in it live**

אני 589 נאם 5002 אדני 136 יהוה 3069 אם 518 בנים 1121 ואם 518 בנות 1323 יצילו 5337 המה 1992 לבדם 905 ינצלו 5337
'aniy, na'am 'adonay Yahuah, 'am baniym ua'am banout yatziylu; hemah labadam yinatzelu,
***as* I saith Adonai Yahuah neither sons nor daughters they shall deliver they only shall be delivered**

14:17
והארץ 776 תהיה 1961 שממה 8077: או 176 חרב 2719 אביא 935 על 5921 הארץ 776 ההיא 1931 ואמרתי 559 חרב 2719 תעבר 5674
uaha'aretz tihayeh shamamah. 'au chereb 'abiy'a 'al ha'aretz hahiy'a; ua'amartiy, chereb ta'abor
**but the land shall be desolate Or a sword *if* I bring upon the land that and say Sword go**

14:18
בארץ 776 והכרתי 3772 ממנה 4480 אדם 120 ובהמה 929: ושלשת 7969 האנשים 582 האלה 428 בתוכה 8432 חי 2416 אני 589
ba'aretz, uahikratiy mimenah 'adam uabahemah. uashloshet ha'anashiym ha'aeleh batoukah chay 'aniy,
**through the land so that I cut off from it man and beast Though three men these *were* in it live *as* I**

נאם 5002 אדני 136 יהוה 3069 לא 3808 יצילו 5337 בנים 1121 ובנות 1323 כי 3588 הם 1992 לבדם 905
na'am 'adonay Yahuah, la' yatziylu baniym uabanout; kiy hem labadam
**saith Adonai Yahuah neither they shall deliver sons nor daughters but they only**

14:19
ינצלו 5337: או 176 דבר 1698 אשלח 7971 אל 413 הארץ 776 ההיא 1931 ושפכתי 8210 חמתי 2534 עליה 5921
yinatzelu. 'au deber 'ashalach 'al ha'aretz hahiy'a; uashapakatiy chamatiy 'aleyha
**shall be delivered themselves Or a pestilence *if* I send into the land that and pour out my fury upon it**

14:20
בדם 1818 להכרית 3772 ממנה 4480 אדם 120 ובהמה 929: ונח 5146 דנאל 1840 ואיוב 347 בתוכה 8432 חי 2416 אני 589 נאם 5002 אדני 136
badam, lahakriyt mimenah 'adam uabahemah. uanach dani'al ua'ayoub batoukah chay 'aniy, na'am 'adonay
**in blood to cut off from it man and beast Though Noah Daniel and Job *were* in it live *as* I saith Adonai**

יהוה 3069 אם 518 בן 1121 אם 518 בת 1323 יצילו 5337 המה 1992 בצדקתם 6666 יצילו 5337 נפשם 5315:
Yahuah, 'am ben 'am bat yatziylu; hemah batzidqatam yatziylu napsham.
**Yahuah neither son nor daughter shall deliver they by their righteousness they shall *but* deliver their own souls**

14:21
כי 3588 כה 3541 אמר 559 אדני 136 יהוה 3069 אף 637 כי 3588 ארבעת 702 שפטי 8201 הרעים 7451 חרב 2719 ורעב 7458
kiy koh 'amar 'adonay Yahuah 'ap kiy 'arba'at shapatay hara'aym chereb uara'ab
**For thus saith Adonai Yahuah How much more when my four judgments sore the sword and the famine**

וחיה 2416 רעה 7451 ודבר 1698 שלחתי 7971 אל 413 ירושלם 3389 להכרית 3772 ממנה 4480 אדם 120 ובהמה 929:
uachayah ra'ah uadeber, shilachtiy 'al yarushalaim; lahakriyt mimenah 'adam uabahemah.
**beast and the noisome and the pestilence when I send upon Jerusalem to cut off from it man and beast**

14:22
והנה 2009 נותרה 3498 בה 871a פלטה 6413 המוצאים 3318 בנים 1121 ובנות 1323 הנם 2005
uahineh noutarah bah paletah, hamutza'aym baniym uabanout hinam
**Yet behold shall be left therein a remnant that shall be brought forth *both* sons and daughters behold they**

Eze 14:15 If I cause noisome beasts to pass through the land, and they spoil it, so that it be desolate, that no man may pass through because of the beasts:16 Though these three men were in it, as I live, saith YHUH G-D, they shall deliver neither sons nor daughters; they only shall be delivered, but the land shall be desolate.17 Or if I bring a sword upon that land, and say, Sword, go through the land; so that I cut off man and beast from it:18 Though these three men were in it, as I live, saith YHUH G-D, they shall deliver neither sons nor daughters, but they only shall be delivered themselves.19 Or if I send a pestilence into that land, and pour out my fury upon it in blood, to cut off from it man and beast:20 Though Noah, Daniel, and Job, were in it, as I live, saith YHUH G-D, they shall deliver neither son nor daughter; they shall but deliver their own souls by their righteousness.21 For thus saith YHUH G-D; How much more when I send my four sore judgments upon Jerusalem, the sword, and the famine, and the noisome beast, and the pestilence, to cut off from it man and beast?22 Yet, behold, therein shall be left a remnant that shall be brought forth, both sons and daughters: behold, they shall come forth unto you, and you shall see their way and their doings: and you shall be comforted concerning the evil that I have brought upon Jerusalem,

יוצאים 3318 אליכם 413 וראיתם 7200 את 853 דרכם 1870 ואת 853 עלילותם 5949 ונחמתם 5162 על 5921
youtz'aym 'aleykem, uar'aytem 'at darkam ua'at aliyloutam; uanichamtem, 'al
**shall come forth unto you and you shall see their way *and* their doings and you shall be comforted concerning**

**14:23**
הרעה 7451 אשר 834 הבאתי 935 על 5921 ירושלם 3389 את 853 כל 3605 אשר 834 הבאתי 935 עליה 5921:
hara'ah 'asher hebea'tiy 'al yarushalaim, 'at kal 'asher hebea'tiy 'aleyha.
**the evil that I have brought upon Jerusalem all that I have brought *even* concerning upon it**

ונחמו 5162 אתכם 853 כי 3588 תראו 7200 את 853 דרכם 1870 ואת 853 עלילותם 5949 וידעתם 3045 כי 3588 לא 3808
uanichamu 'atkem, kiy tir'au 'at darkam ua'at aliyloutam; uiyda'tem, kiy la'
**And they shall comfort you when you see their ways *and* their doings and you shall know that not**

חנם 2600 עשיתי 6213 את 853 כל 3605 אשר 834 עשיתי 6213 בה 871a נאם 5002 אדני 136 יהוה 3069:
chinam 'asiytiy 'at kal 'asher 'asiytiy bah, na'am 'adonay Yahuah.
**without cause I have done all that I have done in it saith Adonai Yahuah**

**Ezek 15:1**
ויהי 1961 דבר 1697 יהוה 3068 אלי 413 לאמר 559:
uayahiy dabar Yahuah 'aelay lea'mor.
**And came the word of Yahuah unto me saying**

**15:2**
בן 1121 אדם 120 מה 4100 יהיה 1961 עץ 6086 הגפן 1612
ben 'adam mah yihayeh 'aetz hagapen
**Son of man What is tree the vine**

מכל 3605 עץ 6086 הזמורה 2156 אשר 834 היה 1961 בעצי 6086 היער 3293:
mikal 'aetz; hazamourah 'asher hayah ba'atzey haya'ar.
**more than any tree *or than* a branch which is among the trees of the forest?**

**15:3**
היקח 3947 ממנו 4480 עץ 6086
hayuqach mimenu 'aetz,
**Shall be taken thereof wood**

לעשות 6213 למלאכה 4399 אם 518 יקחו 3947 ממנו 4480 יתד 3489 לתלות 8518 עליו 5921 כל 3605 כלי 3627:
la'asout limala'kah; 'am yiqchu mimenu yated, litlout 'alayu kal keliy.
**to do work? or will men take of it a pin to hang thereof? any vessel**

**15:4**
הנה 2009 לאש 784 נתן 5414
hineh la'aesh nitan
**Behold into the fire it is cast**

לאכלה 402 את 853 שני 8147 קצותיו 7098 אכלה 398 האש 784 ותוכו 8432 נחר 2787 היצלח 6743 למלאכה 4399:
la'akalah 'at shaney qatzoutayu 'akalah ha'aesh uatoukou nachar, hayitzalach limala'kah.
**for fuel both the ends of it devour the fire and the midst of it is burned Is it meet for any work?**

**15:5**
הנה 2009
hineh
**Behold**

בהיותו 1961 תמים 8549 לא 3808 יעשה 6213 למלאכה 4399 אף 637 כי 3588 אש 784 אכלתהו 398 ויחר 2787
bihayotou tamiym, la' ye'aseh limala'kah; 'ap kiy 'aesh 'akalatahu uayechar,
**when it was whole no it was meet for work how much less when the fire has devoured it (*him*) and it is burned?**

ונעשה 6213 עוד 5750 למלאכה 4399:
uana'asah 'aud limala'kah.
**shall it be meet yet for *any* work**

**15:6**
לכן 3651 כה 3541 אמר 559 אדני 136 יהוה 3069 כאשר 834 עץ 6086 הגפן 1612 בעץ 6086
laken, koh 'amar 'adonay Yahuah, ka'asher 'aetz hagapen ba'aetz
**Therefore thus saith Adonai Yahuah As tree the vine among the trees of**

היער 3293 אשר 834 נתתיו 5414 לאש 784 לאכלה 402 כן 3651 נתתי 5414 את 853 ישבי 3427 ירושלם 3389:
haya'ar, 'asher natatiyu la'aesh la'akalah ken natatiy, 'at yoshabey yarushalaim.
**the forest which I have given to the fire for fuel so will I give the inhabitants of Jerusalem**

**15:7**
ונתתי 5414
uanatatiy
**And I will set**

את 853 פני 6440 בהם 871a מהאש 784 יצאו 3318 והאש 784 תאכלם 398 וידעתם 3045 כי 3588
'at panay bahem, meha'aesh yatza'au, uaha'aesh ta'kalem; uiyda'tem kiy
**my face against them from *one* fire they shall go out and *another* fire shall devour them and you shall know that**

Eze 14:22 even concerning all that I have brought upon it.23 And they shall comfort you, when you see their ways and their doings: and you shall know that I have not done without cause all that I have done in it, saith YHUH G-D. **Eze** 15:1 And the word of YHUH came unto me, saying,2 Son of man, What is the vine tree more than any tree, or than a branch which is among the trees of the forest?3 Shall wood be taken thereof to do any work? or will men take a pin of it to hang any vessel thereon?4 Behold, it is cast into the fire for fuel; the fire devour both the ends of it, and the midst of it is burned. Is it meet for any work?5 Behold, when it was whole, it was meet for no work: how much less shall it be meet yet for any work, when the fire has devoured it, and it is burned?6 Therefore thus saith YHUH G-D; As the vine tree among the trees of the forest, which I have given to the fire for fuel, so will I give the inhabitants of Jerusalem.7 And I will set my face against them; they shall go out from one fire, and another fire shall devour them; and you shall know that I am YHUH, when I set my face against them.

אני 589 יהוה 3069 בשומי 7760 את 853 פני 6440 בהם 871a: **15:8** ונתתי 5414 את 853 הארץ 776 שממה 8077 יען 3282
'aniy Yahuah, basumiy 'at panay bahem. uanatatiy 'at ha'aretz shamamah; ya'an
**I *am* Yahuah when I set my face against them And I will make the land desolate because**

מעלו 4603 מעל 4604 נאם 5002 אדני 136 יהוה 3069:
ma'alu ma'al, na'am 'adonay Yahuah.
**they have committed a trespass saith Adonai Yahuah**

**Ezek 16:1** ויהי 1961 דבר 1697 יהוה 3068 אלי 413 לאמר 559: **16:2** בן 1121 אדם 120 הודע 3045 את 853 ירושלם 3389 את 853
uayahiy dabar Yahuah 'aelay lea'mor. ben 'adam houda' 'at yarushalaim 'at
**Again came the word of Yahuah unto me saying Son of man cause to know Jerusalem**

תועבתיה 8441: **16:3** ואמרת 559 כה 3541 אמר 559 אדני 136 יהוה 3069 לירושלם 3389 מכרתיך 4351 ומלדתיך 4138
tou'aboteyha. ua'amarta koh 'amar 'adonay Yahuah liyarushalaim, makorotayik uamoladotayik,
**her abominations And say Thus saith Adonai Yahuah unto Jerusalem Your birth and your nativity**

מארץ 776 הכנעני 3669 אביך 1 האמרי 567 ואמך 517 חתית 2850: **16:4** ומולדותיך 4138 ביום 3117
me'aretz ha'kananiy; 'abiyk ha'amoriy ua'amek chitiyt. uamouladoutayik, bayoum
***is* of the land of Canaan your father *was* an Amorite and your mother an Hittite And *as for* your nativity in the day**

הולדת 3205 אתך 853 לא 3808 כרת 3772 שרך 8270 ובמים 4325 לא 3808 רחצת 7364 למשעי 4935 והמלח 4414 לא 3808
huledet 'atak la' karat sharek, uabmayim la' ruchatzt lamish'ay; uahamaleach la'
**were born you not was cut your navel in water neither were you washed to supple *you;* you were salted nor**

המלחת 4414 והחתל 2853 לא 3808 חתלת 2853: **16:5** לא 3808 חסה 2347 עליך 5921 עין 5869 לעשות 6213 לך 3807a אחת 259 מאלה 428
humlachat, uahachatel la' chutalt. la' chasah 'alayik 'ayin, la'asout lak 'achat me'aeleh
**at all swaddled not at all None pitied to you eye to do unto you any of these**

לחמלה 2550 עליך 5921 ותשלכי 7993 אל 413 פני 6440 השדה 7704 בגעל 1604 נפשך 5315 ביום 3117
lachumlah 'alayik; uatushlakiy 'al paney hasadeh bago'al napshek, bayoum
**to have compassion upon you but you were cast out in open the field to the lothing of your person in the day**

הלדת 63205 אתך 853: **16:6** ואעבר 5674 עליך 5921 ואראך 7200 מתבוססת 947 בדמיך 1818 ואמר 559 לך 3807a
huledet 'atak. ua'a'abor 'alayik ua'ar'aek, mitbouseset badamayik; ua'amar lak
**that were born you And when I passed by you and saw you polluted in your own blood and I said unto you**

בדמיך 1818 חיי 2421 ואמר 559 לך 3807a בדמיך 1818 חיי 2421: **16:7** רבבה 7233 כצמח 6780
badamayik chayiy, ua'amar lak badamayik chayiy. rababah, katzemach
***when you were* in your blood Live yea I said unto you *when you were* in your blood Live to multiply as the bud of**

השדה 7704 נתתיך 5414 ותרבי 7235 ותגדלי 1431 ותבאי 935 בעדי 5716 עדיים 5716 שדים 7699
hasadeh natatiyk, uatirbiy uatigdaliy, uataba'ay ba'adiy 'adayiym; shadayim
**the field I have caused you and you have increased and waxen great and you are come to excellent ornaments *your* breasts**

נכנו 3559 ושערך 8181 צמח 6779 ואת 859 ערם 5903 ועריה 6181: **16:8** ואעבר 5674 עליך 5921
nakonu us'arek tzimeach, ua'at 'aerom ua'aryah. ua'a'abor 'alayik
**are fashioned and your hair is grown (*sprouts*) whereas you *were* naked and bare Now when I passed by you**

Eze 15:8 And I will make the land desolate, because they have committed a trespass, saith YHUH G-D. **Eze** 16:1 Again the word of YHUH came unto me, saying,2 Son of man, cause Jerusalem to know her abominations,3 And say, Thus saith YHUH G-D unto Jerusalem; Thy birth and your nativity is of the land of Canaan; your father was an Amorite, and your mother an Hittite.4 And as for your nativity, in the day you were born your navel was not cut, neither were you washed in water to supple you; you were not salted at all, nor swaddled at all.5 None eye pitied you, to do any of these unto you, to have compassion upon you; but you were cast out in the open field, to the lothing of your person, in the day that you were born.6 And when I passed by you, and saw you polluted in your own blood, I said unto you when you were in your blood, Live; yea, I said unto you when you were in your blood, Live.7 I have caused you to multiply as the bud of the field, and you have increased and waxen great, and you are come to excellent ornaments: your breasts are fashioned, and your hair is grown, whereas you were naked and bare.8 Now when I passed by you, and looked upon you, behold, your time was the time of love; and I spread my skirt over you, and covered your nakedness: yea, I sware unto you and entered into a covenant with you, saith YHUH G-D and you became mine.

| ואראך 7200 | והנה 2009 | עתך 6256 | עת 6256 | דדים 1730 | ואפרש 6566 | כנפי 3671 | עליך 5921 | ואכסה 3680 |
|---|---|---|---|---|---|---|---|---|
| ua'ar'aek, | uahineh | 'atek | 'at | dodiym, | ua'apros | kanapiy | 'alayik, | ua'akaseh |
| **and looked upon you** | **and behold** | **your time** | ***was* the time of** | **love** | **and I spread** | **my skirt** | **over you** | **and covered** |

| ערותך 6172 | ואשבע 7650 | לך 3807a | ואבוא 935 | בברית 1285 | אתך 854 | נאם 5002 | אדני 136 | יהוה 3069 | ותהיי 1961 |
|---|---|---|---|---|---|---|---|---|---|
| 'aruatek; | ua'ashaba' | lak | ua'abou'a | bibriyt | 'atak, | na'am | 'adonay | Yahuah | uatihayiy |
| **your nakedness** | **yea I sware** | **unto you** | **and entered** | **into a covenant** | **with you** | **saith** | **Adonai** | **Yahuah** | **and you became** |

| לי 3807a: | 16:9 | וארחצך 7364 | במים 4325 | ואשטף 7857 | דמיך 1818 | מעליך 5921 | ואסכך 5480 |
|---|---|---|---|---|---|---|---|
| liy. | | ua'archatzek | bamayim, | ua'ashtop | damayik | me'alayik; | ua'asukek |
| **mine** | | **Then washed I you** | **with water** | **yea I throughly washed away** | **your blood** | **from you** | **and I anointed you** |

| בשמן 8081: | 16:10 | ואלבישך 3847 | רקמה 7553 | ואנעלך 5274 | תחש 8476 | ואחבשך 2280 |
|---|---|---|---|---|---|---|
| bashamen. | | ua'albiyshek | riqmah, | ua'an'alek | tachash; | ua'achbashek |
| **with oil** | | **I clothed you also** | ***with* broidered work** | **and shod you** | ***with* badgers' skin** | **and I girded you about** |

| בשש 8336 | ואכסך 3680 | משי 4897: | 16:11 | ואעדך 5710 | עדי 5716 | ואתנה 5414 | צמידים 6781 | על 5921 | ידיך 3027 |
|---|---|---|---|---|---|---|---|---|---|
| bashesh, | ua'akasek | meshiy. | | ua'a'adek | 'adiy; | ua'atnah | tzamiydiym | 'al | yadayik, |
| ***with* fine linen** | **and I covered you** | ***with* silk** | | **I decked you also** | ***with* ornaments** | **and I put** | **bracelets** | **upon** | **your hands** |

| ורביד 7242 | על 5921 | גרונך 1627: | 16:12 | ואתן 5414 | נזם 5141 | על 5921 | אפך 639 | ועגילים 5694 | על 5921 | אזניך 241 | ועטרת 5850 |
|---|---|---|---|---|---|---|---|---|---|---|---|
| uarabiyd | 'al | garounek. | | ua'aten | nezem | 'al | 'apek, | ua'agiyliym | 'al | 'azanayik; | ua'ateret |
| **and a chain** | **on** | **your neck** | | **And I put** | **a jewel** | **on** | **your forehead** | **and earrings** | **in** | **your ears** | **and a crown** |

| תפארת 8597 | בראשך 7218: | 16:13 | ותעדי 5710 | זהב 2091 | וכסף 3701 | ומלבושך 4403 | ששי 8336 | ומשי 4897 |
|---|---|---|---|---|---|---|---|---|
| tip'aret | bara'shek. | | uata'adiy | zahab | uakesep, | uamalbushek | sheshy | uameshiy |
| **beautiful** | **upon your head** | | **Thus were you decked** | ***with* gold** | **and silver** | **and your raiment *was of*** | **fine linen** | **and silk** |

| ורקמה 7553 | סלת 5560 | ודבש 1706 | ושמן 8081 | אכלתי 398 | ותיפי 3302 | במאד 3966 | מאד 3966 |
|---|---|---|---|---|---|---|---|
| uariqmah, | solet | uadbash | uashemen | 'akaltiy | uatiypiy | bim'ad | ma'ad, |
| **and broidered work** | **fine flour** | **and honey** | **and oil** | **you did eat** | **and you were beautiful** | **especially** | **exceedingly** |

| ותצלחי 6743 | למלוכה 4410: | 16:14 | ויצא 3318 | לך 3807a | שם 8034 | בגוים 1471 | ביפיך 3308 | כי 3588 |
|---|---|---|---|---|---|---|---|---|
| uatitzlachiy | limlukah. | | uayetzea' | lak | shem | bagouyim | bayapayek; | kiy |
| **and you did prosper** | **into a kingdom** | | **And went forth** | **to you** | **renown** | **among the heathen** | **for your beauty** | **for** |

| כליל 3632 | הוא 1931 | בהדרי 1926 | אשר 834 | שמתי 7760 | עליך 5921 | נאם 5002 | אדני 136 | יהוה 3068: | 16:15 | ותבטחי 982 |
|---|---|---|---|---|---|---|---|---|---|---|
| kaliyl | hua', | bahadariy | 'asher | samtiy | 'alayik, | na'am | 'adonay | Yahuah. | | uatibtachiy |
| ***was* perfect** | **he** | **it through my comeliness** | **which** | **I had put** | **upon you** | **saith** | **Adonai** | **Yahuah** | | **But you did trust** |

| ביפיך 3308 | ותזני 2181 | על 5921 | שמך 8034 | ותשפכי 8210 | את 853 | תזנותיך 8457 | על 5921 |
|---|---|---|---|---|---|---|---|
| bayapayek, | uatizniy | 'al | shamek; | uatishpakiy | 'at | taznutayik | 'al |
| **in your own beauty** | **and playedst the harlot** | **because of** | **your renown** | **and pouredst out** | | **your fornications** | **on** |

| כל 3605 | עובר 5674 | לו 3807a | יהי 1961: | 16:16 | ותקחי 3947 | מבגדיך 899 | ותעשי 6213 | לך 3807a | במות 1116 |
|---|---|---|---|---|---|---|---|---|---|
| kal | 'auber | lou' | yehiy. | | uatiqchiy | mibagadayik, | uata'asiy | lak | bamout |
| **every one** | **that passed by** | **his** | **it was** | | **And you did take** | **of your garments** | **and decked** | **to your** | **high places** |

Eze 16:9 Then washed I you with water; yea, I throughly washed away your blood from you, and I anointed you with oil.10 I clothed you also with broidered work, and shod you with badgers' skin, and I girded you about with fine linen, and I covered you with silk.11 I decked you also with ornaments, and I put bracelets upon your hands, and a chain on your neck.12 And I put a jewel on your forehead, and earrings in your ears, and a beautiful crown upon your head.13 Thus were you decked with gold and silver; and your raiment was of fine linen, and silk, and broidered work; you did eat fine flour, and honey, and oil: and you were exceeding beautiful, and you did prosper into a kingdom.14 And your renown went forth among the heathen for your beauty: for it was perfect through my comeliness, which I had put upon you, saith YHUH G-D.15 But you did trust in your own beauty, and playedst the harlot because of your renown, and pouredst out your fornications on everyone that passed by; his it was.16 And of your garments you did take, and deckedst your high places with divers colors, and playedst the harlot thereupon: the like things shall not come, neither shall it be so.

טלאות 2921 ותזני 2181 עליהם 5921 לא 3808 באות 935 ולא 3808 יהיה 1961: 16:17
talu'aut, uatizniy 'aleyhem; la' ba'aut uala' yihayeh.
*with* **divers colours and playedst the harlot thereupon not** ***the like things*** **one shall come neither shall it be** ***so***

ותקחי 3947 כלי 3627 תפארתך 8597 מזהבי 2091 ומכספי 3701 אשר 834 נתתי 5414 לך 3807a ותעשי 6213 לך 3807a
uatiqchiy kaley tip'artek, mizhabiy uamikaspiy 'asher natatiy lak, uata'asiy lak
**You have also taken jewels** ***your*** **fair of my gold and of my silver which I had given to you and made to yourself**

צלמי 6754 זכר 2145 ותזני 2181 בם 871a: 16:18 ותקחי 3947 את 853 בגדי 899 רקמתך 7553 ותכסים 3680
tzalmey zakar; uatizniy bam. uatiqchiy 'at bigdey riqmatek uatakasiym;
**images of men and did commit whoredom with them And took garments your broidered and covered them**

ושמני 8081 וקטרתי 7004 נתתי 5414 לפניהם 6440: 16:19 ולחמי 3899 אשר 834 נתתי 5414 לך 3807a סלת 5560 ושמן 8081
uashamniy uaqtaratiy, natatiy lipneyhem. ualachmiy 'asher natatiy lak solet uashemen
**and mine oil and mine incense you have set before them My meat also which I gave to you fine flour and oil**

ודבש 1706 האכלתיך 398 ונתתיהו 5414 לפניהם 6440 לריח 7381 ניחח 5207 ויהי 1961 נאם 5002 אדני 136
uadbash he'akaltiyk, uantatiyhu lipneyhem lareyach niychoach uayehiy; na'am 'adonay
**and honey** ***wherewith*** **I fed you, you have even set it before them for a savour sweet and** ***thus*** **it was saith Adonai**

16:20 יהוה 3069: ותקחי 3947 את 853 בניך 1121 ואת 853 בנותיך 1323 אשר 834 ילדת 3205 לי 3807a
Yahuah. uatiqchiy 'at banayik ua'at banoutayik 'asher yaladt liy,
**Yahuah Moreover you have taken your sons** ***and*** **your daughters whom you have borne unto me**

ותזבחים 2076 להם 3807a לאכול 398 המעט 4592 מתזנתך 8457 16:21
uatizbachiym lahem le'akoul; hama'at mitazntak
**and these have you sacrificed unto them to be devoured a small matter** ***Is this*** **of your whoredoms**

ותשחטי 7819 את 853 בני 1121 ותתנים 5414 בהעביר 5674 אותם 853 להם 3807a: 16:22 ואת 853
uatishchatiy 'at banay; uatitaniym, baha'abiyr 'autam lahem. ua'at
**That you have slain my children and delivered them to cause to pass through them** ***the fire*** **for them?** ***And***

כל 3605 תועבתיך 8441 ותזנתיך 8457 לא 3808 זכרתי 2142 את 853 ימי 3117 נעוריך 5271 בהיותך 1961
kal tou'abotayik uataznutayik, la' zakartiy 'at yamey na'aurayik; bihayoutek
***in*** **all your abominations and your whoredoms not you have remembered the days of your youth when you were**

ערם 5903 ועריה 6181 מתבוססת 947 בדמך 1818 היית 1961: 16:23 ויהי 1961 אחרי 310 כל 3605 רעתך 7451 אוי 188
'aerom ua'aryah, mitbouseset badamek hayiyt. uayahiy 'acharey kal ra'atek; 'auy
**naked and bare polluted in your blood** ***and*** **you were And it came to pass after all your wickedness woe**

אוי 188 לך 3807a נאם 5002 אדני 136 יהוה 3069: 16:24 ותבני 1129 לך 3807a גב 1354 ותעשי 6213 לך 3807a
'auy lak, na'am 'adonay Yahuah. uatibniy lak gab; uata'asiy lak
**woe unto you saith Adonai Yahuah** ***That*** **you have also built unto you an eminent place and have made to you**

רמה 7413 בכל 3605 רחוב 7339: 16:25 אל 413 כל 3605 ראש 7218 דרך 1870 בנית 1129 רמתך 7413
ramah bakal rachoub. 'al kal ra'sh derek, baniyta ramatek,
**an high place in every street at every head of the way You have built your high place**

Eze 16:17 Thou have also taken your fair jewels of my gold and of my silver, which I had given you, and madest to thyself images of men, and did commit whoredom with them,18 And tookest your broidered garments, and coveredst them: and you have set mine oil and mine incense before them.19 My meat also which I gave you, fine flour, and oil, and honey, wherewith I fed you, you have even set it before them for a sweet savour: and thus it was, saith YHUH G-D.20 Moreover you have taken your sons and your daughters, whom you have borne unto me, and these have you sacrificed unto them to be devoured. Is this of your whoredoms a small matter,21 That you have slain my children, and delivered them to cause them to pass through the fire for them?22 And in all your abominations and your whoredoms you have not remembered the days of your youth, when you were naked and bare, and were polluted in your blood.23 And it came to pass after all your wickedness, (woe, woe unto you! saith YHUH G-D;)24 That you have also built unto you an eminent place, and have made you an high place in every street.25 Thou have built your high place at every head of the way, and have made your beauty to be abhorred, and have opened your feet to everyone that passed by, and multiplied your whoredoms.

| ותתעבי 8581 | את 853 | יפיך 3308 | ותפשקי 6589 | את 853 | רגליך 7272 | לכל 3605 | עובר 5674 |
|---|---|---|---|---|---|---|---|
| uatata'abiy | 'at | yapayek, | uatapasqiy | 'at | raglayik | lakal | 'auber; |
| **and have made to be abhorred** | | **your beauty** | **and have opened** | | **your feet** | **to every one** | **that passed by** |

| ותרבי 7235 | את 853 | תזנתך 8457 | 16:26 ותזני 2181 | אל 413 | בני 1121 | מצרים 4714 |
|---|---|---|---|---|---|---|
| uatarbiy | 'at | taznutek | uatizniy | 'al | baney | mitzrayim |
| **and multiplied** | | **your whoredoms** | **You have also committed fornication** | **with** | **sons of** | **the Egyptians** |

| שכניך 7934 | גדלי 1432 | בשר 1320 | ותרבי 7235 | את 853 | תזנתך 8457 | להכעיסני 3707: | 16:27 והנה 2009 |
|---|---|---|---|---|---|---|---|
| shakenayik | gidley | basar; | uatarbiy | 'at | taznutek | lahak'ayseniy. | uahineh |
| **your neighbours** | **great of** | **flesh** | **and have increased** | | **your whoredoms** | **to provoke me to anger** | **Behold therefore** |

| נטיתי 5186 | ידי 3027 | עליך 5921 | ואגרע 1639 | חקך 2706 | ואתנך 5414 | בנפש 5315 |
|---|---|---|---|---|---|---|
| natiytiy | yadiy | 'alayik, | ua'agra' | chuqek; | ua'atanek | banepesh |
| **I have stretched out** | **my hand** | **over you** | **and have diminished** | **your ordinary *food*** | **and delivered you** | **unto the will of** |

| שנאותיך 8130 | בנות 1323 | פלשתים 6430 | הנכלמות 3637 | מדרכך 1870 | זמה 2154: | 16:28 |
|---|---|---|---|---|---|---|
| sona'atayik | banout | palishtiym, | haniklamout | midarkek | zimah. | |
| **them that hate you** | ***the* daughters of** | ***the* Philistines** | **which are ashamed** | **of your way** | **lewd** | |

| ותזני 2181 | אל 413 | בני 1121 | אשור 804 | מבלתי 1115 | שבעתך 7646 |
|---|---|---|---|---|---|
| uatizniy | 'al | baney | 'ashur, | mibiltiy | saba'atek; |
| **You have played the whore also** | **with** | **sons of** | **the Assyrians** | **because you were unsatiable** | **could be satisfied** |

| ותזנים 2181 | וגם 1571 | לא 3808 | שבעת 7654: | 16:29 ותרבי 7235 | את 853 |
|---|---|---|---|---|---|
| uatizniym | ua'gam | la' | saba'at. | uatarbiy | 'at |
| **yea, you have played the harlot with them** | **and yet** | **not** | **could be satisfied** | **You have moreover multiplied** | |

| תזנותך 8457 | אל 413 | ארץ 776 | כנען 3667 | כשדימה 3778 | וגם 1571 | בזאת 2063 | לא 3808 | שבעת 7646: | 16:30 מה 4100 | אמלה 535 |
|---|---|---|---|---|---|---|---|---|---|---|
| taznutek | 'al | 'aretz | kana'an | kasdiymah; | uagam | baza't | la' | saba'at. | mah | 'amulah |
| **your fornication** | **in** | **the land of** | **Canaan** | ***unto* Chaldea** | **and yet** | **herewith** | **not** | **you were satisfied** | **How** | **weak** |

| לבתך 3826 | נאם 5002 | אדני 136 | יהוה 3069 | בעשותך 6213 | את 853 | כל 3605 | אלה 428 | מעשה 4639 | אשה 802 | זונה 2181 | שלטת 7986: | 16:31 |
|---|---|---|---|---|---|---|---|---|---|---|---|---|
| libatek, | na'am | 'adonay | Yahuah; | ba'asoutek | 'at | kal | 'aeleh, | ma'aseh | 'ashah | zounah | shalatet. | |
| ***is* your heart** | **saith** | **Adonai** | **Yahuah** | **seeing you do** | | **all** | **these *things*** | **the work of** | **an woman** | **whorish** | **imperious** | |

| בבנותיך 1129 | גבך 1354 | בראש 7218 | כל 3605 | דרך 1870 | ורמתך 7413 | עשיתי 6213 | בכל 3605 | רחוב 7339 |
|---|---|---|---|---|---|---|---|---|
| bibnoutayik | gabek | bara'sh | kal | derek, | uaramatek | 'asiytiy | bakal | rachoub; |
| **In that you buildest** | **your eminent place** | **in the head of** | **every** | **way** | **and your high place** | **make** | **in every** | **street** |

| ולא 3808 | הייתי 1961 | כזונה 2181 | לקלס 7046 | אתנן 868: | 16:32 האשה 802 | המנאפת 5003 | תחת 8478 |
|---|---|---|---|---|---|---|---|
| uala' | hayiytiy | kazounah | laqales | 'atnan. | ha'ashah | hamana'apet; | tachat |
| **and not** | **I have been** | **as an harlot** | **in that you scornest** | **hire** | ***But as* a wife** | **that commit adultery** | **instead of** |

| אישה 376 | תקח 3947 | את 853 | זרים 2114: | 16:33 לכל 3605 | זנות 2181 | יתנו 5414 | נדה 5078 | ואת 859 | נתת 5414 | את 853 | נדניך 5083 | לכל 3605 |
|---|---|---|---|---|---|---|---|---|---|---|---|---|
| 'ayshah, | tiqach | 'at | zariym. | lakal | zonout | yitanu | nedeh; | ua'at | natat | 'at | nadanayik | lakal |
| **her husband** | ***which* takes** | | **strangers** | **to all** | **whores** | **They give gifts** | | ***but*** | **you give** | | **your gifts** | **to all** |

Eze 16:26 Thou have also committed fornication with the Egyptians your neighbors, great of flesh; and have increased your whoredoms, to provoke me to anger.27 Behold, therefore I have stretched out my hand over you, and have diminished your ordinary food, and delivered you unto the will of them that hate you, the daughters of the Philistines, which are ashamed of your lewd way.28 Thou have played the whore also with the Assyrians, because you were unsatiable; yea, you have played the harlot with them, and yet couldest not be satisfied.29 Thou have moreover multiplied your fornication in the land of Canaan unto Chaldea; and yet you were not satisfied herewith.30 How weak is your heart, saith YHUH G-D, seeing you does all these things, the work of an imperious whorish woman;31 In that you buildest your eminent place in the head of every way, and make your high place in every street; and have not been as an harlot, in that you scornest hire;32 But as a wife that committeth adultery, which take strangers instead of her husband!33 They give gifts to all whores: but you givest your gifts to all your lovers, and hirest them, that they may come unto you on every side for your whoredom.

| מאהביך 157 | ותשחדי 7809 | אותם 853 | לבוא 935 | אליך 413 | מסביב 5439 | בתזנותיך 8457: | 16:34 | ויהי 1961 | בך 871a |
|---|---|---|---|---|---|---|---|---|---|
| ma'ahabayik, | uatishchadiy | 'autam, | labou'a | 'aelayik | misabiyb | bataznutayik. | | uayahiy | bak |
| **your lovers** | **and hirest** | **them** | **that they may come** | **unto you** | **on every side** | **for your whoredom** | | **And is** | **in you** |

| הפך 2016 | מן 4480 | הנשים 802 | בתזנותיך 8457 | ואחריך 310 | לא 3808 | זונה 2181 | ובתתך 5414 |
|---|---|---|---|---|---|---|---|
| hepek | min | hanashiym | bataznutayik, | ua'acharayik | la' | zounah; | uabtitek |
| **the contrary** | **from** | ***other* women** | **in your whoredoms** | **whereas follows you** | **none** | **to commit whoredoms** | **and in that you give** |

| אתנן 868 | ואתנן 868 | לא 3808 | נתן 5414 | לך 3807a | ותהי 1961 | להפך 2016: | 16:35 | לכן 3651 | זונה 2181 | שמעי 8085 | דבר 1697 |
|---|---|---|---|---|---|---|---|---|---|---|---|
| 'atnan, | ua'atnan | la' | nitan | lak | uatahiy | lahepek. | | laken | zounah, | shim'ay | dabar |
| **a reward** | **and reward** | **no** | **is given** | **unto you** | **therefore you are** | **contrary** | | **Wherefore** | **O harlot** | **hear** | **the word of** |

| יהוה 3068: | 16:36 | כה 3541 | אמר 559 | אדני 136 | יהוה 3069 | יען 3282 | השפך 8210 | נחשתך 5178 | ותגלה 1540 | ערותך 6172 |
|---|---|---|---|---|---|---|---|---|---|---|
| Yahuah. | | koh | 'amar | 'adonay | Yahuah | ya'an | hishapek | nachushatek | uatigaleh | 'aruatek, |
| **Yahuah** | | **Thus** | **saith** | **Adonai** | **Yahuah** | **Because** | **was poured out** | **your filthiness** | **and discovered** | **your nakedness** |

| בתזנותיך 8457 | על 5921 | מאהביך 157 | ועל 5921 | כל 3605 | גלולי 1544 | תועבותיך 8441 | וכדמי 1818 |
|---|---|---|---|---|---|---|---|
| bataznutayik | 'al | ma'ahabayik; | ua'al | kal | giluley | tou'aboutayik, | uakidmey |
| **through your whoredoms** | **with** | **your lovers** | **and with** | **all** | **the idols of** | **your abominations** | **and by the blood of** |

| בניך 1121 | אשר 834 | נתת 5414 | להם 3807a: | 16:37 | לכן 3651 | הנני 2005 | מקבץ 6908 | את 853 | כל 3605 | מאהביך 157 | אשר 834 |
|---|---|---|---|---|---|---|---|---|---|---|---|
| banayik, | 'asher | natat | lahem. | | laken | hinniy | maqabetz | 'at | kal | ma'ahabayik | 'asher |
| **your children** | **which** | **you did give** | **unto them** | | **therefore** | **Behold** | **I will gather** | | **all** | **your lovers** | **whom** |

| ערבת 6149 | עליהם 5921 | ואת 853 | כל 3605 | אשר 834 | אהבת 157 | על 5921 | כל 3605 | אשר 834 | שנאת 8130 |
|---|---|---|---|---|---|---|---|---|---|
| 'arabt | 'aleyhem, | ua'at | kal | 'asher | 'ahabt, | 'al | kal | 'asher | sana't; |
| **you have taken pleasure** | **with** | ***and*** | **all *them*** | **that** | **you have loved** | **with** | **all *them*** | **that** | **you have hated** |

| וקבצתי 6908 | אתם 853 | עליך 5921 | מסביב 5439 | וגליתי 1540 | ערותך 6172 | אלהם 413 | וראו 7200 | את 853 |
|---|---|---|---|---|---|---|---|---|
| uaqibatztiy | 'atam | 'alayik | misabiyb, | uagileytiy | 'aruatek | 'alehem, | uar'au | 'at |
| **I will even gather** | **them** | **against you** | **round about** | **and will discover** | **your nakedness** | **unto them** | **that they may see** | |

| כל 3605 | ערותך 6172: | 16:38 | ושפטתיך 8199 | משפטי 4941 | נאפות 5003 | ושפכת 8210 | דם 1818 |
|---|---|---|---|---|---|---|---|
| kal | 'aruatek. | | uashpatatiyk | mishpatey | no'apout, | uashopakot | dam; |
| **all** | **your nakedness** | | **And I will judge you** | **are judged *as*** | **women that break wedlock** | **and shed** | **blood** |

| ונתתיך 5414 | דם 1818 | חמה 2534 | וקנאה 7068: | 16:39 | ונתתי 5414 | אותך 853 | בידם 3027 |
|---|---|---|---|---|---|---|---|
| uantatiyk | dam | chemah | uaqin'ah. | | uanatatiy | autak | bayadam, |
| **and I will give you** | **blood in** | **fury** | **and jealousy** | | **And I will also give** | **you** | **into their hand** |

| והרסו 2040 | גבך 1354 | ונתצו 5422 | רמתיך 7413 | והפשיטו 6584 | אותך 853 |
|---|---|---|---|---|---|
| uaharasu | gabek | uanittzu | ramotayik, | uahipshiytu | 'autak |
| **and they shall throw down** | **your eminent place** | **and shall break down** | **your high places** | **they shall strip also** | **you** |

| בגדיך 899 | ולקחו 3947 | כלי 3627 | תפארתך 8597 | והניחוך 3240 | עירם 5903 | ועריה 6181: | 16:40 | והעלו 5927 | עליך 5921 |
|---|---|---|---|---|---|---|---|---|---|
| bagadayik, | ualaqachu | kaley | tip'artek; | uahiniychuk | 'ayarim | ua'aryah. | | uahe'alu | 'alayik |
| **of your clothes** | **and shall take** | **jewels** | **your fair** | **and leave you** | **naked** | **and bare** | | **They shall also bring up** | **against you** |

Eze 16:34 And the contrary is in you from other women in your whoredoms, whereas none followed you to commit whoredoms: and in that you givest a reward, and no reward is given unto you, therefore you are contrary.35 Wherefore, O harlot, hear the word of YHUH:36 Thus saith YHUH G-D; Because your filthiness was poured out, and your nakedness discovered through your whoredoms with your lovers, and with all the idols of your abominations, and by the blood of your children, which you did give unto them;37 Behold, therefore I will gather all your lovers, with whom you have taken pleasure, and all them that you have loved, with all them that you have hated; I will even gather them round about against you, and will discover your nakedness unto them, that they may see all your nakedness.38 And I will judge you, as women that break wedlock and shed blood are judged; and I will give you blood in fury and jealousy.39 And I will also give you into their hand, and they shall throw down your eminent place, and shall break down your high places: they shall strip you also of your clothes, and shall take your fair jewels, and leave you naked and bare.40 They shall also bring up a company against you, and they shall stone you with stones, and thrust you through with their swords.

| קהל 6951 | ורגמו 7275 | אותך 853 | באבן 68 | ובתקוך 1333 | בחרבותם 2719: | 16:41 ושרפו 8313 |
|---|---|---|---|---|---|---|
| qahal, | uaragamu | autak | ba'aben; | uabitaquk | bacharboutam. | uasarapu |
| **a company** | **and they shall stone** | **you** | **with stones** | **and thrust you through** | **with their swords** | **And they shall burn** |

| בתיך 1004 | באש 784 | ועשו 6213 | בך 871a | שפטים 8201 | לעיני 5869 | נשים 802 | רבות 7227 | והשבתיך 7673 |
|---|---|---|---|---|---|---|---|---|
| batayik | ba'aesh, | ua'asu | bak | shapatiym, | la'aeyney | nashiym | rabout; | uahishbatiyk |
| **your houses** | **with fire** | **and execute** | **upon you** | **judgments** | **in the sight of** | **women** | **many** | **and I will cause you to cease** |

| מזונה 2181 | וגם 1571 | אתנן 868 | לא 3808 | תתני 5414 | עוד 5750: | 16:42 והנחתי 5117 | חמתי 2534 | בך 871a |
|---|---|---|---|---|---|---|---|---|
| mizounah, | uagam | 'atnan | la' | titaniy | 'aud. | uahanichotiy | chamatiy | bak, |
| **from playing the harlot** | **and also** | **hire** | **no** | **you shall give** | **any more** | **So will I make to rest** | **my fury** | **toward you** |

| וסרה 5493 | קנאתי 7068 | ממך 4480 | ושקטתי 8252 | ולא 3808 | אכעס 3707 | עוד 5750: | 16:43 יען 3282 | אשר 834 | לא 3808 |
|---|---|---|---|---|---|---|---|---|---|
| uasarah | qin'atiy | mimek; | uashaqatiy, | uala' | 'aka'as | 'aud. | ya'an, | 'asher | la' |
| **and shall depart** | **my jealousy** | **from you** | **and I will be quiet** | **and no** | **will be angry** | **more** | **Because** | **after** | **not** |

| זכרתי 2142 | את 853 | ימי 3117 | נעוריך 5271 | ותרגזי 7264 | לי 3807a | בכל 3605 | אלה 428 | וגם 1571 | אני 589 | הא 1887 |
|---|---|---|---|---|---|---|---|---|---|---|
| zakartiy | 'at | yamey | na'aurayik, | uatirgaziy | liy | bakal | 'aeleh; | uagam | 'aniy | hea' |
| **you have remembered** | | **the days of** | **your youth** | **but have fretted** | **me** | **in all** | **these *things*** | **therefore also** | **I** | **behold** |

| דרכך 1870 | בראש 7218 | נתתי 5414 | נאם 5002 | אדני 136 | יהוה 3069 | ולא 3808 | עשיתי 6213 | את 853 | הזמה 2154 | על 5921 |
|---|---|---|---|---|---|---|---|---|---|---|
| darkek | bara'sh | natatiy, | na'am | 'adonay | Yahuah, | uala' | 'asiytiy | 'at | hazimah, | 'al |
| **your way** | **upon *your* head** | **will recompense** | **saith** | **Adonai** | **Yahuah** | **and not** | **you shall commit** | | **this lewdness** | **above** |

| כל 3605 | תועבתיך 8441: | 16:44 הנה 2009 | כל 3605 | המשל 4911 | עליך 5921 | ימשל 4911 | לאמר 559 |
|---|---|---|---|---|---|---|---|
| kal | tou'abotayik. | hineh | kal | hamoshel, | 'alayik | yimshol | lea'mor; |
| **all** | **your abominations** | **Behold** | **every one** | **that use proverbs** | **against you** | **shall use *this* proverb** | **saying** |

| כאמה 517 | בתה 1323: | 16:45 בת 1323 | אמך 517 | את 853 | געלת 1602 | אישה 376 | ובניה 1121 |
|---|---|---|---|---|---|---|---|
| ka'amah | bitah. | bat | 'amek | 'at | go'alet | 'ayshah | uabaneyha; |
| **As *is* the mother** | ***so is* her daughter** | **daughter** | ***You are* your mother's** | | **that loth** | **her husband** | **and her children** |

| ואחות 269 | אחותך 269 | את 859 | אשר 834 | געלו 1602 | אנשיהן 582 | ובניהן 1121 | אמכן 517 | חתית 2850 |
|---|---|---|---|---|---|---|---|---|
| ua'achout | 'achoutek | 'at | 'asher | ga'alu | 'ansheyhen | uabneyhen, | 'amken | chitiyt, |
| **and your sisters *are*** | **the sisters of** | ***you*** | **which** | **lothed** | **their husbands** | **and their children** | **your mother** | ***was* an Hittite** |

| ואביכן 1 | אמרי 567: | 16:46 ואחותך 269 | הגדולה 1419 | שמרון 8111 | היא 1931 | ובנותיה 1323 | היושבת 3427 | על 5921 |
|---|---|---|---|---|---|---|---|---|
| ua'abiyken | 'amoriy. | ua'achoutek | hagadoulah | shomaroun | hiy'a | uabnouteyha, | hayoushebet | 'al |
| **and your father** | **an Amorite** | **And sister** | **your elder** | ***is* Samaria** | **she** | **and her daughters** | **that dwell** | **at** |

| שמאולך 8040 | ואחותך 269 | הקטנה 6996 | ממך 4480 | היושבת 3427 | מימינך 3225 | סדם 5467 | ובנותיה 1323: | 16:47 ולא 3808 |
|---|---|---|---|---|---|---|---|---|
| samo'aulek; | ua'achoutek | haqatanah | mimek, | hayoushebet | miymiynek, | sadom | uabnouteyha. | uala' |
| **your left hand** | **and sister** | **younger** | **your** | **that dwell at** | **your right hand** | ***is* Sodom** | **and her daughters** | **Yet not** |

| בדרכיהן 1870 | הלכת 1980 | ובתועבותיהן 8441 | עשיתי 6213 | כמעט 4592 | קט 6962 |
|---|---|---|---|---|---|
| badarkeyhen | halakt, | uabtou'abouteyhen | 'asiytiy | kima'at | qat, |
| **after their ways** | **have you walked** | **nor after their abominations** | **done** | **as *if that were* a little *thing*** | **very** |

Eze 16:41 And they shall burn your houses with fire, and execute judgments upon you in the sight of many women: and I will cause you to cease from playing the harlot, and you also shall give no hire anymore.42 So will I make my fury toward you to rest, and my jealousy shall depart from you, and I will be quiet, and will be no more angry.43 Because you have not remembered the days of your youth, but have fretted me in all these things; behold, therefore I also will recompense your way upon your head, saith YHUH G-D: and you shall not commit this lewdness above all your abominations.44 Behold, everyone that useth proverbs shall use this proverb against you, saying, As is the mother, so is her daughter.45 Thou are your mother's daughter, that lotheth her husband and her children; and you are the sister of your sisters, which lothed their husbands and their children: your mother was an Hittite, and your father an Amorite.46 And your elder sister is Samaria, she and her daughters that dwell at your left hand: and your younger sister, that dwell at your right hand, is Sodom and her daughters.47 Yet have you not walked after their ways, nor done after their abominations: but, as if that were a very little thing, you were corrupted more than they in all your ways.

16:48

ותשחתי 7843 מהן 2004 בכל 3605 דרכיך 1870: חי 2416 אני 589 נאם 5002 אדני 136 יהוה 3069 אם 518 עשתה 6213 סדם 5467
uatashchitiy mehen bakal darakayik. chay 'aniy, na'am 'adonay Yahuah, 'am 'astah sadom
**but you were corrupted more than they in all your ways *As live I* saith Adonai Yahuah not has done Sodom**

16:49

אחותך 269 היא 1931 ובנותיה 1323 כאשר 834 עשית 6213 את 859 ובנותיך 1323: הנה 2009 זה 2088 היה 1961
'achoutek, hiy'a uabnouteyha; ka'asher 'asiyt, 'at uabnoutayik. hineh zeh hayah,
**your sister she nor her daughters as you have done *you* and your daughters Behold this was**

עון 5771 סדם 5467 אחותך 269 גאון 1347 שבעת 7653 לחם 3899 ושלות 7962 השקט 8252 היה 1961 לה 3807a ולבנותיה 1323
'auon sadom 'achoutek; ga'aun sib'at lechem uashaluat hashaqet, hayah lah ualibnouteyha,
**the iniquity of Sodom your sister pride fulness of bread and abundance of idleness was in her and in her daughters**

16:50

ויד 3027 עני 6041 ואביון 34 לא 3808 החזיקה 2388: ותגבהינה 1361 ותעשינה 6213 תועבה 8441
uayad 'aniy ua'abyoun la' hechaziyqah. uatigbaheynah, uata'aseynah tou'aebah
**the hand of the poor and needy neither did she strengthen And they were haughty and committed abomination**

16:51

לפני 6440 ואסיר 5493 אתהן 853 כאשר 834 ראיתי 7200: ושמרון 8111 כחצי 2677 חטאתיך 2403 לא 3808 חטאה 2398
lapanay; ua'asiyr 'athen ka'asher ra'aytiy. uashomaroun, kachatziy chata'tayik la' chata'ah;
**before me therefore I took away them as I saw *good* Samaria half of your sins Neither has committed**

ותרבי 7235 את 853 תועבותיך 8441 מהנה 2007 ותצדקי 6663 את 853 אחותך 269 בכל 3605
uatarbiy 'at tou'aboutayik mehenah, uatatzadqiy 'at 'achoutek bakal
**but you have multiplied your abominations more than they and have justified your sisters in all**

16:52

תועבותיך 8441 אשר 834 עשיתי 6213 גם 1571 את 859 שאי 5375 כלמתך 3639 אשר 834 פללת 6419 לאחותך 269
tou'aboutayik 'asher 'asiytiy gam 'at sa'ay kalimatek, 'asher pilalt la'achoutek,
**your abominations which you have done also *You* bear your own shame which have judged your sisters**

בחטאתיך 2403 אשר 834 התעבת 8581 מהן 2004 תצדקנה 6663 ממך 4480 וגם 1571 את 859
bachata'tayik 'asher hit'abt mehen titzadaqnah mimek; uagam 'at
**for your sins that you have committed more abominable than they they are more righteous than you yea also *you***

16:53

בושי 954 ושאי 5375 כלמתך 3639 בצדקתך 6663 אחיותך 269: ושבתי 7725 את 853
boushiy us'ay kalimatek, batzadeqtek achyoutek. uashabtiy 'at
**be confounded and bear your shame in that you have justified your sisters When I shall bring again**

שביתהן 7622 את 853 שבית 7622 סדם 5467 ובנותיה 1323 ואת 853 שבית 7622 שמרון 8111 ובנותיה 1323
shabiytahen, 'at shebiyt sadom uabnouteyha, ua'at shebiyt shomaroun uabnouteyha;
**your captives the captivity of Sodom and her daughters *and* the captivity of Samaria and her daughters**

16:54

ושבית 7622 שביתיך 7628 בתוכהנה 8432: למען 4616 תשאי 5375 כלמתך 3639
uashebiyt shabiytayik batoukahanah. lama'an tis'ay kalimatek,
**then will I bring again the captivity of your captives in the midst of them That you may bear your own shame**

16:55

ונכלמת 3637 מכל 3605 אשר 834 עשית 6213 בנחמך 5162 אתן 854: ואחותיך 269 סדם 5467
uaniklamt mikol 'asher 'asiyt; banachamek 'atan. ua'achoutayik, sadom
**and may be confounded in all that you have done in that you are a comfort unto them When your sisters Sodom**

Eze 16:48 As I live, saith YHUH G-D, Sodom your sister has not done, she nor her daughters, as you have done, you and your daughters.49 Behold, this was the iniquity of your sister Sodom, pride, fulness of bread, and abundance of idleness was in her and in her daughters, neither did she strengthen the hand of the poor and needy.50 And they were haughty, and committed abomination before me: therefore I took them away as I saw good.51 Neither has Samaria committed half of your sins; but you have multiplied your abominations more than they, and have justified your sisters in all your abominations which you have done.52 Thou also, which have judged your sisters, bear your own shame for your sins that you have committed more abominable than they: they are more righteous than you: yea, be you confounded also, and bear your shame, in that you have justified your sisters.53 When I shall bring again their captivity, the captivity of Sodom and her daughters, and the captivity of Samaria and her daughters, then will I bring again the captivity of your captives in the midst of them:54 That you may bear your own shame, and may be confounded in all that you have done, in that you are a comfort unto them.55 When your sisters, Sodom and her daughters, shall return to their former estate, and Samaria and her daughters shall return to their former estate,

| ובנותיה 1323 | תשבן 7725 | לקדמתן 6927 | ושמרון 8111 | ובנותיה 1323 | תשבן 7725 | לקדמתן 6927 |
|---|---|---|---|---|---|---|
| uabnouteyha | tashobana | laqadmatan, | uashomaroun | uabnouteyha, | tashobana | laqadmatan; |
| **and her daughters** | **shall return** | **to their former estate** | **and Samaria** | **and her daughters** | **shall return** | **to their former estate** |

| ואת 859 | ובנותיך 1323 | תשבינה 7725 | לקדמתכן 6927: | 16:56 | ולוא 3808 | היתה 1961 | סדם 5467 | אחותך 269 | לשמועה 8052 |
|---|---|---|---|---|---|---|---|---|---|
| ua'at | uabnoutayik, | tashubeynah | laqadmataken. | | ualou'a | hayatah | sadom | 'achoutek, | lishmu'ah |
| ***then you*** | **and your daughters** | **shall return** | **to your former estate** | | **For not** | **was** | **Sodom** | **your sister** | **mentioned** |

| בפיך 6310 | ביום 3117 | גאוניך 1347: | 16:57 | בטרם 2962 | תגלה 1540 | רעתך 7451 | כמו 3644 | עת 6256 | חרפת 2781 |
|---|---|---|---|---|---|---|---|---|---|
| bapiyk; | bayoum | ga'anayik. | | baterem | tigaleh | ra'atek | kamou, | 'at | cherpat |
| **by your mouth** | **in the day of** | **your pride** | | **Before** | **was discovered** | **your wickedness** | **as** | **at the time of** | ***your* reproach of** |

| בנות 1323 | ארם 758 | וכל 3605 | סביבותיה 5439 | בנות 1323 | פלשתים 6430 | השאטות 7590 | אותך 853 |
|---|---|---|---|---|---|---|---|
| banout | 'aram, | uakal | sabiybouteyha | banout | palishtiym; | hasha'tout | autak |
| **the daughters of** | **Syria** | **and all** | ***that are* round about her** | **the daughters of** | **the Philistines** | **which despise** | **you** |

| מסביב 5439: | 16:58 | את 853 | זמתך 2154 | ואת 853 | תועבותיך 8441 | את 859 | נשאתים 5375 | נאם 5002 | יהוה 3068: | 16:59 | כי 3588 | כה 3541 | אמר 559 |
|---|---|---|---|---|---|---|---|---|---|---|---|---|---|
| misabiyb. | | 'at | zimatek | ua'at | tou'aboutayik | 'at | nasa'tiym; | na'am | Yahuah. | | kiy | koh | 'amar |
| **round about** | | | **your lewdness *and*** | | **your abominations *You*** | | **have borne** | **saith** | **Yahuah** | | **For** | **thus** | **saith** |

| אדני 136 | יהוה 3069 | ועשית 6213 | אותך 854 | כאשר 834 | עשית 6213 | אשר 834 | בזית 959 | אלה 423 | להפר 6565 |
|---|---|---|---|---|---|---|---|---|---|
| 'adonay | Yahuah, | ua'asiyt | autak | ka'asher | 'asiyt; | 'asher | baziyt | 'alah | lahaper |
| **Adonai** | **Yahuah** | **I will even deal** | **with you** | **as** | **you have done** | **which** | **have despised** | **the oath** | **in breaking** |

| ברית 1285: | 16:60 | וזכרתי 2142 | אני 589 | את 853 | בריתי 1285 | אותך 854 | בימי 3117 | נעוריך 5271 |
|---|---|---|---|---|---|---|---|---|
| bariyt. | | uazakartiy | 'aniy | 'at | bariytiy | autak | biymey | na'aurayik; |
| **the covenant** | | **Nevertheless will remember** | **I** | | **my covenant** | **with you** | **in the days of** | **your youth** |

| והקמותי 6965 | לך 3807a | ברית 1285 | עולם 5769: | 16:61 | וזכרת 2142 | את 853 | דרכיך 1870 | ונכלמת 3637 |
|---|---|---|---|---|---|---|---|---|
| uahaqimoutiy | lak | bariyt | 'aulam. | | uazakart | 'at | derakayik | uaniklamt |
| **and I will establish** | **unto you** | **an covenant** | **everlasting** | | **Then you shall remember** | | **your ways** | **and be ashamed** |

| בקחתך 3947 | את 853 | אחותיך 269 | הגדלות 1419 | ממך 4480 | אל 413 | הקטנות 6996 | ממך 4480 | ונתתי 5414 | אתהן 853 | לך 3807a |
|---|---|---|---|---|---|---|---|---|---|---|
| baqachtek, | 'at | 'achoutayik | hagadolout | mimek, | 'al | haqatanout | mimek; | uanatatiy | 'athen | lak |
| **when you shall receive** | | **your sisters** | **elder** | **your** | ***and* to** | **younger** | **your** | **and I will give** | **them** | **unto you** |

| לבנות 1323 | ולא 3808 | מבריתך 1285: | 16:62 | והקימותי 6965 | אני 589 | את 853 | בריתי 1285 | אתך 854 | וידעת 3045 |
|---|---|---|---|---|---|---|---|---|---|
| labanout | uala' | mibariytek. | | uahaqiymoutiy | 'aniy | 'at | bariytiy | 'atak; | uayada'at |
| **for daughters** | **but not** | **by your covenant** | | **And I will establish** | **I** | | **my covenant** | **with you** | **and you shall know** |

| כי 3588 | אני 589 | יהוה 3068: | 16:63 | למען 4616 | תזכרי 2142 | ובשת 954 | ולא 3808 | יהיה 1961 | לך 3807a | עוד 5750 | פתחון 6610 |
|---|---|---|---|---|---|---|---|---|---|---|---|
| kiy | 'aniy | Yahuah. | | lama'an | tizkariy | uabosht, | uala' | yihayeh | lak | 'aud | pitchoun |
| **that** | **I *am*** | **Yahuah** | | **That** | **you may remember** | **and be confounded** | **and never** | **become** | **to you** | **any more** | **open** |

| פה 6310 | מפני 6440 | כלמתך 3639 | בכפרי 3722 | לך 3807a | לכל 3605 | אשר 834 | עשית 6213 | נאם 5002 | אדני 136 | יהוה 3069: |
|---|---|---|---|---|---|---|---|---|---|---|
| peh, | mipaney | kalimatek; | bakapriy | lak | lakal | 'asher | 'asiyt, | na'am | 'adonay | Yahuah. |
| **mouth** | **because of** | **your shame** | **when I am pacified** | **toward you** | **for all** | **that** | **you have done** | **saith** | **Adonai** | **Yahuah** |

Eze 16:56 For your sister Sodom was not mentioned by your mouth in the day of your pride,57 Before your wickedness was discovered, as at the time of your reproach of the daughters of Syria, and all that are round about her, the daughters of the Philistines, which despise you round about.58 Thou have borne your lewdness and your abominations, saith YHUH.59 For thus saith YHUH G-D; I will even deal with you as you have done, which have despised the oath in breaking the covenant.60 Nevertheless I will remember my covenant with you in the days of your youth, and I will establish unto you an everlasting covenant.61 Then you shall remember your ways, and be ashamed, when you shall receive your sisters, your elder and your younger: and I will give them unto you for daughters, but not by your covenant.62 And I will establish my covenant with you; and you shall know that I am YHUH:63 That you may remember, and be confounded, and never open your mouth anymore because of your shame, when I am pacified toward you for all that you have done, saith YHUH G-D.

**Ezek 17:1** 17:2
ויהי 1961 דבר 1697 יהוה 3068 אלי 413 לאמר 559: בן 1121 אדם 120 חוד 2330 חידה 2420 ומשל 4911 משל 4912 אל 413
uayahiy dabar Yahuah 'aelay lea'mor. ben 'adam chud chiydah uamshol mashal; 'al
**And came the word of Yahuah unto me saying Son of man put forth a riddle and speak a parable unto**

**17:3**
בית 1004 ישראל 3478: ואמרת 559 כה 3541 אמר 559 אדני 136 יהוה 3069 הנשר 5404 הגדול 1419 גדול 1419 הכנפים 3671 ארך 750
beyt yisra'ael. ua'amarta koh 'amar 'adonay Yahuah hanesher hagadoul gagoul hakanapayim 'arek
**the house of Israel And say Thus saith Adonai Yahuah A eagle great *with* great wings long**

האבר 83 מלא 4392 הנוצה 5133 אשר 834 לו 3807a הרקמה 7553 בא 935 אל 413 הלבנון 3844 ויקח 3947 את 853 צמרת 6788
ha'aeber, malea' hanoutzah, 'asher lou' hariqmah; ba' 'al halabanoun, uayiqach 'at tzameret
**pinions full of feathers which had divers colours came unto Lebanon and took the highest branch of**

**17:4**
הארז 730: את 853 ראש 7218 יניקותיו 3242 קטף 6998 ויביאהו 935 אל 413 ארץ 776 כנען 3667 בעיר 5892
ha'arez. 'at ra'sh yaniyqoutayu qatap; uayabiy'ahu 'al 'aretz kana'an, ba'ayr
**the cedar the top of his young twigs He cropped off and carried it into a land of traffick (*Canaan*) in a city of**

**17:5**
רכלים 7402 שמו 7760: ויקח 3947 מזרע 2233 הארץ 776 ויתנהו 5414 בשדה 7704 זרע 2233 קח 3947 על 5921 מים 4325
rokaliym samou. uayiqach mizera' ha'aretz, uayitanehu bisdeh zara'; qach 'al mayim
**merchants he set it He took also of the seed of the land and planted it in a field fruitful he placed *it* by waters**

**17:6**
רבים 7227 צפצפה 6851 שמו 7760: ויצמח 6779 ויהי 1961 לגפן 1612 סרחת 5628 שפלת 8217 קומה 6967 לפנות 6437
rabiym, tzaptzapah samou. uayitzmach uayahiy lagepen sorachat shiplat qoumah, lipnout
**great *as* a willow tree *and* set it And it grew and became a vine of spreading low stature turned**

דליותיו 1808 אליו 413 ושרשיו 8328 תחתיו 8478 יהיו 1961 ותהי 1961 לגפן 1612 ותעש 6213 בדים 905
daliyoutayu 'aelayu, uasharashayu tachtayu yihayu; uatahiy lagepen, uata'as badiym,
**whose branches toward him and the roots thereof under him were so it became a vine and brought forth branches**

**17:7**
ותשלח 7971 פארות 6288: ויהי 1961 נשר 5404 אחד 259 גדול 1419 גדול 1419 כנפים 3671 ורב 7227 נוצה 5133 והנה 2009
uatashalach pa'rout. uayahiy nesher 'achad gadoul, gagoul kanapayim uarab noutzah; uahineh
**and shot forth sprigs There was also eagle another great *with* great wings and many feathers and behold**

הגפן 1612 הזאת 2063 כפנה 3719 שרשיה 8328 עליו 5921 ודליותיו 1808 שלחה 7971 לו 3807a להשקות 8248
hagapen haza't kapanah sharasheyha 'alayu, uadaliyoutayu shilchah lou', lahashqout
**vine this did bend her roots toward him and her branches shot forth toward him that he might water (*irrigate*)**

**17:8**
אותה 853 מערגות 6170 מטעה 4302: אל 413 שדה 7704 טוב 2896 אל 413 מים 4325 רבים 7227 היא 1931 שתולה 8362
'autah, me'arugout mata'ah. 'al sadeh toub 'al mayim rabiym hiy'a shatulah;
**it by the furrows of her plantation in a soil good by waters great It was planted**

**17:9**
לעשות 6213 ענף 6057 ולשאת 5375 פרי 6529 להיות 1961 לגפן 1612 אדרת 155: אמר 559 כה 3541 אמר 559
la'asout 'anap ualasea't pariy, lihayout lagepen 'adaret. 'amor, koh 'amar
**that it might bring forth branches and that it might bear fruit that it might be a vine goodly Say you Thus saith**

אדני 136 יהוה 3069 תצלח 6743 הלוא 3808 את 853 שרשיה 8328 ינתק 5423 ואת 853 פריה 6529 יקוסס 7082
'adonay Yahuah titzlach; halou'a 'at sharasheyha yanateq ua'at piryah yaqouses
**Adonai Yahuah Shall it prosper? not the roots thereof shall he pull up *and* the fruit thereof cut off**

**Eze** 17:1 And the word of YHUH came unto me, saying,2 Son of man, put forth a riddle, and speak a parable unto the house of Israel;3 And say, Thus saith YHUH G-D; A great eagle with great wings, longwinged, full of feathers, which had divers colors, came unto Lebanon, and took the highest branch of the cedar:4 He cropped off the top of his young twigs, and carried it into a land of traffick; he set it in a city of merchants.5 He took also of the seed of the land, and planted it in a fruitful field; he placed it by great waters, and set it as a willow tree.6 And it grew, and became a spreading vine of low stature, whose branches turned toward him, and the roots thereof were under him: so it became a vine, and brought forth branches, and shot forth sprigs.7 There was also another great eagle with great wings and many feathers: and, behold, this vine did bend her roots toward him, and shot forth her branches toward him, that he might water it by the furrows of her plantation.8 It was planted in a good soil by great waters, that it might bring forth branches, and that it might bear fruit, that it might be a goodly vine.9 Say you, Thus saith YHUH G-D; Shall it prosper? shall he not pull up the roots thereof, and cut off the fruit thereof, that it where? it shall where in all the leaves of her spring, even without great power or many people to pluck it up by the roots thereof.

ויבש 3001 כל 3605 טרפי 2964 צמחה 6780 תיבש 3001 ולא 3808 בזרע 2220 גדולה 1419 ובעם 5971 רב 7227 למשאות 5375
uayabesh, kal tarpey tzimchah tiybash, uala' bizroa' gadoulah uab'am rab, lemas'aut
**that it wither? *in* all the leaves of her spring it shall wither even without power great or people many to pluck up**

אותה 853 משרשיה 8328: 17:10 והנה 2009 שתולה 8362 התצלח 6743 הלוא 3808 כגעת 5060 בה 871a רוח 7307 הקדים 6921
'autah misharasheyha. uahineh shatulah hatitzlach; halou'a kaga'at bah ruach haqadiym
**it by the roots thereof Yea behold *being* planted shall it prosper not when touch it? wind the east**

תיבש 3001 יבש 3001 על 5921 ערגת 6170 צמחה 6780 תיבש 3001: 17:11 ויהי 1961 דבר 1697 יהוה 3068 אלי 413
tiybash yabosh, 'al 'arugot tzimchah tiybash. uayahiy dabar Yahuah 'aelay
**shall it utterly wither in the furrows where it grew it shall wither Moreover came the word of Yahuah unto me**

לאמר 559: 17:12 אמר 559 נא 4994 לבית 1004 המרי 4805 הלא 3808 ידעתם 3045 מה 4100 אלה 428 אמר 559 הנה 2009 בא 935
lea'mor. 'amar naa' labeyt hameriy, hala' yada'tem mah 'aeleh; 'amor, hineh ba'
**saying Say now to house the rebellious not Know you what these *things mean*? tell *them* Behold is come**

מלך 4428 בבל 894 ירושלם 3389 ויקח 3947 את 853 מלכה 4428 ואת 853 שריה 8269 ויבא 935 אותם 853 אליו 413
melek babel yarushalaim uayiqach 'at malkah ua'at sareyha, uayabea' 'autam 'aelayu
**the king of Babylon *to* Jerusalem and has taken the king thereof *and* the princes thereof and led them with him**

בבלה 894: 17:13 ויקח 3947 מזרע 2233 המלוכה 4410 ויכרת 3772 אתו 854 ברית 1285 ויבא 935 אתו 853 באלה 423 ואת 853
babelah. uayiqach mizera' hamalukah, uayikrot 'atou bariyt; uayabea' 'atou ba'alah, ua'at
**to Babylon And has taken of seed the king's and made with him a covenant and has taken also an oath of *him***

אילי 352 הארץ 776 לקח 3947: 17:14 להיות 1961 ממלכה 4467 שפלה 8217 לבלתי 1115 התנשא 5375
'aeyley ha'aretz laqach. lihayout mamlakah shapalah, labiltiy hitnasea';
**the mighty of the land he has taken That might be the kingdom base that not it might lift itself up**

לשמר 8104 את 853 בריתו 1285 לעמדה 5975: 17:15 וימרד 4775 בו 871a לשלח 7971 מלאכיו 4397
lishmor 'at bariytou la'amadah. uayimrad bou, lishloach mal'akayu
***but* that by keeping of his covenant it might stand But he rebelled against him in sending his ambassadors into**

מצרים 4714 לתת 5414 לו 3807a סוסים 5483 ועם 5971 רב 7227 היצלח 6743 הימלט 4422 העשה 6213 אלה 428
mitzrayim, latet lou' susiym ua'am rab; hayitzalach hayimalet ha'aseh 'aeleh,
**Egypt that they might give him horses and people much Shall he prosper ? shall he escape that does such *things*?**

והפר 6565 ברית 1285 ונמלט 4422: 17:16 חי 2416 אני 589 נאם 5002 אדני 136 יהוה 3068 אם 518 לא 3808 במקום 4725
uaheper bariyt uanimlat. chay 'aniy, na'am 'adonay Yahuah 'am la', bimqoum
**or shall he break the covenant and be delivered? *As* live I saith Adonai Yahuah surely not in the place**

המלך 4428 הממליך 4427 אתו 853 אשר 834 בזה 959 את 853 אלתו 423 ואשר 834 הפר 6565 את 853 בריתו 1285
hamelek hamamliyk 'atou, 'asher bazah 'at 'alatou, ua'asher heper 'at bariytou;
***where* the king *dwell* that made king him whose he despised *whose* oath and whose he brake covenant**

אתו 854 בתוך 8432 בבל 894 ימות 4191: 17:17 ולא 3808 בחיל 2428 גדול 1419 ובקהל 6951 רב 7227 יעשה 6213
'atou batouk babel yamut. uala' bachayil gadoul uabqahal rab, ya'aseh
***even* with him in the midst of Babylon he shall die Neither with army *his* mighty and company great shall make**

Eze 17:10 Yea, behold, being planted, shall it prosper? shall it not utterly where, when the east wind touch it? it shall where in the furrows where it grew.11 Moreover the word of YHUH came unto me, saying,12 Say now to the rebellious house, Know you not what these things mean? tell them, Behold, the king of Babylon is come to Jerusalem, and has taken the king thereof, and the princes thereof, and led them with him to Babylon;13 And has taken of the king's seed, and made a covenant with him, and has taken an oath of him: he has also taken the mighty of the land:14 That the kingdom might be base, that it might not lift itself up, but that by keeping of his covenant it might stand.15 But he rebelled against him in sending his ambassadors into Egypt, that they might give him horses and much people. Shall he prosper? shall he escape that doeth such things? or shall he break the covenant, and be delivered?16 As I live, saith YHUH G-D, surely in the place where the king dwell that made him king, whose oath he despised, and whose covenant he break, even with him in the midst of Babylon he shall die.17 Neither shall Pharaoh with his mighty army and great company make for him in the war, by casting up mounts, and building forts, to cut off many persons:

אותו 853 פרעה 6547 במלחמה 4421 בשפך 8210 סללה 5550 ובבנות 1129 דיק 1785 להכרית 3772 נפשות 5315 רבות 7227: 17:18
'autou par'ah bamilchamah, bishpok solalah uabibnout dayeq; lahakriyt napashout rabout.
**for him Pharaoh in the war by casting up mounts and building forts to cut off persons many**

ובזה 959 אלה 423 להפר 6565 ברית 1285 והנה 2009 נתן 5414 ידו 3027 וכל 3605 אלה 428 עשה 6213
uabazah 'alah lahaper bariyt; uahineh natan yadou uakal 'aeleh 'asah
**Seeing he despised the oath by breaking the covenant and when lo he had given his hand and all these *things* has done**

לא 3808 ימלט 4422: 17:19 לכן 3651 כה 3541 אמר 559 אדני 136 יהוה 3069 חי 2416 אני 589 אם 518 לא 3808 אלתי 423 אשר 834
la' yimalet. laken koh 'amar 'adonay Yahuah chay 'aniy 'am la', 'alatiy 'asher
**not he shall escape Therefore thus saith Adonai Yahuah *As* live I surely not mine oath that**

בזה 959 ובריתי 1285 אשר 834 הפיר 6331 ונתתיו 5414 בראשו 7218: ופרשתי 6566 17:20
bazah, uabriytiy 'asher hepiyr; uantatiyu bara'shou. uaparastiy
**he has despised and my covenant that he has broken even it will I recompense upon his own head And I will spread**

עליו 5921 רשתי 7568 ונתפש 8610 במצודתי 4686 והביאותיהו 935 בבלה 894 ונשפטתי 8199 אתו 854 שם 8033
'alayu rishtiy, uanitpas bimtzudatiy; uahabiy'autiyhu babelah, uanishpattiy 'atou sham,
**upon him my net and he shall be taken in my snare and I will bring him to Babylon and will plead with him there**

מעלו 4603 אשר 834 מעל 4604 בי 871a: 17:21 ואת 853 כל 3605 מברחו 4015 בכל 3605 אגפיו 102 בחרב 2719 יפלו 5307
ma'alou 'asher ma'al biy. ua'at kal mibarachou bakal 'agapayu bachereb yipolu,
**he has trespass that *for* his trespassed against me *And* all his fugitives with all his bands by the sword shall fall**

והנשארים 7604 לכל 3605 רוח 7307 יפרשו 6566 וידעתם 3045 כי 3588 אני 589 יהוה 3068 דברתי 1696: 17:22
uahanish'arym lakal ruach yiparesu; uiyda'tem kiy 'aniy Yahuah dibartiy.
**and they that remain toward all winds shall be scattered and you shall know that I Yahuah have spoken *it***

כה 3541 אמר 559 אדני 136 יהוה 3069 ולקחתי 3947 אני 589 מצמרת 6788 הארז 730 הרמה 7311 ונתתי 5414 מראש 2718
koh 'amar 'adonay Yahuah, ualaqachtiy 'aniy, mitzameret ha'arez haramah uanatatiy; mera'sh
**Thus saith Adonai Yahuah will also take I of the highest branch of cedar the high and will set *it* from the top of**

ינקותיו 3127 רך 7390 אקטף 6998 ושתלתי 8362 אני 589 על 5921 הר 2022 גבה 1364 ותלול 8524: 17:23
yonaqoutayu rak 'aqtop, uashataltiy 'aniy, 'al har gaboha uatalul.
**his young twigs a tender one I will crop off and will plant *it* I upon an mountain high and eminent**

בהר 2022 מרום 4791 ישראל 3478 אשתלנו 8362 ונשא 5375 ענף 6057 ועשה 6213 פרי 6529 והיה 1961 לארז 730
bahar maroum yisra'ael 'ashtalenu, uanasa' 'anap ua'asah periy, uahayah la'arez
**In the mountain of the height of Israel will I plant it and it shall bring forth boughs and bear fruit and be cedar**

אדיר 117 ושכנו 7931 תחתיו 8478 כל 3605 צפור 6833 כל 3605 כנף 3671 בצל 6738 דליותיו 1808 תשכנה 7931: 17:24
'adiyr; uashakanu tachtayu, kal tzipour kal kanap, batzel daliyoutayu tishkonah.
**goodly and it shall dwell under all fowl of every wing in the shadow of the branches thereof shall they dwell**

וידעו 3045 כל 3605 עצי 6086 השדה 7704 כי 3588 אני 589 יהוה 3068 השפלתי 8213 עץ 6086 גבה 1364 הגבהתי 1361 עץ 6086
uayada'aua kal 'atzey hasadeh, kiy 'aniy Yahuah hishpaltiy 'aetz gaboha, higbahtiy 'aetz
**And shall know all the trees of the field that I Yahuah have brought down tree *the* high have exalted tree**

Eze 17:18 Seeing he despised the oath by breaking the covenant, when, lo, he had given his hand, and has done all these things, he shall not escape.19 Therefore thus saith YHUH G-D; As I live, surely mine oath that he has despised, and my covenant that he has broken, even it will I recompense upon his own head.20 And I will spread my net upon him, and he shall be taken in my snare, and I will bring him to Babylon, and will plead with him there for his trespass that he has trespassed against me.21 And all his fugitives with all his bands shall fall by the sword, and they that remain shall be scattered toward all winds: and you shall know that I YHUH have spoken it.22 Thus saith YHUH G-D; I will also take of the highest branch of the high cedar, and will set it; I will crop off from the top of his young twigs a tender one, and will plant it upon an high mountain and eminent:23 In the mountain of the height of Israel will I plant it: and it shall bring forth boughs, and bear fruit, and be a goodly cedar: and under it shall dwell all fowl of every wing; in the shadow of the branches thereof shall they dwell.24 And all the trees of the field shall know that I YHUH have brought down the high tree, have exalted the low tree, have dried up the green tree, and have made the dry tree to flourish: I YHUH have brought down the high tree, have exalted the low tree,

שפל 8217 הובשתי 3001 עץ 6086 לח 3892 והפרחתי 6524 עץ 6086 יבש 3002 אני 589 יהוה 3068 דברתי 1696
shapal, houbashtiy 'aetz lach, uahiprachtiy 'aetz yabesh; 'aniy Yahuah dibartiy
***the*** **low have dried up tree *the* green and have made to flourish tree *the* dry I Yahuah have brought**

ועשיתי 6213:
ua'asiytiy.
**down the high tree**

**Ezek 18:1** ויהי 1961 דבר 1697 יהוה 3068 אלי 413 לאמר 559: **18:2** מה 4100 לכם 3807a אתם 859 משלים 4911 את 853
uayahiy dabar Yahuah 'aelay lea'mor. mah lakem, 'atem moshaliym 'at
**came again The word of Yahuah unto me saying What *mean* to you *that* you use**

המשל 4912 הזה 2088 על 5921 אדמת 127 ישראל 3478 לאמר 559 אבות 1 יאכלו 398 בסר 1155 ושני 8127 הבנים 1121
hamashal hazeh, 'al 'admat yisra'ael lea'mor; about ya'kalu boser, uashiney habaniym
**proverb this concerning the land of Israel saying The fathers have eaten sour grapes and teeth the children's**

תקהינה 6949: **18:3** חי 2416 אני 589 נאם 5002 אדני 136 יהוה 3069 אם 518 יהיה 1961 לכם 3807a עוד 5750 משל 4911 המשל 4912
tiqheynah. chay 'aniy na'am 'adonay Yahuah; 'am yihayeh lakem 'aud, mashol hamashal
**are set on edge? *As* live I saith Adonai Yahuah not shall have to you *occasion* any more to use proverb**

הזה 2088 בישראל 3478: **18:4** הן 2005 כל 3605 הנפשות 5315 לי 3807a הנה 2005 כנפש 5315 האב 1 וכנפש 5315 הבן 1121
hazeh bayisra'ael. hen kal hanapashout liy henah, kanepesh ha'ab uaknepesh haben
**this in Israel Behold all souls *are* mine they as the soul of the father so also the soul of the son**

לי 3807a הנה 2005 הנפש 5315 החטאת 2398 היא 1931 תמות 4191: **18:5** ואיש 376 כי 3588 יהיה 1961 צדיק 6662 ועשה 6213 משפט 4941
liy henah; hanepesh hachata't hiy'a tamut. ua'aysh kiy yihayeh tzadiyq; ua'asah mishapat
***is* mine they the soul that sin it shall die But if a man if be just and do that which is lawful**

וצדקה 6666: **18:6** אל 413 ההרים 2022 לא 3808 אכל 398 ועיניו 5869 לא 3808 נשא 5375 אל 413 גלולי 1544 בית 1004
uatzdaqah. 'al hehariym la' 'akal, ua'aeynayu la' nasa', 'al giluley beyt
**and right *And* upon the mountains not has eaten his eyes neither has lifted up to the idols of the house of**

ישראל 3478 ואת 853 אשת 802 רעהו 7453 לא 3808 טמא 2930 ואל 413 אשה 802 נדה 5079 לא 3808 יקרב 7126: **18:7**
yisra'ael; ua'at 'aeshet re'aehu la' timea', ua'al 'ashah nidah la' yiqrab.
**Israel *neither* wife his neighbour's neither has defiled to a woman menstruous neither has come near**

ואיש 376 לא 3808 יונה 3238 חבלתו 2258 חוב 2326 ישיב 7725 גזלה 1500 לא 3808 יגזל 1497 לחמו 3899
ua'aysh la' youneh, chabolatou choub yashiyb, gazelah la' yigzol; lachmou
**And any not has oppressed his pledge *to* the debtor *but* has restored by violence none has spoiled his bread**

לרעב 7457 יתן 5414 ועירם 5903 יכסה 3680 בגד 899: **18:8** בנשך 5392 לא 3808 יתן 5414
lara'aeb yiten, ua'aeyrom yakaseh baged. baneshek la' yiten,
**to the hungry has given and the naked has covered *with* a garment upon usury not He *that* has given forth**

ותרבית 8636 לא 3808 יקח 3947 מעול 7566 ישיב 7725 ידו 3027 משפט 4941 אמת 571 יעשה 6213 בין 996 איש 376
uatarbiyt la' yiqach, me'auel yashiyb yadou; mishapat 'amet ya'aseh, beyn 'aysh
***any* increase neither has taken from iniquity *that* has withdrawn his hand judgment true has executed between man**

Eze 17:24 and have made the dry tree to flourish: I YHUH have spoken and have done it. **Eze** 18:1 The word of YHUH came unto me again, saying,2 What mean you, that you use this proverb concerning the land of Israel, saying, The fathers have eaten sour grapes, and the children's teeth are set on edge?3 As I live, saith YHUH G-D, you shall not have occasion anymore to use this proverb in Israel.4 Behold, all souls are mine; as the soul of the father, so also the soul of the son is mine: the soul that sin, it shall die.5 But if a man be just, and do that which is lawful and right,6 And has not eaten upon the mountains, neither has lifted up his eyes to the idols of the house of Israel, neither has defiled his neighbor's wife, neither has come near to a menstruous woman,7 And has not oppressed any, but has restored to the debtor his pledge, has spoiled none by violence, has given his bread to the hungry, and has covered the naked with a garment;8 He that has not given forth upon usury, neither has taken any increase, that has withdrawn his hand from iniquity, has executed true judgment between man and man,

18:9
לאיש 376: בחקותי 2708 יהלך 1980 ומשפטי 4941 שמר 8104 לעשות 6213 אמת 571 צדיק 6662 הוא 1931 חיה 2421 יחיה 2421
la'aysh. bachuqoutay yahalek uamishpatay shamar la'asout 'amet; tzadiyq hua' chayoh yichayeh,
**and man in my statutes Has walked and my judgments has kept to deal truly *is* just he shall surely live**

18:10
נאם 5002 אדני 136 יהוה 3069: והוליד 3205 בן 1121 פריץ 6530 שפך 8210 דם 1818 ועשה 6213 אח 251 מאחד 259
na'am 'adonay Yahuah. uahouliyd ben pariytz shopek dam; ua'asah 'ach, me'achad
**saith Adonai Yahuah If he beget a son *that is* a robber a shedder of blood and *that* does the like to *any* one**

18:11
מאלה 428: והוא 1931 את 853 כל 3605 אלה 428 לא 3808 עשה 6213 כי 3588 גם 1571 אל 413 ההרים 2022 אכל 398 ואת 853
me'aeleh. uahu'a 'at kal 'aeleh la' 'asah; kiy gam 'al heharìym 'akal, ua'at
**of these *things* And that he any of those *duties* not does but even upon the mountains has eaten *and***

18:12
אשת 802 רעהו 7453 טמא 2930: עני 6041 ואביון 34 הונה 3238 גזלות 1500 גזל 1497 חבל 2258 לא 3808
'aeshet re'aehu timea'. 'aniy ua'abyoun hounah, gazelout gazal, chabol la'
**wife his neighbour's defiled the poor and needy Has oppressed by violence has spoiled the pledge not**

18:13
ישיב 7725 ואל 413 הגלולים 1544 נשא 5375 עיניו 5869 תועבה 8441 עשה 6213: בנשך 5392 נתן 5414
yashiyb; ua'al hagiluliym nasa' 'aeynayu, tou'aebah 'asah. baneshek natan
**has restored and to the idols has lifted up his eyes abomination has committed upon usury Has given forth**

ותרבית 8636 לקח 3947 וחי 2425 לא 3808 יחיה 2421 את 853 כל 3605 התועבות 8441 האלה 428 עשה 6213 מות 4194
uatarbiyt laqach uachay; la' yichayeh, 'at kal hatou'aebout ha'aeleh 'asah, mout
**and increase has taken shall he then live? not he shall live all abominations these he has done he shall surely**

18:14
יומת 4191 דמיו 1818 בו 871a יהיה 1961: והנה 2009 הוליד 3205 בן 1121 וירא 7200 את 853 כל 3605 חטאת 2403 אביו 1 אשר 834
yumat, damayu bou yihayeh. uahineh houliyd ben, uayar'a 'at kal chata't 'abiyu 'asher
**die his blood upon him shall be Now lo *if* he beget a son that see all sins his father's which**

18:15
עשה 6213 ויראה 7200 ולא 3808 יעשה 6213 כהן 2004: על 5921 ההרים 2022 לא 3808 אכל 398 ועיניו 5869 לא 3808
'asah; uayir'ah uala' ya'aseh kahen. 'al heharìym la' 'akal, ua'aeynayu la'
**he has done and consider and not does such like *That* upon the mountains not has eaten his eyes neither**

18:16
נשא 5375 אל 413 גלולי 1544 בית 1004 ישראל 3478 את 853 אשת 802 רעהו 7453 לא 3808 טמא 2930: ואיש 376 לא 3808
nasa', 'al giluley beyt yisra'ael; 'at 'aeshet re'aehu la' timea'. ua'aysh la'
**has lifted up to the idols of the house of Israel wife his neighbour's not has defiled any Neither**

הונה 3238 חבל 2258 לא 3808 חבל 2254 וגזלה 1500 לא 3808 גזל 1497 לחמו 3899 לרעב 7457 נתן 5414
hounah, chabol la' chabal, uagzelah la' gazal; lachmou lara'aeb natan,
**has oppressed the pledge not has withholden by violence neither has spoiled his bread to the hungry *but* has given**

18:17
וערום 5903 כסה 3680 בגד 899: מעני 6041 השיב 7725 ידו 3027 נשך 5392 ותרבית 8636 לא 3808
ua'aroum kisah baged. me'aniy heshiyb yadou, neshek uatarbiyt la'
**and the naked has covered *with* a garment *That* from the poor has taken off his hand usury nor increase not**

לקח 3947 משפטי 4941 עשה 6213 בחקותי 2708 הלך 1980 הוא 1931 לא 3808 ימות 4191 בעון 5771 אביו 1
laqach, mishpatay 'asah, bachuqoutay halok; hua', la' yamut ba'auon 'abiyu
***that* has received my judgments has executed in my statutes has walked he not shall die for the iniquity of his father**

Eze 18:9 Hath walked in my statutes, and has kept my judgments, to deal truly; he is just, he shall surely live, saith YHUH G-D.10 If he beget a son that is a robber, a shedder of blood, and that doeth the like to any one of these things,11 And that doeth not any of those duties, but even has eaten upon the mountains, and defiled his neighbor's wife,12 Hath oppressed the poor and needy, has spoiled by violence, has not restored the pledge, and has lifted up his eyes to the idols, has committed abomination,13 Hath given forth upon usury, and has taken increase: shall he then live? he shall not live: he has done all these abominations; he shall surely die; his blood shall be upon him.14 Now, lo, if he beget a son, that see all his father's sins which he has done, and considereth, and doeth not such like,15 That has not eaten upon the mountains, neither has lifted up his eyes to the idols of the house of Israel, has not defiled his neighbor's wife,16 Neither has oppressed any, has not withholden the pledge, neither has spoiled by violence, but has given his bread to the hungry, and has covered the naked with a garment,17 That has taken off his hand from the poor, that has not received usury nor increase, has executed my judgments, has walked in my statutes; he shall not die for the iniquity of his father, he shall surely live.

| חיה 2421 | יחיה 2421: | 18:18 אביו 1 | כי 3588 | עשק 6231 | עשק 6233 | גזל 1497 | גזל 1499 | אח 251 | ואשר 834 |
|---|---|---|---|---|---|---|---|---|---|
| chayoh | yichayeh. | 'abiyu | kiy | 'ashaq | 'asheq, | gazal | gezel | 'ach, | ua'asher |
| **he shall surely** | **live** | ***As for* his father** | **because** | **he oppressed** | **cruelly** | **spoiled** | **by violence** | **his brother *is*** | **and which** |

| לא 3808 | טוב 2896 | עשה 6213 | בתוך 8432 | עמיו 5971 | והנה 2009 | מת 4191 | בעונו 5771: | 18:19 ואמרתם 559 | מדע 4069 | לא 3808 | נשא 5375 |
|---|---|---|---|---|---|---|---|---|---|---|---|
| la' | toub | 'asah | batouk | 'amayu; | uahineh | met | ba'auonou. | ua'amartem | madua' | la' | nasa' |
| **not** | **good** | **did *that*** | **among** | **his people** | **lo even** | **he shall die** | **in his iniquity** | **Yet say you** | **Why?** | **not** | **does bear** |

| הבן 1121 | בעון 5771 | האב 1 | והבן 1121 | משפט 4941 | וצדקה 6666 | עשה 6213 | את 853 | כל 3605 | חקותי 2708 |
|---|---|---|---|---|---|---|---|---|---|
| haben | ba'auon | ha'ab; | uahaben | mishapat | uatzdaqah | 'asah, | 'at | kal | chuqoutay |
| **the son** | **the iniquity of** | **the father?** | **When the son** | **that which is lawful** | **and right** | **has done** | | **all** | **my statutes** |

| שמר 8104 | ויעשה 6213 | אתם 853 | חיה 2421 | יחיה 2421: | 18:20 הנפש 5315 | החטאת 2398 | היא 1931 | תמות 4191 | בן 1121 | לא 3808 |
|---|---|---|---|---|---|---|---|---|---|---|
| shamar | uaya'aseh | 'atam | chayoh | yichayeh. | hanepesh | hachata't | hiy'a | tamut; | ben | la' |
| ***and* has kept** | **and has done** | **them** | **he shall surely** | **live** | **The soul** | **that sin** | **it** | **shall die** | **The son** | **not** |

| ישא 5375 | בעון 5771 | האב 1 | ואב 1 | לא 3808 | ישא 5375 | בעון 5771 | הבן 1121 | צדקת 6666 | הצדיק 6662 |
|---|---|---|---|---|---|---|---|---|---|
| yisa' | ba'auon | ha'ab, | ua'ab | la' | yisa' | ba'auon | haben, | tzadaqta | hatzadiyq |
| **shall bear** | **the iniquity of** | **the father** | **the father** | **neither** | **shall bear** | **the iniquity of** | **the son** | **the righteousness of** | **the righteous** |

| עליו 5921 | תהיה 1961 | ורשעת 7564 | רשע 7563 | עליו 5921 | תהיה 1961: | 18:21 והרשע 7563 | כי 3588 | ישוב 7725 | מכל 3605 |
|---|---|---|---|---|---|---|---|---|---|
| 'alayu | tihayeh, | uarish'at | rasha' | 'alayu | tihayeh. | uaharasha', | kiy | yashub | mikal |
| **upon him** | **shall be** | **and the wickedness of** | **the wicked** | **upon him** | **shall be** | **But if the wicked** | **if** | **will turn** | **from all** |

| חטאתו 2403 | אשר 834 | עשה 6213 | ושמר 8104 | את 853 | כל 3605 | חקותי 2708 | ועשה 6213 | משפט 4941 | וצדקה 6666 | חיה 2421 |
|---|---|---|---|---|---|---|---|---|---|---|
| chata'tou | 'asher | 'asah, | uashamar | 'at | kal | chuqoutay, | ua'asah | mishapat | uatzdaqah; | chayoh |
| **his sins** | **that** | **he has committed** | **and keep** | | **all** | **my statutes** | **and do** | **that which is lawful** | **and right** | **he shall surely** |

| יחיה 2421 | לא 3808 | ימות 4191: | 18:22 כל 3605 | פשעיו 6588 | אשר 834 | עשה 6213 | לא 3808 | יזכרו 2142 | לו 3807a |
|---|---|---|---|---|---|---|---|---|---|
| yichayeh | la' | yamut. | kal | pasha'ay | 'asher | 'asah, | la' | yizakaru | lou'; |
| **live** | **not** | **he shall die** | **All** | **his transgressions** | **that** | **he has committed** | **not** | **they shall be mentioned** | **unto him** |

| בצדקתו 6666 | אשר 834 | עשה 6213 | יחיה 2421: | 18:23 החפץ 2654 | אחפץ 2654 | מות 4194 | רשע 7563 | נאם 5002 |
|---|---|---|---|---|---|---|---|---|
| batzidqatou | 'asher | 'asah | yichayeh. | hechapotz | 'achapotz | mout | rasha', | na'am |
| **in his righteousness** | **that** | **he has done** | **he shall live** | **Have I any pleasure** | **at all** | **that should die?** | **the wicked** | **saith** |

| אדני 136 | יהוה 3069 | הלוא 3808 | בשובו 7725 | מדרכיו 1870 | וחיה 2421: | 18:24 ובשוב 7725 | צדיק 6662 |
|---|---|---|---|---|---|---|---|
| 'adonay | Yahuah; | halou'a | bashubou | midrakayu | uachayah. | uabshub | tzadiyq |
| **Adonai** | **Yahuah** | ***and* not** | **that he should return** | **from his ways** | **and live?** | **But when turned away** | **the righteous** |

| מצדקתו 6666 | ועשה 6213 | עול 5766 | ככל 3605 | התועבות 8441 | אשר 834 | עשה 6213 | הרשע 7563 | יעשה 6213 |
|---|---|---|---|---|---|---|---|---|
| mitzidqatou | ua'asah | 'auel, | kakol | hatou'aebout | 'asher | 'asah | harasha' | ya'aseh |
| **from his righteousness** | **and commit** | **iniquity** | **according to all** | **the abominations** | **that** | ***and* does** | **the wicked** | ***man* does** |

| וחי 2425 | כל 3605 | צדקתו 6666 | אשר 834 | עשה 6213 | לא 3808 | תזכרנה 2142 | במעלו 4603 | אשר 834 |
|---|---|---|---|---|---|---|---|---|
| uachay; | kal | tzidqatou | 'asher | 'asah | la' | tizakarnah, | bama'alou | 'asher |
| **shall he live?** | **All** | **his righteousness** | **that** | **he has done** | **not** | **shall be mentioned** | **in his trespass** | **that** |

Eze 18:18 As for his father, because he cruelly oppressed, spoiled his brother by violence, and did that which is not good among his people, lo, even he shall die in his iniquity.19 Yet say you, Why? doth not the son bear the iniquity of the father? When the son has done that which is lawful and right, and has kept all my statutes, and has done them, he shall surely live.20 The soul that sin, it shall die. The son shall not bear the iniquity of the father, neither shall the father bear the iniquity of the son: the righteousness of the righteous shall be upon him, and the wickedness of the wicked shall be upon him.21 But if the wicked will turn from all his sins that he has committed, and keep all my statutes, and do that which is lawful and right, he shall surely live, he shall not die.22 All his transgressions that he has committed, they shall not be mentioned unto him: in his righteousness that he has done he shall live.23 Have I any pleasure at all that the wicked should die? saith YHUH G-D: and not that he should return from his ways, and live?24 But when the righteous turneth away from his righteousness, and committeth iniquity, and doeth according to all the abominations that the wicked man doeth, shall he live? All his righteousness that he has done shall not be mentioned: in his trespass that he has trespassed, and in his sin that he has sinned, in them shall he die.

18:25
מעל 4604 ובחטאתו 2403 אשר 834 חטא 2398 בם 871a ימות 4191: ואמרתם 559 לא 3808 יתכן 8505 דרך 1870
ma'al uabchata'tou 'asher chata' bam yamut. ua'amartem la' yitaken derek
**he has trespassed and in his sin that he has sinned in them shall he die Yet you say not is equal The way of**

18:26
אדני 136 שמעו 8085 נא 4994 בית 1004 ישראל 3478 הדרכי 1870 לא 3808 יתכן 8505 הלא 3808 דרכיכם 1870 לא 3808 יתכנו 8505:
'adonay; shim'au naa' beyt yisra'ael, hadarkiy la' yitaken, hala' darkeykem la' yitakenu.
**Adonai Hear now O house of Israel my way not Is are not your ways not unequal?**

בשוב 7725 צדיק 6662 מצדקתו 6666 ועשה 6213 עול 5766 ומת 4191 עליהם 5921 בעולו 5766 אשר 834
bashub tzadiyq mitzidqatou ua'asah 'auel uamet 'aleyhem; ba'aualou 'asher
**When turned away a righteous *man* from his righteousness and commit iniquity and die in them for his iniquity that**

18:27
עשה 6213 ימות 4191: ובשוב 7725 רשע 7563 מרשעתו 7564 אשר 834 עשה 6213
'asah yamut. uabshub rasha', merish'atou 'asher 'asah,
**he has done shall he die Again when turned away *the* wicked *man* from his wickedness that he has committed**

18:28
ויעש 6213 משפט 4941 וצדקה 6666 הוא 1931 את 853 נפשו 5315 יחיה 2421: ויראה 7200 וישוב 7725
uaya'as mishapat uatzdaqah; hua' 'at napshou yachayeh. uayir'ah uayashub
**and does that which is lawful and right he his soul shall save alive Because he consider and turned away**

18:29
מכל 3605 פשעיו 6588 אשר 834 עשה 6213 חיו 2421 יחיה 2421 לא 3808 ימות 4191: ואמרו 559 בית 1004
mikal pasha'ay 'asher 'asah; chayou yichayeh la' yamut. ua'amaru beyt
**from all his transgressions that he has committed he shall surely live not he shall die Yet saith the house of**

ישראל 3478 לא 3808 יתכן 8505 דרך 1870 אדני 136 הדרכי 1870 לא 3808 יתכנו 8505 בית 1004 ישראל 3478 הלא 3808 דרכיכם 1870 לא 3808
yisra'ael, la' yitaken derek 'adonay; hadarakay la' yitakanu beyt yisra'ael, hala' darkeykem la'
**Israel not is equal The way of Adonai my ways not are equal? O house of Israel not your ways not**

18:30
יתכן 8505: לכן 3651 איש 376 כדרכיו 1870 אשפט 8199 אתכם 853 בית 1004 ישראל 3478 נאם 5002 אדני 136
yitaken. laken 'aysh kidrakayu 'ashpot 'atkem beyt yisra'ael, na'am 'adonay
**are unequal? Therefore every one according to his ways I will judge you O house of Israel saith Adonai**

18:31
יהוה 3068 שובו 7725 והשיבו 7725 מכל 3605 פשעיכם 6588 ולא 3808 יהיה 1961 לכם 3807a למכשול 4383 עון 5771:
Yahuah; shubu uahashiybu mikal pish'aeykem, uala' yihayeh lakem lamikshoul 'auon.
**Yahuah Repent and turn *yourselves* from all your transgressions so not shall be to your ruin iniquity**

השליכו 7993 מעליכם 5921 את 853 כל 3605 פשעיכם 6588 אשר 834 פשעתם 6586 בם 871a ועשו 6213 לכם 3807a לב 3820
hashliyku me'aleykem, 'at kal pish'aeykem 'asher pasha'atem bam, ua'asu lakem leb
**Cast away from you all your transgressions which you have transgressed in them and make to you a heart**

18:32
חדש 2319 ורוח 7307 חדשה 2319 ולמה 4100 תמתו 4191 בית 1004 ישראל 3478: כי 3588 לא 3808 אחפץ 2654 במות 4194
chadash uaruach chadashah; ualamah tamutu beyt yisra'ael. kiy la' 'achapotz bamout
**new and a spirit new for why will you die O house of Israel? For no I have pleasure in the death of**

המת 4191 נאם 5002 אדני 136 יהוה 3069 והשיבו 7725 וחיו 2421:
hamet, na'am 'adonay Yahuah; uahashiybu uichayu.
**him that die saith Adonai Yahuah wherefore turn *yourselves* and live you**

Eze 18:25 Yet you say, The way of YHUH is not equal. Hear now, O house of Israel; Is not my way equal? are not your ways unequal?26 When a righteous man turneth away from his righteousness, and committeth iniquity, and die in them; for his iniquity that he has done shall he die.27 Again, when the wicked man turneth away from his wickedness that he has committed, and doeth that which is lawful and right, he shall save his soul alive.28 Because he considereth, and turneth away from all his transgressions that he has committed, he shall surely live, he shall not die.29 Yet saith the house of Israel, The way of YHUH is not equal. O house of Israel, are not my ways equal? are not your ways unequal?30 Therefore I will judge you, O house of Israel, everyone according to his ways, saith YHUH G-D. Repent, and turn yourselves from all your transgressions; so iniquity shall not be your ruin.31 Cast away from you all your transgressions, whereby you have transgressed; and make you a new heart and a new spirit: for why will you die, O house of Israel?32 For I have no pleasure in the death of him that die, saith YHUH G-D: wherefore turn yourselves, and live you.

| **Ezek 19:1** | ואתה 859 | שא 5375 | קינה 7015 | אל 413 | נשיאי 5387 | ישראל 3478: | **19:2** | ואמרת 559 | מה 4100 | אמך 517 |
|---|---|---|---|---|---|---|---|---|---|---|
| | ua'atah | sa' | qiynah, | 'al | nasiy'aey | yisra'ael. | | ua'amarta, | mah | 'amaka |
| | **Moreover you** | **take up** | **a lamentation** | **for** | **the princes of** | **Israel** | | **And say** | **What *is*** | **your mother?** |

| לביא 3833 | בין 996 | אריות 738 | רבצה 7257 | בתוך 8432 | כפרים 3715 | רבתה 7235 | גוריה 1482: | **19:3** | ותעל 5927 | אחד 259 |
|---|---|---|---|---|---|---|---|---|---|---|
| labiya', | beyn | arayout | rabatzah; | batouk | kapiriym | ribtah | gureyha. | | uata'al | 'achad |
| **A lioness:** | **among** | **lions** | **she lay down** | **among** | **young lions** | **she nourished** | **her whelps** | | **And she brought up** | **one** |

| מגריה 1482 | כפיר 3715 | היה 1961 | וילמד 3925 | לטרף 2963 | טרף 2964 | אדם 120 | אכל 398: | **19:4** | וישמעו 8085 | אליו 413 |
|---|---|---|---|---|---|---|---|---|---|---|
| migureyha | kapiyr | hayah; | uayilmad | litrap | terep | 'adam | 'akal. | | uayishma'au | 'aelayu |
| **of her whelps** | **a young lion** | **it became** | **and it learned** | **to catch** | **the prey** | **men** | **it devoured** | | **also heard** | **of him** |

| גוים 1471 | בשחתם 7845 | נתפש 8610 | ויבאהו 935 | בחחים 2397 | אל 413 | ארץ 776 | מצרים 4714: | **19:5** |
|---|---|---|---|---|---|---|---|---|
| gouyim | bashachtam | nitapas; | uayabi'ahu | bachachiym | 'al | 'aretz | mitzrayim. | |
| **The nations** | **in their pit** | **he was taken** | **and they brought him** | **with chains** | **unto** | **the land of** | **Egypt** | |

| ותרא 7200 | כי 3588 | נוחלה 3176 | אבדה 6 | תקותה 8615 | ותקח 3947 | אחד 259 | מגריה 1482 | כפיר 3715 |
|---|---|---|---|---|---|---|---|---|
| uatera' | kiy | nouchalah, | 'abadah | tiquatah; | uatiqach | 'achad | migureyha | kapiyr |
| **Now when she saw** | **that** | **she had waited** | **was lost** | ***and* her hope** | **then she took** | **another** | **of her whelps** | **a young lion** |

| שמתהו 7760: | **19:6** | ויתהלך 1980 | בתוך 8432 | אריות 738 | כפיר 3715 | היה 1961 | וילמד 3925 | לטרף 2963 | טרף 2964 |
|---|---|---|---|---|---|---|---|---|---|
| samatahu. | | uayithalek | batouk | arayout | kapiyr | hayah; | uayilmad | litrap | terep |
| ***and* made him** | | **And he went up and down** | **among** | **the lions** | **a young lion** | **he became** | **and learned** | **to catch** | **the prey** |

| אדם 120 | אכל 398: | **19:7** | וידע 3045 | אלמנותיו 490 | ועריהם 5892 | החריב 2717 | ותשם 3456 | ארץ 776 |
|---|---|---|---|---|---|---|---|---|
| 'adam | 'akal. | | uayeda' | almanoutayu, | ua'areyhem | hecheriyb; | uatesham | 'aretz |
| **men** | ***and* devoured** | | **And he knew** | **their desolate palaces** | **and their cities** | **he laid waste** | **and was desolate** | **the land** |

| ומלאה 4393 | מקול 6963 | שאגתו 7581: | **19:8** | ויתנו 5414 | עליו 5921 | גוים 1471 | סביב 5439 | ממדינות 4082 |
|---|---|---|---|---|---|---|---|---|
| uamlo'ah, | miqoul | sha'agatou. | | uayitanu | 'alayu | gouyim | sabiyb | mimadiynout; |
| **and the fulness thereof** | **by the noise of** | **his roaring** | | **Then set** | **against him** | **the nations** | **on every side** | **from the provinces** |

| ויפרשו 6566 | עליו 5921 | רשתם 7568 | בשחתם 7845 | נתפש 8610: | **19:9** | ויתנהו 5414 | בסוגר 5474 | בחחים 2397 | ויבאהו 935 |
|---|---|---|---|---|---|---|---|---|---|
| uayiprasu | 'alayu | rishtam | bashachtam | nitapas. | | uayitanuhu | basugar | bachachiym, | uayabi'ahu |
| **and spread** | **over him** | **their net** | **in their pit** | **he was taken** | | **And they put him** | **in ward** | **in chains** | **and brought him** |

| אל 413 | מלך 4428 | בבל 894 | יבאהו 935 | במצדות 4685 | למען 4616 | לא 3808 | ישמע 8085 | קולו 6963 | עוד 5750 | אל 413 |
|---|---|---|---|---|---|---|---|---|---|---|
| 'al | melek | babel; | yabi'ahu | bamatzodout, | lama'an, | la' | yishama' | qoulou | 'aud | 'al |
| **to** | **the king of** | **Babylon** | **they brought him** | **into holds** | **that** | **no** | **should be heard** | **his voice** | **more** | **upon** |

| הרי 2022 | ישראל 3478: | **19:10** | אמך 517 | כגפן 1612 | בדמך 1818 | על 5921 | מים 4325 | שתולה 8362 | פריה 6509 |
|---|---|---|---|---|---|---|---|---|---|
| harey | yisra'ael. | | 'amaka | kagepen | badamaka | 'al | mayim | shatulah; | poriyah |
| **the mountains of** | **Israel** | | **Your mother** | ***is* like a vine** | **in your blood** | **by** | **the waters** | **planted** | **fruitful** |

| וענפה 6058 | היתה 1961 | ממים 4325 | רבים 7227: | **19:11** | ויהיו 1961 | לה 3807a | מטות 4294 | עז 5797 | אל 413 | שבטי 7626 |
|---|---|---|---|---|---|---|---|---|---|---|
| ua'anepah, | hayatah | mimayim | rabiym. | | uayihayu | lah | matout | 'az, | 'al | shibtey |
| **and full of branches** | **she was** | **by reason of waters** | **many** | | **And had** | **she** | **rods** | **strong** | **for** | **the sceptres of** |

**Eze** 19:1 Moreover take you up a lamentation for the princes of Israel,2 And say, What is your mother? A lioness: she lay down among lions, she nourished her whelps among young lions.3 And she brought up one of her whelps: it became a young lion, and it learned to catch the prey; it devoured men.4 The nations also heard of him; he was taken in their pit, and they brought him with chains unto the land of Egypt.5 Now when she saw that she had waited, and her hope was lost, then she took another of her whelps, and made him a young lion.6 And he went up and down among the lions, he became a young lion, and learned to catch the prey, and devoured men.7 And he knew their desolate palaces, and he laid waste their cities; and the land was desolate, and the fulness thereof, by the noise of his roaring.8 Then the nations set against him on every side from the provinces, and spread their net over him: he was taken in their pit.9 And they put him in ward in chains, and brought him to the king of Babylon: they brought him into holds, that his voice should no more be heard upon the mountains of Israel.10 Thy mother is like a vine in your blood, planted by the waters: she was fruitful and full of branches by reason of many waters.11 And she had strong rods for the sceptres of them that bare rule, and her stature was exalted among the thick branches,

משלים 4910 moshaliym, **them that bare rule** | ותגבה 1361 uatigbah **and was exalted** | קומתו 6967 qoumatou **her stature** | על 5921 'al **on** | בין 996 beyn **among** | עבתים 5688 'abotiym; **the thick branches** | וירא 7200 uayera' **and she appeared** | בגבהו 1363 bagabahou, **in her height**

ברב 7230 barob **with the multitude of** | דליתיו 1808: daliyotayu. **her branches** | **19:12** ותתש 5428 uatutash **But she was plucked up** | בחמה 2534 bachemah **in fury** | לארץ 776 la'aretz **to the ground** | השלכה 7993 hushlakah, **she was cast down** | ורוח 7307 uaruach **and wind**

הקדים 6921 haqadiym **the east** | הוביש 3001 houbiysh **dried up** | פריה 6529 piryah; **her fruit** | התפרקו 6561 hitparaqu **were broken** | ויבשו 3001 uayabeshu **and withered** | מטה 4294 mateh **rods** | עזה 5797 'azah **her strong** | אש 784 'aesh **the fire** | אכלתהו 398: 'akalatahu. **consumed them** | **19:13** ועתה 6258 ua'atah **And now**

שתולה 8362 shatulah **she *is* planted** | במדבר 4057 bamidbar; **in the wilderness** | בארץ 776 ba'aretz **in a ground** | ציה 6723 tziyah **dry** | וצמא 6772: uatzama'. **and thirsty** | **19:14** ותצא 3318 uatetzea' **And is gone out** | אש 784 'aesh **fire** | ממטה 4294 mimateh **of a rod of** | בדיה 905 badeyha **her branches**

פריה 6529 piryah **her fruit** | אכלה 398 'akalah, ***which* has devoured** | ולא 3808 uala' **so that no** | היה 1961 hayah **has** | בה 871a bah **she** | מטה 4294 mateh **rod** | עז 5797 'az **strong** | שבט 7626 shebet ***to be* a sceptre** | למשול 4910 limshoul; **to rule** | קינה 7015 qiynah ***is* a lamentation** | היא 1931 hiy'a **This**

ותהי 1961 uatahiy **and shall be** | לקינה 7015: laqiynah. **for a lamentation**

**Ezek 20:1** ויהי 1961 uayahiy **And it came to pass** | בשנה 8141 bashanah **in year** | השביעית 7637 hashabiy'ayt, **the seventh** | בחמשי 2549 bachamishiy **in the fifth** | בעשור 6218 be'asour ***month* the tenth** | לחדש 2320 lachodesh, ***day* of the month** | באו 935 ba'au ***that* came** | אנשים 582 'anashiym **certain**

מזקני 2205 miziqney **of the elders of** | ישראל 3478 yisra'ael **Israel** | לדרש 1875 lidrosh **to inquire of** | את 853 'at | יהוה 3068 Yahuah; **Yahuah** | וישבו 3427 uayeshabu **and sat** | לפני 6440: lapanay. **before me** | **20:2** ויהי 1961 uayahiy **Then came** | דבר 1697 dabar **the word of** | יהוה 3068 Yahuah **Yahuah** | אלי 413 'aelay **unto me**

לאמר 559: lea'mor. **saying** | **20:3** בן 1121 ben **Son of** | אדם 120 'adam, **man** | דבר 1696 daber **speak unto** | את 853 'at | זקני 2205 ziqney **the elders of** | ישראל 3478 yisra'ael **Israel** | ואמרת 559 ua'amarta **and say** | אלהם 413 'alehem, **unto them** | כה 3541 koh **Thus** | אמר 559 'amar **saith** | אדני 136 'adonay **Adonai** | יהוה 3068 Yahuah, **Yahuah**

הלדרש 1875 halidrosh **to inquire of** | אתי 853 'atiy **me?** | אתם 859 'atem **you** | באים 935 ba'aym; **Are come** | חי 2416 chay **live, *As*** | אני 589 'aniy **I** | אם 518 'am **not** | אדרש 1875 'adaresh **I will be inquired of** | לכם 3807a lakem, **by you** | נאם 5002 na'am **saith** | אדני 136 'adonay **Adonai** | יהוה 3068: Yahuah. **Yahuah** | **20:4**

התשפט 8199 hatishpot **Will you judge** | אתם 853 'atam, **them** | התשפוט 8199 hatishpout **will you judge *them*?** | בן 1121 ben **son of** | אדם 120 'adam; **man** | את 853 'at | תועבת 8441 tou'abot **the abominations of** | אבותם 1 aboutam **their fathers** | הודיעם 3045: houdiy'aem. **cause them to know** | **20:5**

ואמרת 559 ua'amarta **And say** | אליהם 413 'aleyhem, **unto them** | כה 3541 koh **Thus** | אמר 559 'amar **saith** | אדני 136 'adonay **Adonai** | יהוה 3069 Yahuah **Yahuah** | ביום 3117 bayoum **In the day** | בחרי 977 bachariy ***when* I chose** | בישראל 3478 bayisra'ael, **Israel** | ואשא 5375 ua'asa' **and lifted up** | ידי 3027 yadiy, **mine hand**

Eze 19:11 and she appeared in her height with the multitude of her branches.12 But she was plucked up in fury, she was cast down to the ground, and the east wind dried up her fruit: her strong rods were broken and withered; the fire consumed them.13 And now she is planted in the wilderness, in a dry and thirsty ground.14 And fire is gone out of a rod of her branches, which has devoured her fruit, so that she has no strong rod to be a sceptre to rule. This is a lamentation, and shall be for a lamentation. **Eze** 20:1 And it came to pass in the seventh year, in the fifth month, the tenth day of the month, that certain of the elders of Israel came to inquire of YHUH, and sat before me.2 Then came the word of YHUH unto me, saying,3 Son of man, speak unto the elders of Israel, and say unto them, Thus saith YHUH G-D; Are you come to inquire of me? As I live, saith YHUH G-D, I will not be inquired of by you.4 Wilt you judge them, son of man, will you judge them? cause them to know the abominations of their fathers:5 And say unto them, Thus saith YHUH G-D; In the day when I chose Israel, and lifted up mine hand unto the seed of the house of Jacob, and made myself known unto them in the land of Egypt, when I lifted up mine hand unto them, saying, I am YHUH your G-d;

| לזרע 2233 | בית 1004 | יעקב 3290 | ואודע 3045 | להם 3807a | בארץ 776 | מצרים 4714 | ואשא 5375 |
|---|---|---|---|---|---|---|---|
| lazera' | beyt | ya'aqob, | ua'auada' | lahem | ba'aretz | mitzrayim; | ua'asa' |
| **unto the seed of** | **the house of** | **Jacob** | **and made myself known** | **unto them** | **in the land of** | **Egypt** | **when I lifted up** |

| ידי 3027 | להם 3807a | לאמר 559 | אני 589 | יהוה 3068 | אלהיכם 430: | 20:6 | ביום 3117 | ההוא 1931 | נשאתי 5375 | ידי 3027 | להם 3807a |
|---|---|---|---|---|---|---|---|---|---|---|---|
| yadiy | lahem | lea'mor, | 'aniy | Yahuah | 'aloheykem. | | bayoum | hahua', | nasa'tiy | yadiy | lahem, |
| **mine hand** | **unto them** | **saying** | **I *am*** | **Yahuah** | **your Elohim** | | **In the day** | **that** | **I lifted up** | **mine hand** | **unto them** |

| להוציאם 3318 | מארץ 776 | מצרים 4714 | אל 413 | ארץ 776 | אשר 834 | תרתי 8446 | להם 3807a | זבת 2100 | חלב 2461 | ודבש 1706 |
|---|---|---|---|---|---|---|---|---|---|---|
| lahoutziy'am | me'aretz | mitzrayim; | 'al | 'aretz | 'asher | tartiy | lahem, | zabat | chalab | uadbash, |
| **to bring them forth** | **of the land of** | **Egypt** | **into** | **a land** | **that** | **I had espied** | **for them** | **flowing *with*** | **milk** | **and honey** |

| צבי 6643 | היא 1931 | לכל 3605 | הארצות 776: | 20:7 | ואמר 559 | אלהם 413 | איש 376 | שקוצי 8251 | עיניו 5869 | השליכו 7993 |
|---|---|---|---|---|---|---|---|---|---|---|
| tzabiy | hiy'a | lakal | ha'aratzout. | | ua'amar | 'alehem, | 'aysh | shiqutzey | 'aeynayu | hashliyku, |
| ***the* glory** | **which is** | **of all** | **the lands** | | **Then said I** | **unto them** | **every man** | **the abominations of** | **his eyes** | **Cast you away** |

| ובגלולי 1544 | מצרים 4714 | אל 408 | תטמאו 2930 | אני 589 | יהוה 3068 | אלהיכם 430: | 20:8 | וימרו 4784 | בי 871a |
|---|---|---|---|---|---|---|---|---|---|
| uabgiluley | mitzrayim | 'al | titama'au; | 'aniy | Yahuah | 'aloheykem. | | uayamaru | biy, |
| **and with the idols of** | **Egypt** | **not** | **defile yourselves** | **I *am*** | **Yahuah** | **your Elohim** | | **But they rebelled** | **against me** |

| ולא 3808 | אבו 14 | לשמע 8085 | אלי 413 | איש 376 | את 853 | שקוצי 8251 | עיניהם 5869 | לא 3808 | השליכו 7993 | ואת 853 |
|---|---|---|---|---|---|---|---|---|---|---|
| uala' | 'abu | lishmoa' | 'aelay, | 'aysh | 'at | shiqutzey | 'aeyneyhem | la' | hishliyku, | ua'at |
| **and not** | **would** | **listen** | **unto me** | **every man** | | **the abominations of** | **their eyes** | **not** | **they did cast away** | ***neither*** |

| גלולי 1544 | מצרים 4714 | לא 3808 | עזבו 5800 | ואמר 559 | לשפך 8210 | חמתי 2534 | עליהם 5921 | לכלות 3615 | אפי 639 |
|---|---|---|---|---|---|---|---|---|---|
| giluley | mitzrayim | la' | 'azabu; | ua'amar | lishpok | chamatiy | 'aleyhem, | lakalout | 'apiy |
| **the idols of** | **Egypt** | **neither** | **did they forsake** | **then I said** | **I will pour out** | **my fury** | **upon them** | **to accomplish** | **my anger** |

| בהם 871a | בתוך 8432 | ארץ 776 | מצרים 4714: | 20:9 | ואעש 6213 | למען 4616 | שמי 8034 | לבלתי 1115 | החל 2490 |
|---|---|---|---|---|---|---|---|---|---|
| bahem, | batouk | 'aretz | mitzrayim. | | ua'aas | lama'an | shamiy, | labiltiy | hechel |
| **against them** | **in the midst of** | **the land of** | **Egypt** | | **But I wrought** | **the sake** | **my name's** | **that not** | **it should be polluted** |

| לעיני 5869 | הגוים 1471 | אשר 834 | המה 1992 | בתוכם 8432 | אשר 834 | נודעתי 3045 | אליהם 413 | לעיניהם 5869 |
|---|---|---|---|---|---|---|---|---|
| la'aeyney | hagouyim | 'asher | hemah | batoukam; | 'asher | nouda'tiy | 'aleyhem | la'aeyneyhem, |
| **before** | **the heathen** | **whom** | **they *were, in*** | **among** | **whose** | **I made myself known** | **unto them** | **sight** |

| להוציאם 3318 | מארץ 776 | מצרים 4714: | 20:10 | ואוציאם 3318 | מארץ 776 | מצרים 4714 |
|---|---|---|---|---|---|---|
| lahoutziy'am | me'aretz | mitzrayim. | | ua'autziy'aem | me'aretz | mitzrayim; |
| **in bringing them forth** | **out of the land of** | **Egypt** | | **Wherefore I caused them to go forth** | **out of the land of** | **Egypt** |

| ואבאם 935 | אל 413 | המדבר 4057: | 20:11 | ואתן 5414 | להם 3807a | את 853 | חקותי 2708 | ואת 853 | משפטי 4941 | הודעתי 3045 |
|---|---|---|---|---|---|---|---|---|---|---|
| ua'abi'aem | 'al | hamidbar. | | ua'aten | lahem | 'at | chuqoutay, | ua'at | mishpatay | houda'atiy |
| **and brought them** | **into** | **the wilderness** | | **And I gave** | **them** | | **my statutes** | ***them*** | **my judgments** | **and showed** |

| אותם 853 | אשר 834 | יעשה 6213 | אותם 853 | האדם 120 | וחי 2425 | בהם 871a: | 20:12 | וגם 1571 | את 853 | שבתותי 7676 | נתתי 5414 | להם 3807a |
|---|---|---|---|---|---|---|---|---|---|---|---|---|
| 'autam; | 'asher | ya'aseh | 'autam | ha'adam | uachay | bahem. | | ua'gam | 'at | shabtoutay | natatiy | lahem, |
| **them** | **which** | **do *if*** | **them** | **a man** | **he shall even live in them** | | | **Moreover also** | | **my sabbaths** | **I gave** | **them** |

Eze 20:6 In the day that I lifted up mine hand unto them, to bring them forth of the land of Egypt into a land that I had espied for them, flowing with milk and honey, which is the glory of all lands:7 Then said I unto them, Cast you away every man the abominations of his eyes, and defile not yourselves with the idols of Egypt: I am YHUH your G-d.8 But they rebelled against me, and would not hear unto me: they did not every man cast away the abominations of their eyes, neither did they forsake the idols of Egypt: then I said, I will pour out my fury upon them to accomplish my anger against them in the midst of the land of Egypt.9 But I wrought for my name's sake, that it should not be polluted before the heathen, among whom they were, in whose sight I made myself known unto them, in bringing them forth out of the land of Egypt.10 Wherefore I caused them to go forth out of the land of Egypt, and brought them into the wilderness.11 And I gave them my statutes, and showed them my judgments, which if a man do, he shall even live in them.12 Moreover also I gave them my sabbaths, to be a sign between me and them, that they might know that I am YHUH that sanctify them.

20:13
להיות 1961 לאות 226 ביני 996 וביניהם 996 לדעת 3045 כי 3588 אני 589 יהוה 3068 מקדשם 6942: וימרו 4784
lihayout la'aut, beyniy uabeyneyhem; lada'at kiy 'aniy Yahuah maqadsham. uayamaru
**to be a sign between me and them that they might know that I *am* Yahuah that sanctify them But rebelled**

בי 871a בית 1004 ישראל 3478 במדבר 4057 בחקותי 2708 לא 3808 הלכו 1980 ואת 853 משפטי 4941 מאסו 3988
biy beyt yisra'ael bamidbar, bachuqoutay la' halaku ua'at mishpatay ma'asu,
**against me the house of Israel in the wilderness in my statutes not they walked *and* my judgments they despised**

אשר 834 יעשה 6213 אתם 853 האדם 120 וחי 2425 בהם 871a ואת 853 שבתתי 7676 חללו 2490 מאד 3966 ואמר 559
'asher ya'aseh 'atam ha'adam uachay bahem, ua'at shabtotay chillu ma'ad; ua'amar
**which do *if* them a man he shall even live in them *and* my sabbaths they polluted greatly then I said**

20:14
לשפך 8210 חמתי 2534 עליהם 5921 במדבר 4057 לכלותם 3615: ואעשה 6213 למען 4616 שמי 8034 לבלתי 1115
lishpok chamatiy 'aleyhem bamidbar lakaloutam. ua'a'aseh lama'an shamiy; labiltiy
**I would pour out my fury upon them in the wilderness to consume them But I wrought for sake my name's that not**

20:15
החל 2490 לעיני 5869 הגוים 1471 אשר 834 הוצאתים 3318 לעיניהם 5869: וגם 1571 אני 589 נשאתי 5375
hechel la'aeyney hagouyim, 'asher houtzea'tiym la'aeyneyhem. uagam 'aniy, nasa'tiy
**it should be polluted before in the heathen whose I brought them out sight Yet also I I lifted up**

ידי 3027 להם 3807a במדבר 4057 לבלתי 1115 הביא 935 אותם 853 אל 413 הארץ 776 אשר 834 נתתי 5414 זבת 2100
yadiy lahem bamidbar; labiltiy habiy'a 'autam 'al ha'aretz 'asher natatiy, zabat
**my hand unto them in the wilderness that not I would bring them into the land which I had given *them* flowing**

20:16
חלב 2461 ודבש 1706 צבי 6643 היא 1931 לכל 3605 הארצות 776: יען 3282 במשפטי 4941 מאסו 3988 ואת 853
chalab uadbash, tzabiy hiy'a lakal ha'aratzout. ya'an bamishpatay ma'asu, ua'at
***with* milk and honey *is* the glory of which all lands Because my judgments they despised *and***

20:17
חקותי 2708 לא 3808 הלכו 1980 בהם 871a ואת 853 שבתותי 7676 חללו 2490 כי 3588 אחרי 310 גלוליהם 1544 לבם 3820 הלך 1980:
chuqoutay la' halaku bahem, ua'at shabtoutay chilelu; kiy 'acharey giluleyhem libam holek.
***in* my statutes not walked in them *but* my sabbaths polluted for after their idols their heart went**

20:18
ותחס 2347 עיני 5869 עליהם 5921 משחתם 7843 ולא 3808 עשיתי 6213 אותם 853 כלה 3617 במדבר 4057:
uatachas 'aeyniy 'aleyhem mishachatam; uala' 'asiytiy 'autam kalah bamidbar.
**Nevertheless spared mine eye them from destroying them neither did I make them an end of in the wilderness**

ואמר 559 אל 413 בניהם 1121 במדבר 4057 בחוקי 2706 אבותיכם 1 אל 408 תלכו 1980 ואת 853 משפטיהם 4941
ua'amar 'al baneyhem bamidbar, bachuqey abouteykem 'al teleku, ua'at mishpateyhem
**But I said unto their children in the wilderness in the statutes of your fathers not walk you *and* their judgments**

20:19
אל 408 תשמרו 8104 ובגלוליהם 1544 אל 408 תטמאו 2930: אני 589 יהוה 3068 אלהיכם 430 בחקותי 2708 לכו 1980 ואת 853
'al tishmoru; uabgiluleyhem 'al titama'au. 'aniy Yahuah 'aloheykem, bachuqoutay leku; ua'at
**neither observe with their idols nor defile yourselves I *am* Yahuah your Elohim in my statutes walk *and***

20:20
משפטי 4941 שמרו 8104 ועשו 6213 אותם 853: ואת 853 שבתותי 7676 קדשו 6942 והיו 1961 לאות 226 ביני 996
mishpatay shimru ua'asu 'autam. ua'at shabtoutay qadeshu; uahayu la'aut beyniy
**my judgments keep and do them *And* my sabbaths hallow and they shall be a sign between me**

Eze 20:13 But the house of Israel rebelled against me in the wilderness: they walked not in my statutes, and they despised my judgments, which if a man do, he shall even live in them; and my sabbaths they greatly polluted: then I said, I would pour out my fury upon them in the wilderness, to consume them.14 But I wrought for my name's sake, that it should not be polluted before the heathen, in whose sight I brought them out.15 Yet also I lifted up my hand unto them in the wilderness, that I would not bring them into the land which I had given them, flowing with milk and honey, which is the glory of all lands;16 Because they despised my judgments, and walked not in my statutes, but polluted my sabbaths: for their heart went after their idols.17 Nevertheless mine eye spared them from destroying them, neither did I make an end of them in the wilderness.18 But I said unto their children in the wilderness, Walk you not in the statutes of your fathers, neither observe their judgments, nor defile yourselves with their idols:19 I am YHUH your G-d; walk in my statutes, and keep my judgments, and do them;20 And hallow my sabbaths; and they shall be a sign between me and you, that you may know that I am YHUH your G-d.

| וביניכם 996 | לדעת 3045 | כי 3588 | אני 589 | יהוה 3068 | אלהיכם 430: | 20:21 וימרו 4784 | בי 871a |
|---|---|---|---|---|---|---|---|
| uabeyneykem, | lada'at | kiy | 'aniy | Yahuah | 'aloheykem. | uayamaru | biy |
| **and between you** | **that you may know** | **that** | **I *am*** | **Yahuah** | **your Elohim** | **Notwithstanding rebelled** | **against me** |

| הבנים 1121 | בחקותי 2708 | לא 3808 | הלכו 1980 | ואת 853 | משפטי 4941 | לא 3808 | שמרו 8104 | לעשות 6213 | אותם 853 | אשר 834 | יעשה 6213 |
|---|---|---|---|---|---|---|---|---|---|---|---|
| habaniym, | bachuqoutay | la' | halaku | ua'at | mishpatay | la' | shamaru | la'asout | 'autam, | 'asher | ya'aseh |
| **the children** | **in my statutes** | **not** | **they walked** | ***and*** | **my judgments** | **neither** | **kept** | **to do** | **them** | **which** | **do *if*** |

| אותם 853 | האדם 120 | וחי 2425 | בהם 871a | את 853 | שבתותי 7676 | חללו 2490 | ואמר 559 | לשפך 8210 | חמתי 2534 |
|---|---|---|---|---|---|---|---|---|---|
| 'autam | ha'adam | uachay | bahem, | 'at | shabtoutay | chilelu; | ua'amar | lishpok | chamatiy |
| **them** | **a man** | **he shall even live** | **in them** | | **my sabbaths** | **they polluted** | **then I said** | **I would pour out** | **my fury** |

| עליהם 5921 | לכלות 3615 | אפי 639 | בם 871a | במדבר 4057: | 20:22 והשבתי 7725 | את 853 | ידי 3027 |
|---|---|---|---|---|---|---|---|
| 'aleyhem, | lakalout | 'apiy | bam | bamidbar. | uahashibotiy | 'at | yadiy, |
| **upon them** | **to accomplish** | **my anger** | **against them** | **in the wilderness** | **Nevertheless I withdrew** | | **mine hand** |

| ואעש 6213 | למען 4616 | שמי 8034 | לבלתי 1115 | החל 2490 | לעיני 5869 | הגוים 1471 | אשר 834 | הוצאתי 3318 | אותם 853 |
|---|---|---|---|---|---|---|---|---|---|
| ua'aas | lama'an | shamiy; | labiltiy | hechel | la'aeyney | hagouyim, | 'asher | houtzea'tiy | 'autam |
| **and wrought** | **for sake** | **my name's** | **that not** | **it should be polluted** | **in the sight of** | **the heathen** | **whose** | **I brought forth** | **them** |

| לעיניהם 5869: | 20:23 גם 1571 | אני 589 | נשאתי 5375 | את 853 | ידי 3027 | להם 3807a | במדבר 4057 | להפיץ 6327 | אתם 853 |
|---|---|---|---|---|---|---|---|---|---|
| la'aeyneyhem. | gam | 'aniy, | nasa'tiy | 'at | yadiy | lahem | bamidbar; | lahapiytz | 'atam |
| **in sight** | **also** | **I** | **I lifted up** | | **mine hand** | **unto them** | **in the wilderness** | **that I would scatter** | **them** |

| בגוים 1471 | ולזרות 2219 | אותם 853 | בארצות 776: | 20:24 יען 3282 | משפטי 4941 | לא 3808 | עשו 6213 |
|---|---|---|---|---|---|---|---|
| bagouyim, | ualzarout | 'autam | ba'aratzout. | ya'an | mishpatay | la' | 'asu |
| **among the heathen** | **and disperse** | **them** | **through the countries** | **Because** | **my judgments** | **not** | **they had executed** |

| וחקותי 2708 | מאסו 3988 | ואת 853 | שבתותי 7676 | חללו 2490 | ואחרי 310 | גלולי 1544 | אבותם 1 | היו 1961 | עיניהם 5869: | 20:25 |
|---|---|---|---|---|---|---|---|---|---|---|
| uachuqoutay | ma'asu, | ua'at | shabtoutay | chilelu; | ua'acharey | giluley | aboutam, | hayu | 'aeyneyhem. | |
| **but my statutes** | **had despised** | ***and*** | **my sabbaths** | **had polluted** | **and after** | **idols** | **their fathers'** | **were** | **their eyes** | |

| וגם 1571 | אני 589 | נתתי 5414 | להם 3807a | חקים 2706 | לא 3808 | טובים 2896 | ומשפטים 4941 | לא 3808 | יחיו 2421 |
|---|---|---|---|---|---|---|---|---|---|
| uagam | 'aniy | natatiy | lahem, | chuqiym | la' | toubiym; | uamishpatiym, | la' | yichayu |
| **Wherefore also** | **I** | **gave** | **them** | **statutes *that were*** | **not** | **good** | **and judgments** | **not** | **they should live** |

| בהם 871a: | 20:26 ואטמא 2930 | אותם 853 | במתנותם 4979 | בהעביר 5674 | כל 3605 | פטר 6363 |
|---|---|---|---|---|---|---|
| bahem. | ua'atamea' | 'autam | bamatnoutam, | baha'abiyr | kal | peter |
| **whereby** | **And I polluted** | **them** | **in their own gifts** | **in that they caused to pass through *the fire*** | **all** | **that open** |

| רחם 7356 | למען 4616 | אשמם 8074 | למען 4616 | אשר 834 | ידעו 3045 | אשר 834 | אני 589 | יהוה 3068: | 20:27 לכן 3651 |
|---|---|---|---|---|---|---|---|---|---|
| racham; | lama'an | 'ashimem, | lama'an | 'asher | yeda'au, | 'asher | 'aniy | Yahuah. | laken |
| **the womb** | **that** | **I might make them desolate** | **to the end** | **that** | **they might know** | **that** | **I *am*** | **Yahuah** | **Therefore** |

| דבר 1696 | אל 413 | בית 1004 | ישראל 3478 | בן 1121 | אדם 120 | ואמרת 559 | אליהם 413 | כה 3541 | אמר 559 | אדני 136 | יהוה 3069 | עוד 5750 | זאת 2063 |
|---|---|---|---|---|---|---|---|---|---|---|---|---|---|
| daber | 'al | beyt | yisra'ael | ben | 'adam, | ua'amarta | 'aleyhem, | koh | 'amar | 'adonay | Yahuah; | 'aud, | za't |
| **speak** | **unto** | **the house of** | **Israel** | **son of** | **man** | **and say** | **unto them** | **Thus** | **saith** | **Adonai** | **Yahuah** | **Yet *in*** | **this** |

Eze 20:21 Notwithstanding the children rebelled against me: they walked not in my statutes, neither kept my judgments to do them, which if a man do, he shall even live in them; they polluted my sabbaths: then I said, I would pour out my fury upon them, to accomplish my anger against them in the wilderness.22 Nevertheless I withdrew mine hand, and wrought for my name's sake, that it should not be polluted in the sight of the heathen, in whose sight I brought them forth.23 I lifted up mine hand unto them also in the wilderness, that I would scatter them among the heathen, and disperse them through the countries;24 Because they had not executed my judgments, but had despised my statutes, and had polluted my sabbaths, and their eyes were after their fathers' idols.25 Wherefore I gave them also statutes that were not good, and judgments whereby they should not live;26 And I polluted them in their own gifts, in that they caused to pass through the fire all that openeth the womb, that I might make them desolate, to the end that they might know that I am YHUH.27 Therefore, son of man, speak unto the house of Israel, and say unto them, Thus saith YHUH G-D; Yet in this your fathers have blasphemed me, in that they have committed a trespass against me.

| גדפו 1442 | אותי 853 | אבותיכם 1 | במעלם 4604 | בי 871a | מעל 4603: | 20:28 |
|---|---|---|---|---|---|---|
| gidpu | 'autiy | abouteykem, | bama'alam | biy | ma'al. | |
| **have blasphemed** | **me** | **your fathers** | **a trespass** | **against me *in that*** | **they have committed** | |

| ואביאם 935 | אל 413 | הארץ 776 | אשר 834 | נשאתי 5375 | את 853 | ידי 3027 | לתת 5414 | אותה 853 | להם 3807a |
|---|---|---|---|---|---|---|---|---|---|
| ua'abiy'aem | 'al | ha'aretz, | 'asher | nasa'tiy | 'at | yadiy, | latet | 'autah | lahem; |
| ***For* when I had brought them** | **into** | **the land** | ***for* the which** | **I lifted up** | | **mine hand** | **to give** | **it** | **to them** |

| ויראו 7200 | כל 3605 | גבעה 1389 | רמה 7311 | וכל 3605 | עץ 6086 | עבת 5687 | ויזבחו 2076 | שם 8033 | את 853 | זבחיהם 2077 |
|---|---|---|---|---|---|---|---|---|---|---|
| uayir'au | kal | gib'ah | ramah | uakal | 'aetz | 'abot, | uayizbachu | sham | 'at | zibcheyhem |
| **then they saw** | **every** | **hill** | **high** | **and all** | **trees** | ***the* thick** | **and they offered** | **there** | | **their sacrifices** |

| ויתנו 5414 | שם 8033 | כעס 3708 | קרבנם 7133 | וישימו 7760 | שם 8033 | ריח 7381 | ניחוחיהם 5207 | ויסיכו 5258 |
|---|---|---|---|---|---|---|---|---|
| uayitanu | sham | ka'as | qarabanam, | uayasiymu | sham, | reyach | niychoucheyhem, | uayasiyku |
| **and they presented** | **there** | **the provocation of** | **their offering** | **also they made** | **there** | **savour** | **their sweet** | **and poured out** |

| שם 8033 | את 853 | נסכיהם 5262: | 20:29 | ואמר 559 | אלהם 413 | מה 4100 | הבמה 1116 | אשר 834 | אתם 859 | הבאים 935 | שם 8033 |
|---|---|---|---|---|---|---|---|---|---|---|---|
| sham | 'at | niskeyhem. | | ua'amar | 'alehem, | mah | habamah, | 'asher | 'atem | haba'aym | sham; |
| **there** | | **their drink offerings** | | **Then I said** | **unto them** | **What** | ***is* the high place** | **whereunto** | **you** | **go?** | **there** |

| ויקרא 7121 | שמה 8034 | במה 1117 | עד 5704 | היום 3117 | הזה 2088: | 20:30 | לכן 3651 | אמר 559 | אל 413 | בית 1004 | ישראל 3478 | כה 3541 |
|---|---|---|---|---|---|---|---|---|---|---|---|---|
| uayiqarea' | shamah | bamah, | 'ad | hayoum | hazeh. | | laken | 'amor | 'al | beyt | yisra'ael, | koh |
| **And is called** | **the name thereof** | **Bamah** | **unto** | **day** | **this** | | **Wherefore** | **say** | **unto** | **the house of** | **Israel** | **Thus** |

| אמר 559 | אדני 136 | יהוה 3069 | הבדרך 1870 | אבותיכם 1 | אתם 859 | נטמאים 2930 | ואחרי 310 | שקוציהם 8251 | אתם 859 |
|---|---|---|---|---|---|---|---|---|---|
| 'amar | 'adonay | Yahuah, | habderek | abouteykem | 'atem | nitma'aym; | ua'acharey | shiqutzeyhem | 'atem |
| **saith** | **Adonai** | **Yahuah** | ***after* the manner of** | **your fathers** | **you** | **Are polluted** | **and after** | **their abominations?** | **you** |

| זנים 2181: | 20:31 | ובשאת 5375 | מתנתיכם 4979 | בהעביר 5674 | בניכם 1121 | באש 784 | אתם 859 |
|---|---|---|---|---|---|---|---|
| zoniym. | | uabis'aet | matnoteykem | baha'abiyr | baneykem | ba'aesh | 'atem |
| **commit whoredom** | | **For when you offer** | **your gifts** | **when you make to pass** | **your sons** | **through the fire** | **you** |

| נטמאים 2930 | לכל 3605 | גלוליכם 1544 | עד 5704 | היום 3117 | ואני 589 | אדרש 1875 | לכם 3807a | בית 1004 | ישראל 3478 | חי 2416 |
|---|---|---|---|---|---|---|---|---|---|---|
| nitma'aym | lakal | giluleykem | 'ad | hayoum, | ua'aniy | 'adaresh | lakem | beyt | yisra'ael; | chay |
| **pollute yourselves** | **with all** | **your idols** | **even unto** | **this day** | **and I** | **shall be inquired of** | **by you** | **O house of** | **Israel?** | **live, *As*** |

| אני 589 | נאם 5002 | אדני 136 | יהוה 3069 | אם 518 | אדרש 1875 | לכם 3807a: | 20:32 | והעלה 5927 | על 5921 | רוחכם 7307 | היו 1961 |
|---|---|---|---|---|---|---|---|---|---|---|---|
| 'aniy, | na'am | 'adonay | Yahuah, | 'am | 'adaresh | lakem. | | uaha'alah | 'al | ruchakem, | hayou |
| **I** | **saith** | **Adonai** | **Yahuah** | **not** | **I will be inquired of** | **by you** | | **And that which comes** | **into** | **your mind** | **shall** |

| לא 3808 | תהיה 1961 | אשר 834 | אתם 859 | אמרים 559 | נהיה 1961 | כגוים 1471 | כמשפחות 4940 | הארצות 776 | לשרת 8334 | עץ 6086 |
|---|---|---|---|---|---|---|---|---|---|---|
| la' | tihayeh; | 'asher | 'atem | 'amariym, | nihayeh | kagouyim | kamishpachout | ha'aratzout, | lasharet | 'aetz |
| **not** | **be at all** | **that** | **you** | **say** | **We will be** | **as the heathen** | **as the families of** | **the countries** | **to serve** | **wood** |

| ואבן 68: | 20:33 | חי 2416 | אני 589 | נאם 5002 | אדני 136 | יהוה 3069 | אם 518 | לא 3808 | ביד 3027 | חזקה 2389 | ובזרוע 2220 | נטויה 5186 |
|---|---|---|---|---|---|---|---|---|---|---|---|---|
| ua'aben. | | chay | 'aniy | na'am | 'adonay | Yahuah; | 'am | la' | bayad | chazaqah | uabizroua' | natuyah |
| **and stone** | | ***As* live I** | | **saith** | **Adonai Yahuah** | | **surely** | **not** | **with a hand mighty** | | **and with a arm stretched out** | |

Eze 20:28 For when I had brought them into the land, for the which I lifted up mine hand to give it to them, then they saw every high hill, and all the thick trees, and they
offered there their sacrifices, and there they presented the provocation of their offering: there also they made their sweet savour, and poured out there their drink offerings.29
Then I said unto them, What is the high place whereunto you go? And the name thereof is called Bamah unto this day.30 Wherefore say unto the house of Israel, Thus saith
YHUH G-D; Are you polluted after the manner of your fathers? and commit you whoredom after their abominations?31 For when you offer your gifts, when you make your
sons to pass through the fire, you pollute yourselves with all your idols, even unto this day: and shall I be inquired of by you, O house of Israel? As I live, saith YHUH G-D, I
will not be inquired of by you.32 And that which cometh into your mind shall not be at all, that you say, We will be as the heathen, as the families of the countries, to serve
wood and stone.33 As I live, saith YHUH G-D, surely with a mighty hand, and with a stretched out arm, and with fury poured out, will I rule over you:

ובחמה 2534 שפוכה 8210 אמלוך 4427 עליכם 5921: **20:34** והוצאתי 3318 אתכם 853 מן 4480 העמים 5971 וקבצתי 6908 אתכם 853
uabchemah shapukah 'amlok 'aleykem. uahoutzea'tiy 'atkem min ha'amiym, uaqibatztiy 'atkem,
**and with fury poured out will I rule over you And I will bring out you from the people and will gather you**

מן 4480 הארצות 776 אשר 834 נפוצתם 6327 בם 871a ביד 3027 חזקה 2389 ובזרוע 2220 נטויה 5186 ובחמה 2534
min ha'aratzout, 'asher napoutzotem bam; bayad chazaqah uabizroua' natuyah, uabchemah
**out of the countries wherein you are scattered there with a hand mighty and with a arm stretched out and with fury**

שפוכה 8210: **20:35** והבאתי 935 אתכם 853 אל 413 מדבר 4057 העמים 5971 ונשפטתי 8199 אתכם 854 שם 8033 פנים 6440 אל 413
shapukah. uahebea'tiy 'atkem, 'al midbar ha'amiym; uanishpattiy 'atakem sham, paniym 'al
**poured out And I will bring you into the wilderness of the people and will I plead with you there face to**

פנים 6440: **20:36** כאשר 834 נשפטתי 8199 את 854 אבותיכם 1 במדבר 4057 ארץ 776 מצרים 4714 כן 3651 אשפט 8199 אתכם 854
paniym. ka'asher nishpattiy 'at abouteykem, bamidbar 'aretz mitzrayim; ken 'ashapet 'atakem,
**face Like as I pleaded *with* your fathers in the wilderness of the land of Egypt so will I plead with you**

נאם 5002 אדני 136 יהוה 3069: **20:37** והעברתי 5674 אתכם 853 תחת 8478 השבט 7626 והבאתי 935 אתכם 853 במסרת 4562
na'am 'adonay Yahuah. uaha'abartiy 'atkem tachat hashabet; uahebea'tiy 'atkem bamasoret
**saith Adonai Yahuah And I will cause to pass you under the rod and I will bring you into the bond of**

הברית 1285: **20:38** וברותי 1305 מכם 4480 המרדים 4775 והפושעים 6586 בי 871a
habariyt. uabaroutiy mikem, hamoradiym uahapousha'aym biy,
**the covenant And I will purge out from among you the rebels and them that transgress against me**

מארץ 776 מגוריהם 4033 אוציא 3318 אותם 853 ואל 413 אדמת 127 ישראל 3478 לא 3808 יבוא 935
me'aretz magureyhem 'autziy'a 'autam, ua'al 'admat yisra'ael la' yabou'a;
**out of the country where they sojourn I will bring forth them and into the land of Israel not they shall enter**

וידעתם 3045 כי 3588 אני 589 יהוה 3068: **20:39** ואתם 859 בית 1004 ישראל 3478 כה 3541 אמר 559 אדני 136 יהוה 3069 איש 376
uiyda'tem kiy 'aniy Yahuah. ua'atem beyt yisra'ael koh 'amar 'adonay Yahuah 'aysh
**and you shall know that I *am* Yahuah As for you O house of Israel thus saith Adonai Yahuah every one**

גלוליו 1544 לכו 1980 עבדו 5647 ואחר 310 אם 518 אינכם 369 שמעים 8085 אלי 413 ואת 853 שם 8034 קדשי 6944 לא 3808
gilulayu laku 'abodu, ua'achar 'am 'aeynakem shoma'aym 'aelay; ua'at shem qadashiy la'
**his idols Go you serve you and hereafter *also* if not you will listen unto me *but* name my holy no**

תחללו 2490 עוד 5750 במתנותיכם 4979 ובגלוליכם 1544: **20:40** כי 3588 בהר 2022 קדשי 6944 בהר 2022 מרום 4791
tachallu 'aud, bamatnouteykem uabgiluleykem. kiy bahar qadashiy bahar maroum
**pollute you more with your gifts and with your idols For in mountain mine holy in the mountain of the height of**

ישראל 3478 נאם 5002 אדני 136 יהוה 3069 שם 8033 יעבדני 5647 כל 3605 בית 1004 ישראל 3478 כלה 3605 בארץ 776 שם 8033
yisra'ael, na'am 'adonay Yahuah, sham ya'abduniy kal beyt yisra'ael kuloh ba'aretz; sham
**Israel saith Adonai Yahuah there shall serve me all the house of Israel all of them in the land there**

ארצם 7521 ושם 8033 אדרוש 1875 את 853 תרומתיכם 8641 ואת 853 ראשית 7225 משאותיכם 4864 בכל 3605
'artzem, uasham 'adroush 'at tarumoteykem, ua'at rea'shiyt masa'auteykem bakal
**will I accept them and there will I require your offerings *and* the firstfruits of your oblations with all**

Eze 20:34 And I will bring you out from the people, and will gather you out of the countries wherein you are scattered, with a mighty hand, and with a stretched out arm, and with fury poured out.35 And I will bring you into the wilderness of the people, and there will I plead with you face to face.36 Like as I pleaded with your fathers in the wilderness of the land of Egypt, so will I plead with you, saith YHUH G-D.37 And I will cause you to pass under the rod, and I will bring you into the bond of the covenant:38 And I will purge out from among you the rebels, and them that transgress against me: I will bring them forth out of the country where they sojourn, and they shall not enter into the land of Israel: and you shall know that I am YHUH.39 As for you, O house of Israel, thus saith YHUH G-D; Go you, serve you everyone his idols, and hereafter also, if you will not hear unto me: but pollute you my holy name no more with your gifts, and with your idols.40 For in mine holy mountain, in the mountain of the height of Israel, saith YHUH G-D, there shall all the house of Israel, all of them in the land, serve me: there will I accept them, and there will I require your offerings, and the firstfruits of your oblations, with all your holy things.

20:41

קדשיכם 6944: בריח 7381 ניחח 5207 ארצה 7521 אתכם 853 בהוציאי 3318 אתכם 853 מן 4480 העמים 5971 וקבצתי 6908
qadasheykem. bareyach niychoach 'artzeh 'atkem bahoutziy'ay 'atkem min ha'amiym, uaqibatztiy
**your holy things with savour *your* sweet I will accept you when I bring out you from the people and gather**

אתכם 853 מן 4480 הארצות 776 אשר 834 נפצתם 6327 בם 871a ונקדשתי 6942 בכם 871a לעיני 5869
'atkem, min ha'aratzout, 'asher napotzotem bam; uaniqdashtiy bakem la'aeyney
**you out of the countries wherein you have been scattered there and I will be sanctified in you before**

20:42

הגוים 1471: וידעתם 3045 כי 3588 אני 589 יהוה 3068 בהביאי 935 אתכם 853 אל 413 אדמת 127 ישראל 3478 אל 413
hagouyim. uiyda'tem kiy 'aniy Yahuah, bahabiy'ay 'atkem 'al 'admat yisra'ael; 'al
**the heathen And you shall know that I *am* Yahuah when I shall bring you into the land of Israel into**

20:43

הארץ 776 אשר 834 נשאתי 5375 את 853 ידי 3027 לתת 5414 אותה 853 לאבותיכם 1: וזכרתם 2142 שם 8033
ha'aretz, 'asher nasa'tiy 'at yadiy, latet 'autah la'abouteykem. uazkartem sham,
**the country *for* the which I lifted up mine hand to give it to your fathers And shall you remember there**

את 853 דרכיכם 1870 ואת 853 כל 3605 עלילותיכם 5949 אשר 834 נטמאתם 2930 בם 871a ונקטתם 6962
'at darkeykem ua'at kal aliylouteykem, 'asher nitmea'tem bam; uanqototem
**your ways *and* all your doings wherein you have been defiled in them and you shall lothe yourselves**

20:44

בפניכם 6440 בכל 3605 רעותיכם 7451 אשר 834 עשיתם 6213: וידעתם 3045 כי 3588 אני 589 יהוה 3068
bipaneykem, bakal ra'auteykem 'asher 'asiytem. uiyda'tem kiy 'aniy Yahuah,
**in your own sight for all your evils that you have committed And you shall know that I *am* Yahuah**

בעשותי 6213 אתכם 854 למען 4616 שמי 8034 לא 3808 כדרכיכם 1870 הרעים 7451 וכעלילותיכם 5949
ba'asoutiy 'atakem lama'an shamiy; la' kadarkeykem hara'aym uaka'aliylouteykem
**when I have wrought with you for sake my name's not according to your ways wicked nor according to your doings**

20:45

הנשחתות 7843 בית 1004 ישראל 3478 נאם 5002 אדני 136 יהוה 3069: ויהי 1961 דבר 1697 יהוה 3068 אלי 413
hanishchatout beyt yisra'ael, na'am 'adonay Yahuah. uayahiy dabar Yahuah 'aelay
**corrupt O you house of Israel saith Adonai Yahuah Moreover came *the* word of Yahuah unto me**

20:46

לאמר 559: בן 1121 אדם 120 שים 7760 פניך 6440 דרך 1870 תימנה 8486 והטף 5197 אל 413 דרום 1864 והנבא 5012
lea'mor. ben 'adam, siym paneyka derek teymanah, uahatep 'al daroum; uahinabea'
**saying Son of man set your face toward *the* south and drop *your word* toward *the* south and prophesy**

20:47

אל 413 יער 3293 השדה 7704 נגב 5045: ואמרת 559 ליער 3293 הנגב 5045 שמע 8085 דבר 1697 יהוה 3068 כה 3541 אמר 559
'al ya'ar hasadeh negeb. ua'amarta laya'ar hanegeb, shama' dabar Yahuah; koh 'amar
**against the forest of the field south And say to the forest of the south Hear the word of Yahuah Thus saith**

אדני 136 יהוה 3069 הנני 2005 מצית 3341 בך 871a אש 784 ואכלה 398 בך 871a כל 3605 עץ 6086 לח 3892 וכל 3605 עץ 6086 יבש 3002
'adonay Yahuah hinniy matztzit baka 'aesh ua'akalah baka kal 'aetz lach uakal 'aetz yabesh
**Adonai Yahuah Behold I will kindle in you a fire and it shall devour in you every tree green and every tree dry**

לא 3808 תכבה 3518 להבת 3852 שלהבת 7957 ונצרבו 6866 בה 871a כל 3605 פנים 6440 מנגב 5045
la' tikbeh lahebet shalhebet, uanitzrabu bah kal paniym minegeb
**not shall be quenched *the* flaming flame and shall be burned therein all faces from the south to**

Eze 20:41 I will accept you with your sweet savour, when I bring you out from the people, and gather you out of the countries wherein you have been scattered; and I will be sanctified in you before the heathen.42 And you shall know that I am YHUH, when I shall bring you into the land of Israel, into the country for the which I lifted up mine hand to give it to your fathers.43 And there shall you remember your ways, and all your doings, wherein you have been defiled; and you shall lothe yourselves in your own sight for all your evils that you have committed.44 And you shall know that I am YHUH, when I have wrought with you for my name's sake, not according to your wicked ways, nor according to your corrupt doings, O you house of Israel, saith YHUH G-D.45 Moreover the word of YHUH came unto me, saying,46 Son of man, set your face toward the south, and drop your word toward the south, and prophesy against the forest of the south field;47 And say to the forest of the south, Hear the word of YHUH; Thus saith YHUH G-D; Behold, I will kindle a fire in you, and it shall devour every green tree in you, and every dry tree: the flaming flame shall not be quenched, and all faces from the south to the north shall be burned therein.

20:48 / 20:49
צפונה 6828: וראו 7200 כל 3605 בשר 1320 כי 3588 אני 589 יהוה 3068 בערתיה 1197 לא 3808 תכבה 3518:
tzapounah. uar'au kal basar, kiy 'aniy Yahuah bi'artiyha; la' tikbeh.
**the north And shall see all flesh that I *am* Yahuah have kindled it not it shall be quenched**

ואמר 559 אהה 162 אדני 136 יהוה 3069 המה 1992 אמרים 559 לי 3807a הלא 3808 ממשל 4911 משלים 4912 הוא 1931:
ua'amar 'ahah 'adonay Yahuah; hemah 'amariym liy, hala' mamashel mashaliym hua'.
**Then said I Ah Adonai Yahuah they say of me not Does speak parables? he**

Ezek 21:1 / 21:2
ויהי 1961 דבר 1697 יהוה 3068 אלי 413 לאמר 559: בן 1121 אדם 120 שים 7760 פניך 6440 אל 413 ירושלם 3389
uayahiy dabar Yahuah 'aelay lea'mor. ben 'adam, siym paneyka 'al yarushalaim,
**And came the word of Yahuah unto me saying Son of man set your face toward Jerusalem**

21:3
והטף 5197 אל 413 מקדשים 4720 והנבא 5012 אל 413 אדמת 127 ישראל 3478: ואמרת 559 לאדמת 127
uahatep 'al miqadashiym; uahinabea' 'al 'admat yisra'ael. ua'amarta la'admat
**and drop *your word* toward the holy places and prophesy against the land of Israel And say to the land of**

ישראל 3478 כה 3541 אמר 559 יהוה 3068 הנני 2005 אליך 413 והוצאתי 3318 חרבי 2719 מתערה 8593 והכרתי 3772
yisra'ael, koh 'amar Yahuah, hinniy 'aelayik, uahoutzea'tiy charbiy mita'arah; uahikratiy
**Israel Thus saith Yahuah Behold I *am* against you and will draw forth my sword out of his sheath and will cut off**

21:4
ממך 4480 צדיק 6662 ורשע 7563: יען 3282 אשר 834 הכרתי 3772 ממך 4480 צדיק 6662 ורשע 7563
mimek tzadiyq uarashaa'. ya'an 'asher hikratiy mimek tzadiyq uarashaa';
**from you the righteous and the wicked Seeing then that I will cut off from you the righteous and the wicked**

21:5
לכן 3651 תצא 3318 חרבי 2719 מתערה 8593 אל 413 כל 3605 בשר 1320 מנגב 5045 צפון 6828: וידעו 3045
laken tetzea' charbiy mita'arah 'al kal basar minegeb tzapoun. uayada'aua
**therefore shall go forth my sword out of his sheath against all flesh from the south to the north That may know**

21:6
כל 3605 בשר 1320 כי 3588 אני 589 יהוה 3068 הוצאתי 3318 חרבי 2719 מתערה 8593 לא 3808 תשוב 7725 עוד 5750:
kal basar, kiy 'aniy Yahuah, houtzea'tiy charbiy mita'arah; la' tashub 'aud.
**all flesh that I Yahuah have drawn forth my sword out of his sheath not it shall return any more**

ואתה 859 בן 1121 אדם 120 האנח 584 בשברון 7670 מתנים 4975 ובמרירות 4814 תאנח 584
ua'atah ben 'adam he'anach; bashibroun matanayim uabimariyrut, te'anach
**therefore you son of man Sigh with the breaking of *your* loins and with bitterness you shall sigh**

21:7
לעיניהם 5869: והיה 1961 כי 3588 יאמרו 559 אליך 413 על 5921 מה 4100 אתה 859 נאנח 584 ואמרת 559
la'aeyneyhem. uahayah kiy ya'maru 'aeleyka, 'al mah 'atah ne'anach; ua'amarta
**before their eyes And it shall be when they say unto you Wherefore how long you? sighest that you shall answer**

אל 413 שמועה 8052 כי 3588 באה 935 ונמס 4549 כל 3605 לב 3820 ורפו 7503 כל 3605 ידים 3027 וכהתה 3543 כל 3605
'al shamu'ah kiy ba'ah uanames kal leb uarapu kal yadayim uakihatah kal
**For the tidings because it comes and shall melt every heart and shall be feeble all hands and shall faint every**

רוח 7307 וכל 3605 ברכים 1290 תלכנה 1980 מים 4325 הנה 2009 באה 935 ונהיתה 1961 נאם 5002 אדני 136 יהוה 3069:
ruach, uakal birkayim telaknah mayim, hineh ba'ah uanihayatah, na'am 'adonay Yahuah.
**spirit and all knees shall be weak *as* water behold it comes and shall be brought to pass saith Adonai Yahuah**

Eze 20:48 And all flesh shall see that I YHUH have kindled it: it shall not be quenched.49 Then said I, Ah Adonai G-D! they say of me, Does he not speak parables? **Eze** 21:1 And the word of YHUH came unto me, saying,2 Son of man, set your face toward Jerusalem, and drop your word toward the holy places, and prophesy against the land of Israel,3 And say to the land of Israel, Thus saith YHUH; Behold, I am against you, and will draw forth my sword out of his sheath, and will cut off from you the righteous and the wicked.4 Seeing then that I will cut off from you the righteous and the wicked, therefore shall my sword go forth out of his sheath against all flesh from the south to the north:5 That all flesh may know that I YHUH have drawn forth my sword out of his sheath: it shall not return anymore.6 Sigh therefore, you son of man, with the breaking of your loins; and with bitterness sigh before their eyes.7 And it shall be, when they say unto you, Wherefore sighest you? that you shall answer, For the tidings; because it cometh: and every heart shall melt, and all hands shall be feeble, and every spirit shall faint, and all knees shall be weak as water: behold, it cometh, and shall be brought to pass, saith YHUH G-D.

**21:8** … **21:9**

ויהי 1961 דבר 1697 יהוה 3068 אלי 413 לאמר 559: בן 1121 אדם 120 הנבא 5012 ואמרת 559 כה 3541 אמר 559 אדני 136 אמר 559

uayahiy dabar Yahuah 'aelay lea'mor. ben 'adam hinabea' ua'amarta, koh 'amar 'adonay; 'amor

**Again came the word of Yahuah unto me saying Son of man prophesy and say Thus saith Adonai Say**

**21:10**

חרב 2719 חרב 2719 הוחדה 2300 וגם 1571 מרוטה 4803: למען 4616 טבח 2874 טבח 2873 הוחדה 2300 למען 4616 היה 1961

chereb chereb huchadah uagam marutah. lama'an taboch tebach huchadah, lama'an hayeh

**A sword a sword is sharpened and also furbished to that make a sore slaughter It is sharpened that it may**

**21:11**

לה 3807a ברק 1300 מרטה 4803 או 176 נשיש 7797 שבט 7626 בני 1121 מאסת 3988 כל 3605 עץ 6086:

lah baraq moratah; 'au nasiys, shebet baniy mo'aset kal 'aetz.

**to glitter it is furbished then we make mirth? the rod of my son it contemneth *as* every tree**

ויתן 5414 אתה 853 למרטה 4803 לתפש 8610 בכף 3709 היא 1931 הוחדה 2300 חרב 2719 והיא 1931 מרטה 4803 לתת 5414

uayiten 'atah lamaratah litpos bakap; hiy'a huchadah chereb uahiy'a moratah, latet

**And he has given it to be furbished may be handled in hand this is sharpened sword and it is furbished to give**

**21:12**

אותה 853 ביד 3027 הורג 2026: זעק 2199 והילל 3213 בן 1121 אדם 120 כי 3588 היא 1931 היתה 1961 בעמי 5971 היא 1931

'autah bayad houreg. za'aq uaheylel ben 'adam, kiy hiy'a haytah ua'amiy, hiy'a

**it into the hand of the slayer Cry and howl son of man for it shall be upon my people it**

בכל 3605 נשיאי 5387 ישראל 3478 מגורי 4048 אל 413 חרב 2719 היו 1961 את 854 עמי 5971 לכן 3651 ספק 5606 אל 413

bakal nasiy'aey yisra'ael; magurey 'al chereb hayu 'at 'amiy, laken sapoq 'al

***shall be* upon all the princes of Israel terrors by reason of the sword shall be *upon* my people therefore smite upon**

**21:13**

ירך 3409: כי 3588 בחן 974 ומה 4100 אם 518 גם 1571 שבט 7626 מאסת 3988 לא 3808 יהיה 1961 נאם 5002 אדני 136

yarek. kiy bochan, uamah 'am gam shebet mo'aset la' yihayeh; na'am 'adonay

***your* thigh Because *it is* a trial and what if even the rod? *the sword* contemn no *more* it shall be saith Adonai**

**21:14**

יהוה 3069: ואתה 859 בן 1121 אדם 120 הנבא 5012 והך 5221 כף 3709 אל 413 כף 3709 ותכפל 3717 חרב 2719

Yahuah. ua'atah ben 'adam, hinabea' uahak kap 'al kap; uatikapel chereb

**Yahuah You therefore son of man prophesy and smite *your* hands together palm and let be doubled the sword of**

שלישתה 7992 חרב 2719 חללים 2491 היא 1931 חרב 2719 חלל 2491 הגדול 1419

shaliyshitah chereb chalaliym, hiy'a, chereb chalal hagadoul,

**the third time the sword of the slain it *is* the sword of *men that are* slain the great**

**21:15**

החדרת 2314 להם 3807a: למען 4616 למוג 4127 לב 3820 והרבה 7235 המכשלים 4383

hachoderet lahem. lama'an lamug leb, uaharbeh hamiksholiym,

**which enter into their privy chambers their that may faint *their* heart and be multiplied *their* ruins**

על 5921 כל 3605 שעריהם 8179 נתתי 5414 אבחת 19 חרב 2719 אח 253 עשויה 6213 לברק 1300 מעטה 4593

'al kal sha'areyhem, natatiy 'abchat chareb; 'ach 'asuyah labaraq ma'atah

**against all their gates I have set the point (*slaughter*) of the sword ah *it is* made bright *it is* wrapped up**

**21:16**

לטבח 2874: התאחדי 258 הימני 3231 השימי 7760 השמילי 8041 אנה 575 פניך 6440

latabach. hit'achadiy heyminiy hasiymiy hasamiyliy; 'anah panayik

**for the slaughter Go you one way or other *either on* the right hand *or* on the left whithersoever your face**

Eze 21:8 Again the word of YHUH came unto me, saying,9 Son of man, prophesy, and say, Thus saith YHUH; Say, A sword, a sword is sharpened, and also furbished:10 It is sharpened to make a sore slaughter; it is furbished that it may glitter: should we then make mirth? it contemneth the rod of my son, as every tree.11 And he has give it to be furbished, that it may be handled: this sword is sharpened, and it is furbished, to give it into the hand of the slayer.12 Cry and howl, son of man: for it shall be upon my people, it shall be upon all the princes of Israel: terrors by reason of the sword shall be upon my people: smite therefore upon your thigh.13 Because it is a trial, and what if the sword contemn even the rod? it shall be no more, saith YHUH G-D.14 Thou therefore, son of man, prophesy, and smite your hands together, and let the sword be doubled the third time, the sword of the slain: it is the sword of the great men that are slain, which entereth into their privy chambers.15 I have set the point of the sword against all their gates, that their heart may faint, and their ruins be multiplied: ah! it is made bright, it is wrapped up for the slaughter.16 Go you one way or other, either on the right hand, or on the left, whithersoever your face is set.

מעדות 3259: 21:17 וגם 1571 אני 589 אכה 5221 כפי 3709 אל 413 כפי 3709 והנחתי 5117 חמתי 2534 אני 589 יהוה 3068
mu'adout. uagam 'aniy, 'akeh kapiy 'al kapiy, uahanichotiy chamatiy; 'aniy Yahuah
**is set also I will also smite mine hands to gether and I will cause to rest my fury I Yahuah**

דברתי 1696: 21:18 ויהי 1961 דבר 1697 יהוה 3068 אלי 413 לאמר 559: 21:19 ואתה 859 בן 1121 אדם 120 שים 7760 לך 3807a
dibartiy. uayahiy dabar Yahuah 'aelay lea'mor. ua'atah ben 'adam siym laka
**have said *it* came again The word of Yahuah unto me saying Also you son of man appoint to you**

שנים 8147 דרכים 1870 לבוא 935 חרב 2719 מלך 4428 בבל 894 מארץ 776 אחד 259 יצאו 3318 שניהם 8147
shanayim darakiym, labou'a chereb melek babel, me'aretz 'achad yetza'ua shaneyhem;
**two ways that may come the sword of the king of Babylon out of land one shall come forth both twain**

ויד 3027 ברא 1254 בראש 7218 דרך 1870 עיר 5892 ברא 1254: 21:20 דרך 1870 תשים 7760 לבוא 935 חרב 2719
uayad barea', bara'sh derek 'ayr barea'. derek tasiym, labou'a chereb,
**and a place choose you *it* at the head of the way to the city choose a way Appoint that may come the sword *to***

את 853 רבת 7237 בני 1121 עמון 5983 ואת 853 יהודה 3063 בירושלם 3389 בצורה 1219: 21:21 כי 3588 עמד 5975 מלך 4428
'at rabat baney 'amoun; ua'at yahudah biyarushalaim batzurah. kiy 'amad melek
**Rabbath of the sons of the Ammonites *and* to Judah in Jerusalem the defenced For stood the king of**

בבל 894 אל 413 אם 517 הדרך 1870 בראש 7218 שני 8147 הדרכים 1870 לקסם 7080 קסם 7081 קלקל 7043 בחצים 2671
babel 'al 'am haderek, bara'sh shaney hadarakiym liqsam qasem; qilqal bachitziym
**Babylon at the parting of the way at the head of two the ways to use divination he made bright *his* arrows**

שאל 7592 בתרפים 8655 ראה 7200 בכבד 3516: 21:22 בימינו 3225 היה 1961 הקסם 7081 ירושלם 3389 לשום 7760
sha'al batarapiym, ra'ah bakabed. biymiynou hayah haqesem yarushalaim, lasum
**he consulted with images he looked in the liver At his right hand was the divination *for* Jerusalem to appoint**

כרים 3733 לפתח 6605 פה 6310 ברצח 7524 להרים 7311 קול 6963 בתרועה 8643 לשום 7760 כרים 3733 על 5921 שערים 8179
kariym liptoach peh baretzach, lahariym qoul bitaru'ah; lasum kariym 'al sha'ariym,
**captains to open the mouth in the slaughter to lift up the voice with shouting to appoint *battering* rams against the gates**

לשפך 8210 סללה 5550 לבנות 1129 דיק 1785: 21:23 והיה 1961 להם 3807a כקסום 7080 שוא 7723 בעיניהם 5869
lishpok solalah libnout dayeq. uahayah lahem kiqsoum shau'a ba'aeyneyhem,
**to cast a mount *and* to build a fort And it shall be unto them as a divination false in their sight**

שבעי 7650 שבעות 7621 להם 3807a והוא 1931 מזכיר 2142 עון 5771 להתפש 8610: 21:24 לכן 3651
shabu'aey shabu'aut lahem; uahu'a mazkiyr 'auon lahitapes. laken,
**that have sworn oaths to them but he will call to remembrance the iniquity that they may be taken Therefore**

כה 3541 אמר 559 אדני 136 יהוה 3069 יען 3282 הזכרכם 2142 עונכם 5771 בהגלות 1540
koh 'amar 'adonay Yahuah ya'an, hazakarkem 'auonakem, bahigalout
**thus saith Adonai Yahuah Because you have made to be remembered your iniquity in that are discovered**

פשעיכם 6588 להראות 7200 חטאותיכם 2403 בכל 3605 עלילותיכם 5949 יען 3282
pish'aeykem, lahera'aut chata'ateykem, bakal 'aliylouteykem; ya'an
**your transgressions so that do appear your sins in all your doings because**

Eze 21:17 I will also smite mine hands together, and I will cause my fury to rest: I YHUH have said it.18 The word of YHUH came unto me again, saying,19 Also, you son of man, appoint you two ways, that the sword of the king of Babylon may come: both twain shall come forth out of one land: and choose you a place, choose it at the head of the way to the city.20 Appoint a way, that the sword may come to Rabbath of the Ammonites, and to Judah in Jerusalem the defenced.21 For the king of Babylon stood at the parting of the way, at the head of the two ways, to use divination: he made his arrows bright, he consulted with images, he looked in the liver.22 At his right hand was the divination for Jerusalem, to appoint captains, to open the mouth in the slaughter, to lift up the voice with shouting, to appoint battering rams against the gates, to cast a mount, and to build a fort.23 And it shall be unto them as a false divination in their sight, to them that have sworn oaths: but he will call to remembrance the iniquity, that they may be taken.24 Therefore thus saith YHUH G-D; Because you have made your iniquity to be remembered, in that your transgressions are discovered, so that in all your doings your sins do appear; because, I say, that you are come to remembrance, you shall be taken with the hand.

21:25

הזכרכם 2142 בכף 3709 תתפשו 8610: ואתה 859 חלל 2491 רשע 7563 נשיא 5387
hizakerkem, bakap titapesu. ua'atah chalal rasha', nasiy'a
**_I say_ that you are come to remembrance with the hand you shall be taken And you profane wicked prince of**

21:26

ישראל 3478 אשר 834 בא 935 יומו 3117 בעת 6256 עון 5771 קץ 7093: כה 3541 אמר 559 אדני 136 יהוה 3068 הסיר 5493 המצנפת 4701
yisra'ael; 'asher ba' youmou, ba'aet 'auon qetz. koh 'amar 'adonay Yahuah, hasiyr hamitznepet,
**Israel whose is come day when iniquity _shall have_ an end Thus saith Adonai Yahuah Remove the diadem**

21:27

והרים 7311 העטרה 5850 זאת 2063 לא 3808 זאת 2063 השפלה 8217 הגבה 1361 והגבה 1364 השפיל 8213: עוה 5754
uahariym ha'atarah; za't la' za't, hashapalah hagabeah, uahagaboah hashapiyl. 'auah
**and take off the crown this _shall_ not _be_ the same _him that is_ low exalt and abase _him that is_ high overturn**

עוה 5754 עוה 5754 אשימנה 7760 גם 1571 זאת 2063 לא 3808 היה 1961 עד 5704 בא 935 אשר 834 לו 3807a המשפט 4941
'auah 'auah 'asiymenah; gam za't la' hayah, 'ad ba' 'asher lou' hamishpat
**overturn overturn I will it and also this no _more_ shall be until he come whose it _is_ right**

21:28

ונתתיו 5414: ואתה 859 בן 1121 אדם 120 הנבא 5012 ואמרת 559 כה 3541 אמר 559 אדני 136 יהוה 3069 אל 413 בני 1121
uantatiyu. ua'atah ben 'adam, hinabea' ua'amarta koh 'amar 'adonay Yahuah, 'al baney
**and I will give _him_ And you son of man prophesy and say Thus saith Adonai Yahuah concerning the sons of**

עמון 5983 ואל 413 חרפתם 2781 ואמרת 559 חרב 2719 חרב 2719 פתוחה 6605 לטבח 2874 מרוטה 4803
'amoun ua'al cherpatam; ua'amarta, chereb chereb patuchah latebach marutah,
**the Ammonites and concerning their reproach even say you The sword the sword _is_ drawn for the slaughter _it is_ furbished**

21:29

להכיל 398 למען 4616 ברק 1300: בחזות 2372 לך 3807a שוא 7723 בקסם 7080 לך 3807a כזב 3577 לתת 5414
lahakiyl lama'an baraq. bachazout lak shau'a, biqsam lak kazab; latet
**to consume because of the glittering Whiles they see unto you vanity whiles they divine unto you a lie to bring**

אותך 853 אל 413 צוארי 6677 חללי 2491 רשעים 7563 אשר 834 בא 935 יומם 3117 בעת 6256 עון 5771
autak, 'al tzaua'rey challey rasha'aym, 'asher ba' youmam, ba'aet 'auon
**you upon the necks of _them that are_ slain _of_ the wicked whose is come day when their iniquity**

21:30

קץ 7093: השב 7725 אל 413 תערה 8593 במקום 4725 אשר 834 נבראת 1254 בארץ 776
qetz. hashab 'al ta'arah; bimaqoum 'asher nibrea't ba'aretz
**_shall have_ an end Shall I cause _it_ to return into his sheath? in the place where you were created in the land of**

21:31

מכרותיך 4351 אשפט 8199 אתך 853: ושפכתי 8210 עליך 5921 זעמי 2195 באש 784 עברתי 5678 אפיח 6315
mekuroutayik 'ashpot 'atak. uashapakatiy 'alayik za'amiy, ba'aesh 'abratiy 'apiyach
**your nativity I will judge you And I will pour out upon you mine indignation in the fire of my wrath I will blow**

21:32

עליך 5921 ונתתיך 5414 ביד 3027 אנשים 582 בערים 1197 חרשי 2796 משחית 4889: לאש 784 תהיה 1961
'alayik; uantatiyk, bayad 'anashiym bo'ariym, charashey mashchiyt. la'aesh tihayeh
**against you and deliver you into the hand of men brutish _and_ skilful to destroy to the fire You shall be**

לאכלה 402 דמך 1818 יהיה 1961 בתוך 8432 הארץ 776 לא 3808 תזכרי 2142 כי 3588 אני 589 יהוה 3068 דברתי 1696:
la'akalah damek yihayeh batouk ha'aretz; la' tizakeriy, kiy 'aniy Yahuah dibartiy.
**for fuel your blood shall be in the midst of the land no _more_ you shall be remembered for I Yahuah have spoken _it_**

Eze 21:25 And you, profane wicked prince of Israel, whose day is come, when iniquity shall have an end,26 Thus saith YHUH G-D; Remove the diadem, and take off the crown: this shall not be the same: exalt him that is low, and abase him that is high.27 I will overturn, overturn, overturn, it: and it shall be no more, until he come whose right it is; and I will give it him.28 And you, son of man, prophesy and say, Thus saith YHUH G-D concerning the Ammonites, and concerning their reproach; even say you, The sword, the sword is drawn: for the slaughter it is furbished, to consume because of the glittering:29 Whiles they see vanity unto you, whiles they divine a lie unto you, to bring you upon the necks of them that are slain, of the wicked, whose day is come, when their iniquity shall have an end.30 Shall I cause it to return into his sheath? I will judge you in the place where you were created, in the land of your nativity.31 And I will pour out mine indignation upon you, I will blow against you in the fire of my wrath, and deliver you into the hand of brutish men, and skilful to destroy.32 Thou shall be for fuel to the fire; your blood shall be in the midst of the land; you shall be no more remembered: for I YHUH have spoken it.

**Ezek 22:1** ויהי 1961 | דבר 1697 | יהוה 3068 | אלי 413 | לאמר 559: | **22:2** ואתה 859 | בן 1121 | אדם 120 | התשפט 8199 | התשפט 8199
uayahiy | dabar | Yahuah | 'aelay | lea'mor. | ua'atah | ben | 'adam, | hatishpot | hatishpot
**Moreover came the word of Yahuah unto me saying | Now you son of man will you judge will you judge**

את 853 | עיר 5892 | הדמים 1818 | והודעתה 3045 | את 853 | כל 3605 | תועבותיה 8441: | **22:3** ואמרת 559 | כה 3541 | אמר 559 | אדני 136
'at | 'ayr | hadamiym; | uahouda'tah, | 'at | kal | tou'abouteyha. | ua'amarta, | koh | 'amar | 'adonay
**city? the bloody yea, you shall show her all her abominations | Then say you Thus saith Adonai**

יהוה 3069 | עיר 5892 | שפכת 8210 | דם 1818 | בתוכה 8432 | לבוא 935 | עתה 6256 | ועשתה 6213 | גלולים 1544 | עליה 5921
Yahuah, | 'ayr | shopeket | dam | batoukah | labou'a | 'atah; | ua'asatah | giluliym | 'aleyha
**Yahuah The city sheddeth blood in the midst of it that may come her time and make idols against herself**

לטמאה 2930: | **22:4** בדמך 1818 | אשר 834 | שפכת 8210 | אשמת 816 | ובגלוליך 1544 | אשר 834 | עשית 6213
latama'ah. | badamek | 'asher | shapakt | 'ashamt, | uabgilulayik | 'asher | 'asiyt
**to defile herself | in your blood that you have shed You are become guilty and in your idols which you have made**

טמאת 2930 | ותקריבי 7126 | ימיך 3117 | ותבוא 935 | עד 5704 | שנותיך 8141 | על 5921 | כן 3651
tamea't, | uataqriybiy | yamayik, | uatabou'a | 'ad | shanoutayik; | 'al | ken,
**have defiled *yourself* and you have caused to draw near your days and are come *even* unto your years therefore have**

נתתיך 5414 | חרפה 2781 | לגוים 1471 | וקלסה 7048 | לכל 3605 | הארצות 776: | **22:5** הקרבות 7138 | והרחקות 7350
natatiyk | cherpah | lagouyim, | uaqalasah | lakal | ha'aratzout. | haqarobout | uaharachoqout
**I made you a reproach unto the heathen and a mocking to all countries | *Those that be* near and *those that be* far**

ממך 4480 | יתקלסו 7046 | בך 871a | טמאת 2931 | השם 8034 | רבת 7227 | המהומה 4103: | **22:6** הנה 2009 | נשיאי 5387 | ישראל 3478
mimek | yitqalsu | bak; | tame'at | hashem, | rabat | hamahumah. | hineh | nasiy'aey | yisra'ael,
**from you shall mock *which are* against you infamous named *and* much vexed | Behold the princes of Israel**

איש 376 | לזרעו 2220 | היו 1961 | בך 871a | למען 4616 | שפך 8210 | דם 1818: | **22:7** אב 1 | ואם 517 | הקלו 7043 | בך 871a
'aysh | lizro'au | hayu | bak; | lama'an | shapak | dam. | 'ab | ua'aem | heqalu | bak,
**every one to their power were in you to shed blood | *by* father and mother have they set light In you**

לגר 1616 | עשו 6213 | בעשק 6233 | בתוכך 8432 | יתום 3490 | ואלמנה 490 | הונו 3238
lager | 'asu | ba'asheq | batoukek; | yatoum | ua'almanah | hounu
**with the stranger have they dealt by oppression in the midst of you the fatherless and the widow have they vexed**

בך 871a: | **22:8** קדשי 6944 | בזית 959 | ואת 853 | שבתתי 7676 | חללת 2490: | **22:9** אנשי 582 | רכיל 7400 | היו 1961
bak. | qadashay | baziyt; | ua'at | shabtotay | chilalt. | 'anshey | rakiyl | hayu
**in you | mine holy things You have despised *and* my sabbaths have profaned | men that carry tales are**

בך 871a | למען 4616 | שפך 8210 | דם 1818 | ואל 413 | ההרים 2022 | אכלו 398 | בך 871a | זמה 2154 | עשו 6213 | בתוכך 8432: | **22:10**
bak | lama'an | shapak | dam; | ua'al | hehariym | 'akalu | bak, | zimah | 'asu | batoukek.
**In you to shed blood and upon the mountains they eat in you lewdness they commit in the midst of you**

ערות 6172 | אב 1 | גלה 1540 | בך 871a | טמאת 2931 | הנדה 5079 | ענו 6031 | בך 871a:
'aruat | 'ab | gilah | bak; | tame'at | hanidah | 'anu | bak.
**nakedness *their* fathers' have they discovered In you *for* pollution *her* that was set apart have they humbled in you**

**Eze** 22:1 Moreover the word of YHUH came unto me, saying,2 Now, you son of man, will you judge, will you judge the bloody city? yea, you shall show her all her abominations.3 Then say you, Thus saith YHUH G-D, The city sheddeth blood in the midst of it, that her time may come, and make idols against herself to defile herself.4 Thou are become guilty in your blood that you have shed; and have defiled thyself in your idols which you have made; and you have caused your days to draw near, and are come even unto your years: therefore have I made you a reproach unto the heathen, and a mocking to all countries.5 Those that be near, and those that be far from you, shall mock you, which are infamous and much vexed.6 Behold, the princes of Israel, everyone were in you to their power to shed blood.7 In you have they set light by father and mother: in the midst of you have they dealt by oppression with the stranger: in you have they vexed the fatherless and the widow.8 Thou have despised mine holy things, and have profaned my sabbaths.9 In you are men that carry tales to shed blood: and in you they eat upon the mountains: in the midst of you they commit lewdness.10 In you have they discovered their fathers' nakedness: in you have they humbled her that was set apart for pollution.

22:11
ואיש 376 את 854 אשת 802 רעהו 7453 עשה 6213 תועבה 8441 ואיש 376 את 853 כלתו 3618 טמא 2930
ua'aysh 'at 'aeshet re'aehu, 'asah tou'aebah, ua'aysh 'at kalatou timea'
**And one *with* wife his neighbour's has committed abomination and another his daughter in law has defiled**

בזמה 2154 ואיש 376 את 853 אחתו 269 בת 1323 אביו 1 ענה 6031 בך 871a: 22:12 שחד 7810 לקחו 3947 בך 871a
bazimah; ua'aysh 'at achotou bat 'abiyu 'anah bak. shochad laqachu bak
**lewdly and another his sister daughter *his* father's has humbled in you gifts have they taken In you**

למען 4616 שפך 8210 דם 1818 נשך 5392 ותרבית 8636 לקחת 3947 ותבצעי 1214 רעיך 7453 בעשק 6233
lama'an shapak dam; neshek uatarbiyt laqachat, uatabatza'ay re'ayik ba'asheq,
**to shed blood usury and increase you have taken and you have greedily gained *of* your neighbours by extortion**

ואתי 853 שכחת 7911 נאם 5002 אדני 136 יהוה 3069: 22:13 והנה 2009 הכיתי 5221 כפי 3709 אל 413 בצעך 1215
ua'atiy shakachat, na'am 'adonay Yahuah. uahineh hikeytiy kapiy, 'al bitz'aek
**and me have forgotten saith Adonai Yahuah Behold therefore I have smitten mine hand at your dishonest gain**

אשר 834 עשית 6213 ועל 5921 דמך 1818 אשר 834 היו 1961 בתוכך 8432: 22:14 היעמד 5975 לבך 3820 אם 518
'asher 'asiyt; ua'al damek, 'asher hayu batoukek. haya'amod libek 'am
**which you have made and at your blood which has been in the midst of you Can endure your heart or**

תחזקנה 2388 ידיך 3027 לימים 3117 אשר 834 אני 589 עשה 6213 אותך 854 אני 589 יהוה 3068 דברתי 1696 ועשיתי 6213: 22:15
techazaqnah yadayik, layamiym 'asher 'aniy 'aseh autak; 'aniy Yahuah dibartiy ua'asiytiy.
**can be strong your hands in the days that I shall deal with you? I Yahuah have spoken *it* and will do *it***

והפיצותי 6327 אותך 853 בגוים 1471 וזריתיך 2219 בארצות 776 והתמתי 8552 טמאתך 2932
uahapiytzoutiy 'autak bagouyim, uazeriytiyk ba'aratzout; uahatimoutiy tuma'atek
**And I will scatter you among the heathen and disperse you in the countries and will consume your filthiness**

ממך 4480: 22:16 ונחלת 2490 בך 871a לעיני 5869 גוים 1471 וידעת 3045 כי 3588 אני 589
mimek. uanichalt bach la'aeyney gouyim; uayada'at kiy 'aniy
**out of you And you shall take your inheritance in yourself in the sight of the heathen and you shall know that I *am***

יהוה 3068: 22:17 ויהי 1961 דבר 1697 יהוה 3068 אלי 413 לאמר 559: 22:18 בן 1121 אדם 120 היו 1961 לי 3807a בית 1004 ישראל 3478
Yahuah. uayahiy dabar Yahuah 'aelay lea'mor. ben 'adam hayu liy beyt yisra'ael
**Yahuah And came the word of Yahuah unto me saying Son of man is become to me the house of Israel**

לסוג 5509 כלם 3605 נחשת 5178 ובדיל 913 וברזל 1270 ועופרת 5777 בתוך 8432 כור 3564 סגים 5509 כסף 3701 היו 1961: 22:19
lasug kulam nachoshet uabdiyl uabarzel ua'auperet batouk kur, sigiym kesep hayu.
**dross all they *are* brass and tin and iron and lead in the midst of the furnace *even* the dross of silver they are**

לכן 3651 כה 3541 אמר 559 אדני 136 יהוה 3069 יען 3282 היות 1961 כלכם 3605 לסגים 5509 לכן 3651 הנני 2005 קבץ 6908 אתכם 853
laken, koh 'amar 'adonay Yahuah, ya'an hayout kulkem lasigiym; laken hinniy qobetz 'atkem,
**Therefore thus saith Adonai Yahuah Because you are become all dross therefore behold I will gather you**

אל 413 תוך 8432 ירושלם 3389: 22:20 קבצת 6910 כסף 3701 ונחשת 5178 וברזל 1270 ועופרת 5777 ובדיל 913 אל 413 תוך 8432
'al touk yarushalaim. qabutzat kesep uanchoshet uabarzel ua'auperet uabdiyl 'al touk
**into the midst of Jerusalem *As* they gather silver and brass and iron and lead and tin into the midst of**

Eze 22:11 And one has committed abomination with his neighbor's wife; and another has lewdly defiled his daughter in law; and another in you has humbled his sister, his
father's daughter.12 In you have they taken gifts to shed blood; you have taken usury and increase, and you have greedily gained of your neighbors by extortion, and have
forgotten me, saith YHUH G-D.13 Behold, therefore I have smitten mine hand at your dishonest gain which you have made, and at your blood which has been in the midst of
you.14 Can your heart endure, or can your hands be strong, in the days that I shall deal with you? I YHUH have spoken it, and will do it.15 And I will scatter you among the
heathen, and disperse you in the countries, and will consume your filthiness out of you.16 And you shall take your inheritance in thyself in the sight of the heathen, and you
shall know that I am YHUH.17 And the word of YHUH came unto me, saying,18 Son of man, the house of Israel is to me become dross: all they are brass, and tin, and iron,
and lead, in the midst of the furnace; they are even the dross of silver.19 Therefore thus saith YHUH G-D; Because you are all become dross, behold, therefore I will gather
you into the midst of Jerusalem.20 As they gather silver, and brass, and iron, and lead, and tin, into the midst of the furnace, to blow the fire upon it, to melt it;

כור 3564 לפחת 5301 עליו 5921 אש 784 להנתיך 5413 כן 3651 אקבץ 6908 באפי 639 ובחמתי 2534 והנחתי 3240
kur, lapachat 'aelayu 'aesh lahantiyk; ken 'aqbotz ba'apiy uabachamatiy, uahinachtiy
**the furnace to blow upon it the fire to melt *it* so will I gather *you* in mine anger and in my fury and I will leave**

והתכתי 5413 אתכם 853: 22:21 וכנסתי 3664 אתכם 853 ונפחתי 5301 עליכם 5921 באש 784 עברתי 5678
uahitaktiy 'atkem. uakinastiy 'atkem, uanapachtiy 'aleykem ba'aesh 'abratiy;
***you there* and melt you Yea I will gather you and blow upon you in the fire of my wrath**

ונתכתם 5413 בתוכה 8432: 22:22 כהתוך 2046 כסף 3701 בתוך 8432 כור 3564 כן 3651 תתכו 55413
uanitaktem batoukah. kahituk kesep batouk kur, ken tutaku
**and you shall be melted in the midst thereof As is melted silver in the midst of the furnace so shall you be melted**

בתוכה 8432 וידעתם 3045 כי 3588 אני 589 יהוה 3068 שפכתי 8210 חמתי 2534 עליכם 5921: 22:23 ויהי 1961
batoukah; uiyda'tem kiy 'aniy Yahuah, shapaktiy chamatiy 'aleykem. uayahiy
**in the midst thereof and you shall know that I Yahuah have poured out my fury upon you And came**

דבר 1697 יהוה 3068 אלי 413 לאמר 559: 22:24 בן 1121 אדם 120 אמר 559 לה 3807a את 859 ארץ 776 לא 3808 מטהרה 2891 היא 1931
dabar Yahuah 'aelay lea'mor. ben 'adam 'amar lah 'at 'aretz, la' matoharah hiy'a;
**the word of Yahuah unto me saying Son of man say unto her *You are* the land not is cleansed that**

לא 3808 גשמה 1656 ביום 3117 זעם 2195: 22:25 קשר 7195 נביאיה 5030 בתוכה 8432 כארי 738
la' gushmah bayoum za'am. qesher nabiy'ayha batoukah, ka'ariy
**nor rained upon in the day of indignation *There is* a conspiracy of her prophets in the midst thereof like a lion**

שואג 7580 טרף 2963 טרף 2964 נפש 5315 אכלו 398 חסן 2633 ויקר 3366 יקחו 3947 אלמנותיה 490
shou'aeg torep tarep; nepesh 'akalu, chosen uayqar yiqachu, 'almanouteyha
**roaring ravening the prey souls they have devoured the treasure and precious things they have taken widows**

הרבו 7235 בתוכה 8432: 22:26 כהניה 3548 חמסו 2554 תורתי 8451 ויחללו 2490 קדשי 6944
hirbu batoukah. kohaneyha chamasu touratiy uayachallu qadashay
**they have made her many in the midst thereof Her priests have violated my law and have profaned mine holy things**

בין 996 קדש 6944 לחל 2455 לא 3808 הבדילו 914 ובין 996 הטמא 2931 לטהור 2889 לא 3808
beyn qodesh lachol la' hibdiylu, uabeyn hatamea' latahour la'
**between the holy and profane no they have put difference between the unclean and the clean neither**

הודיעו 3034 ומשבתותי 7676 העלימו 5956 עיניהם 5869 ואחל 2490 בתוכם 8432: 22:27 שריה 8269
houdiy'au; uamishabtoutay he'aliymu 'aeyneyhem, ua'aechal batoukam. sareyha
**have they showed *difference* and from my sabbaths have hid their eyes and I am profaned among them Her princes**

בקרבה 7130 כזאבים 2061 טרפי 2963 טרף 2964 לשפך 8210 דם 1818 לאבד 6 נפשות 5315 למען 4616 בצע 1214
baqirbah, kiz'aebiym torapey tarep; lishpak dam la'abed napashout, lama'an batzoa'
**in the midst thereof *are* like wolves ravening the prey to shed blood *and* to destroy souls to get**

בצע 1215: 22:28 ונביאיה 5030 טחו 2902 להם 3807a תפל 8602 חזים 2374 שוא 7723 וקסמים 7080
batza'. uanbiy'ayha, tachu lahem tapel, choziym shau'a, uaqosamiym
**dishonest gain And her prophets have daubed them *with* untempered *morter* seeing vanity and divining**

Eze 22:20 so will I gather you in mine anger and in my fury, and I will leave you there, and melt you.21 Yea, I will gather you, and blow upon you in the fire of my wrath, and you shall be melted in the midst thereof.22 As silver is melted in the midst of the furnace, so shall you be melted in the midst thereof; and you shall know that I YHUH have poured out my fury upon you.23 And the word of YHUH came unto me, saying,24 Son of man, say unto her, Thou are the land that is not cleansed, nor rained upon in the day of indignation.25 There is a conspiracy of her prophets in the midst thereof, like a roaring lion ravening the prey; they have devoured souls; they have taken the treasure and precious things; they have made her many widows in the midst thereof.26 Her priests have violated my law, and have profaned mine holy things: they have put no difference between the holy and profane, neither have they showed difference between the unclean and the clean, and have hid their eyes from my sabbaths, and I am profaned among them.27 Her princes in the midst thereof are like wolves ravening the prey, to shed blood, and to destroy souls, to get dishonest gain.28 And her prophets have daubed them with untempered morter, seeing vanity, and divining lies unto them, saying, Thus saith YHUH G-D, when YHUH has not spoken.

להם 3807a | כזב 3577 | אמרים 559 | כה 3541 | אמר 559 | אדני 136 | יהוה 3069 | ויהוה 3068 | לא 3808 | דבר 1696: | 22:29 | עם 5971 | הארץ 776
lahem | kazab; | 'amariym, | koh | 'amar | 'adonay | Yahuah, | uaYahuah | la' | diber. | | 'am | ha'aretz
**unto them | lies | saying | Thus | saith | Adonai | Yahuah | and Yahuah | not | has spoken | | The people of | the land**

עשקו 6231 | עשק 6233 | וגזלו 1497 | גזל 1498 | ועני 6041 | ואביון 34 | הונו 3238 | ואת 853 | הגר 1616
'ashaqu | 'asheq, | uagazalu | gazel; | ua'aniy | ua'abyoun | hounu, | ua'at | hager
**they have used | oppression | and exercised | robbery | and the poor | and needy | have vexed | *yea* | the stranger**

עשקו 6231 | בלא 3808 | משפט 4941: | 22:30 | ואבקש 1245 | מהם 1992 | איש 376 | גדר 1443 | גדר 1447
'ashaqu | bala' | mishapat. | | aa'abaqesh | mehem | 'aysh | goder | gader
**they have oppressed | in much | wrongfully | | And I sought for | among them | a man | that should make up | the hedge**

ועמד 5975 | בפרץ 6556 | לפני 6440 | בעד 1157 | הארץ 776 | לבלתי 1115 | שחתה 7843 | ולא 3808 | מצאתי 4672: | 22:31
ua'aumed | baperetz | lapanay | ba'ad | ha'aretz | labiltiy | shachatah; | uala' | matza'tiy.
**and stand | in the gap | before me | for | the land | that not | I should destroy it | but none | I found**

ואשפך 8210 | עליהם 5921 | זעמי 2195 | באש 784 | עברתי 5678 | כליתים 3615 | דרכם 1870
ua'ashpok | 'aleyhem | za'amiy, | ba'aesh | 'abratiy | kiliytiym; | darkam
**Therefore have I poured out | upon them | mine indignation | with the fire of | my wrath | I have consumed them | their own way**

בראשם 7218 | נתתי 5414 | נאם 5002 | אדני 136 | יהוה 3069:
bara'sham | natatiy, | na'am | 'adonay | Yahuah.
**upon their heads | have I recompensed | saith | Adonai | Yahuah**

**Ezek 23:1** | ויהי 1961 | דבר 1697 | יהוה 3068 | אלי 413 | לאמר 559: | 23:2 | בן 1121 | אדם 120 | שתים 8147 | נשים 802 | בנות 1323
uayahiy | dabar | Yahuah | 'aelay | lea'mor. | | ben | 'adam; | shatayim | nashiym, | banout
**came again | The word of | Yahuah | unto me | saying | | Son of | man | two | women | the daughters of**

אם 517 | אחת 259 | היו 1961: | 23:3 | ותזנינה 2181 | במצרים 4714 | בנעוריהן 5271 | זנו 2181
'am | 'achat | hayu. | | uatizneynah | bamitzrayim, | bin'auareyhen | zanu;
**mother | one | there were | | And they committed whoredoms | in Egypt | in their youth | they committed whoredoms**

שמה 8033 | מעכו 4600 | שדיהן 7699 | ושם 8033 | עשו 6213 | דדי 1717 | בתוליהן 1331: | 23:4 | ושמותן 8034
mah | mo'aku | shadeyhen, | uasham | 'asu, | dadey | batuleyhen. | | uashmoutan,
**there | were pressed | their breasts | and there | they bruised | the teats of | their virginity | | And the names of them**

אהלה 170 | הגדולה 1419 | ואהליבה 172 | אחותה 269 | ותהיינה 1961 | לי 3807a | ותלדנה 3205 | בנים 1121 | ובנות 1323
'ahalah | hagadoulah | ua'ahaliybah | achoutah, | uatihayeynah | liy, | uateladnah | baniym | uabanout;
***were* Aholah | the elder | and Aholibah | her sister | and they were | mine | and they bare | sons | and daughters**

ושמותן 8034 | שמרון 8111 | אהלה 170 | וירושלם 3389 | אהליבה 172: | 23:5 | ותזן 2181 | אהלה 170
uashmoutan | shomaroun | 'ahalah, | uiyarushalaim | 'ahaliybah. | | uatizen | 'ahalah
**Thus *were* their names | Samaria | *is* Aholah | and Jerusalem | Aholibah | | And played the harlot | Aholah**

תחתי 8478 | ותעגב 5689 | על 5921 | מאהביה 157 | אל 413 | אשור 804 | קרובים 7138: | 23:6 | לבשי 3847
tachtay; | uata'agab | 'al | ma'ahabeyha, | 'al | 'ashur | qaroubiym. | | labushey
**when she was mine | and she doted | on | her lovers | on | the Assyrians *her* neighbours | | *Which were* clothed with**

Eze 22:29 The people of the land have used oppression, and exercised robbery, and have vexed the poor and needy: yea, they have oppressed the stranger wrongfully.30 And I sought for a man among them, that should make up the hedge, and stand in the gap before me for the land, that I should not destroy it: but I found none.31 Therefore have I poured out mine indignation upon them; I have consumed them with the fire of my wrath: their own way have I recompensed upon their heads, saith YHUH G-D. **Eze** 23:1 The word of YHUH came again unto me, saying,2 Son of man, there were two women, the daughters of one mother:3 And they committed whoredoms in Egypt; they committed whoredoms in their youth: there were their breasts pressed, and there they bruised the teats of their virginity.4 And the names of them were Aholah the elder, and Aholibah her sister: and they were mine, and they bare sons and daughters. Thus were their names; Samaria is Aholah, and Jerusalem Aholibah.5 And Aholah played the harlot when she was mine; and she doted on her lovers, on the Assyrians her neighbors,6 Which were clothed with blue, captains and rulers, all of them desirable young men,

| 8504 תכלת | 6346 פחות | 5461 וסגנים | 970 בחורי | 2531 חמד | 3605 כלם | 6571 פרשים | 7392 רכבי | 5483: סוסים | 23:7 5414 ותתן |
|---|---|---|---|---|---|---|---|---|---|
| takelet | pachout | uasganiym, | bachurey | chemed | kulam; | parashiym | rokabey | susiym. | uatiten |
| **blue** | **captains** | **and rulers** | **young men** | **desirable** | **all of them** | **horsemen** | **riding upon** | **horses** | **Thus she committed** |

| 8457 תזנותיה | 5921 עליהם | 4005 מבחר | 1121 בני | 804 אשור | 3605 כלם | 3605 ובכל | 834 אשר | 5689 עגבה | 3605 בכל |
|---|---|---|---|---|---|---|---|---|---|
| taznuteyha | 'aleyhem, | mibchar | baney | 'ashur | kulam; | uabkol | 'asher | 'agabah | bakal |
| **her whoredoms** | **with them** | ***that were* the chosen** | **men of** | **Assyria** | ***with* all them** | **and with all** | ***on* whom** | **she doted** | **with all** |

| 1544 גלוליהם | 2930: נטמאה | 23:8 853 ואת | 8457 תזנותיה | 4714 ממצרים | 3808 לא | 5800 עזבה | 3588 כי | 854 אותה | 7901 שכבו |
|---|---|---|---|---|---|---|---|---|---|
| giluleyhem | nitma'ah. | ua'at | taznuteyha | mimitzrayim | la' | 'azabah, | kiy | 'autah | shakabu |
| **their idols** | **she defiled herself** | ***and*** | **her whoredoms** | ***brought* from Egypt** | **Neither** | **left she** | **for** | **with her** | **they lay** |

| 5271 בנעוריה | 1992 והמה | 6213 עשו | 1717 דדי | 1331 בתוליה | 8210 וישפכו | 8457 תזנותם | 5921: עליה | 23:9 3651 לכן |
|---|---|---|---|---|---|---|---|---|
| bin'aureyha, | uahemah | 'asu | dadey | batuleyha; | uayishpaku | taznutam | 'aeleyha. | laken |
| **in her youth** | **and they** | **bruised** | **the breasts of** | **her virginity** | **and poured** | **their whoredom** | **upon her** | **Wherefore** |

| 5414 נתתיה | 3027 ביד | 157 מאהביה | 3027 ביד | 1121 בני | 804 אשור | 834 אשר | 5689 עגבה | 5921: עליהם | 23:10 |
|---|---|---|---|---|---|---|---|---|---|
| natatiyha | bayad | ma'ahabeyha; | bayad | baney | 'ashur, | 'asher | 'agabah | 'aleyhem. | |
| **I have delivered her** | **into the hand of** | **her lovers** | **into the hand of** | **the sons of** | **Assyrians** | **whom** | **she doted** | **upon** | |

| 1992 המה | 1540 גלו | 6172 ערותה | 1121 בניה | 1323 ובנותיה | 3947 לקחו | 853 ואותה | 2719 בחרב | 2026 הרגו | 1961 ותהי |
|---|---|---|---|---|---|---|---|---|---|
| hemah | gilu | 'aruatah | baneyha | uabnouteyha | laqachu, | ua'atah | bachereb | haragu; | uatahiy |
| **These** | **discovered** | **her nakedness** | **her sons** | **and her daughters** | **they took** | **and her** | **with the sword** | **slew** | **became** |

| 8034 שם | 802 לנשים | 8196 ושפוטים | 6213 עשו | 871a: בה | 23:11 7200 ותרא | 269 אחותה |
|---|---|---|---|---|---|---|
| shem | lanashiym, | uashputiym | 'asu | bah. | uatera' | achoutah |
| **and she became famous** | **among women** | **judgment** | **for they had executed** | **upon her** | **And when saw *this*** | **her sister** |

| 172 אהליבה | 7843 ותשחת | 5691 עגבתה | 4480 ממנה | 853 ואת | 8457 תזנותיה | 2183 מזנוני |
|---|---|---|---|---|---|---|
| 'ahaliybah, | uatashchet | 'agbatah | mimenah; | ua'at | taznuteyha, | miznuney |
| **Aholibah** | **she was more corrupt in** | **her inordinate love** | **than she** | ***and*** | ***in* her whoredoms** | ***in her* whoredoms** |

| 269: אחותה | 23:12 413 אל | 1121 בני | 804 אשור | 5689 עגבה | 6346 פחות | 5461 וסגנים | 7138 קרבים | 3847 לבשי | 4358 מכלול |
|---|---|---|---|---|---|---|---|---|---|
| achoutah. | 'al | baney | 'ashur | 'agabah | pachout | uasganiym | qarobiym | labushey | mikloul, |
| ***more than* her sister** | **upon** | **sons of** | **Assyrians** | **She doted** | **captains** | **and rulers** | ***her* neighbours** | **clothed** | **most gorgeously** |

| 6571 פרשים | 7392 רכבי | 5483 סוסים | 970 בחורי | 2531 חמד | 3605: כלם | 23:13 7200 ואראה | 3588 כי | 2930 נטמאה | 1870 דרך | 259 אחד |
|---|---|---|---|---|---|---|---|---|---|---|
| parashiym | rokbey | susiym; | bachurey | chemed | kulam. | ua'aera' | kiy | nitma'ah; | derek | 'achad |
| **horsemen** | **riding upon** | **horses** | **young men** | **desirable** | **all of them** | **Then I saw** | **that** | **she was defiled** | **way** | **one** |

| 8147: לשתיהן | 23:14 3254 ותוסף | 413 אל | 8457 תזנותיה | 7200 ותרא | 582 אנשי | 2707 מחקה | 5921 על | 7023 הקיר |
|---|---|---|---|---|---|---|---|---|
| lishteyhen. | uatousep | 'al | taznuteyha; | uatera', | 'anshey | machuqeh | 'al | haqiyr, |
| ***that* they *took* both** | **And *that* she increased** | **about** | **her whoredoms** | **for when she saw** | **men** | **pourtrayed** | **upon** | **the wall** |

| 6754 צלמי | 3778 כשדיים | 2710 חקקים | 8350: בששר | 23:15 2289 חגורי | 232 אזור | 4975 במתניהם | 5628 סרוחי |
|---|---|---|---|---|---|---|---|
| tzalmey | kasdiyiym | chaquqiym | bashashar. | chagourey | 'aezour | bamataneyhem, | saruchey |
| **the images of** | **the Chaldeans** | **pourtrayed** | **with vermilion** | **Girded** | **with girdles** | **upon their loins** | **exceeding in** |

Eze 23:6 horsemen riding upon horses.7 Thus she committed her whoredoms with them, with all them that were the chosen men of Assyria, and with all on whom she doted: with all their idols she defiled herself.8 Neither left she her whoredoms brought from Egypt: for in her youth they lay with her, and they bruised the breasts of her virginity, and poured their whoredom upon her.9 Wherefore I have delivered her into the hand of her lovers, into the hand of the Assyrians, upon whom she doted.10 These discovered her nakedness: they took her sons and her daughters, and slew her with the sword: and she became famous among women; for they had executed judgment upon her.11 And when her sister Aholibah saw this, she was more corrupt in her inordinate love than she, and in her whoredoms more than her sister in her whoredoms.12 She doted upon the Assyrians her neighbors, captains and rulers clothed most gorgeously, horsemen riding upon horses, all of them desirable young men.13 Then I saw that she was defiled, that they took both one way,14 And that she increased her whoredoms: for when she saw men pourtrayed upon the wall, the images of the Chaldeans pourtrayed with vermilion,15 Girded with girdles upon their loins, exceeding in dyed attire upon their heads, all of them princes to look to, after the manner of the Babylonians of Chaldea,

| 2871 טבולים | 7218 בראשיהם | 4758 מראה | 7991 שלשים | 3605 כלם | 1823 דמות | 1121 בני | 894 בבל | 3778 כשדים |
|---|---|---|---|---|---|---|---|---|
| tabuliym | bara'sheyhem, | mar'aeh | shalishiym | kulam; | damut | baney | babel | kasdiym, |
| **dyed attire** | **upon their heads** | **to look to** | **princes** | **all of them** | ***after* the manner of** | **sons of** | **Babylonians of** | **Chaldea** |

| 776 ארץ | 4138: מולדתם | **23:16** 5689 ותעגב | 5921 עליהם | 4758 למראה | 5869 עיניה | 7971 ותשלח | 4397 מלאכים |
|---|---|---|---|---|---|---|---|
| 'aretz | mouladtam. | uata'agab | 'aleyhem | lamar'ah | 'aeyneyha; | uatishlach | mal'akiym |
| **the land of** | **their nativity** | **And she doted upon him** | **them** | ***with* as soon as she saw** | **her eyes** | **and sent** | **messengers** |

| 413 אליהם | 3778: כשדימה | **23:17** 935 ויבאו | 413 אליה | 1121 בני | 894 בבל | 4904 למשכב | 1730 דדים | 2930 ויטמאו | 853 אותה |
|---|---|---|---|---|---|---|---|---|---|
| 'aleyhem | kasdiymah. | uayabo'au | 'aeleyha | baney | babel | lamishkab | dodiym, | uayatam'au | 'autah |
| **upon them** | **into Chaldea** | **And came** | **to her** | **sons of** | **Babylonians** | **into the bed of** | **love** | **and they defiled** | **her** |

| 8457 בתזנותם | 2930 ותטמא | 871a בם | 3363 ותקע | 5315 נפשה | 1992: מהם | **23:18** 1540 ותגל |
|---|---|---|---|---|---|---|
| bataznutam; | uatitma' | bam, | uateqa' | napshah | mehem. | uatagal |
| **with their whoredom** | **and she was polluted** | **with them** | **and was alienated** | **her mind** | **from them** | **So she discovered** |

| 8457 תזנותיה | 1540 ותגל | 853 את | 6172 ערותה | 3363 ותקע | 5315 נפשי | 5921 מעליה | 834 כאשר | 5361 נקעה | 5315 נפשי |
|---|---|---|---|---|---|---|---|---|---|
| taznuteyha, | uatagal | 'at | 'aruatah; | uateqa' | napshiy | me'aleyha, | ka'asher | naqa'ah | napshiy |
| **her whoredoms** | **and discovered** | | **her nakedness** | **then was alienated** | **my mind** | **from her** | **like as** | **was alienated** | **my mind** |

| 5921 מעל | 269: אחותה | **23:19** 7235 ותרבה | 853 את | 8457 תזנותיה | 2142 לזכר | 853 את | 3117 ימי | 5271 נעוריה |
|---|---|---|---|---|---|---|---|---|
| me'al | achoutah. | uatarbeh | 'at | taznuteyha; | lizkor | 'at | yamey | na'aureyha, |
| **from** | **her sister** | **Yet she multiplied** | | **her whoredoms** | **in calling to remembrance** | | **the days of** | **her youth** |

| 834 אשר | 2181 זנתה | 776 בארץ | 4714: מצרים | **23:20** 5689 ותעגבה | 5921 על | 6370 פלגשיהם | 834 אשר | 1320 בשר |
|---|---|---|---|---|---|---|---|---|
| 'asher | zanatah | ba'aretz | mitzrayim. | uata'agabah, | 'al | pilagsheyhem; | 'asher | basar |
| **wherein** | **she had played the harlot** | **in the land of** | **Egypt** | **For she doted** | **upon** | **their paramours** | **whose** | **flesh** |

| 2543 חמורים | 1320 בשרם | 2231 וזרמת | 5483 סוסים | 2231: זרמתם | **23:21** 6485 ותפקדי | 853 את |
|---|---|---|---|---|---|---|
| chamouriym | basaram, | uazirmat | susiym | zirmatam. | uatipqadiy, | 'at |
| **asses** | ***is as* the flesh of** | **and whose issue** | **horses** | ***is like* the issue of** | **Thus you called to remembrance *the*** | |

| 2154 זמת | 5271 נעוריך | 6213 בעשות | 4714 ממצרים | 1717 דדיך | 4616 למען | 7699 שדי | 5271: נעוריך | **23:22** 3651 לכן | 172 אהליבה |
|---|---|---|---|---|---|---|---|---|---|
| zimat | na'aurayik; | ba'asout | mimitzrayim | dadayik, | lama'an | shadey | na'aurayik. | laken | 'ahaliybah, |
| **lewdness of** | **your youth** | **in bruising** | **by the Egyptians** | **your teats** | **for** | **the paps of** | **your youth** | **Therefore** | **O Aholibah** |

| 3541 כה | 559 אמר | 136 אדני | 3069 יהוה | 2005 הנני | 5782 מעיר | 853 את | 157 מאהביך | 5921 עליך | 853 את | 834 אשר | 5361 נקעה | 5315 נפשך |
|---|---|---|---|---|---|---|---|---|---|---|---|---|
| koh | 'amar | 'adonay | Yahuah | hinniy | me'ayr | 'at | ma'ahabayik | 'alayik, | 'at | 'asher | naqa'ah | napshek |
| **thus** | **saith** | **Adonai** | **Yahuah** | **Behold I** | **will raise up** | | **your lovers** | **against you** | ***from*** | **whom** | **is alienated** | **your mind** |

| 1992 מהם | 935 והבאתים | 5921 עליך | 5439: מסביב | **23:23** 1121 בני | 894 בבל | 3605 וכל | 3778 כשדים | 6489 פקוד |
|---|---|---|---|---|---|---|---|---|
| mehem; | uahabea'tiym | 'alayik | misabiyb. | baney | babel | uakal | kasdiym, | paqoud |
| **from them** | **and I will bring them** | **against you** | **on every side** | **sons of** | **Babylonians** | **and all** | **the Chaldeans** | **Pekod** |

| 7772 ושוע | 6970 וקוע | 3605 כל | 1121 בני | 804 אשור | 854 אותם | 970 בחורי | 2531 חמד | 6346 פחות | 5461 וסגנים | 3605 כלם | 7991 שלשים |
|---|---|---|---|---|---|---|---|---|---|---|---|
| uashoua' | uaqoua', | kal | baney | 'ashur | 'autam; | bachurey | chemed | pachout | uasganiym | kulam, | shalishiym |
| **and Shoa** | **and Koa *and*** | **all** | **sons of** | **Assyrians** | **with them** | **young men** | **desirable** | **captains** | **and rulers** | **all of them** | **great lords** |

Eze 23:15 the land of their nativity:16 And as soon as she saw them with her eyes, she doted upon them, and sent messengers unto them into Chaldea.17 And the Babylonians came to her into the bed of love, and they defiled her with their whoredom, and she was polluted with them, and her mind was alienated from them.18 So she discovered her whoredoms, and discovered her nakedness: then my mind was alienated from her, like as my mind was alienated from her sister.19 Yet she multiplied her whoredoms, in calling to remembrance the days of her youth, wherein she had played the harlot in the land of Egypt.20 For she doted upon their paramours, whose flesh is as the flesh of asses, and whose issue is like the issue of horses.21 Thus you called to remembrance the lewdness of your youth, in bruising your teats by the Egyptians for the paps of your youth.22 There, O Aholibah, thus saith YHUH G-D; Behold, I will raise up your lovers against you, from whom your mind is alienated, and I will bring them against you on every side;23 The Babylonians, and all the Chaldeans, Pekod, and Shoa, and Koa, and all the Assyrians with them: all of them desirable young men, captains and rulers, great lords and renowned, all of them riding upon horses.

| וקראים 7121 | רכבי 7392 | סוסים 5483 | כלם 3605: | 23:24 | ובאו 935 | עליך 5921 | הצן 2021 | רכב 7393 | וגלגל 1534 |
|---|---|---|---|---|---|---|---|---|---|
| uaqru'aym, | rokbey | susiym | kulam. | | uaba'au | 'alayik | hotzen | rekeb | uagalgal |
| **and renowned** | **riding upon** | **horses** | **all of them** | | **And they shall come** | **against you** | ***with* chariots** | **wagons** | **and wheels** |

| ובקהל 6951 | עמים 5971 | צנה 6793 | ומגן 4043 | וקובע 6959 | ישימו 7760 | עליך 5921 | סביב 5439 | ונתתי 5414 |
|---|---|---|---|---|---|---|---|---|
| uabiqhal | 'amiym, | tzinah | uamagen | uaqouba', | yasiymu | 'alayik | sabiyb; | uanatatiy |
| **and with an assembly of** | **people** | **buckler** | **and shield** | **and helmet** | ***which* shall set** | **against you** | **round about** | **and I will set** |

| לפניהם 6440 | משפט 4941 | ושפטוך 8199 | במשפטיהם 4941: | 23:25 | ונתתי 5414 | קנאתי 7068 | בך 871a |
|---|---|---|---|---|---|---|---|
| lipneyhem | mishapat, | uashpatuk | bamishpateyhem. | | uanatatiy | qin'atiy | bak, |
| **before them** | **judgment** | **and they shall judge you** | **according to their judgments** | | **And I will set** | **my jealousy** | **against you** |

| ועשו 6213 | אותך 854 | בחמה 2534 | אפך 639 | ואזניך 241 | יסירו 5493 | ואחריתך 319 | בחרב 2719 |
|---|---|---|---|---|---|---|---|
| ua'asu | 'autak | bachemah, | 'apek | ua'azanayik | yasiyru, | ua'achariytech | bachereb |
| **and they shall deal** | **with you** | **furiously** | **your nose** | **and your ears** | **they shall take away** | **and your remnant** | **by the sword** |

| תפול 5307 | המה 1992 | בניך 1121 | ובנותיך 1323 | יקחו 3947 | ואחריתך 319 | תאכל 398 | באש 784: | 23:26 |
|---|---|---|---|---|---|---|---|---|
| tipoul; | hemah, | banayik | uabnoutayik | yiqachu, | ua'achariytech | te'akel | ba'aesh. | |
| **shall fall** | **they** | **your sons** | **and your daughters** | **shall take** | **and your residue** | **shall be devoured** | **by the fire** | |

| והפשיטוך 6584 | את 853 | בגדיך 899 | ולקחו 3947 | כלי 3627 | תפארתך 8597: | 23:27 | והשבתי 7673 |
|---|---|---|---|---|---|---|---|
| uahipshiytuk | 'at | bagadayik; | ualaqachu | kaley | tip'artek. | | uahishbatiy |
| **They shall also strip you** | | **out of your clothes** | **and take away** | **jewels** | **your fair** | | **Thus will I make to cease** |

| זמתך 2154 | ממך 4480 | ואת 853 | זנותך 2184 | מארץ 776 | מצרים 4714 | ולא 3808 | תשאי 5375 | עיניך 5869 |
|---|---|---|---|---|---|---|---|---|
| zimatek | mimek, | ua'at | zanutek | me'aretz | mitzrayim; | uala' | tis'ay | 'aeynayik |
| **your lewdness** | **from you** | ***and*** | **your whoredom** | ***brought* from the land of** | **Egypt** | **so that not** | **you shall lift up** | **your eyes** |

| אליהם 413 | ומצרים 4714 | לא 3808 | תזכרי 2142 | עוד 5750: | 23:28 | כי 3588 | כה 3541 | אמר 559 | אדני 136 | יהוה 3068 | הנני 2005 | נתנך 5414 |
|---|---|---|---|---|---|---|---|---|---|---|---|---|
| 'aleyhem, | uamitzrayim | la' | tizkariy | 'aud. | | kiy | koh | 'amar | 'adonay | Yahuah, | hinniy | notanak, |
| **unto them** | **Egypt** | **nor** | **remember** | **any more** | | **For** | **thus** | **saith** | **Adonai** | **Yahuah** | **Behold I** | **will deliver you** |

| ביד 3027 | אשר 834 | שנאת 8130 | ביד 3027 | אשר 834 | נקעה 5361 | נפשך 5315 | מהם 1992: | 23:29 | ועשו 6213 |
|---|---|---|---|---|---|---|---|---|---|
| bayad | 'asher | sana't; | bayad | 'asher | naqa'ah | napshek | mehem. | | ua'asu |
| **into the hand *of them*** | **whom** | **you hate** | **into the hand** | **whom** | **is alienated** | **your mind** | ***of them* whom** | | **And they shall deal** |

| אותך 854 | בשנאה 8135 | ולקחו 3947 | כל 3605 | יגיעך 3018 | ועזבוך 5800 | עירם 5903 | ועריה 6181 | ונגלה 1540 |
|---|---|---|---|---|---|---|---|---|
| autak | basin'ah, | ualaqachu | kal | yagiy'aek, | ua'azabuk | 'ayarim | ua'aryah; | uaniglah |
| **with you** | **hatefully** | **and shall take away** | **all** | **your labour** | **and shall leave you** | **naked** | **and bare** | **and shall be discovered** |

| ערות 6172 | זנוניך 2183 | וזמתך 2154 | ותזנותיך 8457: | 23:30 | עשה 6213 | אלה 428 | לך 3807a |
|---|---|---|---|---|---|---|---|
| 'aruat | zanunayik, | uazimatek | uataznutayik. | | 'asoh | 'aeleh | lak; |
| **the nakedness of** | **your whoredoms** | **both your lewdness** | **and your whoredoms** | | **I will do** | **these *things*** | **unto you** |

| בזנותך 2181 | אחרי 310 | גוים 1471 | על 5921 | אשר 834 | נטמאת 2930 | בגלוליהם 1544: | 23:31 | בדרך 1870 |
|---|---|---|---|---|---|---|---|---|
| biznoutek | 'acharey | gouyim, | 'al | 'asher | nitme'at | bagiluleyhem. | | baderek |
| **because you have gone a whoring** | **after** | ***and* the heathen** | **on** | **because** | **you are polluted** | **with their idols** | | **in the way of** |

Eze 23:24 And they shall come against you with chariots, wagons, and wheels, and with an assembly of people, which shall set against you buckler and shield and helmet round about: and I will set judgment before them, and they shall judge you according to their judgments.25 And I will set my jealousy against you, and they shall deal furiously with you: they shall take away your nose and your ears; and your remnant shall fall by the sword: they shall take your sons and your daughters; and your residue shall be devoured by the fire.26 They shall also strip you out of your clothes, and take away your fair jewels.27 Thus will I make your lewdness to cease from you, and your whoredom brought from the land of Egypt: so that you shall not lift up your eyes unto them, nor remember Egypt anymore.28 For thus saith YHUH G-D; Behold, I will deliver you into the hand of them whom you hate, into the hand of them from whom your mind is alienated:29 And they shall deal with you hatefully, and shall take away all your labour, and shall leave you naked and bare: and the nakedness of your whoredoms shall be discovered, both your lewdness and your whoredoms.30 I will do these things unto you, because you have gone a whoring after the heathen, and because you are polluted with their idols.31 Thou have walked in the way of your sister;

| | | | | | | | | | |
|---|---|---|---|---|---|---|---|---|---|
| 269 אחותך | 1980 הלכת | 5414 ונתתי | 3563 כוסה | 3027 בידך: | 23:32 | 3541 כה | 559 אמר | 136 אדני | 3069 יהוה | 3563 כוס |
| 'achoutek | halakt; | uanatatiy | kousah | bayadek. | | koh | 'amar | 'adonay | Yahuah, | kous |
| **your sister** | **You have walked** | **therefore will I give** | **her cup** | **into your hand** | | **Thus** | **saith** | **Adonai** | **Yahuah** | **cup** |

| | | | | | | | |
|---|---|---|---|---|---|---|---|
| 269 אחותך | 8354 תשתי | 6013 העמקה | 7342 והרחבה | 1961 תהיה | 6712 לצחק | 3932 וללעג | 4767 מרבה |
| achoutek | tishtiy, | ha'amuqah | uaharachabah; | tihayeh | litzchoq | ualla'ag | mirbah |
| **your sister's** | **You shall drink of** | **deep** | **and large** | **you shall be** | **laughed to scorn** | **and had in derision** | **much** |

| | | | | | | | |
|---|---|---|---|---|---|---|---|
| 3557 להכיל: | 23:33 | 7943 שכרון | 3015 ויגון | 4390 תמלאי | 3563 כוס | 8047 שמה | 8077 ושממה |
| lahakiyl. | | shikaroun | uayagoun | timale'ay; | kous | shamah | uashmamah, |
| **it containeth** | | ***with* drunkenness** | **and sorrow** | **You shall be filled** | ***with* the cup of** | **astonishment** | **and desolation** |

| | | | | | | | | |
|---|---|---|---|---|---|---|---|---|
| 3563 כוס | 269 אחותך | 8111 שמרון: | 23:34 | 8354 ושתית | 853 אותה | 4680 ומצית | 853 ואת | 2789 חרשיה |
| kous | 'achoutek | shomaroun. | | uashatiyt | 'autah | uamatziyt, | ua'at | charaseyha |
| ***with* the cup of** | **your sister** | **Samaria** | | **You shall even drink** | **it** | **and suck *it* out** | ***and*** | **the sherds thereof** |

| | | | | | | | | | | | |
|---|---|---|---|---|---|---|---|---|---|---|---|
| 1633 תגרמי | 7699 ושדיך | 5423 תנתקי | 3588 כי | 589 אני | 1696 דברתי | 5002 נאם | 136 אדני | 3069 יהוה: | 23:35 | 3651 לכן | 3541 כה |
| tagaremiy | uashadayik | tenateqiy; | kiy | 'aniy | dibartiy, | na'am | 'adonay | Yahuah. | | laken, | koh |
| **you shall break** | **and your own breasts** | **pluck off** | **for** | **I** | **have spoken** | ***it* saith** | **Adonai** | **Yahuah** | | **Therefore** | **thus** |

| | | | | | | | | | | | | |
|---|---|---|---|---|---|---|---|---|---|---|---|---|
| 559 אמר | 136 אדני | 3069 יהוה | 3282 יען | 7911 שכחת | 853 אותי | 7993 ותשליכי | 853 אותי | 310 אחרי | 1458 גוך | 1571 וגם | 859 את | 5375 שאי |
| 'amar | 'adonay | Yahuah, | ya'an | shakachat | 'autiy, | uatashliykiy | 'autiy | 'acharey | gauek; | uagam | 'at | sa'ay |
| **saith** | **Adonai** | **Yahuah** | **Because** | **you have forgotten** | **me** | **and cast** | **me** | **behind** | **your back** | **therefore also** | ***you*** | **bear** |

| | | | | | | | | | | | |
|---|---|---|---|---|---|---|---|---|---|---|---|
| 2154 זמתך | 853 ואת | 8457 תזנותיך: | 23:36 | 559 ויאמר | 3068 יהוה | 413 אלי | 1121 בן | 120 אדם | 8199 התשפוט | 853 את | 170 אהלה |
| zimatek | ua'at | taznutayik. | | uaya'mer | Yahuah | 'aelay, | ben | 'adam | hatishpout | 'at | 'ahalah |
| **your lewdness** | ***and*** | **your whoredoms** | | **said moreover** | **Yahuah** | **unto me** | **Son of** | **man** | **will you judge** | | **Aholah** |

| | | | | | | | | | |
|---|---|---|---|---|---|---|---|---|---|
| 853 ואת | 172 אהליבה | 5046 והגד | 3807a להן | 853 את | 8441 תועבותיהן: | 23:37 | 3588 כי | 5003 נאפו | 1818 ודם |
| ua'at | 'ahaliybah; | uahaged | lahen, | 'at | tou'abouteyhen. | | kiy | ni'apu, | uadam |
| ***and*** | **Aholibah?** | **yea, declare** | **unto them** | | **their abominations** | | **That** | **they have committed adultery** | **and blood** |

| | | | | | | | | |
|---|---|---|---|---|---|---|---|---|
| 3027 בידיהן | 854 ואת | 1544 גלוליהן | 5003 נאפו | 1571 וגם | 853 את | 1121 בניהן | 834 אשר | 3205 ילדו |
| biydeyhen, | ua'at | giluleyhen | ni'apu; | ua'gam | 'at | baneyhen | 'asher | yaldu |
| ***is* in their hands** | ***and with*** | **their idols** | **have they committed adultery** | **and also** | | **their sons** | **whom** | **they bare** |

| | | | | | | | | |
|---|---|---|---|---|---|---|---|---|
| 3807a לי | 5674 העבירו | 3807a להם | 402 לאכלה: | 23:38 | 5750 עוד | 2063 זאת | 6213 עשו | 3807a לי |
| liy, | he'abiyru | lahem | la'akalah | | 'aud | za't | 'asu | liy; |
| **unto me *the fire*** | **have caused to pass through** | **for them** | **to devour them** | | **Moreover** | **this** | **they have done** | **unto me** |

| | | | | | | | | | |
|---|---|---|---|---|---|---|---|---|---|
| 2930 טמאו | 853 את | 4720 מקדשי | 3117 ביום | 1931 ההוא | 853 ואת | 7676 שבתותי | 2490 חללו: | 23:39 | 7819 ובשחטם |
| tima'au | 'at | miqadashiy | bayoum | hahua', | ua'at | shabtoutay | chilelu. | | uabshachatam |
| **they have defiled** | | **my sanctuary** | **in day** | **the same** | ***and*** | **my sabbaths** | **have profaned** | | **For when they had slain** |

| | | | | | | | | | | |
|---|---|---|---|---|---|---|---|---|---|---|
| 853 את | 1121 בניהם | 1544 לגלוליהם | 935 ויבאו | 413 אל | 4720 מקדשי | 3117 ביום | 1931 ההוא | 2490 לחללו | 2009 והנה | 3541 כה |
| 'at | baneyhem | lagiluleyhem, | uayabo'au | 'al | miqadashiy | bayoum | hahua' | lachallou; | uahineh | koh |
| | **their children** | **to their idols** | **then they came into** | | **my sanctuary** | **day** | **the same** | **to profane it** | **and lo** | **thus** |

Eze 23:31 therefore will I give her cup into your hand.32 Thus saith YHUH G-D; Thou shall drink of your sister's cup deep and large: you shall be laughed to scorn and had in derision; it containeth much.33 Thou shall be filled with drunkenness and sorrow, with the cup of astonishment and desolation, with the cup of your sister Samaria.34 Thou shall even drink it and suck it out, and you shall break the sherds thereof, and pluck off your own breasts: for I have spoken it, saith YHUH G-D.35 Therefore thus saith YHUH G-D; Because you have forgotten me, and cast me behind your back, therefore bear you also your lewdness and your whoredoms.36 YHUH said moreover unto me; Son of man, will you judge Aholah and Aholibah? yea, declare unto them their abominations;37 That they have committed adultery, and blood is in their hands, and with their idols have they committed adultery, and have also caused their sons, whom they bare unto me, to pass for them through the fire, to devour them.38 Moreover this they have done unto me: they have defiled my sanctuary in the same day, and have profaned my sabbaths.39 For when they had slain their children to their idols, then they came the same day into my sanctuary to profane it; and, lo, thus have they done in the midst of mine house.

עשו 6213 | בתוך 8432 | ביתי 1004: | 23:40 ואף 637 | כי 3588 | תשלחנה 7971 | לאנשים 582 | באים 935 | ממרחק 4801
'asu | batouk | beytiy. | ua'ap, | kiy | tishlachnah | la'anashiym, | ba'aym | mimerchaq;
**have they done | in the midst of | mine house | And furthermore | that | you have sent | for men | to come | from far**

אשר 834 | מלאך 4397 | שלוח 7971 | אליהם 413 | והנה 2009 | באו 935 | לאשר 834 | רחצת 7364 | כחלת 3583 | עיניך 5869
'asher | mal'ak | shaluach | 'aleyhem | uahineh | ba'au, | la'asher | rachatzt | kachalt | 'aeynayik
**whom | a messenger | *was* sent | unto whom | and lo | they came | for whom | you did wash | *yourself* paintedst | your eyes**

ועדית 5710 | עדי 5716: | 23:41 וישבת 3427 | על 5921 | מטה 4296 | כבודה 3520 | ושלחן 7979 | ערוך 6186 | לפניה 6440 | וקטרתי 7004
ua'adiyt | 'adiy. | uayashabt | 'al | mitah | kabudah, | uashulchan | 'aruk | lapaneyha; | uaqtaratiy
**and decked *yourself with* ornaments | | And sat | upon | a bed | stately | and a table | prepared | before it | mine incense**

ושמני 8081 | שמת 7760 | עליה 5921: | 23:42 וקול 6963 | המון 1995 | שלו 7961 | בה 871a | ואל 413 | אנשים 582
uashamniy | samta | 'aleyha. | uaqoul | hamoun | shaleu | bah | ua'al | 'anashiym
**and mine oil | you have set | whereupon | And a voice of | a multitude | being at ease | *was* with her | and with | the men**

מרב 7230 | אדם 120 | מובאים 935 | סובאים 5433 | ממדבר 4057 | ויתנו 5414 | צמידים 6781 | אל 413 | ידיהן 3027 | ועטרת 5850
merob | 'adam, | muba'aym | suaba'aym | mimidbar; | uayitanu | tzamiydiym | 'al | yadeyhen, | ua'ateret
**of the common | sort | *were* brought | Sabeans | from the wilderness | which put | bracelets | upon | their hands | and crowns**

תפארת 8597 | על 5921 | ראשיהן 7218: | 23:43 ואמר 559 | לבלה 1087 | נאופים 5004 | עת 6258 | יזנה 2181
tip'aret | 'al | rasheyhen. | ua'amar | labalah | ni'aupiym; | 'ata | yiznuh
**beautiful | upon | their heads | Then said I | unto *her that was* old | *in* adulteries | now | Will they commit**

תזנותה 8457 | והיא 1931: | 23:44 ויבוא 935 | אליה 413 | כבוא 935 | אל 413 | אשה 802
taznuteha | uahiy'a. | uayabou'a | 'aeleyha, | kabou'a | 'al | 'ashah
**whoredoms *with her* | and she *with them*? | Yet they went in | unto her | as they go in | unto | a woman**

זונה 2181 | כן 3651 | באו 935 | אל 413 | אהלה 170 | ואל 413 | אהליבה 172 | אשת 802 | הזמה 2154: | 23:45 ואנשים 582 | צדיקם 6662
zounah; | ken | ba'au, | 'al | 'ahalah | ua'al | 'ahaliybah, | 'ashot | hazimah. | ua'anashiym | tzadiyqiym,
**that playeth the harlot | so | went they in unto | Aholah and unto | Aholibah | women | the lewd | And the men | righteous**

המה 1992 | ישפטו 8199 | אותהם 853 | משפט 4941 | נאפות 5003 | ומשפט 4941 | שפכות 8210 | דם 1818 | כי 3588
hemah | yishpatu | 'autahem, | mishapat | no'apout, | uamishpat | shopakout | dam; | kiy
**they | shall judge | them | *after* the manner of | adulteresses | and after the manner of | women that shed | blood | because**

נאפת 5003 | הנה 2007 | ודם 1818 | בידיהן 3027: | 23:46 כי 3588 | כה 3541 | אמר 559 | אדני 136 | יהוה 3069 | העלה 5927 | עליהם 5921
no'apot | henah, | uadam | biydeyhen. | kiy | koh | 'amar | 'adonay | Yahuah; | ha'aleh | 'aleyhem
***are* adulteresses | they | and blood | *is* in their hands | For | thus | saith | Adonai | Yahuah | I will bring up | upon them**

קהל 6951 | ונתן 5414 | אתהן 853 | לזעוה 2189 | ולבז 957: | 23:47 ורגמו 7275 | עליהן 5921 | אבן 68 | קהל 6951
qahal, | uanaton | 'athen | laza'auah | ualabaz. | uaragamu | 'aleyhen | 'aben | qahal,
**a company | and will give | them | to be removed | and spoiled | And shall stone | them *with* | stones | the company**

וברא 1254 | אותהן 853 | בחרבותם 2719 | בניהם 1121 | ובנותיהם 1323 | יהרגו 2026 | ובתיהן 1004 | באש 784
uabarea' | 'othen | bacharboutam; | baneyhem | uabnouteyhem | yaharogu, | uabateyhen | ba'aesh
**and dispatch them | with their swords | their sons | and their daughters | they shall slay | and their houses | with fire**

Eze 23:40 And furthermore, that you have sent for men to come from far, unto whom a messenger was sent; and, lo, they came: for whom you did wash thyself, paintedst your eyes, and deckedst thyself with ornaments,41 And satest upon a stately bed, and a table prepared before it, whereupon you have set mine incense and mine oil.42 And a voice of a multitude being at ease was with her: and with the men of the common sort were brought Sabeans from the wilderness, which put bracelets upon their hands, and beautiful crowns upon their heads.43 Then said I unto her that was old in adulteries, Will they now commit whoredoms with her, and she with them?44 Yet they went in unto her, as they go in unto a woman that playeth the harlot: so went they in unto Aholah and unto Aholibah, the lewd women.45 And the righteous men, they shall judge them after the manner of adulteresses, and after the manner of women that shed blood; because they are adulteresses, and blood is in their hands.46 For thus saith YHUH G-D; I will bring up a company upon them, and will give them to be removed and spoiled.47 And the company shall stone them with stones, and dispatch them with their swords; they shall slay their sons and their daughters, and burn up their houses with fire.

**23:48**

ישרפו 8313: והשבתי 7673 זמה 2154 מן 4480 הארץ 776 ונוסרו 3256 כל 3605 הנשים 802 ולא 3808 תעשינה 6213

yisropu. uahishbatiy zimah min ha'aretz; uaniuasru kal hanashiym, uala' ta'aseynah

**burn up Thus will I cause to cease lewdness out of the land that may be taught all women and not to do**

**23:49**

כזמתכנה 2154: ונתנו 5414 זמתכנה 2154 עליכן 5921 וחטאי 2399 גלוליכן 1544 תשאינה 5375

kazimatkenah. uanatanu zimatkenah 'aleyken, uachata'aey giluleyken tisa'ynah;

**after your lewdness And they shall recompense your lewdness upon you the sins of your idols and you shall bear**

וידעתם 3045 כי 3588 אני 589 אדני 136 יהוה 3069:

uiyda'tem kiy *'aniy* 'adonay Yahuah.

**and you shall know that *I am* Adonai Yahuah**

**Ezek 24:1**

ויהי 1961 דבר 1697 יהוה 3068 אלי 413 בשנה 8141 התשיעית 8671 בחדש 2320 העשירי 6224 בעשור 6218 לחדש 2320

uayahiy dabar Yahuah 'aelay bashanah hatashiy'ayt bachodesh ha'asiyriy, be'asour lachodesh

**Again came the word of Yahuah unto me in year the ninth in month the tenth in the tenth *day* of the month**

**24:2**

לאמר 559: בן 1121 אדם 120 כתוב 3789 לך 3807a את 853 שם 8034 היום 3117 את 853 עצם 6106 היום 3117 הזה 2088 סמך 5564 מלך 4428

lea'mor. ben 'adam, katub laka 'at shem hayoum, 'at 'atzem hayoum hazeh; samak melek

**saying Son of man write for you the name of the day same day *even of* this set the king of**

**24:3**

בבל 894 אל 413 ירושלם 3389 בעצם 6106 היום 3117 הזה 2088: ומשל 4911 אל 413 בית 1004 המרי 4805 משל 4912 ואמרת 559

babel 'al yarushalaim, ba'atzem hayoum hazeh. uamshol 'al beyt hameriy mashal, ua'amarta

**Babylon *himself* against Jerusalem same day this And utter unto house the rebellious a parable and say**

**24:4**

אליהם 413 כה 3541 אמר 559 אדני 136 יהוה 3069 שפת 8239 הסיר 5518 שפת 8239 וגם 1571 יצק 3332 בו 871a מים 4325: אסף 622

'aleyhem, koh 'amar 'adonay Yahuah; shapot hasiyr shapot, uagam yatzoq bou mayim. 'asop

**unto them Thus saith Adonai Yahuah Set on a pot set *it* on and also pour into it water Gather**

**24:5**

נתחיה 5409 אליה 413 כל 3605 נתח 5409 טוב 2896 ירך 3409 וכתף 3802 מבחר 4005 עצמים 6106 מלא 4390:

natacheyha 'aeleyha, kal netach toub yarek uakatep; mibchar 'atzamiym malea'.

**the pieces thereof into it *even* every piece good the thigh and the shoulder *it* with the choice bones fill**

מבחר 4005 הצאן 6629 לקוח 3947 וגם 1571 דור 1754 העצמים 6106 תחתיה 8478 רתח 7571 רתחיה 7570 גם 1571 בשלו 1310

mibchar hatza'an laqouach, ua'gam dur ha'atzamiym tachteyha; ratach ratacheyha, gam bashalu

**the choice of the flock Take and also burn the bones under it well *and* make it boil moreover let them see**

**24:6**

עצמיה 6106 בתוכה 8432: לכן 3651 כה 3541 אמר 559 אדני 136 יהוה 3069 אוי 188 עיר 5892 הדמים 1818 סיר 5518 אשר 834

'atzameyha batoukah. laken koh 'amar 'adonay Yahuah 'auy 'ayr hadamiym siyr 'asher

**the bones of it therein Wherefore thus saith Adonai Yahuah Woe to city the bloody *to* the pot whose**

חלאתה 2457 בה 871a וחלאתה 2457 לא 3808 יצאה 3318 ממנה 4480 לנתחיה 5409 לנתחיה 5409 הוציאה 3318 לא 3808 נפל 5307

chel'atah bah, uachel'atah, la' yatz'ah mimenah; linatacheyha linatacheyha houtziy'ah, la' napal

**scum of her therein *is* and whose scum of her not is gone out of it piece by piece bring it out no let fall**

**24:7**

עליה 5921 גורל 1486: כי 3588 דמה 1818 בתוכה 8432 היה 1961 על 5921 צחיח 6706 סלע 5553 שמתהו 7760 לא 3808

'aeleyha goural. kiy damah batoukah hayah, 'al tzachiyach sela' samatahu; la'

**up on lot For her blood is in the midst of her is upon the top of a rock she set it not**

Eze 23:48 Thus will I cause lewdness to cease out of the land, that all women may be taught not to do after your lewdness.49 And they shall recompense your lewdness upon you, and you shall bear the sins of your idols: and you shall know that I am YHUH G-D. **Eze** 24:1 Again in the ninth year, in the tenth month, in the tenth day of the month, the word of YHUH came unto me, saying,2 Son of man, write you the name of the day, even of this same day: the king of Babylon set himself against Jerusalem this same day.3 And utter a parable unto the rebellious house, and say unto them, Thus saith YHUH G-D; Set on a pot, set it on, and also pour water into it:4 Gather the pieces thereof into it, even every good piece, the thigh, and the shoulder; fill it with the choice bones.5 Take the choice of the flock, and burn also the bones under it, and make it boil well, and let them seethe the bones of it therein.6 Wherefore thus saith YHUH G-D; Woe to the bloody city, to the pot whose scum is therein, and whose scum is not gone out of it! bring it out piece by piece; let no lot fall up on it.7 For her blood is in the midst of her; she set it upon the top of a rock; she poured it not upon the ground, to cover it with dust;

24:8
שפכתהו 8210 על 5921 הארץ 776 לכסות 3680 עליו 5921 עפר 6083: להעלות 5927 חמה 2534 לנקם 5358 נקם 5359
shapakatahu 'al ha'aretz, lakasout 'alayu 'apar. laha'alout chemah linqom naqam,
**she poured it upon the ground to cover it *with* dust That it might cause to come up fury to take vengeance**

24:9
נתתי 5414 את 853 דמה 1818 על 5921 צחיח 6706 סלע 5553 לבלתי 1115 הכסות 3680: לכן 3651 כה 3541 אמר 559 אדני 136
natatiy 'at damah 'al tzachiyach sala'; labiltiy hikasout. laken, koh 'amar 'adonay
**I have set her blood upon the top of a rock that not it should be covered Therefore thus saith Adonai**

24:10
יהוה 3068 אוי 188 עיר 5892 הדמים 1818 גם 1571 אני 589 אגדיל 1431 המדורה 4071: הרבה 7235 העצים 6086 הדלק 1814 האש 784
Yahuah, 'auy 'ayr hadamiym; gam 'aniy 'agdiyl hamadurah. harbeh ha'aetziym hadaleq ha'aesh,
**Yahuah Woe to city the bloody even I will make great the pile for fire Heap on wood kindle the fire**

24:11
התם 8552 הבשר 1320 והרקח 7543 המרקחה 4841 והעצמות 6106 יחרו 2787: והעמידה 5975 על 5921 גחליה 1513 רקה 7386
hatem habasar; uaharqach hamerqachah, uaha'atzamout yecharu. uaha'amydeha 'al gechaleyha reqah;
**consume the flesh and spice it well and the bones let be burned Then set it upon the coals thereof empty**

למען 4616 תחם 3179 וחרה 2787 נחשתה 5178 ונתכה 5413 בתוכה 8432 טמאתה 2932 תתם 8552
lama'an techam uacharah nachushtah, uanitkah batoukah tum'atah, titum
**that may be hot and may burn the brass of it and may be molten in it *that* the filthiness may be consumed**

24:12
חלאתה 2457: תאנים 8383 הלאת 3811 ולא 3808 תצא 3318 ממנה 4480 רבת 7227 חלאתה 2457
chel'atah. ta'aniym hela'at; uala' tetzea' mimenah rabat chel'atah,
***that* the scum of it (*her*) *herself* with lies She has wearied and not went forth out of her great her scum**

24:13
באש 784 חלאתה 2457: בטמאתך 2932 זמה 2154 יען 3282 טהרתיך 2891 ולא 3808 טהרת 2891
ba'aesh chel'atah. batum'atek zimah; ya'an tihartiyk uala' tahart,
***shall be* in the fire her scum In your filthiness *is* lewdness because I have purged you and not you were purged**

24:14
מטמאתך 2932 לא 3808 תטהרי 2891 עוד 5750 עד 5704 הניחי 5117 את 853 חמתי 2534 בך 871a: אני 589
mitum'atek la' titahariy 'aud, 'ad haniychiy 'at chamatiy bak. 'aniy
**from your filthiness not you shall be purged any more till I have caused to rest my fury upon you I**

יהוה 3068 דברתי 1696 באה 935 ועשיתי 6213 לא 3808 אפרע 6544 ולא 3808 אחוס 2347 ולא 3808
Yahuah dibartiy ba'ah ua'asiytiy, la' 'apra' uala' 'achus uala'
**Yahuah have spoken *it:* it shall come to pass and I will do *it* not I will go back and neither will I spare neither**

24:15
אנחם 5162 כדרכיך 1870 וכעלילותיך 5949 שפטוך 8199 נאם 5002 אדני 136 יהוה 3069:
'anachem; kidrakayik uaka'aliyloutayik shapatuk, na'am 'adonay Yahuah.
**will I repent according to your ways and according to your doings shall they judge you saith Adonai Yahuah**

24:16
ויהי 1961 דבר 1697 יהוה 3068 אלי 413 לאמר 559: בן 1121 אדם 120 הנני 2005 לקח 3947 ממך 4480 את 853 מחמד 4261
uayahiy dabar Yahuah 'aelay lea'mor. ben 'adam hinniy loqeach mimaka 'at machmad
**Also came the word of Yahuah unto me saying Son of man behold I take away from you the desire of**

24:17
עיניך 5869 במגפה 4046 ולא 3808 תספד 5594 ולא 3808 תבכה 1058 ולוא 3808 תבוא 935 דמעתך 1832: האנק 602
'aeyneyka bamagepah; uala' tispod uala' tibkeh, ualou'a tabou'a dim'ateka. he'aneq
**your eyes with a stroke yet neither shall you mourn nor weep neither shall run down your tears to cry**

Eze 24:8 That it might cause fury to come up to take vengeance; I have set her blood upon the top of a rock, that it should not be covered.9 Therefore thus saith YHUH G-D; Woe to the bloody city! I will even make the pile for fire great.10 Heap on wood, kindle the fire, consume the flesh, and spice it well, and let the bones be burned.11 Then set it empty upon the coals thereof, that the brass of it may be hot, and may burn, and that the filthiness of it may be molten in it, that the scum of it may be consumed.12 She has wearied herself with lies, and her great scum went not forth out of her: her scum shall be in the fire.13 In your filthiness is lewdness: because I have purged you, and you were not purged, you shall not be purged from your filthiness anymore, till I have caused my fury to rest upon you.14 I YHUH have spoken it: it shall come to pass, and I will do it; I will not go back, neither will I spare, neither will I repent; according to your ways, and according to your doings, shall they judge you, saith YHUH G-D.15 Also the word of YHUH came unto me, saying,16 Son of man, behold, I take away from you the desire of your eyes with a stroke: yet neither shall you mourn nor weep, neither shall your tears run down.

דם 1826 מתים 4191 אבל 60 לא 3808 תעשה 6213 פארך 6287 חבוש 2280 עליך 5921 ונעליך 5275 תשים 7760
dom, metiym 'abel la' ta'aseh, pa'aeraka chaboush 'alayik, uan'aleyka tasiym
**Forbear *for* the dead mourning no make the tire *of your head* bind upon you and your shoes put on**

ברגליך 7272 ולא 3808 תעטה 5844 על 5921 שפם 8222 ולחם 3899 אנשים 582 לא 3808 תאכל 398: 24:18 ואדבר 1696 אל 413 העם 5971
baragleyka; uala' ta'ateh 'al sapam, ua'alechem 'anashiym la' ta'kel. ua'adaber 'al ha'am
**upon your feet and no cover on *your* lips and the bread of men not eat So I spoke unto the people**

בבקר 1242 ותמת 4191 אשתי 802 בערב 6153 ואעש 6213 בבקר 1242 כאשר 834 צויתי 6680: 24:19 ויאמרו 559 אלי 413
baboqer, uatamat 'ashtiy ba'areb; ua'aas baboqer ka'asher tzueytiy. uaya'maru 'aelay
**in the morning and died my wife at even and I did in the morning as I was commanded And said unto me**

העם 5971 הלא 3808 תגיד 5046 לנו 3807a מה 4100 אלה 428 לנו 3807a כי 3588 אתה 859 עשה 6213: 24:20 ואמר 559 אליהם 413
ha'am; hala' tagiyd lanu mah 'aeleh lanu, kiy 'atah 'aseh. ua'amar 'aleyhem;
**the people not Will you tell us what these *things are* to us that you do *so*? Then I answered them**

דבר 1697 יהוה 3068 היה 1961 אלי 413 לאמר 559: 24:21 אמר 559 לבית 1004 ישראל 3478 כה 3541 אמר 559 אדני 136 יהוה 3069
dabar Yahuah, hayah 'aelay lea'mor. 'amor labeyt yisra'ael, koh 'amar 'adonay Yahuah
**The word of Yahuah came unto me saying Speak unto the house of Israel Thus saith Adonai Yahuah**

הנני 2005 מחלל 2490 את 853 מקדשי 4720 גאון 1347 עזכם 5797 מחמד 4261 עיניכם 5869 ומחמל 4263
hinniy machalel 'at miqadashiy ga'aun 'azkem, machmad 'aeyneykem uamachmal
**Behold I will profane my sanctuary the excellency of your strength the desire of your eyes and that which pities**

נפשכם 5315 ובניכם 1121 ובנותיכם 1323 אשר 834 עזבתם 5800 בחרב 2719 יפלו 5307: 24:22 ועשיתם 6213 כאשר 834
napshakem; uabneykem uabnouteykem 'asher 'azabtem bachereb yipolu. ua'asiytem ka'asher
**your soul and your sons and your daughters whom you have left by the sword shall fall And you shall do as**

עשיתי 6213 על 5921 שפם 8222 לא 3808 תעטו 5844 ולחם 3899 אנשים 582 לא 3808 תאכלו 398: 24:23 ופארכם 6287
'asiytiy; 'al sapam la' ta'atu, ua'alechem 'anashiym la' ta'kelu. uap'aerekem
**I have done on *your* lips not you shall cover and the bread of men nor you eat And your tires *shall be***

על 5921 ראשיכם 7218 ונעליכם 5275 ברגליכם 7272 לא 3808 תספדו 5594 ולא 3808 תבכו 1058 ונמקתם 4743
'al ra'sheykem, uana'aleykem baragleykem, la' tispadu uala' tibku; uanmaqotem
**upon your heads and your shoes upon your feet not you shall mourn nor weep but you shall pine away**

בעונתיכם 5771 ונהמתם 5098 איש 376 אל 413 אחיו 251: 24:24 והיה 1961 יחזקאל 3168 לכם 3807a למופת 4159 ככל 3605 אשר 834
ba'auonoteykem, uanhamtem 'aysh 'al 'achiyu. uahayah yachezqea'l lakem lamoupet, kakol 'asher
**for your iniquities and mourn one toward another Thus is Ezekiel unto you a sign according to all that**

עשה 6213 תעשו 6213 בבאה 935 וידעתם 3045 כי 3588 אני 589 אדני 136 יהוה 3069: 24:25 ואתה 859 בן 1121
'asah ta'asu; babo'ah uiyda'tem kiy 'aniy 'adonay Yahuah. ua'atah ben
**he has done shall you do when this comes and you shall know that I *am* Adonai Yahuah Also you son of**

אדם 120 הלוא 3808 ביום 3117 קחתי 3947 מהם 1992 את 853 מעוזם 4581 משוש 4885 תפארתם 8597 את 853 מחמד 4261
'adam, halou'a, bayoum qachtiy mehem 'at ma'uzam, masous tip'artam; 'at machmad
**man *shall it* not *be* in the day *when* I take from them their strength the joy of their glory the desire of**

Eze 24:17 Forbear to cry, make no mourning for the dead, bind the tire of your head upon you, and put on your shoes upon your feet, and cover not your lips, and eat not the bread of men.18 So I spoke unto the people in the morning: and at even my wife died; and I did in the morning as I was commanded.19 And the people said unto me, Wilt you not tell us what these things are to us, that you does so?20 Then I answered them, The word of YHUH came unto me, saying,21 Speak unto the house of Israel, Thus saith YHUH G-D; Behold, I will profane my sanctuary, the excellency of your strength, the desire of your eyes, and that which your soul pitieth; and your sons and your daughters whom you have left shall fall by the sword.22 And you shall do as I have done: you shall not cover your lips, nor eat the bread of men.23 And your tires shall be upon your heads, and your shoes upon your feet: you shall not mourn nor weep; but you shall pine away for your iniquities, and mourn one toward another.24 Thus Ezekiel is unto you a sign: according to all that he has done shall you do: and when this cometh, you shall know that I am YHUH G-D.25 Also, you son of man, shall it not be in the day when I take from them their strength, the joy of their glory, the desire of their eyes, and that whereupon they set their minds, their sons and their daughters,

עיניהם 5869 ואת 853 משא 4853 נפשם 5315 בניהם 1121 ובנותיהם 1323: 24:26 ביום 3117 ההוא 1931 יבוא 935
'aeyneyhem ua'at masa' napsham, baneyhem uabnouteyhem. bayoum hahua', yabou'a
**their eyes *and* *that whereupon* they set their minds their sons and their daughters *That* in day that shall come**

הפליט 6412 אליך 413 להשמעות 2045 אזנים 241: 24:27 ביום 3117 ההוא 1931 יפתח 6605 פיך 6310 את 853
hapaliyt 'aeleyka; lahashma'aut 'azanayim. bayoum hahua', yipatach piyka 'at
**he that escape unto you to cause *you* to hear *it with your* ears? In day that shall be opened your mouth**

הפליט 6412 ותדבר 1696 ולא 3808 תאלם 481 עוד 5750 והיית 1961 להם 3807a למופת 4159
hapaliyt, uatdaber uala' te'alem 'aud; uahayiyta lahem lamoupet,
**to him which is escaped and you shall speak and no be dumb more and you shall be unto them a sign**

וידעו 3045 כי 3588 אני 589 יהוה 3068:
uayada'aua kiy 'aniy Yahuah.
**and they shall know that I *am* Yahuah**

**Ezek 25:1** ויהי 1961 דבר 1697 יהוה 3068 אלי 413 לאמר 559: 25:2 בן 1121 אדם 120 שים 7760 פניך 6440 אל 413 בני 1121
uayahiy dabar Yahuah 'aelay lea'mor. ben 'adam siym paneyka 'al baney
**came again The word of Yahuah unto me saying Son of man set your face against the sons of**

עמון 5983 והנבא 5012 עליהם 5921: 25:3 ואמרת 559 לבני 1121 עמון 5983 שמעו 8085 דבר 1697 אדני 136 יהוה 3069
'amoun; uahinabea' 'aleyhem. ua'amarta libney 'amoun, shim'au dabar 'adonay Yahuah;
**the Ammonites and prophesy against them And say to the sons of the Ammonites Hear the word of Adonai Yahuah**

כה 3541 אמר 559 אדני 136 יהוה 3069 יען 3282 אמרך 559 האח 1889 אל 413 מקדשי 4720 כי 3588 נחל 2490 ואל 413 אדמת 127
koh 'amar 'adonay Yahuah ya'an 'amarek he'ach 'al miqadashiy kiy nichal, ua'al 'admat
**Thus saith Adonai Yahuah Because you said Aha against my sanctuary when it was profaned and against the land of**

ישראל 3478 כי 3588 נשמה 8074 ואל 413 בית 1004 יהודה 3063 כי 3588 הלכו 1980 בגולה 1473: 25:4 לכן 3651 הנני 2005
yisra'ael kiy nashamah, ua'al beyt yahudah, kiy halaku bagoulah. laken hinniy
**Israel when it was desolate and against the house of Judah when they went into captivity therefore Behold I**

נתנך 5414 לבני 1121 קדם 6924 למורשה 4181 וישבו 3427 טירותיהם 2918 בך 871a ונתנו 5414 בך 871a
notanak libney qedem lamourashah, uayishbu tiyrouteyhem bak, uanatanu bak
**will deliver you to the men of the east for a possession and they shall set their palaces in you and make in you**

משכניהם 4908 המה 1992 יאכלו 398 פריך 6529 והמה 1992 ישתו 8354 חלבך 2461: 25:5 ונתתי 5414 את 853 רבה 7237 לנוה 5116
mishkaneyhem; hemah ya'kalu piryek, uahemah yishtu chalabek. uanatatiy 'at rabah linueh
**their dwellings they shall eat your fruit and they shall drink your milk And I will make Rabbah a stable**

גמלים 1581 ואת 853 בני 1121 עמון 5983 למרבץ 4769 צאן 6629 וידעתם 3045 כי 3588 אני 589 יהוה 3068: 25:6 כי 3588
gamaliym, ua'at baney 'amoun lamirbatz tza'n; uiyda'tem kiy 'aniy Yahuah. kiy
***for* camels *and* the sons of the Ammonites a couchingplace *for* flocks and you shall know that I *am* Yahuah For**

כה 3541 אמר 559 אדני 136 יהוה 3069 יען 3282 מחאך 4222 יד 3027 ורקעך 7554 ברגל 7272 ותשמח 8055 בכל 3605
koh 'amar 'adonay Yahuah, ya'an macha'aka yad, uaraq'aka baragel; uatismach bakal
**thus saith Adonai Yahuah Because you have clapped *your* hands and stamped with the feet and rejoiced with all**

Eze 24:26 That he that escapeth in that day shall come unto you, to cause you to hear it with your ears?27 In that day shall your mouth be opened to him which is escaped, and you shall speak, and be no more dumb: and you shall be a sign unto them; and they shall know that I am YHUH. **Eze** 25:1 The word of YHUH came again unto me, saying,2 Son of man, set your face against the Ammonites, and prophesy against them;3 And say unto the Ammonites, Hear the word of YHUH G-D; Thus saith YHUH G-D; Because you saidst, Aha, against my sanctuary, when it was profaned; and against the land of Israel, when it was desolate; and against the house of Judah, when they went into captivity;4 Behold, therefore I will deliver you to the men of the east for a possession, and they shall set their palaces in you, and make their dwellings in you: they shall eat your fruit, and they shall drink your milk.5 And I will make Rabbah a stable for camels, and the Ammonites a couchingplace for flocks: and you shall know that I am YHUH.6 For thus saith YHUH G-D; Because you have clapped your hands, and stamped with the feet, and rejoiced in heart with all your despite against the land of Israel;

25:7
שאטך 7589 בנפש 5315 אל 413 אדמת 127 ישראל 3478: לכן 3651 הנני 2005 נטיתי 5186 את 853 ידי 3027 עליך 5921
sha'taka banepesh, 'al 'admat yisra'ael. laken hinniy natiytiy 'at yadiy 'alayik,
**your despite in heart against the land of Israel therefore Behold I will stretch out mine hand upon you**

ונתתיך 5414 לבג 897 לגוים 1471 והכרתיך 3772 מן 4480 העמים 5971 והאבדתיך 6 מן 4480
uantatiyka labag lagouyim, uahikratiyka min ha'amiym, uaha'abadtiyka min
**and will deliver you for a spoil to the heathen and I will cut you off from the people and I will cause you to perish out of**

25:8
הארצות 776 אשמידך 8045 וידעת 3045 כי 3588 אני 589 יהוה 3068: כה 3541 אמר 559 אדני 136 יהוה 3069 יען 3282 אמר 559
ha'aratzout; 'ashmiydaka, uayada'ata kiy 'aniy Yahuah. koh 'amar 'adonay Yahuah; ya'an, 'amor
**the countries I will destroy you and you shall know that I *am* Yahuah Thus saith Adonai Yahuah Because do say**

25:9
מואב 4124 ושעיר 8165 הנה 2009 ככל 3605 הגוים 1471 בית 1004 יהודה 3063: לכן 3651 הנני 2005 פתח 6605 את 853
mou'ab uase'ayr, hineh kakal hagouyim beyt yahudah. laken hinniy poteach 'at
***that* Moab and Seir Behold *is* like unto all the heathen the house of Judah Therefore behold I will open**

כתף 3802 מואב 4124 מהערים 5892 מעריו 5892 מקצהו 7097 צבי 6643 ארץ 776 בית 1020
ketep mou'ab mehe'ariym, me'arayu miqatzehu; tzabiy, 'aretz beyt
**the side of Moab from the cities from his cities of him *which are* on his frontiers the glory of the country Beth**

25:10
הישימת 3451 בעל 1186 מעון 4583 וקריתמה 7156 לבני 1121 קדם 6924 על 5921 בני 1121 עמון 5983
hayashimout, ba'al ma'aun uaqiryatamah libney qedem 'al baney 'amoun,
**jeshimoth Baal meon and Kiriathaim Unto the men of the east with the sons of the Ammonites**

25:11
ונתתיה 5414 למורשה 4181 למען 4616 לא 3808 תזכר 2142 בני 1121 עמון 5983 בגוים 1471:
uantatiyha lamourashah; lama'an la' tizaker baney 'amoun bagouyim.
**and will give them in possession that not may be remembered the sons of the Ammonites among the nations**

25:12
ובמואב 4124 אעשה 6213 שפטים 8201 וידעו 3045 כי 3588 אני 589 יהוה 3068: כה 3541 אמר 559 אדני 136 יהוה 3069
uabmou'ab 'aaseh shapatiym; uayada'aua kiy 'aniy Yahuah. koh 'amar 'adonay Yahuah,
**And upon Moab I will execute judgments and they shall know that I *am* Yahuah Thus saith Adonai Yahuah**

יען 3282 עשות 6213 אדום 123 בנקם 5358 נקם 5359 לבית 1004 יהודה 3063 ויאשמו 816 אשום 816
ya'an asout 'adoum binqom naqam labeyt yahudah; uaye'ashmu 'ashoum
**Because has dealt *that* Edom by taking vengeance against the house of Judah and has greatly offended**

25:13
ונקמו 5358 בהם 871a: לכן 3651 כה 3541 אמר 559 אדני 136 יהוה 3069 ונטתי 5186 ידי 3027 על 5921
uaniqmu bahem. laken, koh 'amar 'adonay Yahuah, uanatiytiy yadiy 'al
**and revenged himself upon them Therefore thus saith Adonai Yahuah I will also stretch out mine hand upon**

אדום 123 והכרתי 3772 ממנה 4480 אדם 120 ובהמה 929 ונתתיה 5414 חרבה 2723 מתימן 8487 ודדנה 1719
'adoum, uahikratiy mimenah 'adam uabahemah; uantatiyha charabah miteyman, uadadaneh
**Edom and will cut off from it man and beast and I will make it desolate from Teman and they of Dedan**

25:14
בחרב 2719 יפלו 5307: ונתתי 5414 את 853 נקמתי 5360 באדום 123 ביד 3027 עמי 5971 ישראל 3478
bachereb yipolu. uanatatiy 'at niqmatiy be'adoum, bayad 'amiy yisra'ael,
**by the sword shall fall And I will lay my vengeance upon Edom by the hand of my people Israel**

Eze 25:7 Behold, therefore I will stretch out mine hand upon you, and will deliver you for a spoil to the heathen; and I will cut you off from the people, and I will cause you to perish out of the countries: I will destroy you; and you shall know that I am YHUH.8 Thus saith YHUH G-D; Because that Moab and Seir do say, Behold, the house of Judah is like unto all the heathen;9 Therefore, behold, I will open the side of Moab from the cities, from his cities which are on his frontiers, the glory of the country, Beth-jeshimoth, Baal-meon, and Kiriathaim,10 Unto the men of the east with the Ammonites, and will give them in possession, that the Ammonites may not be remembered among the nations.11 And I will execute judgments upon Moab; and they shall know that I am YHUH.12 Thus saith YHUH G-D; Because that Edom has dealt against the house of Judah by taking vengeance, and has greatly offended, and revenged himself upon them;13 Therefore thus saith YHUH G-D; I will also stretch out mine hand upon Edom, and will cut off man and beast from it; and I will make it desolate from Teman; and they of Dedan shall fall by the sword.14 And I will lay my vengeance upon Edom by the hand of my people Israel: and they shall do in Edom according to mine anger and according to my fury; and they shall know my vengeance, saith YHUH G-D.

ועשו 6213 באדום 123 כאפי 639 וכחמתי 2534 וידעו 3045 את 853 נקמתי 5360

ua'asu be'adoum, ka'apiy uakachamatiy; uayada'aua 'at niqmatiy,

**and they shall do in Edom according to mine anger and according to my fury and they shall know my vengeance**

נאם 5002 אדני 136 יהוה 3068: **25:15** כה 3541 אמר 559 אדני 136 יהוה 3069 יען 3282 עשות 6213 פלשתים 6430 בנקמה 5360 וינקמו 5358

na'am 'adonay Yahuah. koh 'amar 'adonay Yahuah, ya'an asout palishtiym binqamah; uayinaqamu

**saith Adonai Yahuah Thus saith Adonai Yahuah Because have dealt the Philistines by revenge and have taken**

נקם 5359 בשאט 7589 בנפש 5315 למשחית 4889 איבת 342 עולם 5769: **25:16** לכן 3651 כה 3541 אמר 559 אדני 136 יהוה 3069 הנני 2005

naqam bish'at banepesh, lamashchiyt 'aeybat 'aulam. laken, koh 'amar 'adonay Yahuah, hinniy

**vengeance with a despiteful heart to destroy *it* hatred for the old Therefore thus saith Adonai Yahuah Behold**

נוטה 5186 ידי 3027 על 5921 פלשתים 6430 והכרתי 3772 את 853 כרתים 3774 והאבדתי 6 את 853 שארית 7611

nouteh yadiy 'al palishtiym, uahikratiy 'at karetiym; uaha'abadtiy, 'at sha'aeriyt

**I will stretch out mine hand upon the Philistines and I will cut off the Cherethims and destroy the remnant of**

חוף 2348 הים 3220: **25:17** ועשיתי 6213 בם 871a נקמות 5360 גדלות 1419 בתוכחות 8433 חמה 2534 וידעו 3045 כי 3588

choup hayam. ua'asiytiy bam naqamout gadolout, batoukachout chemah; uayada'aua kiy

**coast the sea And I will execute upon them vengeance great with rebukes furious and they shall know that**

אני 589 יהוה 3068 בתתי 5414 את 853 נקמתי 5360 בם 871a:

'aniy Yahuah, batitiy 'at niqmatiy bam.

**I *am* Yahuah when I shall lay my vengeance upon them**

**Ezek 26:1**

ויהי 1961 בעשתי 6249 עשרה 6240 שנה 8141 באחד 259 לחדש 2320 היה 1961 דבר 1697 יהוה 3068

uayahiy ba'ashtey 'asreh shanah ba'achad lachodesh; hayah dabar Yahuah

**And it came to pass in one ten year in the first *day* of the month came *that* the word of Yahuah**

אלי 413 לאמר 559: **26:2** בן 1121 אדם 120 יען 3282 אשר 834 אמרה 559 צר 6865 על 5921 ירושלם 3389 האח 1889 נשברה 7665

'aelay lea'mor. ben 'adam, ya'an 'asher 'amarah tzor 'al yarushalaim he'ach, nishbarah

**unto me saying Son of man because that has said Tyrus against Jerusalem Aha she is broken**

דלתות 1817 העמים 5971 נסבה 5437 אלי 413 אמלאה 4390 החרבה 2717: **26:3** לכן 3651 כה 3541

daltout ha'amiym nasebah 'aelay; 'amala'ah hacharabah. laken, koh

***that was* the gates of the people she is turned unto me I shall be replenished *now* she is laid waste Therefore thus**

אמר 559 אדני 136 יהוה 3069 הנני 2005 עליך 5921 צר 6865 והעליתי 5927 עליך 5921 גוים 1471 רבים 7227

'amar 'adonay Yahuah, hinniy 'alayik tzor; uaha'aleytiy 'alayik gouyim rabiym,

**saith Adonai Yahuah Behold I *am* against you O Tyrus and will cause to come up against you nations many**

כהעלות 5927 הים 3220 לגליו 1530: **26:4** ושחתו 7843 חמות 2346 צר 6865 והרסו 2040 מגדליה 4026

kaha'alout hayam lagalayu. uashichatu choumot tzor, uaharasu migdaleyha,

**cause to come up as the sea his waves And they shall destroy the walls of Tyrus and break down her towers**

וסחיתי 5500 עפרה 6083 ממנה 4480 ונתתי 5414 אותה 853 לצחיח 6706 סלע 5553: **26:5** משטח 4894 חרמים 2764

uasicheytiy 'aparah mimenah; uanatatiy 'autah litzchiyach sala'. mishtach charamiym

**I will also scrape her dust from her and make her like the top of a rock *a place for* the spreading of nets**

Eze 25:15 Thus saith YHUH G-D; Because the Philistines have dealt by revenge, and have taken vengeance with a despiteful heart, to destroy it for the old hatred;16 Therefore thus saith YHUH G-D; Behold, I will stretch out mine hand upon the Philistines, and I will cut off the Cherethims, and destroy the remnant of the sea coast.17 And I will execute great vengeance upon them with furious rebukes; and they shall know that I am YHUH, when I shall lay my vengeance upon them. **Eze** 26:1 And it came to pass in the eleventh year, in the first day of the month, that the word of YHUH came unto me, saying,2 Son of man, because that Tyrus has said against Jerusalem, Aha, she is broken that was the gates of the people: she is turned unto me: I shall be replenished, now she is laid waste:3 Therefore thus saith YHUH G-D; Behold, I am against you, O Tyrus, and will cause many nations to come up against you, as the sea causeth his waves to come up.4 And they shall destroy the walls of Tyrus, and break down her towers: I will also scrape her dust from her, and make her like the top of a rock.5 It shall be a place for the spreading of nets in the midst of the sea: for I have spoken it, saith YHUH G-D: and it shall become a spoil to the nations.

| תהיה 1961 | בתוך 8432 | הים 3220 | כי 3588 | אני 589 | דברתי 1696 | נאם 5002 | אדני 136 | יהוה 3069 | והיתה 1961 | לבז 957 |
|---|---|---|---|---|---|---|---|---|---|---|
| tihayeh | batouk | hayam, | kiy | 'aniy | dibartiy, | na'am | 'adonay | Yahuah; | uahayatah | labaz |
| **It shall be** | **in the midst of** | **the sea** | **for** | **I** | **have spoken** | ***it* saith** | **Adonai** | **Yahuah** | **and it shall become** | **a spoil** |

| לגוים 1471: | 26:6 | ובנותיה 1323 | אשר 834 | בשדה 7704 | בחרב 2719 | תהרגנה 2026 | וידעו 3045 | כי 3588 | אני 589 |
|---|---|---|---|---|---|---|---|---|---|
| lagouyim. | | uabnouteyha | 'asher | basadeh, | bachereb | teharagnah; | uayada'aua | kiy | 'aniy |
| **to the nations** | | **And her daughters** | **which** | ***are* in the field** | **by the sword** | **shall be slain** | **and they shall know** | **that** | **I *am*** |

| יהוה 3068: | 26:7 | כי 3588 | כה 3541 | אמר 559 | אדני 136 | יהוה 3069 | הנני 2005 | מביא 935 | אל 413 | צר 6865 | נבוכדראצר 5019 | מלך 4428 | בבל 894 |
|---|---|---|---|---|---|---|---|---|---|---|---|---|---|
| Yahuah. | | kiy | koh | 'amar | 'adonay | Yahuah, | hinniy | mebiy'a | 'al | tzor, | nabukadra'tzar | melek | babel |
| **Yahuah** | | **For** | **thus** | **saith** | **Adonai** | **Yahuah** | **Behold I** | **will bring** | **upon** | **Tyrus** | **Nebuchadrezzar** | **king of** | **Babylon** |

| 26:8 | מצפון 6828 | מלך 4428 | מלכים 4428 | בסוס 5483 | וברכב 7393 | ובפרשים 6571 | וקהל 6951 | ועם 5971 | רב 7227: |
|---|---|---|---|---|---|---|---|---|---|
| | mitzapoun | melek | melakiym; | basus | uabrekeb | uabparashiym | baqahal | ua'am | rab. |
| | **from the north** | **a king of** | **kings** | **with horses** | **and with chariots** | **and with horsemen** | **and companies** | **and people** | **much** |

| בנותיך 1323 | בשדה 7704 | בחרב 2719 | יהרג 2026 | ונתן 5414 | עליך 5921 | דיק 1785 | ושפך 8210 | עליך 5921 |
|---|---|---|---|---|---|---|---|---|
| banoutayik | basadeh | bachereb | yaharog; | uanatan | 'alayik | dayeq, | uashapak | 'alayik |
| **your daughters** | **in the field** | **with the sword** | **He shall slay** | **and he shall make** | **against you** | **a fort** | **and cast** | **against you** |

| סללה 5550 | והקים 6965 | עליך 5921 | צנה 6793: | 26:9 | ומחי 4239 | קבלו 6904 | יתן 5414 | בחמותיך 2346 | ומגדלתיך 4026 |
|---|---|---|---|---|---|---|---|---|---|
| solalah, | uaheqiym | 'alayik | tzinah. | | uamchiy | qabalou, | yiten | bachomoutayik; | uamigdalotayik, |
| **a mount** | **and lift up** | **against you** | **the buckler** | | **And engines of** | **war** | **he shall set** | **against your walls** | **and your towers** |

| יתץ 5422 | בחרבותיו 2719: | 26:10 | משפעת 8229 | סוסיו 5483 | יכסך 3680 | אבקם 80 |
|---|---|---|---|---|---|---|
| yitotz | bacharboutayu. | | miship'at | susayu | yakasek | 'abaqam; |
| **he shall break down** | **with his axes** | | **By reason of the abundance of** | **his horses** | **shall cover you** | **their dust** |

| מקול 6963 | פרש 6571 | וגלגל 1534 | ורכב 7393 | תרעשנה 7493 | חומותיך 2346 | בבאו 935 |
|---|---|---|---|---|---|---|
| miqoul | parash | uagalgal | uarekeb, | tir'ashnah | choumoutayik, | babo'au |
| **at the noise of** | **the horsemen** | **and of the wheels** | **and of the chariots** | **shall shake** | **your walls** | **when he shall enter** |

| בשעריך 8179 | כמבואי 3996 | עיר 5892 | מבקעה 1234: | 26:11 | בפרסות 6541 | סוסיו 5483 | ירמס 7429 |
|---|---|---|---|---|---|---|---|
| bish'arayik, | kimbou'aey | 'ayr | mabuqa'ah. | | baparsout | susayu, | yirmos |
| **into your gates** | **as men enter into** | **a city** | **wherein is made a breach** | | **With the hoofs of** | **his horses** | **shall he tread down** |

| את 853 | כל 3605 | חוצותיך 2351 | עמך 5971 | בחרב 2719 | יהרג 2026 | ומצבות 4676 | עזך 5797 | לארץ 776 |
|---|---|---|---|---|---|---|---|---|
| 'at | kal | chutzoutayik; | 'amek | bachereb | yaharog, | uamatzabout | 'azek | la'aretz |
| | **all** | **your streets** | **your people** | **by the sword** | **he shall slay** | **and garrisons** | **your strong** | **to the ground** |

| תרד 3381: | 26:12 | ושללו 7997 | חילך 2428 | ובזזו 962 | רכלתך 7404 |
|---|---|---|---|---|---|
| tered. | | uashalalu | cheylek, | uabazazu | rakulatek, |
| **shall go down** | | **And they shall make a spoil of** | **your riches** | **and make a prey of** | **your merchandise** |

| והרסו 2040 | חומותיך 2346 | ובתי 1004 | חמדתך 2532 | יתצו 5422 | ואבניך 68 | ועציך 6086 | ועפרך 6083 |
|---|---|---|---|---|---|---|---|
| uaharasu | choumoutayik, | uabatey | chemdatek | yitotzu; | ua'abanayik | ua'aetzayik | ua'aparek, |
| **and they shall break down** | **your walls** | **and houses** | **your pleasant** | **destroy** | **and your stones** | **and your timber** | **and your dust** |

Eze 26:6 And her daughters which are in the field shall be slain by the sword; and they shall know that I am YHUH.7 For thus saith YHUH G-D; Behold, I will bring upon Tyrus Nebuchadrezzar king of Babylon, a king of kings, from the north, with horses, and with chariots, and with horsemen, and companies, and much people.8 He shall slay with the sword your daughters in the field: and he shall make a fort against you, and cast a mount against you, and lift up the buckler against you.9 And he shall set engines of war against your walls, and with his axes he shall break down your towers.10 By reason of the abundance of his horses their dust shall cover you: your walls shall shake at the noise of the horsemen, and of the wheels, and of the chariots, when he shall enter into your gates, as men enter into a city wherein is made a breach.11 With the hoofs of his horses shall he tread down all your streets: he shall slay your people by the sword, and your strong garrisons shall go down to the ground.12 And they shall make a spoil of your riches, and make a prey of your merchandise: and they shall break down your walls, and destroy your pleasant houses: and they shall lay your stones and your timber and your dust in the midst of the water.

8432 בתוך | 4325 מים | 7760: ישימו | 26:13 7673 והשבתי | 1995 המון | 7892 שיריך | 6963 וקול | 3658 כנוריך
batouk mayim yasiymu. uahishbatiy hamoun shiyrayik; uaqoul kinorayik,
**in the midst of the water they shall lay And I will cause to cease the noise of your songs and the sound of your harps**

3808 לא | 8085 ישמע | 5750: עוד | 26:14 5414 ונתתיך | 6706 לצחיח | 5553 סלע | 4894 משטח | 2764 חרמים
la' yishama' 'aud. uantatiyk litzchiyach sela', mishtach charamiym
**no shall be heard more And I will make you like the top of a rock *a place* to sread upon nets**

1961 תהיה | 3808 לא | 1129 תבנה | 5750 עוד | 3588 כי | 589 אני | 3069 יהוה | 1696 דברתי | 5002 נאם | 136 אדני | 3068: יהוה | 26:15 3541 כה | 559 אמר
tihayeh, la' tibaneh 'aud; kiy 'aniy Yahuah dibartiy, na'am 'adonay Yahuah. koh 'amar
**you shall be no you shall be built more for I Yahuah have spoken *it* saith Adonai Yahuah Thus saith**

136 אדני | 3069 יהוה | 6865 לצור | 3808 הלא | 6963 מקול | 4658 מפלתך | 602 באנק | 2491 חלל | 2026 בהרג | 2027 הרג
'adonay Yahuah latzour; hala' miqoul mapaltek, be'anoq chalal behareg hereg
**Adonai Yahuah to Tyrus not at the sound of your fall when cry *the* wounded when is made the slaughter**

8432 בתוכך | 7493 ירעשו | 339: האיים | 26:16 3381 וירדו | 5921 מעל | 3678 כסאותם | 3605 כל | 5387 נשיאי | 3220 הים
batoukek, yir'ashu ha'ayiym. uayaradu me'al kis'autam, kal nasiy'aey hayam,
**in the midst of you? Shall shake the isles Then shall come down from their thrones all the princes of the sea**

5493 והסירו | 853 את | 4598 מעיליהם | 853 ואת | 899 בגדי | 7553 רקמתם | 6584 יפשטו | 2731 חרדות | 3847 ילבשו
uahesiyru 'at ma'ayleyhem, ua'at bigdey riqmatam yipshotu; charadout yilbashu
**and lay away their robes *and* garments their broidered put off *with* trembling they shall clothe themselves**

5921 על | 776 הארץ | 3427 ישבו | 2729 וחרדו | 7281 לרגעים | 8074 ושממו | 5921: עליך | 26:17 5375 ונשאו
'al ha'aretz yeshebu, uacharadu lirga'aym, uashamamu 'alayik. uanasa'au
**upon the ground they shall sit and shall tremble at *every* moment and be astonished at you And they shall take up**

5921 עליך | 7015 קינה | 559 ואמרו | 3807a לך | 349 איך | 6 אבדת | 3427 נושבת | 3220 מימים | 5892 העיר | 1984 ההללה
'alayik qiynah ua'amaru lak, 'aeyk 'abadt, noushebet miyamiym; ha'ayr hahulalah,
**for you a lamentation and say to you How are you destroyed *that were* inhabited of seafaring men city the renowned**

834 אשר | 1961 היתה | 2389 חזקה | 3220 בים | 1931 היא | 3427 וישביה | 834 אשר | 5414 נתנו | 2851 חתיתם | 3605 לכל | 3427: יושביה | 26:18
'asher hayatah chazaqah bayam hiy'a uayoshabeyha, 'asher natanu chitiytam lakal youshibyah.
**which were strong in the sea she and her inhabitants which cause their terror *to be* on all that haunt it**

6258 עתה | 2729 יחרדו | 339 האין | 3117 יום | 4658 מפלתך | 926 ונבהלו | 339 האיים | 834 אשר | 3220 בים
'atah yechradu ha'ayin, youm mapaltek; uanibhalu ha'ayiym 'asher bayam
**Now shall tremble the isles in the day of your fall yea shall be troubled the isles that *are* in the sea**

3318: מצאתך | 26:19 3588 כי | 3541 כה | 559 אמר | 136 אדני | 3069 יהוה | 5414 בתתי | 854 אתך | 5892 עיר | 2717 נחרבת | 5892 כערים
mitzeatek. kiy koh 'amar 'adonay Yahuah, batitiy 'atak 'ayr necherebet, ke'ariym
**at your departure For thus saith Adonai Yahuah When I shall make you a city desolate like the cities**

834 אשר | 3808 לא | 3427 נושבו | 5927 בהעלות | 5921 עליך | 853 את | 8415 תהום | 3680 וכסוך | 4325 המים | 7227: הרבים
'asher la' noushabu; beha'alout 'alayik 'at tahoum, uakisuk hamayim harabiym.
**that not are inhabited when I shall bring up upon you the deep and shall cover you waters great**

Eze 26:13 And I will cause the noise of your songs to cease; and the sound of your harps shall be no more heard.14 And I will make you like the top of a rock: you shall be a place to spread nets upon; you shall be built no more: for I YHUH have spoken it, saith YHUH G-D.15 Thus saith YHUH G-D to Tyrus; Shall not the isles shake at the sound of your fall, when the wounded cry, when the slaughter is made in the midst of you?16 Then all the princes of the sea shall come down from their thrones, and lay away their robes, and put off their broidered garments: they shall clothe themselves with trembling; they shall sit upon the ground, and shall tremble at every moment, and be astonished at you.17 And they shall take up a lamentation for you, and say to you, How are you destroyed, that were inhabited of seafaring men, the renowned city, which were strong in the sea, she and her inhabitants, which cause their terror to be on all that haunt it!18 Now shall the isles tremble in the day of your fall; yea, the isles that are in the sea shall be troubled at your departure.19 For thus saith YHUH G-D; When I shall make you a desolate city, like the cities that are not inhabited; when I shall bring up the deep upon you, and great waters shall cover you;

**26:20** והורדתיך 3381 את 854 יורדי 3381 בור 953 אל 413 עם 5971 עולם 5769 והושבתיך 3427
uahouradtiyk 'at youradey bour 'al 'am 'aulam, uahoshabtiyk
**When I shall bring you down *with* them that descend into *the* pit with the people of old time and shall set you**

בארץ 776 תחתיות 8482 כחרבות 2723 מעולם 5769 את 854 יורדי 3381 בור 953 למען 4616 לא 3808 תשבי 3427
ba'aretz tachtiyout kacharabout me'aulam 'at youradey bour, lama'an la' tashebiy;
**in the earth the low parts *of* in places desolate of old *with* them that go down to *the* pit that not you be inhabited**

ונתתי 5414 צבי 6643 בארץ 776 חיים 2416: **26:21** בלהות 1091 אתנך 5414 ואינך 369
uanatatiy tzabiy ba'aretz chayiym. balahout 'atnek ua'aeynek;
**and I shall set glory in the land of the living a terror I will make you and you *shall be* no**

ותבקשי 1245 ולא 3808 תמצאי 4672 עוד 5750 לעולם 5769 נאם 5002 אדני 136 יהוה 3069:
uatbuqshiy, uala' timatza'ay 'aud la'aulam, na'am 'adonay Yahuah.
***more* though you be sought for yet never shall you be found again again saith Adonai Yahuah**

**Ezek 27:1** ויהי 1961 דבר 1697 יהוה 3068 אלי 413 לאמר 559: **27:2** ואתה 859 בן 1121 אדם 120 שא 5375 על 5921 צר 6865
uayahiy dabar Yahuah 'aelay lea'mor. ua'atah ben 'adam, sa 'al tzor
**came again The word of Yahuah unto me saying Now you son of man take up for Tyrus**

קינה 7015: **27:3** ואמרת 559 לצור 6865 הישבתי 3427 על 5921 מבואת 3996 ים 3220 רכלת 7402
qiynah. ua'amarta latzour, hayoshebetey 'al mabou'at yam, rokelet
**a lamentation And say unto Tyrus O you that are situate at the entrance of the sea *which are* a merchant of**

העמים 5971 אל 413 איים 339 רבים 7227 כה 3541 אמר 559 אדני 136 יהוה 3068 צור 6865 את 859 אמרת 559 אני 589 כלילת 3632 יפי 3308: **27:4**
ha'amiym, 'al 'ayiym rabiym; koh 'amar 'adonay Yahuah, tzour 'at 'amart, 'aniy kaliylat yopiy.
**the people for isles many Thus saith Adonai Yahuah O Tyrus *you* have said I *am* *of* perfect beauty**

בלב 3820 ימים 3220 גבוליך 1366 בניך 1129 כללו 3634 יפיך 3308: **27:5** ברושים 1265 משניר 8149
baleb yamiym gabulayik; bonayik kalu yapayek. baroushiym misaniyr
***are* in the midst of the seas Your borders your builders have perfected your beauty fir trees of Senir**

בנו 1129 לך 3807a את 853 כל 3605 לחתים 3871 ארז 730 מלבנון 3844 לקחו 3947 לעשות 6213 תרן 8650
ba'nu lak, 'at kal luchotayim; 'arez milabanoun laqachu, la'asout toren
**They have made for you all your *ship* boards of cedars from Lebanon they have taken to make masts**

עליך 5921: **27:6** אלונים 437 מבשן 1316 עשו 6213 משוטיך 4880 קרשך 7175 עשו 6213 שן 8127
'alayik. 'alouniym mibashan, 'asu mishoutayik; qarshek 'asu shen
**for you *Of* the oaks of Bashan have they made your oars your benches have made *of* ivory**

בת 1323 אשרים 839 מאיי 339 כתים 3794 **27:7** שש 8336 ברקמה 7553
bat 'ashuriym, me'ayey kitiym shesh bariqmah
**the company of (*daughter*) the Ashurites *brought* out of the isles of Chittim Fine linen with broidered work**

ממצרים 4714 היה 1961 מפרשך 4666 להיות 1961 לך 3807a לנס 5251 תכלת 8504 וארגמן 713 מאיי 339 אלישה 473
mimitzrayim hayah miprasek, lihayout lak lanes; takelet ua'argaman me'ayey 'aliyshah
**from Egypt was that which you spreadest forth to be to you sail blue and purple from the isles of Elishah**

Eze 26:20 When I shall bring you down with them that descend into the pit, with the people of old time, and shall set you in the low parts of the earth, in places desolate of old, with them that go down to the pit, that you be not inhabited; and I shall set glory in the land of the living;21 I will make you a terror, and you shall be no more: though you be sought for, yet shall you never be found again, saith YHUH G-D. **Eze** 27:1 The word of YHUH came again unto me, saying,2 Now, you son of man, take up a lamentation for Tyrus;3 And say unto Tyrus, O you that are situate at the entry of the sea, which are a merchant of the people for many isles, Thus saith YHUH G-D; O Tyrus, you have said, I am of perfect beauty.4 Thy borders are in the midst of the seas, your builders have perfected your beauty.5 They have made all your ship boards of fir trees of Senir: they have taken cedars from Lebanon to make masts for you.6 Of the oaks of Bashan have they made your oars; the company of the Ashurites have made your benches of ivory, brought out of the isles of Chittim.7 Fine linen with broidered work from Egypt was that which you spreadest forth to be your sail; blue and purple from the isles of Elishah was that which covered you.

27:8

היה 1961 מכסך 4374: ישבי 3427 צידון 6721 וארוד 719 היו 1961 שטים 7751 לך 3807a חכמיך 2450 צור 6865

hayah makasek. yoshabey tziydoun ua'aruad, hayu shatiym lak; chakamayik tzour

**was that which covered you The inhabitants of Zidon and Arvad were mariners to you your wise *men* O Tyrus**

27:9

היו 1961 בך 871a המה 1992 חבליך 2259: זקני 2205 גבל 1380 וחכמיה 2450 היו 1961 בך 871a מחזיקי 2388

hayu bak, hemah chobalayik. ziqney gabal uachakameyha hayu bak, machaziyqey

***that* were in you *were* they your pilots The ancients of Gebal and the wise men thereof were in you repairing**

27:10

בדקך 919 כל 3605 אניות 591 הים 3220 ומלחיהם 4419 היו 1961 בך 871a לערב 6148 מערבך 4627: פרס 6539

bidqek; kal aniyout hayam uamalacheyhem hayu bak, la'arob ma'arabek. paras

**your calkers All the ships of the sea with their mariners were in you to occupy your merchandise *They of* Persia**

ולוד 3865 ופוט 6316 היו 1961 בחילך 2428 אנשי 582 מלחמתך 4421 מגן 4043 וכובע 3553 תלו 8518 בך 871a המה 1992

ua'lud uaput hayu bacheylek, 'anshey milchamtek; magen uakouba' tilu bak, hemah

**and of Lud and of Phut were in your army your men of war the shield and helmet they hanged in you they**

27:11

נתנו 5414 הדרך 1926: בני 1121 ארוד 719 וחילך 2428 על 5921 חומותיך 2346 סביב 5439

natanu hadarek. baney 'aruad uacheylek, 'al choumoutayik sabiyb,

**set forth your comeliness The men of Arvad with your army *were* upon your walls round about**

וגמדים 1575 במגדלותיך 4026 היו 1961 שלטיהם 7982 תלו 8518 על 5921 חומותיך 2346 סביב 5439 המה 1992

uagamadiym, bamigdaloutayik hayu; shilteyhem tilu 'al choumoutayik sabiyb, hemah

**and the Gammadims in your towers were their shields they hanged upon your walls round about they**

27:12

כללו 3634 יפיך 3308: תרשיש 8659 סחרתך 5503 מרב 7230 כל 3605 הון 1952

kalu yapayek. tarshiysh sochartek merob kal houn;

**have made perfect your beauty Tarshish *was* your merchant by reason of the multitude of all *kind of* riches**

27:13

בכסף 3701 ברזל 1270 בדיל 913 ועופרת 5777 נתנו 5414 עזבוניך 5801: יון 3120 תבל 8422 ומשך 4902 המה 1992

bakesep barzel badiyl ua'auperet, natanu 'azbounayik. yauan tubal uameshek, hemah

**with silver iron tin and lead they traded in your fairs Javan Tubal and Meshech they**

27:14

רכליך 7402 בנפש 5315 אדם 120 וכלי 3627 נחשת 5178 נתנו 5414 מערבך 4627: מבית 1004

rokalayik; banepesh 'adam uakley nachoshet, natanu ma'arabek. mibeyt

***were* your merchants the persons of men and vessels of brass they traded *in* your market *They* of the house of**

27:15

תוגרמה 8425 סוסים 5483 ופרשים 6571 ופרדים 6505 נתנו 5414 עזבוניך 5801: בני 1121 דדן 1719 רכליך 7402

tougarmah; susiym uaparashiym uapradiym, natanu 'azbounayik. baney dadan rokalayik,

**Togarmah *with* horses and horsemen and mules traded in your fairs The men of Dedan *were* your merchants**

27:16

איים 339 רבים 7227 סחרת 5506 ידך 3027 קרנות 7161 שן 8127 והובנים 1894 השיבו 7725 אשכרך 814: ארם 758

'ayiym rabiym sachorat yadek; qarnout shen uahoubniym heshiybu 'ashkarek. 'aram

**isles many *were* the merchandise of your hand horns of ivory and ebony they brought you *for* a present Syria**

סחרתך 5503 מרב 7230 מעשיך 4639 בנפך 5306 ארגמן 713 ורקמה 7553

sochartek merob ma'asayik; banopek 'argaman uariqmah

***was* your merchant by reason of the multitude of *the* wares of your making with emeralds purple and broidered work**

Eze 27:8 The inhabitants of Zidon and Arvad were your mariners: your wise men, O Tyrus, that were in you, were your pilots.9 The ancients of Gebal and the wise men thereof were in you your calkers: all the ships of the sea with their mariners were in you to occupy your merchandise.10 They of Persia and of Lud and of Phut were in your army, your men of war: they hanged the shield and helmet in you; they set forth your comeliness.11 The men of Arvad with your army were upon your walls round about, and the Gammadims were in your towers: they hanged their shields upon your walls round about; they have made your beauty perfect.12 Tarshish was your merchant by reason of the multitude of all kind of riches; with silver, iron, tin, and lead, they traded in your fairs.13 Javan, Tubal, and Meshech, they were your merchants: they traded the persons of men and vessels of brass in your market.14 They of the house of Togarmah traded in your fairs with horses and horsemen and mules.15 The men of Dedan were your merchants; many isles were the merchandise of your hand: they brought you for a present horns of ivory and ebony.16 Syria was your merchant by reason of the multitude of the wares of your making: they occupied in your fairs with emeralds, purple, and broidered work, and fine linen, and coral, and agate.

27:17
ובוץ 948 וראמת 7215 וכדכד 3539 נתנו 5414 בעזבוניך 5801: יהודה 3063 וארץ 776 ישראל 3478 המה 1992
uabutz uara'mot uakadkod, natanu ba'azbounayik. yahudah ua'aretz yisra'ael, hemah
**and fine linen and coral and agate they occupied in your fairs Judah and the land of Israel they**

27:18
רכליך 7402 בחטי 2406 מנית 4511 ופנג 6436 ודבש 1706 ושמן 8081 וצרי 6875 נתנו 5414 מערבך 4627:
rokalayik; bachitey miniyt uapanag uadbash uashemen uatzoriy, natanu ma'arabek.
***were* your merchants wheat of Minnith and Pannag and honey and oil and balm they traded in your market**

דמשק 1834 סחרתך 5503 ברב 7230 מעשיך 4639 מרב 7230 כל 3605 הון 1952 ביין 3196
dameseq sochartek barob ma'asayik merob kal houn; bayeyn
**Damascus *was* your merchant in the multitude of the wares of your making for the multitude of all riches in the wine of**

27:19
חלבון 2463 וצמר 6785 צחר 6713: ודן 1835 ויון 3120 מאוזל 235 בעזבוניך 5801 נתנו 5414 ברזל 1270 עשות 6219 קדה 6916
chelboun uatzemer tzachar. uadan uayauan ma'auzal, be'azbounayik natanu; barzel asout qidah
**Helbon and wool white Dan also and Javan going to and fro in your fairs occupied iron bright cassia**

27:20 27:21
וקנה 7070 במערבך 4627 היה 1961: דדן 1719 רכלתך 7402 בבגדי 899 חפש 2667 לרכבה 7396: ערב 6152 וכל 3605
uaqaneh, bama'arabek hayah. dadan rokaltek, babigdey chopesh larikbah. 'arab uakal
**and calamus in your market were Dedan *was* your merchant in clothes precious for chariots Arabia and all**

27:22
נשיאי 5387 קדר 6938 המה 1992 סחרי 5503 ידך 3027 בכרים 3733 ואילים 352 ועתודים 6260 בם 871a סחריך 5503:
nasiy'aey qedar, hemah socharey yadek; bakariym ua'aeyliym ua'atudiym, bam socharayik.
**the princes of Kedar they occupied with you in lambs and rams and goats in these *were they* your merchants**

רכלי 7402 שבא 7614 ורעמה 7484 המה 1992 רכליך 7402 בראש 7218 כל 3605 בשם 1314 ובכל 3605 אבן 68
rokaley shaba' uara'mah, hemah rokalayik; bara'sh kal boshem uabkal 'aben
**The merchants of Sheba and Raamah they *were* your merchants with chief of all spices and with all stones**

27:23
יקרה 3368 וזהב 2091 נתנו 5414 עזבוניך 5801: חרן 2771 וכנה 3656 ועדן 5729 רכלי 7402 שבא 7614 אשור 804
yaqarah uazahab, natanu 'azbounayik. charan uakaneh ua'aden, rokaley shaba'; 'ashur
**precious and gold they occupied in your fairs Haran and Canneh and Eden the merchants of Sheba Asshur**

27:24
כלמד 3638 רכלתך 7402: המה 1992 רכליך 7402 במכללים 4360 בגלומי 1545 תכלת 8504
kilmad rokaltek. hemah rokalayik bamakluliym, bigloumey takelet
***and* Chilmad *were* your merchants These *were* your merchants in all sorts *of things* in clothes blue**

ורקמה 7553 ובגנזי 1595 ברמים 1264 בחבלים 2256 חבשים 2280 וארזים 729
uariqmah, uabginzey baromiym; bachabaliym chabushiym ua'aruziym
**and broidered work and in chests of rich apparel with cords bound and made of cedar**

27:25
במרכלתך 4819: אניות 591 תרשיש 8659 שרותיך 7788 מערבך 4627 ותמלאי 4390
bamarkultek. aniyout tarshiysh, sharoutayik ma'arabek; uatimal'ay
**among your merchandise The ships of Tarshish did sing of you in your market and you were replenished**

27:26
ותכבדי 3513 מאד 3966 בלב 3820 ימים 3220: במים 4325 רבים 7227 הביאוך 935 השטים 7751 אתך 853 רוח 7307
uatikbadiy ma'ad baleb yamiym. bamayim rabiym hebiy'auk, hashatiym 'atak; ruach
**and made glorious very in the midst of the seas into waters great have brought Your rowers you wind**

Eze 27:17 Judah, and the land of Israel, they were your merchants: they traded in your market wheat of Minnith, and Pannag, and honey, and oil, and balm.18 Damascus was your merchant in the multitude of the wares of your making, for the multitude of all riches; in the wine of Helbon, and white wool.19 Dan also and Javan going to and fro occupied in your fairs: bright iron, cassia, and calamus, were in your market.20 Dedan was your merchant in precious clothes for chariots.21 Arabia, and all the princes of Kedar, they occupied with you in lambs, and rams, and goats: in these were they your merchants.22 The merchants of Sheba and Raamah, they were your merchants: they occupied in your fairs with chief of all spices, and with all precious stones, and gold.23 Haran, and Canneh, and Eden, the merchants of Sheba, Assur, and Chilmad, were your merchants.24 These were your merchants in all sorts of things, in blue clothes, and broidered work, and in chests of rich apparel, bound with cords, and made of cedar, among your merchandise.25 The ships of Tarshish did sing of you in your market: and you were replenished, and made very glorious in the midst of the seas.26 Thy rowers have brought you into great waters: the east wind has broken you in the midst of the seas.

| הקדים 6921 | שברך 7665 | בלב 3820 | ימים 3220: | 27:27 הונך 1952 | ועזבוניך 5801 | מערבך 4627 | מלחיך 4419 |
|---|---|---|---|---|---|---|---|
| haqadiym, | shabarek | baleb | yamiym. | hounek | ua'azbounayik, | ma'arabek | malachayik |
| **the east** | **has broken you** | **in the midst of** | **the seas** | **Your riches** | **and your fairs** | **your merchandise** | **your mariners** |

| וחבליך 2259 | מחזיקי 2388 | בדקך 919 | וערבי 6148 | מערבך 4627 | וכל 3605 | אנשי 582 | מלחמתך 4421 | אשר 834 |
|---|---|---|---|---|---|---|---|---|
| uachobalayik; | machaziyqey | bidqek | ua'arabey | ma'arabek | uakal | 'anshey | milchamtek | 'asher |
| **and your pilots** | **repairers** | **of your calkers** | **and the occupiers of** | **your merchandise** | **and all** | **your men of** | **war** | **that** |

| בך 871a | ובכל 3605 | קהלך 6951 | אשר 834 | בתוכך 8432 | יפלו 5307 | בלב 3820 | ימים 3220 | ביום 3117 |
|---|---|---|---|---|---|---|---|---|
| bak, | uabkal | qahalek | 'asher | batoukek, | yiplu | baleb | yamiym, | bayoum |
| ***are* in you** | **and in all** | **your company** | **which** | ***is* in the midst of you** | **shall fall** | **into the midst of** | **the seas** | **in the day of** |

| מפלתך 4658: | 27:28 לקול 6963 | זעקת 2201 | חבליך 2259 | ירעשו 7493 | מגרשות 4054: | 27:29 וירדו 3381 |
|---|---|---|---|---|---|---|
| mapaltek. | laqoul | za'aqat | chobalayik; | yir'ashu | migroshout. | uayaradu |
| **your ruin** | **at the sound of** | **the cry of** | **your pilots** | **shall shake** | **The suburbs** | **And shall come down** |

| מאניותיהם 591 | כל 3605 | תפשי 8610 | משוט 4880 | מלחים 4419 | כל 3605 | חבלי 2259 | הים 3220 | אל 413 | הארץ 776 | יעמדו 5975: | 27:30 |
|---|---|---|---|---|---|---|---|---|---|---|---|
| me'aniyouteyhem, | kal | topasey | mashout, | malachiym | kal | chobaley | hayam; | 'al | ha'aretz | ya'amodu. | |
| **from their ships** | **all** | **that handle** | **the oar** | **the mariners *and*** | **all** | **the pilots of** | **the sea** | **upon** | **the land** | **they shall stand** | |

| והשמיעו 8085 | עליך 5921 | בקולם 6963 | ויזעקו 2199 | מרה 4751 | ויעלו 5927 | עפר 6083 | על 5921 | ראשיהם 7218 |
|---|---|---|---|---|---|---|---|---|
| uahishmiy'au | 'alayik | baqoulam, | uayiz'aqu | marah; | uaya'alu | 'apar | 'al | ra'sheyhem, |
| **And shall cause to be heard** | **against you** | **their voice** | **and shall cry** | **bitterly** | **and shall cast up** | **dust** | **upon** | **their heads** |

| באפר 665 | יתפלשו 6428: | 27:31 והקריחו 7139 | אליך 413 | קרחה 7144 | וחגרו 2296 |
|---|---|---|---|---|---|
| ba'aeper | yitpalashu. | uahiqriychu | 'aelayik | qarachah, | uachagaru |
| **in the ashes** | **they shall wallow themselves** | **And they shall make themselves bald** | **for you** | **utterly** | **and gird them with** |

| שקים 8242 | ובכו 1058 | אליך 413 | במר 4751 | נפש 5315 | מספד 4553 | מר 4751: | 27:32 ונשאו 5375 | אליך 413 |
|---|---|---|---|---|---|---|---|---|
| saqiym; | uabaku | 'aelayik | bamar | nepesh | misped | mar. | uanasa'au | 'alayik |
| **sackcloth** | **and they shall weep** | **for you** | **with bitterness of** | **heart** | **wailing** | ***and* bitter** | **And they shall take up** | **for you** |

| בניהם 5204 | קינה 7015 | וקוננו 6969 | עליך 5921 | מי 4310 | כצור 6865 | כדמה 1822 | בתוך 8432 |
|---|---|---|---|---|---|---|---|
| banyhem | qiynah, | uaqounanu | 'alayik; | miy' | katzour, | kadumah | batouk |
| **in their wailing** | **a lamentation** | **and lament** | **over you *saying*** | **What** | ***city is* like Tyrus** | **like the destroyed** | **in the midst of** |

| הים 3220: | 27:33 בצאת 3318 | עזבוניך 5801 | מימים 3220 | השבעת 7646 | עמים 5971 | רבים 7227 | ברב 7230 | הוניך 1952 |
|---|---|---|---|---|---|---|---|---|
| hayam. | batzea't | 'azbounayik | miyamiym, | hisba'at | 'amiym | rabiym; | barob | hounayik |
| **the sea?** | **When went forth** | **your wares** | **out of the seas** | **you filled** | **people** | **many** | **with the multitude of** | **your riches** |

| ומערביך 4627 | העשרת 6238 | מלכי 4428 | ארץ 776: | 27:34 עת 6256 | נשברת 7665 | מימים 3220 |
|---|---|---|---|---|---|---|
| uama'arabayik, | he'ashart | malkey | 'aretz. | 'at | nishberet | miyamiym |
| **and of your merchandise** | **you did enrich** | **the kings of** | **the earth** | **In the time** | ***when* you shall be broken** | **by the seas** |

| במעמקי 4615 | מים 4325 | מערבך 4627 | וכל 3605 | קהלך 6951 | בתוכך 8432 | נפלו 5307: | 27:35 כל 3605 |
|---|---|---|---|---|---|---|---|
| bama'amaqey | mayim; | ma'arabek | uakal | qahalek | batoukek | napalu. | kal |
| **in the depths of** | **the waters** | **your merchandise** | **and all** | **your company** | **in the midst of you** | **shall fall** | **All** |

Eze 27:27 Thy riches, and your fairs, your merchandise, your mariners, and your pilots, your calkers, and the occupiers of your merchandise, and all your men of war, that are in you, and in all your company which is in the midst of you, shall fall into the midst of the seas in the day of your ruin.28 The suburbs shall shake at the sound of the cry of your pilots.29 And all that handle the oar, the mariners, and all the pilots of the sea, shall come down from their ships, they shall stand upon the land;30 And shall cause their voice to be heard against you, and shall cry bitterly, and shall cast up dust upon their heads, they shall wallow themselves in the ashes:31 And they shall make themselves utterly bald for you, and gird them with sackcloth, and they shall weep for you with bitterness of heart and bitter wailing.32 And in their wailing they shall take up a lamentation for you, and lament over you, saying, What city is like Tyrus, like the destroyed in the midst of the sea?33 When your wares went forth out of the seas, you filledst many people; you did enrich the kings of the earth with the multitude of your riches and of your merchandise.34 In the time when you shall be broken by the seas in the depths of the waters your merchandise and all your company in the midst of you shall fall.

ישבי 3427 האיים 339 שממו 8074 עליך 5921 ומלכיהם 4428 שערו 8175 שער 8178 רעמו 7481
yoshabey ha'ayiym, shamamu 'alayik; uamalkeyhem sa'arou sa'ar, ra'amu
**the inhabitants of the isles shall be astonished at you and their kings afraid shall be sore they shall be troubled in**

פנים 6440: **27:36** סחרים 5503 בעמים 5971 שרקו 8319 עליך 5921 בלהות 1091 היית 1961 ואינך 369 עד 5704
paniym. sochariym ba'amiym, sharaqu 'alayik; balahout hayiyt, ua'aeynek 'ad
***their* countenance The merchants among the people shall hiss at you a terror you shall be and never until**

עולם 5769:
'aulam.
***shall be* any more**

**Ezek 28:1** ויהי 1961 דבר 1697 יהוה 3068 אלי 413 לאמר 559: **28:2** בן 1121 אדם 120 אמר 559 לנגיד 5057 צר 6865 כה 3541
uayahiy dabar Yahuah 'aelay lea'mor. ben 'adam 'amor lingiyd tzor koh
**came again The word of Yahuah unto me saying Son of man say unto the prince of Tyrus Thus**

אמר 559 אדני 136 יהוה 3069 יען 3282 גבה 1361 לבך 3820 ותאמר 559 אל 410 אני 589 מושב 4186 אלהים 430 ישבתי 3427
'amar 'adonay Yahuah ya'an gabah libaka uata'mer 'ael 'aniy, moushab 'alohiym yashabtiy
**saith Adonai Yahuah Because *is* lifted up your heart and you have said *am a* El I *in* the seat of Elohim I sit**

בלב 3820 ימים 3220 ואתה 859 אדם 120 ולא 3808 אל 410 ותתן 5414 לבך 3820 כלב 3820 אלהים 430: **28:3** הנה 2009
baleb yamiym; ua'atah 'adam uala' 'ael, uatiten libaka kaleb 'alohiym. hineh
**in the midst of the seas yet you *are* a man and not El though you set your heart as the heart of Elohim Behold *are***

חכם 2450 אתה 859 מדנאל 1840 כל 3605 סתום 5640 לא 3808 עממוך 6004: **28:4** בחכמתך 2451
chakam 'atah midani'al kal satum la' 'amamuka. bachakamataka
**wiser you than Daniel any of secret *there is* no that they can hide from you With your wisdom**

ובתבונתך 8394 עשית 6213 לך 3807a חיל 2428 ותעש 6213 זהב 2091 וכסף 3701 באוצרותיך 214: **28:5**
uabitabunataka, 'ashiyta laka chayil; uata'as zahab uakesep ba'autzarouteyka.
**and with your understanding you have gotten for you riches and have gotten gold and silver into your treasures**

ברב 7230 חכמתך 2451 ברכלתך 7404 הרבית 7235 חילך 2428 ויגבה 1361 לבבך 3824
barob chakamataka birkulataka hirbiyta cheyleka; uayigbah lababka
**By great your wisdom *and* by your traffick have you increased your riches and is lifted up your heart**

בחילך 2428: **28:6** לכן 3651 כה 3541 אמר 559 אדני 136 יהוה 3069 יען 3282 תתך 5414 את 853 לבבך 3824 כלב 3820
bacheyleka. laken koh 'amar 'adonay Yahuah; ya'an titaka 'at lababka kaleb
**because of your riches Therefore thus saith Adonai Yahuah Because you have set your heart as the heart of**

אלהים 430: **28:7** לכן 3651 הנני 2005 מביא 935 עליך 5921 זרים 2114 עריצי 6184 גוים 1471 והריקו 7324
'alohiym. laken, hinniy mebiy'a 'alayik zariym, 'ariytzey gouyim; uaheriyqu
**Elohim therefore Behold I will bring upon you strangers the terrible of the nations and they shall draw**

חרבותם 2719 על 5921 יפי 3308 חכמתך 2451 וחללו 2490 יפעתך 3314: **28:8** לשחת 7845
charboutam 'al yapiy chakamateka, uachillu yip'ateka. lashachat
**their swords against the beauty of your wisdom and they shall defile your brightness to the pit**

Eze 27:35 All the inhabitants of the isles shall be astonished at you, and their kings shall be sore afraid, they shall be troubled in their countenance.36 The merchants among the people shall hiss at you; you shall be a terror, and never shall be anymore. **Eze** 28:1 The word of YHUH came again unto me, saying,2 Son of man, say unto the prince of Tyrus, Thus saith YHUH G-D; Because your heart is lifted up, and you have said, I am a G-d, I sit in the seat of G-d, in the midst of the seas; yet you are a man, and not G-d, though you set your heart as the heart of G-d:3 Behold, you are wiser than Daniel; there is no secret that they can hide from you:4 With your wisdom and with your understanding you have gotten you riches, and have gotten gold and silver into your treasures:5 By your great wisdom and by your traffick have you increased your riches, and your heart is lifted up because of your riches:6 Therefore thus saith YHUH G-D; Because you have set your heart as the heart of G-d;7 Behold, therefore I will bring strangers upon you, the terrible of the nations: and they shall draw their swords against the beauty of your wisdom, and they shall defile your brightness.8 They shall bring you down to the pit, and you shall die the deaths of them that are slain in the midst of the seas.

| יורדוך 3381 | ומתה 4191 | ממותי 4463 | חלל 2491 | בלב 3820 | ימים 3220: | 28:9 האמר 559 |
|---|---|---|---|---|---|---|
| youriduka; | uamatah | mamoutey | chalal | baleb | yamiym. | he'amour |
| **They shall bring you down** | **and the deaths** | **you shall die of *them that are*** | **slain** | **in the midst of** | **the seas** | **Will you yet** |

| תאמר 559 | אלהים 430 | אני 589 | לפני 6440 | הרגך 2026 | ואתה 859 | אדם 120 | ולא 3808 | אל 410 | ביד 3027 |
|---|---|---|---|---|---|---|---|---|---|
| ta'mar | 'alohiym | 'aniy, | lipney | horageka; | ua'atah | 'adam | uala' | 'al | bayad |
| **say *am*** | **god?** | **I** | **before** | **him that slay you** | **but you *shall be*** | **a man** | **and no** | **El** | **in the hand of** |

| מחלליך 2490: | 28:10 מותי 4194 | ערלים 6189 | תמות 4191 | ביד 3027 | זרים 2114 | כי 3588 | אני 589 | דברתי 1696 |
|---|---|---|---|---|---|---|---|---|
| machalaleyka. | moutey | 'areliym | tamut | bayad | zariym; | kiy | 'aniy | dibartiy, |
| **him that slay you** | **the deaths of** | **the uncircumcised** | **You shall die** | **by the hand of** | **strangers** | **for** | **I** | **have spoken** |

| נאם 5002 | אדני 136 | יהוה 3069: | 28:11 ויהי 1961 | דבר 1697 | יהוה 3068 | אלי 413 | לאמר 559: | 28:12 בן 1121 | אדם 120 | שא 5375 |
|---|---|---|---|---|---|---|---|---|---|---|
| na'am | 'adonay | Yahuah. | uayahiy | dabar | Yahuah | 'aelay | lea'mor. | ben | 'adam | sa' |
| ***it* saith** | **Adonai** | **Yahuah** | **Moreover came** | **the word of** | **Yahuah** | **unto me** | **saying** | **Son of** | **man** | **take up** |

| קינה 7015 | על 5921 | מלך 4428 | צור 6865 | ואמרת 559 | לו 3807a | כה 3541 | אמר 559 | אדני 136 | יהוה 3069 | אתה 859 | חותם 2356 | תכנית 8508 | מלא 4392 |
|---|---|---|---|---|---|---|---|---|---|---|---|---|---|
| qiynah | 'al | melek | tzour; | ua'amarta | lou', | koh | 'amar | 'adonay | Yahuah, | 'atah | choutam | takniyt, | malea' |
| **a lamentation** | **upon** | **the king of** | **Tyrus** | **and say** | **unto him** | **Thus** | **saith** | **Adonai** | **Yahuah** | **You** | **seal up** | **the sum** | **full of** |

| חכמה 2451 | וכליל 3632 | יפי 3308: | 28:13 בעדן 5731 | גן 1588 | אלהים 430 | היית 1961 | כל 3605 | אבן 68 | יקרה 3368 |
|---|---|---|---|---|---|---|---|---|---|
| chakamah | uakliyl | yopiy. | ba'aeden | gan | 'alohiym | hayiyta, | kal | 'aben | yaqarah |
| **wisdom** | **and perfect in** | **beauty** | **in Eden** | **the garden of** | **Elohim** | **You have been** | **every** | **stone** | **precious** |

| מסכתך 4540 | אדם 124 | פטדה 6357 | ויהלם 3095 | תרשיש 8658 | שהם 7718 | וישפה 3471 | ספיר 5601 | נפך 5306 |
|---|---|---|---|---|---|---|---|---|
| mesuchaTecha | 'adem | pitdah | uayahalom, | tarshiysh | shoham | uayashapeh, | sapiyr | nopek, |
| ***was* your covering** | **the sardius** | **topaz** | **and the diamond** | **the beryl** | **the onyx** | **and the jasper** | **the sapphire** | **the emerald** |

| וברקת 1304 | וזהב 2091 | מלאכת 4399 | תפיך 8596 | ונקביך 5345 | בך 871a | ביום 3117 | הבראך 1254 |
|---|---|---|---|---|---|---|---|
| uabaraqat | uazahab; | mala'ket | tupeyka | uanqabeyka | bak, | bayoum | hibara'aka |
| **and the carbuncle** | **and gold** | **the workmanship of** | **your tabrets** | **and of your pipes** | **in you** | **in the day** | **that you were created** |

| כוננו 3559: | 28:14 את 859 | כרוב 3742 | ממשח 4473 | הסוכך 5526 | ונתתיך 5414 | בהר 2022 | קדש 6944 | אלהים 430 |
|---|---|---|---|---|---|---|---|---|
| kounanu. | 'at | karub, | mimshach | hasoukek; | uantatiyka, | bahar | qodesh | 'alohiym |
| **was prepared** | ***You*** | **cherub** | ***are* the anointed** | **that cover** | **and I have set you** | **upon mountain of** | ***the* holy** | **Elohim** |

| היית 1961 | בתוך 8432 | אבני 68 | אש 784 | התהלכת 1980: | 28:15 תמים 8549 | אתה 859 | בדרכיך 1870 |
|---|---|---|---|---|---|---|---|
| hayiyta, | batouk | 'abney | 'aesh | hithalakata. | tamiym | 'atah | bidarakeyka, |
| ***so* you were** | **in the midst of** | **the stones of** | **fire** | **you have walked up and down** | ***were* perfect** | **You** | **in your ways** |

| מיום 3117 | הבראך 1254 | עד 5704 | נמצא 4672 | עולתה 5766 | בך 871a: | 28:16 ברב 7230 | רכלתך 7404 |
|---|---|---|---|---|---|---|---|
| miyoum | hibara'ak; | 'ad | nimtza' | 'aualatah | bak. | barob | rakulataka, |
| **from the day** | **that you were created** | **till** | **was found** | **iniquity** | **in you** | **By the multitude of** | **your merchandise** |

| מלו 4390 | תוכך 8432 | חמס 2555 | ותחטא 2398 | ואחללך 2490 |
|---|---|---|---|---|
| malu | toukaka | chamas | uatechata'; | ua'achalelaka |

**they have filled the midst of you *with* violence and you have sinned therefore I will cast you as profane**

Eze 28:9 Wilt you yet say before him that slayeth you, I am G-d? but you shall be a man, and no G-d, in the hand of him that slayeth you.10 Thou shall die the deaths of the uncircumcised by the hand of strangers: for I have spoken it, saith YHUH G-D.11 Moreover the word of YHUH came unto me, saying,12 Son of man, take up a lamentation upon the king of Tyrus, and say unto him, Thus saith YHUH G-D; Thou sealest up the sum, full of wisdom, and perfect in beauty.13 Thou have been in Eden the garden of G-d; every precious stone was your covering, the sardius, topaz, and the diamond, the beryl, the onyx, and the jasper, the sapphire, the emerald, and the carbuncle, and gold: the workmanship of your tabrets and of your pipes was prepared in you in the day that you were created.14 Thou are the anointed cherub that covereth; and I have set you so: you were upon the holy mountain of G-d; you have walked up and down in the midst of the stones of fire.15 Thou were perfect in your ways from the day that you were created, till iniquity was found in you.16 By the multitude of your merchandise they have filled the midst of you with violence, and you have sinned: therefore I will cast you as profane out of the mountain of G-d: and I will destroy you, O covering cherub, from the midst of the stones of fire.

| מהר 2022 | אלהים 430 | ואבדך 6 | כרוב 3742 | הסכך 5526 | מתוך 8432 | אבני 68 | אש 784: | 28:17 |
|---|---|---|---|---|---|---|---|---|
| mehar | 'alohiym | ua'abedaka | karub | hasokek, | mitouk | 'abney | 'aesh. | |
| **out of the mountain of** | **Elohim** | **and I will destroy you** | **O cherub** | **covering** | **from the midst of** | **the stones of** | **fire** | |

| גבה 1361 | לבך 3820 | ביפיך 3308 | שחת 7843 | חכמתך 2451 | על 5921 | יפעתך 3314 | על 5921 |
|---|---|---|---|---|---|---|---|
| gabah | libaka | bayapayeka, | shichata | chakamataka | 'al | yip'ateka; | 'al |
| **was lifted up** | **Thine heart** | **because of your beauty** | **you have corrupted** | **your wisdom** | **by reason of** | **your brightness** | **to** |

| ארץ 776 | השלכתיך 7993 | לפני 6440 | מלכים 4428 | נתתיך 5414 | לראוה 7200 | בך 871a: | 28:18 | מרב 7230 |
|---|---|---|---|---|---|---|---|---|
| 'aretz | hishlaktiyka, | lipney | malakiym | natatiyka | lara'auah | bak. | | merob |
| **the ground** | **I will cast you** | **before** | **kings** | **I will lay you** | **that they may behold** | **in you** | | **by the multitude of** |

| עוניך 5771 | בעול 5766 | רכלתך 7404 | חללת 2490 | מקדשיך 4720 | ואוצא 3318 | אש 784 |
|---|---|---|---|---|---|---|
| 'aboneyka, | ba'auel | rakulataka, | chilalta | miqadasheyka; | ua'autza' | 'aesh |
| **your iniquities** | **by the iniquity of** | **your traffick** | **You have defiled** | **your sanctuaries** | **therefore will I bring forth** | **a fire** |

| מתוכך 8432 | היא 1931 | אכלתך 398 | ואתנך 5414 | לאפר 665 | על 5921 | הארץ 776 | לעיני 5869 | כל 3605 |
|---|---|---|---|---|---|---|---|---|
| mitoukaka | hiy'a | 'akalataka, | ua'atenaka | la'aeper | 'al | ha'aretz, | la'aeyney | kal |
| **from the midst of you** | **it (*she*)** | **shall devour you** | **and I will bring you** | **to ashes** | **upon** | **the earth** | **in the sight of** | **all** |

| ראיך 7200: | 28:19 | כל 3605 | יודעיך 3045 | בעמים 5971 | שממו 8074 | עליך 5921 | בלהות 1091 | היית 1961 |
|---|---|---|---|---|---|---|---|---|
| ro'ayka. | | kal | youda'ayka | ba'amiym, | shamamu | 'alayik; | balahout | hayiyta, |
| **them that behold you** | | **All** | **they that know you** | **among the people** | **shall be astonished** | **at you** | **a terror** | **you shall be** |

| ואינך 369 | עד 5704 | עולם 5769: | 28:20 | ויהי 1961 | דבר 1697 | יהוה 3068 | אלי 413 | לאמר 559: | 28:21 | בן 1121 | אדם 120 |
|---|---|---|---|---|---|---|---|---|---|---|---|
| ua'aeynaka | 'ad | 'aulam. | | uayahiy | dabar | Yahuah | 'aelay | lea'mor. | | ben | 'adam |
| **and never** | **until** | ***shall you be* any more** | | **Again came** | **the word of** | **Yahuah** | **unto me** | **saying** | | **Son of** | **man** |

| שים 7760 | פניך 6440 | אל 413 | צידון 6721 | והנבא 5012 | עליה 5921: | 28:22 | ואמרת 559 | כה 3541 | אמר 559 | אדני 136 | יהוה 3069 | הנני 2005 |
|---|---|---|---|---|---|---|---|---|---|---|---|---|
| siym | paneyka | 'al | tziydoun; | uahinabea' | 'aleyha. | | ua'amarta, | koh | 'amar | 'adonay | Yahuah, | hinniy |
| **set** | **your face** | **against** | **Zidon** | **and prophesy** | **against it** | | **And say** | **Thus** | **saith** | **Adonai** | **Yahuah** | **Behold I** |

| עליך 5921 | צידון 6721 | ונכבדתי 3513 | בתוכך 8432 | וידעו 3045 | כי 3588 | אני 589 | יהוה 3068 |
|---|---|---|---|---|---|---|---|
| 'alayik | tziydoun, | uanikbadtiy | batoukek; | uayada'aua | kiy | 'aniy | Yahuah |
| ***am* against you** | **O Zidon** | **and I will be glorified** | **in the midst of you** | **and they shall know** | **that** | **I *am*** | **Yahuah** |

| בעשותי 6213 | בה 871a | שפטים 8201 | ונקדשתי 6942 | בה 871a: | 28:23 | ושלחתי 7971 | בה 871a | דבר 1698 |
|---|---|---|---|---|---|---|---|---|
| ba'asoutiy | bah | shapatiym | uanipdashtiy | bah. | | uashilachtiy | bah | deber |
| **when I shall have executed** | **in her** | **judgments** | **and shall be sanctified** | **in her** | | **For I will send** | **into her** | **pestilence** |

| ודם 1818 | בחוצותיה 2351 | ונפלל 5307 | חלל 2491 | בתוכה 8432 | בחרב 2719 | עליה 5921 | מסביב 5439 |
|---|---|---|---|---|---|---|---|
| uadam | bachutzouteyha, | uaniplal | chalal | batoukah, | bachereb | 'aleyha | misabiyb; |
| **and blood** | **into her streets** | **and shall be judged** | **the wounded** | **in the midst of her** | **by the sword** | **upon her** | **on every side** |

| וידעו 3045 | כי 3588 | אני 589 | יהוה 3068: | 28:24 | ולא 3808 | יהיה 1961 | עוד 5750 | לבית 1004 | ישראל 3478 | סלון 5544 | ממאיר 3992 |
|---|---|---|---|---|---|---|---|---|---|---|---|
| uayada'aua | kiy | 'aniy | Yahuah. | | uala' | yihayeh | 'aud | labeyt | yisra'ael, | siloun | mam'ayr |
| **and they shall know that** | | **I *am*** | **Yahuah** | | **And no** | **there shall be** | **more** | **unto the house of** | **Israel** | **a brier** | **pricking** |

Eze 28:17 Thine heart was lifted up because of your beauty, you have corrupted your wisdom by reason of your brightness: I will cast you to the ground, I will lay you before kings, that they may behold you.18 Thou have defiled your sanctuaries by the multitude of your iniquities, by the iniquity of your traffick; therefore will I bring forth a fire from the midst of you, it shall devour you, and I will bring you to ashes upon the earth in the sight of all them that behold you.19 All they that know you among the people shall be astonished at you: you shall be a terror, and never shall you be anymore.20 Again the word of YHUH came unto me, saying,21 Son of man, set your face against Zidon, and prophesy against it,22 And say, Thus saith YHUH G-D; Behold, I am against you, O Zidon; and I will be glorified in the midst of you: and they shall know that I am YHUH, when I shall have executed judgments in her, and shall be sanctified in her.23 For I will send into her pestilence, and blood into her streets; and the wounded shall be judged in the midst of her by the sword upon her on every side; and they shall know that I am YHUH.24 And there shall be no more a pricking brier unto the house of Israel, nor any grieving thorn of all that are round about them, that despised them; and they shall know that I am YHUH G-D.

וקוץ 6975 מכאב 3510 מכל 3605 סביבתם 5439 השאטים 7590 אותם 853 וידעו 3045 כי 3588 אני 589 אדני 136
uaqoutz mak'ab, mikol sabiybotam, hasha'tiym 'autam; uayada'au, kiy 'aniy 'adonay
**nor thorn *any* grieving of all *that are* round about them that despised them and they shall know that I *am* Adonai**

יהוה 3069: **28:25** כה 3541 אמר 559 אדני 136 יהוה 3068 בקבצי 6908 את 853 בית 1004 ישראל 3478 מן 4480 העמים 5971
Yahuah. koh 'amar 'adonay Yahuah baqabtziy 'at beyt yisra'ael, min ha'amiym
**Yahuah Thus saith Adonai Yahuah When I shall have gathered the house of Israel from the people**

אשר 834 נפצו 6327 בם 871a ונקדשתי 6942 בם 871a לעיני 5869 הגוים 1471 וישבו 3427
'asher napotzu bam, uanipdashtiy bam la'aeyney hagouyim; uayashabu
***among* whom they are scattered in them and shall be sanctified in them in the sight of the heathen then shall they dwell**

על 5921 אדמתם 127 אשר 834 נתתי 5414 לעבדי 5650 ליעקב 3290: **28:26** וישבו 3427 עליה 5921 לבטח 983 ובנו 1129
'al 'admatam, 'asher natatiy la'abdiy laya'aqob. uayashabu 'aleyha labetach uabanu
**in their land that I have given to my servant Jacob And they shall dwell therein safely and shall build**

בתים 1004 ונטעו 5193 כרמים 3754 וישבו 3427 לבטח 983 בעשותי 6213 שפטים 8201 בכל 3605
batiym uanata'au karamiym, uayashabu labetach; ba'asoutiy shapatiym, bakal
**houses and plant vineyards yea they shall dwell with confidence when I have executed judgments upon all**

השאטים 7590 אתם 853 מסביבותם 5439 וידעו 3045 כי 3588 אני 589 יהוה 3068 אלהיהם 430:
hasha'tiym 'atam misabiyboutam, uayada'au, kiy 'aniy Yahuah 'aloheyhem.
**those that despise them round about them and they shall know that I *am* Yahuah their Elohim**

**Ezek 29:1** בשנה 8141 העשירית 6224 בעשרי 6224 בשנים 8147 עשר 6240 לחדש 2320 היה 1961 דבר 1697 יהוה 3068 אלי 413
bashanah ha'asiyriyt, ba'asiyriy bishneym 'asar lachodesh; hayah dabar Yahuah 'aelay
**In year the tenth in the tenth *month* in *the* two ten *day* of the month came the word of Yahuah unto me**

לאמר 559: **29:2** בן 1121 אדם 120 שים 7760 פניך 6440 על 5921 פרעה 6547 מלך 4428 מצרים 4714 והנבא 5012 עליו 5921 ועל 5921
lea'mor. ben 'adam siym paneyka, 'al par'ah melek mitzrayim; uahinabea' 'alayu, ua'al
**saying Son of man set your face against Pharaoh king of Egypt and prophesy against him and against**

מצרים 4714 כלה 3605: **29:3** דבר 1696 ואמרת 559 כה 3541 אמר 559 אדני 136 יהוה 3069 הנני 2005 עליך 5921 פרעה 6547 מלך 4428 מצרים 4714
mitzrayim kulah. daber ua'amarta koh 'amar 'adonay Yahuah hinniy 'alayik par'ah melek mitzrayim,
**Egypt all Speak and say Thus saith Adonai Yahuah Behold I *am* against you Pharaoh king of Egypt**

התנים 8577 הגדול 1419 הרבץ 7257 בתוך 8432 יאריו 2975 אשר 834 אמר 559 לי 3807a יארי 2975 ואני 589
hataniym hagadoul, harobetz batouk ya'arayu; 'asher 'amar liy ya'ariy ua'aniy
**dragon the great that lies in the midst of his rivers which has said *is* mine own My river and I**

עשיתני 6213: **29:4** ונתתי 5414 חחיים 2397 בלחייך 3895 והדבקתי 1692 דגת 1710 יאריך 2975
'asiytiniy. uanatatiy chachiyiym bilchayeyka, uahidbaqtiy dagat ya'areyka
**have made it for myself But I will put hooks in your jaws and I will cause to stick the fish of your rivers**

בקשקשתיך 7193 והעליתיך 5927 מתוך 8432 יאריך 2975 ואת 853 כל 3605 דגת 1710 יאריך 2975 בקשקשתיך 7193
baqasqasoteyka; uaha'aliytiyka mitouk ya'areyka, ua'at kal dagat ya'areyka, baqasqasoteyka
**unto your scales and I will bring you up out of the midst of your rivers *and* all the fish of your rivers unto your scales**

Eze 28:25 Thus saith YHUH G-D; When I shall have gathered the house of Israel from the people among whom they are scattered, and shall be sanctified in them in the sight of the heathen, then shall they dwell in their land that I have given to my servant Jacob.26 And they shall dwell safely therein, and shall build houses, and plant vineyards; yea, they shall dwell with confidence, when I have executed judgments upon all those that despise them round about them; and they shall know that I am YHUH their G-d. **Eze** 29:1 In the tenth year, in the tenth month, in the twelfth day of the month, the word of YHUH came unto me, saying,2 Son of man, set your face against Pharaoh king of Egypt, and prophesy against him, and against all Egypt:3 Speak, and say, Thus saith YHUH G-D; Behold, I am against you, Pharaoh king of Egypt, the great dragon that lie in the midst of his rivers, which has said, My river is mine own, and I have made it for myself.4 But I will put hooks in your jaws, and I will cause the fish of your rivers to stick unto your scales, and I will bring you up out of the midst of your rivers, and all the fish of your rivers shall stick unto your scales.

29:5

תדבק 1692: ונטשתיך 5203 המדברה 4057 אותך 853 ואת 853 כל 3605 דגת 1710 יאריך 2975 על 5921 פני 6440

tidbaq. uantashtiyka hamidbarah, 'autaka ua'at kal dagat ya'areyka, 'al paney

**shall stick And I will leave you *thrown into* the wilderness you *and* all the fish of your rivers upon open**

השדה 7704 תפול 5307 לא 3808 תאסף 622 ולא 3808 תקבץ 6908 לחית 2416 הארץ 776 ולעוף 5775

hasadeh tipoul, la' te'asep uala' tiqabetz; lachayat ha'aretz ual'aup

**the fields you shall fall not you shall be brought together nor gathered to the beasts of the field and to the fowls of**

29:6

השמים 8064 נתתיך 5414 לאכלה 402: וידעו 3045 כל 3605 ישבי 3427 מצרים 4714 כי 3588 אני 589 יהוה 3068

hashamayim natatiyka la'akalah uayada'aua kal yoshabey mitzrayim, kiy 'aniy Yahuah;

**the heaven I have given you for meat And shall know all the inhabitants of Egypt that I *am* Yahuah**

29:7

יען 3282 היותם 1961 משענת 4938 קנה 7070 לבית 1004 ישראל 3478: בתפשם 8610 בך 871a בכפך 3709

ya'an hayoutam mish'anet qaneh labeyt yisra'ael. batapasam baka bakapka

**because they have been a staff of reed to the house of Israel When they took hold of you by your hand**

תרוץ 7533 ובקעת 1234 להם 3807a כל 3605 כתף 3802 ובהשענם 8172 עליך 5921 תשבר 7665 והעמדת 5975

teroutz, uabaqa'ata lahem kal katep; uabhisha'anam 'aleyik tishaber, uaha'amadta

**you did break and rend their all shoulder and when they leaned upon you, you brake and made to be at a stand**

29:8

להם 3807a כל 3605 מתנים 4975: לכן 3651 כה 3541 אמר 559 אדני 136 יהוה 3069 הנני 2005 מביא 935 עליך 5921 חרב 2719 והכרתי 3772

lahem kal matanayim. laken, koh 'amar 'adonay Yahuah, hinniy mebiy'a 'alayik chareb; uahikratiy

**their all loins Therefore thus saith Adonai Yahuah Behold I will bring upon you a sword and cut off**

29:9

ממך 4480 אדם 120 ובהמה 929: והיתה 1961 ארץ 776 מצרים 4714 לשממה 8077 וחרבה 2723 וידעו 3045 כי 3588

mimek 'adam uabahemah. uahayatah 'aretz mitzrayim lishmamah uacharabah, uayada'au kiy

**out of you man and beast And will be the land of Egypt shall be desolate and waste and they shall know that**

29:10

אני 589 יהוה 3068 יען 3282 אמר 559 יאר 2975 לי 3807a ואני 589 עשיתי 6213: לכן 3651 הנני 2005 אליך 413

'aniy Yahuah; ya'an 'amar ya'ar liy ua'aniy 'asiytiy. laken hinniy 'aeleyka

**I *am* Yahuah because he has said The river *is* mine and I have made *it* therefore Behold I *am* against you**

ואל 413 יאריך 2975 ונתתי 5414 את 853 ארץ 776 מצרים 4714 לחרבות 2723 חרב 2721 שממה 8077 ממגדל 4024

ua'al ya'areyka; uanatatiy 'at 'aretz mitzrayim, lacharabout choreb shamamah, mimigdol

**and against your rivers and I will make the land of Egypt waste utterly *and* desolate from the tower of**

29:11

סונה 5482 ועד 5704 גבול 1366 כוש 3568: לא 3808 תעבר 5674 בה 871a רגל 7272 אדם 120 ורגל 7272 בהמה 929 לא 3808

saueneh ua'ad gabul kush. la' ta'abar bah regel 'adam, uaregel bahemah la'

**Syene even unto the border of Ethiopia No shall pass through it foot of man foot of beast nor**

29:12

תעבר 5674 בה 871a ולא 3808 תשב 3427 ארבעים 705 שנה 8141: ונתתי 5414 את 853 ארץ 776 מצרים 4714

ta'abar bah; uala' tesheb 'arba'aym shanah. uanatatiy 'at 'aretz mitzrayim

**shall pass through it neither shall it be inhabited forty years And I will make the land of Egypt**

שממה 8077 בתוך 8432 ארצות 776 נשמות 8074 ועריה 5892 בתוך 8432 ערים 5892 מחרבות 2717 תהיין 1961

shamamah batouk 'aratzout nashamout, ua'areyha batouk 'ariym macharabout tihayeyna

**desolate in the midst of the countries *that are* desolate and her cities among the cities *that are* laid waste shall be**

Eze 29:5 And I will leave you thrown into the wilderness, you and all the fish of your rivers: you shall fall upon the open fields; you shall not be brought together, nor gathered: I have given you for meat to the beasts of the field and to the fowls of the heaven.6 And all the inhabitants of Egypt shall know that I am YHUH, because they have been a staff of reed to the house of Israel.7 When they took hold of you by your hand, you did break, and rend all their shoulder: and when they leaned upon you, you brakest, and madest all their loins to be at a stand.8 Therefore thus saith YHUH G-D; Behold, I will bring a sword upon you, and cut off man and beast out of you.9 And the land of Egypt shall be desolate and waste; and they shall know that I am YHUH: because he has said, The river is mine, and I have made it.10 Behold, therefore I am against you, and against your rivers, and I will make the land of Egypt utterly waste and desolate, from the tower of Syene even unto the border of Ethiopia.11 No foot of man shall pass through it, nor foot of beast shall pass through it, neither shall it be inhabited forty years.12 And I will make the land of Egypt desolate in the midst of the countries that are desolate, and her cities among the cities that are laid waste shall be desolate forty years: and I will scatter the Egyptians among the nations, and will disperse them through the countries.

| 8077 שממה | 705 ארבעים | 8141 שנה | 6327 והפצתי | 853 את | 4714 מצרים | 1471 בגוים | 2219 וזריתים |
|---|---|---|---|---|---|---|---|
| shamamah, | 'arba'aym | shanah; | uahapitzotiy | 'at | mitzrayim | bagouyim, | uazeriytiym |
| **desolate** | **forty** | **years** | **and I will scatter** | | **the Egyptians** | **among the nations** | **and will disperse them** |

| 776: בארצות | 29:13 | 3588 כי | 3541 כה | 559 אמר | 136 אדני | 3069 יהוה | 7093 מקץ | 705 ארבעים | 8141 שנה | 6908 אקבץ | 853 את |
|---|---|---|---|---|---|---|---|---|---|---|---|
| ba'aratzout. | | kiy | koh | 'amar | 'adonay | Yahuah; | miqetz | 'arba'aym | shanah | 'aqabetz | 'at |
| **through the countries** | | **Yet** | **thus** | **saith** | **Adonai** | **Yahuah** | **At the end of** | **forty** | **years** | **will I gather** | |

| 4714 מצרים | 4480 מן | 5971 העמים | 834 אשר | 6327 נפצו | 8033: שמה | 29:14 | 7725 ושבתי | 853 את | 7622 שבות |
|---|---|---|---|---|---|---|---|---|---|
| mitzrayim, | min | ha'amiym | 'asher | napotzu | shamah. | | uashabtiy | 'at | shabut |
| **the Egyptians** | **from** | **the people** | **where** | **they were scattered** | **there** | | **And I will bring again** | | **the captivity of** |

| 4714 מצרים | 7725 והשבתי | 853 אתם | 776 ארץ | 6624 פתרוס | 5921 על | 776 ארץ | 4351 מכורתם | 1961 והיו |
|---|---|---|---|---|---|---|---|---|
| mitzrayim, | uahashibotiy | 'atam | 'aretz | patrous, | 'al | 'aretz | makuratam; | uahayu |
| **Egypt** | **and will cause to return** | **them** | ***into* the land of** | **Pathros** | **into** | **the land of** | **their habitation** | **and they shall be** |

| 8033 שם | 4467 ממלכה | 8217: שפלה | 29:15 | 4480 מן | 4467 הממלכות | 1961 תהיה | 8217 שפלה | 3808 ולא | 5375 תתנשא | 5750 עוד | 5921 על |
|---|---|---|---|---|---|---|---|---|---|---|---|
| sham | mamlakah | shapalah. | | min | hamamlakout | tihayeh | shapalah, | uala' | titnasea' | 'aud | 'al |
| **there** | **a kingdom** | **base** | | **of** | **the kingdoms** | **It shall be** | **the basest** | **neither** | **shall it exalt itself** | **any more** | **above** |

| 1471 הגוים | 4591 והמעטתים | 1115 לבלתי | 7287 רדות | 1471: בגוים | 29:16 | 3808 ולא | 1961 יהיה | 5750 עוד |
|---|---|---|---|---|---|---|---|---|
| hagouyim; | uahim'attiym, | labiltiy | radout | bagouyim. | | uala' | yihayeh | 'aud |
| **the nations** | **for I will diminish them** | **that no more** | **they shall rule** | **over the nations** | | **And no** | **it shall be** | **more** |

| 1004 לבית | 3478 ישראל | 4009 למבטח | 2142 מזכיר | 5771 עון | 6437 בפנותם | 310 אחריהם |
|---|---|---|---|---|---|---|
| labeyt | yisra'ael | lamibtach | mazkiyr | 'auon, | bipanoutam | 'achareyhem; |
| **of the house of** | **Israel** | **the confidence** | **which bring to remembrance** | ***their* iniquity** | **when they shall look** | **after them** |

| 3045 וידעו | 3588 כי | 589 אני | 136 אדני | 3068: יהוה | 29:17 | 1961 ויהי | 6242 בעשרים | 7651 ושבע | 8141 שנה | 7223 בראשון |
|---|---|---|---|---|---|---|---|---|---|---|
| uayada'au, | kiy | 'aniy | 'adonay | Yahuah. | | uayahiy, | ba'asriym | uasheba' | shanah, | bara'shoun |
| **but they shall know** | **that** | **I *am*** | **Adonai** | **Yahuah** | | **And it came to pass** | **in twentieth** | **and the seven** | **year** | **in the first** |

| 259 באחד | 2320 לחדש | 1961 היה | 1697 דבר | 3068 יהוה | 413 אלי | 559: לאמר | 29:18 | 1121 בן | 120 אדם | 5019 נבוכדראצר |
|---|---|---|---|---|---|---|---|---|---|---|
| ba'achad | lachodesh; | hayah | dabar | Yahuah | 'aelay | lea'mor. | | ben | 'adam, | nabukadra'tzar |
| ***month* in the first** | ***day* of the month** | **came** | **the word of** | **Yahuah** | **unto me** | **saying** | | **Son of** | **man** | **Nebuchadrezzar** |

| 4428 מלך | 894 בבל | 5647 העביד | 853 את | 2428 חילו | 5656 עבדה | 1419 גדלה | 413 אל | 6865 צר | 3605 כל | 7218 ראש | 7139 מקרח | 3605 וכל |
|---|---|---|---|---|---|---|---|---|---|---|---|---|
| melek | babel | he'abiyd | 'at | cheylou | 'abodah | gadolah | 'al | tzor, | kal | ra'sh | muqrach, | uakal |
| **king of** | **Babylon** | **cause to serve** | | **his army** | **a service** | **great** | **against** | **Tyrus** | **every** | **head** | ***was* made bald** | **and every** |

| 3802 כתף | 4803 מרוטה | 7939 ושכר | 3808 לא | 1961 היה | 3807a לו | 2428 ולחילו | 6865 מצר | 5921 על | 5656 העבדה | 834 אשר | 5647 עבד |
|---|---|---|---|---|---|---|---|---|---|---|---|
| katep | marutah; | uasakar | la' | hayah | lou' | ualcheylou | mitzor, | 'al | ha'abodah | 'asher | 'abad |
| **shoulder** | ***was* peeled** | **yet wages** | **no** | **had** | **he** | **nor his army** | **for Tyrus** | **for** | **the service** | **that** | **he had served** |

| 5921: עליה | 29:19 | 3651 לכן | 3541 כה | 559 אמר | 136 אדני | 3069 יהוה | 2005 הנני | 5414 נתן | 5019 לנבוכדראצר | 4428 מלך | 894 בבל | 853 את |
|---|---|---|---|---|---|---|---|---|---|---|---|---|
| 'aleyha. | | laken, | koh | 'amar | 'adonay | Yahuah, | hinniy | noten | linabukadra'tzar | melek | babel | 'at |
| **against it** | | **Therefore** | **thus** | **saith** | **Adonai** | **Yahuah** | **Behold I** | **will give** | **unto Nebuchadrezzar** | **king of** | **Babylon** | |

Eze 29:13 Yet thus saith YHUH G-D; At the end of forty years will I gather the Egyptians from the people whither they were scattered:14 And I will bring again the captivity of Egypt, and will cause them to return into the land of Pathros, into the land of their habitation; and they shall be there a base kingdom.15 It shall be the basest of the kingdoms; neither shall it exalt itself anymore above the nations: for I will diminish them, that they shall no more rule over the nations.16 And it shall be no more the confidence of the house of Israel, which bring their iniquity to remembrance, when they shall look after them: but they shall know that I am YHUH G-D.17 And it came to pass in the seven and twentieth year, in the first month, in the first day of the month, the word of YHUH came unto me, saying,18 Son of man, Nebuchadrezzar king of Babylon caused his army to serve a great service against Tyrus: every head was made bald, and every shoulder was peeled: yet had he no wages, nor his army, for Tyrus, for the service that he had served against it:19 Therefore thus saith YHUH G-D; Behold, I will give the land of Egypt unto Nebuchadrezzar king of Babylon; and he shall take her multitude, and take her spoil, and take her prey; and it shall be the wages for his army.

| ארץ 776 | מצרים 4714 | ונשא 5375 | המנה 1995 | ושלל 7997 | שללה 7998 | ובזז 962 | בזה 957 | והיתה 1961 | שכר 7939 |
|---|---|---|---|---|---|---|---|---|---|
| 'aretz | mitzrayim; | uanasa' | hamonah | uashalal | shalalah | uabazaz | bizah, | uahayatah | sakar |
| **the land of** | **Egypt** | **and he shall take** | **her multitude** | **and take** | **her spoil** | **and take** | **her prey** | **and it shall be** | **the wages** |

| לחילו 2426: | **29:20** פעלתו 6468 | אשר 834 | עבד 5647 | בה 871a | נתתי 5414 | לו 3807a | את 853 | ארץ 776 | מצרים 4714 | אשר 834 |
|---|---|---|---|---|---|---|---|---|---|---|
| lacheylou. | pa'alatou | 'asher | 'abad | bah, | natatiy | lou' | 'at | 'aretz | mitzrayim; | 'asher |
| **for his army** | ***for* his labour** | **wherewith** | **he served** | **against it** | **I have given** | **him** | | **the land of** | **Egypt** | **because** |

| עשו 6213 | לי 3807a | נאם 5002 | אדני 136 | יהוה 3069: | **29:21** ביום 3117 | ההוא 1931 | אצמיח 6779 | קרן 7161 | לבית 1004 |
|---|---|---|---|---|---|---|---|---|---|
| 'asu | liy, | na'am | 'adonay | Yahuah. | bayoum | hahua', | 'atzmiyach | qeren | labeyt |
| **they wrought** | **for me** | **saith** | **Adonai** | **Yahuah** | **In day** | **that** | **will I cause to bud forth** | **the horn** | **of the house of** |

| ישראל 3478 | ולך 3807a | אתן 5414 | פתחון 6610 | פה 6310 | בתוכם 8432 | וידעו 3045 | כי 3588 | אני 589 | יהוה 3068: |
|---|---|---|---|---|---|---|---|---|---|
| yisra'ael, | ualaka | 'aten | pitchoun | peh | batoukam; | uayada'aua | kiy | 'aniy | Yahuah. |
| **Israel** | **and you** | **I will give** | **the opening of** | **the mouth** | **in the midst of them** | **and they shall know** | **that** | **I *am*** | **Yahuah** |

| **Ezek 30:1** ויהי 1961 | דבר 1697 | יהוה 3068 | אלי 413 | לאמר 559: | **30:2** בן 1121 | אדם 120 | הנבא 5012 | ואמרת 559 | כה 3541 | אמר 559 | אדני 136 |
|---|---|---|---|---|---|---|---|---|---|---|---|
| uayahiy | dabar | Yahuah | 'aelay | lea'mor. | ben | 'adam | hinabea' | ua'amarta, | koh | 'amar | 'adonay |
| **came again** | **The word of** | **Yahuah** | **unto me** | **saying** | **Son of** | **man** | **prophesy** | **and say** | **Thus** | **saith** | **Adonai** |

| יהוה 3069 | הילילו 3213 | הה 1929 | ליום 3117: | **30:3** כי 3588 | קרוב 7138 | יום 3117 | וקרוב 7138 | יום 3117 | ליהוה 3068 | יום 3117 | ענן 6051 | עת 6256 |
|---|---|---|---|---|---|---|---|---|---|---|---|---|
| Yahuah; | heyliylu | hah | layoum. | kiy | qaroub | youm, | uaqaroub | youm | laYahuah; | youm | 'anan, | 'at |
| **Yahuah** | **Howl you** | **Woe *worth*** | **the day** | **For** | ***is* near** | **the day** | **even *is* near** | **the day** | **of Yahuah** | **a day** | **cloudy** | **the time of** |

| גוים 1471 | יהיה 1961: | **30:4** ובאה 935 | חרב 2719 | במצרים 4714 | והיתה 1961 | חלחלה 2479 | בכוש 3568 | בנפל 5307 |
|---|---|---|---|---|---|---|---|---|
| gouyim | yihayeh. | uaba'ah | chereb | bamitzrayim, | uahayatah | chalchalah | bakush, | binpol |
| **the heathen** | **it shall be** | **And shall come** | **the sword** | **upon Egypt** | **and shall be** | **great pain** | **in Ethiopia** | **when shall fall** |

| חלל 2491 | במצרים 4714 | ולקחו 3947 | המונה 1995 | ונהרסו 2040 | יסודתיה 3247: | **30:5** כוש 3568 |
|---|---|---|---|---|---|---|
| chalal | bamitzrayim; | ualaqachu | hamounah, | uanehersu | yasoudoteyha. | kush |
| **the slain** | **in Egypt** | **and they shall take away** | **her multitude** | **and shall be broken down** | **her foundations** | **Ethiopia** |

| ופוט 6316 | ולוד 3865 | וכל 3605 | הערב 6154 | וכוב 3552 | ובני 1121 | ארץ 776 | הברית 1285 | אתם 854 |
|---|---|---|---|---|---|---|---|---|
| uaput | ua'lud | uakal | ha'areb | uakub, | uabney | 'aretz | habariyt; | 'atam |
| **and Libya** | **and Lydia** | **and all** | **the mingled people** | **and Chub** | **and the men of** | **the land** | ***that is* in league** | **with them** |

| בחרב 2719 | יפלו 5307: | **30:6** כה 3541 | אמר 559 | יהוה 3069 | ונפלו 5307 | סמכי 5564 | מצרים 4714 | וירד 3381 |
|---|---|---|---|---|---|---|---|---|
| bachereb | yipolu. | koh | 'amar | Yahuah, | uanapalu | somakey | mitzrayim, | uayarad |
| **by the sword** | **shall fall** | **Thus** | **saith** | **Yahuah** | **They also shall fall** | **that uphold** | **Egypt** | **and shall come down** |

| גאון 1347 | עזה 5797 | ממגדל 4024 | סונה 5482 | בחרב 2719 | יפלו 5307 | בה 871a | נאם 5002 | אדני 136 | יהוה 3068: **30:7** |
|---|---|---|---|---|---|---|---|---|---|
| ga'aun | 'azah; | mimigdol | saueneh, | bachereb | yiplu | bah, | na'am | 'adonay | Yahuah. |
| **the pride of** | **her power** | **from the tower of** | **Syene** | **by the sword** | **shall they fall** | **in it** | **saith** | **Adonai** | **Yahuah** |

| ונשמו 8074 | בתוך 8432 | ארצות 776 | נשמות 8074 | ועריו 5892 | בתוך 8432 | ערים 5892 |
|---|---|---|---|---|---|---|
| uanashamu | batouk | 'aratzout | nashamout; | ua'arayu | batouk | 'ariym |

**And they shall be desolate in the midst of the countries *that are* desolate and her cities in the midst of the cities**

Eze 30:20 I have given him the land of Egypt for his labour wherewith he served against it, because they wrought for me, saith YHUH G-D.21 In that day will I cause the horn of the house of Israel to bud forth, and I will give you the opening of the mouth in the midst of them; and they shall know that I am YHUH. **Eze** 30:1 The word of YHUH came again unto me, saying,2 Son of man, prophesy and say, Thus saith YHUH G-D; Howl you, Woe worth the day 3 For the day is near, even the day of YHUH is near, a cloudy day; it shall be the time of the heathen.4 And the sword shall come upon Egypt, and great pain shall be in Ethiopia, when the slain shall fall in Egypt, and they shall take away her multitude, and her foundations shall be broken down.5 Ethiopia, and Libya, and Lydia, and all the mingled people, and Chub, and the men of the land that is in league, shall fall with them by the sword.6 Thus saith YHUH; They also that uphold Egypt shall fall; and the pride of her power shall come down: from the tower of Syene shall they fall in it by the sword, saith YHUH G-D.7 And they shall be desolate in the midst of the countries that are desolate, and her cities shall be in the midst of the cities that are wasted.

| נחרבות 2717 | תהיינה 1961: | 30:8 | וידעו 3045 | כי 3588 | אני 589 | יהוה 3068 | בתתי 5414 | אש 784 | במצרים 4714 |
|---|---|---|---|---|---|---|---|---|---|
| nacharabout | tihayeynah. | | uayada'aua | kiy | 'aniy | Yahuah; | batitiy | 'aesh | bamitzrayim, |
| ***that are* wasted** | **shall be** | | **And they shall know** | **that** | **I *am*** | **Yahuah** | **when I have set** | **a fire** | **in Egypt** |

| ונשברו 7665 | כל 3605 | עזריה 5826: | 30:9 | ביום 3117 | ההוא 1931 | יצאו 3318 | מלאכים 4397 | מלפני 6440 | בצים 6716 |
|---|---|---|---|---|---|---|---|---|---|
| uanishbaru | kal | 'azareyha. | | bayoum | hahua', | yetza'ua | mal'akiym | milapanay | batziym, |
| **and shall be destroyed** | ***when* all** | **her helpers** | | **In day** | **that** | **shall go forth** | **messengers** | **from me** | **in ships** |

| להחריד 2729 | את 853 | כוש 3568 | בטח 983 | והיתה 1961 | חלחלה 2479 | בהם 871a | ביום 3117 | מצרים 4714 | כי 3588 | הנה 2009 |
|---|---|---|---|---|---|---|---|---|---|---|
| lahachariyd | 'at | kush | betach; | uahayatah | chalchalah | bahem | bayoum | mitzrayim, | kiy | hineh |
| **to make afraid** | | **Ethiopians** | **the careless** | **and shall come** | **great pain** | **upon them** | ***as* in the day of** | **Egypt** | **for** | **lo** |

| באה 935: | 30:10 | כה 3541 | אמר 559 | אדני 136 | יהוה 3069 | והשבתי 7673 | את 853 | המון 1995 | מצרים 4714 | ביד 3027 |
|---|---|---|---|---|---|---|---|---|---|---|
| ba'ah. | | koh | 'amar | 'adonay | Yahuah; | uahishbatiy | 'at | hamoun | mitzrayim, | bayad |
| **it comes** | | **Thus** | **saith** | **Adonai** | **Yahuah** | **I will also make to cease** | | **the multitude of** | **Egypt** | **by the hand of** |

| נבוכדראצר 5019 | מלך 4428 | בבל 894: | 30:11 | הוא 1931 | ועמו 5971 | אתו 854 | עריצי 6184 | גוים 1471 | מובאים 935 |
|---|---|---|---|---|---|---|---|---|---|
| nabukadra'tzar | melek | babel. | | hua' | ua'amou | 'atou | 'ariytzey | gouyim, | muba'aym |
| **Nebuchadrezzar** | **king of** | **Babylon** | | **He** | **and his people** | **with him** | **the terrible of** | **the nations** | **shall be brought** |

| לשחת 7843 | הארץ 776 | והריקו 7324 | חרבותם 2719 | על 5921 | מצרים 4714 | ומלאו 4390 | את 853 | הארץ 776 | חלל 2491: | 30:12 |
|---|---|---|---|---|---|---|---|---|---|---|
| lashachet | ha'aretz; | uaheriyqu | charboutam | 'al | mitzrayim, | uamal'au | 'at | ha'aretz | chalal. | |
| **to destroy** | **the land** | **and they shall draw** | **their swords** | **against** | **Egypt** | **and fill** | | **the land** | ***with* the slain** | |

| ונתתי 5414 | יארים 2975 | חרבה 2724 | ומכרתי 4376 | את 853 | הארץ 776 | ביד 3027 | רעים 7451 | והשמתי 8074 | ארץ 776 |
|---|---|---|---|---|---|---|---|---|---|
| uanatatiy | ya'ariym | charabah, | uamakartiy | 'at | ha'aretz | bayad | ra'aym; | uahashimotiy | 'aretz |
| **And I will make** | **the rivers** | **dry** | **and sell** | | **the land** | **into the hand of** | **the wicked** | **and I will make waste** | **the land** |

| ומלאה 4393 | ביד 3027 | זרים 2114 | אני 589 | יהוה 3068 | דברתי 1696: | 30:13 | כה 3541 | אמר 559 | אדני 136 | יהוה 3069 |
|---|---|---|---|---|---|---|---|---|---|---|
| uamlo'ah | bayad | zariym, | 'aniy | Yahuah | dibartiy. | | koh | 'amar | 'adonay | Yahuah |
| **and all that is therein** | **by the hand of** | **strangers** | **I** | **Yahuah** | **have spoken *it*** | | **Thus** | **saith** | **Adonai** | **Yahuah** |

| והאבדתי 6 | גלולים 1544 | והשבתי 7673 | אלילים 457 | מנף 5297 | ונשיא 5387 | מארץ 776 | מצרים 4714 | לא 3808 |
|---|---|---|---|---|---|---|---|---|
| uaha'abadatiy | giluliym | uahishbatiy | 'aliyliym | minop, | uanasiy'a | me'eretz | mitzrayim | la' |
| **I will also destroy** | **the idols** | **and I will cause to cease** | ***their* images** | **out of Noph** | **and a prince** | **of the land of** | **Egypt** | **no** |

| יהיה 1961 | עוד 5750 | ונתתי 5414 | יראה 3374 | בארץ 776 | מצרים 4714: | 30:14 | והשמתי 8074 | את 853 | פתרוס 6624 |
|---|---|---|---|---|---|---|---|---|---|
| yihayeh | 'aud; | uanatatiy | yir'ah | ba'aretz | mitzrayim. | | uahashimotiy | 'at | patrous, |
| **there shall be** | **more** | **and I will put** | **a fear** | **in the land of** | **Egypt** | | **And I will make desolate** | | **Pathros** |

| ונתתי 5414 | אש 784 | בצען 6814 | ועשיתי 6213 | שפטים 8201 | בנא 4996: | 30:15 | ושפכתי 8210 | חמתי 2534 | על 5921 | סין 5512 | מעוז 4581 |
|---|---|---|---|---|---|---|---|---|---|---|---|
| uanatatiy | 'aesh | batzo'an; | ua'asiytiy | shapatiym | banu. | | uashapakatiy | chamatiy, | 'al | siyn | ma'auz |
| **and will set fire** | | **in Zoan** | **and will execute** | **judgments** | **in No** | | **And I will pour** | **my fury** | **upon** | **Sin** | **the strength of** |

| מצרים 4714 | והכרתי 3772 | את 853 | המון 1995 | נא 4996: | 30:16 | ונתתי 5414 | אש 784 | במצרים 4714 | חול 2342 | תחיל 2342 |
|---|---|---|---|---|---|---|---|---|---|---|
| mitzrayim; | uahikratiy | 'at | hamoun | na'. | | uanatatiy | 'aesh | bamitzrayim, | choul | tachiyl |
| **Egypt** | **and I will cut off** | | **the multitude of** | **No** | | **And I will set fire** | | **in Egypt** | **shall have great** | **pain** |

Eze 30:8 And they shall know that I am YHUH, when I have set a fire in Egypt, and when all her helpers shall be destroyed.9 In that day shall messengers go forth from me in ships to make the careless Ethiopians afraid, and great pain shall come upon them, as in the day of Egypt: for, lo, it cometh.10 Thus saith YHUH G-D; I will also make the multitude of Egypt to cease by the hand of Nebuchadrezzar king of Babylon.11 He and his people with him, the terrible of the nations, shall be brought to destroy the land: and they shall draw their swords against Egypt, and fill the land with the slain.12 And I will make the rivers dry, and sell the land into the hand of the wicked: and I will make the land waste, and all that is therein, by the hand of strangers: I YHUH have spoken it.13 Thus saith YHUH G-D; I will also destroy the idols, and I will cause their images to cease out of Noph; and there shall be no more a prince of the land of Egypt: and I will put a fear in the land of Egypt.14 And I will make Pathros desolate, and will set fire in Zoan, and will execute judgments in No.15 And I will pour my fury upon Sin, the strength of Egypt; and I will cut off the multitude of No.16 And I will set fire in Egypt: Sin shall have great pain, and No shall be rent asunder, and Noph shall have distresses daily.

סין 5512 ונא 4996 תהיה 1961 להבקע 1234 ונף 5297 צרי 6862 יומם 3119: 30:17 בחורי 970 און 206 ופי 6364
siyn, banu tihayeh lahibaqea'; uanop tzarey youmam. bachurey 'auen uapiy
**Sin and No shall be rent asunder and Noph *shall have* distresses daily *The* young men of Aven and of Pi**

בסת 6364 בחרב 2719 יפלו 5307 והנה 2007 בשבי 7628 תלכנה 1980: 30:18 ובתחפנחס 8471 חשך 2821 היום 3117
beset bachereb yipolu; uahenah bashabiy telaknah. uabitachapnaches chasak hayoum,
**beseth by the sword shall fall and these into captivity *cities* shall go At Tehaphnehes also will be dark the day**

בשברי 7665 שם 8033 את 853 מטות 4133 מצרים 4714 ונשבת 7673 בה 871a גאון 1347 עזה 5797 היא 1931
bashibriy sham 'at motout mitzrayim, uanishbat bah ga'aun 'azah; hiy'a
**when I shall break there the yokes of Egypt and shall cease in her the pomp of her strength *as for* her**

ענן 6051 יכסנה 3680 ובנותיה 1323 בשבי 7628 תלכנה 1980: 30:19 ועשיתי 6213 שפטים 8201 במצרים 4714
'anan yakasenah, uabnouteyha bashabiy telaknah. ua'asiytiy shapatiym bamitzrayim;
**a cloud shall cover her and her daughters into captivity shall go Thus will I execute judgments in Egypt**

וידעו 3045 כי 3588 אני 589 יהוה 3068: 30:20 ויהי 1961 באחת 259 עשרה 6240 שנה 8141 בראשון 7223
uayada'aua kiy 'aniy Yahuah. uayahiy, ba'achat 'asreh shanah, bara'shoun
**and they shall know that I *am* Yahuah And it came to pass in one of ten year in the first**

בשבעה 7651 לחדש 2320 היה 1961 דבר 1697 יהוה 3068 אלי 413 לאמר 559: 30:21 בן 1121 אדם 120 את 853
bashib'ah lachodesh; hayah dabar Yahuah 'aelay lea'mor. ben 'adam 'at
***month* in the seventh *day* of the month came *that* the word of Yahuah unto me saying Son of man**

זרוע 2220 פרעה 6547 מלך 4428 מצרים 4714 שברתי 7665 והנה 2009 לא 3808 חבשה 2280 לתת 5414 רפאות 7499 לשום 7760 חתול 2848
zaroua' par'ah melek mitzrayim shabaratiy; uahineh la' chubshah latet rapu'aut lasum chitul
**the arm of Pharaoh king of Egypt I have broken and lo not it shall be bound up to be healed to put a roller**

לחבשה 2280 לחזקה 2388 לתפש 8610 בחרב 2719: 30:22 לכן 3651 כה 3541 אמר 559 אדני 136 יהוה 3069 הנני 2005 אל 413
lachabashah lachazaqah litpos bechareb. laken koh 'amar 'adonay Yahuah hinniy 'al
**to bind it to make it strong to hold the sword Therefore thus saith Adonai Yahuah Behold I *am* against**

פרעה 6547 מלך 4428 מצרים 4714 ושברתי 7665 את 853 זרעתיו 2220 את 853 החזקה 2389 ואת 853 הנשברת 7665
par'ah melek mitzrayim, uashabartiy 'at zaro'atayu, 'at hachazaqah ua'at hanishbaret;
**Pharaoh king of Egypt and will break his arms the strong *and* that which was broken**

והפלתי 5307 את 853 החרב 2719 מידו 3027: 30:23 והפצותי 6327 את 853 מצרים 4714 בגוים 1471
uahipaltiy 'at hachereb miyadou. uahapitzoutiy 'at mitzrayim bagouyim;
**and I will cause to fall the sword out of his hand And I will scatter the Egyptians among the nations**

וזריתם 2219 בארצות 776: 30:24 וחזקתי 2388 את 853 זרעות 2220 מלך 4428 בבל 894 ונתתי 5414
uazeriytim ba'aratzout. uachizaqtiy, 'at zaro'aut melek babel, uanatatiy
**and will disperse them through the countries And I will strengthen the arms of the king of Babylon and put**

את 853 חרבי 2719 בידו 3027 ושברתי 7665 את 853 זרעות 2220 פרעה 6547 ונאק 5008 נאקות 5009
'at charbiy bayadou; uashabartiy 'at zero'aut par'ah, uana'aq na'aqout
**my sword in his hand but I will break arms Pharaoh's and he shall groan *with* the groanings of**

Eze 30:17 The young men of Aven and of Pi-beseth shall fall by the sword: and these cities shall go into captivity.18 At Tehaphnehes also the day shall be darkened, when I shall break there the yokes of Egypt: and the pomp of her strength shall cease in her: as for her, a cloud shall cover her, and her daughters shall go into captivity.19 Thus will I execute judgments in Egypt: and they shall know that I am YHUH.20 And it came to pass in the eleventh year, in the first month, in the seventh day of the month, that the word of YHUH came unto me, saying,21 Son of man, I have broken the arm of Pharaoh king of Egypt; and, lo, it shall not be bound up to be healed, to put a roller to bind it, to make it strong to hold the sword.22 Therefore thus saith YHUH G-D; Behold, I am against Pharaoh king of Egypt, and will break his arms, the strong, and that which was broken; and I will cause the sword to fall out of his hand.23 And I will scatter the Egyptians among the nations, and will disperse them through the countries.24 And I will strengthen the arms of the king of Babylon, and put my sword in his hand: but I will break Pharaoh's arms, and he shall groan before him with the groanings of a deadly wounded man.

30:25

חלל 2491 | לפניו 6440: | 30:25 והחזקתי 2388 | את 853 | זרעות 2220 | מלך 4428 | בבל 894 | וזרעות 2220
chalal | lapanayu. | uahachazaqtiy, | 'at | zaro'aut | melek | babel, | uazro'aut
**a deadly wounded *man* | before him | But I will strengthen | the arms of | the king of | Babylon | and the arms of**

פרעה 6547 | תפלנה 5307 | וידעו 3045 | כי 3588 | אני 589 | יהוה 3068 | בתתי 5414 | חרבי 2719 | ביד 3027 | מלך 4428
par'ah | tipolanah; | uayada'aua | kiy | 'aniy | Yahuah | batitiy | charbiy | bayad | melek
**Pharaoh | shall fall down | and they shall know | that | I *am* | Yahuah | when I shall put | my sword | into the hand of | the king of**

בבל 894 | ונטה 5186 | אותה 853 | אל 413 | ארץ 776 | מצרים 4714: | 30:26 והפצותי 6327 | את 853 | מצרים 4714
babel, | uanatah | 'autah | 'al | 'aretz | mitzrayim. | uahapitzoutiy | 'at | mitzrayim
**Babylon | and he shall stretch out | it | upon | the land of | Egypt | And I will scatter | | the Egyptians**

בגוים 1471 | וזריתי 2219 | אותם 853 | בארצות 776 | וידעו 3045 | כי 3588 | אני 589 | יהוה 3068:
bagouyim, | uazeriytiy | 'autam | ba'aratzout; | uayada'aua | kiy | 'aniy | Yahuah.
**among the nations | and disperse them | | among the countries | and they shall know that | | I *am* | Yahuah**

**Ezek 31:1**
ויהי 1961 | באחת 259 | עשרה 6240 | שנה 8141 | בשלישי 7992 | באחד 259 | לחדש 2320 | היה 1961
uayahiy, | ba'achat | 'asreh | shanah, | bashaliyshiy | ba'achad | lachodesh; | hayah
**And it came to pass | in one of | ten | year | in the third *month* | the first | *day* of the month | came**

דבר 1697 | יהוה 3068 | אלי 413 | לאמר 559: | 31:2 בן 1121 | אדם 120 | אמר 559 | אל 413 | פרעה 6547 | מלך 4428 | מצרים 4714 | ואל 413 | המונו 1995
dabar | Yahuah | 'aelay | lea'mor. | ben | 'adam | 'amor | 'al | par'ah | melek | mitzrayim | ua'al | hamounou;
***that* the word of | Yahuah | unto me | saying | Son of | man | speak | unto | Pharaoh | king of | Egypt | and to | his multitude**

אל 413 | מי 4310 | דמית 1819 | בגדלך 1433: | 31:3 הנה 2009 | אשור 804 | ארז 730 | בלבנון 3844 | יפה 3303 | ענף 6057
'al | miy' | damiyta | bagadaleka. | hineh | 'ashur | 'arez | balabanoun, | yapeh | 'anap
**to | Whom | are you like | in your greatness? | Behold | the Assyrian | *was* a cedar | in Lebanon | *with* fair | branches**

וחרש 2793 | מצל 6751 | וגבה 1362 | קומה 6967 | ובין 996 | עבתים 5688 | היתה 1961 | צמרתו 6788: | 31:4 מים 4325
uachoresh | metzal | uagbah | qoumah; | uabeyn | 'abotiym, | hayatah | tzamaratou. | mayim
**and with a shroud | shadowing | and of an high | stature | and among | the thick boughs | was | his top | The waters**

גדלוהו 1431 | תהום 8415 | רממתהו 7311 | את 854 | נהרתיה 5104 | הלך 1980 | סביבות 5439 | מטעה 4302 | ואת 853 | תעלתיה 8585
gidluhu, | tahoum | romamatahu; | 'at | naharoteyha, | halok | sabiybout | mata'ah, | ua'at | ta'aloteyha
**made him great | the deep | set him up on high | *with* | her rivers | running | round about | his plants | *and* | her little rivers**

שלחה 7971 | אל 413 | כל 3605 | עצי 6086 | השדה 7704: | 31:5 על 5921 | כן 3651 | גבהא 1361 | קמתו 6967 | מכל 3605 | עצי 6086 | השדה 7704
shilchah, | 'al | kal | 'atzey | hasadeh. | 'al | ken | gabaha' | qomatou, | mikol | 'atzey | hasadeh;
**sent out | unto | all | the trees of | the field | Therefore | after that | was exalted | his height | above all | the trees of | the field**

ותרבינה 7235 | סרעפתיו 5634 | ותארכנה 748 | פארתו 6288 | ממים 4325 | רבים 7227 | בשלחו 7971: | 31:6
uatirbeynah | sara'apotayu | uate'araknah | po'arotou | mimayim | rabiym | bashalchou.
**and were multiplied | his boughs | and became long | his branches | because of waters | the multitude of | when he shot forth**

בסעפתיו 5589 | קננו 7077 | כל 3605 | עוף 5775 | השמים 8064 | ותחת 8478 | פארתיו 6288 | ילדו 3205 | כל 3605
bisa'apotayu | qinnu | kal | 'aup | hashamayim, | uatachat | po'arotayu | yaladu, | kal
**in his boughs | made their nests | All | the fowls of | heaven | and under | his branches | did bring forth their young | all**

Eze 30:25 But I will strengthen the arms of the king of Babylon, and the arms of Pharaoh shall fall down; and they shall know that I am YHUH, when I shall put my sword into the hand of the king of Babylon, and he shall stretch it out upon the land of Egypt.26 And I will scatter the Egyptians among the nations, and disperse them among the countries; and they shall know that I am YHUH. **Eze** 31:1 And it came to pass in the eleventh year, in the third month, in the first day of the month, that the word of YHUH came unto me, saying,2 Son of man, speak unto Pharaoh king of Egypt, and to his multitude; Whom are you like in your greatness?3 Behold, the Assyrian was a cedar in Lebanon with fair branches, and with a shadowing shroud, and of an high stature; and his top was among the thick boughs.4 The waters made him great, the deep set him up on high with her rivers running round about his plants, and sent out her little rivers unto all the trees of the field.5 Therefore his height was exalted above all the trees of the field, and his boughs were multiplied, and his branches became long because of the multitude of waters, when he shot forth.6 All the fowls of heaven made their nests in his boughs, and under his branches did all the beasts of the field bring forth their young, and under his shadow dwelt all great nations.

| חית 2416<br>chayat<br>**the beasts of** | השדה 7704<br>hasadeh;<br>**the field** | ובצלו 6738<br>uabtzilou<br>**and under his shadow** | ישבו 3427<br>yeshabu,<br>**dwelt** | כל 3605<br>kal<br>**all** | גוים 1471<br>gouyim<br>**nations** | רבים 7227:<br>rabiym.<br>**great** | **31:7** | וייף 3302<br>uayayip<br>**Thus was he fair** | בגדלו 1433<br>bagadalou,<br>**in his greatness** |
|---|---|---|---|---|---|---|---|---|---|

| בארך 753<br>ba'arek<br>**in the length of** | דליותיו 1808<br>daliyoutayu;<br>**his branches** | כי 3588<br>kiy<br>**for** | היה 1961<br>hayah<br>**was** | שרשו 8328<br>sharashou<br>**his root** | אל 413<br>'al<br>**by** | מים 4325<br>mayim<br>**waters** | רבים 7227:<br>rabiym.<br>**great** | **31:8** | ארזים 730<br>'araziym<br>**The cedars** | לא 3808<br>la'<br>**not** | עממהו 6004<br>'amamuhu<br>**could hide him** |
|---|---|---|---|---|---|---|---|---|---|---|---|

| בגן 1588<br>began<br>**in the garden of** | אלהים 430<br>'alohiym<br>**Elohim** | ברושים 1265<br>baroushiym,<br>**the fir trees** | לא 3808<br>la'<br>**not** | דמו 1818<br>damou<br>**were like** | אל 413<br>'al<br>**with** | סעפתיו 5589<br>sa'apotayu,<br>**his boughs** | וערמנים 6196<br>ua'armoniym<br>**and the chesnut trees** | לא 3808<br>la'<br>**not** | היו 1961<br>hayu<br>**were** | כפארתיו 6288<br>kapo'arotayu;<br>**like his branches** |
|---|---|---|---|---|---|---|---|---|---|---|

| כל 3605<br>kal<br>**any** | עץ 6086<br>'aetz<br>**tree** | בגן 1588<br>bagan<br>**in the garden of** | אלהים 430<br>'alohiym,<br>**Elohim** | לא 3808<br>la'<br>**nor** | דמה 1819<br>damah<br>**was like** | אליו 413<br>'aelayu<br>**unto him** | ביפיו 3308:<br>bayapayou.<br>**in his beauty** | **31:9** | יפה 3303<br>yapeh<br>**fair** | עשיתיו 6213<br>'asiytiyu,<br>**I have made him** |
|---|---|---|---|---|---|---|---|---|---|---|

| ברב 7230<br>barob<br>**by the multitude of** | דליותיו 1808<br>daliyoutayu;<br>**his branches** | ויקנאהו 7065<br>uayaqan'ahu<br>**so that envied him** | כל 3605<br>kal<br>**all** | עצי 6086<br>'atzey<br>**the trees of** | עדן 5731<br>'aeden,<br>**Eden** | אשר 834<br>'asher<br>**that** | בגן 1588<br>bagan<br>***were* in the garden of** | האלהים 430:<br>ha'alohiym.<br>**Elohim** | **31:10** |
|---|---|---|---|---|---|---|---|---|---|

| לכן 3651<br>laken,<br>**Therefore** | כה 3541<br>koh<br>**thus** | אמר 559<br>'amar<br>**saith** | אדני 136<br>'adonay<br>**Adonai** | יהוה 3068<br>Yahuah,<br>**Yahuah** | יען 3282<br>ya'an<br>**Because** | אשר 834<br>'asher<br>**which** | גבהת 1361<br>gabahta<br>**you have lifted up yourself** | בקומה 6967<br>baqoumah;<br>**in height** | ויתן 5414<br>uayiten<br>**and he has shot up** |
|---|---|---|---|---|---|---|---|---|---|

| צמרתו 6788<br>tzamaratou<br>**his top** | אל 413<br>'al<br>**to** | בין 996<br>beyn<br>**among** | עבותים 5688<br>aboutiym,<br>**the thick boughs** | ורם 7311<br>uaram<br>**and is lifted up** | לבבו 3824<br>lababou<br>**his heart** | בגבהו 1363:<br>bagabahou.<br>**in his height** | **31:11** | ואתנהו 5414<br>ua'atanehu,<br>**I have therefore delivered him** |
|---|---|---|---|---|---|---|---|---|

| ביד 3027<br>bayad<br>**into the hand of** | איל 410<br>'aeyl<br>**the mighty one of** | גוים 1471<br>gouyim;<br>**the heathen** | עשו 6213<br>asou<br>**he shall surely** | יעשה 6213<br>ya'aseh<br>**deal** | לו 3807a<br>lou',<br>**with him** | כרשעו 7562<br>karish'au<br>**for his wickedness** |
|---|---|---|---|---|---|---|

| גרשתהו 1644:<br>gerashtihu.<br>**I have driven him out** | **31:12** | ויכרתהו 3772<br>uayikratuhu<br>**And have cut him off** | זרים 2114<br>zariym<br>**strangers** | עריצי 6184<br>'ariytzey<br>**the terrible of** | גוים 1471<br>gouyim<br>**the nations** | ויטשהו 5203<br>uayitshuhu;<br>**and have left him** | אל 413<br>'al<br>**upon** |
|---|---|---|---|---|---|---|---|

| ההרים 2022<br>hehariym<br>**the mountains** | ובכל 3605<br>uabkal<br>**and in all** | גאיות 1516<br>ge'ayout<br>**the valleys** | נפלו 5307<br>naplu<br>**are fallen** | דליותיו 1808<br>daliyoutayu,<br>**his branches** | ותשברנה 7665<br>uatishabarnah<br>**and are broken** | פארתיו 6288<br>po'arotayu<br>**his boughs (*branches*)** | בכל 3605<br>bakol<br>**by all** | אפיקי 650<br>'apiyqey<br>**the rivers of** |
|---|---|---|---|---|---|---|---|---|

| הארץ 776<br>ha'aretz,<br>**the land** | וירדו 3381<br>uayeradu<br>**and are gone down** | מצלו 6738<br>mitzilou<br>**from his shadow** | כל 3605<br>kal<br>**all** | עמי 5971<br>'amey<br>**the people of** | הארץ 776<br>ha'aretz<br>**the earth** | ויטשהו 5203:<br>uayitshuhu.<br>**and have left him** | **31:13** | על 5921<br>'al<br>**Upon** | מפלתו 4658<br>mapaltou<br>**his ruin** |
|---|---|---|---|---|---|---|---|---|---|

| ישכנו 7931<br>yishkanu<br>**shall remain** | כל 3605<br>kal<br>**all** | עוף 5775<br>'aup<br>**the fowls of** | השמים 8064<br>hashamayim;<br>**the heaven** | ואל 413<br>ua'al<br>**and upon** | פארתיו 6288<br>po'arotayu<br>**his branches** | היו 1961<br>hayu,<br>**shall be** | כל 3605<br>kal<br>**all** | חית 2416<br>chayat<br>**the beasts of** | השדה 7704:<br>hasadeh.<br>**the field** |
|---|---|---|---|---|---|---|---|---|---|

Eze 31:7 Thus was he fair in his greatness, in the length of his branches: for his root was by great waters.8 The cedars in the garden of G-d could not hide him: the fir trees were not like his boughs, and the chestnut trees were not like his branches; nor any tree in the garden of G-d was like unto him in his beauty.9 I have made him fair by the multitude of his branches: so that all the trees of Eden, that were in the garden of G-d, envied him.10 Therefore thus saith YHUH G-D; Because you have lifted up thyself in height, and he has shot up his top among the thick boughs, and his heart is lifted up in his height;11 I have therefore delivered him into the hand of the mighty one of the heathen; he shall surely deal with him: I have driven him out for his wickedness.12 And strangers, the terrible of the nations, have cut him off, and have left him: upon the mountains and in all the valleys his branches are fallen, and his boughs are broken by all the rivers of the land; and all the people of the earth are gone down from his shadow, and have left him.13 Upon his ruin shall all the fowls of the heaven remain, and all the beasts of the field shall be upon his branches:

**31:14** למען 4616 | אשר 834 | לא 3808 | יגבהו 1361 | בקומתם 6967 | כל 3605 | עצי 6086 | מים 4325 | ולא 3808 | יתנו 5414 | את 853
lama'an 'asher la' yigbahu baqoumatam kal 'atzey mayim, uala' yitanu 'at
**To the end that none exalt themselves for their height *of* all the trees *by* the waters neither shoot up**

צמרתם 6788 | אל 413 | בין 996 | עבתים 5688 | ולא 3808 | יעמדו 5975 | אליהם 352 | בגבהם 1363 | כל 3605 | שתי 8354 | מים 4325 | כי 3588 | כלם 3605
tzamaratam 'al beyn 'abotiym, uala' ya'amdu 'aeleyhem bagabaham kal shotey mayim; kiy kulam
**their top to among the thick boughs neither stand up their trees in their height all that drink water for they all**

נתנו 5414 | למות 4194 | אל 413 | ארץ 776 | תחתית 8482 | בתוך 8432 | בני 1121 | אדם 120 | אל 413
nitanu lamauet 'al 'aretz tachtiyt, batouk baney 'adam 'al
**are delivered unto death to the earth *the* lower parts of in the midst of the children of men with**

יורדי 3381 | בור 953: **31:15** כה 3541 | אמר 559 | אדני 136 | יהוה 3068 | ביום 3117 | רדתו 3381 | שאולה 7585
youradey bour. koh 'amar 'adonay Yahuah bayoum ridtou sha'aulah
**them that go down to the pit Thus saith Adonai Yahuah In the day when he went down to the grave**

האבלתי 56 | כסתי 3680 | עליו 5921 | את 853 | תהום 8415 | ואמנע 4513 | נהרותיה 5104 | ויכלאו 3607 | מים 4325 | רבים 7227
he'abaltiy kisetiy 'aelayu 'at tahoum, ua'amna' naharouteyha, uayikala'au mayim rabiym;
**I caused a mourning I covered for him the deep and I restrained the floods thereof and were stayed waters *the* great**

ואקדר 6937 | עליו 5921 | לבנון 3844 | וכל 3605 | עצי 6086 | השדה 7704 | עליו 5921 | עלפה 5969: **31:16** מקול 6963 | מפלתו 4658
ua'aqdir 'aelayu labanoun, uakal 'atzey hasadeh 'alayu 'alpeh. miqoul mapaltou
**and I caused to mourn for him Lebanon and all the trees of the field for him fainted at the sound of his fall**

הרעשתי 7493 | גוים 1471 | בהורדי 3381 | אתו 853 | שאולה 7585 | את 854 | יורדי 3381 | בור 953
hir'ashtiy gouyim, bahouridiy 'atou sha'aulah 'at youradey bour;
**I made to shake the nations when I cast down to him hell *with* them that descend into the pit**

וינחמו 5162 | בארץ 776 | תחתית 8482 | כל 3605 | עצי 6086 | עדן 5731 | מבחר 4005 | וטוב 2896 | לבנון 3844 | כל 3605
uayinachamu ba'aretz tachtiyt kal 'atzey 'aeden, mibchar uatoub labanoun kal
**and shall be comforted in the earth *the* lower parts of all the trees of Eden the choice and best of Lebanon all**

שתי 8354 | מים 4325: **31:17** גם 1571 | הם 1992 | אתו 854 | ירדו 3381 | שאולה 7585 | אל 413 | חללי 2491 | חרב 2719
shotey mayim. gam hem, 'atou yaradu sha'aulah 'al challey chareb;
**that drink water also They with him went down into hell unto *them that be* slain *with* the sword**

וזרעו 2220 | ישבו 3427 | בצלו 6738 | בתוך 8432 | גוים 1471: **31:18** אל 413 | מי 4310 | דמית 1819 | ככה 3602
uazro'au yashabu batzilou batouk gouyim. 'al miy' damiyta kakah
**and *they that were* his arm *that* dwelt under his shadow in the midst of the heathen To whom are you thus like**

בכבוד 3519 | ובגדל 1433 | בעצי 6086 | עדן 5731 | והורדת 3381 | את 854 | עצי 6086 | עדן 5731 | אל 413 | ארץ 776
bakaboud uabgodel ba'atzey 'aeden; uahuradta 'at 'atzey 'aeden 'al 'aretz
**in glory and in greatness among the trees of Eden? yet shall you be brought down *with* the trees of Eden unto the earth**

תחתית 8482 | בתוך 8432 | ערלים 6189 | תשכב 7901 | את 854 | חללי 2491 | חרב 2719 | הוא 1931 | פרעה 6547
tachtiyt, batouk 'areliym tishkab 'at challey chereb, hua' par'ah
***the* nether parts of in the midst of the uncircumcised you shall lie *with* *them that be* slain by the sword This *is* Pharaoh**

Eze 31:14 To the end that none of all the trees by the waters exalt themselves for their height, neither shoot up their top among the thick boughs, neither their trees stand up in their height, all that drink water: for they are all delivered unto death, to the nether parts of the earth, in the midst of the children of men, with them that go down to the pit.15 Thus saith YHUH G-D; In the day when he went down to the grave I caused a mourning: I covered the deep for him, and I restrained the floods thereof, and the great waters were stayed: and I caused Lebanon to mourn for him, and all the trees of the field fainted for him.16 I made the nations to shake at the sound of his fall, when I cast him down to hell with them that descend into the pit: and all the trees of Eden, the choice and best of Lebanon, all that drink water, shall be comforted in the nether parts of the earth.17 They also went down into hell with him unto them that be slain with the sword; and they that were his arm, that dwelt under his shadow in the midst of the heathen.18 To whom are you thus like in glory and in greatness among the trees of Eden? yet shall you be brought down with the trees of Eden unto the nether parts of the earth: you shall lie in the midst of the uncircumcised with them that be slain by the sword. This is Pharaoh and all his multitude, saith YHUH G-D.

וכל 3605 המונה 1995 נאם 5002 אדני 136 יהוה 3069:
uakal hamounoh, na'am 'adonay Yahuah.
**and all his multitude saith Adonai Yahuah**

**Ezek 32:1**
ויהי 1961 בשתי 8147 עשרה 6240 שנה 8141 בשני 8147 עשר 6240 חדש 2320 באחד 259 לחדש 2320 היה 1961
uayahiy bishtey 'asreh shanah, bishney 'asar chodesh ba'achad lachodesh; hayah
**And it came to pass in two of ten year in two of *the* ten month in the first *day* of the month came**

דבר 1697 יהוה 3068 אלי 413 לאמר 559: **32:2** בן 1121 אדם 120 שא 5375 קינה 7015 על 5921 פרעה 6547 מלך 4428 מצרים 4714
dabar Yahuah 'aelay lea'mor. ben 'adam, sa qiynah 'al par'ah melek mitzrayim,
***that* the word of Yahuah unto me saying Son of man take up a lamentation for Pharaoh king of Egypt**

ואמרת 559 אליו 413 כפיר 3715 גוים 1471 נדמית 1819 ואתה 859 כתנים 8577 בימים 3220 ותגח 1518
ua'amarta 'aelayu, kapiyr gouyim nidmeyta; ua'atah kataniym bayamiym, uatagach
**and say unto him a young lion of the nations You are like and you *are* as a whale in the seas and you came forth**

בנהרותיך 5104 ותדלח 1804 מים 4325 ברגליך 7272 ותרפס 7515 נהרותם 5104: **32:3** כה 3541 אמר 559 אדני 136 יהוה 3069
banaharouteyka, uatidlach mayim baragleyka, uatirpos naharoutam. koh 'amar 'adonay Yahuah,
**with your rivers and troubled the waters with your feet and fouled their rivers Thus saith Adonai Yahuah**

ופרשתי 6566 עליך 5921 את 853 רשתי 7568 בקהל 6951 עמים 5971 רבים 7227 והעלוך 5927
uaparastiy 'alayik 'at rishtiy, biqahal 'amiym rabiym; uahe'aluka
**I will therefore spread out over you my net with a company of people many and they shall bring you up**

בחרמי 2764: **32:4** ונטשתיך 5203 בארץ 776 על 5921 פני 6440 השדה 7704 אטילך 2904 והשכנתי 7931
bachermiy. uantashtiyka ba'aretz, 'al paney hasadeh 'atiyleka; uahishkantiy
**in my net Then will I leave you upon the land upon open the field I will cast you forth and will cause to remain**

עליך 5921 כל 3605 עוף 5775 השמים 8064 והשבעתי 7646 ממך 4480 חית 2416 כל 3605 הארץ 776: **32:5** ונתתי 5414 את 853
'alayik kal 'aup hashamayim, uahisba'atiy mimaka chayat kal ha'aretz. uanatatiy 'at
**upon you all the fowls of the heaven and I will fill with you the beasts of whole the earth And I will lay**

בשרך 1320 על 5921 ההרים 2022 ומלאתי 4390 הגאיות 1516 רמותך 7419: **32:6** והשקיתי 8248 ארץ 776 צפתך 6824
basarka 'al hehariym; uamilea'tiy hage'ayout ramuteka. uahishqeytiy 'aretz tzapataka
**your flesh upon the mountains and fill the valleys *with* your height I will also water the land wherein you swim**

מדמך 1818 אל 413 ההרים 2022 ואפקים 650 ימלאון 4390 ממך 4480: **32:7** וכסיתי 3680 בכבותך 3518
midamaka 'al hehariym; ua'apiqiym yimala'aun mimeka. uakiseytiy bakaboutaka
***with* your blood *even* to the mountains and the rivers shall be full of you And I will cover when I shall put you out**

שמים 8064 והקדרתי 6937 את 853 ככביהם 3556 שמש 8121 בענן 6051 אכסנו 3680 וירח 3394 לא 3808 יאיר 215
shamayim, uahiqdartiy 'at kokabeyhem; shemesh be'anan 'akasenu, uayareach la' ya'ayr
**the heaven and make dark the stars thereof the sun with a cloud I will cover and the moon not shall give**

אורו 216: **32:8** כל 3605 מאורי 3974 אור 216 בשמים 8064 אקדירם 6937 עליך 5921 ונתתי 5414 חשך 2822 על 5921 ארצך 776 נאם 5002
'auru. kal ma'aurey 'aur bashamayim, 'aqdiyrem 'alayik; uanatatiy choshek 'al 'artzaka, na'am
**her light All *the* bright lights of heaven will I make dark over you and set darkness upon your land saith**

**Eze** 32:1 And it came to pass in the twelfth year, in the twelfth month, in the first day of the month, that the word of YHUH came unto me, saying,2 Son of man, take up a lamentation for Pharaoh king of Egypt, and say unto him, Thou are like a young lion of the nations, and you are as a whale in the seas: and you came forth with your rivers, and troubledst the waters with your feet, and fouledst their rivers.3 Thus saith YHUH G-D; I will therefore spread out my net over you with a company of many people; and they shall bring you up in my net.4 Then will I leave you upon the land, I will cast you forth upon the open field, and will cause all the fowls of the heaven to remain upon you, and I will fill the beasts of the whole earth with you.5 And I will lay your flesh upon the mountains, and fill the valleys with your height.6 I will also water with your blood the land wherein you swimmest, even to the mountains; and the rivers shall be full of you.7 And when I shall put you out, I will cover the heaven, and make the stars thereof dark; I will cover the sun with a cloud, and the moon shall not give her light.8 All the bright lights of heaven will I make dark over you, and set darkness upon your land, saith YHUH G-D.

32:9
אדני 136 יהוה 3069: והכעסתי 3707 לב 3820 עמים 5971 רבים 7227 בהביאי 935 שברך 7667 בגוים 1471
'adonay Yahuah. uahik'astiy, leb 'amiym rabiym; bahabiy'ay shibraka bagouyim,
**Adonai Yahuah I will also vex the hearts of people many when I shall bring your destruction among the nations**

32:10
על 5921 ארצות 776 אשר 834 לא 3808 ידעתם 3045: והשמותי 8074 עליך 5921 עמים 5971 רבים 7227 ומלכיהם 4428
'al 'aratzout 'asher la' yada'atam. uahashimoutiy 'aleyka 'amiym rabiym, uamalkeyhem
**into the countries which not you have known Yea I will make amazed at you people many and their kings**

ישערו 8175 עליך 5921 שער 8178 בעופפי 5774 חרבי 2719 על 5921 פניהם 6440 וחרדו 2729 לרגעים 7281
yis'aru 'aleyka sa'ar, ba'aupapiy charbiy 'al paneyhem; uacharadu lirga'aym
**shall be afraid for you horribly when I shall brandish my sword before them and they shall tremble at *every* moment**

32:11
איש 376 לנפשו 5315 ביום 3117 מפלתך 4658: כי 3588 כה 3541 אמר 559 אדני 136 יהוה 3068 חרב 2719 מלך 4428
'aysh lanapshou, bayoum mapalteka. kiy koh 'amar 'adonay Yahuah; chereb melek
**every man for his own life in the day of your fall For thus saith Adonai Yahuah The sword of the king of**

32:12
בבל 894 תבואך 935: בחרבות 2719 גבורים 1368 אפיל 5307 המונך 1995 עריצי 6184
babel tabou'aka. bacharbout gibouriym 'apiyl hamouneka, 'ariytzey
**Babylon shall come upon you By the swords of *the* mighty will I cause to fall your multitude the terrible of**

גוים 1471 כלם 3605 ושדדו 7703 את 853 גאון 1347 מצרים 4714 ונשמד 8045 כל 3605
gouyim kulam; uashadadu 'at ga'aun mitzrayim, uanishmad kal
**the nations all of them and they shall spoil the pomp of Egypt and shall be destroyed all**

32:13
המונה 1995: והאבדתי 6 את 853 כל 3605 בהמתה 929 מעל 5921 מים 4325 רבים 7227 ולא 3808
hamounah. uaha'abadatiy 'at kal bahemtah, me'al mayim rabiym; uala'
**the multitude thereof I will destroy also all the beasts thereof from beside waters *the* great neither**

32:14
תדלחם 1804 רגל 7272 אדם 120 עוד 5750 ופרסות 6541 בהמה 929 לא 3808 תדלחם 1804: אז 227 אשקיע 8257
tidlachem regel 'adam 'aud, uaparsout bahemah la' tidlachem. 'az 'ashqiya'
**shall trouble them the foot of man any more the hoofs of beasts nor trouble them Then will I make deep**

32:15
מימיהם 4325 ונהרותם 5104 כשמן 8081 אוליך 1980 נאם 5002 אדני 136 יהוה 3069: בתתי 5414 את 853 ארץ 776
meymeyhem, uanaharoutam kashemen 'auliyk; na'am 'adonay Yahuah. batitiy 'at 'aretz
**their waters and their rivers like oil cause to run saith Adonai Yahuah When I shall make the land of**

מצרים 4714 שממה 8077 ונשמה 8074 ארץ 776 ממלאה 4393 בהכותי 5221 את 853 כל 3605
mitzrayim shamamah uanshamah, 'aretz mimalo'ah, bahakoutiy 'at kal
**Egypt desolate and shall be destitute the country of that whereof it was full when I shall smite all**

32:16
יושבי 3427 בה 871a וידעו 3045 כי 3588 אני 589 יהוה 3068: קינה 6969 היא 1931
youshabey bah; uayada'aua kiy 'aniy Yahuah. qiynah hiy'a
**them that dwell therein then shall they know that I *am* Yahuah *wherewith* they shall lament her This**

וקוננוה 7015 בנות 1323 הגוים 1471 תקוננה 6969 אותה 853 על 5921 מצרים 4714 ועל 5921 כל 3605 המונה 1995
uaqounanuha, banout hagouyim taqounenah 'autah; 'al mitzrayim ua'al kal hamounah
***is* the lamentation the daughters of the nations shall lament her *even* for Egypt and for all multitude**

Eze 32:9 I will also vex the hearts of many people, when I shall bring your destruction among the nations, into the countries which you have not known.10 Yea, I will make many people amazed at you, and their kings shall be horribly afraid for you, when I shall brandish my sword before them; and they shall tremble at every moment, every man for his own life, in the day of your fall.11 For thus saith YHUH G-D; The sword of the king of Babylon shall come upon you.12 By the swords of the mighty will I cause your multitude to fall, the terrible of the nations, all of them: and they shall spoil the pomp of Egypt, and all the multitude thereof shall be destroyed.13 I will destroy also all the beasts thereof from beside the great waters; neither shall the foot of man trouble them anymore, nor the hoofs of beasts trouble them.14 Then will I make their waters deep, and cause their rivers to run like oil, saith YHUH G-D.15 When I shall make the land of Egypt desolate, and the country shall be destitute of that whereof it was full, when I shall smite all them that dwell therein, then shall they know that I am YHUH.16 This is the lamentation wherewith they shall lament her: the daughters of the nations shall lament her: they shall lament for her, even for Egypt, and for all her multitude, saith YHUH G-D.

| תקוננה 6969 | אותה 853 | נאם 5002 | אדני 136 | יהוה 3069: | 32:17 | ויהי 1961 | בשתי 8147 | עשרה 6240 | שנה 8141 | בחמשה 2568 |
|---|---|---|---|---|---|---|---|---|---|---|
| taqounenah | 'autah, | na'am | 'adonay | Yahuah. | | uayahiy | bishtey | 'asreh | shanah, | bachamishah |
| **they shall lament *for*** | **her** | **saith** | **Adonai** | **Yahuah** | | **It came to pass also** | **in two** | ***the* ten** | **year** | **in the five** |

| עשר 6240 | לחדש 2320 | היה 1961 | דבר 1697 | יהוה 3068 | אלי 413 | לאמר 559: | 32:18 | בן 1121 | אדם 120 | נהה 5091 | על 5921 | המון 1995 |
|---|---|---|---|---|---|---|---|---|---|---|---|---|
| 'asar | lachodesh; | hayah | dabar | Yahuah | 'aelay | lea'mor. | | ben | 'adam | naheh | 'al | hamoun |
| **ten *day*** | **of the month** | **came** | ***that* the word of** | **Yahuah** | **unto me** | **saying** | | **Son of** | **man** | **wail** | **for** | **the multitude of** |

| מצרים 4714 | והורדהו 3381 | אותה 853 | ובנות 1323 | גוים 1471 | אדרם 117 | אל 413 | ארץ 776 | תחתיות 8482 | את 854 |
|---|---|---|---|---|---|---|---|---|---|
| mitzrayim | uahouridehu; | otah | uabnout | gouyim | 'adirim | 'al | 'aretz | tachtiyout | 'at |
| **Egypt** | **and cast them down** | ***even* her** | **and the daughters of** | **nations** | ***the* famous** | **unto** | **the earth** | ***the* lower parts of** | ***with*** |

| יורדי 3381 | בור 953: | 32:19 | ממי 4310 | נעמת 5276 | רדה 3381 | והשכבה 7901 | את 854 | ערלים 6189: | 32:20 |
|---|---|---|---|---|---|---|---|---|---|
| youradey | bour. | | mimiy | na'amata; | radah | uahashkabah | 'at | 'areliym. | |
| **them that go down** | **into the pit** | | **Whom do you pass in beauty?** | | **go down** | **and be you laid** | ***with*** | **the uncircumcised** | |

| בתוך 8432 | חללי 2491 | חרב 2719 | יפלו 5307 | חרב 2719 | נתנה 5414 | משכו 4900 | אותה 853 | וכל 3605 |
|---|---|---|---|---|---|---|---|---|
| batouk | challey | chereb | yipolu; | chereb | nitanah, | mashachu | 'autah | uakal |
| **in the midst of** | ***them that are* slain** | ***by* the sword** | **They shall fall** | **to the sword** | **she is delivered** | **draw** | **her** | **and all** |

| המוניה 1995: | 32:21 | ידברו 1696 | לו 3807a | אלי 410 | גבורים 1368 | מתוך 8432 | שאול 7585 | את 854 |
|---|---|---|---|---|---|---|---|---|
| hamouneyha. | | yadabru | lou' | 'aley | gibouriym | mitouk | sha'aul | 'at |
| **her multitudes** | | **shall speak** | **to him** | **The strong among** | **the mighty** | **out of the midst of** | **hell (*grave*)** | ***with*** |

| עזריו 5826 | ירדו 3381 | שכבו 7901 | הערלים 6189 | חללי 2491 | חרב 2719: | 32:22 | שם 8033 | אשור 804 | וכל 3605 |
|---|---|---|---|---|---|---|---|---|---|
| 'azarayu; | yaradu | shakabu | ha'areliym | challey | chareb. | | sham | 'ashur | uakal |
| **them that help him** | **they are gone down** | **they lie** | **uncircumcised** | **slain by** | **the sword** | | ***is* there** | **Asshur** | **and all** |

| קהלה 6951 | סביבותיו 5439 | קברתיו 6913 | כלם 3605 | חללים 2491 | הנפלים 5307 | בחרב 2719: | 32:23 | אשר 834 | נתנו 5414 | קברתיה 6913 |
|---|---|---|---|---|---|---|---|---|---|---|
| qahalah, | sabiyboutayu | qibrotayu; | kulam | chalaliym, | hanopliym | bechareb. | | 'asher | nitanu | qibroteyha |
| **her company** | ***are* about him** | **his graves** | **all of them** | **slain** | **fallen** | **by the sword** | | **whose** | **are set** | **graves** |

| בירכתי 3411 | בור 953 | ויהי 1961 | קהלה 6951 | סביבות 5439 | קברתה 6900 | כלם 3605 | חללים 2491 | נפלים 5307 | בחרב 2719 | אשר 834 |
|---|---|---|---|---|---|---|---|---|---|---|
| bayarkatey | bour, | uayahiy | qahalah, | sabiybout | qaburatah; | kulam | chalaliym | nopaliym | bachereb, | 'asher |
| **in the sides of** | **the pit** | **and is** | **her company** | **round about** | **her grave** | **all of them** | **slain** | **fallen** | **by the sword** | **which** |

| נתנו 5414 | חתית 2851 | בארץ 776 | חיים 2416: | 32:24 | שם 8033 | עילם 5867 | וכל 3605 | המונה 1995 | סביבות 5439 | קברתה 6900 | כלם 3605 |
|---|---|---|---|---|---|---|---|---|---|---|---|
| natanu | chitiyt | ba'aretz | chayiym. | | sham | 'aeylam | uakal | hamounah, | sabiybout | qaburatah; | kulam |
| **caused** | **terror** | **in the land of** | **the living** | | **There *is*** | **Elam** | **and all** | **her multitude** | **round about** | **her grave** | **all of them** |

| חללים 2491 | הנפלים 5307 | בחרב 2719 | אשר 834 | ירדו 3381 | ערלים 6189 | אל 413 | ארץ 776 | תחתיות 8482 | אשר 834 | נתנו 5414 |
|---|---|---|---|---|---|---|---|---|---|---|
| chalaliym | hanopliym | bachereb | 'asher | yaradu | 'areliym | 'al | 'aretz | tachtiyout, | 'asher | natanu |
| **slain** | **fallen** | **by the sword** | **which** | **are gone down** | **uncircumcised** | **into** | **the earth** | ***the* lower parts of** | **which** | **caused** |

| חתיתם 2851 | בארץ 776 | חיים 2416 | וישאו 5375 | כלמתם 3639 | את 853 | יורדי 3381 | בור 953: |
|---|---|---|---|---|---|---|---|
| chitiytam | ba'aretz | chayiym, | uayis'au | kalimatam | 'at | youradey | bour. |
| **their terror** | **in the land of** | **the living** | **yet have they borne** | **their shame** | ***with*** | **them that go down to** | **the pit** |

Eze 32:17 It came to pass also in the twelfth year, in the fifteenth day of the month, that the word of YHUH came unto me, saying,18 Son of man, wail for the multitude of Egypt, and cast them down, even her, and the daughters of the famous nations, unto the nether parts of the earth, with them that go down into the pit.19 Whom dost you pass in beauty? go down, and be you laid with the uncircumcised.20 They shall fall in the midst of them that are slain by the sword: she is delivered to the sword: draw her and all her multitudes.21 The strong among the mighty shall speak to him out of the midst of hell with them that help him: they are gone down, they lie uncircumcised, slain by the sword.22 Asshur is there and all her company: his graves are about him: all of them slain, fallen by the sword:23 Whose graves are set in the sides of the pit, and her company is round about her grave: all of them slain, fallen by the sword, which caused terror in the land of the living.24 There is Elam and all her multitude round about her grave, all of them slain, fallen by the sword, which are gone down uncircumcised into the nether parts of the earth, which caused their terror in the land of the living; yet have they borne their shame with them that go down to the pit.

**32:25**
בתוך 8432 חללים 2491 נתנו 5414 משכב 4904 לה 3807a בכל 3605 המונה 1995 סביבותיו 5439 קברתה 6913
batouk chalaliym natanu mishkab lah bakal hamounah, sabiyboutayu qibroteha;
**in the midst of the slain They have set a bed her with all her multitude *are* round about him her graves**

כלם 3605 ערלים 6189 חללי 2491 חרב 2719 כי 3588 נתן 5414 חתיתם 2851 בארץ 776 חיים 2416 וישאו 5375
kulam 'areliym challey chereb kiy nitan chitiytam ba'aretz chayiym, uayis'au
**all of them uncircumcised slain by the sword though was caused their terror in the land of the living yet have they borne**

כלמתם 3639 את 854 יורדי 3381 בור 953 בתוך 8432 חללים 2491 נתן 5414: **32:26** שם 8033 משך 4902 תבל 8422
kalimatam 'at youradey bour, batouk chalaliym nitan. sham meshek tubal
**their shame *with* them that go down to the pit in the midst of *them that be* slain he is put There *is* Meshech Tubal**

וכל 3605 המונה 1995 סביבותיו 5439 קברותיה 6913 כלם 3605 ערלים 6189 מחללי 2490 חרב 2719 כי 3588 נתנו 5414
uakal hamounah, sabiyboutayu qibrouteyha; kulam 'areliym machulaley chereb, kiy natanu
**and all her multitude *are* round about him her graves all of them uncircumcised slain by the sword though they caused**

חתיתם 2851 בארץ 776 חיים 2416: **32:27** ולא 3808 ישכבו 7901 את 854 גבורים 1368 נפלים 5307 מערלים 6189
chitiytam ba'aretz chayiym. uala' yishkabu 'at gibouriym, nopaliym me'areliym;
**their terror in the land of the living And not they shall lie *with* the mighty *that are* fallen of the uncircumcised**

אשר 834 ירדו 3381 שאול 7585 בכלי 3627 מלחמתם 4421 ויתנו 5414 את 853 חרבותם 2719 תחת 8478
'asher yaradu sha'aul bikaley milchamtam uayitanu 'at charboutam tachat
**which are gone down to hell (*grave*) with their weapons of war and they have laid their swords under**

ראשיהם 7218 ותהי 1961 עונתם 5771 על 5921 עצמותם 6106 כי 3588 חתית 2851 גבורים 1368 בארץ 776
ra'sheyhem, uatahiy 'auonotam 'al atzmoutam, kiy chitiyt gibouriym ba'aretz
**their heads but shall be their iniquities upon their bones though *they were* the terror of the mighty in the land of**

חיים 2416: **32:28** ואתה 859 בתוך 8432 ערלים 6189 תשבר 7665 ותשכב 7901 את 854 חללי 2491
chayiym. ua'atah, batouk 'areliym tishabar uatishkab 'at challey
**the living Yea you in the midst of the uncircumcised shall be broken and shall lie *with them that are* slain**

חרב 2719: **32:29** שמה 8033 אדום 123 מלכיה 4428 וכל 3605 נשיאיה 5387 אשר 834 נתנו 5414 בגבורתם 1369 את 854
chareb. shamah 'adoum, malakeyha uakal nasiy'ayha, 'asher nitanu bigburatam 'at
***with* the sword There *is* Edom her kings and all her princes which are laid with their might *by***

חללי 2491 חרב 2719 המה 1992 את 854 ערלים 6189 ישכבו 7901 ואת 854 ירדי 3381 בור 953: **32:30**
challey chareb; hemah 'at 'areliym yishkabu ua'at yoradey bour.
***them that were* slain *by* the sword they *with* the uncircumcised shall lie *and with* them that go down to the pit**

שמה 8033 נסיכי 5257 צפון 6828 כלם 3605 וכל 3605 צדני 6722 אשר 834 ירדו 3381 את 854 חללים 2491
shamah nasiykey tzapoun kulam uakal tzidoniy; 'asher yaradu 'at chalaliym,
**There *be* the princes of the north all of them and all the Zidonians which are gone down *with* the slain**

בחתיתם 2851 מגבורתם 1369 בושים 954 וישכבו 7901 ערלים 6189 את 854 חללי 2491 חרב 2719 וישאו 5375
bachitiytam; migburatam boushiym, uayishkabu 'areliym 'at challey chereb, uayis'au
**with their terror of their might they are ashamed and they lie uncircumcised *with them that be* slain *by* the sword and bear**

Eze 32:25 They have set her a bed in the midst of the slain with all her multitude: her graves are round about him: all of them uncircumcised, slain by the sword: though their terror was caused in the land of the living, yet have they borne their shame with them that go down to the pit: he is put in the midst of them that be slain.26 There is Meshech, Tubal, and all her multitude: her graves are round about him: all of them uncircumcised, slain by the sword, though they caused their terror in the land of the living.27 And they shall not lie with the mighty that are fallen of the uncircumcised, which are gone down to hell with their weapons of war: and they have laid their swords under their heads, but their iniquities shall be upon their bones, though they were the terror of the mighty in the land of the living.28 Yea, you shall be broken in the midst of the uncircumcised, and shall lie with them that are slain with the sword.29 There is Edom, her kings, and all her princes, which with their might are laid by them that were slain by the sword: they shall lie with the uncircumcised, and with them that go down to the pit.30 There be the princes of the north, all of them, and all the Zidonians, which are gone down with the slain; with their terror they are ashamed of their might; and they lie uncircumcised with them that be slain by the sword, and bear their shame with them that go down to the pit.

| כלמתם 3639 | את 854 | יורדי 3381 | בור 953: | **32:31** | אותם 853 | יראה 7200 | פרעה 6547 | ונחם 5162 | על 5921 | כל 3605 |
|---|---|---|---|---|---|---|---|---|---|---|
| kalimatam | 'at | youradey | bour. | | 'autam | yir'ah | par'ah, | uanicham | 'al | kal |
| **their shame** | ***with*** | **them that go down to** | **the pit** | | **them** | **shall see** | **Pharaoh** | **and shall be comforted** | **over** | **all** |

| המונה 1995 | חללי 2491 | חרב 2719 | פרעה 6547 | וכל 3605 | חילו 2428 | נאם 5002 | אדני 136 | יהוה 3069: | **32:32** | כי 3588 | נתתי 5414 | את 853 |
|---|---|---|---|---|---|---|---|---|---|---|---|---|
| hamounoh | challey | chereb | par'ah | uakal | cheylou, | na'am | 'adonay | Yahuah. | | kiy | natatiy | 'at |
| **his multitude** | **slain by** | **the sword** | ***even* Pharaoh** | **and all** | **his army** | **saith** | **Adonai** | **Yahuah** | | **For** | **I have caused** | |

| חתיתו 2851 | בארץ 776 | חיים 2416 | והשכב 7901 | בתוך 8432 | ערלים 6189 | את 854 | חללי 2491 |
|---|---|---|---|---|---|---|---|
| chitiytou | ba'aretz | chayiym; | uahushkab | batouk | 'areliym | 'at | challey |
| **my terror** | **in the land of** | **the living** | **and he shall be laid** | **in the midst of** | **the uncircumcised** | ***with*** | ***them that are* slain** |

| חרב 2719 | פרעה 6547 | וכל 3605 | המונה 1995 | נאם 5002 | אדני 136 | יהוה 3069: |
|---|---|---|---|---|---|---|
| chereb, | par'ah | uakal | hamounoh, | na'am | 'adonay | Yahuah. |
| ***with* the sword** | ***even* Pharaoh** | **and all** | **his multitude** | **saith** | **Adonai** | **Yahuah** |

| **Ezek 33:1** | ויהי 1961 | דבר 1697 | יהוה 3068 | אלי 413 | לאמר 559: | **33:2** | בן 1121 | אדם 120 | דבר 1696 | אל 413 | בני 1121 | עמך 5971 |
|---|---|---|---|---|---|---|---|---|---|---|---|---|
| | uayahiy | dabar | Yahuah | 'aelay | lea'mor. | | ben | 'adam, | daber | 'al | baney | 'amaka |
| | **Again came** | **the word of** | **Yahuah** | **unto me** | **saying** | | **Son of** | **man** | **speak** | **to** | **the children of** | **your people** |

| ואמרת 559 | אליהם 413 | ארץ 776 | כי 3588 | אביא 935 | עליה 5921 | חרב 2719 | ולקחו 3947 | עם 5971 | הארץ 776 | איש 376 | אחד 259 | מקציהם 7097 |
|---|---|---|---|---|---|---|---|---|---|---|---|---|
| ua'amarta | 'aleyhem, | 'aretz | kiy | 'abiy'a | 'aleyha | chareb; | ualaqachu | 'am | ha'aretz | 'aysh | 'achad | miqtzeyhem, |
| **and say** | **unto them** | **a land** | **When** | **I bring** | **upon** | **the sword** | **if take** | **the people of** | **the land** | **man of** | **a** | **their coasts** |

| ונתנו 5414 | אתו 853 | להם 3807a | לצפה 6822: | **33:3** | וראה 7200 | את 853 | החרב 2719 | באה 935 | על 5921 | הארץ 776 | ותקע 8628 | בשופר 7782 |
|---|---|---|---|---|---|---|---|---|---|---|---|---|
| uanatanu | 'atou | lahem | latzopeh. | | uara'ah | 'at | hachereb | ba'ah | 'al | ha'aretz; | uataqa' | bashoupar |
| **and set** | **him** | **their** | **for watchman** | | **If when he see** | | **the sword** | **come** | **upon** | **the land** | **and he blow** | **the trumpet** |

| והזהיר 2094 | את 853 | העם 5971: | **33:4** | ושמע 8085 | השמע 8085 | את 853 | קול 6963 | השופר 7782 | ולא 3808 | נזהר 2094 | ותבוא 935 |
|---|---|---|---|---|---|---|---|---|---|---|---|
| uahizhiyr | 'at | ha'am. | | uashama' | hashomea' | 'at | qoul | hashoupar | uala' | nizhar, | uatabou'a |
| **and warn** | | **the people** | | **Then whosoever hear** | | | **the sound of** | **the trumpet** | **and not** | **takes warning** | **if come** |

| חרב 2719 | ותקחהו 3947 | דמו 1818 | בראשו 7218 | יהיה 1961: | **33:5** | את 853 | קול 6963 | השופר 7782 | שמע 8085 | ולא 3808 |
|---|---|---|---|---|---|---|---|---|---|---|
| chereb | uatiqachehu; | damou | bara'shou | yihayeh. | | 'at | qoul | hashoupar | shama' | uala' |
| **the sword** | **and take him away** | **his blood** | **upon his own head** | **shall be** | | | **the sound of** | **the trumpet** | **He heard** | **not** |

| נזהר 2094 | דמו 1818 | בו 871a | יהיה 1961 | והוא 1931 | נזהר 2094 | נפשו 5315 | מלט 4422: | **33:6** | והצפה 6822 | כי 3588 |
|---|---|---|---|---|---|---|---|---|---|---|
| nizhar, | damou | bou | yihayeh; | uahu'a | nizhar | napshou | milet. | | uahatzpeh | kiy |
| **took warning** | **his blood** | **upon him** | **shall be** | **But he** | **that takes warning** | **his soul** | **shall deliver** | | **But if the watchman** | **if** |

| יראה 7200 | את 853 | החרב 2719 | באה 935 | ולא 3808 | תקע 8628 | בשופר 7782 | והעם 5971 | לא 3808 | נזהר 2094 | ותבוא 935 | חרב 2719 | ותקח 3947 |
|---|---|---|---|---|---|---|---|---|---|---|---|---|
| yir'ah | 'at | hachereb | ba'ah, | uala' | taqa' | bashoupar | uaha'am | la' | nizhar, | uatabou'a | chereb, | uatiqach |
| **see** | | **the sword** | **come** | **and not** | **blow** | **the trumpet** | **and the people** | **not** | **be warned** | **if come** | **the sword** | **and take** |

| מהם 1992 | נפש 5315 | הוא 1931 | בעונו 5771 | נלקח 3947 | ודמו 1818 | מיד 3027 | הצפה 6822 | אדרש 1875: |
|---|---|---|---|---|---|---|---|---|
| mehem | napesh; | hua' | ba'auonou | nilqach, | uadamou | miyad | hatzopeh | 'adrosh. |
| **from among them** | ***any* person** | **he** | **in his iniquity** | **is taken away** | **but his blood** | **at hand** | **the watchman's** | **will I require** |

Eze 33:31 Pharaoh shall see them, and shall be comforted over all his multitude, even Pharaoh and all his army slain by the sword, saith YHUH G-D.32 For I have caused my terror in the land of the living: and he shall be laid in the midst of the uncircumcised with them that are slain with the sword, even Pharaoh and all his multitude, saith YHUH G-D. **Eze** 33:1 Again the word of YHUH came unto me, saying,2 Son of man, speak to the children of your people, and say unto them, When I bring the sword upon a land, if the people of the land take a man of their coasts, and set him for their watchman:3 If when he see the sword come upon the land, he blow the trumpet, and warn the people;4 Then whosoever hear the sound of the trumpet, and take not warning; if the sword come, and take him away, his blood shall be upon his own head.5 He heard the sound of the trumpet, and took not warning; his blood shall be upon him. But he that take warning shall deliver his soul.6 But if the watchman see the sword come, and blow not the trumpet, and the people be not warned; if the sword come, and take any person from among them, he is taken away in his iniquity; but his blood will I require at the watchman's hand.

| 33:7 | | | | | | | | |
|---|---|---|---|---|---|---|---|---|
| ואתה 859 | בן 1121 | אדם 120 | צפה 6822 | נתתיך 5414 | לבית 1004 | ישראל 3478 | ושמעת 8085 | מפי 6310 |
| ua'atah | ben | 'adam, | tzopeh | natatiyka | labeyt | yisra'ael; | uashama'ta | mipiy |
| **So you** | **O son of** | **man** | **a watchman** | **I have set you** | **unto the house of** | **Israel** | **therefore you shall hear** | **at my mouth** |

| | | | | 33:8 | | | | | |
|---|---|---|---|---|---|---|---|---|---|
| דבר 1697 | והזהרת 2094 | אתם 853 | ממני 4480: | באמרי 559 | לרשע 7563 | רשע 7563 | מות 4194 | תמות 4191 | ולא 3808 |
| dabar, | uahizharta | 'atam | mimeniy. | ba'amariy | larasha', | rasha' | mout | tamut, | uala' |
| **the word** | **and warn** | **them** | **from me** | **When I say** | **unto the wicked** | **O wicked** | ***man* you shall surely** | **die** | **if not** |

| | | | | | | | | | |
|---|---|---|---|---|---|---|---|---|---|
| דברת 1696 | להזהיר 2094 | רשע 7563 | מדרכו 1870 | הוא 1931 | רשע 7563 | בעונו 5771 | ימות 4191 | ודמו 1818 | מידך 3027 |
| dibarta, | lahazhiyr | rasha' | midarkou; | hua' | rasha' | ba'auonou | yamut, | uadamou | miyadaka |
| **you do speak** | **to warn** | **the wicked** | **from his way** | **that** | **wicked** | **in his iniquity** | ***man* shall die** | **but his blood** | **at your hand** |

| | 33:9 | | | | | | | | | |
|---|---|---|---|---|---|---|---|---|---|---|
| אבקש 1245: | ואתה 859 | כי 3588 | הזהרת 2094 | רשע 7563 | מדרכו 1870 | לשוב 7725 | ממנה 4480 | ולא 3808 | שב 7725 | מדרכו 1870 |
| 'abaqesh. | ua'atah | kiy | hizharta | rasha' | midarkou | lashub | mimenah, | uala' | shab | midarkou; |
| **will I require** | **Nevertheless you** | **if** | **warn** | **the wicked** | **of his way** | **to turn** | **from it** | **if not** | **he do turn** | **from his way** |

| | | | | | | 33:10 | | | | |
|---|---|---|---|---|---|---|---|---|---|---|
| הוא 1931 | בעונו 5771 | ימות 4191 | ואתה 859 | נפשך 5315 | הצלת 5337: | ואתה 859 | בן 1121 | אדם 120 | אמר 559 | אל 413 |
| hua' | ba'auonou | yamut, | ua'atah | napshaka | hitzalta. | ua'atah | ben | 'adam, | 'amor | 'al |
| **he** | **in his iniquity** | **shall die** | **but you** | **your soul** | **have delivered** | **Therefore O you** | **son of** | **man** | **speak** | **unto** |

| | | | | | | | | | | |
|---|---|---|---|---|---|---|---|---|---|---|
| בית 1004 | ישראל 3478 | כן 3651 | אמרתם 559 | לאמר 559 | כי 3588 | פשעינו 6588 | וחטאתינו 2403 | עלינו 5921 | ובם 871a | אנחנו 587 |
| beyt | yisra'ael, | ken | 'amartem | lea'mor, | kiy | pasha'aeynu | uachata'teynu | 'aleynu; | uabam | 'anachnu |
| **the house of** | **Israel** | **Thus** | **you speak** | **saying** | **If** | **our transgressions** | **and our sins** | ***be* upon us** | **and in them** | **we** |

| | | | 33:11 | | | | | | | | |
|---|---|---|---|---|---|---|---|---|---|---|---|
| נמקים 4743 | ואיך 349 | נחיה 2421: | אמר 559 | אליהם 413 | חי 2416 | אני 589 | נאם 5002 | אדני 136 | יהוה 3069 | אם 518 | אחפץ 2654 |
| namaqiym | ua'aeyk | nichayeh. | 'amor | 'aleyhem | chay | 'aniy | na'am | 'adonay | Yahuah | 'am | 'achapotz |
| **pine away** | **how then** | **should we live?** | **Say** | **unto them** | **live** | ***As* I** | **saith** | **Adonai** | **Yahuah** | **no** | **I have pleasure** |

| | | | | | | | | | | |
|---|---|---|---|---|---|---|---|---|---|---|
| במות 4194 | הרשע 7563 | כי 3588 | אם 518 | בשוב 7725 | רשע 7563 | מדרכו 1870 | וחיה 2421 | שובו 7725 | שובו 7725 | מדרכיכם 1870 |
| bamout | harasha', | kiy | 'am | bashub | rasha' | midarkou | uachayah; | shubu | shubu | midarkeykem |
| **in the death of** | **the wicked** | **but** | **no** | **turn** | ***that* the wicked** | **from his way** | **and live** | **turn you** | **turn you** | **from ways** |

| | | | | | 33:12 | | | | | |
|---|---|---|---|---|---|---|---|---|---|---|
| הרעים 7451 | ולמה 4100 | תמותו 4191 | בית 1004 | ישראל 3478: | ואתה 859 | בן 1121 | אדם 120 | אמר 559 | אל 413 | בני 1121 |
| hara'aym | ualamah | tamutu | beyt | yisra'ael. | ua'atah | ben | 'adam, | 'amor | 'al | baney |
| **your evil** | **for why** | **will you die** | **O house of** | **Israel?** | **Therefore you** | **son of** | **man** | **say** | **unto** | **the children of** |

| | | | | | | |
|---|---|---|---|---|---|---|
| עמך 5971 | צדקת 6666 | הצדיק 6662 | לא 3808 | תצילנו 5337 | ביום 3117 | פשעו 6588 |
| 'amaka | tzidqat | hatzadiyq, | la' | tatziylenu | bayoum | pish'au, |
| **your people** | **The righteousness of** | **the righteous** | **not** | **shall deliver him** | **in the day of** | **his transgression** |

| | | | | | | | | |
|---|---|---|---|---|---|---|---|---|
| ורשעת 7564 | הרשע 7563 | לא 3808 | יכשל 3782 | בה 871a | ביום 3117 | שובו 7725 | מרשעו 7562 | וצדיק 6662 |
| uarish'at | harasha' | la' | yikashel | bah, | bayoum | shubou | merish'au; | uatzadiyq, |
| **as for the wickedness of** | **the wicked** | **not** | **he shall fall** | **thereby** | **in the day** | **that he turned** | **from his wickedness** | **the righteous** |

| | | | | | | 33:13 | |
|---|---|---|---|---|---|---|---|
| לא 3808 | יוכל 3201 | לחיות 2421 | בה 871a | ביום 3117 | חטאתו 2398: | באמרי 559 | לצדיק 6662 |
| la' | yukal | lichayout | bah | bayoum | chata'tou. | ba'amariy | latzadiyq |
| **neither** | **shall be able** | **to live** | **for his** | ***righteousness* in the day** | **that he sin** | **When I shall say** | **to the righteous** |

Eze 33:7 So you, O son of man, I have set you a watchman unto the house of Israel; therefore you shall hear the word at my mouth, and warn them from me.8 When I say unto the wicked, O wicked man, you shall surely die; if you dost not speak to warn the wicked from his way, that wicked man shall die in his iniquity; but his blood will I require at your hand.9 Nevertheless, if you warn the wicked of his way to turn from it; if he do not turn from his way, he shall die in his iniquity; but you have delivered your soul.10 Therefore, O you son of man, speak unto the house of Israel; Thus you speak, saying, If our transgressions and our sins be upon us, and we pine away in them, how should we then live?11 Say unto them, As I live, saith YHUH G-D, I have no pleasure in the death of the wicked; but that the wicked turn from his way and live: turn you, turn you from your evil ways; for why will you die, O house of Israel?12 Therefore, you son of man, say unto the children of your people, The righteousness of the righteous shall not deliver him in the day of his transgression: as for the wickedness of the wicked, he shall not fall thereby in the day that he turneth from his wickedness; neither shall the righteous be able to live for his righteousness in the day that he sin.

חיה 2421 יחיה 2421 והוא 1931 בטח 982 על 5921 צדקתו 6666 ועשה 6213 עול 5766 כל 3605 צדקתו 6666 לא 3808
chayoh yichayeh, uahu'a batach 'al tzidqatou ua'asah 'auel; kal tzidqatou la'
**_that_ he shall surely live if he trust to his own righteousness and commit iniquity all his righteousness not**

תזכרנה 2142 ובעולו 5766 אשר 834 עשה 6213 בו 871a ימות 4191: 33:14 ובאמרי 559 לרשע 7563
tizakarnah, uab'aulou 'asher 'asah bou yamut. uab'amariy larasha'
**shall be remembered but for his iniquity that he has committed for it he shall die Again when I say unto the wicked**

מות 4194 תמות 4191 ושב 7725 מחטאתו 2403 ועשה 6213 משפט 4941 וצדקה 6666: 33:15 חבל 2258 ישיב 7725
mout tamut; uashab mechata'tou, ua'asah mishapat uatzdaqah. chabol yashiyb
**You shall surely die if he turn from his sin and do that which is lawful and right _If_ the pledge restore**

רשע 7563 גזלה 1500 ישלם 7999 בחקות 2708 החיים 2416 הלך 1980 לבלתי 1115 עשות 6213 עול 5766 חיו 2421
rasha' gazelah yashalem, bachuqout hachayiym halak, labiltiy asout 'auel; chayou
**the wicked that he had robbed give again in the statutes of life walk without committing iniquity he shall surely**

יחיה 2421 לא 3808 ימות 4191: 33:16 כל 3605 חטאתו 2403 אשר 834 חטא 2398 לא 3808 תזכרנה 2142 לו 3807a
yichayeh la' yamut. kal chata'tou 'asher chata', la' tizakarnah lou';
**live not he shall die None of his sins that he has committed not shall be mentioned unto him**

משפט 4941 וצדקה 6666 עשה 6213 חיו 2421 יחיה 2421: 33:17 ואמרו 559 בני 1121 עמך 5971 לא 3808
mishapat uatzdaqah 'asah chayou yichayeh. ua'amaru baney 'amaka, la'
**that which is lawful and right he has done he shall surely live Yet say the children of your people not**

יתכן 8505 דרך 1870 אדני 136 והמה 1992 דרכם 1870 לא 3808 יתכן 8505: 33:18 בשוב 7725 צדיק 6662
yitaken derek 'adonay; uahemah darkam la' yitaken. bashub tzadiyq
**is equal The way of Adonai but as for them their way not is equal When turned the righteous**

מצדקתו 6666 ועשה 6213 עול 5766 ומת 4191 בהם 871a: 33:19 ובשוב 7725 רשע 7563 מרשעתו 7564
mitzidqatou ua'asah 'auel; uamet bahem. uabshub rasha' merish'atou,
**from his righteousness and commit iniquity he shall even die thereby But if turn the wicked from his wickedness**

ועשה 6213 משפט 4941 וצדקה 6666 עליהם 5921 הוא 1931 יחיה 2421: 33:20 ואמרתם 559 לא 3808 יתכן 8505 דרך 1870 אדני 136
ua'asah mishapat uatzdaqah; 'aleyhem hua' yichayeh. ua'amartem la' yitaken derek 'adonay;
**and do that which is lawful and right thereby he shall live Yet you say not is equal The way of Adonai**

איש 376 כדרכיו 1870 אשפוט 8199 אתכם 853 בית 1004 ישראל 3478: 33:21 ויהי 1961 בשתי 8147 עשרה 6240 שנה 8141
'aysh kidrakayu 'ashpout 'atkem beyt yisra'ael. uayahiy bishtey 'asreh shanah,
**every one after his ways I will judge you O house of Israel And it came to pass in two of _the_ ten year**

בעשרי 6224 בחמשה 2568 לחדש 2320 לגלותנו 1546 בא 935 אלי 413 הפליט 6412 מירושלם 3389
ba'asiyriy bachamishah lachodesh lagalutenu; ba' 'aelay hapaliyt miyarushalaim
**in the tenth _month_ in the fifth _day_ of the month of our captivity came unto me _that_ one that had escaped out of Jerusalem**

לאמר 559 הכתה 5221 העיר 5892: 33:22 ויד 3027 יהוה 3068 היתה 1961 אלי 413 בערב 6153 לפני 6440 בוא 935
lea'mor huktah ha'ayr. uayad Yahuah hayatah 'aelay ba'areb, lipney bou'a
**saying is smitten The city Now the hand of Yahuah was upon me in the evening afore came**

Eze 33:13 When I shall say to the righteous, that he shall surely live; if he trust to his own righteousness, and commit iniquity, all his righteousnesses shall not be remembered; but for his iniquity that he has committed, he shall die for it.14 Again, when I say unto the wicked, Thou shall surely die; if he turn from his sin, and do that which is lawful and right;15 If the wicked restore the pledge, give again that he had robbed, walk in the statutes of life, without committing iniquity; he shall surely live, he shall not die.16 None of his sins that he has committed shall be mentioned unto him: he has done that which is lawful and right; he shall surely live.17 Yet the children of your people say, The way of YHUH is not equal: but as for them, their way is not equal.18 When the righteous turneth from his righteousness, and committeth iniquity, he shall even die thereby.19 But if the wicked turn from his wickedness, and do that which is lawful and right, he shall live thereby.20 Yet you say, The way of YHUH is not equal. O you house of Israel, I will judge you everyone after his ways.21 And it came to pass in the twelfth year of our captivity, in the tenth month, in the fifth day of the month, that one that had escaped out of Jerusalem came unto me, saying, The city is smitten.22 Now the hand of YHUH was upon me in the evening, afore he that was escaped came; and had opened my mouth,

הפליט 6412 ויפתח 6605 את 853 פי 6310 עד 5704 בוא 935 אלי 413 בבקר 1242 ויפתח 6605 פי 6310
hapaliyt, uayiptach 'at piy, 'ad bou'a 'aelay baboqer; uayipatach piy,
**he that was escaped and had opened my mouth until he came to me in the morning and was opened my mouth**

ולא 3808 נאלמתי 481 עוד 5750: 33:23 ויהי 1961 דבר 1697 יהוה 3068 אלי 413 לאמר 559: 33:24 בן 1121 אדם 120 ישבי 3427
uala' ne'alamtiy 'aud. uayahiy dabar Yahuah 'aelay lea'mor. ben 'adam, yoshabey
**and no I was dumb more Then came the word of Yahuah unto me saying Son of man they that inhabit**

החרבות 2723 האלה 428 על 5921 אדמת 127 ישראל 3478 אמרים 559 לאמר 559 אחד 259 היה 1961 אברהם 85 ויירש 3423 את 853 הארץ 776
hecharabout ha'aeleh 'al 'admat yisra'ael 'amariym lea'mor, 'achad hayah 'abraham, uayiyrash 'at ha'aretz;
**wastes those of the land of Israel speak saying one was Abraham and he inherited the land**

ואנחנו 587 רבים 7227 לנו 3807a נתנה 5414 הארץ 776 למורשה 4181: 33:25 לכן 3651 אמר 559 אליהם 413 כה 3541 אמר 559 אדני 136
ua'anachnu rabiym, lanu nitanah ha'aretz lamourashah. laken 'amor 'aleyhem koh 'amar 'adonay
**but we *are* many us is given the land for inheritance Wherefore say unto them Thus saith Adonai**

יהוה 3068 על 5921 הדם 1818 תאכלו 398 ועינכם 5869 תשאו 5375 אל 413 גלוליכם 1544 ודם 1818 תשפכו 8210 והארץ 776
Yahuah 'al hadam ta'kelu ua'aeynekem tis'au 'al giluleykem uadam tishpoku; uaha'aretz
**Yahuah with the blood You eat and your eyes lift up toward your idols and blood shed and the land?**

תירשו 3423: 33:26 עמדתם 5975 על 5921 חרבכם 2719 עשיתן 6213 תועבה 8441 ואיש 376 את 853 אשת 802 רעהו 7453
tiyrashu. 'amadtem 'al charbakem 'asiyten tou'aebah, ua'aysh 'at 'aeshet re'aehu
**shall you possess You stand upon your sword you work abomination and every one wife his neighbour's**

טמאתם 2930 והארץ 776 תירשו 3423: 33:27 כה 3541 תאמר 559 אלהם 413 כה 3541 אמר 559 אדני 136 יהוה 3069 חי 2416 אני 589 אם 518
timea'tam; uaha'aretz tiyrashu. koh ta'mar 'alehem koh 'amar 'adonay Yahuah chay 'aniy 'am
**you defile and the land? shall you possess Thus Say you unto them Thus saith Adonai Yahuah live *As* I surely**

לא 3808 אשר 834 בחרבות 2723 בחרב 2719 יפלו 5307 ואשר 834 על 5921 פני 6440 השדה 7704 לחיה 2416 נתתיו 5414
la' 'asher becharabout bachereb yipolu, ua'asher 'al paney hasadeh, lachayah natatiyu
**not that *are* in the wastes by the sword they shall fall and him that *is* in open the field to the beasts will I give**

לאכלו 398 ואשר 834 במצדות 4686 ובמערות 4631 בדבר 1698 ימותו 4191: 33:28 ונתתי 5414 את 853 הארץ 776
la'akalou; ua'asher bamatzadout uabama'arout badeber yamutu. uanatatiy 'at ha'aretz
**to be devoured and they that *be* in the forts and in the caves of the pestilence shall die For I will lay the land**

שממה 8077 ומשמה 4923 ונשבת 7673 גאון 1347 עזה 5797 ושממו 8074 הרי 2022 ישראל 3478 מאין 369
shamamah uamshamah, uanishbat ga'aun 'azah; uashamamu harey yisra'ael me'ayn
**waste and desolate and shall cease the pomp of her strength and shall be desolate the mountains of Israel that none**

עובר 5674: 33:29 וידעו 3045 כי 3588 אני 589 יהוה 3068 בתתי 5414 את 853 הארץ 776 שממה 8077 ומשמה 4923
'auber. uayada'aua kiy 'aniy Yahuah; batitiy 'at ha'aretz shamamah uamshamah,
**shall pass through Then shall they know that I *am* Yahuah when I have laid the land waste and desolate**

על 5921 כל 3605 תועבתם 8441 אשר 834 עשו 6213: 33:30 ואתה 859 בן 1121 אדם 120 בני 1121 עמך 5971
'al kal tou'abotam 'asher 'asu. ua'atah ben 'adam, baney 'amaka,
**because of all their abominations which they have committed Also you son of man the children of your people**

Eze 33:22 until he came to me in the morning; and my mouth was opened, and I was no more dumb.23 Then the word of YHUH came unto me, saying,24 Son of man, they that inhabit those wastes of the land of Israel speak, saying, Abraham was one, and he inherited the land: but we are many; the land is given us for inheritance.25 Wherefore say unto them, Thus saith YHUH G-D; You eat with the blood, and lift up your eyes toward your idols, and shed blood: and shall you possess the land?26 You stand upon your sword, you work abomination, and you defile everyone his neighbor's wife: and shall you possess the land?27 Say you thus unto them, Thus saith YHUH G-D; As I live, surely they that are in the wastes shall fall by the sword, and him that is in the open field will I give to the beasts to be devoured, and they that be in the forts and in the caves shall die of the pestilence.28 For I will lay the land most desolate, and the pomp of her strength shall cease; and the mountains of Israel shall be desolate, that none shall pass through.29 Then shall they know that I am YHUH, when I have laid the land most desolate because of all their abominations which they have committed.30 Also, you son of man, the children of your people still are talking against you by the walls and in the doors of the houses, and speak one to another, everyone to his brother, saying, Come, I pray you,

הנדברים 1696 בך 871a אצל 681 הקירות 7023 ובפתחי 6607 הבתים 1004 ודבר 1696 חד 2297 את 853 אחד 259 איש 376 את 854
hanidbariym baka 'aetzel haqiyrout, uabpitchey habatiym; uadiber chad 'at 'achad, 'aysh 'at
***still*** **are talking against you by the walls and in the doors of the houses and speak one to another every one** ***to***

33:31
אחיו 251 לאמר 559 באו 935 נא 4994 ושמעו 8085 מה 4100 הדבר 1697 היוצא 3318 מאת 853 יהוה 3068: ויבואו 935
'achiyu lea'mor, bo'au naa' uashim'au, mah hadabar, hayoutzea' me'at Yahuah. uayabou'au
**his brother saying Come I pray you and hear what** ***is*** **the word that comes forth from Yahuah And they come as**

אליך 413 כמבוא 3996 עם 5971 וישבו 3427 לפניך 6440 עמי 5971 ושמעו 8085 את 853 דבריך 1697 ואותם 853 לא 3808
'aeleyka kimbou'a 'am uayeshabu lapaneyka 'amiy, uashama'au 'at debareyka, ua'atam la'
**unto you comes** ***the*** **people and they sit before you** ***as*** **my people and they hear your words but them not**

33:32
יעשו 6213 כי 3588 עגבים 5690 בפיהם 6310 המה 1992 עשים 6213 אחרי 310 בצעם 1215 לבם 3820 הלך 1980:
ya'asu; kiy 'agabiym bapiyhem hemah 'asiym, 'acharey bitz'am libam holek.
**they will do for much love with their mouth they show after their covetousness** ***but*** **their heart goes**

והנך 2005 להם 3807a כשיר 7892 עגבים 5690 יפה 3303 קול 6963 ומטב 2895 נגן 5059
uahinaka lahem kashiyr 'agabiym, yapeh qoul uametib nagen;
**And lo you** ***are*** **unto them as a song of very lovely** ***one that has*** **a pleasant voice and well can play** ***on*** **an instrument**

33:33
ושמעו 8085 את 853 דבריך 1697 ועשים 6213 אינם 369 אותם 853: ובבאה 935 הנה 2009 באה 935
uashama'au 'at debareyka, ua'asiym 'aeynam 'autam. uabbo'ah; hineh ba'ah,
**for they hear** ***them*** **your words but they do not them And when this comes to pass lo it will come**

וידעו 3045 כי 3588 נביא 5030 היה 1961 בתוכם 8432:
uayada'au, kiy nabiy'a hayah batoukam.
**then shall they know that a prophet has been among them**

**Ezek 34:1** ויהי 1961 דבר 1697 יהוה 3068 אלי 413 לאמר 559: **34:2** בן 1121 אדם 120 הנבא 5012 על 5921 רועי 7462 ישראל 3478
uayahiy dabar Yahuah 'aelay lea'mor. ben 'adam hinabea' 'al ro'aey yisra'ael;
**And came the word of Yahuah unto me saying Son of man prophesy against the shepherds of Israel**

הנבא 5012 ואמרת 559 אליהם 413 לרעים 7462 כה 3541 אמר 559 אדני 136 יהוה 3069 הוי 1945 רעי 7462 ישראל 3478
hinabea' ua'amarta 'aleyhem laro'aym koh 'amar 'adonay Yahuah houy ro'aey yisra'ael
**prophesy and say unto them unto the shepherds Thus saith Adonai Yahuah Woe** ***be*** **to** ***the*** **shepherds of Israel**

34:3
אשר 834 היו 1961 רעים 7462 אותם 853 הלוא 3808 הצאן 6629 ירעו 7462 הרעים 7462: את 853 החלב 2459 תאכלו 398 ואת 853
'asher hayu ro'aym 'autam, halou'a hatza'an, yir'au haro'aym. 'at hacheleb ta'kelu ua'at
**that do feed themselves not the flocks? should feed the shepherds the fat You eat** ***and***

34:4
הצמר 6785 תלבשו 3847 הבריאה 1277 תזבחו 2076 הצאן 6629 לא 3808 תרעו 7462: את 853 הנחלות 2470 לא 3808
hatzemer tilbashu, habariy'ah tizbachu; hatza'an la' tir'au. 'at hanachalout la'
***with*** **the wool you clothe you them that are fed you kill the flock not** ***but*** **you feed The diseased not**

חזקתם 2388 ואת 853 החולה 2470 לא 3808 רפאתם 7495 ולנשברת 7665 לא 3808
chizaqtem ua'at hachoulah la' ripea'tem, ualanishberet la'
**have you strengthened** ***neither*** **that which was sick neither have you healed** ***that which was*** **broken neither**

Eze 34:30 and hear what is the word that cometh forth from YHUH.31 And they come unto you as the people cometh, and they sit before you as my people, and they hear your words, but they will not do them: for with their mouth they show much love, but their heart go after their covetousness.32 And, lo, you are unto them as a very lovely song of one that has a pleasant voice, and can play well on an instrument: for they hear your words, but they do them not.33 And when this cometh to pass, (lo, it will come,) then shall they know that a prophet has been among them. **Eze** 34:1 And the word of YHUH came unto me, saying,2 Son of man, prophesy against the shepherds of Israel, prophesy, and say unto them, Thus saith YHUH G-D unto the shepherds; Woe be to the shepherds of Israel that do feed themselves! should not the shepherds feed the flocks?3 You eat the fat, and you clothe you with the wool, you kill them that are fed: but you feed not the flock.4 The diseased have you not strengthened, neither have you healed that which was sick, neither have you bound up that which was broken, neither have you brought again that which was driven away, neither have you sought that which was lost; but with force and with cruelty have you ruled them.

| חבשתם 2280 | ואת 853 | הנדחת 5080 | לא 3808 | השבתם 7725 | ואת 853 | האבדת 6 |
|---|---|---|---|---|---|---|
| chabashtem, | ua'at | hanidachat | la' | hashebotem, | ua'at | ha'abedet |
| **have you bound up** | ***neither*** | **that which was driven away** | **neither** | **have you brought again** | ***neither*** | **that which was lost** |

| לא 3808 | בקשתם 1245 | ובחזקה 2394 | רדיתם 7287 | אתם 853 | ובפרך 6531: | 34:5 | ותפוצינה 6327 |
|---|---|---|---|---|---|---|---|
| la' | biqashtem; | uabchazaqah | radiytem | 'atam | uabparek. | | uataputzeynah |
| **neither** | **have you sought** | **but with force** | **have you ruled** | **them** | **and with cruelty** | | **And they were scattered** |

| מבלי 1097 | רעה 7462 | ותהיינה 1961 | לאכלה 402 | לכל 3605 | חית 2416 | השדה 7704 | ותפוצינה 6327: | 34:6 |
|---|---|---|---|---|---|---|---|---|
| mibaliy | ro'ah; | uatihayeynah | la'akalah | lakal | chayat | hasadeh | uataputzeynah. | |
| **because *there is* no** | **shepherd** | **and they became** | **meat** | **to all** | **the beasts of** | **the field** | **when they were scattered** | |

| ישגו 7686 | צאני 6629 | בכל 3605 | ההרים 2022 | ועל 5921 | כל 3605 | גבעה 1389 | רמה 7311 | ועל 5921 | כל 3605 | פני 6440 | הארץ 776 |
|---|---|---|---|---|---|---|---|---|---|---|---|
| yishgu | tza'niy | bakal | hehariym, | ua'al | kal | gib'ah | ramah; | ua'al | kal | paney | ha'aretz |
| **wandered** | **My sheep** | **through all** | **the mountains** | **and upon yea** | **every** | **hill** | **high** | **upon** | **all** | **the face of** | **the earth** |

| נפצו 6327 | צאני 6629 | ואין 369 | דורש 1875 | ואין 369 | מבקש 1245: | 34:7 | לכן 3651 | רעים 7462 | שמעו 8085 | את 853 |
|---|---|---|---|---|---|---|---|---|---|---|
| napotzu | tza'niy, | ua'aeyn | douresh | ua'aeyn | mabaqesh. | | laken | ro'aym, | shim'au | 'at |
| **was scattered** | **my flock** | **and none** | **did search** | **or** | **seek *after them*** | | **Therefore** | **you shepherds** | **hear** | |

| דבר 1697 | יהוה 3068: | 34:8 | חי 2416 | אני 589 | נאם 5002 | אדני 136 | יהוה 3069 | אם 518 | לא 3808 | יען 3282 | היות 1961 | צאני 6629 | לבז 957 |
|---|---|---|---|---|---|---|---|---|---|---|---|---|---|
| dabar | Yahuah. | | chay | 'aniy | na'am | 'adonay | Yahuah | 'am | la' | ya'an | hayout | tza'niy | labaz |
| **the word of** | **Yahuah** | | **live** | ***As* I** | **saith** | **Adonai** | **Yahuah** | **surely** | **not** | **because** | **become of** | **my flock** | **a prey** |

| ותהיינה 1961 | צאני 6629 | לאכלה 402 | לכל 3605 | חית 2416 | השדה 7704 | מאין 369 | רעה 7462 | ולא 3808 | דרשו 1875 | רעי 7462 |
|---|---|---|---|---|---|---|---|---|---|---|
| uatihayeynah | tza'niy | la'akalah | lakal | chayat | hasadeh | me'ayn | ro'ah, | uala' | darashu | ro'aey |
| **become** | **my flock** | **meat** | **to every** | **beast of** | **the field** | **because *there was* no** | **shepherd** | **neither** | **did search** | **my shepherds** |

| את 853 | צאני 6629 | וירעו 7462 | הרעים 7462 | אותם 853 | ואת 853 | צאני 6629 | לא 3808 | רעו 7462: | 34:9 | לכן 3651 | הרעים 7462 |
|---|---|---|---|---|---|---|---|---|---|---|---|
| 'at | tza'niy; | uayir'au | haro'aym | 'autam, | ua'at | tza'niy | la' | ra'au. | | laken | haro'aym, |
| | ***for* my flock** | **but fed** | **the shepherds** | **themselves** | ***and*** | **my flock** | **not** | **fed** | | **Therefore** | **O you shepherds** |

| שמעו 8085 | דבר 1697 | יהוה 3068: | 34:10 | כה 3541 | אמר 559 | אדני 136 | יהוה 3068 | הנני 2005 | אל 413 | הרעים 7462 | ודרשתי 1875 |
|---|---|---|---|---|---|---|---|---|---|---|---|
| shim'au | dabar | Yahuah. | | koh | 'amar | 'adonay | Yahuah | hinniy | 'al | haro'aym | uadarashtiy |
| **hear** | **the word of** | **Yahuah** | | **Thus** | **saith** | **Adonai** | **Yahuah** | **Behold I *am*** | **against** | **the shepherds** | **and I will require** |

| את 853 | צאני 6629 | מידם 3027 | והשבתים 7673 | מרעות 7462 | צאן 6629 | ולא 3808 | ירעו 7462 | עוד 5750 | הרעים 7462 |
|---|---|---|---|---|---|---|---|---|---|
| 'at | tzea'niy | miyadam, | uahishbatiym | mera'aut | tza'n, | uala' | yir'au | 'aud | haro'aym |
| | **my flock** | **at their hand** | **and cause them to cease** | **from feeding** | **the flock** | **neither** | **shall feed** | **any more** | **the shepherds** |

| אותם 853 | והצלתי 5337 | צאני 6629 | מפיהם 6310 | ולא 3808 | תהיין 1961 | להם 3807a | לאכלה 402: | 34:11 | כי 3588 | כה 3541 | אמר 559 |
|---|---|---|---|---|---|---|---|---|---|---|---|
| 'autam; | uahitzaltiy | tza'niy | mipiyhem, | uala' | tihayeyna | lahem | la'akalah | | kiy | koh | 'amar |
| **themselves** | **for I will deliver** | **my flock** | **from their mouth** | **that not** | **they may be** | **for them** | **meat** | | **For** | **thus** | **saith** |

| אדני 136 | יהוה 3069 | הנני 2005 | אני 589 | ודרשתי 1875 | את 853 | צאני 6629 | ובקרתים 1239: | 34:12 | כבקרת 1243 | רעה 7462 |
|---|---|---|---|---|---|---|---|---|---|---|
| 'adonay | Yahuah; | hinniy | 'aniy | uadarashtiy | 'at | tza'niy | uabiqartiym. | | kabaqarat | ro'ah |
| **Adonai** | **Yahuah** | **Behold I *even*** | **I** | **will both search** | | **my sheep** | **and seek them out** | | **As seek out** | **a shepherd** |

Eze 34:5 And they were scattered, because there is no shepherd: and they became meat to all the beasts of the field, when they were scattered.6 My sheep wandered through all the mountains, and upon every high hill: yea, my flock was scattered upon all the face of the earth, and none did search or seek after them.7 Therefore, you shepherds, hear the word of YHUH;8 As I live, saith YHUH G-D, surely because my flock became a prey, and my flock became meat to every beast of the field, because there was no shepherd, neither did my shepherds search for my flock, but the shepherds fed themselves, and fed not my flock;9 Therefore, O you shepherds, hear the word of YHUH;10 Thus saith YHUH G-D; Behold, I am against the shepherds; and I will require my flock at their hand, and cause them to cease from feeding the flock; neither shall the shepherds feed themselves anymore; for I will deliver my flock from their mouth, that they may not be meat for them.11 For thus saith YHUH G-D; Behold, I, even I, will both search my sheep, and seek them out.12 As a shepherd seek out his flock in the day that he is among his sheep that are scattered; so will I seek out my sheep, and will deliver them out of all places where they have been scattered in the cloudy and dark day.

| עדרו 5739 | ביום 3117 | היותו 1961 | בתוך 8432 | צאנו 6629 | נפרשות 6567 | כן 3651 | אבקר 1239 | את 853 | צאני 6629 | והצלתי 5337 |
|---|---|---|---|---|---|---|---|---|---|---|
| 'adrou | bayoum | heyoutou | batouk | tza'nou | niprashout, | ken | 'abaqer | 'at | tza'niy; | uahitzaltiy |
| **his flock** | **in the day** | **that he is** | **among** | **his sheep** | ***that are* scattered** | **so** | **will I seek out** | | **my sheep** | **and will deliver** |

| אתהם 853 | מכל 3605 | המקומת 4725 | אשר 834 | נפצו 6327 | שם 8033 | ביום 3117 | ענן 6051 | וערפל 6205: | 34:13 |
|---|---|---|---|---|---|---|---|---|---|
| 'athem, | mikal | hamaqoumot | 'asher | napotzu | sham, | bayoum | 'anan | ua'arapel. | |
| **them** | **out of all** | **places** | **where** | **they have been scattered** | **there** | **in day** | **the cloudy** | **and dark** | |

| והוצאתים 3318 | מן 4480 | העמים 5971 | וקבצתים 6908 | מן 4480 | הארצות 776 | והביאתים 935 | אל 413 | אדמתם 127 |
|---|---|---|---|---|---|---|---|---|
| uahoutzea'tiym | min | ha'amiym, | uaqibatztiym | min | ha'aratzout, | uahabiy'atiym | 'al | 'admatam; |
| **And I will bring them out** | **from** | **the people** | **and gather them** | **from** | **the countries** | **and will bring them** | **to** | **their own land** |

| ורעיתים 7462 | אל 413 | הרי 2022 | ישראל 3478 | באפיקים 650 | ובכל 3605 | מושבי 4186 | הארץ 776: | 34:14 |
|---|---|---|---|---|---|---|---|---|
| uar'aytiym | 'al | harey | yisra'ael, | ba'apiyqiym | uabkol | moushabey | ha'aretz. | |
| **and feed them** | **upon** | **the mountains of** | **Israel** | **by the rivers** | **and in all** | **the inhabited places of** | **the country** | |

| במרעה 4829 | טוב 2896 | ארעה 7462 | אתם 853 | ובהרי 2022 | מרום 4791 | ישראל 3478 | יהיה 1961 | נוהם 5116 | שם 8033 | תרבצנה 7257 |
|---|---|---|---|---|---|---|---|---|---|---|
| bamir'ah | toub | 'ar'ah | 'atam, | uabharey | maroum | yisra'ael | yihayeh | nauehem; | sham | tirbatzanah |
| **in a pasture** | **good** | **I will feed** | **them** | **and upon mountains of** | ***the* high** | **Israel** | **shall be** | **their fold** | **there** | **shall they lie** |

| בנוה 5116 | טוב 2896 | ומרעה 4829 | שמן 8082 | תרעינה 7462 | אל 413 | הרי 2022 | ישראל 3478: | 34:15 | אני 589 | ארעה 7462 | צאני 6629 |
|---|---|---|---|---|---|---|---|---|---|---|---|
| banaueh | toub, | uamir'ah | shamen | tir'aynah | 'al | harey | yisra'ael. | | 'aniy | 'ar'ah | tza'niy |
| **in a fold** | **good** | **and *in* a pasture** | **fat** | **shall they feed** | **upon** | **the mountains of** | **Israel** | | **I** | **will feed** | **my flock** |

| ואני 589 | ארביצם 7257 | נאם 5002 | אדני 136 | יהוה 3069: | 34:16 | את 853 | האבדת 6 | אבקש 1245 | ואת 853 |
|---|---|---|---|---|---|---|---|---|---|
| ua'aniy | 'arbiytzem, | na'am | 'adonay | Yahuah. | | 'at | ha'abedet | 'abaqesh | ua'at |
| **and I** | **will cause them to lie down** | **saith** | **Adonai** | **Yahuah** | | | **that which was lost** | **I will seek** | ***and*** |

| הנדחת 5080 | אשיב 7725 | ולנשברת 7665 | אחבש 2280 | ואת 853 | החולה 2470 | אחזק 2388 |
|---|---|---|---|---|---|---|
| hanidachat | 'ashiyb, | ualanishberet | 'achebosh, | ua'at | hachoulah | 'achazeq; |
| **that which was driven away** | **bring again** | **and broken** | **will bind up *that which was*** | **and** | **that which was sick** | **will strengthen** |

| ואת 853 | השמנה 8082 | ואת 853 | החזקה 2389 | אשמיד 8045 | ארענה 7462 | במשפט 4941: | 34:17 | ואתנה 859 | צאני 6629 | כה 3541 |
|---|---|---|---|---|---|---|---|---|---|---|
| ua'at | hashamenah | ua'at | hachazaqah | 'ashmiyd | 'ar'anah | bamishpat. | | ua'atenah | tza'niy, | koh |
| ***but*** | **the fat** | ***and*** | **the strong** | **I will destroy** | **I will feed them** | **with judgment** | | **And *as for* you** | **O my flock** | **thus** |

| אמר 559 | אדני 136 | יהוה 3069 | הנני 2005 | שפט 8199 | בין 996 | שה 7716 | לשה 7716 | לאילים 352 | ולעתודים 6260: | 34:18 |
|---|---|---|---|---|---|---|---|---|---|---|
| 'amar | 'adonay | Yahuah; | hinniy | shopet | beyn | seh | laseh, | la'aeyliym | uala'atudiym. | |
| **saith** | **Adonai** | **Yahuah** | **Behold I** | **judge** | **between** | **cattle** | **and cattle** | **between the rams** | **and the he goats** | |

| המעט 4592 | מכם 4480 | המרעה 4829 | הטוב 2896 | תרעו 7462 | ויתר 3499 | מרעיכם 4829 | תרמסו 7429 |
|---|---|---|---|---|---|---|---|
| hama'at | mikem, | hamir'ah | hatoub | tir'au, | uayeter | mir'aeykem, | tirmasu |
| ***Seem it* a small thing** | **unto you** | **pasture** | **the good** | **to have eaten up** | **but the residue of** | **your pasture?** | **you must tread down** |

| ברגליכם 7272 | ומשקע 4950 | מים 4325 | תשתו 8354 | ואת 853 | הנותרים 3498 | ברגליכם 7272 | תרפשון 7515: |
|---|---|---|---|---|---|---|---|
| baragleykem; | uamishqa' | mayim | tishtu, | ua'at | hanoutariym, | baragleykem | tirposun. |
| **with your feet** | **the deep** | **waters** | **to have drunk of** | ***but*** | **the residue** | **with your feet?** | **you must foul** |

Eze 34:13 And I will bring them out from the people, and gather them from the countries, and will bring them to their own land, and feed them upon the mountains of Israel by the rivers, and in all the inhabited places of the country.14 I will feed them in a good pasture, and upon the high mountains of Israel shall their fold be: there shall they lie in a good fold, and in a fat pasture shall they feed upon the mountains of Israel.15 I will feed my flock, and I will cause them to lie down, saith YHUH G-D.16 I will seek that which was lost, and bring again that which was driven away, and will bind up that which was broken, and will strengthen that which was sick: but I will destroy the fat and the strong; I will feed them with judgment.17 And as for you, O my flock, thus saith YHUH G-D; Behold, I judge between cattle and cattle, between the rams and the he goats.18 Seem it a small thing unto you to have eaten up the good pasture, but you must tread down with your feet the residue of your pastures? and to have drunk of the deep waters, but you must foul the residue with your feet?

34:19 וצאני 6629 מרמס 4823 רגליכם 7272 תרעינה 7462 ומרפש 4833
uatza'niy; mirmas ragleykem tir'aynah, uamirpas
**And *as for* my flock that which you have trodden with your feet they eat and that which you have fouled with**

רגליכם 7272 תשתינה 8354: 34:20 לכן 3651 כה 3541 אמר 559 אדני 136 יהוה 3069 אליהם 413 הנני 2005 אני 589 ושפטתי 8199 בין 996
ragleykem tishteynah. laken, koh 'amar 'adonay Yahuah 'aleyhem; hinniy 'aniy uashapattiy beyn
**your feet they drink Therefore thus saith Adonai Yahuah unto them Behold I *even* I will judge between**

שה 7716 בריה 1277 ובין 996 שה 7716 רזה 7330: 34:21 יען 3282 בצד 6654 ובכתף 3802 תהדפו 1920 ובקרניכם 7161
seh biryah, uabeyn seh razah. ya'an, batzad uabkatep tahadopu, uabqarneykem
**cattle *the* fat and between cattle the lean Because with side and with shoulder you have thrust and with your horns**

תנגחו 5055 כל 3605 הנחלות 2470 עד 5704 אשר 834 הפיצותם 6327 אותנה 853 אל 413 החוצה 2351: 34:22 והושעתי 3467 לצאני 6629
tanagchu kal hanachalout; 'ad 'asher hapitzoutem 'autanah 'al hachutzah. uahousha'atiy latza'niy,
**pushed all the diseased till which you have scattered them to abroad Therefore will I save my flock**

ולא 3808 תהיינה 1961 עוד 5750 לבז 957 ושפטתי 8199 בין 996 שה 7716 לשה 7716: 34:23 והקמתי 6965 עליהם 5921 רעה 7462
uala' tihayeynah 'aud labaz; uashapatiy, beyn seh laseh. uahaqimotiy 'aleyhem ro'ah
**and no they shall more be a prey and I will judge between cattle and cattle And I will set up over them shepherd**

אחד 259 ורעה 7462 אתהן 853 את 853 עבדי 5650 דויד 1732 הוא 1931 ירעה 7462 אתם 853 והוא 1931 יהיה 1961 להן 3807a
'achad uara'ah 'athen, 'at 'abdiy dauiyd; hua' yir'ah 'atam, uahu'a yihayeh lahen
**one and he shall feed them *even* my servant David he shall feed them and he shall be their**

לרעה 7462: 34:24 ואני 589 יהוה 3068 אהיה 1961 להם 3807a לאלהים 430 ועבדי 5650 דוד 1732 נשיא 5387 בתוכם 8432 אני 589 יהוה 3068
laro'ah. ua'aniy Yahuah 'ahayeh lahem le'alohiym, ua'abdiy dauid nasiy'a batoukam; 'aniy Yahuah
**shepherd And I Yahuah will be their to Elohim and my servant David a prince among them I Yahuah**

דברתי 1696: 34:25 וכרתי 3772 להם 3807a ברית 1285 שלום 7965 והשבתי 7673 חיה 2416 רעה 7451 מן 4480
dibartiy. uakaratiy lahem bariyt shaloum, uahishbatiy chaiyah ra'ah min
**have spoken *it* And I will make them a covenant of peace and will cause to cease beasts *the* evil from out of**

הארץ 776 וישבו 3427 במדבר 4057 לבטח 983 וישנו 3462 ביערים 3293: 34:26 ונתתי 5414 אותם 853
ha'aretz; uayashabu bamidbar labetach, uayashanu baya'ariym. uanatatiy 'autam
**the land and they shall dwell in the wilderness safely and sleep in the woods And I will make them**

וסביבות 5439 גבעתי 1389 ברכה 1293 והורדתי 3381 הגשם 1653 בעתו 6256 גשמי 1653 ברכה 1293
uasbiybout gib'atiy barakah; uahouradtiy hageshem ba'atou, gishmey barakah
**and the places round about my hill a blessing and I will cause to come down the shower in his season showers of blessing**

יהיו 1961: 34:27 ונתן 5414 עץ 6086 השדה 7704 את 853 פריו 6529 והארץ 776 תתן 5414 יבולה 2981
yihayu. uanatan 'aetz hasadeh 'at piryou, uaha'aretz titen yabulah,
**there shall be And shall yield the tree of the field her fruit and the earth shall yield her increase**

והיו 1961 על 5921 אדמתם 127 לבטח 983 וידעו 3045 כי 3588 אני 589 יהוה 3068 בשברי 7665 את 853 מטות 4133
uahayu 'al 'admatam labetach; uayada'aua kiy 'aniy Yahuah bashibriy 'at motout
**and they shall be in their land safe and shall know that I *am* Yahuah when I have broken the bands of**

Eze 34:19 And as for my flock, they eat that which you have trodden with your feet; and they drink that which you have fouled with your feet.20 Therefore thus saith YHUH G-D unto them; Behold, I, even I, will judge between the fat cattle and between the lean cattle.21 Because you have thrust with side and with shoulder, and pushed all the diseased with your horns, till you have scattered them abroad;22 Therefore will I save my flock, and they shall no more be a prey; and I will judge between cattle and cattle.23 And I will set up one shepherd over them, and he shall feed them, even my servant David; he shall feed them, and he shall be their shepherd.24 And I YHUH will be their G-d, and my servant David a prince among them; I YHUH have spoken it.25 And I will make with them a covenant of peace, and will cause the evil beasts to cease out of the land: and they shall dwell safely in the wilderness, and sleep in the woods.26 And I will make them and the places round about my hill a blessing; and I will cause the shower to come down in his season; there shall be showers of blessing.27 And the tree of the field shall yield her fruit, and the earth shall yield her increase, and they shall be safe in their land, and shall know that I am YHUH, when I have broken the bands of their yoke, and delivered them out of the hand of those that served themselves of them.

34:28
עלם 5923 והצלתים 5337 מיד 3027 העבדים 5647 בהם 871a: ולא 3808 יהיו 1961 עוד 5750
'alam, uahitzaltiym, miyad ha'abadiym bahem. uala' yihayu 'aud
**their yoke and delivered them out of the hand of those that served themselves of them And no they shall be more**

בז 957 לגוים 1471 וחית 2416 הארץ 776 לא 3808 תאכלם 398 וישבו 3427 לבטח 983 ואין 369
baz lagouyim, uachayat ha'aretz la' ta'kalem; uayashabu labetach ua'aeyn
**a prey to the heathen the beast of the land will neither shall devour them but they shall dwell safely and none**

34:29
מחריד 2729: והקמתי 6965 להם 3807a מטע 4302 לשם 8034 ולא 3808 יהיו 1961 עוד 5750 אספי 622
machariyd. uahaqimotiy lahem mata' lashem; uala' yihayu 'aud 'asupey
**shall make *them* afraid And I will raise up for them a plant of renown and no they shall be more consumed with**

34:30
רעב 7458 בארץ 776 ולא 3808 ישאו 5375 עוד 5750 כלמת 3639 הגוים 1471: וידעו 3045 כי 3588 אני 589 יהוה 3068
ra'ab ba'aretz, uala' yis'au 'aud kalimat hagouyim. uayada'aua, kiy 'aniy Yahuah
**hunger in the land neither bear any more the shame of the heathen Thus shall they know that I Yahuah**

34:31
אלהיהם 430 אתם 854 והמה 1992 עמי 5971 בית 1004 ישראל 3478 נאם 5002 אדני 136 יהוה 3069: ואתן 859
'aloheyhem 'atam; uahemah, 'amiy beyt yisra'ael, na'am 'adonay Yahuah. ua'aten
**their Elohim *am* with them and *that* they *are* my people *even* the house of Israel saith Adonai Yahuah And you**

צאני 6629 צאן 6629 מרעיתי 4830 אדם 120 אתם 859 אני 589 אלהיכם 430 נאם 5002 אדני 136 יהוה 3069:
tza'niy tza'n mara'aytiy 'adam 'atem; 'aniy 'aloheykem, na'am 'adonay Yahuah.
**my flock the flock of my pasture *are* men you I *am* your Elohim saith Adonai Yahuah**

**Ezek 35:1** 35:2
ויהי 1961 דבר 1697 יהוה 3068 אלי 413 לאמר 559: בן 1121 אדם 120 שים 7760 פניך 6440 על 5921 הר 2022
uayahiy dabar Yahuah 'aelay lea'mor. ben 'adam siym paneyka 'al har
**Moreover came the word of Yahuah unto me saying Son of man set your face against mount**

35:3
שעיר 8165 והנבא 5012 עליו 5921: ואמרת 559 לו 3807a כה 3541 אמר 559 אדני 136 יהוה 3069 הנני 2005 אליך 413 הר 2022
se'ayr; uahinabea' 'alayu. ua'amarta lou', koh 'amar 'adonay Yahuah, hinniy 'aeleyka har
**Seir and prophesy against it And say unto it Thus saith Adonai Yahuah Behold I *am* against you O mount**

35:4
שעיר 8165 ונטיתי 5186 ידי 3027 עליך 5921 ונתתיך 5414 שממה 8077 ומשמה 4923: עריך 5892 חרבה 2723
se'ayr; uanatiytiy yadiy 'aleyka, uantatiyka shamamah uamshamah. 'areyka charabah
**Seir and I will stretch out mine hand against you and I will make you waste and desolate your cities waste**

35:5
אשים 7760 ואתה 859 שממה 8077 תהיה 1961 וידעת 3045 כי 3588 אני 589 יהוה 3068: יען 3282 היות 1961 לך 3807a איבת 342
'asiym, ua'atah shamamah tihayeh; uayada'ata kiy 'aniy Yahuah. ya'an, hayout laka 'aeybat
**I will lay and you desolate shall be and you shall know that I *am* Yahuah Because have had for you hatred**

עולם 5769 ותגר 5064 את 853 בני 1121 ישראל 3478 על 5921 ידי 3027 חרב 2719 בעת 6256
'aulam, uatager 'at baney yisra'ael 'al yadey chareb; ba'aet
**a perpetual and have shed *the blood of* the children of Israel by the force of the sword in the time of**

35:6
אידם 343 בעת 6256 עון 5771 קץ 7093: לכן 3651 חי 2416 אני 589 נאם 5002 אדני 136 יהוה 3068 כי 3588
'aeydam, ba'aet 'auon qetz. laken chay 'aniy, na'am 'adonay Yahuah, kiy
**their calamity in the time *that their* iniquity *had* an end Therefore live *as* I saith Adonai Yahuah for**

Eze 34:28 And they shall no more be a prey to the heathen, neither shall the beast of the land devour them; but they shall dwell safely, and none shall make them afraid.29 And I will raise up for them a plant of renown, and they shall be no more consumed with hunger in the land, neither bear the shame of the heathen anymore.30 Thus shall they know that I YHUH their G-d am with them, and that they, even the house of Israel, are my people, saith YHUH G-D.31 And you my flock, the flock of my pasture, are men, and I am your G-d, saith YHUH G-D. **Eze** 35:1 Moreover the word of YHUH came unto me, saying,2 Son of man, set your face against mount Seir, and prophesy against it,3 And say unto it, Thus saith YHUH G-D; Behold, O mount Seir, I am against you, and I will stretch out mine hand against you, and I will make you most desolate.4 I will lay your cities waste, and you shall be desolate, and you shall know that I am YHUH.5 Because you have had a perpetual hatred, and have shed the blood of the children of Israel by the force of the sword in the time of their calamity, in the time that their iniquity had an end:6 Therefore, as I live, saith YHUH G-D, I will prepare you unto blood, and blood shall pursue you: sith you have not hated blood, even blood shall pursue you.

| לדם 1818 | אעשך 6213 | ודם 1818 | ירדפך 7291 | אם 518 | לא 3808 | דם 1818 | שנאת 8130 | ודם 1818 |
|---|---|---|---|---|---|---|---|---|
| ladam | 'a'asaka | uadam | yirdapeka; | 'am | la' | dam | sanea'ta | uadam |
| **unto blood** | **I will prepare you** | **and blood** | **shall pursue you** | **sith** | **not** | **blood** | **you have hated** | **even blood** |

| ירדפך 7291: | 35:7 | ונתתי 5414 | את 853 | הר 2022 | שעיר 8165 | לשממה 8077 | ושממה 8077 | והכרתי 3772 | ממנו 4480 | עבר 5674 |
|---|---|---|---|---|---|---|---|---|---|---|
| yirdapeka. | | uanatatiy | 'at | har | se'ayr, | lashimah | uashmamah; | uahikratiy | mimenu | 'aber |
| **shall pursue you** | | **Thus will I make** | | **mount Seir** | | **most** | **desolate** | **and cut off from it** | | **him that passed out** |

| ושב 7725: | 35:8 | ומלאתי 4390 | את 853 | הריו 2022 | חלליו 2491 | גבעותיך 1389 | וגאותיך 1516 | וכל 3605 |
|---|---|---|---|---|---|---|---|---|
| uashab. | | uamilea'tiy | 'at | harayu | chalalayu; | gib'ateyka | uage'auteyka | uakal |
| **and him that return** | | **And I will fill** | | **his mountains** | ***with* his slain** | ***men* in your hills** | **and in your valleys** | **and in all** |

| אפיקיך 650 | חללי 2491 | חרב 2719 | יפלו 5307 | בהם 871a: | 35:9 | שממות 8077 | עולם 5769 | אתנך 5414 | ועריך 5892 | לא 3808 |
|---|---|---|---|---|---|---|---|---|---|---|
| 'apiyqeyka, | challey | chereb | yiplu | bahem. | | shimamout | 'aulam | 'atenaka, | ua'areyka | la' |
| **your rivers** | **that are slain with** | **the sword** | **shall fall** | **they** | | **desolations** | **perpetual** | **I will make you** | **and your cities** | **not** |

| תישבנה 3427 | וידעתם 3045 | כי 3588 | אני 589 | יהוה 3068: | 35:10 | יען 3282 | אמרך 559 | את 853 | שני 8147 | הגוים 1471 | ואת 853 |
|---|---|---|---|---|---|---|---|---|---|---|---|
| tayshabnah | uiyda'tem | kiy | 'aniy | Yahuah. | | ya'an | 'amaraka | 'at | shaney | hagouyim | ua'at |
| **shall return** | **and you shall know** | **that** | **I *am*** | **Yahuah** | | **Because** | **you have said** | | ***These* two** | **nations** | ***and*** |

| שתי 8147 | הארצות 776 | לי 3807a | תהיינה 1961 | וירשנוה 3423 | ויהוה 3068 | שם 8033 | היה 1961: | 35:11 | לכן 3651 | חי 2416 | אני 589 |
|---|---|---|---|---|---|---|---|---|---|---|---|
| shatey | ha'aratzout | liy | tihayeynah | uiyrashnuha; | uaYahuah | sham | hayah. | | laken | chay | 'aniy, |
| ***these* two** | **countries** | **mine** | **shall be** | **and we will possess it** | **whereas Yahuah** | **there** | **was** | | **Therefore** | **live *as*** | **I** |

| נאם 5002 | אדני 136 | יהוה 3069 | ועשיתי 6213 | כאפך 639 | וכקנאתך 7068 | אשר 834 | עשיתה 6213 |
|---|---|---|---|---|---|---|---|
| na'am | 'adonay | Yahuah | ua'asiytiy, | ka'apaka | uakqin'ataka, | 'asher | 'asiytah, |
| **saith** | **Adonai** | **Yahuah** | **I will even do** | **according to your anger** | **and according to your envy** | **which** | **you have used** |

| משנאתיך 8135 | בם 871a | ונודעתי 3045 | בם 871a | כאשר 834 | אשפטך 8199: | 35:12 |
|---|---|---|---|---|---|---|
| misin'ateyka | bam; | uanouda'atiy | bam | ka'asher | 'ashpateka. | |
| **out of your hatred** | **against them** | **and I will make myself known** | **among them** | **when** | **I have judged you** | |

| וידעת 3045 | כי 3588 | אני 589 | יהוה 3068 | שמעתי 8085 | את 853 | כל 3605 | נאצותיך 5007 | אשר 834 | אמרת 559 |
|---|---|---|---|---|---|---|---|---|---|
| uayada'ata | kiy | 'aniy | Yahuah | shama'atiy | 'at | kal | na'atzouteyka, | 'asher | 'amarta |
| **And you shall know** | **that** | **I** | ***am* Yahuah** | ***and that* I have heard** | | **all** | **your blasphemies** | **which** | **you have spoken** |

| על 5921 | הרי 2022 | ישראל 3478 | לאמר 559 | שממה 8074 | לנו 3807a | נתנו 5414 | לאכלה 402: | 35:13 |
|---|---|---|---|---|---|---|---|---|
| 'al | harey | yisra'ael | lea'mor | shamemah | lanu | nitanu | la'akalah | |
| **against** | **the mountains of** | **Israel** | **saying** | **they are laid desolate** | **us** | **they are given** | **to consume** | |

| ותגדילו 1431 | עלי 5921 | בפיכם 6310 | והעתרתם 6280 | עלי 5921 | דבריכם 1697 | אני 589 |
|---|---|---|---|---|---|---|
| uatagdiylu | 'alay | bapiykem, | uaha'atartem | 'alay | dibreykem; | 'aniy |
| **Thus you have boasted** | **against me** | **with your mouth** | **and have multiplied** | **against me** | **your words** | **I** |

| שמעתי 8085: | 35:14 | כה 3541 | אמר 559 | אדני 136 | יהוה 3069 | כשמח 8055 | כל 3605 | הארץ 776 | שממה 8077 | עשה 6213 | לך 3807a: |
|---|---|---|---|---|---|---|---|---|---|---|---|
| shama'atiy. | | koh | 'amar | 'adonay | Yahuah; | kismoach | kal | ha'aretz, | shamamah | 'aaseh | lak. |
| **have heard *them*** | | **Thus** | **saith** | **Adonai** | **Yahuah** | **When rejoice** | **whole** | **the earth** | **desolate** | **I will make** | **to you** |

Eze 35:7 Thus will I make mount Seir most desolate, and cut off from it him that pass out and him that returneth.8 And I will fill his mountains with his slain men: in your hills, and in your valleys, and in all your rivers, shall they fall that are slain with the sword.9 I will make you perpetual desolations, and your cities shall not return: and you shall know that I am YHUH.10 Because you have said, These two nations and these two countries shall be mine, and we will possess it; whereas YHUH was there:11 Therefore, as I live, saith YHUH G-D, I will even do according to your anger, and according to your envy which you have used out of your hatred against them; and I will make myself known among them, when I have judged you.12 And you shall know that I am YHUH, and that I have heard all your blasphemies which you have spoken against the mountains of Israel, saying, They are laid desolate, they are given us to consume.13 Thus with your mouth you have boasted against me, and have multiplied your words against me: I have heard them.14 Thus saith YHUH G-D; When the whole earth rejoice, I will make you desolate.

**35:15**

| כשמחתך 8057 | לנחלת 5159 | בית 1004 | ישראל 3478 | על 5921 | אשר 834 | שממה 8074 | כן 3651 | אעשה 6213 |
|---|---|---|---|---|---|---|---|---|
| kasimchataka | lanachalat | beyt | yisra'ael | 'al | 'asher | shamemah | ken | 'aaseh |
| **As you did rejoice** | **at the inheritance of** | **the house of** | **Israel** | **because** | **which** | **it was desolate** | **so** | **will I do** |

| לך 3807a | שממה 8077 | תהיה 1961 | הר 2022 | שעיר 8165 | וכל 3605 | אדום 123 | כלה 3605 | וידעו 3045 | כי 3588 | אני 589 | יהוה 3068: |
|---|---|---|---|---|---|---|---|---|---|---|---|
| lak; | shamamah | tihayeh | har | se'ayr | uakal | 'adoum | kulah, | uayada'aua | kiy | 'aniy | Yahuah. |
| **unto you** | **desolate** | **you shall be** | **O mount Seir** | | **and all** | **Idumea *even*** | **all of it** | **and they shall know** | **that** | **I *am*** | **Yahuah** |

**Ezek 36:1**

| ואתה 859 | בן 1121 | אדם 120 | הנבא 5012 | אל 413 | הרי 2022 | ישראל 3478 | ואמרת 559 | הרי 2022 | ישראל 3478 |
|---|---|---|---|---|---|---|---|---|---|
| ua'atah | ben | 'adam, | hinabea' | 'al | harey | yisra'ael; | ua'amarta, | harey | yisra'ael, |
| **Also you** | **son of** | **man** | **prophesy** | **unto** | **the mountains of** | **Israel** | **and say** | **You mountains of** | **Israel** |

| שמעו 8085 | דבר 1697 | יהוה 3068: | **36:2** כה 3541 | אמר 559 | אדני 136 | יהוה 3069 | יען 3282 | אמר 559 | האויב 341 | עליכם 5921 | האח 1889 |
|---|---|---|---|---|---|---|---|---|---|---|---|
| shim'au | dabar | Yahuah. | koh | 'amar | 'adonay | Yahuah, | ya'an | 'amar | ha'auyeb | 'aleykem | he'ach; |
| **hear** | **the word of** | **Yahuah** | **Thus** | **saith** | **Adonai** | **Yahuah** | **Because** | **has said** | **the enemy** | **against you** | **Aha** |

| ובמות 1116 | עולם 5769 | למורשה 4181 | היתה 1961 | לנו 3807a: | **36:3** לכן 3651 | הנבא 5012 | ואמרת 559 | כה 3541 | אמר 559 | אדני 136 | יהוה 3069 |
|---|---|---|---|---|---|---|---|---|---|---|---|
| uabamout | 'aulam, | lamourashah | hayatah | lanu. | laken | hinabea' | ua'amarta, | koh | 'amar | 'adonay | Yahuah; |
| **even high places** | ***the* ancient** | **in possession** | **are** | **ours** | **Therefore** | **prophesy** | **and say** | **Thus** | **saith** | **Adonai** | **Yahuah** |

| יען 3282 | ביען 3282 | שמות 8074 | ושאף 7602 | אתכם 853 | מסביב 5439 | להיותכם 1961 | מורשה 4181 |
|---|---|---|---|---|---|---|---|
| ya'an | baya'an | shamout | uasha'ap | 'atkem | misabiyb, | lihayoutakem | mourashah |
| **Because** | **reason** | **they have made *you* desolate** | **and swallowed up** | **you** | **on every side** | **that you might be** | **a possession** |

| לשארית 7611 | הגוים 1471 | ותעלו 5927 | על 5921 | שפת 8193 | לשון 3956 | ודבת 1681 | עם 5971: | **36:4** |
|---|---|---|---|---|---|---|---|---|
| lish'aeriyt | hagouyim, | uate'alu | 'al | sapat | lashoun | uadibat | 'am. | |
| **unto the residue of** | **the heathen** | **and you are taken up** | **in** | **the lips of** | **talkers** | **and *are* an infamy of** | **the people** | |

| לכן 3651 | הרי 2022 | ישראל 3478 | שמעו 8085 | דבר 1697 | אדני 136 | יהוה 3068 | כה 3541 | אמר 559 | אדני 136 | יהוה 3068 | להרים 2022 |
|---|---|---|---|---|---|---|---|---|---|---|---|
| laken | harey | yisra'ael, | shim'au | dabar | 'adonay | Yahuah; | koh | 'amar | 'adonay | Yahuah | lahariym |
| **Therefore** | **you mountains of** | **Israel** | **hear** | **the word of** | **Adonai** | **Yahuah** | **Thus** | **saith** | **Adonai** | **Yahuah** | **to the mountains** |

| ולגבעות 1389 | לאפיקים 650 | ולגאיות 1516 | ולחרבות 2723 | השממות 8076 | ולערים 5892 | הנעזבות 5800 | אשר 834 | היו 1961 |
|---|---|---|---|---|---|---|---|---|
| ualagaba'aut | la'apiyqiym | ualage'ayout, | ualechrabout | hashomamout | uale'ariym | hane'azabout, | 'asher | hayu |
| **and to the hills** | **to the rivers** | **and to the valleys** | **and to wastes** | **the desolate** | **and to the cities** | **that are forsaken** | **which** | **became** |

| לבז 957 | וללעג 3933 | לשארית 7611 | הגוים 1471 | אשר 834 | מסביב 5439: | **36:5** לכן 3651 | כה 3541 | אמר 559 | אדני 136 | יהוה 3068 |
|---|---|---|---|---|---|---|---|---|---|---|
| labaz | ualla'ag, | lish'aeriyt | hagouyim | 'asher | misabiyb. | laken, | koh | 'amar | 'adonay | Yahuah |
| **a prey** | **and derision** | **to the residue of** | **the heathen** | **that** | ***are* round about** | **Therefore** | **thus** | **saith** | **Adonai** | **Yahuah** |

| אם 518 | לא 3808 | באש 784 | קנאתי 7068 | דברתי 1696 | על 5921 | שארית 7611 | הגוים 1471 | ועל 5921 | אדום 123 | כלא 3605 | אשר 834 |
|---|---|---|---|---|---|---|---|---|---|---|---|
| 'am | la' | ba'aesh | qin'atiy | dibartiy | 'al | sha'aeriyt | hagouyim | ua'al | 'adoum | kula'; | 'asher |
| **Surely** | **not** | **in the fire of** | **my jealousy** | **have I spoken** | **against** | **the residue of** | **the heathen** | **and against** | **Idumea** | **all** | **which** |

| נתנו 5414 | את 853 | ארצי 776 | להם 1992 | למורשה 4181 | בשמחת 8057 | כל 3605 | לבב 3824 | בשאט 7589 | נפש 5315 | למען 4616 |
|---|---|---|---|---|---|---|---|---|---|---|
| natanu | 'at | 'artziy | lahem | lamourashah | basimchat | kal | labab | bish'at | nepesh, | lama'an |
| **have appointed** | | **my land** | **into their** | **possession** | **with the joy of** | **all** | ***their* heart** | **with despiteful** | **minds** | **to** |

Eze 35:15 As you did rejoice at the inheritance of the house of Israel, because it was desolate, so will I do unto you: you shall be desolate, O mount Seir, and all Idumea, even all of it: and they shall know that I am YHUH. **Eze** 36:1 Also, you son of man, prophesy unto the mountains of Israel, and say, You mountains of Israel, hear the word of YHUH:2 Thus saith YHUH G-D; Because the enemy has said against you, Aha, even the ancient high places are ours in possession:3 Therefore prophesy and say, Thus saith YHUH G-D; Because they have made you desolate, and swallowed you up on every side, that you might be a possession unto the residue of the heathen, and you are taken up in the lips of talkers, and are an infamy of the people:4 Therefore, you mountains of Israel, hear the word of YHUH G-D; Thus saith YHUH G-D to the mountains, and to the hills, to the rivers, and to the valleys, to the desolate wastes, and to the cities that are forsaken, which became a prey and derision to the residue of the heathen that are round about;5 Therefore thus saith YHUH G-D; Surely in the fire of my jealousy have I spoken against the residue of the heathen, and against all Idumea, which have appointed my land into their possession with the joy of all their heart, with despiteful minds, to cast it out for a prey.

מגרשה 4054 לבז 957: 36:6 לכן 3651 הנבא 5012 על 5921 אדמת 127 ישראל 3478 ואמרת 559 להרים 2022 ולגבעות 1389
migrashah labaz. laken hinabea' 'al 'admat yisra'ael; ua'amarta lehariym ualagaba'aut
**cast it out for a prey Therefore Prophesy concerning the land of Israel and say unto the mountains and to the hills**

לאפיקים 650 ולגאיות 1516 כה 3541 אמר 559 אדני 136 יהוה 3069 הנני 2005 בקנאתי 7068 ובחמתי 2534 דברתי 1696 יען 3282
la'apiyqiym ualage'ayout koh 'amar 'adonay Yahuah hinniy baqin'atiy uabachamatiy dibartiy, ya'an
**to the rivers and to the valleys Thus saith Adonai Yahuah Behold I in my jealousy and in my fury have spoken because**

כלמת 3639 גוים 1471 נשאתם 5375: 36:7 לכן 3651 כה 3541 אמר 559 אדני 136 יהוה 3069 אני 589 נשאתי 5375 את 853 ידי 3027
kalimat gouyim nasa'tem. laken, koh 'amar 'adonay Yahuah, 'aniy nasa'tiy 'at yadiy;
**the shame of the heathen you have borne Therefore thus saith Adonai Yahuah I have lifted up mine hand**

אם 518 לא 3808 הגוים 1471 אשר 834 לכם 3807a מסביב 5439 המה 1992 כלמתם 3639 ישאו 5375: 36:8 ואתם 859 הרי 2022 ישראל 3478
'am la' hagouyim 'asher lakem misabiyb, hemah kalimatam yisa'au. ua'atem harey yisra'ael
**Surely not the heathen that to you *are* about they their shame shall bear But you O mountains of Israel**

ענפכם 6057 תתנו 5414 ופריכם 16529 תשאו 5375 לעמי 5971 ישראל 3478 כי 3588 קרבו 7126 לבוא 935: 36:9
'anpakem titenu, uaperyakem tis'au la'amiy yisra'ael; kiy qereabu labou'a.
**your branches you shall shoot forth and your fruit yield to my people of Israel for they are at hand to come**

כי 3588 הנני 2005 אליכם 413 ופניתי 6437 אליכם 413 ונעבדתם 5647 ונזרעתם 2232: 36:10 והרביתי 7235
kiy hinniy 'aleykem; uapaniytiy 'aleykem, uane'abadtem uanizra'atem. uahirbeytiy
**For behold I *am* for you and I will turn unto you and you shall be tilled and sown And I will multiply**

עליכם 5921 אדם 120 כל 3605 בית 1004 ישראל 3478 כלה 3605 ונשבו 3427 הערים 5892 והחרבות 2723
'aleykem 'adam, kal beyt yisra'ael kuloh; uanoshabu he'ariym, uahecharabout
**upon you men all the house of Israel *even* all of it and shall be inhabited the cities and the wastes**

תבנינה 1129: 36:11 והרביתי 7235 עליכם 5921 אדם 120 ובהמה 929 ורבו 7235 ופרו 6509
tibaneynah. uahirbeytiy 'aleykem 'adam uabahemah uarabu uaparu;
**shall be builded And I will multiply upon you man and beast and they shall increase and bring fruit**

והושבתי 3427 אתכם 853 כקדמותיכם 6927 והטבתי 2895 מראשתיכם 7221 וידעתם 3045 כי 3588
uahoushabtiy 'atkem kaqadmouteykem, uahetibotiy mera'shoteykem, uiyda'tem kiy
**and I will settle you after your old estates and will do better *unto you* than at your beginnings and you shall know that**

אני 589 יהוה 3068: 36:12 והולכתי 1980 עליכם 5921 אדם 120 את 853 עמי 5971 ישראל 3478 וירשוך 3423
'aniy Yahuah. uahoulaktiy 'aleykem 'adam 'at 'amiy yisra'ael uiyreshuka,
**I *am* Yahuah Yea I will cause to walk upon you men *even* my people Israel and they shall possess you**

והיית 1961 להם 3807a לנחלה 5159 ולא 3808 תוסף 3254 עוד 5750 לשכלם 7921: 36:13 כה 3541 אמר 559 אדני 136
uahayiyta lahem lanachalah; uala' tousip 'aud lashaklam. koh 'amar 'adonay
**and you shall be their inheritance and no you shall more henceforth bereave them *of men* Thus saith Adonai**

יהוה 3069 יען 3282 אמרים 559 לכם 3807a אכלת 398 אדם 120 אתי 859 ומשכלת 7921 גויך 1471 היית 1971:
Yahuah, ya'an 'amariym lakem, 'akelet 'adam 'atiy uamshakelet gouyek hayiyt.
**Yahuah Because they say unto you *land* devourest up men you and bereaved your nations has become**

Eze 36:6 Prophesy therefore concerning the land of Israel, and say unto the mountains, and to the hills, to the rivers, and to the valleys, Thus saith YHUH G-D; Behold, I have spoken in my jealousy and in my fury, because you have borne the shame of the heathen:7 Therefore thus saith YHUH G-D; I have lifted up mine hand, Surely the heathen that are about you, they shall bear their shame.8 But you, O mountains of Israel, you shall shoot forth your branches, and yield your fruit to my people of Israel; for they are at hand to come.9 For, behold, I am for you, and I will turn unto you, and you shall be tilled and sown:10 And I will multiply men upon you, all the house of Israel, even all of it: and the cities shall be inhabited, and the wastes shall be built:11 And I will multiply upon you man and beast; and they shall increase and bring fruit: and I will settle you after your old estates, and will do better unto you than at your beginnings: and you shall know that I am YHUH.12 Yea, I will cause men to walk upon you, even my people Israel; and they shall possess you, and you shall be their inheritance, and you shall no more henceforth bereave them of men.13 Thus saith YHUH G-D; Because they say unto you, Thou land devourest up men, and have bereaved your nations;

**36:14**
לכן 3651 אדם 120 לא 3808 תאכלי 398 עוד 5750 וגויך 1471 לא 3808 תכשלי 3782 עוד 5750 נאם 5002 אדני 136
laken, 'adam la' ta'kaliy 'aud, uagouyek la' takasheliy 'aud; na'am 'adonay
**Therefore men no you shall devour more your nations neither bereave any more saith Adonai**

**36:15**
יהוה 3069: ולא 3808 אשמיע 8085 אליך 413 עוד 5750 כלמת 3639 הגוים 1471 וחרפת 2781 עמים 5971
Yahuah. uala' 'ashmiya' 'aleyka 'aud kalimat hagouyim, uacherapat 'amiym
**Yahuah Neither will I cause *men* to hear in you any more the shame of the heathen the reproach of the people**

לא 3808 תשאי 5375 עוד 5750 וגויך 1471 לא 3808 תכשלי 3782 עוד 5750 נאם 5002 אדני 136 יהוה 3069: **36:16**
la' tis'ay 'aud; uagouyek la' takshiliy 'aud, na'am 'adonay Yahuah.
**neither shall you bear any more your nations neither shall you cause to fall any more saith Adonai Yahuah**

ויהי 1961 דבר 1697 יהוה 3068 אלי 413 לאמר 559: **36:17** בן 1121 אדם 120 בית 1004 ישראל 3478 ישבים 3427 על 5921
uayahiy dabar Yahuah 'aelay lea'mor. ben 'adam, beyt yisra'ael yoshbiym 'al
**Moreover came the word of Yahuah unto me saying Son of man the house of Israel dwelt in**

אדמתם 127 ויטמאו 2930 אותה 853 בדרכם 1870 ובעלילותם 5949 כטמאת 2932 הנדה 5079
'admatam, uayatam'au 'autah, badarkam uaba'aliyloutam; katum'at hanidah,
**their own land when they defiled it by their own way and by their doings as the uncleanness of a removed woman**

היתה 1961 דרכם 1870 לפני 6440: **36:18** ואשפך 8210 חמתי 2534 עליהם 5921 על 5921 הדם 1818 אשר 834 שפכו 8210 על 5921
hayatah darkam lapanay. ua'ashpok chamatiy 'aleyhem, 'al hadam 'asher shapaku 'al
**was their way before me Wherefore I poured my fury upon them for the blood that they had shed upon**

הארץ 776 ובגלוליהם 1544 טמאוה 2930: **36:19** ואפיץ 6327 אתם 853 בגוים 1471
ha'aretz; uabgiluleyhem tima'auha. ua'apiytz 'atam bagouyim,
**the land and for their idols *wherewith* they had polluted *it* And I scattered them among the heathen**

ויזרו 2219 בארצות 776 כדרכם 1870 וכעלילותם 5949 שפטתים 8199: **36:20**
uayizaru ba'aratzout; kadarkam uaka'aliyloutam shapatiym.
**and they were dispersed through the countries according to their way and according to their doings I judged them**

ויבוא 935 אל 413 הגוים 1471 אשר 834 באו 935 שם 8033 ויחללו 2490 את 853 שם 8034 קדשי 6944 באמר 559
uayabou'a, 'al hagouyim 'asher ba'au sham, uayachallu 'at shem qadashiy be'amor
**And when they entered unto the heathen where they went there they profaned name my holy when they said**

להם 3807a עם 5971 יהוה 3068 אלה 428 ומארצו 776 יצאו 3318: **36:21** ואחמל 2550 על 5921 שם 8034 קדשי 6944
lahem 'am Yahuah 'aeleh, uame'artzou yatza'au. ua'achmol 'al shem qadashiy
**to them *are* the people of Yahuah These and out of his land are gone forth But I had pity for name mine holy**

אשר 834 חללוהו 2490 בית 1004 ישראל 3478 בגוים 1471 אשר 834 באו 935 שמה 8033: **36:22** לכן 3651 אמר 559
'asher chilluhu beyt yisra'ael, bagouyim 'asher ba'au shamah. laken 'amor
**which had profaned the house of Israel among the heathen where they went there Therefore say**

לבית 1004 ישראל 3478 כה 3541 אמר 559 אדני 136 יהוה 3069 לא 3808 למענכם 4616 אני 589 עשה 6213 בית 1004 ישראל 3478 כי 3588
labeyt yisra'ael, koh 'amar 'adonay Yahuah, la' lama'anakem 'aniy 'aseh beyt yisra'ael; kiy
**unto the house of Israel Thus saith Adonai Yahuah not *this* for your sake I do O house of Israel but**

Eze 36:14 Therefore you shall devour men no more, neither bereave your nations anymore, saith YHUH G-D.15 Neither will I cause men to hear in you the shame of the heathen anymore, neither shall you bear the reproach of the people anymore, neither shall you cause your nations to fall anymore, saith YHUH G-D.16 Moreover the word of YHUH came unto me, saying,17 Son of man, when the house of Israel dwelt in their own land, they defiled it by their own way and by their doings: their way was before me as the uncleanness of a removed woman.18 Wherefore I poured my fury upon them for the blood that they had shed upon the land, and for their idols wherewith they had polluted it:19 And I scattered them among the heathen, and they were dispersed through the countries: according to their way and according to their doings I judged them.20 And when they entered unto the heathen, whither they went, they profaned my holy name, when they said to them, These are the people of YHUH, and are gone forth out of his land.21 But I had pity for mine holy name, which the house of Israel had profaned among the heathen, whither they went.22 Therefore say unto the house of Israel, Thus saith YHUH G-D; I do not this for your sakes, O house of Israel, but for mine holy name's sake, which you have profaned among the heathen, whither you went.

36:23
שם 8033: באתם 935 אשר 834 בגוים 1471 חללתם 2490 אשר 834 קדשי 6944 לשם 8034 אם 518
sham. ba'tem 'asher bagouyim chilaltem, 'asher qadashiy lashem 'am
**there you went where among the heathen you have profaned which mine holy *sake* for name's rather**

חללתם 2490 אשר 834 בגוים 1471 המחלל 2490 הגדול 1419 שמי 8034 את 853 וקדשתי 6942
chilaltem 'asher bagouyim, hamachulal hagadoul, shamiy 'at uaqidashtiy
**you have profaned which among the heathen which was profaned great my name And I will sanctify**

בהקדשי 6942 יהוה 3069 אדני 136 נאם 5002 יהוה 3068 אני 589 כי 3588 הגוים 1471 וידעו 3045 בתוכם 8432
bahiqadashiy Yahuah, 'adonay na'am Yahuah 'aniy kiy hagouyim uayada'aua batoukam;
**when I shall be sanctified Yahuah Adonai saith Yahuah *I am* that the heathen and shall know in the midst of them**

36:24
הארצות 776 מכל 3605 אתכם 853 וקבצתי 6908 הגוים 1471 מן 4480 אתכם 853 ולקחתי 3947 לעיניהם 5869: בכם 871a
ha'aratzout; mikal 'atkem uaqibatztiy hagouyim, min 'atkem ualaqachtiy la'aeyneyhem. bakem
**countries out of all you and gather the heathen from among you For I will take before their eyes in you**

36:25
וטהרתם 2891 טהורים 2889 מים 4325 עליכם 5921 וזרקתי 2236 אדמתכם 127: אל 413 אתכם 853 והבאתי 935
uathartem; tahouriym mayim 'aleykem uazaraqtiy 'admatkem. 'al 'atkem uahebea'tiy
**and you shall be clean clean water upon you Then will I sprinkle your own land into you and will bring**

36:26
חדש 2319 לב 3820 לכם 3807a ונתתי 5414 אתכם 853: אטהר 2891 גלוליכם 1544 ומכל 3605 טמאותיכם 2932 מכל 3605
chadash, leb lakem uanatatiy 'atkem. 'ataher giluleykem uamikal tuma'auteykem mikol
**new A heart to you also will I give you will I cleanse your idols and from all your filthiness from all**

ונתתי 5414 מבשרכם 1320 האבן 68 לב 3820 את 853 והסרתי 5493 בקרבכם 7130 אתן 5414 חדשה 2319 ורוח 7307
uanatatiy mibasarkem, ha'aben leb 'at uahasirotiy baqirbakem; 'aten chadashah uaruach
**and I will give out of your flesh the stony heart and I will take away within you will I put new and a spirit**

36:27
תלכו 1980 בחקי 2706 אשר 834 את 853 ועשיתי 6213 בקרבכם 7130 אתן 5414 רוחי 7307 ואת 853 בשר 1320: לב 3820 לכם 3807a
teleku, bachuqay 'asher 'at ua'asiytiy, baqirbakem; 'aten ruchiy ua'at basar. leb lakem
**to walk in my statutes which and cause within you I will put my spirit *And* flesh an heart of to you**

36:28
לאבתיכם 1 נתתי 5414 אשר 834 בארץ 776 וישבתם 3427 ועשיתם 6213: תשמרו 8104 ומשפטי 4941
la'aboteykem; natatiy 'asher ba'aretz, uiyshabtem ua'asiytem. tishmaru uamishpatay
**to your fathers I gave that in the land And you shall dwell and do *them* you shall keep and my judgments**

36:29
מכל 3605 אתכם 853 והושעתי 3467 לאלהים 430: לכם 3807a אהיה 1961 ואנכי 595 לעם 5971 לי 3807a והייתם 1961
mikol 'atkem, uahousha'atiy le'alohiym. lakem 'ahayeh ua'anokiy, la'am, liy uihayiytem
**from all you I will also save to Elohim to your will be and I people my and you shall be**

36:30
רעב 7458: עליכם 5921 אתן 5414 ולא 3808 אתו 853 והרביתי 7235 הדגן 1715 אל 413 וקראתי 7121 טמאותיכם 2932
ra'ab. 'aleykem 'aten uala' 'atou, uahirbeytiy hadagan 'al uaqara'tiy tuma'auteykem;
**famine upon you lay and no it and will increase the corn for and I will call your uncleannesses**

עוד 5750 תקחו 3947 לא 3808 אשר 834 למען 4616 השדה 7704 ותנובת 8570 העץ 6086 פרי 6529 את 853 והרביתי 7235
'aud tiqchu la' 'asher lama'an, hasadeh; uatnubat ha'aetz, pariy 'at uahirbeytiy
**more you shall receive no after so that the field and the increase of the tree the fruit of And I will multiply**

Eze 36:23 And I will sanctify my great name, which was profaned among the heathen, which you have profaned in the midst of them; and the heathen shall know that I am YHUH, saith YHUH G-D, when I shall be sanctified in you before their eyes.24 For I will take you from among the heathen, and gather you out of all countries, and will bring you into your own land.25 Then will I sprinkle clean water upon you, and you shall be clean: from all your filthiness, and from all your idols, will I cleanse you.26 A new heart also will I give you, and a new spirit will I put within you: and I will take away the stony heart out of your flesh, and I will give you an heart of flesh.27 And I will put my spirit within you, and cause you to walk in my statutes, and you shall keep my judgments, and do them.28 And you shall dwell in the land that I gave to your fathers; and you shall be my people, and I will be your G-d.29 I will also save you from all your uncleannesses: and I will call for the corn, and will increase it, and lay no famine upon you.30 And I will multiply the fruit of the tree, and the increase of the field, that you shall receive no more reproach of famine among the heathen.

| חרפת 2781 | רעב 7458 | בגוים 1471: | 36:31 וזכרתם 2142 | את 853 | דרכיכם 1870 | הרעים 7451 | ומעלליכם 4611 |
|---|---|---|---|---|---|---|---|
| cherpat | ra'ab | bagouyim. | uazkaratem | 'at | darkeykem | hara'aym, | uama'alleykem |
| **reproach of** | **famine** | **among the heathen** | **Then shall you remember** | | **your own ways** | **evil** | **and your doings** |

| אשר 834 | לא 3808 | טובים 2896 | ונקטתם 6962 | בפניכם 6440 | על 5921 | עונתיכם 5771 | ועל 5921 |
|---|---|---|---|---|---|---|---|
| 'asher | la' | toubiym; | uanqototem | bipneykem, | 'al | 'auonoteykem, | ua'al |
| **that** | ***were* not** | **good** | **and shall lothe yourselves** | **in your own sight** | **for** | **your iniquities** | **and for** |

| תועבותיכם 8441: | 36:32 לא 3808 | למענכם 4616 | אני 589 | עשה 6213 | נאם 5002 | אדני 136 | יהוה 3069 | יודע 3045 | לכם 3807a | בושו 954 |
|---|---|---|---|---|---|---|---|---|---|---|
| tou'abouteykem. | la' | lama'anakem | 'aniy | 'aseh, | na'am | 'adonay | Yahuah, | yiuada' | lakem; | boushu |
| **your abominations** | **Not** | **for your sakes** | **I *this*** | **do** | **saith** | **Adonai** | **Yahuah** | **be it known** | **unto you** | **be ashamed** |

| והכלמו 3637 | מדרכיכם 1870 | בית 1004 | ישראל 3478: | 36:33 כה 3541 | אמר 559 | אדני 136 | יהוה 3069 | ביום 3117 |
|---|---|---|---|---|---|---|---|---|
| uahikalamu | midarkeykem | beyt | yisra'ael. | koh | 'amar | 'adonay | Yahuah, | bayoum |
| **and confounded** | **for your own ways** | **O house of** | **Israel** | **Thus** | **saith** | **Adonai** | **Yahuah** | **In the day** |

| טהרי 2891 | אתכם 853 | מכל 3605 | עונותיכם 5771 | והושבתי 3427 | את 853 | הערים 5892 |
|---|---|---|---|---|---|---|
| tahariy | 'atkem, | mikol | auonouteykem; | uahoushabtiy | 'at | he'ariym, |
| **that I shall have cleansed** | **you** | **from all** | **your iniquities** | **I will also cause *you* to dwell in** | | **the cities** |

| ונבנו 1129 | החרבות 2723: | 36:34 והארץ 776 | הנשמה 8074 | תעבד 5647 | תחת 8478 | אשר 834 | היתה 1961 | שממה 8077 |
|---|---|---|---|---|---|---|---|---|
| uanibnu | hecharabout. | uaha'aretz | hanashamah | te'abed; | tachat | 'asher | hayatah | shamamah, |
| **and shall be builded** | **the wastes** | **And land** | **the desolate** | **shall be tilled** | **whereas** | **after** | **it lay** | **desolate** |

| לעיני 5869 | כל 3605 | עובר 5674: | 36:35 ואמרו 559 | הארץ 776 | הלזו 1977 | הנשמה 8074 | היתה 1961 | כגן 1588 |
|---|---|---|---|---|---|---|---|---|
| la'aeyney | kal | 'auber. | ua'amaru, | ha'aretz | halezu | hanashamah, | hayatah | kagan |
| **in the sight of** | **all** | **that passed by** | **And they shall say** | **the land** | **This** | **that was desolate** | **is become** | **like the garden of** |

| עדן 5731 | והערים 5892 | החרבות 2720 | והנשמות 8074 | והנהרסות 2040 | בצורות 1219 | ישבו 3427: | 36:36 וידעו 3045 |
|---|---|---|---|---|---|---|---|
| 'aeden; | uahe'ariym | hecharebout | uahanashamout | uahaneherasout | batzurout | yashabu. | uayada'aua |
| **Eden** | **and cities** | **the waste** | **and desolate** | **and ruined** | ***are become* fenced** | ***and* are inhabited** | **Then you shall know** |

| הגוים 1471 | אשר 834 | ישארו 7604 | סביבותיכם 5439 | כי 3588 | אני 589 | יהוה 3068 | בניתי 1129 | הנהרסות 2040 | נטעתי 5193 |
|---|---|---|---|---|---|---|---|---|---|
| hagouyim, | 'asher | yisha'aru | sabiybouteykem | kiy | 'aniy | Yahuah | baniytiy | haneherasout, | nata'atiy |
| **the heathen** | **that** | **are left** | **round about** | **that** | **I** | **Yahuah** | **build** | **the ruined** | ***places and* plant that** |

| הנשמה 8074 | אני 589 | יהוה 3068 | דברתי 1696 | ועשיתי 6213: | 36:37 כה 3541 | אמר 559 | אדני 136 | יהוה 3069 | עוד 5750 | זאת 2063 |
|---|---|---|---|---|---|---|---|---|---|---|
| hanashamah; | 'aniy | Yahuah | dibartiy | ua'asiytiy. | koh | 'amar | 'adonay | Yahuah, | 'aud, | za't |
| **that was desolate** | **I** | **Yahuah** | **have spoken *it*** | **and I will do *it*** | **Thus** | **saith** | **Adonai** | **Yahuah** | **yet *for*** | **this** |

| אדרש 1875 | לבית 1004 | ישראל 3478 | לעשות 6213 | להם 3807a | ארבה 7235 | אתם 853 | כצאן 6629 | אדם 120: | 36:38 |
|---|---|---|---|---|---|---|---|---|---|
| 'adaresh | labeyt | yisra'ael | la'asout | lahem; | 'arbeh | 'atam | katza'n | 'adam. | |
| **I will be inquired of** | **by the house of** | **Israel** | **to do *it*** | **for them** | **I will increase** | **them** | **like a flock** | ***with* men** | |

| כצאן 6629 | קדשים 6944 | כצאן 6629 | ירושלם 3389 | במועדיה 4150 | כן 3651 | תהיינה 1961 | הערים 5892 | החרבות 2720 | מלאות 4392 |
|---|---|---|---|---|---|---|---|---|---|
| katza'n | qadashiym, | katza'n | yarushalaim | bamou'adeyha, | ken | tihayeynah | he'ariym | hecharebout, | mele'aut |
| **As the flock of** | ***the* holy** | **flock** | **Jerusalem** | **in her solemn feasts** | **so** | **shall be** | **cities** | **the waste** | **ones filled with** |

Eze 36:31 Then shall you remember your own evil ways, and your doings that were not good, and shall lothe yourselves in your own sight for your iniquities and for your abominations.32 Not for your sakes do I this, saith YHUH G-D, be it known unto you: be ashamed and confounded for your own ways, O house of Israel.33 Thus saith YHUH G-D; In the day that I shall have cleansed you from all your iniquities I will also cause you to dwell in the cities, and the wastes shall be built.34 And the desolate land shall be tilled, whereas it lay desolate in the sight of all that passed by.35 And they shall say, This land that was desolate is become like the garden of Eden; and the waste and desolate and ruined cities are become fenced, and are inhabited.36 Then the heathen that are left round about you shall know that I YHUH build the ruined places, and plant that that was desolate: I YHUH have spoken it, and I will do it.37 Thus saith YHUH G-D; I will yet for this be inquired of by the house of Israel, to do it for them; I will increase them with men like a flock.38 As the holy flock, as the flock of Jerusalem in her solemn feasts; so shall the waste cities be filled with flocks of men: and they shall know that I am YHUH.

צאן 6629 אדם 120 וידעו 3045 כי 3588 אני 589 יהוה 3068:
tza'n 'adam; uayada'aua kiy 'aniy Yahuah.
**flocks of men and they shall know that I *am* Yahuah**

**Ezek 37:1** היתה 1961 עלי 5921 יד 3027 יהוה 3068 ויוצאני 3318 ברוח 7307 יהוה 3068 ויניחני 5117
hayatah 'alay yad Yahuah uayoutzi'aeniy uaruach Yahuah, uayaniycheniy
**was upon me The hand of Yahuah and carried me out in the spirit of Yahuah and set me down**

בתוך 8432 הבקעה 1237 והיא 1931 מלאה 4392 עצמות 6106: **37:2** והעבירני 5674 עליהם 5921 סביב 5439 סביב 5439
batouk habiq'ah; uahiy'a male'ah 'atzmout. uahe'abiyraniy 'aleyhem sabiyb sabiyb;
**in the midst of the valley which *was* full of bones And caused me to pass by them round about**

והנה 2009 רבות 7227 מאד 3966 על 5921 פני 6440 הבקעה 1237 והנה 2009 יבשות 3002 מאד 3966: **37:3** ויאמר 559 אלי 413
uahineh rabout ma'ad 'al paney habiq'ah, uahineh yabeshout ma'ad. uaya'mer 'aelay,
**and behold many *there were* very in open the valley and lo dry *they were* very And he said unto me**

בן 1121 אדם 120 התחיינה 2421 העצמות 6106 האלה 428 ואמר 559 אדני 136 יהוה 3069 אתה 859 ידעת 3045: **37:4** ויאמר 559
ben 'adam hatichayeynah ha'atzamout ha'aeleh; ua'amar 'adonay Yahuah 'atah yada'ta. uaya'mer
**Son of man can live? bones these And I answered O Adonai Yahuah You know Again he said**

אלי 413 הנבא 5012 על 5921 העצמות 6106 האלה 428 ואמרת 559 אליהם 413 העצמות 6106 היבשות 3002 שמעו 8085 דבר 1697
'aelay, hinabea' 'al ha'atzamout ha'aeleh; ua'amarta 'aleyhem, ha'atzamout hayabeshout, shim'au dabar
**unto me Prophesy upon bones these and say unto them bones O you dry hear the word of**

יהוה 3068: **37:5** כה 3541 אמר 559 אדני 136 יהוה 3069 לעצמות 6106 האלה 428 הנה 2009 אני 589 מביא 935 בכם 871a רוח 7307
Yahuah. koh 'amar 'adonay Yahuah, la'atzamout ha'aeleh; hineh 'aniy mebiy'a bakem ruach
**Yahuah Thus saith Adonai Yahuah unto bones these Behold I will cause to enter into you breath**

וחייתם 2421: **37:6** ונתתי 5414 עליכם 5921 גדים 1517 והעלתי 5927 עליכם 5921 בשר 1320 וקרמתי 7159 עליכם 5921 עור 5785
uichayiytem. uanatatiy 'aleykem gidiym uaha'aletiy 'aleykem basar, uaqaramtiy 'aleykem 'aur,
**and you shall live And I will lay upon you sinews and will bring up upon you flesh and cover with you skin**

ונתתי 5414 בכם 871a רוח 7307 וחייתם 2421 וידעתם 3045 כי 3588 אני 589 יהוה 3068: **37:7** ונבאתי 5012 כאשר 834
uanatatiy bakem ruach uichayiytem; uiyda'tem kiy 'aniy Yahuah. uanibea'tiy ka'asher
**and put in you breath and you shall live and you shall know that I *am* Yahuah So I prophesied as**

צויתי 6680 ויהי 1961 קול 6963 כהנבאי 5012 והנה 2009 רעש 7494 ותקרבו 7126 עצמות 6106 עצם 6106
tzueytiy; uayahiy qoul kahinaba'ay uahineh ra'ash, uatiqrabu 'atzmout, 'atzem
**I was commanded and there was a noise and as I prophesied and behold a shaking and came together the bones bone**

אל 413 עצמו 6106: **37:8** וראיתי 7200 והנה 2009 עליהם 5921 גדים 1517 ובשר 1320 עלה 5927 ויקרם 7159 עליהם 5921 עור 5785
'al atzamou. uara'aytiy uahineh 'aleyhem gidiym uabasar 'alah, uayiqram 'aleyhem 'aur
**to his bone when I beheld And lo on them the sinews and the flesh came up and covered upon them the skin**

מלמעלה 4605 ורוח 7307 אין 369 בהם 871a: **37:9** ויאמר 559 אלי 413 הנבא 5012 אל 413 הרוח 7307 הנבא 5012 בן 1121 אדם 120
milma'alah; uaruach 'aeyn bahem. uaya'mer 'aelay, hinabea' 'al haruach; hinabea' ben 'adam
**above but breath *there was* no in them Then said he unto me Prophesy unto the wind prophesy son of man**

**Eze** 37:1 The hand of YHUH was upon me, and carried me out in the spirit of YHUH, and set me down in the midst of the valley which was full of bones,2 And caused me to pass by them round about: and, behold, there were very many in the open valley; and, lo, they were very dry.3 And he said unto me, Son of man, can these bones live? And I answered, O Adonai G-D, you know.4 Again he said unto me, Prophesy upon these bones, and say unto them, O you dry bones, hear the word of YHUH.5 Thus saith YHUH G-D unto these bones; Behold, I will cause breath to enter into you, and you shall live:6 And I will lay sinews upon you, and will bring up flesh upon you, and cover you with skin, and put breath in you, and you shall live; and you shall know that I am YHUH.7 So I prophesied as I was commanded: and as I prophesied, there was a noise, and behold a shaking, and the bones came together, bone to his bone.8 And when I beheld, lo, the sinews and the flesh came up upon them, and the skin covered them above: but there was no breath in them.9 Then said he unto me, Prophesy unto the wind, prophesy, son of man, and say to the wind, Thus saith YHUH G-D; Come from the four winds, O breath, and breathe upon these slain, that they may live.

| 559 ואמרת | 413 אל | 7307 הרוח | 3541 כה | 559 אמר | 136 אדני | 3068 יהוה | 702 מארבע | 7307 רוחות | 935 באי | 7307 הרוח | 5301 ופחי | 2026 בהרוגים |
|---|---|---|---|---|---|---|---|---|---|---|---|---|
| ua'amarta | 'al | haruach | koh | 'amar | 'adonay | Yahuah | me'arba' | ruchout | bo'ay | haruach, | uapchiy | baharugiym |
| **and say** | **to** | **the wind** | **Thus** | **saith** | **Adonai** | **Yahuah** | **from the four** | **winds** | **Come** | **O breath** | **and breathe** | **upon slain** |

| 428 האלה | 2421: ויחיו | 37:10 | 5012 והנבאתי | 834 כאשר | 6680 צוני | 935 ותבוא | 871a בהם | 7307 הרוח | 2421 ויחיו |
|---|---|---|---|---|---|---|---|---|---|
| ha'aeleh | uayichayu. | | uahinabea'tiy | ka'asher | tziuaniy; | uatabou'a | bahem | haruach | uayichayu, |
| **these** | **that they may live** | | **So I prophesied** | **as** | **he commanded me** | **and came** | **into them** | **the breath** | **and they lived** |

| 5975 ויעמדו | 5921 על | 7272 רגליהם | 2428 חיל | 1419 גדול | 3966 מאד | 3966: מאד | 37:11 | 559 ויאמר | 413 אלי | 1121 בן | 120 אדם |
|---|---|---|---|---|---|---|---|---|---|---|---|
| uaya'amdu | 'al | ragleyhem, | chayil | gadoul | ma'aud | ma'ad. | | uaya'mer | 'aelay | ben | 'adam |
| **and stood up** | **upon** | **their feet** | **an army** | **great** | **exceedingly** | **an exceedingly** | | **Then he said** | **unto me** | **Son of** | **man** |

| 6106 העצמות | 428 האלה | 3605 כל | 1004 בית | 3478 ישראל | 1992 המה | 2009 הנה | 559 אמרים | 3001 יבשו | 6106 עצמותינו | 6 ואבדה | 8615 תקותנו |
|---|---|---|---|---|---|---|---|---|---|---|---|
| ha'atzamout | ha'aeleh, | kal | beyt | yisra'ael | hemah; | hineh | 'amariym, | yabashu | atzmouteynu | ua'abadah | tiquatenu |
| **bones** | **these** | ***are* the whole** | **house of** | **Israel** | **they** | **behold** | **they say** | **are dried** | **Our bones** | **and is lost** | **our hope** |

| 1504 נגזרנו | 3807a: לנו | 37:12 | 3651 לכן | 5012 הנבא | 559 ואמרת | 413 אליהם | 3541 כה | 559 אמר | 136 אדני | 3069 יהוה | 2009 הנה | 589 אני |
|---|---|---|---|---|---|---|---|---|---|---|---|---|
| nigzarnu | lanu. | | laken | hinabea' | ua'amarta | 'aleyhem, | koh | 'amar | 'adonay | Yahuah | hineh | 'aniy |
| **we are cut off** | **for our parts** | | **Therefore** | **prophesy** | **and say** | **unto them** | **Thus** | **saith** | **Adonai** | **Yahuah** | **Behold** | **I** |

| 6605 פתח | 853 את | 6913 קברותיכם | 5927 והעליתי | 853 אתכם | 6913 מקברותיכם | 5971 עמי | 935 והבאתי | 853 אתכם | 413 אל |
|---|---|---|---|---|---|---|---|---|---|
| poteach | 'at | qibrouteykem, | uaha'aleytiy | 'atkem | miqibrouteykem | 'amiy; | uahebea'tiy | 'atkem | 'al |
| **will open** | | **your graves** | **and cause to come up** | **you** | **out of your graves** | **O my people** | **and bring** | **you** | **into** |

| 127 אדמת | 3478: ישראל | 37:13 | 3045 וידעתם | 3588 כי | 589 אני | 3068 יהוה | 6605 בפתחי | 853 את | 6913 קברותיכם |
|---|---|---|---|---|---|---|---|---|---|
| 'admat | yisra'ael. | | uiyda'tem | kiy | 'aniy | Yahuah; | bapitchiy | 'at | qibrouteykem, |
| **the land of** | **Israel** | | **And you shall know** | **that** | **I *am*** | **Yahuah** | **when I have opened** | | **your graves** |

| 5927 ובהעלותי | 853 אתכם | 6913 מקברותיכם | 5971: עמי | 37:14 | 5414 ונתתי | 7307 רוחי | 871a בכם | 2421 וחייתם |
|---|---|---|---|---|---|---|---|---|
| uabha'aloutiy | 'atkem | miqibrouteykem | 'amiy. | | uanatatiy | ruchiy | bakem | uichayiytem, |
| **and brought up** | **you** | **out of your graves** | **O my people** | | **And shall put** | **my spirit** | **in you** | **and you shall live** |

| 3240 והנחתי | 853 אתכם | 5921 על | 127 אדמתכם | 3045 וידעתם | 3588 כי | 589 אני | 3068 יהוה | 1696 דברתי | 6213 ועשיתי |
|---|---|---|---|---|---|---|---|---|---|
| uahinachtiy | 'atkem | 'al | 'admatkem; | uiyda'tem | kiy | 'aniy | Yahuah | dibartiy | ua'asiytiy |
| **and I shall place** | **you** | **in** | **your own land** | **then shall you know** | **that** | **I** | **Yahuah** | **have spoken *it*** | **and performed** |

| 5002 נאם | 3068: יהוה | 37:15 | 1961 ויהי | 1697 דבר | 3068 יהוה | 413 אלי | 559: לאמר | 37:16 | 859 ואתה | 1121 בן | 120 אדם | 3947 קח |
|---|---|---|---|---|---|---|---|---|---|---|---|---|
| na'am | Yahuah. | | uayahiy | dabar | Yahuah | 'aelay | lea'mor. | | ua'atah | ben | 'adam, | qach |
| ***it* saith** | **Yahuah** | | **came again** | **The word of** | **Yahuah** | **unto me** | **saying** | | **Moreover you** | **son of** | **man** | **take** |

| 3807a לך | 6086 עץ | 259 אחד | 3789 וכתב | 5921 עליו | 3063 ליהודה | 1121 ולבני | 3478 ישראל | 2270 חברו | 3947 ולקח | 6086 עץ |
|---|---|---|---|---|---|---|---|---|---|---|
| laka | 'aetz | 'achad, | uaktob | 'aelayu | liyahudah, | ualibney | yisra'ael | chaberou | ualqach | 'aetz |
| **for you** | **stick** | **one** | **and write** | **upon it** | **For Judah** | **and for the children of** | **Israel** | **his companions** | **then take** | **stick** |

| 259 אחד | 3789 וכתוב | 5921 עליו | 3130 ליוסף | 6086 עץ | 669 אפרים | 3605 וכל | 1004 בית | 3478 ישראל | 2270 חברו |
|---|---|---|---|---|---|---|---|---|---|
| 'achad, | uaktoub | 'alayu, | layousep | 'aetz | 'aprayim, | uakal | beyt | yisra'ael | chaberou |
| **another** | **and write** | **upon it** | **For Joseph** | **the stick of** | **Ephraim** | **and *for* all** | **the house of** | **Israel** | **his companions** |

Eze 37:10 So I prophesied as he commanded me, and the breath came into them, and they lived, and stood up upon their feet, an exceeding great army.11 Then he said unto me, Son of man, these bones are the whole house of Israel: behold, they say, Our bones are dried, and our hope is lost: we are cut off for our parts.12 Therefore prophesy and say unto them, Thus saith YHUH G-D; Behold, O my people, I will open your graves, and cause you to come up out of your graves, and bring you into the land of Israel.13 And you shall know that I am YHUH, when I have opened your graves, O my people, and brought you up out of your graves,14 And shall put my spirit in you, and you shall live, and I shall place you in your own land: then shall you know that I YHUH have spoken it, and performed it, saith YHUH.15 The word of YHUH came again unto me, saying,16 Moreover, you son of man, take you one stick, and write upon it, For Judah, and for the children of Israel his companions: then take another stick, and write upon it, For Joseph, the stick of Ephraim, and for all the house of Israel his companions:

7:17 ... 37:18

וקרב 7126 אתם 853 אחד 259 אל 413 אחד 259 לך 3807a לעץ 6086 אחד 259 והיו 1961 לאחדים 259 בידך 3027:

uaqarab 'atam 'achad 'al 'achad laka la'aetz 'achad; uahayu la'achadiym bayadeka.

**And join them one to another for you into stick one and they shall become one in your hand**

וכאשר 834 יאמרו 559 אליך 413 בני 1121 עמך 5971 לאמר 559 הלוא 3808 תגיד 5046 לנו 3807a מה 4100 אלה 428

uaka'asher ya'maru 'aeleyka, baney 'amaka lea'mor; halou'a tagiyd lanu mah 'aeleh

**And when shall speak unto you the children of your people saying not Will you show us what *meanest by* these?**

37:19

לך 3807a: דבר 1696 אלהם 413 כה 3541 אמר 559 אדני 136 יהוה 3069 הנה 2009 אני 589 לקח 3947 את 853 עץ 6086 יוסף 3130 אשר 834

lak daber 'alehem, koh 'amar 'adonay Yahuah hineh 'aniy loqeach 'at 'aetz yousep 'asher

**to you Say unto them Thus saith Adonai Yahuah Behold I will take the stick of Joseph which**

ביד 3027 אפרים 669 ושבטי 7626 ישראל 3478 חברו 2270 ונתתי 5414 אותם 853 עליו 5921 את 854 עץ 6086

bayad 'aprayim, uashibtey yisra'ael chabrou uanatatiy 'autam 'aelayu 'at 'aetz

***is* in the hand of Ephraim and the tribes of Israel his fellows and will put them *even* with him *with* the stick of**

37:20

יהודה 3063 ועשיתם 6213 לעץ 6086 אחד 259 והיו 1961 אחד 259 בידי 3027: והיו 1961 העצים 6086 אשר 834

yahudah, ua'asiytim la'aetz 'achad, uahayu 'achad bayadiy. uahayu ha'aetziym 'asher

**Judah and make them stick one and they shall be one in mine hand And shall be the sticks whereon**

37:21

תכתב 3789 עליהם 5921 בידך 3027 לעיניהם 5869: ודבר 1696 אליהם 413 כה 3541 אמר 559 אדני 136 יהוה 3069 הנה 2009 אני 589

tiktob 'aleyhem bayadaka la'aeyneyhem. uadaber 'aleyhem, koh 'amar 'adonay Yahuah hineh 'aniy

**you write whereon in your hand before their eyes And say unto them Thus saith Adonai Yahuah Behold I**

לקח 3947 את 853 בני 1121 ישראל 3478 מבין 996 הגוים 1471 אשר 834 הלכו 1980 שם 8033 וקבצתי 6908 אתם 853

loqeach 'at baney yisra'ael, mibeyn hagouyim 'asher halaku sham; uaqibatztiy 'atam

**will take the children of Israel from among the heathen where they be gone there and will gather them**

37:22

מסביב 5439 והבאתי 935 אותם 853 אל 413 אדמתם 127: ועשיתי 6213 אתם 853 לגוי 1471 אחד 259 בארץ 776

misabiyb, uahebea'tiy 'autam 'al 'admatam. ua'asiytiy 'atam lagouy 'achad ba'aretz

**on every side and bring them into their own land And I will make them nation one in the land**

בהרי 2022 ישראל 3478 ומלך 4428 אחד 259 יהיה 1961 לכלם 3605 למלך 4428 ולא 3808 יהיה 1961 עוד 5750 לשני 8147 גוים 1471

baharey yisra'ael, uamelek 'achad yihayeh lakulam lamelek; uala' yihayeh 'aud lishney gouyim,

**upon the mountains of Israel and king one shall be to them all king and no they shall be more two nations**

37:23

ולא 3808 יחצו 2673 עוד 5750 לשתי 8147 ממלכות 4467 עוד 5750: ולא 3808 יטמאו 2930 עוד 5750

uala' yechatzu 'aud lishtey mamlakout 'aud. uala' yitam'au 'aud,

**neither shall they be divided any more into two kingdoms at all Neither shall they defile themselves any more**

בגלוליהם 1544 ובשקוציהם 8251 ובכל 3605 פשעיהם 6588 והושעתי 3467 אתם 853 מכל 3605

bagiluleyhem uabshiqutzeyhem, uabkol pish'aeyhem; uahousha'atiy 'atam, mikol

**with their idols nor with their detestable things nor with any of their transgressions but I will save them out of all**

מושבתיהם 4186 אשר 834 חטאו 2398 בהם 871a וטהרתי 2891 אותם 853 והיו 1961 לי 3807a לעם 5971 ואני 589

moushaboteyhem 'asher chata'au bahem, uatihartiy 'autam uahayu liy la'am, ua'aniy

**their dwellingplaces wherein they have sinned in them and will cleanse them so shall they be my people and I**

Eze 37:17 And join them one to another into one stick; and they shall become one in your hand.18 And when the children of your people shall speak unto you, saying, Wilt you not show us what you meanest by these?19 Say unto them, Thus saith YHUH G-D; Behold, I will take the stick of Joseph, which is in the hand of Ephraim, and the tribes of Israel his fellows, and will put them with him, even with the stick of Judah, and make them one stick, and they shall be one in mine hand.20 And the sticks whereon you writest shall be in your hand before their eyes.21 And say unto them, Thus saith YHUH G-D; Behold, I will take the children of Israel from among the heathen, whither they be gone, and will gather them on every side, and bring them into their own land:22 And I will make them one nation in the land upon the mountains of Israel; and one king shall be king to them all: and they shall be no more two nations, neither shall they be divided into two kingdoms anymore at all:23 Neither shall they defile themselves anymore with their idols, nor with their detestable things, nor with any of their transgressions: but I will save them out of all their dwellingplaces, wherein they have sinned, and will cleanse them: so shall they be my people, and I will be their G-d.

37:24
אהיה 1961 להם 3807a לאלהים 430: ועבדי 5650 דוד 1732 מלך 4428 עליהם 5921 ורועה 7462 אחד 259 יהיה 1961
'ahayeh lahem le'alohiym. ua'abdiy dauid melek 'aleyhem, uarou'ah 'achad yihayeh
**will be their to Elohim And my servant David *shall be* king over them and shepherd one they shall have**

37:25
לכלם 3605 ובמשפטי 4941 ילכו 1980 וחקתי 2708 ישמרו 8104 ועשו 6213 אותם 853: וישבו 3427 על 5921
lakulam; uabmishpatay yeleku, uachuqotay yishmaru ua'asu 'autam. uayashabu 'al
**all also in my judgments they shall walk and my statutes observe and do them And they shall dwell in**

הארץ 776 אשר 834 נתתי 5414 לעבדי 5650 ליעקב 3290 אשר 834 ישבו 3427 בה 871a אבותיכם 1 וישבו 3427
ha'aretz, 'asher natatiy la'abdiy laya'aqob, 'asher yashabu bah abouteykem; uayashabu
**the land that I have given my servant unto Jacob wherein have dwelt in your fathers and they shall dwell**

עליה 5921 המה 1992 ובניהם 1121 ובני 1121 בניהם 1121 עד 5704 עולם 5769 ודוד 1732 עבדי 5650 נשיא 5387
'aleyha hemah uabneyhem uabney baneyhem 'ad 'aulam, uadauid 'abdiy, nasiy'a
**therein *even* they and their children and their children's children for ever and David my servant prince *shall be***

37:26
להם 3807a לעולם 5769: וכרתי 3772 להם 3807a ברית 1285 שלום 7965 ברית 1285 עולם 5769 יהיה 1961
lahem la'aulam. uakaratiy lahem bariyt shaloum, bariyt 'aulam yihayeh
**their for ever Moreover I will make with them a covenant of peace an covenant everlasting it shall be**

אותם 854 ונתתים 5414 והרביתי 7235 אותם 853 ונתתי 5414 את 853 מקדשי 4720 בתוכם 8432
'autam; uantatiym uahirbeytiy 'autam, uanatatiy 'at miqadashiy batoukam
**with them and I will place them and multiply them and will set my sanctuary in the midst of them**

37:27
לעולם 5769: והיה 1961 משכני 4908 עליהם 5921 והייתי 1961 להם 3807a לאלהים 430 והמה 1992 יהיו 1961 לי 3807a
la'aulam. uahayah mishkaniy 'aleyhem, uahayiytiy lahem le'alohiym; uahemah yihayu liy
**for evermore also shall be My tabernacle with them yea I will be their to Elohim and they shall be my**

37:28
לעם 5971: וידעו 3045 הגוים 1471 כי 3588 אני 589 יהוה 3068 מקדש 6942 את 853 ישראל 3478 בהיות 1961 מקדשי 4720
la'am. uayada'aua hagouyim, kiy 'aniy Yahuah, maqadesh 'at yisra'ael; bihayout miqadashiy
**people And shall know the heathen that I *am* Yahuah do sanctify Israel when shall be my sanctuary**

בתוכם 8432 לעולם 5769:
batoukam la'aulam.
**in the midst of them for evermore**

**Ezek 38:1**
ויהי 1961 דבר 1697 יהוה 3068 אלי 413 לאמר 559:
38:2
בן 1121 אדם 120 שים 7760 פניך 6440 אל 413 גוג 1463 ארץ 776
uayahiy dabar Yahuah 'aelay lea'mor. ben 'adam, siym paneyka 'al goug 'aretz
**And came the word of Yahuah unto me saying Son of man set your face against Gog the land of**

38:3
המגוג 4031 נשיא 5387 ראש 7218 משך 4902 ותבל 8422 והנבא 5012 עליו 5921: ואמרת 559 כה 3541 אמר 559 אדני 136 יהוה 3069
hamagoug, nasiy'a ra'sh meshek uatubal; uahinabea' 'alayu. ua'amarta, koh 'amar 'adonay Yahuah;
**Magog prince of *the* chief Meshech and Tubal and prophesy against him And say Thus saith Adonai Yahuah**

38:4
הנני 2005 אליך 413 גוג 1463 נשיא 5387 ראש 7218 משך 4902 ותבל 8422: ושובבתיך 7725 ונתתי 5414 חחים 2397
hinniy 'aeleyka goug, nasiy'a ra'sh meshek uatubal. uashoubtiyka, uanatatiy chachiym
**Behold I *am* against you O Gog prince of *the* chief Meshech and Tubal And I will turn you back and put hooks**

Eze 37:24 And David my servant shall be king over them; and they all shall have one shepherd: they shall also walk in my judgments, and observe my statutes, and do them.25 And they shall dwell in the land that I have given unto Jacob my servant, wherein your fathers have dwelt; and they shall dwell therein, even they, and their children, and their children's children forever: and my servant David shall be their prince forever.26 Moreover I will make a covenant of peace with them; it shall be an everlasting covenant with them: and I will place them, and multiply them, and will set my sanctuary in the midst of them forevermore.27 My tabernacle also shall be with them: yea, I will be their G-d, and they shall be my people.28 And the heathen shall know that I YHUH do sanctify Israel, when my sanctuary shall be in the midst of them forevermore. **Eze** 38:1 And the word of YHUH came unto me, saying,2 Son of man, set your face against Gog, the land of Magog, the chief prince of Meshech and Tubal, and prophesy against him,3 And say, Thus saith YHUH G-D; Behold I am against you, O Gog, the chief prince of Meshech and Tubal:4 And I will turn you back, and put hooks into your jaws, and I will bring you forth, and all your army, horses and horsemen, all of them clothed with all sorts of armor, even a great company with bucklers and shields, all of them handling swords:

בלחייך 3895 והוצאתי 3318 אותך 853 ואת 853 כל 3605 חילך 2428 סוסים 5483 ופרשים 6571 לבשי 3847
bilchayeyka; uahoutzea'tiy 'autaka ua'at kal cheyleka susiym uaparashiym, labushey
**into your jaws and I will bring forth you *and* all your army horses and horsemen clothed with**

מכלול 4358 כלם 3605 קהל 6951 רב 7227 צנה 6793 ומגן 4043 תפשי 8610 חרבות 2719 כלם 3605: 38:5 פרס 6539
mikloul kulam, qahal rab tzinah uamagen, topasey charabout kulam. paras
**all sorts of *armour even* all of them a company great *with* bucklers and shields handling swords all of them Persia**

כוש 3568 ופוט 6316 אתם 854 כלם 3605 מגן 4043 וכובע 3553: 38:6 גמר 1586 וכל 3605 אגפיה 102 בית 1004 תוגרמה 8425
kush uaput 'atam; kulam magen uakouba'. gomer uakal 'agapeyha, beyt tougarmah,
**Ethiopia and Libya with them all of them *with* shield and helmet Gomer and all his bands the house of Togarmah**

ירכתי 3411 צפון 6828 ואת 853 כל 3605 אגפיו 102 עמים 5971 רבים 7227 אתך 854: 38:7 הכן 3559 והכן 3559 לך 3807a
yarkatey tzapoun ua'at kal 'agapayu; 'amiym rabiym 'atak. hikon uahaken laka,
**quarters *of the* north *and* all his bands people *and* many with you Be you prepared and prepare for yourself**

אתה 859 וכל 3605 קהלך 6951 הנקהלים 6950 עליך 5921 והיית 1961 להם 3807a למשמר 4929: 38:8 מימים 3117 רבים 7227
'atah uakal qahaleka haniqhaliym 'aleyka; uahayiyta lahem lamishmar. miyamiym rabiym
**you and all your company that are assembled unto you and be you unto them a guard After days many**

תפקד 6485 באחרית 319 השנים 8141 תבוא 935 אל 413 ארץ 776 משובבת 7725 מחרב 2719 מקבצת 6908
tipaqed ba'achariyt hashaniym tabou'a 'al 'aretz mashoubebet mechereb, maqubetzet
**you shall be visited in latter the years you shall come into the land *that is* brought back from the sword *and is* gathered**

מעמים 5971 רבים 7227 על 5921 הרי 2022 ישראל 3478 אשר 834 היו 1961 לחרבה 2723 תמיד 8548 והיא 1931 מעמים 5971
me'amiym rabiym, 'al harey yisra'ael, 'asher hayu lacharabah tamiyd; uahiy'a me'amiym
**out of people many against the mountains of Israel which have been waste always but it out of the nations**

הוצאה 3318 וישבו 3427 לבטח 983 כלם 3605: 38:9 ועלית 5927 כשאה 7722 תבוא 935 כענן 6051 לכסות 3680
hutza'ah, uayashabu labetach kulam. ua'aliyta kasho'ah tabou'a, ke'anan lakasout
**is brought forth and they shall dwell safely all of them You shall ascend like a storm *and* come like a cloud to cover**

הארץ 776 תהיה 1961 אתה 859 וכל 3605 אגפיך 102 ועמים 5971 רבים 7227 אותך 854: 38:10 כה 3541 אמר 559 אדני 136 יהוה 3068
ha'aretz tihayeh; 'atah uakal 'agapeyka, ua'amiym rabiym autak. koh 'amar 'adonay Yahuah;
**the land you shall be you and all your bands and people many with you Thus saith Adonai Yahuah**

והיה 1961 ביום 3117 ההוא 1931 יעלו 5927 דברים 1697 על 5921 לבבך 3824 וחשבת 2803 מחשבת 4284
uahayah bayoum hahua', ya'alu dabariym 'al lababeka, uachashabta machashebet
**It shall also come to pass *that* at time the same shall come things into your mind and you shall think an thought**

רעה 7451: 38:11 ואמרת 559 אעלה 5927 על 5921 ארץ 776 פרזות 6519 אבוא 935 השקטים 8252 ישבי 3427
ra'ah. ua'amarta, 'a'aleh 'al 'aretz parazout, abou'a hashoqatiym, yoshabey
**evil And you shall say I will go up to the land of unwalled villages I will go to them that are at rest that dwell**

לבטח 983 כלם 3605 ישבים 3427 באין 369 חומה 2346 ובריח 1280 ודלתים 1817 אין 369 להם 3807a: 38:12 לשלל 7997 שלל 7998 ולבז 962
labetach; kulam, yoshbiym ba'aeyn choumah, uabriyach uadlatayim 'aeyn lahem. lishlol shalal ualaboz
**safely all of them dwelling without walls and bars nor gates neither having To take a spoil and to take**

Eze 38:5 Persia, Ethiopia, and Libya with them; all of them with shield and helmet:6 Gomer, and all his bands; the house of Togarmah of the north quarters, and all his bands: and many people with you.7 Be you prepared, and prepare for thyself, you, and all your company that are assembled unto you, and be you a guard unto them.8 After many days you shall be visited: in the latter years you shall come into the land that is brought back from the sword, and is gathered out of many people, against the mountains of Israel, which have been always waste: but it is brought forth out of the nations, and they shall dwell safely all of them.9 Thou shall ascend and come like a storm, you shall be like a cloud to cover the land, you, and all your bands, and many people with you.10 Thus saith YHUH G-D; It shall also come to pass, that at the same time shall things come into your mind, and you shall think an evil thought:11 And you shall say, I will go up to the land of unwalled villages; I will go to them that are at rest, that dwell safely, all of them dwelling without walls, and having neither bars nor gates,12 To take a spoil, and to take a prey; to turn your hand upon the desolate places that are now inhabited, and upon the people that are gathered out of the nations, which have gotten cattle and goods, that dwell in the midst of the land.

| בז 957 | להשיב 7725 | ידך 3027 | על 5921 | חרבות 2723 | נושבת 3427 | ואל 413 | עם 5971 | מאסף 622 |
|---|---|---|---|---|---|---|---|---|
| baz; | lahashiyb | yadaka | 'al | charabout | noushabot, | ua'al | 'am | ma'asap |
| **a prey** | **to turn** | **your hand** | **upon** | **the desolate places** | ***that are now* inhabited** | **and upon** | **the people** | ***that are* gathered** |

| מגוים 1471 | עשה 6213 | מקנה 4735 | וקנין 7075 | ישבי 3427 | על 5921 | טבור 2872 | הארץ 776: | 38:13 | שבא 7614 | ודדן 1719 |
|---|---|---|---|---|---|---|---|---|---|---|
| migouyim, | 'aseh | miqneh | uaqinyan, | yoshabey | 'al | tabur | ha'aretz. | | shaba' | uadadan |
| **out of the nations** | **which have gotten** | **cattle** | **and goods** | **that dwell** | **in** | **the midst of** | **the land** | | **Sheba** | **and Dedan** |

| וסחרי 5503 | תרשיש 8659 | וכל 3605 | כפריה 3715 | יאמרו 559 | לך 3807a | הלשלל 7997 | שלל 7998 | אתה 859 | בא 935 |
|---|---|---|---|---|---|---|---|---|---|
| uasocharey | tarshiysh | uakal | kapireyha | ya'maru | laka, | halishlol | shalal | 'atah | ba', |
| **and the merchants of** | **Tarshish** | **with all** | **the young lions thereof** | **shall say** | **unto you** | **to take** | **a spoil?** | **you** | **Are come** |

| הלבז 962 | בז 957 | הקהלת 6950 | קהלך 6951 | לשאת 5375 | כסף 3701 | וזהב 2091 | לקחת 3947 | מקנה 4735 | וקנין 7075 | לשלל 7997 |
|---|---|---|---|---|---|---|---|---|---|---|
| halaboz | baz | hiqhalta | qahaleka; | lasea't | kesep | uazahab, | laqachat | miqneh | uaqinyan, | lishlol |
| **to take** | **a prey?** | **have you gathered** | **your company** | **to carry away** | **silver** | **and gold** | **to take away** | **cattle** | **and goods** | **to take** |

| שלל 7998 | גדול 1419: | 38:14 | לכן 3651 | הנבא 5012 | בן 1121 | אדם 120 | ואמרת 559 | לגוג 1463 | כה 3541 | אמר 559 | אדני 136 | יהוה 3069 | הלוא 3808 | ביום 3117 |
|---|---|---|---|---|---|---|---|---|---|---|---|---|---|---|
| shalal | gadoul. | | laken | hinabea' | ben | 'adam, | ua'amarta | lagoug, | koh | 'amar | 'adonay | Yahuah; | halou'a | bayoum |
| **a spoil?** | **great** | | **Therefore** | **prophesy** | **son of** | **man** | **and say** | **unto Gog** | **Thus** | **saith** | **Adonai** | **Yahuah** | **not** | **In day** |

| ההוא 1931 | בשבת 3427 | עמי 5971 | ישראל 3478 | לבטח 983 | תדע 3045: | 38:15 | ובאת 935 | ממקומך 4725 |
|---|---|---|---|---|---|---|---|---|
| hahua', | bashebet | 'amiy | yisra'ael | labetach | teda'. | | uaba'ta | mimaqoumaka |
| **that** | **when dwell** | **my people of** | **Israel** | **safely** | **shall you know *it*?** | | **And you shall come** | **from your place** |

| מירכתי 3411 | צפון 6828 | אתה 859 | ועמים 5971 | רבים 7227 | אתך 854 | רכבי 7392 | סוסים 5483 | כלם 3605 | קהל 6951 | גדול 1419 | וחיל 2428 |
|---|---|---|---|---|---|---|---|---|---|---|---|
| miyarkatey | tzapoun, | 'atah | ua'amiym | rabiym | 'atak; | rokbey | susiym | kulam, | qahal | gadoul | uachayil |
| **out of parts** | ***the* north** | **you** | **and people** | **many** | **with you** | **riding upon** | **horses** | **all of them** | **a company** | **great** | **and a army** |

| רב 7227: | 38:16 | ועלית 5927 | על 5921 | עמי 5971 | ישראל 3478 | כענן 6051 | לכסות 3680 | הארץ 776 | באחרית 319 | הימים 3117 |
|---|---|---|---|---|---|---|---|---|---|---|
| rab. | | ua'aliyta | 'al | 'amiy | yisra'ael, | ke'anan | lakasout | ha'aretz; | ba'achariyt | hayamiym |
| **mighty** | | **And you shall come up** | **against** | **my people of** | **Israel** | **as a cloud** | **to cover** | **the land** | **in latter** | **the days** |

| תהיה 1961 | והבאותיך 935 | על 5921 | ארצי 776 | למען 4616 | דעת 3045 | הגוים 1471 | אתי 853 | בהקדשי 6942 | בך 871a |
|---|---|---|---|---|---|---|---|---|---|
| tihayeh, | uahabi'autiyka | 'al | 'artziy, | lama'an | da'at | hagouyim | 'atiy, | bahiqadashiy | baka |
| **it shall be** | **and I will bring you** | **against** | **my land** | **that** | **may know** | **the heathen** | **me** | **when I shall be sanctified** | **in you** |

| לעיניהם 5869 | גוג 1463: | 38:17 | כה 3541 | אמר 559 | אדני 136 | יהוה 3069 | האתה 859 | הוא 1931 | אשר 834 | דברתי 1696 | בימים 3117 | קדמונים 6931 |
|---|---|---|---|---|---|---|---|---|---|---|---|---|
| la'aeyneyhem | goug. | | koh | 'amar | 'adonay | Yahuah | ha'atah | hua' | 'asher | dibartiy | bayamiym | qadmouniym, |
| **before their eyes** | **O Gog** | | **Thus** | **saith** | **Adonai** | **Yahuah** | ***are* you** | **he** | **of whom** | **I have spoken** | **in time** | **old** |

| ביד 3027 | עבדי 5650 | נביאי 5030 | ישראל 3478 | הנבאים 5012 | בימים 3117 | ההם 1992 | שנים 8141 | להביא 935 | אתך 853 |
|---|---|---|---|---|---|---|---|---|---|
| bayad | 'abaday | nabiy'aey | yisra'ael, | haniba'aym | bayamiym | hahem | shaniym; | lahabiy'a | 'atka |
| **by** | **my servants** | **the prophets of** | **Israel** | **which prophesied** | **in days** | **those** | ***many* years** | **that I would bring** | **you** |

| עליהם 5921: | 38:18 | והיה 1961 | ביום 3117 | ההוא 1931 | ביום 3117 | בוא 935 | גוג 1463 | על 5921 | אדמת 127 | ישראל 3478 |
|---|---|---|---|---|---|---|---|---|---|---|
| 'aleyhem. | | uahayah | bayoum | hahua', | bayoum | bou'a | goug | 'al | 'admat | yisra'ael, |
| **against them?** | | **And it shall come to pass** | **at time** | **the same** | **when** | **shall come** | **Gog** | **against** | **the land of** | **Israel** |

Eze 38:13 Sheba, and Dedan, and the merchants of Tarshish, with all the young lions thereof, shall say unto you, Art you come to take a spoil? have you gathered your company to take a prey? to carry away silver and gold, to take away cattle and goods, to take a great spoil?14 Therefore, son of man, prophesy and say unto Gog, Thus saith YHUH G-D; In that day when my people of Israel dwell safely, shall you not know it?15 And you shall come from your place out of the north parts, you, and many people with you, all of them riding upon horses, a great company, and a mighty army:16 And you shall come up against my people of Israel, as a cloud to cover the land; it shall be in the latter days, and I will bring you against my land, that the heathen may know me, when I shall be sanctified in you, O Gog, before their eyes.17 Thus saith YHUH G-D; Art you he of whom I have spoken in old time by my servants the prophets of Israel, which prophesied in those days many years that I would bring you against them?18 And it shall come to pass at the same time when Gog shall come against the land of Israel, saith YHUH G-D, that my fury shall come up in my face.

| נאם 5002 | אדני 136 | יהוה 3069 | תעלה 5927 | חמתי 2534 | באפי 639: | 38:19 | ובקנאתי 7068 | באש 784 | עברתי 5678 |
|---|---|---|---|---|---|---|---|---|---|
| na'am | 'adonay | Yahuah; | ta'aleh | chamatiy | ba'apiy. | | uabqin'atiy | ba'aesh | 'abratiy |
| **saith** | **Adonai** | **Yahuah** | **shall come up** | ***that* my fury** | **in my face** | | **For in my jealousy** | ***and* in the fire of** | **my wrath** |

| דברתי 1696 | אם 518 | לא 3808 | ביום 3117 | ההוא 1931 | יהיה 1961 | רעש 7494 | גדול 1419 | על 5921 | אדמת 127 | ישראל 3478: | 38:20 |
|---|---|---|---|---|---|---|---|---|---|---|---|
| dibartiy; | 'am | la' | bayoum | hahua', | yihayeh | ra'ash | gadoul, | 'al | 'admat | yisra'ael. | |
| **have I spoken** | **Surely** | **not** | **in day** | **that** | **there shall be** | **a shaking** | **great** | **in** | **the land of** | **Israel** | |

| ורעשו 7493 | מפני 6440 | דגי 1709 | הים 3220 | ועוף 5775 | השמים 8064 | וחית 2416 | השדה 7704 | וכל 3605 |
|---|---|---|---|---|---|---|---|---|
| uara'ashu | mipanay | dagey | hayam | ua'aup | hashamayim | uachayat | hasadeh, | uakal |
| **So that shall shake** | **the face of** | **the fishes of** | **the sea** | **and the fowls of** | **the heaven** | **and the beasts of** | **the field** | **and all** |

| הרמש 7431 | הרמש 7430 | על 5921 | האדמה 127 | וכל 3605 | האדם 120 | אשר 834 | על 5921 | פני 6440 | האדמה 127 |
|---|---|---|---|---|---|---|---|---|---|
| haremes | haromes | 'al | ha'adamah, | uakol | ha'adam, | 'asher | 'al | paney | ha'adamah; |
| **creeping things** | **that creep** | **upon** | **the earth** | **and all** | **the men** | **that *are*** | **upon** | **at my presence of** | **the earth** |

| ונהרסו 2040 | ההרים 2022 | ונפלו 5307 | המדרגות 4095 | וכל 3605 | חומה 2346 | לארץ 776 | תפול 5307: | 38:21 |
|---|---|---|---|---|---|---|---|---|
| uanehersu | hehariym, | uanapalu | hamadaregout, | uakal | choumah | la'aretz | tipoul. | |
| **and shall be thrown down** | **the mountains** | **and shall fall** | **the steep places** | **and every** | **wall** | **to the ground** | **shall fall** | |

| וקראתי 7121 | עליו 5921 | לכל 3605 | הרי 2022 | חרב 2719 | נאם 5002 | אדני 136 | יהוה 3069 | חרב 2719 | איש 376 |
|---|---|---|---|---|---|---|---|---|---|
| uaqara'tiy | 'aelayu | lakal | haray | chereb, | na'am | 'adonay | Yahuah; | chereb | 'aysh |
| **And I will call for** | **against him** | **throughout all** | **my mountains** | **a sword** | **saith** | **Adonai** | **Yahuah** | **sword** | **every man's** |

| באחיו 251 | תהיה 1961: | 38:22 | ונשפטתי 8199 | אתו 853 | בדבר 1698 | ובדם 1818 | וגשם 1653 | שוטף 7857 |
|---|---|---|---|---|---|---|---|---|
| ba'achiyu | tihayeh. | | uanishpattiy | 'atou | badeber | uabdam; | uageshem | shoutep |
| **against his brother** | **shall be** | | **And I will plead against** | **him** | **with pestilence** | **and with blood** | **and shower** | **overflowing** |

| ואבני 68 | אלגביש 417 | אש 784 | וגפרית 1614 | אמטיר 4305 | עליו 5921 | ועל 5921 | אגפיו 102 | ועל 5921 | עמים 5971 | רבים 7227 | אשר 834 |
|---|---|---|---|---|---|---|---|---|---|---|---|
| ua'abney | 'algabiysh | 'aesh | uagapariyt, | 'amtiyr | 'alayu | ua'al | 'agapayu, | ua'al | 'amiym | rabiym | 'asher |
| **and great** | **hail stones** | **fire** | **and brimstone** | **I will rain** | **upon him** | **and upon** | **his bands** | **and upon** | **people** | ***the* many** | **that *are*** |

| אתו 854: | 38:23 | והתגדלתי 1431 | והתקדשתי 6942 | ונודעתי 3045 | לעיני 5869 | גוים 1471 | רבים 7227 |
|---|---|---|---|---|---|---|---|
| 'atou. | | uahitgadiltiy | uahitqadishtiy, | uanouda'atiy, | la'aeyney | gouyim | rabiym; |
| **with him** | | **Thus will I magnify myself** | **and sanctify myself** | **and I will be known** | **in the eyes of** | **nations** | **many** |

| וידעו 3045 | כי 3588 | אני 589 | יהוה 3068: |
|---|---|---|---|
| uayada'aua | kiy | 'aniy | Yahuah. |
| **and they shall know that** | **I** | ***am*** | **Yahuah** |

| Ezek 39:1 | ואתה 859 | בן 1121 | אדם 120 | הנבא 5012 | על 5921 | גוג 1463 | ואמרת 559 | כה 3541 | אמר 559 | אדני 136 | יהוה 3069 | הנני 2005 |
|---|---|---|---|---|---|---|---|---|---|---|---|---|
| | ua'atah | ben | 'adam | hinabea' | 'al | goug, | ua'amarta, | koh | 'amar | 'adonay | Yahuah; | hinniy |
| | **Therefore you** | **son of** | **man** | **prophesy** | **against** | **Gog** | **and say** | **Thus** | **saith** | **Adonai** | **Yahuah** | **Behold I *am*** |

| אליך 413 | גוג 1463 | נשיא 5387 | ראש 7218 | משך 4902 | ותבל 8422: | 39:2 | ושבבתיך 7725 | וששאתיך 8338 |
|---|---|---|---|---|---|---|---|---|
| 'aeleyka | goug, | nasiy'a | ra'sh | meshek | uatubal. | | uashobabtiyka | uashishea'tiyka, |
| **against you** | **O Gog** | **prince of** | ***the* chief** | **Meshech** | **and Tubal** | | **And I will turn you back** | **and leave but the sixth part of you** |

Eze 38:19 For in my jealousy and in the fire of my wrath have I spoken, Surely in that day there shall be a great shaking in the land of Israel;20 So that the fishes of the sea, and the fowls of the heaven, and the beasts of the field, and all creeping things that creep upon the earth, and all the men that are upon the face of the earth, shall shake at my presence, and the mountains shall be thrown down, and the steep places shall fall, and every wall shall fall to the ground.21 And I will call for a sword against him throughout all my mountains, saith YHUH G-D: every man's sword shall be against his brother.22 And I will plead against him with pestilence and with blood; and I will rain upon him, and upon his bands, and upon the many people that are with him, an overflowing rain, and great hailstones, fire, and brimstone.23 Thus will I magnify myself, and sanctify myself; and I will be known in the eyes of many nations, and they shall know that I am YHUH. **Eze** 39:1 Therefore, you son of man, prophesy against Gog, and say, Thus saith YHUH G-D; Behold, I am against you, O Gog, the chief prince of Meshech and Tubal:2 And I will turn you back, and leave but the sixth part of you, and will cause you to come up from the north parts, and will bring you upon the mountains of Israel:

והעליתיך 5927 מירכתי 3411 צפון 6828 והבאותך 935 על 5921 הרי 2022 ישראל 3478: 39:3
uaha'aliytiyka miyarkatey tzapoun; uahabi'autika 'al harey yisra'ael.
**and will cause you to come up from parts *the* north and will bring you upon the mountains of Israel**

והכיתי 5221 קשתך 7198 מיד 3027 שמאולך 8040 וחציך 2671 מיד 3027 ימינך 3225 אפיל 5307: 39:4 על 5921
uahikeytiy qashtaka miyad sama'uleka; uachitzeyka miyad yamiynaka 'apiyl. 'al
**And I will smite your bow out of hand your left and your arrows out of hand your right will cause to fall upon**

הרי 2022 ישראל 3478 תפול 5307 אתה 859 וכל 3605 אגפיך 102 ועמים 5971 אשר 834 אתך 854 לעיט 5861
harey yisra'ael tipoul, 'atah uakal 'agapeyka, ua'amiym 'asher 'atak; la'aeyt
**the mountains of Israel You shall fall you and all your bands and the people that *is* with you unto the ravenous**

צפור 6833 כל 3605 כנף 3671 וחית 2416 השדה 7704 נתתיך 5414 לאכלה 402: 39:5 על 5921 פני 6440 השדה 7704 תפול 5307 כי 3588
tzipour kal kanap uachayat hasadeh natatiyka la'akalah 'al paney hasadeh tipoul; kiy
**birds of every sort and *to* the beasts of the field I will give to be devoured upon open the field You shall fall for**

אני 589 דברתי 1696 נאם 5002 אדני 136 יהוה 3069: 39:6 ושלחתי 7971 אש 784 במגוג 4031 ובישבי 3427 האיים 339
'aniy dibartiy, na'am 'adonay Yahuah. uashilachtiy 'aesh bamagoug, uabyoshabey ha'ayiym
**I have spoken *it* saith Adonai Yahuah And I will send a fire on Magog and among them that dwell *in* the isles**

לבטח 983 וידעו 3045 כי 3588 אני 589 יהוה 3068: 39:7 ואת 853 שם 8034 קדשי 6944 אודיע 3045 בתוך 8432 עמי 5971
labetach; uayada'aua kiy 'aniy Yahuah. ua'at shem qadashiy 'audiya', batouk 'amiy
**carelessly and they shall know that I *am* Yahuah So name my holy will I make known in the midst of my people**

ישראל 3478 ולא 3808 אחל 2490 את 853 שם 8034 קדשי 6944 עוד 5750 וידעו 3045 הגוים 1471 כי 3588 אני 589 יהוה 3068
yisra'ael, uala' 'achel 'at shem qadashiy 'aud; uayada'aua hagouyim kiy 'aniy Yahuah,
**Israel and not *let them* I will pollute name my holy any more and shall know the heathen that I *am* Yahuah**

קדוש 6918 בישראל 3478: 39:8 הנה 2009 באה 935 ונהיתה 1961 נאם 5002 אדני 136 יהוה 3068 הוא 1931 היום 3117 אשר 834
qadoush bayisra'ael. hineh ba'ah uanihayatah, na'am 'adonay Yahuah; hua' hayoum 'asher
***the* Holy One in Israel Behold it is come and it is done saith Adonai Yahuah this *is* the day whereof**

דברתי 1696: 39:9 ויצאו 3318 ישבי 3427 ערי 5892 ישראל 3478 ובערו 1197 והשיקו 5400 בנשק 5402
dibartiy. uayatza'au yoshabey 'arey yisra'ael, uabi'aru uahisiyqu banesheq
**I have spoken And shall go forth they that dwell in the cities of Israel and shall set on fire and burn the weapons**

ומגן 4043 וצנה 6793 בקשת 7198 ובחצים 2671 ובמקל 4731 יד 3027 וברמח 7420 ובערו 1197
uamagen uatzinah baqeshet uabchitziym, uabmaqel yad uabromach; uabi'aru
**both the shields and the bucklers the bows and the arrows and the staves hand and the spears and they shall burn**

בהם 871a אש 784 שבע 7651 שנים 8141: 39:10 ולא 3808 ישאו 5375 עצים 6086 מן 4480 השדה 7704 ולא 3808 יחטבו 2404 מן 4480
bahem 'aesh sheba' shaniym. uala' yis'au 'aetziym min hasadeh, uala' yachtabu min
**them *with* fire seven years So that no they shall take wood out of the field neither cut down *any* out of**

היערים 3293 כי 3588 בנשק 5402 יבערו 1197 אש 784 ושללו 7997 את 853 שלליהם 7997 ובזזו 962 את 853
haya'ariym, kiy banesheq yaba'aru 'aesh; uashalalu 'at sholaleyhem, uabazazu 'at
**the forests for the weapons they shall burn *with* fire and they shall spoil those that spoiled them and rob**

Eze 39:3 And I will smite your bow out of your left hand, and will cause your arrows to fall out of your right hand.4 Thou shall fall upon the mountains of Israel, you, and all your bands, and the people that is with you: I will give you unto the ravenous birds of every sort, and to the beasts of the field to be devoured.5 Thou shall fall upon the open field: for I have spoken it, saith YHUH G-D.6 And I will send a fire on Magog, and among them that dwell carelessly in the isles: and they shall know that I am YHUH.7 So will I make my holy name known in the midst of my people Israel; and I will not let them pollute my holy name anymore: and the heathen shall know that I am YHUH, the Holy One in Israel.8 Behold, it is come, and it is done, saith YHUH G-D; this is the day whereof I have spoken.9 And they that dwell in the cities of Israel shall go forth, and shall set on fire and burn the weapons, both the shields and the bucklers, the bows and the arrows, and the handstaves, and the spears, and they shall burn them with fire seven years:10 So that they shall take no wood out of the field, neither cut down any out of the forests; for they shall burn the weapons with fire: and they shall spoil those that spoiled them, and rob those that robbed them, saith YHUH G-D.

39:11
בזזיהם 962 נאם 5002 אדני 136 יהוה 3069: והיה 1961 ביום 3117 ההוא 1931 אתן 5414 לגוג 1463
bozazeyhem, na'am 'adonay Yahuah. uahayah bayoum hahua' 'aten lagoug
**those that robbed them saith Adonai Yahuah And it shall come to pass in day that *that* I will give unto Gog**

מקום 4725 שם 8033 קבר 6913 בישראל 3478 גי 1516 העברים 5674 קדמת 6926 הים 3220 וחסמת 2629 היא 1931 את 853
maqoum sham qeber bayisra'ael, gey ha'abariym qidmat hayam, uachosemet hiy'a 'at
**a place there *of* graves in Israel the valley of the passengers *on* the east of the sea and shall stop it**

העברים 5674 וקברו 6912 שם 8033 את 853 גוג 1463 ואת 853 כל 3605 המונה 1995 וקראו 7121
ha'abariym; uaqabaru sham, 'at goug ua'at kal hamounoh, uaqara'au,
**the *noses* of the passengers and shall they bury there Gog *and* all his multitude and they shall call**

39:12
גיא 1516 המון 1996 גוג 1463: וקברום 6912 בית 1004 ישראל 3478 למען 4616 טהר 2891 את 853
gey'a hamoun goug. uaqbarum beyt yisra'ael, lama'an taher 'at
***it* The valley of Hamon gog And shall be burying of them the house of Israel that they may cleanse**

39:13
הארץ 776 שבעה 7651 חדשים 2320: וקברו 6912 כל 3605 עם 5971 הארץ 776 והיה 1961 להם 3807a לשם 8034
ha'aretz; shib'ah chadashiym. uaqabaru kal 'am ha'aretz, uahayah lahem lashem;
**the land seven months Yea shall bury *them* all the people of the land and it shall be to them a renown**

39:14
יום 3117 הכבדי 3513 נאם 5002 אדני 136 יהוה 3069: ואנשי 582 תמיד 8548 יבדילו 914
youm hikabadiy, na'am 'adonay Yahuah. ua'anshey tamiyd yabdiylu
**the day that I shall be glorified saith Adonai Yahuah And men of continual employment they shall sever out**

עברים 5674 בארץ 776 מקברים 6912 את 853 העברים 5674 את 853 הנותרים 3498 על 5921 פני 6440 הארץ 776 לטהרה 2891
'abariym ba'aretz, maqabriym 'at ha'abariym, 'at hanoutariym 'al paney ha'aretz lataharah;
**passing through the land to bury *with* the passengers those that remain upon the face of the earth to cleanse it**

39:15
מקצה 7097 שבעה 7651 חדשים 2320 יחקרו 2713: ועברו 5674 העברים 5674 בארץ 776 וראה 7200
miqtzeh shib'ah chadashiym yachqoru. ua'abaru ha'abariym ba'aretz, uara'ah
**after the end of seven months shall they search And the passengers *that* pass through the land when *any* see**

עצם 6106 אדם 120 ובנה 1129 אצלו 681 ציון 6726 עד 5704 קברו 6912 אתו 853 המקברים 6912 אל 413 גיא 1516 המון 1996
'atzem 'adam, uabanah 'atzlou tziyun; 'ad qabaru 'atou hamaqabriym, 'al gey'a hamoun
**a bone man's then shall he set up by it a sign till the buriers it have buried in the valley of Hamon**

39:16
39:17
גוג 1463: וגם 1571 שם 8034 עיר 5892 המונה 1997 וטהרו 2891 הארץ 776: ואתה 859 בן 1121 אדם 120
goug. ua'gam shem 'ayr hamounah uatiharu ha'aretz. ua'atah ben 'adam
**gog And also the name of the city *shall be* Hamonah Thus shall they cleanse the land And you son of man**

כה 3541 אמר 559 אדני 136 יהוה 3069 אמר 559 לצפור 6833 כל 3605 כנף 3671 ולכל 3605 חית 2416 השדה 7704 הקבצו 6908
koh 'amar 'adonay Yahuah 'amor latzipour kal kanap ualkal chayat hasadeh, hiqabatzu
**thus saith Adonai Yahuah Speak unto fowl every feathered and to every beast of the field Assemble yourselves**

ובאו 935 האספו 622 מסביב 5439 על 5921 זבחי 2077 אשר 834 אני 589 זבח 2076 לכם 3807a זבח 2077 גדול 1419
uaba'au he'asapu misabiyb, 'al zibchiy, 'asher 'aniy zobeach lakem zebach gadoul,
**and come gather yourselves on every side to my sacrifice that I do sacrifice for you *even* a sacrifice great**

Eze 39:11 And it shall come to pass in that day, that I will give unto Gog a place there of graves in Israel, the valley of the passengers on the east of the sea: and it shall stop the noses of the passengers: and there shall they bury Gog and all his multitude: and they shall call it The valley of Hamon-gog.12 And seven months shall the house of Israel be burying of them, that they may cleanse the land.13 Yea, all the people of the land shall bury them; and it shall be to them a renown the day that I shall be glorified, saith YHUH G-D.14 And they shall sever out men of continual employment, passing through the land to bury with the passengers those that remain upon the face of the earth, to cleanse it: after the end of seven months shall they search.15 And the passengers that pass through the land, when any see a man's bone, then shall he set up a sign by it, till the buriers have buried it in the valley of Hamon-gog.16 And also the name of the city shall be Hamonah. Thus shall they cleanse the land.17 And, you son of man, thus saith YHUH G-D; Speak unto every feathered fowl, and to every beast of the field, Assemble yourselves, and come; gather yourselves on every side to my sacrifice that I do sacrifice for you, even a great sacrifice upon the mountains of Israel, that you may eat flesh, and drink blood.

39:18
על 5921 הרי 2022 ישראל 3478 ואכלתם 398 בשר 1320 ושתיתם 8354 דם 1818: בשר 1320 גבורים 1368 תאכלו 398
'al harey yisra'ael; ua'akaltem basar uashtiytem dam. basar gibouriym ta'kelu,
**upon the mountains of Israel that you may eat flesh and drink blood the flesh of the mighty You shall eat**

ודם 1818 נשיאי 5387 הארץ 776 תשתו 8354 אילים 354 כרים 3733 ועתודים 6260 פרים 6499 מריאי 4806 בשן 1316
uadam nasiy'aey ha'aretz tishtu; 'aeyliym kariym ua'atudiym pariym, mariy'aey bashan
**and the blood of the princes of the earth drink *of* rams *of* lambs and of goats *of* bullocks fatlings of Bashan**

39:19
כלם 3605: ואכלתם 398 חלב 2459 לשבעה 7654 ושתיתם 8354 דם 1818 לשכרון 7943 מזבחי 2077 אשר 834
kulam. ua'akaltem cheleb lasaba'ah, uashtiytem dam lashikaroun; mizibchiy 'asher
**all of them And you shall eat fat till you be full and drink blood till you be drunken of my sacrifice which**

39:20
זבחתי 2076 לכם 3807a: ושבעתם 7646 על 5921 שלחני 7979 סוס 5483 ורכב 7393 גבור 1368
zabachtiy lakem. uasba'atem 'al shulchaniy sus uarekeb, gibour
**I have sacrificed for you Thus you shall be filled at my table *with* horses and chariots *with* mighty men**

39:21
וכל 3605 איש 376 מלחמה 4421 נאם 5002 אדני 136 יהוה 3069: ונתתי 5414 את 853 כבודי 3519 בגוים 1471 וראו 7200
uakal 'aysh milchamah; na'am 'adonay Yahuah. uanatatiy 'at kaboudiy bagouyim; uar'au
**and with all men of war saith Adonai Yahuah And I will set my glory among the heathen and shall see**

39:22
כל 3605 הגוים 1471 את 853 משפטי 4941 אשר 834 עשיתי 6213 ואת 853 ידי 3027 אשר 834 שמתי 7760 בהם 871a:
kal hagouyim, 'at mishpatiy 'asher 'asiytiy, ua'at yadiy 'asher samtiy bahem.
**all the heathen my judgment that I have executed *and* my hand that I have laid upon them**

39:23
וידעו 3045 בית 1004 ישראל 3478 כי 3588 אני 589 יהוה 3068 אלהיהם 430 מן 4480 היום 3117 ההוא 1931 והלאה 1973:
uayada'aua beyt yisra'ael, kiy 'aniy Yahuah 'aloheyhem; min hayoum hahua' uahal'ah.
**So shall know the house of Israel that I *am* Yahuah their Elohim from day that and forward**

וידעו 3045 הגוים 1471 כי 3588 בעונם 5771 גלו 1540 בית 1004 ישראל 3478 על 5921 אשר 834
uayada'aua hagouyim kiy ba'auonam galu beyt yisra'ael, 'al 'asher
**And shall know the heathen that for their iniquity went into captivity the house of Israel because which**

מעלו 4603 בי 871a ואסתר 5641 פני 6440 מהם 1992 ואתנם 5414 ביד 3027 צריהם 6862
ma'alu biy, ua'astir panay mehem; ua'atanem bayad tzareyhem,
**they trespassed against me therefore hid I my face from them and gave them into the hand of their enemies**

39:24
ויפלו 5307 בחרב 2719 כלם 3605: כטמאתם 2932 וכפשעיהם 6588
uayiplu bachereb kulam. katum'atam uakpish'aeyhem
**and so fell they by the sword all According to their uncleanness and according to their transgressions**

39:25
עשיתי 6213 אתם 853 ואסתר 5641 פני 6440 מהם 1992: לכן 3651 כה 3541 אמר 559 אדני 136 יהוה 3068 עתה 6258
'asiytiy 'atam; ua'astir panay mehem. laken, koh 'amar 'adonay Yahuah, 'atah,
**have I done unto them and hid my face from them Therefore thus saith Adonai Yahuah Now**

אשיב 7725 את 853 שבית 7622 יעקב 3290 ורחמתי 7355 כל 3605 בית 1004 ישראל 3478 וקנאתי 7065
'ashiyb 'at shebiyt ya'aqob, uarichamtiy kal beyt yisra'ael; uaqinea'tiy
**will I bring again the captivity of Jacob and have mercy upon the whole house of Israel and will be jealous**

Eze 39:18 You shall eat the flesh of the mighty, and drink the blood of the princes of the earth, of rams, of lambs, and of goats, of bullocks, all of them fatlings of Bashan.19 And you shall eat fat till you be full, and drink blood till you be drunken, of my sacrifice which I have sacrificed for you.20 Thus you shall be filled at my table with horses and chariots, with mighty men, and with all men of war, saith YHUH G-D.21 And I will set my glory among the heathen, and all the heathen shall see my judgment that I have executed, and my hand that I have laid upon them.22 So the house of Israel shall know that I am YHUH their G-d from that day and forward.23 And the heathen shall know that the house of Israel went into captivity for their iniquity: because they trespassed against me, therefore hid I my face from them, and gave them into the hand of their enemies: so fell they all by the sword.24 According to their uncleanness and according to their transgressions have I done unto them, and hid my face from them.25 Therefore thus saith YHUH G-D; Now will I bring again the captivity of Jacob, and have mercy upon the whole house of Israel, and will be jealous for my holy name;

| לשם 8034 | קדשי 6944: | 39:26 ונשו 5375 | את 853 | כלמתם 3639 | ואת 853 | כל 3605 | מעלם 4603 | אשר 834 |
|---|---|---|---|---|---|---|---|---|
| lashem | qadashiy | uanasu | 'at | kalimatam, | ua'at | kal | ma'aulam | 'asher |
| **for name** | **my holy** | **After that they have borne** | | **their shame** | ***and*** | **all** | **they have trespassed** | **whereby** |

| מעלו 4604 | בי 871a | בשבתם 3427 | על 5921 | אדמתם 127 | לבטח 983 | ואין 369 | מחריד 2729: | 39:27 |
|---|---|---|---|---|---|---|---|---|
| ma'alu | biy; | bashibtam | 'al | 'admatam | labetach | ua'aeyn | machariyd. | |
| **their trespasses** | **against me** | **when they dwelt** | **in** | **their land** | **safely** | **and none** | **made *them* afraid** | |

| בשובבי 7725 | אותם 853 | מן 4480 | העמים 5971 | וקבצתי 6908 | אתם 853 | מארצות 776 | איביהם 341 | ונקדשתי 6942 |
|---|---|---|---|---|---|---|---|---|
| bashoubabiy | 'autam | min | ha'amiym, | uaqibatztiy | 'atam, | me'artzout | 'ayabeyhem; | uanipdashtiy |
| **When I have brought again** | **them** | **from** | **the people** | **and gathered** | **them** | **out of lands** | **their enemies'** | **and am sanctified** |

| בם 871a | לעיני 5869 | הגוים 1471 | רבים 7227: | 39:28 וידעו 3045 | כי 3588 | אני 589 | יהוה 3068 | אלהיהם 430 |
|---|---|---|---|---|---|---|---|---|
| bam, | la'aeyney | hagouyim | rabiym. | uayada'aua, | kiy | 'aniy | Yahuah | 'aloheyhem, |
| **in them** | **in the sight of** | **nations** | **many** | **Then shall they know** | **that** | **I *am*** | **Yahuah** | **their Elohim** |

| בהגלותי 1540 | אתם 853 | אל 413 | הגוים 1471 | וכנסתים 3664 | על 5921 | אדמתם 127 | ולא 3808 |
|---|---|---|---|---|---|---|---|
| bahagaloutiy | 'atam | 'al | hagouyim, | uakinastiym | 'al | 'admatam; | uala' |
| **which caused to be led into captivity** | **them** | **among** | **the heathen** | **but I have gathered them** | **unto** | **their own land** | **and none** |

| אותיר 3498 | עוד 5750 | מהם 1992 | שם 8033: | 39:29 ולא 3808 | אסתיר 5641 | עוד 5750 | פני 6440 | מהם 1992 | אשר 834 | שפכתי 8210 | את 853 |
|---|---|---|---|---|---|---|---|---|---|---|---|
| 'atiyr | 'aud | mehem | sham. | uala' | 'astiyr | 'aud | panay | mehem; | 'asher | shapaktiy | 'at |
| **I have left any more of them there** | | | | **Neither** | **will I hide any more** | | **my face from them** | | **for** | **I have poured out** | |

| רוחי 7307 | על 5921 | בית 1004 | ישראל 3478 | נאם 5002 | אדני 136 | יהוה 3069: |
|---|---|---|---|---|---|---|
| ruchiy | 'al | beyt | yisra'ael, | na'am | 'adonay | Yahuah. |
| **my spirit upon** | | **the house of** | **Israel** | **saith** | **Adonai Yahuah** | |

| Ezek 40:1 | בעשרים 6242 | וחמש 2568 | שנה 8141 | לגלותנו 1546 | בראש 7218 | השנה 8141 | בעשור 6218 | לחדש 2320 |
|---|---|---|---|---|---|---|---|---|
| | ba'asriym | uachamesh | shanah | lagalutenu | bara'sh | hashanah | be'asour | lachodesh, |
| | **In twentieth** | **and the five** | **year** | **of our captivity** | **in the beginning of** | **the year** | **in the tenth** | ***day* of the month** |

| בארבע 702 | עשרה 6240 | שנה 8141 | אחר 310 | אשר 834 | הכתה 5221 | העיר 5892 | בעצם 6106 | היום 3117 | הזה 2088 | היתה 1961 | עלי 5921 | יד 3027 |
|---|---|---|---|---|---|---|---|---|---|---|---|---|
| ba'arba | 'asreh | shanah, | 'achar | 'asher | huktah | ha'ayr; | ba'atzem | hayoum | hazeh, | hayatah | 'alay | yad |
| **in the four ten** | | **year** | **after** | **that** | **was smitten the city** | | **in the selfsame day** | | **this** | **was** | **upon me** | **the hand of** |

| יהוה 3068 | ויבא 935 | אתי 853 | שמה 8033: | 40:2 במראות 4759 | אלהים 430 | הביאני 935 | אל 413 | ארץ 776 | ישראל 3478 |
|---|---|---|---|---|---|---|---|---|---|
| Yahuah, | uayabea' | 'atiy | shamah. | bamar'aut | 'alohiym, | habiy'aniy | 'al | 'aretz | yisra'ael; |
| **Yahuah** | **and brought** | **me** | **there** | **In the visions of** | **Elohim** | **brought he me** | **into** | **the land of** | **Israel** |

| ויניחני 5117 | אל 413 | הר 2022 | גבה 1364 | מאד 3966 | ועליו 5921 | כמבנה 4011 | עיר 5892 | מנגב 5045: | 40:3 ויביא 935 |
|---|---|---|---|---|---|---|---|---|---|
| uayaniycheniy, | 'al | har | gaboah | ma'ad, | ua'alayu | kamibneh | 'ayr | minegeb. | uayabey'a |
| **and set me** | **upon** | **a mountain** | **high** | **very** | **by which** | ***was* as the frame of** | **a city** | **on the south** | **And he brought** |

| אותי 853 | שמה 8033 | והנה 2009 | איש 376 | מראהו 4758 | כמראה 4758 | נחשת 5178 | ופתיל 6616 |
|---|---|---|---|---|---|---|---|
| 'autiy | shamah, | uahineh | 'aysh | mar'aehu | kamar'aeh | nachoshet, | uaptiyl |
| **me** | **there** | **and behold *there was*** | **a man** | **whose appearance *was*** | **like the appearance of** | **brass** | **with a line of** |

Eze 39:26 After that they have borne their shame, and all their trespasses whereby they have trespassed against me, when they dwelt safely in their land, and none made them afraid.27 When I have brought them again from the people, and gathered them out of their enemies' lands, and am sanctified in them in the sight of many nations;28 Then shall they know that I am YHUH their G-d, which cause them to be led into captivity among the heathen: but I have gathered them unto their own land, and have left none of them anymore there.29 Neither will I hide my face anymore from them: for I have poured out my spirit upon the house of Israel, saith YHUH G-D. **Eze** 40:1 In the five and twentieth year of our captivity, in the beginning of the year, in the tenth day of the month, in the fourteenth year after that the city was smitten, in the selfsame day the hand of YHUH was upon me, and brought me thither.2 In the visions of G-d brought he me into the land of Israel, and set me upon a very high mountain, by which was as the frame of a city on the south.3 And he brought me thither, and, behold, there was a man, whose appearance was like the appearance of brass, with a line of flax in his hand, and a measuring reed; and he stood in the gate.

פשתים 6593 בידו 3027 וקנה 7070 המדה 4060 והוא 1931 עמד 5975 בשער 8179: 40:4 וידבר 1696 אלי 413 האיש 376 בן 1121 אדם 120 ראה 7200
pishtiym bayadou uaqneh hamidah; uahu'a 'amed basha'ar. uaydaber 'aelay ha'aysh, ben 'adam ra'aeh
**flax in his hand and a reed measuring and he stood in the gate And said unto me the man Son of man behold**

בעיניך 5869 ובאזניך 241 שמע 8085 ושים 7760 לבך 3820 לכל 3605 אשר 834 אני 589 מראה 7200 אותך 853 כי 3588 למען 4616
ba'aeyneyka uab'azaneyka shama' uasiym libaka, lakol 'asher 'aniy mar'aeh autak, kiy lama'an
**with your eyes and with your ears hear and set your heart upon all that I shall show you for to the intent**

הראותכה 7200 הבאתה 935 הנה 2008 הגד 5046 את 853 כל 3605 אשר 834 אתה 859 ראה 7200 לבית 1004
hara'autakah huba'atah henah; haged 'at kal 'asher 'atah ro'ah labeyt
**that I might show *them* unto you *are* you brought here declare all that you see to the house of**

ישראל 3478: 40:5 והנה 2009 חומה 2346 מחוץ 2351 לבית 1004 סביב 5439 סביב 5439 וביד 3027 האיש 376 קנה 7070
yisra'ael. uahineh choumah michutz labayit sabiyb sabiyb; uabyad ha'aysh qaneh
**Israel And behold a wall on the outside of the house round about and in hand the man's a reed of**

המדה 4060 שש 8337 אמות 520 באמה 520 וטפח 2948 וימד 4058 את 853 רחב 7341 הבנין 1146 קנה 7070
hamidah, shesh 'amout ba'amah uatopach, uayamad 'at rochab habinyan qaneh
**measuring six cubits *long* by the cubit and an hand breadth so he measured the breadth of the building reed**

אחד 259 וקומה 6967 קנה 7070 אחד 259: 40:6 ויבוא 935 אל 413 שער 8179 אשר 834 פניו 6440 דרך 1870 הקדימה 6921 ויעל 5927
'achad, uaqoumah qaneh 'achad. uayabou'a, 'al sha'ar 'asher panayu derek haqadiymah, uaya'al
**one and the height reed one Then came he unto the gate which looks toward the east and went up**

במעלותו 4609 וימד 4058 את 853 סף 5592 השער 8179 קנה 7070 אחד 259 רחב 7341 ואת 853
bama'aloutou uayamad 'at sap hasha'ar, qaneh 'achad rochab, ua'at
**the stairs thereof and measured the threshold of the gate reed *which was* one broad *and***

סף 5592 אחד 259 קנה 7070 אחד 259 רחב 7341: 40:7 והתא 8372 קנה 7070 אחד 259 ארך 753
sap 'achad, qaneh 'achad rochab. uahata', qaneh 'achad 'arek
**threshold *of the gate which was the* other reed one broad And *every* little chamber reed and *was* one long**

וקנה 7070 אחד 259 רחב 7341 ובין 996 התאים 8372 חמש 2568 אמות 520 וסף 5592 השער 8179 מאצל 681
uaqaneh 'achad rochab, uabeyn hata'aym chamesh 'amout; uasap hasha'ar me'aetzel
**reed one broad and between the little chambers *were* five cubits and the threshold of the gate by**

אולם 197 השער 8179 מהבית 1004 קנה 7070 אחד 259: 40:8 וימד 4058 את 853 אלם 197 השער 8179 מהבית 1004 קנה 7070
'aulam hasha'ar mehabayit qaneh 'achad. uayamad 'at 'alam hasha'ar mehabayit qaneh
**the porch of the gate within reed *was* one He measured also the porch of the gate within reed**

אחד 259: 40:9 וימד 4058 את 853 אלם 197 השער 8179 שמנה 8083 אמות 520 ואילו 352 שתים 8147 אמות 520
'achad. uayamad 'at 'alam hasha'ar shamoneh 'amout, ua'aeylau shatayim 'amout
**one Then measured he the porch of the gate eight cubits and the post thereof two cubits**

ואלם 197 השער 8179 מהבית 1004 40:10 ותאי 8372 השער 8179 דרך 1870 הקדים 6921 שלשה 7969 מפה 6311
ua'atam hasha'ar mehabayit uata'aey hasha'ar derek haqadiym, shaloshah mipoh
**and the porch of the gate *was* inward And the little chambers of the gate toward the east *were* three on this side**

Eze 40:4 And the man said unto me, Son of man, behold with your eyes, and hear with your ears, and set your heart upon all that I shall show you; for to the intent that I might show them unto you are you brought hither: declare all that you seest to the house of Israel.5 And behold a wall on the outside of the house round about, and in the man's hand a measuring reed of six cubits long by the cubit and an hand breadth: so he measured the breadth of the building, one reed; and the height, one reed.6 Then came he unto the gate which look toward the east, and went up the stairs thereof, and measured the threshold of the gate, which was one reed broad; and the other threshold of the gate, which was one reed broad.7 And every little chamber was one reed long, and one reed broad; and between the little chambers were five cubits; and the threshold of the gate by the porch of the gate within was one reed.8 He measured also the porch of the gate within, one reed.9 Then measured he the porch of the gate, eight cubits; and the posts thereof, two cubits; and the porch of the gate was inward.10 And the little chambers of the gate eastward were three on this side, and three on that side; they three were of one measure: and the posts had one measure on this side and on that side.

ושלשה 7969 מפה 6311 מדה 4060 אחת 259 לשלשתם 7969 ומדה 4060 אחת 259 לאילם 352 מפה 6311
uashloshah mipoh, midah 'achat lishalashatam; uamidah 'achat la'aeylim mipoh
**and three on that side *were* of measure one *they* three and measure *had* one the posts on this side**

ומפו 6311: 40:11 וימד 4058 את 853 רחב 7341 פתח 6607 השער 8179 עשר 6235 אמות 520 ארך 753
uamipou. uayamad 'at rochab petach hasha'ar 'aser 'amout; 'arek
**and on this side And he measured the breadth of the entry of the gate ten cubits *and* the length of**

השער 8179 שלוש 7969 עשרה 6240 אמות 520: 40:12 וגבול 1366 לפני 6440 התאות 8372 אמה 520 אחת 259 ואמה 520
hasha'ar, shaloush 'asreh 'amout. augbul lipney hata'aut 'amah 'achat, ua'amah
**the gate three ten cubits The space also before the little chambers cubit *on this side* *was* one cubit *was***

אחת 259 גבול 1366 מפה 6311 והתא 8372 שש 8337 אמות 520 מפו 6311 ושש 8337 אמות 520 מפו 6311: 40:13
'achat gabul mipoh; uahata' shesh 'amout mipou, uashesh 'amout mipou.
**one the space on that side and the little chambers *were* six cubits on this side and six cubits on this side**

וימד 4058 את 853 השער 8179 מגג 1406 התא 8372 לגגו 1406 רחב 7341 עשרים 6242
uayamad 'at hasha'ar, migag hata lagagou, rochab 'asriym
**He measured then the gate from the roof of *one* little chamber to the roof of another the breadth twenty**

וחמש 2568 אמות 520 פתח 6607 נגד 5048 פתח 6607: 40:14 ויעש 6213 את 853 אילים 352 ששים 8346 אמה 520 ואל 413 איל 352
uachamesh 'amout; petach neged patach. uaya'as 'at 'aeyliym shishiym 'amah; ua'al 'aeyl
***was* five and cubits door against door He made also posts of threescore cubits even unto the post of**

החצר 2691 השער 8179 סביב 5439 סביב 5439: 40:15 ועל 5921 פני 6440 השער 8179 היאתון 2978 על 5921 לפני 6440 אלם 197
hechatzer, hasha'ar sabiyb sabiyb. ua'al, paney hasha'ar ha'yatoun 'al lipney 'alam
**the court the gate round about And from the face of the gate of the entrance unto the face of the porch of**

השער 8179 הפנימי 6442 חמשים 2572 אמה 520: 40:16 וחלנות 2474 אטמות 331 אל 413 התאים 8372 ואל 413
hasha'ar hapaniymiy; chamishiym 'amah. uachalonout atumout 'al hata'aym ua'ael
**gate the inner *were* fifty cubits And windows *there were* narrow to the little chambers and to**

אליהמה 352 לפנימה 6441 לשער 8179 סביב 5439 סביב 5439 וכן 3651 לאלמות 361 וחלונות 2474 סביב 5439 סביב 5439 לפנימה 6441
'aeleyhemah lipniymah lasha'ar sabiyb sabiyb, uaken la'aelamout; uachalounout sabiyb sabiyb lipniymah,
**their posts within the gate round about and likewise to the arches and windows *were* around about inward**

ואל 408 איל 352 תמרים 8561: 40:17 ויביאני 935 אל 413 החצר 2691 החיצונה 2435 והנה 2009 לשכות 3957
ua'al 'ayil timoriym. uayabiy'aeniy, 'al hechatzer hachiytzounah, uahineh lashakout
**and upon *each* post *were* palm trees Then brought he me into court the outward and lo *there were* chambers**

ורצפה 7531 עשוי 6213 לחצר 2691 סביב 5439 סביב 5439 שלשים 7970 לשכות 3957 אל 413 הרצפה 7531: 40:18
uaritzpah, 'asuy lechatzer sabiyb sabiyb; shaloshiym lashakout 'al haritzpah.
**and a pavement made for the court round about thirty chambers *were* upon the pavement**

והרצפה 7531 אל 413 כתף 3802 השערים 8179 לעמת 5980 ארך 753 השערים 8179 הרצפה 7531 התחתונה 8481:
uaharitzpah 'al ketep hasha'ariym, la'amat 'arek hasha'ariym; haritzpah hatachatounah.
**And the pavement by the side of the gates over against the length of the gates pavement *was* the lower**

Eze 40:11 And he measured the breadth of the entry of the gate, ten cubits; and the length of the gate, thirteen cubits.12 The space also before the little chambers was one cubit on this side, and the space was one cubit on that side: and the little chambers were six cubits on this side, and six cubits on that side.13 He measured then the gate from the roof of one little chamber to the roof of another: the breadth was five and twenty cubits, door against door.14 He made also posts of threescore cubits, even unto the post of the court round about the gate.15 And from the face of the gate of the entrance unto the face of the porch of the inner gate were fifty cubits.16 And there were narrow windows to the little chambers, and to their posts within the gate round about, and likewise to the arches: and windows were round about inward: and upon each post were palm trees.17 Then brought he me into the outward court, and, lo, there were chambers, and a pavement made for the court round about: thirty chambers were upon the pavement.18 And the pavement by the side of the gates over against the length of the gates was the lower pavement.

**40:19** וימד 4058 רחב 7341 מלפני 6440 השער 8179 התחתונה 8481 לפני 6440 החצר 2691
uayamad rochab milipney hasha'ar hatachatounah lipney hechatzer
**Then he measured the breadth from the forefront of gate the lower unto the forefront of court**

הפנימי 6442 מחוץ 2351 מאה 3967 אמה 520 הקדים 6921 והצפון 6828: **40:20** והשער 8179 אשר 834 פניו 6440 דרך 1870 הצפון 6828
hapaniymiy michutz me'ah 'amah; haqadiym uahatzapoun. uahasha'ar, 'asher panayu derek hatzapoun,
**the inner without an hundred cubits eastward and northward And the gate of that looked toward the north**

לחצר 2691 החיצונה 2435 מדד 4058 ארכו 753 ורחבו 7341: **40:21** ותאו 8372
lechatzer hachiytzounah; madad arakou uarachabou. uata'au
**court the outward he measured the length thereof and the breadth thereof And the little chambers thereof**

שלושה 7969 מפו 6311 ושלשה 7969 מפו 6311 ואילו 352 ואלמו 361 היה 1961 כמדת 4060
shaloushah mipou uashloshah mipou, ua'aeylau ua'aelamou hayah, kamidat
***were* three on this side and three on that side and the post thereof and the arches thereof were after the measure of**

השער 8179 הראשון 7223 חמשים 2572 אמה 520 ארכו 753 ורחב 7341 חמש 2568 ועשרים 6242 באמה 520: **40:22**
hasha'ar hara'shoun; chamishiym 'amah arakou, uarochab chamesh ua'asriym ba'amah.
**gate the first *was* fifty cubits the length thereof and the breadth five and twenty cubits**

וחלונו 2474 ואלמו 361 ותמרו 8561 כמדת 4060 השער 8179 אשר 834 פניו 6440 דרך 1870
uachalounou ua'aelamou uatimorou kamidat hasha'ar, 'asher panayu derek
**And their windows and their arches and their palm trees *were* after the measure of the gate that looks toward**

הקדים 6921 ובמעלות 4609 שבע 7651 יעלו 5927 בו 871a ואילמו 361 לפניהם 6440: **40:23** ושער 8179
haqadiym; uabma'alout sheba' ya'alu bou, ua'aeylamou lipneyhem. uasha'ar
**the east and by steps seven they went up unto it and the arches thereof *were* before them And the gate of**

לחצר 2691 הפנימי 6442 נגד 5048 השער 8179 לצפון 6828 ולקדים 6921 וימד 4058 משער 8179 אל 413
lechatzer hapaniymiy, neged hasha'ar, latzapoun ualaqadiym; uayamad misha'ar 'al
**court the inner *was* over against the gate toward the north and toward the east and he measured from gate to**

שער 8179 מאה 3967 אמה 520: **40:24** ויולכני 1980 דרך 1870 הדרום 1864 והנה 2009 שער 8179 דרך 1870 הדרום 1864
sha'ar me'ah 'amah. uayoulikeniy derek hadaroum, uahineh sha'ar derek hadaroum;
**gate an hundred cubits After that he brought me me toward the south and behold a gate toward the south**

ומדד 4058 אילו 352 ואילמו 361 כמדות 4060 האלה 428: **40:25** וחלונים 2474
uamadad 'aeylou ua'aeylamou kamidout ha'aeleh. uachalouniym
**and he measured the posts thereof and the arches thereof according to measures these And *there were* windows**

לו 3807a ולאילמו 361 סביב 5439 סביב 5439 כהחלנות 2474 האלה 428 חמשים 2572 אמה 520 ארך 753 ורחב 7341
lou' ual'aeylamou sabiyb sabiyb, kahachalonout ha'aeleh; chamishiym 'amah 'arek, uarochab
**in it and in the arches thereof round about like windows those *was* fifty cubits the length and the breadth**

חמש 2568 ועשרים 6242 אמה 520: **40:26** ומעלות 4609 שבעה 7651 עלותו 5930 ואלמו 361 לפניהם 6440
chamesh ua'asriym 'amah. uama'alout shib'ah 'aloutou ua'aelamou lipneyhem;
**five and twenty cubits And steps *there were* seven to go up to it and the arches thereof *were* before them**

Eze 40:19 Then he measured the breadth from the forefront of the lower gate unto the forefront of the inner court without, an hundred cubits eastward and northward.20 And the gate of the outward court that looked toward the north, he measured the length thereof, and the breadth thereof.21 And the little chambers thereof were three on this side and three on that side; and the posts thereof and the arches thereof were after the measure of the first gate: the length thereof was fifty cubits, and the breadth five and twenty cubits.22 And their windows, and their arches, and their palm trees, were after the measure of the gate that look toward the east; and they went up unto it by seven steps; and the arches thereof were before them.23 And the gate of the inner court was over against the gate toward the north, and toward the east; and he measured from gate to gate an hundred cubits.24 After that he brought me toward the south, and behold a gate toward the south: and he measured the posts thereof and the arches thereof according to these measures.25 And there were windows in it and in the arches thereof round about, like those windows: the length was fifty cubits, and the breadth five and twenty cubits.26 And there were seven steps to go up to it, and the arches thereof were before them: and it had palm trees, one on this side, and another on that side, upon the posts thereof.

| 8561 ותמרים | 3807a לו | 259 אחד | 6311 מפו | 259 ואחד | 6311 מפו | 413 אל | 352 אילו | 40:27 8179 ושער |
|---|---|---|---|---|---|---|---|---|
| uatimoriym | lou', | 'achad | mipou | ua'achad | mipou | 'al | 'aeylou | uasha'ar |
| **and palm trees** | **it had** | **one** | **on this side** | **and another** | **on that side** | **upon** | **the post thereof** | **And *there was* a gate** |

| 2691 לחצר | 6442 הפנימי | 1870 דרך | 1864 הדרום | 4058 וימד | 8179 משער | 413 אל | 8179 השער | 1870 דרך | 1864 הדרום | 3967 מאה |
|---|---|---|---|---|---|---|---|---|---|---|
| lechatzer | hapaniymiy | derek | hadaroum; | uayamad | misha'ar | 'al | hasha'ar | derek | hadaroum | me'ah |
| **in court** | **the inner** | **toward** | **the south** | **and he measured** | **from gate** | **to** | **gate** | **toward** | **the south** | **an hundred** |

| 520: אמות | 40:28 935 ויביאני | 413 אל | 2691 חצר | 6442 הפנימי | 8179 בשער | 1864 הדרום | 4058 וימד | 853 את | 8179 השער | 1864 הדרום |
|---|---|---|---|---|---|---|---|---|---|---|
| 'amout. | uayabiy'aeniy | 'al | chatzer | hapaniymiy | basha'ar | hadaroum; | uayamad | 'at | hasha'ar | hadaroum, |
| **cubits** | **And he brought me** | **to** | **court** | **the inner** | **by gate** | **the south** | **and he measured** | | **gate** | **the south** |

| 4060 כמדות | 428: האלה | 40:29 8372 ותאו | 352 ואילו | 361 ואלמו |
|---|---|---|---|---|
| kamidout | ha'aeleh. | uata'au | ua'aeylau | ua'aelamou |
| **according to measures** | **these** | **And the little chambers thereof** | **and the post thereof** | **and the arches thereof** |

| 4060 כמדות | 428 האלה | 2474 וחלונות | 3807a לו | 361 ולאלמו | 5439 סביב | 5439 סביב | 2572 חמשים |
|---|---|---|---|---|---|---|---|
| kamidout | ha'aeleh, | uachalounout | lou' | ual'aelamou | sabiyb | sabiyb; | chamishiym |
| **according to these measures** | **these** | **and *there were* windows** | **in it** | **and in the arches thereof** | **round** | **about** | ***it was* fifty** |

| 520 אמה | 753 ארך | 7341 ורחב | 6242 עשרים | 2568 וחמש | 520: אמות | 40:30 361 ואלמות | 5439 סביב | 5439 סביב | 753 ארך | 2568 חמש | 6242 ועשרים |
|---|---|---|---|---|---|---|---|---|---|---|---|
| 'amah | 'arek, | uarochab | 'asriym | uachamesh | 'amout. | ua'aelamout | sabiyb | sabiyb; | 'arek, | chamesh | ua'asriym |
| **cubits** | **long** | **and broad** | **twenty** | **and five** | **cubits** | **And the arches** | **round** | **about** | **long** | ***were* five** | **and twenty** |

| 520 אמה | 7341 ורחב | 2568 חמש | 520: אמות | 40:31 361 ואלמו | 413 אל | 2691 חצר | 2435 החצונה | 8561 ותמרים |
|---|---|---|---|---|---|---|---|---|
| 'amah, | uarochab | chamesh | 'amout. | ua'aelamau, | 'al | chatzer | hachitzounah, | uatimoriym |
| **cubits** | **and broad** | **five** | **cubits** | **And the arches thereof** | ***were* toward** | **court** | **the utter** | **and palm trees** |

| 413 אל | 352 אילו | 4609 ומעלות | 8083 שמונה | 4608 מעלו | 40:32 935 ויביאני | 413 אל | 2691 החצר | 6442 הפנימי |
|---|---|---|---|---|---|---|---|---|
| 'al | 'aeylou | uama'alout | shamouneh | ma'alou | uayabiy'aeniy | 'al | hechatzer | hapaniymiy |
| ***were* upon** | **the post thereof** | **and steps** | ***had* eight** | **the going up to it** | **And he brought me** | **into** | **court** | **the inner** |

| 1870 דרך | 6921 הקדים | 4058 וימד | 853 את | 8179 השער | 4060 כמדות | 428: האלה | 40:33 8372 ותאו |
|---|---|---|---|---|---|---|---|
| derek | haqadiym; | uayamad | 'at | hasha'ar, | kamidout | ha'aeleh. | uata'au |
| **toward** | **the east** | **and he measured** | | **the gate** | **according to measures** | **these** | **And the little chambers thereof** |

| 352 ואלו | 361 ואלמו | 4060 כמדות | 428 האלה | 2474 וחלונות | 3807a לו |
|---|---|---|---|---|---|
| ua'aelou | ua'aelamou | kamidout | ha'aeleh, | uachalounout | lou' |
| **and the post thereof** | **and the arches thereof** | ***were* according to measures** | **these** | **and *there were* windows** | **therein** |

| 361 ולאלמו | 5439 סביב | 5439 סביב | 753 ארך | 2572 חמשים | 520 אמה | 7341 ורחב | 2568 חמש | 6242 ועשרים | 520: אמה | 40:34 |
|---|---|---|---|---|---|---|---|---|---|---|
| ual'aelamou | sabiyb | sabiyb; | 'arek | chamishiym | 'amah, | uarochab | chamesh | ua'asriym | 'amah. | |
| **and in the arches thereof** | **round** | **about** | **long** | ***it was* fifty** | **cubits** | **and broad** | **five** | **and twenty** | **cubits** | |

| 361 ואלמו | 2691 לחצר | 2435 החיצונה | 8561 ותמרים | 413 אל | 352 אלו | 6311 מפו |
|---|---|---|---|---|---|---|
| ua'aelamou | lechatzer | hachiytzounah, | uatimoriym | 'al | 'alou | mipou |
| **And the arches thereof *were*** | **toward court** | **the outward** | **and palm trees *were*** | **upon** | **the post thereof** | **on this side** |

Eze 40:27 And there was a gate in the inner court toward the south: and he measured from gate to gate toward the south an hundred cubits.28 And he brought me to the inner court by the south gate: and he measured the south gate according to these measures;29 And the little chambers thereof, and the posts thereof, and the arches thereof, according to these measures: and there were windows in it and in the arches thereof round about: it was fifty cubits long, and five and twenty cubits broad.30 And the arches round about were five and twenty cubits long, and five cubits broad.31 And the arches thereof were toward the utter court; and palm trees were upon the posts thereof: and the going up to it had eight steps.32 And he brought me into the inner court toward the east: and he measured the gate according to these measures.33 And the little chambers thereof, and the posts thereof, and the arches thereof, were according to these measures: and there were windows therein and in the arches thereof round about: it was fifty cubits long, and five and twenty cubits broad.34 And the arches thereof were toward the outward court; and palm trees were upon the posts thereof, on this side, and on that side: and the going up to it had eight steps.

| ומפו 6311 | ושמנה 8083 | מעלות 4609 | מעלו 4608 | 40:35 | ויביאני 935 | אל 413 | שער 8179 | הצפון 6828 |
|---|---|---|---|---|---|---|---|---|
| uamipou; | uashmoneh | ma'alout | ma'alou | | uayabiy'aeniy | 'al | sha'ar | hatzapoun; |
| **and on that side** | **and eight** | **steps** | **the going up to it *had*** | | **And he brought me** | **to** | **gate** | **the north** |

| ומדד 4058 | כמדות 4060 | האלה 428: | 40:36 | תאו 8372 | אלו 352 | ואלמו 361 |
|---|---|---|---|---|---|---|
| uamadad | kamidout | ha'aeleh. | | ta'au | 'aelou | ua'aelamou |
| **and measured *it*** | **according to measures** | **these** | | **The little chambers thereof** | **the post thereof** | **and the arches thereof** |

| וחלונות 2474 | לו 3807a | סביב 5439 | סביב 5439 | ארך 753 | חמשים 2572 | אמה 520 | ורחב 7341 | חמש 2568 | ועשרים 6242 | אמה 520: | 40:37 |
|---|---|---|---|---|---|---|---|---|---|---|---|
| uachalounout | lou' | sabiyb | sabiyb; | 'arek | chamishiym | 'amah, | uarochab | chamesh | ua'asriym | 'amah. | |
| **and the windows** | **to it** | **round** | **about** | **the length** | ***was* fifty** | **cubits** | **and the breadth** | **five** | **and twenty** | **cubits** | |

| ואילו 352 | לחצר 2691 | החיצונה 2435 | ותמרים 8561 | אל 413 | אילו 352 | מפו 6311 |
|---|---|---|---|---|---|---|
| ua'aeylau | lechatzer | hachiytzounah, | uatimoriym | 'al | 'aeylou | mipou |
| **And the post thereof *were*** | **toward court** | **the utter** | **and palm trees** | ***were* upon** | **the post thereof** | **on this side** |

| ומפו 6311 | ושמנה 8083 | מעלות 4609 | מעלו 4608 | 40:38 | ולשכה 3957 | ופתחה 6607 |
|---|---|---|---|---|---|---|
| uamipou; | uashmoneh | ma'alout | ma'alou | | ualishkah | uapiytchah, |
| **and on that side** | **and eight** | **steps** | **the going up to it *had*** | | **And the chambers** | **and the entries thereof** |

| באילים 352 | השערים 8179 | שם 8033 | ידיחו 1740 | את 853 | העלה 5930: | 40:39 | ובאלם 197 | השער 8179 | שנים 8147 |
|---|---|---|---|---|---|---|---|---|---|
| be'aeyliym | hasha'ariym; | sham | yadiychu | 'at | ha'aelah. | | uab'alam | hasha'ar, | shanayim |
| ***were* by the posts of** | **the gates** | **where** | **they washed** | | **the burnt offering** | | **And in the porch of** | **the gate** | ***were* two** |

| שלחנות 7979 | מפו 6311 | ושנים 8147 | שלחנות 7979 | מפה 6311 | לשחוט 7819 | אליהם 413 | העולה 5930 | והחטאת 2403 |
|---|---|---|---|---|---|---|---|---|
| shulchanout | mipou, | uashnayim | shulchanout | mipoh; | lishkout | 'aleyhem | ha'aulah, | uahachata't |
| **tables** | **on this side** | **and two** | **tables** | **on that side** | **to slay** | **thereon** | **the burnt offering** | **and the sin offering** |

| והאשם 817: | 40:40 | ואל 413 | הכתף 3802 | מחוצה 2351 | לעולה 5927 | לפתח 6607 | השער 8179 | הצפונה 6828 | שנים 8147 |
|---|---|---|---|---|---|---|---|---|---|
| uaha'asham. | | ua'al | hakatep | michutzah, | la'auleh | lapetach | hasha'ar | hatzapounah, | shanayim |
| **and the trespass offering** | | **And at** | **the side** | **without** | **as one goes up** | **to the entry of** | **gate** | **the north** | ***were* two** |

| שלחנות 7979 | ואל 413 | הכתף 3802 | האחרת 312 | אשר 834 | לאלם 197 | השער 8179 | שנים 8147 | שלחנות 7979: | 40:41 | ארבעה 702 |
|---|---|---|---|---|---|---|---|---|---|---|
| shulchanout; | ua'al | hakatep | ha'acheret, | 'asher | la'aulam | hasha'ar, | shanayim | shulchanout. | | 'arba'ah |
| **tables** | **and on** | **side** | **the other** | **which** | ***was* at the porch of** | **the gate** | ***were* two** | **tables** | | **Four** |

| שלחנות 7979 | מפה 6311 | וארבעה 702 | שלחנות 7979 | מפה 6311 | לכתף 3802 | השער 8179 | שמונה 8083 | שלחנות 7979 | אליהם 413 |
|---|---|---|---|---|---|---|---|---|---|
| shulchanout | mipoh, | ua'arbah | shulchanout | mipoh | laketep | hasha'ar; | shamouneh | shulchanout | 'aleyhem |
| **tables *were*** | **on this side** | **and four** | **tables** | **on that side** | **by the side of** | **the gate** | **eight** | **tables** | **whereupon** |

| ישחטו 7819: | 40:42 | וארבעה 702 | שלחנות 7979 | לעולה 5930 | אבני 68 | גזית 1496 | ארך 753 | אמה 520 | אחת 259 |
|---|---|---|---|---|---|---|---|---|---|
| yishchatu. | | ua'arbah | shulchanout | la'alah | 'abney | gaziyt, | 'arek | 'amah | 'achat |
| **they slew their sacrifices** | | **And the four** | **tables** | **for the burnt offering** | **stone** | ***were* of hewn** | **long** | **cubit** | ***of* a** |

| וחצי 2677 | ורחב 7341 | אמה 520 | אחת 259 | וחצי 2677 | וגבה 1363 | אמה 520 | אחת 259 | אליהם 413 | ויניחו 3240 | את 853 | הכלים 3627 |
|---|---|---|---|---|---|---|---|---|---|---|---|
| uachetziy | uarochab | 'amah | 'achat | uachetziy, | uagobah | 'amah | 'achat; | 'aleyhem, | uayaniychu | 'at | hakeliym |
| **and an half** | **and broad** | **cubit** | **a** | **and an half** | **and high** | **cubit** | **one** | **whereupon** | **also they laid** | | **the instruments** |

Eze 40:35 And he brought me to the north gate, and measured it according to these measures;36 The little chambers thereof, the posts thereof, and the arches thereof, and the windows to it round about: the length was fifty cubits, and the breadth five and twenty cubits.37 And the posts thereof were toward the utter court; and palm trees were upon the posts thereof, on this side, and on that side: and the going up to it had eight steps.38 And the chambers and the entries thereof were by the posts of the gates, where they washed the burnt offering.39 And in the porch of the gate were two tables on this side, and two tables on that side, to slay thereon the burnt offering and the sin offering and the trespass offering.40 And at the side without, as one go up to the entry of the north gate, were two tables; and on the other side, which was at the porch of the gate, were two tables.41 Four tables were on this side, and four tables on that side, by the side of the gate; eight tables, whereupon they slew their sacrifices.42 And the four tables were of hewn stone for the burnt offering, of a cubit and an half long, and a cubit and an half broad, and one cubit high: whereupon also they laid the instruments wherewith they slew the burnt offering and the sacrifice.

40:43

אשר 834 ישחטו 7819 את 853 העולה 5930 בם 871a והזבח 2077: והשפתים 8240 טפח 2948 אחד 259 מוכנים 3559
'asher yishchatu 'at ha'aulah bam uahazabach. uahashapatayim, topach 'achad mukaniym
**wherewith they slew the burnt offering in them and the sacrifice And hooks hand broad an fastened**

40:44

בבית 1004 סביב 5439 סביב 5439 ואל 413 השלחנות 7979 בשר 1320 הקרבן 7133: ומחוצה 2351 לשער 8179 הפנימי 6442
babayit sabiyb sabiyb; ua'al hashulchanout basar haqaraban. uamichutzah lasha'ar hapaniymiy
**within *were* round about and upon the tables *was* the flesh of the offering And without gate the inner**

לשכות 3957 שרים 7891 בחצר 2691 הפנימי 6442 אשר 834 אל 413 כתף 3802 שער 8179 הצפון 6828 ופניהם 6440
lishkout shariym, bechatzer hapaniymiy 'asher, 'al ketep sha'ar hatzapoun, uapneyhem
***were* the chambers of the singers in court the inner which *was* at the side of gate the north and their prospect**

40:45

דרך 1870 הדרום 1864 אחד 259 אל 413 כתף 3802 שער 8179 הקדים 6921 פני 6440 דרך 1870 הצפן 6828: וידבר 1696
derek hadaroum; 'achad, 'al ketep sha'ar haqadiym, paney derek hatzapon. uaydaber
***was* toward the south one at the side of gate the east *having* the prospect toward the north And he said**

40:46

אלי 413 זה 2090 הלשכה 3957 אשר 834 פניה 6440 דרך 1870 הדרום 1864 לכהנים 3548 שמרי 8104 משמרת 4931 הבית 1004:
'aelay; zoh halishkah, 'asher paneyha derek hadaroum, lakohaniym, shomrey mishmeret habayit.
**unto me This chamber whose prospect *is* toward the south *is* for the priests the keepers of the charge of the house**

והלשכה 3957 אשר 834 פניה 6440 דרך 1870 הצפון 6828 לכהנים 3548 שמרי 8104 משמרת 4931 המזבח 4196 המה 1992
uahalishkah, 'asher paneyha derek hatzapoun, lakohaniym, shomrey mishmeret hamizbeach; hemah
**And the chamber whose prospect *is* toward the north *is* for the priests the keepers of the charge of the altar these**

40:47

בני 1121 צדוק 6659 הקרבים 7131 מבני 1121 לוי 3878 אל 413 יהוה 3068 לשרתו 8334: וימד 4058
baney tzadouq, haqarebiym mibney leuiy 'al Yahuah lasharatou. uayamad
***are* the sons of Zadok which come near among the sons of Levi to Yahuah to minister unto him So he measured**

את 853 החצר 2691 ארך 753 מאה 3967 אמה 520 ורחב 7341 מאה 3967 אמה 520 מרבעת 7251 והמזבח 4196 לפני 6440
'at hechatzer 'arek me'ah 'amah, uarochab me'ah 'amah maruba'at; uahamizbeach lipney
**the court long an hundred cubits and broad an hundred cubits foursquare and the altar *that was* before**

40:48

הבית 1004: ויבאני 935 אל 413 אלם 197 הבית 1004 וימד 4058 אל 352 אלם 197 חמש 2568 אמות 520
habayit. uayabi'aeniy 'al 'alam habayit uayamad 'al 'alam, chamesh 'amout
**the house And he brought me to the porch of the house and measured *each* post of the porch five cubits**

מפה 6311 וחמש 2568 אמות 520 מפה 6311 ורחב 7341 השער 8179 שלש 7969 אמות 520 מפו 6311 ושלש 7969 אמות 520
mipoh, uachamesh 'amout mipoh; uarochab hasha'ar, shalosh 'amout mipou, uashalosh 'amout
**on this side and five cubits on that side and the breadth of the gate *was* three cubits on this side and three cubits**

40:49

מפו 6311: ארך 753 האלם 197 עשרים 6242 אמה 520 ורחב 7341 עשתי 6249 עשרה 6240 אמה 520
mipou. 'arek ha'alam 'asriym 'amah, uarochab 'ashtey 'asreh 'amah,
**on that side The length of the porch *was* twenty cubits and the breadth one of ten cubits**

ובמעלות 4609 אשר 834 יעלו 5927 אליו 413 ועמדים 5982 אל 413 האילים 352 אחד 259 מפה 6311
uabama'alout, 'asher ya'alu 'aelayu; ua'amudiym 'al ha'aeyliym, 'achad mipoh
**and *he brought me* by the steps whereby they went up to it and *there were* pillars by the posts one on this side**

Eze 40:43 And within were hooks, an hand broad, fastened round about: and upon the tables was the flesh of the offering.44 And without the inner gate were the chambers of the singers in the inner court, which was at the side of the north gate; and their prospect was toward the south: one at the side of the east gate having the prospect toward the north.45 And he said unto me, This chamber, whose prospect is toward the south, is for the priests, the keepers of the charge of the house.46 And the chamber whose prospect is toward the north is for the priests, the keepers of the charge of the altar: these are the sons of Zadok among the sons of Levi, which come near to YHUH to minister unto him.47 So he measured the court, an hundred cubits long, and an hundred cubits broad, foursquare; and the altar that was before the house.48 And he brought me to the porch of the house, and measured each post of the porch, five cubits on this side, and five cubits on that side: and the breadth of the gate was three cubits on this side, and three cubits on that side.49 The length of the porch was twenty cubits, and the breadth eleven cubits; and he brought me by the steps whereby they went up to it: and there were pillars by the posts, one on this side, and another on that side.

ואחד 259 מפה 6311:
ua'achad mipoh.
**and another on that side**

**Ezek 41:1** ויביאני 935 אל 413 ההיכל 1964 וימד 4058 את 853 האילים 352 שש 8337 אמות 520 רחב 7341
uayabiy'aeniy 'al haheykal; uayamad 'at ha'aeyliym, shesh 'amout rochab
**Afterward he brought me to the temple and measured the posts six cubits broad**

מפו 6311 ושש 8337 אמות 520 רחב 7341 מפו 6311 רחב 7341 האהל 168: **41:2** ורחב 7341
mipou uashesh 'amout rochab mipou rochab ha'ahel. uarochab
**on the one side and six cubits broad on the other side *which was* the breadth of the tabernacle And the breadth of**

הפתח 6607 עשר 6235 אמות 520 וכתפות 3802 הפתח 6607 חמש 2568 אמות 520 מפו 6311 וחמש 2568 אמות 520 מפו 6311
hapetach 'aser 'amout uakitpout hapetach, chamesh 'amout mipou, uachamesh 'amout mipou;
**the door *was* ten cubits and the sides of the door *were* five cubits on the one side and five cubits on the other side**

וימד 4058 ארכו 753 ארבעים 705 אמה 520 ורחב 7341 עשרים 6242 אמה 520: **41:3** ובא 935 לפנימה 6441
uayamad arakou 'arba'aym 'amah, uarochab 'asriym 'amah. uaba' lipniymah,
**and he measured the length thereof forty cubits and the breadth twenty cubits Then went he inward**

וימד 4058 איל 352 הפתח 6607 שתים 8147 אמות 520 והפתח 6607 שש 8337 אמות 520 ורחב 7341 הפתח 6607 שבע 7651
uayamad 'aeyl hapetach shatayim 'amout; uahapetach shesh 'amout, uarochab hapetach sheba'
**and measured the post of the door two cubits and the door six cubits and the breadth of the door seven**

אמות 520: **41:4** וימד 4058 את 853 ארכו 753 עשרים 6242 אמה 520 ורחב 7341 עשרים 6242 אמה 520 אל 413 פני 6440
'amout. uayamad 'at arakou 'asriym 'amah, uarochab 'asriym 'amah 'al paney
**cubits So he measured the length thereof twenty cubits and the breadth twenty cubits to before**

ההיכל 1964 ויאמר 559 אלי 413 זה 2088 קדש 6944 הקדשים 6944: **41:5** וימד 4058 קיר 7023 הבית 1004 שש 8337
haheykal; uaya'mer 'aelay, zeh qodesh haqadashiym. uayamad qiyr habayit shesh
**the temple and he said unto me This This *is* the most holy place After he measured the wall of the house six**

אמות 520 ורחב 7341 הצלע 6763 ארבע 702 אמות 520 סביב 5439 סביב 5439 לבית 1004 סביב 5439: **41:6**
'amout; uarochab hatzela' 'arba 'amout sabiyb sabiyb labayit sabiyb.
**cubits and the breadth of *every* side chamber four cubits round about the house about on every side**

והצלעות 6763 צלע 6763 אל 413 צלע 6763 שלוש 7969 ושלשים 7970 פעמים 6471 ובאות 935 בקיר 7023 אשר 834
uahatzala'aut tzela' 'al tzela' shaloush uashloshiym pa'amiym, uaba'aut baqiyr 'asher
**And the side chambers one over another *were* three and thirty in order and they entered into the wall which**

לבית 1004 לצלעות 6763 סביב 5439 סביב 5439 להיות 1961 אחוזים 270 ולא 3808 יהיו 1961 אחוזים 270
labayit latztzela'aut sabiyb sabiyb lihayout 'achuziym; uala' yihayu 'achuziym
***was* of the house for the side chambers round about that they might have hold but not they had hold**

בקיר 7023 הבית 1004: **41:7** ורחבה 7337 ונסבה 5437 למעלה 4605 למעלה 4605
baqiyr habayit. uarachabah uanasabah lama'alah lama'alah
**in the wall of the house And *there was* an enlarging and a winding about *still* up went still upward**

**Eze** 41:1 Afterward he brought me to the temple, and measured the posts, six cubits broad on the one side, and six cubits broad on the other side, which was the breadth of the tabernacle.2 And the breadth of the door was ten cubits; and the sides of the door were five cubits on the one side, and five cubits on the other side: and he measured the length thereof, forty cubits: and the breadth, twenty cubits.3 Then went he inward, and measured the post of the door, two cubits; and the door, six cubits; and the breadth of the door, seven cubits.4 So he measured the length thereof, twenty cubits; and the breadth, twenty cubits, before the temple: and he said unto me, This is the most holy place.5 After he measured the wall of the house, six cubits; and the breadth of every side chamber, four cubits, round about the house on every side.6 And the side chambers were three, one over another, and thirty in order; and they entered into the wall which was of the house for the side chambers round about, that they might have hold, but they had not hold in the wall of the house.7 And there was an enlarging, and a winding about still upward to the side chambers: for the winding about of the house went still upward round about the house: therefore the breadth of the house was still upward, and so increased from the lowest chamber to the highest by the midst.

6763 לצלעות 3588 כי 4141 מוסב 1004 הבית 4605 למעלה 4605 למעלה 5439 סביב 5439 סביב 1004 לבית 5921 על 3651 כן
latzla'aut, kiy musab habayit lama'alah lama'alah sabiyb sabiyb labayit, 'al ken
**to the side chambers for the winding about of the house *went* still upward round about the house therefore thus**

7341 רחב 1004 לבית 4605 למעלה 3651 וכן 8481 התחתונה 5927 יעלה 5921 על 5945 העליונה 8484: לתיכונה **41:8**
rochab labayit lama'alah; uaken hatachatounah ya'aleh 'al ha'alyounah latiykounah.
**the breadth of the house was still upward and so *from* the lowest *chamber* increased to the highest by the midst**

7200 ואראיתי 1004 לבית 1363 גבה 5439 סביב 5439 סביב 3245 מיסדות 6763 הצלעות 4393 מלו 7070 הקנה 8337 שש 520 אמות
uara'aytiy labayit gobah sabiyb sabiyb; meysadout hatzala'at malou haqaneh, shesh 'amout
**I saw also of the house the height round about the foundations of the side chambers *were* a full reed of six cubits**

679: אצילה **41:9** 7341 רחב 7023 הקיר 834 אשר 6763 לצלע 413 אל 2351 החוץ 2568 חמש 520 אמות 834 ואשר
'atziylah. rochab haqiyr 'asher latzela' 'al hachutz chamesh 'amout; ua'asher
**great The thickness of the wall which *was* for the side chamber with out *was* five cubits and *that* which**

3240 מנח 1004 בית 6763 צלעות 834 אשר 1004: לבית **41:10** 996 ובין 3957 הלשכות 7341 רחב
munach, beyt tzala'aut 'asher labayit. uabeyn halashakout rochab
***was* left *was* the place of the side chambers that *were* within And between the chambers *was* the wideness of**

6242 עשרים 520 אמה 5439 סביב 1004 לבית 5439 סביב 5439: סביב **41:11** 6607 ופתח 6763 הצלע
'asriym 'amah sabiyb labayit sabiyb sabiyb. uapetach hatzela'
**twenty cubits round about the house on every side And the doors of the side chambers**

3240 למנח 6607 פתח 259 אחד 1870 דרך 6828 הצפון 6607 ופתח 259 אחד 1864 לדרום 7341 ורחב
lamunach, petach 'achad derek hatzapoun, uapetach 'achad ladaroum; uarochab
***were* toward *the place that was* left door one toward the north and door another toward the south and the breadth of**

4725 מקום 3240 המנח 2568 חמש 520 אמות 5439 סביב 5439: סביב **41:12** 1146 והבנין 834 אשר 413 אל 6440 פני 1508 הגזרה
maqoum hamunach, chamesh 'amout sabiyb sabiyb. uahabinyan 'asher 'al paney hagizrah
***the* place that was left *was* five cubits round about Now the building that *was* to before the separate place at**

6285 פאת 1870 דרך 3220 הים 7341 רחב 7657 שבעים 520 אמה 7023 וקיר 1146 הבנין 2568 חמש 520 אמות 7341 רחב 5439 סביב 5439 סביב
pa'at derek hayam, rochab shib'aym 'amah, uaqiyr habinyan chamesh 'amout rochab sabiyb sabiyb;
**the end toward the west broad *was* seventy cubits and the wall of the building *was* five cubits thick round about**

753 וארכו 8673 תשעים 520: אמה **41:13** 4058 ומדד 853 את 1004 הבית 753 ארך 3967 מאה 520 אמה
ua'arakou tish'aym 'amah. uamadad 'at habayit, 'arek me'ah 'amah;
**and the length thereof ninety cubits So he measured the house long an hundred cubits**

1508 והגזרה 1140 והבניה 7023 וקירותיה 753 ארך 3967 מאה 520: אמה **41:14** 7341 ורחב
uahagizrah uahabinyah uaqiyrouteyha, 'arek me'ah 'amah. uarochab
**and the separate place and the building with the walls thereof long an hundred cubits Also the breadth of**

6440 פני 1004 הבית 1508 והגזרה 6921 לקדים 3967 מאה 520: אמה **41:15** 4058 ומדד 753 ארך
paney habayit uahagizrah laqadiym me'ah 'amah. uamadad 'arek
**the face of the house and of the separate place toward the east an hundred cubits And he measured the length of**

Eze 41:8 I saw also the height of the house round about: the foundations of the side chambers were a full reed of six great cubits.9 The thickness of the wall, which was for the side chamber without, was five cubits: and that which was left was the place of the side chambers that were within.10 And between the chambers was the wideness of twenty cubits round about the house on every side.11 And the doors of the side chambers were toward the place that was left, one door toward the north, and another door toward the south: and the breadth of the place that was left was five cubits round about.12 Now the building that was before the separate place at the end toward the west was seventy cubits broad; and the wall of the building was five cubits thick round about, and the length thereof ninety cubits.13 So he measured the house, an hundred cubits long; and the separate place, and the building, with the walls thereof, an hundred cubits long;14 Also the breadth of the face of the house, and of the separate place toward the east, an hundred cubits.15 And he measured the length of the building over against the separate place which was behind it, and the galleries thereof on the one side and on the other side, an hundred cubits, with the inner temple, and the porches of the court;

1146 הבנין 413 אל 6440 פני 1508 הגזרה 834 אשר 5921 על 310 אחריה 862 ואתוקיהא 6311 מפו
habinyan 'al paney hagizrah 'asher 'al 'achareyha ua'atuqeyha mipou
**the building over against the separate place which *was* on behind it and the galleries thereof on the one side**

6311 ומפו 3967 מאה 520 אמה 1964 וההיכל 6442 הפנימי 197 ואלמי 2691: החצר **41:16** 5592 הספים
uamipou me'ah 'amah; uahaheykal hapaniymiy, ua'alamey hechatzer. hasipiym
**and on the other side an hundred cubits with temple the inner and the porches of the court The door posts**

2474 והחלונים 331 האטמות 862 והאתיקים 5439 סביב 7969 לשלשתם 5048 נגד 5592 הסף 7824 שחיף 6086 עץ
uahachalouniym ha'atumout uaha'atiyqiym sabiyb lishalashatam, neged hasap sachiyp 'aetz
**and windows the narrow and the galleries round about on their three stories over against the door cieled with wood**

5439 סביב 5439 סביב 776 והארץ 5704 עד 2474 החלנות 2474 והחלנות 3680: מכסות **41:17** 5921 על 5921 מעל
sabiyb sabiyb; uaha'aretz 'ad hachalonout, uahachalonout makusout. 'al me'al
**round about and from the ground up to the windows and the windows *were* covered To *that* above**

6607 הפתח 5704 ועד 1004 הבית 6442 הפנימי 2351 ולחוץ 413 ואל 3605 כל 7023 הקיר 5439 סביב 5439 סביב 6442 בפנימי 2435 ובחיצון
hapetach ua'ad habayit hapaniymiy ualachutz ua'al kal haqiyr sabiyb sabiyb bapaniymiy uabachiytzoun
**the door even unto house the inner and without and by all the wall round about within and without**

4060: מדות **41:18** 6213 ועשוי 3742 כרובים 8561 ותמרים 8561 ותמרה 996 בין 3742 כרוב 3742 לכרוב
midout. ua'asuy karubiym uatimoriym; uatimorah beyn karub likrub,
***by* measure And *it was* made *with* cherubims and palm trees so that a palm tree *was* between a cherub and a cherub**

8147 ושנים 6440 פנים 3742: לכרוב **41:19** 6440 ופני 120 אדם 413 אל 8561 התמרה 6311 מפו
uashnayim paniym lakrub. uapaney 'adam 'al hatimorah mipou,
**and two faces *every* cherub *had* So that the face of a man *was* toward the palm tree on the one side**

6440 ופני 3715 כפיר 413 אל 8561 התמרה 6311 מפו 6213 עשוי 413 אל 3605 כל 1004 הבית 5439 סביב
uapaney kapiyr 'al hatimorah mipou; 'asuy 'al kal habayit sabiyb
**and the face of a young lion toward the palm tree on the other side *it was* made through all the house round**

5439: סביב **41:20** 776 מהארץ 5704 עד 5921 מעל 6607 הפתח 3742 הכרובים 8561 והתמרים 6213 עשוים 7023 וקיר
sabiyb. meha'aretz 'ad me'al hapetach, hakarubiym uahatimoriym 'asuyim; uaqiyr
**about From the ground unto above the door *were* cherubims and palm trees made and *on* the wall of**

1964: ההיכל **41:21** 1964 ההיכל 4201 מזוזת 7251 רבעה 6440 ופני 6944 הקדש 4758 המראה
haheykal haheykal mazuzat rabu'ah; uapaney haqodesh, hamar'ah
**the temple the temple The posts of *were* squared *and* the face of the sanctuary the appearance *of the one***

4758: כמראה **41:22** 4196 המזבח 6086 עץ 7969 שלוש 520 אמות 1364 גבה 753 וארכו 8147 שתים 520 אמות
kamar'ah. hamizbeach 'aetz shalouosh 'amout gaboah ua'arakou shetayim 'amout,
**as the appearance *of the other* The altar of wood *was* three cubits high and the length thereof two cubits**

4740 ומקצועותיו 3807a לו 753 וארכו 7023 וקירתיו 6086 עץ 1696 וידבר 413 אלי 2088 זה 7979 השלחן
uamiqtzo'autayu lou', ua'arakou uaqiyrotayu 'aetz; uaydaber 'aelay, zeh hashulchan,
**and the corners thereof and the length thereof and the walls thereof *were of* wood and he said unto me This *is* the table**

Eze 41:16 The door posts, and the narrow windows, and the galleries round about on their three stories, over against the door, cieled with wood round about, and from the ground up to the windows, and the windows were covered;17 To that above the door, even unto the inner house, and without, and by all the wall round about within and without, by measure.18 And it was made with cherubims and palm trees, so that a palm tree was between a cherub and a cherub; and every cherub had two faces;19 So that the face of a man was toward the palm tree on the one side, and the face of a young lion toward the palm tree on the other side: it was made through all the house round about.20 From the ground unto above the door were cherubims and palm trees made, and on the wall of the temple.21 The posts of the temple were squared, and the face of the sanctuary; the appearance of the one as the appearance of the other.22 The altar of wood was three cubits high, and the length thereof two cubits; and the corners thereof, and the length thereof, and the walls thereof, were of wood: and he said unto me, This is the table that is before YHUH.

41:23 41:24

אשר 834 לפני 6440 יהוה 3069: ושתים 8147 דלתות 1817 להיכל 1964 ולקדש 6944: ושתים 8147 דלתות 1817 לדלתות 1817
'asher lipney Yahuah. uashtayim dalatout laheykal ualaqodesh. uashtayim dalatout ladlatout;
**that *is* before Yahuah And two doors the temple and the sanctuary *had* And two the doors leaves *apiece***

41:25

שתים 8147 מוסבות 4142 דלתות 1817 שתים 8147 לדלת 1817 אחת 259 ושתי 8147 דלתות 1817 לאחרת 312: ועשויה 6213
shatayim musabout dalatout, shatayim ladelet 'achat, uashtey dalatout la'acheret. ua'asuyah
***had* two turning leaves two *leaves* for door *the* one and two door leaves for the other *door* And *there were* made**

אליהן 413 אל 413 דלתות 1817 ההיכל 1964 כרובים 3742 ותמרים 8561 כאשר 834 עשוים 6213 לקירות 7023
'aleyhen 'al daltout haheykal karubiym uatimoriym, ka'asher 'asuyim laqiyrout;
**on them on the doors of the temple cherubims and palm trees like as *were* made upon the walls**

41:26

ועב 5646 עץ 6086 אל 413 פני 6440 האולם 197 מהחוץ 2351: וחלונים 2474 אטמות 331
ua'ab 'aetz 'al paney ha'aulam mehachutz. uachalouniym atumout
**and *there were* thick planks wood upon the face of the porch without And windows *there were* narrow**

ותמרים 8561 מפו 6311 ומפו 6311 אל 413 כתפות 3802 האולם 197 וצלעות 6763 הבית 1004
uatimoriym mipou uamipou, 'al katpout ha'aulam; uatzal'aut habayit
**and palm trees on the one side and on the other side on *the* sides of the porch and *upon* the side chambers of the house**

והעבים 5646:
uaha'abiym.
**and thick planks**

**Ezek 42:1**

ויוצאני 3318 אל 413 החצר 2691 החיצונה 2435 הדרך 1870 דרך 1870 הצפון 6828 ויבאני 935 אל 413
uayoutzi'aeniy, 'al hechatzer hachiytzounah, haderek derek hatzapoun; uayabi'aeniy 'al
**Then he brought me forth into court the utter the way toward the north and he brought me into**

42:2

הלשכה 3957 אשר 834 נגד 5048 הגזרה 1508 ואשר 834 נגד 5048 הבנין 1146 אל 413 הצפון 6828: אל 413
halishkah, 'asher neged hagizrah ua'asher neged habinyan 'al hatzapoun. 'al
**the chamber that *was* over against the separate place and which *was* before the building toward the north to**

42:3

פני 6440 ארך 753 אמות 520 המאה 3967 פתח 6607 הצפון 6828 והרחב 7341 חמשים 2572 אמות 520: נגד 5048
paney 'arek 'amout hame'ah, petach hatzapoun; uaharochab chamishiym 'amout. neged
**Before the length of an cubits the hundred door *was* the north and the breadth *was* fifty cubits Over against**

העשרים 6242 אשר 834 לחצר 2691 הפנימי 6442 ונגד 5048 רצפה 7531 אשר 834 לחצר 2691 החיצונה 2435
ha'asriym, 'asher lechatzer hapaniymiy, uaneged ritzpah, 'asher lechatzer hachiytzounah;
**the twenty *cubits* which *were* for court the inner and over against *the* pavement which *was* for court the utter**

42:4

אתיק 862 אל 413 פני 6440 אתיק 862 בשלשים 7992: ולפני 6440 הלשכות 3957 מהלך 4109 עשר 6235 אמות 520 רחב 7341 אל 413
'atiyq 'al paney 'atiyq bashalishiym. ualipaney halashakout mahalak 'aser 'amout rochab 'al
***was* gallery to against gallery in three *stories* And before the chambers *was* a walk of ten cubits breadth an**

42:5

הפנימית 6442 דרך 1870 אמה 520 אחת 259 ופתחיהם 6607 לצפון 6828: והלשכות 3957 העליונת 5945 קצרות 7114 כי 3588
hapaniymiyt, derek 'amah 'achat; uapiytcheyhem latzapoun. uahalashakout ha'alyounot qatzurout; kiy
**inward a way of cubit one and their doors toward the north Now chambers the upper *were* shorter for**

Eze 41:23 And the temple and the sanctuary had two doors.24 And the doors had two leaves apiece, two turning leaves; two leaves for the one door, and two leaves for the other door.25 And there were made on them, on the doors of the temple, cherubims and palm trees, like as were made upon the walls; and there were thick planks upon the face of the porch without.26 And there were narrow windows and palm trees on the one side and on the other side, on the sides of the porch, and upon the side chambers of the house, and thick planks. **Eze** 42:1 Then he brought me forth into the utter court, the way toward the north: and he brought me into the chamber that was over against the separate place, and which was before the building toward the north.2 Before the length of an hundred cubits was the north door, and the breadth was fifty cubits.3 Over against the twenty cubits which were for the inner court, and over against the pavement which was for the utter court, was gallery against gallery in three stories.4 And before the chambers was a walk of ten cubits breadth inward, a way of one cubit; and their doors toward the north.5 Now the upper chambers were shorter: for the galleries were higher than these, than the lower, and than the middlemost of the building.

42:6

יוכלו 3201 אתיקים 862 מהנה 2007 מהתחתנות 8481 ומהתכנות 8484 בנין 1146: כי 3588 משלשות 8027
youkalu 'atiyqiym mehenah, mehatachatonout uamehatikonout binyan. kiy mashulashout
**were higher *the* galleries than these than the lower and than the middlemost of the building For *were in* three *stories***

הנה 2007 ואין 369 להן 3807a עמודים 5982 כעמודי 5982 החצרות 2691 על 5921 כן 3651 נאצל 680
henah, ua'aeyn lahen 'amudiym, ka'amudey hachatzerout; 'al ken ne'atzal,
**they but not had pillars as the pillars of the courts therefore after that *the building* was straitened**

42:7

מהתחתונות 8481 ומהתיכנות 8484 מהארץ 776: וגדר 1447 אשר 834 לחוץ 2351 לעמת 5980 הלשכות 3957
mehatachatounout uamehatiykonout meha'aretz. uagader 'asher lachutz la'amat halashakout,
**more than the lowest and the middlemost from the ground And the wall that *was* without over against the chambers**

42:8

דרך 1870 החצר 2691 החיצונה 2435 אל 413 פני 6440 הלשכות 3957 ארכו 753 חמשים 2572 אמה 520: כי 3588
derek hechatzer hachiytzounah 'al paney halashakout; arakou chamishiym 'amah. kiy
**toward court the utter on the forepart of the chambers the length thereof *was* fifty cubits For**

ארך 753 הלשכות 3957 אשר 834 לחצר 2691 החצונה 2435 חמשים 2572 אמה 520 והנה 2009 על 5921 פני 6440 ההיכל 1964
'arek halashakout, 'asher lechatzer hachiytzounah chamishiym 'amah; uahineh 'al paney haheykal
**the length of the chambers that *were* in court the utter *was* fifty cubits and lo on before the temple**

42:9

מאה 3967 אמה 520: ומתחתה 8478 לשכות 3957 האלה 428 המבוא 3996 מהקדים 6921 בבאו 935 להנה 2007
me'ah 'amah. uamitachatah halashakout ha'aeleh; hamabou'a mehaqadiym, babo'au lahenah,
***were* an hundred cubits And from under chambers these *was* the entry on the east side as one goes into them**

42:10

מהחצר 2691 החצנה 2435: ברחב 7341 גדר 1444 החצר 2691 דרך 1870 הקדים 6921 אל 413 פני 6440
mehechatzer hachitzonah. barochab geder hechatzer, derek haqadiym 'al paney
**from court the utter *were* in the thickness of the wall of the court toward the east over against**

42:11

הגזרה 1508 ואל 413 פני 6440 הבנין 1146 לשכות 3957: ודרך 1870 לפניהם 6440 כמראה 4758
hagizrah ua'al paney habinyan lashakout. uaderek lipneyhem, kamar'aeh
**the separate place and over against the building The chambers And the way before them *was* like the appearance of**

הלשכות 3957 אשר 834 דרך 1870 הצפון 6828 כארכן 753 כן 3651 רחבן 7341 וכל 3605 מוצאיהן 4161
halashakout, 'asher derek hatzapoun, ka'arakan ken rachaban; uakol moutza'aeyhen,
**the chambers which *were* toward the north as long as they *and* so as broad as they and all their goings out**

42:12

וכמשפטיהן 4941 וכפתחיהן 6607: וכפתחי 6607 הלשכות 3957 אשר 834
uakmishpateyhen uakpitcheyhen. uakpitchey halashakout, 'asher
***were* both according to their fashions and according to their doors And according to the doors of the chambers that**

דרך 1870 הדרום 1864 פתח 6607 בראש 7218 דרך 1870 דרך 1870 בפני 6440 הגדרת 1448 הגינה 1903 דרך 1870 הקדים 6921
derek hadaroum, petach bara'sh darek; derek, bipaney hagaderet hagiynah, derek haqadiym
***were* toward the south *was* a door in the head of the way *even* the way before the wall directly toward the east**

42:13

בבואן 935: ויאמר 559 אלי 413 לשכות 3957 הצפון 6828 לשכות 3957 הדרום 1864 אשר 834 אל 413 פני 6440
babou'an. uaya'mer 'aelay, lishkout hatzapoun lishkout hadaroum 'asher 'al paney
**as one enter into them Then said he unto me chambers The north chambers *and* the south which *are* to before**

Eze 42:6 For they were in three stories, but had not pillars as the pillars of the courts: therefore the building was straitened more than the lowest and the middlemost from the ground.7 And the wall that was without over against the chambers, toward the utter court on the forepart of the chambers, the length thereof was fifty cubits.8 For the length of the chambers that were in the utter court was fifty cubits: and, lo, before the temple were an hundred cubits.9 And from under these chambers was the entry on the east side, as one go into them from the utter court.10 The chambers were in the thickness of the wall of the court toward the east, over against the separate place, and over against the building.11 And the way before them was like the appearance of the chambers which were toward the north, as long as they, and as broad as they: and all their goings out were both according to their fashions, and according to their doors.12 And according to the doors of the chambers that were toward the south was a door in the head of the way, even the way directly before the wall toward the east, as one entereth into them.13 Then said he unto me, The north chambers and the south chambers, which are before the separate place, they be holy chambers, where the priests that approach unto YHUH shall eat the most holy things: there shall they lay the most holy things, and the meat offering,

הגזרה 1508 הנה 2007 לשכות 3957 הקדש 6944 אשר 834 יאכלו 398 שם 8033 הכהנים 3548 אשר 834 קרובים 7138 ליהוה 3069 קדשי 6944
hagizrah henah lishkout haqodesh, 'asher ya'kalu sham hakohaniym 'asher qaroubiym laYahuah qadashey
**the separate place they chambers *be* holy where shall eat there the priests that approach Yahuah the most**

הקדשים 6944 שם 8033 יניחו 3240 קדשי 6944 הקדשים 6944 והמנחה 4503 והחטאת 2403 והאשם 817
haqadashiym; sham yaniychu qadashey haqadashiym, uahaminchah uahachata't uaha'asham,
**holy things there shall they lay the most holy things and the meat offering and the sin offering and the trespass offering**

כי 3588 המקום 4725 קדש 6918: 42:14 בבאם 935 הכהנים 3548 ולא 3808 יצאו 3318 מהקדש 6944 אל 413 החצר 2691
kiy hamaqoum qadosh. babo'am hakohaniym, uala' yetza'ua mehaqodesh 'al hechatzer
**for the place *is* holy When enter therein the priests then not shall they go out of the holy *place* into court**

החיצונה 2435 ושם 8033 יניחו 3240 בגדיהם 899 אשר 834 ישרתו 8334 בהן 871a כי 3588 קדש 6944 הנה 2007 ילבשו 3847
hachiytzounah, uasham yaniychu bigadeyhem 'asher yasharatu bahen kiy qodesh henah; yilbeshu
**the utter but there they shall lay their garments wherein they minister therein for *are* holy they and shall put on**

בגדים 899 אחרים 312 וקרבו 7126 אל 413 אשר 834 לעם 5971: 42:15 וכלה 3615
bagadiym 'acheriym, uaqarabu 'al 'asher la'am. uakilah,
**garments other and shall approach to *those things* which *are* for the people Now when he had made an end of**

את 853 מדות 4060 הבית 1004 הפנימי 6442 והוציאני 3318 דרך 1870 השער 8179 אשר 834 פניו 6440 דרך 1870 הקדים 6921
'at midout habayit hapaniymiy, uahoutziy'aniy derek hasha'ar, 'asher panayu derek haqadiym;
**measuring house the inner he brought me forth toward the gate whose prospect *is* toward the east**

ומדדו 4058 סביב 5439 סביב 5439: 42:16 מדד 4058 רוח 7307 הקדים 6921 בקנה 7070 המדה 4060 חמש 2568 אמות 520
uamdadou sabiyb sabiyb. madad ruach haqadiym biqneh hamidah; chamesh 'amout
**and measured it round about He measured side the east with reed the measuring five hundred (*cubits*)**

קנים 7070 בקנה 7070 המדה 4060 סביב 5439: 42:17 מדד 4058 רוח 7307 הצפון 6828 חמש 2568 מאות 3967 קנים 7070 בקנה 7070
qaniym biqneh hamidah sabiyb. madad ruach hatzapoun; chamesh me'aut qaniym biqneh
**reeds with reed the measuring round about He measured side the north five hundred reeds with reed**

המדה 4060 סביב 5439: 42:18 את 853 רוח 7307 הדרום 1864 מדד 4058 חמש 2568 מאות 3967 קנים 7070 בקנה 7070
hamidah sabiyb. 'at ruach hadaroum madad; chamesh me'aut qaniym biqneh
**the measuring round about side the south He measured five hundred reeds with reed**

המדה 4060: 42:19 סבב 5437 אל 413 רוח 7307 הים 3220 מדד 4058 חמש 2568 מאות 3967 קנים 7070 בקנה 7070
hamidah. sabab 'al ruach hayam; madad chamesh me'aut qaniym biqneh
**the measuring He turned about to side the west *and* measured five hundred reeds with reed**

המדה 4060: 42:20 לארבע 702 רוחות 7307 מדדו 4058 חומה 2346 לו 3807a סביב 5439 סביב 5439 ארך 753 חמש 2568 מאות 3967
hamidah. la'arba' ruchout madadou, choumah lou' sabiyb sabiyb, 'arek chamesh me'aut,
**the measuring by the four sides He measured it a wall it had round about *reeds* long five hundred**

ורחב 7341 חמש 2568 מאות 3967 להבדיל 914 בין 996 הקדש 6944 לחל 2455:
uarochab chamesh me'aut; lahabdiyl beyn haqodesh lachol.
**and broad five hundred to make a separation between the sanctuary and the profane place**

Eze 42:13 and the trespass offering; for the place is holy.14 When the priests enter therein, then shall they not go out of the holy place into the utter court, but there they shall lay their garments wherein they minister; for they are holy; and shall put on other garments, and shall approach to those things which are for the people.15 Now when he had made an end of measuring the inner house, he brought me forth toward the gate whose prospect is toward the east, and measured it round about.16 He measured the east side with the measuring reed, five hundred reeds, with the measuring reed round about.17 He measured the north side, five hundred reeds, with the measuring reed round about.18 He measured the south side, five hundred reeds, with the measuring reed.19 He turned about to the west side, and measured five hundred reeds with the measuring reed.20 He measured it by the four sides: it had a wall round about, five hundred reeds long, and five hundred broad, to make a separation between the sanctuary and the profane place.

| **Ezek 43:1** וילכני 1980 | אל 413 | השער 8179 | שער 8179 | אשר 834 | פנה 6437 | דרך 1870 | הקדים 6921: | **43:2** והנה 2009 |
|---|---|---|---|---|---|---|---|---|
| uayoulikeniy | 'al | hasha'ar; | sha'ar | 'asher | poneh | derek | haqadiym. | uahineh, |
| **Afterward he brought me** | **to** | **the gate** | ***even* the gate** | **that** | **looks** | **toward** | **the east** | **And behold** |

| כבוד 3519 | אלהי 430 | ישראל 3478 | בא 935 | מדרך 1870 | הקדים 6921 | וקולו 6963 | כקול 6963 | מים 4325 | רבים 7227 |
|---|---|---|---|---|---|---|---|---|---|
| kaboud | 'alohey | yisra'ael, | ba' | miderek | haqadiym; | baqoulou, | kaqoul | mayim | rabiym, |
| **the glory of** | **the Elohim of** | **Israel** | **came** | **from the way of** | **the east** | **and his voice** | ***was* like a noise of** | **waters** | **many** |

| והארץ 776 | האירה 215 | מכבדו 3519: | **43:3** וכמראה 4758 | המראה 4758 | אשר 834 | ראיתי 7200 |
|---|---|---|---|---|---|---|
| uaha'aretz | he'ayrah | mikdodou. | uakmar'aeh | hamar'ah | 'asher | ra'aytiy, |
| **and the earth** | **shined** | **with his glory** | **And *it was* according to the appearance of** | **the vision** | **which** | **I saw** |

| כמראה 4758 | אשר 834 | ראיתי 7200 | בבאי 935 | לשחת 7843 | את 853 | העיר 5892 | ומראות 4758 | כמראה 4758 |
|---|---|---|---|---|---|---|---|---|
| kamara'ah | 'asher | ra'aytiy | babo'ay | lashachet | 'at | ha'ayr, | umar'aut | kamara'ah |
| ***even* according to the vision** | **that** | **I saw** | **when I came** | **to destroy** | | **the city** | **like the visions *were*** | **like the vision** |

| אשר 834 | ראיתי 7200 | אל 413 | נהר 5104 | כבר 3529 | ואפל 5307 | אל 413 | פני 6440: | **43:4** וכבוד 3519 | יהוה 3068 | בא 935 | אל 413 | הבית 1004 |
|---|---|---|---|---|---|---|---|---|---|---|---|---|
| 'asher | ra'aytiy | 'al | nahar | kabar; | ua'apol | 'al | panay. | uakaboud | Yahuah | ba' | 'al | habayit; |
| **that** | **I saw** | **by** | ***the* river** | **Chebar** | **and I fell** | **upon** | **my face** | **And the glory of** | **Yahuah** | **came** | **into** | **the house** |

| דרך 1870 | שער 8179 | אשר 834 | פניו 6440 | דרך 1870 | הקדים 6921: | **43:5** ותשאני 5375 | רוח 7307 | ותביאני 935 | אל 413 | החצר 2691 |
|---|---|---|---|---|---|---|---|---|---|---|
| derek | sha'ar, | 'asher | panayu | derek | haqadiym. | uatisa'aeniy | ruach, | uatabiy'aeniy | 'al | hechatzer |
| ***by* the way of** | **the gate** | **whose** | **prospect** | ***is* toward** | **the east** | **So took me up** | **the spirit** | **and brought me** | **into** | **court** |

| הפנימי 6442 | והנה 2009 | מלא 4390 | כבוד 3519 | יהוה 3068 | הבית 1004: | **43:6** ואשמע 8085 | מדבר 1696 | אלי 413 | מהבית 1004 |
|---|---|---|---|---|---|---|---|---|---|
| hapaniymiy; | uahineh | malea' | kaboud | Yahuah | habayit. | ua'ashma' | midaber | 'aelay | mehabayit; |
| **the inner** | **and behold** | **filled** | **the glory of** | **Yahuah** | **the house** | **And I heard** | ***him* speaking** | **unto me** | **out of the house** |

| ואיש 376 | היה 1961 | עמד 5975 | אצלי 681: | **43:7** ויאמר 559 | אלי 413 | בן 1121 | אדם 120 | את 853 | מקום 4725 | כסאי 3678 | ואת 853 |
|---|---|---|---|---|---|---|---|---|---|---|---|
| ua'aysh | hayah | 'amed | 'atzliy. | uaya'mer | 'aelay, | ben | 'adam | 'at | maqoum | kis'ay, | ua'at |
| **and the man** | **become** | **stood** | **by me** | **And he said** | **unto me** | **Son of** | **man** | | **the place of** | **my throne** | ***and*** |

| מקום 4725 | כפות 3709 | רגלי 7272 | אשר 834 | אשכן 7931 | שם 8033 | בתוך 8432 | בני 1121 | ישראל 3478 | לעולם 5769 | ולא 3808 |
|---|---|---|---|---|---|---|---|---|---|---|
| maqoum | kapout | raglay, | 'asher | 'ashkan | sham | batouk | baney | yisra'ael | la'aulam; | uala' |
| **the place of** | **the soles of** | **my feet** | **where** | **I will dwell** | **there** | **in the midst of** | **the children of** | **Israel** | **for ever** | **and no** |

| יטמאו 2930 | עוד 5750 | בית 1004 | ישראל 3478 | שם 8034 | קדשי 6944 | המה 1992 | ומלכיהם 4428 | בזנותם 2184 |
|---|---|---|---|---|---|---|---|---|
| yatam'au | 'aud | beyt | yisra'ael | shem | qadashiy | hemah | uamalkeyhem | biznutam, |
| **shall defile** | **more** | **the house of** | **Israel** | **name** | **my holy** | ***neither* they** | **nor their kings** | **by their whoredom** |

| ובפגרי 6297 | מלכיהם 4428 | במותם 1116: | **43:8** בתתם 5414 | ספם 5592 | את 853 | ספי 5592 |
|---|---|---|---|---|---|---|
| uabpigrey | malkeyhem | bamoutam. | batitam | sipam | 'at | sipiy, |
| **nor by the carcases of** | **their kings** | **in their high places** | **In their setting of** | **their threshold *by*** | | **my thresholds** |

| ומזוזתם 4201 | אצל 681 | מזוזתי 4201 | והקיר 7023 | ביני 996 | וביניהם 996 | וטמאו 2930 | את 853 | שם 8034 | קדשי 6944 |
|---|---|---|---|---|---|---|---|---|---|
| uamzuzatam | 'aetzel | mazuzatiy, | uahaqiyr | beyniy | uabeyneyhem; | uatim'au | 'at | shem | qadashiy |
| **and their post by** | | **my posts** | **and the wall** | **between me** | **and them** | **they have even defiled** | | **name** | **my holy** |

**Eze** 43:1 Afterward he brought me to the gate, even the gate that look toward the east:2 And, behold, the glory of the G-d of Israel came from the way of the east: and his voice was like a noise of many waters: and the earth shined with his glory.3 And it was according to the appearance of the vision which I saw, even according to the vision that I saw when I came to destroy the city: and the visions were like the vision that I saw by the river Chebar; and I fell upon my face.4 And the glory of YHUH came into the house by the way of the gate whose prospect is toward the east.5 So the spirit took me up, and brought me into the inner court; and, behold, the glory of YHUH filled the house.6 And I heard him speaking unto me out of the house; and the man stood by me.7 And he said unto me, Son of man, the place of my throne, and the place of the soles of my feet, where I will dwell in the midst of the children of Israel forever, and my holy name, shall the house of Israel no more defile, neither they, nor their kings, by their whoredom, nor by the carcases of their kings in their high places.8 In their setting of their threshold by my thresholds, and their post by my posts, and the wall between me and them, they have even defiled my holy name by their abominations that they have committed: wherefore I have consumed them in mine anger.

| בתועבותם 8441 | אשר 834 | עשו 6213 | ואכל 3615 | אתם 853 | באפי 639: | 43:9 | עתה 6258 |
|---|---|---|---|---|---|---|---|
| batou'aboutam | 'asher | 'asu, | ua'akal | 'atam | ba'apiy. | | 'atah |
| **by their abominations** | **that** | **they have committed** | **wherefore I have consumed** | **them** | **in mine anger** | | **Now** |

| ירחקו 7368 | את 853 | זנותם 2184 | ופגרי 6297 | מלכיהם 4428 | ממני 4480 | ושכנתי 7931 | בתוכם 8432 |
|---|---|---|---|---|---|---|---|
| yarachaqu | 'at | zanutam | uapigrey | malkeyhem | mimeniy; | uashakantiy | batoukam |
| **let them put away far** | | **their whoredom** | **and the carcases of** | **their kings** | **from me** | **and I will dwell** | **in the midst of them** |

| לעולם 5769: | 43:10 | אתה 859 | בן 1121 | אדם 120 | הגד 5046 | את 853 | בית 1004 | ישראל 3478 | את 853 | הבית 1004 | ויכלמו 3637 |
|---|---|---|---|---|---|---|---|---|---|---|---|
| la'aulam. | | 'atah | ben | 'adam, | haged | 'at | beyt | yisra'ael | 'at | habayit, | uayikalamu |
| **for ever** | | **You** | **son of** | **man** | **show** | | **the house** | **Israel** | | ***to* the house of** | **that they may be ashamed** |

| מעונותיהם 5771 | ומדדו 4058 | את 853 | תכנית 8508: | 43:11 | ואם 518 | נכלמו 3637 | מכל 3605 | אשר 834 | עשו 6213 |
|---|---|---|---|---|---|---|---|---|---|
| me'auonouteyhem; | uamadadu | 'at | takniyt. | | ua'am | niklamu | mikol | 'asher | 'asu, |
| **of their iniquities** | **and let them measure** | | **the pattern** | | **And if** | **they be ashamed** | **of all** | **that** | **they have done** |

| צורת 6699 | הבית 1004 | ותכונתו 8498 | ומוצאיו 4161 | ומובאיו 4126 | וכל 3605 |
|---|---|---|---|---|---|
| tzurat | habayit | uatkunatou | uamoutza'ayu | uamouba'ayu | uakal |
| **the form of** | **the house** | **and the fashion thereof** | **and the goings out thereof** | **and the comings in thereof** | **and all** |

| צורתו 6699 | ואת 853 | כל 3605 | חקתיו 2708 | וכל 3605 | צורתי 6699 | וכל 3605 | תורתו 8451 | הודע 3045 | אותם 853 |
|---|---|---|---|---|---|---|---|---|---|
| tzurotau | ua'at | kal | chuqotayu | uakal | tzurotay | uakal | tourotau | houda' | 'autam, |
| **the forms thereof** | ***and*** | **all** | **the ordinances thereof** | **and all** | **the forms thereof** | **and all** | **the laws thereof** | **show** | **them** |

| וכתב 3789 | לעיניהם 5869 | וישמרו 8104 | את 853 | כל 3605 | צורתו 6699 | ואת 853 | כל 3605 | חקתיו 2708 | ועשו 6213 |
|---|---|---|---|---|---|---|---|---|---|
| uaktob | la'aeyneyhem; | uayishmaru | 'at | kal | tzuratou | ua'at | kal | chuqotayu | ua'asu |
| **and write *it*** | **in their sight** | **that they may keep** | | **the whole** | **form thereof** | ***and*** | **all** | **the ordinances thereof** | **and do** |

| אותם 853: | 43:12 | זאת 2063 | תורת 8451 | הבית 1004 | על 5921 | ראש 7218 | ההר 2022 | כל 3605 | גבלו 1366 | סביב 5439 | סביב 5439 |
|---|---|---|---|---|---|---|---|---|---|---|---|
| 'autam. | | za't | tourat | habayit; | 'al | ra'sh | hahar | kal | gabulou | sabiyb | sabiyb |
| **them** | | **This** | ***is* the law of** | **the house** | **Upon** | **the top of** | **the mountain** | **the whole** | **limit thereof** | **round** | **about** |

| קדש 6944 | קדשים 6944 | הנה 2009 | זאת 2063 | תורת 8451 | הבית 1004: | 43:13 | ואלה 428 | מדות 4060 | המזבח 4196 |
|---|---|---|---|---|---|---|---|---|---|
| qodesh | qadashiym, | hineh | za't | tourat | habayit. | | ua'aleh | midout | hamizbeach |
| ***shall be* most** | **holy** | **Behold** | **this** | ***is* the law of** | **the house** | | **And these** | ***are* the measures of** | **the altar** |

| באמות 520 | אמה 520 | אמה 520 | וטפח 2948 | וחיק 2436 | האמה 520 | ואמה 520 | רחב 7341 |
|---|---|---|---|---|---|---|---|
| ba'amout, | 'amah | 'amah | uatopach; | uacheyq | ha'amah | ua'amah | rochab, |
| **after the cubits** | **The cubit** | ***is* a cubit** | **and an hand breadth** | **even the bottom** | ***shall be* a cubit** | **a cubit** | **the breadth** |

| וגבולה 1366 | אל 413 | שפתה 8193 | סביב 5439 | זרת 2239 | האחד 259 | וזה 2088 | גב 1354 |
|---|---|---|---|---|---|---|---|
| augbulah | 'al | sapatah | sabiyb | zeret | ha'achad, | uazeh | gab |
| **and the border thereof** | **by** | **the edge thereof** | **round about** | **span** | ***shall be* a** | **and this** | ***shall be* the higher place of** |

| המזבח 4196: | 43:14 | ומחיק 2436 | הארץ 776 | עד 5704 | העזרה 5835 | התחתונה 8481 | שתים 8147 | אמות 520 |
|---|---|---|---|---|---|---|---|---|
| hamizbeach. | | uamecheyq | ha'aretz | 'ad | ha'azarah | hatachatounah | shatayim | 'amout, |
| **the altar** | | **And from the bottom** | ***upon* the ground *even*** | **to** | **settle** | **the lower** | ***shall be* two** | **cubits** |

Eze 43:9 Now let them put away their whoredom, and the carcases of their kings, far from me, and I will dwell in the midst of them forever.10 Thou son of man, show the house to the house of Israel, that they may be ashamed of their iniquities: and let them measure the pattern.11 And if they be ashamed of all that they have done, show them the form of the house, and the fashion thereof, and the goings out thereof, and the comings in thereof, and all the forms thereof, and all the ordinances thereof, and all the forms thereof, and all the laws thereof: and write it in their sight, that they may keep the whole form thereof, and all the ordinances thereof, and do them.12 This is the law of the house; Upon the top of the mountain the whole limit thereof round about shall be most holy. Behold, this is the law of the house.13 And these are the measures of the altar after the cubits: The cubit is a cubit and an hand breadth; even the bottom shall be a cubit, and the breadth a cubit, and the border thereof by the edge thereof round about shall be a span: and this shall be the higher place of the altar.14 And from the bottom upon the ground even to the lower settle shall be two cubits, and the breadth one cubit; and from the lesser settle even to the greater settle shall be four cubits, and the breadth one cubit.

ורחב 7341 אמה 520 אחת 259 ומהעזרה 5835 הקטנה 6996 עד 5704 העזרה 5835 הגדולה 1419 ארבע 702 אמות 520
uarochab 'amah 'achat; uameha'azarah haqatanah 'ad ha'azarah hagadoulah 'arba 'amout,
**and the breadth cubit one and from settle the lesser to settle *even* the greater *shall be* four cubits**

ורחב 7341 האמה 520: **43:15** וההראל 741 ארבע 702 אמות 520 ומהאריאל 741 ולמעלה 4605 הקרנות 7161
uarochab ha'amah. uahahar'ael 'arba 'amout; uameha'ari'ayl ualma'alah, haqaranout
**and the breadth *one* cubit So the altar *shall be* four cubits and from the altar and upward horns**

ארבע 702: **43:16** והאריאל 741 שתים 8147 עשרה 6240 ארך 753 בשתים 8147 עשרה 6240 רחב 7341 רבוע 7251 אל 413 ארבעת 702
'arba. uaha'ariy'ael shateym 'asreh 'arek, bishteym 'asreh rochab; rabua' 'al 'arba'at
***shall be* four And the altar *shall be* two ten *cubits* long two ten broad square in *the* four**

רבעיו 7253: **43:17** והעזרה 5835 ארבע 702 עשרה 6240 ארך 753 בארבע 702 עשרה 6240 רחב 7341 אל 413 ארבעת 702
raba'ayu. uaha'azarah 'arba 'asreh 'arek, ba'arba 'asreh rochab, 'al 'arba'at
**squares thereof And the settle *shall be* four ten *cubits* long four ten broad in *the* four**

רבעיה 7253 והגבול 1366 סביב 5439 אותה 853 חצי 2677 האמה 520 והחיק 2436 לה 3807a אמה 520 סביב 5439
raba'ayha; uahagabul sabiyb 'autah chatziy ha'amah, uahacheyq lah 'amah sabiyb,
**squares thereof and the border about it *shall be* half a cubit and the bottom thereof *shall be* a cubit about**

ומעלתהו 4609 פנות 6437 קדים 6921: **43:18** ויאמר 559 אלי 413 בן 1121 אדם 120 כה 3541 אמר 559 אדני 136 יהוה 3069 אלה 428
uama'alotehu panout qadiym. uaya'mer 'aelay, ben 'adam koh 'amar 'adonay Yahuah, 'aeleh
**and his stairs shall look *toward* the east And he said unto me Son of man thus saith Adonai Yahuah These**

חקות 2708 המזבח 4196 ביום 3117 העשותו 6213 להעלות 5927 עליו 5921 עולה 5930 ולזרק 2236
chuqout hamizbeach, bayoum he'asoutou; leha'alout 'alayu aulah, ualizroq
***are* the ordinances of the altar in the day when they shall make it to offer thereon burnt offerings and to sprinkle**

עליו 5921 דם 1818: **43:19** ונתתה 5414 אל 413 הכהנים 3548 הלוים 3881 אשר 834 הם 1992 מזרע 2233 צדוק 6659 הקרבים 7138
'alayu dam. uanatatah 'al hakohaniym halauiyim 'asher hem mizera' tzadouq haqarobiym
**thereon blood And you shall give to the priests the Levites that *be* they of the seed of Zadok which approach**

אלי 413 נאם 5002 אדני 136 יהוה 3068 לשרתני 8334 פר 6499 בן 1121 בקר 1241 לחטאת 2403: **43:20** ולקחת 3947
'aelay, na'am 'adonay Yahuah lasharateniy; par ben baqar lachata't. ualaqachta
**unto me saith Adonai Yahuah to minister unto me a bullock young bull for a sin offering And you shall take**

מדמו 1818 ונתתה 5414 על 5921 ארבע 702 קרנתיו 7161 ואל 413 ארבע 702 פנות 6438 העזרה 5835 ואל 413 הגבול 1366
midamou, uanatatah 'al 'arba qarnotayu ua'al 'arba pinout ha'azarah, ua'al hagabul
**of the blood thereof and put *it* on *the* four horns of it and on *the* four corners of the settle and upon the border**

סביב 5439 וחטאת 2398 אותו 853 וכפרתהו 3722: **43:21** ולקחת 3947 את 853 הפר 6499 החטאת 2403
sabiyb; uachitea'ta 'autou uakipartahu. ualaqachta, 'at hapar hachata't;
**round about thus shall you cleanse it and purge You shall take also the bullock of the sin offering**

ושרפו 8313 במפקד 4662 הבית 1004 מחוץ 2351 למקדש 4720: **43:22** וביום 3117 השני 8144 תקריב 7126
uasrapou bamipqad habayit, michutz lamiqdash. uabayoum hasheniy, taqriyb
**and he shall burn it in the appointed place of the house without the sanctuary And on day the second you shall offer**

Eze 43:15 So the altar shall be four cubits; and from the altar and upward shall be four horns.16 And the altar shall be twelve cubits long, twelve broad, square in the four squares thereof.17 And the settle shall be fourteen cubits long and fourteen broad in the four squares thereof; and the border about it shall be half a cubit; and the bottom thereof shall be a cubit about; and his stairs shall look toward the east.18 And he said unto me, Son of man, thus saith YHUH G-D; These are the ordinances of the altar in the day when they shall make it, to offer burnt offerings thereon, and to sprinkle blood thereon.19 And you shall give to the priests the Levites that be of the seed of Zadok, which approach unto me, to minister unto me, saith YHUH G-D, a young bullock for a sin offering.20 And you shall take of the blood thereof, and put it on the four horns of it, and on the four corners of the settle, and upon the border round about: thus shall you cleanse and purge it.21 Thou shall take the bullock also of the sin offering, and he shall burn it in the appointed place of the house, without the sanctuary.22 And on the second day you shall offer a kid of the goats without blemish for a sin offering; and they shall cleanse the altar, as they did cleanse it with the bullock.

שעיר 8163 עזים 5795 תמים 8549 לחטאת 2403 וחטאו 2398 את 853 המזבח 4196 כאשר 834 חטאו 2398
sa'ayr aziym tamiym lachata't; uachit'au 'at hamizbeach, ka'asher chit'au
**a kid of the goats without blemish for a sin offering and they shall cleanse the altar as they did cleanse**

בפר 6499: **43:23** בכלותך 3615 מחטא 2398 תקריב 7126 פר 6499 בן 1121 בקר 1241
bapar. bakaloutaka mechatea'; taqriyb par ben baqar
***it* with the bullock When you have made an end of cleansing *it* you shall offer a bullock young bull**

תמים 8549 ואיל 352 מן 4480 הצאן 6629 תמים 8549: **43:24** והקרבתם 7126 לפני 6440 יהוה 3068 והשליכו 7993
tamiym, ua'ayil min hatza'an tamiym. uahiqrabtam lipney Yahuah; uahishliyku
**without blemish and a ram out of the flock without blemish And you shall offer them before Yahuah and shall cast**

הכהנים 3548 עליהם 5921 מלח 4417 והעלו 5927 אותם 853 עלה 5930 ליהוה 3068: **43:25** שבעת 7651 ימים 3117
hakohaniym 'aleyhem melach, uahe'alu 'autam 'alah laYahuah. shib'at yamiym,
**the priests upon them salt and they shall offer up them *for* a burnt offering unto Yahuah Seven days**

תעשה 6213 שעיר 8163 חטאת 2403 ליום 3117 ופר 6499 בן 1121 בקר 1241 ואיל 352 מן 4480 הצאן 6629
ta'aseh sa'ayr chata't layoum; uapar ben baqar ua'ayil min hatza'an
**shall you prepare they shall a goat *for* a sin offering every day also a bullock young bull and a ram out of the flock**

תמימים 8549 יעשו 6213: **43:26** שבעת 7651 ימים 3117 יכפרו 3722 את 853 המזבח 4196 וטהרו 2891 אתו 853
tamiymiym ya'asu. shib'at yamiym, yakaparu 'at hamizbeach, uatiharu 'atou;
**without blemish prepare Seven days shall they purge the altar and purify it**

ומלאו 4390 ידו 3027 **43:27** ויכלו 3615 את 853 הימים 3117 והיה 1961 ביום 3117
umil'au yadau uiykalu 'at hayamiym; uahayah bayoum
**and they shall consecrate themselves And when are expired these days and it shall be *that* upon day**

השמיני 8066 והלאה 1973 יעשו 6213 הכהנים 3548 על 5921 המזבח 4196 את 853 עולותיכם 5930 ואת 853 שלמיכם 8002
hashamiyniy uahal'ah, ya'asu hakohaniym 'al hamizbeach 'at 'aulouteykem ua'at shalmeykem,
**the eighth and *so* forward shall make the priests upon the altar your burnt offerings *and* your peace offerings**

ורצאתי 7521 אתכם 853 נאם 5002 אדני 136 יהוה 3069:
uaratza'tiy 'atkem, na'am 'adonay Yahuah.
**and I will accept you saith Adonai Yahuah**

**Ezek 44:1** וישב 7725 אתי 853 דרך 1870 שער 8179 המקדש 4720 החיצון 2435 הפנה 6437 קדים 6921
uayasheb 'atiy, derek sha'ar hamiqdash hachiytzoun, haponeh qadiym;
**Then he brought back me *the* way of the gate of sanctuary the outward which looks toward the east**

והוא 1931 סגור 5462: **44:2** ויאמר 559 אלי 413 יהוה 3068 השער 8179 הזה 2088 סגור 5462 יהיה 1961 לא 3808 יפתח 6605 ואיש 376
uahu'a sagur. uaya'mer 'aelay Yahuah hasha'ar hazeh sagur yihayeh la' yipateach, ua'aysh
**and it *was* shut Then said unto me Yahuah gate This shall be shut it shall be not opened and man**

לא 3808 יבא 935 בו 871a כי 3588 יהוה 3068 אלהי 430 ישראל 3478 בא 935 בו 871a והיה 1961 סגור 5462:
la' yaba' bou, kiy Yahuah 'alohey yisra'ael ba' bou; uahayah sagur.
**no shall enter in by it because Yahuah the Elohim of Israel has entered in by it therefore it shall be shut**

Eze 43:23 When you have made an end of cleansing it, you shall offer a young bullock without blemish, and a ram out of the flock without blemish.24 And you shall offer them before YHUH, and the priests shall cast salt upon them, and they shall offer them up for a burnt offering unto YHUH.25 Seven days shall you prepare every day a goat for a sin offering: they shall also prepare a young bullock, and a ram out of the flock, without blemish.26 Seven days shall they purge the altar and purify it; and they shall consecrate themselves.27 And when these days are expired, it shall be, that upon the eighth day, and so forward, the priests shall make your burnt offerings upon the altar, and your peace offerings; and I will accept you, saith YHUH G-D. **Eze** 44:1 Then he brought me back the way of the gate of the outward sanctuary which look toward the east; and it was shut.2 Then said YHUH unto me; This gate shall be shut, it shall not be opened, and no man shall enter in by it; because YHUH, the G-d of Israel, has entered in by it, therefore it shall be shut.

**44:3**
את 853 הנשיא 5387 נשיא 5387 הוא 1931 ישב 3427 בו 871a לאכול 398 לחם 3899 לפני 6440 יהוה 3068 מדרך 1870 אלם 197
'at hanasiy'a, nasiy'a hua' yesheb bou le'akoul lachem lipney Yahuah; miderek 'alam
**_It is_ the prince the prince he shall sit in it to eat bread before Yahuah by the way of the porch of**

**44:4**
השער 8179 יבוא 935 ומדרכו 1870 יצא 3318: ויביאני 935 דרך 1870 שער 8179 הצפון 6828 אל 413
hasha'ar yabou'a, uamidarkou yetzea'. uayabiy'aeniy derek sha'ar hatzapoun 'al
***that* gate he shall enter and by the way of the same shall go out Then brought he me the way of gate the north to**

פני 6440 הבית 1004 וארא 7200 והנה 2009 מלא 4390 כבוד 3519 יהוה 3068 את 853 בית 1004 יהוה 3068 ואפל 5307 אל 413
paney habayit ua'aera' uahineh malea' kaboud Yahuah 'at beyt Yahuah; ua'apol 'al
**before the house and I looked and behold filled the glory of Yahuah the house of Yahuah and I fell upon**

**44:5**
פני 6440: ויאמר 559 אלי 413 יהוה 3068 בן 1121 אדם 120 שים 7760 לבך 3820 וראה 7200 בעיניך 5869 ובאזניך 241 שמע 8085
panay. uaya'mer 'aelay Yahuah ben 'adam siym libaka uar'aeh ba'aeyneyka uab'azaneyka shama',
**my face And said unto me Yahuah Son of man mark well and behold with your eyes and with your ears hear**

את 853 כל 3605 אשר 834 אני 589 מדבר 1696 אתך 853 לכל 3605 חקות 2708 בית 1004 יהוה 3068 ולכל 3605 תורתו 8451
'at kal 'asher 'aniy madaber 'atak, lakal chuqout beyt Yahuah ualkal tourotou
**all that I say unto you concerning all the ordinances of the house of Yahuah and all the laws thereof**

**44:6**
ושמת 7760 לבך 3820 למבוא 3996 הבית 1004 בכל 3605 מוצאי 4161 המקדש 4720: ואמרת 559 אל 413
uasamta libaka limbou'a habayit, bakol moutza'aey hamiqdash. ua'amarta 'al
**and mark well the entering in of the house with every going forth of the sanctuary And you shall say to**

מרי 4805 אל 413 בית 1004 ישראל 3478 כה 3541 אמר 559 אדני 136 יהוה 3069 רב 7227 לכם 3807a מכל 3605
meriy 'al beyt yisra'ael, koh 'amar 'adonay Yahuah; rab lakem mikal
**the rebellious _even_ to the house of Israel Thus saith Adonai Yahuah let it suffice to you of all**

**44:7**
תועבותיכם 8441 בית 1004 ישראל 3478: בהביאכם 935 בני 1121 נכר 5236
tou'abouteykem beyt yisra'ael. bahabiy'akem baney nekar,
**your abominations O you house of Israel In that you have brought _into my sanctuary_ strangers alien**

ערלי 6189 לב 3820 וערלי 6189 בשר 1320 להיות 1961 במקדשי 4720 לחללו 2490 את 853 ביתי 1004
'arley leb ua'arley basar, lihayout bamiqdashiy lachallou 'at beytiy;
**uncircumcised in heart and uncircumcised in flesh to be in my sanctuary to pollute it _even_ my house**

בהקריבכם 7126 את 853 לחמי 3899 חלב 2459 ודם 1818 ויפרו 6565 את 853 בריתי 1285 אל 413 כל 3605
bahaqriybakem 'at lachmiy cheleb uadam, uayaperu 'at bariytiy, 'al kal
**when you offer my bread the fat and the blood and they have broken my covenant because _of_ all**

**44:8**
תועבותיכם 8441: ולא 3808 שמרתם 8104 משמרת 4931 קדשי 6944 ותשימון 7760 לשמרי 8104 משמרתי 4931
tou'abouteykem. uala' shamartem mishmeret qadashay; uatasiymun, lashomarey mishmartiy
**your abominations And not you have kept the charge of mine holy things but you have set keepers of my charge**

**44:9**
במקדשי 4720 לכם 3807a: כה 3541 אמר 559 אדני 136 יהוה 3068 כל 3605 בן 1121 נכר 5236 ערל 6189 לב 3820
bamiqdashiy lakem. koh 'amar 'adonay Yahuah kal ben nekar, 'arel leb
**in my sanctuary for yourselves Thus saith Adonai Yahuah of all the children of stanger uncircumcised in heart**

Eze 44:3 It is for the prince; the prince, he shall sit in it to eat bread before YHUH; he shall enter by the way of the porch of that gate, and shall go out by the way of the same.4 Then brought he me the way of the north gate before the house: and I looked, and, behold, the glory of YHUH filled the house of YHUH: and I fell upon my face.5 And YHUH said unto me, Son of man, mark well, and behold with your eyes, and hear with your ears all that I say unto you concerning all the ordinances of the house of YHUH, and all the laws thereof; and mark well the entering in of the house, with every going forth of the sanctuary.6 And you shall say to the rebellious, even to the house of Israel, Thus saith YHUH G-D; O you house of Israel, let it suffice you of all your abominations,7 In that you have brought into my sanctuary strangers, uncircumcised in heart, and uncircumcised in flesh, to be in my sanctuary, to pollute it, even my house, when you offer my bread, the fat and the blood, and they have broken my covenant because of all your abominations.8 And you have not kept the charge of mine holy things: but you have set keepers of my charge in my sanctuary for yourselves.9 Thus saith YHUH G-D; No stranger, uncircumcised in heart, nor uncircumcised in flesh, shall enter into my sanctuary, of any stranger that is among the children of Israel.

וערל 6189 בשר 1320 לא 3808 יבוא 935 אל 413 מקדשי 4720 לכל 3605 בן 1121 נכר 5236 אשר 834 בתוך 8432 בני 1121
ua'arel basar, la' yabou'a 'al miqadashiy; lakal ben nekar, 'asher batouk baney
**nor uncircumcised in flesh no shall enter into my sanctuary of any the sons of stanger that *is* among the children of**

ישראל 3478: 44:10 כי 3588 אם 518 הלוים 3881 אשר 834 רחקו 7368 מעלי 5921 בתעות 8582 ישראל 3478 אשר 834
yisra'ael. kiy 'am halauiyim, 'asher rachaqu me'alay, bit'aut yisra'ael 'asher
**Israel *And* but rather the Levites that are gone away far from me when went astray Israel which**

תעו 8582 מעלי 5921 אחרי 310 גלוליהם 1544 ונשאו 5375 עונם 5771: 44:11 והיו 1961 במקדשי 4720
ta'au me'alay, 'acharey giluleyhem; uanasa'au 'auonam. uahayu bamiqdashiy
**went astray away from me after their idols they shall even bear their iniquity Yet they shall be in my sanctuary**

משרתים 8334 פקדות 6486 אל 413 שערי 8179 הבית 1004 ומשרתים 8334 את 853 הבית 1004 המה 1992 ישחטו 7819 את 853
masharatiym, paqudout 'al sha'arey habayit, uamsharatiym 'at habayit; hemah yishchatu 'at
**ministers *having* charge at the gates of the house and ministering to the house they shall slay**

העלה 5930 ואת 853 הזבח 2077 לעם 5971 והמה 1992 יעמדו 5975 לפניהם 6440 לשרתם 8334: 44:12 יען 3282
ha'aelah ua'at hazebach la'am, uahemah ya'amdu lipneyhem lasharatam. ya'an,
**the burnt offering *and* the sacrifice for the people and they shall stand before them to minister unto them Because**

אשר 834 ישרתו 8334 אותם 853 לפני 6440 גלוליהם 1544 והיו 1961 לבית 1004 ישראל 3478 למכשול 4383 עון 5771 על 5921
'asher yasharatu 'autam lipney giluleyhem, uahayu labeyt yisra'ael lamikshoul 'auon; 'al
**which they ministered unto them before their idols and caused the house of Israel to fall into iniquity therefore**

כן 3651 נשאתי 5375 ידי 3027 עליהם 5921 נאם 5002 אדני 136 יהוה 3069 ונשאו 5375 עונם 5771: 44:13 ולא 3808
ken nasa'tiy yadiy 'aleyhem, na'am 'adonay Yahuah, uanasa'au 'auonam. uala'
**after that have I lifted up mine hand against them saith Adonai Yahuah and they shall bear their iniquity And not**

יגשו 5066 אלי 413 לכהן 3547 לי 3807a ולגשת 5066 על 5921 כל 3605 קדשי 6944 אל 413
yigshu 'aelay lakahen liy, ualageshet 'al kal qadashay, 'al
**they shall come near unto me to do the office of a priest unto me nor to come near to any of my holy things in**

קדשי 6944 הקדשים 6944 ונשאו 5375 כלמתם 3639 ותועבותם 8441 אשר 834 עשו 6213: 44:14
qadashey haqadashiym; uanasa'au kalimatam, uatou'aboutam 'asher 'asu.
**most consecrated the holy *place* but they shall bear their shame and their abominations which they have committed**

ונתתי 5414 אותם 853 שמרי 8104 משמרת 4931 הבית 1004 לכל 3605 עבדתו 5656 ולכל 3605 אשר 834 יעשה 6213
uanatatiy 'autam, shomrey mishmeret habayit; lakol abodatou, ualkol 'asher ye'aseh
**But I will make them keepers of the charge of the house of all the service thereof and for all that shall be done**

בו 871a: 44:15 והכהנים 3548 הלוים 3881 בני 1121 צדוק 6659 אשר 834 שמרו 8104 את 853 משמרת 4931 מקדשי 4720
bou. uahakohaniym halauiyim baney tzadouq, 'asher shamaru 'at mishmeret miqadashiy
**therein But the priests the Levites the sons of Zadok that kept the charge of my sanctuary**

בתעות 8582 בני 1121 ישראל 3478 מעלי 5921 המה 1992 יקרבו 7126 אלי 413 לשרתני 8334 ועמדו 5975
bit'aut baney yisra'ael me'alay, hemah yiqrabu 'aelay lasharateniy; ua'amadu
**when went astray the children of Israel from me they shall come near to me to minister unto me and they shall stand**

Eze 44:10 And the Levites that are gone away far from me, when Israel went astray, which went astray away from me after their idols; they shall even bear their iniquity.11 Yet
they shall be ministers in my sanctuary, having charge at the gates of the house, and ministering to the house: they shall slay the burnt offering and the sacrifice for the people,
and they shall stand before them to minister unto them.12 Because they ministered unto them before their idols, and caused the house of Israel to fall into iniquity; therefore
have I lifted up mine hand against them, saith YHUH G-D, and they shall bear their iniquity.13 And they shall not come near unto me, to do the office of a priest unto me, nor
to come near to any of my holy things, in the most holy place: but they shall bear their shame, and their abominations which they have committed.14 But I will make them
keepers of the charge of the house, for all the service thereof, and for all that shall be done therein.15 But the priests the Levites, the sons of Zadok, that kept the charge of my
sanctuary when the children of Israel went astray from me, they shall come near to me to minister unto me, and they shall stand before me to offer unto me the fat and the
blood, saith YHUH G-D:

| לפני 6440 | להקריב 7126 | לי 3807a | חלב 2459 | ודם 1818 | נאם 5002 | אדני 136 | יהוה 3069: | 44:16 | המה 1992 | יבאו 935 | אל 413 | מקדשי 4720 |
|---|---|---|---|---|---|---|---|---|---|---|---|---|
| lapanay, | lahaqriyb | liy | cheleb | uadam, | na'am | 'adonay | Yahuah. | | hemah | yabo'au | 'al | miqadashiy, |
| **before me** | **to offer** | **unto me** | **the fat** | **and the blood** | **saith** | **Adonai** | **Yahuah** | | **They** | **shall enter** | **into** | **my sanctuary** |

| והמה 1992 | יקרבו 7126 | אל 413 | שלחני 7979 | לשרתני 8334 | ושמרו 8104 | את 853 | משמרתי 4931: | 44:17 |
|---|---|---|---|---|---|---|---|---|
| uahemah | yiqrabu | 'al | shulchaniy | lasharateniy; | uashamaru | 'at | mishmartiy. | |
| **and they** | **shall come near** | **to** | **my table** | **to minister unto me** | **and they shall keep** | | **my charge** | |

| והיה 1961 | בבואם 935 | אל 413 | שערי 8179 | החצר 2691 | הפנימית 6442 | בגדי 899 | פשתים 6593 |
|---|---|---|---|---|---|---|---|
| uahayah, | babou'am | 'al | sha'arey | hechatzer | hapaniymiyt, | bigdey | pishtiym |
| **And it shall come to pass *that*** | **when they enter in** | **at** | **the gates of** | **court** | **the inner** | **garments** | ***with* linen** |

| ילבשו 3847 | ולא 3808 | יעלה 5927 | עליהם 5921 | צמר 6785 | בשרתם 8334 | בשערי 8179 | החצר 2691 | הפנימית 6442 |
|---|---|---|---|---|---|---|---|---|
| yilbashu; | uala' | ya'aleh | 'aleyhem | tzemer, | basharatam, | basha'arey | hechatzer | hapaniymiyt |
| **they shall be clothed** | **and no** | **shall come** | **upon them** | **wool** | **whiles they minister** | **in the gates of** | **court** | **the inner** |

| וביתה 1004: | 44:18 | פארי 6287 | פשתים 6593 | יהיו 1961 | על 5921 | ראשם 7218 | ומכנסי 4370 | פשתים 6593 | יהיו 1961 | על 5921 |
|---|---|---|---|---|---|---|---|---|---|---|
| uabayatah. | | pa'arey | pishtiym | yihayu | 'al | ra'sham, | umiknasey | pishtiym, | yihayu | 'al |
| **and within** | | **bonnets** | **linen** | **They shall have** | **upon** | **their heads** | **and breeches** | **linen** | **shall have** | **upon** |

| מתניהם 4975 | לא 3808 | יחגרו 2296 | ביזע 3154: | 44:19 | ובצאתם 3318 | אל 413 | החצר 2691 |
|---|---|---|---|---|---|---|---|
| mataneyhem; | la' | yachgaru | bayaza'. | | 'aubtzea'tam | 'al | hechatzer |
| **their loins** | **not** | **they shall gird *themselves* with any thing that cause sweat** | | | **And when they go forth** | **into** | **court** |

| החיצונה 2435 | אל 413 | החצר 2691 | החיצונה 2435 | אל 413 | העם 5971 | יפשטו 6584 | את 853 | בגדיהם 899 | אשר 834 | המה 1992 |
|---|---|---|---|---|---|---|---|---|---|---|
| hachiytzounah | 'al | hechatzer | hachiytzounah | 'al | ha'am | yipshatu | 'at | bigadeyhem, | 'asher | hemah |
| **the utter *even*** | **into** | **court** | **the utter** | **to** | **the people** | **they shall put off** | | **their garments** | **wherein** | **they** |

| משרתם 8334 | בם 871a | והניחו 3240 | אותם 853 | בלשכת 3957 | הקדש 6944 | ולבשו 3847 | בגדים 899 | אחרים 312 | ולא 3808 |
|---|---|---|---|---|---|---|---|---|---|
| masharatiym | bam, | uahiniychu | 'autam | balishkot | haqodesh; | ualabashu | bagadiym | 'acheriym, | uala' |
| **ministered** | **therein** | **and lay** | **them** | **in chambers** | **the holy** | **and they shall put on** | **garments** | **other** | **and not** |

| יקדשו 6942 | את 853 | העם 5971 | בבגדיהם 899: | 44:20 | וראשם 7218 | לא 3808 | יגלחו 1548 | ופרע 6545 | לא 3808 |
|---|---|---|---|---|---|---|---|---|---|
| yaqadshu | 'at | ha'am | babigdeyhem. | | uara'sham | la' | yagalechu, | uapera' | la' |
| **they shall sanctify** | | **the people** | **with their garments** | | **their heads** | **Neither** | **shall they shave** | **their locks** | **nor** |

| ישלחו 7971 | כסום 3697 | יכסמו 3697 | את 853 | ראשיהם 7218: | 44:21 | ויין 3196 | לא 3808 | ישתו 8354 | כל 3605 | כהן 3548 |
|---|---|---|---|---|---|---|---|---|---|---|
| yashalechu; | kasoum | yiksamu | 'at | ra'sheyhem. | | uayayin | la' | yishtu | kal | kohen; |
| **suffer to grow long** | **they shall** | **only** | | **polltheir heads** | | **wine** | **Neither** | **shall drink** | **any** | **priest** |

| בבואם 935 | אל 413 | החצר 2691 | הפנימית 6442: | 44:22 | ואלמנה 490 | וגרושה 1644 | לא 3808 | יקחו 3947 | להם 3807a |
|---|---|---|---|---|---|---|---|---|---|
| babou'am | 'al | hechatzer | hapaniymiyt. | | ua'almanah | uagrushah, | la' | yiqchu | lahem |
| **when they enter** | **into** | **court** | **the inner** | | **a widow** | **nor her that is put away** | **Neither** | **shall they take** | **their** |

| לנשים 802 | כי 3588 | אם 518 | בתולת 1330 | מזרע 2233 | בית 1004 | ישראל 3478 | והאלמנה 490 | אשר 834 | תהיה 1961 | אלמנה 490 | מכהן 3548 |
|---|---|---|---|---|---|---|---|---|---|---|---|
| lanashiym; | kiy | 'am | batulot, | mizera' | beyt | yisra'ael, | uaha'almanah | 'asher | tihayeh | 'almanah, | mikohen |
| **for wives** | **but** | **rather** | **maidens of** | **the seed of** | **the house of** | **Israel** | **or the offspring** | **that** | **had** | **a widow** | **a priest** |

Eze 44:16 They shall enter into my sanctuary, and they shall come near to my table, to minister unto me, and they shall keep my charge.17 And it shall come to pass, that when they enter in at the gates of the inner court, they shall be clothed with linen garments; and no wool shall come upon them, whiles they minister in the gates of the inner court, and within.18 They shall have linen bonnets upon their heads, and shall have linen breeches upon their loins; they shall not gird themselves with anything that causeth sweat.19 And when they go forth into the utter court, even into the utter court to the people, they shall put off their garments wherein they ministered, and lay them in the holy chambers, and they shall put on other garments; and they shall not sanctify the people with their garments.20 Neither shall they shave their heads, nor suffer their locks to grow long; they shall only poll their heads.21 Neither shall any priest drink wine, when they enter into the inner court.22 Neither shall they take for their wives a widow, nor her that is put away: but they shall take maidens of the seed of the house of Israel, or a widow that had a priest before.

| יקחו 3947: | 44:23 | ואת 853 | עמי 5971 | יורו 3384 | בין 996 | קדש 6944 | לחל 2455 | ובין 996 |
|---|---|---|---|---|---|---|---|---|
| yiqachu. | | ua'at | 'amiy | youru, | beyn | qodesh | lachol; | uabeyn |
| **_before_ they shall take** | | **_And_** | **my people** | **they shall teach** | **_the difference_ between** | **the holy** | **and profane** | **and between** |

| טמא 2931 | לטהור 2889 | יודעם 3045: | 44:24 | ועל 5921 | ריב 7379 | המה 1992 | יעמדו 5975 | לשפט 8199 |
|---|---|---|---|---|---|---|---|---|
| tamea' | latahour | youdi'am. | | ua'al | riyb, | hemah | ya'amdu | lishpat |
| **the unclean** | **_and_ the clean** | **cause them to discern** | | **And in** | **controversy** | **they** | **shall stand** | **in judgment** |

| במשפטי 4941 | ושפטהו 8199 | ואת 853 | תורתי 8451 | ואת 853 | חקתי 2708 | בכל 3605 | מועדי 4150 |
|---|---|---|---|---|---|---|---|
| bamishpatay | uashapathu | ua'at | tourotay | ua'at | chuqotay | bakal | mou'aday |
| **according to my judgments** | **_and_ they shall judge it** | **_and_** | **my laws** | **_and_** | **my statutes** | **in all** | **mine assemblies** |

| ישמרו 8104 | ואת 853 | שבתותי 7676 | יקדשו 6942: | 44:25 | ואל 413 | מת 4191 | אדם 120 | לא 3808 | יבוא 935 | לטמאה 2930 |
|---|---|---|---|---|---|---|---|---|---|---|
| yishmoru, | ua'at | shabtoutay | yaqadeshu. | | ua'al | met | 'adam, | la' | yabou'a | latama'ah; |
| **they shall keep** | **_and_** | **my sabbaths** | **they shall hallow** | | **And at** | **dead** | **person** | **no** | **they shall come** | **to defile themselves** |

| כי 3588 | אם 518 | לאב 1 | ולאם 517 | ולבן 1121 | ולבת 1323 | לאח 251 | ולאחות 269 | אשר 834 | לא 3808 | היתה 1961 | לאיש 376 |
|---|---|---|---|---|---|---|---|---|---|---|---|
| kiy | 'am | la'ab | ual'am | ualben | ualbat | la'ach, | ual'achout | 'asher | la' | hayatah | la'aysh |
| **but** | **rather** | **for father** | **or for mother** | **or for son** | **or for daughter** | **for brother** | **or for sister** | **that** | **no** | **has had** | **husband** |

| יטמאו 2930: | 44:26 | ואחרי 310 | טהרתו 2893 | שבעת 7651 | ימים 3117 | יספרו 5608 | לו 3807a: | 44:27 |
|---|---|---|---|---|---|---|---|---|
| yitama'au. | | ua'acharey | taharatou; | shib'at | yamiym | yisparu | lou'. | |
| **they may defile themselves** | | **And after** | **he is cleansed** | **seven** | **days** | **they shall reckon** | **unto him** | |

| וביום 3117 | באו 935 | אל 413 | הקדש 6944 | אל 413 | החצר 2691 | הפנימית 6442 | לשרת 8334 | בקדש 6944 | יקריב 7126 |
|---|---|---|---|---|---|---|---|---|---|
| uabyoum | bo'au | 'al | haqodesh | 'al | hechatzer | hapaniymiyt | lasharet | baqodesh, | yaqriyb |
| **And in the day** | **that he goes** | **into** | **the sanctuary** | **unto** | **court** | **the inner** | **to minister** | **in the sanctuary** | **he shall offer** |

| חטאתו 2403 | נאם 5002 | אדני 136 | יהוה 3069: | 44:28 | והיתה 1961 | להם 3807a | לנחלה 5159 | אני 589 | נחלתם 5159 |
|---|---|---|---|---|---|---|---|---|---|
| chata'tou; | na'am | 'adonay | Yahuah. | | uahayatah | lahem | lanachalah, | 'aniy | nachalatam; |
| **his sin offering** | **saith** | **Adonai** | **Yahuah** | | **And it shall be** | **unto them** | **for an inheritance** | **I _am_** | **their inheritance** |

| ואחזה 272 | לא 3808 | תתנו 5414 | להם 3807a | בישראל 3478 | אני 589 | אחזתם 272: | 44:29 | המנחה 4503 | והחטאת 2403 |
|---|---|---|---|---|---|---|---|---|---|
| aa'achuzah, | la' | titanu | lahem | bayisra'ael, | 'aniy | 'achuzatam. | | haminchah | uahachata't |
| **and possession** | **no** | **you shall give** | **them** | **in Israel** | **I _am_** | **their possession** | | **the meat offering** | **and the sin offering** |

| והאשם 817 | המה 1992 | יאכלום 398 | וכל 3605 | חרם 2764 | בישראל 3478 | להם 3807a | יהיה 1961: | 44:30 | וראשית 7225 |
|---|---|---|---|---|---|---|---|---|---|
| uaha'asham, | hemah | ya'kalum; | uakal | charim | bayisra'ael | lahem | yihayeh. | | uarea'shiyt |
| **and the trespass offering** | **They** | **shall eat** | **and every** | **dedicated thing** | **in Israel** | **theirs** | **shall be** | | **And the first of** |

| כל 3605 | בכורי 1061 | כל 3605 | וכל 3605 | תרומת 8641 | כל 3605 | מכל 3605 | תרומותיכם 8641 | לכהנים 3548 | יהיה 1961 |
|---|---|---|---|---|---|---|---|---|---|
| kal | bikurey | kal | uakal | tarumat | kol, | mikol | tarumouteykem, | lakohaniym | yihayeh; |
| **all** | **the firstfruits of** | **all _things_** | **and every** | **oblation of** | **all** | **of every _sort of_** | **your oblations** | **the priest's** | **shall be** |

| וראשית 7225 | ערסותיכם 6182 | תתנו 5414 | לכהן 3548 | להניח 5117 | ברכה 1293 | אל 413 | ביתך 1004: |
|---|---|---|---|---|---|---|---|
| uarea'shiyt | arisouteykem | titanu | lakohen, | lahaniyach | barakah | 'al | beytaka. |
| **also the first of** | **your dough** | **you shall give** | **unto the priest** | **to rest** | **that he may cause the blessing** | **on** | **your house** |

Eze 30:23 And they shall teach my people the difference between the holy and profane, and cause them to discern between the unclean and the clean.24 And in controversy they shall stand in judgment; and they shall judge it according to my judgments: and they shall keep my laws and my statutes in all mine assemblies; and they shall hallow my sabbaths.25 And they shall come at no dead person to defile themselves: but for father, or for mother, or for son, or for daughter, for brother, or for sister that has had no husband, they may defile themselves.26 And after he is cleansed, they shall reckon unto him seven days.27 And in the day that he go into the sanctuary, unto the inner court, to minister in the sanctuary, he shall offer his sin offering, saith YHUH G-D.28 And it shall be unto them for an inheritance: I am their inheritance: and you shall give them no possession in Israel: I am their possession.29 They shall eat the meat offering, and the sin offering, and the trespass offering; and every dedicated thing in Israel shall be theirs.30 And the first of all the firstfruits of all things, and every oblation of all, of every sort of your oblations, shall be the priest's: you shall also give unto the priest the first of your dough, that he may cause the blessing to rest in your house.

**44:31**

כל 3605 נבלה 5038 וטרפה 2966 מן 4480 העוף 5775 ומן 4480 הבהמה 929 לא 3808 יאכלו 398 הכהנים 3548:

kal nabelah uatrepah, min ha'aup uamin habehemah; la' ya'kalu hakohaniym.

**any thing that is dead of itself or torn whether *it be* fowl or beast not shall eat of The priests**

**Ezek 45:1**

ובהפילכם 5307 את 853 הארץ 776 בנחלה 5159 תרימו 7311 תרומה 8641 ליהוה 3068

uabhapiylakem 'at ha'aretz banachalah, tariMu tarumah laYahuah

**Moreover when you shall divide by lot the land for inheritance you shall offer an oblation unto Yahuah**

קדש 6944 מן 4480 הארץ 776 ארך 753 חמשה 2568 ועשרים 6242 אלף 505 ארך 753 ורחב 7341

qodesh min ha'aretz 'arek, chamishah ua'asriym 'alep 'arek, uarochab

**an holy portion of the land the length *shall be* of five and twenty thousand *reeds* the length and the breadth**

**45:2**

עשרה 6235 אלף 505 קדש 6944 הוא 1931 בכל 3605 גבולה 1366 סביב 5439: יהיה 1961 מזה 2088 אל 413

'asarah 'alep; qodesh hua' bakal gabulah sabiyb. yihayeh mizeh 'al

***shall be* ten thousand *shall be* holy This in all the borders thereof round about there shall be Of this for**

הקדש 6944 חמש 2568 מאות 3967 בחמש 2568 מאות 3967 מרבע 7251 סביב 5439 וחמשים 2572 אמה 520

haqodesh, chamesh me'aut bachamesh me'aut maruba' sabiyb; uachamishiym 'amah,

**the sanctuary five hundred *in length* with five hundred *in breadth* square round about and fifty cubits**

**45:3**

מגרש 4054 לו 3807a סביב 5439: ומן 4480 המדה 4060 הזאת 2063 תמוד 4058 ארך 753 חמש 2568 ועשרים 6242

migrash lou' sabiyb. uamin hamidah haza't tamoud, 'arek, chamesh ua'asriym

**for the suburbs thereof round about And of measure this shall you measure the length of five and twenty**

**45:4**

אלף 505 ורחב 7341 עשרת 6235 אלפים 505 ובו 871a יהיה 1961 המקדש 4720 קדש 6944 קדשים 6944: קדש 6944

'alep, uarochab 'aseret 'alapiym; uabou yihayeh hamiqdash qodesh qadashiym. qodesh

**thousand and the breadth of ten thousand and in it shall be the sanctuary *and* the most holy place *The* holy**

מן 4480 הארץ 776 הוא 1931 לכהנים 3548 משרתי 8334 המקדש 4720 יהיה 1961 הקרבים 7131 לשרת 8334

min ha'aretz hua', lakohaniym masharatey hamiqdash yihayeh, haqarebiym lasharet

***portion* of the land he for the priests the ministers of the sanctuary shall be which shall come near to minister unto**

**45:5**

את 853 יהוה 3068 והיה 1961 להם 3807a מקום 4725 לבתים 1004 ומקדש 4720 למקדש 4720: וחמשה 2568 ועשרים 6242

'at Yahuah; uahayah lahem maqoum labatiym, uamiqdash lamiqdash. uachamishah ua'asriym

**Yahuah and it shall be their a place for houses and an holy place for the sanctuary And the five and twenty**

אלף 505 ארך 753 ועשרת 6235 אלפים 505 רחב 7341 יהיה 1961 ללוים 3881 משרתי 8334 הבית 1004 להם 1992

'alep 'arek, ua'aseret 'alapiym rochab; yihayeh lalauiyim masharatey habayit lahem

**thousand of length and the ten thousand of breadth shall also have the Levites the ministers of the house for themselves**

**45:6**

לאחזה 272 עשרים 6242 לשכת 3957: ואחזת 272 העיר 5892 תתנו 5414 חמשת 2568 אלפים 505 רחב 7341

la'achuzah 'asriym lashakot. ua'achuzat ha'ayr titanu, chameshet 'alapiym rochab,

**for a possession *for* twenty chambers And the possession of the city you shall appoint five thousand broad**

וארך 753 חמשה 2568 ועשרים 6242 אלף 505 לעמת 5980 תרומת 8641 הקדש 6944 לכל 3605 בית 1004 ישראל 3478

ua'arek, chamishah ua'asriym 'alep, la'amat tarumat haqodesh; lakal beyt yisra'ael

**and long five and twenty thousand over against the oblation of the holy *portion* for the whole house of Israel**

Eze 44:31 The priests shall not eat of anything that is dead of itself, or torn, whether it be fowl or beast. **Eze** 45:1 Moreover, when you shall divide by lot the land for inheritance, you shall offer an oblation unto YHUH, an holy portion of the land: the length shall be the length of five and twenty thousand reeds, and the breadth shall be ten thousand. This shall be holy in all the borders thereof round about.2 Of this there shall be for the sanctuary five hundred in length, with five hundred in breadth, square round about; and fifty cubits round about for the suburbs thereof.3 And of this measure shall you measure the length of five and twenty thousand, and the breadth of ten thousand: and in it shall be the sanctuary and the most holy place.4 The holy portion of the land shall be for the priests the ministers of the sanctuary, which shall come near to minister unto YHUH: and it shall be a place for their houses, and an holy place for the sanctuary.5 And the five and twenty thousand of length, and the ten thousand of breadth, shall also the Levites, the ministers of the house, have for themselves, for a possession for twenty chambers.6 And you shall appoint the possession of the city five thousand broad, and five and twenty thousand long, over against the oblation of the holy portion: it shall be for the whole house of Israel.

| יהיה 1961: | 45:7 ולנשיא 5387 | מזה 2088 | ומזה 2088 | לתרומת 8641 | הקדש 6944 |
|---|---|---|---|---|---|
| yihayeh. | ualanasiy'a | mizeh | uamizeh | litrumat | haqodesh |
| **it shall be** | **And a *portion shall be* for the prince** | **on the one *side*** | **and on the other *side*** | **of the oblation of** | **the holy** |

| ולאחזת 272 | העיר 5892 | אל 413 | פני 6440 | תרומת 8641 | הקדש 6944 | ואל 413 | פני 6440 | אחזת 272 |
|---|---|---|---|---|---|---|---|---|
| uala'achuzat | ha'ayr, | 'al | paney | tarumat | haqodesh | ua'al | paney | 'achuzat |
| ***portion* and of the possession of** | **the city** | **to** | **before** | **the oblation of** | **the holy *portion*** | **and to** | **before** | **the possession of** |

| העיר 5892 | מפאת 6285 | ים 3220 | ימה 3220 | ומפאת 6285 | קדמה 6924 | קדימה 6921 | וארך 753 | לעמות 5980 | אחד 259 |
|---|---|---|---|---|---|---|---|---|---|
| ha'ayr, | mip'at | yam | yamah, | uamipa'at | qedamah | qadiymah; | ua'arek, | la'umout | 'achad |
| **the city** | **from side** | **the west** | **westward** | **and from side** | **the east** | **eastward** | **and the length** | ***shall be* over against** | **one of** |

| החלקים 2506 | מגבול 1366 | ים 3220 | אל 413 | גבול 1366 | קדימה 6921: | 45:8 לארץ 776 | יהיה 1961 | לו 3807a | לאחזה 272 | בישראל 3478 | ולא 3808 |
|---|---|---|---|---|---|---|---|---|---|---|---|
| hachalaqiym, | migbul | yam | 'al | gabul | qadiymah. | la'aretz | yihayeh | lou' | la'achuzah | bayisra'ael; | uala' |
| **the portions** | **from border** | ***the* west** | **unto** | **border** | ***the* east** | **In the land** | **shall be** | **his** | **possession** | **in Israel** | **and no** |

| יונו 3238 | עוד 5750 | נשיאי 5387 | את 853 | עמי 5971 | והארץ 776 | יתנו 5414 | לבית 1004 | ישראל 3478 |
|---|---|---|---|---|---|---|---|---|
| younu | 'aud | nasiy'ay | 'at | 'amiy, | uaha'aretz | yitanu | labeyt | yisra'ael |
| **shall oppress** | **more** | **my princes** | | **my people** | **and *the rest of* the land** | **shall they give** | **to the house of** | **Israel** |

| לשבטיהם 7626: | 45:9 כה 3541 | אמר 559 | אדני 136 | יהוה 3069 | רב 7227 | לכם 3807a | נשיאי 5387 | ישראל 3478 | חמס 2555 | ושד 7701 |
|---|---|---|---|---|---|---|---|---|---|---|
| lashibteyhem. | koh | 'amar | 'adonay | Yahuah | rab | lakem | nasiy'aey | yisra'ael, | chamas | uashod |
| **according to their tribes** | **Thus** | **saith** | **Adonai** | **Yahuah** | **Let it suffice** | **to you** | **O princes of** | **Israel** | **violence** | **and spoil** |

| הסירו 5493 | ומשפט 4941 | וצדקה 6666 | עשו 6213 | הרימו 7311 | גרשתיכם 1646 | מעל 5921 | עמי 5971 | נאם 5002 | אדני 136 | יהוה 3069: 45:10 |
|---|---|---|---|---|---|---|---|---|---|---|
| hasiyru, | uamishpat | uatzdaqah | 'asu; | hariymu | garushoteykem | me'al | 'amiy, | na'am | 'adonay | Yahuah. |
| **remove** | **and judgment** | **and justice** | **execute** | **take away** | **your exactions** | **from** | **my people** | **saith** | **Adonai** | **Yahuah** |

| מאזני 3976 | צדק 6664 | ואיפת 374 | צדק 6664 | ובת 1324 | צדק 6664 | יהי 1961 | לכם 3807a: | 45:11 האיפה 374 | והבת 1324 | תכן 8506 | אחד 259 |
|---|---|---|---|---|---|---|---|---|---|---|---|
| ma'zaney | tzedeq | ua'aeypat | tzedeq | uaba'at | tzedeq | yahiy | lakem. | ha'aeypah | uahabat, | token | 'achad |
| **balances** | **just** | **and a ephah** | **just** | **and a bath** | **just** | **shall have** | **to you** | **The ephah** | **and the bath** | **measure *of*** | **one** |

| יהיה 1961 | לשאת 5375 | מעשר 4643 | החמר 2563 | הבת 1324 | ועשירת 6224 | החמר 2563 | האיפה 374 | אל 413 | החמר 2563 |
|---|---|---|---|---|---|---|---|---|---|
| yihayeh, | lasea't | ma'asar | hachamor | habat; | ua'asiyriyt | hachamor | ha'aeypah, | 'al | hachamor |
| **shall be** | **that may contain** | ***the* tenth part of** | **an homer** | **the bath** | **the tenth part of** | **an homer** | **the ephah** | **after** | **the homer** |

| יהיה 1961 | מתכנתו 4971: | 45:12 והשקל 8255 | עשרים 6242 | גרה 1626 | עשרים 6242 | שקלים 8255 | חמשה 2568 | ועשרים 6242 |
|---|---|---|---|---|---|---|---|---|
| yihayeh | matkuntou. | uahasheqel | 'asriym | gerah; | 'asriym | shaqaliym | chamishah | ua'asriym |
| **shall be** | **the measure thereof** | **And the sheqel** | ***shall be* twenty** | **gerahs** | **twenty** | **shekels** | **five** | **and twenty** |

| שקלים 8255 | עשרה 6235 | וחמשה 2568 | שקל 8255 | המנה 4488 | יהיה 1961 | לכם 3807a: | 45:13 זאת 2063 | התרומה 8641 | אשר 834 | תרימו 7311 |
|---|---|---|---|---|---|---|---|---|---|---|
| shaqaliym, | 'asarah | uachamishah | sheqel, | hamaneh | yihayeh | lakem. | za't | hatarumah | 'asher | tariymu; |
| **shekels** | **ten** | **five** | **shekels** | **maneh** | **shall be** | **to your** | **This** | ***is* the oblation** | **that** | **you shall offer** |

| ששית 8345 | האיפה 374 | מחמר 2563 | החטים 2406 | וששיתם 8341 | האיפה 374 | מחמר 2563 |
|---|---|---|---|---|---|---|
| shishiyt | ha'aeypah | mechomer | hachitiym, | uashishiytem | ha'aeypah, | mechomer |
| ***the* sixth part of** | **an ephah** | **of an homer of** | **wheat** | **and you shall give the sixth part of** | **an ephah** | **of an homer of** |

Eze 45:7 And a portion shall be for the prince on the one side and on the other side of the oblation of the holy portion, and of the possession of the city, before the oblation of the holy portion, and before the possession of the city, from the west side westward, and from the east side eastward: and the length shall be over against one of the portions, from the west border unto the east border.8 In the land shall be his possession in Israel: and my princes shall no more oppress my people; and the rest of the land shall they give to the house of Israel according to their tribes.9 Thus saith YHUH G-D; Let it suffice you, O princes of Israel: remove violence and spoil, and execute judgment and justice, take away your exactions from my people, saith YHUH G-D.10 You shall have just balances, and a just ephah, and a just bath. I 11 The ephah and the bath shall be of one measure, that the bath may contain the tenth part of an homer, and the ephah the tenth part of an homer: the measure thereof shall be after the homer.12 And the shekel shall be twenty gerahs: twenty shekels, five and twenty shekels, fifteen shekels, shall be your manneh.13 This is the oblation that you shall offer; the sixth part of an ephah of an homer of wheat, and you shall give the sixth part of an ephah of an homer of barley:

| השערים 8184: | 45:14 וחק 2706 | השמן 8081 | הבת 1324 | השמן 8081 | מעשר 4643 | הבת 1324 |
|---|---|---|---|---|---|---|
| hasa'ariym. | uachoq | hashemen | habat | hashemen, | ma'asar | habat |
| **barley** | **Concerning the ordinance of** | **oil** | **the bath of** | **oil** | ***you shall offer* the tenth part of** | **a bath** |

| מן 4480 | הכר 3734 | עשרת 6235 | הבתים 1324 | חמר 2563 | כי 3588 | עשרת 6235 | הבתים 1324 | חמר 2563: | 45:15 ושה 7716 | אחת 259 | מן 4480 |
|---|---|---|---|---|---|---|---|---|---|---|---|
| min | hakor, | 'aseret | habatiym | chamor; | kiy | 'aseret | habatiym | chamor. | uaseh | 'achat | min |
| **out of** | **the cor *which is of*** | **ten** | **baths** | **an homer** | **for** | **ten** | **baths** | ***are* an homer** | **And lamb** | **one** | **out of** |

| הצאן 6629 | מן 4480 | המאתים 3967 | ממשקה 4945 | ישראל 3478 | למנחה 4503 | ולעולה 5930 |
|---|---|---|---|---|---|---|
| hatza'an | min | hama'tayim | mimashqeh | yisra'ael, | laminchah | ual'aulah |
| **the flock** | **out of** | **two hundred** | **out of the fat pastures of** | **Israel** | **for a meat offering** | **and for a burnt offering** |

| ולשלמים 8002 | לכפר 3722 | עליהם 5921 | נאם 5002 | אדני 136 | יהוה 3069: | 45:16 כל 3605 | העם 5971 | הארץ 776 |
|---|---|---|---|---|---|---|---|---|
| ualishlamiym; | lakaper | 'aleyhem, | na'am | 'adonay | Yahuah. | kal | ha'am | ha'aretz, |
| **and for peace offerings** | **to make reconciliation** | **for them** | **saith** | **Adonai** | **Yahuah** | **All** | **the people *of*** | **the land** |

| יהיו 1961 | אל 413 | התרומה 8641 | הזאת 2063 | לנשיא 5387 | בישראל 3478: | 45:17 ועל 5921 | הנשיא 5387 | יהיה 1961 |
|---|---|---|---|---|---|---|---|---|
| yihayu | 'al | hatarumah | haza't; | lanasiy'a | bayisra'ael. | ua'al | hanasiy'a | yihayeh, |
| **shall give** | **to** | **oblation** | **this** | **for the prince** | **in Israel** | **And on** | **the prince's** | **it shall be** |

| העולות 5930 | והמנחה 4503 | והנסך 5262 | בחגים 2282 | ובחדשים 2320 | ובשבתות 7676 |
|---|---|---|---|---|---|
| ha'aulout | uahaminchah | uahanesek | bachagiym | uabechadashiym | uabashabatout, |
| ***part to give* burnt offerings** | **and meat offerings** | **and drink offerings** | **in the feasts** | **and in the new moons** | **and in the sabbaths** |

| בכל 3605 | מועדי 4150 | בית 1004 | ישראל 3478 | הוא 1931 | יעשה 6213 | את 853 | החטאת 2403 | ואת 853 | המנחה 4503 | ואת 853 |
|---|---|---|---|---|---|---|---|---|---|---|
| bakal | mou'adey | beyt | yisra'ael; | hua' | ya'aseh | 'at | hachata't | ua'at | haminchah, | ua'at |
| **in all** | **solemnities of** | **the house of** | **Israel** | **he** | **shall prepare** | | **the sin offering** | ***and*** | **the meat offering** | ***and*** |

| העולה 5930 | ואת 853 | השלמים 8002 | לכפר 3722 | בעד 1157 | בית 1004 | ישראל 3478: | 45:18 כה 3541 | אמר 559 |
|---|---|---|---|---|---|---|---|---|
| ha'aulah | ua'at | hashalamiym, | lakaper | ba'ad | beyt | yisra'ael. | koh | 'amar |
| **the burnt offering** | ***and*** | **the peace offerings** | **to make reconciliation** | **for** | **the house of** | **Israel** | **Thus** | **saith** |

| אדני 136 | יהוה 3068 | בראשון 7223 | באחד 259 | לחדש 2320 | תקח 3947 | פר 6499 | בן 1121 | בקר 1241 | תמים 8549 |
|---|---|---|---|---|---|---|---|---|---|
| 'adonay | Yahuah | bara'shoun | ba'achad | lachodesh, | tiqach | par | ben | baqar | tamiym; |
| **Adonai** | **Yahuah** | **In the first *month*** | **in the first *day*** | **of the month** | **you shall take** | **a bullock** | **young** | **bull** | **without blemish** |

| וחטאת 2398 | את 853 | המקדש 4720: | 45:19 ולקח 3947 | הכהן 3548 | מדם 1818 | החטאת 2403 | ונתן 5414 | אל 413 | מזוזת 4201 |
|---|---|---|---|---|---|---|---|---|---|
| uachitea'ta | 'at | hamiqdash. | ualaqach | hakohen | midam | hachata't, | uanatan | 'al | mazuzat |
| **and cleanse** | | **the sanctuary** | **And shall take** | **the priest** | **of the blood of** | **the sin offering** | **and put *it*** | **upon** | **the posts of** |

| הבית 1004 | ואל 413 | ארבע 702 | פנות 6438 | העזרה 5835 | למזבח 4196 | ועל 5921 | מזוזת 4201 | שער 8179 | החצר 2691 |
|---|---|---|---|---|---|---|---|---|---|
| habayit, | ua'al | 'arba | pinout | ha'azarah | lamizabeach; | ua'al | mazuzat, | sha'ar | hechatzer |
| **the house** | **and upon** | ***the* four** | **corners of** | **the settle** | **of the altar** | **and upon** | **the posts of** | **the gate of** | **court** |

| הפנימית 6442: | 45:20 וכן 3651 | תעשה 6213 | בשבעה 7651 | בחדש 2320 | מאיש 376 | שגה 7686 | ומפתי 6612 |
|---|---|---|---|---|---|---|---|
| hapaniymiyt. | uaken | ta'aseh | bashib'ah | bachodesh, | me'aysh | shogeh | uamipetiy; |
| **the inner** | **And so** | **you shall do *the*** | **seventh *day*** | **of the month** | **for every one** | **that err** | **and for *him that is* simple** |

Eze 45:14 Concerning the ordinance of oil, the bath of oil, you shall offer the tenth part of a bath out of the cor, which is an homer of ten baths; for ten baths are an homer:15 And one lamb out of the flock, out of two hundred, out of the fat pastures of Israel; for a meat offering, and for a burnt offering, and for peace offerings, to make reconciliation for them, saith YHUH G-D.16 All the people of the land shall give this oblation for the prince in Israel.17 And it shall be the prince's part to give burnt offerings, and meat offerings, and drink offerings, in the feasts, and in the new moons, and in the sabbaths, in all solemnities of the house of Israel: he shall prepare the sin offering, and the meat offering, and the burnt offering, and the peace offerings, to make reconciliation for the house of Israel.18 Thus saith YHUH G-D; In the first month, in the first day of the month, you shall take a young bullock without blemish, and cleanse the sanctuary:19 And the priest shall take of the blood of the sin offering, and put it upon the posts of the house, and upon the four corners of the settle of the altar, and upon the posts of the gate of the inner court.20 And so you shall do the seventh day of the month foreveryone that erreth, and for him that is simple: so shall you reconcile the house.

| וכפרתם 3722 | את 853 | הבית 1004: | **45:21** בראשון 7223 | בארבעה 702 | עשר 6240 | יום 3117 | לחדש 2320 | יהיה 1961 | לכם 3807a |
|---|---|---|---|---|---|---|---|---|---|
| uakipartem | 'at | habayit. | bara'shoun | ba'arbah | 'asar | youm | lachodesh, | yihayeh | lakem |
| **so shall you reconcile** | | **the house** | **In the first *month*** | **in the four** | **ten** | **day** | **of the month** | **shall have** | **to you** |

| הפסח 6453 | חג 2282 | שבעות 7620 | ימים 3117 | מצות 4682 | יאכל 398: | **45:22** ועשה 6213 | הנשיא 5387 | ביום 3117 |
|---|---|---|---|---|---|---|---|---|
| hapasach; | chag | shabu'aut | yamiym, | matzout | ye'akel. | ua'asah | hanasiy'a | bayoum |
| **the passover** | **a feast of** | **seven** | **days** | **unleavened bread** | **shall be eaten** | **And shall prepare** | **the prince** | **upon day** |

| ההוא 1931 | בעדו 1157 | ובעד 1157 | כל 3605 | עם 5971 | הארץ 776 | פר 6499 | חטאת 2403: | **45:23** ושבעת 7651 | ימי 3117 | החג 2282 |
|---|---|---|---|---|---|---|---|---|---|---|
| hahua', | ba'adou | uab'ad | kal | 'am | ha'aretz; | par | chata't. | uashib'at | yamey | hechag |
| **that** | **for himself** | **and for** | **all** | **the people of** | **the land** | **a bullock** | ***for* a sin offering** | **And seven** | **days of** | **the feast** |

| יעשה 6213 | עולה 5930 | ליהוה 3068 | שבעת 7651 | פרים 6499 | ושבעת 7651 | אילים 352 | תמימם 8549 | ליום 3117 | שבעת 7651 |
|---|---|---|---|---|---|---|---|---|---|
| ya'aseh | aulah | laYahuah | shib'at | pariym | uashib'at | 'aeyliym | tamiymim | layoum, | shib'at |
| **he shall prepare** | **a burnt offering** | **to Yahuah** | **seven** | **bullocks** | **and seven** | **rams** | **without blemish** | **daily** | **seven** |

| הימים 3117 | וחטאת 2403 | שעיר 8163 | עזים 5795 | ליום 3117: | **45:24** ומנחה 4503 | איפה 374 | לפר 6499 | ואיפה 374 |
|---|---|---|---|---|---|---|---|---|
| hayamiym; | uachata't | sa'ayr | aziym | layoum. | uaminchah, | 'aeypah | lapar | ua'aeypah |
| **the days** | **and a sin offering** | **a kid of** | **the goats** | **daily *for*** | **And a meat offering of** | **an ephah** | **for a bullock** | **and an ephah** |

| לאיל 352 | יעשה 6213 | ושמן 8081 | הין 1969 | לאיפה 374: | **45:25** בשביעי 7651 | בחמשה 2568 | עשר 6240 | יום 3117 | לחדש 2320 |
|---|---|---|---|---|---|---|---|---|---|
| la'ayil | ya'aseh; | uashemen | hiyn | la'aeypah. | bashabiy'ay | bachamishah | 'asar | youm | lachodesh |
| **for a ram** | **he shall prepare** | **and oil** | **an hin of** | **for an ephah** | **In the seventh *month*** | **five** | **ten** | **day** | **of the month** |

| בחג 2282 | יעשה 6213 | כאלה 428 | שבעת 7651 | הימים 3117 | כחטאת 2403 | כעלה 5930 |
|---|---|---|---|---|---|---|
| bachag, | ya'aseh | ka'aeleh | shib'at | hayamiym; | kachata't | ka'aulah, |
| **in the feast of** | **shall he do** | **the like** | **seven** | **the days** | **according to the sin offering** | **according to the burnt offering** |

| וכמנחה 4503 | וכשמן 8081: |
|---|---|
| uakaminchah | uakashamen. |
| **and according to the meat offering** | **and according to the oil** |

**Ezek 46:1**

| כה 3541 | אמר 559 | אדני 136 | יהוה 3069 | שער 8179 | החצר 2691 | הפנימית 6442 | הפנה 6437 | קדים 6921 | יהיה 1961 | סגור 5462 |
|---|---|---|---|---|---|---|---|---|---|---|
| koh | 'amar | 'adonay | Yahuah | sha'ar | hechatzer | hapaniymiyt | haponeh | qadiym, | yihayeh | sagur, |
| **Thus** | **saith** | **Adonai** | **Yahuah** | **The gate of** | **court** | **the inner** | **that looks toward** | **the east** | **shall be** | **shut** |

| ששת 8337 | ימי 3117 | המעשה 4639 | וביום 3117 | השבת 7676 | יפתח 6605 | וביום 3117 | החדש 2320 |
|---|---|---|---|---|---|---|---|
| sheshet | yamey | hama'aseh; | uabyoum | hashabat | yipateach, | uabyoum | hachodesh |
| **six** | **days** | **the working** | **and in the day of** | **the sabbath** | **it shall be opened** | **and in the day of** | **the new moon** |

| יפתח 6605: | **46:2** ובא 935 | הנשיא 5387 | דרך 1870 | אולם 197 | השער 8179 | מחוץ 2351 | ועמד 5975 | על 5921 |
|---|---|---|---|---|---|---|---|---|
| yipateach. | uaba' | hanasiy'a | derek | 'ualam | hasha'ar | michutz, | ua'amad | 'al |
| **it shall be opened** | **And shall enter** | **the prince** | ***by* the way of** | **the porch of** | ***that* gate** | **without** | **and shall stand** | **by** |

| מזוזת 4201 | השער 8179 | ועשו 6213 | הכהנים 3548 | את 853 | עולתו 5930 | ואת 853 | שלמיו 8002 | והשתחוה 7812 |
|---|---|---|---|---|---|---|---|---|
| mazuzat | hasha'ar, | ua'asu | hakohaniym, | 'at | alatou | ua'at | shalamayu, | uahishtachauah |
| **the post of** | **the gate** | **and shall prepare** | **the priests** | | **his burnt offering *and*** | | **his peace offerings** | **and he shall worship** |

Eze 45:21 In the first month, in the fourteenth day of the month, you shall have the passover, a feast of seven days; unleavened bread shall be eaten.22 And upon that day shall the prince prepare for himself and for all the people of the land a bullock for a sin offering.23 And seven days of the feast he shall prepare a burnt offering to YHUH, seven bullocks and seven rams without blemish daily the seven days; and a kid of the goats daily for a sin offering.24 And he shall prepare a meat offering of an ephah for a bullock, and an ephah for a ram, and an hin of oil for an ephah.25 In the seventh month, in the fifteenth day of the month, shall he do the like in the feast of the seven days, according to the sin offering, according to the burnt offering, and according to the meat offering, and according to the oil. **Eze** 46:1 Thus saith YHUH G-D; The gate of the inner court that look toward the east shall be shut the six working days; but on the Sabbath it shall be opened, and in the day of the new moon it shall be opened.2 And the prince shall enter by the way of the porch of that gate without, and shall stand by the post of the gate, and the priests shall prepare his burnt offering and his peace offerings, and he shall worship at the threshold of the gate: then he shall go forth; but the gate shall not be shut until the evening.

על 5921 | מפתן 4670 | השער 8179 | ויצא 3318 | והשער 8179 | לא 3808 | יסגר 5462 | עד 5704 | הערב 6153: | 46:3
'al | miptan | hasha'ar | uayatza'; | uahasha'ar | la' | yisager | 'ad | ha'areb.
**at | the threshold of | the gate | then he shall go forth | but the gate | not | shall be shut | until | the evening**

והשתחוו 7812 | עם 5971 | הארץ 776 | פתח 6607 | השער 8179 | ההוא 1931 | בשבתות 7676 | ובחדשים 2320 | לפני 6440
uahishtachauu | 'am | ha'aretz, | petach | hasha'ar | hahua', | bashabatout | uabechadashiym; | lipney
**Likewise shall worship | the people of | the land *at* | the door of | gate | this | in the sabbaths | and in the new moons | before**

יהוה 3068: | 46:4 | והעלה 5930 | אשר 834 | יקרב 7126 | הנשיא 5387 | ליהוה 3068 | ביום 3117 | השבת 7676 | ששה 8337 | כבשים 3532
Yahuah. | uaha'alah, | 'asher | yaqriyb | hanasiy'a | laYahuah; | bayoum | hashabat, | shishah | kabasiym
**Yahuah | And the burnt offering | that | shall offer | the prince | unto Yahuah | in day | the sabbath | *shall be* six | lambs**

תמימם 8549 | ואיל 352 | תמים 8549: | 46:5 | ומנחה 4503 | איפה 374 | לאיל 352 | ולכבשים 3532
tamiymim | ua'ayil | tamiym. | uaminchah | 'aeypah | la'ayil, | ualakbasiym
**without blemish | and a ram | without blemish | And the meat offering | *shall be* an ephah | for a ram | and for the lambs**

מנחה 4503 | מתת 4991 | ידו 3027 | ושמן 8081 | הין 1969 | לאיפה 374: | 46:6 | וביום 3117
minchah | matat | yadou; | uashemen | hiyn | la'aeypah. | uabyoum
**the meat offering | to give | as he shall be able | and oil | an hin of | to an ephah | And in the day of**

החדש 2320 | פר 6499 | בן 1121 | בקר 1241 | תמימם 8549 | וששת 8337 | כבשם 3532 | ואיל 352 | תמימם 8549
hachodesh, | par | ben | baqar | tamiymim; | uasheshet | kabasiym | ua'ayil | tamiymim
**the new moon *it shall be* | a bullock | young | bull | without blemish | and six | lambs | and a ram | without blemish**

יהיו 1961: | 46:7 | ואיפה 374 | לפר 6499 | ואיפה 374 | לאיל 352 | יעשה 6213 | מנחה 4503 | ולכבשים 3532
yihayu. | ua'aeypah | lapar | ua'aeypah | la'ayil | ya'aseh | minchah, | ualakbasiym,
**they shall be | And an ephah | for a bullock | and an ephah | for a ram | he shall prepare | a meat offering | and for the lambs**

כאשר 834 | תשיג 5381 | ידו 3027 | ושמן 8081 | הין 1969 | לאיפה 374: | 46:8 | ובבוא 935 | הנשיא 5387 | דרך 1870
ka'asher | tasiyg | yadou; | uashemen | hiyn | la'aeypah. | uabba' | hanasiy'a; | derek
**according as | shall attain unto | his hand | and oil | an hin of | to an ephah | And when shall enter | the prince | *by* the way of**

אולם 197 | השער 8179 | יבוא 935 | ובדרכו 1870 | יצא 3318: | 46:9 | ובבוא 935 | עם 5971
'ualam | hasha'ar | yabou'a, | uabdarkou | yetzea'. | uabba' | 'am
**the porch of | *that* gate | he shall go in | and by the way thereof | he shall go forth | But when shall come | the people of**

הארץ 776 | לפני 6440 | יהוה 3068 | במועדים 4150 | הבא 935 | דרך 1870 | שער 8179 | צפון 6828 | להשתחות 7812 | יצא 3318
ha'aretz | lipney | Yahuah | bamou'adiym | haba' | derek | sha'ar | tzapoun | lahishtachauot, | yetzea'
**the land | before | Yahuah | in the solemn feasts | he that enter in | *by* the way of | gate | *the* north | to worship | shall go out**

דרך 1870 | שער 8179 | נגב 5045 | והבא 935 | דרך 1870 | שער 8179 | נגב 5045 | יצא 3318 | דרך 1870 | שער 8179
derek | sha'ar | negeb, | uahaba' | derek | sha'ar | negeb, | yetzea' | derek | sha'ar
***by* the way of | gate | *the* south | and he that enter | *by* the way of | gate | *the* south | shall go forth | *by* the way of | gate**

צפונה 6828 | לא 3808 | ישוב 7725 | דרך 1870 | השער 8179 | אשר 834 | בא 935 | בו 871a | כי 3588 | נכחו 5226 | יצאו 3318
tzapounah; | la' | yashub, | derek | hasha'ar | 'asher | ba' | bou, | kiy | nikchou | yetza'au
***the* north | not | he shall return | *by* the way of | the gate | whereby | he came | in | but | over against it | shall go forth**

Eze 46:3 Likewise the people of the land shall worship at the door of this gate before YHUH in the sabbaths and in the new moons.4 And the burnt offering that the prince shall offer unto YHUH in the Sabbath day shall be six lambs without blemish, and a ram without blemish.5 And the meat offering shall be an ephah for a ram, and the meat offering for the lambs as he shall be able to give, and an hin of oil to an ephah.6 And in the day of the new moon it shall be a young bullock without blemish, and six lambs, and a ram: they shall be without blemish.7 And he shall prepare a meat offering, an ephah for a bullock, and an ephah for a ram, and for the lambs according as his hand shall attain unto, and an hin of oil to an ephah.8 And when the prince shall enter, he shall go in by the way of the porch of that gate, and he shall go forth by the way thereof.9 But when the people of the land shall come before YHUH in the solemn feasts, he that entereth in by the way of the north gate to worship shall go out by the way of the south gate; and he that entereth by the way of the south gate shall go forth by the way of the north gate: he shall not return by the way of the gate whereby he came in, but shall go forth over against it.

46:10 ... 46:11

והנשיא 5387 בתוכם 8432 בבואם 935 יבוא 935 ובצאתם 3318 יצאו 3318:
uahanasiy'a; batoukam babou'am yabou'a, uabtzea'tam yetze'au.
**And the prince in the midst of them when they go in shall go in and when they go forth shall go forth**

ובחגים 2282 ובמועדים 4150 תהיה 1961 המנחה 4503 איפה 374 לפר 6499 ואיפה 374 לאיל 352
uabachagiym uabamou'adiym, tihayeh haminchah 'aeypah lapar ua'aeypah la'ayil,
**And in the feasts and in the solemnities shall be the meat offering an ephah to a bullock and ephah to a ram**

46:12
ולכבשים 3532 מתת 4991 ידו 3027 ושמן 8081 הין 1969 לאיפה 374: וכי 3588 יעשה 6213 הנשיא 5387 נדבה 5071
ualakbasiym matat yadou; uashemen hiyn la'aeypah. uakiy ya'aseh hanasiy'a nadabah
**and to the lambs to give as he is able and oil an hin of to an ephah Now when shall prepare the prince a voluntary**

עולה 5930 או 176 שלמים 8002 נדבה 5071 ליהוה 3068 ופתח 6605 לו 3807a את 853 השער 8179 הפנה 6437
aulah 'au shalamiym nadabah laYahuah uapatach lou', 'at hasha'ar haponeh
**burnt offering or peace offerings voluntarily unto Yahuah *one* shall then open him the gate that looks toward**

קדים 6921 ועשה 6213 את 853 עלתו 5930 ואת 853 שלמיו 8002 כאשר 834 יעשה 6213 ביום 3117 השבת 7676
qadiym, ua'asah 'at alatou ua'at shalamayu, ka'asher ya'aseh bayoum hashabat;
**the east and he shall prepare his burnt offering *and* his peace offerings as he did on day the sabbath**

46:13
ויצא 3318 וסגר 5462 את 853 השער 8179 אחרי 310 צאתו 3818: וכבש 3532 בן 1121 שנתו 8141
uayatza' uasagar 'at hasha'ar 'acharey tze'atou. uakebes ben shanatou
**then he shall go forth and shall shut the gate after his going forth *one* *of* a lamb of *the* first year**

46:14
תמים 8549 תעשה 6213 עולה 5930 ליום 3117 ליהוה 3068 בבקר 1242 בבקר 1242 תעשה 6213 אתו 853:
tamiym, ta'aseh aulah layoum laYahuah; baboqer baboqer ta'aseh 'atou.
**without blemish You shall prepare a burnt offering daily unto Yahuah every morning you shall prepare it**

ומנחה 4503 תעשה 6213 עליו 5921 בבקר 1242 בבקר 1242 ששית 8345 האיפה 374 ושמן 8081 שלישית 7992
uaminchah ta'aseh 'alayu baboqer baboqer shishiyt ha'aeypah, uashemen shalishiyt
**And a meat offering you shall prepare for it every morning the sixth part of an ephah and oil *the* third part of**

46:15
ההין 1969 לרס 7450 את 853 הסלת 5560 מנחה 4503 ליהוה 3068 חקות 2708 עולם 5769 תמיד 8548:
hahiyn laros 'at hasolet; minchah laYahuah, chuqout 'aulam tamiyd.
**an hin of to temper the fine flour a meat offering unto Yahuah *by* a ordinance perpetual continually**

ועשו 6213 את 853 הכבש 3532 ואת 853 המנחה 4503 ואת 853 השמן 8081 בבקר 1242 בבקר 1242 עולת 5930
ua'asu 'at hakebes ua'at haminchah ua'at hashemen baboqer baboqer; 'aulot
**Thus shall they prepare the lamb *and* the meat offering *and* the oil every morning *for* a burnt offering**

46:16
תמיד 8548: כה 3541 אמר 559 אדני 136 יהוה 3068 כי 3588 יתן 5414 הנשיא 5387 מתנה 4979 לאיש 376 מבניו 1121 נחלתו 5159
tamiyd. koh 'amar 'adonay Yahuah kiy yiten hanasiy'a matanah la'aysh mibanayu, nachalatou
**continual Thus saith Adonai Yahuah If give the prince a gift unto any of his sons the inheritance thereof**

46:17
היא 1931 לבניו 1121 תהיה 1961 אחזתם 272 היא 1931 בנחלה 5159: וכי 3588 יתן 5414 מתנה 4979 מנחלתו 5159
hiy'a labanayu tihayeh; 'achuzatam hiy'a banachalah. uakiy yiten matanah minachalatou,
**it his sons' shall be *shall be* their possession he by inheritance But if he give a gift of his inheritance**

Eze 46:10 And the prince in the midst of them, when they go in, shall go in; and when they go forth, shall go forth.11 And in the feast and in the solemnities the meat offering shall be an ephah to a bullock, and ephah to a ram, and to the lambs as he is able to give, and an hin of oil to an ephah.12 Now when the prince shall prepare a voluntary burnt offering or peace offerings voluntarily unto YHUH, one shall then open him the gate that look toward the east, and he shall prepare his burnt offering and his peace offerings, as he did on the Sabbath day: then he shall go forth; and after his going forth one shall shut the gate.13 Thou shall daily prepare a burnt offering unto YHUH of a lamb of the first year without blemish: you shall prepare it every morning.14 And you shall prepare a meat offering for it every morning, the sixth part of an ephah, and the third part of an hin of oil, to temper with the fine flour; a meat offering continually by a perpetual ordinance unto YHUH.15 Thus shall they prepare the lamb, and the meat offering, and the oil, every morning for a continual burnt offering.16 Thus saith YHUH G-D; If the prince give a gift unto any of his sons, the inheritance thereof shall be his sons'; it shall be their possession by inheritance.17 But if he give a gift of his inheritance to one of his servants, then it shall be his to the year of liberty; after it shall return to the prince:

| לאחד 259 | מעבדיו 5650 | והיתה 1961 | לו 3807a | עד 5704 | שנת 8141 | הדרור 1865 | ושבת 7725 | לנשיא 5387 | אך 389 |
|---|---|---|---|---|---|---|---|---|---|
| la'achad | me'abadayu, | uahayatah | lou' | 'ad | shanat | hadarour, | uashabat | lanasiy'a; | 'ak |
| **to one** | **of his servants** | **then it shall be** | **his** | **to until** | **year of** | **the liberty** | **after it shall return** | **to the prince** | **but** |

| נחלתו 5159 | בניו 1121 | להם 1992 | תהיה 1961: | **46:18** | ולא 3808 | יקח 3947 | הנשיא 5387 | מנחלת 5159 | העם 5971 |
|---|---|---|---|---|---|---|---|---|---|
| nachalatou, | banayu | lahem | tihayeh. | | uala' | yiqach | hanasiy'a | minachalat | ha'am, |
| **his inheritance** | **his sons'** | **for them** | **shall be** | | **Moreover not** | **shall take** | **the prince** | **of inheritance** | **the people's** |

| להונתם 3238 | מאחזתם 272 | מאחזתו 272 | ינחל 5157 | את 853 | בניו 1121 |
|---|---|---|---|---|---|
| lahounotam | me'achuzatam, | me'achuzatou | yanchiyl | 'at | banayu; |
| **by oppression, to thrust them out** | **of their possession** | **out of his own possession** | ***but* he shall give inheritance** | | **his sons** |

| למען 4616 | אשר 834 | לא 3808 | יפצו 6327 | עמי 5971 | איש 376 | מאחזתו 272: | **46:19** | ויביאני 935 | במבוא 3996 |
|---|---|---|---|---|---|---|---|---|---|
| lama'an | 'asher | la' | yaputzu | 'amiy, | 'aysh | me'achuzatou. | | uayabiy'aeniy | bamabou'a |
| **that** | **after** | **not** | **be scattered** | **my people** | **every man** | **from his possession** | | **After he brought me** | **through the entry** |

| אשר 834 | על 5921 | כתף 3802 | השער 8179 | אל 413 | הלשכות 3957 | הקדש 6944 | אל 413 | הכהנים 3548 | הפנות 6437 | צפונה 6828 |
|---|---|---|---|---|---|---|---|---|---|---|
| 'asher | 'al | ketep | hasha'ar | 'al | halishkout | haqodesh | 'al | hakohaniym, | haponout | tzapounah; |
| **which *was*** | **at** | **the side of** | **the gate** | **into** | **chambers** | **the holy** | **of** | **the priests** | **which looked toward** | **the north** |

| והנה 2009 | שם 8033 | מקום 4725 | בירכתם 3411 | ימה 3220: | **46:20** | ויאמר 559 | אלי 413 | זה 2088 | המקום 4725 | אשר 834 | יבשלו 1310 |
|---|---|---|---|---|---|---|---|---|---|---|---|
| uahineh | sham | maqoum, | bayarkatim | yamah. | | uaya'mer | 'aelay, | zeh | hamaqoum, | 'asher | yabashlu |
| **and behold** | **there** | ***was* a place** | **on the two sides** | **westward** | | **Then said he** | **unto me** | **This** | ***is* the place** | **where** | **shall boil** |

| שם 8033 | הכהנים 3548 | את 853 | האשם 817 | ואת 853 | החטאת 2403 | אשר 834 | יאפו 644 | את 853 | המנחה 4503 | לבלתי 1115 |
|---|---|---|---|---|---|---|---|---|---|---|
| sham | hakohaniym, | 'at | ha'asham | ua'at | hachata't; | 'asher | ya'pu | 'at | haminchah, | labiltiy |
| **there** | **the priests** | | **the trespass offering** | ***and*** | **the sin offering** | **where** | **they shall bake** | | **the meat offering** | **that not** |

| הוציא 3318 | אל 413 | החצר 2691 | החיצונה 2435 | לקדש 6942 | את 853 | העם 5971: | **46:21** | ויוציאני 3318 | אל 413 |
|---|---|---|---|---|---|---|---|---|---|
| houtziy'a | 'al | hechatzer | hachiytzounah | laqadesh | 'at | ha'am. | | uayoutziy'aeniy, | 'al |
| **they bear out *them*** | **into** | **court** | **the utter** | **to sanctify** | | **the people** | | **Then he brought me forth** | **into** |

| החצר 2691 | החיצנה 2435 | ויעבירני 5674 | אל 413 | ארבעת 702 | מקצועי 4740 | החצר 2691 | והנה 2009 | חצר 2691 | במקצע 4740 |
|---|---|---|---|---|---|---|---|---|---|
| hechatzer | hachiytzonah, | uaya'abiyreniy, | 'al | 'arba'at | miqtzou'aey | hechatzer; | uahineh | chatzer | bamiqtzoa' |
| **the court** | **the utter** | **and caused me to pass** | **by** | ***the* four** | **corners of** | **the court** | **and behold** | ***there was* a court** | **in every** |

| החצר 2691 | חצר 2691 | במקצע 4740 | החצר 2691: | **46:22** | בארבעת 702 | מקצעות 4740 | החצר 2691 | חצרות 2691 | קטרות 7000 |
|---|---|---|---|---|---|---|---|---|---|
| hechatzer, | chatzer | bamiqtzoa' | hechatzer. | | ba'arba'at | miktzo'aut | hechatzer | chatzerout | qaturout, |
| **the court** | **of the court** | **corner of** | ***there was* a court** | | **In the four** | **corners of** | **the court** | ***there were* courts** | **joined of** |

| ארבעים 705 | ארך 753 | ושלשים 7970 | רחב 7341 | מדה 4060 | אחת 259 | לארבעתם 702 | מהקצעות 7106: | **46:23** | וטור 2905 |
|---|---|---|---|---|---|---|---|---|---|
| 'arba'aym | 'arek, | uashloshiym | rochab; | midah | 'achat, | la'arba'atam | mahuqatza'aut | | uatur |
| **forty** | ***cubits* long** | **and thirty** | **broad** | **measure** | ***were of* one** | **these four** | **corners** | | **And *there was* a row** |

| סביב 5439 | בהם 871a | סביב 5439 | לארבעתם 702 | ומבשלות 4018 | עשוי 6213 | מתחת 8478 | הטירות 2918 |
|---|---|---|---|---|---|---|---|
| sabiyb | bahem | sabiyb | la'arba'atam; | uambashlout | 'asuy, | mitachat | hatiyrout |
| ***of building* round about** | **in them** | **round about them** | **four** | **and boiling places** | ***it was* made** | ***with*** | **under the rows** |

Eze 46:17 but his inheritance shall be his sons' for them.18 Moreover the prince shall not take of the people's inheritance by oppression, to thrust them out of their possession; but he shall give his sons inheritance out of his own possession: that my people be not scattered every man from his possession.19 After he brought me through the entry, which was at the side of the gate, into the holy chambers of the priests, which looked toward the north: and, behold, there was a place on the two sides westward.20 Then said he unto me, This is the place where the priests shall boil the trespass offering and the sin offering, where they shall bake the meat offering; that they bear them not out into the utter court, to sanctify the people.21 Then he brought me forth into the utter court, and caused me to pass by the four corners of the court; and, behold, in every corner of the court there was a court.22 In the four corners of the court there were courts joined of forty cubits long and thirty broad: these four corners were of one measure.23 And there was a row of building round about in them, round about them four, and it was made with boiling places under the rows round about.

סביב 5439: | **46:24** ויאמר 559 | אלי 413 | אלה 428 | בית 1004 | המבשלים 1310 | אשר 834 | יבשלו 1310 | שם 8033 | משרתי 8334
sabiyb. | uaya'mer | 'aelay; | 'aeleh | beyt | hamabashliym, | 'asher | yabashlu | sham | masharatey
**round about | Then said he | unto me | These *are* the places of | them that boil | where | shall boil | there | the ministers of**

הבית 1004 | את 853 | זבח 2077 | העם 5971:
habayit | 'at | zebach | ha'am.
**the house | | the sacrifice of | the people**

**Ezek 47:1** וישבני 7725 | אל 413 | פתח 6607 | הבית 1004 | והנה 2009 | מים 4325 | יצאים 3318 | מתחת 8478
uayashibeniy | 'al | petach | habayit | uahineh | mayim | yotza'aym, | mitachat
**Afterward he brought me again | unto | the door of | the house | and behold | waters | issued out | from under**

מפתן 4670 | הבית 1004 | קדימה 6921 | כי 3588 | פני 6440 | הבית 1004 | קדים 6921 | והמים 4325 | ירדים 3381
miptan | habayit | qadiymah, | kiy | paney | habayit | qadiym; | uahamayim | yordiym,
**the threshold of | the house | eastward | for | the forefront of | the house | *stood toward* the east | and the waters | came down**

מתחת 8478 | מכתף 3802 | הבית 1004 | הימנית 3233 | מנגב 5045 | למזבח 4196: | **47:2** ויוצאני 3318 | דרך 1870
mitachat | miketep | habayit | hayamaniyt, | minegeb | lamizabeach. | uayoutzi'aeniy | derek
**from under | from side of | the house | the right | at the south | *side* of the altar | Then brought he me out of | the way of**

שער 8179 | צפונה 6828 | ויסבני 5437 | דרך 1870 | חוץ 2351 | אל 413 | שער 8179 | החוץ 2351 | דרך 1870 | הפונה 6437 | קדים 6921 | והנה 2009
sha'ar | tzapounah | uayasibeniy | derek | chutz, | 'al | sha'ar | hachutz, | derek | hapouneh | qadiym; | uahineh
**the gate | northward | and led me about | the way | without | unto | gate | the utter *by* the way | | that looks | eastward | and behold**

מים 4325 | מפכים 6349 | מן 4480 | הכתף 3802 | הימנית 3233: | **47:3** בצאת 3318 | האיש 376 | קדים 6921 | וקו 6957 | בידו 3027
mayim | mapakiym, | min | hakatep | hayamaniyt. | batzea't | ha'aysh | qadiym | uaqau | bayadou;
**waters | unstable | on | side | the right | when went forth | the man | eastward | *that had* the line | in his hand**

וימד 4058 | אלף 505 | באמה 520 | ויעברני 5674 | במים 4325 | מי 4325 | אפסים 657: | **47:4**
uayamad | 'alep | ba'amah, | uaya'abireniy | bamayim | mey | 'apasayim.
**And he measured | a thousand | cubits | and he brought me | through the waters | the waters | *were to* the ankles**

וימד 4058 | אלף 505 | ויעברני 5674 | במים 4325 | מים 4325 | ברכים 1290 | וימד 4058
uayamad | 'alep, | uaya'abireniy | bamayim | mayim | birkayim; | uayamad
**Again he measured | a thousand | and brought me | through the waters | the waters | *were to* the knees | Again he measured**

אלף 505 | ויעברני 5674 | מי 4325 | מתנים 4975: | **47:5** וימד 4058 | אלף 505 | נחל 5158
'alep, | uaya'abireniy | mey | matanayim. | uayamad | 'alep, | nachal
**a thousand | and brought me through | *the* waters | *were to* the loins | Afterward he measured | a thousand | *and it was* a river**

אשר 834 | לא 3808 | אוכל 3201 | לעבר 5674 | כי 3588 | גאו 1342 | המים 4325 | מי 4325 | שחו 7813 | נחל 5158 | אשר 834 | לא 3808
'asher | la' | 'aukal | la'abor; | kiy | ga'au | hamayim | mey | sachu, | nachal | 'asher | la'
**that | not | I could | pass over | for | were risen | the waters | waters to | swim *in* | a river | that | not**

יעבר 5674: | **47:6** ויאמר 559 | אלי 413 | הראית 7200 | בן 1121 | אדם 120 | ויולכני 1980
ya'abor. | uaya'mer | 'aelay | hara'ayta | ben | 'adam; | uayoulikeniy
**could be passed over | And he said unto me | | have you seen *this*? | Son of | man | Then he brought me**

Eze 46:24 Then said he unto me, These are the places of them that boil, where the ministers of the house shall boil the sacrifice of the people. **Eze** 47:1 Afterward he brought me again unto the door of the house; and, behold, waters issued out from under the threshold of the house eastward: for the forefront of the house stood toward the east, and the waters came down from under from the right side of the house, at the south side of the altar.2 Then brought he me out of the way of the gate northward, and led me about the way without unto the utter gate by the way that look eastward; and, behold, there ran out waters on the right side.3 And when the man that had the line in his hand went forth eastward, he measured a thousand cubits, and he brought me through the waters; the waters were to the ancles.4 Again he measured a thousand, and brought me through the waters; the waters were to the knees. Again he measured a thousand, and brought me through; the waters were to the loins.5 Afterward he measured a thousand; and it was a river that I could not pass over: for the waters were risen, waters to swim in, a river that could not be passed over.6 And he said unto me, Son of man, have you seen this? Then he brought me, and caused me to return to the brink of the river.

וישבני 7725 | שפת 8193 | הנחל 5158: | 47:7 בשובני 7725 | והנה 2009 | אל 413 | שפת 8193 | הנחל 5158 | עץ 6086
uayashibeniy | sapat | hanachal. | bashubeniy | uahineh | 'al | sapat | hanachal, | 'aetz
**and caused me to return to | the brink of | the river | when I had returned | Now behold | at | the bank of | the river | trees**

רב 7227 | מאד 3966 | מזה 2088 | ומזה 2088: | 47:8 ויאמר 559 | אלי 413 | המים 4325 | האלה 428 | יוצאים 3318 | אל 413 | הגלילה 1552
rab | ma'ad; | mizeh | uamizeh. | uaya'mer | 'aelay, | hamayim | ha'aeleh | youtz'aym, | 'al | hagaliylah
**many *were* very | on the one *side* | and on the other | Then said he | unto me | waters | These | issue out | toward | country**

הקדמונה 6930 | וירדו 3381 | על 5921 | הערבה 6160 | ובאו 935 | הימה 3220 | אל 413 | הימה 3220 | המוצאים 3318 | ונרפאו 7495
haqadmounah, | uayaradu | 'al | ha'arabah; | uaba'au | hayamah, | 'al | hayamah | hamutza'aym | uanirpe'au
**the east | and go down | into | the desert | and go into | the sea | into | the sea | *which being* brought forth | shall be healed**

המים 4325: | 47:9 והיה 1961 | כל 3605 | נפש 5315 | חיה 2416 | אשר 834 | ישרץ 8317 | אל 413 | כל 3605 | אשר 834 | יבוא 935
hamayim. | uahayah | kal | nepesh | chayah | 'asher | yishrotz | 'al | kal | 'asher | yabou'a
**the waters | And it shall come to pass *that* | every | thing | that live | which | moves | in | every | which | shall come**

שם 8033 | נחלים 5158 | יחיה 2421 | והיה 1961 | הדגה 1710 | רבה 7227 | מאד 3966 | כי 3588 | באו 935 | שמה 8033
sham | nachalayim | yichayeh, | uahayah | hadagah | rabah | ma'ad; | kiy | ba'au | shamah
**whithersoever | the rivers | shall live | and there shall be | a fish | great *multitude of* | very | because | shall come | there**

המים 4325 | האלה 428 | וירפאו 7495 | וחי 2425 | כל 3605 | אשר 834 | יבוא 935 | שמה 8033 | הנחל 5158: | 47:10
hamayim | ha'aeleh, | uayerapa'au | uachay, | kal | 'asher | yabou'a | shamah | hanachal.
**waters | these | for they shall be healed | and shall live | every thing | which | comes | there | the river**

והיה 1961 | יעמדו 5975 | עליו 5921 | דוגים 1728 | מעין 5872 | גדי 1423 | ועד 5704 | עין 5882 | עגלים 5695
uahayah | ya'amadu | 'alayu | dauagiym, | me'ayn | gadiy | ua'ad | 'aeyn | 'aglayim,
**And it shall come to pass *that* | shall stand | upon it *that* | the fishers | from En | gedi | even unto | En | eglaim**

משטוח 4894 | לחרמים 2764 | יהיו 1961 | למינה 4327 | תהיה 1961 | דגתם 1710 | כדגת 1710 | הים 3220 | הגדול 1419
mishatouach | lacharamiym | yihayu; | lamiynah | tihayeh | dagatam, | kidgat | hayam | hagadoul
***a place* to spread forth | nets | they shall be | according to their kinds | shall be | their fish | as the fish of | the sea | the great**

רבה 7227 | מאד 3966: | 47:11 בצאתו 1207 | וגבאיו 1360 | ולא 3808 | ירפאו 7495 | למלח 4417
rabah | ma'ad. | batzea'tou | uagba'ayn | uala' | yerapa'au | lamelach
**many | exceeding | But the miry places thereof | and the marishes thereof | not | shall be healed | to salt**

נתנו 5414: | 47:12 ועל 5921 | הנחל 5158 | יעלה 5927 | על 5921 | שפתו 8193 | מזה 2088 | ומזה 2088 | כל 3605 | עץ 6086
nitanu. | ua'al | hanachal | ya'aleh | 'al | sapatou | mizeh | uamizeh | kal | 'aetz
**they shall be given | And by | the river | shall grow | upon | the bank thereof | on this side | and on that side | all | trees**

מאכל 3978 | לא 3808 | יבול 5034 | עלהו 5929 | ולא 3808 | יתם 8552 | פריו 6529 | לחדשיו 2320
ma'akal | la' | yiboul | 'alehu | uala' | yitom | piryou, | lachadashayu
***for* meat | not | shall fade | whose leaf | neither | shall be consumed | the fruit thereof | according to his months**

יבכר 1069 | כי 3588 | מימיו 4325 | מן 4480 | המקדש 4720 | המה 1992 | יוצאים 3318 | והיו 1961 | פריו 6529
yabaker, | kiy | meymayu, | min | hamiqdash | hemah | youtz'aym; | uahayu | piryou
**it shall bring forth new fruit | because | their waters | of | the sanctuary | they | issued out | and shall be | the fruit thereof**

Eze 47:7 Now when I had returned, behold, at the bank of the river were very many trees on the one side and on the other.8 Then said he unto me, These waters issue out toward the east country, and go down into the desert, and go into the sea: which being brought forth into the sea, the waters shall be healed.9 And it shall come to pass, that everything that live, which moveth, whithersoever the rivers shall come, shall live: and there shall be a very great multitude of fish, because these waters shall come thither: for they shall be healed; and everything shall live whither the river cometh.10 And it shall come to pass, that the fishers shall stand upon it from En-gedi even unto En-eglaim; they shall be a place to spread forth nets; their fish shall be according to their kinds, as the fish of the great sea, exceeding many.11 But the miry places thereof and the marishes thereof shall not be healed; they shall be given to salt.12 And by the river upon the bank thereof, on this side and on that side, shall grow all trees for meat, whose leaf shall not fade, neither shall the fruit thereof be consumed: it shall bring forth new fruit according to his months, because their waters they issued out of the sanctuary: and the fruit thereof shall be for meat, and the leaf thereof for medicine.

למאכל 3978 ועלהו 5929 לתרופה 8644: **47:13** כה 3541 אמר 559 אדני 136 יהוה 3069 גה 1454 גבול 1366 אשר 834
lama'akal, ua'alehu litrupah. koh 'amar 'adonay Yahuah, geh gabul 'asher
**for meat and the leaf thereof for medicine Thus saith Adonai Yahuah This *shall be* the border whereby**

תתנחלו 5157 את 853 הארץ 776 לשני 8147 עשר 6240 שבטי 7626 ישראל 3478 יוסף 3130 חבלים 2256: **47:14**
titnachalu 'at ha'aretz, lishney 'asar shibtey yisra'ael; yousep chabaliym.
**you shall inherit the land according to two ten tribes of Israel Joseph *shall have two* portions**

ונחלתם 5157 אותה 853 איש 376 כאחיו 251 אשר 834 נשאתי 5375 את 853 ידי 3027 לתתה 5414
uanchaltem 'autah 'aysh ka'achiyu, 'asher nasa'tiy 'at yadiy, latitah
**And you shall inherit it one as well as another *concerning the* which I lifted up mine hand to give it**

לאבתיכם 1 ונפלה 5307 הארץ 776 הזאת 2063 לכם 3807a בנחלה 5159: **47:15** וזה 2088 גבול 1366 הארץ 776
la'aboteykem; uanapalah ha'aretz haza't lakem banachalah. uazeh gabul ha'aretz;
**unto your fathers and shall fall the land this unto you for inheritance And this *shall be* the border of the land**

לפאת 6285 צפונה 6828 מן 4480 הים 3220 הגדול 1419 הדרך 1870 חתלן 2855 לבוא 935 צדדה 6657: **47:16** חמת 2574 ברותה 1268 סברים 5453
lip'at tzapounah min hayam hagadoul haderek chetlon labou'a tzadadah. chamat beroutah sibrayim,
**toward side the north from the sea the great the way of Hethlon *as men* go to Zedad Hamath Berothah Sibraim**

אשר 834 בין 996 גבול 1366 דמשק 1834 ובין 996 גבול 1366 חמת 2574 חצר 2694 התיכון 8484 אשר 834 אל 413 גבול 1366
'asher beyn gabul dameseq, uabeyn gabul chamat; chatzer hatiykon, 'asher 'al gabul
**which *is* between the border of Damascus and between the border of Hamath Hazar hatticon which *is* by the coast of**

חורן 2362: **47:17** והיה 1961 גבול 1366 מן 4480 הים 3220 חצר 2603 עינון 5869 גבול 1366 דמשק 1834 וצפון 6828 צפונה 6828
chauran. uahayah gabul min hayam, chatzar 'aeynoun gabul dameseq, uatzapoun tzapounah
**Hauran And shall be the border from the sea Hazar enan the border of Damascus and the north northward**

וגבול 1366 חמת 2574 ואת 853 פאת 6285 צפון 6828: **47:18** ופאת 6285 קדים 6921 מבין 996 חורן 2362 ומבין 996 דמשק 1834
augbul chamat; ua'at pa'at tzapoun. uapa'at qadiym mibeyn chauran uamibeyn dameseq
**and the border of Hamath *And* side *this is* *the* north And side *the* east from Hauran and from Damascus**

ומבין 996 הגלעד 5168 ומבין 996 ארץ 776 ישראל 3478 הירדן 3383 מגבול 1366 על 5921 הים 3220 הקדמוני 6931
uamibeyn hagil'ad uamibeyn 'aretz yisra'ael hayarden, migbul 'al hayam haqadmouniy
**and from Gilead and from the land of Israel *by* the Jordan from the border unto the sea the east**

תמדו 4058 ואת 853 פאת 6285 קדימה 6921: **47:19** ופאת 6285 נגב 5045 תימנה 8486 מתמר 8559 עד 5704 מי 4325
tamodu; ua'at pa'at qadiymah. uapa'at negeb teymanah, mitamar, 'ad mey
**you shall measure *And* side *this is* *the* east And side *the* south southward from Tamar *even* to the waters of**

מריבות 4808 קדש 6946 נחלה 5158 אל 413 הים 3220 הגדול 1419 ואת 853 פאת 6285 תימנה 8486 נגבה 5045: **47:20** ופאת 6285 ים 3220
mariybout qadesh, nachalah 'al hayam hagadoul; ua'at pe'at teymanah negbah. uapa'at yam
**strife *in* Kadesh the river to the sea the great *And* side *this is the* south southward *The* side also west**

הים 3220 הגדול 1419 מגבול 1366 עד 5704 נכח 5227 לבוא 935 חמת 2574 זאת 2063 פאת 6285 ים 3220:
hayam hagadoul, migbul 'ad nokach labou'a chamat; za't pa'at yam.
**the sea *shall be* the great from the border till over against *a man* come Hamath This side *is the* west**

Eze 47:13 Thus saith YHUH G-D; This shall be the border, whereby you shall inherit the land according to the twelve tribes of Israel: Joseph shall have two portions.14 And you shall inherit it, one as well as another: concerning the which I lifted up mine hand to give it unto your fathers: and this land shall fall unto you for inheritance.15 And this shall be the border of the land toward the north side, from the great sea, the way of Hethlon, as men go to Zedad;16 Hamath, Berothah, Sibraim, which is between the border of Damascus and the border of Hamath; Hazar-hatticon, which is by the coast of Hauran.17 And the border from the sea shall be Hazar-enan, the border of Damascus, and the north northward, and the border of Hamath. And this is the north side.18 And the east side you shall measure from Hauran, and from Damascus, and from Gilead, and from the land of Israel by Jordan, from the border unto the east sea. And this is the east side.19 And the south side southward, from Tamar even to the waters of strife in Kadesh, the river to the great sea. And this is the south side southward.20 The west side also shall be the great sea from the border, till a man come over against Hamath. This is the west side.

**47:21** וחלקתם 2505 את 853 הארץ 776 הזאת 2063 לכם 3807a לשבטי 7626 ישראל 3478: **47:22**
uachilaqtem 'at ha'aretz haza't lakem lashibtey yisra'ael.
**So shall you divide the land this unto you according to the tribes of Israel**

והיה 1961 תפלו 5307 אותה 853 בנחלה 5159 לכם 3807a ולהגרים 1616 הגרים 1481
uahayah, tapiylu 'autah banachalah lakem, ualhageriym hagariym
**And it shall come to pass *that* you shall divide by lot it for an inheritance unto you and to the strangers that sojourn**

בתוככם 8432 אשר 834 הולדו 3205 בנים 1121 בתוככם 8432 והיו 1961 לכם 3807a כאזרח 249
batoukakem, 'asher houlidu baniym batoukakem; uahayu lakem, ka'azrach
**among you which shall beget children among you and they shall be unto you as born in the country**

בבני 1121 ישראל 3478 אתכם 854 יפלו 5307 בנחלה 5159 בתוך 8432 שבטי 7626 ישראל 3478: **47:23**
bibney yisra'ael, 'atakem yiplu banachalah, batouk shibtey yisra'ael.
**among the children of Israel with you they shall have inheritance among the tribes of Israel**

והיה 1961 בשבט 7626 אשר 834 גר 1481 הגר 1616 אתו 854 שם 8033 תתנו 5414 נחלתו 5159
uahayah bashebet, 'asher gar hager 'atou; sam titanu nachalatou,
**And it shall come to pass *that* in tribe what sojourneth the stranger for there shall you give *him* his inheritance**

נאם 5002 אדני 136 יהוה 3068:
na'am 'adonay Yahuah.
**saith Adonai Yahuah**

**Ezek 48:1** ואלה 428 שמות 8034 השבטים 7626 מקצה 7097 צפונה 6828 אל 413 יד 3027 דרך 1870 חתלן 2855
ua'aleh shemout hashabatiym; miqtzeh tzapounah 'al yad derek chetlon
**Now these *are* the names of the tribes From end the north to the coast of the way of Hethlon**

לבוא 935 חמת 2574 חצר 2704 עינן 5881 גבול 1366 דמשק 1834 צפונה 6828 אל 413 יד 3027 חמת 2574 והיו 1961 לו 3807a
labou'a chamat chatzar 'aeynan gabul dameseq tzapounah 'al yad chamat, uahayu lou'
**as one goes to Hamath Hazar enan the border of Damascus northward to the coast of Hamath for these are his**

פאת 6285 קדים 6921 הים 3220 דן 1835 אחד 259: **48:2** ועל 5921 גבול 1366 דן 1835 מפאת 6285 קדים 6921 עד 5704 פאת 6285 ימה 3220
pa'at qadiym hayam dan 'achad. ua'al gabul dan, mip'at qadiym 'ad pa'at yamah
**sides east *and* west *portion for* Dan a And by the border of Dan from side *the* east unto side *the* west**

אשר 836 אחד 259: **48:3** ועל 5921 גבול 1366 אשר 836 מפאת 6285 קדימה 6921 ועד 5704 פאת 6285 ימה 3220
'asher 'achad. ua'al gabul 'asher, mip'at qadiymah ua'ad pa'at yamah
***portion for* Asher a And by the border of Asher from side *the* east even unto side *the* west**

נפתלי 5321 אחד 259: **48:4** ועל 5921 גבול 1366 נפתלי 5321 מפאת 6285 קדמה 6921 עד 5704 פאת 6285 ימה 3220
naptaliy 'achad. ua'al gabul naptaliy, mip'at qadimah 'ad pa'at yamah
***portion for* Naphtali a And by the border of Naphtali from side *the* east unto side *the* west**

מנשה 4519 אחד 259: **48:5** ועל 5921 גבול 1366 מנשה 4519 מפאת 6285 קדמה 6921 עד 5704 פאת 6285 ימה 3220
manasheh 'achad. ua'al gabul manasheh, mip'at qadimah 'ad pa'at yamah
***portion for* Manasseh a And by the border of Manasseh from side *the* east unto side *the* west**

Eze 47:21 So shall you divide this land unto you according to the tribes of Israel.22 And it shall come to pass, that you shall divide it by lot for an inheritance unto you, and to the strangers that sojourn among you, which shall beget children among you: and they shall be unto you as born in the country among the children of Israel; they shall have inheritance with you among the tribes of Israel.23 And it shall come to pass, that in what tribe the stranger sojourneth, there shall you give him his inheritance, saith YHUH G-D. **Eze** 48:1 Now these are the names of the tribes. From the north end to the coast of the way of Hethlon, as one go to Hamath, Hazar-enan, the border of Damascus northward, to the coast of Hamath; for these are his sides east and west; a portion for Dan.2 And by the border of Dan, from the east side unto the west side, a portion for Asher.3 And by the border of Asher, from the east side even unto the west side, a portion for Naphtali.4 And by the border of Naphtali, from the east side unto the west side, a portion for Manasseh.5 And by the border of Manasseh, from the east side unto the west side, a portion for Ephraim.

| | | | | | | | | | | |
|---|---|---|---|---|---|---|---|---|---|---|
| אפרים 669 | אחד 259: | 48:6 | ועל 5921 | גבול 1366 | אפרים 669 | מפאת 6285 | קדים 6921 | ועד 5704 | פאת 6285 | ימה 3220 |
| 'aprayim | 'achad. | | ua'al | gabul | 'aprayim, | mip'at | qadiym | ua'ad | pa'at | yamah |
| **portion *for* Ephraim** | **a** | | **And by** | **the border of** | **Ephraim** | **from side** | ***the* east** | **even unto** | **side** | ***the* west** |

| | | | | | | | | | | | | |
|---|---|---|---|---|---|---|---|---|---|---|---|---|
| ראובן 7205 | אחד 259: | 48:7 | ועל 5921 | גבול 1366 | ראובן 7205 | מפאת 6285 | קדים 6921 | עד 5704 | פאת 6285 | ימה 3220 | יהודה 3063 |
| ra'uben | 'achad. | | ua'al | gabul | ra'uben, | mip'at | qadiym | 'ad | pa'at | yamah | yahudah |
| **portion *for* Reuben** | **a** | | **And by** | **the border of** | **Reuben** | **from side** | ***the* east** | **unto** | **side** | ***the* west** | **portion *for* Judah** |

| | | | | | | | | | | | | |
|---|---|---|---|---|---|---|---|---|---|---|---|---|
| אחד 259: | 48:8 | ועל 5921 | גבול 1366 | יהודה 3063 | מפאת 6285 | קדים 6921 | עד 5704 | פאת 6285 | ימה 3220 | תהיה 1961 | התרומה 8641 | אשר 834 |
| 'achad. | | ua'al | gabul | yahudah, | mip'at | qadiym | 'ad | pa'at | yamah; | tihayeh | hatarumah | 'asher |
| **a** | | **And by** | **the border of** | **Judah** | **from side** | ***the* east** | **unto** | **side** | ***the* west** | **shall be** | **the offering** | **which** |

| | | | | | | | | | |
|---|---|---|---|---|---|---|---|---|---|
| תרימו 7311 | חמשה 2568 | ועשרים 6242 | אלף 505 | רחב 7341 | וארך 753 | כאחד 259 | החלקים 2506 | מפאת 6285 |
| tariymu | chamishah | ua'asriym | 'alep | rochab, | ua'arek | ka'achad | hachalaqiym | mip'at |
| **you shall offer of** | **five** | **and twenty** | **thousand** | ***reeds in* breadth** | **and *in* length** | **as one of** | **the *other* parts** | **side from** |

| | | | | | | | | | | | |
|---|---|---|---|---|---|---|---|---|---|---|---|
| קדימה 6921 | עד 5704 | פאת 6285 | ימה 3220 | והיה 1961 | המקדש 4720 | בתוכו 8432: | 48:9 | התרומה 8641 | אשר 834 | תרימו 7311 |
| qadiymah | 'ad | pa'at | yamah, | uahayah | hamiqdash | batoukou. | | hatarumah | 'asher | tariymu |
| ***the* east** | **unto** | **side** | ***the* west** | **and shall be** | **the sanctuary** | **in the midst of it** | | **The oblation** | **that** | **you shall offer** |

| | | | | | | | | | | |
|---|---|---|---|---|---|---|---|---|---|---|
| ליהוה 3068 | ארך 753 | חמשה 2568 | ועשרים 6242 | אלף 505 | ורחב 7341 | עשרת 6235 | אלפים 505: | 48:10 | ולאלה 428 | תהיה 1961 |
| laYahuah; | 'arek, | chamishah | ua'asriym | 'alep, | uarochab | 'aseret | 'alapiym. | | ual'aeleh | tihayeh |
| **unto Yahuah** | ***in* length** | ***shall be of* five** | **and twenty** | **thousand** | **and breadth** | ***of* ten** | **thousand *in*** | | **And for them** | **shall be** |

| | | | | | | | |
|---|---|---|---|---|---|---|---|
| תרומת 8641 | הקדש 6944 | לכהנים 3548 | צפונה 6828 | חמשה 2568 | ועשרים 6242 | אלף 505 | וימה 3220 |
| tarumat | haqodesh | lakohaniym | tzapounah | chamishah | ua'asriym | 'alep, | uayamah |
| **oblation** | ***this* holy** | ***even* for the priests** | **toward the north** | **five** | **and twenty** | **thousand** | ***in length* and toward the west** |

| | | | | | | | | | | |
|---|---|---|---|---|---|---|---|---|---|---|
| רחב 7341 | עשרת 6235 | אלפים 505 | וקדימה 6921 | רחב 7341 | עשרת 6235 | אלפים 505 | ונגבה 5045 | ארך 753 | חמשה 2568 |
| rochab | 'aseret | 'alapiym, | uaqadiymah, | rochab | 'aseret | 'alapiym, | uanegbah | 'arek | chamishah |
| ***in* breadth** | **ten** | **thousand** | **and toward the east** | ***in* breadth** | **ten** | **thousand** | **and toward the south** | ***in* length** | **five** |

| | | | | | | | |
|---|---|---|---|---|---|---|---|
| ועשרים 6242 | אלף 505 | והיה 1961 | מקדש 4720 | יהוה 3069 | בתוכו 8432: | 48:11 | לכהנים 3548 |
| ua'asriym | 'alep; | uahayah | miqdash | Yahuah | batoukou. | | lakohaniym |
| **and twenty** | **thousand** | **and shall be** | ***the* sanctuary of** | **Yahuah** | **in the midst thereof** | | ***It shall be* for the priests** |

| | | | | | | | | | | | |
|---|---|---|---|---|---|---|---|---|---|---|---|
| המקדש 6942 | מבני 1121 | צדוק 6659 | אשר 834 | שמרו 8104 | משמרתי 4931 | אשר 834 | לא 3808 | תעו 8582 | בתעות 8582 | בני 1121 |
| hamaqudash | mibney | tzadouq, | 'asher | shamaru | mishmartiy; | 'asher | la' | ta'au, | bita'aut | baney |
| **that are sanctified** | **of the sons of** | **Zadok** | **which** | **have kept** | **my charge** | **who** | **not** | **went** | **astray** | ***the* children of** |

| | | | | | | | | | | |
|---|---|---|---|---|---|---|---|---|---|---|
| ישראל 3478 | כאשר 834 | תעו 8582 | הלוים 3881: | 48:12 | והיתה 1961 | להם 3807a | תרומיה 8642 | מתרומת 8641 | הארץ 776 |
| yisra'ael, | ka'asher | ta'au | halauiyim. | | uahayatah | lahem | tarumiyah | mitrumat | ha'aretz |
| **Israel** | **as** | **when went astray** | **the Levites** | | **And shall be** | **unto them** | ***this* oblation of** | **that is offered** | **the land** |

| | | | | | | | | | | |
|---|---|---|---|---|---|---|---|---|---|---|
| קדש 6944 | קדשים 6944 | אל 413 | גבול 1366 | הלוים 3881: | 48:13 | והלוים 3881 | לעמת 5980 | גבול 1366 | הכהנים 3548 |
| qodesh | qadashiym; | 'al | gabul | halauiyim. | | uahalauiyim, | la'amat | gabul | hakohaniym, |
| **a thing** | **most holy** | **by** | **the border of** | **the Levites** | | **And the Levites** | **over against** | **the border of** | **the priests** |

Eze 48:6 And by the border of Ephraim, from the east side even unto the west side, a portion for Reuben.7 And by the border of Reuben, from the east side unto the west side, a portion for Judah.8 And by the border of Judah, from the east side unto the west side, shall be the offering which you shall offer of five and twenty thousand reeds in breadth, and in length as one of the other parts, from the east side unto the west side: and the sanctuary shall be in the midst of it.9 The oblation that you shall offer unto YHUH shall be of five and twenty thousand in length, and of ten thousand in breadth.10 And for them, even for the priests, shall be this holy oblation; toward the north five and twenty thousand in length, and toward the west ten thousand in breadth, and toward the east ten thousand in breadth, and toward the south five and twenty thousand in length: and the sanctuary of YHUH shall be in the midst thereof.11 It shall be for the priests that are sanctified of the sons of Zadok; which have kept my charge, which went not astray when the children of Israel went astray, as the Levites went astray.12 And this oblation of the land that is offered shall be unto them a thing most holy by the border of the Levites.13 And over against the border of the priests the Levites shall have five and twenty thousand in length, and ten thousand in breadth:

| 2568 חמשה | 6242 ועשרים | 505 אלף | 753 ארך | 7341 ורחב | 6235 עשרת | 505 אלפים | 3605 כל | 753 ארך | 2568 חמשה | 6242 ועשרים |
|---|---|---|---|---|---|---|---|---|---|---|
| chamishah | ua'asriym | 'alep | 'arek, | uarochab | 'aseret | 'alapiym; | kal | 'arek, | chamishah | ua'asriym |
| ***shall have* five** | **and twenty** | **thousand** | ***in* length** | **and breadth** | **ten** | **thousand** | ***in* all** | **the length** | ***shall be* five** | **and twenty** |

| 505 אלף | 7341 ורחב | 6235 עשרת | 505: אלפים | 48:14 3808 ולא | 4376 ימכרו | 4480 ממנו | 3808 ולא | 4171 ימר | 3808 ולא | 5674 יעבור |
|---|---|---|---|---|---|---|---|---|---|---|
| 'alep, | uarochab | 'aseret | 'alapiym. | uala' | yimkaru | mimenu, | uala' | yamer | uala' | ya'abur |
| **thousand** | **and the breadth** | **ten** | **thousand** | **And not** | **they shall sell** | **of it** | **neither** | **exchange** | **nor** | **alienate** |

| 7225 ראשית | 776 הארץ | 3588 כי | 6944 קדש | 3068: ליהוה | 48:15 2568 וחמשת | 505 אלפים | 3498 הנותר | 7341 ברחב | 5921 על | 6440 פני |
|---|---|---|---|---|---|---|---|---|---|---|
| ra'shiyt | ha'aretz; | kiy | qodesh | laYahuah. | uachameshet | 'alapiym | hanoutar | barochab, | 'al | paney |
| **the firstfruits of** | **the land** | **for** | ***it is* holy** | **unto Yahuah** | **And the five** | **thousand** | **that are left** | **in the breadth** | **over** | **against** |

| 2568 חמשה | 6242 ועשרים | 505 אלף | 2455 חל | 1931 הוא | 5892 לעיר | 4186 למושב | 4054 ולמגרש | 1961 והיתה |
|---|---|---|---|---|---|---|---|---|
| chamishah | ua'asriym | 'alep, | chol | hua' | la'ayr, | lamoushab | ualmigrash; | uahayatah |
| **the five** | **and twenty** | **thousand** | ***shall be* a profane *place*** | **he** | **for the city** | **for dwelling** | **and for suburbs** | **and shall be** |

| 5892 העיר | 8432 בתוכה | 48:16 428 ואלה | 4060 מדותיה | 6285 פאת | 6828 צפון | 2568 חמש | 3967 מאות | 702 וארבעת |
|---|---|---|---|---|---|---|---|---|
| ha'ayr | batoukoh | ua'aeleh | midouteyha | pa'at | tzapoun, | chamesh | me'aut | ua'arba'at |
| **the city** | **in the midst thereof** | **And these *shall be*** | **the measures thereof** | **side** | ***the* north** | **five** | **hundred** | **and four** |

| 505 אלפים | 6285 ופאת | 5045 נגב | 2568 חמש | 2568 חמש | 3967 מאות | 702 וארבעת | 505 אלפים | 6285 ומפאת | 6921 קדים | 2568 חמש | 3967 מאות | 702 וארבעת |
|---|---|---|---|---|---|---|---|---|---|---|---|---|
| 'alapiym, | uapa'at | negeb | chamesh | chamesh | me'aut | ua'arba'at | 'alapiym; | uamipa'at | qadiym, | chamesh | me'aut | ua'arba'at |
| **thousand** | **and side** | ***the* south** | **five** | **five** | **hundred** | **and four** | **thousand** | **and on side** | ***the* east** | **five** | **hundred** | **and four** |

| 505 אלפים | 6285 ופאת | 3220 ימה | 2568 חמש | 3967 מאות | 702 וארבעת | 505: אלפים | 48:17 1961 והיה | 4054 מגרש | 5892 לעיר |
|---|---|---|---|---|---|---|---|---|---|
| 'alapiym, | uapa'at | yamah | chamesh | me'aut | ua'arba'at | 'alapiym. | uahayah | migrash | la'ayr |
| **thousand** | **and from side** | ***the* west** | **five** | **hundred** | **and four** | **thousand** | **And shall be** | **the suburbs** | **of the city** |

| 6828 צפונה | 2572 חמשים | 3967 ומאתים | 5045 ונגבה | 2572 חמשים | 3967 ומאתים | 6921 וקדימה |
|---|---|---|---|---|---|---|
| tzapounah | chamishiym | uama'tayim, | uanegbah | chamishiym | uama'tayim; | uaqadiymah |
| **toward the north** | **fifty** | **and two hundred** | **and toward the south** | **fifty** | **and two hundred** | **and toward the east** |

| 2572 חמשים | 3967 ומאתים | 3220 וימה | 2572 חמשים | 3967: ומאתים | 48:18 3498 והנותר | 753 בארך |
|---|---|---|---|---|---|---|
| chamishiym | uama'tayim, | uayamah | chamishiym | uama'tayim. | uahanoutar | ba'arek |
| **fifty** | **and two hundred** | **and toward the west** | **fifty** | **and two hundred** | **And the residue** | **in length** |

| 5980 לעמת | 8641 תרומת | 6944 הקדש | 6235 עשרת | 505 אלפים | 6921 קדימה | 6235 ועשרת | 505 אלפים | 3220 ימה | 1961 והיה |
|---|---|---|---|---|---|---|---|---|---|
| la'amat | tarumat | haqodesh, | 'aseret | 'alapiym | qadiymah | ua'aseret | 'alapiym | yamah, | uahayah |
| **over against** | **the oblation of** | **the holy** | ***portion shall be* ten** | **thousand** | **eastward** | **and ten** | **thousand** | **westward** | **and it shall be** |

| 5980 לעמת | 8641 תרומת | 6944 הקדש | 1961 והיתה | 8393 תבואתה | 3899 ללחם | 5647 לעבדי | 5892: העיר | 48:19 |
|---|---|---|---|---|---|---|---|---|
| la'amat | tarumat | haqodesh; | uahayatah | tabu'atoh | lalechem, | la'abadey | ha'ayr. | |
| **over against** | **the oblation of** | **the holy *portion*** | **and shall be** | **the increase thereof** | **for food** | **unto them that serve** | **the city** | |

| 5647 והעבד | 5892 העיר | 5647 יעבדוהו | 3605 מכל | 7626 שבטי | 3478: ישראל | 48:20 3605 כל | 8641 התרומה | 2568 חמשה | 6242 ועשרים |
|---|---|---|---|---|---|---|---|---|---|
| uaha'abed | ha'ayr; | ya'abduhu | mikol | shibtey | yisra'ael. | kal | hatarumah, | chamishah | ua'asriym |
| **And they that serve** | **the city** | **shall serve it** | **out of all** | **the tribes of** | **Israel** | **All** | **the oblation** | ***shall be* five** | **and twenty** |

Eze 48:13 all the length shall be five and twenty thousand, and the breadth ten thousand.14 And they shall not sell of it, neither exchange, nor alienate the firstfruits of the land: for it is holy unto YHUH.15 And the five thousand, that are left in the breadth over against the five and twenty thousand, shall be a profane place for the city, for dwelling, and for suburbs: and the city shall be in the midst thereof.16 And these shall be the measures thereof; the north side four thousand and five hundred, and the south side four thousand and five hundred, and on the east side four thousand and five hundred, and the west side four thousand and five hundred.17 And the suburbs of the city shall be toward the north two hundred and fifty, and toward the south two hundred and fifty, and toward the east two hundred and fifty, and toward the west two hundred and fifty.18 And the residue in length over against the oblation of the holy portion shall be ten thousand eastward, and ten thousand westward: and it shall be over against the oblation of the holy portion; and the increase thereof shall be for food unto them that serve the city.19 And they that serve the city shall serve it out of all the tribes of Israel.20 All the oblation shall be five and twenty thousand by five and twenty thousand: you shall offer the holy oblation foursquare, with the possession of the city.

אלף 505 בחמשה 2568 ועשרים 6242 אלף 505 רביעית 7243 תרימו 7311 את 853 תרומת 8641 הקדש 6944 אל 413 אחזת 272
'alep, bachamishah ua'asriym 'alep; rabiy'ayt, tariymu 'at tarumat haqodesh, 'al 'achuzat
**thousand by five and twenty thousand foursquare you shall offer oblation the holy with the possession of**

48:21
העיר 5892: והנותר 3498 לנשיא 5387 מזה 2088 ומזה 2088 לתרומת 8641 הקדש 6944
ha'ayr. uahanoutar lanasiy'a mizeh uamizeh litrumat haqodesh
**the city And the residue *shall be* for the prince on the one side and on the other of oblation the holy**

ולאחזת 272 העיר 5892 אל 413 פני 6440 חמשה 2568 ועשרים 6242 אלף 505 תרומה 8641 עד 5704 גבול 1366 קדימה 6921
uala'achuzat ha'ayr 'al paney chamishah ua'asriym 'alep tarumah 'ad gabul qadiymah
**and of the possession of the city over against the five and twenty thousand of the oblation toward border *the* east**

וימה 3220 על 5921 פני 6440 חמשה 2568 ועשרים 6242 אלף 505 על 5921 גבול 1366 ימה 3220 לעמת 5980 חלקים 2506
uayamah, 'al paney chamishah ua'asriym 'alep 'al gabul yamah, la'amat chalaqiym
**and westward against over the five and twenty thousand toward border *the* west over against the portions**

48:22
לנשיא 5387 והיתה 1961 תרומת 8641 הקדש 6944 ומקדש 4720 הבית 1004 בתוכה 8432
lanasiy'a; uahayatah tarumat haqodesh, uamiqdash habayit batoukoh
**for the prince and it shall be oblation the holy and the sanctuary of the house *shall be* in the midst thereof**

ומאחזת 272 הלוים 3881 ומאחזת 272 העיר 5892 בתוך 8432 אשר 834
uame'achuzat halauiyim uame'achuzat ha'ayr, batouk 'asher
**Moreover from the possession of the Levites and from the possession of the city *being* in the midst *of that* which**

48:23
לנשיא 5387 יהיה 1961 בין 996 גבול 1366 יהודה 3063 ובין 996 גבול 1366 בנימן 1144 לנשיא 5387 יהיה 1961:
lanasiy'a yihayeh; beyn gabul yahudah, uabeyn gabul binyamin, lanasiy'a yihayeh.
**the prince's is between the border of Judah and between the border of Benjamin for the prince shall be**

48:24
ויתר 3499 השבטים 7626 מפאת 6285 קדימה 6921 עד 5704 פאת 6285 ימה 3220 בנימן 1144 אחד 259: ועל 5921
uayeter hashabatiym; mip'at qadiymah 'ad pa'at yamah binyamin 'achad. ua'al
**As for the rest of the tribes from side *the* east unto side *the* west Benjamin *shall have* a *portion* And by**

48:25
גבול 1366 בנימן 1144 מפאת 6285 קדימה 6921 עד 5704 פאת 6285 ימה 3220 שמעון 8095 אחד 259: ועל 5921
gabul binyamin, mip'at qadiymah 'ad pa'at yamah shim'aun 'achad. ua'al
**the border of Benjamin from side *the* east unto side *the* west Simeon *shall have* a *portion* And by**

48:26
גבול 1366 שמעון 8095 מפאת 6285 קדימה 6921 עד 5704 פאת 6285 ימה 3220 ישׂשכר 3485 אחד 259: ועל 5921
gabul shim'aun, mip'at qadiymah 'ad pa'at yamah yisaskar 'achad. ua'al
**the border of Simeon from side *the* east unto side *the* west Issachar *shall have* a *portion* And by**

48:27
גבול 1366 יששכר 3485 מפאת 6285 קדימה 6921 עד 5704 פאת 6285 ימה 3220 זבולן 2074 אחד 259: ועל 5921 גבול 1366
gabul yisaskar, mip'at qadiymah 'ad pa'at yamah zabulun 'achad. ua'al gabul
**the border of Issachar from side *the* east unto side the west Zebulun *shall have* a *portion* And by the border of**

48:28
זבולן 2074 מפאת 6285 קדמה 6921 עד 5704 פאת 6285 ימה 3220 גד 1410 אחד 259: ועל 5921 גבול 1366 גד 1410 אל 413
zabulun, mip'at qadimah 'ad pa'at yamah gad 'achad. ua'al gabul gad, 'al
**Zebulun from side *the* east unto side *the* west Gad *shall have* a *portion* And by *the* border of Gad at**

Eze 48:21 And the residue shall be for the prince, on the one side and on the other of the holy oblation, and of the possession of the city, over against the five and twenty thousand of the oblation toward the east border, and westward over against the five and twenty thousand toward the west border, over against the portions for the prince: and it shall be the holy oblation; and the sanctuary of the house shall be in the midst thereof.22 Moreover from the possession of the Levites, and from the possession of the city, being in the midst of that which is the prince's, between the border of Judah and the border of Benjamin, shall be for the prince.23 As for the rest of the tribes, from the east side unto the west side, Benjamin shall have a portion.24 And by the border of Benjamin, from the east side unto the west side, Simeon shall have a portion.25 And by the border of Simeon, from the east side unto the west side, Issachar a portion.26 And by the border of Issachar, from the east side unto the west side, Zebulun a portion.27 And by the border of Zebulun, from the east side unto the west side, Gad a portion.28 And by the border of Gad, at the south side southward, the border shall be even from Tamar unto the waters of strife in Kadesh, and to the river toward the great sea.

פאת 6285 נגב 5045 תימנה 8486 והיה 1961 גבול 1366 מתמר 8559 מי 4325 מריבת 4808 קדש 6943 נחלה 5158
pa'at negeb teymanah; uahayah gabul mitamar, mey mariybat qadesh, nachalah
**side *the* south southward shall be even the border from Tamar *unto* the waters of strife *in* Kadesh *and* to the river**

על 5921 הים 3220 הגדול 1419: **48:29** זאת 2063 הארץ 776 אשר 834 תפילו 5307 מנחלה 5159 לשבטי 7626 ישראל 3478
'al hayam hagadoul. za't ha'aretz 'asher tapiylu minachalah lashibtey yisra'ael;
**toward the sea the great This *is* the land which you shall divide by lot for inheritance unto the tribes of Israel**

ואלה 428 מחלקותם 4256 נאם 5002 אדני 136 יהוה 3069: **48:30** ואלה 428 תוצאת 8444 העיר 5892 מפאת 6285 צפון 6828
ua'aleh machlaqoutam, na'am 'adonay Yahuah. ua'aleh toutza'at ha'ayr; mip'at tzapoun,
**and these *are* their portions saith Adonai Yahuah And these *are* the goings out of the city on side *the* north**

חמש 2568 מאות 3967 וארבעת 702 אלפים 505 מדה 4060: **48:31** ושערי 8179 העיר 5892 על 5921 שמות 8034 שבטי 7626
chamesh me'aut ua'arba'at 'alapiym midah. uasha'arey ha'ayr, 'al shemout shibtey
**five hundred and four thousand measures And the gates of the city *shall be* after the names of the tribes of**

ישראל 3478 שערים 8179 שלושה 7969 צפונה 6828 שער 8179 ראובן 7205 אחד 259 שער 8179 יהודה 3063 אחד 259 שער 8179 לוי 3878 אחד 259: **48:32**
yisra'ael, sha'ariym shaloushah tzapounah; sha'ar ra'uben 'achad, sha'ar yahudah 'achad, sha'ar leuiy 'achad.
**Israel gates three northward gate of Reuben one gate of Judah one gate of Levi one**

ואל 413 פאת 6285 קדימה 6921 חמש 2568 מאות 3967 וארבעת 702 אלפים 505 ושערים 8179 שלשה 7969 ושער 8179 יוסף 3130 אחד 259 שער 8179
ua'al pa'at qadiymah, chamesh me'aut ua'arba'at 'alapiym, uash'ariym shaloshah; uasha'ar yousep 'achad, sha'ar
**And at side *the* east five hundred and four thousand and gates three and gate of Joseph one gate of**

בנימן 1144 אחד 259 שער 8179 דן 1835 אחד 259: **48:33** ופאת 6285 נגבה 5045 חמש 2568 מאות 3967 וארבעת 702 אלפים 505 מדה 4060 ושערים 8179
binyamin 'achad, sha'ar dan 'achad. uapa'at negbah, chamesh me'aut ua'arba'at 'alapiym midah, uash'ariym
**Benjamin one gate of Dan one And side *at the* south five hundred and four thousand measures and gates**

שלשה 7969 שער 8179 שמעון 8095 אחד 259 שער 8179 יששכר 3485 אחד 259 שער 8179 זבולן 2074 אחד 259: **48:34** פאת 6285 ימה 3220 חמש 2568
shaloshah; sha'ar shim'aun 'achad, sha'ar yisaskar 'achad, sha'ar zabulun 'achad. pa'at yamah, chamesh
**three gate of Simeon one gate of Issachar one gate of Zebulun one *At the* side west five**

מאות 3967 וארבעת 702 אלפים 505 שעריהם 8179 שלשה 7969 שער 8179 גד 1410 אחד 259 שער 8179 אשר 836 אחד 259 שער 8179 נפתלי 5321
me'aut ua'arba'at 'alapiym, sha'areyhem shaloshah; sha'ar gad 'achad, sha'ar 'asher 'achad, sha'ar naptaliy
**hundred and four thousand gates *with their* three gate of Gad one gate of Asher one gate of Naphtali**

אחד 259: **48:35** סביב 5439 שמנה 8083 עשר 6240 אלף 505 ושם 8034 העיר 5892 מיום 3117
'achad. sabiyb shamonah 'asar 'alep; uashem ha'ayr miyoum
**one *It was* round about eight ten thousand *measures* and the name of the city from *that* day *shall be***

יהוה 3068 שמה 8033:
Yahuah shamah.
**Yahuah *is* there**

Eze 48:29 This is the land which you shall divide by lot unto the tribes of Israel for inheritance, and these are their portions, saith YHUH G-D.30 And these are the goings out of the city on the north side, four thousand and five hundred measures.31 And the gates of the city shall be after the names of the tribes of Israel: three gates northward; one gate of Reuben, one gate of Judah, one gate of Levi.32 And at the east side four thousand and five hundred: and three gates; and one gate of Joseph, one gate of Benjamin, one gate of Dan.33 And at the south side four thousand and five hundred measures: and three gates; one gate of Simeon, one gate of Issachar, one gate of Zebulun.34 At the west side four thousand and five hundred, with their three gates; one gate of Gad, one gate of Asher, one gate of Naphtali.35 It was round about eighteen thousand measures: and the name of the city from that day shall be, YHUH is there.

# DANIEL
## (*Daniyeal*)

Daniel 9:2 and 10:2 identifies the Prophet Daniel as the author and Y'shua also mentions Daniel as the author in Matt 24:15. Daniel's Hebrew name means *Yah is my judge* and it is believed that the book may have been written originally in Aramaic approximately between 540 and 530 B.C. In 605 B.C., Nebuchadnezzar King of Babylon had conquered Jerusalem and the House of Judah and deported the survivors to Babylon, including Daniel, who would serve in the royal court of Nebuchadnezzar. The book is a record of miraculous events, prophecies and visions of the Prophet Daniel from their time in captivity to when the messiah would come in the end. Much of the book has been fulfilled perfectly down to the intricate detail Daniel was given, so we should rest knowing that everything that is yet to come true will come true just as Yahuah has declared through His Prophet Daniel.

| **Dan 1:1** | | | | | | | | | |
|---|---|---|---|---|---|---|---|---|---|
| 8141 בשנת | 7969 שלוש | 4438 למלכות | 3079 יהויקים | 4428 מלך | 3063 יהודה | 935 בא | 5019 נבוכדנאצר | 4428 מלך | 894 בבל |
| bishnat | shaloush, | lamalkut | yahouyaqiym | melek | yahudah; | ba' | unabukadra'tzar | melek | babel |
| **In year** | ***the* third** | **of the reign of** | **Jehoiakim** | **king of** | **Judah** | **came** | **Nebuchadnezzar** | **king of** | **Babylon** |

| | | | 1:2 | | | | | | | |
|---|---|---|---|---|---|---|---|---|---|---|
| 3389 ירושלם | 6696 ויצר | 5921: עליה | 5414 ויתן | 136 אדני | 3027 בידו | 853 את | 3079 יהויקים | 4428 מלך | 3063 יהודה | 7117 ומקצת |
| yarushalaim | uayatzar | 'aleyha. | uayiten | 'adonay | bayadou | 'at | yahouyaqiym | melek | yahudah, | uamiqtzat |
| ***unto* Jerusalem** | **and besieged** | **it** | **And gave** | **Adonai** | **into his hand** | | **Jehoiakim** | **king of** | **Judah** | **with part of** |

| 3627 כלי | 1004 בית | 430 האלהים | 935 ויביאם | 776 ארץ | 8152 שנער | 1004 בית | 430 אלהיו | 853 ואת | 3627 הכלים |
|---|---|---|---|---|---|---|---|---|---|
| kaley | beyt | ha'alohiym, | uayabiy'aem | 'aretz | shin'ar | beyt | 'alohayu; | ua'at | hakeliym |
| **the vessels of** | **the house of** | **Elohim** | **which he carried into** | **the land of** | **Shinar** | ***to* the house of** | **his god** | ***and*** | **the vessels** |

| | | | | 1:3 | | | | |
|---|---|---|---|---|---|---|---|---|
| 935 הביא | 1004 בית | 214 אוצר | 430: אלהיו | 559 ויאמר | 4428 המלך | 828 לאשפנז | 7227 רב | 5631 סריסיו |
| habiy'a, | beyt | 'autzar | 'alohayu. | uaya'mer | hamelek, | la'ashpanaz | rab | sariysayu; |
| **he brought into** | **house** | ***the* treasure of** | **his god** | **And spoke** | **the king** | **unto Ashpenaz** | **the master of** | **his eunuchs** |

| | | | | | | | 1:4 | |
|---|---|---|---|---|---|---|---|---|
| 935 להביא | 1121 מבני | 3478 ישראל | 2233 ומזרע | 4410 המלוכה | 4480 ומן | 6579: הפרתמים | 3206 ילדים | 834 אשר |
| lahabiy'a | mibney | yisra'ael | uamizera' | hamalukah | uamin | hapartamiym. | yaladiym | 'asher |
| **that he should bring** | ***certain* of the children of** | **Israel** | **and of seed** | **the king's** | **and of** | **the princes** | **Children** | **whom** |

| 369 אין | 871a בהם | 3605 כל | 3971 מאום | 2896 וטובי | 4758 מראה | 7919 ומשכילים | 3605 בכל | 2451 חכמה | 3045 וידעי | 1847 דעת |
|---|---|---|---|---|---|---|---|---|---|---|
| 'aeyn | bahem | kal | ma'um | uatoubey | mar'aeh | uamaskiyliym | bakal | chakamah | uayoda'aey | da'at |
| **was no** | **in whom** | **every** | **blemish** | **but well** | **favoured** | **and skilful** | **in all** | **wisdom** | **and cunning in** | **knowledge** |

| 995 ומביני | 4093 מדע | 834 ואשר | 3581 כח | 871a בהם | 5975 לעמד | 1964 בהיכל | 4428 המלך | 3925 וללמדם |
|---|---|---|---|---|---|---|---|---|
| uambiyney | mada', | ua'asher | koach | bahem, | la'amod | baheykal | hamelek; | ualalamdam |
| **and understanding** | **science** | **and such as *had*** | **ability** | **in them** | **to stand** | **in palace** | **the king's** | **and whom they might teach** |

| | | | 1:5 | | | | | | |
|---|---|---|---|---|---|---|---|---|---|
| 5612 ספר | 3956 ולשון | 3778: כשדים | 4487 וימן | 3807a להם | 4428 המלך | 1697 דבר | 3117 יום | 3117 ביומו | 6598 מפת |
| seper | ualshoun | kasdiym. | uayaman | lahem | hamelek | dabar | youm | bayoumou, | mipat |
| **the learning** | **and the tongue of** | **the Chaldeans** | **And appointed** | **them** | **the king** | **a provision of** | **day** | **to day** | **meat** |

| 6598 בג | 4428 המלך | 3196 ומיין | 4960 משתיו | 1431 ולגדלם | 8141 שנים | 7969 שלוש | 7117 ומקצתם |
|---|---|---|---|---|---|---|---|
| bag | hamelek | uamiyeyn | mishtayu, | ualgadlam | shaniym | shaloush; | uamiqtzatam, |
| **from** | **the king's** | **and of the wine** | **which he drank** | **so nourishing them** | **years** | **three** | **that at the end thereof** |

| | | | 1:6 | | | | | | |
|---|---|---|---|---|---|---|---|---|---|
| 5975 יעמדו | 6440 לפני | 4428: המלך | 1961 ויהי | 871a בהם | 1121 מבני | 3063 יהודה | 1840 דניאל | 2608 חנניה | 4332 מישאל |
| ya'amdu | lipney | hamelek. | uayahiy | bahem | mibney | yahudah; | daniyea'l | chananyah, | misha'ael |
| **they might stand** | **before** | **the king** | **Now were** | **among these** | **of the children of** | **Judah** | **Daniel** | **Hananiah** | **Mishael** |

**Daniel** 1:1 In the third year of the reign of Jehoiakim king of Judah came Nebuchadnezzar king of Babylon unto Jerusalem, and besieged it.2 And YHUH gave Jehoiakim king of Judah into his hand, with part of the vessels of the house of G-d: which he carried into the land of Shinar to the house of his god; and he brought the vessels into the treasure house of his god.3 And the king spoke unto Ashpenaz the master of his eunuchs, that he should bring certain of the children of Israel, and of the king's seed, and of the princes;4 Children in whom was no blemish, but well favoured, and skilful in all wisdom, and cunning in knowledge, and understanding science, and such as had ability in them to stand in the king's palace, and whom they might teach the learning and the tongue of the Chaldeans.5 And the king appointed them a daily provision of the king's meat, and of the wine which he drank: so nourishing them three years, that at the end thereof they might stand before the king.6 Now among these were of the children of Judah, Daniel, Hananiah, Mishael, and Azariah:

1:7

ועזריה 5838: וישם 7760 להם 1992 שר 8269 הסריסים 5631 שמות 8034 וישם 7760 לדניאל 1840 בלטשאצר 1095
ua'azaryah. uayasem lahem sar hasariysiym shemout; uayasem ladaniyea'l beltasha'tzar,
**and Azariah gave Unto whom the prince of the eunuchs names for he gave unto Daniel *the name of* Belteshazzar**

1:8

ולחנניה 2608 שדרך 7714 ולמישאל 4332 מישך 4335 ולעזריה 5838 עבד 5650 נגו 5664: וישם 7760 דניאל 1840 על 5921
ualachananyah shadrak, ualmiysha'ael meyshak, uala'azaryah 'abed nagou. uayasem daniyea'l 'al
**and to Hananiah *of* Shadrach and to Mishael *of* Meshach and to Azariah *of* Abed nego But purposed Daniel in**

לבו 3820 אשר 834 לא 3808 יתגאל 1351 בפתבג 6598 המלך 4428 וביין 3196 משתיו 4960
libou, 'asher la' yitga'al bapatbag hamelek uabyeyn mishtayu;
**his heart that not he would defile himself with the portion of meat the king's nor with the wine which he drank**

1:9

ויבקש 1245 משר 8269 הסריסים 5631 אשר 834 לא 3808 יתגאל 1351: ויתן 5414 האלהים 430
uayabaqesh misar hasariysiym, 'asher la' yitga'al. uayiten ha'alohiym
**therefore he requested of the prince of the eunuchs that not he might defile himself Now had brought the Elohim**

1:10

את 853 דניאל 1840 לחסד 2617 ולרחמים 7356 לפני 6440 שר 8269 הסריסים 5631: ויאמר 559 שר 8269 הסריסים 5631
'at daniyea'l, lachesed ualrachamiym; lipney sar hasariysiym. uaya'mer sar hasariysiym
**Daniel into favor and tender love with the prince of the eunuchs And said the prince of the eunuchs**

לדניאל 1840 ירא 3373 אני 589 את 853 אדני 113 המלך 4428 אשר 834 מנה 4487 את 853 מאכלכם 3978 ואת 853 משתיכם 4960 אשר 834
ladaniyea'l, yarea' 'aniy 'at 'adoniy hamelek, 'asher minah, 'at ma'akalkem ua'at mishteykem; 'asher
**unto Daniel fear I my adonai the king who has appointed your meat *and* your drink for**

למה 4100 יראה 7200 את 853 פניכם 6440 זעפים 2196 מן 4480 הילדים 3206 אשר 834 כגילכם 1524
lamah yir'ah 'at paneykem zo'apiym, min hayladiym 'asher kagiylakem,
**why should he see your faces worse liking than the children which *are* of your sort?**

1:11

וחיבתם 2325 את 853 ראשי 7218 למלך 4428: ויאמר 559 דניאל 1840 אל 413 המלצר 4453 אשר 834 מנה 4487
uachiyabtem 'at ra'shiy lamelek. uaya'mer daniyea'l 'al hameltzar; 'asher minah
**then shall you make me endanger my head to the king Then said Daniel to Melzar whom had set**

1:12

שר 8269 הסריסים 5631 על 5921 דניאל 1840 חנניה 2608 מישאל 4332 ועזריה 5838: נס 5254 נא 4994 את 853 עבדיך 5650
sar hasariysiym, 'al daniyea'l chananyah, misha'ael ua'azaryah. nas naa' 'at 'abadeyka
**the prince of the eunuchs over Daniel Hananiah Mishael and Azariah Prove I beseech you your servants**

1:13

ימים 3117 עשרה 6235 ויתנו 5414 לנו 3807a מן 4480 הזרעים 2235 ונאכלה 398 ומים 4325 ונשתה 8354: ויראו 7200
yamiym 'asarah; uayitanu lanu min hazeroayIm uana'kalah uamayim uanishteh. uayera'au
**days ten and let them give us some pulse to eat and water to drink Then let be looked upon**

לפניך 6440 מראינו 4758 ומראה 4758 הילדים 3206 האכלים 398 את 853 פתבג 6598 המלך 4428
lapaneyka mar'aeynu, uamara'aeh hayladiym, ha'akaliym, 'at patbag hamelek;
**before you our countenances and the countenance of the children that eat of the portion of meat the king's**

1:14

וכאשר 834 תראה 7200 עשה 6213 עם 5973 עבדיך 5650: וישמע 8085 להם 3807a לדבר 1697 הזה 2088 וינסם 5254 ימים 3117
uaka'asher tir'ah, 'aseh 'am 'abadeyka. uayishma' lahem ladabar hazeh; uaynasem yamiym
**and as you see deal with your servants So he consented to them in matter this and proved them days**

Dan 1:7 Unto whom the prince of the eunuchs gave names: for he gave unto Daniel the name of Belteshazzar; and to Hananiah, of Shadrach; and to Mishael, of Meshach; and to Azariah, of Abed-nego.8 But Daniel purposed in his heart that he would not defile himself with the portion of the king's meat, nor with the wine which he drank: therefore he requested of the prince of the eunuchs that he might not defile himself.9 Now G-d had brought Daniel into favor and tender love with the prince of the eunuchs.10 And the prince of the eunuchs said unto Daniel, I fear my lord the king, who has appointed your meat and your drink: for why should he see your faces worse liking than the children which are of your sort? then shall you make me endanger my head to the king.11 Then said Daniel to Melzar, whom the prince of the eunuchs had set over Daniel, Hananiah, Mishael, and Azariah,12 Prove your servants, I beseech you, ten days; and let them give us pulse to eat, and water to drink.13 Then let our countenances be looked upon before you, and the countenance of the children that eat of the portion of the king's meat: and as you seest, deal with your servants.14 So he consented to them in this matter, and proved them ten days.

| 6235: עשרה | 1:15 | 7117 ומקצת | 3117 ימים | 6235 עשרה | 7200 נראה | 4758 מראיהם | 2896 טוב | 1277 ובריאי | 1320 בשר | 4480 מן | 3605 כל |
|---|---|---|---|---|---|---|---|---|---|---|---|
| 'asarah. | | uamiqtzat | yamiym | 'asarah, | nir'ah | mar'aeyhem | toub, | uabriy'aey | basar; | min | kal |
| **ten** | | **And at the end of** | **days** | **ten** | **appeared** | **their countenances** | **fairer** | **and fatter** | **in flesh** | **than** | **all** |

| 3206 הילדים | 398 האכלים | 853 את | 6598 פתבג | 4428: המלך | 1:16 | 1961 ויהי | 4453 המלצר | 5375 נשא | 853 את |
|---|---|---|---|---|---|---|---|---|---|
| hayladiym, | ha'akaliym, | 'at | patbag | hamelek. | | uayahiy | hameltzar, | nosea' | 'at |
| **the children** | **which did eat** | | **the portion of meat** | **the king's** | | **Thus** | **Melzar** | **took away** | |

| 6598 פתבגם | 3196 ויין | 4960 משתיהם | 5414 ונתן | 3807a להם | 2235: זרענים | 1:17 | 3206 והילדים | 428 האלה |
|---|---|---|---|---|---|---|---|---|
| patbagam, | uayeyn | mishteyhem; | uanoten | lahem | zera'aniym. | | uahayaladiym | ha'aeleh |
| **the portion of their meat** | **and the wine** | **that they should drink** | **and gave** | **them** | **pulse** | | **As for children** | **these** |

| 702 ארבעתם | 5414 נתן | 3807a להם | 430 האלהים | 4093 מדע | 7919 והשכל | 3605 בכל | 5612 ספר | 2451 וחכמה | 1840 ודניאל | 995 הבין |
|---|---|---|---|---|---|---|---|---|---|---|
| 'arba'tam, | natan | lahem | ha'alohiym | mada' | uahaskel | bakal | seper | uachakamah; | uadaniyea'l | hebiyn, |
| **four** | **gave** | **them** | **Elohim** | **knowledge** | **and skill** | **in all** | **learning** | **and wisdom** | **and Daniel** | **had understanding** |

| 3605 בכל | 2377 חזון | 2472: וחלמות | 1:18 | 7117 ולמקצת | 3117 הימים | 834 אשר | 559 אמר | 4428 המלך | 935 להביאם |
|---|---|---|---|---|---|---|---|---|---|
| bakal | chazoun | bachalomout. | | ualmiqtzat | hayamiym, | 'asher | 'amar | hamelek | lahabiy'am; |
| **in all** | **visions** | **and dreams** | | **Now at the end of** | **the days** | **that** | **had said** | **the king** | **he should bring them in** |

| 935 ויביאם | 8269 שר | 5631 הסריסים | 6440 לפני | 5019: נבכדנצר | 1:19 | 1696 וידבר | 854 אתם | 4428 המלך |
|---|---|---|---|---|---|---|---|---|
| uayabiy'aem | sar | hasariysiym, | lipney | nabukadnetzar. | | uaydaber | 'atam | hamelek |
| **then brought them in** | **the prince of** | **the eunuchs** | **before** | **Nebuchadnezzar** | | **And communed** | **with them** | **the king** |

| 3808 ולא | 4672 נמצא | 3605 מכלם | 1840 כדניאל | 2608 חנניה | 4332 מישאל | 5838 ועזריה | 5975 ויעמדו | 6440 לפני |
|---|---|---|---|---|---|---|---|---|
| uala' | nimtza' | mikulam, | kadaniyea'l | chananyah, | misha'ael | ua'azaryah; | uaya'amdu | lipney |
| **and none** | **was found** | **among them all** | **like Daniel** | **Hananiah** | **Mishael** | **and Azariah** | **therefore stood they** | **before** |

| 4428: המלך | 1:20 | 3605 וכל | 1697 דבר | 2451 חכמת | 998 בינה | 834 אשר | 1245 בקש | 1992 מהם | 4428 המלך | 4672 וימצאם | 6235 עשר |
|---|---|---|---|---|---|---|---|---|---|---|---|
| hamelek. | | uakol, | dabar | chakamat | biynah, | 'asher | biqesh | mehem | hamelek; | uayimtza'aem | 'aser |
| **the king** | | **And in all** | **matters of** | **wisdom** | ***and* understanding** | **that** | **inquired of them** | | **the king** | **he found them** | **ten** |

| 3027 ידות | 5921 על | 3605 כל | 2748 החרטמים | 825 האשפים | 834 אשר | 3605 בכל | 4438: מלכותו | 1:21 | 1961 ויהי | 1840 דניאל |
|---|---|---|---|---|---|---|---|---|---|---|
| yadout, | 'al | kal | hachartumiym | ha'ashapiym, | 'asher | bakal | malkutou. | | uayahiy | daniyea'l, |
| **times** | **better than** | **all** | **the magicians** | ***and* astrologers** | **that *were*** | **in all** | **his realm** | | **And continued *even*** | **Daniel** |

| 5704 עד | 8141 שנת | 259 אחת | 3566 לכורש | 4428: המלך |
|---|---|---|---|---|
| 'ad | shanat | 'achat | lakouresh | hamelek. |
| **unto** | **year** | ***the* first of** | **Cyrus** | **king** |

| **Dan 2:1** | 8141 ובשנת | 8147 שתים | 4438 למלכות | 5019 נבכדנצר | 2492 חלם | 5019 נבכדנצר | 2472 חלמות |
|---|---|---|---|---|---|---|---|
| | uabishnat | shatayim, | lamalkut | nabukadnetzar, | chalam | nabukadnetzar | chalomout; |
| | **And in the year** | **second** | **of the reign of** | **Nebuchadnezzar** | **dreamed** | **Nebuchadnezzar** | **dreams** |

| 6470 ותתפעם | 7307 רוחו | 8142 ושנתו | 1961 נהיתה | 5921: עליו | 2:2 | 559 ויאמר | 4428 המלך | 7121 לקרא | 2748 לחרטמים |
|---|---|---|---|---|---|---|---|---|---|
| uatitpa'am | ruachou, | uashnatou | nihyatah | 'alayu. | | uaya'mer | hamelek | liqra' | lachartumiym |
| **wherewith was troubled** | **his spirit** | **and his sleep** | **brake** | **from him** | | **Then commanded** | **the king** | **to call** | **the magicians** |

Eze 1:15 And at the end of ten days their countenances appeared fairer and fatter in flesh than all the children which did eat the portion of the king's meat.16 Thus Melzar took away the portion of their meat, and the wine that they should drink; and gave them pulse.17 As for these four children, G-d gave them knowledge and skill in all learning and wisdom: and Daniel had understanding in all visions and dreams.18 Now at the end of the days that the king had said he should bring them in, then the prince of the eunuchs brought them in before Nebuchadnezzar.19 And the king communed with them; and among them all was found none like Daniel, Hananiah, Mishael, and Azariah: therefore stood they before the king.20 And in all matters of wisdom and understanding, that the king inquired of them, he found them ten times better than all the magicians and astrologers that were in all his realm.21 And Daniel continued even unto the first year of king Cyrus. **Dan** 2:1 And in the second year of the reign of Nebuchadnezzar Nebuchadnezzar dreamed dreams, wherewith his spirit was troubled, and his sleep break from him.2 Then the king commanded to call the magicians, and the astrologers, and the sorcerers, and the Chaldeans, for to show the king his dreams. So they came and stood before the king.

ולאשפים 825 ולמכשפים 3784 ולכשדים 3778 להגיד 5046 למלך 4428 חלמתיו 2472 ויבאו 935 ויעמדו 5975 לפני 6440
uala'ashapiym, ualamakashapiym ualakasdiym, lahagiyd lamelek chalomotayu; uayabo'au uaya'amdu lipney
**and the astrologers and the sorcerers and the Chaldeans to show for the king his dreams So they came and stood before**

המלך 4428: 2:3 ויאמר 559 להם 1992 המלך 4428 חלום 2472 חלמתי 2492 ותפעם 6470 רוחי 7307 לדעת 3045 את 853 החלום 2472: 2:4
hamelek. uaya'mer lahem hamelek chaloum chalamatiy; uatipa'am ruchiy, lada'at 'at hachaloum.
**the king And said unto them the king a dream I have dreamed and was troubled my spirit to know the dream**

וידברו 1696 הכשדים 3778 למלך 4428 ארמית 762 מלכא 4430 לעלמין 5957 חיי 2418 אמר 560 חלמא 2493 לעבדיך 5649
uayadabru hakasdiym lamelek 'aramiyt; malka' la'alamiyn chayiy, 'amar chelma' la'abadayik
**Then spoke the Chaldeans to the king in Syriack O king for ever live tell the dream your servant**

ופשרא 6591 נחוא 2324: 2:5 ענה 6032 מלכא 4430 ואמר 560 לכשדיא 3779 מלתא 4406 מני 4481 אזדא 230
uapishra' nachauea'. 'aneh malka' ua'amar lakasdaya' milea'ta miniy 'azda';
**and the interpretation we will show answered The king and said to the Chaldean The thing (*matter*) from me is gone**

הן 2006 לא 3809 תהודעונני 3046 חלמא 2493 ופשרה 6591 הדמין 1917 תתעבדון 5648
hen la' tahouda'aunaniy chelma' uapishreh, hadamiyn tit'abdun,
**if not you will make known unto me the dream with the interpretation thereof pieces you shall be cut in**

ובתיכון 1005 נולי 5122 יתשמון 7761: 2:6 והן 2006 חלמא 2493 ופשרה 6591 תהחון 2324 מתנן 4978
uabateykoun naualiy yitsamun. uahen chelma' uapishreh tahachauon, matanan
**and your houses a dunghill shall be made But if the dream and the interpretation thereof you show gifts**

ונבזבה 5023 ויקר 3367 שגיא 7690 תקבלון 6902 מן 4481 קדמי 6925 להן 2006 חלמא 2493 ופשרה 6591
uanbizbah uayqar sagiy'a, taqablun min qadamay; lahen chelma' uapishreh
**and rewards and honor great you shall receive of me therefore the dream and the interpretation thereof**

החוני 2324: 2:7 ענו 6032 תנינות 8579 ואמרין 560 מלכא 4430 חלמא 2493 יאמר 560 לעבדוהי 5649 ופשרה 6591
hachauoniy. 'anou tinyanut ua'amariyn; malka' chelma' yea'mar la'abdouhiy uapishrah
**show me They answered again and said the king the dream Let tell his servants and the interpretation of it**

נהחוה 2324: 2:8 ענה 6032 מלכא 4430 ואמר 560 מן 4481 יציב 3330 ידע 3046 אנה 576 די 1768 עדנא 5732 אנתון 608 זבנין 2084 כל 3605
nahachaueh. 'aneh malka' ua'amar, min yatziyb yada' 'anah, diy 'adana' 'antun zabaniyn; kal
**we will show answered The king and said of certainty know I that the time you would gain all**

קבל 6903 די 1768 חזיתון 2370 די 1768 אזדא 230 מני 4481 מלתא 4406: 2:9 די 1768 הן 2006 חלמא 2493 לא 3809
qabel diy chazeytoun, diy 'azda' miniy milta'. diy hen chelma' la'
**according to forasmuch you see forasmuch is gone from me the thing But if the dream not**

תהודענני 3046 חדה 2298 היא 1932 דתכון 1882 ומלה 4406 כדבה 3538 ושחיתה 7844 הזמנתון 2164
tahouda'aunaniy chadah hiy'a datakoun, uamilah kidbah uashchiytah hazmintun
**you will make known unto *there is but* one me decree for you for words lying and corrupt you have prepared**

למאמר 560 קדמי 6925 עד 5704 די 1768 עדנא 5732 ישתנא 8133 להן 2006 חלמא 2493 אמרו 560 לי 3807a ואנדע 3046 די 1768
lamemar qadamay, 'ad diy 'adana' yishtanea'; lahen, chelma' 'amaru liy, ua'anda' diy
**to speak before me till forasmuch the time be changed therefore me the dream tell me and I shall know that**

Dan 2:3 And the king said unto them, I have dreamed a dream, and my spirit was troubled to know the dream.4 Then spoke the Chaldeans to the king in Syriack, O king, live forever: tell your servants the dream, and we will show the interpretation.5 The king answered and said to the Chaldeans, The thing is gone from me: if you will not make known unto me the dream, with the interpretation thereof, you shall be cut in pieces, and your houses shall be made a dunghill.6 But if you show the dream, and the interpretation thereof, you shall receive of me gifts and rewards and great honor: therefore show me the dream, and the interpretation thereof.7 They answered again and said, Let the king tell his servants the dream, and we will show the interpretation of it.8 The king answered and said, I know of certainty that you would gain the time, because you see the thing is gone from me.9 But if you will not make known unto me the dream, there is but one decree for you: for you have prepared lying and corrupt words to speak before me, till the time be changed: therefore tell me the dream, and I shall know that you can show me the interpretation thereof.

| 6591 פשרה | 2324: תהחונני | 2:10 | 6032 ענו | 3779 כשדיא | 6925 קדם | 4430 מלכא | 560 ואמרין | 3809 לא | 383 איתי |
|---|---|---|---|---|---|---|---|---|---|
| pishreh | tahachaunaniy. | | 'anou | kasdaya | qadam | malka' | ua'amariyn, | la' | 'aytay |
| **the interpretation thereof** | **you can show me** | | **answered** | **the Chaldeans** | **before** | **the king** | **and said** | **not** | **There is** |

| 606 אנש | 5922 על | 3007 יבשתא | 1768 די | 4406 מלת | 4430 מלכא | 3202 יוכל | 2324 להחויה | 3606 כל | 6903 קבל | 1768 די | 3606 כל | 4430 מלך |
|---|---|---|---|---|---|---|---|---|---|---|---|---|
| 'anash | 'al | yabeshta', | diy | milat | malka', | yukal | lahachauayah; | kal | qabel, | diy | kal | melek |
| **a man** | **upon** | **the earth** | **that** | **matter** | ***the* king's** | **can** | **show** | **at any** | **according to** | **therefore *there is*** | **no** | **king** |

| 7229 רב | 7990 ושליט | 4406 מלה | 1836 כדנה | 3809 לא | 7593 שאל | 3605 לכל | 2749 חרטם | 826 ואשף | 3779: וכשדי | 2:11 | 4406 ומלתא | 1768 די |
|---|---|---|---|---|---|---|---|---|---|---|---|---|
| rab | uashaliyt, | milah | kidnah | la' | sha'ael, | lakal | chartom | ua'ashap | uakasday. | | uamilta' | diy |
| **adonai** | **nor ruler** | **things** | **such** | **no** | ***that* asked** | **at any** | **magician** | **or astrologer** | **or Chaldean** | | **And *it is* a thing** | **that** |

| 4430 מלכה | 7593 שאל | 3358 יקירה | 321 ואחרן | 3809 לא | 383 איתי | 1768 די | 2324 יחונה | 6925 קדם | 4430 מלכא | 3861 להן | 426 אלהין | 1768 די | 4070 מדרהון |
|---|---|---|---|---|---|---|---|---|---|---|---|---|---|
| malkah | sha'ael | yaqiyrah, | ua'acharan | la' | 'aytay, | diy | yachauinah | qadam | malka'; | lahen | 'alahiyn, | diy | madarahoun, |
| **the king** | **require** | **rare** | **and other** | **none** | **there is** | **that** | **can show it** | **before** | **the king** | **except** | **the gods** | **whose** | **dwelling** |

| 5974 עם | 1321 בשרא | 3809 לא | 383: איתוהי | 2:12 | 3606 כל | 6903 קבל | 1836 דנה | 4430 מלכא | 1149 בנס | 7108 וקצף | 7690 שגיא |
|---|---|---|---|---|---|---|---|---|---|---|---|
| 'am | bisra' | la' | 'aytouhiy. | | kal | qabel | danah, | malka' | banas | uaqtzap | sagiy'a; |
| **with** | **flesh** | **not** | **is of him** | | ***For* cause** | **according to** | **this** | **the king** | **was angry** | **and furious** | **very** |

| 560 ואמר | 7 להובדה | 3606 לכל | 2445 חכימי | 895: בבל | 2:13 | 1882 ודתא | 5312 נפקת | 2445 וחכימיא |
|---|---|---|---|---|---|---|---|---|
| ua'amar | lahoubadah, | lakol | chakiymey | babel. | | uadata' | nepqat, | uachakiymaya' |
| **and commanded** | **to destroy** | **all** | **the wise *men* of** | **Babylon** | | **And the decree** | **went forth** | **that the wise** |

| 6992 מתקטלין | 1156 ובעו | 1841 דניאל | 2269 וחברוהי | 6992: להתקטלה | 2:14 | 116 באדין | 1841 דניאל | 8421 התיב | 5843 עטא |
|---|---|---|---|---|---|---|---|---|---|
| mitqataliyn; | uab'au | daniyea'l | uachabrouhiy | lahitqatalah. | | bea'dayin | daniyea'l, | hatiyb | 'ata' |
| ***men* should be slain** | **and they sought** | **Daniel** | **and his fellows** | **to be slain** | | **Then** | **Daniel** | **answered with** | **counsel** |

| 2942 וטעם | 746 לאריוך | 7229 רב | 2877 טבחיא | 1768 די | 4430 מלכא | 1768 די | 5312 נפק | 6992 לקטלה | 2445 לחכימי | 895: בבל | 2:15 |
|---|---|---|---|---|---|---|---|---|---|---|---|
| uat'aem, | la'aryouk | rab | tabachaya' | diy | malka'; | diy | napaq | laqtalah, | lachakiymey | babel. | |
| **and wisdom** | **to Arioch** | **the captain** | **guard** | **of** | ***the* king's** | **which** | **was gone forth** | **to slay** | **the wise *men* of** | **Babylon** | |

| 6032 ענה | 560 ואמר | 746 לאריוך | 7990 שליטא | 1768 די | 4430 מלכא | 5922 על | 4100 מה | 1882 דתא | 2685 מהחצפה | 4481 מן | 6925 קדם |
|---|---|---|---|---|---|---|---|---|---|---|---|
| 'aneh | ua'amar, | la'aryouk | shaliyta' | diy | malka', | 'al | mah | data' | mahachtzapah | min | qadam |
| **He answered** | **and said** | **to Arioch** | **captain** | **forasmuch** | ***the* king's** | **for** | **why** | ***is* the decree *so*** | **hasty** | **according** | **from** |

| 4430 מלכא | 116 אדין | 4406 מלתא | 3046 הודע | 746 אריוך | 1841: לדניאל | 2:16 | 1841 ודניאל | 5954 על | 1156 ובעה | 4481 מן | 4430 מלכא | 1768 די |
|---|---|---|---|---|---|---|---|---|---|---|---|---|
| malka'; | 'adayin | milta', | houda' | aryouk | ladaniyea'l. | | uadaniyea'l, | 'al | uab'ah | min | malka'; | diy |
| **the king?** | **Then** | **the thing** | **made known** | **Arioch** | **to Daniel** | | **Then Daniel** | **went in** | **and desired** | **of** | ***the* king** | **that** |

| 2166 זמן | 5415 ינתן | 3807a לה | 6591 ופשרא | 2324 להחויה | 4430: למלכא | 2:17 | 116 אדין | 1841 דניאל | 1005 לביתה | 236 אזל |
|---|---|---|---|---|---|---|---|---|---|---|
| zaman | yinten | leh, | uapishra' | lahachauayah | lamalka'. | | 'adayin | daniyea'l | labayateh | 'azal; |
| **time** | **he would give** | **and him** | **the interpretation** | **that he would show** | **the king** | | **Then** | **Daniel** | **to his house** | **went** |

| 2608 ולחנניה | 4333 מישאל | 5839 ועזריה | 2269 חברוהי | 4406 מלתא | 3046: הודע | 2:18 | 7359 ורחמין | 1156 למבעא |
|---|---|---|---|---|---|---|---|---|
| ualachananyah | misha'el | ua'azaryah | chabrouhiy | milta' | houda'. | | uarachamiyn, | lamib'aa' |
| **and to Hananiah** | **Mishael** | **and Azariah** | **his companions** | **the thing** | **made known** | | **That mercies** | **they would desire** |

Dan 2:10 The Chaldeans answered before the king, and said, There is not a man upon the earth that can show the king's matter: therefore there is no king, lord, nor ruler, that asked such things at any magician, or astrologer, or Chaldean.11 And it is a rare thing that the king requireth, and there is none other that can show it before the king, except the gods, whose dwelling is not with flesh.12 For this cause the king was angry and very furious, and commanded to destroy all the wise men of Babylon.13 And the decree went forth that the wise men should be slain; and they sought Daniel and his fellows to be slain.14 Then Daniel answered with counsel and wisdom to Arioch the captain of the king's guard, which was gone forth to slay the wise men of Babylon:15 He answered and said to Arioch the king's captain, Why is the decree so hasty from the king? Then Arioch made the thing known to Daniel.16 Then Daniel went in, and desired of the king that he would give him time, and that he would show the king the interpretation.17 Then Daniel went to his house, and made the thing known to Hananiah, Mishael, and Azariah, his companions:18 That they would desire mercies of the G-d of heaven concerning this secret; that Daniel and his fellows should not perish with the rest of the wise men of Babylon.

מן 4481 קדם 6925 אלה 426 שמיא 8065 על 5922 רזה 7328 דנה 1836 די 1768 לא 3809 יהבדון 7 דניאל 1841 וחברוהי 2269 עם 5974
min qadam 'alah shamaya', 'al razah danah; diy la' yahobadun daniyea'l uachabrouhiy, 'am
**according of the El heaven concerning secret this that not should perish Daniel and his fellows with**

שאר 7606 חכימי 2445 בבל 895: אדין 116 לדניאל 1841 בחזוא 2376 די 1768 ליליא 3916 רזה 7328 גלי 1541 אדין 116
sha'ar chakiymey babel. 'adayin, ladaniyea'l bachezua' diy leylaya' razah galiy; 'adayin
**the rest of the wise *men* of Babylon 2:19 Then unto Daniel in a vision in night the secret was revealed Then**

דניאל 1841 ברך 1289 לאלה 426 שמיא 8065: ענה 6032 דניאל 1841 ואמר 560 להוא 1934 שמה 8036 די 1768 אלהא 426 מברך 1289 מן 4481
daniyea'l, barik le'alah shamaya'. 'aneh daniyea'l ua'amar, lehauea' shameh diy 'alaha' mabarak, min
**Daniel blessed the El of heaven 2:20 answered Daniel and said be the name of Elohim Blessed for**

עלמא 5957 ועד 5705 עלמא 5957 די 1768 חכמתא 2452 וגבורתא 1370 די 1768 לה 3807a היא 1932: והוא 1932 מהשנא 8133 עדניא 5732
'alma' ua'ad 'alma'; diy chakmata' uagburata' diy leh hiy'a. uahu'a mahashnea' 'adanaya'
**ever and unto ever for wisdom and might *are* that to him are 2:21 And he who changes the times**

וזמניא 2166 מהעדה 5709 מלכין 4430 ומהקים 6966 מלכין 4430 יהב 3052 חכמתא 2452 לחכימין 2445 ומנדעא 4486 לידעי 3046
uazimnaya', maha'adeh malkiyn uamhaqeym malkiyn; yaheb chakmata' lachakiymiyn, uamanda'a' layada'aey
**and the seasons he remove kings and set up kings he gives wisdom unto the wise and knowledge to them that know**

בינה 999: הוא 1931 גלא 1541 עמיקתא 5994 ומסתרתא 5642 ידע 3046 מה 4100 בחשוכא 2816 ונהירא 5094 עמה 5974
biynah. hua' galea' amiyqata' uamsatrata'; yada' mah bachashouka', uanehiyra' 'ameh
**understanding 2:22 He reveal the deep and secret things he knows what *is* in the darkness and the light with him**

שרא 8271: לך 3807a אלה 426 אבהתי 2 מהודא 3029 ומשבח 7624 אנה 576 די 1768 חכמתא 2452 וגבורתא 1370 יהבת 3052 לי 3807a
sharea'. lak 'alah 'abahatiy, mahoudea' uamshabach 'anah, diy chakmata' uagburata' yahabt liy;
**dwell 2:23 to you O El of my fathers thank and praise *you* I who wisdom and might have given me**

וכען 3705 הודעתני 3046 די 1768 בעינא 1156 מנך 4481 די 1768 מלת 4406 מלכא 4430
uak'an houda'ataniy diy ba'aeyna' minak, diy milat malka'
**and now have made known unto me what we desired of you for matter *the* king's**

הודעתנא 3046: כל 3606 קבל 6903 דנה 1836 דניאל 1841 על 5954 על 5922 אריוך 746 די 1768 מני 4483
houda'atena'. kal qabel danah, daniyea'l 'al 'al aryouk, diy maniy
**you have *now* made known unto us 2:24 all according to Therefore Daniel went in unto Arioch whom had ordained**

מלכא 4430 להובדה 7 לחכימי 2445 בבל 895 אזל 236 וכן 3652 אמר 560 לה 3807a לחכימי 2445 בבל 895 אל 409 תהובד 7
malka', lahoubadah lachakiymey babel; 'azal uaken 'amar leh, lachakiymey babel 'al tahoubed,
**the king to destroy the wise *men* of Babylon he went and thus said unto him the wise *men* of Babylon not Destroy**

העלני 5954 קדם 6925 מלכא 4430 ופשרא 6591 למלכא 4430 אחוא 2324: אדין 116 אריוך 746 בהתבהלה 927 הנעל 5954
ha'aelaniy qadam malka', uapishra' lamalka' 'achauea'. 'adayin 'aryouk bahitbahalah, han'ael
**bring me in before the king and the interpretation unto the king I will show 2:25 Then Arioch in haste brought**

לדניאל 1841 קדם 6925 מלכא 4430 וכן 3652 אמר 560 לה 3807a די 1768 השכחת 7912 גבר 1400 מן 4481 בני 1121 גלותא 1547 די 1768 יהוד 3061 די 1768
ladaniyea'l qadam malka'; uaken 'amar leh, diy hashkachat gabar min baney galuta' diy yahud, diy
**in Daniel before the king and thus said unto him whom I have found a man of *the* child captivity of Judah that**

Dan 2:19 Then was the secret revealed unto Daniel in a night vision. Then Daniel blessed the G-d of heaven.20 Daniel answered and said, Blessed be the name of G-d forever and ever: for wisdom and might are his:21 And he changeth the times and the seasons: he removeth kings, and set up kings: he give wisdom unto the wise, and knowledge to them that know understanding:22 He revealeth the deep and secret things: he know what is in the darkness, and the light dwell with him.23 I thank you, and praise you, O you G-d of my fathers, who have given me wisdom and might, and have made known unto me now what we desired of you: for you have now made known unto us the king's matter.24 Therefore Daniel went in unto Arioch, whom the king had ordained to destroy the wise men of Babylon: he went and said thus unto him; Destroy not the wise men of Babylon: bring me in before the king, and I will show unto the king the interpretation.25 Then Arioch brought in Daniel before the king in haste and said thus unto him, I have found a man of the captives of Judah, that will make known unto the king the interpretation.

| פשרא 6591 | למלכא 4430 | יהודע 3046: | 2:26 | ענה 6032 | מלכא 4430 | ואמר 560 | לדניאל 1841 | די 1768 | שמה 8036 |
|---|---|---|---|---|---|---|---|---|---|
| pishra' | lamalka' | yahouda'. | | 'aneh | malka' | ua'amar | ladaniyea'l, | diy | shameh |
| **the interpretation** | **unto the king** | **will make known** | | **answered** | **The king** | **and said** | **to Daniel** | **whose** | **name** |

| בלטשאצר 1096 | האיתיך 383 | כהל 3546 | להודעתני 3046 | חלמא 2493 | די 1768 | חזית 2370 |
|---|---|---|---|---|---|---|
| beltasha'tzar; | ha'aytayik | kahel, | lahouda'ataniy | chelma' | diy | chazeyt |
| ***was* Belteshazzar** | **are you** | **able** | **to make known unto me** | **the dream** | **which** | **I have seen** |

| ופשרה 6591: | 2:27 | ענה 6032 | דניאל 1841 | קדם 6925 | מלכא 4430 | ואמר 560 | רזה 7328 | די 1768 | מלכא 4430 |
|---|---|---|---|---|---|---|---|---|---|
| uapishreh. | | 'aneh | daniyea'l | qadam | malka' | ua'amar; | razah | diy | malka' |
| **and the interpretation thereof?** | | **answered** | **Daniel** | **in the presence of** | **the king** | **and said** | **The secret** | **which** | **the king** |

| שאל 7593 | לא 3809 | חכימין 2445 | אשפין 826 | חרטמין 2749 | גזרין 1505 | יכלין 3202 | להחויה 2324 |
|---|---|---|---|---|---|---|---|
| sha'ael, | la' | chakiymiyn | 'ashapiyn, | chartumiyn | gazariyn, | yakaliyn | lahachauayah |
| **has demanded** | **cannot** | ***the* wise** | ***men* the astrologers** | **the magicians** | **the soothsayers** | **cannot** | **show** |

| למלכא 4430: | 2:28 | ברם 1297 | איתי 383 | אלה 426 | בשמיא 8065 | גלא 1541 | רזין 7328 | והודע 3046 | למלכא 4430 | נבוכדנצר 5020 | מה 4101 |
|---|---|---|---|---|---|---|---|---|---|---|---|
| lamalka'. | | baram | 'aytay | 'alah | bishmaya' | galea' | raziyn, | uahouda', | lamalka' | nabukadnetzar, | mah |
| **unto the king** | | **But** | **there is a** | **El** | **in heaven** | **that reveal** | **secrets** | **and make known** | **to the king** | **Nebuchadnezzar** | **what** |

| די 1768 | להוא 1934 | באחרית 320 | יומיא 3118 | חלמך 2493 | וחזוי 2376 | ראשך 7217 | על 5922 | משכבך 4903 | דנה 1836 | הוא 1932: | 2:29 |
|---|---|---|---|---|---|---|---|---|---|---|---|
| diy | lehauea' | ba'achariyt | youmaya'; | chelmak | uachezuey | rea'shak | 'al | mishkabak | danah | hua'. | |
| **that** | **shall be** | **in the latter** | **days** | **Your dream** | **and the visions of** | **your head** | **upon** | **your bed** | ***are* these** | **it** | |

| אנתה 607 | מלכא 4430 | רעיונך 7476 | על 5922 | משכבך 4903 | סלקו 5559 | מה 4101 | די 1768 | להוא 1934 | אחרי 311 |
|---|---|---|---|---|---|---|---|---|---|
| 'antah | malka', | ra'younak | 'al | mishkabak | saliqu, | mah | diy | lehauea' | 'acharey |
| **As for you** | **O king** | **your thoughts** | ***into your mind* upon** | **your bed** | **came** | **what** | **as much** | **should come to pass** | **here** |

| דנה 1836 | וגלא 1541 | רזיא 7328 | הודעך 3046 | מה 4101 | די 1768 | להוא 1934: | 2:30 | ואנה 576 | לא 3809 |
|---|---|---|---|---|---|---|---|---|---|
| danah; | uagalea' | razaya' | houda'ak | mah | diy | lehauea'. | | ua'anah, | la' |
| **after** | **and he that reveal** | **secrets** | **make known to you** | **what** | **forasmuch** | **shall come to pass** | | **But as for me** | **not** |

| בחכמה 2452 | די 1768 | איתי 383 | בי 871a | מן 4481 | כל 3605 | חייא 2417 | רזא 7328 | דנה 1836 | גלי 1541 | לי 3807a | להן 3861 | על 5922 | דברת 1701 |
|---|---|---|---|---|---|---|---|---|---|---|---|---|---|
| bachakamah | diy | 'aytay | biy | min | kal | chayaya', | raza' | danah | galiy | liy; | lahen, | 'al | dibrat |
| **for *any* wisdom** | **that** | **I have** | **to me** | **more than** | **any** | **living** | **secret** | **this** | **is revealed** | **to** | **but** | **for** | ***their* sakes** |

| די 1768 | פשרא 6591 | למלכא 4430 | יהודעון 3046 | ורעיוני 7476 | לבבך 3825 | תנדע 3046: | 2:31 | אנתה 607 |
|---|---|---|---|---|---|---|---|---|
| diy | pishra' | lamalka' | yahouda'aun, | uara'youney | libbak | tinda'. | | 'antah |
| **that** | **the interpretation** | **to the king** | **shall make known** | **and the thoughts of** | **your heart** | **that you might know** | | **You** |

| מלכא 4430 | חזה 2370 | הוית 1934 | ואלו 431 | צלם 6755 | חד 2298 | שגיא 7690 | צלמא 6755 | דכן 1797 | רב 7229 | וזיוה 2122 | יתיר 3493 | קאם 6966 |
|---|---|---|---|---|---|---|---|---|---|---|---|---|
| malka', | chazeh | hauayata | ua'alu | tzalem | chad | sagiy'a, | tzalma' | diken | rab | uaziyueh | yatiyr | qa'aem |
| **O king** | **saw** | **become** | **and behold** | **image** | **a single** | **great** | **image** | **This** | **great** | **whose brightness** | ***was* excellent** | **stood** |

| לקבלך 6903 | ורוה 7299 | דחיל 1763: | 2:32 | הוא 1932 | צלמא 6755 | ראשה 7217 | די 1768 | דהב 1722 | טב 2869 | חדוהי 2306 | ודרעוהי 1872 |
|---|---|---|---|---|---|---|---|---|---|---|---|
| laqabalak; | uareueh | dachiyl. | | hua' | tzalma', | rea'sheh | diy | dahab | tab, | chadouhiy | uadra'auhiy |
| **before you** | **and the form thereof** | ***was* terrible** | | **This** | **image's** | **head** | ***was* of** | **gold** | **fine** | **his breast** | **and his arms** |

Dan 2:26 The king answered and said to Daniel, whose name was Belteshazzar, Art you able to make known unto me the dream which I have seen, and the interpretation thereof?27 Daniel answered in the presence of the king, and said, The secret which the king has demanded cannot the wise men, the astrologers, the magicians, the soothsayers, show unto the king;28 But there is a G-d in heaven that revealeth secrets, and make known to the king Nebuchadnezzar what shall be in the latter days. Thy dream, and the visions of your head upon your bed, are these;29 As for you, O king, your thoughts came into your mind upon your bed, what should come to pass hereafter: and he that revealeth secrets make known to you what shall come to pass.30 But as for me, this secret is not revealed to me for any wisdom that I have more than any living, but for their sakes that shall make known the interpretation to the king, and that you might know the thoughts of your heart.31 Thou, O king, saw, and behold a great image. This great image, whose brightness was excellent, stood before you; and the form thereof was terrible.32 This image's head was of fine gold, his breast and his arms of silver, his belly and his thighs of brass,

די 1768 כסף 3702 מעוהי 4577 וירכתה 3410 די 1768 נחש 5174: **2:33** שקוהי 8243 די 1768 פרזל 6523 רגלוהי 7271 מנהון 4481 די 1768 פרזל 6523
diy kasap; ma'auhiy uayarkateh diy nachash. shaqouhiy diy parzel; raglouhiy minhoun diy parzel,
**of silver his belly and his thighs of brass His legs of iron his feet part of iron**

ומנהון 4481 די 1768 חסף 2635: **2:34** חזה 2370 הוית 1934 עד 5704 די 1768 התגזרת 1505 אבן 69 די 1768 לא 3809 בידין 3028 ומחת 4223
uaminhoun diy chasap. chazeh hauayata, 'ad diy hitgazeret 'aben diy la' biydayin, uamchat
**and part of clay saw You till that was cut out a stone of without hands which smote**

לצלמא 6755 על 5922 רגלוהי 7271 די 1768 פרזלא 6523 וחספא 2635 והדקת 1855 המון 1994: **2:35** באדין 116 דקו 1855
latzalma' 'al raglouhiy, diy parzala' uakaspa'; uahadeqet himoun. bea'dayin daqu
**the image upon his feet *that were* of iron and clay and break to pieces them Then was broken to pieces**

כחדה 2298 פרזלא 6523 חספא 2635 נחשא 5174 כספא 3702 ודהבא 1722 והוו 1934 כעור 5784 מן 4481 אדרי 147 קיט 7007
kachadah parzala' chaspa' nachasha' kaspa' uadahaba', uahauou ka'aur min 'adrey qayit,
**together the iron the clay the brass the silver and the gold and became like the chaff of threshingfloors the summer**

ונשא 5376 המון 1994 רוחא 7308 וכל 3606 אתר 870 לא 3809 השתכח 7912 להון 3807b ואבנא 69 די 1768 מחת 4223 לצלמא 6755 הות 1934
uansa' himoun rucha', uakal 'atar la' hishtakach lahoun; ua'abna' diy machat latzalma', hauat
**and carried away them the wind that place no was found for them and the stone that smote the image became**

לטור 2906 רב 7229 ומלת 4391 כל 3606 ארעא 772: **2:36** דנה 1836 חלמא 2493 ופשרה 6591 נאמר 560 קדם 6925
latur rab uamlat kal 'ar'aa'. danah chelma', uapishreh nea'mar qadam
**a mountain great and filled the whole earth This *is* the dream and the interpretation thereof we will tell before**

מלכא 4430: **2:37** אנתה 607 מלכא 4430 מלך 4430 מלכיא 4430 די 1768 אלה 426 שמיא 8065 מלכותא 4437 חסנא 2632 ותקפא 8632 ויקרא 3367
malka'. 'antah malka', melek malkaya'; diy 'alah shamaya', malkuta' chisna' uataqapa' uiyqara'
**the king You O king *are* a king of kings for the El of heaven a kingdom power and strength and glory**

יהב 3052 לך 3807a: **2:38** ובכל 3606 די 1768 דארין 1753 בני 1123 אנשא 606 חיות 2423 ברא 1251 ועוף 5776
yahab lak. uabkal diy da'ariyn baney 'anasha' cheyuat bara' ua'aup
**has given to you And wheresoever that dwell the children of men the beasts of the field and the fowls of**

שמיא 8065 יהב 3052 בידך 3028 והשלטך 7981 בכלהון 3606 אנתה 607 הוא 1931 ראשה 7217 די 1768 דהבא 1722: **2:39**
shamaya' yahab biydak, uahashlatak bakalahoun; 'antah hua', rea'shah diy dahaba'.
**the heaven has he given into your hand and has made you ruler over them all You *are* this head of gold**

ובתרך 870 תקום 6966 מלכו 4437 אחרי 317 ארעא 772 מנך 4481 ומלכו 4437 תליתיא 8523 אחרי 317 די 1768 נחשא 5174 די 1768
uabatarak, taqum malku 'achariy 'ara minak; uamalku taliytaya' 'achariy diy nachasha', diy
**And after you shall arise kingdom another inferior to you and kingdom third another of brass which**

תשלט 7981 בכל 3605 ארעא 772: **2:40** ומלכו 4437 רביעיה 7244 תהוא 1934 תקיפה 8624 כפרזלא 6523 כל 3606 קבל 6903
tishlat bakal 'ar'aa'. uamalku rabiy'ayah tehauea' taqiypah kaparzala'; kal qabel,
**shall bear rule over all the earth And kingdom *the* fourth shall be strong as iron forasmuch according to**

די 1768 פרזלא 6523 מהדק 1855 וחשל 2827 כלא 3606 וכפרזלא 6523 די 1768 מרעע 7490 כל 3606 אלין 459 תדק 1855
diy parzala' mahadeq uachashel kol'a, uakparzala' diy mara'a' kal 'aleyn tadiq
**as iron break in pieces and subdue all *things* and as iron that break all these shall it break in pieces**

Dan 2:33 His legs of iron, his feet part of iron and part of clay.34 Thou saw till that a stone was cut out without hands, which smote the image upon his feet that were of iron and clay, and break them to pieces.35 Then was the iron, the clay, the brass, the silver, and the gold, broken to pieces together, and became like the chaff of the summer threshingfloors; and the wind carried them away, that no place was found for them: and the stone that smote the image became a great mountain, and filled the whole earth.36 This is the dream; and we will tell the interpretation thereof before the king.37 Thou, O king, are a king of kings: for the G-d of heaven has given you a kingdom, power, and strength, and glory.38 And wheresoever the children of men dwell, the beasts of the field and the fowls of the heaven has he given into your hand, and has made you ruler over them all. Thou are this head of gold.39 And after you shall arise another kingdom inferior to you, and another third kingdom of brass, which shall bear rule over all the earth.40 And the fourth kingdom shall be strong as iron: forasmuch as iron breaketh in pieces and subdueth all things: and as iron that breaketh all these, shall it break in pieces and bruise.

| ותרע 7490: | 2:41 ודי 1768 | חזיתה 2370 | רגליא 7271 | ואצבעתא 677 | מנהון 4481 | חסף 2635 | די 1768 | פחר 6353 | ומנהון 4481 | פרזל 6523 |
|---|---|---|---|---|---|---|---|---|---|---|
| uateroa'. | uadiy | chazaytah | raglaya' | ua'atzbe'ata', | minhoun | chasap | diy | pechar | uaminhoun | parzel, |
| **and bruise** | **And whereas** | **you saw** | **the feet** | **and toes** | **part** | **clay** | **of** | **potters'** | **a part of** | **iron** |

| מלכו 4437 | פליגה 6386 | תהוה 1934 | ומן 4481 | נצבתא 5326 | די 1768 | פרזלא 6523 | להוא 1934 | בה 871a | כל 3605 | קבל 6903 | די 1768 |
|---|---|---|---|---|---|---|---|---|---|---|---|
| malku | paliygah | tehaueh, | uamin | nitzbata' | diy | parzala' | lehauea' | bah; | kal | qabel | diy |
| **the kingdom** | **divided** | **shall be** | **but of** | **the strength** | **of** | **the iron** | **there shall be** | **in it** | **forasmuch** | **according to** | **as** |

| חזיתה 2370 | פרזלא 6523 | מערב 6151 | בחסף 2635 | טינא 2917: | 2:42 ואצבעת 677 | רגליא 7271 | מנהון 4481 | פרזל 6523 | ומנהון 4481 | חסף 2635 |
|---|---|---|---|---|---|---|---|---|---|---|
| chazaytah, | parzala', | ma'arab | bachasap | tiyna'. | ua'atzba'at | raglaya', | minhoun | parzel | uaminhoun | chasap; |
| **you saw** | **the iron** | **mixed** | **with clay** | **miry** | **And *as* the toes of** | **the feet *were*** | **part of** | **iron** | **and part of** | **clay** |

| מן 4481 | קצת 7118 | מלכותא 4437 | תהוה 1934 | תקיפה 8624 | ומנה 4481 | תהוה 1934 | תבירה 8406: | 2:43 די 1768 | חזית 2370 | פרזלא 6523 | מערב 6151 |
|---|---|---|---|---|---|---|---|---|---|---|---|
| min | qatzat | malkuta' | tehaueh | taqiypah, | uaminah | tehaueh | tabiyrah. | diy | chazayta, | parzala' | ma'arab |
| **partly *so*** | **and part** | **the kingdom** | **shall be** | **strong** | **and part of it** | | **broken** | **And whereas** | **you saw** | **iron** | **mixed** |

| בחסף 2635 | טינא 2917 | מתערבין 6151 | להון 1934 | בזרע 2234 | אנשא 606 | ולא 3809 | להון 1934 | דבקין 1693 | דנה 1836 | עם 5974 | דנה 1836 |
|---|---|---|---|---|---|---|---|---|---|---|---|
| bachasap | tiyna', | mit'arabiyn | lehauon | bizra' | 'anasha', | uala' | lehauon | dabaqiyn | danah | 'am | danah; |
| **with clay** | **miry** | **mingled themselves** | **they shall** | **with the seed of** | **men** | **but not** | **they** | **shall cleave** | **one** | **to** | **another** |

| הא 1888 | כדי 1768 | פרזלא 6523 | לא 3809 | מתערב 6151 | עם 5974 | חספא 2635: | 2:44 וביומיהון 3118 | די 1768 | מלכיא 4430 | אנון 581 | יקים 6966 | אלה 426 |
|---|---|---|---|---|---|---|---|---|---|---|---|---|
| hea' | kadiy | parzala', | la' | mit'arab | 'am | chaspa'. | uabyoumeyhon | diy | malkaya' | 'anun, | yaqiym | 'alah |
| **even** | **as** | **iron** | **not** | **is mixed** | **with** | **clay** | **And in the days** | **of** | **kings** | **these** | **shall set up** | **the El of** |

| שמיא 8065 | מלכו 4437 | די 1768 | לעלמין 5957 | לא 3809 | תתחבל 2255 | ומלכותה 4437 | לעם 5972 | אחרן 321 | לא 3809 | תשתבק 7662 |
|---|---|---|---|---|---|---|---|---|---|---|
| shamaya' | malku | diy | la'alamiyn | la' | titchabal, | uamalkutah, | la'am | 'acharan | la' | tishtabiq; |
| **heaven** | **a kingdom** | **which** | **for ever** | **not** | **shall be destroyed** | **and the kingdom** | **people** | **other** | **not** | **shall be left** |

| תדק 1855 | ותסיף 5487 | כל 3606 | אלין 459 | מלכותא 4437 | והיא 1932 | תקום 6966 | לעלמיא 5957: | 2:45 כל 3606 | קבל 6903 |
|---|---|---|---|---|---|---|---|---|---|
| tadiq | uataseyp | kal | 'aleyn | malkauata', | uahiy'a | taqum | la'alamaya'. | kal | qabel |
| ***but* it break in pieces** | **and consume** | **all** | **these** | **kingdoms** | **and it** | **shall stand** | **for ever** | **Forasmuch** | **according to** |

| די 1768 | חזית 2370 | די 1768 | מטורא 2906 | אתגזרת 1505 | אבן 69 | די 1768 | לא 3809 | בידין 3028 | והדקת 1855 |
|---|---|---|---|---|---|---|---|---|---|
| diy | chazayta | diy | mitura' | 'atgazeret | 'aben | diy | la' | biydayin, | uahadeqet |
| **as** | **you saw** | **that** | **out of the mountain** | **he cut** | **the stone** | **forasmuch** | **without** | **hands** | **and that it brake in pieces** |

| פרזלא 6523 | נחשא 5174 | חספא 2635 | כספא 3702 | ודהבא 1722 | אלה 426 | רב 7229 | הודע 3046 | למלכא 4430 | מה 4100 | די 1768 |
|---|---|---|---|---|---|---|---|---|---|---|
| parzala' | nachasha' | chaspa' | kaspa' | uadahaba', | 'alah | rab | houda' | lamalka', | mah | diy |
| **the iron** | **the brass** | **the clay** | **the silver** | **and the gold** | **El** | ***the* great** | **has made known** | **to the king** | **what** | **forasmuch** |

| להוא 1934 | אחרי 311 | דנה 1836 | ויציב 3330 | חלמא 2493 | ומהימן 540 | פשרה 6591: | 2:46 באדין 116 |
|---|---|---|---|---|---|---|---|
| lehauea' | 'acharey | danah; | uayatziyb | chelma' | uamheyman | pishreh. | bea'dayin |
| **shall come to pass** | **the future** | **hereafter** | **and certain** | **the dream *is*** | **and sure** | **the interpretation thereof** | **Then** |

| מלכא 4430 | נבוכדנצר 5020 | נפל 5308 | על 5922 | אנפוהי 600 | ולדניאל 1841 | סגד 5457 | ומנחה 4504 | וניחחין 5208 | אמר 560 |
|---|---|---|---|---|---|---|---|---|---|
| malka' | nabukadnetzar | napal | 'al | anpouhiy, | ualdaniyea'l | sagid; | uaminchah | uaniychochiyn, | 'amar |
| **the king** | **Nebuchadnezzar** | **fell** | **upon** | **his face** | **and Daniel** | **worshipped** | **and an oblation** | **and sweet odours** | **commanded** |

Dan 2:41 And whereas you saw the feet and toes, part of potters' clay, and part of iron, the kingdom shall be divided; but there shall be in it of the strength of the iron, forasmuch as you saw the iron mixed with miry clay.42 And as the toes of the feet were part of iron, and part of clay, so the kingdom shall be partly strong, and partly broken.43 And whereas you saw iron mixed with miry clay, they shall mingle themselves with the seed of men: but they shall not cleave one to another, even as iron is not mixed with clay.44 And in the days of these kings shall the G-d of heaven set up a kingdom, which shall never be destroyed: and the kingdom shall not be left to other people, but it shall break in pieces and consume all these kingdoms, and it shall stand forever.45 Forasmuch as you saw that the stone was cut out of the mountain without hands, and that it break in pieces the iron, the brass, the clay, the silver, and the gold; the great G-d has made known to the king what shall come to pass hereafter: and the dream is certain, and the interpretation thereof sure.46 Then the king Nebuchadnezzar fell upon his face, and worshipped Daniel, and commanded that they should offer an oblation and sweet odours unto him.

לנסכה 5260 | לה 3807a: | **2:47** ענה 6032 | מלכא 4430 | לדניאל 1841 | ואמר 560 | מן 4481 | קשט 7187 | די 1768 | אלהכון 426 | הוא 1932
lanasakah | leh. | 'aneh | malka' | ladaniyea'l | ua'amar, | min | qashot | diy | 'alahakoun, | hua'
**that they should offer unto him | answered The king unto Daniel and said Of | a truth *it is* that your Elohim is | he**

אלה 426 | אלהין 426 | ומרא 4756 | מלכין 4430 | וגלה 1541 | רזין 7328 | די 1768 | יכלת 3202 | למגלא 1541 | רזה 7328 | דנה 1836: | **2:48** אדין 116
'alah | 'alahiyn | uamarea' | malkiyn | uagaleh | raziyn; | diy | yakelata, | lamiglea' | razah | danah. | 'adayin
**El of | gods | and a Adonai of | kings | and a revealer of | secrets | seeing | you could | reveal | secret | this | Then**

מלכא 4430 | לדניאל 1841 | רבי 7236 | ומתנן 4978 | רברבן 7260 | שגיאן 7690 | יהב 3052 | לה 3807a | והשלטה 7981 | על 5922 | כל 3606
malka' | ladaniyea'l | rabiy, | uamatanan | rabraban | sagiy'an | yahab | leh, | uahashlateh, | 'al | kal
**the king | of Daniel | made a great man | and gifts | great | many | gave | him | and made him ruler | over | the whole**

מדינת 4083 | בבל 895 | ורב 7229 | סגנין 5460 | על 5922 | כל 3606 | חכימי 2445 | בבל 895: | **2:49** ודניאל 1841 | בעא 1156 | מן 4481
madiynat | babel; | uarab | signiyn, | 'al | kal | chakiymey | babel. | uadaniyea'l | ba'aa' | min
**province of | Babylon | and chief of | the governors | over | all | the wise *men* of | Babylon | Then Daniel | requested | of**

מלכא 4430 | ומני 4483 | על 5922 | עבידתא 5673 | די 1768 | מדינת 4083 | בבל 895 | לשדרך 7715 | מישך 4336 | ועבד 5665 | נגו 5665 | ודניאל 1841
malka', | uamaniy, | 'al | 'abiydata' | diy | madiynat | babel, | lashadrak | meyshak | ua'abed | nagou; | uadaniyea'l
**the king | and he set | over | the affairs | of | the province of | Babylon | Shadrach | Meshach | and Abed | nego | but Daniel**

בתרע 8651 | מלכא 4430:
bitra' | malka'.
***sat* in the gate of | the king**

**Dan 3:1** נבוכדנצר 5020 | מלכא 4430 | עבד 5648 | צלם 6755 | די 1768 | דהב 1722 | רומה 7314 | אמין 521 | שתין 8361
nabukadnetzar | malka', | 'abad | tzalem | diy | dahab, | rumeh | 'amiyn | shitiyn,
**Nebuchadnezzar | the king | made | an image | of | gold | whose height | cubits | *was* threescore**

פתיה 6613 | אמין 521 | שת 8353 | אקימה 6966 | בבקעת 1236 | דורא 1757 | במדינת 4083 | בבל 895: | **3:2**
patayeh | 'amiyn | shit; | 'aqiymeh | babiq'at | dura', | bimdiynat | babel.
***and* the breadth thereof | cubits | six | he set it up | in the plain of | Dura | in the province of | Babylon**

ונבוכדנצר 5020 | מלכא 4430 | שלח 7972 | למכנש 3673 | לאחשדרפניא 324 | סגניא 5460 | ופחותא 6347 | אדרגזריא 148
uanabukadnetzar | malka' | shalach | lamiknash | la'achashdarpanaya' | signaya' | uapachauata' | 'adargazaraya'
**Then Nebuchadnezzar | the king | sent | to gather together | the princes | the governors | and the captains | the judges**

גדבריא 1411 | דתבריא 1884 | תפתיא 8614 | וכל 3606 | שלטני 7984 | מדינתא 4083 | למתא 858 | לחנכת 2597 | צלמא 6755 | די 1768
gadabaraya' | databaraya' | tiptayea', | uakol | shiltoney | madiynata'; | lametea' | lachanukat | tzalma', | diy
**the treasurers | the counsellors | the sheriffs | and all | the rulers of | the provinces | to come | to the dedication of | the image | which**

הקים 6966 | נבוכדנצר 5020 | מלכא 4430: | **3:3** באדין 116 | מתכנשין 3673 | אחשדרפניא 324 | סגניא 5460 | ופחותא 6347
haqiym | nabukadnetzar | malka'. | bea'dayin | mitkanshiyn | 'achashdarpanaya' | signaya' | uapachauata'
**had set up | Nebuchadnezzar | the king | Then | were gathered together | the princes | the governors | and captains**

אדרגזריא 148 | גדבריא 1411 | דתבריא 1884 | תפתיא 8614 | וכל 3606 | שלטני 7984 | מדינתא 4083 | לחנכת 2597 | צלמא 6755
'adargazaraya' | gadabaraya' | databaraya' | tiptayea', | uakol | shiltoney | madiynata', | lachanukat | tzalma',
**the judges | the treasurers | the counsellors | the sheriffs | and all | the rulers of | the provinces | unto the dedication of | the image**

Dan 2:47 The king answered unto Daniel, and said, Of a truth it is, that your G-d is a G-d of gods, and a Adonai of kings, and a revealer of secrets, seeing you couldest reveal this secret.48 Then the king made Daniel a great man, and gave him many great gifts, and made him ruler over the whole province of Babylon, and chief of the governors over all the wise men of Babylon.49 Then Daniel requested of the king, and he set Shadrach, Meshach, and Abed-nego, over the affairs of the province of Babylon: but Daniel sat in the gate of the king. **Dan** 3.1 Nebuchadnezzar the king made an image of gold, whose height was threescore cubits, and the breadth thereof six cubits: he set it up in the plain of Dura, in the province of Babylon.2 Then Nebuchadnezzar the king sent to gather together the princes, the governors, and the captains, the judges, the treasurers, the counsellers, the sheriffs, and all the rulers of the provinces, to come to the dedication of the image which Nebuchadnezzar the king had set up.3 Then the princes, the governors, and captains, the judges, the treasurers, the counsellers, the sheriffs, and all the rulers of the provinces, were gathered together unto the dedication of the image that Nebuchadnezzar the king had set up; and they stood before the image that Nebuchadnezzar had set up.

| די 1768 | הקים 6966 | נבוכדנצר 5020 | מלכא 4430 | וקאמין 6966 | לקבל 6903 | צלמא 6755 | די 1768 | הקים 6966 | נבוכדנצר 5020: | 3:4 |
|---|---|---|---|---|---|---|---|---|---|---|
| diy | haqiym | nabukadnetzar | malka'; | uaqa'amiyn | laqabel | tzalma', | diy | haqeym | nabukadnetzar. | |
| **that** | **had set up** | **Nebuchadnezzar** | **the king** | **and they stood** | **before** | **the image** | **that** | **had set up** | **Nebuchadnezzar** | |

| וכרוזא 3744 | קרא 7123 | בחיל 2429 | לכון 3807a | אמרין 560 | עממיא 5972 | אמיא 524 | ולשניא 3961: | 3:5 | בעדנא 5732 | די 1768 |
|---|---|---|---|---|---|---|---|---|---|---|
| uakarouza' | qarea' | bachayil; | lakoun | 'amariyn | 'amamaya', | 'amaya' | ualishanaya'. | | ba'adana' | diy |
| **Then an herald** | **cried** | **aloud** | **To you** | **it is commanded** | **O people** | **nations** | **and languages** | | ***That* at time** | **what** |

| תשמעון 8086 | קל 7032 | קרנא 7162 | משרוקיתא 4953 | קיתרוס 7030 | סבכא 5443 | פסנתרין 6460 | סומפניה 5481 | וכל 3606 | זני 2178 | זמרא 2170 |
|---|---|---|---|---|---|---|---|---|---|---|
| tishma'aun | qal | qarna' | mashrouqiyta' | qiytarous | sabaka' | pasanteriyn | sumponayah, | uakol | zaney | zamara'; |
| **you hear** | **the sound of** | **the cornet** | **flute** | **harp** | **sackbut** | **psaltery** | **dulcimer** | **and all** | **kinds of** | **music** |

| תפלון 5308 | ותסגדון 5457 | לצלם 6755 | דהבא 1722 | די 1768 | הקים 6966 | נבוכדנצר 5020 | מלכא 4430: | 3:6 | ומן 4479 | די 1768 | לא 3809 |
|---|---|---|---|---|---|---|---|---|---|---|---|
| tiplun | uatisgadun | latzelem | dahaba', | diy | haqiym | nabukadnetzar | malka'. | | uman | diy | la' |
| **you fall down** | **and worship** | **image** | ***the* golden** | **that** | **has set up** | **Nebuchadnezzar** | **the king** | | **And who** | **soever** | **not** |

| יפל 5308 | ויסגד 5457 | בה 871a | שעתא 8160 | יתרמא 7412 | לגוא 1459 | אתון 861 | נורא 5135 | יקדתא 3345: | 3:7 | כל 3605 | קבל 6903 |
|---|---|---|---|---|---|---|---|---|---|---|---|
| yipel | uayisgud; | bah | sha'ata' | yitramea', | lagou'a | 'atun | nura' | yaqidta'. | | kal | qabel |
| **fall down** | **and worship** | **the same** | **hour** | **shall be cast** | **into the midst of** | **a furnace** | **fiery** | **burning** | | **There** | **fore** |

| דנה 1836 | בה 871a | זמנא 2166 | כדי 1768 | שמעין 8086 | כל 3605 | עממיא 5972 | קל 7032 | קרנא 7162 | משרוקיתא 4953 | קיתרס 7030 | שבכא 5443 |
|---|---|---|---|---|---|---|---|---|---|---|---|
| danah | beh | zimna' | kadiy | shama'ayn | kal | 'amamaya' | qal | qarna' | mashrouqiyta' | qiytaros | sabaka' |
| **after** | **at that** | **time** | **when** | **heard** | **all** | **the people** | **the sound of** | **the cornet** | **flute** | **harp** | **sackbut** |

| פסנטרין 6460 | וכל 3606 | זני 2178 | זמרא 2170 | נפלין 5308 | כל 3606 | עממיא 5972 | אמיא 524 | ולשניא 3961 | סגדין 5457 | לצלם 6755 |
|---|---|---|---|---|---|---|---|---|---|---|
| pasanteriyn, | uakol | zaney | zamara'; | napaliyn | kal | 'amamaya' | 'amaya' | ualishanaya', | sagadiyn | latzelem |
| **psaltery** | **and all** | **kinds of** | **music** | **fell down** | **all** | **the people** | **the nations** | **and the languages** | ***and* worshipped** | **image** |

| דהבא 1722 | די 1768 | הקים 6966 | נבוכדנצר 5020 | מלכא 4430: | 3:8 | כל 3606 | קבל 6903 | דנה 1836 | בה 871a | זמנא 2166 | קרבו 7127 | גברין 1400 |
|---|---|---|---|---|---|---|---|---|---|---|---|---|
| dahaba', | diy | haqiym | nabukadnetzar | malka'. | | kal | qabel | danah | beh | zimna', | qaribu | gubriyn |
| ***the* golden** | **that** | **had set up** | **Nebuchadnezzar** | **the king** | | **Where** | **fore** | **after** | **at that** | **time** | **came near** | **certain** |

| כשדאין 3779 | ואכלו 399 | קרציהון 7170 | די 1768 | יהודיא 3062: | 3:9 | ענו 6032 | ואמרין 560 | לנבוכדנצר 5020 | מלכא 4430 | מלכא 4430 |
|---|---|---|---|---|---|---|---|---|---|---|
| kasda'ayn; | ua'akalu | qartzeyhoun | diy | yahudayea'. | | 'anou | ua'amariyn, | linabukadnetzar | malka'; | malka' |
| **Chaldeans** | **and brought** | **accused** | **against** | **the Jews** | | **They spoke** | **and said** | **to Nebuchadnezzar** | **the king** | **O king** |

| לעלמין 5957 | חיי 2418: | 3:10 | אנתה 607 | מלכא 4430 | שמת 7761 | טעם 2942 | די 1768 | כל 3605 | אנש 606 | די 1768 | ישמע 8086 | קל 7032 | קרנא 7162 |
|---|---|---|---|---|---|---|---|---|---|---|---|---|---|
| la'alamiyn | chayiy. | | 'antah | malka' | samta | ta'aem | diy | kal | 'anash | diy | yishma' | qal | qarna' |
| **for ever** | **live** | | **You** | **O king** | **have made** | **a decree** | **that** | **every** | **man** | **that** | **shall hear** | **the sound of** | **the cornet** |

| משרקיתא 4953 | קיתרס 7030 | שבכא 5443 | פסנתרין 6460 | וסיפניה 5481 | וכל 3606 | זני 2178 | זמרא 2170 | יפל 5308 | ויסגד 5457 | לצלם 6755 |
|---|---|---|---|---|---|---|---|---|---|---|
| mashrouqiyta' | qiytaros | sabaka' | pasanteriyn | uasiyponayah | uakol | zaney | zamara'; | yipel | uayisgud | latzelem |
| **flute** | **harp** | **sackbut** | **psaltery** | **and dulcimer** | **and all** | **kinds of** | **music** | **shall fall down** | **and worship** | **image** |

| דהבא 1722: | 3:11 | ומן 4479 | די 1768 | לא 3809 | יפל 5308 | ויסגד 5457 | יתרמא 4412 | לגוא 1459 | אתון 861 | נורא 5135 |
|---|---|---|---|---|---|---|---|---|---|---|
| dahaba'. | | uman | diy | la' | yipel | uayisgud; | yitramea' | lagou'a | 'atun | nura' |
| ***the* golden** | | **And who** | **that** | **not** | **fall down** | **and worship** | ***that* he should be cast** | **into the midst of** | **a furnace** | **fiery** |

Dan 3:4 Then an herald cried aloud, To you it is commanded, O people, nations, and languages,5 That at what time you hear the sound of the cornet, flute, harp, sackbut, psaltery, dulcimer, and all kinds of musick, you fall down and worship the golden image that Nebuchadnezzar the king has set up:6 And whoso fall not down and worshippeth shall the same hour be cast into the midst of a burning fiery furnace.7 Therefore at that time, when all the people heard the sound of the cornet, flute, harp, sackbut, psaltery, and all kinds of musick, all the people, the nations, and the languages, fell down and worshipped the golden image that Nebuchadnezzar the king had set up.8 Wherefore at that time certain Chaldeans came near, and accused the Jews.9 They spoke and said to the king Nebuchadnezzar, O king, live forever.10 Thou, O king, have made a decree, that every man that shall hear the sound of the cornet, flute, harp, sackbut, psaltery, and dulcimer, and all kinds of musick, shall fall down and worship the golden image:11 And whoso fall not down and worshippeth, that he should be cast into the midst of a burning fiery furnace.

3:12

יקדתא 3345: איתי 383 גברין 1400 יהודאין 3062 די 1768 מנית 4483 יתהון 3487 על 5922 עבידת 5673 מדינת 4083 בבל 895
yaqidta'. 'aytay gubriyn yahuda'yin, diy maniyta yatahoun 'al 'abiydat madiynat babel,
**burning There are certain Jews that you have set whom over the affairs of the province of Babylon**

שדרך 7715 מישך 4336 ועבד 5665 נגו 5665 גבריא 1400 אלך 479 לא 3809 שמו 7761 עליך 5922 מלכא 4430 טעם 2942 לאלהיך 426 לא 3809
shadrak meyshak ua'abed nagou; gubraya' 'alek, la' samu 'alayik malka' ta'aem, lalahayik la'
**Shadrach Meshach and Abed nego men these not have regarded to you O king regarded your Elohim not**

3:13

פלחין 6399 ולצלם 6755 דהבא 1722 די 1768 הקימת 6966 לא 3809 סגדין 5457: באדין 116 נבוכדנצר 5020 ברגז 7266 וחמה 2528
palachiyn, ualtzelem dahaba' diy haqeymata la' sagadiyn. bea'dayin nabukadnetzar birgaz uachamah,
**they serve image *the* golden which you have set up nor worship Then Nebuchadnezzar in *his* rage and fury**

3:14

אמר 560 להיתיה 858 לשדרך 7715 מישך 4336 ועבד 5665 נגו 5665 באדין 116 גבריא 1400 אלך 479 היתיו 858 קדם 6925 מלכא 4430:
'amar lahayatayah, lashadrak meyshak ua'abed nagou; bea'dayin gubraya' 'alek, heytayu qadam malka'.
**commanded to bring Shadrach Meshach and Abed nego Then men these they brought before the king**

ענה 6032 נבכדנצר 5020 ואמר 560 להון 3807b הצדא 6656 שדרך 7715 מישך 4336 ועבד 5665 נגו 5665 לאלהי 426 לא 3809
'aneh nabukadnetzar ua'amar lahoun, hatzada' shadrak meyshak ua'abed nagou; le'alahay, la'
**spoke Nebuchadnezzar and said unto them, *Is it* true O Shadrach Meshach and Abed nego my gods not**

3:15

איתיכון 383 פלחין 6399 ולצלם 6755 דהבא 1722 די 1768 הקימת 6966 לא 3809 סגדין 5457: כען 3705 הן 2006 איתיכון 838 עתידין 6263 די 1768
'ayteykoun palachiyn, ualtzelem dahaba' diy haqeymet la' sagadiyn. ka'an hen 'ayteykoun 'atiydiyn, diy
**do you serve image *the* golden which I have set up? nor worship Now if you be ready that**

בעדנא 5732 די 1768 תשמעון 8086 קל 7032 קרנא 7162 משרוקיתא 4953 קיתרס 7030 שבכא 5443 פסנתרין 6460 וסומפניה 5481 וכל 3605
ba'adana' diy tishma'aun qal qarna' mashrouqiyta' qiytaros sabaka' pasanteriyn uasumaponayah uakol
**at time what you hear the sound of the cornet flute harp sackbut psaltery and dulcimer and all**

זני 2178 זמרא 2170 תפלון 5308 ותסגדון 5457 לצלמא 6755 די 1768 עבדת 5648 והן 2006 לא 3809 תסגדון 5457 בה 871a שעתה 8160
zaney zamara', tiplun uatisgadun latzalma' diy 'abdet uahen la' tisgadun, bah sha'atah
**kinds of music you fall down and worship the image which I have made *well* but if not you worship the same hour**

תתרמון 7412 לגוא 1459 אתון 861 נורא 5135 יקדתא 3345 ומן 4479 הוא 1932 אלה 426 די 1768 ישיזבנכון 7804 מן 4481
titramoun, lagou'a 'atun nura' yaqidta'; uman hua' 'alah, diy yasheyzabinkoun min
**you shall be cast into the midst of a furnace fiery burning and who *is* that El that shall deliver you out of**

3:16

ידי 3028: ענו 6032 שדרך 7715 מישך 4336 ועבד 5665 נגו 5665 ואמרין 560 למלכא 4430 נבוכדנצר 5020 לא 3809 חשחין 2818
yaday. 'anou, shadrak meyshak ua'abed nagou, ua'amariyn lamalka'; nabukadnetzar, la' chashchiyn
**my hand? answered Shadrach Meshach and Abed nego and said to the king O Nebuchadnezzar *are* not careful**

3:17

אנחנה 586 על 5922 דנה 1836 פתגם 6600 להתבותך 8421: הן 2006 איתי 383 אלהנא 426 די 1768 אנחנא 586 פלחין 6399 יכל 3202
'achnah 'al danah pitgam lahatabutak. hen 'aytay, 'alahana' diy 'anachna' palachiyn, yakiyl
**we in this matter to answer you If it be *so* our Elohim whom we serve is able**

3:18

לשיזבותנא 7804 מן 4481 אתון 861 נורא 5135 יקדתא 3345 ומן 4481 ידך 3028 מלכא 4430 ישיזב 7804: והן 2006 לא 3809 ידיע 3046
lasheyzabutana'; min 'atun nura' yaqidta' uamin yadak malka' yasheyzib. uahen la', yadiya'
**to deliver us from furnace fiery *the* burning and out of your hand O king he will deliver *us* But if not known**

Dan 3:12 There are certain Jews whom you have set over the affairs of the province of Babylon, Shadrach, Meshach, and Abed-nego; these men, O king, have not regarded you: they serve not your gods, nor worship the golden image which you have set up.13 Then Nebuchadnezzar in his rage and fury commanded to bring Shadrach, Meshach, and Abed-nego. Then they brought these men before the king.14 Nebuchadnezzar spoke and said unto them, Is it true, O Shadrach, Meshach, and Abed-nego, do not you serve my gods, nor worship the golden image which I have set up?15 Now if you be ready that at what time you hear the sound of the cornet, flute, harp, sackbut, psaltery, and dulcimer, and all kinds of musick, you fall down and worship the image which I have made; well: but if you worship not, you shall be cast the same hour into the midst of a burning fiery furnace; and who is that G-d that shall deliver you out of my hands?16 Shadrach, Meshach, and Abed-nego, answered and said to the king, O Nebuchadnezzar, we are not careful to answer you in this matter.17 If it be so, our G-d whom we serve is able to deliver us from the burning fiery furnace, and he will deliver us out of your hand, O king.18 But if not, be it known unto you, O king, that we will not serve your gods, nor worship the golden image which you have set up.

להוא 1934 לך 3807a מלכא 4430 די 1768 לאלהיך 426 לא 3809 איתינא 383 פלחין 6399 ולצלם 6755 דהבא 1722 די 1768 הקימת 6966 לא 3809
lehauea' lak malka'; diy le'lahayk la' 'aytayna' palachiyn, ualtzelem dahaba' diy haqeymata la'
**be it unto you O king that your gods not we will serve image *the* golden which you have set up nor**

נסגד 5457: 3:19 באדין 116 נבוכדנצר 5020 התמלי 4391 חמא 2528 וצלם 6755 אנפוהי 600 אשתנו 8133 על 5922 שדרך 7715
nisgud. bea'dayin nabukadnetzar hitmaliy chama', uatzlem anpouhiy 'ashtanu 'al shadrak
**worship Then Nebuchadnezzar was full of fury and the form of his visage was changed against Shadrach**

מישך 4336 ועבד 5665 נגו 5665 ענה 6032 ואמר 560 למזא 228 לאתונא 861 חד 2298 שבעה 7655 על 5922
meyshak ua'abed nagou; 'aneh ua'amar lamezea' la'atuna', chad shib'ah, 'al
**Meshach and Abed nego *therefore* he spoke and commanded that they should heat the furnace one seven times more**

די 1768 חזה 2370 למזיה 228: 3:20 ולגברין 1400 גברי 1401 חיל 2429 די 1768 בחילה 2429 אמר 560 לכפתה 3729 לשדרך 7715
diy chazeh lamezayeh. ualgubriyn gibarey chayil diy bachayaleh, 'amar lakapatah, lashadrak
**than it was wont to be heated And men mighty *the* most that *were* in his army he commanded to bind Shadrach**

מישך 4336 ועבד 5665 נגו 5665 למרמא 7412 לאתון 861 נורא 5135 יקדתא 3345: 3:21 באדין 116 גבריא 1400 אלך 479 כפתו 3729
meyshak ua'abed nagou; lamirmea' la'atun nura' yaqidta'. bea'dayin gubraya' 'alek, kapitu
**Meshach and Abed nego *and* to cast *them* into furnace fiery *the* burning Then men these were bound**

בסרבליהון 5622 פטישיהון 6361 וכרבלתהון 3737 ולבשיהון 3831 ורמיו 7412 לגוא 1459 אתון 861 נורא 5135
basarbaleyhoun patiysheyhoun uakarbalatahoun ualbusheyhoun; uarmiyu lagou'a 'atun nura'
**in their coats the hosen and their hats and their *other* garments and were cast into the midst of furnace fiery**

יקדתא 3345: 3:22 כל 3606 קבל 6903 דנה 1836 מן 4481 די 1768 מלת 4406 מלכא 4430 מחצפה 2685 ואתונא 861 אזה 228 יתירא 3493
yaqidta'. kal qabel danah, min diy milat malka' machtzapah, ua'atuna' 'aezeh yatiyra';
***the* burning There fore this because that commandment *the* king's was urgent and the furnace hot exceeding**

גבריא 1400 אלך 479 די 1768 הסקו 5267 לשדרך 7715 מישך 4336 ועבד 5665 נגו 5665 קטל 6992 המון 1994 שביבא 7631 די 1768 נורא 5135: 3:23 וגבריא 1400
gubraya' 'alek, diy hasiqu lashadrak meyshak ua'abed nagou, qatil himoun, shabiyba' diy nura'. uagubraya'
**men those that took up Shadrach Meshach and Abed nego slew those the flame of the fire And men**

אלך 479 תלתהון 8532 שדרך 7715 מישך 4336 ועבד 5665 נגו 5665 נפלו 5308 לגוא 1459 אתון 861 נורא 5135 יקדתא 3345 מכפתין 3729:
'alek talatehoun, shadrak meyshak ua'abed nagou; napalu lagou'a 'atun nura' yaqidta' makaptiyn.
**these three Shadrach Meshach and Abed nego fell down into the midst of furnace fiery *the* burning bound**

3:24 אדין 116 נבוכדנצר 5020 מלכא 4430 תוה 8429 וקם 6966 בהתבהלה 927 ענה 6032 ואמר 560 להדברוהי 1907
'adayin nabukadnetzar malka', tauah uaqam bahitbahalah; 'aneh ua'amar lahadabarouhiy,
**Then Nebuchadnezzar the king was astonied and rose up in haste *and* spoke and said unto his counsellors**

הלא 3809 גברין 1400 תלתא 8532 רמינא 7412 לגוא 1459 נורא 5135 מכפתין 3729 ענין 6032 ואמרין 560 למלכא 4430 יציבא 3330
hala' gubriyn talata' rameyna' lagou'a nura' makaptiyn, 'anayin ua'amariyn lamalka', yatziyba'
**not men three Did we cast into the midst of the fire? bound Then answered and said unto the king TRUE**

מלכא 4430: 3:25 ענה 6032 ואמר 560 הא 1888 אנה 576 חזה 2370 גברין 1400 ארבעה 703 שרין 8271 מהלכין 1981 בגוא 1459 נורא 5135
malka'. 'aneh ua'amar, ha' 'anah chazeh gubriyn 'arba'ah, sharayin mahlakiyn bagou'a nura',
**O king He answered and said Lo I see men four loose walking in the midst of the fire**

Dan 3:19 Then was Nebuchadnezzar full of fury, and the form of his visage was changed against Shadrach, Meshach, and Abed-nego: therefore he spoke, and commanded that they should heat the furnace one seven times more than it was wont to be heated.20 And he commanded the most mighty men that were in his army to bind Shadrach, Meshach, and Abed-nego, and to cast them into the burning fiery furnace.21 Then these men were bound in their coats, their hosen, and their hats, and their other garments, and were cast into the midst of the burning fiery furnace.22 Therefore because the king's commandment was urgent, and the furnace exceeding hot, the flame of the fire slew those men that took up Shadrach, Meshach, and Abed-nego.23 And these three men, Shadrach, Meshach, and Abed-nego, fell down bound into the midst of the burning fiery furnace.24 Then Nebuchadnezzar the king was astonied, and rose up in haste, and spoke, and said unto his counsellers, Did not we cast three men bound into the midst of the fire? They answered and said unto the king, True, O king.25 He answered and said, Lo, I see four men loose, walking in the midst of the fire, and they have no hurt; and the form of the fourth is like the Son of G-d.

וחבל 2257 לא 3809 איתי 383 בהון 871b ורוה 7299 די 1768 רביעיא 7244 דמה 1821 לבר 1247 אלהין 426: באדין 116 קרב 7127

3:26

uachabal la' 'aytay bahoun; uareueh diy rabiy'aya dameh labar 'alahiyn. bea'dayin qareb

**and hurt no have they and the form of the fourth is like the Son of Elohim Then came near**

נבוכדנצר 5020 לתרע 8651 אתון 861 נורא 5135 יקדתא 3345 ענה 6032 ואמר 560 שדרך 7715 מישך 4336 ועבד 5665 נגו 5665

nabukadnetzar, litra' 'atun nura' yaqidta' 'aneh ua'amar, shadrak meyshak ua'abed nagou

**Nebuchadnezzar to the mouth of furnace fiery *the* burning *and* spoke and said Shadrach Meshach and Abed nego**

עבדוהי 5649 די 1768 אלהא 426 עליא 5943 פקו 5312 ואתו 858 באדין 116 נפקין 5312 שדרך 7715 מישך 4336 ועבד 5665

abdouhiy diy 'alaha' 'ala'ya puqu ua'atou; bea'dayin napaqiyn, shadrak meyshak ua'abed

**you servants of Elohim the most high come forth and come you *here* Then came forth Shadrach Meshach and Abed**

נגו 5665 מן 4481 גוא 1459 נורא 5135: ומתכנשין 3673 אחשדרפניא 324 סגניא 5460 ופחותא 6347

3:27

nagou min goua' nura'. uamitkanshiyn 'achashdarpanaya' signaya' uapachauata'

**nego of the midst of the fire And being gathered together the princes governors and captains**

והדברי 1907 מלכא 4430 חזין 2370 לגבריא 1400 אלך 479 די 1768 לא 3809 שלט 7981 נורא 5135 בגשמהון 1655 ושער 8177 ראשהון 7217

uahadabrey malka' chazayin lagubraya' 'alek diy la' shalet nura' bageshmahoun, us'ar rea'shahoun

**and counsellors *the* king's saw men these whose no had power the fire upon bodies an hair of their head**

לא 3809 התחרך 2761 וסרבליהון 5622 לא 3809 שנו 8133 וריח 7382 נור 5135 לא 3809 עדת 5709 בהון 871b: ענה 6032

3:28

la' hitcharak, uasarabaleyhoun la' shanou; uareyach nur, la' 'adat bahoun. 'aneh

**nor was singed their coats neither were changed the smell of fire nor had passed on them *Then* spoke**

נבוכדנצר 5020 ואמר 560 בריך 1289 אלההון 426 די 1768 שדרך 7715 מישך 4336 ועבד 5665 נגו 5665 די 1768 שלח 7972 מלאכה 4398

nabukadnetzar ua'amar, bariyk 'alahahoun diy shadrak meyshak ua'abed nagou, diy shalach mal'akeh

**Nebuchadnezzar and said Blessed *be* the Elohim of Shadrach Meshach and Abed nego who has sent his angel**

ושיזב 7804 לעבדוהי 5649 די 1768 התרחצו 7365 עלוהי 5922 ומלת 4406 מלכא 4430 שניו 8133 ויהבו 3052 גשמיהון 1655 די 1768

uasheyzib la'abdouhiy, diy hitrachitzu 'alouhiy; uamilat malka' shaniyu, uayhabu geshmeyhoun diy

**and delivered his servants that trusted in him and word *the* king's have changed and yielded their bodies that**

לא 3809 יפלחון 6399 ולא 3809 יסגדון 5457 לכל 3606 אלה 426 להן 3861 לאלההון 426: ומני 4481 שים 7761 טעם 2942 די 1768 כל 3606

3:29

la' yiplachun uala' yisgadun lakal 'alah, lahen le'alahahoun. uaminiy siym ta'aem diy kal

**they might serve nor worship any god except their own Elohim Therefore I make a decree That every**

עם 5972 אמה 524 ולשן 3961 די 1768 יאמר 560 שלה 7955 על 5922 אלההון 426 די 1768 שדרך 7715 מישך 4336 ועבד 5665 נגוא 5665

'am 'amah ualishan, diy yea'mar shalah 'al 'alahahoun, diy shadrak meyshak ua'abed nagou'a

**people nation and language which speak anything amiss against the Elohim of Shadrach Meshach and Abed nego**

הדמין 1917 יתעבד 5648 וביתה 1005 נולי 5122 ישתוה 7739 כל 3606 קבל 6903 די 1768 לא 3809 איתי 383 אלה 426 אחרן 321 די 1768

hadamiyn yit'abed, uabayteh naualiy yishtaueh; kal qabel, diy la' 'aytay 'alah 'acharan, diy

***in* pieces shall be cut and their houses a dunghill shall be made because there is that no there is El other that**

יכל 3202 להצלה 5338 כדנה 1836: באדין 116 מלכא 4430 הצלח 6744 לשדרך 7715 מישך 4336 ועבד 5665 נגו 5665 במדינת 4083

3:30

yikul lahatzalah kidanah. bea'dayin malka', hatzalach lashadrak meyshak ua'abed nagou bimdiynat

**can deliver after this sort Then the king promoted Shadrach Meshach and Abed nego in the province of**

Dan 3:26 Then Nebuchadnezzar came near to the mouth of the burning fiery furnace, and spoke, and said, Shadrach, Meshach, and Abed-nego, you servants of the most high G-d, come forth, and come hither. Then Shadrach, Meshach, and Abed-nego, came forth of the midst of the fire.27 And the princes, governors, and captains, and the king's counsellers, being gathered together, saw these men, upon whose bodies the fire had no power, nor was an hair of their head singed, neither were their coats changed, nor the smell of fire had passed on them.28 Then Nebuchadnezzar spoke, and said, Blessed be the G-d of Shadrach, Meshach, and Abed-nego, who has sent his angel, and delivered his servants that trusted in him, and have changed the king's word, and yielded their bodies, that they might not serve nor worship any god, except their own G-d.29 Therefore I make a decree, That every people, nation, and language, which speak anything amiss against the G-d of Shadrach, Meshach, and Abed-nego, shall be cut in pieces, and their houses shall be made a dunghill: because there is no other G-d that can deliver after this sort.30 Then the king promoted Shadrach, Meshach, and Abed-nego, in the province of Babylon.

בבל 895:
babel.
**Babylon**

**Dan 4:1** נבוכדנצר 5020 מלכא 4430 לכל 3605 עממיא 5972 אמיא 524 ולשניא 3961 די 1768 דארין 1753 בכל 3606 ארעא 772 שלמכון 8001
nabukadnetzar malka', lakal 'amamaya' 'amaya' ualishanaya' diy da'ariyn bakal 'ar'aa' shalamakoun
**Nebuchadnezzar the king unto all people nations and languages that dwell in all the earth Peace**

ישגא 7680: **4:2** אתיא 852 ותמהיא 8540 די 1768 עבד 5648 עמי 5974 אלהא 426 עליא 5943 שפר 8232 קדמי 6925
yisgea'. 'ataya' uatimhaya', diy 'abad 'amiy, 'alaha' 'ala'ya shapar qadamay
**be multiplied unto you the signs and wonders that has wrought toward me Elohim *the* high it good I thought**

להחויה 2324: **4:3** אתוהי 852 כמה 4101 רברבין 7260 ותמהוהי 8540 כמה 4101 תקיפין 8624 מלכותה 4437 מלכות 4437 עלם 5957
lahachauayah. 'atouhiy kamah rabrabiyn, uatimhouhiy kamah taqiypiyn; malkuteh malkut 'alam,
**to show *are* his signs How great and his wonders how mighty *are* his kingdom *is* an kingdom everlasting**

ושלטנה 7985 עם 5974 דר 1859 ודר 17859: **4:4** אנה 576 נבוכדנצר 5020 שלה 7954 הוית 1934 בביתי 1005 ורענן 7487
uashalataneh 'am dar uadar. 'anah nabukadnetzar, shaleh haueyt babeytiy, uara'anan
**and his dominion *is* from generation to generation I Nebuchadnezzar at rest was in mine house and flourishing**

בהיכלי 1965: **4:5** חלם 2493 חזית 2370 וידחלנני 1763 והרהרין 2031 על 5922 משכבי 4903 וחזוי 2376 ראשי 7217
baheykaliy. chelem chazeyt uiydachalinaniy; uaharhoriyn 'al mishkabiy, uachezuey rea'shiy
**in my palace a dream I saw which made me afraid and the thoughts upon my bed and the visions of my head**

יבהלנני 927: **4:6** ומני 4481 שים 7761 טעם 2942 להנעלה 5954 קדמי 6925 לכל 3606 חכימי 2445 בבל 895 די 1768
yabahalunaniy. uaminiy siym ta'aem, lahana'alah qadamay, lakol chakiymey babel; diy
**troubled me Therefore made I a decree to bring in before me all the wise *men* of Babylon that**

פשר 6591 חלמא 2493 יהודענני 3046: **4:7** באדין 116 עללין 5954 חרטמיא 2749 אשפיא 826
pashar chelma' yahouda'ananiy. bea'dayin 'alaliyn chartumaya' 'ashapaya',
**the interpretation of the dream they might make known unto me Then came in the magicians the astrologers**

כשדיא 3779 וגזריא 1505 וחלמא 2493 אמר 560 אנה 576 קדמיהון 6925 ופשרה 6591 לא 3809
kasdaya uagazaraya'; uachelma', 'amar 'anah qadameyhoun, uapishreh la'
**the Chaldeans and the soothsayers and the dream told I before them but the interpretation thereof not**

מהודעין 3046 לי 3807a: **4:8** ועד 5705 אחרין 318 על 5954 קדמי 6925 דניאל 1841 די 1768 שמה 8036 בלטשאצר 1096
mahouda'ayn liy. ua'ad 'achareyn 'al qadamay daniyea'l diy shameh beltasha'tzar
**they did make known unto me But at the last came in before me Daniel whose name *was* Belteshazzar**

כשם 8036 אלהי 426 ודי 1768 רוח 7308 אלהין 426 קדישין 6922 בה 871a וחלמא 2493 קדמוהי 6925
kashum 'alahiy, uadiy ruach 'alahiyn qadiyshiyn beh; uachelma' qadamouhiy
**according to the name of my god and whom *is* the spirit of God *the* holy in whom and the dream before him**

אמרת 560: **4:9** בלטשאצר 1096 רב 7229 חרטמיא 2749 די 1768 אנה 576 ידעת 3046 די 1768 רוח 7308 אלהין 426 קדישין 6922 בך 871a
'amret. beltasha'tzar rab chartumaya' diy 'anah yid'aet, diy ruach 'alahiyn qadiyshiyn bak,
**I told O Belteshazzar master of the magicians because I know that the spirit of God *the* holy *is* in you**

**Dan** 4:1 Nebuchadnezzar the king, unto all people, nations, and languages, that dwell in all the earth; Peace be multiplied unto you.2 I thought it good to show the signs and wonders that the high G-d has wrought toward me.3 How great are his signs! and how mighty are his wonders! his kingdom is an everlasting kingdom, and his dominion is from generation to generation.4 I Nebuchadnezzar was at rest in mine house, and flourishing in my palace:5 I saw a dream which made me afraid, and the thoughts upon my bed and the visions of my head troubled me.6 Therefore made I a decree to bring in all the wise men of Babylon before me, that they might make known unto me the interpretation of the dream.7 Then came in the magicians, the astrologers, the Chaldeans, and the soothsayers: and I told the dream before them; but they did not make known unto me the interpretation thereof.8 But at the last Daniel came in before me, whose name was Belteshazzar, according to the name of my god, and in whom is the spirit of the holy gods: and before him I told the dream, saying,9 O Belteshazzar, master of the magicians, because I know that the spirit of the holy gods is in you, and no secret trouble you, tell me the visions of my dream that I have seen, and the interpretation thereof.

4:10

וכל 3606 רז 7328 לא 3809 אנס 598 לך 3807a חזוי 2376 חלמי 2493 די 1768 חזית 2370 ופשרה 6591 אמר 560:

uakal raz la' 'anes lak; chezuey chelmiy diy chazeyt uapishreh 'amar.

**and all secret no trouble to you me the visions of my dream that I have seen and the interpretation thereof you tell**

וחזוי 2376 ראשי 7217 על 5922 משכבי 4903 חזה 2370 הוית 1934 ואלו 431 אילן 363 בגוא 1459 ארעא 772

uachezuey rea'shiy 'al mishkabiy; chazeh haueyt, ua'alu 'aylan bagou'a 'ar'aa'

**Thus *were* the visions of mine head in my bed saw I and behold a tree in the midst of the earth**

4:11

ורומה 7314 שגיא 7690: רבה 7236 אילנא 363 ותקף 8631 ורומה 7314 ימטא 4291 לשמיא 8065

uarumeh sagiy'a. rabah 'aylana' uatqip; uarumeh yimtea' lishmaya',

**and the height thereof *was* great grew The tree and was strong and the height thereof reached unto heaven**

4:12

וחזותה 2379 לסוף 5491 כל 3605 ארעא 772: עפיה 6074 שפיר 8209 ואנבה 4 שגיא 7690

uachazouteh lasoup kal 'ar'aa'. 'apayeh shapiyr ua'anbeh sagiy'a,

**and the sight thereof to the end of all the earth The leaves thereof *were* fair and the fruit thereof much**

ומזון 4203 לכלא 3606 בה 871a תחתוהי 8460 תטלל 2927 חיות 2423 ברא 1251 ובענפוהי 6056 ידרון 1753 צפרי 6853

uamazoun lakola' beh; tachotohiy tatalel cheyuat bara', uab'anpouhiy yaduran tziparey

**and meat for all in it *was* under it had shadow the beasts of the field and in the boughs thereof dwell the fowls of**

4:13

שמיא 8065 ומנה 4481 יתזין 2110 כל 3606 בשרא 1321: חזה 2370 הוית 1934 בחזוי 2376 ראשי 7217 על 5922 משכבי 4903 ואלו 431

shamaya', uamineh yitaziyn kal bisra'. chazeh haueyt bachezuey rea'shiy 'al mishkabiy; ua'alu

**the heaven and of it was fed all flesh saw I in the visions of my head upon my bed and behold**

4:14

עיר 5894 וקדיש 6922 מן 4481 שמיא 8065 נחת 5182: קרא 7123 בחיל 2429 וכן 3652 אמר 560 גדו 1414 אילנא 363 וקצצו 7113

'ayr uaqadiysh, min shamaya' nachit. qarea' bachayil uaken 'amar, godu 'aylana' uaqatzitzu

**a watcher and an holy one from heaven came down He cried aloud and thus said Hew down the tree and cut off**

ענפוהי 6056 אתרו 5426 עפיה 6074 ובדרו 921 אנבה 4 תנד 5111 חיותא 2423 מן 4481 תחתוהי 8479 וצפריא 6853 מן 4481

anpouhiy, 'ataru 'apayeh uabadaru 'anbeh; tanud cheyuata' min tachatouhiy, uatzipraya' min

**his branches shake off you his leaves and scatter his fruit let get away the beasts from under it and the fowls from**

4:15

ענפוהי 6056: ברם 1297 עקר 6136 שרשוהי 8330 בארעא 772 שבקו 7662 ובאסור 613 די 1768 פרזל 6523 ונחש 5174

anpouhiy. baram 'aqar sharashouhiy ba'ar'aa' shabuqu, uabe'asur diy parzel uanchash,

**his branches Nevertheless the stump of his roots in the earth leave even with a band of iron and brass**

בדתאא 1883 די 1768 ברא 1251 ובטל 2920 שמיא 8065 יצטבע 6647 ועם 5974 חיותא 2423 חלקה 2508 בעשב 6211

badit'aa' diy bara'; uabtal shamaya' yitzataba', ua'am chayuata' chalaqeh ba'asab

**in the tender grass of the field with the dew of heaven let it be wet and with the beasts *let* his portion *be* in the grass of**

4:16

ארעא 772: לבבה 3825 מן 4481 אנושא 606 ישנון 8133 ולבב 3825 חיוה 2423 יתיהב 3052 לה 3807a ושבעה 7655 עדנין 5732

'ar'aa'. libbeh min 'anasha' yashanoun, ualbab cheyuah yityahib leh; uashib'ah 'adaniyn

**the earth his heart from man's Let be changed and a heart beast's let be given unto him and seven times**

4:17

יחלפון 2499 עלוהי 5922: בגזרת 1510 עירין 5894 פתגמא 6600 ומאמר 3983 קדישין 6922 שאלתא 7595 עד 5704

yachlapun 'alouhiy. bigzerat 'ayriyn pitgama', uamea'mar qadiyshiyn sha'aelata'; 'ad

**let pass over him *is* by the decree of the watchers This matter and the word of the holy ones the demand *by* to**

Dan 4:10 Thus were the visions of mine head in my bed; I saw, and behold a tree in the midst of the earth, and the height thereof was great.11 The tree grew, and was strong, and the height thereof reached unto heaven, and the sight thereof to the end of all the earth:12 The leaves thereof were fair, and the fruit thereof much, and in it was meat for all: the beasts of the field had shadow under it, and the fowls of the heaven dwelt in the boughs thereof, and all flesh was fed of it.13 I saw in the visions of my head upon my bed, and, behold, a watcher and an holy one came down from heaven;14 He cried aloud, and said thus, Hew down the tree, and cut off his branches, shake off his leaves, and scatter his fruit: let the beasts get away from under it, and the fowls from his branches:15 Nevertheless leave the stump of his roots in the earth, even with a band of iron and brass, in the tender grass of the field; and let it be wet with the dew of heaven, and let his portion be with the beasts in the grass of the earth:16 Let his heart be changed from man's, and let a beast's heart be given unto him; and let seven times pass over him.17 This matter is by the decree of the watchers, and the demand by the word of the holy ones: to the intent that the living may know that the most High rule in the kingdom of men, and give it to whomsoever he will, and set up over it the basest of men.

| 1701 דברת | 1768 די | 3046 ינדעון | 2417 חייא | 1768 די | 7990 שליט | 5943 עליא | 4437 במלכות | 606 אנושא | 4479 ולמן | 1768 די |
|---|---|---|---|---|---|---|---|---|---|---|
| dibrat | diy | yinda'aun | chayaya' | diy | shaliyt | 'ala'ya | bamalkut | 'anasha' | ualman | diy |
| **the intent** | **that** | **may know** | **the living** | **that** | **rule** | **the most high** | **in the kingdom of** | **men** | **and to whomsoever** | **that** |

| 6634 יצבא | 5415 יתננה | 8215 ושפל | 606 אנשים | 6966 יקים | 5922 עליה | 4:18 1836 דנה | 2493 חלמא | 2370 חזית | 576 אנה | 4430 מלכא | 5020 נבוכדנצר |
|---|---|---|---|---|---|---|---|---|---|---|---|
| yitzabea' | yitninah, | uashpal | 'anashiym | yaqiym | 'alayah | danah | chelma' | chazeyt, | 'anah | malka' | nabukadnetzar; |
| **he will** | **gives it** | **the basest of** | **men** | **set up** | **over it** | **This** | **dream** | **have seen** | **I** | **king** | **Nebuchadnezzar** |

| 607 ואנתה | 1096 בלטשאצר | 6591 פשרא | 560 אמר | 3606 כל | 6903 קבל | 1768 די | 3606 כל | 2445 חכימי | 4437 מלכותי |
|---|---|---|---|---|---|---|---|---|---|
| ua'antah | beltasha'tzar | pishrea' | 'amar, | kal | qabel | diy | kal | chakiymey | malkutiy, |
| **Now you** | **O Belteshazzar** | **the interpretation thereof** | **declare** | **all** | **forasmuch** | **as** | **all** | **the wise *men* of** | **my kingdom** |

| 3809 לא | 3202 יכלין | 6591 פשרא | 3046 להודעתני | 607 ואנתה | 3546 כהל | 1768 די | 7308 רוח | 426 אלהין | 6922 קדישין |
|---|---|---|---|---|---|---|---|---|---|
| la' | yakaliyn | pishra' | lahouda'ataniy, | ua'antah | kahel, | diy | ruach | 'alahiyn | qadiyshiyn |
| **not** | **are able** | **the interpretation** | **to make known unto me** | **but you** | ***are* able** | **for** | **the spirit of** | **God** | ***the* holy** |

| 871a: בך | 4:19 116 אדין | 1841 דניאל | 1768 די | 8036 שמה | 1096 בלטשאצר | 8075 אשתומם | 8160 כשעה | 2298 חדה | 7476 ורעינהי | 927 יבהלנה |
|---|---|---|---|---|---|---|---|---|---|---|
| bak. | 'adayin | daniyea'l | diy | shameh | beltasha'tzar, | 'ashtoumam | kasha'ah | chadah, | uara'yonohiy | yabahaluneh; |
| ***is* in you** | **Then** | **Daniel** | **whose** | **name** | ***was* Belteshazzar** | **was astonied** | **for hour** | **one** | **and his thoughts** | **troubled him** |

| 6032 ענה | 4430 מלכא | 560 ואמר | 1096 בלטשאצר | 2493 חלמא | 6591 ופשרא | 409 אל | 927 יבהלך | 6032 ענה | 1096 בלטשאצר |
|---|---|---|---|---|---|---|---|---|---|
| 'aneh | malka' | ua'amar, | beltasha'tzar | chelma' | uapishrea' | 'al | yabahalak, | 'aneh | beltasha'tzar |
| **spoke** | **The king** | **and said** | **Belteshazzar** | **the dream** | **or the interpretation thereof** | **not** | **trouble you** | **answered** | **Belteshazzar** |

| 560 ואמר | 4756 מראי | 2493 חלמא | 8131 לשנאיך | 6591 ופשרה | 6146: לעריך | 4:20 363 אילנא |
|---|---|---|---|---|---|---|
| ua'amar, | maray | chelma' | lasana'ayak | uapishreh | la'arayak | 'aylana' |
| **and said** | **My adonai** | **the dream *be*** | **to them that hate you** | **you and the interpretation thereof** | **to your enemies** | **The tree** |

| 1768 די | 2370 חזית | 1768 די | 7236 רבה | 8631 ותקף | 7314 ורומה | 4291 ימטא | 8065 לשמיא | 2379 וחזותה | 3606 לכל |
|---|---|---|---|---|---|---|---|---|---|
| diy | chazayta, | diy | rabah | uatqip; | uarumeh | yimtea' | lishmaya', | uachazouteh | lakal |
| **that** | **you saw** | **which** | **grew** | **and was strong** | **whose height** | **reached** | **unto the heaven** | **and the sight thereof** | **to all** |

| 772: ארעא | 4:21 6074 ועפיה | 8209 שפיר | 4 ואנבה | 7690 שגיא | 4203 ומזון | 3606 לכלא | 871a בה | 8460 תחתוהי | 1753 תדור |
|---|---|---|---|---|---|---|---|---|---|
| 'ar'aa'. | ua'apayeh | shapiyr | ua'anbeh | sagiy'a, | uamazoun | lakola' | beh; | tachotohiy, | tadur |
| **the earth** | **Whose leaves *were*** | **fair** | **and the fruit thereof** | **much** | **and meat** | **for all** | **in it *was*** | **under** | **which dwelt** |

| 2423 חיות | 1251 ברא | 6050 ובענפוהי | 7932 ישכנן | 6853 צפרי | 8065: שמיא | 4:22 607 אנתה | 1932 הוא | 4430 מלכא |
|---|---|---|---|---|---|---|---|---|
| cheyuat | bara', | uab'anpouhiy | yishkanan | tziparey | shamaya'. | 'antah | hua' | malka', |
| **the beasts of** | **the field** | **and upon whose branches** | **had their habitation** | **the fowls of** | **the heaven** | ***is* you** | **It** | **O king** |

| 1768 די | 7236 רבית | 8631 ותקפת | 7238 ורבותך | 7236 רבת | 4291 ומטת | 8065 לשמיא | 7985 ושלטנך | 5491 לסוף |
|---|---|---|---|---|---|---|---|---|
| diy | rabayt | uatqept; | uarbutak | rabat | uamtat | lishmaya', | uashalatanak | lasoup |
| **that** | **are grown** | **and become strong** | **for your greatness** | **is grown** | **and reached** | **unto heaven** | **and your dominion** | **to the end of** |

| 772: ארעא | 4:23 1768 ודי | 2370 חזה | 4430 מלכא | 5894 עיר | 6922 וקדיש | 5182 נחת | 4481 מן | 8065 שמיא | 560 ואמר | 1414 גדו |
|---|---|---|---|---|---|---|---|---|---|---|
| 'ar'aa'. | uadiy | chazah | malka' | 'ayr | uaqadiysh | nachit | min | shamaya' | ua'amar | godu |
| **the earth** | **And whereas** | **saw** | **the king** | **a watcher** | **and an holy one** | **coming down** | **from** | **heaven** | **and saying** | **Cut down** |

Dan 4:18 This dream I king Nebuchadnezzar have seen. Now you, O Belteshazzar, declare the interpretation thereof, forasmuch as all the wise men of my kingdom are not able to make known unto me the interpretation: but you are able; for the spirit of the holy gods is in you.19 Then Daniel, whose name was Belteshazzar, was astonied for one hour, and his thoughts troubled him. The king spoke, and said, Belteshazzar, let not the dream, or the interpretation thereof, trouble you. Belteshazzar answered and said, My lord, the dream be to them that hate you, and the interpretation thereof to your enemies.20 The tree that you saw, which grew, and was strong, whose height reached unto the heaven, and the sight thereof to all the earth;21 Whose leaves were fair, and the fruit thereof much, and in it was meat for all; under which the beasts of the field dwelt, and upon whose branches the fowls of the heaven had their habitation:22 It is you, O king, that are grown and become strong: for your greatness is grown, and reacheth unto heaven, and your dominion to the end of the earth.23 And whereas the king saw a watcher and an holy one coming down from heaven, and saying, Hew the tree down, and destroy it; yet leave the stump of the roots thereof in the earth, even with a band of iron and brass, in the tender grass of the field; and let it be wet with the dew of heaven,

| | | | | | | | | | |
|---|---|---|---|---|---|---|---|---|---|
| 363 אילנא | 2255 והחבלוהי | 1297 ברם | 6136 עקר | 8330 שרשוהי | 772 בארעא | 7662 שבקו | 613 ובאסור | 1768 די | 6523 פרזל |
| 'aylana' | uachabluhiy, | baram | 'aqar | sharashouhiy | ba'ar'aa' | shabuqu, | uabe'asur | diy | parzel |
| **the tree** | **and destroy it** | **yet** | **the stump of** | **the roots thereof** | **in the earth** | **leave** | **even with a band** | **of** | **iron** |

| | | | | | | | | | |
|---|---|---|---|---|---|---|---|---|---|
| 5174 ונחש | 1883 בדתאא | 1768 די | 1251 ברא | 2920 ובטל | 8065 שמיא | 6647 יצטבע | 5974 ועם | 2423 חיות | 1251 ברא |
| uanchash, | badit'aa' | diy | bara'; | uabtal | shamaya' | yitzataba', | ua'am | cheyuat | bara' |
| **and brass** | **in the tender grass** | **of** | **the field** | **and with the dew of** | **heaven** | **let it be wet** | **and with** | **the beasts of** | **the field** |

| | | | | | | | | | | |
|---|---|---|---|---|---|---|---|---|---|---|
| 2508 חלקה | 5704 עד | 1768 די | 7655 שבעה | 5732 עדנין | 2499 יחלפון | 5922: עלוהי | 4:24 | 1836 דנה | 6591 פשרא | 4430 מלכא |
| chalaqeh, | 'ad | diy | shib'ah | 'adaniyn | yachlapun | 'alouhiy. | | danah | pishra' | malka'; |
| ***let* his portion *be*** | **till** | **that** | **seven** | **times** | **pass** | **over him** | | **This** | ***is* the interpretation** | **O king** |

| | | | | | | | | | | |
|---|---|---|---|---|---|---|---|---|---|---|
| 1510 וגזרת | 5943 עליא | 1932 היא | 1768 די | 4291 מטת | 5922 על | 4756 מראי | 4430: מלכא | 4:25 | 3807a ולך | 2957 טרדין | 4481 מן |
| uagazerat | 'ala'ya | hiy'a, | diy | matat | 'al | mar'ay | malka'. | | ualak | taradiyn | min |
| **and the decree of** | **the most high** | **this *is*** | **which** | **is come** | **upon** | **my adoni** | **the king** | | **That you** | **they shall drive** | **from** |

| | | | | | | | | | |
|---|---|---|---|---|---|---|---|---|---|
| 606 אנשא | 5974 ועם | 2423 חיות | 1251 ברא | 1934 להוה | 4070 מדרך | 6211 ועשבא | 8450 כתורין | 3807a לך | 2939 יטעמון |
| 'anasha' | ua'am | cheyuat | bara' | lehaueh | madorak | ua'asba' | katouriyn | lak | yata'amun, |
| **men** | **and with** | **the beasts of** | **the field** | **shall be** | **your dwelling** | **and grass** | **as oxen** | **to you** | **they shall make to eat** |

| | | | | | | | | | | | |
|---|---|---|---|---|---|---|---|---|---|---|---|
| 2920 ומטל | 8065 שמיא | 3807a לך | 6647 מצבעין | 7655 ושבעה | 5732 עדנין | 2499 יחלפון | 5922 עליך | 5705 עד | 1768 די | 3046 תנדע | 1768 די |
| uamital | shamaya' | lak | matzab'ayn, | uashib'ah | 'adaniyn | yachlapun | 'alayik | 'ad | diy | tinda', | diy |
| **and with the dew of** | **heaven** | **to you** | **they shall wet** | **and seven** | **times** | **shall pass** | **over you** | **till** | **that** | **you know** | **that** |

| | | | | | | | | | |
|---|---|---|---|---|---|---|---|---|---|
| 7990 שליט | 5943 עליא | 4437 במלכות | 606 אנשא | 4479 ולמן | 1768 די | 6634 יצבא | 5415: יתננה | 4:26 | 1768 ודי |
| shaliyt | 'ala'ya | bamalkut | 'anasha', | ualman | diy | yitzabea' | yitninah. | | uadiy |
| **rule** | **the most high** | **in the kingdom of** | **men** | **and to whomsoever** | **that** | **he will** | **gives it** | | **And whereas** |

| | | | | | | | | | | |
|---|---|---|---|---|---|---|---|---|---|---|
| 560 אמרו | 7662 למשבק | 6136 עקר | 8330 שרשוהי | 1768 די | 363 אילנא | 4437 מלכותך | 3807a לך | 7011 קימה | 4481 מן | 1768 די |
| 'amaru, | lamishbaq | 'aqar | sharashouhiy | diy | 'aylana', | malkutak | lak | qayamah; | min | diy |
| **they commanded** | **to leave** | **the stump** | **roots** | **of** | **the tree** | **your kingdom** | **unto you** | ***shall be* sure** | **after** | **that** |

| | | | | | | | | | |
|---|---|---|---|---|---|---|---|---|---|
| 3046 תנדע | 1768 די | 7990 שלטן | 8065: שמיא | 4:27 | 3861 להן | 4430 מלכא | 4431 מלכי | 8232 ישפר | 5922 עליך |
| tinda', | diy | shalitin | shamaya'. | | lahen | malka', | milkiy | yishpar | 'alayik |
| **you shall have known** | **that** | **do rule** | **the heavens** | | **Wherefore** | **O king** | **my counsel** | **let be acceptable** | **unto you** |

| | | | | | | | | |
|---|---|---|---|---|---|---|---|---|
| 2408 וחטיך | 6665 בצדקה | 6562 פרק | 5758 ועויתך | 2604 במחן | 6033 ענין | 2006 הן | 1934 תהוא | 754 ארכה |
| uachatayak | batzidqah | paruq, | ua'auayatak | bamichan | 'anayin; | hen | tehauea' | 'arkah |
| **and your sins** | **by righteousness** | **break off** | **and your iniquities** | **by shewing mercy to** | **the poor** | **if** | **it may be** | **a lengthening** |

| | | | | | | | | | | |
|---|---|---|---|---|---|---|---|---|---|---|
| 7963: לשלותך | 4:28 | 3606 כלא | 4291 מטא | 5922 על | 5020 נבוכדנצר | 4430: מלכא | 4:29 | 7118 לקצת | 3393 ירחין | 8648 תרי | 6236 עשר |
| lishleuatak. | | kol'a | mata', | 'al | nabukadnetzar | malka'. | | liqtzat | yarchiyn | tarey | 'asar; |
| **of your tranquillity** | | **All** | **this came** | **upon** | **Nebuchadnezzar** | **the king** | | **At the end of** | **months** | **two** | **ten** |

| | | | | | | | | | | | | |
|---|---|---|---|---|---|---|---|---|---|---|---|---|
| 5922 על | 1965 היכל | 4437 מלכותא | 1768 די | 895 בבל | 1981 מהלך | 1934: הוה | 4:30 | 6032 ענה | 4430 מלכא | 560 ואמר | 3809 הלא | 1668 דא | 1932 היא |
| 'al | heykal | malkuta' | diy | babel | mahalek | hauah. | | 'aneh | malka' | ua'amar, | hala' | da | hiy'a |
| **in** | **the palace of** | **the kingdom of** | | **Babylon** | **walking** | **he** | | **spoke** | **The king** | **and said** | ***Is* not** | **this** | **she** |

Dan 4:23 and let his portion be with the beasts of the field, till seven times pass over him;24 This is the interpretation, O king, and this is the decree of the most High, which is come upon my lord the king:25 That they shall drive you from men, and your dwelling shall be with the beasts of the field, and they shall make you to eat grass as oxen, and they shall wet you with the dew of heaven, and seven times shall pass over you, till you know that the most High rule in the kingdom of men, and give it to whomsoever he will.26 And whereas they commanded to leave the stump of the tree roots; your kingdom shall be sure unto you, after that you shall have known that the heavens do rule.27 Wherefore, O king, let my counsel be acceptable unto you, and break off your sins by righteousness, and your iniquities by shewing mercy to the poor; if it may be a lengthening of your tranquillity.28 All this came upon the king Nebuchadnezzar.29 At the end of twelve months he walked in the palace of the kingdom of Babylon.30 The king spoke, and said, Is not this great Babylon, that I have built for the house of the kingdom by the might of my power, and for the honor of my majesty?

בבל 895 | רבתא 7229 | די 1768 | אנה 576 | בניתה 1124 | לבית 1005 | מלכו 4437 | בתקף 8632 | חסני 2632 | וליקר 3367
babel rabata'; diy 'anah banayatah labeyt malku, bitqap chisniy ualiyqar
**Babylon great that I have built for the house of the kingdom by the might of my power and for the honor of**

הדרי 1923: | 4:31 עוד 5751 | מלתא 4406 | בפם 6433 | מלכא 4430 | קל 7032 | מן 4481 | שמיא 8065 | נפל 5308 | לך 3807a | אמרין 560
hadriy. 'aud, milta' bapum malka', qal min shamaya' napal; lak 'amariyn
**my majesty? While the word *was* in the mouth king's a voice from heaven there fell to you it is spoken**

נבוכדנצר 5020 | מלכא 4430 | מלכותה 4437 | עדת 5709 | מנך 4481: | 4:32 ומן 4481 | אנשא 606 | לך 3807a | טרדין 2957 | ועם 5974
nabukadnetzar malka', malkutah 'adat minak. uamin 'anasha' lak taradiyn ua'am
**Nebuchadnezzar *saying* O king The kingdom is departed from you And from men to you they shall drive and with**

חיות 2423 | ברא 1251 | מדרך 4070 | עשבא 6211 | כתורין 8450 | לך 3807a | יטעמון 2939 | ושבעה 7655 | עדנין 5732 | יחלפון 2499
cheyuat bara' madorak, 'asba' katouriyn lak yata'amun, uashib'ah 'adaniyn yachlapun
**the beasts of the field your dwelling *shall be* grass as oxen to you they shall make to eat and seven times shall pass**

עליך 5922 | עד 5705 | די 1768 | תנדע 3046 | די 1768 | שליט 7990 | עליא 5943 | במלכות 4437 | אנשא 606 | ולמן 4479 | די 1768
'alayik 'ad diy tinda', diy shaliyt 'ala'ya bamalkut 'anasha', ualman diy
**over you until forasmuch you know that rule *the* most high in the kingdom of men and to whomsoever that**

יצבא 6634 | יתננה 5415: | 4:33 בה 871a | שעתא 8160 | מלתא 4406 | ספת 5487 | על 5922 | נבוכדנצר 5020 | ומן 4481 | אנשא 606 | טריד 2957
yitzabea' yitninah. bah sha'ata', milta' sapat 'al nabukadnetzar uamin 'anasha' tariyd,
**he will gives it The same hour the thing was fulfilled upon Nebuchadnezzar and from men he was driven**

ועשבא 6211 | כתורין 8450 | יאכל 399 | ומטל 2920 | שמיא 8065 | גשמה 1655 | יצטבע 6647 | עד 5704 | די 1768 | שערה 8177 | כנשרין 5403 | רבה 7236
ua'asba' katouriyn yea'kul, uamital shamaya' gishmeh yitzataba'; 'ad diy sa'areh kanishriyn rabah
**and grass as oxen did eat and with the dew of heaven his body was wet till that his hairs like eagles' were grown**

וטפרוהי 2953 | כצפרין 6853: | 4:34 ולקצת 7118 | יומיה 3118 | אנה 575 | נבוכדנצר 5020 | עיני 5870 | לשמיא 8065
uatiprouhiy katzipriyn. ualiqtzat youmayah 'anah nabukadnetzar 'ayanay lishmaya'
***feathers* and his nails like birds' *claws* And at the end of the days I Nebuchadnezzar mine eyes unto heaven**

נטלת 5191 | ומנדעי 4486 | עלי 5922 | יתוב 8421 | ולעליא 5943 | ברכת 1289 | ולחי 2417 | עלמא 5957 | שבחת 7624
nitlet, uamanda'ay 'alay yatub, ual'alaya baraket, ualchay 'alama' shabchet
**lifted up and mine understanding unto me returned and most high I blessed *the* and him that live for ever I praised**

והדרת 1922 | די 1768 | שלטנה 7985 | שלטן 7985 | עלם 5957 | ומלכותה 4437 | עם 5974 | דר 1859 | ודר 1859: | 4:35 וכל 3606
uahadret; diy shaltaneh shalatan 'alam, uamalkuteh 'am dar uadar. uakal
**and honoured whose dominion *is* an dominion everlasting and his kingdom *is* from generation to generation And all**

דארי 1753 | ארעא 772 | כלה 3809 | חשיבין 2804 | וכמצביה 6634 | עבד 5648 | בחיל 2429 | שמיא 8065
da'arey 'ar'aa' kalah chashiybiyn, uakmitzabayeh, 'abed bacheyl shamaya',
**the inhabitants of the earth as nothing *are* reputed and according to his will he does in the army of heaven**

ודארי 1753 | ארעא 772 | ולא 3809 | איתי 383 | די 1768 | ימחא 4223 | בידה 3028 | ויאמר 560 | לה 3807a | מה 4101 | עבדת 5648:
uada'arey 'ar'aa'; uala' 'aytay diy yamachea' biydeh, uayea'mar leh mah 'abadt.
**and among the inhabitants of the earth and none can that stay his hand or say unto him What do you?**

Dan 4:31 While the word was in the king's mouth, there fell a voice from heaven, saying, O king Nebuchadnezzar, to you it is spoken; The kingdom is departed from you.32 And they shall drive you from men, and your dwelling shall be with the beasts of the field: they shall make you to eat grass as oxen, and seven times shall pass over you, until you know that the most High rule in the kingdom of men, and give it to whomsoever he will.33 The same hour was the thing fulfilled upon Nebuchadnezzar: and he was driven from men, and did eat grass as oxen, and his body was wet with the dew of heaven, till his hairs were grown like eagles' feathers, and his nails like birds' claws.34 And at the end of the days I Nebuchadnezzar lifted up mine eyes unto heaven, and mine understanding returned unto me, and I blessed the most High, and I praised and honoured him that live forever, whose dominion is an everlasting dominion, and his kingdom is from generation to generation:35 And all the inhabitants of the earth are reputed as nothing: and he doeth according to his will in the army of heaven, and among the inhabitants of the earth: and none can stay his hand, or say unto him, What does you?

**4:36**
בה 871a זמנא 2166 מנדעי 4486 יתוב 8421 עלי 5922 וליקר 3367 מלכותי 4437 הדרי 1923 וזוי 2122
beh zimna' manda'ay yatub 'alay, ualiyqar malkutiy hadriy uaziuiy
**At the same time my reason returned unto me and for the glory of my kingdom mine honor and brightness**

יתוב 8421 עלי 5922 ולי 3807a הדברי 1907 ורברבני 7261 יבעון 1156 ועל 5922 מלכותי 4437 התקנת 8627 ורבו 7238
yatub 'alay, ualiy hadabaray uarabrabanay yaba'aun; ua'al malkutiy hatqanat, uarbu
**returned unto me and unto me my counsellors and my lords sought and in my kingdom I was established and majesty**

**4:37**
יתירה 3493 הוספת 3255 לי 3807a: כען 3705 אנה 576 נבוכדנצר 5020 משבח 7624 ומרומם 7313 ומהדר 1922 למלך 4430 שמיא 8065
yatiyrah husapat liy. ka'an 'anah nabukadnetzar, mashabach uamroumem uamhadar lamelek shamaya',
**excellent was added unto me Now I Nebuchadnezzar praise and extol and honor the King of heaven**

די 1768 כל 3605 מעבדוהי 4567 קשט 7187 וארחתה 735 דין 1780 ודי 1768 מהלכין 1981 בגוה 1467 יכל 3202 להשפלה 8214:
diy kal ma'abadouhiy qashot, ua'arachateh diyn; uadiy mahlakiyn bageuah, yakiyl lahashapalah.
**whose all works *are* truth and his ways judgment and those that walk in pride he is able to abase**

**Dan 5:1** ... **5:2**
בלשאצר 1113 מלכא 4430 עבד 5648 לחם 3900 רב 7229 לרברבנוהי 7261 אלף 506 ולקבל 6903 אלפא 506 חמרא 2562 שתה 8355:
belesha'tzar malka', 'abad lachem rab, larabrabanouhiy 'alap; ualaqabel 'alpa' chamra' shateh.
**Belshazzar the king made a feast great to of his lords a thousand and before the thousand wine drank**

בלשאצר 1113 אמר 560 בטעם 2939 חמרא 2562 להיתיה 858 למאני 3984 דהבא 1722 וכספא 3702 די 1768 הנפק 5312 נבוכדנצר 5020
belesha'tzar 'amar bit'aem chamra', lahayatayah lama'ney dahaba' uakaspa', diy hanapeq nabukadnetzar
**Belshazzar commanded while he eat the wine to bring vessels the golden and silver which had taken Nebuchadnezzar**

אבוהי 2 מן 4481 היכלא 1965 די 1768 בירושלם 3390 וישתון 8355 בהון 871b מלכא 4430 ורברבנוהי 7261 שגלתה 7695
'abuhiy, min heykala' diy biyarushalem; uayishtoun bahoun, malka' uarabrabanouhiy, shegalateh
**his father out of the temple which *was* in Jerusalem that might drink therein the king and his princes and his wives**

**5:3**
ולחנתה 3904: באדין 116 היתיו 858 מאני 3984 דהבא 1722 די 1768 הנפקו 5312 מן 4481 היכלא 1965 די 1768 בית 1005
ualchenateh. bea'dayin, hayatiyu ma'ney dahaba', diy hanapiqu, min heykala' diy beyt
**and his concubines Then they brought vessels *the* golden that were taken out of the temple of the house of**

**5:4**
אלהא 426 די 1768 בירושלם 3390 ואשתיו 8355 בהון 871b מלכא 4430 ורברבנוהי 7261 שגלתה 7695 ולחנתה 3904: אשתיו 8355
'alaha' diy biyarushalem; ua'ashtiyu bahoun, malka' uarabrabanouhiy, shegalateh ualchenateh. 'ashtiyu
**Elohim which *was* at Jerusalem and drank in them the king and his princes his wives and his concubines They drank**

**5:5**
חמרא 2562 ושבחו 7624 לאלהי 426 דהבא 1722 וכספא 3702 נחשא 5174 פרזלא 6523 אעא 636 ואבנא 69: בה 871a שעתה 8160
chamra'; uashabachu le'alahey dahaba' uakaspa' nachasha' parzala' 'a'aa ua'abna'. bah sha'atah,
**wine and praised the gods of gold and of silver *of* brass *of* iron *of* wood and of stone In the same hour**

נפקו 5312 אצבען 677 די 1768 יד 3028 אנש 606 וכתבן 3790 לקבל 6903 נברשתא 5043 על 5922 גירא 1528 די 1768 כתל 3797 היכלא 1965
napaqu 'atzba'an diy yad 'anash, uakataban laqabel nebrashta', 'al giyra' diy katal heykala'
**came forth fingers of a hand man's and wrote over against the candlestick upon the plaister of the wall palace**

**5:6**
די 1768 מלכא 4430 ומלכא 4430 חזה 2370 פס 6447 ידה 3028 די 1768 כתבה 3790: אדין 116 מלכא 4430 זיוהי 2122
diy malka'; uamalka' chazeh, pas yadah diy katabah. 'adayin malka' ziyuohiy
**of *the* king's and the king saw the part of the hand that wrote Then the king's countenance**

Dan 4:36 At the same time my reason returned unto me; and for the glory of my kingdom, mine honor and brightness returned unto me; and my counsellers and my lords sought unto me; and I was established in my kingdom, and excellent majesty was added unto me.37 Now I Nebuchadnezzar praise and extol and honor the King of heaven, all whose works are truth, and his ways judgment: and those that walk in pride he is able to abase. **Dan** 5:1 Belshazzar the king made a great feast to a thousand of his lords, and drank wine before the thousand.2 Belshazzar, whiles he tasted the wine, commanded to bring the golden and silver vessels which his father Nebuchadnezzar had taken out of the temple which was in Jerusalem; that the king, and his princes, his wives, and his concubines, might drink therein.3 Then they brought the golden vessels that were taken out of the temple of the house of G-d which was at Jerusalem; and the king, and his princes, his wives, and his concubines, drank in them.4 They drank wine, and praised the gods of gold, and of silver, of brass, of iron, of wood, and of stone.5 In the same hour came forth fingers of a man's hand, and wrote over against the candlestick upon the plaister of the wall of the king's palace: and the king saw the part of the hand that wrote. 6 Then the king's countenance was changed, and his thoughts troubled him,

| 8133 שנוהי | 7476 ורעינהי | 927 יבהלונה | 7001 וקטרי | 2783 חרצה | 8271 משתרין | 755 וארכבתה | 1668 דא | 1668 לדא |
|---|---|---|---|---|---|---|---|---|
| shanouhiy, | uara'yonohiy | yabahaluneh; | uaqitrey | chartzeh | mishtarayin, | ua'arkubateh, | da' | lada' |
| **was changed** | **and his thoughts** | **troubled him** | **so that the joints of** | **his loins** | **were loosed** | **and his knees** | **one** | **against another** |

| 5368: נקשן | 5:7 7123 קרא | 4430 מלכא | 2429 בחיל | 5954 להעלה | 826 לאשפיא | 3779 כשדיא | 1505 וגזריא | 6032 ענה | 4430 מלכא |
|---|---|---|---|---|---|---|---|---|---|
| naqashan. | qarea' | malka' | bachayil, | lahe'alah | la'ashapaya', | kasdaya | uagazaraya'; | 'aneh | malka' |
| **smote** | **cried** | **The king** | **aloud** | **to bring** | **in the astrologers** | **the Chaldeans** | **and the soothsayers** | **spoke** | ***And* the king** |

| 560 ואמר | 2445 לחכימי | 895 בבל | 1768 די | 3605 כל | 606 אנש | 1768 די | 7123 יקרה | 3792 כתבה | 1836 דנה | 6591 ופשרה |
|---|---|---|---|---|---|---|---|---|---|---|
| ua'amar | lachakiymey | babel, | diy | kal | 'anash | diy | yiqreh | katabah | danah, | uapishreh |
| **and said** | **to the wise *men* of** | **Babylon** | **that** | **any of** | **Whosoever** | **that** | **shall read** | **writing** | **this** | **and the interpretation thereof** |

| 2324 יחוינני | 711 ארגונא | 3848 ילבש | 2002 והמונכא | 1768 די | 1722 דהבא | 5922 על | 6676 צוארה | 8523 ותלתי | 4437 במלכותא |
|---|---|---|---|---|---|---|---|---|---|
| yachauinaniy, | 'argauana' | yilbash, | uahamounka' | diy | dahaba' | 'al | tzauareh, | uataltiy | bamalkuta' |
| **show me** | **scarlet** | **shall be clothed with** | **and have a chain** | **of** | **gold** | **about** | **his neck** | **and third** | **in the kingdom** |

| 7981: ישלט | 5:8 116 אדין | 5954 עללין | 3606 כל | 2445 חכימי | 4430 מלכא | 3809 ולא | 3546 כהלין | 3792 כתבא | 7123 למקרא |
|---|---|---|---|---|---|---|---|---|---|
| yishlat. | 'adayin | 'alaliyn | kal | chakiymey | malka'; | uala' | kahaliyn | kataba' | lamiqrea', |
| **shall be ruler *the*** | **Then** | **came in** | **all** | **wise *men*** | ***the* king's** | **but not** | **they could** | **the writing** | **read** |

| 6591 ופשרא | 3046 להודעה | 4430: למלכא | 5:9 116 אדין | 4430 מלכא | 1113 בלשאצר | 7690 שגיא | 927 מתבהל |
|---|---|---|---|---|---|---|---|
| uapishra | lahouda'ah | lamalka'. | 'adayin | malka' | belsha'tzar | sagiy'a | mitbahal, |
| **nor the interpretation thereof** | **make known** | **to the king** | **Then** | **king** | **Belshazzar** | **greatly** | **was troubled** |

| 2122 וזיוהי | 8133 שנין | 5922 עלוהי | 7261 ורברבנוהי | 7672: משתבשין | 5:10 4433 מלכתא | 6903 לקבל | 4406 מלי |
|---|---|---|---|---|---|---|---|
| uaziyuohiy | shanayin | 'alouhiy; | uarabrabanouhiy | mishtabshiyn. | malkta' | laqabel | miley |
| **and his countenance** | **was changed** | **in him** | **and his lords** | **were astonied** | ***Now* the queen** | **by reason of** | **the words of** |

| 4430 מלכא | 7261 ורברבנוהי | 1005 לבית | 4961 משתיא | 5954 עללת | 6032 ענת | 4433 מלכתא | 560 ואמרת | 4430 מלכא | 5957 לעלמין | 2418 חיי | 409 אל |
|---|---|---|---|---|---|---|---|---|---|---|---|
| malka' | uarabrabanouhiy, | labeyt | mishtaya' | 'alalat | 'anat | malkta' | ua'ameret, | malka' | la'alamiyn | chayiy, | 'al |
| **the king** | **and his lords** | **into house** | ***the* banquet** | **came** | **spoke** | ***and* the queen** | **and said** | **O king** | **for ever** | **live** | **not** |

| 927 יבהלוך | 7476 רעיונך | 2122 וזיויך | 409 אל | 8133: ישתנו | 5:11 383 איתי | 1400 גבר | 4437 במלכותך | 1768 די |
|---|---|---|---|---|---|---|---|---|
| yabahaluk | ra'younak, | uaziyuayk | 'al | yishtanou. | 'aytay | gabar | bamalkutak, | diy |
| **let trouble you** | **your thoughts** | **your countenance** | **nor** | **let be changed** | **There is** | **a man** | **in your kingdom** | **in whom** |

| 7308 רוח | 426 אלהין | 6922 קדישין | 871a בה | 3118 וביומי | 2 אבוך | 5094 נהירו | 7924 ושכלתנו | 2452 וחכמה |
|---|---|---|---|---|---|---|---|---|
| ruach | 'alahiyn | qadiyshiyn | beh | uabyoumey | 'abuk, | nahiyru | uasaklatanu | uachakamah |
| ***is* the spirit of** | **God** | ***the* holy** | | **and in the days** | **of your father** | **light** | **and understanding** | **and wisdom** |

| 2452 כחכמת | 426 אלהין | 7912 השתכחת | 871a בה | 4430 ומלכא | 5020 נבכדנצר | 2 אבוך | 7229 רב | 2749 חרטמין |
|---|---|---|---|---|---|---|---|---|
| kachakamat | 'alahiyn | hishtakachat | beh; | uamalka' | nabukadnetzar | 'abuk, | rab | chartumiyn |
| **like the wisdom of** | **the gods** | **was found** | **in him** | **whom the king** | **Nebuchadnezzar** | **your father** | **master of** | **the magicians** |

| 826 אשפין | 3779 כשדאין | 1505 גזרין | 6966 הקימה | 2 אבוך | 4430: מלכא | 5:12 3606 כל | 6903 קבל | 1768 די | 7308 רוח | 3493 יתירה |
|---|---|---|---|---|---|---|---|---|---|---|
| 'ashapiyn, | kasda'ayn | gazariyn, | haqiymeh | 'abuk | malka'. | kal | qabel | diy | ruach | yatiyrah |
| **astrologers** | **Chaldeans** | ***and* soothsayers** | **made** | ***I say* your father** | **the king** | **all** | **Foreasmuch** | **that** | **an spirit** | **excellent** |

Dan 5:6 so that the joints of his loins were loosed, and his knees smote one against another.7 The king cried aloud to bring in the astrologers, the Chaldeans, and the soothsayers. And the king spoke, and said to the wise men of Babylon, Whosoever shall read this writing, and show me the interpretation thereof, shall be clothed with scarlet, and have a chain of gold about his neck, and shall be the third ruler in the kingdom.8 Then came in all the king's wise men: but they could not read the writing, nor make known to the king the interpretation thereof.9 Then was king Belshazzar greatly troubled, and his countenance was changed in him, and his lords were astonied.10 Now the queen, by reason of the words of the king and his lords, came into the banquet house: and the queen spoke and said, O king, live forever: let not your thoughts trouble you, nor let your countenance be changed:11 There is a man in your kingdom, in whom is the spirit of the holy gods; and in the days of your father light and understanding and wisdom, like the wisdom of the gods, was found in him; whom the king Nebuchadnezzar your father, the king, I say, your father, made master of the magicians, astrologers, Chaldeans, and soothsayers;12 Forasmuch as an excellent spirit, and knowledge, and understanding, interpreting of dreams, and shewing of hard sentences, and dissolving of doubts,

| ומנדע 4486 | ושכלתנו 7924 | מפשר 6590 | חלמין 2493 | ואחוית 263 | אחידן 280 | ומשרא 8271 | קטרין 7001 |
|---|---|---|---|---|---|---|---|
| uamanda' | uasaklatanu | mapashar | chelmiyn | ua'achauayat | 'achiydan | uamsharea' | qitriyn, |
| **and knowledge** | **and understanding** | **interpreting of** | **dreams** | **and shewing of** | **hard sentences** | **and dissolving of** | **doubts** |

| השתכחת 7912 | בה 871a | בדניאל 1841 | די 1768 | מלכא 4430 | שם 7761 | שמה 8036 | בלטשאצר 1096 | כען 3705 | דניאל 1841 | יתקרי 7123 |
|---|---|---|---|---|---|---|---|---|---|---|
| hishtakachat | beh | badaniyea'l, | diy | malka' | sam | shameh | beltasha'tzar; | ka'an | daniyea'l | yitqarey |
| **were found** | **in the same** | **Daniel** | **whom** | **the king** | **command** | **named** | **Belteshazzar** | **now** | **Daniel** | **let be called** |

| ופשרה 6591 | יהחוה 2324: | 5:13 באדין 116 | דניאל 1841 | העל 5954 | קדם 6925 | מלכא 4430 | ענה 6032 | מלכא 4430 | ואמר 560 |
|---|---|---|---|---|---|---|---|---|---|
| uapishrah | yahachaueh. | bea'dayin | daniyea'l, | hu'al | qadam | malka'; | 'aneh | malka' | ua'amar |
| **and the interpretation** | **he will show** | **Then** | **Daniel** | **was brought in** | **before** | **the king** | **spoke** | ***And* the king** | **and said** |

| לדניאל 1841 | אנתה 607 | הוא 1932 | דניאל 1841 | די 1768 | מן 4481 | בני 1123 | גלותא 1547 | די 1768 | יהוד 3061 | די 1768 | היתי 858 | מלכא 4430 |
|---|---|---|---|---|---|---|---|---|---|---|---|---|
| ladaniyea'l, | 'antah | hua' | daniyea'l | diy | min | baney | galuta' | diy | yahud, | diy | hayatiy | malka' |
| **unto Daniel** | ***Are* you** | **that** | **Daniel** | **that** | ***are* of** | **the children of** | **the captivity** | **of** | **Judah** | **whom** | **brought** | **the king** |

| אבי 2 | מן 4481 | יהוד 3061: | 5:14 ושמעת 8086 | עליך 5922 | די 1768 | רוח 7308 | אלהין 426 | בך 871a | ונהירו 5094 |
|---|---|---|---|---|---|---|---|---|---|
| 'abiy | min | yahud. | uashim'aet | 'alayik | diy | ruach | 'alahiyn | bak; | uanahiyru |
| **my father** | **out of** | **Judah?** | **I have even heard** | **of you** | **that** | **the spirit of** | **the God** | ***is* in you** | **and *that* light** |

| ושכלתנו 7924 | וחכמה 2452 | יתירה 3493 | השתכחת 7912 | בך 871a: | 5:15 וכען 3705 | העלו 5954 | קדמי 6925 | חכימיא 2445 |
|---|---|---|---|---|---|---|---|---|
| uasaklatanu | uachakamah | yatiyrah | hishtakachat | bak. | uak'an | hu'alu | qadamay, | chakiymaya' |
| **and understanding** | **and wisdom** | **excellent** | **is found** | **in you** | **And now** | **have been brought in** | **before me** | ***the* wise** |

| אשפיא 826 | די 1768 | כתבה 3792 | דנה 1836 | יקרון 7123 | ופשרה 6591 | להודעתני 3046 | ולא 3809 |
|---|---|---|---|---|---|---|---|
| 'ashapaya', | diy | katabah | danah | yiqroun, | uapishreh | lahouda'ataniy; | uala' |
| ***men* the astrologers** | **that** | **writing** | **this** | **they should read** | **and the interpretation thereof** | **make known unto me** | **but not** |

| כהלין 3546 | פשר 6591 | מלתא 4406 | להחויה 2324: | 5:16 ואנה 576 | שמעת 8086 | עליך 5922 | די 1768 | תוכל 3202 | פשרין 6591 |
|---|---|---|---|---|---|---|---|---|---|
| kahaliyn | pashar | milta' | lahachauayah. | ua'anah | shima'aet | 'alayik | diy | tukal | pishriyn |
| **they could** | **the interpretation of** | **the thing** | **show** | **And I** | **have heard** | **of you** | **that** | **you can** | **interpretations** |

| למפשר 6590 | וקטרין 7001 | למשרא 8271 | כען 3705 | הן 2006 | תוכל 3202 | כתבא 3792 | למקרא 7123 | ופשרה 6591 |
|---|---|---|---|---|---|---|---|---|
| lamipshar | uaqitriyn | lamishrea'; | ka'an | hen | tukal | kataba' | lamiqrea', | uapishreh |
| **make** | **and doubts** | **dissolve** | **now** | **if** | **you can** | **the writing** | **read** | **and the interpretation thereof** |

| להודעתני 3046 | ארגונא 711 | תלבש 3848 | והמונכא 2002 | די 1768 | דהבא 1722 | על 5922 | צוארך 6676 | ותלתא 8531 |
|---|---|---|---|---|---|---|---|---|
| lahouda'ataniy, | 'argauana' | tilbash, | uahamounka' | diy | dahaba' | 'al | tzaua'rak, | uatalta' |
| **make known to me** | **scarlet** | **you shall be clothed with** | **and have a chain** | **of** | **gold** | **about** | **your neck** | **and third** |

| במלכותא 4437 | תשלט 7981: | 5:17 באדין 116 | ענה 6032 | דניאל 1841 | ואמר 560 | קדם 6925 | מלכא 4430 | מתנתך 4978 | לך 3807a |
|---|---|---|---|---|---|---|---|---|---|
| bamalkuta' | tishlat. | bea'dayin | 'aneh | daniyea'l, | ua'amar | qadam | malka', | matnatak | lak |
| **in the kingdom** | **shall be ruler *the*** | **Then** | **answered** | **Daniel** | **and said** | **before** | **the king** | **your gifts** | **to yourself** |

| להוין 1934 | ונבזביתך 5023 | לאחרן 321 | הב 3052 | ברם 1297 | כתבא 3792 | אקרא 7123 | למלכא 4430 | ופשרא 6591 |
|---|---|---|---|---|---|---|---|---|
| leheuayan, | uanbazbayatak | la'acharan | hab; | baram, | kataba' | 'aqrea' | lamalka', | uapishra' |
| **Let be** | **and your rewards** | **to another** | **give** | **yet** | **the writing** | **I will read** | **unto the king** | **and the interpretation** |

Dan 5:12 were found in the same Daniel, whom the king named Belteshazzar: now let Daniel be called, and he will show the interpretation.13 Then was Daniel brought in before the king. And the king spoke and said unto Daniel, Art you that Daniel, which are of the children of the captivity of Judah, whom the king my father brought out of Jewry?14 I have even heard of you, that the spirit of the gods is in you, and that light and understanding and excellent wisdom is found in you.15 And now the wise men, the astrologers, have been brought in before me, that they should read this writing, and make known unto me the interpretation thereof: but they could not show the interpretation of the thing:16 And I have heard of you, that you canst make interpretations, and dissolve doubts: now if you canst read the writing, and make known to me the interpretation thereof, you shall be clothed with scarlet, and have a chain of gold about your neck, and shall be the third ruler in the kingdom.17 Then Daniel answered and said before the king, Let your gifts be to thyself, and give your rewards to another; yet I will read the writing unto the king, and make known to him the interpretation.

5:18

אהודענה 3046: אנתה 607 מלכא 4430 אלהא 426 עליא 5943 מלכותא 4437 ורבותא 7238 ויקרא 3367 והדרה 1923 יהב 3052
'ahouda'aneh. 'antah malka'; 'alaha' 'ala'ya malkuta' uarbuta' uiyqara' uahadrah, yahab
**make known to him O you king Elohim *the* most high a kingdom and majesty and glory and honor gave**

5:19

לנבכדנצר 5020 אבוך 2: ומן 4481 רבותא 7238 די 1768 יהב 3052 לה 3807a כל 3606 עממיא 5972 אמיא 524 ולשניא 3961
unabukadra'tzar 'abuk. uamin rabuta' diy yahab leh, kal 'amamaya', 'amaya' ualishanaya',
**Nebuchadnezzar your father And for the majesty that he gave him all people nations and languages**

הוו 1934 זאעין 2112 ודחלין 1763 מן 4481 קדמוהי 6925 די 1768 הוה 1934 צבא 6634 הוא 1934 קטל 6992 ודי 1768 הוה 1934 צבא 6634 הוה 1934
hauou' za'a'ayn uadachaliyn min qadamouhiy; diy hauah tzabea' haua' qatel, uadiy hauah tzabea' hauah
**become trembled and feared before him whom he would he killed and whom he would he**

5:20

מחא 2418 ודי 1768 הוה 1934 צבא 6634 הוה 1934 מרים 4813 ודי 1768 הוה 1934 צבא 6634 הוה 1934 משפיל 8214: וכדי 1768 רם 7313
machea', uadiy hauah tzabea' hauah mariym, uadiy hauah tzabea' hauah mashpiyl. uakdiy rim
**kept alive and whom he would he set up and whom he would he put down But when was lifted up**

5:21

לבבה 3825 ורוחה 7308 תקפת 8631 להזדה 2103 הנחת 5182 מן 4481 כרסא 3764 מלכותה 4437 ויקרה 3367 העדיו 5709 מנה 4481:
libbeh, uarucheh tiqpat lahazadah; hanachat min karasea' malkuteh, uiyqarah he'adiyu mineh.
**his heart and his mind hardened in pride he was deposed from throne his kingly and his glory they took from him**

ומן 4481 בני 1123 אנשא 606 טריד 2957 ולבבה 3825 עם 5974 חיותא 2423 שוי 7739 ועם 5974 ערדיא 6167 מדורה 4070
uamin baney 'anasha' tariyd ualibbeh 'am chayuata' shauiy ua'am 'aradaya' madoureh,
**And from the sons of men he was driven and his heart like the beasts was make *was* with the wild asses his dwelling**

עשבא 6211 כתורין 8450 יטעמונה 2939 ומטל 2920 שמיא 8065 גשמה 1655 יצטבע 6647 עד 5705 די 1768 ידע 3046 די 1768 שליט 7990
'asba' katouriyn yata'amuneh, uamital shamaya' gishmeh yitzataba'; 'ad diy yada', diy shaliyt
***with* grass like oxen they fed him and with the dew of heaven his body was wet till forasmuch he knew that ruled**

5:22

אלהא 426 עליא 5943 במלכות 4437 אנשא 606 ולמן 4479 די 1768 יצבה 6634 יהקים 6966 עליה 5922 ואנתה 607
'alaha' 'ala'ya bamalkut 'anasha', ualman diy yitzabeh yahaqeym 'alayeh ua'antah
**Elohim *the* most high in the kingdom of men and whomsoever that he will he appointeth over it And you**

5:23

ברה 1247 בלשאצר 1113 לא 3809 השפלת 8214 לבבך 3825 כל 3605 קבל 6903 די 1768 כל 3606 דנה 1836 ידעת 3046: ועל 5922 מרא 4756
bareh belesha'tzar, la' hashpelt libbak; kal qabel diy kal danah yada'ata. ua'al mare
**his son O Belshazzar not has humbled your heart all though even all this you knew But against Adonai**

שמיא 8065 התרוממת 7313 ולמאניא 3984 די 1768 ביתה 1005 היתיו 858 קדמיך 6925 ואנתה 607 ורברבניך 7261
shamaya' hitroumamta ualma'naya' diy bayateh hayatiyu qadamayik ua'antah veravrevanayich
**of heaven have lifted up yourself and the vessels of his house they have brought before you and you and your adonai's**

שגלתך 7695 ולחנתך 3904 חמרא 2562 שתין 8355 בהון 871b ולאלהי 426 כספא 3702 ודהבא 1722 נחשא 5174 פרזלא 6523 אעא 636
shegalatak ualchenatak chamra' shatayin bahoun uale'alahey kaspa' uadahaba' nachasha' parzala' 'a'aa
**your wives and your concubines wine have drunk in them and the gods of silver and gold *of* brass iron wood**

ואבנא 69 די 1768 לא 3809 חזין 2370 ולא 3809 שמעין 8086 ולא 3809 ידעין 3046 שבחת 7624 ולאלהא 426 די 1768 נשמתך 5396
ua'abna', diy la' chazayin uala' shama'ayn uala' yada'ayn shabachta; uale'alaha' diy nishmatak
**and stone which not see nor hear nor know you have praised and the Elohim in whose your breath**

Dan 5:18 O you king, the most high G-d gave Nebuchadnezzar your father a kingdom, and majesty, and glory, and honor:19 And for the majesty that he gave him, all people, nations, and languages, trembled and feared before him: whom he would he slew; and whom he would he kept alive; and whom he would he set up; and whom he would he put down.20 But when his heart was lifted up, and his mind hardened in pride, he was deposed from his kingly throne, and they took his glory from him:21 And he was driven from the sons of men; and his heart was made like the beasts, and his dwelling was with the wild asses: they fed him with grass like oxen, and his body was wet with the dew of heaven; till he knew that the most high G-d ruled in the kingdom of men, and that he appointeth over it whomsoever he will.22 And you his son, O Belshazzar, have not humbled your heart, though you knew all this;23 But have lifted up thyself against YHUH of heaven; and they have brought the vessels of his house before you, and you, and your lords, your wives, and your concubines, have drunk wine in them; and you have praised the gods of silver, and gold, of brass, iron, wood, and stone, which see not, nor hear, nor know: and the G-d in whose hand your breath is, and whose are all your ways, have you not glorified:

בידה 3028 וכל 3606 ארחתך 735 לה 3807a לא 3809 הדרת 1922: **5:24** באדין 116 מן 4481 קדמוהי 6925 שליח 7972 פסא 6447 די 1768
biydeh uakal 'archatak leh la' hadarta. bea'dayin min qadamouhiy, shaliyach pasa' diy
***is* hand and all your ways whose *are* not have you glorified Then from him was sent the part of**

ידא 3028 וכתבא 3792 דנה 1836 רשים 7560: **5:25** ודנה 1836 כתבא 3792 די 1768 רשים 7560 מנא 4484 מנא 4484 תקל 8625
yada'; uaktaba' danah rashiym. uadnah kataba' diy rashiym; manea' manea' taqel
**the hand and writing this was written And this *is* the writing that was written MENE MENE TEKEL**

ופרסין 6537: **5:26** דנה 1836 פשר 6591 מלתא 4406 מנא 4484 מנה 4483 אלהא 426 מלכותך 4437 והשלמה 8000: **5:27**
uaparsiyn. danah pashar milta'; manea' menah 'alaha' malkutak uahashlamah.
**UPHARSIN This *is* the interpretation of the thing MENE has numbered Elohim your kingdom and finished it!**

תקל 8625 תקילתה 8625 במאזניא 3977 והשתכחת 7912 חסיר 2627: **5:28** פרס 6537 פריסת 6537 מלכותך 4437 ויהיבת 3052
taqel; taqiylatah bama'zanya' uahishtakachat chasiyr. pares; pariysat malkutak, uaiyhiybat
**TEKEL You are weighed in the balances and are found wanting PERES is divided Your kingdom and given**

למדי 4076 ופרס 6540: **5:29** באדין 116 אמר 560 בלשאצר 1113 והלבישו 3848 לדניאל 1841 ארגונא 711 והמונכא 2002
lamaday uaparas. bea'dayin 'amar belesha'tzar, uahalbiyshu ladaniyea'l 'argauana', uahamounka'
**to the Medes and Persians Then commanded Belshazzar and they clothed to Daniel *with* scarlet and put a chain**

די 1768 דהבא 1722 על 5922 צוארה 6676 והכרזו 3745 עלוהי 5922 די 1768 להוא 1934 שליט 7990 תלתא 8531
diy dahaba' 'al tzauareh; uahakrizu 'alouhiy, diy lehauea' shaliyt talta'
**of gold about his neck and made a proclamation concerning him that he should be ruler *the* third**

במלכותא 4437: **5:30** בה 871a בליליא 3916 קטיל 6992 בלאשצר 1113 מלכא 4430 כשדיא 3779 **5:31** ודריוש 1868 מדיא 4077
bamalkuta'. beh baleylaya', qatiyl bela'shatzar malka' kasdaya uadarayauesh madaya
**in the kingdom In that night was slain Belshazzar the king of the Chaldeans And Darius the Median**

קבל 6902 מלכותא 4437 כבר 1247 שנין 8140 שתין 8361 ותרתין 8648:
qabel malkuta'; kabar shaniyn shitiyn uatarteyn.
**took the kingdom *being* about old years threescore and two**

**Dan 6:1** שפר 8232 קדם 6925 דריוש 1868 והקים 6966 על 5922 מלכותא 4437 לאחשדרפניא 324 מאה 3969 ועשרין 6243 די 1768
shapar qadam darayauesh, uahaqiym 'al malkuta', la'achashdarpanaya' ma'ah ua'asriyn; diy
**It pleased before Darius to set over the kingdom princes an hundred and twenty which**

להון 1934 בכל 3606 מלכותא 4437: **6:2** ועלא 5924 מנהון 4481 סרכין 5632 תלתא 8532 די 1768 דניאל 1841 חד 2298 מנהון 4481 די 1768
lehauon bakal malkuta'. ua'aela' minhoun sarakiyn talata', diy daniyea'l chad minhoun; diy
**should be over the whole kingdom And over these presidents three of whom Daniel *was* first whom that**

להון 1934 אחשדרפניא 324 אלין 459 יהבין 3052 להון 3807b טעמא 2941 ומלכא 4430 לא 3809 להוא 1934 נזק 5142: **6:3** אדין 116 דניאל 1841
lehauon 'achashdarpanaya' 'aleyn, yahabiyn lahoun ta'ma', uamalka' la' lehauea' naziq. 'adayin daniyea'l
**might the princes that give unto them accounts and the king no should have damage Then Daniel**

דנה 1836 הוא 1934 מתנצח 5330 על 5922 סרכיא 5632 ואחשדרפניא 324 כל 3606 קבל 6903 די 1768 רוח 7308 יתירא 3493 בה 871a
danah, haua' mitnatzach, 'al sarakaya' ua'achashdarpanaya'; kal qabel, diy ruach yatiyra' beh,
**this was preferred above the presidents and princes the whole because that an spirit excellent *was* in him**

Dan 5:24 Then was the part of the hand sent from him; and this writing was written.25 And this is the writing that was written, MENE, MENE, TEKEL, UPHARSIN.26 This is the interpretation of the thing: MENE; G-d has numbered your kingdom, and finished it.27 TEKEL; Thou are weighed in the balances, and are found wanting.28 PERES; Thy kingdom is divided, and given to the Medes and Persians.29 Then commanded Belshazzar, and they clothed Daniel with scarlet, and put a chain of gold about his neck, and made a proclamation concerning him, that he should be the third ruler in the kingdom.30 In that night was Belshazzar the king of the Chaldeans slain.31 And Darius the Median took the kingdom, being about threescore and two years old. **Dan** 6:1 It pleased Darius to set over the kingdom an hundred and twenty princes, which should be over the whole kingdom;2 And over these three presidents; of whom Daniel was first: that the princes might give accounts unto them, and the king should have no damage.3 Then this Daniel was preferred above the presidents and princes, because an excellent spirit was in him; and the king thought to set him over the whole realm.

ומלכא 4430 עשית 6246 להקמותה 6966 על 5922 כל 3606 מלכותא 4437: 6:4 אדין 116 סרכיא 5632 ואחשדרפניא 324 הוו 1934
uamalka' 'ashiyt, lahaqamuteh 'al kal malkuta'. 'adayin sarakaya' ua'achashdarpanaya', hauou'
**and the king thought to set him over the whole realm Then the presidents and princes they were**

בעין 1156 עלה 5931 להשכחה 7912 לדניאל 1841 מצד 6655 מלכותא 4437 וכל 3606 עלה 5931 ושחיתה 7844 לא 3809 יכלין 3202
ba'ayin 'alah lahashkachah ladaniyea'l mitzad malkuta'; uakal 'alah uashchiytah la' yakaliyn
**sought occasion to find against Daniel concerning the kingdom but occasion nor fault none they could**

להשכחה 7912 כל 3606 קבל 6903 די 1768 מהימן 540 הוא 1932 וכל 3606 שלו 7960 ושחיתה 7844 לא 3809 השתכחת 7912 עלוהי 5922: 6:5
lahashkachah, kal qabel diy maheyman hua', uakal shilou uashchiytah, la' hishtakachat 'alouhiy.
**find all of forasmuch as *was* faithful he any error or fault neither was there found in him**

אדין 116 גבריא 1400 אלך 479 אמרין 560 די 1768 לא 3808 נהשכח 7912 לדניאל 1841 דנה 1836 כל 3606 עלא 5931 להן 3861 השכחנה 7912 עלוהי 5922
'adayin gubraya' 'alek 'amariyn, diy la' nahashkach ladaniyea'l danah kal 'ala'; lahen hashkachnah 'alouhiy
**Then men these said that not We shall find to Daniel this any occasion except we find *it* against**

בדת 1882 אלהה 426: 6:6 אדין 116 סרכיא 5632 ואחשדרפניא 324 אלן 459 הרגשו 7284 על 5922 מלכא 4430
badat 'alaheh. 'adayin sarakaya' ua'achashdarpanaya' 'alen, hargishu 'al malka';
**concerning the law of his Elohim Then presidents and princes these assembled together to the king**

וכן 3652 אמרין 560 לה 3807a דריוש 1868 מלכא 4430 לעלמין 5957 חיי 2418: 6:7 אתיעטו 3272 כל 3606 סרכי 5632
uaken 'amariyn leh, darayauesh malka' la'alamiyn chayiy. 'atya'atu kal sarakey
**and thus said unto him Darius King for ever live they have consulted together All the presidents of**

מלכותא 4437 סגניא 5460 ואחשדרפניא 324 הדבריא 1907 ופחותא 6347 לקימה 6966 קים 7010 מלכא 4430
malkuta', signaya' ua'achashdarpanaya' hadabaraya' uapachauata', laqayamah qayam malka',
**the kingdom the governors and the princes the counsellors and the captains to establish a statute royal**

ולתקפה 8631 אסר 633 די 1768 כל 3606 די 1768 יבעה 1156 בעו 1159 מן 4481 כל 3606 אלה 426 ואנש 606 עד 5705 יומין 3118 תלתין 8533
ualtaqapah 'asar; diy kal diy yib'aeh ba'au min kal 'alah ua'anash 'ad youmiyn talatiyn,
**and to make firm a decree that whosoever that shall ask a petition of any El or man for days thirty**

להן 3861 מנך 4481 מלכא 4430 יתרמא 4412 לגב 1358 אריותא 744: 6:8 כען 3705 מלכא 4430 תקים 6966 אסרא 633 ותרשם 7560
lahen minak malka', yitramea' lagob 'aryauata'. ka'an malka', taqiym 'asara' uatirshum
**save of you O king he shall be cast into the den of lions Now O king establish the decree and sign**

כתבא 3792 די 1768 לא 3809 להשניה 8133 כדת 1882 מדי 4076 ופרס 6540 די 1768 לא 3809 תעדא 5709: 6:9
kataba'; diy la' lahashanayah kadat maday uaparas diy la' te'adea'.
**the writing that not it be changed according to the law of the Medes and Persians which not altered (*pass away*)**

כל 3606 קבל 6903 דנה 1836 מלכא 4430 דריוש 1868 רשם 7560 כתבא 3792 ואסרא 633: 6:10 ודניאל 1841 כדי 1768 ידע 3046 די 1768
kal qabel danah; malka' darayauesh, rasham kataba' ua'asara'. uadaniyea'l kadiy yada' diy
**all Where fore king Darius signed the writing and the decree Now Daniel when knew that**

רשים 7560 כתבא 3792 על 5954 לביתה 1005 וכוין 3551 פתיחן 6606 לה 3807a בעליתה 5952 נגד 5049 ירושלם 3390
rashiym kataba' 'al labayateh, uakauiyn patiychan leh ba'aliyteh, neged yarushalem;
**was signed the writing he went into his house and his windows *being* open his in his chamber toward Jerusalem**

Dan 6:4 Then the presidents and princes sought to find occasion against Daniel concerning the kingdom; but they could find none occasion nor fault; forasmuch as he was faithful, neither was there any error or fault found in him.5 Then said these men, We shall not find any occasion against this Daniel, except we find it against him concerning the law of his G-d.6 Then these presidents and princes assembled together to the king, and said thus unto him, King Darius, live forever.7 All the presidents of the kingdom, the governors, and the princes, the counsellers, and the captains, have consulted together to establish a royal statute, and to make a firm decree, that whosoever shall ask a petition of any G-d or man for thirty days, save of you, O king, he shall be cast into the den of lions.8 Now, O king, establish the decree, and sign the writing, that it be not changed, according to the law of the Medes and Persians, which altereth not.9 Wherefore king Darius signed the writing and the decree.10 Now when Daniel knew that the writing was signed, he went into his house; and his windows being open in his chamber toward Jerusalem, he kneeled upon his knees three times a day, and prayed, and gave thanks before his G-d, as he did aforetime.

וזמנין 2166 תלתה 8532 ביומא 3118 הוא 1932 ברך 1289 על 5922 ברכוהי 1291 ומצלא 6739 ומודא 3029 קדם 6925 אלהה 426 כל 3606 קבל 6903
uazimniyn talatah bayouma' hua' barek 'al birkouhiy, uamtzalea' uamoudea' qadam 'alaheh, kal qabel
**times three a day he kneeled upon his knees and prayed and gave thanks before his Elohim all as**

די 1768 הוא 1934 עבד 5648 מן 4481 קדמת 6928 דנה 1836: 6:11 אדין 116 גבריא 1400 אלך 479 הרגשו 7284 והשכחו 7912 לדניאל 1841 בעא 1156
diy haua' 'abed, min qadmat danah. 'adayin gubraya' 'alek hargishu, uahashkachu ladaniyea'l; ba'aa'
**that he did from afore time Then men these assembled and found to Daniel praying**

ומתחנן 2604 קדם 6925 אלהה 426: 6:12 באדין 116 קריבו 7127 ואמרין 560 קדם 6925 מלכא 4430 על 5922 אסר 633
uamitchanan qadam 'alaheh. bea'dayin qariybu ua'amariyn qadam malka' 'al 'asar
**and making supplication before his Elohim Then they came near and spoke before the king concerning decree**

מלכא 4430 הלא 3809 אסר 633 רשמת 7560 די 1768 כל 3606 אנש 606 די 1768 יבעה 1156 מן 4481 כל 3606 אלה 426 ואנש 606 עד 5705
malka' hala' 'asar rashamta, diy kal 'anash diy yib'aeh min kal 'alah ua'anash 'ad
***the* king's not a decree Have you signed that every man that shall ask *a petition* of any El or man within**

יומין 3118 תלתין 8533 להן 3861 מנך 4481 מלכא 4430 יתרמא 4412 לגוב 1358 אריותא 744 ענה 6032 מלכא 4430 ואמר 560 יציבא 3330
youmiyn talatiyn, lahen minak malka', yitramea' lagoub aryauta'; 'aneh malka' ua'amar, yatziyba'
**days thirty save of you O king shall be cast into the den of lions? answered The king and said *is* true**

מלתא 4406 כדת 1882 מדי 4076 ופרס 6540 די 1768 לא 3809 תעדא 5709: 6:13 באדין 116 ענו 6032 ואמרין 560
milta' kadat maday uaparas diy la' te'adea'. bea'dayin 'anou ua'amariyn
**The thing according to the law of the Medes and Persians which not altereth Then answered they and said**

קדם 6925 מלכא 4430 די 1768 דניאל 1841 די 1768 מן 4481 בני 1123 גלותא 1547 די 1768 יהוד 3061 לא 3809 שם 7761 עליך 5922 מלכא 4430
qadam malka' diy daniyea'l diy min baney galuta' diy yahud, la' sam 'alayik malka'
**before the king That Daniel which *is* of the children of the captivity of Judah not regard to you O king**

טעם 2942 ועל 5922 אסרא 633 די 1768 רשמת 7560 וזמנין 2166 תלתה 8532 ביומא 3118 בעא 1156 בעותה 1159: 6:14 אדין 116 מלכא 4430
ta'aem, ua'al 'asara' diy rashamta; uazimniyn talatah bayouma', ba'aa' ba'auteh. 'adayin malka'
**decree nor the interdict that you have signed but times three a day make his petition Then the king**

כדי 1768 מלתא 4406 שמע 8086 שגיא 7690 באש 888 עלוהי 5922 ועל 5922 דניאל 1841 שם 7761 בל 1079 לשיזבותה 7804 ועד 5705
kadiy milta' shama', sagiy'a ba'aesh 'alouhiy, ua'al daniyea'l sam bal lasheyzabuteh; ua'ad
**when *these* words he heard sore was displeased with himself and on Daniel set *his* heart to deliver him and till**

מעלי 4606 שמשא 8122 הוא 1934 משתדר 7712 להצלותה 5338: 6:15 באדין 116 גבריא 1400 אלך 479 הרגשו 7284 על 5922 מלכא 4430
me'aley shimasha', haua' mishtadar lahatzaluteh. bea'dayin gubraya' 'alek, hargishu 'al malka';
**the going down of the sun he labored to deliver him Then men these assembled unto the king**

ואמרין 560 למלכא 4430 דע 3046 מלכא 4430 די 1768 דת 1882 למדי 4076 ופרס 6540 די 1768 כל 3606 אסר 633 וקים 7010 די 1768
ua'amariyn lamalka', da' malka' diy dat lamaday uaparas, diy kal 'asar uaqyam diy
**and said unto the king Know O king that the law of the Medes and Persians *is* That no decree nor statute which**

מלכא 4430 יהקים 6966 לא 3809 להשניה 8133: 6:16 באדין 116 מלכא 4430 אמר 560 והיתיו 858 לדניאל 1841 ורמו 7412
malka' yahaqeym la' lahashanayah. bea'dayin malka' 'amar, uahayatiyu ladaniyea'l, uarmou
**the king establish or even may be changed Then the king commanded and they brought to Daniel and cast**

Dan 6:11 Then these men assembled, and found Daniel praying and making supplication before his G-d.12 Then they came near, and spoke before the king concerning the king's decree; Hast you not signed a decree, that every man that shall ask a petition of any G-d or man within thirty days, save of you, O king, shall be cast into the den of lions? The king answered and said, The thing is true, according to the law of the Medes and Persians, which altereth not.13 Then answered they and said before the king, That Daniel, which is of the children of the captivity of Judah, regardeth not you, O king, nor the decree that you have signed, but make his petition three times a day.14 Then the king, when he heard these words, was sore displeased with himself, and set his heart on Daniel to deliver him: and he laboured till the going down of the sun to deliver him.15 Then these men assembled unto the king, and said unto the king, Know, O king, that the law of the Medes and Persians is, That no decree nor statute which the king establisheth may be changed.16 Then the king commanded, and they brought Daniel, and cast him into the den of lions. Now the king spoke and said unto Daniel, Thy G-d whom you servest continually, he will deliver you.

לגבא 1358 די 1768 אריותא 744 ענה 6032 מלכא 4430 ואמר 560 לדניאל 1841 אלהך 426 די 1768 אנתה 607 פלח 6399 לה 3807a
laguba' diy 'aryauata'; 'aneh malka' ua'amar ladaniyea'l, 'alahak, diy 'antah palach leh
***him*** **into the den of lions spoke *Now* the king and said unto Daniel Your Elohim whom you servest to him**

6:17
בתדירא 8411 הוא 1932 ישיזבנך 7804: והיתית 858 אבן 69 חדה 2298 ושמת 7761 על 5922 פם 6433 גבא 1358 וחתמה 2857
bitdiyra', hua' yasheyzabinak. uaheytayit 'aben chadah, uasumat 'al pum guba'; uachatmah
**continually he will deliver you And was brought stone a and laid upon the mouth of the den and sealed it**

מלכא 4430 בעזקתה 5824 ובעזקת 5824 רברבנוהי 7261 די 1768 לא 3809 תשנא 8133 צבו 6640
malka' ba'azqateh, uab'azqat rabrabanouhiy, diy la' tishnea' tzabu
**the king with his own signet and with the signet of his lords that not might be changed the purpose**

6:18
בדניאל 1841: אדין 116 אזל 236 מלכא 4430 להיכלה 1965 ובת 956 טות 2908 ודחון 1761 לא 3809
badaniyea'l. 'adayin 'azal malka' laheykaleh uaba'at tauat, uadachauan la'
**concerning Daniel Then went the king to his palace and passed the night fasting instruments of music neither**

6:19
הנעל 5954 קדמוהי 6925 ושנתה 8139 נדת 5075 עלוהי 5922: באדין 116 מלכא 4430 בשפרפרא 8238 יקום 6966 בנגהא 5053
hana'ael qadamouhiy; uashinteh nadat 'alouhiy. bea'dayin malka', bishparpara' yaqum banagaha';
**were brought him before and his sleep went from him Then the king very early arose in the morning**

6:20
ובהתבהלה 927 לגבא 1358 די 1768 אריותא 744 אזל 236: וכמקרבה 7127 לגבא 1358 לדניאל 1841 בקל 7032 עציב 6088
uabhitbahalah, laguba' diy 'aryauata' 'azal. uakmiqrabeh laguba', ladaniyea'l, baqal 'atziyb
**and in haste unto the den of lions went And when he came to the den unto Daniel with a voice lamentable**

זעק 2200 ענה 6032 מלכא 4430 ואמר 560 לדניאל 1841 דניאל 1841 עבד 5649 אלהא 426 חיא 2417 אלהך 426 די 1768 אנתה 607 פלח 6399
za'aq; 'aneh malka' ua'amar ladaniyea'l, daniyea'l 'abed 'alaha' chaya', 'alahak, diy 'antah palach
**he cried spoke *and* the king and said to Daniel O Daniel servant of Elohim *the* living your Elohim whom you servest**

6:21
לה 3807a בתדירא 8411 היכל 3202 לשיזבותך 7804 מן 4481 אריותא 744: אדין 116 דניאל 1841 עם 5974 מלכא 4430 מלל 4449 מלכא 4430 לעלמין 5957
leh bitdiyra', hayakil lasheyzabutak min 'aryauata'. 'adayin daniyea'l, 'am malka' malil; malka' la'alamiyn
**whom continually is able to deliver you from *the* lions? Then Daniel unto the king said O king for ever**

6:22
חיי 2418: אלהי 426 שלח 7972 מלאכה 4398 וסגר 5463 פם 6433 אריותא 744 ולא 3809 חבלוני 2255 כל 3606 קבל 6903 די 1768
chayiy. 'alahiy shalach mal'akeh, usagar pum 'aryauata' uala' chabaluniy; kal qabel, diy
**live My Elohim has sent his angel and has shut mouths *the* lions' that not they have hurt me for asmuch as**

6:23
קדמוהי 6925 זכו 2136 השתכחת 7912 לי 3807a ואף 638 קדמיך 6925 מלכא 4430 חבולה 2248 לא 3809 עבדת 5648: באדין 116 מלכא 4430
qadamouhiy zaku hishtakachat liy, ua'ap qadamayik malka', chabulah la' 'abdet. bea'dayin malka',
**before him innocency was found in me and also before you O king hurt no have I done Then the king**

שגיא 7690 טאב 2868 עלוהי 5922 ולדניאל 1841 אמר 560 להנסקה 5267 מן 4481 גבא 1358 והסק 5267 דניאל 1841
sagiy'a ta'aeb 'alouhiy, ualdaniyea'l, 'amar lahanasaqah min guba'; uahusaq daniyea'l
**exceeding was glad for him and Daniel commanded that they should take up out of the den So was taken up Daniel**

6:24
מן 4481 גבא 1358 וכל 3606 חבל 2257 לא 3809 השתכח 7912 בה 871a די 1768 הימן 540 באלהה 426: ואמר 560
min guba', uakal chabal la' hishtakach beh, diy heymin be'alaheh. ua'amar
**out of the den and manner of hurt no was found upon him because he believed in his Elohim And commanded**

Dan 6:17 And a stone was brought and laid upon the mouth of the den; and the king sealed it with his own signet, and with the signet of his lords; that the purpose might not be changed concerning Daniel.18 Then the king went to his palace, and passed the night fasting: neither were instruments of musick brought before him: and his sleep went from him.19 Then the king arose very early in the morning, and went in haste unto the den of lions.20 And when he came to the den, he cried with a lamentable voice unto Daniel: and the king spoke and said to Daniel, O Daniel, servant of the living G-d, is your G-d, whom you servest continually, able to deliver you from the lions?21 Then said Daniel unto the king, O king, live forever.22 My G-d has sent his angel, and has shut the lions' mouths, that they have not hurt me: forasmuch as before him innocency was found in me; and also before you, O king, have I done no hurt.23 Then was the king exceeding glad for him, and commanded that they should take Daniel up out of the den. So Daniel was taken up out of the den, and no manner of hurt was found upon him, because he believed in his G-d.24 And the king commanded, and they brought those men which had accused Daniel, and they cast them into the den of lions, them, their children, and their wives;

| מלכא 4430 | והיתיו 858 | גבריא 1400 | אלך 479 | די 1768 | אכלו 399 | קרצוהי 7170 | די 1768 | דניאל 1841 | ולגב 1358 | אריותא 744 |
|---|---|---|---|---|---|---|---|---|---|---|
| malka', | uahayatiyu | gubraya' | 'alek | diy | 'akalu | qartzouhiy | diy | daniyea'l, | ualagob | 'aryauata' |
| **the king** | **and they brought** | **men** | **those** | **which** | **had accuse** | **him** | **that** | **Daniel** | **and into the den of** | **lions** |

| רמו 7412 | אנון 581 | בניהון 1123 | ונשיהון 5389 | ולא 3809 | מטו 4291 | לארעית 773 | גבא 1358 | עד 5704 | די 1768 |
|---|---|---|---|---|---|---|---|---|---|
| ramou, | 'anun | baneyhoun | uansheyhoun; | uala' | matou | la'ar'ayt | guba', | 'ad | diy |
| **they cast *them*** | **sons of them** | **their children** | **and their wives** | **and or ever** | **they came** | **at the bottom of** | **the den** | **till** | **that** |

| שלטו 7981 | בהון 871b | אריותא 744 | וכל 3606 | גרמיהון 1635 | הדקו 1855: | **6:25** באדין 116 | דריוש 1868 | מלכא 4430 | כתב 3790 | לכל 3606 |
|---|---|---|---|---|---|---|---|---|---|---|
| shalitu | bahoun | 'aryauata', | uakal | garmeyhoun | hadiqu. | bea'dayin | darayauesh | malka', | katab | lakal |
| **had the mastery** | **of them** | ***the* lions** | **and all** | **their bones** | **broke in pieces** | **Then** | **Darius** | **king** | **wrote** | **unto all** |

| עממיא 5972 | אמיא 524 | ולשניא 3961 | די 1768 | דארין 1753 | בכל 3606 | ארעא 772 | שלמכון 8001 | ישגא 7680: | **6:26** מן 4481 | קדמי 6925 |
|---|---|---|---|---|---|---|---|---|---|---|
| 'amamaya' | 'amaya' | ualishanaya' | diy | da'ariyn | bakal | 'ar'aa' | shalamakoun | yisgea'. | min | qadamay |
| **people** | **nations** | **and languages** | **that** | **dwell** | **in all** | **the earth** | **Peace unto you** | **be multiplied** | **according** | **I** |

| שים 7761 | טעם 2942 | די 1768 | בכל 3606 | שלטן 7985 | מלכותי 4437 | להון 1934 | זאעין 2112 | ודחלין 1763 | מן 4481 | קדם 6925 | אלהה 426 |
|---|---|---|---|---|---|---|---|---|---|---|---|
| siym | ta'aem | diy | bakal | shalatan | malkutiy, | lehauon | za'a'ayn | uadachaliyn, | min | qadam | 'alaheh |
| **make** | **a decree** | **That** | **in every** | **dominion of** | **my kingdom *men*** | **become** | **tremble** | **and fear** | **according** | **before** | **the Elohim** |

| די 1768 | דניאל 1841 | די 1768 | הוא 1932 | אלהא 426 | חיא 2417 | וקים 7011 | לעלמין 5957 | ומלכותה 4437 | די 1768 | לא 3809 |
|---|---|---|---|---|---|---|---|---|---|---|
| diy | daniyea'l; | diy | hua' | 'alaha' | chaya', | uaqayam | la'alamiyn, | uamalkuteh | diy | la' |
| **of** | **Daniel** | **for** | **he** | **Elohim** | ***is* the living** | **and stedfast** | **for ever** | **and his kingdom** | ***that* which** | **not** |

| תתחבל 2255 | ושלטנה 7985 | עד 5705 | סופא 5491: | **6:27** משיזב 7804 | ומצל 5338 | ועבד 5648 | אתין 852 |
|---|---|---|---|---|---|---|---|
| titchabal, | uashalataneh | 'ad | soupa'. | masheyzib | uamatzil, | ua'abed | 'atiyn |
| **shall be destroyed** | **and his dominion** | ***shall be even* unto** | **the end** | **He deliver** | **and rescueth** | **and he work** | **signs** |

| ותמהין 8540 | בשמיא 8065 | ובארעא 772 | די 1768 | שיזיב 7804 | לדניאל 1841 | מן 4481 | יד 3028 | אריותא 744: | **6:28** ודניאל 1841 | דנה 1836 |
|---|---|---|---|---|---|---|---|---|---|---|
| uatimhiyn, | bishmaya' | uab'ar'aa'; | diy | sheyziyb | ladaniyea'l, | min | yad | 'aryauata'. | uadaniyea'l | danah, |
| **and wonders** | **in heaven** | **and in earth** | **who** | **has delivered** | **to Daniel** | **from** | **the power of** | ***the* lions** | **So Daniel** | **this** |

| הצלח 6744 | במלכות 4437 | דריוש 1868 | ובמלכות 4437 | כורש 3567 | פרסיא 6543 |
|---|---|---|---|---|---|
| hatzalach | bamalkut | darayauesh; | uabmalkut | kouresh | parasaya' |
| **prospered** | **in the reign of** | **Darius** | **and in the reign of** | **Cyrus** | **the Persian** |

**Dan 7:1**

| בשנת 8140 | חדה 2298 | לבלאשצר 1113 | מלך 4430 | בבל 895 | דניאל 1841 | חלם 2493 | חזה 2370 | וחזוי 2376 | ראשה 7217 | על 5922 | משכבה 4903 |
|---|---|---|---|---|---|---|---|---|---|---|---|
| bishnat | chadah, | label'ashatzar | melek | babel, | daniyea'l | chelem | chazah, | uachezuey | rea'sheh | 'al | mishkabeh; |
| **In year** | ***the* first of** | **Belshazzar** | **king of** | **Babylon** | **Daniel** | **a dream** | **had** | **and visions of** | **his head** | **upon** | **his bed** |

| באדין 116 | חלמא 2493 | כתב 3790 | ראש 7217 | מלין 4406 | אמר 560: | **7:2** ענה 6032 | דניאל 1841 | ואמר 560 | חזה 2370 | הוית 1934 | בחזוי 2376 |
|---|---|---|---|---|---|---|---|---|---|---|---|
| bea'dayin | chelma' | katab, | rea'sh | miliyn | 'amar. | 'aneh | daniyea'l | ua'amar, | chazeh | haueyt | bachezuiy |
| **then** | **the dream** | **he wrote** | **the sum of** | **the matters** | ***and* told** | **spoke** | **Daniel** | **and said** | **saw** | **I** | **in my vision** |

| עם 5974 | ליליא 3916 | וארו 718 | ארבע 703 | רוחי 7308 | שמיא 8065 | מגיחן 1519 | לימא 3221 | רבא 7229: | **7:3** וארבע 703 | חיון 2423 |
|---|---|---|---|---|---|---|---|---|---|---|
| 'am | leylaya'; | ua'aru, | 'arba | ruchey | shamaya', | magiychan | layama' | raba'. | ua'arba' | cheyuan |
| **by** | **night** | **and behold *the*** | **four** | **winds of** | **the heaven** | **strove** | **upon sea** | ***the* great** | **And four** | **beasts** |

Dan 6:24 and the lions had the mastery of them, and break all their bones in pieces or ever they came at the bottom of the den.25 Then king Darius wrote unto all people, nations, and languages, that dwell in all the earth; Peace be multiplied unto you.26 I make a decree, That in every dominion of my kingdom men tremble and fear before the G-d of Daniel: for he is the living G-d, and stedfast forever, and his kingdom that which shall not be destroyed, and his dominion shall be even unto the end.27 He delivereth and rescueth, and he worketh signs and wonders in heaven and in earth, who has delivered Daniel from the power of the lions.28 So this Daniel prospered in the reign of Darius, and in the reign of Cyrus the Persian. **Dan** 7:1 In the first year of Belshazzar king of Babylon Daniel had a dream and visions of his head upon his bed: then he wrote the dream, and told the sum of the matters.2 Daniel spoke and said, I saw in my vision by night, and, behold, the four winds of the heaven strove upon the great sea.3 And four great beasts came up from the sea, diverse one from another.

רברבן 7260 סלקן 5559 מן 4481 ימא 3221 שנין 8133 דא 1668 מן 4481 דא 1668: 7:4 קדמיתא 6933 כאריה 744 וגפין 1611 די 1768 נשר 5403 לה 3807a
rabraban, salaqan min yama'; shanayan da' min da'. qadmayata' ka'aryeh, uagapiyn diy nashar lah;
**great came up from the sea diverse one from another The first *was* like a lion and wings that eagle's had**

חזה 2370 הוית 1934 עד 5705 די 1768 מריטו 4804 גפיה 1611 ונטילת 5191 מן 4481 ארעא 772 ועל 5922 רגלין 7271 כאנש 606
chazeh haueyt 'ad diy mariytu gapayh uantiylat min 'ar'aa', ua'al raglayin ke'anash
**beheld I till that were plucked the wings thereof and it was lifted up from the earth and upon the feet as a man**

הקימת 6966 ולבב 3825 אנש 606 יהיב 3052 לה 3807a: 7:5 וארו 718 חיוה 2423 אחרי 317 תנינה 8578 דמיה 1821 לדב 1678 ולשטר 7859
haqiymat, ualbab 'anash yahiyb lah. ua'aru cheyuah 'achariy tinyanah damayah ladob, ualistar
**made stand and a heart man's was given to it And behold beast another a second like to a bear and on side**

חד 2298 הקמת 6966 ותלת 8532 עלעין 5967 בפמה 6433 בין 997 שניה 8128 וכן 3652 אמרין 560 לה 3807a
chad haqimat, uatlat 'ala'ayn bapumah beyn shinaiyah uaken 'amariyn lah,
**one it raised up itself and *it had* three ribs in the mouth of it between the teeth of it and thus they said unto it**

קומי 6966 אכלי 399 בשר 1321 שגיא 7690: 7:6 באתר 870 דנה 1836 חזה 2370 הוית 1934 וארו 718 אחרי 317 כנמר 5245 ולה 3807a גפין 1611
quamiy 'akuliy basar sagiy'a. batar danah chazeh haueyt, ua'aru 'achariy kinmar, ualah gapiyn
**Arise devour flesh much After place of this beheld I and lo another like a leopard which of it wings**

ארבע 703 די 1768 עוף 5776 על 5922 גביה 1355 וארבעה 703 ראשין 7217 לחיותא 2423 ושלטן 7985 יהיב 3052 לה 3807a: 7:7
'arba diy 'aup 'al gabayah ua'arb'ah rea'shiyn lacheyuata', uashalatan yahiyb lah.
**four of a fowl *had* upon the back *had* also four heads the beast and dominion was given to it**

באתר 870 דנה 1836 חזה 2370 הוית 1934 בחזוי 2376 ליליא 3916 וארו 718 חיוה 2423 רביעיה 7244 דחילה 1763 ואימתני 574 ותקיפא 8624
batar danah chazeh haueyt bachezuey leylaya', ua'aru cheyuah rabiy'ayah dachiylah ua'aeymataniy uataqiypa'
**After place of this saw I in visions *the* night and behold a beast fourth dreadful and terrible and strong**

יתירא 3493 ושנין 8128 די 1768 פרזל 6523 לה 3807a רברבן 7260 אכלה 399 ומדקה 1855 ושארא 7606 ברגליה 7271
yatiyra', uashinayin diy parzel lah rabraban, 'akalah uamadeqah, uash'ara' beraglaiyah
**exceedingly and teeth that iron it had great it devoured and brake in pieces and the residue with the feet of it**

רפסה 7512 והיא 1932 משניה 8133 מן 4481 כל 3606 חיותא 2423 די 1768 קדמיה 6925 וקרנין 7162 עשר 6236 לה 3807a: 7:8 משתכל 7920 הוית 1934
rapasah; uahiy'a mashanyah, min kal cheyuata' diy qadamayh, uaqarnayin 'asar lah. mistakal haueyt
**stamped and it *was* diverse from all the beasts that *were* before it and horns *had* ten it considered I was**

בקרניא 7162 ואלו 431 קרן 7162 אחרי 317 זעירה 2192 סלקת 5559 ביניהון 997 ותלת 8532 מן 4481 קרניא 7162 קדמיתא 6933
baqarnaya', ua'alu qeren 'achariy za'aeyrah silqat beyneyhoun uatlat, min qarnaya' qadmayata',
**the horns and behold horn another little there came up among them three of horns in *the* first**

אתעקרו 6132 מן 4481 קדמיה 6925 ואלו 431 עינין 5870 כעיני 5870 אנשא 606 בקרנא 7162 דא 1668
'at'aqaru min qadamaiyah ua'alu 'ayaniyn ka'ayaney 'anasha' baqarna' da',
**there were pluck up by the roots according before whom and behold *were* eyes of like the eyes of man horn this**

ופם 6433 ממלל 4449 רברבן 7260: 7:9 חזה 2370 הוית 1934 עד 5705 די 1768 כרסון 3764 רמיו 7412 ועתיק 6268 יומין 3118
uapum mamalil rabraban. chazeh haueyt, 'ad diy karasauan ramiyu, ua'atiyq youmiyn
**and a mouth speaking great things beheld I till that the thrones were cast down and the Ancient of days**

Dan 7:4 The first was like a lion, and had eagle's wings: I beheld till the wings thereof were plucked, and it was lifted up from the earth, and made stand upon the feet as a man, and a man's heart was given to it.5 And behold another beast, a second, like to a bear, and it raised up itself on one side, and it had three ribs in the mouth of it between the teeth of it: and they said thus unto it, Arise, devour much flesh.6 After this I beheld, and lo another, like a leopard, which had upon the back of it four wings of a fowl; the beast had also four heads; and dominion was given to it.7 After this I saw in the night visions, and behold a fourth beast, dreadful and terrible, and strong exceedingly; and it had great iron teeth: it devoured and break in pieces, and stamped the residue with the feet of it: and it was diverse from all the beasts that were before it; and it had ten horns.8 I considered the horns, and, behold, there came up among them another little horn, before whom there were three of the first horns plucked up by the roots: and, behold, in this horn were eyes like the eyes of man, and a mouth speaking great things.9 I beheld till the thrones were cast down, and the Ancient of days did sit, whose garment was white as snow, and the hair of his head like the pure wool: his throne was like the fiery flame, and his wheels as burning fire.

יתב 3488 לבושה 3831 כתלג 8517 חור 2358 ושער 8177 ראשה 7217 כעמר 6015 נקא 5343 כרסיה 3764 שביבין 7631 די 1768
yatib; labusheh kitlag chiuar, us'ar rea'sheh ka'amar naqea', karsayeh shabiybiyn diy
**did sit whose garment as snow *was* white and the hair of his head like the wool pure his throne flame *and* *was like* that**

נור 5135 גלגלוהי 1535 נור 5135 דלק 1815: 7:10 נהר 5103 די 1768 נור 5135 נגד 5047 ונפק 5312 מן 4481 קדמוהי 6925 אלף 506
nur, galgilouhiy nur daliq. nahar diy nur, naged uanapeq min qadamouhiy, 'alep
**fiery his wheels fire *as* burning A stream that fiery issued and came forth from before him thousand**

אלפים 506 ישמשונה 8120 ורבו 7240 רבון 7240 קדמוהי 6925 יקומון 6966 דינא 1780 יתב 3488
'alpiym yashamashuneh, uaribou rabeuan qadamouhiy yaqumun; diyna' yatib
**thousands ministered unto him and ten thousand times ten thousand before him stood the judgment was set**

וספרין 5609 פתיחו 6606: 7:11 חזה 2370 הוית 1934 באדין 116 מן 4481 קל 7032 מליא 4406 רברבתא 7260 די 1768 קרנא 7162
uasipriyn patiychu. chazeh haueyt, bea'dayin, min qal milaya' rabrabata', diy qarna'
**and the books were opened beheld I then because of the voice of words *the* great which the horn**

ממללה 4449 חזה 2370 הוית 1934 עד 5704 די 1768 קטילת 6992 חיותא 2423 והובד 7 גשמה 1655 ויהיבת 3052 ליקדת 3346 אשא 785: 7:12
mamalalah; chazeh haueyt 'ad diy qatiylat cheyuata' uahubad gishmah, uaiyhiybat liyqedat 'asha'.
**spoke beheld I *even* till that was slain the beast and destroyed his body and given to the burning flame**

ושאר 7606 חיותא 2423 העדיו 5709 שלטנהון 7985 וארכה 754 בחיין 2417 יהיבת 3052 להון 3807b עד 5705
uash'ar cheyuata', he'diyu shalatanahoun; ua'arkah bachayiyn yahiybat lahoun 'ad
**As concerning the rest of the beasts they had taken away their dominion yet prolonged lives were given their for**

זמן 2166 ועדן 5732: 7:13 חזה 2370 הוית 1934 בחזוי 2376 ליליא 3916 וארו 718 עם 5974 ענני 6050 שמיא 8065 כבר 1247
zaman ua'adan. chazeh haueyt bachezuey leylaya', ua'aru 'am 'ananey shamaya', kabar
**a season and time saw I in visions *the* night and behold with the clouds of heaven *one* like the Son of**

אנש 606 אתה 858 הוה 1934 ועד 5705 עתיק 6268 יומיא 3118 מטה 4291 וקדמוהי 6925 הקרבוהי 7127: 7:14 ולה 3807a
'anash 'ateh hauah; ua'ad 'atiyq youmaya' metah, uaqdamouhiy haqrabuhiy. ualeh
**man came he and to the Ancient of days came and before him they brought him near And him**

יהיב 3052 שלטן 7985 ויקר 3367 ומלכו 4437 וכל 3606 עממיא 5972 אמיא 524 ולשניא 3961 לה 3807a יפלחון 6399
yahiyb shalatan uayqar uamalku, uakol 'amamaya', 'amaya' ualishanaya' leh yiplachun;
**there was given dominion and glory and a kingdom that all people nations and languages him should serve**

שלטנה 7985 שלטן 7985 עלם 5957 די 1768 לא 3809 יעדה 5709 ומלכותה 4437 די 1768 לא 3809 תתחבל 2255:
shalataneh shalatan 'alam diy la' ye'adeh, uamalkuteh diy la' titchabal.
**his dominion *is* an dominion everlasting which not shall pass away and his kingdom *that* which not shall be destroyed**

7:15 אתכרית 3735 רוחי 7308 אנה 576 דניאל 1841 בגוא 1459 נדנה 5085 וחזוי 2376 ראשי 7217 יבהלנני 927: 7:16
'atkariyat ruchiy 'anah daniyea'l bagou'a nidneh; uachezuey rea'shiy yabahalunaniy.
**was grieved in my spirit I Daniel in the midst of *my* body and the visions of my head troubled me**

קרבת 7127 על 5922 חד 2298 מן 4481 קאמיא 6966 ויציבא 3330 אבעא 1156 מנה 4481 על 5922 כל 3606 דנה 1836 ואמר 560 לי 3807a
qirbet, 'al chad min qa'amaya', uayatziyba' 'ab'aa' mineh 'al kal danah; ua'amar liy
**I came near unto one of them that stood by and the truth asked him of all this So he told me**

Dan 7:10 A fiery stream issued and came forth from before him: thousand thousands ministered unto him, and ten thousand times ten thousand stood before him: the judgment was set, and the books were opened.11 I beheld then because of the voice of the great words which the horn spoke: I beheld even till the beast was slain, and his body destroyed, and given to the burning flame.12 As concerning the rest of the beasts, they had their dominion taken away: yet their lives were prolonged for a season and time.13 I saw in the night visions, and, behold, one like the Son of man came with the clouds of heaven, and came to the Ancient of days, and they brought him near before him.14 And there was given him dominion, and glory, and a kingdom, that all people, nations, and languages, should serve him: his dominion is an everlasting dominion, which shall not pass away, and his kingdom that which shall not be destroyed.15 I Daniel was grieved in my spirit in the midst of my body, and the visions of my head troubled me.16 I came near unto one of them that stood by, and asked him the truth of all this. So he told me, and made me know the interpretation of the things.

6591 ופשר · 4406 מליא · 3046 יהודענני: · **7:17** 459 אלין · 2423 חיותא · 7260 רברבתא · 1768 די · 581 אנין · 703 ארבע · 703 ארבעה · 4430 מלכין
uapshar milaya' yahouda'ananiy. 'aleyn cheyuata' rabrabata', diy 'aniyn 'arba; 'arba'ah malkiyn
**and the interpretation of the things made me know These beasts great that which *are* four *are* four kings**

6966 יקומון · 4481 מן · 772 ארעא: · **7:18** 6902 ויקבלון · 4437 מלכותא · 6922 קדישי · 5946 עליונין · 2631 ויחסנון · 4437 מלכותא
yaqumun min 'ar'aa'. uiyqabalun malkuta', qadiyshey 'alyouniyn; uayachsanun malkuta'
***which* shall arise out of the earth But shall take the kingdom the saints of *the* most High and possess the kingdom**

5705 עד · 5957 עלמא · 5705 ועד · 5957 עלם · 5957 עלמיא: · **7:19** 116 אדין · 6634 צבית · 3321 ליצבא · 5922 על · 2423 חיותא · 7244 רביעיתא · 1768 די · 1934 הות
'ad 'alma', ua'ad 'alam 'alamaya'. 'adayin, tzabiyt layatzaba', 'al cheyuata' rabiy'ayata', diy hauat
**for ever and even ever for ever Then I would *know* the truth of beast *the* fourth which was**

8133 שניה · 4481 מן · 3606 כלהון · 1763 דחילה · 3493 יתירה · 8128 שניה · 1768 די · 6523 פרזל · 2953 וטפריה · 1768 די · 5174 נחש · 399 אכלה
shanayah min kalahoun dachiylah yatiyrah, shinaiyah diy parzel uatiprayh diy nachash, 'akalah
**diverse from all the others dreadful exceeding teeth whose *were of* iron and his nails that *of* brass *which* devoured**

1855 מדקה · 7606 ושארא · 7271 ברגליה · 7512 רפסה: · **7:20** 5922 ועל · 7162 קרניא · 6236 עשר · 1768 די · 7217 בראשה · 317 ואחרי
madaqah, uash'ara' baraglayh rapasah. ua'al qarnaya' 'asar diy barea'shah, ua'achariy
**brake in pieces and the residue with his feet stamped And of horns *the* ten that *were* in his head and *of* the other**

1768 די · 5559 סלקת · 5308 ונפלו · 4481 מן · 6925 קדמיה · 8532 תלת · 7162 וקרנא · 1797 דכן · 5870 ועינין · 3807a לה · 6433 ופם · 4449 ממלל
diy silqat, uanpalu min qadamaiyah talat; uaqarna' diken ua'ayniyn lah, uapum mamalil
**which came up and fell than before *whom* three even horn *of* that that eyes had and a mouth that spoke**

7260 רברבן · 2376 וחזוה · 7229 רב · 4481 מן · 2273 חברתה: · **7:21** 2370 חזה · 1934 הוית · 7162 וקרנא · 1797 דכן · 5648 עבדה · 7129 קרב · 5974 עם
rabraban, uachezuah rab min chabratah. chazeh haueyt, uaqarna' diken, 'abadah qarab 'am
**very great things whose look *was* more stout than his fellows beheld I and horn *the* same made war with**

6922 קדישין · 3202 ויכלה · 3807b להון: · **7:22** 5705 עד · 1768 די · 858 אתה · 6268 עתיק · 3118 יומיא · 1780 ודינא · 3052 יהב
qadiyshiyn; uayakalah lahoun. 'ad diy 'atah, 'atiyq youmaya', uadiyna' yahib,
**the saints and prevailed against them Until that came the Ancient of days and judgment was given**

6922 לקדישי · 5946 עליונין · 2166 וזמנא · 4291 מטה · 4437 ומלכותא · 2631 החסנו · 6922 קדישין: · **7:23** 3652 כן · 560 אמר · 2423 חיותא
laqadiyshey 'alyouniyn; uazimna' matah, uamalkuta' hechasinu qadiyshiyn. ken 'amar cheyuata'
**to the saints of the most High and the time came that the kingdom possessed the saints Thus he said beast**

7244 רביעיתא · 4437 מלכו · 7244 רביעיא · 1934 תהוא · 772 בארעא · 1768 די · 8133 תשנא · 4481 מן · 3606 כל · 4437 מלכותא · 399 ותאכל
rabiy'ayata', malku rabiy'aya tehauea' ua'ar'aa', diy tishnea' min kal malkauata'; uatea'kul
***The* fourth kingdom *the* fourth shall be upon earth which shall be diverse from all kingdoms and shall devour**

3606 כל · 772 ארעא · 1759 ותדושנה · 1855 ותדקנה: · **7:24** 7162 וקרניא · 6236 עשר · 4481 מנה · 4437 מלכותה · 6236 עשרה
kal 'ar'aa', uatdushinah uatadqinah. uaqarnaya' 'asar, minah malkutah, 'asrah
**the whole earth and shall tread it down and break it in pieces And horns *the* ten out of this kingdom *are* ten**

4430 מלכין · 6966 יקמון · 321 ואחרן · 6966 יקום · 311 אחריהון · 1932 והוא · 8133 ישנא · 4481 מן · 6933 קדמיא · 8532 ותלתה · 4430 מלכין
malkiyn yaqumun; ua'acharan yaqum 'achareyhon, uahu'a yishna' min qadmayea', uatlatah malkiyn
**kings *that* shall arise and another shall rise after them and he shall be diverse from the first and three kings**

Dan 7:17 These great beasts, which are four, are four kings, which shall arise out of the earth.18 But the saints of the most High shall take the kingdom, and possess the kingdom forever, even forever and ever.19 Then I would know the truth of the fourth beast, which was diverse from all the others, exceeding dreadful, whose teeth were of iron, and his nails of brass; which devoured, break in pieces, and stamped the residue with his feet;20 And of the ten horns that were in his head, and of the other which came up, and before whom three fell; even of that horn that had eyes, and a mouth that spoke very great things, whose look was more stout than his fellows.21 I beheld, and the same horn made war with the saints, and prevailed against them;22 Until the Ancient of days came, and judgment was given to the saints of the most High; and the time came that the saints possessed the kingdom.23 Thus he said, The fourth beast shall be the fourth kingdom upon earth, which shall be diverse from all kingdoms, and shall devour the whole earth, and shall tread it down, and break it in pieces.24 And the ten horns out of this kingdom are ten kings that shall arise: and another shall rise after them; and he shall be diverse from the first, and he shall subdue three kings.

7:25

יהשפל 8214: ומלין 4406 לצד 6655 עליא 5943 ימלל 4449 ולקדישי 6922 עליונין 5946 יבלא 1080
yahashpil. uamiliyn, latzad 'ala'ya yamalil, ualqadiyshey 'alyouniyn yabalea';
**he shall subdue And words against the most high he shall speak *great* and the saints of the most High shall wear out**

ויסבר 5452 להשניה 8133 זמנין 2166 ודת 1882 ויתיהבון 3052 בידה 3028 עד 5705 עדן 5732 ועדנין 5732 ופלג 6387
uayisbar, lahashanayah zimniyn uadat, uayityahabun biydeh, 'ad 'adan ua'adaniyn uaplag
**and think to change times and laws and they shall be given into his hand until a time and times and the dividing of**

7:26

עדן 5732: ודינא 1780 יתב 3488 ושלטנה 7985 יהעדון 5709 להשמדה 8046 ולהובדה 7 עד 5705
'adan. uadiyna' yitib; uashalataneh yaha'adoun, lahashamadah ualhouadah 'ad
**time But the judgment shall sit and his dominion they shall take away to consume and to destroy *it* unto**

7:27

סופא 5491: ומלכותה 4437 ושלטנא 7985 ורבותא 7238 די 1768 מלכות 4437 תחות 8460 כל 3606 שמיא 8065
soupa'. uamalkutah uashalatana' uarbuta', diy malkauat tachout kal shamaya',
**the end And the kingdom and dominion and the greatness of the kingdom under the whole heaven**

יהיבת 3052 לעם 5972 קדישי 6922 עליונין 5946 מלכותה 4437 מלכות 4437 עלם 5957 וכל 3606 שלטניא 7985
yahiybat la'am qadiyshey 'alyouniyn; malkuteh malkut 'alam, uakol shalatanaya',
**shall be given to the people of the saints of the most High whose kingdom *is* an kingdom everlasting and all dominions**

7:28

לה 3807a יפלחון 6399 וישתמעון 8086: עד 5705 כה 3542 סופא 5491 די 1768 מלתא 4406 אנה 576 דניאל 1841 שגיא 7690 רעיוני 7476
leh yiplachun uayishtama'aun. 'ad kah soupa' diy milta'; 'anah daniyea'l sagiy'a ra'younay
**him shall serve and obey Hereto this *is* the end of the matter As for me Daniel much my cogitations**

יבהלנני 927 וזיוי 2122 ישתנון 8133 עלי 5922 ומלתא 4406 בלבי 3821 נטרת 5202:
yabahalunaniy, uaziyuay yishtanoun 'alay, uamilta' balibiy nitret.
**troubled me and my countenance changed in me but the matter in my heart I kept**

**Dan 8:1**

בשנת 8141 שלוש 7969 למלכות 4438 בלאשצר 1112 המלך 4428 חזון 2377 נראה 7200 אלי 413 אני 589 דניאל 1840 אחרי 310
bishnat shaloush, lamalkut bela'shatzar hamelek; chazoun nir'ah 'aelay 'aniy daniyea'l, 'acharey
**In year *the* third of the reign of Belshazzar king a vision appeared unto me *even unto* me Daniel after**

8:2

הנראה 7200 אלי 413 בתחלה 8462: ואראה 7200 בחזון 2377 ויהי 1961 בראתי 7200 ואני 589 בשושן 7800
hanir'ah 'aelay batachilah. ua'ar'ah bechazoun uayahiy bir'atiy, ua'aniy bashushan
**that which appeared unto me at the first And I saw in a vision and it came to pass when I saw that I *was* at Shushan**

8:3

הבירה 1002 אשר 834 בעילם 5867 המדינה 4082 ואראה 7200 בחזון 2377 ואני 589 הייתי 1961 על 5921 אובל 180 אולי 195:
habiyrah, 'asher ba'aeylam hamadiynah; ua'ar'ah bechazoun, ua'aniy hayiytiy 'al 'uabal 'aulay.
***in* the palace which *is* in Elam the province of and I saw in a vision and I was by the river of Ulai**

ואשא 5375 עיני 5869 ואראה 7200 והנה 2009 איל 352 אחד 259 עמד 5975 לפני 6440 האבל 180 ולו 3807a קרנים 7161
ua'asa' 'aeynay ua'ar'ah, uahineh 'ayil 'achad, 'amed lipney ha'abal ualou qaranayim;
**Then I lifted up mine eyes and saw and behold ram a there stood before the river which had *two* horns**

8:4

והקרנים 7161 גבהות 1364 והאחת 259 גבהה 1364 מן 4480 השנית 8145 והגבהה 1364 עלה 5927 באחרנה 314: ראיתי 7200 את 853
uahaqaranayim gabohout, uaha'achat gabohah min hasheniyt, uahagabohah, 'alah ba'acharonah. ra'aytiy 'at
**and the *two* horns *were* high but the one *was* higher than the other and the higher came up last I saw**

Dan 7:25 And he shall speak great words against the most High, and shall wear out the saints of the most High, and think to change times and laws: and they shall be given into his hand until a time and times and the dividing of time.26 But the judgment shall sit, and they shall take away his dominion, to consume and to destroy it unto the end.27 And the kingdom and dominion, and the greatness of the kingdom under the whole heaven, shall be given to the people of the saints of the most High, whose kingdom is an everlasting kingdom, and all dominions shall serve and obey him.28 Hitherto is the end of the matter. As for me Daniel, my cogitations much troubled me, and my countenance changed in me: but I kept the matter in my heart. **Dan** 8:1 In the third year of the reign of king Belshazzar a vision appeared unto me, even unto me Daniel, after that which appeared unto me at the first.2 And I saw in a vision; and it came to pass, when I saw, that I was at Shushan in the palace, which is in the province of Elam; and I saw in a vision, and I was by the river of Ulai.3 Then I lifted up mine eyes, and saw, and, behold, there stood before the river a ram which had two horns: and the two horns were high; but one was higher than the other, and the higher came up last.4 I saw the ram pushing westward, and northward, and southward;

| האיל 352 | מנגח 5055 | ימה 3220 | וצפונה 6828 | ונגבה 5045 | וכל 3605 | חיות 2416 | לא 3808 | יעמדו 5975 | לפניו 6440 | ואין 369 |
|---|---|---|---|---|---|---|---|---|---|---|
| ha'ayil | manageach | yamah | uatzapounah | uanegbah, | uakal | chayout | la' | ya'amdu | lapanayu, | ua'aeyn |
| **the ram** | **pushing** | **westward** | **and northward** | **and southward** | **so that** | **beasts** | **no** | **might stand** | **before him** | **neither** |

| מציל 5337 | מידו 3027 | ועשה 6213 | כרצנו 7522 | והגדיל 1431: | 8:5 | ואני 589 | הייתי 1961 |
|---|---|---|---|---|---|---|---|
| matziyl | miyadou; | ua'asah | kirtzonou | uahigdiyl. | | ua'aniy | hayiytiy |
| ***was there any* that could deliver** | **out of his hand** | **but he did** | **according to his will** | **and became great** | | **as I** | **was** |

| מבין 995 | והנה 2009 | צפיר 6842 | העזים 5795 | בא 935 | מן 4480 | המערב 4628 | על 5921 | פני 6440 | כל 3605 | הארץ 776 | ואין 369 | נוגע 5060 |
|---|---|---|---|---|---|---|---|---|---|---|---|---|
| mebiyn, | uahineh | tzapiyr | ha'aziym | ba' | min | hama'arab | 'al | paney | kal | ha'aretz, | ua'aeyn | nougea' |
| **considering** | **And behold** | **an he** | **goat** | **came** | **from** | **the west** | **on** | **the face of** | **whole** | **the earth** | **and not** | **touched** |

| בארץ 776 | והצפיר 6842 | קרן 7161 | חזות 2380 | בין 996 | עיניו 5869: | 8:6 | ויבא 935 | עד 5704 | האיל 352 | בעל 1167 | הקרנים 7161 | אשר 834 |
|---|---|---|---|---|---|---|---|---|---|---|---|---|
| ba'aretz; | uahatzapiyr, | qeren | chazut | beyn | 'aeynayu. | | uayaba', | 'ad | ha'ayil | ba'al | haqaranayim, | 'asher |
| **the ground** | **and the goat *had*** | **a horn** | **notable** | **between** | **his eyes** | | **And he came to** | | **the ram** | **that had** | ***two* horns** | **which** |

| ראיתי 7200 | עמד 5975 | לפני 6440 | האבל 180 | וירץ 7323 | אליו 413 | בחמת 2534 | כחו 3581: | 8:7 | וראיתיו 7200 | מגיע 5060 | אצל 681 |
|---|---|---|---|---|---|---|---|---|---|---|---|
| ra'aytiy, | 'amed | lipney | ha'abal; | uayaratz | 'aelayu | bachamat | kochou. | | uar'aytiyu | magiya' | 'aetzel |
| **I had seen** | **standing** | **before** | **the river** | **and ran** | **unto him** | **in the fury** | **of his power** | | **And I saw him** | **come** | **close unto** |

| האיל 352 | ויתמרמר 4843 | אליו 413 | ויך 5221 | את 853 | האיל 352 | וישבר 7665 | את 853 | שתי 8147 | קרניו 7161 | ולא 3808 |
|---|---|---|---|---|---|---|---|---|---|---|
| ha'ayil, | uayitmarmar | 'aelayu | uayak | 'at | ha'ayil, | uayashaber | 'at | shatey | qaranayu, | uala' |
| **the ram** | **and he was moved with choler** | **against him** | **and smote** | | **the ram** | **and brake** | | **two** | **his horns** | **and no** |

| היה 1961 | כח 3581 | באיל 352 | לעמד 5975 | לפניו 6440 | וישליכהו 7993 | ארצה 776 | וירמסהו 7429 | ולא 3808 |
|---|---|---|---|---|---|---|---|---|
| hayah | koach | ba'ayil | la'amod | lapanayu; | uayashliykehu | 'artzah | uayirmasehu, | uala' |
| **there was** | **power** | **in the ram** | **to stand** | **before him** | **but he cast him down to** | **the ground** | **and stamped upon him** | **and none** |

| היה 1961 | מציל 5337 | לאיל 352 | מידו 3027: | 8:8 | וצפיר 6842 | העזים 5795 | הגדיל 1431 | עד 5704 | מאד 3966 |
|---|---|---|---|---|---|---|---|---|---|
| hayah | matziyl | la'ayil | miyadou. | | uatzpiyr | ha'aziym | higdiyl | 'ad | ma'ad; |
| **there was** | **that could deliver** | **the ram** | **out of his hand** | | **Therefore the he** | **goat** | **waxed great** | **against** | **very** |

| וכעצמו 6105 | נשברה 7665 | הקרן 7161 | הגדולה 1419 | ותעלנה 5927 | חזות 2380 | ארבע 702 | תחתיה 8478 | לארבע 702 |
|---|---|---|---|---|---|---|---|---|
| uak'atzamou, | nishbarah | haqeren | hagadoulah, | uata'alenah | chazut | 'arba | tachteyha, | la'arba' |
| **and when he was strong** | **was broken** | **horn** | **the great** | **and for it came up** | **notable ones** | **four** | **for place** | **toward the four** |

| רוחות 7307 | השמים 8064: | 8:9 | ומן 4480 | האחת 259 | מהם 1992 | יצא 3318 | קרן 7161 | אחת 259 | מצעירה 4704 | ותגדל 1431 | יתר 3499 |
|---|---|---|---|---|---|---|---|---|---|---|---|
| ruchout | hashamayim. | | uamin | ha'achat | mehem, | yatza' | qeren | 'achat | mitza'ayrah; | uatigdal | yeter |
| **winds of** | **heaven** | | **And out of** | **one** | **of them** | **came forth** | **horn** | **a** | **little** | **which waxed great** | **exceeding** |

| אל 413 | הנגב 5045 | ואל 413 | המזרח 4217 | ואל 413 | הצבי 6643: | 8:10 | ותגדל 1431 | עד 5704 | צבא 6635 | השמים 8064 |
|---|---|---|---|---|---|---|---|---|---|---|
| 'al | hanegeb | ua'al | hamizrach | ua'al | hatzebiy. | | uatigdal | 'ad | tzaba' | hashamayim; |
| **toward** | **the south** | **and toward** | **the east** | **and toward** | **the pleasant *land*** | | **And it waxed great *even*** | **to** | **host of** | **the heaven** |

| ותפל 5307 | ארצה 776 | מן 4480 | הצבא 6635 | ומן 4480 | הכוכבים 3556 | ותרמסם 7429: | 8:11 | ועד 5704 |
|---|---|---|---|---|---|---|---|---|
| uatapel | 'artzah | min | hatzaba' | uamin | hakoukabiym | uatirmasem. | | ua'ad |
| **and it cast down to** | **the ground *some*** | **of** | **the host** | **and some of** | **the stars** | **and stamped upon them** | | **Yea even to** |

Dan 8:4 so that no beasts might stand before him, neither was there any that could deliver out of his hand; but he did according to his will, and became great.5 And as I was considering, behold, an he goat came from the west on the face of the whole earth, and touched not the ground: and the goat had a notable horn between his eyes.6 And he came to the ram that had two horns, which I had there seen standing before the river, and ran unto him in the fury of his power.7 And I saw him come close unto the ram, and he was moved with choler against him, and smote the ram, and break his two horns: and there was no power in the ram to stand before him, but he cast him down to the ground, and stamped upon him: and there was none that could deliver the ram out of his hand.8 Therefore the he goat waxed very great: and when he was strong, the great horn was broken; and for it came up four notable ones toward the four winds of heaven.9 And out of one of them came forth a little horn, which waxed exceeding great, toward the south, and toward the east, and toward the pleasant land.10 And it waxed great, even to the host of heaven; and it cast down some of the host and of the stars to the ground, and stamped upon them. 11 Yea, he magnified himself even to the prince of the host, and by him the daily sacrifice was taken away, and the place of his sanctuary was cast down.

שר 8269 הצבא 6635 הגדיל 1431 וממנו 4480 הרים 7311 התמיד 8548 והשלך 7993 מכון 4349
sar hatzaba' higdiyl; uamimenu heriym hatamiyd, uahushlak makoun
**the prince of the host he magnified *himself* and by him *sacrifice* was taken away the daily and was cast down the place of**

8:12
מקדשו 4720: וצבא 6635 תנתן 5414 על 5921 התמיד 8548 בפשע 6588 ותשלך 7993
miqadashou. uatzaba' tinaten 'al hatamiyd bapasha'; uatashlek
**his sanctuary And an host was given *him* against the daily *sacrifice* by reason of transgression and it cast down**

8:13
אמת 571 ארצה 776 ועשתה 6213 והצליחה 6743: ואשמעה 8085 אחד 259 קדוש 6918 מדבר 1696 ויאמר 559 אחד 259 קדוש 6918
'amet 'artzah, ua'asatah uahitzliychah. ua'ashma'ah 'achad qadoush madaber; uaya'mer 'achad qadoush
**the truth *to* the ground and it practised and prospered Then I heard one saint speaking and said another saint**

לפלמוני 6422 המדבר 1696 עד 5704 מתי 4970 החזון 2377 התמיד 8548 והפשע 6588
lapalmouniy hamadaber, 'ad matay hechazoun hatamiyd uahapesha'
**unto that certain *saint* which spoke How long *shall be* the vision *concerning* the daily *sacrifice* and the transgression of**

8:14
שמם 8074 תת 5414 וקדש 6944 וצבא 6635 מרמס 4823: ויאמר 559 אלי 413 עד 5704 ערב 6153
shomem, tet uaqodesh uatzaba' mirmas. uaya'mer 'aelay, 'ad 'areb
**desolation to give both the sanctuary and the host to be trodden under foot? And he said unto me Unto days**

8:15
בקר 1242 אלפים 505 ושלש 7969 מאות 3967 ונצדק 6663 קדש 6944: ויהי 1961 בראתי 7200
boqer, 'alpayim uashlosh me'aut; uanitzdaq qodesh. uayahiy, bir'atiy
**mornings two thousand and three hundred then shall be cleansed the sanctuary And it came to pass when I had seen**

אני 589 דניאל 1840 את 853 החזון 2377 ואבקשה 1245 בינה 998 והנה 2009 עמד 5975 לנגדי 5048 כמראה 4758
'aniy daniyea'l 'at hechazoun; ua'abaqshah biynah, uahineh 'amed lanegdiy kamar'aeh
***even* I Daniel the vision and sought for the meaning and then behold there stood before me as the appearance of**

8:16
גבר 1397: ואשמע 8085 קול 6963 אדם 120 בין 996 אולי 195 ויקרא 7121 ויאמר 559 גבריאל 1403 הבן 995
gaber. ua'ashma' qoul 'adam beyn 'aulay; uayiqra' uaya'mar, gabriy'ael haben
**a man And I heard a voice man's between *the banks of* Ulai which called and said Gabriel make to understand**

8:17
להלז 1975 את 853 המראה 4758: ויבא 935 אצל 681 עמדי 5975 ובבאו 935 נבעתי 1204 ואפלה 5307 על 5921 פני 6440
lahalaz 'at hamar'ah. uayaba' 'aetzel 'amadiy, uabbo'au nib'atiy, ua'apalah 'al panay;
**this *man* the vision So he came near *where* I stood and when he came I was afraid and fell upon my face**

8:18
ויאמר 559 אלי 413 הבן 995 בן 1121 אדם 120 כי 3588 לעת 6256 קץ 7093 החזון 2377:
uaya'mer 'aelay haben ben 'adam, kiy la'et qetz hechazoun.
**but he said unto me Understand O son of man for at the time of the end *shall be* the vision**

ובדברו 1696 עמי 5973 נרדמתי 7290 על 5921 פני 6440 ארצה 776 ויגע 5060 בי 871a
uabdabrou 'amiy, nirdamtiy 'al panay 'aratzah; uayiga' biy,
**Now as he was speaking with me I was in a deep sleep on my face toward the ground but he touched me**

8:19
ויעמידני 5975 על 5921 עמדי 5975: ויאמר 559 הנני 2005 מודיעך 3045 את 853 אשר 834 יהיה 1961 באחרית 319
uaya'amiydeniy 'al 'amadiy. uaya'mer hinniy moudiy'aka, 'at 'asher yihayeh ba'achariyt
**and set up right And he said Behold I will make you know what shall be in the last end of**

Dan 8:12 And an host was given him against the daily sacrifice by reason of transgression, and it cast down the truth to the ground; and it practised, and prospered.13 Then I heard one saint speaking, and another saint said unto that certain saint which spoke, How long shall be the vision concerning the daily sacrifice, and the transgression of desolation, to give both the sanctuary and the host to be trodden under foot?14 And he said unto me, Unto two thousand and three hundred days; then shall the sanctuary be cleansed.15 And it came to pass, when I, even I Daniel, had seen the vision, and sought for the meaning, then, behold, there stood before me as the appearance of a man.16 And I heard a man's voice between the banks of Ulai, which called, and said, Gabriel, make this man to understand the vision.17 So he came near where I stood: and when he came, I was afraid, and fell upon my face: but he said unto me, Understand, O son of man: for at the time of the end shall be the vision.18 Now as he was speaking with me, I was in a deep sleep on my face toward the ground: but he touched me, and set me upright.19 And he said, Behold, I will make you know what shall be in the last end of the indignation:

| הזעם 2195 | כי 3588 | למועד 4150 | קץ 7093: | 8:20 | האיל 352 | אשר 834 | ראית 7200 | בעל 1167 | הקרנים 7161 |
|---|---|---|---|---|---|---|---|---|---|
| haza'am; | kiy | lamou'aed | qetz. | | ha'ayil | 'asher | ra'ayta | ba'al | haqaranayim; |
| **the indignation** | **for** | **at the time appointed** | **the end *shall be*** | | **The ram** | **which** | **you saw** | **having** | ***two* horns** |

| מלכי 4428 | מדי 4074 | ופרס 6539: | 8:21 | והצפיר 6842 | השעיר 8163 | מלך 4428 | יון 3120 | והקרן 7161 | הגדולה 1419 | אשר 834 | בין 996 |
|---|---|---|---|---|---|---|---|---|---|---|---|
| malkey | maday | uaparas. | | uahatzapiyr | hasa'ayr | melek | yauan; | uahaqeren | hagadoulah | 'asher | beyn |
| ***are* the kings of** | **Media** | **and Persia** | | **And goat** | **the rough** | ***is* the king of** | **Grecia** | **and horn** | **the great** | **that *is*** | **between** |

| עיניו 5869 | הוא 1931 | המלך 4428 | הראשון 7223: | 8:22 | והנשברת 7665 | ותעמדנה 5975 | ארבע 702 | תחתיה 8478 | ארבע 702 | מלכיות 4438 |
|---|---|---|---|---|---|---|---|---|---|---|
| 'aeynayu, | hua' | hamelek | hara'shoun. | | uahanishberet, | uata'amodnah | 'arba | tachteyha; | 'arba | malkuyout |
| **his eyes** | **he** | **king** | ***is* the first** | | **Now that being broken** | **whereas stood up** | **four** | **for it** | **four** | **kingdoms** |

| מגוי 1471 | יעמדנה 5975 | ולא 3808 | בכחו 3581: | 8:23 | ובאחרית 319 | מלכותם 4438 | כהתם 8552 |
|---|---|---|---|---|---|---|---|
| migouy | ya'amodanah | uala' | bakochou. | | uab'achariyt | malkutam, | kahatem |
| **out of the nation** | **shall stand up** | **but not** | **in his power** | | **And in the latter time of** | **their kingdom** | **when are come to the full** |

| הפשעים 6586 | יעמד 5975 | מלך 4428 | עז 5794 | פנים 6440 | ומבין 995 | חידות 2420: | 8:24 | ועצם 6105 |
|---|---|---|---|---|---|---|---|---|
| haposha'aym; | ya'amod | melek | 'az | paniym | uamebiyn | chiydout. | | ua'atzam |
| **the transgressors** | **shall stand up** | **a king of** | **fierce** | **countenance** | **and understanding** | **dark sentences** | | **And shall be mighty** |

| כחו 3581 | ולא 3808 | בכחו 3581 | ונפלאות 6381 | ישחית 7843 | והצליח 6743 | ועשה 6213 | והשחית 7843 |
|---|---|---|---|---|---|---|---|
| kochou | uala' | bakochou, | uanipla'aut | yashchiyt | uahitzliyach | ua'asah; | uahishchiyt |
| **his power** | **but not** | **by his own power** | **and wonderfully** | **he shall destroy** | **and shall prosper** | **and practise** | **and shall destroy** |

| עצומים 6099 | ועם 5971 | קדשים 6918: | 8:25 | ועל 5921 | שכלו 7922 | והצליח 6743 | מרמה 4820 | בידו 3027 |
|---|---|---|---|---|---|---|---|---|
| 'atzumiym | ua'am | qadoshiym. | | ua'al | siklou, | uahitzliyach | mirmah | bayadou, |
| **the mighty** | **and people** | ***the* holy** | | **And through also** | **his policy** | **also he shall cause to prosper** | **craft** | **in his hand** |

| ובלבבו 3824 | יגדיל 1431 | ובשלוה 7962 | ישחית 7843 | רבים 7227 | ועל 5921 | שר 8269 | שרים 8269 |
|---|---|---|---|---|---|---|---|
| uabilbabou | yagdiyl, | uabshaluah | yashchiyt | rabiym; | ua'al | sar | sariym |
| **and in his heart** | **he shall magnify *himself*** | **and by peace** | **shall destroy** | **many** | **and against** | **the Prince of** | **princes** |

| יעמד 5975 | ובאפס 657 | יד 3027 | ישבר 7665: | 8:26 | ומראה 4758 | הערב 6153 | והבקר 1242 | אשר 834 |
|---|---|---|---|---|---|---|---|---|
| ya'amod, | uab'apes | yad | yishaber. | | uamara'aeh | ha'areb | uahaboqer | 'asher |
| **he shall also stand up** | **but without** | **hand** | **he shall be broken** | | **And the vision of** | **the evening** | **and the morning** | **which** |

| נאמר 559 | אמת 571 | הוא 1931 | ואתה 859 | סתם 5640 | החזון 2377 | כי 3588 | לימים 3117 | רבים 7227: | 8:27 | ואני 589 | דניאל 1840 | נהייתי 1961 |
|---|---|---|---|---|---|---|---|---|---|---|---|---|
| ne'amar | 'amet | hua'; | ua'atah | satom | hechazoun, | kiy | layamiym | rabiym. | | ua'aniy | daniyea'l, | nihayeytiy |
| **was told** | ***is* true** | **it** | **wherefore you** | **shut up** | **the vision** | **for *shall be*** | **for days** | **many** | | **And I** | **Daniel** | **fainted** |

| ונחליתי 2470 | ימים 3117 | ואקום 6965 | ואעשה 6213 | את 853 | מלאכת 4399 | המלך 4428 | ואשתומם 8074 | על 5921 | המראה 4758 |
|---|---|---|---|---|---|---|---|---|---|
| uanechaleytiy | yamiym, | ua'aqum | ua'a'aseh | 'at | mala'ket | hamelek; | ua'ashtoumem | 'al | hamar'ah |
| **and was sick** | ***certain* days** | **afterward I rose up** | **and did** | | **business** | **the king's** | **and I was astonished** | **at** | **the vision** |

| ואין 369 | מבין 995: |
|---|---|
| ua'aeyn | mebiyn. |
| **but none** | **understood *it*** |

Dan 8:19 for at the time appointed the end shall be.20 The ram which you saw having two horns are the kings of Media and Persia.21 And the rough goat is the king of Grecia: and the great horn that is between his eyes is the first king.22 Now that being broken, whereas four stood up for it, four kingdoms shall stand up out of the nation, but not in his power.23 And in the latter time of their kingdom, when the transgressors are come to the full, a king of fierce countenance, and understanding dark sentences, shall stand up.24 And his power shall be mighty, but not by his own power: and he shall destroy wonderfully, and shall prosper, and practise, and shall destroy the mighty and the holy people.25 And through his policy also he shall cause craft to prosper in his hand; and he shall magnify himself in his heart, and by peace shall destroy many: he shall also stand up against the Prince of princes; but he shall be broken without hand.26 And the vision of the evening and the morning which was told is true: wherefore shut you up the vision; for it shall be for many days.27 And I Daniel fainted, and was sick certain days; afterward I rose up, and did the king's business; and I was astonished at the vision, but none understood it.

| **Dan 9:1** | | | | | | | | | |
|---|---|---|---|---|---|---|---|---|---|
| בשנת 8141 | אחת 259 | לדריוש 1867 | בן 1121 | אחשורוש 325 | מזרע 2233 | מדי 4074 | אשר 834 | המלך 4427 | על 5921 |
| bishnat | 'achat, | ladarayauesh | ben | achashuerous h | mizera' | maday; | 'asher | hamalak, | 'al |
| **In year** | ***the* first** | **of Darius** | **the son of** | **Ahasuerus** | **of the seed of** | **the Medes** | **which** | **was made king** | **over** |

| מלכות 4438 | כשדים 3778: | **9:2** בשנת 8141 | אחת 259 | למלכו 4427 | אני 589 | דניאל 1840 | בינתי 995 | בספרים 5612 | מספר 4557 |
|---|---|---|---|---|---|---|---|---|---|
| malkut | kasdiym. | bishnat | 'achat | lamalakou, | 'aniy | daniyea'l, | biynotiy | basapariym; | mispar |
| **the realm of** | **the Chaldeans** | **In year** | ***the* first** | **of his reign** | **I** | **Daniel** | **understood** | **by books** | **the number of** |

| השנים 8141 | אשר 834 | היה 1961 | דבר 1697 | יהוה 3068 | אל 413 | ירמיה 3414 | הנביא 5030 | למלאות 4390 | לחרבות 2723 |
|---|---|---|---|---|---|---|---|---|---|
| hashaniym, | 'asher | hayah | dabar | Yahuah | 'al | yirmiyah | hanabiy'a, | lamala'ut | lacharabout |
| **the years** | **whereof** | **came** | **the word of** | **Yahuah** | **to** | **Jeremiah** | **the prophet** | **that he would accomplish** | **in the desolations of** |

| ירושלם 3389 | שבעים 7657 | שנה 8141: | **9:3** ואתנה 5414 | את 853 | פני 6440 | אל 413 | אדני 136 | האלהים 430 | לבקש 1245 | תפלה 8605 | ותחנונים 8469 |
|---|---|---|---|---|---|---|---|---|---|---|---|
| yarushalaim | shib'aym | shanah. | ua'atnah | 'at | panay, | 'al | 'adonay | ha'alohiym, | labaqesh | tapilah | uatachanuniym; |
| **Jerusalem** | **seventy** | **years** | **And I set** | | **my face** | **unto** | **Adonai** | **Elohim** | **to seek by** | **prayer** | **and supplications** |

| בצום 6685 | ושק 8242 | ואפר 665: | **9:4** ואתפללה 6419 | ליהוה 3068 | אלהי 430 | ואתודה 3034 | ואמרה 559 |
|---|---|---|---|---|---|---|---|
| batzoum | uasaq | ua'aper. | ua'atpallah | laYahuah | 'alohay | ua'atuadeh; | ua'amrah, |
| **with fasting** | **and sackcloth** | **and ashes** | **And I prayed** | **unto Yahuah** | **my Elohim** | **and made my confession** | **and said** |

| אנא 577 | אדני 136 | האל 410 | הגדול 1419 | והנורא 3372 | שמר 8104 | הברית 1285 | והחסד 2617 | לאהביו 157 |
|---|---|---|---|---|---|---|---|---|
| 'ana' | 'adonay | ha'ael | hagadoul | uahanoura', | shomer | habariyt | uahachesed, | la'ahabayu |
| **O I beseech you** | **Adonai** | **the El** | **the great** | **and dreadful** | **keeping** | **the covenant** | **and mercy** | **to them that love him** |

| ולשמרי 8104 | מצותיו 4687: | **9:5** חטאנו 2398 | ועוינו 5753 | והרשענו 7561 |
|---|---|---|---|---|
| ualshomarey | mitzuotayu. | chata'nu | ua'auiynu | uahirsha'nu |
| **and to them that keep** | **his commandments** | **We have sinned** | **and have committed iniquity** | **and have done wickedly** |

| ומרדנו 4775 | וסור 5493 | ממצותך 4687 | וממשפטיך 4941: | **9:6** ולא 3808 | שמענו 8085 | אל 413 |
|---|---|---|---|---|---|---|
| uamaradanu; | uasour | mimitzuoteka | uamimishpateyka. | uala' | shama'anu | 'al |
| **and have rebelled** | **even by departing** | **from your precepts** | **and from your judgments** | **Neither** | **have we hearkened** | **unto** |

| עבדיך 5650 | הנביאים 5030 | אשר 834 | דברו 1696 | בשמך 8034 | אל 413 | מלכינו 4428 | שרינו 8269 | ואבתינו 1 | ואל 413 | כל 3605 |
|---|---|---|---|---|---|---|---|---|---|---|
| 'abadeyka | hanabiy'aym, | 'asher | dibru | bashimka, | 'al | malakeynu | sareynu | ua'aboteynu; | ua'ael | kal |
| **your servants** | **the prophets** | **which** | **spoke** | **in your name** | **to** | **our kings** | **our princes** | **and our fathers** | **and to** | **all** |

| עם 5971 | הארץ 776: | **9:7** לך 3807a | אדני 136 | הצדקה 6666 | ולנו 3807a | בשת 1322 | הפנים 6440 | כיום 3117 | הזה 2088 |
|---|---|---|---|---|---|---|---|---|---|
| 'am | ha'aretz. | laka | 'adonay | hatzadaqah, | ualanu | boshet | hapaniym | kayoum | hazeh; |
| **the people of** | **the land** | ***belongs* unto you** | **O Adonai** | **righteousness** | **but unto us** | **confusion of** | **faces** | **as day** | ***at* this** |

| לאיש 376 | יהודה 3063 | וליושבי 3427 | ירושלם 3389 | ולכל 3605 | ישראל 3478 | הקרבים 7138 | והרחקים 7350 |
|---|---|---|---|---|---|---|---|
| la'aysh | yahudah | ualyoushabey | yarushalaim, | ualkal | yisra'ael | haqarobiym | uaharachoqiym, |
| **to the men of** | **Judah** | **and to the inhabitants of** | **Jerusalem** | **and unto all** | **Israel** | ***that are* near** | **and *that are* far off** |

| בכל 3605 | הארצות 776 | אשר 834 | הדחתם 5080 | שם 8033 | במעלם 4604 | אשר 834 | מעלו 4603 |
|---|---|---|---|---|---|---|---|
| bakal | ha'aratzout | 'asher | hidachtam | sham, | bama'alam | 'asher | ma'alu |
| **through all** | **the countries** | **where** | **you have driven them** | **where** | **becauseof their trespass** | **that** | **they have trespassed** |

**Dan** 9:1 In the first year of Darius the son of Ahasuerus, of the seed of the Medes, which was made king over the realm of the Chaldeans;2 In the first year of his reign I Daniel
understood by books the number of the years, whereof the word of YHUH came to Jeremiah the prophet, that he would accomplish seventy years in the desolations of
Jerusalem.3 And I set my face unto YHUH G-d, to seek by prayer and supplication, with fasting, and sackcloth, and ashes:4 And I prayed unto YHUH my G-d, and made my
confession, and said, O Adonai, the great and dreadful G-d, keeping the covenant and mercy to them that love him, and to them that keep his commandments;5 We have
sinned, and have committed iniquity, and have done wickedly, and have rebelled, even by departing from your precepts and from your judgments:6 Neither have we hearkened
unto your servants the prophets, which spoke in your name to our kings, our princes, and our fathers, and to all the people of the land.7 O Adonai, righteousness belong unto
you, but unto us confusion of faces, as at this day; to the men of Judah, and to the inhabitants of Jerusalem, and unto all Israel, that are near, and that are far off, through all the
countries whither you have driven them, because of their trespass that they have trespassed against you.

| בך 871a: | 9:8 יהוה 3068 | לנו 3807a | בשת 1322 | הפנים 6440 | למלכינו 4428 | לשרינו 8269 | ולאבתינו 1 | אשר 834 |
|---|---|---|---|---|---|---|---|---|
| bak. | Yahuah | lanu | boshet | hapaniym, | limlakeynu | lasareynu | uala'aboteynu; | 'asher |
| **against you** | **Yahuah** | **to us *belongs*** | **confusion of** | **face** | **to our kings** | **to our princes** | **and to our fathers** | **because** |

| חטאנו 2398 | לך 3807a: | 9:9 לאדני 136 | אלהינו 430 | הרחמים 7356 | והסלחות 5547 | כי 3588 | מרדנו 4775 |
|---|---|---|---|---|---|---|---|
| chata'nu | lak. | la'adonay | 'aloheynu, | harachamiym | uahasalichout; | kiy | maradnu |
| **we have sinned** | **against you** | **To Adonai** | **our Elohim** | ***belong* mercies** | **and forgivenesses** | **though** | **we have rebelled** |

| בו 871a: | 9:10 ולא 3808 | שמענו 8085 | בקול 6963 | יהוה 3069 | אלהינו 430 | ללכת 1980 | בתורתיו 8451 | אשר 834 | נתן 5414 | לפנינו 6440 |
|---|---|---|---|---|---|---|---|---|---|---|
| bou. | uala' | shama'anu, | baqoul | Yahuah | 'aloheynu; | laleket | batourotayu | 'asher | natan | lapaneynu, |
| **against him** | **Neither** | **have we obeyed** | **the voice of** | **Elohim** | **our Elohim** | **to walk** | **in his laws** | **which** | **he set** | **before us** |

| ביד 3027 | עבדיו 5650 | הנביאים 5030: | 9:11 וכל 3605 | ישראל 3478 | עברו 5674 | את 853 | תורתך 8451 | וסור 5493 | לבלתי 1115 |
|---|---|---|---|---|---|---|---|---|---|
| bayad | 'abadayu | hanabiy'aym. | uakal | yisra'ael, | 'abaru | 'at | tourateka, | uasour | labiltiy |
| **by** | **his servants** | **the prophets** | **Yea all** | **Israel** | **have transgressed** | | **your law** | **even by departing** | **that not** |

| שמוע 8085 | בקלך 6963 | ותתך 5413 | עלינו 5921 | האלה 423 | והשבעה 7621 | אשר 834 | כתובה 3789 | בתורת 8451 | משה 4872 |
|---|---|---|---|---|---|---|---|---|---|
| shamoua' | baqouleka; | uatitak | 'aleynu | ha'aelah | uahashabu'ah, | 'asher | katubah | batourat | mosheh |
| **they might obey** | **your voice** | **therefore is poured** | **upon us** | **the curse** | **and the oath** | **that *is*** | **written** | **in the law of** | **Moses** |

| עבד 5650 | האלהים 430 | כי 3588 | חטאנו 2398 | לו 3807a: | 9:12 ויקם 6965 | את 853 | דבריו 1697 | אשר 834 | דבר 1696 |
|---|---|---|---|---|---|---|---|---|---|
| 'abed | ha'alohiym, | kiy | chata'nu | lou'. | uayaqem | 'at | dabarayu | 'asher | diber |
| **the servant of** | **Elohim** | **because** | **we have sinned** | **against him** | **And he has confirmed** | | **his words** | **which** | **he spoke** |

| עלינו 5921 | ועל 5921 | שפטינו 8199 | אשר 834 | שפטונו 8199 | להביא 935 | עלינו 5921 | רעה 7451 | גדלה 1419 | אשר 834 | לא 3808 | נעשתה 6213 |
|---|---|---|---|---|---|---|---|---|---|---|---|
| 'aleynu, | ua'al | shopateynu | 'asher | shapatunu, | lahabiy'a | 'aleynu | ra'ah | gadolah; | 'asher | la' | ne'astah, |
| **against us** | **and against** | **our judges** | **that** | **judged us** | **by bringing** | **upon us** | **a evil** | **great** | **for** | **not** | **has been done** |

| תחת 8478 | כל 3605 | השמים 8064 | כאשר 834 | נעשתה 6213 | בירושלם 3389: | 9:13 כאשר 834 | כתוב 3789 | בתורת 8451 | משה 4872 | את 853 | כל 3605 |
|---|---|---|---|---|---|---|---|---|---|---|---|
| tachat | kal | hashamayim, | ka'asher | ne'astah | biyarushalaim. | ka'asher | katub | batourat | mosheh, | 'at | kal |
| **under** | **whole** | **the heaven** | **as** | **has been done** | **upon Jerusalem** | **As *it is*** | **written** | **in the law of** | **Moses** | | **all** |

| הרעה 7451 | הזאת 2063 | באה 935 | עלינו 5921 | ולא 3808 | חלינו 2470 | את 854 | פני 6440 | יהוה 3068 | אלהינו 430 | לשוב 7725 |
|---|---|---|---|---|---|---|---|---|---|---|
| hara'ah | haza't | ba'ah | 'aleynu; | uala' | chiliynu | 'at | paney | Yahuah | 'aloheynu, | lashub |
| **evil** | **this** | **is come** | **upon us** | **yet not** | **made we our prayer** | | **before** | **Yahuah** | **our Elohim** | **that we might turn** |

| מעוננו 5771 | ולהשכיל 7919 | באמתך 571: | 9:14 וישקד 8245 | יהוה 3068 | על 5921 | הרעה 7451 | ויביאה 935 | עלינו 5921 |
|---|---|---|---|---|---|---|---|---|
| me'auonenu, | ualhaskiyl | ba'amiteka. | uayishqod | Yahuah | 'al | hara'ah, | uayabiy'aha | 'aleynu; |
| **from our iniquities** | **and understand** | **your truth** | **Therefore has watched** | **Yahuah** | **upon** | **the evil** | **and brought it** | **upon us** |

| כי 3588 | צדיק 6662 | יהוה 3068 | אלהינו 430 | על 5921 | כל 3605 | מעשיו 4639 | אשר 834 | עשה 6213 | ולא 3808 | שמענו 8085 | בקלו 6963: | 9:15 ועתה 6258 |
|---|---|---|---|---|---|---|---|---|---|---|---|---|
| kiy | tzadiyq | Yahuah | 'aloheynu, | 'al | kal | ma'asayu | 'asher | 'asah, | uala' | shama'anu | baqolou. | ua'atah |
| **for** | ***is* righteous** | **Yahuah** | **our Elohim** | **in** | **all** | **his works** | **which** | **he does** | **for not** | **we obeyed** | **his voice** | **And now** |

| אדני 136 | אלהינו 430 | אשר 834 | הוצאת 3318 | את 853 | עמך 5971 | מארץ 776 | מצרים 4714 | ביד 3027 | חזקה 2389 |
|---|---|---|---|---|---|---|---|---|---|
| 'adonay | 'aloheynu, | 'asher | houtzea'ta | 'at | 'amaka | me'aretz | mitzrayim | bayad | chazaqah, |
| **O Adonai** | **our Elohim** | **that** | **you have brought forth** | | **your people** | **out of the land of** | **Egypt** | **with a hand** | **mighty** |

Dan 9:8 O Adonai, to us belong confusion of face, to our kings, to our princes, and to our fathers, because we have sinned against you.9 To YHUH our G-d belong mercies and forgivenesses, though we have rebelled against him;10 Neither have we obeyed the voice of YHUH our G-d, to walk in his laws, which he set before us by his servants the prophets.11 Yea, all Israel have transgressed your law, even by departing, that they might not obey your voice; therefore the curse is poured upon us, and the oath that is written in the law of Moses the servant of G-d, because we have sinned against him.12 And he has confirmed his words, which he spoke against us, and against our judges that judged us, by bringing upon us a great evil: for under the whole heaven has not been done as has been done upon Jerusalem.13 As it is written in the law of Moses, all this evil is come upon us: yet made we not our prayer before YHUH our G-d, that we might turn from our iniquities, and understand your truth.14 Therefore has YHUH watched upon the evil, and brought it upon us: for YHUH our G-d is righteous in all his works which he doeth: for we obeyed not his voice.15 And now, O Adonai our G-d, that have brought your people forth out of the land of Egypt with a mighty hand, and have gotten you renown, as at this day; we have sinned, we have done wickedly.

| ותעש 6213 | לך 3807a | שם 8034 | כיום 3117 | הזה 2088 | חטאנו 2398 | רשענו 7561: | 9:16 אדני 136 | ככל 3605 |
|---|---|---|---|---|---|---|---|---|
| uata'as | laka | shem | kayoum | hazeh; | chata'nu | rasha'anu. | 'adonay, | kakal |
| **and have gotten** | **for you** | **renown** | **as day** | ***at* this** | **we have sinned** | **we have done wickedly** | **O Adonai** | **according to all** |

| צדקתך 6666 | ישב 7725 | נא 4994 | אפך 639 | וחמתך 2534 | מעירך 5892 | ירושלם 3389 | הר 2022 |
|---|---|---|---|---|---|---|---|
| tzidqoteka | yashob | naa' | 'apaka | uachamataka, | me'ayraka | yarushalaim | har |
| **your righteousness** | **let be turned away** | **I beseech you** | **your anger** | **and your fury** | **from your city** | **Jerusalem** | **mountain** |

| קדשך 6944 | כי 3588 | בחטאינו 2399 | ובעונות 5771 | אבתינו 1 | ירושלם 3389 | ועמך 5971 | לחרפה 2781 |
|---|---|---|---|---|---|---|---|
| qadasheka | kiy | bachata'aeynu | uba'auonout | 'aboteynu, | yarushalaim | ua'amaka | lacherpah |
| **your holy** | **because** | **for our sins** | **and for the iniquities of** | **our fathers** | **Jerusalem** | **and your people** | ***are become* a reproach** |

| לכל 3605 | סביבתינו 5439: | 9:17 ועתה 6258 | שמע 8085 | אלהינו 430 | אל 413 | תפלת 8605 | עבדך 5650 | ואל 413 | תחנוניו 8469 |
|---|---|---|---|---|---|---|---|---|---|
| lakal | sabiyboteynu. | ua'atah | shama' | 'aloheynu, | 'al | tapilat | 'abdaka | ua'al | tachanunayu, |
| **to all** | ***that are* about us** | **Now therefore** | **hear** | **O our Elohim** | **to** | **the prayer of** | **your servant** | **and to** | **his supplications** |

| והאר 215 | פניך 6440 | על 5921 | מקדשך 4720 | השמם 8076 | למען 4616 | אדני 136: | 9:18 הטה 5186 | אלהי 430 | אזנך 241 |
|---|---|---|---|---|---|---|---|---|---|
| uaha'aer | paneyka, | 'al | miqdashaka | hashamem; | lama'an | 'adonay. | hateh | 'alohay | 'aznaka |
| **and cause to shine** | **your face** | **upon** | **your sanctuary** | **that is desolate** | **for sake** | **Adonai's** | **incline** | **O my Elohim** | **your ear** |

| ושמע 8085 | פקחה 6491 | עיניך 5869 | וראה 7200 | שממתינו 8077 | והעיר 5892 | אשר 834 | נקרא 7121 | שמך 8034 | עליה 5921 | כי 3588 | לא 3808 | על 5921 |
|---|---|---|---|---|---|---|---|---|---|---|---|---|
| uashama' | piqchah | 'ayneyka, | uar'aeh | shomamoteynu, | uaha'ayr | 'asher | niqra' | shimka | 'aleyha; | kiy | la' | 'al |
| **and hear** | **open** | **your eyes** | **and behold** | **our desolations** | **and the city** | **which** | **is called** | **your name** | **by** | **for** | **not** | **for** |

| צדקתינו 6666 | אנחנו 587 | מפילים 5307 | תחנונינו 8469 | לפניך 6440 | כי 3588 | על 5921 | רחמיך 7356 | הרבים 7227: | 9:19 אדני 136 |
|---|---|---|---|---|---|---|---|---|---|
| tzidqoteynu, | 'anachnu | mapiyliym | tachanuneynu | lapaneyka, | kiy | 'al | rachameyka | harabiym. | 'adonay |
| **our righteousnesses** | **we** | **do present** | **our supplications** | **before you** | **but** | **for** | **your mercies** | **great** | **O Adonai** |

| שמעה 8085 | אדני 136 | סלחה 5545 | אדני 136 | הקשיבה 7181 | ועשה 6213 | אל 408 | תאחר 309 | למענך 4616 | אלהי 430 | כי 3588 | שמך 8034 |
|---|---|---|---|---|---|---|---|---|---|---|---|
| shama'ah | 'adonay | salachah, | 'adonay | haqashiybah | ua'aseh | 'al | ta'achar; | lama'anaka | 'alohay, | kiy | shimka |
| **hear** | **O Adonai** | **forgive** | **O Adonai** | **listen** | **and do** | **not** | **defer** | **for your own sake** | **O my Elohim** | **for** | **your name** |

| נקרא 7121 | על 5921 | עירך 5892 | ועל 5921 | עמך 5971: | 9:20 ועוד 5750 | אני 589 | מדבר 1696 | ומתפלל 6419 | ומתודה 3034 | חטאתי 2403 |
|---|---|---|---|---|---|---|---|---|---|---|
| niqra', | 'al | 'ayraka | ua'al | 'ameka. | ua'aud | 'aniy | madaber | uamitpalel, | uamituadeh | chata'tiy, |
| **are called** | **by** | **your city** | **and to** | **your people** | **And whiles** | **I** | ***was* speaking** | **and praying** | **and confessing** | **my sin** |

| וחטאת 2403 | עמי 5971 | ישראל 3478 | ומפיל 5307 | תחנתי 8467 | לפני 6440 | יהוה 3068 | אלהי 430 | על 5921 | הר 2022 | קדש 6944 |
|---|---|---|---|---|---|---|---|---|---|---|
| uachata't | 'amiy | yisra'ael; | uamapiyl | tachinatiy, | lipney | Yahuah | 'alohay, | 'al | har | qodesh |
| **and the sin of** | **my people** | **Israel** | **and presenting** | **my supplication** | **before** | **Yahuah** | **my Elohim** | **for** | **mountain *the*** | **holy of** |

| אלהי 430: | 9:21 ועוד 5750 | אני 589 | מדבר 1696 | בתפלה 8605 | והאיש 376 | גבריאל 1403 | אשר 834 | ראיתי 7200 | בחזון 2377 |
|---|---|---|---|---|---|---|---|---|---|
| 'alohay. | ua'aud | 'aniy | madaber | batapilah; | uaha'aysh | gabriy'ael | 'asher | ra'aytiy | bechazoun |
| **my Elohim** | **Yea whiles** | **I** | ***was* speaking** | **in prayer** | **even the man** | **Gabriel** | **whom** | **I had seen** | **in the vision** |

| בתחלה 8462 | מעף 3286 | ביעף 3288 | נגע 5060 | אלי 413 | כעת 6256 | מנחת 4503 | ערב 6153: | 9:22 ויבן 995 |
|---|---|---|---|---|---|---|---|---|
| batachilah | mu'ap | biy'ap, | nogea' | 'aelay, | ka'aet | minchat | 'areb. | uayaben |
| **at the beginning** | **being caused to fly** | **swiftly** | **touched me** | **about the time of** | **oblation *the*** | **evening** | | **And he informed** |

Dan 9:16 O Adonai, according to all your righteousness, I beseech you, let your anger and your fury be turned away from your city Jerusalem, your holy mountain: because for our sins, and for the iniquities of our fathers, Jerusalem and your people are become a reproach to all that are about us.17 Now therefore, O our G-d, hear the prayer of your servant, and his supplications, and cause your face to shine upon your sanctuary that is desolate, for the Adonai's sake.18 O my G-d, incline your ear, and hear; open your eyes, and behold our desolations, and the city which is called by your name: for we do not present our supplications before you for our righteousnesses, but for your great mercies.19 O Adonai, hear; O Adonai, forgive; O Adonai, hear and do; defer not, for your own sake, O my G-d: for your city and your people are called by your name.20 And whiles I was speaking, and praying, and confessing my sin and the sin of my people Israel, and presenting my supplication before YHUH my G-d for the holy mountain of my G-d;21 Yea, whiles I was speaking in prayer, even the man Gabriel, whom I had seen in the vision at the beginning, being caused to fly swiftly, touched me about the time of the evening oblation.22 And he informed me, and talked with me, and said, O Daniel, I am now come forth to give you skill and understanding.

| וידבר 1696 | עמי 5973 | ויאמר 559 | דניאל 1840 | עתה 6258 | יצאתי 3318 | להשכילך 7919 | בינה 998: | 9:23 |
|---|---|---|---|---|---|---|---|---|
| uaydaber | 'amiy; | uaya'mar | daniyea'l | 'atah | yatza'tiy | lahaskiylaka | biynah. | |
| ***me* and talked** | **with me** | **and said** | **O Daniel** | **now** | **I am come forth** | **to give you skill** | ***and* understanding** | |

| בתחלת 8462 | תחנוניך 8469 | יצא 3318 | דבר 1697 | ואני 589 | באתי 935 | להגיד 5046 | כי 3588 | חמודות 2532 |
|---|---|---|---|---|---|---|---|---|
| bitchilat | tachanuneyka | yatza' | dabar, | ua'aniy | ba'tiy | lahagiyd, | kiy | chamudout |
| **At the beginning of** | **your supplications** | **came forth** | **the commandment** | **and I** | **I *am* come** | **to show you** | **for *are*** | **greatly beloved** |

| אתה 859 | ובין 995 | בדבר 1697 | והבן 995 | במראה 4758: | 9:24 | שבעים 7620 | שבעים 7657 | נחתך 2852 | על 5921 | עמך 5971 |
|---|---|---|---|---|---|---|---|---|---|---|
| 'atah; | uabiyn | badabar, | uahaben | bamar'ah. | | shabu'aym | shib'aym | nechtak | 'al | 'ameka |
| **you** | **therefore understand** | **the matter** | **and consider** | **the vision** | | **weeks** | **Seventy** | **are determined** | **upon** | **your people** |

| ועל 5921 | עיר 5892 | קדשך 6944 | לכלא 3607 | הפשע 6588 | ולחתם 2856 | חטאות 2403 | ולכפר 3722 |
|---|---|---|---|---|---|---|---|
| ua'al | 'ayr | qadasheka | lakalea' | hapesha' | ualachtom | chata'ut | ualkaper |
| **and upon** | **city** | **your holy** | **to finish** | **the transgression** | **and to make an end of** | **sins** | **and to make reconciliation for** |

| עון 5771 | ולהביא 935 | צדק 6664 | עלמים 5769 | ולחתם 2856 | חזון 2377 | ונביא 5030 | ולמשח 4886 | קדש 6944 |
|---|---|---|---|---|---|---|---|---|
| 'auon, | ualhabiy'a | tzedeq | 'aulamiym; | ualachtom | chazoun | uanabiy'a, | ualimshoach | qodesh |
| **iniquity** | **and to bring in** | **righteousness** | **everlasting** | **and to seal up** | **the vision** | **and prophecy** | **and to anoint** | ***the* most** |

| קדשים 6944: | 9:25 | ותדע 3045 | ותשכל 7919 | מן 4480 | מצא 4161 | דבר 1697 | להשיב 7725 | ולבנות 1129 |
|---|---|---|---|---|---|---|---|---|
| qadashiym. | | uateda' | uataskel | min | moutza' | dabar, | lahashiyb | ualibnout |
| **Holy** | | **Know therefore** | **and understand *that*** | **from** | **the going forth of** | **the commandment** | **to restore** | **and to build** |

| ירושלם 3389 | עד 5704 | משיח 4899 | נגיד 5057 | שבעים 7620 | שבעה 7651 | ושבעים 7620 | ששים 8346 | ושנים 8147 | תשוב 7725 | ונבנתה 1129 |
|---|---|---|---|---|---|---|---|---|---|---|
| yarushalaim | 'ad | mashiyach | nagiyd, | shabu'aym | shib'ah; | uashabu'aym | shishiym | uashnayim, | tashub | uanibnatah |
| **Jerusalem** | **until** | **the Messiah** | **the Prince** | **weeks *shall be*** | **seven** | **and weeks** | **threescore** | **and two** | **again** | **shall be built** |

| רחוב 7339 | וחרוץ 2742 | ובצוק 6695 | העתים 6256: | 9:26 | ואחרי 310 | השבעים 7620 | ששים 8346 | ושנים 8147 | יכרת 3772 |
|---|---|---|---|---|---|---|---|---|---|
| rachoub | uacharutz, | uabtzouq | ha'atiym. | | ua'acharey | hashabu'aym | shishiym | uashnayim, | yikaret |
| **the street** | **and the wall** | **even in troublous** | **times** | | **And after** | **weeks** | **threescore** | **and two** | **shall be cut off** |

| משיח 4899 | ואין 369 | לו 3807a | והעיר 5892 | והקדש 6944 | ישחית 7843 | עם 5971 | נגיד 5057 | הבא 935 |
|---|---|---|---|---|---|---|---|---|
| mashiyach | ua'aeyn | lou'; | uaha'ayr | uahaqodesh | yashchiyt | 'am | nagiyd | haba' |
| **Messiah** | **but not** | **for himself** | **and the city** | **and the sanctuary** | **shall destroy** | **the people of** | **the prince** | **that shall come** |

| וקצו 7093 | בשטף 7858 | ועד 5704 | קץ 7093 | מלחמה 4421 | נחרצת 2782 | שממות 8074: | 9:27 |
|---|---|---|---|---|---|---|---|
| uaqitzou | bashetep, | ua'ad | qetz | milchamah, | necharetzet | shomemout. | |
| **and the end thereof** | ***shall be* with a flood** | **and unto** | **the end of** | **the war** | **are determined** | **desolations** | |

| והגביר 1396 | ברית 1285 | לרבים 7227 | שבוע 7620 | אחד 259 | וחצי 2677 | השבוע 7620 | ישבית 7673 |
|---|---|---|---|---|---|---|---|
| uahigbiyr | bariyt | larabiym | shabua' | 'achad; | uachatziy | hashabua' | yashbiyt |
| **And he shall confirm** | **the covenant** | **with many** | **week** | ***for* one** | **and in the midst of** | **the week** | **he shall cause to cease** |

| זבח 2077 | ומנחה 4503 | ועל 5921 | כנף 3671 | שקוצים 8251 | משמם 8074 | ועד 5704 |
|---|---|---|---|---|---|---|
| zebach | uaminchah, | ua'al | kanap | shiqutziym | mashomem, | ua'ad |
| **the sacrifice** | **and the oblation** | **and for** | **the overspreading of** | **abominations** | **he shall make *it* desolate** | **even until** |

Dan 9:23 At the beginning of your supplications the commandment came forth, and I am come to show you; for you are greatly beloved: therefore understand the matter, and consider the vision.24 Seventy weeks are determined upon your people and upon your holy city, to finish the transgression, and to make an end of sins, and to make reconciliation for iniquity, and to bring in everlasting righteousness, and to seal up the vision and prophecy, and to anoint the most Holy.25 Know therefore and understand, that from the going forth of the commandment to restore and to build Jerusalem unto the Messiah the Prince shall be seven weeks, and threescore and two weeks: the street shall be built again, and the wall, even in troublous times.26 And after threescore and two weeks shall Messiah be cut off, but not for himself: and the people of the prince that shall come shall destroy the city and the sanctuary; and the end thereof shall be with a flood, and unto the end of the war desolations are determined.27 And he shall confirm the covenant with many for one week: and in the midst of the week he shall cause the sacrifice and the oblation to cease, and for the overspreading of abominations he shall make it desolate, even until the consummation, and that determined shall be poured upon the desolate.

כלה 3617 ונחרצה 2782 תתך 5413 על 5921 שמם 8074:
kalah uanecharatzah, titak 'al shomem.
**the consummation and that determined shall be poured upon the desolate**

**Dan 10:1**
בשנת 8141 שלוש 7969 לכורש 3566 מלך 4428 פרס 6539 דבר 1697 נגלה 1540 לדניאל 1840 אשר 834 נקרא 7121 שמו 8034
bishnat shaloush, lakouresh melek paras, dabar niglah ladaniyea'l, 'asher niqra' shamou
**In year *the* third of Cyrus king of Persia a thing was revealed unto Daniel whose was called name**

בלטשאצר 1095 ואמת 571 הדבר 1697 וצבא 6635 גדול 1419 ובין 995 את 853 הדבר 1697
beltasha'tzar; ua'amet hadabar uatzaba' gadoul, uabiyn 'at hadabar,
**Belteshazzar *was* true the thing *was* but the time appointed *was* long and he understood the thing**

ובינה 998 לו 3807a במראה 4758: **10:2** בימים 3117 ההם 1992 אני 589 דניאל 1840 הייתי 1961 מתאבל 56 שלשה 7969 שבעים 7620
uabiynah lou' bamar'ah. bayamiym hahem; 'aniy daniyea'l hayiytiy mit'abel, shaloshah shabu'aym
**and understanding had of the vision In days those I Daniel was mourning three weeks**

ימים 3117: **10:3** לחם 3899 חמדות 2532 לא 3808 אכלתי 398 ובשר 1320 ויין 3196 לא 3808 בא 935 אל 413 פי 6310 וסוך 5480 לא 3808
yamiym. lechem chamudout la' 'akaltiy, uabasar uayayin la' ba' 'al piy uasouk la'
**full bread pleasant no I ate flesh nor wine neither came in my mouth did I anoint neither**

סכתי 5480 עד 5704 מלאת 4390 שלשת 7969 שבעים 7620 ימים 3117: **10:4** וביום 3117 עשרים 6242 וארבעה 702 לחדש 2320 הראשון 7223
sakatiy; 'ad mal'at shaloshet shabu'aym yamiym. uabyoum 'asriym ua'arbah lachodesh hara'shoun;
**myself at all till were fulfilled three weeks whole And in the day twentieth and four of month the first**

ואני 589 הייתי 1961 על 5921 יד 3027 הנהר 5104 הגדול 1419 הוא 1931 חדקל 2313: **10:5** ואשא 5375 את 853 עיני 5869 וארא 7200
ua'aniy, hayiytiy 'al yad hanahar hagadoul hua' chidaqel. ua'asa' 'at 'aeynay ua'aera',
**as I was by the side of river the great which *is* Hiddekel Then I lifted up mine eyes and looked**

והנה 2009 איש 376 אחד 259 לבוש 3847 בדים 906 ומתניו 4975 חגרים 2296 בכתם 3800 אופז 210: **10:6** וגויתו 1472
uahineh 'aysh 'achad labush badiym; uamatanayu chaguriym baketem 'uapaz. uaguiyatou
**and behold a man certain clothed in linen whose loins *were* girded with fine gold of Uphaz His body also *was***

כתרשיש 8658 ופניו 6440 כמראה 4758 ברק 1300 ועיניו 5869 כלפידי 3940 אש 784 וזרעתיו 2220 ומרגלתיו 4772
katarshiysh, uapanayu kamar'aeh baraq ua'aeynayu kalapiydey 'aesh, uazro'atayu uamargalotayu,
**like the beryl and his face as the appearance of lightning and his eyes as lamps of fire and his arms and his feet**

כעין 5869 נחשת 5178 קלל 7044 וקול 6963 דבריו 1697 כקול 6963 המון 1995: **10:7** וראיתי 7200 אני 589 דניאל 1840
ka'aeyn nachoshet qalal; uaqoul dabarayu kaqoul hamoun. uara'aytiy 'aniy daniyea'l
**like in colour to brass polished and the voice of his words like the voice of a multitude And saw I Daniel**

לבדי 905 את 853 המראה 4759 והאנשים 582 אשר 834 היו 1961 עמי 5973 לא 3808 ראו 7200 את 853 המראה 4759 אבל 61 חרדה 2731 גדלה 1419 נפלה 5307
labadiy 'at hamar'ah, uaha'anashiym 'asher hayu 'amiy, la' ra'au 'at hamar'ah; 'abal, charadah gadolah naplah
**alone the vision for the men that were with me not saw the vision but a quaking great fell**

עליהם 5921 ויברחו 1272 בהחבא 2244: **10:8** ואני 589 נשארתי 7604 לבדי 905 ואראה 7200 את 853 המראה 4759
'aleyhem, uayibrachu bahechabea'. ua'aniy nish'artiy labadiy, ua'ar'ah, 'at hamar'ah
**upon them so that they fled to hide themselves Therefore I I was left alone and saw vision**

**Dan** 10:1 In the third year of Cyrus king of Persia a thing was revealed unto Daniel, whose name was called Belteshazzar; and the thing was true, but the time appointed was long: and he understood the thing, and had understanding of the vision.2 In those days I Daniel was mourning three full weeks.3 I ate no pleasant bread, neither came flesh nor wine in my mouth, neither did I anoint myself at all, till three whole weeks were fulfilled.4 And in the four and twentieth day of the first month, as I was by the side of the great river, which is Hiddekel;5 Then I lifted up mine eyes, and looked, and behold a certain man clothed in linen, whose loins were girded with fine gold of Uphaz:6 His body also was like the beryl, and his face as the appearance of lightning, and his eyes as lamps of fire, and his arms and his feet like in colour to polished brass, and the voice of his words like the voice of a multitude.7 And I Daniel alone saw the vision: for the men that were with me saw not the vision; but a great quaking fell upon them, so that they fled to hide themselves.8 Therefore I was left alone, and saw this great vision, and there remained no strength in me: for my comeliness was turned in me into corruption, and I retained no strength.

הגדלה 1419 הזאת 2063 ולא 3808 נשאר 7604 בי 871a כח 3581 והודי 1935 נהפך 2015 עלי 5921 למשחית 4889 ולא 3808
hagadolah haza't, uala' nish'ar biy koch; uahoudiy, nehapak 'alay lamashchiyt, uala'
**great this and no there remained in me strength for my comeliness was turned in me into corruption and no**

10:9
עצרתי 6113 כח 3581: ואשמע 8085 את 853 קול 6963 דבריו 1697 וכשמעי 8085 את 853 קול 6963 דבריו 1697 ואני 589
'atzartiy koach. ua'ashma' 'at qoul dabarayu; uakshama'ay 'at qoul dabarayu, ua'aniy,
**I retained strength Yet heard I the voice of his words and when I heard the voice of his words then I**

10:10
הייתי 1961 נרדם 7290 על 5921 פני 6440 ופני 6440 ארצה 776: והנה 2009 יד 3027 נגעה 5060 בי 871a
hayiytiy nirdam 'al panay uapanay 'aratzah. uahineh yad naga'ah biy;
**was in a deep sleep on my face and my face toward the ground And behold an hand touched me**

10:11
ותניעני 5128 על 5921 ברכי 1290 וכפות 3709 ידי 3027: ויאמר 559 אלי 413 דניאל 1840 איש 376 חמדות 2532
uataniy'aeniy 'al birkay uakapout yaday. uaya'mer 'aelay daniyea'l 'aysh chamudout
**which set me upon my knees and *upon* the palms of my hands And he said unto me O Daniel a man greatly beloved**

הבן 995 בדברים 1697 אשר 834 אנכי 595 דבר 1696 אליך 413 ועמד 5975 על 5921 עמדך 5975 כי 3588 עתה 6258 שלחתי 7971 אליך 413
haben badabariym 'asher 'anokiy dober 'aeleyka ua'amod 'al 'amadeka, kiy 'atah shulachtiy 'aeleyka;
**understand the words that I speak unto you and stand you up right for now am I sent unto you**

10:12
ובדברו 1696 עמי 5973 את 853 הדבר 1697 הזה 2088 עמדתי 5975 מרעיד 7460: ויאמר 559 אלי 413 אל 408 תירא 3372
uabdabrou 'amiy 'at hadabar hazeh 'amadtiy mar'ayd. uaya'mer 'aelay 'al tiyraa'
**And when he had spoken unto me word this and stood trembling Then said he unto me not Fear**

דניאל 1840 כי 3588 מן 4480 היום 3117 הראשון 7223 אשר 834 נתת 5414 את 853 לבך 3820 להבין 995 ולהתענות 6031 לפני 6440
daniyea'l kiy min hayoum hara'shoun, 'asher natata 'at libaka lahabiyn ualhit'anout lipney
**Daniel for from day the first that you did set your heart to understand and to chasten yourself before**

10:13
אלהיך 430 נשמעו 8085 דבריך 1697 ואני 589 באתי 935 בדבריך 1697: ושר 8269 מלכות 4438 פרס 6539
'aloheyka nishma'au dabareyka; ua'aniy ba'tiy bidbareyka. uasar malkut paras,
**your Elohim were heard your words and I I am come for your words But the prince of the kingdom of Persia**

עמד 5975 לנגדי 5048 עשרים 6242 ואחד 259 יום 3117 והנה 2009 מיכאל 4317 אחד 259 השרים 8269 הראשנים 7223 בא 935 לעזרני 5826 ואני 589
'amed lanegdiy 'asriym ua'achad youm, uahineh miyka'ael, 'achad hasariym hara'shoniym ba' la'azareniy; ua'aniy
**withstood against me twenty and one days but lo Michael one *of* princes the chief came to help me and I**

10:14
נותרתי 3498 שם 8033 אצל 681 מלכי 4428 פרס 6539: ובאתי 935 להבינך 995 את 853 אשר 834 יקרה 7136
noutartiy' sham, 'aetzel malkey paras. uaba'tiy lahabiynaka, 'at 'asher yiqrah
**remained there with the kings of Persia Now I am come to make you understand what shall befall**

10:15
לעמך 5971 באחרית 319 הימים 3117 כי 3588 עוד 5750 חזון 2377 לימים 3117: ובדברו 1696 עמי 5973
la'amaka ba'achariyt hayamiym; kiy 'aud chazoun layamiym. uabdabrou 'amiy,
**your people in latter the days for yet the vision *is* for *many* days And when he had spoken unto me**

10:16
כדברים 1697 האלה 428 נתתי 5414 פני 6440 ארצה 776 ונאלמתי 481: והנה 2009 כדמות 1823
kadabariym ha'aeleh; natatiy panay 'artzah uane'alamatiy. uahineh, kidmut
**words such I set my face toward the ground and I became dumb And behold *one* like the similitude of**

Dan 10:9 Yet heard I the voice of his words: and when I heard the voice of his words, then was I in a deep sleep on my face, and my face toward the ground.10 And, behold, an hand touched me, which set me upon my knees and upon the palms of my hands.11 And he said unto me, O Daniel, a man greatly beloved, understand the words that I speak unto you, and stand upright: for unto you am I now sent. And when he had spoken this word unto me, I stood trembling.12 Then said he unto me, Fear not, Daniel: for from the first day that you did set your heart to understand, and to chasten thyself before your G-d, your words were heard, and I am come for your words.13 But the prince of the kingdom of Persia withstood me one and twenty days: but, lo, Michael, one of the chief princes, came to help me; and I remained there with the kings of Persia.14 Now I am come to make you understand what shall befall your people in the latter days: for yet the vision is for many days.15 And when he had spoken such words unto me, I set my face toward the ground, and I became dumb.16 And, behold, one like the similitude of the sons of men touched my lips: then I opened my mouth, and spoke, and said unto him that stood before me, O my lord, by the vision my sorrows are turned upon me, and I have retained no strength.

בני 1121 אדם 120 נגע 5060 על 5921 שפתי 8193 ואפתח 6605 פי 6310 ואדברה 1696 ואמרה 559 אל 413 העמד 5975 לנגדי 5048
baney 'adam, nogea' 'al sapatay; ua'aptach piy, ua'adabarah ua'amrah 'al ha'aumed lanegdiy,
**the sons of men touched on my lips then I opened my mouth and spoke and said unto him that stood before me**

אדני 113 במראה 4759 נהפכו 2015 צירי 6735 עלי 5921 ולא 3808 עצרתי 6113 כח 3581: 10:17 והיך 1963 יוכל 3201
'adoniy, bamar'ah nehepku tziyray 'alay, uala' 'atzartiy koach. uaheyk yukal,
**O my adonai by the vision are turned my sorrows upon me and no I have retained strength For how can**

עבד 5650 אדני 113 זה 2088 לדבר 1696 עם 5973 אדני 113 זה 2088 ואני 589 מעתה 6258 לא 3808 יעמד 5975 בי 871a
'abed 'adoniy zeh, ladaber 'am 'adoniy zeh; ua'aniy me'atah la' ya'amad biy
**the servant of my adonai this talk with my adonai? this for as for me straightway no there remained in me**

כח 3581 ונשמה 5397 לא 3808 נשארה 7604 בי 871a: 10:18 ויסף 3254 ויגע 5060 בי 871a כמראה 4758
koach, uanshamah la' nish'arah biy. uayosep uayiga' biy kamar'aeh
**strength breath neither is there left in me Then there came again and touched me *one* like the appearance of**

אדם 120 ויחזקני 2388: 10:19 ויאמר 559 אל 408 תירא 3372 איש 376 חמדות 2532 שלום 7965 לך 3807a חזק 2388
'adam uayachazqeniy. uaya'mer 'al tiyraa' 'aysh chamudout shaloum lak chazaq
**a man and he strengthened me And said not fear O man greatly beloved peace *be* unto you be strong**

וחזק 2388 ובדברו 1696 עמי 5973 התחזקתי 2388 ואמרה 559 ידבר 1696 אדני 113 כי 3588
uachazaq; uakdabrou 'amiy hitchazaqtiy, ua'amarah yadaber 'adoniy kiy
**yea be strong And when he had spoken unto me I was strengthened and said Let speak my adonai for**

חזקתני 2388: 10:20 ויאמר 559 הידעת 3045 למה 4100 באתי 935 אליך 413 ועתה 6258 אשוב 7725 להלחם 3898
chizqtaniy. uaya'mer, hayada'ata lamah ba'tiy 'aeleyka, ua'atah 'ashub, lahilachem
**you have strengthened me Then said he Know you wherefore I come unto you? and now will I return to fight**

עם 5973 שר 8269 פרס 6539 ואני 589 יוצא 3318 והנה 2009 שר 8269 יון 3120 בא 935: 10:21 אבל 61 אגיד 5046
'am sar paras; ua'aniy youtzea', uahineh sar yauan ba'. 'abal 'agiyd
**with the prince of Persia and when I am gone forth and lo the prince of Grecia shall come But I will show**

לך 3807a את 853 הרשום 7559 בכתב 3791 אמת 571 ואין 369 אחד 259 מתחזק 2388 עמי 5973 על 5921 אלה 428 כי 3588
laka, 'at harashum biktab 'amet; ua'aeyn 'achad mitchazeq 'amiy 'al 'aeleh, kiy
**to you that which is noted in the scripture of truth and *there is* none that holds with me in these things for**

אם 518 מיכאל 4317 שרכם 8269:
'am miyka'ael sarkem.
**but Michael your prince**

**Dan 11:1** ואני 589 בשנת 8141 אחת 259 לדריוש 1867 המדי 4075 עמדי 5975 למחזיק 2388 ולמעוז 4581 לו 3807a: **11:2**
ua'aniy bishnat 'achat, ladarayauesh hamadiy; 'amadiy lamachaziyq ualma'auz lou'.
**Also I in year *the* first of Darius the Mede, *even I* stood to confirm and to strengthen him**

ועתה 6258 אמת 571 אגיד 5046 לך 3807a הנה 2009 עוד 5750 שלשה 7969 מלכים 4428 עמדים 5975 לפרס 6539 והרביעי 7243
ua'atah 'amet 'agiyd lak; hineh 'aud shaloshah malakiym 'amdiym laparas, uaharabiy'ay
**And now *the* truth will I show to you Behold yet three kings there shall stand up in Persia and the fourth**

Dan 10:17 For how can the servant of this my lord talk with this my lord? for as for me, straightway there remained no strength in me, neither is there breath left in me.18 Then there came again and touched me one like the appearance of a man, and he strengthened me,19 And said, O man greatly beloved, fear not: peace be unto you, be strong, yea, be strong. And when he had spoken unto me, I was strengthened, and said, Let my lord speak; for you have strengthened me.20 Then said he, Know you wherefore I come unto you? and now will I return to fight with the prince of Persia: and when I am gone forth, lo, the prince of Grecia shall come.21 But I will show you that which is noted in the scripture of truth: and there is none that holdeth with me in these things, but Michael your prince. **Dan** 11:1 Also I in the first year of Darius the Mede, even I, stood to confirm and to strengthen him.2 And now will I show you the truth. Behold, there shall stand up yet three kings in Persia; and the fourth shall be far richer than they all: and by his strength through his riches he shall stir up all against the realm of Grecia.

| יעשיר 6238 | עשר 6239 | גדול 1419 | מכל 3605 | ובחזקתו 2393 | בעשרו 6239 | יעיר 5782 | הכל 3605 |
|---|---|---|---|---|---|---|---|
| ya'ashiyr | 'asher | gadoul | mikol, | uakchezqatou | ba'asharou, | ya'ayr | hakol, |
| **shall be richer** | **through his riches** | **far** | **than *they* all** | **and by his strength** | **through his riches** | **he shall stir up** | **all *against*** |

| את 853 | מלכות 4438 | יון 3120: | 11:3 | ועמד 5975 | מלך 4428 | גבור 1368 | ומשל 4910 | ממשל 4474 | רב 7227 | ועשה 6213 |
|---|---|---|---|---|---|---|---|---|---|---|
| 'at | malkut | yauan. | | ua'amad | melek | gibour; | uamashal | mimshal | rab, | ua'asah |
| | **the realm of** | **Grecia** | | **And shall stand up** | **a king** | **mighty** | **that shall rule** | **dominion** | ***with* great** | **and do** |

| כרצונו 7522: | 11:4 | וכעמדו 5975 | תשבר 7665 | מלכותו 4438 | ותחץ 2673 | לארבע 702 |
|---|---|---|---|---|---|---|
| kirtzounou. | | uak'amadou | tishaber | malkutou, | uatechatz | la'arba' |
| **according to his will** | | **And when he shall stand up** | **shall be broken** | **his kingdom** | **and shall be divided** | **toward the four** |

| רוחות 7307 | השמים 8064 | ולא 3808 | לאחריתו 319 | ולא 3808 | כמשלו 4915 | אשר 834 | משל 4910 | כי 3588 | תנתש 5428 |
|---|---|---|---|---|---|---|---|---|---|
| ruchout | hashamayim; | uala' | la'achariytou, | uala' | kamashalou | 'asher | mashal, | kiy | tinatesh |
| **winds of** | **heaven** | **and not** | **to his posterity** | **nor** | **according to his dominion** | **which** | **he ruled** | **for** | **shall be plucked up** |

| מלכותו 4438 | ולאחרים 312 | מלבד 905 | אלה 428: | 11:5 | ויחזק 2388 | מלך 4428 | הנגב 5045 | ומן 4480 | שריו 8269 |
|---|---|---|---|---|---|---|---|---|---|
| malkutou, | uala'achriym | milabad | 'aeleh. | | uayechazaq | melek | hanegeb | uamin | sarayu; |
| **his kingdom** | **even for others** | **beside** | **those** | | **And shall be strong** | **the king of** | **the south** | **and *one* of** | **his princes** |

| ויחזק 2388 | עליו 5921 | ומשל 4910 | ממשל 4474 | רב 7227 | ממשלתו 4475: | 11:6 | ולקץ 7093 |
|---|---|---|---|---|---|---|---|
| uayechazaq | 'alayu | uamashal, | mimshal | rab | memshaltou. | | ualqetz |
| **and he shall be strong** | **above him** | **and have dominion** | **his dominion** | **great *shall be*** | **a dominion** | | **And in the end of** |

| שנים 8141 | יתחברו 2266 | ובת 1323 | מלך 4428 | הנגב 5045 | תבוא 935 | אל 413 | מלך 4428 | הצפון 6828 |
|---|---|---|---|---|---|---|---|---|
| shaniym | yitchabaru, | uaba'at | melek | hanegeb, | tabou'a | 'al | melek | hatzapoun, |
| **years** | **they shall join themselves together** | **for daughter** | ***the* king's of** | **the south** | **shall come** | **to** | **the king of** | **the north** |

| לעשות 6213 | מישרים 4339 | ולא 3808 | תעצר 6113 | כוח 3581 | הזרוע 2220 | ולא 3808 | יעמד 5975 | וזרעו 2220 |
|---|---|---|---|---|---|---|---|---|
| la'asout | meyshariym; | uala' | ta'tzor | koach | hazaroa', | uala' | ya'amod | uazro'au, |
| **to make** | **an agreement** | **but not** | **she shall retain** | **the power of** | **the arm** | **neither** | **shall he stand** | **nor his arm** |

| ותנתן 5414 | היא 1931 | ומביאיה 935 | והילדה 3205 | ומחזקה 2388 |
|---|---|---|---|---|
| uatinaten | hiy'a | uambiy'ayha | uahayoladah, | uamachaziqah |
| **but she shall be given up** | **she** | **and they that brought her** | **and he that begat her** | **and he that strengthened her** |

| בעתים 6256: | 11:7 | ועמד 5975 | מנצר 5342 | שרשיה 8328 | כנו 3653 | ויבא 935 | אל 413 | החיל 2428 |
|---|---|---|---|---|---|---|---|---|
| ba'atiym. | | ua'amad | minetzer | sharasheyha | kanou; | uayaba' | 'al | hachayil, |
| **in *these* times** | | **But shall *one* stand up** | **out of a branch of** | **her roots** | ***in* his estate** | **which shall come** | **with** | **an army** |

| ויבא 935 | במעוז 4581 | מלך 4428 | הצפון 6828 | ועשה 6213 | בהם 871a | והחזיק 2388: | 11:8 | וגם 1571 |
|---|---|---|---|---|---|---|---|---|
| uayaba' | bama'auz | melek | hatzapoun, | ua'asah | bahem | uahechaziyq. | | ua'gam |
| **and shall enter** | **into the fortress of** | **the king of** | **the north** | **and shall deal** | **against them** | **and shall prevail** | | **And also** |

| אלהיהם 430 | עם 5973 | נסכיהם 5257 | עם 5973 | כלי 3627 | חמדתם 2532 | כסף 3701 | וזהב 2091 | בשבי 7628 | יבא 935 | מצרים 4714 | והוא 1931 |
|---|---|---|---|---|---|---|---|---|---|---|---|
| 'aloheyhem | 'am | nasikeyhem | 'am | kaley | chemdatam | kesep | uazahab | bashabiy | yaba' | mitzrayim; | uahu'a |
| **their gods** | **with** | **their princes *and*** | **with** | **vessels of** | **their precious** | **silver** | **and of gold** | **captives** | **shall carry *into*** | **Egypt** | **and he** |

Dan 11:3 And a mighty king shall stand up, that shall rule with great dominion, and do according to his will.4 And when he shall stand up, his kingdom shall be broken, and shall be divided toward the four winds of heaven; and not to his posterity, nor according to his dominion which he ruled: for his kingdom shall be plucked up, even for others beside those.5 And the king of the south shall be strong, and one of his princes; and he shall be strong above him, and have dominion; his dominion shall be a great dominion.6 And in the end of years they shall join themselves together; for the king's daughter of the south shall come to the king of the north to make an agreement: but she shall not retain the power of the arm; neither shall he stand, nor his arm: but she shall be given up, and they that brought her, and he that begat her, and he that strengthened her in these times.7 But out of a branch of her roots shall one stand up in his estate, which shall come with an army, and shall enter into the fortress of the king of the north, and shall deal against them, and shall prevail:8 And shall also carry captives into Egypt their gods, with their princes, and with their precious vessels of silver and of gold; and he shall continue more years than the king of the north.

| שנים 8141 | יעמד 5975 | ממלך 4428 | הצפון 6828: | 11:9 ובא 935 | במלכות 4438 | מלך 4428 | הנגב 5045 |
|---|---|---|---|---|---|---|---|
| shaniym | ya'amod, | mimelek | hatzapoun | uaba', | bamalkut | melek | hanegeb, |
| ***more* years** | **shall continue** | **than the king of** | **the north** | **So shall come** | **into *his* kingdom** | **the king of** | **the south** |

| ושב 7725 | אל 413 | אדמתו 127: | 11:10 ובנו 1121 | יתגרו 1624 | ואספו 622 | המון 1995 | חילים 2428 |
|---|---|---|---|---|---|---|---|
| uashab | 'al | 'admatou. | uabnou | yitgaru, | ua'asapu | hamoun | chayaliym |
| **and shall return** | **into** | **his own land** | **But his sons** | **shall be stirred up** | **and shall assemble** | **a multitude of** | **forces** |

| רבים 7227 | ובא 935 | בוא 935 | ושטף 7857 | ועבר 5674 | וישב 7725 | ויתגרו 1624 | עד 5704 |
|---|---|---|---|---|---|---|---|
| rabiym, | uaba' | bou' | uashatap | ua'abar; | uayashob | uayitgaru | 'ad |
| **great** | **and *one* shall certainly** | **come** | **and overflow** | **and pass through** | **then shall he return** | **and be stirred up *even*** | **to** |

| מעזה 4581: | 11:11 ויתמרמר 4843 | מלך 4428 | הנגב 5045 | ויצא 3318 | ונלחם 3898 | עמו 5973 | עם 5973 |
|---|---|---|---|---|---|---|---|
| ma'azu. | uayitmarmar | melek | hanegeb, | uayatza' | uanilcham | 'amou | 'am |
| **his fortress** | **And shall be moved with choler** | **the king of** | **the south** | **and shall come forth** | **and fight** | **with him** | ***even* with** |

| מלך 4428 | הצפון 6828 | והעמיד 5975 | המון 1995 | רב 7227 | ונתן 5414 | ההמון 1995 | בידו 3027: | 11:12 |
|---|---|---|---|---|---|---|---|---|
| melek | hatzapoun; | uahe'amiyd | hamoun | rab, | uanitan | hehamoun | bayadou. | |
| **the king of** | **the north** | **and he shall set forth** | **a multitude** | **great** | **but shall be given** | **the multitude** | **into his hand** | |

| ונשא 5375 | ההמון 1995 | ירום 7311 | לבבו 3824 | והפיל 5307 | רבאות 7239 |
|---|---|---|---|---|---|
| uanisa' | hehamoun | yarum | lababou; | uahipiyl | ribo'aut |
| ***And* when he has taken away** | **the multitude** | **shall be lifted up** | **his heart** | **and he shall cast down** | ***many* ten thousands** |

| ולא 3808 | יעוז 5810: | 11:13 ושב 7725 | מלך 4428 | הצפון 6828 | והעמיד 5975 | המון 1995 | רב 7227 |
|---|---|---|---|---|---|---|---|
| uala' | ya'auz. | uashab | melek | hatzapoun, | uahe'amiyd | hamoun, | rab |
| ***by it.* but not** | **he shall be strengthened** | **For shall return** | **the king of** | **the north** | **and shall set forth** | **a multitude** | **greater** |

| מן 4480 | הראשון 7223 | ולקץ 7093 | העתים 6256 | שנים 8141 | יבוא 935 | בוא 935 | בחיל 2428 | גדול 1419 | וברכוש 7399 | רב 7227: | 11:14 |
|---|---|---|---|---|---|---|---|---|---|---|---|
| min | hara'shoun; | ualqetz | ha'atiym | shaniym | yabou'a | bou', | bachayil | gadoul | uabirkush | rab. | |
| **than** | **the former** | **and after** | **certain** | **years** | **shall certainly** | **come** | **with a army** | **great** | **and with riches** | **much** | |

| ובעתים 6256 | ההם 1992 | רבים 7227 | יעמדו 5975 | על 5921 | מלך 4428 | הנגב 5045 | ובני 1121 | פריצי 6530 | עמך 5971 |
|---|---|---|---|---|---|---|---|---|---|
| uaba'atiym | hahem, | rabiym | ya'amdu | 'al | melek | hanegeb; | uabaniy | pariytzey | 'ameka, |
| **And in times** | **those** | **many** | **there shall stand up** | **against** | **the king of** | **the south** | **and also** | **the robbers of** | **your people** |

| ינשאו 5375 | להעמיד 5975 | חזון 2377 | ונכשלו 3782: | 11:15 ויבא 935 | מלך 4428 | הצפון 6828 | וישפך 8210 |
|---|---|---|---|---|---|---|---|
| yinas'au | laha'amiyd | chazoun | uanikshalu. | uayaba' | melek | hatzapoun, | uayishpok |
| **shall exalt themselves** | **to establish** | **the vision** | **but they shall fall** | **So shall come** | **the king of** | **the north** | **and cast up** |

| סוללה 5550 | ולכד 3920 | עיר 5892 | מבצרות 4013 | וזרעות 2220 | הנגב 5045 | לא 3808 | יעמדו 5975 | ועם 5971 | מבחריו 4005 |
|---|---|---|---|---|---|---|---|---|---|
| soulalah, | ualakad | 'ayr | mibatzarout; | uazro'aut | hanegeb | la' | ya'amodu, | ua'am | mibcharayu, |
| **a mount** | **and take** | **cities** | ***the* most fenced** | **and the arms of** | **the south** | **not** | **shall withstand** | **people** | ***neither* his chosen** |

| ואין 369 | כח 3581 | לעמד 5975: | 11:16 ויעש 6213 | הבא 935 | אליו 413 | כרצונו 7522 |
|---|---|---|---|---|---|---|
| ua'aeyn | koach | la'amod. | uaya'as | haba' | 'aelayu | kirtzounou, |
| **neither *shall there be any*** | **strength** | **to withstand** | **But shall do** | **he that comes** | **against him** | **according to his own will** |

Dan 11:9 So the king of the south shall come into his kingdom, and shall return into his own land.10 But his sons shall be stirred up, and shall assemble a multitude of great forces: and one shall certainly come, and overflow, and pass through: then shall he return, and be stirred up, even to his fortress.11 And the king of the south shall be moved with choler, and shall come forth and fight with him, even with the king of the north: and he shall set forth a great multitude; but the multitude shall be given into his hand.12 And when he has taken away the multitude, his heart shall be lifted up; and he shall cast down many ten thousands: but he shall not be strengthened by it.13 For the king of the north shall return, and shall set forth a multitude greater than the former, and shall certainly come after certain years with a great army and with much riches.14 And in those times there shall many stand up against the king of the south: also the robbers of your people shall exalt themselves to establish the vision; but they shall fall.15 So the king of the north shall come, and cast up a mount, and take the most fenced cities: and the arms of the south shall not withstand, neither his chosen people, neither shall there be any strength to withstand.16 But he that cometh against him shall do according to his own will, and none shall stand before him:

| ואין 369 | עומד 5975 | לפניו 6440 | ויעמד 5975 | בארץ 776 | הצבי 6643 | וכלה 3615 | בידו 3027: | 11:17 |
|---|---|---|---|---|---|---|---|---|
| ua'aeyn | aumed | lapanayu; | uaya'amod | ba'aretz | hatzabiy | uakalah | bayadou. | |
| **and none** | **shall stand** | **before him** | **and he shall stand** | **in land** | **the glorious** | **which shall be consumed** | **by his hand** | |

| וישם 7760 | פניו 6440 | לבוא 935 | בתקף 8633 | כל 3605 | מלכותו 4438 | וישרים 3477 | עמו 5973 | ועשה 6213 |
|---|---|---|---|---|---|---|---|---|
| uayasem | panayu | labou'a | batoqep | kal | malkutou | uiyshariym | 'amou | ua'asah; |
| **He shall also set** | **his face** | **to enter** | **with the strength of** | **whole** | **his kingdom** | **and upright ones** | **with him** | **thus shall he do** |

| ובת 1323 | הנשים 802 | יתן 5414 | לו 3807a | להשחיתה 7843 | ולא 3808 | תעמד 5975 | ולא 3808 | לו 3807a |
|---|---|---|---|---|---|---|---|---|
| uaba'at | hanashiym | yiten | lou' | lahashchiytah, | uala' | ta'amod | uala' | lou' |
| **and daughter of** | **the women** | **he shall give** | **him** | **corrupting her** | **but not** | **she shall stand *on his side*** | **not neither** | **for him** |

| תהיה 1961: | 11:18 | וישב 7725 | פניו 6440 | לאיים 339 | ולכד 3920 | רבים 7227 | והשבית 7673 | קצין 7101 |
|---|---|---|---|---|---|---|---|---|
| tihayeh. | | uayasheb | panayu | la'ayiym | ualakad | rabiym; | uahishbiyt | qatziyn |
| **be** | | **After this shall he turn** | **his face** | **unto the isles** | **and shall take** | **many** | **but shall cause to cease** | **a prince** |

| חרפתו 2781 | לו 3807a | בלתי 1115 | חרפתו 2781 | ישיב 7725 | לו 3807a: | 11:19 |
|---|---|---|---|---|---|---|
| cherpatou | lou', | biltiy | cherpatou | yashiyb | lou'. | |
| **the reproach *offered by him*** | **for his own behalf** | **without** | **his own reproach** | **he shall cause *it* to turn** | **upon him** | |

| וישב 7725 | פניו 6440 | למעוזי 4581 | ארצו 776 | ונכשל 3782 | ונפל 5307 | ולא 3808 | ימצא 4672: | 11:20 |
|---|---|---|---|---|---|---|---|---|
| uayasheb | panayu, | lama'auzey | artzou; | uanikshal | uanapal | uala' | yimatzea'. | |
| **Then he shall turn** | **his face** | **toward the fort of** | **his own land** | **but he shall stumble** | **and fall** | **and not** | **be found** | |

| ועמד 5975 | על 5921 | כנו 3653 | מעביר 5674 | נוגש 5065 | הדר 1925 | מלכות 4438 | ובימים 3117 | אחדים 259 |
|---|---|---|---|---|---|---|---|---|
| ua'amad | 'al | kanou | ma'abiyr | nouges | heder | malkut; | uabyamiym | 'achadiym |
| **Then shall stand up** | **in** | **his estate** | **a raiser of** | **taxes** | ***in* the glory of** | **the kingdom** | **but within days** | **few** |

| ישבר 7665 | ולא 3808 | באפים 639 | ולא 3808 | במלחמה 4421: | 11:21 | ועמד 5975 | על 5921 | כנו 3653 | נבזה 959 | ולא 3808 |
|---|---|---|---|---|---|---|---|---|---|---|
| yishaber, | uala' | ba'apayim | uala' | bamilchamah. | | ua'amad | 'al | kanou | nibzeh, | uala' |
| **he shall be destroyed** | **neither** | **in anger** | **nor** | **in battle** | | **And shall stand up** | **in** | **his estate** | **a vile person** | **not** |

| נתנו 5414 | עליו 5921 | הוד 1935 | מלכות 4438 | ובא 935 | בשלוה 7962 | והחזיק 2388 | מלכות 4438 |
|---|---|---|---|---|---|---|---|
| natanu | 'alayu | houd | malkut; | uaba' | bashaluah, | uahecheziyq | malkut |
| **they shall give** | **to whom** | **the honor of** | **the kingdom** | **but he shall come in** | **peaceably** | **and obtain** | **the kingdom** |

| בחלקלקות 2519: | 11:22 | וזרעות 2220 | השטף 7858 | ישטפו 7857 | מלפניו 6440 | וישברו 7665 | וגם 1571 |
|---|---|---|---|---|---|---|---|
| bachalaqlaqout. | | uazro'aut | hashetep | yishatapu | milpanayu | uayishaberu; | ua'gam |
| **by flatteries** | | **And with the arms of** | **a flood** | **shall they be overflown** | **from before him** | **and shall be broken** | **yea also** |

| נגיד 5057 | ברית 1285: | 11:23 | ומן 4480 | התחברות 2266 | אליו 413 | יעשה 6213 | מרמה 4820 | ועלה 5927 |
|---|---|---|---|---|---|---|---|---|
| nagiyd | bariyt. | | uamin | hitchabrut | 'aelayu | ya'aseh | mirmah; | ua'alah |
| **the prince of** | **the covenant** | | **And after** | **the league** | ***made* with him** | **he shall work** | **deceitfully** | **for he shall come up** |

| ועצם 6105 | במעט 4592 | גוי 1471: | 11:24 | בשלוה 7962 | ובמשמני 4924 | מדינה 4082 | יבוא 935 |
|---|---|---|---|---|---|---|---|
| ua'atzam | bim'at | gouy. | | bashaluah | uabmishmaney | madiynah | yabou'a |
| **and shall become strong with** | **small a** | **people** | | **peaceably even** | **upon the fattest places of** | **the province** | **He shall enter** |

Dan 11:16 and he shall stand in the glorious land, which by his hand shall be consumed.17 He shall also set his face to enter with the strength of his whole kingdom, and upright ones with him; thus shall he do: and he shall give him the daughter of women, corrupting her: but she shall not stand on his side, neither be for him.18 After this shall he turn his face unto the isles, and shall take many: but a prince for his own behalf shall cause the reproach offered by him to cease; without his own reproach he shall cause it to turn upon him.19 Then he shall turn his face toward the fort of his own land: but he shall stumble and fall, and not be found.20 Then shall stand up in his estate a raiser of taxes in the glory of the kingdom: but within few days he shall be destroyed, neither in anger, nor in battle.21 And in his estate shall stand up a vile person, to whom they shall not give the honor of the kingdom: but he shall come in peaceably, and obtain the kingdom by flatteries.22 And with the arms of a flood shall they be overflown from before him, and shall be broken; yea, also the prince of the covenant.23 And after the league made with him he shall work deceitfully: for he shall come up, and shall become strong with a small people.24 He shall enter peaceably even upon the fattest places of the province; and he shall do that which his fathers have not done, nor his fathers' fathers;

| ועשה 6213 | אשר 834 | לא 3808 | עשו 6213 | אבתיו 1 | ואבות 1 | אבתיו 1 | בזה 961 | ושלל 7998 | ורכוש 7399 | להם 1992 |
|---|---|---|---|---|---|---|---|---|---|---|
| ua'asah, | 'asher | la' | 'asu | 'abotayu | ua'about | 'abotayu, | bizah | uashalal | uarkush | lahem |
| **and he shall do *that*** | **which** | **not** | **have done** | **his fathers** | **nor fathers'** | **his fathers** | **the prey** | **and spoil** | **and riches** | **among them** |

| יבזור 967 | ועל 5921 | מבצרים 4013 | יחשב 2803 | מחשבתיו 4284 | ועד 5704 | עת 6256: | 11:25 | ויער 5782 |
|---|---|---|---|---|---|---|---|---|
| yibzour; | ua'al | mibatzariym | yachasheb | machshabotayu | ua'ad | 'aet. | | uaya'aer |
| **he shall scatter *yea*** | **and against** | **the strong holds** | **he shall forecast** | **his devices** | **even for** | **a time** | | **And he shall stir up** |

| כחו 3581 | ולבבו 3824 | על 5921 | מלך 4428 | הנגב 5045 | בחיל 2428 | גדול 1419 | ומלך 4428 | הנגב 5045 | יתגרה 1624 |
|---|---|---|---|---|---|---|---|---|---|
| kochou | ualbabou | 'al | melek | hanegeb | bachayil | gadoul | uamelek | hanegeb, | yitgareh |
| **his power** | **and his courage** | **against** | **the king of** | **the south** | **with a army** | **great** | **and the king of** | **the south** | **shall be stirred up** |

| למלחמה 4421 | בחיל 2428 | גדול 1419 | ועצום 6099 | עד 5704 | מאד 3966 | ולא 3808 | יעמד 5975 | כי 3588 | יחשבו 2803 | עליו 5921 |
|---|---|---|---|---|---|---|---|---|---|---|
| lamilchamah, | bachayil | gadoul | ua'atzum | 'ad | ma'ad; | uala' | ya'amod, | kiy | yachshabu | 'alayu |
| **to battle** | **with a army** | **great** | **and mighty** | **with** | **very** | **but not** | **he shall stand** | **for** | **they shall forecast** | **against him** |

| מחשבות 4284: | 11:26 | ואכלי 398 | פת 6598 | בגו 6598 | ישברוהו 7665 | וחילו 2428 | ישטוף 7857 |
|---|---|---|---|---|---|---|---|
| machashabout. | | ua'akaley | pat | bagou | yishbaruhu | uacheylou | yishtoup; |
| **devices** | | **Yea they that feed of** | **the portion** | **of his meat** | **shall destroy him** | **and his army** | **shall overflow** |

| ונפלו 5307 | חללים 2491 | רבים 7227: | 11:27 | ושניהם 8147 | המלכים 4428 | לבבם 3824 | למרע 4827 | ועל 5921 | שלחן 7979 | אחד 259 |
|---|---|---|---|---|---|---|---|---|---|---|
| uanapalu | chalaliym | rabiym. | | uashneyhem | hamalakiym | lababam | lamera', | ua'al | shulchan | 'achad |
| **and shall fall down** | **slain** | **many** | | **And both** | **these kings'** | **hearts *shall be*** | **to do mischief** | **and at** | **table** | **one** |

| כזב 3577 | ידברו 1696 | ולא 3808 | תצלח 6743 | כי 3588 | עוד 5750 | קץ 7093 | למועד 4150: | 11:28 |
|---|---|---|---|---|---|---|---|---|
| kazab | yadaberu; | uala' | titzlach, | kiy | 'aud | qetz | lamou'aed. | |
| **lies** | **and they shall speak** | **but not** | **it shall prosper** | **for** | **yet** | **the end *shall be*** | **at the time appointed** | |

| וישב 7725 | ארצו 776 | ברכוש 7399 | גדול 1419 | ולבבו 3824 | על 5921 | ברית 1285 | קדש 6944 | ועשה 6213 |
|---|---|---|---|---|---|---|---|---|
| uayashob | artzou | birkush | gadoul, | ualbabou | 'al | bariyt | qodesh; | ua'asah |
| **Then shall he return into** | **his land** | **with riches** | **great** | **and his heart *shall be*** | **against** | **covenant** | ***the* holy** | **and he shall do** |

| ושב 7725 | לארצו 776: | 11:29 | למועד 4150 | ישוב 7725 | ובא 935 | בנגב 5045 | ולא 3808 |
|---|---|---|---|---|---|---|---|
| uashab | la'artzou. | | lamou'aed | yashub | uaba' | banegeb; | uala' |
| ***exploits* and return** | **to his own land** | | **At the time appointed** | **he shall return** | **and come** | **toward the south** | **but not** |

| תהיה 1961 | כראשנה 7223 | וכאחרנה 314: | 11:30 | ובאו 935 | בו 871a | ציים 6716 | כתים 3794 | ונכאה 3512 |
|---|---|---|---|---|---|---|---|---|
| tihayeh | kara'shonah | uaka'acharonah. | | uaba'au | bou | tziyiym | kitiym | uanik'ah, |
| **it shall be** | **as the former** | **or as the latter** | | **For shall come** | **against him** | **the ships of** | **Chittim** | **therefore he shall be grieved** |

| ושב 7725 | וזעם 2194 | על 5921 | ברית 1285 | קודש 6944 | ועשה 6213 | ושב 7725 | ויבן 995 |
|---|---|---|---|---|---|---|---|
| uashab | uaza'am | 'al | bariyt | qoudesh | ua'asah; | uashab | uayaben, |
| **and return** | **and have indignation** | **against** | **covenant** | ***the* holy** | **so shall he do** | **he shall even return** | **and have intelligence** |

| על 5921 | עזבי 5800 | ברית 1285 | קדש 6944: | 11:31 | וזרעים 2220 | ממנו 4480 | יעמדו 5975 | וחללו 2490 | המקדש 4720 |
|---|---|---|---|---|---|---|---|---|---|
| 'al | 'azabey | bariyt | qodesh. | | uazro'aym | mimenu | ya'amodu; | uachillu | hamiqdash |
| **with them** | **that forsake** | **covenant** | ***the* holy** | | **And arms** | **on his part** | **shall stand** | **and they shall pollute** | **the sanctuary of** |

Dan 11:24 he shall scatter among them the prey, and spoil, and riches: yea, and he shall forecast his devices against the strong holds, even for a time.25 And he shall stir up his power and his courage against the king of the south with a great army; and the king of the south shall be stirred up to battle with a very great and mighty army; but he shall not stand: for they shall forecast devices against him.26 Yea, they that feed of the portion of his meat shall destroy him, and his army shall overflow: and many shall fall down slain.27 And both these kings' hearts shall be to do mischief, and they shall speak lies at one table; but it shall not prosper: for yet the end shall be at the time appointed.28 Then shall he return into his land with great riches; and his heart shall be against the holy covenant; and he shall do exploits, and return to his own land.29 At the time appointed he shall return, and come toward the south; but it shall not be as the former, or as the latter.30 For the ships of Chittim shall come against him: therefore he shall be grieved, and return, and have indignation against the holy covenant: so shall he do; he shall even return, and have intelligence with them that forsake the holy covenant.31 And arms shall stand on his part, and they shall pollute the sanctuary of strength, and shall take away the daily sacrifice, and they shall place the abomination that make desolate.

**11:32**

המעוז 4581 והסירו 5493 התמיד 8548 ונתנו 5414 השקוץ 8251 משומם 8074:
hamma'auz uahesiyru hatamiyd, uanatanu hashiqutz mashoumem.
**strength and shall take away the daily *sacrifice* and they shall place the abomination that make desolate**

ומרשיעי 7561 ברית 1285 יחניף 2610 בחלקות 2514 ועם 5971 ידעי 3045 אלהיו 430
uamarshiy'aey bariyt, yachaniyp bachalaqout; ua'am yoda'aey 'alohayu
**And such as do wickedly against the covenant shall he corrupt by flatteries but the people that do know their Elohim**

יחזקו 2388 ועשו 6213: **11:33** ומשכילי 7919 עם 5971 יבינו 995 לרבים 7227 ונכשלו 3782
yachaziqu ua'asu. uamaskiyley 'am, yabiynu larabiym; uanikshalu
**shall be strong and do *exploits* And they that understand among the people shall instruct many yet they shall fall**

בחרב 2719 ובלהבה 3852 בשבי 7628 ובבזה 961 ימים 3117: **11:34** ובהכשלם 3782 יעזרו 5826
bachereb uablehabah bishbiy uabbizah yamiym. uabhikashalam, ye'azaru
**by the sword and by flame by captivity and by spoil *many* days Now when they shall fall they shall be holpen with**

עזר 5828 מעט 4592 ונלוו 3867 עליהם 5921 רבים 7227 בחלקלקות 2519: **11:35** ומן 4480 המשכילים 7919 יכשלו 3782
'azer ma'at; uaniluu 'aleyhem rabiym bachalaqlaqout. uamin hamaskiyliym yikashalu,
**a help little but shall cleave to them many with flatteries And *some* of them of understanding shall fall**

לצרוף 6884 בהם 871a ולברר 1305 וללבן 3835 עד 5704 עת 6256 קץ 7093 כי 3588 עוד 5750
litzroup bahem ualbarer ualalben 'ad 'at qetz; kiy 'aud
**to try them and to purge and to make *them* white *even* to the time of the end because *it is* yet**

למועד 4150: **11:36** ועשה 6213 כרצונו 7522 המלך 4428 ויתרומם 7311 ויתגדל 1431 על 5921
lamou'aed. ua'asah kirtzounou hamelek, uayitroumem uayitgadel 'al
**for a time appointed And shall do according to his will the king and he shall exalt himself and magnify himself above**

כל 3605 אל 410 ועל 5921 אל 410 אלים 410 ידבר 1696 נפלאות 6381 והצליח 6743 עד 5704 כלה 3615 זעם 2195
kal al, ua'al 'al 'aeliym, yadaber nipla'aut; uahitzliyach 'ad kalah za'am,
**every god against *the* El *of* gods shall speak marvellous things and shall prosper till be accomplished the indignation**

כי 3588 נחרצה 2782 נעשתה 6213: **11:37** ועל 5921 אלהי 430 אבתיו 1 לא 3808 יבין 995 ועל 5921
kiy necharatzah ne'asatah. ua'al 'alohey 'abotayu la' yabiyn, ua'al
**for that that is determined shall be done And neither the Elohim of his fathers nor shall he regard above**

חמדת 2532 נשים 802 ועל 5921 כל 3605 אלוה 433 לא 3808 יבין 995 כי 3588 על 5921 כל 3605 יתגדל 1431: **11:38**
chemdat nashiym ua'al kal 'alouah la' yabiyn; kiy 'al kal yitgadal.
**the desire of women above any god nor regard for above all he shall magnify himself**

ולאלה 433 מעזים 4581 על 5921 כנו 3653 יכבד 3513 ולאלוה 433 אשר 834 לא 3808 ידעהו 3045 אבתיו 1 יכבד 3513
uale'aloah ma'aziym, 'al kanou yakabed; uale'alouah 'asher la' yada'ahu 'abotayu, yakabed
**But the Elohim of forces in his estate shall he honor and a god whom not knew his fathers shall he honor**

בזהב 2091 ובכסף 3701 ובאבן 68 יקרה 3368 ובחמדות 2532: **11:39** ועשה 6213 למבצרי 4013 מעזים 4581 עם 5973
bazahab uabkesep uab'aben yaqarah uabachamudout. ua'asah lamibtzarey ma'aziym 'am
**with gold and silver and with stones precious and pleasant things Thus shall he do in the holds most strong with**

Dan 11:32 And such as do wickedly against the covenant shall he corrupt by flatteries: but the people that do know their G-d shall be strong, and do exploits.33 And they that understand among the people shall instruct many: yet they shall fall by the sword, and by flame, by captivity, and by spoil, many days.34 Now when they shall fall, they shall be holpen with a little help: but many shall cleave to them with flatteries.35 And some of them of understanding shall fall, to try them, and to purge, and to make them white, even to the time of the end: because it is yet for a time appointed.36 And the king shall do according to his will; and he shall exalt himself, and magnify himself above every god, and shall speak marvellous things against the G-d of gods, and shall prosper till the indignation be accomplished: for that that is determined shall be done.37 Neither shall he regard the G-d of his fathers, nor the desire of women, nor regard any god: for he shall magnify himself above all.38 But in his estate shall he honor the G-d of forces: and a god whom his fathers knew not shall he honor with gold, and silver, and with precious stones, and pleasant things.39 Thus shall he do in the most strong holds with a strange god, whom he shall acknowledge and increase with glory: and he shall cause them to rule over many, and shall divide the land for gain.

| | | | | | | | |
|---|---|---|---|---|---|---|---|
| אלוה 433 | נכר 5236 | אשר 834 | הכיר 5234 | ירבה 7235 | כבוד 3519 | והמשילם 4910 | ברבים 7227 |
| 'alouah | nekar, | 'asher | hikiyr | yarbeh | kaboud; | uahimshiylam | barabiym, |
| **a god** | **strange** | **whom** | **he shall acknowledge** | ***and* increase with** | **glory** | **and he shall cause them to rule over** | **many** |

| | | | | | | | | | |
|---|---|---|---|---|---|---|---|---|---|
| ואדמה 127 | יחלק 2505 | במחיר 4242: | **11:40** | ובעת 6256 | קץ 7093 | יתנגח 5055 | עמו 5973 | מלך 4428 | הנגב 5045 |
| ua'adamah | yachaleq | bimachiyr. | | uab'aet | qetz, | yitnagach | 'amou | melek | hanegeb, |
| **and the land** | **shall divide** | **for gain** | | **And at the time of** | **the end** | **shall push** | **at him** | **the king of** | **the south** |

| | | | | | | | |
|---|---|---|---|---|---|---|---|
| וישתער 8175 | עליו 5921 | מלך 4428 | הצפון 6828 | ברכב 7393 | ובפרשים 6571 | ובאניות 591 | רבות 7227 |
| uayista'aer | 'alayu | melek | hatzapoun, | barekeb | uabparashiym, | uaba'aniyout | rabout; |
| **and shall come a whirlwind** | **against him *like*** | **the king of** | **the north** | **with chariots** | **and with horsemen** | **and in ships** | **many** |

| | | | | | | | |
|---|---|---|---|---|---|---|---|
| ובא 935 | בארצות 776 | ושטף 7857 | ועבר 5674: | **11:41** | ובא 935 | בארץ 776 | הצבי 6643 |
| uaba' | ba'aratzout | uashatap | ua'abar. | | uaba' | ba'aretz | hatzabiy, |
| **and he shall enter** | **into the countries** | **and shall overflow** | **and pass over** | | **He shall enter also** | **into land** | **the glorious** |

| | | | | | | | |
|---|---|---|---|---|---|---|---|
| ורבות 7227 | יכשלו 3782 | ואלה 428 | ימלטו 4422 | מידו 3027 | אדום 123 | ומואב 4124 | וראשית 7225 |
| uarabout | yikashelu; | ua'aleh | yimalatu | miyadou, | 'adoum | uamou'ab, | uarea'shiyt |
| **and many** | ***countries* shall be overthrown** | **but these** | **shall escape** | **out of his hand** | ***even* Edom** | **and Moab** | **and the chief of** |

| | | | | | | | | |
|---|---|---|---|---|---|---|---|---|
| בני 1121 | עמון 5983: | **11:42** | וישלח 7971 | ידו 3027 | בארצות 776 | וארץ 776 | מצרים 4714 | לא 3808 |
| baney | 'amoun. | | uayishlach | yadou | ba'aratzout; | ua'aretz | mitzrayim, | la' |
| **the children of** | **Ammon** | | **He shall stretch forth also** | **his hand** | **upon the countries** | **and the land of** | **Egypt** | **not** |

| | | | | | | | |
|---|---|---|---|---|---|---|---|
| תהיה 1961 | לפליטה 6413: | **11:43** | וממשל 4910 | במכמני 4362 | הזהב 2091 | והכסף 3701 | ובכל 3605 |
| tihayeh | lipleytah. | | uamashal, | bamikmaney | hazahab | uahakesep, | uabkol |
| **shall** | **escape** | | **But he shall have power** | **over the treasures of** | **gold** | **and of silver** | **and over all** |

| | | | | | | |
|---|---|---|---|---|---|---|
| חמדות 2532 | מצרים 4714 | ולבים 3864 | וכשים 3569 | במצעדיו 4703: | **11:44** | ושמעות 8052 |
| chamudout | mitzrayim; | ualubiym | uakushiym | bamitz'adayu. | | ushmu'aut |
| **the precious things of** | **Egypt** | **and the Libyans** | **and the Ethiopians** | ***shall be* at his steps** | | **But tidings** |

| | | | | | | |
|---|---|---|---|---|---|---|
| יבהלהו 926 | ממזרח 4217 | ומצפון 6828 | ויצא 3318 | בחמא 2534 | גדלה 1419 | להשמיד 8045 |
| yabahaluhu, | mimizrach | uamitzapoun; | uayatza' | bachema' | gadolah, | lahashamiyd |
| **shall trouble him** | **out of the east** | **and out of the north** | **therefore he shall go forth** | **with fury** | **great** | **to destroy** |

| | | | | | | | | |
|---|---|---|---|---|---|---|---|---|
| ולהחרים 2763 | רבים 7227: | **11:45** | ויטע 5193 | אהלי 168 | אפדנו 643 | בין 996 | ימים 3220 | להר 2022 |
| ualhachariym | rabiym. | | uayita' | 'ahaley | apadnou, | beyn | yamiym | lahar |
| **and utterly to make away** | **many** | | **And he shall plant** | **the tabernacles of** | **his palace** | **between** | **the seas** | **in mountain** |

| | | | | | | | |
|---|---|---|---|---|---|---|---|
| צבי 6643 | קדש 6944 | ובא 935 | עד 5704 | קצו 7093 | ואין 369 | עוזר 5826 | לו 3807a: |
| tzabiy | qodesh; | uaba' | 'ad | qitzou, | ua'aeyn | 'auzer | lou'. |
| ***the* glorious holy** | | **yet he shall come to** | | **his end and none** | | **shall help him** | |

| | | | | | | | | | | |
|---|---|---|---|---|---|---|---|---|---|---|
| **Dan 12:1** | ובעת 6256 | ההיא 1931 | יעמד 5975 | מיכאל 4317 | השר 8269 | הגדול 1419 | העמד 5975 | על 5921 | בני 1121 | עמך 5971 |
| | uaba'aet | hahiy'a | ya'amod | miyka'el | hasar | hagadoul, | ha'aumed | 'al | baney | 'ameka |
| | **And at time that** | | **shall stand up** | **Michael** | **prince** | **the great** | **which stands for** | | **the children of** | **your people** |

Dan 11:40 And at the time of the end shall the king of the south push at him: and the king of the north shall come against him like a whirlwind, with chariots, and with horsemen, and with many ships; and he shall enter into the countries, and shall overflow and pass over.41 He shall enter also into the glorious land, and many countries shall be overthrown: but these shall escape out of his hand, even Edom, and Moab, and the chief of the children of Ammon.42 He shall stretch forth his hand also upon the countries: and the land of Egypt shall not escape.43 But he shall have power over the treasures of gold and of silver, and over all the precious things of Egypt: and the Libyans and the Ethiopians shall be at his steps.44 But tidings out of the east and out of the north shall trouble him: therefore he shall go forth with great fury to destroy, and utterly to make away many.45 And he shall plant the tabernacles of his palace between the seas in the glorious holy mountain; yet he shall come to his end, and none shall help him. **Dan** 12:1 And at that time shall Michael stand up, the great prince which stand for the children of your people: and there shall be a time of trouble, such as never was since there was a nation even to that same time: and at that time your people shall be delivered, everyone that shall be found written in the book.

והיתה 1961 עת 6256 צרה 6869 אשר 834 לא 3808 נהיתה 1961 מהיות 1961 גוי 1471 עד 5704 העת 6256 ההיא 1931
uahayatah 'at tzarah, 'asher la' nihyatah mihyout gouy, 'ad ha'aet hahiy'a;
**and there shall be a time of trouble such as never was since there was a nation *even* to time that same**

12:2
ובעת 6256 ההיא 1931 ימלט 4422 עמך 5971 כל 3605 הנמצא 4672 כתוב 3789 בספר 5612: ורבים 7227
uaba'aet hahiy'a yimalet 'amaka, kal hanimtza' katub baseper. uarabiym
**and at time that shall be delivered your people every one that shall be found written in the book And many of**

מישני 3463 אדמת 127 עפר 6083 יקיצו 6974 אלה 428 לחיי 2416 עולם 5769 ואלה 428 לחרפות 2781 לדראון 1860
miyasheney 'admat 'apar yaqiytzu; 'aeleh lachayey 'aulam, ua'aleh lacharapout ladir'aun
**them that sleep in the earth the dust of shall awake some to life everlasting and some to shame contempt**

12:3
עולם 5769: והמשכלים 7919 יזהרו 2094 כזהר 2096 הרקיע 7549
'aulam. uahamaskiliym, yazhiru kazohar haraqiya';
***and* everlasting And they that be wise shall shine as the brightness of the firmament**

12:4
ומצדיקי 6663 הרבים 7227 ככוכבים 3556 לעולם 5769 ועד 5703: ואתה 859 דניאל 1840 סתם 5640 הדברים 1697
uamatzdiyqey harabiym, kakoukabiym la'aulam ua'ad. ua'atah daniyea'l, satom hadabariym
**and they that turn to righteousness many as the stars for ever and ever But you O Daniel shut up the words**

12:5
וחתם 2856 הספר 5612 עד 5704 עת 6256 קץ 7093 ישטטו 7751 רבים 7227 ותרבה 7235 הדעת 1847:
uachatom haseper 'ad 'at qetz; yashotatu rabiym uatirbeh hada'at.
**and seal the book *even* to the time of the end shall run to and fro many and shall be increased knowledge**

וראיתי 7200 אני 589 דניאל 1840 והנה 2009 שנים 8147 אחרים 312 עמדים 5975 אחד 259 הנה 2008 לשפת 8193 היאר 2975
uara'aytiy 'aniy daniyea'l, uahineh shanayim 'acheriym 'amdiym; 'achad henah lispat haya'ar,
**Then looked I Daniel and behold two other there stood the one on this *side* of the bank of the river**

12:6
ואחד 259 הנה 2008 לשפת 8193 היאר 2975: ויאמר 559 לאיש 376 לבוש 3847 הבדים 906 אשר 834 ממעל 4605
ua'achad henah lispat haya'ar. uaya'mer, la'aysh labush habadiym, 'asher mima'al
**and the other on that *side* of the bank of the river And *one* said to the man clothed in linen which *was* upon**

12:7
למימי 4325 היאר 2975 עד 5704 מתי 4970 קץ 7093 הפלאות 6382: ואשמע 8085 את 853 האיש 376 לבוש 3847
lameymey haya'ar; 'ad matay qetz hapala'aut. ua'ashma' 'at ha'aysh labush
**the waters of the river How long *shall it be to* the end of these wonders? And I heard the man clothed in**

הבדים 906 אשר 834 ממעל 4605 למימי 4325 היאר 2975 וירם 7311 ימינו 3225 ושמאלו 8040 אל 413 השמים 8064
habadiym, 'asher mima'al lameymey haya'ar uayarem yamiynou uasma'lou 'al hashamayim,
**linen which *was* upon the waters of the river when he held up his right hand and his left hand unto heaven**

וישבע 7650 בחי 2416 העולם 5769 כי 3588 למועד 4150 מועדים 4150 וחצי 2677 וככלות 3615
uayishaba' bachey ha'aulam; kiy lamou'aed mou'adiym uachetziy, uakkalout
**and sware by him that live for ever that *it shall be* for a time times and an half and when he shall have accomplished**

12:8
נפץ 5310 יד 3027 עם 5971 קדש 6944 תכלינה 3615 כל 3605 אלה 428: ואני 589 שמעתי 8085 ולא 3808 אבין 995
napetz yad 'am qodesh tikleynah kal 'aeleh. ua'aniy shama'atiy uala' 'abiyn;
**to scatter the power of people *the* holy *things* shall be finished all these And I heard but not I understood**

Dan 12:2 And many of them that sleep in the dust of the earth shall awake, some to everlasting life, and some to shame and everlasting contempt.3 And they that be wise shall shine as the brightness of the firmament; and they that turn many to righteousness as the stars forever and ever.4 But you, O Daniel, shut up the words, and seal the book, even to the time of the end: many shall run to and fro, and knowledge shall be increased.5 Then I Daniel looked, and, behold, there stood other two, the one on this side of the bank of the river, and the other on that side of the bank of the river.6 And one said to the man clothed in linen, which was upon the waters of the river, How long shall it be to the end of these wonders?7 And I heard the man clothed in linen, which was upon the waters of the river, when he held up his right hand and his left hand unto heaven, and sware by him that live forever that it shall be for a time, times, and an half; and when he shall have accomplished to scatter the power of the holy people, all these things shall be finished.8 And I heard, but I understood not: then said I, O my Adonai, what shall be the end of these things?

| ואמרה 559 | אדני 113 | מה 4100 | אחרית 319 | אלה 428: | 12:9 | ויאמר 559 | לך 1980 | דניאל 1840 | כי 3588 |
|---|---|---|---|---|---|---|---|---|---|
| ua'amarah, | 'adoniy | mah | 'achariyt | 'aeleh. | | uaya'mer | lek | daniyea'l; | kiy |
| **then said I** | **O my Adonai** | **what** | ***shall be* the end of** | **these *things*?** | | **And he said** | **Go your way** | **Daniel** | **for** |

| סתמים 5640 | וחתמים 2856 | הדברים 1697 | עד 5704 | עת 6256 | קץ 7093: | 12:10 | יתבררו 1305 | ויתלבנו 3835 | ויצרפו 6884 | רבים 7227 |
|---|---|---|---|---|---|---|---|---|---|---|
| satumiym | uachatumiym | hadabariym | 'ad | 'aet | qetz. | | yitbararu | uayitlabnu | uayitzarapu | rabiym, |
| ***are* closed up** | **and sealed** | **the words** | **till** | **the time of** | **the end** | | **shall be purified** | **and made white** | **and tried** | **Many** |

| והרשיעו 7561 | רשעים 7563 | ולא 3808 | יבינו 995 | כל 3605 | רשעים 7563 | והמשכלים 7919 | יבינו 995: | 12:11 |
|---|---|---|---|---|---|---|---|---|
| uahirshiy'au | rasha'aym, | uala' | yabiynu | kal | rasha'aym; | uahamaskiliym | yabiynu. | |
| **but shall do wickedly** | **the wicked** | **and none of** | **shall understand** | **none of** | **the wicked** | **but the wise** | **shall understand** | |

| ומעת 6256 | הוסר 5493 | התמיד 8548 | ולתת 5414 | שקוץ 8251 | שמם 8074 | ימים 3117 |
|---|---|---|---|---|---|---|
| uame'aet | husar | hatamiyd, | ualatet | shiqutz | shomem; | yamiym |
| **And from the time** | ***sacrifice* shall be taken away** | ***that* the daily** | **and set up** | **the abomination** | **that make desolate** | **days** |

| אלף 505 | מאתים 3967 | ותשעים 8673: | 12:12 | אשרי 835 | המחכה 2442 | ויגיע 5060 | לימים 3117 | אלף 505 | שלש 7969 |
|---|---|---|---|---|---|---|---|---|---|
| 'alep | ma'tayim | uatish'aym. | | 'ashrey | hamachakeh | uayagiya'; | layamiym | 'alep | shalosh |
| ***there shall be* a thousand** | **two hundred** | **and ninety** | | **Blessed** | ***is* he that wait** | **and comes** | **to days** | ***the* thousand** | **three** |

| מאות 3967 | שלשים 7970 | וחמשה 2568: | 12:13 | ואתה 859 | לך 1980 | לקץ 7093 | ותנוח 5117 | ותעמד 5975 | לגרלך 1486 |
|---|---|---|---|---|---|---|---|---|---|
| me'aut | shaloshiym | uachamishah. | | ua'atah | lek | laqetz; | uatanuach | uata'amod | lagoralaka |
| **hundred** | ***and* thirty** | **and five** | | **But you** | **go your way** | **till the end** | ***be* for you shall rest** | **and stand** | **in your lot** |

| לקץ 7093 | הימין 3117: |
|---|---|
| laqetz | hayamiyn. |
| **at the end of** | **the days** |

Dan 12:9 And he said, Go your way, Daniel: for the words are closed up and sealed till the time of the end.10 Many shall be purified, and made white, and tried; but the wicked shall do wickedly: and none of the wicked shall understand; but the wise shall understand.11 And from the time that the daily sacrifice shall be taken away, and the abomination that make desolate set up, there shall be a thousand two hundred and ninety days.12 Blessed is he that waiteth, and cometh to the thousand three hundred and five and thirty days.13 But go you your way till the end be: for you shall rest, and stand in your lot at the end of the days.

# HOSEA
## (*Houshea*)

The Book of Hosea begins the **Minor Prophets** in the Tanakh from Hosea through Malachi. Verse one identifies the author of the book as the Prophet Hosea whose name in Hebrew means *salvation.* It is Hosea's personal account of his prophetic messages he delivered to the **House of Israel**. Hosea, the son of Beeri, prophesied from 785 to 725 B.C. and the book was written approximately between 755 and 725 B.C. Hosea's life story is a rich metaphor displayed as a long-suffering husband who took back his unfaithful wife which was a direct reflection of the relationship of the Messiah and His sinful bride whom He would provide a way to receive her back and forgive her sins through His sacrifice at Calvary. This story has served as a constant reminder to the idolatrous actions of the Israelites which eventually brought judgment upon the entire nation including the House of Judah.

| **Hos 1:1** | דבר 1697 | יהוה 3068 | אשר 834 | היה 1961 | אל 413 | הושע 1954 | בן 1121 | בארי 882 | בימי 3117 | עזיה 5818 | יותם 3147 | אחז 271 |
|---|---|---|---|---|---|---|---|---|---|---|---|---|
| | dabar | Yahuah | 'asher | hayah, | 'al | houshea' | ben | ba'aeriy, | biymey | 'aziyah | youtam | 'achaz |
| | **The word of** | **Yahuah** | **that** | **came** | **unto** | **Hosea** | **the son of** | **Beeri** | **in the days of** | **Uzziah** | **Jotham** | **Ahaz** |

| יחזקיה 2396 | מלכי 4428 | יהודה 3063 | ובימי 3117 | ירבעם 3379 | בן 1121 | יואש 3101 | מלך 4428 | ישראל 3478: | **1:2** | תחלת 8462 |
|---|---|---|---|---|---|---|---|---|---|---|
| yachizqiyah | malkey | yahudah; | uabiymey | yarab'am | ben | you'ash | melek | yisra'ael. | | tachilat |
| **Hezekiah** | **kings of** | **Judah** | **and in the days of** | **Jeroboam** | **the son of** | **Joash** | **king of** | **Israel** | | **The beginning of** |

| דבר 1696 | יהוה 3068 | בהושע 1954 | ויאמר 559 | יהוה 3068 | אל 413 | הושע 1954 | לך 1980 | קח 3947 | לך 3807a | אשת 802 | זנונים 2183 |
|---|---|---|---|---|---|---|---|---|---|---|---|
| diber | Yahuah | bahoushea'; | uaya'mer | Yahuah | 'al | houshea', | lek | qach | laka | 'aeshet | zanuniym |
| **the word of** | **Yahuah** | **by Hosea** | **And said** | **Yahuah** | **to** | **Hosea** | **Go you** | **take** | **unto you** | **a wife of** | **whoredoms** |

| וילדי 3206 | זנונים 2183 | כי 3588 | זנה 2181 | תזנה 2181 | הארץ 776 | מאחרי 310 | יהוה 3068: | **1:3** | וילך 3212 | ויקח 3947 |
|---|---|---|---|---|---|---|---|---|---|---|
| uayaldey | zanuniym, | kiy | zanoh | tizneh | ha'aretz, | me'acharey | Yahuah. | | uayelek | uayiqach, |
| **and children of** | **whoredoms** | **for** | **has committed** | **great whoredom** | **the land** | ***departing* from** | **Yahuah** | | **So he went** | **and took** |

| את 853 | גמר 1586 | בת 1323 | דבלים 1691 | ותהר 2029 | ותלד 3205 | לו 3807a | בן 1121: | **1:4** | ויאמר 559 | יהוה 3068 | אליו 413 | קרא 7121 |
|---|---|---|---|---|---|---|---|---|---|---|---|---|
| 'at | gomer | bat | diblayim; | uatahar | uateled | lou' | ben. | | uaya'mer | Yahuah | 'aelayu, | qara' |
| | **Gomer** | **the daughter of** | **Diblaim** | **which conceived** | **and bare** | **him** | **a son** | | **And said** | **Yahuah** | **unto him** | **Call** |

| שמו 8034 | יזרעאל 3157 | כי 3588 | עוד 5750 | מעט 4592 | ופקדתי 6485 | את 853 | דמי 1818 | יזרעאל 3157 | על 5921 | בית 1004 | יהוא 3058 |
|---|---|---|---|---|---|---|---|---|---|---|---|
| shamou | yizra'ael; | kiy | 'aud | ma'at, | uapaqadtiy | 'at | damey | yizra'ael | 'al | beyt | yehu'a, |
| **his name** | **Jezreel** | **for** | **yet** | **a little *while*** | **and I will avenge** | | **the blood of** | **Jezreel** | **upon** | **the house of** | **Jehu** |

| והשבתי 7673 | ממלכות 4468 | בית 1004 | ישראל 3478: | **1:5** | והיה 1961 | ביום 3117 | ההוא 1931 |
|---|---|---|---|---|---|---|---|
| uahishbatiy, | mamlakut | beyt | yisra'ael. | | uahayah | bayoum | hahua'; |
| **and will cause to cease** | **the kingdom of** | **the house of** | **Israel** | | **And it shall come to pass** | **at day** | **that** |

| ושברתי 7665 | את 853 | קשת 7198 | ישראל 3478 | בעמק 6010 | יזרעאל 3157: | **1:6** | ותהר 2029 | עוד 5750 | ותלד 3205 | בת 1323 |
|---|---|---|---|---|---|---|---|---|---|---|
| uashabartiy | 'at | qeshet | yisra'ael, | ba'aemeq | yizra'ael. | | uatahar | 'aud | uateled | bat, |
| **that I will break** | | **the bow of** | **Israel** | **in the valley of** | **Jezreel** | | **And she conceived** | **again** | **and bare** | **a daughter** |

| ויאמר 559 | לו 3807a | קרא 7121 | שמה 8034 | לא 3819 | רחמה 7355 | כי 3588 | לא 3808 | אוסיף 3254 | עוד 5750 | ארחם 7355 | את 853 |
|---|---|---|---|---|---|---|---|---|---|---|---|
| uaya'mer | lou', | qara' | shamah | la' | ruchamah; | kiy | la' | 'ausiyp | 'aud, | 'arachem | 'at |
| **And *Elohim* said** | **unto him** | **Call** | **her name** | **Lo** | **ruhamah** | **for** | **no** | **I will** | **more** | **have mercy upon** | |

| בית 1004 | ישראל 3478 | כי 3588 | נשא 5375 | אשא 5375 | להם 3807a: | **1:7** | ואת 853 | בית 1004 | יהודה 3063 | ארחם 7355 |
|---|---|---|---|---|---|---|---|---|---|---|
| beyt | yisra'ael, | kiy | nasoa' | 'asa' | lahem. | | ua'at | beyt | yahudah | 'arachem, |
| **the house of** | **Israel** | **but** | **I will utterly** | **take away** | **them** | | **But** | **the house of** | **Judah** | **I will have mercy upon** |

**Hosea** 1:1 The word of YHUH that came unto Hosea, the son of Beeri, in the days of Uzziah, Jotham, Ahaz, and Hezekiah, kings of Judah, and in the days of Jeroboam the son of Joash, king of Israel.2 The beginning of the word of YHUH by Hosea. And YHUH said to Hosea, Go, take unto you a wife of whoredoms and children of whoredoms: for the land has committed great whoredom, departing from YHUH.3 So he went and took Gomer the daughter of Diblaim; which conceived, and bare him a son.4 And YHUH said unto him, Call his name Jezreel; for yet a little while, and I will avenge the blood of Jezreel upon the house of Jehu, and will cause to cease the kingdom of the house of Israel.5 And it shall come to pass at that day, that I will break the bow of Israel in the valley of Jezreel.6 And she conceived again, and bare a daughter. And G-d said unto him, Call her name Lo-ruhamah: for I will no more have mercy upon the house of Israel; but I will utterly take them away.7 But I will have mercy upon the house of Judah,

והושעתים 3467 | ביהוה 3068 | אלהיהם 430 | ולא 3808 | אושיעם 3467 | בקשת 7198 | ובחרב 2719 | ובמלחמה 4421 | בסוסים 5483
uahousha'atiym | baYahuah | 'aloheyhem; | uala' | 'aushiy'aem, | baqeshet | uabchereb | uabmilchamah, | basusiym
**and will save them | by Yahuah | their Elohim | and not | will save them | by bow | nor by sword | nor by battle | by horses**

ובפרשים 6571: | **1:8** ותגמל 1580 | את 853 | לא 3819 | רחמה 7355 | ותהר 2029 | ותלד 3205 | בן 1121: | **1:9** ויאמר 559
uabparashiym. | uatigmol | 'at | la' | ruchamah; | uatahar | uateled | ben. | uaya'mer
**nor by horsemen | Now when she had weaned | Lo ruhamah | she conceived and bare a son | Then said *Elohim***

קרא 7121 | שמו 8034 | לא 3834 | עמי 5971 | כי 3588 | אתם 859 | לא 3808 | עמי 5971 | ואנכי 595 | לא 3808 | אהיה 1961 | לכם 3807a: | **1:10** והיה 1961
qara' | shamou | la' | 'amiy; | kiy | 'atem | la' | 'amiy, | ua'anokiy | la' | 'ahayeh | lakem. | uahayah
**Call | his name | Lo ammi | for | you | *are* not | my people | and I | not | will be | your *Elohim* | Yet shall be**

מספר 4557 | בני 1121 | ישראל 3478 | כחול 2344 | הים 3220 | אשר 834 | לא 3808 | ימד 4058 | ולא 3808 | יספר 5608
mispar | baney | yisra'ael | kachoul | hayam, | 'asher | la' | yimad | uala' | yisaper;
**the number of | the children of | Israel | as the sand of | the sea | which | cannot | be measured | nor | numbered**

והיה 1961 | במקום 4725 | אשר 834 | יאמר 559 | להם 1992 | לא 3808 | עמי 5971 | אתם 859 | יאמר 559
uahayah | bimqoum | 'asher | ye'amer | lahem | la' | 'amiy | 'atem, | ye'amer
**and it shall come to pass *that* | in the place | where | it was said | unto them | not | my people | You *are* | *there* it shall be said**

להם 1992 | בני 1121 | אל 410 | חי 2416: | **1:11** ונקבצו 6908 | בני 1121 | יהודה 3063 | ובני 1121
lahem | baney | 'ael | chay. | uaniqbatzu | baney | yahudah | uabaney
**unto them | *You are* the sons of | El | *the* living | Then shall be gathered | the children of | Judah | and the children of**

ישראל 3478 | יחדו 3162 | ושמו 7760 | להם 3807a | ראש 7218 | אחד 259 | ועלו 5927 | מן 4480 | הארץ 776 | כי 3588 | גדול 1419
yisra'ael | yachdau, | uasamu | lahem | ra'sh | 'achad | ua'alu | min | ha'aretz; | kiy | gadoul
**Israel | together | and appoint | themselves | head | one | and they shall come up | out of | the land | for | great**

יום 3117 | יזרעאל 3157:
youm | yizra'ael.
***shall be* the day of | Jezreel**

**Hos 2:1** אמרו 559 | לאחיכם 251 | עמי 5971 | ולאחותיכם 269 | רחמה 7355: | **2:2** ריבו 7378 | באמכם 517 | ריבו 7378 | כי 3588
'amru | la'acheykem | 'amiy; | uala'achouteykem | ruchamah. | riybu | ba'amakem | riybu, | kiy
**Say you | unto your brethren | Ammi | and to your sisters | Ruhamah | Plead | with your mother | plead | for**

היא 1931 | לא 3808 | אשתי 802 | ואנכי 595 | לא 3808 | אישה 376 | ותסר 5493 | זנוניה 2183 | מפניה 6440
hiy'a | la' | 'ashtiy, | ua'anokiy | la' | 'ayshah; | uataser | zanuneyha | mipaneyha,
**she *is* | not | my wife | *am* I | neither | her husband | let her therefore put away | her whoredoms | out of her sight**

ונאפופיה 5005 | מבין 996 | שדיה 7699: | **2:3** פן 6435 | אפשיטנה 6584 | ערמה 6174 | והצגתיה 3322 | כיום 3117 | הולדה 3205
uana'apupeyha | mibeyn | shadeyha. | pen | 'apshytenah | 'arumah, | uahitzagtiyha, | kayoum | hiualadah;
**and her adulteries | from between | her breasts | Lest | I strip her | naked | and set her | as in the day | that she was born**

ושמתיה 7760 | כמדבר 4057 | ושתה 7896 | כארץ 776 | ציה 6723 | והמתיה 4191 | בצמא 6772: | **2:4** ואת 853 | בניה 1121 | לא 3808
uasamtiyha | kamidbar, | uashatiha | ka'aretz | tziyah, | uahamitiyha | batzama'. | ua'at | baneyha | la'
**and make her | as a wilderness | and set her | like land a dry | and slay her | with thirst | *And* | her children not**

Hos 1:7 and will save them by YHUH their G-d, and will not save them by bow, nor by sword, nor by battle, by horses, nor by horsemen.8 Now when she had weaned Lo-ruhamah, she conceived, and bare a son.9 Then said G-d, Call his name Lo-ammi: for you are not my people, and I will not be your G-d.10 Yet the number of the children of Israel shall be as the sand of the sea, which cannot be measured nor numbered; and it shall come to pass, that in the place where it was said unto them, You are not my people, there it shall be said unto them, You are the sons of the living G-d.11 Then shall the children of Judah and the children of Israel be gathered together, and appoint themselves one head, and they shall come up out of the land: for great shall be the day of Jezreel. **Hos** 2:1 Say you unto your brethren, Ammi; and to your sisters, Ru-hamah.2 Plead with your mother, plead: for she is not my wife, neither am I her husband: let her therefore put away her whoredoms out of her sight, and her adulteries from between her breasts;3 Lest I strip her naked, and set her as in the day that she was born, and make her as a wilderness, and set her like a dry land, and slay her with thirst.4 And I will not have mercy upon her children; for they be the children of whoredoms.

ארחם 7355 כי 3588 בני 1121 זנונים 2183 המה 1992: **2:5** כי 3588 זנתה 2181 אמם 517
'arachem; kiy baney zanuniym hemah. kiy zanatah 'amam,
**I will have mercy upon for *be* the children of whoredoms they For has played the harlot their mother**

הבישה 3001 הורתם 2029 כי 3588 אמרה 559 אלכה 1980 אחרי 310 מאהבי 157 נתני 5414 לחמי 3899
hobiyshah houratam; kiy 'amarah, 'aelakah 'acharey ma'ahabay notaney lachmiy
**she has done shamefully that conceived them for she said I will go after my lovers that give *me* my bread**

ומימי 4325 צמרי 6785 ופשתי 6593 שמני 8081 ושקויי 8250: **2:6** לכן 3651 הנני 2005 שך 7753 את 853 דרכך 1870 בסירים 5518
uameymay, tzamriy uapiyshtiy, shamniy uashiquyay. laken hinniy sach 'at darkek basiyriym;
**and my water my wool and my flax mine oil and my drink Therefore behold I will hedge up *your* way with thorns**

וגדרתי 1443 את 853 גדרה 1448 ונתיבותיה 5410 לא 3808 תמצא 4672: **2:7** ורדפה 7291 את 853 מאהביה 157 ולא 3808
uagadartiy 'at gaderah, uantiybouteyha la' timtzaa'. uaridpah 'at ma'ahabeyha uala'
**and make a wall her paths not *that* she shall find And she shall follow after her lovers but not**

תשיג 5381 אתם 853 ובקשתם 1245 ולא 3808 תמצא 4672 ואמרה 559 אלכה 1980 ואשובה 7725 אל 413
tasiyg 'atam, uabiqshatam uala' timtzaa'; ua'amarah, 'aelakah ua'ashubah 'al
**she shall overtake them and she shall seek them but not shall find *them* then shall she say I will go and return to**

אישי 376 הראשון 7223 כי 3588 טוב 2896 לי 3807a אז 227 מעתה 6258: **2:8** והיא 1931 לא 3808 ידעה 3045 כי 3588 אנכי 595 נתתי 5414 לה 3807a
'ashiy hara'shoun, kiy toub liy 'az me'atah. uahiy'a la' yada'ah, kiy 'anokiy natatiy lah,
**my husband first for *was it* better with me then than now For she not did know that I gave her**

הדגן 1715 והתירוש 8492 והיצהר 3323 וכסף 3701 הרביתי 7235 לה 3807a וזהב 2091 עשו 6213 לבעל 1168: **2:9** לכן 3651
hadagan uahatiyroush uahayitzhar; uakesep hirbeytiy lah uazahab 'asu laba'al. laken
**corn and wine and oil and silver multiplied her and gold *which* they prepared for Baal Therefore**

אשוב 7725 ולקחתי 3947 דגני 1715 בעתו 6256 ותירושי 8492 במועדו 4150 והצלתי 5337 צמרי 6785
'ashub, ualaqachtiy daganiy ba'atou, uatiyroushiy bamou'adou; uahitzaltiy tzamriy
**will I return and take away my corn in the time thereof and my wine in the season thereof and will recover my wool**

ופשתי 6593 לכסות 3680 את 853 ערותה 6172: **2:10** ועתה 6258 אגלה 1540 את 853 נבלתה 5040 לעיני 5869
uapiyshtiy, lakasout 'at 'aruatah. ua'atah 'agaleh 'at nablutah la'aeyney
**and my flax *given* to cover her nakedness And now will I discover her lewdness in the sight of**

מאהביה 157 ואיש 376 לא 3808 יצילנה 5337 מידי 3027: **2:11** והשבתי 7673 כל 3605 משושה 4885
ma'ahabeyha; ua'aysh la' yatziylenah miyadiy. uahishbatiy kal masousah,
**her lovers and man no shall deliver her out of mine hand I will also cause to cease all her mirth**

חגה 2282 חדשה 2320 ושבתה 7676 וכל 3605 מועדה 4150: **2:12** והשמתי 8074 גפנה 1612 ותאנתה 8384
chagah chadashah uashabatah; uakol mou'adah. uahashimotiy, gapnah uat'aenatah,
**her feast days her new moons and her sabbaths and all her solemn feasts And I will destroy her vines and her fig trees**

אשר 834 אמרה 559 אתנה 866 המה 1992 לי 3807a אשר 834 נתנו 5414 לי 3807a מאהבי 157 ושמתים 7760 ליער 3293
'asher 'amarah, 'atnah hemah liy, 'asher natenu liy ma'ahabay; uasamatiym laya'ar,
**whereof she has said rewards These *are* my that have given me my lovers and I will make a forest**

Hos 2:5 For their mother has played the harlot: she that conceived them has done shamefully: for she said, I will go after my lovers, that give me my bread and my water, my wool and my flax, mine oil and my drink.6 Therefore, behold, I will hedge up your way with thorns, and make a wall, that she shall not find her paths.7 And she shall follow after her lovers, but she shall not overtake them; and she shall seek them, but shall not find them: then shall she say, I will go and return to my first husband; for then was it better with me than now.8 For she did not know that I gave her corn, and wine, and oil, and multiplied her silver and gold, which they prepared for Baal.9 Therefore will I return, and take away my corn in the time thereof, and my wine in the season thereof, and will recover my wool and my flax given to cover her nakedness.10 And now will I discover her lewdness in the sight of her lovers, and none shall deliver her out of mine hand.11 I will also cause all her mirth to cease, her feast days, her new moons, and her sabbaths, and all her solemn feasts.12 And I will destroy her vines and her fig trees, whereof she has said, These are my rewards that my lovers have given me: and I will make them a forest, and the beasts of the field shall eat them.

| 398 ואכלתם | 2416 חית | 7704: השדה | 2:13 | 6485 ופקדתי | 5921 עליה | 853 את | 3117 ימי | 1168 הבעלים | 834 אשר |
|---|---|---|---|---|---|---|---|---|---|
| ua'akalatam | chayat | hasadeh. | | uapaqadtiy | 'aleyha, | 'at | yamey | haba'aliym | 'asher |
| **and shall eat them** | **the beasts of** | **the field** | | **And I will visit** | **upon her** | | **days of** | **the Baalim** | **wherein** |

| 6999 תקטיר | 1992 להם | 5710 ותעד | 5141 נזמה | 2484 וחליתה | 1980 ותלך | 310 אחרי | 157 מאהביה |
|---|---|---|---|---|---|---|---|
| taqtiyr | lahem, | uata'ad | nizmah | uachelyatah, | uatelek | 'acharey | ma'ahabeyha; |
| **she burned incense** | **to them** | **and she decked herself** | ***with* her earrings** | **and her jewels** | **and she went** | **after** | **her lovers** |

| 853 ואתי | 7911 שכחה | 5002 נאם | 3068: יהוה | 2:14 | 3651 לכן | 2009 הנה | 595 אנכי | 6601 מפתיה | 1980 והלכתיה | 4057 המדבר |
|---|---|---|---|---|---|---|---|---|---|---|
| ua'atiy | shakachah | na'am | Yahuah. | | laken, | hineh | 'anokiy | mapateyha, | uaholaktiyha | hamidbar; |
| **and me** | **forgot** | **saith** | **Yahuah** | | **Therefore** | **behold** | **I** | **will allure her** | **and bring her** | ***into* the wilderness** |

| 1696 ודברתי | 5921 על | 3820: לבה | 2:15 | 5414 ונתתי | 3807a לה | 853 את | 3754 כרמיה | 8033 משם | 853 ואת | 6010 עמק | 5911 עכור |
|---|---|---|---|---|---|---|---|---|---|---|---|
| uadibartiy | 'al | libah. | | uanatatiy | lah | 'at | karameyha | misham, | ua'at | 'ameq | 'achour |
| **and speak** | **unto *her*** | **comfortably** | | **And I will give** | **her** | | **her vineyards** | **from there** | ***and*** | **the valley of** | **Achor** |

| 6607 לפתח | 8615 תקוה | 6030 וענתה | 8033 שמה | 3117 כימי | 5271 נעוריה | 3117 וכיום | 5927 עלתה |
|---|---|---|---|---|---|---|---|
| lapetach | tiquah; | ua'anatah | shamah | kiymey | na'aureyha, | yakyoum | 'alotah |
| **for a door of** | **hope** | **and she shall sing** | **there** | **as in the days of** | **her youth** | **and as in the day when** | **she came up** |

| 776 מארץ | 4714: מצרים | 2:16 | 1961 והיה | 3117 ביום | 1931 ההוא | 5002 נאם | 3068 יהוה | 7121 תקראי | 376 אישי | 3808 ולא |
|---|---|---|---|---|---|---|---|---|---|---|
| me'eretz | mitzrayim. | | uahayah | bayoum | hahua' | na'am | Yahuah, | tiqra'ay | 'ashiy; | uala' |
| **out of the land of** | **Egypt** | | **And it shall be** | **at day** | **that** | **saith** | **Yahuah** | ***that* you shall call me** | **Ishi** | **and no** |

| 7121 תקראי | 3807a לי | 5750 עוד | 1180: בעלי | 2:17 | 5493 והסרתי | 853 את | 8034 שמות | 1168 הבעלים | 6310 מפיה | 3808 ולא |
|---|---|---|---|---|---|---|---|---|---|---|
| tiqra'ay | liy | 'aud | ba'liy. | | uahasirotiy | 'at | shamout | haba'aliym | mipiyha; | uala' |
| **you shall call** | **me** | **more** | **Baali** | | **For I will take away** | | **names of** | **the Baalim** | **out of her mouth** | **and no** |

| 2142 יזכרו | 5750 עוד | 8034: בשמם | 2:18 | 3772 וכרתי | 3807a להם | 1285 ברית | 3117 ביום | 1931 ההוא | 5973 עם |
|---|---|---|---|---|---|---|---|---|---|
| yizakaru | 'aud | bishmam. | | uakaratiy | lahem | bariyt | bayoum | hahua', | 'am |
| **they shall be remembered** | **more** | **by their name** | | **And will I make** | **for them** | **a covenant** | **in day** | **that** | **with** |

| 2416 חית | 7704 השדה | 5973 ועם | 5775 עוף | 8064 השמים | 7431 ורמש | 127 האדמה | 7198 וקשת |
|---|---|---|---|---|---|---|---|
| chayat | hasadeh | ua'am | 'aup | hashamayim, | uaremes | ha'adamah; | uaqeshet |
| **the beasts of** | **the field** | **and with** | **the fowls of** | **heaven** | **and *with* the creeping things of** | **the ground** | **and the bow** |

| 2719 וחרב | 4421 ומלחמה | 7665 אשבור | 4480 מן | 776 הארץ | 7901 והשכבתים | 983: לבטח | 2:19 |
|---|---|---|---|---|---|---|---|
| uachereb | uamilchamah | 'ashbour | min | ha'aretz, | uahishkabtiym | labetach. | |
| **and the sword** | **and the battle** | **I will break** | **out of** | **the earth** | **and will make them to lie down** | **safely** | |

| 781 וארשתיך | 3807a לי | 5769 לעולם | 781 וארשתיך | 3807a לי | 6664 בצדק | 4941 ובמשפט |
|---|---|---|---|---|---|---|
| ua'aerastiyk | liy | la'aulam; | ua'aerastiyk | liy | batzedeq | uabmishpat, |
| **And I will betroth you** | **unto me** | **for ever** | **yea I will betroth you** | **unto me** | **in righteousness** | **and in judgment** |

| 2617 ובחסד | 7356: וברחמים | 2:20 | 781 וארשתיך | 3807a לי | 530 באמונה | 3045 וידעת | 853 את |
|---|---|---|---|---|---|---|---|
| uabchesed | uabrachamiym. | | ua'aerastiyk | liy | be'amunah; | uayada'at | 'at |
| **and in lovingkindness** | **and in mercies** | | **I will even betroth you** | **unto me** | **in faithfulness** | **and you shall know** | |

Hos 2:13 And I will visit upon her the days of Baalim, wherein she burned incense to them, and she decked herself with her earrings and her jewels, and she went after her lovers, and forgot me, saith YHUH.14 Therefore, behold, I will allure her, and bring her into the wilderness, and speak comfortably unto her.15 And I will give her her vineyards from thence, and the valley of Achor for a door of hope: and she shall sing there, as in the days of her youth, and as in the day when she came up out of the land of Egypt.16 And it shall be at that day, saith YHUH, that you shall call me Ishi; and shall call me no more Baali.17 For I will take away the names of Baalim out of her mouth, and they shall no more be remembered by their name.18 And in that day will I make a covenant for them with the beasts of the field, and with the fowls of heaven, and with the creeping things of the ground: and I will break the bow and the sword and the battle out of the earth, and will make them to lie down safely.19 And I will betroth you unto me forever; yea, I will betroth you unto me in righteousness, and in judgment, and in lovingkindness, and in mercies.20 I will even betroth you unto me in faithfulness: and you shall know YHUH.

| יהוה 3068: | 2:21 | והיה 1961 | ביום 3117 | ההוא 1931 | אענה 6030 | נאם 5002 | יהוה 3068 | אענה 6030 | את 853 | השמים 8064 | והם 1992 |
|---|---|---|---|---|---|---|---|---|---|---|---|
| Yahuah. | | uahayah | bayoum | hahua' | 'a'aneh | na'am | Yahuah, | 'a'aneh | 'at | hashamayim; | uahem |
| **Yahuah** | | **And it shall come to pass** | **in day** | **that** | **I will hear** | **saith** | **Yahuah** | **I will hear** | | **the heavens** | **and they** |

| יענו 6030 | את 853 | הארץ 776: | 2:22 | והארץ 776 | תענה 6030 | את 853 | הדגן 1715 | ואת 853 | התירוש 8492 | ואת 853 | היצהר 3323 | והם 1992 | יענו 6030 |
|---|---|---|---|---|---|---|---|---|---|---|---|---|---|
| ya'anu | 'at | ha'aretz. | | uaha'aretz | ta'aneh, | 'at | hadagan | ua'at | hatiyroush | ua'at | hayitzhar; | uahem | ya'anu |
| **shall hear** | | **the earth** | | **And the earth** | **shall hear** | | **the corn** | ***and*** | **the wine** | ***and*** | **the oil** | **and they** | **shall hear** |

| את 853 | יזרעאל 3157: | 2:23 | וזרעתיה 2232 | לי 3807a | בארץ 776 | ורחמתי 7355 | את 853 | לא 3808 |
|---|---|---|---|---|---|---|---|---|
| 'at | yizra'ael. | | uazra'atiyha | liy | ba'aretz, | uarichamtiy | 'at | la' |
| | **Jezreel** | | **And I will sow her** | **unto me** | **in the earth** | **and I will have mercy that had** | | **not** |

| רחמה 3819 | ואמרתי 559 | ללא 3818 | עמי 5971 | עמי 5971 | אתה 859 | והוא 1931 | יאמר 559 |
|---|---|---|---|---|---|---|---|
| ruchamah; | ua'amartiy | lala' | 'amiy | 'amiy | 'atah, | uahu'a | ya'mar |
| ***upon* her obtained mercy** | **and I will say** | **to *them which were* not** | **my people** | **my people** | **You *are*** | **and they** | **shall say** |

| אלהי 430: |
|---|
| 'alohay. |
| ***You are* my Elohim** |

| Hos 3:1 | ויאמר 559 | יהוה 3068 | אלי 413 | עוד 5750 | לך 1980 | אהב 157 | אשה 802 | אהבת 157 | רע 7453 | ומנאפת 5003 |
|---|---|---|---|---|---|---|---|---|---|---|
| | uaya'mer | Yahuah | 'aelay, | 'aud | lek | 'ahab | 'ashah, | 'ahubat | rea' | uamna'apet; |
| | **Then said** | **Yahuah** | **unto me** | **yet** | **Go you** | **love** | **a woman** | **beloved of** | ***her* friend** | **yet an adulteress** |

| כאהבת 160 | יהוה 3068 | את 853 | בני 1121 | ישראל 3478 | והם 1992 | פנים 6437 | אל 413 | אלהים 430 | אחרים 312 | ואהבי 157 |
|---|---|---|---|---|---|---|---|---|---|---|
| ka'ahabat | Yahuah | 'at | baney | yisra'ael, | uahem, | poniym | 'al | 'alohiym | 'acheriym, | ua'ahabey |
| **according to the love of** | **Yahuah** | | **toward the children of** | **Israel** | **who** | **look** | **to** | **gods** | **other** | **and love** |

| אשישי 809 | ענבים 6025: | 3:2 | ואכרה 3739 | לי 3807a | בחמשה 2568 | עשר 6240 | כסף 3701 | וחמר 2563 | שערים 8184 |
|---|---|---|---|---|---|---|---|---|---|
| 'ashiyshey | 'anabiym. | | ua'akreha | liy, | bachamishah | 'asar | kasep; | uachomer | sa'ariym |
| **flagons of** | **wine** | | **So I bought her** | **to me** | **five** | **ten** | ***pieces* of silver** | **and *for* an homer of** | **barley** |

| ולתך 3963 | שערים 8184: | 3:3 | ואמר 559 | אליה 413 | ימים 3117 | רבים 7227 | תשבי 3427 | לי 3807a | לא 3808 |
|---|---|---|---|---|---|---|---|---|---|
| ualetek | sa'ariym. | | ua'amar | 'aeleyha, | yamiym | rabiym | teshabiy | liy, | la' |
| **and an half homer of** | **barley** | | **And I said** | **unto her** | **days** | **many** | **You shall abide** | **for me** | **not** |

| תזני 2181 | ולא 3808 | תהיי 1961 | לאיש 376 | וגם 1571 | אני 589 | אליך 413: | 3:4 | כי 3588 | ימים 3117 | רבים 7227 |
|---|---|---|---|---|---|---|---|---|---|---|
| tizniy, | uala' | tihayiy | la'aysh; | uagam | 'aniy | 'aelayik. | | kiy | yamiym | rabiym, |
| **you shall play the harlot** | **and not** | **you shall be** | **for *another* man** | **so also *will*** | **I** | ***be* for you** | | **For** | **days** | **many** |

| ישבו 3427 | בני 1121 | ישראל 3478 | אין 369 | מלך 4428 | ואין 369 | שר 8269 | ואין 369 | זבח 2077 | ואין 369 | מצבה 4676 |
|---|---|---|---|---|---|---|---|---|---|---|
| yeshabu | baney | yisra'ael, | 'aeyn | melek | ua'aeyn | saar, | ua'aeyn | zebach | ua'aeyn | matzebah; |
| **shall abide** | **the children of** | **Israel** | **without** | **a king** | **and without** | **a prince** | **and without** | **a sacrifice** | **and without** | **an image** |

| ואין 369 | אפוד 646 | ותרפים 8655: | 3:5 | אחר 310 | ישבו 7725 | בני 1121 | ישראל 3478 | ובקשו 1245 | את 853 | יהוה 3069 |
|---|---|---|---|---|---|---|---|---|---|---|
| ua'aeyn | 'aepoud | uatrapiym. | | 'achar, | yashubu | baney | yisra'ael, | uabiqshu | 'at | Yahuah |
| **and without** | **an ephod** | **and *without* teraphim** | | **Afterward** | **shall return** | **the children of** | **Israel** | **and seek** | | **Yahuah** |

Hos 2:21 And it shall come to pass in that day, I will hear, saith YHUH, I will hear the heavens, and they shall hear the earth;22 And the earth shall hear the corn, and the wine, and the oil; and they shall hear Jezreel.23 And I will sow her unto me in the earth; and I will have mercy upon her that had not obtained mercy; and I will say to them which were not my people, Thou are my people; and they shall say, Thou are my G-d. **Hos** 3:1 Then said YHUH unto me, Go yet, love a woman beloved of her friend, yet an adulteress, according to the love of YHUH toward the children of Israel, who look to other gods, and love flagons of wine.2 So I bought her to me for fifteen pieces of silver, and for an homer of barley, and an half homer of barley:3 And I said unto her, Thou shall abide for me many days; you shall not play the harlot, and you shall not be for another man: so will I also be for you.4 For the children of Israel shall abide many days without a king, and without a prince, and without a sacrifice, and without an image, and without an ephod, and without teraphim:5 Afterward shall the children of Israel return, and seek YHUH their G-d, and David their king; and shall fear YHUH and his goodness in the latter days.

אלהיהם 430 ואת 853 דוד 1732 מלכם 4428 ופחדו 6342 אל 413 יהוה 3069 ואל 413 טובו 2898 באחרית 319 הימים 3117:
'aloheyhem, ua'at dauid malkam; uapachadu 'al Yahuah ua'al tubou ba'achariyt hayamiym.
**their Elohim *and* David their king and shall fear unto Yahuah and to his goodness in latter the days**

**Hos 4:1** שמעו 8085 דבר 1697 יהוה 3068 בני 1121 ישראל 3478 כי 3588 ריב 7379 ליהוה 3068 עם 5973
shim'au dabar Yahuah baney yisra'ael; kiy riyb laYahuah 'am
**Hear the word of Yahuah *you* children of Israel for has a controversy unto Yahuah with**

יושבי 3427 הארץ 776 כי 3588 אין 369 אמת 571 ואין 369 חסד 2617 ואין 369 דעת 1847 אלהים 430 בארץ 776: **4:2**
youshabey ha'aretz, kiy 'aeyn 'amet ua'aeyn chesed ua'aeyn da'at 'alohiym ba'aretz.
**the inhabitants of the land because *there is* no truth nor mercy nor knowledge of Elohim in the land**

אלה 422 וכחש 3584 ורצח 7523 וגנב 1589 ונאף 5003 פרצו 6555 ודמים 1818 בדמים 1818 נגעו 5060: **4:3**
'aloh uakachesh, uaratzoach uaganob uana'ap; paratzu uadamiym badamiym naga'au.
***By* swearing and lying and killing and stealing and committing adultery they break out and blood in blood touch**

על 5921 כן 3651 תאבל 56 הארץ 776 ואמלל 535 כל 3605 יושב 3427 בה 871a בחית 2416 השדה 7704
'al ken te'abal ha'aretz, ua'amlal kal yousheb bah, bachayat hasadeh
**Therefore after that shall mourn the land and shall languish every one that dwell therein with the beasts of the field**

ובעוף 5775 השמים 8064 וגם 1571 דגי 1709 הים 3220 יאספו 622: **4:4** אך 389 איש 376 אל 408 ירב 7378 ואל 408
uab'aup hashamayim; uagam dagey hayam ye'asepu. 'ak 'aysh 'al yareb ua'al
**and with the fowls of heaven yea also the fishes of the sea shall be taken away Yet man no let strive nor**

יוכח 3198 איש 376 ועמך 5971 כמריבי 7378 כהן 3548: **4:5** וכשלת 3782 היום 3117 וכשל 3782
youkach 'aysh; ua'amaka kimriybey kohen. uakashalta hayoum, uakashal
**reprove another for your people *are* as they that strive with the priest Therefore shall you fall *in* the day and shall fall**

גם 1571 נביא 5030 עמך 5973 לילה 3915 ודמיתי 1820 אמך 517: **4:6** נדמו 1820 עמי 5971 מבלי 1097 הדעת 1847
gam nabiy'a 'amaka layalah; uadamiytiy 'ameka. nidmu 'amiy mibaliy hada'at;
**also the prophet with you *in* the night and I will destroy your mother are destroyed My people for lack of knowledge**

כי 3588 אתה 859 הדעת 1847 מאסת 3988 ואמאסאך 3988 מכהן 3547 לי 3807a ותשכח 7911
kiy 'atah hada'at ma'asta, ua'am'asa'ka mikahen liy, uatishkach
**because you knowledge have rejected I will also reject you *that* you shall be no priest to me seeing you have forgotten**

תורת 8451 אלהיך 430 אשכח 7911 בניך 1121 גם 1571 אני 589: **4:7** כרבם 7235 כן 3651 חטאו 2398 לי 3807a
tourat 'aloheyka, 'ashkach baneyka gam 'aniy. karubam ken chata'au liy;
**the law of your Elohim will forget your children also I As they were increased so they sinned against me**

כבודם 3519 בקלון 7036 אמיר 4171: **4:8** חטאת 2403 עמי 5971 יאכלו 398 ואל 413 עונם 5771 ישאו 5375
kaboudam baqaloun 'amiyr. chata't 'amiy ya'kelu; ua'al 'auonam yis'au
**their glory into shame *therefore* will I change the sin of my people They eat up and on their iniquity they set**

נפשו 5315: **4:9** והיה 1961 כעם 5971 ככהן 3548 ופקדתי 6485 עליו 5921 דרכיו 1870 ומעלליו 4611 אשיב 7725
napshou. uahayah ka'am kakohen; uapaqadtiy 'alayu darakayu, uama'alalayu 'ashiyb
**their heart And there shall be like people like priest and I will punish them for their ways and their doings reward**

**Hos** 4:1 Hear the word of YHUH, you children of Israel: for YHUH has a controversy with the inhabitants of the land, because there is no truth, nor mercy, nor knowledge of G-d in the land.2 By swearing, and lying, and killing, and stealing, and committing adultery, they break out, and blood touch blood.3 Therefore shall the land mourn, and everyone that dwell therein shall languish, with the beasts of the field, and with the fowls of heaven; yea, the fishes of the sea also shall be taken away.4 Yet let no man strive, nor reprove another: for your people are as they that strive with the priest.5 Therefore shall you fall in the day, and the prophet also shall fall with you in the night, and I will destroy your mother.6 My people are destroyed for lack of knowledge: because you have rejected knowledge, I will also reject you, that you shall be no priest to me: seeing you have forgotten the law of your G-d, I will also forget your children.7 As they were increased, so they sinned against me: therefore will I change their glory into shame.8 They eat up the sin of my people, and they set their heart on their iniquity.9 And there shall be, like people, like priest: and I will punish them for their ways, and reward them their doings.

4:10
לו 3807a: | ואכלו 398 | ולא 3808 | ישבעו 7646 | הזנו 2181 | ולא 3808 | יפרצו 6555 | כי 3588 | את 853
lou'. | ua'akalu | uala' | yisba'au, | hiznu | uala' | yiprotzu; | kiy | 'at
**them | For they shall eat | and not | have enough | they shall commit whoredom | and not | shall increase | because**

4:11 4:12
יהוה 3068 | עזבו 5800 | לשמר 8104: | זנות 2184 | ויין 3196 | ותירוש 8492 | יקח 3947 | לב 3820: | עמי 5971
Yahuah | 'azabu | lishmor. | zanut | uayayin | uatiyroush | yiqach | leb. | 'amiy
**Yahuah | they have left off | to take heed to | Whoredom | and wine | and new wine | take away | the heart | My people**

בעצו 6086 | ישאל 7592 | ומקלו 4731 | יגיד 5046 | לו 3807a | כי 3588 | רוח 7307 | זנונים 2183 | התעה 8582
ba'aetzou | yish'al, | uamaqlou | yagiyd | lou'; | kiy | ruach | zanuniym | hit'ah,
**at their stocks | ask counsel | and their staff | declareth | unto them | for | the spirit of | whoredoms | has caused *them* to err**

4:13
ויזנו 2181 | מתחת 8478 | אלהיהם 430: | על 5921 | ראשי 7218 | ההרים 2022 | יזבחו 2076 | ועל 5921
uayiznu | mitachat | 'aloheyhem. | 'al | ra'shey | hehariym | yazabechu, | ua'al
**and they have gone a whoring | from under | their Elohim | upon | the tops of | the mountains | They sacrifice | upon**

הגבעות 1389 | יקטרו 6999 | תחת 8478 | אלון 437 | ולבנה 3839 | ואלה 424 | כי 3588 | טוב 2896 | צלה 6738 | על 5921 | כן 3651
hagaba'aut | yaqateru, | tachat | 'aloun | ualibneh | ua'aelah | kiy | toub | tzilah; | 'al | ken,
**the hills | *and* burn incense | under | oaks | and poplars | and elms | because | *is* good | the shadow thereof | therefore | after that**

4:14
תזנינה 2181 | בנותיכם 1323 | וכלותיכם 3618 | תנאפנה 5003: | לא 3808 | אפקוד 6485 | על 5921
tizneynah | banouteykem, | uakalouteykem | tana'apnah. | la' | 'apqoud | 'al
**shall commit whoredom | your daughters | and your spouses | shall commit adultery | not | I will punish | on**

בנותיכם 1323 | כי 3588 | תזנינה 2181 | ועל 5921 | כלותיכם 3618 | כי 3588 | תנאפנה 5003 | כי 3588 | הם 1992 | עם 5973
banouteykem | kiy | tizneynah, | ua'al | kalouteykem | kiy | tana'apnah, | kiy | hem | 'am
**your daughters | when | they commit whoredom | nor | your spouses | when | they commit adultery | for | themselves | with**

4:15
הזנות 2181 | יפרדו 6504 | ועם 5973 | הקדשות 6948 | יזבחו 2076 | ועם 5971 | לא 3808 | יבין 995 | ילבט 3832:
hazonout | yaparedu, | ua'am | haqadeshout | yazabechu; | ua'am | la' | yabiyn | yilabet.
**whores | are separated | and with | harlots | they sacrifice | therefore the people | not | *that* does understand | shall fall**

אם 518 | זנה 2181 | אתה 859 | ישראל 3478 | אל 408 | יאשם 816 | יהודה 3063 | ואל 408 | תבאו 935 | הגלגל 1537 | ואל 408 | תעלו 5927
'am | zoneh | 'atah | yisra'ael, | 'al | ye'asham | yahudah; | ua'al | tabo'au | hagilgal, | ua'al | ta'alu
**Though | play the harlot | you | Israel | not | *yet* let offend | Judah | and not | come you | *unto* Gilgal | neither | go you up to**

4:16
בית 1007 | און 205 | ואל 408 | תשבעו 7650 | חי 2416 | יהוה 3069: | כי 3588 | כפרה 6510 | סררה 5637 | סרר 5637 | ישראל 3478 | עתה 6258 | ירעם 7462
beyt | 'auen, | ua'al | tishab'au | chay | Yahuah. | kiy | kaparah | sorerah, | sarar | yisra'ael; | 'atah | yir'aem
**Beth aven | nor | swear | live | Yahuah | For | as heifer | slideth back | a backsliding | Israel | now | will feed them**

4:17 4:18
יהוה 3068 | ככבש 3532 | במרחב 4800: | חבור 2266 | עצבים 6091 | אפרים 669 | הנח 3240 | לו 3807a: | סר 5493 | סבאם 5435
Yahuah, | kakebes | bamerchab. | chabur | 'atzabiym | 'aprayim | hanach | lou'. | sar | saba'am;
**Yahuah | as a lamb | in a large place | *is* joined to | idols | Ephraim | let alone | him | is sour | Their drink**

4:19
הזנה 2181 | הזנו 2181 | אהבו 157 | הבו 3051 | קלון 7036 | מגניה 4043: | צרר 6887 | רוח 7307 | אותה 853
hazneh | hiznu, | 'ahabu | hebu | qaloun | magineyha. | tzarar | ruach | 'autah
**they have committed whoredom | continually | do love | Give you | *with* shame | her rulers | has bound up | The wind | her**

Hos 4:10 For they shall eat, and not have enough: they shall commit whoredom, and shall not increase: because they have left off to take heed to YHUH.11 Whoredom and wine and new wine take away the heart.12 My people ask counsel at their stocks, and their staff declareth unto them: for the spirit of whoredoms has caused them to err, and they have gone a whoring from under their G-d.13 They sacrifice upon the tops of the mountains, and burn incense upon the hills, under oaks and poplars and elms, because the shadow thereof is good: therefore your daughters shall commit whoredom, and your spouses shall commit adultery.14 I will not punish your daughters when they commit whoredom, nor your spouses when they commit adultery: for themselves are separated with whores, and they sacrifice with harlots: therefore the people that doth not understand shall fall.15 Though you, Israel, play the harlot, yet let not Judah offend; and come not you unto Gilgal, neither go you up to Beth-aven, nor swear, YHUH live.16 For Israel slideth back as a backsliding heifer: now YHUH will feed them as a lamb in a large place.17 Ephraim is joined to idols: let him alone.18 Their drink is sour: they have committed whoredom continually: her rulers with shame do love, Give you.19 The wind has bound her up in her wings,

בכנפיה 3671 ויבשו 954 מזבחותם 2077:
biknapeyha; uayeboshu mizibchoutam.
**in her wings and they shall be ashamed because of their sacrifices**

**Hos 5:1** שמעו 8085 זאת 2063 הכהנים 3548 והקשיבו 7181 בית 1004 ישראל 3478 ובית 1004 המלך 4428 האזינו 238 כי 3588
shim'au za't hakohaniym uahaqshiybu beyt yisra'ael, uabeyt hamelek ha'aziynu, kiy
**Hear you this O priests and listen *you* house of Israel O house of the king give you ear for**

לכם 3807a המשפט 4941 כי 3588 פח 6341 הייתם 1961 למצפה 4709 ורשת 7568 פרושה 6566 על 5921 תבור 8396: **5:2**
lakem hamishpat; kiy pach heyiytem lamitzpah, uareshet parusah 'al tabour.
***is* toward you judgment because a snare you have been on Mizpah and a net spread upon Tabor**

ושחטה 7819 שטים 7846 העמיקו 6009 ואני 589 מוסר 4148 לכלם 3605: **5:3** אני 589 ידעתי 3045 אפרים 669
uashachatah setiym he'amiyqu; ua'aniy musar lakulam. 'aniy yada'tiy 'aprayim,
**And make slaughter the revolters are profound *to* though I *have been* a rebuker of them all I know Ephraim**

וישראל 3478 לא 3808 נכחד 3582 ממני 4480 כי 3588 עתה 6258 הזנית 2181 אפרים 669 נטמא 2930 ישראל 3478: **5:4** לא 3808
uayisra'ael la' nikchad mimeniy; kiy 'atah hizneyta 'aprayim, nitma' yisra'ael. la'
**and Israel not is hid from me for now you committest whoredom O Ephraim is defiled *and* Israel not**

יתנו 5414 מעלליהם 4611 לשוב 7725 אל 413 אלהיהם 430 כי 3588 רוח 7307 זנונים 2183 בקרבם 7130 ואת 853
yitanu ma'alleyhem, lashub 'al 'aloheyhem; kiy ruach zanuniym baqirbam, ua'at
**They will frame their doings to turn unto their Elohim for the spirit of whoredoms *is* in the midst of them *and***

יהוה 3068 לא 3808 ידעו 3045: **5:5** וענה 6030 גאון 1347 ישראל 3478 בפניו 6440 וישראל 3478 ואפרים 669
Yahuah la' yada'au. ua'anah ga'aun yisra'ael bapanayu; uayisra'ael ua'aprayim,
**Yahuah not they have known And does testify the pride of Israel to his face therefore Israel and Ephraim**

יכשלו 3782 בעונם 5771 כשל 3782 גם 1571 יהודה 3063 עמם 5973: **5:6** בצאנם 6629 ובבקרם 1241 ילכו 1980 לבקש 1245
yikashalu ba'auonam, kashal gam yahudah 'amam. batza'nam uabibqaram, yelaku labaqesh
**shall fall in their iniquity fall also Judah with them with their flocks and with their herds They shall go to seek**

את 853 יהוה 3068 ולא 3808 ימצאו 4672 חלץ 2502 מהם 1992: **5:7** ביהוה 3068 בגדו 898
'at Yahuah uala' yimtza'au; chalatz mehem. baYahuah bagadu,
**Yahuah but not they shall find *him* he has withdrawn from them against Yahuah They have dealt treacherously**

כי 3588 בנים 1121 זרים 2114 ילדו 3205 עתה 6258 יאכלם 398 חדש 2320 את 854 חלקיהם 2506: **5:8** תקעו 8628 שופר 7782
kiy baniym zariym yaladu; 'atah ya'kalem chodesh 'at chelqeyhem. tiq'au shoupar
**for children strange they have begotten now shall devour them a month *with* their portions Blow you the cornet**

בגבעה 1390 חצצרה 2689 ברמה 7414 הריעו 7321 בית 1007 און 205 אחריך 310 בנימין 1144: **5:9** אפרים 669 לשמה 8047 תהיה 1961
bagiba'ah, chatzoarah baramah; hariy'au beyt 'auen, 'achareyka binyamiyn. 'aprayim lashamah tihayeh,
**in Gibeah *and* the trumpet in Ramah cry aloud *at* Beth aven after you O Benjamin Ephraim desolate shall be**

ביום 3117 תוכחה 8433 בשבטי 7626 ישראל 3478 הודעתי 3045 נאמנה 539: **5:10** היו 1961
bayoum toukechah; bashibtey yisra'ael, houda'atiy ne'amanah. hayu
**in the day of rebuke among the tribes of Israel have I made known that which shall surely be were**

Hos 4:19 and they shall be ashamed because of their sacrifices. **Hos** 5:1 Hear you this, O priests; and hear, you house of Israel; and give you ear, O house of the king; for judgment is toward you, because you have been a snare on Mizpah, and a net spread upon Tabor.2 And the revolters are profound to make slaughter, though I have been a rebuker of them all.3 I know Ephraim, and Israel is not hid from me: for now, O Ephraim, you committest whoredom, and Israel is defiled.4 They will not frame their doings to turn unto their G-d. for the spirit of whoredoms is in the midst of them, and they have not known YHUH.5 And the pride of Israel doth testify to his face: therefore shall Israel and Ephraim fall in their iniquity; Judah also shall fall with them.6 They shall go with their flocks and with their herds to seek YHUH; but they shall not find him; he has withdrawn himself from them.7 They have dealt treacherously against YHUH: for they have begotten strange children: now shall a month devour them with their portions.8 Blow you the cornet in Gibeah, and the trumpet in Ramah: cry aloud at Beth-aven, after you, O Benjamin.9 Ephraim shall be desolate in the day of rebuke: among the tribes of Israel have I made known that which shall surely be.10 The princes of Judah were like them that remove the bound: therefore I will pour out my wrath upon them like water.

שרי 8269 יהודה 3063 כמסיגי 5253 גבול 1366 עליהם 5921 אשפוך 8210 כמים 4325 עברתי 5678: **5:11**
sarey yahudah, kamasiygey gabul; 'aleyhem 'ashpouk kamayim 'abratiy.
**The princes of Judah like them that remove the bound upon them *therefore* I will pour out like water my wrath**

עשוק 6217 אפרים 669 רצוץ 7533 משפט 4941 כי 3588 הואיל 2974 הלך 1980 אחרי 310 צו 6673: **5:12**
'ashuq 'aprayim ratzutz mishapat; kiy hou'ayl, halok 'acharey tzau.
***is* oppressed Ephraim *and* broken *in* judgment because willingly he walked after *the* commandment**

ואני 589 כעש 6211 לאפרים 669 וכרקב 7538 לבית 1004 יהודה 3063: **5:13** וירא 7200 אפרים 669 את 853
ua'aniy ka'ash la'aprayim; uakaraqab labeyt yahudah. uayar'a 'aprayim 'at
**Therefore *will* I as a moth *be* unto Ephraim and as rottenness to the house of Judah When saw Ephraim**

חליו 2483 ויהודה 3063 את 853 מזרו 4205 וילך 1980 אפרים 669 אל 413 אשור 804 וישלח 7971 אל 413 מלך 4428 ירב 3377 והוא 1931
chalayou, uayahudah 'at mazorou, uayelek 'aprayim 'al 'ashur, uayishlach 'al melek yareb; uahu'a,
**his sickness and Judah *saw* his wound then went Ephraim to the Assyrian and sent to king Jareb yet he**

לא 3808 יוכל 3201 לרפא 7495 לכם 3807a ולא 3808 יגהה 1455 מכם 4480 מזור 4205: **5:14** כי 3588 אנכי 595 כשחל 7826 לאפרים 669
la' yukal lirpa' lakem, uala' yigheh mikem mazour. kiy 'anokiy kashachal la'aprayim,
**not could heal to you nor cure from you *of* your wound For I as a lion *will be* unto Ephraim**

וככפיר 3715 לבית 1004 יהודה 3063 אני 589 אני 589 אטרף 2963 ואלך 1980 אשא 5375 ואין 369 מציל 5337: **5:15**
uakakpiyr labeyt yahudah; 'aniy 'aniy 'atrop ua'aelek, 'asa' ua'aeyn matziyl.
**and as a young lion to the house of Judah I *even* I will tear and go away I will take and none shall rescue *him***

אלך 1980 אשובה 7725 אל 413 מקומי 4725 עד 5704 אשר 834 יאשמו 816 ובקשו 1245 פני 6440 בצר 6862 להם 1992
'aelek 'ashubah 'al maqoumiy, 'ad 'asher ya'shamu uabiqshu panay; batzar lahem
**I will go *and* return to my place till which they acknowledge their offence and seek my face in affliction their**

ישחרנני 7836:
yashacharuniy.
**they will seek me early**

**Hos 6:1** לכו 1980 ונשובה 7725 אל 413 יהוה 3068 כי 3588 הוא 1931 טרף 2963 וירפאנו 7495 יך 5221
laku uanashubah 'al Yahuah, kiy hua' tarap uayirpa'aenu; yak
**Come and let us return unto Yahuah for he has torn and he will heal us he has smitten**

ויחבשנו 2280: **6:2** יחינו 2421 מימים 3117 ביום 3117 השלישי 7992 יקמנו 6965 ונחיה 2421
uayachbashenu. yachayenu miyomayim; bayoum hashaliyshiy, yaqimenu uanichayeh
**and he will bind us up will he revive us After two days *in* the third *day* he will raise us up and we shall live**

לפניו 6440: **6:3** ונדעה 3045 נרדפה 7291 לדעת 3045 את 853 יהוה 3068 כשחר 7837 נכון 3559 מוצאו 4161
lapanayu. uaned'ah nirdapah, lada'at 'at Yahuah, kashachar nakoun moutza'au;
**in his sight Then shall we know *if* we follow on to know Yahuah as the morning is prepared his going forth**

ויבוא 935 כגשם 1653 לנו 3807a כמלקוש 4456 יורה 3138 ארץ 776: **6:4** מה 4100 אעשה 6213 לך 3807a אפרים 669
uayabou'a kageshem lanu, kamalqoush youreh 'aretz. mah 'aaseh laka 'aprayim,
**and he shall come as the rain unto us as the latter *and* former rain *unto the* earth what shall I do unto you? O Ephraim**

Hos 5:11 Ephraim is oppressed and broken in judgment, because he willingly walked after the commandment.12 Therefore will I be unto Ephraim as a moth, and to the house of Judah as rottenness.13 When Ephraim saw his sickness, and Judah saw his wound, then went Ephraim to the Assyrian, and sent to king Jareb: yet could he not heal you, nor cure you of your wound.14 For I will be unto Ephraim as a lion, and as a young lion to the house of Judah: I, even I, will tear and go away; I will take away, and none shall rescue him.15 I will go and return to my place, till they acknowledge their offence, and seek my face: in their affliction they will seek me early. **Hos** 6:1 Come, and let us return unto YHUH: for he has torn, and he will heal us; he has smitten, and he will bind us up.2 After two days will he revive us: in the third day he will raise us up, and we shall live in his sight.3 Then shall we know, if we follow on to know YHUH: his going forth is prepared as the morning; and he shall come unto us as the rain, as the latter and former rain unto the earth.4 O Ephraim, what shall I do unto you? O Judah, what shall I do unto you? for your goodness is as a morning cloud, and as the early dew it go away.

6:5
מה 4100 אעשה 6213 לך 3807a יהודה 3063 וחסדכם 2617 כענן 6051 בקר 1242 וכטל 2919 משכים 7925 הלך 1980:
mah 'aaseh laka yahudah; uachasdakem ka'anan boqer, uakatal mashkiym holek.
**what shall I do unto you? O Judah for your goodness *is* as a cloud morning and as the dew early it goes away**

על 5921 כן 3651 חצבתי 2630 בנביאים 5030 הרגתים 2060 באמרי 561 פי 6310 ומשפטיך 4941
'al ken, chatzabtiy banabiy'aym, haragtiym ba'amrey piy; uamishpateyka
**Therefore after that have I hewed *them* by the prophets I have slain them by the words of my mouth and your judgments**

אור 216 יצא 3318: 6:6 כי 3588 חסד 2617 חפצתי 2654 ולא 3808 זבח 2077 ודעת 1847 אלהים 430
'aur yetzea'. kiy chesed chapatztiy uala' zabach; uada'at 'alohiym
***are as* the light *that* goes forth For mercy I desired and not sacrifice and the knowledge of Elohim**

מעלות 5930: 6:7 והמה 1992 כאדם 121 עברו 5674 ברית 1285 שם 8033 בגדו 898
me'alout. uahemah ka'adam 'abaru bariyt; sham bagadu
***more* than burnt offerings But they like men have transgressed the covenant there have they dealt treacherously**

בי 871a: 6:8 גלעד 1568 קרית 7151 פעלי 6466 און 205 עקבה 6121 מדם 1818: 6:9 וכחכי 2442 איש 376
biy. gil'ad qiryat po'aley 'auen; 'aqubah midam. uakchakey 'aysh
**against me Gilead *is* a city of them that work iniquity *and is* polluted with blood And as wait for a man**

גדודים 1416 חבר 2267 כהנים 3548 דרך 1870 ירצחו 7523 שכמה 7926 כי 3588 זמה 2154 עשו 6213: 6:10
gadudiym, cheber kohaniym, derek yaratztzchu shekmah; kiy zimah 'asu.
**troops of robbers *so* the company of priests *in the* way murder to consent for lewdness they commit**

בבית 1004 ישראל 3478 ראיתי 7200 שעריריה 8186 שם 8033 זנות 2184 לאפרים 669 נטמא 2930 ישראל 3478: 6:11 גם 1571
babeyt yisra'ael, ra'aytiy sha'aririyah sam zanut la'aprayim, nitma' yisra'ael. gam
**in the house of Israel I have seen an horrible thing there *is the* whoredom of Ephraim is defiled Israel Also**

יהודה 3063 שת 7896 קציר 7105 לך 3807a בשובי 7725 שבות 7622 עמי 5971:
yahudah shat qatziyr lak; bashubiy shabut 'amiy.
**O Judah he has set an harvest for you when I returned the captivity of my people**

Hos 7:1
כרפאי 7495 לישראל 3478 ונגלה 1540 עון 5771 אפרים 669 ורעות 7451
karapa'iy layisra'ael, uaniglah 'auon 'aprayim uara'aut
**When I would have healed Israel then was discovered the iniquity of Ephraim and the wickedness of**

שמרון 8111 כי 3588 פעלו 6466 שקר 8267 וגנב 1590 יבוא 935 פשט 6584 גדוד 1416 בחוץ 2351: 7:2 ובל 1077
shomaroun, kiy pa'alu shaqer; uaganab yabou'a, pashat gadud bachutz. uabal
**Samaria for they commit falsehood and the thief comes in spoil *and* the troop of robbers without And not**

יאמרו 559 ללבבם 3824 כל 3605 רעתם 7451 זכרתי 2142 עתה 6258 סבבום 5437 מעלליהם 4611 נגד 5048
ya'maru lilbabam, kal ra'atam zakaratiy; 'atah sababum ma'alleyhem, neged
**they consider in their hearts all their wickedness *that* I remember now have beset them about their own doings before**

פני 6440 היו 1961: 7:3 ברעתם 7451 ישמחו 8055 מלך 4428 ובכחשיהם 3585 שרים 8269: 7:4 כלם 3605
panay hayu. bara'atam yasamchu melek; uabkachasheyhem sariym. kulam
**my face they are with their wickedness They make glad the king and with their lies the princes They *are* all**

Hos 6:5 Therefore have I hewed them by the prophets; I have slain them by the words of my mouth: and your judgments are as the light that go forth.6 For I desired mercy, and not sacrifice; and the knowledge of G-d more than burnt offerings.7 But they like men have transgressed the covenant: there have they dealt treacherously against me.8 Gilead is a city of them that work iniquity, and is polluted with blood.9 And as troops of robbers wait for a man, so the company of priests murder in the way by consent: for they commit lewdness.10 I have seen an horrible thing in the house of Israel: there is the whoredom of Ephraim, Israel is defiled.11 Also, O Judah, he has set an harvest for you, when I returned the captivity of my people. **Hos** 7:1 When I would have healed Israel, then the iniquity of Ephraim was discovered, and the wickedness of Samaria: for they commit falsehood; and the thief cometh in, and the troop of robbers spoileth without.2 And they consider not in their hearts that I remember all their wickedness: now their own doings have beset them about; they are before my face.3 They make the king glad with their wickedness, and the princes with their lies.4 They are all adulterers, as an oven heated by the baker, who ceaseth from raising after he has kneeded the dough, until it be leavened.

מנאפים 5003 כמו 3644 תנור 8574 בערה 1197 מאפה 644 ישבות 7673 מעיר 5782 מלוש 3888 בצק 1217 עד 5704
mana'apiym, kamou tanur, bo'aerah me'opeh; yishbout me'ayr, milush batzeq 'ad
**adulterers as an oven heated by the baker *who* cease from raising after he has kneaded the dough until**

חמצתו 2556: 7:5 יום 3117 מלכנו 4428 החלו 2470 שרים 8269 חמת 2534 מיין 3196 משך 4900 ידו 3027 את 854
chumtzatou. youm malkenu, hechelu sariym chamat miyayin; mashach yadou 'at
**it be leavened *In the* day of our king have made *him* sick the princes bottle of wine he stretched out his hand *with***

לצצים 3945: 7:6 כי 3588 קרבו 7126 כתנור 8574 לבם 3820 בארבם 693 כל 3605 הלילה 3915 ישן 3462 אפהם 644
lotzatziym. kiy qereabu katanur libam ba'arabam; kal halayalah yashen 'aphem,
**scorners For they have made ready like an oven their heart whiles they lie in wait all the night sleep their baker**

בקר 1242 הוא 1931 בער 1197 כאש 784 להבה 3852: 7:7 כלם 3605 יחמו 2552 כתנור 8574 ואכלו 398 את 853 שפטיהם 8199
boqer hua' bo'aer ka'aesh lehabah. kulam yechamu katanur, ua'akalu 'at shopateyhem;
***in the* morning it burn as a fire the flaming They all are hot as an oven and have devoured their judges**

כל 3605 מלכיהם 4428 נפלו 5307 אין 369 קרא 7121 בהם 871a אלי 413: 7:8 אפרים 669 בעמים 5971 הוא 1931
kal malkeyhem napalu, 'aeyn qorea' bahem 'aelay. 'aprayim ba'amiym hua'
**all their kings are fallen *there is* none that call among them unto me Ephraim among the people he**

יתבולל 1101 אפרים 669 היה 1961 עגה 5692 בלי 1097 הפוכה 2015: 7:9 אכלו 398 זרים 2114 כחו 3581 והוא 1931 לא 3808
yitboulal; 'aprayim hayah 'agah baliy hapukah. 'akalu zariym kochou, uahu'a la'
**has mixed himself Ephraim is a cake not turned have devoured Strangers his strength and he not**

ידע 3045 גם 1571 שיבה 7872 זרקה 2236 בו 871a והוא 1931 לא 3808 ידע 3045: 7:10 וענה 6030 גאון 1347 ישראל 3478
yada'; gam seybah zaraqah bou, uahu'a la' yada'. ua'anah ga'aun yisra'ael
**knows *it* yea gray hairs are here and there upon him yet he not knows And testifies the pride of Israel**

בפניו 6440 ולא 3808 שבו 7725 אל 413 יהוה 3068 אלהיהם 430 ולא 3808 בקשהו 1245 בכל 3605 זאת 2063: 7:11 ויהי 1961 אפרים 669
bapanayu; uala' shabu 'al Yahuah 'aloheyhem, uala' biqshuhu bakal za't. uayahiy 'aprayim,
**to his face and not they do return to Yahuah their Elohim nor seek him for all this also is Ephraim**

כיונה 3123 פותה 6601 אין 369 לב 3820 מצרים 4714 קראו 7121 אשור 804 הלכו 1980: 7:12 כאשר 834 ילכו 1980 אפרוש 6566 עליהם 5921
kayounah poutah 'aeyn leb; mitzrayim qara'au 'ashur halaku. ka'asher yeleku, 'aprous 'aleyhem
**like a dove silly without heart *to* Egypt they call *to* Assyria they go When they shall go I will spread upon them**

רשתי 7568 כעוף 5775 השמים 8064 אורידם 3381 איסרם 3256 כשמע 8088 לעדתם 5712: 7:13 אוי 188
rishtiy, ka'aup hashamayim 'auriydem; 'ayasirem kashema' la'adatam. 'auy
**my net as the fowls of the heaven I will bring them down I will chastise them has heard as their congregation Woe**

להם 1992 כי 3588 נדדו 5074 ממני 4480 שד 7701 להם 1992 כי 3588 פשעו 6586 בי 871a ואנכי 595
lahem kiy nadadu mimeniy, shod lahem kiy pasha'au biy; ua'anokiy
**unto them for they have fled from me destruction unto them because they have transgressed against me though I**

אפדם 6299 והמה 1992 דברו 1696 עלי 5921 כזבים 3577: 7:14 ולא 3808 זעקו 2199 אלי 413 בלבם 3820
'apdem, uahemah dibru 'alay kazabiym. uala' za'aqu 'aelay balibam,
**have redeemed them yet they have spoken against me lies And not they have cried unto me with their heart**

Hos 7:5 In the day of our king the princes have made him sick with bottles of wine; he stretched out his hand with scorners.6 For they have made ready their heart like an oven, whiles they lie in wait: their baker sleep all the night; in the morning it burneth as a flaming fire.7 They are all hot as an oven, and have devoured their judges; all their kings are fallen: there is none among them that call unto me.8 Ephraim, he has mixed himself among the people; Ephraim is a cake not turned.9 Strangers have devoured his strength, and he know it not: yea, gray hairs are here and there upon him, yet he know not.10 And the pride of Israel testifieth to his face: and they do not return to YHUH their G-d, nor seek him for all this.11 Ephraim also is like a silly dove without heart: they call to Egypt, they go to Assyria.12 When they shall go, I will spread my net upon them; I will bring them down as the fowls of the heaven; I will chastise them, as their congregation has heard.13 Woe unto them! for they have fled from me: destruction unto them! because they have transgressed against me: though I have redeemed them, yet they have spoken lies against me.14 And they have not cried unto me with their heart, when they howled upon their beds: they assemble themselves for corn and wine, and they rebel against me.

7:15
3588 כי 3213 יילילו 5921 על 4904 משכבותם 5921 על 1715 דגן 8492 ותירוש 1481 יתגוררו 5493 יסורו 871a בי:
kiy yayeliylu 'al mishkaboutam; 'al dagan uatiyroush yitgouraru yasuru biy.
**when they howled upon their beds for corn and wine they assemble themselves *and* they rebel against me**

7:16
589 ואני 3256 יסרתי 2388 חזקתי 2220 זרועתם 413 ואלי 2803 יחשבו 7451 רע: 7725 ישובו 3808 לא
ua'aniy yisartiy, chizaqtiy zarou'atam; ua'aelay yachashbu ra'. yashubu la'
**Though I have bound *and* strengthened their arms yet against me do they imagine mischief They return *but* not**

5920 על 1961 היו 7198 כקשת 7423 רמיה 5307 יפלו 2719 בחרב 8269 שריהם 2195 מזעם 3956 לשונם 2097 זו
'aal, hayu kaqeshet ramiyah, yiplu bachereb sareyhem miza'am lashounam; zou
***to the* most High they are like a bow deceitful shall fall by the sword their princes for the rage of their tongue this**

3933 לעגם 776 בארץ 4714 מצרים:
la'gam ba'aretz mitzrayim.
***shall be* their derision in the land of Egypt**

**Hos 8:1**
413 אל 2441 חכך 7782 שפר 5404 כנשר 5921 על 1004 בית 3068 יהוה 3282 יען
'al chikka shopar, kanesher 'al beyt Yahuah; ya'an
***Set the* to your mouth trumpet *He shall come* as an eagle against the house of Yahuah because**

8:2
5674 עברו 1285 בריתי 5921 ועל 8451 תורתי 6586 פשעו: 3807a לי 2199 יזעקו 430 אלהי 3045 ידענוך
'abaru bariytiy, ua'al touratiy pasha'au. liy yiz'aqu; 'alohay yada'anuka
**they have transgressed my covenant and against my law trespassed unto me shall cry My Elohim we know you**

8:3
3478 ישראל: 2186 זנח 3478 ישראל 2896 טוב 341 אויב 7291 ירדפו:
yisra'ael. zanach yisra'ael toub; auyeb yirdapou
**Israel has cast off Israel *the thing that is* good the enemy shall pursue him**

8:4
1992 הם 4427 המליכו 3808 ולא
hem himliyku uala'
**They have set up kings but not**

4480 ממני 8323 השירו 3808 ולא 3045 ידעתי 3701 כספם 2091 וזהבם 6213 עשו 3807a להם 6091 עצבים 4616 למען
mimeniy, hesiyru uala' yadaa'tiy; kaspam uazhabam, 'asu lahem 'atzabiym, lama'an
**by me they have made princes did not I knew *it of* their silver and their gold have they made them idols that**

8:5
3772 יכרת: 2186 זנח 5695 עגלך 8111 שמרון 2734 חרה 639 אפי 871a בם 5704 עד 4970 מתי 3808 לא
yikaret. zanach 'aglek shomaroun, charah 'apiy bam; 'ad matay la'
**they may be cut off has cast *you* off Your calf O Samaria is kindled mine anger against them how long *will it be* ere**

8:6
3201 יוכלו 5356 נקין: 3588 כי 3478 מישראל 1931 והוא 2796 חרש 6213 עשהו 3808 ולא 430 אלהים 1931 הוא 3588 כי
yukalu niqayon. kiy miyisra'ael uahu'a, charash 'asahu, uala' 'alohiym hua'; kiy
**they attain to innocency? For from Israel *was* it also the workman made it therefore not Elohim it *is* but**

8:7
7616 שבבים 1961 יהיה 5695 עגל 8111 שמרון: 3588 כי 7307 רוח 2232 יזרעו 5492 וסופתה 7114 יקצרו
shababiym yihayeh, 'aegel shomaroun. kiy ruach yizra'au uasupatah yiqtzoru;
**broken in pieces shall be the calf of Samaria For the wind they have sown and the whirlwind they shall reap**

7054 קמה 369 אין 3807a לו 6780 צמח 1097 בלי 6213 יעשה 7058 קמח 194 אולי 6213 יעשה 2114 זרים 1104 יבלעהו:
qamah 'aeyn lou', tzemach baliy ya'aseh qemach, 'aulay ya'aseh, zariym yibla'ahu.
**stalk has no it the bud (*branch*) no shall yield meal if so be it yield the strangers shall swallow it up**

Hos 7:15 Though I have bound and strengthened their arms, yet do they imagine mischief against me.16 They return, but not to the most High: they are like a deceitful bow: their princes shall fall by the sword for the rage of their tongue: this shall be their derision in the land of Egypt. **Hos** 8:1 Set the trumpet to your mouth. He shall come as an eagle against the house of YHUH, because they have transgressed my covenant, and trespassed against my law.2 Israel shall cry unto me, My G-d, we know you.3 Israel has cast off the thing that is good: the enemy shall pursue him.4 They have set up kings, but not by me: they have made princes, and I knew it not: of their silver and their gold have they made them idols, that they may be cut off.5 Thy calf, O Samaria, has cast you off; mine anger is kindled against them: how long will it be ere they attain to innocency?6 For from Israel was it also: the workman made it; therefore it is not G-d: but the calf of Samaria shall be broken in pieces.7 For they have sown the wind, and they shall reap the whirlwind: it has no stalk: the bud shall yield no meal: if so be it yield, the strangers shall swallow it up.

**8:8** **8:9**

נבלע 1104 ישראל 3478 עתה 6258 היו 1961 בגוים 1471 ככלי 3627 אין 369 חפץ 2656 בו 871a: כי 3588 המה 1992

nibla' yisra'ael; 'atah hayu bagouyim, kikliy 'aeyn chepetz bou. kiy hemah

**is swallowed up Israel now shall they be among the Gentiles as a vessel *is* no pleasure wherein For they**

**8:10**

עלו 5927 אשור 804 פרא 6501 בודד 909 לו 3807a אפרים 669 התנו 8566 אהבים 158: גם 1571 כי 3588 יתנו 5566

'alu 'ashur, pera' bouded lou'; 'aprayim hitnu 'ahabiym. gam kiy yitanu

**are gone up *to* Assyria a wild ass alone by himself Ephraim has hired lovers Yea though they have hired**

**8:11**

בגוים 1471 עתה 6258 אקבצם 6908 ויחלו 2490 מעט 4592 ממשא 4853 מלך 4428 שרים 8269:

bagouyim 'atah 'aqabtzem; uayachelu ma'at, mimasa' melek sariym.

**among the nations now will I gather them and they shall sorrow a little for the burden of the king of princes**

**8:12**

כי 3588 הרבה 7235 אפרים 669 מזבחת 4196 לחטא 2398 היו 1961 לו 3807a מזבחות 4196 לחטא 2398: אכתוב 3789 לו 3807a

kiy hirbah 'aprayim mizbachot lachata'; hayu lou' mizbachout lachata'. 'aktoub lou',

**Because has made many Ephraim altars to sin shall be unto him altars to sin I have written to him**

**8:13**

רבו 7239 רבו 7239 תורתי 8451 כמו 3644 זר 2114 נחשבו 2803: זבחי 2077 הבהבי 1890

ribou rubey touratiy; kamou zar nechshabu. zibchey habahabay,

**the things of great my law as a strange thing *but* they were counted *for the* sacrifices of mine offerings**

יזבחו 2076 בשר 1320 ויאכלו 398 יהוה 3069 לא 3808 רצם 7521 עתה 6258 יזכר 2142 עונם 5771 ויפקד 6485

yizbachu basar uaya'kelu, Yahuah la' ratzam; 'atah yizkor 'auonam uayipqod

**They sacrifice flesh and eat it *but* Yahuah not accept them now will he remember their iniquity and visit**

**8:14**

חטאותם 2403 המה 1992 מצרים 4714 ישובו 7725: וישכח 7911 ישראל 3478 את 853 עשהו 6213 ויבן 1129 היכלות 1964 ויהודה 3063

chata'utam, hemah mitzrayim yashubu. uayishkach yisra'ael 'at 'asehu, uayiben heykalout, uayahudah

**their sins they *to* Egypt shall return For has forgotten Israel his Maker and builds temples and Judah**

הרבה 7235 ערים 5892 בצרות 1219 ושלחתי 7971 אש 784 בעריו 5892 ואכלה 398 ארמנתיה 759:

hirbah 'ariym batzurout; uashilachtiy 'aesh ba'arayu, ua'akalah 'armanoteyha.

**has multiplied cities fenced but I will send a fire upon his cities and it shall devour the palaces thereof**

**Hos 9:1**

אל 408 תשמח 8055 ישראל 3478 אל 413 גיל 1524 כעמים 5971 כי 3588 זנית 2181 מעל 5921 אלהיך 430

'al tismach yisra'ael 'al gil ka'amiym, kiy zaniyta me'al 'aloheyka;

**not Rejoice O Israel for joy as *other* people for you have gone a whoring from your Elohim**

**9:2**

אהבת 157 אתנן 868 על 5921 כל 3605 גרנות 1637 דגן 1715: גרן 1637 ויקב 3342 לא 3808 ירעם 7462

'ahabta 'atnan, 'al kal garanout dagan. goren uayeqeb la' yir'aem;

**you have loved a reward upon every floor corn The floor and the winepress not shall feed them**

**9:3**

ותירוש 8492 יכחש 3584 בה 871a: לא 3808 ישבו 3427 בארץ 776 יהוה 3069 ושב 7725 אפרים 669 מצרים 4714

uatiyroush yakachesh bah. la' yeshabu ba'aretz Yahuah; uashab 'aprayim mitzrayim,

**and the new wine shall fail in her not They shall dwell in land Yahuah but shall return Ephraim *to* Egypt**

**9:4**

ובאשור 804 טמא 2931 יאכלו 398: לא 3808 יסכו 5258 ליהוה 3068 יין 3196 ולא 3808

uab'ashur tamea' ya'kelu. la' yisachu laYahuah yayin uala'

**and in Assyria unclean *things* they shall eat not They shall offer *offerings* to Yahuah wine neither**

Hos 8:8 Israel is swallowed up: now shall they be among the Gentiles as a vessel wherein is no pleasure.9 For they are gone up to Assyria, a wild ass alone by himself: Ephraim has hired lovers.10 Yea, though they have hired among the nations, now will I gather them, and they shall sorrow a little for the burden of the king of princes.11 Because Ephraim has made many altars to sin, altars shall be unto him to sin.12 I have written to him the great things of my law, but they were counted as a strange thing.13 They sacrifice flesh for the sacrifices of mine offerings, and eat it; but YHUH accepteth them not; now will he remember their iniquity, and visit their sins: they shall return to Egypt.14 For Israel has forgotten his Maker, and buildeth temples; and Judah has multiplied fenced cities: but I will send a fire upon his cities, and it shall devour the palaces thereof. **Hos** 9:1 Rejoice not, O Israel, for joy, as other people: for you have gone a whoring from your G-d, you have loved a reward upon every cornfloor.2 The floor and the winepress shall not feed them, and the new wine shall fail in her.3 They shall not dwell in YHUH's land; but Ephraim shall return to Egypt, and they shall eat unclean things in Assyria.4 They shall not offer wine offerings to YHUH, neither shall they be pleasing unto him: their sacrifices shall be unto them as the bread of mourners;

| | | | | | | | |
|---|---|---|---|---|---|---|---|
| יערבו 6148 | לו 3807a | זבחיהם 2077 | כלחם 3899 | אונים 205 | להם 3807a | כל 3605 | אכליו 398 |
| ye'arbu | lou' | zibcheyhem, | kalechem | 'auniym | lahem, | kal | 'aklayu |
| **shall they be pleasing** | **unto him** | **their sacrifices** | **as the bread of** | **mourners *shall be*** | **unto them** | **all** | **that eat thereof** |

| | | | | | | | | | | | |
|---|---|---|---|---|---|---|---|---|---|---|---|
| יטמאו 2930 | כי 3588 | לחמם 3899 | לנפשם 5315 | לא 3808 | יבוא 935 | בית 1004 | יהוה 3068: | 9:5 | מה 4100 | תעשו 6213 | ליום 3117 |
| yitama'au; | kiy | lachmam | lanapsham, | la' | yabou'a | beyt | Yahuah. | | mah | ta'asu | layoum |
| **shall be polluted** | **for** | **their bread** | **for their soul** | **not** | **shall come into** | **the house of** | **Yahuah** | | **What** | **will you do** | **in day** |

| | | | | | | | | | |
|---|---|---|---|---|---|---|---|---|---|
| מועד 4150 | וליום 3117 | חג 2282 | יהוה 3068: | 9:6 | כי 3588 | הנה 2009 | הלכו 1980 | משד 7701 | מצרים 4714 |
| mou'aed; | ualyoum | chag | Yahuah. | | kiy | hineh | halaku | mishod, | mitzrayim |
| ***the* solemn** | **and in the day of** | **the feast of** | **Yahuah?** | | **For** | **lo** | **they are gone** | **because of destruction** | **Egypt** |

| | | | | | | | |
|---|---|---|---|---|---|---|---|
| תקבצם 6908 | מף 4644 | תקברם 6912 | מחמד 4261 | לכספם 3701 | קמוש 7057 | יירשם 3423 | חוח 2336 |
| taqabtzem | mop | taqabrem; | machmad | lakaspam, | qimous | yirashem, | chouach |
| **shall gather them up** | **Memphis** | **shall bury them** | ***the* pleasant** | ***places* for their silver** | **nettles** | **shall possess them** | **thorns** |

| | | | | | | | | | |
|---|---|---|---|---|---|---|---|---|---|
| באהליהם 168: | 9:7 | באו 935 | ימי 3117 | הפקדה 6486 | באו 935 | ימי 3117 | השלם 7966 | ידעו 3045 | ישראל 3478 |
| ba'ahaleyhem. | | ba'au | yamey | hapaqudah, | ba'au | yamey | hashilum, | yeda'au | yisra'ael; |
| ***shall be* in their tabernacles** | | **are come** | **The days of** | **visitation** | **are come** | **the days of** | **recompence** | **shall know *it*** | **Israel** |

| | | | | | | | | | | |
|---|---|---|---|---|---|---|---|---|---|---|
| אויל 191 | הנביא 5030 | משגע 7696 | איש 376 | הרוח 7307 | על 5921 | רב 7230 | עונך 5771 | ורבה 7227 | משטמה 4895: | 9:8 |
| 'auiyl | hanabiy'a, | mashuga' | 'aysh | haruach, | 'al | rob | 'auonaka, | uarabah | mastemah. | |
| ***is* a fool** | **the prophet** | ***is* mad** | **man** | **the spiritual** | **for** | **the multitude of** | **your iniquity** | **and the great** | **hatred** | |

| | | | | | | | | | | |
|---|---|---|---|---|---|---|---|---|---|---|
| צפה 6822 | אפרים 669 | עם 5973 | אלהי 430 | נביא 5030 | פח 6341 | יקוש 3352 | על 5921 | כל 3605 | דרכיו 1870 | משטמה 4895 |
| tzopeh | 'aprayim | 'am | 'alohay; | nabiy'a | pach | yaqoush | 'al | kal | darakayu, | mastemah |
| **The watchman of** | **Ephraim** | ***was* with** | **my Elohim** | ***but* the prophet** | ***is* a snare of** | **a fowler** | **in** | **all** | **his ways** | ***and* hatred** |

| | | | | | | |
|---|---|---|---|---|---|---|
| בבית 1004 | אלהיו 430: | 9:9 | העמיקו 6009 | שחתו 7843 | כימי 3117 | הגבעה 1390 |
| babeyt | 'alohayu. | | he'amiyqu | shichetu | kiymey | hagib'ah; |
| **in the house of** | **his Elohim** | | **deeply** | **They have corrupted** | ***themselves* as in the days of** | **Gibeah** |

| | | | | | | | | |
|---|---|---|---|---|---|---|---|---|
| יזכור 2142 | עונם 5771 | יפקוד 6485 | חטאותם 2403: | 9:10 | כענבים 6025 | במדבר 4057 | מצאתי 4672 | ישראל 3478 |
| yizkour | 'auonam, | yipqoud | chata'utam. | | ka'anabiym | bamidbar, | matza'tiy | yisra'ael, |
| ***therefore* he will remember** | **their iniquity** | **he will visit** | **their sins** | | **like grapes** | **in the wilderness** | **I found** | **Israel** |

| | | | | | | | | |
|---|---|---|---|---|---|---|---|---|
| כבכורה 1063 | בתאנה 8384 | בראשיתה 7225 | ראיתי 7200 | אבותיכם 1 | המה 1992 | באו 935 | בעל 1187 | פעור 6465 |
| kabikurah | bit'aenah | barea'shiytah, | ra'aytiy | abouteykem; | hemah | ba'au | ba'al | pa'aur, |
| **as the firstripe** | **in the fig tree** | **at her first time** | **I saw** | **your fathers** | ***but* they** | **went** | ***to* Baal** | **peor** |

| | | | | | | |
|---|---|---|---|---|---|---|
| וינזרו 5144 | לבשת 1322 | ויהיו 1961 | שקוצים 8251 | כאהבם 157: | 9:11 | אפרים 669 |
| uayinazaru | laboshet, | uayihayu | shiqutziym | ka'ahabam. | | 'aprayim |
| **and separated themselves** | **unto *that* shame** | **and were** | ***their* abominations** | **according as they loved** | | ***As for* Ephraim** |

| | | | | | | | | |
|---|---|---|---|---|---|---|---|---|
| כעוף 5775 | יתעופף 5774 | כבודם 3519 | מלדה 3205 | ומבטן 990 | ומהריון 2032: | 9:12 | כי 3588 | אם 518 |
| ka'aup | yit'aupep | kaboudam; | miledah | uamibeten | uameherayoun. | | kiy | 'am |
| **like a bird** | **shall fly away** | **their glory** | **from the birth** | **and from the womb** | **and from the conception** | | **Though** | **lo** |

Hos 9:4 all that eat thereof shall be polluted: for their bread for their soul shall not come into the house of YHUH.5 What will you do in the solemn day, and in the day of the feast of YHUH?6 For, lo, they are gone because of destruction: Egypt shall gather them up, Memphis shall bury them: the pleasant places for their silver, nettles shall possess them: thorns shall be in their tabernacles.7 The days of visitation are come, the days of recompence are come; Israel shall know it: the prophet is a fool, the spiritual man is mad, for the multitude of your iniquity, and the great hatred.8 The watchman of Ephraim was with my G-d: but the prophet is a snare of a fowler in all his ways, and hatred in the house of his G-d.9 They have deeply corrupted themselves, as in the days of Gibeah: therefore he will remember their iniquity, he will visit their sins.10 I found Israel like grapes in the wilderness; I saw your fathers as the firstripe in the fig tree at her first time: but they went to Baal-peor, and separated themselves unto that shame; and their abominations were according as they loved.11 As for Ephraim, their glory shall fly away like a bird, from the birth, and from the womb, and from the conception.12 Though they bring up their children, yet will I bereave them, that there shall not be a man left: yea, woe also to them when I depart from them!

יגדלו 1431 | את 853 | בניהם 1121 | ושכלתים 7921 | מאדם 120 | כי 3588 | גם 1571 | אוי 188 | להם 3807a
yagadlu | 'at | baneyhem, | uashikaltiym | me'adam; | kiy | gam | 'auy | lahem
**they bring up | their children | yet will I bereave them | *that there shall* not *be* a man | *left* yea | also | woe | to them**

בשורי 5493 | מהם 1992: | 9:13 אפרים 669 | כאשר 834 | ראיתי 7200 | לצור 6865 | שתולה 8362 | בנוה 5116 | ואפרים 669
basuriy | mehem. | 'aprayim | ka'asher | ra'aytiy | latzour | shatulah | banaueh; | ua'aprayim
**when I depart | from them | Ephraim | as | I saw | Tyrus | *is* planted | in a pleasant place | but Ephraim**

להוציא 3318 | אל 413 | הרג 2026 | בניו 1121: | 9:14 תן 5414 | להם 3807a | יהוה 3068 | מה 4100 | תתן 5414 | תן 5414 | להם 3807a | רחם 7358
lahoutziy'a | 'al | horeg | banayu. | ten | lahem | Yahuah | mah | titen; | ten | lahem | rechem
**shall bring forth | to | the murderer | his children | Give | them | O Yahuah | what | will you give? | give | them | a womb**

משכיל 7921 | ושדים 7699 | צמקים 6784: | 9:15 כל 3605 | רעתם 7451 | בגלגל 1537 | כי 3588 | שם 8033 | שנאתים 8130 | על 5921
mashkiyl, | uashadayim | tzomaqiym. | kal | ra'atam | bagilgal | kiy | sham | sanea'tiym, | 'al
**miscarrying | and breasts | dry | All | their wickedness | *is* in Gilgal | for | there | I hated them | for**

רע 7455 | מעלליהם 4611 | מביתי 1004 | אגרשם 1644 | לא 3808 | אוסף 3254 | אהבתם 160 | כל 3605 | שריהם 8269
roa' | ma'alleyhem, | mibeytiy | 'agarashem; | la' | 'ausep | 'ahabatam, | kal | sareyhem
**the wickedness of | their doings | of mine house | I will drive them out | no | more | I will love them | all | their princes**

סררים 5637: | 9:16 הכה 5221 | אפרים 669 | שרשם 8328 | יבש 3001 | פרי 6529 | בלי 1097 | יעשון 6213 | גם 1571 | כי 3588 | ילדון 3205
sorariym. | hukah | 'aprayim, | sharasham | yabesh | pariy | baliy | ya'asun; | gam | kiy | yeledun,
***are* revolters | is smitten | Ephraim | their root | is dried up | fruit | no | they shall bear | yea | though | they bring forth**

והמתי 4191 | מחמדי 4261 | בטנם 990: | 9:17 ימאסם 3988 | אלהי 430 | כי 3588 | לא 3808 | שמעו 8085
uahematiy | machamadey | bitnam. | yim'asem | 'alohay, | kiy | la' | shama'au
**yet will I slay | *even* the beloved | *fruit* of their womb | will cast them away | My Elohim | because | not | they did listen**

לו 3807a | ויהיו 1961 | נדדים 7074 | בגוים 1471:
lou'; | uayihayu | nodadiym | bagouyim.
**unto him | and they shall be | wanderers among the nations**

**Hos 10:1** גפן 1612 | בוקק 1238 | ישראל 3478 | פרי 6529 | ישוה 7737 | לו 3807a | כרב 7230 | לפריו 6529
gepen | bouqeq | yisra'ael, | pariy | yashaueh | lou'; | karob | lapiryou,
***is* an vine | empty | Israel | fruit | he bring forth | unto himself | according to the multitude | of his fruit**

הרבה 7235 | למזבחות 4196 | כטוב 2896 | לארצו 776 | היטיבו 3190 | מצבות 4676: | 10:2 חלק 2505
hirbah | lamizbachout, | katoub | la'artzou, | heytiybu | matzabout. | chalaq
**he has increased | the altars | according to the goodness of | his land | they have made goodly | images | is divided**

לבם 3820 | עתה 6258 | יאשמו 816 | הוא 1931 | יערף 6202 | מזבחותם 4196 | ישדד 7703 | מצבותם 4676: | 10:3 כי 3588
libam | 'atah | ye'ashamu; | hua' | ya'arop | mizbachoutam, | yashoded | matzeboutam. | kiy
**Their heart | now | shall they be found faulty | he | shall break down | their altars | he shall spoil | their images | For**

עתה 6258 | יאמרו 559 | אין 369 | מלך 4428 | לנו 3807a | כי 3588 | לא 3808 | יראנו 3372 | את 853 | יהוה 3068 | והמלך 4428 | מה 4100 | יעשה 6213
'atah | ya'maru, | 'aeyn | melek | lanu; | kiy | la' | yarea'nu | 'at | Yahuah, | uahamelek | mah | ya'aseh
**now | they shall say | no | king | We have | because | not | we feared | Yahuah | then a king | what | should do**

Hos 9:13 Ephraim, as I saw Tyrus, is planted in a pleasant place: but Ephraim shall bring forth his children to the murderer.14 Give them, O YHUH: what will you give? give them a miscarrying womb and dry breasts.15 All their wickedness is in Gilgal: for there I hated them: for the wickedness of their doings I will drive them out of mine house, I will love them no more: all their princes are revolters.16 Ephraim is smitten, their root is dried up, they shall bear no fruit: yea, though they bring forth, yet will I slay even the beloved fruit of their womb.17 My G-d will cast them away, because they did not hear unto him: and they shall be wanderers among the nations. **Hos** 10:1 Israel is an empty vine, he bring forth fruit unto himself: according to the multitude of his fruit he has increased the altars; according to the goodness of his land they have made goodly images.2 Their heart is divided; now shall they be found faulty: he shall break down their altars, he shall spoil their images.3 For now they shall say, We have no king, because we feared not YHUH; what then should a king do to us?

| לנו 3807a: | 10:4 דברו 1696 | דברים 1697 | אלות 422 | שוא 7723 | כרת 3772 | ברית 1285 | ופרח 6524 | כראש 7219 | משפט 4941 | על 5921 |
|---|---|---|---|---|---|---|---|---|---|---|
| lanu. | dibru | dabariym, | 'alout | shau'a | karot | bariyt; | uaparach | kara'sh | mishapat, | 'al |
| **to us?** | **They have spoken** | **words** | **swearing** | **falsely** | **in making** | **a covenant** | **thus spring up** | **as hemlock** | **judgment** | **in** |

| תלמי 8525 | שדי 7704: | 10:5 לעגלות 5697 | בית 1007 | און 205 | יגורו 1481 | שכן 7934 | שמרון 8111 | כי 3588 |
|---|---|---|---|---|---|---|---|---|
| talmey | saday. | la'aglout | beyt | 'auen, | yaguru | shakan | shomaroun; | kiy |
| **the furrows of** | **the field** | **because of the calves of** | **Beth** | **aven** | **shall fear** | **The inhabitants of** | **Samaria** | **for** |

| אבל 56 | עליו 5921 | עמו 5971 | וכמריו 3649 | עליו 5921 | יגילו 1523 | על 5921 | כבודו 3519 | כי 3588 |
|---|---|---|---|---|---|---|---|---|
| 'abal | 'alayu | 'amou, | uakmarayu | 'alayu | yagiylu, | 'al | kaboudou | kiy |
| **shall mourn** | **over it** | **the people thereof** | **and the priests thereof** | **on it** | ***that* rejoiced** | **for** | **the glory thereof** | **because** |

| גלה 1540 | ממנו 4480: | 10:6 גם 1571 | אותו 853 | לאשור 804 | יובל 2986 | מנחה 4503 | למלך 4428 | ירב 3377 | בשנה 1317 | אפרים 669 |
|---|---|---|---|---|---|---|---|---|---|---|
| galah | mimenu. | gam | 'autou | la'ashur | yubal, | minchah | lamelek | yareb; | bashanah | 'aprayim |
| **it is departed** | **from it** | **also** | **It** | **unto Assyria** | **shall be carried** | ***for* a present** | **to king** | **Jareb** | **shame** | **Ephraim** |

| יקח 3947 | ויבוש 954 | ישראל 3478 | מעצתו 6098: | 10:7 נדמה 1820 | שמרון 8111 | מלכה 4428 | כקצף 7110 | על 5921 |
|---|---|---|---|---|---|---|---|---|
| yiqach, | uayeboush | yisra'ael | me'atzatou. | nidmeh | shomaroun | malkah; | kaqetzep | 'al |
| **shall receive** | **and shall be ashamed of** | **Israel** | **his own counsel** | ***As for* is cut off** | **Samaria** | **her king** | **as the foam** | **on** |

| פני 6440 | מים 4325: | 10:8 ונשמדו 8045 | במות 1116 | און 205 | חטאת 2403 | ישראל 3478 | קוץ 6975 | ודרדר 1863 |
|---|---|---|---|---|---|---|---|---|
| paney | mayim. | uanishmadu | bamout | 'auen, | chata't | yisra'ael, | qoutz | uadardar, |
| **upon** | **the water** | **also shall be destroyed** | **The high places of** | **Aven** | **the sin of** | **Israel** | **the thorn** | **and the thistle** |

| יעלה 5927 | על 5921 | מזבחותם 4196 | ואמרו 559 | להרים 2022 | כסונו 3680 | ולגבעות 1389 | נפלו 5307 | עלינו 5921: | 10:9 |
|---|---|---|---|---|---|---|---|---|---|
| ya'aleh | 'al | mizbachoutam; | ua'amaru | lehariym | kasunu, | ualagaba'aut | niplu | 'aleynu. | |
| **shall come up** | **on** | **their altars** | **and they shall say** | **to the mountains** | **Cover us** | **and to the hills** | **Fall** | **on us** | |

| מימי 3117 | הגבעה 1390 | חטאת 2398 | ישראל 3478 | שם 8033 | עמדו 5975 | לא 3808 | תשיגם 5381 | בגבעה 1390 | מלחמה 4421 |
|---|---|---|---|---|---|---|---|---|---|
| miymey | hagib'ah, | chata'ta | yisra'ael; | sham | 'amadu, | la' | tasiygem | bagib'ah | milchamah |
| **from the days of** | **Gibeah** | **you have sinned** | **O Israel** | **there** | **they stood** | **not** | **did overtake them** | **in Gibeah** | **the battle** |

| על 5921 | בני 1121 | עלוה 5932: | 10:10 באותי 185 | ואסרם 3256 | ואספו 622 | עליהם 5921 |
|---|---|---|---|---|---|---|
| 'al | baney | 'aluah. | ba'auatiy | ua'asarem; | ua'aspu | 'aleyhem |
| **against** | **the children of** | **iniquity** | ***It is* in my desire** | **that I should chastise them** | **and shall be gathered** | **against them** |

| עמים 5971 | באסרם 631 | לשתי 8147 | עינתם 5869 | 10:11 ואפרים 669 | עגלה 5697 | מלמדה 3925 |
|---|---|---|---|---|---|---|
| 'amiym, | ba'asaram | lishtey | 'aynotam | ua'aprayim | 'aglah | malumadah |
| **the people** | **when they shall bind themselves** | **in two** | **their furrows** | **And Ephraim** | ***is as* an heifer** | ***that is* taught** |

| אהבתי 157 | לדוש 1758 | ואני 589 | עברתי 5674 | על 5921 | טוב 2898 | צוארה 6676 | ארכיב 7392 | אפרים 669 | יחרוש 2790 | יהודה 3063 |
|---|---|---|---|---|---|---|---|---|---|---|
| 'ahabtiy | ladush, | ua'aniy | 'abartiy, | 'al | toub | tzaua'rah; | 'arkiyb | 'aprayim | yacharoush | yahudah, |
| ***and* love** | **to tread out *the corn*** | **but I** | **passed over** | **upon** | **fair** | **her neck** | **I will make to ride** | **Ephraim** | **shall plow** | **Judah** |

| ישדד 7702 | לו 3807a | יעקב 3290: | 10:12 זרעו 2232 | לכם 3807a | לצדקה 6666 | קצרו 7114 | לפי 6310 | חסד 2617 | נירו 5214 | לכם 3807a |
|---|---|---|---|---|---|---|---|---|---|---|
| yasaded | lou' | ya'aqob. | zir'au | lakem | litzdaqah | qitzru | lapiy | chesed, | niyru | lakem |
| **shall break clods** | **his** | ***and* Jacob** | **Sow** | **to yourselves** | **in righteousness** | **reap** | **in** | **mercy** | **break up** | **to your** |

Hos 10:4 They have spoken words, swearing falsely in making a covenant: thus judgment spring up as hemlock in the furrows of the field.5 The inhabitants of Samaria shall fear because of the calves of Beth-aven: for the people thereof shall mourn over it, and the priests thereof that rejoiced on it, for the glory thereof, because it is departed from it.6 It shall be also carried unto Assyria for a present to king Jareb: Ephraim shall receive shame, and Israel shall be ashamed of his own counsel.7 As for Samaria, her king is cut off as the foam upon the water.8 The high places also of Aven, the sin of Israel, shall be destroyed: the thorn and the thistle shall come up on their altars; and they shall say to the mountains, Cover us; and to the hills, Fall on us.9 O Israel, you have sinned from the days of Gibeah: there they stood: the battle in Gibeah against the children of iniquity did not overtake them.10 It is in my desire that I should chastise them; and the people shall be gathered against them, when they shall bind themselves in their two furrows.11 And Ephraim is as an heifer that is taught, and love to tread out the corn; but I passed over upon her fair neck: I will make Ephraim to ride; Judah shall plow, and Jacob shall break his clods.12 Sow to yourselves in righteousness, reap in mercy; break up your fallow ground:

נִיר 5215 niyr; fallow ground | ועת 6256 ua'at for it is time | לדרוש 1875 lidroush to seek | את 853 'at | יהוה 3069 Yahuah, Yahuah | עד 5704 'ad till | יבוא 935 yabou'a he come | וירה 3384 uayoreh and rain | צדק 6664 tzedeq righteousness | לכם 3807a: lakem. upon you

10:13 חרשתם 2790 charashtem You have plowed | רשע 7562 resha' wickedness | עולתה 5766 'aualatah iniquity | קצרתם 7114 qatzartem you have reaped | אכלתם 398 'akaltem you have eaten | פרי 6529 pariy the fruit of | כחש 3585 kachash; lies | כי 3588 kiy because | בטחת 982 batachta you did trust | בדרכך 1870 badarkaka in your way | ברב 7230 barob in the multitude of | גבוריך 1368: giboureyka. your mighty men

10:14 וקאם 6965 uaqam Therefore shall arise | שאון 7588 sha'aun a tumult | בעמך 5971 ba'ameka among your people | וכל 3605 uakal and all | מבצריך 4013 mibtzareyka your fortresses | יושד 7703 yushad, shall be spoiled | כשד 7701 kashod as spoiled | שלמן 8020 shalman Shalman | בית 1009 beyt Beth | ארבאל 695 'arbea'l arbel | ביום 3117 bayoum in the day of | מלחמה 4421 milchamah; battle | אם 517 'aem the mother | על 5921 'al upon | בנים 1121 baniym *her* children | רטשה 7376: rutashah. was dashed in pieces

10:15 ככה 3602 kakah, So | עשה 6213 'asah shall do | לכם 3807a lakem unto you | בית 1008 beyt Beth | אל 352 'ael, el | מפני 6440 mipaney because of | רעת 7451 ra'at your great | רעתכם 7451 ra'atakem; wickedness | בשחר 7837 bashachar in a morning | נדמה 1820 nidmoh shall utterly | נדמה 1820 nidmah be cut off | מלך 4428 melek the king of | ישראל 3478: yisra'ael. Israel

Hos 11:1 כי 3588 kiy When | נער 5288 na'ar *was* a child | ישראל 3478 yisra'ael Israel | ואהבהו 157 ua'ahabehu; then I loved him | וממצרים 4714 uamimitzrayim and out of Egypt | קראתי 7121 qaraa'tiy called | לבני 1121: libniy. my son

11:2 קראו 7121 qara'au *As* they called | להם 3807a lahem; them | כן 3651 ken so | הלכו 1980 halaku they went | מפניהם 6440 mipaneyhem, from them | לבעלים 1168 laba'aliym unto Baalim | יזבחו 2076 yazabechu, they sacrificed | ולפסלים 6456 ualapasiliym and to graven images | יקטרון 6999: yaqaterun. burned incense

11:3 ואנכי 595 ua'anokiy I also | תרגלתי 7270 tirgaltiy taught to go | לאפרים 669 la'aprayim, Ephraim | קחם 3947 qacham taking them | על 5921 'al by | זרועתיו 2220 zarou'autayu; their arms | ולא 3808 uala' but not | ידעו 3045 yada'au they knew | כי 3588 kiy that | רפאתים 7495: rapa'tiym. I healed them

11:4 בחבלי 2256 bachabley with cords of | אדם 120 'adam a man | אמשכם 4900 'amshakem I drew them | בעבתות 5688 ba'abotout with bands of | אהבה 160 'ahabah, love | ואהיה 1961 ua'ahayeh and I was | להם 3807a lahem to them | כמרימי 7311 kimriymey as they that take off | על 5923 'al the yoke | על 5921 'al on | לחיהם 3895 lacheyhem; their jaws | ואט 5186 ua'at and I laid | אליו 413 'aelayu unto them | אוכיל 398: 'auchiyl. meat

11:5 לא 3808 la' not | ישוב 7725 yashub He shall return | אל 413 'al into | ארץ 776 'aretz the land of | מצרים 4714 mitzrayim, Egypt | ואשור 804 ua'ashur but the Assyrian | הוא 1931 hua' *shall be* he | מלכו 4428 malkou; his king | כי 3588 kiy because | מאנו 3985 me'anu they refused | לשוב 7725: lashub. to return

11:6 וחלה 2342 uakalah And shall abide | חרב 2719 chereb the sword | בעריו 5892 ba'arayu, on his cities | וכלתה 3615 uakiltah and shall consume | בדיו 905 badayu his branches | ואכלה 398 ua'akalah; and devour

Hos 10:12 for it is time to seek YHUH, till he come and rain righteousness upon you.13 You have plowed wickedness, you have reaped iniquity; you have eaten the fruit of lies: because you did trust in your way, in the multitude of your mighty men.14 Therefore shall a tumult arise among your people, and all your fortresses shall be spoiled, as Shalman spoiled Beth-arbel in the day of battle: the mother was dashed in pieces upon her children.15 So shall Bethel do unto you because of your great wickedness: in a morning shall the king of Israel utterly be cut off. **Hos** 11:1 When Israel was a child, then I loved him, and called my son out of Egypt.2 As they called them, so they went from them: they sacrificed unto Baalim, and burned incense to graven images.3 I taught Ephraim also to go, taking them by their arms; but they knew not that I healed them.4 I drew them with cords of a man, with bands of love: and I was to them as they that take off the yoke on their jaws, and I laid meat unto them.5 He shall not return into the land of Egypt, but the Assyrian shall be his king, because they refused to return.6 And the sword shall abide on his cities, and shall consume his branches, and devour them, because of their own counsels.

11:7

ממעצותיהם 4156: ועמי 5971 תלואים 8511 למשובתי 4878 ואל 413 על 5920
mimo'atzouteyhem. ua'amiy talu'aym limshubatiy; ua'al 'al
**them because of their own counsels And my people are bent to backsliding from me though to the most High**

11:8

יקראהו 7121 יחד 3162 לא 3808 ירומם 7311: איך 349 אתנך 5414 אפרים 669 אמגנך 4042 ישראל 3478
yiqra'ahu, yachad la' yaroumem 'aeyk 'atenaka 'aprayim, 'amagenka yisra'ael,
**they called them at all none would exalt *him* How shall I give you up Ephraim? *how* shall I deliver you Israel?**

איך 349 אתנך 5414 כאדמה 126 אשימך 7760 כצבאים 6636 נהפך 2015 עלי 5921 לבי 3820 יחד 3162 נכמרו 3648
'aeyk 'atenaka ka'admah, 'asiymaka kitzba'yim; nehapak 'alay libiy, yachad nikmaru
**how shall I make you as Admah? *how* shall I set you as Zeboim? is turned within me mine heart together are kindled**

11:9

נחומי 5150: לא 3808 אעשה 6213 חרון 2740 אפי 639 לא 3808 אשוב 7725 לשחת 7843 אפרים 669 כי 3588 אל 410
nichumay. la' 'aaseh charoun 'apiy, la' 'ashub lashachet 'aprayim; kiy 'ael
**my repentings not I will execute the fierceness of mine anger not I will return to destroy Ephraim for *am* El**

11:10

אנכי 595 ולא 3808 איש 376 בקרבך 7130 קדוש 6918 ולא 3808 אבוא 935 בעיר 5892: אחרי 310 יהוה 3068
'anokiy uala' 'aysh, baqirbaka qadoush, uala' abou'a ba'ayr. 'acharey Yahuah
**I and not man in the midst of you *the* Holy One and not I will enter into the city after Yahuah**

11:11

ילכו 1980 כאריה 738 ישאג 7580 כי 3588 הוא 1931 ישאג 7580 ויחרדו 2729 בנים 1121 מים 3220:
yelaku ka'aryeh yish'ag; kiy hua' yish'ag, uayecherdu baniym miyam.
**They shall walk like a lion he shall roar when he shall roar then shall tremble the children from the west**

יחרדו 2729 כצפור 6833 ממצרים 4714 וכיונה 3123 מארץ 776 אשור 804 והושבתים 3427 על 5921 בתיהם 1004
yecheradu katzipour mimitzrayim, uakyounah me'aretz 'ashur; uahoushabtiym 'al bateyhem
**They shall tremble as a bird out of Egypt and as a dove out of the land of Assyria and I will place them in their houses**

11:12

נאם 5002 יהוה 3068: סבבני 5437 בכחש 3585 אפרים 669 ובמרמה 4820 בית 1004 ישראל 3478 ויהודה 3063 עד 5750 רד 7300
na'am Yahuah. sababuniy bakachash 'aprayim, uabmirmah beyt yisra'ael; uayahudah, 'aud rad
**saith Yahuah compass me about with lies Ephraim and with deceit the house of Israel but Judah yet rule**

עם 5973 אל 410 ועם 5973 קדושים 6918 נאמן 539:
'am al, ua'am qadoushiym ne'aman.
**with El and with the saints is faithful**

**Hos 12:1**

אפרים 669 רעה 7462 רוח 7307 ורדף 7291 קדים 6921 כל 3605 היום 3117 כזב 3577 ושד 7701 ירבה 7235
'aprayim ro'ah ruach uarodep qadiym, kal hayoum kazab uashod yarbeh;
**Ephraim feed on wind and follows after the east wind he daily lies and desolation heincrease**

12:2

וברית 1285 עם 5973 אשור 804 יכרתו 3772 ושמן 8081 למצרים 4714 יובל 2986: וריב 7379 ליהוה 3069
uabriyt 'am 'ashur yikrotu, uashemen lamitzrayim yubal. uariyb laYahuah
**and a covenant with the Assyrians they do make and oil into Egypt is carried *has* also a controversy Yahuah**

עם 5973 יהודה 3063 ולפקד 6485 על 5921 יעקב 3290 כדרכיו 1870 כמעלליו 4611 ישיב 7725 לו 3807a:
'am yahudah; ualipqod 'al ya'aqob kidrakayu, kama'alalayu yashiyb lou'.
**with Judah and will punish on Jacob according to his ways according to his doings will he recompense him**

Hos 11:7 And my people are bent to backsliding from me: though they called them to the most High, none at all would exalt him.8 How shall I give you up, Ephraim? how shall I deliver you, Israel? how shall I make you as Admah? how shall I set you as Zeboim? mine heart is turned within me, my repentings are kindled together.9 I will not execute the fierceness of mine anger, I will not return to destroy Ephraim: for I am G-d, and not man; the Holy One in the midst of you: and I will not enter into the city.10 They shall walk after YHUH: he shall roar like a lion: when he shall roar, then the children shall tremble from the west.11 They shall tremble as a bird out of Egypt, and as a dove out of the land of Assyria: and I will place them in their houses, saith YHUH.12 Ephraim compass me about with lies, and the house of Israel with deceit: but Judah yet rule with G-d, and is faithful with the saints. **Hos** 12:1 Ephraim feedeth on wind, and followed after the east wind: he daily increaseth lies and desolation; and they do make a covenant with the Assyrians, and oil is carried into Egypt.2 YHUH has also a controversy with Judah, and will punish Jacob according to his ways; according to his doings will he recompense him.

| 12:3 בבטן 990 | עקב 6117 | את 853 | אחיו 251 | ובאונו 202 | שרה 8280 | את 854 | אלהים 430: 12:4 |
|---|---|---|---|---|---|---|---|
| babeten | 'aqab | 'at | 'achiyu; | uab'aunou | sarah | 'at | 'alohiym. |
| **in the womb** | **He took by the heel** | | **his brother** | **and by his strength** | **he had power** | ***with*** | **Elohim** |

| וישר 7786 | אל 413 | מלאך 4397 | ויכל 3201 | בכה 1058 | ויתחנן 2603 | לו 3807a | בית 1008 | אל 410 | ימצאנו 4672 |
|---|---|---|---|---|---|---|---|---|---|
| uayasar | 'al | mal'ak | uayakal, | bakah | uayitchanen | lou'; | beyt | 'ael | yimtza'anu, |
| **Yea he had power** | **over** | **the angel** | **and prevailed** | **he wept** | **and made supplication** | **unto him** | ***in* Beth** | **el** | **he found him** |

| ושם 8033 | ידבר 1696 | עמנו 5973: | 12:5 ויהוה 3068 | אלהי 430 | הצבאות 6635 | יהוה 3068 | זכרו 2143: | 12:6 ואתה 859 | באלהיך 430 |
|---|---|---|---|---|---|---|---|---|---|
| uasham | yadaber | 'amanu. | uaYahuah | 'alohey | hatzaba'aut; | Yahuah | zikrou. | ua'atah | be'aloheyka |
| **and there** | **he spoke** | **with us** | **Even Yahuah** | **Elohim** | **of hosts** | **Yahuah** | ***is* his memorial** | **you** | **you to your Elohim** |

| תשוב 7725 | חסד 2617 | ומשפט 4941 | שמר 8104 | וקוה 6960 | אל 413 | אלהיך 430 | תמיד 8548: | 12:7 כנען 3667 | בידו 3027 |
|---|---|---|---|---|---|---|---|---|---|
| tashub; | chesed | uamishpat | shamor, | uaqaueh | 'al | 'aloheyka | tamiyd. | kana'an, | bayadou |
| **Therefore turn** | **mercy** | **and judgment** | **keep** | **and wait** | **on** | **your Elohim** | **continually** | ***He is* a merchant** | ***are* in his hand** |

| מאזני 3976 | מרמה 4820 | לעשק 6231 | אהב 157: | 12:8 ויאמר 559 | אפרים 669 | אך 389 | עשרתי 6238 | מצאתי 4672 | און 202 |
|---|---|---|---|---|---|---|---|---|---|
| ma'zaney | mirmah | la'ashoq | 'aheb. | uaya'mer | 'aprayim, | 'ak | 'ashartiy, | matza'tiy | 'auen |
| **the balances of** | **deceit** | **to oppress** | **he love** | **And said** | **Ephraim** | **Yet** | **I am become rich** | **I have found out** | **substance** |

| לי 3807a | כל 3605 | יגיעי 3018 | לא 3808 | ימצאו 4672 | לי 3807a | עון 5771 | אשר 834 | חטא 2399: | 12:9 ואנכי 595 | יהוה 3068 | אלהיך 430 |
|---|---|---|---|---|---|---|---|---|---|---|---|
| liy; | kal | yagiy'ay | la' | yimtz'au | liy | 'auon | 'asher | chet'a. | ua'anokiy | Yahuah | 'aloheyka |
| **me** | ***in* all** | **my labours** | **none** | **they shall find** | **in me** | **iniquity** | **that** | ***were* sin** | **And I *that am*** | **Yahuah** | **your Elohim** |

| מארץ 776 | מצרים 4714 | עד 5704 | אושיבך 3427 | באהלים 168 | כימי 3117 | מועד 4150: 12:10 |
|---|---|---|---|---|---|---|
| me'aretz | mitzrayim; | 'aud | 'aushiybaka | ba'ahaliym | kiymey | mou'aed. |
| **from the land of** | **Egypt** | **yet** | **will make you to dwell** | **in tabernacles** | **as in the days of** | **the solemn feast** |

| ודברתי 1696 | על 5921 | הנביאים 5030 | ואנכי 595 | חזון 2377 | הרביתי 7235 | וביד 3027 | הנביאים 5030 |
|---|---|---|---|---|---|---|---|
| uadibartiy | 'al | hanabiy'aym, | ua'anokiy | chazoun | hirbeytiy; | uabyad | hanabiy'aym |
| **I have also spoken** | **by** | **the prophets** | **and I** | **visions** | **have multiplied** | **and by the ministry of** | **the prophets** |

| אדמה 1819: | 12:11 אם 518 | גלעד 1568 | און 205 | אך 389 | שוא 7723 | היו 1961 | בגלגל 1537 | שורים 7794 | זבחו 2076 | גם 1571 |
|---|---|---|---|---|---|---|---|---|---|---|
| 'adameh. | 'am | gil'ad | 'auen | 'ak | shau'a | hayu, | bagilgal | shauariym | zibechu; | gam |
| **used similitudes** | ***Is there* in** | **Gilead?** | **iniquity** | **surely** | **vanity** | **they are** | **in Gilgal** | **bullocks** | **they sacrifice** | **yea** |

| מזבחותם 4196 | כגלים 1530 | על 5921 | תלמי 8525 | שדי 7704: | 12:12 ויברח 1272 | יעקב 3290 | שדה 7704 | ארם 758 | ויעבד 5647 |
|---|---|---|---|---|---|---|---|---|---|
| mizbachoutam | kagaliym, | 'al | talmey | saday. | uayibrach | ya'aqob | sadeh | 'aram; | uaya'abod |
| **their altars** | ***are* as heaps** | **in** | **the furrows of** | **the fields** | **And fled** | **Jacob** | ***into the* country of** | **Syria** | **and served** |

| ישראל 3478 | באשה 802 | ובאשה 802 | שמר 8104: | 12:13 ובנביא 5030 | העלה 5927 | יהוה 3068 | את 853 | ישראל 3478 | ממצרים 4714 |
|---|---|---|---|---|---|---|---|---|---|
| yisra'ael | ba'ashah, | uab'ashah | shamar. | uabnabiy'a | he'alah | Yahuah | 'at | yisra'ael | mimitzrayim; |
| **Israel** | **for a wife** | **and for a wife** | **he kept *sheep*** | **And by a prophet** | **brought** | **Yahuah** | | **Israel** | **out of Egypt** |

| ובנביא 5030 | נשמר 8104: | 12:14 הכעיס 3707 | אפרים 669 | תמרורים 8563 | ודמיו 1818 | עליו 5921 |
|---|---|---|---|---|---|---|
| uabnabiy'a | nishmar. | hik'ays | 'aprayim | tamaruriym; | uadamayu | 'alayu |
| **and by a prophet was he preserved** | | **provoked *him* to anger** | **Ephraim** | **most bitterly** | **therefore his blood** | **upon him** |

Hos 12:3 He took his brother by the heel in the womb, and by his strength he had power with G-d:4 Yea, he had power over the angel, and prevailed: he wept, and made
supplication unto him: he found him in Bethel, and there he spoke with us;5 Even YHUH G-d of hosts; YHUH is his memorial.6 Therefore turn you to your G-d: keep mercy
and judgment, and wait on your G-d continually.7 He is a merchant, the balances of deceit are in his hand: he love to oppress.8 And Ephraim said, Yet I am become rich, I have
found me out substance: in all my labours they shall find none iniquity in me that were sin.9 And I that am YHUH your G-d from the land of Egypt will yet make you to dwell
in tabernacles, as in the days of the solemn feast.10 I have also spoken by the prophets, and I have multiplied visions, and used similitudes, by the ministry of the prophets.11 Is
there iniquity in Gilead? surely they are vanity: they sacrifice bullocks in Gilgal; yea, their altars are as heaps in the furrows of the fields.12 And Jacob fled into the country of
Syria, and Israel served for a wife, and for a wife he kept sheep.13 And by a prophet YHUH brought Israel out of Egypt, and by a prophet was he preserved.14 Ephraim
provoked him to anger most bitterly: therefore shall he leave his blood upon him, and his reproach shall his Adonai return unto him.

יטוש 5203 וחרפתו 2781 ישיב 7725 לו 3807a אדניו 113:
yitoush, uacherpatou, yashiyb lou' 'adonayu.
**shall he leave and his reproach shall return unto him his Adonai**

**Hos 13:1** כדבר 1696 אפרים 669 רתת 7578 נשא 5375 הוא 1931 בישראל 3478 ויאשם 813 בבעל 1168 וימת 4191: **13:2**
kadaber 'aprayim ratet, nasa' hua' bayisra'ael; uaye'asham baba'al uayamot.
**When spoke Ephraim trembling exalted himself he in Israel but when he offended in Baal he died**

ועתה 6258 יוספו 3254 לחטא 2398 ויעשו 6213 להם 3807a מסכה 4541 מכספם 3701
ua'atah yousipu lachata', uaya'asu lahem masekah mikaspam
**And now more and more they sin and have made them molten images of their silver**

כתבונם 8394 עצבים 6091 מעשה 4639 חרשים 2796 כלה 3605 להם 3807a הם 1992 אמרים 559
kitbunam 'atzabiym, ma'aseh charashiym kuloh; lahem hem 'amariym,
**according to their own understanding *and* idols the work of the craftsmen all of it of them they say**

זבחי 2076 אדם 120 עגלים 5695 ישקון 5401: **13:3** לכן 3651 יהיו 1961 כענן 6051 בקר 1242 וכטל 2919 משכים 7925
zobachey 'adam, 'agaliym yishaqun. laken, yihayu ka'anan boqer, uakatal mashkiym
**Let that sacrifice the men the calves kiss Therefore they shall be as the cloud morning and as the dew early**

הלך 1980 כמץ 4671 יסער 5590 מגרן 1637 וכעשן 6227 מארבה 699: **13:4**
halok; kamotz yaso'aer migoren, uak'ashan me'arubah.
**that passed away as the chaff *that* is driven with the whirlwind out of the floor and as the smoke out of the chimney**

ואנכי 595 יהוה 3068 אלהיך 430 מארץ 776 מצרים 4714 ואלהים 430 זולתי 2108 לא 3808 תדע 3045 ומושיע 3467 אין 369
ua'anokiy Yahuah 'aloheyka me'aretz mitzrayim; ua'alohiym zulatiy la' teda', uamoushiya' 'ayin
**Yet I *am* Yahuah your Elohim from the land of Egypt and god but me no you shall know for saviour *there is* no**

בלתי 1115: **13:5** אני 589 ידעתיך 3045 במדבר 4057 בארץ 776 תלאבות 8514: **13:6** כמרעיתם 4830
biltiy. 'aniy yada'atiyka bamidbar; ba'aretz tal'about. kamar'aytam
**beside me I did know you in the wilderness in the land of great drought According to their pasture**

וישבעו 7646 שבעו 7646 וירם 7311 לבם 3820 על 5921 כן 3651 שכחוני 7911: **13:7**
uayisba'au, saba'au uayaram libam; 'al ken shakechuniy.
**so were they filled they were filled and was exalted their heart therefore after that have they forgotten me**

ואהי 1961 להם 3807a כמו 3644 שחל 7826 כנמר 5246 על 5921 דרך 1870 אשור 7789: **13:8** אפגשם 6298
ua'ahiy lahem kamou shachal; kanamer 'al derek 'ashur. 'apgashem
**Therefore I will be unto them as a lion as a leopard by the way will I observe them I will meet them**

כדב 1677 שכול 7909 ואקרע 7167 סגור 5458 לבם 3820 ואכלם 398 שם 8033 כלביא 3833 חית 2416
kadob shakul, ua'aqra' sagour libam; ua'akalem sham kalabiy', chayat
**as a bear *that is* bereaved *of her whelps* and will rend the caul of their heart and will I devour them there like a lion beast**

השדה 7704 תבקעם 1234: **13:9** שחתך 7843 ישראל 3478 כי 3588 בי 871a בעזרך 5828: **13:10** אהי 165 מלכך 4428
hasadeh tabaq'aem. shichetaka yisra'ael kiy biy ba'azreka. 'ahiy malkaka
**the wild shall tear them you have destroyed yourself O Israel but in me *is* your help I will be your king**

**Hos** 13:1 When Ephraim spoke trembling, he exalted himself in Israel; but when he offended in Baal, he died.2 And now they sin more and more, and have made them molten images of their silver, and idols according to their own understanding, all of it the work of the craftsmen: they say of them, Let the men that sacrifice kiss the calves.3 Therefore they shall be as the morning cloud, and as the early dew that pass away, as the chaff that is driven with the whirlwind out of the floor, and as the smoke out of the chimney.4 Yet I am YHUH your G-d from the land of Egypt, and you shall know no god but me: for there is no savior beside me.5 I did know you in the wilderness, in the land of great drought.6 According to their pasture, so were they filled; they were filled, and their heart was exalted; therefore have they forgotten me.7 Therefore I will be unto them as a lion: as a leopard by the way will I observe them:8 I will meet them as a bear that is bereaved of her whelps, and will rend the caul of their heart, and there will I devour them like a lion: the wild beast shall tear them.9 O Israel, you have destroyed thyself; but in me is your help.

אפוא 645 ויושיעך 3467 בכל 3605 עריך 5892 ושפטיך 8199 אשר 834 אמרת 559 תנה 5414 לי 3807a מלך 4428
aepou'a, uayoushiy'aka bakal 'areyka; uashopateyka, 'asher 'amarta, tanah liy melek
**where *is any other* that may save in all your cities? and your judges of whom you said Give me a king**

ושרים 8269: 13:11 אתן 5414 לך 3807a מלך 4428 באפי 639 ואקח 3947 בעברתי 5678: 13:12 צרור 6887 עון 5771
uasariym. 'aten laka melek ba'apiy, ua'aqach ba'abratiy. tzarur 'auon
**and princes? I gave to you a king in mine anger and took *him* away in my wrath *is* bound up The iniquity of**

אפרים 669 צפונה 6845 חטאתו 2403: 13:13 חבלי 2256 יולדה 3205 יבאו 935 לו 3807a הוא 1931 בן 1121 לא 3808 חכם 2450
'aprayim, tzapunah chata'tou. chebley youledah yabo'au lou'; hua' ben la' chakam,
**Ephraim *is* hid his sin The sorrows of a travailing woman shall come upon him he *is* son not wise**

כי 3588 עת 6256 לא 3808 יעמד 5975 במשבר 4866 בנים 1121: 13:14 מיד 3027 שאול 7585
kiy 'at la' ya'amod bamishbar baniym. miyad sha'al
**for long not he should stay in *the place of* the breaking forth of children from the power of the grave**

אפדם 6299 ממות 4194 אגאלם 1350 אהי 165 דבריך 1698 מות 4194 אהי 165 קטבך 6987 שאול 7585
'apdem, mimauet 'ag'alem; 'ahiy dabareyka mauet, 'ahiy qatabaka sha'aul,
**I will ransom them from death I will redeem them I will be your plagues O death I will be your destruction O grave**

נחם 5164 יסתר 5641 מעיני 5869: 13:15 כי 3588 הוא 1931 בן 996 אחים 251 יפריא 6500 יבוא 935 קדים 6921
nocham yisater me'aeynay. kiy hua', ben 'achiym yapriy; yabou'a qadiym
**repentance shall be hid from mine eyes Though he among *his* brethren be fruitful shall come an east wind**

רוח 7307 יהוה 3068 ממדבר 4057 עלה 5927 ויבוש 954 מקורו 4726 ויחרב 2717 מעינו 4599
ruach Yahuah mimidbar 'aleh, uayeboush maqourou uayecharab ma'ayanou,
**the wind of Yahuah from the wilderness shall come up and shall become dry his spring and shall be dried up his fountain**

הוא 1931 ישסה 8154 אוצר 214 כל 3605 כלי 3627 חמדה 2532: 13:16 תאשם 816 שמרון 8111 כי 3588 מרתה 4784
hua' yishseh, 'autzar kal kaliy chemdah. te'asham shomaroun, kiy maratah
**he shall spoil the treasure of all vessels pleasant shall become desolate Samaria for she has rebelled**

באלהיה 430 בחרב 2719 יפלו 5307 עלליהם 5768 ירטשו 7376 והריותיו 2030
be'aloheyha; bachereb yipolu, 'alaleyhem yarutashu, uahariyoutayu
**against her Elohim by the sword they shall fall their infants shall be dashed in pieces and their women with child**

יבקעו 1234:
yabuqa'au.
**shall be ripped up**

**Hos 14:1** שובה 7725 ישראל 3478 עד 5704 יהוה 3068 אלהיך 430 כי 3588 כשלת 3782 בעונך 5771: 14:2 קחו 3947 עמכם 5973
shubah yisra'ael, 'ad Yahuah 'aloheyka; kiy kashalta ba'auoneka. qachu 'amakem
**return O Israel unto Yahuah your Elohim for you have fallen by your iniquity Take with you**

דברים 1697 ושובו 7725 אל 413 יהוה 3068 אמרו 559 אליו 413 כל 3605 תשא 5375 עון 5771 וקח 3947 טוב 2896 ונשלמה 7999
dabariym, uashubu 'al Yahuah; 'amru 'aelayu, kal tisa' 'auon uaqach toub, uanshalmah
**words and turn to Yahuah say unto him all Take away iniquity and receive *us* graciously so will we render**

Hos 13:10 I will be your king: where is any other that may save you in all your cities? and your judges of whom you saidst, Give me a king and princes?11 I gave you a king in mine anger, and took him away in my wrath.12 The iniquity of Ephraim is bound up; his sin is hid.13 The sorrows of a travailing woman shall come upon him: he is an unwise son; for he should not stay long in the place of the breaking forth of children.14 I will ransom them from the power of the grave; I will redeem them from death: O death, I will be your plagues; O grave, I will be your destruction: repentance shall be hid from mine eyes.15 Though he be fruitful among his brethren, an east wind shall come, the wind of YHUH shall come up from the wilderness, and his spring shall become dry, and his fountain shall be dried up: he shall spoil the treasure of all pleasant vessels.16 Samaria shall become desolate; for she has rebelled against her G-d: they shall fall by the sword: their infants shall be dashed in pieces, and their women with child shall be ripped up. **Hos** 14:1 O Israel, return unto YHUH your G-d; for you have fallen by your iniquity.2 Take with you words, and turn to YHUH: say unto him, Take away all iniquity, and receive us graciously: so will we render the calves of our lips.

| פרים 6499 | שפתינו 8193: | 14:3 אשור 804 | לא 3808 | יושיענו 3467 | על 5921 | סוס 5483 | לא 3808 | נרכב 7392 | ולא 3808 | נאמר 559 | עוד 5750 |
|---|---|---|---|---|---|---|---|---|---|---|---|
| pariym | sapateynu. | 'ashur | la' | youshiy'aenu, | 'al | sus | la' | nirkab, | uala' | na'mar | 'aud |
| **the calves of** | **our lips** | **Asshur** | **not** | **shall save us** | **upon** | **horses** | **not** | **we will ride** | **neither** | **will we say** | **any more** |

| אלהינו 430 | למעשה 4639 | ידינו 3027 | אשר 834 | בך 871a | ירחם 7355 | יתום 3490: | 14:4 ארפא 7495 | משובתם 4878 |
|---|---|---|---|---|---|---|---|---|
| 'aloheynu | lama'aseh | yadeynu; | 'asher | baka | yarucham | yatoum. | 'arpa' | mashubatam, |
| ***You are* our gods** | **to the work of** | **our hands** | **for** | **in you** | **finds mercy** | **the fatherless** | **I will heal** | **their backsliding** |

| אהבם 157 | נדבה 5071 | כי 3588 | שב 7725 | אפי 639 | ממנו 4480: | 14:5 אהיה 1961 | כטל 2919 | לישראל 3478 | יפרח 6524 |
|---|---|---|---|---|---|---|---|---|---|
| 'ahabem | nadabah; | kiy | shab | 'apiy | mimenu. | 'ahayeh | katal | layisra'ael, | yiprach |
| **I will love them** | **freely** | **for** | **is turned away** | **mine anger** | **from him** | **I will be** | **as the dew** | **unto Israel** | **he shall grow** |

| כשושנה 7799 | ויך 5221 | שרשיו 8328 | כלבנון 3844: | 14:6 ילכו 1980 | ינקותיו 3127 | ויהי 1961 | כזית 2132 | הודו 3035 |
|---|---|---|---|---|---|---|---|---|
| kashoushanah; | uayak | sharashayu | kalabanoun. | yelaku | yonaqoutayu, | uiyhiy | kazayit | houdou; |
| **as the lily** | **and cast forth** | **his roots** | **as Lebanon** | **shall spread** | **His branches** | **and shall be** | **as the olive tree** | **his beauty** |

| וריח 7381 | לו 3807a | כלבנון 3844: | 14:7 ישבו 3427 | ישבי 3427 | בצלו 6738 | יחיו 2421 | דגן 1715 | ויפרחו 6524 |
|---|---|---|---|---|---|---|---|---|
| uareyach | lou' | kalabanoun. | yashubu | yoshabey | batzilou, | yachayu | dagan | uayiprachu |
| **and smell** | **his** | **as Lebanon** | **shall return** | **They that dwell** | **under his shadow** | **they shall revive** | ***as the* corn** | **and grow** |

| כגפן 1612 | זכרו 2143 | כיין 3196 | לבנון 3844: | 14:8 אפרים 669 | מה 4100 | לי 3807a | עוד 5750 |
|---|---|---|---|---|---|---|---|
| kagapen; | zikrou | kayeyn | labanoun. | 'aprayim | mah | liy | 'aud |
| **the vine** | **the scent thereof** | ***shall be* as the wine of** | **Lebanon** | **Ephraim *shall say*** | **What *have*** | **I *to do*** | **any more** |

| לעצבים 6091 | אני 589 | עניתי 6030 | ואשורנו 7789 | אני 589 | כברוש 1265 | רענן 7488 | ממני 4480 | פריך 6529 | נמצא 4672: | 14:9 מי 4310 |
|---|---|---|---|---|---|---|---|---|---|---|
| la'atzabiym; | 'aniy | 'aniytiy | ua'ashurenu, | 'aniy | kibroush | ra'anan, | mimeniy | peryaka | nimtza'. | miy' |
| **with idols?** | **I** | **have heard *him*** | **and observed him** | **I *am*** | **like a fir tree** | **green** | **From me** | **your fruit** | **is found** | **Who *is*** |

| חכם 2450 | ויבן 995 | אלה 428 | נבון 995 | וידעם 3045 | כי 3588 | ישרים 3477 | דרכי 1870 | יהוה 3069 |
|---|---|---|---|---|---|---|---|---|
| chakam | uayaben | 'aeleh, | naboun | uayeda'aem; | kiy | yashariym | darkey | Yahuah |
| **wise** | **and he shall understand** | **these *things*?** | **prudent** | **and he shall know them?** | **for** | ***are* right** | **the ways of** | **Yahuah** |

| וצדקים 6662 | ילכו 1980 | בם 871a | ופשעים 6586 | יכשלו 3782 | בם 871a: |
|---|---|---|---|---|---|
| uatzadiqiym | yelaku | bam, | uaposha'aym | yikasheluu | bam. |
| **and the just** | **shall walk** | **in them** | **but the transgressors** | **shall fall** | **therein** |

Hos 14:3 Asshur shall not save us; we will not ride upon horses: neither will we say anymore to the work of our hands, You are our gods: for in you the fatherless findeth mercy.4 I will heal their backsliding, I will love them freely: for mine anger is turned away from him.5 I will be as the dew unto Israel: he shall grow as the lily, and cast forth his roots as Lebanon.6 His branches shall spread, and his beauty shall be as the olive tree, and his smell as Lebanon.7 They that dwell under his shadow shall return; they shall revive as the corn, and grow as the vine: the scent thereof shall be as the wine of Lebanon.8 Ephraim shall say, What have I to do anymore with idols? I have heard him, and observed him: I am like a green fir tree. From me is your fruit found.9 Who is wise, and he shall understand these things? prudent, and he shall know them? for the ways of YHUH are right, and the just shall walk in them: but the transgressors shall fall therein.

# JOEL
## (*Youael*)

The Book of Joel states the author was the Prophet Joel in the first verse. Joel's name in Hebrew means *Yah is El*. The book was written approximately between 835 and 800 B.C. as Joel was called as a prophet to the **House of Judah**. During this time Israel is devastated by an invasion of locusts which destroys everything from the fields of grain, vineyards, to the gardens and the trees. Joel claims the locust is divine judgment coming against the nation for their sins. Joel also prophesies about the outpouring of the Spirit of Elohim and is quoted by Peter in Acts 2 as having taken place at Pentecost.

| **Joel 1:1** | דבר 1697 | יהוה 3068 | אשר 834 | היה 1961 | אל 413 | יואל 3100 | בן 1121 | פתואל 6602: | **1:2** שמעו 8085 | זאת 2063 | הזקנים 2205 |
|---|---|---|---|---|---|---|---|---|---|---|---|
| | dabar | Yahuah | 'asher | hayah, | 'al | you'ael | ben | petu'ael. | shim'au | za't | hazaqeniym, |
| | **The word of** | **Yahuah** | **that** | **came** | **to** | **Joel** | **the son of** | **Pethuel** | **Hear** | **this** | **you old men** |

| והאזינו 238 | כל 3605 | יושבי 3427 | הארץ 776 | ההיתה 1961 | זאת 2063 | בימיכם 3117 | ואם 518 | בימי 3117 | אבתיכם 1: | **1:3** |
|---|---|---|---|---|---|---|---|---|---|---|
| uaha'aziynu, | kal | youshabey | ha'aretz; | hehayatah | za't | biymeykem, | ua'am | biymey | 'aboteykem. | |
| **and give ear** | **all** | **you inhabitants of** | **the land** | **Has been** | **this** | **in your days** | **or even** | **in the days of** | **your fathers'** | |

| עליה 5921 | לבניכם 1121 | ספרו 5608 | ובניכם 1121 | לבניהם 1121 | ובניהם 1121 | לדור 1755 | אחר 312: | **1:4** |
|---|---|---|---|---|---|---|---|---|
| 'aleyha | libneykem | saperu; | uabneykem | libneyhem, | uabneyhem | ladour | 'acher. | |
| **of it** | **your children** | **Tell you** | **and *let* your children** | ***tell* their children** | **and their children** | **generation** | **another** | |

| יתר 3499 | הגזם 1501 | אכל 398 | הארבה 697 | ויתר 3499 | הארבה 697 | אכל 398 | הילק 3218 |
|---|---|---|---|---|---|---|---|
| yeter | hagazam | 'akal | ha'arbeh, | uayeter | ha'arbeh | 'akal | hayaleq; |
| **That which has left** | **the palmerworm** | **has eaten** | **the locust** | **and that which has left** | **the locust** | **has eaten** | **the cankerworm** |

| ויתר 3499 | הילק 3218 | אכל 398 | החסיל 2625: | **1:5** הקיצו 6974 | שכורים 7910 | ובכו 1058 | והיללו 3213 | כל 3605 |
|---|---|---|---|---|---|---|---|---|
| uayeter | hayeleq, | 'akal | hechasiyl. | haqiytzu | shikouriym | uabku, | uaheylilu | kal |
| **and that which has left** | **the cankerworm** | **has eaten** | **the caterpiller** | **Awake** | **you drunkards** | **and weep** | **and howl** | **all** |

| שתי 8354 | יין 3196 | על 5921 | עסיס 6071 | כי 3588 | נכרת 3772 | מפיכם 6310: | **1:6** כי 3588 | גוי 1471 | עלה 5927 | על 5921 |
|---|---|---|---|---|---|---|---|---|---|---|
| shotey | yayin; | 'al | 'asiys | kiy | nikrat | mipiykem. | kiy | gouy | 'alah | 'al |
| **you drinkers of** | **wine** | **because of** | **the new wine** | **for** | **it is cut off** | **from your mouth** | **For** | **a nation** | **is come up** | **upon** |

| ארצי 776 | עצום 6099 | ואין 369 | מספר 4557 | שניו 8127 | שני 8127 | אריה 738 | ומתלעות 4973 | לביא 3833 | לו 3807a: | **1:7** |
|---|---|---|---|---|---|---|---|---|---|---|
| 'artziy, | 'atzum | ua'aeyn | mispar; | shinayu | shiney | 'aryeh, | uamtal'aut | labiy'a | lou'. | |
| **my land** | **strong** | **and without** | **number** | **whose teeth** | ***are* the teeth of** | **a lion** | **and the cheek teeth of** | **a great lion** | **he has** | |

| שם 7760 | גפני 1612 | לשמה 8047 | ותאנתי 8384 | לקצפה 7111 | חשף 2834 | חשפה 2834 | והשליך 7993 | הלבינו 3835 |
|---|---|---|---|---|---|---|---|---|
| sam | gapniy | lashamah, | uat'aenatiy | liqtzapah; | chasop | chasapah | uahishliyk, | hilabiynu |
| **He has laid** | **my vine** | **waste** | **and my fig tree** | **barked** | **he has made it** | **clean bare** | **and cast *it* away** | **are made white** |

| שריגיה 8299: | **1:8** אלי 421 | כבתולה 1330 | חגרת 2296 | שק 8242 | על 5921 | בעל 1167 | נעוריה 5271: | **1:9** הכרת 3772 |
|---|---|---|---|---|---|---|---|---|
| sariygeyha. | 'aliy | kibtulah | chagurat | saq | 'al | ba'al | na'aureyha. | hakarat |
| **the branches thereof** | **Lament** | **like a virgin** | **girded with** | **sackcloth** | **for** | **the husband of** | **her youth** | **is cut off** |

| מנחה 4503 | ונסך 5262 | מבית 1004 | יהוה 3068 | אבלו 56 | הכהנים 3548 | משרתי 8334 | יהוה 3068: | **1:10** שדד 7703 |
|---|---|---|---|---|---|---|---|---|
| minchah | uanesek | mibeyt | Yahuah; | 'abalu | hakohaniym, | masharatey | Yahuah. | shudad |
| **The meat offering** | **and the drink offering** | **from the house of** | **Yahuah** | **mourn** | **the priests** | **ministers** | **Yahuah's** | **is wasted** |

**Joel** 1:1 The word of YHUH that came to Joel the son of Pethuel.2 Hear this, you old men, and give ear, all you inhabitants of the land. Hath this been in your days, or even in the days of your fathers?3 Tell you your children of it, and let your children tell their children, and their children another generation.4 That which the palmerworm has left has the locust eaten; and that which the locust has left has the cankerworm eaten; and that which the cankerworm has left has the caterpiller eaten.5 Awake, you drunkards, and weep; and howl, all you drinkers of wine, because of the new wine; for it is cut off from your mouth.6 For a nation is come up upon my land, strong, and without number, whose teeth are the teeth of a lion, and he has the cheek teeth of a great lion.7 He has laid my vine waste, and barked my fig tree: he has made it clean bare, and cast it away; the branches thereof are made white.8 Lament like a virgin girded with sackcloth for the husband of her youth.9 The meat offering and the drink offering is cut off from the house of YHUH; the priests, YHUH's ministers, mourn.10 The field is wasted, the land mourn; for the corn is wasted: the new wine is dried up, the oil languisheth.

| | | | | | | | | | | 1:11 |
|---|---|---|---|---|---|---|---|---|---|---|
| שדה 7704 | אבלה 56 | אדמה 127 | כי 3588 | שדד 7703 | דגן 1715 | הוביש 3001 | תירוש 8492 | אמלל 536 | יצהר 3323: | הבישו 954 |
| sadeh, | 'abalah | 'adamah; | kiy | shudad | dagan, | houbiysh | tiyroush | 'amlal | yitzhar. | hobiyshu |
| **The field** | **mourns** | **the land** | **for** | **is wasted** | **the corn** | **is dried up** | **the new wine** | **languish** | **the oil** | **Be you ashamed** |

| | | | | | | | | | |
|---|---|---|---|---|---|---|---|---|---|
| אכרים 406 | הילילו 3213 | כרמים 3755 | על 5921 | חטה 2406 | ועל 5921 | שערה 8184 | כי 3588 | אבד 6 | קציר 7105 |
| 'akariym, | heyliylu | koramiym, | 'al | chitah | ua'al | sa'arah; | kiy | 'abad | qatziyr |
| **O you husbandmen** | **howl** | **O you vinedressers** | **for** | **the wheat** | **and for** | **the barley** | **because** | **is perished** | **the harvest of** |

| | 1:12 | | | | | | | |
|---|---|---|---|---|---|---|---|---|
| שדה 7704: | הגפן 1612 | הובישה 3001 | והתאנה 8384 | אמללה 535 | רמון 7416 | גם 1571 | תמר 8558 | ותפוח 8598 |
| sadeh. | hagapen | houbiyshah, | uahata'aenah | 'amlalah; | rimoun | gam | tamar | uatapuach, |
| **the field** | **The vine** | **is dried up** | **and the fig tree** | **languish** | **the pomegranate tree** | **also** | **the palm tree** | **and the apple tree** |

| | | | | | | | | | | 1:13 |
|---|---|---|---|---|---|---|---|---|---|---|
| כל 3605 | עצי 6086 | השדה 7704 | יבשו 3001 | כי 3588 | הביש 3001 | ששון 8342 | מן 4480 | בני 1121 | אדם 120: | חגרו 2296 |
| kal | 'atzey | hasadeh | yabeshu, | kiy | hobiysh | sasoun | min | baney | 'adam. | chigru |
| ***even* all** | **the trees of** | **the field** | **are withered** | **because** | **is withered away** | **joy** | **from** | **the sons of** | **men** | **Gird yourselves** |

| | | | | | | | | | |
|---|---|---|---|---|---|---|---|---|---|
| וספדו 5594 | הכהנים 3548 | הילילו 3213 | משרתי 8334 | מזבח 4196 | באו 935 | לינו 3885 | בשקים 8242 | משרתי 8334 | אלהי 430 |
| uasipdu | hakohaniym, | heyliylu | masharatey | mizbeach, | bo'au | liynu | basaqiym, | masharatey | 'alohay; |
| **and lament** | **you priests** | **howl** | **you ministers of** | **the altar** | **come** | **lie all night** | **in sackcloth** | **you ministers of** | **my Elohim** |

| | | | | | | 1:14 | |
|---|---|---|---|---|---|---|---|
| כי 3588 | נמנע 4513 | מבית 1004 | אלהיכם 430 | מנחה 4503 | ונסך 5262: | קדשו 6942 | צום 6685 |
| kiy | nimna' | mibeyt | 'aloheykem | minchah | uanasek. | kaddeshu | tzoum |
| **for** | **is withholden** | **from the house of** | **your Elohim** | **the meat offering** | **and the drink offering** | **Sanctify you** | **a fast** |

| | | | | | | | | | |
|---|---|---|---|---|---|---|---|---|---|
| קראו 7121 | עצרה 6116 | אספו 622 | זקנים 2205 | כל 3605 | ישבי 3427 | הארץ 776 | בית 1004 | יהוה 3068 | אלהיכם 430 |
| qara'au | 'atzarah, | 'aspu | zaqeniym, | kal | yoshabey | ha'aretz, | beyt | Yahuah | 'aloheykem; |
| **call** | **a solemn assembly** | **gather** | **the elders** | ***and* all** | **the inhabitants of** | **the land** | ***into the* house of** | **Yahuah** | **your Elohim** |

| | | | 1:15 | | | | | | | |
|---|---|---|---|---|---|---|---|---|---|---|
| וזעקו 2199 | אל 413 | יהוה 3068: | אהה 162 | ליום 3117 | כי 3588 | קרוב 7138 | יום 3117 | יהוה 3068 | וכשד 7701 | משדי 7706 |
| uaza'aqu | 'al | Yahuah. | 'ahah | layoum; | kiy | qaroub | youm | Yahuah, | uakshod | mishaday |
| **and cry** | **unto** | **Yahuah** | **Alas** | **for the day** | **for** | ***is* at hand** | **the day of** | **Yahuah** | **and as a destruction** | **from the Almighty** |

| | 1:16 | | | | | | | | | 1:17 |
|---|---|---|---|---|---|---|---|---|---|---|
| יבוא 935: | הלוא 3808 | נגד 5048 | עינינו 5869 | אכל 400 | נכרת 3772 | מבית 1004 | אלהינו 430 | שמחה 8057 | וגיל 1524: | |
| yabou'a. | halou'a | neged | 'aeyneynu | 'akel | nikrat; | mibeyt | 'aloheynu | simchah | uagiyl. | |
| **shall it come** | **not** | **before** | **our eyes** | **the meat** | **Is cut off** | **from the house of** | **our Elohim?** | ***yea* joy** | **and gladness** | |

| | | | | | | | | | |
|---|---|---|---|---|---|---|---|---|---|
| עבשו 5685 | פרדות 6507 | תחת 8478 | מגרפתיהם 4053 | נשמו 8074 | אצרות 214 | נהרסו 2040 | ממגרות 4460 | כי 3588 | הביש 3001 |
| 'abashu | parudout, | tachat | megrapoteyhem, | nashamu | 'atzarout, | nehersu | mamagurout; | kiy | hobiysh |
| **is rotten** | **The seed** | **under** | **their clods** | **are laid desolate** | **the garners** | **are broken down** | **the barns** | **for** | **is withered** |

| | 1:18 | | | | | | | | | | |
|---|---|---|---|---|---|---|---|---|---|---|---|
| דגן 1715: | מה 4100 | נאנחה 584 | בהמה 929 | נבכו 943 | עדרי 5739 | בקר 1241 | כי 3588 | אין 369 | מרעה 4829 | להם 1992 | גם 1571 |
| dagan. | mah | ne'anchah | bahemah, | naboku | 'adrey | baqar, | kiy | 'aeyn | mir'ah | lahem; | gam |
| **the corn** | **How** | **do groan** | **the beasts** | **are perplexed** | **the herds of** | **cattle** | **because** | **they have no** | **pasture** | **for them** | **yea** |

| | | | 1:19 | | | | | | |
|---|---|---|---|---|---|---|---|---|---|
| עדרי 5739 | הצאן 6629 | נאשמו 816: | אליך 413 | יהוה 3068 | אקרא 7121 | כי 3588 | אש 784 | אכלה 398 | נאות 4999 |
| 'adrey | hatza'an | ne'ashamu. | 'aeleyka | Yahuah | 'aqraa'; | kiy | 'aesh, | 'akalah | na'aut |
| **flocks of** | **the sheep** | **are made desolate** | **to you** | **O Yahuah** | **will I cry** | **for** | **the fire** | **has devoured** | **the pastures of** |

1:11 Be you ashamed, O you husbandmen; howl, O you vinedressers, for the wheat and for the barley; because the harvest of the field is perished.12 The vine is dried up, and the fig tree languisheth; the pomegranate tree, the palm tree also, and the apple tree, even all the trees of the field, are withered: because joy is withered away from the sons of men.13 Gird yourselves, and lament, you priests: howl, you ministers of the altar: come, lie all night in sackcloth, you ministers of my G-d: for the meat offering and the drink offering is withholden from the house of your G-d.14 Sanctify you a fast, call a solemn assembly, gather the elders and all the inhabitants of the land into the house of YHUH your G-d, and cry unto YHUH,15 Alas for the day! for the day of YHUH is at hand, and as a destruction from the Almighty shall it come.16 Is not the meat cut off before our eyes, yea, joy and gladness from the house of our G-d?17 The seed is rotten under their clods, the garners are laid desolate, the barns are broken down; for the corn is withered.18 How do the beasts groan! the herds of cattle are perplexed, because they have no pasture; yea, the flocks of sheep are made desolate.19 O YHUH, to you will I cry: for the fire has devoured the pastures of the wilderness, and the flame has burned all the trees of the field.

מדבר 4057 | ולהבה 3852 | להטה 3857 | כל 3605 | עצי 6086 | השדה 7704: | **1:20** גם 1571 | בהמות 929 | שדה 7704 | תערוג 6165 | אליך 413

midbar, | ualehabah, | lihatah | kal | 'atzey | hasadeh. | gam | bahamout | sadeh | ta'aroug | 'aeleyka;

**the wilderness | and the flame | has burned | all | the trees of | the field | also | The beasts of | the field | cry | unto you**

כי 3588 | יבשו 3001 | אפיקי 650 | מים 4325 | ואש 784 | אכלה 398 | נאות 4999 | המדבר 4057:

kiy | yabashu | 'apiyqey | mayim, | ua'aesh | 'akalah | na'aut | hamidbar.

**for | are dried up | the rivers of | waters | and the fire | has devoured | the pastures of | the wilderness**

**Joel 2:1** תקעו 8628 | שופר 7782 | בציון 6726 | והריעו 7321 | בהר 2022 | קדשי 6944 | ירגזו 7264 | כל 3605 | ישבי 3427

tiq'au | shoupar | batziyoun, | uahariy'au | bahar | qadashiy | yirgazu | kal | yoshabey

**Blow you | the trumpet | in Zion | and sound an alarm | in mountain | my holy | let tremble | all | the inhabitants of**

הארץ 776 | כי 3588 | בא 935 | יום 3117 | יהוה 3068 | כי 3588 | קרוב 7138: | **2:2** יום 3117 | חשך 2822 | ואפלה 653 | יום 3117 | ענן 6051

ha'aretz; | kiy | ba' | youm | Yahuah | kiy | qaroub. | youm | choshek | ua'apelah, | youm | 'anan

**the land | for | comes | the day of | Yahuah | for | *it is* near at hand | A day of | darkness | and of gloominess | a day of | clouds**

וערפל 6205 | כשחר 7837 | פרש 6566 | על 5921 | ההרים 2022 | עם 5971 | רב 7227 | ועצום 6099 | כמהו 3644 | לא 3808

ua'arapel, | kashachar | parus | 'al | heháriym; | 'am | rab | ua'atzum, | kamohu, | la'

**and of thick darkness | as the morning | spread | upon | the mountains | a people | great | and a strong | the like | not**

נהיה 1961 | מן 4480 | העולם 5769 | ואחריו 310 | לא 3808 | יוסף 3254 | עד 5704 | שני 8147 | דור 1755 | ודור 1755: | **2:3**

nihayah | min | ha'aulam, | ua'acharayu | la' | yousep, | 'ad | shaney | dour | uadour.

**there has been | from | ever | after it | neither | *shall be* any more | *even* to | the years of | many | to generations**

לפניו 6440 | אכלה 398 | אש 784 | ואחריו 310 | תלהט 3857 | להבה 3852 | כגן 1588 | עדן 5731 | הארץ 776 | לפניו 6440

lapanayu | 'akalah | 'aesh, | ua'acharayu | talahet | lehabah; | kagan | 'aeden | ha'aretz | lapanayu,

**before them | devour | A fire | and behind them | burn | a flame | *is* as the garden of | Eden | the land | before them**

ואחריו 310 | מדבר 4057 | שממה 8077 | וגם 1571 | פליטה 6413 | לא 3808 | היתה 1961 | לו 3807a: | **2:4** כמראה 4758 | סוסים 5483

ua'acharayu | midbar | shamamah, | uagam | paleytah | la' | hayatah | lou'. | kamar'aeh | susiym

**and behind them | wilderness | a desolate | yea all | escape | nothing | shall | them | The appearance of them *is* | of horses**

מראהו 4758 | וכפרשים 6571 | כן 3651 | ירוצון 7323: | **2:5** כקול 6963 | מרכבות 4818 | על 5921 | ראשי 7218 | ההרים 2022

mar'aehu; | uakparashiym | ken | yarutzun. | kaqoul | markabout, | 'al | ra'shey | hehariym

**as the appearance of | and as horsemen | so | shall they run | Like the noise of | chariots | on | the tops of | mountains**

ירקדון 7540 | כקול 6963 | להב 3851 | אש 784 | אכלה 398 | קש 7179 | כעם 5971 | עצום 6099 | ערוך 6186 | מלחמה 4421: | **2:6**

yaraqedun, | kaqoul | lahab | 'aesh, | 'akalah | qash; | ka'am | 'atzum, | 'aruk | milchamah.

**shall they leap | like the noise of | a flame of | fire | that devour | the stubble | as a people | strong | set array | in battle**

מפניו 6440 | יחילו 2342 | עמים 5971 | כל 3605 | פנים 6440 | קבצו 6908 | פארור 6289: | **2:7** כגבורים 1368 | ירצון 7323

mipanayu | yachiylu | 'amiym; | kal | paniym | qibtzu | pa'rur. | kagibouriym | yarutzun,

**Before their face | shall be much pained | the people | all | faces | shall gather | blackness | like mighty men | They shall run**

כאנשי 582 | מלחמה 4421 | יעלו 5927 | חומה 2346 | ואיש 376 | בדרכיו 1870 | ילכון 1980 | ולא 3808 | יעבטון 5670

ka'anshey | milchamah | ya'alu | choumah; | ua'aysh | bidrakayu | yelekun, | uala' | ya'abtun

**like men of war | they shall climb | the wall | every one | on his ways | they shall march | and not | they shall break**

1:20 The beasts of the field cry also unto you: for the rivers of waters are dried up, and the fire has devoured the pastures of the wilderness. **Joel** 2:1 Blow you the trumpet in Zion, and sound an alarm in my holy mountain: let all the inhabitants of the land tremble: for the day of YHUH cometh, for it is nigh at hand;2 A day of darkness and of gloominess, a day of clouds and of thick darkness, as the morning spread upon the mountains: a great people and a strong; there has not been ever the like, neither shall be anymore after it, even to the years of many generations.3 A fire devour before them; and behind them a flame burneth: the land is as the garden of Eden before them, and behind them a desolate wilderness; yea, and nothing shall escape them.4 The appearance of them is as the appearance of horses; and as horsemen, so shall they run.5 Like the noise of chariots on the tops of mountains shall they leap, like the noise of a flame of fire that devour the stubble, as a strong people set in battle array.6 Before their face the people shall be much pained: all faces shall gather blackness.7 They shall run like mighty men; they shall climb the wall like men of war; and they shall march everyone on his ways, and they shall not break their ranks:

| ארחותם 734: | 2:8 | ואיש 376 | אחיו 251 | לא 3808 | ידחקון 1766 | גבר 1397 | במסלתו 4546 | ילכון 1980 | ובעד 1157 | השלח 7973 |
|---|---|---|---|---|---|---|---|---|---|---|
| 'arachoutam. | | ua'aysh | 'achiyu | la' | yidchaqun, | geber | bimsilatou | yelekun; | uab'ad | hashelach |
| **their ranks** | | **one** | **another** | **Neither** | **shall thrust** | **every one** | **in his path** | **they shall walk** | **and through** | **the sword** |

| יפלו 5307 | לא 3808 | יבצעו 1214: | 2:9 | בעיר 5892 | ישקו 8264 | בחומה 2346 | ירצון 7323 |
|---|---|---|---|---|---|---|---|
| yipolu | la' | yibtza'au. | | ba'ayr | yashoqu, | bachoumah | yarutzun, |
| ***when* they fall upon** | **not** | **they shall be wounded** | | **in the city** | **They shall run to and fro** | **upon the wall** | **they shall run** |

| בבתים 1004 | יעלו 5927 | בעד 1157 | החלונים 2474 | יבאו 935 | כגנב 1590: | 2:10 | לפניו 6440 | רגזה 7264 |
|---|---|---|---|---|---|---|---|---|
| babatiym | ya'alu; | ba'ad | hachalouniym | yabo'au | kaganab. | | lapanayu | ragazah |
| **upon the houses** | **they shall climb up** | **at** | **the windows** | **they shall enter in** | **like a thief** | | **before them** | **shall quake** |

| ארץ 776 | רעשו 7493 | שמים 8064 | שמש 8121 | וירח 3394 | קדרו 6937 | וכוכבים 3556 | אספו 622 | נגהם 5051: | 2:11 |
|---|---|---|---|---|---|---|---|---|---|
| 'aretz, | ra'ashu | shamayim; | shemesh | uayareach | qadaru, | uakoukabiym | 'asapu | nagaham. | |
| **The earth** | **shall tremble** | **the heavens** | **the sun** | **and the moon** | **shall be dark** | **and the stars** | **shall withdraw** | **their shining** | |

| ויהוה 3069 | נתן 5414 | קולו 6963 | לפני 6440 | חילו 2426 | כי 3588 | רב 7227 | מאד 3966 | מחנהו 4264 | כי 3588 | עצום 6099 | עשה 6213 | דברו 1697 |
|---|---|---|---|---|---|---|---|---|---|---|---|---|
| uaYahuah | natan | qoulou | lipney | cheylou, | kiy | rab | ma'ad | machanehu, | kiy | 'atzum | 'aseh | dabarou; |
| **And Yahuah** | **shall utter** | **his voice** | **before** | **his army** | **for** | **great** | ***is* very** | **his camp** | **for *he is*** | **strong** | **that execute** | **his word** |

| כי 3588 | גדול 1419 | יום 3117 | יהוה 3069 | ונורא 3372 | מאד 3966 | ומי 4310 | יכילנו 3557: | 2:12 | וגם 1571 | עתה 6258 | נאם 5002 | יהוה 3068 |
|---|---|---|---|---|---|---|---|---|---|---|---|---|
| kiy | gadoul | youm | Yahuah | uanoura' | ma'ad | uamiy | yakiylenu. | | uagam | 'atah | na'am | Yahuah, |
| **for** | ***is* great** | **the day of** | **Yahuah** | **and terrible** | **very** | **and who** | **can abide it?** | | **Therefore also** | **now** | **saith** | **Yahuah** |

| שבו 7725 | עדי 5704 | בכל 3605 | לבבכם 3824 | ובצום 6685 | ובבכי 1065 | ובמספד 4553: | 2:13 | וקרעו 7167 | לבבכם 3824 |
|---|---|---|---|---|---|---|---|---|---|
| shubu | 'aday | bakal | lababkem; | uabtzoum | uabbakiy | uabmisped. | | uaqir'au | lababkem |
| **turn you** | ***even* to me** | **with all** | **your heart** | **and with fasting** | **and with weeping** | **and with mourning** | | **And rend** | **your heart** |

| ואל 408 | בגדיכם 899 | ושובו 7725 | אל 413 | יהוה 3068 | אלהיכם 430 | כי 3588 | חנון 2587 | ורחום 7349 | הוא 1931 | ארך 750 | אפים 639 |
|---|---|---|---|---|---|---|---|---|---|---|---|
| ua'al | bigdeykem, | uashubu | 'al | Yahuah | 'aloheykem; | kiy | chanun | uarachum | hua', | 'arek | 'apayim |
| **and not** | **your garments** | **and turn** | **unto** | **Yahuah** | **your Elohim** | **for** | **he *is* gracious** | **and merciful** | **he** | **slow to** | **anger** |

| ורב 7227 | חסד 2617 | ונחם 5162 | על 5921 | הרעה 7451: | 2:14 | מי 4310 | יודע 3045 | ישוב 7725 | ונחם 5162 | והשאיר 7604 | אחריו 310 |
|---|---|---|---|---|---|---|---|---|---|---|---|
| uarab | chesed, | uanicham | 'al | hara'ah. | | miy' | youdea' | yashub | uanicham; | uahish'ayr | 'acharayu |
| **and of great** | **kindness** | **and repent him** | **of** | **the evil** | | **Who** | **knows *if*** | **he will return** | **and repent** | **and leave** | **behind him** |

| ברכה 1293 | מנחה 4503 | ונסך 5262 | ליהוה 3068 | אלהיכם 430: | 2:15 | תקעו 8628 | שופר 7782 | בציון 6726 |
|---|---|---|---|---|---|---|---|---|
| barakah, | minchah | uanesek, | laYahuah | 'aloheykem. | | tiq'au | shoupar | batziyoun; |
| **a blessing** | ***even* a meat offering** | **and a drink offering** | **unto Yahuah** | **your Elohim?** | | **Blow** | **the trumpet** | **in Zion** |

| קדשו 6942 | צום 6685 | קראו 7121 | עצרה 6116: | 2:16 | אספו 622 | עם 5971 | קדשו 6942 | קהל 6951 | קבצו 6908 | זקנים 2205 | אספו 622 |
|---|---|---|---|---|---|---|---|---|---|---|---|
| qadashu | tzoum | qara'au | 'atzarah. | | 'aspu | 'am | qadashu | qahal | qibtzu | zaqeniym, | 'aspu |
| **sanctify** | **a fast** | **call** | **a solemn assembly** | | **Gather** | **the people** | **sanctify** | **the congregation** | **assemble** | **the elders** | **gather** |

| עוללים 5768 | וינקי 3243 | שדים 7699 | יצא 3318 | חתן 2860 | מחדרו 2315 | וכלה 3618 | מחפתה 2646: |
|---|---|---|---|---|---|---|---|
| 'aulaliym, | uayonaqey | shadayim; | yetzea' | chatan | mechedrou, | uakalah | mechupatah. |
| **the children** | **and those that suck** | **the breasts** | **let go forth** | **the bridegroom** | **of his chamber** | **and the bride** | **out of her closet** |

2:8 Neither shall one thrust another; they shall walk everyone in his path: and when they fall upon the sword, they shall not be wounded.9 They shall run to and fro in the city; they shall run upon the wall, they shall climb up upon the houses; they shall enter in at the windows like a thief.10 The earth shall quake before them; the heavens shall tremble: the sun and the moon shall be dark, and the stars shall withdraw their shining:11 And YHUH shall utter his voice before his army: for his camp is very great: for he is strong that executeth his word: for the day of YHUH is great and very terrible; and who can abide it?12 Therefore also now, saith YHUH, turn you even to me with all your heart, and with fasting, and with weeping, and with mourning:13 And rend your heart, and not your garments, and turn unto YHUH your G-d: for he is gracious and merciful, slow to anger, and of great kindness, and repenteth him of the evil.14 Who know if he will return and repent, and leave a blessing behind him; even a meat offering and a drink offering unto YHUH your G-d?15 Blow the trumpet in Zion, sanctify a fast, call a solemn assembly:16 Gather the people, sanctify the congregation, assemble the elders, gather the children, and those that suck the breasts: let the bridegroom go forth of his chamber, and the bride out of her closet.

2:17 בין 996 האולם 197 ולמזבח 4196 יבכו 1058 הכהנים 3548 משרתי 8334 יהוה 3068 ויאמרו 559 חוסה 2347 יהוה 3068
beyn ha'aulam ualamizbeach, yibku hakohaniym, masharatey Yahuah; uaya'maru chusah Yahuah
**between the porch and the altar Let weep the priests the ministers of Yahuah and let them say Spare O Yahuah**

על 5921 עמך 5971 ואל 408 תתן 5414 נחלתך 5159 לחרפה 2781 למשל 4910 בם 871a גוים 1471 למה 4100
'al 'ameka, ua'al titen nachalataka lacherpah limshol bam gouyim, lamah
**over your people and not give your heritage to reproach should rule over them *that* the heathen wherefore**

יאמרו 559 בעמים 5971 איה 346 אלהיהם 430: 2:18 ויקנא 7065 יהוה 3068 לארצו 776 ויחמל 2550 על 5921
ya'maru ba'amiym, 'ayeh 'aloheyhem. uayaqanea' Yahuah la'artzou; uayachmol 'al
**should they say among the people Where *is* their Elohim? Then will be jealous Yahuah for his land and pity on**

עמו 5971: 2:19 ויען 6030 יהוה 3068 ויאמר 559 לעמו 5971 הנני 2005 שלח 7971 לכם 3807a את 853 הדגן 1715 והתירוש 8492
'amou. uaya'an Yahuah uaya'mer la'amou, hinniy sholeach lakem 'at hadagan uahatiyroush
**his people Yea will answer Yahuah and say unto his people Behold I will send to you corn and wine**

והיצהר 3323 ושבעתם 7646 אתו 854 ולא 3808 אתן 5414 אתכם 853 עוד 5750 חרפה 2781 בגוים 1471: 2:20
uahayitzhar, uasba'atem 'atou; uala' 'aten 'atkem 'aud cherpah bagouyim.
**and oil and you shall be satisfied with him and no I will make you more a reproach among the heathen**

ואת 853 הצפוני 6830 ארחיק 7368 מעליכם 5921 והדחתיו 5080 אל 413 ארץ 776 ציה 6723 ושממה 8077 את 854
ua'at hatzapouniy 'archiyq me'aleykem, uahidachtiyu 'al 'aretz tziyah uashmamah 'at
**But the northern *army* I will remove far off from you and will drive him into a land barren and desolate *with***

פניו 6440 אל 413 הים 3220 הקדמני 6931 וספו 5490 אל 413 הים 3220 האחרון 314 ועלה 5927 באשו 889
panayu, 'al hayam haqadmoniy, uasopou 'al hayam ha'acharoun; ua'alah ba'ashou,
**his face toward the sea the east and his hinder part toward the sea the utmost and shall come up his stink**

ותעל 5927 צחנתו 6709 כי 3588 הגדיל 1431 לעשות 6213: 2:21 אל 408 תיראי 3372 אדמה 127 גילי 1523 ושמחי 2055 כי 3588
uata'al tzachanatou, kiy higdiyl la'asout. 'al tiyr'ay 'adamah; giyliy uasmachiy, kiy
**and shall come up his ill savour because he great things has done not Fear O land be glad and rejoice for**

הגדיל 1431 יהוה 3068 לעשות 6213: 2:22 אל 408 תיראו 3372 בהמות 929 שדי 7704 כי 3588 דשאו 1876 נאות 4999 מדבר 4057
higdiyl Yahuah la'asout. 'al tiyra'au bahamout saday, kiy dasha'au na'aut midbar;
**great things Yahuah will do not Be afraid you beasts of the field for do spring the pastures of the wilderness**

כי 3588 עץ 6086 נשא 5375 פריו 6529 תאנה 8384 וגפן 1612 נתנו 5414 חילם 2426: 2:23 ובני 1121 ציון 6726 גילו 1523
kiy 'aetz nasa' piryou, ta'aenah uagepen natanu cheylam. uabney tziyoun, giylu
**for the tree bear her fruit the fig tree and the vine do yield their strength then you children of Zion Be glad**

ושמחו 8055 ביהוה 3068 אלהיכם 430 כי 3588 נתן 5414 לכם 3807a את 853 המורה 4175 לצדקה 6666
uasimchu baYahuah 'aloheykem, kiy natan lakem 'at hamoureh litzdaqah;
**and rejoice in Yahuah your Elohim for he has given to you the former rain moderately**

ויורד 3381 לכם 3807a גשם 1653 מורה 4175 ומלקוש 4456 בראשון 7223: 2:24 ומלאו 4390
uayoured lakem, geshem moureh uamalqoush bara'shoun. uamal'au
**and he will cause to come down for you the rain the former rain and the latter rain in the first *month* And shall be full**

2:17 Let the priests, the ministers of YHUH, weep between the porch and the altar, and let them say, Spare your people, O YHUH, and give not your heritage to reproach, that the heathen should rule over them: wherefore should they say among the people, Where is their G-d?18 Then will YHUH be jealous for his land, and pity his people.19 Yea, YHUH will answer and say unto his people, Behold, I will send you corn, and wine, and oil, and you shall be satisfied therewith: and I will no more make you a reproach among the heathen:20 But I will remove far off from you the northern army, and will drive him into a land barren and desolate, with his face toward the east sea, and his hinder part toward the utmost sea, and his stink shall come up, and his ill savour shall come up, because he has done great things.21 Fear not, O land; be glad and rejoice: for YHUH will do great things.22 Be not afraid, you beasts of the field: for the pastures of the wilderness do spring, for the tree beareth her fruit, the fig tree and the vine do yield their strength.23 Be glad then, you children of Zion, and rejoice in YHUH your G-d: for he has given you the former rain moderately, and he will cause to come down for you the rain, the former rain, and the latter rain in the first month. 24 And the floors shall be full of wheat, and the fats shall overflow with wine and oil.

2:25
הגרנות 1637 בר 1250 והשיקו 7783 היקבים 3342 תירוש 8492 ויצהר 3323: ושלמתי 7999 לכם 3807a את 853 השנים 8141
hagaranout bar; uaheshiyqu hayaqabiym tiyroush uayitzhar. uashilamtiy lakem 'at hashaniym,
**the floors of wheat and shall overflow the fats *with* wine and oil And I will restore to you the years**

אשר 834 אכל 398 הארבה 697 הילק 3218 והחסיל 2625 והגזם 1501 חילי 2426 הגדול 1419 אשר 834 שלחתי 7971
'asher 'akal ha'arbeh, hayeleq uahechasiyl uahagazam; cheyliy hagadoul, 'asher shilachtiy
**that has eaten the locust the cankerworm and the caterpiller and the palmerworm my army great which I sent**

2:26
בכם 871a: ואכלתם 398 אכול 398 ושבוע 7646 והללתם 1984 את 853 שם 8034 יהוה 3068 אלהיכם 430 אשר 834
bakem. ua'akaltem 'akoul uasaboua', uahilaltem, 'at shem Yahuah 'aloheykem, 'asher
**among you And you shall eat in plenty and be satisfied and praise the name of Yahuah your Elohim that**

2:27
עשה 6213 עמכם 5973 להפליא 6381 ולא 3808 יבשו 954 עמי 5971 לעולם 5769: וידעתם 3045 כי 3588 בקרב 7130
'asah 'amakem lahapliy'a; uala' yeboshu 'amiy la'aulam. uiyda'tem, kiy uaqereb
**has dealt with you wondrously and not be ashamed my people shall never And you shall know that *am* in the midst of**

2:28
ישראל 3478 אני 589 ואני 589 יהוה 3068 אלהיכם 430 ואין 369 עוד 5750 ולא 3808 יבשו 954 עמי 5971 לעולם 5769:
yisra'ael 'aniy, ua'aniy Yahuah 'aloheykem ua'aeyn 'aud; uala' yeboshu 'amiy la'aulam.
**Israel I and *that* I *am* Yahuah your Elohim and none else and not be ashamed my people shall never**

והיה 1961 אחרי 310 כן 3651 אשפוך 8210 את 853 רוחי 7307 על 5921 כל 3605 בשר 1320 ונבאו 5012
uahayah 'acharey ken, 'ashpouk 'at ruchiy 'al kal basar, uaniba'au
**And it shall come to pass afterward this *that* I will pour out my spirit upon all flesh and shall prophesy**

2:29
בניכם 1121 ובנותיכם 1323 זקניכם 2205 חלמות 2492 יחלמון 2472 בחוריכם 970 חזינות 2384 יראו 7200: וגם 1571
baneykem uabnouteykem; ziqneykem chalomout yachalomun, bachureykem, chezyonout yir'au. ua'gam
**your sons and your daughters your old men shall dream dreams your young men visions shall see And also**

2:30
על 5921 העבדים 5650 ועל 5921 השפחות 8198 בימים 3117 ההמה 1992 אשפוך 8210 את 853 רוחי 7307: ונתתי 5414
'al ha'abadiym ua'al hashapachout; bayamiym hahemah, 'ashpouk 'at ruchiy. uanatatiy
**upon the servants and upon the handmaids in days those will I pour out my spirit And I will show**

2:31
מופתים 4159 בשמים 8064 ובארץ 776 דם 1818 ואש 784 ותימרות 8490 עשן 6227: השמש 8121 יהפך 2015
moupatiym, bashamayim uaba'aretz; dam ua'ash, uatiymarout 'ashan. hashemesh yehapek
**wonders in the heavens and in the earth blood and fire and pillars of smoke The sun shall be turned**

2:32
לחשך 2822 והירח 3394 לדם 1818 לפני 6440 בוא 935 יום 3117 יהוה 3068 הגדול 1419 והנורא 3372:
lachoshek, uahayareach ladam; lipney, bou'a youm Yahuah, hagadoul uahanoura'.
**into darkness and the moon into blood before come day of Yahuah the great and the terrible**

והיה 1961 כל 3605 אשר 834 יקרא 7121 בשם 8034 יהוה 3068 ימלט 4422 כי 3588 בהר 2022 ציון 6726
uahayah, kal 'asher yiqra' bashem Yahuah yimalet; kiy bahar tziyoun
**And it shall come to pass *that* whosoever whom shall call on the name of Yahuah shall be delivered for in mount Zion**

ובירושלם 3389 תהיה 1961 פליטה 6413 כאשר 834 אמר 559 יהוה 3068 ובשרידים 8300 אשר 834 יהוה 3068 קרא 7121:
uabiyarushalaim tihayeh paleytah, ka'asher 'amar Yahuah, uabasriydiym, 'asher Yahuah qorea'.
**and in Jerusalem shall be deliverance as has said Yahuah and in the remnant whom Yahuah shall call**

2:25 And I will restore to you the years that the locust has eaten, the cankerworm, and the caterpiller, and the palmerworm, my great army which I sent among you.26 And you shall eat in plenty, and be satisfied, and praise the name of YHUH your G-d, that has dealt wondrously with you: and my people shall never be ashamed.27 And you shall know that I am in the midst of Israel, and that I am YHUH your G-d, and none else: and my people shall never be ashamed.28 And it shall come to pass afterward, that I will pour out my spirit upon all flesh; and your sons and your daughters shall prophesy, your old men shall dream dreams, your young men shall see visions:29 And also upon the servants and upon the handmaids in those days will I pour out my spirit.30 And I will show wonders in the heavens and in the earth, blood, and fire, and pillars of smoke.31 The sun shall be turned into darkness, and the moon into blood, before the great and the terrible day of YHUH come.32 And it shall come to pass, that whosoever shall call on the name of YHUH shall be delivered: for in mount Zion and in Jerusalem shall be deliverance, as YHUH has said, and in the remnant whom YHUH shall call.

**Joel 3:1**

כי 3588 הנה 2009 בימים 3117 ההמה 1992 ובעת 6256 ההיא 1931 אשר 834 אשוב 7725 את 853 שבות 7622 יהודה 3063

kiy, hineh bayamiym hahemah uaba'aet hahiy'a; 'asher 'ashub 'at shabut yahudah

**For behold in those days those and in time that when I shall bring again the captivity of Judah**

**3:2**

וירושלם 3389: וקבצתי 6908 את 853 כל 3605 הגוים 1471 והורדתים 3381 אל 413 עמק 6010 יהושפט 3092

uiyarushalaim. uaqibatztiy 'at kal hagouyim, uahouradtiym, 'al 'ameq yahoushapat;

**and Jerusalem I will also gather all nations and will bring them down into the valley of Jehoshaphat**

ונשפטתי 8199 עמם 5973 שם 8033 על 5921 עמי 5971 ונחלתי 5159 ישראל 3478 אשר 834 פזרו 6340

uanishpattiy 'amam sham, 'al 'amiy uanachalatiy yisra'ael 'asher pizru

**and will plead with them there for my people and *for* my heritage Israel whom they have scattered**

**3:3**

בגוים 1471 ואת 853 ארצי 776 חלקו 2505: ואל 413 עמי 5971 ידו 3032 גורל 1486 ויתנו 5414 הילד 3206

bagouyim, ua'at 'artziy chilequ. ua'al 'amiy yadu goural; uayitanu hayeled

**among the nations *and* my land parted And for my people they have cast lots and have given a boy**

**3:4**

בזונה 2181 והילדה 3207 מכרו 4376 ביין 3196 וישתו 8354: וגם 1571 מה 4100 אתם 859 לי 3807a צר 6865

bazounah, uahayaldah makaru bayayin uayishtu. uagam mah 'atem liy tzor

**for an harlot and a girl sold for wine that they might drink Yea and what *have* you *to do* with me O Tyre**

וצידון 6721 וכל 3605 גלילות 1552 פלשת 6429 הגמול 1576 אתם 859 משלמים 7999 עלי 5921 ואם 518 גמלים 1580 אתם 859 עלי 5921

uatziydoun, uakol galiylout palashet; hagamul, 'atem mashalamiym 'alay, ua'am gomaliym 'atem 'alay,

**and Zidon and all the coasts of Palestine? a recompence? you will render me and if recompense you me**

**3:5**

קל 7031 מהרה 4120 אשיב 7725 גמלכם 1576 בראשכם 7218: אשר 834 כספי 3701 וזהבי 2091 לקחתם 3947

qal maherah, 'ashiyb gamulkem bara'shkem. 'asher kaspiy uazhabiy laqachtem;

**swiftly *and* speedily will I return your recompense upon your own head Because my silver and my gold you have taken**

**3:6**

ומחמדי 4261 הטבים 2896 הבאתם 935 להיכליכם 1964: ובני 1121 יהודה 3063 ובני 1121

uamachamaday hatobiym, habea'tem laheykleykem. uabney yahudah uabney

**and my pleasant things goodly have carried into your temples The children also of Judah and the children of**

**3:7**

ירושלם 3389 מכרתם 4376 לבני 1121 היונים 3125 למען 4616 הרחיקם 7368 מעל 5921 גבולם 1366: הנני 2005

yarushalaim, makartem libney hayauaniym; lama'an harchiyqam me'al gabulam. hinniy

**Jerusalem have you sold unto the Grecians that you might remove them far from their border Behold I**

מעירם 5782 מן 4480 המקום 4725 אשר 834 מכרתם 4376 אתם 853 שמה 8033 והשבתי 7725 גמלכם 1576

ma'ayram, min hamaqoum, 'asher makartem 'atam shamah; uahashibotiy gamulkem

**will raise them out of the place where you have sold them there and will return your recompence**

**3:8**

בראשכם 7218: ומכרתי 4376 את 853 בניכם 1121 ואת 853 בנותיכם 1323 ביד 3027 בני 1121 יהודה 3063

bara'shkem. uamakartiy 'at baneykem ua'at banouteykem, bayad baney yahudah,

**upon your own head And I will sell your sons *and* your daughters into the hand of the children of Judah**

**3:9**

ומכרום 4376 לשבאים 7615 אל 413 גוי 1471 רחוק 7350 כי 3588 יהוה 3068 דבר 1696: קראו 7121 זאת 2063

uamkarum lishaba'yim 'al gouy rachouq; kiy Yahuah diber. qara'au za't

**and they shall sell them to the Sabeans to a people far off for Yahuah has spoken *it* Proclaim you this**

**Joel** 3:1 For, behold, in those days, and in that time, when I shall bring again the captivity of Judah and Jerusalem,2 I will also gather all nations, and will bring them down into the valley of Jehoshaphat, and will plead with them there for my people and for my heritage Israel, whom they have scattered among the nations, and parted my land.3 And they have cast lots for my people; and have given a boy for an harlot, and sold a girl for wine, that they might drink.4 Yea, and what have you to do with me, O Tyre, and Zidon, and all the coasts of Palestine? will you render me a recompence? and if you recompence me, swiftly and speedily will I return your recompence upon your own head;5 Because you have taken my silver and my gold, and have carried into your temples my goodly pleasant things:6 The children also of Judah and the children of Jerusalem have you sold unto the Grecians, that you might remove them far from their border.7 Behold, I will raise them out of the place whither you have sold them, and will return your recompence upon your own head:8 And I will sell your sons and your daughters into the hand of the children of Judah, and they shall sell them to the Sabeans, to a people far off: for YHUH has spoken it. 9 Proclaim you this among the Gentiles;

| בגוים 1471 | קדשו 6942 | מלחמה 4421 | העירו 5782 | הגבורים 1368 | יגשו 5066 | יעלו 5927 | כל 3605 | אנשי 582 |
|---|---|---|---|---|---|---|---|---|
| bagouyim, | qadashu | milchamah; | ha'ayru | hagibouriym, | yigshu | ya'alu, | kal | 'anshey |
| **among the Gentiles** | **Prepare** | **war** | **wake up** | **the mighty men** | **let draw near** | **let them come up** | **all** | **the men of** |

| המלחמה 4421: | 3:10 כתו 3807 | אתיכם 855 | לחרבות 2719 | ומזמרתיכם 4211 | לרמחים 7420 | החלש 2523 | יאמר 559 | גבור 1368 |
|---|---|---|---|---|---|---|---|---|
| hamilchamah. | kotu | 'ateykem | lacharabout, | uamazmaroteykem | lirmachiym; | hachalash, | ya'mar | gibour |
| **war** | **Beat** | **your plowshares** | **into swords** | **and your pruninghooks** | **into spears** | **the weak** | **let say** | ***am* strong** |

| אני 589: | 3:11 עושו 5789 | ובאו 935 | כל 3605 | הגוים 1471 | מסביב 5439 | ונקבצו 6908 | שמה 8033 |
|---|---|---|---|---|---|---|---|
| 'aniy. | 'aushu | uaba'au | kal | hagouyim | misabiyb | uaniqbatzu; | shamah |
| **I** | **Assemble yourselves** | **and come** | **all** | **you heathen** | **round about** | **and gather yourselves together** | **there** |

| הנחת 5181 | יהוה 3068 | גבוריך 1368: | 3:12 יעורו 5782 | ויעלו 5927 | הגוים 1471 | אל 413 | עמק 6010 |
|---|---|---|---|---|---|---|---|
| hanachat | Yahuah | giboureyka. | ye'auru | uaya'alu | hagouyim, | 'al | 'aemeq |
| **cause to come down** | **O Yahuah** | **your mighty ones** | **Let be wakened** | **and come up** | **the heathen** | **to** | **the valley of** |

| יהושפט 3092 | כי 3588 | שם 8033 | אשב 3427 | לשפט 8199 | את 853 | כל 3605 | הגוים 1471 | מסביב 5439: | 3:13 שלחו 7971 | מגל 4038 | כי 3588 | בשל 1310 |
|---|---|---|---|---|---|---|---|---|---|---|---|---|
| yahoushapat; | kiy | sham, | 'aesheb | lishpat | 'at | kal | hagouyim | misabiyb. | shilchu | magal, | kiy | bashal |
| **Jehoshaphat** | **for** | **there** | **will I sit** | **to judge** | | **all** | **the heathen** | **round about** | **Put you** | ***in* the sickle** | **for** | **is ripe** |

| קציר 7105 | באו 935 | רדו 3381 | כי 3588 | מלאה 4390 | גת 1660 | השיקו 7783 | היקבים 3342 | כי 3588 | רבה 7227 | רעתם 7451: 3:14 |
|---|---|---|---|---|---|---|---|---|---|---|
| qatziyr; | bo'au | radu | kiy | mal'ah | gat, | heshiyqu | hayaqabiym, | kiy | rabah | ra'atam. |
| **the harvest** | **come** | **get you down** | **for** | **is full** | **the press** | **overflow** | **the fats** | **for** | ***is* great** | **their wickedness** |

| המונים 1995 | המונים 1995 | בעמק 6010 | החרוץ 2742 | כי 3588 | קרוב 7138 | יום 3117 | יהוה 3068 | בעמק 6010 | החרוץ 2742: | 3:15 שמש 8121 |
|---|---|---|---|---|---|---|---|---|---|---|
| hamouniym | hamouniym, | ba'aemeq | hecharutz; | kiy | qaroub | youm | Yahuah, | ba'aemeq | hecharutz. | shemesh |
| **Multitudes** | **multitudes** | **in the valley of** | **decision** | **for** | ***is* near** | **the day of** | **Yahuah** | **in the valley of** | **decision** | **The sun** |

| וירח 3394 | קדרו 6937 | וכוכבים 3556 | אספו 622 | נגהם 5051: | 3:16 ויהוה 3068 | מציון 6726 | ישאג 7580 |
|---|---|---|---|---|---|---|---|
| uayareach | qadaru; | uakoukabiym | 'asapu | nagaham. | uaYahuah | mitziyoun | yish'ag, |
| **and the moon** | **shall be darkened** | **and the stars** | **shall withdraw** | **their shining** | **Yahuah also** | **out of Zion** | **shall roar** |

| ומירושלם 3389 | יתן 5414 | קולו 6963 | ורעשו 7493 | שמים 8064 | וארץ 776 | ויהוה 3068 | מחסה 4268 | לעמו 5971 |
|---|---|---|---|---|---|---|---|---|
| uamiyarushalaim | yiten | qoulou, | uara'ashu | shamayim | ua'aretz; | uaYahuah | machaseh | la'amou, |
| **and from Jerusalem** | **utter** | **his voice** | **and shall shake** | **the heavens** | **and the earth** | **but Yahuah** | ***will be* the hope** | **of his people** |

| ומעוז 4581 | לבני 1121 | ישראל 3478: | 3:17 וידעתם 3045 | כי 3588 | אני 589 | יהוה 3068 | אלהיכם 430 | שכן 7931 | בציון 6726 |
|---|---|---|---|---|---|---|---|---|---|
| uama'auz | libney | yisra'ael. | uiyda'tem, | kiy | 'aniy | Yahuah | 'aloheykem, | shoken | batziyoun |
| **and the strength of** | **the children of** | **Israel** | **So shall you know** | **that** | **I *am*** | **Yahuah** | **your Elohim** | **dwelling** | **in Zion** |

| הר 2022 | קדשי 6944 | והיתה 1961 | ירושלם 3389 | קדש 6944 | וזרים 2114 | לא 3808 | יעברו 5674 | בה 871a | עוד 5750: 3:18 |
|---|---|---|---|---|---|---|---|---|---|
| har | qadashiy | uahayatah | yarushalaim | qodesh, | uazariym | la' | ya'abru | bah | 'aud. |
| **mountain** | **my holy** | **then shall be** | **Jerusalem** | **holy** | **and strangers** | **no** | **there shall pass through** | **her** | **any more** |

| והיה 1961 | ביום 3117 | ההוא 1931 | יטפו 5197 | ההרים 2022 | עסיס 6071 | והגבעות 1389 | תלכנה 1980 | חלב 2461 |
|---|---|---|---|---|---|---|---|---|
| uahayah | bayoum | hahua' | yitapu | hehariym | 'asiys, | uahagaba'aut | telaknah | chalab, |
| **And it shall come to pass** | **in day** | **that** | **shall drop down *that*** | **the mountains** | **new wine** | **and the hills** | **shall flow *with*** | **milk** |

Joel 3:9 Prepare war, wake up the mighty men, let all the men of war draw near; let them come up:10 Beat your plowshares into swords, and your pruninghooks into spears: let the weak say, I am strong.11 Assemble yourselves, and come, all you heathen, and gather yourselves together round about: thither cause your mighty ones to come down, O YHUH.12 Let the heathen be wakened, and come up to the valley of Jehoshaphat: for there will I sit to judge all the heathen round about.13 Put you in the sickle, for the harvest is ripe: come, get you down; for the press is full, the fats overflow; for their wickedness is great.14 Multitudes, multitudes in the valley of decision: for the day of YHUH is near in the valley of decision.15 The sun and the moon shall be darkened, and the stars shall withdraw their shining.16 YHUH also shall roar out of Zion, and utter his voice from Jerusalem; and the heavens and the earth shall shake: but YHUH will be the hope of his people, and the strength of the children of Israel.17 So shall you know that I am YHUH your G-d dwelling in Zion, my holy mountain: then shall Jerusalem be holy, and there shall no strangers pass through her anymore.18 And it shall come to pass in that day, that the mountains shall drop down new wine, and the hills shall flow with milk,

| וכל 3605 | אפיקי 650 | יהודה 3063 | ילכו 1980 | מים 4325 | ומעין 4599 | מבית 1004 | יהוה 3068 | יצא 3318 | והשקה 8248 |
|---|---|---|---|---|---|---|---|---|---|
| uakal | 'apiyqey | yahudah | yelaku | mayim; | uama'ayan, | mibeyt | Yahuah | yetzea', | uahishqah |
| **and all** | **the rivers of** | **Judah** | **shall flow** | ***with* waters** | **and a fountain** | **of the house of** | **Yahuah** | **shall come forth** | **and shall water** |

| את 853 | נחל 5158 | השטים 7851: | **3:19** | מצרים 4714 | לשממה 8077 | תהיה 1961 | ואדום 123 | למדבר 4057 | שממה 8077 | תהיה 1961 | מחמס 2555 |
|---|---|---|---|---|---|---|---|---|---|---|---|
| 'at | nachal | hashitiym. | | mitzrayim | lishmamah | tihayeh, | ua'adoum | lamidbar | shamamah | tihayeh; | mechamas |
| | **valley of** | **the Shittim** | | **Egypt** | **a desolation** | **shall be** | **and Edom** | **wilderness** | **a desolate** | **shall be** | **for the violence** |

| בני 1121 | יהודה 3063 | אשר 834 | שפכו 8210 | דם 1818 | נקיא 5355 | בארצם 776: | **3:20** | ויהודה 3063 | לעולם 5769 | תשב 3427 |
|---|---|---|---|---|---|---|---|---|---|---|
| baney | yahudah, | 'asher | shapaku | dam | naqiy'a | ba'artzam. | | uayahudah | la'aulam | tesheb; |
| ***against* the children of** | **Judah** | **because** | **they have shed** | **blood** | **innocent** | **in their land** | | **But Judah** | **for ever** | **shall dwell** |

| וירושלם 3389 | לדור 1755 | ודור 1755: | **3:21** | ונקיתי 5352 | דמם 1818 | לא 3808 | נקיתי 5352 | ויהוה 3068 |
|---|---|---|---|---|---|---|---|---|
| uiyarushalaim | ladour | uadour. | | uaniqeytiy | damam | la' | niqeytiy; | uaYahuah |
| **and Jerusalem** | **from generation** | **to generation** | | **For I will cleanse** | **their blood** | **not** | ***that* I have cleansed** | **for Yahuah** |

| שכן 7931 | בציון 6726: |
|---|---|
| shoken | batziyoun. |
| **dwell** | **in Zion** |

Joel 3:18 and all the rivers of Judah shall flow with waters, and a fountain shall come forth of the house of YHUH, and shall water the valley of Shittim.19 Egypt shall be a desolation, and Edom shall be a desolate wilderness, for the violence against the children of Judah, because they have shed innocent blood in their land.20 But Judah shall dwell forever, and Jerusalem from generation to generation.21 For I will cleanse their blood that I have not cleansed: for YHUH dwell in Zion.

# AMOS
## (*Amous*)

Verse one identifies the author as the Prophet Amos. The book was written approximately between 760 and 753 B.C. Amos name in Hebrew means *Burden.* He was called as a prophet to the northern kingdom, the **House of Israel**. At the time Elohim calls him Amos is a shepherd and a fruit picker from the Judean village of Tekoa and lacks an education or a priestly background. His messages of impending doom and captivity for the House of Israel because of her sins are largely unpopular and ignored because not since the days of Solomon had times been so good in Israel. Amos' ministry takes place while Jeroboam II reigns over Israel and Uzziah reigns over Judah but his prophecies of doom are against the House of Judah as well and surrounding nations for sins Amos exposes rather uniquely.

**Amos 1:1**
1697 דברי 5986 עמוס 834 אשר 1961 היה 5349 בנקדים 8620 מתקוע 834 אשר 2372 חזה 5921 על 3478 ישראל
dibrey 'amous, 'asher hayah banoqadiym mitaqoua'; 'asher chazah 'al yisra'ael
**The words of Amos who was among the herdmen of Tekoa which he saw concerning Israel**

3117 בימי 5818 עזיה 4428 מלך 3063 יהודה 3117 ובימי 3379 ירבעם 1121 בן 3101 יואש 4428 מלך 3478 ישראל 8141 שנתים 6440 לפני
biymey 'aziyah melek yahudah, uabiymey yarab'am ben you'ash melek yisra'ael, shanatayim lipney
**in the days of Uzziah king of Judah and in the days of Jeroboam the son of Joash king of Israel two years before**

7494 הרעש: **1:2** 559 ויאמר 3068 יהוה 6726 מציון 7580 ישאג 3389 ומירושלם 5414 יתן 6963 קולו 56 ואבלו
hara'ash. uaya'mar Yahuah mitziyoun yish'ag, uamiyarushalaim yiten qoulou; ua'abalu
**the earthquake And he said Yahuah from Zion will roar and from Jerusalem utter his voice and shall mourn**

4999 נאות 7462 הרעים 3001 ויבש 7218 ראש 3760 הכרמל: **1:3** 3541 כה 559 אמר 3068 יהוה 5921 על 7969 שלשה
na'aut haro'aym, uayabesh ra'sh hakarmel. koh 'amar Yahuah, 'al shaloshah
**the habitations of the shepherds and shall wither of top the Carmel Thus saith Yahuah For three**

6588 פשעי 1834 דמשק 5921 ועל 702 ארבעה 3808 לא 7725 אשיבנו 5921 על 1758 דושם
pish'aey dameseq, ua'al 'arba'ah la' 'ashiybenu; 'al dusham
**transgressions of Damascus and for four not I will turn away *the punishment* thereof because they have threshed**

2742 בחרצות 1270 הברזל 853 את 5168 הגלעד: **1:4** 7971 ושלחתי 784 אש 1004 בבית 2371 חזאל
bacharutzout habarzel 'at hagil'ad. uashilachtiy 'aesh babeyt chaza'ael;
**with threshing instruments of iron Gilead But I will send a fire into the house of Hazael**

398 ואכלה 759 ארמנות 1130 בן 1908 הדד: **1:5** 7665 ושברתי 1280 בריח 1834 דמשק 3772 והכרתי 3427 יושב
ua'akalah 'armanout ben hadad. uashabartiy bariyach dameseq, uahikratiy yousheb
**which shall devour the palaces of Ben hadad I will break also the bar of Damascus and cut off the inhabitant**

1237 מבקעת 206 און 8551 ותומך 7626 שבט 1004 מבית 5730 עדן 1540 וגלו 5971 עם 758 ארם
mibiq'at 'auen, uatoumek shebet mibeyt 'aden; uagalu 'am 'aram
**from the plain of Aven and him that holds the sceptre from Beth eden and shall go into captivity the people of Syria**

7024 קירה 559 אמר 3068 יהוה: **1:6** 3541 כה 559 אמר 3068 יהוה 5921 על 7969 שלשה 6588 פשעי 5804 עזה 5921 ועל 702 ארבעה 3808 לא
qiyrah 'amar Yahuah. koh 'amar Yahuah, 'al shaloshah pish'aey 'azah, ua'al 'arba'ah la'
**unto Kir saith Yahuah Thus saith Yahuah For three transgressions of Gaza and for four not**

7725 אשיבנו 5921 על 1540 הגלותם 1546 גלות 8003 שלמה 5462 להסגיר
'ashiybenu; 'al hagaloutam galut shalemah lahasgiyr
**I will turn away *the punishment* thereof because they carried away captive captivity the whole to deliver *them* up**

**Amos** 1:1 The words of Amos, who was among the herdman of Tekoa, which he saw concerning Israel in the days of Uzziah king of Judah, and in the days of Jeroboam the son of Joash king of Israel, two years before the earthquake.2 And he said, YHUH will roar from Zion, and utter his voice from Jerusalem; and the habitations of the shepherds shall mourn, and the top of Carmel shall where.3 Thus saith YHUH; For three transgressions of Damascus, and for four, I will not turn away the punishment thereof; because they have threshed Gilead with threshing instruments of iron:4 But I will send a fire into the house of Hazael, which shall devour the palaces of Ben-hadad.5 I will break also the bar of Damascus, and cut off the inhabitant from the plain of Aven, and him that holdeth the sceptre from the house of Eden: and the people of Syria shall go into captivity unto Kir, saith YHUH.6 Thus saith YHUH; For three transgressions of Gaza, and for four, I will not turn away the punishment thereof;

לאדום 123: | 1:7 ושלחתי 7971 | אש 784 | בחומת 2346 | עזה 5804 | ואכלה 398 | ארמנתיה 759: | 1:8 והכרתי 3772
le'adoum. | uashilachtiy | 'aesh | bachoumat | 'azah; | ua'akalah | 'armanoteyha. | uahikratiy
**to Edom | But I will send | a fire | on the wall of | Gaza | which shall devour | the palaces thereof | And I will cut off**

יושב 3427 | מאשדוד 795 | ותומך 8551 | שבט 7626 | מאשקלון 831 | והשיבותי 7725 | ידי 3027 | על 5921 | עקרון 6138
yousheb | me'ashdoud, | uatoumek | shebet | me'ashqaloun; | uahashiyboutiy | yadiy | 'al | aqroun,
**the inhabitant | from Ashdod | and him that holds | the sceptre | from Ashkelon | and I will turn | mine hand | against | Ekron**

ואבדו 6 | שארית 7611 | פלשתים 6430 | אמר 559 | אדני 136 | יהוה 3069: | 1:9 כה 3541 | אמר 559 | יהוה 3068 | על 5921 | שלשה 7969
ua'abadu | sha'aeriyt | palishtiym, | 'amar | 'adonay | Yahuah. | koh | 'amar | Yahuah, | 'al | shaloshah
**and shall perish | the remnant of | the Philistines | saith | Adonai | Yahuah | Thus | saith | Yahuah | For | three**

פשעי 6588 | צר 6865 | ועל 5921 | ארבעה 702 | לא 3808 | אשיבנו 7725 | על 5921 | הסגירם 5462
pish'aey | tzor, | ua'al | 'arba'ah | la' | 'ashiybenu; | 'al | hasagiyram
**transgressions of | Tyrus | and for | four | not | I will turn away *the punishment* thereof | because | they delivered up**

גלות 1546 | שלמה 8003 | לאדום 123 | ולא 3808 | זכרו 2142 | ברית 1285 | אחים 251: | 1:10 ושלחתי 7971 | אש 784 | בחומת 2346 | צר 6865
galut | shalemah | le'adoum, | uala' | zakaru | bariyt | 'achiym. | uashilachtiy | 'aesh | bachoumat | tzor;
**captivity | the whole | to Edom | and not | remembered | covenant | the brotherly | But I will send | a fire | on the wall of | Tyrus**

ואכלה 398 | ארמנתיה 759: | 1:11 כה 3541 | אמר 559 | יהוה 3069 | על 5921 | שלשה 7969 | פשעי 6588 | אדום 123 | ועל 5921
ua'akalah | 'armanoteyha. | koh | 'amar | Yahuah, | 'al | shaloshah | pish'aey | 'adoum, | ua'al
**which shall devour | the palaces thereof | Thus | saith | Yahuah | For | three | transgressions of | Edom | and for**

ארבעה 702 | לא 3808 | אשיבנו 7725 | על 5921 | רדפו 7291 | בחרב 2719 | אחיו 251 | ושחת 7843
'arba'ah | la' | 'ashiybenu; | 'al | radapou | bachereb | 'achiyu | uashichet
**four | not | I will turn away *the punishment* thereof | because | he did pursue | with the sword | his brother | and did cast off**

רחמיו 7356 | ויטרף 2963 | לעד 5703 | אפו 639 | ועברתו 5678 | שמרה 8104 | נצח 5331: | 1:12 ושלחתי 7971 | אש 784 | בתימן 8487
rachamayu, | uayitrop | la'ad | 'apou, | ua'abratou | shamarah | netzach. | uashilachtiy | 'aesh | bateyman;
***all* pity | and did tear | perpetually | his anger | and his wrath | he kept | for ever | But I will send | a fire | upon Teman**

ואכלה 398 | ארמנות 759 | בצרה 1224: | 1:13 כה 3541 | אמר 559 | יהוה 3068 | על 5921 | שלשה 7969 | פשעי 6588 | בני 1121
ua'akalah | 'armanout | batzrah | koh | 'amar | Yahuah, | 'al | shaloshah | pish'aey | baney
**which shall devour | the palaces of | Bozrah | Thus | saith | Yahuah | For | three | transgressions of | the children of**

עמון 5983 | ועל 5921 | ארבעה 702 | לא 3808 | אשיבנו 7725 | על 5921 | בקעם 1234
'amoun, | ua'al | 'arba'ah | la' | 'ashiybenu; | 'al | biq'am
**Ammon | and for | four | not | I will turn away *the punishment* thereof | because | they have ripped up**

הרות 2030 | הגלעד 5168 | למען 4616 | הרחיב 7337 | את 853 | גבולם 1366: | 1:14 והצתי 3341 | אש 784 | בחומת 2346
harout | hagil'ad, | lama'an | harchiyb | 'at | gabulam. | uahitzatiy | 'aesh | bachoumat
**the women with child | *of* Gilead | that | they might enlarge | their border | But I will kindle | a fire | in the wall of**

רבה 7237 | ואכלה 398 | ארמנותיה 759 | בתרועה 8643 | ביום 3117 | מלחמה 4421 | בסער 5591 | ביום 3117
rabah, | ua'akalah | armanouteyha; | bitaru'ah | bayoum | milchamah, | basa'ar | bayoum
**Rabbah | and it shall devour | the palaces thereof | with shouting | in the day of | battle | with a tempest | in the day of**

Amos 1:6 because they carried away captive the whole captivity, to deliver them up to Edom:7 But I will send a fire on the wall of Gaza, which shall devour the palaces thereof:8 And I will cut off the inhabitant from Ashdod, and him that holdeth the sceptre from Ashkelon, and I will turn mine hand against Ekron: and the remnant of the Philistines shall perish, saith YHUH G-D. 9 Thus saith YHUH; For three transgressions of Tyrus, and for four, I will not turn away the punishment thereof; because they delivered up the whole captivity to Edom, and remembered not the brotherly covenant:10 But I will send a fire on the wall of Tyrus, which shall devour the palaces thereof.11 Thus saith YHUH; For three transgressions of Edom, and for four, I will not turn away the punishment thereof; because he did pursue his brother with the sword, and did cast off all pity, and his anger did tear perpetually, and he kept his wrath forever:12 But I will send a fire upon Teman, which shall devour the palaces of Bozrah.13 Thus saith YHUH; For three transgressions of the children of Ammon, and for four, I will not turn away the punishment thereof; because they have ripped up the women with child of Gilead, that they might enlarge their border:14 But I will kindle a fire in the wall of Rabbah, and it shall devour the palaces thereof, with shouting in the day of battle,

1:15

סופה 5492: והלך 1980 מלכם 4428 בגולה 1473 הוא 1931 ושריו 8269 יחדו 3162 אמר 559 יהוה 3068:
supah. uahalak malkam bagoulah; hua' uasarayu yachdau 'amar Yahuah.
**the whirlwind And shall go their king into captivity he and his princes together saith Yahuah**

**Amos 2:1**

כה 3541 אמר 559 יהוה 3068 על 5921 שלשה 7969 פשעי 6588 מואב 4124 ועל 5921 ארבעה 702 לא 3808
koh 'amar Yahuah, 'al shaloshah pish'aey mou'ab, ua'al 'arba'ah la'
**Thus saith Yahuah For three transgressions of Moab and for four not**

2:2

אשיבנו 7725 על 5921 שרפו 8313 עצמות 6106 מלך 4428 אדום 123 לשיד 7875: ושלחתי 7971
'ashiybenu; 'al sarapou atzmout melek 'adoum lasiyd. uashilachtiy
**I will turn away *the punishment* thereof because he burned the bones of the king of Edom into lime But I will send**

אש 784 במואב 4124 ואכלה 398 ארמנות 759 הקריות 7152 ומת 4191 בשאון 7588 מואב 4124 בתרועה 8643
'aesh bamou'ab, ua'akalah 'armanout haqariyout; uamet basha'aun mou'ab, bitaru'ah
**a fire upon Moab and it shall devour palaces of the Kerioth and shall die with tumult Moab with shouting**

2:3

בקול 6963 שופר 7782: והכרתי 3772 שופט 8199 מקרבה 7130 וכל 3605 שריה 8269
baqoul shoupar. uahikratiy shoupet miqirbah; uakal sareyha
***and* with the sound of the trumpet And I will cut off the judge from the midst thereof and all the princes thereof**

2:4

אהרוג 2026 עמו 5973 אמר 559 יהוה 3068: כה 3541 אמר 559 יהוה 3069 על 5921 שלשה 7969 פשעי 6588 יהודה 3063 ועל 5921 ארבעה 702
'aharoug 'amou 'amar Yahuah. koh 'amar Yahuah, 'al shaloshah pish'aey yahudah, ua'al 'arba'ah
**will slay with him saith Yahuah Thus saith Yahuah For three transgressions of Judah and for four**

לא 3808 אשיבנו 7725 על 5921 מאסם 3988 את 853 תורת 8451 יהוה 3069 וחקיו 2706
la' 'ashiybenu; 'al ma'asam 'at tourat Yahuah uachuqayu
**not I will turn away *the punishment* thereof because they have despised the law of Yahuah and his commandments**

2:5

לא 3808 שמרו 8104 ויתעום 8582 כזביהם 3577 אשר 834 הלכו 1980 אבותם 1 אחריהם 310: ושלחתי 7971
la' shamaru, uayat'aum kizbeyhem, 'asher halaku aboutam 'achareyhem. uashilachtiy
**not have kept and caused them to err their lies the which have walked their fathers after But I will send**

2:6

אש 784 ביהודה 3063 ואכלה 398 ארמנות 759 ירושלם 3389: כה 3541 אמר 559 יהוה 3068 על 5921 שלשה 7969
'aesh biyahudah; ua'akalah 'armanout yarushalaim. koh 'amar Yahuah, 'al shaloshah
**a fire upon Judah and it shall devour the palaces of Jerusalem Thus saith Yahuah For three**

פשעי 6588 ישראל 3478 ועל 5921 ארבעה 702 לא 3808 אשיבנו 7725 על 5921 מכרם 4376 בכסף 3701
pish'aey yisra'ael, ua'al 'arba'ah la' 'ashiybenu; 'al mikram bakesep
**transgressions of Israel and for four not I will turn away *the punishment* thereof because they sold for silver**

2:7

צדיק 6662 ואביון 34 בעבור 5668 נעלים 5275: השאפים 7602 על 5921 עפר 6083 ארץ 776 בראש 7218 דלים 1800
tzadiyq, ua'abyoun ba'abur na'alayim. hasho'apiym 'al 'apar 'aretz bara'sh daliym,
**the righteous and the poor for a pair of shoes That pant after the dust of the earth on the head of the poor**

ודרך 1870 ענוים 6035 יטו 5186 ואיש 376 ואביו 1 ילכו 1980 אל 413 הנערה 5291 למען 4616 חלל 2490 את 853 שם 8034
uaderek 'anauiym yatu; ua'aysh ua'abiyu, yelaku 'al hana'arah, lama'an chalel 'at shem
**and the way of the meek turn aside and a man and his father will go in unto the *same* maid to profane name**

Amos 1:14 with a tempest in the day of the whirlwind:15 And their king shall go into captivity, he and his princes together, saith YHUH. **Amos** 2:1 Thus saith YHUH; For three transgressions of Moab, and for four, I will not turn away the punishment thereof; because he burned the bones of the king of Edom into lime: But I will send a fire upon Moab, and it shall devour the palaces of Kerioth: and Moab shall die with tumult, with shouting, and with the sound of the trumpet:3 And I will cut off the judge from the midst thereof, and will slay all the princes thereof with him, saith YHUH.4 Thus saith YHUH; For three transgressions of Judah, and for four, I will not turn away the punishment thereof; because they have despised the law of YHUH, and have not kept his commandments, and their lies caused them to err, after the which their fathers have walked:5 But I will send a fire upon Judah, and it shall devour the palaces of Jerusalem.6 Thus saith YHUH; For three transgressions of Israel, and for four, I will not turn away the punishment thereof; because they sold the righteous for silver, and the poor for a pair of shoes;7 That pant after the dust of the earth on the head of the poor, and turn aside the way of the meek: and a man and his father will go in unto the same maid, to profane my holy name:

| | | | | | | | | | |
|---|---|---|---|---|---|---|---|---|---|
| קדשי 6944: | 2:8 | ועל 5921 | בגדים 899 | חבלים 2254 | יטו 5186 | אצל 681 | כל 3605 | מזבח 4196 | ויין 3196 |
| qadashiy | | ua'al | bagadiym | chabuliym | yatu, | 'aetzel | kal | mizbeach; | uayeyn |
| **my holy** | | **And upon** | **clothes** | **laid to pledge** | **they lay *themselves* down** | **by** | **every** | **altar** | **and the wine of** |

| | | | | | | | | | | | |
|---|---|---|---|---|---|---|---|---|---|---|---|
| ענושים 6064 | ישתו 8354 | בית 1004 | אלהיהם 430: | 2:9 | ואנכי 595 | השמדתי 8045 | את 853 | האמרי 567 | מפניהם 6440 | אשר 834 | כגבה 1363 |
| 'anushiym | yishtu, | beyt | 'aloheyhem. | | ua'anokiy | hishmadtiy | 'at | ha'amoriy | mipaneyhem, | 'asher | kagobah |
| **the condemned** | **they drink *in*** | **the house** | **of their god** | | **Yet I** | **destroyed** | | **the Amorite** | **before them** | **whose** | **height** |

| | | | | | | | | |
|---|---|---|---|---|---|---|---|---|
| ארזים 730 | גבהו 1363 | וחסן 2634 | הוא 1931 | כאלונים 437 | ואשמיד 8045 | פריו 6529 | ממעל 4605 | ושרשיו 8328 |
| 'araziym | gabahou, | uachason | hua' | ka'alouniym; | ua'ashmiyd | piryou | mima'al, | uasharashayu |
| **of the cedars** | ***was* like the height of** | **and strong** | **he *was*** | **as the oaks** | **yet I destroyed** | **his fruit** | **from above** | **and his roots** |

| | | | | | | | | | |
|---|---|---|---|---|---|---|---|---|---|
| מתחת 8478: | 2:10 | ואנכי 595 | העליתי 5927 | אתכם 853 | מארץ 776 | מצרים 4714 | ואולך 1980 | אתכם 853 | במדבר 4057 |
| mitachat. | | ua'anokiy | he'aleytiy | 'atkem | me'aretz | mitzrayim; | ua'aulek | 'atkem | bamidbar |
| **from beneath** | | **Also I** | **brought up** | **you** | **from the land of** | **Egypt** | **and led** | **you** | **through the wilderness** |

| | | | | | | | | | |
|---|---|---|---|---|---|---|---|---|---|
| ארבעים 705 | שנה 8141 | לרשת 3423 | את 853 | ארץ 776 | האמרי 567: | 2:11 | ואקים 6965 | מבניכם 1121 | לנביאים 5030 |
| 'arba'aym | shanah, | lareshet | 'at | 'aretz | ha'amoriy. | | ua'aqiym | mibneykem | linabiy'aym, |
| **forty** | **years** | **to possess** | | **the land of** | **the Amorite** | | **And I raised up** | **of your sons** | **for prophets** |

| | | | | | | | | | |
|---|---|---|---|---|---|---|---|---|---|
| ומבחוריכם 970 | לנזרים 5139 | האף 637 | אין 369 | זאת 2063 | בני 1121 | ישראל 3478 | נאם 5002 | יהוה 3068: | 2:12 |
| uamibachureykem | linaziriym; | ha'ap | 'aeyn | za't | baney | yisra'ael | na'am | Yahuah. | |
| **and of your young men** | **for Nazarites** | **even** | ***Is it* not** | **thus** | **O you children of** | **Israel?** | **said** | **Yahuah** | |

| | | | | | | | | | | | |
|---|---|---|---|---|---|---|---|---|---|---|---|
| ותשקו 8248 | את 853 | הנזרים 5139 | יין 3196 | ועל 5921 | הנביאים 5030 | צויתם 6680 | לאמר 559 | לא 3808 | תנבאו 5012: | 2:13 | הנה 2009 |
| uatashqu | 'at | hanaziriym | yayin; | ua'al | hanabiy'aym | tziuiytem | lea'mor, | la' | tinaba'au. | | hineh |
| **But you gave to drink** | | **the Nazarites** | **wine** | **and on** | **the prophets** | **commanded** | **saying** | **not** | **Prophesy** | | **Behold** |

| | | | | | | | | | | | |
|---|---|---|---|---|---|---|---|---|---|---|---|
| אנכי 595 | מעיק 5781 | תחתיכם 8478 | כאשר 834 | תעיק 5781 | העגלה 5699 | המלאה 4395 | לה 3807a | עמיר 5995: | 2:14 | ואבד 6 | מנוס 4498 |
| 'anokiy | me'ayq | tachteykem; | ka'asher | ta'ayq | ha'agalah, | hamla'ah | lah | 'amiyr. | | ua'abad | manous |
| **I** | **am pressed** | **under you** | **as that** | **is pressed** | **a cart *is*** | **full of** | **with** | **sheaves** | | **Therefore shall perish** | **the flight** |

| | | | | | | | | | | |
|---|---|---|---|---|---|---|---|---|---|---|
| מקל 7031 | וחזק 2389 | לא 3808 | יאמץ 553 | כחו 3581 | וגבור 1368 | לא 3808 | ימלט 4422 | נפשו 5315: | 2:15 | ותפש 8610 |
| miqal, | uachazaq | la' | ya'ametz | kochou; | uagibour | la' | yamalet | napshou. | | uatopes |
| **from the swift** | **and the strong** | **not** | **shall strengthen** | **his force** | **the mighty** | **neither** | **shall deliver** | **himself** | | **that handle** |

| | | | | | | | | | |
|---|---|---|---|---|---|---|---|---|---|
| הקשת 7198 | לא 3808 | יעמד 5975 | וקל 7031 | ברגליו 7272 | לא 3808 | ימלט 4422 | ורכב 7392 | הסוס 5483 | לא 3808 |
| haqeshet | la' | ya'amod, | uaqal | baraglayu | la' | yamalet; | uarokeb | hasus, | la' |
| **the bow** | **Neither** | **shall he stand** | **and *he that is* swift** | **of foot** | **not** | **shall deliver *himself*** | **he that ride** | **the horse** | **neither** |

| | | | | | | | | | | |
|---|---|---|---|---|---|---|---|---|---|---|
| ימלט 4422 | נפשו 5315: | 2:16 | ואמיץ 533 | לבו 3820 | בגבורים 1368 | ערום 6174 | ינוס 5127 | ביום 3117 | ההוא 1931 | נאם 5002 |
| yamalet | napshou. | | ua'amiytz | libou | bagibouriym; | 'aroum | yanus | bayoum | hahua' | na'am |
| **shall deliver** | **himself** | | **And is courageous** | **he that** | **among the mighty** | **naked** | **shall flee away** | **in day** | **that** | **saith** |

| |
|---|
| יהוה 3068: |
| Yahuah. |
| **Yahuah** |

Amos 1:8 And they lay themselves down upon clothes laid to pledge by every altar, and they drink the wine of the condemned in the house of their god.9 Yet destroyed I the Amorite before them, whose height was like the height of the cedars, and he was strong as the oaks; yet I destroyed his fruit from above, and his roots from beneath.10 Also I brought you up from the land of Egypt, and led you forty years through the wilderness, to possess the land of the Amorite.11 And I raised up of your sons for prophets, and of your young men for Nazarites. Is it not even thus, O you children of Israel? saith YHUH.12 But you gave the Nazarites wine to drink; and commanded the prophets, saying, Prophesy not.13 Behold, I am pressed under you, as a cart is pressed that is full of sheaves.14 Therefore the flight shall perish from the swift, and the strong shall not strengthen his force, neither shall the mighty deliver himself:15 Neither shall he stand that handleth the bow; and he that is swift of foot shall not deliver himself: neither shall he that rideth the horse deliver himself.16 And he that is courageous among the mighty shall flee away naked in that day, saith YHUH.

**Amos 3:1** שמעו 8085 את 853 הדבר 1697 הזה 2088 אשר 834 דבר 1696 יהוה 3068 עליכם 5921 בני 1121 ישראל 3478 על 5921 כל 3605
shim'au 'at hadabar hazeh, 'asher diber Yahuah 'aleykem baney yisra'ael; 'al kal
**Hear word this that has spoken Yahuah against you O children of Israel against whole**

המשפחה 4940 אשר 834 העליתי 5927 מארץ 776 מצרים 4714 לאמר 559: **3:2** רק 7535 אתכם 853 ידעתי 3045 מכל 3605
hamishpachah, 'asher he'aleytiy me'aretz mitzrayim lea'mor. raq 'atkem yada'tiy, mikol
**the family which I brought up from the land of Egypt saying only You have I known of all**

משפחות 4940 האדמה 127 על 5921 כן 3651 אפקד 6485 עליכם 5921 את 853 כל 3605 עונתיכם 5771: **3:3** הילכו 1980 שנים 8147
mishpachout ha'adamah; 'al ken 'apqod 'aleykem, 'at kal 'auonoteykem. hayelaku shanayim
**the families of the earth therefore after that I will punish on you *for* all your iniquities Can walk two**

יחדו 3162 בלתי 1115 אם 518 נועדו 3259: **3:4** הישאג 7580 אריה 738 ביער 3293 וטרף 2964 אין 369 לו 3807a היתן 5414 כפיר 3715
yachdau; biltiy 'am nou'adu. hayish'ag 'aryeh baya'ar, uaterep 'aeyn lou'; hayiten kapiyr
**together except lo they be agreed? Will roar a lion in the forest when prey? has no he will cry out a young lion**

קולו 6963 ממענתו 4585 בלתי 1115 אם 518 לכד 3920: **3:5** התפל 5307 צפור 6833 על 5921 פח 6341 הארץ 776 ומוקש 4170
qoulou mima'anatou, biltiy 'am lakad. hatipol tzipour 'al pach ha'aretz, uamouqesh
**his voice of his den unless if he have taken *nothing*? Can fall a bird in a snare *upon* the earth gin *where***

אין 369 לה 3807a היעלה 5927 פח 6341 מן 4480 האדמה 127 ולכוד 3920 לא 3808 ילכוד 3920: **3:6** אם 518 יתקע 8628 שופר 7782
'aeyn lah; haya'aleh pach min ha'adamah, ualakoud la' yilkoud. 'am yitaqa' shoupar
**no *is* for him? shall *one* take up a snare from the earth and have taken nothing at all? Shall be blown a trumpet**

בעיר 5892 ועם 5971 לא 3808 יחרדו 2729 אם 518 תהיה 1961 רעה 7451 בעיר 5892 ויהוה 3068 לא 3808 עשה 6213: **3:7** כי 3588
ba'ayr, ua'am la' yecharadu; 'am tihayeh ra'ah ba'ayr, uaYahuah la' 'asah. kiy
**in the city and the people not be afraid? shall there be evil in a city and Yahuah not has done it? Surely**

לא 3808 יעשה 6213 אדני 136 יהוה 3069 דבר 1697 כי 3588 אם 518 גלה 1540 סודו 5475 אל 413 עבדיו 5650 הנביאים 5030: **3:8** אריה 738
la' ya'aseh 'adonay Yahuah dabar; kiy 'am galah soudou, 'al 'abadayu hanabiy'aym. 'aryeh
**nothing will do Adonai Yahuah thing but when he reveal his secret unto his servants the prophets The lion**

שאג 7580 מי 4310 לא 3808 יירא 3372 אדני 136 יהוה 3068 דבר 1696 מי 4310 לא 3808 ינבא 5012: **3:9** השמיעו 8085 על 5921 ארמנות 759
sha'ag miy' la' yiyra'; 'adonay Yahuah diber, miy' la' yinabea'. hashmiy'au 'al 'armanout
**has roared who not will fear? Adonai Yahuah has spoken who but can prophesy? Publish in the palaces**

באשדוד 795 ועל 5921 ארמנות 759 בארץ 776 מצרים 4714 ואמרו 559 האספו 622 על 5921 הרי 2022 שמרון 8111
ba'ashdoud, ua'al 'armanout ba'aretz mitzrayim; ua'amru, he'asapu 'al harey shomaroun,
**at Ashdod and in the palaces in the land of Egypt and say Assemble yourselves upon the mountains of Samaria**

וראו 7200 מהומת 4103 רבות 7227 בתוכה 8432 ועשוקים 6217 בקרבה 7130: **3:10** ולא 3808 ידעו 3045 עשות 6213
uar'au mahumot rabout batoukah, ua'ashuqiym baqirbah. uala' yada'au asout
**and behold tumults *the* great in the midst thereof and the oppressed in the midst thereof For not they know to do**

נכחה 5229 נאם 5002 יהוה 3068 האוצרים 686 חמס 2555 ושד 7701 בארמנותיהם 759: **3:11** לכן 3651 כה 3541 אמר 559 אדני 136
nakochah na'am Yahuah; ha'autzariym chamas uashod ba'armanouteyhem. laken, koh 'amar 'adonay
**right saith Yahuah who store up violence and robbery in their palaces Therefore thus saith Adonai**

**Amos** 3:1 Hear this word that YHUH has spoken against you, O children of Israel, against the whole family which I brought up from the land of Egypt, saying,2 You only have I known of all the families of the earth: therefore I will punish you for all your iniquities.3 Can two walk together, except they be agreed?4 Will a lion roar in the forest, when he has no prey? will a young lion cry out of his den, if he have taken nothing?5 Can a bird fall in a snare upon the earth, where no gin is for him? shall one take up a snare from the earth, and have taken nothing at all?6 Shall a trumpet be blown in the city, and the people not be afraid? shall there be evil in a city, and YHUH has not done it?7 Surely YHUH G-D will do nothing, but he revealeth his secret unto his servants the prophets.8 The lion has roared, who will not fear? YHUH G-D has spoken, who can but prophesy?9 Publish in the palaces at Ashdod, and in the palaces in the land of Egypt, and say, Assemble yourselves upon the mountains of Samaria, and behold the great tumults in the midst thereof, and the oppressed in the midst thereof.10 For they know not to do right, saith YHUH, who store up violence and robbery in their palaces.11 Therefore thus saith YHUH G-D; An adversary there shall be even round about the land; and he shall bring down your strength from you, and your palaces shall be spoiled.

יהוה 3069 צר 6862 וסביב 5439 הארץ 776 והורד 3381 ממך 4480 עזך 5797
Yahuah, tzar uasbiyb ha'aretz; uahourid mimek 'azek,
**Yahuah An adversary *there shall be* even round about the land and he shall bring down from you your strength**

ונבזו 962 ארמנותיך 759: **3:12** כה 3541 אמר 559 יהוה 3068 כאשר 834 יציל 5337 הרעה 7462 מפי 6310 הארי 738
uanabozu armanoutayik. koh 'amar Yahuah ka'asher yatziyl hara'ah mipiy ha'ariy
**and shall be spoiled your palaces Thus saith Yahuah As takes the shepherd outof the mouth of the lion**

שתי 8147 כרעים 3767 או 176 בדל 915 אזן 241 כן 3651 ינצלו 5337 בני 1121 ישראל 3478 הישבים 3427 בשמרון 8111
shatey kara'ayim 'au badal 'azen; ken yinatzalu baney yisra'ael, hayoshbiym bashomaroun,
**two legs or a piece of an ear so shall be taken out the children of Israel that dwell in Samaria**

בפאת 6285 מטה 4296 ובדמשק 1833 ערש 6210: **3:13** שמעו 8085 והעידו 5749 בבית 1004 יעקב 3290 נאם 5002
bip'at mitah uabidamesheq 'ares. shim'au uaha'aydu babeyt ya'aqob; na'am
**in the corner (*edge*) of a bed and in Damascus *in* a couch Hear you and testify in the house of Jacob saith**

אדני 136 יהוה 3069 אלהי 430 הצבאות 6635: **3:14** כי 3588 ביום 3117 פקדי 6485 פשעי 6588 ישראל 3478 עליו 5921
'adonay Yahuah 'alohey hatzaba'aut. kiy, bayoum paqadiy pish'aey yisra'ael 'alayu;
**Adonai Yahuah the Elohim of hosts That in the day I shall visit the transgressions of Israel upon him**

ופקדתי 6485 על 5921 מזבחות 4196 בית 1008 אל 410 ונגדעו 1438 קרנות 7161 המזבח 4196 ונפלו 5307 לארץ 776: **3:15**
uapaqadtiy 'al mizbachout beyt 'ael, uanigda'au qarnout hamizbeach, uanapalu la'aretz.
**I will also visit that the altars of Beth el and shall be cut off the horns of the altar and fall to the ground**

והכיתי 5221 בית 1004 החרף 2779 על 5921 בית 1004 הקיץ 7019 ואבדו 6 בתי 1004 השן 8127 וספו 5486
uahikeytiy beyt hachorep 'al beyt haqayitz; ua'abadu batey hashen, uasapu
**And I will smite house the winter with house the summer and shall perish houses of the ivory and shall have an end**

בתים 1004 רבים 7227 נאם 5002 יהוה 3068:
batiym rabiym na'am Yahuah.
**houses *the* great saith Yahuah**

**Amos 4:1**
שמעו 8085 הדבר 1697 הזה 2088 פרות 6510 הבשן 1316 אשר 834 בהר 2022 שמרון 8111 העשקות 6231 דלים 1800
shim'au hadabar hazeh, parout habashan 'asher bahar shomaroun, ha'ashaqout daliym,
**Hear word this *you* kine of Bashan that *are* in the mountain of Samaria which oppress the poor**

הרצצות 7533 אביונים 34 האמרת 559 לאדניהם 113 הביאה 935 ונשתה 8354: **4:2** נשבע 7650 אדני 136 יהוה 3069
harotzatzout 'abyouniym; ha'amarout la'adoneyhem habiy'a'ah uanishteh. nishba' 'adonay Yahuah
**which crush the needy which ones say to their masters Bring and let us drink has sworn Adonai Yahuah**

בקדשו 6944 כי 3588 הנה 2009 ימים 3117 באים 935 עליכם 5921 ונשא 5375 אתכם 853 בצנות 6793 ואחריתכן 319
baqadashou, kiy hineh yamiym ba'aym 'aleykem; uanisa' 'atkem batzinout, ua'achariytaken
**by his holiness that lo the days shall come upon you that he will take away you with hooks and your posterity**

בסירות 5518 דוגה 1729: **4:3** ופרצים 6556 תצאנה 3318 אשה 802 נגדה 5048 והשלכתנה 7993
basiyrout dugah. uapratziym tetza'nah 'ashah negdah; uahishlaktenah
**with hooks fish And the breaches you shall go out *at* every *cow at that which* is before her and you shall cast**

Amos 3:12 Thus saith YHUH; As the shepherd take out of the mouth of the lion two legs, or a piece of an ear; so shall the children of Israel be taken out that dwell in Samaria in the corner of a bed, and in Damascus in a couch.13 Hear you, and testify in the house of Jacob, saith YHUH G-D, the G-d of hosts,14 That in the day that I shall visit the transgressions of Israel upon him I will also visit the altars of Bethel: and the horns of the altar shall be cut off, and fall to the ground.15 And I will smite the winter house with the summer house; and the houses of ivory shall perish, and the great houses shall have an end, saith YHUH. **Amos** 4:1 Hear this word, you kine of Bashan, that are in the mountain of Samaria, which oppress the poor, which crush the needy, which say to their masters, Bring, and let us drink.2 The Adonai G-D has sworn by his holiness, that, lo, the days shall come upon you, that he will take you away with hooks, and your posterity with fishhooks.3 And you shall go out at the breaches, every cow at that which is before her; and you shall cast them into the palace, saith YHUH.

| ההרמונה 2038 | נאם 5002 | יהוה 3068: | 4:4 באו 935 | בית 1008 | אל | ופשעו 6586 | הגלגל 1537 | הרבו 7235 | לפשע 6586 | והביאו 935 |
|---|---|---|---|---|---|---|---|---|---|---|
| haharmounah | na'am | Yahuah. | bo'au | beyt | 'ael | uapiysh'au, | hagilgal | harbu | lipshoa'; | uahabiy'au |
| ***them* into the palace** | **saith** | **Yahuah** | **Come *to*** | **Beth** | **el** | **and transgress** | **at Gilgal** | **multiply** | **transgression** | **and bring** |

| לבקר 1242 | זבחיכם 2077 | לשלשת 7969 | ימים 3117 | מעשרתיכם 4643: | 4:5 וקטר 6999 | מחמץ 2557 | תודה 8426 |
|---|---|---|---|---|---|---|---|
| laboqer | zibcheykem, | lishloshet | yamiym | ma'saroteykem. | uaqater | mechametz | toudah, |
| ***every* morning** | **your sacrifices** | **after three** | **years** | ***and* your tithes** | **And offer** | **with leaven** | **a sacrifice of thanksgiving** |

| וקראו 7121 | נדבות 5071 | השמיעו 8085 | כי 3588 | כן 3651 | אהבתם 157 | בני 1121 | ישראל 3478 | נאם 5002 | אדני 136 | יהוה 3068: 4:6 |
|---|---|---|---|---|---|---|---|---|---|---|
| uaqir'au | nadabout | hashmiy'au; | kiy | ken | 'ahabtem | baney | yisra'ael, | na'am | 'adonay | Yahuah. |
| **and proclaim** | **the free offerings** | ***and* publish** | **for** | **this** | **like you** | **O you children of** | **Israel** | **saith** | **Adonai** | **Yahuah** |

| וגם 1571 | אני 589 | נתתי 5414 | לכם 3807a | נקיון 5356 | שנים 8147 | בכל 3605 | עריכם 5892 | וחסר 2640 | לחם 3899 | בכל 3605 | מקומתיכם 4725 |
|---|---|---|---|---|---|---|---|---|---|---|---|
| uagam | 'aniy | natatiy | lakem | niqyoun | shinayim | bakal | 'areykem, | uachoser | lechem, | bakol | maqoumoteykem; |
| **And also** | **I** | **have given** | **to you** | **cleanness of** | **teeth** | **in all** | **your cities** | **and want of** | **bread** | **in all** | **your places** |

| ולא 3808 | שבתם 7725 | עדי 5704 | נאם 5002 | יהוה 3068: | 4:7 וגם 1571 | אנכי 595 | מנעתי 4513 | מכם 4480 | את 853 | הגשם 1653 |
|---|---|---|---|---|---|---|---|---|---|---|
| uala' | shabtem | 'aday | na'am | Yahuah. | ua'gam | 'anokiy | mana'atiy | mikem | 'at | hageshem, |
| **yet not** | **have you returned** | **unto Me** | **saith** | **Yahuah** | **And also** | **I** | **have withholden** | **from you** | | **the rain** |

| בעוד 5750 | שלשה 7969 | חדשים 2320 | לקציר 7105 | והמטרתי 4305 | על 5921 | עיר 5892 | אחת 259 | ועל 5921 | עיר 5892 |
|---|---|---|---|---|---|---|---|---|---|
| ba'aud | shaloshah | chadashiym | laqatziyr, | uahimtartiy | 'al | 'ayr | 'achat, | ua'al | 'ayr |
| **when *there were* yet** | **three** | **months** | **to the harvest** | **and I caused it to rain** | **upon** | **city** | **one** | **and upon** | **city** |

| אחת 259 | לא 3808 | אמטיר 4305 | חלקה 2513 | אחת 259 | תמטר 4305 | וחלקה 2513 | אשר 834 | לא 3808 | תמטיר 4305 | עליה 5921 |
|---|---|---|---|---|---|---|---|---|---|---|
| 'achat | la' | 'amtiyr; | chelqah | 'achat | timater, | uachelqah | 'asher | la' | tamtiyr | 'aleyha |
| **another** | **not** | **and caused it to rain** | **piece** | **one** | **was rained upon** | **and the piece** | **whereupon** | **not** | **it rained** | **on** |

| תיבש 3001: | 4:8 ונעו 5128 | שתים 8147 | שלש 7969 | ערים 5892 | אל 413 | עיר 5892 | אחת 259 | לשתות 8354 | מים 4325 | ולא 3808 | ישבעו 7646 | ולא 3808 |
|---|---|---|---|---|---|---|---|---|---|---|---|---|
| tiybash. | uana'au | shatayim | shalosh | 'ariym | 'al | 'ayr | 'achat | lishtout | mayim | uala' | yisba'au; | uala' |
| **withered** | **So wandered** | **two** | ***or* three** | **cities** | **unto** | **city** | **one** | **to drink** | **water** | **but not** | **they were satisfied** | **yet not** |

| שבתם 7725 | עדי 5704 | נאם 5002 | יהוה 3068: | 4:9 הכיתי 5221 | אתכם 853 | בשדפון 7711 | ובירקון 3420 | הרבות 7235 |
|---|---|---|---|---|---|---|---|---|
| shabtem | 'aday | na'am | Yahuah. | hikeytiy | 'atkem | bashidapoun | uabayeraqoun | harabout |
| **have you returned** | **unto me** | **saith** | **Yahuah** | **I have smitten** | **you** | **with blasting** | **and mildew** | **when increased** |

| גנותיכם 1593 | וכרמיכם 3754 | ותאניכם 8384 | וזיתיכם 2132 | יאכל 398 | הגזם 1501 | ולא 3808 |
|---|---|---|---|---|---|---|
| ganouteykem | uakarmeykem | uat'aeneykem | uazeyteykem | ya'kal | hagazam; | uala' |
| **your gardens** | **and your vineyards** | **and your fig trees** | **and your olive trees** | **devoured *them*** | **the palmerworm** | **yet not** |

| שבתם 7725 | עדי 5704 | נאם 5002 | יהוה 3068: | 4:10 שלחתי 7971 | בכם 871a | דבר 1698 | בדרך 1870 | מצרים 4714 |
|---|---|---|---|---|---|---|---|---|
| shabtem | 'aday | na'am | Yahuah. | shilachtiy | bakem | deber | baderek | mitzrayim, |
| **have you not returned** | **unto me** | **saith** | **Yahuah** | **I have sent** | **among you** | **the pestilence** | **after the manner of** | **Egypt** |

| הרגתי 2026 | בחרב 2719 | בחוריכם 970 | עם 5973 | שבי 7628 | סוסיכם 5483 | ואעלה 5927 | באש 889 |
|---|---|---|---|---|---|---|---|
| haragtiy | bachereb | bachureykem, | 'am | shabiy | suseykem; | ua'aleh | ba'ash |
| **have I slain** | **with the sword** | **your young men** | **with** | **have taken away** | **your horses** | **and I have made to come up** | **the stink of** |

Amos 4:4 Come to Bethel, and transgress; at Gilgal multiply transgression; and bring your sacrifices every morning, and your tithes after three years:5 And offer a sacrifice of thanksgiving with leaven, and proclaim and publish the free offerings: for this liketh you, O you children of Israel, saith YHUH G-D.6 And I also have given you cleanness of teeth in all your cities, and want of bread in all your places: yet have you not returned unto me, saith YHUH.7 And also I have withholden the rain from you, when there were yet three months to the harvest: and I caused it to rain upon one city, and caused it not to rain upon another city: one piece was rained upon, and the piece whereupon it rained not withered.8 So two or three cities wandered unto one city, to drink water; but they were not satisfied: yet have you not returned unto me, saith YHUH.9 I have smitten you with blasting and mildew: when your gardens and your vineyards and your fig trees and your olive trees increased, the palmerworm devoured them: yet have you not returned unto me, saith YHUH.10 I have sent among you the pestilence after the manner of Egypt: your young men have I slain with the sword, and have taken away your horses; and I have made the stink of your camps to come up unto your nostrils: yet have you not returned unto me, saith YHUH.

4264 מחניכם 639 ובאפכם 3808 ולא 7725 שבתם 5704 עדי 5002 נאם 3068 יהוה: **4:11** 2015 הפכתי 871a בכם
machaneykem uab'apkhem, uala' shabtem 'aday na'am Yahuah. hapaktiy bakem,
**your camps unto your nostrils yet not have you returned unto me saith Yahuah I have overthrown *some* of you**

4114 כמהפכת 430 אלהים 853 את 5467 סדם 853 ואת 6017 עמרה 1961 ותהיו 181 כאוד 5337 מצל 8316 משרפה 3808 ולא
kamahpekat 'alohiym 'at sadom ua'at 'amorah, uatihayu ka'aud mutzal misrepah; uala'
**overthrew Elohim Sodom *and* Gomorrah and you were as a firebrand plucked out of the burning yet not**

7725 שבתם 5704 עדי 5002 נאם 3068 יהוה: **4:12** 3651 לכן 3541 כה 6213 אעשה 3807a לך 3478 ישראל 6118 עקב 3588 כי 2063 זאת
shabtem 'aday na'am Yahuah. laken koh 'aaseh laka yisra'ael; 'aeqeb kiy za't
**have you returned unto me saith Yahuah Therefore thus will I do unto you O Israel *and* because for this**

6213 אעשה 3807a לך 3559 הכון 7125 לקראת 430 אלהיך 3478 ישראל: **4:13** 3588 כי 2009 הנה 3335 יוצר 2022 הרים 1254 ובורא
'aaseh lak, hikoun liqra't 'aloheyka yisra'ael. kiy hineh youtzer hariym uaborea'
**I will do unto you prepare to meet your Elohim O Israel For lo he that form the mountains and createth**

7307 רוח 5046 ומגיד 120 לאדם 4100 מה 7808 שחו 6213 עשה 7837 שחר 5890 עיפה 1869 ודרך 5921 על 1116 במתי
ruach, uamagiyd la'adam mah sechou, 'aseh shachar 'aeypah, uadorek 'al bamatey
**the wind and declareth unto man what *is* his thought that make the morning darkness and tread upon the high places of**

776 ארץ 3068 יהוה 430 אלהי 6635 צבאות 8034 שמו:
'aretz; Yahuah 'alohey tzaba'aut shamou.
**the earth Yahuah The Elohim of hosts *is* his name**

**Amos 5:1** 8085 שמעו 853 את 1697 הדבר 2088 הזה 834 אשר 595 אנכי 5375 נשא 5921 עליכם 7015 קינה 1004 בית 3478 ישראל: **5:2**
shim'au 'at hadabar hazeh, 'asher 'anokiy nosea' 'aleykem qiynah beyt yisra'ael.
**Hear you word this which I take up against you *even* a lamentation O house of Israel**

5307 נפלה 3808 לא 3254 תוסיף 6965 קום 1330 בתולת 3478 ישראל 5203 נטשה 5921 על 127 אדמתה 369 אין 6965 מקימה: **5:3**
naplah la' tousiyp qum, batulat yisra'ael; nitshah 'al 'admatah 'aeyn maqiymah.
**is fallen no she shall more rise The virgin of Israel she is forsaken upon her land *there is* none to raise her up**

3588 כי 3541 כה 559 אמר 136 אדני 3069 יהוה 5892 העיר 3318 היצאת 505 אלף 7604 תשאיר 3967 מאה
kiy koh 'amar 'adonay Yahuah, ha'ayr hayotza't 'alep tash'ayr me'ah;
**For thus saith Adonai Yahuah The city the one went out *by* a thousand shall leave an hundred**

3318 והיוצאת 3967 מאה 7604 תשאיר 6235 עשרה 1004 לבית 3478 ישראל: **5:4** 3588 כי 3541 כה 559 אמר
uahayoutzea't me'ah tash'ayr 'asarah labeyt yisra'ael. kiy koh 'amar
**and that one which went forth *by* an hundred shall one leave ten to the house of Israel For thus saith**

3068 יהוה 1004 לבית 3478 ישראל 1875 דרשוני 2421 וחיו: **5:5** 408 ואל 1875 תדרשו 1008 בית 410 אל 1537 והגלגל 3808 לא
Yahuah labeyt yisra'ael; dirshuniy uichayu. ua'al tidrashu beyt 'ael, uahagilgal la'
**Yahuah unto the house of Israel Seek you me and you shall live But not seek Beth el and Gilgal nor**

935 תבאו 884 ובאר 7651 שבע 3808 לא 5674 תעברו 3588 כי 1537 הגלגל 1540 גלה 1540 יגלה 1008 ובית 410 אל 1961 יהיה
tabo'au, uab'aer sheba' la' ta'aboru; kiy hagilgal galoh yigleh, uabeyt 'ael yihayeh
**enter into and Beer sheba not pass to for Gilgal shall surely go into captivity and Beth el shall come**

Amos 4:11 I have overthrown some of you, as G-d overthrew Sodom and Gomorrah, and you were as a firebrand plucked out of the burning: yet have you not returned unto me, saith YHUH.12 Therefore thus will I do unto you, O Israel: and because I will do this unto you, prepare to meet your G-d, O Israel.13 For, lo, he that formeth the mountains, and createth the wind, and declareth unto man what is his thought, that make the morning darkness, and treadeth upon the high places of the earth, The YHUH, The G-d of hosts, is his name. **Amos** 5:1 Hear you this word which I take up against you, even a lamentation, O house of Israel.2 The virgin of Israel is fallen; she shall no more rise: she is forsaken upon her land; there is none to raise her up.3 For thus saith YHUH G-D; The city that went out by a thousand shall leave an hundred, and that which went forth by an hundred shall leave ten, to the house of Israel.4 For thus saith YHUH unto the house of Israel, Seek you me, and you shall live:5 But seek not Bethel, nor enter into Gilgal, and pass not to Beer-sheba: for Gilgal shall surely go into captivity, and Bethel shall come to nought.

לאון 205: 5:6 דרשו 1875 את 853 יהוה 3069 וחיו 2421 פן 6435 יצלח 6743 כאש 784 בית 1004 יוסף 3130 ואכלה 398
la'auen. dirshu 'at Yahuah uachayu; pen yitzlach ka'aesh beyt yousep, ua'akalah
**to nought Seek Yahuah and you shall live lest he break out like fire *in* the house of Joseph and devour *it***

ואין 369 מכבה 3518 לבית 1008 אל 410: 5:7 ההפכים 2015 ללענה 3939 משפט 4941 וצדקה 6666 לארץ 776
ua'aeyn makabeh labeyt 'ael. hahopakiym lala'anah mishapat; uatzdaqah la'aretz
**and *there be* none to quench *it* in Beth el You who turn to wormwood judgment righteousness in the earth**

הניחו 3240: 5:8 עשה 6213 כימה 3598 וכסיל 3685 והפך 2015 לבקר 1242 צלמות 6757
hiniychu. 'aseh kiymah uakasiyl, uahopek laboqer tzalmauet,
**leave off *Seek him* that make the seven stars (*Pleiades*) and Orion and turned into the morning the shadow of death**

ויום 3117 לילה 3915 החשיך 2821 הקורא 7121 למי 4325 הים 3220 וישפכם 8210 על 5921 פני 6440 הארץ 776 יהוה 3068
uayoum layalah hechshiyk; haqourea' lamey hayam, uayishpakem 'al paney ha'aretz Yahuah
**and the day *with* night make dark that call for the waters of the sea and pour them out upon the face of the earth Yahuah**

שמו 8034: 5:9 המבליג 1082 שד 7701 על 5921 עז 5794 ושד 7701 על 5921 מבצר 4013 יבוא 935: 5:10
shamou. hamabliyg shod 'al 'az; uashod 'al mibtzar yabou'a.
***is* his name That strengthen the spoiled against the strong so that the spoiled against the fortress shall come**

שנאו 8130 בשער 8179 מוכיח 3198 ודבר 1696 תמים 8549 יתעבו 8581: 5:11 לכן 3651 יען 3282 בושסכם 1318
sana'au basha'ar moukiyach; uadober tamiym yata'aebu. laken ya'an boushaskem
**They hate in the gate him that rebuke and him that speak uprightly they abhor therefore Forasmuch as your treading**

על 5921 דל 1800 ומשאת 4864 בר 1250 תקחו 3947 ממנו 4480 בתי 1004 גזית 1496 בניתם 1129 ולא 3808 תשבו 3427
'al dal, umas'at bar tiqchu mimenu, batey gaziyt baniytem uala' teshabu
***is* upon the poor and burdens of wheat you take from him houses of hewn stone you have built but not you shall dwell**

בם 871a כרמי 3754 חמד 2531 נטעתם 5193 ולא 3808 תשתו 8354 את 853 יינם 3196: 5:12 כי 3588 ידעתי 3045 רבים 7227
bam; karmey chemed nata'atem, uala' tishtu 'at yeynam. kiy yada'tiy rabiym
**in them vineyards pleasant you have planted but not you shall drink wine of them For I know manifold**

פשעיכם 6588 ועצמים 6099 חטאתיכם 2403 צררי 6887 צדיק 6662 לקחי 3947 כפר 3724 ואביונים 34 בשער 8179
pish'aeykem, ua'atzumiym chata'teykem; tzorarey tzadiyq loqchey koper, ua'abyouniym basha'ar
**your transgressions and mighty your sins they afflict the just they take a bribe and the poor in the gate *from their right***

הטו 5186: 5:13 לכן 3651 המשכיל 7919 בעת 6256 ההיא 1931 ידם 1826 כי 3588 עת 6256 רעה 7451 היא 1931: 5:14 דרשו 1875
hitu. laken, hamaskiyl ba'aet hahiy'a yidom; kiy 'at ra'ah hiy'a. dirshu
**they turn aside Therefore the prudent in time that shall keep silence for time *is* an evil it Seek**

טוב 2896 ואל 408 רע 7451 למען 4616 תחיו 2421 ויהי 1961 כן 3651 יהוה 3068 אלהי 430 צבאות 6635 אתכם 854 כאשר 834
toub ua'al ra' lama'an tichayu; uiyhiy ken Yahuah 'alohey tzaba'aut 'atakem ka'asher
**good and not evil that you may live and shall be so Yahuah the Elohim of hosts with you as**

אמרתם 559: 5:15 שנאו 8130 רע 7451 ואהבו 157 טוב 2896 והציגו 3322 בשער 8179 משפט 4941 אולי 194 יחנן 2603
'amartem. sin'au ra' ua'ahabu toub, uahatziygu basha'ar mishapat; 'aulay, yechenan
**you have spoken Hate the evil and love the good and establish in the gate judgment it may be that will be gracious**

Amos 5:6 Seek YHUH, and you shall live; lest he break out like fire in the house of Joseph, and devour it, and there be none to quench it in Bethel.7 You who turn judgment to wormwood, and leave off righteousness in the earth,8 Seek him that make the seven stars and Orion, and turneth the shadow of death into the morning, and make the day dark with night: that call for the waters of the sea, and poureth them out upon the face of the earth: YHUH is his name:9 That strengtheneth the spoiled against the strong, so that the spoiled shall come against the fortress.10 They hate him that rebuketh in the gate, and they abhor him that speaketh uprightly.11 Forasmuch therefore as your treading is upon the poor, and you take from him burdens of wheat: you have built houses of hewn stone, but you shall not dwell in them; you have planted pleasant vineyards, but you shall not drink wine of them.12 For I know your manifold transgressions and your mighty sins: they afflict the just, they take a bribe, and they turn aside the poor in the gate from their right.13 Therefore the prudent shall keep silence in that time; for it is an evil time.14 Seek good, and not evil, that you may live: and so YHUH, the G-d of hosts, shall be with you, as you have spoken.15 Hate the evil, and love the good, and establish judgment in the gate: it may be that YHUH G-d of hosts will be gracious unto the remnant of Joseph.

| יהוה 3068 | אלהי 430 | צבאות 6635 | שארית 7611 | יוסף 3130: | 5:16 לכן 3651 | כה 3541 | אמר 559 | יהוה 3068 | אלהי 430 | צבאות 6635 |
|---|---|---|---|---|---|---|---|---|---|---|
| Yahuah | 'alohey | tzaba'aut | sha'aeriyt | yousep. | laken | koh | 'amar | Yahuah | 'alohey | tzaba'aut |
| **Yahuah** | **Elohim** | **of hosts *unto*** | **the remnant of** | **Joseph** | **Therefore** | **thus** | **saith** | **Yahuah** | **the Elohim** | **of hosts** |

| אדני 136 | בכל 3605 | רחבות 7339 | מספד 4553 | ובכל 3605 | חוצות 2351 | יאמרו 559 | הו 1930 | הו 1930 | וקראו 7121 |
|---|---|---|---|---|---|---|---|---|---|
| 'adonay, | bakal | rachobout | misped, | uabkal | chutzout | ya'maru | hou | hou; | uaqar'au |
| **Adonai *shall be*** | **in all** | **streets** | **Wailing** | **in all** | **the highways** | **they shall say** | **Alas** | **alas** | **and they shall call** |

| אכר 406 | אל 413 | אבל 60 | ומספד 4553 | אל 413 | יודעי 3045 | נהי 5092: | 5:17 ובכל 3605 | כרמים 3754 |
|---|---|---|---|---|---|---|---|---|
| 'akar | 'al | 'aebel, | uamisped | 'al | youda'aey | nehiy. | uabkal | karamiym |
| **the husbandman** | **to** | **mourning** | **and wailing** | **to** | **such as are skilful of** | **lamentation** | **And in all** | **vineyards** |

| מספד 4553 | כי 3588 | אעבר 5674 | בקרבך 7130 | אמר 559 | יהוה 3068: | 5:18 הוי 1945 | המתאוים 183 | את 853 | יום 3117 | יהוה 3068 |
|---|---|---|---|---|---|---|---|---|---|---|
| misped; | kiy | 'aabor | baqirbaka | 'amar | Yahuah. | houy | hamit'auiym | 'at | youm | Yahuah; |
| ***shall be* wailing** | **for** | **I will pass** | **through you** | **saith** | **Yahuah** | **Woe unto you** | **ones that desire** | | **the day of** | **Yahuah** |

| למה 4100 | זה 2088 | לכם 3807a | יום 3117 | יהוה 3068 | הוא 1931 | חשך 2822 | ולא 3808 | אור 216: | 5:19 כאשר 834 | ינוס 5127 | איש 376 | מפני 6440 |
|---|---|---|---|---|---|---|---|---|---|---|---|---|
| lamah | zeh | lakem | youm | Yahuah | hua' | choshek | uala' | 'aur. | ka'asher | yanus | 'aysh | mipaney |
| **to what end *is*** | **it** | **for you?** | **the day of** | **Yahuah** | ***is* he** | **darkness** | **and not** | **light** | **As if** | **did flee** | **a man** | **from** |

| הארי 738 | ופגעו 6293 | הדב 1677 | ובא 935 | הבית 1004 | וסמך 5564 | ידו 3027 | על 5921 | הקיר 7023 | ונשכו 5391 | הנחש 5175: | 5:20 |
|---|---|---|---|---|---|---|---|---|---|---|---|
| ha'ariy, | uapga'au | hadob; | uaba' | habayit, | uasamak | yadou | 'al | haqiyr, | uanshakou | hanachash. | |
| **a lion** | **and met him** | **a bear** | **or went into** | **the house** | **and leaned** | **his hand** | **on** | **the wall** | **and bit him** | **a serpent** | |

| הלא 3808 | חשך 2822 | יום 3117 | יהוה 3068 | ולא 3808 | אור 216 | ואפל 651 | ולא 3808 | נגה 5051 | לו 3807a: | 5:21 שנאתי 8130 | מאסתי 3988 |
|---|---|---|---|---|---|---|---|---|---|---|---|
| hala' | choshek | youm | Yahuah | uala' | 'aur; | ua'apel | uala' | nogah | lou'. | sanea'tiy | ma'astiy |
| ***Shall* not** | ***be* darkness** | **the day of** | **Yahuah** | **and not** | **light?** | **even very dark** | **and no** | **brightness** | **in it?** | **I hate** | **I despise** |

| חגיכם 2282 | ולא 3808 | אריח 7306 | בעצרתיכם 6116: | 5:22 כי 3588 | אם 518 | תעלו 5927 | לי 3807a | עלות 5930 |
|---|---|---|---|---|---|---|---|---|
| chageykem; | uala' | 'ariyach | ba'atzroteykem. | kiy | 'am | ta'alu | liy | 'alout |
| **your feast days** | **and not** | **I will smell** | **in your solemn assemblies** | **Though** | **if** | **you offer** | **me** | **burnt offerings** |

| ומנחתיכם 4503 | לא 3808 | ארצה 7521 | ושלם 8002 | מריאיכם 4806 | לא 3808 | אביט 5027: | 5:23 |
|---|---|---|---|---|---|---|---|
| uaminchoteykem | la' | 'artzeh; | uashelem | mariy'aeykem | la' | 'abiyt. | |
| **and your meat offerings** | **not** | **I will accept *them*** | **the peace offerings of** | **your fat beasts** | **neither** | **will I regard** | |

| הסר 5493 | מעלי 5921 | המון 1995 | שריך 7892 | וזמרת 2172 | נבליך 5035 | לא 3808 | אשמע 8085: | 5:24 ויגל 1556 |
|---|---|---|---|---|---|---|---|---|
| haser | me'alay | hamoun | shireyka; | uazimrat | nabaleyka | la' | 'ashma. | uayigal |
| **Take you away** | **from me** | **the noise of** | **your songs** | **for the melody of** | **your viols** | **not** | **I will hear** | **But let run down** |

| כמים 4325 | משפט 4941 | וצדקה 6666 | כנחל 5158 | איתן 386: | 5:25 הזבחים 2077 | ומנחה 4503 | הגשתם 5066 | לי 3807a |
|---|---|---|---|---|---|---|---|---|
| kamayim | mishapat; | uatzdaqah | kanachal | 'aeytan. | hazabachiym | uaminchah | higashtem | liy |
| **as waters** | **judgment** | **and righteousness** | **as a stream** | **mighty** | **sacrifices** | **and offerings** | **Have you offered** | **unto me** |

| במדבר 4057 | ארבעים 705 | שנה 8141 | בית 1004 | ישראל 3478: | 5:26 ונשאתם 859 | את 853 | סכות 5522 | מלככם 4428 | ואת 853 |
|---|---|---|---|---|---|---|---|---|---|
| bamidbar | 'arba'aym | shanah | beyt | yisra'ael. | uansa'tem, | 'at | sikut | malkakem, | ua'at |
| **in the wilderness** | **forty** | **years** | **O house of** | **Israel?** | **But you have borne** | | **the tabernacle of** | **Moloch** | ***and*** |

Amos 5:16 Therefore YHUH, the G-d of hosts, the Adonai, saith thus; Wailing shall be in all streets; and they shall say in all the highways, Alas! alas! and they shall call the husbandman to mourning, and such as are skilful of lamentation to wailing.17 And in all vineyards shall be wailing: for I will pass through you, saith YHUH.18 Woe unto you that desire the day of YHUH! to what end is it for you? the day of YHUH is darkness, and not light.19 As if a man did flee from a lion, and a bear met him; or went into the house, and leaned his hand on the wall, and a serpent bit him.20 Shall not the day of YHUH be darkness, and not light? even very dark, and no brightness in it?21 I hate, I despise your feast days, and I will not smell in your solemn assemblies.22 Though you offer me burnt offerings and your meat offerings, I will not accept them: neither will I regard the peace offerings of your fat beasts.23 Take you away from me the noise of your songs; for I will not hear the melody of your viols.24 But let judgment run down as waters, and righteousness as a mighty stream.25 Have you offered unto me sacrifices and offerings in the wilderness forty years, O house of Israel?26 But you have borne the tabernacle of your Moloch and Chiun your images, the star of your god, which you made to yourselves.

| כיון 3594 | צלמיכם 6754 | כוכב 3556 | אלהיכם 430 | אשר 834 | עשיתם 6213 | לכם 3807a: | **5:27** והגליתי 1540 |
|---|---|---|---|---|---|---|---|
| kiyun | tzalmeykem; | koukab | 'aloheykem, | 'asher | 'asiytem | lakem. | uahigleytiy |
| **Chiun** | **your images** | **the star of** | **your god** | **which** | **you made** | **to yourselves** | **Therefore will I cause to go into captivity** |

| אתכם 853 | מהלאה 1973 | לדמשק 1834 | אמר 559 | יהוה 3068 | אלהי 430 | צבאות 6635 | שמו 8034: |
|---|---|---|---|---|---|---|---|
| 'atkem | mehala'ah | ladamaseq; | 'amar | Yahuah | 'alohey | tzaba'aut | shamou. |
| **you** | **beyond** | **Damascus** | **saith** | **Yahuah *is*** | **The Elohim of hosts** | | **whose name** |

**Amos 6:1**

| הוי 1945 | השאננים 7600 | בציון 6726 | והבטחים 982 | בהר 2022 | שמרון 8111 | נקבי 5344 |
|---|---|---|---|---|---|---|
| houy | hasha'ananiym | batziyoun, | uahabotachiym | bahar | shomaroun; | naqubey |
| **Woe** | **to them *that are* at ease** | **in Zion** | **and trust** | **in the mountain of** | **Samaria** | ***which are* named** |

| ראשית 7225 | הגוים 1471 | ובאו 935 | להם 1992 | בית 1004 | ישראל 3478: | **6:2** עברו 5674 | כלנה 3641 | וראו 7200 | ולכו 1980 | משם 8033 |
|---|---|---|---|---|---|---|---|---|---|---|
| ra'shiyt | hagouyim, | uaba'au | lahem | beyt | yisra'ael. | 'abru | kalneh | uar'au, | ualku | misham |
| **chief of** | **the nations** | **came** | **to whom** | **the house of** | **Israel** | **Pass you unto** | **Calneh** | **and see** | **and go you** | **from there *to*** |

| חמת 2574 | רבה 7274 | ורדו 3381 | גת 1661 | פלשתים 6430 | הטובים 2896 | מן 4480 | הממלכות 4467 | האלה 428 | אם 518 | רב 7227 |
|---|---|---|---|---|---|---|---|---|---|---|
| chamat | rabah; | uardu | gat | palishtiym, | hatoubiym | min | hamamlakout | ha'aeleh, | 'am | rab |
| **Hamath** | **the great** | **then go down** | ***to* Gath** | **of the Philistines** | ***be they* better** | **than** | **kingdoms?** | **these** | **or** | **greater** |

| גבולם 1366 | מגבלכם 1366: | **6:3** המנדים 5077 | ליום 3117 | רע 7451 | ותגישון 5066 | שבת 3427 | חמס 2555: |
|---|---|---|---|---|---|---|---|
| gabulam | migabulkem. | hamanadiym | layoum | ra'; | uatagiyshun | shebet | chamas. |
| **their border** | **than your border?** | **You that put far away** | **day** | ***the* evil** | **and cause to come near** | **the seat of** | **violence** |

**6:4**

| השכבים 7901 | על 5921 | מטות 4296 | שן 8127 | וסרחים 5628 | על 5921 | ערשותם 6210 | ואכלים 398 | כרים 3733 | מצאן 6629 |
|---|---|---|---|---|---|---|---|---|---|
| hashokabiym | 'al | mitout | shen, | uasruchiym | 'al | 'arsoutam; | ua'akaliym | kariym | mitza'n, |
| **That lie** | **upon** | **beds of** | **ivory** | **and stretch themselves** | **upon** | **their couches** | **and eat** | **the lambs** | **out of the flock** |

| ועגלים 5695 | מתוך 8432 | מרבק 4770: | **6:5** הפרטים 6527 | על 5921 | פי 6310 | הנבל 5035 | כדויד 1732 | חשבו 2803 | להם 1992 |
|---|---|---|---|---|---|---|---|---|---|
| ua'agaliym | mitouk | marbeq. | haporatiym | 'al | piy | hanabel; | kadauiyd | chashabu | lahem |
| **and the calves** | **out of the midst of** | **the stall** | **That chant to** | | **the sound of** | **the viol** | **like David *and*** | **invent** | **to themselves** |

| כלי 3627 | שיר 7892: | **6:6** השתים 8354 | במזרקי 4219 | יין 3196 | וראשית 7225 | שמנים 8081 | ימשחו 4886 | ולא 3808 |
|---|---|---|---|---|---|---|---|---|
| kaley | shiyr. | hashotiym | bamizraqey | yayin, | uarea'shiyt | shamaniym | yimashachu; | uala' |
| **instruments of** | **music** | **That drink** | **in bowls** | **wine** | **and chief** | **ointments** | **anoint themselves *with the*** | **but not** |

| נחלו 2470 | על 5921 | שבר 7667 | יוסף 3130: | **6:7** לכן 3651 | עתה 6258 | יגלו 1540 | בראש 7218 | גלים 1540 |
|---|---|---|---|---|---|---|---|---|
| nechlu | 'al | sheber | yousep. | laken | 'atah | yiglu | bara'sh | goliym; |
| **they are grieved** | **for** | **the affliction of** | **Joseph** | **Therefore** | **now** | **shall they go captive** | **with the first** | **that go captive** |

| וסר 5493 | מרזח 4794 | סרוחים 5628: | **6:8** נשבע 7650 | אדני 136 | יהוה 3069 | בנפשו 5315 | נאם 5002 |
|---|---|---|---|---|---|---|---|
| uasar | mirzach | saruchiym. | nishba' | 'adonay | Yahuah | banapshou, | na'am |
| **and shall be removed** | **the banquet of** | **them that stretched themselves** | **has sworn** | **Adonai** | **Yahuah** | **by himself** | **saith** |

| יהוה 3068 | אלהי 430 | צבאות 6635 | מתאב 8374 | אנכי 595 | את 853 | גאון 1347 | יעקב 3290 | וארמנותיו 759 | שנאתי 8130 |
|---|---|---|---|---|---|---|---|---|---|
| Yahuah | 'alohey | tzaba'aut, | mata'aeb | 'anokiy | 'at | ga'aun | ya'aqob, | ua'armanotayu | sanea'tiy; |
| **Yahuah** | **the Elohim of hosts** | | **abhor** | **I** | | **the excellency of** | **Jacob** | **and his palaces** | **hate** |

Amos 5:27 Therefore will I cause you to go into captivity beyond Damascus, saith YHUH, whose name is The G-d of hosts. **Amos** 6:1 Woe to them that are at ease in Zion, and trust in the mountain of Samaria, which are named chief of the nations, to whom the house of Israel came!2 Pass you unto Calneh, and see; and from thence go you to Hamath the great: then go down to Gath of the Philistines: be they better than these kingdoms? or their border greater than your border?3 You that put far away the evil day, and cause the seat of violence to come near;4 That lie upon beds of ivory, and stretch themselves upon their couches, and eat the lambs out of the flock, and the calves out of the midst of the stall;5 That chant to the sound of the viol, and invent to themselves instruments of musick, like David;6 That drink wine in bowls, and anoint themselves with the chief ointments: but they are not grieved for the affliction of Joseph.7 Therefore now shall they go captive with the first that go captive, and the banquet of them that stretched themselves shall be removed.8 The Adonai G-D has sworn by himself, saith YHUH the G-d of hosts, I abhor the excellency of Jacob, and hate his palaces: therefore will I deliver up the city with all that is therein.

6:9

והסגרתי 5462 עיר 5892 ומלאה 4393: והיה 1961 אם 518 יותרו 3498 עשרה 6235 אנשים 582
uahisgartiy 'ayr uamlo'ah. uahayah, 'am yiuataru 'asarah 'anashiym
**therefore will I deliver up the city with all that is therein And it shall come to pass if there remain ten men**

6:10

בבית 1004 אחד 259 ומתו 4191: ונשאו 5375 דודו 1730 ומסרפו 5635 להוציא 3318 עצמים 6106
babayit 'achad uametu. uansa'au doudou uamsarapou, lahoutziy'a 'atzamiym
**in house one that they shall die And shall take him up a man's uncle and he that burn him to bring out the bones**

מן 4480 הבית 1004 ואמר 559 לאשר 834 בירכתי 3411 הבית 1004 העוד 5750 עמך 5973 ואמר 559 אפס 657
min habayit ua'amar la'asher bayarkatey habayit ha'aud 'amak ua'amar 'apes;
**out of the house and shall say unto him that *is* by the sides of the house *Is there* yet *any* with you? and he shall say No**

6:11

ואמר 559 הס 2013 כי 3588 לא 3808 להזכיר 2142 בשם 8034 יהוה 3068: כי 3588 הנה 2009 יהוה 3068
ua'amar has, kiy la' lahazkiyr bashem Yahuah. kiy hineh Yahuah
**Then shall he say Hold your tongue for not we may make mention of the name of Yahuah For behold Yahuah**

6:12

מצוה 6680 והכה 5221 הבית 1004 הגדול 1419 רסיסים 7447 והבית 1004 הקטן 6996 בקעים 1233: הירצון 7323 בסלע 5553
matzaueh, uahikah habayit hagadoul rasiysiym; uahabayit haqaton baqi'aym. hayarutzun basela'
**command and he will smite house the great *with* breaches and house the little *with* clefts Shall run upon the rock?**

סוסים 5483 אם 518 יחרוש 2790 בבקרים 1241 כי 3588 הפכתם 2015 לראש 7219 משפט 4941 ופרי 6529 צדקה 6666
susiym, 'am yacharoush babaqariym; kiy hapaktem lara'sh mishapat, uapariy tzadaqah
**horses lo will one plow *there* with oxen? for you have turned into gall judgment and the fruit of righteousness**

6:13

ללענה 3939: השמחים 8055 ללא 3808 דבר 1697 האמרים 559 הלוא 3808 בחזקנו 2392 לקחנו 3947 לנו 3807a
lala'anah. hasamechiym lala' dabar; ha'amariym, halou'a bachazaqenu, laqachnu lanu
**into hemlock You which rejoice of nought in a thing which say Have we not by our own strength taken to us**

6:14

קרנים 7161: כי 3588 הנני 2005 מקים 6965 עליכם 5921 בית 1004 ישראל 3478 נאם 5002 יהוה 3068 אלהי 430 הצבאות 6635 גוי 1471
qarnayim. kiy hinniy meqym 'aleykem beyt yisra'ael, na'am Yahuah 'alohey hatzaba'aut gouy;
**horns But behold I will raise up against you O house of Israel saith Yahuah the Elohim of hosts a nation**

ולחצו 3905 אתכם 853 מלבוא 935 חמת 2574 עד 5704 נחל 5158 הערבה 6160:
ualachatzu 'atkem milbou' chamat 'ad nachal ha'arabah.
**and they shall afflict you from the entering in *of* Hamath unto the river of the wilderness**

**Amos 7:1**

כה 3541 הראני 7200 אדני 136 יהוה 3069 והנה 2009 יוצר 3335 גבי 1462 בתחלת 8462
koh hir'aniy 'adonay Yahuah, uahineh youtzer gobay, bitchilat
**Thus has showed unto me Adonai Yahuah and behold he formed grasshoppers in the beginning of**

7:2

עלות 5927 הלקש 3954 והנה 2009 לקש 3954 אחר 310 גזי 1488 המלך 4428: והיה 1961
'alout halaqesh; uahineh leqesh, 'achar gizey hamelek. uahayah,
**the shooting up *of* the latter growth and lo *it was* the latter growth after mowings the king's And it came to pass *that***

אם 518 כלה 3615 לאכול 398 את 853 עשב 6212 הארץ 776 ואמר 559 אדני 136 יהוה 3068 סלח 5545 נא 4994
'am kilah le'akoul 'at 'aeseb ha'aretz, ua'amar, 'adonay Yahuah salach na,
**when when they had made an end of eating the grass of the land then I said O Adonai Yahuah forgive I beseech you**

Amos 6: 9 And it shall come to pass, if there remain ten men in one house, that they shall die.10 And a man's uncle shall take him up, and he that burneth him, to bring out the bones out of the house, and shall say unto him that is by the sides of the house, Is there yet any with you? and he shall say, No. Then shall he say, Hold your tongue: for we may not make mention of the name of YHUH.11 For, behold, YHUH commandeth, and he will smite the great house with breaches, and the little house with clefts.12 Shall horses run upon the rock? will one plow there with oxen? for you have turned judgment into gall, and the fruit of righteousness into hemlock:13 You which rejoice in a thing of nought, which say, Have we not taken to us horns by our own strength?14 But, behold, I will raise up against you a nation, O house of Israel, saith YHUH the G-d of hosts; and they shall afflict you from the entering in of Hamath unto the river of the wilderness. **Amos** 7:1 Thus has YHUH G-D showed unto me; and, behold, he formed grasshoppers in the beginning of the shooting up of the latter growth; and, lo, it was the latter growth after the king's mowings.2 And it came to pass, that when they had made an end of eating the grass of the land, then I said, O Adonai G-D, forgive, I beseech you: by whom shall Jacob arise? for he is small.

מי 4310 יקום 6965 יעקב 3290 כי 3588 קטן 6996 הוא 1931: 7:3 נחם 5162 יהוה 3068 על 5921 זאת 2063 לא 3808 תהיה 1961 אמר 559 7:4 יהוה 3068:
miy' yaqum ya'aqob; kiy qaton hua'. nicham Yahuah 'al za't; la' tihayeh 'amar Yahuah.
**by whom shall arise? Jacob for *is* small he repented Yahuah for this not shall be saith Yahuah**

כה 3541 הראני 7200 אדני 136 יהוה 3069 והנה 2009 קרא 7121 לרב 7378 באש 784 אדני 136 יהוה 3069 ותאכל 398 את 853
koh hir'aniy 'adonay Yahuah, uahineh qorea' larib ba'aesh 'adonay Yahuah; uata'kal 'at
**Thus has showed unto me Adonai Yahuah and behold called to contend by fire Adonai Yahuah and it devoured**

תהום 8415 רבה 7227 ואכלה 398 את 853 החלק 2506: 7:5 ואמר 559 אדני 136 יהוה 3069 חדל 2308 נא 4994 מי 4310
tahoum rabah, ua'akalah 'at hacheleq. ua'amar, 'adonay Yahuah chadal na, miy'
**the deep *the* great and did eat up a part Then said I O Adonai Yahuah cease I beseech you by whom**

יקום 6965 יעקב 3290 כי 3588 קטן 6996 הוא 1931: 7:6 נחם 5162 יהוה 3068 על 5921 זאת 2063 גם 1571 היא 1931 לא 3808 תהיה 1961 אמר 559 אדני 136
yaqum ya'aqob; kiy qaton hua'. nicham Yahuah 'al za't; gam hiy'a la' tihayeh, 'amar 'adonay
**shall arise? Jacob for *is* small he repented Yahuah for this This also not shall be saith Adonai**

יהוה 3069: 7:7 כה 3541 הראני 7200 והנה 2009 אדני 136 נצב 5324 על 5921 חומת 2346 אנך 594 ובידו 3027
Yahuah. koh hir'aniy, uahineh 'adonay nitzab 'al choumat 'anak; uabyadou
**Yahuah Thus he showed me and behold Adonai stood upon a wall *made by* a plumbline in his hand**

אנך 594: 7:8 ויאמר 559 יהוה 3068 אלי 413 מה 4100 אתה 859 ראה 7200 עמוס 5986 ואמר 559 אנך 954 ויאמר 559 אדני 136
'anak. uaya'mer Yahuah 'aelay, mah 'atah ro'ah 'amous, ua'amar 'anak; uaya'mer 'adonay,
***with* a plumbline And said Yahuah unto me what you? see Amos And I said A plumbline Then said Adonai**

הנני 2005 שם 7760 אנך 594 בקרב 7130 עמי 5971 ישראל 3478 לא 3808 אוסיף 3254 עוד 5750 עבור 5674 לו 3807a: 7:9
hinniy sam 'anak baqereb 'amiy yisra'ael, la' 'ausiyp 'aud 'abour lou'.
**Behold I will set a plumbline in the midst of my people Israel not again any more I will pass by them**

ונשמו 8074 במות 1116 ישחק 3446 ומקדשי 4720 ישראל 3478 יחרבו 2717 וקמתי 6965 על 5921
uanashamu bamout yischaq, uamiqdashey yisra'ael yecherabu; uaqamtiy 'al
**And shall be desolate the high places of Isaac and the sanctuaries of Israel shall be laid waste and I will rise against**

בית 1004 ירבעם 3379 בחרב 2719: 7:10 וישלח 7971 אמציה 558 כהן 3548 בית 1008 אל 410 אל 413 ירבעם 3379 מלך 4428
beyt yarab'am bechareb. uayishlach, 'amatzayah kohen beyt 'ael, 'al yarab'am melek
**the house of Jeroboam with the sword Then sent Amaziah the priest of Beth el to Jeroboam king of**

ישראל 3478 לאמר 559 קשר 7194 עליך 5921 עמוס 5986 בקרב 7130 בית 1004 ישראל 3478 לא 3808 תוכל 3201 הארץ 776 להכיל 3557
yisra'ael lea'mor; qashar 'aleyka 'amous, baqereb beyt yisra'ael, la' tukal ha'aretz, lahakiyl
**Israel saying has conspired against you Amos in the midst of the house of Israel not is able the land to bear**

את 853 כל 3605 דבריו 1697: 7:11 כי 3588 כה 3541 אמר 559 עמוס 5986 בחרב 2719 ימות 4191 ירבעם 3379 וישראל 3478 גלה 1540
'at kal dabarayu. kiy koh 'amar 'amous, bachereb yamut yarab'am; uayisra'ael, galoh
**all his words For thus saith Amos by the sword shall die Jeroboam and Israel shall surely**

יגלה 1540 מעל 5921 אדמתו 127: 7:12 ויאמר 559 אמציה 558 אל 413 עמוס 5986 חזה 2374 לך 1980 ברח 1272 לך 3807a אל 413
yigleh me'al 'admatou. uaya'mer 'amatzayah 'al 'amous, chozeh lek barach laka 'al
**be led away captive out of their own land Also said Amaziah unto Amos O seer go you flee away for you into**

Amos 7:3 YHUH repented for this: It shall not be, saith YHUH.4 Thus has YHUH G-D showed unto me: and, behold, YHUH G-D called to contend by fire, and it devoured the great deep, and did eat up a part.5 Then said I, O Adonai G-D, cease, I beseech you: by whom shall Jacob arise? for he is small.6 YHUH repented for this: This also shall not be, saith YHUH G-D.7 Thus he showed me: and, behold, YHUH stood upon a wall made by a plumbline, with a plumbline in his hand.8 And YHUH said unto me, Amos, what seest you? And I said, A plumbline. Then said the Adonai, Behold, I will set a plumbline in the midst of my people Israel: I will not again pass by them anymore:9 And the high places of Isaac shall be desolate, and the sanctuaries of Israel shall be laid waste; and I will rise against the house of Jeroboam with the sword.10 Then Amaziah the priest of Bethel sent to Jeroboam king of Israel, saying, Amos has conspired against you in the midst of the house of Israel: the land is not able to bear all his words.11 For thus Amos saith, Jeroboam shall die by the sword, and Israel shall surely be led away captive out of their own land.12 Also Amaziah said unto Amos, O you seer, go, flee you away into the land of Judah, and there eat bread, and prophesy there:

7:13

ארץ 776 יהודה 3063 ואכל 398 שם 8033 לחם 3899 ושם 8033 תנבא 5012: ובית 1008 אל 410 לא 3808 תוסיף 3254 עוד 5750 להנבא 5012
'aretz yahudah; ua'akol sham lechem, uasham tinabea'. uabeyt 'ael, la' tousiyp 'aud lahinabea';
**the land of Judah and eat there bread and there prophesy But Beth el not again any more *at* prophesy**

7:14

כי 3588 מקדש 4720 מלך 4428 הוא 1931 ובית 1004 ממלכה 4467 הוא 1931: ויען 6030 עמוס 5986 ויאמר 559 אל 413 אמציה 558
kiy miqdash melek hua', uabeyt mamlakah hua'. uaya'an 'amous uaya'mer 'al 'amatzayah,
**for chapel *is the* king's it and court *is the* king's it Then answered Amos and said to Amaziah**

לא 3808 נביא 5030 אנכי 595 ולא 3808 בן 1121 נביא 5030 אנכי 595 כי 3588 בוקר 951 אנכי 595 ובולס 1103
la' nabiy'a 'anokiy, uala' ben nabiy'a 'anokiy; kiy bouqer 'anokiy uaboules
**no prophet I *was* neither son a prophet's *was* I but *was* an herdman I and a gatherer of**

7:15

שקמים 8256: ויקחני 3947 יהוה 3068 מאחרי 310 הצאן 6629 ויאמר 559 אלי 413 יהוה 3068 לך 1980 הנבא 5012 אל 413
shiqmiym. uayiqacheniy Yahuah, me'acharey hatza'an; uaya'mer 'aelay Yahuah, lek hinabea' 'al
**sycomore fruit And took me Yahuah *as I* followed the flock and said unto me Yahuah Go you prophesy unto**

7:16

עמי 5971 ישראל 3478: ועתה 6258 שמע 8085 דבר 1697 יהוה 3068 אתה 859 אמר 559 לא 3808 תנבא 5012 על 5921 ישראל 3478
'amiy yisra'ael. ua'atah shama' dabar Yahuah; 'atah 'amer, la' tinabea' 'al yisra'ael,
**my people Israel Now therefore hear you the word of Yahuah You say not Prophesy against Israel**

7:17

ולא 3808 תטיף 5197 על 5921 בית 1004 ישחק 3446: לכן 3651 כה 3541 אמר 559 יהוה 3068 אשתך 802 בעיר 5892
uala' tatiyp 'al beyt yischaq. laken koh 'amar Yahuah 'ashtaka ba'ayr
**and not *your word* drop against the house of Isaac Therefore thus saith Yahuah Your wife in the city**

תזנה 2181 ובניך 1121 ובנתיך 1323 בחרב 2719 יפלו 5307 ואדמתך 127 בחבל 2256 תחלק 2505 ואתה 859
tizneh uabaneyka uabnoteyka bachereb yipolu, ua'admataka bachebel tachulaq; ua'atah,
**shall be an harlot and your sons and your daughters by the sword shall fall and your land by line shall be divided and you**

על 5921 אדמה 127 טמאה 2931 תמות 4191 וישראל 3478 גלה 1540 יגלה 1540 מעל 5921 אדמתו 127:
'al 'adamah tame'ah tamut, uayisra'ael, galoh yigleh me'al 'admatou.
**in land a polluted shall die and Israel shall surely go into captivity forth of his land**

**Amos 8:1**

8:2

כה 3541 הראני 7200 אדני 136 יהוה 3069 והנה 2009 כלוב 3619 קיץ 7019: ויאמר 559 מה 4100 אתה 859
koh hir'aniy 'adonay Yahuah; uahineh kalub qayitz. uaya'mer, mah 'atah
**Thus has showed unto me Adonai Yahuah and behold a basket of summer fruit And he said what you?**

ראה 7200 עמוס 5986 ואמר 559 כלוב 3619 קיץ 7019 ויאמר 559 יהוה 3068 אלי 413 בא 935 הקץ 7093 אל 413 עמי 5971
ro'ah 'amous, ua'amar kalub qayitz; uaya'mer Yahuah 'aelay, ba' haqetz 'al 'amiy
**see Amos And I said A basket of summer fruit Then said Yahuah unto me is come The end upon my people of**

8:3

ישראל 3478 לא 3808 אוסיף 3254 עוד 5750 עבור 5674 לו 3807a: והילילו 3213 שירות 7892 היכל 1964 ביום 3117 ההוא 1931
yisra'ael, la' 'ausiyp 'aud 'abour lou'. uaheyliylu shiyrout heykal bayoum hahua',
**Israel not I will again any more pass by them And shall be howlings the songs of the temple in day that**

8:4

נאם 5002 אדני 136 יהוה 3068 רב 7227 הפגר 6297 בכל 3605 מקום 4725 השליך 7993 הס 2013: שמעו 8085
na'am 'adonay Yahuah; rab hapeger, bakal maqoum hishliyk has. shim'au
**saith Adonai Yahuah *there shall be* many dead bodies in every place they shall cast *them* forth *with* silence Hear**

Amos 7:13 But prophesy not again anymore at Bethel: for it is the king's chapel, and it is the king's court.14 Then answered Amos, and said to Amaziah, I was no prophet, neither was I a prophet's son; but I was an herdman, and a gatherer of sycomore fruit:15 And YHUH took me as I followed the flock, and YHUH said unto me, Go, prophesy unto my people Israel.16 Now therefore hear you the word of YHUH: Thou say, Prophesy not against Israel, and drop not your word against the house of Isaac.17 Therefore thus saith YHUH; Thy wife shall be an harlot in the city, and your sons and your daughters shall fall by the sword, and your land shall be divided by line; and you shall die in a polluted land: and Israel shall surely go into captivity forth of his land. **Amos** 8:1 Thus has YHUH G-D showed unto me: and behold a basket of summer fruit.2 And he said, Amos, what seest you? And I said, A basket of summer fruit. Then said YHUH unto me, The end is come upon my people of Israel; I will not again pass by them anymore.3 And the songs of the temple shall be howlings in that day, saith YHUH G-D: there shall be many dead bodies in every place; they shall cast them forth with silence.4 Hear this, O you that swallow up the needy, even to make the poor of the land to fail,

| זאת 2063 | השאפים 7602 | אביון 34 | ולשבית 7673 | ענוי 6035 | ארץ 776: | 8:5 לאמר 559 | מתי 4970 | יעבר 5674 |
|---|---|---|---|---|---|---|---|---|
| za't | hasho'apiym | abyoun; | ualashbiyt | 'anuey | 'aretz. | lea'mor, | matay | ya'abor |
| **this** | **O you that swallow up** | **the needy** | **even to make to fail** | **the poor of** | **the land** | **Saying** | **When** | **will be gone** |

| החדש 2320 | ונשבירה 7666 | שבר 7668 | והשבת 7676 | ונפתחה 6605 | בר 1250 | להקטין 56994 | איפה 374 | ולהגדיל 1431 |
|---|---|---|---|---|---|---|---|---|
| hachodesh | uanashbiyrah | sheber, | uahashabat | uaniptachah | bar; | lahaqtiyn | 'aeypah | ualhagdiyl |
| **the new moon** | **that we may sell** | **corn?** | **and the sabbath** | **that we may set forth** | **wheat** | **making small** | **the ephah** | **and great** |

| שקל 8255 | ולעות 5791 | מאזני 3976 | מרמה 4820: | 8:6 לקנות 7069 | בכסף 3701 | דלים 1800 | ואביון 34 | בעבור 5668 |
|---|---|---|---|---|---|---|---|---|
| sheqel, | ual'auet | ma'zaney | mirmah. | liqnout | bakesep | daliym, | ua'abyoun | ba'abur |
| **the shekel** | **and falsifying** | **the balances** | **by deceit?** | **That we may buy** | **for silver** | **the poor** | **and the needy** | **for** |

| נעלים 5275 | ומפל 4651 | בר 1250 | נשביר 7666: | 8:7 נשבע 7650 | יהוה 3068 | בגאון 1347 | יעקב 3290 | אם 518 | אשכח 7911 |
|---|---|---|---|---|---|---|---|---|---|
| na'alayim; | uamapal | bar | nashbiyr. | nishba' | Yahuah | big'aun | ya'aqob; | 'am | 'ashkach |
| **a pair of shoes** | **the refuse of the wheat?** | ***yea* and sell** | | **has sworn** | **Yahuah** | **by the excellency of** | **Jacob** | **Surely** | **I will forget** |

| לנצח 5331 | כל 3605 | מעשיהם 4639: | 8:8 העל 5921 | זאת 2063 | לא 3808 | תרגז 7264 | הארץ 776 | ואבל 56 | כל 3605 | יושב 3427 | בה 871a |
|---|---|---|---|---|---|---|---|---|---|---|---|
| lanetzach | kal | ma'aseyhem. | ha'al | za't | la' | tirgaz | ha'aretz, | ua'abal | kal | yousheb | bah; |
| **never** | **any of** | **their works** | **Shall for** | **this** | **not** | **tremble** | **the land** | **and mourn** | **every one** | **that dwell** | **therein?** |

| ועלתה 5927 | כאר 216 | כלה 3605 | ונגרשה 1644 | ונשקה 8248 | כיאור 2975 | מצרים 4714: 8:9 |
|---|---|---|---|---|---|---|
| ua'alatah | ka'aur | kulah, | uanigrashah | uanishqa'ah | kiya'aur | mitzrayim. |
| **and it shall rise up** | **as a flood** | **wholly** | **and it shall be cast out** | **and drowned** | **as by the flood of** | **Egypt** |

| והיה 1961 | ביום 3117 | ההוא 1931 | נאם 5002 | אדני 136 | יהוה 3069 | והבאתי 935 | השמש 8121 | בצהרים 6672 |
|---|---|---|---|---|---|---|---|---|
| uahayah | bayoum | hahua', | na'am | 'adonay | Yahuah, | uahebea'tiy | hashemesh | batzaharayim; |
| **And it shall come to pass** | **in day** | **that** | **saith** | **Adonai** | **Yahuah** | **that I will cause to go down** | **the sun** | **at noon** |

| והחשכתי 2821 | לארץ 776 | ביום 3117 | אור 216: | 8:10 והפכתי 2015 | חגיכם 2282 | לאבל 60 | וכל 3605 | שיריכם 7892 |
|---|---|---|---|---|---|---|---|---|
| uahachashaktiy | la'aretz | bayoum | 'aur. | uahapaktiy | chageykem | la'aebel, | uakal | shiyreykem |
| **and I will darken** | **the earth** | **in day** | ***the* clear** | **And I will turn** | **your feasts** | **into mourning** | **and all** | **your songs** |

| לקינה 7015 | והעליתי 5927 | על 5921 | כל 3605 | מתנים 4975 | שק 8242 | ועל 5921 | כל 3605 | ראש 7218 | קרחה 7144 | ושמתיה 7760 |
|---|---|---|---|---|---|---|---|---|---|---|
| laqiynah, | uaha'aleytiy | 'al | kal | matanayim | saq, | ua'al | kal | ra'sh | qarachah; | uasamtiyha |
| **into lamentation** | **and I will bring up** | **upon** | **all** | **loins** | **sackcloth** | **upon** | **every** | **head** | **baldness** | **and I will make it** |

| כאבל 60 | יחיד 3173 | ואחריתה 319 | כיום 3117 | מר 4751: | 8:11 הנה 2009 | ימים 3117 | באים 935 | נאם 5002 | אדני 136 | יהוה 3069 |
|---|---|---|---|---|---|---|---|---|---|---|
| ka'aebel | yachiyd, | ua'achariytah | kayoum | mar. | hineh | yamiym | ba'aym, | na'am | 'adonay | Yahuah, |
| **as the mourning of** | **an only *son*** | **and the end thereof** | **as a day** | **bitter** | **Behold** | **the days** | **come** | **saith** | **Adonai** | **Yahuah** |

| והשלחתי 7971 | רעב 7458 | בארץ 776 | לא 3808 | רעב 7458 | ללחם 3899 | ולא 3808 | צמא 6772 | למים 4325 | כי 3588 | אם 518 | לשמע 8085 | את 853 |
|---|---|---|---|---|---|---|---|---|---|---|---|---|
| uahishlachtiy | ra'ab | ba'aretz; | la' | ra'ab | lalechem | uala' | tzama' | lamayim, | kiy | 'am | lishmoa', | 'at |
| **that I will send** | **a famine** | **in the land** | **not** | **a famine** | **of bread** | **nor** | **a thirst** | **for water** | **but** | **of** | **hearing** | |

| דברי 1697 | יהוה 3068: | 8:12 ונעו 5128 | מים 3220 | עד 5704 | ים 3220 | ומצפון 6828 | ועד 5704 | מזרח 4217 |
|---|---|---|---|---|---|---|---|---|
| dibrey | Yahuah. | uana'au | miyam | 'ad | yam, | uamitzapoun | ua'ad | mizrach; |
| **the words of** | **Yahuah** | **And they shall wander** | **from sea** | **to** | **sea** | **and from the north** | **even to** | **the east** |

Amos 8:5 Saying, When will the new moon be gone, that we may sell corn? and the Sabbath, that we may set forth wheat, making the ephah small, and the shekel great, and falsifying the balances by deceit?6 That we may buy the poor for silver, and the needy for a pair of shoes; yea, and sell the refuse of the wheat?7 YHUH has sworn by the excellency of Jacob, Surely I will never forget any of their works.8 Shall not the land tremble for this, and everyone mourn that dwell therein? and it shall rise up wholly as a flood; and it shall be cast out and drowned, as by the flood of Egypt.9 And it shall come to pass in that day, saith YHUH G-D, that I will cause the sun to go down at noon, and I will darken the earth in the clear day:10 And I will turn your feasts into mourning, and all your songs into lamentation; and I will bring up sackcloth upon all loins, and baldness upon every head; and I will make it as the mourning of an only son, and the end thereof as a bitter day.11 Behold, the days come, saith YHUH G-D, that I will send a famine in the land, not a famine of bread, nor a thirst for water, but of hearing the words of YHUH:12 And they shall wander from sea to sea, and from the north even to the east, they shall run to and fro to seek the word of YHUH, and shall not find it.

8:13

ישוטטו 7751 לבקש 1245 את 853 דבר 1697 יהוה 3068 ולא 3808 ימצאו 4672: ביום 3117 ההוא 1931 תתעלפנה 5968 הבתולת 1330
yashoutatu labaqesh 'at dabar Yahuah uala' yimtza'au. bayoum hahua' tit'alapnah habatulot
**they shall run to and fro to seek the word of Yahuah and not shall find *it* In day that shall faint virgins**

8:14

היפות 3303 והבחורים 970 בצמא 6772: הנשבעים 7650 באשמת 819 שמרון 8111 ואמרו 559 חי 2416 אלהיך 430 דן 1835 וחי 2416
hayapout uahabachuriym batzama'. hanishba'aym ba'ashmat shomaroun, ua'amaru, chey 'aloheyka dan, uachey
**the fair and young men for thirst They that swear by the sin of Samaria and say live Your god O Dan and live**

דרך 1870 באר 884 שבע 7651 ונפלו 5307 ולא 3808 יקומו 6965 עוד 5750:
derek ba'aer sheba'; uanapalu uala' yaqumu 'aud.
**The manner of Beer sheba even they shall fall and never rise up again**

Amos 9:1

ראיתי 7200 את 853 אדני 136 נצב 5324 על 5921 המזבח 4196 ויאמר 559 הך 5221 הכפתור 3730 וירעשו 7493
ra'aytiy 'at 'adonay nitzab 'al hamizbeach, uaya'mer hak hakapatour uayir'ashu
**I saw Adonai standing upon the altar and he said Smite the lintel of the door that may shake**

הספים 5592 ובצעם 1214 בראש 7218 כלם 3605 ואחריתם 319 בחרב 2719 אהרג 2026 לא 3808 ינוס 5127
hasipiym, uabtza'am bara'sh kulam, ua'achariytam bachereb 'aharog; la' yanus
**the posts and cut them in the head all of them and the last of them with the sword I will slay not he that flee shall**

9:2

להם 3807a נס 5127 ולא 3808 ימלט 4422 להם 3807a פליט 6412: אם 518 יחתרו 2864 בשאול 7585 משם 8033 ידי 3027
lahem nas, uala' yimalet lahem paliyt. 'am yachtaru bisha'aul, misham yadiy
**of them flee away not shall be delivered of them he that escape Though they dig into heli (*grave*) there mine hand**

9:3

תקחם 3947 ואם 518 יעלו 5927 השמים 8064 משם 8033 אורידם 3381: ואם 518
tiqachem; ua'am ya'alu hashamayim, misham 'auriydem. ua'am
**shall take them and though they climb up *to* heaven there will I bring them down And though**

יחבאו 2244 בראש 7218 הכרמל 3760 משם 8033 אחפש 2664 ולקחתים 3947 ואם 518 יסתרו 5641 מנגד 5048
yechaba'au bara'sh hakarmel, misham 'achapes ualqachtiym; ua'am yisataru mineged
**they hide themselves in the top of Carmel there I will search and take them out and though they be hid from**

9:4

עיני 5869 בקרקע 7172 הים 3220 משם 8033 אצוה 6680 את 853 הנחש 5175 ונשכם 5391: ואם 518 ילכו 1980
'aeynay baqarqa' hayam, misham 'atzaueh 'at hanachash uanshakam. ua'am yelaku
**my sight in the bottom of the sea there will I command the serpent and he shall bite them And though they go**

בשבי 7628 לפני 6440 איביהם 341 משם 8033 אצוה 6680 את 853 החרב 2719 והרגתם 2026 ושמתי 7760 עיני 5869
bashabiy lipney 'ayabeyhem, misham 'atzaueh 'at hachereb uaharagatam; uasamtiy 'aeyniy
**into captivity before their enemies there will I command the sword and it shall slay them and I will set mine eyes**

9:5

עליהם 5921 לרעה 7451 ולא 3808 לטובה 2896: ואדני 136 יהוה 3069 הצבאות 6635 הנוגע 5060 בארץ 776 ותמוג 4127
'aleyhem lara'ah uala' latoubah. ua'adonay Yahuah hatzaba'aut, hanougea' ba'aretz uatamoug,
**upon them for evil and not for good And Adonai Yahuah of hosts *is* he that touch the land and it shall melt**

ואבלו 56 כל 3605 יושבי 3427 בה 871a ועלתה 5927 כיאר 2975 כלה 3605 ושקעה 8257 כיאר 2975
ua'abalu kal youshabey bah; ua'alatah kaya'ar kulah, uashaqa'ah kiy'ar
**and shall mourn all that dwell therein and it shall rise up like a flood wholly and shall be drowned as *by* the flood of**

Amos 8:13 In that day shall the fair virgins and young men faint for thirst.14 They that swear by the sin of Samaria, and say, Thy god, O Dan, live; and, The manner of Beer-sheba live; even they shall fall, and never rise up again.**Amos** 9:1 I saw YHUH standing upon the altar: and he said, Smite the lintel of the door, that the posts may shake: and cut them in the head, all of them; and I will slay the last of them with the sword: he that fleeth of them shall not flee away, and he that escapeth of them shall not be delivered.2 Though they dig into hell, thence shall mine hand take them; though they climb up to heaven, thence will I bring them down:3 And though they hide themselves in the top of Carmel, I will search and take them out thence; and though they be hid from my sight in the bottom of the sea, thence will I command the serpent, and he shall bite them:4 And though they go into captivity before their enemies, thence will I command the sword, and it shall slay them: and I will set mine eyes upon them for evil, and not for good.5 And YHUH G-D of hosts is he that touch the land, and it shall melt, and all that dwell therein shall mourn: and it shall rise up wholly like a flood; and shall be drowned, as by the flood of Egypt.

9:6
מצרים 4714: הבונה 1129 בשמים 8064 מעלותו 4609 ואגדתו 92 על 5921 ארץ 776 יסדה 3245 הקרא 7121
mitzrayim. habouneh bashamayim ma'aloutau ua'agudatou 'al 'aretz yasadah; haqourea'
**Egypt *It is* he that builds in the heaven his stories and his troop in the earth has founded he that call**

9:7
למי 4325 הים 3220 וישפכם 8210 על 5921 פני 6440 הארץ 776 יהוה 3068 שמו 8034: הלוא 3808 כבני 1121
lamey hayam, uayishpakem 'al paney ha'aretz Yahuah shamou. halou'a kibney
**for the waters of the sea and pour them out upon the face of the earth Yahuah *is* his name *Are* not as children of**

כשיים 3569 אתם 859 לי 3807a בני 1121 ישראל 3478 נאם 5002 יהוה 3068 הלוא 3808 את 853 ישראל 3478 העליתי 5927
kushiyiym 'atem liy baney yisra'ael na'am Yahuah; halou'a 'at yisra'ael, he'aleytiy
**the Ethiopians you unto me O children of Israel? said Yahuah not Israel Have I brought up**

9:8
מארץ 776 מצרים 4714 ופלשתיים 6430 מכפתור 3731 וארם 758 מקיר 7024: הנה 2009 עיני 5869 אדני 136
me'aretz mitzrayim, uapalishtiyiym mikaptour ua'aram miqiyr. hineh 'aeyney 'adonay
**out of the land of Egypt? and the Philistines from Caphtor and the Syrians from Kir? Behold the eyes of Adonai**

יהוה 3069 בממלכה 4467 החטאה 2403 והשמדתי 8045 אתה 859 מעל 5921 פני 6440 האדמה 127 אפס 657 כי 3588 לא 3808
Yahuah bamamlakah hachata'ah, uahishmadtiy 'atah, me'al paney ha'adamah; 'apes, kiy la'
**Yahuah are upon the kingdom sinful and I will destroy it from off the face of the earth saving that not**

9:9
השמיד 8045 אשמיד 8045 את 853 בית 1004 יעקב 3290 נאם 5002 יהוה 3068: כי 3588 הנה 2009 אנכי 595 מצוה 6680 והנעותי 5128
hashameyd 'ashmiyd 'at beyt ya'aqob na'am Yahuah. kiy hineh 'anokiy matzaueh, uahani'autiy
**I will utterly destroy the house of Jacob saith Yahuah For lo I will command and I will sift**

בכל 3605 הגוים 1471 את 853 בית 1004 ישראל 3478 כאשר 834 ינוע 5128 בכברה 3531 ולא 3808 יפול 5307 צרור 6872
bakal hagouyim 'at beyt yisra'ael; ka'asher yinoua' bakabarah, uala' yipoul tzarour
**among all nations the house of Israel like as *corn* is sifted in a sieve yet not shall fall the least grain**

9:10
ארץ 776: בחרב 2719 ימותו 4191 כל 3605 חטאי 2400 עמי 5971 האמרים 559 לא 3808 תגיש 5066 ותקדים 6923 בעדינו 1157
'aretz. bachereb yamutu, kol chata'aey 'amiy; ha'amariym, la' tagiysh uataqdiym ba'adeynu
**the earth by the sword shall die All the sinners of my people which say not shall overtake nor prevent against us**

9:11
הרעה 7451: ביום 3117 ההוא 1931 אקים 6965 את 853 סכת 5521 דויד 1732 הנפלת 5307 וגדרתי 1443 את 853
hara'ah. bayoum hahua', 'aqiym 'at sukat dauiyd hanopelet; uagadartiy 'at
**The evil In day that will I raise up the tabernacle of David that is fallen and close up**

9:12
פרציהן 6556 והרסתיו 2034 אקים 6965 ובניתיה 1129 כימי 3117 עולם 5769: למען 4616 יירשו 3423
pirtzeyhen, uaharisotayu 'aqiym, uabniytiyha kiymey 'aulam. lama'an yiyrashu
**the breaches thereof and his ruins I will raise up and I will build it as in the days of old That they may possess**

את 853 שארית 7611 אדום 123 וכל 3605 הגוים 1471 אשר 834 נקרא 7121 שמי 8034 עליהם 5921 נאם 5002 יהוה 3068 עשה 6213 זאת 2063:
'at sha'aeriyt 'adoum uakal hagouyim, 'asher niqra' shamiy 'aleyhem; na'am Yahuah 'asheh za't.
**the remnant of Edom and of all the heathen which are called my name by saith Yahuah that does this**

9:13
הנה 2009 ימים 3117 באים 935 נאם 5002 יהוה 3068 ונגש 5066 חורש 2790 בקצר 7114 ודרך 1869 ענבים 6025
hineh yamiym ba'aym na'am Yahuah, uanigash chouresh baqotzer, uadorek 'anabiym
**Behold the days come saith Yahuah that shall overtake the plowman the reaper and the treader of grapes**

Amos 9:6 It is he that buildeth his stories in the heaven, and has founded his troop in the earth; he that call for the waters of the sea, and poureth them out upon the face of the earth: YHUH is his name.7 Are you not as children of the Ethiopians unto me, O children of Israel? saith YHUH. Have not I brought up Israel out of the land of Egypt?7 and the Philistines from Caphtor, and the Syrians from Kir?8 Behold, the eyes of YHUH G-D are upon the sinful kingdom, and I will destroy it from off the face of the earth; saving that I will not utterly destroy the house of Jacob, saith YHUH.9 For, lo, I will command, and I will sift the house of Israel among all nations, like as corn is sifted in a sieve, yet shall not the least grain fall upon the earth.10 All the sinners of my people shall die by the sword, which say, The evil shall not overtake nor prevent us.11 In that day will I raise up the tabernacle of David that is fallen, and close up the breaches thereof; and I will raise up his ruins, and I will build it as in the days of old:12 That they may possess the remnant of Edom, and of all the heathen, which are called by my name, saith YHUH that doeth this.13 Behold, the days come, saith YHUH, that the plowman shall overtake the reaper, and the treader of grapes him that soweth seed; and the mountains shall drop sweet wine, and all the hills shall melt.

9:14

במשך 4900 הזרע 2233 והטיפו 5197 ההרים 2022 עסיס 6071 וכל 3605 הגבעות 1389 תתמוגגנה 4127: ושבתי 7725

bamoshek hazara'; uahitiypu hehariym 'asiys, uakal hagaba'aut titmougagnah. uashabtiy

**him that sow seed and shall drop the mountains sweet wine and all the hills shall melt And I will bring again**

את 853 שבות 7622 עמי 5971 ישראל 3478 ובנו 1129 ערים 5892 נשמות 8074 וישבו 3427 ונטעו 5193

'at shabut 'amiy yisra'ael uabanu 'ariym nashamout uayashabu, uanata'au

**the captivity of my people of Israel and they shall build cities *the* waste and inhabit *them* and they shall plant**

9:15

כרמים 3754 ושתו 8354 את 853 יינם 3196 ועשו 6213 גנות 1593 ואכלו 398 את 853 פריהם 6529:

karamiym, uashatu 'at yeynam; ua'asu ganout, ua'akalu 'at pariyhem.

**vineyards and drink the wine thereof they shall also make gardens and eat the fruit of them**

ונטעתים 5193 על 5921 אדמתם 127 ולא 3808 ינתשו 5428 עוד 5750 מעל 5921 אדמתם 127 אשר 834 נתתי 5414 להם 1992

uanta'atiym 'al 'admatam; uala' yinatashu 'aud, me'al 'admatam 'asher natatiy lahem,

**And I will plant them upon their land and no they shall be pulled up more out of their land which I have given them**

אמר 559 יהוה 3069 אלהיך 430:

'amar Yahuah 'aloheyka.

**saith Yahuah your god**

Amos 9:14 And I will bring again the captivity of my people of Israel, and they shall build the waste cities, and inhabit them; and they shall plant vineyards, and drink the wine thereof; they shall also make gardens, and eat the fruit of them.15 And I will plant them upon their land, and they shall no more be pulled up out of their land which I have given them, saith YHUH your G-d.

# OBADIAH
## (*Abadyah*)

Verse one identifies the author as the Prophet Obadiah and is the shortest book in the Tanakh with only 21 verses. The name Obadiah in Hebrew means *Servant of Yah.* From the historical references in the book, we can locate Obadiah's ministry in Judah during the reign of Jehoram (848-841 B.C.), son of Jehoshaphat. The Book of Obadiah pronounces judgment on Edom for all of their treacheries. Malachi 1:2-5 clearly indicates the same. Obadiah is a prophet called by Elohim to condemn Edom for sins against both Elohim and Israel. The Edomites are descendants of Esau and the Israelites are descendants of his twin brother, Jacob. A quarrel between the brothers has affected their descendants for over 1,000 years up to the time of the writing of this prophecy and still continues to this day. Edom (*Esau*) is indicted because of his violence against his brother Jacob. Both 2 Kings and 2 Chronicles inform of the war and rebellion of Edom in the days of Jehoram when Edom, after a fierce struggle, threw off the yoke of Judah (2 Kings 8:20-22 and 2 Chron 21:8-10) as prophesied by Isaac to Esau (Gen 27:38-40). After the revolt of Edom, according to 2 Chron 21:16, the Philistines and Arabians attacked Judah and carried off all the goods found in the king's palace, together with his sons and wives. Instead of helping Judah, Edom joined in and helped loot Jerusalem. This best fits the statements in Obadiah, verses 11-14. When the Philistines, Arabians, and Edomites entered Jerusalem, they cast lots to decide which portions of the city would be granted to each contingent for the purpose of plunder. The Edomites went through periods of submission and freedom. But when the Babylonians fought against and defeated the nation of Israel, the Edomites were able to rejoice over the victory for they had allied themselves with the Babylonians and could celebrate the victory. Thus, Edom finally broke the yoke from their neck. The capital of the Edomites was Petra and it was a magnificent city but today it is nothing but ruins.

**Obadiah 1:1**
2377 חזון 5662 עבדיה 3541 כה 559 אמר 136 אדני 3068 יהוה 123 לאדום 8052 שמועה 8085 שמענו 853 מאת
chazoun 'abadyah; koh 'amar 'adonay Yahuah le'adoum, shamu'ah shama'anu me'at
**The vision of Obadiah Thus saith Adonai Yahuah concerning Edom a rumour We have heard from**

3069 יהוה 6735 וציר 1471 בגוים 7971 שלח 6965 קומו 6965 ונקומה 5921 עליה 4421 למלחמה: **1:2** 2009 הנה
Yahuah uatziyr bagouyim shulach, qumu uanaqumah 'aleyha lamilchamah. hineh
**Yahuah and an ambassador among the heathen is sent Arise you and let us rise up against her in battle Behold**

6996 קטן 5414 נתתיך 1471 בגוים 959 בזוי 859 אתה 3966 מאד: **1:3** 2087 זדון 3820 לבך 5377 השיאך
qaton natatiyka bagouyim; bazuy 'atah ma'ad. zadoun libaka hishiy'aka,
**small I have made you among the heathen are despised you greatly The pride of your heart has deceived you**

7931 שכני 2288 בחגוי 5553 סלע 4791 מרום 3427 שבתו 559 אמר 3820 בלבו 4310 מי 3381 יורדני
shokaniy bachaguey sela' meroum shibtou; 'amer balibou, miy' yourideniy
***you* that dwell in the clefts of the rock *is* high whose habitation that saith in his heart Who shall bring me down *to the***

776 ארץ: **1:4** 518 אם 1361 תגביה 5404 כנשר 518 ואם 996 בין 3556 כוכבים 7760 שים 7064 קנך 8033 משם
'aretz. 'am tagbiyah kanesher, ua'am beyn koukabiym siym qineka; misham
**ground? Though you exalt *yourself* as the eagle and though among the stars you set your nest there**

3381 אורידך 5002 נאם 3068 יהוה: **1:5** 518 אם 1590 גנבים 935 באו 3807a לך 518 אם 7703 שודדי 3915 לילה 349 איך 1820 נדמיתה
'auriydaka na'am Yahuah. 'am ganabiym ba'au laka 'am shoudadey layalah, 'aeyk nidmeytah,
**will I bring you down saith Yahuah If thieves came to you if robbers by night how are you cut off**

3808 הלוא 1589 יגנבו 1767 דים 518 אם 1219 בצרים 935 באו 3807a לך 3808 הלוא 7604 ישאירו
halou'a yignabu dayam; 'am botzriym ba'au lak, halou'a yash'ayru
**not would they have stolen till they had enough? if the grapegatherers came to you not would they leave *some***

5955 עללות: **1:6** 349 איך 2664 נחפשו 6215 עשו 1158 נבעו 4710 מצפניו: **1:7** 5704 עד 1366 הגבול
'alalout. 'aeyk nechpasu 'aesau, nib'au matzpunayu. 'ad hagabul
**grapes? How are searched out *the things* of Esau *how* are sought up his hidden *things* to the border *even***

**Obadiah** 1:1 The vision of Obadiah. Thus saith YHUH G-D concerning Edom; We have heard a rumour from YHUH, and an ambassador is sent among the heathen, Arise you, and let us rise up against her in battle.2 Behold, I have made you small among the heathen: you are greatly despised.3 The pride of your heart has deceived you, you that dwellest in the clefts of the rock, whose habitation is high; that saith in his heart, Who shall bring me down to the ground?4 Though you exalt thyself as the eagle, and though you set your nest among the stars, thence will I bring you down, saith YHUH.5 If thieves came to you, if robbers by night, (how are you cut off!) would they not have stolen till they had enough? if the grapegatherers came to you, would they not leave some grapes?6 How are the things of Esau searched out! how are his hidden things sought up!

| שלחוך 7971 | כל 3605 | אנשי 582 | בריתך 1285 | השיאוך 5377 | יכלו 3201 | לך 3807a | אנשי 582 |
|---|---|---|---|---|---|---|---|
| shilchuka, | kal | 'anshey | bariyteka, | hishiy'auka | yukalu | laka | 'anshey |
| **have brought you** | **All** | **the men** | **of your confederacy** | **have deceived you** | ***and* prevailed** | **against you** | **the men** |

| שלמך 7965 | לחמך 3899 | ישימו 7760 | מזור 4204 | תחתיך 8478 | אין 369 | תבונה 8394 |
|---|---|---|---|---|---|---|
| shalomeka; | lachmaka, | yasiymu | mazour | tachteyka, | 'aeyn | tabunah |
| **that were at peace with you** | ***they that eat* your bread** | **have laid** | **a wound** | **under you *there is*** | **none else** | **understanding** |

| בו 871a: | 1:8 | הלוא 3808 | ביום 3117 | ההוא 1931 | נאם 5002 | יהוה 3068 | והאבדתי 6 | חכמים 2450 | מאדום 123 | ותבונה 8394 |
|---|---|---|---|---|---|---|---|---|---|---|
| bou. | | halou'a | bayoum | hahua' | na'am | Yahuah; | uaha'abadatiy | chakamiym | me'adoum, | uatbunah |
| **in him** | | **not** | **in day** | **that** | **saith** | **Yahuah** | **Shall I even destroy** | **the wise *men*** | **out of Edom** | **and understanding** |

| מהר 2022 | עשו 6215: | 1:9 | וחתו 2865 | גבוריך 1368 | תימן 8487 | למען 4616 | יכרת 3772 | איש 376 |
|---|---|---|---|---|---|---|---|---|
| mehar | 'aesau. | | uachatu | giboureyka | teyman; | lama'an | yikaret | 'aysh |
| **out of the mount of** | **Esau?** | | **And shall be dismayed** | **your mighty *men*** | **O Teman** | **to the end that** | **may be cut off** | **every one** |

| מהר 2022 | עשו 6215 | מקטל 6993: | 1:10 | מחמס 2555 | אחיך 251 | יעקב 3290 | תכסך 3680 | בושה 955 |
|---|---|---|---|---|---|---|---|---|
| mehar | 'aesau | miqatel. | | mechamas | 'achiyka | ya'aqob | takaska | bushah; |
| **of the mount of** | **Esau** | **by slaughter** | | **For *your* violence** | ***against* your brother** | **Jacob** | **shall cover you** | **shame** |

| ונכרת 3772 | לעולם 5769: | 1:11 | ביום 3117 | עמדך 5975 | מנגד 5048 | ביום 3117 | שבות 7617 |
|---|---|---|---|---|---|---|---|
| uanikrata | la'aulam. | | bayoum | 'amadaka | mineged, | bayoum | shabout |
| **and you shall be cut off** | **for ever** | | **In the day** | ***that* you stoodest** | **on the other side** | **in the day** | **carried away captive** |

| זרים 2114 | חילו 2428 | ונכרים 5237 | באו 935 | שערו 8179 | ועל 5921 | ירושלם 3389 | ידו 3032 | גורל 1486 | גם 1571 | אתה 859 |
|---|---|---|---|---|---|---|---|---|---|---|
| zariym | cheylou; | uanakariym | ba'au | sa'arou | ua'al | yarushalaim | yadu | goural, | gam | 'atah |
| ***that* the strangers** | **his forces** | **and foreigners** | **entered into** | **his gates** | **and upon** | **Jerusalem** | **cast** | **lots** | **even** | **you** |

| כאחד 259 | מהם 1992: | 1:12 | ואל 408 | תרא 7200 | ביום 3117 | אחיך 251 | ביום 3117 | נכרו 5235 |
|---|---|---|---|---|---|---|---|---|
| ka'achad | mehem. | | ua'al | tera' | bayoum | 'achiyka | bayoum | nakarou, |
| ***were* as one** | **of them** | | **But not** | **you should have looked** | **on the day of** | **your brother** | **in the day** | **that he became a stranger** |

| ואל 408 | תשמח 8055 | לבני 1121 | יהודה 3063 | ביום 3117 | אבדם 6 | ואל 408 | תגדל 1431 |
|---|---|---|---|---|---|---|---|
| ua'al | tismach | libney | yahudah | bayoum | 'abadam; | ua'al | tagdel |
| **neither** | **should you have rejoiced** | **over the children of** | **Judah** | **in the day of** | **their destruction** | **neither** | **proudly** |

| פיך 6310 | ביום 3117 | צרה 6869: | 1:13 | אל 408 | תבוא 935 | בשער 8179 | עמי 5971 | ביום 3117 |
|---|---|---|---|---|---|---|---|---|
| piyka | bayoum | tzarah. | | 'al | tabou'a | basha'ar | 'amiy | bayoum |
| **should you have spoken** | **in the day of** | **distress** | | **not** | **You should have entered** | **into the gate** | **of my people** | **in the day of** |

| אידם 343 | אל 408 | תרא 7200 | גם 1571 | אתה 859 | ברעתו 7451 | ביום 3117 | אידו 343 | ואל 408 | תשלחנה 7971 |
|---|---|---|---|---|---|---|---|---|---|
| 'aeydam, | 'al | tera' | gam | 'atah | bara'atou | bayoum | 'aeydou; | ua'al | tishlachnah |
| **their calamity** | **not** | **you should have looked** | **yea** | **you** | **on their affliction** | **in the day of** | **their calamity** | **nor** | **have laid** |

| בחילו 2428 | ביום 3117 | אידו 343: | 1:14 | ואל 408 | תעמד 5975 | על 5921 | הפרק 6563 | להכרית 3772 |
|---|---|---|---|---|---|---|---|---|
| bacheylou | bayoum | 'aeydou. | | ua'al | ta'amod | 'al | hapereq, | lahakriyt |
| ***hand* on their substance** | **in the day of** | **their calamity** | | **Neither** | **should you have stood in** | | **the crossway** | **to cut off** |

Obad 1:7 All the men of your confederacy have brought you even to the border: the men that were at peace with you have deceived you, and prevailed against you; they that eat your bread have laid a wound under you: there is none understanding in him.8 Shall I not in that day, saith YHUH, even destroy the wise men out of Edom, and understanding out of the mount of Esau?9 And your mighty men, O Teman, shall be dismayed, to the end that everyone of the mount of Esau may be cut off by slaughter.10 For your violence against your brother Jacob shame shall cover you, and you shall be cut off forever.11 In the day that you stoodest on the other side, in the day that the strangers carried away captive his forces, and foreigners entered into his gates, and cast lots upon Jerusalem, even you were as one of them.12 But you should not have looked on the day of your brother in the day that he became a stranger; neither should you have rejoiced over the children of Judah in the day of their destruction; neither should you have spoken proudly in the day of distress.13 Thou should not have entered into the gate of my people in the day of their calamity; yea, you should not have looked on their affliction in the day of their calamity, nor have laid hands on their substance in the day of their calamity;14 Neither should you have stood in the crossway, to cut off those of his that did escape;

| את 853 | פליטיו 6412 | ואל 408 | תסגר 5462 | שרידיו 8300 | ביום 3117 |
|---|---|---|---|---|---|
| 'at | paliytayu; | ua'al | tasger | sariydayu | bayoum |
| | **those of his that did escape** | **neither** | **should you have delivered up** | **those of his that did remain** | **in the day of** |

| צרה 6869: | 1:15 | כי 3588 | קרוב 7138 | יום 3117 | יהוה 3068 | על 5921 | כל 3605 | הגוים 1471 | כאשר 834 | עשית 6213 | יעשה 6213 | לך 3807a |
|---|---|---|---|---|---|---|---|---|---|---|---|---|
| tzarah. | | kiy | qaroub | youm | Yahuah | 'al | kal | hagouyim; | ka'asher | 'ashiyta | ye'aseh | lak, |
| **distress** | | **For** | ***is* near** | **the day of** | **Yahuah** | **upon** | **all** | **the heathen** | **as** | **you have done** | **it shall be done** | **unto you** |

| גמלך 1576 | ישוב 7725 | בראשך 7218: | 1:16 | כי 3588 | כאשר 834 | שתיתם 8354 | על 5921 | הר 2022 | קדשי 6944 | ישתו 8354 |
|---|---|---|---|---|---|---|---|---|---|---|
| gamulka | yashub | bara'sheka. | | kiy, | ka'asher | shatiytem | 'al | har | qadashiy | yishtu |
| **your reward** | **shall return** | **upon your own head** | | **For** | **as** | **you have drunk** | **upon** | **my mountain** | **holy *so*** | **shall drink** |

| כל 3605 | הגוים 1471 | תמיד 8548 | ושתו 8354 | ולעו 3886 | והיו 1961 | כלוא 3808 |
|---|---|---|---|---|---|---|
| kal | hagouyim | tamiyd; | uashatu | uala'au, | uahayu | kalou'a |
| **all** | **the heathen** | **yea continually** | **and drink** | **and they shall swallow down** | **and they shall be** | **as though not** |

| היו 1961: | 1:17 | ובהר 2022 | ציון 6726 | תהיה 1961 | פליטה 6413 | והיה 1961 | קדש 6944 | וירשו 3423 | בית 1004 |
|---|---|---|---|---|---|---|---|---|---|
| hayu. | | uabhar | tziyoun | tihayeh | paleytah | uahayah | qodesh; | uayarashu | beyt |
| **they had been** | | **But upon mount** | **Zion** | **shall be** | **deliverance** | **and there shall be** | **holiness** | **and shall possess** | **the house of** |

| יעקב 3290 | את 853 | מורשיהם 4180: | 1:18 | והיה 1961 | בית 1004 | יעקב 3290 | אש 784 | ובית 1004 | יוסף 3130 | להבה 3852 |
|---|---|---|---|---|---|---|---|---|---|---|
| ya'aqob, | 'at | mourasheyhem | | uahayah | beyt | ya'aqob | 'aesh | uabeyt | yousep | lehabah, |
| **Jacob** | | **their possessions** | | **And shall be** | **the house of** | **Jacob** | **a fire** | **and the house of** | **Joseph** | **a flame** |

| ובית 1004 | עשו 6215 | לקש 7179 | ודלקו 1814 | בהם 871a | ואכלום 398 | ולא 3808 | יהיה 1961 |
|---|---|---|---|---|---|---|---|
| uabeyt | 'aesau | laqash, | uadalaqu | bahem | ua'akalum; | uala' | yihayeh |
| **and the house of** | **Esau** | **for stubble** | **and they shall kindle** | **in them** | **and devour them** | **and not** | **there shall be** |

| שריד 8300 | לבית 1004 | עשו 6215 | כי 3588 | יהוה 3068 | דבר 1696: | 1:19 | וירשו 3423 | הנגב 5045 | את 853 |
|---|---|---|---|---|---|---|---|---|---|
| sariyd | labeyt | 'aesau, | kiy | Yahuah | diber. | | uayarashu | hanegeb | 'at |
| ***any* remaining of** | **the house of** | **Esau** | **for** | **Yahuah** | **has spoken *it*** | | **And shall possess** | ***they of* the south** | |

| הר 2022 | עשו 6215 | והשפלה 8219 | את 853 | פלשתים 6430 | וירשו 3423 | את 853 | שדה 7704 | אפרים 669 | ואת 853 |
|---|---|---|---|---|---|---|---|---|---|
| har | 'aesau, | uahashapelah | 'at | palishtiym, | uayarashu | 'at | sadeh | 'aprayim, | ua'at |
| **the mount of** | **Esau** | **and *they of* the plain** | | **the Philistines** | **and they shall possess** | | **the fields of** | **Ephraim** | ***and*** |

| שדה 7704 | שמרון 8111 | ובנימן 1144 | את 853 | הגלעד 5168: | 1:20 | וגלת 1546 | החל 2426 | הזה 2088 | לבני 1121 |
|---|---|---|---|---|---|---|---|---|---|
| sadeh | shomaroun; | uabinyamin | 'at | hagil'ad. | | uagalut | hachel | hazeh | libney |
| **the fields of** | **Samaria** | **and Benjamin** | ***shall possess*** | **Gilead** | | **And the captivity of** | **host of** | **this** | **the children of** |

| ישראל 3478 | אשר 834 | כנענים 3669 | עד 5704 | צרפת 6886 | וגלת 1546 | ירושלם 3389 | אשר 834 | בספרד 5614 |
|---|---|---|---|---|---|---|---|---|
| yisra'ael | 'asher | kana'aniym | 'ad | tzarapat, | uagalut | yarushalaim | 'asher | bisaparad; |
| **Israel** | ***shall possess* that of** | **the Canaanites *even*** | **unto** | **Zarephath** | **and the captivity of** | **Jerusalem** | **which *is*** | **in Sepharad** |

| ירשו 3423 | את 853 | ערי 5892 | הנגב 5045: | 1:21 | ועלו 5927 | מושעים 3467 | בהר 2022 | ציון 6726 | לשפט 8199 | את 853 | הר 2022 |
|---|---|---|---|---|---|---|---|---|---|---|---|
| yirshu | 'at | 'arey | hanegeb. | | ua'alu | moushi'aym | bahar | tziyoun, | lishpat | 'at | har |
| **shall possess** | | **the cities of** | **the south** | | **And shall come up** | **saviours** | **on mount** | **Zion** | **to judge** | | **the mount of** |

Obad 1:14 neither should you have delivered up those of his that did remain in the day of distress.15 For the day of YHUH is near upon all the heathen: as you have done, it shall be done unto you: your reward shall return upon your own head.16 For as you have drunk upon my holy mountain, so shall all the heathen drink continually, yea, they shall drink, and they shall swallow down, and they shall be as though they had not been.17 But upon mount Zion shall be deliverance, and there shall be holiness; and the house of Jacob shall possess their possessions.18 And the house of Jacob shall be a fire, and the house of Joseph a flame, and the house of Esau for stubble, and they shall kindle in them, and devour them; and there shall not be any remaining of the house of Esau; for YHUH has spoken it.19 And they of the south shall possess the mount of Esau; and they of the plain the Philistines: and they shall possess the fields of Ephraim, and the fields of Samaria: and Benjamin shall possess Gilead.20 And the captivity of this host of the children of Israel shall possess that of the Canaanites, even unto Zarephath; and the captivity of Jerusalem, which is in Sepharad, shall possess the cities of the south.21 And saviours shall come up on mount Zion to judge the mount of Esau;

| | | | |
|---|---|---|---|
| 𐤏𐤔𐤅 | 𐤅𐤄𐤉𐤕𐤄 | 𐤋𐤉𐤄𐤅𐤄 | 𐤄𐤌𐤋𐤅𐤊𐤄 |
| עשו 6215 | והיתה 1961 | ליהוה 3068 | המלוכה 4410: |
| 'aesau; | uahayatah | laYahuah | hamalukah. |
| **Esau** | **and shall be** | **Yahuah's** | **the kingdom** |

Obad 1:21 and the kingdom shall be YHUH's.

# JONAH
## (*Younah*)

Verse one specifically identifies Jonah as the author. The book was written approximately between 793 and 758 B.C. The name of Jonah in Hebrew means *dove*. Jonah's disobedience and the repentance and revival of Nineveh are the key themes of the book. Jonah's refusal to obey the call of Elohim causes his own death by being swallowed by a great fish which is then followed by Elohim's mercy as he repents and is delivered to then be obedient. It is said that the revival which Jonah brings to Nineveh could have been the greatest evangelistic efforts of all time and shows insight as to how Elohim desires both repentance and salvation to everyone.

| **Jonah 1:1** ויהי 1961 | דבר 1697 | יהוה 3068 | אל 413 | יונה 3124 | בן 1121 | אמתי 573 | לאמר 559: | **1:2** קום 6965 | לך 1980 | אל 413 | נינוה 5210 |
|---|---|---|---|---|---|---|---|---|---|---|---|
| uayahiy | dabar | Yahuah, | 'al | younah | ben | 'amitay | lea'mor. | qum | lek | 'al | nynabuh |
| **Now came** | **the word of** | **Yahuah** | **unto** | **Jonah** | **the son of** | **Amittai** | **saying** | **Arise** | **go you** | **to** | **Nineveh** |

| העיר 5892 | הגדולה 1419 | וקרא 7121 | עליה 5921 | כי 3588 | עלתה 5927 | רעתם 7451 | לפני 6440: | **1:3** ויקם 6965 | יונה 3124 | לברח 1272 |
|---|---|---|---|---|---|---|---|---|---|---|
| ha'ayr | hagadoulah | uaqra' | 'aeleyha; | kiy | 'alatah | ra'atam | lapanay. | uayaqam | younah | libroach |
| **that city** | **great** | **and cry** | **against it** | **for** | **is come up** | **their wickedness** | **before me** | **But rose up** | **Jonah** | **to flee** |

| תרשישה 8659 | מלפני 6440 | יהוה 3068 | וירד 3381 | יפו 3305 | וימצא 4672 | אניה 591 | באה 935 | תרשיש 8659 | ויתן 5414 |
|---|---|---|---|---|---|---|---|---|---|
| tarshiyshah, | milipney | Yahuah; | uayered | yapou | uayimtza' | 'aniyah | ba'ah | tarshiysh, | uayiten |
| **unto Tarshish** | **from the presence of** | **Yahuah** | **and went down to** | **Joppa** | **and he found** | **a ship** | **going** | ***to* Tarshish** | **so he paid** |

| שכרה 7939 | וירד 3381 | בה 871a | לבוא 935 | עמהם 5973 | תרשישה 8659 | מלפני 6440 | יהוה 3068: | **1:4** ויהוה 3068 |
|---|---|---|---|---|---|---|---|---|
| sakarah | uayered | bah | labou'a | 'amahem | tarshiyshah, | milipney | Yahuah. | uaYahuah |
| **the fare thereof** | **and went down** | **into it** | **to go** | **with them** | **unto Tarshish** | **from the presence of** | **Yahuah** | **But Yahuah** |

| הטיל 2904 | רוח 7307 | גדולה 1419 | אל 413 | הים 3220 | ויהי 1961 | סער 5591 | גדול 1419 | בים 3220 | והאניה 591 | חשבה 2803 | להשבר 7665: | **1:5** |
|---|---|---|---|---|---|---|---|---|---|---|---|---|
| hetiyl | ruach | gadoulah | 'al | hayam, | uayahiy | sa'ar | gadoul | bayam; | uaha'aniyah, | chishbah | lahishaber. | |
| **sent out** | **a wind** | **great** | **into** | **the sea** | **and there was** | **a tempest** | **mighty** | **in the sea** | **so that the ship** | ***was* like** | **to be broken** | |

| ויראו 3372 | המלחים 4419 | ויזעקו 2199 | איש 376 | אל 413 | אלהיו 430 | ויטלו 2904 | את 853 | הכלים 3627 | אשר 834 | באניה 591 |
|---|---|---|---|---|---|---|---|---|---|---|
| uayiyra'au | hamalachiym, | uayiz'aqu | 'aysh | 'al | 'alohayu | uayatilu | 'at | hakeliym | 'asher | ba'aniyah |
| **Then were afraid** | **the mariners** | **and cried** | **every man** | **unto** | **his god** | **and cast forth** | | **the wares** | **that** | ***were* in the ship** |

| אל 413 | הים 3220 | להקל 7043 | מעליהם 5921 | ויונה 3124 | ירד 3381 | אל 413 | ירכתי 3411 | הספינה 5600 | וישכב 7901 |
|---|---|---|---|---|---|---|---|---|---|
| 'al | hayam, | lahaqel | me'aleyhem; | uayounah, | yarad | 'al | yarkatey | hasapiynah, | uayishkab |
| **into** | **the sea** | **to lighten *it*** | **of them** | **But Jonah** | **was gone down** | **into** | **the sides of** | **the ship** | **and he lay** |

| וירדם 7290: | **1:6** ויקרב 7126 | אליו 413 | רב 7227 | החבל 2259 | ויאמר 559 | לו 3807a | מה 4100 | לך 3807a | נרדם 7290 | קום 6965 |
|---|---|---|---|---|---|---|---|---|---|---|
| uayeradam. | uayiqrab | 'aelayu | rab | hachobel, | uaya'mer | lou' | mah | laka | nirdam; | qum |
| **and was fast asleep** | **So came** | **to him** | **master** | **the ship** | **and said** | **unto him** | **What** | ***meanest* to you** | **O sleeper?** | **arise** |

| קרא 7121 | אל 413 | אלהיך 430 | אולי 194 | יתעשת 6245 | האלהים 430 | לנו 3807a | ולא 3808 | נאבד 6: | **1:7** ויאמרו 559 | איש 376 |
|---|---|---|---|---|---|---|---|---|---|---|
| qara' | 'al | 'aloheyka, | 'aulay | yit'ashet | ha'alohiym | lanu | uala' | na'bed. | uaya'maru | 'aysh |
| **call** | **upon** | **your Elohim** | **if so be that** | **will think upon** | **Elohim** | **us** | **not** | ***that* we perish** | **And they said** | **every one** |

| אל 413 | רעהו 7453 | לכו 1980 | ונפילה 5307 | גורלות 1486 | ונדעה 3045 | בשלמי 7945 | הרעה 7451 | הזאת 2063 | לנו 3807a | ויפלו 5307 |
|---|---|---|---|---|---|---|---|---|---|---|
| 'al | re'aehu, | laku | uanapiylah | gouralout, | uaned'ah, | bashelmiy | hara'ah | haza't | lanu; | uayapilu |
| **to** | **his fellow** | **Come** | **and let us cast lots** | | **that we may know** | **for whose cause** | **evil** | **this *is*** | **upon us** | **So they cast** |

**Jonah** 1:1 Now the word of YHUH came unto Jonah the son of Amittai, saying,2 Arise, go to Nineveh, that great city, and cry against it; for their wickedness is come up before me.3 But Jonah rose up to flee unto Tarshish from the presence of YHUH, and went down to Joppa; and he found a ship going to Tarshish: so he paid the fare thereof, and went down into it, to go with them unto Tarshish from the presence of YHUH.4 But YHUH sent out a great wind into the sea, and there was a mighty tempest in the sea, so that the ship was like to be broken.5 Then the mariners were afraid, and cried every man unto his god, and cast forth the wares that were in the ship into the sea, to lighten it of them. But Jonah was gone down into the sides of the ship; and he lay, and was fast asleep.6 So the shipmaster came to him, and said unto him, What meanest you, O sleeper? arise, call upon your G-d, if so be that G-d will think upon us, that we perish not.7 And they said everyone to his fellow, Come, and let us cast lots, that we may know for whose cause this evil is upon us. So they cast lots, and the lot fell upon Jonah.

1:8

גורלות 1486 ויפל 5307 הגורל 1486 על 5921 יונה 3124: ויאמרו 559 אליו 413 הגידה 5046 נא 4994 לנו 3807a באשר 834 למי 4310

gouralout, uayipol hagoural 'al younah. uaya'maru 'aelayu, hagiydah naa' lanu, ba'asher lamiy

**lots fell and lot upon Jonah Then said they unto him Tell we pray you us for cause whose**

הרעה 7451 הזאת 2063 לנו 3807a מה 4100 מלאכתך 4399 ומאין 370 תבוא 935 מה 4100 ארצך 776 ואי 335 מזה 2088 עם 5971

hara'ah haza't lanu; mah mala'aktaka uame'ayin tabou'a, mah 'artzeka, ua'aey mizeh 'am

**evil this *is* upon us What *is* your occupation? and where come you? what *is* your country? and what of this people**

1:9

אתה 859: ויאמר 559 אליהם 413 עברי 5680 אנכי 595 ואת 853 יהוה 3068 אלהי 430 השמים 8064 אני 589 ירא 3373 אשר 834

'atah. uaya'mer 'aleyhem 'abriy 'anokiy; ua'at Yahuah 'alohey hashamayim 'aniy yarea', 'asher

***are* you? And he said unto them *am* an Hebrew I *and* Yahuah the Elohim of heaven I fear which**

1:10

עשה 6213 את 853 הים 3220 ואת 853 היבשה 3004: וייראו 3372 האנשים 582 יראה 3373 גדולה 1419 ויאמרו 559 אליו 413

'asah 'at hayam ua'at hayabashah. uayiyra'au ha'anashiym yir'ah gadoulah, uaya'maru 'aelayu

**has made the sea *and* the dry land Then were fearing the men afraid exceedingly and said unto him**

מה 4100 זאת 2063 עשית 6213 כי 3588 ידעו 3045 האנשים 582 כי 3588 מלפני 6440 יהוה 3069 הוא 1931 ברח 1272 כי 3588

mah za't 'ashiyta; kiy yada'au ha'anashiym, kiy milipney Yahuah hua' boreach, kiy

**Why this? have you done For knew the men that from the presence of Yahuah he fled because**

1:11

הגיד 5046 להם 1992: ויאמרו 559 אליו 413 מה 4100 נעשה 6213 לך 3807a וישתק 8367 הים 3220 מעלינו 5921 כי 3588

higiyd lahem. uaya'maru 'aelayu mah na'aseh lak, uayishtoq hayam me'aleynu; kiy

**he had told them Then said they unto him What shall we do unto you that may be calm the sea unto us? for**

1:12

הים 3220 הולך 1980 וסער 5590: ויאמר 559 אליהם 413 שאוני 5375 והטילני 2904 אל 413 הים 3220

hayam houlek uaso'aer. uaya'mer 'aleyhem, sa'auniy uahatiyluniy 'al hayam,

**the sea wrought and was tempestuous And he said unto them Take me up and cast me forth into the sea**

1:13

וישתק הים 3220 מעליכם 5921 כי 3588 יודע 3045 אני 589 כי 3588 בשלי 7945 הסער 8367 הגדול 1419 הזה 2088 עליכם 5921:

uayishtoq hayam me'aleykem; kiy youdea' 'aniy, kiy basheliy, hasa'ar hagadoul hazeh 'aleykem.

**so shall be calm the sea unto you for know I that for my sake tempest *is* great this upon you**

ויחתרו 2864 האנשים 582 להשיב 7725 אל 413 היבשה 3004 ולא 3808 יכלו 3201 כי 3588 הים 3220 הולך 1980

uayachtaru ha'anashiym, lahashiyb 'al hayabashah uala' yakolu; kiy hayam, houlek

**Nevertheless rowed hard the men to bring *it* to the land but not they could for the sea wrought**

1:14

וסער 5590 עליהם 5921: ויקראו 7121 אל 413 יהוה 3068 ויאמרו 559 אנה 575 יהוה 3068 אל 408

uaso'aer 'aleyhem. uayiqra'au 'al Yahuah uaya'maru, 'anah Yahuah 'al

**and was tempestuous against them Wherefore they cried unto Yahuah and said We beseech you O Yahuah not**

נא 4994 נאבדה 6 בנפש 5315 האיש 376 הזה 2088 ואל 408 תתן 5414 עלינו 5921 דם 1818 נקיא 5355 כי 3588 אתה 859 יהוה 3068 כאשר 834

naa' na'badah, banepesh ha'aysh hazeh, ua'al titen 'aleynu dam naqiy'a; kiy 'atah Yahuah, ka'asher

**we beseech you let us perish for life man's this not and lay upon us blood innocent for you O Yahuah as**

1:15

חפצת 2654 עשית 6213: וישאו 5375 את 853 יונה 3124 ויטלהו 2904 אל 413 הים 3220 ויעמד 5975 הים 3220

chapatzta 'ashiyta. uayis'au 'at younah, uayatiluhu 'al hayam; uaya'amod hayam

**it pleased you have done So they took up Jonah and cast him forth into the sea and ceased the sea**

Jonah 1:8 Then said they unto him, Tell us, we pray you, for whose cause this evil is upon us; What is your occupation? and whence come you? what is your country? and of what people are you?9 And he said unto them, I am an Hebrew; and I fear YHUH, the G-d of heaven, which has made the sea and the dry land.10 Then were the men exceedingly afraid, and said unto him, Why have you done this? For the men knew that he fled from the presence of YHUH, because he had told them.11 Then said they unto him, What shall we do unto you, that the sea may be calm unto us? for the sea wrought, and was tempestuous.12 And he said unto them, Take me up, and cast me forth into the sea; so shall the sea be calm unto you: for I know that for my sake this great tempest is upon you.13 Nevertheless the men rowed hard to bring it to the land; but they could not: for the sea wrought, and was tempestuous against them.14 Wherefore they cried unto YHUH, and said, We beseech you, O YHUH, we beseech you, let us not perish for this man's life, and lay not upon us innocent blood: for you, O YHUH, have done as it pleased you.15 So they took up Jonah, and cast him forth into the sea: and the sea ceased from her raging.

| | 1:16 | | | | | | | | | |
|---|---|---|---|---|---|---|---|---|---|---|
| מזעפו 2197: | | וייראו 3372 | האנשים 582 | יראה 3373 | גדולה 1419 | את 853 | יהוה 3068 | ויזבחו 2076 | זבח 2077 | ליהוה 3068 |
| miza'apou. | | uayiyra'au | ha'anashiym | yir'ah | gadoulah | 'at | Yahuah; | uayizbachu | zebach | laYahuah, |
| **from her raging** | | **Then feared** | **the men** | **afraid** | **exceedingly** | | **Yahuah** | **and offered** | **a sacrifice** | **unto Yahuah** |

| | | 1:17 | | | | | | | | |
|---|---|---|---|---|---|---|---|---|---|---|
| וידרו 5087 | נדרים 5088: | | וימן 4487 | יהוה 3068 | דג 1709 | גדול 1419 | לבלע 1104 | את 853 | יונה 3124 | ויהי 1961 | יונה 3124 |
| uayidru | nadariym. | | uayaman | Yahuah | dag | gadoul, | libloa' | 'at | younah; | uayahiy | younah |
| **and made** | **vows** | | **Now had prepared** | **Yahuah** | **a fish** | **great** | **to swallow up** | | **Jonah** | **And was** | **Jonah** |

| | | | | | |
|---|---|---|---|---|---|
| במעי 4578 | הדג 1709 | שלשה 7969 | ימים 3117 | ושלשה 7969 | לילות 3915: |
| bim'aey | hadag, | shaloshah | yamiym | uashloshah | leylout. |
| **in the belly of** | **the fish** | **three** | **days** | **and three** | **nights** |

| Jonah 2:1 | | | | | | | 2:2 | | |
|---|---|---|---|---|---|---|---|---|---|
| | ויתפלל 6419 | יונה 3124 | אל 413 | יהוה 3068 | אלהיו 430 | ממעי 4578 | הדגה 1710: | ויאמר 559 | קראתי 7121 |
| | uayitpalel | younah, | 'al | Yahuah | 'alohayu; | mim'aey | hadagah. | uaya'mer, | qara'tiy |
| | **Then prayed** | **Jonah** | **unto** | **Yahuah** | **his Elohim** | **out of belly** | **the fish's** | **And said** | **I cried** |

| | | | | | | | | |
|---|---|---|---|---|---|---|---|---|
| מצרה 6869 | לי 3807a | אל 413 | יהוה 3068 | ויענני 6030 | מבטן 990 | שאול 7585 | שועתי 7768 | שמעת 8085 |
| mitzarah | liy | 'al | Yahuah | uaya'aneniy; | mibeten | sha'aul | shiua'atiy | shama'ata |
| **by reason of affliction** | **mine** | **unto** | **Yahuah** | **and he heard me** | **out of the belly of** | **hell (*grave*)** | **cried I** | ***and* you heard** |

| | 2:3 | | | | | | | |
|---|---|---|---|---|---|---|---|---|
| קולי 6963: | | ותשליכני 7993 | מצולה 4688 | בלבב 3824 | ימים 3220 | ונהר 5104 | יסבבני 5437 | כל 3605 |
| qouliy. | | uatashliykeniy | matzulah | bilbab | yamiym, | uanahar | yasobbeniy; | kal |
| **my voice** | | **For you had cast me** | ***into the* deep** | **in the midst of** | **the seas** | **and the floods** | **compassed me about** | **all** |

| | | | | 2:4 | | | | | | |
|---|---|---|---|---|---|---|---|---|---|---|
| משבריך 4867 | וגליך 1530 | עלי 5921 | עברו 5674: | ואני 589 | אמרתי 559 | נגרשתי 1644 | מנגד 5048 | עיניך 5869 | אך 389 | אוסיף 3254 |
| mishbareyka | uagaleyka | 'alay | 'abaru. | ua'aniy | 'amartiy, | nigrashtiy | mineged | 'ayneyka; | 'ak | 'ausiyp |
| **your billows** | **and your waves** | **me** | **passed over** | **Then I** | **said** | **I am cast out** | **of** | **your sight** | **yet** | **I will again** |

| | | | | 2:5 | | | | | |
|---|---|---|---|---|---|---|---|---|---|
| להביט 5027 | אל 413 | היכל 1964 | קדשך 6944: | אפפוני 661 | מים 4325 | עד 5704 | נפש 5315 | תהום 8415 | יסבבני 5437 |
| lahabiyt, | 'al | heykal | qadasheka | 'apapuniy | mayim | 'ad | nepesh, | tahoum | yasobbeniy; |
| **look** | **toward** | **temple** | **your holy** | **compassed me about** | **The waters** | ***even* to** | **the soul** | **the depth** | **closed me round about** |

| | | | 2:6 | | | | |
|---|---|---|---|---|---|---|---|
| סוף 5488 | חבוש 2280 | לראשי 7218: | לקצבי 7095 | הרים 2022 | ירדתי 3381 | הארץ 776 | ברחיה 1280 |
| sup | chabush | lara'shiy. | laqitzbey | hariym | yaradtiy, | ha'aretz | barcheyha |
| **the weeds** | **were wrapped** | **about my head** | **to the bottoms of** | **the mountains** | **I went down** | **the earth** | **with her bars *was*** |

| | | | | | | | 2:7 | |
|---|---|---|---|---|---|---|---|---|
| בעדי 1157 | לעולם 5769 | ותעל 5927 | משחת 7845 | חיי 2416 | יהוה 3068 | אלהי 430: | בהתעטף 5848 | עלי 5921 |
| ba'adiy | la'aulam; | uata'al | mishachat | chayay | Yahuah | 'alohay. | bahit'atep | 'alay |
| **about me** | **for ever** | **yet have you brought up** | **from corruption** | **my life** | **O Yahuah** | **my Elohim** | **When fainted** | **within me** |

| | | | | | | | | | | 2:8 |
|---|---|---|---|---|---|---|---|---|---|---|
| נפשי 5315 | את 853 | יהוה 3069 | זכרתי 2142 | ותבוא 935 | אליך 413 | תפלתי 8605 | אל 413 | היכל 1964 | קדשך 6944: | משמרים 8104 |
| napshiy, | 'at | Yahuah | zakaratiy; | uatabou'a | 'aeleyka | tapilatiy, | 'al | heykal | qadasheka | mashamriym |
| **my soul** | | **Yahuah** | **I remembered** | **and came in** | **unto you** | **my prayer** | **into** | **temple** | **your holy** | **They that observe** |

| | | | | 2:9 | | | | | |
|---|---|---|---|---|---|---|---|---|---|
| הבלי 1892 | שוא 7723 | חסדם 2617 | יעזבו 5800: | ואני 589 | בקול 6963 | תודה 8426 | אזבחה 2076 | לך 3807a | אשר 834 |
| habley | shau'a; | chasdam | ya'azobu. | ua'aniy, | baqoul | toudah | 'azbachah | lak, | 'asher |
| **vanities** | **lying** | **their own mercy** | **forsake** | **But I** | **with the voice of** | **thanksgiving** | **will sacrifice** | **unto you** | **that** |

Jonah 1:16 Then the men feared YHUH exceedingly, and offered a sacrifice unto YHUH, and made vows.17 Now YHUH had prepared a great fish to swallow up Jonah. And Jonah was in the belly of the fish three days and three nights. **Jonah** 2:1 Then Jonah prayed unto YHUH his G-d out of the fish's belly,2 And said, I cried by reason of mine affliction unto YHUH, and he heard me; out of the belly of hell cried I, and you heardest my voice.3 For you had cast me into the deep, in the midst of the seas; and the floods compassed me about: all your billows and your waves passed over me.4 Then I said, I am cast out of your sight; yet I will look again toward your holy temple.5 The waters compassed me about, even to the soul: the depth closed me round about, the weeds were wrapped about my head.6 I went down to the bottoms of the mountains; the earth with her bars was about me forever: yet have you brought up my life from corruption, O YHUH my G-d.7 When my soul fainted within me I remembered YHUH: and my prayer came in unto you, into your holy temple.8 They that observe lying vanities forsake their own mercy.9 But I will sacrifice unto you with the voice of thanksgiving; I will pay that that I have vowed. Salvation is of YHUH.

נדרתי 5087 אשלמה 7999 ישועתה 3444 ליהוה 3068: **2:10** ויאמר 559 יהוה 3068 לדג 1709 ויקא 6958 את 853 יונה 3124
nadartiy 'ashalemah; yashu'atah laYahuah. uaya'mer Yahuah ladag; uayaqea' 'at younah
***that* I have vowed I will pay Salvation *is* of Yahuah And spoke Yahuah unto the fish and it vomited out Jonah**

אל 413 היבשה 3004:
'al hayabashah.
**upon the dry land**

**Jonah 3:1** ויהי 1961 דבר 1697 יהוה 3068 אל 413 יונה 3124 שנית 8145 לאמר 559: **3:2** קום 6965 לך 1980 אל 413 נינוה 5210 העיר 5892
uayahiy dabar Yahuah 'al younah sheniyt lea'mor. qum lek 'al nynabuh ha'ayr
**And came the word of Yahuah unto Jonah the second time saying Arise go you unto Nineveh that city**

הגדולה 1419 וקרא 7121 אליה 413 את 853 הקריאה 7150 אשר 834 אנכי 595 דבר 1696 אליך 413: **3:3** ויקם 6965 יונה 3124 וילך 1980 אל 413
hagadoulah; uaiqra' 'aeleyha 'at haqariy'ah, 'asher 'anokiy dober 'aeleyka. uayaqam younah, uayelek 'al
**great and preach unto it the preaching that I bid you So arose Jonah and went unto**

נינוה 5210 כדבר 1697 יהוה 3068 ונינוה 5210 היתה 1961 עיר 5892 גדולה 1419 לאלהים 430 מהלך 4109 שלשת 7969
nynabuh kidbar Yahuah; uaniynaueh, hayatah 'ayr gadoulah le'alohiym, mahalak shaloshet
**Nineveh according to the word of Yahuah Now Nineveh was an city great exceeding of journey three**

ימים 3117: **3:4** ויחל 2490 יונה 3124 לבוא 935 בעיר 5892 מהלך 4109 יום 3117 אחד 259 ויקרא 7121 ויאמר 559 עוד 5750 ארבעים 705 יום 3117
yamiym. uayachel younah labou'a ba'ayr, mahalak youm 'achad; uayiqra' uaya'mar, 'aud 'arba'aym youm,
**days' And began Jonah to enter into the city journey day's a and he cried and said Yet forty days**

ונינוה 5210 נהפכת 2015: **3:5** ויאמינו 539 אנשי 582 נינוה 5210 באלהים 430 ויקראו 7121 צום 6685 וילבשו 3847
uaniynaueh nehapaket. uaya'amiynu 'anshey niynaueh be'alohiym; uayiqra'au tzoum uayilbashu
**and Nineveh shall be overthrown So believed the people of Nineveh in Elohim and proclaimed a fast and put on**

שקים 8242 מגדולם 1419 ועד 5704 קטנם 6996: **3:6** ויגע 5060 הדבר 1697 אל 413 מלך 4428 נינוה 5210 ויקם 6965
saqiym, migdoulam ua'ad qatanam. uayiga' hadabar 'al melek niynaueh, uayaqam
**sackcloth from the greatest of them even to the least of them For came word unto the king of Nineveh and he arose**

מכסאו 3678 ויעבר 5674 אדרתו 155 מעליו 5921 ויכס 3680 שק 8242 וישב 3427 על 5921 האפר 665: **3:7**
mikis'au, uaya'aber 'adartou me'alayu; uayakas saq, uayesheb 'al ha'aeper.
**from his throne and he laid his robe from him and covered *him with* sackcloth and sat in ashes**

ויזעק 2199 ויאמר 559 בנינוה 5210 מטעם 2940 המלך 4428 וגדליו 1419 לאמר 559 האדם 120
uayaz'aeq, uaya'mer baniynaueh, mita'am hamelek uagdolayu lea'mor; ha'adam
**And he caused *it* to be proclaimed and published through Nineveh by the decree of the king and his nobles saying man**

והבהמה 929 הבקר 1241 והצאן 6629 אל 408 יטעמו 2938 מאומה 3972 אל 408 ירעו 7462 ומים 4325 אל 408 ישתו 8354: **3:8**
uahabahemah habaqar uahatza'n, 'al yit'amu ma'aumah, 'al yir'au, uamayim 'al yishtu.
**nor beast herd nor flock neither Let taste any thing not let them feed water nor drink**

ויתכסו 3680 שקים 8242 האדם 120 והבהמה 929 ויקראו 7121 אל 413 אלהים 430 בחזקה 2394 וישבו 7725 איש 376
uayitkasu saqiym, ha'adam uahabahemah, uayiqra'au 'al 'alohiym bachazaqah; uayashubu, 'aysh
**But let be covered *with* sackcloth man and beast and cry unto Elohim mightily *yea* let them turn every one**

Jonah 2:10 And YHUH spoke unto the fish, and it vomited out Jonah upon the dry land. **Jonah** 3:1 And the word of YHUH came unto Jonah the second time, saying,2 Arise, go unto Nineveh, that great city, and preach unto it the preaching that I bid you.3 So Jonah arose, and went unto Nineveh, according to the word of YHUH. Now Nineveh was an exceeding great city of three days' journey.4 And Jonah began to enter into the city a day's journey, and he cried, and said, Yet forty days, and Nineveh shall be overthrown.5 So the people of Nineveh believed G-d, and proclaimed a fast, and put on sackcloth, from the greatest of them even to the least of them.6 For word came unto the king of Nineveh, and he arose from his throne, and he laid his robe from him, and covered him with sackcloth, and sat in ashes.7 And he caused it to be proclaimed and published through Nineveh by the decree of the king and his nobles, saying, Let neither man nor beast, herd nor flock, taste anything: let them not feed, nor drink water:8 But let man and beast be covered with sackcloth, and cry mightily unto G-d: yea, let them turn everyone from his evil way, and from the violence that is in their hands.

מדרכו 1870 | הרעה 7451 | ומן 4480 | החמס 2555 | אשר 834 | בכפיהם: | **3:9** | מי 4310 | יודע 3045 | ישוב 7725 | ונחם 5162 | האלהים 430

midarkou hara'ah, uamin hechamas 'asher bakapeyhem. miy' youdea' yashub, uanicham ha'alohiym;

**from his way evil and from the violence that *is* in their hands Who can tell will turn and repent *if* Elohim**

ושב 7725 | מחרון 2740 | אפו 639 | ולא 3808 | נאבד 6: | **3:10** | וירא 7200 | האלהים 430 | את 853 | מעשיהם 4639 | כי 3588 | שבו 7725

uashab mecharoun 'apou uala' na'bed. uayar'a ha'alohiym 'at ma'aseyhem, kiy shabu

**and turn away from fierce his anger not? *that* we perish And saw Elohim their works that they turned**

מדרכם 1870 | הרעה 7451 | וינחם 5162 | האלהים 430 | על 5921 | הרעה 7451 | אשר 834 | דבר 1696 | לעשות 6213 | להם 1992 | ולא 3808

midarkam hara'ah; uayinachem ha'alohiym, 'al hara'ah 'asher diber la'asout lahem uala'

**from their way evil and repented Elohim of the evil that he had said *that* he would do unto them and not**

עשה 6213:

'asah.

**he did *it***

**Jonah 4:1** | וירע 7489 | אל 413 | יונה 3124 | רעה 7451 | גדולה 1419 | ויחר 2734 | לו 3807a: | **4:2** | ויתפלל 6419 | אל 413

uayera' 'al younah ra'ah gadoulah; uayichar lou'. uayitpalel 'al

**But it displeased about Jonah adversity exceedingly and was very angry he And he prayed unto**

יהוה 3069 | ויאמר 559 | אנה 577 | יהוה 3069 | הלוא 3808 | זה 2088 | דברי 1697 | עד 5704 | היותי 1961 | על 5921 | אדמתי 127 | על 5921 | כן 3651

Yahuah uaya'mar, 'anah Yahuah halou'a zeh dabariy, 'ad hayoutiy 'al 'admatiy, 'al ken

**Yahuah and said I pray you Yahuah *was* not this my saying when yet I was in my country? Therefore so**

קדמתי 6923 | לברח 1272 | תרשישה 8659 | כי 3588 | ידעתי 3045 | כי 3588 | אתה 859 | אל 410 | חנון 2587 | ורחום 7349 | ארך 750 | אפים 639 | ורב 7227

qidamtiy libroach tarshiyshah; kiy yada'tiy, kiy 'atah 'al chanun uarachum, 'arek 'apayim uarab

**I before fled unto Tarshish for I knew that you *are a* El gracious and merciful slow to anger and of great**

חסד 2617 | ונחם 5162 | על 5921 | הרעה 7451: | **4:3** | ועתה 6258 | יהוה 3068 | קח 3947 | נא 4994 | את 853 | נפשי 5315 | ממני 4480 | כי 3588

chesed, uanicham 'al hara'ah. ua'atah Yahuah, qach naa' 'at napshiy mimeniy; kiy

**kindness and repent you of the evil Therefore now O Yahuah take I beseech you my life from me for**

טוב 2896 | מותי 4194 | מחיי 2416: | **4:4** | ויאמר 559 | יהוה 3068 | ההיטב 3190 | חרה 2734 | לך 3807a: | **4:5** | ויצא 3318 | יונה 3124 | מן 4480

toub moutiy mechayay. uaya'mer Yahuah, haheyteb charah lak. uayetzea' younah min

***it is* better for me to die than to live Then said Yahuah Do well *to be* angry? to you So went out Jonah of**

העיר 5892 | וישב 3427 | מקדם 6924 | לעיר 5892 | ויעש 6213 | לו 3807a | שם 8033 | סכה 5521 | וישב 3427 | תחתיה 8478 | בצל 6738 | עד 5704 | אשר 834

ha'ayr, uayesheb miqedem la'ayr; uaya'as lou' sham sukah, uayesheb tachteyha batzel, 'ad 'asher

**the city and sat on the east side of the city and made him there a booth and sat under it in the shadow till he**

יראה 7200 | מה 4100 | יהיה 1961 | בעיר 5892: | **4:6** | וימן 4487 | יהוה 3068 | אלהים 430 | קיקיון 7021 | ויעל 5927 | מעל 5921

yir'ah, mah yihayeh ba'ayr. uayaman Yahuah 'alohiym qiyqayoun uaya'al me'al

**might see what would become of the city And prepared Yahuah Elohim a gourd and made *it* to come up over**

ליונה 3124 | להיות 1961 | צל 6738 | על 5921 | ראשו 7218 | להציל 5337 | לו 3807a | מרעתו 7451 | וישמח 8055 | יונה 3124 | על 5921 | הקיקיון 7021

layounah, lihayout tzel 'al ra'shou, lahatziyl lou' mera'atou; uayismach younah 'al haqiyqayoun

**Jonah that it might be a shadow over his head to deliver him from his grief So was glad Jonah of the gourd**

Jonah 3:9 Who can tell if G-d will turn and repent, and turn away from his fierce anger, that we perish not?10 And G-d saw their works, that they turned from their evil way; and G-d repented of the evil, that he had said that he would do unto them; and he did it not. **Jonah** 4:1 But it displeased Jonah exceedingly, and he was very angry.2 And he prayed unto YHUH, and said, I pray you, O YHUH, was not this my saying, when I was yet in my country? Therefore I fled before unto Tarshish: for I knew that you are a gracious G-d, and merciful, slow to anger, and of great kindness, and repentest you of the evil.3 Therefore now, O YHUH, take, I beseech you, my life from me; for it is better for me to die than to live.4 Then said YHUH, Doest you well to be angry?5 So Jonah went out of the city, and sat on the east side of the city, and there made him a booth, and sat under it in the shadow, till he might see what would become of the city.6 And YHUH G-d prepared a gourd, and made it to come up over Jonah, that it might be a shadow over his head, to deliver him from his grief. So Jonah was exceeding glad of the gourd.

| שמחה 8056 | גדולה 1419: | 4:7 וימן 4487 | האלהים 430 | תולעת 8438 | בעלות 5927 | השחר 7837 | למחרת 4283 | ותך 5221 | את 853 |
|---|---|---|---|---|---|---|---|---|---|
| simchah | gadoulah. | uayaman | ha'alohiym | toula'at, | ba'alout | hashachar | lamacharat; | uatak | 'at |
| **glad** | **exceedingly** | **But prepared** | **Elohim** | **a worm** | **when rose** | **the morning** | **the next day** | **and it smote** | |

| הקיקיון 7021 | וייבש 3001: | 4:8 ויהי 1961 | כזרח 2224 | השמש 8121 | וימן 4487 | אלהים 430 | רוח 7307 | קדים 6921 |
|---|---|---|---|---|---|---|---|---|
| haqiyqayoun | uayiybash. | uayahiy | kizroach | hashemesh, | uayaman | 'alohiym | ruach | qadiym |
| **the gourd** | **that it withered** | **And it came to pass** | **when did arise** | **the sun** | **that prepared** | **Elohim** | **a wind** | **east** |

| חרישית 2759 | ותך 5221 | השמש 8121 | על 5921 | ראש 7218 | יונה 3124 | ויתעלף 5968 | וישאל 7592 | את 853 | נפשו 5315 | למות 4191 | ויאמר 559 |
|---|---|---|---|---|---|---|---|---|---|---|---|
| chariyshiyt, | uatak | hashemesh | 'al | ra'sh | younah | uayit'alap; | uayish'al | 'at | napshou | lamut, | uaya'mer |
| **vehement** | **and beat** | **the sun** | **upon** | **the head of** | **Jonah** | **that he fainted** | **and wished** | | **in himself** | **to die** | **and said** |

| טוב 2896 | מותי 4191 | מחיי 2416: | 4:9 ויאמר 559 | אלהים 430 | אל 413 | יונה 3124 | ההיטב 3190 | חרה 2734 | לך 3807a | על 5921 | הקיקיון 7021 |
|---|---|---|---|---|---|---|---|---|---|---|---|
| toub | moutiy | mechayay. | uaya'mer | 'alohiym | 'al | younah, | haheyteb | charah | laka | 'al | haqiyqayoun; |
| ***It is* better** | **for me to die** | **than to live** | **And said** | **Elohim** | **to** | **Jonah** | **Do well** | ***to be* angry** | **to you** | **for** | **the gourd?** |

| ויאמר 559 | היטב 3190 | חרה 2734 | לי 3807a | עד 5704 | מות 4194: | 4:10 ויאמר 559 | יהוה 3068 | אתה 859 | חסת 2347 | על 5921 | הקיקיון 7021 |
|---|---|---|---|---|---|---|---|---|---|---|---|
| uaya'mer | heyteb | charah | liy | 'ad | mauet. | uaya'mer | Yahuah, | 'atah | chasta | 'al | haqiyqayoun, |
| **And he said** | **do well** | ***to be* angry** | **I** | ***even* unto** | **death** | **Then said** | **Yahuah** | **You** | **have had pity** | **on** | **the gourd** |

| אשר 834 | לא 3808 | עמלת 5998 | בו 871a | ולא 3808 | גדלתו 1431 | שבן 1121 | לילה 3915 | היה 1961 | ובן 1121 | לילה 3915 |
|---|---|---|---|---|---|---|---|---|---|---|
| 'asher | la' | 'amalta | bou | uala' | gidaltou; | shebin | layalah | hayah | uabin | layalah |
| ***for the* which** | **not** | **you have laboured** | **in him** | **neither** | **made it grow** | **which in** | **a night** | **came up** | **and in** | **a night** |

| אבד 6: | 4:11 ואני 589 | לא 3808 | אחוס 2347 | על 5921 | נינוה 5210 | העיר 5892 | הגדולה 1419 | אשר 834 | יש 3426 | בה 871a | הרבה 7235 | משתים 8147 |
|---|---|---|---|---|---|---|---|---|---|---|---|---|
| 'abad. | ua'aniy | la' | 'achus, | 'al | niynaueh | ha'ayr | hagadoulah; | 'asher | yesh | bah | harbeh | mishteym |
| **perished** | **And I** | **not** | **should spare** | **over** | **Nineveh** | **that city** | **great** | **who** | **are** | **wherein** | **more than** | **two** |

| עשרה 6240 | רבו 7239 | אדם 120 | אשר 834 | לא 3808 | ידע 3045 | בין 996 | ימינו 3225 | לשמאלו 8040 | ובהמה 929 | רבה 7227: |
|---|---|---|---|---|---|---|---|---|---|---|
| 'asreh | ribou | 'adam, | 'asher | la' | yada' | beyn | yamiynou | lisma'lou, | uabhemah | rabah. |
| **ten** | **ten thousand** | **persons** | **that** | **cannot** | **discern** | **between** | **their right *hand*** | **and their left *hand*** | **and *also* cattle?** | **much** |

Jonah 4:7 But G-d prepared a worm when the morning rose the next day, and it smote the gourd that it withered.8 And it came to pass, when the sun did arise, that G-d prepared a vehement east wind; and the sun beat upon the head of Jonah, that he fainted, and wished in himself to die, and said, It is better for me to die than to live.9 And G-d said to Jonah, Doest you well to be angry for the gourd? And he said, I do well to be angry, even unto death.10 Then said YHUH, Thou have had pity on the gourd, for the which you have not laboured, neither madest it grow; which came up in a night, and perished in a night:11 And should not I spare Nineveh, that great city, wherein are more than sixscore thousand persons that cannot discern between their right hand and their left hand; and also much cattle?

# MICAH
## (*Miykah*)

The first verse tells us the author of the book was the Prophet Micah. The Book of Micah was written approximately between 735 and 700 B.C. The Hebrew name Micah means *Who is like Yah*. The book has also been called "*Isaiah in miniature*" because it is essentially the same message as the prophecy of Isaiah. Micah was sent to prophesy to all 12 tribes of both the **House of Judah** (*Jacob*) and the **House of Israel** of coming judgment for the sins of corrupt leadership and idolatry but promises hope if they will repent. The prophet condemns the rulers, priests and prophets of Israel who exploit and mislead the people and claims it is because of their deeds that Jerusalem will be invaded and destroyed. Micah has very powerful prophecies concerning Y'shua the Messiah.

**Micah 1:1**
דבר 1697 יהוה 3068 אשר 834 היה 1961 אל 413 מיכה 4318 המרשתי 4183 בימי 3117 יותם 3147 אחז 271 יחזקיה 2396
dabar Yahuah 'asher hayah, 'al miykah hamorashtiy, biymey youtam 'achaz yachizqiyah
**The word of Yahuah that came to Micah the Morasthite in the days of Jotham Ahaz *and* Hezekiah**

מלכי 4428 יהודה 3063 אשר 834 חזה 2372 על 5921 שמרון 8111 וירושלם 3389: **1:2** שמעו 8085 עמים 5971 כלם 3605 הקשיבי 7181 ארץ 776
malkey yahudah; 'asher chazah 'al shomaroun uiyarushalaim. shim'au 'amiym kulam, haqashiybiy 'aretz
**kings of Judah which he saw concerning Samaria and Jerusalem Hear people all you listen O earth**

ומלאה 4393 ויהי 1961 אדני 136 יהוה 3069 בכם 871a לעד 5707 אדני 136 מהיכל 1964 קדשו 6944: **1:3** כי 3588 הנה 2009
uamlo'ah; uiyhiy 'adonay Yahuah bakem la'aed, 'adonay meheykal qadashou. kiy hineh
**and all that therein is and let be Adonai Yahuah against you witness Adonai from temple his holy For behold**

יהוה 3068 יצא 3318 ממקומו 4725 וירד 3381 ודרך 1869 על 5921 במותי 1116 ארץ 776: **1:4**
Yahuah yotzea' mimaqoumou; uayarad uadarak 'al bamutey 'aretz.
**Yahuah comes forth out of his place and will come down and tread upon the high places of the earth**

ונמסו 4549 ההרים 2022 תחתיו 8478 והעמקים 6010 יתבקעו 1234 כדונג 1749 מפני 6440 האש 784 כמים 4325
uanamasu heharyim tachtayu, uaha'amaqiym yitabaqa'au; kadounag mipaney ha'aesh, kamayim
**And shall be molten the mountains under him and the valleys shall be cleft as wax before the fire *and* as the waters**

מגרים 5064 במורד 4174: **1:5** בפשע 6588 יעקב 3290 כל 3605 זאת 2063 ובחטאות 2403 בית 1004
mugariym bamourad. bapesha' ya'aqob kal za't, uabchata'ut beyt
***that are* poured down a steep place For the transgression of Jacob *is* all this and for the sins of the house of**

ישראל 3478 מי 4310 פשע 6588 יעקב 3290 הלוא 3808 שמרון 8111 ומי 4310 במות 1116 יהודה 3063 הלוא 3808
yisra'ael; miy' pesha' ya'aqob, halou'a shomaroun, uamiy bamout yahudah, halou'a
**Israel What *is* the transgression of Jacob? Is it not Samaria? and what *are* the high places of Judah? *are they* not**

ירושלם 3389: **1:6** ושמתי 7760 שמרון 8111 לעי 5856 השדה 7704 למטעי 4302 כרם 3754
yarushalaim. uasamtiy shomaroun la'ay hasadeh lamata'aey karem;
**Jerusalem? Therefore I will make Samaria as an heap of the field *and* as plantings of a vineyard**

והגרתי 5064 לגי 1516 אבניה 68 ויסדיה 3247 אגלה 1540: **1:7** וכל 3605
uahigartiy lagay 'abaneyha, uiysodeyha 'agaleh. uakal
**and I will pour down into the valley the stones thereof and the foundations thereof I will discover And all**

פסיליה 6456 יכתו 3807 וכל 3605 אתנניה 868 ישרפו 8313 באש 784 וכל 3605
pasiyleyha yukatu, uakal 'atnaneyha yisarapu ba'ash, uakal
**the graven images thereof shall be beaten to pieces and all the hires thereof shall be burned with the fire and all**

**Micah** 1:1 The word of YHUH that came to Micah the Morasthite in the days of Jotham, Ahaz, and Hezekiah, kings of Judah, which he saw concerning Samaria and Jerusalem.2 Hear, all you people; hear, O earth, and all that therein is: and let YHUH G-D be witness against you, YHUH from his holy temple.3 For, behold, YHUH cometh forth out of his place, and will come down, and tread upon the high places of the earth.4 And the mountains shall be molten under him, and the valleys shall be cleft, as wax before the fire, and as the waters that are poured down a steep place.5 For the transgression of Jacob is all this, and for the sins of the house of Israel. What is the transgression of Jacob? is it not Samaria? and what are the high places of Judah? are they not Jerusalem?6 Therefore I will make Samaria as an heap of the field, and as plantings of a vineyard: and I will pour down the stones thereof into the valley, and I will discover the foundations thereof.7 And all the graven images thereof shall be beaten to pieces, and all the hires thereof shall be burned with the fire, and all the idols thereof will I lay desolate:

| עצביה 6091 | אשים 7760 | שממה 8077 | כי 3588 | מאתנן 868 | זונה 2181 | קבצה 6908 | ועד 5704 | אתנן 868 | זונה 2181 |
|---|---|---|---|---|---|---|---|---|---|
| 'atzabeyha | 'asiym | shamamah; | kiy | me'atnan | zounah | qibatzah, | ua'ad | 'atnan | zounah |
| **the idols thereof** | **will I lay** | **desolate** | **for** | **of the hire of** | **an harlot** | **she gathered *it*** | **and to** | **the hire of** | **an harlot** |

| ישובו 7725: | 1:8 | על 5921 | זאת 2063 | אספדה 5594 | ואילילה 3213 | אילכה 1980 | שילל 7758 | וערום 6174 | אעשה 6213 | מספד 4553 |
|---|---|---|---|---|---|---|---|---|---|---|
| yashubu. | | 'al | za't | 'aspadah | ua'aeyliylah, | 'aeylakah | shiylal | ua'aroum; | 'aaseh | misped |
| **they shall return** | | **Therefore** | **this** | **I will wail** | **and howl** | **I will go** | **stripped** | **and naked** | **I will make** | **a wailing** |

| כתנים 8577 | ואבל 60 | כבנות 1323 | יענה 3284: | 1:9 | כי 3588 | אנושה 605 | מכותיה 4347 | כי 3588 | באה 935 | עד 5704 | יהודה 3063 |
|---|---|---|---|---|---|---|---|---|---|---|---|
| kataniym, | ua'abel | kibanout | ya'anah. | | kiy | 'anushah | makouteyha; | kiy | ba'ah | 'ad | yahudah, |
| **like the dragons** | **and mourning** | **company of** | **owls** | | **For** | ***is* incurable** | **her wound** | **for** | **it is come** | **unto** | **Judah** |

| נגע 5060 | עד 5704 | שער 8179 | עמי 5971 | עד 5704 | ירושלם 3389: | 1:10 | בגת 1661 | אל 408 | תגידו 5046 | בכו 1058 | אל 408 | תבכו 1058 |
|---|---|---|---|---|---|---|---|---|---|---|---|---|
| naga' | 'ad | sha'ar | 'amiy | 'ad | yarushalaim. | | bagat | 'al | tagiydu, | bakou | 'al | tibku; |
| **he is come** | **unto** | **the gate of** | **my people** | ***even* to** | **Jerusalem** | | **at Gath *it*** | **not** | **Declare you** | **weep you** | **not** | **at all** |

| בבית 1004 | לעפרה 1036 | עפר 6083 | התפלשתי 6428 | 1:11 | עברי 5674 | לכם 3807a | יושבת 3427 | שפיר 8208 | עריה 6181 |
|---|---|---|---|---|---|---|---|---|---|
| babeyt | la'aprah, | 'apar | hitpalashetiy | | 'abriy | lakem | youshebet | shapiyr | 'aryah |
| **in the house** | **of Aphrah** | **in the dust** | **roll yourself** | | **Pass away** | **to you** | **you inhabitant of** | **Saphir** | **naked** |

| בשת 1322 | לא 3808 | יצאה 3318 | יושבת 3427 | צאנן 6630 | מספד 5594 | בית 1018 | האצל 681 | יקח 3947 | מכם 4480 |
|---|---|---|---|---|---|---|---|---|---|
| boshet; | la' | yatz'ah | youshebet | tza'anan, | mispad | beyt | ha'aetzel, | yiqach | mikem |
| ***having* your shame** | **not** | **came forth** | **the inhabitant of** | **Zaanan** | **in the mourning of** | **Beth** | **ezel** | **he shall receive** | **of you** |

| עמדתו 5979: | 1:12 | כי 3588 | חלה 2470 | לטוב 2896 | יושבת 3427 | מרות 4796 | כי 3588 | ירד 3381 | רע 7451 | מאת 853 | יהוה 3069 |
|---|---|---|---|---|---|---|---|---|---|---|---|
| 'amdatou. | | kiy | chalah | latoub | youshebet | marout; | kiy | yarad | ra' | me'aet | Yahuah, |
| **his standing** | | **For** | **waited carefully** | **for good** | **the inhabitant of** | **Maroth** | **but** | **came down** | **evil** | **from** | **Yahuah** |

| לשער 8179 | ירושלם 3389: | 1:13 | רתם 7573 | המרכבה 4818 | לרכש 7409 | יושבת 3427 | לכיש 3923 | ראשית 7225 |
|---|---|---|---|---|---|---|---|---|
| lasha'ar | yarushalaim. | | ratom | hamerkabah | larekesh | youshebet | lakiysh; | ra'shiyt |
| **unto the gate of** | **Jerusalem** | | **bind** | **the chariot** | **to the swift beast** | **O you inhabitant of** | **Lachish** | ***is* the beginning of** |

| חטאת 2403 | היא 1931 | לבת 1323 | ציון 6726 | כי 3588 | בך 871a | נמצאו 4672 | פשעי 6588 | ישראל 3478: | 1:14 | לכן 3651 |
|---|---|---|---|---|---|---|---|---|---|---|
| chata't | hiy'a | labat | tziyoun, | kiy | bak | nimtza'au | pish'aey | yisra'ael. | | laken |
| **the sin** | **she** | **to the daughter of** | **Zion** | **for** | **in you** | **were found** | **for the transgressions of** | **Israel** | | **Therefore** |

| תתני 5414 | שלוחים 7964 | על 5921 | מורשת 4182 | גת 1661 | בתי 1004 | אכזיב 392 | לאכזב 391 | למלכי 4428 | ישראל 3478: | 1:15 | עד 5750 |
|---|---|---|---|---|---|---|---|---|---|---|---|
| titaniy | shiluchiym, | 'al | moureshet | gat; | batey | 'akziyb | la'akzab, | lamalkey | yisra'ael. | | 'aud, |
| **shall you give** | **presents** | **to** | **Moresheth** | **gath** | **the houses of** | **Achzib** | ***shall be* a lie** | **to the kings of** | **Israel** | | **Yet** |

| הירש 3423 | אבי 935 | לך 3807a | יושבת 3427 | מרשה 4762 | עד 5704 | עדלם 5725 | יבוא 935 | כבוד 3519 | ישראל 3478: | 1:16 |
|---|---|---|---|---|---|---|---|---|---|---|
| hayouresh | 'abiy | lak, | youshebet | mareshah; | 'ad | 'adulam | yabou'a | kaboud | yisra'ael. | |
| **an heir** | **will I bring** | **unto you** | **O inhabitant of** | **Mareshah** | **unto** | **Adullam** | **he shall come** | **the glory of** | **Israel** | |

| קרחי 7139 | וגזי 1494 | על 5921 | בני 1121 | תענוגיך 8588 | הרחבי 7337 | קרחתך 7144 | כנשר 5404 | כי 3588 |
|---|---|---|---|---|---|---|---|---|
| qarachiy | uagoziy, | 'al | baney | ta'anugayik; | harachibiy | qarachatek | kanesher, | kiy |
| **Make you bald** | **and poll you** | **for** | **children** | **your delicate** | **enlarge** | **your baldness** | **as the eagle** | **for** |

Micah 1:7 for she gathered it of the hire of an harlot, and they shall return to the hire of an harlot.8 Therefore I will wail and howl, I will go stripped and naked: I will make a wailing like the dragons, and mourning as the owls.9 For her wound is incurable; for it is come unto Judah; he is come unto the gate of my people, even to Jerusalem.10 Declare you it not at Gath, weep you not at all: in the house of Aphrah roll thyself in the dust.11 Pass you away, you inhabitant of Saphir, having your shame naked: the inhabitant of Zaanan came not forth in the mourning of Beth-ezel; he shall receive of you his standing.12 For the inhabitant of Maroth waited carefully for good: but evil came down from YHUH unto the gate of Jerusalem.13 O you inhabitant of Lachish, bind the chariot to the swift beast: she is the beginning of the sin to the daughter of Zion: for the transgressions of Israel were found in you.14 Therefore shall you give presents to Moresheth-gath: the houses of Achzib shall be a lie to the kings of Israel.15 Yet will I bring an heir unto you, O inhabitant of Mareshah: he shall come unto Adullam the glory of Israel.16 Make you bald, and poll you for your delicate children; enlarge your baldness as the eagle; for they are gone into captivity from you.

גלו 1540 ממך 4480:
galu mimek.
**they are gone into captivity from you**

**Mic 2:1**
הוי 1945 חשבי 2803 און 205 ופעלי 6466 רע 7451 על 5921 משכבותם 4904 באור 216 הבקר 1242 יעשוה 6213
houy choshbey 'auen uapo'aley ra' 'al mishkaboutam; ba'aur haboqer ya'asuha,
**Woe to them that devise iniquity and work evil upon their beds when is light the morning they practise it**

כי 3588 יש 3426 לאל 410 ידם 3027: **2:2** וחמדו 2530 שדות 7704 וגזלו 1497 ובתים 1004
kiy yesh la'ael yadam. uachamadu sadout uagazalu, uabatiym
**because it is in *the* power (*El*) *of* their hand And they covet fields and take *them* by violence and houses**

ונשאו 5375 ועשקו 6231 גבר 1397 וביתו 1004 ואיש 376 ונחלתו 5159: **2:3** לכן 3651 כה 3541 אמר 559 יהוה 3068
uanasa'au; ua'ashaqu geber uabeytou, ua'aysh uanachalatou. laken, koh 'amar Yahuah,
**and take *them* away so they oppress a man and his house even a man and his heritage Therefore thus saith Yahuah**

הנני 2005 חשב 2803 על 5921 המשפחה 4940 הזאת 2063 רעה 7451 אשר 834 לא 3808 תמישו 4185 משם 8033 צוארתיכם 6677 ולא 3808
hinniy chosheb 'al hamishpachah haza't ra'ah; 'asher la' tamiyshu misham tzau'aroteykem, uala'
**Behold do I devise against family this an evil which not you shall remove from your necks neither**

תלכו 1980 רומה 7317 כי 3588 עת 6256 רעה 7451 היא 1931: **2:4** ביום 3117 ההוא 1931 ישא 5375 עליכם 5921 משל 4912
telaku roumah, kiy 'aet ra'ah hiy'a. bayoum hahua' yisa' 'aleykem mashal,
**shall you go haughtily for time *is* evil this In day that shall *one* take up against you a parable**

ונהה 5091 נהי 5093 נהיה 5092 אמר 559 שדוד 7703 נשדנו 7703 חלק 2506 עמי 5971 ימיר 4171 איך 349
uanahah nahiy nihayah 'amar shadoud nashadunu, cheleq 'amiy yamiyr; 'aeyk
**and lament with a doleful lamentation We be *and* say utterly spoiled the portion of my people he has changed how**

ימיש 4185 לי 3807a לשובב 7728 שדינו 7704 יחלק 2505: **2:5** לכן 3651 לא 3808 יהיה 1961 לך 3807a משליך 7993
yamiysh liy, lashoubeb sadeynu yachaleq. laken la' yihayeh laka, mashliyk
**has he removed *it* from me turning away our fields he has divided Therefore none will have to you that shall cast**

חבל 2256 בגורל 1486 בקהל 6951 יהוה 3068: **2:6** אל 408 תטפו 5197 יטיפון 5197 לא 3808
chebel bagoural; biqahal Yahuah. 'al tatipu yatiypun; la'
**a cord by lot in the congregation of Yahuah not Prophesy you *say they to them that* prophesy not**

יטפו 5197 לאלה 428 לא 3808 יסג 5253 כלמות 3639: **2:7** האמור 559 בית 1004 יעקב 3290
yatipu la'aleh, la' yisag kalimout. he'amur beyt ya'aqob,
**they shall prophesy to them not *that* they shall take shame O *you that are* named the house of Jacob**

הקצר 7114 רוח 7307 יהוה 3068 אם 518 אלה 428 מעלליו 4611 הלוא 3808 דברי 1697 ייטיבו 3190 עם 5973 הישר 3477
haqatzar ruach Yahuah, 'am 'aeleh ma'alalayu; halou'a dabaray yeytiybu, 'am hayashar
**is straitened? the spirit of Yahuah *are* if these his doings? *do* not my words do good to uprightly?**

הולך 1980: **2:8** ואתמול 865 עמי 5971 לאויב 341 יקומם 6965 ממול 4136 שלמה 8008 אדר 145 תפשטון 6584
houlek. ua'atamul, 'amiy la'auyeb yaqoumem, mimul salmah, 'ader tapshitun;
**him that walk Even of late my people as an enemy is risen up with the garment the robe you pull off**

**Micah** 2:1 Woe to them that devise iniquity, and work evil upon their beds! when the morning is light, they practise it, because it is in the power of their hand.2 And they covet fields, and take them by violence; and houses, and take them away: so they oppress a man and his house, even a man and his heritage.3 Therefore thus saith YHUH; Behold, against this family do I devise an evil, from which you shall not remove your necks; neither shall you go haughtily: for this time is evil.4 In that day shall one take up a parable against you, and lament with a doleful lamentation, and say, We be utterly spoiled: he has changed the portion of my people: how has he removed it from me! turning away he has divided our fields.5 Therefore you shall have none that shall cast a cord by lot in the congregation of YHUH.6 Prophesy you not, say they to them that prophesy: they shall not prophesy to them, that they shall not take shame.7 O you that are named the house of Jacob, is the spirit of YHUH straitened? are these his doings? do not my words do good to him that walk uprightly?8 Even of late my people is risen up as an enemy: you pull off the robe with the garment from them that pass by securely as men averse from war.

2:9
מעברים 5674 בטח 983 שובי 7725 מלחמה 4421: נשי 802 עמי 5971 תגרשון 1644 מבית 1004
me'abariym betach, shubey milchamah. nashey 'amiy tagarashun, mibeyt
**from them that pass by securely *as* men averse from war The women of my people have you cast out from houses**

2:10
תענגיה 8588 מעל 5921 עלליה 5768 תקחו 3947 הדרי 1926 לעולם 5769: קומו 6965 ולכו 1980 כי 3588 לא 3808 זאת 2063
ta'anugeyha; me'al 'alaleyha, tiqchu hadariy la'aulam. qumu ualku, kiy la' za't
**their pleasant from their children have you taken away my glory for ever Arise you and depart for no this *is***

2:11
המנוחה 4496 בעבור 5668 טמאה 2930 תחבל 2254 וחבל 2256 נמרץ 4834: לו 3863 איש 376 הלך 1980 רוח 7307
hamanuchah; ba'abur tama'ah tachabel uachebel nimratz. lou' 'aysh halek ruach
***your* rest because it is polluted it shall destroy *you* even destruction with a sore If a man walking in the spirit**

ושקר 8267 כזב 3576 אטף 5197 לך 3807a לייז 3196 ולשכר 7941 והיה 1961 מטיף 5197
uasheqer kizeb, 'atip laka, layayin ualashekar; uahayah matiyp
**and falsehood do lie *saying* I will prophesy unto you of wine and of strong drink he shall even be the prophet of**

2:12
העם 5971 הזה 2088: אסף 622 אאסף 622 יעקב 3290 כלך 3605 קבץ 6908 אקבץ 6908 שארית 7611 ישראל 3478 יחד 3162
ha'am hazeh. 'asoup 'a'asop ya'aqob kulak, qabetz 'aqabetz sha'aeriyt yisra'ael, yachad
**the people this I will surely assemble O Jacob all of you I will surely gather the remnant of Israel together**

אשימנו 7760 כצאן 6629 בצרה 1223 כעדר 5739 בתוך 8432 הדברו 1699 תהימנה 1949
'asiymenu katza'n batzarah ka'aeder batouk hadabarou, tahiymenah
**I will put them as the sheep Bozrah as the flock in the midst of their fold they shall make great noise**

2:13
מאדם 120: עלה 5927 הפרץ 6555 לפניהם 6440 פרצו 6555 ויעברו 5674
me'adam. 'alah haporetz lipneyhem, paratzu uaya'aboru,
**by reason of *the multitude of* men is come up The breaker before them they have broken up and have passed through**

שער 8179 ויצאו 3318 בו 871a ויעבר 5674 מלכם 4428 לפניהם 6440 ויהוה 3068 בראשם 7218:
sha'ar uayetzea'u bou; uaya'abor malkam lipneyhem, uaYahuah bara'sham.
**the gate and are gone out by it and shall pass their king before them and Yahuah on the head of them**

**Mic 3:1**
ואמר 559 שמעו 8085 נא 4994 ראשי 7218 יעקב 3290 וקציני 7101 בית 1004 ישראל 3478 הלוא 3808 לכם 3807a
ua'amar, shim'au naa' ra'shey ya'aqob, uaqtziyney beyt yisra'ael; halou'a lakem,
**And I said Hear I pray you O heads of Jacob and you princes of the house of Israel *Is it* not for you**

3:2
לדעת 3045 את 853 המשפט 4941: שנאי 8130 טוב 2896 ואהבי 157 רעה 7451 גזלי 1497 עורם 5785 מעליהם 5921 ושארם 7607
lada'at 'at hamishpat. sona'aey toub ua'ahabey ra'ah gozaley auram me'aleyhem, usha'aeram
**to know judgment? Who hate the good and love the evil who pluck off their skin from off them and their flesh**

3:3
מעל 5921 עצמותם 6106: ואשר 834 אכלו 398 שאר 7607 עמי 5971 ועורם 5785 מעליהם 5921 הפשיטו 6584 ואת 853
me'al atzmoutam. ua'asher 'akalu sha'aer 'amiy ua'auram me'aleyhem hipshiytu, ua'at
**from off their bones Who also eat the flesh of my people and their skin from off them flay *and***

3:4
עצמתיהם 6106 פצחו 6476 ופרשו 6566 כאשר 834 בסיר 5518 וכבשר 1320 בתוך 8432 קלחת 7037: אז 227 יזעקו 2199
'atzmouteyhem pitzechu; uaparasu ka'asher basiyr, uakbasar batouk qalachat. 'az yiz'aqu
**their bones they break and chop them in pieces as for the pot and as flesh within the caldron Then shall they cry**

Micah 2:9 The women of my people have you cast out from their pleasant houses; from their children have you taken away my glory forever.10 Arise you, and depart; for this is not your rest: because it is polluted, it shall destroy you, even with a sore destruction.11 If a man walking in the spirit and falsehood do lie, saying, I will prophesy unto you of wine and of strong drink; he shall even be the prophet of this people.12 I will surely assemble, O Jacob, all of you; I will surely gather the remnant of Israel; I will put them together as the sheep of Bozrah, as the flock in the midst of their fold: they shall make great noise by reason of the multitude of men.13 The breaker is come up before them: they have broken up, and have passed through the gate, and are gone out by it: and their king shall pass before them, and YHUH on the head of them. **Micah** 3:1 And I said, Hear, I pray you, O heads of Jacob, and you princes of the house of Israel; Is it not for you to know judgment?2 Who hate the good, and love the evil; who pluck off their skin from off them, and their flesh from off their bones;3 Who also eat the flesh of my people, and flay their skin from off them; and they break their bones, and chop them in pieces, as for the pot, and as flesh within the caldron.4 Then shall they cry unto YHUH, but he will not hear them:

| אל 413 | יהוה 3068 | ולא 3808 | יענה 6030 | אותם 853 | ויסתר 5641 | פניו 6440 | מהם 1992 | בעת 6256 | ההיא 1931 | כאשר 834 |
|---|---|---|---|---|---|---|---|---|---|---|
| 'al | Yahuah, | uala' | ya'aneh | 'autam; | uayaster | panayu | mehem | ba'aet | hahiy'a, | ka'asher |
| **unto** | **Yahuah** | **but not** | **he will hear** | **them** | **he will even hide** | **his face** | **from them** | **at time** | **that** | **as** |

| הרעו 7489 | מעלליהם 4611: | 3:5 | כה 3541 | אמר 559 | יהוה 3068 | על 5921 | הנביאים 5030 | המתעים 8582 | את 853 |
|---|---|---|---|---|---|---|---|---|---|
| here'au | ma'alleyhem. | | koh | 'amar | Yahuah, | 'al | hanabiy'aym | hamat'aym | 'at |
| **they have behaved themselves ill** | **in their doings** | | **Thus** | **saith** | **Yahuah** | **concerning** | **the prophets** | **that make err** | |

| עמי 5971 | הנשכים 5391 | בשניהם 8127 | וקראו 7121 | שלום 7965 | ואשר 834 | לא 3808 | יתן 5414 | על 5921 | פיהם 6310 | וקדשו 6942 |
|---|---|---|---|---|---|---|---|---|---|---|
| 'amiy; | hanoshakiym | bashineyhem | uaqar'au | shaloum, | ua'asher | la' | yiten | 'al | piyhem, | uaqidshu |
| **my people** | **that bite** | **with their teeth** | **and cry** | **Peace** | **and who** | **not** | **he that put** | **into** | **their mouths** | **they even prepare** |

| עליו 5921 | מלחמה 4421: | 3:6 | לכן 3651 | לילה 3915 | לכם 3807a | מחזון 2377 | וחשכה 2821 | לכם 3807a |
|---|---|---|---|---|---|---|---|---|
| 'alayu | milchamah. | | laken | layalah | lakem | mechazoun, | uachashakah | lakem |
| **against him** | **war** | | **Therefore** | **night *shall be*** | **unto you** | ***that you shall* not have a vision** | **and it shall be dark** | **unto you** |

| מקסם 7080 | ובאה 935 | השמש 8121 | על 5921 | הנביאים 5030 | וקדר 6937 | עליהם 5921 | היום 3117: | 3:7 |
|---|---|---|---|---|---|---|---|---|
| miqsom; | uaba'ah | hashemesh | 'al | hanabiy'aym, | uaqadar | 'aleyhem | hayoum. | |
| ***that you shall* not divine** | **and shall go down** | **the sun** | **over** | **the prophets** | **and shall be dark** | **over them** | **the day** | |

| ובשו 954 | החזים 2374 | וחפרו 2659 | הקסמים 7080 | ועטו 5844 | על 5921 | שפם 8222 | כלם 3605 | כי 3588 |
|---|---|---|---|---|---|---|---|---|
| uaboshu | hachoziym, | uachaparu | haqosamiym, | ua'atou | 'al | sapam | kulam; | kiy |
| **Then shall be ashamed** | **the seers** | **and confounded** | **the diviners** | **yea they shall cover** | **over** | **their lips** | **will all** | **for** |

| אין 369 | מענה 4617 | אלהים 430: | 3:8 | ואולם 199 | אנכי 595 | מלאתי 4390 | כח 3581 | את 853 | רוח 7307 | יהוה 3068 | ומשפט 4941 |
|---|---|---|---|---|---|---|---|---|---|---|---|
| 'aeyn | ma'aneh | 'alohiym. | | ua'aulam, | 'anokiy | malea'tiy | koach | 'at | ruach | Yahuah, | uamishpat |
| ***there is* no** | **answer of** | **Elohim** | | **But truly** | **I** | **am full of** | **power *by*** | | **the spirit of** | **Yahuah** | **and of judgment** |

| וגבורה 1369 | להגיד 5046 | ליעקב 3290 | פשעו 6588 | ולישראל 3478 | חטאתו 2403: | 3:9 | שמעו 8085 | נא 4994 | זאת 2063 | ראשי 7218 |
|---|---|---|---|---|---|---|---|---|---|---|
| uagaburah; | lahagiyd | laya'aqob | pish'au, | ualyisra'ael | chata'tou. | | shim'au | naa' | za't, | ra'shey |
| **and of might** | **to declare** | **unto Jacob** | **his transgression** | **and to Israel** | **his sin** | | **Hear you** | **I pray you** | **this** | **heads of** |

| בית 1004 | יעקב 3290 | וקציני 7101 | בית 1004 | ישראל 3478 | המתעבים 8581 | משפט 4941 | ואת 853 | כל 3605 | הישרה 3477 | יעקשו 6140: | 3:10 |
|---|---|---|---|---|---|---|---|---|---|---|---|
| beyt | ya'aqob, | uaqtziyney | beyt | yisra'ael; | hamata'abiym | mishapat, | ua'at | kal | hayasharah | ya'aqeshu. | |
| **the house of** | **Jacob** | **and princes of** | **the house of** | **Israel** | **that abhor** | **judgment *and*** | | **all** | **equity** | **pervert** | |

| בנה 1129 | ציון 6726 | בדמים 1818 | וירושלם 3389 | בעולה 5766: | 3:11 | ראשיה 7218 | בשחד 7810 | ישפטו 8199 |
|---|---|---|---|---|---|---|---|---|
| boneh | tziyoun | badamiym; | uiyarushalaim | ba'aulah. | | ra'sheyha | bashochad | yishpotu, |
| **They build up** | **Zion** | **with blood** | **and Jerusalem** | **with iniquity** | | **The heads thereof** | **for reward** | **judge** |

| וכהניה 3548 | במחיר 4242 | יורו 3384 | ונביאיה 5030 | בכסף 3701 | יקסמו 7080 | ועל 5921 | יהוה 3068 | ישענו 8172 |
|---|---|---|---|---|---|---|---|---|
| uakohaneyha | bimachiyr | youru, | uanbiy'ayha | bakesep | yiqasomu; | ua'al | Yahuah | yisha'aenu |
| **and the priests thereof** | **for hire** | **teach** | **and the prophets thereof** | **for money** | **divine** | **yet upon** | **Yahuah** | **will they lean** |

| לאמר 559 | הלוא 3808 | יהוה 3068 | בקרבנו 7130 | לא 3808 | תבוא 935 | עלינו 5921 | רעה 7451: | 3:12 | לכן 3651 | בגללכם 1558 | ציון 6726 | שדה 7704 |
|---|---|---|---|---|---|---|---|---|---|---|---|---|
| lea'mor, | halou'a | Yahuah | baqirbenu, | la' | tabou'a | 'aleynu | ra'ah. | | laken | biglalakem, | tziyoun | sadeh |
| **say** | ***Is* not none** | **Yahuah** | **among us?** | **will not** | **can come** | **upon us** | **evil** | | **Therefore** | **for your sake** | **Zion** | ***as* a field** |

Micah 3:4 he will even hide his face from them at that time, as they have behaved themselves ill in their doings.5 Thus saith YHUH concerning the prophets that make my people err, that bite with their teeth, and cry, Peace; and he that put not into their mouths, they even prepare war against him.6 Therefore night shall be unto you, that you shall not have a vision; and it shall be dark unto you, that you shall not divine; and the sun shall go down over the prophets, and the day shall be dark over them.7 Then shall the seers be ashamed, and the diviners confounded: yea, they shall all cover their lips; for there is no answer of G-d.8 But truly I am full of power by the spirit of YHUH, and of judgment, and of might, to declare unto Jacob his transgression, and to Israel his sin.9 Hear this, I pray you, you heads of the house of Jacob, and princes of the house of Israel, that abhor judgment, and pervert all equity.10 They build up Zion with blood, and Jerusalem with iniquity.11 The heads thereof judge for reward, and the priests thereof teach for hire, and the prophets thereof divine for money: yet will they lean upon YHUH, and say, Is not YHUH among us? none evil can come upon us.12 Therefore shall Zion for your sake be plowed as a field, and Jerusalem shall become heaps, and the mountain of the house as the high places of the forest.

תחרש 2790 וירושלם 3389 עיין 5856 תהיה 1961 והר 2022 הבית 1004 לבמות 1116 יער 3293:
techaresh; uiyarushalaim 'ayiyn tihayeh, uahar habayit labamout ya'ar.
**shall be plowed and Jerusalem heaps shall become and the mountain of the house as the high places of the forest**

**Mic 4:1**
והיה 1961 באחרית 319 הימים 3117 יהיה 1961 הר 2022 בית 1004 יהוה 3068 נכון 3559
uahayah ba'achariyt hayamiym, yihayeh har beyt Yahuah nakoun
**But in the last days it shall come to pass *that* the mountain of the house of Yahuah established**

בראש 7218 ההרים 2022 ונשא 5375 הוא 1931 מגבעות 1389 ונהרו 5102 עליו 5921 עמים 5971: **4:2** והלכו 1980
bara'sh heharim, uanisa' hua' migba'aut; uanaharu 'alayu 'amiym uahalaku
**in the top of the mountains and shall be exalted it above the hills and shall flow unto it people And shall come**

גוים 1471 רבים 7227 ואמרו 559 לכו 1980 ונעלה 5927 אל 413 הר 2022 יהוה 3069 ואל 413 בית 1004 אלהי 430 יעקב 3290
gouyim rabiym, ua'amaru laku uana'aleh 'al har Yahuah ua'al beyt 'alohey ya'aqob,
**nations many and say Come and let us go up to the mountain of Yahuah and to the house of the Elohim of Jacob**

ויורנו 3384 מדרכיו 1870 ונלכה 1980 בארחתיו 734 כי 3588 מציון 6726 תצא 3318 תורה 8451 ודבר 1697
uayourenu midrakayu, uanelakah ba'arachotayu; kiy mitziyoun tetzea' tourah, uadbar
**and he will teach us of his ways and we will walk in his paths for of Zion shall go forth the law and the word of**

יהוה 3069 מירושלם 3389: **4:3** ושפט 8199 בין 996 עמים 5971 רבים 7227 והוכיח 3198 לגוים 1471 עצמים 6099 עד 5704 רחוק 7350
Yahuah miyarushalaim. uashapat, beyn 'amiym rabiym, uahoukiyach lagouyim 'atzumiym 'ad rachouq;
**Yahuah from Jerusalem And he shall judge among people many and rebuke nations strong afar off**

וכתתו 3807 חרבתיהם 2719 לאתים 855 וחניתתיהם 2595 למזמרות 4211 לא 3808 ישאו 5375 גוי 1471 אל 413
uakitatu charboteyhem la'atiym, uachaniytoteyhem lamazmerout, la' yis'au gouy 'al
**and they shall beat their swords into plowshares and their spears into pruninghooks not shall lift up nation against**

גוי 1471 חרב 2719 ולא 3808 ילמדון 3925 עוד 5750 מלחמה 4421: **4:4** וישבו 3427 איש 376 תחת 8478 גפנו 1612 ותחת 8478
gouy chereb, uala' yilmadun 'aud milchamah. uayashabu, 'aysh tachat gapnou uatachat
**nation a sword and neither shall they learn any more war But they shall sit every man under his vine and under**

תאנתו 8384 ואין 369 מחריד 2729 כי 3588 פי 6310 יהוה 3068 צבאות 6635 דבר 1696: **4:5** כי 3588 כל 3605 העמים 5971
ta'aenatou ua'aeyn machariyd; kiy piy Yahuah tzaba'aut diber. kiy kal ha'amiym,
**his fig tree and none shall make *them* afraid for the mouth of Yahuah of hosts has spoken *it* For all people**

ילכו 1980 איש 376 בשם 8034 אלהיו 430 ואנחנו 587 נלך 1980 בשם 8034 יהוה 3068 אלהינו 430 לעולם 5769 ועד 5703: **4:6**
yelaku 'aysh bashem 'alohayu; ua'anachnu, nelek bashem Yahuah 'aloheynu la'aulam ua'ad.
**will walk every one in the name of his god and we will walk in the name of Yahuah our Elohim for ever and ever**

ביום 3117 ההוא 1931 נאם 5002 יהוה 3068 אספה 622 הצלעה 6760 והנדחה 5080 אקבצה 6908 ואשר 834
bayoum hahua' na'am Yahuah 'asapah hatzole'ah, uahanidachah 'aqabetzah; ua'asher
**In day that saith Yahuah will I assemble her that halteth and her that is driven out I will gather and her that**

הרעתי 7489: **4:7** ושמתי 7760 את 853 הצלעה 6760 לשארית 7611 והנהלאה 1972 לגוי 1471 עצום 6099
hare'atiy. uasamtiy 'at hatzole'ah lish'aeriyt, uahanahala'ah lagouy 'atzum;
**I have afflicted And I will make her that halted a remnant and her that was cast far off a nation strong**

**Micah** 4:1 But in the last days it shall come to pass, that the mountain of the house of YHUH shall be established in the top of the mountains, and it shall be exalted above the hills; and people shall flow unto it.2 And many nations shall come, and say, Come, and let us go up to the mountain of YHUH, and to the house of the G-d of Jacob; and he will teach us of his ways, and we will walk in his paths: for the law shall go forth of Zion, and the word of YHUH from Jerusalem.3 And he shall judge among many people, and rebuke strong nations afar off; and they shall beat their swords into plowshares, and their spears into pruninghooks: nation shall not lift up a sword against nation, neither shall they learn war anymore.4 But they shall sit every man under his vine and under his fig tree; and none shall make them afraid: for the mouth of YHUH of hosts has spoken it.5 For all people will walk everyone in the name of his god, and we will walk in the name of YHUH our G-d forever and ever.6 In that day, saith YHUH, will I assemble her that halteth, and I will gather her that is driven out, and her that I have afflicted;7 And I will make her that halted a remnant, and her that was cast far off a strong nation: and YHUH shall reign over them in mount Zion from henceforth, even forever.

ומלך 4427 יהוה 3068 עליהם 5921 בהר 2022 ציון 6726 מעתה 6258 ועד 5704 עולם 5769: **4:8** ואתה 859 מגדל 4026 עדר 5739
uamalak Yahuah 'aleyhem bahar tziyoun, me'atah ua'ad 'aulam. ua'atah migdal 'aeder,
**and shall reign Yahuah over them in mount Zion from henceforth and even forever And you O tower of the flock**

עפל 6076 בת 1323 ציון 6726 עדיך 5704 תאתה 857 ובאה 935 הממשלה 4475 הראשנה 7223 ממלכת 4467
'apel bat tziyoun 'adeyka tea'teh; uaba'ah, hamemshalah hara'shonah, mamleket
**the strong hold of the daughter of Zion unto you shall it come even shall come dominion the first the kingdom**

לבת 1323 ירושלם 3389: **4:9** עתה 6258 למה 4100 תריעי 7321 רע 7452 המלך 4428 אין 369 בך 871a אם 518 יועצך 3289
labat yarushalaim. 'atah lamah tariy'ay rea'; hamelek 'aeyn bak, 'am you'atzek
**to the daughter of Jerusalem Now why do you cry out aloud? king is there no in you? or your counsellor**

אבד 6 כי 3588 החזיקך 2388 חיל 2427 כיולדה 3205: **4:10** חולי 2342 וגחי 1518 בת 1323
'abad, kiy hecheziyqek chiyl kayouledah. chuliy uagochiy bat
**is perished? for have taken you pangs as a woman in travail Be in pain and labour to bring forth O daughter of**

ציון 6726 כיולדה 3205 כי 3588 עתה 6258 תצאי 3318 מקריה 7151 ושכנת 7931 בשדה 7704
tziyoun kayouledah; kiy 'atah tetza'ay miqiryah uashakant basadeh,
**Zion like a woman in travail for now shall you go forth out of the city and you shall dwell in the field**

ובאת 935 עד 5704 בבל 894 שם 8033 תנצלי 5337 שם 8033 יגאלך 1350 יהוה 3068 מכף 3709
uaba'at 'ad babel sham tinatzeliy, sam yig'alek Yahuah, mikap
**and you shall go *even* to Babylon there shall you be delivered there shall redeem you Yahuah from the hand of**

איביך 341: **4:11** ועתה 6258 נאספו 622 עליך 5921 גוים 1471 רבים 7227 האמרים 559 תחנף 2610 ותחז 2372 בציון 6726
'ayabayik. ua'atah ne'aspu 'aleyka gouyim rabiym; ha'amariym techanap, uatachaz batziyoun
**your enemies Now also are gathered against you nations many that say Let her be defiled and let look upon Zion**

עינינו 5869: **4:12** והמה 1992 לא 3808 ידעו 3045 מחשבות 4284 יהוה 3068 ולא 3808 הבינו 995 עצתו 6098 כי 3588
'aeyneynu. uahemah, la' yada'au machashabout Yahuah, uala' hebiynu atzatou; kiy
**our eye But they not know the thoughts of Yahuah neither understand they his counsel for**

קבצם 6908 כעמיר 5995 גרנה 1637: **4:13** קומי 6965 ודושי 1758 בת 1323 ציון 6726 כי 3588 קרנך 7161
qibtzam ke'amiyr goranah. quamiy uadoushiy bat tziyoun, kiy qarnek
**he shall gather them as the sheaves into the floor Arise and thresh O daughter of Zion for your horn**

אשים 7760 ברזל 1270 ופרסתיך 6541 אשים 7760 נחושה 5154 והדקות 1854 עמים 5971 רבים 7227 והחרמתי 2763
'asiym barzel uaparsotayik 'asiym nachushah, uahadiqout 'amiym rabiym; uahacharamtiy
**I will make iron and your hoofs I will make brass and you shall beat in pieces people many and I will consecrate**

ליהוה 3068 בצעם 1214 וחילם 2428 לאדון 113 כל 3605 הארץ 776:
laYahuah bitz'am, uacheylam la'adon kal ha'aretz.
**unto Yahuah their gain and their substance unto Adonai of whole the earth**

**Mic 5:1** עתה 6258 תתגדדי 1413 בת 1323 גדוד 1416 מצור 4692 שם 7760 עלינו 5921 בשבט 7626 יכו 5221
'atah titgodadiy bat gadud, matzour sam 'aleynu; bashebet yaku
**Now gather yourself in troops O daughter troops siege he has laid against us with a rod they shall smite**

Micah 4:8 And you, O tower of the flock, the strong hold of the daughter of Zion, unto you shall it come, even the first dominion; the kingdom shall come to the daughter of Jerusalem.9 Now why dost you cry out aloud? is there no king in you? is your counselor perished? for pangs have taken you as a woman in travail.10 Be in pain, and labour to bring forth, O daughter of Zion, like a woman in travail: for now shall you go forth out of the city, and you shall dwell in the field, and you shall go even to Babylon; there shall you be delivered; there YHUH shall redeem you from the hand of your enemies.11 Now also many nations are gathered against you, that say, Let her be defiled, and let our eye look upon Zion.12 But they know not the thoughts of YHUH, neither understand they his counsel: for he shall gather them as the sheaves into the floor.13 Arise and thresh, O daughter of Zion: for I will make your horn iron, and I will make your hoofs brass: and you shall beat in pieces many people: and I will consecrate their gain unto YHUH, and their substance unto YHUH of the whole earth. **Micah** 5:1 Now gather thyself in troops, O daughter of troops: he has laid siege against us: they shall smite the judge of Israel with a rod upon the cheek.

| על 5921 | הלחי 3895 | את 853 | שפט 8199 | ישראל 3478: | 5:2 ואתה 859 | בית 1035 | לחם 3899 | אפרתה 672 | צעיר 6810 | להיות 1961 |
|---|---|---|---|---|---|---|---|---|---|---|
| 'al | halachiy, | 'at | shopet | yisra'ael. | ua'atah | beyt | lachem | 'apratah, | tza'ayr | lihayout |
| **upon** | **the cheek** | | **the judge of** | **Israel** | **But you** | **Beth** | **lehem** | **Ephratah** | **little *though*** | **you be** |

| באלפי 505 | יהודה 3063 | ממך 4480 | לי 3807a | יצא 3318 | להיות 1961 | מושל 4910 | בישראל 3478 |
|---|---|---|---|---|---|---|---|
| ba'alpey | yahudah, | mimaka | liy | yetzea', | lihayout | moushel | bayisra'ael; |
| **among the thousands of** | **Judah** | ***yet* out of you** | **unto me** | **shall he come forth** | ***that is* to be** | **ruler** | **in Israel** |

| ומוצאתיו 4163 | מקדם 6924 | מימי 3117 | עולם 5769: | 5:3 לכן 3651 | יתנם 5414 | עד 5704 | עת 6256 |
|---|---|---|---|---|---|---|---|
| uamoutza'atayu | miqedem | miymey | 'aulam. | laken | yitanem, | 'ad | 'at |
| **whose goings forth of him** | ***have been* from of old** | **from days of** | **everlasting** | **Therefore** | **will he give them up** | **until** | **the time** |

| יולדה 3205 | ילדה 3205 | ויתר 3499 | אחיו 251 | ישובון 7725 | על 5921 | בני 1121 | ישראל 3478: 5:4 |
|---|---|---|---|---|---|---|---|
| youledah | yaladah; | uayeter | 'achiyu, | yashubun | 'al | baney | yisra'ael. |
| ***that* she which travail** | **has brought forth** | **then the remnant of** | **his brethren** | **shall return** | **unto** | **the children of** | **Israel** |

| ועמד 5975 | ורעה 7462 | בעז 5797 | יהוה 3069 | בגאון 1347 | שם 8034 | יהוה 3069 | אלהיו 430 |
|---|---|---|---|---|---|---|---|
| ua'amad, | uara'ah | ba'az | Yahuah, | big'aun | shem | Yahuah | 'alohayu; |
| **And he shall stand** | **and feed** | **in the strength of** | **Yahuah** | **in the majesty of** | **the name of** | **Yahuah** | **his Elohim** |

| וישבו 3427 | כי 3588 | עתה 6258 | יגדל 1431 | עד 5704 | אפסי 657 | ארץ 776: | 5:5 והיה 1961 | זה 2088 | שלום 7965 |
|---|---|---|---|---|---|---|---|---|---|
| uayashabu | kiy | 'atah | yigdal | 'ad | 'apsey | 'aretz. | uahayah | zeh | shaloum; |
| **and they shall abide** | **for** | **now** | **shall he be great** | **unto** | **the ends of** | **the earth** | **And shall be** | **this** | ***man* the peace** |

| אשור 804 | כי 3588 | יבוא 935 | בארצנו 776 | וכי 3588 | ידרך 1869 | בארמנתינו 759 | והקמנו 6965 | עליו 5921 |
|---|---|---|---|---|---|---|---|---|
| 'ashur | kiy | yabou'a | ba'artzenu, | uakiy | yidrok | ba'armanoteynu, | uahaqemonu | 'alayu |
| **the Assyrian** | **when** | **shall come** | **into our land** | **and when** | **he shall tread** | **in our palaces** | **then shall we raise** | **against him** |

| שבעה 7651 | רעים 7462 | ושמנה 8083 | נסיכי 5257 | אדם 120: | 5:6 ורעו 7462 | את 853 | ארץ 776 | אשור 804 | בחרב 2719 | ואת 853 |
|---|---|---|---|---|---|---|---|---|---|---|
| shib'ah | ro'aym, | uashmonah | nasiykey | 'adam. | uar'au | 'at | 'aretz | 'ashur | bachereb, | ua'at |
| **seven** | **shepherds** | **and eight** | **principal** | **men** | **And they shall waste** | | **the land of** | **Assyria** | **with the sword** | ***and*** |

| ארץ 776 | נמרד 5248 | בפתחיה 6607 | והציל 5337 | מאשור 804 | כי 3588 | יבוא 935 | בארצנו 776 |
|---|---|---|---|---|---|---|---|
| 'aretz | nimrod | bipatacheyha; | uahitziyl | me'ashur, | kiy | yabou'a | ba'artzenu, |
| **the land of** | **Nimrod** | **in the entrances thereof** | **thus shall he deliver** | ***us* from the Assyrian** | **when** | **he comes** | **into our land** |

| וכי 3588 | ידרך 1869 | בגבולנו 1366: | 5:7 והיה 1961 | שארית 7611 | יעקב 3290 | בקרב 7130 | עמים 5971 | רבים 7227 | כטל 2919 |
|---|---|---|---|---|---|---|---|---|---|
| uakiy | yidrok | bigabulenu. | uahayah | sha'aeriyt | ya'aqob, | baqereb | 'amiym | rabiym, | katal |
| **and when** | **he tread** | **within our borders** | **And shall be** | **the remnant of** | **Jacob** | **in the midst of** | **people** | **many** | **as a dew** |

| מאת 853 | יהוה 3068 | כרביבים 7241 | עלי 5921 | עשב 6212 | אשר 834 | לא 3808 | יקוה 6960 | לאיש 376 | ולא 3808 | ייחל 3176 | לבני 1121 | אדם 120: 5:8 |
|---|---|---|---|---|---|---|---|---|---|---|---|---|
| me'at | Yahuah, | kirbiybiym | 'aley | 'aeseb; | 'asher | la' | yaqaueh | la'aysh, | uala' | yayachel | libney | 'adam. |
| **from** | **Yahuah** | **as the showers** | **upon** | **the grass** | **that** | **not** | **tarry** | **for man** | **nor** | **wait** | **for the sons of** | **men** |

| והיה 1961 | שארית 7611 | יעקב 3290 | בגוים 1471 | בקרב 7130 | עמים 5971 | רבים 7227 | כאריה 738 | בבהמות 929 |
|---|---|---|---|---|---|---|---|---|
| uahayah | sha'aeriyt | ya'aqob | bagouyim, | baqereb | 'amiym | rabiym, | ka'aryeh | babahamout |
| **And shall be** | **the remnant of** | **Jacob** | **among the Gentiles** | **in the midst of** | **people** | **many** | **as a lion** | **among the beasts of** |

Micah 5:2 But you, Bethlehem Ephratah, though you be little among the thousands of Judah, yet out of you shall he come forth unto me that is to be ruler in Israel; whose goings forth have been from of old, from everlasting.3 Therefore will he give them up, until the time that she which travaileth has brought forth: then the remnant of his brethren shall return unto the children of Israel.4 And he shall stand and feed in the strength of YHUH, in the majesty of the name of YHUH his G-d; and they shall abide: for now shall he be great unto the ends of the earth.5 And this man shall be the peace, when the Assyrian shall come into our land: and when he shall tread in our palaces, then shall we raise against him seven shepherds, and eight principal men.6 And they shall waste the land of Assyria with the sword, and the land of Nimrod in the entrances thereof: thus shall he deliver us from the Assyrian, when he cometh into our land, and when he treadeth within our borders.7 And the remnant of Jacob shall be in the midst of many people as a dew from YHUH, as the showers upon the grass, that tarried not for man, nor waiteth for the sons of men.8 And the remnant of Jacob shall be among the Gentiles in the midst of many people as a lion among the beasts of the forest, as a young lion among the flocks of sheep:

| יער 3293 | ככפיר 3715 | בעדרי 5739 | צאן 6629 | אשר 834 | אם 518 | עבר 5674 | ורמס 7429 | וטרף 2963 |
|---|---|---|---|---|---|---|---|---|
| ya'ar, | kikapiyr | be'adrey | tza'n; | 'asher | 'am | 'abar | uaramas | uatarap |
| **the forest** | **as a young lion** | **among the flocks of** | **sheep** | **who** | **if** | **he go through** | **both tread down** | **and tear in pieces** |

| ואין 369 | מציל 5337: | 5:9 | תרם 7311 | ידך 3027 | על 5921 | צריך 6862 | וכל 3605 | איביך 341 | יכרתו 3772: | 5:10 |
|---|---|---|---|---|---|---|---|---|---|---|
| ua'aeyn | matziyl. | | tarom | yadaka | 'al | tzareyka; | uakal | 'ayabeyka | yikaretu. | |
| **and none** | **can deliver** | | **shall be lifted up** | **Thine hand** | **upon** | **your adversaries** | **and all** | **your enemies** | **shall be cut off** | |

| והיה 1961 | ביום 3117 | ההוא 1931 | נאם 5002 | יהוה 3068 | והכרתי 3772 | סוסיך 5483 | מקרבך 7130 |
|---|---|---|---|---|---|---|---|
| uahayah | bayoum | hahua' | na'am | Yahuah, | uahikratiy | suseyka | miqirbeka; |
| **And it shall come to pass** | **in day** | **that** | **saith** | **Yahuah** | **that I will cut off** | **your horses** | **out of the midst of you** |

| והאבדתי 6 | מרכבתיך 4818: | 5:11 | והכרתי 3772 | ערי 5892 | ארצך 776 | והרסתי 2040 | כל 3605 | מבצריך 4013: | 5:12 |
|---|---|---|---|---|---|---|---|---|---|
| uaha'abadatiy | markaboteyka. | | uahikratiy | 'arey | 'artzeka; | uaharastiy | kal | mibtzareyka. | |
| **and I will destroy** | **your chariots** | | **And I will cut off** | **the cities of** | **your land** | **and throw down** | **all** | **your strong holds** | |

| והכרתי 3772 | כשפים 3785 | מידך 3027 | ומעוננים 6049 | לא 3808 | יהיו 1961 | לך 3807a: | 5:13 | והכרתי 3772 |
|---|---|---|---|---|---|---|---|---|
| uahikratiy | kashapiym | miyadeka; | uama'aunaniym | la' | yihayu | lak. | | uahikratiy |
| **And I will cut off** | **witchcrafts** | **out of your hand *more*** | **and soothsayers** | **no** | **shall have** | **to you** | | **also will I cut off** |

| פסיליך 6456 | ומצבותיך 4676 | מקרבך 7130 | ולא 3808 | תשתחוה 7812 | עוד 5750 | למעשה 4639 |
|---|---|---|---|---|---|---|
| pasiyleyka | uamatzebouteyka | miqirbeka; | uala' | tishtachaueh | 'aud | lama'aseh |
| **Your graven images** | **and your standing images** | **out of the midst of you** | **and no** | **you shall worship** | **more** | **the work of** |

| ידיך 3027: | 5:14 | ונתשתי 5428 | אשיריך 842 | מקרבך 7130 | והשמדתי 8045 | עריך 5892: | 5:15 | ועשיתי 6213 |
|---|---|---|---|---|---|---|---|---|
| yadeyka. | | uanatashtiy | 'asheyreyka | miqirbeka; | uahishmadtiy | 'areyka. | | ua'asiytiy |
| **your hands** | | **And I will pluck up** | **your groves** | **out of the midst of you** | **so will I destroy** | **your cities** | | **And I will execute** |

| באף 639 | ובחמה 2534 | נקם 5359 | את 853 | הגוים 1471 | אשר 834 | לא 3808 | שמעו 8085: |
|---|---|---|---|---|---|---|---|
| ba'ap | uabchemah | naqam | 'at | hagouyim; | 'asher | la' | shame'au. |
| **in anger** | **and fury** | **vengeance** | ***upon*** | **the heathen** | **such as** | **not** | **they have heard** |

| Mic 6:1 | שמעו 8085 | נא 4994 | את 853 | אשר 834 | יהוה 3068 | אמר 559 | קום 6965 | ריב 7378 | את 854 | ההרים 2022 | ותשמענה 8085 | הגבעות 1389 |
|---|---|---|---|---|---|---|---|---|---|---|---|---|
| | shim'au | naa' | 'at | 'asher | Yahuah | 'amer; | qum | riyb | 'at | hehariym, | uatishma'nah | hagaba'aut |
| | **Hear you** | **now** | | **what** | **Yahuah** | **saith** | **Arise** | **contend you** | ***before*** | **the mountains** | **and let hear** | **the hills** |

| קולך 6963: | 6:2 | שמעו 8085 | הרים 2022 | את 853 | ריב 7379 | יהוה 3069 | והאתנים 386 | מסדי 4146 | ארץ 776 | כי 3588 |
|---|---|---|---|---|---|---|---|---|---|---|
| qouleka. | | shim'au | hariym | 'at | riyb | Yahuah, | uaha'aetaniym | Mosedei | 'aretz; | kiy |
| **your voice** | | **Hear you** | **O mountains** | | **controversy** | **Yahuah** | **and you strong** | **foundations of** | **the earth** | **for** |

| ריב 7379 | ליהוה 3069 | עם 5973 | עמו 5971 | ועם 5973 | ישראל 3478 | יתוכח 3198: | 6:3 | עמי 5971 | מה 4100 | עשיתי 6213 | לך 3807a |
|---|---|---|---|---|---|---|---|---|---|---|---|
| riyb | laYahuah | 'am | 'amou, | ua'am | yisra'ael | yituakach. | | 'amiy | meh | 'asiytiy | laka |
| **has a controversy** | **Yahuah** | **with his** | **people** | **and with** | **Israel** | **he will plead** | | **O my people** | **what** | **have I done** | **unto you?** |

| ומה 4100 | הלאתיך 3811 | ענה 6030 | בי 871a: | 6:4 | כי 3588 | העלתיך 5927 | מארץ 776 | מצרים 4714 |
|---|---|---|---|---|---|---|---|---|
| uamah | hel'aetiyka; | 'aneh | biy. | | kiy | he'alitiyka | me'aretz | mitzrayim, |
| **and wherein** | **have I wearied you?** | **testify** | **against me** | | **For** | **I brought you up** | **out of the land of** | **Egypt** |

Micah 5:8 who, if he go through, both treadeth down, and teareth in pieces, and none can deliver.9 Thine hand shall be lifted up upon your adversaries, and all your enemies shall be cut off.10 And it shall come to pass in that day, saith YHUH, that I will cut off your horses out of the midst of you, and I will destroy your chariots:11 And I will cut off the cities of your land, and throw down all your strong holds:12 And I will cut off witchcrafts out of your hand; and you shall have no more soothsayers:13 Thy graven images also will I cut off, and your standing images out of the midst of you; and you shall no more worship the work of your hands.14 And I will pluck up your groves out of the midst of you: so will I destroy your cities.15 And I will execute vengeance in anger and fury upon the heathen, such as they have not heard. **Micah** 6:1 Hear you now what YHUH saith; Arise, contend you before the mountains, and let the hills hear your voice.2 Hear you, O mountains, YHUH's controversy, and you strong foundations of the earth: for YHUH has a controversy with his people, and he will plead with Israel.3 O my people, what have I done unto you? and wherein have I wearied you? testify against me.4 For I brought you up out of the land of Egypt, and redeemed you out of the house of servants; and I sent before you Moses, Aaron, and Miriam.

| ומבית 1004 | עבדים 5650 | פדיתיך 6299 | ואשלח 7971 | לפניך 6440 | את 853 | משה 4872 | אהרן 175 | ומרים 4813: | 6:5 |
|---|---|---|---|---|---|---|---|---|---|
| uamibeyt | 'abadiym | padiytiyka; | ua'ashlach | lapaneyka, | 'at | mosheh | 'aharon | uamiryam. | |
| **and out of the house of** | **servants** | ***and* redeemed you** | **and I sent** | **before you** | | **Moses** | **Aaron** | **and Miriam** | |

| עמי 5971 | זכר 2142 | נא 4994 | מה 4100 | יעץ 3289 | בלק 1111 | מלך 4428 | מואב 4124 | ומה 4100 | ענה 6030 | אתו 853 | בלעם 1109 | בן 1121 |
|---|---|---|---|---|---|---|---|---|---|---|---|---|
| 'amiy, | zakar | naa' | mah | ya'atz, | balaq | melek | mou'ab, | umeh | 'anah | 'atou | bil'am | ben |
| **O my people** | **remember** | **now** | **what** | **consulted** | **Balak** | **king of** | **Moab** | **and what** | **answered** | **him** | **Balaam** | **the son of** |

| בעור 1160 | מן 4480 | השטים 7851 | עד 5704 | הגלגל 1537 | למען 4616 | דעת 3045 | צדקות 6666 | יהוה 3068: | 6:6 | במה 1400 |
|---|---|---|---|---|---|---|---|---|---|---|
| ba'aur; | min | hashitiym | 'ad | hagilgal, | lama'an | da'at | tzidqout | Yahuah. | | bamah |
| **Beor** | **from** | **Shittim** | **unto** | **Gilgal** | **that** | **you may know** | **the righteousness of** | **Yahuah** | | **Wherewith** |

| אקדם 6923 | יהוה 3068 | אכף 3721 | לאלהי 430 | מרום 4791 | האקדמנו 6923 | בעולות 5930 |
|---|---|---|---|---|---|---|
| 'aqadem | Yahuah, | 'akap | le'alohey | maroum; | ha'aqadmenu | ua'alout, |
| **shall I come before** | **Yahuah** | ***and* bow myself** | **before Elohim?** | ***the* high** | **shall I come before him** | **with burnt offerings** |

| בעגלים 5695 | בני 1121 | שנה 8141: | 6:7 | הירצה 7521 | יהוה 3068 | באלפי 505 | אילים 352 | ברבבות 7233 | נחלי 5158 |
|---|---|---|---|---|---|---|---|---|---|
| ua'agaliym | baney | shanah. | | hayirtzeh | Yahuah | ba'alpey | 'aeyliym, | baribbout | nachaley |
| **with calves** | **of old?** | **a year** | | **Will be pleased** | **Yahuah** | **with thousands of** | **rams** | ***or* with ten thousands of** | **rivers of** |

| שמן 8081 | האתן 5414 | בכורי 1060 | פשעי 6588 | פרי 6529 | בטני 990 | חטאת 2403 | נפשי 5315: | 6:8 | הגיד 5046 |
|---|---|---|---|---|---|---|---|---|---|
| shamen; | ha'aten | bakouriy | pish'ay, | pariy | bitniy | chata't | napshiy. | | higiyd |
| **anointing oil?** | **shall I give** | **my firstborn *for*** | **my transgression** | **the fruit of** | **my body *for*** | **the sin of** | **my soul?** | | **He has showed** |

| לך 3807a | אדם 120 | מה 4100 | טוב 2896 | ומה 4100 | יהוה 3068 | דורש 1875 | ממך 4480 | כי 3588 | אם 518 | עשות 6213 | משפט 4941 | ואהבת 160 | חסד 2617 |
|---|---|---|---|---|---|---|---|---|---|---|---|---|---|
| laka | 'adam | mah | toub; | uamah | Yahuah | douresh | mimaka, | kiy | 'am | asout | mishapat | ua'ahabat | chesed, |
| **to you** | **O man** | **what** | ***is* good** | **and what** | **Yahuah** | **does require** | **of you** | **but** | **if** | **to do** | **justly** | **and to love** | **mercy** |

| והצנע 6800 | לכת 1980 | עם 5973 | אלהיך 430: | 6:9 | קול 6963 | יהוה 3068 | לעיר 5892 | יקרא 7121 | ותושיה 8454 | יראה 7200 |
|---|---|---|---|---|---|---|---|---|---|---|
| uahatznea' | laket | 'am | 'aloheyka. | | qoul | Yahuah | la'ayr | yiqra', | uatushiyah | yir'ah |
| **and humbly** | **walk** | **with** | **your Elohim?** | | **voice** | **Yahuah's** | **unto the city** | **cry** | **and *the man of* wisdom** | **shall see** |

| שמך 8034 | שמעו 8085 | מטה 4294 | ומי 4310 | יעדה 3259: | 6:10 | עוד 5750 | האש 786 | בית 1004 | רשע 7563 |
|---|---|---|---|---|---|---|---|---|---|
| shameka; | shim'au | mateh | uamiy | ya'adah. | | 'aud, | ha'aysh | beyt | rasha', |
| **your name** | **hear you** | **the rod** | **and who** | **has appointed it** | | **yet** | **Are there burning** | **in the house of** | **the wicked** |

| אצרות 214 | רשע 7562 | ואיפת 374 | רזון 7332 | זעומה 2194: | 6:11 | האזכה 2135 | במאזני 3976 |
|---|---|---|---|---|---|---|---|
| 'atzarout | resha'; | ua'aeypat | razoun | za'aumah. | | ha'azkeh | bama'zaney |
| **the treasures of** | **wickedness** | **and the measure** | **scant** | ***that is* abominable?** | | **Shall I count *them* pure** | **with the balances** |

| רשע 7562 | ובכיס 3599 | אבני 68 | מרמה 4820: | 6:12 | אשר 834 | עשיריה 6223 | מלאו 4390 | חמס 2555 |
|---|---|---|---|---|---|---|---|---|
| resha'; | uabkiys | 'abney | mirmah. | | 'asher | 'ashiyreyha | mala'au | chamas, |
| **wicked** | **and with the bag of** | **weights?** | **deceitful** | | **For** | **the rich men thereof** | **are full of** | **violence** |

| וישביה 3427 | דברו 1696 | שקר 8267 | ולשונם 3956 | רמיה 7423 | בפיהם 6310: | 6:13 | וגם 1571 | אני 589 |
|---|---|---|---|---|---|---|---|---|
| uayoshabeyha | dibru | shaqer; | ualshounam | ramiyah | bapiyhem. | | uagam | 'aniy |
| **and the inhabitants thereof** | **have spoken lies** | | **and their tongue *is* deceitful** | | **in their mouth** | | **Therefore also I** | |

Micah 6:5 O my people, remember now what Balak king of Moab consulted, and what Balaam the son of Beor answered him from Shittim unto Gilgal; that you may know the righteousness of YHUH.6 Wherewith shall I come before YHUH, and bow myself before the high G-d? shall I come before him with burnt offerings, with calves of a year old?7 Will YHUH be pleased with thousands of rams, or with ten thousands of rivers of oil? shall I give my firstborn for my transgression, the fruit of my body for the sin of my soul?8 He has showed you, O man, what is good; and what doth YHUH require of you, but to do justly, and to love mercy, and to walk humbly with your G-d?9 The YHUH's voice crieth unto the city, and the man of wisdom shall see your name: hear you the rod, and who has appointed it.10 Are there yet the treasures of wickedness in the house of the wicked, and the scant measure that is abominable?11 Shall I count them pure with the wicked balances, and with the bag of deceitful weights?12 For the rich men thereof are full of violence, and the inhabitants thereof have spoken lies, and their tongue is deceitful in their mouth.13 Therefore also will I make you sick in smiting you, in making you desolate because of your sins.

6:14

החליתי 2470 הכותך 5221 השמם 8074 על 5921 חטאתך 2403: אתה 859 תאכל 398 ולא 3808 תשבע 7646
hachilotiy hakouteka; hashamem 'al chata'teka. 'atah ta'kal uala' tisba',
**will make *you* sick in smiting you in making *you* desolate because of your sins You shall eat but not be satisfied**

וישחך 3445 בקרבך 7130 ותסג 5253 ולא 3808 תפליט 6403 ואשר 834 תפלט 6403
uayeshchaka baqirbeka; uataseg uala' tapliyt, ua'asher tapalet
**and your casting down *shall be* in the midst of you and you shall take hold but not shall deliver and *that* what you deliverest**

6:15

לחרב 2719 אתן 5414: אתה 859 תזרע 2232 ולא 3808 תקצור 7114 אתה 859 תדרך 1869 זית 2132 ולא 3808 תסוך 5480
lachereb 'aten. 'atah tizra' uala' tiqtzour; 'atah tidrok zayit uala' tasuk
**to the sword will I give up You shall sow but not you shall reap you shall tread the olives but not you shall anoint**

6:16

שמן 8081 ותירוש 8492 ולא 3808 תשתה 8354 יין 3196: וישתמר 8104 חקות 2708 עמרי 6018 וכל 3605 מעשה 4639
shemen, uatiyroush uala' tishteh yayin. uayishtamer chuqout 'amariy, uakol ma'aseh
***you with* oil and sweet wine but not shall drink wine For are kept the statutes of Omri and all the works of**

בית 1004 אחאב 256 ותלכו 1980 במעצותם 4156 למען 4616 תתי 5414 אתך 853 לשמה 8047 וישביה 3427
beyt 'ach'ab, uatelaku bamo'atzoutam; lama'an titiy 'atka lashamah, uayoshabeyha
**the house of Ahab and you walk in their counsels that I should make you a desolation and the inhabitants thereof**

לשרקה 8322 וחרפת 2781 עמי 5971 תשאו 5375:
lishreqah, uacherapat 'amiy tisa'au.
**an hissing thereof the reproach of my people you shall bear**

**Mic 7:1**

אללי 480 לי 3807a כי 3588 הייתי 1961 כאספי 625 קיץ 7019 כעללת 5955 בציר 1210
'alalay liy, kiy hayiytiy ka'asapey qayitz, ka'allot batziyr;
**Woe is me for I am as when they have gathered the summer fruits as the grapegleanings of the vintage**

7:2

אין 369 אשכול 811 לאכול 398 בכורה 1063 אותה 853 נפשי 5315: אבד 6 חסיד 2623 מן 4480 הארץ 776 וישר 3477
'aeyn ashkoul le'akoul, bikurah 'auatah napshiy. 'abad chasiyd min ha'aretz, uayashar
***there is* no cluster to eat the firstripe fruit desired my soul *man* is perished The good out of the earth and upright**

7:3

באדם 120 אין 369 כלם 3605 לדמים 1818 יארבו 693 איש 376 את 853 אחיהו 251 יצודו 6679 חרם 2764: על 5921
ba'adam 'ayin; kulam ladamiym ye'arobu, 'aysh 'at 'achiyhu yatzudu cherem. 'al
**among men *there is* none they all for blood lie in wait every man his brother they hunt *with* a net That**

הרע 7451 כפים 3709 להיטיב 3190 השר 8269 שאל 7592 והשפט 8199 בשלום 7966 והגדול 1419 דבר 1696
hara' kapayim laheytiyb, hasar sho'ael, uahashopet bashilum; uahagadoul, dober
***they may do* evil *with* both hands earnestly the prince ask and the judge *ask* for a reward and the great *man* he utter**

7:4

הות 1942 נפשו 5315 הוא 1931 ויעבתוה 5686: טובם 2896 כחדק 2312 ישר 3477
hauat napshou hua' uaya'abatuha. toubam kachedeq, yashar
**mischievous desire his so they wrap it up The best of them *is* as a brier *the most* upright**

ממסוכה 4534 יום 3117 מצפיך 6822 פקדתך 6486 באה 935 עתה 6258 תהיה 1961 מבוכתם 3998:
mimasukah; youm matzapeyka paqudataka ba'ah, 'atah tihayeh mabukatam.
***is sharper* than a thorn hedge the day of your watchmen *and* your visitation comes now shall be their perplexity**

Micah 6:14 Thou shall eat, but not be satisfied; and your casting down shall be in the midst of you; and you shall take hold, but shall not deliver; and that which you deliverest will I give up to the sword.15 Thou shall sow, but you shall not reap; you shall tread the olives, but you shall not anoint you with oil; and sweet wine, but shall not drink wine.16 For the statutes of Omri are kept, and all the works of the house of Ahab, and you walk in their counsels; that I should make you a desolation, and the inhabitants thereof an hissing: therefore you shall bear the reproach of my people. **Micah** 7:1 Woe is me! for I am as when they have gathered the summer fruits, as the grapegleanings of the vintage: there is no cluster to eat: my soul desired the firstripe fruit.2 The good man is perished out of the earth: and there is none upright among men: they all lie in wait for blood; they hunt every man his brother with a net.3 That they may do evil with both hands earnestly, the prince asketh, and the judge asketh for a reward; and the great man, he uttereth his mischievous desire: so they wrap it up.4 The best of them is as a brier: the most upright is sharper than a thorn hedge: the day of your watchmen and your visitation cometh; now shall be their perplexity.

| 7:5 אל 408 | תאמינו 539 | ברע 7453 | אל 408 | תבטחו 982 | באלוף 441 | משכבת 7901 | חיקך 2436 | שמר 8104 | פתחי 6607 |
|---|---|---|---|---|---|---|---|---|---|
| 'al | ta'amiynu | barea', | 'al | tibtachu | ba'alup; | mishokebet | cheyqeka, | shamor | pitchey |
| **not** | **Trust you** | **in a friend** | **not** | **put you confidence** | **in a guide** | **her that lies** | **in your bosom** | **keep from** | **the doors** |

| פיך 6310: | 7:6 כי 3588 | בן 1121 | מנבל 5034 | אב 1 | בת 1323 | קמה 6965 | באמה 517 | כלה 3618 |
|---|---|---|---|---|---|---|---|---|
| piyka. | kiy | ben | manabel | 'ab, | bat | qamah | ua'amah, | kalah |
| **of your mouth** | **For** | **the son** | **dishonors** | **the father** | **the daughter** | **rise up** | **against her mother** | **the daughter in law** |

| בחמתה 2545 | איבי 341 | איש 376 | אנשי 582 | ביתו 1004: | 7:7 ואני 589 | ביהוה 3068 | אצפה 6822 | אוחילה 3176 |
|---|---|---|---|---|---|---|---|---|
| bachamotah; | 'ayabey | 'aysh | 'anshey | beytou. | ua'aniy | baYahuah | 'atzapeh, | 'auchiylah |
| **against her mother in law** | **enemies** | **a man's** | ***are* the men of** | **his own house** | **Therefore I** | **unto Yahuah** | **will look** | **I will wait** |

| לאלהי 430 | ישעי 3468 | ישמעני 8085 | אלהי 430: | 7:8 אל 408 | תשמחי 8056 | איבתי 341 | לי 3807a | כי 3588 | נפלתי 5307 |
|---|---|---|---|---|---|---|---|---|---|
| le'alohey | yish'ay; | yishma'aeniy | 'alohay. | 'al | tismachiy | 'ayabtiy | liy, | kiy | napaltiy |
| **for the Elohim** | **of my salvation** | **will hear me** | **my Elohim** | **not** | **Rejoice** | **O mine enemy** | **against me** | **when** | **I fall** |

| קמתי 6965 | כי 3588 | אשב 3427 | בחשך 2822 | יהוה 3068 | אור 216 | לי 3807a: | 7:9 זעף 2197 | יהוה 3068 | אשא 5375 | כי 3588 |
|---|---|---|---|---|---|---|---|---|---|---|
| qamatiy; | kiy | 'aesheb | bachoshek, | Yahuah | 'aur | liy. | za'ap | Yahuah | 'asa', | kiy |
| **I shall arise** | **when** | **I sit** | **in darkness** | **Yahuah** | ***shall be* a light** | **unto me** | **the indignation of** | **Yahuah** | **I will bear** | **because** |

| חטאתי 2398 | לו 3807a | עד 5704 | אשר 834 | יריב 7378 | ריבי 7379 | ועשה 6213 | משפטי 4941 | יוציאני 3318 | לאור 216 |
|---|---|---|---|---|---|---|---|---|---|
| chata'tiy | lou'; | 'ad | 'asher | yariyb | riybiy | ua'asah | mishpatiy, | youtziy'aeniy | la'aur, |
| **I have sinned** | **against him** | **until** | **which** | **he plead** | **my cause** | **and execute** | **judgment for me** | **he will bring me forth** | **to the light** |

| אראה 7200 | בצדקתו 6666: | 7:10 ותרא 7200 | איבתי 341 | ותכסה 3680 | בושה 955 | האמרה 559 |
|---|---|---|---|---|---|---|
| 'ar'ah | batzidqatou. | uatera' | 'ayabtiy | uatkaseha | bushah, | ha'amarah |
| ***and* I shall behold** | **his righteousness** | **Then shall see *it*** | ***she that is* mine enemy** | **and shall cover her** | **shame** | **which said** |

| אלי 413 | איו 346 | יהוה 3068 | אלהיך 430 | עיני 5869 | תראינה 7200 | בה 871a | עתה 6258 | תהיה 1961 | למרמס 4823 | כטיט 2916 |
|---|---|---|---|---|---|---|---|---|---|---|
| 'aelay, | 'ayou | Yahuah | 'alohayik; | 'aeynay | tir'aynah | bah, | 'atah | tihayeh | lamirmas | katiyt |
| **unto me** | **Where** | ***is* Yahuah** | **your Elohim?** | **my eyes** | **shall behold** | **her** | **now** | **shall she be** | **trodden down** | **as the mire of** |

| חוצות 2351: | 7:11 יום 3117 | לבנות 1129 | גדריך 1447 | יום 3117 | ההוא 1931 | ירחק 7368 | חק 2706: | 7:12 יום 3117 | הוא 1931 |
|---|---|---|---|---|---|---|---|---|---|
| chutzout. | youm | libnout | gaderayik; | youm | hahua' | yirchaq | choq. | youm | hua' |
| **the streets** | ***In* the day** | **that are to be built** | **your walls** | **day *in*** | **that** | **shall be far removed** | **the decree** | ***In* day** | **that** |

| ועדיך 5704 | יבוא 935 | למני 4480 | אשור 804 | וערי 5892 | מצור 4693 | ולמני 4480 | מצור 4693 | ועד 5704 | נהר 5104 |
|---|---|---|---|---|---|---|---|---|---|
| ua'adeyka | yabou'a, | laminiy | 'ashur | ua'arey | matzour; | ualminiy | matzour | ua'ad | nahar, |
| **even to you** | ***also* he shall come** | **from** | **Assyria** | **the cities** | ***from the* fortified** | **and from** | **the fortress** | **even to** | **the river** |

| וים 3220 | מים 3220 | והר 2022 | ההר 2022: | 7:13 והיתה 1961 | הארץ 776 | לשממה 8077 | על 5921 |
|---|---|---|---|---|---|---|---|
| uayam | miyam | uahar | hahar. | uahayatah | ha'aretz | lishmamah | 'al |
| **and from sea** | **to sea** | **and *from* mountain** | **to mountain** | **Notwithstanding shall be** | **the land** | **desolate** | **because of** |

| ישביה 3427 | מפרי 6529 | מעלליהם 4611: | 7:14 רעה 7462 | עמך 5971 | בשבטך 7626 | צאן 6629 | נחלתך 5159 |
|---|---|---|---|---|---|---|---|
| yoshabeyha; | mipriy | ma'alleyhem. | ra'aeh | 'ameka | bashibteka, | tza'n | nachalateka, |
| **them that dwell therein** | **for the fruit of** | **their doings** | **Feed** | **your people** | **with your rod** | **the flock of** | **your heritage** |

Micah 7:5 Trust you not in a friend, put you not confidence in a guide: keep the doors of your mouth from her that lie in your bosom.6 For the son dishonoureth the father, the daughter rise up against her mother, the daughter in law against her mother in law; a man's enemies are the men of his own house.7 Therefore I will look unto YHUH; I will wait for the G-d of my salvation: my G-d will hear me.8 Rejoice not against me, O mine enemy: when I fall, I shall arise; when I sit in darkness, YHUH shall be a light unto me.9 I will bear the indignation of YHUH, because I have sinned against him, until he plead my cause, and execute judgment for me: he will bring me forth to the light, and I shall behold his righteousness.10 Then she that is mine enemy shall see it, and shame shall cover her which said unto me, Where is YHUH your G-d? mine eyes shall behold her: now shall she be trodden down as the mire of the streets.11 In the day that your walls are to be built, in that day shall the decree be far removed.12 In that day also he shall come even to you from Assyria, and from the fortified cities, and from the fortress even to the river, and from sea to sea, and from mountain to mountain.13 Notwithstanding the land shall be desolate because of them that dwell therein, for the fruit of their doings.14 Feed your people with your rod, the flock of your heritage,

| שכני 7931 | לבדד 910 | יער 3293 | בתוך 8432 | כרמל 3760 | ירעו 7462 | בשן 1316 | וגלעד 1568 | כימי 3117 |
|---|---|---|---|---|---|---|---|---|
| shokaniy | labadad, | ya'ar | batouk | karmel; | yir'au | bashan | uagil'ad | kiymey |
| **which dwell** | **solitarily** | ***in* the wood** | **in the midst of** | **Carmel** | **let them feed** | ***in* Bashan** | **and Gilead** | **as in the days of** |

| עולם 5769: | 7:15 | כימי 3117 | צאתך 3318 | מארץ 776 | מצרים 4714 | אראנו 7200 |
|---|---|---|---|---|---|---|
| 'aulam. | | kiymey | tzea'taka | me'aretz | mitzrayim; | 'ar'anu |
| **old** | | **According to the days of** | **your coming** | **out of the land of** | **Egypt** | **will I show unto him** |

| נפלאות 6381: | 7:16 | יראו 7200 | גוים 1471 | ויבשו 954 | מכל 3605 | גבורתם 1369 | ישימו 7760 | יד 3027 | על 5921 |
|---|---|---|---|---|---|---|---|---|---|
| nipla'aut. | | yir'au | gouyim | uayeboshu, | mikol | gaburatam; | yasiymu | yad | 'al |
| **marvellous things** | | **shall see** | **The nations** | **and be confounded** | **at all** | **their might** | **they shall lay** | ***their* hand** | **upon** |

| פה 6310 | אזניהם 241 | תחרשנה 2790: | 7:17 | ילחכו 3897 | עפר 6083 | כנחש 5175 | כזחלי 2119 | ארץ 776 | ירגזו 7264 |
|---|---|---|---|---|---|---|---|---|---|
| peh, | 'azaneyhem | techerashnah. | | yalachaku | 'apar | kanachash, | kazochaley | 'aretz, | yirgazu |
| ***their* mouth** | **their ears** | **shall be deaf** | | **They shall lick** | **the dust** | **like a serpent** | **like worms of** | **the earth** | **they shall move** |

| ממסגרתיהם 4526 | אל 413 | יהוה 3068 | אלהינו 430 | יפחדו 6342 | ויראו 3372 | ממך 4480: | 7:18 | מי 4310 | אל 410 |
|---|---|---|---|---|---|---|---|---|---|
| mimisgaroteyhem; | 'al | Yahuah | 'aloheynu | yipchadu, | uayir'au | mimeka. | | miy' | 'al |
| **out of their holes** | **of** | **Yahuah** | **our Elohim** | **they shall be afraid** | **and shall fear** | **because of you** | | **Who** | ***is a* El** |

| כמוך 3644 | נשא 5375 | עון 5771 | ועבר 5674 | על 5921 | פשע 6588 | לשארית 7611 | נחלתו 5159 | לא 3808 | החזיק 2388 |
|---|---|---|---|---|---|---|---|---|---|
| kamouka, | nosea' | 'auon | ua'aber | 'al | pesha', | lish'aeriyt | nachalatou; | la' | hechaziyq |
| **like unto you** | **that pardoneth** | **iniquity** | **and passed** | **by** | **the transgression** | **of the remnant** | **of his heritage?** | **not** | **he retain** |

| לעד 5703 | אפו 639 | כי 3588 | חפץ 2654 | חסד 2617 | הוא 1931: | 7:19 | ישוב 7725 | ירחמנו 7355 | יכבש 3533 |
|---|---|---|---|---|---|---|---|---|---|
| la'ad | 'apou, | kiy | chapetz | chesed | hua'. | | yashub | yarachamenu, | yikbosh |
| **for ever** | **his anger** | **because** | **delight** | ***in* mercy** | **he** | | **He will turn again** | **he will have compassion upon us** | **he will subdue** |

| עונתינו 5771 | ותשליך 7993 | במצלות 4688 | ים 3220 | כל 3605 | חטאותם 2403: | 7:20 | תתן 5414 | אמת 571 | ליעקב 3290 |
|---|---|---|---|---|---|---|---|---|---|
| 'auonoteynu; | uatashliyk | bimatzulout | yam | kal | chata'utam. | | titen | 'amet | laya'aqob, |
| **our iniquities** | **and you will cast** | **into the depths of** | **the sea** | **all** | **their sins** | | **You will perform** | **the truth** | **to Jacob** |

| חסד 2617 | לאברהם 85 | אשר 834 | נשבעת 7650 | לאבתינו 1 | מימי 3117 | קדם 6924: |
|---|---|---|---|---|---|---|
| chesed | la'abraham; | 'asher | nishba'ta | la'aboteynu | miymey | qedem. |
| ***and* the mercy** | **to Abraham** | **which** | **you have sworn** | **unto our fathers** | **from the days of** | **old** |

Micah 7:14 which dwell solitarily in the wood, in the midst of Carmel: let them feed in Bashan and Gilead, as in the days of old.15 According to the days of your coming out of the land of Egypt will I show unto him marvellous things.16 The nations shall see and be confounded at all their might: they shall lay their hand upon their mouth, their ears shall be deaf.17 They shall lick the dust like a serpent, they shall move out of their holes like worms of the earth: they shall be afraid of YHUH our G-d, and shall fear because of you.18 Who is a G-d like unto you, that pardoneth iniquity, and pass by the transgression of the remnant of his heritage? he retaineth not his anger forever, because he delighteth in mercy.19 He will turn again, he will have compassion upon us; he will subdue our iniquities; and you will cast all their sins into the depths of the sea.20 Thou will perform the truth to Jacob, and the mercy to Abraham, which you have sworn unto our fathers from the days of old.

# NAHUM
## (*Nachum*)

Verse one identifies the author as Nahum and his name in Hebrew means *Consoler* or *Comforter*. The book was probably written approximately between 663 and 612 B.C. Nahum did not prophesy a warning or call to repentance the people of Nineveh because Yahuah had already done this by sending them the prophet Jonah 150 years earlier which caused them to repent at that time but with a promise of what would happen if they turned back to their evil ways. Nahum was sent to the **House of Judah** to tell them not to despair because Yahuah had pronounced judgment on the Assyrians which came true in 612 B.C. There are many theories as to where the city was located. One such theory is that it was Capernaum, which means *the village of Nahum* on the Sea of Galilee.

| **Nahum 1:1** | | | | | | **1:2** | | | |
|---|---|---|---|---|---|---|---|---|---|
| משא 4853 | נינוה 5210 | ספר 5612 | חזון 2377 | נחום 5151 | האלקשי 512: | | אל 410 | קנוא 7072 | ונקם 5358 |
| masa' | niynaueh; | seper | chazoun | nachum | ha'alqoshiy. | | 'ael | qanou'a | uanoqem |
| **The burden of** | **Nineveh** | **The book of** | **the vision of** | **Nahum** | **the Elkoshite** | | **El** | ***is* jealous** | **and revenge** |

| | | | | | | | | | |
|---|---|---|---|---|---|---|---|---|---|
| יהוה 3069 | נקם 5358 | יהוה 3069 | ובעל 1167 | חמה 2534 | נקם 5358 | יהוה 3069 | לצריו 6862 | ונוטר 5201 | הוא 1931 |
| Yahuah, | naqam | Yahuah | uaba'al | chemah; | noqem | Yahuah | latzarayu, | uanouter | hua' |
| **Yahuah** | **revenge** | **Yahuah** | **and *is* furious** | **wrath** | **will take vengeance** | **Yahuah** | **on his adversaries** | **and reserve** | **he** |

| | **1:3** | | | | | | | | | |
|---|---|---|---|---|---|---|---|---|---|---|
| לאיביו 341: | | יהוה 3068 | ארך 750 | אפים 639 | וגדול 1419 | כח 3581 | ונקה 5352 | לא 3808 | ינקה 5352 | יהוה 3068 |
| la'ayabayu. | | Yahuah | 'arek | 'apayim | uagedoul | koach, | uanaqeh | la' | yanaqeh; | Yahuah |
| ***wrath* for his enemies** | | **Yahuah** | ***is* slow** | **to anger** | **and great in** | **power** | **and will at all** | **not** | **acquit** | ***the wicked* Yahuah** |

| | | | | | | **1:4** | | |
|---|---|---|---|---|---|---|---|---|
| בסופה 5492 | ובשערה 8183 | דרכו 1870 | וענן 6051 | אבק 80 | רגליו 7272: | גוער 1605 | בים 3220 | ויבשהו 3001 |
| basupah | uabis'arah | darkou, | ua'anan | 'abaq | raglayu. | gou'aer | bayam | uayabshehu, |
| **in the whirlwind** | **and in the storm** | ***has* his way** | **and the clouds** | ***are* the dust** | **of his feet** | **He rebuke** | **the sea** | **and make it dry** |

| | | | | | | | | | **1:5** | |
|---|---|---|---|---|---|---|---|---|---|---|
| וכל 3605 | הנהרות 5104 | החריב 2717 | אמלל 536 | בשן 1316 | וכרמל 3760 | ופרח 6525 | לבנון 3844 | אמלל 536: | הרים 2022 | רעשו 7493 |
| uakal | hanaharout | hecheriyb; | 'amlal | bashan | uakarmel, | uaperach | labanoun | 'amlal. | hariym | ra'ashu |
| **and all** | **the rivers** | **dry up** | **languish** | **Bashan** | **and Carmel** | **and the flower of** | **Lebanon** | **languish** | **The mountains** | **quake** |

| | | | | | | | | | | **1:6** |
|---|---|---|---|---|---|---|---|---|---|---|
| ממנו 4480 | והגבעות 1389 | התמגגו 4127 | ותשא 5375 | הארץ 776 | מפניו 6440 | ותבל 8398 | וכל 3605 | ישבי 3427 | בה 871a: | לפני 6440 |
| mimenu, | uahagaba'aut | hitmogagu; | uatisa' | ha'aretz | mipanayu, | uatebel | uakal | yoshabey | bah. | lipney |
| **at him** | **and the hills** | **melt** | **and is burned** | **the earth** | **at his presence** | **yea the world** | **and all** | **that dwell** | **therein** | **before** |

| | | | | | | | | | |
|---|---|---|---|---|---|---|---|---|---|
| זעמו 2195 | מי 4310 | יעמוד 5975 | ומי 4310 | יקום 6965 | בחרון 2740 | אפו 639 | חמתו 2534 | נתכה 5413 | כאש 784 |
| za'amou | miy' | ya'amoud, | uamiy | yaqum | bacharoun | 'apou; | chamatou | nitkah | ka'aesh, |
| **his indignation?** | **Who** | **can stand** | **and who** | **can abide** | **in the fierceness of** | **his anger?** | **his fury** | **is poured out** | **like fire** |

| | | | **1:7** | | | | | | |
|---|---|---|---|---|---|---|---|---|---|
| והצרים 6697 | נתצו 5422 | ממנו 4480: | | טוב 2896 | יהוה 3068 | למעוז 4581 | ביום 3117 | צרה 6869 | וידע 3045 |
| uahatzuriym | nittzu | mimenu. | | toub | Yahuah, | lama'auz | bayoum | tzarah; | uayodea' |
| **and the rocks** | **are thrown down** | **by him** | | ***is* good** | **Yahuah** | **a strong hold** | **in the day of** | **trouble** | **and he knows** |

| | | **1:8** | | | | | | |
|---|---|---|---|---|---|---|---|---|
| חסי 2620 | בו 871a: | | ובשטף 7858 | עבר 5674 | כלה 3617 | יעשה 6213 | מקומה 4725 | ואיביו 341 |
| chosey | bou. | | uabshetep | 'aber, | kalah | ya'aseh | maqoumah; | ua'ayabayu |
| **them that trust** | **in him** | | **But with flood** | **an overrunning** | **an utter end of** | **he will make** | **the place thereof** | **and his enemies** |

| | | **1:9** | | | | | | | | | |
|---|---|---|---|---|---|---|---|---|---|---|---|
| ירדף 7291 | חשך 2822: | | מה 4100 | תחשבון 2803 | אל 413 | יהוה 3068 | כלה 3617 | הוא 1931 | עשה 6213 | לא 3808 | תקום 6965 |
| yaradep | choshek | | mah | tachashbun | 'al | Yahuah, | kalah | hua' | 'aseh; | la' | taqum |
| **shall pursue** | **darkness** | | **What** | **do you imagine** | **against** | **Yahuah?** | **an utter end** | **he** | **will make** | **not** | **shall rise up** |

**Nahum** 1:1 The burden of Nineveh. The book of the vision of Nahum the Elkoshite.2 G-d is jealous, and YHUH revengeth; YHUH revengeth, and is furious; YHUH will take vengeance on his adversaries, and he reserveth wrath for his enemies.3 YHUH is slow to anger, and great in power, and will not at all acquit the wicked: YHUH has his way in the whirlwind and in the storm, and the clouds are the dust of his feet.4 He rebuketh the sea, and make it dry, and drieth up all the rivers: Bashan languisheth, and Carmel, and the flower of Lebanon languisheth.5 The mountains quake at him, and the hills melt, and the earth is burned at his presence, yea, the world, and all that dwell therein.6 Who can stand before his indignation? and who can abide in the fierceness of his anger? his fury is poured out like fire, and the rocks are thrown down by him.7 YHUH is good, a strong hold in the day of trouble; and he know them that trust in him.8 But with an overrunning flood he will make an utter end of the place thereof, and darkness shall pursue his enemies.9 What do you imagine against YHUH? he will make an utter end: affliction shall not rise up the second time.

פעמים 6471 | צרה 6869: | **1:10** כי 3588 | עד 5704 | סירים 5518 | סבכים 5440 | וכסבאם 5435 | סבואים 5433
pa'amayim tzarah. kiy 'ad siyriym sabukiym, uaksaba'am sabu'aym;
**the second time affliction For while *as* thorns *they be* folden together and while they are drunken *as* drunkards**

אכלו 398 | קקש 7179 | יבש 3001 | מלא 4390: | **1:11** ממך 4480 | יצא 3318 | חשב 2803 | על 5921 | יהוה 3068 | רעה 7451
'aklu, kaqash yabesh malea'. mimek yatza', chosheb 'al Yahuah ra'ah;
**they shall be devoured as stubble dry fully of you There is *one* come out that imagineth against Yahuah evil**

יעץ 3289 | בליעל 1100: | **1:12** כה 3541 | אמר 559 | יהוה 3068 | אם 518 | שלמים 8003 | וכן 3651 | רבים 7227 | וכן 3651 | נגזו 1494
yo'aetz baliya'al. koh 'amar Yahuah 'am shalemiym uaken rabiym, uaken nagozu
**a counsellor wicked Thus saith Yahuah Though *they* be quiet and likewise many yet thus shall they be cut down**

ועבר 5674 | וענתך 6031 | לא 3808 | אענך 6031 | עוד 5750: | **1:13** ועתה 6258 | אשבר 7665 | מטהו 4132
ua'abar; ua'anitik, la' 'a'anek 'aud. ua'atah 'ashbor motehu
**when he shall pass through. Though I have afflicted you no I will afflict the more For now will I break his yoke**

מעליך 5921 | ומוסרתיך 4147 | אנתק 5423: | **1:14** וצוה 6680 | עליך 5921 | יהוה 3068 | לא 3808
me'alayik; uamousarotayik 'anateq. uatziuah 'aleyka Yahuah, la'
**from off you and your bonds will I burst in sunder And has given a commandment concerning you Yahuah *that* no**

יזרע 2232 | משמך 8034 | עוד 5750 | מבית 1004 | אלהיך 430 | אכרית 3772 | פסל 6459 | ומסכה 4541 | אשים 7760
yizara' mishimka 'aud; mibeyt 'aloheyka 'akriyt pesel uamasekah 'asiym
**be sown of your name more out of the house of your gods will I cut off the graven image and the molten image I will make**

קברך 6913 | כי 3588 | קלות 7043: | **1:15** הנה 2009 | על 5921 | ההרים 2022 | רגלי 7272 | מבשר 1319 | משמיע 8085
qibreka kiy qalouta. hineh 'al hehariym ragley mabaser mashmiya'
**your grave for you are vile Behold upon the mountains the feet of him that bring good tidings that publisheth**

שלום 7965 | חגי 2287 | יהודה 3063 | חגיך 2282 | שלמי 7999 | נדריך 5088 | כי 3588 | לא 3808 | יוסיף 3254 | עוד 5750 | לעבור 5674 | בך 871a
shaloum, chagiy yahudah chagayik shalmiy nadarayik; kiy la' yousiyp 'aud la'abour bach
**peace keep O Judah your solemn feasts perform your vows for no more again shall pass through you**

בליעל 1100 | כלה 3605 | נכרת 3772:
baliya'al kuloh nikrat.
**the wicked he is utterly cut off**

**Nah 2:1** עלה 5927 | מפיץ 6327 | על 5921 | פניך 6440 | נצור 5341 | מצרה 4694 | צפה 6822 | דרך 1870 | חזק 2388 | מתנים 4975
'alah mepiytz 'al panayik natzour matzurah; tzapeh derek chazeq matanayim,
**is come up He that dash in pieces before your face keep the munition watch the way make strong *your* loins**

אמץ 553 | כח 3581 | מאד 3966: | **2:2** כי 3588 | שב 7725 | יהוה 3068 | את 853 | גאון 1347 | יעקב 3290 | 1347 | ישראל 3478
'ametz koach ma'ad. kiy shab Yahuah 'at ga'aun ya'aqob, kig'aun yisra'ael;
**fortify *your* power mightily For has turned away Yahuah the excellency of Jacob as the excellency of Israel**

כי 3588 | בקקום 1238 | בקקים 1238 | וזמריהם 2156 | שחתו 7843: | **2:3** מגן 4043 | גבריהו 1368 | מאדם 119
kiy baqaqum baqaqiym, uazmoreyhem shichetu. magen giboreyhu ma'adam,
**for the emptiers have emptied them out and their vine branches marred The shield of his mighty men is made red**

Nahum 1:10 For while they be folden together as thorns, and while they are drunken as drunkards, they shall be devoured as stubble fully dry.11 There is one come out of you, that imagineth evil against YHUH, a wicked counselor.12 Thus saith YHUH: Though they be quiet, and likewise many, yet thus shall they be cut down, when he shall pass through. Though I have afflicted you, I will afflict you no more.13 For now will I break his yoke from off you, and will burst your bonds in sunder.14 And YHUH has given a commandment concerning you, that no more of your name be sown: out of the house of your gods will I cut off the graven image and the molten image: I will make your grave; for you are vile.15 Behold upon the mountains the feet of him that bring good tidings, that publisheth peace! O Judah, keep your solemn feasts, perform your vows: for the wicked shall no more pass through you; he is utterly cut off. **Nahum** 2:1 He that dasheth in pieces is come up before your face: keep the munition, watch the way, make your loins strong, fortify your power mightily.2 For YHUH has turned away the excellency of Jacob, as the excellency of Israel: for the emptiers have emptied them out, and marred their vine branches.3 The shield of his mighty men is made red, the valiant men are in scarlet:

| אנשי 582 | חיל 2428 | מתלעים 8529 | באש 784 | פלדות 6393 | הרכב 7393 | ביום 3117 | הכינו 3559 | והברשים 1265 |
|---|---|---|---|---|---|---|---|---|
| 'anshey | chayil | matula'aym, | ba'aesh | paladout | harekeb | bayoum | hakiynou; | uahabroshiym |
| **men** | ***the* valiant** | ***are* in scarlet** | **flaming *shall be*** | **with torches** | **the chariots** | **in the day of** | **his preparation** | **and the fir trees** |

| הרעלו 7477: | 2:4 | בחוצות 2351 | יתהוללו 1984 | הרכב 7393 | ישתקשקון 8264 | ברחבות 7339 |
|---|---|---|---|---|---|---|
| hara'alu. | | bachutzout | yithoulalu | harekeb, | yishtaqshaqun | barachobout; |
| **shall be terribly shaken** | | **in the streets** | **shall rage** | **The chariots** | **they shall justle one against another** | **in the broad ways** |

| מראיהן 4758 | כלפידם 3940 | כברקים 1300 | ירוצצו 7323: | 2:5 | יזכר 2142 | אדיריו 117 | יכשלו 3782 |
|---|---|---|---|---|---|---|---|
| mar'aeyhen | kalapiydim, | kabraqiym | yaroutzetzu. | | yizkor | 'adiyrayu, | yikashalu |
| **they shall seem** | **like torches** | **like the lightnings** | **they shall run** | | **He shall recount** | **his worthies** | **they shall stumble** |

| בהלכותם 1979 | ימהרו 4116 | חומתה 2346 | והכן 3559 | הסכך 5526: | 2:6 | שערי 8179 | הנהרות 5104 |
|---|---|---|---|---|---|---|---|
| bahaliykatam | yamaharu | choumatah, | uahkan | hasokek. | | sha'arey | hanaharout |
| **in their walk** | **they shall make haste** | ***to* the wall thereof** | **and shall be prepared** | **the defence** | | **The gates of** | **the rivers** |

| נפתחו 6605 | וההיכל 1964 | נמוג 4127: | 2:7 | והצב 5324 | גלתה 1540 | העלתה 5927 |
|---|---|---|---|---|---|---|
| niptachu; | uahaheykal | namoug. | | uahutzab | gultah | ho'alatah; |
| **shall be opened** | **and the palace** | **shall be dissolved** | | **And Huzzab** | **shall be led away captive** | **she shall be brought up** |

| ואמהתיה 519 | מנהגות 5090 | כקול 6963 | יונים 3123 | מתפפת 8608 | על 5921 | לבבהן 3824: | 2:8 | ונינוה 5210 | כברכת 1295 |
|---|---|---|---|---|---|---|---|---|---|
| ua'amhoteyha, | manahagout | kaqoul | youniym, | matopapot | 'al | libabehen. | | uaniynaueh | kibrekat |
| **and her maids** | **shall lead** | ***her* as with the voice of** | **doves** | **tabering** | **upon** | **their breasts** | | **But Nineveh** | **like a pool of** |

| מים 4325 | מימי 3117 | היא 1931 | והמה 1992 | נסים 5127 | עמדו 5975 | עמדו 5975 | ואין 369 | מפנה 6437: | 2:9 |
|---|---|---|---|---|---|---|---|---|---|
| mayim | miymey | hiy'a; | uahemah | nasiym, | 'amadu | 'amodu | ua'aeyn | mapneh. | |
| **water** | ***is* of old** | **he** | **yet they** | **shall flee away** | **Stand** | **stand** | ***shall they cry* but none** | **shall look back** | |

| בזו 962 | כסף 3701 | בזו 962 | זהב 2091 | ואין 369 | קצה 7097 | לתכונה 8498 | כבד 3519 | מכל 3605 | כלי 3627 |
|---|---|---|---|---|---|---|---|---|---|
| bozu | kesep | bozu | zahab; | ua'aeyn | qetzeh | latakunah, | kabod | mikol | kaliy |
| **Take you the spoil** | **of silver** | **take the spoil** | **of gold** | **for *there is* none** | **end of** | **the store** | ***and* glory** | **out of all** | **furniture** |

| חמדה 2532: | 2:10 | בוקה 950 | ומבוקה 4003 | ומבלקה 1110 | ולב 3820 | נמס 4549 | ופק 6375 | ברכים 1290 | וחלחלה 2479 |
|---|---|---|---|---|---|---|---|---|---|
| chemdah. | | buqah | uambuqah | uambulaqah; | ualeb | names | uapiq | birkayim, | uachalchalah |
| ***the* pleasant** | | **She is empty** | **and void** | **and waste** | **and the heart** | **melt** | **and smite together** | **the knees** | **and much pain *is*** |

| בכל 3605 | מתנים 4975 | ופני 6440 | כלם 3605 | קבצו 6908 | פארור 6289: | 2:11 | איה 346 | מעון 4583 | אריות 738 | ומרעה 4829 |
|---|---|---|---|---|---|---|---|---|---|---|
| bakal | matanayim, | uapaney | kulam | qibtzu | pa'rur. | | 'ayeh | ma'aun | arayout, | uamir'ah |
| **in all** | **loins** | **and the faces of them all** | | **gather** | **blackness** | | **Where *is*** | **the dwelling of** | **the lions** | **and the feedingplace** |

| הוא 1931 | לכפרים 3715 | אשר 834 | הלך 1980 | אריה 738 | לביא 3833 | שם 8033 | גור 1482 | אריה 738 | ואין 369 |
|---|---|---|---|---|---|---|---|---|---|
| hua' | lakapiriym; | 'asher | halak | 'aryeh | labiy'a | sham | gur | 'aryeh | ua'aeyn |
| **he** | **of the young lions** | **where** | **walked** | **the lion** | ***even* the old lion** | **there** | **whelp** | ***and* the lion's** | **and none** |

| מחריד 2729: | 2:12 | אריה 738 | טרף 2963 | בדי 1767 | גרותיו 1484 | ומחנק 2614 | ללבאתיו 3833 | וימלא 4390 |
|---|---|---|---|---|---|---|---|---|
| machariyd. | | 'aryeh | torep | badey | goroutayu, | uamchaneq | lalib'atayu; | uayamalea' |
| **made *them* afraid?** | | **The lion** | **did tear in pieces** | **enough for** | **his whelps** | **and strangled** | **for his lionesses** | **and filled** |

Nahum 2:3 the chariots shall be with flaming torches in the day of his preparation, and the fir trees shall be terribly shaken.4 The chariots shall rage in the streets, they shall justle one against another in the broad ways: they shall seem like torches, they shall run like the lightnings.5 He shall recount his worthies: they shall stumble in their walk; they shall make have to the wall thereof, and the defence shall be prepared.6 The gates of the rivers shall be opened, and the palace shall be dissolved.7 And Huzzab shall be led away captive, she shall be brought up, and her maids shall lead her as with the voice of doves, tabering upon their breasts.8 But Nineveh is of old like a pool of water: yet they shall flee away. Stand, stand, shall they cry; but none shall look back.9 Take you the spoil of silver, take the spoil of gold: for there is none end of the store and glory out of all the pleasant furniture.10 She is empty, and void, and waste: and the heart melteth, and the knees smite together, and much pain is in all loins, and the faces of them all gather blackness.11 Where is the dwelling of the lions, and the feedingplace of the young lions, where the lion, even the old lion, walked, and the lion's whelp, and none made them afraid?12 The lion did tear in pieces enough for his whelps, and strangled for his lionesses, and filled his holes with prey, and his dens with ravin.

| | | | | 2:13 | | | | | | |
|---|---|---|---|---|---|---|---|---|---|---|
| טרף 2964 | חריו 2356 | ומענתיו 4585 | טרפה 2966: | | הנני 2005 | אליך 413 | נאם 5002 | יהוה 3068 | צבאות 6635 | והבערתי 1197 |
| terep | chorayu, | uam'anotayu | tarepah. | | hinniy | 'aeleyka, | na'am | Yahuah | tzaba'aut, | uahib'artiy |
| **with prey** | **his holes** | **and his dens** | **with ravin** | | **Behold I *am*** | **against you** | **saith** | **Yahuah** | **of hosts** | **and I will burn** |

| | | | | | | | | |
|---|---|---|---|---|---|---|---|---|
| בעשן 6227 | רכבה 7393 | וכפיריך 3715 | תאכל 398 | חרב 2719 | והכרתי 3772 | מארץ 776 | טרפך 2964 | ולא 3808 |
| be'ashan | rikbah, | uakpiyrayik | ta'kal | chareb; | uahikratiy | me'aretz | tarpek, | uala' |
| **in the smoke** | **her chariots** | **and your young lions** | **shall devour** | **the sword** | **and I will cut off** | **from the earth** | **your prey** | **and no** |

| | | | |
|---|---|---|---|
| ישמע 8085 | עוד 5750 | קול 6963 | מלאככה 4397: |
| yishama' | 'aud | qoul | mal'akekeh. |
| **shall be heard** | **more** | **the voice of** | **your messengers** |

| Nah 3:1 | | | | | | | | | | | 3:2 | |
|---|---|---|---|---|---|---|---|---|---|---|---|---|
| | הוי 1945 | עיר 5892 | דמים 1818 | כלה 3605 | כחש 3585 | פרק 6563 | מלאה 4395 | לא 3808 | ימיש 4185 | טרף 2964: | קול 6963 | שוט 7752 |
| | houy | 'ayr | damiym; | kulah, | kachash | perek | male'ah, | la' | yamiysh | tarep. | qoul | shout, |
| | **Woe** | **city** | ***to* the bloody** | ***it is* all** | **lies** | ***and* robbery** | **full of** | **not** | **depart** | **the prey** | **The noise of** | **a whip** |

| | | | | | | | 3:3 |
|---|---|---|---|---|---|---|---|
| וקול 6963 | רעש 7494 | אופן 212 | וסוס 5483 | דהר 1725 | ומרכבה 4818 | מרקדה 7540: | פרש 6571 |
| uaqoul | ra'ash | 'aupan; | uasus | doher, | uamerkabah | maraqedah. | parash |
| **and the noise of** | **the rattling of** | **the wheels** | **and of horses** | **the pransing** | **chariots** | **and of the jumping** | **The horseman** |

| | | | | | | | |
|---|---|---|---|---|---|---|---|
| מעלה 5927 | ולהב 3851 | חרב 2719 | וברק 1300 | חנית 2595 | ורב 7230 | חלל 2491 | וכבד 3514 |
| ma'aleh, | ualahab | chereb | uabraq | chaniyt, | uarob | chalal | uakobed |
| **lift up** | **both the bright** | **sword** | **and the glittering** | **spear** | **and *there is* a multitude of** | **slain** | **and a great number of** |

| | | | | | | 3:4 |
|---|---|---|---|---|---|---|
| פגר 6297 | ואין 369 | קצה 7097 | לגויה 1472 | יכשלו 3782 | בגויתם 1472: | מרב 7230 |
| pager; | ua'aeyn | qetzeh | lagauiyah, | yikshelu | bigauiyatam. | merob |
| **carcases** | **and *there is* none** | **end** | **of *their* corpses** | **they stumble** | **upon their corpses** | **Because of the multitude of** |

| | | | | | | | | |
|---|---|---|---|---|---|---|---|---|
| זנוני 2181 | זונה 2181 | טובת 2896 | חן 2580 | בעלת 1172 | כשפים 3785 | המכרת 4376 | גוים 1471 | בזנוניה 2183 |
| zanuney | zounah, | toubat | chen | ba'alat | kashapiym; | hamokeret | gouyim | bizanuneyha, |
| **the whoredoms of** | **harlot** | **the well** | **favored** | **the mistress of** | **witchcrafts** | **that sell** | **nations** | **through her whoredoms** |

| | | 3:5 | | | | | | |
|---|---|---|---|---|---|---|---|---|
| ומשפחות 4940 | בכשפיה 3785: | הנני 2005 | אליך 413 | נאם 5002 | יהוה 3068 | צבאות 6635 | וגליתי 1540 | שוליך 7757 |
| uamishpachout | bikshapeyha. | hinniy | 'aleyka, | na'am | Yahuah | tzaba'aut, | uagileytiy | shulayik |
| **and families** | **through her witchcrafts** | **Behold I *am*** | **against you** | **saith** | **Yahuah** | **of hosts** | **and I will discover** | **your skirts** |

| | | | | | | | 3:6 | |
|---|---|---|---|---|---|---|---|---|
| על 5921 | פניך 6440 | והראיתי 7200 | גוים 1471 | מערך 4626 | וממלכות 4467 | קלונך 7036: | והשלכתי 7993 | עליך 5921 |
| 'al | panayik; | uahar'aeytiy | gouyim | ma'arek, | uamamlakout | qalounek. | uahishlachtiy | 'aleyka |
| **upon** | **your face** | **and I will show** | **the nations** | **your nakedness** | **and the kingdoms** | **your shame** | **And I will cast** | **upon you** |

| | | | | 3:7 | |
|---|---|---|---|---|---|
| שקצים 8251 | ונבלתיך 5034 | ושמתיך 7760 | כראי 7210: | והיה 1961 | כל 3605 |
| shiqtziym | uanibaltiyk; | uasamtiyk | kara'ay. | uahayah | kal |
| **abominable filth** | **and make you vile** | **and will set you** | **as a gazingstock** | **And it shall come to pass *that*** | **all** |

| | | | | | | | | | | | |
|---|---|---|---|---|---|---|---|---|---|---|---|
| ראיך 7200 | ידוד 5074 | ממך 4480 | ואמר 559 | שדדה 7703 | נינוה 5210 | מי 4310 | ינוד 5110 | לה 3807a | מאין 370 | אבקש 1245 |
| ro'ayik | yidoud | mimek, | ua'amar | shadadah | niynaueh, | miy' | yanud | lah; | me'ayin | 'abaqesh |
| **they that look upon you** | **shall flee** | **from you** | **and say** | **is laid waste** | **Nineveh** | **who** | **will bemoan** | **her?** | **where** | **shall I seek** |

Nahum 2:13 Behold, I am against you, saith YHUH of hosts, and I will burn her chariots in the smoke, and the sword shall devour your young lions: and I will cut off your prey from the earth, and the voice of your messengers shall no more be heard. **Nahum** 3:1 Woe to the bloody city! it is all full of lies and robbery; the prey departeth not;2 The noise of a whip, and the noise of the rattling of the wheels, and of the pransing horses, and of the jumping chariots.3 The horseman lift up both the bright sword and the glittering spear: and there is a multitude of slain, and a great number of carcases; and there is none end of their corpses; they stumble upon their corpses:4 Because of the multitude of the whoredoms of the wellfavoured harlot, the mistress of witchcrafts, that sell nations through her whoredoms, and families through her witchcrafts.5 Behold, I am against you, saith YHUH of hosts; and I will discover your skirts upon your face, and I will show the nations your nakedness, and the kingdoms your shame.6 And I will cast abominable filth upon you, and make you vile, and will set you as a gazingstock.7 And it shall come to pass, that all they that look upon you shall flee from you, and say, Nineveh is laid waste: who will bemoan her? whence shall I seek comforters for you?

| מנחמים 5162 | לך 3807a: | 3:8 התיטבי 3190 | מנא 4996 | אמון 527 | הישבה 3427 | ביארים 2975 | מים 4325 |
|---|---|---|---|---|---|---|---|
| manachamiym | lak. | hateytabiy | mina' | 'amoun, | hayoshabah | baya'ariym, | mayim |
| **comforters** | **for you?** | **Are you better** | **than No** | **populous** | **that was situate** | **among the rivers** | ***that had* the waters** |

| סביב 5439 | לה 3807a | אשר 834 | חיל 2426 | ים 3220 | מים 4325 | חומתה 2346: | 3:9 כוש 3568 | עצמה 6109 | ומצרים 4714 |
|---|---|---|---|---|---|---|---|---|---|
| sabiyb | lah; | 'asher | cheyl | yam, | miyam | choumatah. | kush | 'atzamah | uamitzrayim |
| **round about it** | | **whose** | **rampart** | ***was* the sea** | ***was* from the sea?** | ***and* her wall** | **Ethiopia** | ***were* her strength** | **and Egypt** |

| ואין 369 | קצה 7097 | פוט 6316 | ולובים 3864 | היו 1961 | בעזרתך 5833: | 3:10 גם 1571 | היא 1931 | לגלה 1473 | הלכה 1980 | בשבי 7628 | גם 1571 |
|---|---|---|---|---|---|---|---|---|---|---|---|
| ua'aeyn | qetzeh; | put | ualubiym, | hayu | ba'azratek. | gam | hiy'a, | lagolah | halakah | bashebiy, | gam |
| **and it was** | **infinite** | **Put** | **and Lubim** | **were** | **your helpers** | **Yet** | ***was* she** | **carried away** | **she went** | **into captivity** | **also** |

| עלליה 5768 | ירטשו 7376 | בראש 7218 | כל 3605 | חוצות 2351 | ועל 5921 | נכבדיה 3513 | ידו 3032 | גורל 1486 | וכל 3605 |
|---|---|---|---|---|---|---|---|---|---|
| 'alaleyha | yarutshu | bara'sh | kal | chutzout; | ua'al | nikbadeyha | yadu | goural, | uakal |
| **her young children** | **were dashed in pieces** | **at the top of** | **all** | **the streets** | **and for** | **her honorable men** | **they cast** | **lots** | **and all** |

| גדוליה 1419 | רתקו 7576 | בזקים 2131: | 3:11 גם 1571 | את 859 | תשכרי 7937 | תהי 1961 | נעלמה 5956 | גם 1571 | את 859 | תבקשי 1245 |
|---|---|---|---|---|---|---|---|---|---|---|
| gadouleyha | rutqu | baziqiym. | gam | 'at | tishkariy, | tahiy | na'alamah; | gam | 'at | tabaqshiy |
| **her great men** | **were bound** | **in chains** | **also** | ***You*** | **shall be drunken** | **you shall be** | **hid** | **also** | ***you*** | **shall seek** |

| מעוז 4581 | מאויב 341: | 3:12 כל 3605 | מבצריך 4013 | תאנים 8384 | עם 5973 | בכורים 1061 | אם 518 |
|---|---|---|---|---|---|---|---|
| ma'auz | me'auyeb. | kal | mibtzarayik, | ta'aeniym | 'am | bikuriym; | 'am |
| **strength** | **because of the enemy** | **All** | **your strong holds** | ***shall be like* fig trees** | **with** | **the firstripe figs** | **if** |

| ינועו 5128 | ונפלו 5307 | על 5921 | פי 6310 | אוכל 398: | 3:13 הנה 2009 | עמך 5973 | נשים 802 | בקרבך 7130 |
|---|---|---|---|---|---|---|---|---|
| yinou'au | uanapalu | 'al | piy | 'aukel. | hineh | 'amek | nashiym | baqirbek, |
| **they be shaken** | **they shall even fall** | **into** | **the mouth of** | **the eater** | **Behold** | **your people** | ***are* women** | **in the midst of you** |

| לאיביך 341 | פתוח 6605 | נפתחו 6605 | שערי 8179 | ארצך 776 | אכלה 398 | אש 784 | בריחיך 1280: | 3:14 מי 4325 | מצור 4692 |
|---|---|---|---|---|---|---|---|---|---|
| la'ayabayik, | patouach | niptachu | sha'arey | 'artzek; | 'akalah | 'aesh | bariychayik. | mey | matzour |
| **unto your enemies** | **shall be set wide** | **open** | **the gates** | **of your land** | **shall devour** | **the fire** | **your bars** | **waters** | **the siege** |

| שאבי 7579 | לך 3807a | חזקי 2388 | מבצריך 4013 | באי 935 | בטיט 2916 | ורמסי 7429 | בחמר 2563 | החזיקי 2388 | מלבן 4404: | 3:15 שם 8033 |
|---|---|---|---|---|---|---|---|---|---|---|
| sha'abiy | lak, | chazqiy | mibtzarayik; | bo'ay | batiyt | uarimsiy | bachomer | hachaziyqiy | malben. | sam |
| **Draw** | **you for** | **fortify** | **your strong holds** | **go** | **into clay** | **and tread** | **the morter** | **make strong** | **the brickkiln** | **There** |

| תאכלך 398 | אש 784 | תכריתך 3772 | חרב 2719 | תאכלך 398 | כילק 3218 | התכבד 3513 |
|---|---|---|---|---|---|---|
| ta'kalek | 'aesh, | takriytek | chereb, | ta'kalek | kayaleq; | hitkabed |
| **shall devour you** | **the fire** | **shall cut you off** | **the sword** | **it shall eat you up** | **like the cankerworm** | **make yourself many** |

| כילק 3218 | התכבדי 3513 | כארבה 697: | 3:16 הרבית 7235 | רכליך 7402 | מכוכבי 3556 |
|---|---|---|---|---|---|
| kayeleq, | hitkabdiy | ka'arbeh. | hirbeyt | rokalayik, | mikoukabey |
| **as the cankerworm** | **make yourself many** | **as the locusts** | **You have multiplied** | **your merchants** | **above the stars of** |

| השמים 8064 | ילק 3218 | פשט 6584 | ויעף 5774: | 3:17 מנזריך 4502 | כארבה 697 | וטפסריך 2951 | כגוב 1462 |
|---|---|---|---|---|---|---|---|
| hashamayim; | yeleq | pashat | uaya'ap. | minzarayik | ka'arbeh, | uatapsarayik | kagoub |
| **heaven** | **the cankerworm** | **spoil** | **and flies away** | **Your crowned *are*** | **as the locusts** | **and your captains** | **as the great** |

Nahum 3:8 Art you better than populous No, that was situate among the rivers, that had the waters round about it, whose rampart was the sea, and her wall was from the sea?9 Ethiopia and Egypt were her strength, and it was infinite; Put and Lubim were your helpers.10 Yet was she carried away, she went into captivity: her young children also were dashed in pieces at the top of all the streets: and they cast lots for her honourable men, and all her great men were bound in chains.11 Thou also shall be drunken: you shall be hid, you also shall seek strength because of the enemy.12 All your strong holds shall be like fig trees with the firstripe figs: if they be shaken, they shall even fall into the mouth of the eater.13 Behold, your people in the midst of you are women: the gates of your land shall be set wide open unto your enemies: the fire shall devour your bars.14 Draw you waters for the siege, fortify your strong holds: go into clay, and tread the morter, make strong the brickkiln.15 There shall the fire devour you; the sword shall cut you off, it shall eat you up like the cankerworm: make thyself many as the cankerworm, make thyself many as the locusts.16 Thou have multiplied your merchants above the stars of heaven: the cankerworm spoileth, and flieth away.17 Thy crowned are as the locusts, and your captains as the great grasshoppers,

| | | | | | | | | | |
|---|---|---|---|---|---|---|---|---|---|
| גבי 1462 | החונים 2583 | בגדרות 1448 | ביום 3117 | קרה 7135 | שמש 8121 | זרחה 2224 | ונודד 5074 | ולא 3808 | נודע 3045 |
| gobay; | hachouniym | bagaderout | bayoum | qarah, | shemesh | zarachah | uanoudad, | uala' | nouda' |
| **grasshoppers** | **which camp** | **in the hedges** | **in day** | ***the* cold** | **the sun** | ***but* when arise** | **and they flee away** | **and not** | **is known** |

| | | | | | | | | | |
|---|---|---|---|---|---|---|---|---|---|
| מקומו 4725 | אים 335: | **3:18** | נמו 5123 | רעיך 7462 | מלך 4428 | אשור 804 | ישכנו 7931 | אדיריך 117 | נפשו 6335 |
| maqoumou | 'ayam. | | namu | ro'ayka | melek | 'ashur, | yishkanu | 'adiyreyka; | naposhu |
| **their place** | **where they *are*** | | **slumber** | **Your shepherds** | **O king of** | **Assyria** | **shall dwell *in the dust*** | **your nobles** | **is scattered** |

| | | | | | | | | | | |
|---|---|---|---|---|---|---|---|---|---|---|
| עמך 5971 | על 5921 | ההרים 2022 | ואין 369 | מקבץ 6908: | **3:19** | אין 369 | כהה 3545 | לשברך 7667 | נחלה 2470 | מכתך 4347 |
| 'amaka | 'al | hehariym | ua'aeyn | maqabetz. | | 'aeyn | kehah | lashibreka, | nachalah | makateka; |
| **your people** | **upon** | **the mountains** | **and no man** | **gathered *them*** | | ***There is* no** | **healing of** | **your bruise** | **is grievous** | **your wound** |

| | | | | | | | | | | | |
|---|---|---|---|---|---|---|---|---|---|---|---|
| כל 3605 | שמעי 8085 | שמעך 8088 | תקעו 8628 | כף 3709 | עליך 5921 | כי 3588 | על 5921 | מי 4310 | לא 3808 | עברה 5674 | רעתך 7451 |
| kal | shoma'aey | shim'aka, | taqa'au | kap | 'aleyka, | kiy, | 'al | miy' | la' | 'abarah | ra'ataka |
| **all** | **that hear** | **the bruit of you** | **shall clap** | **the hands** | **over you** | **for** | **upon** | **whom** | **not** | **has passed** | **your wickedness** |

| |
|---|
| תמיד 8548: |
| tamiyd. |
| **continually?** |

Nahum 3:17 which camp in the hedges in the cold day, but when the sun arise they flee away, and their place is not known where they are.18 Thy shepherds slumber, O king of Assyria: your nobles shall dwell in the dust: your people is scattered upon the mountains, and no man gathereth them.19 There is no healing of your bruise; your wound is grievous: all that hear the bruit of you shall clap the hands over you: for upon whom has not your wickedness passed continually?

# HABAKKUK
## (*Chabaquq*)

Verse one identifies the author as an oracle from the Prophet Habakkuk, whose name in Hebrew means *to embrace*. Habakkuk was a prophet sent to the **House of Judah** after the destruction of Nineveh. The book was written approximately between 610 and 605 B.C. and is a conversation between Habakkuk and Elohim as to why His chosen people were suffering at the hands of their enemies. Elohim answers Habakkuk and faith is restored.

| **Habakkuk 1:1** | המשא 4853 | אשר 834 | חזה 2372 | חבקוק 2265 | הנביא 5030: | **1:2** | עד 5704 | אנה 575 | יהוה 3068 | שועתי 7768 | ולא 3808 |
|---|---|---|---|---|---|---|---|---|---|---|---|
| | hamasa' | 'asher | chazah, | chabaquq | hanabiy'a. | | 'ad | 'anah | Yahuah | shiua'atiy | uala' |
| | **The burden** | **which** | **did see** | **Habakkuk** | **the prophet** | | **how** | **long** | **O Yahuah** | **shall I cry** | **and not** |

| תשמע 8085 | אזעק 2199 | אליך 413 | חמס 2555 | ולא 3808 | תושיע 3467: | **1:3** | למה 4100 | תראני 7200 | און 205 | ועמל 5999 |
|---|---|---|---|---|---|---|---|---|---|---|
| tishma'; | 'az'aq | 'aeleyka | chamas | uala' | toushiya'. | | lamah | tar'aeniy | 'auen | ua'amal |
| **you will hear** | ***even* cry out** | **unto you** | ***of* violence** | **and not** | **you will save** | | **Why** | **do you show me** | **iniquity** | **and grievance?** |

| תביט 5027 | ושד 7701 | וחמס 2555 | לנגדי 5048 | ויהי 1961 | ריב 7379 | ומדון 4066 | ישא 5375: | **1:4** | על 5921 |
|---|---|---|---|---|---|---|---|---|---|
| tabiyt, | uashod | uachamas | lanegdiy; | uayahiy | riyb | uamadoun | yisa'. | | 'al |
| **cause *me* to behold** | **for spoiling** | **and violence** | ***are* before me** | **and there are *that*** | **strife** | **and contention** | **raise up** | | **Therefore** |

| כן 3651 | תפוג 6313 | תורה 8451 | ולא 3808 | יצא 3318 | לנצח 5331 | משפט 4941 | כי 3588 | רשע 7563 | מכתיר 3803 | את 853 |
|---|---|---|---|---|---|---|---|---|---|---|
| ken | tapug | tourah, | uala' | yetzea' | lanetzach | mishapat; | kiy | rasha' | machtiyr | 'at |
| **after that** | **is slacked** | **the law** | **and not** | **does go forth** | **never** | **and judgment** | **for** | **the wicked** | **does compass about** | |

| הצדיק 6662 | על 5921 | כן 3651 | יצא 3318 | משפט 4941 | מעקל 6127: | **1:5** | ראו 7200 | בגוים 1471 | והביטו 5027 | והתמהו 8539 |
|---|---|---|---|---|---|---|---|---|---|---|
| hatzadiyq, | 'al | ken | yetzea' | mishapat | ma'aqal. | | ra'au | bagouyim | uahabiytu, | uahitamhu |
| **the righteous** | **therefore** | **after that** | **proceed** | **judgment** | **wrong** | | **Behold you** | **among the heathen** | **and regard** | **and wonder** |

| תמהו 8539 | כי 3588 | פעל 6467 | פעל 6466 | בימיכם 3117 | לא 3808 | תאמינו 539 | כי 3588 | יספר 5608: | **1:6** | כי 3588 | הנני 2005 |
|---|---|---|---|---|---|---|---|---|---|---|---|
| tamahu; | kiy | po'al | po'ael | biymeykem, | la' | ta'amiynu | kiy | yasupar. | | kiy | hinniy |
| **marvellously** | **for** | **a work** | **I will work** | **in your days** | **not** | ***which* you will believe** | **though** | **it be told *you*** | | **For** | **lo, I** |

| מקים 6965 | את 853 | הכשדים 3778 | הגוי 1471 | המר 4751 | והנמהר 4116 | ההולך 1980 | למרחבי 4800 | ארץ 776 | לרשת 3423 |
|---|---|---|---|---|---|---|---|---|---|
| meqym | 'at | hakasdiym, | hagouy | hamar | uahanimhar; | hahoulek | lamerchabey | 'aretz, | lareshet |
| **raise up** | | **the Chaldeans** | **nation** | ***that* bitter** | **and hasty** | **which shall march** | **through the breadth of** | **the land** | **to possess** |

| משכנות 4908 | לא 3808 | לו 3807a: | **1:7** | אים 366 | ונורא 3372 | הוא 1931 | ממנו 4480 | משפטו 4941 | ושאתו 7613 |
|---|---|---|---|---|---|---|---|---|---|
| mishkanout | la' | lou'. | | 'ayom | uanoura' | hua'; | mimenu | mishpatou | use'aetou |
| **the dwellingplaces *that are*** | **not** | **theirs** | | ***are* terrible** | **and dreadful** | **They** | **of themselves** | **their judgment** | **and their dignity** |

| יצא 3318: | **1:8** | וקלו 7043 | מנמרים 5246 | סוסיו 5483 | וחדו 2300 | מזאבי 2061 | ערב 6153 |
|---|---|---|---|---|---|---|---|
| yetzea'. | | uaqalu | minameriym | susayu, | uachadu | miza'aebey | 'areb, |
| **shall proceed** | | **also are swifter** | **than the leopards** | **Their horses** | **and are fierce** | **more than wolves** | **the evening** |

| ופשו 6335 | פרשיו 6571 | ופרשיו 6571 | מרחוק 7350 | יבאו 935 | יעפו 5774 | כנשר 5404 | חש 2363 |
|---|---|---|---|---|---|---|---|
| uapashu | parashayu; | uaparashayu | merachouq | yabo'au, | ya'apu | kanesher | chash |
| **and shall spread *themselves*** | **their horsemen** | **and their horsemen** | **from far** | **shall come** | **they shall fly** | **as the eagle *that*** | **hasten** |

**Habakkuk** 1:1 The burden which Habakkuk the prophet did see.2 O YHUH, how long shall I cry, and you will not hear! even cry out unto you of violence, and you will not save!3 Why dost you show me iniquity, and cause me to behold grievance? for spoiling and violence are before me: and there are that raise up strife and contention.4 Therefore the law is slacked, and judgment doth never go forth: for the wicked doth compass about the righteous; therefore wrong judgment proceed.5 Behold you among the heathen, and regard, and wonder marvellously: for I will work a work in your days, which you will not believe, though it be told you.6 For, lo, I raise up the Chaldeans, that bitter and hasty nation, which shall march through the breadth of the land, to possess the dwellingplaces that are not theirs.7 They are terrible and dreadful: their judgment and their dignity shall proceed of themselves.8 Their horses also are swifter than the leopards, and are more fierce than the evening wolves: and their horsemen shall spread themselves, and their horsemen shall come from far; they shall fly as the eagle that hasteth to eat.

1:9

לאכול 398: כלה 3605 לחמס 2555 יבוא 935 מגמת 4041 פניהם 6440 קדימה 6921 ויאסף 622 כחול 2344
le'akoul. kuloh lachamas yabou'a, magamat paneyhem qadiymah; uaya'asop kachoul
**to eat all for violence They shall come shall sup up their faces *as* the east wind and they shall gather as the sand**

1:10

שבי 7628: והוא 1931 במלכים 4428 יתקלס 7046 ורזנים 7336 משחק 4890 לו 3807a הוא 1931 לכל 3605 מבצר 4013
shebiy. uahu'a bamalakiym yitqalas, uarozaniym mischaq lou'; hua' lakal mibtzar
**the captivity And they at the kings shall scoff and the princes *shall be* a scorn unto them every strong hold**

1:11

ישחק 7832 ויצבר 6651 עפר 6083 וילכדה 3920: אז 227 חלף 2498 רוח 7307 ויעבר 5674 ואשם 816
yischaq, uayitzbor 'apar uayilkadah. 'az chalap ruach uaya'abor ua'ashem;
**they shall deride for they shall heap dust and take it Then shall change *his* mind and he shall pass over and offend**

1:12

זו 2098 כחו 3581 לאלהו 433: הלוא 3808 אתה 859 מקדם 6924 יהוה 3069 אלהי 430 קדשי 6918 לא 3808
zu kokou le'alohou. halou'a 'atah miqedem, Yahuah 'alohay qadoshiy la'
***imputing* this his power unto his god *Are* not you from everlasting Yahuah my Elohim my Holy One? not**

נמות 4191 יהוה 3069 למשפט 4941 שמתו 7760 וצור 6697 להוכיח 3198
namut; Yahuah lamishpat samtou, uatzur lahoukiyach
**we shall die Yahuah for judgment you have ordained them and O mighty *Elohim* for correction**

1:13

יסדתו 3245: טהור 2890 עינים 5869 מראות 7200 רע 7451 והביט 5027 אל 413 עמל 5999 לא 3808 תוכל 3201
yasadtou. tahour 'aeynayim mera'aut ra', uahabiyt 'al 'amal la' tukal;
**you have established them *You are* of purer eyes than to behold evil and look on iniquity not and can**

למה 4100 תביט 5027 בוגדים 898 תחריש 2790 בבלע 1104 רשע 7563
lamah tabiyt bougadiym, tachariysh babala' rasha'
**wherefore look you upon them that deal treacherously *and* hold your tongue when devour the wicked**

1:14

צדיק 6662 ממנו 4480: ותעשה 6213 אדם 120 כדגי 1709 הים 3220 כרמש 7431 לא 3808
tzadiyq mimenu. uata'aseh 'adam kidgey hayam; karemes la'
**righteous *the man that is* more than he? And make men as the fishes of the sea as the creeping things *that have* no**

1:15

משל 4910 בו 871a: כלה 3605 בחכה 2443 העלה 5927 יגרהו 1641 בחרמו 2764 ויאספהו 622
moshel bou. kuloh bachakah he'alah, yagorehu bachermou, uaya'aspehu
**ruler over them? all of them with the angle They take up they catch them in their net and gather them**

1:16

במכמרתו 4365 על 5921 כן 3651 ישמח 8055 ויגיל 1523: על 5921 כן 3651 יזבח 2076 לחרמו 2764
bamikmartou; 'al ken yismach uayagiyl. 'al ken yazabeach lachermou,
**in their drag therefore after that they rejoice and are glad Therefore after that they sacrifice unto their net**

1:17

ויקטר 6999 למכמרתו 4365 כי 3588 בהמה 1992 שמן 8082 חלקו 2506 ומאכלו 3978 בראה 1277: העל 5921 כן 3651
uiyqater lamikmartou; kiy bahemah shamen chelqou, uama'akalou bari'ah. ha'al ken
**and burn incense unto their drag because by them *is* fat their portion and their meat plenteous therefore after that**

יריק 7324 חרמו 2764 ותמיד 8548 להרג 2026 גוים 1471 לא 3808 יחמול 2550:
yariyq chermou; uatamiyd laharog gouyim la' yachmoul.
**Shall they empty their net and continually to slay nations not spare**

Hab 1:9 They shall come all for violence: their faces shall sup up as the east wind, and they shall gather the captivity as the sand.10 And they shall scoff at the kings, and the princes shall be a scorn unto them: they shall deride every strong hold; for they shall heap dust, and take it.11 Then shall his mind change, and he shall pass over, and offend, imputing this his power unto his god.12 Art you not from everlasting, O YHUH my G-d, mine Holy One? we shall not die. O YHUH, you have ordained them for judgment; and, O mighty G-d, you have established them for correction.13 Thou are of purer eyes than to behold evil, and canst not look on iniquity: wherefore lookest you upon them that deal treacherously, and holdest your tongue when the wicked devour the man that is more righteous than he?14 And make men as the fishes of the sea, as the creeping things, that have no ruler over them?15 They take up all of them with the angle, they catch them in their net, and gather them in their drag: therefore they rejoice and are glad.16 Therefore they sacrifice unto their net, and burn incense unto their drag; because by them their portion is fat, and their meat plenteous.17 Shall they therefore empty their net, and not spare continually to slay the nations?

| Hab 2:1 5921 על | 4931 משמרתי | 5975 אעמדה | 3320 ואתיצבה | 5921 על | 4692 מצור | 6822 ואצפה | 7200 לראות | 4100 מה | 1696 ידבר |
|---|---|---|---|---|---|---|---|---|---|
| 'al | mishmartiy | 'a'amodah, | ua'atyatzabah | 'al | matzour; | ua'atzapeh, | lera'aut | mah | yadaber |
| **upon** | **my watch** | **I will stand** | **and I am setting myself** | **upon** | **the tower** | **and will watch** | **to see** | **what** | **he will say** |

| 871a בי | 4100 ומה | 7725 אשיב | 5921 על | 8433: תוכחתי | 2:2 6030 ויענני | 3068 יהוה | 559 ויאמר | 3789 כתוב | 2377 חזון |
|---|---|---|---|---|---|---|---|---|---|
| biy, | uamah | 'ashiyb | 'al | toukachatiy. | uaya'aneniy | Yahuah | uaya'mer, | katoub | chazoun, |
| **unto me** | **and what** | **I shall answer** | **when** | **I am reproved** | **And answered me** | **Yahuah** | **and said** | **Write** | **the vision** |

| 874 ובאר | 5921 על | 3871 הלחות | 4616 למען | 7323 ירוץ | 7121 קורא | 871a: בו | 2:3 3588 כי | 5750 עוד | 2377 חזון | 4150 למועד |
|---|---|---|---|---|---|---|---|---|---|---|
| uaba'aer | 'al | haluchot; | lama'an | yarutz | qourea' | bou. | kiy | 'aud | chazoun | lamou'aed, |
| **and make *it* plain** | **upon** | **tables** | **that** | **he may run** | **that read** | **it** | **For** | ***is* yet** | **the vision** | **for an appointed time** |

| 6315 ויפח | 7093 לקץ | 3808 ולא | 3576 יכזב | 518 אם | 4102 יתמהמה | 2442 חכה | 3807a לו | 3588 כי | 935 בא | 935 יבא | 3808 לא |
|---|---|---|---|---|---|---|---|---|---|---|---|
| uayapeach | laqetz | uala' | yakazeb; | 'am | yitmahmah | chakeh | lou', | kiy | ba' | yaba' | la' |
| **but it shall speak** | **at the end** | **and not** | **and lie** | **though** | **it tarry** | **wait for** | **it** | **because** | **it will surely** | **come** | **not** |

| 309: יאחר | 2:4 2009 הנה | 6075 עפלה | 3808 לא | 3474 ישרה | 5315 נפשו | 871a בו | 6662 וצדיק | 530 באמונתו | 2421: יחיה | 2:5 637 ואף |
|---|---|---|---|---|---|---|---|---|---|---|
| ya'acher. | hineh | 'aplah, | la' | yasharah | napshou | bou; | uatzadiyq | be'amunatou | yichayeh. | ua'ap |
| **it will tarry** | **Behold** | ***which* is lifted up** | **not** | **is upright** | **his soul** | **in him** | **but the just** | **by his faith** | **shall live** | **Yea also** |

| 3588 כי | 3196 היין | 898 בוגד | 1397 גבר | 3093 יהיר | 3808 ולא | 5115 ינוה | 834 אשר | 7337 הרחיב | 7585 כשאול | 5315 נפשו | 1931 והוא |
|---|---|---|---|---|---|---|---|---|---|---|---|
| kiy | hayayin | bouged, | geber | yahiyr | uala' | yinueh; | 'asher | hirchiyb | kiysha'aul | napshou, | uahu'a |
| **because** | **by wine** | **he transgress** | ***he is* a man** | **proud** | **neither** | **keep at home** | **who** | **enlarge** | **as hell** | **his desire** | **and he** |

| 4194 כמות | 3808 ולא | 7650 ישבע | 622 ויאסף | 413 אליו | 3605 כל | 1471 הגוים | 6908 ויקבץ | 413 אליו | 3605 כל | 5971: העמים 2:6 |
|---|---|---|---|---|---|---|---|---|---|---|
| kamauet | uala' | yisba', | uaya'asop | 'aelayu | kal | hagouyim, | uayiqbotz | 'aelayu | kal | ha'amiym. |
| ***is* as death** | **and cannot** | **be satisfied** | **but gathered** | **unto him** | **all** | **nations** | **and heapeth** | **unto him** | **all** | **people** |

| 3808 הלוא | 428 אלה | 3605 כלם | 5921 עליו | 4912 משל | 5375 ישאו | 4426 ומליצה | 2420 חידות | 3807a לו | 559 ויאמר | 1945 הוי |
|---|---|---|---|---|---|---|---|---|---|---|
| halou'a | 'aeleh | kulam, | 'alayu | mashal | yisa'au, | uamliytzah | chiydout | lou'; | uaya'mar, | houy |
| **not** | **these** | **all** | **against him** | **a parable** | **Shall take up** | **and a taunting** | **proverb** | **against him** | **and say** | **Woe** |

| 7235 המרבה | 3808 לא | 3807a לו | 5704 עד | 4970 מתי | 3513 ומכביד | 5921 עליו | 5671: עבטיט | 2:7 3808 הלוא | 6621 פתע |
|---|---|---|---|---|---|---|---|---|---|
| hamarbeh | la' | lou', | 'ad | matay | uamakbiyd | 'alayu | 'abtiyt. | halou'a | peta', |
| **to him that increase *that which is*** | **not** | **his** | **how** | **long?** | **and that laden** | **himself** | **with thick clay** | **not** | **suddenly** |

| 6965 יקומו | 5391 נשכיך | 6974 ויקצו | 2111 מזעזעיך | 1961 והיית | 4933 למשסות | 3807a: למו | 2:8 3588 כי |
|---|---|---|---|---|---|---|---|
| yaqumu | noshakeyka, | uayiqtzu | maza'za'ayka; | uahayiyta | limshisout | lamou. | kiy |
| **Shall they rise up** | **that shall bite you** | **and awake** | **that shall vex you** | **and you shall be** | **for booties** | **unto them** | **Because** |

| 859 אתה | 7997 שלות | 1471 גוים | 7227 רבים | 7997 ישלוך | 3605 כל | 3499 יתר | 5971 עמים | 1818 מדמי | 120 אדם |
|---|---|---|---|---|---|---|---|---|---|
| 'atah | shalouta | gouyim | rabiym, | yashaluka | kal | yeter | 'amiym; | midmey | 'adam |
| **you** | **have spoiled** | **nations** | **many** | **shall spoil you** | **all** | **the remnant of** | **the people** | **because of blood** | **men's** |

| 2555 וחמס | 776 ארץ | 7151 קריה | 3605 וכל | 3427 ישבי | 871a: בה | 2:9 1945 הוי | 1214 בצע | 1215 בצע | 7451 רע |
|---|---|---|---|---|---|---|---|---|---|
| uachamas | 'aretz, | qiryah | uakal | yoshabey | bah. | houy, | botzea' | betza' | ra' |
| **and *for* the violence of** | **the land** | **of the city** | **and of all** | **that dwell** | **therein** | **Woe** | **to him that covet** | **covetousness** | **an evil** |

**Hab** 2:1 I will stand upon my watch, and set me upon the tower, and will watch to see what he will say unto me, and what I shall answer when I am reproved.2 And YHUH answered me, and said, Write the vision, and make it plain upon tables, that he may run that readeth it.3 For the vision is yet for an appointed time, but at the end it shall speak, and not lie: though it tarry, wait for it; because it will surely come, it will not tarry.4 Behold, his soul which is lifted up is not upright in him: but the just shall live by his faith.5 Yea also, because he transgresseth by wine, he is a proud man, neither keep at home, who enlargeth his desire as hell, and is as death, and cannot be satisfied, but gathereth unto him all nations, and heapeth unto him all people:6 Shall not all these take up a parable against him, and a taunting proverb against him, and say, Woe to him that increaseth that which is not his! how long? and to him that ladeth himself with thick clay!7 Shall they not rise up suddenly that shall bite you, and awake that shall vex you, and you shall be for booties unto them?8 Because you have spoiled many nations, all the remnant of the people shall spoil you; because of men's blood, and for the violence of the land, of the city, and of all that dwell therein.9 Woe to him that coveteth an evil covetousness to his house,

| לביתו 1004 | לשום 7760 | במרום 4791 | קנו 7064 | להנצל 5337 | מכף 3709 | רע 7451: | 2:10 יעצת 3289 |
|---|---|---|---|---|---|---|---|
| labeytou; | lasum | bamaroum | qinou, | lahinatzel | mikap | ra'. | ya'atzata |
| **to his house** | **that he may set** | **on high** | **his nest** | **that he may be delivered** | **from the power of** | **evil** | **You have consulted** |

| בשת 1322 | לביתך 1004 | קצות 7096 | עמים 5971 | רבים 7227 | וחוטא 2398 | נפשך 5315: | 2:11 כי 3588 | אבן 68 | מקיר 7023 |
|---|---|---|---|---|---|---|---|---|---|
| boshet | labeyteka; | qatzout | 'amiym | rabiym | uachoutea' | napsheka. | kiy | 'aben | miqiyr |
| **shame** | **to your house** | **by cutting off** | **people** | **many** | **and have sinned** | ***against* your soul** | **For** | **the stone** | **out of the wall** |

| תזעק 2199 | וכפיס 3714 | מעץ 6086 | יעננה 6030: | 2:12 הוי 1945 | בנה 1129 | עיר 5892 | בדמים 1818 | וכונן 3559 |
|---|---|---|---|---|---|---|---|---|
| tiz'aq; | uakapiys | me'aetz | ya'anenah. | houy | boneh | 'ayr | badamiym; | uakounen |
| **shall cry** | **and the beam** | **out of the timber** | **shall answer it** | **Woe** | **to him that builds** | **a town** | **with blood** | **and stablisheth** |

| קריה 7151 | בעולה 5766: | 2:13 הלוא 3808 | הנה 2009 | מאת 853 | יהוה 3068 | צבאות 6635 | וייגעו 3021 | עמים 5971 | בדי 1767 | אש 784 |
|---|---|---|---|---|---|---|---|---|---|---|
| qiryah | ba'aulah. | halou'a | hineh, | me'at | Yahuah | tzaba'aut; | uayiyga'au | 'amiym | badey | 'aesh, |
| **a city** | **by iniquity** | ***is it* not** | **Behold** | **of the** | **Yahuah** | **of hosts** | **that shall labour** | **the people** | **in the very** | **fire** |

| ולאמים 3816 | בדי 1767 | ריק 7385 | יעפו 3286: | 2:14 כי 3588 | תמלא 4390 | הארץ 776 | לדעת 3045 | את 853 |
|---|---|---|---|---|---|---|---|---|
| uala'amiym | badey | riyq | yi'apu. | kiy | timalea' | ha'aretz, | lada'at | 'at |
| **and the people** | **for very** | **vanity?** | **shall weary themselves** | **For** | **shall be filled with** | **the earth** | **the knowledge of** | |

| כבוד 3519 | יהוה 3068 | כמים 4325 | יכסו 3680 | על 5921 | ים 3220: | 2:15 הוי 1945 | משקה 8248 | רעהו 7453 | מספח 5596 |
|---|---|---|---|---|---|---|---|---|---|
| kaboud | Yahuah; | kamayim | yakasu | 'al | yam. | houy | mashqeh | re'aehu, | masapeach |
| **the glory of** | **Yahuah** | **as the waters** | **cover** | **over** | **the sea** | **Woe** | **unto him that gives drink** | **his neighbour** | **that put** |

| חמתך 2573 | ואף 637 | שכר 7937 | למען 4616 | הביט 5027 | על 5921 | מעוריהם 4589: | 2:16 שבעת 7646 |
|---|---|---|---|---|---|---|---|
| chamataka | ua'ap | shaker; | lama'an | habiyt | 'al | ma'aureyhem. | saba'ata |
| **your bottle** | ***to him* and also** | **make *him* drunken** | **that** | **you may look** | **on** | **their nakedness** | **You are filled with** |

| קלון 7036 | מכבוד 3519 | שתה 8354 | גם 1571 | אתה 859 | והערל 6188 | תסוב 5437 | עליך 5921 | כוס 3563 | ימין 3225 |
|---|---|---|---|---|---|---|---|---|---|
| qaloun | mikaboud, | shateh | gam | 'atah | uahe'arel; | tisoub | 'aleyka, | kous | yamiyn |
| **shame** | **for glory** | **drink you** | **also** | **yourself** | **and let foreskin be uncovered** | **shall be turned** | **unto you** | **the cup of** | **right hand** |

| יהוה 3068 | וקיקלון 7022 | על 5921 | כבודך 3519: | 2:17 כי 3588 | חמס 2555 | לבנון 3844 | יכסך 3680 |
|---|---|---|---|---|---|---|---|
| Yahuah, | uaqiyqaloun | 'al | kaboudeka. | kiy | chamas | labanoun | yakaseka, |
| **Yahuah's** | **and shameful spewing** | ***shall be* on your** | **glory** | **For** | **the violence of** | **Lebanon** | **shall cover you** |

| ושד 7701 | בהמות 929 | יחיתן 2865 | מדמי 1818 | אדם 120 | וחמס 2555 | ארץ 776 | קריה 7151 |
|---|---|---|---|---|---|---|---|
| uashod | bahemout | yachiytan; | midmey | 'adam | uachamas | 'aretz, | qiryah |
| **and the spoil of** | **beasts** | ***which* made them afraid** | **because of blood** | **men's** | **and for the violence of** | **the land** | **of the city** |

| וכל 3605 | ישבי 3427 | בה 871a: | 2:18 מה 4100 | הועיל 3276 | פסל 6459 | כי 3588 | פסלו 6458 | יצרו 3336 |
|---|---|---|---|---|---|---|---|---|
| uakal | yoshabey | bah. | mah | hou'ayl | pesel, | kiy | pasalou | yotzarou, |
| **and of all** | **that dwell** | **therein** | **What** | **profiteth** | **the graven image** | **that** | **has graven it** | **the maker thereof** |

| מסכה 4541 | ומורה 3384 | שקר 8267 | כי 3588 | בטח 982 | יצר 3335 | יצרו 3335 | עליו 5921 | לעשות 6213 | אלילים 457 | אלמים 483: |
|---|---|---|---|---|---|---|---|---|---|---|
| masekah | uamoureh | shaqer; | kiy | batach | yotzer | yitzrou | 'alayu, | la'asout | 'aliyliym | 'almiym. |
| **the molten image** | **and a teacher of** | **lies** | **that** | **trust** | **the maker of** | **his work** | **therein** | **to make** | **idols?** | **dumb** |

Hab 2:9 that he may set his nest on high, that he may be delivered from the power of evil! 10 Thou have consulted shame to your house by cutting off many people, and have sinned against your soul. 11 For the stone shall cry out of the wall, and the beam out of the timber shall answer it. 12 Woe to him that buildeth a town with blood, and stablisheth a city by iniquity! 13 Behold, is it not of YHUH of hosts that the people shall labour in the very fire, and the people shall weary themselves for very vanity? 14 For the earth shall be filled with the knowledge of the glory of YHUH, as the waters cover the sea. 15 Woe unto him that give his neighbor drink, that puttest your bottle to him, and make him drunken also, that you may look on their nakedness! 16 Thou are filled with shame for glory: drink you also, and let your foreskin be uncovered: the cup of YHUH's right hand shall be turned unto you, and shameful spewing shall be on your glory. 17 For the violence of Lebanon shall cover you, and the spoil of beasts, which made them afraid, because of men's blood, and for the violence of the land, of the city, and of all that dwell therein. 18 What profiteth the graven image that the maker thereof has graven it; the molten image, and a teacher of lies, that the maker of his work trusteth therein, to make dumb idols?

2:19
הוי 1945 אמר 559 לעץ 6086 הקיצה 6974 עורי 5782 לאבן 68 דומם 1748 הוא 1931 יורה 3384 הנה 2009 הוא 1931 תפוש 8610
houy 'amer la'aetz haqiytzah, 'auriy la'aben dumam; hua' youreh, hineh hua', tapus
**Woe *unto* him that saith to wood Awake Arise to the stone dumb it shall teach Behold it *is* laid over**

זהב 2091 וכסף 3701 וכל 3605 רוח 7307 אין 369 בקרבו 7130: 2:20 ויהוה 3068 בהיכל 1964 קדשו 6944
zahab uakesep, uakal ruach 'aeyn baqirbou. uaYahuah baheykal qadashou;
**with gold and silver and *there is* no breath and there is no in the midst of it But Yahuah *is* in temple his holy**

הס 2013 מפניו 6440 כל 3605 הארץ 776:
has mipanayu kal ha'aretz.
**let keep silence before him all the earth**

Hab 3:1
תפלה 8605 לחבקוק 2265 הנביא 5030 על 5921 שגינות 7692: 3:2 יהוה 3068 שמעתי 8085 שמעך 8088 יראתי 3372
tapilah lachabaquq hanabiy'a; 'al shigayonout. Yahuah shama'atiy shim'aka yarea'tiy
**A prayer of Habakkuk the prophet upon Shigionoth O Yahuah I have heard your speech *and* was afraid**

יהוה 3068 פעלך 6467 בקרב 7130 שנים 8141 חייהו 2421 בקרב 7130 שנים 8141 תודיע 3045 ברגז 7267 רחם 7355
Yahuah pa'laka baqereb shaniym chayeyhu, baqereb shaniym toudiya'; barogez rachem
**O Yahuah your work in the midst of the years revive in the midst of the years make known in wrath mercy**

תזכור 2142: 3:3 אלוה 433 מתימן 8487 יבוא 935 וקדוש 6918 מהר 2022 פארן 6290 סלה 5542 כסה 3680 שמים 8064 הודו 3035
tizkour. 'alouah miteyman yabou'a, uaqadoush mehar pa'ran selah; kisah shamayim houdou,
**remember Elohim from Teman came and the Holy One from mount Paran Selah covered the heavens His glory**

ותהלתו 8416 מלאה 4390 הארץ 776: 3:4 ונגה 5051 כאור 216 תהיה 1961 קרנים 7161 מידו 3027 לו 3807a
uatahilatou mal'ah ha'aretz. uanogah ka'aur tihayeh, qarnayim miyadou lou';
**and his praise was full of the earth And *his* brightness as the light was he had horns *coming* out of hand his**

ושם 8033 חביון 2253 עזה 5797: 3:5 לפניו 6440 ילך 1980 דבר 1698 ויצא 3318 רשף 7565 לרגליו 7272: 3:6
uasham chebyoun 'azoh lapanayu yelek daber; uayetzea' reshep laraglayu.
**and there *was* the hiding of his power Before him went the pestilence went forth and burning coals at his feet**

עמד 5975 וימדד 4058 ארץ 776 ראה 7200 ויתר 5425 גוים 1471 ויתפצצו 6327 הררי 2042 עד 5703
'amad uayamoded 'aretz, ra'ah uayater gouyim, uayitpotzatzu hararey 'ad,
**He stood and measured the earth he beheld and drove asunder the nations and were scattered mountains the everlasting**

שחו 7817 גבעות 1389 עולם 5769 הליכות 1979 עולם 5769 לו 3807a: 3:7 תחת 8478 און 205 ראיתי 7200 אהלי 168 כושן 3572
shachu gib'aut 'aulam; haliykout 'aulam lou' tachat 'auen, ra'aytiy 'ahaley kushan;
**did bow hills the perpetual ways *are* everlasting his in affliction I saw the tents of Cushan**

ירגזון 7264 יריעות 3407 ארץ 776 מדין 4080: 3:8 הבנהרים 5104 חרה 2734 יהוה 3068 אם 518 בנהרים 5104
yirgazun yariy'aut 'aretz midyan. habinahariym charah Yahuah, 'am banahariym
**did tremble *and* the curtains of the land of Midian against the rivers? Was displeased Yahuah or against the rivers?**

אפך 639 אם 518 בים 3220 עברתך 5678 כי 3588 תרכב 7392 על 5921 סוסיך 5483 מרכבתיך 4818
'apeka, 'am bayam 'abrateka; kiy tirkab 'al suseyka, markaboteyka
***was* your anger or against the sea *was* your wrath that you did ride upon your horses *and* your chariots of**

Hab 2:19 Woe unto him that saith to the wood, Awake; to the dumb stone, Arise, it shall teach! Behold, it is laid over with gold and silver, and there is no breath at all in the midst of it.20 But YHUH is in his holy temple: let all the earth keep silence before him. **Hab** 3:1 A prayer of Habakkuk the prophet upon Shigionoth.2 O YHUH, I have heard your speech, and was afraid: O YHUH, revive your work in the midst of the years, in the midst of the years make known; in wrath remember mercy.3 G-d came from Teman, and the Holy One from mount Paran. Selah. His glory covered the heavens, and the earth was full of his praise.4 And his brightness was as the light; he had horns coming out of his hand: and there was the hiding of his power.5 Before him went the pestilence, and burning coals went forth at his feet.6 He stood, and measured the earth: he beheld, and drove asunder the nations; and the everlasting mountains were scattered, the perpetual hills did bow: his ways are everlasting.7 I saw the tents of Cushan in affliction: and the curtains of the land of Midian did tremble.8 Was YHUH displeased against the rivers? was your anger against the rivers? was your wrath against the sea, that you did ride upon your horses and your chariots of salvation?

ישועה 3444: | 3:9 עריה 6181 | תעור 5783 | קשתך 7198 | שבעות 7621 | מטות 4294 | אמר 562 | סלה 5542 | נהרות 5104
yashu'ah. | 'aryah | te'aur | qashtekha, | shabu'aut | matout | 'amer | selah; | naharout
**salvation? | quite | was made naked | Your bow | *according* to the oaths of | the tribes | *even your* word | Selah | with rivers**

תבקע 1234 | ארץ 776: | 3:10 ראוך 7200 | יחילו 2342 | הרים 2022 | זרם 2230 | מים 4325 | עבר 5674 | נתן 5414
tabaqa' | 'aretz. | ra'auka | yachiylu | hariym, | zerem | mayim | 'abar; | natan
**You did cleave | the earth | saw you | *and* they trembled | The mountains | the overflowing of | the water | passed by | uttered**

תהום 8415 | קולו 6963 | רום 7315 | ידיהו 3027 | נשא 5375: | 3:11 שמש 8121 | ירח 3394 | עמד 5975 | זבלה 2073 | לאור 216
tahoum | qoulou, | roum | yadeyhu | nasa'. | shemesh | yareach | 'amad | zabulah; | la'aur
**the deep | his voice | on high | his hands | *and* lifted up | The sun | *and* moon | stood still | in their habitation | at the light of**

חציך 2671 | יהלכו 1980 | לנגה 5051 | ברק 1300 | חניתך 2595: | 3:12 בזעם 2195 | תצעד 6805 | ארץ 776
chitzeyka | yahaleku, | lanogah | baraq | chaniyteka. | baza'am | titz'ad | 'aretz;
**your arrows | they went | *and* at the shining of | your glittering spear | in indignation | You did march through | the land**

באף 639 | תדוש 1758 | גוים 1471: | 3:13 יצאת 3318 | לישע 3468 | עמך 5973 | לישע 3468 | את 853
ba'ap | tadush | gouyim. | yatza'ta | layesha' | 'ameka, | layesha' | 'at
**in anger | you did thresh | the heathen | You went forth | for the salvation of | your people | *even* for salvation**

משיחך 4899 | מחצת 4272 | ראש 7218 | מבית 1004 | רשע 7563 | ערות 6168 | יסוד 3247 | עד 5704 | צואר 6677
mashiycheka; | machatzata | ra'sh | mibeyt | rasha', | 'arout | yasoud | 'ad | tzaua'ar
**with your anointed | you wounded | the head | out of the house of | the wicked | by discovering | the foundation | unto | the neck**

סלה 5542: | 3:14 נקבת 5344 | במטיו 4294 | ראש 7218 | פרזו 6518 | יסערו 5590 | להפיצני 6327
selah. | naqabta | bamatayu | ra'sh | parazou | yis'aru | lahapiytzeniy;
**Selah | You did strike through | with his staves | the head | of his villages | they came out as a whirlwind | to scatter me**

עליצתם 5951 | כמו 3644 | לאכל 398 | עני 6041 | במסתר 4565: | 3:15 דרכת 1869 | בים 3220 | סוסיך 5483 | חמר 2563
'aliytzutam, | kamou | le'akol | 'aniy | bamistar. | darakta | bayam | suseyka; | chamor
**their rejoicing *was* as | to devour | poor | the secretly | You did walk through | the sea | with your horses | *through* the heap of**

מים 4325 | רבים 7227: | 3:16 שמעתי 8085 | ותרגז 7264 | בטני 990 | לקול 6963 | צללו 6750 | שפתי 8193 | יבוא 935 | רקב 7538 | בעצמי 6106
mayim | rabiym. | shama'atiy | uatirgaz | bitniy, | laqoul | tzalalu | sapatay, | yabou'a | raqab | ba'atzamay
**waters | great | I heard | When trembled | my belly | at the voice | quivered | my lips | entered | rottenness | into my bones**

ותחתי 8478 | ארגז 7264 | אשר 834 | אנוח 5117 | ליום 3117 | צרה 6869 | לעלות 5927 | לעם 5971
uatachtay | 'argaz; | 'asher | 'anuach | layoum | tzarah, | la'alout | la'am
**and in myself | I trembled | that | I might rest | in the day of | trouble | when he comes up | unto the people**

יגודנו 1464: | 3:17 כי 3588 | תאנה 8384 | לא 3808 | תפרח 6524 | ואין 369 | יבול 2981 | בגפנים 1612
yagudenu. | kiy | ta'aenah | la' | tiprach, | ua'aeyn | yabul | bagapaniym,
**he will invade them *with his troops* | Although | the fig tree | not | shall blossom | and neither | *shall* fruit | *be* in the vines**

כחש 3584 | מעשה 4639 | זית 2132 | ושדמות 7709 | לא 3808 | עשה 6213 | אכל 400 | גזר 1504 | ממכלה 4356 | צאן 6629
kichesh | ma'aseh | zayit, | uashdemout | la' | 'asah | 'akel; | gazar | mimiklah | tza'n,
**shall fail | the labour of | the olive | and the fields | no | shall yield | meat | shall be cut off | from the fold | the flock**

Hab 3:9 Thy bow was made quite naked, according to the oaths of the tribes, even your word. Selah. Thou did cleave the earth with rivers.10 The mountains saw you, and they trembled: the overflowing of the water passed by: the deep uttered his voice, and lifted up his hands on high.11 The sun and moon stood still in their habitation: at the light of your arrows they went, and at the shining of your glittering spear.12 Thou did march through the land in indignation, you did thresh the heathen in anger.13 Thou went forth for the salvation of your people, even for salvation with your anointed; you woundedst the head out of the house of the wicked, by discovering the foundation unto the neck. Selah.14 Thou did strike through with his staves the head of his villages: they came out as a whirlwind to scatter me: their rejoicing was as to devour the poor secretly.15 Thou did walk through the sea with your horses, through the heap of great waters.16 When I heard, my belly trembled; my lips quivered at the voice: rottenness entered into my bones, and I trembled in myself, that I might rest in the day of trouble: when he cometh up unto the people, he will invade them with his troops.17 Although the fig tree shall not blossom, neither shall fruit be in the vines; the labour of the olive shall fail, and the fields shall yield no meat; the flock shall be cut off from the fold,

| 𐤅𐤀𐤉𐤍 | 𐤁𐤒𐤓 | 𐤁𐤓𐤐𐤕𐤉𐤌 | **3:18** | 𐤅𐤀𐤍𐤉 | 𐤁𐤉𐤄𐤅𐤄 | 𐤀𐤏𐤋𐤅𐤆𐤄 | 𐤀𐤂𐤉𐤋𐤄 | 𐤁𐤀𐤋𐤄𐤉 | 𐤉𐤔𐤏𐤉 | **3:19** |
|---|---|---|---|---|---|---|---|---|---|---|
| ואין 369 | בקר 1241 | ברפתים 7517: | | ואני 589 | ביהוה 3068 | אעלוזה 5937 | אגילה 1523 | באלהי 430 | ישעי 3468: | |
| ua'aeyn | baqar | barapatiym. | | ua'aniy | baYahuah | a'alouzah; | 'agiylah | be'alohey | yish'ay. | |
| **and *there shall be* no** | **herd** | **in the stalls** | | **Yet I** | **in Yahuah** | **will rejoice** | **I will joy** | **in the Elohim** | **of my salvation** | |

| 𐤉𐤄𐤅𐤄 | 𐤀𐤃𐤍𐤉 | 𐤇𐤉𐤋𐤉 | 𐤅𐤉𐤔𐤌 | 𐤓𐤂𐤋𐤉 | 𐤊𐤀𐤉𐤋𐤅𐤕 | 𐤅𐤏𐤋 | 𐤁𐤌𐤅𐤕𐤉 | 𐤉𐤃𐤓𐤊𐤍𐤉 |
|---|---|---|---|---|---|---|---|---|
| יהוה 3069 | אדני 136 | חילי 2428 | וישם 7760 | רגלי 7272 | כאילות 355 | ועל 5921 | במותי 1116 | ידרכני 1869 |
| Yahuah | 'adonay | cheyliy, | uayasem | raglay | ka'ayalout, | ua'al | bamoutay | yadrikeniy; |
| **Yahuah** | **Adonai *is*** | **my strength** | **and he will make** | **my feet** | **like hinds' *feet*** | **and upon** | **mine high places** | **he will make me to walk** |

| 𐤋𐤌𐤍𐤑𐤇 | 𐤁𐤍𐤂𐤉𐤍𐤅𐤕𐤉 |
|---|---|
| למנצח 5329 | בנגינותי 5058: |
| lamanatzeach | binagiynoutay. |
| **To the chief singer** | **on my stringed instruments** |

Hab 3:17 and there shall be no herd in the stalls:18 Yet I will rejoice in YHUH, I will joy in the G-d of my salvation.19 YHUH G-d is my strength, and he will make my feet like hinds' feet, and he will make me to walk upon mine high places. To the chief singer on my stringed instruments.

# ZEPHANIAH
## (*Tzapanyah*)

Verse one identifies the author as the Prophet Zephaniah and his name in Hebrew means "*Defended by Yah.*" The book was written to the **House of Judah** sometime between 735 and 725 B.C. Zephaniah's message is three fold: 1) Yahuah is sovereign over all the nations of the earth. 2) The wicked will be punished and the righteous will be vindicated on judgment day. 3) Yahuah always blesses those who repent and trust in Him. Zephaniah prophesies judgment on the whole earth and on all nations on what is called the Day of the Yahuah. He follows it up with prophecies of coming blessing on all nations, especially on the faithful remnant of His people, which are yet to be fulfilled.

**Zephaniah 1:1**

| דבר 1697 | יהוה 3068 | אשר 834 | היה 1961 | אל 413 | צפניה 6846 | בן 1121 | כושי 3569 | בן 1121 | גדליה 1436 | בן 1121 |
|---|---|---|---|---|---|---|---|---|---|---|
| dabar | Yahuah | 'asher | hayah, | 'al | tzapanyah | ben | kushiy | ben | gadalyah, | ben |
| **The word of** | **Yahuah** | **which** | **came** | **unto** | **Zephaniah** | **the son of** | **Cushi** | **the son of** | **Gedaliah** | **the son of** |

| אמריה 568 | בן 1121 | חזקיה 2396 | בימי 3117 | יאשיהו 2977 | בן 1121 | אמון 526 | מלך 4428 | יהודה 3063: | **1:2** | אסף 622 | אסף 622 |
|---|---|---|---|---|---|---|---|---|---|---|---|
| 'amaryah | ben | chizqiyah; | biymey | ya'shiyahu | ben | 'amoun | melek | yahudah. | | 'asoup | 'asep |
| **Amariah** | **the son of** | **Hizkiah** | **in the days of** | **Josiah** | **the son of** | **Amon** | **king of** | **Judah** | | **I will utterly** | **consume** |

| כל 3605 | מעל 5921 | פני 6440 | האדמה 127 | נאם 5002 | יהוה 3068: | **1:3** | אסף 622 | אדם 120 | ובהמה 929 | אסף 622 | עוף 5775 |
|---|---|---|---|---|---|---|---|---|---|---|---|
| kol, | me'al | paney | ha'adamah | na'am | Yahuah. | | 'asep | 'adam | uabahemah, | 'asep | 'aup |
| **all things** | **from** | **off the face** | **the land** | **saith** | **Yahuah** | | **I will consume** | **man** | **and beast** | **I will consume** | **the fowls of** |

| השמים 8064 | ודגי 1709 | הים 3220 | והמכשלות 4384 | את 853 | הרשעים 7563 | והכרתי 3772 | את 853 | האדם 120 | מעל 5921 |
|---|---|---|---|---|---|---|---|---|---|
| hashamayim | uadgey | hayam, | uahamakshelout | 'at | harasha'aym; | uahikratiy | 'at | ha'adam, | me'al |
| **the heaven** | **and the fishes of** | **the sea** | **and the stumblingblocks** | ***with*** | **the wicked** | **and I will cut off** | | **man** | **from** |

| פני 6440 | האדמה 127 | נאם 5002 | יהוה 3068: | **1:4** | ונטיתי 5186 | ידי 3027 | על 5921 | יהודה 3063 | ועל 5921 | כל 3605 | יושבי 3427 |
|---|---|---|---|---|---|---|---|---|---|---|---|
| paney | ha'adamah | na'am | Yahuah. | | uanatiytiy | yadiy | 'al | yahudah, | ua'al | kal | youshabey |
| **off** | **the land** | **saith** | **Yahuah** | | **I will also stretch out** | **mine hand** | **upon** | **Judah** | **and upon** | **all** | **the inhabitants of** |

| ירושלם 3389 | והכרתי 3772 | מן 4480 | המקום 4725 | הזה 2088 | את 853 | שאר 7605 | הבעל 1168 | את 853 | שם 8034 | הכמרים 3649 |
|---|---|---|---|---|---|---|---|---|---|---|
| yarushalaim; | uahikratiy | min | hamaqoum | hazeh | 'at | sha'ar | haba'al, | 'at | shem | hakamariym |
| **Jerusalem** | **and I will cut off** | **from** | **place** | **this** | | **the remnant of** | **Baal** | | ***and*** **the name of** | **the Chemarims** |

| עם 5973 | הכהנים 3548: | **1:5** | ואת 853 | המשתחוים 7812 | על 5921 | הגגות 1406 | לצבא 6635 | השמים 8064 | ואת 853 | המשתחוים 7812 |
|---|---|---|---|---|---|---|---|---|---|---|
| 'am | hakohaniym. | | ua'at | hamishtachauiym | 'al | hagagout | litzaba' | hashamayim; | ua'at | hamishtachauiym |
| **with** | **the priests** | | ***And*** | **them that worship** | **upon** | **the housetops** | **the host of** | **heaven** | ***and*** | **them that worship** |

| הנשבעים 7650 | ליהוה 3068 | והנשבעים 7650 | במלכם 4428: | **1:6** | ואת 853 | הנסוגים 5472 | מאחרי 310 | יהוה 3069 |
|---|---|---|---|---|---|---|---|---|
| hanishba'aym | laYahuah, | uahanishba'aym | bamalkam. | | ua'at | hanasougiym | me'acharey | Yahuah; |
| ***and*** **that swear** | **by Yahuah** | **and that swear** | **by Milcom** | | ***And*** | **them that are turned back** | **from** | **Yahuah** |

| ואשר 834 | לא 3808 | בקשו 1245 | את 853 | יהוה 3069 | ולא 3808 | דרשהו 1875: | **1:7** | הס 2013 | מפני 6440 | אדני 136 |
|---|---|---|---|---|---|---|---|---|---|---|
| ua'asher | la' | biqshu | 'at | Yahuah | uala' | darashuhu. | | has | mipaney | 'adonay |
| **and** ***those*** **that** | **not** | **have sought** | | **Yahuah** | **nor** | **inquired for him** | | **Hold your peace** | **at the presence of** | **Adonai** |

| יהוה 3069 | כי 3588 | קרוב 7138 | יום 3117 | יהוה 3068 | כי 3588 | הכין 3559 | יהוה 3068 | זבח 2077 | הקדיש 6942 | קראיו 7121: |
|---|---|---|---|---|---|---|---|---|---|---|
| Yahuah; | kiy | qaroub | youm | Yahuah, | kiy | hekiyn | Yahuah | zebach | hiqdiysh | qaru'ayu. |
| **Yahuah** | **for** | ***is*** **at hand** | **the day of** | **Yahuah** | **for** | **has prepared** | **Yahuah** | **a sacrifice** | **he has bid** | **his guests** |

**Zephaniah** 1:1 The word of YHUH which came unto Zephaniah the son of Cushi, the son of Gedaliah, the son of Amariah, the son of Hizkiah, in the days of Josiah the son of Amon, king of Judah.2 I will utterly consume all things from off the land, saith YHUH.3 I will consume man and beast; I will consume the fowls of the heaven, and the fishes of the sea, and the stumblingblocks with the wicked; and I will cut off man from off the land, saith YHUH.4 I will also stretch out mine hand upon Judah, and upon all the inhabitants of Jerusalem; and I will cut off the remnant of Baal from this place, and the name of the Chemarims with the priests;5 And them that worship the host of heaven upon the housetops; and them that worship and that swear by YHUH, and that swear by Malcham;6 And them that are turned back from YHUH; and those that have not sought YHUH, nor inquired for him.7 Hold your peace at the presence of YHUH G-D: for the day of YHUH is at hand: for YHUH has prepared a sacrifice, he has bid his guests.

1:8
והיה 1961 ביום 3117 זבח 2077 יהוה 3068 ופקדתי 6485 על 5921 השרים 8269 ועל 5921 בני 1121
uahayah, bayoum zebach Yahuah, uapaqadtiy 'al hasariym ua'al baney
**And it shall come to pass in the day of sacrifice Yahuah's that I will punish on the princes and on children**

1:9
המלך 4428 ועל 5921 כל 3605 הלבשים 3847 מלבוש 4403 נכרי 5237: ופקדתי 6485 על 5921 כל 3605 הדולג 1801 על 5921
hamelek; ua'al kal halobashiym malbush nakariy. uapaqadtiy, 'al kal hadouleg 'al
**the king's and on all such as are clothed apparel *with* strange also will I punish and on all those that leap on**

1:10
המפתן 4670 ביום 3117 ההוא 1931 הממלאים 4390 בית 1004 אדניהם 113 חמס 2555 ומרמה 4820: והיה 1961
hamiptan bayoum hahua'; hamamal'aym beyt 'adoneyhem chamas uamirmah. uahayah
**the threshold In the day same which fill houses their masters' *with* violence and deceit And it shall come to pass**

ביום 3117 ההוא 1931 נאם 5002 יהוה 3068 קול 6963 צעקה 6818 משער 8179 הדגים 1709 ויללה 3215 מן 4480
bayoum hahua' na'am Yahuah qoul tza'aqah misha'ar hadagiym, uiylalah min
**in day that saith Yahuah *that there shall be* the noise of a cry from gate the fish and an howling from**

1:11
המשנה 4932 ושבר 7667 גדול 1419 מהגבעות 1389: הילילו 3213 ישבי 3427 המכתש 4389 כי 3588 נדמה 1820 כל 3605 עם 5971
hamishneh; uasheber gadoul mehagaba'aut. heyliylu yoshabey hamaktesh; kiy nidmah kal 'am
**the second and crashing a great from the hills Howl you inhabitants of Maktesh for are cut down all people**

1:12
כנען 3667 נכרתו 3772 כל 3605 נטילי 5187 כסף 3701: והיה 1961 בעת 6256 ההיא 1931 אחפש 2664 את 853
kana'an, nikratu kal natiyley kasep. uahayah ba'aet hahiy'a, 'achapes 'at
**the merchant are cut off all they that bear silver And it shall come to pass at time that *that* I will search**

ירושלם 3389 בנרות 5216 ופקדתי 6485 על 5921 האנשים 582 הקפאים 7087 על 5921 שמריהם 8105 האמרים 559 בלבבם 3824 לא 3808
yarushalaim banerout; uapaqadtiy 'al ha'anashiym, haqopa'aym 'al shimreyhem, ha'amariym bilbabam, la'
**Jerusalem with candles and punish on the men that are settled on their lees that say in their heart not**

1:13
ייטיב 3190 יהוה 3068 ולא 3808 ירע 7489: והיה 1961 חילם 2428 למשסה 4933 ובתיהם 1004 לשממה 8077
yeytiyb Yahuah uala' yarea'. uahayah cheylam limshisah, uabateyhem lishmamah;
**will do good Yahuah neither will he do evil Therefore shall become their goods a booty and their houses a desolation**

ובנו 1129 בתים 1004 ולא 3808 ישבו 3427 ונטעו 5193 כרמים 3754 ולא 3808 ישתו 8354 את 853
uabanu batiym uala' yeshebu, uanata'au karamiym, uala' yishtu 'at
**they shall also build houses but not inhabit *them* and they shall plant vineyards but not drink**

1:14
יינם 3196: קרוב 7138 יום 3117 יהוה 3068 הגדול 1419 קרוב 7138 ומהר 4118 מאד 3966 קול 6963 יום 3117 יהוה 3068
yeynam. qaroub youm Yahuah hagadoul, qaroub uamaher ma'ad; qoul youm Yahuah,
**the wine thereof *is* near day of Yahuah The great *it is* near and hasten greatly *even* the voice of the day of Yahuah**

1:15
מר 4751 צרח 6873 שם 8033 גבור 1368: יום 3117 עברה 5678 היום 3117 ההוא 1931 יום 3117 צרה 6869 ומצוקה 4691 יום 3117
mar tzoreach sham gibour. youm 'abrah hayoum hahua'; youm tzarah uamtzuqah, youm
**bitterly shall cry there the mighty man day wrath *is* a day of That a day of trouble and distress a day of**

1:16
שאה 7722 ומשואה 4875 יום 3117 חשך 2822 ואפלה 653 יום 3117 ענן 6051 וערפל 6205: יום 3117 שופר 7782
sho'ah uamshou'ah, youm choshek ua'apelah, youm 'anan ua'arapel. youm shoupar
**wasteness and desolation a day of darkness and gloominess a day of clouds and thick darkness A day of the trumpet**

Zeph 1:8 And it shall come to pass in the day of YHUH's sacrifice, that I will punish the princes, and the king's children, and all such as are clothed with strange apparel.9 In the same day also will I punish all those that leap on the threshold, which fill their masters' houses with violence and deceit.10 And it shall come to pass in that day, saith YHUH, that there shall be the noise of a cry from the fish gate, and an howling from the second, and a great crashing from the hills.11 Howl, you inhabitants of Maktesh, for all the merchant people are cut down; all they that bear silver are cut off.12 And it shall come to pass at that time, that I will search Jerusalem with candles, and punish the men that are settled on their lees: that say in their heart, YHUH will not do good, neither will he do evil.13 Therefore their goods shall become a booty, and their houses a desolation: they shall also build houses, but not inhabit them; and they shall plant vineyards, but not drink the wine thereof.14 The great day of YHUH is near, it is near, and hasteth greatly, even the voice of the day of YHUH: the mighty man shall cry there bitterly.15 That day is a day of wrath, a day of trouble and distress, a day of wasteness and desolation, a day of darkness and gloominess, a day of clouds and thick darkness,

| ותרועה 8643 | על 5921 | הערים 5892 | הבצרות 1219 | ועל 5921 | הפנות 6438 | הגבהות 1364: | 1:17 | והצרתי 6887 | לאדם 120 |
|---|---|---|---|---|---|---|---|---|---|
| uatru'ah; | 'al | he'ariym | habatzurout, | ua'al | hapinout | hagabohout. | | uahatzerotiy | la'adam, |
| **and alarm** | **against** | **cities** | **the fenced** | **and against** | **towers** | **the high** | | **And I will bring distress** | **upon men** |

| והלכו 1980 | כעורים 5787 | כי 3588 | ליהוה 3068 | חטאו 2398 | ושפך 8210 | דמם 1818 | כעפר 6083 |
|---|---|---|---|---|---|---|---|
| uahalaku | ka'auariym, | kiy | laYahuah | chata'au; | uashupak | damam | ke'apar, |
| **that they shall walk** | **like blind men** | **because** | **against Yahuah** | **they have sinned** | **and shall be poured out** | **their blood** | **as dust** |

| ולחמם 3894 | כגללים 1561: | 1:18 | גם 1571 | כספם 3701 | גם 1571 | זהבם 2091 | לא 3808 | יוכל 3201 | להצילם 5337 | ביום 3117 |
|---|---|---|---|---|---|---|---|---|---|---|
| ualchumam | kaglaliym. | | gam | kaspam | gam | zahabam | la' | yukal | lahatziylam, | bayoum |
| **and their flesh** | **as the dung** | | **Neither** | **their silver** | **nor** | **their gold** | **not** | **shall be able** | **to deliver them** | **in the day of** |

| עברת 5678 | יהוה 3068 | ובאש 784 | קנאתו 7068 | תאכל 398 | כל 3605 | הארץ 776 | כי 3588 | כלה 3617 | אך 389 | נבהלה 926 |
|---|---|---|---|---|---|---|---|---|---|---|
| 'abrat | Yahuah, | uab'aesh | qin'atou, | te'akel | kal | ha'aretz; | kiy | kalah | 'ak | nibhalah |
| **wrath** | **Yahuah's** | **but by the fire of** | **his jealousy** | **shall be devoured** | **whole** | **the land** | **for** | **riddance of** | **even** | **a speedy** |

| יעשה 6213 | את 853 | כל 3605 | ישבי 3427 | הארץ 776: |
|---|---|---|---|---|
| ya'aseh, | 'at | kal | yoshabey | ha'aretz. |
| **he shall make** | | **all** | **them that dwell *in* the land** | |

| **Zeph 2:1** | התקוששו 7197 | וקושו 7197 | הגוי 1471 | לא 3808 | נכסף 3700: | 2:2 | בטרם 2962 | לדת 3205 | חק 2706 |
|---|---|---|---|---|---|---|---|---|---|
| | hitqoushashu | uaqoushu; | hagouy | la' | niksap. | | baterem | ledet | choq, |
| | **Gather yourselves together** | **yea gather together** | **O nation** | **not** | **desired** | | **Before** | **bring forth** | **the decree** |

| כמץ 4671 | עבר 5674 | יום 3117 | בטרם 2962 | לא 3808 | יבוא 935 | עליכם 5921 | חרון 2740 | אף 639 | יהוה 3068 | בטרם 2962 | לא 3808 | יבוא 935 |
|---|---|---|---|---|---|---|---|---|---|---|---|---|
| kamotz | 'abar | youm; | baterem | la' | yabou'a | 'aleykem, | charoun | 'ap | Yahuah, | baterem | la' | yabou'a |
| **as the chaff** | **pass** | ***before* the day** | **before** | **not** | **come** | **upon you** | ***the* fierce** | **anger of** | **Yahuah** | **before** | **not** | **come** |

| עליכם 5921 | יום 3117 | אף 639 | יהוה 3068: | 2:3 | בקשו 1245 | את 853 | יהוה 3068 | כל 3605 | ענוי 6035 | הארץ 776 | אשר 834 | משפטו 4941 |
|---|---|---|---|---|---|---|---|---|---|---|---|---|
| 'aleykem, | youm | 'ap | Yahuah. | | baqashu | 'at | Yahuah | kal | 'anuey | ha'aretz, | 'asher | mishpatou |
| **upon you** | **the day of** | **anger** | **Yahuah's** | | **Seek you** | | **Yahuah** | **all** | **you meek of** | **the earth** | **which** | **his judgment** |

| פעלו 6466 | בקשו 1245 | צדק 6664 | בקשו 1245 | ענוה 6038 | אולי 194 | תסתרו 5641 | ביום 3117 | אף 639 | יהוה 3068: | 2:4 | כי 3588 |
|---|---|---|---|---|---|---|---|---|---|---|---|
| pa'alu; | baqashu | tzedeq | baqashu | 'anauah, | 'aulay | tisataru, | bayoum | 'ap | Yahuah. | | kiy |
| **have wrought** | **seek** | **righteousness** | **seek** | **meekness** | **it may be** | **you shall be hid** | **in the day of** | **anger** | **Yahuah's** | | **For** |

| עזה 5804 | עזובה 5800 | תהיה 1961 | ואשקלון 9831 | לשממה 8077 | אשדוד 795 | בצהרים 6672 | יגרשוה 1644 | ועקרון 6138 |
|---|---|---|---|---|---|---|---|---|
| 'azah | 'azubah | tihayeh, | ua'ashqaloun | lishmamah; | 'ashdoud, | batzaharayim | yagarashuha, | ua'aqroun |
| **Gaza** | **forsaken** | **shall be** | **and Ashkelon** | **a desolation** | **Ashdod** | **at the noonday** | **they shall drive out** | **and Ekron** |

| תעקר 6131: | 2:5 | הוי 1945 | ישבי 3427 | חבל 2256 | הים 3220 | גוי 1471 | כרתים 3774 | דבר 1697 | יהוה 3068 |
|---|---|---|---|---|---|---|---|---|---|
| te'aqer. | | houy, | yoshabey | chebel | hayam | gouy | karetiym; | dabar | Yahuah |
| **shall be rooted up** | | **Woe** | ***unto* the inhabitants of** | **coast** | **the sea** | **the nation of** | **the Cherethites** | **the word of** | **Yahuah** |

| עליכם 5921 | כנען 3667 | ארץ 776 | פלשתים 6430 | והאבדתיך 6 | מאין 369 | יושב 3427: |
|---|---|---|---|---|---|---|
| 'aleykem, | kana'an | 'aretz | palishtiym, | uaha'abadtiyk | me'ayn | yousheb. |
| ***is* against you** | **O Canaan** | **the land of** | **the Philistines** | **I will even destroy you** | **that there shall be no** | **inhabitant** |

Zeph 1:16 A day of the trumpet and alarm against the fenced cities, and against the high towers.17 And I will bring distress upon men, that they shall walk like blind men, because they have sinned against YHUH: and their blood shall be poured out as dust, and their flesh as the dung.18 Neither their silver nor their gold shall be able to deliver them in the day of YHUH's wrath; but the whole land shall be devoured by the fire of his jealousy: for he shall make even a speedy riddance of all them that dwell in the land. **Zeph** 2:1 Gather yourselves together, yea, gather together, O nation not desired;2 Before the decree bring forth, before the day pass as the chaff, before the fierce anger of YHUH come upon you, before the day of YHUH's anger come upon you.3 Seek you YHUH, all you meek of the earth, which have wrought his judgment; seek righteousness, seek meekness: it may be you shall be hid in the day of YHUH's anger.4 For Gaza shall be forsaken, and Ashkelon a desolation: they shall drive out Ashdod at the noon day, and Ekron shall be rooted up.5 Woe unto the inhabitants of the sea coast, the nation of the Cherethites! the word of YHUH is against you; O Canaan, the land of the Philistines, I will even destroy you, that there shall be no inhabitant.

| 2:6 והיתה 1961 | חבל 2256 | הים 3220 | נות 5116 | כרת 3741 | רעים 7462 | וגדרות 1448 | צאן 6629: | 2:7 והיה 1961 | חבל 2256 |
|---|---|---|---|---|---|---|---|---|---|
| uahayatah | chebel | hayam, | nauot | qara'ut | ro'aym | uagidrout | tza'n. | uahayah | chebel, |
| **And shall be** | **coast** | **the sea** | **dwellings** | ***and* cottages** | ***for* shepherds** | **and folds for** | **flocks** | **And shall be** | **the coast** |

| לשארית 7611 | בית 1004 | יהודה 3063 | עליהם 5921 | ירעון 7462 | בבתי 1004 | אשקלון 831 | בערב 6153 |
|---|---|---|---|---|---|---|---|
| lish'aeriyt | beyt | yahudah | 'aleyhem | yir'aun; | babatey | 'ashqaloun, | ba'areb |
| **for the remnant of** | **the house of** | **Judah** | **thereupon** | **they shall feed** | **in the houses of** | **Ashkelon** | **in the evening** |

| ירבצון 7257 | כי 3588 | יפקדם 6485 | יהוה 3068 | אלהיהם 430 | ושב 7725 | שבותם 7622 | 2:8 שמעתי 8085 |
|---|---|---|---|---|---|---|---|
| yirbatzun, | kiy | yipqadem | Yahuah | 'aloheyhem | uashab | shebutam | shama'atiy |
| **shall they lie down** | **for** | **shall visit them** | **Yahuah** | **their Elohim** | **and turn away** | **their captivity** | **I have heard** |

| חרפת 2781 | מואב 4124 | וגדופי 1421 | בני 1121 | עמון 5983 | אשר 834 | חרפו 2778 | את 853 | עמי 5971 |
|---|---|---|---|---|---|---|---|---|
| cherpat | mou'ab, | uagidupey | baney | 'amoun; | 'asher | cherapu | 'at | 'amiy, |
| **the reproach of** | **Moab** | **and the revilings of** | **the children of** | **Ammon** | **whereby** | **they have reproached** | | **my people** |

| ויגדילו 1431 | על 5921 | גבולם 1366: | 2:9 לכן 3651 | חי 2416 | אני 589 | נאם 5002 | יהוה 3068 | צבאות 6635 | אלהי 430 | ישראל 3478 |
|---|---|---|---|---|---|---|---|---|---|---|
| uayagdiylu | 'al | gabulam. | laken | chay | 'aniy | na'am | Yahuah | tzaba'aut | 'alohey | yisra'ael, |
| **and magnified *themselves*** | **against** | **their border** | **Therefore** | **live *as*** | **I** | **saith** | **Yahuah** | **of hosts** | **the Elohim of** | **Israel** |

| כי 3588 | מואב 4124 | כסדם 5467 | תהיה 1961 | ובני 1121 | עמון 5983 | כעמרה 6017 | ממשק 4476 | חרול 2738 | ומכרה 4379 | מלח 4417 |
|---|---|---|---|---|---|---|---|---|---|---|
| kiy | mou'ab | kisadom | tihayeh | uabney | 'amoun | ka'amorah, | mimshaq | charul | uamikreh | melach |
| **Surely** | **Moab** | **as Sodom** | **shall be** | **and the children of** | **Ammon** | **as Gomorrah** | ***even and* the breeding** | **nettles** | **and pits** | **salt** |

| ושממה 8077 | עד 5704 | עולם 5769 | שארית 7611 | עמי 5971 | יבזום 962 | ויתר 3499 | גוי 1471 |
|---|---|---|---|---|---|---|---|
| uashmamah | 'ad | 'aulam; | sha'aeriyt | 'amiy | yabazum, | uayeter | gouy |
| **and a desolation** | **until** | **perpetual** | **the residue of** | **my people** | **shall spoil them** | **and the remnant of** | **my people** |

| ינחלום 5157: | 2:10 זאת 2063 | להם 1992 | תחת 8478 | גאונם 1347 | כי 3588 | חרפו 2778 | ויגדלו 1431 |
|---|---|---|---|---|---|---|---|
| yinchalum. | za't | lahem | tachat | ga'aunam; | kiy | cherapu | uayagdilu, |
| **shall possess them** | **This** | **shall they have** | **for** | **their pride** | **because** | **they have reproached** | **and magnified *themselves*** |

| על 5921 | עם 5971 | יהוה 3069 | צבאות 6635: | 2:11 נורא 3372 | יהוה 3068 | עליהם 5921 | כי 3588 | רזה 7329 | את 853 | כל 3605 | אלהי 430 |
|---|---|---|---|---|---|---|---|---|---|---|---|
| 'al | 'am | Yahuah | tzaba'aut. | noura' | Yahuah | 'aleyhem, | kiy | razah, | 'at | kal | 'alohey |
| **against** | **the people of** | **Yahuah** | **of hosts** | ***will be* terrible** | **Yahuah** | **unto them** | **for** | **he will famish** | | **all** | **the gods of** |

| הארץ 776 | וישתחוו 7812 | לו 3807a | איש 376 | ממקומו 4725 | כל 3605 | איי 339 | הגוים 1471: | 2:12 גם 1571 | אתם 859 |
|---|---|---|---|---|---|---|---|---|---|
| ha'aretz; | uayishatachauu | lou' | 'aysh | mimaqoumou, | kal | 'ayey | hagouyim. | gam | 'atem |
| **the earth** | **and *men* shall worship** | **him** | **every one** | **from his place** | ***even*all** | **the isles of** | **the heathen** | **also** | **You** |

| כושים 3569 | חללי 2491 | חרבי 2719 | המה 1992: | 2:13 ויט 5186 | ידו 3027 | על 5921 | צפון 6828 | ויאבד 6 | את 853 |
|---|---|---|---|---|---|---|---|---|---|
| kushiym, | challey | charbiy | hemah. | uayet | yadou | 'al | tzapoun, | uiy'abed | 'at |
| **Ethiopians** | **you *shall be* slain** | ***by* my sword** | **they** | **And he will stretch out** | **his hand** | **against** | **the north** | **and destroy** | |

| אשור 804 | וישם 7760 | את 853 | נינוה 5210 | לשממה 8077 | ציה 6723 | כמדבר 4057: | 2:14 ורבצו 7257 | בתוכה 8432 |
|---|---|---|---|---|---|---|---|---|
| 'ashur; | uayasem | 'at | niynaueh | lishmamah, | tziyah | kamidbar. | uarabatzu | batoukah |
| **Assyria** | **and will make** | | **Nineveh** | **a desolation** | ***and* dry** | **like a wilderness** | **And shall lie down** | **in the midst of her** |

Zeph 2:6 And the sea coast shall be dwellings and cottages for shepherds, and folds for flocks.7 And the coast shall be for the remnant of the house of Judah; they shall feed thereupon: in the houses of Ashkelon shall they lie down in the evening: for YHUH their G-d shall visit them, and turn away their captivity.8 I have heard the reproach of Moab, and the revilings of the children of Ammon, whereby they have reproached my people, and magnified themselves against their border.9 Therefore as I live, saith YHUH of hosts, the G-d of Israel, Surely Moab shall be as Sodom, and the children of Ammon as Gomorrah, even the breeding of nettles, and saltpits, and a perpetual desolation: the residue of my people shall spoil them, and the remnant of my people shall possess them.10 This shall they have for their pride, because they have reproached and magnified themselves against the people of YHUH of hosts.11 YHUH will be terrible unto them: for he will famish all the gods of the earth; and men shall worship him, everyone from his place, even all the isles of the heathen.12 You Ethiopians also, you shall be slain by my sword.13 And he will stretch out his hand against the north, and destroy Assyria; and will make Nineveh a desolation, and dry like a wilderness.

עדרים 5739 כל 3605 חיתו 2416 גוי 1471 גם 1571 קאת 6893 גם 1571 קפד 7090 בכפתריה 3730 ילינו 3885
'adariym kal chaytou gouy, gam qa'at gam qipod, bakaptoreyha yaliynu;
**flocks all the beasts of the nations both the cormorant also the bittern in the upper lintels of it shall lodge**

קול 6963 ישורר 7891 בחלון 2474 חרב 2721 בסף 5592 כי 3588 ארזה 731 ערה 6168: **2:15** זאת 2063
qoul yashourer bachaloun choreb basap, kiy 'arzah 'aerah. za't
***their* voice shall sing in the windows desolation *shall be* in the thresholds for the cedar work he shall uncover This**

העיר 5892 העליזה 5947 היושבת 3427 לבטח 983 האמרה 559 בלבבה 3824 אני 589 ואפסי 657 עוד 5750 איך 349
ha'ayr ha'aliyzah hayoushebet labetach, ha'amarah bilbabah, 'aniy ua'apsiy 'aud; 'aeyk
**city *is* the rejoicing that dwelt carelessly that said in her heart I *am* and *there is* none besides *me* how**

היתה 1961 לשמה 8047 מרבץ 4769 לחיה 2416 כל 3605 עובר 5674 עליה 5921 ישרק 8319 יניע 5128 ידו 3027:
hayatah lashamah, marbetz lachayah, kal 'auber 'aleyha, yishroq yaniya' yadou.
**is she become a desolation a place to lie down in for beasts every one that passed by her shall hiss *and* wag his hand**

**Zeph 3:1** הוי 1945 מראה 4754 ונגאלה 1351 העיר 5892 היונה 3238: **3:2** לא 3808 שמעה 8085 בקול 6963 לא 3808
houy mor'ah uanig'alah; ha'ayr hayounah. la' sham'ah baqoul, la'
**Woe to her that is filthy and polluted city to the oppressing not She obeyed the voice not**

לקחה 3947 מוסר 4148 ביהוה 3068 לא 3808 בטחה 982 אל 413 אלהיה 430 לא 3808 קרבה 7126: **3:3** שריה 8269 בקרבה 7130
laqchah musar; baYahuah la' batachah, 'al 'aloheyha la' qarebah. sareyha baqirbah,
**she received correction in Yahuah not she trusted to her Elohim not she drew near Her princes within her**

אריות 738 שאגים 7580 שפטיה 8199 זאבי 2061 ערב 6153 לא 3808 גרמו 1633 לבקר 1242: **3:4** נביאיה 5030 פחזים 6348
arayout sho'agiym; shopateyha za'aebey 'areb, la' garamu laboqer. nabiy'ayha pochaziym,
**lions *are* roaring her judges wolves *are* evening not they gnaw the bones till the morrow Her prophets *are* light**

אנשי 582 בגדות 900 כהניה 3548 חללו 2490 קדש 6944 חמסו 2554 תורה 8451: **3:5** יהוה 3068 צדיק 6662
'anshey bogadout; kohaneyha chillu qodesh, chamasu tourah. Yahuah tzadiyq
**persons *and* treacherous her priests have polluted the sanctuary they have done violence to the law Yahuah The just**

בקרבה 7130 לא 3808 יעשה 6213 עולה 5766 בבקר 1242 בבקר 1242 משפטו 4941 יתן 5414 לאור 216 לא 3808 נעדר 5737 ולא 3808
baqirbah, la' ya'aseh 'aulah; baboqer baboqer mishpatou yiten la'aur la' ne'adar, uala'
***is* in the midst thereof not he will do iniquity every morning his judgment does he bring to light not he fail but no**

יודע 3045 עול 5767 בשת 1322: **3:6** הכרתי 3772 גוים 1471 נשמו 8074 פנותם 6438 החרבתי 2717 חוצותם 2351 מבלי 1097
youdea' 'aual boshet. hikratiy gouyim, nashamu pinoutam, hecharabtiy chutzoutam mibaliy
**knows the unjust shame I have cut off the nations are desolate their towers I made waste their streets that none**

עובר 5674 נצדו 6658 עריהם 5892 מבלי 1097 איש 376 מאין 369 יושב 3427: **3:7** אמרתי 559 אך 389 תיראי 3372
'auber; nitzadu 'areyhem mibaliy 'aysh me'ayn yousheb. 'amartiy 'ak tiyr'ay
**passed by are destroyed their cities so that there is no man that there is none inhabitant I said Surely you will fear**

אותי 853 תקחי 3947 מוסר 4148 ולא 3808 יכרת 3772 מעונה 4585 כל 3605 אשר 834 פקדתי 6485 עליה 5921 אכן 403
'autiy tiqchiy musar, uala' yikaret ma'anah, kal 'asher paqadtiy 'aleyha; 'aken
**me you will receive instruction so not should be cut off their dwelling howsoever which I punished them but**

Zeph 2:14 And flocks shall lie down in the midst of her, all the beasts of the nations: both the cormorant and the bittern shall lodge in the upper lintels of it; their voice shall sing in the windows; desolation shall be in the thresholds: for he shall uncover the cedar work.15 This is the rejoicing city that dwelt carelessly, that said in her heart, I am, and there is none beside me: how is she become a desolation, a place for beasts to lie down in! everyone that pass by her shall hiss, and wag his hand. **Zeph** 3:1 Woe to her that is filthy and polluted, to the oppressing city!2 She obeyed not the voice; she received not correction; she trusted not in YHUH; she drew not near to her G-d.3 Her princes within her are roaring lions; her judges are evening wolves; they gnaw not the bones till the morrow.4 Her prophets are light and treacherous persons: her priests have polluted the sanctuary, they have done violence to the law.5 The just YHUH is in the midst thereof; he will not do iniquity: every morning doth he bring his judgment to light, he faileth not; but the unjust know no shame.6 I have cut off the nations: their towers are desolate; I made their streets waste, that none pass by: their cities are destroyed, so that there is no man, that there is none inhabitant.7 I said, Surely you will fear me, you will receive instruction; so their dwelling should not be cut off, howsoever I punished them:

| השכימו 7925 | השחיתו 7843 | כל 3605 | עלילותם 5949: | 3:8 לכן 3651 | חכו 2442 | לי 3807a | נאם 5002 | יהוה 3068 | ליום 3117 |
|---|---|---|---|---|---|---|---|---|---|
| hishkiymu | hishchiytu, | kal | aliyloutam. | laken | chaku | liy | na'am | Yahuah, | layoum |
| **they rose early** | ***and* corrupted** | **all** | **their doings** | **Therefore** | **wait you** | **upon me** | **saith** | **Yahuah** | ***until* the day** |

| קומי 6965 | לעד 5706 | כי 3588 | משפטי 4941 | לאסף 622 | גוים 1471 | לקבצי 6908 | ממלכות 4467 | לשפך 8210 |
|---|---|---|---|---|---|---|---|---|
| qumiy | la'ad; | kiy | mishpatiy | le'asop | gouyim | laqabatziy | mamlakout, | lishpok |
| **that I rise up** | **to the prey** | **for** | **my determination** | ***is* to gather** | **the nations** | **that I may assemble** | **the kingdoms** | **to pour** |

| עליהם 5921 | זעמי 2195 | כל 3605 | חרון 2740 | אפי 639 | כי 3588 | באש 784 | קנאתי 7068 | תאכל 398 | כל 3605 |
|---|---|---|---|---|---|---|---|---|---|
| 'aleyhem | za'amiy | kal | charoun | 'apiy, | kiy | ba'aesh | qin'atiy, | te'akel | kal |
| **upon them** | **mine indignation** | ***even* all** | **fierce** | **my anger** | **for** | **with the fire of** | **my jealousy** | **shall be devoured** | **all** |

| הארץ 776: | 3:9 כי 3588 | אז 227 | אהפך 2015 | אל 413 | עמים 5971 | שפה 8193 | ברורה 1305 | לקרא 7121 | כלם 3605 | בשם 8034 |
|---|---|---|---|---|---|---|---|---|---|---|
| ha'aretz. | kiy | 'az | 'ahpok | 'al | 'amiym | sapah | barurah; | liqra' | kulam | bashem |
| **the earth** | **For** | **then** | **will I turn** | **to** | **the people** | **a language** | **pure** | **that they may call** | **all** | **upon the name of** |

| יהוה 3068 | לעבדו 5647 | שכם 7926 | אחד 259: | 3:10 מעבר 5676 | לנהרי 5104 | כוש 3568 | עתרי 6282 | בת 1323 |
|---|---|---|---|---|---|---|---|---|
| Yahuah, | la'abadou | shakem | 'achad. | me'aeber | lanaharey | kush; | 'ataray | bat |
| **Yahuah** | **to serve him** | **consent** | ***with* one** | **From beyond** | **the rivers of** | **Ethiopia** | **my suppliants** | ***even* the daughter** |

| פוצי 6327 | יובלון 2986 | מנחתי 4503: | 3:11 ביום 3117 | ההוא 1931 | לא 3808 | תבושי 954 | מכל 3605 | עלילתיך 5949 | אשר 834 |
|---|---|---|---|---|---|---|---|---|---|
| putzay, | youbilun | minchatiy. | bayoum | hahua', | la' | teboushiy | mikol | 'aliylotayik, | 'asher |
| **of my dispersed** | **shall bring** | **mine offering** | **In day** | **that** | **not** | **shall you be ashamed** | **for all** | **your doings** | **wherein** |

| פשעת 6586 | בי 871a | כי 3588 | אז 227 | אסיר 5493 | מקרבך 7130 | עליזי 5947 | גאותך 1346 |
|---|---|---|---|---|---|---|---|
| pasha'at | biy; | kiy | 'az | 'asiyr | miqirbek, | 'aliyzey | ga'auatek, |
| **you have transgressed** | **against me** | **for** | **then** | **I will take away** | **out of the midst of you** | **them that rejoice** | **in your pride** |

| ולא 3808 | תוספי 3254 | לגבהה 1361 | עוד 5750 | בהר 2022 | קדשי 6944: | 3:12 והשארתי 7604 | בקרבך 7130 | עם 5971 |
|---|---|---|---|---|---|---|---|---|
| uala' | tousipiy | lagabahah | 'aud | bahar | qadashiy | uahish'artiy | baqirbek, | 'am |
| **no** | **more** | **you shall be haughty** | **further** | **because of mountain** | **my holy** | **I will also leave** | **in the midst of you** | **people** |

| עני 6041 | ודל 1800 | וחסו 2620 | בשם 8034 | יהוה 3068: | 3:13 שארית 7611 | ישראל 3478 | לא 3808 | יעשו 6213 | עולה 5766 |
|---|---|---|---|---|---|---|---|---|---|
| 'aniy | uadal; | uachasu | bashem | Yahuah. | sha'aeriyt | yisra'ael | la' | ya'asu | 'aulah |
| **an afflicted** | **and poor** | **and they shall trust** | **in the name of** | **Yahuah** | **The remnant of** | **Israel** | **not** | **shall do** | **iniquity** |

| ולא 3808 | ידברו 1696 | כזב 3577 | ולא 3808 | ימצא 4672 | בפיהם 6310 | לשון 3956 | תרמית 8656 | כי 3588 | המה 1992 | ירעו 7462 | ורבצו 7257 |
|---|---|---|---|---|---|---|---|---|---|---|---|
| uala' | yadabru | kazab, | uala' | yimatzea' | bapiyhem | lashoun | tarmiyt; | kiy | hemah | yir'au | uarabatzu |
| **nor** | **speak** | **lies** | **neither** | **shall be found** | **in their mouth** | **a tongue** | **deceitful** | **for** | **they** | **shall feed** | **and lie down** |

| ואין 369 | מחריד 2729: | 3:14 רני 7442 | בת 1323 | ציון 6726 | הריעו 7321 | ישראל 3478 | שמחי 8055 | ועלזי 5937 | בכל 3605 |
|---|---|---|---|---|---|---|---|---|---|
| ua'aeyn | machariyd. | raniy | bat | tziyoun, | hariy'au | yisra'ael; | simchiy | ua'alaziy | bakal |
| **and none** | **shall make *them* afraid** | **Sing** | **O daughter of** | **Zion** | **shout** | **O Israel** | **be glad** | **and rejoice** | **with all** |

| לב 3820 | בת 1323 | ירושלם 3389: | 3:15 הסיר 5493 | יהוה 3068 | משפטיך 4941 | פנה 6437 | איבך 341 | מלך 4428 |
|---|---|---|---|---|---|---|---|---|
| leb, | bat | yarushalaim. | hesiyr | Yahuah | mishpatayik, | pinah | 'ayabek; | melek |
| **the heart** | **O daughter of** | **Jerusalem** | **has taken away** | **Yahuah** | **your judgments** | **he has cast out** | **your enemy** | **the king of** |

Zeph 3:7 but they rose early, and corrupted all their doings.8 Therefore wait you upon me, saith YHUH, until the day that I rise up to the prey: for my determination is to gather the nations, that I may assemble the kingdoms, to pour upon them mine indignation, even all my fierce anger: for all the earth shall be devoured with the fire of my jealousy.9 For then will I turn to the people a pure language, that they may all call upon the name of YHUH, to serve him with one consent.10 From beyond the rivers of Ethiopia my suppliants, even the daughter of my dispersed, shall bring mine offering.11 In that day shall you not be ashamed for all your doings, wherein you have transgressed against me: for then I will take away out of the midst of you them that rejoice in your pride, and you shall no more be haughty because of my holy mountain.12 I will also leave in the midst of you an afflicted and poor people, and they shall trust in the name of YHUH.13 The remnant of Israel shall not do iniquity, nor speak lies; neither shall a deceitful tongue be found in their mouth: for they shall feed and lie down, and none shall make them afraid.14 Sing, O daughter of Zion; shout, O Israel; be glad and rejoice with all the heart, O daughter of Jerusalem.15 YHUH has taken away your judgments, he has cast out your enemy: the king of Israel, even YHUH, is in the midst of you:

| ישראל 3478 | יהוה 3068 | בקרבך 7130 | לא 3808 | תיראי 3372 | רע 7451 | עוד 5750: | 3:16 | ביום 3117 | ההוא 1931 | יאמר 559 |
|---|---|---|---|---|---|---|---|---|---|---|
| yisra'ael | Yahuah | baqirbek, | la' | tiyr'ay | ra' | 'aud. | | bayoum | hahua', | ye'amer |
| **Israel *even*** | **Yahuah** | ***is* in the midst of you** | **not** | **you shall see** | **evil** | **any more** | | **In day** | **that** | **it shall be said** |

| לירושלם 3389 | אל 408 | תיראי 3372 | ציון 6726 | אל 408 | ירפו 7503 | ידיך 3027: | 3:17 | יהוה 3068 | אלהיך 430 | בקרבך 7130 |
|---|---|---|---|---|---|---|---|---|---|---|
| liyarushalaim | 'al | tiyra'ay; | tziyoun | 'al | yirpu | yadayik. | | Yahuah | 'alohayik | baqirbek |
| **to Jerusalem** | **not** | **Fear you** | ***and to* Zion** | **not** | **Let be slack** | **your hands** | | **Yahuah** | **your Elohim** | **in the midst of you** |

| גבור 1368 | יושיע 3467 | ישיש 7797 | עליך 5921 | בשמחה 8057 | יחריש 2790 | באהבתו 160 | יגיל 1523 | עליך 5921 | ברנה 7440: | 3:18 |
|---|---|---|---|---|---|---|---|---|---|---|
| gibour | youshiya'; | yasiys | 'aleyka | basimchah, | yachariysh | ba'ahabatou, | yagiyl | 'alayik | barinah. | |
| ***is* mighty** | **he will save** | **he will rejoice** | **over you** | **with joy** | **he will rest** | **in his love** | **he will joy** | **over you** | **with singing** | |

| נוגי 3013 | ממועד 4150 | אספתי 622 | ממך 4480 | היו 1961 | משאת 4864 | עליה 5921 | חרפה 2781: | 3:19 |
|---|---|---|---|---|---|---|---|---|
| nugey | mimou'aed | 'asaptiy | mimek | hayu; | mas'aet | 'aleyha | cherpah. | |
| ***them that are* sorrowful** | **for the solemn assembly** | **I will gather** | **of you** | ***who* are** | ***of it was* a burden** | **to whom** | **the reproach** | |

| הנני 2005 | עשה 6213 | את 853 | כל 3605 | מעניך 6031 | בעת 6256 | ההיא 1931 | והושעתי 3467 | את 853 | הצלעה 6760 |
|---|---|---|---|---|---|---|---|---|---|
| hinniy | 'aseh | 'at | kal | ma'anayik | ba'aet | hahiy'a; | uahousha'atiy | 'at | hatzole'ah, |
| **Behold I** | **will undo** | | **all** | **that afflict you** | **at time** | **that** | **and I will save her** | | **that halteth** |

| והנדחה 5080 | אקבץ 6908 | ושמתים 7760 | לתהלה 8416 | ולשם 8034 | בכל 3605 | הארץ 776 |
|---|---|---|---|---|---|---|
| uahanidachah | 'aqabetz, | uasamatiym | lithilah | ualshem, | bakal | ha'aretz |
| **and her that was driven out** | **gather** | **and I will get them** | **praise** | **and fame** | **in every** | **the land** |

| בשתם 1322: | 3:20 | בעת 6256 | ההיא 1931 | אביא 935 | אתכם 853 | ובעת 6256 | קבצי 6908 | אתכם 853 | כי 3588 |
|---|---|---|---|---|---|---|---|---|---|
| bashatam. | | ba'aet | hahiy'a | 'abiy'a | 'atkem, | uaba'aet | qabtziy | 'atkem; | kiy |
| **where they have been put to shame** | | **At time** | **that** | **will I bring you *again*** | | **even in the time that I gather you** | | | **for** |

| אתן 5414 | אתכם 853 | לשם 8034 | ולתהלה 8416 | בכל 3605 | עמי 5971 | הארץ 776 | בשובי 7725 | את 853 | שבותיכם 7622 |
|---|---|---|---|---|---|---|---|---|---|
| 'aten | 'atkem | lashem | ualitahilah, | bakal | 'amey | ha'aretz, | bashubiy | 'at | shabuteykem |
| **I will make** | **you** | **a name** | **and a praise** | **among all** | **my people of** | **the earth** | **when I turn back** | | **your captivity** |

| לעיניכם 5869 | אמר 559 | יהוה 3068: |
|---|---|---|
| la'ayneykem | 'amar | Yahuah. |
| **before your eyes** | **saith** | **Yahuah** |

Zeph 3:16 you shall not see evil anymore.16 In that day it shall be said to Jerusalem, Fear you not: and to Zion, Let not your hands be slack.17 YHUH your G-d in the midst of you is mighty; he will save, he will rejoice over you with joy; he will rest in his love, he will joy over you with singing.18 I will gather them that are sorrowful for the solemn assembly, who are of you, to whom the reproach of it was a burden.19 Behold, at that time I will undo all that afflict you: and I will save her that halteth, and gather her that was driven out; and I will get them praise and fame in every land where they have been put to shame.20 At that time will I bring you again, even in the time that I gather you: for I will make you a name and a praise among all people of the earth, when I turn back your captivity before your eyes, saith YHUH.

# HAGGAI
## (*Chagay*)

Verse one identifies the author as the Prophet Haggai, whose Hebrew name means *Feast*. The Prophet Haggi was sent to the Exiles of the **House of Judah** living in Babylon and was written in approximately 520 B.C. Haggai challenge the people not to be discouraged and to examine their priorities and to glorify Elohim with reverence and with determination to the restoration of the Temple in spite of any opposition. He also urged them to turn from their sinfulness and to trust in Elohim's sovereign power to accomplish their goals. The book records the problems they faced at this time and how the people courageously overcame and accomplished their goals in spite of the opposition round about by believing and trusting Elohim would provide for all their needs as long as they strived to be obedient.

**Haggai 1:1**
בשנת 8141 שתים 8147 לדריוש 1867 המלך 4428 בחדש 2320 הששי 8345 ביום 3117 אחד 259 לחדש 2320 היה 1961 דבר 1697
bishnat shatayim ladarayauesh hamelek, bachodesh hashishiy, bayoum 'achad lachodesh; hayah dabar
**In year *the* second of Darius the king in month *the* sixth in day *the* first of the month came the word of**

יהוה 3068 ביד 3027 חגי 2292 הנביא 5030 אל 413 זרבבל 2216 בן 1121 שאלתיאל 7597 פחת 6346 יהודה 3063 ואל 413 יהושע 3091 בן 1121
Yahuah bayad chagay hanabiy'a, 'al zarubabel ben sha'altiy'ael pachat yahudah, ua'al yahousha' ben
**Yahuah by Haggai the prophet unto Zerubbabel the son of Shealtiel governor of Judah and to Joshua the son of**

1:2
יהוצדק 3087 הכהן 3548 הגדול 1419 לאמר 559: כה 3541 אמר 559 יהוה 3068 צבאות 6635 לאמר 559 העם 5971 הזה 2088 אמרו 559 לא 3808 עת 6256
yahoutzadaq hakohen hagadoul lea'mor. koh 'amar Yahuah tzaba'aut lea'mor; ha'am hazeh 'amaru, la' 'at
**Josedech priest the high saying Thus speak Yahuah of hosts saying the people This say not The time**

1:3
בא 935 עת 6256 בית 1004 יהוה 3068 להבנות 1129: ויהי 1961 דבר 1697 יהוה 3068 ביד 3027 חגי 2292 הנביא 5030
ba' 'at beyt Yahuah lahibanout. uayahiy dabar Yahuah, bayad chagay hanabiy'a
**is come the time house *that* Yahuah's should be built Then came the word of Yahuah by Haggai the prophet**

1:4
1:5
לאמר 559: העת 6256 לכם 3807a אתם 859 לשבת 3427 בבתיכם 1004 ספונים 5603 והבית 1004 הזה 2088 חרב 2720: ועתה 6258 כה 3541
lea'mor. ha'aet lakem 'atem, lashabet babateykem sapuniym; uahabayit hazeh chareb. ua'atah koh
**saying *Is it* time for you O you to dwell in houses your ceiled and house this lie waste? Now therefore thus**

1:6
אמר 559 יהוה 3068 צבאות 6635 שימו 7760 לבבכם 3824 על 5921 דרכיכם 1870: זרעתם 2232 הרבה 7235 והבא 935 מעט 4592 אכול 398
'amar Yahuah tzaba'aut; siymu lababkem 'al darkeykem. zara'atem harbeh uahabea' ma'at, 'akoul
**saith Yahuah of hosts Consider your heart on your ways You have sown much and bring in little you eat**

ואין 369 לשבעה 7654 שתו 8354 ואין 369 לשכרה 7937 לבוש 3847 ואין 369 לחם 2527 לו 3807a
ua'aeyn lasaba'ah shatou ua'aeyn lashakarah, laboush ua'aeyn lachom lou';
**but not you have enough you drink but not you are filled with drink you clothe but there is none warm you**

1:7
והמשתכר 7936 משתכר 7936 אל 413 צרור 6872 נקוב 5344: כה 3541 אמר 559 יהוה 3068 צבאות 6635 שימו 7760 לבבכם 3824
uahamistaker, mistaker 'al tzarour naqub. koh 'amar Yahuah tzaba'aut; siymu lababkem
**and he that earn wages earn wages *to put it* into a bag with holes Thus saith Yahuah of hosts Consider your heart**

1:8
על 5921 דרכיכם 1870: עלו 5927 ההר 2022 והבאתם 935 עץ 6086 ובנו 1129 הבית 1004 וארצה 7521 בו 871a
'al darkeykem. 'alu hahar uahabea'tem 'aetz uabanu habayit; ua'artzeh bou
**on your ways Go up to the mountain and bring wood and build the house and I will take pleasure in it**

**Haggai** 1:1 In the second year of Darius the king, in the sixth month, in the first day of the month, came the word of YHUH by Haggai the prophet unto Zerubbabel the son of Shealtiel, governor of Judah, and to Joshua the son of Josedech, the high priest, saying,2 Thus speaketh YHUH of hosts, saying, This people say, The time is not come, the time that YHUH's house should be built.3 Then came the word of YHUH by Haggai the prophet, saying,4 Is it time for you, O you, to dwell in your cieled houses, and this house lie waste?5 Now therefore thus saith YHUH of hosts; Consider your ways.6 You have sown much, and bring in little; you eat, but you have not enough; you drink, but you are not filled with drink; you clothe you, but there is none warm; and he that earneth wages earneth wages to put it into a bag with holes.7 Thus saith YHUH of hosts; Consider your ways.8 Go up to the mountain, and bring wood, and build the house; and I will take pleasure in it, and I will be glorified, saith YHUH.

ואכבד 3513 | אמר 559 יהוה 3068: | **1:9** פנה 6437 | אל 413 | הרבה 7235 | והנה 2009 | למעט 4592 | והבאתם 935 | הבית 1004
ua'akabad 'amar Yahuah. panoh 'al harbeh uahineh lim'at, uahabea'tem habayit
**and I will be glorified saith Yahuah** ***You*** **looked for much and lo** ***it came*** **to little and when you brought** ***it*** **home**

ונפחתי 5301 | בו 871a | יען 3282 | מה 4100 | נאם 5002 | יהוה 3069 | צבאות 6635 | יען 3282 | ביתי 1004 | אשר 834 | הוא 1931 | חרב 2720 | ואתם 859
uanapachtiy bou; ya'an meh, na'am Yahuah tzaba'aut, ya'an, beytiy 'asher hua' chareb, ua'atem
**I did blow upon it because of Why? saith Yahuah of hosts Because of mine house that he** ***is*** **waste and you**

רצים 7323 | איש 376 | לביתו 1004: | **1:10** על 5921 | כן 3651 | עליכם 5921 | כלאו 3607 | שמים 8064 | מטל 2919 | והארץ 776
ratziym 'aysh labeytou. 'al ken 'aleykem, kala'au shamayim mital; uaha'aretz
**run every man unto his own house Therefore after that over you is stayed the heaven from dew and the earth**

כלאה 3607 | יבולה 2981: | **1:11** ואקרא 7121 | חרב 2721 | על 5921 | הארץ 776 | ועל 5921 | ההרים 2022 | ועל 5921 | הדגן 1715
kala'ah yabulah. ua'aqra' choreb 'al ha'aretz ua'al heha riym, ua'al hadagan
**is stayed** ***from*** **her fruit And I called for a drought upon the land and upon the mountains and upon the corn**

ועל 5921 | התירוש 8492 | ועל 5921 | היצהר 3323 | ועל 5921 | אשר 834 | תוציא 3318 | האדמה 127 | ועל 5921 | האדם 120 | ועל 5921
ua'al hatiyroush ua'al hayitzhar, ua'al 'asher toutziy'a ha'adamah; ua'al ha'adam ua'al
**and upon the new wine and upon the oil and upon** ***that*** **which you bring forth the ground and upon men and upon**

הבהמה 929 | ועל 5921 | כל 3605 | יגיע 3018 | כפים 3709: | **1:12** וישמע 8085 | זרבבל 2216 | בן 1121 | שלתיאל 7597 | ויהושע 3091
habehemah, ua'al kal yagiya' kapayim. uayishma' zarubabel ben shaltiy'ael uayahoushua'
**cattle and upon all the labour of the hands Then obeyed Zerubbabel the son of Shealtiel and Joshua**

בן 1121 | יהוצדק 3087 | הכהן 3548 | הגדול 1419 | וכל 3605 | שארית 7611 | העם 5971 | בקול 6963 | יהוה 3068 | אלהיהם 430 | ועל 5921
ben yahoutzadaq hakohen hagadoul uakol sha'aeriyt ha'am, baqoul Yahuah 'aloheyhem, ua'al
**the son of Josedech priest the high with all the remnant of the people the voice of Yahuah their Elohim and on**

דברי 1697 | חגי 2292 | הנביא 5030 | כאשר 834 | שלחו 7971 | יהוה 3068 | אלהיהם 430 | וייראו 3372 | העם 5971 | מפני 6440 | יהוה 3068: | **1:13**
dibrey chagay hanabiy'a, ka'asher shalachou Yahuah 'aloheyhem; uayiyra'au ha'am mipaney Yahuah.
**the words of Haggai the prophet as had sent him Yahuah their Elohim and did fear the people before Yahuah**

ויאמר 559 | חגי 2292 | מלאך 4397 | יהוה 3068 | במלאכות 4400 | יהוה 3068 | לעם 5971 | לאמר 559 | אני 589 | אתכם 854 | נאם 5002 | יהוה 3068: | **1:14**
uaya'mer chagay mal'ak Yahuah bamal'akut Yahuah la'am lea'mor; 'aniy 'atakem na'am Yahuah.
**Then spoke Haggai messenger Yahuah's in message Yahuah's unto the people saying I** ***am*** **with you saith Yahuah**

ויער 5782 | יהוה 3068 | את 853 | רוח 7307 | זרבבל 2216 | בן 1121 | שלתיאל 7597 | פחת 6346 | יהודה 3063 | ואת 853 | רוח 7307
uaya'ar Yahuah 'at ruach zarubabel ben shaltiy'ael pachat yahudah, ua'at ruach
**And stirred up Yahuah the spirit of Zerubbabel the son of Shealtiel governor of Judah** ***and*** **the spirit of**

יהושע 3091 | בן 1121 | יהוצדק 3087 | הכהן 3548 | הגדול 1419 | ואת 853 | רוח 7307 | כל 3605 | שארית 7611 | העם 5971 | ויבאו 935
yahousha' ben yahoutzadaq hakohen hagadoul, ua'at ruach, kal sha'aeriyt ha'am; uayabo'au
**Joshua the son of Josedech priest the high** ***and*** **the spirit of all the remnant of the people and they came**

ויעשו 6213 | מלאכה 4399 | בבית 1004 | יהוה 3068 | צבאות 6635 | אלהיהם 430: | **1:15** ביום 3117 | עשרים 6242 | וארבעה 702 | לחדש 2320
uaya'asu mala'kah, babeyt Yahuah tzaba'aut 'aloheyhem. bayoum 'asriym ua'arbah lachodesh
**and did work in the house of Yahuah of hosts their Elohim In the day twentieth and** ***the*** **four the month**

Hag 1:9 You looked for much, and, lo, it came to little; and when you brought it home, I did blow upon it. Why? saith YHUH of hosts. Because of mine house that is waste, and you run every man unto his own house.10 Therefore the heaven over you is stayed from dew, and the earth is stayed from her fruit.11 And I called for a drought upon the land, and upon the mountains, and upon the corn, and upon the new wine, and upon the oil, and upon that which the ground bring forth, and upon men, and upon cattle, and upon all the labour of the hands.12 Then Zerubbabel the son of Shealtiel, and Joshua the son of Josedech, the high priest, with all the remnant of the people, obeyed the voice of YHUH their G-d, and the words of Haggai the prophet, as YHUH their G-d had sent him, and the people did fear before YHUH.13 Then spoke Haggai YHUH's messenger in YHUH's message unto the people, saying, I am with you, saith YHUH.14 And YHUH stirred up the spirit of Zerubbabel the son of Shealtiel, governor of Judah, and the spirit of Joshua the son of Josedech, the high priest, and the spirit of all the remnant of the people; and they came and did work in the house of YHUH of hosts, their G-d,15 In the four and twentieth day of the sixth month, in the second year of Darius the king.

8345 בששי 8141 בשנת 8147 שתים 1867 לדריוש 4428 המלך:
bashishiy; bishnat shatayim ladarayauesh hamelek.
**sixth in year *the* second of Darius the king**

**Hag 2:1**
7637 בשביעי 6242 בעשרים 259 ואחד 2320 לחדש 1961 היה 1697 דבר 3068 יהוה 3027 ביד 2292 חגי 5030 הנביא
bashabiy'ay ba'asriym ua'achad lachodesh; hayah dabar Yahuah, bayad chagay hanabiy'a
**In the seventh *month* in twentieth *the* one *day* of the month came the word of Yahuah by Haggai the prophet**

559 לאמר: **2:2** 559 אמר 4994 נא 413 אל 2216 זרבבל 1121 בן 7597 שלתיאל 6346 פחת 3063 יהודה 413 ואל 3091 יהושע 1121 בן
lea'mor. 'amar na, 'al zarubabel ben shaltiy'ael pachat yahudah, ua'al yahousha' ben
**saying Speak now to Zerubbabel the son of Shealtiel governor of Judah and to Joshua the son of**

3087 יהוצדק 3548 הכהן 1419 הגדול 413 ואל 7611 שארית 5971 העם 559 לאמר: **2:3** 4310 מי 871a בכם 7604 הנשאר 834 אשר 7200 ראה
yahoutzadaq hakohen hagadoul; ua'al sha'aeriyt ha'am lea'mor. miy' bakem hanisha'ar, 'asher ra'ah
**Josedech priest the high and to the residue of the people saying Who among you *is* left that saw**

853 את 1004 הבית 2088 הזה 3519 בכבודו 7223 הראשון 4100 ומה 859 אתם 7200 ראים 853 אתו 6258 עתה 3808 הלוא 3644 כמהו
'at habayit hazeh, bikboudou hara'shoun; uamah 'atem ro'aym 'atou 'atah, halou'a kamohu
**house this in her glory? first and how you do see it now? *is it* not in comparison of it**

369 כאין 5869 בעיניכם: **2:4** 6258 ועתה 2388 חזק 2216 זרבבל 5002 נאם 3068 יהוה 2388 וחזק 3091 יהושע 1121 בן 3087 יהוצדק
ka'ayin ba'aeyneykem. ua'atah chazaq zarubabel na'am Yahuah uachazaq yahousha' ben yahoutzadaq
**as nothing? in your eyes Yet now be strong O Zerubbabel saith Yahuah and be strong O Joshua son of Josedech**

3548 הכהן 1419 הגדול 2388 וחזק 3605 כל 5971 עם 776 הארץ 5002 נאם 3068 יהוה 6213 ועשו 3588 כי 589 אני 854 אתכם 5002 נאם
hakohen hagadoul uachazaq kal 'am ha'aretz na'am Yahuah ua'asu; kiy 'aniy 'atakem, na'am
**priest the high and be strong all *you* people of the land saith Yahuah and work for I *am* with you saith**

3068 יהוה 6635 צבאות: **2:5** 853 את 1697 הדבר 834 אשר 3772 כרתי 854 אתכם 3318 בצאתכם 4714 ממצרים 7307 ורוחי
Yahuah tzaba'aut. 'at hadabar 'asher karatiy 'atakem batza'takem mimitzrayim, uaruchiy
**Yahuah of hosts *According to* the word that I covenanted with you when you came out of Egypt so my spirit**

5975 עמדת 8432 בתוככם 408 אל 3372 תיראו: **2:6** 3588 כי 3541 כה 559 אמר 3068 יהוה 6635 צבאות 5750 עוד 259 אחת 4592 מעט 1931 היא 589 ואני
'amedet batoukakem; 'al tiyra'au. kiy koh 'amar Yahuah tzaba'aut, 'aud 'achat ma'at hiy'a; ua'aniy,
**remains among you not fear you For thus saith Yahuah of hosts Yet once a little *while* it *is* and I**

7493 מרעיש 853 את 8064 השמים 853 ואת 776 הארץ 853 ואת 3220 הים 853 ואת 2724 החרבה: **2:7** 7493 והרעשתי 853 את 3605 כל 1471 הגוים
mar'aysh 'at hashamayim ua'at ha'aretz, ua'at hayam ua'at hecharabah. uahir'ashtiy 'at kal hagouyim,
**will shake the heavens *and* the earth *and* the sea *and* the dry *land* And I will shake all nations**

935 ובאו 2532 חמדת 3605 כל 1471 הגוים 4390 ומלאתי 853 את 1004 הבית 2088 הזה 3519 כבוד 559 אמר 3068 יהוה 6635 צבאות: **2:8**
uaba'au chemdat kal hagouyim; uamilea'tiy 'at habayit hazeh kaboud, 'amar Yahuah tzaba'aut.
**shall come and the desire of all nations and I will fill house this *with* glory saith Yahuah of hosts**

3807a לי 3701 הכסף 3807a ולי 2091 הזהב 5002 נאם 3068 יהוה 6635 צבאות: **2:9** 1419 גדול 1961 יהיה 3519 כבוד 1004 הבית 2088 הזה
liy hakesep ualiy hazahab; na'am Yahuah tzaba'aut. gadoul yihayeh kaboud habayit hazeh
***is* mine The silver *is* mine and the gold saith Yahuah of hosts greater shall be The glory of house this**

**Hag** 2:1 In the seventh month, in the one and twentieth day of the month, came the word of YHUH by the prophet Haggai, saying,2 Speak now to Zerubbabel the son of Shealtiel, governor of Judah, and to Joshua the son of Josedech, the high priest, and to the residue of the people, saying,3 Who is left among you that saw this house in her first glory? and how do you see it now? is it not in your eyes in comparison of it as nothing?4 Yet now be strong, O Zerubbabel, saith YHUH; and be strong, O Joshua, son of Josedech, the high priest; and be strong, all you people of the land, saith YHUH, and work: for I am with you, saith YHUH of hosts:5 According to the word that I covenanted with you when you came out of Egypt, so my spirit remain among you: fear you not.6 For thus saith YHUH of hosts; Yet once, it is a little while, and I will shake the heavens, and the earth, and the sea, and the dry land;7 And I will shake all nations, and the desire of all nations shall come: and I will fill this house with glory, saith YHUH of hosts.8 The silver is mine, and the gold is mine, saith YHUH of hosts.9 The glory of this latter house shall be greater than of the former, saith YHUH of hosts: and in this place will I give peace, saith YHUH of hosts.

האחרון 314 מן 4480 הראשון 7223 אמר 559 יהוה 3068 צבאות 6635 ובמקום 4725 הזה 2088 אתן 5414 שלום 7965 נאם 5002 יהוה 3068 צבאות 6635:
ha'acharoun min hara'shoun, 'amar Yahuah tzaba'aut; uabamaqoum hazeh 'aten shaloum, na'am Yahuah tzaba'aut.
**latter than of the former saith Yahuah of hosts and in place this will I give peace saith Yahuah of hosts**

2:10
בעשרים 6242 וארבעה 702 לתשיעי 8671 בשנת 8141 שתים 8147 לדריוש 1867 היה 1961 דבר 1697 יהוה 3069 אל 413
ba'asriym ua'arbah latashiy'ay, bishnat shatayim ladarayauesh; hayah dabar Yahuah, 'al
**In twentieth and *the* four *day* of the ninth *month* in year of *the* second Darius came the word of Yahuah by**

חגי 2292 הנביא 5030 לאמר 559: 2:11 כה 3541 אמר 559 יהוה 3068 צבאות 6635 שאל 7592 נא 4994 את 853 הכהנים 3548 תורה 8451
chagay hanabiy'a lea'mor. koh 'amar Yahuah tzaba'aut; sha'al naa' 'at hakohaniym tourah
**Haggai the prophet saying Thus saith Yahuah of hosts Ask now the priests *concerning* the law**

לאמר 559: 2:12 הן 2005 ישא 5375 איש 376 בשר 1320 קדש 6944 בכנף 3671 בגדו 899 ונגע 5060 בכנפו 3671 אל 413 הלחם 3899
lea'mor. hen yisaa' 'aysh basar qodesh biknap bigdou, uanaga' biknapou 'al halechem
**saying If bear one flesh holy in the skirt of his garment and do touch with his skirt or bread**

ואל 413 הנזיד 5138 ואל 413 היין 3196 ואל 413 שמן 8081 ואל 413 כל 3605 מאכל 3978 היקדש 6942 ויענו 6030 הכהנים 3548
ua'al hanaziyd ua'al hayayin ua'al shemen ua'al kal ma'akal hayiqdash; uaya'anu hakohaniym
**and or pottage and or wine and or oil and or any meat shall it be holy? And answered? the priests**

ויאמרו 559 לא 3808: 2:13 ויאמר 559 חגי 2292 אם 518 יגע 5060 טמא 2931 נפש 5315 בכל 3605 אלה 428 היטמא 2930
uaya'maru la'. uaya'mer chagay, 'am yiga' tamea' nepesh bakal 'aeleh hayitma';
**and said No Then said Haggai If touch *one that is* unclean by a dead body any of these shall it be unclean?**

ויענו 6030 הכהנים 3548 ויאמרו 559 יטמא 2930: 2:14 ויען 6030 חגי 2292 ויאמר 559 כן 3651 העם 5971 הזה 2088
uaya'anu hakohaniym uaya'maru yitama'. uaya'an chagay uaya'mer, ken ha'am hazeh
**And answered the priests and said It shall be unclean Then answered Haggai and said So the people *is* this**

וכן 3651 הגוי 1471 הזה 2088 לפני 6440 נאם 5002 יהוה 3068 וכן 3651 כל 3605 מעשה 4639 ידיהם 3027 ואשר 834 יקריבו 7126 שם 8033
uaken hagouy hazeh lapanay na'am Yahuah, uaken kal ma'aseh yadeyhem; ua'asher yaqriybu sham
**and so nation *is* this before me saith Yahuah and so *is* every work of their hands and that which they offer there**

טמא 2931 הוא 1931: 2:15 ועתה 6258 שימו 7760 נא 4994 לבבכם 3824 מן 4480 היום 3117 הזה 2088 ומעלה 4605 מטרם 2962 שום 7760
tamea' hua'. ua'atah siymu naa' lababkem, min hayoum hazeh uama'alah; miterem sum
***is* unclean he And now consider you I pray your heart from day this and upward from before was laid**

אבן 68 אל 413 אבן 68 בהיכל 1964 יהוה 3068: 2:16 מהיותם 1961 בא 935 אל 413 ערמת 6194 עשרים 6242
'aben 'al 'aben baheykal Yahuah. mihayoutam ba' 'al 'aremat 'asriym,
**a stone upon a stone in the temple of Yahuah Since those *days* were when *one* came to an heap of twenty *measures***

והיתה 1961 עשרה 6235 בא 935 אל 413 היקב 3342 לחשף 2834 חמשים 2572 פורה 6333 והיתה 1961
uahayatah 'asarah; ba' 'al hayeqeb, lachasop chamishiym pu'rah, uahayatah
**there were *but* ten when *one* came to the pressfat for to draw out fifty *vessels out of* the press there were**

עשרים 6242: 2:17 הכיתי 5221 אתכם 853 בשדפון 7711 ובירקון 3420 ובברד 1259 את 853 כל 3605 מעשה 4639 ידיכם 3027
'asriym. hikeytiy 'atkem bashidapoun uabayeraqoun uababarad, 'at kal ma'aseh yadeykem;
***but* twenty I smote you with blasting and with mildew and with hail *in* all the labours of your hands**

Hag 2:10 In the four and twentieth day of the ninth month, in the second year of Darius, came the word of YHUH by Haggai the prophet, saying,11 Thus saith YHUH of hosts; Ask now the priests concerning the law, saying,12 If one bear holy flesh in the skirt of his garment, and with his skirt do touch bread, or pottage, or wine, or oil, or any meat, shall it be holy? And the priests answered and said, No.13 Then said Haggai, If one that is unclean by a dead body touch any of these, shall it be unclean? And the priests answered and said, It shall be unclean.14 Then answered Haggai, and said, So is this people, and so is this nation before me, saith YHUH; and so is every work of their hands; and that which they offer there is unclean.15 And now, I pray you, consider from this day and upward, from before a stone was laid upon a stone in the temple of YHUH:16 Since those days were, when one came to an heap of twenty measures, there were but ten: when one came to the pressfat for to draw out fifty vessels out of the press, there were but twenty.17 I smote you with blasting and with mildew and with hail in all the labours of your hands; yet you turned not to me, saith YHUH.

ואין 369 אתכם 853 אלי 413 נאם 5002 יהוה 3068: **2:18** שימו 7760 נא 4994 לבבכם 3824 מן 4480 היום 3117 הזה 2088 ומעלה 4605 מיום 3117
ua'aeyn 'atkem 'aelay na'am Yahuah. siymu naa' lababkem, min hayoum hazeh uama'alah; miyoum
**yet not you *turned* to me saith Yahuah Concider now your heart from day this and upward day of**

עשרים 6242 וארבעה 702 לתשיעי 8671 למן 4480 היום 3117 אשר 834 יסד 3245 היכל 1964 יהוה 3068 שימו 7760
'asriym ua'arbah latashiy'ay, lamin hayoum 'asher yusad heykal Yahuah siymu
**twentieth and *the* four the ninth *month even* from the day that the foundation of was laid temple Yahuah's concider**

לבבכם 3824: **2:19** העוד 5750 הזרע 2233 במגורה 4035 ועד 5704 הגפן 1612 והתאנה 8384 והרמון 7416 ועץ 6086
lababkem. ha'aud hazera' bamagurah, ua'ad hagapen uahata'aenah uaharimoun ua'aetz
**your heart *it* Is still the seed in the barn? yea, as yet the vine and the fig and the pomegranate tree**

הזית 2132 לא 3808 נשא 5375 מן 4480 היום 3117 הזה 2088 אברך 1288: **2:20** ויהי 1961 דבר 1697 יהוה 3068 שנית 8145
lazayit la' nasa'; min hayoum hazeh 'abarek. uayahiy dabar Yahuah sheniyt
***and* the olive tree not has brought forth from day this will I bless *you* And came the word of Yahuah again**

אל 413 חגי 2292 בעשרים 6242 וארבעה 702 לחדש 2320 לאמר 559: **2:21** אמר 559 אל 413 זרבבל 2216 פחת 6346 יהודה 3063 לאמר 559
'al chagay, ba'asriym ua'arbah lachodesh lea'mor. 'amor 'al zarubabel pachat yahudah lea'mor;
**unto Haggai in twentieth and *the* four *day* of the month saying Speak to Zerubbabel governor of Judah saying**

אני 589 מרעיש 7493 את 853 השמים 8064 ואת 853 הארץ 776: **2:22** והפכתי 2015 כסא 3678 ממלכות 4467 והשמדתי 8045
'aniy mar'aysh, 'at hashamayim ua'at ha'aretz. uahapaktiy kisea' mamlakout, uahishmadtiy,
**I will shake the heavens *and* the earth And I will overthrow the throne of kingdoms and I will destroy**

חזק 2392 ממלכות 4467 הגוים 1471 והפכתי 2015 מרכבה 4818 ורכביה 7392
chozeq mamlakout hagouyim; uahapaktiy merkabah uarokabeyha,
**the strength of the kingdoms of the heathen and I will overthrow the chariots and those that ride in them**

וירדו 3381 סוסים 5483 ורכביהם 7392 איש 376 בחרב 2719 אחיו 251: **2:23** ביום 3117 ההוא 1931 נאם 5002 יהוה 3068
uayaradu susiym uarokabeyhem, 'aysh bachereb 'achiyu. bayoum hahua' na'am Yahuah
**and shall come down the horses and their riders every one by the sword of his brother In day that saith Yahuah**

צבאות 6635 אקחך 3947 זרבבל 2216 בן 1121 שאלתיאל 7597 עבדי 5650 נאם 5002 יהוה 3068 ושמתיך 7760 כחותם 2368
tzaba'aut 'aqachaka zarubabel ben sha'altiy'ael 'abdiy na'am Yahuah, uasamtiyka kachoutam;
**of hosts will I take you O Zerubbabel the son of Shealtiel my servant saith Yahuah and will make you as a signet**

כי 3588 בך 871a בחרתי 977 נאם 5002 יהוה 3068 צבאות 6635:
kiy baka bachartiy, na'am Yahuah tzaba'aut.
**for in you I have chosen saith Yahuah of hosts**

Hag 2:18 Consider now from this day and upward, from the four and twentieth day of the ninth month, even from the day that the foundation of YHUH's temple was laid, consider it.19 Is the seed yet in the barn? yea, as yet the vine, and the fig tree, and the pomegranate, and the olive tree, has not brought forth: from this day will I bless you.20 And again the word of YHUH came unto Haggai in the four and twentieth day of the month, saying,21 Speak to Zerubbabel, governor of Judah, saying, I will shake the heavens and the earth;22 And I will overthrow the throne of kingdoms, and I will destroy the strength of the kingdoms of the heathen; and I will overthrow the chariots, and those that ride in them; and the horses and their riders shall come down, everyone by the sword of his brother.23 In that day, saith YHUH of hosts, will I take you, O Zerubbabel, my servant, the son of Shealtiel, saith YHUH, and will make you as a signet: for I have chosen you, saith YHUH of hosts.

# ZECHARIAH
## (*Zakaryah*)

Verse one identifies the author as the Prophet Zechariah whose name in Hebrew means *Yah remembers*. The book was written in two primary parts, between 520 and 470 B.C. to the **House of Judah** and Zechariah was one of those who returned from Babylon to Jerusalem and he emphasized a tone of encouragement to the struggling Israelites trying to rebuild their temple. Zechariah was born in Babylon during the 70 years of exile and like Ezekiel and Jeremiah he was both a prophet and a priest and much of the prophetic events prophesied are yet to be fulfilled. Zechariah's dated visions and messages in chapters (Zech 1–8) all take place in the same general time period as Haggai's, beginning in 520 BC with a call for the people of Judah to repent (Zech 1:1). Though his final messages in chapters (Zech 9–14) go undated, the mention of Greece in (Zech 9:13) suggests the prophecies came much later in his life, presumably sometime in the 480 BC, before Ezra (458 BC) and Nehemiah (444 BC) arrived to again revitalize the Jewish people. The book of Zechariah contains the clearest and the largest number of Messianic passages among the Minor Prophets. Zechariah pictures Y'shua our Messiah in both His first coming (Zech 9:9) and His second coming (Zech 9:10–10:12). Y'shua will come, according to Zechariah, as Savior, Judge, and ultimately, as the righteous King ruling His people from Jerusalem (Zech 14:8–9).

| **Zechariah 1:1** | 2320 בחדש | 8066 השמיני | 8141 בשנת | 8147 שתים | 1867 לדריוש | 1961 היה | 1697 דבר | 3068 יהוה | 413 אל | 2148 זכריה |
|---|---|---|---|---|---|---|---|---|---|---|
| | bachodesh | hashamiyniy, | bishnat | shatayim | ladarayauesh; | hayah | dabar | Yahuah | 'al | zakaryah |
| | **In month** | **the eighth** | **in year** | **the second** | **of Darius** | **came** | **the word of** | **Yahuah** | **unto** | **Zechariah** |

| 1121 בן | 1296 ברכיה | 1121 בן | 5714 עדו | 5030 הנביא | 559: לאמר | **1:2** | 7107 קצף | 3068 יהוה | 5921 על | 1 אבותיכם | 7110: קצף | **1:3** |
|---|---|---|---|---|---|---|---|---|---|---|---|---|
| ben | berekyah, | ben | 'adou | hanabiy'a | lea'mor. | | qatzap | Yahuah | 'al | abouteykem | qatzep. | |
| **the son of** | **Berechiah** | **the son of** | **Iddo** | **the prophet** | **saying** | | **displeased** | **Yahuah** | **with** | **your fathers** | **has been sore** | |

| 559 ואמרת | 413 אלהם | 3541 כה | 559 אמר | 3068 יהוה | 6635 צבאות | 7725 שובו | 413 אלי | 5002 נאם | 3068 יהוה | 6635 צבאות | 7725 ואשוב |
|---|---|---|---|---|---|---|---|---|---|---|---|
| ua'amarta | 'alehem, | koh | 'amar | Yahuah | tzaba'aut, | shubu | 'aelay, | na'am | Yahuah | tzaba'aut; | ua'ashub |
| **Therefore say you** | **unto them** | **Thus** | **saith** | **Yahuah** | **of hosts** | **Turn you** | **unto me** | **saith** | **Yahuah** | **of hosts** | **and I will turn** |

| 413 אליכם | 559 אמר | 3068 יהוה | 6635: צבאות | **1:4** | 408 אל | 1961 תהיו | 1 כאבתיכם | 834 אשר | 7121 קראו | 413 אליהם | 5030 הנביאים |
|---|---|---|---|---|---|---|---|---|---|---|---|
| 'aleykem, | 'amar | Yahuah | tzaba'aut. | | 'al | tihayu | ka'aboteykem | 'asher | qara'au | 'aleyhem | hanabiy'aym |
| **unto you** | **saith** | **Yahuah** | **of hosts** | | **not** | **Be you** | **as your fathers** | **unto whom** | **have cried** | **to them** | **the prophets** |

| 7223 הראשנים | 559 לאמר | 3541 כה | 559 אמר | 3068 יהוה | 6635 צבאות | 7725 שובו | 4994 נא | 1870 מדרכיכם | 7451 הרעים | 4611 ומעליליכם |
|---|---|---|---|---|---|---|---|---|---|---|
| hara'shoniym | lea'mor, | koh | 'amar | Yahuah | tzaba'aut, | shubu | naa' | midarkeykem | hara'aym, | uama'alileiykem |
| **the former** | **saying** | **Thus** | **saith** | **Yahuah** | **of hosts** | **Turn you** | **now** | **from your ways** | **evil** | **and *from* your doings** |

| 7451 הרעים | 3808 ולא | 8085 שמעו | 3808 ולא | 7181 הקשיבו | 413 אלי | 5002 נאם | 3068: יהוה | **1:5** | 1 אבותיכם | 346 איה | 1992 הם |
|---|---|---|---|---|---|---|---|---|---|---|---|
| hara'aym; | uala' | shama'au | uala' | hiqshiybu | 'aelay | na'am | Yahuah. | | abouteykem | 'ayeh | hem; |
| **evil** | **but not** | **they did hear** | **nor** | **listen** | **unto me** | **saith** | **Yahuah** | | **Your fathers** | **where** | ***are* they?** |

| 5030 והנבאים | 5769 הלעולם | 2421: יחיו | **1:6** | 389 אך | 1697 דברי | 2706 וחקי | 834 אשר | 6680 צויתי | 853 את | 5650 עבדי |
|---|---|---|---|---|---|---|---|---|---|---|
| uahanabi'aym, | hal'aulam | yichayu. | | 'ak | dabaray | uachuqay, | 'asher | tziuiytiy | 'at | 'abaday |
| **and the prophets** | **for ever?** | **do they live** | | **But** | **my words** | **and my statutes** | **which** | **I commanded** | | **my servants** |

| 5030 הנביאים | 3808 הלוא | 5381 השיגו | 1 אבתיכם | 7725 וישובו | 559 ויאמרו | 834 כאשר | 2161 זמם | 3068 יהוה | 6635 צבאות |
|---|---|---|---|---|---|---|---|---|---|
| hanabiy'aym, | halou'a | hisiygu | 'aboteykem; | uayashubu | uaya'maru, | ka'asher | zamam | Yahuah | tzaba'aut |
| **the prophets** | **not** | **did they take hold of** | **your fathers?** | **and they returned** | **and said** | **Like as** | **thought** | **Yahuah** | **of hosts** |

**Zechariah** 1:1 In the eighth month, in the second year of Darius, came the word of YHUH unto Zechariah, the son of Berechiah, the son of Iddo the prophet, saying,2 YHUH has been sore displeased with your fathers.3 Therefore say you unto them, Thus saith YHUH of hosts; Turn you unto me, saith YHUH of hosts, and I will turn unto you, saith YHUH of hosts.4 Be you not as your fathers, unto whom the former prophets have cried, saying, Thus saith YHUH of hosts; Turn you now from your evil ways, and from your evil doings: but they did not hear, nor hear unto me, saith YHUH.5 Your fathers, where are they? and the prophets, do they live forever?6 But my words and my statutes, which I commanded my servants the prophets, did they not take hold of your fathers? and they returned and said, Like as YHUH of hosts thought to do unto us, according to our ways, and according to our doings, so has he dealt with us.

לעשות 6213 לנו 3807a כדרכינו 1870 וכמעללינו 4611 כן 3651 עשה 6213 אתנו 854: 1:7 ביום 3117

la'asout lanu, kidrakeynu uakma'alaleynu, ken 'asah 'atanu. bayoum

**to do unto us according to our ways and according to our doings so has he dealt with us Upon the day of**

עשרים 6242 וארבעה 702 לעשתי 6249 עשר 6240 חדש 2320 הוא 1931 חדש 2320 שבט 7626 בשנת 8141 שתים 8147 לדריוש 1867 היה 1961

'asriym ua'arbah la'ashtey 'asar chodesh hua' chodesh shabat, bishnat shatayim ladarayauesh; hayah

**twentieth and four for one ten month which *is* the month Sebat in year the second of Darius came**

דבר 1697 יהוה 3068 אל 413 זכריה 2148 בן 1121 ברכיהו 1296 בן 1121 עדוא 5714 הנביא 5030 לאמר 559: 1:8 ראיתי 7200 הלילה 3915

dabar Yahuah 'al zakaryah ben berekyahu, ben 'adou'a hanabiy'a lea'mor. ra'aytiy halayalah,

**the word of Yahuah unto Zechariah the son of Berechiah the son of Iddo the prophet saying I saw by night**

והנה 2009 איש 376 רכב 7392 על 5921 סוס 5483 אדם 122 והוא 1931 עמד 5975 בין 996 ההדסים 1918 אשר 834 במצלה 4699 ואחריו 310

uahineh 'aysh rokeb 'al sus 'adom, uahu'a 'amed, beyn hahadasiym 'asher bamatzulah; ua'acharayu

**and behold a man riding upon a horse red and he stood among the myrtle *trees* that *were* in the bottom and behind**

סוסים 5483 אדמים 122 שרקים 8320 ולבנים 3836: 1:9 ואמר 559 מה 4100 אלה 428 אדני 113 ויאמר 559 אלי 413

susiym 'adumiym, saruqiym ualbaniym. ua'amar mah 'aeleh 'adoniy; uaya'mer 'aelay,

**horses *him were there* red speckled and white Then said I what *are* these? O my adonai And said unto me**

המלאך 4397 הדבר 1697 בי 871a אני 589 אראך 7200 מה 4100 המה 1992 אלה 428: 1:10 ויען 6030 האיש 376 העמד 5975 בין 996

hamal'ak hadober biy, 'aniy 'ar'aka mah hemah 'aeleh. uaya'an, ha'aysh ha'aumed beyn

**the angel that talked with me I will show you what they these be And answered the man that stood among**

ההדסים 1918 ויאמר 559 אלה 428 אשר 834 שלח 7971 יהוה 3068 להתהלך 1980 בארץ 776: 1:11

hahadasiym uaya'mar; 'aeleh 'asher shalach Yahuah, lahithalek ba'aretz.

**the myrtle *trees* and said These *are they* whom has sent Yahuah to walk to and fro through the earth**

ויענו 6030 את 853 מלאך 4397 יהוה 3069 העמד 5975 בין 996 ההדסים 1918 ויאמרו 559 התהלכנו 1980

uaya'anu 'at mal'ak Yahuah ha'aumed beyn hahadasiym, uaya'maru hithalaknu

**And they answered the angel of Elohim that stood among the myrtle *trees* and said We have walked to and fro**

בארץ 776 והנה 2009 כל 3605 הארץ 776 ישבת 3427 ושקטת 8252: 1:12 ויען 6030 מלאך 4397 יהוה 3068 ויאמר 559

ba'aretz; uahineh kal ha'aretz yoshebet uashoqatet. uaya'an mal'ak Yahuah uaya'mar

**through the earth and behold all the earth sit still and is at rest Then answered the angel of Yahuah and said**

יהוה 3068 צבאות 6635 עד 5704 מתי 4970 אתה 859 לא 3808 תרחם 7355 את 853 ירושלם 3389 ואת 853 ערי 5892 יהודה 3063

Yahuah tzaba'aut, 'ad matay, 'atah la' tarachem 'at yarushalaim, ua'at 'arey yahudah;

**O Yahuah of hosts how long you not will you have mercy Jerusalem *and* on the cities of Judah**

אשר 834 זעמתה 2194 זה 2088 שבעים 7657 שנה 8141: 1:13 ויען 6030 יהוה 3068 את 853

'asher za'amtah, zeh shib'aym shanah. uaya'an Yahuah 'at

***against* which you have had indignation these threescore and ten (*seventy*) years? And answered Yahuah**

המלאך 4397 הדבר 1696 בי 871a דברים 1697 טובים 2896 דברים 1697 נחמים 5150: 1:14 ויאמר 559 אלי 413 המלאך 4397

hamal'ak hadober biy dabariym toubiym; dabariym nichumiym. uaya'mer 'aelay, hamal'ak

**the angel that talked with me words *with* good words *and* comfortable So said unto me the angel**

Zech 1:7 Upon the four and twentieth day of the eleventh month, which is the month Sebat, in the second year of Darius, came the word of YHUH unto Zechariah, the son of Berechiah, the son of Iddo the prophet, saying,8 I saw by night, and behold a man riding upon a red horse, and he stood among the myrtle trees that were in the bottom; and behind him were there red horses, speckled, and white.9 Then said I, O my lord, what are these? And the angel that talked with me said unto me, I will show you what these be.10 And the man that stood among the myrtle trees answered and said, These are they whom YHUH has sent to walk to and fro through the earth.11 And they answered the angel of YHUH that stood among the myrtle trees, and said, We have walked to and fro through the earth, and, behold, all the earth sitteth still, and is at rest.12 Then the angel of YHUH answered and said, O YHUH of hosts, how long will you not have mercy on Jerusalem and on the cities of Judah, against which you have had indignation these threescore and ten years?13 And YHUH answered the angel that talked with me with good words and comfortable words.14 So the angel that communed with me said unto me, Cry you, saying, Thus saith YHUH of hosts; I am jealous for Jerusalem and for Zion with a great jealousy.

| הדבר 1696 | בי 871a | קרא 7121 | לאמר 559 | כה 3541 | אמר 559 | יהוה 3068 | צבאות 6635 | קנאתי 7065 | לירושלם 3389 | ולציון 6726 |
|---|---|---|---|---|---|---|---|---|---|---|
| hadober | biy, | qara' | lea'mor, | koh | 'amar | Yahuah | tzaba'aut; | qinea'tiy | liyarushalaim | ualtziyoun |
| **that communed** | **with me** | **Cry you** | **saying** | **Thus** | **saith** | **Yahuah** | **of hosts** | **I am jealous** | **for Jerusalem** | **and for Zion** |

| קנאה 7068 | גדולה 1419: | 1:15 וקצף 7110 | גדול 1419 | אני 589 | קצף 7107 | על 5921 | הגוים 1471 | השאננים 7600 | אשר 834 | אני 589 |
|---|---|---|---|---|---|---|---|---|---|---|
| qin'ah | gadoulah. | uaqetzep | gadoul | 'aniy | qotzep, | 'al | hagouyim | hasha'ananiym; | 'asher | 'aniy |
| **with a jealousy** | **great** | **And am sore** | **very** | **I** | **displeased** | **with** | **the heathen** | ***that are* at ease** | **for** | **I** |

| קצפתי 7107 | מעט 4592 | והמה 1992 | עזרו 5826 | לרעה 7451: | 1:16 לכן 3651 | כה 3541 | אמר 559 | יהוה 3068 | שבתי 7725 |
|---|---|---|---|---|---|---|---|---|---|
| qatzaptiy | ma'at, | uahemah | 'azaru | lara'ah. | laken | koh | 'amar | Yahuah | shabtiy |
| **was displeased** | ***but* a little** | **and they** | **helped** | ***forward* the affliction** | **Therefore** | **thus** | **saith** | **Yahuah** | **I am returned** |

| לירושלם 3389 | ברחמים 7356 | ביתי 1004 | יבנה 1129 | בה 871a | נאם 5002 | יהוה 3068 | צבאות 6635 | וקוה 6961 | ינטה 5186 | על 5921 |
|---|---|---|---|---|---|---|---|---|---|---|
| liyarushalaim | barachamiym, | beytiy | yibaneh | bah, | na'am | Yahuah | tzaba'aut; | uaqauah | yinateh | 'al |
| **to Jerusalem** | **with mercies** | **my house** | **shall be built** | **in it** | **saith** | **Yahuah** | **of hosts** | **and a line** | **shall be stretched forth** | **upon** |

| ירושלם 3389: | 1:17 עוד 5750 | קרא 7121 | לאמר 559 | כה 3541 | אמר 559 | יהוה 3068 | צבאות 6635 | עוד 5750 | תפוצינה 6327 | ערי 5892 |
|---|---|---|---|---|---|---|---|---|---|---|
| yarushalaim. | 'aud | qara' | lea'mor, | koh | 'amar | Yahuah | tzaba'aut, | 'aud | taputzeynah | 'aray |
| **Jerusalem** | **yet** | **Cry** | **saying** | **Thus** | **saith** | **Yahuah** | **of hosts** | **yet** | **shall be spread abroad** | **My cities** |

| מטוב 2896 | ונחם 5162 | יהוה 3068 | עוד 5750 | את 853 | ציון 6726 | ובחר 977 | עוד 5750 | בירושלם 3389: | 1:18 |
|---|---|---|---|---|---|---|---|---|---|
| mitoub; | uanicham | Yahuah | 'aud | 'at | tziyoun, | uabachar | 'aud | biyarushalaim. | |
| **through prosperity** | **and shall comfort** | **Yahuah** | **yet** | | **Zion** | **and shall choose** | **yet** | **Jerusalem** | |

| ואשא 5375 | את 853 | עיני 5869 | וארא 7200 | והנה 2009 | ארבע 702 | קרנות 7161: | 1:19 ואמר 559 | אל 413 | המלאך 4397 | הדבר 1696 | בי 871a |
|---|---|---|---|---|---|---|---|---|---|---|---|
| ua'asa' | 'at | 'aeynay | ua'aera'; | uahineh | 'arba | qarnout. | ua'amar, | 'al | hamal'ak | hadober | biy |
| **Then lifted I up** | | **mine eyes** | **and saw** | **and behold** | **four** | **horns** | **And I said** | **unto** | **the angel** | **that talked** | **with me** |

| מה 4100 | אלה 428 | ויאמר 559 | אלי 413 | אלה 428 | הקרנות 7161 | אשר 834 | זרו 2219 | את 853 | יהודה 3063 | את 853 | ישראל 3478 |
|---|---|---|---|---|---|---|---|---|---|---|---|
| mah | 'aeleh; | uaya'mer | 'aelay, | 'aeleh | haqaranout | 'asher | zeru | 'at | yahudah, | 'at | yisra'ael |
| **What *be*** | **these?** | **And he answered** | **me** | **These** | ***are* the horns** | **which** | **have scattered** | | **Judah** | | **Israel** |

| וירושלם 3389: | 1:20 ויראני 7200 | יהוה 3068 | ארבעה 702 | חרשים 2796: | 1:21 ואמר 559 | מה 4100 | אלה 428 | באים 935 | לעשות 6213 |
|---|---|---|---|---|---|---|---|---|---|
| uiyarushalaim | uayar'aeniy | Yahuah, | 'arba'ah | charashiym. | ua'amar | mah | 'aeleh | ba'aym | la'asout; |
| **and Jerusalem** | **And showed me** | **Yahuah** | **four** | **carpenters** | **Then said I** | **What** | **these** | **come** | **to do?** |

| ויאמר 559 | לאמר 559 | אלה 428 | הקרנות 7161 | אשר 834 | זרו 2219 | את 853 | יהודה 3063 | כפי 6310 | איש 376 | לא 3808 | נשא 5375 | ראשו 7218 |
|---|---|---|---|---|---|---|---|---|---|---|---|---|
| uaya'mer | lea'mor, | 'aeleh | haqaranout | 'asher | zeru | 'at | yahudah, | kapiy | 'aysh | la' | nasa' | ra'shou, |
| **And he spoke** | **saying** | **These** | ***are* the horns** | **which** | **have scattered** | | **Judah** | **so that** | **man** | **no** | **did lift up** | **his head** |

| ויבאו 935 | אלה 428 | להחריד 2729 | אתם 853 | לידות 3034 | את 853 | קרנות 7161 | הגוים 1471 | הנשאים 5375 | קרן 7161 | אל 413 |
|---|---|---|---|---|---|---|---|---|---|---|
| uayabo'au | 'aeleh | lahachariyd | 'atam, | layadout | 'at | qarnout | hagouyim, | hanos'aym | qeren | 'al |
| **but are come** | **these** | **to fray** | **them** | **to cast out** | | **the horns of** | **the Gentiles** | **which lifted up** | ***their* horn** | **over** |

| ארץ 776 | יהודה 3063 | לזרותה 2219: |
|---|---|---|
| 'aretz | yahudah | lazaroutah. |
| **the land of** | **Judah** | **to scatter it** |

Zech 1:15 And I am very sore displeased with the heathen that are at ease: for I was but a little displeased, and they helped forward the affliction.16 Therefore thus saith YHUH; I am returned to Jerusalem with mercies: my house shall be built in it, saith YHUH of hosts, and a line shall be stretched forth upon Jerusalem.17 Cry yet, saying, Thus saith YHUH of hosts; My cities through prosperity shall yet be spread abroad; and YHUH shall yet comfort Zion, and shall yet choose Jerusalem.18 Then lifted I up mine eyes, and saw, and behold four horns.19 And I said unto the angel that talked with me, What be these? And he answered me, These are the horns which have scattered Judah, Israel, and Jerusalem.20 And YHUH showed me four carpenters.21 Then said I, What come these to do? And he spoke, saying, These are the horns which have scattered Judah, so that no man did lift up his head: but these are come to fray them, to cast out the horns of the Gentiles, which lifted up their horn over the land of Judah to scatter it.

**Zech 2:1** ואשא 5375 עיני 5869 וארא 7200 והנה 2009 איש 376 ובידו 3027 חבל 2256 מדה 4060: **2:2** ואמר 559 אנה 575
ua'asa' 'aeynay ua'aera' uahineh 'aysh; uabyadou chebel midah. ua'amar 'anah
**I lifted up mine eyes *again* and looked and behold a man in his hand *with* a line measuring Then said I Where**

אתה 859 הלך 1980 ויאמר 559 אלי 413 למד 4058 את 853 ירושלם 3389 לראות 7200 כמה 4100 רחבה 7341 וכמה 4100
'atah halok; uaya'mer 'aelay, lamod 'at yarushalaim, lir'aut kamah rachbah uakamah
**you? go And he said unto me To measure Jerusalem to see what *is* the breadth thereof and what *is***

ארכה 753: **2:3** והנה 2009 המלאך 4397 הדבר 1697 בי 871a יצא 3318 ומלאך 4397 אחר 312 יצא 3318 לקראתו 7125: **2:4**
'arakah. uahineh, hamal'ak hadober biy yotzea'; uamal'ak 'acher, yotzea' liqra'tou.
**the length thereof And behold the angel that talked with me went forth and angel another went out to meet him**

ויאמר 559 אלו 413 רץ 7323 דבר 1696 אל 413 הנער 5288 הלז 1975 לאמר 559 פרזות 6519 תשב 3427 ירושלם 3389
uaya'mer 'aelayu, rutz, daber 'al hana'ar halaz lea'mor; parazout tesheb yarushalaim,
**And said unto him Run speak to young man this saying *as* towns without walls shall be inhabited Jerusalem**

מרב 7230 אדם 120 ובהמה 929 בתוכה 8432: **2:5** ואני 589 אהיה 1961 לה 3807a נאם 5002 יהוה 3069 חומת 2346 אש 784 סביב 5439
merob 'adam uabahemah batoukah. ua'aniy 'ahayeh lah na'am Yahuah, choumat 'aesh sabiyb;
**for the multitude of men and cattle therein For I will be unto her saith Yahuah a wall of fire round about**

ולכבוד 3519 אהיה 1961 בתוכה 8432: **2:6** הוי 1945 הוי 1945 ונסו 5127 מארץ 776 צפון 6828 נאם 5002 יהוה 3068
ualkaboud 'ahayeh batoukah. houy houy, uanusu me'aretz tzapoun na'am Yahuah;
**and the glory will be in the midst of her Ho ho *come forth* and flee from the land of the north saith Yahuah**

כי 3588 כארבע 702 רוחות 7307 השמים 8064 פרשתי 6566 אתכם 853 נאם 5002 יהוה 3068: **2:7** הוי 1945 ציון 6726 המלטי 4422
kiy ka'arba' ruchout hashamayim perastiy 'atkem na'am Yahuah. houy tziyoun himaltiy;
**for as the four winds of the heaven I have spread abroad you saith Yahuah Woe Zion Deliver yourself**

יושבת 3427 בת 1323 בבל 894: **2:8** כי 3588 כה 3541 אמר 559 יהוה 3068 צבאות 6635 אחר 310 כבוד 3519 שלחני 7971 אל 413
youshebet bat babel. kiy koh 'amar Yahuah tzaba'aut 'achar kaboud, shalachaniy 'al
**that dwell *with* the daughter of Babylon For thus saith Yahuah of hosts After the glory has he sent me unto**

הגוים 1471 השללים 7997 אתכם 853 כי 3588 הנגע 5060 בכם 871a נגע 5060 בבבת 892 עינו 5869: **2:9** כי 3588 הנני 2005 מניף 5130 את 853
hagouyim hasholaliym 'atkem; kiy hanogea' bakem, nogea' bababat 'aeynou. kiy hinniy meniyp 'at
**the nations which spoiled you for he that touch you touch the apple of his eye For behold I will shake**

ידי 3027 עליהם 5921 והיו 1961 שלל 7998 לעבדיהם 5650 וידעתם 3045 כי 3588 יהוה 3068 צבאות 6635
yadiy 'aleyhem, uahayu shalal la'abdeyhem; uiyda'tem kiy Yahuah tzaba'aut
**mine hand upon them and they shall be a spoil to their servants and you shall know that Yahuah of hosts**

שלחני 7971: **2:10** רני 7442 ושמחי 2055 בת 1323 ציון 6726 כי 3588 הנני 2005 בא 935 ושכנתי 7931 בתוכך 8432 נאם 5002
shalachaniy. raniy uasimchiy bat tziyoun; kiy hinniy ba' uashakantiy batoukek na'am
**has sent me Sing and rejoice O daughter of Zion for lo I come and I will dwell in the midst of you saith**

יהוה 3068: **2:11** ונלוו 3867 גוים 1471 רבים 7227 אל 413 יהוה 3068 ביום 3117 ההוא 1931 והיו 1961 לי 3807a לעם 5971 ושכנתי 7931
Yahuah. uaniluu gouyim rabiym 'al Yahuah bayoum hahua', uahayu liy la'am; uashakantiy
**Yahuah And shall be joined nations many to Yahuah in day that and shall be my people and I will dwell**

**Zech** 2:1 I lifted up mine eyes again, and looked, and behold a man with a measuring line in his hand.2 Then said I, Whither go you? And he said unto me, To measure Jerusalem, to see what is the breadth thereof, and what is the length thereof.3 And, behold, the angel that talked with me went forth, and another angel went out to meet him,4 And said unto him, Run, speak to this young man, saying, Jerusalem shall be inhabited as towns without walls for the multitude of men and cattle therein:5 For I, saith YHUH, will be unto her a wall of fire round about, and will be the glory in the midst of her.6 Ho, ho, come forth, and flee from the land of the north, saith YHUH: for I have spread you abroad as the four winds of the heaven, saith YHUH.7 Deliver thyself, O Zion, that dwellest with the daughter of Babylon.8 For thus saith YHUH of hosts; After the glory has he sent me unto the nations which spoiled you: for he that touch you touch the apple of his eye.9 For, behold, I will shake mine hand upon them, and they shall be a spoil to their servants: and you shall know that YHUH of hosts has sent me.10 Sing and rejoice, O daughter of Zion: for, lo, I come, and I will dwell in the midst of you, saith YHUH.11 And many nations shall be joined to YHUH in that day, and shall be my people:

בתוכך 8432 וידעת 3045 כי 3588 יהוה 3068 צבאות 6635 שלחני 7971 אליך 413: **2:12** ונחל 5157 יהוה 3068 את 853
batoukek, uayada'at kiy Yahuah tzaba'aut shalachaniy 'alayik. uanachal Yahuah 'at
**in the midst of you and you shall know that Yahuah of hosts has sent me unto you And shall inherit Yahuah**

יהודה 3063 חלקו 2506 על 5921 אדמת 127 הקדש 6944 ובחר 977 עוד 5750 בירושלם 3389: **2:13** הס 2013 כל 3605 בשר 1320 מפני 6440
yahudah chelqou, 'al 'admat haqodesh; uabachar 'aud biyarushalaim. has kal basar mipaney
**Judah his portion in land the holy and shall choose again Jerusalem Be silent all O flesh before**

יהוה 3068 כי 3588 נעור 5782 ממעון 4583 קדשו 6944:
Yahuah; kiy ne'aur mim'aun qadashou.
**Yahuah for he is raised up out of habitation his holy**

**Zech 3:1** ויראני 7200 את 853 יהושע 3091 הכהן 3548 הגדול 1419 עמד 5975 לפני 6440 מלאך 4397 יהוה 3068 והשטן 7854 עמד 5975
uayar'aeniy, 'at yahousha' hakohen hagadoul, 'amed lipney mal'ak Yahuah; uahasatan 'amed
**And he showed me Joshua priest the high standing before the angel of Yahuah and Satan standing**

על 5921 ימינו 3225 לשטנו 7853: **3:2** ויאמר 559 יהוה 3068 אל 413 השטן 7854 יגער 1605 יהוה 3068 בך 871a השטן 7854 ויגער 1605
'al yamiynou lasitnou. uaya'mer Yahuah 'al hasatan, yig'ar Yahuah baka hasatan, uayig'ar
**at his right hand to resist him And said Yahuah unto the Satan rebuke Yahuah against you O Satan even rebuke**

יהוה 3068 בך 871a הבחר 977 בירושלם 3389 הלוא 3808 זה 2088 אוד 181 מצל 5337 מאש 784: **3:3** ויהושע 3091 היה 1961
Yahuah baka, habocher biyarushalaim; halou'a zeh 'aud mutzal me'aesh. uiyahoushua' hayah
**Yahuah against you that has chosen Jerusalem *is* not this a brand plucked out of the fire? Now Joshua was**

לבש 3847 בגדים 899 צואים 6674 ועמד 5975 לפני 6440 המלאך 4397: **3:4** ויען 6030 ויאמר 559 אל 413 העמדים 5975
labush bagadiym tzu'aym; ua'aumed lipney hamal'ak. uaya'an uaya'mer, 'al ha'amadiym
**clothed with garments filthy and stood before the angel And he answered and spoke unto those that stood**

לפניו 6440 לאמר 559 הסירו 5493 הבגדים 899 הצאים 6674 מעליו 5921 ויאמר 559 אליו 413 ראה 7200 העברתי 5674
lapanayu lea'mor, hasiyru habagadiym hatzo'aym me'alayu; uaya'mer 'aelayu, ra'aeh he'abartiy
**before him saying Take away the garments filthy from him And he said unto him Behold I have caused to pass**

מעליך 5921 עונך 5771 והלבש 3847 אתך 853 מחלצות 4254: **3:5** ואמר 559 ישימו 7760 צניף 6797 טהור 2889 על 5921
me'aleyka 'auoneka, uahalabesh 'atka machalatzout. ua'amar yasiymu tzaniyp tahour 'al
**from you your iniquity and I will clothe you with change of raiment And I said Let them set a mitre fair upon**

ראשו 7218 וישימו 7760 הצניף 6797 הטהור 2889 על 5921 ראשו 7218 וילבשהו 3847 בגדים 899 ומלאך 4397 יהוה 3068
ra'shou; uayasiymu hatzaniyp hatahour 'al ra'shou, uayalabishuhu bagadiym, uamal'ak Yahuah
**his head So they set a mitre fair upon his head and clothed him with garments And the angel of Yahuah**

עמד 5975: **3:6** ויעד 5749 מלאך 4397 יהוה 3069 ביהושע 3091 לאמר 559: **3:7** כה 3541 אמר 559 יהוה 3068 צבאות 6635 אם 518 בדרכי 1870
'amed. uaya'ad mal'ak Yahuah, biyahoushua' lea'mor. koh 'amar Yahuah tzaba'aut, 'am bidrakay
**stood by And protested the angel of Yahuah unto Joshua saying Thus saith Yahuah of hosts If in my ways**

תלך 1980 ואם 518 את 853 משמרתי 4931 תשמר 8104 וגם 1571 אתה 859 תדין 1777 את 853 ביתי 1004 וגם 1571 תשמר 8104 את 853
telek ua'am 'at mishmartiy tishmor, uagam 'atah tadiyn 'at beytiy, ua'gam tishmor 'at
**you will walk and if my charge you will keep then also you shall judge my house and also shall keep**

Zech 2:11 and I will dwell in the midst of you, and you shall know that YHUH of hosts has sent me unto you.12 And YHUH shall inherit Judah his portion in the holy land, and shall choose Jerusalem again.13 Be silent, O all flesh, before YHUH: for he is raised up out of his holy habitation. **Zech** 3:1 And he showed me Joshua the high priest standing before the angel of YHUH, and Satan standing at his right hand to resist him.2 And YHUH said unto Satan, YHUH rebuke you, O Satan; even YHUH that has chosen Jerusalem rebuke you: is not this a brand plucked out of the fire?3 Now Joshua was clothed with filthy garments, and stood before the angel.4 And he answered and spoke unto those that stood before him, saying, Take away the filthy garments from him. And unto him he said, Behold, I have caused your iniquity to pass from you, and I will clothe you with change of raiment.5 And I said, Let them set a fair mitre upon his head. So they set a fair mitre upon his head, and clothed him with garments. And the angel of YHUH stood by.6 And the angel of YHUH protested unto Joshua, saying,7 Thus saith YHUH of hosts; If you will walk in my ways, and if you will keep my charge, then you shall also judge my house, and shall also keep my courts, and I will give you places to walk among these that stand by.

3:8

חצרי 2691 ונתתי 5414 לך 3807a מהלכים 1980 בין 996 העמדים 5975 האלה 428: שמע 8085 נא 4994 יהושע 3091 הכהן 3548 הגדול 1419
chatzeray; uanatatiy laka mahlakiym, beyn ha'amadiym ha'aeleh. shama' naa' yahousha' hakohen hagadoul,
**my courts and I will give to you *places* to walk among that stand by these Hear now O Joshua priest the high**

אתה 859 ורעיך 7453 הישבים 3427 לפניך 6440 כי 3588 אנשי 582 מופת 4159 המה 1992 כי 3588 הנני 2005 מביא 935 את 853
'atah uare'ayka hayoshbiym lapaneyka, kiy 'anshey moupet hemah; kiy hinniy mebiy'a 'at
**you and your fellows that sit before you for *are* men wondered at they for behold I will bring forth**

3:9

עבדי 5650 צמח 6780: כי 3588 הנה 2009 האבן 68 אשר 834 נתתי 5414 לפני 6440 יהושע 3091 על 5921 אבן 68 אחת 259 שבעה 7651
'abdiy tzemach. kiy hineh ha'aben, 'asher natatiy lipney yahousha', 'al 'aben 'achat shib'ah
**my servant the BRANCH For behold the stone that I have laid before Joshua upon stone one *shall be* seven**

עינים 5869 הנני 2005 מפתח 6605 פתחה 6603 נאם 5002 יהוה 3068 צבאות 6635 ומשתי 4185 את 853 עון 5771
'aeynayim; hinniy mapateach pituchah, na'am Yahuah tzaba'aut, uamashtiy 'at 'auon
**eyes behold I will engrave the graving thereof saith Yahuah of hosts and I will remove the iniquity of**

3:10

הארץ 776 ההיא 1931 ביום 3117 אחד 259: ביום 3117 ההוא 1931 נאם 5002 יהוה 3068 צבאות 6635 תקראו 7121 איש 376 לרעהו 7453 אל 413
ha'aretz hahiy'a bayoum 'achad. bayoum hahua', na'am Yahuah tzaba'aut, tiqraa'au 'aysh lare'aehu; 'al
**the land that in day one In day that saith Yahuah of hosts shall you call every man his neighbour to**

תחת 8478 גפן 1612 ואל 413 תחת 8478 תאנה 8384:
tachat gepen ua'al tachat ta'aenah.
**under the vine and to under the fig tree**

**Zech 4:1** 4:2

וישב 7725 המלאך 4397 הדבר 1696 בי 871a ויעירני 5782 כאיש 376 אשר 834 יעור 5782 משנתו 8142:
uayashab hamal'ak hadober biy; uaya'ayreniy ka'aysh 'asher ya'aur mishanatou.
**And came again the angel that talked with me and waked me as a man that is wakened out of his sleep**

ויאמר 559 אלי 413 מה 4100 אתה 859 ראה 7200 ויאמר 559 ראיתי 7200 והנה 2009 מנורת 4501 זהב 2091 כלה 3605 וגלה 1543 על 5921
uaya'mer 'aelay, mah 'atah ro'ah; uaya'mer ra'aytiy uahineh manourat zahab kulah uagulah 'al
**And said unto me What you? see And I said I have looked and behold a candlestick *of* gold all with a bowl upon**

ראשה 7218 ושבעה 7651 נרתיה 5216 עליה 5921 שבעה 7651 ושבעה 7651 מוצקות 4166 לנרות 5216 אשר 834 על 5921
ra'shah, uashib'ah neroteyha 'aleyha, shib'ah uashib'ah mutzaqout, lanerout 'asher 'al
**the top of it and his seven lamps thereon *and* seven and his seven pipes to the lamps which *are* upon**

4:3

ראשה 7218: ושנים 8147 זיתים 2132 עליה 5921 אחד 259 מימין 3225 הגלה 1543 ואחד 259 על 5921
ra'shah. uashnayim zeytiym 'aleyha; 'achad miymiyn hagulah, ua'achad 'al
**the top thereof And two olive *trees* by it one upon the right *side* of the bowl and the other upon**

4:4 4:5

שמאלה 8040: ויען 6030 ואמר 559 אל 413 המלאך 4397 הדבר 1696 בי 871a לאמר 559 מה 4100 אלה 428 אדני 113:
sama'lah. ua'aan ua'amar, 'al hamal'ak hadober biy lea'mor; mah 'aeleh 'adoniy.
**the left side thereof So I answered and spoke to the angel that talked with me saying What *are* these my adonai?**

ויען 6030 המלאך 4397 הדבר 1696 בי 871a ויאמר 559 אלי 413 הלוא 3808 ידעת 3045 מה 4100 המה 1992
uaya'an hamal'ak hadober biy uaya'mer 'aelay, halou'a yada'ta mah hemah
**Then answered the angel that talked with me and said unto me not Know you what they**

Zech 3:8 Hear now, O Joshua the high priest, you, and your fellows that sit before you: for they are men wondered at: for, behold, I will bring forth my servant the BRANCH.9
For behold the stone that I have laid before Joshua; upon one stone shall be seven eyes: behold, I will engrave the graving thereof, saith YHUH of hosts, and I will remove the
iniquity of that land in one day.10 In that day, saith YHUH of hosts, shall you call every man his neighbor under the vine and under the fig tree. **Zech** 4:1 And the angel that
talked with me came again, and waked me, as a man that is wakened out of his sleep,2 And said unto me, What seest you? And I said, I have looked, and behold a candlestick
all of gold, with a bowl upon the top of it, and his seven lamps thereon, and seven pipes to the seven lamps, which are upon the top thereof:3 And two olive trees by it, one
upon the right side of the bowl, and the other upon the left side thereof.4 So I answered and spoke to the angel that talked with me, saying, What are these, my lord?5 Then the
angel that talked with me answered and said unto me, Know you not what these be? And I said, No, my lord.

4:6

אלה 428 ואמר 559 לא 3808 אדני 113: ויען 6030 ויאמר 559 אלי 413 לאמר 559 זה 2088 דבר 1697 יהוה 3068 אל 413

'aeleh; ua'amar la' 'adoniy. uaya'an uaya'mer 'aelay lea'mor, zeh dabar Yahuah, 'al

**these be? And I said No my adonai Then he answered and spoke unto me saying This *is* the word of Yahuah unto**

4:7

זרבבל 2216 לאמר 559 לא 3808 בחיל 2428 ולא 3808 בכח 3581 כי 3588 אם 518 ברוחי 7307 אמר 559 יהוה 3068 צבאות 6635: מי 4310 אתה 859

zarubabel lea'mor; la' bachayil uala' uakoach, kiy 'am baruchiy, 'amar Yahuah tzaba'aut. miy' 'atah

**Zerubbabel saying Not by might nor by power but rather by my spirit saith Yahuah of hosts Who *are* you**

הר 2022 הגדול 1419 לפני 6440 זרבבל 2216 למישר 4334 והוציא 3318 את 853 האבן 68 הראשה 7222

har hagadoul lipney zarubabel lamiyshor; uahoutziy'a 'at ha'aben hara'shah,

**O mountain? great before Zerubbabel *you shall become* a plain and he shall bring forth the stone the head**

4:8 4:9

תשאות 8663 חן 2580 חן 2580 לה 3807a: ויהי 1961 דבר 1697 יהוה 3068 אלי 413 לאמר 559:

teshu'aut chen chen lah. uayahiy dabar Yahuah 'aelay lea'mor.

***thereof with* shoutings *crying* Grace grace unto it Moreover came the word of Yahuah unto me saying**

ידי 3027 זרבבל 2216 יסדו 3245 הבית 1004 הזה 2088 וידיו 3027 תבצענה 1214 וידעת 3045

yadey zarubabel, yisdu habayit hazeh uayadayu tabatza'anah; uayada'ata,

**The hands of Zerubbabel have laid the foundation of house this his hands also shall finish it and you shall know**

4:10

כי 3588 יהוה 3068 צבאות 6635 שלחני 7971 אליכם 413: כי 3588 מי 4310 בז 937 ליום 3117 קטנות 6996 ושמחו 8055

kiy Yahuah tzaba'aut shalachaniy 'aleykem. kiy miy' baz layoum qatanout uasamaku,

**that Yahuah of hosts has sent me unto you For who has despised the day of small *things*? for they shall rejoice**

וראו 7200 את 853 האבן 68 הבדיל 913 ביד 3027 זרבבל 2216 שבעה 7651 אלה 428 עיני 5869 יהוה 3068 המה 1992

uar'au 'at ha'aben habdiyl bayad zarubabel shib'ah 'aeleh; 'aeyney Yahuah, hemah

**and shall see the stones the plummet in the hand of Zerubbabel seven *with* those *are* the eyes of Yahuah they**

4:11

משוטטים 7751 בכל 3605 הארץ 776: ואען 6030 ואמר 559 אליו 413 מה 4100 שני 8147 הזיתים 2132 האלה 428

mashoutatiym bakal ha'aretz. ua'aan ua'amar 'aelayu; mah shaney hazeytiym ha'aeleh,

**which run to and fro throughout whole the earth Then answered I and said unto him What two olive *trees are* these**

4:12

על 5921 ימין 3225 המנורה 4501 ועל 5921 שמאולה 8040: ואען 6030 שנית 8145 ואמר 559 אליו 413 מה 4100

'al yamiyn hamanourah ua'al sama'aulah. ua'aan sheniyt, ua'amar 'aelayu; mah

**upon the right *side* of the candlestick and upon the left side thereof? And I answered again and said unto him What**

4:13

שתי 8147 שבלי 7641 הזיתים 2132 אשר 834 ביד 3027 שני 8147 צנתרות 6804 הזהב 2091 המריקים 7324 מעליהם 5921 הזהב 2091:

shatey shibaley hazeytiym, 'asher bayad, shaney tzantarout hazahab, hamariyqiym me'aleyhem hazahab.

***be these* two branches olive which through the two pipes golden empty out of themselves? the golden *oil***

4:14

ויאמר 559 אלי 413 לאמר 559 הלוא 3808 ידעת 3045 מה 4100 אלה 428 ואמר 559 לא 3808 אדני 113: ויאמר 559 אלה 428

uaya'mer 'aelay lea'mor, halou'a yada'ta mah 'aeleh; ua'amar la' 'adoniy. uaya'mer 'aeleh

**And he answered me and said not Know you what these *be*? And I said No my adonai Then said he These**

שני 8147 בני 1121 היצהר 3323 העמדים 5975 על 5921 אדון 113 כל 3605 הארץ 776:

shaney baney hayitzhar; ha'amadiym 'al 'adoun kal ha'aretz.

**two *are* ones the anointed that stand by Adonai of whole the earth**

Zech 4:6 Then he answered and spoke unto me, saying, This is the word of YHUH unto Zerubbabel, saying, Not by might, nor by power, but by my spirit, saith YHUH of hosts.7 Who are you, O great mountain? before Zerubbabel you shall become a plain: and he shall bring forth the headstone thereof with shoutings, crying, Grace, grace unto it.8 Moreover the word of YHUH came unto me, saying,9 The hands of Zerubbabel have laid the foundation of this house; his hands shall also finish it; and you shall know that YHUH of hosts has sent me unto you.10 For who has despised the day of small things? for they shall rejoice, and shall see the plummet in the hand of Zerubbabel with those seven; they are the eyes of YHUH, which run to and fro through the whole earth.11 Then answered I, and said unto him, What are these two olive trees upon the right side of the candlestick and upon the left side thereof?12 And I answered again, and said unto him, What be these two olive branches which through the two golden pipes empty the golden oil out of themselves?13 And he answered me and said, Know you not what these be? And I said, No, my lord.14 Then said he, These are the two anointed ones, that stand by YHUH of the whole earth.

**Zech 5:1** ... **5:2**

ואשוב 7725 ואשא 5375 עיני 5869 ואראה 7200 והנה 2009 מגלה 4039 עפה 5774: ויאמר 559 אלי 413 מה 4100
ua'ashub ua'asa' 'aeynay ua'ar'ah; uahineh magilah 'apah. uaya'mer 'aelay, mah
**Then I turned and lifted up mine eyes and looked and behold a roll flying And he said unto me What**

אתה 859 ראה 7200 ואמר 559 אני 589 ראה 7200 מגלה 4039 עפה 5774 ארכה 753 עשרים 6242 באמה 520 ורחבה 7341
'atah ro'ah; ua'amar, 'aniy ro'ah magilah 'apah, 'arakah 'asriym ba'amah, uarachabah
**you? see And I answered I see a roll flying the length thereof *is* twenty cubits and the breadth thereof**

**5:3**

עשר 6235 באמה 520: ויאמר 559 אלי 413 זאת 2063 האלה 423 היוצאת 3318 על 5921 פני 6440 כל 3605 הארץ 776 כי 3588
'aser ba'amah. uaya'mer 'aelay, za't ha'aelah, hayoutzea't 'al paney kal ha'aretz; kiy
**ten cubits Then said he unto me This *is* the curse that goes forth over the face of whole the earth for**

כל 3605 הגנב 1589 מזה 2088 כמוה 3644 נקה 5352 וכל 3605 הנשבע 7650 מזה 2088 כמוה 3644
kal hagoneb, mizeh kamouha niqah, uakal hanishba', mizeh kamouha
**every one that steal *as* on this *side* according to it shall be cut off and every one that swears *as* on that *side* according to it**

**5:4**

נקה 5352: הוצאתיה 3318 נאם 5002 יהוה 3069 צבאות 6635 ובאה 935 אל 413 בית 1004 הגנב 1590 ואל 413
niqah. houtzea'tiyha, na'am Yahuah tzaba'aut, uaba'ah 'al beyt haganab, ua'al
**shall be cut off I will bring it forth saith Yahuah of hosts and it shall enter into the house of the thief and into**

בית 1004 הנשבע 7650 בשמי 8034 לשקר 8267 ולנה 3885 בתוך 8432 ביתו 1004 וכלתו 3615 ואת 854
beyt hanishba' bishmiy lashaqer; ualaneh batouk beytou, uakilatu ua'at
**the house of him that swears by my name falsely and it shall remain in the midst of his house and shall consume it *with***

**5:5**

עציו 6086 ואת 854 אבניו 68: ויצא 3318 המלאך 4397 הדבר 1697 בי 871a ויאמר 559 אלי 413 שא 5375
'aetzayu ua'at 'abanayu. uayetzea' hamal'ak hadober biy; uaya'mer 'aelay, sa'
**the timber thereof *and* the stones thereof Then went forth the angel that talked with me and said unto me Lift up**

**5:6**

נא 4994 עיניך 5869 וראה 7200 מה 4100 היוצאת 3318 הזאת 2063: ואמר 559 מה 4100 היא 1931 ויאמר 559 זאת 2063 האיפה 374
naa' 'ayneyka uar'aeh, mah hayoutzea't haza't. ua'amar mah hiy'a; uaya'mer, za't ha'aeypah
**now your eyes and see what that goes forth *is* this And I said What *is* it? And he said This *is* an ephah**

**5:7**

היוצאת 3318 ויאמר 559 זאת 2063 עינם 5869 בכל 3605 הארץ 776: והנה 2009 ככר 3603 עפרת 5777
hayoutzea't, uaya'mer za't 'aeynam bakal ha'aretz. uahineh kikar 'aperet
**that goes forth He said moreover This *is* their resemblance through all the earth And behold a talent of lead**

**5:8**

נשאת 5375 וזאת 2063 אשה 802 אחת 259 יושבת 3427 בתוך 8432 האיפה 374: ויאמר 559 זאת 2063 הרשעה 7564
nisea't; uaza't 'ashah 'achat, youshebet batouk ha'aeypah. uaya'mer za't harish'ah,
**there was lifted up and this woman *is* a that sit in the midst of the ephah And he said This *is* wickedness**

**5:9**

וישלך 7993 אתה 853 אל 413 תוך 8432 האיפה 374 וישלך 7993 את 853 אבן 68 העפרת 5777 אל 413 פיה 6310:
uayashlek 'atah 'al touk ha'aeypah; uayashlek 'at 'aben ha'aperet 'al piyha.
**And he cast it into the midst of the ephah and he cast the weight of lead upon the mouth**

ואשא 5375 עיני 5869 וארא 7200 והנה 2009 שתים 8147 נשים 802 יוצאות 3318 ורוח 7307 בכנפיהם 3671
ua'asa' 'aeynay ua'aera', uahineh shatayim nashiym youtza'aut uaruach bakanpeyhem,
**Then lifted I up mine eyes and looked and behold two women there came out and the wind *was* in their wings**

**Zech** 5:1 Then I turned, and lifted up mine eyes, and looked, and behold a flying roll.2 And he said unto me, What seest you? And I answered, I see a flying roll; the length thereof is twenty cubits, and the breadth thereof ten cubits.3 Then said he unto me, This is the curse that go forth over the face of the whole earth: foreveryone that stealeth shall be cut off as on this side according to it; and everyone that sweareth shall be cut off as on that side according to it.4 I will bring it forth, saith YHUH of hosts, and it shall enter into the house of the thief, and into the house of him that sweareth falsely by my name: and it shall remain in the midst of his house, and shall consume it with the timber thereof and the stones thereof.5 Then the angel that talked with me went forth, and said unto me, Lift up now your eyes, and see what is this that go forth.6 And I said, What is it? And he said, This is an ephah that go forth. He said moreover, This is their resemblance through all the earth.7 And, behold, there was lifted up a talent of lead: and this is a woman that sitteth in the midst of the ephah.8 And he said, This is wickedness. And he cast it into the midst of the ephah; and he cast the weight of lead upon the mouth thereof.9 Then lifted I up mine eyes, and looked, and, behold, there came out two women, and the wind was in their wings; for they had wings like the wings of a stork:

ולהנה 2007 כנפים 3671 ככנפי 3671 החסידה 2624 ותשאנה 5375 את 853 האיפה 374 בין 996 הארץ 776 ובין 996
ualahenah kanapayim kakanpey hachasiydah; uatisa'nah 'at ha'aeypah, beyn ha'aretz uabeyn
**for they had wings like the wings of a stork and they lifted up the ephah between the earth and between**

5:10 5:11
השמים 8064: ואמר 559 אל 413 המלאך 4397 הדבר 1697 בי 871a אנה 575 המה 1992 מולכות 1980 את 853 האיפה 374:
hashamayim. ua'amar 'al hamal'ak hadober biy; 'anah hemah moulikout 'at ha'aeypah.
**the heaven Then said I to the angel that talked with me Where these do bear the ephah?**

ויאמר 559 אלי 413 לבנות 1129 לה 3807a בית 1004 בארץ 776 שנער 8152 והוכן 3559 והניחה 3240 שם 8033 על 5921
uaya'mer 'aelay, libnout lah bayit ba'aretz shin'ar; uahukan uahuniychah sham 'al
**And he said unto me To build it an house in the land of Shinar and it shall be established and set there upon**

מכנתה 4369:
makunatah.
**her own base**

**Zech 6:1**
ואשב 7725 ואשא 5375 עיני 5869 ואראה 7200 והנה 2009 ארבע 702 מרכבות 4818 יצאות 3318 מבין 996
ua'ashub, ua'asa' 'aeynay ua'ar'ah, uahineh 'arba markabout yotze'aut, mibeyn
**And I turned and lifted up mine eyes and looked and behold four chariots there came out from between**

6:2
שני 8147 ההרים 2022 וההרים 2022 הרי 2022 נחשת 5178: במרכבה 4818 הראשנה 7223 סוסים 5483 אדמים 122
shaney hehariym; uaheharivm harey nachoshet. bamerkabah hara'shonah susiym 'adumiym;
**two mountains and the mountains *were* mountains of brass In chariot the first horses *were* red**

6:3
ובמרכבה 4818 השנית 8145 סוסים 5483 שחרים 7838: ובמרכבה 4818 השלשית 7992 סוסים 5483 לבנים 3836 ובמרכבה 4818 הרבעית 7243
uabamerkabah hasheniyt susiym shachoriym. uabamerkabah hashalishiyt susiym labaniym; uabamerkabah harabi'ayt,
**and in chariot the second horses black And in chariot the third horses white and in chariot the fourth**

6:4
סוסים 5483 ברדים 1261 אמצים 554: ואען 6030 ואמר 559 אל 413 המלאך 4397 הדבר 1696 בי 871a מה 4100 אלה 428
susiym barudiym 'amutziym. ua'aan ua'amar, 'al hamal'ak hadober biy; mah 'aeleh
**horses grisled *and* bay Then I answered and said unto the angel that talked with me What *are* these**

6:5
אדני 113: ויען 6030 המלאך 4397 ויאמר 559 אלי 413 אלה 428 ארבע 702 רחות 7307 השמים 8064 יוצאות 3318
'adoniy. uaya'an hamal'ak uaya'mer 'aelay; 'aeleh, 'arba ruchout hashamayim, yotza'aut
**my adonai? And answered the angel and said unto me These *are* the four spirits of the heavens *which* go forth**

6:6
מהתיצב 3320 על 5921 אדון 113 כל 3605 הארץ 776: אשר 834 בה 871a הסוסים 5483 השחרים 7838 יצאים 3318 אל 413 ארץ 776
mehityatzeb 'al 'adoun kal ha'aretz. 'asher bah hasusiym hashachoriym, yotza'aym 'al 'aretz
**from standing before Adonai of all the earth which *are* therein horses The black go forth into country**

6:7
צפון 6828 והלבנים 3836 יצאו 3318 אל 413 אחריהם 310 והברדים 1261 יצאו 3318 אל 413 ארץ 776 התימן 8486: והאמצים 554
tzapoun, uahalabaniym, yatza'ua 'al 'achareyhem; uahabarudiym, yatza'ua 'al 'aretz hateyman. uaha'amutziym
**the north and the white go forth toward after them and the grisled go forth into country the south And the bay**

יצאו 3318 ויבקשו 1245 ללכת 1980 להתהלך 1980 בארץ 776 ויאמר 559 לכו 1980
yatza'ua, uayabaqshu laleket lahithalek ba'aretz, uaya'mer laku
**went forth and sought to go that they might walk to and fro through the earth and he said Get you there**

Zech 5:9 and they lifted up the ephah between the earth and the heaven.10 Then said I to the angel that talked with me, Whither do these bear the ephah?11 And he said unto me, To build it an house in the land of Shinar: and it shall be established, and set there upon her own base. **Zech** 6:1 And I turned, and lifted up mine eyes, and looked, and, behold, there came four chariots out from between two mountains; and the mountains were mountains of brass.2 In the first chariot were red horses; and in the second chariot black horses;3 And in the third chariot white horses; and in the fourth chariot grisled and bay horses.4 Then I answered and said unto the angel that talked with me, What are these, my lord?5 And the angel answered and said unto me, These are the four spirits of the heavens, which go forth from standing before YHUH of all the earth.6 The black horses which are therein go forth into the north country; and the white go forth after them; and the grisled go forth toward the south country.7 And the bay went forth, and sought to go that they might walk to and fro through the earth: and he said, Get you hence, walk to and fro through the earth. So they walked to and fro through the earth.

התהלכו 1980 בארץ 776 ותתהלכנה 1980 בארץ 776: 6:8 ויזעק 2199 אתי 854 וידבר 1696 אלי 413
hithalaku ba'aretz; uatithalaknah ba'aretz. uayaz'aeq 'atiy, uaydaber 'aelay
**walked to and fro through the earth So they walked to and fro through the earth Then cried unto me and spoke unto me**

לאמר 559 ראה 7200 היוצאים 3318 אל 413 ארץ 776 צפון 6828 הניחו 5117 את 853 רוחי 7307 בארץ 776 צפון 6828: 6:9 ויהי 1961
lea'mor; ra'aeh, hayoutza'aym 'al 'aretz tzapoun, heniychu 'at ruchiy ba'aretz tzapoun. uayahiy
**saying Behold these that go toward country in the north have quieted my spirit country the north And came**

דבר 1697 יהוה 3068 אלי 413 לאמר 559: 6:10 לקוח 3947 מאת 853 הגולה 1473 מחלדי 2469 ומאת 853 טוביה 2900 ומאת 853
dabar Yahuah 'aelay lea'mor. laqouach me'at hagoulah, mechelday uame'aet toubiyah uame'aet
**the word of Yahuah unto me saying Take of *them of* the captivity *even* of Heldai and of Tobijah and of**

ידעיה 3048 ובאת 935 אתה 859 ביום 3117 ההוא 1931 ובאת 935 בית 1004 יאשיה 2977 בן 1121 צפניה 6846 אשר 834 באו 935
yada'yah; uaba'ta 'atah bayoum hahua', uaba'ta, beyt ya'shiyah ben tzapanyah, 'asher ba'au
**Jedaiah are come you the day the same and come the house of Josiah the son of Zephaniah which and go into**

מבבל 894: 6:11 ולקחת 3947 כסף 3701 וזהב 2091 ועשית 6213 עטרות 5850 ושמת 7760 בראש 7218 יהושע 3091 בן 1121
mibabel. ualaqachta kesep uazahab ua'asiyta atarout; uasamta, bara'sh yahousha' ben
**from Babylon Then take silver and gold and make crowns and set *them* upon the head of Joshua the son of**

יהוצדק 3087 הכהן 3548 הגדול 1419: 6:12 ואמרת 559 אליו 413 לאמר 559 כה 3541 אמר 559 יהוה 3068 צבאות 6635 לאמר 559 הנה 2009 איש 376
yahoutzadaq hakohen hagadoul. ua'amarta 'aelayu lea'mor, koh 'amar Yahuah tzaba'aut lea'mor; hineh 'aysh
**Josedech priest the high And speak unto him saying Thus speak Yahuah of hosts saying Behold the man**

צמח 6780 שמו 8034 ומתחתיו 8478 יצמח 6779 ובנה 1129 את 853 היכל 1964 יהוה 3068: 6:13
tzemach shamou uamitachtayu yitzmach, uabanah 'at heykal Yahuah.
***is* The BRANCH whose name and out of his place he shall grow up and he shall build the temple of Yahuah**

והוא 1931 יבנה 1129 את 853 היכל 1964 יהוה 3068 והוא 1931 ישא 5375 הוד 1935 וישב 3427 ומשל 4910 על 5921 כסאו 3678
uahu'a yibneh 'at heykal Yahuah uahu'a yisa' houd, uayashab uamashal 'al kis'au;
**Even he shall build the temple of Yahuah and he shall bear the glory and shall sit and rule upon his throne**

והיה 1961 כהן 3548 על 5921 כסאו 3678 ועצת 6098 שלום 7965 תהיה 1961 בין 996 שניהם 8147: 6:14 והעטרת 5850
uahayah kohen 'al kis'au, ua'atzat shaloum, tihayeh beyn shaneyhem. uaha'atarot,
**and he shall be a priest upon his throne and the counsel of peace shall be between them both And the crowns**

תהיה 1961 לחלם 2494 ולטוביה 2900 ולידעיה 3048 ולחן 2581 בן 1121 צפניה 6846 לזכרון 2146 בהיכל 1964
tihayeh lachelem ualtoubiyah ualiyada'yah, ualchen ben tzapanyah; lazikaroun baheykal
**shall be to Helem and to Tobijah and to Jedaiah and to Hen the son of Zephaniah for a memorial in the temple of**

יהוה 3068: 6:15 ורחוקים 7350 יבאו 935 ובנו 1129 בהיכל 1964 יהוה 3068 וידעתם 3045 כי 3588 יהוה 3068
Yahuah. uarchouqiym yabo'au, uabanu baheykal Yahuah, uiyda'tem kiy Yahuah
**Yahuah And far off they shall come *that are* and build in the temple of Yahuah and you shall know that Yahuah**

צבאות 6635 שלחני 7971 אליכם 413 והיה 1961 אם 518 שמוע 8085 תשמעון 8085 בקול 6963 יהוה 3068
tzaba'aut shalachaniy 'aleykem; uahayah 'am shamoua' tishma'aun, baqoul Yahuah
**of hosts has sent me unto you And *this* shall come to pass if you will diligently obey the voice of Yahuah**

Zech 6:8 Then cried he upon me, and spoke unto me, saying, Behold, these that go toward the north country have quieted my spirit in the north country.9 And the word of YHUH came unto me, saying,10 Take of them of the captivity, even of Heldai, of Tobijah, and of Jedaiah, which are come from Babylon, and come you the same day, and go into the house of Josiah the son of Zephaniah;11 Then take silver and gold, and make crowns, and set them upon the head of Joshua the son of Josedech, the high priest;12 And speak unto him, saying, Thus speaketh YHUH of hosts, saying, Behold the man whose name is The BRANCH; and he shall grow up out of his place, and he shall build the temple of YHUH:13 Even he shall build the temple of YHUH; and he shall bear the glory, and shall sit and rule upon his throne; and he shall be a priest upon his throne: and the counsel of peace shall be between them both.14 And the crowns shall be to Helem, and to Tobijah, and to Jedaiah, and to Hen the son of Zephaniah, for a memorial in the temple of YHUH.15 And they that are far off shall come and build in the temple of YHUH, and you shall know that YHUH of hosts has sent me unto you. And this shall come to pass, if you will diligently obey the voice of YHUH your G-d.

אלהיכם 430:
'aloheykem.
**your Elohim**

**Zech 7:1** ויהי 1961 | בשנת 8141 | ארבע 702 | לדריוש 1867 | המלך 4428 | היה 1961 | דבר 1697 | יהוה 3068 | אל 413 | זכריה 2148
uayahiy | bishnat | 'arba, | ladarayauesh | hamelek; | hayah | dabar | Yahuah | 'al | zakaryah,
**And it came to pass | in year of *the* fourth | Darius | king | came | *that* the word of | Yahuah | unto | Zechariah**

בארבעה 702 | לחדש 2320 | התשעי 8671 | בכסלו 3691: | 7:2 וישלח 7971 | בית 1008 | אל 410 | שר 8272 | אצר 687
ba'arbah | lachodesh | hatashi'ay | bakisleu. | uayishlach | beyt | 'ael, | sar | 'atzer
**in the fourth | month | *day of* the ninth | *even* in Chisleu | When they had sent | unto the house of | El | Sher | ezer**

ורגם 7278 | מלך 4428 | ואנשיו 582 | לחלות 2470 | את 853 | פני 6440 | יהוה 3069: | 7:3 לאמר 559 | אל 413 | הכהנים 3548 | אשר 834
uaregem | melek | ua'anashayu; | lakalout | 'at | paney | Yahuah. | lea'mor, | 'al | hakohaniym | 'asher
**and Regem | melek | and their men | to pray | | before | Yahuah | *And* to speak | unto | the priests | which**

לבית 1004 | יהוה 3068 | צבאות 6635 | ואל 413 | הנביאים 5030 | לאמר 559 | האבכה 1058 | בחדש 2320 | החמשי 2549
labeyt | Yahuah | tzaba'aut, | ua'al | hanabiy'aym | lea'mor; | ha'abkeh | bachodesh | hachamiyshiy,
***were* in the house of | Yahuah | of hosts | and to | the prophets | saying | Should I weep | in month | the fifth**

הנזר 5144 | כאשר 834 | עשיתי 6213 | זה 2088 | כמה 4100 | שנים 8141: | 7:4 ויהי 1961 | דבר 1697 | יהוה 3068 | צבאות 6635 | אלי 413
hinazer | ka'asher | 'asiytiy, | zeh | kameh | shaniym. | uayahiy | dabar | Yahuah | tzaba'aut | 'aelay
**separating *myself* | as | I have done | these | so many | years? | Then came | the word of | Yahuah | of hosts | unto me**

לאמר 559: | 7:5 אמר 559 | אל 413 | כל 3605 | עם 5971 | הארץ 776 | ואל 413 | הכהנים 3548 | לאמר 559 | כי 3588 | צמתם 6684 | וספוד 5594
lea'mor. | 'amor | 'al | kal | 'am | ha'aretz, | ua'al | hakohaniym | lea'mor; | kiy | tzamtem | uasapoud
**saying | Speak | unto | all | the people of | the land | and to | the priests | saying | When | you fasted | and mourned**

בחמישי 2549 | ובשביעי 7637 | וזה 2088 | שבעים 7657 | שנה 8141 | הצום 6684 | צמתני 6684 | אני 589: | 7:6 וכי 3588
bachamiyshiy | uabashbiy'ay, | uazeh | shib'aym | shanah, | hatzoum | tzamtuniy | 'aniy. | uakiy
**in the fifth | and seventh *month* | even those | seventy | years | did you at all | fast unto me *even* | to me? | And when**

תאכלו 398 | וכי 3588 | תשתו 8354 | הלוא 3808 | אתם 859 | האכלים 398 | ואתם 859 | השתים 8354: | 7:7
ta'kalu | uakiy | tishtu; | halou'a | 'atem | ha'akaliym, | ua'atem | hashotiym.
**you did eat | and when | you did drink | not | you | did eat *for yourselves* | and you | drink *for yourselves*?**

הלוא 3808 | את 853 | הדברים 1697 | אשר 834 | קרא 7121 | יהוה 3068 | ביד 3027 | הנביאים 5030 | הראשנים 7223 | בהיות 1961 | ירושלם 3389
halou'a | 'at | hadabariym, | 'asher | qara' | Yahuah | bayad | hanabiy'aym | hara'shoniym, | bihayout | yarushalaim
***Should you* not *hear* | | the words | which | has cried | Yahuah | by | the prophets | former | when was | Jerusalem**

ישבת 3427 | ושלוה 7961 | ועריה 5892 | סביבתיה 5439 | והנגב 5045 | והשפלה 8219 | ישב 3427: | 7:8
yoshebet | uashleuah, | ua'areyha | sabiyboteyha; | uahanegeb | uahashapelah | yosheb.
**inhabited | and in prosperity | and the cities thereof | round about her | the south | and the plain? | when *men* inhabited**

ויהי 1961 | דבר 1697 | יהוה 3068 | אל 413 | זכריה 2148 | לאמר 559: | 7:9 כה 3541 | אמר 559 | יהוה 3068 | צבאות 6635 | לאמר 559 | משפט 4941 | אמת 571
uayahiy | dabar | Yahuah, | 'al | zakaryah | lea'mor. | koh | 'amar | Yahuah | tzaba'aut | lea'mor; | mishapat | 'amet
**And came | the word of | Yahuah | unto | Zechariah | saying | Thus | speak | Yahuah | of hosts | saying | judgment | true.**

**Zech** 7:1 And it came to pass in the fourth year of king Darius, that the word of YHUH came unto Zechariah in the fourth day of the ninth month, even in Chisleu;2 When they had sent unto the house of G-d Sherezer and Regem-melech, and their men, to pray before YHUH,3 And to speak unto the priests which were in the house of YHUH of hosts, and to the prophets, saying, Should I weep in the fifth month, separating myself, as I have done these so many years?4 Then came the word of YHUH of hosts unto me, saying,5 Speak unto all the people of the land, and to the priests, saying, When you fasted and mourned in the fifth and seventh month, even those seventy years, did you at all fast unto me, even to me?6 And when you did eat, and when you did drink, did not you eat for yourselves, and drink for yourselves?7 Should you not hear the words which YHUH has cried by the former prophets, when Jerusalem was inhabited and in prosperity, and the cities thereof round about her, when men inhabited the south and the plain?8 And the word of YHUH came unto Zechariah, saying,

| 8199 שפטו | 2617 וחסד | 7356 ורחמים | 6213 עשו | 376 איש | 854 את | 251 אחיו: | 7:10 | 490 ואלמנה | 3490 ויתום |
|---|---|---|---|---|---|---|---|---|---|
| shapotu, | uachesed | uarachamiym, | 'asu | 'aysh | 'at | 'achiyu. | | ua'almanah | uayatoum |
| **Execute** | **mercy** | **and compassions** | **and show** | **every man** | ***to*** | **his brother** | | **And the widow** | **nor the fatherless** |

| 1616 גר | 6041 ועני | 408 אל | 6231 תעשקו | 7451 ורעת | 376 איש | 251 אחיו | 408 אל | 2803 תחשבו | 3824: בלבבכם | 7:11 |
|---|---|---|---|---|---|---|---|---|---|---|
| ger | ua'aniy | 'al | ta'ashoqu; | uara'at | 'aysh | 'achiyu, | 'al | tachshabu | bilbabkem. | |
| **the stranger** | **nor the poor** | **not** | **oppress** | **and evil** | **of man** | ***against* his brother** | **none** | **let you imagine** | **in your heart** | |

| 3985 וימאנו | 7181 להקשיב | 5414 ויתנו | 3802 כתף | 5637 סררת | 241 ואזניהם | 3513 הכבידו | 8085: משמוע | 7:12 |
|---|---|---|---|---|---|---|---|---|
| uayama'anu | lahaqshiyb, | uayitanu | katep | soraret; | ua'azaneyhem | hikbiydu | mishmoua'. | |
| **But they refused** | **to listen** | **and pulled away** | **the shoulder** | **stubborn** | **and their ears** | **stopped** | **that they should not hear** | |

| 3820 ולבם | 7760 שמו | 8068 שמיר | 8085 משמוע | 853 את | 8451 התורה | 853 ואת | 1697 הדברים | 834 אשר | 7971 שלח |
|---|---|---|---|---|---|---|---|---|---|
| ualibam | samu | shamiyr, | mishmoua' | 'at | hatourah | ua'at | hadabariym | 'asher | shalach |
| **Yea their hearts** | **they made** | ***as* an adamant stone** | ***lest* they should hear** | | **the law** | ***and*** | **the words** | **which** | **has sent** |

| 3068 יהוה | 6635 צבאות | 7307 ברוחו | 3027 ביד | 5030 הנביאים | 7223 הראשנים | 1961 ויהי | 7110 קצף | 1419 גדול | 853 מאת | 3068 יהוה |
|---|---|---|---|---|---|---|---|---|---|---|
| Yahuah | tzaba'aut | baruchou, | bayad | hanabiy'aym | hara'shoniym; | uayahiy | qetzep | gadoul, | me'at | Yahuah |
| **Yahuah** | **of hosts** | **in his spirit** | **by** | **the prophets** | **the former** | **therefore came** | **a wrath** | **great** | **from** | **Yahuah** |

| 6635: צבאות | 7:13 | 1961 ויהי | 834 כאשר | 7121 קרא | 3808 ולא | 8085 שמעו | 3651 כן | 7121 יקראו | 3808 ולא |
|---|---|---|---|---|---|---|---|---|---|
| tzaba'aut. | | uayahiy | ka'asher | qara' | uala' | shame'au; | ken | yiqra'au | uala' |
| **of hosts** | | **Therefore it is come to pass *that*** | **as** | **he cried** | **and not** | **they would hear** | **so** | **they cried** | **and not** |

| 8085 אשמע | 559 אמר | 3068 יהוה | 6635: צבאות | 7:14 | 5590 ואסערם | 5921 על | 3605 כל | 1471 הגוים | 834 אשר | 3808 לא |
|---|---|---|---|---|---|---|---|---|---|---|
| 'ashma, | 'amar | Yahuah | tzaba'aut. | | ua'aesa'arem, | 'al | kal | hagouyim | 'asher | la' |
| **I would hear** | **saith** | **Yahuah** | **of hosts** | | **But I scattered them with a whirlwind** | **among** | **all** | **the nations** | **whom** | **not** |

| 3045 ידעום | 776 והארץ | 8074 נשמה | 310 אחריהם | 5674 מעבר | 7725 ומשב | 7760 וישימו | 776 ארץ | 2532 חמדה |
|---|---|---|---|---|---|---|---|---|
| yada'aum, | uaha'aretz | nashamah | 'achareyhem, | me'abor | uamishab; | uayasiymu | 'aretz | chemdah |
| **they knew** | **Thus the land** | **desolate** | **after them** | ***that no man* passed through** | **nor returned** | **for they laid** | **land** | ***the* pleasant** |

| 8047: לשמה |
|---|
| lashamah. |
| **was desolate** |

| **Zech 8:1** | 1961 ויהי | 1697 דבר | 3068 יהוה | 6635 צבאות | 559: לאמר | 8:2 | 3541 כה | 559 אמר | 3068 יהוה | 6635 צבאות | 7065 קנאתי | 6726 לציון |
|---|---|---|---|---|---|---|---|---|---|---|---|---|
| | uayahiy | dabar | Yahuah | tzaba'aut | lea'mor. | | koh | 'amar | Yahuah | tzaba'aut, | qinea'tiy | latziyoun |
| | **Again came *to me*** | **the word of** | **Yahuah** | **of hosts** | **saying** | | **Thus** | **saith** | **Yahuah** | **of hosts** | **I was jealous** | **for Zion** |

| 7068 קנאה | 1419 גדולה | 2534 וחמה | 1419 גדולה | 7065 קנאתי | 3807a: לה | 8:3 | 3541 כה | 559 אמר | 3068 יהוה | 7725 שבתי | 413 אל | 6726 ציון |
|---|---|---|---|---|---|---|---|---|---|---|---|---|
| qin'ah | gadoulah; | uachemah | gadoulah | qinea'tiy | lah. | | koh | 'amar | Yahuah, | shabtiy | 'al | tziyoun, |
| **jealousy** | ***with* great** | **and fury** | ***with* great** | **I was jealous** | **for her** | | **Thus** | **saith** | **Yahuah** | **I am returned** | **unto** | **Zion** |

| 7931 ושכנתי | 8432 בתוך | 3389 ירושלם | 7121 ונקראה | 3389 ירושלם | 5892 עיר | 571 האמת | 2022 והר | 3068 יהוה |
|---|---|---|---|---|---|---|---|---|
| uashakantiy | batouk | yarushalaim; | uaniqra'ah | yarushalaim | 'ayr | ha'amet, | uahar | Yahuah |
| **and will dwell** | **in the midst of** | **Jerusalem** | **and shall be called** | **Jerusalem** | **a city of** | **the truth** | **and the mountain of** | **Yahuah** |

Zech 7:9 Thus speaketh YHUH of hosts, saying, Execute true judgment, and show mercy and compassions every man to his brother:10 And oppress not the widow, nor the fatherless, the stranger, nor the poor; and let none of you imagine evil against his brother in your heart.11 But they refused to hear, and pulled away the shoulder, and stopped their ears, that they should not hear.12 Yea, they made their hearts as an adamant stone, lest they should hear the law, and the words which YHUH of hosts has sent in his spirit by the former prophets: therefore came a great wrath from YHUH of hosts.13 Therefore it is come to pass, that as he cried, and they would not hear; so they cried, and I would not hear, saith YHUH of hosts:14 But I scattered them with a whirlwind among all the nations whom they knew not. Thus the land was desolate after them, that no man passed through nor returned: for they laid the pleasant land desolate. **Zech** 8:1 Again the word of YHUH of hosts came to me, saying,2 Thus saith YHUH of hosts; I was jealous for Zion with great jealousy, and I was jealous for her with great fury.3 Thus saith YHUH; I am returned unto Zion, and will dwell in the midst of Jerusalem: and Jerusalem shall be called a city of truth; and the mountain of YHUH of hosts the holy mountain.

8:4

צבאות 6635 הר 2022 הקדש 6944: כה 3541 אמר 559 יהוה 3068 צבאות 6635 עד 5704 ישבו 3427 זקנים 2205 וזקנות 2205
tzaba'aut har haqodesh. koh 'amar Yahuah tzaba'aut, 'aud yeshabu zaqeniym uazqenout,
**of hosts mountain the holy Thus saith Yahuah of hosts yet There shall dwell old men and old women**

8:5

ברחבות 7339 ירושלם 3389 ואיש 376 משענתו 4938 בידו 3027 מרב 7230 ימים 3117: ורחבות 7339 העיר 5892
birchobout yarushalaim; ua'aysh mish'antou bayadou merob yamiym. uarchobout ha'ayr
**in the streets of Jerusalem and every man with his staff in his hand for very age And the streets of the city**

8:6

ימלאו 4390 ילדים 3206 וילדות 3207 משחקים 7832 ברחבתיה 7339: כה 3541 אמר 559 יהוה 3069 צבאות 6635 כי 3588
yimala'au, yaladiym uiyladout; masachaqiym birchoboteyha. koh 'amar Yahuah tzaba'aut, kiy
**shall be full of boys and girls playing in the streets thereof Thus saith Yahuah of hosts If**

יפלא 6381 בעיני 5869 שארית 7611 העם 5971 הזה 2088 בימים 3117 ההם 1992 גם 1571 בעיני 5869
yipalea', ba'aeyney sha'aeriyt ha'am hazeh, bayamiym hahem; gam ba'aeynay
**it be marvellous in the eyes of the remnant of the people this in days these also in my eyes?**

8:7

יפלא 6381 נאם 5002 יהוה 3069 צבאות 6635: כה 3541 אמר 559 יהוה 3068 צבאות 6635 הנני 2005 מושיע 3467 את 853 עמי 5971
yipalea', na'am Yahuah tzaba'aut. koh 'amar Yahuah tzaba'aut, hinniy moushiya' 'at 'amiy
**should it be marvellous said Yahuah of hosts Thus saith Yahuah of hosts Behold I will save my people**

8:8

מארץ 776 מזרח 4217 ומארץ 776 מבוא 3996 השמש 8121: והבאתי 935 אתם 853 ושכנו 7931 בתוך 8432
me'aretz mizrach; uame'aretz mabou'a hashamesh. uahebea'tiy 'atam, uashakanu batouk
**from country the east and from country entry the west And I will bring them and they shall dwell in the midst of**

8:9

ירושלם 3389 והיו 1961 לי 3807a לעם 5971 ואני 589 אהיה 1961 להם 3807a לאלהים 430 באמת 571 ובצדקה 6666: כה 3541
yarushalaim; uahayu liy la'am, ua'aniy 'ahayeh lahem le'alohiym, be'amet uabitzdaqah. koh
**Jerusalem and they shall be my people and I will be their to Elohim in truth and in righteousness Thus**

אמר 559 יהוה 3068 צבאות 6635 תחזקנה 2388 ידיכם 3027 השמעים 8085 בימים 3117 האלה 428 את 853 הדברים 1697 האלה 428
'amar Yahuah tzaba'aut techzaqnah yadeykem, hashom'aym bayamiym ha'aeleh, 'at hadabariym ha'aeleh;
**saith Yahuah of hosts Let be strong your hands you that hear in days these words these**

מפי 6310 הנביאים 5030 אשר 834 ביום 3117 יסד 3245 בית 1004 יהוה 3068 צבאות 6635
mipiy hanabiy'aym, 'asher bayoum yusad beyt Yahuah tzaba'aut
**by the mouth of the prophets which *were* in the day *that* the foundation of was laid the house of Yahuah of hosts**

8:10

ההיכל 1964 להבנות 1129: כי 3588 לפני 6440 הימים 3117 ההם 1992 שכר 7939 האדם 120 לא 3808 נהיה 1961 ושכר 7939 הבהמה 929
haheykal lahibanout. kiy, lipney hayamiym hahem, sakar ha'adam la' nihayah, uaskar habahemah
**the temple that might be built For before days these hire *for* man no there was hire *for* beast**

איננה 369 וליוצא 3318 ולבא 935 אין 369 שלום 7965 מן 4480 הצר 6862 ואשלח 7971 את 853 כל 3605
'aeynenah; ualayoutzea' ualaba' 'aeyn shaloum min hatzar, ua'ashalach 'at kal
**nor any to him that went out or came in neither *was there any* peace because of the affliction for I set all**

8:11

האדם 120 איש 376 ברעהו 7453: ועתה 6258 לא 3808 כימים 3117 הראשנים 7223 אני 589 לשארית 7611 העם 5971
ha'adam 'aysh bare'aehu. ua'atah, la' kayamiym hara'shoniym 'aniy, lish'aeriyt ha'am
**men every one against his neighbour But now not as in days the former I *will be* unto the residue of the people**

Zech 8:4 Thus saith YHUH of hosts; There shall yet old men and old women dwell in the streets of Jerusalem, and every man with his staff in his hand for very age.5 And the streets of the city shall be full of boys and girls playing in the streets thereof.6 Thus saith YHUH of hosts; If it be marvellous in the eyes of the remnant of this people in these days, should it also be marvellous in mine eyes? saith YHUH of hosts.7 Thus saith YHUH of hosts; Behold, I will save my people from the east country, and from the west country;8 And I will bring them, and they shall dwell in the midst of Jerusalem: and they shall be my people, and I will be their G-d, in truth and in righteousness.9 Thus saith YHUH of hosts; Let your hands be strong, you that hear in these days these words by the mouth of the prophets, which were in the day that the foundation of the house of YHUH of hosts was laid, that the temple might be built.10 For before these days there was no hire for man, nor any hire for beast; neither was there any peace to him that went out or came in because of the affliction: for I set all men everyone against his neighbor.11 But now I will not be unto the residue of this people as in the former days, saith YHUH of hosts.

8:12
הזה 2088 נאם 5002 יהוה 3068 צבאות 6635: כי 3588 זרע 2233 השלום 7965 הגפן 1612 תתן 5414 פריה 6529 והארץ 776
hazeh; na'am Yahuah tzaba'aut. kiy zera' hashaloum, hagapen titen piryah uaha'aretz
**this saith Yahuah of hosts For the seed *shall be* prosperous the vine shall give her fruit and the ground**

תתן 5414 את 853 יבולה 2981 והשמים 8064 יתנו 5414 טלם 2919 והנחלתי 5157 את 853 שארית 7611 העם 5971
titen 'at yabulah, uahashamayim yitanu talam; uahinachaltiy, 'at sha'aeriyt ha'am
**shall give her increase and the heavens shall give their dew and I will cause to possess the remnant of the people**

8:13
הזה 2088 את 853 כל 3605 אלה 428: והיה 1961 כאשר 834 הייתם 1961 קללה 7045 בגוים 1471 בית 1004
hazeh 'at kal 'aeleh. uahayah ka'asher heyiytem qalalah bagouyim, beyt
**this all these *things* And it shall come to pass *that* as you were a curse among the heathen O house of**

יהודה 3063 ובית 1004 ישראל 3478 כן 3651 אושיע 3467 אתכם 853 והייתם 1961 ברכה 1293 אל 408 תיראו 3372 תחזקנה 2388
yahudah uabeyt yisra'ael, ken 'aushiya 'atkem, uihyiytem barakah; 'al tiyra'au techzaqnah
**Judah and house of Israel so will I save you and you shall be a blessing not fear *but* let be strong**

8:14
ידיכם 3027: כי 3588 כה 3541 אמר 559 יהוה 3068 צבאות 6635 כאשר 834 זממתי 2161 להרע 7489 לכם 3807a בהקציף 7107
yadeykem. kiy koh 'amar Yahuah tzaba'aut ka'asher zamamtiy lahara' lakem, bahaqtziyp
**your hands For thus saith Yahuah of hosts As I thought to punish to you when provoked to wrath**

8:15
אבתיכם 1 אתי 853 אמר 559 יהוה 3068 צבאות 6635 ולא 3808 נחמתי 5162: כן 3651 שבתי 7725 זממתי 2161 בימים 3117 האלה 428
'aboteykem 'atiy, 'amar Yahuah tzaba'aut; uala' nichamatiy. ken shabtiy zamamtiy bayamiym ha'aeleh,
**your fathers me saith Yahuah of hosts and not I repented So again have I thought in days these**

8:16
להיטיב 3190 את 853 ירושלם 3389 ואת 853 בית 1004 יהודה 3063 אל 408 תיראו 3372: אלה 428 הדברים 1697 אשר 834
laheytiyb 'at yarushalaim ua'at beyt yahudah; 'al tiyra'au. 'aeleh hadabariym 'asher
**to do well *unto* Jerusalem *and to* the house of Judah not fear you These *are* the things that**

תעשו 6213 דברו 1696 אמת 571 איש 376 את 854 רעהו 7453 אמת 571 ומשפט 4941 שלום 7965 שפטו 8199
ta'asu; dabaru 'amet 'aysh 'at re'aehu, 'amet uamishpat shaloum, shiptu
**you shall do Speak you the truth every man *to* his neighbour truth the judgment of *and* peace execute**

8:17
בשעריכם 8179: ואיש 376 את 853 רעת 7451 רעהו 7453 אל 408 תחשבו 2803 בלבבכם 3824 ושבעת 7621 שקר 8267
basha'areykem. ua'aysh 'at ra'at re'aehu, 'al tachshabu bilbabkem, uashbu'at sheqer
**in your gates And of you none evil *against* his neighbour none let imagine in your hearts and oath false**

8:18
אל 408 תאהבו 157 כי 3588 את 853 כל 3605 אלה 428 אשר 834 שנאתי 8130 נאם 5002 יהוה 3068: ויהי 1961 דבר 1697 יהוה 3068
'al te'ahabu; kiy 'at kal 'aeleh 'asher sanea'tiy na'am Yahuah. uayahiy dabar Yahuah
**no love for all these *are things* that I hate saith Yahuah And came the word of Yahuah**

8:19
צבאות 6635 אלי 413 לאמר 559: כה 3541 אמר 559 יהוה 3068 צבאות 6635 צום 6685 הרביעי 7243 וצום 6685 החמישי 2549
tzaba'aut 'aelay lea'mor. koh 'amar Yahuah tzaba'aut, tzoum harbiy'ay uatzoum hachamiyshiy
**of hosts unto me saying Thus saith Yahuah of hosts The fast of the fourth *month* and the fast of the fifth**

וצום 6685 השביעי 7637 וצום 6685 העשירי 6224 יהיה 1961 לבית 1004 יהודה 3063 לששון 8342 ולשמחה 8057 ולמעדים 4150
uatzoum hashabiy'ay uatzoum ha'asiyriy, yihayeh labeyt yahudah lasasoun ualsimchah, ualmo'adiym
**and the fast of the seventh and the fast of the tenth shall be to the house of Judah joy and gladness and feasts**

Zech 8:12 For the seed shall be prosperous; the vine shall give her fruit, and the ground shall give her increase, and the heavens shall give their dew; and I will cause the remnant of this people to possess all these things.13 And it shall come to pass, that as you were a curse among the heathen, O house of Judah, and house of Israel; so will I save you, and you shall be a blessing: fear not, but let your hands be strong.14 For thus saith YHUH of hosts; As I thought to punish you, when your fathers provoked me to wrath, saith YHUH of hosts, and I repented not:15 So again have I thought in these days to do well unto Jerusalem and to the house of Judah: fear you not.16 These are the things that you shall do; Speak you every man the truth to his neighbor; execute the judgment of truth and peace in your gates:17 And let none of you imagine evil in your hearts against his neighbor; and love no false oath: for all these are things that I hate, saith YHUH.18 And the word of YHUH of hosts came unto me, saying,19 Thus saith YHUH of hosts; The fast of the fourth month, and the fast of the fifth, and the fast of the seventh, and the fast of the tenth, shall be to the house of Judah joy and gladness, and cheerful feasts; therefore love the truth and peace.

8:20
טובים 2896 והאמת 571 והשלום 7965 אהבו 157: כה 3541 אמר 559 יהוה 3068 צבאות 6635 עד 5704 אשר 834
toubiym; uaha'amet uahashaloum 'ahabu. koh 'amar Yahuah tzaba'aut; 'ad 'asher
**cheerful therefore the truth and peace love Thus saith Yahuah of hosts *It shall* yet *come to pass* that**

8:21
יבאו 935 עמים 5971 וישבי 3427 ערים 5892 רבות 7227: והלכו 1980 ישבי 3427 אחת 259 אל 413 אחת 259
yabo'au 'amiym, uayoushabey 'ariym rabout. uahalaku yoshabey 'achat 'al 'achat
**there shall come people and the inhabitants of cities many And shall go the inhabitants of one *city* to another**

8:22
לאמר 559 נלכה 1980 הלוך 1980 לחלות 2470 את 853 פני 6440 יהוה 3068 ולבקש 1245 את 853 יהוה 3068 צבאות 6635 אלכה 1980 גם 1571 אני 589:
lea'mor, nelakah halouk lachalout 'at paney Yahuah, ualbaqesh 'at Yahuah tzaba'aut; 'aelakah gam 'aniy.
**saying Let us go speedily to pray before Yahuah and to seek Yahuah of hosts will go also I**

ובאו 935 עמים 5971 רבים 7227 וגוים 1471 עצומים 6099 לבקש 1245 את 853 יהוה 3068 צבאות 6635 בירושלם 3389 ולחלות 2470 את 853
uaba'au 'amiym rabiym uagouyim 'atzumiym, labaqesh 'at Yahuah tzaba'aut biyarushalaim; ualchalout 'at
**Yea shall come people many and nations strong to seek Yahuah of hosts in Jerusalem and to pray**

8:23
פני 6440 יהוה 3068: כה 3541 אמר 559 יהוה 3068 צבאות 6635 בימים 3117 ההמה 1992 אשר 834 יחזיקו 2388 עשרה 6235
paney Yahuah. koh 'amar Yahuah tzaba'aut bayamiym hahemah, 'asher yachaziyqu 'asarah
**before Yahuah Thus saith Yahuah of hosts In days *it shall come to pass* those that shall take hold ten**

אנשים 582 מכל 3605 לשנות 3956 הגוים 1471 והחזיקו 2388 בכנף 3671 איש 376 יהודי 3064 לאמר 559 נלכה 1980
'anashiym, mikol lashonout hagouyim; uahecheziyqu biknap 'aysh yahudiy lea'mor, nelakah
**men out of all languages of the nations even shall take hold of the skirt of him that *is* a Jew saying We will go**

עמכם 5973 כי 3588 שמענו 8085 אלהים 430 עמכם 5973:
'amakem, kiy shama'anu 'alohiym 'amakem.
**with you for we have heard *that* Elohim with you**

**Zech 9:1**
משא 4853 דבר 1697 יהוה 3068 בארץ 776 חדרך 2317 ודמשק 1834 מנחתו 4496 כי 3588
masa' dabar Yahuah ba'aretz chadrak, uadameseq manuchatou; kiy
**The burden of the word of Yahuah in the land of Hadrach and Damascus *shall be* the rest thereof when**

9:2
ליהוה 3068 עין 5869 אדם 120 וכל 3605 שבטי 7626 ישראל 3478: וגם 1571 חמת 2574 תגבל 1379 בה 871a צר 6865
laYahuah 'aeyn 'adam, uakol shibtey yisra'ael. uagam chamat tigbal bah; tzor
***shall be* toward Yahuah the eyes of man *as of* all the tribes of Israel And also Hamath shall border thereby Tyrus**

9:3
וצידון 6721 כי 3588 חכמה 2449 מאד 3966: ותבן 1129 צר 6865 מצור 4692 לה 3807a ותצבר 6651 כסף 3701 כעפר 6083
uatziydoun, kiy chakamah ma'ad. uatiben tzor matzour lah; uatitzbar kesep ke'apar,
**and Zidon though it be wise very And did build Tyrus a strong hold herself and heaped up silver as the dust**

9:4
וחרוץ 2742 כטיט 2916 חוצות 2351: הנה 2009 אדני 136 יורשנה 3423 והכה 5221 בים 3220 חילה 2428 והיא 1931
uacharutz katiyt chutzout. hineh 'adonay yourishenah, uahikah bayam cheylah; uahiy'a
**and fine gold as the mire of the streets Behold Adonai will cast her out and he will smite in the sea her power and she**

9:5
באש 784 תאכל 398: תרא 7200 אשקלון 831 ותירא 3372 ועזה 5804 ותחיל 2342 מאד 3966 ועקרון 6138
ba'aesh te'akel. tera' 'ashqaloun uatiyra', ua'azah uatachiyl ma'ad, ua'aqroun
**with fire shall be devoured shall you see *it* Ashkelon and fear Gaza also *shall see it* and be sorrowful very and Ekron**

Zech 9:20 Thus saith YHUH of hosts; It shall yet come to pass, that there shall come people, and the inhabitants of many cities:21 And the inhabitants of one city shall go to another, saying, Let us go speedily to pray before YHUH, and to seek YHUH of hosts: I will go also.22 Yea, many people and strong nations shall come to seek YHUH of hosts in Jerusalem, and to pray before YHUH.23 Thus saith YHUH of hosts; In those days it shall come to pass, that ten men shall take hold out of all languages of the nations, even shall take hold of the skirt of him that is a Jew, saying, We will go with you: for we have heard that G-d is with you. **Zech** 9:1 The burden of the word of YHUH in the land of Hadrach, and Damascus shall be the rest thereof: when the eyes of man, as of all the tribes of Israel, shall be toward YHUH.2 And Hamath also shall border thereby; Tyrus, and Zidon, though it be very wise.3 And Tyrus did build herself a strong hold, and heaped up silver as the dust, and fine gold as the mire of the streets.4 Behold, YHUH will cast her out, and he will smite her power in the sea; and she shall be devoured with fire.5 Ashkelon shall see it, and fear; Gaza also shall see it, and be very sorrowful, and Ekron; for her expectation shall be ashamed; and the king shall perish from Gaza, and Ashkelon shall not be inhabited.

| כי 3588 | הביש 954 | מבטה 4007 | ואבד 6 | מלך 4428 | מעזה 5804 | ואשקלון 831 | לא 3808 | תשב 3427: | 9:6 |
|---|---|---|---|---|---|---|---|---|---|
| kiy | hobiysh | mebatah; | ua'abad | melek | me'azah, | ua'ashqaloun | la' | tesheb. | |
| **for** | **shall be ashamed** | **her expectation** | **and shall perish** | **the king** | **from Gaza** | **and Ashkelon** | **not** | **shall be inhabited** | |

| וישב 3427 | ממזר 4464 | באשדוד 795 | והכרתי 3772 | גאון 1347 | פלשתים 6430: | 9:7 | והסרתי 5493 | דמיו 1818 |
|---|---|---|---|---|---|---|---|---|
| uayashab | mamzer | ba'ashdoud; | uahikratiy | ga'aun | palishtiym. | | uahasirotiy | damayu |
| **And shall dwell** | **a bastard** | **in Ashdod** | **and I will cut off** | **the pride of** | **the Philistines** | | **And I will take away** | **his blood** |

| מפיו 6310 | ושקציו 8251 | מבין 996 | שניו 8127 | ונשאר 7604 | גם 1571 | הוא 1931 | לאלהינו 430 |
|---|---|---|---|---|---|---|---|
| mipiyu, | uashiqutzayu | mibeyn | shinayu, | uanish'ar | gam | hua' | le'aloheynu; |
| **out of his mouth** | **and his abominations** | **from between** | **his teeth** | **but he that remains** | **even** | **he** | ***shall be* for our Elohim** |

| והיה 1961 | כאלף 441 | ביהודה 3063 | ועקרון 6138 | כיבוסי 2983: | 9:8 | וחניתי 2583 | לביתי 1004 |
|---|---|---|---|---|---|---|---|
| uahayah | ka'alup | biyahudah, | ua'aqroun | kiyabusiy. | | uachaniytiy | labeytiy |
| **and he shall be** | **as a governor** | **in Judah** | **and Ekron** | **as a Jebusite** | | **And I will encamp about** | **mine house** |

| מצבה 4675 | מעבר 5674 | ומשב 7725 | ולא 3808 | יעבר 5674 | עליהם 5921 |
|---|---|---|---|---|---|
| mitzabah | me'abor | uamishab, | uala' | ya'abor | 'aleyhem |
| **because of the army** | **because of him that passed by** | **and because of him that return** | **and no** | **shall pass** | **through them** |

| עוד 5750 | נגש 5065 | כי 3588 | עתה 6258 | ראיתי 7200 | בעיני 5869: | 9:9 | גילי 1523 | מאד 3966 | בת 1323 | ציון 6726 | הריעי 7321 |
|---|---|---|---|---|---|---|---|---|---|---|---|
| 'aud | noges; | kiy | 'atah | ra'aytiy | ba'aeynay. | | giyliy | ma'ad | bat | tziyoun, | hariy'ay |
| **any more** | **oppressor** | **for** | **now** | **have I seen** | **with mine eyes** | | **Rejoice** | **greatly** | **O daughter of** | **Zion** | **shout** |

| בת 1323 | ירושלם 3389 | הנה 2009 | מלכך 4428 | יבוא 935 | לך 3807a | צדיק 6662 | ונושע 3467 | הוא 1931 | עני 6041 | ורכב 7392 |
|---|---|---|---|---|---|---|---|---|---|---|
| bat | yarushalaim, | hineh | malkek | yabou'a | lak, | tzadiyq | uanousha' | hua'; | 'aniy | uarokeb |
| **O daughter of** | **Jerusalem** | **behold** | **your King** | **comes** | **unto you** | ***is* just** | **and having salvation** | **he** | **lowly** | **and riding** |

| על 5921 | חמור 2543 | ועל 5921 | עיר 5895 | בן 1121 | אתנות 860: | 9:10 | והכרתי 3772 | רכב 7393 | מאפרים 669 | וסוס 5483 |
|---|---|---|---|---|---|---|---|---|---|---|
| 'al | chamour, | ua'al | 'ayir | ben | 'atonout. | | uahikratiy | rekeb | me'aprayim, | uasus |
| **upon** | **an ass** | **and upon** | **a colt** | **the foal of** | **his ass** | | **And I will cut off** | **the chariot** | **from Ephraim** | **and the horse** |

| מירושלם 3389 | ונכרתה 3772 | קשת 7198 | מלחמה 4421 | ודבר 1696 | שלום 7965 | לגוים 1471 | ומשלו 4915 |
|---|---|---|---|---|---|---|---|
| miyarushalaim, | uanikratah | qeshet | milchamah, | uadiber | shaloum | lagouyim; | uamashalou |
| **from Jerusalem** | **and shall be cut off** | **bow** | **the battle** | **and he shall speak** | **peace** | **unto the heathen** | **and his dominion** |

| מים 3220 | עד 5704 | ים 3220 | ומנהר 5104 | עד 5704 | אפסי 657 | ארץ 776: | 9:11 | גם 1571 | את 859 | בדם 1818 |
|---|---|---|---|---|---|---|---|---|---|---|
| miyam | 'ad | yam, | uaminahar | 'ad | 'apsey | 'aretz. | | gam | 'at | badam |
| ***shall be* from sea** | ***even* to** | **sea** | **and from the river *even*** | ***to* the** | **ends of the** | **earth** | | **As for also** | ***you*** | **by the blood** |

| בריתך 1285 | שלחתי 7971 | אסיריך 615 | מבור 953 | אין 369 | מים 4325 | בו 871a: | 9:12 | שובו 7725 | לבצרון 1225 |
|---|---|---|---|---|---|---|---|---|---|
| bariytek, | shilachtiy | 'asiyrayik | mibour, | 'aeyn | mayim | bou. | | shubu | labitzaroun, |
| **of your covenant** | **I have sent forth** | **your prisoners** | **out of the pit** | ***is* no** | **water** | **wherein** | | **Turn you** | **to the strong hold** |

| אסירי 615 | התקוה 8615 | גם 1571 | היום 3117 | מגיד 5046 | משנה 4932 | אשיב 7725 | לך 3807a: | 9:13 | כי 3588 | דרכתי 1869 | לי 3807a |
|---|---|---|---|---|---|---|---|---|---|---|---|
| 'asiyrey | hatiquah; | gam | hayoum | magiyd | mishneh | 'ashiyb | lak. | | kiy | daraktiy | liy |
| **you prisoners of** | **hope** | **even** | **to day** | **do I declare** | **double** | ***that* I will render** | **unto you** | | **When** | **I have bent** | **for me** |

Zech 9:6 And a bastard shall dwell in Ashdod, and I will cut off the pride of the Philistines.7 And I will take away his blood out of his mouth, and his abominations from between his teeth: but he that remain, even he, shall be for our G-d, and he shall be as a governor in Judah, and Ekron as a Jebusite.8 And I will encamp about mine house because of the army, because of him that pass by, and because of him that returneth: and no oppressor shall pass through them anymore: for now have I seen with mine eyes.9 Rejoice greatly, O daughter of Zion; shout, O daughter of Jerusalem: behold, your King cometh unto you: he is just, and having salvation; lowly, and riding upon an ass, and upon a colt the foal of an ass.10 And I will cut off the chariot from Ephraim, and the horse from Jerusalem, and the battle bow shall be cut off: and he shall speak peace unto the heathen: and his dominion shall be from sea even to sea, and from river even to the ends of the earth.11 As for you also, by the blood of your covenant I have sent forth your prisoners out of the pit wherein is no water.12 Turn you to the strong hold, you prisoners of hope: even today do I declare that I will render double unto you;13 When I have bent Judah for me, filled the bow with Ephraim, and raised up your sons, O Zion, against your sons, O Greece, and made you as the sword of a mighty man.

יהודה 3063 קשת 7198 מלאתי 4390 אפרים 669 ועוררתי 5782 בניך 1121 ציון 6726 על 5921 בניך 1121 יון 3120 ושמתיך 7760
yahudah, qeshet milea'tiy 'aprayim, ua'aurartiy banayik tziyoun, 'al banayik yauan; uasamtiyk
**Judah the bow filled with Ephraim and raised up your sons O Zion against your sons O Greece and made you**

כחרב 2719 גבור 1368: **9:14** ויהוה 3068 עליהם 5921 יראה 7200 ויצא 3318 כברק 1300 חצו 2671
kachereb gibour. uaYahuah 'aleyhem yera'ah, uayatza' kabaraq chitzou;
**as the sword of a mighty man And Yahuah over them shall be seen and shall go forth as the lightning his arrow**

ואדני 136 יהוה 3069 בשופר 7782 יתקע 8628 והלך 1980 בסערות 5591 תימן 8486: **9:15** יהוה 3069 צבאות 6635 יגן 1598
ua'adonay Yahuah bashoupar yitqa', uahalak basa'arout teyman. Yahuah tzaba'aut yagen
**and Adonai Yahuah the trumpet shall blow and shall go with whirlwinds of the south Yahuah of hosts shall defend**

עליהם 5921 ואכלו 398 וכבשו 3533 אבני 68 קלע 7050 ושתו 8354 המו 1993 כמו 3644 יין 3196
'aleyhem ua'akalu, uakabashu 'abney qela', uashatu hamu kamou yayin;
**them and they shall devour and subdue stones *with* sling and they shall drink *and* make a noise as *through* wine**

ומלאו 4390 כמזרק 4219 כזויות 2106 מזבח 4196: **9:16** והושיעם 3467 יהוה 3068 אלהיהם 430 ביום 3117
uamala'au kamizraq, kazauiyout mizbeach. uahoushiy'am Yahuah 'aloheyhem bayoum
**and they shall be filled like bowls *and* as the corners of the altar And shall save them Yahuah their Elohim in day**

ההוא 1931 כצאן 6629 עמו 5971 כי 3588 אבני 68 נזר 5145 מתנוססות 5264 על 5921 אדמתו 127: **9:17**
hahua' katza'n 'amou; kiy 'abney nezer, mitnousout 'al 'admatou.
**that as the flock of his people for they *shall be as* the stones of a crown lifted up as an ensign upon his land**

כי 3588 מה 4100 טובו 2898 ומה 4100 יפיו 3308 דגן 1715 בחורים 970 ותירוש 8492 ינובב 5107
kiy mah tubou uamah yapayou; dagan bachuriym, uatiyroush yanoubeb
**For how *great is* his goodness and how *great is* his beauty corn the young men and new wine shall make cheerful**

בתלות 1330:
batulout.
**the maids**

**Zech 10:1** שאלו 7592 מיהוה 3069 מטר 4306 בעת 6256 מלקוש 4456 יהוה 3069 עשה 6213 חזיזים 2385 ומטר 4306
sha'alu meYahuah matar ba'aet malqoush, Yahuah 'aseh chaziyziym; uamtar
**Ask you of Yahuah rain in the time of the latter rain *so* Yahuah shall make bright clouds and showers of**

גשם 1653 יתן 5414 להם 1992 לאיש 376 עשב 6212 בשדה 7704: **10:2** כי 3588 התרפים 8655 דברו 1696 און 205 והקוסמים 7080 חזו 2372
geshem yiten lahem, la'aysh 'aeseb basadeh. kiy hatarapiym dibru 'auen, uahaqousamiym chazu
**rain give them to every one grass in the field For the idols have spoken vanity and the diviners have seen**

שקר 8267 וחלמות 2472 השוא 7723 ידברו 1696 הבל 1892 ינחמון 5162 על 5921 כן 3651 נסעו 5265 כמו 3644 צאן 6629
sheqer, uachalomout hashab yadaberu, hebel yanachemun; 'al ken nasa'au kamou tza'n,
**a lie and dreams false have told in vain they comfort therefore after that they went their way as a flock**

יענו 6031 כי 3588 אין 369 רעה 7462: **10:3** על 5921 הרעים 7462 חרה 2734 אפי 639 ועל 5921
ya'anu kiy 'aeyn ro'ah. 'al haro'aym charah 'apiy, ua'al
**they were troubled because *there was* no shepherd against the shepherds was kindled Mine anger and against**

Zech 9:14 And YHUH shall be seen over them, and his arrow shall go forth as the lightning: and YHUH G-D shall blow the trumpet, and shall go with whirlwinds of the south.15 YHUH of hosts shall defend them; and they shall devour, and subdue with sling stones; and they shall drink, and make a noise as through wine; and they shall be filled like bowls, and as the corners of the altar.16 And YHUH their G-d shall save them in that day as the flock of his people: for they shall be as the stones of a crown, lifted up as an ensign upon his land.17 For how great is his goodness, and how great is his beauty! corn shall make the young men cheerful, and new wine the maids. **Zech** 10 10:1 Ask you of YHUH rain in the time of the latter rain; so YHUH shall make bright clouds, and give them showers of rain, to everyone grass in the field.2 For the idols have spoken vanity, and the diviners have seen a lie, and have told false dreams; they comfort in vain: therefore they went their way as a flock, they were troubled, because there was no shepherd.3 Mine anger was kindled against the shepherds, and I punished the goats: for YHUH of hosts has visited his flock the house of Judah, and has made them as his goodly horse in the battle.

העתודים 6260 אפקוד 6485 כי 3588 פקד 6485 יהוה 3068 צבאות 6635 את 853 עדרו 5739 את 853 בית 1004 יהודה 3063 ושם 7760 אותם 853
ha'atudiym 'apqoud; kiy paqad Yahuah tzaba'aut 'at 'adrou 'at beyt yahudah, uasam 'autam,
**the goats I punished for has visited Yahuah of hosts his flock the house of Judah and has made them**

כסוס 5483 הודו 3035 במלחמה 4421: 10:4 ממנו 4480 פנה 6438 ממנו 4480 יתד 3489 ממנו 4480 קשת 7198 מלחמה 4421 ממנו 4480
kasus houdou bamilchamah. mimenu pinah mimenu yated, mimenu qeshet milchamah; mimenu
**as horse his goodly in the battle Out of him the corner out of him the nail out of him bow the battle out of him**

יצא 3318 כל 3605 נוגש 5065 יחדו 3162: 10:5 והיו 1961 כגברים 1368 בוסים 947 בטיט 2916
yetzea' kal nouges yachdau. uahayu kagiboriym bousiym batiyt
**came forth every oppressor together And they shall be as mighty *men* which tread down *their enemies* in the mire of**

חוצות 2351 במלחמה 4421 ונלחמו 3898 כי 3588 יהוה 3068 עמם 5973 והבישו 3001 רכבי 7392
chutzout bamilchamah, uanilchamu, kiy Yahuah 'amam; uahobiyshu rokabey
**the streets in the battle and they shall fight because Yahuah *is* with them and shall be confounded the riders**

סוסים 5483: 10:6 וגברתי 1396 את 853 בית 1004 יהודה 3063 ואת 853 בית 1004 יוסף 3130 אושיע 3467
susiym. uagibartiy 'at beyt yahudah, ua'at beyt yousep 'aushiya,
***on* horses And I will strengthen the house of Judah *and* the house of Joseph I will save**

והושבותים 7725 כי 3588 רחמתים 7355 והיו 1961 כאשר 834 לא 3808
uahoushaboutiym kiy richamtiym, uahayu ka'asher la'
**and I will bring them again *to place them* for I have mercy upon them and they shall be as though not**

זנחתים 2186 כי 3588 אני 589 יהוה 3068 אלהיהם 430 ואענם 6030: 10:7 והיו 1961 כגבור 1368
zanachtiym; kiy, 'aniy Yahuah 'aloheyhem ua'a'anem. uahayu kagibour
**I had cast them off for I *am* Yahuah their Elohim and will hear them And shall be like a mighty man**

אפרים 669 ושמח 8055 לבם 3820 כמו 3644 יין 3196 ובניהם 1121 יראו 7200 ושמחו 8056 יגל 1523
'aprayim, uasamach libam kamou yayin; uabneyhem yir'au uasamechu, yagel
***they of* Ephraim and shall rejoice their heart as *through* wine yea their children shall see *it* and be glad shall rejoice**

לבם 3820 ביהוה 3068: 10:8 אשרקה 8319 להם 3807a ואקבצם 6908 כי 3588 פדיתים 6299 ורבו 7235 כמו 3644
libam baYahuah. 'ashraqah lahem ua'aqabtzem kiy padiytiym; uarabu kamou
**their heart in Yahuah I will hiss for them and gather them for I have redeemed them and they shall increase as**

רבו 7235: 10:9 ואזרעם 2232 בעמים 5971 ובמרחקים 4801 יזכרוני 2142
rabu. ua'azra'aem ba'amiym, uabamerchaqiym yizkaruniy;
**they have increased And I will sow them among the people and in far countries they shall remember me**

וחיו 2421 את 854 בניהם 1121 ושבו 7725: 10:10 והשיבותים 7725 מארץ 776 מצרים 4714
uachayu 'at baneyhem washabu. uahashiyboutiym me'aretz mitzrayim,
**and they shall live *with* their children and turn again I will bring them again also out of the land of Egypt**

ומאשור 804 אקבצם 6908 ואל 413 ארץ 776 גלעד 1568 ולבנון 3844 אביאם 935 ולא 3808 ימצא 4672
uame'ashur 'aqabtzem; ua'al 'aretz gil'ad ualabanoun 'abiy'aem, uala' yimatzea'
**and out of Assyria gather them and into the land of Gilead and Lebanon I will bring them and not *place* shall be found**

Zech 10:4 Out of him came forth the corner, out of him the nail, out of him the battle bow, out of him every oppressor together.5 And they shall be as mighty men, which tread down their enemies in the mire of the streets in the battle: and they shall fight, because YHUH is with them, and the riders on horses shall be confounded.6 And I will strengthen the house of Judah, and I will save the house of Joseph, and I will bring them again to place them; for I have mercy upon them: and they shall be as though I had not cast them off: for I am YHUH their G-d, and will hear them.7 And they of Ephraim shall be like a mighty man, and their heart shall rejoice as through wine: yea, their children shall see it, and be glad; their heart shall rejoice in YHUH.8 I will hiss for them, and gather them; for I have redeemed them: and they shall increase as they have increased.9 And I will sow them among the people: and they shall remember me in far countries; and they shall live with their children, and turn again.10 I will bring them again also out of the land of Egypt, and gather them out of Assyria; and I will bring them into the land of Gilead and Labanon; and place shall not be found for them.

10:11

להם 3807a: ועבר 5674 בים 3220 צרה 6869 והכה 5221 בים 3220 גלים 1530 והבישו 3001 כל 3605

lahem. ua'abar bayam tzarah, uahikah bayam galiym, uahobiyshu kal

**for them And he shall pass through the sea *with* affliction and shall smite in the sea the waves and shall dry up all**

10:12

מצולות 4688 יאר 2975 והורד 3381 גאון 1347 אשור 804 ושבט 7626 מצרים 4714 יסור 5493:

matzulout ya'ar; uahurad ga'aun 'ashur, uashebet mitzrayim yasur.

**the deeps of the river and shall be brought down the pride of Assyria and the sceptre of Egypt shall depart away**

וגברתים 1396 ביהוה 3068 ובשמו 8034 יתהלכו 1980 נאם 5002 יהוה 3068:

uagibartiym baYahuah, uabishmou yithalaku; na'am Yahuah.

**And I will strengthen them in Yahuah and in his name they shall walk up and down saith Yahuah**

**Zech 11:1** 11:2

פתח 6605 לבנון 3844 דלתיך 1817 ותאכל 398 אש 784 בארזיך 730: הילל 3213 ברוש 1265 כי 3588 נפל 5307

patach labanoun dalateyka; uata'kal 'aesh ba'arazeyka. heylel baroush kiy napal

**Open O Lebanon your doors that may devour the fire your cedars Howl fir tree for is fallen**

1:3

ארז 730 אשר 834 אדרים 117 שדדו 7703 הילילו 3213 אלוני 437 בשן 1316 כי 3588 ירד 3381 יער 3293 הבצור 1219

'arez, 'asher 'adiriym shudadu; heyliylu 'alouney bashan, kiy yarad ya'ar habatzur

**the cedar because the mighty are spoiled howl, O you oaks of Bashan for is come down the forest of the vintage**

קול 6963 יללת 3215 הרעים 7462 כי 3588 שדדה 7703 אדרתם 155 קול 6963 שאגת 7581 כפירים 3715 כי 3588

qoul yillat haro'aym, kiy shuddah 'adartam; qoul sha'agat kapiyriym, kiy

***There is* a voice of the howling of the shepherds for is spoiled their glory a voice of the roaring of young lions for**

11:4 11:5

שדד 7703 גאון 1347 הירדן 3383: כה 3541 אמר 559 יהוה 3068 אלהי 430 רעה 7462 את 853 צאן 6629 ההרגה 2028: אשר 834

shudad ga'aun hayarden. koh 'amar Yahuah 'alohay; ra'aeh 'at tza'n haharegah. 'asher

**is spoiled pride of the Jordan Thus saith Yahuah my Elohim Feed the flock of the slaughter Whose**

קניהן 7069 יהרגן 2026 ולא 3808 יאשמו 816 ומכריהן 4376 יאמר 559 ברוך 1288 יהוה 3068 ואעשר 6238

qoneyhen yahargun uala' ye'ashamu, uamokareyhen ya'mar, baruk Yahuah ua'ashir;

**possessors slay them and not hold themselves guilty and they that sell them say Blessed *be* Yahuah for I am rich**

11:6

ורעיהם 7462 לא 3808 יחמול 2550 עליהן 5921: כי 3588 לא 3808 אחמול 2550 עוד 5750 על 5921 ישבי 3427 הארץ 776

uaro'aeyhem, la' yachmoul 'aleyhen. kiy la' 'achmoul 'aud 'al yoshabey ha'aretz

**and their own shepherds not pity them For no I will pity more on the inhabitants of the land**

נאם 5002 יהוה 3068 והנה 2009 אנכי 595 ממציא 4672 את 853 האדם 120 איש 376 ביד 3027 רעהו 7453 וביד 3027 מלכו 4428

na'am Yahuah; uahineh 'anokiy mamtziy'a 'at ha'adam, 'aysh bayad re'aehu uabyad malkou,

**saith Yahuah but lo I will deliver the men every one into hand his neighbour's and into the hand of his king**

11:7

וכתתו 3807 את 853 הארץ 776 ולא 3808 אציל 5337 מידם 3027: וארעה 7462 את 853 צאן 6629

uakitatu 'at ha'aretz, uala' 'atziyl miyadam. ua'ar'ah 'at tza'n

**and they shall smite the land not I will deliver *them* out of their hand And I will feed the flock of**

ההרגה 2028 לכן 3651 עניי 6041 הצאן 6629 ואקח 3947 לי 3807a שני 8147 מקלות 4731 לאחד 259 קראתי 7121 נעם 5278

haharegah, laken 'aniyey hatza'an; ua'aqach liy shaney maqlout, la'achad qaraa'tiy no'am

**slaughter *even you* therefore O poor of the flock And I took unto me two staves the one I called Beauty**

Zech 10:11 And he shall pass through the sea with affliction, and shall smite the waves in the sea, and all the deeps of the river shall dry up: and the pride of Assyria shall be brought down, and the sceptre of Egypt shall depart away.12 And I will strengthen them in YHUH; and they shall walk up and down in his name, saith YHUH. **Zech** 11:1 Open your doors, O Lebanon, that the fire may devour your cedars.2 Howl, fir tree; for the cedar is fallen; because the mighty are spoiled: howl, O you oaks of Bashan; for the forest of the vintage is come down.3 There is a voice of the howling of the shepherds; for their glory is spoiled: a voice of the roaring of young lions; for the pride of Jordan is spoiled.4 Thus saith YHUH my G-d; Feed the flock of the slaughter;5 Whose possessors slay them, and hold themselves not guilty: and they that sell them say, Blessed be YHUH; for I am rich: and their own shepherds pity them not.6 For I will no more pity the inhabitants of the land, saith YHUH: but, lo, I will deliver the men everyone into his neighbor's hand, and into the hand of his king: and they shall smite the land, and out of their hand I will not deliver them.7 And I will feed the flock of slaughter, even you, O poor of the flock. And I took unto me two staves; the one I called Beauty, and the other I called Bands; and I fed the flock.

| 259 ולאחד | 7121 קראתי | 2254 חבלים | 7462 וארעה | 853 את | 6629: הצאן | 11:8 3582 ואכחד | 853 את | 7969 שלשת | 7462 הרעים | 3391 בירח | 259 אחד |
|---|---|---|---|---|---|---|---|---|---|---|---|
| ual'achad | qaraa'tiy | chobaliym, | ua'ar'ah | 'at | hatza'an. | ua'akchid | 'at | shaloshet | haro'aym | bayerach | 'achad; |
| **and the other** | **I called** | **Bands** | **and I fed** | | **the flock** | **also I cut off** | | **Three** | **shepherds** | **in month** | **one** |

| 7114 ותקצר | 5315 נפשי | 871a בהם | 1571 וגם | 5315 נפשם | 973 בחלה | 871a: בי | 11:9 559 ואמר | 3808 לא | 7462 ארעה | 853 אתכם | 4191 המתה |
|---|---|---|---|---|---|---|---|---|---|---|---|
| uatiqtzar | napshiy | bahem, | uagam | napsham | bachalah | biy. | ua'amar | la' | 'ar'ah | 'atkem; | hametah |
| **and lothed** | **my soul** | **them** | **and also** | **their soul** | **abhorred** | **me** | **Then said I** | **not** | **I will feed** | **you** | **that that die** |

| 4191 תמות | 3582 והנכחדת | 3582 תכחד | 7604 והנשארות | 398 תאכלנה | 802 אשה | 853 את | 1320 בשר | 7468: רעותה 11:10 |
|---|---|---|---|---|---|---|---|---|
| tamut, | uahanikchedet | tikached, | uahanish'arout, | ta'kalnah | 'ashah | 'at | basar | ra'utah. |
| **let it die** | **and that that is to be cut off** | **let it be cut off** | **and the rest** | **let eat** | **every one** | | **the flesh of** | **another** |

| 3947 ואקח | 853 את | 4731 מקלי | 853 את | 5278 נעם | 1438 ואגדע | 853 אתו | 6565 להפיר | 853 את | 1285 בריתי | 834 אשר |
|---|---|---|---|---|---|---|---|---|---|---|
| ua'aqach | 'at | maqliy | 'at | no'am, | ua'agda' | 'atou; | lahapeyr | 'at | bariytiy, | 'asher |
| **And I took** | | **my staff *it*** | | ***even* Beauty** | **and cut asunder** | **him** | **that I might break** | | **my covenant** | **which** |

| 3772 כרתי | 854 את | 3605 כל | 5971: העמים | 11:11 6565 ותפר | 3117 ביום | 1931 ההוא | 3045 וידעו | 3651 כן | 6041 עניי | 6629 הצאן |
|---|---|---|---|---|---|---|---|---|---|---|
| karatiy | 'at | kal | ha'amiym. | uatupar | bayoum | hahua'; | uayeda'au | ken | 'aniyey | hatza'an |
| **I had made** | ***with*** | **all** | **the people** | **And it was broken** | **in day** | **that** | **and knew** | **so** | **the poor of** | **the flock** |

| 8104 השמרים | 853 אתי | 3588 כי | 1697 דבר | 3068 יהוה | 1931: הוא | 11:12 559 ואמר | 413 אליהם | 518 אם | 2896 טוב | 5869 בעיניכם |
|---|---|---|---|---|---|---|---|---|---|---|
| hashomariym | 'atiy, | kiy | dabar | Yahuah | hua'. | ua'amar | 'aleyhem, | 'am | toub | ba'aeyneykem |
| **that waited upon** | **me** | **that** | ***was* the word of** | **Yahuah** | **it** | **And I said** | **unto them** | **If** | **good** | **you think** |

| 3051 הבו | 7939 שכרי | 518 ואם | 3808 לא | 2308 חדלו | 8254 וישקלו | 853 את | 7939 שכרי | 7970 שלשים | 3701: כסף | 11:13 559 ויאמר |
|---|---|---|---|---|---|---|---|---|---|---|
| habu | sakariy | ua'am | la' | chadalu; | uayishqalu | 'at | sakariy | shaloshiym | kasep. | uaya'mer |
| **give** | ***me* my price** | **and if** | **not** | **forbear** | **So they weighed** | | ***for* my price** | **thirty** | ***pieces of* silver** | **And said** |

| 3069 יהוה | 413 אלי | 7993 השליכהו | 413 אל | 3335 היוצר | 145 אדר | 3366 היקר | 834 אשר | 3365 יקרתי | 5921 מעליהם | 3947 ואקחה | 7970 שלשים |
|---|---|---|---|---|---|---|---|---|---|---|---|
| Yahuah | 'aelay, | hashaliykehu | 'al | hayoutzer, | 'aeder | hayaqar, | 'asher | yaqartiy | me'aleyhem; | ua'aqchah | shaloshiym |
| **Yahuah** | **unto me** | **Cast it** | **unto** | **the potter** | **goodly** | **a price** | **that** | **I was prised at** | **of them** | **And I took** | **thirty** |

| 3701 הכסף | 7993 ואשליך | 853 אתו | 1004 בית | 3069 יהוה | 413 אל | 3335: היוצר | 11:14 1438 ואגדע | 853 את | 4731 מקלי |
|---|---|---|---|---|---|---|---|---|---|
| hakesep, | ua'ashliyk | 'atou | beyt | Yahuah | 'al | hayoutzer. | ua'agda' | 'at | maqliy |
| ***pieces of* the silver** | **and cast** | **them** | **in the house of** | **Yahuah** | **to** | **the potter** | **Then I cut asunder** | | **staff** |

| 8145 השני | 853 את | 2254 החבלים | 6565 להפר | 853 את | 264 האחוה | 996 בין | 3063 יהודה | 996 ובין |
|---|---|---|---|---|---|---|---|---|
| hasheniy, | 'at | hachobaliym; | lahaper | 'at | ha'achauah, | beyn | yahudah | uabeyn |
| **mine other *even*** | | **Bands** | **that I might break** | | **the brotherhood** | **between** | **Judah** | **and between** |

| 3478: ישראל | 11:15 559 ויאמר | 3068 יהוה | 413 אלי | 5750 עוד | 3947 קח | 3807a לך | 3627 כלי | 7462 רעה | 196: אולי | 11:16 3588 כי |
|---|---|---|---|---|---|---|---|---|---|---|
| yisra'ael. | uaya'mer | Yahuah | 'aelay; | 'aud | qach | laka, | kaliy | ro'ah | 'auiliy. | kiy |
| **Israel** | **And said** | **Yahuah** | **unto me** | **yet** | **Take** | **unto you** | **the instruments of** | **a shepherd** | **foolish** | **For** |

| 2009 הנה | 595 אנכי | 6965 מקים | 7462 רעה | 776 בארץ | 3582 הנכחדות | 3808 לא | 6485 יפקד | 5288 הנער | 3808 לא |
|---|---|---|---|---|---|---|---|---|---|
| hineh | 'anokiy | meqym | ro'ah | ba'aretz, | hanikchadout | la' | yipqod | hana'ar | la' |
| **lo** | **I** | **will raise up** | **a shepherd** | **in the land** | **those that be cut off** | **not** | ***which* shall visit** | **the young one** | **neither** |

Zech 11:8 Three shepherds also I cut off in one month; and my soul lothed them, and their soul also abhorred me.9 Then said I, I will not feed you: that that die, let it die; and that that is to be cut off, let it be cut off; and let the rest eat everyone the flesh of another.10 And I took my staff, even Beauty, and cut it assunder, that I might break my covenant which I had made with all the people.11 And it was broken in that day: and so the poor of the flock that waited upon me knew that it was the word of YHUH.12 And I said unto them, If you think good, give me my price; and if not, forbear. So they weighed for my price thirty pieces of silver.13 And YHUH said unto me, Cast it unto the potter: a goodly price that I was prised at of them. And I took the thirty pieces of silver, and cast them to the potter in the house of YHUH.14 Then I cut asunder mine other staff, even Bands, that I might break the brotherhood between Judah and Israel.15 And YHUH said unto me, Take unto you yet the instruments of a foolish shepherd.16 For, lo, I will raise up a shepherd in the land, which shall not visit those that be cut off, neither shall seek the young one, nor heal that that is broken, nor feed that that stand still: but he shall eat the flesh of the fat, and tear their claws in pieces.

יבקש 1245 והנשברת 7665 לא 3808 ירפא 7495 הנצבה 5324 לא 3808 יכלכל 3557 ובשר 1320 הבריאה 1277 יאכל 398
yabaqesh, uahanishberet la' yarapea'; hanitzabah la' yakalkel, uabsar habariy'ah ya'kal,
**shall seek that that is broken nor heal that that stands still nor feed but the flesh of the fat he shall eat**

**11:17**
ופרסיהן 6541 יפרק 6561: הוי 1945 רעי 7473 האליל 457 עזבי 5800 הצאן 6629 חרב 2719 על 5921 זרועו 2220
uaparseyhen yapareq. houy ro'aey ha'aliyl 'azabiy hatza'an, chereb 'al zarou'au
**and their claws tear in pieces Woe to shepherd the idol that leave the flock the sword *shall be* upon his arm**

ועל 5921 עין 5869 ימינו 3225 זרעו 2220 יבוש 3001 תיבש 3001 ועין 5869 ימינו 3225 כהה 3543 תכהה 3543:
ua'al 'aeyn yamiynou; zaro'au yaboush tiybash, ua'aeyn yamiynou kahoh tikheh.
**and upon eye his right his arm shall be clean dried up and eye his right shall be utterly darkened**

**Zech 12:1**
משא 4853 דבר 1697 יהוה 3068 על 5921 ישראל 3478 נאם 5002 יהוה 3068 נטה 5186 שמים 8064
masa' dabar Yahuah 'al yisra'ael; na'am Yahuah noteh shamayim
**The burden of the word of Yahuah for Israel saith Yahuah which stretch forth the heavens**

**12:2**
ויסד 3245 ארץ 776 ויצר 3335 רוח 7307 אדם 120 בקרבו 7130: הנה 2009 אנכי 595 שם 7760 את 853
uayosed 'aretz, uayotzer ruach 'adam baqirbou. hineh 'anokiy sam 'at
**and lay the foundation of the earth and form the spirit of man within him Behold I will make**

ירושלם 3389 סף 5592 רעל 7478 לכל 3605 העמים 5971 סביב 5439 וגם 1571 על 5921 יהודה 3063 יהיה 1961 במצור 4692
yarushalaim sap ra'al lakal ha'amiym sabiyb; ua'gam 'al yahudah yihayeh bamatzour
**Jerusalem a cup of trembling unto all the people round about when both against Judah *and* they shall be in the siege**

**12:3**
על 5921 ירושלם 3389: והיה 1961 ביום 3117 ההוא 1931 אשים 7760 את 853 ירושלם 3389 אבן 68 מעמסה 4614 לכל 3605 העמים 5971 כל 3605
'al yarushalaim. uahayah bayoum hahu' 'asiym 'at yarushalaim 'aben ma'amasah lakal ha'amiym, kal
**against Jerusalem And will I in day that make Jerusalem a stone burdensome for all people all**

עמסיה 6006 שרוט 8295 ישרטו 8295 ונאספו 622 עליה 5921 כל 3605 גויי 1471
'amaseyha sarout yisaretu; uane'aspu 'aleyha, kal gouyey
**that burden themselves with it shall be cut in pieces be gathered together against it *through* all the people of**

**12:4**
הארץ 776: ביום 3117 ההוא 1931 נאם 5002 יהוה 3068 אכה 5221 כל 3605 סוס 5483 בתמהון 8541 ורכבו 7392 בשגעון 7697
ha'aretz. bayoum hahua' na'am Yahuah 'akeh kal sus batimahoun, uarokabou bashiga'aun;
**the earth In day that saith Yahuah I will smite every horse with astonishment and his rider with madness**

**12:5**
ועל 5921 בית 1004 יהודה 3063 אפקח 6491 את 853 עיני 5869 וכל 3605 סוס 5483 העמים 5971 אכה 5221 בעורון 5788:
ua'al beyt yahudah 'apqach 'at 'aeynay, uakol sus ha'amiym, 'akeh ba'auaroun.
**and upon the house of Judah I will open mine eyes and every horse of the people will smite with blindness**

ואמרו 559 אלפי 441 יהודה 3063 בלבם 3820 אמצה 556 לי 3807a ישבי 3427 ירושלם 3389 ביהוה 3068
ua'amaru 'alupey yahudah balibam; 'amtzah liy yoshabey yarushalaim, baYahuah
**And shall say the governors of Judah in their heart strength *shall be* my The inhabitants of Jerusalem in Yahuah**

**12:6**
צבאות 6635 אלהיהם 430: ביום 3117 ההוא 1931 אשים 7760 את 853 אלפי 441 יהודה 3063 ככיור 3595 אש 784
tzaba'aut 'aloheyhem. bayoum hahua' 'asiym 'at 'alupey yahudah kakiyour 'aesh
**of hosts their Elohim In day that will I make the governors of Judah like an hearth of fire**

Zech 11:17 Woe to the idol shepherd that leaveth the flock! the sword shall be upon his arm, and upon his right eye: his arm shall be clean dried up, and his right eye shall be utterly darkened. **Zech** 12:1 The burden of the word of YHUH for Israel, saith YHUH, which stretcheth forth the heavens, and layeth the foundation of the earth, and formeth the spirit of man within him.2 Behold, I will make Jerusalem a cup of trembling unto all the people round about, when they shall be in the siege both against Judah and against Jerusalem.3 And in that day will I make Jerusalem a burdensome stone for all people: all that burden themselves with it shall be cut in pieces, though all the people of the earth be gathered together against it.4 In that day, saith YHUH, I will smite every horse with astonishment, and his rider with madness: and I will open mine eyes upon the house of Judah, and will smite every horse of the people with blindness.5 And the governors of Judah shall say in their heart, The inhabitants of Jerusalem shall be my strength in YHUH of hosts their G-d.6 In that day will I make the governors of Judah like an hearth of fire among the wood, and like a torch of fire in a sheaf; and they shall devour all the people round about, on the right hand and on the left: and Jerusalem shall be inhabited again in her own place, even in Jerusalem.

| בעצים 6086 | וכלפיד 3940 | אש 784 | בעמיר 5995 | ואכלו 398 | על 5921 | ימין 3225 | ועל 5921 | שמאול 8040 | את 853 |
|---|---|---|---|---|---|---|---|---|---|
| ba'aetziym, | uaklapiyd | 'aesh | ba'amiyr, | ua'akalu | 'al | yamiyn | ua'al | sama'ul | 'at |
| **among the wood** | **and like a torch of** | **fire** | **in a sheaf** | **and they shall devour** | **on** | **the right hand** | **and on** | **the left** | |

| כל 3605 | העמים 5971 | סביב 5439 | וישבה 3427 | ירושלם 3389 | עוד 5750 | תחתיה 8478 | בירושלם 3389: | 12:7 |
|---|---|---|---|---|---|---|---|---|
| kal | ha'amiym | sabiyb; | uayashabah | yarushalaim | 'aud | tachteyha | biyarushalaim. | |
| **all** | **the people** | **round about** | **and shall be inhabited** | **Jerusalem** | **again** | **in her own place** | ***even* in Jerusalem** | |

| והושיע 3467 | יהוה 3068 | את 853 | אהלי 168 | יהודה 3063 | בראשנה 7223 | למען 4616 | לא 3808 | תגדל 1431 | תפארת 8597 |
|---|---|---|---|---|---|---|---|---|---|
| uahoushiya' | Yahuah | 'at | 'ahaley | yahudah | bara'shonah; | lama'an | la' | tigdal | tip'aret |
| **also shall save** | **Yahuah** | | **the tents of** | **Judah** | **first** | **that** | **not** | **do magnify *themselves*** | **the glory of** |

| בית 1004 | דויד 1732 | ותפארת 8597 | ישב 3427 | ירושלם 3389 | על 5921 | יהודה 3063: | 12:8 ביום 3117 | ההוא 1931 | יגן 1598 |
|---|---|---|---|---|---|---|---|---|---|
| beyt | dauiyd, | uatip'aret | yosheb | yarushalaim | 'al | yahudah. | bayoum | hahua', | yagen |
| **the house of** | **David** | **and the glory of** | **the inhabitants of** | **Jerusalem** | **against** | **Judah** | **In day** | **that** | **shall defend** |

| יהוה 3068 | בעד 1157 | יושב 3427 | ירושלם 3389 | והיה 1961 | הנכשל 3782 | בהם 871a | ביום 3117 | ההוא 1931 | כדויד 1732 |
|---|---|---|---|---|---|---|---|---|---|
| Yahuah | ba'ad | yousheb | yarushalaim, | uahayah | hanikshal | bahem | bayoum | hahua' | kadauiyd; |
| **Yahuah** | **about** | **the inhabitants of** | **Jerusalem** | **and he that is** | **feeble** | **among them** | **at day** | **that** | ***shall be* as David** |

| ובית 1004 | דויד 1732 | כאלהים 430 | כמלאך 4397 | יהוה 3068 | לפניהם 6440: | 12:9 והיה 1961 | ביום 3117 |
|---|---|---|---|---|---|---|---|
| uabeyt | dauiyd | kealohym, | kamal'ak | Yahuah | lipneyhem. | uahayah | bayoum |
| **and the house of** | **David** | ***shall be* as Elohim** | **as the angel of** | **Yahuah** | **before them** | **And it shall come to pass** | **in day** |

| ההוא 1931 | אבקש 1245 | להשמיד 8045 | את 853 | כל 3605 | הגוים 1471 | הבאים 935 | על 5921 | ירושלם 3389: | 12:10 ושפכתי 8210 | על 5921 |
|---|---|---|---|---|---|---|---|---|---|---|
| hahua'; | 'abaqesh, | lahashamiyd | 'at | kal | hagouyim, | haba'aym | 'al | yarushalaim. | uashapakatiy | 'al |
| **that** | ***that* I will seek** | **to destroy** | | **all** | **the nations** | **that come** | **against** | **Jerusalem** | **And I will pour** | **upon** |

| בית 1004 | דויד 1732 | ועל 5921 | יושב 3427 | ירושלם 3389 | רוח 7307 | חן 2580 | ותחנונים 8469 | והביטו 5027 |
|---|---|---|---|---|---|---|---|---|
| beyt | dauiyd | ua'al | yousheb | yarushalaim, | ruach | chen | uatachanuniym, | uahibiytu |
| **the house of** | **David** | **and upon** | **the inhabitants of** | **Jerusalem** | **the spirit of** | **grace** | **and of supplications** | **and they shall look** |

| אלי 413 | את 853 | אשר 834 | דקרו 1856 | וספדו 5594 | עליו 5921 | כמספד 5594 | על 5921 | היחיד 3173 |
|---|---|---|---|---|---|---|---|---|
| 'aelay | 'at | 'asher | daqaru; | uasapadu | 'alayu, | kamisped | 'al | hayachiyd, |
| **upon me** | | **whom** | **they have pierced** | **and they shall mourn** | **for him** | **as one mourns** | **for** | ***his* only** |

| והמר 4843 | עליו 5921 | כהמר 4843 | על 5921 | הבכור 1060: | 12:11 ביום 3117 | ההוא 1931 |
|---|---|---|---|---|---|---|
| uahamer | 'alayu | kahamer | 'al | habakour. | bayoum | hahua', |
| ***son* and shall be in bitterness** | **for him** | **as one that is in bitterness** | **for** | ***his* firstborn** | **In day** | **that** |

| יגדל 1431 | המספד 4553 | בירושלם 3389 | כמספד 4553 | הדד 1910 | רמון 7417 | בבקעת 1237 | מגדון 4023: | 12:12 |
|---|---|---|---|---|---|---|---|---|
| yigdal | hamisped | biyarushalaim, | kamispad | hadad | rimoun | babiq'at | magidoun. | |
| **great *shall there be*** | **a mourning** | **in Jerusalem** | **as the mourning of** | **Hadad** | **rimmon** | **in the valley of** | **Megiddon** | |

| וספדה 5594 | הארץ 776 | משפחות 4940 | משפחות 4940 | לבד 905 | משפחת 4940 | בית 1004 | דויד 1732 | לבד 905 | ונשיהם 802 | לבד 905 |
|---|---|---|---|---|---|---|---|---|---|---|
| uasapadah | ha'aretz, | mishpachout | mishpachout | labad; | mishpachat | beyt | dauiyd | labad | uansheyhem | labad, |
| **And shall mourn** | **the land** | **every** | **family** | **apart** | **the family of** | **the house of** | **David** | **apart** | **and their wives** | **apart** |

Zech 12:7 YHUH also shall save the tents of Judah first, that the glory of the house of David and the glory of the inhabitants of Jerusalem do not magnify themselves against Judah.8 In that day shall YHUH defend the inhabitants of Jerusalem; and he that is feeble among them at that day shall be as David; and the house of David shall be as G-d, as the angel of YHUH before them.9 And it shall come to pass in that day, that I will seek to destroy all the nations that come against Jerusalem.10 And I will pour upon the house of David, and upon the inhabitants of Jerusalem, the spirit of grace and of supplications: and they shall look upon me whom they have pierced, and they shall mourn for him, as one mourn for his only son, and shall be in bitterness for him, as one that is in bitterness for his firstborn.11 In that day shall there be a great mourning in Jerusalem, as the mourning of Hadadrimmon in the valley of Megiddon.12 And the land shall mourn, every family apart; the family of the house of David apart, and their wives apart; the family of the house of Nathan apart, and their wives apart;

משפחת 4940 בית 1004 נתן 5416 לבד 905 ונשיהם 802 לבד 905: **12:13** משפחת 4940 בית 1004 לוי 3878 לבד 905
mishpachat beyt natan labad, uansheyhem labad. mishpachat beyt leuiy labad,
**the family of the house of Nathan apart and their wives apart The family of the house of Levi apart**

ונשיהם 802 לבד 905 משפחת 4940 השמעי 8097 לבד 905 ונשיהם 802 לבד 905: **12:14** כל 3605 המשפחות 4940 הנשארות 7604
uansheyhem labad; mishpachat hashim'ay labad, uansheyhem labad. kol, hamishpachout hanish'arout,
**and their wives apart the family of Shimei apart and their wives apart All the families that remain**

משפחת 4940 משפחת 4940 לבד 905 ונשיהם 802 לבד 905:
mishpachot mishpachat labad; uansheyhem labad.
**every family apart and their wives apart**

**Zech 13:1** ביום 3117 ההוא 1931 יהיה 1961 מקור 4726 נפתח 6605 לבית 1004 דויד 1732 ולישבי 3427 ירושלם 3389
bayoum hahua', yihayeh maqour niptach, labeyt dauiyd ualyoshabey yarushalaim;
**In day that there shall be a fountain opened to the house of David and to the inhabitants of Jerusalem**

לחטאת 2403 ולנדה 5079: **13:2** והיה 1961 ביום 3117 ההוא 1931 נאם 5002 יהוה 3068 צבאות 6635 אכרית 3772
lachata't ualnidah. uahayah bayoum hahua' na'am Yahuah tzaba'aut, 'akriyt
**for sin and for uncleanness And it shall come to pass in day that saith Yahuah of hosts *that* I will cut off**

את 853 שמות 8034 העצבים 6091 מן 4480 הארץ 776 ולא 3808 יזכרו 2142 עוד 5750 וגם 1571 את 853 הנביאים 5030 ואת 853
'at shemout ha'atzabiym min ha'aretz, uala' yizakaru 'aud; ua'gam 'at hanabiy'aym ua'at
**the names of the idols out of the land and no they shall be remembered more and also the prophets *and***

רוח 7307 הטמאה 2932 אעביר 5674 מן 4480 הארץ 776: **13:3** והיה 1961 כי 3588 ינבא 5012 איש 376
ruach hatum'ah 'aabiyr min ha'aretz. uahayah, kiy yinabea' 'aysh
**spirit the unclean I will cause to pass out of the land And it shall come to pass *that* when shall prophesy any**

עוד 5750 ואמרו 559 אליו 413 אביו 1 ואמו 517 ילדיו 3205 לא 3808 תחיה 2421 כי 3588 שקר 8267 דברת 1696
'aud ua'amaru 'aelayu 'abiyu ua'amou yoladayu la' tichayeh, kiy sheqer dibarta
**yet then shall say unto him his father and his mother that begat him not You shall live for lies you speak**

בשם 8034 יהוה 3068 ודקרהו 1856 אביהו 1 ואמו 517 ילדיו 3205 בהנבאו 5012: **13:4**
bashem Yahuah; uadqaruhu 'abiyhu ua'amou yoladayu bahinaba'au.
**in the name of Yahuah and shall thrust him through his father and his mother that begat him when he prophesieth**

והיה 1961 ביום 3117 ההוא 1931 יבשו 954 הנביאים 5030 איש 376 מחזינו 2384
uahayah bayoum hahua', yeboshu hanabiy'aym 'aysh mechezyonou
**And it shall come to pass in day that shall be ashamed *that* the prophets every one of his vision**

בהנבאתו 5012 ולא 3808 ילבשו 3847 אדרת 155 שער 8181 למען 4616 כחש 3584: **13:5** ואמר 559 לא 3808 נביא 5030
bahinaba'atou; uala' yilbshu 'aderet se'ar lama'an kachesh. ua'amar la' nabiy'a
**when he has prophesied neither shall they wear a garment rough to deceive But he shall say no prophet**

אנכי 595 איש 376 עבד 5647 אדמה 127 אנכי 595 כי 3588 אדם 120 הקנני 7069 מנעורי 5271: **13:6** ואמר 559
'anokiy; 'aysh 'abed 'adamah 'anokiy, kiy 'adam hiqnaniy mina'auray. ua'amar
**I *am* man serve husband I *am* for man taught me to keep cattle from my youth And *one* shall say**

Zech 12:13 The family of the house of Levi apart, and their wives apart; the family of Shimei apart, and their wives apart;14 All the families that remain, every family apart, and their wives apart. **Zech** 13:1 In that day there shall be a fountain opened to the house of David and to the inhabitants of Jerusalem for sin and for uncleanness.2 And it shall come to pass in that day, saith YHUH of hosts, that I will cut off the names of the idols out of the land, and they shall no more be remembered: and also I will cause the prophets and the unclean spirit to pass out of the land.3 And it shall come to pass, that when any shall yet prophesy, then his father and his mother that begat him shall say unto him, Thou shall not live; for you speak lies in the name of YHUH: and his father and his mother that begat him shall thrust him through when he prophesieth.4 And it shall come to pass in that day, that the prophets shall be ashamed everyone of his vision, when he has prophesied; neither shall they wear a rough garment to deceive:5 But he shall say, I am no prophet, I am an husbandman; for man taught me to keep cattle from my youth.

| אליו 413 | מה 4100 | המכות 4347 | האלה 428 | בין 996 | ידיך 3027 | ואמר 559 | אשר 834 | הכיתי 5221 |
|---|---|---|---|---|---|---|---|---|
| 'aelayu, | mah | hamakout | ha'aeleh | beyn | yadeyka; | ua'amar | 'asher | hukeytiy |
| **unto him** | **What** | **wounds** | ***are* these** | **in** | **your hands?** | **Then he will answer, *Those*** | **with which** | **I was wounded** |

| בית 1004 | מאהבי 157: | 13:7 חרב 2719 | עורי 5782 | על 5921 | רעי 7473 | ועל 5921 | גבר 1397 | עמיתי 5997 | נאם 5002 | יהוה 3069 |
|---|---|---|---|---|---|---|---|---|---|---|
| beyt | ma'ahabay. | chereb, | 'auriy | 'al | ro'aey | ua'al | geber | 'amiytiy, | na'am | Yahuah |
| ***in* the house of** | **my friends** | **O sword** | **Awake** | **against** | **my shepherd** | **and against** | **the man *that is*** | **my fellow** | **saith** | **Yahuah** |

| צבאות 6635 | הך 5221 | את 853 | הרעה 7462 | ותפוצין 6327 | הצאן 6629 | והשבתי 7725 | ידי 3027 | על 5921 | הצערים 6819: | 13:8 |
|---|---|---|---|---|---|---|---|---|---|---|
| tzaba'aut; | hak | 'at | hara'ah | uatputzeyna | hatza'an, | uahashibotiy | yadiy | 'al | hatzo'ariym. | |
| **of hosts** | **smite** | | **the shepherd** | **and shall be scattered** | **the sheep** | **and I will turn** | **mine hand** | **upon** | **the little ones** | |

| והיה 1961 | בכל 3605 | הארץ 776 | נאם 5002 | יהוה 3068 | פי 6310 | שנים 8147 | בה 871a | יכרתו 3772 | יגועו 1478 |
|---|---|---|---|---|---|---|---|---|---|
| uahayah | bakal | ha'aretz | na'am | Yahuah, | piy | shanayim | bah, | yikaratu | yigua'au; |
| **And it shall come to pass *that*** | **in all** | **the land** | **saith** | **Yahuah** | **parts** | **two** | **therein** | **shall be cut off** | ***and* die** |

| והשלשית 7992 | יותר 3498 | בה 871a: | 13:9 והבאתי 935 | את 853 | השלשית 7992 | באש 784 | וצרפתים 6884 |
|---|---|---|---|---|---|---|---|
| uahashalishiyt | yiuater | bah. | uahebea'tiy | 'at | hashalishiyt | ba'aesh, | uatzraptiym |
| **but the third** | **shall be left** | **therein** | **And I will bring** | | **the third *part*** | **through the fire** | **and will refine them** |

| כצרף 6884 | את 853 | הכסף 3701 | ובחנתים 974 | כבחן 974 | את 853 | הזהב 2091 | הוא 1931 | יקרא 7121 | בשמי 8034 | ואני 589 | אענה 6030 | אתו 853 |
|---|---|---|---|---|---|---|---|---|---|---|---|---|
| kitzrop | 'at | hakesep, | uabchantiym | kibchon | 'at | hazahab; | hua' | yiqra' | bishmiy, | ua'aniy | 'a'aneh | 'atou, |
| **as is refined** | | **silver** | **and will try them** | **as is tried** | | **gold** | **they** | **shall call on** | **my name** | **and I** | **will hear** | **them** |

| אמרתי 559 | עמי 5971 | הוא 1931 | והוא 1931 | יאמר 559 | יהוה 3068 | אלהי 430: |
|---|---|---|---|---|---|---|
| 'amartiy | 'amiy | hua', | uahu'a | ya'mar | Yahuah | 'alohay. |
| **I will say** | ***is* my people** | **It** | **and they** | **shall say** | **Yahuah *is*** | **my Elohim** |

| **Zech 14:1** הנה 2009 | יום 3117 | בא 935 | ליהוה 3068 | וחלק 2505 | שללך 7998 | בקרבך 7130: | 14:2 ואספתי 622 |
|---|---|---|---|---|---|---|---|
| hineh | youm | ba' | laYahuah; | uachulaq | shalalek | baqirbek. | ua'asaptiy |
| **Behold** | **the day of** | **comes** | **of Yahuah** | **and shall be divided** | **your spoil** | **in the midst of you** | **For I will gather** |

| את 853 | כל 3605 | הגוים 1471 | אל 413 | ירושלם 3389 | למלחמה 4421 | ונלכדה 3920 | העיר 5892 | ונשסו 8155 | הבתים 1004 | והנשים 802 |
|---|---|---|---|---|---|---|---|---|---|---|
| 'at | kal | hagouyim | 'al | yarushalaim | lamilchamah | uanilkadah | ha'ayr, | uanashasu | habatiym, | uahanashiym |
| | **all** | **nations** | **against** | **Jerusalem** | **to battle** | **and shall be taken** | **the city** | **and rifled** | **the houses** | **and the women** |

| תשגלנה 7693 | ויצא 3318 | חצי 2677 | העיר 5892 | בגולה 1473 | ויתר 3499 | העם 5971 | לא 3808 | יכרת 3772 | מן 4480 |
|---|---|---|---|---|---|---|---|---|---|
| tishagalnah | uayatza' | chatziy | ha'ayr | bagoulah, | uayeter | ha'am, | la' | yikaret | min |
| **ravished** | **and shall go forth** | **half of** | **the city** | **into captivity** | **and the residue of** | **the people** | **not** | **shall be cut off** | **from** |

| העיר 5892: | 14:3 ויצא 3318 | יהוה 3069 | ונלחם 3898 | בגוים 1471 | ההם 1992 | כיום 3117 | הלחמו 3898 | ביום 3117 | קרב 7128: | 14:4 |
|---|---|---|---|---|---|---|---|---|---|---|
| ha'ayr. | uayatza' | Yahuah, | uanilcham | bagouyim | hahem; | kayoum | hilachamou | bayoum | qarab. | |
| **the city** | **Then shall go forth** | **Yahuah** | **and fight** | **against nations** | **those** | **as when** | **he fought** | **in the day of** | **battle** | |

| ועמדו 5975 | רגליו 7272 | ביום 3117 | ההוא 1931 | על 5921 | הר 2022 | הזתים 2132 | אשר 834 | על 5921 | פני 6440 | ירושלם 3389 | מקדם 6924 |
|---|---|---|---|---|---|---|---|---|---|---|---|
| ua'amadu | raglayu | bayoum | hahu' | 'al | har | hazetiym | 'asher | 'al | paney | yarushalaim | miqedem |
| **And shall stand** | **his feet** | **in day** | **that** | **upon** | **mount of** | **the Olives** | **which** | ***is* on** | **before** | **Jerusalem** | **on the east** |

Zech 13:6 And one shall say unto him, What are these wounds in your hands? Then he shall answer, Those with which I was wounded in the house of my friends.7 Awake, O sword, against my shepherd, and against the man that is my fellow, saith YHUH of hosts: smite the shepherd, and the sheep shall be scattered: and I will turn mine hand upon the little ones.8 And it shall come to pass, that in all the land, saith YHUH, two parts therein shall be cut off and die; but the third shall be left therein.9 And I will bring the third part through the fire, and will refine them as silver is refined, and will try them as gold is tried: they shall call on my name, and I will hear them: I will say, It is my people: and they shall say, YHUH is my G-d. **Zech** 14:1 Behold, the day of YHUH cometh, and your spoil shall be divided in the midst of you.2 For I will gather all nations against Jerusalem to battle; and the city shall be taken, and the houses rifled, and the women ravished; and half of the city shall go forth into captivity, and the residue of the people shall not be cut off from the city.3 Then shall YHUH go forth, and fight against those nations, as when he fought in the day of battle.4 And his feet shall stand in that day upon the mount of Olives, which is before Jerusalem on the east, and the mount of Olives shall cleave in the midst thereof toward the east and toward the west,

| | | | | | | |
|---|---|---|---|---|---|---|
| 1234 ונבקע | 2022 הר | 2132 הזיתים | 2677 מחציו | 4217 מזרחה | 3220 וימה | 1516 גיא |
| uanibqa' | har | hazeytiym | mechetzyou | mizrachah | uayamah, | gey'a |
| **and shall cleave** | **mount of** | **the Olives** | **in the midst thereof** | **toward the east** | **and toward the west** ***and there shall be*** | **a valley** |

| | | | | | | | | 14:5 |
|---|---|---|---|---|---|---|---|---|
| 1419 גדולה | 3966 מאד | 4185 ומש | 2677 חצי | 2022 ההר | 6828 צפונה | 2677 וחציו | 5045: נגבה | |
| gadoulah | ma'ad; | uamash | chatziy | hahar | tzapounah | uachetzyou | negbah. | |
| **great** | **very** | **and shall remove** | **half of** | **the mountain** | **toward the north** | **and half** | ***of it*** **toward the south** | |

| | | | | | | | | | |
|---|---|---|---|---|---|---|---|---|---|
| 5127 ונסתם | 1516 גיא | 2022 הרי | 3588 כי | 5060 יגיע | 1516 גי | 2022 הרים | 413 אל | 682 אצל | 5127 ונסתם |
| uanastem | gey'a | haray, | kiy | yagiya' | gey | hariym | 'al | 'atzal | uanastem, |
| **And you shall flee** ***to*** | **the valley of** | **the mountains** | **for** | **shall reach** | **the valley of** | **the mountains** | **unto** | **Azal** | **yea you shall flee** |

| | | | | | | | | | | |
|---|---|---|---|---|---|---|---|---|---|---|
| 834 כאשר | 5127 נסתם | 6440 מפני | 7494 הרעש | 3117 בימי | 5818 עזיה | 4428 מלך | 3063 יהודה | 935 ובא | 3068 יהוה | 430 אלהי |
| ka'asher | nastem | mipaney | hara'ash, | biymey | 'aziyah | melek | yahudah; | uaba' | Yahuah | 'alohay, |
| **like as** | **you fled** | **from before** | **the earthquake** | **in the days of** | **Uzziah** | **king of** | **Judah** | **and shall come** | **Yahuah** | **my Elohim** |

| | | | 14:6 | | | | | | | |
|---|---|---|---|---|---|---|---|---|---|---|
| 3605 כל | 6918 קדשים | 5973: עמך | 1961 והיה | 3117 ביום | 1931 ההוא | 3808 לא | 1961 יהיה | 216 אור | 3368 יקרות | 7087 יקפאון |
| kal | qadoshiym | 'amak. | uahayah | bayoum | hahua'; | la' | yihayeh | 'aur, | yaqarout | yaqpa'un |
| ***and*** **all** | **the saints** | **with you** | **And it shall come to pass** | **in day** | **that** | **not** | **shall be** | ***that*** **the light** | **clear** | ***nor*** **dark** |

| 14:7 | | | | | | | | | | |
|---|---|---|---|---|---|---|---|---|---|---|
| | 1961 והיה | 3117 יום | 259 אחד | 1931 הוא | 3045 יודע | 3068 ליהוה | 3808 לא | 3117 יום | 3808 ולא | 3915 לילה |
| | uahayah | youm | 'achad, | hua' | yiuada' | laYahuah | la' | youm | uala' | layalah; |
| | **But it shall be** | **day** | **one** | **which** | **shall be known** | **to Yahuah** | **not** | **day** | **nor** | **night** |

| | | | | | 14:8 | | | | |
|---|---|---|---|---|---|---|---|---|---|
| 1961 והיה | 6256 לעת | 6153 ערב | 1961 יהיה | 216: אור | 1961 והיה | 3117 ביום | 1931 ההוא | 3318 יצאו | 4325 מים |
| uahayah | la'et | 'areb | yihayeh | 'aur. | uahayah | bayoum | hahua', | yetza'ua | mayim |
| **but it shall come to pass** ***that*** | **at time** | **evening** | **it shall be** | **light** | **And it shall be** | **in day** | **that** | **shall go out** | **waters** |

| | | | | | | | | | |
|---|---|---|---|---|---|---|---|---|---|
| 2416 חיים | 3389 מירושלם | 2677 חצים | 413 אל | 3220 הים | 6931 הקדמוני | 2671 וחצים | 413 אל | 3220 הים | 314 האחרון |
| chayiym | miyarushalaim, | chetzyam, | 'al | hayam | haqadmouniy, | uachetzyam | 'al | hayam | ha'acharoun; |
| ***that*** **living** | **from Jerusalem** | **half of them** | **toward** | **the sea** | **former** | **and half of them** | **toward** | **the sea** | **the hinder** |

| | | | 14:9 | | | | | | | | |
|---|---|---|---|---|---|---|---|---|---|---|---|
| 7019 בקיץ | 2779 ובחרף | 1961: יהיה | 1961 והיה | 3068 יהוה | 4428 למלך | 5921 על | 3605 כל | 776 הארץ | 3117 ביום | 1931 ההוא | 1961 יהיה |
| baqayitz | uabachorep | yihayeh. | uahayah | Yahuah | lamelek | 'al | kal | ha'aretz; | bayoum | hahua', | yihayeh |
| **in summer** | **and in winter** | **shall it be** | **And shall be** | **Yahuah** | **king** | **over** | **all** | **the earth** | **in day** | **that** | **shall there be** |

| | | | | 14:10 | | | | | | |
|---|---|---|---|---|---|---|---|---|---|---|
| 3068 יהוה | 259 אחד | 8034 ושמו | 259: אחד | 5437 יסוב | 3605 כל | 776 הארץ | 6160 כערבה | 1387 מגבע | 7417 לרמון | 5045 נגב |
| Yahuah | 'achad | uashmou | 'achad. | yisoub | kal | ha'aretz | ka'arabah | migeba' | larimoun, | negeb |
| **Yahuah** | **one** | **and his name** | **one** | **shall be turned** | **All** | **the land** | **as a plain** | **from Geba** | **to Rimmon** | **south of** |

| | | | | | | | | | |
|---|---|---|---|---|---|---|---|---|---|
| 3389 ירושלם | 7213 וראמה | 3427 וישבה | 8478 תחתיה | 8179 למשער | 1144 בנימן | 5704 עד | 4725 מקום | 8179 שער | 7223 הראשון |
| yarushalaim; | uara'amah | uayashabah | tachteyha | lamisha'ar | binyamin, | 'ad | maqoum | sha'ar | hara'shoun |
| **Jerusalem** | **and it shall be lifted up** | **and inhabited** | **in her place** | **from gate** | **Benjamin's** | **unto** | **the place of** | **gate** | **the first** |

| | | | | | | | | 14:11 | |
|---|---|---|---|---|---|---|---|---|---|
| 5704 עד | 8179 שער | 6434 הפנים | 4028 ומגדל | 2606 חננאל | 5704 עד | 3342 יקבי | 4428: המלך | 3427 וישבו | 871a בה |
| 'ad | sha'ar | hapiniym, | uamigdal | chanan'ael, | 'ad | yiqbey | hamelek. | uayashabu | bah, |
| **unto** | **gate** | **the corner** | **and** ***from*** **the tower of** | **Hananeel** | **unto** | **winepresses** | **the king's** | **And** ***men*** **shall dwell** | **in it** |

Zech 14:4 and there shall be a very great valley; and half of the mountain shall remove toward the north, and half of it toward the south.5 And you shall flee to the valley of the mountains; for the valley of the mountains shall reach unto Azal: yea, you shall flee, like as you fled from before the earthquake in the days of Uzziah king of Judah: and YHUH my G-d shall come, and all the saints with you.6 And it shall come to pass in that day, that the light shall not be clear, nor dark:7 But it shall be one day which shall be known to YHUH, not day, nor night: but it shall come to pass, that at evening time it shall be light.8 And it shall be in that day, that living waters shall go out from Jerusalem; half of them toward the former sea, and half of them toward the hinder sea: in summer and in winter shall it be.9 And YHUH shall be king over all the earth: in that day shall there be one YHUH, and his name one.10 All the land shall be turned as a plain from Geba to Rimmon south of Jerusalem: and it shall be lifted up, and inhabited in her place, from Benjamin's gate unto the place of the first gate, unto the corner gate, and from the tower of Hananeel unto the king's winepresses.

| | | | | | | | | |
|---|---|---|---|---|---|---|---|---|
| 2764 וחרם | 3808 לא | 1961 יהיה | 5750 עוד | 3427 וישבה | 3389 ירושלם | 983: לבטח | 14:12 2063 וזאת | 1961 תהיה |
| uacherem | la' | yihayeh | 'aud; | uayashabah | yarushalaim | labetach. | uaza't | tihayeh |
| **and utter destruction** | **no** | **there shall be** | **more** | **but shall be inhabited** | **Jerusalem** | **safely** | **And this** | **shall be** |

| | | | | | | | | | | |
|---|---|---|---|---|---|---|---|---|---|---|
| 4046 המגפה | 834 אשר | 5062 יגף | 3068 יהוה | 853 את | 3605 כל | 5971 העמים | 834 אשר | 6633 צבאו | 5921 על | 3389 ירושלם |
| hamagepah, | 'asher | yigop | Yahuah | 'at | kal | ha'amiym, | 'asher | tzaba'au | 'al | yarushalaim; |
| **the plague** | **wherewith** | **will smite** | **Yahuah** | | **all** | **the people** | **that** | **have fought** | **against** | **Jerusalem** |

| | | | | | | | | |
|---|---|---|---|---|---|---|---|---|
| 4743 המק | 1320 בשרו | 1931 והוא | 5975 עמד | 5921 על | 7272 רגליו | 5869 ועיניו | 4743 תמקנה | 2356 בחריהן |
| hameq | basarou, | uahu'a | 'amed | 'al | raglayu, | ua'aeynayu | timaqnah | bachoreyhen, |
| **shall consume away** | **Their flesh** | **while they** | **stand** | **upon** | **their feet** | **and their eyes** | **shall consume away** | **in their holes** |

| | | | | | | | |
|---|---|---|---|---|---|---|---|
| 3956 ולשונו | 4743 תמק | 6310: בפיהם | 14:13 1961 והיה | 3117 ביום | 1931 ההוא | 1961 תהיה | 4103 מהומת |
| ualshounou | timaq | bapiyhem. | uahayah | bayoum | hahua', | tihayeh | mahumat |
| **and their tongue** | **shall consume away** | **in their mouth** | **And it shall come to pass** | **in day** | **that** | **shall be *that*** | **a tumult** |

| | | | | | | | | |
|---|---|---|---|---|---|---|---|---|
| 3068 יהוה | 7227 רבה | 871a בהם | 2388 והחזיקו | 376 איש | 3027 יד | 7453 רעהו | 5927 ועלתה | 3027 ידו |
| Yahuah | rabah | bahem; | uahecheziyqu, | 'aysh | yad | re'aehu, | ua'alatah | yadou |
| ***from* Yahuah** | **great** | **among them** | **and they shall lay hold on** | **every one** | **the hand of** | **his neighbour** | **and shall rise up** | **his hand** |

| | | | | | | | |
|---|---|---|---|---|---|---|---|
| 5921 על | 3027 יד | 7453: רעהו | 14:14 1571 וגם | 3063 יהודה | 3898 תלחם | 3389 בירושלם | 622 ואסף |
| 'al | yad | re'aehu. | ua'gam | yahudah, | tilachem | biyarushalaim; | ua'usap |
| **against** | **the hand of** | **his neighbour** | **And also** | **Judah** | **shall fight** | **at Jerusalem** | **and shall be gathered together** |

| | | | | | | | | | | |
|---|---|---|---|---|---|---|---|---|---|---|
| 2428 חיל | 3605 כל | 1471 הגוים | 5439 סביב | 2091 זהב | 3701 וכסף | 899 ובגדים | 7230 לרב | 3966: מאד | 14:15 3651 וכן | 1961 תהיה |
| cheyl | kal | hagouyim | sabiyb, | zahab | uakesep | uabgadiym | larob | ma'ad. | uaken | tihayeh |
| **the wealth of** | **all** | **the heathen** | **round about** | **gold** | **and silver** | **and apparel** | **in abundance** | **great** | **And so** | **shall be** |

| | | | | | | | | | | |
|---|---|---|---|---|---|---|---|---|---|---|
| 4046 מגפת | 5483 הסוס | 6505 הפרד | 1581 הגמל | 2543 והחמור | 3605 וכל | 929 הבהמה | 834 אשר | 1961 יהיה | 4264 במחנות | 1992 ההמה |
| magepat | hasus, | hapered | hagamal | uahachamour, | uakal | habehemah, | 'asher | yihayeh | bamachanout | hahemah; |
| **the plague of** | **the horse** | **of the mule** | **of the camel** | **and of the ass** | **and of all** | **the beasts** | **that** | **shall be** | **in tents** | **these** |

| | | | | | | | | |
|---|---|---|---|---|---|---|---|---|
| 4046 כמגפה | 2063: הזאת | 14:16 1961 והיה | 3605 כל | 3498 הנותר | 3605 מכל | 1471 הגוים | 935 הבאים | 5921 על |
| kamagepah | haza't. | uahayah, | kal | hanoutar | mikal | hagouyim, | haba'aym | 'al |
| **as plague** | **this** | **And it shall come to pass *that*** | **every one** | **that is left** | **of all** | **the nations** | **which came** | **against** |

| | | | | | | | | | | |
|---|---|---|---|---|---|---|---|---|---|---|
| 3389 ירושלם | 5927 ועלו | 1767 מדי | 8141 שנה | 8141 בשנה | 7812 להשתחות | 4428 למלך | 3068 יהוה | 6635 צבאות | 2287 ולחג | 853 את |
| yarushalaim; | ua'alu | midey | shanah | bashanah, | lahishtachauot | lamelek | Yahuah | tzaba'aut, | ualachog | 'at |
| **Jerusalem** | **shall even go up** | **from** | **year** | **to year** | **to worship** | **the King** | **Yahuah** | **of hosts** | **and to keep** | |

| | | | | | | | | | |
|---|---|---|---|---|---|---|---|---|---|
| 2282 חג | 5521: הסכות | 14:17 1961 והיה | 834 אשר | 3808 לא | 5927 יעלה | 853 מאת | 4940 משפחות | 776 הארץ | 413 אל |
| chag | hasukout. | uahayah | 'asher | la' | ya'aleh | me'at | mishpachout | ha'aretz | 'al |
| **the feast of** | **tabernacles** | **And it shall be *that*** | **whoso** | **not** | **will come up** | **of *all*** | **the families of** | **the earth** | **unto** |

| | | | | | | | | | | |
|---|---|---|---|---|---|---|---|---|---|---|
| 3389 ירושלם | 7812 להשתחות | 4428 למלך | 3068 יהוה | 6635 צבאות | 3808 ולא | 5921 עליהם | 1961 יהיה | 1653: הגשם | 14:18 518 ואם | 4940 משפחת |
| yarushalaim, | lahishtachauot, | lamelek | Yahuah | tzaba'aut; | uala' | 'aleyhem | yihayeh | hagashem. | ua'am | mishpachat |
| **Jerusalem** | **to worship** | **the King** | **Yahuah** | **of hosts** | **even no** | **upon them** | **shall be** | **rain** | **And if** | **the family of** |

Zech 14:11 And men shall dwell in it, and there shall be no more utter destruction; but Jerusalem shall be safely inhabited.12 And this shall be the plague wherewith YHUH will smite all the people that have fought against Jerusalem; Their flesh shall consume away while they stand upon their feet, and their eyes shall consume away in their holes, and their tongue shall consume away in their mouth.13 And it shall come to pass in that day, that a great tumult from YHUH shall be among them; and they shall lay hold everyone on the hand of his neighbor, and his hand shall rise up against the hand of his neighbor.14 And Judah also shall fight at Jerusalem; and the wealth of all the heathen round about shall be gathered together, gold, and silver, and apparel, in great abundance.15 And so shall be the plague of the horse, of the mule, of the camel, and of the ass, and of all the beasts that shall be in these tents, as this plague.16 And it shall come to pass, that everyone that is left of all the nations which came against Jerusalem shall even go up from year to year to worship the King, YHUH of hosts, and to keep the feast of tabernacles.17 And it shall be, that whoso will not come up of all the families of the earth unto Jerusalem to worship the King, YHUH of hosts, even upon them shall be no rain.18 And if the family of Egypt go not up, and come not, that have no rain;

| מצרים 4714 | לא 3808 | תעלה 5927 | ולא 3808 | באה 935 | ולא 3808 | עליהם 5921 | תהיה 1961 | המגפה 4046 | אשר 834 | יגף 5062 | יהוה 3068 |
|---|---|---|---|---|---|---|---|---|---|---|---|
| mitzrayim | la' | ta'aleh | uala' | ba'ah | uala' | 'aleyhem; | tihayeh | hamagepah, | 'asher | yigop | Yahuah |
| **Egypt** | **not** | **go up** | **and not** | **come** | **that *have* no *rain*** | **on them** | **there shall be** | **the plague** | **wherewith** | **will smite** | **Yahuah** |

| את 853 | הגוים 1471 | אשר 834 | לא 3808 | יעלו 5927 | לחג 2287 | את 853 | חג 2282 | הסכות 5521: | **14:19** | זאת 2063 | תהיה 1961 | חטאת 2403 |
|---|---|---|---|---|---|---|---|---|---|---|---|---|
| 'at | hagouyim, | 'asher | la' | ya'alu, | lachog | 'at | chag | hasukout. | | za't | tihayeh | chata't |
| | **the heathen** | **that** | **not** | **come up** | **to keep** | | **feast of** | **the tabernacles** | | **This** | **shall be** | **the punishment of** |

| מצרים 4714 | וחטאת 2403 | כל 3605 | הגוים 1471 | אשר 834 | לא 3808 | יעלו 5927 | לחג 2287 | את 853 | חג 2282 | הסכות 5521: | **14:20** |
|---|---|---|---|---|---|---|---|---|---|---|---|
| mitzrayim; | uachata't | kal | hagouyim, | 'asher | la' | ya'alu, | lachog | 'at | chag | hasukout. | |
| **Egypt** | **and the punishment of** | **all** | **nations** | **that** | **not** | **come up** | **to keep** | | **feast of** | **the tabernacles** | |

| ביום 3117 | ההוא 1931 | יהיה 1961 | על 5921 | מצלות 4698 | הסוס 5483 | קדש 6944 | ליהוה 3068 | והיה 1961 | הסירות 5518 |
|---|---|---|---|---|---|---|---|---|---|
| bayoum | hahua', | yihayeh | 'al | matzilout | hasus, | qodesh | laYahuah; | uahayah | hasiyrout |
| **In day** | **that** | **shall there be** | **upon** | **the bells of** | **the horses** | **HOLINESS** | **UNTO THE YAHUAH** | **and shall be** | **the pots** |

| בבית 1004 | יהוה 3068 | כמזרקים 4219 | לפני 6440 | המזבח 4196: | **14:21** | והיה 1961 | כל 3605 | סיר 5518 | בירושלם 3389 | וביהודה 3063 | קדש 6944 |
|---|---|---|---|---|---|---|---|---|---|---|---|
| babeyt | Yahuah, | kamizraqiym | lipney | hamizbeach. | | uahayah | kal | siyr | biyarushalaim | uabiyahudah, | qodesh |
| **in house** | **Yahuah's** | **like the bowls** | **before** | **the altar** | | **Yea shall be** | **Every** | **pot** | **in Jerusalem** | **and in Judah** | **holiness** |

| ליהוה 3068 | צבאות 6635 | ובאו 935 | כל 3605 | הזבחים 2076 | ולקחו 3947 | מהם 1992 | ובשלו 1310 | בהם 871a | ולא 3808 | יהיה 1961 |
|---|---|---|---|---|---|---|---|---|---|---|
| laYahuah | tzaba'aut, | uaba'au | kal | hazobachiym, | ualaqachu | mehem | uabishlu | bahem; | uala' | yihayeh |
| **unto Yahuah** | **of hosts** | **and shall come** | **all** | **that sacrifice** | **and take** | **they of them** | **and see** | **therein** | **and no** | **there shall be** |

| כנעני 3669 | עוד 5750 | בבית 1004 | יהוה 3068 | צבאות 6635 | ביום 3117 | ההוא 1931: |
|---|---|---|---|---|---|---|
| kana'aniy | 'aud | babeyt | Yahuah | tzaba'aut | bayoum | hahua'. |
| **the Canaanite** | **more** | **in the house of** | **Yahuah** | **of hosts** | **in day** | **that** |

Zech 14:18 there shall be the plague, wherewith YHUH will smite the heathen that come not up to keep the feast of tabernacles.19 This shall be the punishment of Egypt, and the punishment of all nations that come not up to keep the feast of tabernacles.20 In that day shall there be upon the bells of the horses, HOLINESS UNTO THE YHUH; and the pots in YHUH's house shall be like the bowl's before the altar.21 Yea, every pot in Jerusalem and in Judah shall be holiness unto YHUH of hosts: and all they that sacrifice shall come and take of them, and seethe therein: and in that day there shall be no more the Canaanite in the house of YHUH of hosts.

# MALACHI
## (*Malakiy*)

Verse one identifies the author as the Prophet Malachi whose name in Hebrew means *My Messenger*. The book was written approximately between 440 and 400 B.C. approximately 100 years after the **House of Judah** returned to Jerusalem to rebuild the temple. Malachi's message to the House of Judah was a warning to the people to repent and turn back to Elohim. The priests were accepting blemished sacrifices from the people and the people were not paying their tithes, as well as marrying outside their own people to pagans. Malachi rebukes his people and reiterates Elohim's love for His people and His promises of a coming Messenger who will prepare the way for יהוה.

**Malachi 1:1**
משא 4853 דבר 1697 יהוה 3068 אל 413 ישראל 3478 ביד 3027 מלאכי 4401: 1:2 אהבתי 157 אתכם 853 אמר 559 יהוה 3068
masa' dabar Yahuah 'al yisra'ael; bayad mal'akiy. 'ahabtiy 'atkem 'amar Yahuah,
**The burden of the word of Yahuah to Israel by Malachi I have loved you say Yahuah**

ואמרתם 559 במה 1400 אהבתנו 157 הלוא 3808 אח 251 עשו 6215 ליעקב 3290 נאם 5002 יהוה 3068 ואהב 157 את 853 יעקב 3290: 1:3
ua'amartem bamah 'ahabtanu; halou'a 'ach 'aesau laya'aqob na'am Yahuah, ua'ahab 'at ya'aqob.
**Yet you say Wherein have you loved us? *Was* not brother? Esau Jacob's saith Yahuah yet I loved Jacob**

ואת 853 עשו 6215 שנאתי 8130 ואשים 7760 את 853 הריו 2022 שממה 8077 ואת 853 נחלתו 5159 לתנות 8568 מדבר 4057: 1:4
ua'at 'aesau sanea'tiy; ua'asiym 'at harayu shamamah, ua'at nachalatou latanout midbar.
***And* Esau I hated and laid his mountains waste *and* his heritage for the dragons of the wilderness**

כי 3588 תאמר 559 אדום 123 רששנו 7567 ונשוב 7725 ונבנה 1129 חרבות 2723 כה 3541 אמר 559 יהוה 3068
kiy ta'mar 'adoum rushashnu, uanashub uanibneh charabout, koh 'amar Yahuah
**Whereas saith Edom We are impoverished but we will return and build the desolate places thus saith Yahuah**

צבאות 6635 המה 1992 יבנו 1129 ואני 589 אהרוס 2040 וקראו 7121 להם 3807a גבול 1366 רשעה 7564 והעם 5971
tzaba'aut, hemah yibnu ua'aniy 'aharous; uaqar'au lahem gabul rish'ah, uaha'am
**of hosts They shall build but I will throw down and they shall call them The border of wickedness and, the people**

אשר 834 זעם 2194 יהוה 3068 עד 5704 עולם 5769: 1:5 ועיניכם 5869 תראינה 7200 ואתם 859 תאמרו 559 יגדל 1431
'asher za'am Yahuah 'ad 'aulam. ua'aeyneykem tir'aynah; ua'atem ta'maru yigdal
***against* whom has indignation Yahuah for ever And your eyes shall see and you shall say will be magnified**

יהוה 3068 מעל 5921 לגבול 1366 ישראל 3478: 1:6 בן 1121 יכבד 3513 אב 1 ועבד 5650 אדניו 113 ואם 518 אב 1 אני 589
Yahuah, me'al ligbul yisra'ael. ben yakabed 'ab ua'abed 'adonayu; ua'am 'ab 'aniy
**Yahuah from the border of Israel A son honors *his* father and a servant his master if then *be* a father I**

איה 346 כבודי 3519 ואם 518 אדונים 113 אני 589 איה 346 מוראי 4172 אמר 559 יהוה 3068 צבאות 6635 לכם 3807a הכהנים 3548 בוזי 959
'ayeh kaboudiy ua'am adouniym 'aniy 'ayeh moura'ay 'amar Yahuah tzaba'aut, lakem hakohaniym bouzey
**where *is* my honor? and if *be* a master I where *is* my fear? say Yahuah of hosts unto you O priests that despise**

שמי 8034 ואמרתם 559 במה 1400 בזינו 959 את 853 שמך 8034: 1:7 מגישים 5066 על 5921 מזבחי 4196 לחם 3899 מגאל 1351
shamiy, ua'amartem bameh baziynu 'at shameka. magishiym 'al mizbachiy lachem mago'al,
**my name And you say Wherein have we despised your name? You offer upon mine altar bread polluted**

ואמרתם 559 במה 1400 גאלנוך 1351 באמרכם 559 שלחן 7979 יהוה 3068 נבזה 959 הוא 1931: 1:8 וכי 3588
ua'amartem bameh ge'alnuka; be'amarakem shulchan Yahuah nibzeh hua'. uakiy
**and you say Wherein have we polluted you? In that you say The table of Yahuah *is* contemptible he And if**

**Malachi** 1:1 The burden of the word of YHUH to Israel by Malachi.2 I have loved you, saith YHUH. Yet you say, Wherein have you loved us? Was not Esau Jacob's brother? saith YHUH: yet I loved Jacob,3 And I hated Esau, and laid his mountains and his heritage waste for the dragons of the wilderness.4 Whereas Edom saith, We are impoverished, but we will return and build the desolate places; thus saith YHUH of hosts, They shall build, but I will throw down; and they shall call them, The border of wickedness, and, The people against whom YHUH has indignation forever.5 And your eyes shall see, and you shall say, YHUH will be magnified from the border of Israel.6 A son honoureth his father, and a servant his master: if then I be a father, where is mine honor? and if I be a master, where is my fear? saith YHUH of hosts unto you, O priests, that despise my name. And you say, Wherein have we despised your name?7 You offer polluted bread upon mine altar; and you say, Wherein have we polluted you? In that you say, The table of YHUH is contemptible.

| תגשון 5066 | עור 5787 | לזבח 2076 | אין 369 | רע 7451 | וכי 3588 | תגישו 5066 | פסח 6455 | וחלה 2470 | אין 369 | רע 7451 | הקריבהו 7126 | נא 4994 |
|---|---|---|---|---|---|---|---|---|---|---|---|---|
| tagishun | 'auer | lizboach | 'aeyn | ra', | uakiy | tagiyshu | piseach | uacholeh | 'aeyn | ra'; | haqariybehu | naa' |
| **you offer** | **the blind** | **for sacrifice** | **it it not** | **evil?** | **and if** | **your offer** | **the lame** | **and sick** | **is it not** | **evil?** | **offer *it*** | **now** |

| לפחתך 6346 | הירצך 7521 | או 176 | הישא 5375 | פניך 6440 | אמר 559 | יהוה 3069 | צבאות 6635: | 1:9 ועתה 6258 | חלו 2470 |
|---|---|---|---|---|---|---|---|---|---|
| lapechateka, | hayirtzaka | 'au | hayisa' | paneyka, | 'amar | Yahuah | tzaba'aut. | ua'atah | chalu |
| **unto your governor** | **will he be pleased with you** | **or** | **accept** | **your person?** | **saith** | **Yahuah** | **of hosts** | **And now** | **beseech** |

| נא 4994 | פני 6440 | אל 410 | ויחננו 2603 | מידכם 3027 | היתה 1961 | זאת 2063 | הישא 5375 | מכם 4480 | פנים 6440 |
|---|---|---|---|---|---|---|---|---|---|
| naa' | paney | 'al | uiychanenu; | miyedkem | hayatah | za't, | hayisa' | mikem | paniym, |
| **I pray you** | **before** | **El** | **that he will be gracious unto us** | **by your means** | **has been** | **this** | **will he regard** | **your** | **persons?** |

| אמר 559 | יהוה 3068 | צבאות 6635: | 1:10 מי 4310 | גם 1571 | בכם 871a | ויסגר 5462 | דלתים 1817 | ולא 3808 |
|---|---|---|---|---|---|---|---|---|
| 'amar | Yahuah | tzaba'aut. | miy' | gam | bakem | uayisgor | dalatayim, | uala' |
| **saith** | **Yahuah** | **of hosts** | **Who *is there*** | **even** | **among you** | **that would shut** | **the doors *for nought*?** | **neither** |

| תאירו 215 | מזבחי 4196 | חנם 2600 | אין 369 | לי 3807a | חפץ 2656 | בכם 871a | אמר 559 | יהוה 3068 | צבאות 6635 | ומנחה 4503 |
|---|---|---|---|---|---|---|---|---|---|---|
| ta'ayru | mizbachiy | chinam; | 'aeyn | liy | chepetz | bakem, | 'amar | Yahuah | tzaba'aut, | uaminchah |
| **you shall kindle (*light*) *fire on*** | **mine altar** | **for nought** | **have no** | **I** | **pleasure** | **in you** | **saith** | **Yahuah** | **of hosts** | **an offering** |

| לא 3808 | ארצה 7521 | מידכם 3027: | 1:11 כי 3588 | ממזרח 4217 | שמש 8121 | ועד 5704 | מבואו 935 | גדול 1419 |
|---|---|---|---|---|---|---|---|---|
| la' | 'artzeh | miyedkem. | kiy | mimizrach | shemesh | ua'ad | mabou'au, | gadoul |
| **neither** | **will I accept** | **at your hand** | **For** | **from the rising of** | **the sun** | **even unto** | **the going down** | ***shall be* great** |

| שמי 8034 | בגוים 1471 | ובכל 3605 | מקום 4725 | מקטר 6999 | מגש 5066 | לשמי 8034 | ומנחה 4503 |
|---|---|---|---|---|---|---|---|
| shamiy | bagouyim, | uabkal | maqoum, | muqtar | mugash | lishmiy | uaminchah |
| ***of the same* my name** | **among the Gentiles** | **and in every** | **place** | **incense** | ***shall be* offered** | **unto my name** | **and a offering** |

| טהורה 2889 | כי 3588 | גדול 1419 | שמי 8034 | בגוים 1471 | אמר 559 | יהוה 3068 | צבאות 6635: | 1:12 ואתם 859 | מחללים 2490 | אותו 853 |
|---|---|---|---|---|---|---|---|---|---|---|
| tahourah; | kiy | gadoul | shamiy | bagouyim, | 'amar | Yahuah | tzaba'aut. | ua'atem | machalaliym | 'autou; |
| **pure** | **for** | ***shall be* great** | **my name** | **among the heathen** | **saith** | **Yahuah** | **of hosts** | **But you** | ***have* profaned** | **it** |

| באמרכם 559 | שלחן 7979 | אדני 136 | מגאל 1351 | הוא 1931 | וניבו 5108 | נבזה 959 | אכלו 400: | 1:13 ואמרתם 559 |
|---|---|---|---|---|---|---|---|---|
| be'amarakem, | shulchan | 'adonay | mago'al | hua', | uaniybou | nibzeh | akalou. | ua'amartem |
| **in that you say** | **The table of** | **Adonai** | ***is* polluted** | **he** | **and the fruit thereof** | ***is* contemptible** | ***even* his meat** | **You said also** |

| הנה 2009 | מתלאה 4972 | והפחתם 5301 | אותו 853 | אמר 559 | יהוה 3068 | צבאות 6635 | והבאתם 935 | גזול 1497 |
|---|---|---|---|---|---|---|---|---|
| hineh | matala'ah | uahipachtem | 'autou, | 'amar | Yahuah | tzaba'aut, | uahabea'tem | gazul, |
| **behold** | **what a weariness *is it*** | **and you have snuffed at** | **it** | **saith** | **Yahuah** | **of hosts** | **and you brought** | ***that which was* torn** |

| ואת 853 | הפסח 6455 | ואת 853 | החולה 2470 | והבאתם 935 | את 853 | המנחה 4503 | הארצה 7521 | אותה 853 | מידכם 3027 | אמר 559 |
|---|---|---|---|---|---|---|---|---|---|---|
| ua'at | hapiseach | ua'at | hachouleh, | uahabea'tem | 'at | haminchah; | ha'artzeh | 'autah | miyedkem | 'amar |
| ***and*** | **the lame** | ***and*** | **the sick** | **thus you brought** | | **an offering** | **should I accept** | **this** | **of your hand?** | **saith** |

| יהוה 3068: | 1:14 וארור 779 | נוכל 3230 | ויש 3426 | בעדרו 5739 | זכר 2145 | ונדר 5087 | וזבח 2076 | משחת 7843 | לאדני 136 |
|---|---|---|---|---|---|---|---|---|---|
| Yahuah. | ua'arur | noukel, | uayesh | ba'adrou | zakar, | uanoder | uazobeach | mashachat | la'adonay; |
| **Yahuah** | **But cursed *be*** | **the deceiver** | **which has** | **in his flock** | **a male** | **and vowed** | **and sacrifice** | **a corrupt thing** | **unto Adonai** |

Mal 1:8 And if you offer the blind for sacrifice, is it not evil? and if you offer the lame and sick, is it not evil? offer it now unto your governor; will he be pleased with you, or accept your person? saith YHUH of hosts.9 And now, I pray you, beseech G-d that he will be gracious unto us: this has been by your means: will he regard your persons? saith YHUH of hosts.10 Who is there even among you that would shut the doors for nought? neither do you kindle fire on mine altar for nought. I have no pleasure in you, saith YHUH of hosts, neither will I accept an offering at your hand.11 For from the rising of the sun even unto the going down of the same my name shall be great among the Gentiles; and in every place incense shall be offered unto my name, and a pure offering: for my name shall be great among the heathen, saith YHUH of hosts.12 But you have profaned it, in that you say, The table of YHUH is polluted; and the fruit thereof, even his meat, is contemptible.13 You said also, Behold, what a weariness is it! and you have snuffed at it, saith YHUH of hosts; and you brought that which was torn, and the lame, and the sick; thus you brought an offering: should I accept this of your hand? saith YHUH.14 But cursed be the deceiver, which has in his flock a male, and voweth, and sacrificeth unto YHUH a corrupt thing:

כי 3588 מלך 4428 גדול 1419 אני 589 אמר 559 יהוה 3068 צבאות 6635 ושמי 8034 נורא 3372 בגוים 1471:
kiy melek gadoul 'aniy, 'amar Yahuah tzaba'aut, uashmiy noura' bagouyim.
**for *am* a King great I saith Yahuah of hosts and my name *is* dreadful among the heathen**

**Mal 2:1** ... **2:2**
ועתה 6258 אליכם 413 המצוה 4687 הזאת 2063 הכהנים 3548: אם 518 לא 3808 תשמעו 8085 ואם 518 לא 3808
ua'atah, 'aleykem hamitzuah haza't hakohaniym. 'am la' tishma'au ua'am la'
**And now *is* for you commandment this O you priests If not you will hear and if not**

תשימו 7760 על 5921 לב 3820 לתת 5414 כבוד 3519 לשמי 8034 אמר 559 יהוה 3068 צבאות 6635 ושלחתי 7971 בכם 871a את 853
tasiymu 'al leb latet kaboud lishmiy, 'amar Yahuah tzaba'aut, uashilachtiy bakem 'at
**you will lay *it* to heart to give glory unto my name saith Yahuah of hosts I will even send upon you**

המארה 3994 וארותי 779 את 853 ברכותיכם 1293 וגם 1571 ארותיה 779 כי 3588 אינכם 369 שמים 7760 על 5921
hama'aerah, ua'aroutiy 'at birkouteykem; ua'gam 'aroutiyha, kiy 'aeynakem samiym 'al
**a curse and I will curse your blessings and yea I have cursed them *already* because *it* not you do lay to**

**2:3**
לב 3820: הנני 2005 גער 1605 לכם 3807a את 853 הזרע 2233 וזריתי 2219 פרש 6569 על 5921 פניכם 6440 פרש 6569
leb. hinniy gou'aer lakem 'at hazera', uazeriytiy paresh 'al paneykem, peresh
**heart Behold I will corrupt to your seed and spread dung upon your faces *even* the dung**

**2:4**
חגיכם 2282 ונשא 5375 אתכם 853 אליו 413: וידעתם 3045 כי 3588 שלחתי 7971 אליכם 413 את 853
chageykem; uanasa' 'atkem 'aelayu. uiyda'tem kiy shilachtiy 'aleykem, 'at
**of your solemn feasts and *one* shall take away you with it And you shall know that I have sent unto you**

**2:5**
המצוה 4687 הזאת 2063 להיות 1961 בריתי 1285 את 854 לוי 3878 אמר 559 יהוה 3068 צבאות 6635: בריתי 1285 היתה 1961
hamitzuah haza't; lihayout bariytiy 'at leuiy, 'amar Yahuah tzaba'aut. bariytiy hayatah
**commandment this might be *that* my covenant *with* Levi saith Yahuah of hosts My covenant was**

אתו 854 החיים 2416 והשלום 7965 ואתנם 5414 לו 3807a מורא 4172 וייראני 3372 ומפני 6440 שמי 8034
'atou, hachayiym uahashaloum, ua'atanem lou' moura' uayiyra'aeniy; uamipaney shamiy
**with him of life and peace and I gave them to him *for* the fear *wherewith* he feared me and before my name**

**2:6**
נחת 2865 הוא 1931: תורת 8451 אמת 571 היתה 1961 בפיהו 6310 ועולה 5766 לא 3808 נמצא 4672 בשפתיו 8193 בשלום 7965
nichat hua'. tourat 'amet hayatah bapiyhu, ua'aulah la' nimtza' bispatayu; bashaloum
**was afraid he The law of truth was in his mouth and iniquity not was found in his lips in peace**

**2:7**
ובמישור 4334 הלך 1980 אתי 854 ורבים 7227 השיב 7725 מעון 5771: כי 3588 שפתי 8193 כהן 3548 ישמרו 8104
uabmiyshour halak 'atiy, uarabiym heshiyb ma'aun. kiy siptey kohen yishmeru
**and equity he walked with me and many did turn away from iniquity For lips the priest's should keep**

**2:8**
דעת 1847 ותורה 8451 יבקשו 1245 מפיהו 6310 כי 3588 מלאך 4397 יהוה 3068 צבאות 6635 הוא 1931: ואתם 859
da'at, uatourah yabaqshu mipiyhu; kiy mal'ak Yahuah tzaba'aut hua'. ua'atem
**knowledge and the law they should seek at his mouth for *is* the messenger of Yahuah of hosts he But you**

סרתם 5493 מן 4480 הדרך 1870 הכשלתם 3782 רבים 7227 בתורה 8451 שחתם 7843 ברית 1285 הלוי 3878
sartem min haderek, hikshaltem rabiym batourah; shichatem bariyt haleuiy,
**are departed out of the way you have caused to stumble many at the law you have corrupted the covenant of Levi**

Mal 1:14 for I am a great King, saith YHUH of hosts, and my name is dreadful among the heathen. **Mal** 2:1 And now, O you priests, this commandment is for you.2 If you will not hear, and if you will not lay it to heart, to give glory unto my name, saith YHUH of hosts, I will even send a curse upon you, and I will curse your blessings: yea, I have cursed them already, because you do not lay it to heart.3 Behold, I will corrupt your seed, and spread dung upon your faces, even the dung of your solemn feasts; and one shall take you away with it.4 And you shall know that I have sent this commandment unto you, that my covenant might be with Levi, saith YHUH of hosts.5 My covenant was with him of life and peace; and I gave them to him for the fear wherewith he feared me, and was afraid before my name.6 The law of truth was in his mouth, and iniquity was not found in his lips: he walked with me in peace and equity, and did turn many away from iniquity.7 For the priest's lips should keep knowledge, and they should seek the law at his mouth: for he is the messenger of YHUH of hosts.8 But you are departed out of the way; you have caused many to stumble at the law; you have corrupted the covenant of Levi, saith YHUH of hosts.

2:9

אמר 559 יהוה 3068 צבאות 6635: וגם 1571 אני 589 נתתי 5414 אתכם 853 נבזים 959 ושפלים 8217 לכל 3605 העם 5971

'amar Yahuah tzaba'aut. uagam 'aniy natatiy 'atkem nibziym uashpaliym lakal ha'am;

**saith Yahuah of hosts Therefore also I have made you contemptible and base before all the people**

2:10

כפי 6310 אשר 834 אינכם 369 שמרים 8104 את 854 דרכי 1870 ונשאים 5375 פנים 6440 בתורה 8451: הלוא 3808 אב 1 אחד 259

kapiy, 'asher 'aeynakem shomariym 'at darakay, uanos'aym paniym batourah. halou'a 'ab 'achad

**according as not you have kept my ways but have been partial in the law not father? one**

לכלנו 3605 הלוא 3808 אל 410 אחד 259 בראנו 1254 מדוע 4069 נבגד 898 איש 376 באחיו 251

lakulanu, halou'a 'ael 'achad bara'anu; madua', nibgad 'aysh ba'achiyu,

**Have we all *have* not El one created us? why do we deal treacherously every man against his brother**

2:11

לחלל 2490 ברית 1285 אבתינו 1: בגדה 898 יהודה 3063 ותועבה 8441 נעשתה 6213

lachalel bariyt 'aboteynu. bagadah yahudah, uatou'abah ne'astah

**by profaning the covenant of our fathers? has dealt treacherously Judah and an abomination is committed**

בישראל 3478 ובירושלם 3389 כי 3588 חלל 2490 יהודה 3063 קדש 6944 יהוה 3068 אשר 834 אהב 157 ובעל 1166

bayisra'ael uabiyarushalaim; kiy chilel yahudah, qodesh Yahuah 'asher 'aheb, uaba'al

**in Israel and in Jerusalem for has profaned Judah the holiness of Yahuah which he loved and has married**

2:12

בת 1323 אל 410 נכר 5236: יכרת 3772 יהוה 3069 לאיש 376 אשר 834 יעשנה 6213 ער 5782 וענה 6030

bat 'ael nekar. yakret Yahuah la'aysh 'asher ya'asenah 'aer ua'aneh,

**the daughter of a god strange will cut off Yahuah the man that does *this* the master and the scholar**

2:13

מאהלי 168 יעקב 3290 ומגיש 5066 מנחה 4503 ליהוה 3069 צבאות 6635: וזאת 2063 שנית 8145

me'ahaley ya'aqob; uamagiysh minchah, laYahuah tzaba'aut. uaza't sheniyt

**out of the tabernacles of Jacob and him that offer an offering unto Yahuah of hosts And this again**

תעשו 6213 כסות 3680 דמעה 1832 את 853 מזבח 4196 יהוה 3068 בכי 1065 ואנקה 603 מאין 369 עוד 5750

ta'asu, kasout dim'ah 'at mizbach Yahuah, bakiy ua'anaqah; me'ayn 'aud,

**have you done covering *with* tears the altar of Yahuah *with* weeping and with crying out not any more**

2:14

פנות 6437 אל 413 המנחה 4503 ולקחת 3947 רצון 7522 מידכם 3027: ואמרתם 559 על 5921 מה 4100 על 5921

panout 'al haminchah, ualaqachat ratzoun miyedkem. ua'amartem 'al mah; 'al

***insomuch that* he regard about the offering or receive *it with* good will at your hand Yet you say fore? Where on**

כי 3588 יהוה 3068 העיד 5749 בינך 996 ובין 996 אשת 802 נעוריך 5271 אשר 834 אתה 859

kiy Yahuah he'ayd beynaka uabeyn 'aeshet na'aureyka, 'asher 'atah

**Because Yahuah has been witness between you and between the wife of your youth *against* whom you**

2:15

בגדתה 898 בה 871a והיא 1931 חברתך 2278 ואשת 802 בריתך 1285: ולא 3808 אחד 259 עשה 6213

bagadtah bah, uahiy'a chabertaka ua'aeshet bariyteka. uala' 'achad 'asah,

**have dealt treacherously yet *is* she your companion and the wife of your covenant And not one? did he make**

ושאר 7605 רוח 7307 לו 3807a ומה 4100 האחד 259 מבקש 1245 זרע 2233 אלהים 430 ונשמרתם 8104

uash'ar ruach lou', uamah ha'achad, mabaqesh zera' 'alohiym; uanishmartem

**Yet the residue of the spirit had he And wherefore one? That he might seek a seed godly Therefore take heed to**

Mal 2:9 Therefore have I also made you contemptible and base before all the people, according as you have not kept my ways, but have been partial in the law.10 Have we not all one father? has not one G-d created us? why do we deal treacherously every man against his brother, by profaning the covenant of our fathers?11 Judah has dealt treacherously, and an abomination is committed in Israel and in Jerusalem; for Judah has profaned the holiness of YHUH which he loved, and has married the daughter of a strange god.12 YHUH will cut off the man that doeth this, the master and the scholar, out of the tabernacles of Jacob, and him that offereth an offering unto YHUH of hosts.13 And this have you done again, covering the altar of YHUH with tears, with weeping, and with crying out, insomuch that he regardeth not the offering anymore, or receive it with good will at your hand.14 Yet you say, Wherefore? Because YHUH has been witness between you and the wife of your youth, against whom you have dealt treacherously: yet is she your companion, and the wife of your covenant.15 And did not he make one? Yet had he the residue of the spirit. And wherefore one? That he might seek a godly seed. Therefore take heed to your spirit, and let none deal treacherously against the wife of his youth.

7307 ברוחכם 802 ובאשת 5271 נעוריך 408 אל 898 יבגד: **2:16** 3588 כי 8130 שנא 7971 שלח 559 אמר
baruchakem, uab'aeshet na'aureyka 'al yibgod. kiy sanea' shalach, 'amar
**your spirit against the wife of his youth none and let deal treacherously For *that* he hate putting away saith**

3068 יהוה 430 אלהי 3478 ישראל 3680 וכסה 2555 חמס 5921 על 3830 לבושו 559 אמר 3068 יהוה 6635 צבאות 8104 ונשמרתם
Yahuah 'alohey yisra'ael, uakisah chamas 'al labushou, 'amar Yahuah tzaba'aut; uanishmartem
**Yahuah the Elohim of Israel for *one* cover violence with his garment saith Yahuah of hosts therefore take heed to**

7307 ברוחכם 3808 ולא 898 תבגדו: **2:17** 3021 הוגעתם 3068 יהוה 1697 בדבריכם 559 ואמרתם 1400 במה
baruchakem uala' tibgodu. houga'atem Yahuah badibreykem, ua'amartem bamah
**your spirit not *that* you deal treacherously You have wearied Yahuah with your words Yet you say Wherein**

3021 הוגענו 559 באמרכם 3605 כל 6213 עשה 7451 רע 2896 טוב 5869 בעיני 3068 יהוה 871a ובהם 1931 הוא 2654 חפץ
houga'anu; be'amarakem, kal 'asheh ra' toub ba'aeyney Yahuah uabahem hua' chapetz,
**have we wearied *him*? When you say Every one that does evil *is* good in the sight of Yahuah in them he and delight**

176 או 346 איה 430 אלהי 4941 המשפט:
'au 'ayeh 'alohey hamishpat.
**or Where *is* the Elohim of judgment?**

**Mal 3:1** 2005 הנני 7971 שלח 4397 מלאכי 6437 ופנה 1870 דרך 6440 לפני 6597 ופתאם 935 יבוא 413 אל 1964 היכלו
hinniy sholeach mal'akiy, uapinah derek lapanay; uapit'am yabou'a 'al heykalou
**Behold I will send my messenger and he shall prepare the way before me suddenly shall come to his temple**

113 האדון 834 אשר 859 אתם 1245 מבקשים 4397 ומלאך 1285 הברית 834 אשר 859 אתם 2655 חפצים 2009 הנה 935 בא
ha'adoun 'asher 'atem mabaqshiym, uamal'ak habariyt 'asher 'atem chapetziym hineh ba',
**and Adonai whom you seek even the messenger of the covenant whom you delight in behold he shall come**

559 אמר 3068 יהוה 6635 צבאות: **3:2** 4310 ומי 3557 מכלכל 853 את 3117 יום 935 בואו 4310 ומי 5975 העמד 7200 בהראותו 3588 כי
'amar Yahuah tzaba'aut. uamiy makalkel 'at youm bo'au, uamiy ha'aumed behera'atou; kiy
**saith Yahuah of hosts But who may abide the day of his coming and who shall stand when he appear? for**

1931 הוא 784 כאש 6884 מצרף 1287 וכברית 3526 מכבסים: **3:3** 3427 וישב 6884 מצרף 2891 ומטהר 3701 כסף
hua' ka'aesh matzarep, uakboriyt makabsiym. uayashab matzarep uamtaher kesep,
**he *is* like a fire refiner's and like soap fullers' And he shall sit *as* a refiner and purifier of silver**

2891 וטהר 853 את 1121 בני 3878 לוי 2212 וזקק 853 אתם 2091 כזהב 3701 וככסף 1961 והיו 3068 ליהוה 5066 מגישי
uatihar 'at baney leuiy uaziqaq 'atam, kazahab uakakasep; uahayu laYahuah, magiyshey
**and he shall purify the sons of Levi and purge them as gold and silver that they may unto Yahuah offer**

4503 מנחה 6666 בצדקה: **3:4** 6149 וערבה 3068 ליהוה 4503 מנחת 3063 יהודה 3389 וירושלם 3117 כימי
minchah bitzadaqah. ua'arabah laYahuah, minchat yahudah uiyarushalaim; kiymey
**an offering in righteousness Then shall be pleasant unto Yahuah the offering of Judah and Jerusalem as in the days of**

5769 עולם 8141 וכשנים 6931 קדמניות: **3:5** 7126 וקרבתי 413 אליכם 4941 למשפט 1961 והייתי 5704 עד 4116 ממהר
'aulam, uakshaniym qadmoniyout. uaqarabtiy 'aleykem lamishpat uahayiytiy 'aed mamaher,
**old and as years *in* former And I will come near to you to judgment and I will be a witness swift**

Mal 2:16 For YHUH, the G-d of Israel, saith that he hateth putting away: for one covereth violence with his garment, saith YHUH of hosts: therefore take heed to your spirit, that you deal not treacherously.17 You have wearied YHUH with your words. Yet you say, Wherein have we wearied him? When you say, Every one that doeth evil is good in the sight of YHUH, and he delighteth in them; or, Where is the G-d of judgment? **Mal** 3:1 Behold, I will send my messenger, and he shall prepare the way before me: and the Adonai, whom you seek, shall suddenly come to his temple, even the messenger of the covenant, whom you delight in: behold, he shall come, saith YHUH of hosts.2 But who may abide the day of his coming? and who shall stand when he appeareth? for he is like a refiner's fire, and like fullers' soap:3 And he shall sit as a refiner and purifer of silver: and he shall purify the sons of Levi, and purge them as gold and silver, that they may offer unto YHUH an offering in righteousness.4 Then shall the offering of Judah and Jerusalem be pleasant unto YHUH, as in the days of old, and as in former years.5 And I will come near to you to judgment; and I will be a swift witness against the sorcerers, and against the adulterers, and against false swearers, and against those that oppress the hireling in his wages, the widow, and the fatherless,

| במכשפים 3784 | ובמנאפים 5003 | ובנשבעים 7650 | לשקר 8267 | ובעשקי 6231 | שכר 7939 |
|---|---|---|---|---|---|
| bamakashpiym | uabamana'apiym, | uabanishba'aym | lashaqer; | uab'ashaqey | sakar |
| **against the sorcerers** | **and against the adulterers** | **and against swearers** | **false** | **and against those that oppress** | ***in his* wages** |

| שכיר 7916 | אלמנה 490 | ויתום 3490 | ומטי 5186 | גר 1616 | ולא 3808 | יראוני 3372 | אמר 559 | יהוה 3068 |
|---|---|---|---|---|---|---|---|---|
| sakiyr | 'almanah | uayatoum | uamatey | ger | uala' | yera'aniy, | 'amar | Yahuah |
| **the hireling** | **the widow** | **and the fatherless** | **and that turn aside** | **the stranger** | ***from his right* and not** | **fear me** | **saith** | **Yahuah** |

| צבאות 6635: | 3:6 | כי 3588 | אני 589 | יהוה 3068 | לא 3808 | שניתי 8138 | ואתם 859 | בני 1121 | יעקב 3290 | לא 3808 | כליתם 3615: | 3:7 |
|---|---|---|---|---|---|---|---|---|---|---|---|---|
| tzaba'aut. | | kiy | 'aniy | Yahuah | la' | shaniytiy; | ua'atem | baney | ya'aqob | la' | kaliytem. | |
| **of hosts** | | **For** | **I *am*** | **Yahuah** | **not** | **I change** | **therefore you** | **sons of** | **Jacob** | **not** | **are consumed** | |

| למימי 3117 | אבתיכם 1 | סרתם 5493 | מחקי 2706 | ולא 3808 | שמרתם 8104 | שובו 7725 | אלי 413 |
|---|---|---|---|---|---|---|---|
| lamiymey | 'aboteykem | sartem | mechuqay | uala' | shamartem, | shubu | 'aelay |
| **Even from the days** | **of your fathers** | **you are gone away** | **from mine ordinances** | **not** | **and have kept *them*** | **Return** | **unto me** |

| ואשובה 7725 | אליכם 413 | אמר 559 | יהוה 3068 | צבאות 6635 | ואמרתם 559 | במה 1400 | נשוב 7725: | 3:8 | היקבע 6906 | אדם 120 | אלהים 430 |
|---|---|---|---|---|---|---|---|---|---|---|---|
| ua'ashubah | 'aleykem, | 'amar | Yahuah | tzaba'aut; | ua'amartem | bameh | nashub. | | hayiqba' | 'adam | 'alohiym, |
| **and I will return** | **unto you** | **saith** | **Yahuah** | **of hosts** | **But you said** | **Wherein** | **shall we return?** | | **Will rob** | **a man** | **Elohim?** |

| כי 3588 | אתם 859 | קבעים 6906 | אתי 853 | ואמרתם 559 | במה 1400 | קבענוך 6906 | המעשר 4643 | והתרומה 8641: | 3:9 | במארה 3994 | אתם 859 |
|---|---|---|---|---|---|---|---|---|---|---|---|
| kiy | 'atem | qoba'aym | 'atiy, | ua'amartem | bameh | qaba'anuka; | hama'aser | uahatarumah. | | bama'aerah | 'atem |
| **Yet** | **you** | **have robbed me** | | **But you say** | **Wherein** | **have we robbed you?** | ***In* tithes** | **and offerings** | | **with a curse** | **You** |

| נארים 779 | ואתי 853 | אתם 859 | קבעים 6906 | הגוי 1471 | כלו 3605: | 3:10 | הביאו 935 | את 853 | כל 3605 | המעשר 4643 | אל 413 | בית 1004 | האוצר 214 |
|---|---|---|---|---|---|---|---|---|---|---|---|---|---|
| nea'ariym, | ua'atiy | 'atem | qoba'aym; | hagouy | kulou. | | habiy'au | 'at | kal | hama'aser | 'al | beyt | ha'autzar, |
| ***are* cursed** | **for me** | **you** | **have robbed *even*** | **this nation** | **whole** | | **Bring you** | | **all** | **the tithes** | **into** | **house** | **the store** |

| ויהי 1961 | טרף 2964 | בביתי 1004 | ובחנוני 974 | נא 4994 | בזאת 2063 | אמר 559 | יהוה 3068 | צבאות 6635 | אם 518 | לא 3808 | אפתח 6605 |
|---|---|---|---|---|---|---|---|---|---|---|---|
| uiyhiy | terep | babeytiy, | uabchanuniy | naa' | baza't, | 'amar | Yahuah | tzaba'aut; | 'am | la' | 'aptach |
| **that there may be** | **meat** | **in my house** | **and prove me** | **now** | **herewith** | **saith** | **Yahuah** | **of hosts** | **if** | **not** | **I will open** |

| לכם 3807a | את 853 | ארבות 699 | השמים 8064 | והריקתי 7324 | לכם 3807a | ברכה 1293 | עד 5704 | בלי 1097 |
|---|---|---|---|---|---|---|---|---|
| lakem, | 'at | aroubout | hashamayim, | uahariyqotiy | lakem | barakah | 'ad | baliy |
| **to you** | | **the windows of** | **heaven** | **and pour out** | **to you** | **a blessing *that there shall*** | **until** | **not** |

| די 1767: | 3:11 | וגערתי 1605 | לכם 3807a | באכל 398 | ולא 3808 | ישחת 7843 | לכם 3807a | את 853 |
|---|---|---|---|---|---|---|---|---|
| day. | | uaga'artiy | lakem | ba'akel, | uala' | yashchit | lakem | 'at |
| ***be room* enough *to receive it*** | | **And I will rebuke** | **for your sakes** | **the devourer** | **and not** | **he shall destroy** | **for you** | |

| פרי 6529 | האדמה 127 | ולא 3808 | תשכל 7921 | לכם 3807a | הגפן 1612 | בשדה 7704 | אמר 559 | יהוה 3068 |
|---|---|---|---|---|---|---|---|---|
| pariy | ha'adamah; | uala' | tashakel | lakem | hagapen | basadeh, | 'amar | Yahuah |
| **the fruits of** | ***your* ground** | **neither** | **shall cast her fruit before the time** | **to your** | **vine** | **in the field** | **saith** | **Yahuah** |

| צבאות 6635: | 3:12 | ואשרו 833 | אתכם 853 | כל 3605 | הגוים 1471 | כי 3588 | תהיו 1961 | אתם 859 | ארץ 776 | חפץ 2656 | אמר 559 | יהוה 3068 |
|---|---|---|---|---|---|---|---|---|---|---|---|---|
| tzaba'aut. | | ua'ashru | 'atkem | kal | hagouyim; | kiy | tihayu | 'atem | 'aretz | chepetz, | 'amar | Yahuah |
| **of hosts** | | **And shall call blessed** | **you** | **all** | **nations** | **for** | **shall be** | **you** | **a land** | **delightsome** | **saith** | **Yahuah** |

Mal 3:5 and that turn aside the stranger from his right, and fear not me, saith YHUH of hosts.6 For I am YHUH, I change not; therefore you sons of Jacob are not consumed.7 Even from the days of your fathers you are gone away from mine ordinances, and have not kept them. Return unto me, and I will return unto you, saith YHUH of hosts. But you said, Wherein shall we return?8 Will a man rob G-d? Yet you have robbed me. But you say, Wherein have we robbed you? In tithes and offerings.9 You are cursed with a curse: for you have robbed me, even this whole nation.10 Bring you all the tithes into the storehouse, that there may be meat in mine house, and prove me now herewith, saith YHUH of hosts, if I will not open you the windows of heaven, and pour you out a blessing, that there shall not be room enough to receive it.11 And I will rebuke the devourer for your sakes, and he shall not destroy the fruits of your ground; neither shall your vine cast her fruit before the time in the field, saith YHUH of hosts.12 And all nations shall call you blessed: for you shall be a delightsome land, saith YHUH of hosts.

| צבאות 6635: | 3:13 | חזקו 2388 | עלי 5921 | דבריכם 1697 | אמר 559 | יהוה 3068 | ואמרתם 559 | מה 4100 | נדברנו 1696 |
|---|---|---|---|---|---|---|---|---|---|
| tzaba'aut. | | chazaqu | 'alay | dibreykem | 'amar | Yahuah; | ua'amartem | mah | nidbarnu |
| **of hosts** | | **have been stout** | **against me** | **Your words** | **saith** | **Yahuah** | **Yet you say** | **What** | **have we spoken *so much*** |

| עליך 5921: | 3:14 | אמרתם 559 | שוא 7723 | עבד 5647 | אלהים 430 | ומה 4100 | בצע 1215 | כי 3588 | שמרנו 8104 | משמרתו 4931 | וכי 3588 |
|---|---|---|---|---|---|---|---|---|---|---|---|
| 'aleyka. | | 'amartem | shau'a | 'abod | 'alohiym; | uamah | betza', | kiy | shamarnu | mishmartou, | uakiy |
| **against you?** | | **You have said** | ***It is* vain** | **to serve** | **Elohim** | **and what** | **profit** | ***is it* that** | **we have kept** | **his ordinance** | **and that** |

| הלכנו 1980 | קדרנית 6941 | מפני 6440 | יהוה 3069 | צבאות 6635: | 3:15 | ועתה 6258 | אנחנו 587 | מאשרים 833 | זדים 2086 | גם 1571 | נבנו 1129 |
|---|---|---|---|---|---|---|---|---|---|---|---|
| halaknu | qadoranniyt, | mipaney | Yahuah | tzaba'aut. | | ua'atah | 'anachnu | ma'ashriym | zediym; | gam | nibnu |
| **we have walked** | **mournfully** | **before** | **Yahuah** | **of host?** | | **And now** | **we** | **call happy** | **the proud** | **yea** | **are set up** |

| עשי 6213 | רשעה 7564 | גם 1571 | בחנו 974 | אלהים 430 | וימלטו 4422: | 3:16 | אז 227 | נדברו 1696 | יראי 3372 | יהוה 3068 |
|---|---|---|---|---|---|---|---|---|---|---|
| 'asey | rish'ah, | gam | bachanu | 'alohiym | uayimaletu. | | 'az | nidbaru | yira'aey | Yahuah |
| **they that work** | **wickedness** | **yea** | ***they that* tempt** | **Elohim** | **are even delivered** | | **Then** | **spoke** | **they that feared** | **Yahuah** |

| איש 376 | את 854 | רעהו 7453 | ויקשב 7181 | יהוה 3068 | וישמע 8085 | ויכתב 3789 | ספר 5612 | זכרון 2146 | לפניו 6440 |
|---|---|---|---|---|---|---|---|---|---|
| 'aysh | 'at | re'aehu; | uayaqsheb | Yahuah | uayishma', | uayikateb | seper | zikaroun | lapanayu |
| ***often* one** | ***to*** | **another** | **and hearkened** | **Yahuah** | **and heard *it*** | **and was written** | **a book of** | **remembrance** | **before him** |

| ליראי 3372 | יהוה 3068 | ולחשבי 2803 | שמו 8034: | 3:17 | והיו 1961 | לי 3807a | אמר 559 | יהוה 3068 | צבאות 6635 |
|---|---|---|---|---|---|---|---|---|---|
| layir'aey | Yahuah, | ualchoshabey | shamou. | | uahayu | liy, | 'amar | Yahuah | tzaba'aut, |
| **for them that feared** | **Yahuah** | **and that thought upon** | **his name** | | **And they shall be** | **mine** | **saith** | **Yahuah** | **of hosts** |

| ליום 3117 | אשר 834 | אני 589 | עשה 6213 | סגלה 5459 | וחמלתי 2550 | עליהם 5921 | כאשר 834 | יחמל 2550 | איש 376 | על 5921 | בנו 1121 | העבד 5647 |
|---|---|---|---|---|---|---|---|---|---|---|---|---|
| layoum | 'asher | 'aniy | 'aseh | sagulah; | uachamalatiy | 'aleyhem, | ka'asher | yachmol | 'aysh, | 'al | banou | ha'abed |
| **in that day** | **when** | **I** | **make up** | ***my* jewels** | **and I will spare** | **them** | **as** | **spares** | **a man** | **for** | **his own son** | **that serve** |

| אתו 853: | 3:18 | ושבתם 7725 | וראיתם 7200 | בין 996 | צדיק 6662 | לרשע 7563 | בין 996 | עבד 5647 | אלהים 430 |
|---|---|---|---|---|---|---|---|---|---|
| 'atou. | | uashabtem | uar'aytem, | beyn | tzadiyq | larasha'; | beyn | 'abed | 'alohiym, |
| **him** | | **Then shall you return** | **and discern** | **between** | **the righteous** | **and the wicked** | **between** | **him that serve** | **Elohim** |

| לאשר 834 | לא 3808 | עבדו 5647: |
|---|---|---|
| la'asher | la' | abadou. |
| ***and* him that** | **not** | **serve him** |

| **Mal 4:1** | כי 3588 | הנה 2009 | היום 3117 | בא 935 | בער 1197 | כתנור 8574 | והיו 1961 | כל 3605 | זדים 2086 | וכל 3605 | עשה 6213 |
|---|---|---|---|---|---|---|---|---|---|---|---|
| | kiy | hineh | hayoum | ba', | bo'aer | katanur; | uahayu | kal | zediym | uakal | 'aseh |
| | **For** | **behold** | **the day** | **comes** | **that shall burn** | **as an oven** | **and they become** | **all** | **the proud** | ***yea* and all** | **that do** |

| רשעה 7564 | קש 7179 | ולהט 3857 | אתם 853 | היום 3117 | הבא 935 | אמר 559 | יהוה 3069 | צבאות 6635 | אשר 834 | לא 3808 | יעזב 5800 |
|---|---|---|---|---|---|---|---|---|---|---|---|
| rish'ah | qash, | ualihat | 'atam | hayoum | haba', | 'amar | Yahuah | tzaba'aut, | 'asher | la' | ya'azob |
| **wickedly** | **shall be stubble** | **and shall burn up** | **them** | **the day** | **that comes** | **saith** | **Yahuah** | **of hosts** | **that** | **neither** | **it shall leave** |

| להם 1992 | שרש 8328 | וענף 6057: | 4:2 | וזרחה 2224 | לכם 3807a | יראי 3373 | שמי 8034 | שמש 8121 | צדקה 6666 | ומרפא 4832 |
|---|---|---|---|---|---|---|---|---|---|---|
| lahem | shoresh | ua'anap. | | uazarachah | lakem | yira'aey | shamiy | shemesh | tzadaqah, | uamarpea' |
| **them** | **root** | **nor branch** | | **But shall arise** | **unto you** | **that fear** | **my name** | **the Sun of** | **righteousness** | **with healing** |

Mal 3:13 Your words have been stout against me, saith YHUH. Yet you say, What have we spoken so much against you?14 You have said, It is vain to serve G-d: and what profit is it that we have kept his ordinance, and that we have walked mournfully before YHUH of hosts?15 And now we call the proud happy; yea, they that work wickedness are set up; yea, they that tempt G-d are even delivered.16 Then they that feared YHUH spoke often one to another: and YHUH hearkened, and heard it, and a book of remembrance was written before him for them that feared YHUH, and that thought upon his name.17 And they shall be mine, saith YHUH of hosts, in that day when I make up my jewels; and I will spare them, as a man spareth his own son that serveth him.18 Then shall you return, and discern between the righteous and the wicked, between him that serveth G-d and him that serveth him not. **Mal** 4:1 For, behold, the day cometh, that shall burn as an oven; and all the proud, yea, and all that do wickedly, shall be stubble: and the day that cometh shall burn them up, saith YHUH of hosts, that it shall leave them neither root nor branch.2 But unto you that fear my name shall the Sun of righteousness arise with healing in his wings; and you shall go forth, and grow up as calves of the stall.

בכנפיה 3671 ויצאתם 3318 ופשתם 6335 כעגלי 5695 מרבק 4770: **4:3** ועסותם 6072 רשעים 7563 כי 3588
biknapeyha; uaytza'tem uapishtem ka'agley marbeq. ua'asoutem rasha'aym, kiy
**in his wings and you shall go forth and grow up as calves of the stall And you shall tread down the wicked for**

יהיו 1961 אפר 665 תחת 8478 כפות 3709 רגליכם 7272 ביום 3117 אשר 834 אני 589 עשה 6213 אמר 559 יהוה 3068 צבאות 6635: **4:4**
yihayu 'aeper, tachat kapout ragleykem; bayoum 'asher 'aniy 'aseh, 'amar Yahuah tzaba'aut.
**they shall be ashes under the soles of your feet in the day that I shall do *this* saith Yahuah of hosts**

זכרו 2142 תורת 8451 משה 4872 עבדי 5650 אשר 834 צויתי 6680 אותו 853 בחרב 2722 על 5921 כל 3605 ישראל 3478
zikru tourat mosheh 'abdiy; 'asher tziuiytiy 'autou bachoreb 'al kal yisra'ael,
**Remember you the law of Moses my servant which I commanded *unto* him in Horeb for all Israel**

חקים 2706 ומשפטים 4941: **4:5** הנה 2009 אנכי 595 שלח 7971 לכם 3807a את 853 אליה 452 הנביא 5030 לפני 6440 בוא 935 יום 3117
chuqiym uamishpatiym. hineh 'anokiy sholeach lakem, 'at 'aeliyah hanabiy'a; lipney, bou'a youm
***with* the statutes and judgments Behold I will send to you Elijah the prophet before the coming of day of**

יהוה 3068 הגדול 1419 והנורא 3372: **4:6** והשיב 7725 לב 3820 אבות 1 על 5921 בנים 1121 ולב 3820
Yahuah, hagadoul uahanoura'. uaheshiyb leb about 'al baniym, ualeb
**Yahuah the great and dreadful And he shall turn the heart of the fathers to the children of and the heart of**

בנים 1121 על 5921 אבותם 1 פן 6435 אבוא 935 והכיתי 5221 את 853 הארץ 776 חרם 2764:
baniym 'al aboutam; pen abou'a uahikeytiy 'at ha'aretz cherem.
**the children to their fathers lest I come and smite the earth *with* a curse**

Mal 4:3 And you shall tread down the wicked; for they shall be ashes under the soles of your feet in the day that I shall do this, saith YHUH of hosts.4 Remember you the law of Moses my servant, which I commanded unto him in Horeb for all Israel, with the statutes and judgments.5 Behold, I will send you Elijah the prophet before the coming of the great and dreadful day of YHUH:6 And he shall turn the heart of the fathers to the children, and the heart of the children to their fathers, lest I come and smite the earth with a curse. THE END OF THE PROPHETS.

# PARSHAS FESTIVAL READINGS

**PARSHA EREV HANUKKAH** (*Feast of Dedication*) (Numbers 7:1-8:4)

**Brit Chadasha** (*feast of Dedication*) (John 10:22-39)

**PARSHA EREV PESACH** (*Passover eve*) (Lev 23:4-8, Exo 33:12-34:26, Num 28:16-31)

**Brit Chadasha** (*Passover eve*) (John 13:1-17:26)

**PARSHA YOM PESACH** (*Passover day*) (Leviticus 23:4-8)

**Brit Chadasha** (*Passover day*) (John 18:1-19:42)

**PARSHA PESACH SHABBATH** (*Passover Sabbath*) (Exo 33:12-34:26, Num 28:16-31, Eze 36:37-37:14)

**PARSHA SHAVUOT** (*Pentecost/feast of Weeks*) (Exo 19:1-20:23, Lev 23:15-21, Num 28:26-31, Deut 14:22-16:17, Eze 1:1-28 & 3:12, Hab 3:1-19)

**Brit Chadasha** (*Pentecost/feast of Weeks*) (Acts 2:1-21 & 37:41)

**PARSHA ROSH HASHANA** (*Feast of Trumpets*) (Gen 21:1-34, Num 29:1-6, I Sam 1:1-2:10)

**Brit Chadasha** (*feast of Trumpets*) (I Thess 4:13-18)

**PARSHA YOM KIPPUR** (*Day of Atonement*) (Lev 16:1-34 & 18:1-30, Num 29:7-11, Isa 57:14-58:14)

**Brit Chadasha** (*Day of Atonement*) (Rom 3:21-26, II Cor 5:10-21)

**PARSHA EREV SUKKOT** (*eve of Tabernacles or Tabernacles Sabbath*) (Exo 33:12-34:26, Num 29:17-25, Eze 38:18-39:16)

**Brit Chadasha** (*eve of Tabernacles or Tabernacles Sabbath*) (John 7:37-44)

**PARSHA SUKKOT DAY 1** (*Feast of Tabernacles*) (Lev 22:26-23:44, Num 29:12-16, Zech 14:1-21)

**Brit Chadasha Day 1** (*feast of Tabernacles*) (Revelation 21:1-7)

**PARSHA HOSHANAH RABBAH** (*great supplication*) (Numbers 29:26-34)

**Brit Chadasha Hoshanah Rabbah** (*great supplication*) (John 7:1-2 & 37-44)

**PARSHA SUKKOT DAY 8** (*Feast of Tabernacles*) (Deut 14:22-16:8, Num 29:35-30:1, I Kings 8:54-66)

**Brit Chadasha Day 8** (*Feast of Tabernacles*) (Matthew 17:1-9, Mark 12:28-33)

# CHART ONE: Paleo and Modern Hebrew Letter Meanings

| Pictograph | Name | Meaning | Pictograph | Name | Meaning |
|---|---|---|---|---|---|
|  | Aleph<br>א | Ox Head/Provide<br>Strength/Unity<br>First/Crown |  | Lamed<br>ל | Staff/Shepherd<br>Authority/Protect<br>Control/Teach |
|  | Beit<br>ב | House/Family<br>Inside Of<br>Body/Woman |  | Mem<br>מ - ם | Water/Wash<br>Chaos/Mighty<br>Birth/Blood |
|  | Gimmel<br>ג | Lift Up/Carry<br>Camel/Walk<br>Ascend/Descend |  | Nun<br>נ - ן | Seed/Heir<br>Fish Darting<br>Imparting Life |
|  | Dalet<br>ד | Door/Pathway<br>Access/Enter<br>Hang |  | Samekh<br>ס | Hand on Staff<br>Support/Prop<br>Vine/Protect |
|  | Hey<br>ה | Window/Glory<br>Behold/Breath<br>Reveal/Sign |  | Ayin<br>ע | Eye/See/Watch<br>Experience<br>Discernment |
|  | Vav-U<br>ו | Hook/Man<br>Nail/Bridge<br>Secure/Add |  | Peh<br>פ - ף | Mouth/Word<br>Speak/Watch<br>Communicate |
|  | Zayin<br>ז | Plow/Food<br>Weapon/Kill<br>Cut off/Death |  | Tzadhe<br>צ - ץ | Righteous/Hunt<br>Desire/Need<br>Fishhook/Capture |
|  | Chet-Heth<br>ח | Protect/Enclose<br>Fence/Wall<br>Separation/Open |  | Qoph<br>ק | Back of Head<br>Horizon/Behind<br>To Rise Up |
|  | Tet<br>ט | Snake/Seal<br>Basket/Set Apart<br>Surround/ Mark |  | Resh<br>ר | Head/Face<br>Exalted/Top<br>Chief/Beginning |
|  | Yod<br>י | Hand/Grasp<br>Work/Make<br>Deed/Create |  | Shin<br>ש | Eat/Teeth<br>Consume/Give<br>Destroy/Fire |
|  | Kaph<br>כ - ך | Palm of Hand<br>To Open/Cover<br>Allow/Anoint |  | Tav<br>ת | Mark/Sacrifice<br>Sign/Judgment<br>Covenant/Save |

MATS www.AlephTavScriptures.com William Sanford WHSanford@aol.com

# CHART TWO:Paleo and Modern Hebrew Codes

| Pictograph | Name | Symbol | Pictograph | Name | Symbol |
|---|---|---|---|---|---|
| | Aleph (1) א | A | | Lamed (30) ל | L |
| | Beit (2) ב | B | | Mem (40) מ - ם | M |
| | Gimmel (3) ג | G | | Nun (50) נ - ן | N |
| | Dalet (4) ד | D | | Samekh (60) ס | S |
| | Hey (5) ה | H | | Ayin (70) ע | A |
| | Uau (6) ו | U | | Pey (80) פ - ף | P |
| | Zayin (7) ז | Z | | Tzadhe (90) צ - ץ | Tz |
| | Chet-Heth (8) ח | Ch | | Qoph (100) ק | Q |
| | Tet (9) ט | T | | Reysh (200) ר | R |
| | Yod (10) י | Y | | Shen (300) ש | S/Sh |
| | Kaph (20) כ - ך | K | | Ta (400) ת | T/Th |

MATS www.AlephTavScriptures.com William Sanford WHSanford@aol.com

CPSIA information can be obtained
at www.ICGtesting.com
Printed in the USA
BVHW052015250321
603422BV00002B/45